FACETS VIDEO ENCYCLOPEDIA

Catherine Foley and Milos Stehlik, Editors

Facets Multi-Media, Inc.

Distributed by Academy Chicago Publishers

Published by Facets Multi-Media, Inc., 1517 West Fullerton Avenue, Chicago, IL 60614

Printed and bound in the U.S.A.

Cover, title, section pages and catalog design by Stuart Cohn

Database management by MKS Composing

Composition and electronic production by Point West, Inc.

Catalog database computer programs by Jim Bash

Printed and bound by Ripon Printers

Library of Congress Cataloging-in-Publication Data
Foley, Catherine, 1952-
Facets video encyclopedia/Catherine Foley and Milos Stehlik.
p. cm,
ISBN 0-89733-467-1
1. Motion pictures Catalogs. 2. Video Recordings Catalogs.
I. Stehlik, Milos, II Title.
PN1998.F635 1999
016.79143'75–dc21

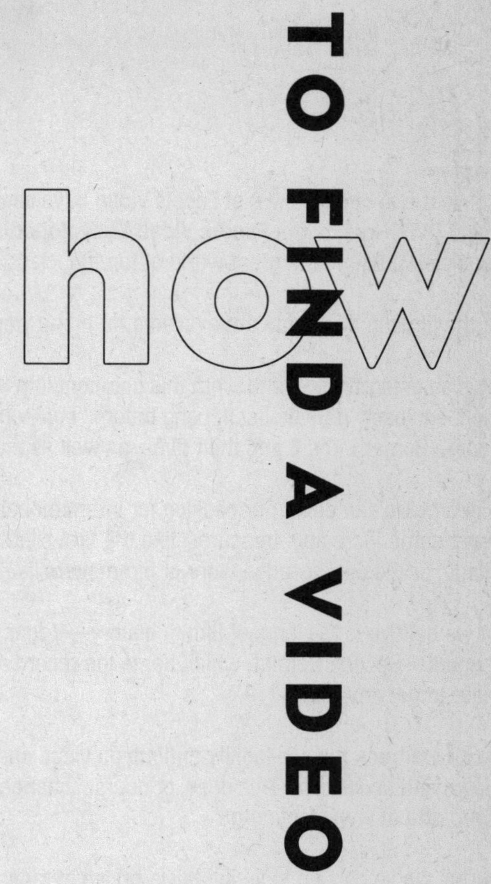

Alphabetically

Check the Title Index, which begins on page 959

If the film or video is a short which is a part of a compilation, check the Short Film Index on page 875

By director

Check the Director Index, which begins on page 899

By country or language

Check the Table of Contents or Subject Area Contents on the following pages.

By genre

See the Table of Contents.

Short films

Check the Short Film Index on page 875

Upfront

For the last two decades, we at Facets Video have searched far and wide for the rare, the unusual and the exciting on video, laser disc and DVD. Here, in the **Facets Video Encyclopedia**, you'll find the fruit of our twenty years of loving labor—what we truly believe is an unparalleled guide to the great world of foreign, classic American, silent, documentary, experimental, fine arts and children's films on video.

All of the films in this guide are available for home viewing on video cassette, DVD or laser disc.

What is so astonishing—and what this compendium of the world's cinematic treasure suggests—is that the film world, like the world of fashion, endlessly repeats itself. Long before "independents" like Quentin Tarantino, there were independent pioneers like Maurice Engel or George Romero. You'll find their films, as well as those of Tarantino, listed and described in the **Facets Video Encyclopedia.**

No video guide can equal our passion for international cinema, and alongside popular, well-known directors like Truffaut or Bergman, you'll discover some incredible treasures, like the first silent French version of Casanova, or Les Vampires, the beautifully restored serial by Louis Feuillade, or the cutting-edge work of filmmakers like Valie Export, Jean-Luc Godard or Chantal Akerman.

What we believe is the longest film in history—Edgar Reitz's monumental Heimat—which clocks in at 15½ hours is here, as well as the sequel—Second Heimat, which beats the record at a little over 26 hours in length. Best of all, it's riveting viewing—once hooked, it's hard to get any sleep.

Because we track the availability of films on video and disc very closely, we concentrated only on films on tape or disc which are available and accessible. This does, of course, change. You can always get free, up-to-the-minute information on availability by checking our web-site at www.facts.org

Likewise, we've chosen to include sale prices of tapes or discs, which were current at press time. Fortunately, prices of videos mostly go down, rarely up. Again, you can check the latest price at www.facets.org

Each film in the **Facets Video Encyclopedia** is accompanied by an informed description and director, country of origin, and running time. Our approach in this guide has been cinematic; we focused on each tape's artistic or dramatic film values. A number of the tapes included in the Facets Video Encyclopedia are segregated in terms of director: those people whose body of work stands on its own, artists whose singular vision is spotlighted within their prospective countries. Included are filmmakers who have left us, from pioneers Griffith, Murneau, Eisenstein to Fassbinder, Tarkovsky, Pasolini, Kurosawa, Bunuel and Kubrick. Highlighted are visionaries who continue to open our eyes in new ways: giants like Jean-Luc Godard, Robert Altman and Michaelangelo Antonioni. We felt it was important to be comprehensive and inclusive—to write about the "body of work" of these key figures so that their work can be appreciated in all its richness.

We welcome your comments, and sincerely wish this guide allows you to spend many enjoyable hours watching what these thousands of talented filmmakers have accomplished.

Where To Buy or Rent Tapes

An increasing number of video stores throughout the country are venturing outside the blockbuster mentality and stock foreign, experimental, fine arts, and independent features and documentaries.

If your video store is not one of these progressive outlets, you can purchase any tape or laser disc in this book which is currently in print directly from Facets Video. To order, within the United States, call toll-free at 800-331-6197, (outside of U.S. call 773-281-9075), fax at 773-929-5437, email sales@facets.org or secure online ordering at www.facets.org or write: Facets Video, 1517 West Fullerton Avenue, Chicago, Illinois 60614. The "S" numbers at the end of each video description in this book refer to Facets Video's sales order numbers.

Facets Video also offers a rent-by-mail service within the continental United States. For rent-by-mail membership information, contact Facets (see above).

To Order Additional Copies of This Book

To order additional copies of this book, you may call Academy Chicago Publishers at 1-800-248-7323 or e-mail academy363@aol.com or visit the Academy Chicago web-site at www.academychicago.com Or send $17.95 plus $3.75 for each copy to Academy Chicago Publishers, 363 West Erie Street, Chicago, IL 60610.

table of contents

INTERNATIONAL CINEMA 1

RECENT FRENCH CINEMA 2
- CUTTING EDGE FRENCH FILMMAKERS 7
- JEAN-LUC GODARD 9
- CHRIS MARKER 10
- MAURICE PIALAT 10
- JACQUES RIVETTE 10
- RAUL RUIZ 11
- BERTRAND TAVERNIER 11
- BERTRAND BLIER 11
- ALAIN RESNAIS 12
- CLAUDE CHABROL 12
- LOUIS MALLE 13
- ERIC ROHMER 13
- AGNES VARDA 14
- FRANCOIS TRUFFAUT 14
- ROBERT BRESSON 15
- BARBET SCHROEDER 15
- JEAN ROUCH 16
- MARCEL OPHULS 16
- JEAN-JACQUES ANNAUD 16
- FRENCH COMEDY 16

FRENCH CLASSICS 19
- MARCEL CARNE 24
- RENE CLAIR 25
- HENRI-GEORGES CLOUZOT 25
- JEAN-PIERRE MELVILLE 25
- JEAN VIGO 25
- JEAN RENOIR 25
- MARCEL PAGNOL 26
- MAX OPHULS 27
- JEAN COCTEAU 27
- ALBERTO CAVALCANTI 28
- JACQUES TATI 28
- THE FRENCH LANDSCAPE 28

BELGIAN CINEMA 29
CHANTAL AKERMAN 29
SWISS CINEMA 30
ALAIN TANNER 30
DUTCH CINEMA 30

RECENT ITALIAN CINEMA 32
- BERNARDO BERTOLUCCI 35
- TAVIANI BROTHERS 35
- MICHELANGELO ANTONIONI 35
- ETTORE SCOLA 36
- FEDERICO FELLINI 36
- PIER PAOLO PASOLINI 37
- VITTORIO DE SICA 37
- ROBERTO ROSSELLINI 38
- LUCHINO VISCONTI 39
- SERGIO LEONE 39

ITALIAN CLASSICS 40
- SWORD & SANDAL EPICS 42
- ITALIAN ISSUES 42

SPANISH CINEMA 44
- CARLOS SAURA 45
- ALMODOVAR 46
- LUIS BUNUEL 46
- SPANISH ISSUES 47
- PORTUGUESE FILMS 48

LATIN AMERICAN CINEMA 49
- TOMAS GUTIERREZ ALEA 53
- BRAZILIAN CINEMA 53
- CARIBBEAN CINEMA 54
- THE HISPANIC WORLD 55

RECENT GERMAN CINEMA 63
- RAINER WERNER FASSBINDER 66
- WERNER HERZOG 67
- WIM WENDERS 67

GERMAN CLASSICS 68
- FRITZ LANG 71
- FRIEDRICH MURNAU 73
- GERMAN SIGHTS & SOUNDS 73
- AUSTRIAN CINEMA 74
- AUSTRIAN VIEWS 74

SCANDINAVIAN CINEMA 75
- INGMAR BERGMAN 77
- JAN TROELL 79
- AKI & MIKA KAURISMAKI 79
- CARL THEODOR DREYER 79
- VICTOR SJOSTROM 79
- SCANDINAVIAN WORLD 79

RUSSIAN CINEMA 80
- ANDREI TARKOVSKY 84
- SERGEI PARADJANOV 84
- ANDREI KONCHALOVSKY 84
- EARLY SOVIET CINEMA 85
- SERGEI EISENSTEIN 86
- DZIGA VERTOV 86
- UKRAINIAN FILMS 86
- BALTIC FILMS 86
- THROUGH RUSSIAN EYES 87
- EASTERN EUROPE/SOVIET UNION 89

POLISH CINEMA 90
- YOUNG POLISH DIRECTORS TO WATCH 95
- KRZYSZTOF KIESLOWSKI 95
- AGNIESZKA HOLLAND 96
- ANDRZEJ WAJDA 96
- JERZY SKOLIMOWSKI 97
- ROMAN POLANSKI 97
- POLAND: PAST AND PRESENT 98

CZECH CINEMA 99
- MILOS FORMAN 100
- JAN NEMEC 101
- JAN KADAR 101
- CZECH REPORT 101

HUNGARIAN CINEMA 101
- ISTVAN SZABO 103
- HUNGARIAN ISSUES 103

YUGOSLAV CINEMA 103
- DUSAN MAKAVEJEV 104
- EMIR KUSTURICA 104

ROMANIAN CINEMA 104
BULGARIAN CINEMA 104
GREEK CINEMA 104
- MICHAEL CACOYANNIS 105
- COSTA-GAVRAS 105

TURKISH CINEMA 106
IRANIAN CINEMA 106
ISRAELI CINEMA 107
ISRAELI CULTURE 109
MIDEAST: THE CHALLENGE OF CHANGE 110
YIDDISH & JEWISH CINEMA 111
THE WORLD OF JUDAISM 113
NORTH AFRICAN FILMS 116

CHINESE CINEMA 117
- ZHANG YIMOU 118
- HONG KONG CINEMA 118
- HONG KONG ACTION CINEMA 124
- JACKIE CHAN 133
- CHINESE CULTURE & POLITICS 135
- TAIWANESE CINEMA 136

KOREAN CINEMA 136

JAPANESE CINEMA 137
- JUZO ITAMI 140
- SHOHEI IMAMURA 141
- NAGISA OSHIMA 141
- KON ICHIKAWA 141
- HIROSHI TESHIGAHARA 141
- AKIRA KUROSAWA 142
- KENJI MIZOGUCHI 143
- YASUJIRO OZU 143
- JAPANESE ISSUES 144

OTHER ASIAN FILMS 144
ASIAN WORLD 145
FILIPINO CINEMA 145
FILIPINO PERSPECTIVES 146
INDIAN CINEMA 146
INDIAN ISSUES 148
BUDDHISM & EASTERN RELIGIONS 149

AFRICAN CINEMA 150
SOUTH AFRICAN CINEMA 150
AFRICAN SPOTLIGHT 151

VERY SPECIAL 153
EUROPEAN SILENT CINEMA 153
LANGUAGE INSTRUCTION 154

BRITISH CINEMA 157

RECENT BRITISH CINEMA 158
- PETER GREENAWAY 165
- MIKE LEIGH 165
- KEN LOACH 166
- STEPHEN FREARS 166
- NICOLAS ROEG 166
- KEN RUSSELL 167
- DEREK JARMAN 167
- TERRY GILLIAM 168
- PETER WATKINS 168
- WORLD OF JAMES BOND 168
- BRITISH CULTURE 169

BRITISH CLASSICS 171
- DAVID LEAN 180
- POWELL/PRESSBURGER 180
- BRITISH COMEDY 181
- SHERLOCK HOLMES MYSTERIES 185

BRITISH TELEVISION 188
- MONTY PYTHON 198
- DR. WHO 199

IRISH FEATURES 202
IRISH PERSPECTIVES 202

AUSTRALIAN CINEMA 205
- PETER WEIR 207
- NEW ZEALAND CINEMA 208
- AUSTRALIAN/NEW ZEALAND ISSUES 209

CANADIAN CINEMA 210
- ATOM EGOYAN 212
- DAVID CRONENBERG 212
- QUEBECOIS CINEMA 213

AMERICAN FILM 215

RECENT AMERICAN CINEMA 216
- MARTIN SCORSESE 253
- ROBERT ALTMAN 254
- JONATHAN DEMME 255
- TIM BURTON 255
- STANLEY KUBRICK 255
- CLINT EASTWOOD 256
- DAVID LYNCH 257
- ALAN RUDOLPH 257
- ARTHUR PENN 257
- STEVEN SPIELBERG 258
- JAMES IVORY 258
- FRANCIS F. COPPOLA 259
- SAM SHEPARD 260

AMERICAN COMEDY 261
- WOODY ALLEN 288

AMERICAN WESTERNS 290
- THE AMERICAN WEST 298

LITERATURE ON SCREEN 300
- WRITERS & THEIR WORKS 302
- MARK TWAIN ADAPTATIONS 308
- THEATRE ON SCREEN 310
- PERFORMING ARTS INSTRUCTION 316
- AMERICAN MUSICALS 319
- MOVIES ABOUT MOVIES 332

CLASSIC AMERICAN CINEMA 340
- JOHN FORD 340
- SAM FULLER 341

HOWARD HAWKS 341
DOUGLAS SIRK 342
GEORGE STEVENS 342
WILLIAM WYLER 343
ORSON WELLES 344
ERNST LUBITSCH 345
BILLY WILDER 345
PRESTON STURGES 346
NICHOLAS RAY 346
SAM PECKINPAH 347
JOSEF VON STERNBERG 347
ERICH VON STROHEIM 348
JOHN HUSTON 348
GEORGE CUKOR 349
FRANK CAPRA 350
ALFRED HITCHCOCK 351
JOSEPH LOSEY 353
BLAKE EDWARDS 353
CECIL B. DEMILLE 354
RELIGIOUS FEATURES & EPICS 355
AMERICAN CLASSICS 356

SILENT AMERICAN CINEMA 395
CHARLES CHAPLIN 407
BUSTER KEATON 408
HAROLD LLOYD 409
SILENT COMEDY 410
D.W. GRIFFITH 412

TELEVISION SHOWS 414

INDEPENDENT SPIRITS 425

INDEPENDENT AMERICAN CINEMA 426
JOHN CASSAVETES 440
JOHN SAYLES 440
GUS VAN SANT 440
COEN BROTHERS 441
QUENTIN TARANTINO 441
JON JOST 441
HAL HARTLEY 442
JILL GODMILOW 442
JIM JARMUSCH 442
JONAS MEKAS 442
STEVEN SODERBERGH 443
MONTE HELLMAN 443
AFRICAN-AMERICAN INDEPENDENTS 443
SPIKE LEE 446
EARLY BLACK CINEMA 447
AFRICAN-AMERICAN ISSUES 449
ASIAN-AMERICAN INDEPENDENTS 455

GAY & LESBIAN CINEMA 456

DOCUMENTARY CINEMA 468
LES BLANK 480
EMILE DE ANTONIO 481
DANNY LYON 481
ERROL MORRIS 481

EXPERIMENTAL CINEMA & VIDEO 482
JAMES BROUGHTON 492
BARBARA HAMMER 492

GUILTY PLEASURES 493

SCI-FI ON VIDEO 494

CULT FILMS 503
RUSS MEYER 513
ROGER CORMAN 513
JOHN WATERS 514
PAUL MORRISSEY 514
ED WOOD, JR. 514
HORROR FLICKS 516
BLAXPLOITATION FILMS 531
COMEDY ACTS 534
ELVIS PRESLEY 536
SERIALS 537
TRAILERS & COMMERCIALS 539
COMICS & THEIR CREATORS 541

FINE ARTS ON VIDEO 543

ART ON VIDEO 544
PHOTOGRAPHY 558
APPLIED ART 560
ART TECHNIQUES 562
ARCHITECTURE 565
PERFORMANCE ART 566
DANCE ON VIDEO 568

MUSIC ON VIDEO 577
OPERA 577
CLASSICAL MUSIC 586
CLASSICAL VOICE 595
WORLD MUSIC 600
FOLK & COUNTRY MUSIC 604
GOSPEL MUSIC 606
JAZZ, BLUES & R&B 608
OTHER MUSIC 616
ROCK PORTRAITS & SUPERSTARS 618
MUSIC INSTRUCTION 623

CHILDREN'S VIDEO 627

CHILDREN'S VIDEO 628
FAIRY TALES 645
PRE-SCHOOL VIDEO 649
WONDERWORKS 660
FEATURE FILMS FOR KIDS 661
CHILDREN'S ACTIVITIES 668
FOREIGN LANGUAGES FOR CHILDREN 671

ANIMATION 675

HOLLYWOOD STUDIO ANIMATION 676
WALT DISNEY FILMS 690
TV ANIMATION 694
INTERNATIONAL & INDEPENDENT ANIMATION 704
LARRY JORDAN 718

JAPANESE ANIMATION 719

NON-FICTION VIDEO 755

HISTORICAL DOCUMENTARY 756
WORLD WAR II 765
THE HOLOCAUST 774
THE VIETNAM WAR 777
THE CIVIL WAR 779

CULTURAL DOCUMENTARY 781
ANCIENT CIVILIZATIONS 784
IDEAS & PHILOSOPHY 785
NATIVE AMERICAN CULTURE 786
RELIGION 789
BIOGRAPHY & MEMOIRS 793
THE KENNEDYS 797
POLITICAL & CONTEMPORARY EVENTS 798
ENVIRONMENTAL & GLOBAL ISSUES 801
EDUCATION & HISTORY 807

NATURE VIDEOS 812
SPORTS & THE OUTDOORS 825
TRAVEL 828
AIDS 833
SCIENCE 835
MATHEMATICS 838
SPACE EXPLORATION 838
TRANSPORTATION 841
COMPUTERS 845

PERSONAL GROWTH 847
PARENTING & THE HOME 857
TEST PREPARATION 858
LANGUAGE ARTS 859
OTHER EDUCATIONAL VIDEOS 860
OCCULT/NEW AGE 861
UNIDENTIFIED FLYING OBJECTS 862

CD ROMS 863

Short Film Index 875
Director Index 899
Title Index 959

subject area contents

Acting instruction 316–319
Actor biographies 332–339
African-American independents 443–447
African-American cinema, early 447–449
African cinema 150–151
AIDS 833–835
Airplanes, air travel 841–845
Algerian films 116
American cinema 215–541
American cinema, documentary 468–481
American cinema, independent 426–446
American comedy 261–289
American musicals 319–331
American silents 395–413
American West 298–299
American westerns 290–298
Ancient civilizations 784–785
Animals 812–825
Animation 676–753
Animation, Hollywood studio 676–704
Animation, international & independent 704–718
Animation, Japanese 719–753
Animation, TV 676–704
Anime 719–753
Apartheid 150–153
Archeology 781–785
Architecture 565–566
Art, applied 560–562
Art on video 544–566
Art techniques 562–565
Asian-American independents 455
Asian cinema 117–149
Asian world 145
Astronomy 838–841
Athletics 825–828
Australian cinema 205–209
Austrian cinema 74
Automobiles 841–845
Avant-garde cinema 482–492
Ballet 568–576
Baltic films 86
Belgian cinema 29, 116
Bengali cinema 146
Biography 793–798, 332–339
Blaxploitation films 531–534
Blues (music) 608–616
Bond, James—films 168
Brazilian cinema 53–54
British cinema 158–187
British classics 171–181
British culture 169–170
British silents 153
British television 188–202
Buddhism 149–150
Bulgarian cinema 104
Burkina Faso films 150
Cambodian films 144–145
Cameroon films 150
Canadian cinema 210–213
Caribbean cinema 54–55
Cartoons 676–753
Cartoons, children's 676–704
CD ROMS 863–874
Celtic culture 202–204
Child development 857
Children's activity videos 668
Children's feature films 660
Children's films—foreign language 671
Children's video 628–674
Chinese cinema 117–136
Cinema history 332–339
Civil rights (history) 449–455
Civil War 779–780
Classic American cinema 356–394
Comedy acts 534–536
Comedy, American 261–289
Comedy, British 181–185
Comedy, French 16–18
Comedy, silent 395–412
Comics & their creators 541
Commercials 539–541
Communism 86–89
Computers 845–846
Cuban cinema 49–55
Cult films 503–515
Cultural documentary 781–811
Czech cinema 99–101
Czechoslovak cinema 99–101
Dance 568–576
Danish films 75–79
Disarmament 798
Disney films 690
Documentary films 468–481
Documentary, cultural 781–811
Documentary, historical 756–801, 807–811
Dr. Who 199–202
Drama instruction 316
Drama performances 310–316
Dutch cinema 30–31
Eastern Europe 89–104
Educational & instructional 756–859
Educational films, history 807–811
Educational videos, other 845–859
Elvis Presley 536–537
English films 158–187
English language instruction 858
Environment 801–807
Estonian films 86
Ethiopian films 150
European cinema 2–105
Experimental films & video 482–492
Exploitation films 503–515, 531
Fairy Tales 645
Filipino cinema 145–146
Film history 332–339
Film production techniques 316–318
Filmmaker biographies 332–339
Fine arts 544–626
Finnish films 77, 79
Folk music 604–606
Foreign films 2–214
Foreign language for children 671
Foreign language instruction 154
French cinema 2–30
French classics 19–30
French comedy 16–18
French silents 153
Gay films 456–457
German cinema 63–73
German classics 68–73
Global issues 801–807
Gospel Music 606–608
Greek cinema 104–106
Guilty pleasures 494–531
Health videos 847
Hebrew language 107, 111, 113
Hindi cinema 146
Historical documentary 756–801, 807–811
Holland—films 30–31
Holocaust 774–777
Home economics 857
Hong Kong action cinema 124–135
Hong Kong cinema 118–124
Horror flicks 516–531
Hungarian cinema 101–103
Icelandic cinema 75–
Independents, African-American 443–447
Independents, American 426–447
Independents, Asian-American 455
Indian cinema 146–149
Instructional 756–860
International cinema 1–213
Iranian cinema 106–107
Irish features 202–204
Israeli cinema 107–110
Italian cinema 32–42
Italian classics 40–42
Italian silents 153
Ivory coast films 150
Japanese cinema 137–144
Japanimation 719–753
Jewish cinema 111–116
Judaism 111
Kennedys 797–798
Kids films 628–674
Korean cinema 136
Language arts 859–861
Language instruction 154–155
Latin American cinema 49–62
Latvian films 87
Lebanese cinema 116
Lesbian films 456–467
Libyan films 116
Literary adaptations 300–309
Literary documentaries 300–309
Lithuanian films 87
Malayalam cinema 145
Malaysian films 144
Mark Twain adaptations 308–309
Martial arts videos 124–135
Mathematics 838
Memoirs 793–798
Mideast, the 110
Monty Python 198–199
Movie previews 540–541

Movies about movies.......................... 332–339
Music instruction.............................. 623–625
Music on video 577–625
Music, blues...................................... 608–616
Music, folk.. 604–606
Music, gospel 606–608
Music, jazz, blues & r&b 608–616
Music, rhythm & blues...................... 608–616
Music, popular................................... 616–618
Music, rock 'n roll............................. 618–623
Music, other...................................... 616–618
Music, classical.................................. 586–595
Music, classical voice......................... 595–600
Music, country................................... 604–606
Music, world...................................... 600–604
Musicals.. 319–331
Native American culture 786–789
Nature 812–825
Netherlands—films.............................. 30–31
New age videos 847–862
New Zealand cinema 208–209
Nigerian films.................................... 151–152
North African films............................. 116–
Norwegian films 76–79
Nuclear arms race 801
Occult videos..................................... 861–862
Olympics 825
Opera 577–586
Outdoors 812–825
Outer Space 835–841
Painters, painting............................... 544–565
Parenting 857
Peace studies 857–858
Performance art.................................. 566–567
Performing arts instruction 316
Personal growth 847–857
Philippines, films 145–146
Philosophy... 785–786
Photography 558–560
Plays (filmed) 310
Playwrights 310
Poets & their works.................................. 302
Polish cinema.. 90–99
Politics 798–801
Pop music 616–618
Portuguese films... 48
Pre-school videos...................................... 649
Psychology 785
Quebecois cinema 213
Railroads.. 841–845
Rain forests 801–807
Religion 789–793
Religions, Eastern 149–150
Religious features 355–356
Rhythm & Blues.................................. 606–616
Rock 'n roll 618–623
Romanian cinema 104
Russian cinema 80–89
Russian documentaries........................... 87–89
Scandinavian cinema............................... 75–79
Sci-Fi films... 494–502
Science... 835–838
Scotland 169
Screen writing.. 316
Sculpture on video 544–558
Sengalese films 150
Serials 537–539
Sherlock Holmes mysteries 185–187
Ships, shipping.................................... 841–845
Silent cinema, American 395–413
Silent cinema, European 153–154
Silent cinema, Russian 85–86, 154
Silent comedy 395–412
Sing-a-longs 668
Social issues.. 798–811
South African cinema......................... 150–153
South American cinema 44–48
Soviet cinema.. 80–89
Space exploration 838–841
Spanish cinema 44–48
Spanish Civil War 48
Spiritual growth 847–857
Sports 825–828
Stagecraft 316
Swedish films 75–79
Swiss cinema 30
Sword & sandal epics 42
Taiwanese cinema 136
Television, American.......................... 414–423
Television, British 188–202
Television, commercials 539–541
Test preparation 858–859
Theatre training... 316
Theatre on screen....................................... 310
Trailers.. 539–541
Transportation 841–845
Travel.. 828–833
Tunisian cinema... 116
Turkish cinema 106
Ukrainian films.. 86
Unidentified Flying Objects....................... 862
Video art... 482–492
Vietnam war 777
Vietnamese films... 145
Visual arts 544–565
Wales 169–170
War documentaries 765–780
West, (American) films about............. 298–299
Westerns 290–298
Wonderworks 660
World War II 765–777
Writers & their works 302
Writing instruction 859
Yiddish cinema 111–116
Yugoslav cinema................................. 103–104
Zaire films 150
Zimbabwe films 152

CINEMA international

recent french cinema

The 317th Platoon
A brilliant evocation of the senselessness of war during the last days of the French occupation of Indochina, based on the director's own experiences of being taken prisoner at Dien Buen Phu. The film tells of the platoon's retreat, focusing on a career soldier and the commanding young lieutenant as they make their way through ambushes, betrayals, rain, jungle, villages, pain, disease and inexorable fatigue to inevitable annihilation. With awesome cinematography by Raoul Coutard. With Jacques Perrin, Bruno Cremer, Pierre Fabre and Manuel Zarzo. French with English subtitles.
VHS: S13224. $59.95.
Pierre Schoendoerffer, France, 1965, 100 mins.

36 Filette
On a Biarritz family vacation, the 14-year old daughter, a very bored teenager, falls in love with an older man, who takes her to discos, seduces and abandons her. Catherine Breillat in her third feature fashions an insightful drama about sexual politics and male hypocrisy. With Jean-Pierre Leaud and Jean-Francois Stevenin. French with English subtitles.
VHS: S12993. $19.98.
Catherine Breillat, France, 1988, 86 mins.

A la Mode
An adorable French romantic comedy tells the rags-to-riches tale of a talented young fashion designer who turns Paris on its ear at the same time that he's winning the hearts of the city's loveliest women. French with English subtitles.
VHS: S23479. $19.95.
Laser: Letterboxed. **LD74810. $39.99.**
Remy Duchemin, France, 1993, 89 mins.

Act of Aggression
Catherine Deneuve and Jean-Louis Trintignant star in this diabolical film about a man whose wife is murdered and who is driven to near-insanity until he tries to take revenge by his own hand. A tense, action-packed mystery. French with English subtitles.
VHS: S00016. $59.95.
Gerard Pires, France, 1982, 94 mins.

All the Mornings in the World
This film combines the fervor of passionate music making and young love in 17th century France in the story of cellist Marin Marais and his learning at the hands of teacher/composer Sainte-Colombe. Gerard Depardieu and his son Guillaume star as a musician in different stages of life, who must choose between his devotion to his instructor, his love for this instructor's daughter, and his art. French with English subtitles.
Laser: LD74487. $39.99.
Alain Corneau, France, 1992, 110 mins.

And God Created Woman
The first feature film by Vadim, and the spectacular debut of Brigitte Bardot as a blond orphan girl. English dubbed.
VHS: S00047. $29.98.
Roger Vadim, France, 1957, 90 mins.

Anderson Platoon
One of the great films about Vietnam, directed by Pierre Schoendoerffer, the documentary focuses on an integrated combat unit led by Black West Pointer Lt. Joseph B. Anderson, and captures the tension, anger, hopelessness and pathos of armed conflict. Winner of the Academy Award for Best Documentary Feature.
VHS: S02404. $19.95.
Pierre Schoendoerffer, France, 1967, 65 mins.

Augustin
Jean-Chretien Sibertin Blanc stars as a man with a peculiar job offset by dreams of greatness. During the day he investigates brain dead cases for an insurance company, but his own dream is to succeed as an actor. This comedy of aspirations takes on a hopeful complication when he gets a part opposite a French film idol. He will play a waiter, and in order to prepare, he actually works as one, which results in humorous consequences. *Omnibus*, the short which won both an Academy Award and a Palme D'Or, is also on this video. French with English subtitles.
VHS: S28387. $59.95.
Anne Fontaine, France, 1995, 61 mins.

Award Winning French Shorts
Three shorts from the 8th International Festival at Oberhausen: *Le The a la Menthe*, directed by Pierre Kafien, with some French dialog but no subtitles; *End of Summer*, from the National Film Board of Canada, in French with subtitles and English narration; and *Le Poulet*, a comedy from Claude Berri. France/Canada, 1962.
VHS: S02583. $29.95.

Barbarella
The film Jane Fonda most wants to forget. On the planet Sogo, where sin is at a discount, Barbarella (Fonda) runs athwart an evil queen (Anita Pallenberg) and her petty henchman (Milo O'Shea), who threaten our heroine's less-than-intact virtue with an overdose of pleasure. But to the rescue flies an oak tree masquerading as an angel (John Phillip Law), and in the end goodness triumphs, sort of. Fonda sheds her clothes, Law flaps his wings, and in general, everyone acts dotty in this film adaptation of the popular French comic strip. Script by Terry Southern, imaginative sets and top-notch camerawork by Claude Renoir.
VHS: S00095. $19.95.
Laser: Widescreen. **LD75155. $34.98.**
Roger Vadim, France, 1968, 98 mins.

Barocco
Isabelle Adjani and Gerard Depardieu are a terrific couple. Depardieu is a thief who kills a man and takes his place, including his girlfriend. The two plot blackmail and other intrigues that can only go bad. This over-the-top thriller achieves a singular stylistic unity. French with English subtitles.
VHS: S23291. $79.95.
Andre Techine, France, 1976, 102 mins.

Beaumarchais
From the director of *La Cage aux Folles* comes an elegant, wicked, witty portrait of the legendary French playwright Pierre-Augustin Caron de Beaumarchais. Author of the comic plays *The Marriage of Figaro* and *The Barber of Seville*, which were made into operas by Mozart and Rossini, Beaumarchais was also an inventor, playwright, diplomat, playboy and Royal spy. With Fabrice Luchini, Manuel Blanc, Sandrine Kiberlain and Michel Serrault. "Glorious! Giddy! Inspired! Light and fanciful... sparkles with wit" (*LA Times*). French with English subtitles.
VHS: S34734. $94.98.
Edouard Molinaro, France, 1997, 100 mins.

The Best Way
Marc, the aggressive athletic director at a boys' summer camp, discovers the drama teacher dressed in women's clothes, and is shocked by his attraction to him. Their tense confrontation results in Marc forcing him to confront his suppressed sexuality. French with English subtitles.
VHS: S00120. $49.95.
Claude Miller, France, 1982, 85 mins.

Between Heaven and Earth
A fable with serious overtones. Carmen Maura plays Maria, an ambitious television journalist who has a series of surreal dreams. She falls into a profound moral and spiritual crisis when she communicates with her unborn child and believes the baby is unprepared and unwilling to be born. A prominent scientist and a young man in her apartment building try to help her decide the child's fate. "Entertaining and provocative, Carmen Maura is great" (Paul Wunder, WBAI Radio). With Jean-Pierre Cassel, Didier Bezace, Samuel Mussen and Andre Delvaux. French with English subtitles.
VHS: S20076. $79.95.
Marion Hansel, France, 1993, 80 mins.

Bim, the Little Donkey and Dream of the Wild Horses
The first film by the director of *The Red Balloon, Bim* is a delightful story of a lovable donkey who is taken away from a small boy to become the pet of a very rich family. The boy's efforts to get his donkey back lead to all sorts of adventures. *Dream of the Wild Horses* is a landmark short film by Georges Franju.
VHS: S01691. $29.95.
Albert Lamorisse, France, 1948, 45 mins.

Blue Jeans
A young boy is sent to England to improve his English, where he has his first experience with the opposite sex. When his girl friend takes up with a more experienced young man, the young boy confides in one of his supervisors and is taken advantage of. French with English subtitles.
VHS: S00158. $59.95.
Hugues des Roziers, France, 1978, 80 mins.

By the Blood of Others
Directed by Marc Simenon, the son of the famous mystery novelist, with Mariangela Melato. In a small village, a deranged man is holding two women hostage in an abandoned farmhouse. The whole village faces the problem of how to free the women without spilling blood. More than just a tense mystery, the film is an acute study of moral responsibility and a detailed picture of small-town French provincial life. French with English subtitles.
VHS: S06502. $59.95.
Marc Simenon, France, 1973, 90 mins.

Bye Bye
Reminiscent of *Kids, Salaam Bombay* and *Pixote*, this realistic slice of urban teen life in modern-day France is a serious yet sensitive tale of two young French-Arab brothers dealing with the clash of cultures and generations in Marseilles. After a family tragedy, Ismael and Mouloud leave Paris and end up on the doorstep of their uncle and family. Once there, the two brothers are pulled apart as one is seduced by the streets and its life of drugs and crime, while the other desperately seeks to rescue him without falling to its temptations. French with English subtitles.
VHS: S31670. $19.98.
Karim Dridi, France, 1996, 107 mins.

Camille Claudel
Intense performances by Isabelle Adjani and Gerard Depardieu add fire to this adaptation of the family-"authorized" biography of overlooked sculptress Camille Claudel. After years of living with master sculptor Auguste Rodin (Depardieu) as pupil and lover, Claudel fell into a paranoid depression when he left her. Her disapproving family had her committed to a mental institution, where she wasted away for the remaining 30 years of her life. Adjani won a Cesar for her performance in this tragic story. French with English subtitles.
VHS: S12987. $19.98.
Laser: LD70900. $49.95.
Bruno Nuytten, France, 1990, 149 mins.

Chanel Solitaire
This American-French co-production covers the first 40 years of the life of Coco Chanel, the self-made designer who changed the shape of fashion. Starring Marie-France Pisier, *Chanel Solitaire* interweaves the professional with the personal. With Rutger Hauer, Timothy Dalton, Karen Black and Brigitte Fossey. In English.
VHS: S01509. $19.99.
George Kaczender, France/USA, 1981, 120 mins.

Chasing Butterflies
A whimsical comedy of social decay from one of the least-known masters of world cinema. Set in a charming French village sealed off from modern life, the contemporary world begins to intrude via radio reports of terrorism, foreigners snapping up property and greedy relatives settling in. Narda Blanchett stars in this formally beautiful yet unsentimentally nostalgic film. French with English subtitles.
VHS: S26463. $79.95.
Otar Iosseliani, France, 1993, 115 mins.

The City of Lost Children
This cross between a children's fairy tale and a hellish sci-fi nightmare questions the very nature of dreams, fantasy and the hope of a collective social fabric. Though heavy with ambition, the fantastic sets and backdrops, together with superb effects, animate a truly engrossing cast of characters. These range from a villainous pair of Siamese twins to hitmen fleas. Amidst the tumult, children struggle in a world dominated by crime and perverse ambitions. Jean-Paul Gaultier did the costumes. French with English subtitles.
VHS: S28392. $99.99.
Laser: Letterboxed. **LD75826. $34.95.**
Jean-Pierre Jeunet/Marc Caro, France, 1995, 112 mins.

Colonel Chabert
Gerard Depardieu stars as the returning war hero who is not supposed to return. Now he faces another battle at home to claim that which is rightfully his. Honore de Balzac's novel is treated to a lush production. Also features Fanny Ardant, Fabrice Luchini and Andre Dussollier. French with English subtitles.
VHS: S24953. $14.95.
Yves Angelo, France, 1992, 111 mins.

Cyrano de Bergerac
Gerard Depardieu is magnificent as the poetic soldier with the prominent proboscis. Based on the classic play by Rostand in which a 17th century swordsman proves inarticulate only when it comes to expressing his love for his cousin Roxanne face to face. Packed with pageantry, poetry and robust performances. With Anne Brochet, Jacques Weber, and some 2000 extras. French with English subtitles.
VHS: S14784. $19.98.
Laser: LD72215. $49.95.
Jean-Paul Rappeneau, France, 1989, 135 mins.

Deadly Sanctuary
Banned in Europe, although now it's difficult to tell why, and based on the writings of the Marquis de Sade, with an international cast including Jack Palance, Klaus Kinski, Sylva Koscina, Akim Tamiroff and Mercedes McCambridge. In English.
VHS: S04784. $39.95.
Jess (Jesus) Franco, France/USA, 1970, 93 mins.

Diva

A breathtaking series of visual images in this stylish romantic thriller; at the heart of the film is an opera-intoxicated 18-year-old mail carrier who becomes unwittingly entangled in a web of murder, intrigue and passion. French dialog with English subtitles.
VHS: S00348. $29.95.
Laser: Widescreen. **LD75998. $69.95.**
DVD: DV60128. $29.98.
Jean-Jacques Beineix, France, 1982, 123 mins.

Dupont Lajoie (Rape of Innocence)

Jean Carmet stars in this tense dramatic film that explores French racism. At a campground where tourists gather, Carnet's character, Lajoie, accidentally kills the girlfriend of his teenage son when she resists his sexual assault. To save his own life he insinuates that Arabs did it, and then begins a hateful campaign of vengeance that has a surprising outcome. French with English subtitles.
VHS: S22680. $59.95.
Yves Boisset, France, 1974, 103 mins.

The Elegant Criminal (L'Elegant Criminel)

Francis Girod's terrifying study of France's most diabolical 19th century serial killer, a charismatic and elusive romantic figure whose constantly shifting persona—poet, thief, killer and hero—thrilled the public. With Daniel Auteuil, Jacques Duby and Jean Davy. French with English subtitles.
VHS: S17706. $19.98.
Francois Girod, France, 1990, 120 mins.

Elle Voit des Nains Partout

A clever adaptation of the Cafe Theatre Show, this is a very modern fairy tale complete with a wild Tom Thumb brought up by the Nuns of Eternal Help, Little Red Riding Hood, who delivers wine for her father's liquor company, and Snow White, who doesn't get to marry Prince Charming. French with English subtitles.
VHS: S00401. $59.95.
Jean-Claude Sussfeld, France, 1983, 83 mins.

Emmanuelle

The first European erotic film to receive critical acclaim and go on to international success, *Emmanuelle* is the story of Sylvia Kristel, the naive, inexperienced wife of a French diplomat, who discovers what life (and sex) is all about when she joins her husband in Bangkok and meets some of his uninhibited friends. French with English subtitles.
VHS: S00406. $19.95.
Just Jaeckin, France, 1974, 94 mins.

Emmanuelle 2

Sylvia Kristel reprises the role that made her an international star, in this classic sequel to the erotic blockbuster hit *Emanuelle*. French with English subtitles.
VHS: S34239. $19.98.
Francis Giacobetti/Francis Leroi, France, 1975, 92 mins.

Entre Nous

Set in Lyons in 1950, two women are drawn together by postwar discontent. Isabelle Huppert and Miou-Miou are both trapped in middle class marriages, and find they can offer each other something their men cannot. Their relationship deepens into a dependency that eventually bursts the confines of the provincial society around them. French with English subtitles.
VHS: S00410. $19.98.
Diane Kurys, France, 1983, 100 mins.

Every Other Weekend

Nathalie Baye stars as a once-famous television actress who gave up her kids to pursue her career. Now she's hoping to revive her relationship with her two young children in this heartbreaking tale of love, loss and the eternal hope for a second chance. "It's a triumph! A tender road picture that's dramatic, intimate and real, in a way American movies rarely are" (Jeff Craig, *Sixty Second Preview*). French with English subtitles.
VHS: S29781. $89.95.
Nicole Garcia, France, 1989, 100 mins.

Farinelli

Farinelli, an 18th-century castrato, was one of Europe's most acclaimed singers. This lavishly designed, brilliantly costumed film focuses on his troubled artistic and personal life as he conquers the opera world and has women faint in his presence, yet needs his brother to consummate his sexual conquests. Corbiau ingeniously recreates the unique castrato sound by electronically blending a male and female voice; Jeroen Krabbe appears as Friedrich Handel. French with English subtitles.
VHS: S26396. $19.95.
Laser: LD75080. $34.95.
Gerard Corbiau, France/Belgium/Italy, 1995, 115 mins.

The Fifth Element

In this haute couture-designed, futuristic tour-de-force from Luc Besson, Bruce Willis stars as a cab driver who becomes an unsuspecting hero when he picks up the kind of fare that only comes along every 5000 years: a perfect being, a perfect beauty, a perfect weapon (Milla Jovovich). Together they must save the world. The most expensive French film in history. With Gary Oldman, Chris Tucker and fashions by Gautier. In English.
VHS: S32390. $19.95.
Laser: LD76371. $39.95.
DVD: DV60158. $24.98.
Luc Besson, France/USA, 1997, 126 mins.

Fort Saganne

This lavish recreation of the Foreign Legion genre stars Gerard Depardieu and Catherine Deneuve in one of the most expensive French films ever made. The epic film follows the story of an extraordinary leader denied the fruits of his labor because of his peasant background. He somehow manages to rise to a position of prominence. Just when he can rightly enjoy the benefits of his rank, the murderous Algerian revolt of 1914 occurs. French with English subtitles.
VHS: S21510. $89.95.
Alain Corneau, France, 1984, 180 mins.

Franz

Two women take up residence at a boarding home that had previously been an all-male residence. One interacts with the group, while the other devotes her attentions to a single man at the home, Jacques Brel. A melodrama that entwines the past and present. French with English subtitles.
VHS: S01668. $19.95.
Jacques Brel, France, 1972, 88 mins.

French Twist

Loli (Victoria Abril) thought she had the perfect marriage until she realized her husband (Alain Chabat) had been cheating on her for years. When Loli takes a mistress herself (Josiane Balasko, the film's director), her philandering husband must pour on the charm to become his own wife's lover again. Also stars Miguel Bose, Catherine Hiegel and many actors from the esteemed Comedie Francaise. French with English subtitles.
VHS: S29824. $99.99.
Laser: LD75966. $39.99.
Josiane Balasko, France, 1996, 100 mins.

Germinal

Gerard Depardieu stars in this sweeping film based on Emile Zola's masterful novel. A simple but honest and charismatic miner takes on a heroic quest for justice that leads him and his entire community to a fateful end. This tale of unforgivable wrongs stirs the soul. French with English subtitles.
VHS: S22537. $19.95.
Laser: LD74612. $39.95.
Claude Berri, France, 1993, 158 mins.

Grain of Sand

An incisive study of a woman's attempt at independence stars Delphine Seyrig as an unemployed woman in Paris who tries to reconcile her past with her present. Solange isolates herself from the world around her and decides to go back into the past, to a town in Corsica where she believes she will find the only man she has ever loved. Based on a true story, *The Grain of Sand* (*Le Grain de Sable*) is a moving film and a stunning directing debut by Pomme Meffre. With Delphine Seyrig, Genevieve Fontanel, Coralie Seyrig and Michel Aumont. French with English subtitles.
VHS: S03718. $59.95.
Pomme Meffre, France, 1984, 90 mins.

The Green House

In the waning days of World War II, a crusty Parisian zoo director weaves a fantastic tale to protect his granddaughter from the horrors of war. Like his classic film, *King of Hearts*, director Philippe De Broca creates a visually stunning fairy tale that tugs at the heart as well as the mind. With Claude Rich. "A brilliant little gem of a movie that will lodge firmly in your heart and head" (Dr. Joy Browne, WOR Radio Network). French with English subtitles.
VHS: S30942. $59.95.
Philippe de Broca, France, 1996, 93 mins.

Hate (La Haine)

Winner of Best Director at the Cannes Film Festival 1995, Mathieu Kassovitz's harsh black-and-white drama of dispossessed urban youth is an unremitting look at the violence, unemployment and racial hatred that divide the young of contemporary France. Set in a Paris suburb over the course of 24 hours, the film is remarkable for the verve of its authentic performances and its gritty, realistic feel. French with English subtitles. Letterboxed.
VHS: S29387. $19.95.
Mathieu Kassovitz, France, 1995, 91 mins.

Her and She and Him

From the Audubon collection, a tale of sex and submission, where young Greta, with nothing but her beauty and guitar, arrives in Paris, and soon finds herself with a lustful, lonely woman. Dubbed in English.
VHS: S34132. $29.95.
Max Pecas, France, 1972, 90 mins.

The Holes (Les Gaspards)

One day a busload of tourists suddenly sinks into the ground. So do a few buildings, most of the police force, and some of the choicest beauties in Paris. With Philippe Noiret, Charles Denner and Gerard Depardieu. Dubbed in English.
VHS: S14553. $59.95.
Pierre Tchernia, France, 1972, 92 mins.

The Horseman on the Roof

In a world ravaged by revolution and a sweeping epidemic, two strangers—a beautiful countess (Juliet Binoche) searching for her family and a handsome renegade (Olivier Martinez) who is being hunted by assassins—discover their only chance for survival is each other. Based on the novel by Jean Giono. "A swashbuckling romance adventure" (*Wall Street Journal*). French with English subtitles.
VHS: S30831. $19.95.
Laser: LD76103. $39.99.
Jean-Paul Rappeneau, France, 1995, 135 mins.

Icy Breasts

A top-notch suspense thriller starring Alain Delon as a detective trying to prevent his lovely psychotic client, Mirelle Darc, from killing her lovers. A well-tooled thriller with a stunning climax. French with English subtitles.
VHS: S04246. $59.95.
Georges Lautner, France, 1975, 105 mins.

Indochine

Regis Wargnier's epic is set during the French occupation of Southeast Asia in the 1930s. Catherine Deneuve plays a plantation owner who searches for her adopted Vietnamese daughter Camille (Linh Dan Pham) after the young woman falls in love and becomes a communist revolutionary. "This intimate and tautly scripted work interweaves layers of deep affection with stirring historical details of 30s French Indochina, maintaining throughout an unshakable tension of a world about to change" (*Toronto Festival of Festivals*). Winner of the 1992 Academy Award for Best Foreign Language Film. French with English subtitles.
VHS: S20220. $19.95.
Laser: LD72330. $39.95.
Regis Wargnier, France, 1992, 160 mins.

Invitation au Voyage

The title comes from the poet Baudelaire, the film tells of a young man's plunge into the twilight world of his own desires as he travels the modern landscape. Winner of special honors at the Cannes Film Festival. French with English subtitles.
VHS: S00635. $19.95.
Peter Del Monte, France, 1982, 90 mins.

Ivan and Abraham

Winner at the Cannes Film Festival, this powerful film is the story of the friendship of Abraham, a volatile Jewish boy, and Ivan, an older Christian boy, who flee 1930s Poland, where political tensions are mounting, to the vast and perilous countryside. The runaways are followed by Aaron, a young Communist outlaw, and Abraham's teenage sister, Rachel, whose love for Aaron has estranged her from her family. Expertly interweaving personal drama and and historical perspective, the film centers on these four outcasts as they try to detach themselves from a world hurtling into chaos and violence. "Dazzling in its beauty, its audacity, its intelligence, its subtlety, its freedom" (Claude Lanzmann, director of *Shoah*). Yiddish, Polish, Russian and Gypsy dialog with English subtitles. Letterboxed.
VHS: S31191. $89.95.
Yolande Zauberman, France, 1993, 105 mins.

Jacques Lacan's Psychoanalysis Part One

A priceless document for anyone interested in contemporary thought and analysis. In interviews with Jacques-Alain Miller, Jacques Lacan, the famous French psychoanalyst called by many the French Freud, exposes with unexpected simplicity his most complex theories of the unconscious; the cure, the difference between psychoanalysis and psychotherapy, love and women. "For anyone hoping to understand the institutionalization of Freudian thought and the challenge Lacan represents, this is an essential work." French with English subtitles.
VHS: S18142. $69.95.
Benoit Jacquot, France, 1974, 60 mins.

Jean de Florette
A marvelous tale of greed and intolerance from the novel by Pagnol about a city hunchback who inherits a valuable piece of property in rural France only to have his efforts thwarted by the villainy of his venal neighbor. With Gerard Depardieu, Yves Montand, Daniel Auteuil, Elisabeth Depardieu and Ernestine Mazurownas as little Manon. French with English subtitles. 122 mins.
VHS: S07522. $19.98.
Claude Berri, France, 1987, 122 mins.

Jean de Florette/Manon of the Spring
Together for the first time on laser disc. *Jean de Florette* is the story of a hunchback farmer battling a drought and struggling against his scheming neighbors. Its sequel, *Manon of the Spring*, is the story of Jean's daughter Manon, the wild shepherdess, repulsed by the attentions of the remorseful Ugolin. Starring Gerard Depardieu, Yves Montand and Emmanuelle Beart.
Laser: Widescreen. **LD74934. $99.99.**
Claude Berri, France, 1987, 235 mins.

Jean Gabin
The great French actor is remembered by some of the writers, directors and co-stars who worked with him through 50 years and 100 films, including Rene Clement, Jean Dellanoy, Denys de la Patelliere, Michel Audiard, Granier Deferre, Jean Desailly, Francois Arnoul, Lino Ventura, Danielle Darrieux and Madeleine Renaud. With clips from *Pepe le Moko, Grande Illusion, La Bete Humaine, Le Chat* and many others. Narrated by Nadia Gray. 1978, 60 mins.
VHS: S31572. $59.95.

Josepha
Michel (Claude Brasseur) and Josepha (Miou-Miou) are husband and wife, actor and actress. On a movie location, Josepha has an affair but then decides to re-join her husband in order to "remake" the man she used to love. A critically-acclaimed, poignant examination of passion and anger. English dubbed.
VHS: S00658. $59.95.
Christopher Frank, France, 1983, 100 mins.

Julia
In this erotic drama, a woman tries to lose her virginity while vacationing in the Swiss Alps. With Silvia Kristel, Jean-Claude Bouillon and Terry Today. In English.
VHS: S35243. $19.95.
Sigi Rothmund, France, 1974, 83 mins.

Justine de Sade
An adaptation of the Marquis de Sade's work *Huguette Boisvert*, depicting the life of a young country girl initiated into the Marquis' inspired practices of sadism. In English.
VHS: S35244. $19.95.
Claude Piersen, France, 1979, 90 mins.

L'Amour en Herbe (Budding Love)
Pascal Meynier and Guilhaine Dubos star in this passionate film about forbidden teenage love. When Pascal's character fails at school, his parents realize he has something on his mind. It turns out to be his lovely 17-year-old friend, Martine. Though forbidden to see her, he remains true to his lover until betrayal intervenes. French with English subtitles.
VHS: S22679. $59.95.
Roger Andrieux, France, 1977, 100 mins.

L'Annee des Meduses
The most erotically charged film since *Last Tango*. A love battle between a nymphet (Valerie Kaprisky) and a gigolo (Bernard Giradeau). The combat is fought on the beaches of the South of France. French with English subtitles.
VHS: S05210. $69.95.
Christopher Frank, France, 1984, 110 mins.

L'Escorte
"Call it Pasolini lite or the gay version of Renoir's *Boudu Sauve des Eaux*, *L'Escorte* is a wry little comedy of manners about how a hustler upsets the lives of a middle-class same-sex couple" (Dimitri Katadotis). French with English subtitles.
VHS: S31736. $79.95.
Denis Langlois, France, 1996, 91 mins.

L'Etat Sauvage
This thriller is set in the 1960s in an African nation, which is struggling to create itself after independence from colonial rule. A UNESCO official returns looking for his wife and finds her living with a powerful black minister in the new government. Racial and sexual prejudices are stripped bare, as the fight begins to end this love affair. With Jacques Dutronc, Marie-Christine Barrault and Michel Piccoli. "Brutally frank!" (Kathleen Carroll, *New York Daily News*). French with English subtitles.
VHS: S14988. $59.95.
Laser: Widescreen. **LD71610. $49.95.**
Francois Girod, France, 1978, 111 mins.

L'Homme Blesse (The Wounded Man)
The sensitive story of a French teenager and his discovery of his own homosexuality, this film directed by Patrice Chereau received the French Cesar. Henri, the teenager, tries to stop an attack on a man in a public toilet, is given a sexy kiss by the attacker, and discovers that he is strongly attracted to men. French with English subtitles.
VHS: S06588. $79.95.
Patrice Chereau, France, 1984, 90 mins.

La Grande Bouffe
Marcello Mastroianni, Philippe Noiret, Ugo Tognazzi and Michel Piccoli star in this strange, depraved comedy which was a 1970's worldwide sensation. The four men—victims of their appetites—retire to a Parisian villa, where they fill their systems with an overload of carnal pleasures until they die in a blow-out of orgiastic over-indulgence. French with English subtitles.
VHS: S26480. $79.95.
Marco Ferreri, France/Italy, 1973, 125 mins.

La Jetee/ An Occurrence at Owl Creek Bridge
One of the most challenging films ever made, Chris Marker's neo-science fiction film is set in a ruined France after World War III, in which a man's vivid childhood experience allows him to travel forward and backward in time. As a grown man, he meets the girl he had glimpsed as a child at the airport, falls in love with her, chooses to remain in the past, but is executed by those who hold power in the future. France, 1962, 29 mins. Also contains *An Occurrence at Owl Creek Bridge*, directed by Robert Enrico and based on a short story by Ambrose Bierce, which tells the tale of a man who is about to be hanged when the rope suddenly snaps and he is able to escape. Unfortunately, his newly found freedom is short-lived. USA, 1962, 27 mins.
VHS: S06274. $39.95.

La Lectrice
The fabulous French actress Miou-Miou has the title role of a woman who makes her living reading to her varied clientele. Playing her role as storyteller with increasing confidence, Miou-Miou becomes teacher, confidant, provocateur and confessor to her clients. A seductive and humorous comedy that has captured the attention of literate movie goers on an international scale. An unusual film directed with a deft, wry touch by Michel Deville. French with English subtitles.
VHS: S10759. $19.98.
Michel Deville, France, 1989, 98 mins.

La Passante
Romy Schneider in a dual role—as Elsa, a German refugee, and as Lina, the wife of a contemporary world leader. A story of two lovers compelled by action, mystery and political drama. With Michel Piccoli and Maria Schell. French with English subtitles.
VHS: Out of print. For rental only.
Laser: LD71087. $49.95.
Jacques Rouffio, France, 1983, 106 mins.

La Petite Sirene
The shocking subject matter of this film—a love affair between a 14 year old girl and a 40 year old man—is handled with a great deal of restraint by French director Roger Andrieux. At first the situation is rather innocent, almost funny. But as the movie progresses things take a dangerous turn, and the climax is jolting. The sex scenes are handled with delicacy; more is suggested than shown. Starring Laura Alexis and Philippe Leotard. French with English subtitles.
VHS: S13818. $19.98.
Roger Andrieux, France, 1985, 104 mins.

La Promesse
Igor and his father Roger run an apartment scam, renting to illegal immigrants and working them illegally. Immigrant Amidou is injured when he falls off a scaffold and Igor makes a promise that exposes the different values of Igor, Roger and Amidou's wife, Assita.
VHS: S34739. $94.98.
Jean-Pierre Dardenne/Luc Dardenne, Belgium/France/Luxembourg, 1996, 90 mins.

La Vie Continue
Annie Girardot stars as a middle aged woman struggling with three children after her husband suddenly dies of a heart attack. With Jean-Pierre Cassel. English dubbed.
VHS: S01709. $59.95.
Moshe Mizrahi, France, 1980

The Last Train
Jean-Louis Trintignant and Romy Schneider star in this dramatic story of longing set just after the onset of World War II. Though the main character sets off in search of his pregnant wife, he finds instead a passionate entanglement with another woman. Based on a George Simenon novel. Dubbed in English.
VHS: S29474. $19.95.
Pierre Granier-Deferre, France, 1973, 101 mins.

Latcho Drom
In Romany, "Latcho Drom" means "safe journey." This haunting, vibrant, seamless, award-winning film is neither a documentary nor a fiction film but a musical that tells the story of the historic odyssey of the Gypsies from India to Egypt and the pain and joy of being in an outsider culture. With gypsy musicians from India, Egypt, Turkey, Romania, Hungary, Slovakia, France and Spain. Winner of the Prix Gervais at the Cannes Film Festival. Romany with English subtitles. "Remarkable…exuberant, passionate…at times ecstatic" (Michael Wilmington, *Chicago Tribune*).
VHS: S29702. $89.95.
Tony Gatlif, France, 1992/93, 103 mins.

Le Complot
Inspired by historical events, Rene Gainville's intelligent political thriller focuses on France's bitter war with Algeria and the group of disenchanted Army officers who opposed DeGaulle's decision to pull out. In a desperate attempt to save the colony, they attempt a coup. Top-notch cast includes Michel Bouquet and Jean Rochefort caught in a cat and mouse game between rebels, politicos and police. French with English subtitles.
VHS: S13281. $29.95.
Rene Gainville, France, 1973, 120 mins.

Le Crabe Tambour
Based on the career of French naval officer Pierre Guillaume and told through the recollections of his fellow officers, *Le Crabe Tambour* covers some 20 years of French history as Guillaume patrolled the Mekong River in Vietnam by boat in the 50's, then, taken prisoner, spent three years in a Vietnamese jail, and finally participated in the unsuccessful 1961 rebellion of French army generals against Charles de Gaulle. Shot by Charles de Gaulle, the film often recalls Joseph Conrad, and is "one of the grandest, most beautiful adventure movies in years…successfully maintains its epic sweep from start to finish" (*N.Y. Times*). French with English subtitles.
VHS: S08513. $59.95.
Pierre Schoendoerffer, France, 1977, 120 mins.

Le Jupon Rouge
In this lesbian menage-a-trois drama, shifting attractions are played out between three women of different ages. The eldest, Bacha (legendary Italian actress Alida Valli), is a human rights activist and concentration camp survivor. Her younger fashion-designer friend Manuela (Marie Christine Barrault) is her primary emotional support. When Manuela meets the beautiful Claude (Guillemette Groban), the two begin a relationship that incites Bacha's intense jealousy. French with English subtitles.
VHS: S32214. $39.99.
Genevieve Lefebvre, France, 1987, 90 mins.

Les Choses de la Vie
A sensitive businessman, injured in an automobile accident, reflects on his wife and his mistress, both of whom he dearly loves. Though a stylishly sophisticated romantic, Les *Choses de la Vie* builds to a deeply moving examination of the fragility of life relationships. "An extraordinary film" (*Le Figaro*). Starring Romy Schneider, Michel Piccoli, Lea Massari. French with English subtitles.
VHS: S12820. $29.95.
Claude Sautet, France, 1970, 90 mins.

Les Miserables
Jean-Paul Belmondo stars as a retired fighter inspired by the Victor Hugo novel. This illiterate boxer does everything he can, at great risk to his own life, to save a desperate Jewish family during the Nazi domination of France. It won a Golden Globe for its grand sweep and epic proportions. French with English subtitles.
VHS: S27648. $29.98.
Laser: LD75557. $39.98.
Claude Lelouch, France, 1995, 175 mins.

Les Violons du Bal
The relationship between art and personal sacrifice is explored in Michel Drach's film about a brilliant young filmmaker obsessed with chronicling his family's extraordinary efforts to escape Nazi-occupied France. Marie-Jose Nat, the director's wife, won the Best Actress Award at Cannes. With Jean-Louis Trintignant. French with English subtitles.
VHS: S17927. $29.95.
Michel Drach, France, 1974, 110 mins.

Life Is a Long Quiet River
An understated social comedy about a nurse who takes revenge on her indifferent lover, a married doctor, by switching two newborn babies. The narrative picks up 12 years later, as the two radically different families adjust to the severe changes when the children are returned to their rightful parents. Chatiliez dissects the mores of the two families, the upper middle class Le Quesnoys and the nefarious, criminal Groseilles. With Benoit Magimel, Helene Vincent and Daniel Gelin. French with English subtitles.
VHS: S18931. $79.95.
Etienne Chatiliez, France, 1987, 90 mins.

The Little Thief
The story of a female teenage delinquent in France who was reformed by the power of the photographic image. Based on a treatment never filmed by the late director Francois Truffaut and completed by Claude Miller. Story mirrors *400 Blows* in tone and subject matter. French with English subtitles.
VHS: S12223. $19.95.
Claude Miller, France, 1989, 100 mins.

Lola
Jacques Demy's *Lola* is a precisely constructed film about love, "with an almost balletic sense of rhythm set against the urban background of Nantes." The beautiful Anouk Aimee plays Lola, a cabaret dancer, who is courted by her childhood friend. But she is still in love with Michel, who had left her with their child when he went off to seek his fortune. After spending the night with another man, Michel reappears, rich, and takes her away. French with English subtitles.
VHS: S10738. $59.95.
Jacques Demy, France, 1961, 91 mins.

Love After Love
Isabelle Huppert stars along with Hippolyte Giradot and Bernard Giraudeau in this complex story of love and sex. A novelist famed for turning her life into salable fiction must confront changing times. As the '70s generation confronts the '90s, this character finds that the expectations of romance and the fundamental needs of love are often contradictory and comic. French with English subtitles.
VHS: S26608. $19.98.
Diane Kurys, France, 1994, 104 mins.

Love and the Frenchwoman
Seven French directors tackle the steamy subject of French women in love in this often witty omnibus film. With a cast of top actors, including Jean-Paul Belmondo, Marie-Jose Nat, Annie Girardot and Martine Carol. Episodes directed by Michel Boisrond, Jean-Paul Le Chanois, Christian-Jaque, Rene Clair, Jean Delannoy, Henri Verneuil and Henri Decoin. France, 1960, 143 mins. English dubbed.
VHS: S00774. $29.95.

Love Without Pity
Hippo is a modern bohemian, a Belmondo for the 90s, no job, no hopes, no cares—until he meets a beautiful and successful graduate student. Thus begins an obsessive and intensely passionate affair that consumes them both. Set in Paris, *Love without Pity* is a hard-edged, existential romance for today, about an alienated generation facing tomorrow. Starring Hippolyte Girardot and Mireille Perrier. This acclaimed film was writer/director Eric Rochant's theatrical debut. French with yellow English subtitles.
VHS: S15271. $19.98.
Laser: LD71618. $39.95.
Eric Rochant, France, 1991, 95 mins.

Lumiere & Company
To commemorate the centennial of the Lumiere brothers' first "motion picture," David Lynch, Spike Lee, Wim Wenders, Zhang Yimou, John Boorman, Arthur Penn, Peter Greenaway, Claude LeLouch, Costa Gavras, James Ivory and a host of leading international filmmakers created their own one-minute Lumiere film. Using the restored original camera, each director offered his own signature style to the film. Sandwiched between these 40 exciting, eclectic shorts are intriguing interviews with the filmmakers. A must-see for all movie fans, *Lumiere & Company* speaks for the passion, beauty and visionary dream of this 100-year-old art form. English and French with English subtitles.
VHS: S30468. $19.98.
DVD: DV60162. $24.98.
Sarah Moon, France, 1996, 88 mins.

Ma Vie en Rose
Ludovic is a seven-year-old boy who dresses, acts like and is convinced he's a girl, and wants to marry his next door neighbor and best friend Jerome—who also happens to be the son of his father's boss. For Ludovic, nothing is more natural than to change his gender, and he truly believes a miracle will happen. But as the innocent Ludovic tries to set things right, he must deal with the gay phobias, fears and prejudices of the adult world. With a wonderful, self-possessed performance by 11-year-old Georges du Fresne. Winner of The Golden Globe for Best Foreign Language Film. "Deft and wildly colorful" (Janet Maslin, *The New York Times*).
VHS: S34329. $98.99.
Alain Berliner, France/Belgium/Great Britain, 1997, 89 mins.

Madame Butterfly
This award-winning film from the popular Puccini opera is the heart-wrenching story of a beautiful young geisha who forsakes her family, and ultimately her life, for her American husband. With an international cast of opera stars, including Ying Huang, Richard Troxell of the New York City Opera, Ning Liang and Richard Cowan. Italian with English subtitles.
VHS: S31204. $24.95.
Frederic Mitterand, France, 1995, 129 mins.

Madame Rosa
Simone Signoret stars in the role of a Holocaust survivor forced into prostitution who befriends and shelters the children of the dispossessed, the prostitutes, Jews and Arabs who can no longer provide or care for their children. With Ben Youb, Claude Dauphin and filmmaker Costa-Gavras. French with English subtitles.
VHS: S00794. $24.95.
Moshe Mizrahi, France, 1977, 104 mins.

Mademoiselle
Tony Richardson's film about sexual obsession is based on a screenplay by Jean Genet. Set in a remote French village, the mayor, chief of police and a virginal school teacher played by Jeanne Moreau are unsettled by the appearance of an Italian guest worker and his teenage son. Moreau's sexual longing for the stranger sets in motion a dark *menage* of betrayal. With Ettore Manni, Keith Skinner and Umberto Orsini. French with English subtitles.
VHS: S20401. $19.98.
Tony Richardson, France, 1966, 105 mins.

Mado
"A beautifully made, complex film about the inter-relationship of love and business," wrote Pauline Kael. Romy Schneider stars as the mysterious woman who belongs to no one. Michel Piccoli and Charles Denner also star. French with English subtitles.
VHS: S00796. $59.95.
Claude Sautet, France, 1979, 130 mins.

A Man and a Woman
The 1966 Academy Award winner, a legendary love story starring Jean-Louis Trintignant as a race car driver who falls in love with Anouk Aimee. Stylish, well-acted and visually dynamic. Available only in a dubbed version.
VHS: S02322. $19.98.
Claude Lelouch, France, 1966, 103 mins.

A Man and a Woman—20 Years Later
Twenty years after the release of *A Man and a Woman*, Lelouch reunites Anouk Aimee and Jean-Louis Trintignant. A hit at numerous film festivals during 1986. French with English subtitles.
VHS: S02323. $19.98.
Claude Lelouch, France, 1986, 112 mins.

Manon of the Spring
Emmanuelle Beart is the grown-up, revenge-seeking daughter of the kindly hunchback who was destroyed by the greed of his neighbors. Yves Montand and his nephew Daniel Auteuil learn the awful truth of their villainy in the conclusion of a classic tale of misinformation and retribution. From the novel by Pagnol. French with English subtitles. 123 mins.
VHS: S07523. $19.98.
Claude Berri, France, 1987, 113 mins.

Monkey People (aka Monkey Folks, Le Peuple Singe)
Five years in the making, this fascinating French documentary about the simian world is narrated by actress Susan Sarandon. There are over 120 species in the tropical forests of Asia, Africa and South America, many of which were captured on film by Gerard Vienne. The film deals with social relations among the animals, using tools to acquire food, and playful activities that prove instructive and entertaining.
VHS: S14575. $19.98.
Gerard Vienne, France, 1989, 85 mins.

The Music Teacher
The music of Verdi, Mahler, Schumann, Mozart, Bellini, Schubert and Offenbach is highlighted in this 1989 Academy Award Nominee for Best Foreign Film. Just before World War I a group of opera students gather to compete to settle a grudge between a retired opera star and a wealthy patron. Lots of emotional fireworks. Called "elegant and cultivated" by the *Boston Globe*. With Jose Van Dam, Joachim Dallyroc and Anne Roussel. French with English subtitles.
VHS: S11535. $19.98.
Gerard Corbiau, France/Belgium, 1989, 100 min.

My Father's Glory
An 11-year-old boy spends an enchanting summer in the rugged French countryside with his family. The experience becomes a turning point in his young life and cements his relationship with his father. From the novel by Marcel Pagnol, a gorgeous film starring Philippe Caubere and Nathalie Roussel. French with English subtitles.
VHS: S16035. $19.98.
Yves Robert, France, 1991, 103 mins.

My Favorite Season (Ma Saison Preferee)
Techine's fascinating, dark and somber story of a middle-aged brother and sister (Catherine Deneuve and Daniel Auteuil), a provincial lawyer and a skilled surgeon, respectively, who begin to come to terms with what they have become professionally and personally when their aging mother (Marthe Villalonge) begins to disintegrate after a stroke. Techine himself describes *Ma Saison Preferee* as a film "about individuality and the frigity of the modern world." French with English subtitles.
VHS: S32613. $89.98.
DVD: DV60165. $29.98.
Andre Techine, France, 1993, 124 mins.

My Life and Times with Antonin Artaud
Gerard Mordillat's intimate portrait of the multifaceted Artaud begins with his release from prison and his return to Paris. This poet, actor, philosopher and all-around man of the theater is viewed through the eyes of Jacques Prevel, Artaud's disciple, pusher and companion. With Sami Frey and Marc Barbet. French with English subtitles.
VHS: S27755. $89.95.
Gerard Mordillat, France, 1995, 93 mins.

My Mother's Castle
In the companion film to *My Father's Glory*, a boy continues his love affair with the wild country of southern France. Through frequent family visits to their summer home, he learns to love and understand his mother's true nature. The heartfelt conclusion to the story by Marcel Pagnol. French with English subtitles.
VHS: S16036. $19.98.
Yves Robert, France, 1991, 117 mins.

Nea
Nea is a story of turbulent erotic passion and a young girl's striving to overcome the hypocrisy and repression of her father's home. 16-year-old Sybille Ashby, the daughter of a wealthy industrialist, has written her first novel, which her publisher believes to be an erotic masterpiece. But to complete it, Sybille convinces the publisher to initiate her sexually. French with English subtitles.
VHS: S00921. $59.95.
Nelly Kaplan, France, 1976, 100 mins.

Nelly and Monsieur Arnaud
In this engaging romance of longing and denial reminiscent of Kieslowski's *Red*, Emmanuelle Beart plays Nelly, who is introduced to the wealthy Arnaud (Michel Serrault) and agrees to transcribe his memoirs. The unlikely couple develop a playful flirtation, which is complicated by Nelly's involvement with Arnaud's charming editor (Jean-Hugues Anglade). What follows is a devastating succession of near-misses and might-have-beens that frame the hesitations and sudden pleasures of unexpected love. "A winning romance! Exceptionally touching and astonishing" (Gary Arnold, *Washington Times*). French with English subtitles.
VHS: S30936. $89.95.
Claude Sautet, France, 1996, 103 mins.

Next Summer
A star-studded French romantic drama which features Claudia Cardinale, Fanny Ardant, Philippe Noiret, Marie Trintignant and Jean-Louis Trintignant in the story of an imaginary family in which family frustrations vie with passions, and the quest for power and beauty. A big hit in France. French with English subtitles.
VHS: S06012. $69.95.
Nadine Trintignant, France, 1984, 120 mins.

Notorious Nobodies (Illustres Inconnus)
Winner of the Camera Award, *Notorious Nobodies*, wrote filmmaker Costa-Gavras, "attempts to describe for us the struggle of men and women around the world to save what is most precious to them: their dignity…neither a plea nor a denunciation but rather an original cinema of exceptional quality, a tragedy about human destiny." Comprised of eight individual stories taking place on the same day in far-flung corners of the globe, *Notorious Nobodies* is "a chronicle of emotions and images of an era, with horror made banal, abrasive humor, and above all, hope dotted throughout. *Notorious Nobodies* is a report both impartial and exhilarating, a film which is humble and ambitious." The eight sequences of the film are set in Prague, Munich, Paris, Vietnam, Geneva, Montevideo, Zaire and France. French with English subtitles.
VHS: S07822. $59.95.
Stanislav Stanojevic, France, 1986, 102 mins.

The Old Lady Who Walked in the Sea
Screen legend Jeanne Moreau is a charming swindler whose roving eye can spot the outlines of a new scam with the greatest of ease. Her latest plan also happens to require a handsome young man. The result is a humorous triangle of tension and desire between her, her partner (Michel Serrault) and the newcomer, all revolving around a large but illicit cash prize. French with English subtitles.
VHS: S28062. $19.98.
Laser: LD75610. $39.99.
Laurent Heynemann, France, 1996, 94 mins.

One Deadly Summer
Psychological thriller features Isabelle Adjani as a mysterious woman who returns to her mother's village to seek revenge on three men who had beaten and raped her mother years before. French with English subtitles.
VHS: S03313. $59.95.
Jean Becker, France, 1983, 134 mins.

Overseas
A stylistically audacious first feature by the talented French actress Brigitte Rouan. Set in the late 40s, *Overseas* traces that opposite fortunes of three wealthy sisters living in French occupied North Africa at the onset of the Algerian war. With Nicole Garcia, Rouan, Marianne Basler and Philippe Galland.
VHS: S16859. $19.98.
Brigitte Rouan, France, 1990, 98 mins.

Paris Vu Par (Six in Parirs)
This omnibus film from the major figures of the French New Wave (Jean-Luc Godard, Claude Chabrol, Eric Rohmer, Jean Douchet, Jean Rouch and Jean-Daniel Pollet) offers a series of witty, wry vignettes about contemporary Paris. Godard's work, Une Femme Est une Femme, is about a young woman who dispatches letters to her two lovers and is concerned she mixed up the contents. With Joanna Shimkus, Nadine Ballot, Barbet Schroeder, Micheline Dax, Claude Melki, Chabrol and Stephane Audran. French with English subtitles. France, 1964, 98 mins.
VHS: S19543. $69.95.

Peppermint Soda
Diane Kurys' autobiographical first feature charts the adventures of two carefree sisters, Anne (Elenore Klarwein), a shy misfit, and Frederique (Odile Michel), a free-spirited extrovert, during the socially turbulent Paris of the early '60s. Living with their divorced Jewish mother, the girls shuttle between a rigid, claustrophobic school and awkward holidays with their father. "The film is a harsh, unsentimental look at adolescence, with the '60s setting serving primarily to define the social and political context of the girls' rites of passage" (*Time Out*). With Anouk Ferjac, Michel Puterflam, Yves Renier and Robert Rimbaud. French with English subtitles.
VHS: S19416. $29.95.
Diane Kurys, France, 1977, 97 mins.

Ponette
Four-year-old wonder Victoire Thivisol, in some of the most extraordinary child acting to grace the big screen, stars as Ponette, who is sent off by her father to live with her relatives after the death of her mother in a car accident. Ponette is inconsolable and will not accept the fact that her mother is never coming back. But ultimately it is her faith, love and strength of character that enable her to triumphantly overcome her tragedy. "Remarkable…one of the most sensitive, luminous films about the very young ever made" (Kevin Thomas, *Los Angeles Times*).
VHS: S33869. $89.98.
DVD: DV60207. $29.98.
Jacques Doillon, France, 1996, 92 mins.

A Pure Formality
Gerard Depardieu faces off against director Roman Polanski in this unsettling mystery from the director of *Cinema Paradiso*. Depardieu plays a man accused of a murder that he doesn't remember committing. He and Polanski play a deadly game of deceptions, distortions and lies where a series of unexpected flashbacks finally reveal the unforseen truth about this intriguing case. With a brilliant performance from Polanski. French with English subtitles.
VHS: S26990. $96.99.
Laser: LD75437. $39.95.
Giuseppe Tornatore, France, 1994, 107 mins.

Queen Margot
Winner of five Cesar Awards, Patrice Chereau's stylish, realistic adaptation Alexander Dumas' tale is set during the Catholic-Protestant wars of 16th-century France. Isabelle Adjani plays Margot, the unwilling daughter of Catherine de Medici (Virna Lisi in a Cannes Festival-winning role), who is married to Protestant leader King Henry of Navarre (Daniel Auteuil). In the film Chereau creates a non-stop series of betrayals, intrigues, plots, poisonings, love affairs and executions as Margot falls for a common soldier (Vincent Perez). French with English subtitles.
VHS: S25051. $19.98.
Laser: LD74955. $39.99.
Patrice Chereau, France, 1994, 144 mins.

Red Kiss
Nadia (Charlotte Valandrey) is fifteen, full of life, and loves the poet Apollinaire, cemeteries, Scarlett O'Hara, and…Stalin. Her parents are Jewish immigrants from Poland. Nadia and her parents believe that the revolution is imminent, that the best doctors come from the USSR and that Soviet children are paid to go to school. At a demonstration, Nadia meets Stephane (French heartthrob Lambert Wilson) and through him discovers another life, another world. French with English subtitles.
VHS: S12992. $19.98.
Vera Belmont, France, 1985, 110 mins.

Rendez Vous
Andre Techine's (*Scene of the Crime*) sexy, stylish melodrama stars Juliette Binoche (*Hail Mary, Unbearable Lightness of Being*) as an actress on a "rendezvous" with destiny, who projects a carnality that drives men wild. The obsessive passion culminates in her relationship with a self-destructive lover. "Sizzles with eroticism." French with English subtitles.
VHS: S11634. $29.95.
Andre Techine, France, 1985, 82 mins.

Rendez-Moi Ma Peau
A modern-day witch loses most of her magical power, but has just enough to mess up the lives of two strangers when she transposes their personalities. The fun begins as a detective tracks down Zora the witch, while Jean-Pierre and Marie are trapped inside each other's bodies. French with English subtitles.
VHS: S01105. $59.95.
Patrick Schulmann, France, 1981, 82 mins.

Return of Martin Guerre
Dramatization of an extraordinary imposture that took place in the 16th century and became a legend; the husband leaves his family and years later, returns. He re-integrates himself into the family and community, but then serious doubts spring up about his identity—is he the real Martin Guerre? With Gerard Depardieu, Nathalie Baye. French with English subtitles.
VHS: S01107. $29.98.
Laser: Widescreen. **LD76003. $69.95.**
DVD: DV60160. $29.98.
Daniel Vigne, France, 1983, 123 mins.

Ridicule
The Oscar-nominated satire of 18th-century French court manners in the reign of Louis XVI directed by Patrice Leconte (*Monsieur Hire*) and written by first-time screenwriter Remi Waterhouse. A young man, in a noble quest to save his hometown, becomes torn between two beautiful women in a triangle of love and deceipt. A beautifully detailed study of court life, manners and wit, directed with a sense of controlled elegance. French with English subtitles.
VHS: S31277. $103.99.
Laser: LD76255. $39.99.
Patrice Leconte, France, 1996, 103 mins.

Sartre by Himself (Sartre par Lui Meme)
A revealing documentary portrait of the existentialist philosopher and writer. The film offers a conversational feast for anyone with an interest in 20th century philosophy, the intellectual ferment of post-war Paris, or the vibrant personalities of Sartre and his long-time friend, Simone de Beauvoir. French with English subtitles.
VHS: S11594. $99.95.
Alexandre Astruc/Michel Contat, France, 1979, 190 mins.

Savage Nights
Cloaked in controversy because its maker and star, Cyril Collard, died of AIDS just days after the film won the coveted Cesar (French Oscar) award, *Savage Nights* is a story of passion and love in the age of HIV. A bisexual photographer finds his life is shared by those he loves in a way that many would find unforgivable. The film provokes and astonishes with its singular perspective; it is all the more incendiary by being rooted in real life. French with English subtitles.
VHS: S22530. $14.95.
Cyril Collard, France, 1993, 126 mins.

Scandal Man
Maurice Ronet plays a photographer who becomes involved in a sensational story when he photographs the daughter of an American Ku Klux Klan leader embracing a black man at a nightclub. French with English subtitles.
VHS: S01964. $19.95.
Richard Balducci, France, 86 mins.

Scene of the Crime
Catherine Deneuve is a strikingly beautiful widow in a tiny French hamlet. She unexpectedly comes across a sexy outlaw played by Danielle Darrieux. This escaped convict brings her to a new sexual awareness in this lyrically paced film. French with English subtitles.
VHS: S25032. $24.95.
Andre Techine, France, 1987, 90 mins.

The Scent of Green Papaya
A moving and undeniably brilliant film by the talented Vietnamese-exile filmmaker Tran Anh Hung, set in 1951 and centered on a young woman who becomes a servant for a turbulent family. The film follows in exquisitely lyrical detail the quiet beauty and stoically accepted hardships of her life as, ten years later, she starts a love affair with her next employer. Shot entirely on a Paris soundstage, this, says critic Roger Ebert, "is a film to cherish." Vietnamese with English subtitles.
VHS: S23925. $19.95.
Laser: LD74799. $34.95.
Tran Anh Hung, Vietnam/France, 1993, 104 mins.

Secret Obsession
Ben Gazzara and Julie Christie star in this dramatic love story set in North Africa and Europe. Ben has an illegitimate son that he won't acknowledge, who grows up to fall in love with Julie Christie, who is already Ben's lover. With Pat Bruel and Jean Carmet. Talk about a family affair. In English.
VHS: S08069. $79.95.
Ridha Behi, France/Tunisia, 1988, 84 mins.

The Seducer's Diary (Le Journal du Seducteur)
Chiara Mastroianni is Claire, a young psychology student who falls under the spell of Gregoire (Melvil Poupard) a troubled philosophy student who successfully seduces women by giving them a copy of Kierkegaard's *Diary of a Seducer*. The Parisian cast of characters also includes Claire's amnesiac shrink (Hubert Saint Macary), an androgynous slacker (Mathieu Amalric) who cons his way into Claire's house and her mother's bed, Gregoire's paranoid grandmother (Micheline Presle), his batty literature professor, Mr. Icon (Jean-Pierre Leaud), and a dead body in the refrigerator. "Dubroux has a light touch, a slow-burning sense of humor and a dark admiration for Cocteau" (Barbara Shulgasser, *San Francisco Examiner*).
VHS: S32680. $89.95.
Daniele Dubroux, France, 1995, 95 mins.

Seven Deadly Sins
Several French and Italian filmmakers, among them Eduardo De Filippo, Yves Allegret, Georges Lacombe and Roberto Rossellini, create separate vignettes that illustrate the dangers and provocations of the seven vices, suffused with a caustic, black wit. With Michele Morgan, Francoise Rosay, Gerard Philipe, and Isabelle Miranda. French and Italian with English subtitles. 1953, 127 mins.
VHS: S18030. $29.95.

Simone de Beauvoir
A candid portrait of a remarkable woman. Simone de Beauvoir discusses her political views, the student uprisings of 1968, sexual fidelity, aging and death. Interwoven with interviews are archival photographs and footage of the events, both personal and historical, that have shaped her thinking. French with English subtitles.
VHS: S08606. $59.95.
Malka Ribowska/Josee Dayan, France, 1982, 110 mins.

A Simple Story
Romy Schneider, in her French Academy Award-winning performance, plays a successful industrial designer disturbed by intangible doubts brought on with the approach of middle age. At the crossroads of her life she must balance her career, a teenage son, an ex-husband, a boyfriend and her peers. French with English subtitles.
VHS: S01205. $29.95.
Claude Sautet, France, 1978, 100 mins.

A Single Girl
This intimate drama shows a day in the life of a young Parisian woman named Valerie, played by newcomer Virginie Ledoyen (*La Ceremonie*). Before her first day at work as a room service waitress at a four-star hotel, Valerie reveals to her boyfriend Remi (Benoit Magimentl), that she is four weeks pregnant. Shot in real time, we follow Valerie around as she meditates on the paths of human nature she crosses, sometimes comic, sometimes hostile, which lead her to make important decisions about her future. "Stunning…remarkable…exerts a hypnotic grip" (Michael Wilmington, *Chicago Tribune*). French with English subtitles.
VHS: S32169. $89.98.
Benoit Jacquot, France, 1996, 90 mins.

Soldier Duroc...It's Your Party
The story of a love-hungry French soldier who crosses German enemy lines in 1944 France to visit his fiancee, only to be trapped by the German soldiers. With Pierre Tornade, Robert Webber, Michel Galabru. French with English subtitles.
VHS: S01225. $39.95.
Michel Serard, France, 95 mins.

Someone Behind the Door
A bizarre psychological drama about a neuropsychiatrist who uses a deranged amnesiac murderer as his tool for revenge in a plot to kill his philandering wife. With Charles Bronson, Anthony Perkins and Jill Ireland. In English.
VHS: S34177. $19.95.
Nicolas Gessner, France, 1971, 97 mins.

Sorceress
An intriguing film about the clash between a dedicated healer and a pursuer of heretics. Truffaut protege and longtime friend Suzanne Schiffman makes her directorial debut with a convincing period piece that raises timely questions on the role of the church and its oppression of women. At once a theological discourse and a story well told, this film illuminates challenges made toward Christianity as early as the Middle Ages.
English Language Version.
VHS: S17691. $29.95.
Subtitled Version.
VHS: S12672. $29.95.
Suzanne Schiffman, France, 1988, 98 mins.

Soviet Spy
Docudrama written by Hans Otto Meissner, Chief of Protocol at the German Embassy in Tokyo during World War II. Story concerns the case of Richard Sorge, a German journalist hanged as a spy in 1944 for warning Moscow that German armies would attack the Soviets. French with English subtitles. France, 1961, 130 mins.
VHS: S01671. $19.95.

Starting Place
Robert Kramer achieved notoriety with his 1969 documentary, *People's War*. After 24 years he returns with a documentary that continues to explore the same subjects and once again reveals the other side of Vietnamese society, rarely seen in this country. It is provocative and elegiac at the same time, reflecting a perspective altered in part by the passing of time and the reasoned expectations of an older, more sober outlook.
VHS: S27649. $39.95.
Robert Kramer, France/Great Britain/Vietnam, 1993, 80 mins.

Stuntwoman
Raquel Welch stars as a stuntwoman whose death-defying job hampers her romantic life. With Jean-Paul Belmondo.
VHS: S35246. $19.95.
Claude Zidi, France, 1981, 95 mins.

Tartuffe
In his first directorial effort, Gerard Depardieu (*Green Card, Cyrano*) breathes new life into Moliere's classic stage masterpiece about religious and sexual hypocrisy. The dazzling cast includes Depardieu, his wife Elizabeth, and renowned classical actor Francois Perier. Based on a stage production directed by Jacques Lasalle of the Theatre National de Strasbourg. "The best production of *Tartuffe* I've seen" (Stanley Kauffmann). French with English subtitles.
VHS: S13590. $79.95.
Gerard Depardieu, France, 1984, 140 mins.

Therese and Isabelle
Based on the novel by Violette Leduc, *Therese and Isabelle* is a story of love between two students at an exclusive girls' school. Filmed in black and white. English dubbed.
VHS: S01320. $29.95.
Radley Metzger, France, 1968, 102 mins.

Thieves
Andre Techine's crime thriller, told from multiple, overlapping points of view, features strong, subtle performances from Daniel Auteuil as tormented Lyon policeman Alex Noel, Didier Bezace as his shady older brother Ivan, and a dazzling Catherine Deneuve as Marie, a lesbian philosophy professor and author. "Techine takes the stuff of slick French cinema and deepens it with every frame" (*New City*). French with English subtitles.
VHS: S31788. $98.99.
Laser: LD76307. $39.95.
Andre Techine, France, 1996, 116 mins.

This Special Friendship
A 16-year-old boy becomes infatuated with a young classmate at a strict Jesuit boarding school. "A masterpiece…shocking in the best sense of the word" (L.A. *Times*). A sensitively directed film with a bravura performance by Didier Haudepin. French with English subtitles.
VHS: S01333. $49.95.
Jean Delannoy, France, 1964, 99 mins.

This Sweet Sickness
A Hitchcockian study of erotic intrigue is freely adapted from a Patricia Highsmith novel. The practical, quiet loner David (Gerard Depardieu) builds an elaborate mountain chalet to seduce Lise (Dominique Laffin), a married woman with whom he's fallen obsessively in love. David rejects the legitimate and honest love of Juliette (Miou-Miou), with tragic repercussions. Former Truffaut and Godard protege Claude Miller charts these emotions with sureness of touch. With Claude Pieplu and Christian Clavier. French with English subtitles.
VHS: S19294. $24.98.
Claude Miller, France, 1977, 107 mins.

Tom and Lola
These beautiful children have damaged immune systems that force them to remain isolated in hermetically sealed plastic bubbles. This isolation cannot inhibit their beguiling spirit, a spirit that manifests itself in a bold bid to free themselves from this claustrophobic environment. French with English subtitles.
VHS: S21543. $69.95.
Bertrand Arthuys, France, 1994, 98 mins.

Un Coeur en Hiver
Claude Sautet's 13th feature is loosely based on Lermontov's novel *A Hero of Our Time*. Two violin makers (Daniel Auteuil and Andre Dussollier) are affected when a beautiful violinist (Emmanuelle Beart) enters their lives. The film addresses the question of whether Auteuil is able to reconcile his cold, rigid nature with his deep, emotional attraction to Beart. With Elizabeth Bourgine, Myriam Boyer, Brigitte Catillon, and Maurice Garrel as a brilliant music teacher. French with English subtitles.
VHS: S20208. $19.98.
Claude Sautet, France, 1991, 100 mins.

Uranus
From Claude Berri, the director of *Jean de Florette* and *Manon of the Spring*. Gerard Depardieu stars in this controversial adaptation of the French novel about a flawed Renaissance man, a poet, philosopher and hustler, entangled with individual heroism, sexual politics and collaboration with the Nazi occupation forces during World War II. French with English subtitles.
VHS: S17401. $19.98.
Claude Berri, France, 1990, 100 mins.

A Very Curious Girl
Nelly Kaplan's sensational sex comedy, with Bernadette Lafont as the town 'loose girl' who, tired of enduring physical and sexual exploitation, begins to charge for her services, accumulating power she never imagined, and 'gets back at her clients' for what they have done unto her. French with English subtitles.
VHS: S01410. $29.95.
Nelly Kaplan, France, 1971, 105 mins.

Vincent, Francois, Paul & the Others
A lyrical homage to male friendship featuring outstanding performances by Yves Montand, Michel Piccoli and Gerard Depardieu. The three men find their friendship sustains them through a series of middle-age crises. "An extraordinary movie fugue on the theme of friendship. Sautet's style is one of the great pleasures of modern movie-going," wrote *The Washington Post*. French with English subtitles.
VHS: S01417. $29.95.
Claude Sautet, France, 1977, 113 mins.

Voyage en Douce
Geraldine Chaplin and Dominique Sanda star in this graceful film about two women who decide to take charge of their lives. Fed up with the men they know, they set off on a journey. In the lush countryside of Southern France they share jokes, meals, and erotic daydreams. French with English subtitles.
VHS: S22443. $79.95.
Michel Deville, France, 1981, 97 mins.

The Wanderer
Alain Fournier's classic novel, *Le Grand Meaulnes*, is interpreted by Albiococco with fantastic imagery and stunning color-in a remarkable recreation of a child's memories and examination of his transition from romantic, idealistic youth to clear-eyed adult. With Jean Blaise and Brigitte Fossey. "Heartbreaking…Romantic" (*L.A. Times*). French with English subtitles.
VHS: S15273. $29.95.
Jean-Gabriel Albicocco, France, 1967, 108 mins.

We Were One Man
A simple French farmer and a wounded, abandoned German soldier are ultimately united in an openly sexual relationship in this award-winning French film. French with English subtitles.
VHS: S01437. $49.95.
Philippe Vallois, France, 1980, 90 mins.

Weapons of the Spirit
Between 1940 and 1944, a small village in the mountains of France, Le Chambon, became Europe's most effective haven for Jews, saving 5,000 men, women and children from the Holocaust. In this extraordinary documentary by Pierre Sauvage, who was born and protected in this peaceful village, the director shares this heartwarming story of the poor farming village of French Protestants who, under the eyes of the German occupation forces and the Vichy government, resisted the violence through "the weapons of the spirit." French with English subtitles.
VHS: S12461. $90.00.
Pierre Sauvage, France/USA, 1986, 91 mins.

When the Cat's Away
The missing cat of a beautiful, young French fashion stylist (Garance Clavel) serves to re-unite a Parisian neighborhood in this intimate drama which features the actual residents of the Bastille section of Paris. The film has an emotional authenticity and "effortlessness that is a rare thing in our time" (*New City*). French with English subtitles.
VHS: S32798. $98.99.
Cedric Klapisch, France, 1997, 91 mins.

Wild Reeds
In 1962, a group of teenagers confront emotional, sexual and political turmoil provoked by both their own personal lives and the larger social framework of a small provincial town affected by the French-Algerian War. This engaging, elegaic film captures both the fleeting nature of youth and the profound turmoil of this intriguing stage of life. French with English subtitles.
VHS: S29407. $29.98.
DVD: DV60168. $29.98.
Andre Techine, France, 1995, 110 mins.

A Woman at Her Window
Romy Schneider plays an aristocratic woman immersed in the despotic world of Greece circa 1936, who pursues shallow affairs with her noble counterparts (Philippe Noiret). When she rescues a political activist (Victor Lanoux) she falls in love and is transformed by new passions. French with English subtitles.
VHS: S21757. $79.95.
Pierre Granier-Deferre, France, 1977, 110 mins.

The Women
Brigitte Bardot stars as a very personal secretary to Maurice Ronet, who is writing his memoirs of his many love affairs. English dubbed.
VHS: S02614. $29.95.
Jean Aurel, France, 1969, 83 mins.

CUTTING EDGE FRENCH FILMMAKERS

Baxter
Beware of the dog who thinks! Before *Look Who's Talking* took Hollywood by storm, *Baxter* came out of the kennel in France with his unique perspective on the strange behavior of the human animal. Shuttled from master to master, Baxter disagrees with an old woman, finds himself charged to the newlywed couple across the way, and ends up with a young master who is obsessed with Hitler. French with English subtitles.
VHS: S16685. $19.98.
Laser: CLV/CAV. **LD72047. $39.95.**
Jerome Boivin, France, 1991, 82 mins.

Chocolat
Claire Denis takes the viewer on an emotional and strikingly visual memory trip back to the colonial Africa of her youth. In her directorial debut, she spins an engaging tale of a small white girl growing up in Cameroon on the isolated compound of her French official father and her lonely gorgeous mother. With Guilia Boschi, Issach de Bankole, Francois Cluzet and Cecile Ducasse. French with English subtitles.
VHS: S11534. $19.98.
Claire Denis, France, 1988, 105 mins.

The Deadly Trap (Death Scream)
Faye Dunaway stars as a woman, neglected by her husband, who starts to believe she is going mad when a series of mishaps occur. Actually, an industrious espionage organization is going after its one-time member (Frank Langella), by harassing his emotionally fragile wife. With Barbara Parkins. In English.
VHS: S35240. $19.95.
Rene Clement, France/Italy, 1971, 97 mins.

Dr. Petiot
Michel Serrault stars in this macabre tale of a doctor who lured desperate Jews into a trap. They sought to escape Nazi-controlled France, but this doctor tricked them and murdered them in his own private crematorium and then stole their belongings. Based on the true story of a French physician. French with English subtitles.
VHS: S21511. $29.95.
Christian de Chalonge, France, 1990, 102 mins.

Field of Honor
During the Napoleonic Wars a French farm boy takes the place of the son of a rich family and begins to rethink the bargain when the bullets start to fly. Chris Campion is the young soldier trying to survive the Prussian advance. An intriguing tale of war, irony, and the people caught between the armies, directed with great sensitivity by Jean-Pierre Denis, one of the most talented young French filmmakers. French with English subtitles.
VHS: S10758. $19.98.
Jean-Pierre Denis, France, 1987, 87 mins.

Franck Goldberg: Sampler
A compilation of short films that includes: "Red Souvenir"—a documentary-style look at kids in New York; "No Sellout"—a rap music video based on Malcolm X's speeches; "Lynch"—the story of the police killing of a young graffiti artists in the New York subway; "Promised Land"—an examination of the purposeless violence of the U.S. as seen by this French video artist.
VHS: S07126. $39.95.
Franck Goldberg, France, 1985-86, 60 mins.

The Hairdresser's Husband
An acclaimed, quirky film about erotic obsession from the director of *Monsieur Hire*. Antoine (Jean Rochefort) is a middle-aged man whose life-long ambition to marry a hairdresser is fulfilled in his tender relationship with the beautiful and graceful Matila (Anna Galiena). With Henri Hocking and Maurice Chevit. French with English subtitles.
VHS: S18680. $19.95.
Laser: LD75204. $34.98.
Patrice Leconte, France, 1990, 84 mins.

I Can't Sleep
Paralleling such recent jigsaw narratives as *Red* and *Pulp Fiction*, Claire Denis weaves together disparate fragments which gradually reveal the underlying connections between a group of disconnected characters: a tall Lithuanian blonde arrives in Paris looking for work as an actress; a West Indian musician pressures his wife to move back to Martinique; the police hunt a serial killer and a beautiful black queen performs in drag at a local nightclub. In a major atmospheric study of contemporary alienation, Denis beautifully captures the psychological undercurrents that haunt the modern urban world. French with English subtitles.
VHS: S28632. $89.95.
Claire Denis, France, 1995, 110 mins.

In the Land of the Deaf
A unique and privileged look inside the world of deaf people. A teacher, a woman treated for mental illness because of her deafness, and a newly wed deaf couple offer compelling portraits from a community estimated to comprise 130 million people worldwide in a film which is revealing, moving and often funny. French and French Sign Language with English subtitles.
VHS: S25993. $79.95.
Nicolas Philibert, France, 1994, 99 mins.

Irma Vep
Olivier Assayas' stylish take on the world of French surrealist film serials stars Hong Kong action film star Maggie Cheung, who, playing herself, is brought to Paris to star in a modern version of the famous silent Feuillade serial, *Les Vampires*. But Jean-Pierre Leaud, who plays the director of the film, is at the end of his emotional rope, and the production becomes a series of emotional entanglements between its protagonists. Assayas' witty, acute observations of people and places touches on the nature of creation in a film which is a favorite of film festivals worldwide. English and French with English subtitles.
VHS: S32984. $89.98.
DVD: DV60286. $29.95.
Olivier Assayas, France, 1996, 97 mins.

La Femme Nikita
A stylish punk thriller from director Luc Besson *(Subway, The Big Blue)* in which a French street junkie (played by the beautiful Anne Parillaud) is arrested and threatened with life imprisonment. She is then allowed to leave if she agrees to go to work for the French secret police as an assassin. This suspenseful film is highlighted by Besson's stylishly decorous visual compositions and innate sense of dramatic pacing. Also starring Tcheky Karyo and Jeanne Moreau. French with English subtitles.
VHS: S14530. $19.95.
Laser: Widescreen. **LD75217. $44.95.**
Luc Besson, France, 1991, 117 mins.

Marquis
An audacious rendering of the political, social and sexual manners of the *ancien regime* and the class division and social disruption that produced the French Revolution. Adapted from the writings of the Marquis de Sade, Henri Xhonneux and Roland Topor's elegantly witty film uses elaborate puppets in human form to act out erotic and sexual decadence. "Elegantly naughty with wry, intellectual satire. The film plays out all manner of human desire" (J. Hoberman). French with English subtitles.
VHS: S18104. $29.95.
Henri Xhonneux, France, 1989, 85 mins.

Mina Tannenbaum
Mousy, introspective Mina and overweight, outgoing Ethel meet at the age of seven, and for the next 25 years their lives are intertwined. They survive adolescence—the humiliations of an ugly duckling childhood, their guilt-happy Jewish mothers—and emerge, Mina as a star of the Paris art world and Ethel as a self-determined woman. Romane Bohringer and Elsa Zylberstein deliver remarkable performances in a powerful, emotional work called the "best foreign film of the year" by the Boston Society of Film Critics. French with English subtitles.
VHS: S28615. $89.95.
Martine Dugowson, France, 1993, 128 mins.

Monsieur Hire
A disturbing and finely crafted thriller about obsession and responsibility. Michel Blanc stars as a reclusive tailor who enjoys watching Sandra Bonnaire undress across the courtyard. When a murder is committed, his peculiarities make him a suspect. Based on a novel by Georges Simeon. With Luc Thuillier and Andre Wilms. Be prepared to be affected. French with English subtitles.
VHS: S13672. $19.98.
Patrice Leconte, France, 1989, 81 mins.

My Sex Life (Or How to Get Into an Argument)
Paul, a 29-year-old assistant professor, cannot complete his dissertation, his arch rival has just been promoted over him to full professor, and he must figure out a way to break up with his girlfriend of 10 years. To complicate matters, he finds himself involved in several simultaneous relationships, including one with his best friend's girlfriend. "Wildly romantic. One of the great French films of the decade" *(Village Voice)*. French with English subtitles. Letterboxed.
VHS: S33351. $89.98.
Arnaud Desplechin, France, 1997, 178 mins.

Nenette and Boni
Gregoire Colin is 19-year-old Boniface Pavone, a sex-starved pizza worker who combats loneliness by conjuring vivid and hilarious fantasies involving the baker's voluptuous wife (Valerie Bruni Tedeschi). When his estranged 15-year-old sister Nenette (Alice Houri) shows up at his doorstep seven months pregnant with a child she doesn't want, the two warily embark on a journey of the spirit that leads them to an unexpected family reunion. French with English subtitles.
VHS: S33879. $89.95.
Claire Denis, France, 1997, 103 mins.

No Fear, No Die
Starring Issach de Bankole, Alex Descas and Jean-Claude Brialy, this film explores a sordid underworld of gambling and desire centered around an illegal cock-fighting club. Two immigrants supply the birds and train them, but the arrangement breaks down when the club owner's mistress (Solveig Dommartin) becomes involved in these murky dealings. From the director of *Chocolat*. French with English subtitles.
VHS: S20785. $29.95.
Claire Denis, France, 1993, 97 mins.

Noir et Blanc
Claire Devers' first critically-acclaimed film tracks the sado-masochistic relationship between a bleached-out accountant and a black masseur. As the masochism of Antoine, the unremarkable young man who is the accountant, grows evermore dependent, the film tracks the relationship to its horrifying climax. French with English subtitles.
VHS: S23599. $79.95.
Claire Devers, France, 1989, 89 mins.

Patrick Bokanowski—Courts-Metrages
Short films by Patrick Bokanowski, including *La Plage* (1991, 12 mins.); *La Femme qui se poudre* (1972, 18 mins.); *Dejeuner du matin* (1974, 12 mins.); and *Au bord du lac* (1993, 6 mins.).
VHS: S35146. $29.95.
Patrick Bokanowski, France, 1972/1974/1991/1993, 48 mins.

Patrick Bokanowski—L'Ange (1977-1982)
"In this Brueghel or Bosch cloaked in 19th-century tailcoat, characters 'a la Boltanski,' infinitely coupled to their either seeming trivial or simply absurd chores, at once mobile… and frozen in a sort of infernal eternity, meet in various parts of an unidentifiable location, on and around, it seems, an immense expressionist staircase which leads, neverthelss, to a final luminous irradiation.…This film…has reached cult status among amateurs of a most deeply disrupting and bewitching cinema" (Dominique Noguez).
VHS: S35145. $29.95.
Patrick Bokanowski, France, 1982, 70 mins.

Pigalle
Called "a punchy, smartly-executed, nocturnal narco-trip" by *Variety*, this bittersweet love story from the talented director of *Bye Bye* is set in the home to pimps, pushers, junkies and petty criminals in an unforgettable valentine to Pigalle, the Parisian boulevard of sin. "The ne plus ultra of risky bohemian adventure" *(New York Times)*. French with English subtitles.
VHS: S33321. $79.95.
Karim Dridi, France/Switzerland, 1994, 93 mins.

The Professional
Jean Reno, of *La Femme Nikita*, Gary Oldman and Danny Aiello star in this hyper fast thriller from French filmmaker Luc Besson in his American debut. A hitman develops an unexpected bond with an orphaned 12-year-old girl. Saddled with this casualty of the business, her father was intimately involved in illicit activity, *The Professional* still manages to keep up a breakneck pace. VHS letterboxed.
VHS: S24663. $19.95.
Laser: LD74902. $34.95.
DVD: DV60231. $24.95.
Luc Besson, USA, 1994, 84 mins.

Remi Lange—Omelette
One day, a young man, tired of writing and rewriting the same screenplay, begins making a film diary. At first, he records everyday events with his Super-8 camera: his parents, his friends, his grandmother, a friend who is HIV positive. He then, camera in hand, lets a skeleton out of the closet before his parents. "The first filmed coming-out in the history of cinema" *(Cosmopolitan)*.
VHS: S35148. $29.95.
Remi Lange, 1993, 75 mins.

Salut Cousin
Merzak Allouache's realistic tale of the OTHER Paris—the poor tenements of the 18th arrondissement. Alilo, just off the plane from Algiers, hooks up with his cousin, a would-be rap star who is also a pathological liar and a guide to the Paris underground scene. French and Arabic with English subtitles.
VHS: S33322. $79.95.
Merzak Allouache, France/Algeria/Belgium/Luxembourg, 1996, 98 mins.

Sand and Blood
With the spectacular landscapes of Southern France as her backdrop, director Jeanne Labrune creates a dazzling, sensual film focusing on eroticism and human intimacy. Using the mystique of bullfighting as a stepping stone to broader issues, Labrune explores the friendship between Francisco, a gifted matador, and Manuel, a cultivated doctor and musician. French with English subtitles.
VHS: S12465. $79.95.
Jeanne Labrune, France, 1987, 101 mins.

A Self-Made Hero
In this droll comedy Matthiew Kassovitz *(Hate)* stars as Albert Dehousse. At once a feeble slave to his mother's madness, history will remember Albert's captivating rise to heroism as a leader of the French Resistance. As brilliantly as de Gaulle eludes his nation's collaboration with the Nazis, so will Albert shed his life of mediocrity in favor of one more fantastical. With Anouk Grinberg and Jean-Louis Trintignant. French with English subtitles.
VHS: S33880. $89.95.
Jacques Audiard, France, 1996, 105 mins.

Son of the Shark
This highly acclaimed French film won the International Critics Prize at the Venice Film Festival. It is based on a true story, and follows a pair of inseparable young brothers. Abandoned by their parents, they terrorize their hometown with acts of desperate violence. Yet some mystical bond keeps this shocking pair oddly in sync. A brilliant feature from one of France's hottest young director-stars. French with English subtitles.
VHS: S26279. $19.98.
Agnes Merlet, France, 1994, 85 mins.

Special Police

This story of intrigue, political scandal, and murder centers on a young woman, Carole Bouquet, as she tries to solve the mystery of her brother's death. A computer expert who works for the police, played by Richard Berry, decides to help her. As they begin to uncover the truth dangerous forces are revealed that threaten them. French with English subtitles.

VHS: S20759. $29.95.
Michel Vianey, France, 1985, 92 mins.

Subway

Besson's stylish, neo-punkish thriller takes its place in the subterranean corners of the Paris subway, as Fred, a casual thief and cool rebel, is on the run. Underground, he encounters a motley collection of subway denizens; a huge European hit, and an intriguing underworld journey. English dubbed.

VHS: S01276. $29.95.
DVD: DV60267. $19.95.
Luc Besson, France, 1985, 104 mins.

JEAN-LUC GODARD

Alphaville

Eddie Constantine is Lemmy Caution, inter-galactic private eye, in this bravura mix of comic strip, science fiction and film noir in what is ultimately a new style of cinema in which form and content are identical. Lemmy sets out to dispose of diabolical scientist Leonard von Braun (a.k.a. Leonard Nosferatu) from Alphaville, the futuristic city run by an electronic brain, where love has been banished. A film in which poetry mixes freely with pulp to create a new dimension, a new cinematic reality. French with English subtitles.

VHS: S07702. $29.95.
Laser: LD75075. $49.95.
Jean-Luc Godard, France, 1965, 100 mins.

Band of Outsiders

Claude Brasseur, Sami Frey and Anna Karina plan to steal money hidden in a house where Karina works, but the robbery is messed up and murder is the result. Godard's thriller is set in the fringe world of *Breathless*—the world of outsiders. Most of the film takes place in a suburb of Paris, and Godard has transformed it into a setting of beauty and poignancy. Godard's three characters are "trembling on the edge of crime…dancing on the edge of the volcano" (Richard Roud). French with English subtitles.

VHS: S00093. $29.95.
Jean-Luc Godard, France, 1964, 97 mins.

Breathless

The landmark French New Wave film by Godard features Jean-Paul Belmondo as a small-time hood on the run from the law, having an affair with an American girl in Paris (Jean Seberg). A film which owes much to American film noir and yet revolutionized the world of film. Remastered. French with English subtitles.

VHS: S08698. $24.95.
Laser: CLV. LD71507. $49.95.
Jean-Luc Godard, France, 1959, 89 mins.

Comment Ca Va? (How Is It Going?)

Co-directed by Anne-Marie Mieville, Jean-Luc Godard's work-combining video and film—is a fascinating dialectic on the dissemination and processing of information, both literary and visual. Two workers of a communist newspaper strike out to make a film and video about the newspaper and the printing plant. One of the workers, Odette (Mieville), has strange ideas about content and form and how the film should be made. *Comment ca va?* is a formally brilliant work about the transmission of ideas by the major media. French with English subtitles.

VHS: S19232. $59.95.
Jean-Luc Godard/Anne-Marie Mieville, France, 1976, 76 mins.

Detective

Jean-Luc Godard's classic crime drama centers around the Hotel Concorde in St. Lazare and an unhappily married couple (Nathalie Baye and Claude Brasseur) who unwittingly become involved with the mob as they try to collect a debt from a boxing manager. A hotel detective tries to solve a two-year-old murder case with his tense nephew. Godard ties the two stories together to present his own views on modern life, ranging from pornography to language to film itself. "A mini-masterpiece…a cross between a *Grand Hotel* for the 1980s and film noir…riotously funny. Built on the charisma of its stars and on the memories of the great thrillers of tne '40s, tenuously held together by Godard's romantic pessimism, curiosity and sense of humor, it's co-dedicated, sensibly, to Clint Eastwood" (Tony Rayns). With Johnny Hakllysay, Jean-Pierre Leaud, Alain Cuny and Laurent Terzieff. French with English subtitles.

VHS: S34641. $49.98.
Jean-Luc Godard, France, 1985, 95 mins.

First Name: Carmen

An important recent film by Jean-Luc Godard; in this gun-crazy romance, Godard re-examines not only his own previous attitudes, but the entire *femme fatale* tradition of Western culture. Based freely on the novel by Prosper Merimee and the opera by Bizet, the film is a cool depiction of a sexually explicit romance between a policeman and a beautiful young woman who leads him into a life of crime and humiliation. With Myriem Roussel, Maruschka Detmers, Jacques Bonnaffre. French with English subtitles.

VHS: S09355. $19.98.
Jean-Luc Godard, France, 1983, 85 mins.

Godard/Truffaut Shorts

A short film by Jean-Luc Godard made prior to his release of *Breathless* entitled *All the Boys Are Called Patrick*, and a short film by Francois Truffaut, *Les Mistons*, a charming evocative film about the arousal of sexual feelings in a group of young boys on summer holiday. French with English subtitles.

VHS: S01777. $29.95.
Jean-Luc Godard/Francois Truffaut, France, 1957

Ici et Ailleurs (Here and Elsewhere)

Jean-Luc Godard initiated his radical video period with this startling film that combines videotape and film, enabling him to superimpose more than two images simultaneously. Made as part of the "Dziga Vertov group," with Jean-Pierre Gorin and Anne-Marie Mieville, the film was commissioned by the Palestinians and originally titled *Until Victory*. The film's original purpose was to examine life in the Palestinian camps. But following the defeat of the Palestine army in the Six Day War, *Ici et Ailleurs* was radically transformed, becoming a meditation on how cinema records history. Godard, Gorin and Mieville contrast a French family ("Here") with an impressionstic portrait of Palestine ("Elsewhere") reflected and transmitted by television, books and pictures. French with English subtitles.

VHS: S19231. $59.95.
Jean-Luc Godard, France/Switzerland, 1970/1976

JLG/JLG

In this autobiographical essay of confessional images, Godard speculates on the oppression of culture from the isolation of his home in Switzerland. Subtitled A *Self-Portrait in December*, Godard plays himself in an effort to explain what he has been doing for the past 30 years. In this unique cinematic self-portrait, Godard is self-absorbed and alone as he mumbles to himself or to his sexy young maid. In this cinematic self-portrait, sequestered from the world and bunkered in a safe and cozy haven with his books, his movie equipment and his eccentricities, he muses upon images of women, receives visits from various government officials and makes references to his past mistakes. French with English subtitles.

VHS: S30000. $89.95.
Jean-Luc Godard, France, 1994, 60 mins.

King Lear

Struggling to re-interpret his famous relative's tragic tale of passion and madness, the young William Shakespeare, Jr. the Fifth encounters a bewildering array of bizarre personalities and cryptic, ritualistic imagery. A surreal examination of The Bard's most powerful drama, from one of the avant-garde's most adventurous filmmakers. Featuring Burgess Meredith, Molly Ringwald, Woody Allen, Norman Mailer and Peter Sellars.

VHS: S16475. $24.95.
Jean-Luc Godard, France, 1987, 91 mins.

Le Gai Savoir

Two alien beings, brought together in an empty earth space, are exposed to our culture via its popular images—a compelling experiment that not only foreshadows the use of these images in Godard's later films but also explains precisely why these images are the building blocks of any film. As Godard explains at the end, "This film is not and cannot be an attempt to explain cinema or embody its object, but merely suggests effective ways to achieve it. This is not the film that should be made, but if a film is to be made it must follow some of the paths shown here." With Jean-Pierre Leaud and Juliet Berto. French with English subtitles.

VHS: S15378. $39.95.
Jean-Luc Godard, France, 1965, 96 mins.

Le Petit Soldat

The debut feature of Anna Karina, and Godard's second feature, this film was banned in France for its razor-sharp reflection of the Algerian war in a politically divided nation. Michel Subor is a French secret agent on an assassination mission. The film's depiction of brutality and torture, used by both sides in this bloody war, infuriated both the Left and the Right. French with English subtitles.

VHS: S08091. $29.95.
Jean-Luc Godard, France, 1960, 88 mins.

Les Carabiniers

One of the important early-period films from Jean-Luc Godard; a parable about the stupidity and ugliness of war. The story revolves around two gullible clodhoppers who set out to fight for their king in exchange for "all the treasures in the world." French with English subtitles.

VHS: S05327. $29.95.
Jean-Luc Godard, France, 1985, 107 mins.

A Married Woman

Godard managed to infuriate Charles de Gaulle with this frank document of a Parisian romantic triangle. Macha Meril is the young wife and mother in love with her husband and her lover. She doesn't want to decide between them because, quite frankly, she enjoys the attention of both. French with English subtitles.

VHS: S00829. $29.95.
Jean-Luc Godard, France, 1964, 94 mins.

Masculine Feminine

A film about the children of Marx and Coca Cola directed by the child of Brecht and Hollywood. Two young lovers attempt to communicate throughout 15 discontinuous, contrapuntal vignettes. Dancing between precision and improvisation, this is one of Godard's most complex films, representing both a search for tenderness and a disheartening foray into the Sex War. With Jean-Pierre Leaud, Chantal Goya, and Catherine-Isabelle Duport. French with English subtitles.

VHS: S00830. $29.95.
Jean-Luc Godard, France, 1966, 103 mins.

My Life to Live

This film in 12 episodes is "one of the most beautiful, touching and original films by Godard, an extremely complex blend of social document, theatricality and interior drama…" (Georges Sadoul). Anna Karina is a salesgirl in a record shop who can't pay her rent, is evicted by her landlady and becomes a prostitute. "It triumphs because it is intelligent, discreet, delicate to the touch. It both edifies and gives pleasure because it is about what is most important…the nature of our humanity" (Susan Sontag). French with English subtitles.

VHS: S00907. $29.95.
Laser: LD76282. $49.95.
Jean-Luc Godard, France, 1962, 85 mins.

Numero Deux

Jean-Luc Godard brilliantly mixes video and film, set in the director's Grenoble studio. The action unfolds on two television monitors. Godard secured the money for the film claiming the project was a remake of *Breathless*. The elusive plot essentially concerns the marital discord—set off by the wife's infidelity—between a young working-class couple (Sandrine Battistella and Pierre Oudry) who live in a claustrophobic, high rise apartment complex. The film, made in collaboration with Anne-Marie Mieville, is a dialectic on the relationship of sex and money. "I think it's something like a masterpiece. *Numero Deux* is among the most visually compelling films Godard has ever made. He uses his video monitors to invent a dozen new ways of splitting the screen or layering the image. Compared to it, every other movie in town is just a cavity on the screen" (J. Hoberman, *The Village Voice*). With Alexandre Rignault and Rachel Stefanopoli. French with English subtitles.

VHS: S19233. $59.95.
Jean-Luc Godard, France/Switzerland, 1976, 88 mins.

Oh Woe Is Me (Helas Pour Moi)

Gerard Depardieu meets Jean-Luc Godard in this gentle Godard fable in which divinity touches everyday life. Godard transposes to Switzerland the Greek myth in which Zeus inhabited Amphitryon's body to seduce a man's wife, with surprising results. Godardian touches like titles on the screen, townspeople who function as a theatrical chorus and music from Bach, Beethoven and Tchaikovsky make this a cerebral but passionate exploration of constancy and cinema. French with English subtitles.

VHS: S26336. $89.95.
Jean-Luc Godard, France, 1994, 84 mins.

Paris Vu Par (Six in Paris)

This omnibus film from the major figures of the French New Wave (Jean-Luc Godard, Claude Chabrol, Eric Rohmer, Jean Douchet, Jean Rouch and Jean-Daniel Pollet) offers a series of witty, wry vignettes about contemporary Paris. Godard's work, *Une Femme Est une Femme*, is about a young woman who dispatches letters to her two lovers and is concerned she mixed up the contents. With Joanna Shimkus, Nadine Ballot, Barbet Schroeder, Micheline Dax, Claude Melki, Chabrol and Stephane Audran. French with English subtitles. France, 1964, 98 mins.

VHS: S19543. $69.95.

Passion

In Godard's satire of filmmaking and lovemaking, Jerzy Radziwilowicz plays a Godard-like director in search of meaning, plagued by professional, financial and personal problems. "Reunited with cameraman Raoul Coutard after 16 years, and with a trio of great actors (Isabelle Huppert, Hanna Schygulla, Michel Piccoli), [Godard] orchestrates his personal passions for classical music, romantic painting, and the business of filmmaking around his favorite theme of how life relates to love…offer(s) sounds and images that astonish the senses and tease the mind" (Martyn Auty). French with English subtitles.

VHS: S34640. $49.98.
Jean-Luc Godard, France, 1982, 88 mins.

Pierrot le Fou

One of the high points of 20th century cinema. Ravishing and moving, the story features Jean-Paul Belmondo as Ferdinand, who one evening leaves his wife in the middle of a boring party. He meets a girl with whom he was in love five years earlier, and who is involved with a gang of criminals. After Ferdinand finds a dead man in her room, they leave Paris for a deserted island. One of Godard's most poetic films, full of the anguish of love, aptly summarized in his own words over the first images of the film, "At the age of fifty, Velasquez no longer painted precise objects; he painted what lay between precise objects." The final murder-suicide sequence on the island is one of the most brilliant Godard has ever created. French with English subtitles.

VHS: S10739. $59.95.

Jean-Luc Godard, France, 1965, 110 mins.

Rogopag

The title reflects four brilliant European directors who contributed short films to this collection: Roberto Rossellini, Jean-Luc Godard, Pier Paolo Pasolini and Ugo Gregoretti. *Virginity*, by Rossellini, is a comic essay on the distinctions between illusion and reality. Orson Welles stars in Pasolini's *La Ricotta*, a satire about the debasement of religion. This film caused Pasolini to be charged and sentenced to prison for "insulting the religion of [Italy]." *The New World*, by Godard, offers a chilling view of Paris after a nuclear war. And in Gregoretti's *The Range Grown Chicken*, a family suffers the ravages of brain-washing consumerism. French and Italian with English subtitles.

VHS: S23995. $24.95.

Roberto Rossellini/Jean-Luc Godard/Pier Paolo Pasolini/Ugo Gregoretti, France/Italy, 1962, 122 mins.

Sympathy for the Devil

The Rolling Stones rehearse "Sympathy for the Devil" as a white revolutionary tries to commit suicide when her boyfriend switches to Black Power in this singular and daring film originally called *One Plus One*. The film, tackling the themes of growth and revolution, is envisioned as a collage which the viewer is challenged to "edit" himself. With The Rolling Stones, Anne Wiazemsky and Iain Quarrier.

VHS: S22456. $29.95.

Jean-Luc Godard, France, 1970, 92 mins.

Two or Three Things I Know About Her

Shot simultaneously with *Made in U.S.A.* (one was filmed mornings, the other in the evenings), this drama focuses on modern life in Paris. Vlady stars as a Parisian housewife who lives in a large housing estate and supplements her husband's income by working as a part-time prostitute. Against an aural backdrop of Beethoven, her life over a 24-hour period is detailed as it speaks about the sale of oneself in the pursuit of happiness. A barrage of words, images and philosophising, with whispering and narration by Godard, this highly inventive and energetic, early "mockumentary" set the standard for such works. French with English subtitles.

VHS: S29507. $89.95.

Jean-Luc Godard, France, 1966, 95 mins.

Weekend

"End of Cinema, end of world," read the titles at the conclusion of Godard's 1967 apocalyptic film *Weekend*. Godard himself described the work as both "a film found on the junk heap," and "a film lost in the cosmos." Presenting a dark, comic vision of the end of capitalist society, *Weekend* reflects the turmoil and chaos of the late sixties better than any Hollywood film from that era. It also stands as the climax to the first phase of Godard's filmmaking career, before he turned to the making of more experimental Marxist films after the social upheavals of 1968. With Mirielle Darc and Jean-Pierre Leaud. French with English subtitles.

VHS: S14572. $29.95.

Jean-Luc Godard, France, 1967, 105 mins.

A Woman Is a Woman

"I conceived this film within the framework of a neo-realist musical: *an absolute contradiction*, but that's the way I wanted to make the film," said Godard. Godard's closely-knit texture of small bistros, striptease joints, political suspicion and conjugal wavering is constantly violated in its naturalistic surface, not just by the comic turns of the plot, but by Godard's reminders not only that the film is a performance, but that the projected images are themselves illusory: "The film has a beauty that is brash and pathetic, like splintered colored glass, fragments that somehow compose a picture while refusing to hold together: musical, sad, uproarious, definitely frail" (Edgardo Cozarinsky). French with English subtitles.

VHS: S08090. $59.95.

Jean-Luc Godard, France, 1961, 85 mins.

CHRIS MARKER

La Jetee

Chris Marker's landmark film is set in postnuclear Paris. The story concerns an astronaut who travels back through time to realize a brief affair with a woman he once glimpsed. With the exception of a haunting shot of the woman blinking, the entire film is composed with still photographs and isolated shots. French with English subtitles.

VHS: S18956. $19.95.

Chris Marker, France, 1962, 29 mins.

La Jetee/ An Occurrence at Owl Creek Bridge

One of the most challenging films ever made, Chris Marker's neo-science fiction film is set in a ruined France after World War III, in which a man's vivid childhood experience allows him to travel forward and backward in time. As a grown man, he meets the girl he had glimpsed as a child at the airport, falls in love with her, chooses to remain in the past, but is executed by those who hold power in the future. France, 1962, 29 mins. Also contains *An Occurrence at Owl Creek Bridge*, directed by Robert Enrico and based on a short story by Ambrose Bierce, which tells the tale of a man who is about to be hanged when the rope suddenly snaps and he is able to escape. Unfortunately, his newly found freedom is short-lived. USA, 1962, 27 mins.

VHS: S06274. $39.95.

Le Joli Mai

Chris Marker's great cinema-verite study of Paris in May, 1962, the month the Algerian War came to an end and France was at peace for the first time since 1939. The first part, "Prayer from the Top of the Eiffel Tower," is about personal happiness and ambition; the second, "The Return of Fantomas," concerned with social and political issues and the relationships of people to each other. A very moving, "personal, and ironic film aided by Pierre Lhomme's superb handling of the 'living camera'" (Georges Sadoul). French with English subtitles.

VHS: S05325. $29.95.

Chris Marker, France, 1962, 180 mins.

Sans Soleil

An audacious and remarkable work from the brilliant essayist and poet Chris Marker, *Sans Soleil* visually interprets a series of letters from a wandering cameraman, based on his travels and experiences from West Africa to Tokyo as he searches for purpose, identity and self-definition through his observations, rituals, speculations, passions and predicaments. "As entertaining as *Zelig*, as visionary as *Blade Runner*" (Jim Hoberman, *Village Voice*). In English.

VHS: S18422. $29.95.

Chris Marker, France, 1983, 100 mins.

MAURICE PIALAT

Loulou

French heartthrob Gerard Depardieu and Isabelle Huppert star in this acclaimed film by Maurice Pialat. Huppert plays Nelly, a married woman who meets Loulou (Depardieu), a charming, leather-jacketed stud in a crowded Paris disco. She can't resist his lustful style and returns home with him. Loulou turns out to be as passionate in bed as on the dance floor, and they embark on a free-wheeling relationship that is a mixture of unabashed eroticism and authentic romance. French with English subtitles.

VHS: S12196. $79.95.

Maurice Pialat, France, 1980, 110 mins.

Police

Gerard Depardieu is a tough French cop who becomes a little too attached to his work. He finds the fine line between cop and criminal is blurred when he meets drug dealer Sophie Marceau. In *Police*, director Maurice Pialat *(Loulou)* subverts the mainstream thriller genre for a personal film that deliberately works against all conventional expectations. A wonderfully spontaneous and authentic film. French with English subtitles.

VHS: S14571. $29.95.

Maurice Pialat, France, 1985, 113 mins.

Under the Sun of Satan

A work of great subtlety and tremendous assurance, the film stars Depardieu in his perhaps most astonishing performance, as a tortured country priest who feels unworthy of God's love. Depardieu's priest encounters the young and beautiful Mouchette, played by Sandrine Bonnaire, who lives in the same town and is a murderess who unwittingly shapes the priest's life. A brilliant new film from one of France's most uncompromising directors. French with English subtitles.

VHS: S10868. $29.95.

Maurice Pialat, France, 1987, 101 mins.

Van Gogh

Maurice Pialat's bold biography of Vincent Van Gogh. The film concentrates on the final three months of Van Gogh's life, the period he spent in Arles. Pialat painstakingly captures the artist's daily life and the private demons that plagued him. Stripped of melodrama, the film offers a different interpretation of Van Gogh's "madness." With Alexandra London, Gerard Sety, Bernard Le Coq, Corrine Bourdona and Elsa Zylberstein. French with English subtitles.

VHS: S19333. $19.95.

Maurice Pialat, France, 1991, 155 mins.

JACQUES RIVETTE

Celine and Julie Go Boating

A most wonderful film from Jacques Rivette, a multi-layered, exuberant lark about two hyperimaginative young ladies (Dominique Labourier and Juliet Berto) involved in a haunted house mystery. Considered by many critics to be the seminal movie of the '70s; a dazzling jack-in-the-box. "The most radical and delightful narrative film since *Citizen Kane*! The experience of a lifetime" (David Thomson, *Soho Weekly*). French with English subtitles.

VHS: S31131. $89.95.

Jacques Rivette, France, 1974, 193 mins.

Divertimento

The cast of Rivette's *La Belle Noiseuse*, Emmanuelle Beart, Jane Birkin and Michel Piccoli, star in this further meditation on the nature of artistic creation. An artist, seemingly past his prime, finds new inspiration in a young woman who inspires him with both her beauty (as expressed through her body) and her soul. French with English subtitles.

VHS: S23997. $89.95.

Jacques Rivette, France/Switzerland, 1990, 126 mins.

Joan the Maid: The Battles

A brilliant interpretation of the story of Joan of Arc by French New Wave and post-New Wave master Jacques Rivette. With a ravishing performance from Sandrine Bonnaire as Joan, this epic about the 15th century teenager who led the French army into battle is a freshly detailed view of the passion and of the complex moral, ecumenical and power issues Joan of Arc forced to the surface. At the same time, Rivette succeeds at humanizing Joan's personal conflict in a very direct yet intimate way. The film follows Joan as she leaves Domremy and tries to convince a captain to take her to the Dauphin, and ends with her first battle, at Orleans. French with English subtitles.

VHS: S35298. $49.95.

Jacques Rivette, France, 1993, 115 mins.

Joan the Maid: The Prisons

In the second part of his film diptych, Jacques Rivette concentrates on Joan of Arc's imprisonment, interrogation and eventual burning at the stake. Rivette emphasizes Joan's marytrdom in a poignant interpretation of her famous line, "I know what I must do but at times I don't know how." Sandrine Bonnaire plays Joan while Rivette himself appears in a cameo as the priest who blesses her just before she leaves home. French with English subtitles.

VHS: S35299. $49.95.

Jacques Rivette, France, 1993, 126 mins.

Joan the Maid: Complete Set

The complete Jacques Rivette two-film set of *Joan the Maid: The Battles* and *Joan the Maid: The Prisons*. French with English subtitles.

VHS: S35300. $89.95.

Jacques Rivette, France, 1993, 241 mins.

La Belle Noiseuse

Jacques Rivette's ambitious masterpiece explores the artistic process in terms of both its transcendent power and its potential for exploitation and destructivness. The core of the film is the confrontation between Frenhofer, a renowned but inactive painter, and a model (played by Emmanuelle Beart). It begins in wary hostility, escalates into a pitched battle of wills, and ends as a true collaboration, with each driving the other to dangerous limits. "One of the finest films ever made about art" (Gene Siskel, *Chicago Tribune*). Winner of the Grand Jury Prize at the Cannes Film Festival. Cinematography by William Lubtchansky. With Michel Piccoli and Bernard Dufour. French with English subtitles.

VHS: S20304. $89.95.

Jacques Rivette, France/Switzerland, 1990, 240 mins.

The Nun (La Religeuse)

Initially banned by the French government, this brilliant adaptation of Diderot's classic 18th century novel explores the moving tale of Suzanne Simonin (Anna Karina, in perhaps her finest screen performance), a 16-year-old girl who is forced by her parents to enter a convent against her will. Unable to bear the hypocrisy and oppression which characterize her new life, Suzanne becomes desperate for freedom. Her attempts first land her in another convent, which, though quite different, is equally constraining. Based on the novel by Diderot. French with English subtitles.

VHS: S13606. $59.95.

Jacques Rivette, France, 1965, 155 mins.

Paris Belongs to Us

Shot on weekends, with no money and no sets, with actors donating their time and Chabrol providing left-over film stock, this film concerns a group of amateurs who come together in Paris to stage a performance of Shakespeare's *Pericles*. But sexual and political tensions develop, their composer dies, the producer kills himself and a fascist conspiracy seems to be lurking in the background. The result of Rivette's two-year struggle is a work of total originality and inventiveness, of amazing depth and independence of vision. French with English subtitles.

VHS: S07472. $59.95.

Jacques Rivette, France, 1958-60, 124 mins.

Up/Down/Fragile

Rivette's luminous romantic musical set in summertime Paris is about three women, an ex-hooker, a former amnesia victim and a librarian, whose lives—which revolve around each other and an opulent nightclub run by a mysterious man—are changed by a mystery, an artist and a gun. Starring Marianne Denicourt, Nathalie Richard and Laurence Cote. "The antithesis of the slick Hollywood musical…graceful" (Kevin Thomas, *L.A. Times*).

VHS: S32500. $89.95.

Jacques Rivette, France/Switzerland, 1995, 169 mins.

RAUL RUIZ

The Golden Boat

This quirky, funny and violent film combines the antics of a homeless, compulsive assassin named Austin, who is desperately in love with a Mexican soap opera star and accompanied by Israel, a philosophy student and part time rock critic for the *Village Voice*, with the fringe of the New York underground. Filmed with the help of the Kitchen, it also includes appearances by such downtown figures as Jim Jarmusch, Vito Acconci, John Zorn, the Wooster Group, and even Annie Sprinkle.

VHS: S18968. $59.95.

Raul Ruiz, USA/Luxembourg/Hong Kong, 1990, 88 mins.

Hypothesis of the Stolen Painting

One of the most important films of the seventies, *The Hypothesis of the Stolen Painting* began as a documentary on writer Pierre Klossowski but soon became, in Ruiz's words, "a fiction about theory." A pompous art collector offers a new history of western art through a guided tour of a fantastic gallery of "living images," all created by the "forgotten" artist, Tonnerr. As our guide drones away about aspects of his collection, the human figures begin to smirk and fidget, emphasizing their play-acting and introducing a new level of spectating into the narrative. Structured as a kind of never-ending detective thriller, Ruiz's film is a daring, fascinating meditation on the relationship between words and images, between works of art and their description or interpretation. Photographed by Sacha Vierny. French with English subtitles.

VHS: S15343. $59.95.

Raul Ruiz, France, 1978, 67 mins.

Life Is a Dream

"If Raul Ruiz wrote novels or poems, he would be a literary celebrity on the short list for the Nobel Prize," said Georgia Brown in *The Village Voice* about this prolific filmmaker of a seemingly unlimited imagination. *Life Is a Dream* is loosely based on the classic play of the same title by Calderon de La Barca. It is a baroque mix of revolutionary politics, pop culture and semiotics that features a Chilean revolutionary using Calderon's play as a mnemonic device. French with English subtitles.

VHS: S26501. $59.95.

Raul Ruiz, France, 1986, 100 mins.

On Top of the Whale

Shot in five languages (one of them imaginary), this film concerns a European anthropological expedition to Patagonia. The ethnologists set out to study a tribe of Indians which now consists of merely two surviving members who speak a strange language made up of only a few phrases (different meanings are produced by varying the inflections). A humorous and intellectual film written and directed by Raul Ruiz, one of the most inventive filmmakers working in Europe today, *On Top of the Whale* is filled with audacious visual ideas, and its cold and misty Northern images often recall Murnau. English, Spanish, French, Dutch and German with English subtitles.

VHS: S13521. $59.95.

Raul Ruiz, Netherlands, 1982, 93 mins.

Three Lives and Only One Death

Marcello Mastroianni in a wonderful, touching and often funny performance as the dissolute husband in Raul Ruiz's inventive, immensely entertaining cinematic game of illusions, assumed personalities and false memories. Banker/arms dealer Luc Allamand is caught in a surrealistic shell game during which the primary players remain a mystery to each other. With Chiara Mastroianni. French with English subtitles.

VHS: S33004. $89.95.

Raul Ruiz, France, 1997, 123 mins.

BERTRAND TAVERNIER

Capitaine Conan

In this brilliantly photographed and acted epic of the Great War, Philippe Torreton stars as a dedicated career soldier and fearless combat officer who leads a band of 50 irregulars. When the Armistice is signed peace does not come easily to Conan and his men, who carry on their killing for nine months after the war has ended. French with English subtitles. Letterboxed.

VHS: S34310. $79.95.

Bertrand Tavernier, France, 1996, 129 mins.

The Clockmaker

Tavernier's debut film, in which Philippe Noiret is the clockmaker whose existence is shattered by the news that his son has been accused of a political murder. Tavernier invests the film with details from the cultural to the personal and domestic. French with English subtitles.

VHS: S00250. $59.95.

Bertrand Tavernier, France, 1975, 105 mins.

Coup de Torchon

Cordier is the only police officer in a small 1938 West African town. He is ridiculed by the local pimps and cuckolded by his wife while his mistress is beaten by her husband. Driven to the brink, he takes revenge on all his enemies. From Jim Thompson's novel *POP 1280*, this darkly funny picture stars Philippe Noiret and Isabelle Huppert. French with English subtitles.

VHS: S00275. $29.95.

Laser: LD75025. $69.95.

Bertrand Tavernier, France, 1981, 128 mins.

Daddy Nostalgie

Dirk Bogarde and Jane Birkin star as a father and daughter who must work through their relationship to arrive at a position of mutual respect and understanding. The painful realization that time is running out makes this scenario all the more compelling. French with English subtitles.

VHS: S20687. $29.98.

Bertrand Tavernier, France, 1990, 105 mins.

Judge and the Assassin

A provocative look at madness and society. In France of the late 19th century, a demented and violent ex-sergeant goes on a rampage of brutal rapes and murders. Philippe Noiret is the clever but ruthless judge who masterminds the capture and interrogation of the murderer, while French comic actor Michel Galabru is the sly psychopath. "Bertrand Tavernier challenges the viewer's reactions, weighing the moral hypocrisy of a self-serving judge against the acts of an insanely murderous victim" (PFA notes). French with English subtitles.

VHS: S11633. $29.95.

Laser: Widescreen. Side 3 CAV. **LD71609. $59.95.**

Bertrand Tavernier, France, 1975, 100 mins.

L.627

The gritty world of Parisian drug culture is revealed in Tavernier's cinema verite style film. L.627 is the name of the special undercover drug squadron in Paris. But Tavernier is not interested in a simple "take" on the hazardous life of a drug cop. He explores the rivalries and loyalties, and the emotional deprivation that becomes a part of a policeman's life as he struggles to balance truth, justice and love in an alien urban world. French with English subtitles.

VHS: S24378. $79.95.

Bertrand Tavernier, France, 1992, 145 mins.

Life and Nothing But

Bertrand Tavernier once again explores the awful legacy of war. Set in 1920, this powerful drama unfolds in post World War I France—a country devastated both physically and spiritually. It tells the story of two women of differing backgrounds who are looking for the missing men they love. Along the way they encounter two French officers, one detailed to identify the dead and the other assigned to choose a body to be honored as France's unknown soldier. Tavernier turns his film into an incredibly moving journey through the postwar landscape of France, touching on the deep psychological scars which the conflict has left behind. With Philippe Noiret, Sabine Azema and Pascale Vidal. French with English subtitles.

VHS: S14787. $19.98.

Bertrand Tavernier, France, 1989, 135 mins.

Mississippi Blues

Tavernier and Parrish approach the Mississippi Delta through its townspeople and its music—Delta Blues and gospel. They explore their own knowledge of this world—Tavernier's from reading Faulkner and Mark Twain, Parrish's from his intimate knowledge of the South. And they skillfully link the drama with such questions as the relationship of the church to politics, and the relationship of music to the life in the Mississippi Delta.

VHS: S09244. $29.95.

Robert Parrish/Bertrand Tavernier, USA/France, 1983, 101 mins.

Round Midnight

Bertrand Tavernier's exquisite homage to jazz—the moving story of a black jazz musician in 1959 Paris, struggling to create the bebop sound. With an Oscar for Herbie Hancock's score, one of the most critically acclaimed films of 1986. English dialog.

VHS: S03495. $19.98.

Laser: LD70669. $29.98.

Bertrand Tavernier, France, 1986, 132 mins.

Spoiled Children

Bertrand Tavernier's autobiographical work about a famous filmmaker (Michel Piccoli) who escapes the disruptions of his home life by renting an apartment in a sleek, highrise building. He is immediately drawn into an obsessive affair with a much younger woman (Christine Pascal), who quickly entangles him in a tenants' fight over the brutal behavior of the landlord. "The film carries the weight of Tavernier's convictions about the injustices everyone is forced to contest, domestically and at work" (*Time Out*). With Michel Aumont, Gerard Jugnot and Arlette Bonnard. French with English subtitles.

VHS: S19460. $79.95.

Bertrand Tavernier, France, 1977, 113 mins.

A Sunday in the Country

Bertrand Tavernier's poetic study of an aging impressionist painter, emotionally withdrawn from his family and disappointed by their accomplishments, who makes one final attempt at reconciliation. With Louis Ducreux, Sabine Azema, Michel Aumont and Genevieve Mnich. French with English subtitles.

VHS: S02934. $29.98.

Bertrand Tavernier, France, 1984, 93 mins.

BERTRAND BLIER

Beau Pere

A wry, sexy, sophisticated comedy that was a major hit in New York, *Beau Pere* stars Patrick Dewaere, Nathalie Baye, Nicole Garcia and Maurice Ronet in the story of a 14-year old girl who, after the death of her mother, has to choose whether to live with her real father or her stepfather. She chooses to live with the stepfather because she is attracted to him. From the Oscar-winning director of *Get Out Your Handkerchiefs*. French with English subtitles.

VHS: S00108. $19.98.

Bertrand Blier, France, 1982, 120 mins.

Buffet Froid

Filled with black humor, Blier's highly original thriller features Gerard Depardieu. Structured as an absurdly hilarious nightmare, the film's logic is twisted and stark: what do you do if you've been unemployed for six months, your wife has disappeared, and you find yourself looking at your own knife sticking out of the belly of a fellow subway passenger—and you can't remember how it got there? French with English subtitles.

VHS: S08257. $19.95.

Bertrand Blier, France, 1980, 95 mins.

Get Out Your Handkerchiefs

Raoul is a doting husband who thinks the best way to pick up his wife's spirits is with an affair. But a menage-a-trois with a bewildered stranger doesn't work, and finally hope arrives with a precocious 13-year-old Christian who achieves the seemingly impossible. An Academy Award winner for "Best Foreign Film". With Gerard Depardieu, Patrick Dewaere, Carole Laure and Michel Serrault. French with English subtitles.

VHS: S00494. $59.95.

Bertrand Blier, France, 1978, 109 mins.

Menage

This black comedy is a brilliant sexual farce. The charismatic, gay thief Bob (Gerard Depardieu) coolly insinuates himself into the troubled lives of Antoine (Michel Blanc) and Monique (Miou-Miou). The film is redolent with Blier's characteristic wit, energy and sexual daring. French with English subtitles.

VHS: S16945. $89.95.

Bertrand Blier, France, 1986, 84 mins.

My Man

A wonderfully irreverent, sexy, provocative film from Bertrand Blier, with the beautiful Anouk Grinberg as a vivacious prostitute with a heart of gold who offers her services for free to those who can return the pleasure, yet who falls for a penniless hustler. Winner of the Best Actress Award at the Berlin Film Festival; a treat of a film about sex, values, identity and trust. "A film that flirts with outrage" (Janet Maslin, *The New York Times*). With Gerard Lanvin, Valeria Bruni Tedeschi and Mathieu Kassovitz. Letterboxed. French with English subtitles.

VHS: S33313. $89.95.

Bertrand Blier, France, 1997, 95 mins.

Too Beautiful for You

Gerard Depardieu stars as a successful car dealer obsessed with his plain temporary secretary much to the displeasure of his stunningly beautiful wife. Bertrand Blier directs this dark comedy that also stars Josiane Balasko and Carole Bouquet. Expect the unexpected in this artful and painfully funny look at adultery. French with English subtitles.
VHS: S13673. $19.98.
Laser: LD71629. $39.95.
Bertrand Blier, France, 1988, 91 mins.

ALAIN RESNAIS

Hiroshima, Mon Amour

From the beginning, in which the love-making of a French actress (Emmanuelle Riva) and a Japanese architect (Eiji Okada) is intercut with newsreel footage of Hiroshima's atomic holocaust and its aftermath, to the couple's painful walk through the reconstructed city, Resnais' film recaptures both the pain and the richness of the war. French with English subtitles.
VHS: S00571. $29.95.
Alain Resnais, France, 1959, 91 mins.

La Guerre Est Finie

This great film by Alain Resnais, scripted by Jorge Semprun, stars Yves Montand, Genevieve Bujold, Ingrid Thulin and Michel Piccoli. Resnais shifts between reality and Montand's mental states in an incisive portrait of an aging Spanish revolutionary exile who is imprisoned by his past as he confronts the failure of his ideas. Resnais explores Montand's insecurities through his relationships with two very different women (Thulin and Bujold). French with English subtitles.
VHS: S23758. $29.95.
Alain Resnais, France, 1966, 120 mins.

Last Year at Marienbad

The strange geometry of a romantic triangle marks the beginning of this elegant, labyrinthine puzzle. Written by French New Wave novelist Alain Robbe-Grillet and from the director of *Hiroshima, Mon Amour, Last Year at Marienbad* is a film classic, the subject of myriad interpretations. Starring Delphine Seyrig, Giorgio Albertazzi, and Sacha Pitoeff. French with English subtitles. New presentation in videoscope.
VHS: S00730. $29.95.
Alain Resnais, France, 1961, 90 mins.

Mon Oncle d'Amerique

Three middle-class French drifters, each convinced they lack definition and excitement, dream about the imaginary and mythic "American Uncle," cross a behavioral scientist who instills in them a sense of wonder and excitement and the mystery of the unknown. The film is structured like a riddle, "one which proves that surrealism lives" *(Time Out)*. With Gerard Depardieu, Nicole Garcia, Roger Pierre and Marie Dubois. French with English subtitles.
VHS: S02141. $29.95.
Alain Resnais, France, 1980, 126 mins.

Muriel

One of the most interesting films from Alain Resnais, a bold and beautiful film, in which Resnais takes an incident from provincial life, the reunion of a middle-aged woman and her old lover at Boulogne. Out of the trivia of everyday life and its anxieties, he creates a mosaic masterpiece that probes the themes of time and memory, and the relationship between personal conscience and public consciousness (the references to the Algerian War). With Delphine Seyrig, Jean-Pierre Kerien, Nina Klein. Music by Hans Werner Henze. French with English subtitles.
VHS: S02079. $59.95.
Alain Resnais, France, 1963, 115 mins.

Night and Fog

A newly mastered version of what Francois Truffaut called "the greatest film of all time": Alain Resnais' incredibly powerful, searing, unforgettable film on Nazi concentration camps, truly a film for all time. Edited by Chris Marker. French with English subtitles.
VHS: S00930. $19.95.
Alain Resnais, France, 1955, 32 mins.

Providence

A famous novelist, suffering from a fatal illness, passes a terrible night hallucinating about various members of his family: his dead wife, his son and daughter-in-law, and his illegitimate son. A brilliant study of memory and reality from Alain Resnais; with John Gielgud, David Warner, Dirk Bogarde, Ellen Burstyn. English dialog.
VHS: S01067. $59.95.
Alain Resnais, Great Britain, 1977, 104 mins.

Stavisky

With *Stavisky*, director Alain Resnais has crafted an extraordinarily beautiful and sophisticated film that requires intense concentration but yields tremendous rewards. The story is that of a French swindler and conman extraordinaire, whose financial manipulations in the 30s brought on riots that helped to topple a government. With Jean-Paul Belmondo, Anny Duperey, Charles Boyer and Gerard Depardieu. Photographed by Sacha Vierny, with a musical score by Stephen Sondheim. French with English subtitles.
VHS: S14986. $59.95.
Alain Resnais, France, 1974, 117 mins.

CLAUDE CHABROL

Betty

Claude Chabrol's masterful tale of alienation stars Stephane Audran as a mysterious woman living in an elegant Versailles hotel, who takes in Marie Trintignant, a wife running away from an emotionless middle class marriage. Set in a world of casual affairs and ice-cold betrayals, *Betty* is a suspenseful, moving psychological study. French with English subtitles.
VHS: S21503. $89.95.
Claude Chabrol, France, 1993, 103 mins.

Blood Relative

The great French director Claude Chabrol directed this Canadian production, which stars Donald Sutherland, Stephane Audran, Donald Pleasance and David Hemmings. The situation is an incestuous relationship which leads to deadly consequences. Chabrol directs with a masterly, cool and detached style that results in a first-rate thriller. Filmed in English.
VHS: S11482. $19.95.
Claude Chabrol, Canada, 1983, 101 mins.

Club Extinction

Previously known as *Dr. M, Club Extinction* is Chabrol's masterful reworking of Fritz Lang's *Dr. Mabuse* scripts. In 21st century Berlin an epidemic of bizarre deaths is sweeping through the city, and a steady stream of propaganda fills the air. Each death serves to further excite Dr. M, who directs the subliminal madness from a hidden fortress above the city. One man, the assassin, stands between freedom and mass destruction. Starring Alan Bates, Jennifer Beals, and Andrew McCarthy.
VHS: S13718. $89.95.
Claude Chabrol, France/Germany, 1989, 105 mins.

The Eye of Vichy

Claude Chabrol strips the mask off a forbidden chapter of French history, the Vichy regime, in this controversial documentary which touches the sensitive subject of French complicity and collaboration with the Nazis during World War II. French with English subtitles.
VHS: S27610. $29.95.
Claude Chabrol, France, 1993, 110 mins.

Horse of Pride

"Too poor that I am to possess another animal, at least 'the horse of pride' will always have a stall in my stable," said Breton peasant Alain Le Goff to his grandson Pierre Jakez-Helias, who grew up to write the best-selling novel, *Horse of Pride*. Director Claude Chabrol was drawn to the story, a calendar of Breton ways and customs from 1905-1920 centering around one family's struggles to rise on the social ladder. The film addresses the Breton's fascination with fantasy through both the energies of the young boy, Pierre, who wishes to carry the daydreams of his loved ones into reality, and the Celtic tradition of storytelling with its emphasis on the sensational, the dramatic, and the intensity of imagination. With Jacques Dufilho and Bernadette Lesache. French with English subtitles.
VHS: S09571. $59.95.
Claude Chabrol, France, 1980, 120 mins.

Innocents with Dirty Hands

One of Chabrol's least-known thrillers. Julie Wormser (stunningly played by Romy Schneider) is an icy wife who plots with her lover, writer and neighbor, Jeff Marle, to get rid of her alcoholic, impotent husband (Rod Steiger) while vacationing in St. Tropez. Fascinatingly ironic and ambiguous with a wonderfully convoluted plot, ever-changing relationsips and intriguing minor characters. "A superbly stylish and baroque crime thriller which marks a return for Chabrol to the bravura incorporation of pulp conventions" *(Time Out)*. French with English subtitles.
VHS: S34651. $79.95.
Claude Chabrol, France/Germany/Italy, 1975, 125 mins.

L'Enfer

Claude Chabrol is in top form in this top-notch thriller—the study of deranged jealousy—based on a script by Henri-Georges *(Diabolique)* Clouzot. Paul Cluzet plays the owner of a small hotel who has everything—a beautiful wife, a new son, and a successful business located on a serene lake. But then he hears voices and begins to question his wife's fidelity, which begins a downward spiral into madness. With Emmanuelle Beart. French with English subtitles.
VHS: S25816. $19.98.
Claude Chabrol, France, 1994, 100 mins.

La Ceremonie

Claude Chabrol returns in great form with this gripping suspense thriller. Sophie (Sandrine Bonnaire, *Monsieur Hire*) is a quiet, eccentric maid, hired by the Lelievres, a fashionable, bourgeoise French family living in a Brittany country estate. When Sophie befriends Jeanne (Isabelle Huppert), a boisterous postal worker who hates the Lelievres, the two misfits form a destructive bond, secured on a similar secret past. French with English subtitles.
VHS: S31550. $89.95.
Claude Chabrol, France, 1996, 111 mins.

La Rupture

One of Claude Chabrol's best films: a taut, diabolical thriller about a woman (Stephane Audran) who leaves her drug-addicted husband (Jean-Claude Drouot) after he violently attacks their child while in a schizophrenic haze. His aristocratic parents hire a brutal private detective (Jean-Pierre Cassel) to turn up incriminating evidence in order to discredit her in a child custody suit. With Michel Bouquet, Catherine Rouvel and Jean Carmet. French with English subtitles.
VHS: S19461. $24.95.
Claude Chabrol, France/Italy/Spain, 1970, 124 mins.

Le Beau Serge

Claude Chabrol's first, great film—one of the landmarks of the French New Wave. Produced on a miniscule budget in the natural setting in Sardent, Francois (Jean-Claude Brialy) is convalescing in his native village to find his childhood friend (Gerard Blain) a drunkard in a bad marriage, and after an affair with Bernadette Lafont, interferes in Serge's life only to finally accept reality and understand. French with English subtitles.
VHS: S03509. $29.95.
Claude Chabrol, France, 1958, 97 mins.

Le Boucher

A first rate psychological thriller from Claude Chabrol about the evolving relationship of a beautiful school teacher and a serial murderer. "In Chabrol's films, the relationships are plotted with a mathematical precision that does not rule out surprising developments" (Roy Armes). With Stephane Audran, Antonio Passallia, Mario Beccaria and Pasquale Ferone. French with English subtitles.
VHS: S16929. $24.95.
Laser: CLV. **LD72051. $39.95.**
Claude Chabrol, France/Italy, 1969, 90 mins.

Les Biches

In Chabrol's New Wave set-piece, Federique is a rich and fashionable lesbian who encounters a young, bohemian sidewalk artist called Why. They escape together to St. Tropez for Christmas where Why ends up in bed with the young architect, Paul. Tension between the three escalates when they co-habit Federique's villa. As Paul's affections lean toward Federique, Why begins a jealous transformation that culminates in a deadly conclusion. French with English subtitles.
VHS: S16167. $24.95.
Claude Chabrol, France, 1968, 104 mins.

Les Bonnes Femmes (The Good Girls)

Bernadette Lafont, Clotilde Joano, Stephane Audran and Lucille Saint-Simon star as four working girls in Paris in this brilliant New Wave thriller by Claude Chabrol. What they hope to find is love, but each ends up in the hands of a killer. As always, Chabrol is interested more in the milieu which supports his characters than in the suspense, as he gives us an intimate look at ordinary lives full of boredom and vague dreams. Cinematography by the great Henri Decae. French with English subtitles.
VHS: S26901. $24.95.
Claude Chabrol, France, 1960, 105 mins.

Les Cousins
One of the great Chabrol early films; Charles (Gerard Blain), a student from the provinces, comes to Paris to live with his sophisticated, bullying cousin Paul, falls in love with Florence, but she becomes Paul's mistress. During their examinations, Paul passes effortlessly while Charles fails, and Charles accidentally kills Paul after trying to kill him. An ingenious, brilliant portrayal of student life in Paris, with great cinematography by Henri Decae. French with English subtitles.
VHS: S04906. $79.95.
Claude Chabrol, France, 1958, 110 mins.

Madame Bovary
The classic 19th century novel by Gustave Flaubert has been masterfully adapted to the screen by veteran filmmaker Claude Chabrol. Isabelle Huppert occupies the erotic title role of Emma Bovary, the unhappily married woman who wants more out of life. With Christophe Malavoy, Jean Yanne, Lucas Belvaux and Christiane Minazolli. French with English subtitles.
VHS: S16504. $14.98.
Laser: LD71454. $39.98.
Claude Chabrol, France, 1991, 130 mins.

Piece of Pleasure
Chabrol's dark vision of the complexities of modern marriage. A story of a couple whose marriage is eroding because of the tyrannical will of the husband. French with English subtitles.
VHS: S01029. $79.95.
Claude Chabrol, France, 1976, 100 mins.

Story of Women
An almost perfect film; Claude Chabrol bases his Venice Film Festival award-winning film on the true story of the last woman to be guillotined in France, at the onset of WWII. Isabelle Huppert delivers a stunning, riveting performance as the wife-abortionist who, despite the compromises she makes for the sake of a "better" life, is redeemed as a true individual at the end. A brilliant film from the hands of a true master. French with English subtitles.
VHS: S12990. $29.95.
Claude Chabrol, France, 1988, 112 mins.

Ten Days' Wonder
Claude Chabrol's elegant transposition of an Ellery Queen thriller—a situation of mental aberration, adultery and blackmail. Featuring Orson Welles, Marlene Jobert, Michel Piccoli and Anthony Perkins, the film is notable for its plumbing the psychological depths of the Oedipal complex within the confines of a terrific thriller. In English.
VHS: S07462. $24.95.
Claude Chabrol, France, 1971, 101 mins.

Who's Got the Black Box?
Murder and intrigue overseas as black boxes are hidden in the heads of statues. The boxes are being used to jam radar signals on Greek missiles. A great spy thriller with a sensational ending involving a mine shaft. With Jean Seberg, Maurice Ronet, Christian Marquand and Saro Urzzil. Dubbed in English.
VHS: S32601. $24.95.
Claude Chabrol, France/Italy/Greece, 1970, 90 mins.

LOUIS MALLE

Alamo Bay
A powerful drama based on actual events on the Texas Gulf coast detailing the conflicts between local shrimp fishermen and Vietnamese refugees. With Ed Harris and Amy Madigan from director Louis Malle. Music by Ry Cooder.
VHS: S00026. $79.95.
Louis Malle, USA, 1985, 99 mins.

Atlantic City
Burt Lancaster delivers a stunning performance as the seemingly washed-up gangster, with Susan Sarandon as his lost-soul companion. A moving portrait of American dreams, contained in the small-world milieu of the slums and the gambling palaces of Atlantic City. Based on the screenplay by John Guare.
VHS: S00073. $14.95.
Louis Malle, Canada/USA, 1981, 101 mins.

Au Revoir les Enfants (Goodbye, Children)
Louis Malle returns to the days of German occupation during World War II to recount the story of the friendship between two schoolboys, one Jewish and the other Catholic. A winner of many awards including Best Picture in France. Familiar themes are explored. Subtitled.
VHS: S08496. $19.98.
Louis Malle, France, 1988, 104 mins.

Calcutta
Louis Malle transforms this recording of his trip through India's great city from a simple travelogue into an intense examination of the minute details that make up the lives of those he encounters. An awesome tapestry emerges, one that joins such disparate strands as Moslems and Hindus, or the protests of a former government official and the building of a skyscraper without modern equipment. English narration.
VHS: S22466. $29.95.
Louis Malle, France, 1976, 99 mins.

Damage
French director Louis Malle's adaptation of Josephine Hart's novel about an upper class Parliament member (Jeremy Irons) who has an affair with an ethereal French woman (Juliette Binoche) who is about to be married to Irons' son (Rupert Graves). Miranda Richardson co-stars as Irons' long-suffering wife. This unrated version contains the excised material the MPAA found objectionable enough to warrant an NC-17 rating.
VHS: S18607. $19.95.
Laser: LD72184. $49.95.
Louis Malle, Great Britain/USA, 1992, 111 mins.

Elevator to the Gallows
A Hitchcock-like romantic thriller from director Louis Malle *(Atlantic City, Au Revoir les Enfants)* which features a terrific early performance by French superstar Jeanne Moreau as a woman waiting for her lover to return from committing the "perfect crime." Malle sets old Hollywood film noir formulas to new rhythms in what is one of the first films of the French New Wave. Original jazz score by the late great Miles Davis. French with English subtitles.
VHS: S15394. $29.95.
Louis Malle, France, 1957, 87 mins.

The Fire Within
Louis Malle's painful and devastating portrait of dissolution and self-destruction, capturing the final two days of a wealthy French writer visiting his friends, following his release from a mental asylum. Brilliantly scored by Erik Satie, the film has a harsh, bleak beauty and despair. With Maurice Ronet, Lena Skerla, Yvonne Clech and Hubert Deschamps. French with English subtitles.
VHS: S17697. $29.95.
Louis Malle, France, 1963, 108 mins.

The Lovers
A landmark of both French cinema and screen eroticism, *The Lovers* stars Jeanne Moreau as a stylish provincial wife whose shallow life changes when she meets an unpretentious young man. The film caused a furor of protest when it was first released; today its tender sensuality and genuine feeling for passion are a welcome relief. Henri Decae's magical photography and Brahm's Second Quartet create an atmosphere of luminous romanticism. French with English subtitles.
VHS: S16078. $29.95.
Louis Malle, France, 1958, 89 mins.

May Fools
A well-to-do family gathers to divide the spoils of a country estate after the death of the ancient matriarch. Michel Piccoli and Miou-Miou star in this satiric portrait of a family and a nation in conflict. With Bruno Carette, Harriet Walter, Dominique Blanc and Michel Duchaussoy. Set during the summer of 1968. French with English subtitles.
VHS: S13675. $19.98.
Laser: LD71621. $39.95.
Louis Malle, France, 1990, 105 mins.

Murmur of the Heart
Louis Malle directed this affectionate story of a young man's coming of age. When a 14-year-old boy from a bourgeois home is sent to a sanitarium for his health, he learns that mother knows best. A comic and, at the time, quite scandalous motion picture. With Benoit Ferreux as the rambunctious kid and Lea Massari as his sensuous mom. Also Daniel Gelin, Marc Winocourt and Michel Lonsdale. Watch for the dinner tennis match. French with English subtitles.
VHS: S11533. $19.98.
Louis Malle, France/Germany/Italy, 1971, 118 mins.

My Dinner with Andre
Nearly two hours of dinner conversation between New York avant-garde theatre director Andre Gregory and playwright Wallace Shawn becomes a fascinating dialog about the meaning of life, a bizarre and entertaining satirical comedy, and one of the most highly praised films of 1982.
VHS: S00905. $29.98.
Louis Malle, USA, 1981, 110 mins.

Pretty Baby
Director Malle has taken a taboo subject, child prostitution, and created a film of humanity and beauty. Brooke Shields plays a young girl in 1917 New Orleans; Keith Carradine is a photographer obsessed with the red light district bewitched by Shields. With Susan Sarandon.
VHS: S01053. $19.95.
Laser: LD75341. $29.98.
Louis Malle, USA, 1978, 109 mins.

Vanya on 42nd Street
Louis Malle returns to the characters of his *My Dinner with Andre* in this very cinematic filming of Andre Gregory's staging of Chekhov's *Uncle Vanya*, in a run-down Broadway theatre for a small, private audience. Wallace Shawn and Julianne Moore star in the melancholy drama, using the new translation by David Mamet. The performances are outstanding, and quite surprisingly, this becomes first-rate Chekhov.
VHS: S25658. $19.95.
Laser: LD74988. $34.95.
Louis Malle, USA, 1994, 119 mins.

A Very Private Affair
Brigitte Bardot and Marcello Mastroianni star in this tale about the trials of movie stardom. A beautifully filmed story by the director of *My Dinner with Andre* and *Atlantic City*. English dialog.
VHS: S01411. $19.98.
Louis Malle, USA, 1962, 94 mins.

Viva Maria
Louis Malle's bawdy, irreverent work about two beautiful entertainers and anarchists (Jeanne Moreau and Brigitte Bardot) who become entangled in the Mexican revolution. With George Hamilton, Gregor Von Rezzori and Paulette Dubost. French with English subtitles.
VHS: S20402. $19.98.
Laser: LD76320. $39.99.
Louis Malle, France/Italy, 1965, 119 mins.

Zazie dans le Metro
Called "an exceedingly funny picture…funny in a bold, delicate, freakish, vulgar, outrageous, and occasionally nightmarish way…From start to finish, the picture is crammed with sight gags and preposterous photographic stunts. *Zazie* is a film like *Alice in Wonderland*; Zazie is a foul-mouthed little cynic, age 11, who comes to Paris for a weekend with her uncle (Philippe Noiret), a female impersonator, and nobody and nothing are quite what they seem" (Pauline Kael). From Louis Malle, the director of *Murmur of the Heart*. French with English subtitles.
VHS: S12991. $29.95.
Louis Malle, France, 1960, 85 mins.

ERIC ROHMER

Chloe in the Afternoon
In *Chloe in the Afternoon*, the last of Eric Rohmer's *Moral Tales* series, Frederic (Bernard Verley) is a married man who fantasizes about the women he sees on the street. When he runs into Bohemian Chloe (Zouzou), an old friend, during his afternoon lunch, he discovers that he may be too squeamish to actually cheat on his wife. "A formal, elegant examination of someone puzzled by marital fidelity, *Chloe in the Afternoon* is a wonderfully cool and lucid expression of the twists and turns of its hero's thoughts." French with English subtitles.
VHS: S06832. $19.98.
DVD: DV60283. $29.95.
Eric Rohmer, France, 1972, 97 mins.

Claire's Knee
Eric Rohmer's most popular work, a vibrant, luscious comedy which focuses on the temptations of a diplomat who visits his childhood home just before he is married to a woman with whom he has lived for six years. Charming and sunny sex comedy. With Jean-Claude Brialy, Lawrence De Monaghan. French with English subtitles.
VHS: S04875. $19.98.
DVD: DV60288. $29.95.
Eric Rohmer, France, 1970, 105 mins.

Eric Rohmer: The Moral Tales Box Set
This five-tape set includes five Rohmer classics: *La Collectionneuse* (1966), *My Night at Maud's* (1969), *Claire's Knee* (1970), *Chloe in the Afternoon* (1972), *The Girl at the Monceau Bakery* and *Suzanne's Career*. French with English subtitles.
VHS: S32178. $79.98.
Eric Rohmer, France, 1962-1972, 402 mins.

Four Adventures of Reinette and Mirabelle
In many ways, Rohmer's most offbeat film since 1978's *Perceval*. The film centers on the relationship between two young women: Reinette, a naive but talented painter from the provinces, and Mirabelle, a worldly Parisian student who meets Reinette during summer vacation and invites her to share an apartment during the upcoming school year. The narrative is partitioned into the four segments of the title, each one yielding a graceful epiphany and playing upon a central theme of the perils of idealism. A delightful comedy enhanced by Rohmer's customary richness of characterization. French with English subtitles.
VHS: S13577. $29.95.
Eric Rohmer, France, 1989, 95 mins.

Full Moon in Paris

A headstrong young woman (Pascale Ogier) moves out on her devoted love and takes her own apartment in Paris in order to "experience" loneliness—instead, she juggles various lovers. A continuing investigation by Rohmer of the morality of love and sex. French with English subtitles.

VHS: S00474. $24.95.

Eric Rohmer, France, 1985, 101 mins.

The Girl at the Monceau Bakery/ Suzanne's Career

"Two delightful short features" (Geoff Andrew) from Eric Rohmer. In *The Girl at the Monceau Bakery* (1962), a young man is drawn to a woman he admires from afar. When she goes away, he seeks comfort in the arms of the girl in the local bakery. *Suzanne's Career* (1963) follows the relationship between two friends when they both become interested in the same girl. This is the first part of Rohmer's *Moral Tales*. French with English subtitles.

VHS: S32177. $19.98.

Eric Rohmer, France, 1962/1963, 78 mins.

La Collectionneuse

This is the third in a series of six films from "The Moral Tales," a group of films by the consummate master of comic French drama. A handsome man onvacation in St. Tropez is unnerved by the sybaritic presence of a fellow guest who is staying at the same pension. He confronts her erotic threat by a renewed commitment to moral turpitude. French with English subtitles.

VHS: S28995. $19.98.

Eric Rohmer, France, 1966, 88 mins.

My Night at Maud's

The third in Rohmer's series of moral tales, the story of Jean-Louis, a devout Catholic who, arriving to start a new job at Clermont-Ferrand, meets an attractive and intelligent divorcee. The next day, Jean-Louis meets a young Catholic woman to whom he is immediately attracted, but when he makes advances to her they are rejected. French with English subtitles.

VHS: S04871. $19.98.
DVD: DV60163. $29.98.

Eric Rohmer, France, 1969, 110 mins.

Pauline at the Beach

Another treat from the director of *My Night at Maud's* and *Claire's Knee*. Rohmer explores the complicated romantic and sexual entanglements of six people on summer holiday. The coincidences, misunderstandings and passionate antics of the adults are observed by teenage Pauline and her first boyfriend. French with English subtitles.

VHS: S01003. $24.95.

Eric Rohmer, France, 1983, 94 mins.

Rendevous in Paris

Through the picturesque cafes and parks of Paris in the springtime, New Wave master Eric Rohmer displays his unique take on the follies and treacheries of the human heart in this witty, enchanting comedy which follows three young couples as they face the vanities, cruelties and deceptions of their romantic entanglements. "The perfect little gift for lovers of film, of Paris and of love!" (Richard Corliss, *Time*). French with English subtitles.

VHS: S31412. $89.95.

Eric Rohmer, France, 1996, 100 mins.

A Tale of Springtime

Eric Rohmer initiates a new cycle, *Tales of the Four Seasons*, with this film about the romantic entanglements between Jeanne, a beautiful philosophy teacher, and Natacha, a younger woman who invites Jeanne to stay at her father's apartment. Natacha tries to manipulate an affair between Jeanne and her father, to get rid of her father's young lover, whom she despises. With Anne Teyssedre, Hugues Quester and Florence Darel. French with English subtitles.

VHS: S18459. $19.98.

Eric Rohmer, France, 1989, 112 mins.

Tale of Winter

Charlotte Very, Michel Voletti, Herve Furic, and Frederic Van Dren Dreissche are cast in this bubbling romantic comedy from Eric Rohmer. Very plays a woman unhappy with her two current lovers. In the pursuit of simplicity, she begins a torrid affair with an old flame. French with English subtitles.

VHS: S26144. $89.95.

Eric Rohmer, France, 1994, 114 mins.

AGNES VARDA

Agnes Varda and Susan Sontag: Lions and Cannibals

This 1969 conversation explores the cinema approaches of film directors Varda and Sontag, who were among the small group of artists represented in the prestigious seventh annual New York Film Festival (1969). Here they discuss their ideas and their films with Jack Kroll, senior editor at *Newsweek*. Discussion covers similarities in their aesthetic and their work, how their new films concern the problems of tortured personalities, politics and the grotesque in everyday matters. 28 mins.

VHS: S31578. $59.95.

Cleo from 5 to 7

Ninety minutes, exactly, in the life of the singer Corinne Marchand, as she waits for the results of a medical test for cancer, and meets a young soldier about to leave for the Algerian war. Because of the anticipation, every trivial incident takes on a new significance. "Produced mainly in the streets of Paris, this is a moving poem of love and death" (Georges Sadoul). With Antoine Bourseiller. French with English subtitles.

VHS: S03510. $29.95.
Laser: Widescreen. **LD76824. $49.95.**

Agnes Varda, France/Italy, 1961, 90 mins.

Jacquot de Nantes

Agnes Varda's loving tribute to her late husband, Jacques Demy, begins in Nantes in 1938 with a boy obsessed with movies. This 8-year-old makes puppets for little operettas. As he grows older his obsession never dies, even though his father makes him study mechanics. A number of happy childhood events animate this captivating film about a man who grows up and yet retains a youthful delight in fantasy that shapes his enduring vision and makes him a master of the French musical. French with English subtitles.

VHS: S20738. $19.95.

Agnes Varda, France, 1991, 118 mins.

Le Bonheur

A beautiful, elegant, romantic film that explores the issue of a man who is trying to love two women. Jean-Claude Drouot plays a happily married carpenter who wants his wife to accept that he can love his mistress at the same time. Controversial because of its exploration of morality and because Drouot's real-life family play his wife and children. Agnes Varda's daring is to explore the nature of relationship from a woman's point of view. French with English subtitles.

VHS: S16188. $29.95.

Agnes Varda, France, 1965, 87 mins.

Lion's Love

Varda's journey into American 60's culture is a comment on the margins of Hollywood with Ragni and Rado (*Hair*) and Warhol's Viva as a menage a trois awaiting discovery and fame in an indifferent Hollywood. Varda also weaves in other material-Michael McClure's avant-garde theatre piece *The Beard*, Shirley Clarke's film experiments and TV news. A film made in response to (or acceptance of) the 60's American social, political and cultural upheavals.

VHS: S22467. $39.95.

Agnes Varda, USA, 1969, 115 mins.

Vagabond

Agnes Varda's extraordinarily bleak account of a young woman's death and life. In a breathtaking performance, Sandrine Bonnaire (*La Ceremonie*) is Mona, a waif who drops out of Parisian society to wander the southwest French countryside, exploring the open spaces and implicit freedom absent in her life. In the opening scene, her body is discovered frozen. Varda expertly recounts her life, carefully dissecting French society. French with English subtitles.

VHS: S02982. $24.95.
Laser: LD71863. $49.95.

Agnes Varda, France, 1986, 105 mins.

FRANCOIS TRUFFAUT

The 400 Blows

One of the landmarks of cinema, which introduced the character of Antoine Doinel, played by Jean-Pierre Leaud, to the world, as the 12-year-old boy left to his own devices in an indifferent adult world. An uncompromising film, winner of innumerable awards. French with English subtitles.

VHS: S00006. $29.95.
Laser: LD70800. $59.95.
DVD: DV60174. $39.95.

Francois Truffaut, France, 1959, 97 mins.

The Bride Wore Black

Francois Truffaut's stylish and suspenseful homage to Hitchcock stars a stone-faced Jeanne Moreau tracking down and killing (each in a unique way) the five men responsible for her husband's accidental death. A very odd and dark film, it contains many masterful stylistic flourishes and is further highlighted by an eerie, atmospheric musical score from Bernard Herrmann. Beautifully photographed by Raoul Coutard. French with English subtitles.

VHS: S14805. $19.99.
Laser: LD72165. $34.95.

Francois Truffaut, France, 1968, 107 mins.

Confidentially Yours

This double tribute to Hitchcock and *film noir* pictures a small town that is overtaken by a series of brutal murders. The first suspect is real estate agent Jean-Louis Trintignant. Fanny Ardant, his secretary, believes he is being framed and sets out to solve the mystery. French with newly translated English subtitles.

VHS: S00263. $29.95.
Laser: CLV. **LD72100. $49.95.**

Francois Truffaut, France, 1983, 110 mins.

Day for Night

Truffaut's love poem to the movies and movie-making features Truffaut playing a director who struggles to complete a film while at the same time handling the emotional problems of staff and crew. Funny and bittersweet, *Day for Night* provides insights into the movie process. Oscar winner for Best Foreign Picture, with Jean-Pierre Leaud, Jacqueline Bisset. English dubbed.

VHS: S00308. $59.95.

Francois Truffaut, France, 1973, 116 mins.

Fahrenheit 451

Truffaut's first English-language production stars Julie Christie and Oskar Werner. Based on Ray Bradbury's masterpiece about a future without books, Werner plays a fireman in charge of burning books who meets a schoolteacher (Christie) who dares to read. In original English language.

VHS: S00425. $59.95.
Laser: LD70028. $34.98.

Francois Truffaut, France, 1966, 112 mins.

Francois Truffaut

A 1977 conversation between Truffaut (speaking in French, with English voice translation) and Richard Roud (then director of the New York Film Festival) about Truffaut's life, work, origin of the auteur theory, and problems and opportunities in the French film scene of the 1950s and '60s. With clips from *The 400 Blows, Jules and Jim, Bed and Board, The Man Who Loved Women* and others. 28 mins.

VHS: S31567. $59.95.

Francois Truffaut: 25 Years, 25 Films

This documentary offers a comprehensive overview of Truffaut's career. Added attractions include his first film, *Les Mistons*, interviews with Truffaut discussing his work, the theatrical trailers of nine films, Jean-Pierre Leaud's audition for *The 400 Blows* and Steven Spielberg's discussion of Truffaut's acting role as the scientist in *Close Encounters of the Third Kind*. With commentary by Truffaut scholar and biographer Annette Insdorf.

Laser: LD71929. $39.95.

Francois Truffaut: Stolen Portraits

A brilliant documentary which provides new insights and revelations. Full of extensive clips and in-depth interviews with dozens of Truffaut's collaborators and friends, including Gerard Depardieu, Eric Rohmer, Marcel Ophuls, Claude Chabrol, Jacques Rivette, Truffaut's daughter and Truffaut's former wife, Madeleine Morgenstern, this remarkable film shines new light on the psychological motivations of Truffaut's life and on his filmmaking career. French with English subtitles.

VHS: S26965. $19.98.

Serge Toubiana/Michel Pascal, France, 1993, 93 mins.

Godard/Truffaut Shorts

A short film by Jean-Luc Godard made prior to his release of *Breathless* entitled *All the Boys Are Called Patrick*, and a short film by Francois Truffaut, *Les Mistons*, a charming evocative film about the arousal of sexual feelings in a group of young boys on summer holiday. French with English subtitles.

VHS: S01777. $29.95.

Jean-Luc Godard/Francois Truffaut, France, 1957

Jules and Jim

Truffaut's famous love triangle stars Henri Serre as Jim and Oskar Werner as Jules, both in love with Catherine (Jeanne Moreau). Their free-wheeling friendship is suspended when Jules marries Catherine and takes her back to Germany. The two friends are separated by World War I, and when they meet again after the war, Catherine changes partners. One of the films that justifies the invention of the movies. Photography by Raoul Coutard; music by Georges Delerue. French with English subtitles.

VHS: S00663. $29.95.
Laser: LD71069. $59.95.

Francois Truffaut, France, 1961, 105 mins.

The Last Metro

Truffaut's poignant, compelling drama, set in Nazi-occupied Paris, unfolds in the Theatre Montmartre, as a group of actors rehearse. But everyone harbors a secret. Catherine Deneuve visits her exiled Jewish husband; the leading man is a member of the Resistance. Touching and tense.

VHS: S00724. $29.95.
Laser: LD71522. $69.95.

Francois Truffaut, France, 1980, 135 mins.

Love on the Run

The latest episode in the life of Truffaut's hero Antoine Doinel begins with our protagonist newly divorced in his thirties and awaiting publication of his first novel. Doinel's incurable romanticism and complicated affairs of the heart make for a funny and bittersweet conclusion With Jean-Pierre Leaud, Marie-France Pisier. French with newly translated English subtitles.

VHS: S00778. $29.95.

Francois Truffaut, France, 1979, 95 mins.

The Man Who Loved Women

More than a comedy of the sexes, this is a touching exploration of the many faces of love. Truffaut's story is of Bertrand Morane, an intelligent and sensitive man who writes his memoirs, remembering all the women he has loved. Starring Charles Denner and featuring Brigitte Fossey, Nathalie Baye and Leslie Caron. English dubbed.

VHS: S00818. $19.98.
Laser: LD76410. $34.98.
Francois Truffaut, France, 1977, 119 mins.

Mississippi Mermaid

Jean-Paul Belmondo plays a wealthy industrialist living on the island of La Reunion, who orders a bride by mail and receives, in place of his intended, the beautiful Catherine Deneuve and a flimsy (but apparently acceptable) explanation. The imposter soon absconds with his bank account and leads him into a murky drama of missing persons and murder. What comes out of this strange mix is a surprisingly powerful adult love story. French with English subtitles.

VHS: S14806. $19.99.
Laser: LD72126. $39.98.
Francois Truffaut, France, 1969, 123 mins.

Shoot the Piano Player

Charles Aznavour is the skilled concert pianist whose role in his wife's suicide has made him hide from life by playing in a bistro. But life and love refuse to pass him by, and inevitably he is drawn back into feeling once again. The film includes many touches of light humor, including Truffaut's homage to American gangster films. French with English subtitles.

VHS: S01192. $29.95.
Laser: LD70461. $49.95.
Francois Truffaut, France, 1960, 80 mins.

Small Change

Small Change presents the viewer with ten boys and girls whose adventures illustrate the different stages of passage from early childhood to adolescence. Some episodes are funny, some serious, some sheer fantasy. Together they animate the notion that childhood is often perilous but also full of grace. French with English subtitles.

VHS: S01216. $19.99.
Laser: LD72156. $34.98.
Francois Truffaut, France, 1976, 106 mins.

The Soft Skin

Truffaut's New Wave classic is a study of a man's first incident of infidelity. Pierre Desailly is the successful publisher who, while often separated from his wife because of business, meets a younger flight attendant, and has an affair. With legendary skill and acute sensitivity, Truffaut rips the mask off the lies, suspicions and guilt that lead to the disintegration of ordinary marriages. French with newly translated English subtitles.

VHS: S01224. $29.95.
Laser: LD76800. $49.95.
Francois Truffaut, France, 1964, 120 mins.

Story of Adele H.

In 1863, the beautiful young daughter of the world-famous writer Victor Hugo crosses the Atlantic in desperate pursuit of the man she believes is her fiance, her lover, her destiny. For months and years she waits for him, harasses him, throws herself in his path. Finally, her intensity gives way to madness. Truffaut called this film the autopsy of a passion. French with English subtitles.

VHS: S01259. $19.99.
Laser: LD71510. $34.98.
Francois Truffaut, France, 1975, 97 mins.

Two English Girls

Based on the only other novel by Henri-Pierre Roche, the author of *Jules and Jim*, the situation is reversed as two sisters are in love with the same man at the turn of the century. Leaud is the young Parisian convalescing at the seaside. Extraordinary mood photography by Almendros. French with English subtitles.

VHS: S01382. $29.95.
Laser: Includes 24 minutes of restored footage. **LD72445. $69.95.**
Francois Truffaut, France, 1971, 108 mins.

The Wild Child

The Wild Child is based on a remarkable journal, the 1806 memoirs of a French physician, a certain Jean Itard. The record begins in 1798, when a child is found living in the forest like an animal. Dr. Itard sets for himself the task of educating this child who is totally alien to civilization. Shot in austere black and white, the film achieves a depth of vision treating anew love, freedom, the nature of childhood and childhood's end. French with English subtitles.

VHS: S14810. $19.99.
Laser: LD75540. $39.98.
Francois Truffaut, France, 1970, 85 mins.

The Woman Next Door

Fanny Ardant and Gerard Depardieu star as former tempestuous lovers now married to other people who suddenly find themselves living next door to one another. Truffaut masterfully guides the couple through a maze of confused feelings, steering them toward their final encounter. French with newly translated English subtitles.

VHS: S01477. $29.95.
Laser: LD76801. $49.95.
Francois Truffaut, France, 1981, 106 mins.

ROBERT BRESSON

The Devil, Probably

Predating the "after the revolution" disillusionment of recent Generation-X films, this film from French new wave master Robert Bresson follows Charles, a modern-day fallen angel, and his quartet of friends, who are all in revolt against the pollution of an industrialized consumer society. Unable to find redemption in revolution, the church, psychoanalysis or even love, Charles makes a desperate bargain with a junkie friend. Originally banned in France for its daring portrait of alienated youth, *The Devil, Probably* "expresses the malaise of our time more profoundly and more magnificently than any work of art in any medium" (Andrew Sarris, *Village Voice*). "A masterpiece! A voluptuous film!" (Francois Truffaut). French with English subtitles.

VHS: S30824. $89.95.
Robert Bresson, France, 1977, 95 mins.

Diary of a Country Priest

The story of an ailing priest who believes he has failed. Pauline Kael said: "*Diary of a Country Priest* is one of the most profound emotional experiences in the history of the cinema." French with English subtitles.

VHS: S19932. $59.95.
Robert Bresson, France, 1951, 116 mins.

L'Argent

The subject of *L'Argent* is materialism, specifically the consequences of the passing of a counterfeit 500-franc note which initiates a chain reaction of corruption and moral error leading to a truly terrifying climax. *L'Argent* is one of Bresson's most perfect works; its subject and form are inseparable; every action leaves a trace, nothing is superfluous. With Christian Patey, Sylvie Van Den Elsen, Michel Briquet and Caroline Lang. French with English subtitles.

VHS: S20302. $59.95.
Robert Bresson, France/Switzerland, 1983, 82 mins.

Lancelot of the Lake

Robert Bresson's masterpiece is set in the last days of the age of chivalry. As the Knights return to King Arthur's Court after a doomed quest for the Holy Grail, they are torn apart by jealousies and rivalries, at the center of which is Lancelot and his relationship with Guinevere. Told in Bresson's austere style, with rich colors and stark images, the film becomes a hypnotic study in the loss of faith, in which reality stands in sharp relief to the spiritual. With Luc Simon, Laura Duc Condominas and Humbert Balsan. French with English subtitles.

VHS: S23284. $79.95.
Robert Bresson, France/Italy, 1975, 80 mins.

Les Dames du Bois de Boulogne

This rarely-seen second feature by Bresson was co-scripted by Jean Cocteau based on an anecdote in a novel by Diderot. Two sophisticated lovers, Helene and Jean, agree to remain friends even when their ardor for one another has died. Helene good naturedly introduces her ex-lover Jean to a new woman and everything seems fine as a new romance begins. But this woman harbors a mysterious past that threatens to unsettle everything. Maria Casares stars in a rigorous, intense film remarkable for Cocteau's layered dialog. French with English subtitles.

VHS: S24045. $59.95.
Robert Bresson, France, 1944, 83 mins.

A Man Escaped

A perfect film, based on the true story of a French Resistance fighter's escape from a Gestapo prison. In Bresson's hands, the narrative of the prison escape just hours before he is executed becomes a transcendental meditation on the meaning of freedom and existence told in light and shadows. "I would like to show this miracle: an invisible hand over the prison, directing what happens…the film is a mystery…The Spirit breathes where it will," said Bresson. Struck from a beautiful, newly mastered print. French with English subtitles.

VHS: S06464. $29.95.
Robert Bresson, France, 1956, 102 mins.

Mouchette

"Bresson constructs a drama of extraordinary tension and adventure," wrote *The New York Times*. "The adventure leads to escape from life, to a moment when nature and the supernatural meet in a fleeting intimation of grace so powerful that even an awareness of what the camera cannot show us is happiness enough." A 14-year-old friendless schoolgirl, Mouchette, lives with her alcoholic bootleg father, and her mother is dying. She is more sensitive than anyone around her and thus, paradoxically, less able to communicate. Based on the novel *La Nouvelle Histoire de Mouchette* by Georges Bernanos, Mouchette, says Bresson, "is found everywhere: wars, concentration camps, tortures, assassinations." French with English subtitles.

VHS: S06465. $24.95.
Robert Bresson, France, 1960, 80 mins.

Pickpocket

Robert Bresson's masterpiece is a magnificent drama about a thief, his techniques, motives and secret existence. Loosely based on *Crime and Punishment*, it tells the compelling story of an insignificant man who drifts into crime. "One of the four or five great dates in the history of cinema! A film with deep inspiration, free, instinctive, burning, bewildering" (Louis Malle). French with English subtitles.

VHS: S29896. $89.95.
Robert Bresson, France, 1959, 75 mins.

Une Femme Douce

Bresson's first film in color, which introduced 20-year-old Dominique Sanda to the world in a haunting transposition of Dostoevsky's story *A Gentle Creature*. Sanda plays the role of a young woman who marries a pawn broker (Guy Frangin) but finds she cannot bring herself to adapt her life to his, and so leaps to her death from a Paris balcony. We-like the husband—don't really know the reason why. As the young woman, Sanda delivers a star-making performance, perhaps the most erotic and natural of all of Bresson's heroines. French with English subtitles.

VHS: S26462. $29.95.
Robert Bresson, France, 1969, 87 mins.

BARBET SCHROEDER

Barfly

Mickey Rourke and Faye Dunaway are superb in this film based on Charles Bukowski's novel; Rourke is the gifted back-alley poet who's not afraid to defend his honor or freedom, but whose lust for life has given him a unique sense of love and romance. Faye Dunaway is the woman who's seen the darkest side of life and finds a rebirth through her new-found barroom bard.

VHS: S06587. $19.98.
Laser: LD70517. $34.98.
Barbet Schroeder, France/USA, 1987, 100 mins.

Before and After

Meryl Streep and Liam Neeson star in this suspense-laden thriller of murder, a suspected murderer and a shadow of a doubt. Streep and Neeson bring their intensity to this frightening, puzzling tale of violence and confusion.

VHS: S29826. $19.98.
Laser: LD75967. $39.99.
Barbet Schroeder, USA, 1996, 108 mins.

Charles Bukowski Tapes

"It's a gem…an outrageously stimulating and unnerving all-night drinking session with a gutter eloquent barroom philosopher who has made his soul your own…One of the most intimate, revelatory and unsparing glimpses any film or video has ever given us of a writer's life and personality," raved Michael Wilmington in *The Los Angeles Times*. Directed by Barbet Schroeder (*Barfly*), a 4-hour video portrait of the renegade poet of contemporary literature.

VHS: S08117. $100.00.
Barbet Schroeder, USA/France, 1987, 240 mins.

Desperate Measures

Andy Garcia is Frank Connor, a San Francisco cop who enlists convicted multiple murderer Peter McCabe (Michael Keaton) as a bone marrow donor in order to save his gravely ill son. When McCabe escapes from the hospital, Connor must pursue and protect the prisoner in order to save his son's life.

VHS: S34087. $104.99.
Laser: LD76841. $39.98.
DVD: DV60250. $24.95.
Barbet Shroeder, USA, 1998, 100 mins.

Kiss of Death

Nicolas Cage and David Caruso are cast in this compelling, effective and superbly acted thriller loosely based on the 1947 film noir classic of the same name. Caruso is a tough ex-con who becomes a police informant. Unfortunately, the criminal underworld is no place to make friends, as Cage's character proves with his violent, psychotic behavior. Samuel L. Jackson is also featured.

VHS: S26293. $96.98.
Laser: LD75071. $39.98.
Barbet Schroeder, USA, 1994, 100 mins.

Reversal of Fortune

Jeremy Irons won an Oscar for his wickedly suave performance as accused socialite Claus von Bulow. The Danish born aristocrat goes from the society page to the front page when his rich American wife suspiciously falls into a coma. The comatose Sunny—played by Glenn Close—narrates much of the film, which also stars Ron Silver as the dynamic appeal lawyer Alan Dershowitz. Based on the book by Dershowitz that was brilliantly adapted for the screen by Nicholas Kazan.

VHS: S13923. $19.95.
Barbet Schroeder, USA, 1990, 112 mins.

Single White Female

Barbet Schroeder directed this brooding psychological thriller about a fashion designer (Bridget Fonda) whose enigmatic roommate (Jennifer Jason Leigh) begins to appropriate her life with frightening ease. With Steven Weber and Peter Friedman.

VHS: S18007. $19.95.
DVD: DV60229. $24.95.
Barbet Schroeder, USA, 1992, 107 mins.

JEAN ROUCH

Le Jaguar

Part fiction, part documentary and part social commentary, *Jaguar* is the story of three young men from the savannah of Niger who leave their homeland to seek wealth and adventure on the coast and in the cities of Ghana. Filmed in the 1950s when no portable synchronized sound equipment was available, Jean Rouch had the main characters of the film improvise a narrative while they viewed the footage which in itself was improvised. The resulting soundtrack consists of remembered dialog, joking and exclamations, and questions and explanations about the action on screen. The three young men, a herdsman, a fisherman and their friend, travel for a month to the coast of Ghana and eventually part to take jobs in the cities. Successful but homesick, they return to Niger; they have become *jaguars* with a knowledge of life in the modern city. English narration.

VHS: S10730. $350.00.
Jean Rouch, France/Niger, 1954, 96 mins.

Les Maitres Fous

Jean Rouch's quintessential film documents the ceremony of a West African religious movement, the Hauku, which was widespread in Niger and Ghana from the 20s to the 50s. In 1954, Rouch was asked by a small group in Ghana to film their annual ceremony in which the participants would enter into a trance and become possessed by a variety of spirits associated with the western colonial powers. Today, *Les Maitres Fous* remains as one of the great works of ethnographic cinema. English narration.

VHS: S10728. $200.00.
Jean Rouch, France/Ghana, 1955, 35 mins.

The Lion Hunters

Filmed in the savannahs of northern Niger and Mali over a seven year period in the 50s and 60s, *The Lion Hunters* follows the Gao hunters on several hunts and explores the relationships between the Songhay tribes and the Fulani herdsmen. When lions raid the cattle of the Fulani herdsmen, the Fulani request the Songhay chiefs to send Gao hunters to their aid. Although lions kill only sick or injured cattle, they will occasionally kill a healthy cow. The Gao are able to determine which lion is responsible since they know each lion's individual characteristics and habits. One of the most important works of Jean Rouch's career. English narration.

VHS: S10729. $300.00.
Jean Rouch, France/Mali, 1965, 68 mins.

MARCEL OPHULS

Costa-Gavras Talks with Marcel Ophuls: Political Films

Two internationally known directors who have made a specialty of films with an outspoken political edge discuss the values and methods in the genre, and the problems they have faced. Costa-Gavras (*Z*) and Ophuls (*The Sorrow and The Pity*) address such themes as the difference between "objective" and "subjective" truth and their personal motives for choosing this form of film art. 1976, 28 mins.

VHS: S31568. $59.95.

Hotel Terminus: The Life and Times of Klaus Barbie

Marcel Ophuls' award-winning documentary spans 70 years and three continents. Culled from 120 hours of interviews, it traces the 40-year-manhunt for Nazi war criminal Klaus Barbie, the ruthless SS interrogator known as "The Butcher of Lyon." "A shocking, unforgettable film" (Ebert and Siskel). Winner of the Academy Award for Best Documentary and the International Critics Prize at the Cannes Film Festival. Original English-language version (includes French, German and Spanish footage subtitled in English). 2 cassettes.

VHS: S10756. $29.98.
Marcel Ophuls, France/USA, 1988, 267 mins.

Sorrow and the Pity

Marcel Ophuls' monumental documentary covering the German occupation of France during World War II. Through poignant interviews and stark newsreel footage, Ophuls creates a sense of living history. "A magnificent epic on the themes of collaboration and resistance. There's nothing comparable to [it]" (Pauline Kael). English dubbed.

VHS: S01233. $59.95.
Marcel Ophuls, France, 1972, 260 mins.

JEAN-JACQUES ANNAUD

The Bear

A rare and wonderful animal adventure story for adults. Based on the novel *The Grizzly King* by Michigan author James Oliver Curwood, Annaud tells the story of an orphaned cub and the wounded kodiak bear who grudgingly befriends the distant relative. They encounter hunters, packs of trained dogs and other dangers and learn to trust each other. With Jack Wallace and Tcheky Karyo as the humans and starring Bart and Douce as the bears. Filmed on location in the Italian Dolemite mountains.

VHS: S12209. $14.95.
Jean-Jacques Annaud, France, 1988, 93 mins.

The Lover

Jean-Jacques Annaud adapts Marguerite Duras' autobiographical novel *L'Amant*: political, social and class tensions and sexual role-playing refracted through an erotic relationship between a beautiful French girl (Jane March) and her older, elegant, aristocratic Chinese lover (Tony Leung). The film is set in French-occupied Indochina during the 1920s. This is the uncut, unrated European version that was initially rated NC-17. Original English dialog.

VHS: S18520. $19.98.
Laser: LD71870. $39.98.
Jean-Jacques Annaud, France/Great Britain, 1991, 113 mins.

Quest for Fire

Eighty thousand years ago the Cro-Magnon equivalents of the Three Stooges set out to find fire. On the way they locate Rae Dawn Chong and invent the missionary position. Less serious than intended, this prehistorical epic does have its moments.

VHS: S04597. $69.98.
Jean-Jacques Annaud, Canada/France, 1981, 100 mins.

Seven Years in Tibet

The true story of Heinrich Harrer (Brad Pitt), an Austrian national and a Nazi sympathizer who leaves Austria in 1939 to climb a mountain in the Himalayas. Through a series of circumstances (including British POW camp), he and mountain-climbing guide Peter Aufschnaiter (David Thewlis (*Naked*) become the only two foreigners in the Tibetan Holy City of Lhasa. There, Heinrich's life changes forever as he witnesses the Tibetan/Chinese confrontation escalating and becomes a close confidant to the Dalai Lama. VHS letterboxed.

VHS: S33693. $105.99.
Laser: LD76780. $34.95.
Jean-Jacques Annaud, USA, 1997, 136 mins.

FRENCH COMEDY

A Pain in the A..

Jacques Brel and Lino Ventura star in this story of a hired killer who becomes entangled in the life of a suicidal shirt salesman while trying to fulfill a contract on a Mob informer. Funny and original. French with English subtitles.

VHS: S00987. $59.95.
Edouard Molinaro, France, 1973, 90 mins.

The Accompanist

Claude Miller's (*The Little Thief*) haunting tale of the love-hate relationship between a shy, unsophisticated pianist and the charismatic singer she idolizes is set against the backdrop of WWII France and features great performances from Richard Bohringer, Elena Safonova and Romane Bohringer. French with English subtitles.

VHS: S21894. $19.95.
Claude Miller, France, 1993, 101 mins.

Alberto Express

An absurdist comedy about the strange predicament of Alberto, a man nearing 40 and broke, whose family's byzantine rules stipulate he must remunerate his parents for the money spent on his upbringing. In this black comedy about the bonds fractured over family and money, Alberto must find the means to pay off his family or risk losing his forthcoming child. With Sergio Castellitto, Nino Manfredi, Marie Trintignant, Michel Aumont and Jeanne Moreau. French and Italian with English subtitles.

VHS: S18859. $19.98.
Arthur Joffe, France/Italy, 1991, 90 mins.

Bandits

Claude Lelouch's comedy thriller about a criminal's return to society. He's bent on finding the culprits responsible for his wife's murder and the estrangement of his daughter. "A gem [that is] effortlessly charming, intelligent and sophisticated" (*New York Post*). With Jean Yanne, Marie-Sophie L., Patrick Bruel and Corrine Marchand. French with English subtitles.

VHS: S19729. $19.98.
Claude Lelouch, France, 1986, 98 mins.

Barjo

A wacky French farce based on the novel by Philip K. Dick, *Barjo* is the "slightly psychotic" story of young, underdeveloped Barjo, who lives near his sister Fanfan, waiting for the UFOs. When he accidentally burns down his house, he moves in with Fanfan, discovers sex, and quietly drives Fanfan's husband insane. Nutty, off-the-wall comedy from the director of *Baxter*. French with English subtitles.

VHS: S20424. $19.95.
Jerome Boivin, France, 1992, 85 mins.

Belmondo Is the Swashbuckler

An action-adventure comedy, starring Jean-Paul Belmondo as the swashbuckler who out-Errols Errol Flynn in a colorful, wild and action-packed romp through the French Revolution. French with English subtitles.

VHS: S04449. $59.95.
Jean-Paul Rappeneau, France, 1975, 100 mins.

The Brain

Gerard Oury's light, French, romantic comedy stars David Niven as a charismatic thief who devises the daring robbery of a train carrying NATO cash. The other players are Jean-Paul Belmondo, Bourvil, Eli Wallach, Silvia Monti and Fernand Valois.

VHS: S16888. $19.95.
Gerard Oury, France, 1969, 100 mins.

Cafe au Lait

In this audacious comedy from Mathieu Kassovitz, director of *La Haine* (*Hate*), an interracial romantic trio comes to grips with joint parenthood. A beautiful, pregnant young West Indian woman has two lovers, an African Muslim law student and a Jewish bicycle messenger, who hate one another. When she refuses to reveal which of them is the father of her expected child, they are forced to get along. French with English subtitles.

VHS: S28397. $89.95.
Mathieu Kassovitz, France, 1994, 94 mins.

Cartouche

An 18th century cooper's son (Jean-Paul Belmondo) becomes a quick-witted and gallant thief in this hilarious spoof of swashbucklers from Philippe de Broca (*King of Hearts*). He and his friends take over the crime syndicate in Paris, and eventually dedicate themselves to avenging the death of their co-leader, Venus. With Claudia Cardinale, Odile Versois and Philippe Lemaire. French with English subtitles.

VHS: S16186. $29.95.
Philippe de Broca, France/Italy, 1964, 115 mins.

Cross My Heart
A French comedy which became a cult hit. Martin (Nicolas Parodi) conceals his mother's death to avoid the soulless French social services or anonymous orphanage. His classmates enter into a pact to withhold the information from the authorities and tension is established through their intricate efforts to preserve all signs of normalcy. "A comic essay on the desperate ingenuity of youth" (*Time Magazine*). Cinematography by Jean-Claude Saillier. With Sylvain Copans, Cecilia Rouaud and Delphine Gouttman. French with English subtitles.
VHS: S18860. $19.98.
Jacques Fansten, France, 1990, 105 mins.

The Daydreamer (Le Distrait)
From the filmmaker of *Tall Blonde Man With One Black Shoe*, a zany comedy in which Pierre Richard plays an absent-minded advertising man, bumbling through an ad agency and reducing it to a shambles. French with English subtitles.
VHS: S03990. $59.95.
Pierre Richard, France, 1977, 90 mins.

Dead Tired (Grosse Fatigue)
Carole Bouquet, Michel Blanc, Philippe Noiret and even Roman Polanski appear in this sinister but darkly comic look at the French film industry. Blanc finds himself in a number of comic situations that are completely inexplicable until he discovers that he has a double. This comic feature shows the seamy underside of the glamorous world of film in France. French with English subtitles.
VHS: S27073. $29.95.
Laser: LD75454. $39.95.
Michel Blanc, France, 1994, 85 mins.

Dear Detective (Tendre Poulet)
Annie Girardot and Philippe Noiret star in this comic thriller about a madcap female police detective. She is investigating the mysterious circumstances surrounding the murders of three senate deputies. Despite this somber focus there is still time for big laughs and even romance. French with English subtitles.
VHS: S22036. $59.95.
Philippe de Broca, France, 1977, 90 mins.

Delicatessen
Imagine the Coen brothers remaking Terry Gilliam's *Brazil* on speed and you get the idea of this film, set in a vaguely post-nuclear Paris. The action unfolds in a decaying building, where a war breaks out between a group of innocents, cannibals and militant vegetarians. French with English subtitles. With Dominique Pinon (*Diva*), Laure Dougnac and Claude Dreyfus.
VHS: S18069. $89.98.
Laser: LD75125. $39.95.
Jean-Marie Jeunet/Marc Caro, France, 1991, 95 mins.

Delusions of Grandeur
A delightful fast-paced comedy of royal intrigue set in 17th century Spain. Louis de Funes is the evil, all-powerful minister of the King of Spain, and Yves Montand is his clever servant. French with English subtitles.
VHS: S00321. $59.95.
Gerard Oury, France, 1976, 85 mins.

Et la Tendresse?...Bordel!
Between a sex crazed criminal, a happily unemployed intellectual, and a young, timid romantic evolve three couples, and three different attitudes toward love. Offering profound criticisms of heterosexual relationships, this is the hilarious film that launched Patrick Schulmann's career. Dubbed in English.
VHS: S00417. $69.95.
Patrick Schulmann, France, 1979, 97 mins.

Et la Tendresse?...Bordel! #2
A delirium of humor describes the relationship between a color blind painter and radio personality in this, Schulmann's third feature. With Diane Bellego, Christian Francois and Fabrice Luchini. French with English subtitles.
VHS: S16190. $69.95.
Patrick Schulmann, France, 1983, 100 mins.

Extenuating Circumstances
A well-known judge and his wife find themselves stranded in an unsavory auberge outside Paris, where a gang of criminals live. The couple hide their identities and inadvertently become accepted by the gang. When they try to convert their new friends into respectable citizens, an ex-con whom the judge once sentenced to prison appears to upset their plans. French with English subtitles.
VHS: S20757. $29.95.
Jean Boyer, France, 1939, 90 mins.

Fernandel the Dressmaker
Comedy directed by one of France's most prolific directors, starring Fernandel, a leading comic for four decades, famous for his long, horse-like face. French with English subtitles.
VHS: S00375. $34.95.
Jean Boyer, France, 1956, 95 mins.

The First Time
Claude Berri's (*Manon of the Spring, Germinal*) breakthrough success stars Alain Cohen and Charles Denner in an uproarious comedy about the traditional rite of passage to manhood, that very first time. A young artist and his buddies are desperate to find girls and maybe even love with endless complications along the way. French with English subtitles.
VHS: S23890. $29.95.
Claude Berri, France, 1967, 83 mins.

Forbidden Fruit
Comic actor Fernandel stars as a simple if lusty country doctor who introduces a pretty young woman into his household as an assistant. Her job is something of a mystery, throwing the doctor's marriage into crisis. This melodrama is based on a novel from George Simenon (*Inspector Maigret*). In English.
VHS: S25925. $24.95.
Henri Verneuil, France, 1952, 97 mins.

French Fried Vacation (Les Bronzes)
This comic spoof pokes fun at the idea of Club Med-style vacations, where grown adults find themselves in exotic locations in search of sexual adventure. Recreation takes precedence over rest. French with English subtitles.
VHS: S22035. $29.95.
Patrice Leconte, France, 1978, 90 mins.

The Infernal Trio
A macabre murder comedy, called "erotic chic" by *Newsweek*, directed by Francis Girod. Michel Piccoli plays a sociopathic lawyer who seduces two sisters (Romy Schneider and Mascha Gomska) and enlists them in a conspiracy to marry and murder victims and defraud their insurance companies. Threatened with exposure, they eliminate the witnesses and destroy the bodies with acid, distracted in the butchery only by their erotic arousal. But when a prospective female victim becomes romantically involved with one of the sisters, the infernal trio must stretch itself into an uneasy quartet. French with English subtitles.
VHS: S10871. $29.95.
Francois Girod, France, 1974, 100 mins.

King of Hearts
Alan Bates stars in this popular cult film as a World War I British soldier involved in the insanity of modern warfare. In the small French village of Marville, the inmates of the local asylum have taken over when the local populace has fled in terror. The soldier finds their company preferable to army life. What is so crazy about that? With Jean-Claude Brialy, Genevieve Bujold, Michel Serrault, Adolfo Celliand and Pierre Brasseur.
VHS: S00680. $19.95.
Laser: Widescreen. **LD71078. $49.95.**
Philippe de Broca, Great Britain/France/Italy, 1967, 100 mins.

La Cage aux Folles
A gay couple in St.Tropez discover their lives are complicated when the son of one of the men wants to marry into a politically repressive family. Ugo Tognazzi and Michel Serrault are Renato and Albin, the owners of the La Cage aux Folles nightclub, which features a popular revue of female impersonation. This surprise international hit was based on the play by Jean Poiret. With Benny Luke and Michael Galabru as the head of the Union of Moral Order. French with English subtitles.
VHS: S00702. $19.95.
Laser: LD70756. $49.95.
Edouard Molinaro, France, 1979, 91 mins.

La Cage aux Folles II
Renato (Ugo Tognazzi) and Albin (Michel Serrault) of *La Cage aux Folles* return as the proprietor and main attraction of the elegant cabaret, La Cage aux Folles. Albin is offended by Renato's suggestion that he is a bit too mature to impersonate the young Marlene Dietrich of the *Blue Angel*, and an incredible series of comic events ensues. English dubbed.
VHS: S00703. $19.98.
Edouard Molinaro, France, 1981, 99 mins.

La Cage aux Folles III
La Cage aux Folles III, The Wedding. The boys are back! The good news is they will inherit a fortune if they marry, but the bad news is they have 18 months to have a baby. English dubbed.
VHS: S00704. $19.95.
Georges Lautner, France, 1986, 88 mins.

La Chevre
The comedy team of Gerard Depardieu and Pierre Richard, who were so successful in *Les Comperes*, bring to the screen another great French farce. Their travels range from the board rooms of a huge multinational conglomerate to the tropics of Mexico, in search of the chairman of the board's missing accident-prone daughter. French with English subtitles.
VHS: S05209. $69.95.
Francis Veber, France, 1985, 91 mins.

La Discrete
Christian Vincent's sophisticated comedy of manners about Antoine (Fabrice Luchini), a parliamentary aide whose plans to end his current relationship are shattered when he discovers his girlfriend embracing another man. Hurt and deeply resentful, he orchestrates a vengeful plot to seduce every woman he meets, abandon her and record the entries in a journal he will publish. "*La Discrete* is an assured and lyrical testament to the old saying, 'Love conquers all'" (*Toronto Festival of Festivals*). With Judith Henry, Maurice Garrel and Marie Bunuel. French with English subtitles.
VHS: S20301. $89.95.
Christian Vincent, France, 1990, 95 mins.

La Grande Vadrouille
In 1943, three allied parachutists land behind enemy lines and end up creating chaos for the conductor and decorator who find them. The only way for this pair to regain their peaceable existence lies in the return of this troublesome trio to a free zone. French with English subtitles.
VHS: S20756. $29.95.
Gerard Oury, France, 1966, 122 mins.

Le Chat
Jean Gabin and Simone Signoret star as a couple whose love has turned to hate after 25 years of marriage. Julien (Jean Gabin) lavishes love on his cat, inciting jealousy in his wife. An award winner at the Chicago International Film Festival and the Berlin Film Festival. French with English subtitles.
VHS: S00221. $59.95.
Pierre Granier-Deferre, France, 1975, 88 mins.

Little Indian, Big City
A Parisian broker finds he has a son raised in the Amazon jungle and returns the youth to civilization with wild consequences. A hit in France, it sparked the American film *Jungle to Jungle*. With Thierry Lhermitte, Patrik Timsit, Ludwig Briand and Miou-Miou. Dubbed in English.
VHS: S33951. $103.99.
Herve Palud, France, 1994, 90 mins.

Mama, There's a Man in Your Bed
From the creator of *Three Men and a Cradle*, this heartwarming film is the story of an unlikely romance between a harried CEO and his financially strapped cleaning woman who is desperately trying to keep her five children from going hungry. Writer/director Coline Serreau has a lot to say about class and color differences in a world none too tolerant of either. Starring Daniel Auteuil, Firmine Richard, Pierre Vernier, and Maxime Leroux. French with English subtitles.
VHS: S13792. $19.98.
Coline Serreau, France, 1989, 111 mins.

The Man in a Raincoat
Fernandel visits a chorus girl who charges for her company, only to have the rendezvous cut short when the woman is murdered while changing her clothes. The innocent-of-murder married man finds his troubles only beginning in this comic-mystery. With John McGiver and Bernard Blier. Dubbed into English. B&W.
VHS: S05696. $29.95.
Julien Duvivier, France/Italy, 1957, 97 mins.

The Red Inn (L'Auberge Rouge)
One of the funniest classic French comedies, starring the great Fernandel. An innkeeper and his wife (Francoise Rosay) hatch a murderous plan for their guests. Only the will of God in the form of an intervening priest (Fernandel) can save them. French with English subtitles.
VHS: S26877. $24.95.
Claude Autant-Lara, France, 1951, 95 mins.

Return of the Tall Blond Man with One Black Shoe
Pierre Richard and Mireille Dare are in love on vacation in Rio and yet again the target of comedic espionage. Hit-men "Prince" and "Charming" have the Tall Blond at the top of their list, but he manages to bumble through showers of bullets unharmed. The whole mad melee culminates in a confrontation at the symphony orchestra as the hilarious *Tall Blond Man with One Black Shoe* meets its rip-roaring sequel. French with English subtitles.
VHS: S16170. $29.95.
Yves Robert, France, 1973, 84 mins.

A Royal Affair
In this elegant sexual farce Maurice Chevalier plays a mythic French king visiting Paris, who becomes entangled in a group of slapstick and frenetic events, the exchange of mistresses and political blackmail. Chevalier performs several songs. French with English subtitles.
VHS: S18171. $24.95.
Marc Gilbert Sauvajon, France, 1950, 100 mins.

Salut d'Artiste (Salute the Artist)

A comedy about two second-rate actors who are trying to make it in the cinema and theater in Paris. Nicolas is 45; he doesn't lack work, but the roles he gets are invariably bottom-drawer. So he continues to dream about stardom as he accepts anything that pays the bills—commercials, even dubbing parrots' voices in cartoons. His friend Clement, faced with similar frustration, ends up giving up acting and taking an executive job. Directed by Yves Robert and starring Marcello Mastroianni and Francoise Fabian. French with English subtitles.

VHS: S13592. $29.95.

Yves Robert, France, 1974, 96 mins.

Senechal the Magnificent

Unable to perform on stage, an actor decides to bring his favorite roles to life—that is, real life. The result is a hilarious string of misunderstandings that end up in court. There he gets a new role, but loses his voice. Fernandel is in top comic form in this comic delight of a film. French with English subtitles.

VHS: S21881. $39.95.

Jean Boyer, France, 1957, 95 mins.

Serious About Pleasure

Jane Birkin stars in this comedy about a romantic trio. Richard Leduc and Michael Lonsdale are the two men who share the love of this woman, despite societal disapproval. On the road a series of quirky adventures tests their patience and Birkin's unexpected pregnancy tests their love. French with English subtitles.

VHS: S22886. $79.95.

Robert Benayoun, France, 1975, 100 mins.

Sheep Has Five Legs

One of the best-loved films of Fernandel. In this film, he plays quintuplets as well as the father of the brood—and also plays the actor Fernandel. A totally, wildly improbable comedy. French with English subtitles.

VHS: S01188. $29.95.

Henri Verneuil, France, 1953, 94 mins.

The Sucker (Le Corniauds)

On his way to a vacation, Antoine Marechal (Bourvil) loses his car in an accident. The offending businessman, Saroyan (famed comic Louis de Funes), gives him a Cadillac so that he can still go on to Italy. Only this car turns Antoine into a smuggler. Antoine is not as naive as he seems however, and he manages to make the most of this ridiculous situation. French with English subtitles.

VHS: S22033. $29.95.

Gerard Oury, France, 1965, 90 mins.

Tall Blond Man with One Black Shoe

A beautifully mastered print of the original French version of Yves Robert's international comedy hit. Rival factions within French intelligence try to pass off a randomly selected dupe as a "superagent." Frizzy-haired Pierre Richard, France's reigning king of comedy, is the concert-violinist turned patsy in love with a very pretty but very married harpist. French with English subtitles.

VHS: S13282. $29.95.
Laser: LD71628. $39.95.

Pierre Richard, France, 1972, 90 mins.

Tall Blond Man with One Black Shoe/Return of the Tall Blond Man

Two of a pair, this is the French comedy that inspired Hollywood to enlist Tom Hanks as *The Man with One Red Shoe*. Capture the laughs at a discount with this specially packaged 2-pack. French with English subtitles.

VHS: S16169. $49.95.

Tatie Danielle

Meet the meanest old lady on earth. She's Auntie—"Tatie"-Danielle, a demanding and manipulative woman who must be waited on hand and foot. When she moves in with her great nephew, he and his wife hope that "Tatie" will be the grandmother the children never had. It doesn't take long, however, for this cantankerous old lady to make everyone's life hell. A clever and darkly hilarious work from director Etienne Chatliez. French with English subtitles.

VHS: S15585. $19.98.

Etienne Chatiliez, France, 1991, 114 mins.

That Man from Rio

Philippe de Broca's caper comedy is a parody of '60s Cold War thrillers. Jean-Paul Belmondo plays an air force pilot who pursues a double agent and thief from Paris to Rio to dense jungles of the Amazon in search of a valuable statuette. "Fantasy takes over, and Belmondo [outdoes] Fairbanks in agility, Lloyd in cliffhanging, and Bond in indestructibility" (Brenda Davies, *Monthly Film Bulletin*). Music by Georges Delerue. With Jean Servais, Francoise Dorleac, Adolfo Celi and Simone Renant. French with English subtitles.

VHS: S20405. $19.98.
Laser: LD76323. $39.99.

Philippe de Broca, France/Italy, 1964, 120 mins.

That Naughty Girl and Love on a Pillow

Two films starring Brigitte Bardot at her sexiest. In the French comedy *That Naughty Girl*, Bardot is the not-so-innocent teenage daughter of a notorious crime boss. In *Love on a Pillow*, Bardot is an heiress who tries to help a young man who has attempted suicide by having an affair with him, despite the pleas of her family and friends. Both dubbed in English. Michel J. Boisrand, France, 1956, 84 mins./Roger Vadim, France, 1964, 102 mins.

VHS: S30030. $19.95.

Three Men and a Cradle

One of the funniest French films in recent years, an unlikely story of three confirmed bachelors who receive a six-month-old roommate. This little bundle of joy can turn into a big bundle of trouble, and chaos of a hilarious kind ensues. French with English subtitles.

VHS: S02266. $14.98.

Coline Serreau, France, 1985, 100 mins.

The Visitors

The biggest-grossing French film comedy in a long time, Alain Terzian's *The Visitors (Les Visiteurs)* is a wacky comedy about two time-travelling medieval knights who get stuck in the 20th century with some nutty results. "Uproarious…a truly hilarious farce" (*Wall Street Journal*). With Christian Claver, Jean Reno and Valerie LeMercier. French with English subtitles.

VHS: S31025. $19.95.
Laser: LD76158. $39.98.

Jean-Marie Poire, France, 1993, 107 mins.

Widow Couderc

A fun French thriller with Simone Signoret the provincial widow whose love affairs lead her to fall in love with an escaped murderer, based on a novel by Georges Simenon. With Alain Delon. French with English subtitles.

VHS: S01458. $59.95.

Pierre Granier-Deferre, France, 1974, 92 mins.

french classics

Abel Gance at Work
Rare production footage showing the creator of *Napoleon* at work—includes footage from *La Roue* and *Napoleon*. 43 mins.
VHS: S13210. $19.95.

Abel Gance's Beethoven
The monumental epic from the director of *Napoleon*, Abel Gance's *Beethoven* offers an extraordinary vision of the romantic artist as a tragic hero. This symphonic film, full of magnificent sequences, features Gance's return to the visual freedom of the silent cinema, while using sound in a daring, expressionistic manner. With Harry Baur, Jean-Louis Barrault, Marcel Dallio. French with English subtitles.
VHS: S13045. $29.95.
Abel Gance, France, 1936, 116 mins.

Adam and Evelyn
Stewart Granger is carefree gambler who must change his ways when a friend dies. Granger is left in charge of a young woman who becomes his daughter. It's a pleasant and cheerful tale of evolving loyalties and maturing tastes. Also features Jean Simmons. French with English subtitles.
VHS: S21562. $24.95.
Harold French, France, 1956, 80 mins.

Adorable Julia
A middle-aged actress decides to take on a younger lover in this humorous sex comedy based on the novel by Somerset Maugham. With Lilli Palmer and Charles Boyer. French with English subtitles.
VHS: S14653. $29.96.
Alfred Weidenmann, France, 1962, 97 mins.

Ali Baba and the Forty Thieves
Ali Baba, played by Fernandel, accidentally discovers the magic hiding place of Abdul and his 40 thieves. With this unexpected treasure he buys a beautiful slave to be his wife, only to find his desires thwarted by the plans of the wronged thieves and the master of his new wife, in this comedy based on the old classic. French with English subtitles.
VHS: S20758. $59.95.
Jacques Becker, France, 92 mins.

The Associate
Michael Serrault (*La Cage aux Folles*) stars in this sexy French comedy about a meek businessman, Julien Pardot, who invents an imaginary English business partner. When his clients, wife and mistress all begin to prefer the imaginary "Mr. Davis" over himself, Pardot devises a plot to kidnap and murder his creation. With Claudine Auger. French with English subtitles. "A small oasis in the arid landscape of French film comedy" (*Variety*).
VHS: S30943. $29.95.
Rene Gainville, France, 1982, 94 mins.

Back to the Wall
An entertaining and suspenseful tale of murder and blackmail starring the great Jeanne Moreau as the adulterous wife in the middle of everything. French with English subtitles.
VHS: S14655. $29.95.
Edouard Molinaro, France, 1958, 94 mins.

Battle of Austerlitz
An epic production with an international cast (Claudia Cardinale, Orson Welles, Vittorio de Sica, Jean-Louis Trintignant) as Abel Gance, the director of *Napoleon*, returns to his character for the most important battle of his career—*The Battle of Austerlitz*. English dubbed.
VHS: S00101. $19.95.
Abel Gance, France, 1960, 118 mins.

Bim, the Little Donkey and Dream of the Wild Horses
The first film by the director of *The Red Balloon*, *Bim* is a delightful story of a lovable donkey who is taken away from a small boy to become the pet of a very rich family. The boy's efforts to get his donkey back lead to all sorts of adventures. *Dream of the Wild Horses* is a landmark short film by Georges Franju.
VHS: S01691. $29.95.
Albert Lamorisse, France, 1948, 45 mins.

Blood and Roses
Roger Vadim's Italian-made adaptation of Sheridan Le Fanu's *Carmilla* is a kinky thriller about a young woman's obsession with her family's perverse association with vampires. The source material was later remade as *The Vampire Lovers* and *The Blood-Spattered Bride*. With Mel Ferrer, Elsa Martinelli, Annette Vadim and Marc Allegret.
VHS: S16886. $19.95.
Roger Vadim, Italy, 1961, 74 mins.

Blood of the Beasts
Contrasting peaceful views of a Parisian suburb with unflinching scenes from a slaughterhouse, this film is a masterpiece that impacted documentary film practice worldwide. Disturbing in its honesty, it challenges a number of banal conceptions seemingly integral to everyday life. French with English subtitles.
VHS: S24076. $14.95.
Georges Franju, France, 1949, 22 mins.

Bomb for a Dictator
Pierre Fresnay and Gregoire Aslan star in this tense tale about an assassination plot. A fanatical terrorist plots the murder of a South American dictator. His plan involves the bombing of an airliner.
VHS: S23797. $24.95.
Alex Joff, France, 1957, 71 mins.

Bride Is Much Too Beautiful
A very early Bardot vehicle—Brigitte Bardot plays the cover girl who is publicized into a fake romance, but she really loves a photographer. With Micheline Presle, Louis Jourdan. English dubbed.
VHS: S05294. $39.95.
Fred Surin, France, 1957, 90 mins.

The Burning Court
A strange film that deals with a number of weird subjects, including occultism, possession, family curses, etc. An unusual and very interesting foreign horror opus, dubbed in English. With Jean-Claude Brialy.
VHS: S15687. $29.95.
Julien Duvivier, France/Italy/Germany, 1961, 113 mins.

Candide
An updated version of Voltaire's classic novella. A modern Candide questioning nothing, and blithely assuming that everything happens for the best in this best of all possible worlds. Starring Jean-Pierre Cassel, Pierre Brasseur and Dahlia Lavi. Dubbed in English.
VHS: S14632. $29.95.
Norbert Carbonnaux, France, 1960, 90 mins.

Carnival in Flanders
In 1616, in a small town in Spanish-occupied Flanders, the city fathers find out that a detachment of Spaniards is arriving and the men leave town. The women, however, join together to seduce and entertain the soldiers. With a script by Charles Spaak and magnificent sets by Lazare Meerson, *Carnival in Flanders* is not only an enjoyable farce, but a rare example of the work of Feyder, a key filmmaker. French with English subtitles.
VHS: S00215. $24.95.
Jacques Feyder, France, 1935, 95 mins.

Charterhouse at Parma
Stendahl's novel of the same name about a young Archbishop in love is adapted for the screen in this film featuring Gerard Philipe. When he wishes to break his vows, an ambitious aunt intervenes to insure his continued progress at the Italian court. French with English subtitles.
VHS: S20773. $39.95.

Classic Foreign Shorts—Volume 3: Un Chant d'Amour, Romance Sentimentale
Un Chant d'Amour is Jean Genet's only film, a legendary and long suppressed film masterpiece. "A song of man's love soaring above the sexual ghetto of prison and non-existence" (*Cahiers du Cinema*). 20 mins. *Romance Sentimentale* is usually attributed to Sergei Eisenstein, and although Eisenstein worked on it, it was probably directed by Grigori Alexandrov. Photographed by Tisse and financed by its only player—a wealthy woman who wanted to appear in an Eisenstein film-*Romance Sentimentale* was filmed in Paris during the winter of 1929-30. The film is a somber experimental poem portraying the emotions aroused in a woman (Mara Gitry) by the realization that love is dead. 20 mins.
VHS: S26947. $29.95.

Club des Femmes
Entertaining yet powerful film about the personal life of women who work in a Parisian nightclub, with Danielle Darrieux and Elsa Argal. The *New York Times* identified the film's message as: "Women of the world unite against men's tyranny and chauvinism." French with English subtitles.
VHS: S00254. $34.95.
Jacques Deval, France, 1936, 90 mins.

Colette: Of the Goncourt Academy
A filmed reading and dramatization starring the famed French author and her work, *La Chevre de Monsieur Seguin*. French with English subtitles.
VHS: S02579. $34.95.
Yannick Bellon, France, 1951, 30 mins.

The Count of Monte Cristo
Alexander Dumas' classic swashbuckling tale of treachery, deceit, betrayal and murder stars Louis Jourdan, Bernard Dheran and Yvonne Furneaux. Dubbed in English. Unedited, widescreen version. Two-tape set.
VHS: S34146. $19.98.
Claude Autant-Lara, France, 1961, 150 mins.

Crainquebille
A great satire based on the classic story by Anatole France, the story of a Parisian street merchant, directed by the legendary Jacques Feyder (*Carnival in Flanders*), and starring Maurice Feraudy. Silent.
VHS: S03170. $17.95.
Jacques Feyder, France, 1923, 50 mins.

Crazy for Love
Brigitte Bardot's first film made for one of France's most prolific directors, Jean Boyer, who turned out over 70 films during his career. It's a comedy about the inheritance of a farm in Normandy. Bourvil co-stars. French with English subtitles.
VHS: S02161. $29.95.
Jean Boyer, France, 1952, 100 mins.

Crime and Punishment
Two of the greatest actors, Harry Baur and Pierre Blanchar, and the master of French poetic realism, Pierre Chenal, join in this masterful adaptation of one of the great works of literature. Hailed worldwide as one of the most imaginative adaptations of Dostoevsky's complex, brooding novel, "Chenal's studio-bound stylization and direction created a feverish climate of airless oppression and suspense. And Blanchar's cat-and-mouse confrontation with the magnificent Harry Baur, as the wily magistrate Porfiry, is one of the great acting setpieces of the French screen" (National Film Theatre). French with English subtitles.
VHS: S09197. $59.95.
Pierre Chenal, France, 1935, 110 mins.

The Crucible
Arthur Miller's dramatic masterpiece; the screenplay and dialogue were written by Jean-Paul Sartre and this French film stars Simone Signoret, Yves Montand and Mylene Demongeot. Set in Salem, Massachusetts, in 1692, the film dramatizes the persecution of witches and serves as a powerful allegory for the anti-communist hysteria of America in the 1950s. French with English subtitles.
VHS: S23571. $39.95.
Raymond Rouleau, France, 1957, 108 mins.

Daniella by Night
Elke Sommer's last French film before her American career is notable for its famous nude scene of Elke, its climax atop the Musee d'Orsay, and a scintillating score by Charles Aznavour. Includes original theatrical trailer. French with English subtitles.
VHS: S33135. $29.95.
Max Pecas, France, 1962, 83 mins.

The Days of Our Years
Jean Cocteau, Marcel Achard, Andre Roussin, Georges Auric and Pierre Fresnay contributed to this documentary about the first 50 years of the 20th century. Air and sea exploration, the opening of King Tut's tomb and the first rocket launch are included alongside footage of artists and scientists like Sarah Bernhardt, Renoir, Pablo Picasso, Shaw, Auguste Rodin, Jean-Paul Sartre and Henri Matisse. English narration.
VHS: S22465. $29.95.

Dedee d'Anvers

Simone Signoret plays a popular Antwerp barfly who is being tormented by her brutal bouncer boyfriend (Dalio). A kindly sea captain offers to make life much easier for Dedee but he is killed by the bouncer. It is up to the owner of the bar, Bernard Blier, to help the barfly gain her freedom. French with English subtitles.
VHS: S03751. $29.95.
Yves Allegret, France, 1949, 95 mins.

Devil in the Flesh

The account of a clandestine love affair between an adolescent schoolboy and the discontented wife of a soldier during World WarI, from the novel by Raymond Radiguet. "It has the beauty and despair of lovers attempting to save something for themselves in a period of hopeless confusion" (Pauline Kael). English dubbed.
VHS: S03749. $34.95.
Claude Autant-Lara, France, 1947, 112 mins.

Diabolically Yours

Poor Alain Delon has lost his memory. But Senta Berger, who claims to be his wife, says everything will be fine once he is out of the hospital and back at his estate. An intricate thriller involving unnatural accidents, murder plots and a lusting Chinese servant. With Sergio Fantoni and Peter Mosbacher as Kim. The last film of Julien Duvivier (*Tales of Manhattan, Flesh and Fantasy*). In English.
VHS: S09316. $59.95.
Julien Duvivier, France, 1968, 90 mins.

Double Agents

A fascinating tale of espionage, mystery and intrigue, set during the Second World War. German spies stationed in England send a woman to France, her mission to deliver British coastal defense secrets to a Nazi lieutenant. Spellbinding. With Marina Vlady and Robert Hossein. Dubbed in English.
VHS: S04366. $29.95.
Robert Hossein, France-Italy, 1959

Duke of the Derby

Veteran actor Jean Gabin stars as a racetrack handicapper used to a lifestyle in excess of his income, which he derives from his daily betting at the track. French with English subtitles.
VHS: S01669. $29.95.
Gilles Grangier, France, 1962, 83 mins.

End of the World

Astronomer Victor Francen announces to the world the arrival of a comet which will strike and destroy the earth in 30 days in this rarest of all finds, Abel Gance's lost science fiction epic *La Fin du Monde*. Unfortunately the original film, running 105 minutes, has been cut to 54 minutes by the U.S. distributor and a silly prologue has been added. But Gance's ending montage of distortion and destruction of the world is nothing short of dazzling. French with English subtitles.
VHS: S23036. $19.98.
Abel Gance, France, 1930, 54 mins.

Eternal Return

Jean Delannoy's modernized version of the legend of Tristan and Isolde. An enormous commercial success during the worst days of the German occupation of France, the film is based on a script by Jean Cocteau, and is the tragic love story of two friends, Patrice and his Uncle Marc, who share a deep friendship. When Patrice falls in love with Marc's wife Nathalie, the loyalty he feels for his uncle prevents him from telling her of his love, only to find that she returns it. French with English subtitles.
VHS: S04914. $29.95.
Jean Delannoy, France, 1943, 100 mins.

The Fabulous Versailles

Shot on location, this stunning recreation of the inhabitants and visitors of Versailles features Orson Welles, Claudette Colbert, Edith Piaf, Sacha Guitry and Jean Marais. Three hundred years of the French monarchy comes to life with such figures as Mme. de Pompadour, Ben Franklin (Welles), Louis XIV (Guitry) and many more. Welles also narrates. Dubbed in English.
VHS: S24011. $19.95.
Sacha Guitry, France, 1954, 103 mins.

Fanfan la Tulipe

Gerard Philipe and Gina Lolabrigida star in this funny and satirical look at military exploits set in the time of Louis XV. Gerard's character narrowly escapes a wedding and finds a new beloved, the army. It seems he was promised both an illustrious career and even a royal match. Oddly enough, his luck holds and he wins more success than even his greatest fans could have imagined. Winner Best Director at Cannes. French with English subtitles.
VHS: S29988. $29.95.
Christian Jaque, France/Italy, 1952, 98 mins.

Films of Georges Melies, Volume 1

These seven Georges Melies early short subjects from 1902 to 1912 feature the elaborate sets and trick photography that make his films so interesting to watch. Included are the groundbreaking classic *A Trip to the Moon* (1902, 9 mins.), about a fantasy rocket trip to the moon, which boasts one of the best prints available; *Melomaniac* (1903, 3 mins.), which features the head of a musical conductor as the musical notes; *The Monster* (1903, 3 mins.), in which an Egyptian magician creates a monster out of thin air; *Terrible Turkish Executioner* (1904, 3 mins.), about four men who are beheaded at one time and manage to restore themselves; *Palace of Arabian Nights* (1905, 13 mins.), a trip to the netherworld; *The Eclipse* (1907, 12 mins.), in which scientists gather to watch a solar eclipse; and *The Conquest of the Pole* (1912, 12 mins.), in which scientists encounter curious creatures at the North Pole. Silent with orchestra score.
VHS: S30160. $19.95.

Forbidden Games

Rene Clement's beautiful allegory is the story of two children orphaned by the war who build a secret cemetery for animals and steal crosses from the church yard to mark the graves. Wonderfully natural performances from Georges Pojouly, whom Clement discovered in a camp, and Brigitte Fossey create a moving film about the effects of war on children. Winner at the Venice Film Festival and Best Foreign Film Oscar. French with English subtitles.
VHS: S00457. $29.95.
Laser: LD70988. $39.95.
Rene Clement, France, 1952, 90 mins.

French Way

Josephine Baker stars in this rare wartime musical comedy. Baker plays Cupid to a would-be Romeo and Juliet while trying to re-open her nightclub. Five extraordinary songs by Baker. French with English subtitles. France, 1940.
VHS: S01627. $34.95.

Gervaise

A perfect example of a polished adaptation of a novel, this one, *L'Assommoir* by Emile Zola. Gervaise is a young woman whose husband becomes an alcoholic after an accident. Notable for a marvelous reconstruction of 19th century Paris. French with English subtitles.
VHS: S00493. $24.95.
Rene Clement, France, 1957, 116 mins.

Golgotha

Robert Levigan stars as Jesus in the first sound film made about the life of Jesus of Nazareth. Jean Gabin is Pontius Pilate, while Harry Bauer appears as King Herod in this early Biblical film. It's a moving and credible account of the story, and it tells this story without any undue flourishes. Dubbed in English.
VHS: S29448. $29.95.
Julien Duvivier, France, 1935, 95 mins.

Grand Melies (Franju) and Melies' Short Films

Famous, stylish docudrama directed by Georges Franju on the life of the pioneering "Magician of the Cinema." With special insights into his early career, how he achieved his spectacular effects and his sad final demise. Featuring Melies' wife (Madame Georges Melies) and son (Andre Melies). Following this rare film we are pleased to present quality recordings of Melies' most famous shorts, including: *The Trip to the Moon, Paris to Monte Carlo, Extraordinary Illusions, The Enchanted Well, The Conquest of the Pole*, and *The Apparition*. English narration. 70 mins.
VHS: S13507. $39.95.

Grisbi (Hands Off the Loot)

Jean Gabin stars in this unorthodox tale as the King of the Parisian underworld. When a gold heist goes bad, the loot is suddenly missing, and there will be no honor among these thieves. The legendary Jeanne Moreau joins Gabin in this thriller/drama. Dubbed.
VHS: S21603. $24.95.
Jacques Becker, France, 1953, 94 mins.

Hail Mafia

This is a terrific film with a top-notch international cast. Jack Klugman and Henry Silva play mafia hitmen ordered to kill Eddie Constantine. Klugman is torn between his orders and his loyalty to his old friend Eddie. An intriguing look at the emotional make-up of mafia hitmen. In English.
VHS: S32600. $24.95.
Raoul J. Levy, France, 1965, 89 mins.

Head Against the Wall

Jean-Pierre Mocky stars as a wild young man in love with Anouk Aimee, who is declared insane and spends time in mental institutions until he escapes and returns to Aimee. A work of strange beauty and power, the first feature by Franju. French with English subtitles.
VHS: S03747. $34.95.
Georges Franju, France, 1958, 98 mins.

Head over Heels

Brigitte Bardot stars as a woman, bored with her marriage, who resumes her career as a model. While on assignment in London she meets a man and is flattered by his attention. Also known as *Two Weeks in September*. From the director of *Sundays and Cybele*. French with English subtitles.
VHS: S01667. $19.95.
Serge Bourguignon, France, 1967, 89 mins.

The Hunchback of Notre Dame

This is no homogenized cartoon version, but a restoration of the previously unavailable, French-made adaptation of Victor Hugo's novel, starring Anthony Quinn as Quasimodo the hunchback bellringer and Gina Lollobrigida as the seductive gypsy Esmeralda. Special 40th anniversary edition.
VHS: S31091. $103.99.
Laser: LD76150. $39.99.
Jean Delannoy, France/Italy, 1957, 104 mins.

I Killed Rasputin

A portrait of the friendship between the men that ended in the betrayal and assassination by Felix Youssoupoff of Rasputin, the "mad monk" who rose to power in Russia before the revolution. Dubbed in English.
VHS: S09247. $19.95.
Robert Hossein, France/Italy, 1967, 95 mins.

Is Paris Burning?

The gripping heroism of the Allied Resistance during the Paris liberation of 1944 is depicted in this multi-storied war epic scripted by Francis Ford Coppola and Gore Vidal. The illustrious international cast includes: Jean-Paul Belmondo, Kirk Douglas, Yves Montand, and Orson Welles.
VHS: S13707. $29.95.
Rene Clement, France/USA, 1968, 173 mins.

J'Accuse (Silent)

Gance's first, silent version of his anti-war story of a young peasant woman, her husband, and the poet who loves her. The two men go to war. While they are gone, the woman is raped by a German soldier and becomes pregnant. When her husband returns he accuses the poet. When the two men discover the truth, they return to the trenches to avenge her. Silent with French titles.
VHS: S30193. $24.95.
Abel Gance, France, 1918

J'Accuse (Sound)

One of the great films by Abel Gance (*Napoleon*) and a powerful statement against war. A strange man, obsessed with the horrors of war, calls upon the millions of dead soldiers from World War I to rise from their graves and march upon the cities of the world. With Victor Francen, Jean Max. French with English subtitles.
VHS: S12329. $29.95.
Abel Gance, France, 1938, 127 mins.

Jailbird's Vacation

Lino Ventura stars in this story of two ex-cons who takes jobs as lumberjacks in an isolated sawmill in order to extract revenge. French with English subtitles.
VHS: S02799. $19.95.
Robert Enrico, France, 1965, 125 mins.

Judex

Franju's homage to early crime serials of Feuilliade. The story is set in 1914 at the castle of a wealthy banker whose many wrongs Judex intends to redress, aided by Cocantin and the Liquorice Kid. In the meantime, the banker's daughter is falling in love with the supersleuth. French with English subtitles.
VHS: S00661. $29.95.
Georges Franju, France, 1963, 103 mins.

Just Another Pretty Face

One of the last appearances of Henri Vidal, the handsome, athletic, leading man in many French films. Vidal plays a detective who solves a jewel smuggling case, and falls in love with a young woman who was involved with the smugglers. French with English subtitles.
VHS: S01675. $19.95.
Marc Allegret, France, 1958, 110 mins.

Juve Contre Fantomas

Made in 1913-14, these short films pitting detective Juve against the criminal master of disguise, Fantomas, were very influential in the Surrealist movement. Silent.
VHS: S00667. $29.95.
Louis Feuillade, France, 1913-14, 64 mins.

Killing Game
Jean-Pierre Cassel, Claudine Auger and Michel Duchaussoy star in this early film by Alain Jessua. Cassel and Auger are cartoonists who meet a wealthy playboy who lives out his fantasies through cartoons and hires them to create a comic strip. As they do, he begins to live the comic strip out—but unfortunately, it involves murder.
VHS: S06333. $39.95.
Alain Jessua, France, 1967, 90 mins.

Kiss for a Killer
At the center of this film is a beautiful woman played by Mylene Demongeot, who is destined to drive men mad. She may look innocent but this appearance only makes her true passion-cold-blooded murder—more achievable. It's a thriller based on the best-selling novel, that also stars Henri Vidal and Isa Miranda. Dubbed in English.
VHS: S21604. $24.95.

L'Ecole Buissoniere
A simple account of how a village school teacher with "modern" ideas inspires his charges with a passion for knowledge that eventually spreads to their aroused, suspicious parents. The drama unfolds in the classroom of a provincial school where the gradual expansion of a reluctant child's mind is depicted as tangibly and fascinatingly as the opening of a flower. A vision of hard-core realism that conveys the importance of children in the community. French with English subtitles.
VHS: S16118. $29.95.
Jean-Paul Le Chanois, France, 1951, 84 mins.

L'Inhumaine
In this early, silent science-fiction film, Einar Norsen (Jaque Catelain) has devised an elaborate system for resurrecting the dead, which he uses to win the object of his unrequited love, Claire Lescaut (Georgette Leblanc), an infamous singer. Critics have regarded this film as an attempt to celebrate film as art and to reconcile the popular with the elitist. Silent with French titles.
VHS: S30194. $24.95.
Marcel L'Herbier, France, 1924

La Chute de la Maison Usher
Though directed by Jean Epstein, this French silent version of the Poe classic is also notable for having given apprenticeship to Luis Bunuel. Henri Langlois of the Cinematheque Francaise wrote, "An absolute mastery of editing and rhythm in which slow motion, super-impressions, moving camera shots, and the mobile camera combine to play a totally ungratuitous role. The lighting of the sets transforms them and imparts a sense of mystery. The actors were merely objects."
VHS: S06223. $59.95.
Jean Epstein, France, 1928

La Maternelle
A compassionate tale of the sad-faced, squalid children of the Paris slums who find daily sanctuary from the ugliness and terror of their home lives at "La Maternelle." The story of a gangly waif named Marie, the film captures the anguish among the spattered flowers of Montmartre. French with English subtitles.
VHS: S16117. $29.95.
Jean Benoit-Levy/Marie Epstein, France, 1933, 83 mins.

La Roue (Wheel of Fate)
In its time, this film had such an impact on French filmmakers that Jean Cocteau supposedly began referring to "a cinema before and after *La Roue*." It is the tragic tale of Sisif (Severin Mars), an engine driver, who saves a girl from a train crash and adopts her, then falls in love with her as she grows up into a beautiful young woman (Ivy Close). He marries her off to a rich railway administrator in an effort to rid himself of temptation and guilt but his torment does not cease. "No film since De Mille's *The Cheat*, not even L'Herbier's *El Dorado*, had so stunned the French filmmakers, critics and cinephiles" (Richard Abel, *French Cinema*). Silent with French titles.
VHS: S30195. $24.95.
Abel Gance, France, 1921, 130 mins.

La Symphonie Pastorale
Based on Andre Gide's introspective short story. Set in a mountain village, the story follows the spiritual growth and decline of a well-meaning pastor (Pierre Blanchar) and Gertrude (Michele Morgan), a blind orphan he takes into his home. Initially, the minister is guided by Christian principles to raise Gertrude with fatherly love, but as she grows into a beautiful woman, he is driven by a passion that destroys the happiness of his wife and son. Digitally mastered with new electronic subtitles. French with English subtitles.
VHS: S30143. $29.95.
Jean Delannoy, France, 1976, 105 mins.

La Terre
In this silent film adaptation of Emile Zola's story of greed and deception among small landowners, Armand Bour stars as Old Fouan, a farmer who is slowly robbed of his land, his farmhouse and his money, by his own sons. Features excellent performances from Comedie Francaise actors and cinematography described by Paul de la Borie as meticulously painterly, almost Millet-like, in its realism. Silent with French titles.
VHS: S30196. $24.95.
Andre Antoine, France, 1921, 97 mins.

Lady Chatterley's Lover
Marc Allegret's version of the D.H. Lawrence novel with Danielle Darrieux as the Lady. Although the film was banned for a number of years by the New York Board of Censors, it is now almost too tasteful in its depiction of Lady Chatterley's sexual awakening. Darrieux delivers a performance of great complexity. French with English subtitles.
VHS: S18172. $24.95.
Marc Allegret, France, 1955, 102 mins.

Lafayette
Michel Le Boyer stars with an all-star international cast, including Orson Welles and Vittorio De Sica, in this biographical film. The great noble Frenchman assisted in the American Revolution and became an outspoken defender of freedom and liberty. He aided the ragged but determined armed forces marshalled by Washington. The relationship between Lafayette and his wife is given special attention in this costume spectacular. Dubbed in English.
VHS: S23991. $24.95.
Jean Dreville, France/Italy, 1963, 84 mins.

The Last Adventure
Alain Delon stars in this story of two friends who are fooled by an insurance scam that almost costs them their lives. When they find the man responsible he tells them about a secret treasure aboard a crashed plane somewhere on the coast of Africa, but their search for riches has unexpected results. French with English subtitles.
VHS: S20771. $29.95.
Robert Enrico, France, 1966, 102 mins.

Le Bourgeois Gentilhomme
Moliere's *Le Bourgeois Gentilhomme*, presented by the Comedie Francaise in the tradition of Commedia Dell'Arte. Music by Jean Baptiste Lully, a contemporary of Moliere's. Lavish costumes, ballets and dances. French with English subtitles.
VHS: S00735. $29.95.
Jean Meyer, France, 1958, 97 mins.

Le Cas du Dr. Laurent
(*The Case of Dr. Laurent*). Jean Gabin delivers a stirring performance as a country doctor who is a dedicated man with an abundance of compassion for his patients in this superb example of the "French cinema of quality."
VHS: S05326. $29.95.
Jean-Paul Le Chanois, France, 1957, 92 mins.

Le Gendarme a New York
A hilarious, wonderful spoof of American culture as seen by the French. Famous French comedian Louis de Funes and his troupe take on Manhattan with madcap adventures around every turn. The second in this popular series. French with English subtitles.
VHS: S33138. $59.95.
Jean Girault, France, 1965, 92 mins.

Le Gendarme de St. Tropez
This is the first of a highly popular series featuring the comic antics of gendarme Ludovic Cruchot. His ambitions are at odds with the laid-back atmosphere of the resort St. Tropez, and his hopes are finally dashed when his daughter has just a little too much fun on the beach. French with English subtitles.
VHS: S20770. $29.95.
Jean Girault, France, 1965, 95 mins.

Le Golem: The Legend of Prague
The first sound version of the Jewish folk legend of the rabbi who brings the Golem back to life in order to frighten the emperor was shot on location in Prague and features a first-rate performance from Harry Baur as the Emperor, along with Roger Karl and Charles Dorat. French with English subtitles.
VHS: S14690. $79.95.
Julien Duvivier, France, 1935, 96 mins.

Le Grand Melies: The Great Melies, Father of Fiction Films
This amazing documentary, by Georges Franju, traces the life and artistic innovation of an early film great. Melies saw the transformative power latent in the new possibilities offered by the motion picture. Andre Melies portrays his father George in this highly regarded tribute to the French innovator. French with English subtitles, 25 mins.
VHS: S22512. $39.95.
Georges Franju, France, 1936, 25 mins.

Les Abysses
Based on the actual 1933 French murder case which inspired Jean Genet to write *The Maids, Les Abysses is an electrifying study of avarice, despair and violence. "The cinema has given us its foremost tragedy" (Jean-Paul Sartre). French with English subtitles.*
VHS: S14640. $29.95.
Nico Papatakis, France, 1963, 90 mins.

Les Liaisons Dangereuses
The first—and certainly the best—version of Laclos' novel, with the incredible Gerard Philipe playing Valmont, and Jeanne Moreau, Madame de Merteuil. Directed by Roger Vadim and updated to 1960, Vadim's exploration of free-thinking attitudes and portrait of the corrupt upper-class society is particularly distinguished through the outstanding performances of both Philipe and Moreau. With Jean-Louis Trintignant, Annette Vadim; music by, among others, Thelonious Monk. French with English subtitles.
VHS: S10740. $59.95.
Roger Vadim, France, 1959, 106 mins.

Les Miserables
This faithful adaptation of Victor Hugo's great novel stars Jean Gabin as the escaped convict Jean Valjean, who is pursued by the relentless Police Inspector Javert. A great cast; Gabin, in particular, is superb. With Bernard Blier, Bourvil, Serge Reggiani and Daniele Delorme. English dubbed.
Part I.
VHS: S02573. $29.95.
Part II.
VHS: S02574. $29.95.
Jean-Paul Le Chanois, France, 1957, 210 mins.

Les Vampires
Feulliade's legendary serial, one of the masterpieces of silent cinema, which figures prominently in Olivier Assayas' film *Irma Vep*, is a thriller about a gang of archcriminals preying on the decadent Parisian bourgeousie. With French actress Musidora as Irma Vep. "Groundbreaking…visionary in its hallucinatory naturalism and still exciting to watch today" (Graham Fuller, *Andy Warhol's Interview*). Remastered boxed set features new music. Ten episodes.
VHS: S34325. $99.95.
Louis Feuillade, France, 1915

The Liars
In this unpretentious, low-keyed mystery a Frenchman, after making his fortune in Africa, returns to Paris, advertises for a wife and is almost taken in (and murdered) by two con artists. Starring Dawn Addams and Jean Servais. French with English subtitles.
VHS: S14641. $29.95.
Edmond T. Greville, France, 1964, 92 mins.

Life Upside Down
This Winner of the Best First Film Award at the Venice Film Festival tells the story of a successful real estate developer (Charles Denner) who withdraws from his perfect life. Between his flighty wife and a round of meaningless events his growing detachment may seem insane at first, but it could also be the only sensible solution. French with English subtitles.
VHS: S20878. $79.95.
Alain Jessua, France, 1965, 115 mins.

Little World of Don Camillo
A priest in a northern Italian town has trouble staying out of mischief in this all-time classic. When the communists are elected to power in the town, he tangles with the mayor of the little hamlet, who is a flag-waving party man. With Fernandel, Gino Cervi. Dubbed in English.
VHS: S13354. $29.95.
Julien Duvivier, France, 1951, 106 mins.

Love of Three Queens
Hedy Lamarr, the voluptuous star of *Ecstasy*, plays an actress who portrays three of the most fascinating women in history. Lamarr is Guenevieve, a saintly countess who tries desperately to save her kingdom; Empress Josephine; and Helen of Troy, the woman whose beauty launched a thousand ships. Massimo Serato is the wealthy nobleman who is hopelessly in love with Lamarr in this stirring drama of passion and pleasure.
VHS: S13667. $29.95.
Marc Allegret, USA, 1954, 80 mins.

Love Play
The lost film of the legendary Jean Seberg, not seen in over 30 years, is based on Francoise Sagan's novel *Bonjour Tristesse*. The radiant Seberg stars as a young American in Paris discovering her sexuality. With Christian Marquand (*And God Created Woman*). In English.
VHS: S33136. $29.95.
Francois Moreuil, France, 1965, 87 mins.

Loves of Casanova
Ivan Mosjoukine stars as the great lover in this silent epic-style romance. Also stars Jeanne Boitel, Marcelle Denya, Michael Simon, Suzanne Bianchetti as Catherine II and Diana Karenne as Maria Mari. Also includes 20-minute Mosjoukine short, *Lord of the Moguls*. Also known as *The Prince of Adventurers*.
VHS: S30191. $24.95.
Alexandre Volkoff, France, 1927, 134 mins.

The Lumiere Brothers' First Films

Narrated by Bertrand Tavernier, this amazing journey through the birth of the motion picture as art form is no ordinary compilation. All of the titles in this series were restored by the Lumiere Institute (of which Tavernier is president) and demonstrate the tremendous breadth of the Lumieres' work—from the first dolly shot to their extraordinary recording of history in Russia, China and the United States. A must for every lover of silent film. In English.
VHS: S32044. $49.95.
Bertrand Tavernier, France, 1996, 70 mins.

Man from Nowhere

A witty and stylish film by Pierre Chenal, and one of the high points of classic French comedy, *The Man from Nowhere* is based on Luigi Pirandello's novel, *The Late Mathias Pascal*. Pierre Blanchar is the henpecked husband who unexpectedly gets a chance to start a new life. A colorful supporting cast, pungent dialog and Chenal's ironic direction combine in a film which mixes melodrama with satire. "A sparkling comic melodrama. Rich characters, luscious turn-of-the-century landscapes and delightful performances are aided by a screenplay which snaps with one witticism after another" (*Detroit News*). French with English subtitles.
VHS: S09198. $59.95.
Pierre Chenal, France, 1937, 98 mins.

Man in the Silk Hat

A moving tribute to the famous french actor of the silent era, Max Linder, whom Chaplin once called "my professor," directed by his daughter. During his lifetime, Linder made some 400-500 short comedies, and came to America to make his only three feature-length films. With numerous excerpts from Linder's films, this is a loving tribute to one of the giants of comedy. Narrated in English by Maud Linder.
VHS: S04870. $24.95.
Maud Linder, France, 1984, 96 mins.

Maria Chapdelaine

The film from which Jean Gabin rose to prominence, from the director of *Pepe Le Moko* and *Poil de Carotte*. One of Duvivier's first great films, which earned him a reputation for his "poetic realism." French with English subtitles.
VHS: S00824. $29.95.
Julien Duvivier, France, 1934, 75 mins.

The Marvelous Life of Joan of Arc

This popular historical reconstruction was de Gastyne's most ambitious, and took him two years to shoot. The life of Joan of Arc is told from her peasant youth at Domremy to her death at the stake in Rouen. Stars Simone Genevois as Jeanne, Philippe Heriat as Gilles de Rais, and Jean Toulot as La Tremouille. Silent with French titles.
VHS: S30198. $24.95.
Marc de Gastyne, France, 1929, 124 mins.

Marvelous Melies

A collection of great films by the great pioneer magician of the cinema, Georges Melies: *A Trip to the Moon, Paris to Monte Carlo, The Doctor's Secret, Kingdom of the Fairies, The Enchanted Well* and *The Conquest of the Pole.*
VHS: S05789. $29.95.
Georges Melies, France, 60 mins.

Max Linder

By 1910 Max Linder was an internationally popular comic, typically playing a dapper dandy of the idle rich. He developed a slapstick style that anticipated Mack Sennett and Chaplin. His popularity was at its peak in 1914, when he was called up for World War I. With original French titles. Silent.
VHS: S00833. $29.95.
Max Linder, France, 1911-13

Mayerling

The romantic, sumptuous film that established Charles Boyer as a screen idol. Set in Vienna in 1883, Boyer plays the Archduke Rudolf, who is madly in love with Maria Vetsera, played by Danielle Darrieux. An opulent romance with a sharp portrait of the Hapsburg court. French with English subtitles.
VHS: S00837. $29.95.
Anatole Litvak, France, 1936, 91 mins.

Melies III: The Search for Munchhausen

A terrific compilation of trick film fantasies from Melies including *Baron Munchhausen's Dream, The Witch's Revenge, The Infernal Caldron, The Damnation of the Monster,* and *The Terrible Turkish Executioners.* 45 mins.
VHS: S14814. $29.95.

Menilmontant

An important film made by Dimitri Kirsanov in France, a silent film done without titles which "is not a melodrama but an antecedent to neo-realism, portraying life itself with a sensitive use of natural sets and a feeling for poetry and truth" (Georges Sadoul). In the film, a young girl is seduced by a young man who deserts her when she is pregnant. She contemplates suicide, meets her sister who's since become a prostitute, and is reconciled with her again.
VHS: S07466. $39.95.
Dimitri Kirsanov, France, 1926, 27 mins

Miracle of Saint Therese

Nearly 100 years ago this Carmelite nun died of tuberculosis after devoting her 24-year-life to the development of her faith. When her autobiography sold over 1,000,000 copies, a public letter campaign asking for sainthood was so successful that the church waved the usual 50-year waiting period for canonization and sainthood. In 1923 Therese de Lisieux was beatified, and then canonized in 1925. This is an affectionate and affecting tribute to the watchmaker's daughter who became the second patroness saint of France. With Frances Descaut, Jean Debucourt and Suzanne Flon. "A studied and reverent re-enactment of the simple, closeted life of a Carmelite nun" (*The New York Times*). Dubbed in English.
VHS: S30734. $29.95.
France, 1959, 90 mins.

Moderato Cantabile

Peter Brook's second feature stars Jeanne Moreau as a bored housewife and Jean-Paul Belmondo as the blue-collar worker she can't resist in Marguerite Duras' story of secrets and hidden passion. French with English subtitles.
VHS: S33137. $59.95.
Peter Brook, France, 1959, 90 mins.

Modigliani (Montparnasse 19)

Jacques Becker inherited this project from Max Ophuls, who co-wrote the screenplay but died before production started. The film is an examination of the art and dissolute life of the 19th-century French painter Modigliani (Gerard Philipe). The story tracks Modigliani's affairs with British poet Beatrice Hastings (Lilli Palmer) and Jeanne (Anouk Aimee), his mistress and model in the final years of his life. "A quiet masterpiece that ultimately soars to sublimity" (Andrew Sarris). With Gerard Sety, Lino Ventura, Lila Kedrova and Lea Padovani. French with English subtitles.
VHS: S19523. $59.95.
Jacques Becker, France, 1958, 110 mins.

Monsieur Vincent

Winner of an Academy Award as Best Foreign Film, Pierre Fresnay gives the characterization of Vincent de Paul an extraordinarily human, emotional portrayal. Based on a scenario by Jean Anouilh, cinematography by Claude Renoir. French with English subtitles.
VHS: S00874. $39.95.
Maurice Cloche, France, 1948

Moore and Thill in Louise

Grace Moore and Georges Thill star in this adaptation of the Charpentier opera. Between domineering parents and her love, a seamstress finds her life severely hemmed in. Confounded, she throws everything aside and confronts the world. French language.
VHS: S25533. $39.95.
Abel Gance, France, 1938, 83 mins.

More Melies

A second companion volume to *Marvelous Melies*, this further compilation of pioneering primitives from Georges Melies includes *The Inn Where No Man Rests, Spiritualist Photographer, The Magic Lantern, Clockmaker's Dream, The Cook in Trouble, The Bob Kick (a.k.a. Mischievous Kid), The Oracle of Delphi, Drawing Lesson, Jupiter's Thunderbolt* and *The Mermaid.* B&W, 60 mins.
VHS: S08047. $29.95.

Ms. Don Juan (Don Juan 73)

Brigitte Bardot and her ex-husband Roger Vadim reteam for this sexy spin-off of the Don Juan legend. Bardot confesses to her cousin, a priest, about all the men she has seduced. With Jane Birkin, Maurice Ronet, Mathieu Carriere and Robert Hossein. Dubbed in English.
VHS: S32952. $19.95.
Roger Vadim, France, 1973, 95 mins.

Nana

Charles Boyer and Martine Carol star in this color version of Emile Zola's famous novel about a girl from the slums who becomes a respectable lady and then sets out to humiliate the class which is responsible for her previous misery. French with English subtitles.
VHS: S00915. $34.95.
Christian Jacque, France, 1955, 120 mins.

Napoleon (Gance)

A masterpiece of world cinema, employing a variety of new techniques, including triple screen and mobile use of the camera by strapping it to a galloping horse. Long thought to be lost, the film has been reconstructed and is presented with a sound track composed by Carmine Coppola.
VHS: S00917. $79.95.
Abel Gance, France, 1927, 235 mins.

Napoleon (Guitry)

Orson Welles, Maria Schell, Yves Montand, and Erich von Stroheim star in Sacha Guitry's classic biography of Napoleon, from his youth as a soldier in the French Army until his exile to the Island of Elba. A monumental production with a cast of thousands, originally shot in Technicolor. English dialog.
VHS: S00918. $29.95.
Laser: LD70061. $89.98.
Sacha Guitry, France, 1955, 115 mins.

The Necklace

Based on the story by Guy de Maupassant. Mathilde Loisel is married to a decent but minor government official. Dreams of a better life are put on hold when she loses a necklace, forcing her into menial work to replace it. Only years later is the shocking meaning behind this necklace revealed. In English. 21 mins.
VHS: S22366. $79.95.

An Occurrence at Owl Creek Bridge

Award winning short film based on a story by Ambrose Bierce about the final moments of a man about to be hung for sabotage during the Civil War. Highly recommended.
VHS: S02247. $19.95.
Robert Enrico, France, 1962, 29 mins.

Panique

A major film by one of the most underrated of early French directors, Panique is the story of a vicious young crook who robs and murders an elderly woman in a fairground and then conspires with his girlfriend to put the blame for the crime on a bearded recluse, played by the great actor Michel Piccoli. Based on the novel by Charles Simenon, with a script by one of the great French screenwriters, Charles Spaak, Panique ends with a harrowing climax in which Simon is hounded to death by an angry mob. French with English subtitles.
VHS: S07099. $29.95.
Julien Duvivier, France, 1946, 87 mins.

Pantaloons (Don Juan)

French comedian Fernandel is mistaken for Don Juan when he is just the servant of the great lover. Didn't Bob Hope make this movie as the servant of Casanova? The Gallic horse-faced farceur makes a convincing swashbuckler much to the rage of Fernando Rey, as a villainous nobleman. Dubbed in English.
VHS: S05439. $29.95.
John Berry, France, 1956, 95 mins.

Paris 1900

Documentary about life in Paris between 1900 and 1914, largely composed of stills from the Cinematheque Francaise. English narration by Monty Woolley. Alain Resnais worked as assistant production supervisor on the film. French songs sung by Claude Dauphin.
VHS: S02578. $29.95.
Nicole Vedres, France, 1948, 50 mins.

Paris Waltz

Considered one of the last *monstres-sacres* of the French musical stage, Yvonne Printemps portrays Jacques Offenbach's beautiful and tempestuous prima donna, Hortense Schneider (1833-1920) in this beautifully photographed film with music by Offenbach and gowns by Dior. Also stars Printemps' real-life husband, Pierre Fresnay, as Offenbach. "Delightful, witty, with 20 songs. In a selection from *Fortunio*, Printemps' is singing that is sensed in the soul" (Stefan Zucker, *Opera Fanatic*). French with English subtitles.
VHS: S28433. $34.95.
Marcel Archard, France, 1948, 92 mins.

Passion for Life

One of the best films by Jean-Paul Le Chanois, and one of the best performances by Bernard Blier; Blier plays a progressive teacher who introduces new teaching methods into a provincial village school, comes into conflict with the traditional parents, but ends up by winning his fight. With Juliette Faber, Edouard Delmont, music by Joseph Kosma. French with English subtitles.
VHS: S06437. $69.95.
Jean-Paul Le Chanois, France, 1948, 89 mins.

Pathe Freres Vol. 1

A collection of early film fantasies from Pathe Freres, including: *The Red Spectre* (hand colored), the imitation of Melies *Trip to the Moon; El Buen Cigario* (attributed by some to Max Linder); *Fantasia Florido, Album Marvilloso, La Ruche Mereilleurs.* 60 mins.
VHS: S05790. $29.95.

Pathe Freres Vol. 2

Ten short films from Pathe Freres, including *The Enchanted House, Pixillation, Posada Mysteriosa, The Invisible Thief, The Yawner, The Poor Coat, Wiffels Wins a Beauty Prize, I Fetch the Bread*, and Zecca's classic *Down in the Deep*. 60 mins.
VHS: S05791. $29.95.

Pattes Blanches

Paul Bernard and Suzy Delair star in this 1949 melodrama, directed by Jean Gremillon, about a reclusive aristocrat ridiculed in the provincial French fishing town where he lives, because of the gaudy white spats he is always so fond of wearing.Adapted from a play by Jean Anouilh."If Emily Bronte had written *The Postman Always Rings Twice*, the result would be the hard-boiled, Gothic *Pattes Blanches*, an extraordinary French film" (Carrie Rickey, *Philadelphia Inquirer*). French with English subtitles.
VHS: S14987. $59.95.
Jean Gremillon, France, 1987, 92 mins.

The Pearls of the Crown

A groundbreaking film with a sharp, satirical underpinning directed by Sacha Guitry and Christian Jacque has Guitry performing four separate roles, stretched out over four centuries, each character feverishly in pursuit of the four pear-shaped pearls aligning the English royal crown."It is an amazing and weirdly fascinating condensation of fact and fiction" (*Stage*).With Jacqueline Delubac, Lyn Harding and Jean Louis Barrault. English, French and Italian with English subtitles.
VHS: S17488. $59.95.
Sacha Guitry/Christian Jacque, France/Italy, 1937, 121 mins.

Pepe le Moko

A gem of French cinema with an unbelievable performance by Jean Gabin as Pepe le Moko, a Parisian gangster hiding out in the Algerian Casbah.A menacing atmosphere full of shadows contributes to the image of Pepe as the outsider/hero who falls in love with a Parisian woman, tries to escape with her and finds his path blocked by the police.The spine-tingling ending is classic. With Mireille Balin and Line Noro. French with English subtitles.
VHS: S01007. $29.95.
Julien Duvivier, France, 1936, 95 mins.

Phedre

"To see Marie Bell in *Phedre* is a unique opportunity to experience fully what is French genius," said Andre Malraux.This film adaptation of Racine's great tragedy stars Bell when she was a remarkably well-preserved 68 years old—but a great actress in a great French classic. French with English subtitles.
VHS: S01022. $29.95.
Pierre Jourdan, France, 1968, 92 mins.

Pilgrimage to Rome

Jean Gabin, one of France's most beloved film actors, stars as an unrepentant gangster who upon release from jail sets off, disguised as a priest, to recover his hidden loot in Rome. International terrorists hijack his plane causing a small detour on this pilgrimage to the object of his veneration. French with English subtitles.
VHS: S20772. $59.95.
Jean Girault, France, 1976, 90 mins.

Poil de Carotte

Duvivier's poignant story about "Carrot Top," an unloved young boy mistreated by his mother. Carrot Top's often-absent father remains unaware but the family faces a crisis when the boy tries suicide.A moving, sensitive film with great performances by Robert Lynen, Harry Baur and Catherine Fonteney. French with English subtitles.
VHS: S01043. $29.95.
Julien Duvivier, France, 1931, 90 mins.

Princess Tam Tam

Perhaps the best of her six features, Josephine Baker stars in this exotic Pygmalion-like musical comedy about a French author who goes to North Africa to write a novel, but becomes distracted—then entranced—by a native girl whom he transforms into a "princess." Shot partly on location in Tunisia, *Princess Tam Tam* allows Josephine a chance to display her impish, comedic charm, as well as her erotic and evocative talents. "Josephine Baker...the one and only...astonishing," wrote *The New York Post*. French with English subtitles.
VHS: S10867. $29.95.
Edmond T. Greville, France, 1935, 77 mins.

Prix de Beaute

Louise Brooks' last starring role in a feature, and her only film made in France, is a tragic drama about a young typist who wins an international beauty contest unknown to her jealous fiance. The film, wrote Andrew Sarris in *The Village Voice* "confirms once more that Louise Brooks was one of the most enduringly fascinating women ever to appear in front of the camera." French with English subtitles.
VHS: S10395. $59.95.
Augusto Genina, France/Italy, 1930, 93 mins.

The Proud Ones (Les Orgueilleux)

Highly suggestive of Albert Camus' *The Plague*, Yves Allegret's grim adaptation of Sartre's novel *L'Amour Redempteur* was virtually unknown in this country until Martin Scorsese "discovered" the work, and organized its re-release. Michele Morgan plays an aristocratic French woman traveling through Mexico whose husband dies from a mysterious disease. Stranded in a decaying Mexican coastal town, Morgan falls for a local doctor (Gerard Philipe) who is distraught over his wife's death. With Carlos Moctezuma, Victor Mendoza andMichele Cardone. French with English subtitles.
VHS: S19518. $59.95.
Yves Allegret, France, 1953, 105 mins.

Purple Noon (Plein Soleil)

Rene Clement's psychological thriller, with the young Alain Delon as a morally bankrupt individual who is stricken with envy of his best friend. He murders him and then takes over his identity, even becoming the lover of his friend's girlfriend. Based on Patricia Highsmith's novel *The Talented Mr. Ripley, Purple Noon* is a startling and disturbing film that elicits audience fascination with a cunning "anti-hero." Stunningly photographed by Henri Decae against the backgrounds of southern Italy. French with English subtitles.
VHS: S30639. $19.95.
Laser: Widescreen. **LD76093. $49.98.**
Rene Clement, France/Italy, 1959, 118 mins.

The Red and the Black

Gerard Philipe stars in this adaptation of the famous novel by Stendhal, cast in the role of the opportunist Julien Sorel; Danielle Darrieux is Madame de Renal. French with English subtitles.
VHS: S06438. $29.95.
Claude Autant-Lara, France, 1953, 140 mins.

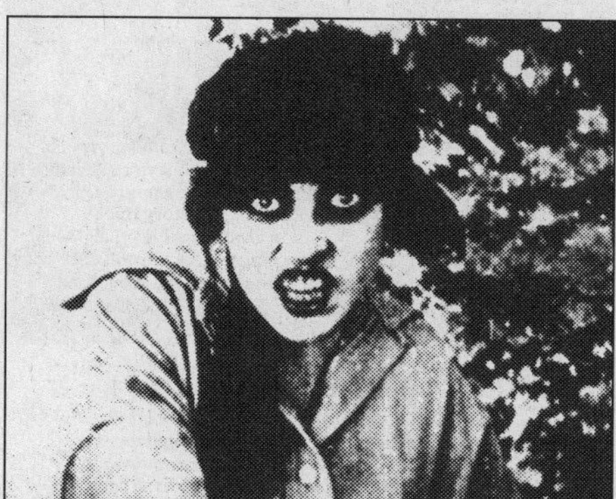

Red Balloon

A classic childhood fantasy with appeal for viewers of every age. This is a story of Pascal, a French boy who befriends a red balloon which follows him everywhere.A touching allegory of the magic powers of love and friendship. No dialog.
VHS: S01098. $14.95.
Albert Lamorisse, France, 1956, 34 mins.

Red Balloon/White Mane

Albert Lamorisse's *Red Balloon* is a priceless classic about a young boy's friendship with a red balloon. 1956, 38 mins. His *White Mane* explores man's relationship to nature; it chronicles the efforts of bandits to capture a wild white stallion, and a young boy who rescues him. Winner of the International Grand Prize, Best Short Film, Cannes Film Festival. 1952, 38 mins.
VHS: S18762. $24.95.
Laser: LD70443. $29.95.

Respectful Prostitute

Jean Paul Sartre's famous existential play is adapted for the screen in an English-language version starring Barbara Laage, Ivan Desny and Walter Bryan.A sensitive and compelling look at racial prejudice in America's Deep South, the plot concerns a black man who is shot by a senator's nephew, and a prostitute who is talked into testifying that the murder was committed in defense of an assault.
VHS: S07458. $19.95.
Charles Brabant/Marcel Pagliero, France, 75 min.

Rififi

Jules Dassin's classic tale, one of the most famous French gangster films ever made, is the story of a gangster who, when sprung from jail, finds his wife living with another man. He returns to his old racket, jewel thievery, and there follows an aftermath of murder, kidnapping and retribution. Steeped in the details of the sleazy Montmartre neighborhood, the film builds incredible suspense, and is particularly famous for its 30-minute, silent bank heist in which the audience is drawn in as participants.This is the complete, 117-minute version, which includes several scenes cut from the film because of sexual or violent content. French with English subtitles.
VHS: S15387. $24.95.
Jules Dassin, France, 1955, 117 mins.

Ruy Blas

Jean Marais plays two roles in Jean Cocteau's adaptation of the Victor Hugo novel. Danielle Darrieux portrays the Queen of Spain in this story of mistaken identity set in the court of Charles II. Revenge and love are the driving forces that set this court aflame with intrigues and romance. French with English subtitles.
VHS: S22034. $59.95.
Pierre Billon, France, 1948, 90 mins.

The Shameless Old Lady

The first feature of theatre designer and director Rene Allio, *The Shameless Old Lady* is an adaptation of Bertolt Brecht's story about a 70-year-old woman who, after 60 years of servitude as dutiful daughter, wife and mother, cuts loose, to the consternation of her stuffy offspring. Madame Bertini, impeccably played by the renowned actress Sylvie, becomes a veritable whirlwind of activity in the final 18 months of her life. French with English subtitles.
VHS: S08124. $39.95.
Rene Allio, France, 1966, 95 mins.

The Sorceress (1956)

A young French engineer is sent to Sweden to build a road.There he encounters an enchanting fairy nymph (Marina Vlady). In reality, she is just a country girl raised in isolation, but the townspeople ostracize her as a witch.These fears spell tragedy for the young love which grows between the Frenchman and the sorceress. French with English subtitles.
VHS: S26874. $69.95.
Andre Michel, France, 1956, 91 mins.

Stormy Waters (Remorques)

Jean Gabin stars as the tough captain of a rescue ship, who has an affair with a beautiful woman (Michele Morgan) he rescues during a fierce gale.Their romance is interrupted when Gabin's wife falls critically ill. English dubbed.
VHS: S01258. $29.95.
Jean Gremillon, France, 1939, 75 mins.

The Story of a Cheat

Sacha Guitry was a seminal influence in French films as an actor, author and producer of over 120 plays, and as a director, screenwriter and actor in 32 movies. Now American audiences can see his work in this classic film. It tells the story of an 11-year-old who discovers that honesty is the best policy. Putting this theory into practice leads to an enchanting tale. Guitry himself is featured. French with English subtitles.
VHS: S22480. $59.95.
Sacha Guitry, France, 1936, 83 mins

Sundays and Cybele

Winner of multiple awards including an Oscar, the moving, intelligently-told account of shell-shocked Hardy Kruger, who finds a source of communication with the outside world through his friendship with the orphaned girl Patricia Gozzi. French with English subtitles.
VHS: S01284. $29.95.
Serge Bourguignon, France, 1962, 110 mins.

Sylvia and the Phantom

An enchanting film that mixes comedy with pathos, the story of a sixteen year old-daughter who has fallen in love with the ghost of her grandmother's lover.The result of this whimsical love affair is a wonderful perspective on first love. French with English subtitles.
VHS: S03308. $24.95.
Claude Autant-Lara, France, 1950, 93 mins.

Tales of Paris

A collection of four short films about Parisian women, made by four talented French directors. Includes *The Tale of Ella*, by Jacques Poitrenaud; *The Tale of Antonia*, by Michel Boisrond; *The Tale of Francoise*, by Claude Barma; and *The Tale of Sophie*, starring Catherine Deneuve, co-written by Roger Vadim, directed by Marc Allegret. France, 1962, 85 mins.
VHS: S15191. $29.95.

That Naughty Girl and Love on a Pillow

Two films starring Brigitte Bardot at her sexiest. In the French comedy *That Naughty Girl*, Bardot is the not-so-innocent teenage daughter of a notorious crime boss. In *Love on a Pillow*, Bardot is an heiress who tries to help a young man who has attempted suicide by having an affair with him, despite the pleas of her family and friends. Both dubbed in English. Michel J. Boisrand, France, 1956, 84 mins./Roger Vadim, France, 1964, 102 mins.
VHS: S30030. $19.95.

Three Waltzes

Yvonne Printemps achieved her greatest theatrical success with this 1938 film, a French adaptation of a Viennese operetta which she performed for nearly two years.The film, spanning three generations from 1867 to 1937, recounts the love story of a ballerina, her daughter and her granddaughter. Music by Oscar Straus, with adaptations of music by Johann Strauss I and Strauss II. French with English subtitles. 101 mins.
VHS: S28434. $34.95.

Time Out for Love

Michele, beautiful and successful fashion executive, tries to commit suicide when she fears that her affair with Pierre, a race car driver, is on the wane. Things are further complicated when the 19-year-old American girl (played by Jean Seberg) trying to nurse her back to health gets in the middle of things by falling for Pierre herself. Photographed by Raoul Coutard. French with English subtitles.

VHS: S14651. $29.95.

Jean Valere, France, 1961, 93 mins.

Torture of Silence

Released in France as *Mater Dolorosa*, Gance made this picture again in 1932. A melodrama about a doctor who neglects his wife because of his work, and she seeks the company of his best friend. Silent with English subtitles.

VHS: S01364. $24.95.

Abel Gance, France, 1917, 55 mins.

The Umbrellas of Cherbourg

Catherine Deneuve stars in this sumptuously photographed romantic musical of two lovers who are split up by the Algerian war. The girl marries another when she discovers she is pregnant. He also marries; yet they meet again. All dialog is sung; with haunting music by Michel LeGrand and lyrics by Demy, including the song, "I Will Wait for You." "A masterpiece! More beautiful and more startling than ever!" (*New York Daily News*). "The kind of movie that audiences will remember all their lives" (*Chicago Tribune*). French with English subtitles.

VHS: S30735. $29.95.

Laser: Widescreen. **LD76164. $49.98.**

DVD: DV60126. $29.98.

Jacques Demy, France/Germany, 1964, 92 mins.

Volpone

Harry Baur plays the raucous old Volpone, Louis Jouvet the shameless, swindling Mosca in this version of the Ben Johnson satire. This was Baur's last film. French with English subtitles.

VHS: S01420. $29.95.

Maurice Tourneur, France, 1939, 95 mins.

Voyage Surprise

A nonsense comedy about a slapstick chase across the beautiful landscape of Haute-Provence, with a script and directed by Pierre Prevert, this film stars Martine Carol and Sioel, in the story of a crazy old man who takes his tourists on a "mystery tour" that collides with a wedding, the police, a brothel, thieves and revolutionaries. French with English subtitles.

VHS: S06440. $79.95.

Pierre Prevert, France, 1946, 108 mins.

Walls of Malapaga

Jean Gabin is a man on the run for killing his mistress. Safely stowed away on a ship, a sudden toothache sends him searching for succor in Genoa. There he meets a lonely waitress with a young daughter. They fall in love, but in this simple tale of desperation and loneliness it may be too late for these sad figures. French with English subtitles.

VHS: S21607. $24.95.

Rene Clement, France/Italy, 1949, 91 mins.

Warrior's Rest

Brigitte Bardot portrays an innocent young woman led to heartbreak by an anarchist student she rescues from suicide and falls in love with. Also known by the title *Love on a Pillow*. French with English subtitles.

VHS: S01673. $19.95.

Roger Vadim, France, 1962, 98 mins.

Will You Dance with Me?

Brigitte Bardot goes undercover as a dance instructor in order to clear her husband of murder charges. With Henri Vidal in the final role of his career. French with English subtitles.

VHS: S01965. $19.95.

Michel Boisrond, France, 1959, 89 mins.

Zorro (Delon)

Alain Delon stars as Zorro, the masked hero who rescues helpless peasants from the clutches of evil despot Colonel Huerta (Stanley Baker), the corrupt governor of Spanish California, in this widescreen version of the swashbuckling adventure. In English.

VHS: S34324. $14.99.

Duccio Tessari, Italy/France, 1974, 124 mins.

Zou Zou

Also featuring Jean Gabin, who was just on the brink of international success, *Zou Zou* is a Warners-style backstage musical in which a talented Cinderella (in this case a laundress played by Josephine Baker) takes the place of the lead on the opening night and saves the show. Clearly a star vehicle for Baker, she appears at her best here, as a glamorous, larger-than-life sophisticate. Watch for her spectacular rendition of "Haiti" that will remain indelible in everyone's memory. French with English subtitles.

VHS: S10866. $29.95.

Marc Allegret, France, 1934, 92 mins.

MARCEL CARNE

Bizarre Bizarre

A complicated mystery-farce about a group of Victorian Englishmen enmeshed in a web of disguises, lies, murders, romances and all-around intrigue. With a marvelous performance by Michel Simon, a collaboration between director Carne and screenwriter Prevert. French with English subtitles.

VHS: S00134. $29.95.

Marcel Carne, France, 1937, 90 mins.

Children of Paradise

Set in the 1840's, when pantomime and melodrama were at their height on Paris' famed theater street, the Boulevard du Crime, Marcel Carne's delicate yet elaborate portrait of the actors and thieves who made the Boulevard their home has all the passion, intelligence and authority of a truly great work of art. "The *Gone with the Wind* of art films" (Andrew Sarris).

VHS: S14499. $39.95.

Laser: CAV/CLV. Includes interview with Carne, treatment and photos. **LD70124. $89.95.**

Marcel Carne, France, 1943-45, 188 mins.

Daybreak (Le Jour Se Leve)

Jean Gabin in perhaps the finest role of his career as a factory worker barricaded against the police after a murder. Through a series of flashbacks he thinks over the events that led him to kill. French with English subtitles.

VHS: S00312. $29.95.

Marcel Carne, France, 1939, 87 mins.

Les Visiteurs du Soir

Marcel Carne's charming fantasy, set in the 15th century, and starring Arletty. The devil sends two envoys to a chateau to intervene in the betrothal of a count and a lady, and the male ghost falls in love with Lady Anne. The Devil himself must intervene. The images and sets often have the charm of medieval miniatures, and *Les Visiteurs du Soir* was a considerable success. French with English subtitles.

VHS: S06439. $29.95.

Marcel Carne, France, 1942, 110 mins.

The Marvelous Visit

An inventive adaptation of H.G. Wells' story about a fallen angel who is discovered by a priest and his assistant. The two care for the angel's rehabilitation. The angel wanders into a sleepy village and his eccentric behavior transforms it. With Gilles Kohler, Deborah Berger and Jean-Pierre Castaldi. French with English subtitles.

VHS: S19499. $59.95.

Marcel Carne, France, 1974, 102 mins.

Misty Wharf (Quai des Brumes)

A deserter, Jean Gabin, arrives at the port looking for a ship in which to escape from the police. He has committed a murder during a fit of temper, and while still searching for a likely ship he falls in love with Michele Morgan and her nostalgic beauty. French with English subtitles.

VHS: S21756. $39.95.

Marcel Carne, France, 1938, 90 mins.

RENE CLAIR

A Nous la Liberte

The inspiration for Chaplin's *Modern Times*, an imaginative social satire about a man who escapes from prison and builds a phonograph business with an assembly line every bit as repressive as the prison he escaped from. With elegantly futuristic sets, and a memorable score. French with English subtitles.

VHS: S19455. $29.98.

Rene Clair, France, 1931, 97 mins.

And Then There Were None

A tense adaptation of Agatha Christie's novel in which ten people are inexplicably invited to a remote island, where they are murdered, one by one. With Walter Huston, Barry Fitzgerald, Roland Young and Judith Anderson.

VHS: S07779. $19.95.

Rene Clair, USA, 1945, 98 mins.

Beauties of the Night (Les Belles de Nuit)

A wonderful romantic fantasy from Rene Clair in which a young music teacher escapes his drab life through a world of dreams. Romantic adventures await him every night with beautiful women. Though these dreams start off with enchantment, they end in disaster, forcing him to accept reality and his own true love. Gerard Philipe, Martine Carol, Gina Lollobrigida and Magali Vendeuil star. French with English subtitles.

VHS: S26157. $29.95.

Rene Clair, France, 1952, 89 mins.

Beauty and the Devil (La Beaute du Diable)

Gerard Philipe, Michel Simon and Simone Valere star in an elaborately costumed, romantic drama from Rene Clair. The result is a film which casts an otherworldly shadow on this tale of love and redemption. Mephisto tempts a young man to sell his soul in return for youth, riches and a young gypsy girl. French with English subtitles.

VHS: S26158. $29.95.

Rene Clair, France, 1950, 97 mins.

Crazy Ray

Clair's first feature film reveals the influences of surrealism in the fantastic story of an inventor who discovers a ray which can put people to sleep, and proceeds to put all of Paris under. Silent, English titles.

VHS: S00278. $29.95.

Rene Clair, France, 1922, 60 mins.

I Married a Witch

A Salem witch and her sorcerer father come back to haunt the descendant of the Puritan who had them burned. This is a delightful comedy by Thorne Smith (*Topper*) and shows Fredric March and Veronica Lake in top form. This pre-*Bewitched* farce also features Susan Hayward and Robert Benchley.

VHS: S02534. $19.98.

Rene Clair, USA, 1942, 82 mins.

The Italian Straw Hat

Pauline Kael called *The Italian Straw Hat* "one of the funniest films ever made and one of the most elegant as well." Based on an immensely popular farce by Eugene Labiche, the plot is a breezy tale about a bridegroom whose horse has a taste for ladies' hats. Rene Clair substituted sight gags for the clever word play, directed the action at a breakneck pace, and "screwball comedy" was born. This version is transferred from the restored negative, with a newly added musical score by Raymond Alessandrini. Starring Albert Prejean. Silent.

VHS: S16562. $39.95.

Rene Clair, France, 1927, 74 mins.

Le Million

A joy of a musical comedy about two penniless artists who win the lottery and become millionaires. But the lottery tickets are in a coat that is stolen, and then the fun begins. Refreshingly original in use of sound in which the music, dialogue and sound effects were recorded on a single track, and in its stylized action. Totally charming. French with English subtitles.

VHS: S19456. $29.98.

Rene Clair, France, 1931, 81 mins.

Le Voyage Imaginaire

This is one of the rarest Rene Clair films. It follows a group of people who experience a series of surrealistic adventures. Chaplin and Jackie Coogan save the adventurers in one episode. It's a valuable example of early silent French cinema.

VHS: S22882. $24.95.

Rene Clair, France, 1925, 62 mins.

Les Grandes Manoeuvres

Brigitte Bardot, Gerard Philipe and Michele Morgan are featured in this star-studded, ironic French comedy about the power of love over pride. Set in a pre-WWI garrison town, a handsome soldier (Philipe) wagers that he can seduce any woman he pleases before leaving for summer maneuvers. The first color feature from master director Rene Clair. Unrated. French with English subtitles.

VHS: S23745. $29.95.

Rene Clair, Italy/France, 1955, 106 mins.

Quatorze Juillet

A rarely seen classic. The simple story highlights the romantic adventures of a Parisian taxi driver and a young girl who sells flowers. After meeting on July 14th (Quatorze Juillet, Bastille Day), the two fall in and out of love as the boy gets involved with gangsters and the girl protects him from the law. Starring Anabella and George Rigaud. French with English subtitles.

VHS: S13669. $29.95.

Rene Clair, France, 1932, 85 mins.

Rene Clair

Regarded for decades as one of the most original of cinema stylists, Rene Clair started in the silent film era and established himself as a master of droll comedy. On this program Clair discusses his silent film career, his ideas about cinema, and his instinct to de-emphasize the spoken word in film. Contains excerpts from Clair's *Le Million* (1931) and *Les Grandes Manoeuvres* (1955). 1958, 28 mins.

VHS: S31579. $59.95.

Two Timid Souls (Les Deux Timides)

Fremissin (Pierre Batcheff), the shy and inexperienced lawyer, defends Garadoux (Jim Gerald), who is charged with spouse abuse. When Fremissin fails, Garadoux is sentenced to prison. Two years later, when the widowed Garadoux is released from prison, he seeks to marry the beautiful Cecile (Vera Flory), but she's in love with Fremissin. With Francoise Rosay and Maurice de Feraudy. Silent with French and German intertitles, music track.

VHS: S33052. $24.95.

Rene Clair, France, 1928, 62 mins.

Under the Roofs of Paris

Clair's poetic exploration of Parisian life evokes his characters' follies with shabby little garrets, cobblestoned streets, bistros, boudoirs and jails, all recreated within the studio. Also notable is Clair's adventuresome use of music. French with English subtitles.

VHS: S01398. $29.95.

Rene Clair, France, 1929, 95 mins.

HENRI-GEORGES CLOUZOT

Diabolique

The sadistic headmaster of a boys school is murdered by his tremulous wife and vengeful mistress in this classic French thriller. They dump the body, but suddenly the deceased appears in a recent school photograph. The suspense builds to an explosive climax. With Simone Signoret, Vera Clouzot, Paul Meurisse and Charles Vanel. Frenchwith English subtitles.

VHS: S00335. $29.95.
Laser: LD70749. $49.95.

Henri-Georges Clouzot, France, 1955, 116 mins.

Jenny Lamour

A fabulous thriller: Suzy Delair plays the music hall girl who believes that she has killed a mean old man. Her husband (Bernard Blier) wanted to kill him, but finds him already dead when he arrives. Each hides their experience from the other, and the husband becomes the suspect. Louis Jouvet is brilliant in his role as the world-weary, wise cop. Clouzot creates a brooding atmosphere and etches indelible psychological portraits of trapped, frail human beings. Original title: *Quai des Orfevres*. English dubbed.

VHS: S03748. $29.95.

Henri-Georges Clouzot, France, 1947, 105 mins.

Karajan: Early Images, Vol. 2 (1965-66)

An anthology of Herbert von Karajan's work with the Vienna Symphony Orchestra. The highlights are Karajan's rehearsal for Schumann's *Symphony No. 4*, and a performance of Mozart's *Concerto for Violin and Orchestra, No. 5*, with Yehudi Menuhin. The film is directed by the important French filmmaker Henri-Georges Clouzot (*The Wages of Fear*).

Laser: LD72002. $34.95.

Henri-Georges Clouzot, France, 89 mins.

Manon

From the novel by Abbe Prevost, this is a modern adaptation of the classic love between Manon Lescaut and the chevalier Des Grieux. The film was set by Clouzot during the German Occupation of France and in the months surrounding D-Day, with Des Grieux a dealer in the Parisian black market and Manon dying in the Palestinian desert. French with English subtitles.

VHS: S03359. $29.95.

Henri-Georges Clouzot, France, 1948, 90 mins.

The Raven (Le Corbeau)

An ingenious, suspenseful thriller, made in wartime occupied France and based on a true story. A small French town is torn asunder by poison pen letters which breed tensions and suicides. The suspects are a doctor, a crippled girl and a sick woman. Ultimately, it is discovered that the criminal is a revered old man. With brilliant performances from Ginette Leclerc and Pierre Fresnay. As the old man says in the film, "You think that goodness is light and darkness is evil. But where is the darkness? Where the light?" French with English subtitles.

VHS: S16563. $59.95.

Henri-Georges Clouzot, France, 1943, 92 mins.

The Wages of Fear

An exercise in terror and suspense, this uncut version stars Yves Montand and Charles Vanel as uncertain comrades—trapped in a South American village—who identify because they are both French and both penniless. Desperate for a job, they agree to drive two trucks filled with nitroglycerine 300 miles over treacherous roads. Basil Wright called this film "the greatest suspense thriller of all time; it is the suspense not of mystery but of Damocles' sword." French with English subtitles.

VHS: S16210. $29.95.
Laser: LD70766. $59.95.

Henri-Georges Clouzot, France, 1953, 148 mins.

JEAN-PIERRE MELVILLE

Bob le Flambeur

An amazing film noir thriller and a film which anticipates the French New Wave with its gritty locations, free-wheeling camera, jump cuts and a musical jazz score. Roger Duchesne plays petty hood and small-time gambler Bob who, newly released from prison, immediately plots to rob the casino at Deauville. Shot between dusk and dawn in Pigalle, this is the quintessential "city at night" film with Bob the kind of a gangster who still has a moral code. Great cinematography by Henri Decae. French with English subtitles.

VHS: S20741. $59.95.

Jean-Pierre Melville, France, 1955, 97 mins.

Le Doulos

A complicated thriller of double and triple crosses, beautiful women and a dark vision of a world in a masterful film noir. Set in the Paris underworld, at the center of which is Jean-Paul Belmondo, a professional informer who maintains his relationship with a police inspector and a burglar just out of jail and afraid he can't hack the criminal life anymore. Famous for its 9½ minute single take—brilliant camerawork from Nicolas Hayer—and terrific performances. With Serge Reggiani, Jean Desailly and Michel Piccoli. French with English subtitles.

VHS: S09905. $59.95.

Jean-Pierre Melville, France, 1962, 108 mins.

Le Samourai

Melville's classic film noir masterpiece stars Alain Delon as a cool and mysterious contract killer who lives by a personal code of *bushido*, moving in and out of shadows in the Parisian rain wearing a trenchcoat and a fedora hiding his eyes. A mythical revenge story with Cathy Rosier as a jazz piano player who witnesses one of his hits but doesn't tell the police. With Nathalie Delon. "The closest thing to a perfect movie that I have ever seen" (John Woo). Letterboxed.

VHS: S32197. $89.95.

Jean-Pierre Melville, France, 1967, 95 mins.

Le Silence de la Mer

An old man and his beautiful niece are forced to endure the presence of a Nazi officer during the German occupation of their small French village. Vowing never to speak to the invader, the couple listen in silence as the officer pours out his ideas and feelings about music, war and his love of France. Just as the officer overcomes their enmity and at the same time discovers the realities of Nazism in France, he is ordered to the eastern front. French with English subtitles.

VHS: S30612. $29.95.

Jean-Pierre Melville, France, 1947, 86 mins.

Leon Morin, Priest

Jean-Pierre Melville's 1961 French/Italian co-production is set in Nazi-occupied France, and details the fascinating and complex relationship formed between a passionate, anticlerical communist Barny (Emmanuelle Riva) and a disarming, young priest (Jean-Paul Belmondo). Photographed by the great Henri Decae. "An intellectual romance, sharp and witty…with vivid wartime backgrounds" (Leslie Halliwell). French with English subtitles.

VHS: S16985. $59.95.

Jean-Pierre Melville, France/Italy, 1961, 118 mins.

Les Enfants Terribles

A lyrical treatment of Jean Cocteau's perverse tribute to rebellious adolescence. Made in 1949, even today it is one of the most electrifying confrontations of normality by abnormality in the cinema. Paul (Edouard Dermithe) and Elisabeth (Nicole Stephane) are born into such extreme wealth that they are immune to the confines and limits of the real world. Their innocence leads them to self-destruction and to crime. Jean Cocteau's claustrophobic drama is brought to the screen by the great Jean-Pierre Melville in this perverse story of love, death and incest. French with English subtitles.

VHS: S01663. $29.95.

Jean-Pierre Melville, France, 1949, 105 mins.

Les Enfants Terribles and Les Parents Terribles

Family affairs abound in this double feature written by Jean Cocteau. *Les Parents Terribles* is the gut-wrenching story of incestuous, emotional rivalries that destroy an already neurotic family. *Les Enfants Terribles* is Cocteau's screen version of his celebrated play about a teenage brother and sister who share an unhealthy obsession with each other. French with English subtitles.

Laser: LD75963. $59.99.

Jean-Pierre Melville/Jean Cocteau, France, 1948/1949, 198 mins.

JEAN VIGO

A Propos de Nice

One of the great works of the cinema, Jean Vigo's "lyrical, violent, and subversive social polemic is full of black humor and biting sarcasm…a short film, but a great one: An example of true cinema, but also an attack on a particular kind of world" (Sadoul). A document with a point of view on the city of Nice, contrasting the hotels with poverty, a film of great contrasts.

VHS: S04841. $24.95.

Jean Vigo, France, 1928, 20 mins.

L'Atalante

The high water mark of French poetic realism, set on a barge plying the Seine. A young barge captain and his bride live on a barge with the eccentric Pere Jules (Michel Simon). With Boris Kauffman's cinematography, which evokes Paris and the Seine with the luminosity of Atget or Cartier-Bresson, and everyday life full of magical moments like Pere Jules' "museum" of exotic marvels and the husband's underwater vision of his lost bride. "May be the greatest film ever made" (Georgia Brown, *The Village Voice*). Initially cut by seven minutes, this version is the fully restored, 89-minute cut. With Dita Parlo, Jean Daste and Michel Simon. French with English subtitles.

VHS: S17696. $59.95.

Jean Vigo, France, 1934, 89 mins.

Zero for Conduct

Based on Vigo's personal childhood experiences, a poetic yet revolutionary portrait of a revolt at a boarding school. Vigo creates a claustrophobic world in which the petty tyrannies of the school regime stand in sharp relief to the tender delirium of the children. Filled with deep psychological insights, this cinematic landmark was banned in France until 1946 on the grounds that it maliciously attacked the French educational system. Music by Maurice Jaubert, photography by Boris Kaufman. With Jean Daste and Louis Lefebvre. French with English subtitles.

VHS: S01500. $29.95.

Jean Vigo, France, 1933, 44 mins.

JEAN RENOIR

Boudu Saved from Drowning

A light comedy as well as a satire on bourgeois lifestyle in France. Michel Simon is Boudu, a scruffy tramp who is saved from his suicide attempt by a bookseller. Boudu insists his rescuer is now responsible for him, and creates chaos in his new home. French with English subtitles.

VHS: S17512. $59.95.
Laser: LD75419. $39.99.

Jean Renoir, France, 1932, 87 mins.

Crime of Monsieur Lange

Based on a scenario of Jacques Prevert, and one of the great films of Jean Renoir, the film sprang from Renoir's belief that the common man, by united action, could overcome tyranny. The head of a small printing press disappears with all the firm's capital. The employees band together, collect some money, and go into business as publishers of the popular novelettes of their neighbor, Monsieur Lange. "The world's greatest…director is Jean Renoir…life is always spilling over a Renoir frame as if the screen were not big enough to encompass all the humanity" (Andrew Sarris, *The Village Voice*). French with English subtitles.

VHS: S05324. $59.95.

Jean Renoir, France, 1936, 90 mins.

Day in the Country

Based on a story by Guy de Maupassant: "An innocent girl comes of age in Jean Renoir's short film. This lyrical tragedy rates with Renoir's greatest… Visually it recaptures the impressionist period" (Pauline Kael). French with English subtitles.

VHS: S19931. $39.95.

Jean Renoir, France, 1935, 40 mins.

Diary of a Chambermaid

Jean Renoir dreamed for ten years about making a film based on the novel by Octave Mirbeau, set in the decadent French upper classes. Paulette Goddard plays the outspoken maid who arouses the enmities of the household. In English.

VHS: S07298. $19.98.

Jean Renoir, USA, 1946, 86 mins.

Elena and Her Men

One of the most important Jean Renoir films, considered by Renoir "une fantasie musicale," the film stars Ingrid Bergman and is a film about the power of love, the power of women, the folly of progress, the beauty of laziness, and the evil of dictators. With Jean Marais, Mel Ferrer, Juliette Greco. French with English subtitles.

VHS: S05992. $59.95.

Jean Renoir, France, 1956, 98 mins.

Elusive Corporal

A story of man's triumph over adversity, set in a P.O.W. camp on the day of the French surrender to Germany in World War II. In many ways an updating of Renoir's 1937 masterpiece *Grand Illusion*. French with English subtitles.

VHS: S17514. $59.95.

Jean Renoir, France, 1962, 109 mins.

French Can Can

"One of the screen's most extraordinarily beautiful displays of late cinematic maturity," said Andrew Sarris about Renoir's film, which stars Jean Gabin as the night club owner who re-discovers the can-can. "Renoir hurls his cancan artists at the viewer, tempting us with the consuming spectacle, which is…inherently kinetic and ineffably voluptuous." French with English subtitles.

VHS: S01662. $59.95.

Jean Renoir, France, 1955, 93 mins.

The Golden Coach

One of the great works of postwar French cinema, Jean Renoir's sublime masterpiece—photographed by his brother Claude—charts the affairs of an 18th-century actress (Anna Magnani) as she travels through colonial Peru with a commedia dell'arte troupe. She is simultaneously pursued by a bullfighter (Ricardo Rioli), a soldier (Paul Campbell) and the Viceroy (Duncan Lamont). With Odoardo Spadaro, Nada Fiorelli and Ralph Truman.

VHS: S19899. $59.95.

Jean Renoir, France/Italy, 1952, 103 mins.

Grand Illusion

A beautifully mastered version of Jean Renoir's great masterpiece, a classic comment on war's fading glory. Set in WW I, the film tells of two French officers captured by German forces. Interred in a prison camp, the two officers encounter Von Rauffenstein, an aristocratic career officer played by von Stroheim. With Jean Gabin, Pierre Fresnay and von Stroheim. French with English subtitles.

VHS: S12469. $29.95.
Laser: LD70373. $89.95.
DVD: DV60170. $39.95.

Jean Renoir, France, 1937, 111 mins.

La Bete Humaine

A psychological drama of murder, revenge, conscience and the eternal triangle, based on a story by Emile Zola. Renoir fills the film with hauntingly beautiful symbolism. French with English subtitles.

VHS: S00700. $24.95.

Jean Renoir, France, 1938, 101 mins.

La Chienne

Jean Renoir's first great sound classic. The scenario is based on a novel by La Foucardiere. It is the story of a cashier who works in a hosiery business and whose sole passion is the painting he does in his spare time. Unhappily married to the widow of a noncommissioned officer who disappeared during the war, he meets a prostitute and becomes tragically involved with her. *La Chienne* combines the best of Renoir's work: the magnificent direction of actors, a subtle and very nuanced portrayal of a rather dubious aspect of French society. French with English subtitles.

VHS: S09570. $59.95.

Jean Renoir, France, 1931, 100 mins.

La Marseillaise

Renoir's remarkable ability to recreate the mood of the past was never more evident than in *La Marseillaise*. A classic tribute to the glory of the French Revolution, the film captures the human values of the struggle as well as the historical perspective. French with English subtitles.

VHS: S17513. $39.95.

Jean Renoir, France, 1938, 131 mins.

La Petite Marchande d'Allumettes (The Little Matchgirl)/La Jetee

Originally this adaptation of a Hans Christian Andersen story was silent and much longer. Now the later sound version is available. A poor young matchgirl falls asleep in the snow. Her dream transforms the people of her everyday life into toys. Though the nature of this dream is enchanting, the overall story has a bitter end. French with English subtitles. Jean Renoir, France, 1928, 29 mins. Also includes *La Jetee*, a challenging science fiction film set in a ruined France after World War III, in which a man's vivid childhood experience allows him to travel forward and backward in time. As a grown man, he meets the girl he had glimpsed as a child at the airport, falls in love with her, chooses to remain in the past, but is executed by those who hold power in the future. Jean Renoir, France, 1962, 29 mins.

VHS: S05521. $29.95.

Le Petit Theatre de Jean Renoir

Jean Renoir's last film is a return, in some ways, to the humanistic themes of his life, in this theatrical wedding of four separate stories. *Le Dernier Reveillon (The Last Christmas Dinner)*, is a highly stylized and expanded version of *The Little Matchgirl; Le Cireuse Electrique (The Electric Floor Waxer)* is a funny comedy sung to music by Joseph Kosma, in which a wife neglects her husband for her vacuum cleaner; *Entr'acte* stars Jeanne Moreau as a turn-of-the century singer; *Le Roi d'Yvetot* is a story of manners and morals in which a middle-aged man with a seductive young wife is teased by the townspeople who suspect that a man of his age with a young wife must be cuckolded. French with English subtitles.

VHS: S07505. $59.95.

Jean Renoir, France, 1969, 100 mins.

Lower Depths

Another classic statement by Renoir about social and economic classes, this time using a story about an impoverished thief (Jean Gabin) who meets and lives with a Baron (Louis Jouvet). Along the way the Baron discovers the joys of living without material wealth. A feast for the eyes and intellect. French with English subtitles.

VHS: S05857. $29.95.

Jean Renoir, France, 1936, 92 mins.

Madame Bovary

Jean Renoir's French version of Flaubert's great novel stars Valentine Tessier "as an anomalous creature, half swan, half goose. This large woman is not at all what one expects, yet she's surprisingly effective. The sunlight and the spaciousness emphasize Emma's loneliness; she's a middle-class woman with an ample figure, drifting along on romantic daydreams" (Pauline Kael). With Pierre Renoir, Jean's brother, as Charles Bovary, Max Dearly as M. Homais. French with English subtitles.

VHS: S01536. $79.95.

Jean Renoir, France, 1934

Picnic on the Grass

One of the wonders of cinema, Jean Renoir's tribute to French Impressionism and a work of almost overpowering lyricism—as a scientific outing turns into a Bacchanal. Shot at Les Collettes, the Renoir family home near Cannes. French with English subtitles.

VHS: S17515. $59.95.

Jean Renoir, France, 1959, 92 mins.

Renoir Silent Shorts

Includes *Little Match Girl* and *Charleston*, a humorous erotic dance fantasy that scandalized viewers of the time with its provocative sexuality, starring Catherine Hessling. With a jazz score and historical introduction. Silent.

VHS: S03703. $49.95.

Jean Renoir, France, 1926, 30 mins.

The River

Renoir's film about India, a film about British colonialism, a film which Jacques Rivette calls "the only example of a film vigorously reflecting itself (turned upon itself), and in which the narrative structure, the metaphysical themes and the sociological descriptions not only answer one another but are in every way interchangeable." In English.

VHS: S01661. $29.95.
Laser: LD71305. $44.95.

Jean Renoir, India, 1950, 99 mins.

Rules of the Game

One of the great films of all time, a satirical anatomy of polite society, with a mixture of farce and bitterness. Set at a weekend party at the chateau of the rich Marquis de la Chayniest, the story concerns complicated love intrigues. French with English subtitles.

VHS: S04456. $29.95.
Laser: LD70446. $89.95.

Jean Renoir, France, 1939, 90 mins.

The Southerner

One of Renoir's American films, the story of a migrant worker (Zachary Scott) who tries to make a go of it on a farm of his own. English dialog.

VHS: S01236. $19.95.

Jean Renoir, USA, 1945, 91 mins.

Testament of Dr. Cordelier

"A fascinating experiment adapting TV techniques—direct recording, multiple cameras, long takes, thorough pre-rehearsal—to the cinema. The Jekyll and Hyde story transposed to a modern setting affords an excuse for an homage to Renoir's beloved actors, and Jean-Louis Barrault is extraordinary as the evil genius, prancing and twitching like some nightmarish faun on an orgy of destruction. Most of the exteriors were shot on location in the streets of Paris, and the intrusion of this creature lends them a bizarre air of menace" (Tom Milne). French with English subtitles.

VHS: S05328. $29.95.

Jean Renoir, France, 1959, 95 mins.

Toni

The story of Italian immigrants working in a quarry, of love, murder and betrayal, Renoir's great film is based on an actual incident and shot on location. The film anticipated the Italian neo-realist movement in its near-documentary approach, its use of non-actors in principal roles, in its deep commitment to common people, their lives and struggles. French with English subtitles.

VHS: S01358. $29.95.

Jean Renoir, France, 1934, 83 mins.

Tournament

Silent period spectacle from Renoir, story is set in 1565 when Catherine de Medici attempted to maintain power while balancing between Catholics and Protestants. Silent.

VHS: S03704. $49.95.

Jean Renoir, France, 1929, 90 mins.

MARCEL PAGNOL

Angele

Considered by many to be the finest work of Marcel Pagnol, the film's innovative use of location shooting is an important precursor to neo-realism. *Angele* combines a melodramatic story of a young girl's seduction, betrayal and redemption by true love with the naturalist settings of Provence. Based on Jean Giono's novel, *Un de Baumugnes*. With Fernandel, Orane Demazis. French with English subtitles.

VHS: S08258. $59.95.

Marcel Pagnol, France, 1934, 150 mins.

Baker's Wife

The earthy comedy to end all earthy comedies; a young wife leaves her husband for a handsome young shepherd—but tragedy of all French tragedies—she happens to be the baker's wife. The baker, too heartsick to bake, throws the town into panic. And the townspeople organize to cajole, lure, or force the young lady in question away from her lover and back to her husband-so they can get back to their bread. French with English subtitles.

VHS: S00088. $59.95.

Marcel Pagnol, France, 1933, 101 mins.

Cesar

The final film of the trilogy begins twenty years after the first, *Marius*. Fanny's husband has died and her son is at last told of his true father. Marius and Fanny are reunited at last. French with English subtitles.

VHS: S00223. $39.95.

Marcel Pagnol, France, 1936, 121 mins.

Fanny

The second in the Marcel Pagnol trilogy begun with *Marius*, in which Marius goes to sea leaving Fanny, his fiancee, pregnant. She in turn marries a sailmaker and rebukes Marius upon his return. Warm comic invention. French with English subtitles.

VHS: S19900. $39.95.

Marc Allegret, France, 1931, 120 mins.

Harvest

A film of utter serenity and great goodness, the story of a scissors grinder and a woman who pass by a deserted town, inhabited by only one man. The woman stays with the man and together they bring new life to the land. Based upon the novel by Jean Giono, featuring Fernandel, Orane Demazis. French with English subtitles.

VHS: S01967. $59.95.

Marcel Pagnol, France, 1937, 128 mins.

Le Schpountz

Fernandel, Charpin and Orane Demazis star in this hilarious comedy about a country bumpkin convinced he is the next great leading man of French film. Once he arrives in Paris, this outsider storms the industry, giving Marcel Pagnol the opportunity to satirize the movie-making industry. French with English subtitles.

VHS: S25107. $59.95.

Marcel Pagnol, France, 1938, 135 mins.

Letters from My Windmill
Three tales from the director of *Baker's Wife* and *Topaze*. In the first the devil takes over the body of a dunce and torments a priest at Christmas eve mass. The second documents the troubles that arise when a community of priests make and sell their own wine. And the last is a story of a miller who pretends to compete with a new steam-driven mill. French with English subtitles.
VHS: S01566. $59.95.
Marcel Pagnol, France, 1954, 134 mins.

Marius
The first film of the celebrated Marcel Pagnol trilogy, famous for its dialog and rich humanity. The story introduces Marius who longs to go to sea in spite of his love for Fanny. Frenchwith English subtitles.
VHS: S00826. $39.95.
Alexander Korda, France, 1931, 120 mins.

Nais
The horse-faced Fernandel stars in this Marcel Pagnol production, a heartrending love story which crosses the class structures in rural Provence; Nais, a beautiful country girl, is in love with the son of a wealthy family. Fernandel is the hunchback who sacrifices his own love for her in order to give Nais her happiness. French with English subtitles. (For several minutes in this film, subtitles are inadequate.) Very rare film.
VHS: S06480. $34.95.
Fernand Lauterier, France, 1945, 95 mins.

Topaze (1933)
Based on Pagnol's play, this early film chronicles the metamorphosis of a timid and persecuted school teacher. The teacher is fired and finds a new job, where he blindly enters into a business scam. Fernandel, Jacqueline Pagnol and Pierre Larquey star in Pagnol's response to an earlier, less faithful, Hollywood adaptation of his play. French with English subtitles.
VHS: S25104. $59.95.
Louis Gasnier, France, 1933, 92 mins.

Topaze (1951)
The third French version of Pagnol's popular comic play, this time starring Fernandel as a naive schoolteacher who is thrust into the world of wealth, sex and crooked business when he unwittingly becomes a pawn in a wealthy baron's game. French with English subtitles.
VHS: S01660. $59.95.
Marcel Pagnol, France, 1951, 92 mins.

The Well-Digger's Daughter
Touching and hilarious story about a young woman who is seduced and then abandoned, and the unpleasant effect this has on her peasant father. With Raimu, Fernandel and Josette Day. French with English subtitles.
VHS: S01565. $29.95.
Marcel Pagnol, France, 1941, 142 mins.

MAX OPHULS

The Bartered Bride and The Last Waltz
The Bartered Bride features Jarmila Novotna and Willi Domgraf-Fassbaender. This 1932 production was directed by Max Ophuls with music by Smetana. "Fans of Novotna will certainly want to watch these over and over again while fans of the filmmaker's art will probably derive even more pleasure than will purely opera connoisseurs" (*H & B Directory*). Sung in German with German dialog (no subtitles). 76 mins. Novotna also stars in *The Last Waltz* (1935), featuring Harry Welchman, with music by Oscar Straus. English. 73 mins.
VHS: S28429. $34.95.

Caught
A dark and compelling story of a girl married to the wrong man who runs away and falls in love with a struggling young ghetto doctor. Chased down by the husband, she is forced to choose between money and love. Robert Ryan gives a strong performance as the vicious, mentally unstable millionaire husband (based on Howard Hughes). With Barbara Bel Geddes and James Mason as the lovers. Intelligently handled by director Ophuls in his most successful American film.
VHS: S00222. $19.95.
Max Ophuls, USA, 1949, 90 mins.

De Mayerling a Sarajevo
The assassination in Sarajevo of the Archduke Franz-Ferdinand and his wife, the Countess Sophie, is the spark that starts World War I. This historical event energizes Max Ophuls' classic tale of romance, power and greed. Casting an ironic eye on the extravagance and absurdity of the ruling class and portraying a bittersweet romance against the background of operas, balls and rides through the woods, Ophuls is at his masterful best. French with English subtitles.
VHS: S30613. $29.95.
Max Ophuls, France, 1940, 89 mins.

Earrings of Madame De...
Max Ophuls' powerful romantic tragedy, starring Charles Boyer, Vittorio de Sica, Danielle Darrieux. A spoiled socialite, married to a general, flirts with an amorous diplomat. As the affair escalates, her passion rips through the glittering facade of their privileged existence, plunging them into disaster as they risk everything for love and honor. Newly mastered. Frenchwith English subtitles.
VHS: S08999. $29.95.
Laser: LD75543. $49.98.
Max Ophuls, France, 1953, 105 mins.

La Ronde
Love as a bitterly comic merry-go-round. Simone Signoret plays a young whore involved with a young soldier who leaves her, setting off a chain of affairs and partners that ends with Signoret again. Based on the play *Reigen* by Arthur Schnitzler. French with English subtitles.
VHS: S00711. $29.95.
Laser: LD75027. $49.95.
Max Ophuls, France, 1950, 97 mins.

La Signora di Tutti
The only film that Ophuls made in Italy, *La Signora di Tutti* features Isa Miranda as Gaby Doriot, a film star at the peak of her popularity with the public and in the depths of despair in her private life. As the film opens, she has attempted suicide. Under ether on the operating table, her life unfolds for her (us) in a series of fragmented flashbacks. A powerful melodrama transcended by sheer stylistic splendor; the visual lyricism of Ophuls' camera movements is at times breathtaking. Italian with English subtitles.
VHS: S01966. $59.95.
Max Ophuls, Italy, 1934, 92 mins.

Le Plaisir
Max Ophuls' ironic, humorous trilogy of De Maupassant short stories stars some of France's greatest stars (Simone Simon, Danielle Darrieux, Jean Gabin, Jean Servais, Madeleine Renaud, Ginette Leclerc, Pierre Brasseur). The three tales are*Le Masque*, in which an old man rediscovers his youth by wearing a mask; *La Maison Tellier*, in which a group of prostitutes go on an annual holiday trip to the country; and *La Modele*, in which an artist who makes mistresses out of his models marries one when she cripples herself while trying to commit suicide. French with English subtitles.
VHS: S00741. $29.95.
Max Ophuls, France, 1952, 94 mins.

Letter from an Unknown Woman
Louis Jourdan is a famed concert pianist who is unaware he has been adored for years by the very shy Joan Fontaine until one very special night of passion that produces a child. Told in a series of flashbacks, Jourdan learns he is a father much too late to do the right thing.
VHS: S07435. $19.95.
Laser: CLV, 1 disc, Criterion. **LD71450. $49.95.**
Max Ophuls, USA, 1948, 87 mins.

Liebelei
The film which established the reputation for Max Ophuls, based on a play by Arthur Schnitzler; the story of a young lieutenant who is in love with a Viennese girl, and is called to account by a baron who believes him to be the lover of the baroness. The military code requires a duel, the lieutenant is killed, and the girl throws herself out the window in despair. "Ophuls' magical adaptation of Schnitzler's mordant love play is a lament to lost innocence, transported by Ophuls' moving camera into the mystical regions of remembrance" (NY Film Festival). German with English subtitles.
VHS: S07820. $39.95.
Max Ophuls, Germany, 1932, 88 mins.

Lola Montes
Ophuls' opulent biography of the famous 19th-century courtesan whose adventures and love affairs with King Ludwig I, Liszt and a student are told in flashback from a circus ring by the ring master, Peter Ustinov. Brilliant use of color and Cinemascope, breathtaking shots and camera movements; Ophuls conjures up a sublime work that is pure cinema. With Martine Carol, Anton Walbrook, Ivan Desny and Oskar Werner. French with English subtitles.
VHS: S02771. $19.98.
Max Ophuls, France, 1955, 110 mins.

Novotna in The Bartered Bride and The Last Waltz
Novotna, the acclaimed singer from 1930's Europe, stars in both these operas. Smetana's music is beautifully realized in German. Then Oscar Straus' work is presented in English. 76 minutes.
VHS: S25534. $39.95.
Max Ophuls/Leo Mittler, Germany/Czechoslovakia, 1932
Gerald Barry, Great Britain/France

JEAN COCTEAU

Beauty and the Beast
Jean Cocteau's superb adaptation of Marie Leprince de Beaumont's dark fairy tale is a ferociously inventive and stylized depiction of erotic obsession, about a young woman's discovery of a ravaged soul beneath a monstrous beast. With Jean Marais, Josette Day and Marcel Andre. Cinematography by Henri Alekan. "A sensuously fascinating film, the visual progression of the fable into a dream-world casts its unpredictable spell" (Bosley Crowther).
VHS: S00110. $24.95.
Laser: CAV. **LD70865. $89.95.**
DVD: DV60175. $39.95.
Jean Cocteau, France, 1946, 93 mins.

Blood of a Poet
The first work of the significant poet, playwright and surrealist Jean Cocteau is one of the most important contributions to early avant-garde cinema—a stunning, primal and powerful work that uses jagged, poetic, harsh and highly personal images, dreams and symbols to reflect an artist's inner life. The work is composed in four illogical, timeless sequences. French with English subtitles.
VHS: S17880. $29.95.
Laser: LD75381. $49.98.
Jean Cocteau, France, 1930, 54 mins.

The Eagle Has Two Heads (L'Aigle A Deux Tetes)
A rarely seen film by Jean Cocteau (*Orpheus, Beauty and the Beast*) based on his own play. Jean Marais plays the poet/anarchist who falls in love with the queen (Edwige Feuillere) he initially sets out to assassinate in Cocteau's high romantic melodrama. With music by the great Georges Auric. French with English subtitles.
VHS: S23863. $29.95.
Jean Cocteau, France, 1948, 93 mins.

Jean Cocteau: Autobiography of an Unknown
Jean Cocteau, one of the 20th century's greatest eclectic artists, in a definitive portrait completed from archival film. Cocteau relates his experiences from earliest childhood through his life as one of the creative circle in Paris at the turn of the century. In an intense personal narration, he describes his family and the inspiration he drew from his circle of friends including Nijinsky, Diaghilev, Renoir, Picasso, Satie, Chaplin and others. A marvelous portrait of a great artist.
VHS: S07597. $19.95.
Edgardo Cozarinsky, France, 1985, 60 mins.

Les Enfants Terribles and Les Parents Terribles
Family affairs abound in this double feature written by Jean Cocteau. *Les Parents Terribles* is the gut-wrenching story of incestuous, emotional rivalries that destroy an already neurotic family. *Les Enfants Terribles* is Cocteau's screen version of his celebrated play about a teenage brother and sister who share an unhealthy obsession with each other. French with English subtitles.
Laser: LD75963. $59.99.
Jean-Pierre Melville/Jean Cocteau, France, 1948/1949, 198 mins.

Les Parents Terribles
This steamy adaptation of Cocteau's own play features Jean Marais as the doting son of a middle-class Parisian family, who falls in love with a young woman (Josette Day), unaware that she is his father's mistress. The riveting psychological drama about the complicated tangle of sexuality, parental rivalry, jealousy and Freudian obsession features a great performance from Marais as a mama's boy in love. French with English subtitles.
VHS: S23864. $29.95.
Jean Cocteau, France, 1948, 98 mins.

Orpheus
Cocteau's famous retelling of the Greek myth, with Jean Marais as Orphee, the successful poet envied and despised, who pushes himself beyond mortality, and Maria Casares as the dark, troubled, passionate Death. A great film. French with English subtitles.
VHS: S00977. $29.95.
Jean Cocteau, France, 1949, 95 mins.

Testament of Orpheus
After 70 years of life and 29 years of filmmaking, Jean Cocteau waves goodbye to films, and this, his last work, is a compendium of his filmic style. We meet Cocteau wandering in the 18th century only to be brought into the 20th where he encounters gypsies, evil omens and the dead poet of *Orpbee*. A great many trick effects and many of Cocteau's collaborators appear in the film: Marais, Leaud, Yul Brynner, Casares. French with English subtitles.
VHS: S01313. $29.95.
Jean Cocteau, France, 1959, 80 mins.

ALBERTO CAVALCANTI

The Life and Adventures of Nicholas Nickleby

Cedric Hardwicke in the Dickens tale of a young boy who tries to save himself and his family from a miserly uncle. Director Cavalcanti was active in the film avant-garde of the 1920's, and gives this film style by paying attention to visual design and lighting.

VHS: S00929. $19.95.

Alberto Cavalcanti, Great Britain, 1947, 105 mins.

Rien Que les Heures

This bold documentary remains a landmark in the tradition of documentary film. The life of Paris is shown over one 24-hour period, including images of the city at work and play. Cinematic effects paint a moody picture resulting in a surrealistic view of this great city. Silent with English intertitles.

VHS: S21080. $19.95.

Alberto Cavalcanti, France, 1926, 45 mins.

Went the Day Well?

Leslie Banks and Elizabeth Allan star in this World War II drama based on a story by Graham Greene. An advance body of German troops secretly occupies a village by posing as Royal Engineers. Eventually they are discovered and a bloody battle follows.

VHS: S23816. $24.95.

Alberto Cavalcanti, Great Britain, 1942, 92 mins.

JACQUES TATI

Gai Dimanche/Swing to the Left

Two rare early short films by Jacques Tati. In *Gai Dimanche* (French with *no* subtitles), Tati and the clown Rhum buy a used bus, pick up sight-seers and tour the countryside. In *Swing to the Left*, Tati plays a farm hand who goes rounds with a professional boxer.

VHS: S04362. $49.95.

Jacques Tati, France, 1931-36

Jour de Fete

The first feature by Jacques Tati. This perceptive and witty village comedy set in Saint-Severe casts Tati as a simple, determined postman trying desperately to modernize his operations, with frightening repercussions. Shot in a splash color format, the film was released in black and white with some hand-tinted color sequences. "Tati was a method, a way of looking at the world to discover comic rhythms never seen before or since in movies" (Vincent Canby). French with English subtitles.

Laser: LD70386. $49.95.

Jacques Tati, France, 1949, 76 mins.

Mon Oncle

A masterpiece by the great French comic Jacques Tati which concentrates on young Gerard Arpel and his Uncle Hulot (Jacques Tati) in a house where gadgets overpower everything. Sound effects, minimal dialog contribute to Tati's wry humor. French with English subtitles.

VHS: S00870. $29.95.

Laser: LD71234. $49.95.

Jacques Tati, France, 1958, 114 mins.

Mr. Hulot's Holiday

Jacques Tati's second film introduces M. Hulot (Tati), a genial, eccentric, middle-class French everyman whose vacation at a seaside French resort in Brittany produces one minor catastrophe after another. Tati's intricate juxtaposing of mime and slapstick is so refined, pure and expressive, there's an extraordinary pain, passion and tenderness that produces laughter and heartbreak. With Nathalie Pascaud, Michele Rolla and Louis Perrault. French with English subtitles.

VHS: S00891. $24.95.

Laser: LD71241. $59.95.

Jacques Tati, France, 1952, 91 mins.

Parade

Parade centers around the lives of two small children gradually brought closer together as they wend their way through the activities of a circus. Director Tati appears in the film as Monsieur Loyal, a circus performer, and presents some of his most unique and best known pieces of mime. Loyal is able to transform the mood of the circus into one of celebration and joy through the various music hall numbers weaved throughout the film.

VHS: S13735. $29.95.

Laser: CLV, 1 disc, Criterion. **LD70431. $49.95.**

Jacques Tati, France, 1974, 85 mins.

Playtime

Called one of the funniest men in the world by the *New York Times*, Jacques Tati's Playtime is an hilarious comedy and satire on coping with the modern world. For Tati's now-legendary character, M. Hulot, everything seems to be against him—a glass-fronted airport, a new restaurant, even a supermarket. Full of visual gags and inventive use of sound, *Playtime* is one of the most imaginative and funniest films ever. Digitally remastered and letterboxed. English dialog.

VHS: S01038. $39.95.

Jacques Tati, France, 1967, 108 mins.

Traffic

Jacques Tati's fifth and final feature, a laugh-filled look at modern society and the automobile, captures the absurdities of human behavior on the street and behind the wheel. Tati's Mr. Hulot is back as an absent-minded inventor trying to transport his ultramodern camper to Amsterdam for an auto show. "Splendidly funny...exuberantly entertaining...*Traffic* is a hilarious highway odyssey, a panorama that unfolds around Mr. Hulot" (Vincent Canby). English language version. Letterboxed.

VHS: S21383. $29.95.

Jacques Tati, France, 1971, 89 mins.

THE FRENCH LANDSCAPE

Bonjour de Paris

Paris, "La Ville Lumiere"—discover Paris with Marina, a teenager, and her uncle Paul, a true Parisian, as he explains the culture and history of the city by visiting the medieval Notre Dame and Conciergerie, Montparnasse, the contemporary Beaubourg and Defense, as well as other sites. 45 mins.

English Narration.

VHS: S06883. $49.95.

French Narration.

VHS: S06882. $49.95.

Chanel, Chanel

The world of fashion has produced no more charismatic figure than Coco Chanel. Her style was stamped on over half a century of fashion—her life spelling out a new blueprint for simplicity and ease. Top designer Karl Lagerfeld, who became head of the house of Chanel in 1983, has brought back the excitement of fashion that Chanel generated during her prime. Rare archive footage tells the fascinating story of her life. 60 minutes.

VHS: S07624. $29.95.

Edith Piaf: I Regret Nothing

A BBC-produced musical biography of Edith Piaf, the most popular French singer of the 20th century. Extensive footage from Piaf's concerts is included, as well as interviews with those who knew her, such as Charles Aznavour.

VHS: S00936. $29.95.

Michael Houldey, Great Britain, 110 mins.

Edith Piaf: La Vie en Rose

Piaf's life story, told through archival footage and the recollections of her friends, from her beginnings as a street singer to stardom in the *boites* of Paris—a warmly nostalgic video that includes Piaf's singing "La Vie en Rose," "Non, je ne regrette rien," and other favorites.

VHS: S05549. $29.95.

The Eiffel Tower

This fascinating story of this engineering marvel and the genius who designed it describes the technological challenges entailed and the outrage the Eiffel Tower faced upon its completion. 50 mins.

VHS: S31240. $29.95.

Eternal France

Visit the Normandy Coast and glide along the canals of Alsace to Strasbourg. Wander inside the majestic cathedrals of Reims and Chartres and watch the artistry of glass-makers in Baccarat, the lace-makers in the Auvergne region and the silk painters in Lyon. 50 mins.

VHS: S12273. $24.95.

France Nobody Knows

Explore the lesser-known regions of France on this unique tour of the French countryside. Visit Alsace, Savoie, Auvergne, Provence, and the island of Corsica. You'll ride through the Alps, visit a Roman arena, see prehistoric relics. 30 mins.

VHS: S08278. $24.95.

French Singers

Edith Piaf, George Brassens and Maurice Chevalier are each captured in live performances and in rare documentary footage.

VHS: S10590. $29.95.

The Hunchback of Notre Dame

To the medieval world he was a hideous living gargoyle. But in the eyes of the woman he loved, his spirit soared like the spires of a great cathedral. An *A & E Biography*.

VHS: S30837. $19.95.

In Love with Paris

The City of Light and food, fashion, history, art, and shopping. See it all, and capture the spirit of Paris on an unforgettable tour. 50 mins.

VHS: S10766. $24.95.

Jacques Brel

The life and music of the inimitable French composer-singer, the tough Parisian with the guitar who looked life in the eye unflinchingly. There are no June/moon/ spoon lyrics here—Brel lives in the modernity of his music about loving and losing and surviving in love.

VHS: S05550. $39.95.

Jacques Prevert

A portrait of the great poet, playwright and novelist, as Prevert discusses religion, the politics of art, and his work. French *without* English subtitles. 53 mins.

Home Video.

VHS: S06957. $59.95.

Public Performance.

VHS: S09502. $100.00.

Jean Genet

Genet had never accepted an interview before a camera. It is thus an event to see him for the first time, speaking in total liberty about his love of the shadows of prison life, and for the light of Greece, and his involvements with the Black Panthers and other groups; finally, he reveals the birth of his vocation as a writer. French *without* English subtitles.

Home Video.

VHS: S06955. $59.95.

Public Performance.

VHS: S08839. $100.00.

Les Antilles: Guadeloupe and Martinique

These Caribbean islands showcase the rich, atmospheric locales that speak to the social and political heritage of French culture. This is indispensable for class discussion for the Francophone. 60 mins.

French Narration.

VHS: S19781. $35.00.

English Narration.

VHS: S19782. $35.00.

Les Chateaux de la Loire

The history of France comes alive as you tour the magnificent chateaux which dot the Loire. A unique opportunity to examine the splendid interiors and classic architecture of these famous sites. 55 mins. English narration.

VHS: S00003. $49.95.

Les Clips Francophones

Popular music is a highly regarded means to unlocking the barriers of language-learning. These clips, representing the best French artists—M.C. Solaar, Patricia Kaas and King Dady Yod- introduce contemporary language usage ("slang") and cultural styles and attitudes. The lyrics of each song, biographies, grammatical commentary and language exercises are included in each text. 30 mins.

VHS: S19783. $49.95.

Masters of the French Stage: Jean-Louis Barrault and Madeline Renaud

Leading figures on the French stage since World War II, director/actor Jean-Louis Barrault and his wife, actress Madeleine Renaud, present the jealousy scene from Moliere's *Le Misanthrope* and recitations from other works of French drama and poetry, including Jacques Prevert's *Bird*, Paul Valois' *Liberte* and a charming fable about animal intelligence. Barrault performs his famous circus horse-riding pantomime and discusses the importance of state subsidies to the theater for the good of the country's intellectual life. Some French dialog.

VHS: S30997. $89.95.

1969, 28 mins.

Maurice Chevalier

A portrait of the charmer in the straw hat, the most beloved of the song-and-dance men, with archival footage tracing his career from Montmartre to Hollywood, and clips from such films as *The Merry Widow*, *Innocents of Paris* and *Gigi*. Among the many songs Chevalier sings is his signature song, "Louise."

VHS: S10047. $39.95.

Michel Tournier

The hermit of the valley of Chevreuse, who lives in his house "like the snail who secretes his house around him, year by year…a very complex shell," speaks about the themes that are dear to him—the Germany of his youth, Tunisia, photography, the vocation of the writer, and above all, childhood in general, the mystery of which he constantly tries to fathom in his novels, such as *Roi des Aulnes* and *Meteores*. French *without* English subtitles.

Home Video.
VHS: S06958. $59.95.
Public Performance.
VHS: S08831. $100.00.

Mon Ane: Au Clair de la Lune

This delightful collection of 15 traditional French songs features colorful animation and French subtitles for sing-alongs. Includes "Au clair de la lune," "Sur le pont d'Avignon" and "Frere Jacques." A fun way to promote oral and listening comprehension for beginning and intermediate students of French. 35 mins.

VHS: S31239. $29.95.

Mont St. Michel

The Cathedral of the Sea has been a site of worship for centuries. Today its collection of religious buildings from the Middle Ages include a treasure of art and architecture. This title, from the series *Spirit of France*, shows the splendor of this unique and holy island. English narration, 56 mins.

VHS: S24935. $29.95.

Montparnasse Revisited

This series captures the history of one of Paris' most colorful and vital districts. The painters, writers, composers, actors, musicians and photographers who made Paris the center of the art world between 1900 and the Second World War defined the avant garde. Together they created modern art as we know it. Each volume is 55 mins. Directed by Matthew Reinders and based on a program by Jean-Marie Drot.

Volume 1: The Brilliant Years, 1900-1914.
VHS: S21041. $29.95.
Volume 2: Artists at War, 1914-1918.
VHS: S21042. $29.95.
Volume 3: Face to Face with Giacometti.
VHS: S21043. $29.95.
Volume 4: A Life in the Day of Man Ray.
VHS: S21044. $29.95.
Volume 5: Who Was Modigliani?
VHS: S21045. $29.95.
Volume 6: The Man Behind Picasso—Daniel-Henry Kahnweiler.
VHS: S21046. $29.95.
Volume 7: Ghosts at the Banquet—The Twenties.
VHS: S21047. $29.95.
Volume 8: Songs and Sentiments—Music Hall.
VHS: S21048. $29.95.
Volume 9: The Composers.
VHS: S21049. $29.95.
Volume 10: Soutine the Obsessed.
VHS: S21050. $29.95.
The Ten-Volume Set.
VHS: S21051. $199.95.

Museum City Videos: Paris, City of Light

Monuments to the glory of France, including the Arc de Triomphe, the Champs Elysees, the Eiffel Tower and the Louvre, are illustrated through the perspectives of such notable Paris citizens as Napoleon and Coco Chanel. 58 mins.

VHS: S29922. $19.98.

Noel a Paris

Follow a Parisian family as it celebrates the holidays. We participate in a festive dinner, exchange gifts, and continue the celebration throughout New Year's Eve. A wonderful presentation of French tradition and culture. 30 mins.

English Narration.
VHS: S05288. $49.95.
French Narration.
VHS: S05287. $49.95.

Rivers of France

Take a luxury cruise on the Seine and experience picturesque Honfleur, the Bayeux tapestry, Monet's Giverny, Normandy's D-Day beaches, Joan of Arc's Rouen, Mont St. Michel, Brittany folklore, Carnac's monolith, ballooning the Loire Valley Chateaux, a canal trip through Burgundy's vineyards, the Louvre's new pyramid entrance, the Musee D'Orsay, and the new Bastille Opera House.

VHS: S32729. $49.95.
Clay Francisco, USA, 1993, 80 mins.

Salamandre: Chateaux of the Loire

A study of France's 18 socially important chateaux uses computer animation technology to study the chateau's evolution from feudal fortresses to expansive manors. French and English dialog.

Laser: LD70308. $49.95.

Simone de Beauvoir

This film is the passionate testimony of a half-century of intellectual and political life, the itinerary of a woman who has covered many fields of human endeavor, yet who reveals herself—in the company of her lover, Jean-Paul Sartre—as human and accessible. French *without* English subtitles.

Home Video.
VHS: S06954. $59.95.
Public Performance.
VHS: S08838. $100.00.

Turckhein et Sa Fete du Vin

This show about the fundamental importance of vineyards and wine in French culture reveals the excitement of the various wine fests in the Alsatian village of Turckhein. In French. With transcript and exercises. 30 mins.

VHS: S19805. $39.95.

Versailles

Perhaps the most famous of all royal palaces—built by Louis XIV in the 17th century. Marvel at the Hall of Mirrors, the royal bedchamber, the spectacle of the fountains and the formal gardens. 55 mins. English narration.

VHS: S05279. $69.95.

Visite en France

This cultural video simulates an actual visit to Paris and the surrounding areas by two young students. The sites also include the Loire Valley, and a Son et Lumiere Festival. Various functions such as socializing, greeting, introducing and leaving are incorporated into the conversation, with other vocabulary and expressions related to the various activities attended by the teenagers. Seven 15-minute segments for advanced-beginning-intermediate. 105 mins.

VHS: S09066. $59.9.

BELGIAN CINEMA

Daens

Nominated for an Academy Award for Best Foreign Language Film in 1992, *Daens* is the story of Father Adolph Daens, a Catholic priest who returns to his village after a long absence, to discover his fellow townspeople living in abject poverty. Called by his conscience to speak out against the miserable working conditions in the factories, Father Daens soon finds himself in a head-to-head battle with not only the businessmen and the monarchy, but Catholic Church officials as well. Based on a true story, Father Daens is later elected to Parliament to represent the workers he risked his reputation to champion. With Jan Declier, Antje de Boeck and Gerard Desarthe. Flemish and French with English subtitles.

VHS: S26963. $19.98.
Stijn Coninx, Belgium/France/Netherlands, 1992, 134 mins.

The Eighth Day

From the director of *Toto the Hero* comes this Belgian cross between *Rain Man* and *Forrest Gump*, the tender story of Harry, a soul-dead Belgian businessman whose life is changed forever when he meets Georges, a man with Downs Syndrome. On the road together, the two men go on a fascinating journey of self-discovery, profoundly touching each other's lives. Outstanding performances by Daniel Auteuil and Pascal Duquenne earned both a Best Actor Award at Cannes—the first time two actors have shared such an award at the Festival. French with English subtitles.

VHS: S31697. $19.95.
Laser: LD76288. $39.99.
Jaco Van Dormael, Belgium, 1996, 108 mins.

Farinelli

Farinelli, an 18th-century castrato, was one of Europe's most acclaimed singers. This lavishly designed, brilliantly costumed film focuses on his troubled artistic and personal life as he conquers the opera world and has women faint in his presence, yet needs his brother to consummate his sexual conquests. Corbiau ingeniously recreates the unique castrato sound by electronically blending a male and female voice; Jeroen Krabbe appears as Friedrich Handel. French with English subtitles.

VHS: S26396. $19.95.
Laser: LD75080. $34.95.
Gerard Corbiau, France/Belgium/Italy, 1995, 115 mins.

La Promesse

Igor and his father Roger run an apartment scam, renting to illegal immigrants and working them illegally. Immigrant Amidou is injured when he falls off a scaffold and Igor makes a promise that exposes the different values of Igor, Roger and Amidou's wife, Assita.

VHS: S34739. $94.98.
Jean-Pierre Dardenne/Luc Dardenne, Belgium/France/Luxembourg, 1996, 90 mins.

Man Bites Dog

An off-center, mock documentary with a profanely serious thrust about a Belgian documentary crew that impassively follows Ben (Benoit Poelvoorde), a pasty-faced, deadpan serial killer. The film is shot in black and white and composed primarily in hand-held shots, as the filmmakers "profile" their remorseless killer. The corpses mount through the killer's lethal strangulations, shootings and stabbings, though the film is primarily concerned with how the media and society are implicated in the horrendous crimes. French with English subtitles. This is the uncut version.

VHS: S18974. $19.98.
Laser: LD76788. $49.95.
Remy Belvaux/Andre Bonzel/Benoit Poelvoorde, Belgium, 1991, 95 mins.

The Music Teacher

The music of Verdi, Mahler, Schumann, Mozart, Bellini, Schubert and Offenbach is highlighted in this 1989 Academy Award Nominee for Best Foreign Film. Just before World War I a group of opera students gather to compete to settle a grudge between a retired opera star and a wealthy patron. Lots of emotional fireworks. Called "elegant and cultivated" by the *Boston Globe*. With Jose Van Dam, Joachim Dallyroc and Anne Roussel. French with English subtitles.

VHS: S11535. $19.98.
Gerard Corbiau, France/Belgium, 1989, 100 min.

The Sexual Life of the Belgians

Belgian filmmaker Jan Bucquoy's autobiographical comedy is a deadpan, satiric account of a young man's sexual awakening from the furtive gropings of his early teen years through his adulthood during the free-love sixties, eventually leading to the final struggle: marriage. A droll, entertaining festival favorite. French with English subtitles.

VHS: S28483. $29.95.
Jan Bucquoy, Belgium, 1995, 85 mins.

Toto the Hero

Winner of the Camera d'Or at the 1991 Cannes Film Festival, this witty and audacious debut film by Belgian director Jaco Van Dormael concerns Thomas, who is convinced he was exchanged at birth with his neighbor Alfred and subsequently condemned to lead an anonymous, insignificant life. Appearing as 'Toto le Heros', the invented secret agent of his adolescence, Thomas undergoes a fantastic odyssey to track Alfred down and uncover his true identity. With Michel Bouquet, Mireille Perrier and Jo de Backer. French with English subtitles.

VHS: S18544. $94.95.
Laser: LD75277. $44.95.
Jaco Van Dormael, Belgium/France/Germany, 1991, 90 mins.

CHANTAL AKERMAN

Akermania, Volume One

A collection of shorter works by Chantal Akerman. Includes *Saute ma Ville*, Akerman's first film (1968) which stars the filmmaker at age 18. Also featured is *I'm Hungry, I'm Cold*, the story of two love-struck Belgian girls on the loose in Paris, and the 1972 New York silent experimental film *Hotel Monterey*. French with English subtitles.

VHS: S16298. $19.98.
Chantal Akerman, France/Belgium, 89 mins.

A Couch in New York

When a frazzled New York psychoanalyst (William Hurt) and a free-spirited dancer in Paris (Juliette Binoche, *The English Patient*) exchange apartments, the resulting switch begins a spiral of comic confusion involving spurned lovers, mistaken identities and a golden retriever.

VHS: S31717. $19.95.
Laser: LD76289. $39.99.
Chantal Akerman, France/Germany, 1996, 104 mins.

The Eighties

"Goofy hypersophisticated," one critic called it. "Goofy formalism," wrote another. "Goofy deconstruction of the musical." It all adds up, to everyone's delight, to pure, playful pleasure. The first hour, shot on video, is a montage of auditions for parts in a musical comedy. Songs and choreography are rehearsed, repeated, and revised by actors responding to offscreen direction by Akerman. The second part, shot in 35mm, is the wonderful, wholly satisfying pay-off; a musical extravaganza set in a shopping mall. French with English subtitles.

VHS: S12610. $79.95.
Chantal Akerman, Belgium/France, 1983, 85 min.

Je, Tu, Il, Elle

Chantal Akerman's first feature moves like a process or a journey, most likely one from youth into adulthood. Akerman stars as the protagonist of the film, whom we first discover in her apartment compulsively eating raw sugar, reading aloud and rearranging her furniture. She hits the road and after various misadventures finds herself at the home of a woman she loves. The heavy silence underscores themes of estrangement and alienation. With Niels Arestrup and Claire Wauthion. French with English subtitles.

VHS: S12562. $29.95.
Chantal Akerman, France, 1974, 90 mins.

News from Home

"Most simply described, the film is a portrait of Manhattan in which a generally static camera presents a succession of geometrically framed streetscapes—it's a spare and ravishing *city symphony* that takes its cues from Manhattan's own relentless grid" (J. Hoberman).
VHS: S13819. $24.95.
Chantal Akerman, USA/Belgium, 1976, 90 mins.

Night and Day (Nuit et Jour)

Chantal Akerman's daring film about sexual independence concerns one woman's simultaneous relationships with two men. Set over a sweltering Paris summer, the story follows Julie (Guilaine Londez), a beautiful young woman who is involved in a passionate relationship with Jack (Thomas Langmann). Completely isolated from the outside world, with no friends or intimates, they engage in marathon bouts of sex. At night, Jack drives a taxi to support them while Julie walks the Paris streets. Julie is inexorably drawn to Joseph (Francois Negret), a solitary young man who drives Jack's cab during the day. French with English subtitles.
VHS: S19974. $19.98.
Chantal Akerman, France/Belgium, 1991, 91 mins.

Rendezvous d'Anna

One of the most important films of the 70's, Chantal Akerman's "laying bare of grim reality". A woman filmmaker floats around Europe while having encounters with several people, both strangers and intimate relations, that reveal her as a catalyst for commitment. Aurore Clement plays Anna in this minimalist experiment that is perhaps the most accessible of Akerman's films, which evokes human needs, fears and subtleties by concentrating on the spaces in between conversation. With Lea Massari, Helmut Griem, Jean-Pierre Cassel. French with English subtitles.
VHS: S09346. $29.95.
Chantal Akerman, France/Belgium, 1978, 122 mins.

Toute Une Nuit

A hot, steamy summer night. All over the city, it's impossible to sleep. So goes the context of Akerman's film, tension fractured by an explosion of amorous comings and goings. A woman leaves her husband's bed to meet her lover. A little girl runs away from home, her cat in her arms. A man gazes longingly through a window at a woman sitting alone. The film is made entirely of fragments such as these, disregarding narrative content yet evoking the best loved conventions of romantic melodrama. Wonderfully moody location shooting. Cast: Angelo Abazoglou, Natalia Ackerman, Veronique Alain. French with English subtitles.
VHS: S12561. $29.95.
Chantal Akerman, France/Belgium, 1982, 89 mins.

Window Shopping

This amusing and romantic film combines the simplicity of a 1940s Hollywood musical with a knowing attitude that allows it to strip away some of the squeaky naivete of such films. It's set on one level of a shopping mall where "romance is in the air." Great fun. French with English subtitles.
VHS: S13820. $29.95.
Chantal Akerman, France, 1986

SWISS CINEMA

The Boat Is Full

It is the summer of 1942 and the Swiss government, alarmed at the vast numbers of people fleeing Nazi Germany, has set up immigration policies so stringent that they have declared the country "a full lifeboat." Complications arise when a Swiss innkeeper's wife takes in a group of frightened refugees. A haunting film from noted Swiss Filmmaker Markus Imhoof. "Virtually a flawless movie....One I will not soon forget!" (Jeffrey Lyons). French and German with English subtitles.
VHS: S00161. $29.95.
Markus Imhoof, Switzerland, 1980, 100 mins.

Ernesto Che Guevara: The Bolivian Diary

An intriguing look inside Cuba's incredible revolutionary leader Che Guevara, who, at age 39, was executed in 1967 by the Bolivian army, aided by the CIA. Guevara's diary, a detailed, personal account of his futile 11-month attempt to foment revolution in Bolivia, is the basis of this moving portrait. Che's relationship with the mysterious Tania, his betrayal by local peasants, his constant battle with asthma, and his distress at the death of comrades are recounted. Interviews with Bolivians who met Che during these final days testify to a man who embraced sacrifice for his ideals. "An understated, stunningly effective portrait" (Michael Wilmington, *Chicago Tribune*). English and Spanish with English subtitles.
VHS: S33355. $29.98.
Richard Dindo, Switzerland, 1997, 94 mins.

Four in a Jeep

Viveca Lindfors, Ralph Meeker and Michael Medwin star in this Berlin Film Festival winner. Vienna is divided among the allied powers, thereby forcing soldiers from the four powers to patrol the streets together. Soon the Russian and American in the group are at odds over a young Austrian woman whose husband has just escaped from a Russian camp.
VHS: S24003. $24.95.
Leopold Lindtberg, Switzerland, 1951, 81 mins.

The Invitation

Claude Goretta (*The Lacemaker*) takes viewers to a garden party that begins respectfully and falls to pieces as the sun and alcohol take their toll. Removed from their office surroundings, the guests let down their reserve until the butler restores the party and people to their proper order. Both charming and insightful, the film wryly observes the impact that time and space have on ordinary people. "One of the most impressive works to come out of Switzerland" (James Monaco, *The Movie Guide*). Digitally mastered with new electronic subtitles. French with English subtitles.
VHS: S30144. $29.95.
Claude Goretta, Switzerland/France, 1973, 100 mins.

Journey of Hope

A naive Kurdish family of refugees from Turkey travel to the Swiss border and are forced to cross the Alps at night during the winter. A grueling tale based on fact, it was awarded an Oscar for Best Foreign Language Film. Turkish, Kurdish and German with English subtitles.
VHS: S15418. $19.98.
Laser: LD75210. $34.98.
Xavier Koller, Switzerland, 1990, 111 minutes.

The Lacemaker

Isabelle Huppert shot from minor actress to international star with a mesmerizing performance as a young woman incapable of escaping anonymity. This acclaimed and beautiful film by Swiss director Claude Goretta is a sad twist on the Cinderella story as Huppert is swept away by Francois, a rich, handsome young student. At first, he is captivated by her graceful movements and enticed by her virginity. But their romance is short-lived; he soon breaks with her and brings about her mental collapse. French with English subtitles.
VHS: S12953. $29.95.
Claude Goretta, Switzerland/France, 1977, 107 mins.

The Last Chance

This innovative Swiss film chronicles the travails of two escaped POW's working their way through Northern Italy to Switzerland. The war in Italy is almost over, but that does not mean everyone they encounter is willing to help these Allied soldiers. E.G. Morrison and John Hoy star in this tense film shot on location in a neo-realist style. English and other languages with English subtitles.
VHS: S23992. $24.95.
Leopold Lindtberg, Switzerland, 1945, 104 mins.

Max Frisch

Performance of scenes from Max Frisch's off-Broadway plays *Andorra* and *I'm Not Stiller*. Interview with the celebrated Swiss novelist and playwright. 1963, 27 mins.
VHS: S32323. $89.95.

ALAIN TANNER

In the White City

When his ship lands in Lisbon, a disconnected sailor drifts through the streets and twisting alleys of the ghostly "white city," recording himself and his impressions with a Super-8 camera. He settles into a room above a saloon, and soon finds himself in an affair with the barmaid. Keeping a diary on film, he lets his world slip away; his ship leaves port without him, and he sends obscure notes (with some of his film) to his wife in Switzerland. A poignant and beautifully acted film starring Bruno Ganz and Teresa Madruga. French, Portuguese, German and English with subtitles.
VHS: S16499. $79.95.
Alain Tanner, France, 1983, 108 mins.

Jonah Who Will Be 25 in the Year 2000

Alain Tanner's masterpiece; a sensitive, literate and engaging comedy follows eight individuals affected by the political events of 1968. Tanner describes the film as "a dramatic tragi-comedy in political science fiction." Stars Myriam Boyer, Jean-Luc Bideau, Roger Jendly, Jacques Denis and Miou-Miou as a lovely supermarket clerk with no qualms about liberating groceries. French with English subtitles.
VHS: S16679. $29.95.
Alain Tanner, Switzerland, 1976, 115 mins.

La Salamandre

A treat: a journalist and his novelist friend research the story of a girl who was accused of shooting and wounding her uncle. Bulle Ogier delivers a disarming performance as the rare but tough and independent factory worker who confounds the two intellectuals with her inner revolt. Priceless for a scene in which Ogier, now a sales girl in a shoe shop, begins to caress the legs of her customers—funny, absurd, shocking, erotic. A unique film. French with English subtitles.
VHS: S21198. $79.95.
Alain Tanner, Switzerland, 1971, 125 mins.

Messidor

Tanner explores one of his favorite themes—the limitations of freedom—in this totally original mixture of experimentation and melodrama. Clementine Amouroux and Catherine Retore are two young women who hitchhike their way through Switzerland, but even their friendship cannot keep the idyllic odyssey free of fear and violence. French with English subtitles.
VHS: S26464. $29.95.
Alain Tanner, Switzerland/France, 1981, 120 mins.

DUTCH CINEMA

1-900

Two busy professionals meet on a telephone sex line for good times. From their initial contact a strange and intense relationship develops that is by turns erotic, funny, frustrating and sinister. 1-900 protocol demands that they never actually meet, nor even discover each other's actual identity. Intimate contact, however, becomes an obsession leading them to explore the boundaries of imagination, fantasy and power. Dutch with English subtitles.
VHS: S29509. $19.98.
Theo Van Gogh, Netherlands, 1995, 80 mins.

Antonia's Line

In this recasting in a woman's image of a story from the book of Genesis, an 88-year-old Dutchwoman recalls her past on the last day of her life, filled with colorful characters like a Russian midwife-undertaker, a Danish recluse, a mentally disabled girl, a village idiot and a mad Madonna who howls at the moon. An Academy Award winner for Best Foreign Language Film, the film also won Best Picture at the Toronto International Film Festival. Dutch with English subtitles.
VHS: S29956. $19.98.
Laser: LD75969. $39.99.
Marleen Gorris, Netherlands, 1995, 102 mins.

The Assault

The 1987 winner of the Oscar for Best Foreign Language Picture, Fons Rademakers' epic tale is of a young boy who witnesses the brutal massacre of his family in the final days of World War II. The only survivor, the nightmarish memory haunts him until he uncovers and faces the truth. English dubbed.
VHS: S03573. $79.95.
Fons Rademakers, Netherlands, 1986, 126 mins.

Ciske the Rat

Dutch singing sensation Danny De Munk stars as a troubled kid in the winds of war between his separated parents in this touching childhood saga set in 1934 Amsterdam. Directed by Guido Peters and based on the best-selling book trilogy by Piet Bakker. Dutch with English subtitles.
VHS: S32016. $59.95.
Guido Peters, Netherlands, 1984, 107 mins.

Crocodiles in Amsterdam

Described as a "slapstick female buddy movie," this Dutch feature stars two friends, Gino and Nina. Though thoroughly different, they manage to wrest friendship from the most inauspicious situations. Nina's rebelliousness and Gino's frivolity place them at each other's mercy, and often in hilarious situations. Dutch with English subtitles.
VHS: S26937. $39.95.
Annette Apon, Netherlands, 1990, 88 mins.

De Overval (Resistance)

Paul Rotha, one of the founders of the modern documentary, turns his attention to the resistance movement in Europe during World War II. The center of this riveting feature deals with the raid on a Dutch prison during the Nazi occupation and the liberation of 50 important political prisoners. With Chris Baay, Hetty Beck and Yoka Berretty. Dutch with English subtitles.
VHS: S33030. $69.95.
Paul Rotha, Netherlands, 1962, 97 mins.

The Dear Boys

A harsh, stylized and feverish piece about dark sexual fantasies and deep romantic longing, the film concerns the romantic and sexual entanglements of a morose, self-absorbed writer and an uninhibited, carefree young man who recklessly pursues thrills and excitement. This groundbreaking, unapologetically gay work is adapted from Gerard Reve's novel. With Hugo Netsers, Hans Dagelet, Bill Van Dijk, and Albert Mol.
VHS: S17444. $69.95.
Paul de Lussanet, Netherlands, 1980, 90 mins.

Egg

A remarkable film from Holland and one of the gems of the Cannes Film Festival in the year of its release, *Egg* is the story of Johan, a quiet, good-hearted, 35-year-old baker who answers a personal ad from a lonely schoolteacher named Eva. When the woman comes to town after an exchange of many letters, contrary to the expectations of the entire village, she decides to stay. *Egg* is a delightfully deadpan romantic fable in the spirit of Buster Keaton and Jacques Tati. Dutch with English subtitles.

VHS: S12330. $59.95.
Laser: LD70260. $34.95.
Danniel Danniel, Netherlands, 1988, 58 mins.

The Eye Above the Well

A poetic depiction of life and ritual in the Indian state of Kerala, this unique film, called "a masterpiece" by Luis Marcorelles, features superb performance footage which shows how song, dance, martial arts and religion are passed from one generation to the next. Malayalam with English subtitles.

VHS: S26503. $59.95.
Johan van der Keuken, Netherlands, 1988, 94 mins.

A Flight of Rainbirds

In this dramatic comedy about love, sex and religion, Jeroen Krabbe stars in a hilarious dual role. As a repressed cell biologist, he dreams he has a week to lose his virginity or he will die. His rakish alter ego tries to help the bumbling Maarten find the lucky woman who can save his life. Dutch with English subtitles.

VHS: S16527. $29.95.
Ate de Jong, Netherlands, 1981, 94 mins.

For a Lost Soldier

This haunting, true story follows a boy's wartime sexual awakening. It's controversial because this 12-year-old falls in love with a Canadian soldier who is in Holland just at the end of World War II. Ballet star Rudi van Danzig recreates this memory from his childhood to show how a boy falls in love with his handsome liberator. Dutch with English subtitles.

VHS: S21831. $19.98.
Roeland Kerbosch, Netherlands, 1993, 95 mins.

The Forbidden Quest

In June 1903 an unremarkable ship called *Holland* departed for Norway. In fact, this ship was secretly headed for the South Pole. Nearly 40 years later, the sole survivor, a ship's carpenter, was finally located in a tiny cottage in Ireland. There, the old man explained how murder, cannibalism and, finally, a spiritual awakening befell the men of that fateful voyage. A harrowing adventure in the tradition of Herman Melville and Joseph Conrad. "Stunning archival footage, an intriguing plot, and a dash of *The Twilight Zone*" (Bill Hoffman, *The New York Post*). Dedicated to Frank Hurley. In English.

VHS: S27563. $59.95.
Peter Delpeut, Netherlands, 1993, 75 mins.

The Fourth Man

Paul Verhoeven's surprise hit is a roller-coaster ride through forbidden sensual pleasure in the context of a kinky thriller. The three men in Christine's past all have one thing in common; they're dead. And when Gerard, seduced by Christine, moves into her life, a grisly series of dreams and visions hints he could be next: the fourth man. English dubbed.

VHS: S00461. $24.95.
Paul Verhoeven, Netherlands, 1984, 104 mins.

Keetje Tippel

Paul Verhoeven's first international success, the story of a young Dutch girl adrift in 1881 Amsterdam, who rises from a life of poverty and prostitution to become a woman of means, education and attainment. This bawdy, tough, and delightful film is a Cinderella tale for intelligent adults. With the sexy Monique van der Ven and Rutger Hauer. Dutch with English subtitles.

VHS: S08998. $29.95.
Paul Verhoeven, Netherlands, 1975, 104 mins.

Lyrical Nitrate

An unusual and moving tribute to early cinema constructed from color-tinted and toned nitrate films found deteriorating in the attic of an Amsterdam movie house. Through meticulous restoration, these prints, dating from the earliest years of the century, are shown in the rich and subtle colors in which they were originally exhibited, accompanied by an evocative soundtrack. "The cumulative effect of *Lyrical Nitrate* is a revelation" (*The New York Post*). Dutch intertitles with English subtitles.

VHS: S27564. $59.95.
Peter Delpeut, Netherlands, 1991, 50 mins.

A Question of Silence

A murder committed by three women, all strangers to each other, leads to a controversial examination of the deep-seated rage—a result of living all their lives in a male-dominated society—which led to the crime. With outstanding performances. Dutch with English subtitles.

VHS: S01081. $29.95.
Marleen Gorris, Netherlands, 1983, 92 mins.

Rare Dutch and Belgian Experimental Program

Includes five short films: *Mystic Lamb* (11 mins.), *Rain* (10 mins.), *New Earth* (23 mins.), *Bridge* (15 mins.) and *Umbrella* (30 mins.)

VHS: S14922. $29.95.

Rembrandt—1669

The final years of the artist's life and varied career, detailing the tension between his egotistical, self-centered celebrity and the contemplation, insight and emotional refinement of his art. An investigation of a man's art and life, the movie reveals the fascinating process and discoveries Rembrandt's art was heir to. "A fascinating life, a near perfect union of form and content" (*Variety*). With Frans Stelling, Tom de Koff and Aye Fil. Dutch with English subtitles.

VHS: S17766. $79.95.
Jos Stelling, Netherlands, 1977, 114 mins.

Spetters (Dubbed)

Violence and tragedy mark this episodic story involving four young people in Holland on a turbulent collision course with their dreams. English dubbed and Dutch with English subtitles.

VHS: S01239. $29.95.
Paul Verhoeven, Netherlands, 1980, 108 mins.

Spetters (Subtitled)

Dutch filmmaker Paul Verhoeven uses a motorcross championship to explore the homoerotic tensions of three young men, each obsessed with a beautiful, enigmatic hot dog stand owner. Verhoeven combines high melodrama with lurid sex sequences and a heightened visual style that's over-the-top romantic. With Ton Scherpenzeel, Kayak Toon Agterberg and Maarten Spanjer. Cameo appearance by Rutger Hauer. Dutch with English subtitles.

VHS: S18627. $39.95.
Paul Verhoeven, Netherlands, 1983, 109 mins.

Suite 16

One trick turns to murder, leaving a handsome young hustler trapped in the luxurious suite of Glover (Pete Postlethwaite, *The Usual Suspects*), a wealthy businessman. Together they seduce sexy young women in a game of voyeurism that leads to murder. The question becomes, which is stronger: money, sex or power—and can one get enough? "Genre fans will appreciate the extra depth in this erotic piece by Dereddere, who makes Zalman King look like Walt Disney" (Buzz McClain, *Video Business*). English, Dutch and French with English subtitles.

VHS: S30247. $14.95.
Dominique Dereddere, Netherlands, 1996, 93 mins.

To Play or to Die

Set in a Dutch boys' school, the introverted and shy Kees enters into a psychosexual battle of wills with his handsome tormentor Charel, the leader of the brutal gang that uses fascist sadomasochistic games to exert their power. With Geert Hunaerts and Tjebbo Gerritsma. Dutch with English subtitles.

VHS: S18587. $29.95.
Frank Krom, USA, 1991, 50 mins.

Turkish Delights

A very amusing, uplifting, and tragic story of a couple madly in love. This Academy Award nominee is a study of two free spirits forced to change by the events of their lives. From the director of *The Fourth Man*. English dubbed.

VHS: S01377. $39.95.
Paul Verhoeven, Netherlands, 1974, 100 mins.

The Vanishing

A young husband descends into the obsessive corners of his mind when his wife Saskla inexplicably vanishes while on holiday in France. This cold-blooded psychological thriller was winner of the 1991 Grand Prize of Dutch Cinema for Best Film. It succeeds the old-fashioned way, by hooking the viewer on the characters and murky undercurrents of the story—seducing us into the midst of a clean, logical nightmare. In the finest tradition of Hitchcock, *The Vanishing* will haunt you long after it is over. "It's unforgettable even if you try to forget it" (*San Francisco Chronicle*). Dutch and French with yellow English subtitles.

VHS: S15444. $19.98.
Laser: LD72197. $39.95.
George Sluizer, Netherlands, 1991, 107 mins.

recent italian cinema

Acla's Descent into Floristella
Sold into servitude by his parents, 12-year-old Acla must work underground in sulfur mines. Repeatedly beaten by his owner, the threat of sexual abuse is also ever-present. When he runs away, there are dire consequences for both him and his family. The story is based on the social mores and disturbing sexual practices found in 1930's Sicily. Italian with English subtitles.
VHS: S21544. $69.95.
Aurelio Grimaldi, Italy, 1987, 86 mins.

Acqua e Sapone
Comedy based on the adventures of a young woman in the high fashion world in Rome. Complications set in when a handsome janitor (played by director Verdone) impersonates her tutor-priest. English title: *Soap and Water*. Italian with English subtitles.
VHS: S00067. $19.95.
Carlo Verdone, Italy, 1983, 100 mins.

Aurora
Sophia Loren is Aurora, a woman who will do anything for her son, Ciro (played by Sophia's son Edoardo Ponti), who was blinded at the age of two and has no real father. When they find out that there is a procedure that will heal him, Aurora sets out to find all the men who could be Ciro's "daddies," to help her finance the operation. Along the way she is reunited with the only man she ever loved and the only man who wants to be Ciro's father. With Daniel J. Travanti. Filmed in Italy. In English.
VHS: S31219. $14.99.
Maurizio Ponzi, Italy, 1984, 91 mins.

Belle Starr
A virtually unclassifiable work by Lina Wertmuller, directed under the pseudonym Nathan Wich. It's a spaghetti western that charts the lawless aggression and sexual anarchy of the notorious bandit queen (Elsa Martinelli). Cinematography by John Alonzo. With Robert Wood, George Eastman, Dan Harrison and Eugene Walter. English dubbed.
VHS: S02190. $59.95.
Lina Wertmuller, Italy, 1979, 90 mins.

Bellissimo: Images of the Italian Cinema
A history of the Italian cinema by Gianfredo Mingozzi, an unprecedented reconstruction of the Italian cinema as a sophisticated art form. This unique film contains clips from the 1940's to the present, including such famous films as *Open City, Divorce Italian Style, 8½* and *Seven Beauties*, and captures the great personalities of Italian filmmaking, including Dino De Laurentiis, Sophia Loren, Bertolucci, Mastroianni, Marco Ferreri, Rossellini, de Sica, Pasolini, Zeffirelli, Fellini, Wertmuller, Monica Vitti, Giancarlo Giannini, and Toto. English and Italian with English subtitles.
VHS: S05170. $29.95.
Gianfranco Mingozzi, Italy, 1987, 110 mins.

Beyond Obsession
From Liliana Cavani (*A Night Porter*) comes this shocker about the strange relationship of a political prisoner (Marcello Mastroianni), his daughter (Eleonora Giorgi), and her obsession with an elusive American (Tom Berenger). With Michel Piccoli. Also known as *Beyond the Door* (1982).
VHS: S17447. $24.95.
Liliana Cavani, Italy, 1982, 116 mins.

Bix
This famed trumpeter revolutionized jazz. In this first-rate musical biography his life and times are recreated based on the known facts. He is seen playing in some of the original locations including spots throughout the Midwest where *Bix* began. Hoagey Carmichael and Pee Wee Russel are just some of the figures seen accompanying him, performing songs like "Dardenella" and "Stardust." In English.
VHS: S20939. $29.95.
Pupi Avati, Italy/USA, 1990, 100 mins.

Bread and Chocolate
Nino Manfredi stars as an Italian immigrant struggling to make a life in the difficult Teutonic world of Switzerland. This comic Everyman finds himself forced into ever more degrading situations, but he never gives up. The result is a comedy with an intense feeling of pathos. With Anna Karina. Italian with English subtitles.
VHS: S27409. $24.95.
Franco Brusati, Italy, 1974, 109 mins.

Brother Sun, Sister Moon
Lavish costume epic depicts the story of St. Francis of Assisi, a man so gentle wild animals would eat from his hand, as he rejects the pomp of the Catholic Church. With some interesting characters working on this production, including Alec Guinness as the Pope, Lina Wertmuller in screenwriting capacity and 60's pop star Donovan supplying the music. English dialog.
VHS: S02623. $14.95.
Franco Zeffirelli, Italy/USA, 1973, 121 mins.

Burn!
Marlon Brando plays Sir William Walker, a cynical freelance secret agent and adventurer hired by the British government to dismantle Portugal's sugar trade monopoly in its Caribbean island colony of Quiemada. "The film soars with the imaginative force of art" (Pauline Kael). English dialog.
VHS: S00192. $19.98.
Laser: CLV. **LD70352. $59.95.**
Gillo Pontecorvo, Italy, 1970, 112 mins.

Caligula
Bob Guccione's entry into filmmaking was a disaster, but nevertheless, *Caligula* has achieved cult status of sorts. This epic of debauchery in Caligula's Rome stars Peter O'Toole, Malcolm McDowell and John Gielgud. English dialog.
VHS: S05788. $59.95.
Tinto Brass, Italy, 1982, 105 mins.

Caro Diario (Dear Diary)
This magical, virtually indescribable comedy by Nanni Moretti won the Best Director Prize at Cannes and follows the travails of a simple man (Moretti) in search of the true meaning of life. The film's three episodes confront, respectively, the changing character of Rome and of Moretti's generation, the possibility (and impossibility) of solitude, and the nature of truth in medicine. Often hilarious, always original, to say that Moretti is the Italian Woody Allen is to underestimate the pathos which underlies the accuracy of his social observations, the incisiveness of his insights. Don't miss. Italian with English subtitles.
VHS: S23967. $19.98.
Nanni Moretti, Italy, 1994, 100 mins.

Cemetery Man (aka Of Death, Of Love)
In this critically acclaimed black comedy, Rupert Everett (*The Madness of King George*) stars as a hapless Italian groundskeeper who has a cemetery full of vengeful dead who won't stay dead, including the woman he loves (Anna Falchi, *The City of Lost Children*). Based on the best-selling novel by Tiziano Sclavi. "Tantalizing! Deliriously original! A movie full of surprises" (Kevin Thomas, *Los Angeles Times*).
VHS: S30242. $95.99.
Laser: LD76041. $39.98.
Michele Soavi, Italy, 1996, 100 mins.

Christopher Columbus
With the 500th anniversary of his voyage to the Americas comes this historically detailed account of Columbus' discoveries. Gabriel Byrne leads this fascinating story of the life, times and voyages of Columbus. Stars Faye Dunaway, Oliver Reed, Max Von Sydow, Eli Wallach and Nicol Williamson.
VHS: S16039. $19.98.
Alberto Lattuada, Italy, 1985, 128 mins.

Ciao, Professore
This brilliant comedy details the outrageous clash between a strict, no-nonsense teacher and his class of rambunctious, street-smart children. Ultimately it's the teacher who ends up learning more about life from his charges than the other way round. Italian with English subtitles.
VHS: S23107. $19.95.
Laser: Letterboxed. **LD74806. $39.99.**
Lina Wertmuller, Italy, 1993, 91 mins.

Cinema Paradiso
An affectionate salute to the magic of the movies and the individuals who spend their lives in the projection booth. This Italian film received an Oscar for Best Foreign Language Film. Philippe Noiret stars as Alfredo, the projectionist for a small Sicilian village movie palace, who opens up new worlds for one very inquisitive child. With Jaques Perrin, Salvatore Cascio, Pupella Maggio and Marco Leonardi. Italian with English subtitles.
VHS: S12603. $19.98.
Giuseppe Tornatore, Italy, 1989, 125 mins.

Collector's Item
Laura Antonelli and Florinda Bolkan make life difficult for Tony Musante as she comes to regret a past seduction in this sexual thriller filmed on location in Paris and the seaside resorts of France. In the tradition of Fatal Attraction and 9½ Weeks, with handcuffs, chains, brass beds and knotted stockings on display. Italian with English subtitles.
VHS: S09850. $39.95.
Giuseppe Patroni-Griffi, Italy/Spain, 1986, 99 mins.

The Conviction
Marco Bellocchio's controversial feature starts with a young woman and a professor who are accidentally locked in a museum overnight. This enforced intimacy devolves into a night of love-making. But in the morning the man reveals he had the keys the entire time. The woman, Clair Nebout, accuses him of rape. The question that dominates the court trial is, "Was it coercion or mutual passion?" Italian with English subtitles.
VHS: S23115. $19.98.
Marco Bellocchio, Italy, 1994, 92 mins.

Corleone
This Italian production traces the rise of Corleone from his humble beginnings in a village near Palermo to his eminence as high priest of organized crime. With Giuliano Gemma (who won Best Actor at the Montreal Film Festival for his performance) and Claudia Cardinale. In English.
VHS: S34178. $19.95.
Pasquale Squitier, Italy, 1977, 109 mins.

Devil in the Flesh
Although the theme has been done many times, Marco Bellocchio managed to shock the international festival circuit with his notoriously explicit oral sex scene between Maruschka Detmers and Federico Pitzalis. *Devil in the Flesh*, wrote *Variety*, is "paradoxically one of the funniest, lightest works Bellocchio has come up with in some time. Yes, eroticism is a key theme, and thanks to an electrifying performance by Detmers, sparks fly in all directions." Andrea is quietly studying in his last year in high school when Giulia (Detmers) comes into his life.
VHS: S09594. $19.98.
Marco Bellocchio, Italy, 1986, 110 mins.

Emmanuelle in Egypt
A group of decadent women determined to possess and conquer the opposite sex soon find themselves consumed by the bizarre exploits of their hosts, in this rollicking sexual adventure starring Laura Gemser, Gabriele Tinti and Susan Scott.
VHS: S34945. $19.95.
Brunello Rondi, Italy, 1977, 88 mins.

Emmanuelle Queen of the Desert
Hell hath no fury like Emanuelle (Laura Gemser) as she deals out revenge to a group of commandos who killed her grandfather and sexually assaulted and killed her sister. With Ivan Rassimov, Giacomo Rossi-Stuart, Gabriele Tinti, Ely Galleani and Chris Avram.
VHS: S34946. $19.95.
Joe D'Amato, Italy, 1983, 90 mins.

Ernesto
A lushly mounted, sensitively directed, complex depiction of homosexuality with Martin Halm as the boy who cooly tries anything and Michele Placido as the older, seducing man. "Genuinely erotic…*Ernesto* reconciles the legacies of Pasolini and Fassbinder." Italian with English subtitles.
VHS: S00416. $49.95.
Salvatore Samperi, Italy, 1983, 98 mins.

Everybody's Fine
A bittersweet story of a father's quest to reunite his five grown children in a film from the director of *Cinema Paradiso*. Marcello Mastroianni plays an elderly widower who decides to surprise his children by touring Italy and finding out how they live. Italian with English subtitles.
VHS: S16569. $19.95.
Giuseppe Tornatore, Italy, 1990, 115 mins.

The Eyes, the Mouth
A critically acclaimed tour-de-force; Lou Castel returns to his home to a family traumatized by suicide and unravelling at the seams in a film which re-established Bellocchio as a major world talent. With stunning performances from Castel, Angela Molina and Emmanuelle Riva. Italian with English subtitles.
VHS: S00424. $19.95.
Marco Bellocchio, Italy, 1982, 100 mins.

Flatfoot
Italian comic Bud Spencer stars in this ridiculous comedy about a maverick cop. He suddenly finds himself on the trail of gangsters who are selling drugs to young school kids. Despite this serious issue, there are hilarious situations and plenty of action. French with English subtitles.
VHS: S23891. $29.95.
Steno, Italy, 1971, 93 mins.

The Flavor of Corn
Lorenzo is a handsome, first-year professor with a quiet demeanor. He brings a passion for teaching to his young charges in a small village. As his relationship with his girlfriend deteriorates, he finds himself spending more time with 12-year-old Duilio. Soon Duilio's stepmother is questioning the nature of this amorous friendship. Italian with English subtitles.
VHS: S21545. $69.95.
Gianni Da Campo, Italy, 1994, 89 mins.

Flight of the Innocent
The ten-year-old son of a brutal kidnapper witnesses his entire family's murder at the hands of a rival gang. He escapes only to find himself being hunted by both these relentless killers and the police. The boy's desperate struggle for survival becomes a path to redemption for the crimes of his father. Italian with English subtitles.
VHS: S21034. $92.95.
Laser: LD72409. $34.98.
Carlo Carlei, Italy, 1993, 105 mins.

Forever Mary
Forever Mary tells the story of an idealistic school teacher trying to make a difference in a rigid reform school. The film works in such a traditional, straightforward style that it's easy to overlook its freshness and imagination. Directed by Marco Risi with passion and grace, *Forever Mary* has all the warmth and easy vitality that make Italian films so beguiling, and it affords its durable star Michele Placido one of his richest roles. Italian with English subtitles.
VHS: S15443. $79.95.
Marco Risi, Italy, 1991, 100 mins.

The Frightened Woman
Sayer, a wealthy, secretive man, gratifies his sadistic fantasies through elaborately staged games of "master and slave." But one weekend, when his regular girl becomes unavailable, Sayer lures a young, beautiful journalist to be his slave, leading to a surprisingly twisted game of terror and pleasure. With Dagmar Lassander and Philippe Leroy-Beaulieu. Dubbed in English.
VHS: S34133. $29.95.
Piero Schivazappia, Italy, 1971, 90 mins.

Henry IV
Pirandello's classic play, directed by Marco Bellocchio (*Fists in the Pocket*), stars Marcello Mastroianni as the aristocrat who falls off a horse and believes himself to be the medieval French Emperor. A fabulous investigation of delusion. With Claudia Cardinale. Italian with English subtitles.
VHS: S04874. $24.95.
Marco Bellocchio, Italy, 1985, 94 mins.

Honey Sweet Love
In this romantic comedy based on a true story, British Colonel Harold Pearson (Ben Cross) gains control of a small Sicilian village during the summer of 1943. He tells the villagers they must cease their semi-illegal activities and elect a mayor. Don Siro (Eli Wallach) arranges the election of the mayor and invites the Colonel to the mayor's house, where the colonel is struck by the mayor's beautiful wife (Jo Champa).
VHS: S33852. $29.95.
Enrico Coletti, France/Italy, 1994, 90 mins.

The Icicle Thief
Maurizio Nichetti presents an energetic send-up of the 1949 Italian neo-realist masterpiece *The Bicycle Thief* while, at the same time, spoofing the ridiculousness of contemporary television commercials. The writer-director takes on a double acting role as a frustrated filmmaker and a fictional glass factory worker who steals a chandelier for his wife. Complications arise when the boundaries between the two stories collide. With Caterina Sylos Labini, Claudio G. Fava and Heidi Komarek. "This hilarious comedy is everything *The Purple Rose of Cairo* should have been and more" (Jonathan Rosenbaum, *Chicago Reader*). Italian with English subtitles.
VHS: S14456. $19.98.
Maurizio Nichetti, Italy, 1989, 93 mins.

Il Postino
Massimo Troisi stars as a humble postman in a small but beautiful Italian village, whose life is transformed by the simple powers of poetry. Pablo Neruda is poet-living-in-exile who gives this bumbling mailman the right words to seduce the woman of his dreams. Troisi died abruptly after completing this role, turning this touching and deeply felt film into a highly apt but wholly unexpected memorial to his skills as a comic actor. With Maria Grazia Cucinotta and Philippe Noiret. Based on the novel *Burning Patience*, by Antonia Skarmenta. Italian with English subtitles.
VHS: S27378. $19.95.
Laser: LD75509. $39.99.
Michael Radford, Italy, 1995, 108 mins.

In the Name of the Pope-King
In Nome del Papa Re is the recipient of three David de Donatello prizes, and stars Nino Manfredi. Set in 1867 as Italian patriots fight to unify the country and Rome stands alone ruled by the Pope, Monsignor Colobo, a magistrate of the Papal State, is about to resign from his office when young terrorists blow up the barracks of the government troops, and the Monsignor discovers that one of the suspects is his own 20-year-old son. A compelling story of intrigue, political conflict and murder unfolds. Italian with English subtitles.
VHS: S05169. $29.95.
Luigi Magni, Italy, 1985, 115 mins.

Johnny Stecchino
A frenetic comedy directed by and starring Roberto Benigni (*Down by Law* and *Night on Earth*). Playing two roles, Benigni is a shy, nervous bus driver who's seduced by a beautiful Italian mistress (Nicoletta Braschi) to stand in for his nefarious look-alike, Johnny, a corrupt Mafiosi who turned state's evidence. Benigni is like Chaplin on speed—colorful, loopy and insanely funny. With Paolo Banacelli and Franco Volpi. Italian with English subtitles.
VHS: S19058. $19.98.
Laser: CLV. **LD72103. $39.99.**
Roberto Benigni, Italy, 1991, 100 mins.

Julia and Julia
Kathleen Turner is a troubled American widow living in Trieste, Italy. She's living two lives as she crosses between two realities, one of which features a live husband and the young child she never had. From the director of *Invitation au Voyage*, a bizarre mystery of unexplained passions. With Gabriel Byrne and Sting. In English.
VHS: S06533. $19.98.
Laser: LD71070. $39.98.
Peter Del Monte, Italy, 1987, 98 mins.

La Scorta
Set in the the Mafia stronghold of Trapani, Sicily, *La Scorta* is a very sophisticated thriller which tells the story of four men assigned to protect an investigating magistrate. Told from the perspective of the bodyguards, this tense, fast-paced film focuses on the magistrate's relentless drive for justice, only to fall victim at the end. Italian with English subtitles.
VHS: S31631. $89.95.
Ricky Tognazzi, Italy, 1993, 92 mins.

Lamerica
Called "one of the great films of the past decade" (Michael Wilmington, *Chicago Tribune*), Gianni Amelio's elaborate fresco-of-a-film is set in Albania. Fiore, an unscrupulous Italian businessman, arrives to grab the spoils of the post-Communist turmoil. He appoints a half-crazy old Albanian man as his patsy to serve as chairman of his fraudulent company. When this puppet slips away from his manipulators, Fiore's cocky assistant Gino is dispatched to track him down. The film takes the form of an odyssey that is also a moral awakening. With Enrico Lo Verso, Michele Placido and Carmelo Di Mazzarelli. Italian with English subtitles.
VHS: S30257. $89.95.
Gianni Amelio, Italy, 1995, 120 mins.

The Last Diva
Born in Florence in 1888, Francesca Bertini made her film debut in a 1907 short about a beauty contestant, *Goddess of the Sea*. Exactly 70 years later she starred in Bernardo Bertolucci's *1900* as Burt Lancaster's mother. Temperamental, capricious, willful, egocentric, amazingly elegant and beautiful, Francesca was one of the silver screen's last divas. In this touching, funny and wondrous portrait of a unique woman, scenes from many of her classic films are juxtaposed with interviews of the geniuses of Italian cinema—such as the late Sergio Leone, whose father, Roberto Roberti, directed some of Bertini's finest performances. Italian with English subtitles.
VHS: S14170. $29.95.
Gianfranco Mingozzi, Italy, 1982, 85 mins.

Lovers and Liars
Goldie Hawn stars as a woman swept away by a mysterious stranger (Giancarlo Giannini) while vacationing in Italy. Searching for adventure, they embark on an odyssey while he uses every lie he can think of to seduce her. Before the truth comes out, many hilarious complications follow in this madcap adventure. With Claudine Auger.
VHS: S06180. $24.95.
Mario Monicelli, Italy, 1980, 96 mins.

Malicious
Laura Antonelli gives a tantalizing performance in this bizarre, kinky Italian sex comedy. Antonelli plays a housekeeper for a widow and his three sons, and she quickly becomes the object of lusty affection of every male in the house including the fourteen year old Nino. Director Samperi masterfully combines amusement with a boy's budding sexual awareness and dramatic sequences bordering on danger and erotic passion. English dubbed.
VHS: S00809. $49.95.
Salvatore Samperi, Italy, 1974, 97 mins.

Mediterraneo
Winner of the 1991 Best Foreign Language Academy Award. A small, eight-man battalion is ordered to secure a strategically unimportant Greek island. They are cut off from their superiors and encounter a liberated, magical community of beautiful women, sad-hearted prostitutes, a sympathetic priest and no resistance. With Diego Abatantuono, Claudio Bigagli and Giuseppe Cederna. Italian with English subtitles.
VHS: S18159. $19.98.
Gabriele Salvatores, Italy, 1991, 99 mins.

Mille Bolle Blu
In this nostalgic comedy the wacky residents of a single block in Rome await the miracle of a solar eclipse even as their lives continue to unfold in maddening vibrancy. Three characters, the engaged Elvira, the escaped convict Caligiuri, and the blind trumpeter Guido, all have a chance for a taste of happiness. Italian with English subtitles.
VHS: S29780. $89.95.
Leone Pompucci, Italy, 1996, 83 mins.

The Monster
A blockbuster runaway hit in Italy, Roberto Benigni (*Down by Law*) directed this hilarious comedy in which he stars as a small-time con-man, pegged as a big-time serial killer, who is forced to find the real murderers before the cops find him. With Roberto Benigni, Michel Blanc and Nicoletta Braschi. "Hysterical...A genius at work" (Kenneth Turan, *Los Angeles Times*). Italian with English subtitles.
VHS: S31417. $98.99.
Roberto Benigni, Italy, 1996, 111 mins.

A Night Full of Rain
Candice Bergen is a feminist. Giancarlo Giannini (*New York Stories*) is a journalist. Their marriage becomes a battle royale of the sexes in this fierce and fun drama which was Lina Wertmuller's first English language film. Shot on location in Italy and San Francisco.
VHS: S13801. $19.98.
Lina Wertmuller, Italy, 1978, 104 mins.

Night Porter
Controversial film about the perverse relationship between a former SS officer from a Nazi concentration camp and a woman, a former inmate at the camp. From one of Italy's few women directors, with Dirk Bogarde and Charlotte Rampling. English dialog. VHS letterboxed.
VHS: S00934. $19.98.
Liliana Cavani, Italy, 1973, 117 mins.

Open Doors
Gian Maria Volonte stars as a conscientious judge assigned to a notorious murder case in Palermo during the reign of Mussolini. He believes there is more to the story than the self-confessed killer of three is willing to admit—and boy, is he right. Starring Ennio Fantastichini, Renzo Giovampietro and Renato Carpentieri. This rewarding, thoughtful drama was nominated for an Oscar as Best Foreign Language Film. Italian with English subtitles.
VHS: S14786. $19.98.
Gianni Amelio, Italy, 1989, 109 mins.

Palombella Rossa
Director Nanni Moretti's political comedy about the fate of Italian communism. The action follows a politician who is injured in a car crash and suffers from amnesia. He awakens to find himself about to play an important water polo match. While his teammates negotiate positions and devise strategies, he leaps out of the pool to interview a succession of bureaucrats, partyhacks and militants. "The scope of its concerns, and Moretti's ability to express these in visual terms, is ambitious and accomplished" (*Toronto Festival of Festivals*). Italian with English subtitles.
VHS: S19975. $19.98.
Nanni Moretti, Italy, 1989, 87 mins.

The Pool Hustlers
Recent Italian comedy about the fascinating world of big time billiards. A small-time wizard with a stick and balls proves to be a great irritation to the established champion, but still has time for romance. With Francesco Nuti, Giuliana de Sio, and Marcello Loti. Italian with English subtitles.
VHS: S08709. $24.95.
Maurizio Ponzi, Italy, 1983, 101 mins.

Rorret
An Italian reconsideration of Michael Powell's classic Peeping Tom and several Hitchcock thrillers, this film concerns the shy, anonymous owner of a repertory theater expressly devoted to thrillers and horror movies. Mr. Rorret lives behind the movie screen, documenting the responses of the women watching the films, and begins to stalk them. The film beautifully recreates moments from Hitchcock's *Psycho, Dial M for Murder,* and *Strangers on a Train*. "Good, creepy fun" (*New York Post*).
VHS: S17396. $29.95.
Fulvio Wetzl, Italy, 1987, 105 mins.

Running Away
Sophia Loren and Sydney Penny star as an Italian mother and daughter who flee World War II Rome in hopes of finding safety in the ancestral mountain village. The journey proves perilous and echoes Loren's Oscar-winning role in *Two Women*. With Robert Loggia, Andrea Occhipinti and Carla Calo. Based on the novel by Alberto Moravia.
VHS: S13271. $89.95.
Dino Risi, Italy/USA, 1989, 101 mins.

Sacco and Vanzetti
The legalized persecution and murder of anarchists Sacco and Vanzetti was an event that stunned the world. A story of rebellion and heroism. A story of an American dream and an American lie. With Gian Maria Valante and Riccardo Cucciola. In English.
VHS: S34204. $19.95.
Giuliano Montaldo, Italy, 1971, 120 mins.

Scent of a Woman (Profumo di Donna)
The original, award-winning Italian version of the comedy-drama was directed by Dino Risi and stars Vittorio Gassman in a tour-de-force performance as a blind and embittered army captain who undertakes a tour of Italy acccompanied by his young aide (Alessandro Momo). At first his adventures seem innocent and amusing, but as the two men travel through Genoa and Rome, a darker purpose is revealed. With Agostina Belli. Italian with English subtitles.
VHS: S08780. $89.95.
Dino Risi, Italy, 1974, 103 mins.

The Seduction of Mimi
Lina Wertmuller's Cannes Award-winning, sexy political farce about Mimi, a Sicilian laborer whose life is turned upside down as a result of not voting for the Mafia's candidate in a local selection. With Giancarlo Giannini. "An extremely funny domestic comedy not to be missed." (*Daily News*). Italian with English subtitles.
VHS: S31674. $29.98.
DVD: DV60281. $29.95.
Lina Wertmuller, Italy, 1972, 89 mins.

Seven Beauties
Giancarlo Giannini plays Pasqualino Frafuso, an aspiring small-time gangster whose moral conscience is constantly overcome by his driving instincts for survival. His efforts lead him from jail to mental hospital to concentration camp, and with each departure he thinks he has left the worst behind. A huge success in the U.S., *Seven Beauties* features first-rate performances from Giannini and Fernando Rey. Italian with English subtitles.
VHS: S01181. $59.95.
Lina Wertmuller, Italy, 1976, 111 mins.

The Sleazy Uncle
Franco Brusati's poetic film about an eccentric man, Luca (Vittorio Gassman), whose charm and grace gain the attention of his emotionally rigid, wealthy nephew, Ricardo (Giancarlo Giannini). With wit and sureness of detail, the old man insinuates himself deeper and deeper into the younger man's life. "Outrageous but poetic" (*The New York Times*). Italian with English subtitles.
VHS: S17363. $89.95.
Franco Brusati, Italy, 1990, 104 mins.

Smugglers
Adventure story of a group of smugglers during the Russian Revolution, who profit from the hardships created by the fighting and must avoid both sides in the conflict. Dubbed in English.
VHS: S04776. $59.95.
Valintino Orsini, Italy, 1975, 110 mins.

Sotto...Sotto
Comedy from Wertmuller commenting on the battle between the sexes, as Oscar's wife tells him she is in love with another. He never suspects it is with her friend Adele. Italian with English subtitles.
VHS: S01234. $19.95.
Lina Wertmuller, Italy, 1984, 104 mins.

The Star Maker
From the director of *Cinema Paradiso* comes this story of Joe Morelli "the Star Maker," a con man who travels from village to village posing as a talent scout for a big movie studio. The chance he offers to simple people causes them to open up and share their innermost feelings. Joe is content to live off the gullible until he meets a woman who changes his life. In Italian with English subtitles.
VHS: S29968. $19.98.
Laser: LD76013. $39.99.
Giuseppe Tornatore, Italy, 1989, 107 mins.

Stephano Quantestorie
Muarizio Nichetti, creator of *The Icicle Thief*, also created this film in which he once again plays a lead comic role. The beautiful prime suspect in a robbery becomes the touchstone for an imaginative policman (Nichetti). Soon he imagines a whole slew of scenarios where his life would be radically different because he cannot reconcile his professional duties with his desires for the female suspect. When these different personas break free, pandemonium results. In Italian with English subtitles.
VHS: S28388. $59.95.
Maurizio Nichetti, Italy, 1993, 90 mins.

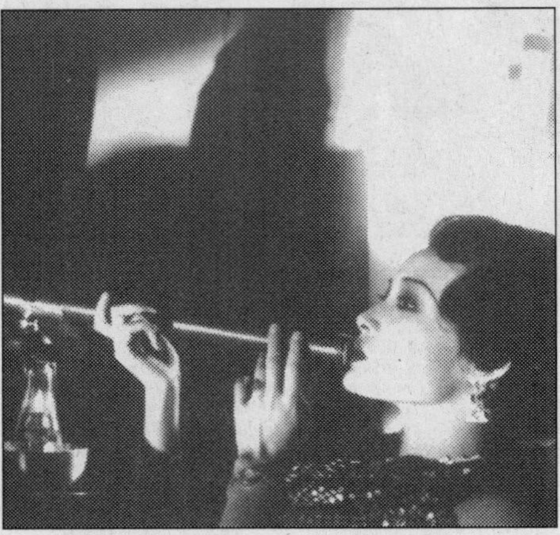

The Story of Boys and Girls
The engagement of two young lovers brings together an intoxicating mix of friends and family. Between the 20 delicious courses and flowing wine, the guests loosen their belts as well as their tongues, spilling family secrets and revealing romantic intrigues. Even the maid gets caught in a lusty tryst that leaves her flushed and rumpled when she serves the next dish. Italian with English subtitles.
VHS: S16525. $19.98.
Pupi Avati, Italy, 1991, 92 mins.

Summer Night (With Greek Profile, Almond Eyes and Scent of Basil)
Director Lina Wertmuller loves those long titles. She also wrote the rest of the script, which concerns a very rich member of the Italian ruling class who kidnaps a noted terrorist and holds *him* for ransom. This change of pace leads to smoldering passion on an island estate. With Mariangela Melato and Michele Placido. Italian with English subtitles.
VHS: S05612. $79.95.
Lina Wertmuller, Italy, 1987, 97 mins.

Swept Away
Raffaella, a rich, beautiful, acid-tongued Milanese who has chartered a yacht, and Gennarino, a swarthy Sicilian deckhand, are marooned on an isolated island in the Mediterranean. She is a capitalist for whom the system has paid off, he is a dedicated Communist. *Swept Away* is the story of their tumultuous courtship, in what one critic described as a "fierce battle of the sexes as witty as it is wise." Letterboxed. Italian with , English subtitles.
VHS: S01290. $29.98.
Laser: LD75999. $49.95.
DVD: DV60125. $29.98.
Lina Wertmuller, Italy, 1975, 116 mins.

Terranova
Set in 1950s Venezuela, *Terranova* captures the intensity of a turning point in the lives of six characters whose often conflictive and painful relationships become a metaphor for the challenges of self-acceptance and the inevitable consequences of self-discovery. With Antonio Banderas. Spanish with English subtitles.
VHS: S31737. $79.95.
Calogero Salvo, Venezuela/Italy, 1991, 96 mins.

Tigers in Lipstick
Veteran Italian comedy director Luigi Zampa in an omnibus of seven stories about aggressive women who take advantage of their men. With Ursula Andress, Monica Vitti, Laura Antonelli, Sylvia Kristel, Michele Placido, Roberto (*Down by Law*) Benigni. In English.
VHS: S07439. $39.95.
Luigi Zampa, Italy, 1979, 83 mins.

Tosca's Kiss
The remarkable film by Daniel Schmid, set in the Casa Verdi, the musicians' retirement home set up by Giuseppe Verdi in 1902. Funny, poignant, sensitive, inspiring—"one of the most insightful, life-affirming and just plain entertaining movies." Italian with English subtitles.
VHS: S01365. $39.95.
Daniel Schmid, Italy, 1985, 87 mins.

The Tree of Wooden Clogs
A passionate, moving film, an epic celebration of an Italian family's indomitable spirit, winner of the Grand Prize at the 1978 Cannes Film Festival. The subject of the film is peasant life in northern Italy at the turn of the century, focusing on about a year in the life of three families living on a feudal estate. "A quiet masterpiece" (*Newsweek*). "The movie, which runs slightly more than three hours, is an accumulation of dozens of experiences of children, adults, old people, village idiots, of harvest times and plantings, of moments of boredom and jealousy, celebrations, fatigue, brief pleasures and mysterious ones. It moves so effortlessly, often with great humor and always with compassion, it seems much shorter than most 90-minute films" (Vincent Canby, *New York Times*). Italian with English subtitles.
VHS: S12946. $19.98.
Ermanno Olmi, Italy, 1978, 185 mins.

Vito and the Others
A chilling depiction of the street life of the neglected who pass through the extreme poverty of Naples. The realistic, documentary-like plot centers on a 12-year-old boy and his friends, drawn into the netherworld of crime, drugs and prostitution. With Nando Triola, Giovanni Bruno and Mario Lentl. Italian with English subtitles.
VHS: S18752. $69.95.
Antonio Capuano, Italy, 1992, 90 mins.

Volere Volare
Maurizio Nichetti collaborated with animator Guido Manuli in this inventive comedy that blends live action and animation. The story concerns the nervous and complicated romance of a shy special effects technician, Maurizio (Nichetti), and Martina (Angela Finocchiaro), a beautiful actress who dramatizes bizarre sexual fantasies for a group of strange clients. Complications ensue when Maurizio's body is transformed into the form and shape of a cartoon, assuming its own will. With Patrizio Roversi and Mariella Valentini. Italian with English subtitles.
VHS: S19205. $19.95.
Laser: CLV. LD72102. $39.95.
Maurizio Nichetti/Guido Manuli, Italy, 1991, 92 mins.

When Women Had Tails
Lina Wertmuller co-wrote the screenplay of this slapstick farce about a group of prehistoric cave dwellers. With Senta Berger, Giuliano Gemma, Frank Wolff and Lando Buzzanca. Italian with English subtitles.
VHS: S17734. $29.95.
Pasquale Festa Campanile, Italy, 1970, 110 mins.

Where's Piccone?
A wonderful, very funny film from the Italian comic genius Nanni Loy, starring the incomparable Giancarlo Giannini. The search is on for Pasquale Piccone, who inexplicably vanishes in an ambulance on the way to the hospital. His wife and small-time hustler Giannini team up to discover the mystery and together find that this respectable man has lead a double life. A fantastic, comic voyage into the Neapolitan underworld. Italian with English subtitles.
VHS: S05168. $29.95.
Nanni Loy, Italy, 1985, 110 mins.

Zuppa di Pesce (Fish Soup)

Set between the 1950s and late '70s against the beauty of the Tuscany seaside, *Fish Soup* offers small sketches of family behavior and psychology, from gatherings to complicated relationships. Narrating with a rare balance of frankness, naturalness and tenderness, Infascelli reveals a Chekhovian understanding of family relationships as we follow the development of Isabella (Chiara Caselli) and her relationship with her father (Philippe Noiret) and family. With Macha Meril, Andrea Prodan, Renzo Montagnani and Fausto Fiorentini. "A family-size *Amarcord* set of recollections" (*L'Avvenire*). Italian with English subtitles.

VHS: S32622. $29.95.
Fiorella Infascelli, Italy/France, 1991, 107 mins.

BERNARDO BERTOLUCCI

1900

Bernardo Bertolucci's opus, a sweeping, epic achievement which chronicles the rise of Fascism and Socialism in Italy through the interlocking stories of family generations. The stellar cast includes Robert De Niro and Gerard Depardieu as two friends torn apart by the political upheavals in their country, Dominique Sanda, Stefania Sandrelli, Donald Sutherland and Alberto Grimaldi. A work of massive scope, brilliance and power, Pauline Kael said Bertolucci "is trying to make a people's film by drawing on the mythology of the movies, as if it were a collective memory. *1900* is a romantic moviegoer's version of the class struggle—a love poem for the movies as well as for the life of those who live communally on the land." English dialog.

VHS: S06845. $29.95.
Bernardo Bertolucci, Italy, 1977, 245 mins.

Before the Revolution

Bernardo Bertolucci's timelessly lyrical affirmation of youth's rites of passage through love and politics. A young man rejects his middle-class surroundings and struggles with the Communist ideology to which he believes himself committed, only to find that he is too deeply involved with the beauty of life as it was before the revolution. Made when Bertolucci was only 22 years old, *Before the Revolution* was the revelation of the 1964 New York Film Festival. Italian with English subtitles.

VHS: S07500. $29.95.
Bernardo Bertolucci, Italy, 1962, 110 mins.

The Conformist

Bertolucci equates the rise of Italian fascism with the psychosexual life of his protagonist, for whom conformity becomes an obsession after a traumatic homosexual experience in his youth. A dazzling descent into the nature of corruption of power, with many now-famous sequences and extraordinary cinematography by Vittorio Storaro. With Jean-Louis Trintignant, Dominique Sanda and Stefania Sandrelli. English dubbed.

Laser: LD75355. $29.98.
Bernardo Bertolucci, Italy, 1970, 108 mins.

The Grim Reaper

Rarely since *Citizen Kane* has a film debut by a director conveyed such promise. Like *Rashomon*, *The Grim Reaper* brilliantly explores the many sides to the truth of a brutal murder of a prostitute in a Rome Park. Bernardo Bertolucci delves into the dark underbelly of brute poverty, creating a tense tapestry of behavior and a challenging puzzle which leaves us celebrating life in all is pain, joy and humor. Italian with English subtitles.

VHS: S13280. $29.95.
Bernardo Bertolucci, Italy, 1962, 100 mins.

The Last Emperor

Bernardo Bertolucci's multiple Academy-award winner, set and shot in Beijing's Forbidden City, stars John Lone as Pu Yi, the last emperor of China who, at the age of three, became the "Lord of 10,000 Years," China's last emperor. In English.

VHS: S07372. $29.98.
Bernardo Bertolucci, Italy/USA, 1987, 140 mins.

Last Tango in Paris

Powerful, explosive, erotic, political film that took the world by storm; Maria Schneider and Marlon Brando co-star in this film of love, sex and will. "The most powerfully erotic film ever made," wrote Pauline Kael. "*Last Tango* is a genuine masterpiece of staggering proportions," said *Newsweek*. English dialog. Uncut, X-rated version.

VHS: S00727. $19.98.
Laser: CLV, 2 discs, Criterion. **LD70412. $69.95.**
Laser: Letterboxed, MGM. **LD71176. $39.98.**
Bernardo Bertolucci, Italy, 1974, 129 mins.

Little Buddha

Keanu Reeves and Bridget Fonda star in this sweeping tale of destiny and mysticism. Chris Isaak is a young American boy whose life is transformed forever when he becomes involved with a prince searching for the reincarnation of his beloved teacher. As these different worlds collide, an extraordinary adventure unfolds.

VHS: S22604. $19.95.
Laser: LD74641. $39.99.
Bernardo Bertolucci, Great Britain, 1994, 123 mins.

Partner

Bertolucci's third feature film is a beautiful, funny adventure that uses sound, silence, music, color and an extremely literary frame of reference to create a two-hour sense of the impression of what it's like to be a romantic in today's world. The screenplay by Bertolucci and Gianni Amico is very freely inspired by Dostoevsky's short novel, *The Double*, about an ineffectual young man who is taken over—and ultimately driven to madness—by his alter ego, who can do all the things he cannot. Italian with English subtitles.

VHS: S08263. $39.95.
Bernardo Bertolucci, Italy, 1968, 112 mins.

The Sheltering Sky

John Malkovich and Debra Winger star as an unfortunate pair of American tourists adrift in the deserts of North Africa. Bernardo Bertolucci brings this Paul Bowles novel to the screen and tries his best to capture in images, the words and intentions of the author. Vincent Canby called this "Bertolucci's most seductive, most hypnotic movie." With Campbell Scott, Jill Bennett, Timothy Spall and Eric Vu-An.

VHS: S13753. $19.98.
Laser: LD70674. $39.98.
Bernardo Bertolucci, USA, 1990, 139 mins.

The Spider's Stratagem

The breakthrough film of Bertolucci is an extremely atmospheric puzzler, based on a short story by Jorge Luis Borges. A young man visits the provincial town where his anti-Fascist father was assassinated 30 years earlier, and is rejected by the populace at every turn. With Giulio Brogi and Alida Valli, and beautiful cinematography by Vittorio Storaro. Italian with English subtitles.

VHS: S12827. $29.95.
Bernardo Bertolucci, Italy, 1970, 97 mins.

Stealing Beauty

Filmed on location in Italy, a beautiful 19-year-old comes to spend the summer with her late mother's friends. Her mission is to consummate her romance with an Italian boy she met four years earlier and to discover her father's identity through clues in her mother's diary. This lushly filmed romantic adventure, written by Susan Minot, co-stars Jeremy Irons and Sinead Cusack.

VHS: S28480. $99.99.
Laser: LD75958. $39.98.
Bernardo Bertolucci, Italy, 1996, 119 mins.

Tragedy of a Ridiculous Man

The seriocomic tale of a sudden kidnapping that jolts a family into togetherness. Ugo Tognazzi portrays the rich Parma dairy farmer forced to sell his possessions to meet the ransom demanded by the terrorist gang holding his son. Bertolucci examines the siege mentality of Italy's leftist brigades and strips the mask off family dynamics hidden behind webs of deceit. "The best Bertolucci movie…in a long time. The best treatment of the generation gap between a father and son that I have yet seen" (Andrew Sarris).

VHS: S13803. $59.99.
Bernardo Bertolucci, Italy, 1981, 116 mins.

TAVIANI BROTHERS

Allonsanfan

Marcello Mastroianni stars in a comic masterpiece making use of bravura lighting and color schemes. Set after Napoleon has fallen in 1816, the film features Martroianni as a disillusioned Jacobin aristocrat released from prison and torn between his revolutionary ideals and comfortable lifestyle. With Laura Betti, Lea Massari. Italian with English subtitles.

VHS: S05167. $29.95.
Paolo Taviani/Vittorio Taviani, Italy, 1984, 115 mins.

Fiorile (Wild Flower)

In the orange groves of Italy, the Benedetti family preserves their time-honored ways, including the curse that has followed them for generations. In this provocative tale, greed, lust, romance and forbidden love stalk the unsuspecting members of this clan in a warmly nostalgic look at the process of history. Italian with English subtitles.

VHS: S21211. $19.95.
Paolo Taviani/Vittorio Taviani, Italy, 1993, 118 mins.

Night of the Shooting Stars

This magical film by the Taviani Brothers is set on the night of the Feast of St. Lawrence during the last days of World War II. A woman recalls her beloved and a night years ago when, on another such night, a group of peasants fled through the Tuscan countryside amid exploding shells lighting up the sky instead of stars. The film is a beautiful tapestry of fact, myth and wartime memory, romantic and intense. Italian with English subtitles.

VHS: S00933. $19.98.
Paolo Taviani/Vittorio Taviani, Italy, 1982, 106 mins.

Padre Padrone

A shepherd boy from the backwaters of Sardinia molds himself into a linguistic scholar. This simple tale forms the foundation of one of the most important recent Italian films—a major statement on the third world cycle of poverty. Using non-actors for its cast, the film won universal acclaim and the Grand Prize at the Cannes Film Festival. Italian with English subtitles.

VHS: S00986. $19.98.
Paolo Taviani/Vittorio Taviani, Italy, 1977, 117 mins.

St. Michael Had a Rooster

The Taviani Brothers construct a powerful parable about revolution and freedom in this beautiful, rarely-seen adaptation of a story by Tolstoy. Set in 19th-century Italy, Giulio Brogi plays Giulio Manieri, a romantic idealist and leader of a group of anarchists. Captured and condemned to death, Manieri firmly believes in his political convictions while in prison. After 10 years, he meets a group of young revolutionaries who tell him the movement has changed and his beliefs are no longer valid. Feeling he has wasted ten years of his life, Manieri finds himself unable to function in the new outside world. Italian with English subtitles.

VHS: S32983. $79.95.
Paolo Taviani/Vittorio Taviani, Italy, 1971, 87 mins.

MICHELANGELO ANTONIONI

Blow-Up

The classic film questioning the relationship between image and reality; David Hemmings plays a fashion photographer who photographs a woman (Vanessa Redgrave) in a park and later comes to believe that he has actually photographed a murder. Through the photograph, Hemmings is lured out of his life to search for the truth. English dialog.

VHS: S00152. $19.98.
Laser: CAV, widescreen, 2 discs, Criterion. **LD70351. $79.95.**
Laser: Extended play, chapter search, MGM. **LD70528. $34.98.**
Michelangelo Antonioni, Great Britain, 1966, 111 mins.

Eclipse

The third of Antonioni's great trilogy, with Monica Vitti the alienated woman among the upper bourgeoisie. A brilliant film, with its stupefying climax of silence, comprised of 58 shots lasting 7 minutes. Italian with English subtitles.

VHS: S00393. $29.95.
Michelangelo Antonioni, Italy, 1966, 123 mins.

Il Grido

Alida Valli and Steve Cochran are featured in the story of a jilted husband who wanders with his daughter from village to village and woman to woman until, after a last gaze at his wife, he falls to his death. Set in the desolate landscapes of Antonioni's own childhood in the Po Valley, the plot "develops no longer explicitly through major events but implicitly in silent interstices between minor events" (Seymour Chatman). A breakthrough work from Antonioni's neo-realist period. Italian with English subtitles.

VHS: S09655. $24.95.
Michelangelo Antonioni, Italy, 1957, 116 mins.

L'Avventura

A film about the fragility of human relationships which established Antonioni as a major talent. A party of rich Italians land on an uninhabited island, and one young woman disappears. "Our drama is non-communication," said Antonioni, "and it is this feeling that dominates the characters in my film." With Monica Vitti. Winner of the Special Jury Award at Cannes. Italian with English subtitles.

VHS: S00696. $29.95.
Laser: LD70342. $124.95.
Michelangelo Antonioni, Italy, 1960, 145 mins.

La Notte

The second installment of Italian director Michelangelo Antonioni's trilogy. Jeanne Moreau plays a bored, dissatisfied woman who abandons her simple minded husband (Marcello Mastroianni), who in turn attempts to seduce a beautiful, vacant woman (Monica Vitti). Moody, introverted and beautiful, brilliantly photographed by Gianni Di Venanzo. Italian with English subtitles.
VHS: S14850. $39.95.
Michelangelo Antonioni, Italy, 1961, 122 mins.

Mystery of Oberwald

A daring—previously unreleased—film experiment, shot by Antonioni on video, then transferred to 35mm. Based on the melodramatic play (on which Cocteau based his *Eagle Has Two Heads*), the central character, the Queen (the great Monica Vitti), is in hiding ten years after the assassination of her husband, Prince Ferdinand. She gives refuge to a fleeing anarchist poet who happens to resembleher dead husband and becomes her "angel of death" and her lover. Italian with English subtitles.
VHS: S35297. $79.95.
Michelangelo Antonioni, Italy, 1980, 129 mins.

Red Desert

Antonioni's masterpiece, with the great Monica Vitti playing the neurotic young woman married to an engineer in the industrial wasteland of northern Italy, searching in vain for meaning in life. Antonioni's first film in color—and what color! One of the most important films of the last half of the century. Italian with English subtitles.
VHS: S02080. $29.95.
Michelangelo Antonioni, Italy, 1964, 116 mins.

Zabriskie Point

Antonioni's portrait of revolutionary America of the 1960's; a disquieting, visually stunning film about two American young people of the 60's, faced with American commercialism, consumerism and the need to find oneself. With Mark Frechette and Daria Halprin. English dialog.
VHS: S01497. $19.98.
Laser: LD70721. $34.98.
Michelangelo Antonioni, USA, 1970, 112 mins.

ETTORE SCOLA

The Family

Nominated for Best Foreign film, this Ettore Scola drama about 80 years in the life of a middle-class family in Rome has absolutely nothing to do with the Charles Bronson mafia movie of the same name. Vittorio Gassman heads an abundant cast of Italian actors that include Stefania Sandrelli and Ricky Tognazzi. Also non-Italian actors like Fanny Ardant and Philippe Noiret. A note of interest: the camera never leaves the house. Italian with English subtitles.
VHS: S08231. $19.98.
Ettore Scola, Italy, 1986, 128 mins.

Le Bal

A unique experiment: adapted freely from an enormously successful French stage play, *Le Bal* is a non-talking movie set in a dance hall over a period of 50 years of French history. Through the marathon of waltzes, foxtrots, tangos, boogie steps, twists, cha-chas, rhumbas, the dancers reflect changing styles and mores in an energetic fresco. French with English subtitles.
VHS: S00733. $79.95.
Ettore Scola, Italy/France, 1982, 112 mins.

Macaroni

Marcello Mastroianni and Jack Lemmon star in this film about two World War II buddies who are re-united in Italy amidst a secret, fictitious love affair Antonio has created for his sister with his American friend. In English and some Italian.
VHS: S04955. $79.95.
Ettore Scola, Italy, 1985, 104 mins.

Passione d'Amore

This story of obsessive love between an ugly spinster and a handsome young officer won the Cannes Special Jury Prize in 1981 and is notable for its strong performances from the sensuous Laura Antonelli and Jean-Louis Trintignant. Mad and consumed by desire, this woman manages to overcome the officer's reservations. Steven Sondheim's Tony-award winning musical *Passion* is based on this story. Italian with English subtitles.
VHS: S22231. $24.95.
Ettore Scola, Italy, 1981, 117 mins.

FEDERICO FELLINI

8½

Fellini's great autobiographical masterpiece, the loose portrayal of a film director during the course of making a film and finding himself trapped by his fears and insecurities. Continually inventive, with the performance of a lifetime from Marcello Mastroianni as Guido, the director, and from Claudia Cardinale, Anouk Aimee and Sandra Milo. Italian with English subtitles.
VHS: S07140. $59.95.
Laser: Widescreen. **LD70806. $59.95.**
Federico Fellini, Italy, 1963, 138 mins.

Amarcord

A film which breathes freedom—a nostalgic, fantastic and funny reminiscence of growing up in Fellini's home town of Rimini—made, Fellini said, to finish with youth and tenderness. Against the comic background are sets of indelible characters and an omnipresent Fascist state. *Amarcord* breathlessly shifts between the melodramatic, the intimate and the burlesque in what is a deeply personal, shared vision. The images—a peacock flying through the snow, a child on his way to school who encounters cows that the early-morning fog has transformed into monsters—are like icons; unforgettable. Italian with English subtitles.
VHS: S00042. $39.95.
Laser: LD75072. $69.95.
DVD: DV60173. $39.95.
Federico Fellini, Italy, 1974, 127 mins.

Ciao Federico!

A revealing portrait of Fellini at work, directing the actors who populate the unreal world of his *Satyricon*. Immersed in the creative process, Fellini moves through the set, a larger than life embodiment of his characters. English and Italian with English subtitles.
VHS: S00242. $19.95.
Gideon Bachmann, Italy, 1971, 55 mins.

City of Women

Federico Fellini's imaginative voyage into the world of women-or, more accurately, into the world of male fantasies about women, set adrift in the threatening seas of middle-age and feminism. Part apocalyptic joyride, part funhouse, part dream, part vaudeville, *City of Women* stars Marcello Mastroianni in an outlandish work of fantasy and humor. Italian with enhanced English subtitles.
VHS: S11591. $79.95.
Federico Fellini, Italy, 1980, 138 mins.

The Clowns

Fellini's homage to circus clowns is in itself a clownish spoof as it invades the screen with three rings of slapstick, spectacle and sensation. "My films owe an enormous amount to the circus," said Fellini. "For me the clowns were always a traumatic visual experience, ambassadors of a vocation of a showman." This affectionate journey to the root of Fellini's inspiration is comic and magically moving, with one of the best musical scores by the great Nino Rota.
VHS: S00253. $34.95.
Federico Fellini, Italy, 1971, 90 mins.

Fellini Satyricon

Federico Fellini freely adapts the work of Petronius Arbiter in this sexual odyssey through ancient Rome. With an emphasis on spectacle and the grotesque, we follow two young Romans in their pursuit of pleasure and personal survival. With Martin Potter, Hiram Keller, Capucine and Luigi Montefiori as the Minotaur. Letterboxed. Italian with English subtitles.
VHS: S06318. $19.98.
Laser: Widescreen. **LD70979. $124.95.**
Federico Fellini, Italy, 1969, 138 mins.

Fellini's Roma

"A story of a city," to quote Fellini. In *Roma*, Fellini strings together a series of images of Rome, and through his eyes this special city becomes a living, breathing organism. *Roma* is quite possibly Fellini's most avowedly autobiographical film to date—a loving document of his own personal encounter with Rome. Starring Fiona Florence, Britta Barnes, Pia de Doses, Marne Maitland and Peter Gonzales as Fellini at 18. Italian with English subtitles.
VHS: S14807. $19.99.
Laser: LD72120. $49.98.
Federico Fellini, Italy, 1972, 128 mins.

Fellini: A Director's Notebook

In this autobiographical work, the touch of Fellini is everywhere. The film begins with a trip to the set of the never-completed *The Voyage of Mastorna*. Then it shows some of the real elements that inspired the later *Satyricon*, including a subway tour of ancient Rome and some odd characters who might be used in the film. In addition, clips from previous works show Gulietta Massina and Marcello Mastroianni.
VHS: S27768. $29.95.
Federico Fellini, USA/Italy, 1970, 60 mins.

Ginger and Fred

A warm, touching satire not only of television, but of lost hopes and idealism, and of the impossibility of love in the face of blatant commercialism. Giulietta Masina and Marcello Mastroianni are two retired Astaire and Rogers imitators who are reunited after thirty years for a nostalgic TV variety show. Italian with English subtitles.
VHS: S02526. $19.98.
Federico Fellini, Italy, 1986, 128 mins.

I Vitelloni

The young, restless men in a small town on the Adriatic are, each in his own way, discontent. They spend their time pursuing diversion and girls, vaguely dreaming impossible pipe dreams. This brilliant, acid-sharp look at a generation nevertheless reveals Fellini's affection for his characters. The film "is the story of adolescents who cannot see anything more in life than satisfying their animal desires, sleeping, eating, fornication. I was trying to say there is something more, there is always more. Life must have a meaning beyond the animal" (Fellini). Italian with English subtitles.
VHS: S00601. $59.95.
Federico Fellini, Italy, 1953, 104 mins.

Il Bidone

Three small-time crooks run scams on the poor by disguising themselves as priests, in this film that begins as a comedy and turns tragic. When one of them tries to double-cross the others, they beat him up and leave him to die on a stony hillside. In a powerful final sequence, he finds salvation before he dies. With Broderick Crawford, Franco Fabrizi, Giulietta Masina and Richard Basehart. English title: *The Swindle*. Italian with English subtitles.
VHS: S10873. $69.95.
Federico Fellini, Italy, 1955, 92 mins.

Intervista

Fellini's movie combines the film-within-a-film, the essay memoir, a playful recollection of previous works and an eerie conflating of the past and present in this surreal and imaginative distillation of a man's life and work. As Fellini prepares to adapt Kafka's *Amerika*, his every move and gesture is captured by a Japanese documentary crew. The structure allows Fellini to delve into his past, with visits from Marcello Mastroianni and Anita Ekberg and profound remembrances of *La Dolce Vita*. "An enchanting work, a magical mixture of recollection, parody, memoir, satire, self-examination, and joyous fantasy with Fellini himself as the master of ceremonies" (Vincent Canby, *New York Times*). Italian with English subtitles.
VHS: S18583. $89.95.
Federico Fellini, Italy, 1987, 109 mins.

Juliet of the Spirits

"Within a simple, naively romantic narrative frame concerning a wife's desperation over her husband's philanderings, director Federico Fellini has put together an imperial-size fantasy of a physical opulence to make the old Vincente Minnelli musicals look like Army training films," wrote Vincent Canby. Newly mastered from a beautiful print. Italian with English subtitles.
VHS: S11178. $29.95.
Federico Fellini, Italy, 1965, 146 mins.

La Dolce Vita

"A landmark of cinematic social comment," wrote one critic about Fellini's journey through a decadent Rome. Banned by the Church in many countries, the sensationalism of the film often obscured its serious intent. *La Dolce Vita* follows a society journalist (Marcello Mastroianni) through a nightmarish world in which emotions have been destroyed by surface realities, moral conventions and unresolved guilt. With Anita Ekberg, Anouk Aimee, Alain Cuny and Nadia Gray. Italian with English subtitles.
VHS: S00705. $24.95.
Federico Fellini, Italy, 1961, 174 mins.

La Strada

Fellini's masterpiece. Giulietta Masina plays Gelsomina, a tragic waif sold to play clown to travelling show strongman Zampano (Anthony Quinn). "Simplicity itself, *La Strada* is a magical tale and an unbearably painful account of loneliness which will always be associated with the sublimely Chaplinesque Masina…but Quinn, too, is superb, particularly in the final revelation of his own heartbreak and isolation." With Richard Basehart and Aldo Silvani. Italian with English subtitles.
VHS: S00712. $29.95.
Laser: LD71088. $49.95.
Federico Fellini, Italy, 1954, 107 mins.

Nights of Cabiria

The third of Fellini's trilogy of solitude, *Nights of Cabiria* features Giuletta Masina as an impoverished prostitute living on the outskirts of Rome, who is betrayed by her faith in human nature. Winner of the Academy Award for Best Foreign Film, Masina's performance is one of the great performances on film. Italian with English subtitles.
VHS: S18582. $39.95.
Federico Fellini, Italy, 1957, 110 mins.

Orchestra Rehearsal

Fellini's comic and controversial made-for-TV vignette depicts the turmoil of Italian society through events that take place during a rehearsal gathering set in a 13th-century chapel. "Gloriously funny... [Fellini's] very best work" (*The New York Times*).
VHS: S32614. $79.98.
DVD: DV60167. $29.98.
Federico Fellini, Italy/Germany, 1979, 72 mins.

Spirits of the Dead

Jane and Peter Fonda, Alain Delon, Brigitte Bardot and Terence Stamp are among the stars cast in this adaptation of three Edgar Allan Poe tales. The three episodes are *Metzerngerstein*, directed by Roger Vadim; *William Wilson*, directed by Louis Malle; and Fellini's brilliant *Toby Dammit*. In the first, the Fonda siblings are involved in a macabre tale built around incestuous desire. The middle work concerns a sadistic fiend (Delon) who, among other things, whips the then-wildly famous Bardot. Finally, Stamp plays a movie star who loses his head and makes a bet with the devil, whom Fellini portrays, in a brilliant master stroke, as a beautiful little girl in a white dress. French with English subtitles.
VHS: S27647. $29.95.
Laser: Letterboxed. **LD76043. $39.98.**
DVD: DV60361. $29.99.
Roger Vadim/Louis Malle/Federico Fellini, France/Italy, 1968, 117 mins.

Variety Lights

Fellini's first, truly wonderful feature is the story of a group of second-rate theatrical performers on tour. The aging manager of the company falls in love with a newcomer, to the chagrin of his faithful mistress (Giulietta Masina). Though co-directed by Alberto Lattuada, "this is Fellini's film rather than Lattuada's. Already present in his special 'universe': his sense of irony, his baroque qualities, his sympathy for and delight in downtrodden eccentrics, and his portrait of 'bidones' striving comically to find themselves" (Georges Sadoul). Italian with English subtitles.
VHS: S07506. $29.95.
Laser: LD76742. $49.95.
Federico Fellini/Alberto Lattuada, Italy, 1952, 86 mins.

White Sheik

When a provincial couple go to Rome for their honeymoon, the bride sneaks off to the movie set where her idol, the White Sheik, is making a film. "Perhaps the freshest and the most tender and naturalistic of Fellini's films" (Pauline Kael). Italian with English subtitles.
VHS: S00135. $29.95.
Federico Fellini, Italy, 1952, 86 mins.

PIER PAOLO PASOLINI

Accatone!

A parable of redemption, set in the slums of Rome, Accatone "The Scrounger" (Franco Citti) lives as a thief, beggar and pimp. This is simply one of the most important films of the last 20 years, and a milestone in Italian filmmaking. He's in love with Stella, tries to reform her, but fails. *Accatone*, the debut film of Pier Paolo Pasolini, is notable for 'its rough-edged style, its cool, unhysterical portrait of corruption, cruelty, and violence, and its quiet lyricism marked one of the most significant directorial debuts of the sixties." (Georges Sadoul).
VHS: S11153. $39.95.
Pier Paolo Pasolini, Italy, 1961, 120 mins.

Arabian Nights

Pasolini's final film of his Trilogy of Life, *Arabian Nights* is a carnal comic tale following the adventures of a slave girl, Pelligrini, as she rises to power. "Rich, romantic and magnificent! Its graphic sex scenes, which have a dreamy kind of beauty to them, are erotic without being pornographic" (Vincent Canby). Italian with English subtitles.
VHS: S07021. $29.95.
Pier Paolo Pasolini, Italy, 1974, 130 mins.

The Canterbury Tales

A film which fits within the context of Pasolini's explorations of bawdy, historical classics (together with *Arabian Nights* and *Decameron*), Pasolini once again seeks out the exotic and controversial aspect of Chaucer's classic. In English.
VHS: S07821. $29.95.
Pier Paolo Pasolini, Italy, 1971, 109 mins.

The Decameron

The first part of Pasolini's great trilogy, based on the ribald tales of Boccaccio, which deal with human sensuality and artistic creation. Pasolini has re-fashioned the 100 tales into a collection of 11 sketches that is at the same time erotic, political, humorous and autobiographical. Pasolini himself appears in the role of the painter Giotto, and continues to use non-professional actors because, he said, he was fed up with the traditional cinema's "false language of realism." Italian with English subtitles.
VHS: S08260. $29.95.
DVD: DV60356. $29.99.
Pier Paolo Pasolini, Italy, 1970, 111 mins.

The Gospel According to St. Matthew

Non-actors, rugged Southern Italian landscapes and towns, cinema-verite techniques, expressive close-ups are some of the elements of Pasolini's moving sacred and mythic epic. His Christ is anguished, determined, a peripatetic preacher against the afflictions of social injustice, whose miracles are matter-of-fact. Italian with English subtitles.
VHS: S18168. $29.95.
Pier Paolo Pasolini, Italy, 1964, 136 mins.

Hawks and Sparrows

A wildly comic fable, with the great Italian stone-faced clown Toto playing Everyman and Ninetto Davoli, his good natured but empty-headed son. Pasolini uses a comic crow, which philosophizes amusingly and pointedly about the passing scene, as a counterpoint to the performers, representing humanity, as they progress down the road of life. The result is a major Pasolini film and a powerful, tragic fable which shows two delightful innocents caught, like many Italians, between the Church and Marxism. "Complex, mystical and fascinating" (*New York Times*). Italian with English subtitles.
VHS: S12351. $29.95.
Pier Paolo Pasolini, Italy, 1964, 88 mins.

Love Meetings

A witty and sensual investigation of sex in Italy, including impressive appearances by famed author Alberto Moravia and noted psychologist Cesare Musatti, conducted by Pier Paolo Pasolini. Pasolini appears as the interviewer with a wide range of individuals who share their tales of love—prostitution, homosexuality, marital and non-marital liaisons. Italian with English subtitles.
VHS: S12352. $29.95.
Pier Paolo Pasolini, Italy, 1964, 90 mins.

Mamma Roma

Anna Magnani gives a terrific performance in the title role of this key film. It was Pasolini's second feature but it is rarely seen. The story revolves around a former prostitute, played by Magnani, who gets a new chance for a different life. She does her best to help her son, Ettore, get ahead. He is mesmerized, however, by the evils of the big city, so she makes one last desperate attempt to get him a respectable job. Italian with English subtitles.
VHS: S26664. $79.95.
Pier Paolo Pasolini, Italy, 1963, 110 mins.

Medea

Soprano Maria Callas in a dramatic, non-musical interpretation of Euripides' tragedy. "Under Pasolini's direction, Callas becomes a fascinating cinematic presence, brilliant and brutal" (*NY Times*). Italian with English subtitles.
VHS: S00841. $49.95.
Pier Paolo Pasolini, Italy, 1970, 100 mins.

Oedipus Rex

One of the great films by Pasolini, which adds a prologue and epilogue to the play by Sophocles, was translated by Pasolini. The film adds much psychoanalytic insight to the Sophocles theme; Pasolini's intent was, he said, "to make a kind of completely metaphoric—and therefore mythicized-autobiography; and second, to confront both the problem of psychoanalysis and the problem of the myth." Italian with English subtitles.
VHS: S07333. $29.95.
Pier Paolo Pasolini, Italy, 1967, 110 mins.

Pigsty

A remarkable, late-period work from Pier Paolo Pasolini, *Pigsty* (*I Porcile*) brilliantly interweaves two storylines. In the first, a man wanders a medieval, war-ravaged countryside devouring the weak; in the second, a German youth's profound alienation leads him into a strange relationship with a group of pigs. With Jean-Pierre Leaud, Ugo Tognazzi, Pierre Clementi and Anne Wiazemsky. Italian with English subtitles. Letterboxed.
VHS: S18063. $29.95.
Pier Paolo Pasolini, USA, 1969, 100 mins.

Rogopag

The title reflects four brilliant European directors who contributed short films to this collection: Roberto Rossellini, Jean-Luc Godard, Pier Paolo Pasolini and Ugo Gregoretti. *Virginity*, by Rossellini, is a comic essay on the distinctions between illusion and reality. Orson Welles stars in Pasolini's *La Ricotta*, a satire about the debasement of religion. This film caused Pasolini to be charged and sentenced to prison for "insulting the religion of [Italy]." *The New World*, by Godard, offers a chilling view of Paris after a nuclear war. And in Gregoretti's *The Range Grown Chicken*, a family suffers the ravages of brain-washing consumerism. French and Italian with English subtitles.
VHS: S23995. $24.95.
Roberto Rossellini/Jean-Luc Godard/Pier Paolo Pasolini/Ugo Gregoretti, France/Italy, 1962, 122 mins.

Salo: 120 Days of Sodom

An extremely controversial film, the last work by Pier Paolo Pasolini. Loosely based on the book by the Marquis de Sade, Pasolini transplanted the setting to Mussolini's post-Nazi-fascist state of Salo. Pasolini creates a symbolic place where sexual joy and normality are punished while perversion is rewarded. The plot concerns eight fascists who round up 16 teenage boys and girls and, in a secluded villa, submit their hostages to various sadistic ordeals including rape, mutilation and murder. "Pasolini has intended the film to work on many different levels: an illustration of the moral anarchy of absolute power; the debasement of sexuality through violence; an exploration of victims as victimizers. The result is, alternately, surreal, harrowing, depressing, repulsive, and fascinating...a hellish journey through a sick soul." Contains nudity, explicit sexual situations and extreme graphic violence; for mature audiences only. Italian with English subtitles.
VHS: S11717. $89.95.
Laser: CLV. **LD72111. $49.95.**
Pier Paolo Pasolini, Italy, 1975, 115 mins.

Teorema

Pier Paolo Pasolini's breakthrough film, predicated on the theorem that "anything done by the bourgeoisie, however sincere and profound, and noble, is on the wrong track." Into the home of a classic bourgeois family walks in Terence Stamp, a stranger. Each one of the family—mother, father, son, daughter, maid-seeks and finds in the stranger a catalyst for the fulfillment of desire denied within the confines of the family structure. "Liberated thus by a moment of authenticity, each is left, on the visitor's departure, with a personal kind of madness, stripped naked in a symbolic desert." Italian with English subtitles.
VHS: S18193. $29.95.
Pier Paolo Pasolini, Italy, 1968, 93 mins.

Whoever Says the Truth Shall Die

A remarkable film on Pier Paolo Pasolini, poet, political personality, aesthetician and director of such important and controversial films as *Gospel According to St. Matthew* and *Oedipus Rex*. Director Bregstein explores whether Pasolini's murder at age 53 in 1975 was by Pino the Frog, a 17-year-old male prostitute, or an assassination by a group of right-wing fascists. English and Italian with English subtitles.
VHS: S02654. $59.95.
Philo Bregstein, Netherlands, 1981, 60 mins.

VITTORIO DE SICA

After the Fox

Peter Sellers is Italy's most wanted criminal, the Fox. He devises a scheme to enlist the aid of an entire coastal village to smuggle gold bullion, by posing as a movie director who needs local talent in his new picture. With Britt Eklund and Victor Mature. Script by Neil Simon.
VHS: S04589. $14.95.
Laser: LD76358. $39.99.
Vittorio de Sica, Great Britain/Italy, 1966, 103 mins.

The Bicycle Thief

Perhaps the single most important and moving film of Italian neo-realism, *Bicycle Thief* tells the deceptively simple story of an unemployed man finding work to paste up signs, work requiring a bicycle, which is then stolen. A landmark of cinema. Italian with English subtitles.
VHS: S00128. $69.95.
Laser: Original Italian dialog with English subtitles; analog track contains the English dubbed soundtrack. Includes theatrical trailer and the English dubbed version. **LD70881. $39.95.**
Vittorio de Sica, Italy, 1948, 90 mins.

Bread, Love, and Dreams

Vittorio de Sica stars as a mature marshall posted to a small Italian village. He soon begins to pursue the devilish Frisky (Gina Lollobrigida). Between her accomplished flirting and his determined courting the town is lost in delightful gossip. This warm comedy also features Marisa Merlini and Roberto Risso. Dubbed in English.

VHS: S23985. $24.95.
Luigi Comencini, Italy, 1954, 91 mins.

The Children Are Watching Us

With his fifth film, Vittorio de Sica surprised everyone by turning into a vicious critic of society. The film, set among the bourgeoisie, focuses on a marital triangle. The mother of a four-year-old boy leaves her husband for another man; the husband, unable to stand the humiliation, commits suicide. The boy, lonely and unwanted, is sent to an orphanage. The script was written by six scenarists, including Cesare Zavattini, who, through the film, emerged as a driving force in Italian cinema for many years to come. B&W. Italian with English subtitles.

VHS: S02077. $29.95.
Vittorio de Sica, Italy, 1944, 92 mins.

The Garden of the Finzi-Continis

Vittorio de Sica's (*The Bicycle Thief, Miracle in Milan*) Academy Award-winning masterpiece is visually restored and remastered in Dolby stereo. Dominique Sanda plays the daughter of a cultured Italian Jewish family of immense wealth, languishing in aristocratic privilege on their estate, oblivious, until the end, to the danger that Fascism poses for their precious world. Italian with English subtitles.

VHS: S00480. $19.95.
Laser: LD71000. $49.95.
Vittorio de Sica, Italy, 1971, 94 mins.

Gold of Naples

Vittorio de Sica directed the four vignettes comprising this famous omnibus film set in the old section of Naples. With a script by Cesare Zavattini, the film exhibits the new style de Sica developed after turning away from neo-realism. *The Racketeer* stars Toto as a poor soul bullied by his wife and children, *Pizza on Credit* stars Sophia Loren as the young wife of a pizza baker; *The Gambler* stars de Sica as a man whose rich wife will not give him money to satisfy his gambling urge, and *Teresa* stars Silvana Mangano as a prostitute trapped into marriage with a strange young gentleman. Italian with English subtitles.

VHS: S06441. $19.95.
Vittorio de Sica, Italy, 1954, 107 mins.

Indiscretion of An American Wife

Neo-realist art film produced by David Selznick, starring Jennifer Jones (Mrs. Selznick) and Montgomery Clift, about a love affair that does not work out. An interesting example of Clift's work.

VHS: S00621. $19.98.
Vittorio de Sica, USA/Italy, 1954, 63 mins.

It Happened in the Park

A story of what goes on during a 24 hour period in the Villa Borghese parks. French with English subtitles.

VHS: S03746. $29.95.
Vittorio de Sica, France/Italy, 1956, 72 mins.

Miracle in Milan

A masterpiece, a key work of Italian neo-realist cinema, a wonderfully inventive and comic film that effectively condemns the inequities that existed for millions of displaced Europeans after World War II. "The rich vein of sly, compassionate humor that Chaplin and Rene Clair used has been tapped by de Sica; the great director has brought up purest gold" (*New York Times*). Grand Award, Cannes Film Festival. Italian with English subtitles.

VHS: S12957. $29.95.
Laser: LD70419. $49.95.
Vittorio de Sica, Italy, 1951, 96 mins.

Roof

A masterpiece of neo-realism, the story concerns a young couple who marry against the wishes of the young woman's father and learn that finding an apartment is more difficult than they thought. Italian with English subtitles.

VHS: S01968. $29.95.
Vittorio de Sica, Italy, 98 mins.

Shoeshine

One of the great films of Italian neo-realism; in Nazi-occupied Rome, two young shoeshine boys get involved in a black market deal in order to raise money for a horse, are caught and sent to prison, and one of them betrays the other. A collaboration between de Sica and the father of neo-realism, Cesare Zavattini, a work of incredible emotion and power. Italian with English subtitles.

VHS: S05869. $79.95.
Vittorio de Sica, Italy, 1947, 90 mins.

Two Women

Sophia Loren won an Academy Award for her portrayal of a mother ravaged by war as she and her 13-year old daughter become the focus of attack by retreating German soldiers. A heartwrenching film—one of the best known—by Vittorio de Sica. Italian with English subtitles.

VHS: S04462. $29.95.
Vittorio de Sica, Italy, 1961, 99 mins.

Umberto D

One of the masterpieces of Italian Neo-Realist cinema— the Italian postwar Renaissance. The story centers on a retired civil servant, living only on his pension, whose best friend is his dog. Unable to survive on his meager income, he sacrifices a part of his pension for his dog, and is evicted by his landlady for non-payment of rent. Italian with English subtitles.

VHS: S01393. $29.95.
Laser: LD70483. $49.95.
Vittorio de Sica, Italy, 1952, 89 mins.

Yesterday, Today and Tomorrow

Sophia Loren and Marcello Mastroianni star in this Oscar-winning film that contains three different comic stories. Loren is great as the skilled temptress who uses sex to get what she wants, and her striptease remains a steamy, unforgettable film achievement.

VHS: S21220. $29.99.
Vittorio de Sica, Italy, 1964, 119 mins.

ROBERTO ROSSELLINI

Age of the Medici

With a script based on 15th century Florentine texts, this three-part film furthers Rossellini's exploration of the artistic, social, economic and political forces in our modern world. The key figures include Cosimo de Medici, son of an important banker, who saw that the major artistic visions should be allowed free rein as long as they operated under the sponsorship of the Medici. "*The Age of the Medici* is an epic representation of a particular time and space—the extensions of which are timeless and boundless" (Eric Sherman). The three parts are: *Cosimo de Medici, The Power of Cosimo*, and *Leon Battista Alberti: Humanism*. One of the major cinematic achievements ever. Available only as a complete, 252 minute set. In English.

VHS: S07384. $149.95.
Roberto Rossellini, Italy, 1973, 252 mins.

Amore

Available for the first time in the original two-part version, *Amore* is Rossellini's homage to the incredible Anna Magnani. In *The Human Voice*, based on Cocteau's one-act drama, Magnani is featured alone onscreen with a telephone, playing to an unseen lover. The interest is centered not so much on her dialog but on her expressive face and her actions—the myriad manifestations of her grief and suffering. *The Miracle*, inspired by a story from Federico Fellini, is a small masterpiece casting Magnani as a simple peasant who must defend her belief that she has given birth to the new Messiah. Condemned by the Catholic Legion of Decency and banned in several American cities at the time of its release, this inspired film was later praised by The Vatican and upheld in a landmark decision by the U.S. Supreme Court. "Excruciatingly passionate" (Peter Rainer, *L.A. Herald*). Italian with English subtitles.

VHS: S14984. $24.95.
Roberto Rossellini, Italy, 1948, 78 mins.

Blaise Pascal

Generally considered the finest of Rossellini's series of history films, this finely detailed portrait of life in seventeenth century France was described by Rossellini as "the drama of a man who develops scientific thought which is in conflict with the dogmatism of his deep religious faith." Rossellini's portrait of the philosopher/scientist is also a speculation on the nature of knowledge, cultural development, substance, space and time. French with English subtitles.

VHS: S06031. $79.95.
Roberto Rossellini, Italy/France, 1971, 131 mins.

Era Notte a Roma

A major film of Roberto Rossellini: three soldiers, an American, Englishman and Russian, having escaped from a concentration camp during the final months of Rome's occupation, are given refuge in a young woman's loft. She and her fiance survive through various black market schemes. A defrocked priest, Tarcisio, suspects the girl's complicity with Allied soldiers, but is willing to go along with it in return for favors. The woman resists, and Tarcisio causes the scattering of the group and the death of the Russian and several compatriots. In his book on Rossellini, Guarner said that from the point of *Era Notte a Roma* Rossellini no longer merely observed, but began to analyze: "Temporal and spatial leaps occur with utter simplicity and bridge ancient and modern cultures." English, Russian, German and Italian with English subtitles.

VHS: S07383. $79.95.
Roberto Rossellini, Italy, 1960, 145 mins.

Europa 51

A profound and sincere diary of an artist confused by the state of the world around him, this Rossellini film stars Ingrid Bergman as an American society woman living in Rome after the suicide of her son, searching for some meaning in the chaotic, postwar world. She discovers poverty and ends up in an asylum, in one of the major, rarely seen works of Roberto Rossellini. In English.

VHS: S06444. $79.95.
Roberto Rossellini, Italy, 1952, 110 mins.

Fear

Rossellini's last and darkest film, with Ingrid Bergman, shows a marriage stumbling across lines of suspicion, mistrust and fear. The husband of the story attempts blackmailing his wife in an effort to force her into a confession. She tolerates this blackmail because of an abstract guilt over her adulterous actions. Rossellini's visual motifs, darkness and shadows, create the moral muddle through which the characters move. Filmed in English.

VHS: S02951. $79.95.
Roberto Rossellini, Italy, 1954, 84 mins.

Flowers of St. Francis

Rossellini's continuing investigation of the nature of history and myth in the re-telling of the story of St. Francis of Assissi and his band of friars, as they attain perfect harmony with nature. This is the British release version, identical to the original Italian release, 10-15 mins. longer than the original U.S. release. Italian with English subtitles.

VHS: S02076. $29.98.
Roberto Rossellini, Italy, 1950, 75 mins.

General Della Rovere

Rossellini's great moral character study is the story of Emmanuele Bardone, a petty con man, who fleeces his victims until persuaded by the Germans to impersonate a partisan leader. He assumes the admirable qualities of the heroic officer. Italian with English subtitles.

VHS: S00484. $29.95.
Roberto Rossellini, Italy, 1960, 139 mins.

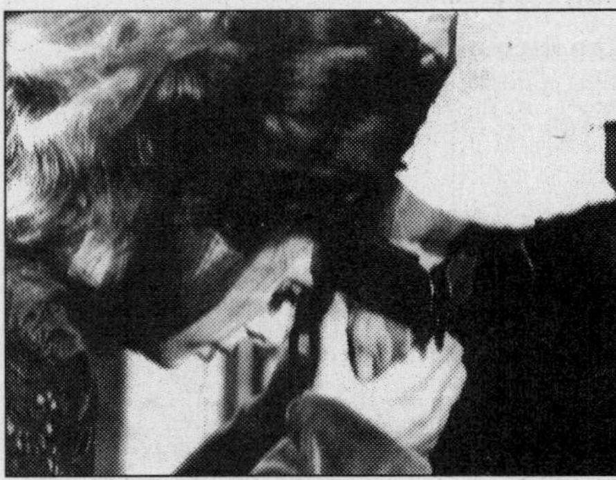

Germany Year Zero

The original edition of Roberto Rossellini's great film—in its German language subtitled version. "The actors were all nonprofessionals. Made in the neo-realist style…his lyrical view of Germany in the immediate postwar period has some magnificent scenes….Among the memorable…are the voice of Hitler on a phonograph among the ruins of the Chancellery, and the death of the hero in a gutted building" (Georges Sadoul).

VHS: S02952. $79.95.
Roberto Rossellini, Germany/Italy, 1947, 75 mins.

Machine to Kill Bad People

One of the rarest and most daring of Rossellini's films. Set shortly after the end of the war, in a small Italian village, a photographer is given a magical camera that has the power to petrify and kill anyone it "shoots." The photographer decides to eliminate all the evil people from the town. But in the process, he learns the difficulty of distinguishing between good and evil. On another level, *Machine to Kill Bad People* is an exploitation of Rossellini's statement that the cinema is unique among the arts because it captures moments of death at work. With Gennaro Pisano, Giovanni Amato and Marilyn Buferd.

VHS: S26382. $29.95.
Roberto Rossellini, Italy, 1948, 80 mins.

Man with a Cross (L'Uomo della Croce)

An extremely rare film by Roberto Rossellini, his third feature, made under the Fascist control of Italy. Basically rejected after the War because of the Fascist content of the film, "Rossellini produces a work which focuses upon the Italian expeditionary forces on the Eastern Front and upon a Catholic chaplain representative of Italy's religious majority…the principal character's humanity and sacrifice seem to prefigure the good-natured priest of *Rome, Open City* who works with leftist Resistance leaders…Rossellini underlines the common humanity in Fascist and Bolshevik alike" (Peter Bonadella, *Italian Cinema from Neo-Realism to Present*). Italian with English subtitles.

VHS: S11170. $69.95.
Roberto Rossellini, Italy, 1943, 76 mins.

Miracle
Brief, sensual and controversial film from Rossellini (source for 1952 Supreme Court case on censorship) starring Anna Magnani as a peasant woman who is convinced she is pregnant with a new Christ child. Based on a story by Federico Fellini, who appears. Italian with English subtitles.
VHS: S00858. $29.95.
Roberto Rossellini, Italy, 1948, 43 mins.

Open City
A beautiful video master, transferred from a new negative, of this key film of Italian Neo-Realism, shot largely during the Nazi occupation of Rome. Two resistance leaders, one a Communist, the other a priest, work toward weakening the German occupation. The cumulative power of Rossellini's feeling for his subject was translated into a visual intensity that makes the picture sometimes almost impossible to watch. With a great performance by Anna Magnani. Italian with English subtitles.
VHS: S13591. $24.95.
Laser: LD75058. $49.95.
Roberto Rossellini, Italy, 1945, 103 mins.

Paisan
One of the landmarks of Italian neo-realism; six episodes of the Battle of Italy from 1943-45. Improvised dialog, non-actors, and the story of the people in the War, the film became a cornerstone of postwar Italian cinema, appropriately called, by many critics, a "revelation…It is a people fighting, as others have done so often, against tyranny and their own weakness, against injustice and poverty." Italian with English subtitles.
VHS: S00989. $29.95.
Roberto Rossellini, Italy, 1946, 115 mins.

Return of the Pilot (Un Pilota Ritorna)
This is Rossellini's second feature and it follows the simple but dramatic tale of an Italian pilot who is interned in a British POW camp. It's a rare work and is easy enough to follow despite the lack of subtitles. In Italian without English subtitles.
VHS: S29892. $59.95.
Roberto Rossellini, Italy, 1942, 87 mins.

The Rise of Louis XIV
Italian master Roberto Rossellini works in a documentary-like naturalism to showcase the peculiar antics, mystery and bizarre nature of the extremely unconventional aristocratic French leader. With Jean-Marie Patte, Raymond Jourdan, Silvagni and Katharina Renn. Produced for French television. French with English subtitles.
VHS: S17845. $24.95.
Roberto Rossellini, France, 1966, 100 mins.

Rogopag
The title reflects four brilliant European directors who contributed short films to this collection: Roberto Rossellini, Jean-Luc Godard, Pier Paolo Pasolini and Ugo Gregoretti. *Virginity*, by Rossellini, is a comic essay on the distinctions between illusion and reality. Orson Welles stars in Pasolini's *La Ricotta*, a satire about the debasement of religion. This film caused Pasolini to be charged and sentenced to prison for "insulting the religion of [Italy]." *The New World*, by Godard, offers a chilling view of Paris after a nuclear war. And in Gregoretti's *The Range Grown Chicken*, a family suffers the ravages of brain-washing consumerism. French and Italian with English subtitles.
VHS: S23995. $24.95.
Roberto Rossellini/Jean-Luc Godard/Pier Paolo Pasolini/Ugo Gregoretti, France/Italy, 1962, 122 mins.

Seven Deadly Sins
Several French and Italian filmmakers, among them Eduardo De Filippo, Yves Allegret, Georges Lacombe and Roberto Rossellini, create separate vignettes that illustrate the dangers and provocations of the seven vices, suffused with a caustic, black wit. With Michele Morgan, Francoise Rosay, Gerard Philipe, and Isabelle Miranda. French and Italian with English subtitles. 1953, 127 mins.
VHS: S18030. $29.95.

Stromboli
A beautiful new video print of Rossellini's brilliant and sensual film. It stars the beautiful Ingrid Bergman (then his wife) as a Lithuanian WWII refugee who marries a fisherman on the island of Stromboli to escape internment, then rebels against the rigidity of the island's laws and traditions. "A great film" (Francois Truffaut). Italian with English subtitles.
VHS: S15272. $24.95.
Roberto Rossellini, Italy, 1949, 107 mins.

Vanina Vanini
Based on a story by Stendhal, set in Risorgimento, Italy, in 1824. Vanina Vanini, the daughter of a Roman aristocrat, falls in love with a wounded patriot hiding out in her father's house, nurses him back to health, and naively follows him to northern Italy where she tries to free him of political commitment which separates them in their love. Rossellini's great achievement is to rediscover a historical past spontaneously, accurately, and in all its complexity. With Sandra Milo, Laurent Terzieff. Italian with English subtitles.
VHS: S04907. $29.95.
Roberto Rossellini, Italy, 1961, 113 mins.

Voyage in Italy
Katherine and Alex Joyce are a sophisticated but strained American couple who take a holiday in Italy on family business. While he remains bored and sarcastic, Katherine experiences a physical and psychological awakening in a fresh world of ancient ruins, natural landscapes and temperamentally different people. They come to the edge of breakup before being momentarily reconciled in what many consider to be Rossellini's most influential film. Starring Ingrid Bergman and George Sanders. Also titled *Strangers*.
VHS: S15669. $24.95.
Roberto Rossellini, Italy, 1953, 83 mins.

LUCHINO VISCONTI

Conversation Piece
Burt Lancaster is the rich, isolated professor whose life is shattered when the beautiful Countess Brumonti and her lovely daughter appear at his home. The Professor gradually becomes entangled in the bizarre plots of the Countess and her daughter. English dubbed.
VHS: S00268. $29.95.
Luchino Visconti, Italy/France, 1974, 112 mins.

The Damned
A gigantic allegory of the rise of Nazism through the decadent Krupp-like family; a baroque film which explores the dark cycles of violence and evil in human history and consciousness with erotic indulgence. With Dirk Bogarde, Ingrid Thulin, Helmut Berger, Charlotte Rampling. English dubbed.
VHS: S00293. $59.95.
Luchino Visconti, Italy/Germany, 1969, 146 mins.

Death in Venice
Visconti's adaptation of the classic Thomas Mann novella was a tremendous triumph; Dirk Bogarde plays the aging artist who, in Venice, becomes obsessed with the ideal beauty of a young boy. With stunning cinematography and Visconti's elegant, operatic touch. English dubbed.
VHS: S00316. $59.95.
Laser: LD76809. $39.99.
Luchino Visconti, Italy, 1971, 130 mins.

The Innocent
An elegant, visually beautiful exploration of the constraints of marriage and its disintegration. Featuring a remarkably sensuous performance by Laura Antonelli, and an equally strong performance from Giancarlo Giannini. "*The Innocent* is one of Visconti's most beautiful films" (Vincent Canby). Italian with English subtitles.
VHS: S00625. $29.95.
Luchino Visconti, Italy, 1976, 125 mins.

Ludwig
Luchino Visconti's legendary epic of (mad) King Ludwig of Bavaria. Visconti focuses on Ludwig's fears and fantasies and his relationship with composer Richard Wagner to create a portrait of a "homosexual recluse whose passions are opera, fairy-tale castles, and exquisite young men. Nothing is more sumptuous than Helmut Berger's performance in the lead, the brooding mad scenes, the deliberately contrived hysterical outbursts" (Tony Rayns). With Romy Schneider, Trevor Howard and Silvana Mangano. This version is longer than the original American theatrical release version by 47 minutes. Letterboxed. Italian with English subtitles.
VHS: S32982. $79.95.
Luchino Visconti, France/Italy/Germany, 1972, 231 mins.

Ossessione
One of the great revelations of the cinema: Luchino Visconti's adaptation of James M. Cain's *The Postman Always Rings Twice*, about the tragic love between a wanderer and the wife of an innkeeper, who murder the husband. For long never shown in the U.S., the film had a profound influence on the course of the cinema, beginning the era that would become Italian neo-realism. A masterpiece. Italian with English subtitles.
VHS: S05922. $29.95.
Luchino Visconti, Italy, 1942, 135 mins.

Rocco and His Brothers
Luchino Visconti's brilliant work concentrates on the dramatic clash between two differing value systems—an intellectual belief in the cause of progress and emotional nostalgia for a decaying past. The struggle is played out by two sons, Rocco (Alain Delon), a gentle boy, who is in conflict with Simone (Renato Salvatori), a loutish boxer. Both are in love with Nadia (Annie Girardot), a prostitute, and are bound by old traditions that neither can escape. Considered by many critics to be Visconti's greatest film. Italian with English subtitles.
VHS: S07471. $79.95.
Luchino Visconti, Italy, 1960, 134 mins.

Sandra of a Thousand Delights
In this searing drama, a woman returns to her home town in order to attend a ceremony commemorating her father. He died like millions of Jews in Nazi concentration camps. This trip rekindles a host of unanswered past memories that hint at betrayal, incest, lost love and the haunting possibilities of what might have been. Italian with English subtitles.
VHS: S22464. $39.95.
Luchino Visconti, Italy, 1965, 100 mins.

Senso
One of Luchino Visconti's greatest films—luscious, operatic, and an extraordinary portrait of a decadent and corrupt aristocracy. Set in Venice of 1866, Alida Valli plays an Italian countess who falls in love with an Austrian officer (Farley Granger). When war breaks out, she is torn between her patriotism and her emotional obsession with the officer. Visconti portrays a milieu in which "Livia's seduction and treachery and Franz's cowardice and deceit are an inevitable result of their environment." Italian with English subtitles.
VHS: S09353. $29.95.
Luchino Visconti, Italy, 1955, 115 mins.

White Nights
Mario, a shy young man, meets a mysterious girl, Natalie, weeping as she stands on a canal bridge. She tells him that she loves a sailor who left on a long journey and promised to return in one year; a year has passed and he still hasn't arrived. Gradually, Mario falls in love with the girl and struggles to persuade her that the sailor will never return. Just when he seems to have convinced her, the man from her past does in fact appear. Based on a story by Fyodor Dostoyevsky. With Marcello Mastroianni, Maria Schell and Jean Marais. Italian with English subtitles.
VHS: S13679. $59.95.
Luchino Visconti, Italy, 1957, 107 mins.

SERGIO LEONE

Fistful of Dollars
Leone's sterling spaghetti Western, starring Clint Eastwood as "the man with no name," is a slick remake of Kurosawa's *Yojimbo*, which was itself based on Dashiell Hammett's novel *Red Harvest*. A superlative soundtrack by Ennio Morricone. English dubbed.
Laser: LD70570. $34.98.
Sergio Leone, Italy, 1964, 96 mins.

A Fistful of Dynamite
This Sergio Leone epic of a revolution in Mexico is also known under the title *Duck, You Sucker*. It follows the exploits of an Irish terrorist, played by James Coburn, who continuously crosses paths with a Mexican bandit family headed by Rod Steiger. They both like explosives and annoying the government troops. The musical score is by Ennio Morricone. English dialog.
VHS: S03672. $19.98.
Laser: Director's cut, widescreen. **LD75542. $49.98.**
Sergio Leone, Italy, 1972, 138 mins.

For a Few Dollars More
The second collaboration of Sergio Leone and Clint Eastwood finds Eastwood reluctantly accompanying a mysterious bounty hunter (Lee Van Cleef) to track a vicious killer and his band of outlaw grotesques. Music by Ennio Morricone. With Gian Maria Volonte and Klaus Kinski.
VHS: S02525. $19.98.
Laser: Letterboxed. **LD71883. $39.98.**
Sergio Leone, Italy/Spain/Germany, 1965, 130 mins.

The Good, The Bad and the Ugly

The third—and best—Sergio Leone "Dollars" Western. Set during the Civil War, three men out on the skids search for a treasure chest of the Confederates, each knowing a little about its whereabouts. A great musical score by Ennio Morricone. With Clint Eastwood, Eli Wallach, Lee Van Cleef. A brilliant spaghetti Western and Leone at his best.

VHS: S11553. $24.98.
Laser: LD70587. $49.98.
DVD: DV60149. $24.98.
Sergio Leone, Italy/Spain, 1967, 161 mins.

Once Upon a Time in America

The complete, uncut version of Leone's epic of American criminal life begins with five young men growing up in Brooklyn during the 1920's and the road that leads each of them to becoming powerful Mob bosses. Stars Robert de Niro, James Woods, Elizabeth McGovern, Treat Williams, Tuesday Weld and others, in a film many critics consider the one important film to be released in 1984.

VHS: S00961. $29.98.
Laser: LD71434. $39.98.
Sergio Leone, Italy, 1984, 227 mins.

Once Upon a Time in the West

A great Western by the great Sergio Leone, uncut. Henry Fonda is the ruthless psychopath, Jason Robards the half-breed falsely accused of a terrible slaughter, and Charles Bronson "The Man" who remembers how his brother was savagely tortured. Brilliant direction by Leone achieves a film of epic significance, shot in dazzling Monument Valley locations.

VHS: S00962. $29.95.
Sergio Leone, USA, 1968, 165 mins.

ITALIAN CLASSICS

1860

One of the first modern Italian films, this daring feature is the story of a Sicilian mountaineer who leaves behind his new bride in order to fight with Garibaldi. *1860* was the first Italian film to use actors from real life, and was shot mostly on locations in Sicily where many of Garibaldi's battles took place. A key film in the evolution of Italian neo-realism. Italian with English subtitles.

VHS: S16119. $29.95.
Alessandro Blasetti, Italian, 1933, 72 mins.

Angel in a Taxi

A charming fable with an ingenious premise. A sweet-faced boy named Marietto stars as a clever, mischievous six-year-old in an orphanage who longs for a mother. "Did Jesus choose his own mother?" he asks a nun. She replies in the affirmative—and so Marietto figures that what was good enough for Jesus is good enough for him. Spotting Camilla, a beautiful ballerina, in a magazine, he decides she is to be his parent and runs away to find her. Vittorio De Sica pops up in a trio of small but important disguises: a sympathetic policeman, a harried messenger, and a philosophical taxi driver. Dubbed in English.

VHS: S13601. $29.95.
Antonio Leonviola, Italy, 1959, 89 mins.

Anna

Anna is a nun on the verge of taking her last vows, whose sinful life as a nightclub entertainer, passion for one man and drive to marry another haunt her. Her old feelings are renewed when her former fiancee is brought to the hospital where she now serves as a nurse after a serious accident. A first-rate performance by Silvana Mangano dominates this powerful drama about the conflict between the flesh and the spirit. With Vittorio Gassman and Raf Vallone. Italian with English subtitles.

VHS: S26387. $29.95.
Alberto Lattuada, Italy, 1952, 111 mins.

Antony and Cleopatra

Produced in Italy in 1913, this rare classic of early Italian cinema starred Amleto Novelli (*Quo Vadis*) and was remarkable for its stunning sets and impressive crowd scenes. 74 mins.

VHS: S29459. $24.95.

Ave Maria

In this 1936 film, Beniamino Gigli is a tenor blackmailed by a woman, who expresses his rage through a performance of *La Traviata*. "Di quella pira," songs and excerpts from *La Boheme* are also performed. "Gigli…is a perfect lover and a fine actor. Beauty of his voice and captivating story keep up the dramatic tension. Photography is outstanding" (*Variety*, 1936). Italian with English subtitles. 76 mins.

VHS: S28425. $34.95.

Bandits of Orgosolo

Set in a remote Sardinian village and cast with local non-professional actors, Vittorio de Seta's first feature explores the moral and social cultures unique to the rural cultures of poverty. A shepherd, Michele, must flee an unjust accusation of theft and murder. Forced into the role of an outlaw to survive, he winds up robbing peasants who are as poor as himself. "This is a western from which all the romantic excitement about toughness has been stripped away, and whose characters, instead of being free and wild, have been humiliated deep within themselves by centuries of feudalism." With Michele Cossu and Peppedu Cuccu. English dubbed.

VHS: S00094. $29.95.
Vittorio de Seta, Sardinia, 1961, 98 mins.

Battle of Algiers

Internationally acclaimed, the staggering newsreel-like authenticity of the staged street riots and vital performances of the actors give *Battle of Algiers* a unique dramatic impact on this detailing of the Algerian revolt against the French. French/Algerian with English subtitles.

VHS: S01976. $29.95.
Gillo Pontecorvo, Italy, 1967, 122 mins.

Big Deal on Madonna Street

A hilarious satire on all burglary capers, Mario Monicelli's stylish film is now a classic account of the misadventures of a group of amateurish crooks (Vittorio Gassman, Marcello Mastroianni, Renato Salvatori, Rossana Rory) as they attempt to rob a store. Italian with English subtitles.

VHS: S01657. $29.95.
Laser: Letterboxed. **LD76174. $49.98.**
Mario Monicelli, Italy, 1956, 91 mins.

The Bird with the Crystal Plumage

An American writer (Tony Musante, TV's *Toma*) traveling in Rome is the only witness to an attempted murder by a sinister man in a raincoat and black leather gloves. When the police fail to make any progress he launches his own personal investigation and nearly loses his life in the process. With Suzy Kendall. Dubbed in English.

VHS: S34290. $19.99.
Dario Argento, Italy/Germany, 1969, 98 mins.

Bitter Rice

In the dreary rice fields of the Po Valley, a thief on the run meets a hard-working, beautiful girl. Silvana Mangano portrays the seductive rice worker who betrays her comrades in order to steal the thief's loot, a role which rocketed her to international stardom. With Vittorio Gassman, Raf Vallone, Doris Dowling and Lia Corelli. Italian with English subtitles.

VHS: S16185. $29.95.
Giuseppe de Santis, Italy, 1949, 96 mins.

Black Jesus

Based on real incidents in the Congo, this film chronicles the downfall of an African leader of national independence. Woody Strode plays Black Jesus, a man betrayed by one of his followers and unwittingly martyred by the men in power. Under cruel interrogation you see the life begin to drain out of the man, his eyes reflecting the horrors of the times. Long after the violence of the film is forgotten, you will remember the look in Strode's eyes. In English. "*Black Jesus* has the impact of *Z*. Strode should get an Academy Award" (ABC-TV).

VHS: S30729. $29.95.
Valerio Zurlini, Italy, 1971, 90 mins.

A Bullet for the General

Gian Maria Volonte and Klaus Kinski are featured in this spaghetti Western of sorts. It actually concerns an American spy who is determined to assassinate a Mexican revolutionary. Before this hired killer can find his mark, he must pose as a sympathetic fighter on the side of the revolutionaries.

VHS: S27889. $19.98.
Damiano Damiani, Italy, 1966, 113 mins.

Cabiria

The most ambitious and spectacular of the historical epics for which Italy was famous before World War I, *Cabiria* set the standard for big budget, feature-length movies and opened the way for Griffith and DeMille. During the war between Carthage and Rome, a girl—Cabiria—is separated from her parents. In her odyssey through the world of ancient Rome, she encounters an erupting volcano, the barbaric splendor of Carthage, human sacrifice and Hannibal crossing the Alps. Mastered from a 35mm archive print using variable speed projection to match the original hand cranked camera, *Cabiria* features a newly recorded soundtrack from the original 1914 score.

VHS: S06218. $39.95.
Giovanni Pastrone, Italy, 1914, 123 mins.

The Christus

The story of Christ is presented in this silent Italian production that was adapted from a poem by Fausto Salvatore. He most likely based his poem on a much more popular source. Filmed closer to the Holy Land than most Hollywood films on the same subject matter. Silent.

VHS: S04813. $24.95.
Guilio Antamoro, Italy, 1917, 90 mins.

Cyrano de Bergerac

Edmond Rostand's enduring love story is given a unique and beautiful incarnation in this hand-tinted silent classic. Pierre Magnier brings true pathos to the chivalrous lover who dares not reveal his face with its monstrous nose to the woman he loves. Carlo Moser's score captures the excitement of this romantic, action-filled film. French and English intertitled.

VHS: S27308. $29.95.
Augusto Genina, Italy/France, 1925, 114 mins.

Divorce—Italian Style

The adult comedy sensation that started it all. Marcello Mastroianni is a Sicilian nobleman who, tiring of his fatuous and fawning wife, begins directing his attentions toward his teenage cousin. In an attempt to end his problems once and for all, he devises a plan to catch his wife cheating so he can kill her…but first he must find her a lover! Italian with English subtitles.

VHS: S15951. $24.95.
Pietro Germi, Italy, 1962, 104 mins.

The Driver's Seat

Elizabeth Taylor stars as a spinster on a bizarre quest. She goes in search of an ideal mate and encounters both a series of outlandish adventures and a mysterious man. A novel from Muriel Sparks is the basis for this unusual film. Andy Warhol makes an appearance. Dubbed in English.

VHS: S27897. $19.98.
Giuseppe Patroni Griffi, Italy, 1975, 90 mins.

Fabiola

An early sound spectacle from Italy of the days of Ancient Rome, focusing on the story of Fabiola, daughter of a Roman senator, who converts to Christianity when her father is killed and his Christian servants accused. With Michel Simon and Henri Vidal. Dubbed in English.

VHS: S14635. $29.95.
Alessandro Blasetti, Italy, 1948, 96 mins.

Fiances (I Fidanzati)

Ermanno Olmi's (*Tree of the Wooden Clogs*) brilliant second feature is the simple story of a young man from Milan who takes a welding job in Sicily which takes him away from his fiancee, because he thinks the separation will be good for their relationship. But loneliness and the strange environment make him turn back to her. Olmi's deep humanism is evident in his moving depiction of the lives of simple people, played by non-professionals. One of the truly great Italian films of the 60's. Italian with English subtitles.

VHS: S26577. $29.95.
Ermanno Olmi, Italy, 1963, 84 mins.

The Forbidden Christ

This only film by Italian writer, journalist and poet Curzio Malaparte, best known for his 1944 novel *Kaputt*, is the story of a soldier who returns from the war after years in a POW camp to find that his younger brother, a Resistance fighter, has been killed by the Nazis. Bent on revenge against the person in his village who betrayed his brother to the enemy, he seeks information from the war-weary townsfolk, but his rage and impatience lead him to kill the wrong man. Italian with English subtitles.

VHS: S30244. $24.95.
Curzio Malaparte, Italy, 1950, 98 mins.

Four Ways Out

Gina Lollobrigida stars in this stark, gritty drama co-authored by Federico Fellini. A group of thieves robs a soccer stadium in broad daylight. In hiding, the thieves begin to whither under the pressure of their crimes. Winner of the Best Italian Film at the 1951 Venice Film Festival. Dubbed in English.

VHS: S24014. $24.95.
Pietro Germi, Italy, 1951, 74 mins.

Frate Francisco
This mammoth, lavish production exemplifies the spectacular Italian historical epics made during the era of silent films. The story is based on the life of the saint. He was born to a life of ease, only to reject everything for a vow of poverty. Alleged to have experienced the stigmata (wounds like those suffered by Christ on the cross), this holy man's spiritual ways remain inspirational. Includes original musical score with sound effects.
VHS: S25866. $24.95.
Guilio Antamoro, Italy, 1927, 75 mins.

Full Hearts and Empty Pockets
The happy-go-lucky adventures of a young, handsome and impoverished gentleman on the loose in Rome. With the kind of luck that only occurs in the Eternal City, he parleys ten lire into a large fortune and a position of power in a seemingly wealthy corporation, becomes the pawn in a struggle between power brokers and blackmailers, and falls in love! With Linda Christian, Gino Cervi, Senta Berger. In English.
VHS: S07508. $29.95.
Camillo Mastrocinque, Germany/Italy, 1963, 88 mins.

Girl with a Suitcase
A girl with nothing except good looks finds herself at the mercy of one man after another until she is finally jilted by a rich young scoundrel. About to be cast adrift in a sea of corruption, she finds her protector in the person of her betrayer's 16-year-old brother. The film reveals the very sensitive area between purity and vice and launched the international career of Claudia Cardinale. With Jaques Perrin. Italian with English subtitles. "Extremely well acted [and] worth seeing" (*1996 Video Movie Guide*).
VHS: S30730. $29.95.
Valerio Zurlini, Italy/France, 1961, 111 mins.

Heart and Soul
Based on the very popular Italian novel *Cuore*, by Edmond de Amicis, this postwar Italian film stars Vittorio de Sica and Maria Mercades in what is a touching portrait of a devoted and philosophical teacher at a boys' school who encounters obstacles, including being suspended for his political beliefs. Italy's answer to *Goodbye Mr. Chips*. Italian with English subtitles.
VHS: S26772. $29.95.
Duilio Coletti, Italy, 1948, 98 mins.

I Sing for You Alone
Tito Schipa plays a tenor whose stage fright causes his voice to break on a high note. The audience boos him and runs him out of town, but he comes back in the end when he sings a concert in this Marx Brothers-like slapstick farce. "[Schipa] is at his most caressing and works magic on eight songs [in this] lovely print" (Stefan Zucker, *Opera Fanatic's Catalog*). In English, with songs in English, Italian, French and Spanish. 57 mins.
VHS: S28426. $34.95.

Il Bell'Antonio
Marcello Mastroianni and Claudia Cardinale star in this passionate story of love and sex which was written by Pier Paolo Pasolini and Gino Visentini. Mastroianni plays the dashing Antonio Magnano, who finally relinquishes his bachelorhood and faces the loss of his libido in this ribald satire of marriage, Catholicism and machismo. Italian with English subtitles.
VHS: S20570. $24.95.
Mauro Bolognini, Italy, 1960, 115 mins.

The Iron Crown
A rare work from Mussolini's Italy; critic Mira Liehm writes, "The center of Blasetti's work lay in the mythological films and films with an openly pro-fascist tendency. In the years 1938-1941 he shot a generally overvalued costume tetralogy, which represents a transition between his fascist films and his work after 1942. The most important of this tetralogy…is *The Iron Crown*, a pseudo-historical fantasy based on a naive plot…which tried to create a kind of Italian saga in the style of *Die Niebelungenlied*…Blasetti, the true eclectic, mixed in everything he could think of, including Ariosto and the Grimm Brothers, while his directing drew heavily on early Fritz Lang." Italian with English subtitles.
VHS: S08781. $69.95.
Alessandro Blasetti, Italy, 1941

Kapo
Gillo Pontecorvo (*Battle of Algiers*) directed this moving study of hope and humiliation in Nazi concentration camps. A Jewish family living in Paris during WWII is arrested by the Nazis and shipped to a labor camp where their ordeal begins. "Stark and terrifying" (*Time*). English and some foreign dialog with English subtitles.
VHS: S14638. $29.95.
Gillo Pontecorvo, Italy, 1959, 116 mins.

Laugh for Joy (Risate di Gioia)
Anna Magnani in one of her greatest roles in this moving, bitter story of a film extra in Rome's Cinecitta Studio who is involved with American film executive Fred Clark and con-man Ben Gazzara. A major film by Mario Monicelli (*The Organizer, Big Deal on Madonna Street*). Cinemascope. Italian with English subtitles.
VHS: S15182. $59.95.
Mario Monicelli, Italy, 1954, 106 mins.

Le Soldatesse
War, prostitution, hunger, compassion, self-respect and the cheapening of life's values are interwoven in this dynamic story of a convoy of Athenian women who are transported for military brothels in the north during the occupation of Greece, accompanied by a greedy sargeant, a bombastic major and a war-sickened lieutenant. With Marie LaForet, Anna Karina, Lea Massari, Mario Adorf and Thomas Milian. Italian with English subtitles.
VHS: S30550. $29.95.
Valerio Zurlini, Italy/France/Yugoslavia, 1964, 97 mins.

The Libertine (La Matriarca)
Initially banned in America and challenged all the way to the Supreme Court, *The Libertine* is the story of Mimi, a young woman who discovers that her recently deceased husband had kept a secret apartment equipped to satisfy his unusual sexual desires. With Catherine Spaak and Jean-Louis Trintignant. Italian with English subtitles.
VHS: S33337. $29.95.
Pasquale Festa Companile, Italy, 1969, 90 mins.

Love in the City
One of the best omnibus films, which brought together the best Italian filmmakers of the 50's. The episodes are: *The Spectator*, by Dino Risi; *When Love Fails*, by Antonioni; *Love Cheerfully Arranged* (also known as *The Matrimonial Agency*), by Fellini; *Paid Love*, by Carlo Lizzani; *The Love of a Mother*, by Zavattini and Maselli and *Italy Turns Around*, by Alberto Lattuada. The inspiration for the film is said to have been Zavattini; particularly notable are the Antonioni episode, in which unsuccessful suicides tell why they blame disappointment in love for trying to end their lives, and the very funny Fellini episode, in which a client (played by Fellini) at a matrimonial agency pretends that he is searching for a wife for a friend who thinks he is a werewolf. 90 mins. Italian with English subtitles.
VHS: S01969. $39.95.

Lure of the Sila
Silvana Mangano, Amedeo Nazzari and Vittorio Gassman star in this sensual tale about unrequited love and passion, revenge and death, set in southern Italy. Gassman, in one of his early appearances, is falsely accused of murder, and years later his sister, now grown up, decides on revenge. Dubbed in English.
VHS: S05602. $29.95.
Duilio Coletti, Italy, 1949, 72 mins.

Mado Robin Live!
Mado Robin (1918-1960) was the preeminent 20th-century French coloratura. This live performance includes selections from *Lakme, Mireille, Rigoletto, Hamlet, Barbiere* and *Lucia*. Be sure to check out the "mad scene" in the latter, in which Robin demonstrates her B-flat above high C which landed her in the *Guinness Book of World Records*. 24 mins.
VHS: S28423. $34.95.

Magnificent Adventurer
A saga about Benvenuto Cellini, the famed Florentine sculptor, whose passion for fine arts was matched only by his love for beautiful women and swordplay. With Brett Halsey, Bernard Blier and Claudia Mori. 1976, 94 mins.
VHS: S11116. $59.95.
Riccardo Freda, Italy/Spain, 1963, 94 mins.

Musica Proibita
A haunting tale of romance, murder, revenge and fate from the period in Italian cinema just prior to Neo-Realism. The story focuses on the son of an opera tenor who must pay for the sins of his father. Italian with English subtitles.
VHS: S00902. $29.95.
Carlo Campogalliani, Italy, 1943, 93 mins.

Non Ti Scordar di Me
In this 1935 hit film, Beniamino Gigli portrays a cuckolded Italian singer, performing "Di quella pira," songs and excerpts from *Rigoletto, Africana, Mignon, Favorita, Marta* and *Elisir* (a total of four high Cs). "This is Gigli's most popular film, lovingly restored" (Steve Cohen, *The Delaware Jewish Voice* and *The Philadelphia Jewish Times*). English. 73 mins.
VHS: S28424. $34.95.

The Organizer
In 19th-century Turin, an itinerant professor unites a ragtag group of textile workers in a strike against their factory. Crippling accidents have become commonplace in a factory where 14-hour shifts are typical, children work side by side with adults, and no safety standards exist. When one man is maimed, the workers draw up a list of demands, which are summarily dismissed by the bosses. It's only when an outsider (Marcello Mastroianni) stumbles into their midst that they are able to focus their efforts and bring about the possibility of change. With Annie Girardot and Bernard Blier. Italian with English subtitles.
VHS: S32494. $24.95.
Mario Monicelli, Italy, 1954, 127 mins.

Pardon My Trunk
An Italian comedy about a member of a royal family who bestows the unusual gift of a pachyderm to one of his subjects as a suitable reward. The cast includes Vittorio De Sica, Maria Mercader, Nando Bruno and Sabu. When elephants are involved it makes sense to hire Sabu, the elephant boy. English dubbed.
VHS: S06163. $29.95.
Gianni Franciolini, Italy, 1952, 85 mins.

Peddlin' in Society
Clearly inspired by the situation of Moliere's *Would-Be-Gentleman, Peddlin' in Society* gives full rein to Anna Magnani's comic talents and Vittorio De Sica's charm. A funny and delightful showcase for both these fine actors. Italian with English subtitles.
VHS: S14644. $29.95.
Gennaro Righelli, Italy, 1947, 90 mins.

The Queen of Sheba
Gino Cervi, Leonora Ruffo, Gino Leurini and Marina Berti are featured in this lavish costume drama set during the reign of King Solomon. There is plenty of desert passion within this plot inspired by the Bible. Intrigues keep the film going, but exotic dancers and a gazelle milk bath have a fascination of their own. Dubbed in English.
VHS: S23990. $24.95.
Pietro Francisi, Italy, 1953, 103 mins.

Quo Vadis?
The first cinematic adaptation of the Henryk Sienkiewicz novel about Nero and ancient Rome, this original Italian large-scale silent epic was probably cinema's first blockbuster. Italian with English titles.
VHS: S06215. $24.95.
Enrico Guazzoni, Italy, 1912, 45 mins.

Rogopag
The title reflects four brilliant European directors who contributed short films to this collection: Roberto Rossellini, Jean-Luc Godard, Pier Paolo Pasolini and Ugo Gregoretti. *Virginity*, by Rossellini, is a comic essay on the distinctions between illusion and reality. Orson Welles stars in Pasolini's *La Ricotta*, a satire about the debasement of religion. This film caused Pasolini to be charged and sentenced to prison for "insulting the religion of [Italy]." *The New World*, by Godard, offers a chilling view of Paris after a nuclear war. And in Gregoretti's *The Range Grown Chicken*, a family suffers the ravages of brain-washing consumerism. French and Italian with English subtitles.
VHS: S23995. $24.95.
Roberto Rossellini/Jean-Luc Godard/Pier Paolo Pasolini/Ugo Gregoretti, France/Italy, 1962, 122 mins.

Seduced and Abandoned
One of the funniest Italian films ever—a comedy about the Sicilian code of honor, in which an unexpected chain of events is set in motion after an equally unexpected seduction, with truly hilarious results. With Stefania Sandrelli. Italian with English subtitles.
VHS: S18170. $29.95.
Pietro Germi, Italy, 1963, 118 mins.

Tigris
Though common today, when this silent film was produced in Italy in 1913, the mounting tension between a villian and his inventive counterspy was new and fascinating. Today the rivalry between these two opponents in both disguises and tricks still offers engaging entertainment. Piano score. 48 mins.
VHS: S29460. $19.95.

Time of Indifference
Francesco Maselli's adaptation of Alberto Moravia's novel examines the spiritual malaise and moral decay of an aristocratic family in 20s Italy. With Rod Steiger, Claudia Cardinale, Shelley Winters and Paulette Goddard. In English.
VHS: S19874. $29.95.
Francesco Maselli, Italy, 1964, 84 mins.

The Unfaithfuls
This multifaceted Italian comedy, produced by Dino de Laurentiis and Carlo Ponti, reveals life among the rich, corrupt society of Rome. An extortionist threatens to expose the extra-marital affairs of the philandering upper-class, with sometimes comical and sometimes tragic results. With Gina Lollobrigida, Mai Britt, Pierre Cressoy and Marina Vlady.
VHS: S34390. $14.99.
Aldo Tonti/Luciano Trasatti, Italy, 1960, 91 mins.

Verdi (The Opera)
Pierre Cressoy and Anna Marie Ferreo star in this story of the life and work of Italian composer Giuseppe Verdi. With Gaby Andr, Irene Genna, Tito Gobbi, Mario del Monaco, Sandro Ruffini and Laura Gobe.
VHS: S30524. $29.95.
Raffaello Matarazzo, Italy, 1953, 120 mins.

We the Living

This Italian war-time production of the classic novel of Ayn Rand, the author of *Fountainhead* and *Atlas Shrugged*, is set in Russia of the early 1920's and follows Kira (Alida Valli) as she gradually copes with Russia's sweeping social and ideological changes in the wake of the Revolution. Literally lost for many years, this film was only recently found by Ayn Rand's supporters in Rome, and re-constructed. "One of the most exciting movies to come along in years. A moving epic in the tradition of *Gone with the Wind*" (*Boston Globe*). Italian with English subtitles.
VHS: S09584. $89.95.
Laser: CLV. **LD70267. $89.00.**
Goffredo Alessandrini, Italy, 1943, 170 mins.

What a Woman!

This comedy stars Charles Boyer as a rakish count who transforms socially-awkward-though-beautiful peasant girl Sophia Loren into a movie star when he secures her picture on the cover of a prestigious magazine. Marcello Mastroianni plays Loren's sophisticated photographer-lover. With Nino Besozzi and Titina De Filippo. English dubbed.
VHS: S19877. $19.95.
Alessandro Blasetti, Italy, 1956, 95 mins.

Where the Hot Wind Blows

"Peyton Place, Italian style!" A fiery Italian soap opera from Jules Dassin, the director of *Never on a Sunday*. Starring tempestuous Gina Lollobrigida, fighting Yves Montand, mysterious Melina Mercouri, and sexy Marcello Mastroianni.
VHS: S01612. $14.99.
Jules Dassin, Italy, 1959, 120 mins.

Woman of Rome

Gina Lollobrigida plays a girl of easy virtue in this film which also stars Daniel Gelin, Franco Fabrizi and Raymond Pellegrin.
VHS: S06854. $34.95.
Luigi Zampa, Italy, 1956, 93 mins.

Women in Prison

In lyric pseudo-documentary style, writer/director/producer Geza von Radvanyi has recreated the humiliation, outrages and sexual frustrations of the women held in detention camps in Italy following the second World War. These women were treated like hardened criminals for the offense of lacking passports or proper identification. An intense and poignant story. Italian, French and English with English subtitles.
VHS: S14652. $29.95.
Geza von Radvanyi, Italy, 1951, 90 mins.

Women Without Names

Simone Simon stars as a woman trapped in a camp for expatriate women left without documents at the end of World War II. She plots to marry a camp worker and gain her freedom. This drama is notable for its examination of a number of themes then considered quite controversial, including sexuality, lesbianism, abortion and human rights. Italian, French and English dialog with English subtitles.
VHS: S22471. $29.95.
Geza von Radvanyi, Italy, 1949, 94 mins.

SWORD & SANDAL EPICS

Caesar the Conquerer

Colorful tale of the legendary ruler of Rome as he leads his legions into battle. He and his armies are pitted against the rebel hordes from Gaul. With Cameron Mitchell and Rik Battaglia. Dubbed in English.
VHS: S32584. $24.95.
Amerigo Anton, Italy, 1961, 103 mins.

David and Goliath

The classic retelling of the age-old fable of David and Goliath. Welles is colorful as King Saul. Ivo Payer is a very masculine David and Kronos is Goliath. With Eleonora Rossi. Dubbed in English.
VHS: S32585. $24.95.
Richard Potter/Ferdinando Baldi, Italy, 1961, 110 mins.

Fury of Hercules

Brad Harris plays the title character. He's pumped up and he's not pleased with the way the little people are being treated in a despot's kingdom. He offers his assistance to the lovely Brigitte Corey and her followers. Cast also includes Mara Berni, Carlo Tamberlani, Serge Gainsbourg and Alan Steel.
VHS: S10391. $19.95.
Gianfranco Parolini, USA, 1961, 95 mins.

Giant of Marathon

Steve Reeves and Mylene Demongeot are featured in this sword and sandal spectacle. Reeves is a courageous Greek hero who frustrates an invading Persian army with his muscle-bound antics. This is one of Reeves' best, with cinematography by Mario Bava.
VHS: S23173. $29.95.
Jacques Tourneur, France/Italy, 1960, 90 mins.

Head of Tyrant

Massimo Girotti, Isabelle Corey and Renato Baldini star in this story of deception and lust set in ancient Assyria. A beautiful, innocent, young girl gives herself to a cruel tyrant who has conquered her city. She plans to gain his affection and then decapitate him. Letterboxed.
VHS: S23174. $24.95.
Fernando Cherchiio, Italy, 1959, 83 mins.

Hercules

Steve Reeves stars in the original, uncut spectacle that brings to life the legendary pagan playgrounds of the mystical Mediterranean. The prototype of all the sword and sandal epics.
VHS: S08040. $19.98.
Pietro Francisi, Italy, 1959, 107 mins.

Hercules Against the Moon Men

A race of evil aliens have landed on the moon in ancient Greece. The queen of Samar makes a pact with the moon men to conquer the world and become the most powerful woman alive. Hercules comes to the rescue to put a stop to the madness. With Alan Steel and Jany Clair. Dubbed in English.
VHS: S34504. $24.95.
Giacomo Gentilomo, France/Italy, 1965, 88 mins.

Hercules Against the Sons of the Sun

Hercules rescues an Inca princess from being sacrificed and replaces the usurper with the rightful heir to the throne. With Giuliano Gemma and Mark Forest. Dubbed in English.
VHS: S34503. $24.95.
Osvaldo Civirani, Italy/Spain, 1964, 80 mins.

Hercules and the Captive Women

Famed Greek Bodybuilder Hercules (Reg Park) travels to Atlantis and is annoyed by his rude treatment by the sadistic Queen Antinea (Fay Spain). In order to rescue his son he must fight dragons and an army of identical men before removing the island from the map. With Ettore Manni and Marlo Petri and probably some captive women.
VHS: S09130. $29.95.
Vittorio Cottafavi, Italy, 1963, 87 mins.

Hercules in the Haunted World

Reg Park plays Mr. Muscles. He and a buddy go to Hell, literally, to fetch a magical plant that will heal an ailing princess. Once in Hades they encounter Christopher Lee as the evil Lichas, a servant of the god Pluto. Also rock men, seas of lava and nubile maidens in chains. With Leonara Ruffo and Giorgio Ardisson.
VHS: S09129. $29.95.
Mario Bava, Italy, 1961, 83 mins.

Hercules Unchained

The Greek hero-god Hercules in further adventures as Steve Reeves once again flexes his muscles in the uncut sequel to *Hercules*.
VHS: S08043. $19.98.
Pietro Francisi, Italy, 1960, 101 mins.

Invincible Brothers

Hordes of leopard men descend upon an innocent woman to bring her to the underground kingdom of a despotic queen. The plan of this ruler is twisted. She actually loves the woman's princely suitor, and hopes her ploy will force him into her lair. Richard Lloyd and Tony Freeman star. Dubbed in English. 1965.
VHS: S29453. $29.95.

Jason and the Argonauts

Special effects wizard Ray Harryhausen provided the effects for this mythological adventure, which stars Todd Armstrong as the sailor and explorer who returns to the kingdom of Thessaly after a 20-year voyage, to make his rightful claim to the throne, but who must first find the magical fleece. Bernard Herrmann wrote the score.
VHS: S08522. $14.95.
Laser: CAV. **LD71557. $99.95.**
Don Chaffey, Great Britain, 1963, 104 mins.

Last Glory of Troy (The Avenger)

Our hero gets involved with Etruscans, Trojans and a princess. With Steve Reeves, Carla Marlier and Giacom Stuart. Dubbed in English.
VHS: S32588. $24.95.
Giorgio Rivalta, France/Italy, 1962, 108 mins.

The Medusa Against the Son of Hercules

In this Italian-Spanish feature, a demi-god battles a hideous, one-eyed monster and her legion of stone men. With Richard Harrison.
VHS: S32946. $19.95.
Alberto de Martino, Spain/Italy, 1962, 95 mins.

The Mongols

Jack Palance plays the son of Genghis Khan, while Anita Ekberg is the lady he lusts for. An elaborate spectacle piece with lots of excitement and plenty of pitched battles. With Andre de Toth. Dubbed in English.
VHS: S32583. $24.95.
Leopoldo Savona, Italy/France, 1960, 115 mins.

Revolt of the Slaves

Set in ancient Roman times, this film stars Rhonda Fleming as the daughter of a wealthy aristocrat. She falls in love with a Christian slave, and because of this affair, becomes mixed up in a scheme to save Christians from certain death in the Coliseum. This classic film makes the most of the outrageous spectacle where Roman Christians are to be killed for public entertainment. Dubbed in English.
VHS: S27903. $19.98.
Nunzio Malasomma, Italy/Germany/Spain, 1961, 102 mins.

Romulus and Remus

Steve Reeves is at the center of this drama based on the mythic twin brothers who founded the city of Rome. It starts with their legendary upbringing by a wild she wolf, and then follows them through battles as their military status grows. All this is put in jeopardy when they fall in love with the same woman, the daughter of the King of the Sabines. Dubbed in English. 1961.
VHS: S29450. $29.95.

Samson

Brad Harris interprets the Biblical role as the strong man with very sensitive hair. Alan Steel is cast as the son of Samson. In this Italian production, the fabled muscle man offers his assistance to the king and confronts many enemies. With Brigitte Corey, Serge Gainsbourg, Carolo Tamberlani and Walter Reeves, who is probably not any relation to George or Steve. In color.
VHS: S10387. $19.95.
Gianfranco Parolini, USA, 1961, 90 mins.

Samson and the 7 Miracles of the World

Considered by many to be one of the great sword and sandal pictures of the 1960s. Samson fights against a murdering horde of Tartar warriors while trying to save the life of a beautiful Chinese princess.
VHS: S15366. $29.95.
Riccardo Freda, France/Italy, 1962, 80 mins.

Sandokan and the Pirates of Malaysia

Steve Reeves stars as Sandokan, the leader of a revolt against the East India company and the White Raj of Sarawak. Sandokan has a very personal reason to oppose this tyrannical group. British troops killed his family. His fight for both justice and revenge makes for a thrilling action adventure film. Dubbed in English.
VHS: S27904. $19.98.
Sergio Sollima, Italy/France/Germany, 1964, 110 mins.

Sins of Rome

A well-made Italian version of the story of the rebel slave Spartacus and his slave revolt against Rome. With Massimo Girotti, Ludmilla Cherina and Gianna Maria Canale. Dubbed in English.
VHS: S32582. $24.95.
Riccardo Freda, Italy, 1954, 95 mins.

Son of Hercules in the Land of Darkness

Argolis, the son of Hercules, rescues peasants held in captivity by the evil Queen of Dem. In this "sword and sandal" spectacle, the heroic exploits of Argolis reach such mighty extremes that he brings fiery destruction upon the city of this diabolical ruler by channeling the forces of nature. With Dan Vadis and Carl Brown. Dubbed in English. 1963.
VHS: S29452. $29.95.

Vulcan, Son of Jupiter

Rod Flash Illush, Bella Cortez and Gordon Mitchell face off against bizarre monsters in this Ancient Greek pastiche of horror and fantasy. Greek gods, lizard-like men and strange underground creatures keep this film humming along through one battle after another. Dubbed in English. 1962.
VHS: S29451. $29.95.

ITALIAN ISSUES

Florence

Robin Williams directs and narrates this journey along the footsteps of Michelangelo through the treasures of Florence: the Medici Palace, Michelangelo's David, as well as the works of Verrocchio, Donatello, Ghilberti's Golden Doors of Paradise, and Brunelleschi's magnificent dome for the Cathedral of Santa Maria del Fiore. Art treasures by Leonardo da Vinci and Botticelli are featured. 50 mins.
VHS: S05049. $29.95.

Florence: Cradle of the Rennaissance

The art and architecture from the hub of the Rennaissance movement continues to impact upon today's modern art scene. This tour is a unique portrait of Florence.
VHS: S16726. $19.98.

Rome
A cultural tour through Rome, narrated by Robin Williams, featuring the art and architecture of the great city, and insights into the ancient world of Rome. Places featured include the Appian Way, the Vatican, the treasures of the Sistine Chapel, The Campidoglio, as well as how Napoleon copied the Roman Forum for the City of Paris. 50 mins.
VHS: S05048. $24.95.

Rome, The Eternal City
Begin your visit to Rome on Palatine Hill, home to emperors, kings and pontiffs. Admire the ruins of the Roman Forum and the colosseum. Go shopping along the Via Condotti, then rest your feet on the Spanish steps. Meet the Romans in Piazza Navona, Campo dei Fiori and at the Trevi Fountain. Tour St. Peter's Basilica, the Sistine Chapel, the Vatican Museums. 55 mins.
VHS: S10771. $24.95.

Vatican City: Art and Glory
There is no other place on the planet that can match the riches of Vatican City. Within its collections there are masterpieces from ancient times, the middle ages and the Renaissance. Only here can one view the Apollo Belvedere, Michelangelo's Sistine Chapel frescoes, and Raphael's masterwork, the School of Athens.
VHS: S24267. $19.98.

Venice: Queen of the Adriatic
Seen through the eyes of artists and architects, this tour of Italy's remarkable "floating" city admires the influence of Venetian culture on western civilization.
VHS: S16725. $19.98.

Vidal in Venice, Part One
Gore Vidal, the celebrated American writer, takes the viewer along the routes of Venice's glorious, mysterious, twisted history. In this beautifully filmed, very personal tour of Venice past and present, Vidal tells about the Venetian people, their Empire, including visits to Crete and Maxos, Venetian strongholds of the past. 55 mins.
VHS: S05050. $29.95.

Vidal in Venice, Part Two
The art treasures, the sumptuous palaces, the literary past, the scandals of yesterday and the touristy Venice of today are all revealed in Vidal's chronicle as he wanders from the canals to the Doge's Palace. 55 mins.
VHS: S05051. $29.95.

spanish cinema

Against the Wind

Antonio Banderas and Emma Suarez star in this story of obsessive and destructive romantic love. They are brother and sister. Juan (Banderas) takes refuge in an isolated area of Andalusia. His exile from home proves useless however, when his sister decides she must see her true love, her brother. Spanish with English subtitles.

VHS: S23959. $19.95.

Paco Perinan, Spain, 1990, 117 mins.

Baton Rouge

Antonio Banderas, Victoria Abril and Carmen Maura star in this sexy thriller loaded with unexpected treachery and passion. Banderas is a gigolo who joins forces with a psychologist to frame a woman for murder. Their victim is experiencing terrible nightmares but she is not so unbalanced as to make the perfect fall gal. Spanish with English subtitles.

VHS: S29864. $89.95.

Rafael Moleon, Spain, 1988, 90 mins.

Belle Epoque

This film won an Oscar as the Best Foreign Language Film in 1994. In this charming romantic comedy, a handsome young soldier flees the Spanish Revolution only to inspire his own sexual revolution. Finding succor in the house of an artist who has four daughters, he proceeds to seduce them all, or is it the other way around? Spanish with English subtitles.

VHS: S22768. $19.95.

Laser: LD74619. $34.95.

Fernando Trueba, Spain, 1992, 109 mins.

Butterfly Wings

This unusual drama about a dysfunctional family registers alternately as sad, horrifying and somber. Carmen hopes her unborn child is a son in order to carry on her husband's name. Guilt and fear prevent her from telling her sensitive and shy six-year-old daughter. The birth of the child triggers a series of nightmarish events. Winner of the Best Picture at the San Sebastian Film Festival. Spanish with English subtitles.

VHS: S20382. $59.95.

Juanma Bajo Ulloa, Spain, 1991, 105 mins.

Colegas

From the director of *El Diputado*, the story of three friends and their transition into adulthood. A crisis comes about when one of the friends becomes pregnant, and the youths resort to street hustling to raise the funds to solve the problem. Spanish with English subtitles.

VHS: S01562. $89.95.

Eloy de la Iglesia, Spain, 117 mins.

Costa Brava (Family Album)

Two women, one a tour guide in Barcelona, the other a Tel Aviv-born, Boston-bred seismic engineer, are engaged in a comic romance that is both warm and convincing. This film won the Audience Award at the Los Angeles Gay and Lesbian Film Festival for Best Feature and the Audience Award for Best Lesbian Feature at the San Francisco Gay and Lesbian Film Festival. Shot on location, in English.

VHS: S29868. $49.95.

Marta Balletbo-Coll, Spain, 1995, 92 mins.

Cronica del Alba

Based on a novel by Ramon Sender, *Cronica del Alba* continues the story that Sender started in his novel, *Valentina*. Pepe, the main character, is balancing his time between University studies and a pharmacy lab apprenticeship. Set in 1919 in Zarazoga, Pepe, like all young Spaniards, is caught up in the building tension of the impending rebellion. More in love than ever with the voluptuously grown Valentina, all access to her is now prohibited by her over-protective mother. Spanish with English subtitles.

VHS: S07589. $49.95.

Antonio J. Betancour, Spain, 1982, 82 mins.

Demons in the Garden

Demons in the Garden presents the ironic chronicle of the emotional education in provincial Spain during the post-war Franco years. The film follows the intricate relationships among two feuding brothers and a sister, an overbearing mother and an adopted daughter (stunningly played by Angela Molina) who has given birth to an illegitimate child, fathered by one of the sons, set against a wealth of rich background detail. "This is probably the best film of Aragon's career...a film of great beauty and sensitivity," wrote *Variety*. Spanish with English subtitles.

VHS: S10869. $29.95.

Manuel Gutierrez Aragon, Spain, 1983, 105 min.

Diamond Plaza

Based on the novel by Merce Rodoreda; this film features two opposing characters—the woman, docile and sensitive, the man, domineering yet childish—who are forced to mature when their lives are shattered by a tragic, cruel and violent civil war. Spanish with English subtitles.

VHS: S07733. $59.95.

Francesco Bertrin, Spain, 1981, 112 mins.

Don Juan, My Love

It is the eve of All Saints Day and the ghost of Don Juan, the world's most legendary lover, is rising from his grave in a cemetery in Seville, Spain. His soul has been trapped in Purgatory for 450 years, and he is returning to earth to perform a good deed which will free him from his phantom existence. "A breathless bedroom farce!" (*New York Daily News*). With Maria Barranco, Rossy De Palma, and Loles Leon, best known for their roles in Almodovar's *Women on the Verge of a Nervous Breakdown*. Spanish with yellow English subtitles.

VHS: S15545. $19.98.

Antonio Mercero, Spain, 1991, 96 mins.

Dream of Light (Quince Tree of the Sun)

An amazingly beautiful, studied film by the Spanish cinematic genius Victor Erice, and one of the most intense, detailed looks at the artistic process. The film follows the creation of a single painting, a still life of a quince tree, by contemporary painter Antonio Lopez Garcia. The film takes the form of a journal as Erice delves inside the very process of artistic creation—"in its own minimalist way [the film] becomes a thoughtful, delicate inquiry into the essence of the artistic process, and a tribute to the beauty and mutability of nature. Erice's film is much bigger than it may appear to be. It is also, like the subject, undeniably one of a kind" (*The New York Times*). Original title: *El Sol del Membrillo*. Winner of the International Critics' Prize at the Cannes Film Festival. Spanish with English subtitles.

VHS: S35296. $79.95.

Victor Erice, Spain, 1991, 128 mins.

El Diputado

A political thriller about a gay man high in the ranks of the Spanish Socialist Party whose love affair with a 16-year-old boy jeopardizes the fate of the nation. The Advocate said the gay love scenes are among the best ever presented in a commercial film. Spanish with English subtitles.

VHS: S00397. $79.95.

Eloy de la Iglesia, Spain, 1983, 111 mins.

El Sacerdote (The Priest)

An early work by Eloy de la Iglesia, this is the shocking story of a troubled priest fighting for his own soul. Father Miguel fights physical and psychic fantasies of sex and suffers from painful memories of a bizarre childhood. Banned at the time of its original release. Spanish with English subtitles.

VHS: S23576. $79.95.

Eloy de la Iglesia, Spain, 1979, 62 mins.

Extramuros

Carmen Maura, famed for her riveting portrayals in *Women on the Verge of a Nervous Breakdown* and *Law of Desire*, plays a nun who is challenged by her irrepressible lesbian desires. Set in a convent during the Spanish Inquisition, the film is not only a depiction of repressed passion, but a sharply critical look at the relationship between the Church and political power as the convent vies for fame and money through the faked visions and stigmata of the lesbian sisters. Spanish with English subtitles.

VHS: S24033. $39.95.

Miguel Picazo, Spain, 1985, 120 mins.

The Fencing Master

An aristocratic swordsman takes on a female pupil, the mysterious Adela de Otero, after she wins him over with her skill and beauty. In their secret lessons, Don Jaime teaches Adela his deadly thrust to the throat and finds himself falling in love. After one of Don Jaime's pupils is found murdered by a thrust to the throat, he soon finds himself drawn into a world of politics and intrigue. With Assumpta Serna, Omero Antonutti and Joaquim de Almeida. Spanish with English subtitles.

VHS: S32963. $89.95.

Pedro Olea, Spain, 1992, 88 mins.

Fortunata y Jacinta

Based on the best-known novel by the great 19th century novelist Benito Perez Galdos, who has been often compared to the Latin equivalent of Flaubert, *Fortunata y Jacinta* is a detailed, keenly observed story of two women who are in love with the same man. Spanish with English subtitles.

VHS: S04609. $39.95.

Angelino Fons, Spain, 1969, 108 mins.

I Don't Want to Talk About It

Marcello Mastroianni stars in Maria-Luisa Bemberg's (*The Official Story*) fairy tale-like film about love. Mastroianni plays a handsome and wealthy European man who picks a rather unlikely object of affection. Bemberg's thought-provoking film poses the question, "How can size matter when it is a question of love?" Spanish with English subtitles.

VHS: S24326. $19.95.

Laser: LD74892. $34.95.

Maria-Luisa Bemberg, Spain, 1994, 102 mins.

I'm the One You're Looking For

Through the exotic streets of Barcelona's underworld, the darker side of love and sexuality comes to life in a taut psychological thriller about a beautiful celebrity model seeking revenge on her rapist. Vengeful desire becomes an uncontrollable obsession when she teams up with a short-tempered taxi driver and a hot-blooded erotic dancer in her frantic search. Based on a short story by Gabriel Garcia Marquez, who also co-wrote the screenplay. Spanish with English subtitles.

VHS: S13842. $19.98.

Jaime Chavarri, Spain, 1988, 85 mins.

In a Glass Cage

A thriller that redefines the horror film. Written and directed by Agustin Villaronga, the story concerns a Nazi concentration camp doctor and his family living in exile in Spain a few years after the war. After a nasty fall leaves him in need of an iron lung, the Nazi finds his new male nurse an indispensable member of the family. With Gunter Meisner, David Sust and Marisa Paredes as Griselda. Spanish with English subtitles.

VHS: S10734. $79.95.

Agustin Villaronga, Spain, 1986, 110 mins.

In Memoriam

Based on a short story by Adolfo Bioy Casares; Geraldine Chaplin and the great Spanish actor Jose Luis Gomez star in the story of a man who has to come to terms with a past he longed to leave behind, only to find out that his inability to express his feelings has caused a great tragedy. Spanish with English subtitles.

VHS: S07734. $39.95.

Enrique Brasso, Spain, 1976, 96 mins.

Intruso

An erotic love triangle with a Hitchcockian twist, *Intruso* tells the story of Luis, Ramiro and Angel, three childhood friends whose lives become strangely entangled as adults. Although Luisa marries Angel, she realizes that she's in love with Ramiro. Angel then suddenly disappears, leaving Luisa and Ramiro free to marry. Years later, Angel returns, drawing them into a swirling vortex of jealousy, love and madness. Starring Victoria Abril (*Tie Me Up, Tie Me Down*). Spanish with English subtitles.

VHS: S32222. $89.95.

Vicente Aranda, Spain, 1993, 90 mins.

It's Raining Money

Eddie Constantine and Elisa Montes star in this Cold War era thriller. Secret agent Lemmy Caution goes to great lengths in order to foil an embezzlement plot in Spain. Dubbed in English.

VHS: S27900. $19.98.

Jose Luis Monter, France/Spain, 1963, 85 mins.

Jamon, Jamon
This winner of the Silver Lion at the Venice Film Festival combines outrageous humor and steamy sex in a quirky movie of mismatched love affairs. Anna Galiena, Stefania Sandrelli, Javier Bardem and Penelope Cruz are all featured in this tale of erotic passions.
VHS: S21097. $19.98.
Bigas Luna, Spain, 1993, 95 mins.

La Memoria del Agua
The story of Joseph Fruferman, whose memories of his childhood in Russia and his adult life in France take up the last moments of his life. Images of his mother, late wife and daughter frame these poignant memories in a haunting black-and-white film in which the narrative is interspliced with documentary fragments. The film centers on the love that makes the impossible possible through its overwhelming power and survives physical death and separation just as water retains its memory even after its molecules separate. Spanish and Russian dialog with English subtitles.
VHS: S27799. $29.95.
Hector Faver, Spain, 1991, 82 mins.

Last Evenings with Teresa (Ultimas Tardes con Teresa)
Based on a novel by Juan Marse; the story of an ill-fated love affair between Teresa, a society girl, and Manolo, an ambitious petty thief. She sees in him an exploited, working class man; for him, she signifies hope. Spanish with English subtitles.
VHS: S07739. $59.95.
Gonzalo Herralde, Spain, 1983, 105 mins.

Lazarillo
This morality tale is set in 17th-century Castile. A fatherless boy is abandoned by his mother and subsequently finds work with a strange succession of employers. A blind beggar, a miserly sacristan, a fake nobleman and even a traveling band of performers all teach him valuable lessons in vanity, cunning, deception and, ultimately, survival. Spanish with English subtitles.
VHS: S21606. $24.95.
Cesar Ardavin, Spain, 1959, 109 mins.

Letters from Alou
Alou is an African immigrant in Spain whose unflagging optimism is unaffected by all the instances of exploitation and discrimination that characterize his new home. This social drama won Best Picture and Best Male Lead at the San Sebastian Film Festival. Spanish, French and Senegalese with English subtitles.
VHS: S20879. $79.95.
Montxo Armendariz, Spain, 1990, 100 mins.

Los Placeres Ocultos
A closeted banker, middle-aged and successful, falls madly in love with a poor but handsome 18-year-old student—with devastating consequences for the young man. Carefully crafted and insightfully scripted, *Los Placeres Ocultos* was the first openly gay film to emerge from Spain following the death of Franco. Virtually unknown to American audiences, this complex updating of *Death in Venice* is among the most powerful affirmations of gay life ever depicted on film. Spanish with English subtitles.
VHS: S11636. $79.95.
Eloy de la Iglesia, Spain, 1977, 97 mins.

Marianela
Based on the novel by Benito Perez Galdos, Marianela is the story of a disfigured orphan girl whose only solace is to serve as a guide to a young and handsome blind man, Pablo. When Pablo recovers his eyesight, Marianela's fragile world is shattered. Spanish with English subtitles.
VHS: S03197. $39.95.
Angelino Fons, Spain, 1972, 105 mins.

Miracle in Rome
Called "a small miracle itself" by the *New York Times, Miracle in Rome* tells the story of Margarito Duarte, a man whose seven-year-old daughter dies suddenly. Upon visiting her grave 12 years later, Margarito finds his daughter's body just as he had left it. His fellow townspeople call the event a miracle, but the town bishop wants the girl reburied. Based on an original story by Gabriel Garcia Marquez, who also co-wrote the screenplay. Spanish with English subtitles.
VHS: S13511. $19.98.
Lisandro Duque Naranjo, Spain, 1988, 76 mins.

Miracle of Marcelino
The classic, immensely popular film of the 50's, set in a rural area of Spain, an emotionally moving story of a young boy discovering faith. Spanish with English subtitles.
VHS: S06478. $59.95.
Ladislao Vajda, Spain, 1956, 88 mins.

Moonchild
Since ancient times an African tribe has awaited the arrival of a white boy who is the Son of the Moon. David, a 12-year-old European orphan, believes he is that child-god. The result is an unexpected fantasy adventure that is beautifully filmed and magically evocative. Spanish with English subtitles.
VHS: S27612. $69.95.
Agustin Villaronga, Spain, 1989, 80 mins.

Mouth to Mouth (Boca a Boca)
A struggling actor takes a job as a phone sex operator to make ends meet, setting in motion a hilariously sexy, madcap adventure. With Almodovar vet Javier Bardem, Josep Maria Flotats and Aitana Sanchez-Gijon. Spanish with English subtitles.
VHS: S34288. $103.99.
Manuel Gomez Pereira, Spain, 1995, 97 mins.

Padre Nuestro
This Bunuelian black comedy is a satirical romp about a cardinal (Fernando Rey) who returns to his native village to prepare final arrangements before his death. He reconciles with his atheist brother (Francisco Rabal) though he's torn about acknowledging his illegitimate daughter (Victoria Abril), a notorious local prostitute known as "La Cardenala." "Mr. Rey and Mr. Rabal sing; the two pros give superlative performances full of shadings and surprises" (Walter Goodman). Spanish with English subtitles.
VHS: S19063. $79.95.
Francisco Regueiro, Spain, 1985, 91 mins.

The Red Squirrel
Jota, a rock musician deserted by his girlfriend, is contemplating suicide when he rushes to the aid of a young woman after her motorcycle crashes. When he discovers she has lost her memory as a result of the accident, he pretends to be her lover and creates a fictitious life for her. *The Daily Telegraph* called this modern-day version of Alfred Hitchcock's masterpiece, *Vertigo*, "as taut and intricate as anything by Hitchcock." Winner of Director's Fortnight at Cannes and Best Young Picture at European Felix Awards. Spanish with English subtitles.
VHS: S30041. $89.95.
Julio Medem, Spain, 1993, 104 mins.

Skyline
Fernando Colombo's unconventional drama about cultural dislocation. The film details the comical day-to-day activities of a resettled Spanish photographer, Gustavo (Antonio Resines), as he attempts to establish his reputation and earn a living in New York. The film has a documentary-style naturalism as Gustavo endures small and private struggles heightened by his unfamiliarity with the language through his determination for self-sufficiency and respect. With Beatriz Perez-Porro, Patricia Cisarano and Jaime Nos. Spanish with English subtitles.
VHS: S01211. $39.95.
Laser: LD71328. $49.95.
Fernando Colomo, Spain, 1983, 90 mins.

Spirit of the Beehive
A landmark Spanish film by Victor Erice, featuring the remarkable Ana Torrent in the story of two little girls growing up after the Spanish Civil War in the countryside. The hypnotic, spellbinding nature of the film is a rare achievement in cinema, as Erice evokes a deep poetry of childhood in a portrait of isolation. Spanish with English subtitles.
VHS: S08104. $29.95.
Victor Erice, Spain, 1973, 95 mins.

Starknight
Harvey Keitel, Klaus Kinski and Fernando Rey star in this unique combination sci-fi/medieval era film. An alien lands in a small village and falls for a young noble woman. With the help of a necromancer, he eventually attains his new earthbound goal, marriage to the young lady. In English.
VHS: S27857. $14.99.
Fernando Colomo, Spain, 1985, 90 mins.

Tombs ofF the Blind Dead
Spanish auteur Ossorio made his name in the '70s Spanish horror genre with this tale of horrific and malefic reanimated mummified corpses of 13th-century Templar knights who seek victims through sound alone and drink human blood in order to sustain their own damned existence. The superb, highly influential score by Anton Garcia Abril helps underline the stunning visuals. Despite the trite storylines and hammy acting, "the Templars make Ossorio's grisly, heart-string quartet more than worth the effort, galloping to the rescue of the viewer's sanity like a spectral cavalry charge" (Nigel J. Burrell, March 1995). Digitally remastered collector's edition presented in its original uncut form. Spanish with English subtitles.
VHS: S31002. $14.98.
Amando de Ossorio, Spain, 1972, 102 mins.

Tu Solo
Traditions like bull fighting inevitably depend on venerable institutions. This graceful art is revealed through a true story set in Spain's most prestigious bull fighting school. Students tell their own side of the story, and in a unique tradition, bare all for a nude bullfighting scene.
VHS: S23743. $79.95.
Teo Escamilla, Spain, 1995, 96 mins.

Umbrella for Three (Paraguas Para Tres)
Daniel and Maria are two recently divorced professionals living in modern Spain who happen to run into each other an awful lot. This is a romantic comedy after all, and though it takes a while for it to dawn on them, they are fated to fall in love. Only after a series of comic misadventures do they come to understand the mysteries of chance and love. In Spanish with English subtitles.
VHS: S26277. $59.95.
Felipe Vega, Spain, 1992, 93 mins.

Wild Horses
When an elderly pensioner (Hector Alterio) resorts to bank robbery to recover his $15,000 nest egg, a young employee (Leonard Sbaraglia) gives him $500,000 and volunteers to be his hostage. The unlikely duo escapes and hits the road to Patagonia. During their flight, Jose and Pedro send videotaped messages to the press detailing the money's illegal origins and their own good intentions. Ordinary citizens soon come to their aid, and Jose and Pedro find themselves in the limelight. With Cecilia Dopazo. "Cut from the same cloth as *Butch Cassidy and the Sundance Kid* and *Thelma and Louise* with a touch of Tarantino thrown in" (*Box Office Magazine*). Spanish with English subtitles.
VHS: S32962. $89.95.
Marcelo Pineyro, Argentina, 1995, 122 mins.

Zafarinas
Filmed within Zafarinas, North Africa, Olea's gripping action thriller concerns the Grupo de Regulares barracks in this ancient walled city. A shoot-out with the military police leads to an investigation of two identical deaths in the same day. Commander Contreras (Oscar Ladoire) releases a prisoner from the stockade to lead the investigation. Suspicion runs rampant and Jaime (Jorge Sanz, *Belle Epoque*) is thrown into the midst of a love triangle where all is not what it seems. Spanish with English subtitles.
VHS: S32173. $89.98.
Pedro Olea, Spain, 1995, 85 mins.

CARLOS SAURA

Ay, Carmela
The always vivacious Carmen Maura, the star of so many films by Pedro Almodovar, plays the title role of an apolitical cabaret performer caught between the combatants of the Spanish Civil War. Maura performs several lively musical numbers in this historical drama directed by Carlos Saura (*Blood Wedding*). With Andres Pajares, Gabino Diego, Miguel Rellan and Maurizio De Razza as the Italian officer in charge of staging a musical revue for a very demanding Fascist audience. In Spanish with English subtitles.
VHS: S15353. $19.95.
Carlos Saura, Spain, 1990, 105 mins.

Blood Wedding
A flamenco ballet version of Federico Garcia Lorca's classic, from the director of *Carmen*. The climax of this dramatic story is a duel to the death between the bridegroom and the bride's former lover. Featuring choreographer Antonio Gades, former director of the National Ballet of Spain. Music by Emilio de Diego. Spanish with English subtitles.
VHS: S00150. $24.95.
Carlos Saura, Spain, 1981, 71 mins.

Cria
A beautifully acted, haunting film—Ana, played by Ana Torrent, is the nine-year-old heroine who has an uncanny talent for observing scenes not meant for her eyes. Carlos Saura fashions a film about the darker side of childhood, about superstition, knowledge, and loss of innocence. Spanish with English subtitles.
VHS: S00279. $49.95.
Carlos Saura, Spain, 1977, 115 mins.

Elisa Vida Mia
Fernando Rey won Best Actor at Cannes for his role in this story about a man estranged from his daughter (Geraldine Chaplin). She has returned to help her ailing father and writes his biography. Eventually her own recollections lead to a deeper understanding that enable the two to reunite. Spanish with English subtitles.
VHS: S21758. $59.95.
Carlos Saura, Spain, 1977, 125 mins.

Garden of Delights
One of Carlos Saura's best films; a terrific black comedy starring the great Spanish actor Jose Luis Lopez Vasquez as the son of a rich family who, in a car accident, develops amnesia. The spendthrift, greedy family is only concerned with supporting their freewheeling habits. But lost in the amnesia is the number of the Swiss bank account which holds the cash, and so the family has to resort to devious means of psychoanalysis in an attempt to "cure" Jose, and get the bank account number at the same time. Truly a wonderful film. Spanish with English subtitles.
VHS: S07575. $29.95.
Carlos Saura, Spain, 1970, 95 mins.

The Hunt
Made under the repressive regime of Franco's Spain, this brilliant allegory deals with four men rabbit-hunting in the country outside Madrid. As the day passes, the sun gets hotter and petty jealousies spark memories and guilt about the Spanish Civil War. The day ends in violence and a shocking climax as the men's seething anger and hatreds are stripped bare. Spanish with English subtitles.
VHS: S20836. $59.95.
Carlos Saura, Spain, 1965, 87 mins.

Outrage
Antonio Banderas stars as a man who falls passionately in love with a circus sharp shooter. He never suspects that his feelings of devotion are a prelude to the emotional and physical nightmare he will soon enter. It all begins when his lover is raped by three mechanics. Mentally disabled by the attack, she launches a series of vengeful killings and ends up in a bloody showdown with justice. Also known as *Dispara* (*Shoot!*). With Francesca Neri, Walter Vidarte and Eulalia Ramon. Spanish with English subtitles.
VHS: S27408. $14.98.
Laser: LD75554. $39.99.
Carlos Saura, Italy/Spain, 1995, 96 mins.

Sevillanas
Seven short flamenco performances, featuring some of Spain's top performers, are collected on this documentary-like work. This film is from the maker of the wildly successful *Carmen*, a dance-laden film featuring spectacular flamenco sequences. In addition to the terrific dance found on this newer work, there is extraordinary music and singing. Spanish with English subtitles.
VHS: S27205. $39.95.
Carlos Saura, Spain, 1992, 55 mins.

The Stilts (Los Zancos)
The Stilts stars Laura del Sol, Fernando Fernan Gomez and Francisco Rabal in a passionate, complex inquiry into the dynamics of the human psyche through the story of a doomed love triangle. Spanish with English subtitles.
VHS: S06843. $24.95.
Carlos Saura, Spain, 1984, 95 mins.

ALMODOVAR

Dark Habits
An outrageous comedy from Pedro Almodovar, set in a convent that's falling apart. Mother Superior is feeling low, the youngest nun has been eaten by cannibals, and the convent hasn't saved a soul in years. But a night club singer on the run has taken refuge in the convent, and the nuns throw their wildest party yet. "Hilarious, irreverent fun," wrote *The Village Voice*, "Part Luis Bunuel, part John Waters camp. Lots of laughs." Spanish with English subtitles.
VHS: S08103. $79.95.
Pedro Almodovar, Spain, 1984, 116 mins.

The Flower of My Secret
Almodovar's fun story of a romance writer, fresh out of inspiration, who goes looking for a real-life love of her own. Starring Marisa Paredes, Juan Echanove, Carmen Elias, Rossy de Palma and Chus Lampreave. "Delicious! Funny! Almodovar returns to the comedy of his earlier, best work" (Caryn James, *The New York Times*). Spanish with English subtitles.
VHS: S30148. $19.95.
Laser: LD75995. $39.95.
Pedro Almodovar, Spain, 1996, 101 mins.

High Heels
Part revenge comedy, thriller and sexual farce, Pedro Almodovar's *High Heels* is a Sirkian melodrama about the bizarre relationship between an aging Spanish movie star and singer (Marisa Paredes) and her daughter, a prominent local television anchor woman (Victoria Abril). Almodovar throws in an acrobatic sex scene, a prison dance number, an on-camera confession, a buried family secret and a final reconciliation. Spanish with English subtitles.
VHS: S16919. $89.95.
Pedro Almodovar, Spain, 1990, 115 mins.

Kika
Pedro Almodovar's offbeat sex farce is the story of Kika, a make-up artist who lives with her lover Ramon, a photographer specializing in women's lingerie. Their maid, Juanita, is madly in love with Kika, while Ramon's stepfather likes to seduce her from time to time. That's only the beginning of the preposterous goings on which really heat up when Pablo, Juanita's brother, an on-the-lam ex-porno star, enters the picture. Spanish with English subtitles.
VHS: S23572. $14.98.
Laser: LD75489. $39.99.
Pedro Almodovar, Spain, 1994, 109 mins.

Labyrinth of Passion
Pedro Almodovar's second feature film features nymphomaniacs, incest victims, transvestites, rock musicians and Iranian fundamentalists living in Madrid. In other words, something for everyone who thinks this filmmaker is the kinkiest and most entertaining modern artist to emerge from the Iberian peninsula since Salvador Dali. Cast includes Cecilia Roth, Helga Line, Marta Fernandez-Mura, Fernando Vivanco and Ruze Neiro as the uncomfortable heir to the Arabian throne. Spanish with English subtitles.
VHS: S12364. $79.95.
Pedro Almodovar, Spain, 1982, 100 mins.

Law of Desire
An entertaining, hedonist film unlike any other. Pablo, the main character, is a filmmaker who lives the high life in Madrid, engaging in casual drugs and homosexual encounters, with the real complications beginning when Pablo brings home Antonio, the government minister's son, who falls madly in love with him. Spanish with English subtitles.
VHS: S06023. $79.95.
Pedro Almodovar, Spain, 1987, 105 mins.

Live Flesh
Set in Madrid, Almodovar's seductive, subversive comedy stars Liberto Rabal as Victor, a pizza delivery man obsessed with Elena (Francesca Neri), a beautiful Italian junkie he met and slept with a few days ago. When his aggressive courting is mistaken for rape, cops David (Javier Bardem) and Sancho (Jose Sancho) show up at the scene, Victor's gun accidentally goes off and the younger David is shot and paralyzed. Four years later David is a wheelchair basketball star, now married to Elena. When Victor is released from prison, their destinies begin to cross again. But nothing is what it seems, and only when Victor turns this world upside down do we see the true picture. Spanish with English subtitles.
VHS: S34669. $99.99.
Laser: LD77020. $39.99.
Pedro Almodovar, Spain/France, 1998, 101 mins.

Matador
From Pedro Almodovar, another excursion into the bizarre and offbeat. A retired bullfighter and a female defense attorney find they share similar interests, which happen to be sex and death. His darkest film yet, but filled with madcap characters and wry humor. With Assumpta Serna, Antonio Banderas, Nacho Martinez, Eva Cobo, Chus Lampreave and Carmen Maura. In Spanish with English subtitles.
VHS: S10733. $79.95.
Pedro Almodovar, Spain, 1986, 115 mins.

Pepi, Luci, Bom and Other Girls
Pedro Almodovar announced his stylistic preoccupations and thematic concerns with his first feature after a series of shorts on Super 8 and 16mm. Luci leaves her psychopathic husband for a lesbian affair. He responds by raping Pepi, whose friends, a motley collection of punks and musicians, come to her aid. With Carmen Maura, Eva Siva, Alaska, Felix Rotaeta, Concha. Spanish with English subtitles.
VHS: S16918. $79.95.
Pedro Almodovar, Spain, 1980, 80 mins.

Tie Me Up, Tie Me Down
The controversial hit by Pedro Almodovar about Ricki, who falls in love with Marina, an ex-porn movie star, and proceeds to capture her and tie her up at her own apartment. She is torn between trying to escape and falling in love with him. "Almodovar's theme is not the domination of women, but the strangeness of love and possessiveness. The performances are outstanding. Antonio Banderas is psychopathic and vulnerable, Victoria Abril is fierce and funny" (*Sight and Sound*). Spanish with English subtitles (only R version available).
VHS: S12994. $19.95.
Pedro Almodovar, Spain, 1990, 103 mins.

What Have I Done to Deserve This?
Carmen Maura stars as a housewife and cleaning woman hooked on no-doz who ends up selling one of her sons to a dentist and killing her husband with a ham bone. "An absolutely wonderful black comedy. A small masterpiece," wrote *The New York Times*. Spanish with English subtitles.
VHS: S08102. $79.95.
Pedro Almodovar, Spain, 1985, 100 mins.

Women on the Verge of a Nervous Breakdown
The latest wacky comedy from Pedro Almodovar once again stars Carmen Maura, his perennial leading lady. She plays a popular Spanish actress driven to distraction when her lover leaves for another woman. She knows she can talk him out of leaving if only she can talk directly to him and not deal with the answering machine. A comedy of errors ensues that involve a drugged pitcher of gazpacho, Shiite terrorists and a mental patient who left the asylum too soon. Spanish with English subtitles.
VHS: S10757. $19.98.
Pedro Almodovar, Spain, 1988, 98 mins.

LUIS BUNUEL

Age of Gold
Bunuel's masterpiece extolls love and attacks religion and the social order in an amazing assemblage of images that remain no less provocative today than they were in 1930. Its central metaphor is a couple making love who are continually disturbed by the intrusions of officialdom, police and the Church. It remains one of the most unashamedly erotic films ever made, with a famous toe-sucking sequence. Financed by the Vicomte de Noailles, who gave Bunuel complete freedom and declared it "exquisite and delicious," the film immediately became the object of right-wing extremists and remained unseen for generations because of the Church's threat to excommunicate the Vicomte if the film were distributed. With Gaston Modot, Lya Lys, Max Ernst and Pierre Prevert. French with English subtitles.
VHS: S00024. $29.95.
Luis Bunuel, France, 1930, 62 mins.

Belle de Jour
A masterpiece from Luis Bunuel in which the cool Catherine Deneuve sparkles as a respectable middle-class wife with a very contented husband, who finds a day job in a brothel that gives her an outlet for deeper, darker passions. "Bunuel constructs both a clear portrait of the bourgeoisie as degenerate, dishonest and directionless, and an unhysterical depiction of Deneuve's inner fantasy life where she entertains dreams of humiliations galore" (Geoff Andrew). French with English subtitles.
VHS: S26707. $19.98.
Laser: LD75380. $49.98.
Luis Bunuel, France, 1967, 100 mins.

The Criminal Life of Archibaldo de la Cruz
Archibaldo believes a musical box he owned as a youth had the power to kill. He still believes he can kill women and, in fact, confesses to several murders. Bunuel delivers a hilarious portrait of a frustrated sadist who "is an artist…His crimes are his very conscious, aesthetic attempts to revive a delicious sensation" (Raymond Durgnat). With Ernesto Alonso, Miroslava and Rita Macedo. Spanish with English subtitles.
VHS: S18118. $29.95.
Luis Bunuel, Mexico, 1955, 91 mins.

Death in the Garden
A thriller with a surrealist's touch, this is one of Bunuel's most accessible and fascinating films. Fleeing a repressive government, a group of misfits (a miner, a prostitute, a priest and a deaf-mute girl) escape through the Amazon jungle. As the journey becomes more arduous, the characters begin to shed their petty differences and work toward a common good. The discovery of a crashed airliner supplying food and money introduces a renewed unpleasantness in the group. With Georges Marchal, Michel Piccoli and Simone Signoret. French with English subtitles.
VHS: S29487. $59.95.
Luis Bunuel, France/Mexico, 1956, 90 mins.

Diary of a Chambermaid
A great Bunuel film in which Bunuel updated the famous Mirabeau novel about the decadent French upper classes of the 19th century to 1928; Jeanne Moreau plays the chambermaid, both demure and cunning, who takes a position in a cheerless chateau, and immediately becomes the newest "objet d'art" for a whole family of perfectly ordinary perverts, from the shoe-fetishist father to the gamekeeper, who is a reactionary and a rapist. French with English subtitles.
VHS: S05990. $24.95.
Luis Bunuel, France, 1964, 97 mins.

The Discreet Charm of the Bourgeoisie
Six characters are forever trying to sit down for a meal, but bizarre events—dreams, fantasies, guests, terrorists—interfere. Bunuel's brilliant satire lampoons the church, diplomats, wealthy socialites and radical terrorists and is a pure joy to watch. With Fernando Rey, Delphine Seyrig, Stephane Audran, Bulle Ogier, Jean-Pierre Cassel and Michel Piccoli. French with English subtitles.
VHS: S00345. $24.95.
Luis Bunuel, France, 1972, 100 mins.

El (This Strange Passion)
The psychological study of a man obsessed. A wealthy, middle-aged man marries a young woman and then develops a paranoid obsession with her supposed infidelity. One of the great films from Bunuel's Mexican period, the black humor of *El* failed to be appreciated by critics at the time of its release. It is now considered one of the most representative of Bunuel's personal mythology. Spanish with English subtitles.
VHS: S13680. $24.95.
Luis Bunuel, Mexico, 1952, 88 mins.

El Bruto

A powerful social melodrama which deals with a corrupt landlord who decides he needs a strong-arm man to intimidate his restless tenants. El Bruto, played by Pedro Armendariz, is the thick-headed slaughterhouse worker loyal to the exploiters. Bruto is lusted after by his employer's frustrated wife and at the same time longs for an innocent girl whose father he unfortunately beat to death. Spanish with English subtitles.
VHS: S06934. $24.95.
Luis Bunuel, Mexico, 1952, 83 mins.

The Exterminating Angel

A metaphorically rich and comic film, *Exterminating Angel* is the story of guests invited to an elegant dinner party who find they are unable to leave at the end of the evening. A mysterious force compels them to stay…and stay…and stay. After several days, their well-heeled social facades collapse as hunger, thirst, fear, and boredom send them into a frenzy. Bunuel stated that this film is "a metaphor, a deeply felt, disturbing reflection of the life of modern man, a witness to the fundamental preoccupations of our time." It is certainly one of Bunuel's greatest achievements. Spanish with English subtitles.
VHS: S00422. $24.95.
Luis Bunuel, Mexico, 1962, 95 mins.

Fever Mounts in El Pao

Gerard Philipe's last film, set on an island off the coast of Latin America. Philipe portrays Vazquez, the idealistic secretary to a corrupt and callous governor. When he eventually becomes governor himself, he betrays his humane idealism. Bunuel skillfully blends melodrama with acute political analysis of how systems subvert individuals. English dubbed.
VHS: S00441. $29.95.
Luis Bunuel, Mexico, 1959, 97 mins.

The Great Madcap (El Gran Calavera)

Bunuel's hilarious portrait of the hypocrisy of the middle class centers on the disastrous results of a wealthy man's spendthrift habits and womanizing on his family. An elegant satire on class, sex, advertising and the reverse exploitation of the ruling elite. Spanish with English subtitles.
VHS: S18117. $29.95.
Luis Bunuel, Mexico, 1949, 90 mins.

Illusion Travels by Streetcar

Shot in something like two weeks, to pay grocery bills (one of five features turned out during Bunuel's very active 1952-53 period), *Illusion* tells the story of two young employees of a municipal public transport company in Mexico City—driver and conductor—who get drunk at a local festival and decide to take the girl on one last trip on a train about to be retired from service. This results in a number of hilarious incidents and unexpected adventures. Spanish with English subtitles.
VHS: S13588. $59.95.
Luis Bunuel, Mexico, 1953, 90 mins.

Land Without Bread

An extraordinary film about the impoverished people living in the Las Hurdes region of Spain. Bunuel constructs the film in the manner of a travelogue. The absurdity of the contrast between narration and image results in a vision so powerful the film seems surreal. Plus a classic short film, *Housing Problems*, directed by A. Elton and E. Anstey. Spanish with English subtitles.
VHS: S00720. $29.95.
Luis Bunuel, Spain, 1932, 45 mins.

Los Olvidados

A milestone of filmmaking; Bunuel's great film looks at the lives of young people growing up in the slums of Mexico, and in particular, at the desperately inevitable process by which an older, more corrupt gang leader, Jacob, hounds and destroys the younger, more innocent Pedro, before being destroyed himself. Spanish with English subtitles.
VHS: S09000. $59.95.
Luis Bunuel, Mexico, 1950, 81 mins.

Mexican Bus Ride

Bunuel, in a relaxed, populist mood, presents this story of a young peasant who is forced to leave his bride on their wedding night to travel to the city to finalize his dying mother's will. On his bus journey he encounters a diverse group of passengers in a picaresque adventure which is not without its anarchic and surreal overtones. Spanish with English subtitles.
VHS: S02664. $29.95.
Luis Bunuel, Mexico, 1951, 85 mins.

Milky Way

Luis Bunuel's truly outrageous and very funny satire on the Catholic church and church ritual, and a road movie in its own right. Two tramps on a pilgrimage encounter the Devil, the Virgin Mary, and different arguments about Catholic doctrine. French with English subtitles.
VHS: S06935. $24.95.
Luis Bunuel, France, 1968, 102 mins.

Nazarin

A simple priest tries to live by Christian precepts in one of Luis Bunuel's best—and most unjustly neglected—films. "I am very much attached to Nazarin," said Bunuel. "He is a priest. He could as well be a hairdresser or a waiter. What interests me about him is that he stands by his ideas, that these ideas are unacceptable to society at large, and that after his adventures with prostitutes, thieves and so forth, they lead him to being irrevocably damned by the prevailing social order." With Francisco Rabal, Marga Lopez and Rita Macedo. Spanish with English subtitles.
VHS: S08695. $69.95.
Luis Bunuel, Mexico, 1958, 92 mins.

Phantom of Liberty

One of Bunuel's masterpieces of surrealism, this loosely structured series of anecdotes deals with the concept of freedom. A daisy-chain of characters move through this cinema of dreams and absurdity, demonstrating the cosmic comedy of humans who constantly enslave themselves in order to be free. The lightest and liveliest of Bunuel's films filled with riddles, jokes and outrageous associations ridiculing the power to reason. French with English subtitles.
VHS: S04869. $24.95.
Luis Bunuel, France, 1974, 102 mins.

Simon of the Desert

Bunuel's outrageous satire of the Church has Simon sitting on top of a pillar in the Mexican desert, haunted by the Devil in all forms. Often called the greatest short film of all time, Bunuel's wit has never been more deadly, his surrealist vision never clearer. Spanish with English subtitles.
VHS: S01204. $29.95.
Luis Bunuel, Mexico, 1965, 40 mins.

Susana

Susana is the story of a delinquent girl who escapes from detention and hides out on a remote finca, where she destroys the rigid, uptight family with her immoral scheming. Despite the conventional melodramatic structure, *Susana* displays Bunuel's surreal fascination with the illusion of conventions. Spanish with English subtitles.
VHS: S05991. $24.95.
Luis Bunuel, Mexico, 1951, 87 mins.

That Obscure Object of Desire

A final masterpiece from Bunuel, in which he uses two actresses playing one role to illustrate the unfathomable nature of sexual obsession. Fernando Rey stars. Nominated for two Academy Awards, including Best Foreign Film. French with English subtitles.
VHS: S01314. $29.95.
Laser: LD70472. $49.95.
Luis Bunuel, France, 1976, 100 mins.

Tristana

The stunning Catherine Deneuve is Tristana, a victim of her own captivating beauty who is desired by two men. The first is her lecherous guardian (played by the great Fernando Rey) who, after raising her from a teenager, takes her as his mistress. The other is a young artist (Franco Nero) who wants to marry her but lacks the courage to free her from the corrupt relationship with her guardian. Set in 1920's Spain, *Tristana* is a scathing examination of moral decay viewed through Bunuel's typically dispassionate and ironic eyes. Spanish with English subtitles. Letterboxed.
VHS: S15344. $24.95.
Laser: LD75490. $49.95.
Luis Bunuel, Spain, 1970, 98 mins.

Un Chien Andalou/Land Without Bread

Two great early films by Luis Bunuel: *Un Chien Andalou* continues to shock audiences today as it did in 1928; *Land Without Bread* is a horrifying account of one of Spain's most desolate regions, a documentary masterpiece made all the more harrowing for its travelogue style.
VHS: S12462. $29.95.
Luis Bunuel, Spain, 1928/32, 42 mins.

Viridiana

Bunuel's outrageous and devastating attack on religion and society. Viridiana, about to take her vows as a nun, takes to the pure Christian life by organizing a haven for a blind man, leper, cripple and beggar. Full of Freudian symbolism, the film ends in a famous orgy of destruction, containing Bunuel's blasphemous scene of the Last Supper. The film that got Bunuel kicked out of Spain. Spanish with English subtitles.
VHS: S01419. $29.95.
Luis Bunuel, Spain, 1961, 90 mins.

A Woman Without Love

Based on a short story by Guy de Maupassant. Set in a decaying mansion, a young wife has a brief secret affair, separates from her lover, and then bears his son. Bunuel makes ample use of the gothic setting in the mansion which is part home, part antiques, part a tomb, in a surrealist plumbing of a bizarre love story. Spanish with English subtitles.
VHS: S06840. $24.95.
Luis Bunuel, Mexico, 1951, 91 mins.

Wuthering Heights

A wonderfully twisted adaption of Emily Bronte's famed novel, set in Mexico. Alternatively titled *The Abyss of Passion*, the film was called "a magical example of how an artist of genius can take someone else's classic work and shape it to fit his own temperament without violating it" (Vincent Canby). Spanish with English subtitles.
VHS: S04876. $24.95.
Luis Bunuel, Mexico, 1953, 90 mins.

The Young One

Luis Bunuel's only American film is a powerful work about racism and sexual exploitation. A northern black jazz clarinetist (Bernie Hamilton) fleeing from false rape charges turns up on a small island off the Carolina coast and finds himself being hunted by a game warden (Zachary Scott). The sheriff's racial bigotry flares openly, though he is concealing his own perverse sexual fixation on a beautiful young nymphet (Kay Meersman). "A film that is realistically simple in all its parts, and realistically complex in its total picture of life and people" (*Newsweek*). With Crahan Denton and Claudio Brook.
VHS: S19462. $59.95.
Luis Bunuel, USA/Mexico, 1960, 95 mins.

SPANISH ISSUES

Barcelona

This city is one of the great Mediterranean cultural centers. Picasso, Miro and Dali all began here. Gaudi, certainly one of the most innovative architects from the turn of the century, added a special touch to Barcelona. This documentary visits some of Gaudi's most famous works, including his unfinished cathedral and Guell Park, as well as other outstanding landmarks in the city, such as the Catalan Museum and early Christian churches. 45 mins.
VHS: S18896. $75.00.

Barcelona: Archive of Courtesy

This video reveals the cultural delights of the capital of Catalonia. The jewel-like architecture of Antonio Gaudi, the art of Joan Miro, and even the contemporary feel of this exciting city make it an unmatched treasure trove of the arts.
VHS: S24265. $19.98.

Cervantes

Horst Buchholz, Gina Lollobrigida, Louis Jourdan, Fernando Rey and Jose Ferrer star in this film based on the life of the author of *Don Quixote*. As a young man, Cervantes left his homeland to become a soldier. The experience was integral to his later artistic development. Dubbed in English. Also known as *Cervantes the Young Rebel*.
VHS: S26876. $24.95.
Vincent Sherman, Spain/France/Italy, 1967, 119 mins.

Cervantes and Friend

Perhaps Spain's greatest author, Cervantes is known worldwide because of his novel *Don Quixote* and its central character. The story of both the author and this memorable old gentleman are revealed in this video. 28 mins.
VHS: S26533. $29.95.

Christmas in Spain

Feliz Navidad! Window shop along Madrid's Plaza Mayor. Join a Spanish family for a special Christmas dinner, and celebrate the Feast of the Three Kings. A wonderful glimpse of Spanish tradition. 30 mins.
English Narration.
VHS: S05263. $49.95.
Spanish Narration.
VHS: S05262. $49.95.

El Escorial and Toledo

Tour the magnificent 16th century palace and monastery built by Phillip II, exhibiting the famous works of Velazquez, Goya and others. Then on to Toledo with its renowned Moorish architecture, the home of El Greco and the legendary fortress of El Alcazar. 40 mins. English narration.
VHS: S05728. $49.95.

"Espana Es..."— The Sights and Sounds of Modern Spain

This program examines the diversity of contemporary Spain, from the fiesta in Seville to the faster pace in the urban center of Madrid. 28 mins.
VHS: S20276. $29.95.

The Good Fight

It was one of history's most dramatic expressions of international solidarity when 40,000 volunteers from around the world went to fight the armies of Franco, Hitler and Mussolini in the Spanish Civil War of 1936-39. *The Good Fight* tells the story of 3,200 Americans who volunteered to fight on the side of the Spanish Republic. This vivid series of portraits with 12 of the survivors (half the Americans lost their lives in Spain) brings to life the reasons for joining the foreign conflict, and what it was to be a part of a people's army against fascism in the war that was the rehearsal for World War II. An absorbing and passionate account full of humor, pride and deep sorrow, their interviews are illustrated with rare archival footage of the Lincoln Brigade in Spain as well as Hollywood films, songs and newsreels with such notables as Hemingway himself and Henry Fonda. Narrated by Studs Terkel.
VHS: S12206. $69.95.
Noel Buckner/Mary Dore/Sam Sills, USA, 1984, 98 mins.

Grandes Festivales de Espana

In Spain, a festival is a representation of the feelings and character of the people and pride in their cities. Each of the festivals— Fallas, Semana Santa, Feria de Abril and La Fiesta de Santiago— invites visitors to become active participants in the celebrations, whether it is the pandemonium of Valencia and Pamplona during Fallas and San Fermin, or the solemnity of Sevilla during Semana Santa. 37 mins.
English Narration.
VHS: S30563. $59.95.
Spanish Narration.
VHS: S30564. $59.95.

Introducing Don Quixote

An introduction to Don Quixote adapted from slide/ film strip shows to video. Covers the role of Miguel Cervantes in Spanish literature, and the essence of Don Quixote. 30 mins.
English Version.
VHS: S06384. $39.95.
Spanish Version.
VHS: S06385. $39.95.

La Gloria de Espana

Once the most powerful nation in the world, witness Spain's Golden Age from the 16th century to the present with its bustling cities and rich countryside. In English and then Spanish. 25 mins. each.
VHS: S05261. $59.95.

La Lengua (The Spanish Language)

Presents an exploration of how the Spanish language came to be such a dominant world language. It explains who speaks Spanish, where and why. English and Spanish as well as Bilingual signs are compared and presented for review and practice. The value of two languages is explained. Spanish and English narration. 55 mins.
VHS: S10320. $32.95.

Loyola, the Soldier Saint

A romantic biography of the founder of the Jesuit movement, this work charts Loyola's brutal war experiences, his spiritual and moral recovery and eventual sainthood. With Raphael Duran. English dubbed.
VHS: S18031. $29.95.
Jose Diaz Morales, Spain/USA, 1952, 93 mins.

Madrid

View the historical splendors of one of the most beautiful cities in Spain. Visit the Plaza Mayor, the Royal Palace and Prado Museum. Then on to modern Madrid with its artists, Flamenco dancers, cafes and bullfights. 57 mins.
English Narration.
VHS: S05260. $49.95.
Spanish Narration.
VHS: S05259. $49.95.

Pamplona/Viva San Fermin

Experience the spectacle, wonder and excitement of Pamplona's traditional running of the Bulls. With a tape script and a teacher's guide. 30 mins.
English Narration.
VHS: S19831. $65.00.
Spanish Narration.
VHS: S19832. $65.00.

Pimpenella: Nuestras Mejores Canciones (Our Favorite Songs)

A concert performance by this acclaimed duo has been captured on videotape. It includes "Ahora Decide", "Valiente", "Solo Tu, Solo Yo", "La Familia" and many more songs. 55 mins.
VHS: S23868. $19.95.

Sabicas: El Maestro de Flamenco

The only video available about the legendary guitarist Agustin Castellon Campos Sabicas, a self-taught child prodigy who became known in Spain as *El Fenomeno*, and who pioneered the use of the flamenco guitar as a solo instrument. This video features four guitar solos played by Sabicas: "Malaguena," "Zapateado del Re," "Sitio de Zaragoza" and "Arabian Dance," as well as a *siguiriya* performed by the late Maria Alba, with guitar accompaniment by Adonis Puertas and vocal accompaniment by Luis Vargas.
VHS: S27204. $34.00.

Salamanca— The Heart of Spain's Golden Age

Salamanca is as old as Spain itself. Its University, founded in 1223, helped fuel artistic, cultural and educational achievements integral to Spain's Golden Age. The city itself stands as a monument to this historic influence. 30 mins.
VHS: S26534. $32.95.

Seville: Jewel of Andalusia

With its exotic Moorish palaces, ancient Catholic churches and intriguing Jewish neighborhoods this ancient city remains unmatched for its unique sights. There are even ruins from the Visigoth, Greek and Roman invaders.
VHS: S24266. $19.98.

Spain: Everything Under the Sun

Tour the colorful Spanish countryside and see all of her most beautiful cities, including Madrid, Segovia, Avila, Seville, Costa del Sol, and more. 50 mins.
VHS: S05771. $24.95.

Spanish Civil War

A major, unparalleled history of this bloody conflict of the 1930's, a war of belief that claimed three million lives, and featured such men on the front lines as Ernest Hemingway and the famous Abraham Lincoln Brigade. This 6-hour, detailed history of the conflict and the political maneuvers behind it is a remarkable, well-researched portrait of one of the key events of the 20th century. 360 mins. Double cassette.
VHS: S04899. $79.95.

Spanish History— A Continent Conquered

From the Caribbean Sea to the tip of the continent of South America, the history, power and culture of Spain lives today. This program presents a look at the Hispanic nations of South America as the 21st century dawns. 28 mins.
VHS: S31892. $29.95.

Spanish History—The Heritage of Rome

This program captures the artistic, political, religious and cultural influence of the Roman conquest on Spanish society. 28 mins.
VHS: S20275. $29.95.

Spanish TV Commercials

Spaniards add their own unique approach to advertising in this series of TV commercials. Compare and contrast their ads with ours. Culturally authentic information about Spain is highlighted throughout the film. Includes script.
VHS: S05275. $49.95.

Spanish TV Commercials—Volume 2

A second program of the unique Spanish approach toward commercials, providing an insight into the daily life of the Spanish people. 45 mins.
VHS: S09051. $49.95.

PORTUGUESE FILMS

The Convent

John Malkovich and Catherine Deneuve are a married couple who become sidetracked from their own relationship while on a professional visit to a Portugese convent. As a professor, Malkovich is determined to prove that Shakespeare was of Spanish Jewish origin. While he searches for evidence in support of his theory, Deneuve becomes enmeshed in a flirtation with their host, the sinister Baltar. Their exchanges bring the battle between good and evil to an intense carnal level through the lure of temptation. English, French and Portuguese with English subtitles.
VHS: S29510. $19.98.
Manuel De Oliveira, Portugal, 1995, 90 mins.

The Jester

This acclaimed Portuguese film, which captured the Grand Prize at the Locarno Film Festival, intertwines excerpts of Alexandre Herculano's classic play *O Bobo*, which chronicles the founding of Portugal's monarchy, with a modern-day drama about Portugal after the loss of Angola, in a brilliant exposition of the rise and fall of empire. Portuguese with English subtitles.
VHS: S26500. $59.95.
Jose Alvano Morais, Portugal, 1987, 127 mins.

The Jew

Set during the Spanish Inquisition, this provocative, unusual Portuguese film is based on the true story of Antonio da Silva, a talented playwright and writer in 18th-century Portugal who is accused of heresy: still secretly being a Jew, even after converting to Catholicism. He must stand up to a ferocious Church hierarchy at odds with a decadent monarchy. "Even more hair-raising than *The Crucible*....An incongruously beautiful period film" (Michael Wilmington, *Chicago Tribune*). Portuguese with English subtitles.
VHS: S32684. $79.95.
Jom Tob Azuley, Portugal/Brazil, 1995, 85 mins.

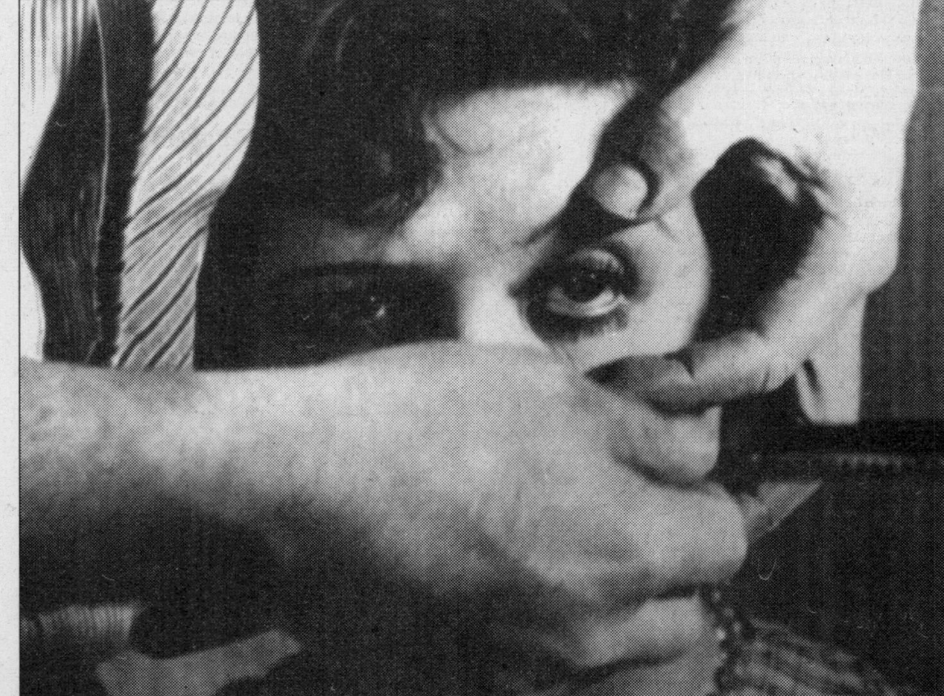

latin american cinema

8-A Ochoa
The Kafka-esque world of Cuba under Castro's rule is brought to light in this reconstruction (including actual footage) of the 1989 trial and firing squad execution of General Arnaldo Ochoa, the highest-ranking general and hero of the revolution, accused of illegal drug trafficking. "In its structure, urgency and tone, *8-A* resembles *Z*" (Emanuel Levy, *Variety*). Spanish with English subtitles.
VHS: S31359. $89.95.
Orlando Jimenez-Leal, Cuba, 84 mins.

Alias, La Gringa
This powerful political drama from Peru follows the adventures and escapades of La Gringa, a charismatic criminal who cannot be incarcerated by any jail. Helped by an imprisoned intellectual, he escapes. Determined to aid his accomplice, he returns to prison in disguise and is trapped by a riot and corruption beyond his grasp. Spanish with English subtitles.
VHS: S20383. $59.95.
Alberto Durant, Peru, 1991, 92 mins.

Argentinisima I
Fernando Ayala directed this film inspired by the poetry of Atahualpa Yupanqui, in a film which alternates reality with fantasy, and is based almost entirely on Argentinian folklore. The soundtrack is drawn from various ethnographic music of Argentina, and the film features spectacular scenery of Argentina. With Atahualpa Rupanqui, Mercedes Sosa, Los Chalchaleros, Eduardo Falu, Ariel Ramirez, Jaime Torres. In Spanish *without* English subtitles.
VHS: S04956. $59.95.
Fernando Ayala/Hector Olivera, Argentina, 115 mins.

Barrocco
A visual and musical history of Latin America from the director of *Frida* and Reed: Insurgent Mexico. The daring film portrays the birth of Latin American identity through the synthesis of African, Mayan, Aztec and Spanish cultures. "A musical dream that explores the beauty, cruelty and mystery of Latin America through sound and image." (*San Francisco Chronicle*).
Spanish with English subtitles.
VHS: S26498. $59.95.
Paul Leduc, Spain/Cuba, 1989, 108 mins.

Bitter Sugar
This visceral, energizing look at contemporary Cuba is an impassioned love story set against the political and economic tensions of Havana. Gustavo, an ideal young Communist with a glorified vision of Castro's regime, falls in love with Yolanda, a disenchanted dancer who longs to escape to Miami. Despite their radically opposed beliefs, the young couple are inseparable. The city begins to erupt around Gustavo when his rebellious musician brother injects himself with the AIDS virus in suicidal protest, and his father realizes that he will earn more money as a hotel bar pianist than as a doctor. Spanish with English subtitles.
VHS: S32391. $89.95.
Leon Ichaso, Cuba, 1996, 102 mins.

Black River
Absolute power corrupts absolutely in the Amazonian jungles of Rio Negro. First, a new governor and his ambitious wife (Angela Molina) successfully confront the brutal local chief, but the era they usher in is one of gambling, prostitution and economic exploitation. Frank Ramirez plays the head of security, who grabs control only to initiate a regime of austerity and restriction as madness buries good intentions. Spanish with English subtitles.
VHS: S27737. $59.95.
Atahualpa Lichy, Venezuela/Spain, 1990, 116 mins.

Cabeza de Vaca
A visually spellbinding biography of the Spanish explorer Nunez Cabeza de Vaca, the sole survivor of a 16th-century Spanish shipwreck off the coast of Florida. Cabeza de Vaca discovers the Iguase, a traditional Indian tribe, which allows Cabeza into their tribe. Over the next eight years, he learns about their mysterious culture and becomes a leader of the group. But his former identity catches up with him when a team of Spanish conquistadors return to colonize the Indians. "Bold and imaginative, the film has ambition, freshness, imagination, mystery and exhilarating reach. It has greatness in it" (Jay Carr, *Boston Globe*). With Juan Diego, Daniel Gimenez Cacho and Roberto Sosa. Spanish and Indian with English subtitles.
VHS: S19356. $29.95.
Nicolas Echevarria, Mexico/Spain, 1991, 109 mins.

Camila
A young Catholic socialite from Buenos Aires falls in love and runs away with a young Jesuit priest. The two find temporary happiness in a small provincial village, but eventually they are recognized and ultimately condemned to death without a trial. Spanish with English subtitles.
VHS: S00209. $59.95.
Maria-Luisa Bemberg, Argentina, 1984, 90 mins.

Celestial Clockwork
With her only dress on her back and a poster of her idol under her arm, a young woman dives into a modern-day fairy tale where dreams really do come true. Pursing her longtime dream in Paris, Ana's adventure is filled with distractions and obstacles, including a gay clairvoyant, an eccentric psychoanalyst, a Puerto Rican witch doctor and a jealous roommate determined to bring her down. But when all is said and done, she will become the belle of the ball. French and Spanish with English subtitles. "Outrageous, funny and a visual delight" (*Siskel & Ebert*).
VHS: S30751. $99.99.
Laser: LD76109. $39.99.
Fina Torres, Venezuela, 1996, 83 mins.

Chicago Latino Cinema Collection: I
The best of contemporary Latin American cinema in six recent feature films as curated in the Chicago Latino Film Festival. The six features in this special collection, each available on a single cassette, are: *Confessing to Laura* (Jaime Osorio Gomez, Colombia); *Tango: Our Dance* (Jorge Zanada, Argentina); *Shoot to Kill* (Carlos Azpurua, Venezuela); *Butterfly Wings* (Juanma Bajo Ulloa, Spain); *Alias, La Gringa* (Alberto Durant, Peru) and *Savage Capitalism* (Andre Klotzel, Brazil). Six-volume set.
VHS: S20598. $299.99.

Chicago Latino Cinema Collection: II
Eight recent Latin American films, including the work of the legendary Argentine director Leopoldo Torre Nilsson and his son, make up this unique retrospective of award-winning contemporary films. The eight feature films in this second collection of Latin American cinema include *Buccaneer Soul* (Carlos Reichenbach, Brazil); *The Love of Silent Movies* (Pablo Torre, Argentina); *Black River* (Atahualpa Lichy, Venezuela/Spain); *We're All Stars* (Felipe Degregori, Peru); *The Day You Love Me* (Sergio Dow, Colombia); *Martin Fierro* (Loepoldo Torre Nilsson, Argentina); *Painted Lips* (*Boquitas Pintadas*) (Leopoldo Torre Nilsson, Argentina) and *The Seven Madmen* (*Los Siete Locos*) (Loepoldo Torre Nilsson, Argentina). Eight-volume set.
VHS: S27831. $349.99.

Chronicle of a Boy Alone
Banned for 30 years by the Argentinian government, *Chronicle of a Boy Alone* is a searing indictment of a fascist regime running roughshod over its children. Focusing on the bleak life of 11-year-old bad boy Polin, who's been abandoned by his family and sent to live in, a state-run orphanage, it is also a moving portrait of the human spirit imprisoned by the chains of well-intentioned fools. A neo-realist masterpiece. Spanish with English subtitles.
VHS: S32018. $59.95.
Leonardo Favio, Argentina, 1964, 86 mins.

The City of the Dogs (La Ciudad de los Perros)
A terrific film adaptation of the great South American novel by Mario Vargas Llosa, *The City of Dogs* is the powerful story of a young man's upbringing in the military academy, and eventual disillusionment with both the military structures, the power which they represent, and the system which they enforce. The original title of Llosa's novel was "Time of the Hero". Spanish with English subtitles.
VHS: S04611. $39.95.
Francisco J. Lombardi, Peru, 1985, 135 mins.

Confessing to Laura
A gut-wrenching drama from Colombia which is set during a raging civil war in the aftermath of the assassination of liberal leader Jorge Elieser Gaitain in 1948. Three people are trapped in Laura's home during a riot, setting the stage for an intense, unforgettable night. Spanish with English subtitles.
VHS: S20379. $59.95.
Jaime Osorio Gomez, Colombia, 1990, 90 mins.

Crecor de Golpe (Growing Up)
Ubaldo Martinez, Julio Cesar Ludeuna and Cecilia Roth star in this touching story about an orphan who finds the paternal love he needs in an old widower. Spanish with NO subtitles.
VHS: S23922. $24.95.
Sergio Renan, Argentina, 1977, 84 mins.

Crepuscolo
The story of an obsessive passion of a man in love with the wife of his best friend, this classic from the Mexican cinema stars Arturo de Cordova, Gloria Marin and Lilia Michel. In Spanish *without* English subtitles.
VHS: S05919. $39.95.
Julio Bracho, Mexico, 1944, 108 mins.

Cronos
An ingenious alchemist creates a device that grants him eternal life. 400 years later an elderly antique dealer discovers the properties of this unique invention. Though he grows younger every time he uses this device, there is a terrible price to pay. Life after death becomes a bloody promise without end. This film won Grand Prize during Critics' Week at Cannes. Spanish with English subtitles.
VHS: S22127. $19.98.
Guillermo Del Toro, Mexico, 1992, 90 mins.

Cuando Viajan las Estrellas
A Hollywood star comes to Mexico to learn flamenco, but rather learns the ways of the genteel "charro" when she falls in love with one, played by Jorge Negrette, the quintessential singing cowboy, and the most romantic idol of the Golden Age of Mexican cinema. With Raquel Rojas, Joaquin Pardave. In Spanish *without* English subtitles.
VHS: S05920. $39.95.
Alberto Gout, Mexico, 1942, ;+4108 mins.

Cuesta Abajo
Rare musical drama featuring the master of the tango, Carlos Gardel, together with Vicente Padula, Anita Camillo. Spanish *without* English subtitles.
VHS: S06034. $54.95.
John Reinhardt, Argentina, 1934, 65 mins.

Danzon
This sensual, exuberant work by the gifted Mexican director Maria Novaro tells the story of Julia (Maria Rojo), a 40-year-old telephone operator and single mother whose emotional life consists of ballroom dancing. When her dancing partner disappears, Julia undertakes a grueling odyssey to locate him. Her search takes her on an extraordinary inner voyage. "One of the most enchanting surprises of the season" (Andrew Sarris). With Carmen Salinas, Blanca Guerra and Tito Vasconcelos. Spanish with English subtitles.
VHS: S19334. $19.95.
Maria Novaro, Mexico, 1991, 96 mins.

Dark Side of the Heart
From the director of *Man Facing Southeast* comes this parable about a narcissistic poet in search of the perfect woman. Claiming he will not "tolerate a woman who cannot fly," young Oliverio rejects potential lovers. When he meets a prostitute named Ana who can actually fly, she prefers to keep their relationship a business arrangement. Tormented and lovelorn, Oliverio must face the consequences of pursuing his dream. An original work of magical realism by Argentina's talented Subiela. With Dario Grandineti, Sandra Ballesteros and Nacha Guevara. "Intoxicatingly lush and sensual" (*Los Angeles Times*). Spanish with English subtitles.
VHS: S32657. $89.95.
Eliseo Subiela, Argentina/Canada, 1992, 127 mins.

The Day You Love Me
Winner of the Casa de las Americas award for Best Latin American feature, this humorous period film recaptures 1935, the year of Juan Vicente Gomez' dictatorship when Venezuela played host to the great tango singer Carlos Gardel as he presented his film *The Day You Love Me*. Romance and politics clash, exposing the lies, hopes and false dreams of an era on the eve of change as a small city meets, for the first time, the King of the Tango. Spanish with English subtitles.
VHS: S27739. $59.95.
Sergio Dow, Colombia, 1986, 80 mins.

Details of a Duel
One morning a teacher and a butcher leave home to go about their business, which, on this day, includes preparing for death. Contrary to their true natures, one must kill the other by mid-afternoon. Egged on by the clergy, the militia and the town's bureaucrats, a private affair becomes a gladiatorial spectacle. A comedy about escalation, anticipation, and manners, this absurdly inexorable process is the subject of Sergio Cabrera's wry first feature. Spanish with English subtitles.
VHS: S14149. $59.95.
Sergio Cabrera, Colombia, 1989, 97 mins.

Diary of the War of Pigs
Based on the novel by Adolfo Bioy Casares; the generation gap is taken to the extreme by a group of young people who have decided to exterminate all senior citizens in this futuristic vision. One of the great films by the neglected Argentinian film master, Leopoldo Torre Nilsson. Spanish with English subtitles.
VHS: S01124. $39.95.
Leopoldo Torre Nilsson, Argentina, 1975, 90 mins.

Don Segundo Sombra
Continuing in the series of adaptations of works from South and Latin American authors, this film is based on an Argentine novel by Riccardo Guiraldes, and is set amidst the life of the Argentine gauchos. Spanish with English subtitles.
VHS: S03199. $59.95.
Manuel Antin, Argentina, 1969, 110 mins.

Dona Barbara
Based on the 1929 novel by Romulo Gallegos, *Dona Barbara* tells of a dramatic confrontation over land and civil rights, notable for its passionate characterizations.
VHS: S04610. $39.95.
Fernando de Fuentes, Mexico, 1943, 138 mins.

Dona Herlinda and Her Son
A delightful, funny film from Mexico called by David Denby of *New York Magazine* a "sly, deadpan comedy. The ultimate gay homage to mom." Spanish with English subtitles.
VHS: S06022. $79.95.
Jaime H. Hermosillo, Mexico, 1986, 90 mins.

El Compadre Mendoza
This rare example of classic Mexican cinema examines the corrupted ideals of the Revolution in the story of an opportunistic landowner who faces the choice of remaining loyal to a general in Zapata's army and being financially ruined or saving his own skin. The character of the general is clearly modeled on Zapata himself. Spanish with English subtitles.
VHS: S26946. $29.95.
Fernando de Fuentes, Mexico, 1933

El Corsario Negro
From the Mexican classic cinema, with fabulous camerawork by the legendary Gabriel Figueroa, in a love, action and adventure story starring Pedro Armendariz and the beautiful Maria Luisa Zea. In Spanish *without* English subtitles.
VHS: S05917. $54.95.
Chano Urueto, Mexico, 1944, 84 mins.

El Dia Que Me Queiras
The tango has always had one voice—the voice is, and has been, the legendary Carlos Gardel. Gardel took an obscure dance born in the brothels of Buenos Aires, sweetened its melody, added lyrics about the life and feelings of a city, culture and people, and gave the tango new dimension. This rare musical drama is one of Gardel's classic films, made in 1935, and stars Rosita Moreno, Tito Lusiardo, Manuel Pelufo. Argentina, 1935, B&W, 95 mins. Spanish *without* English subtitles.
VHS: S05849. $54.95.

El Gran Acontecimiento (The Great Apparition)
The enchanting legend of the Virgin of Guadalupe is brought to life in this animated feature. She is greatly revered both in Mexico, where her shrine is located, and throughout the world. Spanish with NO subtitles.
VHS: S23918. $34.95.

El Grito
The laborers of a sugar plantation face the brutal repression of the ruling power, sacrificing their lives to form the first union in their country, in this powerful film from Peru. Spanish with English subtitles.
VHS: S23477. $39.95.
Alberto Durant, Peru, 1982, 84 mins.

El Muerto
Based on a short story of the same name by Jorge Luis Borges, *El Muerto* traces the life of Benjamin Otalora, in 19th century South America. Otalora, a fugitive, meets the leader of a smuggling ring upon his arrival in Montevideo. The smuggler takes him under his wings, yet when the aging gang leader takes sick, Otalora covertly attempts to claim power within this ring. Spanish with English subtitles.
VHS: S03196. $39.95.
Hector Olivera, Argentina, 1975, 103 mins.

El Mundo del Talisman
In this animated feature, a brother and sister find a virtual world of booby traps in the planet they inherit. Spanish with NO subtitles. 1987, 80 mins.
VHS: S23912. $24.95.

El Super
A hilarious comedy set in New York, but made by two Cuban exiles. Roberto, a Cuban, has been a building superintendent in New York City for ten years but, from his basement-level point of view, he has eyes only for Cuba or Miami, where it doesn't snow. With humor, compassion and accuracy, the film describes Roberto's dream of returning to his crime-free, snow-free homeland. Spanish with English subtitles.
VHS: S11592. $79.95.
Orlando Jimenez-Leal/Leon Ichaso, USA, 1979, 90 mins.

El Tango en Broadway
Carlos Gardel, Trini Ramos, Blanca Vischer, Vicente Padula, Jaime Davesa star in this rare musical comedy starring the incomparable master of the tango, Carlos Gardel. Spanish *without* English subtitles.
VHS: S05850. $54.95.
Louis Gasnier, Argentina, 1934, 95 mins.

Erendira
Based on a section of Gabriel Garcia Marquez' *One Hundred Years of Solitude*, *Erendira* is an erotic black comedy laden with sexual fantasy, surreal pranks and political allegory. Erendira is a teenage girl exploited as a sexual slave by her greedy grandmother. Spanish with English subtitles.
VHS: S00413. $24.95.
Ruy Guerra, Mexico, 1983, 103 mins.

Fable of the Beautiful Pigeon Fancier
Based on a fragment from his novel *Love in the Time of Cholera*, *Fable of the Beautiful Pigeon Fancier* was conceived and co-written by Nobel Prize winner Gabriel Garcia Marquez. Reteaming Garcia Marquez with director Ruy Guerra (who began his career as an actor, starring in Werner Herzog's masterpiece *Aguirre: The Wrath of God*), with whom he'd collaborated on the earlier *Erendira*, *Fable of the Beautiful Pigeon Fancier* tells the story of Orestes, a wealthy factory owner who falls madly in love with a married pigeon breeder. "An elegant Wellesian comedy of fate and manners" (*Los Angeles Times*). Spanish with English subtitles.
VHS: S13692. $19.98.
Ruy Guerra, Mexico/Spain, 1988, 73 mins.

Fabulas de la Selva
Johnny Chuck, Peter Cottontail, Chatterer the Squirrel and all the other characters from Thornton W. Burgess' stories are featured in this animated adaptation of his classic works. Spanish with NO subtitles.
VHS: S23919. $34.95.

Far Away and Long Ago (Alla Lejos y Hace Tiempo)
A poetic rendering of the autobiographical novel by Guillermo Hudson—images of the mystery of the Argentinian pampa, its gauchos, witchcraft and women —perturbing memories that nurtured the writer's childhood. Spanish with English subtitles.
VHS: S07737. $39.95.
Manuel Antin, Argentina, 1974, 91 mins.

Frida
Paul Leduc's widely acclaimed, brilliantly visual tribute to the spirit and determination of Frida Kahlo, who risked her life for her art and love, and became one of the dominant painters of the 20th century. Told in surreal flashbacks reminiscent of her own canvasses, the film remarkably captures the spirit and determination of the woman who made herself into a great artist, a cultural leader, a political activist. With Ofelia Medina, Juan Jose Gurrola, Max Kerlow. Spanish with English subtitles.
VHS: S08997. $29.95.
Paul Leduc, Mexico, 1984, 108 mins.

Fridays of Eternity
Based on the novel by Maria Granata. Immortal love and the supernatural create this light-hearted story of loyalty, infidelity, loves and lovers. With Thelma Biral, Hector Alterio. Spanish with English subtitles.
VHS: S07736. $59.95.
Hector Olivera, Argentina, 1981, 89 mins.

Funny Dirty Little War
An important film from Hector Olivera, the story is a parable of events in Peronist Argentina. The film is a comedy about rightist Peronists who plot to oust the leftist mayor of the town. But the mayor refuses to budge, and a "funny dirty little war" ensues. Federico Luppi is brilliant as the mayor. Spanish with English subtitles.
VHS: S06841. $24.95.
Hector Olivera, Argentina, 1983, 80 mins.

The Garcia Marquez Collection
A compilation of six feature films based on the stories, chronicles and novels written by Nobel Prize winner Gabriel Garcia Marquez, author of *Love in the Time of Cholera*. Includes *Miracle in Rome, Letters from the Park, Fable of the Beautiful Pigeon Fancier, The Summer of Miss Forbes, I'm the One You're Looking For* and *A Very Old Man with Enormous Wings*. All titles are in Spanish with English subtitles.
VHS: S14457. $119.88.

Golden Cockerel (El Gallo de Oro)
Based on a screenplay by Gabriel Garcia Marquez, Carlos Fuentes and Roberto Galvadon, and on a novel by Juan Rulfo. Poor man starts making a fortune with a gamecock, and the greedy owner of the arena, yet their fortune finally severs their relationship. Spanish with English subtitles.
VHS: S07738. $39.95.
Robert Galvadon, Mexico, 1964, 110 mins.

The Green Wall
A breakthrough film from South America, *The Green Wall* is based on Armando Robles Godoy's own experiences of homesteading in the Peruvian jungle. *The Green Wall* is "a bitter and beautiful movie," in which "Godoy translates his experience into film poetry rather than flat reportage and uses the physical environment (exquisitely photographed by his cameraman brother, Mario) as a great natural mystery, idyllic but cruel, rich but unyielding to the will of a handsome young settler (Mexican star Julio Aleman, in a vibrant performance) who is determined to survive there with his family." The idyll is broken both by the bureaucracy in far-off Lima, and at the film's end: "The blow comes from the rain forest near their house, where father and son have constructed a mock city of clay as a symbol of the civilized stupidity they sought to escape. The film's final sequence, an almost wordless funeral, is masterful movie making, a haunting glimpse of humanity that lingers in the mind" (Pauline Kael, *The New Yorker*). "A masterpiece!" (Roger Ebert). Spanish with English subtitles.
VHS: S11250. $79.95.
Armando Robles Godoy, Peru, 1970, 110 mins.

I the Worst of All
Based on the book *Traps of Faith* by Nobel Prize winner Octavio Paz, this is the last film completed by Maria Luisa Bemberg (*Camilla, I Don't Want to Talk About It*) before her death in 1995. The film tells the story of real-life Mexican poet and writer Sister Juana Ines de la Cruz (Assumpta Serna, *Matador*), a target of the Spanish Inquisition, and her passionate relationship with a Viceroy's wife (Dominique Sanda, *The Conformist*), who protects the nun so that she may continue her work. As the Sister's status begins to grow and she is visited in Mexico City by such intellectuals as Siguenza y Gongora as well as nobility from all over the world, the Church attempts to silence the nun. Considered radical for her time, Sister Juana is now recognized as one of Mexico's greatest poets and the first published feminist of the American continent. Spanish with English subtitles.
VHS: S27733. $29.95.
Maria-Luisa Bemberg, Argentina, 1993, 100 mins.

In Love
The story of a rebel soldier who dreams of a Mexico in which all are equal. He falls in love with a woman from the privileged class who considers him beneath her social status. Spanish with English subtitles. Mexico, 81 mins.
VHS: S02854. $24.95.

Johnny 100 Pesos
Based on a true story, this is an offbeat, darkly comic thriller of a bungled heist in the tradition of *Reservoir Dogs* and *Dog Day Afternoon*. Johnny Garcia stars as a teenager whose first armed robbery escalates into a hostage situation when the police surround the building, leaving no escape for Johnny and his accomplices. The event turns into a media circus focusing on Johnny as a symbol of what's wrong with the country. Spanish with English subtitles.
VHS: S28501. $19.98.
Gustavo Graef-Marino, Chile, 1994, 95 mins.

Julio and His Angel
This is the story of a young orphan boy who believes in his heart that he can find his guardian angel. At first his quest seems unimaginable, but ultimately, he finds his angel, and then his adventures truly begin. It is a loving story of faith and growth. Spanish with English subtitles.
VHS: S29944. $59.95.
Jorge Cervera Jr., Mexico, 1995, 98 mins.

Killing Grandpa

The delightfully whimsical story of Don Mariano Aguero (FedericoLuppi), an old engineer who has lost his will to live. Left comatose by a failed suicide attempt, the old man awaits death as his three greedy children await their inheritance. Their plans are thwarted with the arrival of Rosita (Ines Estevez), the beautiful, young half-sister of Don Mariano's handyman. Don Mariano makes a rapid recovery as a result of Rosita's prowess in bed. "A thoroughly entertaining pic, with top-class production values and an excellent cast" (David Stratton, *Variety*). Spanish with English subtitles.

VHS: S31629. $89.95.
Luis Cesar D'Angiolillo, Argentina, 1991, 114 mins.

La Boca del Lobo

Hailed by Judy Stone of the *San Francisco Chronicle* as "a powerful drama" and considered by many to be one of the finest films to emerge from Latin and South America in recent years, *La Boca del Lobo* is the study of a bloody encounter between the Peruvian Army and the Maoist Shining Path. Winner of the Grand Prize at the San Sebastian Film Festival. Spanish with English subtitles.

VHS: S12363. $79.95.
Miguel Pereira, Peru, 1989, 100 mins.

La Dama de las Camelias

Based on Alexander Dumas' *Camille*, a novel about the desperate love between a bullfighter and a stage actress, this classic Mexican film stars Maria Felix and Jorge Mistral. Spanish *without* English subtitles.

VHS: S05918. $54.95.
Roberto Gavaldon, Mexico, 1953, 108 mins.

La Discoteca del Amor

Adolfo Aristarain's Argentinian musical comedy in which a funny detective and his clumsy assistant are the odd couple in charge of solving a case of musical piracy. With Cacho Castana, Monica Gonzaga. *In Spanish without English subtitles.*

VHS: S05046. $39.95.
Adolfo Aristarain, Argentina, 1980, 105 mins.

La Patrilla del Tiempo—1 (Time Patrol—1)

High tech weapons blast the kids from time machine to time machine in this animated feature. Whether they find themselves in prehistoric times or far in the future, it is always a matter of good versus evil. Spanish with NO subtitles. 1986, 95 mins.

VHS: S23916. $34.95.

La Paz

A respected Bolivian heart surgeon returns to his native Bolivia during the summer of 1980, just as a coup has threatened the lives of thousands. He finds himself trapped by a curfew in the very classroom where a mentoring teacher once helped him. As he ponders the now dead teacher, a committed woman journalist appears. Spanish with English subtitles.

VHS: S29878. $14.98.
Jose Sanchez, Bolivia, 1994, 25 mins.

La Regenta

Based on a novel by Leopoldo Clarin, the story is set in 18th century Spain, and investigates the prejudices of a small town against women. Spanish with English subtitles.

VHS: S03198. $39.95.

La Rosa Blanca

Based on a short story by Bruno Traven, the writer of *Treasure of Sierra Madre*, and one of Mexico's quintessential novelists. Spanish with English subtitles.

VHS: S03200. $39.95.
Roberto Gavaldon, Mexico, 1960, 100 mins.

La Tigra

Based on the novella by Jose de La Cuadra, this Ecuadorian feature looks at female identity through the eyes of Latin American machismo culture. The Tigress is the myth of woman: beautiful, sexual, powerful and revered. This film may be the best visual equivalent of literary "magical realism" ever filmed, and was awarded the Best Film Prize at the 1990 Cartagena Film Festival. Spanish with English subtitles.

VHS: S26499. $59.95.
Camilo Luzuriaga, Ecuador, 1990, 80 mins.

Laurel & Hardy in Spanish

NOT dubbed, NOT subtitled, this series of Laurel & Hardy classics feature "El Gordo y El Flaco"—as they are known to the Spanish-speaking world—actually speaking Spanish! These are separate films with different, supporting players than in the American releases; some of these films feature additional gags and even different resolutions to stories in certain cases. This series of films is of special interest because it gives us a rare example of Hollywood's early attempt at internationalizing the talking picture. Completely digitally remastered.

El Gordo y El Flaco: La Vida Nocturna. This expanded version of *Blotto* features some interesting variations on Laurel & Hardy's drunk routine in the nightclub. There are some additional variety acts not seen in the American release version as well. As an additional bonus, Stan Laurel narrates a brief segment about how the foreign versions were made. Included in this tape is an excerpt from the Spanish version of *Pardon Us* (*De Botte y de Botte*), with the missing fire-rescue scene restored. 55 mins.

VHS: S29858. $24.98.

El Gordo y El Flaco: Politiquerias. This Spanish version of *Chickens Come Home* is one of the most interesting of the Spanish series. While the basic story is the same, the addition of vaudeville acts to the party scene are something unique—one of the performers, Hadji Ali, has to be seen to be believed! As an added bonus, a short newsreel clip is included featuring Hadji Ali performing his water routine and Stan Laurel at a swimming contest. 60 mins.

VHS: S29859. $24.98.

El Gordo y El Flaco: Noche de Duendes. The "Laurel-Hardy Murder Case" is combined with "Berth Marks" to form a feature-length scare comedy. When Hardy reads that Ebeneezer Laurel has died and they are looking for the heirs to the multi-million-dollar estate, he and Stan Laurel show up at the old mansion to collect. Locked in by the police, they must stay there overnight with a murderer loose in the house. 51 mins.

VHS: S29860. $24.98.

El Gordo y El Flaco: Los Calaveras. In this offering, *Be Big* is combined with *Laughing Gravy* to form a feature-length comedy. When Stan and Ollie try to sneak out of their homes to attend a lodge meeting, the wives catch them. After the divorce, they are living in a boarding house with a small dog and a landlord who doesn't allow pets. Full of great sight gags, this adaptation is among the most true to the original versions of both films. Still there are a few new gags sprinkled in for good measure. 63 mins.

VHS: S29861. $24.98.

El Gordo y El Flaco: Ladrones. New gags abound, as well as a completely different ending in this expanded Spanish version of *Night Owls*. Also included is *Tiemblea y Titubuea* (*Below Zero*), which contains new footage as well. 63 mins.

VHS: S29862. $24.98.

El Gordo y El Flaco: De Botte en de Botte. Laurel & Hardy's first feature-length movie, *Pardon Us*, was the only one filmed in foreign language editions. Of them, only this Spanish-language re-issue seems to have survived. When Laurel & Hardy try to make their own beer they get arrested and put in prison, where they encounter all sorts of adventures. They finally get pardoned when they save the warden's daughter from the clutches of The Tiger, a ruthless convict bent on escape. 65 mins.

VHS: S29863. $24.98.

Like Water for Chocolate

Immensely popular, magical story of a young girl whose cooking is infused with her emotions as she prepares her meals. Unrequited passions, changing political situations and madness emerge in this highly entertaining, sensual and funny story. Written by Laura Esquivel and directed by her husband. Spanish with English subtitles.

VHS: S21358. $19.95.
Laser: Letterboxed. **LD74638. $39.99.**
Alfonso Arau, Mexico, 1992, 105 mins.

Los Hermanos del Hierro

The lives of two boys are predetermined by their embittered mother upon the death of her husband. Her thirst of vengeance would not be quenched until she brought upon her the darkest day of her life. Antonio Aguilar, Julio Aleman, Columba Dominguez star. In Spanish *without* English subtitles.

VHS: S05921. $24.95.
Ismael Rodriguez, Mexico, 1961, 95 mins.

The Love of Silent Movies

Pablo Torre directs this compelling film about a man who can't function in a world outside the lives of the characters he portrays. Ralph de Palma had his 15 minutes of fame as a Latin Lover in silent Hollywood films. Thirty years have passed and with them the silent movie era. But de Palma recreates his past glories by paying tribute to silent films each night. Spanish with English subtitles.

VHS: S27736. $59.95.
Pablo Torre, Argentina, 1993, 92 mins.

Macario

The talents of top director Roberto Gavaldon, novelist B. Traven (*The Treasure of Sierra Madre*) and cinematographer Gabriel Figueroa combined to produce this gentle, moving fable on human morality. The title of the film comes from the name of a young peasant, despondent over his inability to provide for his family. On the Day of the Dead, he meets Death, disguised as another peasant, who trades him the power to cure the dying for a portion of turkey. Macario's fame soon spreads around the country, and he soon has a flourishing business—until a local doctor decides to call in The Inquisition. Spanish with English subtitles.

VHS: S11180. $79.95.
Roberto Gavaldon, Mexico, 1958, 91 mins.

Man Facing Southeast

In this critically-acclaimed Argentine film a man named Rantes suddenly appears in a Buenos Aires hospital, expertly playing the organ. But who is he—this man with no recorded identity? Doctor Denis dismisses Rantes' claim of being an alien visitor as a simple case of paranoid delusion. Beatriz, his only visitor, sees him as an intimate and knowing companion. The other patients, intrigued by his mysterious intelligence, see him as their only source of hope. Dubbed.

VHS: S05214. $19.95.
Eliseo Subiela, Argentina, 1986, 105 mins.

Maria Candelaria

"The classic and most memorable of all Mexican films" (B. Rayes Nevares, *The Mexican Cinema*). A poignant story starring Dolores del Rio as a young girl mercilessly persecuted by her townspeople because of her mother's immoral behavior. Spanish with English subtitles.

VHS: S02663. $24.95.
Emilio Fernandez, Mexico, 1945, 99 mins.

Martin Fierro

This riveting film by Leopoldo Torre Nilsson deals with the life of Martin Fierro. Drafted into military service, he is assigned to work for the commander. When he returns home, his wife and family are gone. As he descends into depression, he kills a black man during a drunken fight, and is forced to flee. Together with his friend Cruz, he lives in an Indian encampment in relative safety. Spanish with English subtitles.

VHS: S27740. $59.95.
Leopoldo Torre Nilsson, Argentina, 1968, 135 mins.

Mary My Dearest

A petty thief discovers a former flame who, after once jilting him, has suddenly appeared in his apartment wearing a wedding dress. She fascinates him with magic tricks, persuading him to abandon his life of crime and marry her. They form a vaudeville team whose sexual magnetism is more magical than their threadbare illusions. When Maria's car breaks down, she must turn to an insane asylum for a phone, unleashing an absurd nightmare of entrapment and madness. Co-written from the surreal imagination of Gabriel Garcia Marquez. Spanish with English subtitles.

VHS: S15668. $79.95.
Jaime H. Hermosillo, Mexico, 1983, 100 mins.

Midaq Alley (El Callegon de los Milagros)

The most awarded film in Mexican history, based on the Nobel Prize-winning novel by Egyptian writer Naguib Mahfouz. A complex portrait of lives in a Mexico City neighborhood, and the connections between them. Local pub owner Don Ru (Ernesto Gomez Cruz) is tired of marriage to his wife, Eusebia (Delia Casanova), and has feelings for a young clerk. Don Ru's son Chava (Juan Manuel Bernal) runs away to the U.S. after he almost kills Don Ru's lover. Chava's friend Abel (Bruno Bichir) is in love with Alma (Selma Hayek), the daughter of a tarot reader.

VHS: S34879. $89.95.
Jorge Fons, Mexico, 1995, 140 mins.

Miss Mary

From the director of *Camila*, Julie Christie stars as an English governess in Buenos Aires working for a wealthy family bound by a sense of tradition. Director Maria-Luisa Bemberg weaves broad political events together with intimate personal dramas. English language.

VHS: S03461. $19.95.
Maria-Luisa Bemberg, Argentina, 1986, 100 mins.

A Mixed-Up Adventure

In order to raise money to buy the electric guitar of his dreams, 16-year-old Miguel decides to kidnap and ransom 4-year-old Maggie, only to discover how difficult it is to take care of the cute but irrepressible little girl. Abandoning his plan, Miguel is returning Maggie home when she is abducted by another kidnapper. Aided by a group of Maggie's young friends, Miguel and the band of children go after the bad guy to rescue Maggie. A charming, suspenseful and funny, award-winning film that will entertain the whole family. Spanish with English subtitles. Public performance.

VHS: S32121. $99.95.
Juan Carlos Escheverria, Venezuela, 1993, 94 mins.

Narda or the Summer

Based on the short story by Salvador Elizondo, this Mexican drama is the revealing story of two young men who decide to share a woman during the summer. Narda, however, has plans of her own. She will not belong to either one—both will belong to her. Spanish with English subtitles.

VHS: S23476. $39.95.
Juan Guerrero, Mexico, 1968, 82 mins.

Nueba Yol

This charming film about disappointment, triumph and the American dream broke all box office records in the Dominican Republic. When Balbuena (Luisito Marti) moves from Santo Domingo to New York ("Nueba Yol" in Dominican slang) hoping to make a fortune, he is in for a harsh disappointment, but finds the inner resources to succeed and find love in this land of crime, betrayal and strict labor laws. "*Nueba Yol*'s well-placed plot and endearing characters provide a solid foundation for the deeper, more thought-provoking issues it raises. The film addresses not only immigration and crime but also the more universal themes of dreams, disappointment and triumph" (Mary Ann Farley, *Video Business*). Spanish with English subtitles.

VHS: S30285. $19.95.
Angel Muniz, Dominican Republic, 1996, 105 mins.

The Official Story

Winner of the Academy Award for Best Foreign Language Film in 1985, this powerful Argentinean feature is the true story of a comfortable middle-class couple and their adopted daughter. As the film progresses, the couple gradually begin to suspect that their daughter may be one of the many Argentinean children separated from their parents as they are detained or tortured and given away. The wife's journey of self-discovery reveals the horrors of the military dictatorship in Argentina. Directed by Luis Puenzo. With great performances from Hector Alterio and Norma Aleandro. Spanish with English subtitles.

VHS: S00949. $19.98.
Luis Puenzo, Argentina, 1985, 112 mins.

Oriane

A taut, Gothic, Latin American romance, winner of the Camera d'Or at the Cannes Film Festival. Marie returns to a rundown Venezuelan house in the jungle where she spent summers as a child. Her return ignites memories of a summer when her adolescent sexual curiosity led to a surprising encounter. "An exotic *Jane Eyre* set in a jungle-choked hacienda" (*Seattle Weekly*). With Doris Wells and Daniela Silverio. Spanish with English subtitles.

VHS: S27801. $29.95.
Fina Torres, Venezuela, 1991, 92 mins.

Painted Lips (Boquitas Pintadas)

This feature about obsessive love deals with a romantically handsome young man in the later stages of tuberculosis who is furiously fought over by four women. The film tells the story as it is recalled after his death by one of the women, who dies 30 years later, finally "cured" of romance. With Alfredo Alcon, Martha Gonzalez and Luisina Brando. Spanish with English subtitles.

VHS: S27741. $59.95.
Leopoldo Torre Nilsson, Argentina, 1975, 120 mins.

The Pearl

Mexican production of the John Steinbeck story about a poor fisherman who finds a beautiful pearl which changes his life. Pedro Armendariz is the bewildered fisherman who finds it hard to believe the changes that happen to himself and his wife.

VHS: S02560. $74.95.
Emilio Fernandez, USA/Mexico, 1947, 77 mins.

A Place in the World

In a sprawling ranching valley in Argentina, the lives of its inhabitants are forever changed with the arrival of a multinational company that dazzles the impoverished farmers with promises of wealth. Told through the eyes of a young man coming of age, *A Place in the World* is a poignant tale of the inevitable confrontation between traditional values and the inexorable incursions of progress. Spanish with English subtitles.

VHS: S32213. $89.95.
Adolfo Aristarain, Argentina, 1992, 120 mins.

Place Without Limits

From Arturo Ripstein, perhaps Mexico's most interesting filmmaker, a bittersweet dissection of machismo and homophobia in Latin America. La Manuela, a transvestite who lives in a brothel run by his daughter, "emerges as an all-out attack on machismo, suggesting that it can often mask in a man a highly insecure sense of masculinity" (*Los Angeles Times*). Spanish with English subtitles.

VHS: S31134. $79.95.
Arturo Ripstein, Mexico, 1977, 110 mins.

Portrait of Teresa

One of the key Cuban films shot in a fluid style, the film focuses on the stubborn survival of deeply ingrained traditions of machismo and sexism in post-revolutionary society. Teresa, a housewife, incurs the displeasure of her husband because of her involvement in political and cultural groups. Perhaps the most controversial Cuban film to be released in U.S. Spanish with English subtitles.

VHS: S12197. $69.95.
Pastor Vega, Cuba, 1979, 115 mins.

Pubis Angelical

Based on a novel by Manuel (*Kiss of the Spider Woman*) Puig—the poignant story of a dying woman reflecting on her life, intertwining dreams and fantasies of political events with her frustration with the men who stifled her. With Graciella Borges, Alfredo Alcon. Spanish with English subtitles.

VHS: S07740. $39.95.
Raul de la Torre, Argentina, 1983, 117 mins.

Reed: Mexico Insurgente

Paul Leduc's (*Frida Naturelaza Vida*) brilliant first feature focuses on John Reed's experience as an American journalist who covered the Mexican Revolution of 1914. The film shows the Revolution as both mundane and disorganized and poses the question of whether a journalist—surrounded by suffering-can remain an impartial observer. An important milestone in the history of contemporary Latin American cinema, and a powerful, intelligent film. Spanish with English subtitles.

VHS: S25733. $59.95.
Paul Leduc, Mexico, 1971, 106 mins.

Rodrigo D: No Future

A truly powerful film about growing up on the streets in the drug capital of Medelin, Colombia. Shot in quasi-documentary style, many of the young people who appeared in the film are now dead or in jail. In the tradition of *Los Olvidados* and *Pixote*, we meet a variety of young people who will never have to worry about growing old. Spanish with English subtitles.

VHS: S14744. $79.95.
Victor Gaviria, Colombia, 1990, 93 mins.

Romero

Raul Julia gives a compelling performance as the Archbishop of El Salvador, who was murdered for his ability to stir the masses into thoughts of political reform. Oscar Romero was a kind but apolitical churchman until his eyes were opened and he became a powerful voice of the people. With Richard Jordan, Eddie Velez, Tony Plana, Harold Gould and Ana Alicia. A riveting historical lesson from Paulist Pictures. Written by Jon Sacret Young (*Testament*).

VHS: S11582. $29.95.
John Duigan, USA, 1989, 105 mins.

The Roots

This compilation of four short stories by Francisco Gonzales, produced by Manuel Barbachano (*Torero!*), won the International Film Critics Award at Cannes. Includes *The Cows, Our Lady, The One-Eyed Boy* and *The Filly*. Spanish with English subtitles.

VHS: S14645. $29.95.
Benito Alazraki, Mexico, 1958, 85 mins.

Santa Sangre

A startling vision of passion and obsession from the creator of *El Topo*. Guy Stockwell stars as Orgo, a sadistic circus master who brutally disfigures his wife after she catches him with another woman. Witness to the horror is their young son, Fenix. Traumatized, he is committed to an asylum. Freed by his armless mother twelve years later, they forge an unholy alliance. He "gives" her his arms, she takes control of his mind. Together they feed a mounting obsession of desire and revenge. Directed and co-written by Alejandro Jodorowsky, *Santa Sangre* is a film of bold and bizarre images, delicately balanced between the theater of the absurd and a circus of horrors. English language version. Available in both *R* and *NC-17* rated versions.

VHS: S13586. $19.98.
Alejandro Jodorowsky, Mexico/Italy, 1990, 123 mins.

The Seven Madmen (Los Siete Locos)

A daring political thriller set in South America in the 1930s. A failed idealist links up with a strangely assorted group which intends to overthrow the government and install a new regime. But the plan ultimately fails when a military coup beats it to the revolution. With Alfredo Alcon, Norma Aleandro and Thelma Biral. Spanish with English subtitles.

VHS: S27742. $59.95.
Leopoldo Torre Nilsson, Argentina, 1973, 121 mins.

A Shadow You Soon Will Be

Based on the novel by Osvaldo Soriano and directed by Hector Olivera (*Funny Dirty Little War*), this road movie about a group of wandering misfits on their way to nowhere is an allegory of contemporary Argentine society. "A modern-day *Don Quixote* as imagined by Luis Bunuel" (Stephen Holden, *The New York Times*). Spanish with English subtitles.

VHS: S30042. $89.95.
Hector Olivera, Argentina, 1994, 105 mins.

Shattered Cross

Based on the novel by Marcos Aguinis, and winner of the Premio Planeta. A political-ecclesiastical subject of great controversy shapes this film in which a young priest has to face the Church and the Army in order to defend his ideals. With Oscar Martinez, Ana Maria Picchio. Spanish with English subtitles.

VHS: S07735. $59.95.
Mario David, Argentina, 1985, 103 mins.

Shoot to Kill

A mother seeks to clear the damaged reputation of her son when he is murdered during a routine police round-up and condemned as a criminal. She launches a campaign for justice and vindication for her son. "An ambitious suspense thriller which current events in Venezuela make particularly relevant" (*Variety*). Spanish with English subtitles.

VHS: S20381. $59.95.
Carlos Azpurua, Venezuela, 1990, 90 mins.

The Silence of Neto

Mixing magic-realism and historical events, this "fine, richly entertaining film" (Michael Wilmington, *Chicago Tribune*) is the first film produced entirely in Guatemala. Filmed in the colonial city of Antigua, it tells the politically charged story of a young boy striving to follow his dreams while his country struggles to preserve democracy amidst CIA cold-war propaganda. Through the eyes of young Neto, we are given an authentic insider's look at the diverse people of Guatemala and the historical events that have shaped their destiny. Spanish with English subtitles.

VHS: S32224. $49.95.
Luis Argueta, Guatemala, 1994, 106 mins.

Strange Ways

In this gripping thriller filmed in the rugged mountains of Mexico, a college theatre group drives a beat-up van along a dark and winding country road and gets stuck in a wilderness unfamiliar to their pristine ways. Forced to spend time in a small highland village, they stumble across an operation of illegal tree cutting that puts them at odds with the brutal owner of a local lumber business. Soon they realize that their wrong turn may cost them more than a few lost performances. Spanish with English subtitles.

VHS: S32170. $89.98.
Alfonso Corona, Mexico, 1995, 91 mins.

The Summer of Miss Forbes

Written by Nobel prize-winning author Gabriel Garcia Marquez, *The Summer of Miss Forbes* is a wickedly funny black comedy about two children plotting to kill their authoritarian nanny. A biting comedy reminiscent of the work of legendary filmmaker Luis Bunuel, *The Summer of Miss Forbes* was directed by Jaime Humberto Hermosillo, one of Mexico's premier filmmakers. Spanish with English subtitles.

VHS: S13693. $19.98.
Jaime H. Hermosillo, Mex./Spain, 1988, 85 min.

Tango Bar

Carlos Gardel is teamed up with Rosita Moreno in this 1930's Argentinean musical drama. Spanish *without* English subtitles.

VHS: S06035. $54.95.
John Reinhardt, Argentina, 1935, 58 mins.

Tango: Our Dance

The sensuality and stylized rituals popular with the residents of Buenos Aires are part of the complex art form called the tango. Director Jorge Zanada examines the unique role of this dance within Argentina's social and personal landscape, exploring issues of machismo and passion contained within the dance. With a special appearance by Robert Duvall. Spanish with English subtitles.

VHS: S20380. $29.95.
Jorge Zanada, Argentina, 1988, 71 mins.

Time for Revenge

This political thriller captures a brilliant performance from Federico Luppi as a disenchanted demolition worker who rigs a fake industrial accident in order to get back at his corrupt employers. But the plan fails, and in order to protect himself and the scheme, he goes to extraordinary lengths to fulfill his original goal. Spanish with English subtitles.

VHS: S04872. $24.95.
Adolfo Aristarain, Argentina, 1983, 112 mins.

Times to Come
Reminiscent of *Clockwork Orange* and an Argentine *Blade Runner*, this tense thriller was awarded three prestigious ACE awards—Best Director, Best Actor (Hugo Soto) and Best Supporting Actor (Charly Garcia). Spanish with English subtitles.
VHS: S12361. $79.95.
Gustavo Mosquera, Argentina, 1981

The Torch
Paulette Goddard and Gilbert Roland are featured in this tale of love and war. A Mexican revolutionary restores the rule of law to a small town, but the love of a young, aristocratic woman threatens to break his concentration. With Pedro Armendariz and Antonio Kaneen. Cinematography by Gabriel Figueroa.
VHS: S25702. $19.95.
Emilio Fernandez, USA/Mexico, 1949, 83 mins.

The Track of the Ants
"Halfway between *Koyaanisqatsi* and *Brazil*...Dispensing with story and words, Venezuelan filmmaker Rafael Marziano-Tinoco looks at the life of Caracas much as a disenchanted god might survey an ant hill gone awry" (*Village Voice*). A city symphony with a Latin beat, *The Track of the Ants* focuses on the sprawling tropical metropolis of Caracas, Venezuela. Director Marziano-Tinoco captures both the fading splendor and the brilliant promise of a world continually caught in the crossroads of past and present, nature and civilization. Best Documentary, Philadelphia Film Festival. No dialog.
VHS: S27798. $29.95.
Rafael Marziano-Tinoco, Venezuela/Poland, 1993, 54 mins.

Two to Tango
Don Stroud is a professional assassin sent to Buenos Aires by a secret organization known as "The Company". Down Argentine way he falls for the girlfriend of his target. It takes two to tango when a cold-blooded killer meets a hot-blooded dancer. With Adrienne Sachs, Michael Cavanaugh and Duilio Marzio. Based on the novel *Last Days of the Victim*. In English. Produced by Roger Corman.
VHS: S08510. $79.95.
Hector Olivera, USA/Argentina, 1988, 87 mins.

Vamanos con Pancho Villa
The key work of the godfather of Mexican cinema, Fernando de Fuentes, this remarkable feature is the story of a group of friends who decide to join forces with Pancho Villa. Several die heroic but meaningless deaths, and the last three enter Villa's elite force, Los Dorados, the Golden Ones. Fuentes acutely charts the disillusionment, stagnation and corruption which followed the Revolution in what is clearly a milestone of Latin American cinema. With a remarkable performance from Antonio Fraustio. Spanish with English subtitles.
VHS: S24690. $39.95.
Fernando de Fuentes, Mexcio, 1935, 92 mins.

Veronico Cruz
A fascinating film from Argentina, Miguel Pereira's *Veronico Cruz* shows how the Falklands (Malvinas) war affected the life of an Indian boy from one of Argentina's most remote regions. Awarded the Silver Bear at the Berlin Film Festival, *Veronico Cruz* also received four Condors—Best Picture, Best Director, Best Screenplay and Best Supporting Actor from the Argentine Society of Film Critics. Spanish with English subtitles.
VHS: S12362. $79.95.
Miguel Pereira, Argentina, 1989

A Very Old Man with Enormous Wings
Magical realism and comic confusion blend in a startling film about visions and expectations. Amid the debris of a Columbian cyclone lands an old man with enormous wings, whose seemingly miraculous anatomy attracts the curious and devout from around the world. Silent and disheveled, this fantastical "creature" is housed in a chicken coop as his hosts and the onlookers wait for his heavenly message—which turns out to be a very mixed blessing. Original story by Gabriel Garcia Marquez, who also co-wrote the screenplay. Spanish with English subtitles.
VHS: S13841. $19.98.
Fernando Birri, Cuba/Spain, 1988, 90 mins.

We're All Stars
This wacky comedy of errors takes off when the members of the Huambachano family get a chance to win fame and fortune and to appear as the "family of the week" on the popular TV game show, *We're All Stars*. The only catch: the television needs the "perfect" family, so the Huambachanos are forced to cover up the family divorce. Winner of Best Picture awards at three international film festivals. Spanish with English subtitles.
VHS: S27738. $59.95.
Felipe Degregori, Peru, 1993, 80 mins.

Winter Barracks
Based on a novel by Osvaldo Soriano: a tango singer arrives in a village for a temporary engagement. Soon after, he notices the military repression and is subjected to suffer its brutal consequences. Spanish with English subtitles.
VHS: S07766. $39.95.
Lautaro Murua, Argentina, 1984, 116 mins.

Yanco
Stunningly photographed tale of fantasy and folklore. Yanco is a small Indian boy, considered bewitched because of his hypersensitivity to sound. He flees his village to an island and a musical environment. B&W, no dialog, but occasional Spanish with English subtitles.
VHS: S01485. $29.95.
Servando Gonzalez, Mexico, 1960, 85 mins.

TOMAS GUTIERREZ ALEA

Death of a Bureaucrat
With Death of a Bureaucrat, Alea pays homage to the history of film comedy—from the anarchic tradition of Bunuel and Vigo, to the satire of Billy Wilder and the physical comedy of silent greats Harold Lloyd and Buster Keaton. The story of a young man's attempt to fight the system is an entertaining and hilarious account of galloping bureaucracy and the tyranny of red tape. An adventurous mix of slapstick farce and paranoid nightmare make this comedy a rich and enjoyable frenzy of laughter. Spanish with English subtitles.
VHS: S13916. $59.95.
Tomas Gutierrez Alea, Cuba, 1966, 87 mins.

Guantanamera
This road movie, farce, satire, picaresque picture, black comedy, bedroom farce about life in Cuba is the last film by the maestro of Cuban Cinema, Tomas Gutierrez Alea (Strawberry and Chocolate). Intertwining the stories of two groups, members of a funeral procession and some truckdrivers making the journey on the road to Havana, the film stars Alea's widow and leading lady, Mirtha Ibarra, as ex-economics professor Georgina, who, with her husband, bureaucrat Adolfo (Carlos Cruz), tests a new funeral system with the body of Aunt Yoyita, an elderly singing star who returned to Cuba to visit an old flame and dropped dead in his arms.
VHS: S34736. $89.98.
Tomas Gutierrez Alea, Cuba/Spain, 1994, 104 mins.

The Last Supper
A celebrated film from Cuba, photographed with a lush palette, this startlingly beautiful masterpiece is based on an incident from 18th century Cuban history. The film is also a dazzling moral tale of a pious slaveholder who decides to improve his soul and instruct his slaves in the glories of Christianity by inviting 12 of them to participate in a reenactment of the Last Supper. Spanish with English subtitles.
VHS: S12466. $69.95.
Tomas Gutierrez Alea, Cuba, 1976, 101 mins.

Letters from the Park
The enchanting story of two young people too shy to pursue the intimacy they both seek. They independently enlist the help of the local poet to write love letters to each other. The poet writes the letters to make some extra money but also to unburden himself of the unbounded love he feels but for which he has no outlet. When the young woman of the couple becomes the object of his affection, he is confused and faced with a moral and emotional dilemma in this surprising and sweet romance. Based on an original story by Gabriel Garcia Marquez, who also co-wrote the screenplay. Spanish with English subtitles.
VHS: S13510. $19.98.
Tomas Gutierrez Alea, Spain, 1988, 85 mins.

Memories of Underdevelopment
A breakthrough Cuban film, the first Cuban film to be released in the U.S. Set in the 1960s, the film centers on a Europeanized Cuban intellectual, too idealistic (or lazy) to leave for Miami, but too decadent to fit into the new Cuban society. The film is a remarkable demonstration that artistic subtlety, political commitment, and superior entertainment need not be incompatible. Spanish with English subtitles.
VHS: S11593. $59.95.
Tomas Gutierrez Alea, Cuba, 1968, 97 mins.

Strawberry & Chocolate
A sensation from Cuba in which a chance encounter over ice cream between a middle-aged gay man and a young, fervent believer in contemporary Cuban Marxism sets the stage for a funny but serious film about difference and acceptance. Their friendship develops despite official intolerance of homosexuality and it soon withstands that short-sighted policy. This film broke box office attendance records in Cuba and achieved world-wide acclaim. Spanish with English subtitles.
VHS: S26613. $19.95.
Laser: LD75320. $39.98.
Tomas Gutierrez Alea, Cuba, 1994, 104 mins.

Up to a Certain Point
This sly social comedy stars Oscar Alvarez, Mirta Ibarra and Omar Valdes. A married, middle-aged screenwriter is researching the problem of machismo in Cuban society and suddenly falls under the spell of Lina, a strong, self-supporting, young dockworker. Spanish with English subtitles.
VHS: S23285. $79.95.
Tomas Gutierrez Alea, Cuba, 1985, 72 mins.

BRAZILIAN CINEMA

Amor Bandido
A gritty murder mystery from the director of *Dona Flor*, set in the glamorous and seedy Copacabana district of Rio de Janeiro. Christina Ache and Paulo Guarnieri are street people, thrown together by tragedy and eventually torn apart. *Amor* mixes an eerie love triangle of two young lovers and the girl's detective father with the search for a mad killer. Portuguese with English subtitles.
VHS: S12945. $19.98.
Bruno Barreto, Brazil, 1987, 98 mins.

Black God, White Devil
A quintessential film from Brazil's Cinema Novo, this film of immense power from Glauber Rocha is set in the impoverished Northeastern Brazil, and focuses on a poor peasant as he changes from a fanatical preacher into an honorable bandit. A violent yet lyrical portrait of Brazilian society. Portuguese with English subtitles.
VHS: S07299. $79.95.
Glauber Rocha, Brazil, 1964, 102 mins.

Black Orpheus
Marcel Camus' quintessential love story based on the Greek myth of Orpheus and Eurydice is set against the vivid backdrop of carnival in Rio de Janeiro. Orpheus, the streetcar conductor, falls hopelessly in love with Eurydice; winner of the Grand Prize at Cannes as well as an Oscar for Best Foreign Film. Portuguese with English subtitles.
VHS: S00138. $29.95.
Laser: LD70346. $79.95.
Marcel Camus, Brazil, 1958, 103 mins.

Buccaneer Soul
One of Brazil's Cinema Novo's guiding spirits, Carlos Reichenbach, directs this fascinating look at Brazilian love through literature, cinema and music in the story of two friends living through the chaotic 1960s. "One of the most interesting and creative Brazilian filmmakers" (Jonathan Rosenbaum, *Chicago Reader*). Portuguese with English subtitles.
VHS: S27735. $59.95.
Carlos Reichenbach, Brazil, 1993, 116 mins.

Bye Bye Brazil
A small-time travelling sideshow plays over 9,000 miles of backwards Brazil, a mixture of primitivism and progress. One of the most original and entertaining films of recent years, *Bye Bye Brazil* is exotic and exuberant, and often very moving. Portuguese with English subtitles.
VHS: S00198. $19.98.
Carlos Diegues, Brazil, 1980, 110 mins.

The Dolphin
A sensual tale, set on the shores of Brazil, based on the legend of the dolphin-man. On nights with a full moon, a dolphin appears in the form of a handsome young man and seduces women. The local inhabitants are both at odds with and enchanted by the dolphin-man, whose presence scares away the fish, and incites the desires of the town's women and the anxieties of the men. With stunning photography by Pedro Farkas and a strong performance by Cassia Kiss. Portuguese with yellow English subtitles.
VHS: S15546. $19.98.
Walter Lima Jr., Brazil, 1987, 95 mins.

Dona Flor and Her Two Husbands
Funny, sexy and intoxicating! *Dona Flor* is a ribald folktale about a young widow, her respectable new husband, and her dynamic but dead first husband who refuses to stay buried, featuring the sensual Sonia Braga as Dona Flor. Portuguese with English subtitles.
VHS: S00359. $19.98.
Bruno Barreto, Brazil, 1977, 106 mins.

Four Days in September

A first-rate political thriller in the tradition of *Z* from Bruno (*Dona Flor*) Barreto. Based on a true story and set during the days of the military junta, a group of young idealists kidnaps the American ambassador in order to throw attention to the curtailment of freedom in Brazil. Told from the perspective of one of the young revolutionaries, Barreto's controversial film creates a tense atmosphere as he depicts the four days the ambassador was in captivity, and in the process revisits Brazil's all-too-recent political past. With Alan Arkin, Pedro Cardoso and Fernanda Torres. Portuguese with English subtitles.
VHS: S34726. $103.99.
Bruno Barreto, Brazil, 1997, 107 mins.

Happily Ever After

A sizzling sexy drama from Bruno Barreto, the director of *Dona Flor and Her Two Husbands, Happily Ever After* stars Regina Duarte as a seemingly happy mother who is an interior decorator. By chance, she meets the man of her dreams in a nightclub, who turns out to be a transvestite and a bi-sexual. But Fernanda and Miguel develop a steamy affair, and Miguel takes her on a trip into the criminal underworld, away from the safety of her upper-class existence. Portuguese with English subtitles.
VHS: S06014. $69.95.
Bruno Barreto, Brazil, 1986, 106 mins.

Hour of the Star

The brilliant, critically-acclaimed film by Suzana Amaral, winner at the Berlin Film Festival, based on a novel by Clarice Lispector. The neo-realistic story of a young girl who comes to Sao Paolo from the provinces to find work and love, *Hour of the Star* is an often funny, tragi-comic film, the breakthrough work for Suzana Amaral. Portuguese with English subtitles.
VHS: S04720. $79.95.
Suzana Amaral, Brazil, 1977, 85 mins.

How Tasty Was My Little Frenchman

One of the high points of Brazil's Cinema Novo, this wicked black comedy inspired a furor at Cannes. A French explorer is captured by an Amazon tribe and tries desperately to be accepted by his captors. The tribe feeds him well—only at the end does the Frenchman realize why. A brilliant satire on the Colonialist mentality. French and Tupi with English subtitles.
VHS: S25905. $79.95.
Nelson Pereira dos Santos, Brazil, 1971, 80 mins.

Luzia

Set on the vast and beautiful plains of central Brazil, *Luzia* stars the alluring Claudia Ohana (one of Brazil's biggest box-office stars: *Erendira, Fable of the Beautiful Pigeon Fancier*) as a cowgirl caught in a clash between squatters and the powerful ranch owners. Luzia's extraordinary rodeo skills and incredible beauty attract the attention of the landowners, whose history of marauding returns to gain revenge. Portuguese with yellow English subtitles.
VHS: S15004. $19.98.
Fabio Barreto, Brazil, 1988, 112 mins.

Memories of Prison

Based, like his earlier film *Vidas secas*, on a book by Graciliano Ramos, this film is set in the 1930s and is an account of Ramos' imprisonment on the penal island of Ilha Grande. A fictional film with a documentary tone, the film "is meant to be a metaphor for Brazilian society today and a film against prisons in the widest sense of the word...This is a film to look out for." Portuguese with English subtitles.
VHS: S33029. $69.95.
Nelson Pereira dos Santos, Brazil, 1984, 187 mins.

Pixote

This acclaimed feature by Hector Babenco has been out of release for years. Nothing in recent cinema comes close to the devastating account of brutalization and exploitation offered in Babenco's film about a 12-year-old boy who somehow survives the vicious oppression of reform school to escape and find his way into dope-dealing, prostitution and murder on the streets of Sao Paolo, Brazil. Portuguese with English subtitles.
VHS: S30982. $89.95.
Hector Babenco, Brazil, 1981, 127 mins.

Quilombo

From Carlos Diegues, the director of *Bye Bye Brazil* and *Xica*, comes a handsome tale of revolution and conflict set in the mid-1600s. Disgruntled slaves in northeastern Brazil leave their plantations and form Quilombo de Palmares—their own democratic nation in the jungle. But this doesn't sit well with the Portuguese landowners, who send in their troops to restore control. A sequel of sorts to *Ganga Zumba*, this historical saga is a stirring fusion of folklore, political impact and dynamic storytelling, realized in vibrant tropical colors and set to the pulsing beat of Gilberto Gil's musical score. With Antonio Pompeu, Toni Tornado, and the dazzling Zeze Motta as Dandara the temptress. Portuguese with English subtitles.
VHS: S14573. $29.95.
Carlos Diegues, Brazil, 1984, 114 mins.

Savage Capitalism

Brazil's outrageously dramatic tele-novellas inspire this tale of marital infidelity, national betrayal, public scandal, long lost orphans and of course, forbidden love. When a reporter uncovers the truth behind a company's plans to mine in the interior of Brazil it sets in motion a complex tale. Ecological ruin could result if the primal forces of this passionate land are ignored. Portuguese with English subtitles.
VHS: S21133. $59.95.
Andre Klotzel, Brazil, 1993, 86 mins.

The Story of Fausta

Betty Fari—remembered for her miraculous performance in *Bye Bye Brazil*—is Fausta, a quirky cleaning lady whose voluptuous nature opens the door to a more comfortable life with an elderly widower. From the director of *Dona Flor and Her Two Husbands*. Portuguese with English subtitles.
VHS: S15666. $19.98.
Bruno Barreto, Brazil, 1988, 90 mins.

Terra em Transe

The brief story of this important film by Glauber Rocha is the story of a young poet and journalist who is persuaded by his lover to become involved in the politics of his country..."*Terra em Transe* is perhaps Rocha's most personal film and the most politically committed and polemical film of the Brazilian *cinema novo*. In Brazil it was attacked as fascist by the academic left and hailed by the extreme left as a revolutionary film ...full of extremely moving and provocative images—including footage from a Rocha documentary, *Maranhao*" (Georges Sadoul). "For me, my most important film...a more profound expression of my life" (Rocha). Portuguese with English subtitles.
VHS: S08783. $69.95.
Glauber Rocha, Brazil, 1966, 112 mins.

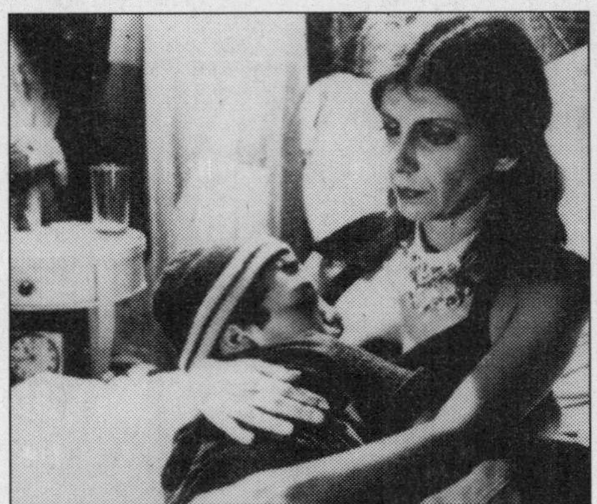

Tieta di Agresta

From the director of *Bye Bye Brazil*. Sonia Braga (*The Kiss of the Spider Woman*) stars as the rich and powerful widow of a Brazilian industrialist who is caught up in the political upheaval of her girlhood village. In the midst of the uproar, she is forced to wrestle with her past and reveal her darkest secrets. Based on a novel by Jorge Amado. Soundtrack by Caetano Veloso. Portuguese with English subtitles.
VHS: S34876. $89.95.
DVD: English subtitles. **DV60375. $29.98.**
Carlos Carlos Diegues, Brazil, 1997, 115 mins.

Xica

Carlos Diegues' comedy concerns Xica (Zeze Motta), a beautiful black slave who uses her sexual charm and savvy to benefit from Brazil's economic emergence. The film is set in the 18th century, when the fantastic wealth produced from the diamond trade transformed Brazil into a decadent hothouse. Xica ascends to the role of unofficial Empress, gleefully mocking her former masters while stockpiling newly found assets and power. "The film marks Diegues as one of Brazil's most innovative directors, who speaks his piece with exuberance, wit and style" (*San Francisco Chronicle*). With Walmor Chagas, Jose Wilker, Marcus Vinicius and Altair Lima. Portuguese with English subtitles.
VHS: S19417. $79.95.
Carlos Diegues, Brazil, 1976, 109 mins.

CARIBBEAN CINEMA

Belly Pain

This hot, sexy comedy from Kingston, Jamaica, is an authentic pleasure. When a child is bad, people say, "Mother band your belly." But in this case it's "Father band your belly." Mom's having an affair and the daughter is pregnant. Who's having sex with whom? Belly pain can drive you insane with desire or laughter.
VHS: S22213. $29.95.
Carl Ross/Keeling Beckford, Jamaica

Caryl Phillips

West Indian-born Caryl Phillips has published six works of fiction including *Cambridge* and *Higher Ground*. He explores provocatively different perspectives of the African diaspora as well as the anatomy of slavery with stylistic virtuosity. On March 7, 1995, Phillips read from *Crossing the River*, a Booker Prize finalist, and spoke with novelist and essayist Pico Iyer in Los Angeles. From the *Lannan Literary Videos* series. 60 mins.
VHS: S32428. $19.95.

Come to Saint Lucia

A look at the cultural and folk life of this attractive Caribbean island. Narrated in English by Von Martin. 25 mins.,
VHS: S06807. $70.00.

Dancehall Queen

This modern-day Cinderella story is the largest grossing Jamaican film ever. Marcia, a single mother, toils the streets of the Kingston ghetto by day as a street vendor; by night, she's the "mystery lady," the new star of the Kingston dancehall. If she can win the dancehall contest, the prize money, and more importantly, her own sense of worth, she will be free of lowlife Larry (who pretends to help her but is actually after her eldest daughter), the murderous thug Priest, and the ghetto itself.
VHS: S32524. $19.95.
DVD: DV60308. $29.95.
Jamaica, 1997, 95 mins.

Divine Horsemen: The Living Gods of Haiti

Posthumously edited by Teiji and Cherel Ito, a remarkable document of the Rada, Petro and Congo cults of Haiti whose devotees commune with cosmic powers through invocations, voodoo dances and ritual ceremonies. The sound track conveys the power of ritual drumming and singing.
VHS: S00349. $29.95.
Maya Deren, USA, 52 mins.

Dominican Republic, Cradle of the Americas

A documentary view of the culture, people, and folk life of the Dominican Republic. Columbus loved this island, naming it "Little Spain" (Hispaniola), but before his arrival Indian cultures flourished which left their mark on the everyday lives of the people. From the Arawaks and Taino pre-hispanic Indians of the area to the coming of the Spanish and on up to today's modern life, the Dominican Republic remains a beautiful island with a rich tradition. Directed by Angel Hurtado. English and Spanish narrations by Herbert Morales. 25 mins.
English Narration.
VHS: S06794. $60.00.
Spanish Narration.
VHS: S06795. $60.00.

Harder They Come

Jimmy Cliff is Ivan, a country boy who comes to the city to make a record and get his share of that pie up in the sky. But it isn't until he shoots a cop and becomes a fugitive from the law that he gets his sought-after notoriety, proving that you can get it if you really want. The pulsating reggae soundtrack features Cliff, Toots and the Maytels, Desmond Decker. The first genuine Jamaican film.
VHS: S00541. $19.95.
Laser: LD70753. $49.95.
Perry Henzell, Jamaica, 1973, 104 mins.

Islands of the Caribbean

A variety of travel adventures, from nightlife to water sports to shopping, in the Dominican Republic and Puerto Rico. 30 mins.
VHS: S14013. $24.95.

Jamaican Heritage

This film covers the people and cultural aspects of the island's heritage, while not missing any of Jamaica's natural beauty. The music and dance that play such a major role in the life of the people are featured, as well as works of local artists and craftsmen. Directed by Angel Hurtado. Narration in English by Megan Thomas. 25 mins.
VHS: S06783. $70.00.

Krik? Krak! Tales of a Nightmare

An innovative feature set in Haiti which blends documentary and fiction scenes to delve into the tormented history of the Black world: Haiti, the terrible experience under Papa Doc Duvalier, and the work of his infamous paramilitary force, the Tontons Macoutes. "Remarkably insightful, original, compassionate picture of the eternal Haiti" (Graham Greene). "Unflinching. Passionate. Creativity and daring in shooting, editing and music are matched by the depth of feeling for the Haitian people" (Jonathan Demme).
VHS: S27807. $29.95.
Vanyoska Gert/Jac Avila, Haiti/USA, 78 mins.

Me Yu an' Mi Taxi
This acclaimed comic production includes a dazzling cast of Jamaica's finest comedians, including the master himself—Oliver Samuels. See the full genius of Jamaica's popular theatre in all its fabulous madness.
VHS: S15331. $29.95.

Nueba Yol
This charming film about disappointment, triumph and the American dream broke all box office records in the Dominican Republic. When Balbuena (Luisito Marti) moves from Santo Domingo to New York ("Nueba Yol" in Dominican slang) hoping to make a fortune, he is in for a harsh disappointment, but finds the inner resources to succeed and find love in this land of crime, betrayal and strict labor laws. "*Nueba Yol*'s well-placed plot and endearing characters provide a solid foundation for the deeper, more thought-provoking issues it raises. The film addresses not only immigration and crime but also the more universal themes of dreams, disappointment and triumph" (Mary Ann Farley, *Video Business*). Spanish with English subtitles.
VHS: S30285. $19.95.
Angel Muniz, Dominican Republic, 1996, 105 mins.

Obeah Wedding
This Jamaican drama tells the story of a middle-class woman who falls victim to a casanova whose only desire is to take advantage of women and then drop them flat. Starring Richard Mullings as Roy Sweetness and Leonie Samuels as Shirley.
VHS: S15333. $29.95.
Jamaica, 1989, 100 mins.

Rhythms of Haiti
With a flood of melody and a rainbow of color that engulfs the traveler in a visit to this small but complex Caribbean country, the film captures the folk life as well as tourist aspects of the island. Many of Haiti's artists are shown at work in their natural environment, bringing their landscapes to life. Directed by Angel Hurtado, 25 mins.
English Narration. Roger Wilkison.
VHS: S06792. $70.00.
French Narration. Max Gautier.
VHS: S06793. $70.00.

Son Son
In *Son Son*, a feature from Jamaica, Keith Sheppard was raised by his mother, Karen Clarke, in the ghettoes of Kingston, Jamaica. This young man has an attitude when it comes to finding a job, as suggested by his mother. Ignoring her pleas, he ends up in the streets, where he learns the harsh reality that a life of crime is no easy way to riches.
VHS: S22203. $29.95.

Stepping Razor Red X: The Peter Tosh Story
Tosh was not just a reggae star, but a Rasta visionary, revolutionary, and Jamaican folk hero. Rare concert footage, interviews and narration from Tosh himself make this a special opportunity to understand this legendary musician. From the slums of Kingston, to stardom, to his brutal murder, it's all here.
VHS: S23329. $29.95.
Nicholas Campbell, USA, 1992, 73 mins.

Sugar Cane Alley
Euzhan Palcy's lyrical village drama set in French-occupied 1930s Martinique. The story examines the relationship of a determined, impoverished 11-year-old and his equally difficult and shrewd grandmother, who sacrifices everything for the boy's happiness. With Darling Legitimus, Garry Cadenat, Routa Seck and Joby Bernabe. French with English subtitles.
VHS: S01278. $29.95.
Euzhan Palcy, France, 1984, 107 mins.

THE HISPANIC WORLD

Abuela's Weave
Esperanza's *abuela*, her grandmother, is unmatched in her weaving skills. She shares the gift of traditional Mayan tapestry with her granddaughter. Together they decide to sell their wares in the market, but Abuela's birthmark may frighten away customers. Esperanza must sell their works alone.
VHS: S21884. $44.95.

Adelante Mujeres!
The National Women's History Project presents this unique view on the history of Mexican-American/Chicana women. Beginning with the Spanish Conquest, it documents a host of major events and personalities. This affirmative history employs hundreds of newly available photographs from archives across the continent. 30 mins.
English Version.
VHS: S26514. $125.00.
Spanish Version.
VHS: S26515. $125.00.

Amazonia: Voices from the Rainforest
For over 500 years the native inhabitants of the Amazon have fought against the invasion and destruction of their homeland. This historic devastation has already resulted in the mass extinction of over 700 tribes. In this stunningly filmed work, the people for whom the Amazon has always been home voice both their fears and their hopes. 70 mins.
VHS: S21571. $95.00.

And the Earth Did Not Swallow Him (...y no se lo trago la tierra)
Based on Tomas Rivera's classic novella, this is the beautiful and moving semi-autobiographical account of 12-year-old Marcos Gonzales (Jose Alcala), the son of Mexican-American migrant workers in the 1950s, and their annual ritual of leaving Crystal City, Texas, for the harvest season work that will take them throughout the midwest during summer and fall. Reminscent of *To Kill a Mockingbird* or *Catcher in the Rye*. "An epic story of survival...affecting and beautifully photographed" (Kevin Thomas, *The Los Angeles Times*).
VHS: S30709. $79.95.
Severo Perez, USA, 1994, 99 mins.

Archeological Yucatan: Mexico
A fascinating travel-view of the legendary ruins of Chichen Itza, Tulum, Uxmal and many other ancient Mayan sites, including visits to Merida, a city of contrasting sights, cultural blends and people.
VHS: S03097. $39.95.

Argentina
Argentina is explored in this documentary, which moves from the Glacier National Park to the desert landscapes, rocky coastline and tropical rain forest. The program also examines the lives of the *gauchos*, Argentina's cowboys. 40 mins.
English Narration.
VHS: S19829. $39.95.
Spanish Narration.
VHS: S19828. $39.95.

Aymaras of Bolivia
With one foot in the world of ancient traditions and the other in contemporary society, the Aymara people of Bolivia straddle centuries. Taped entirely on location in Bolivia, the program looks at a traditional Aymara rite of passage ceremony and the struggle of Aymara women in the capital city of La Paz. Produced by Maryknoll Media. 28 mins.
VHS: S09070. $24.95.

The Aztecs
Established in 1325, Tenochtitlan grew out of religious guidance from the god Huitzilopochtil. Cimalpopoca suffered the burdens of slavery under the lords of Azcapotzalco up to the year 1428, when Itzcoatl gave freedom to his country. Montezuma, Ilhuicamina, Azayacatl, Tizoc and Ahuizotl increased the glory and power of the new Mexican Empire, providing a forum for pursuits in sculpture, architecture and music based around homage for their gods. This is a concise look at the historical and cultural aspects of Aztec society in their varied manifestations. In Spanish, no subtitles. 15 mins.
VHS: S16381. $69.95.

Barry Lopez
In his books *Arctic Dreams, Of Wolves and Men* and *Crossing Open Ground*, Barry Lopez explores man's role in the natural world. On October 5, 1992, he read his essay "Rediscovery of North America" and spoke to Michael Silverblatt. From the *Lannan Literary Videos* series. 60 mins.
VHS: S27137. $19.95.

Battle for the Falklands
As head of the Argentine military junta, Lieutenant General Leopoldo Galtiere stormed the peaceful Falkland Islands after 150 years of British rule. This program shows how Thatcher struck back, the events, the battles and world reaction. 110 mins.
VHS: S13126. $39.98.

Before the Incas
Machu Picchu represents the pinnacle of Inca civilization. Northern Bolivia belies traces of even earlier cultures that predate the Incas. This program explores the lives of a series of peoples that conquered, occupied, absorbed and replaced their predecessors. Sites like Lake Titicaca, Mochica and Chimu yield their secrets to the modern era in this documentary. 43 mins.
VHS: S22927. $29.95.

Belize
The general patterns of the culture of Belize are shown in this account by the Museum of Modern Art of Latin America. English narration. 20 mins.
VHS: S06769. $60.00.

Bilingual Americans
Explores the "melting pot that never happened" in America, and the bilingual-bicultural nature of American society. Bilingual English-Spanish narration.
VHS: S07431. $59.95.

Brazil: Heart of South America
A video tour of Brazil including Bahia, Rio de Janeiro, the Amazon, the Iguazu Falls, and the beat of Sao Paolo. 55 mins.
VHS: S09878. $24.95.

Building Peace in the Midst of War
An inspiring documentary showing how individuals and communities can make a difference in Central America. This tape includes the moving testimonies of both North Americans and Salvadorans as they talk about humanitarian aid to El Salvador organized by ordinary people who care enough to help. 1988, 30 mins.
VHS: S13967. $35.00.

The Buried Mirror
World-renowned author and diplomat Carlos Fuentes explores the diversity that comprises the Hispanic world. From Spain and Portugal to South and Central America, the Caribbean and the U.S., a whole range of peoples, with specific traditions and histories, make up the entity of Hispanidad.
Program I: The Virgin and the Bull. Fuentes examines the mix of people found in contemporary Latin America. Spanish, Arab, Jewish, Indian and African forebears make for a rich, illustrious and vibrant culture. From the shores of Vera Cruz to Spain, with its flamenco and bull-fighting traditions, this author traces that which defines Latin America. 59 mins.
VHS: S21370. $29.95.
Program II: Conflict of the Gods. Modern Mexico City has revealed the Aztec temples and ruins once thought lost. Carlos Fuentes leads the viewer through an exploration of the Indian world that believed the blond exiled god would return. The meeting of Europe and America was bloody, but there is hope in the union of these traditions. 59 mins.
VHS: S21371. $29.95.
Program III: The Age of Gold. Shortly after the conquest Spain and all of Europe felt the rush of enormous treasures from the New World, including not just gold and silver but chocolate, the tomato and the potato. These gifts transformed a world ambivalent about earthly things. Phillip II lived in a monastic-like cell while Cervantes questioned all values in his work. And yet Native Americans transformed the richness of the Baroque into an American idiom. 59 mins.
VHS: S21372. $29.95.
Program IV: The Price of Freedom. One million Mexicans gather in the Zocalo, the central square of Mexico City, to celebrate El Grito, the cry for independence. Beginning here, Fuentes travels south into the rest of Latin America, sifting through the difficulties and failed promises left in the wake of revolutionary independence. 59 mins.
VHS: S21373. $29.95.
Program V: Unfinished Business. This century has brought enormous changes to the Hispanic communities of the world. Today half a million Mexicans brave border patrols to enter the US in search of Gringo gold. In return they bring Latino gold, the riches of centuries of tradition and change. 59 mins.
VHS: S21374. $29.95.
Complete Set. Five tapes.
VHS: S21375. $99.95.

Burning Rivers
Rich rain forests are chopped down, badly polluted rivers burn and pesticides poison farm workers. All this happens in Guatemala. The social and economic conditions that spawn this nightmare scenario impact the environment. Only when these issues are considered together can a solution be found, one which addresses the unequal distribution of wealth that characterizes this country. 28 mins.
VHS: S21578. $85.00.

Call and Response
Volunteers from the U.S. live in Mexico and Guatemala for a few weeks in Maryknoll's Call and Response Program. This video joins a group of Michigan college students in Oaxaca, Mexico, where they meet and serve a variety of people. 29 mins.
VHS: S15863. $19.95.

Carlos Fuentes

In this revealing interview with his wife, the Televisa reporter Sylvia Fuentes, Carlos Fuentes speaks of the Hispanic notion of originality and of the function of time in literature. He recalls his youth in the U.S, the affirmation of his identity in that difficult context and his political formation; discusses his major works and reads from *La Region mas Transparente*. Spanish *without* English subtitles.
Home Video.
VHS: S06966. $59.95.
Public Performance.
VHS: S08829. $100.00.

Carlos Fuentes (Lannan Literary Videos)

Mexico's most celebrated novelist reads from *The Death of Artemio Cruz* and *Christopher Unborn*, as well as unpublished manuscripts, in Los Angeles. It was recorded on October 2, 1989. Lewis MacAdams then interviews this world famous author. From the *Lannan Literary Videos* series. 60 mins.
VHS: S27124. $19.95.

Chicano! History of the Mexican American Civil Rights Movement

Titles on this four-tape set include: *Quest for a Homeland, The Struggle in the Fields, Taking Back the Schools* and *Fighting for Political Power.* Suitable for courses in American History, Chicano Studies, Contemporary Issues, Media Literacy, Social Studies and Geography. Each tape is 60 mins.
VHS: S30416. $69.95.

The Colombian Way of Life

Bogota is the focus of this video. Its history, climate, government, geography and rapidly growing population are all examined. The resulting images counteract stereotypes associated with cocaine, coffee and guerilla violence. 24 mins.
VHS: S23709. $129.95.
Laser: LD74790. $149.95.

Colors of Hope

Narrated by Meryl Streep, *Colors of Hope* tells the story of an Argentine family's incredible ability to maintain hope and closeness in spite of the torture and torment which accompanied their years as political prisoners; the moving, true account of hope and perseverance behind such fictionalized accounts as *The Official Story*. Produced by Amnesty International. 1985, 20 mins.
VHS: S06886. $20.00.

Cosquin, City of Folklore

A visit to the folklore festival which is celebrated annually in Cosquin, Argentina. Narrated in Spanish by Amelia Bence. 14 mins.,
VHS: S06764. $40.00.

Cuba Amor

This beautifully photographed video gives a rare view of Cuba, an island which current U.S. laws prevent most American tourists from visiting. Features glimpses of some of Cuba's renowned beaches, famous tourist sites and street scenes in Havana, Trinidad, Santiago de Cuba, Pinar del Rio and Cien Fuegos, as well as some of Cuba's internationally famous singers and bands. Public performance.
VHS: S32115. $59.95.
Toshi Matsushita, USA, 1995, 38 mins.

The Dark Light of Dawn

Commissioned by the Guatemala Human Rights Commission/U.S.A., this documentary presents a factual overview and moving visual portrait of the recent years of conflict in Guatemala. It traces the manipulation of political power in the country and shows that after the return of civilian rule, military repression has not abated. Human rights violations, especially against the Indian population, are poignantly depicted—and efforts of families to find their "disappeared" relatives are documented.
VHS: S06601. $55.00.
E. Reyes/G. Brown, USA, 1987, 28 mins.

Dateline: San Salvador

For seven years, civil war raged in El Salvador, ravaging the countryside, destroying an already under-developed economy, and placing the country high on the international list of human rights violations. On May 1, 1986, 80,000 Salvadorans, in protest of these conditions, defied the guns of government forces and marched through the streets of their capital, demanding an end to the war. *Dateline: San Salvador* documents this historic march and explores the concerns of the people behind the banners. Spanish with English voice-over.
VHS: S05628. $55.00.
Pamela Cohen, USA, 1987, 28 mins.

David Vinas y Mempo Giardinelli

Subtitled *Senas de exilio*, a liberating discussion about the particular problems of working in exile in this revealing portrait of the writer. Spanish *without* English subtitles. 53 mins.
Home Video.
VHS: S06948. $59.95.
Public Performance.
VHS: S09504. $100.00.

Day of the Dead

The color and spectacle of "The Day of the Dead" rituals and customs are explained by fusing Aztec and European traditions. The celebration is presented in village dances, homes, market places and cemeteries. "A program both entertaining and education and well executed" (*Northeast Newsletter*). 28 mins.
English Narration.
VHS: S19827. $45.00.
Spanish Narration.
VHS: S19826. $45.00.

Death of Che Guevara

In November, 1968, Che Guevara went from Cuba to Bolivia in order to start a new revolutionary movement. But he failed in a dramatic way. This film is an investigation of the capture, and death, of Che Guevara. In Spanish language *without* English subtitles. 92 mins.
VHS: S07996. $59.95.

Did They Buy It?: Nicaragua's 1990 Elections

"A fascinating 45-minute video documentary by Chicagoan Bob Hercules, filmed on location with a crew of four, that concentrates largely on the U.S. media coverage of the Nicaraguan elections. What emerges is not only a sharp piece of alternative news coverage that helps to explain the outcome, but also a revealing and multifaceted (and alternately funny and chilling) look at how the U.S. news about Nicaragua actually gets 'created'" (Jonathan Rosenbaum).
VHS: S15192. $29.95.
Bob Hercules, USA, 1991, 45 mins.

The Disappearance of Garcia Lorca

Haunted by boyhood memories of the great poet Federico Garcia Lorca, a young journalist living in Puerto Rico returns to his Spanish home in search of the truth. With Esai Morales, Edward James Olmos, and Andy Garcia as Federico Garcia Lorca. In English.
VHS: S33018. $104.99.
Marcos Zurinaga, USA, 1996, 114 mins.

Discovering the Music of Latin America

Classical, folk and pre-Columbian instruments all play a large role in the music of Latin America. The many traditions of this diverse region have spawned a rich array of song and dance. 20 mins.
VHS: S23515. $49.95.

The Eagle's Children

Addresses important issues about dance, tracing the origins of the dance "La Danza de la Conquista del Gran Tenochtitlan," and its thousands of adherents in Central Mexico.
VHS: S33894. $24.95.
Bruce Pacho Lane, Mexico, 39 mins.

Eduardo Galeano

Eduardo Galeano, born in Montevideo, Uruguay, is a journalist, historian, caricaturist and political activist best-known for his *Memory of Fire*, a poetic historical trilogy of the Americas from the native creation myths to modern time. The trilogy is a brilliant collage that strives to restore the cultural heritage of Latin America. Mr. Galeano read from *Walking Words, The Book of Embraces*, and spoke with Michael Silverblatt, the host of the radio interview program *Bookworm*. From the *Lannan Literary Videos* series. 60 mins.
VHS: S32431. $19.95.

Egberto Gismonti

Charlie Byrd and Stan Getz pioneered the use of Brazilian rhythms and the bossa nova in American jazz. Brazilian musician Egberto Gismonti lifts the use of these elements to a new plateau, as in this live concert recorded at the 1987 Freiburg Arts Festival. 55 mins.
VHS: S09826. $24.95.

El Charanguero: Jaime Torres, the Charango Player

Argentina's Jaime Torres, the world's foremost charango performer, is presented in a never-before-recorded ritual to Pachamama (Mother Earth) by the indigenous people of the Quebrada, Argentina. Features dances and music performed on traditional instruments and the history of the charango, as well as dramatic concert footage. "An appealing portrait of a man, his music and his culture" (Nancy McCray, *Booklist*).
English Version.
VHS: S30167. $24.99.
Spanish Version.
VHS: S30168. $24.99.
Jeffrey Briggs/Simona Munoz-Briggs, USA, 1995, 58 mins.

El Che: Investigating a Legend

This program examines Che Guevara, the revolutionary who became a symbol of an entire generation. Covers his voyages of discovery through Latin America, his meeting with Castro, his travels around the world as Cuba's ambassador, his days as a victorious leader in guerilla warfare, his various disguises, his disastrous episode in the Congo, and his tragic end in Bolivia at age 39. 90 mins.
VHS: S34720. $19.95.

El Crucero

An in-depth picture of a Nicaraguan coffee plantation shot in September 1984 in four different documentary styles. The first section takes a feminist biographical approach, the second a cinema-verite approach, the third uses Brechtian intertitles while a union organizer speaks on the audio track, and the final segment features two women talking while the image depicts a girl carrying a bucket in slow motion.
VHS: S06310. $69.95.
Julia Lesage, USA, 1987, 59 mins.

El Matador

Narrated by Ricardo Montalban, the life of a young bullfighter, Miguel Espinosa Armillita, as he begins his long years of training to become a premier matador. Insights into the traditions, history and culture of Mexico. 59 mins.
English Narration.
VHS: S06835. $49.95.
Spanish Narration.
VHS: S06834. $49.95.

El Salvador: The Seeds of Liberty

The conflict in this embattled land is explored through interviews with military, government and church leaders in El Salvador and the U.S. The film examines the martyrdom of four North American missionaries and the significance of this pivotal event. It contains scenes of the funeral of assassinated Archbishop Romero and interviews with the poor, who relate their tragedies and hopes for a dignified life and a free society. Produced by Maryknoll Media. 28 mins.
VHS: S04925. $24.95.

Empire in the Sun

This colorful documentary explores some of the strange customs, lifestyles, and oddities of the people of Peru. Italian production with English narration. Italy, 1956, 86 mins.
VHS: S10556. $24.95.
Laser: CAV, widescreen. **LD70565. $69.98.**
Laser: CLV, widescreen. **LD70566. $39.98.**

Environment Under Fire: Ecology and Politics in Central America

Celebrated for its lush tropical forests, today Central America's natural environment is seriously endangered. More than two-thirds of rain forests have been destroyed and deadly pesticides are being exported from U.S. to Central America. This film explores the issues behind the crisis along with potential solutions. Winner of two major festival awards; produced by the Environmental Project on Central America and the Moving Images Video Project. 28 mins.
VHS: S10888. $39.95.

Epic History of the Mexican Revolution

This is the only documentary of the heroic revolution authorized by the Mexican National Defense Department. Newsreel footage helps create an authentic portrait of the battlefield. In Spanish, no subtitles. 80 mins.
VHS: S16379. $39.95.

Ernesto Cardenal

Ernesto Cardenal is an ordained Catholic priest and revolutionary poet who champions the rights of ordinary Nicaraguans. On January 28, 1991, he read from *Cantico Cosmico* in Los Angeles. The English translations were read by Edward Asner and Ruben Martinez (who also interviewed the author). From the *Lannan Literary Videos* series. 60 mins.
VHS: S27130. $19.95.

Ernesto Che Guevara: The Bolivian Diary

An intriguing look inside Cuba's incredible revolutionary leader Che Guevara, who, at age 39, was executed in 1967 by the Bolivian army, aided by the CIA. Guevara's diary, a detailed, personal account of his futile 11-month attempt to foment revolution in Bolivia, is the basis of this moving portrait. Che's relationship with the mysterious Tania, his betrayal by local peasants, his constant battle with asthma, and his distress at the death of comrades are recounted. Interviews with Bolivians who met Che during these final days testify to a man who embraced sacrifice for his ideals. "An understated, stunningly effective portrait" (Michael Wilmington, *Chicago Tribune*). English and Spanish with English subtitles.
VHS: S33355. $29.98.
Richard Dindo, Switzerland, 1997, 94 mins.

Etched in Stone: The Golden Age of Cuban Tobacco Art

The famous "Havana" is treasured by cigar connoisseurs all over the world. In the mid-19th century, the labels, wrappers and bands used to market Cuban tobacco to an international clientele evolved into high art and are now popular collectibles. It was an art of extraordinary detail and beauty, which resulted in what is known as "The Golden Age" of lithography. This entertaining documentary looks at the skill and imagination that created these exquisite gold-embossed and gilded cigar box labels.

VHS: S31854. $19.95.

Evita: Her Real Story

Film clips, newly produced footage, photographs and conversations with historians, experts and family members combine to present the truth about Evita Peron, the woman who captivated Argentina. Features an interview with Madonna. 75 mins.

VHS: S31507. $9.99.

Evita: The Woman Behind the Myth

In this *A & E Biography*, rare photographs and films and accounts from close aides and bitter enemies offer insight into the life of Eva Duarte de Peron, a woman whose political power and prestige nearly eclipsed that of her husband, Argentine president Juan Peron. 50 mins.

VHS: S31415. $19.95.

Experience Brazil: The Northeast

Play soccer on the beach, scale palm trees, dance to Brazilian rhythms and float down the Amazon during a rainstorm. 47 mins.

VHS: S31468. $19.99.

Experience Ecuador and the Galapagos Islands

Soar into the Amazon on an old army plane, ride on the roof of a train, bathe in hot water from a volcano, romp with sea lions, explore the Galapagos and climb 18,000 icy feet. 47 mins.

VHS: S31469. $19.99.

Experience Ruta Maya

Visit the 3,000-year-old culture of Ruta Maya as you drive along unpaved roads to Mayan ruins, scuba dive along a 150-mile barrier reef, swim among dolphins and enter a Mayan tomb. 47 mins.

VHS: S31474. $19.99.

Festivals and Holidays in Latin America

Celebrations, both religious and secular, reflect the different cultures of the many groups inhabiting Latin America. Bilingual English-Spanish narration.

VHS: S07428. $59.95.

Fiesta

Fiestas are the central expression of honor and tradition in most Mexican small towns. They're designed to celebrate the patron saints through an ethnographic tradition of dance, markets, music and the *charredas* (like rodeos). This film shares how people behave in their time of joy and spontaneity. 22 mins.

VHS: S20238. $29.95.

Flavors of South America

This video takes you to an authentic Peruvian restaurant to observe the customs and practices of local chefs. The program takes a journey into the village markets and countryside to learn about the culture and people of this beautiful country. In Spanish. 56 mins.

VHS: S19823. $29.95.

The Forgotten Village

John Steinbeck wrote the story and script for this moving film about the ancient life of Mexico, the story of the little pueblo of Santiago on the skirts of a hill in the mountains. An extremely moving portrait of life in a Mexican village. Narrated by Burgess Meredith.

VHS: S08785. $39.95.

Herbert Kline, USA, 1941

Gabriel Garcia Marquez

Gabriel Garcia Marquez rarely gives interviews and has never before spoken publicly about his involvement in Latin American cinema, so this exclusive and fascinating interview with him is a considerable coup. This program uses material shot in Colombia and Cuba, archive footage of events in the author's life and clips from films he has worked on. Other interviewers in this program include film directors Ruy Guerra and Fernando Birri, who have both directed films based on Marquez's stories. 59 min.

VHS: S18388. $19.95.

Getting to Heaven

This short drama, based on interviews with actual immigrants, portrays Hispanic immigrant workers at a New York City restaurant, depicting their workaday reality and dreams for a better life in the U.S.

VHS: S33378. $39.95.

Alfredo Bejar, USA, 1996, 19 mins.

The Greening of Cuba

Profiles Cuban farmers and scientists working to reinvent a sustainable agriculture, based on ecological principals and local knowledge rather than imported agricultural inputs. High school to adult. Spanish with English subtitles. 1995, 38 mins.

VHS: S31907. $69.95.

Grenada Revisited

This video looks back at what precipitated the deployment of over 5,000 U.S. troops to the small Caribbean island and examines the consequences today. Was the 1983 U.S. invasion of Grenada necessary? USA, 1991, 28 mins.

VHS: S15215. $25.00.

Guatemala, Land of Color

A look at the cultural and folk life aspects of one of the most colorful countries in Central America. We begin our tour in the capital of Guatemala City and from there fly inland to the city of Flores, which lies in the jungle and is our entrance to the ancient Mayan city of Tikal. Traversing the labyrinth of paths, the film explores the temples of this highly developed civilization and travels on to the colonial capital of Antigua, changed little since the time of the Spaniards. The film captures the people as they live, work and celebrate their religious holidays. Directed by Angel Hurtado, 25 mins.

English Narration. Renee Channey.
VHS: S06790. $60.00.
Spanish Narration. Ivan Silva.
VHS: S06791. $60.00.

Guatemala: Jeramias and El Salvador: Flor

Two portraits of contemporary youth in two nations in conflict: In *Guatemala*, an Indian teenager is forced to flee from violence in his village. Now in the city, he is torn by bitter memories and adapting to new values. In *El Salvador*, soldiers obliterate Flor's village and kill her uncle and brother. Flor and the rest of her family are re-located to a temporary shelter in the city. As part of a youth group, she now works for a more peaceful society. Produced by Maryknoll Media.

VHS: S06272. $24.95.

Guatemala: When the People Lead

Follows the long and arduous journey home for tens of thousands of Guatemalans who had been living in Mexican refugee camps. Upon their return home, military action threatens their region. 29 mins.

VHS: S23401. $85.00.

Guelaguetza

Oaxaca is the site of one of Mexico's most fascinating cultural festivals. Held in early July of each year, it started out as a Zapotec celebration in the early 16th century, and has evolved into a truly multicultural event, with Zapotec and Spanish cultural traditions proudly intertwined and presented at one of the most breathtaking sites imaginable. 28 mins.

VHS: S32244. $29.95.

The Havana: Cigar of Connoisseurs

The obsession that linked Winston Churchill, John F. Kennedy, Fidel Castro and Groucho Marx begins with Cuban-grown tobacco. These expensive cigars require three to four years of production, all of which goes up in smoke in 45 minutes or less. Shot on location in Cuba, this documentary details the history and tradition of the world's finest cigar. 59 mins.

VHS: S26810. $24.95.

The Healer

An American missionary who works among the Aymara Indians of Peru finds God in an unexpected way. A film of the relationship between the priest and an Indian holy man. Ancient rites and customs of the Aymara are contrasted with traditional rites of Latin American Catholics. Produced by Maryknoll Media. 24 mins.

VHS: S04928. $24.95.

Hispanic Folk Art and the Environment: A New Mexican Perspective

Produced in cooperation with the Museum of International Folk Art, this interdisciplinary program for Grades K-12 includes a video, a curriculum guide, and a set of 20 color prints to enable students to understand and appreciate past and present Hispanic folk traditions, and to recognize the influences of the natural environment on folk life and folk arts. 29 mins.

VHS: S30019. $85.00.

Hispanic Magazine's Guide to Hispanic Excellence

This three-part series offers role models for Latino students. Each 35-minute tape focuses on a specific area of achievement, including *The Leaders*, *Sports* and *Arts and Entertainment*. This mosaic of excellence comprises Latinos from diverse backgrounds representing different areas of the U.S.

VHS: S21725. $74.85.

Hispanics of Achievement Video Collection

This set compiles compelling biographies of men and women who have contributed to their countries and culture. Figures from South and Central America, Mexico and Spain are included. Period music, historic materials and authoritative opinion make this series an invaluable resource. Each volume is 30 mins.

Cesar Chavez. (1927-1993) Mexican-American labor leader.
VHS: S24449. $39.95.
Ferdinand and Isabella. (1485-1516)/(1451-1504) Spanish monarchs.
VHS: S24452. $39.95.
George Santayana. (1863-1952) Spanish philosopher and poet.
VHS: S24455. $39.95.
Hernan Cortes. (1485-1547) Spanish explorer.
VHS: S24451. $39.95.
Joan Baez. (1941 - Present) Mexican-American folksinger.
VHS: S24447. $39.95.
Juan and Evita Peron. (1895-1974)/(1919-1952) President and First Lady of Argentina.
VHS: S24454. $39.95.
Pablo Neruda. (1904-1973) Chilean poet and diplomat.
VHS: S24453. $39.95.
Pancho Villa. (1878-1923) Mexican revolutionary.
VHS: S24456. $39.95.
Roberto Clemente. (1934-1972) Puerto Rican baseball great.
VHS: S24450. $39.95.
Simon Bolivar. (1783-1830) Latin-American revolutionary.
VHS: S24448. $39.95.
Hispanics of Achievement Video Collection. 10-volume set.
VHS: S24457. $399.50.

Honduras, A World into Itself

A look at the folk life and culture of Honduras, the cradle of the ancient Mayan Empire. A panorama of this lovely Central American country, from the ancient ruins of Copan to the bustling cities of today. The film captures the Honduran people in their daily lives, working, playing and surrounded by the natural beauty of their country. The music of the Caramba, the most ancient of American Indian instruments, is heard in the background. Directed by Angel Hurtado, 20 mins.

English Narration. Herbert Morales.
VHS: S06784. $60.00.
Spanish Narration. Marioano Sanchez.
VHS: S06785. $60.00.

Honduras: Carlos and Nicaragua: Balty

Two portraits of contemporary youth coping in nations in conflict. Poverty has not kept Carlos from studying to be a teacher. Through a theatre group, he reaches out to neighbors displaced by war and economic development. Balty is a young medical student who works in a war zone near the Honduran border in Nicaragua. She finds excitement relating her faith to political commitment in a revolutionary society. Produced by Maryknoll Media.

VHS: S06273. $24.95.

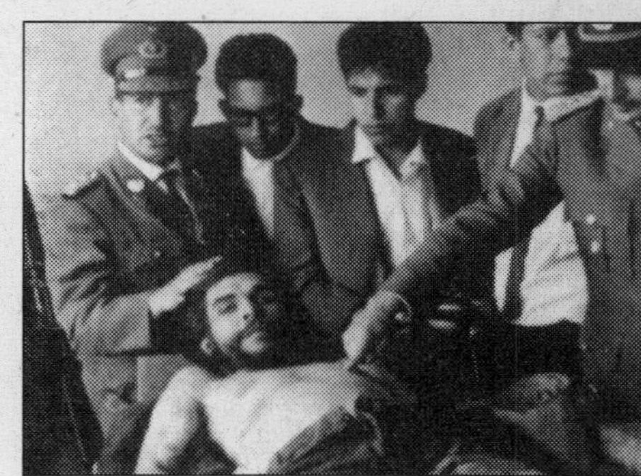

I Like It Like That

A remarkable feature set in the Puerto Rican milieu of the Bronx. Rita Moreno, Lauren Velez and Jon Seda star in a hard-edged comedy about a family struggling to keep it all together. The film is a deft mixture of simple drama with humor, in a kind of slum-glamor romanticism that gives humanity to its realistically-drawn characters. Music from the Bario Boyz.

VHS: S24262. $19.95.
Laser: LD74844. $34.95.
Darnell Martin, USA, 1994, 106 mins.

Imagenes Latino Americanas

This video provides intermediate and advanced instruction on comprehension and practical insights into varied lifestyles of modern Latin American societies. Shot on location, the documentary is a starting point for discussions on Latin America. 25 mins.

VHS: S19842. $39.95.

Images of Mexican Los Angeles

Surveys the history of the Mexican community—its origins, culture, achievements and difficulties—in the Los Angeles basin. Public performance rights included.

VHS: S33383. $59.95.
Antonio Rios-Bustamante, USA, 1992, 28 mins.

Improper Conduct
Controversial, powerful documentary, a series of interviews with fascinating Cuban intellectuals and homosexuals who have been persecuted under the Castro regime. An indictment of Castro, implicating also those who would turn a blind eye toward repression from the left. Spanish with English subtitles.
VHS: S00614. $19.95.
Nestor Almendros, USA, 1984, 112 mins.

In the Shadow of War/O My People!
In the Shadow of War shows how projects supported by Protestant churches are transforming the life of a community in Nicaragua. Narrated by Glenda Jackson. Directed by J. Reiter and W. Tirando. *O My People!* is a slide show on video telling the story of the suffering in El Salvador using voices of witnesses as well as drawings by children. Directed by J. Friedrich.
VHS: S03953. $95.00.
Reiter/Tirando/Friedrich, USA, 1986, 47 mins.

Incas Remembered
An hour long exploration of the Inca civilization. During their pre-Columbian reign, the Incas developed modern irrigation canals, performed brain surgery and were master builders. Edwin Newman provides the introduction.
VHS: S02155. $24.95.
Peter Jarvis, USA, 1986, 60 mins.

Isabel Allende
The best-selling Chilean author (*La Casa de los Espiritus/House of the Spirits*) speaks with the Colombian critic Magdalena Garcia Pinto about the extravagant environment that surrounded her youth, and how she created the great novel, "like a tapestry." She speaks of the relationship of Latin American women to feminism, disputing many facile notions on the subject, and affirms the role of a writer as one capable of understanding both sexes. Spanish *without* English subtitles.
Home Video.
VHS: S06963. $59.95.
Public Performance.
VHS: S08840. $100.00.

The Island of Puerto Rico
The diverse regions and peoples of Puerto Rico are profiled in this geographic look at the island. 28 mins.
VHS: S20239. $29.95.

Joan Baez (1941-Present)—Mexican-American Folksinger
From *The Hispanics of Achievement Video Collection*. Includes music, photographs and commentary on the life of the pioneering folk singer and activist. This biography was designed for classroom use. Ages 10+. 30 minutes. Spanish with NO subtitles.
VHS: S24943. $39.95.

Jorge Luis Borges
The great Argentinian writer has an animated dialogue with his young compatriot, the novelist Reina Roffe. With great lucidity, Borges speaks of his work and the aesthetic and philosophical foundations that support it. We see Borges in the cafes and streets of his Buenos Aires and hear him tell unpublished stories of gaucho exploits in the pampa, evoke the avant-garde movements of the first part of the century, and read five of his poems. Spanish *without* English subtitles.
Home Video.
VHS: S06947. $59.95.
Public Performance.
VHS: S08830. $100.00.

Jorge Luis Borges: Borges and I
Weaves together dramatized sequences from Borges' work with a rare interview with Borges at home, an unpretentious apartment overlooking noisy Buenos Aires. The program relates Borges' profoundly original stories to his personal experience and attempts to reconcile the public and private images of this major 20th century writer. 76 mins.
VHS: S04153. $19.95.

Journey of Carlos Fuentes: Crossing Borders
A biography of Carlos Fuentes, filmed in Mexico, Nicaragua and the United States, the camera follows Fuentes on his travels to Aztec ruins, movie sets and war zones. Along the way this writer/diplomat holds forth on art, sex and politics. The film also features readings by Fuentes. 60 min.
VHS: S18387. $19.95.
Joan Saffa, USA, 60 mins.

Juan Carlos Onetti
The Uruguayan writer, creator of *El Astillero* (The Shipyard), speaks with Jorge Ruffinelli about the influence of Faulkner on Latin American letters and about his own obsessive atmospheric writing, and tells several poignant anecdotes about himself in difficult situations. Spanish *without* English subtitles.
Home Video.
VHS: S06952. $59.95.
Public Performance.
VHS: S08836. $100.00.

Juan Goytisolo
The well-known Spanish author has an open dialogue with the Chilean critic and editor Randolph Pope, in which he recalls a childhood dynamited by the Civil War and a youth in open rebellion against the official mythology of Franco's Spain. He discusses the exacerbated state of exile which led him to create the ultimate hyperbole of the traitor "en grande" as paradoxical redeemer of the sclerotic state of the nation. He reads from *Juan Sin Tierra, Makbara, Senas de Intentidad* and *Paisajes Despues de La Batalla*. Spanish *without* English subtitles.
Home Video.
VHS: S06949. $59.95.
Public Performance.
VHS: S08833. $100.00.

Juan Rulfo
The author of the most important Mexican novel written—*Pedro Parama*—evokes his childhood, with the help of Sylvia Fuentes, in the context of revolutionary Mexico. He describes how a priest's collection of black-listed books introduced him to the world's best writers, as bullets ricocheted through his little town. The presence of death and violence in his fiction is directly related to those difficult years as an orphan. Spanish *without* English subtitles.
Home Video.
VHS: S06965. $59.95.
Public Performance.
VHS: S08835. $100.00.

Julio Cortazar
The author of *Rayuela* (Hopscotch) speaks openly and eloquently with his most rigorous critic, Saul Sosnowski, about the presence of the reader in his fiction and his own trajectory from a kind of literary individualism to a more collective style. He discusses the importance of the Cuban revolution and the tasks he has set for himself as an intellectual in the context of Latin America. He confesses in this last interview before his untimely death in 1986 that he still searches for the "kibbutz of desire, or the center, from which one can imagine, feel and actually live reality in a harmonious manner." Spanish *without* English subtitles.
Home Video.
VHS: S06946. $59.95.
Public Performance.
VHS: S08832. $100.00.

Kids Explore Mexico
The culture, customs and history of Mexico are illustrated in this video aimed at high school students. It makes culture and geography a fun and exciting experience. Lyrics, thought-provoking questions and maps ease class preparation and stimulate class discussion. In English, 34 mins.
VHS: S24790. $49.95.

La Antigua-Guatemala: An American Monument
A documentary on Antigua, the colonial capital of Guatemala. One of the oldest cities in the Americas, it lies in a valley surrounded by volcanoes. Despite volcanic eruptions and earthquakes, it is still much like it would have been found in the days of the early Spaniards. Many of the lovely colonial buildings are preserved, allowing the viewer to go back in history and appreciate the Roman-Arabic architecture that the Spanish have left in Central America. Directed by Angel Hurtado, 25 mins.
English Narration. Renee Channey.
VHS: S06788. $60.00.
Spanish Narration. Andres Morales.
VHS: S06789. $60.00.

La Conquista
The events leading to Spain's emergence as a superpower in the late 15th century—the expulsion of the Moors, the invention of the printing press, and the discovery of the New World. In English and then Spanish. 25 mins. each.
VHS: S05269. $59.95.

Land of the Conquistadors
Extremadura was a province of Western Spain that was home to such Conquistadores as Cortez, Pizarro, Balboa and Hernando de Soto. This program looks at the historical and social importance of Extremadura to the development of modern Spain. 28 mins.
VHS: S20274. $29.95.

Las Nicas and Home Life
Las Nicas is a 45-minute document of interviews with Nicaraguan women, done in 1981 and 1982, in which the women speak about topics of work, sexual politics, religion, family life and social participation. *Home Life* documents a Nicaraguan family in Esteli. Filmmaker is editor of *Jump Cut*. English and Spanish with English subtitles.
VHS: S00722. $69.95.
Julia Lesage, USA, 1985, 72 mins.

Latin American Historical Personalities
Any map of South America will read like a directory of families and towns in Spain. The Spanish conquerors created nations and left their language and culture everywhere in South America. Who were these explorers and the founders of nations? Who led these nations, built capitals and developed the countries we see today? This program introduces the major Hispanic figures of Latin American history. 28 mins.
VHS: S31894. $29.95.

Latin American Trails: Guatemala
Beautifully shot in various regions of Guatemala, this documentary illustrates the history and music traditions, architecture, art and theater of this exotic country where Mayan and other native cultures have lived for many centuries. Narrated by Mexican actress Claudette Maille (*Like Water for Chocolate*).
VHS: S32604. $24.95.
Ariel Zapata, USA/Guatemala, 1997, 40 mins.

The Legend of El Dorado
The myth and reality of gold in the new world as viewed through the pre-Columbian treasures of Bogota's Gold Museum. Pieces from tribes of the Sunu archaeological zone, the Quimbays and the Musicas are featured. Directed by Angel Hurtado, 25 mins.
English Narration.
VHS: S06805. $70.00.
Spanish Narration.
VHS: S06806. $70.00.

Life in Small Hispanic Towns
Between the large metropolitan cities and the rural regions are countless small towns that reflect the history and culture of Latin America. Bilingual English-Spanish narration.
VHS: S07429. $59.95.

Luis J. Rodriguez
Raised in Watts and East Los Angeles, Luis J. Rodriguez speaks from a place which is too often ignored. In this video he reads from *The Concrete River, Poems Across the Pavement* and *Always Running, La Vida Loca: Gang Days in L.A.* The reading took place on December 8, 1992, in Los Angeles. Michael Silverblatt spoke with this innovative author. From the *Lannan Literary Videos* series. 60 mins.
VHS: S27138. $19.95.

Luis Rafael Sanchez
The author of *La Guaracha del Macho Camacho* and, most recently, *La Importancia de Llamarse Daniel Santos* responds to questions by the great translator Gregory Rabassa. He analyzes the essence of his own novels and speaks of the problems of Caribbean identity in the proximity of the United States. He recites popular poetry and reads from *La Guaracha*. Spanish *without* English subtitles.
Home Video.
VHS: S06964. $59.95.
Public Performance.
VHS: S08843. $100.00.

Luisa Valenzuela
Valenzuela is considered by Carlos Fuentes to be the "crown princess" of Latin American letters. She is a "writer's writer," yet her tales of love in repressive societies—especially her native Argentina—touch upon the basic chords of human emotion. She responds to questions by Magdalena Garcia Pinto and describes the need to "name fears" in order to control and exorcise them. Spanish *without* English subtitles.
Home Video.
VHS: S06871. $59.95.
Public Performance.
VHS: S08842. $100.00.

MacMichael on Nicaragua
Dr. David MacMichael has worked for U.S. government agencies as a specialist in counterintelligence in both Vietnam and El Salvador. This is a dramatic and detailed account of MacMichael's report on Nicaragua, where he travelled extensively and studied the election process for three months.
VHS: S03809. $45.00.
Ian Thiermann, USA, 1984, 30 mins.

The Mambo Kings
Arne Glimcher's adaptation of Oscar Hijueles's Pulitzer prize winning-novel *The Mambo Kings Play Songs of Love* about dreamy innocence and protection of the American Dream in post-war America. The film centers on two young immigrant brothers (Armand Assante and Almodovar regular Antonio Banderas) impassioned reach for fame and recognition as pioneers of the sweet, daring, sexy Mambo music. The film also details various sexual and romantic entanglements. With Cathy Moriarty and Maruschka Detmers.
VHS: S17028. $19.98.
Laser: Widescreen. **LD71553. $29.98.**
Arne Glimcher, USA, 1992, 104 mins.

Manuel Puig
In this delightful conversation with Reina Roffe, Puig describes his early need to escape the provincial world of his upbringing in the hinterlands of Argentina, and his entire trajectory as a novelist. He discusses and reads from *La Traicion de Rita Hayworth, The Buenos Aires Affair, Pubis Angelical* and *Sangre de Amor Correspondido*. Spanish *without* English subtitles.
Home Video.
VHS: S06950. $59.95.
Public Performance.
VHS: S08837. $100.00.

Mario Vargas Llosa
Subtitled *Maestro de las voces*, a conversation with the great novelist, author of *City of the Dogs*. Spanish *without* English subtitles. 53 mins.
Home Video.
VHS: S06951. $59.95.
Public Performance.
VHS: S09505. $100.00.

Market Day in a Changing Economy (Latin American Lifestyles)
The traditional market and the role of women in Latin America are explored as the economy of the region develops and expands. Bilingual English-Spanish narration.
VHS: S07427. $59.95.

The Maya Collection
This ten-volume collection examines 35 sites of Mayan architecture, with specially prepared texts and narrative, cinematography, and music by maestro Juan Lino, to express the Maya consciousness of the world. Volumes include: *Uxmal, Palenque, Chichen Itza, Yaxchilan, Tonina, Tulum, Tikal, Copan, Edzna* and *Frederick Catherwood*, English illustrator in Mesoamerica from 1841-1843. 10 hours.
VHS: S31891. $199.00.

The Mayan Mystery
This short film recreates the vibrant life once found at the center of great Mayan cities. Striking visuals and an engaging soundtrack sharpen this experience. 18 mins.
VHS: S23717. $49.95.

Memorias de un Mexicano
This work by Mexican film pioneer Salvador Toscano presents the history of the Mexican Revolution, from the splendor of Porfiriato to the candidacy of Francisco I. It covers Madero, the civil war, Zapata in the South and Villa in the north, and the formation of revolutionary governments with Obregon and Calles. Presented by Carmen Toscano. Video and book set. In Spanish.
VHS: S35016. $89.95.

Men of Horses
This documentary about the "charros" (Mexican Horsemen) highlights the traditional art of "La Charreria," a colorful rodeo involving various crafts and skills. In Spanish, with no subtitles. 10 mins.
VHS: S16367. $29.95.

A Mexican Colonial Tour
Travel to the most fascinating cities in Mexico. We visit Mexico City, go sightseeing in the Zocalo, shop in the Zona Rosa and visit the museums in Chapultepec. In Cuernavaca, we see the cathedral and the Cuahnahuac Museum which houses Diego Rivera's famous murals. We complete our trip in Taxco, a town famous for its silver. 35 mins.
English Narration.
VHS: S05258. $39.95.
Spanish Narration.
VHS: S05257. $39.95.

Mexican Festivals
Every Mexican village or city has a fiesta, a three- or four-day period when its citizenry express their joy, hopes and optimism about their town and community. English narration. 30 mins.
VHS: S19841. $39.95.

Mexican Market
Just outside Mexico City lies a lively market. Families are seen arriving to prepare for a busy day of selling and bartering. 10 mins.
VHS: S23719. $49.95.

Mexican People and Culture
Designed to present material on the Hispanic peoples of America—their origins and their cultural heritage. Presents an overview of the geography and historical development of modern Mexico and Mexican-Americans and their role in contemporary American life. Bilingual—in both Spanish and English.
VHS: S06740. $59.95.

Mexican Pre-Hispanic Cultures
This program emphasizes pre-Hispanic civilization. The video examines Teotihuacan, the Toltecs, the Aztecs and the Mayas, who pioneered studies in math, astronomy and art. The program also provides an overview of the art, ceramics, sculptures and murals that are collected in Mexican museums. 26 mins.
English Version.
VHS: S20236. $29.95.
Spanish Version.
VHS: S20237. $29.95.

A Mexican Pyramid Tour
Relive history as you tour the fascinating archeological sites of Mexico's past civilizations. You will marvel at the beauty of the Pyramid of the Sun and the pyramids at Mitla. Explore Monte Alban, Chichen Itza and Tulum. As a final stop, we see the famous Museum of Anthropology. 35 mins.
English Version.
VHS: S05256. $39.95.
Spanish Version.
VHS: S05255. $39.95.

Mexican River Cruise
This colorful travel essay follows the voyage of the *Pacific Princess* as she lands at exotic Mexican ports of call including Acapulco, Zihautanejo-Ixtapa, Puerto Vallarta, Mazatlan and Cabo San Lucas. Claiming fame as the "Love Boat," the *Princess* lives up to her reputation as stops are made at the world's great hotels, restaurants and resorts on route to Los Angeles.
VHS: S15849. $19.95.

The Mexican Way of Life
Mexico has tremendous variety reflected in its landscape and in its people. There are lavish resorts and simple villages. Snow-covered mountains give way to desolate deserts. Even its history reflects the conflicting influences of Native American civilizations and Spanish conquistadors. 23 mins.
VHS: S23710. $129.95.
Laser: LD74791. $149.95.

Mexican Youth Today
This program illustrates the concerns and attitudes of young Mexicans about the fate of their country, the ecology, their futures, goals and ambitions. The program combines interviews with students, commentary from teachers, images of the school, and the students' appreciation for Mexican culture, with a special emphasis on the last day of school. Spanish with English subtitles. 25 mins.
VHS: S20232. $29.95.

Mexico
A fascinating overview of Mexican culture. We explore the most important aspects of its civilization: Indian and Hispanic. Highlights include: bullfights, charros, the Ballet Folklorico, historic sites and pre-Columbian ruins. Delight in the regional dress and costumes of the people. 55 mins.
English Narration.
VHS: S05277. $49.95.
Spanish Narration.
VHS: S05276. $49.95.

Mexico Before Cortez
Many diverse groups built the cities that comprise contemporary Mexico. Artifacts, manuscripts, sculpture and architecture are combined in this film to trace these pre-Colombian peoples. 14 mins.
VHS: S23718. $49.95.

Mexico City— Metropolis in the Mountains
This program studies the consequences of the shifting population rates in Mexico City, where a projected 25 million people will live by the year 2000. It examines the cultural diversity of urban life, emphasizing the city's architectural splendor and grace. 28 mins.
VHS: S20278. $29.95.

Mexico Is...The Sights and Sounds of Modern Mexico
This video reproduces the spirit and energy of the Mexican people, capturing their lives and social behavior in markets, small towns, fiestas, beautiful countryside and ancient history. With limited narration, the film provides an atmospheric sense of contemporary Mexico. 26 mins.
VHS: S20230. $59.95.

Mexico on Video
This video examines the richness of Mexico and looks at pre-Hispanic civilization, the exuberance of mariachis and charros, the floating gardens at Xochimilco, and bullfights. The program highlights Mexico's cultural traditions, the Folkloric Ballet, and murals from leading artist Diego Rivera. 37 mins.
English Version.
VHS: S20234. $29.95.
Spanish Version.
VHS: S20235. $29.95.

Mexico, Journey to the Sun
Discover Mexico, from its ancient ruins and colorful towns to its intriguing nightlife and sunny beaches. 30 mins.
VHS: S14014. $24.95.

Mi Vida Loca: My Crazy Life
Allison Anders' vibrant feature is set in Echo Park, Los Angeles, where best friends Sad Girl and Mousie are now enemies as they have both become pregnant by the same man, Ernesto, a local drug dealer. A gritty slice of life.
VHS: S23484. $19.95.
Laser: LD75229. $34.98.
Allison Anders, USA, 1994, 94 mins.

Miguel Pinero at Magic Gallery
The late, great Nuyorican poet intones his blistering verse at an East Village art show. 1985, 20 mins.
VHS: S10196. $29.95.

Milagro Beanfield War
Robert Redford's personal fable, set in New Mexico, concerns the "war" between a greedy land-developer and a small-time bean farmer. Steeped in the lore of the Chicano culture, the film unabashedly draws on myth and poetic folklore to evoke the regional culture.
VHS: S07293. $14.98.
Laser: LD70056. $34.95.
Robert Redford, USA, 1988, 112 mins.

Modern Puerto Rico
This program explores the dynamic growth and rich beauty of Puerto Rico. The program is first presented in English and then in Spanish. 40 mins.
VHS: S07430. $59.95.

Mysteries of Peru
This two-part program examines two recurring mysteries of Peru. 120 mins.
Tape 1. Who drew the vast figures seen in the Peruvian desert at Nazca, and why?
VHS: S19548. $19.95.
Tape 2. What happened to the ancient civilization that created Peru's vast and undeveloped coastal canals?
VHS: S19549. $19.95.

Neighbors to Nicaragua
Neighbors to Nicaragua tells the story of Project Minnesota/Leon, a sister-state program between Minnesota and the Department of Leon in Nicaragua. Originally set up by church congregations in the Minneapolis area, PML involves people from all walks of life in the day to day life of their counterparts in the sister state. Directed by Gregory Rutchik and Robert Vaaler. 30 minutes.
VHS: S04308. $29.95.

Nicaragua: For the First Time
Examines the Nicaraguan election process in detail by interviewing international observers, electoral experts, all party candidates, and many segments of the population.
VHS: S03730. $95.00.
Cineaccion, USA, 1985, 58 mins.

Nomads of the Rainforest
Visit a Waironi Indian tribe in Eastern Ecuador in this NOVA video. 60 mins.
VHS: S28647. $19.95.

Octavio Paz
A conversation with the critic, novelist and philosopher. Spanish *without* English subtitles. 53 mins.
Home Video.
VHS: S08467. $59.95.
Public Performance.
VHS: S09503. $100.00.

Octavio Paz (Lannan Literary Videos)
Octavio Paz won the Nobel Prize in 1990. He read on October 18, 1988, from *The Collected Poems of Octavio Paz 1957-1987* at Georgetown University in Washington, D.C., with his translator Eliot Weinberger reading the English versions of his poems. Lewis MacAdams interviews this revered Mexican writer in English while Professor Enrico Santi interviews Paz in Spanish. From the *Lannan Literary Videos* series. 60 mins.
VHS: S27114. $19.95.

Old Gringo
From the director of *The Official Story* comes a tale of romance and revolution set in Mexico during the time of Pancho Villa, based on Carlos Fuentes' monumental novel. Jane Fonda stars as an American spinster who takes on a job as a private tutor with a wealthy Mexican family. Timing is everything in a revolution. She meets a handsome rebel general and a bitter but charming old American and guides their destinies. With Gregory Peck as the title character and Jimmy Smits as General Arroyo.
VHS: S12210. $14.95.
Luis Puenzo, USA, 1989, 119 mins.

The One and Only Lola Beltran
Often called "Lola la Grande" (Lola the Great), this singer is considered by many fans to be the First Lady of Mexican Music. This two-volume video set captures the excitement of her music. Both music videos were filmed in Paris and are in Spanish.
VHS: S29397. $39.90.

The Panama Invasion Revisited
A documentary reviewing the events leading up to the notorious invasion, how the attack was carried out, the resulting casualties, and the impact on life in Panama today. USA, 1991, 28 mins.
VHS: S15216. $25.00.

The Party Line
Rich Maldonado, a 20-something Latino, lives in a world of fantasy. When he calls a phone sex service one evening, only to discover his former high school sweetheart on the other end of the line, this romantic comedy soon transforms into a parable about ethnic identity and self-sacrifice. Public performance rights included.
VHS: S33379. $59.95.
Mario Barrera, USA, 1996, 26 mins.

Paz Si Guerra No
Through narration and Canadian participants, the video is a journey with the International March for Peace across Central America. The march, comprised of 300 individuals from 30 different countries, was organized in support of the Contadora Peace process. Despite being stoned in Costa Rica and rebuffed at the Honduran border, they reached Mexico City, a support of marchers 50,000 strong.
VHS: S03726. $55.00.
Marier/Lucille/Sauriol, Canada, 1986, 59 mins.

Peace Begins Here
Many Americans are concerned about U.S. policy in Central America, but only a small percentage are actively doing something to change it. This provocative video examines the thoughts and motivations of a range of Americans who are taking action. Their personal stories are a powerful inspiration; featured are former Air Force Captain Brian Wilson, who was run over by a train during a protest at Concord Naval Weapons Station, a Presbyterian minister involved in escorting Salvadorans back to their villages, and others. 28 mins.
VHS: S10886. $39.95.

People of the Caribbean
A unique, bi-lingual tape (in Spanish and English) designed to develop concepts regarding the heritage of our minority groups. Highlights the countries that have sent many Black and Spanish-speaking people to the U.S., including Puerto Rico, Dominican Republic, Jamaica, Trinidad and Tobago, Barbados and Cuba. Sound in both English and Spanish.
VHS: S06739. $59.95.

Peru: Inca Heritage
Ruins of the proud Inca people form the backdrop for this video. Peru's contemporary descendants of this ancient civilization are then revealed against these imposing monuments. 17 mins.
VHS: S23714. $49.95.

Photo Album
An original, quirky remembrance of the filmmaker's experiences as a young immigrant from Cuba settling in Boston. This sometimes surreal autobiography stars his real family, and demonstrates Oliver's ability to distinguish between satire and parody. English and Spanish with English subtitles.
VHS: S02906. $29.95.
Enrique Oliver, USA, 1985, 14 mins.

Pictures from a Revolution
A revealing personal document about photojournalist Susan Meiselas, who returned to Nicaragua in 1989, ten years after her groundbreaking photographs on the revolution, to question her subjects and assess the political and social transformation. The film studies the aftermath of events and history, a collision of memory, photography and truth. "Susan Meiselas recalls acts of terrorism and moments of terrible fright" (Vincent Canby).
VHS: S17786. $29.95.
Susan Meiselas/Alfred Guzzetti/Richard P. Rogers, USA, 1991, 92 mins.

Pinatas, Posadas y Pastorelas
Mexico City's neighborhoods are transformed into villages from December 16-25 with the lively and entertaining tradition of *posadas*. See how the religious nature of Mexican life is balanced with Spanish and Indian culture, interweaving customs, theories and modern practices. 25 mins.
English Narration.
VHS: S19840. $49.95.
Spanish Narration.
VHS: S19839. $49.95.

A Place to Call Home
Young people in Veracruz, Mexico face many of the same challenges that young people face in the U.S. Emau—a youth center founded by a Maryknoll priest from New York—offers them friendship, counseling and fun. Look at their lives in the light of *posadas*, the Mexican Christmas commemoration of Mary and Joseph searching out a home for Jesus. 29 mins.
VHS: S15865. $19.95.

Population Explosion and Industrialization (Latin American Lifestyles)
The changes in the environment and society of Latin America are presented as both population and development increases in the 20th century. Bilingual English-Spanish narration.
VHS: S07425. $59.95.

Puerto Cabezas: Our Sister City
A unique and remarkable video on Nicaragua, made by two videomakers from Burlington, Vermont. Burlington's sister city is Puerto Cabezas, Nicaragua, a vital port town on the Atlantic Coast. In the video, the vitality, tenacity and hopes of the Miskito Indians and Cosenos emerge through the words of their leaders, the eyes of their children, and their music—the lilting Caribbean beat in Miskito, Spanish, Creole and English.
VHS: S03727. $50.00.
D. Kraft/M. Fishman, USA, 1985, 22 mins.

Puerto Rico: History and Culture
Designed to develop an appreciation of the rich history and cultural traditions of Puerto Rico. In addition to surveying its history from the 15th century to the present, examples are given of the wide variety of cultural and artistic talent in Puerto Rico's tradition. Specifically designed for social studies and foreign language study. Bilingual, presented in both English and Spanish.
VHS: S06741. $59.95.

The Pyramids of the Sun and the Moon
An important film depicting the growth and development of one of the earliest cultures in Mexico. The people of Teotihuacan constructed the Pyramids of the Sun and the Moon with such exact scientific calculation that only recently have modern scientists been able to appreciate their development. Filmed on location in Mexico, this film is a wonderful introduction to pre-Colombian cultures. Directed by Angel Hurtado, 20 mins.
English Narration. Renee Channey.
VHS: S06802. $60.00.
Spanish Narration. Ivan Silva.
VHS: S06803. $60.00.

Qeros: The Shape of Survival
The Qeros Indians live beneath the Peruvian Andes, where they endure rigorous daily struggles with nature in order to survive. The land was formerly occupied by the Incas, who conquered the rival communities. The Qeros take part in elaborate rituals to the Aukis (spirits) to sustain their continued health and safety. 53 mins.
VHS: S20215. $29.95.

Queremos La Paz (We Want Peace)
Nicaraguans from all walks of life speak directly to the people of North America by directly answering the question, "What is your message to the North American people?" This film provides a refreshing glimpse of the Nicaraguan situation and their hopes for the future. "This video is the next best thing to a visit to Nicaragua" (Pete Seeger).
VHS: S03725. $39.00.
Syracuse Alt. Media Netwk., USA, 1986, 33 mins.

A Question of Conscience
On November 16, 1989, uniformed soldiers entered the Jesuit residence on the grounds of El Salvador's Central American University and murdered six priests, their cook and her daughter. This film tells the story behind this brutal massacre. A moving homage to the murdered priests as well as a study of the power of religious commitment. Directed by Ilan Ziv. 43 mins.
VHS: S14733. $39.95.

Raoni
Introduced and narrated by Marlon Brando. Raoni is the forceful and charismatic Chief of the Txucarramae Indians, an Amazonian tribe indigenous to the Brazilian rain forest. He has achieved international recognition as the spokesman for all of Brazil's surviving Indians. *Raoni* focuses on the heroic conflict that pits a lone Indian Chief against the determined rapacity of multinational corporations and short-sighted governments. Nominated for an Academy Award for Best Documentary.
VHS: S10732. $29.95.
Jean-Pierre Dutilleux, France/USA, 1978, 84 mins.

Return of the Maya
A millennium ago the Maya were one of the most advanced civilizations on the planet. Today, after being treated as second class citizens in their own country and being forced into exile from contemporary Guatemala, they are helping uncover the glory of their heritage at the ancient city of Edzna in Mexico. 28 mins.
VHS: S21591. $85.00.

Return to Aguacayo
A dramatic account of 450 displaced Salvadorans who attempt to return to their homes and farming cooperative in the Guazapa region of El Salvador, after having been forced to leave by the army. The unique footage was acquired by a member of a North American religious delegation which went to El Salvador in the hopes of protecting the displaced from attacks by the Armed Forces on their journey home.
VHS: S11492. $35.00.
Celeste Greco, USA, 1987, 18 mins.

Ricardo Montalban's South America
Although poverty and suffering are associated with Latin America, it is a continent rich in culture and beauty. This film is a graphic tour of several countries south of the Panama Canal, capturing dozens of attractive images, but with special emphasis on music and dance. 28 mins.
VHS: S04933. $24.95.

Roots of Rhythm
Harry Belafonte hosts this globe-trotting, star-studded celebration tracing the history of Latin music. With 40 songs performed by Gloria Estefan, Dizzy Gillespie, Desi Arnaz, Celia Cruz, King Sunny Ade, Celia Cruz, Isaac Oviedo, Ruben Blades and more. Three videos. 57 mins. each.
VHS: S32193. $39.95.

Roses in December
On December 2, 1980, lay missioner Jean Donovan and three American nuns were brutally murdered by members of El Salvador's security forces. With compassion and sensitivity, this film chronicles Jean's brief life—from her affluent childhood in Connecticut, to her decision to volunteer with the Maryknolls in El Salvador, to her tragic death. This award-winning film is an eloquent memorial to a courageous young woman.
VHS: S09442. $39.95.
Ana Carrigan/Bernard Stone, USA, 1982, 56 mins.

Ruben Blades
Robert Mugge's stirring tribute to Ruben Blades, including appearances by Linda Ronstadt and Pete Hamill.
VHS: S05881. $24.95.
Robert Mugge, USA, 1986, 60 mins.

Salsa
The rhythms of salsa, featuring Tito Puente, Charlie Palmieri and Celia Cruz, exploring the connection between salsa and the political and cultural currents in the Latin community. Ruben Blades demonstrates how politics and music work together.
VHS: S08894. $24.95.

School of Assassins
U.S. taxpayers fund some of the worst human rights violators in this hemisphere. Former dictators from throughout South America received their training at the U.S. Army School of the Americas. This documentary reveals the connection between this school and the human rights offenses committed by its graduates in El Salvador. 18 mins.
VHS: S22475. $19.95.

Selena
A music sensation by the age of 23, this young performer's star was rising fast when she was killed by the president of her fan club. Jennifer Lopez and Edward James Olmos star in the true-life drama that charts the musical rise of Selena from Texas barrio to stardom.
VHS: S32066. $19.95.
Laser: LD76314. $39.98.
Gregory Nava, USA, 1997, 128 mins.

Sentinels of Silence: The Ruins of Ancient Mexico
Filmed almost entirely from helicopter, this documentary presents spectacular views of the seven most important archaeological sites in Mexico: Teotihuacan, Monte Alban, Mitla, Tulum, Palenque, Chichen Itza and Uxmal. Narrated in English by Orson Welles, and in Spanish by Ricardo Montalban. 18 mins.
English Version.
VHS: S16376. $39.95.
Spanish Version.
VHS: S16377. $39.95.

Severo Sarduy
The leader of the avant-garde in Latin America speaks from his estate in Chantilly with the Cuban critic Roberto Gonzalez Echevarria. The range of subjects is great, from Sarduy's humble beginnings as a student and his role as a bard of the provincial Camaguey, to the highly original response to the Cuban revolution embodied in *Gestos* and later in *De Donde son los Cantates*. They explore Sarduy's influential role in introducing such writers as Gabriel Garcia Marquez into the international community from his position at Editions Seuil in Paris, and his relationship to French structuralism. Spanish *without* English subtitles.
Home Video.
VHS: S06962. $59.95.
Public Performance.
VHS: S08841. $100.00.

Shotguns and Accordions
Nationally-aired PBS documentary gives a street-level perspective of the music of the marijuana growing regions of Colombia with a behind-the-scenes tour of the provocative culture. From *Beats of the Heart* series.
VHS: S12607. $19.95.

Si o No?
This program examines the issue of statehood for Puerto Rico: its impact on island life and its consequences for the United States. The program studies the history of the island during the past century, contrasting life on the island and mainland. 28 mins.
VHS: S20279. $29.95.

The Sights and Sounds of South America
The beautiful sights of the Hispanic colonial capitals and the the sounds of. Spanish and Indian voices and music are captured on this tape. 28 mins.
VHS: S31893. $29.95.

Simon Bolivar
Maximilian Schell stars as Simon Bolivar, the legendary leader who unites various groups of revolutionaries under his command and in a series of fierce battles proclaims his country's freedom. 120 mins.
VHS: S11111. $49.95.

Sonia Sanchez
This dynamic poet, playwright, activist and teacher stresses African-American unity. On this video she reads from *homegirls & handgrenades* and *Under a Soprano Sky*. Lewis MacAdams then interviews her. This tape was recorded on September 17, 1990, at Georgetown University in Washington, D.C. From the *Lannan Literary Videos* series. 60 mins.
VHS: S27128. $19.95.

The Sounds of Mexico
Mexican music is as diverse and wide-ranging as its geography, and every region has its peculiar rhythms and preferred instruments. This documentary celebrates the richness of the sound and the originality of its voice. In Spanish. 45 mins.
VHS: S19833. $39.95.

Spanish Club: Fiesta!
A live-action video featuring Senora Reyes and her Spanish language club as they explore the meaning of fiesta. The program uses traditional Hispanic songs and stories to teach culture as well as language. For children ages 2-8.
VHS: S21923. $19.95.

Spanish Club: Los Animales!
Senora Reyes and the Spanish Club Kids explore the world of animals in Volume 2 of this series, which uses traditional Hispanic songs and stories for children ages 2-8.
VHS: S21924. $19.95.

Spirit of Samba
Nationally-aired PBS documentary gives a street-level perspective of the black music of Brazil, with a behind-the-scenes tour of the provocative culture. From *Beats of the Heart* series.
VHS: S12606. $19.95.

Stairway to the Mayan Gods
Joseph Campbell wrote the narration for this journey to the ceremonial center of the Mayan Indians of Central America and Mexico. 28 mins.
VHS: S06490. $89.95.

Stairways to the Gods: On the Trail of the Jaguar
The jaguar is the recurrent symbol of the ancient Native American cultures of Central America. Beginning and ending at the sacred pyramid in Tikal, called the Temple of the Great Jaguar, this program follows the symbol of the jaguar across a number of archeological sites, explaining its varied meanings and the light it casts on the peoples of Mesoamerica. 43 mins.
VHS: S22925. $19.95.

Stand and Deliver
Edward James Olmos brings the story of Jaime Escalante and his progress in teaching calculus to unmotivated barrio students to life. An inspirational true-to-life educational miracle set at Garfield High in Los Angeles in 1982. Cast includes Rosana De Soto, Andy Garcia and Lou Diamond Phillips as the gang kid who wants to learn.
VHS: S07925. $14.95.
Laser: LD70683. $24.98.
Ramon Menendez, USA, 1988, 103 mins.

Symphony of Mexico
Symphony of the New World by composer Anton Dvorak provides the rhythm and mood for this fast-paced documentary on modern Mexico. Without words, the program relays the complexities of Mexican culture, bringing the audience on trip that transcends consciousness. 20 mins.
VHS: S16369. $29.95.

Tales from the Latin American Indians
Five magical tales from the Latin American Indians, including *The Magic of the Quetzal Bird, The Legend of Mexico City (Eagle and Snake), The Legend of Quezalcohuatl* and *The Legend of Loiza*. 30 mins.
English Version.
VHS: S20240. $29.95.
Spanish Version.
VHS: S20241. $29.95.

This Is Mexico
This documentary provides an ideological history of Mexico from ancient times to the present. Images of Indian monuments, dances and dress demonstrate Mexico's rich cultural foundation which then evolved by Spanish influence. This amalgam of culture provides the diverse nature of Mexico today. No narration. 20 mins.
VHS: S16370. $29.95.

This Land Is Our Land
Small family farmers in southern Brazil struggle in grass-roots organizations to gain title to land. Some families are displaced by huge dams, others face bank foreclosures, still others camp out for years in plastic tents to pressure the government to release unused land owned by a small minority. The video contains stories of perseverance, courage and hope in the face of violence and overwhelming odds. Produced by Maryknoll Media. 28 mins.
VHS: S11716. $24.95.

Threads of Tradition
Documents the rebirth of the traditional crafts of weaving and embroidery in the Hispanic culture of southern Colorado. Carding, spinning, dyeing, weaving are shown, as well as many examples of folk art. 14 mins.
VHS: S07637. $29.95.

Touring Mexico
A journey through the clash of climates, cultures and geographical extremes of Mexico, including Mexico City, the Yucatan, the classic Mayan civilization at Uxmal, Chichen Itza, the city of Merida, and the Olmecs of La Venta, the pyramid of Tijan and the mysteries of Monte Alban in Oaxaca. Other features include the City of the Gods at Teotihuacan, the colossi of Tula, the Floating Gardens of Xochimilco and more. 60 mins.
VHS: S09906. $29.95.

The Tree of Knowledge
Set in Huehuetla, in Eastern Mexico, the film contrasts the Mexican national school system's campaign to integrate Indian pupils, with the Indian Huehues dance, which shows young Indians how to learn from whites yet not lose their identity.
VHS: S33893. $24.95.
Bruce Pacho Lane, Mexico, 1988, 25 mins.

Tree of Life
More than just an anthropological documentary, this rare, beautifully made document of the Voladar ritual as performed by the Totonac Indians of Huehuetla, Mexico, brings alive the mythic dimensions of ritual communal celebration. The Voladores (Flyers) ritual is perhaps the oldest surviving dance in the Western Hemisphere, dating back to 500 A.D. It is accompanied by flute and drum music and narration taken from 15th-century Nahuatl poetry.
VHS: S09294. $24.95.

Troubadours: A Musical Performance by Groupo Camayoc
Taped in Esteli, Nicaragua, the program features a unique musical performance by the Nicaraguan folk singing group Camayoc, which means "messenger" in Nahuatl, the language of many Central American indigenous people. They play and sing their own songs and those of Carlos Meija Godoy and Pablo Milanes. Lyrics translated into English by Humberto Estrada.
VHS: S11181. $49.95.
Julia Lesage, USA/Nicaragua, 1987, 49 mins.

TV Commercials
See the innovative approach to advertising in a group of Mexican television commercials that introduce authentic cultural information. 45 mins.
VHS: S19830. $45.00.

Un Dia Cualquiera
This video features daily events in Honduras, including a pick-up soccer game, a party and a wedding, to give viewers the sense and concepts of specific situations. The workbook includes cultural information, oral and written exercises and tests. In Spanish. 30 mins.
VHS: S19820. $49.95.

Unheard Voices
For 10 years civil war raged in El Salvador. Yet rarely do we hear the voices of those who have suffered the most: the children, who make up nearly 1/2 the country's population. Many live in poverty, raised in orphanages or refugee camps. *Unheard Voices* is a poignant, emotional look at these young, forgotten victims. 1990, 16 mins.
VHS: S13966. $29.95.

Victor Hernandez Cruz
The African, Indian and Spanish cultures of Victor Hernandez Cruz's native Puerto Rico infuse his work. He has been the World Heavyweight Poetry Bout champion twice. On this video he reads from *Rhythm, Content and Flavor* and *By Lingual Wholes*. It was recorded in Los Angeles on April 17, 1989. Lewis MacAdams conducted the interview. From the *Lannan Literary Videos* series. 60 mins.
VHS: S27119. $19.95.

Video Visits: Argentina, Land of Natural Wonder
Explore Patagonia, Glacier National Park, Perito Moreno Glacier, the resort towns of San Martin and Bariloche, the Arrayanes Forest and the rainforests and jungles of Misiones Province, and hear the legacy of the *gaucho* on this video trip to Argentina. 51 mins.
VHS: S31452. $24.99.

Video Visits: Costa Rica, The Land of Pure Life
Visit the ruins of this land's pre-Columbian past, the Pacific Coast beaches and the central valley that first attracted Spanish settlers to this bountiful land. 56 mins.
VHS: S31454. $24.99.

Video Visits: Cuba, Island of Dreams
History infuses every element of this tropical paradise. Rugged mountains, beautiful beaches and historic sites in Havana, Trinidad and Santiago are all shown on this video. For centuries, Cuba has drawn adventurers and visitors ranging from Christopher Columbus to Ernest Hemingway and the infamous Al Capone. 52 mins.
VHS: S29828. $24.95.

Video Visits: Peru, A Golden Treasure

Travel to Lima's colonial mansions, beaches and Gold Museum, the oceanside resort of Las Dunas, "the City of Kings" and the Nazca lines, and explore the legacy of the Incas in Cuzo. 53 mins.
VHS: S31461. $24.99.

Voice of the Voiceless

Over half a million El Salvadoran refugees live in the United States. The war which has driven them here and their struggle to survive amidst poverty and fear of deportation is chronicled in this moving documentary, filmed in the Los Angeles refugee community. 60 mins.
VHS: S04307. $39.95.

War in El Cedro: American Veterans in Nicaragua

A revealing look at the realities of war through the eyes of combat veterans, and an eloquent plea, by those who have been there, to avoid military intervention in the affairs of other countries. Determined to make a positive contribution to a war-torn country, ten American veterans of World War II, Korea and Vietnam travelled to the village of El Cedro to help rebuild a health clinic destroyed by the Contras.
VHS: S11490. $39.95.
Don North, USA, 1987, 50 mins.

Warriors of the Amazon

This NOVA video catches a rare glimpse into the lives of the Yanomami, who live in a remote part of the Amazon rain forest. 60 mins.
VHS: S28646. $19.95.

We Are Guatemalans

After 12 years in Mexico a group of Guatemalan refugees returned home. Forced to flee the ethnic cleansing of their homeland, this documentary tells a tale of renewed commitment to the future of their country. It centers on the town Cuarto Pueblo and the dramatic ordeals faced by its inhabitants. 28 mins.
VHS: S22474. $19.95.

A Week in the Life of a Mexican Student

Xavier Sierra is a 14-year-old student shown at work, in class and at home in this video. 24 mins.
VHS: S23721. $99.95.

Where Land Is Life

For the indigenous people of Peru's Altiplano, the rugged land around Lake Titanica is more than soil. Centuries of conquest and exploitation have forced the Aymara and Quechua people to give up the land that has sustained them. Today, despite various setbacks, they are reclaiming the land of their birthright, and at the same time rediscovering the traditional methods of agriculture that made this region the breadbasket of Peru. 28 mins.
VHS: S13249. $24.95.

Zocalo—The Heart of Mexico

This program charts 24 hours in the frantic life of Zocalo, Mexico City's central plaza, that mirrors the people, their attitudes, and the cultural, social and life conditions of contemporary Mexico. 23 mins.
VHS: S20233. $59.95.

Zoot Suit

A stylized musical about the arrest of Chicano gang members in Los Angeles in 1942 and the resulting controversial trial. Written and directed by Luis Valdez, based on his own play. Starring Daniel Valdez, Tyne Daly, Mike Gomez, Abel Franco and Edward James Olmos as El Pachuco, the spirit of the Zoot Suit experience.
VHS: S14453. $14.98.
Luis Valdez, USA, 1981, 103 mins.

recent german cinema

All of Me
Georgette Dee, the famed transvestite cabaret star from Germany, stars as Orlanda. On a concert tour, Orlanda and his/her wife Elisabeth both fall for the same Polish man. This scenario makes for a witty film, and the musical numbers, particularly the title tune, are terrific. German with English subtitles.
VHS: S26867. $39.95.
Bettina Wilhelm, Germany, 1990, 76 mins.

All-Round Reduced Personality
A key work of the new German cinema, in which Helke Sander constructs a justly celebrated portrait of Edda, a free-lance photojournalist, and the divided city of Berlin. The film is a wryly funny but serious commentary on contemporary life, and a poignant look at a single woman trying to make a go of it. Sander, a leading figure of the German women's movement, is the film's writer, director and star, who bravely portrays Edda as an individual straddling multiple worlds—work, womanhood, motherhood, East, West, capitalism and socialism. Also known under the British-release title *Redupers*. German with English subtitles.
VHS: S34334. $59.95.
Helke Sander, Germany, 1977, 98 mins.

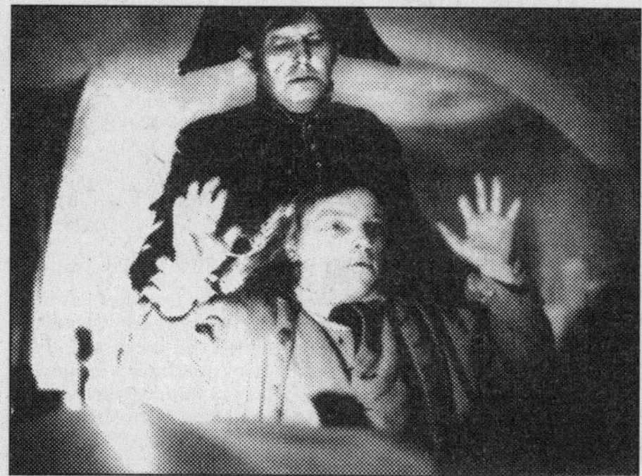

Anita, Dances of Vice
Anita Berber, the notorious "naked" dancer of Berlin of the Weimar era, comes alive in the visions of an old woman who claims to be Anita in Rosa von Praunheim's truly original film. The police commit her to a mental institution where in the old woman's dreams and exchanges with the staff, scenes from Anita's life appear. "Huber is irresistibly funny as the city's pugnacious doyenne of sin," wrote *The Village Voice*. German with English subtitles.
VHS: S09349. $39.95.
Rosa von Praunheim, Germany, 1987, 85 mins

Bagdad Cafe
From Percy Adlon, the director of *Sugarbaby*, an English-language film about a friendship between two women at a desert truck stop motel and diner. One is black and overworked. The other is German and overdressed. A haunting musical score and a top notch supporting cast which includes Jack Palance makes this sweet comedy starring C.C. Pounder and Marianne Sagebrecht a delight. In English.
VHS: S07965. $14.98.
Laser: LD75953. $34.95.
Percy Adlon, USA, 1988, 91 mins.

Black and White as Day and Night
Bruno Ganz stars in this feature, from the director of *Das Boot*, about a man obsessed. Ganz's character devotes himself to computers when he fails at chess. When the machine he works on loses, he becomes determined to best the offending world chess champion himself. Sadly the stress takes an unforeseen toll on his health, leading to a surprise ending. German with English subtitles.
VHS: S23194. $29.95.
Wolfgang Petersen, Germany, 1963, 103 mins.

The Blue Hour
The third feature by Swiss-born Marcel Gisler tells the story of an odd affair between two Berliners: Theo, a hip young callboy, and Marie, his French neighbor. The *Blue Hour* is a look at male prostitution and at gay men who sleep with women. With Andreas Herder, Dina Leipzig and Cyrill Rey-Coquais. German with English subtitles.
VHS: S19446. $29.95.
Marcel Gisler, Germany, 1991, 87 mins.

The Bridge (Die Brucke)
A powerful, deeply moving classic of German cinema. Set in 1945, seven German boys defend an insignificant bridge from an American attack. Based on the autobiographical novel of Manfred Gregor, this searing film was nominated for an Oscar and won a Golden Globe award. Its depiction of futile valor and wasted youth touched audiences the world over. German with English subtitles.
VHS: S26597. $39.95.
Bernhard Wicki, Germany, 1959, 102 mins.

Brother of Sleep
From the director of *Stalingrad* comes this "haunting, highly entertaining and visually stunning" (Paul Wunder, WBAI) portrait of a young musical prodigy torn between his musical gift and the woman he loves. Based on the best-selling novel by Robert Schneider. With Andre Eisermann (*Kaspar Hauser*) and Dana Vavrova (*Autumn Milk*). German with English subtitles.
VHS: S31544. $98.99.
Laser: LD76243. $34.95.
Joseph Vilsmaier, Germany, 1996, 133 mins.

Celeste
From the director of *Bagdad Cafe* and *Sugar Baby* comes one of those rare films to successfully portray the creative and emotional life of an artist. Marcel Proust, the celebrated author of *Remembrance of Things Past*, is seen through the young eyes of Celeste Albaret, who for nine years before the author's death was his cook, companion, secretary, friend and surrogate mother. Award-winning actress Eva Mattes delivers a flawless performance in this stunning and witty love story. Written and directed by Percy Adlon. German with English subtitles.
VHS: S13915. $29.95.
Percy Adlon, Germany, 1981, 107 mins.

Das Boot: The Director's Cut
Wolfgang Petersen's riveting, claustrophobic, German U-Boat warfare drama is presented in its original widescreen theatrical release ratio. This version also includes a newly redesigned digital soundtrack. With Juergen Prochnow, Herbert Gruenemeyer and Klaus Wennemann. Presented on two cassettes. German with English subtitles.
VHS: S14834. $24.95.
Laser: 3 sides. **LD72444. $39.95.**
DVD: DV60159. $24.98.
Wolfgang Petersen, Germany, 1981, 209 mins.

Der Sprinter
In order to please his parents, who are distressed because of his preference for other men, Wieland takes up track and field and is surprised to find himself attracted to a female shot-putter. German with English subtitles.
VHS: S02187. $59.95.
Christopher Boll, Germany, 1983, 90 mins.

Dragon Chow
A beautiful and moving film, *Dragon Chow* tells the story of Asian political refugees living on the edge of deportation in the land of economic miracles, West Germany. The film's hero, Shezad, a gentle but resourceful Pakistani, lands a job in a second-rate Chinese restaurant, where he befriends an Oriental waiter named Xiao (Ric Young of *The Last Emperor*). Together they attempt to storm the citadel of Western capitalism by opening a restaurant of their own. German, Urdu and Mandarin with English subtitles.
VHS: S12468. $69.95.
Jan Schutte, Germany, 1987, 75 mins.

East Side Story
A unique documentary about the world of Communist musicals—a world unknown in the West. Hearty peasants and workers sing and dance their way through fields and factories in films which border on campiness, in this unorthodox view of socialist propaganda. "Bright as a spangled sputnik. Don't dream of missing *East Side Story*, with its beach blanket bingo, Bulgarian-style" (Janet Maslin, *New York Times*).
VHS: S33314. $59.95.
Dana Ranga, Germany, 1997, 77 mins.

Fast Buck
A young man's fascination with love turns to tragedy. German with English subtitles. 90 mins.
VHS: S04775. $59.95.
Renate Stegmuller/Raimund Koplin, Germany, 1983, 95 mins.

Female Misbehavior
Monika Treut's kinky exploration of nonconformist women combines two older short films, *Bondage* (1983), about a sadomasochistic lesbian, and *Annie* (1989), a portrait of former porno star Annie Sprinkle, with two recent documentaries, *Dr. Paglia* and *Max*. The former is a witty send-up of controversial academic Camille Paglia; the latter, a look at a lesbianNative American that shows her transsexual change from woman to man. "Treut is a sexual-political provocateur who in her explorations of the sexual fringe takes us where few filmmakers visit" (*New York Post*).
VHS: S19558. $29.95.
Monika Treut, Germany/USA, 1992, 80 mins.

Film Before Film
A truly unique film by German filmmaker Werner Nekes, who owns one of the world's great collections of primitive motion picture and photographic equipment. In this fascinating documentary, Nekes explores how scientific advances in the 19th century—particularly developments in optics, theories of light, seeing and perception—aided the development of the moving image. But *Film before Film* is *not* a "documentary" in the traditional sense of the term—it's a great deal of fun and exploration of how moving images function through actual illustration of rare photographic and motion picture equipment. German with English subtitles.
VHS: S08946. $29.95.
Werner Nekes, Germany, 1987, 90 mins.

Flaming Ears
This edgy, sci-fi lesbian fantasy follows the lives of three women: a comic book artist, a performance artist/pyromaniac and and amoral alien who likes lizards. In this cyberdyke movie, love and revenge vie for supremacy amidst violence and ennui in an anti-romantic plea for love of all kinds. German with English subtitles.
VHS: S26936. $39.95.
Angela Hans Sheirl/Ursula Purrer/Dietmar Schipek, Austria, 1991, 84 mins.

Forget Mozart
Beginning in Vienna, Dec. 5, 1791, this German film reconstructs the life and times of the genius composer. As friends and associates gather at his deathbed, the extraordinary arc of his career is laid out, placed in the context of his art and life. He's portrayed as a complicated, difficult artist trying desperately to reconcile his personal life and private obsessions. German with English subtitles.
VHS: S16699. $29.95.
Salvo Luther, Germany, 1986, 93 mins.

Germany Pale Mother
A beautiful, moving account of the filmmaker's own childhood, made for her own daughter, which traces the history of Germany from an extremely personal, intimate point of view. The film begins on the eve of the German invasion of Poland, as a young woman sees her husband go off to the German army. She and her daughter struggle for survival during the war, only to face a husband who, when he returns, wreaks emotional havoc on the family. Brilliant performances from Eva Mattes, Ernst Jacobi and Elisabeth Stepanek. German with English subtitles.
VHS: S35301. $79.95.
Helma Sanders-Brahms, Germany, 1980, 109 mins.

Halfmoon
Three of legendary writer Paul Bowles' greatest and strangest stories are presented in this winner of the Critic's Prize (1995 Berlin Film Festival). *Merkala Beach* tells the story of two young Moroccan men whose friendship is tested by the appearance of a beautiful temptress; *Call at Corazon* joins a honeymooning couple as they travel the Amazon; *Allal* is a supernatural, surreal exchange between a young orphan and a poisonous cobra. In English and Arabic with English subtitles.
VHS: S28616. $29.95.
Frieder Schlaich/Irene von Alberti, Germany, 1995, 90 mins.

Hans Richter: Give Chance a Chance
Richter talks of how World War I led to the Surrealist movement, the artists of the period, his early training, Dada, Bauhaus, the antagonism of the Third Reich toward experimentation, crossover from painting to film and experiments with music. With clips from films *Ghosts Before Breakfast*, *Rhythm 21*, *8 X 8* and others. 28 mins, 1973.
VHS: S31591. $59.95.

Heimat

While America watched *Roots*, Germany watched *Heimat* with the same mixture of pride and shame that held a nation spellbound. The riveting 16-hour film, presented as a 9-tape boxed set, was the sensation of the Munich, London and Venice Film Festivals and a huge hit in France and Germany. It is the incredible interlocking saga of a German family from the end of World War I to 1982. Ambitious, grand, yet very intimate, *Heimat* is an incredible motion picture chronicle—an immersion in the lives, loves and tragedies of the extended Simon family. Shot over two years, the film features 28 leading performers, 140 speaking roles and a cast of 5,000 non-professional actors. German with English subtitles.

VHS: S27403. $149.95.
Edgar Reitz, Germany, 1984, 924 mins.

Heimat II

"Staggeringly rich....*The Second Heimat*, which runs 25½ hours, forms, with its predecessor, a magnificent, nearly unprecedented 'film novel': a portrait of Germany in the 20th century with few equals in either film or literature...outlandishly ambitious...an often dazzling success. That [Edgar] Reitz is able to sustain growth and tension, inexorable flow and translucent clarity through the entire vast length, and hold audiences rapt...seems something of a miracle. The story is of Maria's son, Herrmann Simon, and his life in Munich from 1960 to 1970. There, a brilliant young modernist musician and composer, he falls in with an incandescent circle of young students, artists, rebels and lovers—all brought shatteringly to life by Reitz and a splendid cast of actors and musicians...*The Second Heimat* may be the screen's finest portrayal of youth in the '60s" (Michael Wilmington, *Chicago Tribune*). German with clear English subtitles.

VHS: S27808. $249.95.
Edgar Reitz, Germany, 1994, 1416 mins.

Heimat Set

Includes *Heimat* and *The Second Heimat*.

VHS: S30170. $349.95.
Edgar Reitz, Germany, 1984/1994, 2340 mins.

I Am My Own Woman

The exceptional life of Eastern-bloc transvestite Charlotte von Mahlsdorf is the subject of this film. Her story symbolizes both political resistance and sexual difference under a repressive regime. It's a documentary with a touch of Brecht that features a true queer free spirit. German with English subtitles.

VHS: S22670. $19.95.
Rosa von Praunheim, Germany, 1993, 91 mins.

Ironhand

Costume adventure story set during the Middle Ages about two friends who grow to serve opposing masters, during a period of conflict between Church and State. German with English subtitles. Germany, 120 mins.

VHS: S04774. $59.95.
Wolfgang Liebeneizer, Germany, 1978, 103 mins.

Jumper

An unusual and disquieting film, in which a collection of tragi-comic characters all seem to lose their footing in the struggle of life without direction. German with English subtitles.

VHS: S02188. $59.95.
Benno Trachtmann, Germany, 1985, 90 mins.

Just a Gigolo

Actor David Hemmings directed this post-World War I melodrama starring David Bowie as a veteran looking for work in Berlin. He finds he is best at entertaining lonely older women with too much money. Cast includes Kim Novak, Maria Schell, Sydne Rome, Curt Jurgens, David Hemmings and Marlene Dietrich, who sings the title tune and shows her age. Hemmings debut as director. In English.

VHS: Out of print. For rental only.
Laser: CLV. **LD70268. $39.95.**
David Hemmings, Germany, 1979, 98 mins.

Kaspar Hauser

One of the greatest mysteries of his age: a 16-year-old youth was found abandoned in Nuremberg, Germany, unable to walk, write or speak. He became renowned as "a wild child," and as the object of scientific study. The case inspired over 2,000 books as well as the acclaimed film by Werner Herzog, *Every Man for Himself and God Against All*. Now filmmaker Peter Sehr makes a compelling film which looks at Kaspar Hauser in a social and historical context: as the crown prince of Baden, abducted as a child in the name of political intrigue, and raised in a dungeon. "A tour de force of wit, originality and poignancy" (Kevin Thomas, *Los Angeles Times*). German with English subtitles.

VHS: S31105. $79.95.
Peter Sehr, Germany, 1994, 137 mins.

Killing Cars

Jurgen Prochnow, the captain of *Das Boot*, now plays a brilliant automotive engineer who has designed and built an automobile that runs on cellular energy. This greatly annoys members of the oil cartel and rival gas guzzling car makers. A thriller set in Europe and the Middle East. With Senta Berger, Daniel Gelin and William Conrad as Mahoney. In English.

VHS: S05931. $79.95.
Michael Verhoeven, Germany, 1985, 104 min.

Knife in the Head

Bruno Ganz stars as a scientist in this murky political thriller, one of the most interesting films to emerge from the German New Wave. He sets off in search of his estranged wife, but is sidetracked when he loses his speech and memory in a bizarre accident. As the plot develops, a strange and unexpected twist throws him even further off balance. German with English subtitles.

VHS: S20870. $79.95.
Reinhard Hauff, Germany, 1978, 113 mins.

The Last Five Days

In 1943 a young woman (Lena Stolze), part of a group of students who formed a covert opposition group, the White Rose, that decried German crimes, was discovered by the Nazis and sentenced to death. The film explores her confinement, her relationship with a cellmate, the repercussions of her martyrdom, and her heroism and struggle against monumental darkness and depravity. With Lena Stolze and Irm Hermann. German with English subtitles.

VHS: S17632. $79.95.
Percy Adlon, Germany, 1982, 112 mins.

Leni Riefenstahl

This 1973 documentary includes Riefenstahl talking of her life as a dancer, a star of "mountain films," her relationship to Third Reich leaders, her search for the primitive, development as a director, new film techniques, editing, film music, being a woman in a man's film world and her discovery of the Nuba people of the Sudan. With many clips from her films *Blaue Licht*, *Triumph des Willens*, *Olympia* and *Tiefland*, and many photos from her own archives. Filmed in her Munich studio and in the Alps. 60 mins.

VHS: S31564. $59.95.

Love and Anarchy

Giancarlo Giannini (*Seven Beauties*) is Tunin, an oppressed Italian peasant out to assassinate Mussolini in the early 1930s. His plans are subverted when he takes residence in a brothel and finds love, in this wild and sexy political comedy. Italian with English subtitles. "Passionate and stirring" (*The New York Times*).

VHS: S31546. $29.98.
Lina Wertmuller, Italy, 1973, 129 mins.

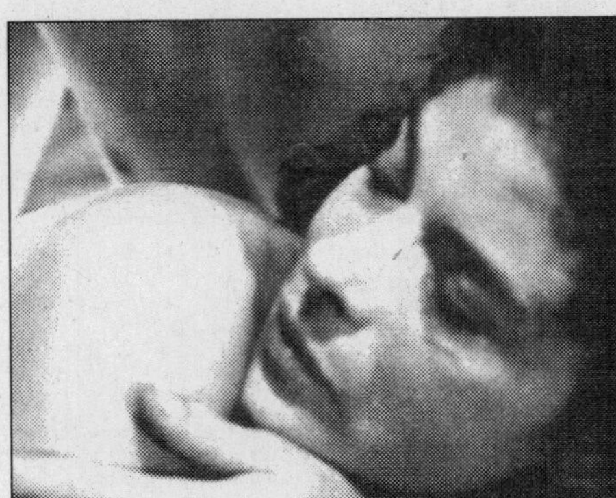

Makin' Up

This German film was a surprise hit and won a Student Academy Award. Frenzy is a harried cartoonist who relies on her friend Maischa, a date-crazy person, for inspiration. Maischa has hit a dry patch so in search of inspiration Frenzy must fix Maischa up and inadvertently finds herself on a double date. Includes the short film *The Most Beautiful Breasts in the World*. German with English subtitles.

VHS: S24671. $59.95.
Katia Von Garnier, Germany, 1993, 68 mins.

Marianne and Juliane

Barbara Sukowa, Jutta Lampe and Rudiger Vogler star in this drama which chronicles the story of two sisters. One is a left-wing editor, while the other became a communist terrorist who ends up in prison. This film offers a chilling personal account that illustrates the political turmoil that afflicted West Germany in the 1970s. German with English subtitles.

VHS: S21504. $59.95.
Margarethe von Trotta, Germany, 1980, 106 mins.

Maybe...Maybe Not

Germany's highest grossing film ever is the story of Axel (German box-office hunk Til Schwiger), a handsome, open-minded heterosexual whose girlfriend, Doro (Katja Reimann), kicks him out for cheating on her. Axel finds the only place he has to sleep is at the apartment of Norbert (Joachim Krol), a gay acquaintance who would like nothing better than to seduce Axel. The hunter now becomes the prey and the consequences are comical as Axel tries to fend off the advances of Norbert and a host of other male suitors while trying to win back the heart of Doro. German with English subtitles. "Riotous gender-bender! Outspoken and wickedly wild!" (*The New York Observer*).

VHS: S30615. $96.98.
Sonke Wortmann, Germany, 1996, 93 mins.

Me and Him

Griffin Dunne thought he had problems dating in the Big Apple in *After Hours*. That was before he found his male member not only had a mind of its own but a voice as well. Billed as the ultimate buddy picture, this unusual comedy from Doris Dorrie (*Men*) was based on a novel by Alberto Moravia. Cast includes Ellen Greene, Carey Lowell, Kelly Bishop, Craig T. Nelson and Mark Linn-Baker as the voice of Griffin's little friend.

VHS: S11575. $89.95.
Doris Dorrie, USA, 1989, 95 mins.

Mein Krieg (My Private War)

An eerie compilation of home movies and oral histories of six Wehrmacht soldiers who were involved in the Nazi invasion of the former Soviet Union. The images of the war (soldiers swimming in the Black Sea, bombed out landscapes and literally thousands of dead bodies) are contrasted with the soldiers' memories and reminiscences of their experiences. "*Mein Krieg* is annotated only by the veterans themselves as they explicate the material they produced nearly a half-century before" (J. Hoberman, *The Village Voice*).

VHS: S19859. $79.95.
Harriet Eder/Thomas Kufus, Germany, 1990, 90 mins.

Men

Doris Dorrie's runaway hit of a screwball comedy about a businessman (Heiner Lauterbach) who discovers his wife is having an affair with a Bohemian artist. Disguised as the artist's roommate, Lauterbach watches, waits, and plots a strange reversal on the unsuspecting couple. German with English subtitles.

VHS: S20591. $29.95.
Doris Dorrie, Germany, 1985, 99 mins.

Mozart: A Childhood Chronicle

A profound and witty account of Mozart's life from child prodigy to mature composer. "Should not be missed by anyone who has even a passing interest in Mozart," wrote The New York Times. German with English subtitles.

VHS: S04730. $79.95.
Klaus Kirschner, Germany, 1976, 224 mins.

My Father Is Coming

An adventurous German woman receives word from her Bavarian father of his intentions to visit her in New York, where she must pull off an elaborate facade of being married and successful. Her gay roommate poses as her husband but complications ensue when a string of bizarre circumstances result in her father's transformation into an underground sexual icon. With Shelly Kastner, Alfred Edel and Annie Sprinkle.

VHS: S18412. $29.95.
Monika Treut, USA/Germany, 1991, 83 mins.

The Nasty Girl

When Sonja investigates the secret past of her home town, she uncovers more than she expected—and more than the townsfolk want revealed. Before she knows it, she is nicknamed "the nasty girl" and her trouble really begins. This provocative comedy about secrets and surprises features a fabulous performance by Lena Stolze and is based on a true story. "One of the best films of the year!" (*Los Angeles Daily News*). German with yellow English subtitles. Presented in letterbox format.

VHS: S15354. $19.95.
Michael Verhoeven, Germany, 1991, 94 mins.

Neurosia

A sort of *Citizen Queer* in which Orson Welles meets John Waters; this irreverent docu-autobiography shamelessly celebrates gay filmmaker Rosa von Praunheim's life, recapping five decades of activism, guerilla filmmaking and camp by recalling his oeuvre of over 50 films and his role in the birth of the gay rights movement in the 1970s. After Rosa is shot onstage while hosting a tribute to himself, a tabloid reporter travels from Germany to New York to find the motive—and the body. English/German with English subtitles.

VHS: S31351. $29.95.
Rosa von Praunheim, Germany, 1995, 87 mins.

Oppermann Family

Two-cassette mammoth West German TV production based on the novel by Lion Feuchtwanger about the Oppermann family, starting in the Nazi years of 1932, and their attempt to survive in Berlin against the forces of the Hitler regime. German with English subtitles.

VHS: S02005. $99.95.
Egon Monk, Germany, 1982, 238 mins.

Parsifal (Syberberg)

Syberberg's (*Our Hitler*) remarkable homage to Richard Wagner, with Edith Clever. Syberberg explores Wagner's last, mystic opera, with a challenging style, using Wagner's face as a set. The actors perform to a recording expressly made for the film. German lyrics with English subtitles.

VHS: S00995. $79.95.
Hans Jurgen Syberberg, Germany, 1982, 255 mins.

Positive

The New York City gay community's response to the AIDS crisis is powerfully documented in *Positive*. Rosa von Praunheim has captured the spirit of activism generated by playwright Larry Kramer, musician and co-founder of People With AIDS Coalition (PWA) Michael Callen, and New York filmmaker and journalist Phil Zwickler. They have chosen to act and speak out, refusing to be "AIDS victims." Having neither the time nor the patience to mince words, their groups, like ACT-UP and Queer Nation, demand a response to the epidemic that has threatened to annihilate them. An immensely important historical document.
VHS: S14152. $29.95.
Rosa von Praunheim/Phil Zwickler, USA, 1990, 80 mins.

The Promise

In this love story the Berlin wall separates two young lovers. They first fall for each other in their teens and their passion stretches over 28 years until the wall no longer presents an obstacle to their joint happiness. It's an epic story about the endurance of love. German with English subtitles.
VHS: S27255. $19.98.
Laser: LD75471. $39.99.
Margarethe von Trotta, Germany, 1995, 115 mins.

Rosa Luxemburg

Rosa Luxemburg's amazing life as a political radical and fiercely independent woman is brought to life in this sweeping biography starring the acclaimed actress Barbara Sukowa. From war and revolution to Luxemburg's tempestuous personal life, including her love affairs and numerous jail sentences, this charismatic figure stayed true to her ideals. German with English subtitles.
VHS: S20595. $29.95.
Margarethe von Trotta, Germany, 1985, 122 mins.

Rosalie Goes Shopping

The wonderfully comic Marianne Sagebrecht plays the calculating German war bride of an Arkansas crop duster. Rosalie Greenspan has 37 credit cards and she isn't afraid of pushing them all over the posted limit. Brad Davis and Judge Reinhold costar in this very original black comedy about achieving the American dream through misrepresentation.
VHS: S12516. $89.95.
Percy Adlon, Germany, 1989, 94 mins.

Salmonberries

German director Percy Adlon's political thriller features k.d. lang in her film debut. The story concerns a repressed East German librarian who escapes her oppressive surroundings after her lover is killed trying to scale the Berlin Wall. Devastated and grief stricken, Roswitha (Rosel Zech) travels to Alaska. Trapped in a grim, remote Eskimo outpost, she finds comfort and emotional fulfillment with the sexually ambiguous lang.
VHS: S18844. $29.95.
Percy Adlon, Canada/Germany, 1991, 94 mins.

Schramm

Nekromantik's director Jorg Buttgereit depicts the world of a serial killer in this hypnotizing orgy of sex and violence. It's all seen through the eyes of the killer, Lothar Schramm (Florian Koemer von Gustorf). He is fascinated by a prostitute (Monika M.) and obsessed with death. The result is a well-crafted, surreal vision of love and desire.
VHS: S27510. $29.95.
Jorg Buttgereit, Germany, 90 mins.

The Second Awakening of Christa Klages

Von Trotta's first solo directorial effort without husband Volker Schlondorff is the story of Christa (Tina Engel), a young divorced mother who, to finance her day-care center, robs a bank with two male accomplices and then finds that her associates at the center will not accept the stolen money. An unpredictable, didactic and profoundly political film. "*Christa Klages* is about friendships and bonds of identification between women…it's the film that the touted *Girl Friends* and *One Sings, The Other Doesn't* claimed to be but never got around to" (*Chicago Reader*). German with English subtitles.
VHS: S32175. $39.95.
Margarethe von Trotta, Germany, 1977, 93 mins.

Seduction: The Cruel Woman

Pina Bausch dancer Mechtild Grossman plays Wanda, a dominatrix whose troupe services customers and elaborately stages S&M performances in this "stunning" film from German filmmakers Elfi Mikesch and Monika Treut (*Virgin Machine*). Much more important to Mikesch's insinuating camera than the petty tortures are the settings, costumes, and look of each encounter. This is S&M by Avedon, outfits by Dior…By the way, on her off hours, of which there are few, Wanda prefers women. German with English subtitles.
VHS: S12460. $29.95.
Elfi Mikesch/Monika Treut, Germany, 1985, 84 mins.

Sheer Madness

In this intellectually complex and exhilarating film, von Trotta maps the destructive side of heterosexual politics as she explores the relationship of two profoundly enmeshed women. Olga (Hanna Schygulla), a professor of women's literature, saves Ruth (Angela Winkler), an artist, from suicide and tries to free her from going into the dark places of the self. "A moving and first-rate piece of work" (Barbara Koenig Quart, *Cineaste*). German with English subtitles.
VHS: S32176. $39.95.
Margarethe von Trotta, Germany, 1982, 107 mins.

Silence=Death

This film serves as an important historical document, exploring the reactions of New York's artistic community to the ravages of AIDS. Responses range from David Wojnorowicz' venomous proclamations and paintings, and painter Rafael Gambas' seething indictment of homophobic bigotry, to Keith Haring's nostalgic longing for the days of care-free sex, and Allen Ginsberg's musing upon his shyer attitude about experimenting sexually. Even with the gentler voices, the film's undercurrent is an angry demand for action and recognition. "Best AIDS film to date…" (*The Guardian*).
VHS: S14148. $29.95.
Rosa von Praunheim/Phil Zwickler, USA, 1990, 60 mins.

Sisters, Or the Balance of Happiness

Von Trotta's stunning story of two sisters: the orderly and efficient Maria (Jutta Lampe), and the dependent and resentful Anna (Gudrun Gabriel), who studies biology at university while Maria foots the tuition and bills. Though they are physical and emotional opposites, they can live neither with nor without each other. When Anna commits suicide, Maria attempts to reinvent Anna through Miriam, a lively typist in the office secretarial pool, who obliges Maria to weigh the balance inside herself instead of searching out opposite types to stabilize her needs. "Beautifully visualized, intelligently written, von Trotta's movie is a stunning achievement" (Carrie Rickey, *Village Voice*). German with English subtitles.
VHS: S32174. $39.95.
Margarethe von Trotta, Germany, 1979, 97 mins.

Stalingrad

From the same production team that brought the world *Das Boot*, this film brings the bloodiest battle in the history of warfare to the screen: the legendary battle of Stalingrad. With German forces following Hitler's orders to neither retreat nor surrender, over two million Russians and Germans lost their lives in what came to be a turning point in the defeat of Germany in the Second World War. One of the most unflinchingly realistic war films ever made, *Stalingrad* stands alone in its searing, unforgettable imagery, "powerfully underscoring the adage that war is hell" (*The New York Times*). German with English subtitles. Letterboxed.
VHS: S30467. $29.95.
Joseph Vilsmaier, Germany, 1996, 150 mins.

Street Kid

Peter Kern's story about a 14-year-old street walker and male prostitute who becomes a pawn in a nasty dysfunctional family and their weird games of domination. Filled with stark imagery, powerful performances and a gritty authenticity that "challenges the taboos and constraints of mainstream Hollywood filmmaking." With Winfried Glatzeder, Max Kellerman, Daniel Aminatey and Nicole Weber. German with English subtitles.
VHS: S17778. $69.95.
Peter Kern, Germany, 1991, 89 mins.

Swann in Love

Jeremy Irons, Ornella Muti, Alain Delon star in Schlondorff's engrossing, sexy film based on Proust's monumental modern novel, centering on a wealthy gentleman who thrives in the finest circles of high society and risks everything for his erotic obsession. English dialog.
VHS: S01289. $24.95.
Volker Schlondorff, Germany/France, 1984, 110 mins.

Taxi Zum Klo

A smash hit at the Berlin and New York Film Festivals in 1981, *Taxi Zum Klo* is an autobiographical examination of the director's own sexual escapades and fantasies. Frank Ripploh explores every aspect of gay life in Berlin, with hilarious results. German with English subtitles.
VHS: S01304. $39.95.
Frank Ripploh, Germany, 1981

Tears in Florence

A love story between a woman who has had a disfiguring auto accident and the man who struck her. As their love blossoms they learn that they are in fact brother and sister. Then the woman discovers she is pregnant. German with English subtitles.
VHS: S02186. $59.95.
Marianne Schafer, Germany, 1982, 90 mins.

The Tin Drum

The 1979 Academy Award winner for Best Foreign Film. *The Tin Drum* is a masterpiece of dazzling exuberance and originality adapted from the novel by Gunter Grass. The film is a stunning parable of modern society in violent transition narrated by a unique hero for our times—Oskar, a boy who decides at three not to grow any older. VHS letterboxed. German with English subtitles.
VHS: S01349. $39.95.
Laser: LD76415. $69.99.
Volker Schlondorff, Germany, 1979, 142 min.

Tonio Kroger

A brilliant adaptation of Thomas Mann's 1903 novel about a young writer torn between contradictory desires for security and luxury as well as the carefree, passionate life. Fluid time structure, eerie music, and black and white evoke a dream-like world. German with English subtitles.
VHS: S01360. $29.95.
Rolf Thiele, Germany, 1965, 92 mins.

Via Appia

A complex film about gay desire and paranoia. A former German steward travels to Rio to find a mysterious man who left a cryptic message, "Welcome to the AIDS Club," following a sexual encounter. "Via Appia, the nickname of a Rio district where male prostitutes hang out, becomes a grim guided tour of the city's gay subculture, its bars, discos, streets and a beach known as the AIDS farm. The documentary-within-the film-format justifies this material" (Vincent Canby). With Peter Senner, Guilherme de Padua and Yves Jansen. German and Spanish with English subtitles.
VHS: S18693. $39.95.
Jochen Hick, Germany/Brazil, 1992, 90 mins.

Virgin Machine

Called "steamy" by *The San Francisco Chronicle* and "a lesbian *Candide*…deliriously obscene" by *The San Francisco Examiner*, *Virgin Machine* is an offbeat black and white comedy about a journalist researching romantic love. The study takes her from German endocrinologists to San Francisco's porn district where she meets Susie Sexpert, a woman who lectures on the relative merits of various strippers and demonstrates dildos the way some women handle tupperware. German with English subtitles.
VHS: S10940. $29.95.
Monika Treut, Germany, 1988, 90 mins.

A Virus Knows No Morals

A black comedy filled with the worst fears, a savagely funny burlesque on the AIDS crisis, irreverent yet deadly serious. Nurses on the night shift roll dice to see which AIDS patient will die next. An epidemic victim is harassed by a reporter on his death bed—he sticks her with a contaminated syringe. The government opens a quarantine called Hell Gay Land. Gay terrorists capture the Minister of Health. An outrageous and yet extremely honest film by von Praunheim, this controversial film shook West Germany. German with English subtitles.
VHS: S09350. $39.95.
Rosa von Praunheim, Germany, 1985, 82 mins.

Voyager

Volker Schlondorff's adaptation of Max Frisch's novel stars Sam Shepard as Walter Faber, a peripatetic American engineer whose travels reunite him with a woman (Barbara Sukowa) from his past. He then meets a beautiful young German woman (Julie Delpy), who represents his past and future. Schlondorff's film mixes European style with an elliptical American narrative, switching from black and white to color.
VHS: S16550. $19.98.

Wannsee Conference

An acclaimed film that reenacts the fateful January 1942 meeting of the Nazi party and top German officials that set in motion "The Final Solution," the destruction of European Jewry. "It is mesmerizing for seeming to be so commonplace. *The Wannsee Conference* finds a voice for dealing with matters that are, after all, not unspeakable" (Vincent Canby). With Dietrich Mattausch, Gerd Bockmann, Friedrich Beckhaus and Gunter Sporrle. German with English subtitles.
VHS: S07395. $19.95.
Heinz Schirk, Germany, 1984, 87 mins.

Westler: East of the Wall

Before the wall separating East and West Germany came down it divided not just a nation but thousands of families. This film tells a story about the nearly impossible romance between two gay men on opposite sides of the wall. German with English subtitles.
VHS: S24836. $39.95.
Wieland Speck, Germany, 1986, 94 mins.

Whisky and Sofa (Operation Moonlight)

Maria Schell, Carl Michaels and Nadja Gray star in this sparkling romantic comedy. Schell is a beautiful and determined architect who is set on winning a major architectural competition. She even tries to flirt with a rival in order to ensure her success. Naturally this harmless maneuver leads to unforseen romantic consequences. Dubbed in English.

VHS: S23802. $24.95.

Gunter Grawert, Germany, 1963, 85 mins.

The Wonderful, Horrible Life of Leni Riefenstahl

An exhaustive, infuriating and unforgettable documentary about Leni Riefenstahl at age 90: actress, filmmaker (*Olympia, Triumph of the Will*), propagandist, personal friend of Goebbels and Hitler, photographer, explorer. Filmmaker Ray Mueller confronts Leni as she seeks to remold her image from that of a master propagandist and Nazi to that of a noble and heroic victim of history. Essential viewing. German with English subtitles.

VHS: S23996. $39.95.

Laser: LD75388. $69.99.

Ray Mueller, Germany, 1993, 180 mins.

RAINER WERNER FASSBINDER

Ali: Fear Eats the Soul

A major film by Fassbinder, Ali is the outrageous, touching story of the bumpy love affair between a sixtyish German floorwasher and an inarticulate Arab mechanic barely half her age. A moving romance, a perverse social comedy, a biting drama of racial prejudice, Ali: Fear Eats the Soul is all these things, although in Fassbinder's freewheeling vision it is not always easy to tell where one leaves off and another begins. Winner of the International Critics Prize, Cannes Film Festival. German with enhanced English subtitles.

VHS: S11590. $29.95.

Rainer W. Fassbinder, Germany, 1974, 94 mins.

The American Soldier

Fassbinder's homage to Hollywood gangster films is updated for the seventies. Murder is still for sale, but crime is organized by the state, not by the mob. Ricky—hired first by the U.S. to fight in Vietnam, and now by the German police—follows orders to kill: kill soldiers, kill strangers, kill even his girlfriend. Although Ricky wears a soft fedora (as well as a white double-breasted suit), it is Fassbinder who tips his hat, with secondary characters named Walsh and Fuller. Stars Karl Scheydt, Fassbinder, Margarethe von Trotta and Kurt Raab. German with English subtitles.

VHS: S16498. $29.95.

Rainer W. Fassbinder, Germany, 1970, 80 mins.

Beware of a Holy Whore

Hanna Schygulla and Rainer Werner Fassbinder are both featured in this film about a doomed film production unit. Both the crew and cast are besieged by every conceivable problem in a luxurious seaside hotel. As they wait for the director to show up and the producer scrambles to procure more cash, they are forced to confront themselves and each other. German with English subtitles.

VHS: S24950. $19.98.

Rainer W. Fassbinder, Germany, 1970, 103 mins.

The Bitter Tears of Petra Von Kant

"A tragi-comic love story disguised as a lesbian slumber party in high-camp drag" (Molly Haskell), the film makes us a witness to the struggles for domination among three lesbians: a successful and "liberated" fashion designer, her contented and silent slave girl, and a sultry but cruel model who ends up making the master her slave. The dynamics of their interrelationships are played out in this claustrophobic, self-contained little world, accompanied only by the music of The Platters and Giuseppe Verdi. A riveting chamber drama of style. With Margit Carstensen, Hanna Schygulla, Eva Mattes and Irm Hermann. German with English subtitles.

VHS: S13914. $29.95.

Rainer W. Fassbinder, Germany, 1972, 124 mins.

Chinese Roulette

A brilliant social satire from the director of The Marriage of Maria Braun. When a businessman, his wife, and their lovers are forced by the couple's paraplegic daughter to participate in a rigorous game of truth-telling, latent hatreds within the family are revealed, speeding the way toward the film's shocking climax. Starring Anna Karina and Ulli Lommel. German with English subtitles.

VHS: S12821. $29.95.

Rainer W. Fassbinder, Germany, 1976, 96 mins.

Effi Briest

Fassbinder's masterpiece is the German Madame Bovary. Hanna Schygulla plays the inexperienced, beautiful and naive woman who marries a much older Prussian diplomat, falls prey to a charming, shrewd womanizer, and suffers the consequences of an unforgiving society. Beautifully shot in black and white with elegant framing, the film is both a very accurate adaptation of the novel by Theodor Fontane, and a critical re-analysis. With Wolfgang Schenck and Ulli Lommel. German with English subtitles.

VHS: S17620. $59.95.

Rainer W. Fassbinder, Germany, 1974, 140 mins.

Fox and His Friends

A lower-class carnival entertainer professionally known as Fox the Talking Head strikes it rich, after a life of hard knocks, by winning the lottery. His new-found wealth attracts an elegant bourgeois lover, who proceeds to vamp Fox as thoroughly and unthinkingly as Lola Lola or Theda Bara. This ill-fated romance between "the capitalist and the lottery queen" makes for one of Fassbinder's most skillfully wrought films, expertly evoking a brittle, upper-class gay milieu where, as one character puts it, "God's dressed up like Marlene Dietrich, holding his nose." German with English subtitles. Electronically subtitled.

VHS: S06443. $29.95.

Rainer W. Fassbinder, Germany, 1975, 123 mins.

Germany in Autumn

Eleven leading filmmakers collaborated on this protest against Fascist tendencies in West Germany by reflecting on the tragic events of Autumn, 1977, when public official Hanns Martin Schleyer was kidnapped and murdered by the Baader-Meinhof group, whose members mysteriously died in prison. The film's contents range from an elegiac sequence of the burial of the prisoners to newsreel clips of Rommel's cortege and a fictitious argument among TV executives about a controversial production of Antigone. In the amazing Fassbinder sequence, he interviews his mother, who first endorses the dictatorship and then physically abuses her boyfriend. The contradictions in the film "belong to one nation: only if all the country's contradictions are together, can you accept this history and understand it" (Alexander Kluge). Screenplay by Heinrich Boll and Peter Steinbach. Directed by Alf Brusellin, Bernhard Sinkel, Rainer W. Fassbinder, Alexander Kluge, Beate Mainka-Jellinghaus, Maximiliane Mainka, Peter Schubert, Edgar Reitz, Katja Rupe, Hans Peter Cloos and Volker Schloendorff. Germany, 1978, 134 mins.

VHS: S20729. $29.95.

Rainer W. Fassbinder, et al., Germany, 1978, 134 mins.

Gods of the Plague

Fassbinder's third feature, about a petty criminal who plans to rob a supermarket, only to be betrayed by the two women who love him. "Fassbinder's gangster film doesn't happen on the level of black limousines, bursts of machine-gun fire, blinking blondes and detective brilliance; it uses more lower-class people and shoplifters; 'little' girls who do all that for love of the great glamour" (Goethe Institute). With Hanna Schygulla, Harry Baer and Margarethe von Trotta. German with English subtitles.

VHS: S11149. $29.95.

Rainer W. Fassbinder, Germany, 1969, 92 mins.

I Only Want You to Love Me (Ich Will Doch Nur, Dass Ihr Mich Liebt)

Fassbinder's striking tale of a young man's desire to be loved is the story of a man who is saddled by debts and troubled by his unfulfilling home life. In this dark melodrama, his wife and parents seem indifferent to him and to his pain. His unhappy life is significantly altered for the worse when, one night, in a drunken stupor, he kills a bar-keeper, mistaking him for his distant father. German with English subtitles.

VHS: S27665. $39.95.

Rainer W. Fassbinder, Germany, 1976, 100 mins.

In a Year of Thirteen Moons

One of Fassbinder's most unusual and daring films, In a Year of Thirteen Moons stars Erwin Spengler as a man desperately in love with his business partner. He decides to have a sex change operation, becomes Elvira, but this fails to attract the love of his beloved. Instead, the new "she" finds a series of damaging relationships and betrayals. Fassbinder uses harsh color, asymmetrical sets, a dissonant sound track and alternating narrative techniques to evoke the pain of Erwin/Elvira in a film that stretches the boundaries of conventional storytelling. German with English subtitles.

VHS: S23998. $29.95.

Rainer W. Fassbinder, Germany, 1979, 129 mins.

A Man Like Eva

A film based on the life of Rainer Werner Fassbinder, the enfant terrible of the new German cinema. Eva Mattes, one of Fassbinder's own stars, is Fassbinder (in drag) in this film in what Vincent Canby in The New York Times called "A stunning performance…a blood-curdling homage…a hypnotic, unorthodox, appropriately paean to Fassbinder, the great German filmmaker who died in 1982." German with English subtitles.

VHS: S06589. $79.95.

Radu Gabrea, Germany, 1983, 92 mins.

The Marriage of Maria Braun

Hanna Schygulla stars in Fassbinder's spectacular weaving of soap opera, comedy, history, politics and social satire into a lucid whole. Maria marries Hermann Braun the night before he is called to the front in WWII Germany. Soon he's believed to be dead, and Maria starts working her way up through the bedrooms of the social elite. When her husband suddenly returns, a fight ensues and she ends up clobbering her lover to death. At the American war trial, Hermann accepts blame and prison sentence, while Maria is left to deal with her uncertain pregnancy and promiscuous nature in this darkly humorous metaphor for the German post-war national spirit. German with English subtitles.

VHS: S01909. $29.95.

Rainer W. Fassbinder, Germany, 1979, 120 mins.

Merchant of Four Seasons

A climax in the prolific career of Rainer Werner Fassbinder. The story, that of a fruit peddler who watches his unexceptional life disintegrate, sounds like a slice-of-life melodrama gone slightly amok, but the treatment is everything; a virtuoso balance of soap opera, social comedy, irony, politics, farce and brilliant ensemble acting. German with English subtitles. With Irm Hermann, Hanna Schygulla.

VHS: S12467. $29.95.

Rainer W. Fassbinder, Germany, 1972, 88 mins.

Mother Kusters Goes to Heaven

A major Fassbinder film. Mother Kusters finds herself suddenly widowed. Her husband was a factory worker who one day goes berserk, killing the boss' son and throwing himself into the machinery. Her daughter, a would-be chanteuse, moves in with a muckraking journalist to further her career. Soon the dead man's life is distorted throughout pages of a cheap tabloid. Fassbinder paints a world where the honest and the good fall prey to a system of corrupt media and politics, a world where only small kindnesses carry relief to overwhelming suffering. German with English subtitles.

VHS: S16695. $29.95.

Rainer W. Fassbinder, Germany, 1975, 108 mins.

Querelle

Brad Davis, Jeanne Moreau and Franco Nero star in Rainer Werner Fassbinder's final film, adapted from Jean Genet's great novel, Querelle de Brest. The film focuses on a beautiful but callous and tough young French sailor whose beauty and heartlessness both attract and repell all who meet him. English dialog.

VHS: S01080. $19.95.

Rainer W. Fassbinder, Germany/France, 1982, 106 mins.

Satan's Brew

Kurt Raab stars as a would-be poet and revolutionary whose imagination overreaches his talents. Forced into betrayal, he hurts those around him and ultimately starts to believe that he is the reincarnation of the 19th-century German romantic poet Stefan George. This black comedy is a biting satire about the cult of the individual artist. German with English subtitles.

VHS: S24949. $19.98.

Rainer W. Fassbinder, Germany, 1976, 112 mins.

Shadow of Angels

Rainer Werner Fassbinder collaborated with director Daniel Schmid on this film adaptation of Fassbinder's controversial play The Garbage, the City and Death. Much controversy surrounded one character in particular: a Jewish businessman (Klaus Lowitsch), who is always referred to as "the rich Jew." Ultimately, the story is more concerned with the outsider status of this businessman and the prostitute (Ingrid Caven) whom he hires to listen to him (and, on occasion, to perform in a mock wedding ceremony). Both find themselves out of place in a milieu dominated by prostitutes, pimps, corrupt policemen and perverse businessmen. Fassbinder appears as the prostitute's sadistic, gay pimp. German with English subtitles.

VHS: S27664. $39.95.

Daniel Schmid, Germany, 1976, 105 mins.

The Stationmaster's Wife

Elisabeth Trissenaar is the bored wife whose flamboyant affairs epitomize the fake bourgeois morality and buried social and political resentments within German society. Her pleasant, attentive husband (Kurt Raab) is no match for the succession of oppressive lovers she falls prey to. Fassbinder dramatizes this through a Sirkian deployment of bold, ironic colors, brisk melodrama and tight framing. With Bernard Helfrich, Karl Heinz-von Hassel and Udo Kier. German with English subtitles.

VHS: S18933. $29.95.

Rainer W. Fassbinder, Germany, 1977, 113 mins.

Why Does Herr R. Run Amok?

Herr R., a likable office worker with a family, calmly picks up an ornate lamp one evening and bludgeons to death his wife, child and neighbor. One of Fassbinder's most notorious films, full of brilliant insights into the loneliness of existence, the terrors and anxieties of middle-class life. With Lilith Ungerer, Amadeus Fengler, Franz Maron and Hanna Schygulla. German with English subtitles.

VHS: S20306. $59.95.

Rainer W. Fassbinder, Germany, 1969, 87 mins.

WERNER HERZOG

Aguirre: The Wrath of God

"One of the great, mad, passionate, foolhardy masterpieces-as reckless and as brilliant as Greed or Apocalypse Now" (Roger Ebert). Shot on location in the Amazon, Klaus Kinski is Aguirre searching for El Dorado—the mythical City of Gold. German with English subtitles.

VHS: S00025. $29.95.

Werner Herzog, Germany, 1972, 94 mins.

Heart of Glass

Werner Herzog's brilliant, sensual, hypnotic film about the magical and desperate attempts of the people in a small village to learn the formula for making special glass, supplied by a wandering herdsman with extraordinary powers. An apocalyptic movie with stunning imagery (cinematography by Jorg Schmidt-Reitwin) that achieves a mystical, surreal power. With Josef Bierbichler, Stefan Guttler, Clemens Scheitz, and Sepp Muller. Music by Popol Vuh. German with English subtitles.

VHS: S17397. $29.95.

Werner Herzog, Germany, 1976, 94 mins.

Herdsmen of the Sun

Herzog's fascination with the natural world at its most enduringly strange led him to the southern Sahara for Herdsmen of the Sun, "a startling anthropological documentary about the nomadic members of the Wodaabe Tribe" (Janet Maslin). Once a year, the men decorate themselves with beads and blue lipstick and festive hats to participate in what amounts to a beauty pageant. French, English and Peul with English subtitles.

VHS: S16054. $59.95.

Werner Herzog, Germany, 1988, 52 mins.

The Mystery of Kaspar Hauser

In 1828, a young man appeared in the town square of Nuremberg, his origins unknown, having apparently been kept in solitary confinement all his life; five years later he was murdered by an unidentified assailant. Kaspar's brief, enigmatic destiny becomes a powerful metaphor for life in Werner Herzog's vision of the extreme edges of existence. Former mental patient Bruno S. delivers a sympathetic and powerful performance. "Herzog achieves a visionary, overcast style" (Pauline Kael, The New Yorker). Also known as Every Man for Himself and God against All. With Walter Ladengast, Brigitte Mira, Hans Musaus and Willy Semmelrogge. German with English subtitles.

VHS: S20303. $29.95.

Werner Herzog, Germany, 1974, 110 mins.

Nosferatu the Vampyre

Herzog's terrific remake of Murnau's 1922 silent original stars Klaus Kinski as the title character and Isabelle Adjani as the beautiful object of his bloodlust, Lucy Parker. This unique film is a must-see for horror fans. German with English subtitles.

Laser: LD76377. $49.95.

Werner Herzog, Germany/France, 1979, 107 mins.

Signs of Life

The breakthrough first feature from Werner Herzog. A young German soldier is stationed on a small Greek island, cut off from the larger traumatic events of the Second World War. The island's beauty tempts him with the promise of peace, but ultimately he cannot accept the potential of this enchanting place. German with English subtitles.

VHS: S26146. $69.95.

Werner Herzog, Germany, 1968, 90 mins.

Stroszek

The adventures of Herzog's alter-ego, Bruno S., continue as a former mental patient and Berlin street singer joins with a whore and an aging eccentric to emigrate to Wisconsin in search of the American dream. "Surprisingly positive, tragicomic, poetic narrative" (Leonard Maltin). With Eva Mattes and Clemens Scheitz. English and German with English subtitles.

VHS: S12826. $29.95.

Werner Herzog, Germany, 1977, 108 mins.

Where the Green Ants Dream

Two tribes of Aborigines, the Wororas and the Riratjingus, preserve their ancient legends, songs and laws of creation in the heart of Australia. They come into conflict with the laws of modern Australia when a large company tries to mine uranium in one of their holy places, the place where the "Green Ants Dream." With Bruce Spence, Wandjuk Marika, Roy Marika. English dialog.

VHS: S07103. $24.95.

Werner Herzog, Germany/Australia, 1985, 99 mins.

Woyzeck

Woyzeck represents one of the most extraordinary events in the history of literature. Written in 1836, just before its author's death at the age of 23, Buchner's drama anticipates by some 50 to 100 years the literary movements of the 20th century. Herzog's version of Woyzeck is a film without shadows. This caustic tragedy of an ordinary man's headlong plunge into madness and murder is filmed with a terrible clarity, punctuated by bursts of unexpected lyricism. In the title role, Klaus Kinski delivers a harrowing and unforgettable performance, as stark and unsentimental as the razor with which the hero carries out his chilling destiny. With Eva Mattes. German with English subtitles.

VHS: S12989. $59.95.

Werner Herzog, Germany, 1978, 82 mins.

WIM WENDERS

The American Friend

Using Patricia Highsmith's novel *Ripley's Game*, Wenders has made a spellbinding existential thriller which moves from the docks of Hamburg to the streets of New York. Dennis Hopper plays the gambler who lures Bruno Ganz deeper and deeper into international intrigue and murder. With cameo appearances by Sam Fuller, Nicholas Ray, Gerard Blain and Daniel Schmid. English and German dialog.

VHS: S00043. $29.95.

Wim Wenders, Germany, 1977, 127 mins.

The End of Violence

Mike (Bill Pullman) is a successful Hollywood producer who makes explosive action blockbusters. Ray (Gabriel Byrne) is a NASA-trained surveillance expert who is engaged in a top-secret FBI project that will place hidden cameras throughout Los Angeles to catch criminals in action. Paige (Andie MacDowell) is Mike's estranged wife, who stands to inherit his empire. When Max himself becomes the victim of violence, their stories converge and collide.

VHS: S33428. $99.99.

Laser: LD76810. $39.99.

Wim Wenders, Germany/USA, 1997, 122 mins.

Faraway, So Close

Otto Sander, Nastassia Kinski, Willem Dafoe and Peter Falk are joined by Lou Reed as himself and a Mikhail Gorbachev look-alike for another angel's view of Berlin. When an angel loses his wings, the temptations of earthly life inevitably tempt Satan and lead to bad memories and gangster inspired violence. English and German with English subtitles.

VHS: S21353. $94.95.

Laser: LD74473. $39.95.

Wim Wenders, Germany, 1993, 146 mins.

Lisbon Story

Wenders' elegiac docudrama is a declaration of love for the city of Lisbon and an elegant play with the camera. Rudiger Volger is Phillip Winter, a soundman who travels to Lisbon at the request of a friend, the elusive and mysterious filmmaker Friedrich Monroe (Patrick Bauchau). When he arrives at Friedrich's flat, he discovers his friend has vanished but left behind some silent footage from a film the two were working on. Phillip strikes up a relationship with a group of Portuguese children and starts to rove the streets of Lisbon to record sound for his friend's images. With an appearance by Manuel de Oliveira. English, German and Portuguese with English subtitles.

VHS: S32681. $89.95.

Wim Wenders, Germany/Portugal, 1994, 100 mins.

Notebook on Cities and Clothes

A provocative documentary by Wim Wenders about high fashion designer Yohji Yamamoto. The film is frequently a passionate and compelling essay about a time (Paris), architecture, language and the creative process. Made during the editing of Wenders' epic *Until the End of the World*. Shot by several cameramen, including Wenders' usual collaborator Robby Muller. Japanese, German, French and English with English subtitles.

VHS: S18192. $59.95.

Wim Wenders, France, 1990, 80 mins.

Paris, Texas

A film by German director Wim Wenders, written by Sam Shepard, photography by Robby Muller, music by Ry Cooder and starring Harry Dean Stanton and Nastassia Kinski! A contemporary story of a man's journey, actual and psychological, to recover his past.

VHS: S00993. $19.98.

Wim Wenders, USA, 1984, 145 mins.

Until the End of the World

Wim Wenders filmed this epic, futuristic drama in fifteen cities in eight countries around the world. The year is 1999. Solveig Dommartin, the enchanting trapeze artist from *Wings of Desire*, pursues William Hurt, who helped himself to stolen money she was guarding for some very nice criminals. She also just might be in love with the mysterious Hurt who is on a secret mission for Max Von Sydow, his even more mysterious father who lives in an underground laboratory in the middle of Australia. Also along for the global chase are boyfriend Sam Neill, and detectives Rudiger Vogler and Ernie Dingo. This ambitious work explores the potential end of the world and the incredible power of our dreams. The tape is presented in a letter-boxed format with Surround Sound and employs state-of-the-art High-Definition video technology.

VHS: S16633. $19.98.

Laser: LD71505. $34.98.

Wim Wenders, France/Germany/Australia, 1991, 178 min.

Wings of Desire

"The first time I saw the film I thought it was a knockout; on second viewing it already seemed a classic," wrote J. Hoberman of Wim Wenders' re-examination of the divided city of Berlin. Daniel, played by Bruno Ganz, is the angel who has grown tired and frustrated at his inability to affect people's lives. When he falls in love with a beautiful trapeze artist, he decides to leave the heavens and enter the mortal world. With incredible cinematography by Henri Alekan, *Wings of Desire* is one of the rare movies of the past decade that actually stretch, break and re-form the boundaries of the medium" (David Denby, *New York Magazine*). German with yellow English subtitles.

VHS: S09593. $19.98.

Wim Wenders, Germany, 1988, 110 mins.

german classics

Alraune (aka Unholy Love)
This silent film is the best of the three versions of this film based on Hanns Heinz Ewer's popular novel about Alraune (Brigitte Helm, *Metropolis*), the offspring of a prostitute artificially inseminated by a mad doctor (Paul Wegener) with the semen of a hanged man. German with English titles.
VHS: S30190. $24.95.
Henrik Galeen, Germany, 1928, 97 mins.

Backstairs
A first-rate example of German Expressionist cinema in the story of a maid who is having an affair with a man who disappears one day without warning and leaves her waiting anxiously for a letter from him. With Henry Porten, Fritz Kortner and William Dieterle. Silent.
VHS: S03344. $29.95.
Leopold Jessner, Germany, 1921, 44 mins.

Barcarole
The remarkable Edwige Feuillere stars as a young man who accepts a wager to seduce a married woman. The plot backfires when he finds himself in love and has to accept the penalty of death rather than betray her. An early film in color. German *without* English subtitles.
VHS: S24129. $29.95.
Gerhard Lamprecht, Germany, 1935, 78 mins.

Baron Munchausen
Only the fourth color film made in Germany, *Munchausen* employs a wide range of sensational special effects which amaze and amuse in the recounting of the adventures of the legendary hero Baron von Munchausen. The action ranges from Venice to St. Petersburg to the moon and back, as the Baron (Hans Albers) travels by horse, balloon and cannonball. The film was recently reconstructed by the Friedrich Murnau Foundation. German with English subtitles.
VHS: S00097. $69.95.
Josef von Baky, Germany, 1943, 110 mins.

Berlin, Symphony of a Great City
Walter Ruttmann's great documentary is a dynamic vision of Berlin, unfolding from dawn until midnight. Ruttmann captured the city's expressive poetry by concealing his camera in vans and suitcases to capture a portrait of the city and its people. Music composed and conducted by Timothy Brock, performed by the Olympia Chamber Orchestra. On the same program is *Opus 1*, a ten-minute essay Ruttman shot in 1922.
VHS: S01931. $24.95.
Walter Ruttmann, Germany, 1927, 62 mins.

The Bird with the Crystal Plumage
An American writer (Tony Musante, TV's *Toma*) traveling in Rome is the only witness to an attempted murder by a sinister man in a raincoat and black leather gloves. When the police fail to make any progress he launches his own personal investigation and nearly loses his life in the process. With Suzy Kendall. Dubbed in English.
VHS: S34290. $19.99.
Dario Argento, Italy/Germany, 1969, 98 mins.

Black Roses
Near the end of her life, Lilian Harvey asked to see only one of her films, *Black Roses*. A search of the major archives turned up nothing, and she was never again to see her favorite work. Set in 1900's Russia, Harvey (a ballerina) must sleep with the Tsarist governor in order to save the life of her true love. Dennis Hoey also stars. Mastered from the only known nitrate print. Produced in Germany in 1935, and then remade in Germany and Great Britain in 1936.
VHS: S10964. $29.95.
Paul Martin, Germany/Great Britain, 1936, 79 mins.

Blue Light
A painter falls in love with a young girl whom the villagers fear as a witch because only she can reach the dangerous mountain peak. When the painter discovers her secret route, she jumps off a cliff. Riefenstahl's first film as director was shot on location and emphasizes the romantic mysticism of the mountains and the transmuting power of nature. The film so impressed Hitler he asked her to make films for the Nazis. Co-scripted by Bela Balasz. German with English subtitles.
VHS: S00159. $29.95.
Leni Riefenstahl, Germany, 1932, 77 mins.

Blum Affair
An important postwar German film, directed by Erich Engel. On the surface a fast-paced exciting thriller, the film reveals the whole horrible relation of fascism, business and anti-Semitism in Germany of the late 20's. An unemployed man kills an accountant for money. He is caught, brought to a police inspector who, it turns out, served in the same *Freikorps* regiment—the murdered man worked for Blum, a Jewish industrialist, who perhaps knew something of tax fraud at the company. The case becomes a right versus left political drama. With Hans Christian Blech, Gisela Trowe, Kurt Ehrhardt. German with English subtitles.
VHS: S06853. $39.95.
Erich Engel, Germany, 1948, 109 mins.

The Broken Jug
Based on the immensely popular comedy by Heinrich von Kleist about a village judge who has his own sense of dispensing justice during the 18th century, this classic production features Emil Jannings, Angela Salloker and Paul Dahlke, and was adapted by Thea von Harbou. German with English subtitles.
VHS: S24126. $29.95.
Gustav Ucicky, Germany, 1935, 82 mins.

The Brothers Schellenberg
In his last German-made film, Conrad Veidt gives a sensitive performance in dual roles as two brothers. The younger brother, a wealthy financier, is a womanizer who nearly ruins a young woman's life. The older brother, a philanthropist, operates a welfare center for needy persons and saves a woman's life. The film tries to depict through realism how miserable life was in the post-war Germany of the early 1920s. With Lil Dagover, Freida Richard and Lianne Haid. Silent, German titles.
VHS: S33058. $24.95.
Karl Grunne, Germany, 1926, 82 mins.

Cabinet of Dr. Caligari
The great Expressionist classic with Werner Krauss as Caligari, the fairground showman who hypnotizes his servant (Conrad Veidt) into committing murder at night. Famous for its distorted painted sets, its grotesque camera angles and its atmospheric horror, this cinematic landmark is now newly mastered from a 35mm archive print with an orchestral score. English intertitles.
VHS: S10765. $29.95.
Laser: LD75516. $49.99.
DVD: DV60034. $29.95.
Robert Wiene, Germany, 1919, 52 mins.

Cafe Electric
In this early silent film Marlene Dietrich plays the daughter of a rich building contractor who slums with her gigolo boyfriend at the Cafe Electric, a hole-in-the-wall joint where prostitutes and pimps gather. With Willi Forst, Fritz Alberti and Anny Coty. German with English titles.
VHS: S33056. $24.95.
Gustav Ucicky, Austria, 1927, 80 mins.

Captain from Koepenick
A big success, this German comedy about a cobbler, who in order to free himself from the dehumanizing effects of petty bureaucracy on the common man impersonates an army officer, is a funny social satire. German with English subtitles.
VHS: S06442. $39.95.
Helmut Kautner, Germany, 1957, 88 mins.

Cesare Borgia
The bloodthirsty reign of Cesare and Lucrezia Borgia is at the center of this long-lost, silent classic film. Conrad Veidt plays one of the descendants of Pope Alexander VI. This ruthless historical character is said to have murdered several people, including his own brother Juan Borgia, and to have committed incest with his sister Lucretia. This careful psychological study of these figures is a thought-provoking examination of greed, lust and evil. Silent with English intertitles.
VHS: S21608. $24.95.
Richard Oswald, Germany, 1923, 83 mins.

Clothes Make the Man
Heinz Ruhmann stars in this Nazi-era feature adapted from a novella by Gottfried Keller about the adventures of a young seamstress in a small town during the Victorian period and her encounters with a tailor who is so well dressed that he's mistaken for a count. Produced in 1940, the film is a rare example of the kind of escapist filmmaking in Nazi Germany. German with English subtitles.
VHS: S24122. $29.95.
Helmut Kautner, Germany, 1940

The Confessions of Felix Krull
Horst Buchholz stars as the charming but devious con-artist who quickly rises in rank as a Parisian hotel employee. A rarely seen adaptation of the famous Thomas Mann novella. Directed by Kurt Hoffman. German with English subtitles.
VHS: S15440. $29.95.
Kurt Hoffman, Germany, 1958, 107 mins.

Congress Dances
Delightful operetta set during the 1815 Congress of Vienna, banned by the Nazis because many of the members of the production crew were Jewish. The film is a fine example of early German sound movie-making. Lilian Harvey plays an ambitious businesswoman who sees potential for financial and romantic opportunities. German with English subtitles.
VHS: S02220. $29.95.
Erik Charell, Germany, 1931, 92 mins.

Danton (aka All for a Woman)
One of the most important achievements of German Expressionism, and one of the rarest, this biographical film about the downfall of the French Revolutionary is particularly notable for its incredible performances from Emil Jannings and Werner Jrauss. With Maly Delschaft, Charlotte Ander and Eduard von Winterstein. English intertitles.
VHS: S30212. $29.95.
Dimitri Buchowetzki, Germany, 1921, 100 mins.

Day of Freedom—Our Fighting Forces
Leni Riefenstahl (*Triumph of the Will*) directs this propaganda documentary on the armed forces of Nazi Germany. Military parades, lots of flags and leaders. Planes fly in a swastika formation. This short film was thought to have been lost. No dialog or narration. Original music score.
VHS: S05504. $19.95.
Leni Riefenstahl, Germany, 1935, 17 mins.

The Day the Sky Exploded
A science fiction spectacular about a missile that explodes in outer space, causing general chaos and an impromptu asteroid shower. Dubbed in English.
VHS: S14669. $29.95.
Paolo Heusch, Germany, 1957, 80 mins.

Der Stern von Africa
The true story of German Luftwaffe World War II Air ace Joachim Marseille, who fought in Africa in an ME 109 fighter against U.S. and British forces. German with English subtitles.
VHS: S32231. $29.95.
Alfred Weidenmann, Germany, 1956, 108 mins.

Der Untertan (The Subject)
Werner Peters and Erich Nadler star in this rarely seen film from post-war Germany. Directed by Wolfgang Staudte. German with English subtitles.
VHS: S15439. $29.95.
Wolfgang Staudte, Germany, 1951

Devil in Silk
This intense psychological thriller concerns a composer who unknowingly marries a fatally jealous woman. In the end he must try to prove to the police that he is innocent when she turns up dead. Dubbed in English.
VHS: S23800. $24.95.
Rolf Hansen, Germany, 1956, 102 mins.

Diary of a Lost Girl
Louise Brooks appears as an innocent girl whose life collapses when she is made pregnant by her father's young assistant. In this follow-up to *Pandora's Box*, Brooks is just as riveting. Unavailable in the U.S. for over 50 years until its theatrical reissue in 1983, this is the most complete version in existence. Piano and jazz ensemble score.
VHS: S00339. $29.95.
G.W. Pabst, Germany, 1929, 100 mins.

Die Deutsche Wochenschau #1 (The German Weekly Newsreel)

Four newsreels from Nazi Germany are presented in this collection now available on video. Combat footage of the Luftwaffe over Greece and Crete. Winter fighting in Finland and Russia. U-Boats in the North Atlantic. Also fabric being made from waste paper. German with no subtitles. WWII as seen from another viewpoint. Germany, 1941, 50 mins.
VHS: S05500. $24.95.

Die Goldene Stadt

Veit Harlan, the notorious Nazi-era director, and Alfred Braun are responsible for this film about a young girl who lives in a small village and dreams of visiting Prague. Her father won't let her go; he wants her to marry Thomas, a noble German farmer boy. With Krista Soderbaum and Rudolf Prack. One of the most interesting examples of entertainment and propaganda under the Nazis. German *without* English subtitles.
VHS: S24128. $29.95.
Veit Harlan, Germany, 1942

Don Quixote

An extremely rare and beautiful film directed by G.W. Pabst (*The Threepenny Opera*) and based on the Cervantes novel. The film, a British production, was shot in Haute-Provence in France, and features the great Russian actor Feodor Chaliapin as well as George Robey and Sidney Fox. Of particular note are Pabst's sequences of tilting at the windmills.
VHS: S06857. $39.95.
G.W. Pabst, Great Britain/France, 1933, 83 mins.

Ecstasy

This unjustly neglected film has suffered from the notoriety of its nude scene with Hedy Lamarr: the Pope denounced it, Hitler banned it, American distributors censored it and Hedy's millionaire German munitions maker husband tried to buy up all the prints and destroy them. Hedy plays a child bride with an impotent husband who has an affair but refuses to go away with her lover when the husband commits suicide. Notable for its use of location sound and its very stylish, lyrical eroticism and images that beg psychoanalytic interpretation. Minimal English dialog.
VHS: S00394. $19.95.
Gustav Machaty, Germany, 1932, 75 mins.

The Eternal Waltz

A candid, forthcoming and fascinating biography of the brilliant composer Johann Strauss, the so-called Waltz King. This German-made work is set off by its stylish decor, elaborate sets, haunting music and excellent performances from Bernhard Wicki, Hilde Krahl and Annemarie Dueringer. 97 mins.
VHS: S17451. $19.95.
Paul Verhoeven, Germany, 1954, 98 mins.

Fahnen Junker

From bayonet fighting to blasting bunkers, glacier climbing to sniper fire, here is the tough training that molded the leaders of Nazi armies. This original 1943 Nazi film depicts the life at German schools for infantry officers. 17 mins. German with English subtitles.
VHS: S08313. $24.95.

Fortune's Fool

Germany's most famous pre-war actor, Emil Jannings, stars in this film about an uneducated butcher who emerges in the chaotic years after World War I to control the meat-packing industry. Silent.
VHS: S01658. $29.95.
Reinhold Schunzel, Germany, 1923

FP-1 Doesn't Answer

This all-German, non-subtitled film starring Hans Albers and a pre-Hollywood Peter Lorre is one of the hardest-to-find Lorre titles in the United States. A pilot is put to the test when Floating Platform 1 (FP-1), a mid-Atlantic fueling station, is threatened by treason. Not to be confused with the English version starring Conrad Veidt.
VHS: S30122. $14.95.
Karl Hartl, Germany, 1932, 74 mins.

Friedemann Bach

This war-time, escapist feature is the rather bizarre story of the eldest son of J.S. Bach, Friedemann. He is a gifted musician, but feels so confined by his autocratic family that he ends up wasting his talent. His life ends tragically, in debauchery and penury. With Gustaf Gundgrens and Eugen Klopfer. German with English subtitles.
VHS: S26065. $29.95.
Traugott Muller, Germany, 1941, 100 mins.

Germany Awake

A documentary on the German motion picture and its use as a tool for propaganda, produced by the great German film historian Erwin Leiser. Among the many feature film excerpts included in this film are *Dawn* (1933), *Jew Suss* (1940), *The Rothschilds* (1940), *The Great King* (1942), and others. English commentary and German with English subtitles.
VHS: S03357. $34.95.
Erwin Leiser, Germany, 1968, 90 mins.

Girl from Flanders

Maximilian Schell, Nicole Berger and Gert Frobe star in this anti-war drama. Schell is a lieutenant sickened by the inanities of war, who finds solace in a young woman. She is a Belgian who detests the German soldiers in her country until she meets this special man. Dubbed in English.
VHS: S23988. $24.95.
Helmut Kautner, Germany, 1956, 91 mins.

The Golden Age of German Cinema

This four-film collection is filled with dazzling imagery and eerie presages of Nazism. (Two of the three directors later worked for Hitler.) Includes Robert Wiene's pioneering expressionist film, *The Cabinet of Dr. Caligari* (1919), with Conrad Veidt; G.W. Pabst's 1927 social decay melodrama, *The Love of Jeanne Ney*; F.W. Murnau's *Faust* (1926) and Walter Ruttmann's *Berlin, Symphony of a Great City* (1927), "the *Koyaanisqatsi* of its day, in which the frenetic rhythm of trains, schoolboys, shop girls and soldiers is brilliantly edited into a tone poem of urban life" (Steven Smith, *Pulse!*). Effectively enhanced with new orchestral scores by composer Timothy Brock.
Laser: LD76000. $99.95.

The Golem

Based on the ancient Jewish legend of the clay figure created by Rabbi Loew in the 16th century to defend the Jews in the Prague ghetto against pogrom. In this great classic famous for its extraordinary crowd scenes and painted sets, the Golem falls in love with the Rabbi's daughter, terrorizes the emperor's court and is subdued by an innocent child. "The alternately terrified and exultant crowd at times recalls the flamboyant outlines and disjointed movement of a painting by El Greco" (Lotte Eisner). With Paul Wegener, Albert Steinbruck and Lyda Salmonova. Silent with music track, English titles.
VHS: S00514. $29.95.
Paul Wegener/Carl Boese, Germany, 1920, 118 mins.

The Green Archer

Well-paced action adapted from the Edgar Wallace novel about a masked archer who eliminates his victims as he baffles police. With Gert Frobe. German with English subtitles.
VHS: S31266. $24.95.
Jurgen Roland, Germany, 1960, 93 mins.

Hamlet

"Dip the flags before her, for she is unique," said the legendary film historian Bela Balasz after seeing Asta Nielsen with her pale face and immense eyes in what is one of the most famous performances on film by this great actress of German expressionism. "In every film this woman who seems the quintessence, the epitome of her era, renews herself. In *Hamlet*, she is as vibrant as a Damascus sabre, the Danish Joan of Arc." Beautiful print. Silent with German intertitles.
VHS: S34254. $24.95.
Sven Gade/Heinz Schall, Germany, 1921, 134 mins.

Homecoming

Joe May's *The Homecoming* was a big success in America, and much of the credit goes to the visionary producer behind this film, as so many other films of the German Expressionist era, Erich Pommer. The story of the film concerns the escape and arduous trek home of two German POW's from a Russian labor camp. Strong performances from Gustav Frolich (Metropolis) and Lars Hanson, as well as Dita Parlo (L'Atalante) as the young wife who welcomes home the wrong man. Silent with English titles.
VHS: S07756. $29.95.
Joe May, Germany, 1928, 74 mins.

The Island of Bliss

A rare production with sets created by the great Max Reinhardt. Directed by Arthur Kahane, this silent film is presented with an accompanying music track. Germany, 1913.
VHS: S15438. $29.95.

Joyless Street

Famous as the film that brought Greta Garbo to international fame, *Joyless Street* draws a powerful depiction of the deteriorating life of the middle class in Austria during the inflationary years. A landmark of the German silent cinema by one of its greatest talents, the film produces "moments of searing pain, mental anguish, and sheer unblemished beauty" (Paul Rotha, *The Film till Now*). Restored with material from the State Museum Munich and Cinematheque Francaise, this version is longer and closer to the original than any available in the U.S. until now. Piano score.
VHS: S01924. $29.95.
G.W. Pabst, Germany, 1925, 96 min.

Jud Suess

Still banned in Germany (except for educational viewings), this scandalous, classic Nazi anti-Semitic propoganda film caused riots at its screenings and disaster for its cast and crew. The Third Reich's most notorious fictional expression of policy, it is the story of a Jew who rises to power under the duchy of Wuerttemberg by abusing and raping Aryans. German with English subtitles.
VHS: S34066. $29.95.
Veit Harlan, Germany, 1940, 100 mins.

Kameradschaft

Based on a true incident, the film depicts a mining disaster on the Franco-German border in 1919, where German miners come to the rescue of their entombed French brothers in defiance of wartime enmities and the interest of their bosses. A daring experience in realistic sound cinema, and a deeply moving assertion of international working class solidarity. German with English subtitles.
VHS: S00669. $39.95.
G.W. Pabst, Germany, 1931, 78 mins.

Kolberg

Commissioned by the Reich Propaganda Minister to "demonstrate…that a people united at home and at the front will overcome the enemy," this bizarre project is based on the resistance of the city of Kolberg to the advance of Napoleon's armies in 1806 and 1807. As the city's military leaders are willing to capitulate, the Mayor sends his father to ask the Queen of Prussia for help while he organizes the citizens into a militia. Goebbels reportedly hoped that *Kolberg* would rival *Gone with the Wind* in grandeur, and so no expense was spared. Ten thousand uniforms were constructed for the film, 200,000 soldiers were withdrawn from service to take part in battle scenes, and trainloads of salt were sent to create snow for several scenes. Ironically, a few days after *Kolberg* opened in the city of Kolberg, Soviet troops entered the city. German with English subtitles.
VHS: S02254. $79.95.
Veit Harlan, Germany, 1945, 99 mins.

The Love of Jeanne Ney

G.W. Pabst's adaptation of Ilya Ehrenberg's novel about Jeanne Ney (Edith Jehanne), a beautiful young German woman who falls in love with the man (Uno Henning) responsible for her father's murder during the Russian Revolution. They marry and resettle in Paris, where they are hounded by an extortionist (Fritz Rasp). With Brigitte Helm. English intertitles.
VHS: S02193. $24.95.
G.W. Pabst, Germany, 1927, 120 mins.

Ludwig II

A penetrating and lively account of the rise and fall of the Bavarian monarch couched between extremes of dream and illogic, with stunning use of Bavarian locations, landscape and architecture. With O.W. Fischer, Ruth Leuwerik and Marianne Koch. German only, with no English subtitles.
VHS: S17230. $39.95.
Erich Kautner, Germany, 1955, 109 mins.

Luis Trenker

A three-part biography of the German actor, producer, novelist and director, using the occasion of his 95th birthday to portray his first break into films, his political persecution, his Hollywood exile, his return to Germany and his continued involvement in the arts. German *without* subtitles.
Part I. 60 mins.
VHS: S17235. $29.95.
Part II. 60 mins.
VHS: S17236. $29.95.
Part III. 60 mins.
VHS: S17237. $29.95.

Luis Trenker Films

Luis Trenker, one of the most prolific and well-known directors, producers and actors of the German sound era, has remained almost unknown in the West until a "Trenker Revival;' at the Telluride Film Festival. This collection of Trenker films is now available in German *without* English subtitles.

His People
In this early drama, Edward Sloman focuses on two sons, Morris the lawyer and Sammy the prizefighter, in lower Manhattan. As both stray from traditions cherished by their first-generation, Russian-immigrant parents, each learns to preserve the family's self-respect. Alternatively titled *Proud Heart, Common People* and *The Jew*. Rudolph Schildkraut, Kate Price, Virginia Brown Faire and Arthur Lubin star. Silent.
VHS: S16314. $72.00.

Der Berg Ruft. Tonio Carrl, an Italian, and Edward Whymer, an Englishman, both want to be the first to climb the Matterhorn. During one attempt, Whymer has an accident, and Tonia saves his life. Later, during another attempt, Wymer gets to the top a few hours before Tonio, but during the descent, three of Whymer's men are fatally injured and Whymer is accused of cutting the rope to save his life. Again, Tonio comes to his rescue. 1937, 95 mins. German *without* English subtitles.
VHS: S07990. $69.95.

Der Feuerteufel. A historical drama about Prussian and Austrian soldiers who fight against Napoleon. A wood cutter from Kaernten becomes a freedom fighter who battles the French Army and the hatred of his compatriots. 1940, 98 mins. German *without* English subtitles.
VHS: S07991. $49.95.

Der Kaiser von Kalifornien. A Luis Trenker film about the pioneering days of the old American west. The story of the Swiss printer Johann Sutter, who settled as a farmer in unknown California, and on whose land gold was first discovered, starting the California gold rush. 1936, 95 mins. German *without* English subtitles.
VHS: S07985. $49.95.

Der Rebell. Luis Trenker stars in this classic patriotic drama, set in 1809. The freedom-loving mountain dwellers of Tyrol are banding together to fight Napoleon's troops, who have overrun their homeland. When Severin Anderlan, one of their own, comes home from the university, he joins them and fights the oppressors to the bitter end. 92 mins. German *without* English subtitles.
VHS: S07987. $69.95.

Der Sohn der Weissen Berge. Hans Turri, the German skiing champion, also works as an Alpine guide. He trains with his comrades for the coming championships, when, just a few days before the event, an engineer named Milacs hires him as a guide. When Turri returns without Milacs, Turri is suspected of murder. Set in the beautiful Swiss Alps. 1930. German *without* English subtitles.
VHS: S07983. $69.95.

Der Verlorene Sohn. Prodigal son story about Tonio, a native son of the Dolomite mountain region, who is catapulted to New York City at the time of the Great Depression. Just as he hits bottom, an old friend discovers and rescues him. Despite his new-found luxury and the affection of his friend's daughter, Tonio returns to his village, his people, and his girl. 90 mins. German *without* English subtitles.
VHS: S07989. $69.95.

Duell in den Bergen. A suspenseful Alpine drama set in the Dolomites. A border patrol officer is sent to a village in the Dolomites to infiltrate a group of dangerous drug smugglers, and a bitter battle erupts between the police and the villains. German *without* English subtitles. 1950.
VHS: S07984. $69.95.

Flucht in die Dolomiten. Luis Trenker and Marianne Holt star in this drama about Giovanni, a family man, who is under suspicion of having killed his brother. He flees his hometown to work at a construction site high up in the Dolomites. Hard and dangerous work are in store for him, but also temptation in the form of a beautiful local girl. His tribulations end when he returns home and learns that he is cleared of the murder charges. 1955, 87 mins. German *without* English subtitles.
VHS: S07988. $69.95.

Im Banne des Monte Miracolo. The Monte Miracolo is reputed to be a cursed mountain, since up to now all attempts to conquer it have failed and resulted in tragedy and death. When two Dutch men succeed in climbing the bewitched mountain for the first time, the spell seems to be broken. Now two engineers who work in the village also plan to climb the mountain, one of whom is experienced and cautious, the other reckless. 85 mins. German *without* English subtitles.
VHS: S07986. $69.95.

Maedchen in Uniform

Legendary film from the German post-Expressionism period, extremely daring for its time in suggesting lesbianism in the story of a young girl whose identity is choked by the authoritarian boarding school she attends. German with English subtitles.
VHS: S02140. $24.95.
Leontine Sagan, Germany, 1931, 87 mins.

Manon Lescaut

Robison (*Warning Shadows*) adapted this film from the tragic romance by Abbe Prevost and the opera by Massenet in one of the rarest achievements of the German silent era. With Lya de Putti and Marlene Dietrich. German with English titles.
VHS: S30197. $24.95.
Arthur Robinson, Germany, 1926, 39 mins.

Men Against Tanks/ Engineers to the Front

A Nazi-produced documentary, as German soldiers re-enact combat exploits for this elaborate and frightening film showing how infantrymen battle Soviet armored attacks. In *Engineers to the Front*, German engineer/soldiers—the men who paved the way for the blitzkrieg—lift mines, build bridges and force river crossings under fire. 58 mins. German with English subtitles.
VHS: S08312. $39.95.

Morgenrot

The grim reality of World War I is the subject of this rare film, produced just before Hitler's ascension to power, which tells the story of a German U-boat and its crew in the struggle against the might of England's sea power. An uncertain blend of pacifism and patriotism, the submarine's sinking of a British cruiser leads to sympathy for the lives of the drowned enemy sailors among family members of the U-boat back in Germany, as the film reflects the changing values in post-war Germany. Rudolf Forester and Adele Sandrick star. German *without* English subtitles.
VHS: S07982. $49.95.
Gustav Ucicky, Germany, 1933, 75 mins.

Mother Krausen's Journey into Happiness

One of the earliest and most visually striking of the German Neo-Realist films based on a Marxist thesis, this film, based on the reminiscences of the Berlin artist Heinrich Zille, is a tragic tale of misery and unhappiness in the Berlin slums and their effect on one house, leading to prison and suicide. German titles.
VHS: S30213. $29.95.
Piel Jutzi, Germany, 1929, 120 mins.

Murderers Are Among Us

A woman returns from her internment in a concentration camp only to find her Berlin apartment occupied by a young doctor. Both end up living there, leading to a complicated series of attachments. The doctor is especially problematic. He is traumatized by his wartime experiences and decides to seek revenge against a former superior. Stars Hildegard Knef and Ernst Wilhelm Borchert. German with English subtitles.
VHS: S29869. $39.95.
Wolfgang Staudte, Germany, 1946, 84 mins.

My Song Goes 'Round the World

The British title of *The Joseph Schmidt Story*, this is the last film done in Germany by the prolific director Richard Oswald. Starring Joseph Schmidt and Charlotte Anders. German with English subtitles.
VHS: S02933. $39.95.
Richard Oswald, Germany, 1934

The Old and the Young King

Emil Jannings stars in this elaborate historical drama about the conflict between Frederick William I of Prussia, whose only love is for his army, and his young and brilliant son, Frederick the Great. German with English subtitles.
VHS: S24124. $29.95.
Hans Steinhoff, Germany, 1935, 88 mins.

Olympia: Festival of Beauty

Part Two of Riefenstahl's extraordinary film about the 1936 Olympics. Engrossingly beautiful, the film provides a glimpse of the Nazi mystique and idealization of the youthful male body. English dialog.
VHS: S00955. $29.95.
Leni Riefenstahl, Germany, 1936, 97 mins.

Olympia: Festival of the People

Leni Riefenstahl was given unlimited resources and full artistic freedom to produce this film of the 1936 Olympic Games in Berlin. *Festival of the People* is Part One. Famous sequences include the men's diving competition, Jesse Owen's sprint races and Riefenstahl's use of telephoto lenses and slow motion. English dialog.
VHS: S00956. $29.95.
Leni Riefenstahl, Germany, 1936, 115 mins.

Olympia: Parts One and Two

Leni Riefenstahl's films of the 1936 Olympic Games in Berlin: *Festival of the People* and *Festival of Beauty*. English dialog.
Laser: LD76220. $99.95.
Leni Riefenstahl, Germany, 1936, 212 mins.

Opium

Causing something of a sensation when first exhibited in Berlin, this long-lost, early silent film deals with the problems and perils of narcotics addiction. Of special note are the scenes that depicted the debauchery of sex and drugs. Conrad Veidt gives a remarkable portrayal of a man who is so consumed by sex that it leads to his tragic death. With Werner Krauss, Eduard von Winterstein and Hanna Ralph. Silent with German titles.
VHS: S33057. $24.95.
Robert Reinert, Germany, 1919, 112 mins.

Orphan Boy of Vienna

Wonderful schmaltz in this story of an orphan boy who is fortunate enough to be accepted by the famous Vienna Choir Boys and finds there the maternal love he lacked in the person of Sister Maria. German with English subtitles, 87 mins.
VHS: S03343. $59.95.

The Oyster Princess

This witty satire on the American businessman and the Prussian aristocracy tells the story of Ossi (Ossi Oswalda), whose American "Oyster King" father promises to buy her a prince to marry. The victim recommended by their marriage broker is Prince Nucki, who lives in a run-down apartment with his friend Josef. What follows is one of the most lavish weddings ever filmed, but the wedding night is not at all what the "princess" had in mind. With Harry Liedtke, Viktor Janson, Julius Falkenstein and Curt Bois. Silent with English intertitles. "A summoning up of everything Lubitsch had learned about the art of comedy" (Herman G. Weinberg, in *The Lubitsch Touch*).
VHS: S30211. $29.95.
Ernst Lubitsch, Germany, 1919, 70 mins.

Pandora's Box

G.W. Pabst's baroque interpretation of Wedekind's *Lulu* plays is an eerie depiction of erotic obsession and sexual abandon. The action moves between Berlin and London, as Lulu (Louise Brooks), a beautiful, charismatic chorus girl, orchestrates a succession of casual affairs until her fateful encounter with Jack the Ripper. With Fritz Kortner, Franz Lederer and Carl Goetz. Silent with music track. English titles.
VHS: S00990. $24.95.
G.W. Pabst, Germany, 1928, 110 mins.

Paracelsus

An interesting film directed by G.W. Pabst, unfortunately not available in a subtitled version. Paracelsus is named the head physician of Basel and orders the city gates to be closed against the plague. He heals the dancer Fliegenbein of the plague, but the authorities don't approve of his healing methods, seek to arrest him, and Fliegenbein helps Paracelsus escape. German *without* English subtitles.
VHS: S07981. $49.95.
G.W. Pabst, Germany, 1943, 100 mins.

The Phoney American

Also known as *Toller Hecht Auf Krummer Tour* and *It's A Great Life*, William Bendix, Christine Kaufmann and Ron Randell star in this charming comedy about a German orphan raised by a masquerading air force pilot. Bendix is great as a blustery but ultimately kind-hearted sergeant. German with English subtitles.
VHS: S23901. $29.95.
Akos Von Ratony, Germany, 1961, 74 mins.

Punishment Battalion 999

Based on the novel by Heinz G. Konsalik, this acclaimed film tells the story of soldiers who are punished by the High Command for ordering retreats to save men's lives and working too hard to discover an anti-gangrene serum. Noted for its unflinching, nightmarish realism, this U.S.-distributed war film is unusual because of its Eastern Front setting. Features Werner Peters, George Thomas and Sonja Ziemann. German with English subtitles.
VHS: S28522. $29.95.
Harald Philipp, Germany, 1959, 103 mins.

Rebel Flight to Cuba

This gem is the inspiration behind the 70's Airport disaster/comedy films. A priest, a minister, a rabbi, an unhappy rich countess, a quibbling couple, a Nazi fugitive and a pregnant woman are just some of the characters that provoke inane subplots and love triangles. The supercool hero even chain smokes. Dubbed in English.
VHS: S22470. $29.95.
Gottfried Reinhardt, Germany, 1959, 90 mins.

Romance in a Minor Key

A wartime feature, this escapist drama stars Marianne Hoppe and Paul Dahlke in the story of a husband who discovers that his wife has somehow acquired a very valuable pearl necklace. A rare example of feature filmmaking under the Nazi regime. German with English subtitles.
VHS: S24120. $29.95.
Helmut Kautner, Germany, 1943

Sacred Mountain/White Flame

Two famous short films by director Riefenstahl. Tremendous music and dance sequences, as well as fluid camera shots of idyllic natural settings. Silent with English subtitles. Music track.
VHS: S01146. $34.95.
Leni Riefenstahl, Germany, 1931, 60 mins.

Secrets of a Soul
A professor is driven into a state of terror by a dream in which he attempts to stab his wife, in this remarkable Expressionist feature, which uses Freud's theories of psychoanalysis to depict the professor's dreams. Superimpositions, symbolic images of razors and knives and menacing shadows create a demented world. With Werner Krauss and Jack Trevor. Silent with music track, English intertitles.
VHS: S03701. $19.95.
G.W. Pabst, Germany, 1926, 94 mins.

Shattered
One of the key films of the German *kammerspiel* movement, this silent work chronicles the tragic repercussions of a furtive love affair between a railway worker's daughter (Edith Posca) and her father's supervisor (Werner Krauss). "This grim, small-scale film…is sparse, naturalistic, dealing in a minimum number of characters and observing the unities of time, place and action" (*The Faber Companion to Foreign Films*). With Paul Otto.
VHS: S19598. $39.95.
Lupu Pick, Germany, 1921, 62 mins.

The Ship of Lost Men
Available for the first time in the United States, this silent film starring Marlene Dietrich and Fritz Kortner is the story of a daring airline pilot who crash-lands in the Atlantic Ocean and is rescued by a strange ship housing a crew of escaped criminals and other dangerous characters.
VHS: S30790. $19.95.
Maurice Tourneur, Germany, 1929, 97 mins.

Stop Train 349 (Delay at Marienborn)
Sean Flynn, Jose Ferrer and Nicole Courcel are featured in this thriller. Aboard an American train going from Berlin to the Western Zone is an East German stowaway. The Russians find out and try to stop the train, setting off a battle between the Commies and the good guys.
VHS: S23323. $24.95.
Rolf Hadrich, Germany/Italy/France, 1963, 92 mins.

Street
Classic drama inaugurated an entire series of German films, known as street films, which explore the allures and dangers of city life. Remarkable for its expressionistic lighting, photography, and hallucinatory images of crowds, fireworks, and autos. Silent.
VHS: S01268. $29.95.
Karl Grune, Germany, 1923, 87 mins.

The Student of Prague (1913)
One of the earliest, most important films in the history of silent German cinema, the film incorporates the myths of the Doppelganger, the Faust legend and the shattered mirror image; often considered the first film to incorporate Expressionist means. Silent with English subtitles.
VHS: S01274. $29.95.
Stellan Rye, Germany, 1913, 45 mins.

The Student of Prague (1926)
Conrad Veidt stars in this haunting tale about an unscrupulous student in the mysterious Czech capital. He is intrigued by that which the devil offers him and decides to sell his soul. Germany, 1926, 84 mins. Silent with English intertitles.
VHS: S23850. $24.95.

The Threepenny Opera (1931)
Lotte Lenya plays Jenny in this famous adaptation of Bertolt Brecht/Kurt Weill's play, freely based on John Gay's *Beggar's Opera*. In London at the turn of the century the best friend of a police chief, the bandit Mack the Knife, marries Polly without the knowledge of her father, Peachum, the king of the beggars, and thus starts a conflict between the beggars and the thieves. A newly remastered version. German with English subtitles.
VHS: S21186. $39.95.
Laser: LD70797. $39.95.
G.W. Pabst, Germany, 1931, 114 mins.

The Threepenny Opera (1962)
A lively adaptation of the famous Brecht/Weill musical. This popular version stars Curt Jergens, Gert Frobe, Hildegard Knef and, believe it or not, Sammy Davis, Jr. In English.
VHS: S14661. $29.95.
Wolfgang Staudte, Germany/France, 1962, 124 mins.

Tiefland
Based on the libretto for D'Abert's opera, Riefenstahl directs and plays a gypsy dancer. Filmed largely between 1940 and 1945, Riefenstahl worked slowly to avoid working on any political films. Released successfully in 1954. German with English subtitles.
VHS: S01343. $34.95.
Leni Riefenstahl, Germany, 1940-45, 98 mins.

Titanic
The anti-British propaganda film that Goebbels banned from Germany to avoid a panic. A spectacular depiction of the *Titanic*'s disastrous voyage, depicting the stories of many passengers, including the British shipowner whose greed is responsible for the disaster, and the ship's German first officer, who tries to forestall it. Scenes of the sinking were used uncredited in the 1958 British film, *A Night to Remember*. German dialog, no English subtitles.
VHS: S33328. $39.95.
Herbert Selpin/Werner Klingler, Germany, 1943, 90 mins.

Triumph of the Will
Enormously controversial film record of a Nazi party solidarity rally at Nuremberg in 1934, crafted by Riefenstahl in her second directorial assignment. A fascinating lesson in the methods used by the Nazis to inspire national support. German with English subtitles.
VHS: S18194. $29.95.
Leni Riefenstahl, Germany, 1936, 80 mins.

Two Stars in the Galaxy
A rare Cinderella-story, Hollywood-style silent Chinese musical. With Chinese and German titles.
VHS: S33932. $24.95.
China, 1931, 88 mins.

Under the Bridge
This 1945 German feature is the story of two bargemen on the River Havel who falls in love with the same woman. With Carl Raddatz, Gustav Knuth and Hannelore Schroth. German with English subtitles.
VHS: S24121. $29.95.
Helmut Kautner, Germany, 1945

Variety
A guided tour through the decadence of postwar Germany, with Emil Jannings as an acrobat, Lya de Putti as his wife, and Werner Krauss, a famous acrobat who seduces the wife and drives the acrobat to suicide. German with English subtitles.
VHS: S01408. $29.95.
E.A. Dupont, Germany, 1925, 79 mins.

Warning Shadows
Directed by Arthur Robinson, an American who lived and worked in Germany during the 1920's, *Warning Shadows* is one of the famous examples of Expressionist cinema. Paul Rotha described the film, which is the story of a count bitterly jealous of his wife, as "a remarkable achievement. Its purely psychological direction, its definite completeness of time and action, its intimate ensemble were new attributes of the cinema. It was a rare instance of complete filmic unity." Extremely rare. Silent with music track.
VHS: S03345. $29.95.
Arthur Robinson, Germany, 1922, 60 mins.

Waxworks
Starring three of Germany's greatest actors of the silent period, *Waxworks* creates a fantastic atmosphere through curiously deformed lighting effects. A poet sees wax figures at a fair and dreams about Jack the Ripper, Ivan the Terrible and an Oriental despot. Silent.
VHS: S01432. $29.95.
Paul Leni, Germany, 1924, 63 mins.

Weird Tales
This extremely rare film from prolific Expressionist-era director Richard Oswald (father of famed director Gerd Oswald) stars Conrad Veidt and Anita Berber in a compilation of stories, including Poe's *The Black Cat*. An early example of the fascination of silent-era German filmmakers with tales of horror and the occult.
VHS: S30121. $14.95.
Richard Oswald, Germany, 1919

Westfront 1918
The life and death of four German soldiers on the French front during the final months of World War I. One of the finest war films ever made, it has little dialog but tremendous use of natural sounds. German with no subtitles.
VHS: S03702. $29.95.
G.W. Pabst, Germany, 1930, 98 mins.

The White Flame
Leni Riefenstahl, the famed German filmmaker from the Nazi era, also made a number of fascinating silent films. This is one. It falls within that uniquely German genre, the Mountain film, and concerns ski racing. English intertitles.
VHS: S23854. $24.95.
Leni Riefenstahl, Germany, 1921, 30 mins.

White Hell of Pitz Palu
An extremely rare film by G.W. Pabst made at the end of the silent era, and a unique obsession with the German obsession during the 20's with idealized mountain films that "were both brilliant documentaries and first-rate melodramas, with very definite if embryonic propaganda content. They were the inspiration and largely the monopoly of Dr. Arnold Fanck, a former geologist who translated his great passion for the mountains into film….*The White Hell of Pitz Palu* was the last of the great silent German mountain films, and one of the best and most successful. Most of the film was shot under freezing conditions and other hardships during a five-month location trip to the 12,000 foot high Pitz Palu, in the Bernina group of the Alps" (William Everson). Complete with alternate ending. Silent with English titles. At 24 fps.
VHS: S11450. $24.95.
G.W. Pabst/Arnold Fanck, Germany, 1929, 95 mins.

Wilhelm Tell
Conrad Veidt stars in this extremely rare, silent German adaptation of the famous story of William Tell, his fight for freedom and his shooting of the apple. William Dieterle, later to become a Hollywood director, appears as an actor in a secondary role. Silent with German and English intertitles.
VHS: S21610. $24.95.

Woman Men Yearn For
A rare and virtually unclassifiable 1928 German silent film with Marlene Dietrich as a beautiful and beguiling temptress. A recently married man falls in love with a woman he sees on a train and gets tangled in a web of murder. With German title cards, though the narrative is simple to follow.
VHS: S17692. $49.95.

FRITZ LANG

The Big Heat
Classic film noir from Fritz Lang. Ruthless criminals, an honest cop, sultry women and a gripping plot are the elements that make up *The Big Heat*. Glenn Ford stars in Lang's best postwar film, with Lee Marvin as a nasty bad guy and a fine performance by Gloria Grahame as his shallow but wily moll.
VHS: S00130. $59.95.
Fritz Lang, USA, 1953, 90 mins.

Clash by Night
Barbara Stanwyck and Paul Douglas head a stellar cast consisting of Robert Ryan, Marilyn Monroe and Keith Andes in the screen version of the Clifford Odets play. Stanwyck returns to the love of a simple fisherman, but it's clear she isn't satisfied with her lot in life, a fact of which the cynical Robert Ryan takes advantage. The resulting melodrama offers competing romantic attractions and tragic results.
VHS: S29444. $19.98.
Fritz Lang, USA, 1952, 105 mins.

Cloak and Dagger
Gary Cooper confronts a maze of intrigue behind enemy lines in World War II Nazi Germany. A tense drama with great performances. With Lilli Palmer. English dialog.
VHS: S03502. $59.95.
Laser: LD71456. $29.98.
Fritz Lang, USA, 1946, 106 mins.

Crimes of Dr. Mabuse
Lang's horror classic is one of the best "mad doctor" movies ever made—the supernatural fantasy about the evil Dr. Mabuse, who terrorizes a German city. With Rudolph Klein Rogge, Oskar Beregi, Camilla Spira and Theodor Loos. Dubbed in English.
VHS: S32567. $24.95.
Fritz Lang, Germany, 1932, 80 mins.

Destiny
Lang's first critical success, also known as *Between Two Worlds* or *Beyond the Wall*, an allegory about a confrontation between Death and a girl's love and devotion. Lang here reveals his mastery of the medium, particularly in the architectural design in the film. Silent.
VHS: S00327. $29.95.
Fritz Lang, Germany, 1921, 95 mins.

Doctor Mabuse

The original, five-hour German version of Lang's highly influential and inventive classic, written by his wife, Thea von Harbou. The film follows the life of crime of raving, gambling, mastermind villain Mabuse (Rudolf Klein-Rogge), whose organization victimizes well-to-do post-war German society. Through hypnosis, Mabuse plays with the fate of his mistress, a public prosecutor, a Countess and her husband, using them for his plan of creative destruction. A pulp-sensation melodrama combined with skillful staging, structuring and social commentary that raises the film above the limitations of the genre. Silent with English titles.

VHS: S34552. $29.95.
Fritz Lang, Germany, 1922, 300 mins.

Dr. Mabuse, the Gambler, Part I

An exciting thriller and social commentary about the evil machinations of the criminal mastermind Mabuse, who in his drive for power manipulates his victims and battles a tenacious investigator. Silent.

VHS: S00363. $29.95.
Fritz Lang, Germany, 1922, 120 mins.

Dr. Mabuse, the Gambler, Part II

Part II, known as *The Inferno*, continues the story of the evil Dr. Mabuse and his attempts on the life of the public prosecutor. The state of upheaval in the world at the time is clearly manifested in the depiction of the police attack on Mabuse's house. Silent.

VHS: S00364. $29.95.
Fritz Lang, Germany, 1922, 122 mins.

Dr. Mabuse, the Gambler, Parts I & II

The set.

VHS: S05400. $59.90.
Fritz Lang, Germany, 1922

The Fatal Passion of Dr. Mabuse

Dr. Mabuse was Lang's super-villain, master of disguise, hypnosis, and deception, who created evil for evil's sake. This Lang's own condensed version of his original two-part epic.

VHS: S05958. $29.95.
Fritz Lang, 1922, Germany, 90 mins.

Fury

Fritz Lang's first Hollywood film after fleeing Nazi Germany is a powerful indictment of mob violence in America. Lang includes some real footage of a 1934 lynching, making *Fury* a frightening document as well as a compelling melodrama. Spencer Tracy portrays a gas station owner who, by a series of coincidences, is accused of a kidnapping and becomes the target of an angry mob which attempts to lynch him and eventually burns down the jailhouse. With Sylvia Sidney and Walter Brennan.

VHS: S15026. $19.98.
Fritz Lang, USA, 1936, 89 mins.

Hangmen Also Die

A great American film by Fritz Lang. Brian Donlevy is the assassin who murders Heydrich, the Nazi ruler of Czechoslovakia, in this deeply-felt, anti-Nazi, Hollywood film. The script was co-written by Lang with Bertolt Brecht, the cinematography is by the great James Wong Howe, music by Hans Eisler.

VHS: S13051. $24.95.
Fritz Lang, USA, 1943, 131 mins.

House by the River

One of Lang's favorite themes was the ruinous effect of a man's lust for a woman. In *House by the River*, a man kills his maid and implicates his own brother in the crime. With Louis Hayward and Lee Bowman.

VHS: S00586. $29.95.
Fritz Lang, USA, 1950, 88 mins.

The Indian Tomb

One of Germany's great adventure films of the late '50s, this second part of Lang's *The Tiger of Eschnapur* follows Berger and Seetha as they flee from the maharaja's palace. They are betrayed and captured and must face the cruelties of the court. German without English subtitles.

VHS: S31638. $79.95.
Fritz Lang, Germany, 1959, 102 mins.

Kriemhilde's Revenge

The second part of Fritz Lang's *Die Nibelungen* focuses on the hero's widow and her attraction to Attila the Hun. Kriemhilde (Margarete Schon) conspires with Attila to invite Gunther (Theodor Loos) and Hagen (Hans Adalbert Schlettow)—her husband's killers—to a banquet that ends up in a bloodbath. Film critic and director Luc Moullet wrote, "The climax is a long battle lasting three-quarters of an hour with encirclements and identical attacks, defenses against the encirclements, and renewed attacks. Lang creates shots with different details and builds a rhythm of variations. It is [at] the same time vehement, dynamic and the opposite." Remastered from a 35mm archive print; organ score.

VHS: S00693. $24.95.
Fritz Lang, Germany, 1924, 90 mins.

Liliom

Fritz Lang, in his first film in exile from Nazi Germany, teamed up with Franz Waxman and Charles Boyer under the producer Erich Pommer in this rare fantasy, the story of a lowlife carnival barker who is given a second chance to help his family after his own death. The film was released in the U.S. in a version cut by 30 minutes, but this is the un-cut, French release version, un-subtitled, but with the story easy to follow. French with no English subtitles.

VHS: S08336. $39.95.
Fritz Lang, France, 1935, 120 mins.

M

A series of schoolgirls are murdered by a psychopath who terrorizes a large city and is hunted by the police through a network of beggars. Inspired by the real-life "vampire of Dusseldorf," Fritz Lang's great film is one of the key films of German Expressionism. Peter Lorre's performance as the murderer is one of the great screen performances of all time. German with English subtitles.

VHS: S00787. $19.95.
Laser: LD76405. $49.95.
Fritz Lang, Germany, 1931, 95 mins.

Metropolis

A newly mastered version of Fritz Lang's great masterpiece, the first classic of the science fiction genre. His depiction of a giant city controlled by an authoritarian industrialist who lives in a paradise-like garden while the workers live and struggle in subterranean sections of the city was as important for its vision of man in the service of those who control technology as for its implicit and moving social message. "A brilliant piece of expressionist design…with moments of almost incredible beauty and power" (Pauline Kael). Silent with music score.

VHS: S10764. $29.95.
Fritz Lang, Germany, 1926, 90 mins.

Ministry of Fear

Ray Milland, released from a mental hospital, becomes the victim of a Nazi spy ring. His life is threatened along with his sanity in this shocker. With Marjorie Reynolds.

VHS: S33914. $14.98.
Fritz Lang, USA, 1944, 87 mins.

Moonfleet

Lang's only feature shot in Cinemascope. Set in Dorset in 1770, a young orphan discovers his guardian is actually a black marketeer who leads a gang of ruthless smugglers. The film is set off by Lang's eye for expressive photography and baroque decor. With Stewart Granger, Jon Whiteley, George Sanders and Joan Greenwood. Letterboxed.

Laser: LD70007. $34.98.
Fritz Lang, USA, 1955, 87 mins.

The Return of Frank James

An early color work by Fritz Lang in his second collaboration with Henry Fonda (*You Only Live Once*), who returns from his role in the 1939 *Jesse James* in this mythic, unsettling and poetic western about a man's determination to avenge his brother's murder. With Gene Tierney, Jackie Cooper and Henry Hull.

VHS: S02368. $14.98.
Fritz Lang, USA, 1940, 92 mins.

Scarlet Street

A great film noir thriller. Edward G. Robinson is the little store cashier who becomes infatuated with and eventually kills a whore (Joan Bennett) and then allows her pimp boyfriend (Dan Duryea) to be executed for the crime. Based on Jean Renoir's *La Chienne* (1931); one of Lang's best works, with brilliant cinematography of New York at night by Milton Krasner.

VHS: S01166. $19.95.
Fritz Lang, USA, 1945, 105 mins.

Secret Beyond the Door

A Freudian psycho-thriller about a husband, obsessed by the connection between architecture and death, who collects rooms where murders have been committed and adds them to his mansion. Fascinating. With Joan Bennett and Michael Redgrave.

VHS: S01172. $19.98.
Fritz Lang, USA, 1948, 99 mins.

Siegfried

The first part of Fritz Lang's *Die Nibelungen*. *Siegfried* concerns one man's heroic efforts to slay an imposing dragon in order to capture the hand of the King's beautiful sister. "*Siegfried* is dominated by architectural structures that often reduce the characters to decorative elements against landscapes or vast buildings. Lang's decorative compositions seem often like frozen bits of life, as if any movement would disturb the geometry" (Georges Sadoul, *Dictionary of Films*). Organ score. Nine of the ten reels of this version were transferred in color from an original tinted print. English inter-titles.

VHS: S01198. $24.95.
Fritz Lang, Germany, 1924, 100 mins.

Spiders

Considered by many to be the real beginning of the golden age of German silent film, Fritz Lang's adventure story is about an organized band of criminals who scheme to dominate the world. Combining a labyrinth of plots with actual exotic locations, Lang succeeded in creating a highly entertaining film, which was reconstructed over a three year period by film historians David and Kimberly Shepard, using original German censorship records and Lang's own instructions for color tinting. Silent with music track.

VHS: S08945. $29.95.
Fritz Lang, Germany, 1919, 137 mins.

Spies (Spione)

Produced just after his epic *Metropolis*, Fritz Lang's *Spies* continues the director's fascination with futuristic technology, expressionistic design and sweeping adventure. Agent #326, Donald Tremaine, leads an army of government operatives in a last ditch effort to destroy the ruthless plans of Haghi, a wheelchair-bound, criminal mastermind whose goal is no less than world domination. Laced with stunning plot twists, seductive femme fatales and an arsenal of imaginative gadgetry, *Spies* was the first true spy movie.

VHS: S01240. $29.95.
Fritz Lang, Germany, 1928, 88 mins.

The Testament of Dr. Mabuse

Although confined to a mental institution, the arch-criminal Dr. Mabuse uses his hypnotic powers to operate his plan for world domination. He is finally defeated by Inspector Lohmann (who hunted Peter Lorre in *M* just the year before). Mabuse's mouthing of Nazi platitudes and Lang's depiction of him were too close for comfort, and Joseph Goebbels asked him to change the last reel, offering him leadership of the German film industry. Instead, Lang left his wife (Thea von Harbou, who had by then joined the Nazi party) and fled Germany overnight. German with English subtitles.

VHS: S04915. $24.95.
Fritz Lang, Germany, 1933, 120 mins.

The Thousand Eyes of Dr. Mabuse (Eyes of Evil)

The last film of Fritz Lang spawned more sequels to the character of the master criminal he created in his early films. In this low-budget classic Gert Frobe (*Goldfinger*) is investigating the mysterious murders in the Hotel Luxor in Berlin, which is filled with hidden cameras and two-way mirrors. With Dawn Addams, Peter Van Eyck and Wolfgang Preiss. Dubbed in English. B&W.

VHS: S07075. $29.95.
Fritz Lang, France/Italy/Germany, 1960, 103 mins.

The Tiger of Eschnapur

This exciting first of two adventure films set in India marked Fritz Lang's return to Germany. Berger, a young engineer, falls desperately in love with Seetha, a beautiful temple dancer coveted by the Maharaja, forcing Berger and Seetha to attempt to escape. While the exteriors were shot in India, the interiors were all studio sets, yet Lotte Eisner found the film was notable for its "formal perfection, the masterly use of decor and spatial structures." Based on a script written by Lang and Thea von Harbou in 1920. German without English subtitles.

VHS: S31637. $79.95.
Fritz Lang, Germany, 1956, 101 mins.

Western Union

A great film, and one of the very best Westerns. Fritz Lang directed Robert Young, Randolph Scott, Dean Jagger, Virginia Gilmore in the complex story about the pioneer progress of telegraphic communication across Indian country from Omaha to Salt Lake City. Based on a Zane Grey novel.

VHS: S11192. $39.98.
Fritz Lang, USA, 1941, 90 mins.

Woman in the Moon

Probably the most realistic expedition to the moon prior to 1969, Fritz Lang's great science fiction epic is based on a melodramatic script by Lang and his wife Thea von Harbou. Much of it deals with the conflicts among the crew of the rocket on its way to the Moon. But the real stars are the imaginative sets, special effects and expressive photography, which incorporates work by the pioneer animator Oskar Fischinger, with such prophetic details as multi-stage rockets, weightlessness and the first countdown! Silent with music score, English titles.

VHS: S01476. $29.95.
Fritz Lang, Germany, 1929, 148 mins.

The Woman in the Window

Edward G. Robinson stars as a naive college professor whose research into criminal behavior leads him to a chance acquaintance with a beautiful woman, Joan Bennett, which, in turn, leads to murder and blackmail. This tense melodrama has a sinister feel nicely offset with intriguing psychological motifs and is often seen as a companion piece to Lang's *Scarlet Street*. Raymond Massey is also featured.

VHS: S27749. $19.98.
Laser: LD76098. $39.98.
Fritz Lang, USA, 1944, 99 mins.

You and Me

One of Fritz Lang's most fascinating films. A romantic crime story laced with comedy and social commentary, as well as choral sequences. Ex-convict parolees Joe Dennis (George Raft) and Helen (Sylvia Sidney) work in Mr. Morris' department store. When Joe's parole is up, he plans to leave for California, but falls in love with Helen, unaware of her prison record.
VHS: S33916. $14.98.
Fritz Lang, USA, 1938, 94 mins.

FRIEDRICH MURNAU

The Burning Soil

This extremely rare film by Murnau is a dramatically adventuresome story of peasants and the land. Wladimir Gaidarow is a proud, ambitious man who becomes secretary to a Count (Werner Krauss). He moves his affections from the Count's daughter (Lya de Putti) to the Count's young second wife (Stella Arbenina) when he realizes she will inherit an estate which stands on a petroleum oil field. Silent with English titles.
VHS: S30205. $24.95.
Friedrich W. Murnau, Germany, 1922, 98 mins.

City Girl

An extremely rare film by Friedrich Murnau, made during his tenure in Hollywood. Originally made as a silent film under the title Our Daily Bread, it was shortened by Fox, the producers, and a soundtrack added, then released in 1930 under the title City Girl. The film, often compared favorably with Sunrise, was shot by Ernest Palmer, and revolves around the intertwined lives of wheat farmers. Silent, music track.
VHS: S02088. $39.95.
Friedrich W. Murnau, USA, 1928, 89 mins.

Faust

Murnau's last German production before going to Hollywood is a lavish one, inspired by Romantic painters like Caspar David Friedrich. Gosta Ekman is the elderly professor who sells his soul to the devil, Emil Jannings plays Mephistopholes and Camilla Horn is Marguerite. This version is mastered from a restored print. Silent with music track, English intertitles.
VHS: S00437. $29.95.
Friedrich W. Murnau, Germany, 1926, 117 mins.

Haunted Castle

An early Expressionist horror/mystery, set in a northern German castle shrouded in a moody atmosphere. The complicated plot involves disguises, jealousies, forbidding dreams and murders. Silent with music track.
VHS: S00547. $34.95.
Friedrich W. Murnau, Germany, 1921, 56 mins.

The Last Laugh

One of the major works of German silent cinema, Murnau's class drama depicts the fall of the respected, aging, hotel doorman (Emil Jannings) of a posh Berlin hotel, who is cruelly stripped of his position and reduced to a bathroom attendant. The film was groundbreaking for its expressive, mobile camera work, which imparts information visually, without subtitles. "The camera on a trolley glides, rises, zooms, or weaves where the story takes it. The camera takes part in the action and becomes a character in the drama" (Marcel Carne). With Max Hiller, Maly Delschaft and Hans Unterkirchen.
VHS: S00723. $24.95.
Laser: Includes new orchestral score. **LD72446. $49.95.**
Friedrich W. Murnau, Germany, 1924, 91 mins.

Nosferatu

One of Murnau's best known films, Nosferatu's eerie telling of the Dracula story was filmed on location in the mountains, towns, and castles of Bavaria. This German Expressionist symphony of horror is brilliantly infused with the subtle tones of nature: both pure and fresh, as well as twisted and sinister. Newly restored and color tinted, this version was remastered from a 35mm negative and includes recently discovered scenes and inter-titles freshly translated from the original German script. At 84 minutes, it is the most complete version available on home video.
VHS: S15038. $29.95.
DVD: DV60031. $29.95.
Friedrich W. Murnau, Germany, 1922, 84 mins.

Nosferatu: The First Vampire

Digitally remastered version of Murnau's Nosferatu: A Symphony of Horror, hosted by David Carradine, with music by Type O Negative and their music video "Black No. 1."
VHS: S34411. $29.95.
Friedrich W. Murnau, Germany/USA, 1922/1997, 75 mins.

Sunrise

Although this was Murnau's first Hollywood film, he scripted it with Carl Mayer while still in Germany. The story concerns the marriage of a peasant couple whose honeymoon in the big city is detoured by a sultry seductress. But the film is neither trite nor melodramatic; Murnau's sets and camera angles imbue the images with a poetic lyricism that reveals the characters' psychological states. Easily his most perfect film, Murnau's Sunrise was named the "Greatest film of all time," in a recent Cahiers du Cinema Critic's Poll. With George O'Brien, Janet Gaynor and Margaret Livingston.
VHS: S07782. $29.95.
Laser: Outtakes, digital transfer. **LD76401. $49.98.**
Friedrich W. Murnau, USA, 1927, 97 mins.

Tabu

Filmed entirely in Tahiti, Tabu represents an unusual collaboration between legendary directors F.W. Murnau and Robert Flaherty. Combining Flaherty's poetic sense of the native people with Murnau's strong filmic sensibilities, the film tells the story of two lovers doomed by a tribal edict decreeing the beautiful princess as "tabu" to all men. "Murnau is one of the great masters. The beautiful restoration of Tabu will enable future generations to enjoy and appreciate his inspiring talent" (Martin Scorsese). Silent with music track.
VHS: S03712. $39.95.
Laser: CLV/CAV. **LD71591. $34.95.**
Friedrich W. Murnau/Robert Flaherty, USA, 1931, 82 mins.

Tartuffe

F.W. Murnau's (Nosferatu, Last Laugh) brilliant adaptation of Moliere's play Tartuffe features the great Emil Jannings in a larger-than-life portrait of the classic hypocrite. Silent, English inter-titles, organ score. Carl Mayer adapted Moliere's play for the screen. With Lil Dagover, Luise Hoflich and Werner Krauss as Orgon.
VHS: S26969. $24.95.
Friedrich W. Murnau, Germany, 1925, 70 mins.

GERMAN SIGHTS & SOUNDS

Berlin Blockade and Airlift

Documentary on the infamous Soviet blockade of Berlin and the Allied airlift. English narrative.
VHS: S30237. $29.95.
Germany, 40 mins.

Berlin: Journey of a City

This documentary from the Armed Forces Radio and Television Service tells the story of the city at the epicenter of the Cold War. Beginning with the Allied Occupation in 1945, the film shows the Berlin Airlift and the rise and fall of the infamous Berlin Wall. 60 mins.
VHS: S27636. $19.95.

Bertolt Brecht Practice Pieces

Lotte Lenya, Roscoe Lee Browne, Micki Grant and Oliver Clark are shown rehearsing two of Bertolt Brecht's largely unknown and seldom performed "Ubungstucke fur Schauspieler" (Practice Pieces for Actors). Brecht wrote these scenes to train actors in his own method for doing classical drama. Contains scenes from Romeo and Juliet and Hamlet and a brief discussion of the theater of Brecht with Lenya and translator Michael Lebeck.
VHS: S30994. $89.95.
1964, 28 mins.

Best of Nightline: East Germany Opens Its Borders

30 mins.
VHS: S14061. $14.98.

Christmas Video (Germany)

This program leads viewers through Nurenberger Chriskindlesmarkt—the monastery in Andechs, Bavaria, famous for the legend of the original Santa Claus—Rothenburg, Dresden, Oberammergau and Neuschwanstein, during the Christmas season in Germany. 52 mins.
VHS: S31242. $39.95.

Fall of the Berlin Wall

This major symbol of the division between East and West came tumbling down in November 1989. See for yourself history in the making in this West German television documentary that covers the wall's construction and destruction.
VHS: S14002. $59.95.
Peter C. Schmidt, Germany, 1990, 49 mins.

From Weimar to Bonn

Documentary on the history of the German Republic from the Weimar years until the formation of the Federal Republic of Germany. Contains rare, historic film material. English narrative.
VHS: S30238. $29.95.
Germany, 40 mins.

German TV Commercials

A collection of TV commercials, prepared by one of the world's leading ad agencies, provides a wonderful insight into contemporary German culture. Features automobile, soap, cereal, cheese, computer and many other products. Includes script. 25 mins.
VHS: S04946. $49.95.

The German Way of Life

Today a new Germany is emerging from the effects of two World Wars and Cold War partition. Germans discuss the effects of this tumultuous history and the role their country played in these momentous events. 25 mins.
VHS: S23706. $129.95.
Laser: LD74788. $149.95.

Germany, A Tapestry of Tradition

West Germany is the land of castles and kings, cathedrals and alpine peaks. Become enveloped in the quiet mystery of the Black forest. Watch a craftsman carve a violin in the village of Mittenwald, and continue on to the awe-inspiring Gothic cathedrals of Wurzburg, Ettal and Nymphenburg. The fairytale castle of Neuschwanstein, built by the eccentric King Ludwig II, comes alive. Join in the Oktoberfest celebration. 55 mins.
VHS: S10769. $24.95.

History of the Federal Republic of Germany

Documentary on the history of the German Republic up to the fall of the Berlin Wall. Contains rare historical material. English narrative.
VHS: S30210. $29.95.
Germany, 60 mins.

Illusions

A Brechtian art piece about performance and spectacle by the German chanteuse Ute Lemper. In an intimate concert setting, she performs cabaret songs made famous by Marlene Dietrich and Edith Piaf, including "La vie en rose", "Falling in Love Again" and "Non, je ne regrette rien". 102 mins.
VHS: S19107. $29.95.
Laser: LD71896. $39.95.

Michael Nyman Songbook: Ute Lemper

Filmmaker Volker Schlondorff directs the gifted singer Ute Lemper in her stylish performances of songs by Michael Nyman. The songs are inspired by a letter from Mozart, two texts from Rimbaud and six songs by Paul Celan, the German poet whose themes touch on the moral consequences for a Holocaust survivor. 54 mins.
VHS: S19752. $29.95.
Laser: LD71961. $29.95.
Volker Schlondorff, Germany, 54 mins.

Oktoberfest in Munich

This program provides an opportunity to experience the joy, wonder, laughter, song and community spectacle of Oktoberfest. 30 mins.
English Narration.
VHS: S19855. $65.00.
German Narration.
VHS: S19856. $65.00.

Romantic Road

This magical journey into the world of Siegfried and the Lorelei offers a compelling introduction to the cultural, artistic and historical significance of traditional German life. 25 mins.
English Narration.
VHS: S19793. $39.95.
German Narration.
VHS: S19792. $39.95.

Then They Came for Me: Intolerance in Modern Germany

Have the horrific excesses of the Third Reich changed Germany into a more tolerant nation? This video shows startling signs of intolerance and suppression unleashed by contemporary upheavals. The end of Communism and the falling of the Berlin Wall have unleashed both hope and fear among Germans, resulting in a growing call for order. 50 mins.
VHS: S26764. $24.95.

Traitors to Hitler

Documentary on the plot to assassinate Hitler in 1944 by his generals and others. Contains extremely rare, previously unreleased footage of the infamous trial of the anti-Nazi plotters. German dialog with English narrative.
VHS: S30236. $29.95.
Great Britain, 69 mins.

AUSTRIAN CINEMA

First Love

Based on Turgenev's story, the bittersweet, sensitive study of a 16-year-old boy who becomes infatuated with an impoverished princess during a time of social upheaval. A moving, sensual love story with Schell, Dominique Sanda and John Mouler Brown. English dubbed.

VHS: S00445. $29.95.

Maximilian Schell, Austria, 1966, 90 mins.

Invisible Adversaries

"A winning combination of sexual frankness and visual wit," wrote J. Hoberman in *The Village Voice*; "Funny, violent, sexual...It makes you reconsider what you and everyone else is doing in life and in art," said Amy Taubin in *Soho Weekly News*. Set in contemporary Vienna, Valie Export's controversial feature has been called a feminist *Invasion of the Body Snatchers*. Anna (Susanne Widl), a Viennese photographer, discovers that extra-terrestrial beings are colonizing the minds of her fellow citizens by raising the human aggression quotient. The outer world immediately becomes disjointed, but the inner world does too, as Anna and her love (Peter Weibel) try to hang onto their deteriorating relationship. A unique and totally original work by Austria's foremost filmmaker, *Invisible Adversaries* is at once philosophical and funny, psychologically revealing and sexually frank—"a witty and visually brilliant essay on gender and experience, culture and environment" (National Film Theatre, London). German with English subtitles.

VHS: S10414. $59.95.

Valie Export, Austria, 1977, 112 mins.

Menschenfrauen

Valie Export's daring film about relationships, *Menschenfrauen* (loosely translated, "humanwomen"), focuses on Franz S., a journalist, and his relationship with four women: the kindergarten nurse Petra, the teacher Gertrude, barmaid Elisabeth and his wife Anna. Franz "doles out honorary pieces of himself to the 'human women' in his seraglio, whispers the same assurances. Eventually, everyone catches on and makes some effort toward independence" (Gary Indiana, *East Village Eye*). "A landmark film...Valie Export achieves in *Menschenfrauen* what Godard strove for but failed in his *Every Man for Himself*—a human view of a woman's place in a man's world...From credits to close, *Menschenfrauen* eludes conventional cinematic vision..." (Seattle Film Festival). German with English subtitles.

VHS: S10416. $59.95.

Valie Export, Austria, 1980, 100 mins.

Moon of Israel

Based on the novel by H. Rider Haggard, this is the original, long-lost London pre-release version of the film that was bought by Paramount because of competition with DeMille's *The Ten Commandments*, which featured similar scenes and locales. "*Moon of Israel* is a spectacular specimen depicting the miracle of the sea more clearly, if less dramatically, than the DeMille's" (*Variety*, June 29, 1927). Also known under the title *The Slave Queen*. Silent with German titles.

VHS: S30199. $24.95.

Michael Curtiz, Austria/Hungary, 1924, 85 mins.

The Practice of Love

"A dazzling cinematic tour-de-force, combining a thriller narrative with experimental images to tell the story of Judith, a journalist, whose investigation of a murder implicates her two male lovers (an arms dealer and a psychiatrist). Through these relationships, Judith discovers that in a world of male power struggles, love is complicit, marginal or impossible. The film makes a stunningly coherent indictment of male-dominated society." (National Film Theatre, London). Valie Export is "one of the five or six truly original filmmakers working in Europe today who have not been recognized widely and turned into classical 'auteurs,' and this is why each of her films seems initially disturbing, jarring, 'difficult'" (Gary Indiana, *East Village Eye*). German with English subtitles.

VHS: S10415. $59.95.

Valie Export, Austria, 1984, 90 mins.

The Seventh Continent

This challenging, widely acclaimed film by Austrian filmmaker Michael Haneke is based on a true story. It charts the unusual progress of a family that seems utterly conventional: life holds no challenge or interest for them—they simply go through the motions of living. *The Seventh Continent* unsentimentally records their descent into despair and joint suicide. Modern life emerges as the ultimate culprit in this obsessive tale of extreme indifference. German with English subtitles.

VHS: S26527. $89.95.

Michael Haneke, Austria, 1989, 111 mins.

Sodom & Gomorrah

The rare, original silent version of this classic by the young Michael Curtiz about the pillar of salt and the destruction of Lot. With a cast of thousands. Stars Lucy Doraine, Erika Wagner, Walter Slezak and Michael Varkonyi. German with English subtitles.

VHS: S30201. $24.95.

Michael Curtiz, Austria/Hungary, 1922

Symphony in the Mountains

A light romance about a public school teacher who teaches singing and skiing instead of the regular advice of his superiors, falls in love with the sister of one of his students. Featuring songs by the Vienna Boys' Choir. German with English subtitles. Austria, 1935, 75 mins.

VHS: S03356. $49.95.

AUSTRIAN VIEWS

Austria, The Land of Music

Begin your Austrian tour in Salzburg, birthplace of Mozart. Take in the magnificent view of the High Alps outside Heiligenblutt and continue on to Vienna, where coffee houses and elegant shops abound. Attend a concert by the famed Vienna Boys Choir, then travel to the Danube wine district, where the harvest is in progress. 55 mins.

VHS: S10768. $24.95.

Touring Austria

The history, intrigue, romance, opera, festivals, old world grandeur of Austria: the Schoenbrunn and Hofburg palaces, St. Stephen's Cathedral, and the Vienna Boys' Choir. Cruise the Danube, walk the Olympic town of Innsbruck, the Tyrol, the forests and medieval castles of Styria. Glide over the Alps, visit Piber, where the Lippizaner stallions are bred, and gaze at mountainous scenery from the Orient Express. 60 mins.

VHS: S09914. $29.95.

Vienna 1900

In 1900 Vienna appeared to be the most carefree place in the world. But beneath this polished surface, the seeds of unrest had been sown by a famous group of disgruntled thinkers including Sigmund Freud, Arnold Schoenberg and Gustav Klimt. *Vienna 1900* explores the lost pleasures of the glittering old empire and the revolution in thought that would change the world forever. 60 mins.

VHS: S11762. $39.95

scandinavian cinema

Babette's Feast
Stephane Audran is Babette, an exiled French cook-housekeeper for a pair of devoutly religious, elderly Danish sisters. When she wins a lottery she asks to prepare a Gallic feast for the women and their friends to show her appreciation. Based on the short story by Karen Blixen (Isak Dinesen). Winner of Academy Award. Danish with English subtitles.
VHS: S08497. $19.98.
Laser: LD70850. $39.99.
Gabriel Axel, Denmark, 1987, 102 mins.

The Best Intentions
Danish filmmaker Bille August (*Pelle the Conquerer*) directs Ingmar Bergman's autobiographical screenplay about the early courtship, marriage and discord of Bergman's parents. Set between 1909 and 1918, *The Best Intentions* follows Henrik Bergman (Samuel Froler), an emotionally neutral Lutheran pastor, and the vivacious Anna Akerblom (Pernilla August). August and Bergman beautifully delineate the conflicts that arise between Henrik's spartan lifestyle and Anna's demands for possessions. Winner of the 1992 Palme d'Or at the Cannes Film festival. Pernilla August won the Best Actress award. Cinematography by Jorgen Persson. With Max von Sydow, Ghita Norby and Lennart Hjulstrom. Swedish with English subtitles.
VHS: S19019. $29.98.
Bille August, Sweden/Denmark, 1992, 182 mins.

Blueprint for a Million
Gunnar Hellstrom is featured in this surprising portrait about a pair of criminals recently escaped from jail. One of the pair, Erick, realizes he must change his life. Just one last caper should give him the wherewithal to leave crime behind for good. The ending is a surprise to everyone concerned. Dubbed in English.
VHS: S24016. $24.95.
Hasse Ekman, Sweden, 1966, 82 mins.

Breaking the Waves
In her incredible film debut, Emily Watson gives an Academy Award-nominated performance as Bess, a naive young woman who marries Jan, a handsome oil-rig worker. For the first time in her life, Bess experiences passion and physical pleasure she never imagined. But her marital bliss is cut short when an accident on the rig leaves Jan paralyzed. Believing she holds the key to his recovery, Bess will stop at nothing—even infidelity—in order to prolong Jan's life. "A powerhouse love story, a kind of miracle" (*Village Voice*). In English. Letterboxed.
VHS: S31256. $19.98.
Laser: LD76284. $69.95.
Lars von Trier, Great Britain/Denmark, 1996, 152 mins.

Children of Nature
Academy Award nominee for Best Foreign Film, *Children of Nature* is an enchanting love story about an elderly farmer, now in an old-age home, who is reunited with his childhood sweetheart. Together, they rekindle the passion of their youth and set off on an incredible adventure. Icelandic with English subtitles.
VHS: S20574. $19.98.
Fridrik Thor Fridriksson, Iceland, 1993, 85 mins.

The Children of Noisy Village
Before World War II, six boisterous children find adventure and old-fashioned fun around their home town of Noisy Village. Simply exploring the lush countryside of fields and woods inspires these kids to invent a slew of imaginative games. The result is a childhood grounded in seemingly endless possibilities. Based on the best-selling novel from author Astrid Lindgren, who also wrote *Pippi Longstocking*.
VHS: S28997. $24.95.
Lasse Hallstrom, Sweden, 1995, 88 mins.

Cold Fever
This wildly successful anomaly stars Japanese actor Masatoshi Nagase in Iceland in a beautiful and austere spiritual journey which is alternately funny and moving. This Japanese-Icelandic road movie was directed by Fridrik Thor Fridriksson, who captures Iceland's stark and beautiful landscape in a film Roger Ebert called "odd and beautiful." English, Japanese and Icelandic with English subtitles.
VHS: S31193. $89.98.
Fridrik Thor Fridriksson, Iceland, 1995, 85 mins.

The Count of the Old Town
Ingrid Bergman plays the role of Elsa Edlund, the daughter of a woman who owns a small bachelor hotel. Against this backdrop of the old city of Stockholm, the film develops as a thriller about the gang of crooks and booze smugglers who hide out at the hotel. See beautiful Ingrid in her early days. Swedish with English subtitles.
VHS: S15065. $19.98.
Elvin Adolphson/Sigurd Wallen, Sweden, 1935, 104 min.

The Dancer
Called "the ballet world's equivalent of *Hoop Dreams*" (*Miami Herald*), this documentary follows young ballerina Katja Bjourner on her journey as a student at The Royal Swedish Ballet School as she develops toward a promising professional career. Swedish with English subtitles.
VHS: S31189. $29.95.
Donya Feuer, Sweden, 1994, 96 mins.

The Doll
A night watchman has one of the loneliest jobs in the world. In this psychologically unsettling film from Arne Mattson, the watchman-hero decides to liven up his boring hours by borrowing some shapely mannequins from the department store which he guards at night. The other folks in his rooming house take a dim view of this flesh-and-wood romance, however, and tragedy looms as the only alternative." With Per Oscarsson. Swedish with English subtitles.
VHS: S07750. $29.95.
Arne Mattson, Sweden, 1962, 94 mins.

Dollar
Ingrid Bergman stars in this rare pre-war Swedish melodrama about three married couples who are confronted by an American millionairess, Miss Johnstone, with their dishonesty and deceit. Swedish with English subtitles,
VHS: S12448. $19.98.
Laser: CLV/CAV. LD70272. $39.95.
Gustaf Molander, Sweden, 1938, 74 mins.

Dreaming of Rita
A surreal story centered on a young mother named Rita (played by the engaging Marika Lagercrantz), who bears a striking resemblance to the haunting Rita Hayworth. When her mother dies, her widowed father becomes obsessed with finding his lost love, the Rita for whom his daughter was named, who also resembles the Hollywood icon. Mixing comic concepts, this screwball romantic comedy is funny, lyrical, and even contemplative. This film also manages to comment on both child rearing and parental responsibility. Swedish with English subtitles.
VHS: S26797. $29.95.
Jon Lindstrom, Sweden, 1994, 108 mins.

The Element of Crime
Winner at the Cannes Film Festival, and a supremely stylish (and terrifying) thriller. Shot entirely in sepia tone, Michael Elphick plays the cop assigned the Lotto Murders—a diabolical slaughter of little girls. Elphick is a man traumatized by grotesque memories of post-nuke Europe, as in the futuristic nightmare *Blade Runner*, and in his ongoing madness, becomes obsessed with the criminal mind. In English.
VHS: S12279. $79.95.
Lars von Trier, Denmark, 1988, 104 mins.

Elvira Madigan
A modern classic. Elvira (Pia Degermark) is a tightrope artist, and Sixten Sparre (Thommy Berggren), an aristocratic army officer who abandons a promising career for a rapturous affair with Elvira. In the idyllic Swedish countryside they are promptly ostracized for breaking the moral code and the film ends tragically. Lyrical, nostalgic and moving, with beautiful use of Mozart's *Piano Concerto No. 21*. Swedish with English subtitles.
VHS: S00404. $24.98.
Bo Widerberg, Sweden, 1967, 95 mins.

Emma's Shadow
Emma, the willful and lonely 11-year-old daughter of a cold aristocratic family in the 1930's, runs away by staging her own kidnapping. She stumbles into an unlikely friendship with an ex-convict sewer worker memorably played by Borje Ahlstedt of *Fanny and Alexander*. This story of the deep trust and love which bonds these social opposites is told with spirit and style, while the handsome cinematography richly evokes the period. Danish with English subtitles.
VHS: S14069. $19.98.
Soeren Kragh-Jacobsen, Denmark, 1988, 93 min.

The Films of Arne Sucksdorff: The Great Adventure Plus Short Subjects
Distinguished Swedish nature cinematographer Arne Sucksdorff brought the vision of a poet to the wildlife around him and the animals and birds became the principal actors in his films, as these four shorts as well as his acclaimed feature film demonstrate. In *The Great Adventure* (1953, 75 mins.), the rhythms of nature are explored through the eyes of children. Two brothers on a Swedish farm rescue and tame an otter which they keep hidden from their parents. We follow the progress of the forest and its denizens as the seasons change. "A sensuous mixture of beauty and cruelty" (Pauline Kael). *Hunter and the Forest—A Story Without Words* (1956, 6 mins.) is the story of an unusual encounter between a hunter and a family of deer in the forest. On the narrative level it is an idyll, providing an exciting stimulus for creative writing. It also raises more profound questions about man's fundamental attitudes toward hunting as a sport, as well as his sentiments about nature and conservation. The beauty and majesty of the forest and its wildlife is intruded upon by man in the dramatic, touching, magnificently photographed short subject *The Shadow of the Hunter* (1957, 10 mins.). The beautifully photographed short *Struggle for Survival* (1950, 10 mins.) depicts the life cycle of the seagull. The snow-covered woods and its animals are captured in *Shadows on the Snow* (circa mid-1950s, 10 mins.), a dramatic, yet beautiful look at nature and the survival of its creatures.
VHS: S30551. $29.95.
Arne Sucksdorff, Sweden, 1950-57, 115 mins.

Freud Leaving Home
This bittersweet comedy is the story of Freud, the nickname of a psychobabbling 25-year-old girl living at home with her Jewish family in Stockholm. As her family comes together for their mother's 60th birthday party, they are faced with the news of the mother's fatal illness. Forced to confront the reality of their relationships and their identities, the family members reach a point of recognition and Freud tries to flee the family drama. "Strikingly original, both in its use of humor and its new twist on the traditional Jewish family" (*Screen International*). Swedish with English subtitles.
VHS: S31188. $59.95.
Suzanne Bier, Sweden, 1991, 100 mins.

Friends Forever
A teenage boy's sexual confusion becomes a catalyst for change in this tender and unpredictable first feature. Kristian, a shy 16-year-old, is starting a new school. An uncertain conformist, he is irresistibly drawn to the two boys who dominate his class. Henrik, whose unyielding independence defies his androgynous sexual charisma, and Patrick—blond, boisterous and moody-who leads a tyrannical band of troublemakers. The boys' friendship instills self-confidence in Kristian, but their relationship is soon put to the test.
VHS: S15821. $69.95.
Stefan Christian Henszelman, Denmark, 1986, 95 mins.

Girl in a Swing
Meg Tilly plays a mysterious German secretary who captures the interest of Rupert Frazer, a repressed, middle-aged, English antiques dealer. He learns it is always better to know a little something about a potential spouse before you get married.
VHS: S12147. $89.99.
Gordon Hessler, Denmark, 1989, 112 mins.

Good Evening Mr. Wallenberg
A moving and sensitive portrait of Raoul Wallenberg, the heroic Swedish businessman who saved thousands of Jews from extermination in Nazi-dominated Hungary. Despite his amazing courage and luck in his self-appointed mission, his own fate remains a mystery. Swedish with English subtitles.
VHS: S20647. $19.98.
Kjell Grede, Sweden, 115 mins.

Gorilla
This Swedish documentary/drama grafts the story of a white hunter and a beautiful Swedish photographer on to some fascinating documentary footage. See dancing Watusis, pygmies in the jungle, elephants, rhinos, snakes, and the 640-pound gorilla that can sit anywhere it wants. Filmed in the Belgian Congo (now Zaire). Swedish with English subtitles. Sven Nykvist co-directs.
VHS: S05480. $29.95.
Lar Henrik Ottoson, Sweden, 1956, 79 mins.

The Hideaway
A 12-year-old boy who is starved for attention catches a young punk hiding in his basement. The 12-year-old agrees to shelter the older boy and is slowly transformed by the relationship. In the end he must risk everything to save his strange new friend. Danish with English subtitles.
VHS: S24734. $59.95.
Niels Grabo, Denmark, 1993, 70 mins.

House of Angels
A sexy nightclub singer is the sole surviving heir to an old Swedish estate. When she returns to a small town to reclaim her inheritance, her big city ways set the townspeople on edge. This comedy of a black sheep who returns to the fold is a clever tale of love and reversal. Swedish with English subtitles.
VHS: S20737. $19.95.
Colin Nutley, Sweden, 1992, 119 mins.

Hunger
Per Oscarsson gives his greatest performance as Pontus, a starving writer in Norway circa 1890, in Henning Carlsen's filming of a Knut Hamsun novel. Pontus stumbles through the streets in search of his own fantasies. His articles are continually refused by editors, and by autumn he is left penniless and without food. "Every tic, every gesture appears to have been with him for years rather than just assumed for a film part" (Peter Cowie). Winner of the Best Actor Award at the Cannes Film Festival. Swedish with English subtitles.
Laser: CLV. **LD72050. $39.95.**
Henning Carlsen, Sweden, 1966, 100 mins.

I Am Curious—Yellow
The film that scandalized America with its (!) sex and nudity is really a pseudo-Freudian look at the relationship between sex, politics and the body. Lena Nyman is the sociologist trying to get a take on the Swedish class structure while carrying on a passionate affair with a casual visitor to her father's apartment in her bedroom, in front of the Royal Palace, in a tree, on the grass, in a lake. Quintessential '60s nostalgia but a film that broke many taboos and served as a vanguard of liberation. Swedish with English subtitles.
VHS: S00595. $24.95.
Vilgot Sjoman, Sweden, 1968, 95 mins.

I, A Woman
This is the Swedish classic that American couples, in search of cinematic titillation, came flocking to in the '60s. Siv, a gorgeous and restless young woman, revolts against her fanatically religious folks and searches for sexual fulfillment. Dubbed in English.
VHS: S23038. $29.95.
Mac Ahlberg, Sweden, 1966, 80 mins.

Intermezzo
The premiere release of the film that discovered Ingrid Bergman, which took more than 50 years to reach American shores. The romantic drama is the story of a world-famous violinist, whose life is turned upside down when he has an affair with a beautiful, aspiring pianist. When David Selznick saw *Intermezzo*, he brought Ingrid Bergman to Hollywood. Swedish with English subtitles.
VHS: S10881. $19.98.
Gustaf Molander, Sweden, 1936, 91 mins.

Jerusalem
Gertrude and Ingmar are deeply in love and Ingmar is expected to take over the family estate and become the village leader. But their happiness fades when a charismatic preacher, Hellgum, turns up and promises salvation to all those who follow him to the Holy Land. Ingmar's older sister Karin is tempted by his promises and sells the family property to the farmer Persson. The devastated Ingmar abandons Gertrude and marries Persson's daughter Barbro in order to save the family farm. Swedish with English subtitles.
VHS: S33872. $89.98.
Bille August, Sweden, 1996, 166 mins.

June Night
One of Ingrid Bergman's first screen appearances features Bergman as a promiscuous young woman exposed when she becomes the victim of a shooting accident in her small town. Swedish with English subtitles.
VHS: S09356. $19.98.
Laser: CLV/CAV. **LD70270. $39.95.**
Per Lindberg, Sweden, 90 mins.

The Kingdom
Lars von Trier's audacious and inspired soap opera is set in Copenhagen's Kingdom Hospital, which is ailing. Once a respected site of healing, it has become a carnival of horrors. A restless ghost haunts its corridors crying for redemption. Patients try seances while doctors turn to exorcism and voodoo. Despite these efforts, the terrible secret at the heart of *The Kingdom* remains and continues to ensnare the innocent. This film mixes a range of influences from the erotic to the sardonic in an unforgettable hybrid of comedy and terror. Danish with English subtitles.
VHS: S27595. $24.98.
Lars von Trier, Denmark, 1994, 265 mins.

Ladies on the Rocks
The "buddies" in this very funny road movie are two self-determined women. Aspiring comediennes Micha and Laura pack up their van and tour rural Denmark with their cabaret act. But the show does not sit too well with Micha's rock musician boyfriend nor Laura's bourgeois husband, and domestic problems invariably arise. Danish with English subtitles.
VHS: S16497. $29.95.
Christian Braad Thomsen, Denmark, 1983, 100 mins.

Lakki: The Boy Who Grew Wings
The bittersweet, lyrical adventures of a lonely 14-year-old boy are at the center of this haunting film. Neglected by his father and ignored by his decadent mother, Lakki takes to the streets. There he befriends a punk rocker who brutalizes him. All the while, mysterious feathers sprout from his back until, confronted by a miraculous transformation, he must fight for his sanity. Norwegian with English subtitles.
VHS: S26712. $69.95.
Svend Wam, Norway, 1992, 104 mins.

The Last Dance
Winner of two Swedish film awards, this is the perversely comic tale of two couples, Claus and Tove and their best friends Lennart and Liselott, who recount their roller coaster relationship and their shared obsession with ballroom competitions. When Liselott's body is found beneath the pier at the Blackstone ballroom, a flashback reveals the animosity and illicit attractions that plague even these best of friends. With Helena Bergstrom, Reine Brynolfsson, Ewa Froling and Peter Andersson.
VHS: S31270. $59.95.
Colin Nutley, Sweden, 1993, 109 mins.

The Littlest Viking
A wacky Icelandic family comedy about a 12-year-old Viking Prince, Sirgard, who takes on fearsome warriors, legendary beasts and far-out characters as he learns about truth, nobility and honor. Dubbed in English.
Laser: LD74838. $34.95.
Knut W. Jorfald/Lars Rasmussen/Paul Trevor Bale, Iceland, 1995, 85 mins.

The Man from Mallorca
The investigation of a Stockholm post office hold-up founders until the two witnesses to the robbery are murdered. Officers Jarnebring and Johansson suspect Berg, a senior police officer with a mysterious source of income and an impessive alibi. Taken off the case, Jarnebring and Johansson continue to investigate on their own, with disturbing results. A police thriller combining suspense and political commentary.
VHS: S33884. $89.95.
Bo Widerberg, Sweden, 1984, 106 mins.

Man on the Roof
Based on the bestselling novel *The Abominable Man*, this unconventional and influential thriller opens with the murder of a sadistic police officer in a Stockholm hospital. Homicide investigator Martin Beck (Carl Gustav Lindstedt) tracks a killer bent on taking revenge against the police. Director Bo Widerberg used hand-held cameras and other photojournalistic techniques rarely employed in detective films of the time in this visually stunning film. With Sven Wollter and Thomas Hellberg. "A first-rate thriller with an almost unbearably tense climax" (*The Hollywood Reporter*). Swedish with English subtitles.
VHS: S32656. $89.95.
Bo Widerberg, Sweden, 1976, 110 mins.

Mazurka (Mazurka Pa Sengekanten)
A Danish sex farce centering on a school dance where, without question, the mazurka will be part of the program. Max, a popular teacher in a boy's school, could be the next dean of students if he gets married and loses his virginity. Those European schools have such strict standards. Dubbed into English. Adults only. Denmark, 1970, 91 mins.
VHS: S05466. $29.95.

Memories of a Marriage
Watch as a lifetime of love unfolds on the screen in this touching Danish love story—a film about the joys and sorrows, victories and defeats, and, above all, the love between a husband and a wife. With Ghita Norby and Frits Helmuth. "A touching portrait of a married life" (*The Wall Street Journal*). "A well crafted and fully realized film" (*New York Post*). Danish with yellow English subtitles.
VHS: S15265. $19.98.
Kaspar Rostrup, Denmark, 1989, 90 mins.

Miss Julie
The definitive version of August Strindberg's riveting play concerning social and sexual domination. Miss Julie is a noblewoman who allows her butler to seduce her after her engagement is broken. With Anita Bjork and Anders Henrikson. Swedish with English subtitles.
VHS: S01720. $29.95.
Alf Sjoberg, Sweden, 1950, 90 mins.

More About the Children of Noisy Village
From Lasse Hallstrom, the director of *What's Eating Gilbert Grape* and *My Life as a Dog*, and Astrid Lindgren, the creator of *Pippi Longstocking*, comes this story of six children who find adventure in their home town, Noisy Village. Set before World War II, the children explore the idyllic countryside, invent wondrous games, and romp and frolic around their tiny village. A delightful tale that brings back an age of simple fun and good times.
VHS: S34982. $24.95.
Lasse Hallstrom, Sweden, 1994, 85 mins.

Mozart Brothers
A Swedish opera director—an anguished, divorce-wracked enfant terrible—has a bizarre vision for a production of Mozart's Don Giovanni. His efforts to stand the revered opera on its head including destroying the stage in order to install a pool, stripping the opera of its libretto, and freeing the artists of their inhibitions and clothing. Wonderful comic performances in a film that's "witty and uproarious" (*New York Times*). Swedish with English subtitles.
VHS: S10930. $59.95.
Suzanne Osten, Sweden, 1985, 98 mins.

My Life as a Dog
More than just a movie, a phenomenon that has captured the hearts of America. A bright, funny, touching tale of one boy's special growing-up year. Bundled off to a rural village while his ill mother recuperates, young Ingermar finds unexpected adventure with the town's warmhearted eccentrics. Swedish with English subtitles.
VHS: S06240. $19.98.
Laser: Subtitled. **LD75232. $34.98.**
Lasse Hallstrom, Sweden, 1987, 101 mins.

Only One Night
Ingrid Bergman stars as Eva, the girlfriend of her guardian, Valdemar Moreaux. Their relationship crashes when Eva discovers that she is disgusted by the physical side of love. A Swedish melodrama starring the beautiful young Bergman. Swedish with English subtitles.
VHS: S12449. $19.98.
Laser: LD70273. $39.95.
Gustaf Molander, Sweden, 1937, 87 mins.

The Only Way
In the tradition of *The Holocaust, The Hiding Place and Playing for Time*, this is the true and magnificent saga of Denmark's valorous actions to save Danish Jews from Nazi extermination at peril of death. With Jane Seymour and Martin Potter.
VHS: S34203. $19.95.
Bent Christensen, Denmark/Great Britain, 1970, 86 mins.

The Ox
Ingmar Bergman's cinematographer Sven Nykvist directed this compelling drama which examines the social and economic disorder of 1860s Sweden. Stellan Skarsgard plays a man who remains in rural Sweden to tend to his drought-stricken farmland while his wife and child emigrate to the United States. With Max Von Sydow, Liv Ullmann, Erland Josephson and Ewa Froling. Swedish with English subtitles.
VHS: S19439. $19.98.
Sven Nykvist, Sweden, 1991, 93 mins.

Pathfinder
Ruthless invaders disrupt the harmony of living in Lapland about a thousand years ago. To save a defenseless village, a young boy takes on the title role in an attempt to mislead the land pirates who made him an orphan. This Oscar-nominated foreign film is a grand adventure told in an epic visual style. A surprise hit in Norway and this country. In Lapp with English subtitles.
VHS: S13843. $19.98.
Nils Gaup, Norway, 1988, 88 mins.

Pretty Boy
In this unflinching and harshly poetic film, the chronicle of a young runaway boy unfolds on the streets of Copenhagen. There he becomes a street hustler. Before the camera, innocence is plundered and finally lost in this compelling exploration of desire. Danish with English subtitles.
VHS: S23290. $69.95.
Carsten Sonder, Denmark, 1993, 87 mins.

Quiet Days in Clichy
Based on Henry Miller's erotic novel written in 1956. Joey, a self-indulgent American choreographer living in Denmark, spends most of his time seducing sexy Parisian girls together with his buddy Cal. "Henry Miller's memoir of friends, women and cheap wine is a relaxed, very sexy outrage..." (Amos Vogel, *Film as a Subversive Art*). With Paul Valjean and Louise White.
VHS: S23039. $19.98.
Jens Jorgen Thorsen, Denmark, 1970, 91 mins.

Remote Control
At the center of this outrageous comedy is a stolen remote control. Soon hostage goldfish, amateur mobsters and a beautiful kidnapee join the plot to thoroughly confound and delight. Between the hoodlum morons and mom everything comes out right in the end. Icelandic with English subtitles.
VHS: S23432. $94.95.
Laser: LD75132. $24.98.
Oskar Jonasson, Iceland, 1992, 85 mins.

Sebastian

From the creators of *Lakki—The Boy Who Grew Wings* comes this sweet story of sexual confusion set in the ultra-liberal social atmosphere of modern Norway. Seventeen-year-old Sebastian and his buddy Ulf are the perfect pals, until one of them decides he wants more. Joy and gentle comedy follow as the boys struggle to understand this new element in their relationship. Norwegian with English subtitles.

VHS: S31414. $59.95.

Svend Wam, Norway, 1995, 88 mins.

Sir Arne's Treasure

Three Scottish mercenaries murder Sir Arne and his household for his gold. Only Elsalil (Mary Johnson) survives. She moves in with relatives in Marsrand, where she meets charming officer Sir Archi (Richard Lund), who turns out to be one of Sir Arne's murderers. Based on the book by Selma Lagerlof. With Erik Stocklassa, Bror Berger and Hjalmar Selander. Long version. Silent with English titles.

VHS: S33937. $24.95.

Mauritz Stiller, Sweden, 1919, 106 mins.

Slingshot

This charming coming-of-age film follows the antic travails of a 12-year-old with a special possession. He makes a slingshot from contraband condoms that brings him fame, fortune, and big trouble with the local police. Based on a true story, it won the Swedish Academy Award for Best Picture. Swedish with English subtitles.

VHS: S23326. $19.95.
Laser: LD74755. $34.95.

Ake Sandgren, Sweden, 1993, 102 mins.

Smilla's Sense of Snow

Julia Ormond and Gabriel Byrne star in Bille August's (*Best Intentions*) thriller based on the best-selling novel. Smilla (Ormond) uses her knowledge of ice and snow to unravel the web of lies and intrigue surrounding the death of her six-year-old neighbor. With Richard Harris, Vanessa Redgrave and Robert Loggia. In English.

VHS: S31521. $99.99.
Laser: LD76239. $49.98.

Bille August, Denmark/Great Britain, 1997, 121 mins.

Sofie

Liv Ullmann's directorial debut is set in Copenhagen in 1886, and deals with the efforts of Sofie (Karen-Lise Mynster), a beautiful, emotionally sheltered, 28-year-old Jewish woman who longs for independence, to fall in love and get married. Though she is attracted to a charismatic painter (Jesper Christensen), she follows her parents' orders and marries her dull cousin (Torben Zeller). With Erland Josephson and Ghita Norby. Swedish with English subtitles.

VHS: S19972. $79.95.

Liv Ullmann, Sweden, 1992, 142 mins.

Sondagsengler (The Other Side of Sunday)

This Academy Award nominee for best foreign language film, set in 1950s Norway, is a lyrical, biting look at a small church community and the grandeur of adolescence. Maria (Marie Theisen), the preacher's daughter, attempts to free herself from the constraints of the community and her cold fish father, who doesn't always practice what he preaches. She finds an ally in the soulful, free-thinking, middle-aged Mrs. Tunheim (Hildegun Riise), who works at the church. Theisen and Riise shared the Best Actress Prize at the Tokyo International Film Festival.

VHS: S34878. $89.98.

Berit Nesheim, Norway, 1996, 103 mins.

Story of Gosta Berling

Greta Garbo in one of her earliest roles. The story follows a pastor, defrocked because of his drinking, as he goes through loves and sorrow. A masterpiece of Scandinavian cinema. Silent.

VHS: S01260. $29.95.

Mauritz Stiller, Sweden, 1924, 93 mins.

Sunday's Children

Ingmar Bergman wrote the screenplay for this haunting film about a 10-year-old boy named Pu. Pu is in the country for the summer with his family. Everything seems peaceful enough until Pu sees his father fighting with his mother. This event inaugurates an emotional time that resonates within all concerned. Swedish with English subtitles.

VHS: S23744. $29.95.

Daniel Bergman, Sweden, 1993, 118 mins.

Swedenhielms

In this classic drama, Ingrid Bergman plays Astrid, the wealthy girlfriend of Bo Swedenhielm, who, together with his aristocratic but impecunious family, is depending on their father winning the Nobel Prize. Swedish with English subtitles.

VHS: S09357. $19.98.
Laser: LD70271. $39.95.

Gustaf Molander, Sweden, 88 mins.

Thomas Graal's Best Child

The comical adventures of Thomas and Bessie are continued in this sequel. The screenwriter has married his secretary who is now acting in his movies. When a child appears in the household the parents are not in agreement as to how to raise a modern youngster. With Victor Sjostrom and Karin Molander. Silent.

VHS: S03707. $29.95.

Mauritz Stiller, Sweden, 1918, 70 mins.

Thomas Graal's Best Film

An astonishingly sophisticated comedy about love and film. Director Stiller was a Russian emigre working in Sweden who discovered Greta Garbo and ultimately went to Hollywood with her. *Thomas Graal* stars director Victor Sjostrom (*The Wind, He Who Gets Slapped*). Silent.

VHS: S03706. $29.95.

Mauritz Stiller, Sweden, 1917, 70 mins.

Torment

The budding love between two students, Jan-Erik and Bertha, is threatened by a sadistic Latin teacher nicknamed "Caligula" who torments Jan-Erik in class. When Jan-Erik finds Bertha dead in her room and Caligula hiding in a closet, he accuses him of causing her death. Based on the (first) script by Ingmar Bergman, the character of Caligula was seen as a symbol of Nazism. The film is remarkable for its expressive style and a powerful performance by Mai Zetterling as Bertha. With Alf Kjellin and Stig Olin. Swedish with English subtitles.

VHS: S04913. $29.95.

Alf Sjoberg, Sweden, 1944, 90 mins.

The Treasure of Arne

With Victor Sjostrom, Mauritz Stiller was the most important early Scandinavian director, with a painterly visual style, graphic naturalism and a real affinity for landscape and geography. This film concerns the fate of a 16th century Scottish mercenary, an escaped prisoner, and the damages wrought against wealthy landowner and his family.

VHS: S03708. $19.95.

Mauritz Stiller, Sweden, 1919, 40 mins.

Walpurgis Night

Ingrid Bergman plays a woman who is secretly in love with her married boss. Her boss, it turns out, is also in love with her. This forbidden love soon triggers a murky and melodramatic series of startling events, including abortion, blackmail, murder and suicide. Swedish with English subtitles.

VHS: S15066. $19.98.

Gustaf Edgren, Sweden, 1935, 75 mins.

The Winter War

This gruelling film is the first made about the tenacious Finnish soldiers who defended the borders of their tiny country for 105 days against the invasion of the overwhelming and massively armed Soviet Red Army in 1939-40 during World War II. Based on Antti Tuuri's book, the film is a tribute to those Finnish heroes, whose points of view allow us to experience the brutality of daily life in the trenches. Finnish with English subtitles.

VHS: S32217. $29.98.

Pekka Parikka, Finland, 1990, 125 mins.

Witchcraft Through the Ages

A rare and extraordinary film from a little-known master of the silent era. A document of witchcraft from the 15th through the 17th century, the film is reminiscent in style of Bosch, Breughel, Callot and Goya. The film concludes with documented scenes of superstition and cases of possession in 1920. Silent with English subtitles.

VHS: S01471. $29.95.

Benjamin Christensen, Denmark, 1920, 82 mins.

Wolf at the Door

Donald Sutherland brings the later years of artist Paul Gauguin to life in a drama filled with fine art and romantic conquests. This Danish-French co-production is filmed in English and although Anthony Quinn looks more like Gauguin, Max Von Sydow is a dead ringer for August Strindberg.

VHS: S05296. $19.95.

Henning Carlsen, France/Denmark, 1987, 90 mins.

A Woman's Face

Ingrid Bergman depicts the troublesome life of young Anna Holm as a woman who has not only lost both her parents in a fire but was also severely burned and left with terrible facial scars. She descends into a lifestyle of despair and cynical blackmailing schemes. Swedish with English subtitles.

VHS: S15067. $19.98.

Gustaf Molander, Sweden, 1938, 104 mins.

The Women on the Roof

A psychological drama set in Stockholm on the eve of World War I, *The Women on the Roof* follows the struggle of two independent New Women seeking adventure and self-fulfillment in the big city. Linnea rents an attic apartment and becomes the neighbor of Anna, an artist-photographer working on fantasy tableaux in the apartment next door. Though Linnea is inexperienced and Anna more worldly, the two become friends and then lovers. When Anna's former boyfriend appears, their relationship is transformed into an even more complex menage a trois. With Helena Bergstrom, Amanda Ooms and Stellan Skarskard (*Breaking the Waves*).

VHS: S32162. $24.95.

Carl-Gustaf Nykvist, Sweden, 1990, 86 mins.

A World of Strangers

Henning Carlsen's adaptation of Nobel prize winning writer Nadine Gordimer's novel demystifies official government reports and media representation to provide a frightening, kaleidoscopic portrait of the faces, events and personalities imprisoned under the iron-clad racial separation laws and fascist ideology of apartheid. Shot surreptitiously on location in South Africa. With Athol Fugard's frequent collaborator Zakes Mokae.

VHS: S17928. $29.95.

Henning Carlsen, South Africa, 1962, 89 mins.

You Are Not Alone

This Danish film honestly explores the boundaries between friendship and love in a boys' school in a film which is full of nuance, gentleness and humor, reminiscent of the early films of Truffaut. Danish with English subtitles.

VHS: S01491. $79.95.

Lasse Nielsen/Ernst Johansen, Denmark, 1982, 90 mins.

Zentropa

Known in Europe as *Europa*, this stylistically daring work is set in a bleak, defeated Germany. A young American of German ancestry apprentices as a railway porter. He is seduced by a mysterious heiress whose father owns the line and becomes a pawn in a mysterious web of intrigue and deceit. With Jean Marc Barr, Barbara Sukowa and Eddie Constantine. Narrated by Max von Sydow. English and German with English subtitles.

VHS: S18368. $19.95.

Lars von Trier, Denmark/France/Sweden/Germany, 1991, 112 mins.

Zero Kelvin

This "gripping…raw-boned polar adventure" (Stephen Holden, *The New York Times*) is an extraordinary story of conflict and survival filmed on location in the wilderness of Greenland. Set in 1925, it tells the story of three men, a poet, a scientist and a sailor, forced to live together in a remote Arctic cabin during a winter working as fur trappers. Totally cut off from civilization, the men face the elements and each other with increasing difficulty, leading to a violent and harrowing climax. Norwegian with English subtitles.

VHS: S32043. $79.95.

Hans Petter Moland, Norway, 1996, 113 mins.

INGMAR BERGMAN

After the Rehearsal

Bergman takes a deeply personal look at the theater and its delusions in this spellbinding chamber play. The action of the film takes place on the bare stage after a rehearsal of Strindberg's *A Dream Play*. Superbly directed and acted, this is a major effort by one of the most renowned directors. Swedish with English subtitles.

VHS: S00022. $19.95.

Ingmar Bergman, Sweden, 1983, 72 mins.

All These Women

A rare comedy for Ingmar Bergman and his first film in color. Music critic Cornelius intends to write a biography of the cellist Felix and tries to gain admittance to the cellist's inner circle—surrounded by women, fountains and fake swans. Full of absurdist barbs, the film stars Bibi Andersson, Eva Dahlbeck, Karin Kavli and Jarl Kulle. Swedish with English subtitles.

VHS: S07499. $34.95.

Ingmar Bergman, Sweden, 1964, 80 mins.

Autumn Sonata

Ingmar Bergman's intense chamber drama was Ingrid Bergman's first Swedish film in almost 40 years and also her last. She plays a famed international concert pianist whose reunion with her daughter quickly deteriorates from euphoria into recriminations over the past. Rivalry, longing and guilt threaten to destroy the bonds that join a mother and her daughter. With Erland Josephson and Gunnar Bjornstrand. Swedish with English subtitles.

VHS: S00078. $39.95.
Laser: Subtitled. **LD70848. $49.95.**

Ingmar Bergman, Sweden, 1978, 97 mins.

Brink of Life

Superb performances by Eva Dahlbeck, Ingrid Thulin, Bibi Andersson and Max von Sydow mark this study of three women facing childbirth during a 24 hour period in a maternity word. Bergman was awarded the Best Director prize at Cannes for this film. Swedish with English subtitles.

VHS: S00182. $29.95.

Ingmar Bergman, Sweden, 1957, 82 mins.

Cries and Whispers

Ingmar Bergman's anguished, searing examination of the lust, envy, betrayal, love and self-mutilation that passes between four women—three sisters and a family provider—in this sculpted, metaphysical drama. "Bergman uses the women as metaphors for humanity, representing how we respond to anxiety, death, and the visitations of what appears to be a wrathful rather than benevolent God" (James Monaco). With Harriet Andersson, Ingrid Thulin and Liv Ullmann. Cinematography by Sven Nykvist. Swedish with English subtitles.

VHS: S00282. $39.95.

Ingmar Bergman, Sweden, 1972, 91 mins.

Devil's Eye

The Devil dispatches Don Juan to seduce a young, beautiful virgin in one of Bergman's rare comedies. The young girl changes Don Juan's lust to love so that he cannot follow through on his seduction. With Bibi Andersson, Jarl Kulle. Swedish with English subtitles.

VHS: S00331. $29.95.

Ingmar Bergman, Sweden, 1960, 90 mins.

Devil's Wanton

Bergman's sixth film, in which many of his themes and cinematic techniques are in evidence. The story revolves around a set of people adrift in a sea of confusion: a film director, a poet, and a prostitute. Swedish with English subtitles.

VHS: S00333. $29.95.

Ingmar Bergman, Sweden, 1949, 78 mins.

Document: Fanny and Alexander

Beginning on the day before shooting his last feature film and continuing through the wrap, Ingmar Bergman presents the making of *Fanny and Alexander*. With his brilliant cameraman, Sven Nykvist, and his troupe of actors, Bergman shows how he works behind the camera to shape his singular vision. Swedish with English subtitles.

VHS: S08939. $29.95.

Ingmar Bergman, Sweden, 1985, 105 mins.

Dreams

A study of sexual obsession as two women, the owner of a modeling agency and her top model, both have strange one day affairs with married men while on a photographic outing. Exquisite scenes of austere romanticism and painful irony. Swedish with English subtitles.

VHS: S00373. $29.95.

Ingmar Bergman, Sweden, 1955, 86 mins.

From the Life of the Marionettes

An underrated recent film by Bergman, the harrowing journey investigating the motivations of a brutal murder and the unnatural rape of an unsuspecting call girl. A compelling psychological study and a shattering personal experience. English dialog.

VHS: S00472. $29.95.

Ingmar Bergman, Sweden, 1980, 105 mins.

Hour of the Wolf

Max von Sydow portrays an artist living with his wife (Liv Ullmann) on a remote island, haunted by darkness, demons and his imagination, in this effective study of the creative process. Bergman brilliantly uses the eerie landscape to show von Sydow's descent into madness as he is haunted by images of the death of a child. Swedish with English subtitles.

VHS: S17862. $39.95.

Ingmar Bergman, Sweden, 1968, 88 mins.

A Lesson in Love

Ingmar Bergman's "comedy for grownups"—Ernemann, a gynecologist, and his wife meet on a train and pretend not to know each other, as Ernemann tries to "recover" his wife, who has been having an affair with a bombastic sculptor. Swedish with English subtitles.

VHS: S03512. $29.95.

Ingmar Bergman, Sweden, 1954, 95 mins.

The Magic Flute

Quite possibly the best opera adaptation ever put on film, Ingmar Bergman's magical, delightful, enchanting version of Mozart's playful opera, sung in Swedish by a remarkably terrific cast. Bergman and Mozart meeting centuries later, in different mediums, is still a meeting of minds. Swedish with English subtitles.

VHS: S00797. $29.95.

Laser: LD75386. $99.95.

Ingmar Bergman, Sweden, 1973, 134 mins.

The Magician

One of Bergman's most compelling films; Max von Sydow plays the wandering magician with a bag of tricks that turn him from magician to savior, then to con-man and finally to an extraordinary artist. The film has been variously interpreted as an intellectual horror film and as a symbolic self-portrait. With Ingrid Thulin, Gunnar Bjornstrand and Bibi Andersson. Swedish with English subtitles.

VHS: S00799. $29.95.

Laser: Widescreen. **LD76089. $49.95.**

Ingmar Bergman, Sweden, 1958, 101 mins.

Monika

The young Harriet Andersson is Monika, the sultry teenager who escapes her poverty together with a young man. They camp out on an island off the Swedish coast, exploring their emotions and sensuality, but when summer ends, hunger, pregnancy and boredom drive her back to her old life. "Harriet Andersson gives a memorably moving performance as a self-centered, self-willed, but erotic adolescent" (Georges Sadoul). Swedish with English subtitles.

VHS: S09354. $29.95.

Ingmar Bergman, Sweden, 1952, 82 mins.

Night Is My Future

A moving drama of a musician blinded in an accident, and forced to adjust to a world of darkness. Driven to despair, the musician regains his faith in life by studying to become a church organist and finding the love of a simple woman. Swedish with English subtitles.

VHS: S00931. $29.95.

Ingmar Bergman, Sweden, 1947, 87 mins.

Persona

Ingmar Bergman's great achievement, a study of madness, breakdown and transference of identity. The story concerns a brilliant actress who unaccountably loses her will to speak and her shifting, intricate and elaborate relationship with the nurse assigned to her rehabilitation. Liv Ullmann is the actress, Harriet Andersson is the nurse. Cinematography by Sven Nykvist. Swedish with English subtitles.

VHS: S17865. $19.98.

Laser: Digital Transfer. **LD74926. $34.98.**

Ingmar Bergman, Sweden, 1967, 81 mins.

The Ritual

This chamber drama stars Gunnar Bjornstrand, Ingrid Thulin and Anders Ek as members of a small touring company of actors who are trapped in a legal nightmare for an allegedly obscene variety show. A sadistic judge uses the opportunity to ruthlessly examine their personal lives. A brilliant look at the relationship of the artist to society, with a powerful performance from Ingrid Thulin as the unhappy, alcoholic actress. Swedish with English subtitles.

VHS: S26061. $39.95.

Ingmar Bergman, Sweden, 1969, 75 mins.

Sawdust and Tinsel

Ingmar Bergman's profound meditation on art and sexual conflict. Set in turn-of-the-century Sweden and centered on a ragged traveling circus, the plot details the private anguish of the ring master (Ake Gronberg), reunited with his former wife (AnnikaTretow) in a provincial town. Complications erupt when Gronberg's mistress (Harriet Andersson) is seduced by a loquacious actor (Hasse Ekman). With Anders Ek and Gudrum Brost. Swedish with English subtitles.

VHS: S01161. $29.95.

Ingmar Bergman, Sweden, 1953, 83 mins.

Scenes from a Marriage

Liv Ullmann stars in this exploration of the relationship between two people over a 20-year period. "Never before has this extraordinary director and writer explored relationships between the sexes with such compassion and humor. *Scenes from a Marriage* seems to be the simplest, most lucid, most spare film that Bergman has ever made," wrote Vincent Canby in *The New York Times*. Roger Ebert calls it "one of the truest, most luminous love stories ever made, an almost heart-breaking masterpiece." With Erland Josephson.

VHS: S26300. $39.95.

Laser: Widescreen. **LD75409. $69.95.**

Ingmar Bergman, Sweden, 1974, 168 mins.

Secrets of Women

Ingmar Bergman's exploration of sexual dynamics. Rakel (Anita Bjork), Marta (Maj-Britt Nilsson) and Karin (Eva Dahlbeck) are married to three brothers. While waiting for their arrival at a summer retreat, each woman relates an elaborate incident; Rakel's attempted seduction by a friend; Marta's experiences with a Swedish artist in Paris; and Karin's liberating moments while stuck in an elevator with her husband. Swedish with English subtitles.

VHS: S01175. $39.95.

Ingmar Bergman, Sweden, 1952, 114 mins.

Serpent's Egg

Set in Berlin in 1923, the film is about a Jewish-American trapeze artist (David Carradine) and his sister-in-law (Liv Ullmann), who are entrapped by a mad doctor—a prophet who dreams of what the Nazis will accomplish in the 30's. The screen is filled with powerful images. English dialog.

VHS: S01179. $39.95.

Ingmar Bergman, Germany, 1980, 119 mins.

The Seventh Seal

Bergman's powerful allegory of man's search for meaning in life is stunningly visualized. A knight, upon return from the Crusades, plays chess with Death while the Plague ravages medieval Europe. With Max von Sydow, Gunnar Bjornstrand, Bibi Andersson. Swedish with English subtitles.

VHS: S01185. $29.95.

Laser: CAV. **LD70453. $79.95.**

Laser: CLV. **LD70454. $49.95.**

Ingmar Bergman, Sweden, 1956, 96 mins.

The Shame

A brilliant young couple, both violinists, attempt to evade a long-raging civil war and retreat to an island off the coast. The war follows them and they're charged with collaborating with the enemy. A visually spare, emotionally powerful work about hopelessness, betrayal and human weakness. With Liv Ullmann, Max Von Sydow and Gunnar Bjornstrand. Cinematography by Sven Nykvist. Swedish with English subtitles.

VHS: S17863. $39.95.

Ingmar Bergman, Sweden, 1968, 103 mins.

Silence

Part of the Bergman trilogy dealing with the existence of God. Two women are stranded in a remote village where the language is incomprehensible. As one of the women slowly slips into death, the other engages the local barman in a frenzied sexual encounter. Swedish with English subtitles.

VHS: S02773. $24.95.

Ingmar Bergman, Sweden, 1963, 95 mins.

Smiles of a Summer Night

Ingmar Bergman's liveliest work concerns the sexual and romantic roundelay of four couples invited to a country mansion for a summer weekend. "The film is erotic and lyrical, full of blithe spirits brilliantly evoked" (James Monaco). With Gunnar Bjornstrand, Eva Dahlbeck, Ulla Jacobsson and Harriet Andersson. Swedish with English subtitles.

VHS: S01219. $29.95.

Laser: LD70465. $49.95.

Ingmar Bergman, Sweden, 1955, 108 mins.

Summer Interlude

Discovering the diary of a former lover, a ballerina recalls a summer affair with its delirious happiness and tragedy; now a star, she travels back in memory to recapture the pleasure and pain of first love and to purge the memories that have shadowed her own life. "This evocation of past happiness is one of Bergman's most moving films" (Georges Sadoul). Swedish with English subtitles.

VHS: S04912. $29.95.

Ingmar Bergman, Sweden, 1950, 95 mins.

Three Strange Loves

Early Bergman psychological drama follows a husband and wife on a train ride across Germany after the War. As the country struggles to recover the couple ponder the state of their marriage. Swedish with English subtitles.

VHS: S02218. $29.95.

Ingmar Bergman, Sweden, 1949, 88 mins.

Through a Glass Darkly

Powerful psychological study of a young woman's descent into madness. Harriet Andersson plays Karin, who has read that she is an incurable schizophrenic and plunges into a visionary world where God is a spider. With Gunnar Bjornstrand and Max von Sydow. Swedish with English subtitles.

VHS: S01339. $29.95.

Laser: Digital transfer. **LD74974. $49.95.**

Ingmar Bergman, Sweden, 1961, 91 mins.

The Virgin Spring

Max von Sydow stars in this exploration of a father's revenge for the rape and murder of his daughter. Highly contrasting black and white images evoke an imaginative, medieval world created by cinematographer Sven Nykvist. A stunning work. Swedish with English subtitles.

VHS: S01418. $29.95.

Laser: LD75073. $49.95.

Ingmar Bergman, Sweden, 1960, 88 mins.

Wild Strawberries

One of the great films of Bergman, with Victor Sjostrom as the aged Stockholm professor who recollects his past experiences and becomes aware, for the first time, of his failings and shortcomings. With Bibi Andersson, Ingrid Thulin, Gunnar Bjornstrand. Swedish with English subtitles.

VHS: S01462. $29.95.

Laser: LD70487. $49.95.

Ingmar Bergman, Sweden, 1957, 95 mins.

Winter Light

Bergman's great film about the meaning of faith features Max von Sydow as a village pastor, empty of faith and desperately unloved, who reveals his bitter failure to offer spiritual consolation to his flock. With Ingrid Thulin, Gunnar Bjornstrand. Swedish with English subtitles.

VHS: S01468. $29.95.

Ingmar Bergman, Sweden, 1962, 80 mins.

JAN TROELL

The Emigrants

Max von Sydow and Liv Ullmann star in this epic pioneer story set during the 1850's. A young Swedish farming family leave their homeland for a new life in America. Realistic in its depiction of the hardships endured by the emigrants in their quest, *The Emigrants* movingly dramatizes the strength and determination that drove America's early immigrants. Nominated for four Academy Awards. Dubbed in English.

VHS: S20683. $29.99.

Jan Troell, Sweden, 1971, 151 mins.

Hamsun

Max Von Sydow (*Hannah and Her Sisters, The Seventh Seal*) stars in this complex portrait of Knut Hamsun, the Nobel Prize-winning Norwegian author who stunned the world by siding with Hitler and the Nazis. With Ghita Norby. Swedish, Danish and Norwegian with English subtitles.

VHS: S34729. $89.95.

Jan Troell, Germany/Norway/Sweden/Denmark, 1996, 154 mins.

The New Land

Shot on locations in Wisconsin and Minnesota, *The New Land* provides a moving portrait of pioneer immigrant life rarely seen in the American cinema: a life of hardship and joys, but also a life which is difficult on the emotional life and stability. The film picks up the story from the ending of *The Emigrants* to follow the lives of Kristina and Oskar as they try to establish a life in the upper Midwest. With Max Von Sydow and Liv Ullmann. Dubbed in English.

VHS: S20684. $29.99.

Jan Troell, Sweden, 1972, 205 mins.

Zandy's Bride

The American debut of the talented Jan Troell, about the quirky relationship between a shy, reclusive, pioneering peasant (Gene Hackman) and his mail order bride (Liv Ullmann). With Harry Dean Stanton, Eileen Heckart and Susan Tyrrell.

VHS: S18612. $19.98.

Jan Troell, USA, 1974, 116 mins.

AKI & MIKA KAURISMAKI

Amazon

Framed against the backdrop of the Brazilian rain forest, *Amazon* traces the lives of a failed businessman, (Kari Vaananen), his relationship with a renegade bush pilot (Robert Davi), and his obsession for a beautiful school teacher (Rae Dawn Chong) in a remote outpost. In English.

VHS: S16861. $89.98.

Laser: LD75143. $34.98.

Mika Kaurismaki, USA, 1992, 88 mins.

Ariel

This biting and funny satire is inspired by European black comedies, American road movies and 1930's gangster films. When a Finnish miner loses his job, he is given a huge white Cadillac convertible and embarks on a cross-country trip that leads to a series of unpredictable adventures. Finnish with English subtitles.

VHS: S14067. $79.95.

Aki Kaurismaki, Finland, 1989, 74 mins.

La Vie de Boheme

Kaurismaki succeeds in creating a wonderfully ironic chamber drama about three rebel, eccentric artists—a poet, a painter and a composer. They all live the "bohemian life" in which their friendship and camaraderie are the most valued characteristics, even as each faces the harsh everyday reality of the outer world. Kaurismaki creates a fabulously artificial milieu in a film of gentle and unexpected humor and warmth. French with English subtitles.

VHS: S21117. $19.98.

Aki Kaurismaki, France, 1993, 100 mins.

Leningrad Cowboys Go America

This sublimely absurd road movie chronicles the world tour of the most mediocre polka band in Siberia. Nine musicians, one venal manager and a very determined village idiot leave the tundra for the United States in search of paying gigs. Watch for the cameo by Jim Jarmusch as a used-car dealer. If nothing else you will remember the Cowboys' unique style of dress and grooming. English and Finnish with English subtitles.

VHS: S14785. $19.98.

Aki Kaurismaki, Finland, 1989, 78 mins.

The Match Factory Girl

The final part of Aki Kaurismaki's "Proletarian Trilogy" is a bleak portrait of contemporary Helsinki. The tale focuses on Iris (Kati Outinen), a sad-eyed factory woman who seeks the ultimate revenge on the caustic parents who brutalized her and the wealthy architect who sexually humiliated her. With Elina Salo, Esko Nikkari, Vesa Vierikko and Reijo Taipole. Finnish with English subtitles. On the same program is *Those Were the Days* (1992, 5 mins.), a video of the idiosyncratic Finnish rockers The Leningrad Cowboys.

VHS: S19415. $79.95.

Aki Kaurismaki, Finland, 1989, 70 mins.

Tigrero: A Film That Was Never Made

In 1954, armed with a 16mm camera, film, two cases of vodka and 75 boxes of cigars, director Sam Fuller went to Brazil scouting locations for the action-adventure film *Tigrero*. Although this Darryl F. Zanuck production was cast with John Wayne, Ava Gardner and Tyrone Power, the film was never shot because of insurance problems. All that remains of *Tigrero* is Fuller's intriguing footage of the Karaja tribe and their Amazon Rain Forest home. Forty years later, director Mika Kaurismaki ventures back to this location with Fuller and director Jim Jarmusch to talk with the Karaja about the changing world, talk amongst themselves about Fuller's films and the principles of filmmaking, and tell the story of the film that was never made. This film won the International Critics Award at the 1994 Berlin Film Festival.

VHS: S27618. $89.95.

Mika Kaurismaki, Finland/United Germany/Brazil, 1994, 75 mins.

Zombie and the Ghost Train

A black comedy from Mika Kaurismaki. Described as part docu-fiction, part *Hamlet*-style tragedy and just a bit screwball, this unusual road movie chases after a punk rock band that's never seen, always heard, all the way from Helsinki to Istanbul. Finnish with English subtitles.

VHS: S23429. $59.95.

Mika Kaurismaki, Finland, 1993, 88 mins.

CARL THEODOR DREYER

Day of Wrath

Day of Wrath premiered during the blackest period of Nazi occupation of Denmark. It tells a story of witchcraft in the Denmark of 1623 with great atmospheric intensity, visual beauty, a sense of nature and a sense of anguish. Danish with English subtitles.

VHS: S00311. $29.95.

Carl Theodor Dreyer, Denmark, 1943, 110 mins.

Gertrude

Dreyer's last film, the story of a woman who is unhappily married to a lawyer, meets a famous poet whom she had loved, has an affair with a young composer, and decides to live alone in Paris. Rigorous, poignant, and profound. Danish with English subtitles.

VHS: S00492. $34.95.

Carl Theodor Dreyer, Denmark, 1964, 116 mins.

Leaves from Satan's Book

Dreyer sketches Satan's path through four historical periods, in each as a disrupter of the social forces through already powerful male leaders. Dreyer associates the figure of Christ with female figures, and the photography and composition anticipates his later *Passion of Joan of Arc*. Silent.

VHS: S03699. $29.95.

Carl Theodor Dreyer, Denmark, 1919, 165 mins.

Master of the House

Also known as *Thou Shalt Honor Thy Wife*, Dreyer's early morality piece, the story of a spoiled husband who abuses his ordinary wife and mother. Silent with English subtitles.

VHS: S00832. $39.95.

Carl Theodor Dreyer, Denmark, 1925, 118 mins.

Ordet

From the director of *Passion of Joan of Arc*, *Ordet* is the story of a theology student who loses his memory and believes he is Christ. Based on a play by Kaj Munk, *Ordet* is Dreyer's portrayal of the conflict between organized religion and personal belief. Danish with English subtitles.

VHS: S00969. $29.95.

Carl Theodor Dreyer, Denmark, 1955, 126 mins.

Passion of Joan of Arc

One of the most poignant, terrifying and unrelenting emotional historical documents ever filmed. Called an austere masterpiece in reference to the stark sets and extreme close-up photography, *Joan of Arc* is brilliantly portrayed by Maria Falconetti. Silent.

VHS: S00998. $29.95.

Carl Theodor Dreyer, France, 1928, 114 mins.

Vampyr

Vampyr tells with extraordinary images the nightmarish story of a young man who unwittingly becomes involved with two sisters and their father, all victims of a vampire. Dreyer has transformed LeFanu's horror tale *Camilla* into an abstract meditation on the theme of death, and his brilliant use of shadow, light, camera movement and settings are as unnerving today as they were upon this sinister film's release 60 years ago. This version is beautifully mastered from a 35mm archive print. "Among the masterpieces of the horror film..." (Carlos Clarens, *An Illustrated History of the Horror Film*). German with English subtitles.

VHS: S01407. $29.95.

Carl Theodor Dreyer, Denmark, 1931, 75 mins.

VICTOR SJOSTROM

He Who Gets Slapped

This great American silent film, directed by Sweden's Victor Sjostrom, is remarkable both for the performances of Lon Chaney and Norma Shearer and for Sjostrom's incredible lighting effects and use of Expressionist devices. Chaney plays the brilliant scientist who has been cheated out of his discovery and only meets with derision when he tries to claim recognition. Dejected, he becomes a clown with a French traveling circus, and finally exacts a spectacular revenge. With John Gilbert, Tully Marshall, Marc McDermott and Ford Sterling. Silent with music score.

VHS: S19530. $29.95.

Victor Sjostrom, USA, 1924, 85 mins.

Outlaw and His Wife

The great breakthrough film of the Swedish cinema, Victor Sjostrom's 1917 story takes place in Iceland during the 19th century, and is the story of a farmer hunted by the police for a petty crime, who, with his wife, must flee into the hills. Eventually the couple, united by their mutual love, succumb to the brutal forces of nature. This version, restored by Bengt Forslund of the Swedish Film Institute, is accompanied by a full orchestral score, and is tinted in various hues to suggest location and time of day.

VHS: S03705. $29.95.

Victor Sjostrom, Sweden, 1917, 109 mins.

Phantom Chariot

Based on the legend that the coachman of Death must be replaced by the last man to die each year, Sjostrom's film is as famous for its realistic depictions of life in the slums as for its fantasy sequences which make use of double exposures. Silent.

VHS: S01017. $29.95.

Victor Sjostrom, Sweden, 1920

Secret of the Monastery

This extremely rare work by Victor Seastrom (*He Who Gets Slapped*) is the story of a Polish nobleman who kills his unfaithful wife and tries to atone for his sins. He later becomes a brother in a monastery and tells his story as an aged man who incessantly looks back on a happier life outside the monastery walls and before the enormity of his sins. Silent with musical accompaniment.

VHS: S29893. $39.95.

Victor Sjostrom, Sweden, 1919, 70 mins.

Under the Red Robe

Conrad Veidt, Raymond Massey and Annabella star in this drama about France's notoriously wicked Cardinal Richelieu. A poor soldier is forced to serve the fiend in his conflicts with the protestant Huguenots. Sadly, the soldier falls in love with one of the Cardinal's victims.

VHS: S23814. $24.95.

Victor Sjostrom, Great Britain, 1937, 85 mins.

The Wind

"*The Wind* is one of the masterpieces of the silent cinema" (Georges Sadoul). Lillian Gish plays a sensitive young girl from Virginia who goes to live with her cousin on the lonely Texas prairie. She survives the threat of an intruder whom she kills in self-defense, a dust storm, and a temporary descent into near madness. The most powerful performance of Gish's career, in which Victor Sjostrom perfectly synthesized the forces of nature and those of human emotion.

VHS: S09283. $29.95.

Victor Sjostrom, USA, 1928, 90 mins.

SCANDINAVIAN WORLD

Finland, Fresh and Original

Begin in the capital city of Helsinki and proceed to visit the neo-classical Senate Square and the striking monument to composer Jean Sibelius; also journey to the unspoiled wilderness of Lapland where reindeer herding is an ongoing tradition. 50 mins.

VHS: S12274. $24.95.

Video Visits: Denmark, The Jewel of Europe

Explore Copenhagen, the Carlsberg brewery, the toy fantasies of Legoland Park and the fishing port of Skagen. 52 mins.

VHS: S31456. $24.99.

Video Visits: Sweden, Nordic Treasure

Explore the islands, farmlands, fjords and mountains of Sweden as you visit Skansen, Stockholm and the Kosta Boda glassworks and visit the world's only surviving 17th-century warship. 53 mins.

VHS: S31462. $24.99.

russian cinema

Adam's Rib
A contemporary Russian social comedy reminiscent of Chekhov. Set in a crowded flat, the great Irina Churikova plays the stressed-out post-Soviet woman taking care of mute, disabled (but opportunistic) Grandma and her own two daughters. She also tries to deal with her crazed ex-husband and to put a little love into her life, with devastating and hilarious results. A warm, wry comedy. Russian with English subtitles.
VHS: S20826. $19.98.
Vyacheslav Kristofovich, Russia, 1992, 77 mins.

The Anna Akhmatova File
A moving portrait of the extraordinary Soviet poet, Anna Akhmatova. Although her work was banned and went unpublished for 17 years, her poem "Requiem" became the underground anthem for the millions who suffered under Stalin. This unique film, which uses Akhmatova's diaries for text, also includes portraits of Akhmatova's friends and contemporaries-Boris Pasternak, Vladimir Mayakovsky, Mikhail Sostchenko. Russian with English subtitles.
VHS: S13313. $29.95.
Semeon Aranovitch, USSR, 1989, 65 mins.

Anna Karenina
Based on Tolstoy's beloved 1870 novel, this Russian production of the classic tale of tragic passion and human morality traces the paths chosen by two different people, Anna and Vronsky. Letterboxed. With Tatyana Samoylova, Nikolai Gritsenko and Vasili Lanovoi. Russian with English subtitles.
VHS: S31780. $19.98.
Alexander Zarkhi, Russia, 1967, 103 mins.

Autumn Marathon
Andrei is a polite and educated man, an excellent translator of Dostoevsky, and at 45, an established man of letters and college professor. Alla, 25, is genuinely in love with him and Andrei feels perfectly at home in her flat. His official domicile, however, is with Nina, 40, attractive and charming, a good mother, excellent housewife, and in need of Andrei. So, you can see that life is hard for Andrei. This Soviet comedy, scripted by popular playwright Alexander Volodin, is one of the most interesting Soviet films of the last 20 years. Russian with English subtitles.
VHS: S12971. $59.96.
Georgi Daniela, USSR, 1979, 100 mins.

Ballad of a Soldier
Grigori Chukrai's poetic and elegiac war story is one of the major works of post-war Russian cinema, detailing the odd, bemused moments of a soldier's earnest seduction of a country girl while visiting his mother. The film is also devastating at capturing the dread, pain and humiliation of war, and its effects on the people. "The picture flows in such a swift, poetic way that the tragedy of it is concealed by a gentle lyric quality" (*New York Times*). With Vladimir Ivashov and Shanna Prokhorenko. Russian with English subtitles.
VHS: S17516. $29.95.
Grigori Chukrai, USSR, 1959, 89 mins.

Baltic Deputy
An aged scientist is criticized by his colleagues for his support of the Revolution of 1917 and finds friendship and support among the sailors of the Baltic Fleet, who elect him as their deputy to the Petrograd Soviet, in this first-rate psychological drama. Nikolai Cherkassov, in his first major role, gives a brilliant portrayal of the 75-year-old professor although he himself was only 32. Russian with English subtitles.
VHS: S01938. $65.00.
Alexander Zharki/Josef Heifitz, USSR, 1937, 95 mins.

Black & White
Lisa is a young Soviet emigre studying medicine in Manhattan. She meets Roy, an African-American man working as a building superintendent on New York's Lower East Side, and the two fall in love. Their story of passion while living on the edges of Manhattan is ultimately the story of breaking down the barriers that separate people, the story of the quest for freedom and identity. With Elena Shevchenko, Gilbert Giles, Patrick Godfrey, Gina Delio, Hayward Boling, Debra Jo Jackson and Stephen Parris. In English.
VHS: S26333. $59.95.
Boris Frumin, USA/Russia, 1991, 96 mins.

Boris Frumin Three-Pack
Includes the films *Viva Castro!*, *Black & White* and *The Errors of Youth* (*Wild Oats*) by acclaimed Russian filmmaker Boris Frumin.
VHS: S26354. $149.95.
Boris Frumin, USA/Russia, 1978-1993, 265 mins.

The Burglar
Music and the problems of the young share center stage in this "punk" Soviet film. Russian rock star Konstantin Kinchev plays the older of two brothers who defiantly use Leningrad's budding punk culture as a haven for their drunken dad and oppressive society. While much of the narrative rests on the slender shoulders of the younger brother, Kinchev's charismatic musical performance carry the picture's rebel yell against totalitarian tedium. Russian with English subtitles.
VHS: S12966. $59.95.
Valeri Ogorodnikov, USSR, 1988, 101 mins.

Burnt by the Sun
This Academy Award-winning feature (Best Foreign Language Film) is a wonderfully intimate, Chekhovian idyll set in Stalinist Russia which, at its conclusion, packs an explosive political climax. Director Nikita Mikhalkov plays a legendary revolutionary hero living in a dacha outside Moscow with family and friends. Most of the film's complex relationships are seen through the innocent eyes of Mikhalkov's (and the hero's) beautiful daughter in a film that gently reveals the tragedy of living under Stalinism. Russian with English subtitles.
VHS: S26809. $19.98.
Laser: LD75391. $39.95.
Nikita Mikhalkov, Russia, 1994, 134 mins.

A Chef in Love
Nana Djordjadze's Academy Award-nominated film features French star Pierre Richard in the richly textured story of a free-spirited French chef whose restaurant and extraordinary love affair are both endangered by the Russian revolution. French, Georgian and Russian with English subtitles.
VHS: S32617. $19.95.
Nana Djordjadze, Georgia/France, 1996, 95 mins.

The Chekist
In 1917, secret police from the KGB forerunner, C.H.E.K.A., unleashed a reign of terror on all those considered enemies of the revolution. A Cheka officer interrogates, judges and then executes a wide variety of people who cannot fit into the new Soviet system, from Christians and Jews to former aristocrats. Russian with English subtitles.
VHS: S29476. $89.95.
Aleksandr Rogozhkin, USSR, 1992, 90 mins.

Circus
Grigori Alexandrov's daring attempt to import the American musical comedy form into the Soviet Union was conceived by its director as "an eccentric comedy…a real side-splitter." Its star is an American circus artiste who has a black baby—a daring conceit for 1936! The only way she can find happiness is among the Soviet people. Lyubov Orlova is the star in this rare comedy. Russian with English subtitles.
VHS: S27216. $29.95.
Grigori Alexandrov, USSR, 1936, 89 mins.

Close to Eden
Also known as *Urga*, Nikita Mikhalkov's film is set in the vast rolling steppes of inner Mongolia. The young Mongolian shepherd Gombo, his wife Pagma and family live a simple, 19th century existence. Their lives are interrupted a Russian truck driver named Sergei who insinuates himself into their protected lives. Sergei alters the family's traditional perspective when he takes Gombo on a revealing and hilarious trek into the city. Cinematography by Villenn Kaluta. With Badema, Bayaerty, Vladimir Gostukhin and Babushka. Russian and Mongolian with English subtitles.
VHS: S19262. $94.95.
Nikita Mikhalkov, Mongolia/USSR/France, 1991, 118 mins.

Come and See
This towering, cathartic experience, described as "142 minutes of raw emotion," won top prizes at the Moscow and Venice film festivals. The story is based on writer Alex Adamovich's WWII memoirs of SS reprisals against partisans. Set in occupied Byelorussia in 1943, the film follows a raw teenager into the swamps and forests of the border provinces, where he undergoes a hell of atrocities, becoming a middle-aged wreck as he tries to survive the carnage. Remarkable acting, camera work, crowd scenes and direction raise the film far beyond anything comparable as director Elem Klimov manages both a savage beauty and an impassioned elegy in this anti-war film. Russian with English subtitles.
VHS: S12963. $59.95.
Elem Klimov, USSR, 1985, 142 mins.

Commissar
One of the most celebrated Soviet films. In 1967, a Soviet filmmaker told a tale of Jewish life, suffering, bravery and fatalism in a movie about a Red Army commissar who finds herself living with a small-town Jewish family while civil war rages around them. The film, an indictment of anti-Semitism, was Askoldov's first and last feature film. Shortly after its completion, Askoldov was fired and the film locked away. Now finally released, the film's "artistic and emotional impact is formidable…Askoldov has mastered a poetic style" (*Sight and Sound*). Russianwith English subtitles.
VHS: S12962. $59.95.
Alexander Askoldov, USSR, 1967-87, 110 mins.

The Cranes Are Flying
A film that marked a radical opening for Soviet cinema; the lighthearted, romantic, lyrical story of a beautiful young girl (Tatiana Samoilova) caught up in the horrors of war. When her fiance (Alexei Batalov) goes off to war, she marries a man whom she does not love and who raped her, is evacuated to Siberia, and after the war, learns of her fiance's death. But she refuses to believe it and waits for his return. A great international success which won the Grand Prix at Cannes. Russian with English subtitles.
VHS: S17517. $59.95.
Mikhail Kalatozov, USSR, 1957, 94 mins.

Creation of Adam
Andrey is a young man who fears his marriage may fall apart because his wife thinks he is gay. A series of events confirm these suspicions as Andrey meets Philip, an enterprising business man who turns his life around. Philip shows Andrey how to love. Russian with English subtitles.
VHS: S26405. $39.95.
Yuri Pavlov, Russia, 1993, 93 mins.

Crime and Punishment
Lev Kulijanov's supremely authentic translation of Dostoevsky's great novel to the screen, with Innokenti Smoktunovsky playing the Police Inspector Porfiry, and Georgi Taratorkin as the impoverished student-murderer Raskolnikov. Perhaps the best performance, however, belongs to Tatyana Bedova as Sonia, the beautiful woman with the power of redemption. Cinemascope. Russian with English subtitles.
VHS: S10718. $29.95.
Lev Kulijanov, USSR, 1970, 220 mins.

Dark Eyes
Marcello Mastroianni, in an Oscar-nominated role, is Romano, a romantic with a wife, a mistress and a deep yearning to find a Russian woman he met at a spa. Based on several short stories by Chekhov. The first western film of director Mikhalkov (*Oblomov*). With Silvan Mangano, Marthe Keller and Elena Sofonova. Subtitled.
VHS: Out of print. For rental only.
Laser: LD76325. $49.95.
Nikita Mikhalkov, Italy, 1987, 117 mins.

Don Quixote
A masterful adaptation of Cervantes' great novel features Nikolai Cherkassov as Quixote, who becomes so impressed with tales of chivalry that he becomes a knight errant, and takes up arms to defend the poor and oppressed. Kozintsev brings to the adaptation a great sense of color, spectacle and comedy, but preserves Don Quixote's dignity. Russian with English subtitles.
VHS: S01551. $59.95.
Grigori Kozintsev, USSR, 1957, 110 mins.

The Errors of Youth (Wild Oats)
Deemed "too close to 'real' life in the former Soviet Union" and thus banned in 1979, *The Errors of Youth* is the story of Dmitri (Stanislav Zhdanko), a former conscript in the Red Army (now a highly-paid construction worker in Siberia), who finds his love affair disintegrating over the question of children. Disillusioned, he moves to Leningrad, falls into a life of black marketeers, and enters into a marriage of expediency. Director Boris Frumin left the unfinished film behind and emigrated to the United States, and in a historic gesture on Russia's part, was invited back to Leningrad 11 years later to complete the film. With Stanislav Zhdanko, Marina Neyelova and Natalia Varley. Russian with English subtitles.
VHS: S26332. $59.95.
Boris Frumin, USSR, 1978-1989, 87 mins.

Freedom Is Paradise

With his mother dead and a missing father that he has never met, 13-year-old Sasha finds himself the unwilling resident of a grim reform school. When Sasha accidentally learns of his father's whereabouts, he sets off on a 1,000 mile odyssey to a gulag-style high security prison. Russian with English subtitles.

VHS: S16260. $69.95.

Sergei Bodrov, USSR, 1989, 75 mins.

Freeze, Die, Come to Life

A brilliant Soviet film about the brutal conditions of life in and around Stalinist labor camps as seen through the eyes of two remarkable children. This first feature by Vitaly Kanevski, who also wrote the screenplay and co-produced the film, is based on some of his own experiences during the eight years he spent growing up outside such a camp. With Pavel Nazarov, Dinara Drukarova, Yelena Popova. Awarded the Camera D'Or for best first film at Cannes. Russian with English subtitles.

VHS: S15941. $19.98.

Vitaly Kanevski, USSR, 1991, 105 mins.

Glasnost Film Festival

This remarkable 12-volume set is a unique opportunity to witness first-hand the contemporary achievements of Soviet filmmakers as they examine a broad range of topics and issues affecting their society.

Glasnost Film Festival Vol. 1: Against the Current and The Wood Goblin. *Against the Current* is a film about ecological crime and how the residents of Kirishi educate themselves to the meaning of citizenship. They are called extremists, but they continue to organize protests of a major synthetic protein plant. "We couldn't breathe, we coughed, we itched, we buried our children...but we can't put up with it any more," a young woman shouts indignantly at a rally. The residents call the illness "Bykov's disease," after the factory's founder, who is now a government minister. Directed by Dmitri Delov, 1988, 27 mins. *The Wood Goblin* focuses on an old man who has lived alone in the woods with a cat and two dogs for 15 years, in a house he built by himself. He commanded a tank company during World War II and after the war was a local Communist Party chief. Fired from his position after a smear campaign, he went away to live in the woods. As he puts it, he "joined the party of the green world", which he now defends against resourceful poachers and woodcutters. Directed by Boris Kustov, 1987, 18 mins. Both films in Russian with English subtitles.

VHS: S11666. $59.95.

Glasnost Film Festival Vol. 2: The Temple. A strikingly beautiful film about the 1000th anniversary of Christianity in Russia and the role of religion in Soviet society, both past and present. The filmmakers interpret the spiritual experience of the nation anew. We attend a holiday celebration at the Trinity-Sergius monastery at Zagorsk, and see how a burned house of worship is restored by an entire community. We talk with a young monk and an 80-year-old parish priest, Nikolai. One Soviet reviewer wrote about this film: "We cannot rewrite history. We can only learn lessons from it." Directed by Vladimir Dyakonov, USSR, 1987, 58 mins. Russian with English subtitles.

VHS: S11667. $59.95.

Glasnost Film Festival Vol. 3: The Tailor and Early on Sunday. *The Tailor* is a sobering look at the spiritual void and disillusionment of the current generation of middle-aged adults. They entered life with faith in their talent, in their destiny, and in love. But by the dawn of the Brezhnev years, they were aged before their time, having lost their preferred work and the opportunity for creative self-realization. Directed by Vladislav Mirzoyan, 1988. 50 mins. *Early on Sunday* is a simple, endearing film. On a Sunday morning in winter, several old village women go to the forest to gather wood. They chop down some sturdy pine trees, build a fire, banter about their life and other things, and finally go home. Their unpretentious observations evoke bursts of laughter, feelings of compassion, and an immense respect for the dignity and patience of these women who are unaware of their own worth. Directed by Murat Mamedov, 1987, 18 mins. Russian with English subtitles.

VHS: S11668. $59.95.

Glasnost Film Festival Vol. 4: Chernobyl and The Bam Zone. *Chernobyl: Chronicle of Difficult Weeks* was made by the first film crew in the disaster zone following the meltdown of the Chernobyl nuclear power plant in 1986. For more than two weeks, they fought for the right to film, then shot continuously for more than three months. A lifeless city. Empty villages. A dead forest. Portions of the film itself are exposed with white blotches—radiation leakage. Various agencies blocked its wider release and Soviet film goers saw the film only after the director's tragic death from radiation poisoning. Directed by Vladimir Shevchenko, 1988, 53 mins. *The Bam Zone: Permanent Residents* is a daring film set in Siberia. The Baikal-Amur Mainline (BAM) Railroad is called the longest monument to the stagnation of the Brezhnev era. "Before filming, we screened miles of BAM films. There were marches and songs, meetings and delegations...But behind the screen, actually, equipment was breaking down, lives were broken and souls became calloused." Directed by Mikhail Pavlov, 1987, 18 mins. Russian with English subtitles.

VHS: S11669. $59.95.

Glasnost Film Festival Vol. 5: Scenes at a Fountain and The Limit. The ironic title of *Scenes* refers to a powerful, rumbling column of fire—the world's largest natural gas fire, which burned over one year on the shores of the Caspian Sea. Flames shot 600 feet high. The film dramatically documents the courageous firemen who risked their lives to cap the howling 600 foot high blaze. Directed by Igor Gonopolsky, 1988, 28 mins. *The Limit* is "a shout of horror about how the terrible catastrophe of drinking condemns a human being." Families are divided, homes are neglected, kids are hungry. A powerful examination of rampant alcoholism in the Soviet Union. Directed by Tatyana Skabard, 1988, 14 mins. Russian with English subtitles.

VHS: S11670. $59.95.

Glasnost Film Festival Vol. 6: And the Past Seems But a Dream and Theatre Square. In 1937, a group of children wrote an idealistic book called "We Are from Igarka." The filmmaker planned to film their touching reunion 50 years later. But a different childhood was revealed than that in the book, "a time that was much more painful than the worst nightmare. It's a film about the collapse of faith, first faith in God, then in Stalin. It's about the slavish need for an idol and the complicated attitudes of people to Stalinism." Directed by Sergei Miroshnichenko. *Theatre Square* focuses on a hunger strike in 1988 staged in Erevan over the disputed Nagorno-Karabkh region, populated by Armenians, but part of the neighboring republic of Azerbaijan. Directed by Grigor Arutnyan, 1988, 28 mins. Russian with English subtitles.

VHS: S11671. $59.95.

Glasnost Film Festival Vol. 7: Black Square and Dialogues. *Black Square* tells the story of Russia's artistic avant-garde from the 1950's to the 1970's, when artists were confronted by semi-official, ideological art. Works could be smashed by bulldozer, flooded with acid, or covered with concrete. *Black Square* is a cinematic appreciation of works only recently allowed to be exhibited, and the story of the artists, many of whom were forced into exile. Directed by Joseph Pasternak. 1988, 56 mins. *Dialogues* features a bacchanal of rock jazz and punk that erupt in an abandoned Leningrad palace. Collective singing, dancing and playing makes the group a community. Directed by Nikolai Obukhovich, 1987, 28 mins. Russian with English subtitles.

VHS: S11672. $59.95.

Glasnost Film Festival Vol. 8: This Is How We Live and Homecoming. A shocking look at the alienation of young people in a daring look at Soviet punks—young people who emulate fascists by wearing swastikas on their sleeves. Directed by Vladimir Oseledchik, 1987, 30 mins. *Homecoming* is a remarkably frank look at the veterans of the Soviet involvement in Afghanistan who return home with unresolved feelings about a demoralizing and unpopular war, not unlike the U.S. involvement in Vietnam. Directed by Tatyana Chubakova, 1987, 17 mins. Russian with English subtitles.

VHS: S11673. $59.95.

Glasnost Film Festival Vol. 9: Marshall Blucher: A Portrait Against the Background of an Epoch. This daring film tries to unlock the riddle of the dramatic 30's in the Soviet Union by studying the fate of the entire country through the biography of one hero. Marshal Vasily Konstantinovich Blucher was one of the best Red Army commanders, a man of irreproachable courage and compassion. Yet in 1938, he was declared an "enemy of the people," and perished in Stalin's torture chambers. Rare archival footage illustrates the excesses of the Stalin era. Directed by Vladimir Eisner, USSR, 1988, 88 mins. Russian with English subtitles.

VHS: S11674. $59.95.

Glasnost Film Festival Vol. 10: The Trial II and Adonis XIV. *The Trial* dramatically chronicles the Stalinist trials of the 30's and 40's, and a court of conscience, putting the epoch of the Stalin personality cult itself on trial. The "Testament" by famed Bolshevik theoretician Nikolai Bukharin, who was executed by Stalin, is revealed here for the first time by his wife Anna. Directed by Igor Belyayev, 1988, 55 mins. *Adonis XIV* is a parable—a goat, its horns ornamented with little bells, leads a herd of sheep, cows and horses to the slaughterhouse. The symbolism was not lost on the censors, who banned the film for over nine years. One director said, "Everyone who sees this short story should look around and ask himself, 'Why did I survive?'" Directed by Bako Sadykov. 1977, 1988, 9 mins. Russian with English subtitles.

VHS: S11675. $59.95.

Glasnost Film Festival Vol. 11: Final Verdict and The Evening Sacrifice. *Final Verdict* is a look at an actual case: a handsome student, on trial, killed a woman and her guest. This remarkable investigation of "in cold blood" tries to understand the motivation behind the tragedy. The killer is a man of intelligence, and during his 20 months on death row discovers he is no longer the person he once was. The film argues the death sentence does not remove the guilt of the killer. Directed by Hertz Frank, 1987, 88 mins. *The Evening Sacrifice* captures the spirit of a crowd. "He placed the camera in the right place and turned it on at the right moment" in this freewheeling example of "underground" filmmaking from the Soviet Union. Directed by Alexander Sokurov, 1987, 17 mins. Russian with English subtitles.

VHS: S11676. $59.95.

Glasnost Film Festival Vol. 12: Are You Going to the Ball? and Tomorrow Is a Holiday. What is the price young athletes pay for their fleeting celebrity? *Are You Going to the Ball?* takes an unprecedented look at one of the Soviet Union's most sacred institutions: its world-famous women's gymnastic team. "It seems to me I gave up all my health for gymnastics," a former champion says in the film, "My entire body is in pain, and now my time is over." Directed by Nadezhda Khvorova, 1987, 28 mins. *Tomorrow Is a Holiday* looks at women whose job is to stuff live chickens into metal containers. The camera observes there is not much difference between the executioners and their victims. The workers' dorms are utilitarian lodgings, sort of containers for people. The women, enraged by their abnormal living conditions, "keep singing songs to avoid crying or swearing." Directed by Sergei Bosukovsky, 1987, 18 mins. Russian with English subtitles.

VHS: S11677. $59.95.

Glasnost Film Festival Complete Set. The complete set of 12 volumes of the Glasnost Film Festival at a special price.

VHS: S11678. $399.99.

The Gorky Trilogy

The renowned Russian film series by director Mark Donskoi, which is based on the autobiography of Maxim Gorky. Here Donskoi re-creates the tone and mood of Gorky's autobiographical stories with an astounding intensity of feeling. "These dramas still retain their vast humanity and optimism, and they remain the best loved of all Soviet films" (David Robinson). Russian with English subtitles. 100 mins. each.

Part 1: My Childhood. The first and most famous part of the trilogy depicts Gorky's early life in the 1870's. At the age of four Gorky is placed in the care of his cruel grandfather and loving grandmother. After experiencing the misery of abuse and poverty with his new family, he is forced into the streets and becomes a wandering beggar. 1938.

VHS: S15372. $39.95.

Part 2: My Apprenticeship. In the second part of the trilogy, Gorky begins earning his living at the age of eight. Becoming an apprentice to a bourgeois family that falsely promises him an education, he secretly learns to read on his own and sets off on a series of land and sea voyages. During these excursions Gorky sees that the poverty and misery he has continually suffered are facts of everyday life for most of the Russian people. With this recognition he encounters the seeds of the coming revolution. 1939.

VHS: S15373. $39.95.

Part 3: My Universities. In the final part of his trilogy, Donskoi deals with Gorky's early manhood. At the University Gorky meets several liberal intellectuals and is introduced to their radical politics. Making his first attempts at writing, Gorky joins the revolution and begins to accept his role in this quickly-changing world as a brand new person, washed clean of a painful and stunted past. 1940.

VHS: S15374. $39.95.

Mark Donskoi, USSR, 1938-1940

House Built on Sand

A slice of life among the Russian intelligentsia on the eve of World War II. Ada and Sonya were both 30 in 1937. Ada and her friends play a practical joke on Sonya, sending her a love letter from a supposed admirer. But history plays its own sadistic practical joke: a haunting reminder of Stalin's psychotic purge of 1938 and the nightmarish German siege of Leningrad. "Beautiful, leisurely and exceedingly subtle" (Kevin Thomas, *Los Angeles Times*). Russian with English subtitles.

VHS: S33361. $59.95.

Niyole Adomenaite, Russia, 1991, 75 mins.

I Am Cuba

The Cuban revolution is at the center of Mikhail Kalatazov's strange, poetic film from 1964 which unites four stories. Originally controversial because of a uniquely Russian view of Cuba, it was not widely seen. Now the film, which features a poem by Yevgeni Yevtushenko, has been re-released to critical acclaim. It offers a uniquely earthy view of Cuba in the early 1960s. Spanish with English subtitles.

VHS: S27339. $29.95.

Mikhail Kalatozov, Cuba/USSR, 1964, 141 mins.

I Was Stalin's Bodyguard

A controversial film that created a storm in Russia by taking the cloak off a violent, repressive era of Soviet history. Filmmaker Semeon Aranovitch found the last surviving personal bodyguard of Josef Stalin, who began to work for him in the 1930s. *I Was Stalin's Bodyguard* weaves together unprecedented, first-hand testimony with rare footage, including Stalin's home movies. What emerges is a singular portrait of a violent and complex era during which Stalin consolidated his power through brutal repression, yet led the Soviet Union to victory in World War II. Russian with English subtitles.

VHS: S13312. $29.95.

Semeon Aranovitch, USSR, 1990, 73 mins.

I Worked for Stalin

Semeon Aranovich's documentary is a brilliant assembly of eyewitness testimony and rare archival photographs and materials. The film records the Machiavellian power plays between Zhdanov, Andreyev, Khrushchev, Malenkov, Suslov and Molotov as they maneuvered for power and prestige to gain the inside track of becoming Stalin's successor. The film is a chilling record of the inner workings of an authoritarian state. Russian with English subtitles.

VHS: S18686. $29.95.

Semeon Aranovitch, USSR, 1990, 67 mins.

Incident at Map Grid 36-80

A Cold War thriller that's a Soviet response to *The Hunt for the Red October*, about an apocalyptic struggle following a Soviet naval squadron's encounter with a disabled American nuclear submarine. The submarine's computer malfunctions, inadvertently launching its nuclear payload. The film is important for its unprecedented portrait of Soviet military life and its modern technology. Russian with English subtitles.

VHS: S12973. $59.95.
Mikhail Tumanshishvili, USSR, 1983, 85 mins.

Inspector General

Gogol's famous play, performed by members of the Moscow Art Theatre, filmed by Vladimir Petrov. Gogol's work is a satire of provincial corruption in Czarist Russia. An entire town mistakes an illiterate worker for the Czar's Inspector General, and the corrupt officials panic as they believe the man has come to check up on them. Russian with English subtitles.

VHS: S00628. $49.95.
Vladimir Petrov, USSR, 1954, 128 mins.

Interpretation of Dreams

Twentieth-century Russia is the less-than-willing subject of this close psychoanalytic interpretation, inspired by Freud's book of the same name. Archival and newsreel footage, together with commentary employing the psychoanalytic method, offer greatinsights which clarify such cataclysmic events as the rise of Stalin and the Cold War. This acclaimed film has been called "truly magical and extraordinary…" and "an astonishing marriage of Freudian thinking and history." Russian with English subtitles.

VHS: S21132. $29.95.
Andrei Zagdansky, Russia, 1994, 50 mins.

Is It Easy to Be Young

A controversial Soviet documentary, made in 1987, the first look at the punk rock subculture in the Soviet Union. Filmmaker Yuri Podniek captures punks cavorting at a concert, being dragged into court for smashing up a train, and telling the camera about the tender hopes and the drab realities of their lives as hospital orderlies, morticians, and drug-addicted, disillusioned Afghanistan veterans. A powerful, disturbing film. Russian with English subtitles.

VHS: S12967. $59.95.
Yuri Podniek, USSR, 1987, 90 mins.

Jazz Comedy (Jolly Fellows)

Grigori Alexandrov's first musical comedy is the rags-to-fame story of a shepherd boy who reaches lofty heights as a jazz-orchestra conductor. The film belongs to its heroine—Lyubov Orlova—who established herself as the first recognized star of Soviet cinema. *Jazz Comedy* is also remarkable for the clever camera work of Vladimir Nilsen, who introduced Western camera tricks to Soviet cinema. Russian with English subtitles.

VHS: S27215. $29.95.
Grigori Alexandrov, USSR, 1934, 98 mins.

Jazzman

Good-natured flights of fancy strive to overcome harsh ideological realities in the light-hearted Soviet film, *The Jazzman*, as a conservatory musician links up with three street musicians. The four try, in the words of the idealogue, to "popularize the monstrous product of a bourgeois culture,"—in other words, to start the first Soviet jazz combo. A charming film with lots of Soviet Dixieland. Russian with English subtitles.

VHS: S12965. $59.95.
Karen Chakhnazarov, USSR, 1983, 95 mins.

Kindergarten

A largely autobiographical memoir directed by poet Yevgeni Yevtushenko, recalling his boyhood years during World War II in Russia while the city of Moscow was being evacuated as the Nazis approached. Told as a picaresque adventure about a little boy who meets carloads of strange characters, the narrative assumes a poetic, experimental form of storytelling as Yevtushenko recreates the overcrowded railroad stations, Nazi planes, black marketeers, women bandits and passengers and villagers. Russian with English subtitles.

VHS: S12974. $59.95.
Yevgeny Yevtushenko, USSR, 1983, 160 mins.

King Lear (Kozintsev)

One of the truly great Soviet films, and possibly the greatest adaptation of Shakespeare to the screen, Grigori Kozintsev's epic adaptation, shot in Lithuania, is a stunningly visual tour-de-force. With screenplay by Boris Pasternak. Russian with English subtitles.

VHS: S03555. $59.95.
Grigori Kozintsev, USSR, 1971, 140 mins.

Lady with the Dog

Based on Chekhov, and directed by the Russian master of Chekhov adaptations, Josef Heifitz, this bittersweet, nostalgic story opens in Yalta at the beginning of the century. A middle-aged bank official on vacation encounters a beautiful young woman named Anna who each day walks her dog along the promenade. They drift into an affair, part, return to their homes and unhappy marriages, but Dmitri is haunted by Anna's memory and the two arrange clandestine meetings, realizing that they are doomed to a life of brief, secret encounters. Russian with English subtitles.

VHS: S01925. $29.95.
Josef Heifitz, USSR, 1960, 86 mins.

Leo Tolstoy

This feature-length film traces the turbulent life of one of the greatest writers of the 19th century, Leo Tolstoy. Follow his life from childhood through his stormy marriage to his death. A vital biography for all who are interested in gaining insight into the driving forces behind Tolstoy's body of work. Russian with English subtitles.

VHS: S13008. $59.95.
Sergei Gerasimov, USSR, 1983, 180 mins.

Lessons at the End of Spring

A young boy's loss of innocence within a pre-perestroika Russian prison is the Kafkaesque premise of this harrowing film. The impressive feature debut of writer-director Oleg Kavun, *Lessons at the End of Spring* immediately places him at the forefront of Russia's groundbreaking new wave of angry young filmmakers. A landmark in the evolution of Soviet cinema. Mature themes and extensive male nudity. Russian with English subtitles.

VHS: S15495. $69.95.
Olag Kavun, USSR, 1989, 75 mins.

Little Vera

The film that took Russia by storm and then sent a second shock wave when its young star, Natalya Negoda, posed nude for *Playboy*, declared "a smash hit" by *Time Magazine* and "Steamy Sex!" by *Los Angeles Times*. Negoda plays Vera, the sullen, sultry teenager who's torn between her brooding husband and her bitter parents in a dead-end town. With her simmering sensuality and brutal candor, *Little Vera* is a seductive Russian film that gave the Russians (and Americans) something which they never expected—a truly new sex kitten. Russian with English subtitles.

VHS: S10576. $29.95.
Laser: CLV. **LD70262. $39.95.**
Vassili Pitchul, USSR, 1988, 135 mins.

Luna Park

A gang of young, tough skinheads make their mark in the chaotic turmoil of post-Communist Russia, where right-wing extremists of all sorts abound. This iron-pumping gang, led by its crazed leader, knows no limits in its terrifying effort to purify the nation. It's a rollercoaster ride of an action film in the tradition of Mad *Max*. Russian with English subtitles.

VHS: S21196. $29.95.
Pavel Lounguine, USSR, 1992, 107 mins.

Magic Horse

The first cartoon feature film from the Soviet Union, based on one of the most popular children's folk tales, about a boy who befriends a magical horse. With sound dubbed into English.

VHS: S00798. $29.95.
Ivanov Vano, USSR, 1941, 56 mins.

Masters of Russian Animation

Animated films produced by Moscow's world renowned Soyuzmultfilm Studio, including 12 award-winning films.

Masters of Russian Animation: Volume 1. Includes *Film Film Film* (Fyodor Khitruk, 1969, 20 mins.); *Girlfriend* (Yelena Gavrilko, 1990, 10 mins.); *Hunt* (Eduard Nazarov, 1979, 10 mins.); and *Ballerina on a Boat* (Lev Atamanov, 1970, 17 mins.). Total length: 57 mins.
VHS: S33844. $24.95.

Masters of Russian Animation: Volume 2. Includes *Island* (Fyodor Khitruk, 1974, 10 mins.); *Singing Teacher* (Lev Atamanov, 3 mins.); *Last Hunt* (Valentine Karavayev, 1984, 10 mins.); *Old Stair* (Alexander Gorlenko, 1995, 7 mins.); and *Liberated Don Quixote* (Vadim Kurchevsky, 18 mins.). Total length: 48 mins.
VHS: S33845. $24.95.

Masters of Russian Animation: Volume 3. Includes *Contact* (Vladimir Tarasov, 1979, 10 mins.); *Travels of an Ant* (Eduard Nazarov, 1984, 10 mins.); *Cat & Company* (Alexander Guriev, 1991, 10 mins.); and *Tale of Tales* (Yuri Norstein, 1980, 30 mins.). Total length: 60 mins.
VHS: S33846. $24.95.

Masters of Russian Animation: Volume 4. Special children's collection includes *Travels of an Ant* (Eduard Nazarov, 1984, 10 mins.); *Ballerina on a Boat* (Lev Atamanov, 1970, 17 mins.); *Last Hunt* (Valentine Karavayev, 1984, 10 mins.); *Cat & Company* (Alexander Guriev, 1991, 10 mins.); and *Hunt* (Eduard Nazarov, 1979 10 mins.). Total length: 57 mins.
VHS: S33847. $24.95.

Masters of Russian Animation: Volume 5. Includes *Battle of Kerjenets* (Yuri Norstein, 1972, 10 mins.); *Seasons* (1970, 10 mins.); *Heron and Crane* (1975, 10 mins.); *Hedgehog in the Fog* (1977, 10 mins.); and *Tale of Tales* (30 mins.). Total length: 70 mins.
VHS: S33848. $24.95.

Masters of Russian Animation: Volume 6—The Works of Fyodor Khitruk & The Works of Eduard Nazarov. Includes the Khitruk short films *Film Film Film* (1969, 20 mins.); *Island* (1974, 10 mins.); *Lion and Ox* (1984, 10 mins.); and the Nazarov films *Hunt* (1979, 10 mins.); *There Was a Dog* (1983, 10 mins.); and *Travels of an Ant* (1984, 10 mins.). Total length: 70 mins.
VHS: S33849. $24.95.

Masters of Russian Animation: Volume 7. Includes *Firing Range* (Anatoly Petrov, 1978, 10 mins.); *Ball of Yarn* (Nikolai Serebriakov, 10 mins.); *Wolf and Calf* (Mikhail Kamanetsky, 1986, 10 mins.); *My Green Crocodile* (Vadim Kurchevsky, 10 mins.); and *Alter Ego* (Nina Shorina, 10 mins.). Total length: 50 mins.
VHS: S33850. $24.95.

Moscow Does Not Believe in Tears

Vladimir Menshov's melodrama about the cruel anonymity of city life is structured in two parts. The first half is set in 1958, as Menshov charts the interlocking romantic fates of three Russian girls shunned to a workers' dormitory. Tonya (Raisa Ryazanova) finds grace and happiness; Ludmila (Irina Muraveva) is trapped in an unhealthy and oppressive marriage; Katerina (Vera Alentova) is crudely abandoned when her lover discovers she's pregnant. The second half resumes their stories and lives 20 years later. Winner of the 1980 Academy Award for Best Foreign Film. With Alexei Batalov, Alexander Fatiushin and Boris Smorchkov. Russian with English subtitles.

VHS: S19053. $59.95.
Vladimir Menshov, USSR, 1980, 148 mins.

Moscow Parade

Ute Lemper stars in this, the first post-Soviet film about the Stalin era. In 1939, she is a young aristocrat married to a hateful chief of the secret police. His forces have murdered her family but she takes advantage of her marriage to enjoy all the luxuries her present lifestyle allows. When she meets a mysterious man and learns of his plans to paint a horse black, her life is thrown into a whirlwind of change. Russian with English subtitles.

VHS: S21091. $29.95.
Ivan Dykhovichny, USSR, 1993, 103 mins.

New Babylon (Novyi Vavilon)

The Paris Commune of 1871 represents a historic moment that could have led to momentous changes had it succeeded. This early silent Soviet production is based on the events of that often overlooked "forgotten revolution." It dramatizes the fight of the Communards through the story of a young woman caught up in the struggle against the bourgeois. Told in eight parts, this silent epic captures the historic sweep of revolutionary Paris. Includes Dmitri Shostakovich's first film score.

VHS: S27374. $29.95.
Grigori Kozintsev/Leonid Trauberg, USSR, 1929

No Greater Love

The powerful story of a Russian woman who turns her villagers into partisans for revenge against the Germans, who have killed her husband and infant son. An important war-time Soviet film made during the War (1943), the film was dubbed into English by the Soviets. Vera Maretskaya gives an incredible performance as the peasant woman. Dubbed in English.

VHS: S03355. $49.95.
Frederic Ermler, USSR, 1943, 74 mins.

Oblomov

A beautiful adaptation of the famous Ivan Goncharov novel by Nikita (*Dark Eyes, Slave of Love*) Mikhalkov. Oblomov owns 350 serfs he's never met, and just lies on his back in a St. Petersburg apartment, sleeping, eating, sleeping some more, watching his finances dwindle and whining at his servant for not being sensitive enough. A detailed, beautifully photographed film. Russian with English subtitles.

VHS: S12969. $59.95.
Nikita Mikhalkov, USSR, 1980, 120 mins.

Orlova Three-Pack

Includes three films starring Lyubov Orlova, the first recognized star of Soviet cinema: *Volga-Volga, Jazz Comedy (Jolly Fellows)* and *Circus*. Russian with English subtitles.

VHS: S27217. $79.95.
Grigori Alexandrov, USSR, 1934-37, 277 mins.

Othello

Russian actor/director Sergei Bondarchuk (*War and Peace*) stars as the Moor of Venice in this very unusual and compelling Russian adaptation of Shakespeare's great play. The film was awarded the Best Director at the Cannes Film Festival. Dubbed in English.

VHS: S23900. $29.95.
Sergei Yutkevich, Russia, 1955, 108 mins.

The Overcoat

Roland Bykov delivers a moving performance as the poor, degraded clerk in 18th century Russia in this version of Nikolai Gogol's famous short story. Expressionistic in tone, but with a strong dose of realism, it is a commendable adaptation of the story. Russian with English subtitles.

VHS: S00985. $39.95.
Alexei Batalov, USSR, 1962, 73 mins.

Patriots

A remarkable film about divided loyalties in a small Russian town during World War I. The film blends comic, ironic and tragic elements to evoke the eccentric inhabitants of the town, with performances full of spontaneity and remarkably naturalistic use of sound. Yelena Kuzmina stars in a comic role with Nikolai Bogolyubov and Nikolai Kryuchov. "There is something of Chekhov's plays…the concealed and repressed emotions of its characters, the pauses and hints, the circumstances and atmosphere of events, the combination of comic and dramatic elements, all building a profound inner rhythm" (O. Borisov). Russian and German with English subtitles.

VHS: S01939. $59.95.
Boris Barnet, USSR, 1934, 82 mins.

People's Gala Concert

A landmark documentary; Semeon Aranovitch explores the roots of Russian anti-Semitism during Stalin's final years, set around the murder of the brilliant actor Solomon Mikhoels and the case of a group of Russian doctors charged with attempting to poison Stalin. Aranovitch draws on rare archival footage and interviews with survivors and their descendants to relate this untold history. Russian with English subtitles.

VHS: S15824. $79.95.
Semeon Aranovitch, Russia, 1991, 143 mins.

Peter the First Part One

A lavish, spectacular production, the first part covers the early years of the reign of Tsar Peter I. Russian with English subtitles.

VHS: S01552. $59.95.
Vladimir Petrov, USSR, 1937, 95 mins.

Peter the First Part Two

The second part of the lavish biography of Peter the First of Russia. Russian with English subtitles.

VHS: S01553. $59.95.
Vladimir Petrov, USSR, 1938, 104 mins.

Planeta Burg

A foreign sci-fi masterpiece! Cosmonauts land on Venus to find themselves in peril by various alien monstrosities. This appears to be the actual print that Roger Corman used to make parts of the negative to *Voyage to the Prehistoric Planet* (the film cans are addressed to Roger). Visually stunning. Based on a story by Stanislav Lem. Russian with English subtitles.

VHS: S15370. $29.95.
Pavel Klushantsev, USSR, 1962, 73 mins.

Prisoner of the Mountains

A tightly executed moral drama of love and war, Sergei Bodrov's Academy Award-nominated film is based on Tolstoy's classic tale and set in the remote, austerely beautiful Caucasus mountains. Sacha, the dashing soldier (Russian heartthrob Oleg Menshikov, *Burnt by the Sun*), and the young recruit Vania (Sergei Bodrov, Jr.) are captured by a Chechen father who holds them hostage in his village home. The father attempts a prisoner exchange for his son, who is held by the Russian army, but is defeated by lackadaisical and inept bureaucracy of the military. As the two Russians await their fate, a love gradually develops between Vania and their captor's daughter. Russian with English subtitles.

VHS: S31726. $95.99.
Laser: LD76294. $39.99.
Sergei Bodrov, USSR, 1996, 99 mins.

Private Life

Nominated for an Academy Award for Best Foreign Film, *Private Life* focuses on an executive who loses his perch in the bureaucracy, and finds out what his family and friends really think of him. An acutely observed portrait of hypocrisy in the Soviet middle-class, with vividly drawn observations. With Mikhail Ulyanov, Ita Sanvina and Irena Gubanova. Russian with English subtitles.

VHS: S12968. $59.95.
Yuli Raizman, USSR, 1983, 103 mins.

The Red Tent

A virtually unknown but first-rate film by Soviet filmmaker Mikhail Kalatozov, *The Red Tent* was an international production funded in Italy, and is the tragic story of General Nobile, the heroic Italian who tried to cross the North Pole on a dirigible in the early years of this century. When the dirigible crashed, no one responded to their desperate SOS calls, and the survivors huddled within their makeshift red canvas dwelling and continued to hope. Peter Finch stars as General Nobile, Sean Connery portrays the renowned Arctic explorer Roald Amundsen. In English.

VHS: S07414. $19.95.
Laser: LD75303. $39.98.
Mikhail Kalatozov, Italy/USSR, 1969, 121 mins.

Revolt of the Fishermen

An extremely rare film: the only cinematic work by the great theater genius Erwin Piscator made in Russia is set on the ship St. Barbara and remarkable for its mixture of naturalism and expressionism. With Alexei Diky, Emma Tseraskaya.

VHS: S24125. $29.95.
Erwin Piscator, USSR, 1935, 60 mins.

Road to Life

Orphaned youths collect into gangs following the turmoil caused by Russia's Revolutionary and Civil wars. Mustafa leads one band sent to be reformed in an experimental program. Despite a caring teacher, change is complicated by new trades and their inescapable criminal pasts. Russian with English subtitles.

VHS: S22473. $39.95.
Nicolai Ekk, USSR, 1931, 100 mins.

Scarecrow

Called the Soviet *Lord of the Flies, Scarecrow* is a haunting and touching film about a little girl who is ostracized by her cruel classmates. She learns about mob psychology the hard way, registering her bitter comprehension with a luminously expressive face. Russian with English subtitles. With Christula Crbakaita, Yuri Nukulin.

VHS: S12964. $59.95.
Rolan Bykov, USSR, 1985, 101 mins.

Seagull

A sensitive, exquisitely acted version of Chekhov's great play, set in provincial Russia, a penetrating study of the languid melancholia of the residents of an isolated country estate. With Alla Demidova, Lyudmila Savelyeva, Yuri Yakovlev. Russian with English subtitles.

VHS: S01170. $29.95.
Yuri Karasik, USSR, 1971, 99 mins.

Second Circle

Susan Sontag calls Alexander Sokurov "perhaps the most ambitious and original serious filmmaker of his generation." In this film, considered Sokurov's best by many critics, a man confronts his father's death in a society cut off from spiritual values. "Rarely has so much visual and emotional power been generated… the film is extreme in its rigor, subtlety and its sublimity" (*Christian Science Monitor*). Russian with English subtitles.

VHS: S26495. $59.95.
Alexander Sokurov, Russia, 1990, 90 mins.

The Shooting Party

Emil Lotenau's adaptation of Chekhov's short story about a passive magistrate whose unconsummated desire for a woodsman's daughter leads to a terrifying act of violence, official approval and attempted cover up. The film is related in flashback, as Lotenau deftly explores the judge's turpitude, and by larger extension, the corrupt pre-czarist culture. "So rich in its imagery, to watch [this film] is a fascinating, almost intoxicating experience" (Vincent Canby). With Galina Belyayeva and Oleg Yankovsky. Russian with English subtitles.

VHS: S19066. $79.95.
Emil Lotenau, USSR, 1977, 105 mins.

Sideburns

Yuri Mamin's bitter, dark satire about the rise of fascism and reactionary elements in Russia concerns The Pushkin Club, a right-wing movement, enlisted by the Party to orchestrate "a social cleaning service," charged with eliminating "the scum of Western influence." The film's goal is "to make people laugh at reality before they die of horror," Mamin says. Russian with English subtitles.

VHS: S16737. $59.95.
Yuri Mamin, USSR, 1991, 110 mins.

Stalin: By Those Who Knew Him

Includes the films *I Was Stalin's Bodyguard, The Anna Akhmatova File* and *I Worked for Stalin*. Russian with English subtitles.

VHS: S31724. $79.95.
Semeon Aranovitch, USSR, 1989-90, 205 mins.

A Summer to Remember

A small, intimate portrait that recounts the adolescence of a young boy growing up in southern Russia, recalling the relationship with his mother and stepfather, and evoking an innocence and atmosphere he cannot reclaim. The boy's stepfather is played by the excellent Russian filmmaker Sergey Bondarchuk (*War and Peace*). Russian with English subtitles.

VHS: S01280. $39.95.
Georgi Danileya/Igor Talankin, USSR, 1960, 78 mins.

Sword and the Dragon

Beautiful fairytale from Soviet director Alexander Ptushko in which a magic potion and a legendary sword lead a simple farmer into battle against the invading Tugars and their evil leader. Amid galloping hooves and clashing swords, Ilya and his mighty warriors battle to defend their homeland. English dubbed.

VHS: S09194. $19.95.
Alexander Ptushko, USSR, 1960, 81 mins.

Taxi Blues

Pavel Lounguine's first feature is a critique of contemporary Soviet society, captured through the bleak and paternalistic relationship of a hard-drinking, fascist, anti-Semitic taxi driver and a dependent, alcoholic Jewish saxophonist. A French/Soviet co-production with excellent lead performances of Piotr Mamonov and Piotr Zaitchenko. Russian with English subtitles.

VHS: S17398. $29.95.
Pavel Lounguine, USSR/France, 1990, 110 mins.

Tchaikovvsky

An opulent biography of the 19th century composer. The film is centered around his antagonistic relationship with his mentor, the pianist Rubenstein, and his long-term benefactor, the Baroness von Meck. The film downplays the composer's homosexuality to develop the tenets of his unhappy marriage. Music arranged and conducted by Dimitri Tiomkin. With Innokenti Smoktunovsky, Antonina Shuranova and Evgeni Leonov. Russian with English subtitles.

VHS: S19056. $59.95.
Igor Talankin, USSR, 1971, 153 mins.

The Theme

Glen Panfilov's daring work was banned by Soviet authorities for eight years. Esenin (Mikhail Ulyanov), a government-approved playwright and functionary, visits his native village for some artistic rejuvenation and falls for a dynamic and brilliant but uncompromising young artist, Sasa (Inna Churikova), who rejects his overtures. Winner of the 1987 Golden Bear winner at the Berlin Film Festival. With Stansilav Lyubshin, Evgeny Vesnik and Sergei Nikonenko. Russian with English subtitles.

VHS: S19054. $59.95.
Gleb Panfilov, USSR, 1979, 98 mins.

To See Paris and Die

Set behind the iron curtain of 1960s Russia, *To See Paris and Die* tells the story of Elena and her obsessive campaign to win a government-sponsored music scholarship for her gifted son, Yuri. Harboring a secret that could hurt Yuri's chances (that he is Jewish), Elena's drive clouds her sense of justice in this paranoid world of political and religious repression. With Tatyana Vasilyeva and Dimitry Malikov. Russian with English subtitles.

VHS: S32223. $89.95.
Alexander Proshkin, USSR, 1993, 110 mins.

The Twelfth Night

Klara Luchko and Alla Larianova star in this masterful Russian adaptation of Shakespeare's great work. All the wit and lyrical humor of this famed play are brilliantly captured in this entertaining and handsome production. Dubbed in English.

VHS: S23906. $29.95.
Yan Fried, Russia, 1956, 88 mins.

An Unfinished Piece for a Mechanical Piano

A bittersweet, humorous tapestry of human folly and lost dreams, loosely based on Chekhov's play *Platonov*. The course of the film takes place during a summer day at a decaying summer dacha. The hero had a spoilt love affair and now meets his old girlfriend, married to another. All his passions and frustrations burst out in the open. The film's leisurely atmosphere belies the intensity of the emotional content underneath, with Mikhalkov revealing profound moments of truth. With Alexander Kalyagin, Yelena Solovieva and Yevgey Glushenko. Russian with English subtitles.

VHS: S18694. $29.95.
Nikita Mikhalkov, USSR, 1977, 100 mins.

Viva Castro!

Set in Russia in the 60's, when Fidel Castro was as popular as Elvis Presley was in America, *Viva Castro!* is a brilliant look at Russia's disaffected generation of the young. The year is 1965 and the setting is a small Russian town. Young Kolya's father flees from his home and his family after stealing some coins from a museum, and Kolya's mother is sent to a labor camp as punishment for her husband's crime. Kolya falls in love with his singing teacher, but when his father returns from exile, he becomes involved with his father's nurse. With Pavel Zharkov, Julia Sobolevskaya and Sergey Dontsov. Russian with English subtitles.

VHS: S26331. $59.95.
Boris Frumin, Russia, 1993, 82 mins.

Volga-Volga
An unseen miracle of 1930's Soviet cinema, *Volga Volga* is a revelation—a classic musical comedy that catapulted Lyubov Orlova into a Russian mega star. The setting is a giant steamboat making its way up the Volga River. On board is a motley collection of amateur singers and dancers travelling to Moscow to take part in a musical contest. At their center is Lyubov Orlova, featured alongside veteran Meyerhold comedian Igor Ilinsky. A triumphant success upon its release, it remains one of the most important and best-loved films produced by the Soviet regime. Russian with English subtitles.
VHS: S27214. $29.95.
Grigori Alexandrov, USSR, 1937, 90 mins.

War and Peace
The definitive version of Sergei Bondarchuk's epic adaptation of Tolstoy's novel. The story concerns how Napoleon's 1912 Russian invasion affected two upper class families. Winner of the 1968 Best Foreign Language Academy award, the film was shot over five years, with a cast of 10,000 soldiers, nearly 300 sets, 2,000 costumes and production design and art direction culled from more than 40 Russian museums. The film is notable for its gritty authenticity and naturalism and its panoramic social and political portraits, especially the battle of Borodino. Three cassettes. With Ludmila Savelyeva, Vyacheslav Tikhonov and Bondarchuk.
Dubbed in English.
VHS: S07683. $99.95.
Russian with English Subtitles.
VHS: S18466. $99.95.
Sergei Bondarchuk, Russia, 1968, 403 mins.

Window to Paris
This wonderfully inventive, wildly hilarious comedy from Yuri Mamin starts in St. Petersburg, where an impoverished music teacher finds that the closet door of his new one-room apartment opens onto a window on the other side of which lies…Paris! Soon the denizens of the Russian flat are busy transporting themselves (and all the goods they can find) over the Paris rooftops into their St. Petersburg apartment. *Window to Paris* is a sharp, witty and totally original satire. Russian with English subtitles.
VHS: S27083. $96.99.
Laser: LD75447. $34.95.
Yuri Mamin, Russia, 1994, 92 mins.

ANDREI TARKOVSKY

Andrei Rublev
The dazzling and harrowing tale of the 15th century icon painter who survives the cruelties of medieval Russia to create works of art. As bloody Tartar raids, religious brutality, and pagan rites work to quell Rublev's desires and needs, he undertakes a spiritual odyssey that affirms man's ability to transcend adversity. This restored director's cut is presented in letterbox format; Russian with English subtitles.
VHS: S16526. $19.98.
Laser: Uncut, 205 mins. Contains behind-the-scenes production footage. **LD72435. $99.95.**
Andrei Tarkovsky, USSR, 1966, 185 mins.

Directed by Andrei Tarkovsky
It was left to a Polish film crew to document this diary-like last will and testament of the late filmmaker Andrei Tarkovsky. The film was shot in Sweden as Tarkovsky, already ill and in excruciating pain, was directing his final film, *The Sacrifice*. In addition to revealing footage of Tarkovsky at work, the film is a moving look at a major artist at the zenith of his career, concerned as much for the future of mankind as for his art. Swedish and Russianwith English subtitles.
VHS: S12972. $29.95.
Michal Leszczylowski, Sweden, 1988, 100 mins.

The Mirror
Tarkovsky's looking glass is not merely cracked but shattered and we see the jagged, jumbled reflections of its shards, images of the director's childhood mixed with fragments of his adult life…a child's wartime exile, a mother's experience with political terror, the breakup of a marriage, life in a country home; all intermingled with slow motion dream sequences and stark newsreel. An essential film whose puzzles provide the key to this intense filmmaker's other works. Russian with English subtitles.
VHS: S13009. $59.95.
Andrei Tarkovsky, USSR, 1985, 101 mins.

My Name Is Ivan
A new print of the first feature film directed by the great Andrei Tarkovsky. This beautiful work, filled with poetic flourishes and an overriding sense of melancholy, immediately placed him in a position of leadership among the young Soviet filmmakers of his era. Set during WW II, it is the story of a young boy who is deprived of his childhood and struggles with the brutal realities of war. The film contains many images that would later become Tarkovsky's trademark, and is a brutally poetic evocation of innocence lost in the face of war. B&W. Russian with English subtitles.
VHS: S14290. $19.98.
Andrei Tarkovsky, USSR, 1962, 84 mins.

Nostalghia
Called not an entertainment, but an article of faith, Tarkovsky's first film made outside his native Russia, in Italy, is the story of a haggard academic, Gorchakov, who comes to Italy to research the life of an obscure Russian composer. His journey becomes one of meditation and a search for the self. With Erland Josephson. Widescreen. "The nearest to poetry that cinema can ever aspire" (*Financial Times*). Russian and Italian with English subtitles.
VHS: S31620. $29.98.
Laser: LD76279. $69.95.
Andrei Tarkovsky, Italy/Russia, 1983, 120 mins.

The Sacrifice
Andrei Tarkovsky's epitaph, a dark and complex film about redemption and nuclear holocaust, filmed in exile from his native Russia in Sweden, and starring Erland Josephson. With cinematography by Sven Nykvist, one of the most daring films of the decade. Swedish with English subtitles.
VHS: S03568. $29.95.
Andrei Tarkovsky, Sweden, 1986, 145 mins.

Solaris
The release of this remarkable science fiction film marked a milestone in Soviet cinema. *Solaris*, adapted from the science fiction novel by respected Polish writer Stanislav Lem, is one of those rare screen works which improves upon and deepens its literary source. The story deals with a series of expeditions to the planet Solaris—closely examining the ways the various earth scientists there interact among themselves and, more importantly, the ways in which they interact with each other's memories. "I find it one of the most original, most poetic, most beautifully paced science-fiction movies I've ever seen" (Jonas Mekas, *The Village Voice*). Presented in letterboxed format. Russian with English subtitles.
VHS: S14289. $19.98.
DVD: DV60342. $29.99.
Andrei Tarkovsky, USSR, 1972, 167 mins.

Stalker
In this eerie, hypnotic and highly symbolic work, shot in painterly images that seamlessly move from black and white to color, a fallen meteorite produces the Zone, a blistered wasteland that's only penetrated by special guides called "Stalkers." Tarkovsky's film concerns a three-man expedition into this surreal, frightening region. A powerful, extraordinary cinematic experience that anticipates the dread of Chernobyl. With Alexander Kaidanovsky, Nikolai Grinko, and Anatoli Solonitsin. Russian with English subtitles.
VHS: S16984. $19.98.
Andrei Tarkovsky, USSR, 1979, 161 mins.

SERGEI PARADJANOV

Ashik Kerib
Ashik Kerib is a wandering minstrel, forbidden to marry the daughter of a powerful merchant, who travels for one thousand days to finance his wedding. In Paradjanov's hands, it becomes a visual opera of costumes, movement and music, in which surreal framing, icons, pomegranates and other mystical symbols fill a living tableau with images that are simply miraculous. Dedicated to Andrei Tarkovsky, the theme of *Ashik Kerib* is the transforming power of art and the tragedy of the artist. Cinematography by Albert Yavuryan. With Yiur Mgoyan, Veronikia Metonidze and Levan Natroshvili. Azerbaijani and Georgian with English subtitles.
VHS: S19055. $29.95.
Sergei Paradjanov, Russia, 1988, 78 mins.

The Color of Pomegranates
Paradjanov's sublime mosaic on the life, art and spiritual odyssey of the 18th-century Armenian poet Sayat Nova. The film is a collection of images and tableaux that interweave landscapes, villages, costumes, props and music to form a metaphorical history of the Armenian nation. The film "achieves a sort of visionary para-surrealism through the most economical means of gesture, props and texture…A sublime and heartbreaking film" (J. Hoberman, *The Village Voice*). This director's cut repositions the shots and images and restores censored footage. With Sofico Chiaureli, M. Aleksanian and V. Galstian. Armenian with English subtitles. On the same program is *Hagop Hovnatanian*, Paradjanov's 12-minute short on the Armenian artist.
VHS: S19064. $29.95.
Sergei Paradjanov, USSR, 1969, 78 mins.

The Legend of Suram Fortress
Based on a Georgian legend, the first feature completed by Sergei Paradjanov after being released from prison. The tale hangs on the self-sacrifice of a young man who agrees to be bricked up in a fortress wall in order to make it impregnable against invaders. Paradjanov divides his film into a series of tableaux, once again using minimal dialog and searing imagery in a film of surreal, almost hypnotic power. Georgian with English subtitles.
VHS: S13007. $29.95.
Sergei Paradjanov, USSR, 1984, 100 mins.

Paradjanov: A Requiem
Features extensive interviews and scenes from the films of the late Sergei Paradjanov, one of the most controversial and stylistically daring filmmakers of our time. Paradjanov talks about his films and his imprisonment at the hands of Soviet authorities.
VHS: S30708. $29.95.
Ron Holloway, Germany, 1994, 57 mins.

Shadows of Forgotten Ancestors
Sergei Paradjanov's masterpiece, a brilliant, epic story of starcrossed lovers set against the ethnographic panorama of the Carpathian Mountains. The film is a visual tour-de-force of symbols, metaphor, lyrical photography and active camera as it interweaves myth and narrative into an elliptical, seamless work of art. Its images "become superimposed on the mind, and will emerge later with a new and more profound meaning, a meaning that escapes logical analysis, that cannot be grasped intellectually, but which calls upon us to respond with feeling" (Robert Walke). With Ivan Nikolaichuk and Larisa Kadochnikova. Ukrainian with English subtitles.
VHS: S07576. $29.95.
Sergei Paradjanov, USSR, 1964, 99 mins.

ANDREI KONCHALOVSKY

Duet for One
A world famous concert violinist played by Julie Andrews finds herself slowly stricken by multiple sclerosis. Andrews shines in an emotional performance as she strives to maintain her marriage and her sense of self-worth. With Max Von Sydow and Alan Bates.
VHS: S03574. $14.95.
Andrei Konchalovsky, USA, 1986, 107 mins.

Inner Circle
Andrei Konchalovsky recreates the terror of the Stalinist years through the eyes of Stalin's personal film projectionist. Tom Hulce stars as Ivan Sanshin, a loyal Communist who screens the latest newsreels and American movies for the man in charge of the Soviet Union, and his close personal friends, without missing a reel change. Lolita Davidovich is memorable as the wife who knows her husband loves Stalin more. With Bob Hoskins as the head of the KGB.
VHS: S16805. $19.95.
Laser: LD71574. $39.95.
Andrei Konchalovsky, USA/USSR, 1991, 134 mins.

Runaway Train
John Voight and Eric Roberts star in this thriller based on a screenplay by Akira Kurosawa, from the director of *Maria's Lovers*. Voight and Roberts play escaped cons in the Northeast wilderness, aboard a speeding train hurtling toward certain derailment.
VHS: S01139. $14.95.
Laser: Letterboxed. **LD72355. $34.98.**
DVD: DV60215. $24.98.
Andrei Konchalovsky, USA, 1985, 112 mins.

Shy People
Andrei Konchalovsky's film is about a chic Manhattan magazine writer and her troubled teenage daughter, who venture deep into the Louisiana bayou, where they find a lot more than their long-lost relatives-violence, mystery and fear.
VHS: S07475. $19.98.
Andrei Konchalovsky, USA, 1987, 119 mins.

Siberiade
Russian history over six decades is revealed through the eyes of two opposing families in this epic film. One proletarian family, the Ustyuzhanins, yearns for change, while the aristocratic Solomins desperately cling to their privileged past. These opposing views finally climax in a battle over oil in Siberia. Winner of the 1979 Jury Prize at Cannes. Russian with English subtitles.
VHS: S21541. $79.95.
Andrei Konchalovsky, USSR, 1979, 190 mins.

EARLY SOVIET CINEMA

Aelita: Queen of Mars

One of the most remarkable discoveries of the Soviet silent cinema, *Aelita* is a stunning big-budget science fiction spectacle. Enormous futuristic sets and radical constructionist costumes were designed by Alexandra Exter to enhance this story of romance, comedy and danger. A Moscow engineer designs a spaceship and travels to Mars to meet the woman who haunts his dreams. He succeeds but finds himself embroiled in a Martian proletarian uprising. *Aelita*, with its exaggerated production design and political undertones, was a profound influence on Fritz Lang's *Metropolis* three years later. Silent, with orchestral score.

VHS: S13826. $29.95.
Yakov Protazanov, USSR, 1924, 113 mins.

Arsenal

A romantic and lyrical masterpiece set during the war of 1914, in the countryside and at the front. *Arsenal* depicts the Revolutionary struggle in Kiev as the arsenal goes on strike and the strikers are defeated. Its great sequences include the symbol of a starving horse, and the death of the Revolutionary hero who, as he struggles forward with open shirt, is riddled with bullets by the Whites. With S. Shavshenko, A. Buchma. Silent with music track, English titles.

VHS: S00069. $29.95.
Alexander Dovzhenko, USSR, 1929, 65 mins.

Bed and Sofa

A landmark of cinema, this brilliant social comedy centers on a menage-a-trois in the midst of a housing shortage in Moscow. The film rejects politics and symbolism for sense of humor and naturalism. It is supposedly based on details in the life of the great poet Mayakovsky; Ludmila Semyonova is the extraordinary actress at the center of the triangle. Her decision at the end of the film symbolizes the liberation of women in the new Soviet society.

VHS: S01933. $29.95.
Abram Room, USSR, 1927, 73 mins.

Chapayev

A stirring account of a beloved hero of the Russian Revolution, an illiterate Russian who served in Czar's army; after the Revolution, formed his own forces and went on the Red Side, fighting the Whites. Full of incredible images, the film was made from personal experience of the filmmakers. Russian with English subtitles.

VHS: S00231. $49.95.
Serge Vasilyev/Georgi Vasilyev, USSR, 1934, 100 mins.

Chess Fever/By the Law

Chess Fever (28 mins.), Pudovkin's first film, is the story of a young chess fanatic (Vladimir Fogel) who misses his wedding appointment. This sends his fiancee, Vera (Anna Zemtsova, a.k.a. Mrs. Vsevolod Pudovkin), into a frustrated rage and she ends their engagement. As the couple contemplates suicide, a chemist (Yakov Protazanov) plays a trick on Vera, drawing her into the world of chess and reuniting her with her fiance. *By the Law* (90 mins.), Lev Kuleshov's great film—and one of the most important of the silent Soviet period—is set in Alaska, where two men are killed in a remote cabin, and the killer is condemned by his two companions.

VHS: S32090. $29.95.
Vsevolod Pudovkin/Lev Kuleshov, USSR, 1925/1926, 118 mins.

The Cigarette Girl of Mosselprom

A delightful and boisterous comedy satirizing Soviet life and filmmaking in the 1920's, *The Cigarette Girl of Mosselprom* is the greatest work of director Zhelyabuzhsky, who began as a cameraman with the famous Russ collective. The story follows the exploits of a young woman who is tossed from street vending into the world of movies when she is cast as the lead in a romantic melodrama. Silent, with orchestral score.

VHS: S13821. $29.95.
Yuri Zhelyabuzhsky, USSR, 1924, 78 mins.

Classics of the Soviet Cinema

Early works from the Golden Age of Soviet Cinema are joined on this laser disc collection. One of its highlights is a version of Vertov's *Man with a Movie Camera*, containing an exclusive second audio track along with a new digital score. Dovzhenko's *Earth*, Pudovkin's *The End of St. Petersburg* and Eisenstein's *Strike* are also featured. 305 mins.

Laser: LD75913. $124.99.

Death of a Swan

A very rare 1917 film made by Yevgeni Bauer, who came to directing from design and excelled at getting great performances from actors. Prolific—he directed some 20 films each year—Bauer focused on contemporary subjects for his films rather than classical themes, and according to historian Jay Leyda, insisted on dressing all of his heroes and heroines in beautiful dress, no matter whom they portrayed. Silent with *German* titles.

VHS: S33935. $24.95.
Yevgeni Bauer, Russia, 1917

Deserter

When offered the chance to live in comfort in another land, a Hamburg dockworker must decide whether or not to abandon his comrades. *Deserter* daringly violated the freshly established law of natural sound with a powerful barrage of aural effects that mirror the film's dynamic style of montage.

VHS: S32092. $29.95.
Vsevolod Pudovkin, USRR, 1933, 105 mins.

Early Russian Cinema: Before the Revolution

An important ten-part video anthology that considers the early thematic, cultural, political and artistic developments of Russian cinema, before the 1917 October Revolution. Music by Neil Brand. Translation by Julian Graffy. "There was the exhilaration of discovery, a vision of marvelous vistas—but also an awesome sense of the vast interior that remains to be explored" (David Robinson, *Sight and Sound*).

Vol. 1: Beginnings. Documentaries like *A Fish Factory in Astrakhan* (1908) preceded the first Russian dramatic production, *Stenka Razin* (Romashkov, 1908). Meanwhile, the Moscow branch of Pathe produced its own version of the film d'art, *Princess Tarankova*, followed with its first of many Chekhov adaptations, *Romance with Double Bass* (Hansen, 1911). 45 mins.
VHS: S17849. $29.95.

Vol. 2: Folklore and Legend. *Drama in a Gypsy Camp* (Siversen, 1908), and the unreleased *Brigand Brothers* (Goncharov, 1912) are typical folklore subjects, while *A 16th Century Russian Wedding* (1909) and *Rusalka* (1910), both directed by the pioneer enthusiast Vasilii Goncharov, show how rapidly Russian cinema espoused national and cultural themes. (55 mins.)
VHS: S17850. $29.95.

Vol. 3: Starewicz's Fantasies. Starewicz's later puppet animation is now better than his brilliant beginnings at the Khazhonkov Studios. He pioneered insect-puppets in *The Ant and the Grasshopper* (1911) before turning to live action fantasy in his version of Gogol's *Christmas Eve* and contributing to the war effort with an anti-German allegory, The Lily of Belgium (1915). 58 mins.
VHS: S17851. $29.95.

Vol. 4: Provincial Variations. Jewish life was one of the exotic subjects covered in provincial films like the Latvian *Wedding Day* (Slovinski, 1912). The remarkably bleak melodrama *Merchant Bashirov's Daughter* (Larin, 1913, set on the Volga) was based on a real murder scandal. (55 mins)
VHS: S17852. $29.95.

Vol. 5: Chardynin's Pushkin. The former touring actor-manager Petr Chardynin made an early name for himself with Pushkin adaptations like *The Queen of Spades* (1910) and *The House of Kolomna* (1913), in which Ivan Mousjoukine played both a dashing officer and a farcical cook in drag. (45 mins.)
VHS: S17853. $29.95.

Vol. 6: Class Distinctions. Despite strict censorship intended to prevent inflammatory material, Goncharov portrayed the hardship of rural life in *The Peasants' Lot* (1912), and an early film by Evgenii Bauer, *The Silent Witnesses* (1914), dealt frankly with servants' views of their masters. (94 mins.)
VHS: S17854. $29.95.

Vol. 7: Evgenii Bauer. The major discovery of the early Russian cinema. In a mere five prolific years, Bauer achieved mastery of several genres, including the social melodrama of *A Child of the Big City* (1913), erotic comedies like *The 1002nd Ruse*, and the psychological gothic drama of *Daydreams*. (95 mins.)
VHS: S17855. $29.95.

Vol. 8: Iakov Protazanov. Protazanov did not shirk controversy or challenge in either his highly successful pre- or post-1917 careers. *The Departure of a Great Old Man* (1912) provoked legal action by the Tolstoy family for its scandalous portrayal of the writer's last days. His *The Queen of Spades* starred Mosjoukine in one of his most compelling roles. (104 mins.)
VHS: S17856. $29.95.

Vol. 9: High Society. A panorama of Russian cinema's social impact: *Antosha Ruined by a Corset* (Puchalski, 1916) is a racy, knowing urban comedy; *A Life for a Life* (1916) marked the pinnacle of Bauer's ambition to equal lavish foreign production standards; and *The Funeral of Vera Kholodnaia* (1919) records the vast public response to the early death of Russia's greatest star. (72 mins.)
VHS: S17857. $29.95.

Vol. 10: The End of an Era. Between 1917's two revolutions, cinema reflected new themes, as in Bauer's *The Revolutionary* (1917), but also pursued the traditional subject of thwarted love in what would be his last film, *For Luck* (1917). A fragment *Behind the Screen* (1917) shows the husband-wife stars Mosjoukine and Lisenko on the eve of their departure into exile. (72 mins.)
VHS: S17858. $29.95.

Early Russian Cinema: Complete Set. All 10 volumes of the Early Russian cinema collection at a special price.
VHS: S17859. $250.00.

Earth

A great masterpiece—the fourth and last silent film by Dovzhenko, a lyrical evocation of his native Ukraine, the theme of the life cycle of man developed through constant juxtaposition and intertwining of images of life and death. Ultimately very moving, a film poem of inestimable beauty. Silent with English subtitles.

VHS: S00389. $29.95.
Alexander Dovzhenko, USSR, 1930, 88 mins.

End of St. Petersburg

Commissioned, as was Eisenstein's *Ten Days That Shook the World*, to celebrate the tenth anniversary of the Russian Revolution, *End of St. Petersburg* shows the basic difference in approach between Eisenstein and Pudovkin. Pudovkin concentrates on a peasant who comes to St. Petersburg for a visit and becomes "politicized," believing in strike and revolution. Pudovkin focuses on the individual, with the emotional power of the film emerging from seeing the effects of the Revolution on common people. With Ivan Chuvelyov and Vera Baranovskaya. English titles.

VHS: S00408. $29.95.
Vsevolod Pudovkin, USSR, 1927, 75 mins.

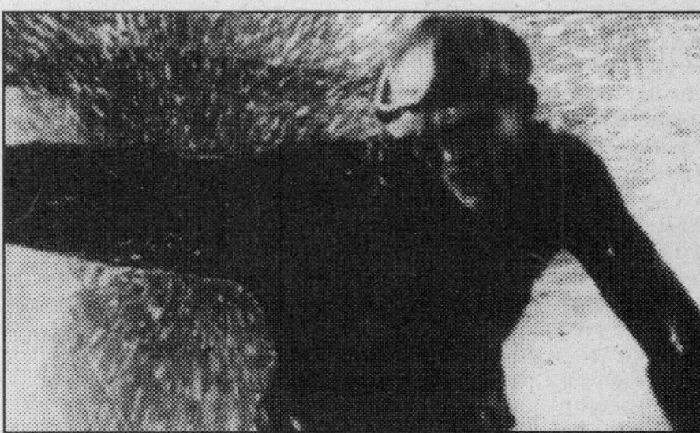

The Extraordinary Adventures of Mr. West in the Land of the Bolsheviks

An inspired satire of America's slanted view of Russia, *Mr. West* is sharply funny as it plays with misconceptions about the Soviet people. A bourgeois American is challenged by his friends to visit those "mad, savage Russians." Once he arrives, he is beset by an onslaught of strange characters and events, thrusting him into a world of danger and intrigue. Soon Mr. West realizes that only through his all-American ingenuity can he survive…then the farce really begins. Silent, with a piano score.

VHS: S03700. $29.95.
Lev Kuleshov, USSR, 1924, 88 mins.

Fall of the Romanov Dynasty

With remarkable historic footage and radical editing, this film stands as a colossal documentary portrait of the collapse of the Czarist regime and the triumphant rise of communist rule. Director Shub, a pioneer in editing and mentor to Sergei Eisenstein (influencing his montage theories), unearthed thousands of films—including personal footage by the Czar's own cameramen—to bring to life a daring and innovative historical drama of the events from 1912 to 1917. Silent, with orchestral score.

VHS: S13822. $29.95.
Esther Shub, USSR, 1927, 90 mins.

Father Sergius

One of the few surviving films from before the October Revolution, *Father Sergius* introduced an anti-religious element into Russian cinema in its realization of Tolstoy's story about an officer who became a monk on the eve of his wedding and suffered tortures of the flesh thereafter. Silent with English subtitles.

VHS: S00435. $29.95.
Yakov Protazanov, USSR, 1917, 81 mins.

Girl with the Hatbox

Moving with the speed and grace of the best American silent comedies, this Russian classic teamed Anna Sten—later a star for Goldwyn in the 1930's—with director Boris Barnet. Sten portrays a working girl who is given a seemingly worthless lottery ticket instead of her wages by her unscrupulous employer. The ticket wins her a fortune, and a madcap chase ensues to possess the ticket—and Anna's love. Silent, with orchestral score.

VHS: S13823. $29.95.
Boris Barnet, USSR, 1927, 67 mins.

Guerilla Brigade

An extremely rare film by Igor Savchenko, the Ukrainian filmmaker who was a contemporary and colleague of both Eisenstein and Dovzhenko. Set in his native Ukraine, *Guerilla Brigade* is set during the Civil War, and is notable for its poetic and epic depiction of the Ukrainian and Russian people joining together in their struggle. Russian with English subtitles.

VHS: S06898. $69.95.
Igor Savchenko, USSR, 1939, 90 mins.

Happiness

Subtitled "A Tale About a Hapless Mercenary Loser, His Wife, His Well-Fed Neighbor and Also About a Priest, a Nun and Other Old Relics," *Happiness* is a slapstick comedy based on old folklore but charged with (often risque) modern satire. Banned in Russia for 40 years, Medvedkin's film offers a parade of comic oddities, from polka-dotted horses to nuns in see-through tunics. Sergei Eisenstein called *Happiness* "a magnificent film" not only for its spy spoofing of Bolshevik values, but for its ability to incite laughter…even from the dourest revolutionary. Silent, with piano score.

VHS: S13824. $29.95.
Alexander Medvedkin, USSR, 1934, 69 mins.

Mother

Pudovkin's great work depicts an aspect of the abortive 1905 revolt, dramatizing the injustices of Czarist life, but focusing on individuals, on human problems with universal meanings. With an incredible performance by Vera Baranovskaya; one of the landmarks of the history of cinema. Silent with English subtitles.

VHS: S00886. $29.95.

Vsevolod Pudovkin, USSR, 1926, 73 mins.

The Mystery of the Leaping Fish and Chess Fever

Two silent film parodies. One of Sherlock Holmes, the other about the Soviet national pastime. Douglas Fairbanks is the scientific detective Coke Ennyday in the bizarre *Mystery of the Leaping Fish*, written by Tod Browning. The second short is a Russian look at the perils of total devotion to a board game.

VHS: S05686. $29.95.

Vsevolod Pudovkin/John Emerson, USA/USSR, 1916-25, 64 mins.

Storm over Asia

Pudovkin's epic of an exploited Mongolian fur trader who becomes involved in the Mongolian uprising against the British during the Civil War period. It is "the film of the destiny of the Occident, although its action takes place in the heart of Asia, on the plateaus of Tibet" (Robert Desnos). Notable for Pudovkin's lyrical/psychological montage which ends in an incredible storm scene which contains "all the dust and debris that Pudovkin could imagine. But how else was Pudovkin to end a film whose attraction for him had been its fable and exotic imagery, except by hyperbole?" (Jay Leyda). With Valeri Inkizhinov, I. Inkizhinov and A. Chistiakov. Silent with music track.

VHS: S01972. $29.95.

Vsevolod Pudovkin, USSR, 1928, 70 mins.

SVD—Club of the Big Deed

This very rare example of an early collaboration between Kozintsev and Trauberg, the originators of F.E.K.S. (Factory of the Eccentric Experimental Actor), is set during the revolutionary period of the Decemberist movement of 1825. Russian with German titles, music track.

VHS: S30202. $24.95.

Grigori Kozintsev/Leonid Trauberg, USSR, 1927, 50 mins.

Three Soviet Masters

Three classic short films from the masters of Soviet cinema: Eisenstein, Vertov and Pudovkin. Includes *Behzin Meadow* (30 mins.), *Kino Pravda* (silent, 14 mins.) and *Chess Fever* (silent, 20 mins.).

VHS: S14921. $29.95.

Turksib/Salt for Svanetia

On one level a gritty and virile documentary on the construction of the Turkestan-Siberia railway, *Turksib* (57 mins.) is also a haunting and meditative attempt by Turin to defy western conventions of plot- and character-driven films and violate the values of studio gloss. With imagery so peculiar that it borders on the surreal, *Salt* (53 mins.) depicts life on the brink of starvation in an isolated village high in the Caucasus Mountains. Not unlike Bunuel's *Land Without Bread* or Welles' *It's All True*, Kalatozov's *Salt* takes the ethnographic documentary to unrealized heights of expression. English titles.

VHS: S32046. $29.95.

Viktor Turin/Mikhail Kalatozov, USSR, 1929/1930, 110 mins.

Zvenigora

Ukrainian director Dovzhenko's first major work lyrically captures the entire history of the Ukraine through a series of folk myths stretching from the Viking invasion to the 1919 Civil War. Silent.

VHS: S01970. $29.95.

Alexander Dovzhenko, USSR, 1928, 73 mins.

SERGEI EISENSTEIN

Alexander Nevsky

Sergei Eisenstein's first sound film, with a brilliant music score by Sergei Prokofiev, in a new, meticulous print and new sound recording of this masterpiece. Russian with English subtitles.

VHS: S12949. $29.95.

Sergei Eisenstein, USSR, 1938, 112 mins.

Alexander Nevsky (New Score)

A newly re-mastered, beautiful print of Eisenstein's masterpiece arrives with the famous Prokofiev score newly recorded by the St. Petersburg Philharmonic Orchestra. Russian with English subtitles.

VHS: S24740. $24.98.

Laser: LD75363. $29.98.

Sergei Eisenstein, USSR, 1938, 110 mins.

Battleship Potemkin

Sergei Eisenstein's depiction of the mutiny of the crew of the *Potemkin* during the insurrection of 1905. The bold imagery, stylized composition and powerful rhythmic editing combine to make it a film consistently voted one of the top ten of all time. Silent, with music by N. Kryukov and a brilliant original music score by Edmund Meisel. Digitally remastered.

VHS: S19293. $29.95.

Sergei Eisenstein, USSR, 1925, 65 mins.

Eisenstein

Soviet documentary about the most famous Russian filmmaker, with rare footage of his early life, first films and famous masterpieces, including *Strike, Potemkin*, and *Ivan the Terrible*. USSR, 1958, 48 mins.

VHS: S01623. $24.95.

General Line

Begun in 1926 after the completion of *Potemkin*, the film uses what Eisenstein called "polyphonic montage" in which the blacks, whites and grays are used like the sounds and tones of a symphony orchestra. Silent.

VHS: S00485. $29.95.

Sergei Eisenstein, USSR, 1929, 90 mins.

Ivan the Terrible, Part I

Huge close-ups, rich decor and Prokofiev's choral music help make this film one of the great achievements of Russian cinema. In part one, Ivan Grozny is proclaimed Czar of all Russia, but faces treachery within his own family. Russian with English subtitles.

VHS: S00645. $29.95.

Sergei Eisenstein, USSR, 1944, 94 mins.

Ivan the Terrible, Part II

After the great success of *Ivan the Terrible, Part I*, Eisenstein rushed to complete *Part II* of what was to be a trilogy. Eisenstein used color in two sequences to signify psychological meaning. Part II details Ivan's revenge on friends who had denounced him. Russian with English subtitles.

VHS: S00646. $29.95.

Sergei Eisenstein, USSR, 1946, 90 mins.

Ivan the Terrible, Parts I & II

Huge close-ups, rich decor and Prokofiev's choral music help make this film one of the great achievements of Russian cinema. In *Part I*, Ivan Grozny is proclaimed Czar of all Russia, but faces treachery within his own family. After the great success of this part, Eisenstein rushed to complete *Part II* of what was to be a trilogy. He used color in two sequences to signify psychological meaning. *Part II* details Ivan's revenge on friends who had denounced him. Russian with English subtitles.

Laser: LD71064. $59.99.

Sergei Eisenstein, USSR, 1944-46, 184 mins.

Que Viva Mexico

Eisenstein's long-lost diamond-in-the-rough, shot by the great Eduard Tisse, and financed by Upton Sinclair. Reconstructed in 1979 by Grigori Alexandrov, the last surviving member of Eisenstein's Mexican team, *Que Viva Mexico* is a silent film narrated in Russian and subtitled in English. Divided into segments: a wedding, a bullfight, a fiesta, a dramatized abortive uprising by peons against feudal masters at the turn of the century. Anyone who has seen the lyrical, ravishing images of Eduard Tisse's *Que Viva Mexico* will revel in the priceless beauty of Eisenstein's incomplete master-work. Russian with English subtitles.

VHS: S12976. $59.95.

Sergei Eisenstein/Grigori Alexandrov, USSR, 1931, 90 mins.

Strike

One of the most original debuts in film history, *Strike* is a brilliant mixture of agit-prop techniques and comic-grotesque stylization in the telling of a factory workers' strike in Czarist Russia in 1912 and the brutal suppression of the strike. Silent.

VHS: S01271. $29.95.

Sergei Eisenstein, USSR, 1924, 75 mins.

Ten Days That Shook the World

Also known as *October*, Eisenstein's famous recreation of the October Revolution during which the Bolsheviks overthrew the Kerensky government. Like his previous work, the film continues Eisenstein's experimental methods. Silent.

VHS: S01306. $29.95.

Sergei Eisenstein, USSR, 1927, 95 mins.

Thunder over Mexico

Also known as *Time in the Sun* and *Eisenstein in Mexico*, this is an edited version of footage from Sergei Eisenstein's unfinished Mexican film, *Que Viva Mexico*. The story has been constructed to focus on the peasant girl and the landowner, and the tragic burial of the two lovers in the sand. Completed by Grigori Alexandrow; cinematography by Eduard Tisse.

VHS: S24123. $29.95.

Sergei Eisenstein, Mexico, 1932

DZIGA VERTOV

Enthusiasm

This tale of coal miners in the Don Basin was made with vivid and unusual use of sound considerably ahead of its time. Upon seeing the film Charles Chaplin wrote: "I would never have believed it possible to assemble mechanical noises to create such beauty. One of the most superb symphonies I have known." English titles.

VHS: S03554. $39.95.

Dziga Vertov, USSR, 1931, 67 mins.

Kino Pravda and Enthusiasm

Two documentaries from the great Soviet polemicist Dziga Vertov, whose avant-garde newsreels known as kino pravda ("film truth") formulated the montage aesthetics of the revolutionary Russian silent cinema of Eisenstein, Kuleshov, Pudovkin and Dovzhenko. Vertov's highly-stylized, non-narrative work produced an anti-formalism which greatly influence Godard.

VHS: S01971. $69.95.

Dziga Vertov, USSR, 1922, 120 mins.

Man with the Movie Camera

Dziga Vertov's masterpiece is an application of "life as it is lived." It makes the cameraman the hero, and is one of the most dynamic experiments with montage; the film also uses trick photography, animation, slow motion and speeded-up shots. It "is a study in film truth on an almost philosophical level…It does deliberately what others try hard to avoid—destroys its own illusions, in the hope that reality will emerge from the process not as a creature of screen illusion but as a liberated spirit" (*Films and Filming*). Silent.

VHS: S00821. $29.95.

Dziga Vertov, USSR, 1928, 69 mins.

Three Songs of Lenin

In this, his last feature film, Vertov paid homage to Russia's great leader with three heartfelt examinations of life in the Soviet Union. "In a Black Prison Was My Face," "We Loved Him" and "In the Great City of Stone" explore the life of Lenin, while showing the effect he had upon the nation and its people. With its exquisite images and masterful editing, *Three Songs of Lenin* paints a living portrait of Vladimir Lenin unequalled by all of the dry rhetoric of history books. Silent, with orchestral score.

VHS: S13825. $29.95.

Dziga Vertov, USSR, 1934, 62 mins.

UKRAINIAN FILMS

Harvest of Despair

A documentary about the Ukrainian "terror famine" of 1923-33, which caused the deaths of 7 million people. Using interviews with survivors and scholars to supplement rare photographic evidence, it establishes that the terror famine was deliberately created by the Soviet government as part of Stalin's decades-long effort to destroy the Ukrainian peasantry who resisted collectivization. Academy Award nomination. Canada, 1984, 55 mins.

VHS: S06254. $39.95.

Video Visits: Ukraine—Ancient Crossroads, Modern Dreams

Marvel at Kiev's Cathedral of St. Sophia, the caves of the Perchersk Monastery, medieval castles, the vacation paradise of Crimea and the heartland city of Lviv. 55 mins.

VHS: S31464. $24.99.

BALTIC FILMS

City Unplugged

Set against the upheaval caused by the collapse of the Soviet Union, this crime story focuses on the forces of greed and evil that erupt when Tovio, a young and innocent engineer who works in the city's electric plant, is recruited by the Russian mob to cause a blackout at the moment the mob plans to rob the National Treasury of $900 million in gold. Tovio must go along with the plan in order to provide for his pregnant wife, but his misdeed leads to complications that will alter his life forever. "Hard-boiled…funny…brutal" (*Toronto Globe and Mail*). Estonian with English subtitles.

VHS: S31012. $59.95.

Ilkka Jrvilaturi, Finland/USA/Sweden/Estonia, 1993, 100 mins.

Estonia: A Tale of Two Nations

Estonia is the smallest republic in the USSR, but along with the other two Baltic republics, it is at the forefront of the independence movement sweeping the Soviet Union. This important film shows history in the making. 1990, 45 mins.

VHS: S13955. $79.95.

Video Visits: Baltic States—Lithuania, Latvia, Estonia

Visit Vilnius, in the heart of Lithuania. See the Gates of Dawn and the restored Traikai Castle. Capture the spirit of Lithuania's past in Klaipeda. Explore Riga's ancient castle, medieval buildings and Doma Baznica, in Latvia. In Estonia, witness the Midsummer's Eve Torch Ceremony procession and visit the Song Festival Amphitheater in Tallinn for an Estonian folk musical festival. 54 mins.
VHS: S31453. $24.99.

THROUGH RUSSIAN EYES

7 Up in the Soviet Union

A Soviet variation of Michael Apted's acclaimed documentary series that chronicles the fears and dreams of seven-year-old children. The ethnic tensions, political uncertainty and poverty impacted on 20 Soviet children are dissected in a film called "Unforgettable" *London Daily Mail*). 70 mins.
VHS: S19243. $19.95.

Anastasia—Dead or Alive?

Evaluate whether modern science has resolved the mystery surrounding Princess Anastasia as NOVA investigates the massacre of Tsar Nicholas and his family. 60 mins.
VHS: S28650. $19.95.

Andrei Voznesensky

Reading from *An Arrow in the Wall* in Los Angeles on November 19, 1990, this Russian poet made clear why he is revered by so many admirers. Among the translators of his work are such literary figures as W.H. Auden, William Jay Smith and Stanley Kunitz. Poet James Ragan reads from Voznesensky's English translations and also interviews this writer. From the *Lannan Literary Videos* series. 60 mins.
VHS: S27129. $19.95.

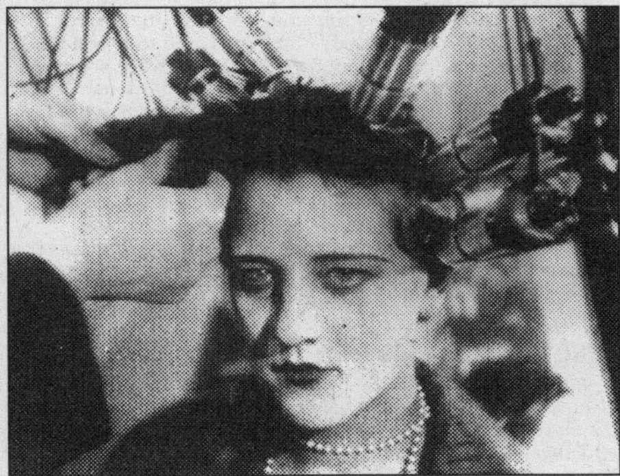

Before Gorbachev—From Stalin to Brezhnev

Made in celebration of the 60th anniversary of the October Revolution, this ambitious film documents the history of the USSR for those 60 years, emphasizing progress and the success of communism. 50 mins.
VHS: S12717. $19.98.

Behind Kremlin Walls

Diane Sawyer and Sam Donaldson host this look inside the Soviet symbol of power, including never-before-allowed looks at Lenin's apartments in the Council of Ministers building, the Grand Kremlin Palace, the Terem Palace, treasures and works of art housed in the Armory Palace and more. 60 mins.
VHS: S12290. $19.98.

Best of Nightline: Chernobyl Nuclear Disaster

30 mins.
VHS: S14042. $14.98.

The Black Tulip

Understanding the impact of the Afghan War on Soviet society is essential to an understanding of glasnost and perestroika. *The Black Tulip* is a remarkable look at the human impact of the war on the Soviet people. 1988, 27 mins.
VHS: S13954. $24.95.

Chernobyl

The graphic and otherwise unavailable facts about the after-effects of Chernobyl—the blast site, the people and areas affected, and the questions: What are the statistical risks? Who will develop cancer? Whose children will be mutants? The Chernobyl accident is expected to cause an additional 20,000 to 200,000 deaths in Western Europe.
VHS: S05281. $29.95.

Danylo Shumuk: Life Sentence

Jailed by the Poles, Nazis and Soviets, Shumuk spent more than 42 years in detention for the non-violent expression of his political opinions. This tape is his life-story, and how the efforts of Amnesty International sustained him throughout all of the impossible years. 1987, 27 mins.
VHS: S06892. $20.00.

Discovering Russian Folk Music

Powerful choruses, plaintive songs, swirling dances and magnificent costumes make this musical tradition both beautiful and distinctive. Viewers will delight in this engaging video. 23 mins.
VHS: S23518. $49.95.

Empire of the Red Bear

This three-volume set from the Discovery Channel explores the Russian wilderness which is home to the red bear. It's a landscape of rugged beauty dominated by oversized features, including active volcanoes. 180 mins.
VHS: S25090. $39.95.

The Face of Russia

This three-part series from producer Michael Gill, hosted and written by James H. Billington, U.S. Librarian of Congress and author of the book by the same title, explores the hearts and minds of the Russian people through their art and culture in a remarkable journey across history, encompassing Russia's grand architecture, icon paintings, music, literature, and cinema. Each tape is 60 mins. Widescreen.

The Face of Russia—Part I: The Face on the Firewood. Reveals the spiritual ideas that have animated Russia for 1,000 years, witnesses recent restorations of churches and monasteries from Kiev to the Kremlin, and looks at icon painting, the first Russian art form.
VHS: S34338. $29.95.

The Face of Russia—Part II: The Facade of Power. Examines Russian architecture, from the Eastern-inspired onion domes on churches to the Western-type palaces of unparalleled splendor. Also looks at the writings of Gogol, including *Dead Souls*, which still influences Russian artists today.
VHS: S34339. $29.95.

The Face of Russia—Part III: Facing the Future. Explores the advance of Russian music and cinema, including the great composer Musorgsky, director Sergei Eisenstein, and looks at how new media forms are shaping Russia during its current time of change.
VHS: S34340. $29.95.

The Face of Russia. Three-part boxed set.
VHS: S34337. $79.95.

Fear and the Muse: The Story of Anna Akhmatova

The great Russian poet is revealed in a video documentary that examines her tragic life in Stalin's Russia, her relationship with poets like Ossip Mandelshtam, and the impact of her poetry, which became a source of strength and inspiration for millions of Russians under Communism. 60 mins.
VHS: S24319. $19.95.

Friends: A Closer Look at the Enemy

Documentary portrait of Betty Petroff, an American teacher/librarian, as she journeys through seven cities in the Soviet Union, eliciting their feelings about the U.S. and the chances for peace in the future. From Leningrad to Red Square, she talks to Soviet citizens of all ages and nationalities to gain their views. Institutional or public performance.
VHS: S06602. $30.00.
G. Shoemaker/B. Petroff, USA, 1987, 30 mins.

From Czar to Stalin

Compiled documentary footage includes World War I, the crowned heads of state in Europe, as well as revolutionary figures in Russia: Lenin, Trotsky and Molotov.
VHS: S03450. $29.98.
Raphael Nussbaum, USA, 1987, 93 mins.

Fun in the U.S.S.R.

Learn how Soviet people spend their weekends. More often than not, what is documented here is the gulf that separates the Soviet people from the Soviet government. A series of whimsical films including *Budget of a Soviet Family* and *Over the Weekend*. 95 mins.
VHS: S12718. $24.98.

Gielgud's Chekhov

Sir John Gielgud hosts and narrates these dramatizations of some of Chekhov's greatest works. 50 minutes each.

Volume 1: *The Fugitive, Desire for Sleep*, and *Rothschild's Violin*.
VHS: S02214. $74.95.
Volume 2: *Volodya* and *The Boarding House*.
VHS: S02215. $74.95.
Volume 3: *The Wallet* and *Revenge*.
VHS: S02216. $74.95

Gogol: Diary of a Madman

An adaptation of the off-Broadway production of the celebrated story by Nicolai Gogol (1809-1852), about a clerk's disintegration into complete madness. Performed by actor and drama teacher William Hickey in a one-man tour-de-force. 1964, 27 mins.
VHS: S32321. $89.95.

Golden Domes of Moscow

This rare look at Moscow includes a tour of Red Square, the Kremlin, the Soviet Space Exhibit, a look at a Soviet wedding, the Bolshoi, and even the Russian circus. 30 mins.
VHS: S08279. $24.95.

Great Crimes and Trials of the 20th Century: The Massacre of the Tsar, Stalin and Katyn

The Tsar and his royal family were not only deposed by Russian Revolutionaries, they were also executed by them. Their story is followed by the intriguing case of 3,000 Polish soldiers whose bodies were found buried in a mass Grave at Katyn. Many could not believe Stalin was responsible, but this video reveals the truth. Narrated by Robert Powell. 52 mins.
VHS: S29975. $19.95.

Habiba: A Sufi Saint from Uzbekistan

Habiba is a Tabib, a Muslim healer. She belongs to the earliest Sufi "Chain of Mystic Transmission," a lineage of teachers whose main representative is a great master, Bahaudin Nacksband. Uzbekistan is a dream-like land, a crossroad of Western and Eastern civilization along the Silk Road. 30 mins.
VHS: S32083. $24.95.

The House with Knights

The story of a grand apartment building, once the residence of rich and privileged families, which turned into a collective housing unit after the revolution of 1917. Through historical footage and personal interviews with former residents, the incredible story comes alive. Russian with English subtitles. 58 mins.
VHS: S23404. $150.00.

If the People Will Lead

The evolution of freedom in the former Soviet Union was critically influenced by the media. Glasnost ushered in a whole new era of self-expression that could not be reversed even by the coup of 1991. Footage from these troubled times details the growth of freedom. The attempted occupation of a Lithuanian TV station by Soviet soldiers offers a chilling example of the people's courage. 58 mins.
VHS: S21592. $95.00.

Inside Russia

A complete survey of Russia prior to WWII, this rare film was completed only weeks before the German invasion of Russia. Included in the rare footage are sequences on the mountain tribes of the Urals, ancient and modern customs in Tiflis, the oil fields of Bakuk, American machinery in Russian coal mines, the site of the Garden of Eden on the Black sea, the Yalta palaces of the Czar and Grand Duke Dmitri, the Red Square, Maxim Gorky's home, the homes of Tolstoy and Gorky, and much more. Some scratches in print. 75 mins.
VHS: S03351. $49.95.

Joseph Brodsky: A Maddening Space

This unique portrait of Nobel prize-winning poet, essayist and controversial former dissident Joseph Brodsky includes an overview of his troubled life in the Soviet Union, his emigration to the U.S. and his devotion to American literature, and is full of examples of both his poetry and his critical essays. 60 mins.
VHS: S24318. $19.95.

KGB: The ÎSoviet Sword and Shield of Action

A three-part exploration of the KGB and Soviet intelligence reveals the details of the objectives and means of Soviet intervention around the world. Narrated by Hugh Marlowe, each volume explores the intelligence network of the KGB and its influence and subversive activities. 60 minutes each volume.

Part 1: The Spies.
VHS: S09966. $14.95.
Part 2: The Secrets.
VHS: S09967. $14.95.
Part 3: The Terrorists.
VHS: S09968. $14.95.

The Kremlin

The rich treasures and history of the Kremlin are revealed in this insightful look at the Kremlin, past and present, in the award-winning series produced by Lucy Jarvis. Introduction by Edwin Newman. 60 mins.
VHS: S05317. $24.95.
Laser: LD70295. $39.95.

Last of the Czars

The Discovery Channel compiled newly available film footage, letters and interviews with survivors from the Czarist era in this finely detailed portrait of the last members of the Romanov family. They ruled Russia for over 300 years, eventually being brought down by a violent revolution that had no place for nobility. 150 mins.

VHS: S27825. $39.95.

Lenin and the Bolsheviks

Two enthusiastic profiles are included on this tape of the Revolutionary leader and Soviet hero, Vladimir Ilyich Lenin. These films emphasize the early years—from the first stirrings of the revolutionary spirit to the victory of the Proletariat in 1917. From the *Inside the Soviet Union* series. 60 mins.

VHS: S12708. $19.95.

Life in the Moscow Circus

These neat little films document various aspects of the circus during the past 30 years—going behind the scenes with the traveling circus, unveiling the anticipated big-top circus tents, and following the development of individual performers. 60 mins.

VHS: S12719. $19.98.

Lucky to Be Born in Russia

The sequel to *The Shattered Mirror*, this video relates the human story behind the October 1993 armed confrontation in Moscow, showing the "inner life" of Russian society during this momentous period. The story of a nation searching for a new way as it moves toward an uncertain future. 58 mins.

VHS: S23403. $150.00.

Moon Heart: The Magical World of Tuvinian Shamans

Moon Heart is a shaman from Tuva, a very powerful healer who speaks to the stars. Tuva is a very ancient country of shamans and throat singers. It lies between the Siberian forests and the Central Asian desert. The high Sayan mountains protect Tuva, keeping it wild and pure. Tuvinian people live in harmony with nature, fearing the rage of the powerful spirits of the mountains. 30 mins.

VHS: S32084. $24.95.

Moscow and Leningrad, The Crown Jewels of Russia

Journey to Moscow, the soul of Mother Russia and home to eight million of its people. Enter the Kremlin, watch the pageantry of Red Square and see the grandeur of St. Basil's Cathedral. 50 mins.

VHS: S12276. $24.95.

The Moscow Circus: Animals Under the Big Top

With a cast of more than 6,000 performers and 7,000 animals, the Moscow Circus blends action, live performance and animals.

VHS: S20183. $14.98.

The Moscow Circus: Dancing Bears and More

The Moscow Circus, which was formed more than 200 years ago by royal decree, blends an astonishing range of animals, fearless tamers and acrobatic entertainers, to stage some amazing physical feats. This program focuses on the theatrical flair of the dancing bears.

VHS: S20182. $14.98.

My Russian Friends

An unprecedented portrait of a people in transition. Using a "verite" camera style with first-person narration, this intimate film confronts political, ideological, and religious issues of concern in the Soviet Union today. 1988, 58 mins.

VHS: S13956. $85.00.

National Geographic Video: Russia's Last Czar

Amid splendor and wealth, Czar Nicholas and Empress Alexandra ruled their immense, but troubled, empire. This video shows long-hidden footage and forgotten photos of the tragic royal family who met their fate during the rise of Soviet Communism. Also included is formerly secret footage of their bones being disinterred. 60 mins.

VHS: S29918. $19.95.

National Geographic Video: Soviet Circus

A rare opportunity to go behind the scenes of this remarkable circus. Revered as an art form, supported by the government and loved by millions, the Soviet circus thrives today within the confines of a strict society. 60 mins.

VHS: S09277. $19.95.

Nicholas and Alexandra

The tragic fate of the last couple in the Russian dynasty is finally exposed to the world. Secrets about their death were maintained by the KGB for decades. This video uses diaries and personal effects from the Imperial Archives to recreate their story. It ends with footage of their woodland grave. 100 mins.

VHS: S25636. $19.95.

Nova—Russian Right Stuff: The Mission

This episode chronicles the arduous training of cosmonauts involved in the Soviet Space Station MIR. 1991, 60 mins.

VHS: S16817. $14.98.

Opiates of the Masses: Religion in the USSR

The battle between church and state was never more profound than in the Soviet block. This film, made just before the Gorbachev reforms, seems to indicate that the church was winning the battle. 105 mins.

VHS: S12716. $24.98.

Our Russian Front

Lewis Milestone produced this World War II documentary narrated by Walter Huston, dealing with the Russian people's determination against the advancing German Army.

VHS: S10583. $19.95.

Poligon

Thousands of residents living near the Soviet nuclear test site of Semipalatinsk were harmed by ambitious Soviet nuclear arms tests. This extraordinary film, shot just before the fall of USSR, reveals the extent of the damage inflicted on this region as well as the rationale behind the development of ever more deadly arms. The last interview given by Andrei Sakharov is also included. 58 mins.

VHS: S21584. $95.00.

Rasputin: Dark Servant of Destiny

In this critically acclaimed HBO original movie, Alan Rickman (*Sense and Sensibility*, *Die Hard*) stars as Rasputin, the man/madman who turns the head of Russia's royal family and the world against him. Also stars Ian McKellen (*Richard III*) as the Tsar and Greta Scacchi (*Presumed Innocent*, *ThePlayer*) as the Tsarina who falls under Rasputin's spell.

VHS: S28497. $19.98.

Uli Edel, Great Britain, 1996, 104 mins.

Realms of the Russian Bear

A remarkable television series produced by the BBC in the advent of perestroika, winner of the Sierra Club Centennial Award and several Emmy awards—an unprecedented look at nature and wildlife inside the vast expanses of Russia.

Volume 1: Green Jewel of the Caspian. Visit Astrakhan, the oldest nature reserve on the Volga Delta, where European, Asian and African species of wildlife mingle. 60 mins.

VHS: S22992. $29.98.

Volume 2: The Arctic Frontier. Take a close look at the home of the great white polar bear encompassing one of Russia's most treasured nature preserves—Wrangel Island—where about 10,000 polar bears roam. 60 mins.

VHS: S22993. $29.98.

Volume 3: The Red Deserts. See the abundant wildlife in the deserts of Central Asia, which cover an area larger than the whole of Western Europe and contain a nature reserve that becomes ablaze with color when melting snows bring poppy fields and pistachio groves to life. 60 mins.

VHS: S22994. $29.98.

Volume 4: The Celestial Mountains. Visit the icy peaks of Tian-Shen, the celestial mountains that run for hundreds of miles along the Central Asian Republics and China, where they give shelter to the elusive snow leopard, the rare white-clawed bear, ibex and Marco Polo sheep. 60 mins.

VHS: S22995. $29.98.

Volume 5: Siberia: The Frozen Forest. Sib ria is the greatest forest on the planet. Its inhabitants survive temperatures that dip to more than -90° F. It also boasts an immense 6,000-mile expanse of fir and spruce as well as Lake Baikal, the oldest and deepest lake on earth. 60 mins.

VHS: S22996. $29.98.

Volume 6: Born of Fire. The Kamchatka Peninsula is two very different worlds: the Arctic and Southeast Asia in a remote and volatile stretch that is home to some of the most active volcanoes on Earth and where the cool Arctic waters mix with warmer southern currents. 60 mins.

VHS: S22997. $29.98.

Realms of the Russian Bear, Six-Volume Set. Approximately 6 hours.

VHS: S22998. $179.98.

Red Empire

An ambitious account of life inside the former Soviet Union. From the political disruptions and vast changes occasioned by the October Revolution of 1917, the ensuing civil war, this series uncovers top secret documents, archival footage, first hand accounts of the rise and fall of the communist state.

Revolutionaries. This film traces the fall of the imperial Tsar to the opposite fortune of Lenin, the hero of the proletariats.

VHS: S16864. $14.98.

Winners and Losers. The ignominy and massive failure of World War I occasions the outbreak of the Civil War and the political rise of the Communist Party.

VHS: S16865. $14.98.

Class Warriors. Josef Stalin seizes control of the party and enacts a fierce socialist platform.

VHS: S16866. $14.98.

Enemies of the People. Paranoid and possibly off-balanced, Stalin consolidates his power and destroys his "opposition," imprisoning his enemies in gulags, and promoting chaos and anarchy by turning the masses on each other.

VHS: S17685. $14.98.

Patriots. With the outbreak of World War II, the prolonged engagement with the Nazis nearly devastates Soviet society and destroys the empire.

VHS: S16867. $14.98.

Survivors. The defeat of the Axis powers launches the political fortunes of Krushchev, creating the Warsaw Pact, and unleashes the Cold War.

VHS: S16868. $14.98.

Prisoners of the Past. Gorbachev rises to power, issuing a series of radical social and economic reforms.

VHS: S16869. $14.98.

Collector's Set.

VHS: S16870. $99.98.

Red Star Rising: The Dawn of the Gorbachev Era

The man who has forever changed the fate of the Soviet Union and the world is Mikhail Gorbachev. The complete story via ABC News. 60 mins.

VHS: S12692. $24.98.

Russia: Then & Now

Travel through Moscow, St. Petersburg, Ukraine, Yalta, Sochi and Samarkand, and see the Trans-Siberian Railroad, Lake Baikal, and more with veteran travel filmmaker Clay Francisco before and after the breakup of the Soviet Union. "Anyone who wants to know more about Russia should not miss Francisco's work" (*ABC News, Hollywood*).

VHS: S32727. $19.95.

Clay Francisco, USA, 1994, 90 mins.

Russian People: Revolution and Evolution

This program explores the history of Russia in the 20th century, and the impact of the changes occurring now under Chairman Gorbachev, as the Soviet Union turns an important corner in the development of their concept of a socialist state. Contains historical material and live footage shot in Moscow, Leningrad and Prague. 45 mins.

VHS: S04166. $39.95.

Savoniha: A Siberian

Savoniha belongs to the "Old Believers," a sect of the Russian Orthodox Church that was exiled to Siberia many centuries ago. 95 years old, she witnessed Stalin's anti-religious campaign, losing her father—one of the main spiritual representatives of the Siberian Old Believers. 30 mins.

VHS: S32082. $24.95.

Sex in the Soviet Union

Ted Koppel, host of ABC's *Nightline*, explores the new sexual mores of the former Soviet Union. Pornography, abortion and prostitution have all exploded because of the headlong rush to enjoy newly found freedoms. 60 mins.

VHS: S23002. $19.98.

The Shattered Mirror

An intimate view of typical Russian life during a period of great social and political change. A remarkable look at the new life, opportunities and challenges that the citizens of Russia now face. Award winner. 58 mins.

VHS: S23402. $150.00.

Solovky Power

Harrowing documentary about the first Soviet prison camp. Aging survivors recall in devastating detail the cruelties and injustice suffered at the hands of their oppressors. Old newsreel footage and recently discovered letters from prisoners further illustrate the bleak conditions. 93 mins.

VHS: S23406. $150.00.

Soviet Armed Forces (I Serve the Soviet Union)

An awesome visual account of Operation Dnieper, the 1967 Soviet military exercise which, involving more than half a million troops, stands as the largest maneuver in world history. Soviet cameras recorded the event as a demonstration of socialist prowess; this version was adapted by the U.S. Department of Defense for internal purposes. The American voice-over offers a comparative evaluation of U.S.-Soviet military capabilities; the remarkable footage documents Soviet military power at its zenith. English voice-over.

VHS: S32074. $19.95.

USSR, 1967, 33 mins.

The Soviet Mind

Student views are presented in this program that reveal the impact of tremendous changes across the vast Soviet Union. Social issues and a comparison of capitalism and socialism provoke challenging discussion. 30 mins.

VHS: S23713. $129.95.

Soviet School Day: Styles in Soviet Education

The film reveals the many faces of Soviet education and the children who participate in it. A Soviet English class discusses Shakespeare and *Catcher in the Rye*, and was produced by the U.S.-USSR Youth Exchange Program.

VHS: S03797. $75.00.

Shirley Ward, USA, 1984, 18 mins.

Soviet Secret Archives

This three-part documentary utilizes rare, never-before-seen footage, personal testimonies and archival materials to relate the evolution of the Red Army. 160 mins.

Red Army Chronicles, Vol. 1. The tragic, brutal history of the Russian Red Army, from the genocidal slaughter of Stalin's top lieutenants during the pre-war purges to the massive casualties they suffered on the Eastern front during the war. 52 mins.

VHS: S19608. $19.95.

Red Navy Chronicles. This documentary probes the extraordinary changes in naval warfare, from Russia's first metal submarine—invented in 1834—through the invention of aircraft carriers and nuclear submarines. 52 mins.

VHS: S19607. $19.95.

The Red Aviator, Vol. 1. This program looks at the profound changes in the development of Russian aviation, from its first full-scale airplane, introduced in 1882, to the World War II-era planes that destroyed 57,000 German aircraft. 52 mins.

VHS: S19606. $19.95.

Soviets on Soviet Jewry

This controversial documentary is intended to explain the Soviet position on Soviet Jews to the outside world. This state-oriented propaganda has biographies on successful Soviet Jews, including a doctor, an engineer and a group of uncensored Jewish poets and writers. The Soviet government warns of the temptation to flee to Israel, but insists that Russia is the "true" homeland. 50 mins.

VHS: S13113. $19.98.

Stalin

An international cast headed by Robert Duvall, authentic Russian locations and superb direction by the Czech emigre Ivan Passer are the hallmarks of this made-for-cable biography of Stalin. The film is an exploration of Stalin's iron-fisted rule. With Jeroen Krabbe, Joan Plowright and Maximilian Schell (as Lenin).

VHS: S18371. $19.98.

Laser: LD74682. $39.98.

Ivan Passer, USA, 1992, 165 mins.

A Taste of Freedom

A chronicle of six weeks in the lives of Sasha and Anya Politkovsky, a prominent TV journalist and his wife, whose daily existence reflects the turmoil and uncertainty of life in contemporary Russia. Russian with English subtitles. 46 min.

VHS: S23405. $150.00.

Ten Days That Shook the World

Not the film by Eisenstein, but a look at the Russian Revolution narrated by Orson Welles. The feelings and events are recreated through a combination of historical footage and interviews with participants in the revolution. 77 mins.

VHS: S09255. $39.95.

Terrorism: The Russian Connection

Ter-ror-ism, n. Use of terror and violence…as a political weapon. —Webster. Andropov, KGB head, becomes Soviet Premier. An Activist Polish Pope is shot by a Turk with Bulgarian connections. US embassies are bombed. Here is the Canadian Broadcasting Company's documentary on the recruitment, training, and techniques of the PLO, other terrorist groups and their Russian connection.

VHS: S03981. $29.95.

Tolstoy

This documentary focuses on the private life of the world-famous author; the descendants of Leo Tolstoy reveal the interesting personal side of the great Russian writer and philosopher.

VHS: S15483. $39.95.

Turgenev's Month in the Country

Suzannah York and Ian McShane star in this fascinating Russian psychological drama of love and passion. England, 90 mins.

VHS: S02752. $74.95.

Video from Russia

Without asking or obtaining permission, an American crew of filmmakers traveled to the Soviet Union and spoke freely with Russian people of all ages and occupations about war, work, friendship and even rock and roll. Translated. English narration by Margot Kidder.

VHS: S02360. $29.95.

Dimitri Devyatkin, USA, 1984, 30 mins.

Vincent Trasov: My Five Years in a Nutshell

From 1969 to 1974, artist Vincent Trasov assumed the identity of Mr. Peanut to examine identity, persona, anthropomorphism and contemporary mythology. In 1974 he ran for mayor of Vancouver as Mr. Peanut with the support of the artistic community on an art platform: P for performance, E for elegance, A for art, N for nonsense, U for unique and T for talent. He received 5% of the vote, but most of the attention from the media. This is his story. 29 mins.

VHS: S12759. $65.00.

Visions of Russia: A Granddaughter Returns

A young American college student, video camera in hand, decides to tour the Soviet Union, birthplace of her grandparents. The result is this charming and spontaneous documentary portrait. 29 mins.

VHS: S14693. $34.95.

The Week That Shook the World: The Soviet Coup

A chronicle that utilizes ABC News' extensive coverage of the attempted Soviet Union coup from August 19-25, 1991. 65 mins.

VHS: S15881. $19.98.

What About the Russians?

"Are the Russians ahead in the nuclear arms race? Why the concern over the MX, the Cruise, the Pershing missiles? Can we trust the Russians to honor a nuclear weapons treaty? How can we end the arms race and maintain our national security?" Government officials including George Kennan, former U.S. ambassador to Russia, Robert McNamara, former Defense secretary, and William Colby, former director of the CIA, discuss these important questions.

VHS: S03803. $45.00.

Ian Thiermann/Vivien Verdon-Roe, USA, 1983, 26 mins.

What Soviet Children Are Saying About Nuclear War

A group of American psychiatrists led by Eric Chivian, M.D., and John Mack, M.D., visited two Soviet Pioneer camps and interviewed Soviet girls and boys aged 10-15. The result is an extraordinary documentary which is informative, refreshing and inspiring.

VHS: S03796. $45.00.

Int'l. Phys. for Prev. Nuc. War, 1983, 22 mins.

EASTERN EUROPE/SOVIET UNION

Crossroads of the Cold War

The 1990's are different from the previous decades, and one of the major changes will be in America's role as a world power. After nearly 50 years of a "Cold War" which has dominated world history, the coming decades will reflect many changes. This program is designed to put the topic into a historical perspective and attempt a critical analysis of this process. 28 mins.

VHS: S10782. $29.95.

Fall of Communism

Whereas Communists predicted a Domino effect of nations falling under Communism, what happened was the exact opposite: one by one leftist nations traded in on their politics for a more democratic future. This video covers everything from the crumbling of the Berlin Wall to independence movements in Poland, Lithuania and Mother Russia herself. 80 mins.

VHS: S13179. $19.98.

The Loss of an Enemy

The Cold War was defined by the fear and loathing of an enemy perceived as powerful and intractable. This documentary explores both the history and long-lasting effects of this legacy with the help of numerous experts, including *Time Magazine* correspondent Strobe Talbot and State Department official Richard Burt. 28 mins.

VHS: S21588. $25.00.

polish cinema

Agent #1
Based on the real-life story of a Polish spy in German-occupied Greece during WWI. Polish with English subtitles.
VHS: S34954. $39.95.
Zbigniew Kuzminski, Poland, 1972, 94 mins.

Akademia Podroze Pana (Mr. Blot's Academy/Travels of Mr. Blot)
Ten-year-old Adam, beginning his education at the Academy, finds the hideout of Bird Matt, who used to be a prince. Touched by his fate, he promises to find the magic button which has the power to restore him to human shape. With Piotr Fronczewski, Leon Niemczyk, Slawek Wronka, Irena Karel and Zdzislawa Sosnicka I Inni. Polish with NO subtitles.
Mr. Blot's Academy, Vol. 1.—Przygody Ksiecia Mateusza. 86 mins.
VHS: S34158. $24.95.
Mr. Blot's Academy, Vol. 2.—Tajemnica Golarza Filipa. 83 mins.
VHS: S34159. $24.95.
Mr. Blot's Academy, Vol. 3.—Wystannicy Bajdacji. 84 mins.
VHS: S34160. $24.95.
Mr. Blot's Academy, Vol. 4.—Wyspa Wynalazcow. 67 mins.
VHS: S34161. $24.95.
Mr. Blot's Academy, The Set.
VHS: S34162. $89.95.
Krzystof Gradowski, Poland, 1983, 85 mins.

All Friends Here
A series of comic situations show the history of Pawlak's and Kargul's families. Funny dialogue, clever situations and famous actors make this a winning film for Polish audiences. Polish with English subtitles.
VHS: S26730. $39.95.
Sylwester Checinski, Poland, 1967, 78 mins.

Apple Tree of Paradise
The sequel to *The Girls of Nowopilki* is set in Warsaw after the First World War, when Poland regained her independence. Again, the film follows the lives of the young heroines. Polish with NO subtitles.
VHS: S11354. $49.95.
Barbara Sass, Poland, 1985, 112 mins.

Aquarium
This psychological spy film is a study of the methods used to shape the personality of an individual working in the service of a totalitarian empire. The film's hero must perform every task assigned to him, in case his orders are checked on by his superiors. When he betrays his friend and protector, he awaits a numbing injection and evacuation to Moscow. Polish with English subtitles.
VHS: S34962. $39.95.
Antoni Krauze, Poland, 1995, 145 mins.

The Art of Loving
Olgierd Pasikonik is a well-known sex therapist who is temporarily impotent. He offers his home to Anna, one of his readers, who is uninterested in sex, but runs the household. His condition is cured by Teresa, the lover of one of his friends. But Teresa never goes to bed twice with the same man and has a strange habit of leaving her fiance at the altar. Polish with English subtitles.
VHS: S34964. $39.95.
Jack Bromski, Poland, 1989

Austeria
Early in World War I, a group of Orthodox Jews flee from the Cossack army in Polish Galicia. A secluded country inn becomes their temporary refuge, where emotional attachments, brief love affairs and even a renewed faith in humankind inspire these desperate individuals. From the director of *Joan of the Angels*. Polish with English subtitles.
VHS: S20839. $59.95.
Jerzy Kawalerowicz, Poland, 1988, 110 mins.

Bad Luck
The odyssey of a man through Poland from 1930 to 1950, in a changing world that seems to have no place for him. We watch him from his childhood to his first love, from his unwilling involvement in Fascist politics to his arrest and imprisonment in a POW camp. Polish with English subtitles.
VHS: S34953. $39.95.
Andrzej Munk, Poland, 1960, 105 mins.

Balance
One of the key films of Krzysztof Zanussi, in which the chance meeting with an old friend causes a woman to confront a painful decision: to stay with her husband and child, or to begin a new life with a new partner. With Maja Komorowska, Marek Piwowski, Halina Mikolajska. Polish with English subtitles.
VHS: S11324. $49.95.
Krzysztof Zanussi, Poland, 1974, 99 mins.

Base of the Dead People
With Emil Karewicz and Zygmunt Kestowicz. Polish with English subtitles.
VHS: S34950. $39.95.
Czeslaw Petelski, Poland, 1959, 81 mins.

Beautiful Stranger
In 1919, during World War I, a young lieutenant confronts the bombastic Rasputin traveling incognito. The General Staff Colonel of the Russian army is impressed with the young man and sends him on a dangerous mission, where he meets a beautiful woman. Now he must choose between his duty and the woman he loves. Polish with English subtitles.
VHS: S21067. $59.95.
Jerzy Hoffman, Poland, 1993, 84 mins.

The Bermuda Triangle
Henry, a doctor from Cracow; Ludwig, a popular lawyer from Lodz; and Jarek, the owner of a car repair shop in Gdansk, have known each other for years. Their friendship has been strengthened by their frequent mountain climbing trips; they can count on and trust each other in every situation. Now, as middleaged men, they have money, social position…but also serious troubles. Henry's daughter is being blackmailed, Ludwig is a victim of the intrigue set up by his wife and her lover and Jarek has enormous financial problems. So the three old friends decide to commit what they think is the "perfect" crime in order to get out of their terrible predicaments. Will they succeed? Polish with English subtitles.
VHS: S14234. $49.95.
Wojciech Wojcik, Poland, 1989, 99 mins.

Between the Cup and the Lip
The young, charismatic count Wentzel Croy-Dulmen falls in love with an enigmatic stranger, a beautiful young woman who's the cousin of his grandfather who lives in Poland. His desire for her necessitates a full-scale reconsidering of his thoughts and ideas about Poland. With Jacek Chmlelnik and Katarzyna Gnlewkowska. Polish with English subtitles.
VHS: S18084. $49.95.
Zbigniew Kuzminski, Poland, 1987, 114 mins.

Big Deal
The continuing comic adventures of Pawlak and Kargul take on an international cast when the two set off for the world's third largest Polish city, Chicago. Polish with English subtitles.
VHS: S26732. $39.95.

Big-Bang
A UFO lands in a small village and the residents prepare to host the terrestrial, acting as representatives of mankind. With Iga Cembrzynska, Ludwik Benoit. Polish with NO subtitles.
VHS: S11359. $39.95.
Andrzej Kondratiuk, Poland, 1986, 98 mins.

The Birthday
The story of a young man in occupied Warsaw whose 23rd birthday falls on the 56th day of the Warsaw Uprising in 1944. With Piotr Lysak, Andrzej Lapicki. Polish with NO subtitles.
VHS: S11350. $49.95.
Ewa & Czeslaw Petelski, Poland, 1980, 99 mins.

The Border
Forbidden love leads to misery and death in this black-and-white Polish film. With E. Barszczewska, L. Zelichowska and J. Pichelski. Polish with English subtitles.
VHS: S34165. $24.95.
Jozef Lejtes, Poland, 1938, 90 mins.

Border Street
A masterpiece of Polish cinema, a tragedy about the Warsaw ghetto involving an old tailor who tries to save his daughters and others. The film culminates with the Warsaw uprising of 1943, when Jews, with the support of the Polish underground, take up arms and die fighting. With passages of visual brilliance. Polish with English subtitles.
VHS: S00169. $59.95.
Aleksandar Ford, Poland, 1948, 101 mins.

Bottom Rock
A contemporary Polish film starring and with the music of Grzegorz Ciechowski, the subject of which is the lack of understanding and hope among young people. Tomasz Hudziec, Jerzy Mercik, Ewa Skibinski star. Polish with English subtitles.
VHS: S12514. $49.95.
Roland Rowinski, Poland, 1987, 83 mins.

By Touch
Two young women, one suffering from cancer and the other a rape victim, seek hope and the will to survive in their friendship in this tautly directed, realistic drama. With Grazyna Szapolowska, Maria Ciunelis. Polish with English subtitles.
VHS: S12359. $49.95.
Magdalena Lazarkiewicz, Poland, 1985, 85 mins.

Caesarian Section
A comedy set in a country hospital, where women compete for the honor of becoming the mother of the millionth inhabitant of the district. Polish with NO subtitles.
VHS: S11343. $49.95.
Stanislaw Moszuk, Poland, 1987, 83 mins.

Call Me Rockefeller
A kind of Polish *Home Alone*. When the Malinowskis go abroad, they leave their children in the care of their housemaid, Misia, who turns out to be a notorious trickster named Jagoda. While the children are at school, Jagoda and her friend Matros loot the Malinowski's apartment and disappear. The children don't report the robbery and instead find creative ways to earn money to replace the stolen property. Their efforts bring them a fortune by the time their parents return. Polish with English subtitles.
VHS: S34957. $39.95.
Waldemar Szarek, Poland, 1990

Camouflage
Zanussi's sixth film, set in an intellectual milieu, tackles the theme of survival in the rat race, and the extent to which one should bend one's principles. Jakub, the past master at survival, assumes the necessary camouflage: "Survive and you win; perish and you're proved wrong." He engages his colleague, the younger Jaroslaw, in a game which ends in desolation and stalemate. With Zbigniew Zapasiewicz and Piotr Garlicki. Polish with English subtitles.
VHS: S11356. $49.95.
Krzysztof Zanussi, Poland, 1977, 106 mins.

Career of Nikodem Dyzma
A 7-part, 3-cassette series based on a novel by Tadeusz Dolega-Mostowicz about a swindler who through pure coincidence reaches prominent government posts, enjoying the support of the aristocratic and government circles taken in by his image of a strong man. Polish with NO subtitles. 3 cassettes.
VHS: S11336. $89.95.
Jan Rybkowski, Poland, 1980, 385 mins.

Casimir the Great
A historical drama that depicts the life of Poland's only king to be dubbed "the Great", for his contribution to the building of the Polish state in the Middle Ages. On two cassettes, in two parts. With Krzysztof Chamiec, Wladyslaw Hancza. Polish with English subtitles.
VHS: S11333. $69.95.

Champion Always Loses
Based on the criminal records of Interpol; two great chess champions in France of the 1930's fall victims to a clever swindle. Polish with NO subtitles.
VHS: S11360. $39.95.
Gregorz Lasota, Poland, 1977, 42 mins.

Chatelaine's Daughter

Set during the 1930's, the film focuses on a young journalist who spends his vacation alone in the Mazurian Lake district. One night while camping, a young girl approaches him and asks him to take her to Warsaw. A romance ensues which evolves into an unexpected conclusion. Polish with NO subtitles.
VHS: S11358. $39.95.
Marek Nowicki, Poland, 1983, 58 mins.

Cheating Flea

A humorous performance about a cheeky, mischievous flea, based on a poem by Jan Brzechwa. Polish with NO subtitles.
VHS: S11295. $39.95.

Children Must Laugh

Aleksandar Ford's powerful documentary, financed by the Jewish labor movement in Poland, is a revealing look at Polish pre-war Jewish life. "Out of the sorrows and shadows of the life of Jewish workers in Poland, a bright ray of hope has come.... Hollywood scouts would do well to locate some of the children... [whose] confidence in their ability to 'build a better world' rises above any language barrier" (*The New York Times*). Polish and Yiddish with English narration and subtitles.
VHS: S19534. $54.00.
Aleksandar Ford, Poland/USA, 1935/65, 64 mins.

Citizen P.

Piszczuk, the hero of Andrzej Munk's *Bad Luck*, appears again, this time striving to adjust to his social environment whatever the price. He yearns to be accepted and appreciated, but always fails. Despite all his hard efforts and good intentions misfortune continues to blight his every move. Starring Jerzy Stuhr. Polish with NO subtitles.
VHS: S14235. $49.95.
Andrzej Kotkowski, Poland, 1989, 112 mins.

Colonel Wolodyjowski

A landmark epic, based on the historical trilogy of Henryk Sienkiewicz. Set in the year 1668, at the time of Turkish invasion of Poland's eastern frontier. With Tadeusz Loniski, Magdalena Zawadzka, Daniel Olbrychski. Polish with English subtitles.
VHS: S11329. $49.95.
Jerzy Hoffman, Poland, 1969, 160 mins.

The Comedienne

A nineteenth century costume drama based on a novel by Wladyslaw Reymont. A young and ambitious provincial girl goes to Warsaw to try her talents as an actress. Polish with NO subtitles.
VHS: S11335. $69.95.
Jerzy Sztwiernia, Poland, 1986, 225 mins.

Commando

This military documentary details the exploits of a brave Polish unit that served with British commandos during World War II. The film follows its training, war-time activities and ultimate fate after 1945. Polish with NO subtitles.
VHS: S16822. $29.95.
Marek Widarski, Poland, 73 mins.

Consul

Based on a true story, the tale of a con artist as an honorary consul. With Piotr Franczewski, Maria Pakulnis, Henryk Bistra and Jerzy Bonczak. Polish with NO subtitles.
VHS: S34151. $29.95.
Miroslaw Bork, Poland, 1989, 100 mins.

Contract

A terrific film by Krzysztof Zanussi. The central characters are Peter, the son of a prominent cardiologist, and Lilka, the daughter of a party dignitary. Their wedding provides a stage for confrontation between their families and friends. With Maja Komorowska and Tadeusz Lomnicki. Polish with NO subtitles.
VHS: S11355. $49.95.
Krzysztof Zanussi, Poland, 1980, 114 mins.

The Countess Cosel (Hrabina Cosel)

Jozef Ignacy Kraszewski's novel serves as the basis for this historical romance. It concerns the Countess Cosel's tragic struggle to marry the man she loved, the father of her children, King August II. Polish with English subtitles.
VHS: S26729. $59.95.
Jerzy Antczak, Poland, 1968, 148 mins.

Coup d'Etat

The military coup in Poland waged by Marshal Jozef Pilsudski is the subject of this film. The film covers the history behind this event, from the Autumn of 1925 to the Brzesc Trial in 1931. Polish with NO subtitles.
VHS: S22210. $39.95.
Ryszard Filipski, Poland, 1981, 158 mins.

Death of the President

This finely acted, detailed and probing film centers around the assassination of Poland's president in 1922. "An historical document coming to life" (*Variety*), the film is a vivid, psychoanalytical look at political assassins and their makeup. Polish with English subtitles.
VHS: S34955. $39.95.
Jerzy Kawalerowicz, Poland, 1977, 144 mins.

The Deluge

The action takes place in the 17th century, the turbulent period of the Polish-Swedish war. The plot is woven around the stormy love of the main character in the film, Andrzej Kmicic (played by Daniel Olbrychski), for a young gentlewoman named Olenka. Based on the novel by Nobel prize-winning author Henryk Sienkiewicz, much of this exciting and romantic film was shot in authentic, ancient Polish castles. Nominated for the Best Foreign Language Film Oscar in 1974. Polish with English subtitles.
VHS: S14230. $79.95.
Jerzy Hoffman, Poland, 1973, 185 mins.

Dismissed from Life

On Christmas Eve 1989, Marek is beaten in the street and left to die in a dump. He survives after the brain surgery, but it leaveshim amnesiac. He wanders through the city, finds shelter with a mad bag lady, and searches for his identity. Meanwhile, his fate is a source of consternation not only to his family, but also to his assailants, who fear Marek will testify against them. Polish with English subtitles.
VHS: S34961. $39.95.
Waldemar Krzystek, Poland, 1992, 90 mins.

The Doll

The emotionally powerful story of an unfulfilled love between a man who is a social climber, and a beautiful but cold woman of aristocratic background, played against a picture of 19th century Poland. Polish with English subtitles.
VHS: S11330. $49.95.
Wojciech J. Has, Poland, 1969, 159 mins.

Dr. Judym

Based on a novel by Stefan Zeromski. The hero is a young doctor of low social origin, who sacrifices his love for his work and for helping the poor, at the turn of the century. Polish with English subtitles.
VHS: S11331. $49.95.
Wlodzimierz Haupe, Poland, 94 mins.

Dziesieciu z Pawiaka

This is the story of a secret underground organization whose mysterious leader takes on a difficult mission. He resolves to save the lives of his soldiers after they have been sentenced to death. Polish with NO subtitles.
VHS: S26654. $24.95.
Ryszard Ordyriski, Poland, 1931, 90 mins.

Egg-Nog (Kogel Mogel)

Kate dreams of a bright career. She wants to study in town but her father, who owns a large farm, has old-fashioned ideas about a woman's place and tries to arrange a marriage for Kate with successful businessman. Instead, she runs away on her wedding day and begins to face the challenges of life in a big and unfriendly city. Will she go to college, return home, or fall in love? Can one escape from one's destiny? Polish with English subtitles.
VHS: S14233. $49.95.
Roman Zaluski, Poland, 1989, 103 mins.

Enigma Secret

The story of the breaking of the Nazi secret coding machine Enigma, by three Polish mathematicians. Tadeusz Borowski, Piotr Fronczewski, Piotr Garlicki star. Polish with English subtitles.
VHS: S11327. $49.95.
Roman Wionczek, Poland, 1979, 158 mins.

Eroica

A truly great film and one of the key works of postwar Polish cinema, this feature by Andrzej Munk is a fine example of the Polish myth of romantic heroism. The Warsaw Uprising is looked at through the eyes of a drunken black marketeer; in the second "movement," Polish prisoners in a German camp fanatically believe in the heroism of their comrade, which, in fact, is a farce. "*Eroica*," wrote Pauline Kael, "is a true black comedy and one of the few modern movies that has something relevant to say about the modern world." Polish with English subtitles.
VHS: S34949. $39.95.
Andrzej Munk, Poland, 1957, 83 mins.

Eve Wants to Sleep

A young woman finds her attempts to secure lodging in the big city frustrated at every turn. The state bureaucracy and the police are the chief culprits. This light comedy was considered quite daring in its time as it is critical of the Polish state. With Barbara Kwiatkowska, Stanislaw Mikulski and Ludwik Benoit. Polish with English subtitles.
VHS: S26649. $29.95.
Tadeusz Chmielewski, Poland, 1958, 97 mins.

The Faithful River

In January 1863, a tragic uprising rocked Poland. This film, based on Stefan Zeromski's novel, shows the heroism which fueled young people at that critical historic moment. It was a struggle that ended for many in death. Polish with English subtitles.
VHS: S26735. $39.95.
Tadeusz Chmielewski, Poland, 1987, 137 mins.

Family Life

One of the key films of the "cinema of moral anxiety." After six years in Warsaw, a design engineer reluctantly returns home to a dilapidated mansion in the country. There he must confront his alcoholic father and a slightly deranged sister, as well as his own life. "At long last, the Polish cinema has a new and important director," wrote Richard Roud. "Very intimate in scale, the film is beautifully acted by Daniel Olbrychski and Jan Kreczmar." Polish with English subtitles.
VHS: S22208. $59.95.
Krzysztof Zanussi, Poland, 1971, 93 mins.

Faustyna

An artistic representation of the mystical life led by Bl. Faustina Kowalska, based upon experiences recorded in her spiritual diary. With Danuta Segda, Danuta Szaflarska and Stanislawa Celinska. Polish with English subtitles.
VHS: S34163. $24.95.
Jerzy Lukasiewicz, Poland, 1995, 84 mins.

Fire in the Steppe

The conclusion of Henryk Sienkiewicz's trilogy brings to an end the saga of the heroines and heroes who lived, loved and died in Poland's most enduring epic. A blend of history and imagination in which the East and West of their era confronted each other in a last stand. Polish with English subtitles. 160 mins.
VHS: S33755. $39.95.

First Day of Freedom

A group of Polish officers, liberated from a German P.O.W. camp, find that freedom is not what they expected. With Elzbieta Czyzewska, Tadusz Fijewski, Tadeusz Lomnicki and Beata Tyszkiewicz. Polish with English subtitles.
VHS: S34956. $39.95.
Aleksander Ford, Poland, 1965, 97 mins.

Florian

A young couple in love find themselves involved in a dangerous plot during the First World War. They must hide an ancient church bell of great historical value. The situation appears desperate until the Polish army appears and helps the patriotic couple. Polish with NO subtitles.
VHS: S26655. $24.95.
Leonard Buczkowski, Poland, 1938, 90 mins.

Forbidden Songs

This was the first movie made in Poland after World War II; it is the story of the songs sung by all of Warsaw during the German occupation. A stirring tale of the heroic underground fighters, their lives and deaths, and those things which sustained them in their epic struggle for freedom. With Danuta Szaflarska and Jerzy Duszynski. Polish with NO English subtitles.
VHS: S15558. $49.95.
Ludwik Starski, Poland, 1947, 100 mins.

Forgotten Melody

The very funny story of love between a young girl and the handsome man who composed a melody for her. With Helena Grossowna and Aleksander Zabczynski. Polish with NO English subtitles.
VHS: S15568. $49.95.
Konrad Tom, Poland, 1938, 80 mins.

Fredro for Adults

A unique erotic comedy by Aleksander Fredro, a classic of Polish comedy, produced for the first time by The Syrena Theatre Company in Warsaw in 1988. 72 mins. Polish with NO subtitles.
VHS: S11371. $39.95.

General Sosabowski
The exploits of the famed Polish military leader. Born in 1892, Sosabowski commanded the First Land Army also known as "The Children of Warsaw," against the Nazi blitzkrieg in 1939. Polish with NO subtitles.
VHS: S16826. $29.95.
E.Z. Szanialawski, Poland, 53 mins.

Girls of Nowopilki
A postwar film version of Pola Gojawiczynska's novel. A lively picture of turn-of-the-century Warsaw as experienced by four young girls. The film begins as the heroines finish primary school and must begin adult life. With Maria Ciunelis, Izabella Drobowitz-Orkisz. Polish with NO subtitles.
VHS: S11353. $49.95.
Barbara Sass, Poland, 1985, 94 mins.

The Glass Menagerie
A television adaptation of Tennessee Williams' famous play. Polish with English subtitles.
VHS: S34951. $39.95.

Gniazdo
A historical film about the beginning of the Polish state under the reign of Mieszko I. The ambitious ruler extends the state borders, allies with Emperor Otto I, is baptized a Roman Catholic and strengthens the country's sovereignty in the victorious battle of Cedynia. With Wojciech Pszoniak, Marek Bargielowski and Franciszek Piecaka. Polish with NO subtitles.
VHS: S34153. $29.95.
Jan Rybkowski, Poland, 1974, 94 mins.

The Great Betrayal
A very accurate description of a selected group from Poland's financial establishment in the early '90s. With Jan Englert, Krzsztof Wakulinski, Marzena Trybata and Ewa Gwaryluk. Polish with NO subtitles.
VHS: S34155. $39.95.
Jan Tominicki, Poland, 1993, 98 mins.

Greta
Krzysztof Gruber directed this moving story about a 10-year-old Polish boy who is a fugitive from a labor camp during WWII. As he makes it to a small town he meets a deserter from the German Army. An SS officer identifies the deserter and shoots him. The boy meets Greta, a girl his own age, and invited to her home, late in the evening he meets Greta's father—the SS officer. With Janusz Grabowski, Agnieszka Kruszewska. Polish with English subtitles.
VHS: S09212. $49.95.
Krzysztof Gruber, Poland, 1986, 60 mins.

Gulag Archipelago
Two powerful documentaries about gulag life and conditions are included on this videocassette: *Gulag Archipelago* and *Exhumation*. From director Jozef Gebski.
VHS: S15567. $39.95.
Jozef Gebski, Poland, 88 mins.

Gypsies
A cinema-verite documentary produced in Poland during the early 60's, which follows a traveling gypsy caravan across rural Poland. Polish with NO subtitles. Produced by the Documentary Film Studio.
VHS: S03354. $39.95.
Wladyslaw Slesicki, Poland, 1961, 30 mins.

H. M. Deserters
This fantastic comedy begins when a bunch of "politically suspected" soldiers of the Austrian-Hungarian empire, whose job it is to guard a camp for Italian POW's, desert from their duties. A long string of adventures soon follows. Polish with NO subtitles.
VHS: S14239. $49.95.
Janusz Majewski, Poland, 1986, 166 mins.

Hallo, Fred the Beard
A delightful musical comedy. The Red Mill theatre is slowly going to ruin. Fred Kampinos, alias Fred the Beard, suddenly appears to pay all the debts and becomes co-owner. Things get complicated, however, when it is revealed that Fred plans to rob the bank located right next door to the small theatre. Polish with NO subtitles.
VHS: S15561. $49.95.
Janusz Rzeszewski, Poland, 1978, 98 mins.

His Excellency the Shop Assistant
A comedy made in 1933 which stars Ina Benita and Eugeniusz Bodo in the story of a shop assistant in a big store who falls in love with the daughter of a VIP. Very funny! Polish with NO subtitles.
VHS: S15569. $49.95.
Michal Waszynski, Poland, 1933, 85 mins.

Hot Thursday
Three 12-year-old friends from a drab mining district accidentally happen upon a plan that could radically improve their lives. A big robbery should grant them the money and success they so desperately crave. In the end, all their hopes don't pan out the way they imagined they would. Polish with English subtitles.
VHS: S26733. $39.95.
Michal Rosa, Poland, 1994, 60 mins.

Hotel Lux
Differences escalate between people for and against a new hotel project into a great finale at the hotel's grand opening. With Ignacy Gogoleski, Henryk Bista, Krzysztof Kolberger and Grazyna Szapotowska. Polish with NO subtitles.
VHS: S34152. $29.95.
Ryszard Ber, Poland, 1979, 90 mins.

Hotel Pacific
The action of this film takes places in the 1930s. Roman Boryczko is looking for a job. He eventually finds employment as a dishwasher in the restaurant of the Pacific Hotel and quickly advances through the hotel hierarchy of posts. But the successive stages of his career also prove to be painful lessons in life. Polish with NO subtitles.
VHS: S15564. $49.95.
Janusz Majewski, Poland, 1975

I Am Who I Am
The first documentary on the issue of homosexuality in Poland. Polish with English subtitles.
VHS: S34164. $24.95.
Ryszard Moch, Poland, 1990, 27 mins.

I Lied
A moving love story made in Poland in 1937, the film stars Jadwiga Smosarska and Eugeniusz Bodo in the story of an attractive young woman forced to navigate in a merciless, male-dominated world. Polish with NO subtitles.
VHS: S11684. $29.00.
Mieczyslaw Krawicz, Poland, 1937, 85 mins.

I Like Bats
A likeable horror story about a beautiful girl—a vampire—who would like to become a human and seeks help from a psychiatrist. Polish with English subtitles.
VHS: S11321. $49.95.
Grzegorz Warchol, Poland, 1985, 90 mins.

Illumination
Krzysztof Zanussi's landmark film is a parable about the limits of rationality. A young scientist believes rational analysis can solve everything until he is confronted by an older woman and the accidental death of a close friend. Zanussi deftly mixes dramatic and documentary footage as he "broke new ground in his cryptic, intelligent, ironic and ethical essays on the scientific mind" (*Faber Companion to Foreign Films*). Polish with English subtitles.
VHS: S26978. $59.95.
Krzysztof Zanussi, Poland, 1973, 91 mins.

In an Old Manor House
Based on a play by the visionary Stanislaw Witkiewicz. The owner of an estate kills his wife after discovering her affair with his son of a previous marriage. Her ghost returns to he manor driving the inhabitants to the verge of insanity in this powerful film. Polish with English subtitles.
VHS: S11319. $49.95.
Andrzej Kotkowski, Poland, 1984, 90 mins.

In Desert and Wilderness
The story of a Polish boy and English girl became the subject of one of the most beautiful adventure books in Polish or perhaps even world literature. Written in 1911 by Henryk Sienkiewicz, the Nobel prize-winning author of *Quo Vadis*, the tale takes place in the late 19th century, relating the adventures of two kidnapped children who escape and find themselves alone in the middle of uncharted Africa. Polish with English subtitles.
VHS: S14238. $49.95.
Wladyslaw Slesicki, Poland, 1973, 144 mins.

Iron Hand
After a power struggle in the 16th century, Stefan Batory won the Polish crown. His right hand man, Mroczek, began to organize a nationwide network of spies to prevent any activities against his King. This film depicts many characters from this important time in Polish history. Polish with English subtitles.
VHS: S22211. $59.95.
Ryszard Ber, Poland, 1989, 103 mins.

Is Lucyna a Girl?
This Polish comedy from the 1930s stars Jadwiga Smosarska as Lucyna, a woman in disguise as a man, who gets a job as an engineer. Once instated, she uses her feminine charm to provoke her colleagues. Polish with NO subtitles.
VHS: S15571. $39.95.
Juliusz Gardan, Poland, 1934, 80 mins.

It'll Be Better
A comic pair of workers from a toy factory in pre-war Lvov are unexpectedly burdened with a nursing job. Great fun! Polish with NO subtitles.
VHS: S15572. $39.95.
Michal Waszynski, Poland, 1936, 92 mins.

Jadzia
A Polish comedy from 1936 about two companies run by a beautiful woman and handsome man. They engage in a competition which sets off a series of funny events. Polish with NO subtitles.
VHS: S15573. $39.95.
Mieczyslaw Krawicz, Poland, 1936, 92 mins.

Jaguar 1936
Set in Vienna, 1936. A Danish businessman buys a Jaguar at an auto dealership, undaunted by the exorbitant price. Two hours later, he sells it for half the price, giving rise to the suspicion of bank fraud in this detective thriller. Polish with NO subtitles.
VHS: S11361. $39.95.
Gregorz Lasota, Poland, 1977, 53 mins.

Janosik
Janosik is a legendary hero of the Tatra Mountains. As the leader of a band of outlaws this mountain robber steals from the rich and helps the poor who are oppressed by the liege lords who rule the countryside. An exciting action film, in the tradition of Robin Hood, full of adventures, fights, duels, pursuits and traps. Polish with English subtitles.
VHS: S14237. $49.95.
Jerzy Passendorfer, Poland, 1973, 144 mins.

Just Beyond This Forest
In 1942 in Warsaw's ghetto, an Aryan washerwoman is rehired by the Jewish woman she worked for before the war, to take her young daughter to the countryside until the war is over. The rude maid takes full advantage of the situation by allowing the desperate woman to shower her with gifts and money before she'll take the child away. The maid and child leave by train, but it's stopped, and they have to proceed on foot. The innocent youngster and the maid begin to develop a strong bond, and by the time they are stopped by a German patrol, the woman is prepared to risk her life for the child. Polish with English subtitles.
VHS: S34965. $39.95.
Jan Lomnicki, Poland, 1991, 90 mins.

Karate Polish Style
A thriller set as two Warsaw artists paint a fresco in the Mazurian Lake District and clash with local thugs. Polish with English subtitles.
VHS: S11320. $49.95.
Jerzy Wojcik, Poland, 1982, 91 mins.

King Boleslaus the Bold
The action of this film is set in 1079, the last year of Boleslaus the Bold's rule. It is the story of conflict between the king and the Bishop of Cracow, a conflict which ended tragically with the bishop's death. Polish with English subtitles.
VHS: S15060. $49.95.
Witold Lesiewicz, Poland, 1972, 105 mins.

The Kingdom of Green Glade
The story of a boy's adventures at the Green Glade. He destroys an ants' nest, tries to kill a spider and gets shrunk to the size of a ladybug. Polish with NO subtitles.
VHS: S34156. $24.95.
Krzysztof Kiwerski, Poland, 1996, 65 mins.

Knights of the Teutonic Order
Certainly one of the highest achievements of the 1960 Polish cinema, and a stirring nationalist epic. Based on the classic novel by Henryk Sienkiewicz, *Krzyzacy* (Knights of the Teutonic Order) is a vivid portrayal of customs and life in medieval Poland, brilliantly directed with epic sweep by Aleksandar Ford. With a cast of thousands, including Andrzej Szalawski and Grazyna Staniszewska. Available in two versions: a Polish-language version with English subtitles, and an English-dubbed version which is shorter by a half-hour. Color.
Knights of the Teutonic Order. English dubbed. 145 mins.
VHS: S12355. $59.95.
Krzyzacy. Polish with English subtitles. 175 mins. 2 cassettes.
VHS: S12354. $59.95.
Aleksandar Ford, Poland, 1960, 142 mins.

Kornblumenblau
Based on a true story about a Polish musician who manages to survive a concentration camp during World War II because he can play the German song "Kornblumenblau" on the accordion. With Adam Kamion. Winner of Poland's A. Munk Award for best debut. Polish with English subtitles.
VHS: S34963. $39.95.
Leszek Wosiewicz, Poland, 1988

La Cuisine Polonaise

A Polish pilot returns home after the Second World War with his English wife and young daughter only to be framed and jailed as a spy. When his wife tries to see him freed, a communist government official demands a high personal price. This deeply emotional historical drama covers the years 1940-1950. With Krystyna Janda, Krzysztof Kolberger, Piotr Machalica, Zbigniew Zamachowski and Marek Kondrat. Polish with NO subtitles.

VHS: S16819. $39.95.
Jacek Bromski, Poland, 1991, 108 mins.

The Last Stage

The horrible lives of female inmates of Auschwitz are chronicled in this chillingly accurate recreation of actual events. Filmed on location at the notorious German concentration camp, it tells the story of one woman's attempts to survive until she is eventually rescued. Based on the experiences of the film's director, Wanda Jakubiowska, as a prisoner of a German concentration camp. With Alina Janowska, Zofia Mrzozowska, Aleksandra Slaska and Edward Dziewonski I Inni. Polish with NO subtitles.

VHS: S34154. $39.95.
Wanda Jakubowska, Poland, 1947, 110 mins.

Leper

A moving, melodramatic story of the forbidden love affair between a wealthy young nobleman and the beautiful teacher of a high society girl. The town folk try to destroy the feelings between these two people of different social positions. With Elzbieta Starostecka and Leszek Teleszynski. Polish with English subtitles.

VHS: S15056. $39.95.
Jerzy Hoffman, Poland, 1976, 100 mins.

Little Prince

A young girl is forced to take up a man's disguise in this classic Polish comedy. Karolina Lubienska stars, and the situation gets more complicated when she meets the man of her dreams. Polish with NO subtitles.

VHS: S15574. $39.95.
T. Szebego/S. Szebego, Poland, 1937, 87 mins.

Love Can Take It All

A Polish film based on the life of the famous cabaret star of pre-war Warsaw, Hanka Ordonowna. With Dorota Staliniska, Stanislawa Celinska, Bozena Dykiel, Piotr Fronczewski and Piotr Garlicki. Polish with NO subtitles.

VHS: S34150. $29.95.
Janusz Rzeszewski, Poland, 1981, 120 mins.

Major Hubal

Legendary Hubal-Major Dobrzanski continued to fight the Nazi occupation of Poland despite the incredible odds against him and his band of soldiers. This war drama is based on a true story. Polish with English subtitles.

VHS: S26734. $39.95.
Bohdan Poreba, Poland, 1973

Man on the Track

Based on a short story by J.S. Stawinski, the film is a study of an old railway worker who cannot fit into the contemporary world and its ideals. Devoting his life to his work, he gives his life to save a train. The film won Munk a director award at the 1957 Karlovy Vary Festival and a Polish Film Critics Prize. With Kazimierz Opalinski, Zygmunt Maciejewski, Zygmunt Zintel, Zygmunt Listkiewicz and Roman Klosowski. Polish with English subtitles.

VHS: S34952. $39.95.
Andrzej Munk, Poland, 1957, 90 mins.

Man/Woman Wanted

A small painting by a relatively unknown local painter disappears from a local museum, prompting a young art historian, afraid that he may be held responsible for it, to disguise himself as a woman and take work as a maid in order to recover the painting. The result is a light-hearted comedy. Wojceich Pokora stars. Polish with English subtitles.

VHS: S14231. $49.95.
Stanislaw Bareja, Poland, 69, mins.

Master and Margarita

A superb adaptation for Polish television of Mikhail Bulgakov's brilliant, troubled novel about Soviet bureaucracy, written during the post-revolutionary years. With Gustaw Holoubek, Zbigniew Zapasiewicz, Anna Dymna. 4 separate cassettes. Polish with English subtitles.

VHS: S12512. $89.95.
Maciej Wojtyszko, Poland, 1990, 373 mins.

Merry Christmas

A comedy set shortly before Christmas, as two men from the countryside go to Warsaw with a truck full of Christmas tress. Polish with NO subtitles.

VHS: S11345. $39.95.
Jerzy Sztwiernia, Poland, 60 mins.

Miss Ewa's Follies

A musical comedy for children based on a novel by Kornel Makuszynski. The story is set in 1932. Following the departure for China of her physican father, 14-year-old Ewa flees the house of her unfriendly guardians and embarks on a series of "follies"—kind-hearted and wise acts that bring happiness to those involved. Polish with NO subtitles.

VHS: S11296. $39.95.

Most Eligible Bachelor

A comedy about a highlander who is the most eligible bachelor in the village, always seeking a suitable wife. Edward Kusztal stars. Polish with NO subtitles.

VHS: S11344. $49.95.
Janusz Kidawa, Poland, 1982, 80 mins.

Mother Joan of the Angels

One of the landmarks of modern Polish cinema, this gripping adaptation of Aldous Huxley's *The Devils of Loudun* (like Ken Russell's *The Devils*), transposes the action to a 17th-century Polish convent, where a priest investigates demonic possession among nuns. But the exorcist finds himself involved in an unavoidable mutual attraction with the Mother Superior. Full of brilliant symbolism, Kawalerowicz weaves a powerful allegory of good vs. evil, chastity vs. eroticism. Polish with English subtitles.

VHS: S22598. $59.95.
Jerzy Kawalerowicz, Poland, 1960, 108 mins.

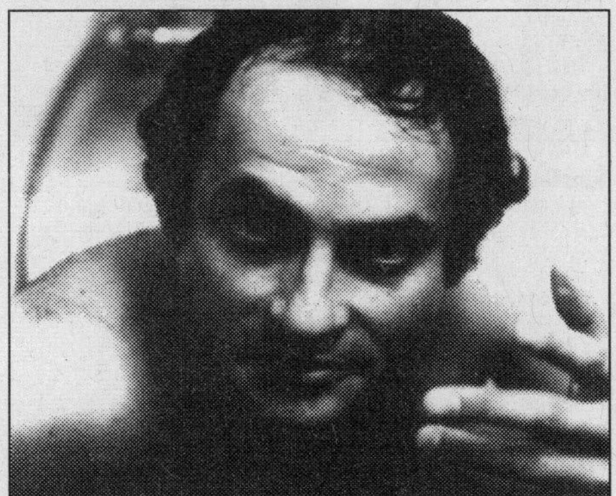

Mother's Heart

Drama unfolds in this early Polish film when two women compete for the same man's attentions. One is the wife, the other is the wife's best friend. When the man unexpectedly dies he leaves behind two grieving woman. There is another unforseen complication. The woman who is not his wife is pregnant. Polish with NO subtitles.

VHS: S26656. $24.95.
Michal Waszynski, Poland, 1938, 84 mins.

Night Train

A classic award-winning film from Jerzy Kawalerowicz (*Mother Joan of the Angels*): a powerful psychological thriller in which a young woman, suffering an inner crisis, buys a ticket from a stranger for a crowded holiday train and finds herself in a "Men Only" sleeper with an unhappy doctor. The police board the train in search of a killer. Winner at the Venice Film Festival. Polish with English subtitles.

VHS: S34143. $39.95.
Jerzy Kawalerowicz, Poland, 1959, 102 mins.

Nights and Days

A family saga based on a novel by Maria Dabrowska. Set in the second half of the 19th century after the failure of he January 1864 Uprising. The film presents a unique portrait of an oppressed society, exile, and the confiscation of property through the loves and struggles of the Niechcic family. With Jadwiga Baranska, Jerzy Binczycki. Polish with English subtitles.

VHS: S11313. $69.95.
Jerzy Antczak, Poland, 1976, 255 mins.

Oh Charles

A young and handsome engineer divides his free time between his wife and several girl friends, each of whom believes she is his one and only, in this comedy which stars Jan Piechocinski and Dorota Kaminska. Polish with NO subtitles.

VHS: S11342. $49.95.
Roman Zaluski, Poland, 1985, 99 mins.

On the Neman River

A 4-part, 2-cassette epic series based on a novel by Eliza Orseszkowa. A historical love story set in the Grodno area after the January 1863 uprising. With Iwona Pawlak, Antoni Marjanski. Polish with English subtitles.

VHS: S11337. $69.95.
Kazimierz Kuzminski, Poland, 1980, 280 mins.

Operation Arsenal

A reconstruction of one of the boldest operations performed by the underground Polish Home Army in occupied Warsaw during World War II. The elite "Gray Ranks" freed 25 prisoners who were being transported to the Pawiak prison. With Cezary Morawski, Jan Englert. Polish with NO subtitles.

VHS: S11351. $49.95.
Jan Lomnicki, Poland, 1977, 96 mins.

The Passenger

A great film by a genius of the Polish cinema of the '60s, Andrzej Munk, who remains too little known only because he died young. On a cruise ship following World War II, a former camp overseer recognizes someone who may or may not have been one of her prisoners in Auschwitz. This chance meeting triggers a series of flashbacks that ultimately speak to the complexities of domination and suffering, but also to the possibilities for resistance. English and Polish with English subtitles.

VHS: S31682. $24.95.
Andrzej Munk, Poland, 1963, 63 mins.

Peach of a Girl

A musical love story set during the 1930's, with lyrics by Julian Tuwim and Ralph Benatzky and music by Wojciech Gluch. Polish with NO subtitles.

VHS: S11370. $39.95.

The Peasants

Based on a nobel prize-winning novel by Wladyslaw Reymont. Set in a small central Polish village at the beginning of the 20th century, the plot revolves around a father and his son's violent love for the same woman—set against the rich detail of country traditions and folklore. 2 tapes, in two parts. Polish with English subtitles. 184 mins.

VHS: S11332. $69.95.

Personal Search

Basia, who is returning from a trip abroad with her young son Peter and beautiful cousin Christine, tries desperately to avoid a search at the Customs desk—yet we do not know what she wants to smuggle. Christine has similar intentions and even fools around with a handsome Customs Officer to get her way. Basia is doing her best to avoid a search, as is Christine, who continues her flirting with the young officer. Both ladies, having nearly succeeded in their subterfuge, forget about little Peter—who is hopelessly in love with Christina. Polish with English subtitles.

VHS: S14232. $49.95.
Witold Leszczynski, Poland, 1974, 71 mins.

Pharaoh

One of the most elaborate, detailed, historically accurate epics and a brilliant expose of the use of power. Young Prince Rameses incurs the wrath of the high priest when he takes a Jewish girl as his mistress, and when he succeeds his father as Rameses III, he battles the high priest for economic and military control of Egypt. With George Zelnik, Barbara Bryl and Krystyna Mikolajewska. Unfortunately this (only available) version has been cut by almost 60 minutes. Dubbed in English.

VHS: S04314. $59.95.
Jerzy Kawalerowicz, Poland, 1966, 125 mins.

Poisonous Plants

Robert Glinski directed this taut drama about a disillusioned journalist who searches for a scoop in a devastated, demoralized, contemporary Polish city. With Boguslaw Linda, Katarzyna Figura. Polish with English subtitles.

VHS: S12513. $39.95.
Robert Glinski, Poland, 1975, 70 mins.

Polanicki's Family

This is a film version of the popular Polish television series *Polanicki Family*. Stan Polanicki is an ambitious young man who meets a lovely young woman called Miss Mary. Her father owes Stan money, but when Stan tries to collect the debt, he discovers his relationship with Miss Mary may suffer. Polish with English subtitles.

VHS: S26979. $39.95.
Jan Rybkowski, Poland, 1983, 104 mins.

Polish Ways

This film displays a large-scale panorama of an anti-Nazi conspiracy in occupied Poland. It represents an innovative attempt to chart the destinies of Polish life in that troubled time. Immensely popular with audiences, this film helped catapult Kazimierz Kaczor to fame. It contains 11 episodes on 11 cassettes. Polish with NO subtitles.

VHS: S26739. $199.95.
Janusz Morgenstern, Poland, 1977, 1026 mins.

Prince Joseph's Soldier

During Napolean's campaign in Poland, a young soldier is accused of desertion. His fiance pleads with the Prince and manages to win him over to her cause. She appeals to Prince Joseph's heart because her cause is love. Polish with NO subtitles.

VHS: S26658. $24.95.
Konrad Tom, Poland, 1938, 85 mins.

Private Investigation

Rafal, with his wife and two children, are returning home from a weekend trip when a tragic car accident leaves his family dead. After a long hospital stay, where he has seen the police investigation come to an impasse, Rafal decides he will find the hit-and-run killer himself and exact his own revenge. With Roman Wilhelmi and Jan Peszek. Polish with English subtitles.

VHS: $15058. $49.95.
Wojciech Wojcik, Poland, 1986, 99 mins.

The Quack

A melodrama based on a novel by Tadeusz Dolega-Mostowicz, set in Poland of the 1930's. A famous surgeon loses his memory and begins wandering alone through Poland's Eastern frontier. Unbelievable happenings abound, including an intriguing amorous adventure. Polish with English subtitles.

VHS: $11312. $49.95.
Jerzy Hoffman, Poland, 1981, 132 mins.

Rosemary Twig

A musical about the Polish Legions. The story of young soldiers of the first skeleton company formed at Oleandry in 1914, performed by the Rozmaitosci Theatre Company in Warsaw in 1988. Polish with NO subtitles.

VHS: $11369. $39.95.

The Saragossa Manuscript

A cult classic, one of the most interesting films to emerge from Eastern Europe, based on the novel *The Manuscript Found in Saragossa*, by Jan Potocki, this romantic, fantastic and witty tale chronicles the adventures of a Walloon guard under the King of Spain. Something of a Don Juan, this colorful 19th-century character must pass numerous tests to prove his courage, honesty and honor in order to become a member of the powerful Mauretanian family. Polish with English subtitles.

VHS: $22596. $59.95.
Wojciech J. Has, Poland, 1965, 174 mins.

Sarah's House

The men whom beautiful Sarah chooses for her lovers are condemned to physical degradation and annihilation under the spell of her charms. But one day she meets her match in this stylish horror film. Polish with English subtitles.

VHS: S09214. $49.95.
Zygmunt Lech, Poland, 1984, 70 mins.

Sauna

A group of intellectuals and professionals from Poland accidentally meet in a sauna in Helsinki, Finland. As they compare stories they find they face an uncertain future since communism is crumbling at home. It was in that quickly vanishing communist world of Poland that their obscure jargon guaranteed them respect and a livelihood. With Boguslaw Linda, Gabriela Kownacka, Marian Opania, Henryk Bista and Piotr Opania I inni. Polish with NO subtitles.

VHS: $26650. $29.95.
Filip Bajon, Poland, 1992, 90 mins.

Second Youth

After 25 years of marriage, a woman leaves her husband to share her life with a much younger man. She travels for several years, loses all her money, and is left by her new beau. Finally, upon her return to Warsaw, she meets her old husband. Polish with NO subtitles.

VHS: $26653. $24.95.
Michal Waszynski, Poland, 1938, 85 mins.

Secret Detective

Set in Cracow during 1936; a precious necklace is ingeniously stolen from a famous jeweler. The police in vain try to catch a pair of cheats: a beautiful woman and a sleuth. Polish with NO subtitles.

VHS: $11362. $39.95.
Gregorz Lasota, Poland, 1977, 50 mins.

Sexmission

A sexy, controversial feature from one of Poland's top filmmakers, and one of the most successful Polish films of the '80s. The legendary box office smash from director Juliusz Machulski is about two men who, after being in voluntary hibernation, awake 50 years later to find the world destroyed by nuclear war and women ruling from the underground. Facing harsh treatment from their female guards, they will do anything to save themselves and to reestablish the male population. Polish with English subtitles.

VHS: $34144. $39.95.
Juliusz Machulski, Poland, 1984, 117 mins.

Siegfried

In 1934, Stefan, an art connoisseur, develops a subtle emotional relationship with homosexual overtones with Siegfried, a young circus acrobat, in this sensitive, daring film. With Gustaw Holoubek, Tomasz Hudziec, Jan Nowicki. Polish with English subtitles.

VHS: $11317. $49.95.
Andrzej Domalik, Poland, 1986, 91 mins.

The Silent Touch

Max Von Sydow and Sarah Miles star in this intriguing film made by Zanussi in Sweden that looks at the creative process of a famous retired composer. His spirit is re-invigorated by the arrival of a young protege, but ultimately he is trapped in an inescapable menage-a-trois. The film deftly merges music and philosophical issues with romance.

VHS: $22063. $92.95.
Krzysztof Zanussi, Sweden, 1994, 92 mins.

Soccer Poker

When the presidents of several soccer clubs get together to fix the final results of a soccer match, a rival club president, an incorruptible ump, a crafty wife and an old soccer pro add to the chaos, and it's anyone's guess how the match will turn out. Polish with English subtitles.

VHS: $34958. $39.95.
Janusz Zaorski, Poland, 1988

Special Mission

A contemporary Polish comedy set in Nazi-occupied Poland. Krzysztof Kowalewski and Dorota Kaminska star in this story about a special mission to intercept a mysterious chest with Himmler's gift to Hitler. Polish with English subtitles.

VHS: $11685. $38.00.
Janusz Rzeszewski, Poland, 1987, 110 mins.

Sportsman Against His Will

A Canadian hockey player is in love with the beautiful Lilly; and their dogs are in love too. A wacky hairstylist is caught in between trying to help all of them. Polish with NO subtitles.

VHS: $15575. $39.95.
Mieczyslaw Krawicz, Poland, 1939, 80 mins.

The Stranger

Winner of the Best Actress Award at the Gdansk Film Festival, and based on Maria Kuncewiszowa's novel. The film is a psychological study of a woman—a gifted violinist whose talent is wasted—spanning the first three decades of this century. An unhappy love, an unsuccessful marriage and lack of understanding with her daughter together present a moving portrait of unfulfilled dreams. With Ewa Wisniewska. Polish with NO subtitles.

VHS: $11338. $49.95.
Ryszard Ber, Poland, 1986, 115 mins.

The Structure of Crystals

Krzysztof Zanussi's debut feature tells the story of a metropolitan member of the scientific elite (Andrzej Zarnecki) who meets with a reclusive old friend (Jan Myslowicz) to convince him to return to the city to resume his work as an important scientist. "It was the first of a series of films [by Zanussi] that look at the scientific community [mainly uncharted territory in the cinema except for science fiction] to make general philosophic points" (*The Faber Companion to Foreign Films*). With Jan Myslowicz, Wladyslaw Jarema and Daniel Olbrychski. Polish with English subtitles.

VHS: $19395. $59.95.
Krzysztof Zanussi, Poland, 1969, 76 mins.

Suspended

Two of Poland's best actors, Krystyna Janda and Jerzy Radziwilowicz, star in this story of a former Polish Home Army officer who is sentenced to death on fabricated charges, escapes from prison, and spend six years in hiding in his fiancee's home during Stalinist times in Poland. Awarded the Best Debut Film Award at the Gdansk Film Festival. Polish with English subtitles.

VHS: $11307. $49.95.
Andrzej Lapicki, Poland, 1986, 92 mins.

Taboo

The talented young Polish director Andrzej Baranski directed this drama about a love triangle set in an austere village. A mother and her daughter are in love with the same man. Polish with English subtitles.

VHS: $11314. $49.95.
Andrzej Baranski, Poland, 1987, 108 mins.

Take It Easy

After the Second World War, two families settle on adjacent land. Their constant bickering provides a pretext for nonstop laughs. A full 18 years after the war, they still feel passionate about an absurd injustice. Polish with English subtitles.

VHS: $26731. $39.95.
Sylwester Checinski, Poland, 1973, 89 mins.

Teddy-Bear

A comedy from Poland, the story of a divorced couple who compete with each other for the money they share in a joint account in a London bank. With Stanislaw Tym, Bronislaw Pawlik. Polish with NO subtitles.

VHS: $11340. $49.95.
Stanislaw Bareja, Poland, 1980, 116 mins.

Thais

In this historical drama, an Alexandrian dancer captures the attention of an ascetic monk. He hopes to save her soul but the very sensuality of her being stands in the way. Anatole France's novel supplies the theme for this beautiful and erotic tale. With Dorota Kwiatkowska, Jerzy Kryszak and Bronislaw Pawlik. Polish with English subtitles.

VHS: $26651. $39.95.
Ryszard Ber, Poland, 1983, 97 mins.

Three Stooges

Musical comedy about three friends who win a big lottery. Polish with English subtitles.

VHS: $34166. $24.95.
Henryk Szaro, Poland, 1937, 84 mins.

The Tramps

Two comic buddies from Lvov take care of a beautiful orphan girl. They make their living singing popular songs that the whole town sings along with them. Watching this film is like taking a journey back to old Lvov. Polish with NO subtitles.

VHS: $15576. $39.95.
Michal Waszynski, Poland, 1939, 99 mins.

The Trial

A full-length documentary film about events which took place in 1949-1956 associated with the trial of General Stanislaw Tatar and others. Polish with NO subtitles.

VHS: $15061. $49.95.
Krzysztof Lang, Poland, 108 mins.

The Trip

A depiction of ethnic animosity toward two women of German ancestry in an old-age home in the Mazurian Lake district. Though they are Mazurians, the daughter Hilda feels Polish; her mother, Augusta, feels German. Hilda doesn't take her mother's talk of returning to their old home seriously until she wakes up one day and sees her mother packed and ready to leave. Best Actress Award for Teresa Budzisz-Krzyzanowska at the 1992 Polish Film Festival in Gdynia. Polish with English subtitles.

VHS: $34959. $39.95.
Magdalena Lazarkiewicz/Piotr Lazarkiewicz, Poland, 1991

A Trip down the River

The first movie in post-war Poland to achieve cult status, this absurd comedy features a group of picturesque characters: a cross-section of Polish society in the late '60s spending their holidays on a boat trip to nowhere. Polish with English subtitles.

VHS: $34247. $29.95.
Mark Piwoski, Poland, 1970, 65 mins.

The Twenties, The Thirties

A handsome, young engineer gets himself into trouble when he tries to cheat on his partners. His attempt to ruin them fails as the cabaret he bought in order to lose them money begins to flourish, and the beautiful actress Liza becomes a star. Starring Grazyna Szapolowski, and Tomasz Stockinger. Polish with NO subtitles.

VHS: $15059. $49.95.
Janusz Rzeszewski, Poland, 1986, 100 mins.

Ty Co w Ostrej Swiecisz Bramie

A young talented Ryszard is kidnapped by his competitors for information. Prayers offered by his fiance to Mother Mary Ostrobramska magically help him see his beloved and his mother once again. Polish with NO subtitles.

VHS: $26657. $24.95.
Jan Nowina Przybylski, Poland, 78 mins.

Upstairs

A classic Polish comedy of errors. Two unrelated men with the same name get involved in a string of bizarre and hilarious adventures. Polish with NO subtitles.

VHS: $15577. $39.95.
Leon Trystan, Poland, 1937, 90 mins.

W Hour

Set in Warsaw on August 1, 1944, when young soldiers from the Home Army units make their last minute preparations for the Warsaw Uprising. Polish with NO subtitles.

VHS: $11349. $39.95.
Janusz Morgenstern, Poland, 85 mins.

What Are You Going to Do to Me, If You Catch Me?

In this comedy the director of a large business tries to save his endangered position by marrying a VIP's daughter, but first he must divorce his current wife. Polish with NO subtitles.

VHS: S11341. $49.95.

Stanislaw Bareja, Poland, 1978, 107 mins.

Without Love

Ewa, a young and ambitious journalist, seeks to advance her career at any cost. Her methods provoke controversies and one of the stories leads to an unexpected tragedy in this film by Barbara Sass. Polish with English subtitles.

VHS: S11325. $49.95.

Barbara Sass, Poland, 1980, 104 mins.

Woman in the Hat

A young actress begins her career seeking her place in life and on stage. An interesting drama, presenting the contemporary Warsaw artistic community. With Hanna Mikuc, Henryk Machalica. Polish with NO subtitles.

VHS: S11357. $49.95.

Stanislaw Rozewicz, Poland, 1984, 116 mins.

YOUNG POLISH DIRECTORS TO WATCH

Baritone

Zbigniew Zapasiewicz stars as a well-known baritone, Taviani, who returns to Poland from abroad for his 50th birthday and promises a grand concert for people in his home town. But shortly before the performance is to begin, he loses his voice. Polish with English subtitles.

VHS: S11311. $49.95.

Janusz Zaorski, Poland, 1985, 100 mins.

Cupid's Bow

A powerful drama about a young married woman who rejects her middle-class conventions and struggles for independence. Set in Cracow after the First World War, the film is based on a novel by Juliusz Kaden Bandrowski, and created a scandal in Poland for its unabashed eroticism. Polish with English subtitles.

VHS: S11318. $49.95.

Jerzy Domaradzki, Poland, 1978, 119 mins.

A Daimler Benz Limousine

On May 5, 1939, in Poznan, two brothers from a Polish-German family steal the car of the Consul General representing the German Reich. This joy ride ends in prison. They are accused of attempted kidnapping and terrorism. One pleads guilty, the other pleads innocent. Now enemies, the two are released and their rivalry takes on a new and cruel dimension. Polish with English subtitles.

VHS: S22212. $59.95.

Filip Bajon, Poland, 1983, 99 mins.

Deja Vu

A period Polish thriller that moves between Chicago and Odessa in 1925. A Chicago mobster and professional hitman is commissioned by the Mafia to track down and kill a traitor who has fled to Odessa. The traitor, Niczypur, uses the newly opened Chicago-Constantinople-Odessa shipping line for an ambitious smuggling operation. The fates of both men will be decided in a violent burst of shoot-outs. With Jerzy Stuhr, Galina Pletrowa, Nikolai Karaczencow and Wladimir Golowin. English, Russian and Polish with English subtitles.

VHS: S19396. $59.95.

Juliusz Machulski, Poland, 1989, 108 mins.

Foul Play

Marek Piwowski directed this detective story, based on a true case from police files, about an armed robbery of a Warsaw department store. A young man is coerced into undercover work for the police, in return for their dropping charges against him. In an interesting twist, the lead roles in the film are played by Olympic Champion boxers Jan Szczepanski and Jerzy Kulej, as the two detectives. Polish with English subtitles.

VHS: S11322. $49.95.

Marek Piwowski, Poland, 1976, 98 mins.

Great Race

One of the most politically daring films to be made in Poland during the 1980's. The subject is a Peace Race, a mass event organized in the spring of 1952. Radek, who runs in the race, wants to win a first prize, and the second wants to win in order to hand a letter to President Bierut, asking for help for his father—a defendant in a political trial. With Tadeusz Bradecki, Krzysztof Pieczynski. Polish with NO subtitles.

VHS: S11347. $49.95.

Jerzy Domaradzki, Poland, 1982, 100 mins.

Hero of the Year

Feliks Falk's updating of the story of Danielak, the hero of his film *Top Dog*. Danielak, in a brilliant performance by Jerzy Stuhr, returns to show business after being sacked from his TV job in 1981, with a series of shows titled "Hero of the Year". A brilliant satire on ruthless corruption. Polish with English subtitles.

VHS: S11309. $49.95.

Feliks Falk, Poland, 1985, 115 mins.

Housemaster

An ailing aristocrat and his house master play a clever game of deception in postwar Poland in this showcase for leading Polish actor Tadeusz Lomnicki, who heads the cast. Although made for Polish television, this is a brilliantly directed piece by one of Poland's most interesting filmmakers, Wojciech Marczewski. Polish with English subtitles.

VHS: S12356. $39.95.

Wojciech Marczewski, Poland, 1979, 85 mins.

Interrogation

The 1990 Cannes Film Festival awarded its Best Actress Award to Krystyna Janda for her performance in this intense drama of a woman victimized by a Stalinist government. The film details the horrible abuse of a cabaret singer in 1950's Warsaw who is arrested after a one night stand with a military officer. Originally banned by the Polish government, *Interrogation* is one of the most powerful films to come out of Poland in the last several decades. Polish with English subtitles.

VHS: S14066. $79.95.

Ryszard Bugajski, Poland, 1982, 118 mins.

Kingsize

This allegory made during the communist era in Poland contrasts two imaginary worlds, one made up of dwarves and the other inhabited by people of normal stature. While the dwarves scheme to get ahead in the meager environment of Drawerland, the Kingsize people magically move from one dimension to the next, granting them many privileges, including the company of women. Polish with English subtitles.

VHS: S20841. $59.95.

Juliusz Machulski, Poland, 1988, 108 mins.

Kung-Fu

A film that remained banned for many years, this contemporary drama by Janusz Kijowski is set in the ambiguous moral climate of 1970's Poland. The story focuses on three university friends who begin their careers at the same time. Daniel Olbrychski, Piotr Fronczewski and Andrzej Seweryn star. Polish with English subtitles.

VHS: S11323. $49.95.

Janusz Kijowski, Poland, 1979, 110 mins.

Little Pendulum

From one of the most interesting filmmakers, a key television film which paints a fascinating, tragic and deeply ironic picture of a man's wasted life during the Stalinist period. Janusz Gajos delivers a stunning performance. Polish with NO subtitles.

VHS: S11346. $39.95.

Filip Bajon, Poland, 60 mins.

The Magnate

A fascinating film by Filip Bajon, the focus of which is on the downfall of the great aristocratic German family of von Teuss in the context of the social and political situation in Europe in the first half of the 20th century. In the authentic scenery of von Teuss's palace in Pszczyna, southern Poland, the film follows the extravagant life of the old prince and his sons in the refined, if risque, atmosphere of family scandals. 2 cassettes. Polish with NO subtitles.

VHS: S11334. $69.95.

Filip Bajon, Poland, 1987, 185 mins.

Masquerade

Janusz Kijowski, one of the boldest members of Poland's film generation of the 1970's, directed this recent film about a famous actor, who, fed up with his popularity, escapes from his conventional career by creating his own theatre, without an audience, where the boundary between the real and the imaginary is obscured. Polish with English subtitles.

VHS: S11316. $49.95.

Janusz Kijowski, Poland, 1986, 102 mins.

Mother of Kings

One of the most highly acclaimed Polish films of recent years, the film is the dramatic story about a poor widow charwoman and mother, shown across the span of the worst moments of Poland's history: the Second World War and the Stalinist times. Filmed in black-and-white to incorporate newsreel footage from Stalinist times, the film won the Grand Prix at the Gdansk Festival. Polish with English subtitles.

VHS: S11306. $49.95.

Janusz Zaorski, Poland, 1982, 126 mins.

Pigs

A harrowing film about the extraordinary social and personal transformation within the break up of Poland's communist society, the story focuses on the efforts of two friends, Olo and Franz, former secret police agents, and their attempt to remain friends and find their place and identity in the rebuilt state. With Boguslaw Linda, Marek Kondrat and Janusz Gajos. Polish with English subtitles.

VHS: S18244. $49.95.

Wladyslaw Pasikowski, Poland, 1992

The Scoundrel

Taken from actual events, this film concerns a circle of Polish fighters in Lodz, 1910. The film explores the shifting relationship between a terrorist and his bitter enemy. With Adam Ferency, Joanna Trzeplecinska and Boguslaw Linda. Polish with English subtitles.

VHS: S18085. $39.95.

Tomasz Wiszniewski, Poland, 1990, 88 mins.

The Story of Sin

The fourth live-action feature by Walerian Borowczyk, *The Story of Sin* is the first feature made in the filmmaker's native land of Poland, where he began his career as an animator in the fifties. The film is a chronicle of a young girl's progress from her strict Victorian upbringing to a love affair with a young man which soon blossoms into passion, jealousy and a final heroically grotesque self-sacrifice. A celebration of *amour fou*, starring Grazyna Dlugolecka and Jerzy Zelnik. Polish with English subtitles.

VHS: S14236. $49.95.

Walerian Borowczyk, Poland, 1975, 128 mins.

Top Dog

One of the key works of the new Polish cinema of the 1970's, a moral investigation of an ambitious individual who rushes into a tangled web of favor-trading, bribery and slander to eliminate his rivals. The film is set with razor-edged realism and specific detail against an unstylish provincial life which becomes grotesque. Polish with English subtitles.

VHS: S02657. $69.95.

Feliks Falk, Poland, 1978, 115 mins.

Train to Hollywood

A very funny, surreal comedy set in a small Polish town, where a beautiful girl dreams of Marilyn Monroe's career. Will the dining car, where she sells beer, take her straight to Hollywood? Polish with English subtitles.

VHS: S11315. $49.95.

Radoslaw Piwowarski, Poland, 1986, 96 mins.

A Woman and a Woman

Ryszard Bugajski created this touching film about friendship. It examines a ten-year period in the lives of Barbara and Irena, two very dear friends. Will their friendship survive the numerous professional and personal conflicts they encounter? Only time will tell. With Halina Labonarska and Anna Romantowska. Polish with English subtitles.

VHS: S15057. $49.95.

Ryszard Bugajski, Poland, 1980, 99 mins.

KRZYSZTOF KIESLOWSKI

Blind Chance

The film presents three different biographies of a man's life, using the "what if" formula. Depicted are the possible careers he could have chosen at the turning point in his life, including that of a physician, a political dissident and a party activist. A brave, probing film. Polish with English subtitles.

VHS: S11308. $49.95.

Krzysztof Kieslowski, Poland, 1982, 122 mins.

Blue

Juliette Binoche stars in this provocative thriller, a role for which she won the Cesar Award and the Venice Film Festival Award as best actress. She becomes entangled in a mysterious web of passion and lies after she digs into the past life of her recently and unexpectedly deceased husband. Part One of Kieslowski's acclaimed trilogy, *Three Colors*.

VHS: S21359. $19.95.
Laser: LD75022. $39.99.

Krzysztof Kieslowski, France, 1993, 98 mins.

Camera Buff (Amator)

In Communist Poland, a young father with a movie camera begins to pose a threat when his initial interest in filmmaking is superceded. He intended to photograph his newborn daughter, but suddenly, this newly formed shutterbug is filming everything in sight, including things the authorities would rather not have exposed. One of the key works of modern Polish cinema. Polish with English subtitles.

VHS: S21197. $79.95.

Krzysztof Kieslowski, Poland, 1979, 112 mins.

The Double Life of Veronique

Two remarkably similar women, in Warsaw and Paris, are acutely aware of each other's existence in this film about the linkage of souls. Veronika is a Polish music student with a beautiful voice and a heart condition. Veronique is a French school teacher paralyzed by doubt. Both roles are played by the beautiful Irene Jacob. Slawomir Idziak's cinematography and Zbigniew Preisner's score are alternately haunting and unforgettable. Polish and French with English subtitles.

VHS: S16928. $89.95.
Laser: LD75182. $34.98.

Krzysztof Kieslowski, Poland/France, 1991, 92 mins.

No End (Without End)

The film's hero, a young libertarian lawyer, dies four days before the film begins, leaving the case of a worker arrested for organizing a strike unresolved. His widow gets involved in the trial while trying to overcome her husband's death but there seems to be no end to his pervasive influence. Krzysztof Kieslowski's powerful portrait of life under martial law in Poland is a film "burning with a passionate engagement with the system" (*Time Out*). With Maria Pakulnis, Aleksander Bardini and Artur Barcis. Polish with English subtitles.

VHS: S20305. $29.95.

Krzysztof Kieslowski, Poland, 1984, 108 mins.

Red

Kieslowski's striking conclusion of his Three Colors trilogy stars Irene Jacob as a model, separated from her lover, who is brought by accident into the life of the aging Jean-Louis Trintignant, retired judge and electronic peeping Tom. As Irene slowly uncovers her lover's secret life, she discovers that her own past is inevitably linked to her destiny. With Jean-Pierre Lorit and Frederique Feder.

VHS: S25606. $19.95.

Laser: Letterboxed. **LD75015. $39.99.**

Krzysztof Kieslowski, Switzerland, 1994, 99 mins.

Subsidiaries (Personel)

At first glance, the conflicts at the theater seem to be related to the generation gap. Later, discussions between the artists and the technical staff reveal vital differences resulting from irreconcilable moral understandings and socio-political views. Polish with English subtitles.

VHS: S26727. $59.95.

Krzysztof Kieslowski, Poland, 1975, 57 mins.

White

The second part of Kieslowski's Blue-White-Red trilogy, based on the concepts of the French tri-colour flag. A Polish man's life disintegrates when his new French bride deserts him after only six months. Forced to begin anew, he returns to Poland and plans a clever scheme of revenge against her. Julie Delpy is great as the young wife. French and Polish with English subtitles.

VHS: S23108. $19.95.

Laser: Letterboxed. **LD74805. $49.95.**

Krzysztof Kieslowski, France/Poland, 1993, 92 mins.

AGNIESZKA HOLLAND

Angry Harvest

Agnieszka Holland's Academy-Award nominated film is a powerful emotional drama set during the German occupation of Poland. The raid on the ghetto, in which a Christian farmer saves a young Jewish woman on the run, and their resulting relationship becomes one of inter-dependent love and ultimate terror that ends in tragedy. A tour-de-force of acting and directing, the film stars Armin Mueller-Stahl, Elisabeth Trissenaar and Wojciech Pszoniak. German with English subtitles.

VHS: S06013. $69.95.

Agnieszka Holland, Germany, 1986, 102 mins.

Europa Europa

The film which took America by storm: Agnieszka Holland's powerful, moving story of a courageous German-Jewish teenager who survived World War II by concealing his identity and living as a Nazi during seven harrowing years through three countries. Based on a true story; a film which changes almost everyone who sees it. "A pure, absurd miracle of history" (*New Yorker Magazine*). Polish, German with English subtitles.

VHS: S16327. $19.98.

Agnieszka Holland, Poland/France, 1991, 100 mins.

Fever

A gripping political thriller, set in 1905. A group of anarchists plots to assassinate the Russian Tsar's governor in Russian-partitioned Poland. A sensitive script subtly probes the psychological motivations of the anarchists as the bomb is passed among them. Banned for many years by Poland's Communist authorities despite its winning the Grand Prize at the Gdansk Film Festival. With Jan Kanty Pawluskiewidz and Barbara Grabowska. Polish with English subtitles.

VHS: S11310. $49.95.

Agnieszka Holland, Poland, 1981, 115 mins.

A Lonely Woman

Agnieszka Holland's last film made in Poland prior to her exile in France—a powerful portrait of a woman raising her child in a small town. Deprived of help and friendship, she is left to her own resources. Will an encounter with a lonely man change her life? Very powerful drama. Polish with English subtitles.

VHS: S11348. $49.95.

Agnieszka Holland, Poland, 1987, 94 mins.

Olivier Olivier

This very unusual story begins when the nine-year-old son of a provincial French family suddenly disappears. Six years later a young man turns up who claims to be the missing youngster, setting off a series of strange reactions from the people he claims as his family. Based, unimaginably, on a true story. With Brigitte Rouan, Jean-Francois Stevenin and Francois Cluzet. French with English subtitles.

VHS: S20708. $19.95.

Laser: LD72381. $34.95.

Agnieszka Holland, France, 1992, 110 mins.

Provincial Actors

This bold first feature is set in the microcosm of a group of actors working in the provinces. While the actors are staging an important Polish play, *Liberation*, ambition, jealousy and betrayal dominate their inter-personal relations. The leading actor longs for stardom but his dreams have placed his marriage into an impossible situation. Polish with English subtitles.

VHS: S25906. $79.95.

Agnieszka Holland, Poland, 1979, 104 mins.

The Secret Garden

Agnieszka Holland's haunting adaptation of Frances Hodgson Burnett's 1909 classic about an orphaned young girl (Kate Maberly) dispatched to her uncle's remote English estate. With the help of her painfully withdrawn cousin (Heydon Prowse) and a local boy (Andrew Knott), she discovers an enchanting garden. Holland beautifully captures the painful social isolation of childhood. Maggie Smith plays the tyrannical housekeeper.

VHS: S20217. $19.98.

Laser: LD72328. $34.98.

DVD: DV60195. $24.98.

Agnieszka Holland, USA, 1993, 102 mins.

To Kill a Priest

Polish filmmaker-in-exile Agnieszka Holland tells the powerfully realistic story of an activist priest who endured the wrath of the secret police for his secular duties. French heartthrob Christopher Lambert is the political cleric in this story based on the true case of Father Jerzy Popieluszko; Ed Harris is the Communist cop out to get him. In English.

VHS: S11786. $89.95.

Agnieszka Holland, USA/France, 1988, 117 mins.

Total Eclipse

Leonardo Di Caprio and David Thewlis star in this film based on the affair between Arthur Rimbaud and Paul Verlaine. Rimbaud left a legacy of brilliant poetry and an example of extreme living that inspired contemporary stars like Jim Morrison. Verlaine, a highly regarded writer in his own right, was an older married man when he became infatuated with Rimbaud. This is a grand film about their passion for love and art, a passion finally doomed by madness. Christopher Hampton wrote the screenplay.

VHS: S27617. $19.98.

Laser: LD75553. $44.95.

Agnieszka Holland, Great Britain/France, 1995, 111 mins.

Washington Square

The meticulous adaptation of Henry James' novel from director Agnieszka Holland. Catherine Sloper (Jennifer Jason Leigh) wants to marry Morris Townsend (Ben Chaplin), but her plans are strongly opposed by her father (Albert Finney), who believes Townsend is only interested in his daughter for her money. But Catherine is determined to follow her heart, even if she loses her inheritance in the process. With Maggie Smith and Judith Ivey.

VHS: S33947. $103.99.

Laser: LD76829. $39.99.

Agnieszka Holland, USA, 1997, 115 mins.

ANDRZEJ WAJDA

Andrzej Wajda Trilogy

Contains *A Generation, Kanal* and *Ashes and Diamonds*.

VHS: S20506. $59.95.

Andrzej Wajda, A Portrait

The famed Polish filmmaker speaks candidly about his life and his relationship to his art. This son of a slain Polish cavalry officer fought in the Resistance before he studied painting in Cracow and filmmaking in Lodz. His films include *Ashes and Diamonds, Kanal, Man of Marble* and *Danton*. The film has been called an "unforgettable and deeply moving experience." Narrated in English.

VHS: S16821. $29.95.

Ewa Lachnit, Poland, 1989, 76 mins.

Ashes and Diamonds

A brilliant statement from Andrzej Wajda, *Ashes and Diamonds* illustrates the conflict of idealism and instinct in this story of a young resistance fighter who assassinates the wrong man at the close of World War II. With Zbigniew Cybulski. Polish with English subtitles.

VHS: S00071. $24.95.

Laser: LD76782. $49.95.

Andrzej Wajda, Poland, 1958, 105 mins.

Birch Wood

One of the most beautiful, reflective films of Andrzej Wajda's great career, *Birch Wood* is the story of two brothers—one seriously ill but full of life, the other a grieving widower, envious of his brother's high spirits in the face of death. Daniel Olbrychski and Olgierd Lukaszewicz star. Polish with English subtitles.

VHS: S11328. $49.95.

Andrzej Wajda, Poland, 1971, 100 mins.

The Conductor

John Gielgud stars as a renowned expatriate Polish conductor who returns home to lead a small, provincial orchestra after a 50-year absence. Though ill and dying Gielgud manages to bring new life to the orchestra, in this sensitive portrayal of a man bent on a final artistic triumph. With Andrej Sewern, winner of the Berlin Film Festival Best Actor Award. English and Polish with English subtitles.

VHS: S20592. $79.95.

Andrzej Wajda, Poland, 1980, 101 mins.

Fury Is a Woman (The Siberian Lady Macbeth)

Andrzej Wajda shot this extraordinary film in Yugoslavia, during a period of self-imposed political exile. *Fury Is a Woman* ranks with Akira Kurosawa's *Throne of Blood* as one of the most successful screen translations of Shakespeare ever made. With Olivera Markovic and Ljuba Tadic. Letterboxed format. Serbian with English subtitles.

VHS: S15510. $59.95.

Andrzej Wajda, Yugoslavia, 1961, 93 mins.

A Generation

Wajda's first feature takes place in 1942 occupied Warsaw, and follows the pursuits of a young man whose life is hardened under the Nazis. When he falls in love with the leader of the Resistance group, he learns to fight back. Stars Tadeusz Lomnicki, Ursula Modrzynska, Zbigniew Cybulski and a very young Roman Polanski. Polish with English subtitles.

VHS: S16189. $24.95.

Andrzej Wajda, Poland, 1954, 90 mins.

Hunting Flies

One of the key films of the Polish film renaissance, this satiric comedy explores the seeming world of emancipated women and emasculated men of Communist Poland. A librarian shares his life and tiny home with his domineering wife. In search of a larger perspective, he has an affair with a beautiful intellectual, who wears fly-shaped glasses. She tries to become the woman behind the great artist. It's a film dedicated to the women of Poland, even as it critiques the relations between the sexes. Polish with English subtitles.

VHS: S23299. $59.95.

Andrzej Wajda, Poland, 1969, 108 mins.

Innocent Sorcerers

This rarely seen film by Andrzej Wajda is reflective of the best of 1960's Polish cinema. The film created a stir with its ironic comic perspective as it focused on young Poles in the 1960's. A bachelor doctor, who is also a jazz musician, can't quite commit himself to his superficial girlfriend. He and his aimless friends find any kind of human contact or emotional commitment a troubling and ultimately uninviting prospect. Polish with English subtitles.

VHS: S22597. $59.95.

Andrzej Wajda, Poland, 1960, 86 mins.

Kanal

Part of the famous Andrzej Wajda trilogy that included *A Generation* and *Ashes and Diamonds*. The almost hallucinatory portrait of a group of Polish citizens and patriots who attempt to flee the Nazis through the sewer system of a war-devastated Warsaw. A film of amazing power and rare courage. Polish with English subtitles.

VHS: S02775. $24.95.

Andrzej Wajda, Poland, 1957, 96 mins.

Korczak

Andrzej Wajda's film chronicles the extraordinary efforts of Dr. Janusz Korczak (Wojciech Pszoniak), a pediatrician and author, to protect a group of abandoned children in the Warsaw Ghetto. On Aug. 6, 1942, he refused an offer from the Nazis to spare his life and accompanied 200 orphans of the Warsaw Ghetto to Treblinka. Agnieszka Holland wrote the screenplay; Robby Muller was the cinematographer. Polish with English subtitles.

VHS: S18932. $79.95.

Andrzej Wajda, Poland/France, 1990, 113 mins.

Land of Promise

Based on the novel by Nobel Prize-winner Wladyslav Reymont, Andrzej Wajda's epic film examines the relationships among three industrialists who own a textile factory in Lodz at the turn of the century. The film is an epic about complex class structures; each man represents a different ethnic group: a Pole (Daniel Olbrychski), a German (Andrzej Seweryn) and a Jew (Wojciech Pszoniak). The drama builds to a climax when the overworked, underpaid workers threaten to revolt. With Anna Nehrebecka. Polish with English subtitles.

VHS: S19397. $79.95.

Andrzej Wajda, Poland, 1974, 178 mins.

Layer Cake

Based on Stanislav Lem's novel, this unusual comic film charts the unlucky life of the fictional race car driver Ryszard Fox. After so many accidents and so many internal organ transplants, he is forced to contemplate exactly how much of his body is really his. Polish with English subtitles.

VHS: S26737. $49.95.

Andrzej Wajda, Poland, 1968, 35 mins.

Lotna

Andrzej Wajda, the son of a Polish cavalry officer killed in the Second World War by Germans, made this film as a tribute to the heroic horsemen who faced off against German tanks. It follows the trajectory of an off-white horse which passes among various military officials until it breaks a leg and is shot. Polish with English subtitles.

VHS: S26728. $59.95.

Andrzej Wajda, Poland, 1959, 89 mins.

Maids of Wilko

Andrzej Wajda's adaptation of Jaroslav Iwaszkiewicz's memoirs is set in the late 1920s. Viktor Ruben (Daniel Olbrychski), a World War I veteran and operator of a small factory, reexamines his life following the death of his friend. Returning to the home of his aunt and uncle, he is drawn into a mysterious web of sexual and romantic longing for the five women he was friends with years before. "Wajda...has made an exquisite period piece which lays bare the futility of attempting to resurrect the past" (*The Faber Companion to Foreign Films*). With Anna Seniuk, Maja Komarowska, Krystyna Zachwatowicz and Christine Pascal. French and Polish with English subtitles.

VHS: S18691. $49.95.

Andrzej Wajda, Poland/France, 1979, 118 mins.

Man of Iron

Made in the center of political events surrounding it, Andrzej Wajda's *Man of Iron* is a powerful sequel to *Man of Marble*. The film merges documentary footage of the Solidarity strike into a fictionalized drama of a disillusioned radio producer (Marian Opania) who is ordered to Gdansk to undermine the reputation of one of the leaders of the worker revolt. "An urgent, nervy narrative conveys all the exhilaration and bewilderment of finding oneself on the very crestline of crucial historical change" (*Time Out*). With Jerzy Radziwilowicz, Krystyna Janda, Irena Byrska and Wieslawa Kosmalska. Winner of the Palme d'Or, 1981 Cannes Film festival. Polish with English subtitles.

VHS: S20403. $19.98.
Laser: LD76328. $49.95.

Andrzej Wajda, Poland, 1981, 152 mins.

Man of Marble

Thirteen years in the making, Wajda's film caused packed houses to rise and sing the Polish national anthem when it finally premiered in Poland in 1977. Denied entrance at Cannes by Polish authorities, it played nonetheless at a commercial theatre there and won the International Critics' Prize. Hailed as "a milestone in Polish cinema" by *Variety*, *Man of Marble* is the story of a young filmmaker trying to reconstruct a truthful picture of the Stalinist past, a past obscured by 20 years of shifting propaganda. Polish with English subtitles.

VHS: S12828. $29.95.

Andrzej Wajda, Poland, 1977, 160 mins.

Samson

Andrzej Wajda's profound psychological study of a man who accidentally kills a schoolmate in a brawl and is imprisoned. He is released with the onset of World War II, only to be locked up once more, but in the Warsaw Ghetto. Again he escapes and finds himself trapped, this time in a world of non-Jews where the threat of capture is ever-present. This powerful film makes extraordinary use of naturalistic symbols and a widescreen format. Polish with English subtitles.

VHS: S23300. $59.95.

Andrzej Wajda, Poland, 1961, 119 mins.

The Wedding

A moving drama of Polish destiny, *The Wedding* is based on a popular nationalistic play (one of the best known literary works in Poland) by Stanislaw Wyspianski about the wedding of a peasant's daughter to a poet. This exceptional work is one of Wajda's most important films; for him it was a synthesis of sorts—a chance to put in one unique metaphor all the ideas and emotions, judgement and love, hate and pride he felt about the country to which he belonged. A landmark in the Polish cinema. Polish with English subtitles.

VHS: S15560. $49.95.

Andrzej Wajda, Poland, 1973, 103 mins.

Without Anesthesia

This contemporary parable offers an unmatched look at the face of Poland before the fall of Communism. A famous Polish foreign correspondent returns home from a successful assignment abroad only to find his marriage and career falling apart. Written by Agnieszka Holland. Polish with English subtitles.

VHS: S22445. $29.95.

Andrzej Wajda, Poland, 1979, 116 mins.

JERZY SKOLIMOWSKI

Hands Up

A legendary film, banned for over a decade in Poland. Jerzy Skolimowski (*Moonlighting*) directed this probing investigation of a group of young physicians who recall their university days during the Stalinist period while meeting at a class reunion. Originally completed in 1967, the film was not released until 1981 and until the director cut it and added a new color sequence. Polish with English subtitles.

VHS: S11326. $49.95.

Jerzy Skolimowski, Poland, 1967-81, 78 mins.

The Lightship

Jerzy Skolimowski's moody film stars Klaus Maria Brandauer and Robert Duvall in the storm-tossed, suffocating world of a lightship in the age-old struggle between good and evil. The ship's captain must somehow protect his men and his rebellious son against an invading gang led by Duvall, who is both cunning and without scruples.

VHS: S03523. $79.95.

Jerzy Skolimowski, USA, 1986, 87 mins.

The Shout

A spellbinding, occult-tinged tape of mind control and superstitions come true, with a top-notch cast, including Alan Bates, Susannah York, John Hurt and Tim Curry. A surrealistic atmosphere pervades this spine-tingler as a mysterious "shout" kills people in the English countryside. Offbeat, psychological thriller that won the Cannes Film Festival.

VHS: S01197. $29.98.

Jerzy Skolimowski, Great Britain, 1978, 90 mins.

Torrents of Spring

A spectacular cast, including Nastassia Kinski, Timothy Hutton and Valeria Golino, star in this visually beautiful, seductive tale based on a story by Turgenev. Kinski is the wife of a Russian landowner who falls in love with and has a passionate affair with Timothy Hutton. In English.

VHS: S12589. $19.98.

Jerzy Skolimowski, France/Italy, 1989, 100 mins.

ROMAN POLANSKI

Bitter Moon

Roman Polanski's story of two different couples whose wild dreams, fantasies and realities collide on a cruise to Istanbul in a tense game of sexual one-upmanship and menage-a-trois features Hugh Grant, Emmanuelle Seigner, Peter Coyote and Kristin Scott Thomas in a film that's been described as "*Love Boat* meets *Last Tango in Paris*."

VHS: S21925. $19.95.
Laser: LD76964. $34.99.

Roman Polanski, France/Britain, 1992, 139 mins.

Chinatown

Jack Nicholson and Faye Dunaway star in Polanski's finely crafted, atmospheric film. What begins as a routine matrimonial snoop job for an average gumshoe mushrooms into a murderous regional and personal scandal told with incredible style, surprises and a gripping narrative line. Outstanding performances by all including John Huston as Dunaway's father and a cameo by Polanski as a great little sleaze.

VHS: S01840. $19.95.
Laser: Widescreen. **LD75371. $49.98.**

Roman Polanski, USA, 1974, 131 mins.

Death and the Maiden

Sigourney Weaver, Ben Kingsley and Stuart Wilson are featured in this adaptation of Ariel Dorfman's acclaimed play. A woman finally has the opportunity to see justice done for the wrong she suffered. She will go to any extreme—after all, her life was destroyed. It's a knockout psychological thriller.

VHS: S25102. $19.98.
Laser: Widescreen. **LD74959. $39.99.**

Roman Polanski, France, 1995, 103 mins.

Diary of Forbidden Dreams

A beautiful girl, lost in a remote area of the Italian Riviera, is constantly besieged and trapped into bizarre incidents as she tries to find her way out. Mastroianni is the nobleman of the villa where she takes refuge until she turns into a tiger and attacks. The beautiful Sydne Rome, Roman Polanski and Mastroianni star in this bizarre fantasy, an Alice in Wonderland of the idle European rich. English dialog.

VHS: S00340. $29.95.

Roman Polanski, Italy/Great Britain, 1981, 94 mins.

Fat and the Lean

A brilliant short film by Roman Polanski, made early in his career; a tour-de-force of abstract, existential allegory.

VHS: S09049. $19.95.

Roman Polanski, France, 1964, 20 mins.

Fearless Vampire Killers

Or *Pardon Me, Your Teeth Are in My Neck*. Roman Polanski directs (and appears in) this cult oddity, a vampire-film spoof that manages both horror and humor. The story involves a professor and his bumbling assistant, who set out to track down a coven of Transylvanian vampires. Cast includes Jack MacGowran, Sharon Tate, Alfie Bass and Terry Downes. This is the restored, original cut.

VHS: S12741. $19.98.
Laser: LD72173. $39.98.

Roman Polanski, USA, 1967, 124 mins.

Frantic

Roman Polanski directs this thriller set in Paris, which finds Harrison Ford more than reasonably concerned when his wife Betty Buckley disappears. A Hitchcock-like plot involves switched luggage and a fetching young courier played by Emmanuelle Seigner. Great scenery and rooftop suspense.

VHS: S07470. $19.98.
Laser: LD70576. $39.98.

Roman Polanski, USA, 1987, 120 mins.

Knife in the Water

Polanski's debut feature film is an incisive study of three people spending a casual weekend on their yacht. A young man, who joined the couple as a hitchhiker, gradually interferes uncomfortably into the couple's lives, and in a brilliant depiction of inter-personal tensions, tests their marriage. Polish with English subtitles.

VHS: S19406. $29.95.
Laser: LD70755. $59.95.

Roman Polanski, Poland, 1960, 90 mins.

Macbeth

Roman Polanski's acclaimed version of Shakespeare's *Macbeth* stars Jon Finch as Macbeth in a beautifully nightmarish vision of the great play. English dialog.

VHS: S00789. $59.95.

Roman Polanski, Great Britain, 1976, 139 mins.

Mammals

A brilliant and rarely seen short film by Roman Polanski, at the height of his mastery. This fourth and final of Polanski's short films won the festivals at Oberhausen and Melbourne.

VHS: S08125. $19.95.

Roman Polanski, Poland, 1963, 10 mins.

Pirates

Comic-adventure film about buccaneers who take on a Spanish galleon filled with Aztec gold. Polanski is said to have spent $30 million on the film, of which $10 million was spent on the replica of the ship *Neptune*. Starring Walter Matthau and Charlotte Lewis.

VHS: S01610. $19.95.

Roman Polanski, France/Tunisia, 1986, 117 mins.

Repulsion

Polanski's first English-language film, a chilling study of madness, stars Catherine Deneuve as a jealously sadistic schizophrenic, terrified of sex. Full of memorable sequences, such as Deneuve's delusions of rape as she sees plaster turn into a clawing hand and walls cracking or overhears the moans of her sister making love. With Yvonne Furneaux and John Fraser. French with English subtitles.

VHS: S01106. $19.95.
Laser: Widescreen. **LD75387. $99.95.**
Roman Polanski, Great Britain, 1965, 105 mins.

Rosemary's Baby

Ira Levin thriller brought to the screen by Roman Polanski, concerning a young wife whose husband becomes involved with a witches' coven. With Mia Farrow and John Cassavetes.

VHS: S02685. $19.95.
Laser: Letterboxed. **LD76433. $39.98.**
Roman Polanski, USA, 1968, 136 mins.

The Tenant

Polanski's most autobiographical film is, like *Repulsion*, a journey through the distorted realm of the human mind. Polanski himself plays Trelkovsky, a nebbish file clerk who moves into the apartment of a young suicide, becomes deeply paranoid, certain that the other tenants are trying to drive *him* to suicide. With Isabelle Adjani, Shelley Winters, Lila Kedrova, Melvyn Douglas. English dialog.

VHS: S01308. $49.95.
Roman Polanski, Great Britain, 1976, 126 mins.

Tess

Winner of three Academy Awards, Polanski's interpretation of Thomas Hardy's novel is a beautiful and timeless masterwork destined to be a classic. Nastassia Kinski stars as Tess against the backdrop of a morally rigid Victorian England. The stunning cinematography is unforgettable. English dialog.

VHS: S01311. $29.95.
Roman Polanski, France/Great Britain, 1980, 170 mins.

Two Men and a Wardrobe

Polanski's award winning short is a bitter parable blending slapstick and the absurd, about two men who emerge from the sea carrying a wardrobe. Made while Polanski was a student at the Polish Film School. Also, *The Fat and the Lean*, another Polanski short, this one an attack on government tyranny. Silent.

VHS: S01936. $49.95.
Roman Polanski, Poland, 1958, 35 mins.

What!

After the macabre twists and psychological terror of his English and Hollywood films, Roman Polanski made this sex farce about a beautiful young woman whose temporary stay at an eccentric millionaire's mansion unleashes a series of strange events. A commercial failure on its initial release, the film was cut to 94 minutes and retitled *Diary of Forbidden Dreams*. This letterboxed version restores the excised material. With Marcello Mastroianni, Hugh Griffith, Sydne Rome, Romoli Valli and Polanski. In English.

VHS: S19876. $29.95.
Roman Polanski, Italy, 1973, 113 mins.

POLAND: PAST AND PRESENT

1000 Years of Polish Cavalry

The history of mounted combat in Poland is addressed in this colorful documentary that begins with the battle of Cedynia in 972 A.D. and concludes with the heroic defense against the blitzkrieg of Nazi tanks and planes in 1939. Polish with NO subtitles.

VHS: S16820. $29.95.
E.Z. Szanialawski, Poland, 51 mins.

About Painting

A special look at the John Paul II painting collection founded by Janina and Karol Porczynski. Also included are three short films about the state of art in Poland. Polish with NO subtitles.

VHS: S16829. $24.95.

As Crosses Are Measure of Freedom

A sensational, deeply moving historical record made in collaboration with and under supervision of the General's closest aide-de-camp: the story of the legendary Polish leader General Anders and the soldiers of the 2nd Corps. English language narration.

VHS: S15578. $39.95.
Krzysztof Szmagier, Poland, 1989, 80 mins.

At the Bottom of the Hell (Dno piekta)

This documentary describes what happened to captured Polish military officers who were tried in Stalinist courts after World War II. It documents the dire conditions in which they were held and the severity of their sentencing. Polish with NO subtitles.

VHS: S16823. $49.95.
Maciej Sienski, Poland, 64 mins.

Best of Kunicka

A recital by the popular Polish singer Halina Kunicka. 98 mins. Polish with NO subtitles.

VHS: S11380. $29.95.

Cracow and Its University

An English language tour of this historically rich Polish city and its more than 600 year old center of learning. You visit the Wawel Castle, the old walls of the city and the famous Cloth House.

VHS: S16828. $24.95.
Fundacia U. Jagiellonskiego, Poland, 1991, 27 mins.

Czeslaw Milosz

Czeslaw Milosz won the Nobel Prize for Literature in 1980. He read from *Selected Poems, The Separate Notebooks* and *Unattainable Earth* in Los Angeles on September 12, 1988. Lewis MacAdams interviewed this poet, novelist, critic and philosopher born in Lithuania. From the *Lannan Literary Videos* series. 60 mins.

VHS: S27113. $19.95.

Far from Poland

A brilliant film: denied a visa to shoot a film in Poland, director Godmilow constructs a film over the bare bones of documentary footage while in New York, resulting in a deft dismemberment of the myth of "documentary truth." The film portrays the birth of the Solidarity movement at the Gdansk shipyards through moving personal testimony and a chilling look at the psychology of a censor.

VHS: S02656. $69.95.
Jill Godmilow, USA, 1984, 106 mins.

Fears

A Polish television special in a 4-part, 2-cassette series about Warsaw cabaret artists in the 1930's. A young actress soon realizes that the price she has to pay for her career is very high. 280 mins. Polish with NO subtitles.

VHS: S11352. $69.95.

Fronczewski—Pietrzak—Smolen Cabaret

A program of songs and sketches originally written for Jan Pietrzak's Warsaw cabaret *Pod Ediga*. A delightful and sharp political satire of life in Poland from the 1950's through the early 80's. Polish with NO subtitles. 120 mins.

VHS: S11375. $29.95.

In the Silence of the Night

27 of the most beautiful Polish Christmas carols, performed by four choirs and soloists, interestingly enough by choirs from Catholic, Evangelist and Orthodox churches. 90 mins. Polish with NO subtitles.

VHS: S11384. $29.95.

Jacek Fedorowicz Cabaret Evening

The leading Polish cabaret satirist, Jacek Fedorowicz, in a cabaret performance satirizing the new political order in Poland. 47 mins.

VHS: S12360. $29.95.

Jan Pietrzak—Mr. Censor

Jan Pietrzak's latest cabaret program, marking his 25 years on the stage, including his now-famous *Zeby Polska byla Polska*. 120 mins. Polish with NO subtitles.

VHS: S11374. $49.95.

Jozef Pilsudzki/Road to Independence

Two historical documentaries from 1937 and 1935 about Poland's fierce road to independence and the funeral of Marshal Pilsudski. Polish with NO subtitles. 112 mins.

VHS: S15563. $39.95.

Kaleidoscope: Polish Folk Dance and Songs

Features songs performed by original folk groups, Polish dances and and colorful costumes from different regions. 68 mins.

VHS: S33754. $29.95.

Land of the White Eagle—Part 1

A series of 10-minute films highlighting Poland's history and traditions, her cultural heritage, architecture and landscape. Part 1 of the series visits Gniezno, Zelazowa Wola, Poznan, Pszczyna, the Pieniny and Beskidy mountains and the Eagle Nest trail between Cracow and Czestochowa. Narration in English. 95 mins.

VHS: S11364. $39.95.

Land of the White Eagle—Part 2

Part 2 of the series visits Warsaw, Cracow, Wieliczke salt mine, Marlbork, Torun, Wroclaw, Lodz, and Szczecin. 90 mins. Narration in English.

VHS: S11365. $39.95.

Land of the White Eagle—Part 3

The last in a series of films about Poland, with visits to Czestochowa, Zamosc, Kalwaria Zebrzydowska, Gdansk and Gdynia. 90 mins. In English.

VHS: S11366. $39.95.

Leszek Dlugosz—It Can Be You

A recital of Leszek Dlugosz, the Cracow-based composer and bard. 97 mins. Polish with NO subtitles.

VHS: S11379. $29.95.

Let's Cotton Together

A show of popular songs from Lvov performed by the Kalambur Theatre of Wroclaw. Polish with NO subtitles. 70 mins.

VHS: S11372. $39.95.

Miners '88

A history-making documentary, this is a detailed look at the workers' strike at the Manifest Lipcowy mine in Poland in August 1988, the final strike that lead to the breakdown of the old politics in Poland. Polish with NO subtitles.

VHS: S16827. $24.95.
Andrzej Piekutowski, Poland, 1988

Nothing to Lose

Beginning in 1988, a young filmmaker traveled throughout Poland documenting the growing unrest and organization that led to the end of Communism in Eastern Europe. It is an amazing inside look at the efforts of ordinary people who changed the course of history. 56 mins.

VHS: S21593. $95.00.
Charles Steiner, USA, 1990, 56 mins.

Order of the White Eagle

A story about the oldest Polish distinction, founded by King August II in 1705, a symbol of Polish tradition and its history. English narration. 45 mins.

VHS: S33756. $24.95.

Ordonka

This is the story of the most famous Polish popular singer from the 1930's. Though she became a well-regarded film star and performer, during the Second World War she was also a good samaritan. Includes original footage of *Ordonka*. Polish with NO subtitles.

VHS: S22209. $24.95.
Maria Kwiatkowska, Poland, 1993, 50 mins.

Paderewski's Return

The last wish of the great Polish pianist and Prime Minister was to be buried in free Poland. Years later, when Poland regained freedom, the coffin of Ignacy Paderewski was transferred from Arlington Cemetery in the U.S. to St. John's Cathedral in Warsaw. English narration. 40 mins.

VHS: S33757. $24.95.

Parada Wspomnien

An insightful documentary about the most exciting years in the Solidarity movement, including conspiracy, famous escapes, and more. Polish with NO subtitles.

VHS: S15565. $29.95.
Bogdan Kosinski/Jacek Petrycki, Poland, 51 mins.

The Pilgrim

An independent documentary made during the first visit of Pope John Paul to Poland in June, 1979. Polish with NO subtitles. 80 mins.

VHS: S11367. $29.95.

Poems for Children

Poems for children written by Jan Brzechwa, Jonstanty Ildefons Galczynski and Julian Tuwim, recited by well-known Polish actors. Polish with NO subtitles. 64 mins.

VHS: S11294. $39.95.

Poland, A Proud Heritage

Journey to Warsaw, filled with newly restored historical buildings, and gaze at the Royal Castle and Sigmund's Column, the symbol of the city. Sunworship in Gdansk along the Baltic Coast, and experience the serenity of the Bialowieza Forest, Europe's last virgin woodland. Walk through the grounds of Auschwitz, and visit the Jasna Gora monastery, where millions of Poles make an annual pilgrimage to the Black Madonna. 55 mins.

VHS: S10772. $24.95.

Polish Christmas Carols

Traditional Polish Christmas carols and pastorales performed by the Children's Choir from Poniatowa, Halina Frackowiak and Krystyna Pronko. 55 mins. Polish with NO subtitles.

VHS: S11385. $37.95.

Polish Songs

From the battle of Grunwald to September 1939: Polish soldiers' songs down the centuries are performed by the Artistic Ensemble of the Polish Army. 90 mins.

VHS: S12357. $29.95.

Prelude
A 6-part series from Polish television for children and teenagers. A story of four children who, unexpectedly left on their own, have to look after their farm. Total length of the two cassettes, 175 mins. Polish with NO subtitles.
VHS: S11363. $69.95.

A Road to Independence
Two documentaries are joined here. One is from 1937, about the Polish road to independence. The other is from 1935 and shows the funeral of Marshal Jozef Pilsudski. B&W. Polish with NO subtitles. Poland, 1935-1937, 112 mins.
VHS: S26976. $29.95.

Royal Castle in Warsaw
A history of the Royal Castle in Warsaw since the 15th century, when Knight Janusz I built the Upper Castle using brick. English narration. 35 mins.
VHS: S33758. $24.95.

Songs and Dance by Slask (Slask Tanczy i Spiewa)
Slask provides 45 minutes of unparalleled entertainment in this dynamic video. It is the best Polish folk music and dancing available. Colorful scenery from the Karlinek region of Silesia is featured. Poland, 45 mins.
VHS: S26736. $29.95.

Stanislaw Moniuszko— The Haunted Manor
One of the best known operas by Stanislaw Moniuszko, performed at the Grand Theatre in Warsaw. Polish with NO subtitles. 135 mins.
VHS: S11368. $39.95.

Sycamore People
A collection of six Polish stories for children, one of which concerns the adventures of *The Sycamore People*. Polish with NO subtitles. 60 mins.
VHS: S16830. $24.95.

Tadeusz Drozda Cabaret
Another in the series of videos presenting outstanding Polish cabaret performers. Tadeusz Drozda is the author of the sketches. 105 mins. Polish with NO subtitles.
VHS: S11377. $29.95.

Thank You Poles
The history of the General Maczek Brigade from 1939 to 1945. The exploits of this crack World War II unit are carefully reconstructed using archival documents, photos and films. Also included rare interviews with German Panzer division officers. Polish with NO subtitles.
VHS: S16825. $29.95.
Wincenty Ronisz, Poland, 95 mins.

The Theatre of Tadeusz Kantor
A unique documentary on the work of a legendary genius of theatre, Tadeusz Kantor. Filmmaker Denis Bablet traces Kantor's roots as a visual artist in Poland and explores his ingenious methods of designing the props which become living sculptures in his extraordinary theatre productions. The program features rare scenes of Kantor at work with the dedicated actors in his troupe, Cricot 2. In a unique scene, Kantor is on-stage and "conducts" the actors much as a symphony conductor leads an orchestra. Extensive segments from some of Kantor's most famous works, *Wielopole, Wielopole* and *The Dead Class*, are also included. Narrated in English. 144 mins.
VHS: S14812. $59.95.

There Was No Room for You
Christmas Carols from Poland performed by Ewa Bem, Andrzej Hiolski, Bernard Ladysz, Janusz Olejniczak, Irena Santor. 90 mins. Polish with NO subtitles.
VHS: S11383. $29.95.

This Is Warsaw
This recent production looks at the Polish capital city, Warsaw. Both the past and the present are covered in this documentary. English narration.
VHS: S26740. $19.95.
Miroslaw Salicki, Poland, 1994, 30 mins.

Two That Stole the Moon
A four-part animated series for children about twin brothers who run away from home in search of Lazyland. Polish with NO subtitles.
VHS: S12358. $29.95.
Leszek Gladys, Poland, 1980, 110 mins.

Two Without a Cox
A cabaret program featuring two popular Polish cabaret performers: Janusz Gajos and Krysztof Jaroszynski, with a guest appearance by singer Danua Blazejczyk. Polish with NO subtitles.
VHS: S11376. $29.95.

Until in Our Hearts
This documentary of recent Polish history is based on the memorabilia and letters accumulated in the Polish Institute and Museum in London. Polish with NO subtitles. Poland, 1987.
VHS: S16824. $29.95.

Virtuiti Militari 1792-1992
Presents the dramatic fate of this period of over 200 years of Polish history. Founded by King Stanislaw August Poniatowski after a victorious battle during Polish-Russian War in 1792. English narration. 50 mins.
VHS: S33759. $24.95.

White Eagle (Orzel Bialy)
An archival television recording of the Representative Artistic Troupe of the Polish Army, initiated in 1943 as front line theater. Here the group performs a popular program about Polish knights and soldiers, at the Teatr Wielki in Lodz. 115 mins.
VHS: S15559. $39.95.

Wilanow— King Jan III Sobieski Residence
This video reveals the opulent baroque home of King Jan III Sobieski. It's a resplendent work of art that was built in honor of the King's wife, Marysienka. Everything from the grand public spaces to the intimate quarters of the royal family and the rooms of the servants are on display in this video. Polish with NO subtitles.
VHS: S26741. $24.95.
Andrzej Lucinski, Poland, 1995, 40 mins.

Wojciech Mlynarski—Lyrical Evening
A recital of lyrical songs written and performed by Wojciech Mlynarski. A variety of songs range from lyrical ballads to love songs and humorous stories. 78 mins. Polish with NO subtitles.
VHS: S11378. $29.95.

Workers '80 (Robotnicy '80)
A series of historical film recordings of the strikes in the shipyards of Gdansk in 1980 make up this portrait of the birth of the Solidarity movement and of its leader, Lech Walesa. Polish with NO subtitles.
VHS: S26977. $14.95.
Andrzej Zajaczkowski, Poland, 1989, 94 mins.
Zenon Laskowik's Benefit—By the Back Door
A cabaret program of Zenon Laskowik, the star of Polish cabaret. 80 mins. Polish with NO subtitles.
VHS: S11373. $39.95.

CZECH CINEMA

All My Good Countrymen
One of the wonders of the Czech New Wave, *All My Good Countrymen* is also one of the least-known films from this miraculous era of Czech filmmaking. The reason is obvious: completed barely before the Soviet invasion of Czechoslovakia in 1968, it was immediately banned and never shown. Despite this, the film won the Special Jury Prize of the Cannes Film Festival, and stylistically is a work of great lyricism, humor and originality. It weaves magical—and very funny—stories about a group of characters in a small Moravian village, immediately following the socialization of Czechoslovakia in 1948. "The film and the milieu it so precisely evokes are not so much nostalgic as they are powerfully remembered and irrevocably lost.... *All My Good Countrymen* reflects the curdled fury of a former true believer" (J. Hoberman, *The Village Voice*). Czech with English subtitles.
VHS: S05252. $59.95.
Vojtech Jasny, Czechoslovakia, 1968, 115 mins.

Boxer and Death
One of the precursor films to the Czech New Wave, this film explores the minds of two men—a prisoner and his keeper—as they try to find fulfillment within the grim confines of a concentration camp. The Nazi commander who has always loved boxing sees a potential in Kopinek, a powerful prisoner who has attempted escape. Czech and German with English subtitles.
VHS: S05893. $29.95.
Peter Solan, Czechoslavakia, 1962, 107 mins.

Cassandra Cat (When the Cat Comes)
A small town is disrupted by a magical cat from a traveling circus who dons special spectacles and transforms people into colors which reveal their true natures. This enchanting fairy tale and moving satire on hypocrisy and folly is a delight for people of all ages. With Jan Werich. English dialog.
VHS: S30549. $29.95.
Vojtech Jasny, Czechoslovakia, 1963, 87 mins.

Closely Watched Trains
An ironic, funny film about a young man on his first job in a small town railroad station, trying to get sexually initiated (in hilarious scenes), who, unwittingly, becomes a tragic hero. Offbeat but tender, *Closely Watched Trains* is a comedy about frustration, eroticism and adventure. Academy Award winner for Best Foreign Picture. With Vaclav Neckar and Jitka Bendova. Czech with English subtitles.
VHS: S00252. $19.98.
Jiri Menzel, Czechoslovakia, 1966, 89 mins.

The Cow
A brilliant achievement from Czech filmmaker Karel Kachyna: the parable about a simple man on a remote mountain top who cares for his ailing mother until he is forced to sell their single cow in order to buy her morphine. The mother dies anyway, but is replaced by a house maid, who in turn is replaced by another woman. This enigmatic fable-like film evokes a sense of hope amidst the most mundane events of an ordinary life in an extraordinary achievement of post-Velvet Revolution Czech cinema. Czech with English subtitles.
VHS: S26411. $89.95.
Karel Kachyna, Czech Republic, 1994, 86 mins.

The Coward
Set in a remote Slovak village during the waning days of World War II, *The Coward* is a probing moral study of heroism. A school teacher and his young wife find a wounded Russian parachutist in their front yard just as the Germans occupy the village; the wife supports the anti-Nazi partisans but her husband collaborates with the Germans. At the end of his humiliation, her husband finds the courage to save his honor and the innocent victims of the Nazis. Czech with English subtitles.
VHS: S27177. $29.95.
Jiri Weiss, Czechoslovakia, 1962, 113 mins.

Dita Saxova
The moving—and beautifully told—tragic story about an 18-year-old girl living in Prague, who seems beautiful and strong to everyone around her, until, a year later, she commits suicide by jumping off a cliff. Based on a novel by Arnost Lustig, *Dita Saxova* deftly explores the psychological contradictions which motivated her. Czech with English subtitles. B&W.
VHS: S04739. $59.95.
Antonin Moskalyk, Czechoslovakia, 1967, 98 mins.

The Elementary School
Jan Sverak's (*Kolya*) wonderful autobiographical mosaic of childhood memories returns to a time when he was ten years old and examining the adult world with great intensity. An artfully simple film rich with surprises and secrets and endowed with intelligent humor and passion toward human weakness. Nominated for Academy Award for Best Foreign Film. Czech with English subtitles.
VHS: S31630. $89.95.
Jan Sverak, Czechoslovakia, 1991, 100 mins.

Erotikon
This forerunner to Machaty's *Ecstacy* examines the moral consequences of a night of unbridled passion between a Prague playboy who is forced to stay the night after missing a train, and a provincial stationmaster's daughter (Ita Rina) who becomes pregnant. With Oleg Fjord and Luiji Serventi. Silent with new English titles.
VHS: S33934. $24.95.
Gustav Machaty, Czechoslovakia, 1929, 88 mins.

Fabulous Adventures of Baron Munchhausen
A masterpiece of animation by Karel Zeman—a fabulous fantasy that mixes live action, antique engravings and animation in a dazzling tour-de-force of fantasy. One of the great works of the cinema. English language version.
VHS: S11474. $29.95.
Karel Zeman, Czechoslovakia, 1965, 75 mins.

The Hard Life of an Adventurer
Karel Stekly (later to become the first Czech to win the Venice Film Festival with *The Strike*) collaborated on the screenplay of this funny send-up of the world of pulp detective stories. A popular mystery writer meets a thief who is a character out of one of his novels. With Otomar Korbelar and Adina Mandlova. Czech with English subtitles.
VHS: S14637. $29.95.
Martin Fric, Czechoslovakia, 1941, 89 mins.

Kolya

A charmer of a movie, due, in no small part, to the wonderful performances of Zdenek Sverak as the confirmed, set-in-his-ways bachelor and Andrej Chalimon as the six-year-old Russian boy stranded in Prague by his mother, who first turns Sverak's life upside down and ultimately wins over his heart. An Oscar- and Golden Globe-winner for Best Foreign Film, this "gem of a film" (*New York Times*) also features political overtones in its whimsical look at a musician reduced to playing at funerals because of his outspokenness and the fact that his brother has emigrated. Czech with English subtitles.

VHS: S31824. $103.99.
Laser: LD76332. $39.99.
Jan Sverak, Czech Republic, 1996, 105 mins.

Larks on a String

From director Jiri Menzel (*Closely Watched Trains*) comes a buoyant and lyrical romantic comedy that was banned in Czechoslovakia until the melt-down of the iron curtain in Europe. While serving time for desertion, and taking steps toward re-education, a rag-tag group of workers unite as a young couple in the camp decides to marry. We soon find that even the prison guards can't resist the unlikely romance, as the wedding and on-site honeymoon unfold in a series of hilarious plot twists. With Vaclav Neckar and Jityka Zelenohorska. Czech with yellow English subtitles.

VHS: S15169. $19.98.
Jiri Menzel, Czechoslovakia, 1969, 96 mins.

The Last Butterfly

Tom Courtenay stars in this beautiful film about an actor forced, by a cruel hoax, to perform for the Nazis. Terezin is a model city that should prove to the world how well the Nazis treat imprisoned Jews. When the curtain goes up, however, there is a surprise that no one expected.

VHS: S22890. $19.98.
Karel Kachyna, Great Britain/Czech Republic, 1994, 106 mins.

Mandragora

Mirek Caslavka stars as a young kid who spurns the workaday robotic lifestyle, continuing from the communist era, which has hung his father out to waste. From his drab origins he is drawn by economic liberties and flashy matrialism to the toxic city of Prague, where everything can be had for a price. He is soon led into the world of male prostitution, teaming up with another boy (David Svec, the film's co-writer) as they try to survive in a world dominated by sex, drugs and teen porn. Czech with English subtitles.

VHS: S33331. $59.95.
Wiktor Grodecki, Czech Republic, 1997, 130 mins.

Murder Czech Style

Jiri Weiss' *Murder Czech Style* features an endearing performance by Rudolf Hrusinsky as a contented, chubby and slightly clumsy office clerk who gets a shot at true love only to eventually discover that his wife is having a torrid affair with the manager of her husband's company. In a film which is one of the often overlooked masterpieces of the Czech New Wave, Weiss shows "Czech indecisiveness, pettiness and opportunism in a mixture of the imaginary and the real." Czech with English subtitles.

VHS: S27178. $29.95.
Jiri Weiss, Czechoslovakia, 1966, 90 mins.

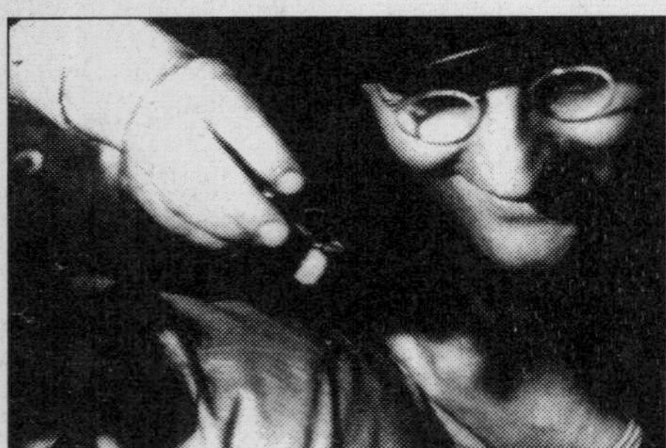

My Sweet Little Village

The overbearing Pavek threatens to replace his sidekick, the simple-minded Otik, but he never does. Instead the two continue to work together in this carefully observed portrait of life in a funny little village. Around this Laurel and Hardy-like pair are a group of eccentrics, all bemusedly following their own quirky obsessions. Czech with English subtitles.

VHS: S26207. $24.95.
Jiri Menzel, Czechoslovakia, 1986, 100 mins.

New Pastures

Early film by Vladimir Cech, who went on to win the Grand Prize at the 1972 Moscow Film Festival for *The Key*. A comedy about three prisoners recently released from jail and their experiences returning home to their small village. Czech with English subtitles.

VHS: S01935. $59.95.
Vladimir Cech, Czechoslovakia, 1962, 92 mins.

Not Angels, But Angels

Young boys in the fast changing world of the Czech Republic find the consumer life is available to them through the sale of their own bodies as prostitutes. This documentary lets them describe their experiences plying the world's oldest trade in a new center for sex tourism. Czech with English subtitles.

VHS: S26404. $39.95.
Wiktor Grodecki, Czech Republic, 1994, 80 mins.

On the Comet

Jules Verne's science fiction adventure is brought to life by Czech animator Karel Zeman. Since the early 1950's Zeman has been directing highly imaginative films that combine animation and live action and are marked by their fantastic trick effects. A film for the whole family! English dialog.

VHS: S00958. $24.95.
Karel Zeman, Czechoslovakia, 76 mins.

A Prayer for Katarina Horovitzova

Originally made in 1969, this powerful film based on Arnost Lustig's award-winning novel was confiscated by the Czech Communist government and kept on the shelf for 21 years. This videotape is literally the re-discovered U.S. and world premiere. Awarded the top prize at the Monte Carlo Film and Television Festival and winner of eight other international prizes, it is the story of a beautiful Polish singer and her passion for life, set against the backdrop of the cruel game of trading Jewish lives for those of Nazi officers imprisoned in American jails. With Jiri Adamira, Lenka Fiserova and Cestmir Randa. Czech with English subtitles. Czechoslovakia, 1991, 60 mins.

VHS: S13695. $59.95.

Romeo, Juliet and Darkness (Sweet Light in a Dark Room)

Romeo, Juliet and Darkness is a radical departure for Czech filmmaking in its unconventional treatment of the Anne Frank theme in a Czech setting. Pavel, a student, hides Hana, a young Jewish girl, in the attic of his apartment building. He is her only link to the outside world, and their growing trust develops into love, until the two are discovered by Pavel's mother. Weiss' double tragedy of young love and the moral question of responsibility to the Jews during the Nazi occupation is treated with poetic restraint. This film is a powerful condemnation of indifference toward force and terrorism. Also known as *Sweet Light in a Dark Room*. Czech with English subtitles.

VHS: S27179. $29.95.
Jiri Weiss, Czechoslovakia, 1959, 96 mins.

Summons for the Queen

A mystery involving murder and a black-market network begins with an anonymous tip to the police about a carefree young woman living far beyond her apparent means. Czech and English dialog.

VHS: S01932. $59.95.
Dusan Klein, Czechoslovakia, 1973, 110 mins.

Tereza

Exciting and complicated murder mystery featuring a female police officer, based on the novel by Anna Sedlmaye Rovia and starring Jirina Svorcova. Czech with English subtitles.

VHS: S01934. $69.95.
Pavel Blumenfeld, Czechoslovakia, 1961, 91 min.

Transport from Paradise

An intense psychological drama set in the Terezin ghetto and based on a novel by Arnost Lustig. Directed by Zbynek Brynych (*The Fifth Horseman Is Fear*), what makes the film remarkable is not only its visual dynamism, but the humanization of its characters, which makes it all the more haunting. Czech with English subtitles. B&W.

VHS: S04738. $59.95.
Zbynek Brynych, Czechoslovakia, 1965, 93 min.

Wolf Trap

A landmark in Czech cinema, *Wolf Trap* is set in a small town in Moravia and focuses on a marital triangle. The town veterinarian is married to an older, domineering yet insecure and needful wife. They adopt an orphaned teenage girl. As the veterinarian gradually falls in love with his adopted daughter, director Jiri Weiss brilliantly constructs a psychological prison of middle class life from which there is no escape. Czech with English subtitles.

VHS: S27176. $29.95.
Jiri Weiss, Czechoslovakia, 1957, 95 mins.

MILOS FORMAN

Amadeus

Milos Forman's adaptation of Peter Shaffer's play is structured as a confession related in flashback, told by the aging court composer, and Mozart's adversary, Salieri (F. Murray Abraham). Cinematographer Miroslav Ondricek finds a baroque, expressionist intensity in the Prague locations. Choreography by Twyla Tharp. With Elizabeth Berridge, Simon Callow, Roy Dotrice, Christine Ebersole and Jeffrey Jones. Winner of eight Academy Awards.

VHS: S00041. $14.98.
Laser: LD75367. $79.95.
Milos Forman, USA, 1984, 160 mins.

Competition

Forman's first film combines two short features, *Do We Need All Those Brass Bands?* and *The Audition*. Both films deal with the generation gap, the first in a band competition which can't overcome its tradition, the second a hilarious look at amateur singers auditioning for a role in a Prague cabaret. Forman's style "was simple: focus the eye of the camera as closely as possible on human detail, and then put on the screen everything that turns up as a result of such a microscopic view" (Antonin Liehm). Co-scripted by Ivan Passer. Czech with English subtitles.

VHS: S14634. $29.95.
Milos Forman, Czechoslovakia, 1963, 84 mins.

Firemen's Ball

One of the hallmarks of the Czech New Wave, Milos Forman's anarchic and freewheeling black comedy is a wry and devastating parable about Stalinist authoritarianism. The inventive story concerns the rituals surrounding a small town's celebration of a retiring fire chief and a bizarre beauty pageant as a trenchant commentary about the social and political order. Screenplay by Ivan Passer and Jaroslav Papousek. Cinematography by Miroslav Ondricek. Forman's last Czech film. Czech with English subtitles.

VHS: S00443. $29.95.
Milos Forman, Czechoslovakia, 1967, 73 mins.

Hair

The first musical about the American anti-war movement of the 1960's. Exceptional adaptation of the musical stars Treat Williams as a hippie who meets John Savage, a youth from Oklahoma bound for Vietnam. Forman moves the story beyond the bounds of the stage play to make a strong statement about war. Choreography by Twyla Tharp.

VHS: S03486. $19.98.
Laser: LD71163. $39.98.
Milos Forman, USA, 1979, 121 mins.

Loves of a Blonde

Milos Forman's great comedy is an acute satire of Czech daily life. The film focuses on the relationship of a factory girl and a touring piano player. After spending a night together in a provincial town, she suddenly appears at the doorstep of his parents' house with devastating results. With Hana Brejchova, Josef Sebanek and Vladimir Pucholt. "Compassionate, painfully true and continually beguiling" (*Time Magazine*). Czech with English subtitles.

VHS: S00781. $29.95.
Milos Forman, Czechoslovakia, 1965, 88 mins.

Milos Forman: The Fourth New York Film Festival

Academy Award-winning Czech director Forman speaks with New York Film Festival director Amos Vogel, discussing his career, his experiences at the big Czech film studio Barandov, the nature of post-Stalinist censorship, and the style of making his early comic masterpiece *Loves of a Blond*. 1966, 28 mins.

VHS: S31575. $59.95.

One Flew Over the Cuckoo's Nest

Milos Forman's sharp adaptation of Ken Kesey's anti-authoritarian novel about a shrewd nonconformist (Jack Nicholson) sentenced to an insane asylum who encourages a group of marginal misfits to assert their rights and independence, over the rigid opposition of the head nurse (Louise Fletcher). Cinematography by Haskell Wexler. With Will Sampson, Brad Dourif, Sydney Lassick, Christopher Lloyd, Danny DeVito and Scatman Crothers. Winner of the five top Academy Awards.

VHS: S18973. $19.98.
DVD: DV60091. $24.98.
Milos Forman, USA, 1975, 134 mins.

The People vs. Larry Flynt

Based on the true story of the controversial *Hustler* magazine publisher, who was sued by the Religious Right and paralyzed by an unknown assassin's bullet, Forman's film focuses on Flynt's (Woody Harrelson) inadvertent crusade for freedom of the press and on his unconventional marriage to an ex-stripper (Courtney Love, in an award-winning performance). With Edward Norton.

VHS: S31292. $19.95.
Laser: LD76206. $39.95.
DVD: DV60137. $24.95.
Milos Forman, USA, 1996, 130 mins.

Ragtime

The lives and loves of a middle class family are set against the scandals and headlines of early 20th-century America. Howard Rollins, Jr., plays the black man involved in murder, Mary Steenburgen is the sweet middle-class woman, and Elizabeth McGovern is the beautiful chorus girl, in Milos Forman's entertaining transposition of the popular best-seller by E.L. Doctorow.

VHS: S01085. $29.95.
Milos Forman, USA, 1983, 155 mins.

Valmont

Milos Forman's adaptation of *Les Liaisons Dangereuses* stars Colin Firth, Annette Bening and Meg Tilly; the script was written by Jean-Claude Carriere, and the cinematography was by Miroslav Ondricek.

VHS: S12418. $14.98.
Milos Forman, USA/France, 1989

JAN NEMEC

Code Name Ruby

A remarkable experiment in non-narrative from Czech New Wave member Jan Nemec, this controversial feature blends documentary, archival footage and fiction into an elliptical narrative in which two young people in Prague, an ancient seat for the practice of alchemy, follow the trail for the mystical philosopher's stone. History and future blend as Nemec, through brilliant montage sequences and fanciful leaps of the imagination, posits crucial questions about the legacy of the past and how it influences the individual's personal freedom and responsibility. With a script by Nemec and Iva Russelakova. With Jan Potmesil and Lucie Rejchrtova. Czech with English subtitles.
VHS: S35302. $29.95.
Jan Nemec, Czech Republic, 1998, 80 mins.

Diamonds of the Night

One of the breakthrough films of the Czech New Wave; based on a short story by Arnost Lustig, and brilliantly directed by Jan Nemec, it is the story of two boys who escape from a Nazi transport train, told in a visual, surrealistic style. On the same tape is Nemec/Lustig's short film *A Loaf of Bread*. Czech with English subtitles. B&W.
VHS: S04737. $59.95.
Jan Nemec, Czechoslovakia, 1964, 71 mins.

Oratorio for Prague

One of the most powerful documentaries ever made and a unique document of the Soviet invasion of Czechoslovakia in 1968, *Oratorio for Prague* "is a film so moving that one is near tears from the first moment after the credits appear. The movie was begun as a documentary about the liberalization of Czechoslovakia and then simply continued when the Russian tanks moved in," wrote Renata Adler in *The New York Times*. The only filmed record of the Soviet invasion of Czechoslovakia, the raw footage for *Oratorio for Prague*, when broadcast by television, was seen by more than 600 million people, and became the first information that the Soviet Army had *not* been "invited" in. Narrated in English.
VHS: S11991. $19.95.
Jan Nemec, Czechoslovakia/France, 1968, 26 mins.

A Report on the Party and the Guests

A miracle of the Czech New Wave, distinguished with being "banned forever" shortly after it was completed. Voted one of the best films of the year by *The New York Times*, it is "an extraordinary allegory…evocative of Kafka or Dostoevsky" (*International Film Guide*). A group of picnickers are led to an elegant banquet, where the "guests" quickly turn collaborators in this brilliant analysis of society and the individual. Czech with English subtitles.
VHS: S05654. $59.95.
Jan Nemec, Czechoslovakia, 1966, 71 mins.

JAN KADAR

Adrift

Jan Kadar's last Czech feature is a brilliant and beautiful film about sexual repression. In the lowlands of the Danube a fisherman rescues a mysterious drowning girl (played by American model Paula Pritchett). The intensity of his feelings conflict with the order of his life as a husband and a father until his passion leads to a tragic climax. Script by Imre Gyongyossy. Czech with English subtitles.
VHS: S23880. $29.95.
Jan Kadar, Czechoslovakia/USA, 1969, 108 mins.

Blue Hotel

From the American Short Story Collection, an adaptation of Stephen Crane's mystery, featuring David Warner and James Keach. Teleplay by Harry Mark Petrakis.
VHS: S00157. $24.95.
Jan Kadar, USA, 1974, 55 mins.

Freedom Road

A made-for-tv movie starring Muhammad Ali as an ex-slave on his way to becoming a U.S. Senator during the Reconstruction Years after the Civil War. Narration by Ossie Davis. Adapted from the Howard Fast novel. With Kris Kristofferson, Ron O'Neal, Barbara O. Jones and Edward Herrmann. Director Jan Kadar's last film.
VHS: S00465. $69.95.
Jan Kadar, USA, 1979, 186 mins.

The Shop on Main Street

A haunting work about the intersecting of the political and personal, developed through the strange yet touching relationship of an elderly Jewish shop owner and a passive carpenter whom the Nazis appoint as her "Aryan controller." Winner of the 1965 Best Foreign Film. With Ida Kaminska and Josef Kroner. "It manages to translate the apocalyptic tragedy of our century into human terms and to do so with laughter and tears, with scorn and passion" (Judith Crist). Slovak with English subtitles.
VHS: S01195. $24.95.
Jan Kadar, Czechoslovakia, 1965, 128 mins.

CZECH REPORT

After the Velvet Revolution

A sobering first-hand look at the impact of democracy on the people of Czechoslovakia after the fall of Communism in 1989. An intimate chronicle of a people and country in transition. 58 mins.
VHS: S23407. $150.00.

Death of Ales Martinu

A disturbing look at the rise in the skinhead movement in the Czech Republic. The film focuses on the story of Ales Martinu, a young Czech skinhead who was killed in a violent confrontation. It vividly illustrates how political changes and economic problems since the fall of Communism have created the climate that breeds fascist movements. 28 mins.
VHS: S23408. $125.00.

Kafka: Nabokov on Kafka

Vladimir Nabokov, widely considered one of the greatest writers of the 20th century, was also a remarkable and legendary professor of literature at Cornell University for many years. Here Christopher Plummer portrays a witty Nabokov providing entertaining insights into Franz Kafka's perplexing novella *The Metamorphosis*. 30 mins.
VHS: S14263. $24.95.

My Prague Spring

This wry, intimate, award-winning portrait of a family was filmed in Prague shortly after the fall of Communism. It examines the effects of this historic transformation through the eyes of a young American of Czech descent and his Czech relations, as they come to terms with the values of capitalism. English and Czech with English subtitles.
VHS: S20733. $89.95.
David Mrazek, USA, 1993, 81 mins.

Video Visits: Czechoslovakia, Triumph and Tradition

Tour Prague and its historic Old Town Square, Prague Castle and the St. Vitus Cathedral. 55 mins.
VHS: S31455. $24.99.

HUNGARIAN CINEMA

Adoption

The breakthrough film for Marta Meszaros (*Diary for All My Children*, a unique mixture of documentary and fictional techniques in the story of Mary, a middle-aged woman, who befriends the younger Julia, who insists on having her child live with her. A film of considerable psychological insight. Hungarian with English subtitles.
VHS: S04726. $69.95.
Marta Meszaros, Hungary, 1975, 89 mins.

After the Revolution

An absurdist peek at the post-Communist Hungarian world. The hero is a writer struggling to complete the great novel, who uses the observations of an extraordinary cat to foment his view of the world. An experimental, tongue-in-cheek feature made in the wake of the cataclysmic political changes in Hungary. Hungarian with English subtitles.
VHS: S15161. $59.95.
Andras Szirtes, Hungary, 1990, 82 mins.

Almanac of Fall

A large, claustrophobic apartment is the setting for this intense chamber-drama from Bela Tarr, one of Europe's most exciting contemporary filmmakers. In this dense setting, the inhabitants of the apartment reveal their darkest secrets, fears, obsessions and hostilities in a style that combines the anguish and existentialism of Bergman with the emotional intensity of Cassavetes. Hungarian with English subtitles.
VHS: S18690. $59.95.
Bela Tarr, Hungary, 119 mins.

The Annunciation

This amazing film, using a cast of children between the ages of 8 and 14, follows the travails of Adam from the Garden of Eden to modern times. Along the way, he becomes a general in Ancient Greece, a Byzantine crusader in Prague, Danton in the French Revolution and a witness to the plague in London. At all times he is tormented and abetted by a young, blond Lucifer. Hungarian with English subtitles.
VHS: S21322. $69.95.
Andras Jeles, Hungary, 1993, 101 mins.

Another Way

Public and private morality collide in this psychological drama about a love triangle during the aftermath of the failed Hungarian uprising in 1956. Livia, the beautiful wife of an army officer, is a reporter at the Budapest newspaper where Eve, an outspoken lesbian journalist, comes to work after two years of politically motivated unemployment. When Eve and Livia fall in love they embark on an affair whose tragic consequences are mirrored by Hungary's oppression under Soviet rule. Based on an autobiographical bestseller. With Jadwiga Jankowska-Kieslak, Grazyna Szapolowska and Josef Kroner. "One of cinema's most truly erotic films" (David Robinson, *The Times*). Hungarian with English subtitles.
VHS: S31358. $89.95.
Karoly Makk, Hungary, 1982, 102 mins.

Bad Guys

A stylistically innovative film from Gyorgy Szomjas, which borrows the conventions of the Western to tell the story of the last days of outlaws in Hungary. In the 1860's, an outlaw and his henchmen hold a reign of terror. But their movement is overtaken by the events of time and a posse is hot on their trail. Hungarian with English subtitles.
VHS: S13344. $69.95.
Gyorgy Szomjas, Hungary, 1979, 93 mins.

Beggar Student

Set in 18th century Cracow, a wonderful Hungarian version of the famous operetta, as General Ollendorf, on the prowl for a brief affair, vows revenge on the lovely Laura, who rejects him by setting up a student to masquerade as the Count Opalinsky. Hungarian with English subtitles.
VHS: S08107. $49.95.
Laszlo Seregi, Hungary, 90 mins.

Bolshe Vita

This acclaimed, multiple-award-winning film centers around a group of young people who meet in a rock pub in Budapest in the summer of 1989 during Hungary's fleeting celebration of Communism's fall. This Pynchonesque crew includes two goofy Russian musicians, an engineer who has been reduced to selling kitchen knives, and two girlfriends, English and American, in search of action. After the fun and romance, they must move on, as the mafia and the onset of new nationalist chaos closes in. Hungarian and Russian with English subtitles.
VHS: S34869. $79.95.
Ibolya Fekete, Hungary, 1996, 90 mins.

Cat's Play

The gifted Hungarian filmmaker Karoly Makk (*Love*) fashions this sharp, observant work about a widowed music teacher's rupture into delusion, obsession and romantic fatalism. The music teacher's ritual weekly dinners with his long-time sweetheart are interrupted by the appearance of the woman's old lover. Hungarian with English subtitles.
VHS: S16930. $59.95.
Karoly Makk, Hungary, 1974, 115 mins.

Cold Days

One of the most important Hungarian films of the 1960's, Andras Kovacs' *Cold Days* was an extremely courageous theme to tackle at the time, in view of the silence which had, until then, shrouded the Hungarian role in World War II. The film is based on the massacre of several thousand Jewish and Serbian people of Novi Sad in 1942. "The film is structured round the memories and self-justifications of four men involved in the massacre as they await trial in 1946. Each, of course, denies his complicity or responsibility…Many of the images in the film remain unforgettable." Hungarian with English subtitles.
VHS: S13338. $59.95.
Andras Kovacs, Hungary, 1966, 102 mins.

Daniel Takes the Train

This acclaimed feature, structured as a nail-biting thriller, confronts one of the most sensitive political periods, 1956, when Hungarians fought Soviet troops in the streets of Budapest. Daniel, hopelessly in love with Marianne, the girl next door, decides to join his friend on a train headed for the Austrian border. The film, in the words of *Variety*, captures "the complexities and passions…a tense and grimly funny experience." Hungarian with English subtitles.
VHS: S27800. $29.95.
Pal Sandor, Hungary, 1983, 90 mins.

The Fifth Seal

A haunting story set at the close of World War II in Hungary, this film begins with an unusual premise. A group of friends are arrested when one of them makes a casual remark that offends a commandant. From this chance event a series of daunting tasks emerge that test their commitment to their moral ideals.
VHS: S20618. $59.95.
Zoltan Fabri, Hungary, 1976, 116 mins.

Flowers of Reverie

This prize-winner at the Berlin International Film Festival combines an examination of inner psychological states with the external political turmoil of the Hungarian Revolution (1848-9). A former soldier named Ferenc is imprisoned for his work in the resistance, leading to a tragic outcome. Hungarian with English subtitles.

VHS: S20617. $59.95.

Laszlo Lugossy, Hungary, 1984, 106 mins.

The Girl

An interesting examination of how the overt repression of women in the older pattern of village life has been replaced by the more subtle sexual and economic exploitation inherent in the apparently freer existence of young girls in the contemporary city. A key film from Marta Meszaros. Hungarian with English subtitles.

VHS: S04727. $69.95.

Marta Meszaros, Hungary, 1968, 89 mins.

A Happy New Year!

The frustrations and emptiness of the lives of the professional class are brought into sharp relief in this brilliant comedy set during the course of one New Year's. As the trio of two men and one woman, all chemical engineers, balance their personal and professional lives on New Year's Eve, their future seems hollow, their chance for happiness and fulfillment elusive. Hungarian with English subtitles.

VHS: S18688. $59.95.

Reszo Szoreny, Hungary, 1979, 84 mins.

A Hungarian Fairy Tale

A strange, beautiful and critically-acclaimed film by Gyula Gazdag, *A Hungarian Fairy Tale* begins at a performance of Mozart's *The Magic Flute* where a beautiful young woman meets a handsome stranger and, transported by the music, they share one night of love. The son born of this magic night is raised by his mother but at the age of three, must be given a father's name, even a fictitious one, according to Hungarian law. Years later, the engaging Andris sets out to find his "father" as his "father" begins a separate journey. "No less resonant than *Wings of Desire*" (J. Hoberman, *The Village Voice*). Hungarian with English subtitles.

VHS: S12365. $19.98.

Gyula Gazdag, Hungary, 1988, 95 mins.

Hungarian Rhapsody

Part of Jancso's proposed trilogy dealing with the relationships between the classes in pre-revolutionary Hungary, *Hungarian Rhapsody* continues the director's highly symbolic and dynamic style which brought him to fame with his early films. Set in 1911, the film follows Istvan, a nobleman who joins ranks with the peasants in opposition to the ruling class in general, and his statesman brother in particular. With Gyorgy Cserhalmi, Lajos Balaszovits and Gabor Koncz. Hungarian with English subtitles.

VHS: S12509. $59.95.

Miklos Jancso, Hungary, 1983, 101 mins.

Lilly in Love

Christopher Plummer is the successful screenwriter who concocts an ingenious plan to test his wife's infidelity in this U.S.-made comedy by Hungarian filmmaker Karoly (*Love*) Makk. Maggie Smith is the wife who is courted by her husband, Plummer, in disguise. In English.

VHS: S00756. $79.95.

Karoly Makk, USA, 1985, 104 mins.

The Little Valentino

A brilliant film debut, and one of the most highly acclaimed European films of recent years, this deceptively simple black and white feature anticipates and stylistically surpasses Jim Jarmusch's *Stranger than Paradise*. The events of the film are concentrated on a single day. The film focuses on Laszlo, a 20-year-old driver's assistant, who spends his day and his money—which he has just stolen—in the aimlessness of everyday life. "It's hard not to be impressed by its on-the-edge assurance" (*Chicago Reader*). Hungarian with English subtitles.

VHS: S13337. $59.95.

Andras Jeles, Hungary, 1979, 102 mins.

Love

Lili Darvas, the famed stage actress and widow of Ferenc Molnar, portrays a bed-ridden old woman in this emotionally precise drama. Her daughter-in-law, whose husband is in jail as a political prisoner, concocts a fictitious story about his life as a filmmaker in America and forges letters from him filled with Hollywood gossip, which the mother devours as she awaits her son's return. When he is finally sprung from prison, it is too late. Hungarian with English subtitles.

VHS: S13659. $59.95.

Karoly Makk, Hungary, 1971, 92 mins.

Magic Hunter

David Bowie lent his name to this film by the talented Hungarian director Ildiko Enyedi (*My Twentieth Century*). The film is an inventive update of a Faustian tale set in modern Hungary, about a Budapest police force sharpshooter (Gary Kemp) who makes a deal with a shady colleague for seven magic bullets guaranteed to hit their target—but there is a price that comes with the seventh bullet that the cop doesn't know about. Hungarian with English subtitles.

VHS: S32026. $79.95.

Ildiko Enyedi, Hungary/Canada, 1996, 106 mins.

Maria's Day

One of the most acclaimed recent Hungarian films, Judit Elek's *Maria's Day* is set 17 years after the failed revolution of 1848. An aristocratic family gathers at the home of Ignac Czendrey to celebrate his youngest daughter's Name Day. In the course of the one day, the unusual past and present of the Czendrey family are unfolded. The family is related to the revolutionary and legendary poet Sandor Petofi and desperately tries to live up to the Petofi myth. They dream of a heroic new epoch, but while they dream, the mundaneness of the present overcomes them. A powerful and moving film. Hungarian with English subtitles.

VHS: S11289. $59.95.

Judit Elek, Hungary, 1985, 113 mins.

The Memories of a River

Judit Ellek's (*Maria's Day*) humanistic, deeply moving moral tale of a Jewish raftsman, accused of drowning a girl in the river Tisza, whose son is forced by the district attorney to testify against him. Winner, Ecumenical Prize, Montreal World Film Festival. Hungarian with English subtitles.

VHS: S34870. $59.95.

Judit Elek, Hungary, 1989, 131 mins.

The Midas Touch

Set on the eve of the Russian invasion in 1956, Geza Beremenyi's fable concerns a merchant who's known as the king of the market for his transcendent ability to transform anything he touches into gold. His abilities are questioned when blood flows through the street. Hungarian with English subtitles.

VHS: S13878. $79.95.

Geza Beremenyi, Hungary, 1989, 100 mins.

My Twentieth Century

At the turn of the century, two identical twins grow up and explore their worlds in very opposite ways. The erotic and playful Dora is a soft and self-indulgent contrast to her bomb-throwing revolutionary sister Lili, who was separated from her at birth. The sisters finally cross paths on the famous Orient Express by sleeping with the same confused man. The beautiful Dortha Segda plays both roles in this witty and sensual film from writer/director Ildiko Enyedi. "The most original, one of a kind, film of the year" (*American Woman*). Hungarian with English subtitles.

VHS: S15264. $19.98.

Ildiko Enyedi, Hungary, 1990, 104 mins.

The Nice Neighbor

Laszlo Szabo stars as a clever but cruel occupant of a Budapest boarding house, one who exercises his exploitative skills to the hilt when the building is torn down and the tenants are allotted new living space. Always playing the role of protector of his fellow tenants, he skillfully manipulates the lot for his own goal: a bigger apartment. Also starring Margit Dayka and Agi Margittay. Hungarian with English subtitles.

VHS: S12510. $59.95.

Zsolt Kezdi-Kovacs, Hungary, 1979, 90 mins.

Nobody's Daughter

This critically acclaimed film follows the tragic life of an eight-year-old orphan girl. Living under a government that sanctions money to foster parents, she finds herself shuffled from family to family; with each move she encounters increasingly brutal abuse. A beautifully acted film with explores an all too real pathos. Hungarian with English subtitles.

VHS: S16500. $59.95.

Lazlo Ranody, Hungary, 1976, 90 mins.

Oh, Bloody Life!

A film of considerable importance from the renowned filmmaker Peter Bacso. Set in the 1950's during the Stalinist era, Bacso's daring film concerns the deportation of Hungarian citizens who have done nothing wrong. Bacso's film is remarkable not only for its courageous depiction of political events, but for his black comedy. Hungarian with English subtitles.

VHS: S08110. $49.95.

Peter Bacso, Hungary, 1985, 115 mins.

A Priceless Day

From the director of *Time Stands Still*, this is a thoughtful, ironic rumination on desire and sexual awakening. A 30-year-old kindergarten teacher visits her lover's wife and the two enter a pact to rid themselves of their men. Based on an idea by Peter Zimre. Cinematography by Lajos Koltai. Music by Gyorgy Selmeczi. Cecilia Esztergalyos, Pat Hetenyi and Judit Pogany. Hungarian with English subtitles.

VHS: S18689. $59.95.

Peter Gothar, Hungary, 1980, 87 mins.

The Red and the White

One of the most original of films, a haunting work about the absurdity and evil of war. Set in Central Russia during the Civil War of 1918, the story details the constant shifting of power between the White guards and the Red soldiers, first at an abandoned monastery, and later, at a field hospital. Using the wide-screen technique consisting of very long takes and a ceaselessly tracking camera movement, Miklos Jancso has fashioned a brilliant visual style which is truly unique in the history of cinema. Hungarian with English subtitles.

VHS: S08940. $79.95.

Miklos Jancso, Hungary, 1968, 92 mins.

Red Earth

A shrewd satire about Communism, Hungarian style. A bauxite mixer discovers his pigs have unearthed high quality bauxite from his back yard. The troubles start when the village bureaucrats and bauxite prospectors insist the discovery was the result of careful, methodical planning. With Imre Nemeth, Sandor Kocsis, Kalman Toronyi and Ferenc Togh. Hungarian with English subtitles.

VHS: S18687. $59.95.

Laszlo Vitezy, Hungary, 105 mins.

Riddance

A young factory worker pretends to be a student in order to impress the boy with whom she is in love, and his snobbish family, in Marta Meszaros' examination of the class and social tensions which still exist within Hungary. Hungarian with English subtitles.

VHS: S04728. $69.95.

Marta Meszaros, Hungary, 1973, 93 mins.

Round Up

One of the greatest films of Miklos Jancso, the brilliant Hungarian filmmaker. A savage, often ironic epic about the effects of imprisonment, fear and torture, set during the 1848 Hungarian Revolution. Several hundred outlaws are captured and in a cat-and-mouse game forced to reveal active rebels by the Austrian police.

VHS: S18585. $59.95.

Miklos Jancso, Hungary, 1965, 87 mins.

Sindbad

One of the most eloquent, beautiful and truly original films of all time. The subject of the film is an aging hedonist concerned only with the sensual pleasures of women, food and drink, who now tries to recapture the memory of these vanished delights. Hungarian with English subtitles.

VHS: S04725. $69.95.

Zoltan Huszarik, Hungary, 1971, 98 mins.

Stand Off

A terrific thriller by Gyula Gazdag. 18-year old Zoltan and his younger brother Istvan have taken 16 girls hostage in a dormitory in a student hostel in a Hungarian border town. They demand a flight out of Budapest and a million dollars. "A devastating expression of the frustration of Eastern Europe" (*L.A. Times*). Intense and powerful performances and a rich musical score. Hungarian with English subtitles.

VHS: S13343. $79.95.

Gyula Gazdag, Hungary, 1989, 97 mins.

Sunday Daughters

A film compared to Truffaut's *400 Blows*, set in an institution for teenage girls, directed with verve and compassion by Janosz Rozsa. Juli, a 16-year-old inmate, seems to be moving toward delinquency, and after repeated rejections from her family, escapes. After a close call with death, she survives and her life brightens when an older woman takes her in, but these hopes are smashed when Juli becomes involved with the woman's son. Using non-professional actors, Rozsa delivers stunning performances in a film that is both endearing and probing. Hungarian with English subtitles.

VHS: S11288. $59.95.

Janosz Rozsa, Hungary, 1980, 100 mins.

A Very Moral Night

A spirited turn-of-the-century tale of a poor medical student lodging cheaply and happily in a bordello. When his widowed mother makes a surprise visit, the madam and the girls set about converting the place into a respectable boarding house. Starring Iren Psota, and Margit Makay as the visiting mother. Hungarian with English subtitles.

VHS: S14822. $59.95.

Karoly Makk, Hungary, 1977, 103 mins.

We Never Die
This independently produced Hungarian comedy became a runaway hit; it's full of sharp barbs about life in the neo-Communist universe. The young hero is turned over to his clever uncle "Juicy", who teaches him how to have fun and survive it all with the help of grub, booze and women. The race track or the bedroom are the places best suited to his golden rule, "Don't take life too seriously." Hungarian with English subtitles.
VHS: S22424. $79.95.
Robert Koltai, Hungary, 1994, 90 mins.

The Witness
Peter Bacso's film was banned for more than nine years. Set in 1949, the film is a political satire that mixes forms and styles, symbolism and screwball farce. The story concerns a functionary who's imprisoned and eventually manipulated into providing testimony against his best friend, a government minister on trial for treason. With Ferenc Kallai, Lajos Oze and Zoltan Fabri. Hungarian with English subtitles.
VHS: S18501. $59.95.
Peter Bacso, Hungary, 1968, 110 mins.

ISTVAN SZABO

25, Firemen's Street
An important film by Istvan Szabo with an intricate flashback structure that recalls Resnais. The setting is an old house on the eve of its demolition; during a hot summer night, the numerous inhabitants indulge in dreams and recollections of the events of the past thirty years. Hungarian with English subtitles.
VHS: S04724. $69.95.
Istvan Szabo, Hungary, 1973, 93 mins.

Father
This sensitive, intelligent study of adolescence and maturation focuses on a young man whose defense mechanism consists of idealizing the memory of his dead father. One of the key films of the Hungarian film renaissance, *Father* is a daring, emotionally charged film. Hungarian with English subtitles.
VHS: S11635. $69.95.
Istvan Szabo, Hungary, 1966, 95 mins.

Hanussen
The third part of Szabo's trilogy (*Mephisto, Colonel Redl*) stars Klaus Maria Brandauer as a charismatic magician and clairvoyant, whose predictions of the future are uncannily accurate. When the Nazis seize power, he is forced to choose between joining them and standing alone. Brilliantly shot, with a riveting performance by Brandauer, Szabo continues to explore the moral issues which shaped the 20th century. Hungarian and German with English subtitles.
VHS: S12496. $19.95.
Istvan Szabo, Hungary/Germany, 1989

Meeting Venus
Istvan Szabo's first English-language film is the erotic story of an opera star/seductress played by Glenn Close who sets her sights on a young conductor played by Niels Arestrup. The torrid romance is played against the romantic music of Richard Wagner and against the world of opera—full of its bizarre characters, power mongering and power plays, lovers, wives, ex-lovers and ex-wives and unabashed melodrama.
VHS: S16161. $19.98.
Laser: Letterboxed. **LD71680. $34.98.**
Istvan Szabo, Hungary/France/Great Britain, 1991, 121 mins.

HUNGARIAN ISSUES

Hungary, Land of Hospitality
In this land of baroque palaces and cobblestone streets, journey to Budapest and to Lake Balaton, stop in the medieval city of Pecs and tour the renowned Zsolnay porcelain factory. 30 mins.
VHS: S12275. $24.95.

Recsk 1953 Documentary of a Hungarian Secret Labor Camp
This powerful film catalogs the atrocities committed by the Stalinist regime of Hungary. With its release, *Recsk* received five major European documentary film awards. In Hungarian with English subtitles.
VHS: S16501. $29.95.
Livia Gyarmathy/Geza Boszormenyi, Hungary, 1989, 100 mins.

YUGOSLAV CINEMA

Balkan Express
A very offbeat, funny comedy. The Balkan Express is a band of roving musicians whose music is just cover for their real work as con men. When the Nazis move in, things take a turn for the worse. Outrageously madcap, full of dramatic twists set against the dark horror of the War. English dubbed. Yugoslavia, 1984, 102 mins.
VHS: S00089. $19.95.

Charuga
The spectacular, true story of a Croatian 1920s Robin Hood, a fanatic ex-soldier and Bolshevik who tried to bring the Revolution to Yugoslavia. A visually complex, engrossing, sensual and unsettling action-adventure movie which is also a serious political drama, Charuga began by robbing from the rich and giving to the poor. But as with many self-styled revolutionaries, he soon robs from everyone and keeps it all for himself. Croatian with English subtitles.
VHS: S27795. $29.95.
Rajko Grlic, Croatia, 1991, 108 mins.

Day That Shook the World (Sarajevsky atentat)
The assassination of Archduke Ferdinand and his wife was an event so monstrous it set the world on fire, igniting the start of World War I. With Christopher Plummer and Maximilian Schell. In English.
VHS: S34199. $19.95.
Veljko Bulajic, Yugoslavia, 1975, 111 mins.

The Harms Case
Based on the life and writing of Daniel Harms, a Russian avant-garde poet of the 1920s who has become a cult figure in Yugoslavia, this challenging film is "an alternately hilarious and unsettling portrait...deliriously surrealistic." Serbo-Croatian with English subtitles.
VHS: S26497. $59.95.
Slobodan Pesic, Yugoslavia, 1988, 90 mins.

Hey Babu Riba
"A magic that is special to movies alone. The greatest pleasure in the world is to walk into a movie you never heard of, by a director you never heard of, and then be overwhelmed by beauty and memory and longing," wrote *The New York Post*. The warm and witty portrait of a close-knit group of Belgrade teenagers in Yugoslavia of the 50's, the magic of Jovan Acin's film focuses on four close-knit friends, all in love with the same girl. A cinematic tribute to a lost time and place, *Hey Babu Riba* was the sleeper hit of the London, Miami, Seattle and San Francisco Film Festivals. Serbian with yellow English subtitles.
VHS: S09592. $19.98.
Jovan Acin, Yugoslavia, 1987, 112 mins.

In the Jaws of Life
At the heart of this disarmingly funny and sexy comedy is a middle-aged woman filmmaker, a bit on the chubby side, with a rather confused personal life, who is making a soap opera titled *The Jaws of Life*. The TV soap opera follows the life of a chubby office clerk not unlike the filmmaker. The two stories unfold side by side until the stories begin to converge. "This sex farce is as rueful as it is funny, as earthy as it is politically astute, as cleverly structured as it is unexpected" (*Village Voice*). Croatian with English subtitles.
VHS: S27796. $29.95.
Rajko Grlic, Yugoslavia, 1984, 95 mins.

The Marathon Family
Full of surprises, full of black humor, this film, called "American gangsterism Balkan style," is set in Serbia between the two world wars. The Topalovic family, five generations of morticians, have questionable ways of keeping up with the competition. But Mirko wants to get out of the business and become a filmmaker. "Sijan has...chronicled the changing climate of a nation of petty-bourgeois businesses which are being revolutionized by new technologies; the era of crematories is on us." With Bogdan Diklic, Danilo Stojkovic, Pavle Vujisic, Mija Aleksic, Mica Tomic and Jelisaveta Sablic. Serbo-Croatian with English subtitles.
VHS: S33028. $69.95.
Slobodan Sijan, Yugoslavia, 1982, 96 mins.

Melody Haunts My Reverie (You Only Love Once)
Voted as the third best Yugoslav film ever made, and an Official Selection at Cannes, this daring film is the story of an idealistic, young, partisan war hero who becomes a leader in the emerging socialist society of a small Croat village, and finds adjustment to the "new Yugoslavia" extremely difficult. He meets and falls in love with a middle-class ballerina, becomes involved with her bourgeois family and is eventually imprisoned. "A highly sensual romance...as passionate as it is politically catastrophic" (*L.A. Times*). Croatian with English subtitles.
VHS: S27797. $29.95.
Rajko Grlic, Yugoslavia, 1981, 103 mins.

Pretty Village, Pretty Flame
Based on an incident that happened in the first winter of the war in Bosnia in 1992, Srdjan Dragojevic's provocative and disturbing movie "unleashes a powerful assault on the insanity of the war" (*New York Times*). Two young boys, Halil, a Muslim, and Milan, a Serb, watch the inauguration of the new Brotherhood and Unity Tunnel in their neighborhood in 1980. Twelve years later, Halil and Milan are now on opposing sides, and Milan lies badly injured alongside wounded Serbs and Muslims in the same hospital as he recalls the events that brought him there. Serbo-Croatian with English subtitles.
VHS: S34229. $89.98.
Srdjan Dragojevic, Yugoslavia, 1996, 125 mins.

The Secret of Nikola Tesla
Nikola Tesla, one of the leading scientific geniuses of the 19th century, whose experiments with alternating current were crucial in the development of electronic technology, found himself locked in a battle with Thomas Edison, George Westinghouse and financier J.P. Morgan. The source of the conflict was Tesla's radical and visionary theories on wireless sources of energy—which intrigued Westinghouse, enraged the conservative Edison and then repelled the formidable Morgan. This film presents Tesla as a tortured, brilliant and complex man of sometimes maddening crochets and quirks (he claimed to be in communication with beings from outer space), as a drama of psychology and issues, and a mystery. This big-budget U.S.-Yugoslavian co-production stars Orson Welles as J.P. Morgan. In English.
VHS: S10800. $79.95.
Krsto Papic, Yugoslavia/USA, 1980, 120 mins.

Someone Else's America
Paskaljevic's tender, funny story of the failed American Dream stars Tom Conti (*Shirley Valentine*) as the Spanish immigrant Alonso, who lives with his blind mother above the dingy bar he owns in Brooklyn. His comic counterpart is Bayo (Miki Monojlovic), an illegal immigrant from Montenegro who toils away at odd jobs in pursuit of the American dream. A rich ensemble piece, it is a heartwarming tale of loss, displacement and, ultimately, the power of friendship. In English and Serbo-Croatian with English subtitles.
VHS: S31784. $89.95.
Goran Paskaljevic, France/Great Britain/Germany/Greece, 1996, 116 mins.

That Summer of White Roses
The very talented Yugoslav filmmaker Rajko Grlic directed this international production which stars Tom Conti, Susan George, Rod Steiger. The idyllic summer is disrupted by the arrival of the German Army, in a story of heroism forged by war and love.
VHS: S13030. $19.98.
Rajko Grlic, USA/Yugoslavia, 1989, 98 mins.

Tito and Me
A poignant comedy set in 1950's Belgrade, Zoran is the 10-year-old boy who adores Yugoslavia's leader Marshall Tito and Jasna, a 12-year-old orphan girl. When Jasna goes on a walking tour of Tito's homeland, Zoran follows with hilariously disastrous results. "A funny, beautifully acted family memoir...*Tito and Me* is the work of a sophisticated comic mind" (Vincent Canby, *The New York Times*). Serbo-Croatian with English subtitles.
VHS: S20425. $19.98.
Goran Markovic, Yugoslavia, 1992, 104 mins.

Vukovar
Filmed in 1933 in the bombed-out city of Vukovar, Yugoslavia, while the war was still raging, *Vukovar* is the award-winning story of two childhood friends—one Croat, the other Serb—who marry, only to be torn apart by a war which ravages their native Yugoslavia. A grim testament to the inexorable effects of war, *Vukovar* was recommended for a White House screening and blocked by the Croatian government from a United Nations screening. Serbo-Croatian with English subtitles.
VHS: S31628. $89.95.
Boro Draskovic, Yugoslavia, 1994, 95 mins.

Ward Six
One of the most powerful stories by Anton Chekhov receives a masterful film adaptation in the hands of Lucian Pintilie, one of the world's foremost directors for the stage as well as screen. The story, set at the turn of the century in a provincial Russian town, concerns a doctor who oversees a grotesque mental ward. The only person he meets with any comprehension of life is one of the inmates. The doctor is reported to the authorities by one of the inmates, is judged mad, and the story's two most humane and intelligent men are locked together in Ward No. 6. A subtle, powerful film based on one of the great literary works of Russian literature. Serbian with English subtitles.
VHS: S10009. $59.95.
Lucien Pintilie, Yugoslavia, 1976, 93 mins.

When I Close My Eyes

Political intrigue meets romantic obsession in this enigmatic thriller. When the rural post office where Ana works is robbed by a young biker, she takes advantage of the confusion after the robbery to steal some money for herself. Despite the suspicions of the police regarding her complicity in the crime, she develops a bizarre attraction to the criminal and becomes increasingly focused on tracking him down, unwittingly delving into a deeper mystery involving her father's death during her childhood. Slovenian with English subtitles.

VHS: S32203. $89.95.

Franci Slak, Yugoslavia, 1993, 94 mins.

Who's Singing Over There?

This subversive, inventive, humorous feature from the talented Slobodan Sijan is set on a bus of provincials who are making their way to Belgrade unaware that tragedy awaits them on April 6, 1941, when Nazi Germany will launch a savage attack on Belgrade. In this film, which helped define the "black cinema" of Yugoslavia, all the passengers are killed except for two gypsy singers who were previously abused and beaten by the passengers, and who, at the end, stand in the rubble singing of the things to come. With Pavle Vujisic, Dragan Nikolic, Aleksander Bercek and Neda Arneric. Serbo-Croatian with English subtitles.

VHS: S33027. $69.95.

Slobodan Sijan, Yugoslavia, 1980, 86 mins.

Yugoslavian Cinema

Contemporary filmmaking is discussed by Dejan Kosanovich and theater critic John Simon. Includes film clips from work by Markovic, Karaklajic, Babic and Papic. 1978, 60 mins.

VHS: S31582. $59.95.

DUSAN MAKAVEJEV

Coca-Cola Kid

Eric Roberts plays a marketing genius sent to boost the Coke company sales in backwoods Australia, only to see his corporate shell penetrated by the gorgeous and very sexy Greta Scacchi. Full of hilarious and memorable scenes, like the kangaroo with an arm in a sling, and a great sex scene full of feathers.

VHS: S00255. $29.98.

Dusan Makavejev, Australia, 1984, 94 mins.

Gorilla Bathes at Noon

An inventive, irreverent and at times touching feature set against the backdrop of post-wall Berlin, winner of the International Critics' Prize at the Berlin Film Festival. The film follows the goofball misadventures of one Russian soldier, stranded in Berlin after his army unit deserts, a kind of "post-Communist Candide" who concocts a fabulous myth that his father was the hero of the liberation of Berlin (brilliantly aided with kitsch archival footage) and is helped in his homesickness by a Siberian tiger at the zoo and a trans-gendered Lenin who knits him a sock, gives him a French kiss and asks him to remove a bullet from his head. English, German and Russian with English subtitles.

VHS: S34333. $59.95.

Dusan Makavejev, Germany/Yugoslavia, 1992, 81 mins.

Innocence Unprotected

In 1942 a professional strong man named Dragoljub Aleksic directed and starred in a trite little melodrama titled *Innocence Unprotected*—the first Serbian talkie. Over 20 years later, Dusan Makavejev retrieved the film from the Archives, tinted many of the sequences by hand, and interviewed Aleksic and his co-workers in present day Yugoslavia 1968. The resulting cinematic collage is a funny and daring (in both content and form) mix of a wide variety of film footage—including documentary, narrative, agitprop, and various other bits and pieces of found footage. Serbian with English subtitles.

VHS: S15487. $59.95.

Dusan Makavejev, Yugoslavia, 1968, 78 mins.

Love Affair: Or, the Case of the Missing Switchboard Operator

A key work of Eastern European cinema, *Love Affair* is a radical investigation of the relationship between sex and politics. The story of a young switchboard operator who falls in love with a sanitary worker until she allows herself to be seduced by a younger, more glamorous man. Told through a daring blend of flashbacks and flashforwards and a mix of documentary and fiction. Serbian with English subtitles.

VHS: S02653. $59.95.

Dusan Makavejev, Yugoslavia, 1967, 70 mins.

Man Is Not a Bird

Man Is Not a Bird is a work of genius which takes place in a mining town in eastern Serbia. The central characters are an engineer in one of the factories and a young hairdresser with whom he has an affair. The film "blends actuality with fiction in a manner so unselfconscious as to seem almost natural. Makavejev brings an instinctive poetry to the editing of the film, intercutting brilliantly Beethoven's *Ode to Joy* being performed inside the copper factory, and Jan and Raika making love together with a quiet, feverish urgency" (*International Film Guide*). Serbian with English subtitles.

VHS: S08265. $59.95.

Dusan Makavejev, Yugoslavia, 1966, 80 mins.

Montenegro

Funny, bizarre, surreal, sensual, unpredictable. Dusan Makavejev's *Montenegro* follows Susan Anspach, a middle-class Swedish housewife who gets embroiled in the free-wheeling sensuality of the Zanzi-Bar in the Yugoslavian-immigrant section of Stockholm in an attempt to discover the meaning of personal choice and freedom. English dialog.

VHS: S00875. $19.98.

Laser: Widescreen. **LD76052. $49.95.**

DVD: DV60287. $29.95.

Dusan Makavejev, Sweden/Great Britain, 1982, 79 mins.

A Night of Love

Alfred Molina, Eric Stoltz, Gabrielle Anwar and Camilla Soeberg star in Dusan Makavejev's inventive adaptation of a story by Emile Zola. Originally titled *Manifesto*, the film is full of gentle, erotic irony as a guard (Molina) must protect a king on a visit to his subjects in a small town. A number of revolutionaries will stop at nothing to get the king. Seduction, misguided faith and sheer incompetence combine to produce a wicked, sexy comedy.

VHS: S26402. $19.98.

Dusan Makavejev, Yugoslavia/USA, 1988, 97 mins.

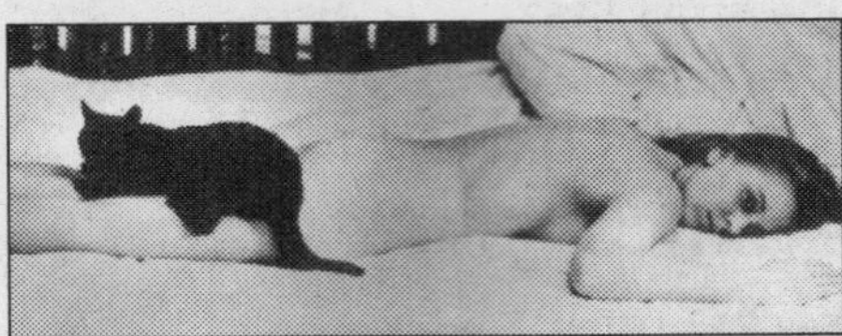

Sweet Movie

The modern cult classic, a hilarious comedy with elements of thriller and horror, "an experience to defy criticism…one of the most challenging, shocking and provocative films of recent years" (Roger Ebert). This daring and totally original film skillfully blends two independent stories with often shocking newsreel footage into a "movie we can't be passive about." The beautiful Carole Laure, winner of the Miss Virginity World contest, is married to Mr. Kapital, a Texas oil billionaire who, instead of consummating their marriage, sterilizes her body with rubbing alcohol. Barely escaping with her life, in Paris Carole has a sexual encounter with El Macho, a rock star at the Eiffel Tower, and ends up in a radical therapy commune. The second story features Anna Prucnal, survivor of The Revolution, now the captain of a boat floating the canals of Amsterdam, whose joyous sexual meeting with a sailor (Pierre Clementi) from the Battleship Potemkin ends up in his murder in a vat of sugar. Pure, unadulterated brilliance, "an audacious attempt…filled with images impossible to forget" (Roger Ebert). English and other languages with English subtitles.

VHS: S10575. $79.95.

Dusan Makavejev, Canada/France, 1975, 97 min.

WR: Mysteries of the Organism

Called "an outrageous, exuberant, marvelous work," by Amos Vogel in *Film Comment* and "a weird and hilarious fantasy…witty and exuberant" by *The New York Times, WR: Mysteries of the Organism* is a unique blend of fact and fiction, and Makavejev's landmark film. It deftly juxtaposes the story of the sexual encounter between the beautiful, liberated Milena and a repressed Soviet figure-skating champion with an exploration of the life and theories of psychoanalyst Wilhelm Reich. The "WR" in the film's title stands for either "Wilhelm Reich" or "World Revolution." Makavejev describes it as "a black comedy, political circus, a fantasy on the fascism and communism of human bodies, the political life of human genitals, a proclamation of the pornographic essence of any system of authority and power over others….If you watch for more than five minutes, you become my accomplice." With Dravic, Jagoda Kaloper, Tuli Kupferberg, Jackie Curtis. English and Serbian with English subtitles.

VHS: S11290. $79.95.

Dusan Makavejev, Yugoslavia/USA, 1971, 84 min.

EMIR KUSTURICA

Arizona Dream

Johnny Depp stars as a young drifter who meets a kindred spirit in Faye Dunaway and unexpectedly falls in love. Between their age differences and the reactions of their dysfunctional families, love is put on trial. Jerry Lewis is great as Depp's car dealership huckstering uncle.

VHS: S23859. $19.98.

Emir Kusturica, USA, 1994, 119 mins.

Do You Remember Dolly Bell?

Kusturica's beautifully modulated tale of a young man's entry into adulthood, his loss of virginity in the company of a B-movie stripper and prostitute. Set in the early 60s, Kusturica grafts the pathos of the Eastern European village movie into a complex tale of intrusive cultures, when Western influences such as fashion and rock and roll and the promise of European socialism threatened to roll over traditional customs, practiced rituals and Tito's political reign. With Slavo Stimac, Slobodan Aligrudic and Ljiljana Blagojevic. Serbo-Croatian with English subtitles.

VHS: S18457. $69.95.

Emir Kusturica, Yugoslavia, 1981, 106 mins.

Time of the Gypsies

A potent mix of comedy, drama and the supernatural, Kusturica's amazingly realistic drama set in the heart of the gypsy culture. Perhan, the hero, is telekinetic and is taken to Italy by the "sheik," where he gets a quick education in gypsy survival skills on the streets of Milan. Warm and affectionate, full of comic scenes, with a great gypsy music sound track. With Dvor Dujmovic and Bora Todorovic. Serbo-Croatian and Romany with English subtitles.

VHS: S12744. $19.95.

Emir Kusturica, Yugoslavia, 1990, 136 mins.

When Father Was Away on Business

Kusturica's Cannes-award winning film is a magical portrait of a boy's coming of age in 50's Yugoslavia. As little Malik takes up sleepwalking and experiences his first love, the family knows the real "business" Father is conducting—in a labor camp for his unrepentant Stalinist leanings and his philandering. Serbo-Croatian with English subtitles.

VHS: S15547. $19.98.

Laser: CAV. **LD72198. $49.95.**

Emir Kusturica, Yugoslavia, 1985, 144 mins.

ROMANIAN CINEMA

The Oak

While Romanian Communism collapses around her, a young woman, the defiant Nela, sets off into the desolate countryside. This apocalyptic road movie, acclaimed at the Cannes Film Festival, evokes a haunting world of extravagant dysfunction and edgy humor. Romanian with English subtitles.

VHS: S20869. $89.95.

Lucien Pintilie, Romania, 1992, 105 mins.

Stone Wedding

Stone Wedding is comprised of two short films based on stories by the classic Romanian writer Igor Agarciceanu, dealing with peasant life and traditions in the Carpathian mountains. Includes: *Fefeleaga* (directed by Mircea Veroiu) and *At a Wedding* (directed by Dan Pita). Romanian with English subtitles.

VHS: S14649. $29.95.

Mircea Veroiu/Dan Pita, Romania, 1972, 90 mins.

An Unforgettable Summer

An unconventional love story from Lucian Pintilie (*The Oak*), featuring a first-rate performance from Kristin Scott-Thomas (*Bitter Moon, Four Weddings and a Funeral*). A recently married army officer and his bride are sent to an army outpost in a backwoods area. The wife tries to establish a genteel, civilized presence there, but conflicts between the couple and both army personnel and the locals of the remote region cause her efforts to be in vain. French, Romanian and Bulgarian with English subtitles.

VHS: S27200. $89.95.

Lucian Pintilie, Romania, 1994, 82 mins.

BULGARIAN CINEMA

Canary Season

The true story of the "lost generation" (1960-1990) of Bulgaria. Angry and defiant upon his release from prison, young Malin confronts his mother, Lily, and violently forces her to reveal the truth of the horrors that she had hoped Malin would never know. Through a series of flashbacks we learn of the repression of the communist regime: rape, prostitution, torture, political murder and a psychiatric asylum. "A film of shattering power. Performances are outstanding" (*Variety*). Bulgarian with English subtitles.

VHS: S34874. $59.95.

Eugeny Mihaylov, Bulgaria, 1993, 133 mins.

The Countess

In this Bulgarian *Drugstore Cowboy*, a teenage girl's rebellion through drugs becomes a metaphor for the struggle between individuality and totalitarianism. Prize winner at the Turin, Angers, Troia and Varna Film Festivals, the film is "starkly beautiful and intensely perceptive" (*Philadelphia City Paper*). Bulgarian with English subtitles.

VHS: S26496. $59.95.

Peter Popzlatev, Bulgaria, 1989, 119 mins.

GREEK CINEMA

Aunt from Chicago

A wonderful, classic Greek comedy. Aunt Calliope is a naturalized American who returns to Greece to put her brother's house in order. Her four nieces are unmarried, and Aunt Calliope sets to fix it. She remodels their house, changes their clothes, struts them around in bikinis and snares everyone a husband-including herself. A wonderful performance from character actress Georgia Vassiliadou as the Aunt. Greek with English subtitles.

VHS: S26386. $29.95.

Alekos Salekarios, Greece, 1959, 72 mins.

Cannon and Nightingale

"Simple yet complicated, satiric yet poignant, Kambanellis' film is memorable, a milestone of the world cinema" *(Film Focus)*. The film, presented in three short segments, covers periods of the occupation of Greece by German, Italian and British forces. Greek with English subtitles.

VHS: S02665. $39.95.
Kambanellis, Greece, 1966, 90 mins.

Delicanis

Everyone expects a young man living in a village in Crete to become a priest, but he turns out to be the most popular lover on the island. Women of all types, including even his widowed aunt, fall prey to his charms until, shunned by his rural neighbors, he must wander alone from place to place. This comedy recalls old romance stories. Greek with English subtitles. Directed by Manolis Skouloudis.

VHS: S21180. $29.98.

The Enchantress

The first fairy tale from the new Greek cinema, winner of many international awards, a journey in the realm of myth, fear and human invincibility. A 17-year old youth, whom nature has endowed with daring and good looks, sets out from his village to find the Enchantress, a beautiful fairy feared by all. He journeys through an enchanted world inhabited by ghosts, spirits, imps and fairies. The world reveals to viewers, young and old, the power of myth, dreams, and enchantment. Greek with NO subtitles.

VHS: S11993. $59.95.
Manoussos Manoussakis, Greece, 1984, 93 mins.

End of the Game (South Wind)

An important film from the New Greek Cinema; three middle-aged couples, once the pillars of the anti-establishment, now live lives compromised to the lifestyle of the bourgeoisie; on a camping trip, their placidity is disturbed by a young nude girl who throws their complacency in turmoil. Greek with English subtitles.

VHS: S05607. $49.95.
Andreas Thomopoulos, Greece, 1984, 85 mins.

Get an Education, My Son

In this stark satire of contemporary Greek life, a teacher in the countryside must deal with the demands of his job, balancing the conservative educational format of the nation with the desires of his students and family. All this is set against the backdrop of the countryside, which is facing rapid depopulation. Greek with English subtitles. Directed by Thodoros Marangos.

VHS: S21175. $29.98.

Heavy Melon

The study of the development of dignity and consciousness of a young man who leaves his village in order to make his living in Athens. Greek with English subtitles. Greece, 1983, 92 mins.

VHS: S01549. $39.95.

Landscape in the Mist

Theo Angelopoulos' moving portrait of two sad-eyed children who traverse Greece in search of their father is a portrayal of loneliness, disillusionment and betrayal and the vision of a world that is both impersonal and unfeeling. The children's painful odyssey is fraught with terrifying figures, allegorical visions (a hand rising from the sea, a dead white horse outlined in the snow) and self-delusion. With Michalis Zeke, Tania Palaiologou, Eva Kotamanidou and Alika Georgouli. Greek with English subtitles.

VHS: S19542. $59.95.
Theo Angelopoulos, Greece/France/Italy, 1988, 125 mins.

Lysistrata

Aristophanes' ancient Greek play is brought to life in this new adaptation starring Jenny Karezi and Costas Kazakos. Lysistrata is the Athenian woman disgusted by the way men have ruined the country with their endless war. Rallying other women, she proposes that they impose an embargo on sexual relations with men as long as the war lasts. The film liberates the action from the stage, places it on location in the acropolis, and renders Aristophanes' plea in a forceful manner. Contains nudity and strong language. Greek with English subtitles.

VHS: S11718. $39.95.
Yiannis Negrepontis, Greece, 1987, 97 mins.

Man with the Red Carnation

A film which broke all box office records in Greece upon its release, *Man with...* is a political drama set in the period after the Civil War. It follows the life of Nikos Beloyannis, a fighter in the guerilla underground. With music composed by Mikis Theodorakis. Greek with English subtitles.

VHS: S02666. $39.95.
Nikos Tzimas, Greece, 1982, 110 mins.

Marching On to Glory

Modern Greek mass culture is skewered in this satiric look at the rise of a popular singing star. Though born in a small village, the hero moves to Athens, where fame awaits him. Despite his success this is not an edifying tale, but a cautionary one. Greek with English subtitles.

VHS: S21177. $29.98.

Parangelia

This old tradition stipulates that only those men who have requested a special song can dance as the tune plays. When an underworld figure is interrupted by three policemen during such a dance, he sets out for revenge, acting out all his anger and frustration built up during a lifetime of repression. Greek with English subtitles.

VHS: S21176. $29.98.
Pavlos Tasios, Greece, 1980, 95 mins.

Path of God

The story of a disillusioned young woman who seeks comfort by entering a convent only to find the same exploitation inside the convent as in the outside world. A thriller that involves adultery, false accusations and murder. Greek with English subtitles. Greece, 1984, 88 mins.

VHS: S01548. $39.95.

Red Lanterns

Just before the law closes down a house of prostitution, a number of dramas unfold. Chief among these is the developing romance between a sailor and a prostitute who wants to begin a new life far from the waterfront. Jenny Karezi stars. Greek with English subtitles.

VHS: S23902. $29.95.
Vassilis Georgiadis, Greece, 1963, 85 mins.

Rembetiko

Rembetiko music is a form of Greek urban blues. *Rembetiko*, winner of the Silver Bear at the Berlin Film Festival, is the story of modern Greece as seen through that music. A highly evocative film which is at once biographical and political. The film's sound is as rich as its color and its characters. Greek with English subtitles.

VHS: S02698. $39.95.
Costas Ferris, Greece, 1983, 101 mins.

Special Request

Based on the true story of Koemtzis, a marginal underworld figure who refused to cooperate with the police during the years of the Junta, and killed two policemen who insulted his brother. He became somewhat of a folk hero while on the run for resisting the dictatorship. "The images, the movement, the poetry all stay with you" (Liberation, Paris). Greek with English subtitles.

VHS: S02667. $39.95.
Pavlos Tassios, Greece, 1980, 96 mins.

Ulysses' Gaze

Theo Angelopoulos' triumphantly haunting Cannes Film Festival Jury Prize-winning film tracing the journey of Greek-American director "Mr. A" (Harvey Keitel) across the Balkans in search of several lost reels of film. Along the way, he has several passionate encounters with various women who have been, or may have been, part of his life. Filled with stunning imagery, the film travels through war-torn Balkans giving a compelling eyewitness account. With Erland Josephson. English and Greek with English subtitles.

VHS: S31800. $29.98.
Theo Angelopoulos, Greece, 1997, 173 mins.

When the Greeks

At the turn of the century a young man from a wealthy family is abducted by a group of bandits intent on a hefty ransom. Succeeding in their plan, they must now confront their role in the emerging bourgeois society that contradicts their traditional ways. Greek with English subtitles.

VHS: S21179. $29.98.
Lakis Papastathis, Greece, 1981, 100 mins.

With Glittering Eyes

This is the story of a mass execution in Greece during the Second World War. An old man must decide which of his three sons will survive. It's a tribute to the traditional family and the values of humanism which have always helped the Greek people survive foreign conquerors. Greek with English subtitles.

VHS: S21178. $29.98.
Panos Glikofridis, Greece

MICHAEL CACOYANNIS

Attila 74

Acclaimed as an "extraordinary and devastatingly powerful film," *Attila 74* confronts the real-life tragedy of the Turkish invasion of Cyprus in 1974. The film "is history in the making. Remarkably, Cacoyannis manages to sustain at once a passionate engagement and a wide historical view—perhaps because he is seeing events always in terms of people" *(Times of London)*. The film, wrote the *L.A. Times*, "is at once a deeply personal record and a formal work of art with a structure and a tragic sense of the inevitable, worthy of Euripides." Greekwith English subtitles.

VHS: S09196. $59.95.
Michael Cacoyannis, Greece/Cyprus, 1974, 103 mins.

The Girl in Black

The Girl in Black "reveals Elli Lambetti as an actress of truly tragic stature." The story of a young Athenian writer on holiday who falls in love with a girl of impoverished gentility and is unable to respond to her. A disaster provoked by spiteful peasants shocks him into a new awareness of his own involvement in life. "The film has a simplicity and a vibrancy that make it stand out from even the best of foreign films. We experience the emotions and temperament of a new film artist who is trying to find his own way," wrote Pauline Kael. Greek with English subtitles.

VHS: S09550. $59.95.
Michael Cacoyannis, Greece, 1956, 104 mins.

A Matter of Dignity

Cacoyannis creates a cynical portrait of Greek upper class life. A wealthy family is on the verge of bankruptcy, and driven by the paranoid and superficial mother, struggle to maintain a facade of security at the cost of strong family bonds. An exceptional drama that is beautifully acted and typical of Cacoyannis' masterful direction. With Ellie Lambetti, George Pappas and Athena Michaelidou. Greek with English subtitles.

VHS: S12511. $59.95.
Michael Cacoyannis, Greece, 1957, 104 mins.

Stella

Melina Mercouri, in her debut film role as a bouzouki singer and dancer who abhors marriage, defies the rules of conventional morality and pays for a freedom denied her by the men who love her, in Michael Cacoyannis' second film. "Melina Mercouri [is] beautifully controlled... There is a pervasive sense of atmosphere that allows the characters to become an organic part of the streets and the houses used for location (the scene with Stella triumphantly riding an open truck to show the neighbors her lover's gift is among the funniest and best observed) and the folklore material (chiefly bouzouki dances and music by Manos Hatzidakis) is dexterously used to enliven the plot" *(International Film Guide)*. Greek with English subtitles.

VHS: S09551. $59.95.
Laser: LD71341. $29.99.
Michael Cacoyannis, Greece, 1957, 95 mins.

Zorba the Greek

Anthony Quinn is Zorba, a crude, sly, lusty lover of life who passes on his passionate philosophy to a young, inexperienced writer (Alan Bates). Based on the novel by Nikos Kazantzakis, music by Mikis Theodorakis. With Irene Papas and Lila Kedrova.

VHS: S01606. $19.98.
Michael Cacoyannis, Greece, 1964, 142 mins.

COSTA-GAVRAS

Betrayed

Greek director Costa-Gavras investigates white hate groups in America in this controversial drama. Debra Winger stars as a novice FBI undercover agent sent to locate and identify rural political unrest in the heartland. She finds there are two sides to the widower father played by Tom Berenger and both are heavily armed. With John Heard and John Mahoney.

VHS: S09919. $19.98.
Costa-Gavras, USA, 1988

Conseil de Famille

Costa-Gavras' *(Z, Mad City, Missing)* turns his attention to comedy in this story of a safe-cracking family who enjoy all the trappings of middle-class success through their sophisticated and dangerous crimes. With French rock star Johnny Hallyday and Fanny Ardant. French with English subtitles.

VHS: S34416. $29.95.
Costa-Gavras, France, 1986, 111 mins.

Costa-Gavras Talks with Marcel Ophuls: Political Films

Two internationally known directors who have made a specialty of films with an outspoken political edge discuss the values and methods in the genre, and the problems they have faced. Costa-Gavras *(Z)* and Ophuls *(The Sorrow and The Pity)* address such themes as the difference between "objective" and "subjective" truth and their personal motives for choosing this form of film art. 1976, 28 mins.

VHS: S31568. $59.95.

Hanna K.

Costa-Gavras' controversial film shot in Israel, starring Jill Clayburgh as the Israeli attorney who takes on the case of a Palestinian accused of terrorism and gets involved in the personal and political struggle between her and her lover, the district attorney. English dialog.

VHS: S00538. $59.95.
Costa-Gavras, France/USA, 1983, 111 mins.

Mad City

Costa-Gavras, in his first movie in six years, skewers TV news in this handsomely mounted anecdote starring Dustin Hoffman as a small-town California local TV reporter trying to make it back to a network. When he stumbles upon a recently fired museum security guard (John Travolta), a shotgun and a bag of dynamite, he blows the incident up into a TV event.

VHS: S33394. $103.99.
DVD: DV60200. $24.98.
Costa-Gavras, USA, 1997, 115 mins.

Missing

Jack Lemmon, Sissy Spacek and John Shea star in Costa-Gavras' political thriller based on the true story of Charles Horman, an American writer who disappears and is killed during the overthrow of Allende's government in Chile. Lemmon is the concerned father whose attempts to learn the truth are stonewalled by bureaucracy and cover-up. English dialog.

VHS: S00862. $24.95.
Costa-Gavras, USA, 1983, 122 mins.

Music Box

Winner of the Golden Bear at the Berlin Film Festival, Costa-Gavras' political thriller stars Jessica Lange as a Chicago attorney defending a Hungarian immigrant (Armin Mueller-Stahl) accused of heinous war crimes more than 50 years ago.

VHS: S12213. $19.95.
Costa-Gavras, USA, 1989, 126 mins.

Z

Academy Award-winning film follows the routine investigation of a seemingly accidental death of a Greek pacifist leader which eventually uncovers a web of violence and terrorist tactics which implicates an entire government in its secret conspiracy to murder an honest man. Dubbed in English.

VHS: S01496. $29.98.
Laser: LD71226. $69.95.
Costa-Gavras, France, 1969, 128 mins.

TURKISH CINEMA

Baba—The Father

Yilmaz Guney *(Yol)* directed this important Turkish film about a desperately poor boatman who agrees to frame himself for a murder in return for the support of his family. But after 24 years at hard labor, he discovers that his sacrifice has been in vain; his daughter has become a prostitute and his son is one of the murderer's henchmen. A powerfully tragic film. Turkishwith English subtitles.

VHS: S15389. $39.95.
Yilmaz Guney, Turkey, 1973, 95 mins.

The Horse

Winner of the prize at the first Tokyo Film Festival, this is an intimate, realistic drama about a father and son confronting the hardships of life in modern Turkey against their own inadequacies, told in lyrical, tragic and compelling fashion reminiscent of *The Bicycle Thief.* Turkish with English subtitles.

VHS: S04734. $69.95.
Ali Ozgenturk, Turkey, 1982, 116 mins.

The Wall

The final film from the director of *Yol*, a harsh but sensitive recreation of the 1976 uprising of the destitute and mistreated children in Turkey's central prison in Ankara. Turkish with English subtitles.

VHS: S04733. $69.95.
Yilmaz Guney, Turkey, 1983, 117 mins.

Yol

Winner at the Cannes Film Festival, a powerful film about five Kurdish prisoners given a week's leave to visit their villages; *Yol* is based on personal experiences of the filmmaker, and is a film about political, religious and sexual oppression. Turkish with English subtitles.

VHS: S01490. $19.95.
Yilmaz Guney, Turkey, 1983, 115 mins.

IRANIAN CINEMA

Bashu, The Little Stranger

Ten-year-old Bashu (Adnan Afravian) is orphaned when his Persian Gulf village is bombed. Hiding in the back of a truck, he is taken north around the Caspian Sea, where he jumps off. The people in this alien land take a dislike to the little stranger and deride his skin and accent. Nai (Susan Taslimi), a woman whose husband is away, finds the boy and accepts him as her own son. "A pure joy in which there are absolutely no false moves" (Kevin Thomas, *Los Angeles Times*). Farsi with English subtitles.

VHS: S33022. $69.95.
Bahram Beyzai, Iran, 1990, 120 mins.

The Cyclist

A visually sophisticated film which deals with the themes of man's exploitation of man and the inequities between rich and poor. The cyclist is Nassim, an Afghan refugee in need of money to pay his wife's medical expenses. With work difficult to come by, a sleazy promoter suggests he undertake a bicycle marathon. Touting him as the Afghani superman, the huckster wagers that Nassim will circle a small area on the outskirts of town, day and night, for a week. Gamblers, bookies and food vendors gather to watch the desperate cyclist from the sidelines, turning his suffering to their own profit. Winner of the Best Film at the Riminicinema Film Festival. Farsi with English subtitles.

VHS: S27790. $29.95.
Mohsen Makhmalbaf, Iran, 1989, 75 mins.

Hamoon

Darioush Mehrjui's bold *Hamoon* not only made it past that country's censors, it was widely shown in Teheran and emerged as one of the year's most popular films, winning six Iranian film awards. A well-to-do Teheran painter (Bita Farrahi), suffering from the seven-year-itch, has an affair with a patron and tells her Western-educated psychiatrist that she wants a divorce and complains bitterly about the Iranian government's treatment of women. Her despondent philosopher husband (Khosro Shakibai), accused of beating his wife, has a breakdown and seeks comfort from his grandmother, and both agree that religion is a fraud. Farsi with English subtitles.

VHS: S33024. $69.95.
Darioush Mehrjui, Iran, 1989, 107 mins.

The Key

Humor, pathos and suspense fill this story of a four-year-old and an infant left home alone while their mother runs out to do some shopping. Young Amir Mohammad has his own ideas about what he wants to do—and watching his baby brother and the meal cooking in the kitchen are not among them. Minor crisis piles on crisis, culminating in the threat of disaster when the cooking pot boils over, dousing the flame on the gas range. As frantic neighbors yell advice to the resourceful youngster, tension mounts. Winner of the award for Best Children's Film at the Berlin Film Festival. Screenplay by Abbas Kiarostami. Farsi with English subtitles.

VHS: S27789. $29.95.
Ebrahim Forouzesh, Iran, 1986, 76 mins.

The Last Act

This highly acclaimed, award-winning debut feature from Karim-Masihi is an atmospheric mystery which unfolds as a play within a play. The action takes place in '30s Tehran, where a sinister brother and sister plot to dispose of their recently widowed sister-in-law in order to obtain her inheritance. They hire a troupe of itinerant performers to pose as servants and stage horrific events. The terrified widow calls on the police for help, but the investigator assigned to the case becomes convinced she is crazy because "evidence" of each "crime" disappears before authorities arrive on the scene. Farsi with English subtitles.

VHS: S35305. $29.95.
Varuzh Karim-Masihi, Iran, 1991, 110 mins.

The Legend of a Sigh

This strikingly feminist film draws on a legend of Azarbayejan province. Ah is a handsome young man who materializes to succor those in need whenever he hears a heartfelt sigh. Milani's protagonist is a woman novelist, suffering from writer's block, who, with the help of Ah, experiences the lives of four women from different social strata. From a wealthy Tehrani who feels unfulfilled by her life, to a poor servant, to a Turkman wife unable to leave the house without her husband's permission, to a rebellious student, the film offers a fascinating portrait of a range of Iranian women and their problems. Farsi with English subtitles.

VHS: S35308. $29.95.
Tahmineh Milani, Iran, 1991, 105 mins.

Life and Nothing More

The film investigates the aftermath of a devastating 1990 earthquake which killed some 50,000 people in northern Iran. This region provided the setting for Kiarostami's *Where Is the Friend's Home.* Kiarostami's search for the two young actors who played central roles in that film becomes the dramatic source of *Life and Nothing More*...as a father and son travel to Quoker, the hometown of the two boys, and along the way meet earthquake survivors who desperately and valiantly work to reconstruct their lives. "...in many ways the most beautiful and powerful Iranian film I've seen" (Jonathan Rosenbaum, *Chicago Reader*). Farsi with English subtitles.

VHS: S27792. $29.95.
Abbas Kiarostami, Iran, 1992, 91 mins.

Nargess

A sharp-edged look at people who live outside the constraints of Islamic law. In her fourth feature, director Rakhshan Bani-etemad tells the tragic story of a love triangle. Afagh, an aging thief who has lost her beauty, is on the verge of losing her young lover, Adel. When Adel meets the beautiful Nargess, he decides to go straight, but honest work does not come by easily, and he decides to go back to the old life for "one last job." "Bani-etemad pushes the Iranian censorship code to the limit, managing to make her outsider characters believable and moving" (Deborah Young, *Variety*). Farsi with English subtitles.

VHS: S35303. $29.95.
Rakhshan Bani-eternad, Iran, 1992, 100 mins.

The Need

"One of those rare works in which the perfect rendering of simple elements produces a small, unforgettable masterpiece. The film's two main characters are boys poised between childhood and manhood. Both are poor. The boy through whose eyes we experience the drama has lost his father in the war and seems to have only the bleakest of prospects, until a relative finds him a choice apprentice's position in a print shop. But there is a catch; another boy coveting the spot has also been taken on, with the better of the two getting the permanent job after a trial period. Thus begins a fierce if somewhat covert rivalry that results in workplace sabotage, fighting and then, very surprisingly, friendship" (Godfrey Cheshire, *Film Comment*). Farsi with English subtitles.

VHS: S27788. $29.95.
Alireza Davudneshad, Iran, 1991, 81 mins.

New Films from Iran

Includes *The Peddler* (Mohsen Makhmalbaf, 1986, 95 mins.), *Where Is the Friend's Home?* (Abbas Kiarostami, 1989, 90 mins.), *The Key* (Ebrahim Forouzesh, 1986, 76 mins.), *The Need* (Alireza Davudneshad, 1991, 81 mins.), *Life and Nothing More* (Abbas Kiarostami, 1992, 91 mins.) and *The Cyclist* (Mohsen Makhmalbaf, 1989, 75 mins.). Farsi with English subtitles.

VHS: S27786. $149.95.

Once Upon a Time, Cinema

A wonderful, fairy tale-like comedy set during the Qajar dynasty, which is a condensed history of Iranian cinema and a love letter to the cinema in general, by the talented and controversial Mohsen Makhmalbaf *(The Peddler, Gabbeh)*. The film tells the story of a Charlie Chaplin-like cinematographer who introduces the magic of movies to the Persian court. The Shah has 84 wives and 200 children, but after a screening he falls desperately in love with the film's heroine. Farsi with English subtitles.

VHS: S35304. $29.95.
Mohsen Makhmalbaf, Iran, 1992, 100 mins.

The Peddler

Shockingly forthright in its view of the social and economic problems of the post-Shah era, *The Peddler* uses a different cameraman and different style for each of three short tales set among the poor of contemporary Tehran. The first episode follows a kindly but naive couple who want someone to adopt their newborn daughter. The second, an astonishing mix of absurdist comedy and the supernatural, concerns a mentally unstable man who lives with his mother in a ramshackle apartment. The final section draws on the American gangster film to show the last hours of a peddler suspected of betraying his friends. Farsi with English subtitles.

VHS: S27787. $29.95.
Mohsen Makhmalbaf, Iran, 1986, 95 mins.

Prince Ehtejab

Based on the classic novel by Houshang Golshiri about the Quajar dynasty, which ruled Persia from 1795-1925, Farmanara's film is "as beautiful as it is tragic" (Kevin Thomas, *Los Angeles Times*). Dying of hereditary tuberculosis, Prince Ehtejab (Jamshid Mashayekhi) shuts himself up in his palace, where he is assailed by the memories and guilt of his family's cruel deeds. Members of his household cannot understand why he lacks the brutality of his ancestors. Then he is visited by the ghost of his father and grandfather, who chide him for not continuing their despotic dynasty. With Fakhri Khorvash. Grand Prix winner, Teheran International Film Festival. Farsi with English subtitles.

VHS: S33026. $69.95.
Bahman Farmanara, Iran, 1974, 93 mins.

The Runner

In this semi-autobiographical coming-of-age story, withdrawn from circulation by Iranian authorities after a short run, Amiro (Majid Mirumand), an illiterate 13-year-old boy, lives alone in a beached ship outside a port city and earns a living selling ice water and shining shoes in a sailors' cafe. The hyperactive and inquisitive boy dreams of journeys and victories, yelling at ships or planes as they pass. His thirst for knowledge is quenched when he attends an evening school, and he attains victory running races with his peers. "An eloquent statement about desire, struggle, and the need for relief" (Georgia Brown, *The Village Voice*). Farsi with English subtitles.
VHS: S33025. $69.95.
Amir Naderi, Iran, 1984, 94 mins.

The Sealed Soil (Khak-e Sar Beh Morh)

The first Iranian feature by a woman, Marva Nabili's brave film focuses on a young woman who is confronted with change in pre-revolutionary Iran. She rejects a number of suitors, inviting the displeasure of her family. Soon the rigid orthodoxies of fundamentalist Islamic life prove too much for her and she faces extreme measures (including an exorcism). This film began shooting just before the revolution and had to be smuggled out for completion and distribution. Farsi with English subtitles.
VHS: S26348. $29.95.
Marva Nabili, Iran/USA, 1977, 90 mins.

The Tenants

In this "bracing social-satire-cum-slapstick-comedy from Iran" *(Motion Picture Guide)*, the landlord of a new apartment building in a suburb of Tehran dies, leaving the ownership of the building up for grabs under Iran's "heir-uncertain" law. The apartment manager transfers the title of the building to his name and tries to evacuate the tenants, but they won't budge. The manager then refuses to make any repairs on the building. When the tenants take the matter into their own hands, their world literally comes crashing down on them. "A fresh breeze from Iran" (Kevin Thomas, *Los Angeles Times*). Farsi with English subtitles.
VHS: S33023. $69.95.
Darioush Mehrjui, Iran, 1991, 110 mins.

Travellers

A daring mix of the traditional Iranian passion play and an experimental narrative style, *Travellers* is the story of a wedding ceremony which turns into a funeral wake when the bride's sister and her entire family are killed in a traffic accident. The film, from director Bahram Beyzai, one of the most talented auteurs of Iranian cinema, is "a brilliant exposition of the themes of death and predestination…[it] incorporates most of Beyzai's stylistic and thematic preoccupations—the alienated identity, theatrical setups, camerawork, sound effects, music, multiplicity of characters, time lapses, etc.—all brought together and unified into a homogeneous whole by the director's unfailing overall control" *(International Film Guide)*. Farsi with English subtitles.
VHS: S35307. $29.95.
Bahram Beyzai, Iran, 1992, 90 mins.

Where Is the Friend's Home?

A lyrical tale about a traveller searching for his friend's home, who finds himself on an excursion through places and moments of great beauty and wonder. The friends are the schoolmates Ahmad and Mohammad Reza. Mohammad Reza's careless attitude towards his homework has drawn several reprimands from their stern teacher, culminating in the threat of expulsion if he does not do his work. When Ahmad prepares to do his own homework, he finds that he has accidentally picked up Mohammad Reza's notebook. Fearing that his friend will be expelled if he cannot submit his lesson the next day, Ahmad defies his parents and sets out to find his friend's home in the neighboring village. Winner of the Bronze Leopard at the Locarno Film Festival. Farsi with English subtitles.
VHS: S27791. $29.95.
Abbas Kiarostami, Iran, 1989, 90 mins.

White Balloon

Winner of the Camera d'Or and co-winner of the International Critic's Prize at the 1995 Cannes Film Festival, this Iranian breakthrough feature tells the story of a young girl's desire for a pretty goldfish to start her New Year's holiday. Snake charmers, a distracted dry cleaner tailor, a lonely and talkative soldier and other assorted adults get in the way of her goal. With a script by Abbas Kiarostami *(Life and Nothing But…)*. "A miracle! Profound!" (Lloyd Sachs, *Chicago Sun-Times*). Farsi with English subtitles.
VHS: S30428. $99.95.
Laser: LD76061. $39.98.
Jafar Panahi, Iran, 1996, 85 mins.

Zinat

A riveting drama about the attempts of Zinat, who runs a health clinic in a remote part of Southern Iran, to break free of the male-dominated rules and regulations that govern life in rural Iran. Though her expertise and hard work make her invaluable to her conservative community, when Zinat becomes engaged to Hamed, his disagreeable mother demands that she quit her job. Zinat tries to be a satisfied wife and daughter-in-law, but when a medical emergency develops in the village, she is forced to choose between her duty to her family and her commitment as a health care provider. "The feminist message is universal" *(Variety)*. Farsi with English subtitles.
VHS: S35306. $29.95.
Ebrahim Mokhtari, Iran, 1994, 88 mins.

ISRAELI CINEMA

The 81st Blow

An historical document made up of footage and stills shot by the Nazis. A compilation of testimony from witnesses who appeared at the Eichmann trial provides a telling narrative. The film's title refers to the story of a Jewish boy in one of the ghettoes, who was struck with 80 blows. He survived and immigrated to Israel, where he found that no one believed his story—which for him was the 81st blow. Academy Award nominee.
VHS: S06570. $79.95.
Jacquot Ehrlich/David Bergman/Haim Gouri, Israel, 1974, 115 mins.

Amazing Grace

A dramatic story is told in this film about the friendship between 18-year-old Jonathon and 30-year-old Thomas. Jonathon places all his hope for happiness in Thomas, who is HIV positive. Winner of the Wolgin Prize at the 1992 Jerusalem Film Festival and Best Film at Turin's Eighth International Gay-Themed Film Festival. Hebrew with English subtitles.
VHS: S22671. $79.95.
Amos Guttman, Israel, 1992, 95 mins.

Atalia

The powerful story, set on kibbutz, of the love between an older woman and a young man. Atalia is a war widow, whose defiant life style is in contradiction to the conventions of kibbutz life. She has become the true outsider, alienated yet psychologically tied to the world of her past, a world she seems unable to leave. Hebrew with English subtitles.
VHS: S15402. $79.95.
Akiva Tevet, Israel, 1985, 90 mins.

Auditions

A provocative portrait of young actors and the struggles behind their success. A passionate and powerful drama about the action beyond the bright lights. Hebrew with English subtitles.
VHS: S34244. $59.95.
Ron Ninio, Israel, 1995, 92 mins.

The Battle of the Chairmanship

They're the kings of the co-op who rule their buildings with an iron hand, and they won't give up their territory without a fight. They're small-time politicians with big egos and when they're up for re-election, anything goes, and it's non-stop comedy every step of the way. Hebrew with English subtitles.
VHS: S34526. $59.95.
Avi Cohen, Israel, 1981, 90 mins.

Because of That War

An extraordinary look at what happens when two of Israel's leading rock musicians, both the children of Holocaust survivors, decide to confront their disturbing past. Exploring the different realities of two generations, haunted by the same horrifying legacy, the film is a stirring tribute to the human spirit, filled with the power and passion of the events that inspired it. Berlin and Leningrad Film Festival winner; voted Israel's best film. "Original, sensitive and beautiful" (Elie Weisel). Hebrew with English subtitles.
VHS: S32020. $89.95.
Orna Ben-Dor Niv, Israel, 1989, 90 mins.

Beyond the Walls

Israel's nominee for Best Foreign Film of 1984 is set within the confines of an overcrowded Israeli prison where hatreds and conflicting ideologies come into sharp focus. When a prison official kills a Jew and blames the Arabs the stage is set. Hebrew with English subtitles.
VHS: S00127. $79.95.
Uri Barabash, Israel, 1984, 103 mins.

But Where Is Daniel Wax?

After years of separation, two men, a doctor and a singer return to Israel and meet at a high school reunion. Both men fantasize about their youth and the admiration they held for the class hero, Daniel Wax. A telling commentary on Israeli society, a Jewish version of *The Big Chill*. Hebrew with English subtitles.
VHS: S12888. $79.95.
Avram Heffner, Israel, 1974, 95 mins.

Crossfire

Based on a true story of war and death and love and passion, Miriam, a beautiful Jewish girl from Tel Aviv, and George, a sophisticated Arab from neighboring Jaffa, meet by chance and fall in love in 1948 Palestine. As Jews and Arabs are busy preparing for the inevitable war to come, the young couple, overwhelmed by their emotions, defy family and friends and secretly carry on their romance, and decide to flee the war-torn land. Hebrew with English subtitles.
VHS: S30529. $59.95.
Gideon Ganani, Israel, 1989, 90 mins.

Cup Final

A political film suffused with humor and wit about an Israeli soldier detained by PLO guerrillas and his shifting relationship with the group's leader, both of whom carry an obsession for the Italian national soccer club. "An uncommon delicacy and wit that's bolstered by the powerful ensemble acting. Like Fuller, Coppola and Kubrick, Eran Riklis brings home the surrealism of war" *(The Village Voice)*. Hebrew with English subtitles.
VHS: S18753. $59.95.
Eran Riklis, Israel, 1992, 107 mins.

Drifting

Controversial Israeli film called "The best gay film ever made," winner of Israeli Oscars for Best Director, Best Actor and Best Cinematography. Hebrew with English subtitles.
VHS: S00376. $69.95.
Amos Guttman, Israel, 1982, 80 mins.

Eagles Attack at Dawn

Rick Jason, Peter Brown and Joseph Shiloal star in this tale of revenge and violence set in the Middle East. An Israeli soldier returns to the prison where he was tortured in order to destroy the sadistic commander of this terrifying place.
VHS: S23889. $29.95.
Menahem Golan, Israel, 1974, 93 mins.

Fictitious Marriage

A high school teacher experiences mid-life crisis when he unexpectedly turns up in Tel Aviv and is mistaken for an Arab laborer. With Shlomo Bar-Aba, Irit Sheleg and Ofra Veingarten. "A human candid camera, an inside look at Israel" *(Hadashot)*. Hebrew with English subtitles.
VHS: S17938. $79.95.
Haim Buzaglo, Israel, 1988, 90 mins.

Going Steady

This Israeli version of *American Graffiti* is a story of teenage love, set to the beat of '50s rock and roll. With Yiftach Katzur, Yvonne Michaels, Zacki Noy, Rachel Steiner, Jonathan Segal and Daphna Armoni. In English.
VHS: S35242. $19.95.
Boaz Davidson, Israel, 1980, 88 mins.

Hamsin (Eastern Wind)

One of the most highly acclaimed and controversial Israeli films, Daniel Wachsmann's drama focuses on a Jewish landowner and his Arab worker. As the two work to build a ranch in Galilee, tensions flair up over the imminent confiscation of Arab lands, and the "hamsin" (the hot wind of the desert) sends tensions soaring to explosive heights. A powerful contemporary drama. With Shlomo Tarshish and Yasin Shawap. Hebrew with English subtitles.
VHS: S11496. $79.95.
Daniel Wachsmann, Israel, 1983, 90 mins.

The Heritage (Ha-Yerusha)

A modern romance is intertwined with a 500-year-old history between a Christian soldier and a young Jewish girl during the Spanish Inquisition. A spellbinding drama, filmed on location in Israel and Spain. Winner of three Israeli Academy Awards. Hebrew with English subtitles.
VHS: S34245. $59.95.
Amnon Rubinstein, Israel, 1993, 89 mins.

Hide and Seek

Now considered a classic of the modern Israeli cinema, this sensitive study of adolescents in the crisis of self-discovery explores the sensitive issue of forbidden love. Can individuals work out their own fate in direct contradiction to a society where only conformity is accepted? Hebrew with English subtitles.
VHS: S06565. $79.95.
Dan Wolman, Israel,.1980, 90 mins.

Hill 24 Doesn't Answer

Four young Zionists are assigned to defend strategic Hill 24 outside Jerusalem, in order to maintain access to the besieged city. Through the diverse personal stories of the defenders, we gain a critical perspective on the birth of Israel and those who risked their lives to insure the State's survival. "The first major success of the young Israeli cinema is superbly directed" (Georges Sadoul). In English.
VHS: S06566. $79.95.
Thorold Dickinson, Israel, 1955, 101 mins.

House on Chelouche Street

Life in Tel Aviv during the period of British rule is told in terms of the maturing of a young man, Sami, the eldest son of a young widow. The film has an authentic flavor that captures the vigor of the new emerging country. Hebrew with English subtitles.
VHS: S00587. $39.95.
Moshe Mizrahi, Israel, 1973, 111 mins.

I Love You Rosa

Jerusalem: 1887. Rosa is a widow at 20, forced to work in a bath house and sew to earn a living. Her husband's only brother is 11-year-old Nessim. The local law demands that a widow marry her late husband's brother, but it will be seven long years before Nessim is a man. Rosa is left to decide whether she will wait or break with tradition and marry a local man instead. An insightful look at the clash of values, feminism, wisdom and tradition. The ending will likely please some and anger others. Nominated for a Best Foreign Film Academy Award in 1973. Dubbed in English.

VHS: S13381. $59.95.

Moshe Mizrahi, Israel, 1973, 90 mins.

Intimate Story

A powerful Israeli drama set on a kibbutz, where Leah and Yaacov are a childless couple failing at childbirth for a second time. Each blames the other for the failure, and the film becomes a powerful metaphor for Israeli society as the supportive atmosphere of the kibbutz is contrasted with its closed community and lack of privacy. Hebrew with English subtitles. With Chava Alberstein and Alex Peleg.

VHS: S11497. $79.95.

Israeli Nadav Levitan, Israel, 1981, 95 mins.

Kazablan

Israel's own *West Side Story* broke all box office records. Starring Yehoram Gaon as the bad boy hero with a heart of gold, and over 1,000 actors, dancers and singers. Hebrew with English subtitles.

VHS: S34524. $59.95.

Menahem Golan, Israel, 1974, 123 mins.

Kuni Lemel in Tel Aviv

A contemporary realization of the story of Kuni Lemel (Mike Burstyn), the Jewish folk hero of the shtetl, about a grandfather's offer to pay his twin grandsons $5 million to marry and return to Israel. The young men are polar opposites, one shy and virtuous, the other outgoing and in love with a shiksa. With Mandy Rice-Davies. Hebrew with English subtitles.

VHS: S17939. $79.95.

Yoel Silberg, Israel, 1977, 90 mins.

Late Summer Blues

A powerful, controversial film from Israel. Drawing on autobiographical details, *Late Summer Blues* looks at a group of seven 18-year-old men and women during the summer break between their final exams and their induction into Israeli Armed Forces as the War of Attrition at the Suez Canal draws on. This summer holiday will cut short their adolescence. First Prize, Israeli Film Awards. Hebrew with English subtitles.

VHS: S12959. $79.95.

Uri Barabash, Israel, 1987, 101 mins.

Laura Adler's Last Love Affair

Rita Zohar stars as Laura Adler, the queen of a shoestring Yiddish theater troupe. She is as deeply loved and worshipped by her diminishing Yiddish-speaking audience as she is by her colleagues. For a brief moment, Laura is on top of the world when she is offered a leading role in an international film and simultaneously has an explosive love affair with a total stranger. However, before her dreams can come to fruition, fate cruelly intervenes. "*Laura Adler* deserves our attention" (*Jerusalem Post*). Hebrew with English subtitles.

VHS: S30528. $59.95.

Avram Heffner, Israel, 1993, 96 mins.

Lupo

Lupo is a furniture dealer with an overflowing zest for life who takes on city officials threatening to demolish his neighborhood in order to put up high-rises. A loving comedy. English dialog.

VHS: S00784. $59.95.

Menahem Golan, Israel, 1970, 100 mins.

My Michael

Two intelligent young adults find each other and marry in a divided Jerusalem of the late 1950's. Michael, a responsible and hard-working scientist, is comfortable in the arrangement, in contrast to Hanna, who finds herself unfulfilled by the petit bourgeois life she is leading. Loneliness and fantasy take over in this gentle yet controversial rendering of the novel by Amos Oz. Hebrew with English subtitles.

VHS: S06569. $79.95.

Dan Wolman, Israel, 1975, 90 mins.

Nadia

A teenage girl wants to be a doctor so she enrolls in a good boarding school as the first step toward this career goal. It would be a simple decision, except that this girl is an Arab from a small town in Israel and the school she chooses is Jewish. Resistance and prejudice strike her from all sides, but she perseveres. B&W, Hebrew with English subtitles.

VHS: S26997. $59.95.

Amnon Rubinstein, Israel, 1987, 90 mins.

Newland

Another outstanding work from Orna Ben-Dor Niv (*Because of That War*). A little girl and her brother travel to Israel after World War II in search of their lost mother and a new life in a new land. Settled in a refugee camp, they are caught in a world of colorful characters and unexpected events. Their story unfolds in a captivating tale of intrigue and expectation and the film's surprise ending is a stunning conclusion to a startling journey. Hebrew with English subtitles.

VHS: S34246. $59.95.

Orna Ben-Dor Niv, Israel, 1994, 107 mins.

Noa at Seventeen

It is 1951 and Noa, a seventeen-year old, struggles for personal autonomy as an ideological debate over the future of kibbutz socialism tears her family apart. Should she finish high school or follow her youth movement friends to kibbutz? Will Israel's labor movement follow Moscow blindly or turn its attention to the West? This sophisticated allegory penetrates the very essence of the bond which fused the personal and the political in the early years of the state of Israel. Hebrew with English subtitles.

VHS: S06568. $79.95.

Isaac Yeshurun, Israel, 1982, 86 mins.

Operation Jonathan

A classic of Israeli cinema, this action-packed story of the incidents at Entebbe is a gripping thriller that only real life could write. Hebrew with English subtitles.

VHS: S34525. $59.95.

Menahem Golan, Israel, 1977, 124 mins.

Over the Ocean

A poignant comedy about a struggling family whose lives are interrupted by the sudden possibility of success. Winner of nine Academy Awards in Israel. Hebrew with English subtitles.

VHS: S34243. $59.95.

Jacob Goldwasser, Israel, 1992, 89 mins.

Saint Clara

Winner of six Israeli Academy Awards, this is the bewitching story of Clara, a 7th-grade Russian emigre at Golda Meier High School in a Negrev town, who has telekinetic and psychic powers. If she falls in love, she will lose her ability to predict winning lottery numbers. Things get complicated when she meets an anarchist rebel hunk at school. Based on a script by Czech playwright/novelist Pavel Kohout. "A knowing, witty homage to adolescence" (Mick LaSalle, *San Francisco Chronicle*). Hebrew with English subtitles.

VHS: S33435. $59.95.

Ari Folman/Uri Sivan, Israel, 1996, 85 mins.

Sallah

Arriving from the Orient as an Israeli immigrant, Sallah is full of expectations. Instead, he lands in a ramshackle transit camp that arouses his disgust. He opts to take on the bureaucracy in his own inimitable fashion, with hilarious results. A very humorous satire and Academy Award nominee. Hebrew with English subtitles.

VHS: S12887. $79.95.

Ephaim Kishon, Israel, 1965, 105 mins.

Shiv'a

Beautiful 25-year-old Gaby works for a catering service specializing in cooking for and giving advice to families during the traditional Jewish seven-day mourning period. The sudden death of a cello player for the Israel Philharmonic Orchestra brings her into a very delicate situation. The spirit of the deceased hovers over all who are present, but Gaby is the only one who truly manages to connect with it. Hebrew with English subtitles.

VHS: S33183. $39.95.

Dina Zvi Riklis, Israel, 1995, 50 mins.

Siege

Set during the Six Day War, this Israeli film, noted for its stark realism, focuses on Tamar, an Israeli woman who loses her husband during the war. Her husband's friends don't want him forgotten, and this forces Tamar to become the ever-grieving widow who, living with her young son, tries to break away from the past, to develop new friends and relationships and establish a new life for herself. With Gilla Almagor and Dahn Ben Amotz. Hebrew with English subtitles.

VHS: S11498. $79.95.

Gilberto Tofano, Israel, 1970, 95 mins.

Song of the Siren

Based on Irit Linur's best-selling novel, this film focuses on the life of 32-year-old Talila Katz. Talia, preoccupied with her turbulent love life, couldn't care less about the wailing sirens which pierce the Tel-Aviv skies during the Gulf War, until she's faced with the reality of the dangers of Saddam Hussein's nightly missiles and marriage to an "unsuitable" suitor. With Dalit Kahan, Boaz Gour-Lavie, Yair Lapid and Orli Zilbershatz. Hebrew with English subtitles.

VHS: S33187. $79.95.

Eytan Fox, Israel, 1994, 91 mins.

Take Two

A sexy comedy from Israel. Assi Doron is an Israeli cinematographer who shoots and directs commercials and documentaries. He lives in a luxurious Tel Aviv penthouse where he conducts his nightly love affairs with models and aspiring actresses who are charmed by the tough, arrogant and cynical divorcee. When he is forced to hire a new assistant, he hires a young American woman. But instead of an assistant, he gets a constant critic of his work, and by all rules, the two conflicting personalities should never fall in love. In English.

VHS: S12947. $79.95.

Baruch Dienar, Israel, 1985, 100 mins.

Three Days and a Child

Old and new relationships are explored in this film based on the classic story by A.B. Yehoshua. A young man returns to his kibbutz after army service to find that the woman with whom he is in love has married someone else. Then, his girlfriend asks him to look after her son for three days. Oded Kotler won a Best Actor award at Cannes for his role in this film. With Illy Gorlitzky and Shuy Osherov. Hebrew with English subtitles.

VHS: S33186. $59.95.

Uri Zohar, Israel, 1967, 105 mins.

Under the Domim Tree

Based on the autobiographical memoir by Gila Almagor (*The Summer of Aviya*), this "gentle, loving film about confronting the past" (*Los Angeles Times*) is the poignant and harrowing story of a group of teenagers living in a youth village for orphans who survived the Nazi concentration camps and other troubled Israeli youths in the 1950s. When life becomes unbearable, the teens find refuge under the beautiful Domim Tree, the only place where they feel at peace. "One of the most beautiful movies of the past 20 years, maybe longer" (*The Record*). Hebrew with English subtitles.

VHS: S30736. $19.98.

Eli Cohen, Israel, 1996, 102 mins.

Wedding in Galilee

An intimate and multi-layered portrait of a Palestinian village under Israeli occupation. The mukhtar of the village wants to hold a traditional wedding for his son, and invites the Israeli military governor as a guest of honor. Beautifully filmed and acted by a cast of non-professionals, the story moves between the alienated grandfather, an angry group of young males prone to violence, an impotent groom and a resourceful bride. Arabic and Hebrew with English subtitles.

VHS: S08938. $24.95.

Michel Kleifi, Israel/Belgium, 1986, 113 mins.

Will My Mother Go Back to Berlin?

Filmmaker Micha Peled's mother escaped Berlin during the Nazi era. She then established herself in Israel. Years later her son travels to the German capital seeking traces of her childhood and returns with a surprise invitation extended to his mother by the mayor of Berlin. Hebrew and German with English subtitles.

VHS: S24715. $59.00.

Micha Peled, Israel/Germany, 60 mins.

Wooden Gun

Set in the tense atmosphere of Tel Aviv of the 1950's, this incisive film focuses on two rival groups of preteens whose behavior, motivated by their interpretations of the concepts of heroism, nationalism and friendship, raise hard questions. Portrayed are first generation sabras (native-born Israelis) who are separated by a tremendous psychological gap from those who came to Israel from Europe, many of them Holocaust survivors. Hebrew with English subtitles.

VHS: S06567. $79.95.

Han Moshenson, Israel, 1979, 91 mins.

You, Me, Jerusalem

Co-directed by an Israeli and a Palestinian, this documentary about Jerusalem's ambulance service has been called "Short Cuts, Jerusalem," and has been likened to TV's *ER*. An Arab doctor and a Jewish paramedic are part of a Jerusalem ambulance team that responds to traffic accidents and terrorist attacks. The pair's daily contact and reliance on each other are hopeful beacons of co-existence in this hostile environment. Arabic and Hebrew with English subtitles. "A political-cinematographic event...infused with humanity and intelligence" (*Liberation*, Paris).

VHS: S30443. $79.00.

Micha X. Peled/George Khleifi, Israel, 1995, 53 mins.

ISRAELI CULTURE

Agadati: Screen of an Artist

This documentary celebrates the life and work of dancer, painter and filmmaker Baruch Agadati, best-known for his film *This Is the Land* (1934), detailing the founding of Tel Aviv, the outbreak of World War I, the Balfour declaration and other important events celebrating 50 years of Jewish growth in Palestine. 37 mins.
VHS: S33185. $39.95.

Amatzia: The Bar Kochba Caves

During troubled times, the Jews of ancient Israel often dwelled in artificial limestone underground caves. The Bar Kochba revolt, which was launched against Rome in 132 C.E., was largely waged from such dwelling places. This video takes us down below, where we view an intricate complex of narrow passageways and tunnels—an enlightening look at of Israel's lesser known, yet more fascinating archeological sites. Color, 12 mins.
VHS: S15405. $29.95.

Bli Sodot—Without Secrets

Winner of Israeli Emmy Awards, this series is designed to teach Hebrew to children. Alphie, an animated host, and his four human friends employ comic sketches, film clips and animations designed to strengthen listening comprehension, vocabulary, grammar, reading and speaking skills. Designed for children of elementary age; each program is approximately 30 mins. The complete 15-volume set includes *Shin/Resh/Lamed; Tav/Intermediate 1/Bet-Hay; Yud-Peh/Alef-Chet/Intermediate 2; Noon-Kaf/Mem-Zayin/Gimel-Shin; Intermediate 3/Bet-Dalet/Samech-Ayin; Tet-Kaf/Intermediate 4/Peh-Vav; Tsadi-Kaf/Intermediate 5/Shvah 1; Shva II, III, IV; Intermediate Shva, Chirik I, II; Chirik III, IV, Intermediate Chirik; Cholam I, II, III; Cholam IV, Intermediate Cholam, Zeireh I; Zeireh II, III, IV; Intermediate Zeireh, Shuruk I, II; and Shuruk III, IV, Intermediate Shuruk. In Hebrew.*
VHS: S24295. $349.95.

Bon Voyage

Over 20 years ago, filmmaker Baruch Dienar created a fun-filled video with a young couple (Gadi Yagil and Shula Chen), travelling by motor scooter, singing their way across Israel. We join them as they tour from Mt. Hermon in the north to Eilat in the south, visiting historic and biblical sites along the way. 30 mins.
VHS: S33172. $29.95.

The Dhimmis: To Be a Jew in Arab Lands

A comprehensive documentary detailing centuries of persecution endured by Jews living in Arab lands. With rare film footage, photographs, maps and interviews, this is a first-rate overview of Jewish life in the midst of ongoing conflict. 29 mins.
VHS: S14692. $34.95.

The Films of Yaacov Ben Dov: Father of the Hebrew Cinema

These film works are a treasure trove of information about Jewish life in Palestine between 1917 and 1933. Within this Zionist vision of Israel a number of important historical figures are captured. Included are Chaim Wiezman, Winston Churchill, Albert Einstein and more. Prepared by the Spielberg Jewish Film Archive in Jerusalem. 30 mins.
VHS: S23245. $39.95.

Flames of Revolt: The Irgun

Examines the role played by the Irgun in the establishment of the State of Israel. Fascinating interviews with former Irgun fighters, British intelligence officers, historians from Israel and England and the late Prime Minister Menachem Begin are interspersed with historic archival footage. The bombing of the British headquarters at the King David Hotel, the breakout from the Acre prison, escapes from detention camps and the sinking of the *Altelena* are but a few of the highlights. 100 mins.
VHS: S33170. $39.95.

The Gevatron—Sing Along

Kibbutz folk singers perform 14 songs on tour. There is also behind-the-scenes footage of these entertainers. Lyrics in Hebrew are translated through English titles. Includes companion booklet. 60 mins.
VHS: S26109. $29.95.

Great Days of History: Exodus and the Birth of Israel

The revelation of the Holocaust did not mean that its survivors would readily be granted asylum in the Promised Land. This riveting chronicle records the dramatic events leading to the establishment of Israel, focusing on Exodus, the clandestine voyage in 1947 of Jewish refugees to Palestine. 55 mins.
VHS: S09436. $29.95.

Homeland

A series of videotapes about the history of the Jewish settlement in the land of Israel in modern times. The series begins in the 19th century and continues through the formation of the modern state of Israel. In Hebrew.
At the Beginning of the Period/Within the Walls of Jerusalem. The first program from Homeland. 44 mins.
VHS: S10567. $39.95.

Inside God's Bunker

This is a chilling and detailed portrait of the Jewish settlers in Hebron just before the infamous 1994 massacre. Religious fervor, vigilante actions and ideological indoctrination helped create the atmosphere that exploded into the world's headlines. Hebrew with English narration and subtitles.
VHS: S24716. $59.00.
Micha Peled, Germany/France/Great Britain, 40 mins.

Israel Sings—Sing Along

This musical travelogue of Israel joins the best sights with popular folk songs. It's sung in Hebrew, but English titles translate each song. Includes companion booklet. 60 mins.
VHS: S26108. $29.95.

Israel—This Land Is Yours!

Explore Israel as it is today, its fascinating peoples and historic sites. Visit Masada, Nazareth, Galilee, Jerusalem and more. 28 mins.
VHS: S06696. $29.95.

Israel: A Nation Is Born

This program about the formation of modern Israel examines the 50-year history of the country and its political, cultural and social heritage. Produced by Moreshet Israel, the documentary presents a diversity of voices, including Harry Truman and Bill Clinton, Anwar Sadat and Itzhak Rabin. It is accompanied by commentary from Abba Eban, Israel's elder statesman, who has been an important personal witness to the struggles and hardships. 300 mins.
VHS: S20196. $149.95.

Israel: The Holy Land

Visit the Holy Land and see the historic religious areas as well as the everyday life and excitement that characterizes the people of Israeli. See Tel Aviv, Nazareth, Jerusalem, Jericho, and more. 60 mins.
VHS: S05778. $24.95.

Israeli Writers

A series of interviews with contemporary Israeli writers, discussing their literary works. Hebrew *without* subtitles. Each program approximately 60 mins.
A.B. Yehoshua.
VHS: S10572. $49.95.
Gershom Scholem on S.Y. Agnon.
VHS: S10573. $59.95.
Moshe Shamir.
VHS: S10571. $49.95.

Jerusalem

Renowned historian Sir Martin Gilbert hosts this two-video set exploration of Jerusalem. He describes the growth of this vital capital from ancient times up to the most recent developments in the Arab-Israeli peace process. Stunning photography, innovative reconstructions and rare footage capture the spirit of this place. 150 mins.
VHS: S29898. $29.95.

Jerusalem Throughout the Ages

Explore Jerusalem, the core of the Jewish, Christian and Muslim faiths, and its profound influence on mankind in this acclaimed five-volume collector's edition video series. Volumes include: Christians and Christianity in Jerusalem (47 mins.), A Walk in Crusader Jerusalem (34 mins.), "Within Thy Gates O Jerusalem:" The City and the Temple (32 mins.), Yearning: Jerusalem of the 19th Century (37 mins.), and Jerusalem Today: City of Neighborhoods (29 mins.). 300 mins.
VHS: S30028. $69.95.

Jerusalem Today: City of Neighborhoods

In the latter half of the 19th century, Jerusalem's inhabitants began to establish their homes beyond the walls of the old city. Since then, scores of neighborhoods have been built. This program examines the Hasidic Beit Ungarin, the Sephardic Ohel Mosche, the Moslem Sheikh Jarach and Talpiot as an example of a garden neighborhood. 29 mins.
VHS: S10600. $29.95.

Jerusalem's Cardo

This journey into the Holy Land roots reveals The Cardo—Jerusalem's ancient, now modern thoroughfare. Walk with Walter Zanger, Israel's favorite tour guide, through the 2000 year-old Roman Gate, on Byzantine paving stones, and in the crusader market. Discover the remnants of a great synagogue and the underground Nea church, the Holy Sepulchre and the multi-level section of the old city. 25 mins.
VHS: S10452. $32.95.

Jerusalem: Gates to the City

Enter Jerusalem through the people who live here through their stories, creations and daily routines. Amid the city's ancient monuments and shrines you'll meet people from many different religions and national and ethnic traditions, all trying to live ordinary lives under extraordinary conditions. High school to adult. 1996, 31 mins.
VHS: S31908. $59.95.

Land of Promise

One of Palestine's earliest sound films, *Land of Promise* utilizes a combination of documentary and travelogue conventions to encourage settlement and investment in the Jewish Homeland. The film portrays Palestine as a land of opportunity for Zionists, a place for fulfilling an ancient dream. English and Hebrew, with narration from David Ross.
VHS: S16316. $72.00.
Juda Leman, Palestine, 1935, 57 mins.

Masada

The story of the siege of 980 Jews who escaped the sacking of Jerusalem by the Romans in 70 A.D. by taking refuge in Herod the Great's winter palace on the mountain of Masada. Made for television, starring Peter O'Toole and Peter Strauss.
VHS: S01717. $19.98.
Boris Sagal, USA, 1980, 131 mins.

Miracle of Survival/The Birth of Israel

This documentary tells the story of the emergent nation of Israel. From the modern military miracle that this country's borders represent, to the continuing everyday survival of the tenacious country, this is a tale of perseverance in the face of the enemy. 60 mins. Includes archival footage.
VHS: S22047. $14.98.

Moshe Dayan

A & E Biography looks at how this master of desert warfare, who transformed a tiny, beleaguered nation into a respected military power, came to champion a different cause: peace. 50 mins.
VHS: S30104. $19.95.

Parpar Nechmad—Lovely Butterfly

This special series designed for children of primary age is entirely in Hebrew, and uses puppets, games, songs and stories to tell children about Jewish holidays and traditions. In elementary Hebrew *without* subtitles. Each program is 30 mins.
Chanukah.
VHS: S10456. $29.95.
Purim.
VHS: S10458. $29.95.
Flowers for the Independence Day.
VHS: S10460. $29.95.

Rabbi Kook

From the series *Jews Who Made History*, produced in Israel, *Rabbi Kook* documents the life of the first Chief Rabbi of the state of Israel, from his childhood in Poland through his immigration to Palestine and his involvement with the secular and religious community in Israel. His philosophy of Jewish life made him a symbol for the Religious Zionist movement and on the other end made him enemies within the Orthodox community. 45 mins. English dialog.
VHS: S11596. $29.95.

Shattered Dreams

A massive, chilling, thoughtful and provocative examination of Israel. Born out of the despair of millions as a utopian haven in the desert, *Shattered Dreams* confronts the realities of Israel today against the background of these utopian beginnings. The film passionately documents what more than 20 years of occupation and expansion have done to the soul of Israel. Provocative and unflinching.
VHS: S12305. $19.98.
Victor Schonfeld, Great Britain, 1988, 173 mins.

Solitary Star: Zehava Ben

The "uncrowned queen" of Oriental and Middle Eastern music has not only captured the hearts of Israelis, but also found new audiences in the Arab world. Her rags-to-riches Cinderella story is told in this powerful musical documentary.
VHS: S33184. $49.95.
Erez Laufer, Israel, 59 mins.

The Unafraid

Writer Meyer Levin captured on film the journey of Jews trying to reach Palestine under the watchful British. Levin returned to Israel 30 years later to find out what had become of the courageous travelers. 35 mins.

VHS: S23253. $29.95.

Underdogs: A Sports (War) Movie

The Hapoel Beit She'an soccer team became the pride of its small town when it made it to the top of the league. In 1996, when the team was on the verge of losing that special status, the entire town was in mourning. The deciding game was against the reigning champion, Maccabi Haifa, and Beit She'an won. More than a film about soccer, this is about the war between the haves and the have-nots, the small town against the big city, the underdog taking on the seasoned champ. Hebrew with English subtitles.

VHS: S33182. $49.95.
Israel, 1996, 85 mins.

Video Visits: Israel, A Land for Everyone

The Wailing Wall, the Church of the Holy Sepulchre and the Al Agsa Mosque reveal the central significance this land holds for three of the world's great religions. Amidst this historic setting, there is a vibrant and diverse modern nation. This video shows the contrasts and the variety that make up modern Israel. 52 mins.

VHS: S29830. $24.95.

Video Visits: Jerusalem, 3,000 Years of Miracles

Beyond the Damascus Gate lies a city dominated by religious treasures and enduring traditions. This video shows numerous key sites, a visit to the Hall of Remembrance and a commemorative site for the Holocaust, as well as a view of the Dead Sea Scrolls. 52 mins.

VHS: S29831. $24.95.

Wall in Jerusalem

Richard Burton narrates this brilliant documentary, which traces the development of Israel into a modern Jewish homeland. Using rare and powerful footage, filmmaker Frederic Rossif documents the earliest settlements, the heavy immigration of the 30's and 40's, the development of the kibbutz, the Balfour Declaration, relations with the League of Nations, confrontations with the Arabs and the British, the incident with the ship *Exodus*, the partition, and the Six Days' War.

VHS: S11231. $24.95.
Frederic Rossif, Great Britain, 1972, 91 mins.

A Woman Called Golda

Ingrid Bergman won an Emmy for her splendid performance as Israeli Prime Minister Golda Meir, a former school teacher from Milwaukee, Wisconsin. Judy Davis and Leonard Nimoy play the young Meirs, who immigrate to Palestine and begin work on a Kibbutz. With Anne Jackson, Ned Beatty, Robert Loggia and Barry Foster.

VHS: S10834. $69.95.
Alan Gibson, USA, 1982, 192 mins.

Yearning: Jerusalem of the 19th Century

The film focuses upon historical developments and changes in Jerusalem of the 19th century, spanning from turn-of-the century Jerusalem, a city on the periphery of the Ottoman Empire, to Allenby's entry into Jerusalem in 1917. 37 mins.

VHS: S10467. $29.95.

Yitzhak Rabin

In this biographical documentary from A&E, the story of Israel's recently assassinated Prime Minister is told in all its complexity. His career paralleled the growth of the state of Israel. Rabin fought for Israeli independence with the Haganah underground army, formulated the Israeli victory in the Six Day War, became Israel's first native-born Prime Minister, and, finally, signed the historic peace treaty with the P.L.O.

VHS: S27211. $19.95.
Bill Harris, USA/Israel, 1995, 50 mins.

MIDEAST: THE CHALLENGE OF CHANGE

17 Days of Terror: The Hijack of TWA 847

In June of 1985, TWA flight was snatched from its course, and its passengers held hostage for 17 days as the world looked on helplessly. From ABC News. 60 mins.

VHS: S12686. $24.98.

444 Days to Freedom: What Really Happened in Iran

A riveting narrative of the Iran hostage saga as seen from the inside out, this award-winning documentary chronicles the events from November 1979 to January 1981, when 52 Americans were held captive by Islamic radicals. A must-see for any student of world affairs. Delivers "an unusual emotional wallop" *(Wall Street Journal)*. 96 mins.

VHS: S31069. $19.98.

The Aftermath of the War with Iraq

An in-depth look at the political impact and unfinished business of the war with Iraq. This highly informative program examines the underlying political and military goals of the war and their impact on the longer term prospects for stability and peace in the Middle East. USA, 1991, 29 mins.

VHS: S15209. $25.00.

America Held Hostage: The Iran Crisis

From ABC News comes the story of the 444 days that changed history. Fanatic supporters of the Ayatollah stormed the US embassy in Tehran and held 52 people captive for over a year. 60 mins.

VHS: S12687. $24.98.

Amnesty International Report on Iran

A documentary on human rights abuses occurring in Iran today, with a commentary on the domestic and international legal standards contravened by these abuses. 1987, 15 mins.

VHS: S06890. $20.00.

Back to Arafat

The first feature-length documentary about the Armenian genocide. 1.5 million Armenians were killed and an entire people driven from their Turkish homeland. *Back to Arafat* also highlights the aspirations of three generations of Armenians scattered throughout the world, who share the dream of returning to the lands surrounding the holy mountain of Arafat. 100 mins.

VHS: S14734. $50.00.

Behind the Flag

A provocative video documentary featuring perspectives largely absent from mainstream media during the Gulf War. While acknowledging the need to resist Iraqi aggression, the video questions whether war was the best alternative, how the allies conducted the war, how the media reported it, and the costs to the U.S., Iraq, and other countries. USA, 1991, 20 mins.

VHS: S15208. $59.95.

Best of Nightline

Assassination of Egyptian President Anwar Sadat. 70 mins.
VHS: S14023. $14.98.
Colonel Muammar Qaddafi. 30 mins.
VHS: S14034. $14.98.
Flight 847 Hijacked. 60 mins.
VHS: S14035. $14.98.
Iranian Jetliner Shot Down by U.S. 30 mins.
VHS: S14054. $14.98.
Massacre of Marines in Beirut. 30 mins.
VHS: S14025. $14.98.
Qaddafi's Warning. 30 mins.
VHS: S14039. $14.98.
The State of Israel Is Recognized by Palestine. 30 mins.
VHS: S14055. $14.98.
Town Meeting—Holy Land. 30 mins.
VHS: S14053. $14.98.
Yasir Arafat. 30 mins.
VHS: S14048. $14.98.

Bethlehem

Palestinian Christians crafted this documentary about the religious history of this holy city. They begin with the story of Jesus' birth, then explore Bethlehem through archeology, architecture, demographics and legends. 41 mins.

VHS: S23001. $19.98.

A Chance for Peace

Produced by CNN, the story of the events leading up to the signing of the historic peace treaty between Israel and the Palestinian Liberation Organization. 60 mins.

VHS: S20511. $14.98.

Christians and Christianity in Jerusalem

The site of Jesus' trial and crucifixion, throughout the centuries Jerusalem has drawn both pilgrims and protectors of its holy places. The Christian presence has had a profound influence on the character of the city. The film traces Christianity's link with Jerusalem from the New Testament to the Crusades. 47 mins.

VHS: S10464. $29.95.

Deadly Currents

"The best film I've ever seen on the Middle East" *(Toronto Star)*—a thoughtful documentary about the Israeli-Palestinian conflict which goes far beyond stereotypes to create an amazing portrait of societies at war. *Deadly Currents* delves deeply into the hearts and minds of the men and women behind the rock-throwing mobs, vigilante posses and political figureheads. Arabic and Hebrew with English voice-over and subtitles.

VHS: S27201. $89.95.
Simcha Jacobovici, Canada, 1992, 115 mins.

Death on the Nile: The Assassination of Anwar Sadat

The Egyptian President turned his back on history and his nation's wishes to pursue peace in the Middle East. He lost his life in the process, cut down by assassin's bullets. From ABC News. 60 mins.

VHS: S12684. $24.98.

Discovering the Music of the Middle East

Islam spread musical traditions from the Middle East as far North as the Balkans. This video introduces a variety of instruments and explains the concepts behind intricate melodic lines and asymmetrical rhythms. 21 mins.

VHS: S23512. $49.95.

Echoes of Conflict

The tensions of the Arab-Israeli conflict are confronted in this showcase of three short films from a new wave of Israeli filmmakers. The titles include *The Movie, Don't Get Involved* and *The Cage*. Witness the turbulence of the Middle East from the perspective of those who face it every day. In Color and B&W. Hebrew with English subtitles.

VHS: S14746. $29.95.
Amit Goren, Israel, 1986-89, 91 mins.

Embroidered Canticles

The Matruz is a unique Moroccan-Jewish music which fuses Hebrew and Arabic texts. Andalusian traditions of music and poetry reflecting the centuries-old link between Jewish and Muslim societies are the vital link to this living musical culture. Live performances and interviews with scholars and performers reveal this musical legacy. French, Arabic and Hebrew with English subtitles.

VHS: S23090. $25.00.
Izza Genini, France, 1991, 26 mins.

Experience Indonesia

Climb an active volcano, snorkel, take part in a tribal ceremony, paddle into the ocean and surf one of the most remote beaches in the world. 47 mins.

VHS: S31470. $19.99.

Farouk: Last of the Pharaohs

An intriguing documentary about Farouk, the last King of Egypt. When he ascended to the throne in 1936, at the age of 16, he was a beloved figure to his country and was expected to accomplish great things. Instead, he became a dissolute playboy, flaunting his love of luxury, huge appetite, gambling and mistresses—all at the expense of his desperately poor countrymen. "Fascinating, frank and fun" (London *Sunday Times*). 50 mins.

VHS: S14516. $29.95.

The Giant Nile

A travelogue that explores the mysteries, beauty, wildlife, landscape, culture and ruins of ancient Egyptian civilization. In this three-part documentary, the viewer is taken on an odyssey of the mind through five countries. 180 mins.

Part One: The Wild River.
VHS: S18276. $19.95.
Part Two: White Nile, Blue Nile.
VHS: S18277. $19.95.
Part Three: Egyptian Journey.
VHS: S18278. $19.95.
Boxed Set. The three-volume, three-hour work is presented in a single, boxed-set edition, including a parchment map.
VHS: S18279. $59.85.

The Gulf Bowl Cabaret

A half-hour tour-de-force satire on the Persian Gulf War, the news media, New Age and the New World Order that acts as an absurdist antidote to the War's fuzzy, feel-good aftermath. Using the anchor desk at Censored Network News as home base, the show includes backdrop footage of the war and its aftermath, musical interludes, reports from "live" correspondents, bizarre and biting commentary, interruptions by "regularly scheduled programming" and commercial parodies. 30 mins.

VHS: S31103. $19.95.

The Gulf Crisis TV Project

The war-maneuvering in the Middle East prompted a group of New York-based TV producers to launch the *Gulf Crisis TV Project*, an effort to put news and views from anti-war activists on television nationwide. The Project contacted 1,000 community groups, from almost every state, to gather videotapes of local activities and demonstrations. The result is this tape, containing four half-hour TV programs entitled "War, Oil and Power;" "Getting Out of the Sand Trap;" "Bring the Troops Home" and "Operation Dissidence." See for yourself! *The Gulf Crisis TV Project* offers another view from America.
VHS: S13775. $29.95.

The Gulf War

Spectacular footage and insider interviews provide a comprehensive look back at "Operation Desert Storm," the Gulf War, as *FRONTLINE* reconstructs the events leading up to the war, as well as the war and its aftermath. 240 mins.
VHS: S28657. $39.95.

Inside Afghanistan

Shot in Kabul, Herat, Kandahar, Spinbuldak and the Afghan countryside in 1987, this film is a look at the other side of war in Afghanistan, the communist government and its supporters. Underscores the chasm between the urbanized, Westernizing supporters of the Communist government and the traditional Muslim of the villages, still based on clan and feudal ties.
VHS: S33896. $24.95.

Inside the West Bank

An in-depth examination of the West Bank, produced as the MPI Video News Magazine, examining the conflict between Israelis and Palestinians in the occupied territories. 90 mins.
VHS: S06545. $19.95.

The Intifada (Palestinian Uprising): A Jewish Eye Witness

A dramatic "photomated" slide presentation on video. "A new perspective on the Intifada—something which generally isn't available in the U.S. American Jews should see this perspective in order to get a more complete picture of the Middle East conflict" (Michael Argamon, Yesh G'vul). 50 mins.
VHS: S31651. $49.95.

Israel and the Occupied Territories

This film details Amnesty International's concern with Israel and the Occupied Territories since the *Intifada*. Interviews with human rights lawyers, doctors, prisoners of conscience and others on beatings, lethal shootings, administrative detention and other issues of concern. 21 mins. 1990.
VHS: S12782. $20.00.

Israel vs. the PLO: The Invasion of Lebanon

Israel's 1982 attempt to obliterate a formidable enemy, the bloody attack on Beirut, and the innocent victims caught in the crossfire. From ABC News. 60 mins.
VHS: S12688. $24.98.

Jerusalem Stories

ABC News' Peter Jennings, who has been reporting on Jerusalem for almost 30 years, goes back to the sacred city to attempt to uncover the mystery of its 4,000-year history. 46 mins.
VHS: S31775. $19.98.

Lifting the Fog: Intrigue in the Middle East

In this panoramic view, the forces that have shaped this dynamic region are brought clearly into focus. History, religion and politics have traditionally shaped this complex area. Today, oil and geopolitics have only deepened its turbulent mix of influences. 60 mins.
VHS: S22999. $29.98.

A Line in the Sand: What Did America Win?

Peter Jennings hosts this special presentation that explores the final effects of the Persian Gulf war. 50 mins.
VHS: S15878. $19.98.

Many Through One

In Cairo, Catholics worship in seven different rites that are reminders of Church history, art and tradition. Priests, bishops and lay people explain the practices and beliefs of their respective rites. 29 mins.
VHS: S15861. $19.95.

Mosque

With recent crises in the Middle East, many misconceptions about Islam have invaded the American psyche. But the understanding of 900 million Muslims and their faith is still a mystery to most. This program, filmed in Cairo, introduces a mosque and shows that Muslim believers are not the fanatics that media reports frequently portray. 29 mins.
VHS: S15859. $19.95.

Mysterious Egypt

From the golden mask of King Tutankhamen in Cairo's museum to Tut's burial site in the Valley of the Kings, this film carefully explores all the most important sites of ancient, mysterious Egypt. A delightful selection of breathtaking visuals. 60 mins.
VHS: S15048. $29.95.

Occupied Palestine

"A complex, sensitive and brutally authentic movie, *Occupied Palestine* delivers its message with unnerving sharpness and accuracy. The simple realities of what it means to live under and to resist occupation have never been so clearly presented to a Western audience," wrote Professor Joel Beinin of Stanford University. *Occupied Palestine* is a film reflecting the Palestinian experience of Zionism and resistance to it. Dramatic, contemporary footage is combined with the testimony of Palestinians as well as Zionist settlers and officials, to develop a fresh perspective on a critical international issue. "Quite simply the best film ever made about the Palestine question" *(Middle East Report)*.
Home Video.
VHS: S10842. $49.95.
Institutional with public performance rights.
VHS: S10847. $99.95.
David Koff, USA/Israel, 1987, 88 mins.

Palestinian Diaries

A unique project in which three young Palestinians, professionally trained and supplied with low-cost cameras, document their lives and the occurrences in their communities, vividly capturing the reality of existence under Israeli occupation. 60 mins.
VHS: S31777. $19.98.

The Persian Gulf: Images of a Conflict

Sold only as a collectible four-volume set. 6 hours 30 mins. *Volume 1: Prelude to War.* This first program prophetically introduces us to Saddam Hussein in a rare interview with Diane Sawyer which predated the invasion of Kuwait by several weeks. The program then takes us on a time trip through the invasion, the UN resolutions, the debates in both Houses, and the war of words between the US and Iraq—finally culminating in the eventful night of January 16, 1991, when the bombs began to fall. *Volume 2: The Allies Strike.* And now the war begins. Some of the footage contained in this volume has not yet been seen on television and includes reports from Saudi Arabia, Baghdad, and other areas of the Middle East as well as reactions at home. *Volume 3: Saddam Hussein vs. the Coalition behind the Military Strategies.* How was the war really fought? What were Hussein's tactics, and where did he fail? This is an analysis that graphically explains the methodology used to wage one of the most comprehensive wars in history. *Volume 4: A Conversation with General Schwarzkopf.* This is an historic interview, conducted by Barbara Walters, which probes the mind and soul of the man who has achieved almost unprecedented historic military status. No other interview with the General, to date, has proven to disclose so much. This last volume is a fitting conclusion to the entire series.
VHS: S14087. $69.98.

Report from Iraq

Produced by award-winning filmmaker John Koop, this video is a document of the journey of a team of Harvard University doctors, lawyers, and students to Iraq—in the aftermath of the Gulf War. USA, 1991, 22 mins.
VHS: S15212. $59.95.

Sadat

Louis Gosset, Jr., portrays the life and career of Egyptian leader Anwar Sadat. This charismatic man began his political career at the helm of an army, but he is best known today as the man who campaigned hard to bring peace to the Middle East. 193 mins.
VHS: S25754. $24.95.

Sandstorm in the Gulf

This video looks back at the mistakes and miscalculations by our government that contributed to the Gulf War, and looks ahead to the major problems in the Middle East that the War hasn't solved: The Arab-Palestinian-Israeli conflict, arms control, regional security, and the gap between rich and poor nations. A provocative discussion of the politics and history of the region. 25 mins.
VHS: S13932. $29.95.

Sea of Galilee

Journey to the ancient waters of Galilee and visit the locales where the Ministry of Jesus actually occurred. Navigating Galilee's waters and traveling its shores, viewers visit Hamat Gader, the world's oldest synagogue, and the ancient world's second largest hot springs. 25 mins.
VHS: S12301. $24.95.

Secret Egypt: A Trance Journey

Egypt's ancient culture merges disparate influences into a vibrant spiritual whole. Healing trance dances occur in ancient tombs just behind the great pyramids. Rituals of exorcism are performed in tents and on crowded city corners. Even cobras are subject to the influences of these old and unfathomable spiritual ways. This documentary shows a side of Egypt rarely revealed to anyone. 50 mins.
VHS: S26719. $29.95.

The Shifting Sands: A History of the Middle East

This video gives the background story every family in America should know. Tracing the history of the Middle East over 5,000 years, NBC News uncovers the delicate balance of power that led to the recent conflict in the Gulf. USA, 60 mins.
VHS: S15217. $19.95.

Sites Unseen: Off the Beaten Track in Jerusalem

A guide to reclusive, obscure and unknown sites of interest in Jerusalem. 45 mins.
VHS: S12907. $39.95.

Stolen Freedom: Occupied Palestine

Casey Kasem (of *America's Top 40* fame) hosts this serious documentary about the plight of the Palestinian people. They have been forced into ghettoes filled with fear and violence. Only the dream of freedom sustains them. 30 mins.
VHS: S23000. $19.98.

Touring Egypt

A fascinating look at Egypt, including walks through the many Cairos of today—the pyramids and Sphinx of Giza, cruising the Nile to Thebes, the Temples of Karnak and Luxor, the temples of Esna and Edfu, Aswan dam and the temple of Isis, the four colossi of Rameses, the Sinai, Suez Canal and the Red Sea, and even El Alamein. 60 mins.
VHS: S09912. $29.95.

Treasures of the Holy Land: Ancient Art from the Israel Museum

Documents the 1986 Metropolitan Museum of Art exhibition. More than 10,000 years of the Holy Land's history are viewed through the objects on display as Philippe de Montebello, the Museum director, guides the viewer through a rich sampling of artifacts, jewelry, inscriptions, mosaics and household objects. 30 mins.
VHS: S03401. $29.95.

Video Visits: Egypt, The Land of Ancient Wonders

Tour Cairo, the Alabster Mosque, the pyramids of Giza, the Sphinx, the Valley of the Kings, the Suez Canal and the port of Alexandria. 58 mins.
VHS: S31457. $24.99.

Video Visits: Jordan, The Desert Kingdom

Visit the modern capital of Amman, the ruins of Jehash, the finest surviving Roman city in the Middle East, biblical sites from the Dead Sea to the Sea of Galilee and the ancient city of Petra, and join scuba divers at Aqaba. 55 mins.
VHS: S31459. $24.99.

War in the Gulf: Answering Children's Questions

Peter Jennings and ABC News correspondents, both in the U.S. and in the Middle East, are joined by Operation Desert Storm military speakers to explain the issues of war to children and their parents. 75 mins.
VHS: S22991. $19.98.

YIDDISH & JEWISH CINEMA

Almonds and Raisins: A History of the Yiddish Cinema

Narrated by Orson Welles, this remarkable documentary is a history of the Yiddish cinema, fascinating and funny, a landmark documentary on the whole lost culture of Yiddish film. Between 1927 and 1940, Yiddish filmmakers made over 100 films in Yiddish, expressing the hopes and fears of the immigrant society— dreams of opportunity, assimilation, social betterment, separation from family and failure. *Almonds and Raisins* lovingly captures the ideas and history of the Yiddish cinema and the richness of the Yiddish language.
VHS: S08101. $59.95.
Russ Karel, Great Britain, 1986, 90 mins.

American Matchmaker (Amerikaner Shadchen)

Edgar G. Ulmer's classic Yiddish film about a dissatisfied man's desire to become a modern day matchmaker after the failure of his most recent marriage, who earmarks for a rival a woman more suited to his own sensibility. With Judith Abarbanel. Yiddish with English subtitles.
VHS: S17937. $69.95.
Edgar G. Ulmer, USA, 1940, 87 mins.

Bent Tree

This charming fable, presented in sand animation, is based on the Yiddish folk tune "Oyfn Veg Shteyt A Boym". The story tells of a small child whose mother tries to prevent him from discovering the world and flying away. 4 mins.
VHS: S12884. $16.95.

Cantor's Son

This is a dramatic film based on the life of its star, Moishe Oysher. A youth leaves his home country to join a troupe of traveling performers. Eventually, he lands in America but is barely able to support himself. On a janitorial job, he is "discovered" as having an unusually fine voice and gains immediate fame. Success does not fulfill him though, and he returns, in the end, to the home of his parents. Yiddish with English subtitles.
VHS: S12885. $79.95.
Ilya Motyleff, USA, 1937, 90 mins.

The Dybbuk

Tragedy, conflict and cultural tension among two families are contrasted in this ambitious work inspired by S. Ansky's ethnographic studies of Jews in the Polish-Russian countryside. "Whatever the movie's original intentions, even have dictated that its theme will be read as harbingers of exile and oblivion" (J. Hoberman, *Village Voice*). With Avrom Marevsky, Isaac Samberg and Moshe Lipman. Yiddish with restored English subtitles.
VHS: S18572. $90.00.
Michal Waszynski, Poland, 1937, 123 mins.

East and West

A comedy about urban Jews who dedicate themselves to traditional *shtetl* life. A New York businessman returns with his daughter to Galicia to attend a family wedding. She's drawn to a charismatic young yeshiva scholar who breaks tradition to court her. With Molly Picon, Jacob Kalish and Sidney M. Goldin. "With broad strokes and plenty of self-parody, it raises the issue of modernity." Silent with Yiddish and English intertitles.
VHS: S18573. $72.00.
Sidney M. Goldin/Ivan Abramson, Austria, 1923, 85 mins.

Eli Eli

Long believed lost, this heartwarming musical drama is the classic Yiddish story of a divided family. While Mom and Dad lose the farm, the family is forced to live apart, but they do it with sadness, humor and music. With Esther Feild (*The Yiddish Mama*), Lazar Fried and Muni Serebroff, with songs by Sholom Secunda. Yiddish with English subtitles.
VHS: S04844. $29.95.
Joseph Seiden, USA, 1940, 85 mins.

God, Man and Devil

A pious Torah scribe is seduced by Satan and transformed into a dishonest factory owner who destroys the religious and communal fabric in this adaptation of Jacob Gordin's play. With Mikhal Mikhalesko, Gustav Berger and Berta Gersten. Yiddish with improved English subtitles.
VHS: S18574. $54.00.
Joseph Seiden, USA, 1949, 100 mins.

Green Fields

A restored Yiddish classic, directed by Edgar G. Ulmer. A pastoral romance based on Peretz Hirschbein's legendary tale of a young student who leaves the Yeshiva to wander across the Pale in search of "true Jews." When the orphaned, otherworldly scholar happens upon a family of Jewish peasants who take him in as a boarder and tutor for their children, an interesting juxtaposition of lifestyles ensues. From the National Center for Jewish Film. Yiddish with English subtitles.
VHS: S11648. $72.00.
Edgar G. Ulmer, USA, 1937, 95 mins.

His Wife's Lover

A charming Yiddish comedy starring the multi-talented Ludwig Satz, about an actor who disguises himself as an old man in order to test his young fiance's fidelity. With Michael Rosenberg and Lucy Levine. Yiddish with English subtitles.
VHS: S14689. $59.95.
Sidney Goldin, USA, 1931, 77 mins.

Horodok

While visiting relatives in Horodok, a Polish *shtetl* between Minsk and Vilna, the American amateur filmmaker Joseph Shapiro recorded his impressions. As he travels the town on foot, he assembles a pastiche of women at work, schools, markets, farm animals, wooden houses and horse-drawn wagons to create a portrait of the people's poor but pious way. Silent.
VHS: S16315. $30.00.
Joseph Shapiro, Poland, 1930, 11 mins.

The Illegals

Author Meyer Levin joined the Haganah's European underground after World War II and recorded on film this fantastic story of the "Aliyah Bet"—the clandestine movement of the Holocaust survivors to Palestine. Made available through the Steven Spielberg Jewish Film Archive in Jerusalem.
VHS: S30526. $39.95.

Isaac Bashevis Singer in America

Isaac Bashevis Singer stars in this latest issue from the *About the Authors* series. This quintessential Jewish writer shares his 80-plus years of experience through memories and interviews. He is seen in his cluttered New York office and on the streets of the city. Narrated by Judd Hirsch. 60 mins.
VHS: S21233. $24.95.

Isaac Bashevis Singer: Champion of Yiddish Literature

Through a series of frank conversations with the Nobel Laureate, we gain an understanding of his life, his great love and devotion to his mother-tongue, his philosophies of writing as well as religion, and his hopes and aspirations for the future of Yiddish. Includes insightful illustrations by Maurice Sendak. In English. 28 mins.
VHS: S15400. $34.95.

The Jester (Der Purimshpiler)

A romantic comedy, in Yiddish, about a drifter who finds temporary peace when he falls in love with a shoemaker's daughter in a small town. A rare example of Yiddish filmmaking in America. Newly mastered and restored. Yiddish with English subtitles.
VHS: S08951. $79.95.
Joseph Green, USA, 1937, 90 mins.

Jewish Life in Bialystok

Two Polish-Jewish brothers, Shaul and Yizhak Goskind, produced six short films about urban Jewish communities within Poland. This film covers the factories and textile workers, synagogues, parks and libraries of Bialystok. Yiddish with new subtitles. 10 mins.
VHS: S18576. $25.00.

Jewish Life in Cracow

This program looks at Cracow's Jewish quarter, juxtaposing footage of the old and new, the streetcars and horse-drawn carriages, merchants conducting business, sporting activities, games and discussions. The work highlights scenes at the Remu Synagogue and Alte Shul. Yiddish with new English subtitles. 10 mins.
VHS: S18577. $25.00.

Jewish Life in Lvov

The program focuses on the architectural and community landmarks, the Yad Haruzim Trade Union Building, the Old Ghetto, the Modern Temple and the Lazarus Hospital and the Nowosci Theater in Lvov. Yiddish with new English subtitles. 10 mins.
VHS: S18578. $25.00.

Jewish Life in Vilna

This rare film document captures the spirit of Jewish life in pre-World War II Vilna. Lively narration and music accompany film sequences of people engaged in the rituals and realities of daily existence—at work, at play, in the synagogue and in school. Vilna's famous landmarks—the Strashun Library, Shripeshiker Cemetery, YIVO Institute—are among the film's highlights. Narrated in Yiddish with new English subtitles.
VHS: S12285. $25.00.
Yitzhak Lerner, Poland, 1939, 10 mins.

Jews of Poland

Five cities: Bialystok, Lvov, Krakow, Vilna and Warsaw. Between 1938 and 1939, two filmmakers visited six Jewish communities in Poland to record the vitality of Jewish life. Little did they know that their film would become one of the last visual accounts of a once vibrant world. They have been preserved by the Spielberg Jewish Film Archive in Jerusalem. 50 mins.
VHS: S12896. $49.95.

Jolly Paupers

A restored Yiddish classic. A musical comedy portraying the relentless efforts of two small-town Jews to escape their misery and achieve fame and fortune. In the face of setbacks, community quarrels and even insanity, they refuse to give in to despair. With violent anti-Semitism intensifying in Poland and Nazism looming on the horizon, their satirical monologues provided Jewish audiences with a rare opportunity to escape through laughter. From the National Center for Jewish Film. Yiddish with English subtitles.
VHS: S11649. $54.00.
Warsaw Art Players, Poland, 1937, 62 mins.

The King and the Fool

Solomon Mikhoels and Benjamin Zuskin, the King and the Fool, created the Yiddish Theater in post-revolutionary Moscow. Stalin put an end to their creative efforts. Their story can now be told with the help of interviews from surviving relatives and excerpts from films and plays in which these two performed. 40 mins.
VHS: S23232. $39.95.

The Last Klezmer

Klezmer music, sometimes called Jewish "soul" music, is a festive Jewish band music which originated in pre-World War II Poland and is enjoying a revival in America, thanks to 69-year-old Klezmer pioneer Leopold Kozlowski. The career of this last of the active Klezmer musicians culminated in roles as actor and musical consultant in *Schindler's List*. 85 mins.
VHS: S27734. $79.95.
Yau Strom

Letter to Mother

One of the most famous of Yiddish-language American films, directed by Joseph Green. Set in the Polish Ukraine and New York City, the film traces the break-up of a family due to stress, poverty, the chaos of war, and the difficulties of immigrant life. With Berta Gerstein, Lucy Gehrman. Newly mastered and restored. Yiddish with English subtitles.
VHS: S08949. $72.00.
Joseph Green, USA, 1938, 100 mins.

A Life of Song: A Portrait of Ruth Rubin

A powerful documentary by Cindy Marshall that explores the life of Ruth Rubin, covering her determination to preserve, collect and transmit the vibrant legacy of Yiddish folksongs. "Inspiring to many people who wonder if there is hope that their own minority music will be able to survive in some way" (Pete Seeger). 38 mins.
VHS: S17934. $34.95.

The Light Ahead

Edgar G. Ulmer directed this adaptation by Mendele Mokher Seforim, the grandfather of "19th century modern Yiddish literature," about a weak man's obsession for a blind woman. The film is considered a "penetrating look at shtetl life," and Mendele's "Eastern European Jewish world." With David Opatoshu, Helen Beverly and Isidore Cashier. "Beverly and Opatoshu are perhaps the most beautiful couple in the history of Yiddish cinema" (J. Hoberman, author of *Bridge of Light*). Yiddish with English subtitles.
VHS: S17936. $69.95.
Edgar G. Ulmer, USA, 1939, 94 mins.

Little Mother (Mamele)

Joseph Green directed this Yiddish-language, American-made film about a young girl (the famous Molly Picon) who is left with the responsibilities of tending house for a helpless and ungrateful family of seven. Newly mastered and restored. Yiddish with English subtitles.
VHS: S08950. $79.95.

Mirele Efros

Berta Gersten plays Mirele, a noble, dignified widow and successful businesswoman who comes into conflict with the daughter-in-law she chose for her eldest son. Set in turn-of-the-century Grodno, and based on the Jacob Gordin play. 1938, 80 mins. Yiddish with English subtitles.
VHS: S12886. $79.95.

Mothers of Today

In this melodrama about a cantor's son gone bad, the promise of American prosperity reveals its downside, that is, the erosion of traditional Jewish values. The cantor's son steals, runs off with a woman of questionable virtue and, worst of all, breaks his mother's heart. Yiddish with English subtitles.
VHS: S26687. $69.95.
Henry Lynn, USA, 1939, 90 mins.

Moving Mountains: The Montreal Yiddish Theatre in the U.S.S.R.

Ina Fichman's remarkable documentary about Dora Wasserman, a Russian-born Jew who returns to her native country, after a 40-year separation, with her talented group of performers to produce the Yiddish play, *Sages of Chelm*.
VHS: S17933. $34.95.
Ina Fichman, USSR, c. 1988, 28 mins.

Nowogrodek

Organized around a visit by Yiddish lexicographer Alexander Harkavy, the activities in Nowogrodek include sporting events, a bustling marketplace, a crowded synagogue courtyard just after Sabbath prayers, the town's fire brigade at work, a children's summer camp and glimpses of the local theater. A lively montage of Poland's medium-sized, Lithuanian-Jewish community. Silent with Yiddish and English intertitles. 1930, 26 mins.
VHS: S16317. $54.00.

Our Children

Suppressed as too Zionist by the Communist Polish government, this film features the comedy team of Dzigan and Schumacher, together with children who survived the Holocaust. The comic actors play all the roles in Sholem Aleichem's *Kasrilevke Brent (Kasrilevke Is Burning)*. They watch as these orphans perform for them. It's a film that explores what to do with nightmares: should they be remembered or forgotten? Yiddish with new English subtitles.
VHS: S23084. $72.00.
Natan Gross/Shaul Goskind, Poland, 1948, 68 mins.

Overture to Glory

Moishe Oysher stars as the Vilner Balabesi, the cantor who leaves his position as Vilna Cantor in order to seek fame and fortune as an opera star in Warsaw. He feels uncomfortable in his new environment and yearns to return home to his wife, child and community. The film provides a wonderful vehicle for Moishe Oysher's rich cantonal voice. With Helen Beverly and Florence Weiss. "An artistic triumph for the Yiddish motion picture industry." *(New York Herald Tribune)*. Yiddish with English subtitles.
VHS: S10256. $79.95.
Max Nosseck, USA, 1940, 85 mins.

Shalom—Songs of Polish Jews

A unique program of songs from the heritage of Polish Jewry, performed in Yiddish and in Hebrew by Slawa Przybylska. 85 mins.
VHS: S11381. $39.95.

The Singing Blacksmith

David Pinski's classic story of a blacksmith who sees too many women and drinks far too much liquor. Then he meets Tamare and his life drastically changes, or does it? In this charming story, set in Eastern Europe but shot in New Jersey, we are treated to a quaintly romantic film in the tradition of classic Yiddish comedy-drama. Directed by the esteemed, expressionist master of low-budget Hollywood cinema Edgar G. Ulmer, this film is definitely worth a look. Yiddish with English subtitles.
VHS: S15401. $79.95.
Edgar G. Ulmer, USA, 1938, 95 mins.

Tevye the Dairyman

This memorable adaptation of Sholem Aleichem's play centers on Tevye, the dairyman, and his daughter Khave, who falls in love with Fedye, the Gentile son of a Ukrainian peasant. Her courtship and marriage pit Tevye's deep-seated faith and loyalty to tradition. Made from a completely restored print. "With all due respect for Zero Mostel and Topol in *Fiddler on the Roof*, it was Maurice Schwartz, the great Yiddish actor/director, who first showed Tevye the Dairyman in his full light as a *mensch* for all seasons. A rare opportunity to see Schwartz in what may have been his most magnificent role" (Judy Stone, *San Francisco Chronicle*). From the National Center for Jewish Film. Yiddish with new English subtitles.
VHS: S12219. $72.00.
Maurice Schwartz, USA, 1939, 96 mins.

The Train to Happiness

In the new era of freedom enjoyed by Russia, the Jewish Shalom Theater has taken root. Against a backdrop where emergent anti-semitic groups are also exercising their newly found freedom to express themselves, this troupe is bringing Jewish culture to Jews who were previously denied their culture and religion by communism. 57 mins.
VHS: S23231. $39.95.

Two Sisters

Betty Glickstein promises her dying mother that she will care for her younger sister, Sally. From the tender age of 13, Betty sacrifices all to fulfill her promise, even forsaking the prospect of her own family and future happiness. Yiddish with new English subtitles.
VHS: S23085. $72.00.
Ben K. Blake, USA, 1938, 82 mins.

Uncle Moses

A historically important adaptation of the Sholom Asch classic, starring legendary Yiddish performer Maurice Schwartz, a driven, unbending despot of his Lower East Side sweatshop who falls in love with the daughter of one of his distraught workers. With Judith Abarbanel and Zvee Scooler. "Immensely entertaining" *(San Francisco Chronicle)*. Yiddish with English subtitles.
VHS: S17935. $59.95.
Sidney Goldin/Aubrey Scotto, USA, 1932, 87 mins.

The Vow

Two friends plan that their unborn children will marry some day. After the friends lose touch with each other, the children, now grown to adulthood, meet and fall in love. Sadly, the father of the boy has already made other plans for his son's future wife. Only the divine intervention of the Prophet Elijah can solve this muddle of human devising. Yiddish with English subtitles.
VHS: S26686. $79.95.
Henryk Szaro, Poland, 1937, 90 mins.

The World of Sholom Aleichem

From the golden age of television, Zero Mostel, Nancy Walker, Charlotte Rae, Jack Gilford and Gertrude Berg all shine in three classic stories told by Sholom Aleichem, the master Yiddish storyteller. "A Tale of Chelm" deals with a bookseller who is sent by his wife to buy a goat in a town full of fools. "Bontche Schweig" follows the path of a poor, defeated man who dies and goes to heaven, and when asked what he would want the most, his answer brings tears to the eyes of angels. "The High School" portrays a couple's efforts to get their son into a non-religious high school and is a story of one small but persistent effort to break out of segregation.
VHS: S30483. $29.95.
1959, 95 mins.

The Yiddish Cinema

A documentary about the vibrant Yiddish film production that flourished in Eastern Europe and the United States between the First and Second World Wars. Employing interviews, music, archival footage and film clips, the program explores the tradition of Yiddish film in expanding culture and language. Narrated by David Mamet.
VHS: S18580. $25.00.
Rich Pontius, USA, 1991, 60 mins.

Yiddish: The Mame-Loshn (The Mother Tongue)

Shot in New York and Los Angeles, this affectionate portrait examines the importance of Yiddish to American Jews today and evokes the language and culture's pleasures through poetry, illustrations, interviews and film clips. Featuring comedian David Steinberg, actor Herschel Bernardi, writers Leo Rosten and Simon Weber, and scholars Joshua Fishman and Saul Goodman.
VHS: S16319. $36.00.
Cordelia Stone/Mary Hardwick, USA, 1980, 58 mins.

Yidl with a Fiddle

The classic Yiddish language musical comedy. Molly Picon plays a shtetl girl who, disguised as a boy, goes off with her father and a band of traveling musicians into the Polish countryside. Made in pre-war Poland, the film provides a warm rendering of Eastern European Jewish life, made all the more fun and wonderful by Molly Picon's unequaled ability to amuse and entertain. Newly mastered and restored. Yiddish with English subtitles.
VHS: S10258. $72.00.
Joseph Green, Poland, 1936, 92 mins.

Zoll Zeyn (Let It Be)

A documentary that assesses the cultural and linguistic impact of Yiddish in modern day Israel, after the early Zionists established Hebrew as a signifier for hope and recovery. Yiddish with English subtitles.
VHS: S18581. $72.00.
H.M. Broder/F. van der Meulen, Israel, 1989, 135 mins.

THE WORLD OF JUDAISM

2,000 Years of Freedom and Honor: The Cochini Jews of India

Jews arrived in India in 72 C.E., soon after the destruction of the Second Temple in Jerusalem. Throughout the years, though deeply loyal to India, they prayed for their return to Zion. This documentary captures the conflicting emotions of two generations of Cochini Jews, and explores their religious, cultural and economic life.
VHS: S33188. $59.95.
Johanna Spector, India, 180 mins.

About the Jews of Yemen: A Vanishing Culture

During their 2000-year-long sojourn in Yemen, Jews developed special traditions, customs, ceremonies, art, music and dance. This documentary captures this rich culture as it is practiced today in modern Israel.
VHS: S33189. $59.95.
Johanna Spector, Yemen, 77 mins.

Alef...Bet...Blast-Off!

This award-winning series will help families discover how traditional Jewish values apply to modern life and fill a child's heart with the pride and joy of being Jewish, as the intrepid Jewish explorer Mitvah Mouse whisks David and Rachel back in time to meet some of the most important people in Jewish history.

Alef...Bet...Blast-Off!: A Whale of a New Year. David and Rachel meet a talented young Russian immigrant, Talli, who tries to teach the kids about freedom. It's hard for the kids to understand how important freedom is until an unexpected twist causes David, Rachel, Talli and Mitzvah Mouse to become personal slaves to the Pharoah (Dom DeLuise). 30 mins.
VHS: S32307. $14.95.

Alef...Bet...Blast-Off!: Lights of Freedom. David is always losing things. Though he tries to improve himself for Rosh Hashana (Jewish New Year), he still manages to lose his sister Rachel's beloved goldfish. Rachel is so upset that she can't forgive David. But thanks to Mitvah Mouse, a trip to a whale's belly, and a heart-to-heart with Jonah himself (Avery Schreiber), David learns to accept responsibility. 30 mins.
VHS: S32306. $14.95.

Argentina's Jews: Days of Awe

Jews came to Argentina and founded the agricultural community of Moiseville. This video provides a history of Argentinian Jewry, counterbalanced with their current battles with anti-Semitism, assimilation and loss of identity. 55 mins.
VHS: S12890. $34.95.

Ashkenaz: Eastern European Jewry

This video offers a nostalgic look at the music of Eastern European Jewry. Yiddish folk songs, liturgical music, Klezmer melodies and even Yiddish theater tunes are all here. The origins of Ashkenazic music are traced with the help of vintage archival footage taken before World War II. 28 mins.
VHS: S21710. $39.95.

Battle for Survival: The Arab-Israeli Six Day War

On June 5, 1967, surrounded and outnumbered three-to-one by Arab troops, Israel had to fight or face destruction. It launched Strike Zion, a top-secret battle plan in which the Israeli airforce attacked air bases and nearly immobilized opposition air power; the tank battle that followed was the biggest in history. This historic film captures fascinating images of the Six Day War, which remains one of the most important battles in recent history and one of the great military victories of all time. Features the rare film documentary *Strike Zion!*. 60 mins.
VHS: S34387. $29.95.

Benjamin and the Miracle of Hanukkah

Herschel Bernardi narrates this video that explains both the story and the history of Hanukkah. This animation also includes a visit to the site of the Hanukkah miracle and a tale detailing the struggle for religious freedom, told by a Russian emigre. 25 mins.
VHS: S26202. $9.95.

The Big Moment

This 1954 classic features three vignettes which illustrate how Jews the world over provide help and support for others. Narrated by Robert Young, with an all-star cast including Donna Reed, John Derek, Thomas Mitchell, Eduard Franz and Forrest Tucker. 30 mins.
VHS: S33171. $19.95.

Branching Out: Tracing Your Jewish Roots

Arthur Kurzweil travels to Ellis Island and other sites in this do-it-yourself video about tracing family trees. This genealogist makes the process clear and understandable to any amateur. 30 mins.
VHS: S23249. $39.95.

Bubbe Meises, Bubbe Stories

Ellen Gould wrote and stars in this one-woman show about her two "Bubbes" (Yiddish for grandmothers). It's a heartwarming concoction made up of humorous but emotional tales from the lives of these women who left the old world and struggled to create a life in the new world. 75 mins.
VHS: S26037. $39.95.

Chanuka at Bubbe's

Delightful Muppet-like characters create an irresistible cast in this program explaining the traditions and significance of Chanuka. Great family entertainment. USA.
VHS: S14949. $19.95.

A Chanukah Adventure
Professor Pellah together with his hungry goldfish goes on a mission to publicize the holiday of Chanukah. He assembles a group of young helpers who come up with some great ideas. The Professor's music video is simply priceless and there are segments of public menorah lightings from all over the world. 30 mins.
VHS: S24675. $19.95.

Children Must Laugh
Aleksandar Ford's powerful documentary, financed by the Jewish labor movement in Poland, is a revealing look at Polish pre-war Jewish life. "Out of the sorrows and shadows of the life of Jewish workers in Poland, a bright ray of hope has come....Hollywood scouts would do well to locate some of the children...[whose] confidence in their ability to 'build a better world' rises above any language barrier" *(The New York Times)*. Polish and Yiddish with English narration and subtitles.
VHS: S19534. $54.00.
Aleksandar Ford, Poland/USA, 1935/65, 64 mins.

Covenant: People of the Living Law
Theodore Bikel leads a panel of experts who examine the flexibility and subsequent longevity of both the U.S. Constitution and Halacha (Jewish Law). 60 mins.
VHS: S24500. $29.95.

A Day in Warsaw
This kaleidoscopic program brings out the diversity of Warsaw, from the Zamenhof and Nalewki streets that were the centerpiece for the city's 400,000 Jews to its study of ancient and contemporary architecture, its theaters, cemeteries and other prominent Jewish institutions. Yiddish with new English subtitles. 10 mins.
VHS: S18579. $100.00.

The Discovery
Josh Saviano, teenage star of the hit TV show *The Wonder Years*, is at the center of this video about bar mitzvah. By questioning friends Josh learns about the ceremony, the heritage it represents, and the responsibilities it confers. 60 mins.
VHS: S24503. $29.95.

Dosvedanya Means Good-bye
Roberta Hantgan's film follows the course of Tamara Okun's life. Tamara is a Russian Jew who waited eight years for an exit visa. From Leningrad to Vienna and finally Washington, D.C., this is a story of perseverance, courage and growing awareness of Jewish identity. 30 mins.
VHS: S23258. $34.95.

The Eternal Jew
Dr. Fritz Hippler was responsible for this vicious anti-Semitic propaganda "documentary." Yiddish with English subtitles.
VHS: S34067. $29.95.
George Roland, USA, 1933, 63 mins.

Eugene
Experience the heartwarming story of Eugene Chernyakhovsky, a boy with cerebral palsy who overcomes many challenges as he prepares for his bar mitzvah. Assisted by a team of experts and volunteers from his community, Eugene transfers his entire *Torah* portion to a computer using only one foot. 60 mins.
VHS: S33743. $34.95.

Europe: Toward the Twentieth Century
Filmed in Vienna and St. Petersburg, this video illustrates the influence that 19th-century European music exerted on Jewish music of that period. Features the Schubert Boys Choir of Vienna, conducted by Matthew Lazar, Cantor Shmuel Barzilai, and Joseph Dorfman. 30 mins.
VHS: S33173. $39.95.

Falashas
Meyer Levin's classic documentary film study of Ethiopian Jewry in 1973. Levin ventured to Ethiopia to record Jews forgotten by the World. We view Jewish rituals and practices as observed for generations in isolation. An important document which became an international event when the Falashas were air-lifted out of Ethiopia in 1984.
VHS: S06578. $34.95.
Meyer Levin, USA, 1973, 27 mins.

Gefilte Fish
Three generations of women share their individual methods for making Gefilte Fish. 15 mins.
VHS: S12870. $25.95.

The Golem (of L.A.)
Ed Asner stars as Rabbi Judah Lowenstein, the elderly Rabbi of Los Angeles' oldest remaining synagogue, in Lewis Schoenbrun's contemporary version of *The Golem*. Twenty-one-year-old David cannot fully comprehend his grandfather's love for the Rabbi's congregation. When the 75-year-old house of worship is about to be demolished to make way for luxury apartments, Grandpa, in a final dramatic act of desperation, enlists the aid of the supernatural in resolving the crisis. Set against the background of urban 1990s America, the story provides keen insight into the modern-day Jewish generation gap. 25 mins.
VHS: S33174. $29.95.

Great Cantors of the Golden Age
In 1931, during the Golden Age of *Chazzanut*, the New York film director Joseph Seiden produced *The Voice of Israel*, the only filmed record of some of the most famous cantors from 1910 to 1940. With restored selections from this footage, Dr. Max Wohlberg describes the history and artistry of these unparalleled vocal talents. Featuring Cantors Mordechai Hershman, Adolph Katchko, David Roitman, Yossele Rosenblatt, Joseph Shlisky and Gershon Sirota.
VHS: S16313. $54.00.
Murray E. Simon, USA, 1990, 54 mins.

Great Sadness of Zohara
Nina Menkes combines sound, image and fragments of poetry in this moving film about the journey of a young Jewish woman who is drawn to explore the world of the spirit. Her journey takes her to remote and increasingly desolate regions of the Arab lands—alienating her from the orthodox Jewish community in Israel. This mystical quest culminates in her return to Israel where, indelibly marked, she confronts her loneliness and a devastating sense of exile.
VHS: S07374. $39.95.
Nina Menkes, USA, 1983, 40 mins.

Guilt and Repentance
The major themes of the High Holy Day service are discussed by a panel of eminent Rabbis and scholars. Translations and interpretations of the texts are also included. 60 mins.
VHS: S24506. $29.95.

The Hasidim
A close look at this Jewish sect which originated in Russia in the 1700s and now has settled in neighborhoods in Brooklyn, NY. With Hasidic songs featured on the soundtrack. 29 mins.
VHS: S15534. $45.00.

Hassidut: Hassidic Music
Music is central for the Hassidic community. Famed Rabbi Nahman of Bratslav taught his students that one can pray not only through word but also through song. Filmed in the Hassidic community, beautiful melodies from prayers, celebrations and other significant events are included. 28 mins.
VHS: S21709. $39.95.

Havana Nagila: The Jews in Cuba
This eye-opening video traces the history and presence of the remaining Jewish community in Cuba. After the 1959 Revolution, 95% of the Cuban Jewish community fled the country. Rich in archival material and Cuban ambience, with fascinating firsthand interviews, we are presented a side of Cuba that has never been seen before. The artful use of Cuban and Jewish music, painting, photography and oral history gives voice to a nearly forgotten community, whose members share a growing national sentiment, that a bridge to Cuba must be built at any cost.
VHS: S30530. $39.95.
Laura Paull, USA, 60 mins.

Hester Street
Set on the Lower East Side of New York in 1896, Gitl and her son reunite with husband Jake, who had previously immigrated from Russia. Jake has completely embraced America by shedding his ethnic heritage, and is embarrassed when Gitl clings to her old country ways. But in this charming and humorous portrait of the Jewish immigrant experience, Gitl finds a way to become victor instead of victim. Carol Kane was nominated for an Oscar for her portrayal of Gitl. With Stephen Keats.
VHS: S00564. $29.95.
Joan Micklin Silver, USA, 1974, 89 mins.

Hot Bagels: The Hole Story
A personable young bagel baker takes us on a tour through the bagel-making process, from its origins to contemporary methods. 12 mins.
VHS: S12869. $25.95.

I Ask for Wonder: Experiencing God
Prayer, study, ritual, tragedy and good deeds can all be pathways to God. Professors and Rabbis join forces to explain the value of these everyday experiences in the practice of Judaism. 60 mins.
VHS: S24504. $29.95.

The Intifada (Palestinian Uprising): A Jewish Eye Witness
A dramatic "photomated" slide presentation on video. "A new perspective on the Intifada—something which generally isn't available in the U.S. American Jews should see this perspective in order to get a more complete picture of the Middle East conflict" (Michael Argamon, Yesh G'vul). 50 mins.
VHS: S31651. $49.95.

Jerusalem: City of Heaven
This program from The Discovery Channel presents a portrait of the complex city claimed by Jews, Muslims and Christians. Filled with the voices of Jerusalem's diverse residents, this documentary uses personal stories and powerful images to show how Jerusalem's remarkable past resonates in the lives of its people today and how anticipation of the Day of Judgement shapes ordinary life as nowhere else on earth. 90 mins.
VHS: S31941. $19.95.

Jewish American Patriots
Jewish American Patriots focuses on the largely neglected history of the contributions of Jews in the United States military. From 1644 through Operation Desert Storm, this documentary details the lives of the vast number of American Jews who fought in defense of their country. Dozens of Jewish patriots are highlighted, from George Washington's close friend, Haym Soloman, to the Jewish Veterans of Operation Desert Storm. 60 mins.
VHS: S27244. $29.95.

Jewish Communities of the Middle Ages
The Jewish communities of Babylonia, Spain and Ashkenaz were once sources for rich and varied Jewish life. This video examines each of these important historical Jewish cultures. 30 mins.
VHS: S23247. $39.95.

The Jewish Holidays Video Guide
The Cohen family invites viewers to experience the cycle of the Jewish calendar with their family. They rediscover the history and customs of the holy days, focusing on songs, stories, meals, games, prayers and rituals. Ed Asner, Theodore Bikel, Monty Hall and Judge Wapner are all featured. 90 mins.
VHS: S23010. $29.95.

A Jewish Perspective on the Environment
In this documentary produced by the Jewish Theological Seminary of America and the Coalition on the Environment and Jewish Life, you'll take a fascinating journey through the Bible and along the Appalachian Trail as experts in the fields of science, religion and philosophy hike, camp and explore the world of nature and share their thoughts and concerns on the intersection of Judaism, the environment and justice. One hour.
VHS: S30960. $34.95.

Jewish Soul Music: The Art of Giora Feldman
Once they wandered all over Europe, small bands of Jewish soul musicians, owning neither land nor property. Musical know-how was passed from father to son, their music based on improvisation and musical skill. Giora Feldman is the fourth generation of such musicians, and his life is the story of the revival of Jewish soul music in our times. After 18 years with the Israel Philharmonic, he decided to return to his roots—to become a klezmer, a Jewish soul musician. This is his incredible story. 50 mins.
VHS: S10257. $39.95.

The Jews of Boston
Native son Leonard Nimoy narrates the vibrant story of America's sixth largest Jewish community, from its tentative roots to its rise to influence in the 20th century. With archival photographs. 60 mins.
VHS: S31423. $19.95.

Jews of Djerba
Djerba, an island off the southeast coast of Tunisia, is home for a small and little known Jewish community. Djerbain Jews see their community as a living remnant of the Babylonian Jewish community created after the destruction of Solomon's temple over 2500 years ago. 26 mins.
VHS: S12895. $34.95.

A Jumping Night in the Garden of Eden
A wonderful documentary on the klezmer bands, Michael Goldman's film focuses on Kapelye of New York and the Klezmer Conservatory Band in Boston in a depiction of this emotional music of Eastern Europe. Klezmer music, played at celebrations of Eastern European Jews, provides a vibrant record of cultures, revealing gypsy, Balkan, Turkish influences. And the current klezmer revival signals a reinventing of the past, as three generations of musicians keep klezmer alive. English and Yiddish with English subtitles.
VHS: S09351. $29.95.
Michael Oldman, USA, 1987, 75 mins.

Keshet ve Anan—Cloud and Rainbow

This series deals with Jewish Holidays, the Jewish calendar and other traditional events, and is primarily designed for children of the elementary and junior high level. Programs are in Hebrew. Each program is approximately 45 mins. Israel, 1989.

New Year and Sukkot.
VHS: S10461. $39.95.
Chanukah.
VHS: S10462. $39.95.
Tu B'Shvat and Purim.
VHS: S10463. $39.95.

Last Jews of Radauti (Song of Radauti)

In this film study of Jews in a small Rumanian town, we meet members of this dwindling community, including the rabbi and shokhet. Observed are the intimate expressions of Jewish life, preparing for the Sabbath, making challah, immersions in the mikveh. 25 mins.
VHS: S12897. $34.95.
Laurence Salzmann, Romania, 25 mins.

Last Journey

Before Nodar Djindjhashvili, a Soviet Jew, left his homeland for the final time, he made an odyssey that took him into 40 communities, spanning 10,000 miles. He recorded Jewish life wherever he found it—in the street, in synagogue, even in cemeteries. What he searches for is the face of Jewish identity. 24 mins.
VHS: S12899. $34.95.

Legendary Voices: Cantors of Yesteryear

In this unique compilation of cantorial greats, we are treated to memorable film recordings of such outstanding voices as David Roitman, Adolph Katchko, Leibele Waldman, Moishe Oysher and Yossele Rosenblatt. A wonderful tribute to a bygone era, and a treasured collector's item for Jewish music lovers everywhere. 45 mins.
VHS: S15406. $49.95.

Lodz Ghetto

This film covers the years 1940-1944 as it chronicles the 200,000 Jews trapped in the Polish ghettos during the German occupation. The film moves from the past and present; the script was developed from the diaries of the survivors and people left behind. Music by Wendy Blackstone. "Your blood turns to ice. To be unmoved by this film is to be made of stone" *(New York Daily News)*.
VHS: S17891. $29.95.
Kathryn Taverna/Alan Adelson, USA, 1991

The Longest Hatred

This stunning, three-part documentary takes an unsparing look at the experience of Jewish people as "the other," from the first century to the present—a revealing history of anti-Semitism with roots long before the Holocaust and branches that continue to sprout in surprising places today. A PBS WGBH Boston Special. 150 mins.
VHS: S33090. $29.95.

Meet Me at Brooklyn and Soto

Harold Gould narrates this nostalgic celebration of the Jewish community of Los Angeles from the 1920s to the 1950s, radiating from the lively corner of Brooklyn Avenue (now Cesar Chavez Avenue) and Soto Street, in East L.A.'s Boyle Heights neighborhood. Major landmarks such as the Breed Street shul, the Soto and Michigan Jewish Community Center and the Old Jewish Home for the Aged in Boyle Heights are fondly remembered. 70 mins.
VHS: S33177. $29.95.

Miracle of Intervale Avenue

This sensitive exploration searches for the secrets of a once thriving Jewish community in the South Bronx that somehow continues despite the decay that surrounds it. The film shows a remarkable reality of Jews, Blacks and Puerto Ricans interacting and helping each other. What makes this film so moving is the cast of vital, complex and moving characters. 65 mins.
VHS: S06576. $59.95.

Molly's Pilgrim

This Academy Award-winning live-action short subject examines the plight of a young Russian Jewish emigrant who has come to the United States to escape religious persecution. It carries a message about American values, Thanksgiving, growing up and religious tolerance. 24 mins.
VHS: S33787. $89.00.

Morocco: The Music of Moroccan Jews

The Moroccan Jews of North Africa created their own unique musical form of expression by borrowing tunes from their Arab neighbors and adding Hebrew. Filmed in Morocco and Israel, this video focuses on the flavor and the poetry, messianic songs and rhythms that evolved into authentic Moroccan-Jewish music. 28 mins.
VHS: S21708. $39.95.

Murray Avenue: A Community in Transition

In this portrait of a vital but changing Jewish neighborhood in Pittsburgh, Sheila Chamovitz focuses on the social and commercial life of three of the neighborhood's traditional businesses: a bakery, a butcher shop and a newsstand. The film offers an appreciation of the intimate, friendly, urban lifestyle common to ethnic neighborhoods and expresses concern about the future survival of these communities. 28 mins.
VHS: S33178. $29.95.

No Shmaltz! My Yiddisheh Cooking Video

Brush up on your Yiddish and your knishes at the same time with this lively cooking video in Yiddish featuring tasty, low-fat international Jewish dishes accompanied by vaudeville humor and Yiddish song. Yiddish actors Shifra Lerer and Hy Wolfe demonstrate the preparation of nine delicious, egg-, dairy- and guilt-free recipes from soups to desserts from Debra Wasserman's *Lowfat Jewish Vegetarian Cookbook*. Yiddish with English subtitles. 30 mins.
VHS: S34936. $24.95.

Now I Know My Aleph Bet

This two-volume set teaches the Hebrew alphabet in a classroom setting through Hebrew songs and Torah tales. Ideal for use in a school setting or at home.
VHS: S24803. $45.00.

An Oasis in Time

Through diaries, journals and personal reminiscences, Jews from many periods and places describe the importance of the Sabbath. There is great value in the age-old practice of one day a week set aside for rest and religious experience. 60 mins.
VHS: S24502. $29.95.

One Word, Many Texts

Edwin Newman hosts this video exploration of the importance placed in text and study within Judaism. Filmed at the Seminary, it shows how traditional texts are read to be relevant for succeeding generations. Includes The Genesis Seminar. 60 mins.
VHS: S24499. $29.95.

Operation Moses: A Documentary

The epic story of the rescue, immigration and absorption of Ethiopian Jewry is told in this gripping documentary. Through testimonials and rare footage, we view the saga of a people saved from extinction by the efforts of the World Jewish community. 27 mins.
VHS: S12892. $29.95.

Passover at Bubbe's

Delightful Muppet-like characters create an irresistible cast in this program explaining the traditions and significance of the Passover holiday. USA.
VHS: S14950. $19.95.

A Passover Seder

Elie Wiesel, acclaimed author of over 30 books, shares his own memories and poetic interpretations regarding this holy ceremony. Mark Podwal provides the illustrations for this animated celebration. 30 mins.
VHS: S23945. $14.95.

Passover: Traditions of Freedom

This holiday commemorates the Jew's journey of freedom from the bonds of Egyptian slavery. History, literature, spirituality and even cooking are combined on this important occasion. Elements of the traditions of Passover are examined, including visits to a matzoh factory and a Passover winery, and four seders with Ashkenazic and Sephardic families.
VHS: S23091. $29.95.
John Nathan, USA, 1994, 57 mins.

Pier Marton: Say I'm a Jew

A collage of interviews with Jews who grew up in post war Europe as they describe their experiences. The film progresses from a "memory" of the Holocaust and early self-denial experiences, to a manifesto-like affirmation of Jewish identity. Directed by Pier Marton. 28 mins.
VHS: S13304. $69.95.
Pier Marton, USA

Pilgrimage of Remembrance: Jews in Poland Today

Of the three and a half million Jews who lived in Poland on the eve of World War II, only 6,000 remain. Yet, each year, more and more Jews from abroad come to pay homage to the birthplace of their ancestors. Filmed on location in 15 different cities and villages, Yaron Shemer's documentary enables us to see what remains of Jewish life in Poland today, while journeying through what was once a rich and glorious era.
VHS: S15404. $49.95.
Yaron Shemer, Poland, 48 mins.

Rambam Cures the King/ Uncle Pinchey Comes Home

Two informative works constructed in combinations of puppet theater and live action. *Rambam Cures the King* is an engaging work about the Biblical scholar Maimonides, who counsels and provides inspiration from advice influenced by the New Testament. *Rambam* is a thoughtful and serious examination of the Jewish pride, religious persecution and cultural identities. In the contemporary *Uncle Pinchey Comes Home*, a Russian immigrant confronts extreme cultural differences and strange adjustments when he goes to live with his Brooklyn relatives. 60 mins.
VHS: S19241. $9.98.

Regression in Time

Regress in time with Dr. Gelberman to the second century, where he reincarnates himself into his *former life*—the author of the Zokar, Rabbi Simeon bar Yohai. 119 mins.
VHS: S10516. $49.95.

The Return

A three-part series covering the story of the Jewish people's dramatic return to their ancestral homeland, culminating in the first Jewish state in 2,000 years. Spans the period from the late 19th century. Includes interviews with founders of the Jewish state, as well as their descendants, including Amos Ben Gurion, son of David Ben Gurion; Ze'ev Jabotinsky, grandson of the spiritual father of Israel's Likud party; the Chelouche family, who helped found Tel Aviv; Shimon Peres; Yitzhak Shamir; and Natan Sharansky. Each tape is 52 minutes. In *Part I: The Birth of a Movement*, Jews make their way to Palestine as a response to anti-Semitism and persecution in Europe. The Dreyfus Affair in France greatly influences Theodore Herzl, who successfully creates Zionism as a political movement. Covers the late 19th century to 1904. *Part II: The Building of a Nation*, covers the founding of Tel Aviv, the Third Aliya, life under the British Mandate and Aliya Bet, and the national liberation movements all dramatically unfold. Details the period through the establishment of the State in 1948. *Part III: The Israeli Experience*, covers the establishment of the State of Israel. Emphasis is placed on the mass immigration of millions of Jews from the world over, from survivors of the Holocaust to a very recent Iraqi immigrant.
VHS: S33169. $115.00.

Return to My Shtetl Delatyn

After 61 years, Berl Nachim Lindwer, accompanied by his son and granddaughter, returns to the shtetl he had loved. Formerly in Galicia and now in Poland/Ukraine, Berl walks the streets and views the houses he was never meant to see again. English narration and Dutch with English subtitles. 60 mins.
VHS: S23239. $39.95.

Return to the Jewish Ghetto of Venice

Of the 1300 Jews who lived in Venice before World War II, only ten families remain. Cut to the rhythm of Italian operas, this video combines Venetian textures with a distinctive Jewish tone that captures the life of this much diminished community. 28 mins.
VHS: S23257. $34.95.

Ritual: Three Portraits of Jewish Life

Morning prayer, the Sukkot festival and a brit milah offer three instances where ritual gives meaning and structure to life. This educational video offers learned opinions from Rabbis and religious experts. 60 mins.
VHS: S24498. $29.95.

Romance of a People: The First 100 Years of Jewish Life in Chicago: 1833-1933

Rare film footage, vintage photos, sound recordings and informative interviews combine to tell the story of the building of Chicago's Jewish community and its impact on the "Windy City." Highlighted is the role of the early German-Jewish settlers in the development of some of the city's major cultural institutions, the arrival of Jews from Eastern Europe, and actual film footage of the Jewish community's pageant "Romance of a People," presented during the Century of Progress Exposition in 1933. With music performed by the Maxwell Street Klezmer Band. 30 mins.
VHS: S33176. $29.95.

Routes of Exile: A Moroccan Jewish Odyssey

This compelling look at the remnant of the Jewish community in Morocco provides a new perspective on the current crisis of Jews in a modern Arab state and in the Middle East. Shot on location, the film vividly portrays the ongoing odyssey of a 2,000 year old community whose remarkable journey is still unfolding. 90 mins.
VHS: S06579. $59.95.

The Sabbath Bride

From sundown on Friday until dusk on Saturday, Jews cherish Shabbat as a sanctuary from the stresses and strains of the working week, a legacy passed from one generation to the next, and a symbol of the enduring strength of the Jewish people.
VHS: S16321. $90.00.
Naomi Gryn, Great Britain, 1987, 52 mins.

Saying Kaddish
Tovah Feldschuh, Phyllis Newman and Stephen Pearlman star in this hour-long drama about a Jewish family affirming life in the face of death. An underlying theme emphasizes the importance of community during times of crises. 60 mins.
VHS: S24505. $29.95.

A Secret Space
The story of David Goodman, the son of liberal, secular parents, who stumbles into an abandoned Lower East Side synagogue being reclaimed by a group of spiritual Jews looking for meaning in their lives. To the dismay of his parents, David becomes increasingly interested in his Jewish roots as he is welcomed into the community of worshipers. 80 mins.
VHS: S12868. $79.95.

Sepharad: Judeo-Spanish Music
Five hundred years after the expulsion of Spanish Jewry, the musical heritage of the Sephardim is alive and well. The film focuses on music first sung by Spanish singers in the Middle Ages, lullabies, wedding tunes, synagogue melodies and songs of mourning, performed in the rich traditional style of the Sephardim. 27 mins.
VHS: S21711. $39.95.

Shalom Shabat
In this delightful program for the whole family, Chaim Topol and Hanny Nachmias perform traditional and contemporary Shabbat songs and stories which have been adapted with modern arrangements and feature color clay animation. Includes "Lecha Dodi," "Shalom Aleichem," "Hinei Ma Tov," "Yedid Nefesh" and 20 other songs as well as the stories "Yosef Mokir Shabbat" and "The Boy with the Prayer." 45 mins. Dialog in English; songs in Hebrew.
VHS: S30866. $24.95.

Shvitz! My Yiddisheh Workout
Tone your muscles while you brush up on your Yiddish with this fun workout tape in Yiddish accompanied by Klezmer music. Veteran actress of the Yiddish stage Shifra Lerer, along with Betty Silberman and Yekhiel Geller-Katz, lead this workout for beginners to buffs. Includes a warm-up and muscle-toning exercises for arms, legs and abdomen. In Yiddish with English subtitles. 30 mins.
VHS: S34937. $24.95.

Sing-Along at Bubbe's
Kids can sing along with their favorite characters from the award-winning *Chanuka at Bubbe's* and *Passover at Bubbe's* as they learn about Jewish holidays. 15 mins.
VHS: S31754. $12.95.

Spirit and Song: The 1997 North American Jewish Choral Festival
Over 500 cantors, musicians, conductors, composers and professional and amateur singers come together at the largest annual gathering of Jewish song and spirit in the U.S. to celebrate the glory of traditional and contemporary music. A five-day musical fest set in the Catskill Mountains. 60 mins.
VHS: S33744. $34.95.

The Star, The Castle and the Butterfly
In the Jewish tradition, Prague is known as *ir va'em b'yisrael* or mother in the family of Israel. A city that has nurtured generations of scholars and sages, Prague's Jewish quarter now only hold memories and monuments to a past full of promise and hope. Hugo Gryn visits some of its most evocative sites.
VHS: S16322. $54.00.
Naomi Gryn, Great Britain, 1990, 25 mins.

The Story of Two Synagogues
In Chodorov, Poland, a 17th-century synagogue was decorated with paintings. Through the perspective of the painter, the lives of that place and time are recalled. Then in Curacao, a synagogue from 1732 serves as a bridge to the small but vibrant community of that tropical Carribean island. 17 mins.
VHS: S23259. $29.95.

Tales of the Days of Awe
Judaism has been described as theology in narrative. Dramatic readings of works by I.L. Peretz, Sholom Aleichem and Elie Wiesel demonstrate this thesis. Robert Blumenfeld and Rochelle Oliver read these legends. 60 mins.
VHS: S24507. $29.95.

The Talmud and the Scholar
Rabbi Adin Steinsaltz' modern translation of the Oral Law has brought this text to a new generation of English speakers. In this portrait, his warm and sensitive ways are revealed along with his singular, inspirational perspective. 58 mins.
VHS: S23261. $34.95.

Teiman: Music of Yemenite Jewry
Yemenite Jews have perfected singing and rhythm, drumming and dancing over centuries. World-renowned vocalists Ofra Haza and Noa (Aicinoam Nini) are just some of the talented performers who illustrate the Yemeni rhythms that have conquered the world stage. 27 mins.
VHS: S21712. $39.95.

There's No Such Thing as a Chanukah Bush, Sandy Goldstein
A young Jewish girl, confronted with Christmas trees and a friend's Chanukah bush, longs to participate in this custom. Fortunately, her grandfather helps her realize the importance of preserving Jewish customs and appreciating other beliefs when he takes her to an office Christmas party. Ideal for studies in Jewish culture. Named Best Short Dramatic Adaptation of the 1993 Charleston Film Fest. 1993, 23 mins.
VHS: S25712. $295.00.

A Tickle in the Heart
A charming portrait of the three Epstein brothers, once the kings of klezmer music. Now retired in Florida and in their 80s, the brothers embark on an international tour. An infectious cinematic snapshot of joie de vivre with "a hearty helping of some of the world's liveliest and most poignant folk music" *(New York Times)*.
VHS: S33315. $59.95.
Stefan Schweitert, USA/Germany, 1997, 83 mins.

Visions of Eden: A Jewish Perspective on the Environment
Take a fascinating journey through the *Bible* and along the Appalachian Trail as experts in the fields of science, religion and philosophy hike, camp, explore the natural world and share their thoughts and concerns on the intersection of Judaism, the environment and justice. 60 mins.
VHS: S33742. $34.95.

Visions: Jewish American Hall of Fame
Since 1969, the Judah Magnes Museum's Jewish American Hall of Fame, under the direction of Mel Wachs, has produced one of the most important series of medals in recent years. A brief history of each of the honorees is accompanied by photos and archival footage. The medals honor such personalities as Haym Salomon, Emma Lazarus, Judah L. Magnes, Henrietta Szold, Golda Meir, Hank Greenberg, Elie Wiesel, Harry Houdini, Barbra Streisand and more. 30 mins.
VHS: S33175. $29.95.

Voices from Sepharad
Five hundred years after Catholic monarchy expelled Jews from the Iberian peninsula, a changed Spain has begun to acknowledge the cultural riches created by coexistence and the contributions made by Jewish communities during the 15 centuries preceding their exile. In this remarkable seven-part series, *Voices from Sepharad* examines Sephardic Jewry from its roots—with a common language based in the cultures of medieval Spain that nurtured a unique style of poetry, music and folklore—to the modern day Sephardic communities scattered about Europe, North Africa, the Middle East and the Americas who have maintained their Hispanic ties.
VHS: S16810. $180.00.
Solly Wolodarsky, Spain/Israel/France, 1992, 364 mins.

West of Hester Street
With great warmth and humor, *West of Hester Street* interweaves the dramatized events of the movement of Jewish immigrants to Galveston, Texas, with the story of a young Jewish peddler who journeys from Russia to Texas. The late Sam Jaffe narrates the heart-warming story of these pioneers.
VHS: S11230. $39.95.
A. & C. Salzman Mondell, USA, 1983, 58 mins.

Where Is My Child?
This moving tale explores tragedy set against the massive exodus of European Jewry into the United States. With Celia Adler, Anna Lillian and Morris Strassberg. "Inevitably there was a price to be paid in terms of health, family ties and religion" *(Kansas City Jewish Chronicle)*.
VHS: S18575. $54.00.
Abraham Left/Harry Lynn, USA, 1937, 92 mins.

Without the Past
The first Jews are said to have arrived in Portugal with the trading expeditions of King Solomon. Isaac Bitton, a descendant of the "Retournados," the Jews who returned to Portugal after the Great Hurricane of 1755, guides us through the fascinating history of Portuguese Jewry, from its very beginnings to today.
VHS: S33190. $34.95.
Johanna Spector, Portugal, 24 mins.

Yehuda Amichai
Poems from *Selected Poetry of Yehuda Amichai* were read by this author on March 15, 1989, at Georgetown University in Washington, D.C. Lewis MacAdams interviewed this German-born Jewish poet who often captures the Jewish past in echoes from the Bible. From the *Lannan Literary Videos* series. 60 mins.
VHS: S27117. $19.95.

The Yiddishe Gauchos
This intriguing documentary tells the nearly forgotten tale of how Jewish immigrants to Argentina became a part of that country's ranching culture. These immigrants built schools, hospitals, libraries, theaters and agricultural coops in the wilderness. Narrated by Eli Wallach.
VHS: S23086. $54.00.
Mark Freeman, USA, 1989, 28 mins.

Zamke: One Story, A Thousand Thoughts
Solly Yellin, or Zamke, as he is known by his childhood friends, born in Poland in the early 1900s, is asked to participate in a dramatic mission to rescue 200 Torah scrolls from Poland during the early 1970s. Disguised as a businessman, Solly leaves his home in South Africa for Poland, motivated by the thought of fulfilling a great Mitzvah. Midway during his mission, he discovers that all is not what it appears to be. 30 mins.
VHS: S33191. $39.95.

Zlateh the Goat
With the holiday season approaching, poor Reuven, the furrier, has no recourse but to sell the family's beloved goat for supplies. But Aaron has other ideas. Story by Isaac B. Singer. Live action. 20 mins.
VHS: S33788. $49.95.

NORTH AFRICAN CINEMA

Halfaouine—Boy of the Terraces
This breakthrough film from North Africa is a charming tale of a young boy's sexual awakening in Muslim Tunisia. Boughedir's style is sensual and full of joy, celebrating the pleasures of everyday life. Arabic with English subtitles. "A source of wonder. Exquisitely sensual. Packed with humor" *(Chicago Reader)*.
VHS: S30707. $79.95.
Ferid Boughedir, Tunisia, 1995, 98 mins.

Lion of the Desert
Moustapha Akkad *(The Message)* returns with this spectacle set in the Libyan desert. Benito Mussolini (Rod Steiger) and General Rodolfo Graziani (Oliver Reed) try to crush the rebellion of Bedouin patriots led by Anthony Quinn against Italian colonialists in 1929 Africa. Includes a "making-of" theatrical short. Two-tape set.
VHS: S34621. $29.98.
DVD: Making of documentary. **DV60426. $29.99.**
Moustapha Akkad, Libya/Great Britain, 1980, 206 mins.

The Message
Originally released under the title Mohammed—Messenger of God, this colossal Panavision effort tells of the origins of Islam, and stars Anthony Quinn and Irene Pappas. After seeing a vision of the Angel Gabriel, Mohammed (Quinn) calls the people of Mecca to cast aside the 300 idols of the Kaaba and worship one God. Also includes the one-hour documentary The Making of an Epic plus the English and Arabic theatrical trailers. Widescreen, digitally remastered. Two-tape set.
VHS: S34622. $29.98.
DVD: Making of documentary. **DV60427. $29.99.**
Moustapha Akkad, Lebanon/Great Britain, 1976, 220 mins.

Salut Cousin
Merzak Allouache's realistic tale of the OTHER Paris—the poor tenements of the 18th arrondissement. Alilo, just off the plane from Algiers, hooks up with his cousin, a would-be rap star who is also a pathological liar and a guide to the Paris underground scene. French and Arabic with English subtitles.
VHS: S33322. $79.95.
Merzak Allouache, France/Algeria/Belgium/Luxembourg, 1996, 98 mins.

Silences of the Palace
This "exquisite, compelling" (Kevin Thomas, *Los Angeles Times*) film is a rare work by a woman filmmaker working in an Arab country, as well as an emotionally powerful look at the role of women in a changing world. Set in Tunisia in the 1950s, Tlatli tells the personal story of servant women living through the last days of French colonial rule, virtual prisoners in the palace of "the beys." Winner of the Camera d'Or at Cannes Film Festival. "A universal coming-of-age story with a feminist twist, a tale that translates effortlessly" (Caryn James, *New York Times*). Arabic and French with English subtitles.
VHS: S31118. $79.95.
Moufida Tlatli, Tunisia, 1996, 127 mins.

chinese cinema

The Blue Kite

Banned by the Chinese government, *The Blue Kite* provides a unique window into contemporary Chinese life and politics. During the Cultural Revolution in China, a man called Teitou, his family and his friends all experienced the political and social upheavals that shook a continent. This scathing indictment of life under Chairman Mao was banned along with the filmmaker. Mandarin with English subtitles.

VHS: S24377. $29.95.
Laser: Widescreen. **LD75374. $49.98.**
Tian Zhuangzhuang, China, 1993, 138 mins.

Blush

The passionate drama from the author of *Raise the Red Lantern*, about the relationship between two close friends and former prostitutes in 1950s Shanghai who fall for the same man. "A sumptuous feast for the eyes while spinning a tale of wives and concubines" (Todd Anthony, *Miami New Times*). Cantonese with English subtitles.

VHS: S32612. $79.95.
Li Shaohong, China/Hong Kong, 1996, 119 mins.

China, My Sorrow

An awestruck 13-year-old boy is arrested by Mao's cultural police for propagating obscene records during the Cultural Revolution. (He composed a love song for a 13-year-old girl.) Isolated in mountain corridors, the young boy befriends another teenage "terrorist" and an elderly Buddhist monk. He imparts on them the need to preserve their family structures and create a greater sense of self. "A deft and oddly lighthearted tribute to the traditions and the spirit of freedom that survived the Cultural Revolution" (Caryn James, *The New York Times*). With Guo Liang Yi and Tieu Quan Nghieu. Mandarin and Shanghaiese with English subtitles.

VHS: S19065. $79.95.
Dai Sijie, China, 1989, 86 mins.

Crows and Sparrows

The most renowned of China's social commentary films of the 1940s. Jay Leyda called it "a milestone in Chinese film history, worthy to be shown alongside the best of international cinema." The tenants of a Shanghai boarding house struggle valiantly to keep their homes, triumphing when the greedy landlord is forced to flee the advancing Red Army. Completed on the eve of the Communist revolution, the film was saved from Kuyomintang confiscation by being hidden in the film studio ceiling. Mandarin with English subtitles.

VHS: S26491. $24.95.
Zheng Junli, China, 1949, 111 mins.

The Day the Sun Turned Cold

A young welder in Northern China transforms the lives of those closest to him when he goes into a police station to accuse someone of having murdered his long-dead father. At first the police are sceptical, but as they listen they become intrigued and reopen the investigation concerning the dead man. This film's beguiling flashback-laden narrative magically captures the harsh reality of the Northern provinces of China. Mandarin with English subtitles.

VHS: S29516. $79.95.
Yim Ho, China, 1994, 99 mins.

Ermo

In this delightful comedy about men and what women want, a humble noodle-maker in a remote Chinese province feels that she is being taken for granted by family and friends. To impress them, she decides to bring home the biggest, most expensive TV she can find-no matter how many noodles she has to peddle to buy it. "A delicious comedy…a terrific surprise" (*New York Times*). Chinese with English subtitles.

VHS: S30577. $99.95.
Laser: LD76170. $39.98.
Zhou Xiaowen, China, 1995, 95 mins.

Farewell My Concubine

This complex story of passion and political intrigue won the Best Film Award at Cannes and is an ambitious historical epic of China in the 20th century. It follows the enduring friendship between two opera stars in old Beijing. As they prosper, the political upheavals of war and revolution take their toll. When a young prostitute threatens their professional and personal union, it becomes just one of many trials which test the enduring strength of art and love that bind these two men.

VHS: S20736. $19.95.
Laser: LD74457. $39.99.
Chen Kaige, China, 1993, 157 mins.

Girl from Hunan

A sweeping portrait of a remote village in turn-of-the-century China struggling to hang on to its feudal traditions. Wedding brings a 12-year-old girl and a breast-fed, two-year-old boy together. As the girl matures, she challenges outlandish ideas of freedom and ends up with an illegitimate child. Her reality is made increasingly complicated as her boy is prepared to marry a few years later, according to tradition. A heightened criticism of feudal attitudes toward women, with a mysterious and affecting focus on the workings of nature; an example of recent Chinese cinema at its finest. Mandarin with English subtitles.

VHS: S15682. $79.95.
Xie Fei/U Lan, China, 1986, 99 mins.

The Horse Thief

The setting is the harsh, barren landscape of Tibet, which on film has a stark beauty not unlike the landscapes of American westerns. Here, amidst a series of tribal and Buddhist rituals captured wordlessly and in great detail, unfolds a tribal drama of theft, ostracism, and terrible retribution. A film of mystical dimensions, *The Horse Thief* is a breathtaking 'Scope epic which concentrates on a primitive way of life and manages to capture it with a surprising degree of sophistication. Mandarin with English subtitles. Full-screen letterbox format.

VHS: S13522. $59.95.
Tian Zhuangzhuang, China, 1987, 88 mins.

Life on a String

Set in a distant, mythological past, this visually impressive film tells the story of a young boy's search for a possible cure for his blindness. He devotes his life to music and to breaking one thousand strings on a banjo. Chinese with English subtitles.

VHS: S17238. $24.95.
Chen Kaige, China, 1990, 110 mins.

Mao's Little Red Video

Propaganda shown to the Chinese population during China's Cultural Revolution, intending to encourage the following behind Chairman Mao. 30 mins.

VHS: S13111. $19.98.

A Mongolian Tale

Driven by a seductive composition, a famous troubadour recounts his true love for the woman he abandoned, in this beautifully simple love story set against the grasslands of Inner Mongolia. With Tengger and Naranhua. "Innocence, betrayal, sacrifice and redemption" (Janet Maslin, *The New York Times*). Mongolian with English subtitles.

VHS: S33005. $89.95.
Xie Sei, China/Hong Kong, 1997, 103 mins.

Path of Glory

We follow a bunch of disparate recruits through police training, as they learn to trust each other and work as a team. Familiar enough territory, but this film retains an emphasis on character development, focusing especially on a traumatized former undercover cop who must undergo training a second time, that sets it apart from its companions in the genre. Mandarin with English subtitles. 1980.

VHS: S24185. $49.95.

Red Cherry

The Chinese nominee for the Oscar is a horrific tale based on a true story about Chuchu and Luo Xiaoman, two Chinese orphans, and their struggle to survive in Russia during World War II as German prisoners. Mandarin with English subtitles.

VHS: S34541. $89.98.
Ye Ying, China, 1995, 120 mins.

Red Firecracker Green Firecracker

A beautiful woman is torn between loyalty to her ancestral heritage and her sensual desire for a rebellious artist. A visually stunning film set against the close of the Ching Dynasty, this tale of forbidden love from award-winning director He Ping ignites the screen with passion. Cantonese with English subtitles.

VHS: S26694. $19.98.
Laser: LD75383. $49.98.
He Ping, China, 1994, 117 mins.

The Reincarnation of Golden Lotus

Joi Wong stars as the Golden Lotus in this feminist reworking of an erotic 12th century Chinese novel. Lotus has the misfortune of her beauty, and becomes the luckless prey of various abusive men. Through carefully threaded flashbacks to the Sung Dynasty, she comes to the realization that she is the reincarnation of the "number one" courtesan of ancient China. Mandarin with English subtitles.

VHS: S16166. $89.95.
Clara Law, China, 1989, 99 mins.

Song of China

A rare film, produced in China during 1936, dealing with a cavalcade of families through three generations. The film is timely in that it deals with the universal problem of the generation gap with great sensitivity. Featuring a native Chinese cast and authentic Chinese music on the soundtrack. With English subtitles. China, 1936, 75 mins.

VHS: S14813. $29.95.

Stage Sisters

Stage Sisters chronicles the fortunes of two actresses in pre-revolutionary China who are separated by money and politics. One accedes to the unscrupulous demands of a wealthy impressario and becomes a famous stage star. The other remains virtuous and joins the revolution. This epic film shows how each lived through the events of civil war and revolution until they are reunited, both on and off the stage. Director Xie Jin has been making films for over 50 years and remains the most popular filmmaker in China. Mandarin with English subtitles.

VHS: S26492. $59.95.
Jin Xie, China, 1965, 112 mins.

The Story of Xinghua

Xinghua is an obedient Chinese wife. Though she never professed love for her husband she married him as she was told to do and then endured his cruelty. Suddenly, this passive position is challenged when she falls passionately in love and begins to dream of the unimaginable, freedom. The official Chinese entry at Cannes. Mandarin with English subtitles.

VHS: S29442. $19.98.
Laser: LD75820. $39.99.
D. Yin Li, China, 1995, 89 mins.

Temptation of a Monk

Joan Chen stars as a beautiful but destructive princess in this epic set in 7th-century China. This story of war, betrayal and merciless revenge is triggered when a general makes a fateful mistake. Now he is relentlessly pursued, as are his mother and his lover (Chen). Based on a book by Lilian Lee, author of *Farewell My Concubine*. Mandarin with English subtitles.

VHS: S26028. $19.98.
DVD: DV60169. $29.98.
Clara Law, China, 1994, 118 mins.

Wicked City

The wicked city of the title is the rough and tumble world of Hong Kong, only this time it's not gangsters but evil aliens who threaten decent people. The reptoids look ordinary as they work alongside humans but their goal would mean the demise of mankind. Based on the anime hit of the same name, this film blends the style of Hong Kong action films and Japanese sci-fi adventures. Cantonese with English subtitles.

VHS: S26607. $19.98.
Peter Mak, China, 1995, 88 mins.

Women from the Lake of Scented Souls

At the center of this moving intergenerational family drama is an old legend about two girls. They drowned themselves in a local lake and were said to have flown away as beautiful birds. A contemporary entrepreneur succeeds in business despite her drunken, abusive husband. Now she faces the chore of putting another woman into an unhappy arranged marriage because her mentally ill son desires a wife. Can this older, wiser woman prevent another drowning? Co-winner of the Golden Bear at the 1993 Berlin Film Festival. Mandarin with English subtitles.

VHS: S25832. $89.95.
Xie Fei, China, 1993, 106 mins.

Women's Story

The plight of Chinese women seen from a woman's point of view. A poignant tale of three peasant women who flee their village to taste freedom in the big city and escape the sexist oppression of rural China. Praised for its feminist viewpoint, Berenice Reynaud calls it "the very stuff every modern woman's life is made of." Special Jury Prize, Paris Women's Film Festival. Mandarin with English subtitles.

VHS: S26493. $59.95.

Peng Xiaolian, China, 1989, 96 mins.

The Wooden Man's Bride

Two lovers are joined in forbidden love in this tempestuous drama. Kui must deliver a beautiful bride to her new family. While she is en route, kidnappers intervene and before she can reach her husband, he dies. Despite this turn of fortune, she must marry him in effigy, forcing her into an illicit affair with the man she really loves. Mandarin with English subtitles.

VHS: S27753. $19.95.

Laser: LD75577. $39.99.

Huang Jianxin, China, 1995, 114 mins.

Yellow Earth

A striking collaboration between two Fifth Generation Chinese filmmakers, director Chen Kaige (*Farewell My Concubine*) and Zhang Yimou (*Raise the Red Lantern*), who photographed the film in deep, stylized colors. Set in spring, 1939, a young soldier researching folk songs enters a small community and gets emotionally entangled with an old man, his 14-year-old daughter and his younger son. The film's conflict is set up by the young woman's attraction to the soldier. With Xue Bai, Wang Xueqi, Tan Tuo and Liu Qiang. Mandarin with English subtitles.

VHS: S19445. $19.98.

Chen Kaige, China, 1984, 89 mins.

ZHANG YIMOU

Ju Dou

The erotic thriller that China didn't want you to see is now on video. An exquisitely photographed and smartly performed drama of secret love and hidden faces. Trouble closely follows passion when a beautiful young bride is drawn to the handsome, strong nephew of her new husband, an ancient and disagreeable owner of an isolated dye factory. With excellent performances by Gong Li, Li Bao-tan, Li Wei and Zhang Li. Mandarin with English subtitles.

VHS: S15072. $19.98.

Zhang Yimou, China/Japan, 1989, 98 mins.

Raise the Red Lantern

The third feature of Zhang Yimou stars the beautiful Gong Li as a 20-year-old college student who leaves school to become the fourth wife of a wealthy, powerful aristocrat. Her presence occasions a series of bitter jealousies and disputes with the three other wives. A fascinating work about sex, oppression and patriarchy. Mandarin with English subtitles.

VHS: S17881. $19.98.

Zhang Yimou, China/Taiwan, 1991, 125 mins.

Red Sorghum

A visually spectacular film which is a sweeping modern-day fable. The first part tells of a nervous young bride's arrival at a remote provincial winery and her takeover of the family business when her older husband is mysteriously murdered. The second half is a heroic and harrowing drama focused on the brutality of the Japanese during their occupation of China, and on partisan resistance. "The film's exoticism is palpable, almost intoxicating" (David Edelstein, *The Village Voice*). Mandarin with yellow English subtitles.

VHS: S15392. $79.95.

Zhang Yimou, China, 1987, 91 mins.

Shanghai Triad

Gong Li is once again the star of a lavish period piece from China's most celebrated director. Li becomes enmeshed in a struggle between vicious, feuding warlords. As the mistress of Shanghai's chief gangster, she doesn't have much say in the matter. Beautiful cinematography, for which this film was nominated for an Academy Award, makes it simply spellbinding. The cause of controversy in China, it offers an unparalleled look at China's enduring power politics. Mandarin with English subtitles.

VHS: S28035. $19.95.

Laser: LD75605. $34.95.

Zhang Yimou, China, 1995, 107 mins.

The Story of Qiu Ju

In this comedy a woman seeks justice for a simple slight against her husband. Along the way, she encounters a welter of bureaucracy and politesse in this well-observed portrait of contemporary Chinese life. Chinese with English subtitles.

VHS: S20709. $19.95.

Laser: LD72382. $34.95.

Zhang Yimou, China, 1993, 100 mins.

To Live

Winner of the 1994 Cannes Palme d'Or, Zhang Yimou's daring political tale of modern China landed him in major difficulties with the Chinese authorities. *To Live* follows a contemporary family across the turbulent face of modern China, from the Japanese invasion through Mao's Great Leap Forward and the Cultural Revolution. The powerful drama is made all the more potent by strong performances from Gong Li. Mandarin Chinese with English subtitles.

VHS: S25900. $19.98.

Zhang Yimou, China, 1994, 132 mins.

HONG KONG CINEMA

3 Wishes

A priest is denied entry into the afterlife because he has been too good. Instead, the gods order the priest back to Earth to take nine lives, thereby balancing his good deeds. Somehow the priest gets stuck in a peculiar container until an unsuspecting tour conductor sets him free. As a sign of his gratitude, the priest grants him three wishes. Hong Kong, Mandarin with English subtitles.

VHS: S27264. $49.95.

4 Faces of Eve

Sandra Ng (*Inspector Wears Skirt* series) is hilariously true to form in her four-part anecdotal portrayal of a weeping call girl, a bored housewife, a lovesick girl and inseparable twins. With Chingmy Yau and Karen Mok. Cantonese with English subtitles. Letterboxed, two-tape set.

VHS: S31947. $89.98.

Kam Kwok Leung, Hong Kong, 1996, 100 mins.

Adventurous Treasure Island

Two brothers find a computer game disk at the seashore, but when they boot it up, strange things occur, and the two boys find themselves in a cyberworld of ships and pirates. With Ng Man Tat, Sik Siu Loong and Fok Siu Man. Cantonese with English subtitles. Letterboxed, two-tape set.

VHS: S31964. $89.95.

Herman Yau, Hong Kong, 1996, 92 mins.

The Age of Miracles

An ordinary family leading a mundane life soon gets a whiff of the extraordinary when their aging mother (Anita Yuen) returns home as a "rejuvenated" woman. With Alan Tam and Jordan Chan. Cantonese with English subtitles. Letterboxed, two-tape set.

VHS: S31967. $89.95.

Chan Ho Sun, Hong Kong, 1996, 100 mins.

Ah Ying

Director Allen Fong's most distinguished work after *Father and Son*. Peter Wang (the director and star of *A Great Wall*) plays a film director trying to start a project in Hong Kong while moonlighting as a lecturer on film. He enters into a Svengali-like relationship with Ah Ying, aspiring actress and fish market vendor. Cantonese with English subtitles.

VHS: S14871. $49.95.

Allen Fong, Hong Kong, 1983, 110 mins.

Alan & Eric—Between Hello and Goodbye

The melodrama of two friends (Alan Tam and Eric Tsang) who are reunited after a long separation. Alan is an aspiring singer about to make it big, while Eric has led an unsettled life as a merchant seaman. They decide to run a poultry farm together, but soon a wedge appears between them in the form of Maggie Cheung. It seems they are destined to be separated once again, until they are unexpectedly reunited in San Francisco. Chinese with English subtitles. Hong Kong, 1991.

VHS: S25927. $49.95.

All About Ah-Long

Chow Yun Fat is a truck driver raising his son alone. This drama is complicated by the return of his former wife. A struggle ensues as the three try to reunify the family. In the end, Chow Yun Fat's character returns to his earlier passion as motorcycle racer for the film's climactic finale. Winner of the 1990 Hong Kong Academy Award for Best Actor. Mandarin with English subtitles.

VHS: S27265. $49.95.

Johnny To, Hong Kong, 1989, 100 mins.

All for the Winner

"What you see in front of you is not concrete, it's money," explains one of the characters in this spoof of the Hong Kong genre of the gambling movie. Naive Stephen Chow is newly arrived in Hong Kong. His opportunistic uncle quickly discovers that Chow has supernatural powers, such as being able to see through cards and predict the winners of races. His uncle promptly gets him involved in a high stakes gambling tournament, through which the insouciant Chow blithely sails, until love threatens to deprive him of his powers. Chinese with English subtitles. Hong Kong, 1990.

VHS: S25928. $49.95.

All's Well, End's Well

The harmonious life of a family is disrupted by a series of romantic complications in the lives of three brothers in this goofy comedy. First, the long-suffering wife of self-centered Raymond Wong leaves, to be replaced by his new girlfriend, less dedicated to maintaining the house than to spending money. Then radio star Stephen Chow gets knocked on the head, sending him into full Jerry Lewis mode, while a frustrated Maggie Cheung tries to figure out how to end this aggravating condition. Finally, there's the reluctant romance between the swishy Leslie Cheung and his butch, motorcycle-riding cousin. Plenty of Hollywood movies get parodied, including *Ghost*, *Pretty Woman* and *The Terminator*. Chinese with English subtitles. Hong Kong, 1992.

VHS: S25930. $99.95.

Angel 2

Moon Lee and her partners, the "Angels" (Alex Wong, Elaine Lui), on vacation in Malaysia, are out to stop a school pal of one of the Angels when they find out he is now a gun-runner plotting a revolution in Malaysia with his private army. Cantonese with English subtitles.

VHS: S33198. $49.95.

Teresa Woo/Raymond Leung, Hong Kong, 1989, 90 mins.

As Tears Go By

This Hong Kong *Mean Streets* is the story of a hot-tempered "little brother" who is constantly being bailed out of trouble by a seasoned street "big brother" who lacks the ambition to rise in the ranks of the triad societies. When big brother falls in love with his cousin from Kowloon, he thinks about leaving "the life." Cantonese with English subtitles.

VHS: S33199. $49.95.

Wong Kar Wai, Hong Kong, 1988

Ashes of Time

This moody costume drama plays out almost entirely in close-up, with dialogue spoken at a whisper. The all-star cast includes Brigette Lin Ching-Hsia, Leslie Cheung Hok-Yau, Tony Leung Kar-Fai, Tony Leung Chiu-Wai, Carina Lau Kar-Ling, Maggie Cheung Man-Yu and Jacky Cheung Hok-Yau. Action directed by Sammo Hung with characters from Jin Yong's *Eagle-Shooting Heroes*. Two-tape set. Letterboxed. Cantonese/Mandarin with English subtitles.

VHS: S30525. $89.95.

Wong Kar-Wai, Hong Kong, 1992-94

Autumn Moon

It all begins when a young Japanese tourist encounters a 15-year-old girl on the streets of Hong Kong. Though the tourist is caught up with shooting video footage and finding bargains, he connects with the girl, in part, because he is also searching for food. Fortunately, the girl's grandmother casts a magic spell that leads the young man into a friendship of deepening intensity with the young woman. Naturally, an erotic interest cannot be avoided. English and Cantonese with English subtitles.

VHS: S26522. $29.95.

Clara Law, Hong Kong, 1992, 108 mins.

An Autumn's Tale

Director Mabel Cheung attended NYU film school, and this bittersweet romantic drama grew out of her own experiences in Manhattan's lower east side. A naive young woman named Jennifer (Cherie Chung) follows her obnoxious boyfriend from Hong Kong to New York only to find him enjoying the affections of an attractive Chinese-American and planning to move to another city. Jennifer is forced to rely on her rough-edged, and often vulgar, older cousin Sampan (Chow Yun Fat) for companionship and advice. Cantonese with English subtitles.

VHS: S13459. $49.95.

Mabel Cheung, Hong Kong, 1987, 98 mins.

Banana Club

Michael, Simon and Eddie are sexist males who get paid for their whining on a popular radio program called "Banana Club." With Michael Chow and Tam Siu Wan. Cantonese with English subtitles. Letterboxed, two-tape set.

VHS: S31958. $89.95.

Sin Chi Wai, Hong Kong, 1996, 96 mins.

The Banquet

Produced to raise money for flood victims in China, this is a comedy about a greedy land developer who convinces his father to live with him as part of a scheme to dupe a Kuwaiti prince. The chief entertainment, however, is the parade of Hong Kong stars making cameo appearances, including Gong Li, Leslie Cheung, Stephen Chow, Michael Hui and John Woo. Among those appearing in the story itself are Andy Lau, Jackie Cheung and Sammo Hung. Chinese with English subtitles. Hong Kong, 1991.

VHS: S25933. $49.95.

BB30

The title of the movie comes from the license of a doctor's car, stolen by a bungling lawyer (Kenny Bee), who wants to buy the car. The budding romance between the lawyer and the doctor is complicated further when he takes a malpractice suit against her partner and a loan shark starts threatening everyone over a debt owed by the lawyer's cousin. Chinese with English subtitles. Hong Kong, 1990.

VHS: S25934. $49.95.

Bitter Taste of Blood
A young man trying to escape a life of crime hides out on a farm on an island after refusing "one last job", while he waits for a friend to arrange a passage for him to Taiwan. He seems to find a place on the farm, falling in love with the daughter of the farm's owner. Unfortunately, he cannot escape his past so easily, as his old gang is looking for him and he is harassed by locals resentful of his relationship with the girl. Chinese with English subtitles. Hong Kong, 1986.
VHS: S25938. $49.95.

The Black Wall
Great location shooting in the crowded streets of Hong Kong marks this pessimistic tale of a young gang member, discontented with the life he is leading, but not knowing how to sever his ties with the gang he has grown up with. Chinese with English subtitles. Hong Kong, 1989.
VHS: S25939. $49.95.

Blue Lightning
After his mother is murdered, a 12-year-old boy must go to live with his estranged father (Danny Lee), an alcoholic ex-cop wallowing in self-pity. Under the influence of the young boy, Lee begins to clean himself up and starts investigating the murder of his ex-wife, assisted by a couple of detectives who have also taken an interest in the boy's welfare, in this glitzy, well-crafted picture. Chinese with English subtitles.
VHS: S25964. $49.95.
Raymond Lee, Hong Kong, 1991

The Bride with White Hair
This 1994 Hong Kong Film Award Winner stars Leslie Cheung and Briget Lin in a beautifully filmed story about a pair of star-crossed lovers. Leslie Cheung has several expertly executed sword-play scenes. Cantonese with English subtitles. Letterboxed.
VHS: S29996. $39.95.
Laser: LD75499. $59.95.
Ronnie Yu, Hong Kong, 1993

The Bride with White Hair 2
Brigitte Lin Ching-Hsia (*Chungking Express*) and Leslie Cheung (*Farewell My Concubine*) return as doomed lovers caught in the crossfire of rival clans in this dazzling sequel to the visually sumptuous epic *The Bride with White Hair*. Letterboxed. Subtitled.
VHS: S30044. $19.99.
Laser: Subtitled/Dubbed. **LD75992. $39.95.**
David Wu, Hong Kong, 1993, 80 mins.

Butterfly and Sword
Joey Wang Hsien-Tsu plays "Butterfly" in this fanciful tale featuring Tony Leung Chiu-Wai and action stars Donny Yen Chi-Tan and Michelle Yeoh Chu-Kheng. The dashing foursome party and thrust their way through a deliriously paced yarn of crossed loves and swords. Cantonese/Mandarin with English subtitles.
VHS: S30309. $49.95.
Laser: Letterboxed. **LD76129. $39.95.**
Tang Chi-Li, Hong Kong, 1992

The Butterfly Murders
A cross between Alfred Hitchcock's *The Birds* and Agatha Christie's *And Then There Were None* about blood-sucking butterflies attacking and killing off the Tien Clan. With Liu Chao-Ko, Mi Hsueh and action director Huang Shu-Tang. Cantonese/Mandarin with English subtitles.
VHS: S30313. $49.95.
Tsui Hark, Hong Kong, 1979

Cageman
A touching, nicely detailed study of a group of long-term inhabitants of a cagehouse, a sort of flophouse where everyone gets an individual cage, little larger than a bed, for themselves. When the building is slated for demolition, the tenants must decide whether to get what compensation they can, or to fight the eviction. The process is complicated by two ambitious local politicians who decide to live for a few days in the cagehouse, now the center of media attention. Chinese with English subtitles. Hong Kong, 1992.
VHS: S25940. $49.95.

Call Girl 1988
A housewife, a runaway and a television star all end up in a call girl ring. This film offers both comedy and serious drama. The male customers search endlessly for satisfaction while the three women reveal the deep sadness involved in their choice of professions. Mandarin with English subtitles.
VHS: S27268. $49.95.
David Lam, Hong Kong, 1988

Chez 'n' Ham
Dicky Cheung Wai-Kin and Eric Tsang Chi-Wei run a disorganized collection agency where they tease the secretary and duck irate Triad hitmen. When they need to infiltrate a rich crook's mansion, Dicky disguises himself as an orphaned schoolboy to gain the sympathy of the lady of the house (Joey Wang Tsu-Hsien) and her maid (Cheung Man). Letterboxed. Cantonese/Mandarin with English subtitles.
VHS: S30337. $49.95.
Herman Yau Lai-To, Hong Kong, 1993

The Chinese Dragon Poses as a Hero
Set in China's Ching Dynasty, a group of greedy foreigners journey to a small village in search of China's national treasures. What they find instead is a creature they've never seen before: the panda, who becomes the center of a battle between local villagers and the money-hungry outsiders. With Xun Cheng Xi, Li Li and Huang Ling. Cantonese with English subtitles.
VHS: S31976. $49.95.
Ni Feng, Hong Kong, 1994, 96 mins.

A Chinese Ghost Story
An entertaining and atmospheric supernatural love story with knock-out special effects. In ancient China, a young scholar takes shelter from the rain in a haunted temple where he falls for a beautiful ghost. With the aid of a Taoist monk, the young couple battle a variety of foes (including a giant tongue which gives new meaning to the expression "I've been slimed") and even storm the gates of Hell. With Leslie Cheung, Wong Tsu Hsien, and Wu Ma. Cantonese with English subtitles.
VHS: S13480. $49.95.
Ching Siu Tung, Hong Kong, 1987, 93 mins.

A Chinese Ghost Story Part II
A love interest between Leslie Cheung (*Farewell My Concubine*) and Joey Wang (*Green Snake*) continues, but this time the heroine is not a ghost. Evil spirits, ghosts and goblins provide an exciting and exotic backdrop in this romantic love story. With Jacky Cheung. Cantonese and Mandarin with English subtitles.
VHS: S30609. $49.95.
Ching Siu Tung, Hong Kong, 1990, 102 mins.

A Chinese Ghost Story Part III
One hundred years have passed since *Chinese Ghost Story II*; Tony Leung is a bumbling monk who gets involved with another ghostly woman, again played by the ethereal Joey Wang. Cantonese/Mandarin with English subtitles.
VHS: S30477. $49.95.
Ching Siu Tung, Hong Kong, 1990, 99 mins.

Christ of Nanking
A tragic love story between a young Japanese novelist (Tony Leung, *The Lovers*) and a religious country girl who is forced to earn a living as a geisha in Nanjing's Red Rose Brothel. Also with Yasuko Tomita. Cantonese with English subtitles. Letterboxed, two-tape set.
VHS: S31957. $89.95.
Tony Au, Hong Kong, 1996, 99 mins.

Chungking Express
From one of the hottest filmmakers on the international film circuit, Wong Kar-Wai, a visually stunning, dream-like valentine to youth and hopeless love. Kar-Wai juxtaposes two quirky, offbeat love stories with beautiful, mysterious women and colorful cops against a backdrop of a Chinese fast-food restaurant. An emotionally intense post-modern romantic comedy. Cantonese with English subtitles.
VHS: S30458. $99.99.
Laser: LD76065. $49.95.
Wong Kar-Wai, Hong Kong, 1996, 102 mins.

City Squeeze
A petty and bullying boss hires an attractive public relations officer in an attempt to cheat on his domineering wife, but his plans are complicated when she must work with his put-upon general manager to secure a large contract for the company. The two are drawn together in spite of the comic conflicts thrown in their way. With Kenny Bee. Semi-letterboxed. Mandarin with English subtitles.
VHS: S24143. $49.95.
Clifton C.S. Ko, Hong Kong, 1989

Comet Butterfly and Sword
This epic battle pits abusive eunuchs against the forces of good. Court intrigues threaten to destroy the Ming Dynasty but a loyal and patriotic farmer, Uncle Lee of the West Wing, teams up with Lady Kao to defeat the forces of chaos. Of course there are plenty of martial arts battles and swordplay on the road to preserving harmony in the Middle Kingdom. Dubbed in English.
VHS: S21828. $49.95.
D J Mike, Hong Kong, 1994

The Contract
Zany Hui Brothers comedy as trio aspires to land contracts for variety shows at TV station. Not so much a plot as a framework on which to hang some fine extended comic sequences. With Michael, Ricky and Samuel Hui. Mandarin with English subtitles (occasionally cropped at edges).
VHS: S24145. $49.95.
Michael Hui, Hong Kong, 1978

Couples, Couples, Couples
Typical romantic comedy about three couples attempting to resolve their difficulties, of course complicating the process along the way. Includes plenty of what passes for humor about AIDS in Hong Kong. Good natured, though. Mandarin with English subtitles (occasionally cropped, but plot easy to follow). 1987.
VHS: S24146. $49.95.

Crossings
A tragic tale of a recent arrival (Anita Yuen Wing-Lee), who unwittingly falls into a drug smuggling scheme with a too-charming countryman (Simon Yam Tak-Wah) and his disturbed girlfriend (Lindzay Chan). Moody lighting and an excellent script by director Evans Chan with Joyce Chan make for a troubling film. Letterboxed. Cantonese/Mandarin with English subtitles.
VHS: S30333. $49.95.
Evans Chan/Joyce Chan, Hong Kong, 1994

Crossline
After suffering years of physical and mental abuse, a woman finally builds up enough strength to kill her demented husband. Is it pre-meditated murder or self-defense? With Chan Chung Wai and Mak Ching Lang. Cantonese with English subtitles. Letterboxed.
VHS: S31993. $49.95.
Jamie Luk, Hong Kong, 1996, 96 mins.

The Crow
Brandon Lee stars in this exciting and mysterious thriller about a man with strange powers. After a terrible crime, only revenge and justice can drive a man to the extremes that define *The Crow*. Brandon Lee, the son of Bruce Lee, is astounding in this, his last film.
VHS: S22157. $19.95.
Alex Proyas, USA, 1993, 100 mins.

The Cruel Kind
This is the Beyond Polanski tale of an erotic photographer in Paris (Chang Kuo-Cu) who slips into madness—or are his visions of a ghost girl (Shi Kai) real? Perhaps his girlfriend-model (Claire LeVert) knows. Cantonese/Mandarin with English subtitles.
VHS: S30321. $49.95.
Ku Wai-Ching, Hong Kong, 1990

Daddy, Father, and Pa Pa
A clever but lonely boy, neglected by his materialistic parents, suddenly finds himself being chased by a criminal gang. Desperate to find him, his mother enlists the aid of two men from her past by telling them that they are each his true father. During the course of the ensuing comic adventures, the three men learn to look beyond their shallow ways. Semi-letterboxed. Mandarin with English subtitles.
VHS: S24149. $49.95.
Clifton C.S. Ko, Hong Kong, 1991

Days of Being Dumb
This charming and hilarious contemporary comedy stars Jacky Cheung Hok-Yau and Tony Leung Chiu-Wai as friends from boyhood who try to enter the Hong Kong underworld as gangsters but end up as jinxes who bring bad luck to every gang they join. When they go into business as pimps and order a woman from Singapore, Tony falls in love with her, and discovers later that she's a lesbian. Letterboxed. Cantonese/Mandarin with English subtitles.
VHS: S30336. $49.95.
Blackie Ko Sau-Leung, Hong Kong, 1993

Days of Being Wild
A critical and commercial success, this award-winning tale binds together the lives of six young people in Hong Kong during the '60s. A sort of Cantonese *Rebel Without a Cause*, but with a more typically Chinese emphasis on the bonds between people. With Maggie Cheung Man-Yu, Andy Lau Tak-Wah, Tony Leung Chiu-Wai, Carina Lau Kar-Ling and Jacky Cheung Hok-Yau. Cantonese/Mandarin with English subtitles.
VHS: S30325. $49.95.
Wong Kar-Wai, Hong Kong, 1990

Deception
Stylish story of various levels of deception, betrayal and murder among three women. A businesswoman finds herself being blackmailed, but who can she trust to help her? Her longtime associate, about to be left behind as the company moves to Canada, or her unscrupulous stockbroker? Interesting also in that virtually all the major roles are played by women. With Joey Wang. Mandarin with English subtitles. 1989.
VHS: S24150. $49.95.

Doctor Mack (aka Mack the Knife)

Dr. Lau Mak (Tony Leung Chiu-Wai), Hong Kong's best coronary surgeon, prefers to work in his own slum clinic. Regulars include a seedy undercover cop (Lau Ching-Wan) and the doctor's young assistant, Andy Hui Chi-On. Mak's old med-schoolmate (Alex To Tak-Wai) tries to steal credit for our hero's surgical procedure while also ripping off their old professor (Richard Ng Yao-Han). Somehow, director Li Chi-Ngai brings it all together, adapting the Japanese *manga* (graphic novel) of Sho Fumimura and Takumi Nagayasu. Letterboxed. Cantonese/Mandarin with English subtitles.

VHS: S30518. $89.95.
Li Chi-Ngai, Hong Kong, 1995

Dream Lovers

This passionate love story, spiced with supernatural elements, alternates between the high fashion/high tech world of contemporary Hong Kong and the mysterious Qin dynasty. When a young orchestra conductor (Chow Yun Fat) meets the daughter of a famous archeologist (Lin Ching-Hsai) at an exhibition of the Qin Emperor's terra cotta army, an affair from the past is reborn and tragedy strikes again. Cantonese with English subtitles.

VHS: S13460. $49.95.
Tony Au, Hong Kong, 1986, 95 mins.

Ebola Syndrome

The team that brought you *The Untold Story* is back again for more blood-curdling gore, with this horrifying tale of one man's mission to kill a deadly disease known as the Ebola Syndrome. With Anthony Wong and Yeung Ming. Cantonese with English subtitles. Letterboxed.

VHS: S31988. $49.95.
Herman Yau, Hong Kong, 1996, 98 mins.

Enigma of Love

When a hard-boiled cop (Maggie Cheung) busts a "gigolo shop," a gangster decides to turn the tables by manipulating Maggie to fall in love with him—instead, he falls for her. Cantonese with English subtitles.

VHS: S33201. $49.95.
Wong Ching-Wah, Hong Kong, 1993

Erotic Ghost Story

Hong Kong bombshell Amy Yip stars as a devilish ghost who, along with her two beautiful sisters, entices and bedazzles all those she touches. Amy Yip and Man Su. Cantonese with English subtitles. Letterboxed.

VHS: S31984. $49.95.
Nam Nai Choi, Hong Kong, 1990, 84 mins.

Escort Girls

A scintillating adult drama delving into the lives and relationships of Hong Kong's escort girls. With Tsang Yuk Yee and Fan Oi Git. Cantonese with English subtitles.

VHS: S32010. $49.95.
Lam Chi Hung, Hong Kong, 1993, 93 mins.

Evening Liaison

Tony Leung (*The Lover*) stars in this captivating love story set in 1930s Shanghai. Leung is a young journalist who accidentally meets and falls in love with a mysterious woman (Mabel Zhang) who claims that she is a ghost. Entranced by their fleeting moment together, he attempts to unravel the secrets of her identity and waits in hope of reliving their first evening liaison. With Kar Fai. Cantonese with English subtitles. Letterboxed, two-tape set.

VHS: S31948. $89.98.
Chen Yi Fei, Hong Kong, 1996, 97 mins.

Fallen Angels

In this neo-noir fantasy, Leon Lai stars as a hitman who is the object of unrequited passion for two women: the female agent (Michele Reis) who hands down his assignments, and an orange-haired punkette name Baby (Karen Mong). "*Fallen Angels* takes every risk known to filmmaking and succeeds triumphantly" (*Sight and Sound*). Letterboxed. Cantonese with English subtitles.

VHS: S34312. $79.95.
Wong Kar-Wai, Hong Kong, 1996, 95 mins.

Fatal Target

Two Hong Kong policewomen (Yukari Oshima and *Angel Terminator*'s Sharon Yeung Pan-pan) on vacation in Manila have to cut their holiday short when the local police need help to stop a ring of arms smugglers. Things get complicated when the ladies realize that the smugglers' leader is Yukari's cousin. Dubbed in English.

VHS: S32693. $14.95.
Godfrey Ho, Hong Kong, 1994, 92 mins.

Feel 100%

A story about friendship, loyalty and devotion between three childhood friends, their lives, struggles and loves. A beautiful and heartwarming tale that brings new meaning to "feeling 100%." With Ekin Cheng and Sammy Cheng. Cantonese with English subtitles. Letterboxed, two-tape set.

VHS: S31959. $89.95.
Ma Wai Ho, Hong Kong, 1996, 96 mins.

Fight Back to School

Action-comedy with current Hong Kong favorite Stephen Chow starring as an impetuous cop whose undisciplined behavior earns him one last chance, going undercover as a high school student to recover a stolen pistol, doubly horrible for Chow since he became a cop because he hated school in the first place. The expected misadventures ensue as Chow goes from loathing the school to becoming an all-too-popular fixture there. Mandarin with English subtitles.

VHS: S24153. $49.95.
Gordon Chan, Hong Kong, 1991

Final Victory

Veering from comedy to pathos, this is the story of the unassertive guy who is given the task of watching over his criminal brothers' mistresses while he serves his jail sentence. Things are complicated when he falls in love with one of the women and must cope with the wrath of his brother, soon to be released from prison. Mandarin with English subtitles.

VHS: S24154. $49.95.
Patrick Tam, Hong Kong, 1987

First Time Is the Last Time

Strong, unsensational drama is set in a woman's prison, focusing chiefly on two of the inmates, one in jail for the first time in order to protect her low-life boyfriend, and another, long-term prisoner with the reputation of being a crazy loner, whose story is told in flashback form, the flashbacks rendered in a vivid, kinetic style which contrasts with the subdued colors and control of the prison. Mandarin with English subtitles (sometimes a bit cropped at the edges). 1989.

VHS: S24156. $49.95.

A Fishy Story

Elegant melodrama of an affair between an aspiring starlet (Maggie Cheung) and a cab driver, set against the backdrop of turbulent 60's Hong Kong. Each must choose between the struggle to maintain their relationship and the easier but less fulfilling paths that are offered them. Mandarin with English subtitles (often chopped on right side—no difficulty following the story though).

VHS: S24155. $49.95.
Anthony Chan, Hong Kong, 1990, 99 mins.

Flirting

Seamy tale of adultery and murder, a mix of straight melodrama and exploitation pic about a dispute between two friends over a Thai wife, which leads to dire consequences. Mandarin with English subtitles (sometimes a bit washed out).

VHS: S24157. $49.95.
Lee Tai Hay, Hong Kong, 1988

Flirting Scholar

Tang Bo Hu (Stephen Chow) is a successful artist and poet who is bored with his many wives and spends all day playing Mah Jongg, until he sees Qiu Xiang (Gong Li) and falls in love with her. He sells himself as a servant to her family, only to find out Qiu Xiang's mother is an old enemy of his family. Cantonese with English subtitles.

VHS: S33202. $49.95.
Lee Lik Chi, Hong Kong, 1993

Flower Drums of Fung Yang

Two lovers are cast out of their village to wander the roads of China. In order to survive, the wife becomes an itinerant singer, until she is kidnapped by bandits terrorizing the region, the leader of whom turns out to be her long-lost brother. Mandarin with English subtitles. 1981.

VHS: S24158. $49.95.

Flying Dagger

In this quintessential *mo ley tow* (makes no sense) comedy, Jacky Cheung Hok-Yau plays a farting forest bandit, Maggie Cheung Man-Yu is a flying catwoman, Tony Leung Kar-Fai turns green from a magic potion and a gay swordsman does a disco number in the lobby of Ng Mang-Dat's inn. Cantonese/Mandarin with English subtitles.

VHS: S30307. $49.95.
Wong Jing, Hong Kong, 1993

For Your Heart Only

Teen romantic comedy, as a group of exuberant boys takes over the apartment of one of the better-off of the gang and a romance evolves between two classmates. Mandarin with English subtitles.

VHS: S24160. $49.95.

Fortune Hunters

A gambling master is deserted by his overanxious disciple, who goes to work for the master's ruthless archrival. Soon the protege finds himself facing his former teacher and romantically linked with his teacher's new student, and he must decide which path is for him. Mandarin with English subtitles. 1987.

VHS: S24162. $49.95.

The Fun, The Luck, and the Tycoon

As a roguish billionaire, Chow Yun Fat is perfect. He manages to bring a light, humorous touch to this comedy about the Lunar New Year. Mandarin with English subtitles.

VHS: S27282. $49.95.
Johnny To, Hong Kong, 1990

Ghost Foot

Lau Zhai (Yuen Biao) is a would-be pupil of Wong Fei Hong who allies with police chief Panther to topple an opium distribution ring. Cantonese with English subtitles.

VHS: S33203. $49.95.
Yuen Woo Ping, Hong Kong, 1993, 93 mins.

Ghost Lantern

Tony Leung Kar-Fai plays a loveable klutz who discovers that his present tribulations are due to problems in his past life. Troubling flashbacks show him (and us) a series of brutal rape-murders ending with the peeling-off of women's skin for use as lantern shades. Also features Chingmy Yau Shuk-Ching and Roy Cheung Yiu-Yeung. Letterboxed. Cantonese/Mandarin with English subtitles.

VHS: S30316. $49.95.
Andrew Lau Wai-Keung, Hong Kong, 1994

Girls Gang

Juvenile delinquency on the ghetto streets of Hong Kong is depicted through five teenage girls. Young and misunderstood, the girls fall prey to drugs and prostitution. With Ng Mui Yee, Tse Man Yee and Tse Pui See. Cantonese with English subtitles. Letterboxed.

VHS: S31994. $49.95.
O Chi Kwan, Hong Kong, 1995, 79 mins.

Gone Forever with My Love

The story of one man's tragedy and the two women whom he loved. With Guo Tao, Xu Fan and Ju Xue. Cantonese with English subtitles.

VHS: S32011. $49.95.
Feng Xiao Gang, Hong Kong, 1994, 95 mins.

Green Snake

Based on an old Chinese fable, this film combines mysticism with romance and climactic battle sequences. Green Snake and Son Ching (Maggie Cheung and Joey Wang) are a pair of snakes who long to be human. Son Ching has been practicing taking human form for 1,000 years and Green Snake for 500 when they are discovered by Fa-Hai, a self-righteous Buddhist monk who finds sin in the snakes' desire to tamper with natural law. In the end, the monk's lack of compassion leads to the destruction of his own ashram and of a nearby town. Cantonese with English subtitles.

VHS: S27271. $49.95.
Laser: LD76115. $69.95.
Tsui Hark, Hong Kong, 1993, 102 mins.

Happy Bigamist

Pleasant romantic comedy. A recently married couple find their lives thrown into turmoil when the husband's first wife, half owner of the house, falls on hard times and is forced to move back. Mandarin with English subtitles.

VHS: S24164. $49.95.

Happy Ghost IV

Teen ghost comedy, as the ghost of a lecherous ancient general keeps interfering in the romantic affairs of the mild-mannered protagonist. Mandarin with English subtitles.

VHS: S24305. $49.97.

Happy Hour

Hong Kong's hottest young heartthrobs, pop-star Andy Hui Chi-On and bad-boy Jordan Chan Siu-Chun, team up with Julian Cheung Chi-Lam as three pub-crawling party animals who pick up a woman in a club and take her home—together. She wakes up thinking she's been gangbanged (she hasn't), and they all end up in court being defended by the redoubtable Lau Ching-Wan, whose tactics would put Johnny Cochran to shame. Two-tape set. Letterboxed. Cantonese/Mandarin with English subtitles.

VHS: S30519. $89.95.
Benny Chan Muk-Sing, Hong Kong, 1995

Happy Together

With gorgeous, saturated images set to an eclectic soundtrack of classic tangos, torch songs and Frank Zappa instrumentals, Wong Kar-Wai chronicles the stormy affair of a gay couple (Hong Kong superstars Tony Leung and Leslie Cheung) living as expatriates in Buenos Aires. "Stylistically brash. Pulsing with life. Captures the restless, open-to-everything spirit of youth" (Stephen Holden, *New York Times*). Letterboxed. Cantonese with English subtitles.
VHS: S34311. $79.95.
Wong Kar-Wai, Hong Kong, 1997, 98 mins.

He Ain't Heavy, He's My Father

Tony Leung Kar-Fai is a wastrel son who looks down at his poor old dad (Tony Leung Chiu-Wai), until he falls into a wishing well during the Autumn Moon Festival and is transported to bygone Hong Kong, where he gets to know his father as a young man and meets a girl who looks just like his own present-day girlfriend. Two-tape set. Letterboxed. Cantonese/Mandarin with English subtitles.
VHS: S30522. $89.95.
Peter Chan Ho-Sun/Li Chi-Ngai, Hong Kong, 1994

He's a Woman, She's a Man

Leslie Cheung Kwok-Wing plays a top record producer who can manufacture Cantonese pop stars overnight. When he resolves to make his next big discovery a male, young hopeful Anita Yuen Wing-Lee cuts her hair and auditions as a teenage boy, winning the job and the heart of the producer, who thinks she's a he! With Carina Lau Kar-Ling. Two-tape set. Letterboxed. Cantonese/Mandarin with English subtitles.
VHS: S30521. $89.95.
Peter Chan Ho-Sun, Hong Kong, 1994

Heart into Hearts

Ad man Alex, facing his impending marriage with trepidation, finds himself drawn to director Joe (Maggie Cheung, in fine form) and must re-evaluate the nature of his relationship with his fiance when they all find themselves in Paris shooting a commercial. Mandarin with English subtitles (occasionally cut off at the ends).
VHS: S24166. $49.95.
Stephen Shin, Hong Kong, 1982

Heartbeat 100

Maggie Cheung is at the center of this peculiar, gory slasher movie and wacky comedy. Cheung is a writer who seeks inspiration for her new screenplay, so she, her sister and a friend travel to a small town that is connected to a recent crime. Instead of inspiration she finds a host of dangers, including haunted houses, corrupt police, a village idiot who carries around poisonous snakes, and his axe-wielding father. When she thinks she witnesses a murder, she decides to investigate on her own, and before long she is helplessly enmeshed in a bizarre concoction that can only lead to mayhem and frustration.
VHS: S27583. $49.95.
Kent Cheng/Lo Kin, Hong Kong, 1986

Heaven Can't Wait

Worthy of Billy Wilder in his prime, this is the tale of a streetwise con man (Tony Leung Chiu-Wai) who meets a spacey young actor (Jordan Chan Siu-Chun) playing Jesus in an avant-garde street theater piece. Tony hits upon the idea to turn Jordan into a pop religious figure and pull in huge donations through media manipulation of the susceptible Hong Kong public. This idea gets a Chinese twist with clever references to the Autumn Moon Festival (when the film was actually released). Letterboxed. Cantonese/Mandarin with English subtitles.
VHS: S30323. $49.95.
Li Chi-Ngai, Hong Kong, 1995

Hello! Who Is It?

Four phone repairmen rape a woman (Anita Lee Yuen-Wah) passing their workstation and accidentally kill her. Her ghost wreaks revenge on them through the telephone system: animating cables to strangle them, leaving death threats on their pagers and pursuing them through crowds by calling the cellular phones of everyone around them. Lau Ching-Wan plays the good-hearted cop who puts her troubled soul to rest. Letterboxed. Cantonese/Mandarin with English subtitles.
VHS: S30343. $49.95.
Jamie Luk Kim-Ming, Hong Kong, 1994

Heroes Among Heroes (aka The Iron Beggar)

Donnie Yen Chi-Tan plays the popular character of Beggar So, one of the famed "Ten Tigers of Canton" featured in numerous popular films during the 1970s. So and his wacky Dad (Ng Mang-Dat) team up with Wong Fei Hung (Do Siu-Jun) to confront the corrupt Twelfth Prince Tao Barac (Hung Yan-Yan). Cantonese/Mandarin with English subtitles.
VHS: S30303. $49.95.
Yuen Woo-Ping/Chan Chin-Chung, Hong Kong, 1993

Heroes Shed No Tears

Woo's homage to *Apocalypse Now* is the story of a team of mercenaries sent by the Thai government to the Vietnam jungle to capture a renegade drug lord alive. Cantonese with English subtitles. Letterboxed.
VHS: S33141. $59.95.
Laser: LD76429. $39.95.
John Woo, Hong Kong, 1985, 93 mins.

Holy Weapon

This unmitigated *mo ley tow* (makes no sense) comedy weaves an absurd fable with seven good girls (including Michelle Yeoh Chu-Kheng, Maggie Cheung Man-Yu, Carol "Dodo" Chen Yu-Ling, Carina Lau Kar-Ling, Sandra Ng Kwan-Yu and Cheung Man) getting together to battle evil. Male co-star Dicky Cheung Wai-Kin even undergoes a magical sex-change to bring the group up to the appropriate mystical number. Also with Ng Mang-Dat, Simon Yam Tak-Wah and Damian Lau Chung-Yun. Letterboxed. Cantonese/Mandarin with English subtitles.
VHS: S30304. $49.95.
Wong Jing, Hong Kong, 1993

Hong Kong 1941

Chow Yun-Fat (*The Replacement Killers, Hard Boiled*) stars in this romantic drama set in war-torn Hong Kong on the eve of the Japanese invasion in 1941. A tragic love story in the tradition of *The English Patient*. Nominated for eight Hong Kong Film Awards, winner of the Taiwan Golden Horse Award for Best Actor (Chow Yun-Fat). Chinese with English subtitles. Letterboxed.
VHS: S34865. $59.95.
Leung Po-Chi, Hong Kong, 1984, 118 mins.

How to Pick Girls Up

Three losers pay an obnoxious talk radio personality to teach them how to court women in this exceptionally silly comedy. The radio host, aside from taking every advantage of his new students, is himself guilty of treating his wife in the shabbiest possible manner. When he discovers he is on the verge of losing her, the former losers, along with their girlfriends, intervene to show their teacher the error of his ways. One of the strangest moments in the film is a scene stolen from *A Clockwork Orange*, in which the radio host forces one of the characters to watch scenes from bad kung fu movies in order to cure him of his aggressive behavior. With Maggie Cheung.
VHS: S27584. $49.95.
Corey Yuen, Hong Kong, 1988, 97 mins.

The Imp

A young female reporter and fellow passengers en route by van to a remote part of China get stuck in the outskirts of town and stay overnight in a small nearby inn. The blood-curdling tale begins when two men from her entourage are mysteriously killed. With Pang Tan and Mark Cheung. Cantonese with English subtitles. Letterboxed.
VHS: S31980. $49.95.
Ivan Lai, Hong Kong, 1996, 98 mins.

The Kid from Tibet

Yuen Biao directs and stars as a naive Tibetan monk sent by his lama to Hong Kong to recover a priceless and powerful ancient relic. Buddhist white magic battles black magic as embodied by the diabolical Yuen Wah and his leather-girl, the ravishing Cheung Man. Letterboxed. Cantonese/Mandarin with English subtitles.
VHS: S30299. $49.95.
Yuen Biao, Hong Kong, 1991

The Kidnap of Wong Chak Fai

Kent Cheng stars in this well-acted thriller as Officer Ching, who unravels a kidnapping just before his retirement, then gets swindled by the man he saved. Now it's time for revenge, and Ching's successor must stop his former boss before it's too late. Cantonese with English subtitles.
VHS: S33204. $49.95.
Ko Sih-Ming, Hong Kong, 1993

Lady Sun

Traditionally told period piece about a man who marries a spirit, only to lose her when he fails to heed her advice and continues to associate with his old friends, whose doubtful character is made clear when he finds himself wrongfully accused of murder and facing execution. Mandarin with English subtitles (occasionally chopped). 1981.
VHS: S24170. $49.95.

Lai Shi: China's Last Eunuch

Lai Shi, a starving child in a poverty-stricken mountain village, implores his father to "snip it off" so that he may attain wealth and status at the Emperor's Court. Unfortunately, Lai Shi undergoes his transformation just before China's turbulent Twenties. An unnerving yet strangely satisfying mix of detailed historical drama, comedy, and pathos. Cantonese with English subtitles.
VHS: S13466. $49.95.
Chan Tsi-liang, Hong Kong, 1988, 100 mins.

Law or Justice

After a model is raped by a psychotic photographer and he is acquitted thanks to a clever (female) lawyer, her schoolgirl sister tries to get revenge, only to find that the rapist has lured her into a trap. The stage is set for another trial, with the lawyer now having second thoughts about representing her client again. With Joey Wang. Mandarin with English subtitles (positioned low at first). 1989.
VHS: S24173. $49.95.

Legal Innocence

A familiar plot pushed to unfamiliar levels of gore. A lawyer (Cecilia Yip) successfully defends an accused killer, then marries him. France Ng Chen-Yu and Leung See-Man are the murder victims; Anthony Wong Chiao-Sun is the cop who figures it all out. Letterboxed. Cantonese/Mandarin with English subtitles.
VHS: S30319. $49.95.
Cha Chuen-Yee, Hong Kong, 1993

Legend of Wisely

A special effects extravaganza in which a group of adventurers journey from Nepal to Egypt to Hong Kong and back again, hot on the trail of a gigantic black pearl stolen from a Himalayan monastery. With Sam Hui, Teddy Robin Kwan and Ti Lung. Cantonese with English subtitles.
VHS: S13464. $49.95.
Teddy Robin Kwan, Hong Kong, 1986, 100 mins.

Life After Life

Well-made occult thriller about a man who feels he is re-living events from a past life, events which ended up in a murder. It's all bound up with some spooky puppets the man is using as part of a fashion show he is producing, while he attempts to make sense out of the obscure portents he is encountering. Mandarin with English subtitles (occasionally chopped but story followable).
VHS: S24175. $49.95.
Peter Wia-Chuen Yung, Hong Kong, 1981, 88 mins.

Love & Sex Among the Ruins

A taxi driver picks up a distraught woman, who confesses her entire life story and ends up in bed with him. This one-night interlude leads to some amusing sexual encounters between five people who are forced to face the complexities of love and sex. With Dayo Wong, Cheung Tat Ming and Choi Siu Fan. Cantonese with English subtitles. Letterboxed, two-tape set.
VHS: S31965. $89.98.
Cheung Chi Sing, Hong Kong, 1996, 100 mins.

Love in Mists

An innocent camping trip leads to a freak accident and a missing girl. She suffers amnesia and is rescued by a stranger, who, unbeknownst to her, is a wanted criminal. With Hung Choi Ling and Wah Lun. Cantonese with English subtitles. Letterboxed.
VHS: S31989. $49.95.
Tong Yee Tun, Hong Kong, 1984, 90 mins.

Love Soldier of Fortune

An eccentric piano tuner named Antonio Go moves into his ancestral home, only to find it haunted by the ghost of his dead uncle. His uncle was a gifted composer who killed himself over an unrequited love, and in order to help young Go win the object of his affections and avoid his uncle's melancholy fate, the uncle gives his nephew songs he has composed. Unfortunately, the nephew, unsure of himself, sells his uncle's songs to an arrogant and talentless pop singer who claims them as his own. To add insult to injury, the pop singer has designs on popular radio journalist Miss So (Maggie Cheung), apparently the hardest working woman in Hong Kong, who is the same woman Go desires. When Go's uncle suddenly disappears, Go realizes he must depend on his own resources to win the affections of Miss So. Hong Kong, 1988, 91 mins.
VHS: S27587. $49.95.

Love unto Waste

Before *Rouge*, Stanley Kwan captured the hedonism, cynicism and ennui of Hong Kong's smart set. Two Taiwanese women on the make in Hong Kong hook up with a young couple for a drunken night and a casual affair. After one of the group is murdered, the remaining members move toward a new and surprising emotional honesty. Cantonese with English subtitles.
VHS: S13473. $49.95.
Stanley Kwan, Hong Kong, 1986, 97 mins.

The Lunatics
This picture follows with the travails of a social worker who deals with mentally disturbed people, most of whom live on the street and refuse to be admitted to shelters or hospitals for treatment. The dedicated but somewhat worn-down social worker is accompanied on his rounds by a reporter doing a sensationalistic story on the mentally ill. The reporter gradually overcomes her preconceived notions about the mentally ill, but not before one of her stories inadvertently sets a tragedy in motion. A strange combination of genuine feeling for the mentally ill and exploitation of them characterizes this movie. The feeling mostly comes about through the generally strong efforts of the cast, including a brief appearance by Chow Yun Fat as one of the street people. Hong Kong, 1986, 87 mins.
VHS: S27588. $49.95.

A Lustful Night
A night of passion leads to murder and a ghost spirit's revenge in this titillating adult drama. With Tsui Bo Lun and Cheung King. Cantonese with English subtitles. Letterboxed.
VHS: S32005. $49.95.
Tsui Kwong Sing, Hong Kong, 1993, 90 mins.

Mainland Dundee
Hilarious satire about the three Chinas learning to coexist, personified by a mainland archeologist (Kenny Bee) and his greedy partner sent to Hong Kong, a pragmatic (and greedy) HK native who lets the archeologist live in his apartment, and their neighbor, who still dreams of raising the nationalist flag over the mainland, although his daughter has different intentions toward the young visitor from the People's Republic. Mandarin with English subtitles (occasionally cropped). 1991.
VHS: S24176. $49.95.

Marriage
In this twisted version of the classic fairy tale *Cinderella*, a forlorn girl hopes to meet her Prince Charming at a grand ball, where they shall share a timeless dance. Cantonese with English subtitles.
VHS: S31990. $49.95.
Chen Kun Kou, Hong Kong, 1984, 80 mins.

Master Wong v. Master Wong
Following hard on the heels of the recent spate of movies about Chinese folk hero Wong Fei Hong comes this especially silly entry, in which Wong is portrayed as a naive bumbler in the company of fools. While Wong tries to escape from his reputation as an invincible martial artist, his cohorts are trying to cash in, imposters are springing up, and an unscrupulous promoter wants to manipulate him for his own ends. Mandarin with English subtitles.
VHS: S24177. $49.95.

The Mermaid
Done in a style reminiscent of traditional Chinese opera, this is the story of a 1000-year-old carp who decides to become human for a while, transforming itself into the double of a spoiled heiress, only to fall in love with a scholar who is patiently awaiting the heiress' hand in marriage, leading to massive confusions when the two women appear in the same place at once, even gaining the attention of the gods. Mandarin with English subtitles (occasionally cropped).
VHS: S24178. $49.95.
Kao Li, Hong Kong, 1985

Mr. Possessed
Unfortunately Ridley (Kenny Bee) has been under a curse since childhood: he literally repels women. When he finally meets someone who can be near him (thanks to her Buddhist charm bracelet) and they fall in love, his mother's meddling sets off a chain of spells and counter-spells, culminating in a Poltergeist-like finale of ghosts and magicians. Mandarin with English subtitles (occasionally cropped or washed out).
VHS: S24181. $49.95.
Wang Tsing, Hong Kong, 1988

Mr. Sunshine
Rotund, upbeat Mr. Mak looses his apartment and his job and moves in with a bickering, dysfunctional family (after causing the eldest daughter to loose her job as well), and proceeds to raise their self-esteem and their awareness of others, all the while searching for a job he and the daughter of the family can hold on to for more than a day. Mandarin with English subtitles. 1989.
VHS: S24182. $49.95.

Mr. Vampire
The first of a popular comedy/horror series featuring the Chinese version of a movie vampire, a more corpse-like creature than his Western counterpart. Mr. Vampire sports long purple fingernails and yellow fangs and, when not levitating, hops like a bunny. Stars Ricky Hui. Cantonese with English subtitles.
VHS: S13445. $49.95.
Lau Kun Wai, Hong Kong, 1986, 99 mins.

Mr. Vampire II
Agile martial arts acrobat Yuen Biao stars in this hilarious romp. Learn more vampire lore, including the salutary effects of holding your breath and having on hand a supply of sticky rice and red-inked sutras. Cantonese with English subtitles.
VHS: S13446. $49.95.
Lau Kun Wai, Hong Kong, 1986, 91 mins.

Mr. Vampire III
Richard Ng stars in Lau Koon Wai's third outing with the Chinese spirit world, which, in addition to vampires, offers a bevy of witches and possessed morticians. Cantonese without English subtitles.
VHS: S13447. $49.95.
Lau Kun Wai, Hong Kong, 1987, 95 mins.

Mr. Vampire IV
More laughs and chills as our favorite Chinese vampires return for action in the fourth installment of Lau Koon Wai's popular genre series. Cantonese without English subtitles.
VHS: S13448. $49.95.
Lau Kun Wai, Hong Kong, 1988, 90 mins.

Muto Bontie
A clever but wicked Japanese fast-food magnate decides to murder his wife for his sexy mistress. His plan comes to a halt when his wife is actually kidnapped. The twist is that the kidnappers are his twin brother and sister-in-law, in cahoots with the law. With Lau Chin Wan and Alice Lau. Cantonese with English subtitles. Letterboxed, two-tape set.
VHS: S31953. $89.98.
Chan Kin Tak, Hong Kong, 1996, 98 mins.

My Beloved
A tale of two lovers forced apart by the man's family once the woman's pregnancy is discovered. She leaves but decides to raise their son by herself. When after a number of years it becomes apparent that the man's new wife cannot bear the child that will continue the family name, they attempt to make the woman turn her child over to them, forcing her to chose between the social advantages her child would enjoy with the well-off family and the intense emotional bond between her and her child. Mandarin with English subtitles.
VHS: S24183. $49.95.
Chu-Huang Chen, Hong Kong, 1988

My Better Half
A funny, surreal adventure which begins during WWI with Flora the whore, who marries a fishmonger and literally screws him to death. His ghost comes back to tell her that the King of Hell will allow him to continue his earthly life if the couple can complete all the sexual positions in one night. They fail, and suddenly it's the '60s, with all new characters, including Kwong, the sickly father of two children, his wife Yin, who's trying to raise $50,000 for his lung operation, and a lecherous chicken-monger who tries to work out a deal with her for sex. Cantonese with English subtitles.
VHS: S33207. $49.95.
Llee Han Chang, Hong Kong, 1993

My Flying Wife
In this witty take on the U.S. film *Ghost*, Sammo Hung plays a street hood who finds he deeply wronged Dodo Cheng Yiu-Yeung in a previous life. Her murder stranded her and their unborn son in the twilight world between heaven and hell—and only an exorcism with the help of Sammo's friend Lam Shing-Ying can give them all a second chance. Letterboxed. Cantonese/Mandarin with English subtitles.
VHS: S30293. $49.95.
O Sing-Pui, Hong Kong, 1991

My Heart Is That Eternal Rose
A woman becomes a gangster's mistress to save her father's life, while her lover must flee the country. Years later they meet again: her father has died and he is a killer doing a job for the gangster. An atmospheric melodrama filled with striking compositions and lurid, tropical colors, tense and melancholy. With Joey Wang, Kenny Bee, Tony Leung. Mandarin with English subtitles (slightly low but readable).
VHS: S24184. $49.95.
Patrick Tam, Hong Kong, 1988

The Naked Killer
Sick action comedy in which a cop falls in love with a woman who joins a team of female hit women who specialize in breaking limbs and castration. With Simon Yam and Carrie Ng. Cantonese with English subtitles.
VHS: S33208. $49.95.
Clarence Ford/Fok Yiu Leung, Hong Kong, 1992, 88 mins.

Naughty! Naughty!
Sam Hui (of the Hui Brothers *Mr. Boo* fame) is a charming young man making a living by his wits and other people's money. It takes a beautiful young woman to bring out the good in him-in spite of himself. Cantonese with English subtitles.
VHS: S14859. $49.95.
Lo Wei, Hong Kong, 119 mins.

The New Legend of Shaolin
Jet Li stars in the fantasy film based on a Chinese legend. The Father Superior of the Shaolin Temple decides to destroy a map to a treasure trove before the evil Manchu rulers find out about it and try to steal it. So as not to lose his way to the treasure, the Father Superior has copies of the map tattooed onto the backs of five young masters of Shaolin. Unfortunately, the Manchus *do* find out about the treasure and come looking for the Shaolin masters. Cantonese and Mandarin with English subtitles.
VHS: S27386. $49.95.
Laser: Letterboxed. **LD76122. $89.95.**
Wong Jing, Hong Kong, 178 mins.

New Tenant
Polanski's *Repulsion* and *The Tenant* meet *Somewhere in Time* and *The Cabinet of Dr. Caligari*. Ex-mental patient Anthony Wong Chau-Sun (also directing) moves into a tenement unit with a mysterous wall clock. When it periodically jams, he joins in a dysfunctional family drama that transpired years past, in the same rooms. Laurence Ng Kai-Wah is a cannibalisitic college professor, Wong Tse-Wah is a fundamentalist Christian psychiatrist, Dolphin Chan Hoi-Hang is a girl named Shark and Lau Ching-Wan is a mental patient named Joe. Letterboxed. Cantonese/Mandarin with English subtitles.
VHS: S30341. $49.95.
Anthony Wong Chau-Sun, Hong Kong, 1995

Ninth of September, The Cursed Day
In the 1930s, a young folk singer committed suicide by throwing herself in the lake on her wedding day. Fifty years later, the cycle begins to repeat itself in the guise of another young singer. With Hilary Tsui, Tung Oi Ling and To Tai Yu. Cantonese with English subtitles. Letterboxed.
VHS: S32012. $49.95.
Chan Siu Cheung, Hong Kong, 1996, 104 mins.

Obsession
A young divorcee falls in love with the wrong man. Her obsession leads to vindication and an explosive fatal attraction. With Maryanna Hung and Chan Wai Man. Cantonese with English subtitles. Letterboxed.
VHS: S31977. $49.95.
Kwok Siu Wai, Hong Kong, 1995, 89 mins.

The Occupant
A woman who is writing her dissertation on Chinese superstition moves into an apartment where a popular singing star was the victim of a murder/suicide. Chow Yun Fat is a policeman who, along with a very superstitious car salesman, comes to the aid of the woman when she becomes possessed by the spirit of the singer. Mandarin with English subtitles.
VHS: S27297. $49.95.
Ronnie Yu, Hong Kong, 1984

The Old Master
Don't be misled by the picture of Jackie Chan on the box cover—it's only a reference to his movie *Young Master* and he doesn't appear in this film. Instead, we have the story of an aging master who travels to Los Angeles to teach, but ends up being manipulated into fighting rival schools in a gambling scheme. A loyal student warns him off this scheme and offers him a place to live in return for being taught kung-fu. While the student practices, the master attempts to adjust to American life, including an extended visit to a disco. Mandarin with English subtitles.
VHS: S27287. $49.95.
Joseph Kuo, Hong Kong, 1980

On the Run
Yuen Biao is a detective who loses his police officer wife just as she is about to solve a crime. Betrayed by his fellow officers, Yuen must now rely on a hired killer from Thailand (Pat Ha), who quickly shows herself to be the only person worthy of his trust. Good performances and a well-crafted violent mood give this film a superior sense of suspense and intrigue. Mandarin with English subtitles.
VHS: S27293. $49.95.
Sammo Hung, Hong Kong, 1988

Operation Pink Squad
A Hong Kong *Police Academy*, in which five guys and four babes play with a Chinese Ouija board, and end up resurrecting an evil spirit bent on possession. Cantonese with English subtitles.
VHS: S33211. $49.95.
Jeff Lau, Hong Kong, 1986

Operation Pink Squad II
Fun mix of ghost comedy and cop action. The scene that parodies *A Better Tomorrow* is particularly hilarious. Cantonese with English subtitles.
VHS: S33212. $49.95.
Jeff Lau, Hong Kong, 1987, 88 mins.

Paper Marriage

This Romantic comedy is set in Canada, where an out-of-work and down-on-his-luck Chinese boxer (Sammo Hung) accepts a promise of payment to go through a form of marriage with a Hong Kong girl (Maggie Cheung) so she can gain citizenship. When the payment fails to materialize, Sammo is forced back into the ring and Maggie even tries mud-wrestling before they ultimately discover their love for each other. Cantonese with English subtitles.

VHS: S13487. $49.95.
Sammo Hung, Hong Kong, 102 mins.

Paradise Hotel

Trouble and chaos take place in the Paradise Hotel when four different groups of Hong Kong neighbors escape to Macau in search of ghosts and romance. With Lee Chun Chau and So Yuk Wah. Cantonese with English subtitles. Letterboxed.

VHS: S31981. $49.95.
Ko Chi Sum, Hong Kong, 1995, 81 mins.

Peace Hotel

Chow Yun Fat stars as the keeper of the mysterious "Peace Hotel," a safe-haven for triad fugitives with an unspoken rule that the hotel would not help escapees flee. Cecilia Yip plays Chow's love interest as the girl for whom he breaks all the rules. Cantonese/Mandarin with English subtitles.

VHS: S30475. $89.95.
Kai-Fei Wai, Hong Kong, 1995, 86 mins.

Perfect Match

Comedy and romance as a boss and one of her managers, a toy designer, share a tempestuous relationship, complicated by the reappearance of her ne'er-do-well cousin and rivals within the company. With Andy Lau. Mandarin with English subtitles. 1989.

VHS: S24186. $49.95.

Pink Bomb

Cynthia Khan, Lee Siu Yin and Fenny Yuen take a tour bus to Thailand, where they pick up a hooker (Gloria Yip) with money stolen from the mob. Thai gangsters want their money back and the tour guide (Waise Lee) helps them fight for their lives. Cantonese with English subtitles.

VHS: S33210. $49.95.
Chiu Sung-Kei, Hong Kong

The Raid

Tsui Hark produced this comic book-styled film starring Jacky Cheung Hok-Yau, Tony Leung Kar-Fai and Joyce Godenzi. Based on the popular "Uncle Choy" picture books of the 1930s, this rambunctious adventure saga is set in the Japanese-occupied Manchuria of that time. Cantonese/Mandarin with English subtitles.

VHS: S30311. $49.95.
Ching Siu-Tung, Hong Kong, 1991

Red to Kill

An unspeakable cesspool of exploitation! "Money" Lo stars as the seemingly benign head of a charitable workhouse for the disabled, who stalks the neighboring tenements by night as a muscle-bound, semi-nude serial rapist/killer. The extensive rape and mayhem are capped by Money's riveting scenes with a nubile, retarded victim, Lily Chung. Two-tape set. Letterboxed. Cantonese/Mandarin with English subtitles.

VHS: S30517. $89.95.
Billy Tang Hin-Sung, Hong Kong, 1995

The Returning

Wu Chien-Lin plays the down-to-earth girlfriend of Tony Leung Chiu-Wai, a journalist who decides to investigate a notorious haunted house by living there. Soon both become enmeshed in the past of the mansion's famous last tenant, a suicidal chanteuse whose hit song echoes endlessly throughout the halls. Two-tape set. Letterboxed. Cantonese/Mandarin with English subtitles.

VHS: S30523. $89.95.
Jacob Cheung Chi-Leung, Hong Kong, 1994

The Roar of the Vietnamese

A violent tale of illegal immigrants being manipulated by criminal gangs, forced to commit crimes in return for supposed passage to the U.S., focusing on a particular group of disparate individuals who bond together under the stress of their situation. More a melancholy action movie than a serious look at the plight of the Vietnamese. Chinese with English subtitles. Hong Kong, 1991.

VHS: S25946. $49.95.

Rose

Maggie Cheung plays Rose, an ace insurance agent beset by insecurities. When a gangster (Roy Cheung) scares away one of her prospective clients, he attempts to make it up to her by taking out a large policy for himself that names Rose as the beneficiary. There is a catch, however: Rose must let him hide out at her place. It doesn't take long for love to develop in this absorbing drama, but the recurring problem of the gangster's violent past is a constant threat to their romantic idyll. Mandarin with English subtitles.

VHS: S27295. $49.95.
Samson Chiu, Hong Kong, 1992, 99 mins.

Rouge

The popular singers/actors Anita Mui and Leslie Cheung are paired in this supernatural love story which alternates between the brothels, theaters and opium dens of Hong Kong in the Thirties, and the cool, detached world of the present day. The ghost of a courtesan appeals to a young journalist to help her find her lost lover who recovered from their joint suicide attempt and thus failed to join her in the spirit world. Cantonese with English subtitles.

VHS: S13465. $49.95.
Stanley Kwan, Hong Kong, 1987, 99 mins.

Run Tiger Run

"Wacky" and "zany" are the adjectives that best describe this bizarre John Woo comedy, done in a *Pee-Wee's Playhouse* style with strange decor and speeded-up, jerky movements. The plot revolves around the nearly identical appearance of two little boys—one the spoiled heir to a large fortune, whose evil uncle wants to do away with him, the other the son of the diminutive but scrappy Teddy Robin Kwan—and the chaos that ensues when everyone ends up in the rich kid's mansion. Mandarin with English subtitles.

VHS: S24192. $49.95.
John Woo, Hong Kong, 1985

Runaway Blues

A young and suave champion race car driver (Andy Lau) accidentally kills an underworld gangster during competition and becomes a fugitive running for his life. Cantonese with English subtitles.

VHS: S31986. $49.95.
David Lau, Hong Kong, 1989, 95 mins.

Saviour of the Soul

In this futuristic tale set in an Art Deco style never-never land, Andy Lau and Anita Mui star as high-flying superheroes stalked by the evil "silver fox" (Aaron Kwok). Cantonese with English subtitles.

VHS: S30756. $49.95.
Cory Yuen, Hong Kong, 1993, 94 mins.

Saviour of the Soul II

Andy Lau and Rosamund Kwan star in this surreal comedy-adventure in which a trio of adventurers quest for the magical "virgin ice" in a spectacular mountain setting, as well as for a mysterious woman one of the men has dreamed of every night of his life. A strange film in which the outlandish plot developments keep changing the direction you think it's going in. Mandarin with English subtitles.

VHS: S24193. $49.95.

Sea Root

A heartwarming story about a young fisherman (Lau Ching Wan) who defied modernization to preserve traditional values passed down from generations of boat people in Hong Kong's Aberden. Sailing gets a little rough when Lotus (Alice Lau) comes aboard. Also with Lee Fung. Cantonese with English subtitles. Letterboxed, two-tape set.

VHS: S31960. $89.95.
Art Concept Creation, Hong Kong, 1996, 92 mins.

Serenade in the Mist

A charming and amusing story about two Hakka duck-breeding families and the emotions and conflicts they encounter along the river bank where they live. With Hong Dou and Ju Xue. Cantonese with Englishsubtitles.

VHS: S31978. $49.95.
Zhang Zi En, Hong Kong, 1993, 94 mins.

Seven Days in Paris

Chinese painter Chie lives in the French countryside and invites his brother Chien from Hong Kong for a visit. When Chien meets the sexy Nina, a romance blossoms. Cantonese with English subtitles.

VHS: S33206. $49.95.
Hong Kong, 1993, 86 mins.

Seven Years Itch

After seven years of marriage a couple find themselves a bit bored with each other, until the husband goes on a business trip to Singapore and gets mixed up with a pretty hustler who knows a sucker when she sees one. Before long, his wife, his leeching brother-in-law, and his shrill mother-in-law are all involved, and the previously quiet marriage is threatened, especially when the obnoxious Mr. Money appears with the offer to take the wife back with him to the U.S. Mandarin with English subtitles.

VHS: S24196. $49.95.
Johnny To, Hong Kong, 1987

The Seventh Curse

Chow Yun Fat appears as the occultist character Wisely, a character first seen in *Legend of Wisely*. This film offers a heady mixture of fantasy, adventure and the supernatural, featuring demons, monsters, flying killer alien-baby monsters and a spinal cord-eating, walking skeleton. Also known as *Dr. Yeun and Wisely*. Mandarin with English subtitles.

VHS: S27272. $49.95.
Nam Nai Choi, Hong Kong, 1986, 88 mins.

Sex and Zen

An unusually high-class, erotic tale, based on the ancient literary classic *The Prayer-Mat of Flesh*. Amy Yip Chi-Mei flaunts her voluptuousness in the face of Lawrence Ng, an easily distracted scholar who has his penis replaced by that of a horse in a Taoist transplantation ritual you'll have to see to believe! Also features Ken Chang and Isabella Chow. Letterboxed. Cantonese/Mandarin with English subtitles.

VHS: S30317. $94.98.
Laser: Letterboxed. **LD76113. $69.95.**
Michael Mak Dong-Kit, Hong Kong, 1993

Sex and Zen II, Parts A & B

Based on a Chinese literary classic, the sequel to this erotic tale continues with Sai Mun Kin, a local merchant whose lascivious escapades with a mysterious woman lead to calamity. Cantonese and Mandarin with English subtitles.

VHS: S31691. $89.95.
Laser: LD76372. $69.98.
Chin Man Kay, Hong Kong, 1996, 88 mins.

Sex and Zen III

Yu Pui Tsuen continues in this spoof with a zany police investigator from the Ming Dynasty who goes undercover in a house of harlots to uncover a fatal love potion. His mission is impeded as he is lost in the pleasure of the beautiful woman he is investigating. With Xu Jin Jiang, Lee Suet Man and Yeung Yuk Mui. Cantonese with English subtitles. Letterboxed, two-tape set.

VHS: S31951. $89.98.
Lai Kay Keung, Hong Kong, 1996, 96 mins.

Sexy & Dangerous

Meet Marble, a teenage girl known on the streets as an arcade game wizard. Teamed up with her girl gang of four, Marble gets into more than a few tight situations, all for the sake of her triad boyfriend, One. With Loletta Lee, Karen Mok and Chan Mui Ying. Cantonese with English subtitles. Letterboxed, two-tape set.

VHS: S31966. $89.95.
Billy Tang, Hong Kong, 1996, 87 mins.

Shanghai 1920

In 1920s Shanghai a Chinese street urchin and the son of a wealthy British trader become fast friends and then become separated. When the Englishman returns years later to start a business, he finds his former friend is now a gangster and their attempts to work together seem destined for failure. The approach of the invading Japanese army to the city throws everyone's lives into confusion, though, and the two find their destinies linked together again. With John Lone. Chinese with English subtitles.

VHS: S27390. $49.95.
Leung Po-Chi, Hong Kong

Struggle for Avengence

Havoc and desolation besiege war-torn China as clans and factions struggle for power in this restless society. This is the story about two neighboring clans who destroy each for the sake of young love. With Man Chung Shan and Yik Yuen. Cantonese with English subtitles.

VHS: S31979. $49.95.
Cheung Mei Kwan, Hong Kong, 1982, 88 mins.

Stunt: A Musical Motion Picture

In this collage of images, representation and meta-reality, the performance artist and stunt man David Leslie orchestrates a spectacular pageant that pays homage to the respective spirits of James Brown, Evel Knievel, Bruce Lee and Julie Andrews. 35 mins.

VHS: S17201. $39.95.

Sweet Peach

An innocent girl falls for the wrong man and is pushed into prostitution and fraud. With Tsui Man Wah and Chan Pui Ki. Cantonese with English subtitles.

VHS: S31997. $49.95.
Lau Fu Keung, Hong Kong, 1994, 95 mins.

Sword of Many Loves

"Cantopop" singing star Lai is featured as a bumptious cart driver who will haul anything for hire, including supplies for an oasis-dwelling witch (Michelle Reis/Li Kar-Yan) who specializes in concocting deadly poisonous charms. He also encounters a stunning bald-headed nun (Cheung Man) who's a bit of a tease. Initially at odds, they unite against an old couple trying to seize supremacy in the world of poisoners and enchanters. Cantonese/Mandarin with English subtitles.
VHS: S30305. $89.99.
Poon Man-Kit, Hong Kong, 1993

Talk to Me, Dicky

Truly ridiculous movie about a couple of detectives tracking down a serial rapist by learning to talk to their penises, which can in turn communicate with the organs of other men, including the rapist. Mandarin with English subtitles. 1992.
VHS: S24199. $49.95.

The Tattoo Connection

A Hong Kong martial arts classic featuring legendary Jim Kelly as a private investigator following the theft of one of the world's biggest diamonds. Dubbed in English.
VHS: S20572. $39.98.
Lee Tse Nam, Hong Kong, 1979, 95 mins.

Teppanyaki

A journey into the strange, silly world of Michael Hui, filled with slapstick, satire and parody. This time he plays a hapless chef attempting to live out his fantasies of escaping to a tropical isle with a pretty stewardess (Sally Yeh). When the chance arises, though, he finds himself accompanied by his bullying wife and father-in-law (and boss), as well as his decrepit father—what would a Michael Hui comedy be without plenty of frustration? Chinese with English subtitles.
VHS: S25949. $49.95.
Michael Hui, Hong Kong, 1983

Thank You Sir

Earnest look at the experiences of a bunch of high school-age cadets in a prestigious police academy. Danny Lee plays the newly appointed deputy commander who tries to bring a more humane approach to training the students, only to run into opposition from other instructors reluctant to change the way things are done. Mandarin with English subtitles.
VHS: S24200. $49.95.
Ivan Lai, Hong Kong, 1989

They Came to Rob Hong Kong

After a violent opening sequence, this turns out to be a silly farce about a group of misfits recruited from mainland China in order to commit a big robbery in Hong Kong. Once they arrive there, however, the group discovers that it is only a pawn in the evil scheme of the master plotter (still coughing up blood after his brawl at the start of the film), and, of course, they band together to foil him. Chinese with English subtitles. Hong Kong, 1989.
VHS: S25950. $49.95.

Those Merry Souls

The nimble Yuen Biao, star of several Jackie Chan action pictures, appears here as a movie stuntman who discovers his late father had been living a secret life. Unbeknownst to him, his father served as a conductor of souls of the newly deceased to the spirit world, and now it is up to Yuen to continue in his father's footsteps. This doesn't sit well with Yuen, who had hoped to live a more ordinary life. With the help of his friends, he attempts to escape his peculiar family legacy. Instead of being an attempt to make a scary ghost picture, this takes a more atmospheric approach, filled with a fondness for Chinese superstition and folklore, as well as plenty of opportunities for Yuen to display his agility. Hong Kong, 1985, 94 mins.
VHS: S27589. $49.95.

Those Were the Days

One day before her wedding, a young bride arranges a reunion with her three high school buddies. Through memorable flashbacks, the girls reminisce about their teenage years together. A sweet story about friendship, hopes and aspirations. With Eric Tsan and Loletta Lee. Cantonese with English subtitles. Letterboxed, two-tape set.
VHS: S31961. $89.95.
Eric Tsang, Hong Kong, 1996, 101 mins.

Tom, Dick & Hairy

Tony Leung Chiu-Wai, Tony Leung Kar-Fai and Lawrence Cheng Tan-Sui play roommates sharing a penthouse bachelor pad in Hong Kong. This crossroads of many lives and loves includes girlfriends Annie Bridgewater/Bai Ahn-Ni and Lau Kam-Ling. When "Hairy" accidentally teaches himself French by watching the wrong TV channel (he thought he was learning English), it makes him a hit with his friends when he orders from the menu in a swank restaurant. Letterboxed. Cantonese/Mandarin with English subtitles.
VHS: S30324. $49.95.
Peter Chan Ho-Sun/Li Chi-Ngai, Hong Kong, 1993

Tri-Star

In this delightful comedy an unorthodox priest tries to help a young prostitute (Anita Yuen) turn her life around. His devotion to the church is compromised when he finds himself falling in love. Co-stars Lau Ching Wan as the wacky cop. Cantonese with English subtitles. Letterboxed, two-tape set.
VHS: S31970. $89.98.
Tsui Hark, Hong Kong, 1996, 109 mins.

Twenty Something (5pm-9am)

The Chinese title, *5pm-9am*, says it all: it's a world where people's lives take place at night, not at their 9-to-5 jobs. In this group tale about Hong Kong's lost generation and their aimless pursuits in the nightclubs and bedrooms of the naked city, Valerie Chow Kar-Ling stars as a movie executive (working at the film's actual production company, UFO), with Jordan Chan Siu-Chun as dissolute party-boy Lam Bo. Teddy Chan Tak-Sum ably directs James Yuen Sai-Sang's incisive script. Two-tape set. Letterboxed. Cantonese/Mandarin with English subtitles.
VHS: S30520. $89.95.
Teddy Chan Tak-Sum, Hong Kong, 1994

Ultracop 2000

In the year 2000, Zorbak, the infamous outlaw from Mars, ignores the Universal Treaty that forbids interplanetary war and goes on a killing spree on Earth. It is up to Nunez (Yukari Oshima) and her fellow Ultracops to stop Zorbak from conquering the Earth. Dubbed in English.
VHS: S32695. $14.95.
Phillip Ko, Hong Kong, 1993, 85 mins.

The Untold Story

Anthony Wong Chiao-Sun won the Hong Kong Best Actor Award for the role of a sociopath who takes over a roast pork shop by grinding up the owner and his family for roast human flesh. He lets it be known that the owner suddenly sold out to him and moved, but his new, pretty assistant and a suspicious cop (Danny Lee Sau-Yin) begin to think otherwise. Letterboxed. Cantonese/Mandarin with English subtitles.
VHS: S30315. $79.95.
Herman Yau Lai-To, Hong Kong, 1993

Wai's Romance

Once a gentleman of wealth, Wai was flocked by many women. Now penniless, he discovers his magnetism has suddenly disappeared. Follow the amusing adventures of Wai and his renewed quest for wealth, romance and love. With Li Li Lee, Tsui Man Wah and Charlie Cho. Cantonese with English subtitles. Letterboxed.
VHS: S32007. $49.95.
To Hoi Sang, Hong Kong, 1994, 96 mins.

Who's the Woman, Who's the Man, Parts A & B

This second take on *He's a Woman, She's a Man* involves an identity crisis arising between a music composer and his live-in girlfriend, a promising young singer. The problem is, she's impersonating a male singer and her newfound fans think he and she are gay. With Leslie Cheung, Anita Mui, Anita Yuen and Eric Tsang. Cantonese and Mandarin with English subtitles.
VHS: S31693. $89.95.

Why Me?

This comedy/drama is the story of a young social worker who takes an interest in Big Cat, a large man who thinks he is a child. The social worker wants to bring both Big Cat and his mother, a street vendor, under the protective wing of the Social Services department, but she must first diffuse their mistrust of the government. Chow Yun Fat is featured as the social worker's more experienced supervisor and love interest. Mandarin with English subtitles.
VHS: S27289. $49.95.
Kent Cheng, Hong Kong, 1985

Witch from Nepal

A man unknowingly inherited a supernatural power from an ancestor, a powerful Nepalese tribal chief, and is hunted by one who wants the power for himself. Cantonese with English subtitles.
VHS: S14857. $49.95.
Ching Siu Ting, Hong Kong, 91 mins.

Women Flowers

Part 3 of the *Feminine Movie Series* by director Wang Jin depicts the lives of Chinese women during the 1900s and a group of women who attempt to strive for freedom of choice. Cantonese with English subtitles. Letterboxed.
VHS: S32013. $49.95.
Wang Jin, Hong Kong, 1994, 95 mins.

Xing Qi Gong Zhi Tan Bi

Qi Gong is an ancient Chinese exercise that helps you feel the air frequency in your body. The male characters in this film show their Qi Gong ability in bringing their female partners to their greatest ecstacy. With Yukari Oshima, Mark Cheng and Wu Fung. Cantonese with English subtitles. Letterboxed.
VHS: S31991. $49.95.
Lam Wah Chuen, Hong Kong, 1993, 83 mins.

You Make Me Laugh

A classic tearjerker starring legendary singer Teresa Tang. With Tsun Han and Ho Chun Hung. Cantonese with English subtitles.
VHS: S31992. $49.95.
Chan Hung Man, Hong Kong, 1981, 73 mins.

Yu Pui Tsuen

Like *Sex & Zen*, this film is an adaptation of the Chinese literary classic. Yu Pui Tsuen is a young man whose sexual fantasies plunge him into a dangerous life of lust and temptation. With Tung Yiu Fai and Yu Chi Wai. Cantonese with English subtitles.
VHS: S31982. $49.95.
Ho Fan, Hong Kong, 1996, 76 mins.

HONG KONG ACTION CINEMA

Aces Go Places II

An extremely likable mixture of Keystone Cops-style slapstick combined with James Bond shenanigans and Cantonese humor, again featuring the fancy-free jewel thief King Kong (Sam Hui). With Sylvia Chang and Carl Mak. Cantonese with English subtitles.
VHS: S13478. $49.95.
Eric Tsang, Hong Kong, 1983, 100 mins.

Aces Go Places III (Our Man from Bond Street)

The third in the popular *Aces Go Places* series, featuring handsome Sam Hui as a debonair master thief. Cantonese with English subtitles.
VHS: S14851. $49.95.
Eric Tsang, Hong Kong, 1982, 94 mins.

All Men Are Brothers—Blood of the Leopard

One of the best of the period sword epics, lavishly produced and photographed in compositions often resembling Chinese landscape paintings come to life. It's the story of an honest general whose sense of duty allows him to be manipulated by scheming courtiers and ambitious rivals. All the while he resists the aid of his sworn brother, a rough-and-tumble monk. With Tony Leung and Joey Wang. Chinese with English subtitles. Hong Kong, 1993.
VHS: S25929. $49.95.
Laser: Letterboxed. **LD76118. $69.95.**

Angel Force

Li Chek Man is a low-ranking woman cop in Hong Kong who finds herself called upon for a secret mission to rescue a fellow agent in Thailand. Her fighting prowess, extended by a crack team of warriors, saves the day in this action-packed film, but not before some serious battles are waged. Dubbed in English.
VHS: S22759. $44.95.
Po-Fa Hwa, Hong Kong, 1994, 95 mins.

Angel of Fury

Martial arts queen Cynthia Rothrock stars as security specialist Nancy Bollins, who is hired to deliver a valuable computer; however, her former lover has plans of his own for the computer.
VHS: S33987. $14.95.
Ackyl Anwary, Indonesia, 1993, 80 mins.

Angel of Kickboxer

High-kicking action and explosive fight scenes abound in this tale of suspense and betrayal in which a kind social worker teams up with a dedicated Hong Kong police inspector to stop a ruthless loan shark who enlists a group of down-and-out Chinese men to rob a prestigious Hong Kong goldsmith. With Yukari Oshima, John Lam, David Koh and Ann Cheung. Dubbed in English.
VHS: S31274. $14.95.
Lee Chiu, Hong Kong, 1989, 100 mins.

Angel on Fire
A beautiful supermodel-turned-gangster doublecrosses her ruthless partners after the gang steals a precious relic from a Manila museum. Now an enterprising young Interpol agent, with the help of a comical taxi driver, must stop the vicious gang and return the relic to its rightful owners. Exciting gunplay and martial arts action with Cynthia Khan, Waise Lee, and Yeung Pan Pan. Dubbed in English.
VHS: S31275. $14.95.
Philip Ko, Hong Kong, 1995, 87 mins.

Angel's Mission
Filled with gun-blasting action and superb martial arts choreography, this is the hard-hitting tale of Cynthia, a beautiful, Japan-based Interpol agent on holiday visiting her mother in Hong Kong. Cynthia's vacation is cut short when her superiors call her in to investigate a Hong Kong-based prostitution ring—in which her mother is a key figure. With Yukari Oshima, Ron Van Lee and Dick Wei. Dubbed in English.
VHS: S31276. $14.95.
Phillip Kao, Hong Kong, 1988, 95 mins.

Angry Young Man
Jealousy leads to misunderstanding and conflict between two college buddies in this classic martial arts actioner. Envious of his friend's newfound popularity in a martial arts club, a young man takes more than a few drastic measures to topple his success. With Pak Ying and Wong Ching Lee. Cantonese with English subtitles.
VHS: S32001. $49.95.
Wong Sing Lui, Hong Kong, 1983, 90 mins.

The Assassin
A reflective tale taking place over a number of years, set in ancient China, about the making of a hero. Stoic Jimmy Wang (Wang Yu) must weigh his filial obligations and the possibilities of living a normal, happy, domestic life against his duties to his country and his desire to fulfill the heroic destiny he feels lies within him, as he decides whether to assassinate a usurping prime minister. Chinese with English subtitles. Hong Kong, 1985.
VHS: S25932. $49.95.

Beach of the War Gods
Another spin on the *Seven Samurai* tale, this time with Ming Dynasty Chinese villagers, led by an itinerant swordsman played by Jimmy Wang (Wang Yu), banding together to fortify their town and throw back invading Japanese. Chinese with English subtitles.
VHS: S25935. $49.95.
Wang Yu, Hong Kong, 1971

The Beautiful Swordswoman
In this classic swordplay drama, the secret life of a beautiful swordswoman is about to be disclosed as she enters into the realm of assassination. With Wong Ling and Yeung Ming. Cantonese with English subtitles.
VHS: S31975. $49.95.
Yeung Kan, Hong Kong, 1983, 88 mins.

Beauty Investigator
In order to capture a serial rapist, two beautiful policewomen go undercover as club hostesses. However, they soon discover that the club owner is actually the head of an arms smuggling syndicate. They decide to take him on, not knowing that he has discovered their identities and hired a Japanese woman assassin to kill them first. With Yukari Oshima and Moon Lee. Dubbed in English.
VHS: S34235. $14.95.
Hsia Hsu, Hong Kong, 1992, 90 mins.

Best Friend of the Cops
Jackie Cheung plays an ex-cop, now a con-man, who dupes a bunch of policemen who are all too ready to be taken in by his scheme. They think they're putting up money to be used as capital in a loan-sharking operation. An off-beat offering in a genre that rarely strays from well-worn paths. Chinese with English subtitles. Hong Kong, 1990.
VHS: S25936. $49.95.

Best of the Best
The story of a policeman in love with the daughter of a gangster, a man who was also once a cop and rival of the hero's father, and who definitely doesn't want his daughter going out with a cop. An above-average mixture of sentiment and violence, filled with a sense of fatalism and funeral images. Chinese with English subtitles.
VHS: S25937. $49.95.
Herman Yau, Hong Kong, 1992

A Better Tomorrow
Kit is an up-and-coming cop, but his brother Ho is a street-hardened criminal. Soon they are both dragged into a savage underworld battle over counterfeit money. Even if Ho wants to go straight, there is a murderous price to pay that forces the brothers into a deadly confrontation.
VHS: S13455. $19.98.
John Woo, Hong Kong, 1986, 90 mins.

A Better Tomorrow—Part II
Although the charismatic gangster Mark, played by Chow Yun Fat, was killed at the end of Part I, Chow returns here as Mark's previously unmentioned twin brother Ken. Ken joins forces with an idealistic cop named Kit (Leslie Cheung) and his now-reformed gangster brother Ti Lung, against another legion of evil criminals. Cantonese with English subtitles.
VHS: S13456. $39.95.
John Woo, Hong Kong, 1988, 100 mins.

A Better Tomorrow—Part III
Chow Yun Fat returns as Mark Gor, the stylish police detective, in this sequel which is actually a prequel. Set in 1974, Gor and his cousin (Tony Leung) want to escape the post-war squalor of Saigon. Unfortunately, both are in love with the same woman (Anita Mui), a gangster moll. This action-filled adventure is loaded with plot twists, outrageously choreographed violent sequences, and a love triangle that leads to tragedy. Also known as *Love and Death in Saigon*. Mandarin with English subtitles.
VHS: S27267. $49.95.
Tsui Hark, Hong Kong, 1989, 114 mins.

Big Bullet
An action drama starring Lau Ching Wan as a misunderstood cop whose honesty leads to a demotion. He makes the best of things as he joins arms with an odd team of four cops to crack down on two high-profile criminals on a killing rampage. Cantonese and Mandarin with English subtitles.
VHS: S31689. $69.95.
Chan Muk Shing, Hong Kong, 1996, 96 mins.

The Big Heat
A seasoned cop is forced to come out of semi-retirement when a friend is brutally murdered. Starring Waise Lee, Joey Wang (*Green Snake*) and Mathew Wong. Cantonese with English subtitles.
VHS: S31983. $49.95.
Johnny To, Hong Kong, 1988, 98 mins.

The Blade
Chiu Man-Cheuk is "Iron Head," a swordfighter in love with his *sifu*'s daughter—as is his best friend. The story heats up when Chiu loses an arm in an ill-advised act of vengeance and must learn a new, one-armed stance. The story harks back to Jimmy Wang Yu's *One-Armed Swordsman*, but the cinematography is in the latest music video style, all snappy camera pans and zooms. Austin Wai Tin-Chi and Valerie Chow Kar-Ling co-star. Two-tape set. Letterboxed. Cantonese/Mandarin with English subtitles.
VHS: S30512. $89.95.
Tsui Hark, Hong Kong, 1995

Bloody Friday
A serial killer is on the loose making his bloody rounds every Friday. It's up to one cop to crack this brutal killing rampage. With Simon Yam, Loletta Lee and Ada Choi. Cantonese with English subtitles. Letterboxed, two-tape set.
VHS: S31952. $89.98.
Danny Ko, Hong Kong, 1996, 94 mins.

Bloody Hero
A group of outlaws from the mainland are given shelter at a wealthy man's house in Hong Kong, then must flee to the Philippines when a counterfeiting deal goes wrong. Once there, they attempt to double-cross their old benefactor, leading to a bloody confrontation. Chinese with English subtitles.
VHS: S25963. $49.95.
Addy Sung, Hong Kong, 1990

Bodyguard from Beijing
Jet Li Lienjie plays a bodyguard trained to protect the highest echelons of China's Communist Party. To protect a beautiful star-witness in a high-powered corruption case (Christy Chung Lai-Tai), the Chinese government loans Jet to Hong Kong, where he gets a bumbling sidekick (Kent Cheng Jut-Si) and an implacable nemesis (Ngai Sing). Two-tape set. Letterboxed. Cantonese/Mandarin with English subtitles.
VHS: S30515. $89.95.
Corey Yuen Kwai, Hong Kong, 1995

Born Invincible
Some nimble kung-fu in this low-budget flick as a series of students attempt to learn enough to overcome an apparently invisible white-haired villain who has only one vulnerable spot on his body (of which no one knows the location). Chinese with English subtitles. Hong Kong, 1983.
VHS: S25965. $49.95.

Brave Young Girls
Several young women fall into the clutches of gangsters, including an illegal immigrant, a karate champ, and a girl sold into prostitution by her mother. Their only hope lies in cooperating with another woman, a tough cop from Japan pursuing arms smugglers. Chinese with English subtitles. Hong Kong, 1990.
VHS: S25966. $49.95.

Bruce Lee and the Green Hornet
A rare screen test of the martial arts icon and charismatic figure Bruce Lee, on the making of the television series *The Green Hornet*, with three complete, uncut episodes and a short film on the making of Robert Clouzet's *Enter the Dragon*, the actor's fullest and most satisfying work. 90 mins.
VHS: S17577. $19.95.

Bruce Lee Gift Set
The charismatic and kinetic kung fu action star Bruce Lee displays his balletic movements in four different works: *The Chinese Connection, Fists of Fury, Return of the Dragon* and *Game of Death*.
VHS: S19096. $49.98.

Bruce Lee: The Immortal Dragon
The story of the man who fought his way from the mean streets of Hong Kong to international stardom as one of the most celebrated kung-fu masters of all time. As Bruce Lee reached the height of fame he was struck down by a mysterious ailment—or was it a family curse? Includes interviews with friends and family, including his late son Brandon, and footage from home movies, screen-tests and his legendary films. 50 mins.
VHS: S32369. $9.95.

Bruce Lee: The Lost Interview
Martial arts expert Lee became world-renowned for his performances in such Kung-fu classics as *Enter the Dragon*. Now his only interview in English is available. Just after the release of his first film, *The Big Boss*, he spoke in Hong Kong with Canada's premiere journalist Pierre Barton. This is the closest one can get to this extraordinary master. 30 mins.
VHS: S23116. $19.95.

Bullet in the Head
John Woo's epic tale of three friends (Tony Leung, Jackie Cheung and Waise Lee) caught up in the turbulent events of the 1960s in Hong Kong and later, in Vietnam, where the three hope to exploit the anarchy and corruption that prevail, only to find themselves in danger of being overwhelmed by it. Their drama is played out in a country captured by such filmic precedents as *The Deer Hunter, Platoon* and *Missing in Action*, seemingly an ideal setting for Woo to explore his themes of loyalty, honor and betrayal. Chinese with English subtitles.
VHS: S20584. $49.95.
Laser: LD76119. $69.95.
John Woo, Hong Kong, 1990

Casino Tycoon II (Part A)
Andy Lau is the general manager of a large casino, adept at balancing the legitimate operations of the casino with the claims of two rival gangs on a part of its profits. When his son is killed, he has to deal with the presence of an unknown rival within his own organization, as well as decide whether to continue his affair with a beautiful reporter (Joey Wang), or remain with his crippled wife. We are unsure what the (*Part A*) of the title refers to, since the movie is complete—normally it would mean that it was part of a two-tape set. Chinese with English subtitles.
VHS: S25942. $49.95.
Wong Jing, Hong Kong, 1992

Catman in Lethal Track
Sam was scratched by a radioactive cat. The result is super human powers. Now this superhero must marshall all his strength to defeat the Asian Mafia in their quest to control all Asia. The mysterious rebel Franco helps Catman in this hyperactive action adventure. Dubbed in English.
VHS: S27877. $19.98.
Alton Cheung, Hong Kong, 1993, 90 mins.

Catman's Boxer's Blow
Sam is a top U.S. agent who develops super-human powers after being scratched by a radioactive cat. Using his laser vision and his overwhelming strength, he fights the less than holy Reverend Cheever. Cheever plans to destroy the world by distributing nuclear devices. It's a sci-fi action flick filled with non-stop violence.
VHS: S27861. $19.98.
Alton Cheung, Hong Kong, 90 mins.

Cheetah on Fire
Two Royal Hong Kong Police inspectors are assigned to help the CIA extradite a suspected criminal back to the U.S. When gunmen from a Golden Triangle drug boss kidnap the criminal to retrieve a secret computer chip from him, the Hong Kong Police and the CIA team up with the local army for a rescue operation, only to make a discovery that threatens the whole unity of their force. Dubbed in English.
VHS: S33876. $14.95.
Tsui Fati, Hong Kong, 1993, 87 mins.

China Heat

A group of aggressively minded women from China's elite task force is selected to capture Hong, a homicidal, international drug lord. Joining them on the hunt are two New York City cops and their stubborn Captain. Powerful fights and exciting stunts. With Sibelle Hu, Alan Lan and Sophia Crawford. Dubbed.

VHS: S34646. $14.95.

William Chang, Hong Kong, 1990, 90 mins.

China O'Brien 2

From the director of *Enter the Dragon*. Cynthia Rothrock is back and deadlier than ever as China O'Brien, who's now Sheriff. Drug Lord Charlie Baskin just blasted his way out of prison and into Sheriff O'Brien's jurisdiction.

VHS: S33988. $14.95.

Robert Clouse, USA, 1989, 85 mins.

Circus Kids

Yuen Biao leads a circus troupe in flight from the Japanese occupation of Shanghai. They return to senior member Wu Ma's home province, but it's now run by a corrupt official, his unwitting henchman (Donnie Yen Chi-Tan), and a kick-fighting hitman (Ken Lo Wai-Kwong). While straightening out Donnie, Biao also falls for Ma's daughter. Letterboxed. Cantonese/Mandarin with English subtitles.

VHS: S30297. $49.95.

Wu Ma, Hong Kong, 1994

City Cops

An FBI informant flees the country for Hong Kong where he is sought by a resourceful FBI agent (Cynthia Rothrock), a couple of HK cops, and a lot of gangsters. The fight sequences involving Rothrock distinguish this picture from a mass of similar stories. Mandarin with English subtitles (occasionally cropped).

VHS: S24141. $49.95.

Lau Kar Wing, Hong Kong

City Kids

Gritty tale of two friends growing up on the mean streets of Hong Kong, attempting to overcome the violence and poverty that form their surroundings. One of them wants to go straight, but will loyalty to his troubled childhood pal drag him down? Mandarin with English subtitles.

VHS: S24142. $49.95.

Poon Man Kit, Hong Kong, 1989

City Ninja

Ben, an evil mastermind of crime, perverts the magical powers of the "Warrior Wizards" by training a gang of Ninja in the techniques of the Ninjitsu. Judy, Lily and Johnny escape from this mastermind's camp but despite the "Thousand Ways" of the Wizards they are in grave danger. Ben is determined to capture them dead or alive. Dubbed in English.

VHS: S27869. $19.98.

Larry Hutton, Hong Kong, 1988, 85 mins.

City on Fire

Cinema City's answer to *The French Connection* stars Chow Yun Fat as a plain-clothes cop out to bust a syndicate of jewel thieves. Cantonese with English subtitles.

VHS: S13477. $49.95.

Ringo Lam, Hong Kong, 1987, 98 mins.

City War

This time the team of Chow Yun Fat and Ti Lung appear on the right side of the law, as a police investigator and a plain-clothes cop who match wits with a vengeful gangster. Cantonese with English subtitles.

VHS: S13469. $49.95.

Sun Chung, Hong Kong, 1989, 100 mins.

Close Escape

Med student finds himself on the run after his brother, unbeknownst to him, rips off stolen diamonds from a mobster, in this above-average crime drama. His friends must locate him before he unwittingly reveals the location of the diamonds. With Aaron Kwok. Mandarin with English subtitles (a bit cropped).

VHS: S24144. $49.95.

Wing Chow, Hong Kong, 1989

A Collection of Chow Yun Fat

Three action-packed films featuring Chow Yun Fat are joined in this video collection. In *Prison on Fire II* a man escapes from prison in order to see his young son. Captured, he must face prison once again, only this time his term is complicated by a new danger. A guard frames him. *Full Contact* follows the story of a gunman double-crossed by a gay villain and a killer. This tale of revenge is tinged with an underlying homoerotic interest. *A Better Tomorrow III* is set in war-ravaged Vietnam. Escape is imperative, but only a gunslinging beauty can help Chow Yun Fat's character leave Vietnam. In Cantonese with English subtitles. The first two are directed by Ringo Lam while the last is directed by Tsui Hark.

VHS: S26517. $79.95.

Cop Image

Anthony Wong Chiao-Sun witnesses a bloody jewelry heist and tries to solve the mystery of the missing loot and a missing cop (Lam Bo-Yi) who has stolen it for himself. Joined by the renegade cop's ex-girlfriend (Wong Sing-Pao) and a petty gangster (pop-star heartthrob Andy Hui Chi-On) in the quest, Anthony finds that Lam Bo-Yi is using the money to emigrate to the U.S. with his secret boyfriend. Written by Lau Wing-Kin. Letterboxed. Cantonese/Mandarin with English subtitles.

VHS: S30332. $49.95.

Herman Lau, Hong Kong, 1994

The Crippled Masters

A ruthless warlord rules his village with an iron fist and punishes those who betray him. One warrior suspected of disloyalty has his arms severed. Another's legs are disfigured. Both are discarded and left to die, but their thirst for revenge is stronger than death. A wise martial arts master convinces the disabled warriors to join forces, and by combining their strengths, they are transformed into an unrelenting, unforgiving, unbeatable killing machine. With Frankie Shum and Jack Conn. Dubbed in English.

VHS: S30886. $14.95.

Joe Law, Hong Kong, 90 mins.

Crocodile Hunter

Andy Lau plays a cop who really should retire, since he's got a bullet lodged in his head. But, no, he's got to come back to track down some dangerous escaped criminals. To make this more difficult, he's saddled with an oafish partner and a couple of obnoxious civilian leads in the case. See chopsticks used as a weapon here. Chinese with English subtitles. Hong Kong, 1989.

VHS: S25943. $49.95.

Crystal Hunt

Lisa (Carrie Ng) hires Professor Lau to find the mysterious Crystal in the forbidden land. However, he is kidnapped by a ruthless gang, which wants Lau to hunt the Crystal for them. Lisa then teams up with Special Police Squad's Madam Wu (Sibelle Hu) and Leung (Donnie Yen) and together they vow to find Professor Lau and the Crystal and fight the bad guys. Dubbed in English.

VHS: S33339. $14.95.

Pak Lam Chui, Hong Kong, 1991, 90 mins.

Curry and Pepper

The Starsky and Hutch of Hong Kong cop movies. The irreverent duo battle criminals and their own superiors, but perhaps the biggest test of their friendship comes when they both vie for the attention of a glamorous reporter doing a documentary on them. 1990.

VHS: S24147. $49.95.

The Cyprus Tigers

On the popular European vacation spot of Cyprus, three of the toughest undercover cops, Dick, Jackie and Bomb (Simon Yam, Collin Cheung and Conan Lee), take on the counterfeiting ringleader Mr. King and his Japanese hoodlums. Watch these three invincible tigers fight for justice with their martial arts skills and their infinite firepower in this roaring action-feast. Also stars Robin Shou from *Mortal Kombat* and the lovely Joey Wang. Dubbed in English.

VHS: S24148. $14.98.

Philip Ko, Hong Kong, 1990, 88 mins.

Dangerous Duty

A police crackdown on a cigarette smuggling ring gets messy when their only witness is hunted down by a professional killer. Hong Kong's finest team up to form the Witness Protection Unit in this action thriller. With Max Mok (*Once upon a Time in China*), Pang Tan and Ng Ngai Cheung. Cantonese with English subtitles. Letterboxed.

VHS: S32002. $49.95.

Tong Wai Shing, Hong Kong, 1996, 90 mins.

The Dead and the Deadly

Vulgar humor, distinctive local color and amazing martial arts sequences distinguish this story of a young man who experiments with the sorcerer's arts. With Sammo Hung and Yuen Biao. Cantonese with English subtitles.

VHS: S13484. $49.95.

Wu Ma, Hong Kong, 1982, 90 mins.

Deadend of Besiegers

Cynthia Khan and Yu Rong Guang star in this interesting match-up of Japanese and Chinese martial arts. Cantonese with English subtitles.

VHS: S33200. $49.95.

Zhang Siu Wan, Hong Kong, 1992, 86 mins.

Deadly Dolls Collection

The deadliest martial arts ever in this new series featuring Michelle Yeoh (*Tomorrow Never Dies, Supercop*), Moon Lee (*Midnight Angels*), Cynthia Rothrock (*China O'Brian*) and others. Includes *Midnight Angels II, Five Lade Venoms* and *Top Fighter II: Deadly China Dolls.*

VHS: S34997. $99.95.

Deadly Target

Yukari Oshima and Sharon Yeung Pan-Pan reprise their roles from *Angel Terminators* as Hong Kong policewomen battling crime, including one of the women's own cousins, a Manila businessman named Hing. The nonstop action includes a subplot with their Philippine counterpart, Eddie, who is kept from his daughter by his mother-in-law, who blames him for the death of her own daughter, his wife. Cantonese/Mandarin with English subtitles.

VHS: S30326. $49.95.

Hong Kong, 1994

Death Rim

The "King of Car Thieves" is determined to retire from a life of crime after a three-year stint in the slammer. His dreams of starting a new life with his family quickly disintegrate when his loyalty toward his gangster brother gets in the way. With Mark Cheng, Yung Kam Cheung and Wong Chi Yeung. Cantonese with English subtitles.

VHS: S32003. $49.95.

Ng Dick Man, Hong Kong, 1996, 85 mins.

Descendant of Wing Chun

Fierce fighting displays the Wing Chun style of kung fu in this this tale of revenge. Evil bandit Ma Lung escapes from prison and seeks revenge on retired Wing Chun teacher Lam Chan, who had helped to imprison him. Dubbed in English.

VHS: S31655. $14.95.

Huang Ha, 1978, Hong Kong, 92 mins.

Devil Hunters

When the most dangerous drug deal of the century is foiled by two mysterious fighters, the warring druglords begin to suspect one another and vow to discover who they are. Little do they know that the fighters are actually part of an alliance of unusual partners, who must now band together again to brave the full-contact fights of their enemies. With Moon Lee, Sibelle Pu, Alex Man and Raymond Lui. Dubbed in English.

VHS: S34236. $14.95.

Tony C.K. Lo, Hong Kong, 1989, 90 mins.

Diary of the Big Man

Major Hong Kong hunk Chow Yun Fat at his most Cary Grant-like. Chow plays an attractive womanizer with two wives and two households. Of course keeping the two separate is more than a full time job, and when Chow finally slips up, comic complications ensue. Cantonese with English subtitles. Hong Kong.

VHS: S14874. $49.95.

Don't Give a Damn

Sammo is a slovenly cop competing with Yuen Biao, a persnickety customs official, to break a criminal smuggling ring. Heartthrob Takeshi Kaneshiro/Kam Shing-Mo gets into the act as Sammo's new boss, a stickler for regulations fresh from the police academy. All resolve their differences in an amazing action finale that moves from a criminal invasion of police HQ to a martial arts blowout in an abandoned warehouse. With kickboxer Ngai Sing. Letterboxed. Cantonese/Mandarin with English subtitles.

VHS: S30292. $49.95.

Sammo Hung, Hong Kong, 1995

Dr. Lam[b]

The good doctor (Simon Yam Tak-Wah) is really a necrophile rapist/murderer who then photographs his victims in this compelling serial killer/police procedure story. Danny Lee Yau-Sin (who also co-directs) is the cop who brings him to justice. Co-starring Kent Cheng Jut-Sui. Letterboxed. Cantonese/Mandarin with English subtitles.

VHS: S30320. $49.95.

Danny Lee Yau-Sin/Billy Tang, Hong Kong, 1992

Dragon Fight

Jet Li plays a member of a touring martial arts team stranded in San Francisco when he tries to stop his teammate (C.L. Tu) from defecting. His friend ends up working for organized crime gangs, though, and Li is drawn toward an ultimate confrontation with his former pal. Nice locations and well-staged action with great stunts by Li. Mandarin with English subtitles (occasionally cropped at edges).

VHS: S24152. $49.95.

Billy Tang, Hong Kong, 1989

Dragon Inn
This rousing epic-adventure is set in a remote inn on China's eastern frontier. The all-star cast includes Tony Leung Kar-Fai, Brigette Lin Chin-Hsia, Maggie Cheung Man-Yu and Donny Yen Chi-Tan. Two-tape set. Cantonese/Mandarin with English subtitles.
VHS: S30510. $89.95.
Laser: Letterboxed. **LD76123. $89.95.**
Raymond Lee Wai-Man/Ching Siu-Tung, Hong Kong, 1992

Dragon: The Bruce Lee Story
An appealing biography of Bruce Lee, the Hong Kong superstar whose mysterious death, at age 33, certified his legend. Jason Scott Lee plays the kung-fu star. With Lauren Holly as Lee's widow Linda.
VHS: S19527. $19.95.
Laser: LD72296. $49.99.
Laser: Widescreen. **LD74836. $69.98.**
DVD: DV60300. $34.98.
Rob Cohen, USA, 1993, 119 mins.

Dragons of the Orient
Key martial arts sites, including Shaolin temple, are visited by a group of reporters in this documentary film. Demonstrations of various feats, including sword swallowing, rolling in glass and fire walking, are included. A short history of the mainland Chinese martial arts champion, Jet Li, is also featured. Mandarin with English subtitles.
VHS: S27296. $49.95.
Rocky Law, Hong Kong, 1993

Drunken Tai-Chi
Chen Nu Tsai is the evil boss of Salt Manor. His son, Chen Duo, is a talented fighter who strives for justice. After he harms an opponent, Chen Duo loses his entire family and emerges penniless and alone. Befriended by a top Tai-Chi master, he triumphs by seeking retribution and learning the lesson of gracious generosity. Dubbed in English.
VHS: S22758. $44.95.
Yuang Ho-Ping, Hong Kong, 1994, 95 mins.

Duel to the Death
The feature film debut by director Ching Siu Tung (*A Chinese Ghost Story*), this swordplay epic is based on the legend of a duel to the death between Japanese Ninjas and Chinese Shaolin monks during the Ming Dynasty to settle the countries' conflicts and stop the bloodshed. Complete with kinetic martial arts choreography, sumptuous photography and nonstop action. With Damian Lau and Norman Tsui Siu-Keung. Cantonese with English subtitles.
VHS: S31110. $59.95.
Laser: LD76172. $39.99.
Ching Siu Tung, Hong Kong, 1982, 90 mins.

The Eagle-Shooting Heroes
Wacky *mo ley tow* (makes no sense) comedy with a shameless cast, a non-stop fairy tale plot and delirious fight sequences staged by Sammo Hung. Starring Brigette Lin Chin-Hsia, Joey Wang Tsu-Hsien, Maggie Cheung Man-Yu, Leslie Cheung Kwok-Wing, Tony Leung Kar-Fai and Tony Leung Chiu-Wai, Jacky Cheung Hok-Yau and Kenny Bee/Cheung Jan-Tao. Two-tape set. Cantonese/Mandarin with English subtitles.
VHS: S30308. $89.95.
Jeff Lau Chun-Wai, Hong Kong, 1993

Eastern Condors
A high-energy Hong Kong version of *The Dirty Dozen*. The U.S. military sends a group of convicts back to Vietnam on a mission to destroy an abandoned ammunition dump before the Viet Cong discover it and use it for their own evil purposes. Stars Sammo Hung, Joyce Godenzi, Yuen Biao and Haing (*The Killing Fields*) Ngor. Letterboxed. Cantonese with English subtitles.
VHS: S13444. $59.95.
Laser: LD76309. $39.95.
Sammo Hung, Hong Kong, 1986, 100 mins.

Eastern Heroes
Hong Kong police inspector Kevin Ma, "The Sweeper," is an expert cop specializing in tackling some of the most vicious gangs in the colony. Kevin learns that the head of Shaw International Enterprises was kidnapped by the Vietnamese. After Kevin kills Tiger, the gang's leader, it's a race against time as Conan, Kevin's brother, travels to Hong Kong to help capture Robin, Tiger's brother, before it's too late. Stars Robin Shou (*Mortal Kombat: The Movie*). Dubbed in English. 91 mins.
VHS: S30140. $34.95.

Eat My Dust
Tired of their lives as gangsters, Tam and Hung decide to leave Hong Kong for South America. But Hung is murdered by one of his fellow men. Years later, Tam returns to Hong Kong and together with Hung's now grown-up son and a gun-wielding female cop they embark on a tough mission to bring in the murderer, who is now the head of a powerful Triad. Dubbed in English.
VHS: S33340. $14.95.
Philip So, Hong Kong, 1993, 94 mins.

Enter the Dragon
Bruce Lee is probably the name that comes to mind for most Americans when they think of martial arts action films. Here the stern-faced Lee infiltrates a strange tournament on an island fortress. With John Saxon and Jim Kelly. In English.
VHS: S14867. $49.95.
Laser: LD72261. $34.98.
Robert Clouse, USA, 1973, 97 mins.

Enter the Dragon—25th Anniversary Special Edition
The quintessential martial arts film that set the standard for all that followed, starring the incomparable Bruce Lee as a British agent who infiltrates the island fortress and brutal martial arts tournament of a death-dealing drug baron. Features three minutes of action footage not seen in previous U.S. version. With *Bruce Lee: In His Own Words* (20 mins.), featuring never-before-seen footage from the Lee family archives, the behind-the-scenes documentary from the original release, *Location: Hong Kong with Enter the Dragon* (7½ mins.), and original theatrical trailer. Digitally restored with all-new stereo soundtrack. Dubbed. Widescreen.
VHS: S34655. $19.98.
DVD: Digitally restored image, never-before-seen footage, English subtitles. **DV60395. 24.98.**
Robert Clouse, Hong Kong/USA, 1973, 103 mins.

Executioners
In a post-nuclear world, water is in short supply. Underworld figures plot to control this precious commodity, but three women stand in their way. These women blaze a trail studded with martial arts feats in their quest to save the world. This sequel to *Heroic Trio* is a must for Hong Kong action and martial arts film enthusiasts. Mandarin with English subtitles.
VHS: S27269. $79.95.
Laser: Please Note: Digital track, Cantonese analog, English dubbed. **LD75825. $39.95.**
DVD: DV60240. $29.95.
Chiung Siu Tung, Hong Kong, 1993

An Eye for an Eye
When an aging crime boss trying to go legit is framed for a murder, his daughter (Joey Wang) is forced to take over the business. She soon finds herself under the control of the men who framed her father in the first place. Meanwhile, she is loved by two detectives investigating the organization, throwing doubt on their ability to objectively pursue the case. Chinese with English subtitles. Hong Kong, 1990.
VHS: S25931. $49.95.

Fatal Chase
Mortal Kombat star Robin Shou stars in this martial arts action thriller. Senior police investigator Marcus Lee and unconventional undercover cop Robin track down the vicious drug dealer Dion in Hong Kong. Robin will stop at nothing to fight for justice and end Dion and his boss Tiger's vicious reign of terror. Dubbed in English. 96 mins.
VHS: S30139. $14.95.

The Fatalist
The story of a hitman with a conscience (Ng Ngai Cheung) who must struggle between good and evil and the cop who will take him down. With Lam Man Lung. Cantonese with English subtitles.
VHS: S31974. $49.95.
Shin Chi Wai, Hong Kong, 1996, 90 mins.

Fate of Lee Khan
A truly astounding martial arts/historical drama from one of the foremost innovators of the *wu xia pian* genre (swordplay film). Lee Khan must accept his destiny as revolution against the Mongol rulers of the Yuan dynasty swirls around him. Cantonese with English subtitles.
VHS: S13485. $49.95.
King Hu, Hong Kong, 1973, 107 mins.

The Fiery Dragon Kid
This entertaining melange of action, romance, and knockabout humor revolves around the duplicitous character of Brigette Lin Ching-Hsia, a government spy trying to unmask a possible rebel, Max Mok Siu-Cheung. They end up part of a provincial carnival run by Sandra Ng Kwan-Yue. Sin Lap-Man plays his evil eunuch with supernatural kung-fu powers. Letterboxed. Cantonese/Mandarin with English subtitles. 1995.
VHS: S30301. $49.95.
Yuen Woo-Ping, Hong Kong, 1995

Final Justice
Stephen Chow Sing-Chi, before he became Hong Kong's biggest comedy star, actually specialized in tough-guy gangster roles—as in John Woo's Just Heroes and his award-winning turn here. He's a petty car thief caught between his gangster boss, Shing Fui-On, and a taciturn cop, Danny Lee Sau-Yin. Co-starring Ken Lo Wai-Kwong. Cantonese/Mandarin with English subtitles.
VHS: S30339. $49.95.
Parkman Wong, Hong Kong, 1988

First Option
The story of the Flying Tigers, an elite group of cops trained like soldiers to combat the most violent of crimes, is told in this action drama. Meet Commander Stone (Michael Wong), a veteran "Tiger" who is tough enough to fight the most hardened criminal, but loses it all to love. With Gigi Leung and Damian Lau. Cantonese with English subtitles. Letterboxed, two-tape set.
VHS: S31949. $89.98.
Gordon Chan, Hong Kong, 1996, 107 mins.

Fist of Legend
A martial arts master is poisoned by Japanese militia who see his academy as an obstacle in their conspiracy to take over China. With Jet Li, Choi Siu Fan and Chin Siu Ho. Cantonese/Mandarin with English subtitles.
VHS: S30476. $89.95.
Gordon Chan, Hong Kong, 1994, 92 mins.

Five Lady Venoms
Five deadly beauties take on the Hong Kong drug cartel. With Elsa Yeung, Eagle Lee, Tattooed Ma, Karen Sun and Merle Kee.
VHS: S34996. $59.95.

Forbidden Arsenal
Decent action flick, utilizing the popular device of cooperation between characters from Hong Kong, Taiwan and the mainland, in this case three cops, whose cultural misunderstandings make some good comic moments. The action scenes are also good. With Cynthia Khan. Mandarin with English subtitles (sometimes chopped at the sides but no difficulty following the plot). 1991.
VHS: S24161. $49.95.

Fox Hunter
Jade Leung Cheng is a metermaid who wants to make it as a real cop. Sent undercover as a bar hostess, she crosses paths with Jordan Chan Siu-Chun, a pimp venal enough to betray his boss, the ruthless crime king Tung. Scenes of Tung coldly shooting Jade's father limb-by-limb before killing him, or escaping from the police after using Jordan (strung with live hand grenades) as a human shield, add to the excitement. Yu Rong-Guang is the dour mainland Chinese cop who's hunting Tung from his own side. Cantonese/Mandarin with English subtitles.
VHS: S30330. $49.95.
Stephen Tung Wai, Hong Kong, 1995

From Beijing with Love (aka From China with Love)
Hong Kong's funny man Stephen Chiau plays a Chinese 007 in this James Bond-like spoof. The story begins when a man with a golden gun steals the cranium bones of China's only dinosaur fossil. With Anita Yuen and Pauline Chan. Cantonese and Mandarin with Chinese and English subtitles.
Part A.
VHS: S30760. $69.95.
Part B.
VHS: S30761. $49.95.
Laser: Parts A and B, letterboxed. **LD76343. $89.98.**
Li Li Chi, Hong Kong, 1994, 89 mins.

Full Contact
A Bangkok nightclub bouncer named Jeff is the hero of this action-filled criminal adventure film. Jeff helps his friend Sam escape from a loan shark only to find that Sam has double-crossed him and marked him for death. With both Sam and Mona, Jeff's girlfriend, convinced that Jeff was killed in an explosion, Jeff escapes to Thailand to recuperate and figure out what to do next. His getaway sets the stage for a variety of surprise appearances as he returns to seek his vengeance. Cantonese with English subtitles.
VHS: S27270. $49.95.
Ringo Lam, Hong Kong, 1992, 99 mins.

Full Throttle
Andy Lau is a misguided youth who has led a life of turmoil since his mother's death. Not caring whether he lives or dies, he spends all his time racing on the dangerous streets of Hong Kong. With David Ng and Leung Wing Kee. Cantonese with English subtitles. Letterboxed, two-tape set.
VHS: S31968. $89.98.
Yee Tung Sing, Hong Kong, 1995, 108 mins.

God of Gamblers

Chow Yun Fat is the suave, almost telepathic God of Gamblers. A blow to the head dissipates his memory and sends him into a childlike frame of mind. Three small-time hustlers parasitically decide to cash in on this state of affairs, but they eventually grow fond of the former God. When his memory returns, Fat can't remember the three hustlers, but despite this complication, the trio comes to his aid as it becomes clear that he is surrounded by enemies. This comic action film was a huge hit and inspired countless imitations, sequels and parodies. With Andy Lau and Joey Wang. Cantonese with English subtitles.

VHS: S27291. $49.95.
Laser: LD76125. $89.95.
Wong Jing, Hong Kong, 1989, 125 mins.

God of Gamblers II

Chow Yun Fat doesn't appear in this film except as the object of veneration to his disciple, The Knight of Gamblers (Andy Lau). Lau, reprising his role from *God of Gamblers*, is joined by the goofy Saint of Gamblers (Stephen Chiau). In this funny, parodic sequel, the two join forces to thwart a plan that would ruin the God of Gamblers' reputation. Cantonese with English subtitles.

VHS: S27292. $49.95.
Wong Jing, Hong Kong, 1989, 103 mins.

Golden Dart Hero

This action-packed, kung fu adventure film follows the rise of an outlaw called Huang Tianba. When Huang's brother is killed, he seeks revenge but is foiled and captured. Then in a complete reversal from his earlier ways, he devotes himself to the court. There his strength serves him well. Dubbed in English.

VHS: S21830. $49.95.
Li Wenhua, Hong Kong, 1994, 98 mins.

Great Hero from China

Wang Fei Hong is a hero to the Chinese people, who runs a martial arts school. When he decides to destroy the opium drug trade, powerful enemies determine that he must be stopped. Against incredible odds he perseveres, resulting in a series of amazing, all-out martial arts battles. Dubbed in English, 90 mins.

VHS: S22610. $39.95.

The Great Jetfoil Robbery

A shipment of $10 million in transit by jetfoil to Hong Kong is seized by three armed men. Through mobile phones, the men coerce the boat's captain to change its course to an unknown destination. The robbery has Hong Kong and Macao's finest on their toes. Cantonese with English subtitles.

VHS: S31995. $49.95.
Kong Ngai, Hong Kong, 1996, 82 mins.

Guardian Angel

Rosa, Candy and Lisa are Interpol officers trained to stage an offensive war against international drug smugglers. However, Rosa is forced against her will to carry out this killing assignment by the ambitious Chan, who had saved her life. This forces Rosa to hunt down the enemies before she becomes the hunted herself. Dubbed in English. Starring Yukari Oshima.

VHS: S32694. $14.95.
Phillip Ko, Hong Kong, 1996, 86 mins.

Gun of Dragon

This smart, tough cop story puts its Hong Kong cop-hero (Ray Lui) and psycho-villain (Mark Cheng Shuk-Wai) in the United States, where both have to operate against an alien backdrop. Meanwhile, the cop has to solve an emotional crisis with his wife (Yvonne Yung). Features Alex Fong and John Sham Ki-Fan. Letterboxed. Cantonese/Mandarin with English subtitles.

VHS: S30335. $49.95.
Tony Leung, Hong Kong, 1994

Handsome Siblings

A great meeting of the martial arts clans leads to a bloody climax of betrayal and counter-betrayal. Starring Andy Lau Tak-Wah as a man called Fishy and Brigette Lin Ching-Hsia playing a woman passing as a man. Will they find that incest is best? With Cheung Man and Ng Mang-Dat. Letterboxed. Cantonese/Mandarin with English subtitles.

VHS: S30310. $49.95.
Eric Tsang Chi-Wai, Hong Kong, 1992

Hard Boiled

This film is an action fan's dream. The seamy underworlds of gun smugglers, mobsters and rebel cops collide in this super-fast paced thriller. A police inspector and a mysterious hit man team up to thwart a dastardly plot hatched by ruthless criminals.
Dubbed Version.

VHS: S21500. $19.98.
Laser: LD74629. $124.95.
DVD: DV60178. $39.95.

Subtitled Version. Letterboxed. Cantonese with English subtitles.

VHS: S24848. $19.98.
John Woo, Hong Kong, 1992, 126 mins.

Hard Target

The American debut of Hong Kong action auteur John Woo (*The Killer, Bullet in the Head*) is an operatic reworking of *The Most Dangerous Game*. Set in New Orleans, the story follows a group of aristocrats who brutally attack homeless Vietnam veterans for sport, cruelly orchestrated by a debonair mercenary (Lance Hendriksen). Jean-Claude Van Damme plays a sea merchant reluctantly drawn into the mix when a beautiful lawyer (Yancy Butler) enlists his support in tracking down her father. With Wilford Brimley.

VHS: S20181. $19.98.
Laser: LD72326. $34.98.
John Woo, USA, 1993

Hard to Die

Dragon Head is the godfather of Hong Kong's biggest criminal gang. When a female police inspector is assigned to arrest him, she getshelp from a dim-witted undercover agent. Filled with gripping gunplay and explosive action. With Sibelle Hu, Carrie Ng and Michiko Nishikawa. Dubbed.

VHS: S34648. $14.95.
Wong Chun-Yeun, Hong Kong, 1993, 90 mins.

He Lives by Night

A strangler is stalking the neon streets of nighttime Hong Kong. A couple of detectives and a late-night DJ team up to stop him, or is it her, before the DJ becomes his next victim. Mandarin with English subtitles (often chopped off at edges). 1982.

VHS: S24165. $49.95.

Hearty Response

An irreverent cop (a breezy Chow Yun Fat) is forced to team up with his boss' rash nephew, who gets him involved with recent illegal immigrant Joey Wang, in a mixture of drama, comedy and intense action scenes. Joey, fearing she might be deported, pretends to believe herself to be Chow's wife, much to his initial irritation, although to his mother's delight. Meanwhile, he continues to chase a drug dealer while she tries to stay clear of a vicious thug involved in her immigration to Hong Kong. Mandarin with English subtitles (sometimes a bit washed out).

VHS: S24168. $49.95.
Low Man, Hong Kong, 1986

Heroic Trio

Three of Hong Kong's biggest female stars, Michelle Yeoh (Khan), Maggie Cheung and Anita Mui, play the leads in this strange tale of competing superheroines thwarting a mysterious series of baby kidnappings, in a comic book style (a la *Batman*). It has been suggested that the film is best read as a political allegory of the three entities of China, Taiwan and Hong Kong having to work together to overcome the many challenges facing them. Mandarin with English subtitles. Letterboxed.

VHS: S24169. $79.95.
Laser: Letterboxed. **LD75501. $59.95.**
Johnny To, Hong Kong, 1992

Honor and Glory

Hard-kicking FBI agent Tracy Pride (Cynthia Rothrock) squares off agaiinst the world's most ruthless hitman. With Robin Shou.

VHS: S33989. $14.95.
Godfrey Hall, USA, 1993, 84 mins.

Hunted in Hong Kong

Dutch and Jim are two American sailors on shore leave in Hong Kong. They soon discover that a little rest and relaxation are off limits when a gang attacks them. With Jim missing, Dutch relies on help from Horatio Lim as he delves into the Hong Kong underworld in search of his friend. Dubbed in English.

VHS: S27880. $19.98.
Lau Shing-Hon, Hong Kong, 1990, 90 mins.

I Love Maria (aka Roboforce)

Lovely songstress Sally Yeh (aka Yeh Ching-Wen) plays an evil superpowered robot, but a mismatched trio of good guys—John Sham Ki-Fan, Tony Leung Chiu-Wai and Tsui Hark—try to harness her powers for good. With Lam Shing-Ying. Action directed by Ching Siu-Tung. Cantonese/Mandarin with English subtitles.

VHS: S30312. $49.95.
David Chung/Tsui Hark, Hong Kong, 1988

The Iceman Cometh

A rip-roaring ride through history with two ancient swordsmen. This thriller comedy includes historic settings in ancient China, promises to be kept to dying martial arts masters, honor to be upheld, special effects, time travel, street life in present-day Hong Kong, a little social commentary, and, of course, good vs. evil. Starring Maggie Cheung and Yuen Biao. Cantonese with English subtitles.

VHS: S14882. $49.95.
Fok Yiu-leung, Hong Kong, 1991, 114 mins.

In the Line of Duty 4 (aka The Witness)

The continuing policewoman-caper, action series starring Cynthia Yang. Cantonese and Mandarin with English subtitles. With Michael Wong and Donnie Yan.

VHS: S30755. $49.95.
Yuen Wo Ping, Hong Kong, 1989

The Inside Story (Triad: The Inside Story)

The oaths of loyalty and bloodshed disclose the secret dealings of the triad world. After the death of his father, a young man who has tried to keep out of the underworld feels obligated to take over the business. With Chow Yun Fat (*The Killer*), Roy Cheung and Shing Fu On. Cantonese with English subtitles.

VHS: S31985. $49.95.
Taylor Wong, Hong Kong, 1990, 94 mins.

Interpol Connection

Law Tak is a vicious international heroin dealer who is being pursued by Hong Kong narcotic bureau officer Ko Pang, a bumbling Philippine policeman, KingKong, and an international police agent named Cynthia (Yukari Oshima). After being captured briefly by KingKong, Law escapes, murdering KingKong's best friend in the process. As KingKong and Ko team up to capture Law, this odd team creates many unexpected and laughable situations. When Cynthia finally joins in to help, it becomes an explosive and deadly battle. Stars Robin Shou (*Mortal Kombat: The Movie*). Dubbed in English. 91 mins.

VHS: S30141. $14.95.

Iron Monkey

Yu Rong-Guang stars as the masked "Iron Monkey." Jean Wang Ching-Ying is his beautiful assistant, young martial artist/actress Tsang Sze-Man crossdresses as the boy Wong Fei-Hung, and Donny Yen Chi-Tan plays Fei-Hung's father. Together they battle corrupt officials in this Tsui Hark production of a Yuen Woo-Ping film. Letterboxed. Cantonese/Mandarin with English subtitles.

VHS: S30513. $89.95.
Yuen Woo-Ping, Hong Kong, 1993

The Iron-Fisted Monk

One of the earliest directorial efforts of Jackie Chan's pal Sammo Hung, who also stars in the film. It's the tale of Shaolin monks who aid villagers to battle the evil Manchus as they swagger through China, raping, looting and pillaging. The mischievous and headstrong Hung, unable to concentrate on his martial arts studies in the temple, sets off on his own to help rid the countryside of the Manchus. Throughout the film he is sometimes aided by his former brethren, the monks, who are more interested in looking out for him than in capturing the Manchus.

VHS: S27585. $49.95.
Sammo Hung, Hong Kong, 1976, 87 mins.

It's a Drink! It's a Bomb!

Two scientists have developed a bomb that's disguised as a popular soft drink. One of the scientists is plagued by second thoughts about selling this weapon to the evil Japanese, so he hides the bomb and flees. Unfortunately, he is quickly hunted down and killed, but not before he passes the secret along to three innocent bystanders. The trio quickly team up for comedy, action and romance, as they try to convince the skeptical police that they aren't simply a bunch of loonies (since no evidence of any kind of crime is to be found).

VHS: S27586. $49.95.
David Chung, Hong Kong, 1985, 87 mins.

Karate Wars

Karate Wars is an all or nothing tournament in which honor, self respect and a million dollars are at stake. Master Oyama trains his students in ancient and secret Kung Fu techniques. His top student, Jason, must face off against his hated rival, but an unforseen complication places this fight outside of the tournament and into the lawless streets. Dubbed in English.

VHS: S27864. $19.98.
David Hue, Hong Kong, 90 mins.

Kickboxer from Hell

Mark Houghton stars as Sean, the American kickboxing champion. In Hong Kong, during preparations for a big match, he becomes involved with a British nun. He joins her and her crusade against Satan and his kickboxing crew led by the damnable Scorpion.

VHS: S27860. $19.98.
Alton Cheung, Hong Kong, 1990, 90 mins.

Kickboxer—The Fighter, the Winner

Illegal kickboxing happens in a world dominated by crime. Prostitution, loan sharking, drugs, and guns dominate. Even before a match starts, opposing crime lords have done their best to affect the outcome. In the end it's all irrelevant. There are two fighters and only one winner.
VHS: S27862. $19.98.
Albert Yu, Hong Kong, 1992, 90 mins.

Kickfighter

When Peter, the Chief Inspector of the Hong Kong Anti-Drug Squad, refuses to "overlook" some illegal drug activity being perpetuated by the exact people appointed to stop it, his family is murdered. Peter escapes to Thailand, only to run into the military drug cartels. He gets help from a prize kickfighter with connections in the Golden Triangle, and together they set out to annihilate one of the deadliest drug-running operations in Asia. With Yukari Oshima. Dubbed in English.
VHS: S34223. $14.95.
Philip Ko, Hong Kong, 1989, 88 mins.

Kill or Be Killed Collection

From the makers of the highly successful Wu-Tang Collection. Four of the deadliest and most anticipated martial arts films ever to hit video.
The 36 Deadly Styles. Pursued by the Silver Fox, the Ghost Faced Killer and Bolo, Jack Long must use what he has learned from the secret book of 36 Deadly Styles to fight them off. Starring Jack Long, Jeannie Chen and Hwang Jang Lee.
VHS: S35001. $19.95.
7 Grand Masters. An aging kung fu master travels the country in an effort to prove himself kung fu grandmaster before he dies. Along the way he takes on a young protege who, upon their return home, challenges the elder for his title. "Generally considered one of the best independently produced chop socky films of the '70s" (*Asian Cult Cinema*). With Jack Long and Lee Yi Min. Directed by Kuo Nai Hong, Hong Kong, 1978, 84 mins.
VHS: S34999. $19.95.
Born Invincible. An entire martial arts academy gets caught up in a conflict between an old man and his daughter in this old-school kung-fu movie with awesome fighting sequences. With Carter Wong. Directed by Joseph Kuo, USA, 1978, 83 mins.
VHS: S35000. $19.95.
Dragon's Claws. The son of the slain Dragon Boxing master prepares to take vengeance upon the man who killed him—the outcast Dragon Claw. Starring Jack Long, Carter Wong, Jimmy Liu and Hwang Jung Li. Dubbed. Directed by Joseph Kuo, Hong Kong, 90 mins.
VHS: S34998. $19.95.

The Killer

John Woo wrote and directed this brilliant gangster drama set in contemporary Hong Kong. The charismatic Chow Yun Fat stars as an amoral hitman who accidentally blinds a young torch singer, agreeing on a final assignment to pay for her surgery. The other plot is Chow's relationship with a tough, uncompromising cop (Danny Lee), as they battle the Hong Kong underworld. *The Killer* is a high-octane mixture of outlandishly stylized camp and outrageously sensational shoot-outs" (J. Hoberman). VHS letterboxed. Chinese with English subtitles.
VHS: S13457. $19.98.
Laser: Director's cut includes trailers from other John Woo films, deleted scenes, commentary from Woo and a guide to Hong Kong cinema. **LD72361. $124.95.**
DVD: DV60177. $39.95.
John Woo, Hong Kong, 1989, 102 mins.

Killer Angels

Meet the "Blue Angels": leader Moon Lee, who goes undercover as a nightclub chanteuse; Yukari Oshima, a jealous, motorcycle-riding bad girl with a shotgun; the cool butch Angel who goes undercover dressed as a man to case the club; and the schoolgirl Angel who beats up the wolfy witness she's protecting. A Hong Kong gal action classic.
VHS: S33205. $14.95.
Lui Jun Go, Hong Kong, 1989, 92 mins.

Killer's Romance

After learning that his father was killed by the notorious Chinatown Triad, Simon Yam becomes a cold-blooded killer determined to get his revenge. When one of his assassinations was witnessed by Joey Wang, Yam plans on silencing her forever. Instead Yam finds himself falling for Wang, and they must now run for their lives from both the cops and the Triad assassins. A suspenseful yarn combined with stylish action, intrigue and romance. Dubbed in English.
VHS: S32623. $14.95.
Philip Ko, Hong Kong, 1991, 91 mins.

Kung Fu the Movie

A feature-length translation of the cult 1970s program about the mysterious, Zen-like actions of Kwai Chang Caine, who gets drawn into an opium plot with an evil warlord (Mako) during the gold rush fever of 1880s California. Brandon Lee, the son of Bruce Lee, co-stars as Caine's adversary. The late Keye Luke appears in flashback as Master Po, Caine's blind instructor.
VHS: S17922. $19.98.
Richard Lang, USA, 1986, 100 mins.

Kung Fu [Cult] Master

The ascent of the native-Chinese Min Dynasty over the Mongol overlords of the Yuan gets blended with elements from the U.S. *Indiana Jones* cycle in an entertaining, if bewildering, extravaganza. Stars Jet Li Lienjie, Chingmy Yau Suk-Ching, Richard Ng Yao-Han, Sammo Hung, Cheung Man and Ngai Sing. Two-tape set. Letterboxed. Cantonese/Mandarin with English subtitles.
VHS: S30516. $89.95.
Wong Jing, Hong Kong, 1993

Lady Killer

After Master Ma kills Old Chin, Chin's wife takes over his gang and expands secretly, hoping to avenge her husband's death. She manages to convince the men in the gang that she will give Ma a fatal heart attack at the most appropriate moment. Her sister joins her in Taiwan from Korea and tries to dissuade her. Cantonese and Mandarin with English subtitles.
VHS: S31690. $34.95.
Lee Chun, Hong Kong, 1996, 77 mins.

Laser Mission

The late Brandon Lee stars with Ernest Borgnine in this intense spy thriller. Lee is a freelance secret agent contracted to save the Laser Master. He must cross an inhospitable part of South Africa to accomplish this mission and then defeat the Soviets who are holding the Laser Master hostage. This is one of Lee's few films, made shortly before his mysterious death on a stage set. 83 mins.
VHS: S27878. $19.98.

The Last Blood

The bodies fly in locations all around Singapore in this over-the-top action film in which an anti-terrorist expert and a headstrong tourist must cooperate to get a rare blood-type donor to a hospital in time to save an important Buddhist monk and the tourist's girlfriend, all the while pursued by terrorists. With Alan Tam and Andy Lau. Mandarin with English subtitles.
VHS: S24171. $49.95.
Wong Ching, Hong Kong, 1991

Last Hero in China

The Wong Fei-Hung franchise ends for Jet Li Lienjie with this serio-comic episode by Wong Jing. Fei-Hung's martial arts academy/clinic, Po Chi Lam (including Dickie Cheung Wai-Kin and Chan Park-Cheung), battles a nefarious prostitution/slavery ring in the heart of Canton. Co-starring Cheung Man. Action directed by Yuen Woo-Ping. Music by James Wong Lin. Cantonese/Mandarin with English subtitles.
VHS: S30314. $49.95.
Wong Jing, Hong Kong, 1992

Last Hurrah for Chivalry

A variation on the classic 1970's style kung-fu flick, starting out as a routine revenge drama, but bringing in a sense of character missing from most of the genre, and progressively veering from the expected development to question the motivations of its main characters, although with plenty of good action along the way, including a classic scene in which the heroes fight the deadly "sleeping watchman." An early exploration by director John Woo of one of his favorite themes, that of loyalty in a chaotic world. Mandarin with English subtitles (occasionally a bit chopped).
VHS: S24172. $59.95.
Laser: LD76274. $39.99.
John Woo, Hong Kong, 1979

Legacy of Rage

Fans of the late Brandon Lee who were disappointed by many of his American films will enjoy this action-drama, in which he agrees to help out a friend, only to find himself in jail for murder, while his deceitful buddy becomes obsessed with his girlfriend. The central portion of the film, where Brandon has to learn to cope with being locked up, is especially strong. Mandarin with English subtitles.
VHS: S24174. $19.95.
Ronny Yu, Hong Kong, 1986

Legend of the Drunken Tiger

It's the year 1898 and government reformists are sought out and publicly executed by the Ching Dynasty officials. Master Wang, a leader of the reformist party, enlists the help of skilled fighters for reinforcements, including Cheong San, a longtime enemy of the treacherous Lord Wing. With the help of Lela Wong, Cheong San's betrothed, Cheong San and Master Wang battle their nemesis to further their cause. Dubbed in English.
VHS: S31654. $14.95.
Robert Tai, 1992, Hong Kong, 98 mins.

Lethal Extortion

A ruthless band of international assassins abducts a whole ensemble of visiting Russian models in Taiwan. When the local police can't seem to make any headway with the extortionists, the sergeant turns to a group of war veterans for help. The highly skilled fighters and the police go head-to-head with the villains in a battle to the death. Dubbed in English.
VHS: S34224. $14.95.
Godfrey Hall, Hong Kong, 1993, 99 mins.

Lethal Girls 2

A chance meeting on the way to handle a case in mainland China leads Hong Kong policeman David Law to a brutal gang of drug smugglers and thrusts him on an unsettling journey to the dark side of Chinese Security Forces. Dubbed in English.
VHS: S31355. $14.95.
Williamson Law, Hong Kong, 1995, 89 mins.

Lethal Match

A murder case and a deadly love triangle prove to be a lethal match in this sizzling actioner. When a cop meets a gangster's mistress, there is more heat than both can handle. With Lam Man Lung and Law Wai Kuen. Cantonese with English subtitles.
VHS: S32004. $49.95.
Jeff Chiang, Hong Kong, 1996, 83 mins.

Lethal Panther

CIA agent Betty Lee is thrust into a quagmire of family rivalry, assassination, betrayal and revenge as she fights to stop Charles Wong, the Chinese boss of the most powerful crime family in the Philippines, from flooding the United States with counterfeit $100 bills. Dubbed in English.
VHS: S31353. $14.95.
Godfrey Ho, Hong Kong, 1991, 89 mins.

Lethal Panther 2

In this explosive tale from the Philippine underworld, Interpol Agent Jane and Hong Kong Police Inspector Dragon travel to the Philippines to investigate the activites of Mitusko, a member of the Yakuza crime organization now operating in Manila. Jane and Dragon join forces with Albert, a bitter Philippine cop who, still reeling from his wife's murder two years earlier, is willing to use any means necessary to capture the killers. Dubbed in English.
VHS: S31354. $14.95.
Cindy Chow, Hong Kong, 1992, 88 mins.

License to Steal

Two daughters of a master thief enter into deadly competition after one of them, envious of her sister's accomplishments, sets her up and has her imprisoned. With her rival out of the way, the bad sister takes over the family's business to become a ruthless jewel thief, until her sibling gets out of jail and the two head for the inevitable showdown. With Yuen Biao. Mandarin with English subtitles. 1990.
VHS: S24205. $49.95.

Love, Guns, and Glass

The "glass" is a chunk of broken window that down-on-his-luck ex-Triad Simon Yam Tak-Wah gives Cecilia Yip/Teh Tong in lieu of a diamond ring. Unfortunately, she's in hock to other, less-adoring Triads. Not to be missed is the gun battle when they try to get their wedding pictures taken, and the blood-splattered portraits they insist on posing for after it's all over. Features Roy Cheung Yiu-Yeung. Letterboxed. Cantonese/Mandarin with English subtitles.
VHS: S30331. $49.95.
Lai Kai-Keung, Hong Kong, 1995

Lucky Stars

One of a popular film series featuring the wild adventures of a team of crazy undercover Hong Kong cops. Starring Sammo Hung and Alan Tam. Cantonese with English subtitles.
VHS: S14884. $49.95.
Eric Tsang, Hong Kong

The Magnificent Butcher

The large Sammo Hung is thoroughly engaging as the butcher Wing, a hapless student of legendary martial arts hero Wong Fei Hong. Wing finds himself dragged into an escalating matrix of violence when his sister-in-law is kidnapped by a thuggish student from a rival school. An itinerant and drunken master provides comic relief as he schools Sammo in various martial arts techniques. Mandarin with English subtitles.
VHS: S27298. $49.95.
Yuen Woo-Ping, Hong Kong, 1979

Magnificent Warriors

Michelle Khan (aka Michelle Yeoh Chu-Kheng) plays a fearless soldier of fortune in World War II Mongolia who heroically tries to save a small village and their wacky leader (Lowell Lo Kuen-Tang) from the approaching Japanese army. Amazing battle scenes. Co-starring Richard Ng Yao-Han. Cantonese/Mandarin with English subtitles.
VHS: S30328. $49.95.
David Chung Chi-Man, Hong Kong, 1986

The Man from Hong Kong

Pedestrian James Bond-style film about a Hong Kong supercop sent to Australia to extradite a criminal, only to get involved in tracking down the mastermind behind a drug-running operation. With Jimmy Wang and George Lazenby (who played Bond in *On Her Majesty's Secret Service*).
VHS: S27380. $49.95.
Brian Trenchard Smith, Australia/Hong Kong, 1975

Man Wanted
Simon Yam (*Bullet in the Head*) is an undercover inspector in Hong Kong's seedy Mongkok district assigned to catch a drug kingpin (Yu Rong Guang, *The East Is Red*) who was previously assumed dead after a sting operation. Cantonese with English subtitles.
VHS: S31633. $59.95.
Laser: LD76248. $39.95.
Benny Chan, Hong Kong, 1995, 92 mins.

Martial Arts Mayhem, Vol. 1
Two hours of board-splitting, bone-breaking violence from '70s Asian Action movies. With trailers from *Fists of Fury, Chinese Connection, Enter the Dragon, Return of the Dragon, 5 Fingers of Death, The Streetfighter* and many more. 120 mins.
VHS: S33260. $24.95.

The Middle Man
A Chinese-American Marine is framed for espionage by a Korean gang, and finds himself hunted by the CIA as well as the gang. Luckily for him, his cousin is acrobatic policewoman Cynthia Kahn, who is reluctantly drawn in to rescue her headstrong relative. Chinese with English subtitles. Hong Kong, 1990.
VHS: S25944. $49.95.

Midnight Angels
Three of Asia's top female action stars lead the way in this thrilling film. Cynthia Luster, Moon Lee and Elaine Lui have the strength and agility for outrageously choreographed fight sequences and shoot-outs. Dubbed in English.
VHS: S27843. $19.95.

Midnight Angels II
While vacationing in Malaysia, a trio of policewomen must use their kung-fu skills to stop a madman who is plotting a revolution. With Moon Lee and Elaine Lui.
VHS: S34994. $59.95.

The Miracle Fighters
Consistently inventive blend of kung-fu and sorcery, often for humorous effect, as a young martial artist finds refuge with a pair of bickering old sorcerers, who take him on as a joint apprentice, teaching him what he needs to overcome an evil magician in pursuit of him. Mandarin with English subtitles (occasionally cropped).
VHS: S24179. $49.95.
Yuen Wo Ping, Hong Kong, 1981

Mission Kill
After a private detective (Moon Lee) helped Interpol crack the biggest cocaine deal in Southeast Asia, the Columbian druglords paid a notorious assassin gang to wipe her out. The FBI counteracted by sending their best agent, Stephen (Simon Yam), to protect her. Little does she know that Stephen is actually on a secret mission to eliminate the Interpol Chief, who is the mastermind behind it all. A sizzling action-thriller filled with mind-blowing martial arts, gunfire action and the cool charms of Simon Yam. Dubbed in English.
VHS: S24180. $14.98.
Lee Chiu, Hong Kong, 1991, 88 mins.

Mission to Kill
A shipment of valuable jewelry has been robbed by an international gang of smugglers. But a member of the group double-crossed them and had the goods deliberately stolen again for himself. The smugglers vow to kill their betraying member and get their jewelry back, while they themselves are being hunted by the police. With Kent Cheng. Dubbed in English.
VHS: S33341. $14.95.
Newton Wang, Hong Kong, 1984, 92 mins.

Mongkok Story
A high school dropout's climb toward power and wealth in the dangerous triad underworld is told in this urban crime thriller set in Hong Kong's crime-ridden Mongkok district. With Edmund Leun, Anthony Wong and Roy Cheung. Cantonese with English subtitles. Letterboxed, two-tape set.
VHS: S31955. $89.98.
Yip Wai Shun, Hong Kong, 1996, 94 mins.

The Moon Warriors
Fun period adventure, featuring some nice settings, as a deposed prince (Kenny Bee), fighting his evil brother for the throne, is rescued by a peasant swordsman (Andy Lau). When the prince sends his new friend to escort his betrothed princess (Anita Mui) back to him, the two fall in love. Meanwhile, there's a spy in the prince's camp. Ably directed by martial arts star Sammo Hung; also featuring Maggie Cheung. Don't miss the sequences involving Andy Lau's best friend, a killer whale. Chinese with English subtitles.
VHS: S25945. $49.95.
Sammo Hung, Hong Kong, 1993

My Father Is a Hero
Jet Li Lienjie plays another of his great Confucian heroes—a secret agent for the mainland Chinese working with Hong Kong to bring down an evil crime boss (Yu Rong-Guang), in this story by Sandy Shaw Li-Qiong. He's abetted by his equally stoic son, Hsieh Miao (from *New Legend of Shaolin*), while the bad guy's goons are Ken Lo Wei-Kwong and Ngai Sing. Anita Mui Ying-Fong plays Inspector "Madam" Wong, Jet's fascinating Hong Kong connection. Two-tape set. Letterboxed. Cantonese/Mandarin with English subtitles.
VHS: S30514. $89.95.
Laser: Letterboxed. **LD76120. $89.95.**
Corey Yuen Kwai, Hong Kong, 1995

Ninja Assassins
Top agents from the KGB and the CIA battle over a momentous new scientific discovery. The outcome of this battle could mean either the end to hunger and war or the triumph of chaos and destruction. CIA agent Tommy leads the good fight, but before he can confront the KGB Ninja organization he needs to learn the secrets of the "Super Ninjitsu Power." Dubbed in English.
VHS: S27872. $19.98.
Tim Ashby, Hong Kong, 1988, 85 mins.

Ninja Empire
Roger Kimsky is dedicated to world domination through his Black Ninja Empire. He will do anything necessary to reach his goal. Drug trafficking gives him nearly limitless resources. Undercover agents sent to infiltrate this group are murdered. Only the Silver Dragon Ninja can fight back and win against this primal evil force. Dubbed in English.
VHS: S27866. $19.98.
Don Kong, Hong Kong, 86 mins.

Ninja Heat
A big city crime lord uses a gang of thugs to spread death and destruction. Two Ninja-trained comrades offer the only opposition to these outlaws. The result is a battle of momentous proportions that spreads action throughout the film. Dubbed in English.
VHS: S27870. $19.98.
Lo Chau Wu, Hong Kong, 1988, 85 mins.

Ninja Hunter
Chuck Norris stars in this martial arts-driven adventure. Evil Ninjas bring death and destruction wherever they go, but Norris is there to throw a wrench in their plans. Together Norris and this violent gang deliver a movie packed with violence and unmatched martial arts sequences.
VHS: S27881. $19.98.

No More Love, No More Death
This prequel to *With or Without You* stars Jacky Cheung as a hitman out for revenge. With Rosamund Kwan and Carina Lau. Cantonese with English subtitles.
VHS: S33209. $49.95.
Hong Kong, 1993

Once Upon a Time in China III
Set in China during the last half of the troubled 1800s, this film centers on the evil Empress Dowager and her eunuch, Li Hung Cheung. The two decide to hold a competition of Lion Dance, a form of martial arts. This leads to much chaos and fighting as the different Lion Dance schools prepare for the competition. Meanwhile, Wong Fei-Hong (Jet Li), China's leading Lion Dancer, is busy defending his father's Lion Dance school against a band of gangsters when his girlfriend (Rosamund Kwan) discovers a Russian plot to assassinate the Lion Dancers. Lots of action, including Club-Foot's gravity-defying feats and a fight against the villains on an oil-covered floor. Cantonese with English subtitles.
VHS: S27285. $49.95.
Laser: Letterboxed. **LD76126. $89.95.**
Tsui Hark, Hong Kong, 1993, 102 mins.

Once Upon a Time in China V
The continuing saga of Wong Fei Hung leads the young Wong through treacherous and maze-like waterways to finally defeat an evil pirate. Set during the tumultuous period of the Qing Dynasty. Stars Chiu Man Chuk as Wong Fei Hung and Rosamund Kwan as Auntie Yee. Cantonese and Mandarin with English subtitles.
Part A.
VHS: S30762. $49.95.
Part B.
VHS: S30763. $49.95.
Tsui Hark, Hong Kong, 1994, 101 mins.

Once Upon a Time in Triad Society II
Triad gangsters prepare for the fight of their lives in this action crime drama. When two rival gangs battle over a piece of turf, a gang fight turns into a dangerous riot that even the cops can't control. With Ng Chun Yu, Roy Cheung and Ada Choi. Cantonese with English subtitles. Letterboxed, two-tape set.
VHS: S31972. $89.98.
Cha Tsuen Yee, Hong Kong, 1996, 90 mins.

The One-Armed Swordsman
Great martial arts action in this story of a young man who loses his arm in a battle but doesn't let this handicap stand in the way of his quest in becoming a great swordsman. With Wang Yu and Chiao Chiao. Cantonese with English subtitles.
VHS: S30754. $49.95.
Chang Chueh, Hong Kong, 1985

Organized Crime & Triad Bureau
Danny Lee stars as a cop who has kidnapped Tung and his girlfriend (played by Cecilia Yip and Anthony Wong), two ringleaders of organized crime. As Lee sets out on his mission to make them pay for their crimes, Yip and Wong are searching for a way out. Chinese with English subtitles.
VHS: S27388. $79.95.
Laser: LD75502. $39.95.
Kirk Wong, Hong Kong, 1993, 91 mins.

The Outlaw Brothers
Yukari Oshima stars opposite writer/director Frankie Chan Fan-Kei, as a martial artist policewoman involved with a suave car thief. Yukari must also confront her nemesis, crime queen Michiko Nishiwaki. Max Mok Siu-Cheung is Frankie's cocky partner. Cantonese/Mandarin with English subtitles.
VHS: S30327. $49.95.
Frankie Chan Fan-Kei, Hong Kong, 1988

Panty Hose Hero
Sammo Hung and Alan Tam are two cops who go undercover as homosexuals to catch a serial killer who murders gay men. This scenario makes the most of lampooning fey ways among the gay men they are trying to save. In addition, there is a violent subplot concerning a drug gang. Mandarin with English subtitles.
VHS: S27281. $49.95.
Sammo Hung, Hong Kong, 1990, 99 mins.

Peacock Prince
An archaeological dig disturbs a menacing evil spirit. Only the young Peacock Prince can battle the evil monster Hell King. He sets off for Tokyo and uses a variety of skills including ESP, martial arts and the mastery of Zen to fight back. Also known as *Peacock King* or *Legend of the Phoenix*. Mandarin with English subtitles.
VHS: S27266. $49.95.
Yuen Biao/Nam Lai Choi, Hong Kong, 1987, 86 mins.

Pedicab Driver
Set in Macao and shot in a ravishing, early 20th century period atmosphere, Sammo Hung's latest Kung fu effort belongs to the class of ingenious boy-girl romance pictures which Hung has been involved in lately as an actor, such as *Painted Faces* and *Eight Taels of Gold*. In those films, Hung forgoes kung fu for character portrayal. Here, he returns to familiar ground, handling action and lightweight comedy romance with ease. Cantonese with English subtitles.
VHS: S14881. $49.95.
Sammo Hung, Hong Kong, 1989, 98 mins.

Peking Opera Blues
Three of the Hong Kong cinema's most popular actresses—Sally Yeh, Cherie Chung, and Lin Ching-Hsai—star in this fast-paced comedy/drama set in turn-of-the-century China. In addition to its stunning art-direction, this film features an assortment of plots and counterplots, assassins, singers, soldiers, and amazing action sequences. Cantonese with English subtitles.
VHS: S13462. $49.95.
Tsui Hark, Hong Kong, 1986, 104 mins.

People's Hero
Ti Lung and Tony Leung star in this thrilling crime drama which borrows liberally from *Dog Day Afternoon*. When two young street punks botch a bank robbery, master criminal Sunny Koo steps in and escalates the theft into a tension-filled hostage situation. Cantonese with English subtitles.
VHS: S13468. $49.95.
Yee Tung-shing, Hong Kong, 1987, 82 mins.

Phantom War
Having relocated to Great Britain's Chinatown after years of fighting his way through Vietcong prison camps, Ken and his wife struggle to make ends meet. But Ken's violent flashbacks make him a prime target for the police, the Mafia druglords and his old wartime nemesis. Now Ken must fight tooth and nail for his life. With Alex Man Chi-Leung, Ben Ng Ngai-Cheung and Yammie Nam Kit-Ying. Dubbed in English.
VHS: S24187. $14.95.
Chow Fung, Hong Kong, 1990, 80 mins.

Pickles Make Me Cry

A low-budget comedy-thriller made in New York by Peter Chow, the Executive Director of Asian Cine-Vision. The title comes from the favorite post love-making snack of William and Jeannie, a young Chinese couple. William and Jeannie also find themselves in something of a pickle when William is shot by a mean Chinatown gang which is trying to extort money from the couple's friends. Cantonese with English subtitles.

VHS: S13479. $49.95.

Peter Chow, USA/Hong Kong, 1988, 85 mins.

Point of No Return

The son and adopted son of an aging hitman, carrying on in their father's footsteps, begin to consider the futility of their way of life once one of them falls in love with the daughter of a policeman, who happens to be their next assignment. With Jackie Cheung and Joey Wang. Mandarin with English subtitles.

VHS: S24188. $49.95.

Guy Y.C. Lai, Hong Kong, 1990

Power Connection

Ray and Jimmy are undercover cops assigned to stop a band of mobsters who are smuggling drugs, counterfeit money and illegal weapons. When their undercover identities are exposed, a powerful Triad syndicate goes all out to eliminate them. Dubbed in English.

VHS: S33875. $14.95.

Phillip Ko, Hong Kong, 1995, 88 mins.

Prince of Portland Street

Dicky Cheung Wai-Kin is "Biggie," a small-time hoodlum in Tsim-Shat-Tsui. He and his best friend, Pao (Simon Yam Tak-Wah), struggle to establish themselves in the brutal world of the Triads, bringing them up against Boss Chi (Tommy Wong Kwong-Leung). You'll also learn why Dicky has that nickname! Letterboxed. Cantonese/Mandarin with English subtitles.

VHS: S30338. $49.95.

David Lam, Hong Kong, 1993

Prison on Fire

A violent prison drama with superstar Chow Yun Fat portraying a cynical gambler serving time for the accidental killing of his adulterous wife. He befriends an innocent and unworldly white collar worker (Leung Ka Fai) who has been framed, and acts as his protector while he adjusts to prison life. Cantonese with English subtitles.

VHS: S13476. $49.95.

Ringo Lam, Hong Kong, 1987, 98 mins.

The Private Eye Blues

Jacky Cheung Hok-Yau does a star turn as a hard-drinking PI investigating a plot full of red herrings, including a psychic girl from the mainland (Cathy Chow) and one of Hong Kong's best plug-uglies, Jean Pol/Lee Kin-Sang. Deftly directed and scripted by Ling Ching-Fong. Letterboxed. Cantonese/Mandarin with English subtitles.

VHS: S30334. $49.95.

Ling Ching-Fong, Hong Kong, 1994

The Prodigal Son

Sammo Hung's martial arts classic is considered by many to be the most authentic kung-fu film ever made. Yuen Biao is a spoiled martial artist-wannabe son whose wealthy father pays others to lose to Yuen during fights. When his father's scheme is revealed to him by a seasoned Peking Opera performer/Wing Chun master (Lam Ching Ying), Yuen vows to learn kung-fu for real. But first he has to pursuade Lam to take him on as a pupil; then there's Lam's rival colleague (Sammo Hung) and a mysterious, fight-seeking challenger to contend with. Cantonese with English subtitles. Widescreen.

VHS: S34237. $59.95.
Laser: LD76943. $39.95.

Sammo Hung, Hong Kong, 1982, 100 mins.

Raped by an Angel (aka Naked Killer 2)

The sequel continues with Mark Cheung as the suave but deadly serial rapist/murderer. The intricate plot shows him worming his way into the lives of Chingmy Yau and Carrie Ng. With Simon Yam (*Full Contact*).

VHS: S30759. $49.95.
Laser: Letterboxed. **LD76111. $69.95.**

Ricky Lau, Hong Kong, 1993, 95 mins.

Red Zone

After years as a stuntman (*Armour of God 2, My Father Is a Hero*), Ken Lo Wai-Kwong broke through to stardom with this film. When a prominent British judge is blown up at the courthouse by a car bomb, Officer Kwong poses as a gangster to get close to Ivy Lau (Valerie Chow Kar-Ling), moll of the underworld kingpin who ordered the hit (Waise Lee Chi-Hung). Fellow officers Kenny Ho Kar-Ling and Yu Rong-Guang provide backup in this taut thriller with an explosive conclusion. Letterboxed. Cantonese/Mandarin with English subtitles.

VHS: S30329. $49.95.

Edward Tang King-Sang, Hong Kong, 1996

Revenge of the Tai-Chi Master

During the Ching dynasty a Tai Chi Master discovers that he and his family will suffer annihilation. In response he sends his son away to be raised by a good friend. Twenty years later, the son is grown and sets out for revenge. The only problem is his father's enemy is still powerful and ruthless. Dubbed in English, 90 mins.

VHS: S22609. $39.95.

Righting Wrongs (aka Above the Law)

Yuen Biao is a lawyer, American martial artist Cynthia Rothrock is a cop. Driven to extremes by an ineffectual justice system, they take matters into their own hands using their kung-fu skills. Tough, gritty martial arts action. Cantonese with English subtitles.

VHS: S30300. $59.95.

Corey Yuen Kwai, Hong Kong, 1986

Road Warriors

An earnest tribute to Hong Kong's unsung heroes, motorcycle traffic cops. In this story, they're trying to stop reckless road racing, especially after the irresponsible son of a publisher runs a school bus off the road, resulting in many casualties. Danny Lee plays the head cop. Mandarin with English subtitles (occasionally cropped).

VHS: S24189. $49.95.

Danny Lee, Hong Kong, 1987

Robo Vampire

Narcotics agent Tom Wilde is shot and killed, but a futuristic experiment gives him a second life as an android robot. In his new role he is sent to the Golden Triangle, where he must rescue the beautiful agent Sophie. Only the drug warlord Mr. Young and his monstrous creation, the Vampire Beast, stand in his way. Dubbed in English.

VHS: S27874. $19.98.

Joe Livingston, Hong Kong, 1993, 90 mins.

Royal Tramp

Visually sumptuous parody of Hong Kong's recent swordplay epics, with smart aleck Stephen Chow as the improbably named Wilson Bond, a fast-thinking lowlife who gets caught up in one tangled court intrigue after another, pledging his loyalty to whoever is threatening him at the moment and playing all sides off against each other while trying to figure a way out of the incredible mess he's in. Great fun. Letterboxed. Mandarin with English subtitles (occasionally washed out but otherwise good). 1991.

VHS: S24190. $49.95.
Laser: Letterboxed. **LD76121. $89.95.**

Royal Tramp II

A continuation of the adventures of Wilson Bond, now a big shot friend of the emperor, still being buffeted by the various factions seeking to overthrow the emperor, and still continuing to aggravate his rivals and bluff or squirm his way out of tight situations. Here he's assigned to escort the emperor's sister, about to be married off to form a political alliance with a treacherous prince, in a worthy sequel to the 1991 hit. Mandarin with English subtitles. 1992.

VHS: S24191. $49.95.

Royal Warriors

After three cops (two from Hong Kong and one from Japan) break up an attempt to rescue a prisoner, the rest of the gang vows revenge. This violent action movie is distinguished by its bruising fights and by the presence of martial arts star Michelle Yeoh (Khan), playing one of the three cops. Also known as *In the Line of Duty II*. Chinese with English subtitles. Hong Kong, 1986.

VHS: S25947. $59.95.
Laser: LD76425. $39.95.
DVD: Filmographies. **$29.95.**

Run and Kill

While drunk, Kent Cheng Jut-Si unwittingly hires a hitman to kill his philandering wife. Sobering up, he finds his wife dead and demented Vietnam war veteran Simon Yam Tak-Wah after him to pay the steep price. When Kent goes to the cops, Simon proceeds to bump off his mom and kid by the most gruesome and graphic means possible. Danny Lee Sau-Yin co-stars in one of his patented turns as Officer "Sir" Lee. Letterboxed. Cantonese/Mandarin with English subtitles.

VHS: S30318. $49.95.

Billy Tang Hin-Sing, Hong Kong, 1993

Seaman No. 7

Jimmy Wang plays the title character, a merchant seaman who accidentally kills a man and flees to Japan, ending up in Kobe, where he is taken in by expatriate Chinese, learns Judo, and has to fight off a bunch of drug-running thugs. Low budget, but it's nice to see a different sort of character in a kung-fu flick as Jimmy Wang's earnest seaman tries to figure out how to get by in a foreign country. Mandarin with English subtitles (occasionally cropped and low).

VHS: S24194. $49.95.

Lo Wei, Hong Kong, 1972

Seeding of a Ghost

In this brutal and explicit tale, a magician helps a man (Philip Ko Chi-Sum) wreak vengeance on everyone even remotely connected with his wife's (Chuan Chi-Hui) rape-murder, resulting in relentless and horrific carnage. Also starring Chu Shao-Chiang. Cantonese/Mandarin with English subtitles.

VHS: S30322. $49.95.

Yan Chuan, Hong Kong, 1986

Semi-Gods and Semi-Devils

Brigitte Lin (as identical twins), Gong Li and Cheung Man alternate as friends and rivals in this funny, flying people/magic/martial arts movie. Based on a Jin Yong story. Cantonese with English subtitles.

VHS: S33213. $49.95.

Andy Chin Wing-Keung, Hong Kong, 1994, 96 mins.

Seven Ninja Kids

Pintsized they may be, but these Ninja Kids go up against the worst odds—and win. It helps that they are on the right side of the law and that their enemies are a buffoonish collection of outlaws. This is an action/adventure film with heart, humor, and seven capable martial arts heroes. Dubbed in English.

VHS: S27868. $19.98.

Seven Warriors

Villagers hire seven soldiers to help get rid of the bandits who have been raiding them, in this entertaining film that owes more to *The Magnificent Seven* than to *The Seven Samurai*, as characters and even entire scenes are transported from the Old West to 1920's China. With Tony Leung as the leader of the soldiers and Jackie Cheung as one of the band. Mandarin with English subtitles.

VHS: S24195. $49.95.

Terry Tong, Hong Kong, 1989

Shadow Ninja

Roy Chiao Hung and Steve Tung Wai star in this martial arts film about an honest cop. This cop stalks a mysterious masked killer, but the path he must follow is strewn with torture and death. He may be gambling his life away in his valorous quest for justice. Dubbed in English. 114 mins.

VHS: S27863. $19.98.

Shanghai Express

An all-star cross between the '60s blockbusters *How the West Was Won* and *It's a Mad, Mad, Mad, Mad World*. Set "way out west" in China, the cast incongruously wear historically accurate American western garb and travel on steam locomotives between dusty clapboard towns straight out of a Sergio Leone movie. Stars Sammo, Yuen Biao, Eric Tsang Chi-Wai, Lam Shing-Ying, Yuen Wah, Richard Ng, Kenny Bee, Rosamund Kwan Chi-Lum, Cynthia Rothrock, Richard Norton and Yukari Oshima. Cantonese/Mandarin with English subtitles.

VHS: S30295. $59.95.

Sammo Hung, Hong Kong, 1986

Shanghai Grand

Two friends destined to rule Shanghai's underworld become enemies when the daughter of a legendary tycoon comes into the picture. A romantic saga immersed in the wheeling and dealing lifestyle of Shanghai in the 1930s. With Leslie Cheung and Andy Lau. Cantonese with English subtitles. Letterboxed, two-tape set.

VHS: S31973. $89.98.

Poon Man Kit, Hong Kong, 1996, 107 mins.

Shaolin Avengers

This classical tale of Shaolin Temple disciples vs. the Manchurian Ching government displays Shaolin martial arts at its best in empty-hand combat. After the siege of the Shaolin Monastery by the Ching government in the 18th century, students of Shaolin, led by Hung See-Kwan, continue to rebel against the Manchus. Dubbed in English.

VHS: S31653. $14.95.

Lee Chiu, Hong Kong, 1992, 98 mins.

Shaolin Collection

From the makers of the *Wu Tang Collection* and the *Kill or Be Killed Collection*.

5 Fighters from Shaolin.

VHS: S34991. $19.95.

Shaolin Temple Strikes Back. A young Ming prince prepares for battle with Manchu invaders by perfecting the drunken lance, 18 bird forms, kicks and lama kung fu techniques. Starring Mark Long, Chang Shan and Chen Chiang Chang. Dubbed. Directed by Joseph Kuo, Hong Kong, 1983, 90 mins.

VHS: S34988. $19.95.

South Shaolin vs. North Shaolin. After completing his training at North Shaolin, a Shaolin monk journeys to the south. On his way, he encounters deadly Ninjas in the employ of the Manchu invaders. Threatened by the proximity of the enemy, he rushes to warn the South Shaolin abbots of the coming Manchu onslaught. Starring Cassanova Wong and Han Ying. Subtitled. Hong Kong, 90 mins.

VHS: S34992. $19.95.

The Buddhist Fist. Two orphans are trained by a Shaolin master in the lethal art of the Buddhist Fist. Separated by fate, they are reunited after a series of disasters and deadly combat. Starring Tsui Sui Ming and Yuen Hsin Yee. Dubbed. Directed by Yuen Woo-Ping, Hong Kong, 1980, 90 mins.
VHS: S34990. $19.95.

The Warrior from Shaolin. Entrusted with intelligence that could win the "Sino Japanese" War for China, a Shaolin monk must fight his way through the enemy in order to deliver the information to its proper destination. Starring Gordon Liu and Lau Kar Wing. Dubbed. Hong Kong, 90 mins.
VHS: S34989. $19.95.

Complete Set. Includes *Shaolin Temple Strikes Back, The Warrior from Shaolin, The Buddhist Fist, South Shaolin vs. North Shaolin* and *5 Fighters from Shaolin*.
VHS: S34993. $99.95.

Shaolin Kung-Fu Kids
A mischievous yet naive monk of the Shaolin Temple gets his first taste of life outside the temple in this light-hearted, modern-day kung-fu comedy. With Roger Kwok, Chu Yan and Lin Ming Yeung. Cantonese with English subtitles.
VHS: S31987. $49.95.
Peter Yuen, Hong Kong, 1995, 92 mins.

Shogun and Little Kitchen
A Capra-esque tale in which Biao starts a popular restaurant in the courtyard of his relative Ng Mang-Dat's tenement building—it features cuisine complete with kung-fu demonstrations by the chef. A subplot involves a revolt by the tenants (including Leon Lai Ming) against heartless developers threatening to level their tenement home. Letterboxed. Cantonese/Mandarin with English subtitles.
VHS: S30298. $49.95.
Donny Yu Jen-Tai, Hong Kong, 1992

The Six Devil Women
Six devilish women journey from the countryside to the big city looking to get rich quick. Their scheme is to pose as sexy hitchhikers and take unsuspecting men for everything they've got. With Pang Dan, Li Suet Man and Leung Yuen Man. Cantonese with English subtitles. Letterboxed.
VHS: S32006. $49.95.
Ma Tin Yiu, Hong Kong, 1996, 89 mins.

Skinny Tiger and Fatty Dragon
This entertaining buddy/cop film is the story of two pals busting up a gang of criminals and cheerfully breaking just about all the rules governing police conduct. A series of well-staged fights and chases are lightened by humor, making this a highly enjoyable film. One of the highlights is a chase sequence where the heroes destroy a villain's Mercedes, bit by bit, for the sole purpose of antagonizing the fiend. Sammo Hung does a continuous Bruce Lee impression throughout the film, despite or because of the fact that there is absolutely no physical resemblance between the wiry Lee and the portly and often mischievous Hung. Cantonese with English subtitles.
VHS: S27288. $49.95.
Lau Kar Wing, Hong Kong, 1990

Slave of the Sword
In this sexy adventure film the innocent daughter of a masterful artist becomes entwined with murderous prostitutes. When the master retires he makes plans that should save her and his three students, but the pull of intrigue and human nature is too great. Before long the greatest assassination plot imaginable will make use of all their charms. Dubbed in English.
VHS: S21829. $49.95.
Chu Yen Ping, Hong Kong, 1994

Slickers vs. Killers
Sammo directs himself in this excellent action/comedy about a beleaguered salesman who is witness to a gangland hit and becomes the next target. He also has to deal with a competitive co-worker (Dodo Cheng Yiu-Yeung), a neurotic psychiatrist and his beautiful policewoman wife. Lam Shing-Ying and Jacky Cheung Hok-Yau are hilarious as the bumbling assassins. With Ngai Sing. Cantonese/Mandarin with English subtitles.
VHS: S30294. $49.95.
Sammo Hung, Hong Kong, 1989

Spider Force
Hong Kong police officers Stuart and Sharon are hot on the trail of drug smugglers from China. When they find out that Sharon's uncle is the head of the drug syndicate, they follow him to a remote island, which turns out to be his headquarters. With Carter Wong, Pauline Chan and Michelle Ko. Dubbed.
VHS: S34647. $14.95.
Kong Yang, Hong Kong, 1992, 90 mins.

Spider Woman
Jade Leung Ching plays twins: the good Kenny Leung and the evil Leung Ken. Enter Officer Edwin Wong (Michael Wong Mun-Tak) to investigate a series of murders that appears to involve at least one of them. He is also on the verge of a divorce from Valerie Chow Kar-Ling. Dayo Wong Chi-Wah co-stars as a macabre coroner always playing practical jokes on his poor assistant Emily Kwan. Letterboxed. Cantonese/Mandarin with English subtitles.
VHS: S30342. $49.95.
Lo Kin, Hong Kong, 1995

Spring Comes Again
An overly zealous man gets more than his feet wet when he packs up with both wife and mistess in this "fatal attraction" adult drama. With Lee To Hung and Lam Kin Ming. Cantonese with English subtitles.
VHS: S31996. $49.95.
Kwan Ching Leung, Hong Kong, 1983, 90 mins.

Street Angels
The owner of a high-class karaoke club is at the top of his game until he falls for one of his club girls. Things start to unravel when he discovers that the girl is actually a spy for a rival club. With Simon Yam Tat Wah (*Full Contact*), Chingmy Yau (*Naked Killer*) and Po Tai Yu. Cantonese with English subtitles. Letterboxed, two-tape set.
VHS: S31969. $89.98.
Billy Tang, Hong Kong, 1996, 91 mins.

Street Gangs of Hong Kong
Ha Chung is a driven young man from a broken home. His passion and his skills as a martial arts expert set him apart as a prospective member of a deadly gang. When this gang commits a crime against Ha Chung's father however, he rebels, and a bloody conflict ensues. Dubbed in English. 104 mins.
VHS: S27879. $19.98.

Street of Fury
Two brothers—one calm and collected, the other strong and impetuous—make waves with the triad society when they hit the ghetto streeets of Hong Kong. Non-stop action. With Louis Koo, Gigi Lai and Teresa Mak. Cantonese with English subtitles. Letterboxed, two-tape set.
VHS: S31954. $89.98.
Billy Tang, Hong Kong, 1996, 90 mins.

The Sword Stained with Royal Blood
Danny Lee Yau-Sin stars as the "Golden Snake Man" caught in a web of multiple vengeance plots involving Yuen Biao, Cheung Man, Ng Mang-Dat and Tsui Kam-Kong. Danny acquits himself nicely as the owner of a huge, magical blade embellished with golden snakes. Letterboxed. Cantonese/Mandarin with English subtitles.
VHS: S30306. $49.95.
Brandy Yuen Chun-Yeung, Hong Kong, 1993

Swordsman
While King Hu is listed as the nominal director of this lavish period epic, the hand of producer Tsui Hark is the dominant influence here. Rousing first entry in the epic *Swordsman* series, carefully detailed, lyrical, and full of fantastic action. Swordsman Ling (Jackie Cheung) and his sidekick "Kiddo" encounter treacherous officials, rebels, and secret sects as the different groups vie to gain possession of a secret scroll stolen from the imperial library. Letterboxed. Mandarin with English subtitles.
VHS: S24197. $49.95.
Laser: LD76117. $69.95.
King Hu, Hong Kong, 1990

Swordsman II
Martial arts star Jet Li takes over the title role in a sequel that's as good as the original, as swordsman Ling continues his adventures in a chaotic world of shifting loyalties and betrayals, the deceiving nature of appearances being exemplified by the evil General Fong, in the midst of transforming himself into a beautiful woman (Briget Lin). With Rosamund Kwan. Mandarin with English subtitles.
VHS: S24198. $49.95.
Ching Siu Tung, Hong Kong, 1991

Swordsman III (aka The East Is Red)
Director Ching Siu-Tung actually surpasses King Hu's sprawling, extravagant original with his second *Swordsman*, an epic tale of flying swordfighters and gender-bending wizardry set in the last days of the Ming Dynasty. Jet Li Lienjie, the original heroic drunken swordsman, faces Brigette Lin Ching-Hsia as "The Invincible Asia," a tyrant who has made the ultimate sacrifice in his grab for power. For the third installment, Lee drops out but Lin returns as the trans-gendered, vengeful Asia, with Joey Wang Tsu-Hsien as her yearningly lesbian lieutenant. Two-tape box set. Letterboxed. Cantonese/Mandarin with English subtitles.
VHS: S30511. $89.95.
Laser: Letterboxed. **LD76127. $89.95.**
Raymond Lee/Cheng Xiaodong, Hong Kong, 1993

Sworn Brother
Brutal but well made drama about two brothers operating on different sides of the law but still maintaining a loyalty to each other, the extent of which is tested when the entire family is drawn into danger once the criminal brother is betrayed by his boss. Chinese with English subtitles.
VHS: S25948. $49.95.
Sammo Hung, Hong Kong, 1986

Tai Chi II
In this kung fu adventure actioner from the director of *Fist of Legend*, martial artists Jacky Wu, Billy Chow and Christy Chung star in a patriotic tale about a young Tai Chi master battling corrupt officials, jealous suitors and evil opium smugglers. Filled with unbelievable fight scenes, *Tai Chi II* is martial arts at its best. Letterboxed. English dubbed or Cantonese/Mandarin with English subtitles.
VHS: S30617. $19.95.
Laser: LD76076. $39.95.
Yuen Wo Ping, Hong Kong, 1996, 95 mins.

The Tai Chi Master
Two monks, friends since childhood, are expelled from the Shaolin monastery for misbehavior. Making their way to the nearest town, one becomes a soldier and the other joins a band of rebels fighting against an oppressive general. The rebel is betrayed by his army friend and can only regain both his sanity and his fighting prowess by rediscovering the Tai-Chi principles of his religious past. Michelle Yeoh is featured in this engaging historical epic. Includes Parts A and B. Mandarin with English subtitles.
VHS: S27283. $49.95.
Laser: Letterboxed. **LD76128. $89.95.**
Yuen Woo Ping, Hong Kong, 1993, 92 mins.

Thunder Cop
Marked for death, a fugitive of the underworld enlists the help of a cop friend. Criminal and cop team up for more than a few compromising situations in this gun-blasting actioner. With Winston Chiao and Nicky Wu. Cantonese with English subtitles. Letterboxed.
VHS: S31998. $49.95.
Clarence Fok, Hong Kong, 1996, 91 mins.

Thunder Ninja Kids: In the Golden Adventure
A mystical golden statue is at the center of this action-laden martial arts adventure. Two gangs of thugs are fighting for possession of this mysterious idol, but the Ninja kids are back to make sure they don't succeed. Even the Mafia can't top these youngsters. Dubbed in English.
VHS: S27873. $19.98.
Charles Lee, Hong Kong, 1992, 90 mins.

Thunder Ninja Kids: Little Kickboxer
Sean Lee is a timid boy continually taunted by his bigger schoolmates. Even so, his mother refuses to let him study Tae Kwondo because his father was killed in a Tae Kwondo match. When she finally relents, Sean makes terrific progress and before long he must face the very man responsible for his father's death. Dubbed in English.
VHS: S27875. $19.98.

Thunder Ninja Kids: The Hunt for the Devil Boxer
All Satan needs to enslave the souls of all mankind is the Sacred Sword. Master William and his son Falcom protect the vital weapon, but Satan has horrible ghouls on his side. Fortunately, a new master, called Samson, takes charge to combat Satan and save the world. Dubbed in English.
VHS: S27871. $19.98.
Alton Cheung, Hong Kong, 1992, 90 mins.

Thunder Ninja Kids: Wonderful Mission
A key spiritual symbol, the revered Buddha of the Capa Ninja Clan, resurfaces after disappearing years ago. The Clan must fight off the Black Ninja Group and another gang led by the notorious Keith in order to recapture their sacred statue. The struggle's outcome depends upon the Thunder Ninja Kids and their supreme martial arts abilities. Dubbed in English.
VHS: S27876. $19.98.
Charles Lee, Hong Kong, 1992, 90 mins.

Thunder Run
Ho and Cheung are partners on the Hong Kong police force taking a vacation in Southeast Asia. However, they soon run into hot water when Ho is mistaken as a drug smuggler in Laos and thrown in jail. Cheung also gets caught in an attempt to rescue Ho and they must execute a risky jailbreak and make a run for their lives, using their cunning instincts and the skills they learned from the force. Dubbed in English.
VHS: S33877. $14.95.
Tsui Pak Lam, Hong Kong, 1991, 91 mins.

Tiger Cage 2
Donnie Yen Chi-Tan, a hair-trigger cop, goes on the lam with Rosamund Kwan Chi-Lum, a prim lawyer, after they witness a botched robbery attempt. The police think they're the perpetrators, while the real crooks (including *Mortal Kombat* star Robin Shou) think they actually got the loot. Cameos by Dodo Cheng Yiu-Yeung and Cynthia Khan/Yeung Lai-Ching. Cantonese/Mandarin with English subtitles.
VHS: S30340. $49.95.
Yuen Woo-Ping, Hong Kong, 1990

Tiger on the Beat II
Danny Lee takes over the Chow Yun Fat role in this sequel, in which his appropriately named nephew Buffalo arrives in Hong Kong to find a wife, but instead falls for a pretty thief who is being chased by a criminal gang which is after a ring she has stolen from them, leading up to a bruising finale in a bus station. Mandarin with English subtitles.
VHS: S24201. $49.95.
Chia Liang Liu, Hong Kong, 1990

The Tigers
Tony Leung and Andy Lau are part of a quintet of cop buddies in what starts out as a routine action film, but which takes an interesting turn when they keep some money they recover in a drug bust and suddenly find themselves both blackmailed by the gangsters and investigated by the internal affairs unit. The situation becomes increasingly grim as pressure from both sides mounts and there seems to be no way out. Mandarin with English subtitles.
VHS: S24202. $49.95.
Eric Tsang, Hong Kong, 1991

To Be No. 1
A fascinating story about life within the triad societies of Hong Kong as seen through the eyes of a legendary overlord and an ambitious but cocky youngster who is recruited into the triad. With Simon Yam, Danny Lee and Cheung Chi Lam. Cantonese with English subtitles. Letterboxed, two-tape set.
VHS: S31962. $89.98.
Lee Wai Man, Hong Kong, 1996, 95 mins.

Top Fighter II: Deadly China Dolls
A look at the deadliest female martial arts stars of the past, present and future. Starring Michelle Yeoh, Moon Lee, Cynthia Rothrock, Angela Mao, Elaine Lui, Amy Yip and Yukari Oshima.
VHS: S34995. $59.95.

Touch and Go
Hard hitting action with the mild-mannered Sammo Hung witnessing a murder and then being pursued by the killers. Things are made worse by a headstrong cop and his reporter sister, who use Sammo as a tool for their own purposes, repeatedly putting him in danger. Some great action sequences with the always surprisingly deft Sammo, well directed by current favorite Ringo Lam. Mandarin with English subtitles.
VHS: S24203. $49.95.
Ringo Lam, Hong Kong, 1991

Tough Beauty and the Sloppy Slob
In this undercover story set in the Philippines, cocky Hong Kong cop Yuen Biao, starchy mainland cop Cynthia Khan/Yang Li-Ching and studly Philippine cop Monsour Del Rosario try to infiltrate a drug ring represented by Waise Lee Chi-Hung. Letterboxed. Cantonese/Mandarin with English subtitles.
VHS: S30296. $49.95.
Yuen Bun/Tsui Chung-Sun, Hong Kong, 1995

Treasure Hunt
Chow Yun Fat is an Americanized CIA agent sent to the Shaolin Temple in mainland China. There he experiences the conflicting pull of modern ways versus ancient Chinese traditions. The plot centers on a psychic link between the CIA agent and a girl held prisoner in the temple. In addition, there are smugglers and agents formulating all kinds of trouble. Filmed on location. Mandarin with English subtitles.
Part A.
VHS: S27300. $49.95.
Part B.
VHS: S28058. $49.95.
Lau Chun-Wai, Hong Kong, 1994

The Valiant Ones
A graceful action film shot almost completely on location, *The Valiant Ones* deals with the preservation of a domestic political force (the Ming Court) against the encroachments of an outside enemy (Japanese pirates) and provides an elemental study of the many facets of the martial arts (displayed by both patriots and pirates). The natural backdrops against which the duel scenes are staged question the relationship between the natural, exterior universe and the mortal (albeit extraordinary) force which is fighting to preserve it. Cantonese with English subtitles.
VHS: S14869. $49.95.
King Hu, Hong Kong

War of the Underworld
Gang warfare explodes when an overzealous member of the Hung Hing triad offends a rival gang leader's son. An action-packed underworld thriller with triad heroes fighting to save their turf from power-hungry gangsters. With Tony Leung Chiu Wai, Jordan Chan and Carmen Lee. Cantonese with English subtitles. Letterboxed, two-tape set.
VHS: S31956. $89.98.
Herman Yau, Hong Kong, 1996, 96 mins.

The Way of the Little Dragon
Though he began as a young street fighter in Hong Kong, Bruce Lee rose to become a master of Jeet Kune Do and an international star. This documentary shows the fascinating story behind the enduring idol. It includes over 30 minutes of rare, unseen footage, including images of a fighting teenage Bruce Lee.
VHS: S27867. $19.98.
J. Silberman, USA, 1966

What Price Survival?
In this modern swordplay remake of the Wang Yu classic *The One-Armed Swordsman*, a duel between two master swordsmen for the hand of a beautiful young maiden leads to a 20-year-old grudge that proves deadly. With Tsui Siu Keung and Lau Chun Yan Ng Hing Kwok. Cantonese and Mandarin with English subtitles.
VHS: S30757. $49.95.
Lee Yan Kwong, Hong Kong, 1994, 96 mins.

White Lotus Cult
Do Siu-Jun stars in this story of the waning of the Ching dynasty. The same fanatical cult featured in *Once Upon a Time in China 2* promises immortality to those who rise against the Europeans in China—resulting in the Boxer Rebellion. The extraordinary martial arts sequences are filmed throughout Beijing, including pavilions deep within the old Forbidden City. Cantonese/Mandarin with English subtitles.
VHS: S30302. $49.95.
Stephen Shin Gei-Yin/Chen Sin-Keng, Hong Kong, 1994

The Wild Couple
In this fast-paced gangster action thriller, a triad leader is stripped of $6 million by a pair of con artists. By the time the cops arrive, the triad boss is left for dead (or so it seems) and the outlaw twosome has narrowly escaped by taking a young girl hostage. With Roy Cheung and Lily Chung. Cantonese with English subtitles. Letterboxed.
VHS: S32009. $49.95.
Tsui Po Wah, Hong Kong, 1996, 97 mins.

Wild Search
Chow Yun Fat is Mew Mew, a cop investigating an arms smuggling ring. One of the smugglers is killed during a raid, leaving her two children orphaned. Mew Mew becomes infatuated with the orphaned older sister and follows the two children to their rural home. A strong visual sense and a highly kinetic style elevate this film above the standard level of police action films. Cantonese with English subtitles.
VHS: S27294. $49.95.
Ringo Lam, Hong Kong, 1989, 95 mins.

Wing Chun
Michelle Yeoh stars as cross-dressing kung fu innovator Yim Wing Chung, who battles the bandit lords and invents a new kungfu style. Don't miss the "tofu fight" and lesbian foot massage scenes. Chinese with English subtitles.
VHS: S27540. $19.95.
Laser: Letterboxed. **LD75500. $59.95.**
Yuen Wo Ping, Hong Kong, 1993

Winner Takes All
A young man sets out to avenge the death of his brother by a criminal gang. His flight from an unsuccessful encounter with the gang leads him into the arms of a young woman. She, in turn, becomes the innocent key to the destruction of the gang when they begin a deadly game in which the winner takes all. Starring Alan Tang, Olivia Cheng and Fung Shui Fan. Cantonese with English subtitles.
VHS: S14873. $49.95.
Stanley Siu, Hong Kong, 94 mins.

Wonder Seven
The Wonder Seven is a group of seven highly trained martial artists and undercover government agents stationed in Hong Kong. The seven have all become assimilated into Hong Kong culture when they receive orders that their government is in trouble. They are assigned to steal two computer disks pertaining to a Sino-Japanese deal, but when they complete their assignment, all sorts of mysterious things begin happening. Cantonese and Mandarin with English subtitles. 90 minutes each.
Part A.
VHS: S27384. $49.95.
Part B.
VHS: S27385. $49.95.
Ching Siu Tung, Hong Kong

Yellow Rain
An action thriller about one man's painful journey into the triad underworld. With Alex Man, Dick Wai and Lo Yui. Cantonese with English subtitles.
VHS: S31999. $49.95.
Lau Chung Pak, Hong Kong, 1990, 81 mins.

Yes Madam
Look out for the high-flying kicks and powerful punches of Lily (Cynthia Khan), the leader of a special operations team, who has been assigned to crack down on an international crime ring. Teamed up with her martial arts instructor boyfriend, the two go after two ruthless criminals. With Cynthia Rothrock and Cheung Ying Chun. Cantonese with English subtitles. Letterboxed.
VHS: S32000. $49.95.
Chan Chun Leung, Hong Kong, 1995, 90 mins.

Yes Madam 5
A computer disk that links a triad gang to a bevy of illegal activity is missing. The search for this highly detrimental item is the cause of a series of thundering battles between cops and gangsters throughout Malaysia and Singapore. Starring Cynthia Yang of the *In the Line of Duty* series. With Chin Siu Ho. Cantonese with English subtitles. Letterboxed.
VHS: S32008. $49.95.
Lau Shing-Hon, Hong Kong, 1996, 90 mins.

Young and Dangerous II, Parts A & B
A powerful struggle between two members of a triad gang causes them to ignore their oaths of loyalty and brotherhood. Keen to the tension, a rival gang stages a bloody attempt to take control. With Jordan Chan, Anthony Wong, Chingmy Yau and Ekin Chang. Cantonese with English subtitles. Letterboxed, two-tape set.
VHS: S31971. $89.98.
Lau Wai Keung, Hong Kong, 1996, 100 mins.

Young and Dangerous III
Part III of this critically acclaimed triad youth series examines the lives of triad gangs, their silent code of honor and those hungry for power in a ruthless and dangerous underworld. An ultra-sleek and ultra-cool action hit in Hong Kong. With Ekin Cheng, Jordan Chan and Karen Mok. Cantonese with English subtitles. Letterboxed, two-tape set.
VHS: S31950. $89.98.
Lau Wai Keung, Hong Kong, 1996, 100 mins.

Zen of Sword
In this Hong Kong action film, masterful martial arts skills are displayed as a prince and princess try to restore their dynasty. With Michele Reis and Cynthia Yang.
VHS: S30758. $49.95.
Yu Ming Shan, Hong Kong, 1992

Zodiac Killers
Pessimistic tale of Chinese living in Tokyo, hoping to beat the intense competition to get ahead in Hong Kong but finding instead that they have few friends and few places to hide when they get involved with Japanese thugs. With Andy Lau. Mandarin with English subtitles. 1991.
VHS: S24204. $49.95.

Zu: Warriors of the Magic Mountain
A mind-boggling adventure/fantasy with impressive special effects including an enormous, pulsing blood monster and a wizard with bushy and infinitely extendable eyebrows. Escaping from the midst of one of ancient China's senseless wars, an unlucky soldier falls through a hole and soon finds himself on a quest to save the earth from evil spirits. Cantonese with English subtitles.
VHS: S13475. $59.95.
Laser: Letterboxed. **LD76373. $39.95.**
Tsui Hark, Hong Kong, 1983, 95 mins.

JACKIE CHAN

The Armour of God
Filmed on location in Yugoslavia, Austria, France and Hong Kong, this fast-moving vehicle for comedy/action star Jackie Chan nearly cost him his life when a relatively simple stunt misfired. Chan plays an adventurer who steals pieces of a prized medieval armour set to sell to rich collectors. But these ancient artifacts are also sought by a criminal cult which will stop at nothing to obtain them. When the cult kidnaps Jackie's former love, Jackie comes up with even more spectacular ways to save the armour and the girl. One of Chan's most thrilling and entertaining films (and with him, that's really saying something). Cantonese with English subtitles.
VHS: S14863. $49.95.
Jackie Chan, Hong Kong, 1986, 100 mins.

Bloodpact
Liu Chia Yung stars in this classic Hong Kong action film. Orphaned when his father is killed, a boy seeks shelter in a monastery only to be shunned by its resident Kung-Fu masters. He must learn the art of fighting from a beggar boy and a wiseman. Chan makes a special appearance.
VHS: S27719. $14.99.
Jackie Chan, Hong Kong, 90 mins.

Crime Story

Jackie Chan is a special agent determined to bring down the crooked cop behind a high-profile kidnapping in this action-packed story based on amazing real-life events.

VHS: S31529. $103.99.

Kirk Wong, Hong Kong, 1997, 104 mins.

Dragon Lord

In this Jackie Chan kung fu classic, Chan demonstrates the agility, humor and awe-inspiring stunts that made him famous. Jackie and his pals combat a group of smugglers selling Chinese cultural treasures abroad, and at the same time, they compete for the affection of a beautiful village maiden. Mandarin with English subtitles.

VHS: S27299. $49.95.

Jackie Chan, Hong Kong, 1982

Dragons Forever

Childhood friends and frequent collaborators Jackie Chan, Sammo Hung and Yuen Biao star in this contemporary comedy with an ecological twist. Big time lawyer Jackie is persuaded to work against a chemical plant, which wants to take over a site used by local fishermen, when he falls for the beautiful cousin of the fishery's owner. In addition to comic bits of kung fu business between the three leads, *Dragons* boasts an amazing fighting finale with Jackie once again pitted against the formidable "Benny." Cantonese with English subtitles.

VHS: S14875. $49.95.

Sammo Hung, Hong Kong, 1988, 88 mins.

Drunken Master (aka Drunken Monkey in a Tiger's Eye)

Jackie Chan stars as Naughty Panther, the practical joker son of a stern and humorless kung fu master. Jackie's training is given over to his uncle, a mighty fighter with a fearsome reputation. Like *Snake in the Eagle's Shadow, Drunken Master* is a transitional film in the development of the Jackie Chan screen persona from ersatz Bruce Lee to kung fu comedian. Of this film, *Inside Kung Fu* proclaimed: "Comedy kung fu has arrived and Jackie is the Chaplinesque champion." Cantonese with English subtitles.

VHS: S14868. $49.95.

Yuen Woo-Ping, Hong Kong, 1978, 90 mins.

Drunken Master II

Jackie Chan stars in this hyperactive but humorous action adventure. The legendary Young Wong Fei Hung finds himself in possession of a jade seal that sets off competing bands of British imperialists and local thugs. It's all part of a plot to rob China of its crown jewels—a plot is so intricately laced with bad guys flying through the air that it takes two parts to resolve. Cantonese and Mandarin with English subtitles.

VHS: S27793. $49.95.

Laser: Letterboxed. **LD76124. $89.95.**

Lau Kar Leung, Hong Kong, 1994, 204 mins.

Drunkenfist Boxing

The title says it all. Jackie Chan smacks his way through this non-stop, martial arts adventure. Dubbed in English.

VHS: S27841. $19.95.

Eagle Shadow Fists

In this action-packed adventure, Chan stars as a famous Chinese actor who joins a group of anti-Japanese commandos to become a guerilla fighter, then leads the commandos to get back the fortune the Japanese have taken as spoils of war. Dubbed in English. 88 mins.

VHS: S30025. $14.98.

Fantasy Mission Force

Jackie Chan joins a crack World War II commando team. Their group leader, the mysterious "Devil Sergeant," pushes his men through vicious battles to retake a fortune stolen by the ruthless Japanese. Just as the commando team is desperate for victory, Chan is trapped in a deadly double cross that leaves him no alternative. He must prevail. Cantonese and Mandarin with English subtitles.

VHS: S27859. $19.98.

Chu Yen Ping, Hong Kong, 1978, 90 mins.

First Strike

It's up to Jackie Chan to save America when members of the Russian mafia pose as KGB agents to steal a nuclear missile and the CIA calls on martial arts master Chan to stop them. Jackie treks the globe by submarine, stilts and snowboards, performing his hilarious heroics along the way—without (as usual) a stunt double.

VHS: S31538. $19.98.

Laser: LD76260. $39.99.

Stanley Tong, Hong Kong, 1997, 85 mins.

Fists of Chan

Exclusive video collection includes Jackie Chan's most stupendous stunts and fight scenes taken from some of his best movies. This collector's item is a must for Chan fans! Dubbed in English. 74 mins.

VHS: S30026. $14.98.

The Hand of Death (aka Countdown in Kung-Fu)

Unremarkable 1970's style kung-fu flick, but notable for being an early effort by renowned director John Woo, and for the presence of Jackie Chan and Sammo Hung. Several men band together to protect a messenger, played by Woo, from corrupt Manchus. Mandarin with English subtitles (occasionally chopped on ends).

VHS: S24163. $49.95.

John Woo, Hong Kong, 1975

Heart of the Dragon

Sammo Hung plays Jackie Chan's backward younger brother, who believes himself to be seven years old, and spends his time playing with real kids until he witnesses a crime and is pursued by gangsters. More a drama than an action movie, focusing on Jackie's frustrations at having to care for his brother and the hurt and bewilderment of Sammo at what he perceives as Jackie's attempts to be rid of him. Mandarin with English subtitles (occasionally cut off at edges).

VHS: S24167. $19.95.

Sammo Hung, Hong Kong, 1985

Invincible Fighter

Jackie Chan is featured in another early martial arts action film. In Mandarin with English subtitles.

VHS: S27842. $19.95.

Island of Fire

Violent, lengthy prison movie following the stories of a number of inmates in a corrupt and brutal prison. Tony Leung Ka Fai stars as an undercover cop investigating the reappearance of supposedly dead prisoners as hitmen. The film also features inmates Jackie Chan and Sammo Hung and crime bosses Wang Yu and Andy Lau. While borrowing liberally from such U.S. staples as *Cool Hand Luke* and *Bad Boys*, this film is held together by its strong cast until its conclusion, a climactic gun battle at a Filipino airport. Chinese with English subtitles.

VHS: S27389. $49.95.

Laser: Letterboxed. **LD76112. $69.95.**

Chu Yen Ping, Hong Kong, 1991

Jackie Chan

In this *A&E Biography*, Hong Kong action movie producer, writer, actor, director and stuntman Jackie Chan talks about his childhood in Peking Opera School where he learned his skills, and his long battle to make it big in America. With clips. 40 mins.

VHS: S33422. $14.95.

Jackie Chan and the 36 Crazy Fists

Chan's character was shunned as a boy by Kung-Fu masters at a famous monastery. Fortunately, this orphan boy was taken in by a wiseman who taught him the techniques of ancient Chinese masters. These dazzling martial arts skills come in handy when he confronts the very men who made him an orphan. This film is an overlooked classic in transition to widespread and renewed popularity. Dubbed in English.

VHS: S28069. $14.98.

Jackie Chan, Hong Kong, 90 mins.

Jackie Chan Best Hits

Renowned and revered the world over, action hero Jackie Chan performs in some of the most amazing fight sequences ever filmed. A number of his best moments have been collected on this video. It's a must for diehard fans. 90 mins.

VHS: S27858. $19.98.

Jackie Chan's Police Force

Chan must face a gang of thugs when he is assigned to protect a witness in a drug case. Chock full of Chan's outrageous stunts and slapstick humor. Dubbed in English.

VHS: S30024. $14.98.

Jackie Chan, 1985, China, 89 mins.

Jackie Chan: My Story

International action superstar Jackie Chan talks about his passions, ambitions and three-decade career in this in-depth documentary which captures Chan's magical mix of mirth, martial arts and madcap motion. Features in-depth interviews and footage from his most popular films. 75 mins.

VHS: S35006. $24.98.

Jackie Chan: Ten Fingers of Death

Jackie Chan is back as a man with a mission. Together with his brother he must avenge the death of their father. Though the odds are against them, the two are driven by an unquenchable thirst for justice. The climactic sequence delivers all the fierce fighting which have made Jackie Chan an international star.

VHS: S18920. $19.98.

Master with Cracked Fingers

A young Jackie Chan stars in this tale of revenge and murder. As a boy, Chan's character sees his father killed. A hermit takes the boy in and trains him to be a fighter. Despite this tutelage, the hermit master does not want his pupil to seek revenge against his father's killers. Dubbed in English.

VHS: S27840. $19.95.

Chin Hsin, Hong Kong, 1971, 79 mins.

Mr. Nice Guy

Jackie Chan (*Rumble in the Bronx, Super Cop*) stars as a TV chef who cooks up his own recipe for justice as he takes on the mob after they kidnap his girlfriend and blow up his apartment. "Jackie Chan remains more fun to watch than all of Hollywood's so-called action heroes put together!" (*Boston Globe*). Dubbed.

VHS: S34868. $103.99.

Sammo Hung, Hong Kong, 1997, 87 mins.

My Lucky Stars

Jackie Chan and Yuen Biao play Hong Kong cops in Japan trying to extradite a notorious criminal. When the Tokyo underworld turns the tables on them, the pair are forced to call for some unconventional reinforcements. With Richard Ng. Cantonese with English subtitles.

VHS: S14862. $49.95.

Sammo Hung, Hong Kong, 99 mins.

Operation Condor

In this daring and stunt-filled adventure, Jackie Chan plays a secret agent on a mission to locate stolen Nazi gold buried deep beneath the Sahara. Dubbed in English.

VHS: S32659. $103.99.

Jackie Chan, Hong Kong, 1997, 90 mins.

Painted Faces

Loosely based on the childhood of Sammo Hung, Jackie Chan and Yuen Biao (now all martial artists/film stars). This compelling and humorous story shows their training at the Peking Opera School run by Yu Jim-yuen. Cantonese with English subtitles.

VHS: S13481. $49.95.

Laser: Letterboxed. **LD76114. $69.95.**

Alex Law, Hong Kong, 1988, 100 mins.

Project A (Part I)

A period comedy chock full of action and suspense. Jackie Chan plays an honest marine cadet in turn-of-the-century Hong Kong, who must do battle with the smugglers and pirate bands operating on the South China Sea. With Sammo Hung and Yuen Biao. Cantonese with English subtitles.

VHS: S13470. $49.95.

Jackie Chan, Hong Kong, 1983, 95 mins.

The Protector

Jackie Chan is a New York cop celebrating his 10th anniversary as an American citizen. The sleazy South Bronx bar where he is sharing an after-shift drink with his partner is raided by a gang of hoodlums. A shoot-out ensues and Jackie's partner is killed. Jackie goes after the gang leader and, in the process, destroys millions of dollars of public property. Now in disgrace, Jackie gets a new partner (Danny Aiello) and a new beat. But where Jackie goes, trouble follows, and the kidnapping of a fashion designer leads Jackie and Danny to Hong Kong and the nastiest drug dealing operation since *The French Connection*. In English.

VHS: S14854. $49.95.

James Glickenhaus, USA, 1985, 94 mins.

Rumble in Hong Kong

In this action-packed martial arts adventure, Jackie Chan is a member of one of Hong Kong's toughest gangs. When a cab driver and a policewoman out for revenge challenge the gang, Jackie Chan proves there is no one better at protecting his boss. Dubbed in English.

VHS: S31862. $14.95.

Hdeng Tsu, Hong Kong, 1989, 75 mins.

Rumble in the Bronx

Jackie Chan stars as a shy relative visiting extended family in New York. Before long the rough-and-tumble world of the Bronx brings out his fighting ability. This martial arts action picture joins the best super-action techniques from Hong Kong with the nastiest villains from New York. Dubbed in English. VHS letterboxed.

VHS: S28049. $19.98.

Laser: LD75608. $39.99.

DVD: DV60055. $24.98.

Stanley Tong, Hong Kong, 1996, 91 mins.

Snake in the Eagle's Shadow

Jackie Chan stars in this unbridled martial arts action film. The title refers to two opposing martial arts schools, the Snake Fist and the Eagle's Claw. Honor and good Hong Kong-style filmmaking demand that their rivalry lead to ever greater clashes. Dubbed in English.

VHS: S27839. $19.95.

Yuen Woo-Ping, Hong Kong, 1971, 90 mins.

Supercop

"Jackie Chan is at his best" (*Chicago Tribune*) as an undercover cop on a mission to put a high-powered drug lord out of business in this non-stop action film. From leaping off a ten-story building onto an airborne helicopter to sailing over speeding trains, Chan performs his own stunts, as usual, but this time he's partnered with Asia's hottest female action star and former Miss Malaysia, Michelle Khan. "Thrills, chills and stunts galore" (*New York Times*).

VHS: S30863. $103.99.

Laser: Widescreen. **LD76168. $49.98.**

Stanley Tong, USA, 1996, 91 mins.

Top Fighter
Top martial arts stars Jean-Claude Van Damme, Jackie Chan, Bruce Lee, Bolo Yeung, Jet Lee, Jim Kelly and others show their fighting best in this compilation of important action sequences. Dubbed in English.
VHS: S27844. $59.95.

Twin Dragons
Jackie Chan plays a pair of twins who miraculously meet after being separated at birth. One is a renowned conductor in New York. The other is a wild martial arts expert who lives the fast life in Hong Kong. When they finally meet, gangsters and the women they love collide in the classic mix of action and absurdity that characterize this popular genre. Dubbed in English.
VHS: S28065. $19.95.
Tsui Hark, Hong Kong, 1993, 100 mins.

Wheels on Meals
Two young entrepreneurs from Hong Kong (Jackie Chan and Yuen Biao) bring Chinese food to the citizens of Barcelona with the aid of their uniquely customized van. They become involved with a young pickpocket who turns out to be the missing heiress sought by their clumsy private detective pal (Sammo Hung). Full of humor, spectacular martial arts scenes, and a bruising final battle between Jackie and bad guy "Benny." Cantonese with English subtitles.
VHS: S14858. $19.98.
Laser: LD76761. $39.95.
Sammo Hung, Hong Kong, 1984, 100 mins.

Will of Iron
Jackie is an illustrator with a serious cocaine habit. Even his friend and dealer, Michael, wants him to quit. Even Jackie's marriage to the long-suffering Carol is on the verge of breaking up as a result of his drug problem. The strong-willed Maggie (Maggie Cheung) arrives for a visit, hoping to put an end to all these problems, but instead insults the ruthless gangster behind it all, putting everyone's lives in danger. Mandarin with English subtitles.
VHS: S27290. $49.95.
John Chiang, Hong Kong, 1990

Winners and Sinners
Laugh-out-loud slapstick and slam-bang action with Sammo Hung and Jackie Chan, highlighted by Jackie's famous roller-skating-under-a-moving-truck stunt. Cantonese with English subtitles. Letterboxed.
VHS: S34645. $19.98.
Sammo Hung, Hong Kong, 1983, 106 mins.

The Young Master
One of Jackie Chan's first films as director/star, it smashed all box office records upon first release and rocketed Jackie to world-wide recognition. This colorful period-comedy follows Jackie as he seeks to restore the honor of his kung fu school and his foster brother. Cantonese with English subtitles.
VHS: S14865. $19.95.
Laser: Letterboxed. **LD76277. $39.99.**
Jackie Chan, Hong Kong, 92 mins.

CHINESE CULTURE & POLITICS

Best of Nightline: Student Protest in China
30 mins.
VHS: S14059. $14.98.

China and the Forbidden City
A very special inside look at the mystery, opulence, grandeur, and thousands-year-old history of China's Forbidden City, one of the most opulent treasures of the world. Winner of the Peabody Award. Introduced by Edwin Newman and Lucy Jarvis. 60 mins.
VHS: S05319. $24.95.

China on the March
Written and narrated by Enakashi Bhavani, this documentary is an intriguing chronicle of the turbulent early years of the Communist revolution.
VHS: S15485. $39.95.
Moan Bhavnani, China, 1949-58

China Rising
For 70 years the "Bamboo Curtain" protected China from the eyes of the West. Now, for the first time, Western filmmakers have been allowed inside the world's most enigmatic country to reveal its secret history. Never-before-seen archival footage-including coverage of the Cultural Revolution—and extraordinary interviews with warlords, revolutionaries and ordinary citizens offer a privileged view of "Asia's sleeping giant." Nominated for the Japan Prize, the world's most prestigous educational award. Includes three 50-minute videos.
VHS: S30151. $49.95.

China—The Cold Red War
The ideological battles between the US and the USSR were nothing compared to the fierce and inter-communistic battles between the Soviets and the People's Republic of China. 70 mins.
VHS: S12713. $19.98.

China: A Century of Revolution
This three-volume, six-hour history of China is a powerful, first-hand look at China's most tumultuous century. An astonishingly candid view of a once-secret nation, featuring eyewitness accounts, rare archival film footage, insightful commentary, historic records and actual Chinese citizens who lived through the century. "Remarkable…a chronicle of achievement, misadventure, cruelty and havoc" (*The New York Times*). 120 minutes each.
China: A Century of Revolution—Born Under the Red Flag. Begins with Mao's death in 1976, continues with the new leadership of Deng Xiaoping, and concludes with the struggle of China's paradoxical goals of economic prosperity and absolute Communist Party control.
VHS: S32999. $19.98.
China: A Century of Revolution—China in Revolution. Begins in 1911, with the fall of the last emperor, and continues through 1949, highlighting four decades of civil war, foreign invasion and the ascension of rival leaders Mao Zedong and Chaing Kai-shek.
VHS: S32997. $19.98.
China: A Century of Revolution—The Mao Years. From the beginning of his rule in 1949 to his death in 1976, Mao Zedong and his colleagues attempted to forge a "new China" from a country mired in poverty and unrest in the aftermath of civil war. Yet "the Mao years" would offer the new "People's Republic of China" little of the stability promised.
VHS: S32998. $19.98.
China: A Century of Revolution—The Set.
VHS: S33000. $49.98.
Sue Williams, USA, 1997, 360 mins.

The Chinese People: A Time of Change
From Hong Kong and Beijing to New York's Chinatown, this program presents an overview of recent Chinese history and a look at present-day China and American-Chinese communities as the political and social revolutions of the 20th century give way to a new role for China on the world scene. Suggested for intermediate and secondary grades as an introduction to the study of modern China and its relationship to the world under a rapidly-changing Communist society. 40 mins. 1996.
VHS: S30498. $39.95.

The Chinese Way of Life
The People's Republic of China combines ancient ways with thoroughly modern ambitions. Beijing's Forbidden City and the Great Wall are historic sites that continue to draw contemporary tourists. This film offers insights into China's rapidly changing culture. 24 mins.
VHS: S23711. $129.95.

Discovering China and Tibet
Enter the Forbidden City of the Ming Dynasty. Travel to Tibet, a Buddhist culture that remains virtually isolated from the rest of the world. Witness the effects of modernization on the Chinese workplace, a growing industry that has transformed China into an awakening giant. 52 mins.
VHS: S10777. $24.95.

The First Emperor of China
An archeological investigation of the magnificent tomb complex of Qin Shi Huang Di, China's emperor in the third century B.C. The program guides its viewers through the actual excavation, an aerial view of the Great Wall, and a guided tour through the Qin Museum.
Laser: LD70004. $99.95.

Forbidden City: The Great Within
For hundreds of years China's emperors used their far flung dominions as resources to embellish this secretive living complex. Cinematographer Zhao Fei shot this revealing look at the palaces, temples and gardens at the very heart of the Chinese Kingdom. Rod Steiger narrates. 50 mins.
VHS: S29426. $19.95.

Generations: A Chinese Family
A warm and unforgettable portrait of a contemporary Chinese family as they embrace traditions and meet new challenges. Doctor Shen Fasheng, a traditional Chinese doctor, introduces us to his wife, mother, children, and grandchildren. Together they relate their family history, and share with the viewer an intimate glimpse of their daily lives. Produced by Maryknoll Media. 28 mins.
VHS: S04926. $24.95.

I Saw Him in the Rice Field
The inspiring story of Bishop James E. Walsh, among the first U.S. missionaries to arrive in China and last to leave when he was released from a Chinese prison in 1970. His love for the Chinese people began the day he arrived there and endured through 12 years of imprisonment. This film traces the career of this remarkable man. Produced by Maryknoll Media. 28 mins.
VHS: S04929. $24.95.

Li-Young Lee
Li-Young Lee has published two books of poetry, *Rose* and *The City in Which I Love You*. Mr. Lee crafts haunting poetry that weaves cultural politics with personal desire and loss. On April 18, 1995, in Los Angeles, Mr. Lee read from his two poetry collections and from *The Winged Seed*, his memoirs of his family's journey from the political turmoil of Indonesia to a small Pennsylvania town. Novelist and editor Shawn Wong talked with Mr. Lee. From the *Lannan Literary Videos* series. 60 mins.
VHS: S32429. $19.95.

Ming Garden
Documents the first cultural exchange between the People's Republic of China and the United States, the installation at the Metropolitan Museum of Art of a Ming-style garden courtyard. These gardens are renowned for their unusual rock formations of naturally eroded limestone, elegant wood architectural elements and fired terra cotta brickwork. 30 mins.
VHS: S03400. $29.95.

Moving the Mountain
The momentous events surrounding the Tiananmen Square uprisings of May 1989 are at the center of this moving film by Michael (*28 Up, 35 Up*) Apted. Part documentary and part dramatization, it captures the feeling of hope and change that inspired the young demonstrators as they sought democracy and confronted a brutal regime. Newsreel footage and powerful personal testimonies of participants in the Tiananmen Square uprisings make this a powerful and compelling film.
VHS: S26863. $99.98.
Laser: LD75418. $39.99.
Michael Apted, USA, 1995, 83 mins.

Religion and Clture in China
China, a growing force in the world scene, has tried to repress all religions. These days, the active practice of religious faith is alive and growing, and its values are clearly in harmony with Chinese culture. Exclusive footage of China provides a background for a discussion of the relationship between faith and culture and the future role of the Catholic church. Produced by Maryknoll Media. 28 mins.
VHS: S06263. $24.95.

The Silk Road I: An Ancient World of Adventure
For thousands of years, the fabled Silk Road, as traveled by Marco Polo, was the major link between the people of Europe and the vast riches of mysterious China. Spanning the deserts, grasslands and seas between Rome, Istanbul and the major cities of China, the Silk Road witnessed an ongoing parade of traders and goods, carrying with them their art, religion and culture. The impact of the Silk Road is immeasurable—giants such as Alexander the Great and tyrants like Genghis Khan created our world's history while striding along its path. This first co-production of China Central TV and the outside world was ten years in the making, and produced at a cost exceeding $50 million. Aired to critical acclaim in over 25 countries, it remains the highest rated series in Japan's television history. With a unique soundtrack by Kitaro, the series is available in six separately packaged volumes.
Across the Taklamakan Desert. Be the first foreign visitor in over 75 years to enter an ancient Buddhist city before attempting to cross the Taklamakan Desert, which means "the place from which nothing living returns." After losing your way in 120 degree heat, you will stumble into an ancient ruin, and then risk a night escape across the desert to safety. 55 mins.
VHS: S13407. $29.95.
In Search of the Kingdom of Lou-Lan. Discover a lost kingdom which vanished into the sands of the desert. Join the first journey in half a century to seek the ruins, in a secure military zone normally forbidden to visitors. You will uncover the Silk Road relics buried over a millenium ago—including a mummy preserved in a secret grave for over 2,000 years. 55 mins.
VHS: S13406. $29.95.
The Art Gallery in the Desert. Tour the world-famous Ma-gao caves, over 30 miles in length, with 3,000 murals and statues—in the middle of the Gobi Desert! Dating from 366 A.D., these caves are a tour-de-force, once-in-a-lifetime dream of art scholars and art lovers alike. 55 mins.
VHS: S13404. $29.95.
The Dark Castle. Encounter a ghost castle in the Gobi Desert, obliterated by Genghis Khan, who exterminated the people who built it. The castle, believed by the Chinese to be cursed, has not been entered for 50 years. You will embark on a Mongol camel journey, cross the desert, and enter the castle gates—alone! 55 mins.
VHS: S13405. $29.95.

Thousand Kilometers Beyond the Yellow River. Cross the Yellow River on a goat-skin raft and gaze in awe at a giant Buddha before entering secret caves never before filmed by a television crew. You will cross the former battlegrounds of the Huns and stroll the streets of a citadel town already hundreds of years old when Marco Polo lived here in the 14th century. 55 mins.
VHS: S13403. $29.95.
The Silk Road, Set 1 (Episodes 1-6). The complete, six-volume set in a gold-embossed slipcase, at a special price. 5½ hours.
VHS: S13408. $149.95.

The Silk Road I, Set 2

This second series of six documentaries follows the Silk Road, the overland path to the Far East made famous by Marco Polo. Produced with the cooperation of China Central Television, this mammoth project took over ten years to complete. It dispels the shroud of mystery surrounding the fabled cities and regions of this ancient way.
A Heat Wave Called Turfan. Between the Tian-Shen Mountains and Taklamakan Desert lies a place called the "Land of Fire." In this inhospitable stretch of the Silk Road, mankind has shaped the surroundings in unique and unusual ways. There are the Thousand Buddha Caves with paintings and carvings dating back hundreds of years, the Jiao-ha Castle carved from living rock atop a cliff, and even the Karez, an underground aqueduct system. 55 mins.
VHS: S20881. $29.95.
Journey into Music—South Through the Tian-Shen Mountains. In this segment the customs of the Uighurs are revealed, while the route rises to meet the high mountain pass at Teinmenquan. In the Kysil Caves a trove of Buddhist art can be seen, dating from the third century. 55 mins.
VHS: S20883. $29.95.
Khotan—Oasis of Silk and Jade. In the Kun-Lun mountains jade has been mined for centuries, while precious jewels have been sought in the riverbeds below. Weavers continue to ply their ancient trade making rugs. And the Buddhist temple city of Dandan Oilik still stands as a testament to the people who live along this way. 55 mins.
VHS: S20880. $29.95.
Through the Tian-Shen Mountains by Rail. This part of *The Silk Road* stretches from Turfan over 300 miles of rail to Korla. Along the way you will pass through the notorious, desiccated Gobi Desert. During the construction of the railway, treasures were uncovered from grave mounds hinting at the long history of this remote region. 55 mins.
VHS: S20882. $29.95.
Two Roads to the Pamirs. Kashgar is a Muslim town which can be seen caught up in the riotous celebration greeting the end of Ramadan. Here master craftsmen still transform silk and wood into precious commodities prized the world over. Finally, a Tajik wedding party shows the people of this often overlooked region engaged in an intimate ceremony which everyone can understand and enjoy. 55 mins.
VHS: S20885. $29.95.
Where Horses Fly Like the Wind. Across the Tian-Shen mountains lies the region inhabited by Kazahks (Cossacks), descendants of the Mongols, former rulers of the great Mongol empire. In the West Land are the very horses used by Ghengis Khan and his men. 55 mins.
VHS: S20884. $29.95.
The Silk Road, Set 2 (Episodes 7-12). Six video cassettes, totalling 5½ hours, in a slipcase.
VHS: S20886. $149.95.

The Silk Road II

The epic journey along the legendary ancient trade route that follows in the footsteps of Alexander the Great and Marco Polo into some of the world's most exotic and inaccessible regions. Six-volume boxed collector's set includes *Across the Pamir, In Search of Wisdom, Beyond Baghdad, The Soghdian Merchants, Across the Karakum Desert* and *All Roads Lead to Rome*. Total running time 15 hours.
VHS: S34222. $149.95.

Video Visits: China, Ancient Rhythms and Modern Currents

Numerous sites from the Middle Kingdom are contained in this awe-inspiring video tour of China. The cities of Beijing and Shanghai, as well as the Great Wall and other sites from the vast expanse of this land are all displayed on this video. 60 mins.
VHS: S29832. $24.95.

TAIWANESE CINEMA

Dust in the Wind

A young man sets out to find work in the big city of Taipei so that he can make money to send home and eventually marry his childhood sweetheart. Marked with great sympathy and understanding for its characters and a spare, unhurried style, *Dust in the Wind* becomes an atmospheric statement on the generation gap and the divide between the village and the city in contemporary Taiwan. From the director of *The Time to Live and the Time to Die* and *A City of Sadness*. Taiwanese dialect with English subtitles.
VHS: S14876. $49.95.
Hou Hsiao-hsien, Taiwan, 1987, 109 mins.

Eat Drink Man Woman

Ang Lee's (The Wedding Banquet) winning blockbuster of a movie about food, sex and independence. Master Chef Chu is Taipei's legendary chef whose extraordinary culinary creations are the center piece of the film. His three beautiful daughters are both sexy and rebellious, but Master Chu holds the family together with his Sunday ritual dinners. But as the generations clash, and Master Chu retires, it's the experienced generation that has the final word in a film that's original, funny, surprising—and delectable. Chinese with English subtitles.
VHS: S24824. $19.98.
Ang Lee, Taiwan/USA, 1994, 104 mins.

Flower Love (aka Love Is Grown with Flowers)

Uneven comedy-drama about a farming village undergoing change, some of the young people wanting to live in the city while others stay on and try to help the older residents adjust to a new scheme to grow flowers to market instead of rice. Mandarin with English subtitles.
VHS: S24159. $49.95.
Tsay Yang-ming, Taiwan, 1989

Outcasts

The most controversial film ever released in Taiwan, Outcasts is the story of teenage boys abandoned by their families because they are gay, and the efforts of an aging photographer to provide a home and family for these young people. Chinese with English subtitles.
VHS: S05987. $49.95.
Yu Kan-Ping, Taiwan, 1986, 102 mins.

Song of the Exile

A memorable film about cultural divisions and alienation. Hueyin is a young Chinese student living in London in 1973. After graduation she returns to Hong Kong because of the job-discrimination she faces in England based on her heritage. Further emotional tensions surface in this touching film after the reunion with her own fragmented family. With Maggie Cheung and Shwu-Fen Chang. Chinese with English subtitles.
VHS: S14745. $79.95.
Ann Hui, Taiwan/China, 1990, 100 mins.

That Day, On the Beach

Generally credited as the film which more than any other marked the launching of the Taiwanese New Wave, That Day, On the Beach mingles the director's own expatriate experience (in the U.S.) with his perceptions of several strata of Taiwanese society. Told in flashbacks, the film begins as two former schoolfriends are reunited after a 13-year separation. One is now a successful concert pianist in Europe; the other has started up a business after the failure of her marriage. The two reminisce about old times, reveal secrets of the past they never dared speak before, and take stock of their present lives. Director Yang weaves several levels of narrative together to create a rich emotional tapestry that reflects the experience of a "lost" generation. Taiwanese dialect with English subtitles.
VHS: S14866. $49.95.
Edward Yang, Taiwan, 1983, 167 mins.

A Time to Live and a Time to Die

Winner of the Golden Bear at the Berlin Film Festival, and directed by one of Asia's most interesting filmmakers, Hou Hsiao-hsien, this film is the story of a family from southern mainland China who migrate to Taiwan in the 1940s to escape financial hardship. Later, they are unable to return and find themselves tragically cut off from their cultural heritage. "Reaches unexpected depths of feeling" (New York Times). Taiwanese with English subtitles.
VHS: S26494. $59.95.
Hou Hsiao-hsien, Taiwan, 1985, 137 mins.

Vive L'Amour

Considered by critics as reminiscent of the best of Michelangelo Antonioni (Blow Up), this "wonderfully evocative" (New York Times) film stars Yan Kuei-Mei and Chen Chao-Jung (both from the hit comedy Eat Drink Man Woman) as May, a chic and seductive real estate agent, and Ah-jong, a street merchant, and their encounters in one of the thousands of vacant, anonymous apartments that fill Taipei, Taiwan. After a chance meeting, the couple use the apartment for their impulsive sexual liaisons, while a shy young gay man hides in the same apartment and spies on the couple, creating a bizarre love triangle. Taiwanese with English subtitles. "A tour de force…tender, stylish" (Amy Taubin, The Village Voice).
VHS: S30884. $19.95.
DVD: DV60285. $29.95.
Tsai Ming-Liang, Taiwan, 1996, 118 mins.

KOREAN CINEMA

301/302

One of the most highly acclaimed films from the new Korean cinema, this provocative, black comedy is winner of Korea's Grand Bell for Best Picture. When the anorexic young woman in apartment 302 mysteriously disappears, a detective visits her neighbor in 301—a newly divorced gourmet cook who's addicted to food—to start the investigation. In flashbacks, the relationship between the two women is seen developing as the startling secret of what happened in 302 is revealed. "The kinkiest variation on the food-obsessed movies that have been filling art houses ever since *Babette's Feast* and *Tampopo* appeared in the 1980s" (John Hartl, *Seattle Times*). Korean with English subtitles.
VHS: S31787. $98.99.
Laser: LD76334. $39.99.
Chul-Soo Park, Korea, 1996, 98 mins.

The Gingko Bed

This rare Korean film, directed by Jacky Kang, is a stylish romantic thriller. The mysteries of reincarnation and past lives are revealed to Su-hyun, a 32-year-old college lecturer, after he purchases an antique gingko bed and returns to his past life as the son of a court musician in love with Princess Mi-dan. "Director Kang serves up a diverting romantic thriller that's at its best" *(Variety)*. Korean with English subtitles.
VHS: S34678. $69.95.
Jacky Kang, Korea, 1996, 88 mins.

Why Has Bodhi-Dharma Left for the East?

An aged monk, his young apprentice and an orphan inhabit a remote monastery. This fascinating Korean film by Bae Yong-kyun focuses on their interaction and, in the process, provokes a contemplation on life, death and enlightenment. A solo effort, the film took ten years to complete. Korean with English subtitles.
VHS: S27338. $79.95.
Laser: LD75463. $69.95.
Bae Yong-kyun, Korea, 1989, 135 mins.

Yongary Monster from the Deep

A Japanese-Korean co-production giant monster movie. The title character, who looks like Godzilla's second cousin, emerges to terrorize Asia after an earthquake in China sets it free. Yongary enjoys drinking gasoline, crushing buildings in Seoul and dancing to rock and roll music. Script by Yungsung Suh.
VHS: S10997. $14.98.
Kidduck Kim, South Korea/Japan, 1967, 100 mins.

japanese cinema

The Adventures of a Blind Man

The astounding martial arts expert and swordsman samurai Zato Ichi is cornered and outnumbered when he goes to Kasama Town to celebrate the New Year. He uncovers a plot of murder and intrigue that involves the corrupt local magistrate. Japanese with English subtitles.

VHS: S26529. $59.95.

Kimoyoshi Yada, Japan, 1965, 86 mins.

Angel Dust

In this Japanese "*Silence of the Lambs* on acid" (Andrew Sarris, *New York Observer*), a mysterious serial killer is murdering women with a lethal needle on the Tokyo subway system. Police psychologist Setsuko has been assigned to the case for her ability to merge her mind with that of the killer's. As she delves deeper into the case, she finds herself in a maze of mind control, hallucination and terror as her ex-boyfriend becomes her prime suspect. A stunningly shot psychological thriller from one of the hottest of "new wave" Japanese filmmakers. Japanese with English subtitles. Letterboxed.

VHS: S31253. $89.95.

Sogo Ishii, Japan, 1997, 116 mins.

Bad Boys

Susumu Hani's first feature film was almost unanimously praised by critics. Based on a collection of papers written by boys at a reform school, this film was shot on location and acted by real inmates who were, in effect, reliving their own experiences. Adding to the gritty realism is the extensive use of 8mm cameras and hand held shots to photograph scenes as an unobtrusive observer. "…among the most talented of the younger generation of film directors from Japan" (Joan Mellen). Japanese with English subtitles.

VHS: S15376. $39.95.

Susumu Hani, Japan, 1960, 90 mins.

Beautiful Mystery

Shinohara is a young bodybuilder who joins a para-military sect in Northern Japan. Amidst the discipline and rigor of the group, his instructor, Takizawa, develops a special interest in this new recruit. Before long, they develop a special and loving relationship. Japanese with English subtitles.

VHS: S29952. $39.95.

Nakamura Genji, Japan, 1983, 60 mins.

Black Lizard

A hilarious caper movie written originally for the stage by Yukio Mishima; the plot concerns a female jewel thief who kidnaps nubile youths and ferries them to a glitzoid secret island. There she turns them into naked love statues—one of them bizarrely played by Mishima himself. Miss Lizard is portrayed by the transvestite actor Akihiro Miwa, who flounces around in an impossible collection of boas and chokers and turns every flourish of her cigarette holder into an over-the-top arabesque. Called "a tale of love, passion, greed and necrophilia" by the *New York Times*, and "Naughty Japanese noir. Like something by Almodovar or John Waters" *(Village Voice)*. Japanese with English subtitles.

VHS: S16261. $79.95.

Kinji Fukasaku, Japan, 1968, 90 mins.

The Blind Swordsman's Cane Sword

Once again the long suffering but incredibly noble and diligent samurai Zato Ichi is back. Swordplay and martial arts, artfully choreographed, make this a standout in the popular series. Japanese with English subtitles.

VHS: S26530. $59.95.

Kimiyoshi Yasuda, Japan, 1967, 93 mins.

The Blind Swordsman's Revenge

When itinerant masseur and master swordsman Zatoichi goes to visit the man who taught him the art of massage, he learns that his old teacher, Hikonoichi, has been murdered while traveling to Kyoto to receive the high rank of Kengyo, master masseur. When Zatochi discovers that Kengyo's daughter Osayo has been taken hostage in a brothel owned by a local gangster boss, Tarsugoro, he vows to rescue Osayo and avenge his mentor's murder. Japanese with English subtitles.

VHS: S28623. $59.95.

Akira Inouye, Japan, 1965, 84 mins.

Blind Woman's Curse

Combing a historical yakuza gangster story with horror film atmosphere makes this film a cult favorite. It follows the chain of mysterious events that unfolds when a woman yakuza boss accidentally blinds a woman from a rival gang. Soon violence threatens to engulf everyone in sight. Japanese with English subtitles.

VHS: S26672. $39.95.

Teruo Ishii, Japan, 1970, 83 mins.

Branded to Kill

The film that led Seijun Suzuki's studio to fire him. Mocking everything from censorship to gangster films, this twisted vision of Japan's underworld follows Hanada Goro, the mob's "No. 3 Killer," as he loses his grip on his career, women and reality and the "No. 1 Killer" makes Goro the target of a cruel cat-and-mouse game. Through it all, Suzuki thwarts logic and convention with stunning visual tricks and disorienting narrative leaps. With its blues score, brilliant black-and-white cinematography and dark humor, *Branded to Kill* is a triumph of style and purpose. "Suzuki's masterwork. Terse, deadpan, and terrific" (Kevin Thomas, *Los Angeles Times*). Japanese with English subtitles. Letterboxed.

VHS: S32968. $29.95.

Seijun Suzuki, Japan, 1967, 91 mins.

Chushingura (The Loyal 47 Retainers)

The *Gone with the Wind* of Japanese cinema, from the director of *The Samurai Trilogy*, set in Japan in 1701. When Lord Asano is forced by a corrupt lord to commit hara kiri, 47 loyal samurai seek vengeance. With Toshiro Mifune, Yuzo Kayama, Chusha Ichikawa and Koshiro Matsumoto. "Spectacle, intrigue and pure pleasure-giving artistry…beautifully photographed in dazzling color" *(San Francisco Chronicle)*. Japanese with English subtitles. Letterboxed. Two cassettes.

VHS: S34629. $29.98.

DVD: DV60456. $34.99.

Hiroshi Inagaki, Japan, 1962, 207 mins.

Double Suicide

Faithful to the Bunraku puppet theatre tradition for which it was originally written, Shinoda's surrealist, overtly sexual and erotic film concerns Jihei, a merchant of paper products, who has neglected his business because of his relentless pursuit of Koharu, a prostitute. Despite the efforts of both his wife and brother to help him, the business is failing, and a business rival wants to buy out his contract. Based on the play by Chikamatsu Monzaemon. Japanese with English subtitles.

VHS: S07362. $29.95.

Laser: LD76987. $49.95.

Masahiro Shinoda, Japan, 1969, 100 mins.

Gate of Hell

An exquisitely stylized tragedy of a warrior's desire for a married noblewoman told in exotic color. Wonderfully choreographed battle scenes, incredible textures and composition. Story is set in 12th century Japan and based on Rape of Lucrece. Japanese with English subtitles.

VHS: S00483. $24.95.

Teinosuke Kinugasa, Japan, 1954

Ghost of Yotsuya

This bizarre, spine-tingling, horrifying tale of the supernatural deals with the psychological torture of the inner mind, and stars Shigeru Amachi and Katsuko Wakasugi. Based on a 250-year-old legend, a masterless samurai must shed his wife and marry a younger and wealthier maiden. Japanese with English subtitles.

VHS: S00497. $59.95.

Nobuo Nakagawa, Japan, 1950, 100 mins.

Giant Robo, Vol. 2

Contains two episodes. In *The Twilight of the Superhero* Giant Robo's punch has no effect on the menacing Eye of the Folger. When the Magnetic Web devices are sabotaged, Taison and Alberto battle for destiny. In *The Truth of Bashtarlle*, inside the fiery Greta Garbo, Daisaku plummets into the icy depths of the Himalayan mountains. As Daisaku lays unconscious, he dreams of his past and the origins of Giant Robo. Japanese with English subtitles. 90 mins.

VHS: S33706. $24.95.

Gonza the Spearman

A beautiful film, set in 18th century Japan. The handsome but overly ambitious Gonza is one of the Matsue clan's most talented lancers. Although he is already engaged to the sister of one of his fellow retainers, Gonza agrees to wed the daughter of his lord to better his position. The fiance's infuriated brother plots against Gonza. This classic tale of conflicts between love and honor, duty and devotion, won a Silver Bear at the Berlin Film Festival. Japanese with English subtitles.

VHS: S12204. $79.95.

Masahiro Shinoda, Japan, 1986, 126 mins.

Grave of the Fireflies

Orphaned and homeless, two children set out to survive on their own in post-World War II Japan. But in the face of a society that is no longer able to help them, they begin to realize that they can never escape the hardships of war, or even find enough to eat. Best Animated Feature, Chicago International Children's Film Festival. "Elegiac and riveting" *(The New York Times)*. Dubbed in English.

VHS: S34783. $29.95.

Isao Takahata, Japan, 1988, 88 mins.

Harikiri

This grim and exquisite film explores the honor in death and the death of honor venerated by the 17th-century samurai. After an unemployed samurai is forced to commit ritual suicide before a feudal lord, his father-in-law returns to the scene, seemingly to commit the same act. Instead this warrior acts out against the cruelly rigid society that enforces such harsh discipline. Japanese with English subtitles.

VHS: S22459. $39.95.

Masaki Kobayashi, Japan, 1962, 135 mins.

Himatsuri

An independent, fortyish lumberjack (Kinya Kitaoji) is outraged by pollution, commercial exploitation and the destruction of wildlife. Believing he's the protector of the mountains through his divine relationship with the goddess of the mountains, he turns to violence against his family to voice his opposition to change and technological intrusion. Awesome sounds and images in a daring film. Japanese with English subtitles.

VHS: S01603. $59.95.

Mitsuo Yanagimachi, Japan, 1985, 120 mins.

Human Condition

One of the great works of Japanese cinema, "this nine and one-half hour long, humanistic anti-war fresco is magnificent, including many forceful scenes that depict the horrors and cruelties of war. Its director, Kobayashi, said, 'I wanted to bring to life the tragedy of men who are forced into war against their will. Kaji is both the oppressor and the oppressed and he learns that he can never stop being an oppressor while he himself is oppressed. Of course I wanted to denounce the crimes of war but I also wanted to show how human society can become inhumane.'" Directed by Masaki Kobayashi, Japan, 1959-61.

Human Condition Part 1 (No Greater Love). The production at mining camps has come to a standstill. Japan is desperate, so Kaji, who believes that war can be won through the hearts and minds of labor, is given authority. 200 mins. B&W. Japanese with English subtitles.

VHS: S08515. $59.95.

Human Condition Part 2 (Road to Eternity). As this sequence opens, Kaji is tortured by the military police for having mistreated the Chinese. Allowed one memorable night with his wife, he is ordered to the front. His records brand him as a "red," and his superiors mistreat him. 180 mins. B&W. Japanese with English subtitles.

VHS: S08516. $59.95.

Human Condition Part 3 (A Soldier's Prayer). Ravaged by hunger and thirst, Kaji awakens to a world gone mad. Surrender? To whom? Americans? Russians? Chiang Kai-shek? Surrendering to avoid needless slaughter, Kaji is force marched to Siberia, where he finds his worst enemy is now a collaborator who brands him a war criminal. Escaping into the wastelands of Siberia, he continues his desperate journey into the ultimate reality of war. 190 mins. B&W. Japanese with English subtitles.

VHS: S08517. $59.95.

Masaki Kobayashi, Japan, 1958-1961

Hunter in the Dark

An elegant, erotic and violent samurai movie set in 18th-century Japan. Upon its 1980 release, the *L.A. Times* wrote that *Hunter in the Dark* is "beautifully mounted and enhanced by exquisite subterranean photography that evokes a midnight world of evil." Tatsuya Nakadai, Tetsuro Tamba and Sonny Chiba star in this digitally remastered and letterboxed version. Japanese with English subtitles.

VHS: S16528. $29.95.

Hideo Gosha, Japan, 1980, 138 mins.

I Bombed Pearl Harbor

Toshiro Mifune, "the Spencer Tracy of Japan," stars in this multi-million-dollar, all-Japanese, Technicolor epic that holds the record for most ships destroyed per minute of film. Filmed 15 years after World War II, these are the events of the war seen through the eyes of the Japanese. The beautifully filmed battle scenes and realistic recreations of several of the Pacific theatre's most important battles make this especially interesting for history buffs. Dubbed in English.

VHS: S30732. $29.95.

Shuei Matsubayashi, Japan, 1960, 98 mins.

I Like You, I Like You Very Much
This is one of the few sexually explicit films available from Japan. Yu has a nice college student boyfriend, but that does not stop him from approaching a sexy stranger waiting for a train one evening. There is only one thing he can say: "I like you, I like you very much." Japanese with English subtitles.
VHS: S29951. $39.95.
Oki Hiroyuki, Japan, 1994, 58 mins.

Incident at Blood Pass
This action-packed epic marks the final appearance of Toshiro Mifune's Yojimbo character. Gentetsu (Katsu Shintaro), a doctor, hires Yojimbo to ambush a Shogunate gold convoy, but all does not go as planned. With Nakamura Kinnosuke. Japanese with English subtitles. Widescreen collector's edition.
VHS: S35008. $29.95.
Inagaki Hiroshi, Japan, 1970, 118 mins.

The Inland Sea
Lucille Carra's interpretation of critic and author Donald Richie's memoir about growing up in Japan's islands is a private odyssey of the inner and outer landscapes. "Conversational and witty, Donald Richie's voice is beautifully full and the film is quiet and hypnotic" *(Honolulu Star-Bulletin)*. Cinematography by Hiro Narita. Score by Toru Takemitsu *(Ran)*.
VHS: S18726. $29.95.
Laser: CLV. **LD72112. $59.95.**
Lucille Carra, Japan, 1992, 57 mins.

Island
Cinematic haiku. A man, his wife and two small boys are the only inhabitants of an island and must, each day, go to the mainland to get their supply of water. The entire story is told without dialog, but rather through visuals, sounds and music. The result is a moving, intensely human allegory for existence with outstanding performances from Nobuko Otowa and Taiji Tonoyama. No dialog.
VHS: S00639. $29.95.
Kaneto Shindo, Japan, 1961, 96 mins.

Kwaidan
Four terrifying tales of the supernatural filmed with visual sensitivity. This is no Japanese monster movie. Rather, it creeps up on you by appealing to human emotions and fears. An Academy Award nominee, this distinctive work is filled with graceful camera movement, unusual colors, haunting sound effects and music. Japanese with English subtitles.
VHS: S00694. $29.95.
Laser: Widescreen. **LD71083. $69.95.**
Masaki Kobayashi, Japan, 1964, 161 mins.

Lady Snowblood— Love Song of Vengeance
Imprisoned and sentenced to hang for the murders she committed to avenge her family, Yuki is given a reprieve by the mysterious Kikui, a secret government agent. In return for her life, Yuki must infiltrate the household of Ransui, an anarchist activist, assassinate him, and recover an important document. Live action. Widescreen. Japanese with English subtitles.
VHS: S33326. $29.95.
Laser: LD76759. $39.95.
Fujita Toshiya, Japan, 1974, 89 mins.

Landlock, Part 1
The story of Luda, a young man who learns to control and utilize the mystical powers of the wind to fight the forces of the evil tyrant Zanark. In the beautiful land of Zaul, Luda enlists the help of some unlikely heroes to avenge his father's murder and save the planet from total destruction. 30 mins.
Dubbed.
VHS: S33704. $19.95.
Subtitled.
VHS: S33705. $24.95.

Late Chrysanthemums
In this adaptation of three Fumiko Hayashi stories, four retired geishas contemplate their past lives and their continuing unequal relationships with men. Filmmaker Mikio Naruse's films center around "women not favored by the traditional family system. They are strong, intelligent women and something in their situation has kept them away from the opportunities for the conventional happy family. They are exiles and they feel their exile keenly" (Audie Bock).
VHS: S17791. $19.98.
Mikio Naruse, Japan, 1954, 101 mins.

Lone Wolf and Cub— Baby Cart at the River Styx
More Samurai graphic violence and sex in this journey of terror along a river of blood! The Yagyu clan has murdered Ogami Itto's wife and stripped him of his position of Official Shogunate Second. Now Ogami Itto and his son Daigoro wander the countryside as the hired assassins known as Lone Wolf and Cub, bent on the desire for revenge upon the Yagyu. Japanese with English subtitles.
VHS: S30767. $29.95.
Misumi Kenji, Japan, 81 mins.

Lone Wolf and Cub—Baby Cart in Peril
Ogami Itto faces his greatest challenge yet: he has been hired to kill Oyuki, tattooed mistress of the martial arts. While searching for Oyuki, Daigor and Itto are separated and Daigor meets Yagyu Gunbei, master swordsman and loser of the duel which won Ogami his position as chief executioner. A duel between the Lone Wolf and his nemesis ensues. Bound by his own code, Ogami must carry out his mission. Japanese with English subtitles.
VHS: S31089. $29.95.
Laser: LD76148. $39.95.
Misumi Kenji, Japan, 81 mins.

Lone Wolf and Cub— Baby Cart in the Land of Demons
Retainers of the Kuroda Clan seek out Ogami Itto, the former Shogunite executioner, to enlist his aid in saving the Clan. Even though the retired Kuroda's true successor is his son, Lord Matsumaru, Kuroda is so besotted with his mistress that he is determined to have her daughter succeed him, passing off the daughter as a boy. Jikei, a high priest Shogunate spy, has been entrusted with Kuroda's plan. Only Ogami has the skill to kill him. Widescreen collector's edition. Japanese with English subtitles.
VHS: S31555. $29.95.
Laser: LD76211. $39.95.
Misumi Kenji, Japan, 1973, 89 mins.

Lone Wolf and Cub—Baby Cart to Hades
Ogami Itto, the official shogunate executioner, is falsely acused of treason and his wife is murdered by the evil Yagyu clan. He now travels the countryside of Japan with his infant son Daigoro accepting jobs as the paid assassins called "Lone Wolf and Cub." He cares for only one thing besides his son: revenge. Based on the successful comic book series. With Wakiyama Tomisaburo as Ogami Itto. "…stunning visual ballet of violence and bloodletting" (Leonard Maltin). Japanese with English subtitles.
VHS: S30478. $29.95.
Misumi Kenji, Japan, 1972, 83 mins.

Lone Wolf and Cub— Sword of Vengeance
As they stalk the countryside of Japan, Ogami gives his infant son Daigoro a terrible choice between a red ball and a sword. To choose the ball means that Daigoro will join his mother in the Void; to choose the sword means he will join his Ronin father, a samurai without a master, in a blood-soaked journey that must end in revenge and death.
VHS: S30865. $29.95.
Laser: LD76079. $39.95.
Misumi Kenji, Japan, 83 mins.

Lone Wolf and Cub: White Heaven and Hell
The Samurai Cinema Saga continues as Yagyu Retsudo, Lord of the Shadow-Yagyu Clan, who framed Ogami Itto, dispatches his daughter Kaoru to face the Lone Wolf and Cub. Widescreen collector's edition. Japanese with English subtitles.
VHS: S31796. $29.95.
Laser: LD76310. $39.95.
Kuroda Yoshiyuki, Japan, 1973, 84 mins.

Maborosi
Acclaimed as one of the finest Japanese films of the decade, Hirokazu Kore-eda's *Maborosi* is a story of great love, inexplicable loss and, at last, hope and regeneration, in which a beautiful young mother struggles to come to terms with the sudden loss of her husband in a remote village on the wild, untamed sea of Japan. Winner, Best Film, Chicago International Film Festival. Japanese with English subtitles.
VHS: S34140. $89.95.
Hirokazu Kore-eda, Japan, 1995, 110 mins.

Masseur Ichi Enters Again
Zatoichi, the blind masseur and gambler, has a chance meeting with master swordsman Yajuro Banno, his former master. Delighted to see his former pupil, Banno invites him to visit his home, which he shares with his sister, Yayoi, who quickly falls in love with the kind and gentle Ichi, much to Banno's chagrin. Things turn out to be not what they seem as Banno is discovered to be involved in a kidnapping and extortion plot. Torn between love and justice, will Ichi's plans of marriage succeed or must he risk all to challenge his old friend and teacher to a duel to the death? Japanese with English subtitles.
VHS: S28624. $59.95.
Tokuzo Tanaka, Japan, 1963, 91 mins.

Masseur Ichi, The Fugitive (Zato Ichi Kyojotabi)
In this martial arts extravaganza the samurai Zato Ichi finds himself trapped between the charms of an old love and his never-ending struggle for survival. Someone has placed a bounty on his head. Japanese with English subtitles.
VHS: S26528. $59.95.
Kimoyoshi Yada, Japan, 1963, 86 mins.

A Matched Set of Razors
All three *Razor* films in one complete widescreen collector's edition. Includes *Sword of Justice, The Snare* and *Who's Got the Gold*. Japanese with English subtitles.
VHS: S31799. $80.00.

Mistress
A deeply moving exploration of love, betrayal and destiny. Japanese with English subtitles.
VHS: S00863. $19.95.
Shiro Toyoda, Japan, 1953, 106 mins.

The Mystery of Rampo
A famous mystery writer continually pushes the bounds of taste with his fiction in this atmospheric thriller from Japan which is filled with eroticism and suspense. As one of the writer's characters suddenly comes to life, he is pushed into ever more surreal and dangerous situations. Japanese with English subtitles.
VHS: S26861. $19.98.
Kazuyoshi Okuyama, Japan, 1994, 101 mins.

Nanami, First Love
A story of passionate desire and psychological turbulence, a troubled young man abandoned early by his mother seeks the love of a nude model and prostitute, Nanami. Fresh and intriguing visuals, creative camera angles and elaborate montage make for a powerful experience. Japanese with English subtitles.
VHS: S02170. $29.95.
Susumu Hani, Japan, 1968, 104 mins.

Narayama Bushi-ko
An old legend, *The Ballad of Narayama*, inspired this moving drama about two elderly people struggling against a harsh but ingrained tradition. Their village home is poor, and as a consequence, upon reaching the age of 70 inhabitants are expected to retreat to an exposed mountain top to meet the gods of Narayama. This prize-winning film combines Kabuki theater with film techniques to render a complex view of fate, duty and despair. Japanese with English subtitles.
VHS: S29517. $79.95.
Keisuke Kinoshita, Japan, 1958, 97 mins.

Okoge
Misa Shimuzu gives a great performance as the lead character Sayoko, a young women who becomes entwined with two gay men having an affair. The lovers, played by Takehiro Murata and Takeo Nakahara, cannot work out their differences despite the best efforts of Sayoko. It is a story that catalogs the sexual politics of contemporary Japan without moralizing. Japanese with English subtitles.
VHS: S20824. $79.95.
Takehiro Nakajima, Japan, 1992, 120 mins.

Onibaba
A stylish Japanese ghost tale, set in medieval Japan. A peasant woman and her daughter manage an existence by impersonating demons—sexually luring soldiers away from their comrades and murdering them. A warrior manages to save his life by seducing the daughter, but the mother's sorcery conjures up a hideous revenge. Mixing graphic violence with sex, *Onibaba* is an exotic, terrifying, supernatural fantasy. Japanese with English subtitles.
VHS: S08691. $29.95.
Laser: LD76985. $49.95.
Kaneto Shindo, Japan, 1964, 103 mins.

A Pack of Wolves
All six *Lone Wolf and Cub* films are collected on this AnimEigo Spine Scene design set. Includes *Sword of Vengeance, Baby Cart at the River Styx, Baby Cart to Hades, Baby Cart in Peril* and *Baby Cart in the Land of Demons*. Widescreen collector's edition. Japanese with English subtitles.
VHS: S31798. $160.00.
Japan

A Page of Madness
Made in 1926 and rediscovered in 1971, this rare Japanese silent film is an hallucinatory study of a janitor of an asylum who attempts to release his wife, who is an inmate there, having been committed after trying to kill herself and her baby. This amazing film by the great Japanese film pioneer Kinugasa relies entirely on visual effects to tell its story. Superimpositions, extreme camera angles and jarring close-ups tell the tale from the janitor's point of view.
VHS: S30189. $24.95.
Teinosuke Kinugasa, Japan, 1926, 75 mins.

The Razor—Sword of Justice
The pulsing '70s soundtrack, soft-core S&M, politically incorrect and misogynist themes and copious buckets of blood make this the most over-the-top Samurai series ever made. Itami "The Razor" Hanzo is the baddest cop in Edo during the late 1800s. His wits are as sharp as his sword and his martial arts skills rival the size of his (ahem) "jurisdiction." He ferrets out corruption high and low and delivers what passes for justice in Edo during the Shogunate period of Japan. A wonderfully guilty pleasure. Japanese with English subtitles.
VHS: S30479. $29.95.
Misumi Kenji, Japan, 1972, 90 mins.

The Razor—The Snare

Sex and violence abound in this Samurai series which warns, "may create feelings of male inadequacy." While investigating the death of a girl during an illegal abortion, Cop Hanzo "Razor" Itami discovers an orgy of wealthy perverts at a convent run by a priestess named Nyokaini. With Katsu Shintaro *(Zatoichi)*, Sato Kel, Nishimura Akira, Kurosawa Toshio and Ineno Kazuko. Japanese with English subtitles.

VHS: S30766. $29.95.

Masumara Yasuzo, Japan, 89 mins.

The Razor—Who's Got the Gold

Hanzo Itami the Edo cop investigates reports of a ghost near the castle moat. Itami captures the woman masquerading as the ghost, who had been hired to scare off anyone who might stumble upon a cache of newly minted gold hidden in the moat, that had been stolen from the Shogunate treasury. Widescreen collector's edition. Japanese with English subtitles.

VHS: S31556. $29.95.
Laser: LD76245. $39.95.

Inyoue Yoshio, Japan, 1974, 84 mins.

Red Lion

The legend returns: Toshiro Mifune is the Red Lion, who, together with his scarlet mane, returns to his village in grand style only to discover that he is the "great one" who will liberate his followers from an oppressive government. With Shima Iwashita. Letterboxed. Japanese with English subtitles.

VHS: S01099. $29.95.

Kihachi Okamoto, Japan, 1969, 115 mins.

Rikisha-Man

A classic film of unrequited love, starring Toshiro Mifune as a feisty rikisha puller who helps raise a young boy after the father has died, loving the boy's mother from a distance that class cannot cross. Winner of the Venice Film Festival Grand Prize. Japanese dialog with English subtitles.

VHS: S02158. $59.95.

Hiroshi Inagaki, Japan, 1958, 105 mins.

Samurai Assassin

Acclaimed by many critics to be the greatest Samurai film of them all, *Samurai Assassin* stars the incomparable Toshiro Mifune as Shino Tsuruchiyo, a samurai whose family stands to lose everything if the plans for the Meiji Restoration proceed. To save his family, he joins forces with the powerful Mito clan and plots to assassinate Lord Ii, one of the Emperor's most trusted advisers. Only too late does he learn that he is in fact Lord Ii'sillegitimate son. Japanese with English subtitles. Widescreen collector's edition.

VHS: S35010. $29.95.

Okamoto Kihachi, Japan, 1965, 122 mins.

Samurai Banners

This epic adventure story, set against the background of great conflict, is based on a best-selling historical novel. Yamamoto Kansuze (Toshiro Mifune, >I>Rashomon) is a fearsome warrior who has risen to the position of Clan Chamberlain through trickery and deceit, but he learns the meaning of honor when he and his lord, Takeda, fall in love with the same woman. One of Mifune's greatest films. Japanese with English subtitles.

VHS: S33002. $34.95.
Laser: LD76426. $59.95.

Hiroshi Inagaki, Japan, 1969, 132 mins.

Samurai I

The first part of Hiroshi Inagaki's trilogy about Japan's most notorious 17th century swordfighter, Mushashi Miyamoto (Toshiro Mifune), details his odyssey from farmer to disaffected killer. Having fought on the losing side during the civil war, he returns as a manic outlaw caught between his feelings for a beautiful village girl and a sympathetic Buddhist priest. "The beauty of wooded sequences, several mass battle scenes and other settings is extraordinary" *(Variety)*. With Rentaro Mikuni, Karuo Yashigusa and Koji Tsurato. Japanese with English subtitles.

VHS: S18905. $29.95.
Laser: LD76789. $49.95.
DVD: DV60339. $29.95.

Hiroshi Inagaki, Japan, 1955, 92 mins.

Samurai II

In the second part, Miyamoto's technical skills are perfected and his transformation to savage warrior is complete. He undergoes a mythic spiritual quest for inner harmony, disrupted by the presence of a rival samurai and the loss of the woman he loved. With Toshiro Mifune, Koji Tsurata and Sachio Sakai. Japanese with English subtitles.

VHS: S18906. $29.95.
Laser: LD76790. $49.95.
DVD: DV60340. $29.95.

Hiroshi Inagaki, Japan, 1955, 102 mins.

Samurai III

In the final part of this samurai trilogy, Miyamoto resolves the personal and professional tensions in his life, confronting the emotional pain of the two women who love him and the roguish swordsman who challenges his domain. With Toshiro Mifune, Koji Tsuruta, Kaoru Uashigusa and Takashi Shimura. Japanese with English subtitles.

VHS: S18907. $29.95.
Laser: LD76791. $49.95.
DVD: DV60341. $29.95.

Hiroshi Inagaki, Japan, 1956, 105 mins.

Samurai Rebellion

This samurai classic, set in 18th-century Japan, combines great acting and thrilling action with thoughtful writing and direction. The magnificent Toshiro Mifune (Seven Samurai, The Samurai Trilogy) stars as Isaburo, a renowned swordsman who takes a heroic but deadly stand for individual freedom. Isaburo is the essence of samurai loyalty until his daughter-in-law is commandeered as mistress for his overlord. The injustice moves him toward a revolt he can never win. Kobayashi creates a bloody climax raging with power and emotion.

VHS: S32163. $29.95.

Masaki Kobayashi, Japan, 1967, 121 mins.

Samurai Trilogy: Complete Set

Three-tape set of *Samurai I, II* and *III*.

VHS: S18908. $69.95.

Shadow of China

A sweeping epic of one man's ascent to power and eventual fall from grace, *Shadow of China* tells the story of a mysterious young tycoon who fights desperately to seize control of Hong Kong—and to hide a past that could destroy him and his empire. Starring John Lone, Sammi Davis, and Vivian Wu, this film, based on the best-selling Japanese novel *Snakehead*, is the English-language film debut by acclaimed Japanese director Mitsuo Yanagimachi. Filmed on location in Hong Kong and Japan. "Elegant, seductive…a modern-day *Casablanca*" (Kevin Thomas, L.A. Times).

VHS: S15074. $9.98.

Mitsuo Yanagimachi, Japan/USA, 1991

Shall We Dance?

Masayuki Suo's charming comedy about Shohei Sugiyama (Koji Yakusyo), a married, middle-aged, workaholic accountant who becomes obsessed with a sad and beautiful dance instructor (Tamiyo Kusakari) he spies through the window of a dance studio. His dull life takes a funny turn when he signs up for ballroom dancing lessons to try to meet the mysterious woman and instead is assigned a plump, middle-aged instructor. But is the mystery woman, as his instructor warns, "all the sweeter when viewed from afar"? Japanese with English subtitles.

VHS: S33346. $103.99.
Laser: LD76819. $39.99.

Masayuki Suo, Japan, 1996, 119 mins.

She and He

Susumu Hani's first attempt to deal with the theme of women's oppression was this Antonioniesque melodrama set in a sterile high rise complex. A woman resident becomes discontent with the empty life she leads with her husband and seeks to make contact with the outside world, so that she may express her inner feelings, which have no outlet within the marriage. When she finally finds a means of expression, her husband's discontent leads to tragedy. A moving story of spiritual rebirth and loss. Japanese with English subtitles.

VHS: S15377. $39.95.

Susumu Hani, Japan, 1963, 110 mins.

The Silk Road

A lavish Japanese epic about warring factions and sacred scrolls in ancient China. More than 100,000 extras were used in the grand scale battle scenes shot on location in the People's Republic of China. Zao Xingte, a failed civil servant, goes west to the kingdom of Xixia, where he is entrusted with a great task that involves a spoiled princess and protecting the hidden library of sacred scriptures. With Koichi Sako, Toshiyuki Nishida and Anna Nakagawa.

VHS: S16712. $89.95.
Laser: LD75258. $34.98.

Junya Sato, Japan, 1988, 99 mins.

Sleepy Eyes of Death—Full Circle Killing

An eerie decapitation on a shadowy street corner sets the stage for the next adventure of the half-breed master swordsman Nemuri Kyoshiro, known as The Sleepy Eyes of Death. Widescreen collector's edition. Japanese with English subtitles.

VHS: S31797. $29.95.
Laser: LD76311. $39.95.

Kimiyoshi Yasuda, Japan, 85 mins.

Sleepy Eyes of Death—Sword of Adventure

While traveling, Nemuri, the son of a Japanese noblewoman and the Christian missionary who raped her, witnesses the public denuding of a young woman. Nemuri befriends an old man who has the duty of taking care of the Shogun's frivolous daughter, Takahime. Nemuri soon finds himself drugged and captured, his destiny to be a sexual toy for the pleasure of the depraved Takahime. Deadly martial arts maneuvers keep the action pumping. Japanese with English subtitles. Letterboxed. 83 mins.

VHS: S31090. $29.95.
Laser: LD76149. $39.95.

Sleepy Eyes of Death—Sword of Fire

Kyoshiro's blazing sword is put to the ultimate test when he gets embroiled in a plot to kill an innocent girl who's posing as a washerwoman. With the help of some unorthodox allies, Kyoshiro is able to deal out his ironic brand of justice to the mob of fanatics who want her dead. Japanese with English subtitles. Widescreen collector's edition.

VHS: S35009. $29.95.

Kenji Misumi, Japan, 1967, 83 mins.

Sleepy Eyes of Death—The Chinese Jade

Nemuri Kyoshiro is a deadly samurai who has no past and wants no future. After disposing of six ambushers, their master, Lord Maeda, sends his ward to seduce him and set him against his enemy, who is trying to protect a document that would cause the downfall of Maeda's clan. Kyoshiro must find a man who is already dead and get him to reveal the secret of the "Chinese Jade." From the novel by Shibata Renzaburo. Widescreen collector's edition. Japanese with English subtitles.

VHS: S30249. $29.95.
Laser: LD76001. $39.95.

Tokuzo Tanaka, Japan, 1963, 82 mins.

Snow Country

Directed by Shiro Toyoda, *Snow Country* focuses on the conflict between Komako, a woman living in the region of northwest Honshu known as the snow country, and Shimamura, a painter in the Nihonga style who feels out of place in Tokyo and wants to escape from the capital, where he only feels alienation. Based on the novel by the same name, *Snow Country* features Ryo Ikebe and Keoko Kishi. Japanese with English subtitles.

VHS: S08518. $29.95.

Shiro Toyoda, Japan, 1967, 144 mins.

The Street Fighter

Sonny Chiba is the martial arts action hero who started the whole outrageous martial arts craze, and this is the film that began his career. He is a violent and ruthless opponent to Japan's evil Yakuza gangs and he will go to any extreme to win. In this classic film he throws someone out of a window, emasculates a rapist, and rips the throat out of an opponent. Includes the original theatrical trailers. Letterboxed. Dubbed in English.

VHS: S27811. $19.98.

Sakae Ozawa, Japan, 1975, 91 mins.

Street Fighter II, Vol. 10—Fight to the Finish, Final Round

This dark, intense, killer animated story continues the journey of young martial artists Ken, Ryu and Chun Li to seek out other street fighters in an effort to improve their skills. 70 mins.

Dubbed.
VHS: S33640. $19.95.
Subtitled.
VHS: S33641. $24.95.

Summer Vacation: 1999

Romantic and beautifully realized, this film tells the story of four boys who experience the adolescent birth pangs of romantic love, sexual awareness and jealousy. Left behind at boarding school during their vacation, the teenagers' summer idyll is disrupted by the arrival of another youth who seems to reincarnate a dead friend. Delicate and provocative, Kaneko's film creates a haunting image of youth suspended between innocence and experience, androgyny and sexual maturity. Japanese with English subtitles.

VHS: S13917. $69.95.

Shusuke Kaneko, Japan, 1988, 90 mins.

Sure Death

In this live-action adventure, Nakamura Mondo, a bumbling constable, is in fact the secret leader of one of several assassination groups in Edo. In his public role, he is investigating a series of freak murders, in which the victims are all themselves assassins. But another group of assassins wants to literally eliminate the competition. Japanese with English subtitles. Widescreen.

VHS: S33327. $29.95.
Laser: LD76760. $39.95.
Sadanaga Masahiso, Japan, 1984, 123 mins.

The Sword of Doom

The legendary Japanese actor and martial artist Toshiro Mifune stars as the instructor of a brash and revenge-bent young Samurai, played by Tatsuya Nakadai. This action-adventure from Toho Films is presented in Japanese with English subtitles. B&W.

VHS: S03635. $29.95.
Laser: Widescreen. **LD75411. $49.95.**
Kihachi Okamoto, Japan, 1967, 120 mins.

Tetsuo: The Iron Man

A post-punk, Japanese film about a man attacked by a feral woman with a metal hand and his bizarre mutation into a perverse combination of man and machine. It's like Godard remaking *Blue Velvet*. With Tomoroh Taguchi, Nobu Kanaoka and Shinya Tsukamoto. Japanese with English subtitles.

VHS: S18410. $19.98.
Shinya Tsukamoto, Japan, 1989, 67 mins.

Tetsuo II: Body Hammer

This Japanese answer to *Blade Runner* and *The Terminator* is a stunning follow-up to the cult classic *Tetsuo: The Iron Man, Body Hammer*. The action in this post-industrial world centers around a stereotypical Tokyo businessman whose body transforms into a gun when seized by his own uncontrollable rage. He is rivaled by "the Guy" (played by director Shinya Tsukamoto), who is the leader of a gang of indoctrinated street thugs. "A delirious ride into surreal and subversive territory. Should not be missed by any sci-fi or horror fan" (Clive Barker). Japanese with English subtitles.

VHS: S32698. $19.95.
Shinya Tsukamoto, Japan, 1997, 83 mins.

Tokyo Decadence

Japanese novelist and filmmaker Ryu Murakami adapts his novel *Topaz*, about a prostitute's (Miho Nikaido) search for redemption. Ai falls under the spell of a charismatic dominatrix and tries desperately to reverse her slide into cocaine dependency and sexual slavery. "Murakami adeptly throws us off balance, with deadpan black humor and a complex politic involving the notion of 'wealth without pride'" (Toronto Film Festival). With Sayoko Amano, Tenmei Kanou and Masahiko Shimada. Japanese with English subtitles.

VHS: S19176. $29.95.
Ryu Murakami, Japan, 1991, 112 mins.

Tokyo Drifter

With its visual daring and breathless action, *Tokyo Drifter* represents the best of Suzuki's outrageously inventive *yazuka* films. The conventional story—about a gangster who honors the old code long after it has been abandoned by the new mob—spins deliriously out of control. Hunted by mobsters and his own bosses, the pop-idol hero pouts, poses and sings through a mad chase across Japan. Disordered, violent and irreverent, *Tokyo Drifter* succeeds marvelously as a thriller and a parody. Japanese with English subtitles. "A jaw-dropping, eye-popping fantasia. Astonishes with style even as it hammers home points about the struggle for individualism" *(LA Weekly)*. Japanese with English subtitles. Letterboxed.

VHS: S32969. $29.95.
Seijun Suzuki, Japan, 1966, 83 mins.

Tokyo Fist

From Shinya Tsuamaoto, the director of *Tetsuo II*, this psycho-kinetic shocker explores a love triangle. Tsuamaoto plays insurance salesman Tsuda, whose life with his fiancee, Hizuru, is turned upside down when he meets his old high school classmate, Takuji, a boxing pro with problems. Bloody, convulsive and darkly comedic. "More power, anger, truth than *Raging Bull*." Japanese with English subtitles.

VHS: S34551. $19.95.
Shinya Tsukamoto, Japan, 1995, 85 mins.

Traffic Jam

A young Tokyo couple are at the center of this dark, comic satire. They take their children to visit the husband's faraway parents, but the long road trip proves to be filled with disastrous incidents. Their journey becomes a metaphor for the gap between young Japanese people and their ancestral roots. Japanese with English subtitles.

VHS: S24731. $29.95.
Mitsuo Kurotsuchi, Japan, 1991, 108 mins.

Traitors of the Blue Castle

Story of samurai plots against the Shogun features action and swordplay. 1958. 100 minutes. Japanese with English subtitles.

VHS: S03004. $59.95.

Village of Dreams

Director Yoichi Higashi masterfully evokes the moods of childhood in the story of identical twin brothers who recall the summer of 1948, when they were eight years old and their Japanese village was a place full of wonder and magic. A visually ravishing hymn to the joys and mysteries of childhood. "Magical! Beautiful! Captures the rhythm and moods of childhood with an intensity that transports you back in time" *(New York Times)*. Japanese with English subtitles. Letterboxed.

VHS: S34722. $89.95.
Yoichi Higashi, Japan, 1995, 112 mins.

When a Woman Ascends the Stairs

Hideko Takamine and Tatsuya Nakadai star in this beautiful, ornate drama about a Ginza bar hostess on the eve of her 30th birthday. The films of Japanese master Mikio Naruse were virtually unknown in the United States until the writings of Donald Ritchie and Audie Bock heralded his contributions as the equal of Kurosawa, Ozu or Mizoguchi.

VHS: S17792. $19.98.
Mikio Naruse, Japan, 1960, 110 mins.

Zatoichi Challenged!

Wandering masseur and swordsman Zatoichi shares a room in an inn with a gravely ill woman and her young son. In her dying breath she pleads with Zatoichi to take her son to his father in Maebara. The boy's father is discovered to be confined and forced by a local gangster to work in an illegal trade. A mysterious master swordsman stands in the way of his rescue. Will Zatoichi risk his life for the helpless boy and his innocent father? Served as the inspiration for *Blind Fury*, starring Rutger Hauer. Japanese with English subtitles.

VHS: S28622. $19.95.
Kenji Misumi, Japan, 1967, 187 mins.

Zatoichi: Masseur Ichi and a Chest of Gold

Zatoichi, the blind gambler and masseur, is caught in a cross-fire of greed and ambition and must clear his name and his long-time friend, the benevolent *yakuza* chief, who was framed in a gold robbery. Japanese with English subtitles.

VHS: S17066. $19.95.
Kazuo Ikehiro, Japan, 1964, 83 mins.

Zatoichi: Masseur Ichi on the Road

As yakuza gangster bosses feud, Ichi ignores their pleas for help because he feels compelled to help a young rich girl on the run. She accidentally injured a powerful lord when he tried to rape her. Her passage is further endangered as rival gangs hope to capture her for ransom. Japanese with English subtitles. 1964, 85 mins.

VHS: S20857. $59.95.

Zatoichi: The Blind Swordsman and the Chess Expert

A tale of friendship, bravery and discipline, this work details the further adventures of Zatoichi, who befriends a master chess player. Zatoichi gambles all of his money to pay for the medical services of a young woman wounded in a sword fight with Japanese gangsters attempting to rob them. Japanese with English subtitles.

VHS: S17067. $19.95.
Kenji Misumi, Japan, 1965, 87 mins.

Zatoichi: The Blind Swordsman and the Fugitives

This samurai drama pits Zatoichi (Shintaro Katsu) against a band of ruffian outlaws. Zatoichi is caught in a sinister web of torture and extortion as local bandits and gangs brutalize the countryside. "The action simply takes your breath away with its speed, surprises and detail" *(The Hawaii Herald)*. With Yumiko Nogawa, Kayo Mikimoto and Kyosuke Machida. Japanese with English subtitles.

VHS: S18911. $59.95.
Kimiyoshi Yasuda, Japan, 1968, 82 mins.

Zatoichi: The Blind Swordsman Samaritan

The fight for justice takes on a personal dimension for the famed blind swordsman when his sister Osode sells herself to pay off her brother's gambling debt. This tragic turn of events is the result of an evil plot, designed by a yakuza boss who desires the charming Osode. Zatoichi's crusade for justice has now become a matter of his own family's honor. Japanese with English subtitles. 1968, 84 mins.

VHS: S20856. $59.95.

Zatoichi: The Blind Swordsman's Vengeance

Zatoichi (Shintaro Katsu) defends a dying man against a group of young gangsters, when he's entangled in a plan to return some money to an isolated village, now overtaken by a band of guerrillas who must be neutralized. With Shigeru Amachi, Mayumi Ogawa, and Kei Sato. Japanese with English subtitles.

VHS: S17068. $59.95.
Tokuzo Tanaka, Japan, 1966, 83 mins.

Zatoichi: The Life and Opinion of Masseur Ichi

Zatoichi is drawn into an epic revenge match between ruthless gangs in the province Shimosa. When one of the lords tries to enlist Zatoichi's services, the other gang boss hires a savage killer. With Masayo Mari, Ryuzo Shimada, Gen Mitamura and Shigeru Amachi. Japanese with English subtitles.

VHS: S18909. $59.95.
Kenji Misumi, Japan, 1962, 96 mins.

Zatoichi: The Return of Masseur Ichi

Masseur Ichi uncovers the crucial secret behind a distinguished lord whom he is hired to massage. Realizing the gravity of the situation, the lord's vassal seeks to silence the blind and seemingly defenseless Ichi. As usual, those who would underestimate this hero pay dearly. Japanese with English subtitles. 1962, 73 mins.

VHS: S20858. $59.95.

Zatoichi: Zatoichi's Flashing Sword

Fleeing brutal gangsters, Zatoichi is embroiled in a feud between completing yakuza bosses. He declares his allegiance to the benevolent Tsumugi and Yasu responds by raising the stakes, deploying bribery, extortion and murder to gain control of a strategically important river. With Naoko Kubo, Mayumi Nagisa, Ryutaro Gomi and Yutaka Nakamura. Japanese with English subtitles.

VHS: S18910. $59.95.
Kazuo Ikehiro, Japan, 1964, 82 mins.

Zero Woman

Extreme sex, guns and violence push the limits in this actioner. Special Agent Rei, code name Zero, is beautiful, strong, seductive and deadly. When the witness of a brutal crime is kidnapped by the Yazuka as soon as Rei is assigned to watch over her, all hell breaks loose as Rei takes on the lethal Japanese mob. Japanese with English subtitles. Widescreen. 90 mins.

VHS: S34693. $29.95.

JUZO ITAMI

The Funeral

Juzo Itami's breakthrough Japanese film is a black comedy concerning the rivalries and hypocrisies of a contemporary Japanese family which is called to the funeral of their father. Itami deftly satirizes contemporary Japanese mores and idiosyncracies. Japanese with English subtitles.

VHS: S07104. $19.98.
Juzo Itami, Japan, 1986, 112 mins.

Minbo—Or the Gentle Art of Japanese Extortion

Juzo Itami turns his acid humor to Japan's infamous institution—the Yakuza gangs—in this film about a courageous attorney who rallies all of the employees at a hotel in an effort to resist the Yakuza blackmail. After the film was completed, thugs viciously attacked the director, forcing him to go into hiding. A brilliant, satirical look at the underbelly of Japanese modern life. Japanese with English subtitles.

VHS: S26090. $29.95.
Juzo Itami, Japan, 1994, 123 mins.

Tampopo

One of the funniest, most enjoyable, satirical comedies is this treasure of a movie the plot of which, loosely, concerns the quest for the perfect Japanese noodle. A mixed-bag of noodle-obsessed men help the heroine of *Tampopo* run the best noodle restaurant in Tokyo, a plan which involves a lot of hilarious mishaps. Japanese with English subtitles.

VHS: S07101. $29.98.
Juzo Itami, Japan, 1987, 114 mins.

Taxing Woman

Juzo Itami's satiric comedy of ambition, greed and the battle of the sexes. A disarming and dedicated woman tax collector meets her match in a millionaire "love hotel" tycoon and tax-evader extraordinaire. Winner of nine Japanese Academy Awards. Japanese with English subtitles.

VHS: S08689. $19.98.
Laser: LD70259. $49.95.
Juzo Itami, Japan, 1987, 127 mins.

A Taxing Woman's Return

In this rousing follow-up to his 1987 hit, *A Taxing Woman*, Juzo Itami brings back his resourceful and charming heroine, tax inspector Ryoko Itakura (described by Vincent Canby of *The New York Times* as "a far more endearing crime buster than Batman") for another battle of wits against the fat cats and swindlers who thrive in Japan's booming economy. Japanese with English subtitles.

VHS: S12195. $29.95.
Juzo Itami, Japan, 1989, 127 mins.

SHOHEI IMAMURA

The Ballad of Narayama

Winner of the Grand Prize at the 1983 Cannes Film Festival, *The Ballad of Narayama* is based on one of the most astonishing of all Japanese legends. A century ago in a remote mountain village, local custom dictated that when a person reached 70 years of age, he was taken to Mount Narayama to die. A brilliant film from director Imamura that delivers a vigorous and beautiful affirmation of family, life and death. "A masterpiece of Japanese Cinema to stand beside *Ugetsu, Tokyo Story,* or *The Seven Samurai*" (M. Wilmington *LA Weekly*). Japanese with English subtitles.

VHS: S14498. $29.95.
Shohei Imamura, Japan, 1983, 129 mins.

Black Rain

A somber, restrained, and very moving story detailing ten years in the life of a family which survived the nuclear bombing of Hiroshima—and the ways in which their bodies and souls were poisoned by the fallout. Filled with haunting images. Japanese with English subtitles. Letterbox format.

VHS: S14068. $19.98.
Shohei Imamura, Japan, 1988, 123 mins.

Eijanaika

Called an "historical documentary", *Eijanaika* is "a sprawling, superb-looking period piece charged with Imamura's characteristically fevered eroticism and underplayed black humor. As spectacle, it's stunning in its dynamism and the last half-hour presents one of the most libidinal depictions of a mass uprising since Eisenstein restaged the storming of the Winter Palace. As in *Vengeance Is Mine*, Imamura imbues the cruelty with virtuoso ferocity and an appalling, visionary beauty" (J. Hoberman, *Village Voice*). Japanese with English subtitles.

VHS: S12205. $79.95.
Shohei Imamura, Japan, 1981, 151 mins.

Vengeance Is Mine

One of the most strikingly original films of the modern cinema, *Vengeance Is Mine* is an "eclectically horrifying portrait of a psychopathic criminal named Iwao Enokizo...(the film) makes every other film on the *In Cold Blood* theme look like child's play," wrote Tom Allen in *The Village Voice*. Enokizu becomes suspect in the murder of two men who work for the government tobacco monopoly. A nationwide dragnet is set up to capture him, but for 78 days he travels throughout Japan committing fraud, cheating women and taking numerous lives. Japanese with English subtitles.

VHS: S09959. $29.95.
Laser: CAV. **LD71391. $89.95.**
Shohei Imamura, Japan, 1979, 112 mins.

NAGISA OSHIMA

Cruel Story of Youth

Oshima's second feature conveys the pent-up sexuality and disillusionment among Japan's postwar generation. Two lovers live outside the boundaries of their society, performing shakedowns on unsuspecting middle-aged men and speeding away on the angry boy's gleaming motorcycle with the goods. With seemingly disconnected details and stark framings, Oshima creates an atmosphere akin to the French New Wave. Japanese with English subtitles.

VHS: S16696. $29.95.
Nagisa Oshima, Japan, 1960, 96 mins.

Empire of Passion (aka In the Realm of Passion)

Oshima follows up his notorious *In the Realm of the Senses* with the story of a peasant woman who, with the help of her lover, kills her husband. Their future hopes wither, however, when the injured party returns from the dead to haunt and endlessly torment them. This sad tale of two lovers consumed by the very passion that they seek is presented to the viewer amidst a somber landscape of embattled moods and emotions, tragic cruelty and overwhelming calm—and the forceful performances and superb photography of this gripping film are unified under Oshima's remarkable lyrical style. *Empire of Passion* earned him the award of Best Director at the 1978 Cannes Film Festival. Starring Kazuko Yoshiyuki, Tatsuya Fuji and Takuzo Kawatani. Japanese with yellow English subtitles.

VHS: S14574. $19.98.
Nagisa Oshima, Japan, 1978, 110 mins.

In the Realm of the Senses

A scandal when it was seized by the New York customs and refused entry into the United States, and the sensation of the New York Film Festival, *In the Realm of the Senses* is, in the words of the Los *Angeles Times*, "probably the most thoughtful work of and on eroticism ever created." Explicit in its depiction of sex, and a film about the literally consuming passions of two people, the film is most infamous for its final castration sequence. Japanese with English subtitles.

VHS: S12222. $19.98.
Nagisa Oshima, Japan, 1971, 100 mins.

Max Mon Amour

A strange sexual farce, this film shows an unhappy housewife who finds an uncomplicated love in the arms of someone new. Only this strong, silent lover is an ape, a chimpanzee to be more specific. The woman's husband, Higgins the diplomat, is quite understanding and even invites the chimp to move in. It's a comedy of manners with a twist. French with English subtitles.

VHS: S20740. $89.95.
Nagisa Oshima, France, 1986, 94 mins.

Merry Christmas Mr. Lawrence

David Bowie delivers a strong performance in Nagisa Oshima's *(In the Realm of the Senses)* apocalyptic tale of a Japanese prison camp during World War II. The film also features To Conti and Ryuichi Sakamoto. English dialog.

VHS: S00850. $29.98.
Nagisa Oshima, Japan/Australia, 1983, 124 mins.

The Sun's Burial

Oshima's most blatantly amoral and extravagantly violent version of the juvenile delinquency drama, set in a world of rival teenage gangs, pimps and prostitutes. Set in a hellish Osaka where an exquisitely cruel femme fatale vies for control of the area's most profitable business with the gangs. Japanese with English subtitles.

VHS: S20596. $29.95.
Nagisa Oshima, Japan, 1960, 87 mins.

Violence at Noon

After investigating the case history of a rapist, Nagisa Oshima created one of the most effective crime films while transcending the genre. The story unfolds through the recollections of two women—the criminal's wife and one of his victims-strangely united in an effort to protect the rapist from capture. Their despair is linked to that of the rapist himself, and ultimately to the failure of the socialist movement in postwar Japan. Oshima masterfully demonstrates the ways in which the compulsion to crime and self-destruction reflects the pathology of the society in which the criminal and victim lives. With Saeda Kawaguchi, Akiko Koyama, Kei Sato and Matsuhiro Toura. Japanese with English subtitles.

VHS: S16037. $79.95.
Nagisa Oshima, Japan, 1966, 100 mins.

KON ICHIKAWA

An Actor's Revenge

A female impersonator in the Kabuki tradition seeks revenge against the villains who caused his parent's death. This complex tale, set in 19th-century Japan, involves numerous plot twists as it blurs the distinctions between illusion and reality. Japanese with English subtitles.

VHS: S20593. $29.95.
Kon Ichikawa, Japan, 1963, 114 mins.

Being Two Isn't Easy

A melancholy work about the joys and mysteries of life as experienced by a two-year-old boy, Taro. Taro is thunderstruck by the small (the climbing of stairs) and the significant (space travel). Ichikawa evokes an impressionistic picture of daily life and inter-family conflicts. The film "catches the fantasy and wonder with which a child must gaze" *(Variety)*. With Fujko Yamamoto, Eiji Funakoshi and Hiroo Suzuki. Japanese with English subtitles.

VHS: S20416. $19.95.
Kon Ichikawa, Japan, 1962, 88 mins.

The Burmese Harp

A Japanese army private in Burma is so revolted by the carnage of war that he refuses to return home. Dressed as a Buddhist monk, he remains to bury the dead. The first Japanese film to stress pacifism, *Burmese Harp* is remarkable for its pulsating black and white images and its humanist fervor. Japanese with English subtitles.

VHS: S00545. $29.95.
Laser: LD72321. $49.95.
Kon Ichikawa, Japan, 1956, 116 mins.

Enjo

A superb adaptation of Mishima's novel *Temple of the Golden Pavillion*, this beautifully photographed, disturbing portrait of a man pushed to extremes is the story of innocence betrayed. The young man (played by Ichikawa) comes to post-war Kyoto to become a monk at a cherished Japanese temple. His miserably poor background and his innocence do not prepare him for the pervasive corruption of the urban world, and in a final desperate and violent act, he makes a plea for a fiery purity by setting fire to the holy temple. Japanese with English subtitles.

VHS: S23756. $79.95.
Kon Ichikawa, Japan, 1958, 98 mins.

Fires on the Plain

Ichikawa's powerful depiction of the inhumanity of war and passionate cry for sanity. A soldier, part of the retreating Japanese army, is forced to hide in the Philippine jungle, where he finds disease, death and cannibalism. Minimal dialog and intense visual images build to a work of immense power.

VHS: S00444. $29.95.
Laser: Widescreen. **LD75074. $49.95.**
Kon Ichikawa, Japan, 1959, 105 mins.

Makioka Sisters

The Makioka Sisters chronicles the life and affairs of four sisters in 20's Japan. An older, conservative sister tries to continue family traditions and pretensions to status, while the younger sisters discover the new freedoms becoming available to them. This battle over traditional ways is set in marked contrast to social and political changes going on in Japan. Japanese with English subtitles.

VHS: Out of print. For rental only.
Laser: CLV. **LD72110. $69.95.**
Kon Ichikawa, Japan, 1983, 130 mins.

Odd Obsession

An elderly Japanese man with a beautiful young wife finds it difficult to reconcile his feelings of desire with his decreasing potency in this "new interpretation of the love-death theme in which some of the most sordid of human actions are captured by means of the sheerest physical beauty...Erotic obsession is presented with such near-claustrophobic intensity that one longs for outdoor scenes...everything is hidden, secreted away" (Donald Richie). Japanese with English subtitles.

VHS: S04463. $29.95.
Kon Ichikawa, Japan, 1960, 96 mins.

Tokyo Olympiad

Utilizing over 100 cameras, the director captures the essence of competition and the beauty of the human form as has never been done before. Ichikawa was commissioned by the Olympic committee to direct a film which would capture the athletic excellence of the event. Not being a sports fan, he chose to present the events in a way which would express the art and beauty involved. Hailed by Gene Siskel as one of his *Top Ten Films I'd Like to See on Video*. Digitally remastered and letterboxed.

VHS: S12572. $49.95.
Laser: CAV, widescreen. **LD71371. $99.95.**
Kon Ichikawa, Japan, 1964, 170 mins.

HIROSHI TESHIGAHARA

Antonio Gaudi

Compelling portrait of Antonio Gaudi (1852-1926), leading proponent of the Art Nouveau movement in architecture in Spain, whose distinctive style is marked by a fluidity of movement, rich color and sensuality of form and texture. Teshigahara's camera examines buildings designed by Gaudi, including Casa Vicens, Crypt of the Colonia Guell and Park Guell, Casa Batlo, Casa Mila and Barcelona's unfinished landmark, Templo de la Sagrada Familia.

VHS: S34740. $89.98.
Hiroshi Teshigahara, Japan, 1984, 72 mins.

Rikyu

Teshigahara presents a poignant film exploring the struggle between art and power. Drinking tea was once a casual ritual around which social and diplomatic relationships were practiced. In the 16th Century, Sen-no Rikyu refined the art of the tea ceremony to aesthetic and spiritual heights. His revolutionary ideas brought him to the forefront of Japanese politics when war lord Hideyoshi Toyotomi confided in him as Tea Master, and together they sought what to each was most high: for Rikyu it was beauty, for Hideyoshi, power. Thoughtful performances from Rentaro Mikune, Tsutomu Yamazaki and Yoshiko Mita bring this historical allegory to its tragic close. Japanese with English subtitles.

VHS: S15684. $79.95.
Laser: CLV. **LD71490. $39.95.**
Hiroshi Teshigahara, Japan, 1990, 116 mins.

Woman in the Dunes

A woman, confined to a deep pit in the sand dunes, where she is fed by neighbors and forced to clear her house of the threatening sands, is joined by a passing photographer whom the villagers have trapped into sharing her work—and bed—forever. This is the situation of Teshigahara's great symbolic and sensual adaptation of Kobo Abe's novel, in which he "builds up the erotic tension...with extreme close-ups that transform the human body into landscape" *(Oxford Companion to Film)*. With Eija Okada and Kyoko Kishida. Japanese with English subtitles. Remastered.
VHS: S13589. $89.98.
Hiroshi Teshigahara, Japan, 1964, 123 mins.

AKIRA KUROSAWA

The Bad Sleep Well

One of Kurosawa's best films, in some ways a prophetic work set in the circles of corporate government and corporations. The film is a black, twisted story of revenge in which a grieving son takes on powerful business and political figures. Set up as a tantalizing thriller, Kurosawa's melodrama is laced with irony and bitter, grotesque humor. Japanese with English subtitles.
VHS: S07334. $29.95.
Laser: LD76988. $69.95.
Akira Kurosawa, Japan, 1959, 151 mins.

Dersu Uzala

Kurosawa's remarkable personal tale of the friendship between a wise old man and a young, Soviet explorer, filmed in the beautiful expanse of Siberia, is a unique story of man's unity with nature, and a powerful testament to faith. Russian dialog with English subtitles.
VHS: S01809. $39.95.
Laser: Widescreen. **LD75028. $69.95.**
Akira Kurosawa, Japan, 1975, 124 mins.

Dodes'ka-den

Unforgettable: Kurosawa's blending of fantasy and reality in the story of a group of Tokyo slum dwellers who, cheated by life, survive on illusion and imagination. A passionate affirmation of life, beautifully photographed. The title of the film comes from the sound of the trolleys. Japanese with English subtitles.
VHS: S00351. $29.95.
Laser: LD75389. $69.99.
Akira Kurosawa, Japan, 1976, 140 mins.

Dreams

From master director Akira Kurosawa *(Rashomon, Kagemusha, Ran)* comes perhaps his most personal film. Eight fascinating episodes dealing with war, childhood fears, the nuclear power question and man's never-ending need to harmonize with nature. Featuring breathtaking visual sequences and Martin Scorsese as Vincent Van Gogh. Japanese with English subtitles.
VHS: S13489. $92.95.
Akira Kurosawa, Japan, 1990, 120 mins.

Drunken Angel

Takashi Shimura plays a doctor who tries to bring about the spiritual and physical recovery of the human debris who live in the ashes of a poor quarter of Tokyo immediately after the war; Toshiro Mifune is an uprooted petty gambler and black-marketeer. One of Kurosawa's classic films in the vein of his love of Dostoevsky. Japanese with English subtitles.
VHS: S00378. $44.95.
Akira Kurosawa, Japan, 1948, 98 mins.

The Hidden Fortress

Set during Japan's feudal wars, this restored version of Akira Kurosawa's drama concerns a gilded princess and her loyal general who undertake a dangerous journey to their homeland, assisted only by a pair of misfits and pursued by warriors and bandits attempting to loot their gold and valuable possessions. Beautifully photographed in widescreen by Ichio Yamazaki. Letterboxed. With Toshiro Mifune, Misa Uehara and Minoru Chiaki. Japanese with English subtitles. With 13 minutes of added footage.
VHS: S00566. $39.95.
Laser: LD71042. $89.95.
Akira Kurosawa, Japan, 1958, 139 mins.

High and Low

Akira Kurosawa's adaptation of an Ed McBain mystery stars two of Japan's greats, Toshiro Mifune and Tatsuya Nakadai, in a riveting American-style thriller set in modern-day Yokohama. Mifune stars as a self-made tycoon targeted by kidnappers. When he realizes they have taken his chauffeur's son and not his own, the millionaire faces a moral dilemma: to save the boy or save his empire from financial ruin. "One of the best detective thrillers ever filmed" *(The New York Times)*. Japanese with new English subtitles. Letterboxed.
VHS: S34781. $29.95.
DVD: DV60365. $39.95.
Akira Kurosawa, Japan, 1963, 142 mins.

I Live in Fear

Toshiro Mifune is cast as the aging head of a Tokyo family who is terrified by the prospect of a nuclear war. The industrialist's large family includes a wife, grandchildren and mistresses, and they bicker greedily over the estate as they bring mental incompetence proceedings against the patriarch. Kurosawa transforms this situation into a powerful humanist statement as *I Live in Fear* projects the end of mankind as a result of man's inhumanity to man. With Toshiro Mifune, Eiko Miyuoshi and Takashi Shimura. Japanese with English subtitles.
VHS: S26383. $29.95.
Akira Kurosawa, Japan, 1955, 105 mins.

The Idiot

Drawing from Fyodor Dostoyevsky, Kurosawa transposes this bitter story to postwar Japan. Kameda, a war criminal sentenced to be shot, has been pardoned at the last moment. The shock makes him into an idiot and prone to epileptic fits. Upon release, he is befriended by the strong and tenacious Akama. When they both fall for the beautiful Takeo Nasu, madness becomes a common denominator in this grossly tragic and haunting film. Japanese with English subtitles.
VHS: S15681. $79.95.
Akira Kurosawa, Japan, 1951, 166 mins.

Ikiru

Akira Kurosawa moved outside his usual stylistic preoccupations to make this poetic and emotionally powerful work about a gravely ill, quiet and dignified civil servant who vows to find grace and purpose in his final months, through the building of a public park. It's a thoughtful, contemplative, lyrical work centered by Takashi Shimura's virtuoso performance. With Nobuo Kaneko, Kyoko Seki and Miki Odagiri. Japanese with English subtitles.
VHS: S00608. $39.95.
Laser: LD70383. $59.95.
Akira Kurosawa, Japan, 1952, 143 mins.

Kagemusha

A masterpiece. Set in 1531 Japan torn by civil strife, *Kagemusha* deals with a mighty Japanese warlord and his commoner look-alike who, after the warlord's death, is used to keep his clan together. Tatsuya Nakadai is superb in the dual role of the war lord and his double, both caught up in the swirl of history as the mighty powers clash in fierce battles and political intrigue. Winner of the Grand Prize at Cannes. Japanese with English subtitles.
VHS: S00668. $29.98.
Laser: CLV. **LD72114. $69.98.**
Akira Kurosawa, Japan, 1980, 159 mins.

The Lower Depths

Akira Kurosawa's masterful reworking of the classic play by Maxim Gorky, using foundations of Japanese Noh theatre, set in Edo during the last Tokugawa period. A rare ensemble effect is achieved from the actors in this moving story of a group of destitute people living in a rooming house. Japanese with English subtitles.
VHS: S03513. $29.95.
Akira Kurosawa, Japan, 1957, 125 mins.

Men Who Tread on Tiger's Tail

A very offbeat Kurosawa film, an adaptation of a popular Kabuki drama about a 12th-century lord who is forced to flee his estate with only six dedicated samurai to guard him. He is hunted by his brother, the Shogun, and is ultimately saved by his chief vassal through a clever disguise. The wartime Japanese government banned the film because it didn't extol the concepts of feudalism and obedience; after the war, the Allied Occupation forces banned it for being pro-feudal. Japanese with English subtitles.
VHS: S00847. $39.95.
Akira Kurosawa, Japan, 1945, 60 mins.

No Regrets for Our Youth

An unusual feminist epic saga which focuses on a charming, talented and self-absorbed Japanese woman, Yukie, who is preparing herself for the role of a spoiled, cultured wife. She flirts with two suitors, one a disaffected leftist, the other a right-wing careerist, though she has no personal interest in politics. The earliest personal and first great film by Kurosawa, with a commanding performance by Setsuko Hara as the complex woman whose life unfolds against the backdrop of Japanese militarist society. Japanese with English subtitles.
VHS: S11176. $29.95.
Akira Kurosawa, Japan, 1946, 110 mins.

Quiet Duel

Based on a play by Kazuo Kikuta, this early Kurosawa film concerns an army surgeon who, during a life-saving operation, contaminates himself with syphilis which, at the time, was virtually incurable. Now suffering with the dreaded disease, he is forced to abandon his fiancee but finds the faith to redouble his work to restore people to health, including the man from whom he contracted the disease. With Toshiro Mifune, Takashi Shimura and Miki Sanjko. Japanese with English subtitles.
VHS: S26384. $29.95.
Akira Kurosawa, Japan, 1949, 95 mins.

Ran

Kurosawa's masterpiece is a decade-in-the-making version of *King Lear* that brilliantly blends Japanese history with Shakespeare's themes. A triumphant film about ruthless ambition, evil plots and "Chaos"—the meaning of the title in Japanese. Japanese with English subtitles. VHS letterboxed.
VHS: S02012. $29.95.
Akira Kurosawa, Japan, 1985, 160 mins.

Rashomon

A cinematic landmark, a brilliant study of the nature of truth. Set in the 12th century. A samurai and his wife are traveling through the woods near Kyoto. They are attacked by a bandit, the wife raped and the husband killed. Four different versions of the incident are told by the participants and a woodcutter who was a witness. Japanese with English subtitles.
VHS: S01092. $29.95.
Laser: LD70440. $49.95.
Akira Kurosawa, Japan, 1951, 89 mins.

Record of a Living Being

An elderly and wealthy industrialist becomes obsessed with a fear of the atomic bomb. In an attempt to save his family, he pressures them to leave Japan. Their refusal brings about his madness and ruin. Another gripping drama from one of Japan's finest living directors. Japanese with English subtitles. Presented in a slightly letterboxed format (1:1.60).
VHS: S15375. $39.95.
Akira Kurosawa, Japan, 1955, 105 mins.

Red Beard

An offbeat, virtually unaccountable work from the Japanese master Akira Kurosawa, mixing the stylizes soap and the action flick, concerns the legendary doctor called Red Beard who attempts to influence his disciples to turn away from private practice to use their skills on the poor and sick. "The film bowls along magnificently in a weird mixture of genuine emotion, absurdity and poetic fantasy" *(Time Out)*. With Toshiro Mifune as Dr. Gillespie, Yuzo Kayama, Yoshio Tsuchiya.
VHS: S02955. $39.95.
Laser: LD70444. $69.95.
Akira Kurosawa, Japan, 1965, 185 mins.

Rhapsody in August

This moving drama, set in Nagasaki, explores the trauma of World War II and the aftereffects of the atomic bomb. Four children on a visit to their grandmother in this historic town get invited to Hawaii to by their American relations, setting off a chain of painful memories that are finally confronted when an American cousin, Richard Gere, arrives. Japanese with English subtitles.
VHS: S21072. $19.98.
Laser: LD74469. $39.99.
Akira Kurosawa, Japan, 1991, 98 mins.

Sanjuro

The hero of Kurosawa's *Yojimbo* returns to help a group of very earnest, very green, very young samurai get their clan rid of corruption. As in *Yojimbo*, much of the comic effect comes from imaginative composition and incongruous movement. With Toshiro Mifune. Japanese with English subtitles.
VHS: S01157. $29.95.
Laser: LD72345. $49.95.
Akira Kurosawa, Japan, 1962, 92 mins.

Sanshiro Sugata

Sanshiro Sugata, like so many of Kurosawa's characters, champions principles against a hostile, established order. In his first film, Kurosawa was already unconventional in style, as the hero advocates the newer art of judo against the traditional and well-entrenched jujitsu masters. Before proving himself, Sanshiro undergoes the long ordeal of learning judo as a discipline in a strikingly visual film extraordinary also for its explosive martial arts choreography. Japanese with English subtitles.
VHS: S03515. $19.95.
Akira Kurosawa, Japan, 1943, 80 mins.

Scandal

Gossip magazines are the target of this film by Kurosawa. A scandal sheet fabricates a romance between Toshiro Mifune, an artist, and a young entertainer. The artist sues the newspaper for libel. But his own lawyer accepts a bribe to ruin the case. *Scandal* is a powerful drama about corruption and redemption. With Mifune, Yoshiko Yamaguchi and Takashi Shimura. Japanese with English subtitles.
VHS: S26385. $29.95.
Akira Kurosawa, Japan, 1950, 105 mins.

Seven Samurai

Set in medieval Japan, Kurosawa's epic centers on a group of impoverished peasants who enlist the protection of seven unemployed samurai to defend their property and harvest from the brutal bandits who terrorize their village. The film is groundbreaking for its visual intensity, stylistic command of movement, space and action, and its expressive emotional range and social criticism. The battle sequences are frightening, devastating and eerie. Cinematography by Asaichi Nakai. With Takashi Shimura, Yoshio Inaba and Toshiro Mifune. Japanese with English subtitles.
VHS: S01182. $34.95.
Laser: CLV, widescreen. **LD70452. $59.95.**
DVD: DV60171. $39.95.
Akira Kurosawa, Japan, 1954, 208 mins.

Stray Dog
A first-rate thriller in which Kurosawa has acknowledged his debt to Georges Simenon. Toshiro Mifune plays rookie Detective Murakami, who loses his gun only to discover that it has fallen into the hands of a killer. Terrified of losing his job, his search takes him into the Tokyo underworld, full of postwar shortages, "divinely hellish under Kurosawa's odd-angled lensing and staccato editing…*Stray Dog* is a Dostoevskian saga of guilt, and expiation, by association" *(Pacific Film Archive)*. Japanese with English subtitles.
VHS: S06462. $24.95.
Laser: LD76989. $69.95.
Akira Kurosawa, Japan, 1949, 122 mins.

Throne of Blood
Kurosawa's brilliant interpretation of Shakespeare's *Macbeth* shifts the action to 16th century feudal Japan, where a samurai is motivated by his ambitious wife and spirit to kill his friend. The movie balances stylized action and movement of the Noh theater with the intensity of the American western. Kurosawa and cinematographer Asaichi Nakai create a foreboding atmosphere in the castles and landscape. With Toshiro Mifune, Isuzu Yamada and Minoru Chiaki. Japanese with English subtitles.
VHS: S01338. $39.95.
Laser: CAV. LD70726. $89.95.
Akira Kurosawa, Japan, 1957, 110 mins.

Yojimbo
Kurosawa's first full-length comedy. Toshiro Mifune is the unemployed samurai warrior who comes to a small village torn apart by two warring factions where he is hired first by one side, then by the other. "Explosively comic and exhilarating," said Pauline Kael. Japanese with English subtitles.
VHS: S01489. $29.95.
Laser: LD70489. $49.95.
Akira Kurosawa, Japan, 1961, 110 mins.

KENJI MIZOGUCHI

47 Ronin
Also known as *A Tale of 47 Loyal Retainers of the Genroku Era*, Mizoguchi's two-part film deals with the vengeance of the retainers of Lord Asano in 1703 following his forced hara-kiri. Mizoguchi's film version is based on a Kabuki version of the story by Seika Mayama. "This is a re-discovered wartime saga of noble samurai sentiments and discreet passions. A girding of the spirit is recommended for this wraparound experience in the same way that the best of the long-form classics are to be savored…", wrote Tom Allen and Andrew Sarris in *The Village Voice*. "Mizoguchi has transformed a basic samurai legend of Japanese folklore into an essential historical drama of Japanese cinema. The boxed courtyards and formal gardens of the 18th century are tracking paradises that Mizoguchi's dolly-and-crane shots exploit fully, and the tale of loyal vassals avenging their lord's honor is rendered subtly throughout by a highly disciplined Expressionism."
Part I. 111 mins.
VHS: S08031. $29.95.
Part II. 108 mins.
VHS: S08032. $29.95.
Kenji Mizoguchi, Japan, 1942

Chikamatsu Monogatari (Crucified Lovers)
One of the masterworks of Kenji Mizoguchi: in 17th century Japan, the illicit love between a merchant's wife and her servant leads to tragedy. Based on a story by Chikamatsu and derived from a Bunraku play, "it is perhaps Mizoguchi's most intense and concentrated study of social mores in feudal Japan and among his most visually sensuous films" (Georges Sadoul). Japanese with English subtitles.
VHS: S09097. $69.95.
Kenji Mizoguchi, Japan, 1954, 110 mins.

A Geisha
A Geisha is a portrait of geisha life, a document about the rise of feminism in post-war Japan and an examination of the evolving relationship of two women. One is a distinguished geisha (Michiyo Kogure), the other, a 16-year-old novice (Ayako Wakao) whom she is training. Kogure is alarmed by the young woman's romantic delusions. "The film's charm is the compassionate but completely unsentimental way it regards the two women's friendship" (Vincent Canby). Japanese with English subtitles.
VHS: S19544. $59.95.
Kenji Mizoguchi, Japan, 1953, 87 mins.

Life of Oharu
An enduring masterpiece of world cinema, from the director of *Ugetsu*. *Life of Oharu* is a poignant, exquisitely filmed portrait of a woman victimized by the brutal strictures of 17th-century feudal Japan. Mizoguchi shows remarkable insight into the psychology of his female protagonist, and photographs her with slow, graceful, hauntingly beautiful camera movements. Japanese with English subtitles.
VHS: S00753. $29.95.
Laser: LD76169. $69.95.
Kenji Mizoguchi, Japan, 1952, 136 mins.

Osaka Elegy
"In 1936 Mizoguchi made his most brilliant pre-war film, *Osaka Elegy*, shot in 20 days and banned after 1940 for 'decadent tendencies,' a euphemism barely concealing the military government's fear of the radicalism of Mizoguchi's satire of the ruthless, all-pervasive Osaka capitalism. In this film the mature Mizoguchi style emerges for the first time as he creates, entirely through visual means, a balance between the fate of the heroine Ayako and the corrupt, degenerate values of Osaka. The plot concerns the seduction of Ayako, a switchboard operator, by her boss" (Joan Mellen, *The Waves at Genji's Door*). Japanese with English subtitles.
VHS: S09958. $29.95.
Laser: LD76799. $49.95.
Kenji Mizoguchi, Japan, 1936, 84 mins.

Princess Yang Kwei Fei
Kenji Mizoguchi's film about a young servant girl who is transformed into a princess and then destroyed by the shifting loyalties, betrayal and revenge around her. Mizoguchi's use of color, decor and diagonal compositions is fluid and baroque and perfectly reflects the characters' emotional conditions. "One of the most beautiful films ever to treat beauty as a subject" *(Andrew Sarris)*. With Masayuki Mori, Machiko Kyo and So Yamamura. Japanese with English subtitles.
VHS: S18421. $29.95.
Kenji Mizoguchi, Japan, 1955, 125 mins.

Sansho the Bailiff
Set in 11th century Japan, the film focuses on a mother who sets off with her two children to find her husband, a former deputy governor, who has been in exile. The family is broken up by a priestess who sells all three to kidnappers, and after many hardships, one of the sons becomes the governor once under Sansho's brutal rule. "Mizoguchi has created a powerful work with strong humanistic overtones. Focusing on the influence the two women in the story have on the hero, the film alternates the idyllic atmosphere of some scenes with the violent cruelty of others" (Georges Sadoul). Japanese with English subtitles.
VHS: S01158. $29.95.
Laser: LD75422. $69.95.
Kenji Mizoguchi, Japan, 1954, 120 mins.

Sisters of Gion
Often considered to be the best pre-war Japanese film, and Mizoguchi's masterpiece, *Sisters of Gion* is set in the red-light district of Kyoto. The film tells of two sisters—the older trained as a geisha in the old tradition, the younger an apprentice devoted to the more progressive ideas. This conflict between the old and the new, wrote Donald Richie in *The Japanese Film*, has become "the protest symbol of modern Japan."
VHS: S03517. $29.95.
Kenji Mizoguchi, Japan, 1936, 69 mins.

Story of the Last Chrysanthemum
Kenji Mizoguchi's chronicle of a Kabuki actor. As the son of a prominent Kabuki family, the young man would be assured eventual fame, but he runs afoul of his father by falling in love with a servant girl, and sets out to make it on his own. Contains some of Mizoguchi's most ethereal imagery, as well as some fascinating use of compositions suggestive of Cinemascope before the widescreen process was invented. Japanese with English subtitles.
VHS: S03516. $29.95.
Kenji Mizoguchi, Japan, 1939, 115 mins.

Street of Shame
The last film by the great Mizoguchi, the story of the dreams and problems of a group of prostitutes living in one gaudy Tokyo brothel, with a remarkable performance by the legendary Machiko Kyo. Japanese with English subtitles.
VHS: S01810. $29.95.
Kenji Mizoguchi, Japan, 1956, 88 mins.

Taira Clan Saga
The last great color film by Mizoguchi. Set in the 12th century as the center of power in Japan shifted from feudal nobility to the Buddhist clergy, the story centers on Kiyomori, scion of the Taira clan of swordsmen. At the beginning of the film he quietly acquiesces to his father's authority; at the end he is in open revolt against it. Mizoguchi describes and analyzes this change in a film that is the work of a major artist in full authority. Japanese with English subtitles.
VHS: S10933. $59.95.
Kenji Mizoguchi, Japan, 1955, 90 mins.

Ugetsu
Kenji Mizoguchi's poetic film is set in feudal, war-ravaged, 16th-century Japan and focuses on the opposite fortunes of two peasants who abandon their families to accumulate wealth and prestige and find emptiness and despair. The film is remarkable for its expressive photography, diagonal compositions and uninterrupted takes. With Machiko Kyo and Masayuki Mori. "Scenes of everyday life alternate with those of a dreamlike, erotic intensity. At the end it is difficult to remember where reality stops and hallucination begins" (*Newsweek*). Japanese with English subtitles. Newly remastered, translated and subtitled print. Presented in original aspect ratio.
VHS: S01390. $24.95.
Laser: LD75412. $49.95.
Kenji Mizoguchi, Japan, 1953, 96 mins.

Utamaro and His Five Women
Mizoguchi's exquisite portrait of the artistic life of Tokyo of the 18th century is a portrait of Edo artist Utamaro (Minnosuke Bando) and his relationship to women. Utamaro stands at the center of the lives of five women who compete for his attention in a film which is remarkably modern for its attitude toward the rights of women. The scenarist, Yoshikata Yoda, stated that the film was an unconscious portrait of Mizoguchi himself. With Kinuyo Tanaka, Kotaro Bando and Hiroko Kawasaki. Japanese with English subtitles.
VHS: S19418. $69.95.
Kenji Mizoguchi, Japan, 1946, 89 mins.

YASUJIRO OZU

An Autumn Afternoon
This profoundly simple and moving film examines changing familial relationships in an increasingly Americanized postwar Tokyo. With his unmistakable and inimitable style, Ozu has created a serenely beautiful film which tells the timeless, moving tale of a father giving up his only daughter in marriage. Both humorous and heartbreaking, *An Autumn Afternoon* was Ozu's 53rd and last film. Japanese with English subtitles.
VHS: S15393. $69.95.
Yasujiro Ozu, Japan, 1952, 112 mins.

Drifting Weeds
A group of travelling actors visits a town where the leading actor's (Ganjiro Nakamura) ex-mistress lives with their son. Nakamura's present lover (Machiko Kyo) is understandably jealous. Brilliant color cinematography by Kazuo Miyagawa; one of Ozu's great films. "A work of subtle genius" *(Film Magazine)*. Also known as *Floating Weeds*. Japanese with English subtitles.
VHS: S00377. $29.95.
Laser: LD70983. $44.95.
Yasujiro Ozu, Japan, 1959, 128 mins.

Early Summer
Director Ozu gracefully portrays the conflicts between three generations in this classic story of a 28-year-old woman who lives with her brother, sister-in-law, nephews and aging parents and must endure their pressure to marry the man of their choice. With Setsuko Hara, Kuniko Miyake and Chishu Ryu. ``A sensitively rendered film about basic human emotions made by a master filmmaker" (Leonard Maltin).
VHS: S06459. $29.95.
Laser: LD76190. $69.95.
Yasujiro Ozu, Japan, 1951, 135 mins.

Equinox Flower
When the daughter of a successful business man defies an arranged marriage and runs off with a pianist, the father refuses to give consent. A warm comedy of reconciliation, this film marks Ozu's first use of color. With Shin Saburi, Kinuyo Tanaka, Ineko Arima and Miyuki Kuwano. Japanese with English subtitles.
VHS: S16079. $69.95.
Yasujiro Ozu, Japan, 1958, 118 mins.

Good Morning (Ohayo)
In this biting comedy, Yasujiro Ozu exposes the hypocrisy of the adult world. When a father (Chishu Ryu, *Tokyo Story*) refuses to buy a television set for his sons, the two small boys take a vow of silence, refusing to say "good morning" to a neighbor. Soon the gossipy apartment complex where they live is in an uproar—the boys' mother must be holding a grudge against her neighbors. Written by Ozu and longtime collaborator Kogo Noda, this witty film makes keen observations about communication and familial relationships. The charming performances of the young leads and a cast of Ozu regulars make it "an all-around pleasure" *(The Faber Companion to Foreign Films)*. Japanese with English subtitles.
VHS: S30740. $29.95.
Laser: LD76986. $49.95.
Yasujiro Ozu, Japan, 1959, 93 mins.

A Hostel in Tokyo (An Inn in Tokyo; Tokyo No Yado)
In this silent Ozu film, a working-class father and his two young sons look for a job and eventually find fleeting companionship with a widow and her little girl. Silent with Chinese and German titles.
VHS: S33936. $24.95.
Yasujiro Ozu, Japan, 1935, 82 mins.

Late Spring
In *Late Spring*, a father feels he is keeping his daughter from marriage; when she is erroneously told that her father is thinking of re-marrying, she agrees to an offer. *Late Spring*, wrote Donald Richie, is "one of the most perfect, most complete, and most successful studies of character ever achieved in the Japanese cinema." With Setsuko Hara, Chishu Ryu. Japanese with English subtitles.
VHS: S21502. $69.95.
Yasujiro Ozu, Japan, 1949, 107 mins.

Record of a Tenement Gentleman

One of Ozu's most wonderful films, a bittersweet comedy about an abandoned child who manages to create a new surrogate family in an unlikely setting from a very unlikely candidate. The surprise ending only reinforces how carefully this film depicts human emotions. Japanese with English subtitles.
VHS: S25907. $69.95.
Yasujiro Ozu, Japan, 1947, 73 mins.

Tokyo Story

One of the legendary classics of humanist cinema, *Tokyo Story* tells the simple, sad story of an elderly couple who travel to Tokyo to visit their two married children, only to find themselves politely ushered off to a hot springs resort. "Ozu's technique, as spare and concentrated as a haiku master's verse, transforms the very banalities of the subject into moments of intimacy and beauty seldom captured on film. As always, the themes go beyond the obvious and are conveyed so gently that only afterwards are many apparent." Japanese with English subtitles. With new electronic subtitles.
VHS: S10919. $69.95.
Yasujiro Ozu, Japan, 1953, 139 mins.

JAPANESE ISSUES

After the Cloud Lifted: Hiroshima's Stories of Recovery

This documentary shows how Hiroshima's atomic bomb survivors overcame personal tragedies and rebuilt their lives, and how their stories of reconciliation continue to inspire the world today. Find out how one survivor used art to help him overcome the horror of having watched his family burn to death, and how a woman swore revenge against the airmen who dropped the bomb and later came face-to-face with the co-pilot of the *Enola Gay*. And meet two disfigured women who chose different paths toward healing. 35 mins.
VHS: S34717. $150.00.

Animated Classics of Japanese Literature Collection 1

The first in a series of works that artfully blends animation with timeless classics of Japanese literature. Japanese with English subtitles.
Animated Classics of Japanese Literature Collection 1, Complete Set.
VHS: S21005. $119.95.

Animated Classics of Japanese Literature Collection 2

This second installment gives the viewer even more opportunities to discern the true heart of Japan via animated versions of the greatest works of Japanese literature ever written. Subtitled in English.
Animated Classics of Japanese Literature Collection 2, Complete Set.
VHS: S21006. $119.95.

The Aroma of Enchantment

From Chip Lord, one of America's premier videomakers, a video essay that investigates the idea of America in Japan by weaving historical material about General Douglas MacArthur with stories told by collectors or practitioners of Americanization in Japan. Lord relates his own feelings of "otherness" and cultural displacement in 1990s Tokyo, connecting these ideas when General MacArthur arrived on Japanese soil in 1946.
VHS: S31254. $59.95.
Chip Lord, USA/Japan, 1992, 55 mins.

Best of Nightline: Akio Morita

30 mins.
VHS: S14064. $14.98.

Daimyo

The unique interaction of the pen and the sword—the civilian and martial arts culture in Japan—is explored in this fascinating program. Feudal landlords, the daimyo owed allegiance to the shogun, defending the land during civil revolution and invasion. As conflicts subsided, the daimyo turned to the peaceful arts to provide balance to the practice of martial arts. Life in medieval Japan is explored, including looks at the tea ceremony, No theatre, calligraphy, swordsmanship and archery from horseback. 30 mins.
VHS: S08475. $29.95.

Discovering the Music of Japan

Set in a beautiful teahouse, this video shows how three major instruments are used. They are the koto, the samisen and the shakuhachi. Historical information and the contemporary role of these instruments are also explained. 22 mins.
VHS: S23514. $49.95.

Empire of the Rising Sun

A two-volume set which chronicles the Japanese Empire from World War I through the end of World War II and Japan's surrender. 120 mins.
VHS: S09204. $49.95.

The Hidden Japan

Drug addicts, alcoholics and homeless people are considered complete outcasts in Japanese society. They are at times blatantly ignored and considered disposable human beings. This film shows how three Maryknoll Fathers, a Maryknoll Sister and Japanese volunteers are responding to the needs of these social exiles. Maryknollers are also helping to operate a seaport hospitality center in northern Japan for transient foreign sailors. 25 mins.
VHS: S13906. $24.95.

Hiroshima - Nagasaki, August 1945

In August 1945 the Japanese government commissioned filmmaker Akira Iwasaki, jailed during WWII for his antiwar beliefs, to document the effects of the new atomic weapon. The U.S. military classified this raw footage—the first shot following the bombings of Hiroshima and Nagasaki—as "secret" for over 20 years before making it public. In 1970, Prof. Barnouw obtained the historic footage and edited together this unforgettable film, adding a factual, eloquently understood narration. "Objective and poetic...strongly moving" *(The Village Voice)*. 17 mins.
VHS: S30093. $79.00.

Japan

Jane Seymour examines how Japan's ancient traditions have blended with new technology and modern trends to shape the society and its people today in this four-volume series. *Volume 1: The Electronic Tribe* focuses on the contrasts between the present day life of factory workers and the inherited religious and rural customs still found in the ordinary home. *Volume 2: The Sword and the Chrysanthemum* takes a close look at what the West sees as a paradox in Japanese society, as represented by the Samurai warrior, who combined an appreciation of beauty and high culture with fighting aggression. *Volume 3: The Legacy of the Shogun* looks at the continuing effect of the 17th century Shogun philosophy of hard work, discipline and hierarchy. It also explores the law-abiding nature of contemporary Japan where Tokyo has one of the lowest crime rates in the world. *Volume 4: A Proper Place in the World* looks at Japan's intervention on the world's stage during the 20th century and its likely future as a world economic superpower. 60 mins. each.
VHS: S16529. $79.98.

Japan: The Island Empire

From the frantic pace of Tokyo to the Great Buddha of Kamakura and the 400-year-old Himeji Castle, this video tour captures the grandeur of Japan. 55 mins.
VHS: S09879. $24.95.

Japanese: Yesterday and Today

Scripted by AP correspondent John Roderick, this two-volume program presents an inside look at Japan. Viewers will learn about the origins of the tea ceremony, Kabuki theater, and haiku poetry as well as about flourishing Japanese industries. Also presented are Japan's prospects for continuing its phenomenal success in the international marketplace. 44 mins.
VHS: S12271. $300.00.

Kabuki Classics: Onoe Baiko VII in The Salt Gatherer

Performance by "living national treasure" Kabuki actor Baiko VII of a famous 18th-century Kabuki dance based on a Noh drama about a simple girl who loves a court noble, a poet, during his exile to a remote island, and her subsequent abandonment. Baiko also grants a rare interview, explains his art and the origin of the dance he performs, and gives notes on technique to his son, also an actor in Kabuki theater. 1972, 27 mins.
VHS: S32332. $89.95.

Kazuo Ishiguro

Kazuo Ishiguro, born in Nagasaki, Japan, and raised in England, is the author of *View of the Hills, An Artist of the Floating World* and *Remains of the Day*, which received the prestigious Booker Prize. Mr. Ishiguro read from his fourth novel, *The Unconsoled*, on October 19, 1995. Pico Iyer, essayist and novelist *(Falling Off the Map)*, talked with Mr. Ishiguo following the reading. From the *Lannan Literary Videos* series. 60 mins.
VHS: S32432. $19.95.

Kendo: The Path of the Sword

Kendo is the original Japanese martial art form. It originates with the sword and the spirit of the warrior. This video shows how practice is performed, the elements of this art including armor and weapons, and the rules governing a match. Interviews help clarify the role of Zen and there is a discussion of the history of this martial art.
VHS: S24860. $29.95.

Kodo: Heartbeat Drummers of Japan

Named after the Japanese word for heartbeat, Kodo is a group of young Asian musicians and dancers who perform traditional and contemporary drumming. 1983, 57 mins.
VHS: S14743. $19.95.

Nagasaki Journey

This compelling production portrays the aftermath of the atomic bomb dropped on the city of Nagasaki from both an American and Japanese perspective, and presents moving personal stories from two Japanese survivors and eyewitness recollections from U.S. Marines. Includes never-before-seen color footage shot during the occupation by Marine cinematographers, as well as striking black-and-white still photos taken the day after the blast by Japanese Army photographer Yosuke Yamahata. 27 mins.
VHS: S30092. $79.00.

National Geographic Video: Living Treasures of Japan

A tribute to the artists who preserve the richness and beauty of ancient Japanese traditions in a special from National Geographic. 60 mins.
VHS: S07392. $19.95.

Shogun

Richard Chamberlain stars in this unedited Emmy Award-winning TV mini-series. Packed with action, romance and adventure, this is the story of a British navigator shipwrecked off the coast of 17th-century feudal Japan. Four cassettes.
VHS: S32180. $249.95.
Jerry London, USA/Japan, 1980, 9 hours, 9 mins.

Survivors

This film presents a remarkable portrait of Japanese-American survivors caught in the atomic bombings of Hiroshima and Nagasaki, as they describe what they saw and felt when the bombs dropped. Also profiled are Americans who face a range of physical, psychological and social problems, corroborated in the video by doctors at the U.S. Public Health Service and Yale University. "Strong...affecting...unsentimental...It's a film every American should see" *(National Catholic News)*. 35 mins.
VHS: S30094. $89.00.

Textile Magicians

A magical journey with five contemporary Japanese fiber artists who left urban centers for cedar forests outside Kyoto in order to live in harmony with nature. With Chiyoko Tanaka, Masakazu Kobayashi, Naomi Kobayashi, Jun Tomita and Hiroyuki Shindo. 58 mins.
VHS: S31849. $29.95.

OTHER ASIAN CINEMA

An Ambition Reduced to Ashes

Directed by H.M. Norodom Sihanouk, the filmmaker King of Cambodia, who also translated the film's subtitles. In an allegory set in contemporary Cambodia, a young prince is told by his Merlin-like guru that he alone can save his country from the tragedies of the past 20 years. When the prince meets a beautiful young girl, the guru warns both that the marriage is impossible: having sexual relations would break the spell preserving the prince's youth, revealing his true 100-year-old self and causing his immediate death. Cambodian with English subtitles.
VHS: S32619. $29.95.
H.M. Norodom Sihanouk, Cambodia, 1995, 44 mins.

Bugis Street

The "alternately funny and gritty, wise and touching" (Kevin Thomas, *Los Angeles Times*) coming-of-age story of Lien, a wide-eyed 16-year-old girl (Hiep Thi Le, *Heaven and Earth*) who comes from a rural village to work in the Sing Sing Hotel, not knowing that the hotel is based in the heart of Singapore's red-light district and all the "female" residents are transvestites and transsexuals. Amid the colorful lives of the "girls," Lien discovers the secrets and pains of love, sexuality and womanhood from her new "sisters." "It's Snow White and the Seven Drag Queens" (Dennis Dermody, *Paper*). English and Cantonese with English subtitles.
VHS: S34318. $79.95.
Yonean, Malaysia, 1994, 110 mins.

Cyclo

Directed by Tran Anh Hung *(The Scent of Green Papaya)*, this gritty tale of innocence lost in the urban jungle of Vietnam fuses the neorealist style of *The Bicycle Thief* with the kinetic energy of *Taxi Driver*. In the heart of Ho Chi Minh City, a young cyclo (pedicab driver) transports passengers through the streets, trying to eke out a meager living for his two sisters and elderly grandfather. When his bicycle is stolen by a local gang, he descends into a crime ring led by the charismatic Poet (Tony Leung, *Chung King Express, Happy Together*), and his older sister turns to prostitution. Vietnamese with English subtitles.

VHS: S32014. $89.95.

Tran Anh Hung, Vietnam, 1996, 123 mins.

The Last Days of Colonel Savath

In this drama about the fall of Phnom Penh in 1973, the Cambodian military abdicates its authority in a disastrous alliance with the Khmer Rouge against King Sandech Sihanouk. The story follows Colonel Savath—who recognizes the folly of his commanding officer, General Nop, but is powerless to stop him—and Savath's father, a retired doctor who returns to surgery only to face Pol Pot's soldiers, who massacre wounded soldiers in hospital beds and operating rooms. Incorporating newsreel footage of the Khmer Rouge, the film stands as a historical document as well as a tragic drama of the Cambodian holocaust. Cambodian with English subtitles.

VHS: S32618. $29.95.

H.M. Norodom Sihanouk, Cambodia, 1995, 34 mins.

Peasants in Distress

Set in 1993 Cambodia, when United Nations troops joined government soldiers in their fight against rebel commandos, *Peasants in Distress* is the story of a battalion commander who falls in love with a young peasant woman after she and her brother send the battalion food. In part out of jealousy over the romance, the commander's deputy defies orders by shooting at a U.N. truck, killing a soldier. The rebels, fearing reprisals from government troops, take the peasants to their jungle encampment, where the commander and the peasant woman marry. Their happiness, however, is short-lived. Cambodian with English subtitles.

VHS: S32620. $29.95.

H.M. Norodom Sihanouk, Cambodia, 1994, 75 mins.

The Scent of Green Papaya

A moving and undeniably brilliant film by the talented Vietnamese-exile filmmaker Tran Anh Hung, set in 1951 and centered on a young woman who becomes a servant for a turbulent family. The film follows in exquisitely lyrical detail the quiet beauty and stoically accepted hardships of her life as, ten years later, she starts a love affair with her next employer. Shot entirely on a Paris soundstage, this, says critic Roger Ebert, "is a film to cherish." Vietnamese with English subtitles.

VHS: S23925. $19.95.

Laser: LD74799. $34.95.

Tran Anh Hung, Vietnam/France, 1993, 104 mins.

ASIAN WORLD

Asia Close-Up

In *Japan*, 13-year-old schoolgirl Satomi Tamura shares details of her life in historic Kyoto, Japan, as viewers follow her to English and character painting classes, her home, a cemetery, and a Shinto shrine. 14 mins. In *Cambodia*, Sok Thea, a 13-year-old Cambodian boy, tells how the loss of his leg to a land mine changed his relationship with his family and friends, as he struggles to use his new prosthesis. One of thousands of Cambodians maimed or killed in the country's genocidal civil war, Sok gives viewers a look into rural Cambodian life. 14 mins.

VHS: S30031. $16.95.

Bali: The Mask of Rangda

Filmed in the remote villages of Bali, this video is an authentic picture of a unique culture. 30 mins.

VHS: S06499. $59.95.

Children of the Earth Series: Asia Close-up, Japan and Cambodia

In the first segment, Satomi Tamura discloses a lifestyle characterized by tradition, strong family ties and education in everything from flower arranging to English lessons. Then in the second segment, Sok Thea, a young Cambodian boy, struggles to adapt to his prosthetic leg. Many have lost limbs in the aftermath of the difficult Cambodian Civil War. 28 mins.

VHS: S27910. $24.95.

Experience Vietnam

Experience Vietnam as you light firecrackers to ring in the new year, fire an AK-47 assault rifle, descend into subterranean tunnels once inhabited by the Vietcong, drink the juice of a snake to ward off sickness, and ride the Reunification Express. 47 mins.

VHS: S31475. $19.99.

Hong Kong: A Family Portrait

In 1997, the British Crown Colony of Hong Kong, a bustling, capitalistic city, will be returned to the People's Republic of China. This video takes a look at the life of a boat family that has made its home in Hong Kong for more than 100 years, now straddling the gap between the modern world and ancient Chinese customs. A National Geographic production. 60 mins.

VHS: S11654. $19.95.

Impressions of Hong Kong and Macau

Savor the delights of this Queen of the Orient and see why Hong Kong is unique. Visit Macau, steeped in history, and go shopping in some of the world's most diverse marketplaces. 25 mins.

VHS: S10776. $24.95.

Kapalana: Death of a Hawaiian Village

Shot over seven years, this award-winning program contains breathtaking footage of a deadly volcanic eruption that spewed ashes and rained destruction on an isolated village. 48 mins.

VHS: S17222. $29.95.

The Mini Dragons Series

A four-part series studying the men and women striving to raise the "mini dragons," four Pacific Rim countries (Singapore, Taiwan, South Korea and Hong Kong), into competitive international players through increased trade, industrial growth and foreign investment. This program studies the individual communities and cultures as well.

Hong Kong.
VHS: S18065. $29.95.
Singapore.
VHS: S18066. $29.95.
South Korea.
VHS: S18067. $29.95.
Taiwan.
VHS: S18068. $29.95.

Mystical Malaysia, Land of Harmony

Discover Malaysia, a country of white sand beaches and virgin jungles, a country rich in culture and traditions. Journey to the island of Penang. Travel to Kota Bhary and witness the traditions of batik printing and kite making. Explore the village of Sarawak, home to the headhunters of Borneo. 45 mins.

VHS: S10779. $24.95.

No Longer Colonies: Hong Kong 1997, Macau 1999

As the timetable toward integration with Mainland Communist China continues to move forward, these last European colonies in Asia are filled with a mixture of hope and trepidation. This documentary looks at the history and the prospects of this fascinating region.

VHS: S21849. $19.95.

Peter Jennings Reporting from the Killing Fields

A powerful television special in which Peter Jennings reports from Cambodia about America's continued role in Southeast Asia, and particularly its support for the genocide by the Khmer Rouge. Includes the heated discussion which followed the original ABC TV newscast. 160 mins.

VHS: S12499. $19.98.

Singapore: Crossroads of Asia

Exotic Singapore, the ancient trading port, in a video visit that captures awe-inspiring sights, from the Temple of Heavenly Happines and the Sultan Mosque to the exotic cuisines. 55 mins.

VHS: S09880. $24.95.

Sri Lanka: A Nation in Anguish

A presentation on *disappearances* and human rights violations committed by the Sri Lankan government, with suggestions for stopping the abuses. Produced by Amnesty International. 18 mins.

VHS: S06891. $20.00.

Taiwan: Exotic Blossom of the Orient

The enchanting island of Taiwan is a land of jade temples, marble cities, sandy beaches. Visit the exquisite National Palace Museum, explore Snake Alley, Tarako Gorge, Wuffeng Temple, and meet the unique people who live here. 50 mins.

VHS: S05763. $34.95.

Touring Korea

Captures the history, legends and drama of the 5,000 year old country, including Chejudo, Korea's own tropical resort, skiing at Dragon Valley, Kyongju, the city of golden treasures, the Mt. Soraksan National Park, the Harvest Moon and Wesak festivals. 60 mins.

VHS: S09909. $29.95.

Video Visits: Indonesia, The Jeweled Archipelago

Visit Java, the Kraton Palace, the ancient man-made mountains of Borobodur, the islands of the famed Komodo Dragon and more. 57 mins.

VHS: S31458. $24.99.

Video Visits: South Korea, Land of Morning Calm

Seoul, like much of Korea, combines modern bustle with ancient sites. Scenic views of Mt. Namsam, Mt. Sorak and the river Han-gang also reveal a landscape where the old and new combine harmoniously. This video displays Korea's treasures to their best advantage. 55 mins.

VHS: S29833. $24.95.

Video Visits: Thailand, The Golden Kingdom

Experience the architectural splendor of the Grand Palace, tour Bangkok's labyrinth of narrow streets, visit Wat Po, where the colossal Reclining Buddha resides, and bask on the beaches of Koko Samui, Phuket and Ko Phi Phi. 56 mins.

VHS: S31463. $24.99.

Video Visits: Vietnam, Land of the Ascending Dragon

Travel the Red River Delta to Hanoi's broad boulevards, celebrate Hung King Festival, marking Vietnam's founding, marvel at Hue's former Imperial City, explore the Huyen Khong Cave and a field hospital, admire Confucian shrines and Buddhist pagodas, tour Ho Chi Minh City, and see the Mekong Delta by boat. 54 mins.

VHS: S31465. $24.99.

FILIPINO CINEMA

Macho Dancer

From world-renowned director Lino Brocka comes a story of sex, violence, and political corruption. Abandoned by his American lover, a handsome teenager from the mountains journeys to Manila in an effort to support his family. With a popular call boy as his mentor, Paul enters the glittering world of the "machodancer"—a world of male strippers, prostitution, drugs, sexual slavery, police corruption and murder. Teeming with sex and erotic Oriental beefcake, *Macho Dancers* is a searing indictment of the hypocrisy and corruption rampant under both the Marcos and Aquino regimes. Uncensored and uncut. Tagalog with English subtitles.

VHS: S14597. $79.95.

Lino Brocka, Philippines, 1988, 136 mins.

Midnight Dancers

Banned in the Philippines, this is the story of three young brothers who are trapped in the world of exotic dancing and prostitution which characterizes much of Manila's gay nighttime scene. Though they struggle along different paths, in the end, the violence of the streets brings them all to the brink of desperation. It is reminiscent of the work of Lino Brocka, though more glossy. Filipino with English subtitles.

VHS: S28048. $29.95.

Mel Chionglo, Philippines, 1995, 118 mins.

Perfumed Nightmare

Called "one of the year's best films" by J. Hoberman in The Village Voice, an enchanting, poignant, and totally original fable by young Philippino filmmaker Kidlat Tahimik, about his awakening to and reaction against American cultural colonialism. Born in 1942 during the Occupation, Tahimik spent the "next 33 typhoon seasons in a cocoon of American dreams." This is his perfumed nightmare: the lotus-land of American technological promise. In his primitive village he worshipped the heroism of the Machine, the sleek beauty of rockets, the efficiency of industrialism. He is the president of his own Werner Von Braun fan club. A bizarre, hallucinatory movie full of dazzling images and outlandish ideas, shot on super 8 for less than $10,000. Winner of the International Critics Award, Berlin Film Festival. English and Tagalog with English subtitles.

VHS: S09300. $59.95.

Kidlat Tahimik, Philippines, 1983, 91 mins.

Rich Boy, Poor Boy

A colleague of the late Filipino director Lino Brocka, Piedro de San Paulo's controversial and banned work rips open the Third World taboo. The story concerns an outlawed relationship between a wealthy, Americanized young man and his strong-willed, quiet farmhand. "Brave and brazen, a bittersweet portrait of friendship and desire" *(Bay Area Reporter)*. With Victor Viller, Edwyn Casas, Cristina Ocampo. Tagalog with English subtitles. On the same program is *A Boy Named Cocoy*, about a mountain boy's quest to find a better life in Manila.

VHS: S17777. $59.95.

Piedro de San Paulo, Philippines, 1991, 94 mins.

Turumba

Set in a tiny Philippine village, Tahimik's *Turumba* focuses on one family which traditionally made papier-mache animals to sell during the Turumba religious festivities. When they get a huge order, the whole life of the family is changed, as Tahimik wryly observes the "creation of the proletariat." Tagalog with English subtitles.

VHS: S013"9. $59.95.

Kidlat Tahimik, Philippines, 1984, 94 mins.

FILIPINO PERSPECTIVES

Best of Nightline: Marcos & Aquino

60 mins.

VHS: S14041. $14.98.

Filipino Americans: Discovering Their Past for the Future

One of the oldest and most influential Asian communities in the U.S., Filipinos have been in this part of the world since 1587, when they were first brought to California by the Spanish. Ever since then, their contributions have been felt in every spectrum of life on this continent. This is their story. 54 mins.

VHS: S21357. $29.95.

First in the Philippines: A Film History of the Second Oregon Volunteer Regiment

A chronicle of the first U.S. war outside the Western Hemisphere. Assembling contemporary newspaper articles, diaries, letters, unit histories and personal interviews, the film tells of the Oregon volunteer regiment, the first ground force to enter combat in the Spanish-American war in 1898.

VHS: S16461. $29.95.

Robert Koglin, USA, 62 mins.

Video Visits: The Philippines, Pearls of the Pacific

The land of the Philippines comprises over 7,000 islands. Ancient tribal customs persist in remote locations, though Spanish colonial architecture can be found in other sites. This video shows both the immense natural beauty and the unique ways of the diverse Filipino landscape. 57 mins.

VHS: S29829. $24.95.

INDIAN CINEMA

1942: A Love Story

An Indian story of music and revolution. With Anil Kapoor, Manisha Koirala, Jackie Shroff, Anupam Kher, and Raghubir Yadav. Music by Rahul Dev Burman. Hindi with English subtitles.

VHS: S35155. $39.95.

Vidhu Vinod Chopra, India, 1994

Aashiq

A classical Indian musical with a super cast, directed by India's great showman Raj Kapoor. Stars Kapoor and Padmini. Hindi with English and Arabic subtitles.

VHS: S22173. $39.95.

Raj Kapoor, India, 1967, 156 mins.

Abhimaan

Showbiz, adultery and one of the great movie scores of the '70s highlight this film starring real-life newlyweds Amitabh Bachchan and Jaya Bhaduri. Subeer Kumar (Amitabh) is on his way to becoming India's top pop singer when he falls in love with religious Uma (Bhaduri), enchanted by her voice. Subeer encourages Uma's singing career, but becomes jealous when it eclipses his own. With Bindu, Asrani. Hindi with English subtitles.

VHS: S33219. $29.95.

Hrishikesh Mukherjee, India, 1973

The Adversary

A young man, graduated from college, is unable to find meaningful employment. His ensuing hardships and personal grief, magnified by the tense and impersonal setting of Calcutta, make for a most devastating film experience. While at times reminiscent of the emotionally wrenching Italian neo-realist classics, this beautiful film often seems to outstrip them with its overwhelming spiritual perspective and astounding depth of feeling. One of Ray's brilliant masterpieces. Bengali with English subtitles.

VHS: S15380. $39.95.

Satyajit Ray, India, 1971, 110 mins.

Agneepath (Path of Fire)

In this Hindi action drama set in the Bombay underworld, young Bhai witnesses the framing of his virtuous schoolmaster father (Alok Nath) in connection with a prostitute. Nath is then lynched by the villagers. Years later Bhai becomes a powerful, ruthless gangster and confronts the main villains. With Mithun Chakraborty and Rohini Hattangadi (winners, Best Supporting Actor, Actress, 1990 Filmfare Award), Amitabh Bachchan, Madhavi and Danny Denzongpa. Music by Laxmikrant Pyarelal. Hindi with English subtitles.

VHS: S35156. $39.95.

Mukul S. Anand, India, 1990, 175 mins.

Amar

In this melodramatic film, said to be Mehboob's favorite, Dilip Kumar stars as Amar, a cowardly lawyer engaged to Anju (Madhubala), who seduces a milkmaid, Sonia (Nimmi), and must face the consequences. Hindi with English subtitles.

VHS: S30077. $29.95.

Mehboob Khan, India, 1954

Amrapali

The story of a very talented daughter, notable for its excellent picturization of classical Indian dances performed by the talented Vijayantimala. Stars Sunil Dutt and Vijayantimala Omdoa. 1969, 172 mins. Hindi with English and Arabic subtitles.

VHS: S22894. $39.95.

Anand

This hit launched a '70s melodrama genre in which the hero endures a terminal illness throughout the length of the film. Rajesh Khanna stars as a man battling terminal intestinal cancer who inspires others with his actions, as he determines to enjoy his remaining days as much as possible, despite his physical pain. Also stars Amitabh Bachchan. Music by Salil Choudhury also contributed to the film's success. Hindi with English subtitles.

VHS: S30068. $29.95.

Hrishkesh Mukherjee, India, 1970

Andaz (A Matter of Style) (Beau Monde)

Raj Kappor, Dilip Kumar and Nargis star in this major musical hit which speaks against the westernizing of Indian women and the mistaken notion of love created by close friendship. Hindi with English subtitles.

VHS: S30066. $29.95.

Mehboob Khan, India, 1949

Antarnaad

The films of Shyam Benegal, a major Indian filmmaker, are often social studies of individuals and class structure. *Antarnaad* is the story of changes that occur in the lives of people living in two villages through *Swadhyaya*—a ceremony that involves the study of self. Five people—including a poor fisherman, a smuggler and a widow looking for revenge after the death of her husband—undergo profound changes. With Shabana Azmi, Om Puri, Kulbhushan Kharbanda. Hindi with English subtitles.

VHS: S22169. $39.95.

Shyam Benegal, India, 1992, 160 mins.

Aparajito

The second part of Satyajit Ray's *Apu* trilogy. *Aparajito* follows Apu (Smaran Ghosal) on his intellectual odyssey from the streets of Benares to the promise and optimism of Calcutta, as he begins his college studies. Music by Ravi Shankar. "It's transitional in structure, rather than dramatic, but it's full of insights and revelations" (Pauline Kael). With Pinaki Sen Gupta, Karuna and Kanu Banerji, and Ramani Sen Gupta. Newly remastered. Bengali with English subtitles.

VHS: S27703. $19.95.

Satyajit Ray, India, 1957, 108 mins.

Arth

Bhatt's breakthrough film of upper-class Bombay life tells the story of Inder Malhotra (Kulbhushan Kharbanda), a filmmaker who leaves his wife, Pooja (Shabana Azmi), for a film star, Kavita (Smitra Paril). Pooja leaves her husband and experiences the struggles of a single working woman. Her dilemmas are intensified as a parallel melodrama is played out by her cleaning lady (Rohini Hattangadi), who kills her husband after he abandons her. The film benefitted from a much-publicized rivalry between actresses Patil and Azmi and gossip suggesting that Bhatt's film was autobiographical. Hindi with English subtitles.

VHS: S30075. $29.95.

Mahesh Bhatt, India, 1982

Aulad

An interesting mix of music and drama in this star-studded feature based on Telegu films. With Jeetendra, Sridevi, Jayapradha, Saeed Jaffrey, Asrani and Vinod Mehra. Music by Lax Ikant Pyarelal. Hindi with English subtitles.

VHS: S35152. $39.95.

Vijay Sadanah, India

Awara

A classical Indian film; an enchanting love story directed by India's greatest showman, Raj Kapoor. The movie presents beautifully the contrast between poor and rich families in India, and is an entertaining mixture full of melodious songs. The story deals with the love of a poor boy for a rich man's daughter. With Raj Kapoor, Nargis, Prithviraj Kapoor. Hindi with English subtitles.

VHS: S22170. $39.95.

Raj Kapoor, India, 1951, 170 mins.

Baazigar

A remake of *Kiss Before Dying* which became quite controversial because the main star takes the role of a murderer, *Baazigar* is also notable for introducing a number of young actors to the Indian cinema. With Rakhee, Shah Rukh Khan, Siddharth, Kajol and Shilpa Shetty. Music by Anu Malik. Hindi with English subtitles.

VHS: S35157. $39.95.

Abbas-Mustan, India, 1993, 90 mins.

Bharamchari

Shammi Kapoor and Rajshree star in this movie for children. A kind-hearted young bachelor takes the responsibility of orphan children. The story includes many songs for children. Hindi with English and Arabic subtitles. India, 1967, 137 mins.

VHS: S22175. $39.95.

Bobby

This kitschy teenage love story was a box-office hit, combining '60s pop sensibility, great music (including the famous love song "Hum tum ek kamre mein band ho," sung by Shailendra Singh and Lata Mangeshkar), and shades of *Romeo & Juliet*, but with a happy ending. Stars Rishi Kapoor, Dimple Kapadia, Premnath, and Durga Khote. Hindi with English subtitles.

VHS: S30070. $29.95.

Raj Kapoor, India, 1973

The Broken Journey

Written by Satyajit Ray and directed by his son, Sandip Ray, *The Broken Journey* is a powerful story of a wealthy doctor who makes a dramatic conversion when confronted with extreme poverty in rural India. Features internationally acclaimed actor Soumitra Chatterji (*The World of Apu, Two Daughters*). Official Selection, Cannes Film Festival. "Eloquent…beautifully composed" (*The Boston Globe*). Hindi with English subtitles.

VHS: S34677. $79.95.

Sandip Ray, India, 1994, 82 mins.

Charulata (The Lonely Wife)

Ray considered this film, structured like a musical rondo, to be his best work. Set in 1879 during the social reform movement in Calcutta, it tells of Charulata (Madhabi Mukherjee, in an exquisitely graceful performance), the bored and neglected upper-class wife of the reformer Bhupati Dutta (Sailen Mukherjee). Wrapped up in the politics of the times, Bhupati is oblivious to his wife's lonelines. When his young cousin Amal (Soumitra Chatterji) arrives, Bhupati hopes that he will encourage Charulata in her reading of literature; instead, she falls in love with the young man. "Gets nearer to the heart of the 'woman's dilemma' than films which see the problem in terms of career possibilities. In so doing, [Ray] has made a film that is extraordinarily contemporary" (Molly Haskell). Fully restored. Bengali with English subtitles.

VHS: S32165. $19.95.

Satyajit Ray, India, 1964, 124 mins.

The Chess Players (Shatranj Ke Khiladi)

Ray's so-called Hindi debut film (it is actually in Urdu with English), although featuring major Hindi stars, was refused a commercial release by local distributors because of Ray's Calcutta art-house reputation. This is a colorful period drama about colonialism and indigenous culture set in 1856 at the court of Wajid Ali Shah in Lucknow. Beginning with an animated cartoon about the British annexation policy (featuring the voice of Amitabh Bachchan), this film features two narratives: the first is based on Premchand's short story about two hookah-smoking zamindars playing interminable games of chess; the second dramatizes the conflict between Wajid and General Charles Outram. Stars Sanjeev Kumar, Saeed Jaffrey, Amjad Khan, Richard Attenborough and Shabana Azmi. Urdu with English subtitles.

VHS: S30069. $29.95.

Satyajit Ray, India, 1977

Days and Nights in the Forest

An incisive and moving study of four men who leave crowded and cold Calcutta for a brief holiday. At their destination, they will each have different, very unique and personal experiences that will alter their lives—a brief love affair, a cheap sexual experience and true love. By the time they leave, each one has been changed in a radical and unique way. Another insightful examination of the human condition from master director Satyajit Ray. Bengali with English subtitles.

VHS: S15379. $39.95.

Satyajit Ray, India, 1970, 120 mins.

Devi
Satyajit Ray broke radically from his humanist, neo-realist style with this sensual, stylized work about Indian superstitiousness, about a wealthy man who attempts to convince his son's young wife she's an incarnate of the goddess Kali. Bengali with English subtitles.
VHS: S16955. $19.95.
Satyajit Ray, India, 1962, 95 mins.

Dhund (Fog)
In this love-triangle suspense film, Zeenat Aman portrays a woman who is married to a vicious, crippled tyrant (Danny Denzongpa). When he is killed, she and her secret lover (Sanjay Khan) are the prime suspects. Hindi with English subtitles.
VHS: S30078. $29.95.
B.R. Chopra, India, 1973

Dil Deke Dehko
An Indian musical that's both a comedy and a tearjerker. With Shashi Kapoor and Asha Parekh. Hindi with English subtitles. India, 1964, 152 mins.
VHS: S22176. $39.95.

Distant Thunder
A moving dramatization of the effects of famine in India during World War II when the government controlled the food supply in order to feed troops, letting common people starve. The film follows the lives of several individuals including a doctor who humbles himself to survive. Bengali with English subtitles.
VHS: S01547. $44.95.
Satyajit Ray, India, 1974, 92 mins.

Do Ankhen Barah Haath
This award-winning Indian film by V. Shantaram is set in an Indian jail. A kind-hearted superintendent changes the lives of the prisoners. With V. Shantaram and Sandhya. Hindi with English and Arabic subtitles.
VHS: S22177. $39.95.
V. Shantaram, India, 1961, 130 mins.

Flames of the Sun (Sholay)
This Hollywood-style "curry western," combining romance, comedy, feudal costume drama and musical elements, broke box-office records in India. It is a revenge story of two adventurous crooks who are hired by an ex-cop to hunt down the man who massacred his family.
VHS: S30071. $29.95.
Ramesh Sippy, India, 1975

Friendship
A crippled boy (Sushil Kumar) and a blind boy (Sudhir Kumar) from Calcutta befriend a sick rich child (Farida) and help each other to survive. Famous for numerous hit songs. Hindi with English subtitles.
VHS: S30079. $29.95.
Satyen Bose, India, 1964

Garam Hava (Hot Winds)
Though never a commercial success, Sathyu's first film received critical acclaim for its masterly handling of the controversial theme of the partition of India during independence from British rule and the Muslim dilemma. The story centers around a middle-aged Muslim shoe manufacturer who must either leave his homeland of Agra, where he has lived for generations, or remain there to face the carnage threatening to ravage the new republic. Although the film's producers anticipated a hostile reception, it went on to win a national award for serving the cause of national integration. "The film remains a landmark for its sensitive portrayal of an essentially human problem emanating from forces of history and politics beyond the individual's control" (Shampa Banerjee, Anil Srivastava, *One Hundred Indian Films*). Urdu with English subtitles.
VHS: S30235. $29.95.
M.S. Sathyu, India, 1975, 136 mins.

Genesis
From one of India's most interesting filmmakers, Mrinal Sen, comes a parable of man's exploitation by his fellow man. A weaver and a farmer live peacefully beyond civilization, until a woman comes into their lives. "It brings home the sparseness, beauty and perils of existence," wrote *The New York Times*. Music by Ravi Shankar. Hindi with English subtitles.
VHS: S26502. $59.95.
Mrinal Sen, India, 1986, 105 mins.

God Is My Witness (Khuda Gawah)
Veteran Indian film actor Amitabh Bachchan stars as the noble Badshah Khan in his 85th film role. Khan meets the lovely Benazir (Sridevi) over a game of Buzkashi in Afghanistan, but before he can marry her, he must go to India and avenge Benazir's father's death. "A three-hour opus about love, prison and a man's word of honor…Spectacular!" (Anon Berger, *LA Weekly*). Winner of nine Indian Academy Awards, including Best Director, Best Cinematography and Best Supporting Actor. Featuring Nagarjun and Shilpa Shirodka. Hindi with English subtitles.
VHS: S25883. $79.95.

Hero
In this independent hit, orphan Jackie (Jackie Shroff) is raised by notorious criminal Pasha (Amrish Puri). When Pasha is arrested, he asks Jackie to silence the main prosecution witness, a retired police officer, Mathur (Shammi Kappor). Jackie kidnaps Mathur's daughter (Meenakshi Sheshadri), who falls in love with Jackie and asks him to give himself up. Hindi with English subtitles.
VHS: S30080. $29.95.
Subhash Ghai, India, 1983

Hum Paanch
Derived from a popular Mahabharata legend set in feudal UP, Bapu's first Hindi film is a remake of Puttanna Kanagal's *Paduvarahalli Pandavaru*. The villainous zamindar Veer Pratap Singh (Amrish Puri) is Duryodhanand, his sidekick Lala, (Kanhaiyalal), is Shakuni. They are opposed by Krishna, a drunken holy man (Sanjeev Kumar), Bhima (Mithun Chakraborty), and Arjun (Raj Babbar). Hindi with English subtitles.
VHS: S30081. $29.95.
Bapu, India, 1980

Imaan
Typical of Sanjeev Kumar's heavy and emotional films of this period, with Johnny Walker providing a comic turn. With Leena Chandavarkar. Hindi with English subtitles.
VHS: S33215. $29.95.
Padamnan, India, 1974

In Custody
Based on the novel by Anita Desai, this comedy has all the delightful details one expects from a Merchant/Ivory production. Surrounded by wine, women and song, a great poet lives his final days in comic self-indulgence. Then an earnest professor changes everything by interviewing him. Winner, National Film of India, Best Picture and Best Actor—Shashi Kapoor. Hindi with English subtitles.
VHS: S23428. $29.95.
Ismail Merchant, India, 1993, 123 mins.

In Praise of Mother Santoshi
This B-movie became the surprise hit of the year when it caused the little-known mother goddess, Santoshi, to become one of the most popular icons among urban working-class women as they began to observe the goddess's ritual fast. The foremost earthly disciple of Santoshi (Anita Guha) is Satyavati (Kanan Kaushal). When Satyavati marries the itinerant Birju, the wives of the celestial trio Brahma, Vishnu, and Shiva create a series of problems intended to test her devotion. Hindi with English subtitles.
VHS: S30082. $29.95.
Vijay Sharma, India, 1975

Jaanam
With Rahul Roy, Pooja Bhat, Paresh Rawal and Rema Lagu. Music by Anu Malik. Hindi with English subtitles.
VHS: S35158. $39.95.
Vikram Bhatt, India

Jalsaghar (The Music Room)
Ray's Chekhovian story of Bishamber Rai, an aging, proud, Indian nobleman who undergoes a slow decline after he, to spite his ambitious businessman neighbor, decides to present a lavish musical fete. "The hero is great *because* he destroys himself; he is also mad….worrying over its faults as a film is like worrying over whether *King Lear* is well constructed; it really doesn't matter" (Pauline Kael). With Chabi Biswas, Ganga Pada Basu, Kali Sarkhar and Padma Devi. Fully restored. Bengali with English subtitles.
VHS: S32166. $19.95.
Satyajit Ray, India, 1958, 100 mins.

Jana Aranya (The Middleman)
When Somnath, a young Calcuttan college graduate, fails to get a job in spite of his qualifications, he breaks with Brahmin tradition and goes into business as a middleman, which, he discovers, imposes a painful choice between morality and survival. Eventually the trafficking of goods becomes the trafficking of human beings as he begins supplying call girls to his clients. With Pradip Mukherjee, Satya Bannerfi, Dipankar Dey, Lily Chakravarti and Aparna Sen. Fully restored. "Under Ray's piercing yet compassionate glance, his characters darken with loss of innocence. The quiet urgency and emotional intensity of the film transcend its context; this is not only a film about India" (New York Film Festival note). Bengali with English subtitles.
VHS: S32168. $19.95.
Satyajit Ray, India, 1975, 131 mins.

Jeevan Dhara
This family drama focuses on a responsible daughter who sacrifices for her family. English subtitles.
VHS: S30073. $29.95.
T. Rama Rao, India, 1982

Jewel Thief
In this cult movie, which determined the look and the fashions of much of late '60s Hindi cinema, Dev Anand stars as the son of a police commissioner (Nasir Hussain), who finds himself mistaken for a notorious jewel thief and a woman's (Vyjayvanthimala) fiance. Features hit songs by Kishore Kumar and Lata Mangeshkar. Hindi with English subtitles.
VHS: S30083. $29.95.
Vijay Anand, India, 1967

Kabhi-Kabhi
A musical social drama dealing with middle class family life in India. The movie consists of songs and a strong performance by India's favorite actor, Amitabh Bachchan. With Rakhi Gulzar and Rishi Kapoor. Hindi with English subtitles. Music by Khayam.
VHS: S22172. $39.95.
Yash Chopra, India, 1978, 152 mins.

Kama Sutra
A seductive tale of love and betrayal in which a king's courtesan is forbidden to embrace her one true love. Trained in the art of pleasure, Maya (Indira Varma), the beautiful servant girl, becomes defiant, rebelling against ancient tradition. As passion takes over, the conflict brings consequences that no one ever envisioned. With Naveen Andrews, Sarita Choudury and Ramon Tiikaram. In English.
VHS: S31738. $99.99.
DVD: DV60306. $24.98.
Mira Nair, India, 1996, 113 mins.

Karma
In this Indian *Dirty Dozen* invoking terrorists backed by neighboring states, Dilip Kumar stars as a benevolent jail warden who feels people become criminals either because they are victims of a corrupt society, or through greed. Hindi with English subtitles.
VHS: S30084. $29.95.
Subhash Ghai, India, 1986

Kashmir Ki Kali
Taking its title from a hit song, this exotic comedy romance stars Shammi Kapoor as a rich youth who spurns his family's wealth and falls in love with a woman not of his social class who isn't interested in his money. Features several Mohammed Rafi hits. Hindi with English subtitles.
VHS: S30085. $29.95.
Shakti Samanta, India, 1964

Katha (The Tale) (The Fable)
This fairly successful musical satire was adapted from Paranjpye's play inspired by the tale of the tortoise and the hare. Rajaram (Naseeruddin Shah) is a slow but steady, upwardly mobile clerk who is in love with Sandhya (Deepti Naval), his neighbor, in a lower-middle-class tenement in Bombay. Rajaram's world is shaken up when the charming Basu (Farouque Shaikh) moves into the tenement and quickly wins three girlfriends, including Sandhya and Rajaram's boss' second wife and daughter. Hindi with English subtitles.
VHS: S30074. $29.95.
Sai Paranjpye, India, 1982

Mahanagar (The Big City)
Madhabi Mukherjee gives a beautiful performance as Arati, a housewife who, upon the urging of her bank clerk husband, takes a job selling knitting machines door to door to help support her family and her husband's extended family. Although the families disapprove of the idea, Arati is successful and finds her strength in the work. Focusing in particular on the role of women in this metaphorphosis, Ray tells a story that is both particular to Calcutta and universally recognizable. Fully restored. "Few directors can match Ray's facility for observation or his perceptiveness in registering those tiny moments of conflict when a casual nuance can drop like a bomb" (David Wilson, *Monthly Film Bulletin*). With Anil Chatterjee, Haradhan Benerjee and Haren Chatterjee. Bengali with English subtitles.
VHS: S32167. $19.95.
Satyajit Ray, India, 1963, 131 mins.

Mard
Amitabh Bachchan stars as Raju Tangewala, the son of a dispossessed rajah, who rebels against British property developers and is given the name "Mard" (man), which he has tattooed on his chest as a sign of virility.
VHS: S30086. $29.95.
Manmohan Desai, India, 1985

Mashall (The Torch)
A likeable masala thriller, written by Javed Akhtar, with a mild political context, starring Dilip Kumar, Anil Kumar, Waheeda Rehman and Rati Agnihotri. Hindi with English subtitles.
VHS: S33214. $29.95.
Yash Chopra, India, 1984

Mere Hazoor
An interesting Indian feature film about Muslim culture, its lifestyles and "etiquettes." Music by Shankar Jaikrishan. With Reaj Kumar, Mala Sinha and Jetinndra. Hindi with English subtitles.
VHS: S22178. $39.95.
Vinod Kumar, India, 1969, 145 mins.

Mere Jeevan Saathi
A highly unusual film from India: a musical-comedy romance, richly detailing a man's rise to success and sudden downfall. A surreal mosaic of colorful images, with flamboyant camera angles and haunting fantasy sequences. In vivid color! Hindi with English subtitles.
VHS: S00849. $29.95.
Ravee Nagaich, India, 1965, 126 mins.

Mohra
An Indian action film with some spectacular action sequences. With Naseerudin Shah, Sunil Shetty, Gulshan Grover, Akshay Kumar and Raveena Tandon. Music by Viju Shah. Hindi with English subtitles.
VHS: S35154. $39.95.
Rajiv Rai, India, 1994

Mother India (Bharat Mata)
This massively successful, award-winning film epic has acquired the status of an Indian *Gone with the Wind*. A color remake of Mehboob's own *Aurat*, the film stars Nargis as an old woman remembering her past and her happy married life with three sons in a rural village. Also stars Raj Kumar, Sunil Dutt and Rajendra Kumar. Hindi with English subtitles.
VHS: S30067. $29.95.
Mehboob Khan, India, 1957

Mughal-E-Azam
A historical Indian masterpiece, considered one of the mega-productions of the Indian screen. The powerful love story portrays a prince who is willing to leave his throne for the woman he loves. With music and songs. Stars Prithviraj Kapoor, Dilip Kumar, Durka Khote. Music by Nashad. Hindi and Urdu with English subtitles.
VHS: S22171. $39.95.
K. Asif, India, 1960, 182 mins.

Pakeezah
An Urdu-language film which stars Meena Kumari, Raj Kumar and Ashok Kumar in a story set in the Muslim culture of India. Much music and dance. Urdu with English subtitles.
VHS: S22179. $39.95.
Kamaal Amrohi, India, 1975, 173 mins.

Pather Panchali
The opening entry of Satyajit Ray's extraordinary *Apu* trilogy, adapted from the epic novel of Bengali writer B.B. Bandapaddhay, is a fiercely naturalistic, devastating portrait of poverty and despair. Ray uses his considerable storytelling powers of detail, incident and observation to interpret the relationship of a young Bengali boy and his family. The film has an emotional rhythm and a fluid, precise lyricism. Winner of the Jury Prize at the 1956 Cannes Film festival. Music composed and performed by Ravi Shankar. With Kanu Banerji, Karuna Banerji, Uma Da Gupta and Chunibala Devi. Newly remastered. Bengali with English subtitles.
VHS: S27702. $19.95.
Satyajit Ray, India, 1955, 112 mins.

Sadma
This remake of Mahendra's classic *Moondram Pirai* stars Kumal Hasan, Sridevi, Gulshan Grover and Silk Smith in one her best roles. Hindi with English subtitles.
VHS: S33216. $29.95.
Balu Mahendra, India, 1983

Saheb
A beautiful family drama about a middle-class family in urban India, featuring talented young actors and great music. English and Arabic subtitles.
VHS: S30076. $29.95.

Satyajit Ray's Apu Trilogy
Lifetime Achievement Award winner Satyajit Ray's three-part masterpiece of a Bengali boy's life from birth through manhood is collected here for the first time for home viewing. *Pather Panchali* (1955, 113 mins.), *Aparajito* (1956, 113 mins.) and *The World of Apu* (1959, 106 mins.), voted Best Foreign Film by the National Board of Review, have all been fully restored to their original beauty and clarity and feature new subtitles for easier viewing, as well as a digitally remixed and remastered soundtrack of Ravi Shankar's original scores. Three-volume box set. Bengali with English subtitles.
VHS: S27701. $59.95.
Satyajit Ray, India, 1995, 332 min.

Shree 420
An epic by the talented showman of Indian cinema Raj Kapoor, full of music and dancing. The movie contrasts the poor and the rich in Indian, culture and stars Kapoor and Nargis. Music by Shankar Jaikrishan. Hindi with English and Arabic subtitles.
VHS: S22180. $39.95.
Raj Kapoor, India, 1959, 157 mins.

Sir
A remake of *The Principal* by director Bhatt, who started making art films but gradually turned more commercial. This film is distinguished by an interesting performance by Pooja Bhat. With Nasserudin Shah and Paresh Rawal. Music by Anu Malik. Hindi with English subtitles.
VHS: S35153. $39.95.
Mahesh Bhatt, India, 1993

Spices
Spices is a spirited, feminist fable from India, where women have few rights and little power. This story of oppression and rebellion was shot in rural Gujarat with both actual villagers and India's top name stars. It explores a community's reaction to a woman's plight as an impoverished beauty named Sonbai spurns the amorous advances of a local tax collector (called sudebars) and takes refuge in a pepper factory. Few of the villagers have the courage to defend her, least of all its men, who are blind to injustice against women. Sonbai's eventual victory is not simply over the villainous sudebar, but over tyranny itself and the subservience that sustains it. The fiery Sonbai was Smita Patil's (two-time winner of India's National Best Actress Award) last role. Originally titled *Mirch Masala*. Hindi with English subtitles.
VHS: S13652. $29.95.
Ketan Mehta, India, 1986, 98 mins.

The Stranger (Agantuk)
Ray's last great masterpiece is the provocative tale of Manmohan, a world traveler who returns to Calcutta after 35 years to visit his niece, Anila. Anila's suspicious husband believes the long-lost uncle to be an imposter who has come to claim an inheritance. As Manmohan's identity is slowly revealed, Anila and her husband must examine their own identities in relation to traditional values and modern civilization. Bengali with English subtitles. "A tour-de-force as the film maestro fathoms his characters psychologically and intellectually…the camera is wielded like a conductor's baton as *Agantuk* strikes chords deep in the mind…a dream of a performance!" *(The Times)*.
VHS: S30611. $59.95.
Satyajit Ray, India, 1991, 120 mins.

Target
Written by Satyajit Ray and directed by his son, Sandip Ray, this powerful and dramatic epic tells the story of an "untouchable" village's struggle against an oppressive landlord. Features celebrated Indian actors Om Puri *(City of Joy, Killing Fields, Ghandi)*, Mohan Agashe *(Salaam Bombay, Mississippi Masala)* and Champa Islam. *"Target's* aim is true. A subtle, unexpectedly powerful movie" *(The Washington Post)*. Hindi with English subtitles.
VHS: S34676. $89.95.
Sandip Ray, India, 1995, 122 mins.

Threshold (aka Dawn) (Umbartha/Subah)
In her best-known screen role, Smita Patil plays Sulabha, the wife of a progressive lawyer (Girish Karnad) who sullies the character of a rape victim in order to benefit his client, the accused rapist. Outraged, Sulabha goes to work in a women's home. When she returns, she discovers her husband has taken a mistress, and determines to leave her home and make a life for herself. Based on an autobiographical work by Shanta Nisal, the film was given a feminist value by Patil's performance and by her use of the film in women's rights campaigns. Marathi/Hindi with English subtitles.
VHS: S30072. $29.95.
Jabbar Parel, India, 1981

Trishul
In this big-budget sequel to *Deewar* (1975), Amitabh Bachchan stars as an Oedipal young man obsessed with his mother, whom he believes has been abandoned by his father (Sanjeev Kumar), and plans a revenge to ruin the prominent businessman.
VHS: S30087. $29.95.
Yash Chopra, India, 1978

Two Daughters
Two wonderfully ironic stories by Ray dealing with the emancipation of women. In the first, a young university graduate rejects his pre-selected bride to marry the village tomboy, who protests. The hero, who does not want to marry a woman he doesn't love, denies the same choice to the girl he does want for his bride. Based on stories by Tagore. With Soumitra Chatterjee, Aparna Das Gupta and Anil Chatterjee. Bengali with English subtitles.
VHS: S04464. $19.95.
Satyajit Ray, India, 1961, 114 mins.

Vidhaata
An Indian *Godfather* with lots of star turns by Indian legends Dilip Kumar and Shammi Kapoor, and the strong young presence of Sanjay Dutt. Hindi with English subtitles.
VHS: S33218. $29.95.
Subhash Ghai, India, 1982

Who Was She?
One of director Khosla's favorites, this rare, big-budget, *Vertigo*-style thriller concerns a young doctor (Manoj Kumar) who is obsessed with a woman who appears to him with different names and guises, making him doubt his senses. Original title: *Woh Kaun Thi*.
VHS: S30088. $29.95.
Raj Khosla, India, 1964

The World of Apu
The final part of Satyajit Ray's *Apu* trilogy, adapted from Bengali writer B.B. Bandapaddhay's epic novel, is a poignant summing up of the earlier films' themes and stylistic preoccupations. Its story traces Apu's leap into adulthood, the consequences of his marriage and birth of his first child. Ray's painterly use of landscape finds a poetry in the incidental, loose textures of daily life. Music by Ravi Shankar. With Soumitra Chatterjee (as Apu), Sharmila Tagore, Alok Chakravarty, and Swapan Mukherji. Newly remastered. Bengali with English subtitles.
VHS: S27704. $19.95.
Satyajit Ray, India, 1959, 105 mins.

Zamaaneko Dikanahai
With Rishi Kapoor, Padmini Kolhapure and Amhad Khan. Hindi with English subtitles.
VHS: S33217. $29.95.
Nasir Husain, India, 1981

INDIAN ISSUES

2,000 Years of Freedom and Honor: The Cochini Jews of India
Jews arrived in India in 72 C.E., soon after the destruction of the Second Temple in Jerusalem. Throughout the years, though deeply loyal to India, they prayed for their return to Zion. This documentary captures the conflicting emotions of two generations of Cochini Jews, and explores their religious, cultural and economic life.
VHS: S33188. $59.95.
Johanna Spector, India, 180 mins.

Best of Nightline: Assassination of Indira Gandhi
30 mins.
VHS: S14032. $14.98.

Brothers in Trouble
Om Puri stars in this vivid portrait of a group of Pakistani illegals in 1960s Britain, in a funny, moving, well-acted film directed by and starring Udayan Prashad, with Om Puri *(City of Joy)* and Angeline Ball *(The Commitments)*. "Has the density and richness of a fine novel" *(Chicago Tribune)*.
VHS: S33319. $79.95.
Udayan Prashad, Great Britain, 1997, 104 mins.

Experience North India
Float along the River Ganges, take a rickshaw ride to the Taj Mahal, learn elephant-riding etiquette, take a Himalayan trek and be a guest at Krishna's 3,500-year birthday party. 47 mins.
VHS: S31472. $19.99.

Great Days of History: Gandhi and India's Independence
This documentary presents a portrait of the architect of India's independence and of the techniques of non-violent resistance. The program documents the reasons for the Indian independence movement, the periodic efforts to thwart or throw off British rule and the nature of British reprisals and Gandhi's role in these events. 52 mins.
VHS: S09435. $29.95.

Hindustani Slide: The Indian Classical Guitar of Debashish Bhattacharya
Northern Indian music has recently added the guitar and slide guitar to a rich musical tradition. Debashish has played since the age of three. The master is accompanied by Kumar Bose to reveal the intricacies and purity of this evolving tradition.
VHS: S25059. $24.95.

India and the Infinite: The Soul of a People
Dr. Huston Smith, author of *The Religions of Man*, joins acclaimed filmmaker Elda Hartley in this award-winning voyage through India's haunting spiritual landscape. Hartley's magnificent images, gathered from Kashmir to Benares, Bombay to Bangalore, combine with Smith's poetic narration in this visual essay of lingering beauty. 30 mins.
VHS: S33853. $19.98.

India, Land of Spirit and Mystique

See the holy city of Varnasi, where pilgrims bathe in the healing waters of the River Ganges. Glide into the past along the canals and lakes of Srinagar. Conclude your visit in Bombay, India's economic hub. 55 mins.
VHS: S10778. $24.95.

Nehru

A fascinating documentary study of the peoples, customs, religions and politics of the "new" India, as told by the descendants of Nehru—the "Father of India."
VHS: S15484. $39.95.
Serge Friendman, USA, 1972

Raga

All the richness of India is in *Raga*. Ravi Shankar returns to Baba, his music guru, after many years of success and acclaim in the West. Indian music had suddenly appeared on the pop scene. And Ravi, who had always wanted to bring his music to the West, is caught up in the whole exuberance of the California sixties music scene. Here we see his popular and triumphant return. Directed by Howard Worth. 95 mins.
VHS: S14716. $19.95.

BUDDHISM AND EASTERN RELIGIONS

The 17th Karrmapa's Return to Tsurphu

The Gyalwa Karmapas were the first Tibetan lamas to be acknowledged as reincarnations and represent some of the most important spiritual figures of Tibet. This program studies the spectacle and circumstances behind the 17th Gyalwa Karmapa's triumphant return to his original seat at the Tsurphu monastery in summer of 1992. The film concludes with the Karmapa's enthronement at the Jokhang Temple. 100 mins.
VHS: S18640. $29.95.

Ancient Futures: Learning from Ladakh

A look at the society of Ladakh, a beautiful, ancient culture high in the Western Himalayas, which until recently was a model of sustainable living. Western style development is now threatening their ecological balance and social harmony. A vivid case study of the potentially harmful impact of "progress". 59 mins.
VHS: S23383. $95.00.

Arising from Flames

The Dalai Lama leads the viewer through the basic precepts of his beliefs in a speech he gave at Tucson, Arizona. He describes how to reduce anger and hatred while simultaneously increasing love and forgiveness. His own experiences as an exile from Tibet offer a perfect example of how trying circumstances can be used for positive results. 60 mins.
VHS: S21188. $29.95.

Bhutan: A Himalayan Cultural Diary

A unique story of the people of Bhutan, their religion and the challenge of dealing with the 20th century. A fascinating look at the easternmost country astride the Himalayas. 35 mins.
VHS: S23346. $29.95.

Buddhism and Black Belts

Filmed in Japan, this video explores the connection between Buddhism and daily activity, the historical relationship of Japanese-style martial arts and the meditation-driven ideas and philosophy of Zen Buddhism.
VHS: S18452. $19.95.

A Change of Heart

Ram Dass, aka Dr. Richard Alpert, a Harvard psychologist, received this new name from his guru on a trip to India. In this documentary, the teaching of service that inspired him there becomes available to a large audience through excerpts from his ten-week "Reaching Out Course." Interviews with other social activists testify to the effectiveness of this spiritual approach to enlightenment.
VHS: S21299. $29.95.

Door of Compassion: An Interview with Zen Meditation Master Thich Nhat Hanh

In this illuminating interview, Hanh, chairman of the Vietnamese Peace Delegation, imparts methods of learning the important skills of mindfulness toward greater self-understanding and peacefulness as he explores the crossroads of holiness and compassion at which the world traditions meet. 42 mins.
VHS: S31553. $24.95.

Exploring the Himalayas, Nepal & Kashmir

This video journey starts in India's state of Kashmir, at Srinagar, on the beautiful Dal Lake, then goes to the ancient trading city of Leh in remote Ladakh and the Annapurna mountains. Raft the Trisuli River, ride the elephant in Chitwan National Park, refuge for the one-horned rhino. Explore the emerald city of Kathmandu, observe the colorful Indra Jatra and meet the engaging Sherpa people living in the shadow of Mt. Everest. 60 mins.
VHS: S12295. $29.95.

The Four Noble Truths

In July 1996, before an audience of 2,500 people at the Barbicon Hall in London, the Dalai Lama taught the most essential lessons of Buddhism for the first time in the west. Produced by award-winning filmmaker David Cherniak, this film shows the Dalai Lama explaining Buddhism in terms of the principles of the independent nature of reality and non-violence. Four-tape boxed set. 6 hours
VHS: S30625. $108.00.

The Good Heart

On this unprecedented video from the 10th annual John Main Seminar in London, the Dalai Lama comments on well-known passages from each of the four Christian Gospels, providing a unique reading of these familiar sources of faith. Four-volume set includes *Day One: St. Matthew's Gospel, Day Two: St. Mark's Gospel, Day Three: St. Luke's Gospel* and *Day Four: St. John's Gospel*. Six hours.
VHS: S31774. $79.98.

H.H. The Dalai Lama on Campus

The Dalai Lama delivers a simple yet profound message of global peace, prosperity and harmony in this 1997 address at UCLA's Pauley Pavilion. Introduced by Richard Gere. 95 mins.
VHS: S33676. $19.98.

The Healers

A fascinating and practical introduction to several Eastern healing techniques and two remarkable men who practice them. Learn about Qi Gong, moxibustion, acupuncture and other methods. Two tapes. 100 mins.
VHS: S32725. $29.95.

Heart of Tibet

This intimate portrait of the 14th Dalai Lama during a visit to Los Angeles reveals His Holiness as a man of simplicity and humor who constantly deals with highly complex ideas and sensitive issues. The program offers a real insight into this remarkable personality, augmented by interviews with the Dalai Lama himself, footage from his visit, and talks with writers, journalists and academicians.
VHS: S15434. $29.95.

David Cherniack, USA, 60 mins.

Himalayan Trekking: Sherpa Expeditions, Nepal
Discover the rugged, remote and stunning high wilderness regions of the Himalayas. Few forms of travel allow close contact with natives and wildlife like trekking. Surprisingly, few treks involve mountaineering ability or specific skills. Local guides strike a path through untamed corners of the world while porters, mules or support vehicles carry the baggage. Walk at your own pace, and enjoy special interests like bird-watching or photography.
VHS: S15845. $19.95.

Human Rights and Moral Practice: The Dalai Lama at Berkeley

This video documents one of the rare occasions on which the Dalai Lama has spoken so forthcomingly about politics. Before an audience of thousands at the University of California in Berkley in 1996, he addressed such themes as birth control, arms trade and the global economy with great insight and sensitivity. 35 mins.
VHS: S31554. $24.95.

Huston Smith: The Mystic's Journey Gift Box Set

Best-selling author Huston Smith *(The World's Religions)* and filmmaker Elda Hartley have each spent decades exploring worldwide spiritual practices. These timeless classics, gathered over 30 years, provide penetrating insights and unprecedented access to some of civilization's most advanced traditions. Includes *The Mystic's Journey, Requiem for a Faith* and *India Infinite*. Each tape is 30 mins.
VHS: S33855. $39.98.

Joseph Campbell: Mythos II

Journey with Joseph Campbell *(The Power of Myth)* as he takes you through the shaping of the eastern tradition and examines spirituality through the mythic images of Hinduism and Buddhism. Hosted by Susan Sarandon. Five-volume set includes *Inward Path, The Enlightened One, Our Eternal Selves, The Way to Illumination* and *The Experience of God*. 280 mins.
VHS: S34728. $99.95.

Kalachakra: The Wheel of Time

This video shows Tibetan Buddhist monks constructing a sand mandala in Ireland according to a 2600-year-old tradition. It is part of the secret Kalachakra initiation rite, which teaches wisdom and compassion. The rite itself is said to affect world peace. 30 mins.
VHS: S26179. $29.95.

Ladakh: In Harmony with the Spirit

Through their belief in tantric Buddism, the people of Ladakh still have strong connections to the psychic energies of gods and demons. This film is a mixture of reality and fiction, history and mythology.
VHS: S16618. $29.95.
Clemens Kuby, USA, 1989, 86 mins.

Mandala: World of Mystic Circle

The mystic uses and scientific possibilities of the mandala are the basis for this examination of the mystic circle used by Tibetan Monks. From a ceremonial dismantling of the sacred Kalachakra mandala to the traces of this eternal pattern found in other historical forms, even in the patterns of matter that make up the universe, this sacred symbol has strange power. 1992, 50 mins.
VHS: S20774. $29.95.

Mind in Tibetan Buddhism

With Ole Nydahl. This Tibetan Buddhist master describes the mind as a pure, limitless field where our thoughts create visions which appear objective to us in sleep and death. 30 mins.
VHS: S08641. $29.95.

Mustang: The Hidden Kingdom

The Dalai Lama's personal emissary acts as guide to this legendary place. Then the ancient elephant routes of India and Bhutan are traversed in the *Queen of Elephants*. Both films are from the Discovery Channel.
VHS: S22543. $19.95.

Nepal: Land of the Gods

A journey to the mountain kingdom of Nepal which explores the Bodhisattva ideals of life, death, karma and rebirth in a land where Tantra is an integral part of daily life, with a unique document of the ancient cultures still thriving in Nepal. 62 mins.
VHS: S00922. $29.95.

Ossian: American Boy/Tibetan Monk

Story of a 12-year-old boy who has lived from age four as a monk in a Tibetan Buddhist monastery in Kathmandu, and is thought to be an incarnation of a High Lama. USA, 1984, 27 mins.
VHS: S02099. $19.95.

Peace Is Every Step

Profiles the full range of the life and work of noted Vietnamese Zen teacher, author and peace activist Thich Nhat Hanh. Features original footage from around the world as well as rare archival scenes from Thich Nhat Hanh's work in the war-torn Vietnam of the 1960s. Directed by award-winning filmmaker Gaetano Kazuo Maida. Narrated by Ben Kingsley. 60 mins.
VHS: S33746. $29.95.

The Reincarnation of Khensur Rinpoche

A Tibetan monk named Choenzy, living in South India, learns about a young boy in Tibet possessed with uncommon qualities that suggest he may be the reincarnation of his spiritual master, Khensur Rinpoche, a revered figure who died four years earlier. "Between Khensur Rinpoche and me, our relationship goes beyond this present lifetime. It's like his body has changed, but inside, the same consciousness has come" (Choenzy). 62 mins.
VHS: S20214. $29.95.

Requiem for a Faith

Witness the last precious vestiges of one of the most spiritual places on earth: Tibet. Acclaimed author Dr. Huston Smith *(The Religions of Man)* provides the moving narration to filmmaker Elda Hartley's remarkable images of a vanished Shangri-La. 30 mins.
VHS: S33854. $19.98.

The Sacred Art of Tibet/ The Visible Compendium

The Sacred Art of Tibet (1972, 28 mins.) was inspired by a gallery showing of unique Tibetan thankas, religious scroll paintings, rupas and other sacred images and artifacts. Jordan set out to present a visual experience of Tibetan Tantric Buddhism, and the resulting film rises above conventional documentary form to become a beautiful and autonomous work of art in its own right. *The Visible Compendium* (1990, 17 mins.) is an animated film that took two years to make and is one of Jordan's most technically refined works to date. It takes the viewer on a trip through idyllic lands where plants smile, an image of a tiger appears in the sun, and nude women wander about comfortably within an enchanted landscape. A beautiful and densely constructed work, rich in enigmatic and allusive images.
VHS: S14552. $59.95.
Larry Jordan, USA, 1972/90, 45 mins.

Sanatan Dharma: Pilgrimage to the Source of Eternal Wisdom

The headwaters to the Mother of India, the Ganges River, are located in the beautiful foothills of the Himalayas. There, Indians and Westerners alike experience the values of truth, simplicity and love that comprise the eternal, universal religion. 43 mins.
VHS: S21230. $29.95.

Secular Meditation
The Dalai Lama addresses the benefits of achieving a state of mental happiness through meditation. 50 mins.
VHS: S31411. $19.98.

Tai Chi: 6 Forms 6 Easy Lessons
Dr. Paul Lam, a Tai Chi master and medical doctor, has combined the best of Eastern and Western traditions. He has distilled the 24 most popular forms of Tai Chi into 6 Forms that are perfect for beginners. Also includes a bonus set of "three in one" Qi Gong exercises. 100 mins.
VHS: S32700. $24.98.

Tantra
An impressionistic video experience that forsakes all language, plunging the viewer without explanation into the sounds and visual splendor of Tantra (a sect of Hinduism) art and ritual. The result is a hypnotic manifestation of faith and experience in poetic form, an interwoven fabric of sound, color, form, emotion and feeling. Directed by Nik Douglas. 1969, 40 mins.
VHS: S14577. $29.95.

Tantra of Gyuto
The Dalai Lama introduces ancient Tantric rituals that use mantric power to transform consciousness, featuring the harmonic chord-chanting of the Gyuto Lamas. Prefaced by rare footage of Tibet narrated by Francis Huxley. 52 mins.
VHS: S01300. $29.95.

Tibet in Exile
This film documents the tragic plight of Tibet, focusing on the nearly 120,000 Tibetans who have escaped from their remote homeland to live in India and Nepal under the guidance of their leader, the Dalai Lama. The video highlights the story of 10 children smuggled out of Tibet by their relatives.
VHS: S15214. $75.00.
B. Banks/M. McLagan, USA, 1991, 30 mins.

Tibet's Holy Mountain
At the intersection of Tibet, Nepal and India is a 22,000'-high mountain believed to house the throne of the foremost gods of Hinduism and Buddhism. This video shows many religious sites on the route to Mt. Kailish, including the 11th-century Tibetan capital of Guge, and Llahsa, the site of rich decorative arts from the Buddhist tradition. 52 mins.
VHS: S22928. $29.95.

Tibet: A Seed for Transformation
This educational video contains information concerning China's takeover of Tibet and how this may affect the rest of the world. Content includes Tibet's Location, Customs and Culture; China's Nuclear Activities; Human Rights Violations; Environmental Destruction; etc. The soundtrack features chanting by the Dalai Lama and Tibetan monks.
VHS: S14538. $49.95.
Wendy Schofield, USA, 29 mins.

Tibet: The Survival of the Spirit
Shot on location in Tibet without Chinese censorship (although the director was arrested three times while filming), this documentary presents a compelling portrayal of conditions in occupied Tibet today. A journal of the Tibetans' unbreakable will to survive, founded on their religious practices.
VHS: S16617. $29.95.
Clemens Kuby, USA, 1991, 92 mins.

Tibetan Buddhist Meditation
With Ole Nydahl. The Tibetan Buddhist meditation master takes us step by step through the teaching—quieting the mind, focusing on motivations for meditation, and taking refuge in the *Buddha*, *Dharma* and *Sangha*. 30 mins.
VHS: S08642. $29.95.

Tibetan Medicine
Ama Lobsang Dolma, Tibet's first woman doctor, heals both the physical and psychic being by treating the patient rather than the disease. Filmed at the Tibetan Medical Center in the Himalayas. 29 mins.
VHS: S01341. $29.95.

Touching Peace
Filmed before an audience of 3,500 in Berkeley, California, Thich Nhat Hanh speaks intimately and insightfully, touching deeply on community building, connecting with your roots, arriving in each moment, and learning true love. 90 mins.
VHS: S33747. $29.95.

A Trek in Nepal
A group of adventurous Americans experience the rugged natural beauty of trekking in Nepal. Highlights include visits to Sherpa homes, the Namche Bazaar, ancient Buddhist temples and the Himalayas. 28 mins.
VHS: S23349. $29.95.

Walking with the Buddha
As immigrants from Southeast Asia continue to come to the U.S., their influence will undoubtedly grow. Theravad Buddhism, with its emphasis on compassion and meditation, offers an example and challenge to all. Filmed in Thailand, this video looks at the Buddha and his followers.
VHS: S21850. $19.95.

Where Eagles Fly: Portraits of Women in Power
An innovative series focusing on powerful, spiritual women.
Nadia Stepanova, Buryatian Shaman. Stepanova is a Buryatian shaman intent on the revival of ceremonies that were performed in the taiga regions of Siberia north of Mongolia. This area is said to be the birthplace of shamanism at the dawn of civilization. This video captures her spiritual mission. 30 mins.
VHS: S26295. $29.95.
We Will Meet Again in the Land of the Dakini. Doljin Kandro Suren is an 80-year-old Buddhist lama and spiritual guide for thousands from Mongolia and Russia. She resisted the anti-religious policies which demoralized her people and now works to combat their despair through ancient spiritual traditions. Now people the world over can hear her teachings through this video. 30 mins.
VHS: S26183. $29.95.

Zen and I: The Life of a Zen Priest
A day in the life of Tachibana Taiki, the most powerful Zen priest in Japan, called "the great turtle priest," Chief Abbot of the Imperial Daitokuji Temple in Kyoto. He discusses the meaning of Zen, its place in the life of the individual, the achievement of enlightenment and the proper way to look on death. Filmed entirely in Japan. With commentary by noted authority on Asian art and Japanese culture Faubion Bowers. 1975, 27 mins.
VHS: S32334. $89.95.

Zen: In Search of Enlightenment
A revealing look at the Japanese form of Buddhism and the determining element in Japanese character. This program explores Zen—a way of life that stresses discipline and self-abnegation and fosters a single-minded devotion to one's goal. 120 mins.
VHS: S20533. $29.95.

Zen: The Best of Alan Watts
Alan Watts has been hailed as both a Zen master and a leading counterculture figure. Now excerpts from films made between 1965 and 1973 have been culled to bring the best of his teachings to new audiences. It all begins when you can conceive of nature as a metaphor. 60 mins.
VHS: S22970. $29.95.

AFRICAN CINEMA

Cinema of Senegal
Senegalese directors Paulin Soumanou Vieyra, Ousmane Sembene and Larry Kardish (Museum of Modern Art Film Department) discuss the need to build an African film audience, the colonial experience, Islam versus native culture, and interpreting the past in film. Includes clips of several films by the participants and by colleagues Samb-Makharam and Traore. 1978, 28 mins. In French with English translation voiceover.
VHS: S31581. $59.95.

Faces of Women
Eugenie Cisse Roland, Sidiki Bakaba and Albertine N'Guessan star in this vibrant, adventurous film about contemporary Africa. Two women try to balance the demands of tradition and modern life in their changing world. It's a sensual, joyous combination of raucous comedy and pulsating African music. In indigenous languages and French with English subtitles.
VHS: S22444. $79.95.
Desire Ecare, Ivory Coast, 1985, 105 mins.

Harvest: 3,000 Years
Haile Gerima *(Sankofa)* returned to his native Ethiopia to make this realistic drama set in contemporary Africa. A peasant family struggles to survive under conditions that remain tied to a feudal past, fighting against the demands of a wealthy and uncaring landowner. Gerima's realism puts the story into the broader historical context of the colonialist African legacy. In Amharic with English subtitles.
VHS: S25565. $59.95.
Haile Gerima, Ethiopia, 1976, 150 mins.

Hyenas
Based on Friedrich Durrenmatt's play *The Visit of the Old Woman*, *Hyenas* is the story of Linguere Ramatou (Ami Diakhate), a woman who returns to the village she was banished from 30 years before. She left poor, unmarried and pregnant, and now returns wealthy, free—and vengeful. Linguere promises the people of the village of Colobane her entire fortune in exchange for the life of Dramaan Drameh (Mansour Diouf), the man who betrayed her and sent her into exile. A brilliant metaphor for post-colonial Africa. "A crowd pleaser…a wicked tale told with wit and irony" (Georgia Brown, *The Village Voice*). In Wolof with English subtitles.
VHS: S31624. $79.95.
Djibril Diop Mambety, Senegal, 1992, 113 mins.

Jit
An old-fashioned romantic comedy from Zimbabwe which features the irresistible beat of African jit-jive in the story of UK, determined to win the heart of Sofi, who is closely guarded by her gangster boyfriend. UK's efforts to win Sofi's heart are hilariously hindered by an ancestral spirit. English language.
VHS: S21893. $29.95.
Michael Raeburn, Zimbabwe, 1993, 98 mins.

Kasarmu Ce: This Land Is Ours
A taut West African thriller that draws on Hausa and western storytelling, centering on the efforts of a young man to avenge the murder of his grandfather by a brutal land baron attempting to seize control of the iron-rich village lands. A politically potent and culturally interesting film, *Kasarmu Ce* is a "penetrating, poetic, joyously contemplative thriller set in a rural backdrop" *(West African Magazine)*. Hausa with English subtitles.
VHS: S18889. $19.95.
Saddik Balewa, Nigeria, 1991, 84 mins.

La Vie Est Belle (Life Is Rosy)
A farce infused with the Zairian sense of belief in Systeme-D or debrouillardise (the art of hustling for survival), this film explores the rich musical world of Kinshasha. It follows a young man who uses wit and guile to trick his greedy boss, attain the woman he loves, and sing his favorite song ("La Vie Est Belle") on national television. French with English subtitles.
VHS: S27561. $59.95.
Ngangura Mweze/Benoit Lamy, Zaire/Belgium, 1987, 85 mins.

Quartier Mozart
Winner of the *Prix Afrique en Creation* at Cannes in 1992, this humorous and magical tale is filled with the sexual antics that enliven a working class neighborhood in Yaounde. A girl takes on the body of a man and learns the true sexual politics of the men around her. In addition, the woman who helps her achieve this transformation metamorphoses herself into Panka, a comic figure who can make a man's penis disappear with a handshake. French with English subtitles.
VHS: S27559. $59.95.
Jean-Pierre Bekolo, Cameroon, 1992, 80 mins.

Tilai
One of the most highly acclaimed contemporary African films. In this troubling drama, a young African man is engaged to the woman he loves until the man's father decides that he should marry this woman himself. This fateful decision forces the young lovers into an illicit affair. On the run, they find tradition and the law will play a large role in their fate. In More with English subtitles.
VHS: S26145. $79.95.
Idrissa Ouedraogo, Burkina Faso, 1990, 81 mins.

Touki Bouki
Mory and his girlfriend Anta imagine an escape from the difficult life they share in Dakar. Paris is their destination, and like the heroes of French New Wave films, they are utterly alienated from their surroundings. A series of adventures ensues as they plot ways to raise money for their trip, but only one can face up to the reality that awaits them. Wolof with English subtitles.
VHS: S27558. $59.95.
Djibril Diop Mambety, Senegal, 1973, 85 mins.

Wend Kuuni (God's Gift)
The measured rhythms and formal compositions of African oral traditions give shape to this metaphoric film about Mossi values. A young mute boy, orphaned when his mother refuses to marry, is found and adopted by a village, which names him "Wend Kuuni," or "God's Gift." This remarkable film won a Cesar and numerous other international awards. More with English subtitles.
VHS: S27560. $59.95.
Gaston Kabore, Burkina Faso, 1982, 70 mins.

SOUTH AFRICAN CINEMA

7 Up in South Africa
A remarkable work that contrasts the lives, attitudes, fears and hopes of 19 South African children caught in oppressive cycles of political violence, tyranny and authoritarian rule. The film documents their determination and hope in spite of the rigid social and political conditions. "A powerful and deeply disturbing comment on the prospects for change in South Africa. The children introduced here are endearingly open and impish" (*The Guardian*).
VHS: S19244. $19.95.
Angus Gibson, South Africa, 1993, 83 mins.

Cry Freedom
An intimate, true tragedy set against the upheavals in South Africa. Tells of the friendship of white journalist Donald Woods (Kevin Kline) and black activist Stephen Biko (Denzel Washington), and the subsequent biography of Biko, championing his cause and telling his story to the world.
VHS: S06820. $14.98.
Laser: LD70021. $39.98.
Richard Attenborough, USA, 1987, 157 mins.

Cry, The Beloved Country

James Earl Jones and Richard Harris star in this adaptation of Alan Paton's famous book. In South Africa two men, one a religious black man and the other a wealthy white farmer, come into conflict over a murder. It's a story which pits family ties and nationalist fervor against the ideals of justice.

VHS: S27846. $19.95.
Laser: LD75928. $39.99.
Darrell Roodt, South Africa, 1995, 120 mins.

A Dry White Season

Donald Sutherland is cast as an incredibly naive South African schoolteacher who has trouble believing his black gardener's son would be arrested for no good reason. Set in the historical perspective of violence and unrest of 1976, director Euzhan Palcy (*Sugar Cane Alley*) uses this basically decent man as a symbol of needed political involvement. A powerful film with a first rate cast that includes Janet Suzman, Susan Sarandon, Winston Ntschone, Zakes Mokae and Marlon Brando as a cynical but able liberal lawyer.

VHS: Out of print. For rental only.
Laser: LD70957. $39.98.
Euzhan Palcy, USA, 1989, 97 mins.

Friends

A brilliant debut feature, this is the story of three South African women who find their friendship put to the test by extreme political circumstances. One of the three, a black activist, is involved in a deadly bomb incident. This sets in motion passionate and blinding forces that threaten to destroy the ideals that originally joined them. With Kerry Fox (*An Angel at My Table*). "Fascinating and bold...has a blazing urgency and passion...boasts a thrilling performance by one of the world's great young actresses, New Zealander Kerry Fox" (Michael Wilmington, *Chicago Tribune*).

VHS: S26870. $59.95.
Elaine Proctor, South Africa, 1994, 109 mins.

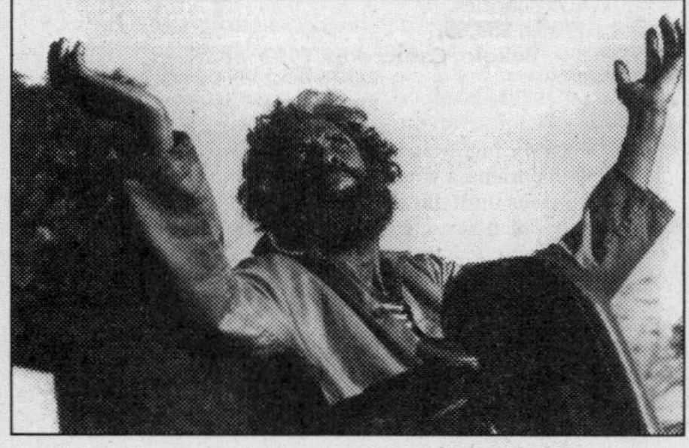

The Gods Must Be Crazy

An international sensation, one of the highest-grossing foreign films in the U.S. and Europe, Jamie Uys' unlikely comedy is the story of an African bushman who discovers a discarded Coke bottle which ultimately brings him face to face with modern man for the first time. Very heartwarming, entertaining, full of non-stop high-jinks, this story about an innocent bushman's encounter with the 20th century has become one of the cult films of the 1980's.

Laser: LD71008. $34.98.
Jamie Uys, South Africa, 1984, 109 mins.

The Gods Must Be Crazy II

Everyone's favorite African Bushman is back in action but this time his mission is personal. When N!Xau finds that his children have been taken for a ride by a pair of unsuspecting poachers, he leaves his village to find them. Along the way he encounters silly white people and other members of the animal kingdom. With Lena Farugia, Hans Strydom and a very tenacious badger.

VHS: S14005. $19.95.
Jamie Uys, USA/Botswana, 1989

The Magic Garden (The Pennywhistle Blues)

An all black cast is featured in this South African musical allegory. Near Johannesburg, a community is affected when some "magic money" is stolen. The film follows those who come in contact with the money from the magic garden. There are many smiles along the way. Filmed in English.

VHS: S05482. $29.95.
Donald Swanson, South Africa, 1960, 63 mins.

Place of Weeping

A powerful human drama of one woman's personal fight for freedom: her bravery, emotional traumas and fight against both the deep-rooted resentment of her people and the violent and oppressive hand of the apartheid system. Starring James Whylie.

VHS: S03037. $19.95.
Darrell Roodt, South Africa, 1986, 90 mins.

Voices of Sarafina

This Tony-Award nominated musical concerns a South African high school class who create their own play about Nelson Mandela. Part documentary, part Broadway show, the energy is infectious and the songs touch the soul. The music is by Mbogeni Ngema and Hugh Masekela. Cast includes Miriam Makeba, Leleti Khumalo, Pat Miaba and Baby Cele.

VHS: S13315. $29.95.
Nigel Noble, USA, 1988, 90 mins.

AFRICAN SPOTLIGHT

Africa Between Myth and Reality

Join artist and art educator Betty LaDuke as she travels to the African country of Eritrea to witness the daily rituals and color of village life that form the basis of her artistic vision. Back in her studio, she reveals how her vision is transformed, stage-by-stage, into figurative and symbolic compositions of myth, magic and reality.

VHS: S31080. $39.99.
1996, 28 mins.

Africa Speaks to the World

At the U.N., a new spotlight has been turned on Africa, but this time by Africans themselves. Acknowledging their mistakes, yet affirming their strengths, they now ask the world's governments and churches to work with them in a new spirit to develop further the many nations on the continent. African leaders from government and church engage in this new dialog, and discuss progress being made, with video input from Tanzania and Zimbabwe. Produced by Maryknoll Media. 28 mins.

VHS: S06269. $24.95.

Africa: Part I

The first two segments of this highly acclaimed series. *Different But Equal* looks at the slave trade in Africa, as Basil Davidson goes back to Africa's origins to show some of the great early civilizations which flourished in Africa; the second segment, *Mastering a Continent*, looks closely at three different communities to examine how African peoples carve out an existence in an often hostile environment. 120 mins.

VHS: S02400. $29.95.

Africa: Part II

The third and fourth segments from the series. In *Caravans of Gold*, Basil Davidson traces the routes of the medieval gold trade which reached from Africa to China and India to Europe; in *Kings and Cities*, the program explores the ways in which African kingdoms functioned as Davidson visits Kano in Nigeria, where a king still holds court in his 15th century palace. 120 mins.

VHS: S02401. $29.95.

Africa: Part III

Segments five and six of the series. *The Bible and the Gun* examines the explorers in Africa, including Stanley and Livingstone and then the missionaries, and finally, men like Cecil Rhodes, who envisioned a diamond-studded empire. *This Magnificent African Cake* looks at the 1800's, when colonialist powers fought over Africa, dramatically altering the face of the continent. 120 mins.

VHS: S02402. $29.95.

Africa: Part IV

Segments seven and eight of Basil Davidson's series. *The Rise of Nationalism* examines the major struggles for African independence—in Ghana, Kenya, Algeria and the Belgian Congo. *The Legacy* looks at Africa in the aftermath of colonial rule, as the continent seeking ways to come to terms with its diverse inheritance. 120 mins.

VHS: S02403. $29.95.

African Art

African art, the booty of colonial wars, emerged in the West as a strange and exotic art form that would influence such modernists as Picasso, Matisse and Modigliani. But, as Kirk Varnedoe, Curator of New York's Museum of Modern Art, and Harvard Professors Henry Louis Gates and Cornel West explain, it is important to view African art within its own cultural context, as we travel to Mali to examine the art of the Bamana, Dogon and Djenne people. From the home of the famous Tyi Warra antelope carvings to the ancient walled city of Djenne, local inhabitants explain the function of art and the role of the artist in their society. "A successful and concise analysis. Fascinating viewing" (*Time Out London*). 47 mins.

VHS: S30786. $29.95.

African Art, Women, History

This documentary is about Luba Art and the relationship between women, art and history. Welcome to the world of Lukasa, a memory board, where kings are born only after their spirits have takenpossession of the body of women. Then watch history come alive. 28 mins.

VHS: S35164. $39.95.

African Ritual and Initiation

Dr. Malidoma Patrice Some explains that during his childhood among the Dagara people, ritual established a link with the worlds of ancestors and spirits. This shaman will lead you to other dimensions of reality. 60 mins.

VHS: S23625. $34.95.

African Safaris

What distinguishes these two videos, which are subtitled "Adventures in Wildlife Observation", is the unique learning approach, looking at animals as does a safari guide, with cues leading the viewer to a better understanding of animal behavior. Consultants include Russell E. Train, founder of the African Wildlife Federation.

Volume 1: Serengeti Migration, Amboseli Elephants. Hundreds of thousands of zebra, wildebeest and Thomson's gazelle follow ancient trails in their annual quest for fresh pasture. Learn how to interpret the cycles that drive animal movements in this guide to the greatest animal migration on earth. Then visit the elephants of Amboseli National Park in Kenya, one of the few parks where elephants have been undisturbed from severe poaching, in an exploration of the behavioral links that bind elephant society. 45 mins.

VHS: S09707. $29.95.

Athol Fugard: Blood Knot

South African playwright, director and actor Athol Fugard has been writing for several decades about the lives of blacks and poor whites in South Africa. *Blood Knot*, Fugard's first important play, was the first performed in South Africa with an interracial cast. This rare filmed recording features excerpts from the original New York production with James Earl Jones and J.D. Cannon.

VHS: S30992. $89.95.
1964, 28 mins.

Belafonte Presents "Fincho"

Harry Belafonte hosts this entertaining look at Nigeria —one primitive village's leap into modern times, in the course of just ten years! 73 minutes.

VHS: S02751. $69.95.

Best of Nightline

Nelson Mandela. 90 mins.
VHS: S14063. $14.98.
South African Debate. 55 mins.
VHS: S14037. $14.98.

Black Man's Land Trilogy, Vol. 1, White Man's Country

Three films on colonialism, nationalism and revolution, called by *The New York Times* "a solid historical document skewed, valuably, to a distinctive African point of view. By affording a forum for black leaders, past and present, it conveys the sense of an enduring dignity that no colonialist rationalizations can eliminate." "A treasure of old stills, buried newsreels, and contemporary interviews, supported by meticulous research and synthesized with the most sensitive acumen. A unique record of what colonialism means in human terms" (Judy Stone, *San Francisco Chronicle*). *White Man's Country* covers the violence of colonial rule, white settlement and African resistance in the story of Kenya, formerly British East Africa, as the British tried to make it a "white man's country" like South Africa or New Zealand. Land was allocated, settlers welcomed, and the "jewel of the British empire," was born. How did Africans confront this process? It was, after all, African land that was taken, African labor that was used to develop it and African taxes that kept the colonial regime solvent. *White Man's Country* combines period photographs and contemporary location footage with the testimony of African and European witnesses, to examine both sides of Europe's "civilizing mission" in Africa. 52 mins.

Home Video.
VHS: S10843. $39.95.
Institutional with public performance rights.
VHS: S10848. $89.95.
David Koff/Anthony Kowarth, Great Britain, 1986

Black Man's Land Trilogy, Vol. 2, Mau Mau

In October 1952 the British government declared a State of Emergency in Kenya. Its object: the defeat of "Mau Mau." In the war that followed, fewer than 40 of 40,000 white settlers were killed while more than 15,000 Africans lost their lives, and hundreds of thousands more were arrested and subjected to a humiliating and often brutal process of "rehabilitation." But what was Mau Mau? A movement based, according to the British Colonial Secretary, on a "perverted nationalism and a sort of nostalgia for barbarism"? Or the Land Freedom Army, an organized political and military response to repression and armed aggression? Using newsreel and previously inaccessible archive footage, and drawing on interviews with participants on both sides, *Mau Mau* examines the myth and reality of Africa's first modern guerrilla war. 52 mins.

Home Video.
VHS: S10844. $39.95.
Institutional with public performance rights.
VHS: S10849. $89.95.
David Koff/Anthony Kowarth, Great Britain, 1986

Black Man's Land Trilogy, Vol. 3, Kenyatta

Jomo Kenyatta's death in 1978 brought to an end a political career that encompassed more than 50 years of African history. Kenyatta entered politics in the mid 1920s and then spent 17 years in exile in Europe. He returned to Kenya in 1946, and was elected President. Arrested in 1952 and imprisoned, he was released in 1961 and two years later became Kenya's first Prime Minister. In power, the man whom Europeans had once reviled as "the leader to darkness and death" was eulogized by them as a pillar of stability. *Kenyatta* weaves archival and contemporary images with interviews with friends and relatives, comrades and opponents, to create a biographical portrait of a key figure in 20th century politics, and a case study of nationalism as a political force in Africa. 52 mins.
Home Video.
VHS: S10845. $39.95.
Institutional with public performance rights.
VHS: S10850. $89.95.
David Koff/Anthony Kowarth, Great Britain, 1986

Children's Stories from Africa

Meet Capusee the Clever Monkey, Bushpig and Warthog, Empesa the Hyena, Infene the Baboon, Gafumbi the Brave Boy and other new friends, in this unique blend of live storytelling, valuable lessons and values, whimsical drawings, African rhythms, and song and dance. Four-tape boxed set. 100 mins.
VHS: S32935. $44.95.

Djabote: Sengalese Drumming & Song from Master Drummer Doudou N'Diaye Rose

This spellbinding film features an Eric Serra audio recording session of Senegalese master drummer Doudou N'Diaye Rose and dozens of other drummers and singers performing as an ensemble.
VHS: S30162. $39.99.
Beatrice Soule/Eric Millot, USA, 1993, 43 mins.

Earthkeepers

Scientists and environmentalists are warning that if people continue to neglect and abuse the Earth, it might become uninhabitable. Men and women in Kenya and Tanzania are working to reverse growing desertification simply by planting trees. This video shows successful programs of ecological healing done by the people of these east African countries. 28 mins.
VHS: S13907. $24.95.

The Elephants of Timbuktu

Five hundred wild elephants make an extraordinary 600-mile migration annually. Despite this vast undertaking, these animals manage to live in harmony with the nomadic Tuareg people. This video presents an unforgettable Smithsonian Expedition. 50 mins.
VHS: S25868. $24.95.

Eritrean Artists in War and Peace

Focuses on the aesthetic development of 12 artist-fighters in Eritrea, northeast Africa, whose unique contemporary art movement was initiated in a war zone by the Eritrean People's Liberation Front during their 30-year struggle for liberation from Ethiopian control. Public performance rights included.
VHS: S33380. $79.95.
Brian Varaday, USA, 1997, 56 mins.

Experience Morocco

Experience Morocco as you zoom down an ancient caravan trail on a Harley, hitch a ride on a farm truck, climb a 14,000-foot mountain, ride a camel and barter in a bazaar. 47 mins.
VHS: S31471. $19.99.

Experience Zimbabwe, Botswana & Namibia

Experience three South African countries as you bungee jump above the Zambezi river, canoe through crocodile-infested waters, swoop over Victoria Falls in a helicopter, take a Chobe safari and sand surf 1000-foot-high sand dunes. 47 mins.
VHS: S31476. $19.99.

Eyewitness South Africa

An American TV journalist is assigned to document this dynamic country. Both black and white audiences share his learning experiences as he explores the multi-faceted nation of South Africa. 35 mins.
VHS: S23712. $129.95.

The First World Festival of Negro Arts

In 1966, in Dakar, Senegal, over 2000 people of the African Diaspora convened to celebrate and debate the world-wide renaissance of Black culture. Poets, musicians, painters, dancers, sculptors, intellectuals and political leaders were in attendance. Aime Cesaire and Alione Diop led the debate about "Negritude", a concept first conceived of by Leopold Senghor. 40 mins.
VHS: S24587. $175.00.

Folks Like Us

The Catholic diocese of Bismarck, North Dakota, has sent four people—a priest, a deacon, a nurse and a speech pathologist-to Bura, Kenya. Filmed in Kenya and North Dakota, this documentary studies the team at work and the impact of their project on families and friends back home. 29 mins.
VHS: S15858. $19.95.

From Sunup

The story of women of black Africa, their strength, courage, daily struggles, concerns and challenges. A candid, authentic picture of the dawn-to-dusk lives of women in the Third World, produced by a Tanzanian woman, Flora M'mbugu, shot in Tanzania with an all-African crew. Portrays the woman's multiple roles as provider, mother, water-carrier, wood-gatherer, cook and entrepreneur, illustrating that the source of her hope and future lies in women's support of each other. 28 mins.
VHS: S04927. $24.95.

Glimpses of West Africa

An ethnographic video that looks at the geography, culture and people of the West African countries of Cote d'Ivoire, Mali and Senegal. The program contains a transcript and lesson plan. 32 mins.
English Narration.
VHS: S19800. $49.95.
French Narration.
VHS: S19799. $49.95.

Jirimpimbira

Kathleen Arnot's *Tale of Temba* inspired this amusing video about a young African boy whose village is experiencing a difficult drought. An old man gives the boy bones which, together with the magic word *Jirimpimbira*, grant him anything he desires. A misadventure follows which gently points out the folly of greed and selfishness. 25 mins.
VHS: S27535. $9.95.

Journey Back to Africa

Katie Couric and Bryant Gumbel experience the diversity of Africa's landscape, from its arid deserts to lush rainforests, snowcapped mountains to coastal plains. Join Bryant as he makes a haunting pilgrimage to Goree Island, last sight of home for the estimated 20 million Africans sold into slavery. 56 mins.
VHS: S34149. $19.95.

Karibu

Although the family is probably the most important social unit in East Africa, urbanization draws young people away from their villages to the big cities. Meaning "welcome" in Swahili, *Karibu* examines parishes in Nairobi that are trying to become "welcoming families" for newcomers. 29 mins.
VHS: S15864. $19.95.

Kenya Safari: Essence of Africa

Traverse the jungles of Kenya and see game reserves, Masai villages, a coffee plantation, and more as you see the essence of African life. 45 mins.
VHS: S05776. $24.95.

Kenyan Youth: Preparing for the Future

For youth the world over, hope is the source of energy and direction. From Kenya, a potential Olympic runner, a budding artist and a family of young musicians tell their stories of determination, hard work and dreams of a bright future, demonstrating their varied skills. Produced by Maryknoll media.
VHS: S06271. $24.95.

Kwanzaa: Echoes of Africa

Kwanzaa, the celebration of "first fruits of harvest" (December 26-January 1) derived from traditions spanning the African continent, has gained considerable popularity among African Americans over recent years. Included is a brief history of the holiday along with inspirational discussion of the meaning of the seven principles of Kwanzaa that are commemorated on each night of the festival. With Dorian Harewood >I>(I'll Fly Away) and singer/actress Mary Catherine.
VHS: S30685. $9.95.
USA, 1996, 30 mins.

Learn to Cook the Easy Way with the Kitchen Divas: Preparing an African Feast

The Shelf sisters (author Angela Shelf Medearis and her sister Marcia Shelf), two culinary divas, demonstrate five traditional African dishes that will take the diner from appetizer to desert. It's a an easy guide to challenging but satisfying recipes.
VHS: S27218. $19.95.

Lions of Dakar

Dakar, Senegal, is the center of Afro Pop, the dynamic mix of traditional West African and contemporary American musical rhythms. This documentary charts the city and its musical influences. With performances by Youssou n'Dour, Ismael Lo and Super Diamono. French narration with English subtitles. 50 mins.
VHS: S19797. $49.95.

Mandela

South African president Nelson Mandela narrates this insightful Academy Award-nominated documentary on his extraordinary life. From his early work protesting the unjust social policies of his homeland to his triumphant election as its leader, *Mandela* offers a fascinating look at one of the greatest figures of the 20th century. Produced by Jonathan Demme. "A fascinating portrait...one of the most inspiring stories of our time" (Roger Ebert, *Chicago Sun-Times*).
VHS: S32339. $19.95.
Laser: LD76350. $39.99.
DVD: DV60228. $29.95.
Jo Menell, USA, 1996, 117 mins.

Mandela's Fight for Freedom

Nelson Mandela has been at the center of South Africa's struggle for justice for many decades. He began as a youthful protestor and evolved over his long prison sentence into a figure for change and progress. This Discovery Channel documentary uses many voices to tell his story. 150 mins.
VHS: S27823. $29.95.

Mandela: The Man and His Country

Morton Dean narrates this emotional examination of Nelson Mandela, the symbolic head of the anti-apartheid movement, who was recently freed from prison after 27 years by the South African government. Includes interviews with Jesse Jackson and James Michener, plus unforgettable footage shot right after Mandela's release. 50 mins.
VHS: S12291. $19.98.

Masters of the Congo Jungle

Produced in 1960 by the Belgian International Scientific Foundation, this is a chronicle of Henri Storck's two-year exploration of the Belgian Congo. Untouched for centuries by outside civilization, the jungle is now disrupted by the invasion of modern man. Storck captures remnants of the ancient African continent, plant and animal life and regional natives co-existing in the simple grandeur and rhythm of the earth.
VHS: S17448. $19.95.

Nelson Mandela 70th Birthday Tribute

A live tribute concert featuring performances by Sting, George Michael, Eurythmics, Tracy Chapman, Peter Gabriel, the Fat Boys and many more. USA, 117 mins.
VHS: S15308. $14.98.

The New Zimbabwe

Blacks and whites once lived in separate societies in colonial Rhodesia and now hope to work together in the new Zimbabwe. They tell of their aspirations and apprehensions in the early years of independence. This film documents the struggle to build a society based on reconciliation and equality while offering historic insights into the problem of achieving that goal. Produced by Maryknoll Media. 28 mins.
VHS: S04930. $24.95.

Nigerian Art—Kindred Spirits

Actress Ruby Dee narrates this journey into Nigerian art and culture. Talented artists from Africa's most populous country share their history and cultural legacy with viewers. 58 mins.
VHS: S29539. $19.98.

"Oba Koso": Nigerian Music and Dance Drama

Excerpts from the famous Yoruba folklore drama about a wicked man who tries to overthrow the king. Intricate dance steps, brilliantly colored costumes and Yoruba instruments and singing. Performance by The National Theater of Nigeria. Commentary and explanation by drama writer Margaret Croyden.
VHS: S30993. $89.95.
1975, 28 mins.

Once Upon a Time

In our fast-changing world, Kenyan storytelling traditions are diminished in their ability to pass on legend and wisdom in society. Uncover why the legacy of diviners, healers, poets, storytellers and singers is finding a home with the Church in Africa. 29 mins.
VHS: S15862. $19.95.

Portrait of Africa
Vangelis, Ladysmith Black Mambazo and Miriam Makeba are featured in these beautifully-shot images of Africa from the producers of the Windham Hill series. From Tanzania's sweeping Serengeti to towering Mt. Kilimanjaro, from Kenya's island of Lamu to striking Lake Turkana, the program presents a remarkable array of people, places and wildlife. 58 mins.
VHS: S11194. $29.95.

Project Tanzania: Part 1: A Response Beyond Charity
When dramatic film reports of the Africa famine shocked the world in 1984, a television station in Raleigh, North Carolina looked for some way to help the people of Africa. What developed not only has helped people in the Shunyanga region of Tanzania. It helped North Carolinians understand the meaning of the word "neighbor." Produced by Maryknoll Media. 28 mins.
VHS: S06262. $24.95.

Project Tanzania: Part 2: A Response Beyond Charity
When WRAL-TV in Raleigh, North Carolina asked its viewers to help the people in Tanzania, it also offered those viewers a chance to enrich their lives. This film looks at what's been the impact of Project Tanzania on North Carolinians. Filmed on location and in Raleigh, N.C. Produced by Maryknoll Media. 28 mins.
VHS: S06264. $24.95.

Rhodes
The 1996 British TV miniseries. From the excitement of the diamond rush to the tragic birth of apartheid, from the intrigues of a Russian princess to dangerous confrontations with local kings, this is the life and legend of Cecil Rhodes (Martin Shaw), the man who changed the face of Africa. By the time he was 40, the country of Rhodesia was named after him. Three-volume set. 336 mins.
VHS: S32796. $59.98.

Shooting Africa
Travel with Ian Thomas, a professional wildlife photographer who lives and works in Africa, on a personal safari to photograph the biggest, fastest, fiercest African animals, filming over 30 animals in their natural environment. 30 mins.
VHS: S09916. $21.95.

Something New Out of Africa
Catholic priests are coming from across the Atlantic again, this time from Nigeria to work among African-American Catholics in southern Louisiana and Texas. The priests and their American parishioners describe how this mix of cultures affects their lives and their Catholic faith. Filmed in Nigeria and the United States, 29 mins.
VHS: S15691. $19.95.

Sons of Bwiregi
This film deals with the efforts of Maryknoll Father Ed Hayes to aid the Tanzanian people, torn between old customs and the modern world, to build a future based on their past. When one member of the tribe wants to remarry after the death of his wife, Father Hayes is given the opportunity to show the people that some traditions must change. Produced by Maryknoll Media. 25 mins.
VHS: S04935. $24.95.

South Africa—The Black Red War
Made in 1978, this film analyzes the apartheid system in South Africa from a communist perspective. The violence of the system is exposed through brutal and graphic footage, and the film does much to expose the barbarism of the ruling parties. 60 mins.
VHS: S12715. $19.98.

The Speeches of Nelson Mandela
Nelson Mandela fought apartheid in South Africa for decades, leading to his conviction and imprisonment for sabotage by the South African government. He won the Nobel Peace Prize for his efforts and was released from prison after 27½ years. Speeches from his long career are collected on this video, which show the depth of his struggle and his triumph as the President of South Africa. From *The Speeches Collection*. USA, 1995, 70 mins.
VHS: S27278. $19.98.

Untamed Africa
Narrated by John Hurt, this two-volume documentary captures the great African migration of grazing animals. *Volume I: The Great Migration Begins* and *Volume II: Survival on the Savannah* show how wildebeests fare with the predators and dangers that haunt them as they wander from the lush Masai Mara to the Serengeti Plain. 120 mins.
VHS: S27827. $39.95.

Video Visits: Morocco, A Bridge Across Time
See old *medinas* (marketplaces), shop for handwoven Berber rugs in Fez and enjoy the outdoor carnival of Marrakesh's Place Jema al-Fna and the annual Moroccan Folklore Festival. 53 mins.
VHS: S31460. $24.99.

Video Visits: Zimbabwe, Africa's Wildlife Sanctuary
Visit Hwange and Mana Pools, Lake Kariba, the capital of Harare, Great Zimbabse and the legendary Victoria Falls. 54 mins.
VHS: S31467. $24.99.

Wild Rapture
This documentary was shot in Equatorial Africa. It contains very unusual footage depicting the customs and lifestyles of some African peoples.
VHS: S23796. $24.95.
Jaques Dupont, USA, 1950, 68 mins.

Witness to Apartheid
This Emmy Award-winning documentary (Best Direction) was shot clandestinely in South Africa during the 1985 State of Emergency. Its interviews of tortured children and their doctors helped galvanize world wide action to change this unjust system.
VHS: S24586. $180.00.
Sharon Sopher, USA, 1986, 56 mins.

Women in Tanzania
From sunup to sundown, women in Tanzania, East Africa, bear the burden of running the household, raising the children and growing the crops. This program looks at the situation of women in Tanzania from the women's perspectives. Includes discussions by a Tanzanian woman who has studied village life and a woman missioner to Tanzania. Produced by Maryknoll Media. 28 mins.
VHS: S06265. $24.95.

Zambian Safari
A fascinating look at the beauty of Zimbabwe, show on location in South Luangwa and Kafue National parks, featuring the exotic wildlife, plants, birds, people, villages, traditional music and dancing of the land of Victoria Falls, the Zambezi River, and many small villages. 40 mins.
VHS: S05871. $24.95.

VERY SPECIAL

Classic Foreign Shorts—Volume 1
Contains three short films, including the classic take-off on Ingmar Bergman, *The Dove; The Existentialist*; and the 1948 short *Loves of Franistan*.
VHS: S09047. $24.95.

Classic Foreign Shorts—Volume 2
Contains Truffaut's early *Les Mistons*; Orson Welles' short *Hearts of Age*; Jean-Luc Godard's *All the Boys Named Patrick*; Roman Polanski's *Fat and the Lean* and *Two Men and a Wardrobe*; and Cavalcanti's *Rien que les Heures*.
VHS: S09048. $24.95.

International Release: A Moving Pictures Magazine
This monthly DVD video magazine navigates the global citizen through the terrain of world cinema with short and feature films, animation, interviews, dance and culture. Features Guatemala's 1995 Academy Award entry for Best Foreign Feature Film, *The Silence of Neto*, plus eight other films.
DVD: DV60264. $19.95.

EUROPEAN SILENT CINEMA

90 Degrees South: With Scott to the Antarctic
Herbert G. Ponting's chronicle of Captain Robert Scott's heroic and ultimately tragic race for the South Pole was originally released in 1913. Ponting, a renowned still photographer, dedicated his life to the memory of Scott, who died with his entire team on the return trip from the pole after losing the race to Amundsen. Twenty years after his friend's death, Ponting added narration to the film, drawing from Scott's diary entries. This is the deeply personal tribute to the heartbreaking last days of the doomed expedition.
VHS: S16434. $39.95.
Laser: CLV/CAV. LD71592. $29.95.
Herbert G. Ponting, Great Britain, 1933, 72 mins.

Antony and Cleopatra
Produced in Italy in 1913, this rare classic of early Italian cinema starred Amleto Novelli *(Quo Vadis)* and was remarkable for its stunning sets and impressive crowd scenes. 74 mins.
VHS: S29459. $24.95.

Cabiria
The most ambitious and spectacular of the historical epics for which Italy was famous before World War I, *Cabiria* set the standard for big budget, feature-length movies and opened the way for Griffith and DeMille. During the war between Carthage and Rome, a girl—Cabiria—is separated from her parents. In her odyssey through the world of ancient Rome, she encounters an erupting volcano, the barbaric splendor of Carthage, human sacrifice and Hannibal crossing the Alps. Mastered from a 35mm archive print using variable speed projection to match the original hand cranked camera, *Cabiria* features a newly recorded soundtrack from the original 1914 score.
VHS: S06218. $39.95.
Giovanni Pastrone, Italy, 1914, 123 mins.

The Christus
The story of Christ is presented in this silent Italian production that was adapted from a poem by Fausto Salvatore. He most likely based his poem on a much more popular source. Filmed closer to the Holy Land than most Hollywood films on the same subject matter. Silent.
VHS: S04813. $24.95.
Guilio Antamoro, Italy, 1917, 90 mins.

Daughters of Eve
Anny Ondra is the starring vamp in this sultry film. She's a showgirl who specializes in leading men astray. Germany, 1928. Silent with English intertitles.
VHS: S23824. $24.95.

David Copperfield
Charles Dickens' unforgettable tale of an orphan vagabond is touchingly realized in this early, silent, color-tinted film. This is the first feature length adaptation of the literary masterwork.
VHS: S23825. $24.95.
Thomas Bentley, Great Britain, 1913, 55 mins.

Frate Francisco
This mammoth, lavish production exemplifies the spectacular Italian historical epics made during the era of silent films. The story is based on the life of the saint. He was born to a life of ease, only to reject everything for a vow of poverty. Alleged to have experienced the stigmata (wounds like those suffered by Christ on the cross), this holy man's spiritual ways remain inspirational. Includes original musical score with sound effects.
VHS: S25866. $24.95.
Guilio Antamoro, Italy, 1927, 75 mins.

Heart of Humanity
Dorothy Philips and Erich von Stroheim star in this silent Canadian production, with Stroheim as a brutal Prussian officer. Silent with music track.
VHS: S07276. $24.95.
Allen Holubar, Canada, 1919, 110 mins.

Kean
An extremely rare example of the legendary actor Ivan Mosjoukine, who stars as the equally famous British stage actor, Edmund Kean.
VHS: S06222. $49.95.
Alexander Volkov, France, 1924

The Lady of the Lake
This silent British feature captures the exciting adventures and freedom of a young girl (Benita Hume) in Scotland. Loosely based from the period that produced Sir Walter Scott's narrative poem, the story concerns the young girl's saving of the life of the King from outlaws.
VHS: S19531. $29.95.
James A. Fitzpatrick, Great Britain, 1928, 60 mins.

Loves of Casanova
Ivan Mosjoukine stars as the great lover in this silent epic-style romance. Also stars Jeanne Boitel, Marcelle Denya, Michael Simon, Suzanne Bianchetti as Catherine II and Diana Karenne as Maria Mari. Also includes 20-minute Mosjoukine short, *Lord of the Moguls*. Also known as *The Prince of Adventurers*.
VHS: S30191. $24.95.
Alexandre Volkoff, France, 1927, 134 mins.

The Lumiere Brothers' First Films
Narrated by Bertrand Tavernier, this amazing journey through the birth of the motion picture as art form is no ordinary compilation. All of the titles in this series were restored by the Lumiere Institute (of which Tavernier is president) and demonstrate the tremendous breadth of the Lumieres' work—from the first dolly shot to their extraordinary recording of history in Russia, China and the United States. A must for every lover of silent film. In English.
VHS: S32044. $49.95.
Bertrand Tavernier, France, 1996, 70 mins.

Man in the Silk Hat

A moving tribute to the famous french actor of the silent era, Max Linder, whom Chaplin once called "my professor," directed by his daughter. During his lifetime, Linder made some 400-500 short comedies, and came to America to make his only three feature-length films. With numerous excerpts from Linder's films, this is a loving tribute to one of the giants of comedy. Narrated in English by Maud Linder.

VHS: S04870. $24.95.

Maud Linder, France, 1984, 96 mins.

Max Linder

By 1910 Max Linder was an internationally popular comic, typically playing a dapper dandy of the idle rich. He developed a slapstick style that anticipated Mack Sennett and Chaplin. His popularity was at its peak in 1914, when he was called up for World War I. With original French titles. Silent.

VHS: S00833. $29.95.

Max Linder, France, 1911-13

Moulin Rouge

Made by German director Dupont *(Variety)* after his move to England in 1927, this is a melodrama set in Paris about a young man who becomes infatuated with the Moulin Rouge star whose daughter he is about to marry. Silent.

VHS: S02160. $29.95.

E.A. Dupont, Great Britain, 1929, 90 mins.

Return of the Rat

In this extremely rare, silent foreign film, the third in "The Rat" series based on the play by Ivor Novello and Constance Collier, the Rat is married to Zelle de Chaumet but she is dallying with an old lover, Henri de Verral. The Rat challenges his rival to a duel and is left for dead. The heartless Zelle gives a costume ball to announce her betrothal to de Verral. The Rat shows up in disguise and a scuffle ensues. When the lights go out, Zelle is stabbed to death and the Rat is the suspect. Stars Ivor Novello, Isabel Jeans, Mabel Poulton, Gordon Harker, Bernard Nadell, Marie Ault, Hazel Terry, Scott Kelly and Gladys Frazin. Silent with music track.

VHS: S30159. $19.95.

Graham Cutts, Great Britain, 1928, 84 mins.

She (1911)

H. Rider Haggard wrote the story on which this early and imaginative silent film is based. It involves the discovery of a lost race. James Cruze and Marguerite Snow star.

VHS: S23846. $24.95.

Theodore Marston/George Nichols, Great Britain, 1911, 20 mins.

She (1925)

H. Rider Haggard's tale of the immortal Queen Ayesha, "She who must be obeyed," is brought to the screen in this early silent version starring Betty Blythe, Carlyle Blackwell and Mary Odette. Silent with musical score. England, 1925, 57 mins.

VHS: S01636. $24.95.

Leander de Cordova, Great Britain, 1925, 57 mins.

Spartacus

An early Italian silent era spectacle, based on the revolt of the gladiators. Also included on this tape is the rare short, *Uncle Tom's Cabin* (1910). 80 mins.

VHS: S07761. $29.95.

Tigris

Though common today, when this silent film was produced in Italy in 1913, the mounting tension between a villian and his inventive counterspy was new and fascinating. Today the rivalry between these two opponents in both disguises and tricks still offers engaging entertainment. Piano score. 48 mins.

VHS: S29460. $19.95.

Trapped by the Mormons

A British thriller about a girl from Manchester who is coerced into joining a secret society. Can the proper authorities find and free her before she develops a fixation for living in Utah? Starring Evelyn Brent as Nora Prescott. With Olive Sloane and Olaf Hytten as Elder Marz. Banned in the US for years. Silent.

VHS: S04812. $29.95.

H.B. Parkinson, Great Britain, 1922, 65 mins.

The Wandering Jew

Rudolph and Joseph Schildkraut star in this silent Austrian film adaptation of the legend concerning the Wandering Jew. 1920, 65 mins. English intertitles.

VHS: S23853. $24.95.

What Do Those Old Films Mean?

Noel Burch's remarkable Channel 4 series, discovering the world of silent cinema never before told.

Volume 1: Great Britain 1900-1912—Along the Great Divide. Using extremely rare films, newly scored music and a lively commentary, film historian Noel Burch explores the contradictions in early British cinema between the "gentlemen inventors of the cinema" and film as an entertainment for the poor. Early films in Britain, says Burch, either showed the poor what bright, happy lives their "betters" led, or held up to them their own, usually drunken, depravity. At the same time, the early filmmakers worked in a climate of fear in an era of panic that "the empire was in danger." By examining the earliest classics, like Cecil Hepworth's *Rescued by Rover* and other, much more obscure films, Burch documents the British filmmakers as the earliest pioneers in the techniques of film editing. 26 mins.

VHS: S08682. $29.95.

Volume 2: U.S.A. 1902-1914—Tomorrow the World. Film historian Noel Burch examines early filmmaking in America against the social background of the immigrant masses streaming into the slums, factories and sweatshops of an industrialized America. It was these immigrants who became the earliest patrons of the nickelodeons, in spite of the fact that many of the earliest films depicted non-Americans as ridiculous or loathsome. But when the middle class discovered the cinema, American movies changed—American film discovered narrative, and at the same time began to censor its own productions, depriving them of social content and criticism. Rare film footage provides the background for this fascinating cinematic and social analysis in this second volume in a remarkable series produced by Britain's Channel Four Television. 26 mins.

VHS: S08683. $29.95.

Volume 3: Denmark 1902-1914—She! Why was Copenhagen the undisputed birthplace of the mature cinema, of psychological realism on the screen, at a time when French or American films were no more than rudimentary melodramas? Film historian Noel Burch examines the Danish silent film phenomenon both from the standpoint of its key figures (the actors Asta Nielsen and Urban Gad, the powerful producer Ole Olsen), and from the social perspective of a Denmark in which women had an advanced position for the time, where feminism was prominent and attitudes toward sexuality liberal. The early Danish cinema was innovative, and in such techniques as lighting, camera angles or editing within one and the same scene, they adopted many techniques before the American directors. As the legendary actress Asta Nielsen wrote in her autobiography, "At a time when almost no one considered that films might be an art, I was determined to put all my energies into the artistic potentialities I had discovered in myself during that first film…If I had had a clear awareness of the terrifying world of unscrupulous businessmen who in those days ran the film industry—I would probably not have embarked on that adventure with such enthusiasm." 26 mins.

VHS: S08684. $29.95.

Volume 4: France 1904-1912—The Enemy Below. "One of the most remarkable features of the seventh art is its unanimous appeal to the masses, with none of the intellectual preparation needed for literature or music," wrote Louis Delluc, and in this fascinating program covering the early years of cinema in France, film historian and critic Noel Burch follows the thesis that the appeal of the silent French cinema was to the working class. "We were attracted to everything denied us by a moral code laid down by others: luxury, wild parties, the great brass band of vices and the image of woman too, but a woman heroized, elevated to adventuress…a generation of young men fell head over heels in love with Musidora in *Les Vampires*," wrote the poet Louis Aragon. 26 mins.

VHS: S08685. $29.95.

Volume 5: U.S.S.R. 1926-1930—Born Yesterday. Amid general poverty, social disorder, an exodus from the rural areas, and the sudden arrival of women in industry, post-Revolutionary Russia was also a period of extraordinary social and cultural experiment. The artists saw art as an instrument of social change, of encouraging new relationships between individuals. The filmmakers and filmmaking groups concentrated on social agitation, on new forms of newsreel, on incorporating into film the great formal experiments of the era. In this fascinating program, film historian Noel Burch focuses on the sexual politics of Soviet cinema—issues such as the collectivization of domestic tasks and child care and the abolition of sexual division of labor in the home. Using rare films which are virtually unknown in the West, Burch provides a unique perspective on this great era of cinema in a climate of virulent change. 26 mins.

VHS: S08686. $29.95.

Volume 6: Germany 1926-1932—Under Two Flags. This volume of *What Do Those Old Films Mean?* focuses on films produced in Germany in the '20s, rarely shown or discussed today. But influenced by the achievements of the young Soviet cinema, the German social workers' movements created the German Workers' Film. Among these early productions were such landmark films as *The Other Side of the Street, Our Daily Bread, Mother Krausen's Journey to Happiness* and *Kuhle Wampe*. This remarkable movement for a "populist" cinema in Germany of the Weimar Republic had much in common with similar efforts in other fields of the arts—for example, the art of Kathe Kollwitz. But it was ultimately replaced by the more palatable—and cheerful—films of Billy Wilder and Robert Siodmak, and, ultimately, by the victory of Nazism. 26 mins.

VHS: S08687. $29.95.

Complete Set. Available at a special price.

VHS: S08688. $149.75.

LANGUAGE INSTRUCTION

Alles Gute!

This new video course from the Goethe Institut and Inter Nationes will help its readers assimilate the language, culture and daily activities of German-speaking countries. 60 mins.

Lessons 1-4.

VHS: S19846. $55.00.

Lessons 5-8.

VHS: S19847. $55.00.

Lessons 9-12.

VHS: S19848. $55.00.

Lessons 13-16.

VHS: S19849. $55.00.

Lessons 17-20.

VHS: S19850. $55.00.

Lessons 21-26.

VHS: S19851. $55.00.

All Six Guides and Videos.

VHS: S19852. $349.75.

Basic Chinese by Video

Pleasure or business travellers will gain a speaking vocabulary of Chinese words and phrases. 90 mins.

VHS: S08277. $74.95.

Basic Hebrew 1 & 2

An introductory course to the Hebrew language, this program is designed to teach Hebrew as a second language. Developed by two professors, *Basic Hebrew* presents vocabulary using live demonstrations, colorful illustrations, graphics, phonetic transcriptions and dramatic scenes with English subtitles. 141 mins. 2 videocassettes and glossary.

VHS: S11595. $95.00.

Contacto

A video course for teaching Spanish to beginning students. The program, a collaboration between North American and Spanish scholars, features methodologies and teaching practices informed by authoritative language and culture from Spain and the larger Hispanic culture. Important grammar concepts are reviewed and repeated on screen with freeze frames and graphics. The text is indexed to each video segment through on-screen cues. 200 mins.

No. 1: Introduction to Verbs, Articles and Greetings.

VHS: S19766. $39.95.

No. 2: Adverbs, Time and Family Relationships.

VHS: S19767. $39.95.

No. 3: Adjectives, Participles, Interrogatives.

VHS: S19768. $39.95.

No. 4: Reflexives, Indefinites, Possession, Holidays.

VHS: S19769. $39.95.

Pupil's Book.

VHS: S19771. $19.95.

Pupil's Workbook.

VHS: S19773. $11.95.

Teachers Book.

VHS: S19772. $11.95.

Contacto, Set of 4 Videos.

VHS: S19770. $195.00.

El Alfabeto Espanol

The role of images in early language acquisition is indisputable. This video combines sound and image to introduce the Spanish alphabet. Useful for native speakers and those learning Spanish for the first time. 17 mins.

VHS: S19819. $59.95.

English Plus

This fast-paced, humorous lesson plan is designed to help students learn the use of spoken, or colloquial, English. The episodes revolve around family, information, food, directions and travel. The booklet contains vocabulary and explanations of each grammatical concept. 62 mins.

VHS: S05988. $59.95.

Ensemble: A Home Video Course for Beginners in French

Designed to provide a survival kit for France. You'll be able to make yourself understood in a variety of situations, and above all, understand what is being said to you. The aim is to equip the viewer to deal with everyday situations. A BBC production. 120 mins.

VHS: S10286. $19.95.

Functional Readings in Spanish—Signs in a Mexican City

Reading signs in Mexico poses complications for Spanish natives, given the subtle differences in vocabulary and the number of Indian words. This program helps improve "sign-reading" capabilities in Mexico. 28 mins.

VHS: S20277. $29.95.

Grammar Music Videos

These videos teach grammatical skills through comic dialogue and lively music. Each 30-minute program isolates specific fundamentals of Spanish. *Trabajamos Commo Burros* introduces the present tense, *Por Que Me Llama?* explores interrogatives, *Ay Ay Ay* teaches the verb plus infinitive constructions, and *Somos Gente del Mundo* compares ser and estar.

Ay Ay Ay.
VHS: S19816. $49.95.
Por Que?
VHS: S19815. $49.95.
Somos Gente.
VHS: S19817. $49.95.
Trabajamos.
VHS: S19814. $49.95.
Grammar Music Videos, Set.
VHS: S19818. $176.00.

Images de France

A complete course for levels I-III of French, which emphasizes conversational French, cultural aspects of France and its people, and specific grammar topics related to the conversations. The films concentrate on a particular theme and include arrival at the airport, at home, at the cafe, etc. After the initial presentation, a commentator explains what occurred during the sequence and provides an in-depth conversation practice session. All four videos are accompanied by a detailed manual which includes bilingual scripts, tests, notes on grammar topics, and a pronunciation guide. Each program averages 77 mins.

Images de France Level 1, Part 1.
VHS: S09059. $39.95.
Images de France Level 1, Part 2.
VHS: S09061. $39.95.
Images de France Level 1 Viewer's Guide.
VHS: S09062. $5.95.
Images de France Level 2-3, Part 1.
VHS: S09063. $39.95.
Images de France Level 2-3, Part 2.
VHS: S09064. $39.95.
Images de France Level 2-3 Viewer's Guide.
VHS: S09065. $5.95.

Kit ou Double

A video notebook composed of six sections about France and French culture designed to help intermediate students. The sections are introduced by puppets. The sections contain specific language goals, created within a realistic cultural or linguistic setting. Each section contains pre-viewing and post-viewing activities and suggestions. 35 mins.
VHS: S19776. $59.95.

L'espace des Francais

A fascinating overview of all the regions of La Belle France, including tourist, historical and economic information. Intermediate level. With accompanying manual containing the script, cultural information, teacher information and pedagogical information. 26 mins.
VHS: S33263. $59.95.

Language in Life

Communicating in Life is a two-phased approach to the problems of human communication, starting with a psychological approach based on recent studies in language acquisition patterns. Part Two provides an entertaining and stimulating study of the basic units of speech: nouns and adjectives, verbs and adverbs, using a Buster Keaton-type actor.
VHS: S02206. $64.95.

Language Tapes

A series of nine tapes.
Basic Arabic by Video. 90 minutes.
VHS: S02980. $74.95.
Basic English for Hispanics by Video. 90 minutes.
VHS: S02310. $19.95.
Basic English Grammar by Video. 73 minutes.
VHS: S02760. $19.95.
Basic French by Video. 90 minutes.
VHS: S02761. $74.95.
Laser: LD70858. $34.95.
Basic German by Video. 90 minutes.
VHS: S02762. $74.95.
Basic Italian by Video. 90 minutes.
VHS: S02763. $74.95.
Basic Japanese by Video. 90 minutes.
VHS: S02981. $74.95.
Basic Russian by Video. 90 minutes.
VHS: S02864. $74.95.
Basic Spanish by Video. 90 minutes.
VHS: S02764. $74.95.

Las Aventuras de Mafalda

Enjoy Malfalda, Susanita, Felipe, Guille and the rest of the *pandilla* in this hilarious introduction to regional language patterns. With 12 five-minute episodes per video.
Volume 1.
VHS: S19837. $39.95.
Volume 2.
VHS: S19838. $39.95.

Le Calendrier des Francais

A month-by-month description of French holidays, including celebrations, sporting events and cultural events that take place during the year. With accompanying manual containing the script, cultural information, teacher information and pedagogical information. Intermediate level. 26 mins.
VHS: S33264. $59.95.

Le Tresor d'Histoires Classiques

A set of four tapes, these animated lessons teach history, culture and language in clear French. Intermediate and advanced students will enjoy seeing and hearing works that they have read. Each tape is 50 mins.
VHS: S24791. $73.95.

Living Language

Essential words and phrases in five scenes to everyone who travels: at the airport, at the hotel, on the street, at the restaurant, and at the department store.
Living Language: French. 60 mins.
VHS: S04356. $29.95.
Living Language: Spanish. 77 mins.
VHS: S04357. $29.95.

Modern Language Instruction

The BBC's specially designed program for quick learning of foreign languages, ideally suited for travelers. Each program contains one video, two audiotapes and two handbooks.
Get By in Italian.
VHS: S19386. $69.95.
Get By in German.
VHS: S19387. $69.95.
Get By in Spanish.
VHS: S19388. $69.95.
Get By in French.
VHS: S19389. $69.95.

Mots Difficiles

A video to teach authentic language and appropriate use of idiomatic expressions to intermediate and advanced French language students, by observing native speakers engaged in realistic, functional dialogs. Rich in scenes and expressions from everyday life. A script is provided.
VHS: S09057. $59.95.

Poesie de la Francophonie

For beginning and intermediate levels, this is a collection of 67 poems that represent the French-speaking portions of the world. With selections by Verlaine, Victor Hugo, Jean de La Fontaine, Maurice Careme and Alfred de Musset. 100 mins.
VHS: S19798. $49.95.

The Russian Language

A collaboration between top Russian linguists and the St. Petersburg's Documentary Film Studio, this program provides extensive lessons in learning, applying and use of the Russian language, conveyed through the circumstances and events of a fictional American businessman and his various encounters in Russian locations. The video includes an illustrated and colorful textbook and audio cassette of the soundtrack portion to aid the listener and viewer.
VHS: S18446. $99.95.

Say It by Signing

The classic Living Language series special video to help people of all ages communicate with the hearing impaired. 60 minutes.
VHS: S01951. $29.95.

Spanish Emergency Lesson Plans: The Video

Filmed on location in South America, these self-contained lessons provide cultural capsules complete with vocabulary and grammar exercises, joined by on-screen multiple choice exercises on travel, communications and animals. In Spanish. 30 mins.
VHS: S19821. $49.95.

Survival Spanish

One of the very best language-learning tapes, this ten-lesson conversational course is designed to teach how to "think" in Spanish, offering humor, enthusiasm and real-life situations for business, money, information, restaurants, family, telephone usage and travel. 60 mins.
VHS: S05989. $69.95.

TV und Texte

A valuable language-teaching video about contemporary German society was created to allow students to become active participants. The contents of a news broadcast are broken down, with the difficult words and phrases highlighted for repetition. Written exercises supplement newspaper articles and comprehension questions reveal the amount of learning and text skills being developed. Each unit contains a series of writing and speaking assignments which provide individual and group work. 71-page text with photos, transcripts and an answer key. 50 mins.
VHS: S19790. $49.95.

british CINEMA

recent british cinema

10 Rillington Place

Richard Attenborough stars in this factual account of the John Christie-Timoth case, while John Hurt and Judy Geeson round out the supporting cast. The Evans murder rocked Britain in the late 1940's. Determined to see justice done, the wrong man was condemned for this crime. This shocking incident led to the end of capital punishment in Great Britain.

VHS: S29498. $19.95.

Richard Fleischer, Great Britain, 1970, 111 mins.

84 Charing Cross Road

A charming adult drama about a 20-year correspondence between a budding New York writer and an English dealer in Antiquarian books. Anne Bancroft and Anthony Hopkins breathe life into this semi-autobiographical film translation of a popular play and novel.

VHS: S04677. $19.95.

David Jones, Great Britain/USA, 1987, 97 mins.

Absolute Beginners: The Musical

When London was starting to swing, they called the first teenagers "Absolute Beginners." David Bowie stars in this film which charts the lives of two lovers who must choose to live by their idealist principles or sell out to get to the top of the fashion world.

VHS: S07699. $14.98.

Julien Temple, Great Britain, 1976, 107 mins.

Absolution

Richard Burton is a strict Catholic school teacher who becomes the victim of a sinister practical joke. A devious mystery written and directed by Anthony Shaffer *(Sleuth)* that was filmed in 1979, but only recently been made available. With Dominic Guard, Dai Bradley, Andrew Keir and Willoughby Gray.

VHS: S07525. $19.95.

Anthony Shaffer, Great Britain, 1981, 95 mins.

The Advocate

This offbeat, lusty period thriller is set during the (believe it or not) Middle Ages. A brilliant young lawyer is sent to the British countryside where he becomes the center of a complicated series of events involving an accusation of murder, witchcraft, Medieval politics and secret societies. Remarkably realistic, *The Advocate* cleverly bridges ethics with historical drama and the pursuit of justice.

VHS: S24322. $19.95.

Laser: Widescreen. **LD74913. $39.99.**

Leslie Megahey, Great Britain, 1994, 102 mins.

An Affair in Mind

Amanda Donohoe and Stephen Dillon star in this gripping psychological thriller produced for the BBC, based on a story by Ruth Rendell. Graham Lanceton is a best-selling novelist who is obsessed with the thoughts of Dru, the rich girl who loves him. From total strangers, they become passionate lovers—the only thing that stands in their way is Dru's husband, Tiny.

VHS: S10437. $19.98.

Michael Baker, Great Britain, 1987, 90 mins.

An African Dream

Kitty Aldridge plays an English schoolteacher who moves to South Africa in 1906 with her husband. She forms a friendship with an educated native named Katana, much to the displeasure of the local community. When rumors of romantic interest start to surface, tempers flair and actions get out of hand. With John Kani, Dominic Jephcott, John Carson, Richard Haines, Joy Stewart and Lyn Hooker. Filmed in Africa by the director of photography for the Indiana Jones movies.

VHS: S12539. $94.95.

John Smallcombe, Great Britain, 1990, 94 mins.

After Darkness

John Hurt is very concerned about his suicidal schizophrenic younger brother, Julian Sands, in this European thriller. He feels guiltier because he already feels responsible for the death of Julian's identical twin brother. With Victoria Abril and Pamela Salem.

VHS: S07783. $79.95.

Dominique Othenin-Girard/Sergio Guerraz, Switzerland/Great Britain, 1985, 104 mins.

After Pilkington

The calm surface of Oxford academic life is shattered for James Westgate by the sudden reappearance of his childhood sweetheart Penny in this award-winning BBC production. James' intense obsession with Penny draws him into a tangle of misunderstanding, intrigue and murder as their involvement in the mysterious disappearance of Pilkington becomes more than just a re-enactment of their childhood adventures. With Bob Peck *(Edge of Darkness)* and Miranda Richardson *(Dance with a Stranger)*.

VHS: S10439. $19.98.

Christopher Morahan, Great Britain, 1987, 99 mins.

Alice's Adventures in Wonderland

An enchanting live-action adaptation of Lewis Carroll's classic novel, with an all-star supporting cast. With Fiona Fullerton, Michael Crawford, Peter Sellers, and Dudley Moore.

VHS: S34206. $19.95.

William Sterling, Great Britain, 1972, 97 mins.

American Friends

An observant social comedy of manners and repression and the collision of sexual awakening and 19th century morality. Set in 1864, a single, middle-aged, Oxford University tutor (Michael Palin), who's studiously avoided romantic relations, encounters two vibrant American women, Caroline Hartley (Connie Booth) and her 17-year-old niece (Trini Alvarado), during his Swiss holiday. He's forced to choose between his long-dormant emotional demands and his academic requirements. With Alfred Molina and David Calder.

VHS: S18996. $92.95.

Laser: LD75144. $34.98.

Tristam Powell, Great Britain, 1991, 95 mins.

Angel Baby

In this critically acclaimed story, John Lynch *(Moll Flanders)* is Harry, a young man who hears voices. Jacqueline McKenzie *(Romper Stomper)* is Kate, who receives messages from an angel who speaks to her through *Wheel of Fortune*. When these two eccentric romantics find and fall for each other, their life outside the bounds of "normal" society is transformed. "Heartbreakingly good" (Janet Maslin, *The New York Times*).

VHS: S31536. $95.99.

Laser: LD76241. $34.99.

Michael Rymer, Great Britain, 1997, 101 mins.

Angels and Insects

Amidst the luxurious world of a wealthy family in Victorian England lies a strange secret involving sex. Kristin Scott Thomas and Patsy Kensit star in this story of a biologist who discovers rare and sultry creatures at the heart of a culture known for an obsession with civility and prudishness. It's a story of erotic decadence and illicit passion.

VHS: S28037. $19.98.

Laser: LD75606. $39.95.

Philip Haas, Great Britain, 1995, 118 mins.

Aria

Ten different directors select a different aria and have free rein to do anything that they want. The world of opera meets the medium of film with an eclectic mix of music and imagery. Robert Altman, Ken Russell, Derek Jarman, Jean-Luc Godard, Nicolas Roeg, Julien Temple, Bill Bryden, Franc Roddam, Charles Sturridge and Bruce Beresford go off in different directions. Cast includes Buck Henry, Theresa Russell, John Hurt, Anita Morris and Peter Fonda's daughter Bridget.

VHS: S07452. $14.98.

Ken Russell, et al., Great Britain, 1988, 90 mins.

An Awfully Big Adventure

Hugh Grant, Alan Rickman and Georgina Cates star in this inventive coming-of-age story about a teenage girl obsessed with the theater. This obsession leads her into the very grown-up world of a Liverpool theater company. Secrets, manipulation, menace and sex dominate. Set just after the Second World War, this film is based on Beryl Bainbridge's popular novel by the same title.

VHS: S26710. $19.95.

Laser: LD75323. $39.98.

Mike Newell, Great Britain, 1995, 113 mins.

BackBeat

Sheryl Lee and Stephen Dorff star in this energetic and exciting drama about a band with a new sound. They are just about to hit it big. In a heady mix of music, youth and love, conflict is inevitable. That's why a band that started out with five members produced only four well-known stars.

VHS: S22079. $94.95.

Laser: LD74595. $34.95.

Iain Softley, Great Britain, 1993, 100 mins.

Bartleby

Paul Scofield delivers a strong performance as the boss who has empathy with Bartleby, the alienated individual of Herman Melville's novel who is slowly giving up on life. With John McEnery.

VHS: S01550. $29.95.

Anthony Friedman, Great Britain, 1970, 79 mins.

Battle of Britain

Not the documentary, but the all-star recreation of the most decisive battle in history. Michael Caine, Robert Shaw, Christopher Plummer, Sir Laurence Olivier, and Sir Ralph Richardson star in this epic drama complete with amazingly filmed fighting sequences featuring authentic Spitfires, Hurricanes and Heinkels.

VHS: S04769. $19.98.

Laser: Widescreen. **LD76005. $49.98.**

Guy Hamilton, Great Britain, 1969, 132 mins.

Bawdy Adventures of Tom Jones

Based on one of the classic staples of English literature, the story of Tom Jones, the 18th century playboy, who makes his way through some of England's most prominent bedrooms in his quest for the woman of his dreams.

VHS: S03024. $59.95.

Cliff Owen, Great Britain, 1976, 89 mins.

Beautiful Thing

One of the best gay films to come out of Britain in years. With Linda Henry, Glen Berry and Scott Neal. "A warm and funny love story. Refreshingly spunky and unsentimental" (Michael Musto, *Village Voice*).

VHS: S31196. $98.99.

Hettie MacDonald, Great Britain, 1996, 90 mins.

Before the Rain

Three intertwined stories are joined in this haunting feature about individuals facing hard choices. Set in the former Yugoslavia and London, it combines ethical and moral quandaries with compelling situations and jarringly striking settings. Academy Award nominee for Best Foreign Language Picture. English and Macedonian with English subtitles.

VHS: S25952. $19.95.

Milcho Manchevski, Great Britain/Macedonia/France, 1994, 115 mins.

Bellman and True

A British thriller that is both a detailed character study and a caper film. A meek computer programmer becomes involved in an elaborate bank heist. He soon finds that his associates in crime are no league of gentlemen. With Bernard Hill, Kieren O'Brien, Frances Tomelty, Richard Hope and Ken Bones.

VHS: S08028. $14.98.

Richard Loncraine, Great Britain, 1988, 112 mins.

Billy Liar

From an unsympathetic, working-class family and an insecure dead-end job, Billy Fisher dreams of escape. Free-wheeling Liz (Julie Christie) comes into his life and gives the harassed hero (Tom Courtenay) one possibility to escape.

VHS: S04453. $19.98.

John Schlesinger, Great Britain, 1963, 94 mins.

Black Windmill

Michael Caine stars in this Donald Siegel thriller about a British agent whose son is kidnapped. Caine ruffles the feathers of friend and foe to accomplish the safe return of his flesh and blood. With Janet Suzman, John Vernon, Donald Pleasance, and Delphine Seyrig.

VHS: S07794. $59.95.

Don Siegel, Great Britain, 1974, 106 mins.

Blunt: The Fourth Man

Anthony Hopkins stars as a spy in this taut thriller based on the actual Guy Burgess-Anthony Blunt spy ring. It involved trusted government workers who relied on England's old boy network to rise to the top. Despite their aristocratic upbringing this spy ring sold British secrets to the Soviet Union, undetected for years. Suddenly their secret is out and they must escape.

VHS: S27660. $14.95.

John Glenister, Great Britain, 1992, 86 mins.

Born of Fire

Peter Firth *(Equus)* is a flautist with a problem. During a London recital he begins to improvise strange melodies. Suzan Crowley is an astronomer who says the music is linked to an upcoming volcanic eruption in Turkey. A tale of the supernatural. With Stefan Kalipha.

VHS: S05222. $79.95.

Jamil Dehlavi, Great Britain/Turkey, 1987, 83 mins.

Brannigan
John Wayne plays the title's tough Chicago cop, who is sent to London to bring back fugitive John Vernon. When his prisoner is hijacked, Wayne finds his stay in jolly old England to be extended, much to the dismay of Scotland Yard. With Richard Attenborough, Judy Geeson, Mel Ferrer, Daniel Pilon and Lesley-Anne Down.
VHS: S12139. $19.95.
Laser: LD76154. $39.98.
Douglas Hickox, Great Britain, 1975, 111 mins.

Breaking Glass
A British drama about a talented young singer and her shot at a show business career. Hazel O'Connor is the rising rock star and Phil Daniels is her youthful manager. With Jon Finch and Jonathan Pryce as a junkie saxophone player. A gritty, tune-filled exploration of the underbelly of success.
VHS: S06121. $49.95.
Brian Gibson, Great Britain, 1980, 93 mins.

Bridge Too Far
A stunning story of one of history's most controversial and disastrous World War II battles, the Allied defeat at Arnhem in 1944. Starring Robert Redford, Michael Caine, Laurence Olivier and Sean Connery. Based on the book by Cornelius Ryan. Letterboxed.
VHS: S12426. $24.98.
Richard Attenborough, Great Britain, 1977, 175 mins.

Brimstone and Treacle
A comic drama with rather bizarre underpinnings features Sting (of the group Police) as a handsome young drifter who gradually takes over the lives of a middle class couple and their paralyzed daughter. Music by Police, Go-Go's and Squeeze.
VHS: S01693. $19.98.
Richard Loncraine, Great Britain, 1983, 85 mins.

Britannia Hospital
A day of celebration turns into an apocalyptic nightmare in Lindsay Anderson's biting social satire. The staff of Britannia Hospital is preparing for its 500th anniversary, the visit of the Queen of England. But all is not well, as the gates are mobbed by protesters, the wards overflow with casualties of terrorist bombings, and the unions threaten to strike. With Malcolm McDowell.
VHS: S00183. $19.98.
Lindsay Anderson, Great Britain, 1983, 116 mins.

Broken Glass
An uplifting and tragically moving film version of Arthur Miller's award-winning psychodrama. In 1938, violent anti-Semitic riots break out in Nazi Germany and a sudden unexplained paralysis grips the legs of Brooklyn Jewish housewife Sylvia Gellburg (Margot Leicester). As Dr. Harry Hyman (Mandy Patinkin) investigates her condition, he learns of her fears for the Jews, and for her marriage to Phillip (Henry Goodman), whose loathing of his Jewishness was extended not only to his position in a WASP bank, but to their bedroom. Determined to restore both health and marriage for the Gellbergs, Dr. Hyman must strip away yearning, sexual denial, guilt and social injustice if he is to bring the couple face-to-face with themselves.
VHS: S30935. $19.98.
David Thacker, Great Britain, 1996, 100 mins.

Brothers in Trouble
Om Puri stars in this vivid portrait of a group of Pakistani illegals in 1960s Britain, in a funny, moving, well-acted film directed by and starring Udayan Prashad, with Om Puri *(City of Joy)* and Angeline Ball *(The Commitments)*. "Has the density and richness of a fine novel" *(Chicago Tribune)*.
VHS: S33319. $79.95.
Udayan Prashad, Great Britain, 1997, 104 mins.

The Browning Version
Albert Finney plays the disliked British don who suffers humiliation as his wife (Greta Scacchi) carries on an affair with Matthew Modine in this first-rate remake based on the Terrence Rattigan play. Finney delivers a nuanced performance as the teacher who has paid for the sublimation of his feelings by becoming a petty tyrant who is unloved by his wife and finds a fleeting human connection with a young student.
VHS: S23936. $19.95.
Laser: Widescreen. **LD75167. $34.98.**
Mike Figgis, Great Britain, 1994, 97 mins.

The Brylcreem Boys
When Canadian airman Miles Keogh (Bill Campbell) and German pilot Rudolph von Stegenbeck (Angus MacFayden) intern in the same camp, run by Commandant Sean O'Brien (Gabriel Byrne) in 1941 Dublin, they soon find that war is not the only battle between them. Both seek the heart of the fiery Irish beauty Mattie (Jean Butler, *Riverdance*, in her film debut).
VHS: S33230. $69.99.
Terence Ryan, Great Britain, 1996, 106 mins.

The Bushbaby
When a young woman's plans to smuggle her six-inch pet lemur, "Bushbaby", into the West are mislaid, she enlists the help of her friend Tembo (Louis Gossett Jr.) to guide her and the animal out of the African bush.
VHS: S19034. $19.98.
John Trent, Great Britain, 1970, 100 mins.

Business as Usual
When a store manager is fired from her job for reporting a case of sexual harassment in the work place, the national media rallies to her cause. A contemporary drama starring Glenda Jackson, John Thaw (Inspector Morse on PBS' *Mystery* series) and Cathy Tyson from *Mona Lisa*.
VHS: S09142. $89.95.
Lezli-Ann Barrett, Great Britain, 1988, 89 mins.

Buster
Phil Collins plays Buster, a small-time thief with a heart of gold. But his dream of the good life becomes a reality when he pulls off the greatest train robbery in history—$7 million in used bank notes. Off to Acapulco, even paradise has problems, though. And when the money disappears, wife June misses the old way of life and realizes all the money in the world can't take the place of the woman Buster loves. "Two Thumbs Up!" (E&S).
VHS: S09288. $89.99.
David Green, Great Britain, 1988, 102 mins.

Butterfly Kiss
In this horrific, comedic and romantic, female-driven alternative drama, the mentally unbalanced and dangerous Eunice (Amanda Plummer) meets a pretty, shy gas station attendant named Miriam (Saskia Reeves), and the two become lovers. Miriam joins Eunice on a murderous road trip across Britain, thinking she can save her friend from her self-destruction. A "twisted British answer to *Thelma & Louise* spiced with dashes of *Heavenly Creatures* and *Natural Born Killers*" *(The New York Times)*.
VHS: S32357. $79.95.
Michael Winterbottom, Great Britain, 1996, 90 mins.

Carrington
Emma Thompson gives a terrific performance as Dora Carrington, an unorthodox, androgynous painter from the early 20th-century Bloomsbury Group, who passionately loves gay writer Giles Lytton-Strachey (Jonathan Pryce). The highly regarded playwright Christopher Hampton *(Les Liaisons Dangereuses)* directs this tight, witty and insightful period piece, set amidst the self-conscious world of broken conventions and sexual eccentricities that come to mind whenever the name of the Bloomsbury Group is uttered.
VHS: S27596. $19.95.
Laser: LD75532. $34.99.
Christopher Hampton, Great Britain, 1995, 116 mins.

The Cement Garden
Andrew Birkin's chilling adaptation of Ian McEwan's *(The Good Son)* 1978 debut novel about incest, *The Cement Garden* is the erotic, macabre story of four young siblings and their attempt to maintain a semblance of normalcy after both parents suddenly die. Left to their own devices, the children begin to give freer expression to their sexuality. "Hypnotic and haunting—a hothouse of sexual tension and secret longing that is hard to shake" (Peter Travers, *Rolling Stone*).
VHS: S30256. $89.95.
Andrew Birkin, Great Britain/France/Germany, 1993, 105 mins.

Chariots of Fire
Drama based on a true story of two young men who run in the 1924 Olympics—a Jewish student from Cambridge and a Scottish missionary. Winner of Oscar for Best Picture, as well as Best Musical Score by Vangelis.
VHS: S00228. $19.98.
Laser: LD70542. $34.98.
DVD: DV60085. $24.98.
Hugh Hudson, Great Britain, 1981, 123 mins.

Charlotte Bronte's Jane Eyre
Love, passion and revenge conspire in this lavish adaptation of Charlotte Bronte's classic tale of the improbable love between a young governess who was once an orphan and her tragic and mysterious employer. From the director of *Fierce Creatures*. Starring Samantha Morton and Ciaran Hinds.
VHS: S32366. $19.95.
Robert Young, Great Britain, 1997, 108 mins.

The Charmer
Nigel Havers is a 1930s con man called Ralph Gorse. Handsome, suave and sophisticated, this charmer is determined to take every opportunity to climb the social ladder. He may very well use every woman in his path. This path however, leads inexorably to graver crimes, including murder.
VHS: S21690. $99.98.
Alan Gibson, Great Britain, 1994, 50 mins.

Circle of Passion
Thomas Murray (Charles Finch), a succesful London banker and devoted husband, is married to Amanda, a beautiful socialite whose father is Thomas' business partner. When Thomas is transferred to Paris, Amanda refuses to join him and Thomas finds the passion he's never known in the lovely and free-spirited Katherine. Torn between love and responsibility, he must choose between the wife who would never leave him and the woman he truly loves. With Sandrine Bonnaire and Jane March.
VHS: S33168. $79.95.
Charles Finch, Great Britain, 1997, 94 mins.

The Clash of the Titans
Portraying the Greek myth, Laurence Olivier is Zeus who sends his mortal son Perseus to face awesome supernatural challenges in pursuit of his destiny. With fantastic effects by Ray Harryhausen which include the taming of Pegasus.
VHS: S16851. $19.98.
Laser: LD72170. $39.98.
Desmond Davis, Great Britain, 1981, 118 mins.

Cold Light of Day
Richard E. Grant *(Portrait of a Lady)* is a police officer who will stop at nothing to catch the serial killer of children in the English countryside, including seducing a single mother (Lindsay Baxter) to use her young daughter as bait for the killer. A chilling tale of murder and suspense.
VHS: S30864. $19.95.
Laser: LD76227. $39.98.
Rudolf Van Den Berg, Great Britain, 1995, 101 mins.

Coming Through
In this biography of D.H. Lawrence the sexual themes of the author are placed in situations taken from his own life. Kenneth Branagh stars as Lawrence with Helen Mirren as Kate, a graduate student that he would seduce. Finally overcome by true love, Lawrence commits himself to choices that lead to scandal and ultimately exile.
VHS: S20808. $19.98.
Peter Barber-Fleming, Great Britain, 1993, 80 mins.

A Dangerous Man: Lawrence After Arabia
Picks up where *Lawrence of Arabia* left off. It's 1919 when T.E. Lawrence (Ralph Fiennes) arrives at the Paris Peace Conference and peace proves to be a harder battle than war, as Lawrence finds himself fighting British and French deception on an urban battlefield, with hidden interests in the new discovery of Middle Eastern oil.
VHS: S33223. $19.98.
Christopher Menaul, Great Britain, 1990, 104 mins.

Dark Obsession
Gabriel Byrne stars as a man tormented by jealousy and guilt, who attempts to escape into a world of obsessive, erotic fantasies. His stunning wife, played by Amanda Donohoe, is slowly pulled under by her husband's dark sex games and deepening madness in this story of obsession and retribution. "Steamy, stylish and chilling" *(LA Times)*. "Plenty of sex and intrigue" *(Daily Variety)*.
VHS: S15181. $24.95.
Nick Broomfield, Great Britain, 1991

The Day of the Jackal
A superior thriller concerning a plot to assassinate General Charles de Gaulle in Paris. Based on the best selling novel by Frederick Forsyth. Edward Fox is the meticulous hitman assigned to do the job. The top notch cast includes Michel Lonsdale, Delphine Seyrig, Alan Badel, Cyril Cusack and Derek Jacobi. A blueprint for murder.
VHS: S07808. $59.95.
DVD: DV60244. $24.98.
Fred Zinnemann, Great Britain/France, 1973, 143 min.

Deadly Advice
Jane Horrocks stars as Jodie, a teenager who is being driven to an early grave by her pesky mother. Help comes in the form of a book on legendary killers. Soon fiends like Jack the Ripper appear with deadly advice. Jonathan Pryce is also featured as the small town doctor who begins to suspect that something is amiss in this deadly comedy.
VHS: S27754. $19.95.
Laser: LD75578. $39.99.
Mandie Fletcher, Great Britain, 1993, 91 mins.

A Deadly Game
Before the fall of the Berlin Wall, a deadly chess game of espionage raged between the East and West—and no bigger pawn existed than Charlie Muffin (David Hemmings). Returning from East Berlin after a perilous mission, he narrowly avoids a death trap set by his own colleagues. Who will be the pawn when the final move is made?
VHS: S14629. $59.99.
Jack Gold, Great Britain, 1979, 104 mins.

Death on the Nile
Peter Ustinov and Mia Farrow star in this adaptation of Agatha Christie's famous mystery, with Hercule Poirot playing detective games with a dozen or so suspects.
VHS: S04542. $19.98.
John Guillermin, Great Britain, 1978, 135 mins.

Different for Girls
When Paul (Rupert Graves) last saw his old school friend he remembered a boy named Karl. Now, 15 years later, he unexpectedly runs into him again, but now she is Kim, a post-operative transsexual. Worlds apart in their attitudes toward life, they no longer appear to have anything in common. But as she teaches him to grow up and he teaches her to have fun, they accidentally fall in love. With Steven Mackintosh as Karl/Kim.
VHS: S34230. $89.98.
Richard Spence, Great Britain, 1996, 101 mins.

Doctor and the Devils
Based on an original screenplay by Dylan Thomas, this dramatic thriller concerns two of the most famous villains in the history of English crime. Broom and Fallon begin working for Dr. Thomas Rock providing bodies for his anatomical research.
VHS: S00352. $79.98.
Freddie Francis, Great Britain, 1985, 93 mins.

Doctor Faustus
Richard Burton stars in this retelling of Christopher Marlowe's cautionary tale of an aging scholar who makes a bargain with the Devil. Inquiring minds want to know if Helen of Troy really looked so much like Elizabeth Taylor. Performed by members of the Oxford University Dramatic Society.
VHS: S03943. $19.95.
Richard Burton/Nevill Coghill, Great Britain, 1968, 93 mins.

The Dogs of War
Christopher Walken is a sentimental mercenary in this film of Frederick Forsyth's novel about a plot by a business conglomerate to overthrow an African government for their own profit. With Tom Berenger, Colin Blakely, Paul Freeman and Jobeth Williams. Lots of action and acting. VHS letterboxed.
VHS: S06994. $14.95.
Laser: LD76363. $39.99.
John Irvin, Great Britain, 1980, 102 mins.

The Dresser
Albert Finney and Tom Courtenay star in this compelling study of the relationship between the leader of a British touring stage company and his dresser. The action of the film takes place as Finney prepares for his 277th performance of *King Lear*. A film rich in comedy, compassion and love for the theater, from the popular London stage play.
VHS: S00374. $14.95.
Peter Yates, Great Britain, 1983, 118 mins.

Dressmaker
Brilliant performances from two of Britain's greatest actresses, Joan Plowright and Billie Whitelaw, as two sisters locked in a love-hate relationship, highlight this critically-acclaimed film by Jim O'Brien. The sisters' simmering bitterness explodes into the open when their shy 17-year-old niece, whom they have raised since childhood, falls in love with an American G.I.
VHS: S11171. $79.95.
Laser: CLV. **LD71589. $39.95.**
Jim O'Brien, Great Britain, 1989, 92 mins.

Duellists
Keith Carradine and Harvey Keitel are two officers in Napoleon's army who violently confront each other in a series of savage duels in Ridley Scott's film about passion and honor, based on a story by Joseph Conrad.
VHS: S00379. $19.95.
Ridley Scott, Great Britain, 1977, 110 mins.

Eden Valley
From Amber Production Team, a Newcastle group of filmmakers, "a stirring British film" (Lisa Katzman, *Village Voice*) that explores the conflict between urban and rural values as mirrored in the lives of a father and his estranged teenaged son. The film was shot as a result of relationships the filmmakers built within the community; they mix professional and non-professional actors in a unique production rooted in English working-class life. With Brian Hogg, Darren Bell and Mike Elliott.
VHS: S31121. $59.95.
Amber Production Team, Great Britain, 1994, 95 mins.

Edge of Darkness
A powerful mystery set in England focusing on a secret government project which leads to nuclear contamination. With Joe Don Baker, Bob Peck.
VHS: S04954. $29.98.
Martin Campbell, Great Britain, 1986, 157 mins.

Emily Bronte's Wuthering Heights
Years before their acclaimed performances in *The English Patient*, Juliette Binoche and Ralph Fiennes starred together in this visually stunning, passionate and eerily atmospheric adaptation of Emily Bronte's timeless tale of two families and the doomed love that entwines them.
VHS: S32511. $92.99.
Peter Kosminsky, Great Britain, 1992, 107 mins.

Emma
Jane Austen's delightfully wicked comedy of love and matchmaking features an acclaimed, star-studded cast, including Kate Beckinsale *(Cold Comfort Farm)* as the clever and beautiful woman who can't resist orchestrating other people's love lives as she risks missing out on her own perfect match. With Prunella Scales *(Howard's End)* and Samantha Bond *(Goldeneye)*.
VHS: S30823. $19.95.
Diarmuid Lawrence, Great Britain, 1996, 108 mins.

Empire State
Docked in a seedy part of London's waterfront, the Empire State harbors a variety of nightclubbers from every walk of life. Ray McAnally ("Cal") is the proprietor of the mysterious realm who is mired in a dirty financial war with a relentless land speculator, Martin Landau.
VHS: S07760. $79.95.
Ron Peck, Great Britain, 1987, 102 mins.

Enchanted April
Mike Newell's wonderfully textured adaptation of Elizabeth von Arnim's 1922 novel about four radically different English women who pool their resources to share the expenses of a breathtaking Italian villa for one month. With Miranda Richardson, Josie Lawrence, Polly Walker and Joan Plowright.
VHS: S18369. $19.95.
Laser: LD75189. $34.98.
Mike Newell, Great Britain, 1991, 93 mins.

FairyTale
When two young girls claim they've photographed fairies, it causes a real-life controversy that fascinates all of wartime England, including Sir Arthur Conan Doyle and Harry Houdini. Starring Peter O'Toole and Harvey Keitel.
VHS: S33401. $99.99.
Charles Sturridge, Great Britain, 1997, 99 mins.

Fall from Grace
James Fox, Michael York, Patsy Kensit and Gary Cole star in this chilling tale of espionage and deception. In 1943 Hitler's forces dominate and terrorize Europe. A crack team of British and American intelligence officers undertake a huge gamble. They must convince Hitler of the impossible. Their success could hasten the end of the war. Failure is unthinkable.
VHS: S26521. $69.99.
Waris Hussein, Great Britain, 1994, 240 mins.

Farewell My Lovely
Dick Richards's British version of Raymond Chandler's novel about a private eye's (Robert Mitchum) search for a gangster's girlfriend. With Charlotte Rampling, John Ireland and Sylvia Miles.
VHS: S02144. $19.95.
Dick Richards, Great Britain, 1975, 95 mins.

Fatal Confinement
Joan Crawford stars in this mysterious portrayal of a mother and her daughter, living in seclusion for 15 years. A large corporation pressures her into selling her land for a factory. A tense and volatile drama, reminiscent of Crawford's real-life role as "Mommie Dearest." Paul Berg, Charles Bickford also star.
VHS: S07459. $19.95.
Robert Guest, Great Britain, 1964, 70 mins.

Feast of July
Embeth Davidtz stars in this engrossing drama set in the 19th-century English countryside. Bella (Davidtz) sets off to find the married man who fathered her stillborn child and ends up in the Wainwright household. Ultimately, she finds more than she bargained for, including a belief in her own resolve which allows her to forge a new life. An exquisitely detailed portrait of a woman's struggle to define and own her life. A Merchant/Ivory production.
VHS: S27523. $19.95.
Laser: LD75548. $39.99.
Christopher Menaul, Great Britain, 1995, 116 mins.

A Foreign Field
Lauren Bacall, Geraldine Chaplin, Jean Moreau and Alec Guiness are all featured in this comedy of undying memory. They reunite at Normandy where they first encountered one another during D-Day. Now 50 years later, old rivalries and even romance are alive once again.
VHS: S21039. $89.98.
Charles Sturridge, Great Britain, 1993, 90 mins.

Fourth Protocol
An adaptation of the Frederick Forsyth spy novel featuring Michael Caine as a British agent out to foil a Russian plot. The Russians plan to drop a nuclear bomb near an American base in England, thereby destroying their friendly relations.
VHS: S07015. $14.95.
John MacKenzie, Great Britain, 1987, 119 mins.

The Franchise Affair
The Franchise—a secluded mansion inhabited by two secretive women. As moonlight strikes the mansion's attic window, a half-naked young girl flees frantically through the woods. What is the secret of The Franchise? The clue is in the attic.... England, 149 mins.
VHS: S14329. $26.98.

French Lesson
A first feature from Brian Gilbert about an English teen visiting Paris and growing from a vulnerable innocent to a charming, witty, young woman. English and French with English subtitles.
VHS: S00467. $19.98.
Brian Gilbert, Great Britain, 1984, 90 mins.

French Lieutenant's Woman
Harold Pinter wrote the screenplay adapted from John Fowles' novel. A hauntingly beautiful film starring Meryl Streep and Jeremy Irons, about a woman ostracized by Victorian society and abandoned by her lover.
VHS: S00468. $19.95.
Laser: LD70140. $39.98.
Karel Reisz, Great Britain, 1981, 124 mins.

Freshkill
Sarita Choudhury *(Mississippi Masala)* and Erin McMurtry are two young, lesbian parents caught up in a global exchange of industrial waste via contaminated sushi in Manhattan. The crisis escalates when a multinational corporation is implicated and the couple's infant daughter mysteriously vanishes. "Vibrant...capturing succintly both the vitality and absurdity of modern life" (Kevin Thomas, *Los Angeles Times*).
VHS: S33134. $39.99.
Shu Lea Cheang, Great Britain, 1997, 80 mins.

Gandhi
Richard Attenborough's dream project realized in epic style with Ben Kingsley as Gandhi in an Oscar winning performance, and a cast including Candice Bergen, Martin Sheen and John Gielgud.
VHS: S02022. $29.95.
Laser: LD72202. $49.95.
Richard Attenborough, Great Britain, 1982, 187 mins.

Glass Mountain
Many singers from La Scala appear in the opera sequence of this inspiring film about a British composer who writes an opera about the Italian Alps. With Valentina Cortese and Sebastian Shaw.
VHS: S26381. $29.95.
Henry Cass, Great Britain, 1950, 94 mins.

The Great Train Robbery
Sean Connery heads a team of criminals that includes Lesley-Anne Down and Donald Sutherland. They scheme to snatch a fortune in gold from a moving train in 1840's England. Michael Crichton's novel is based on fact. A delightful tongue-in-cheek caper film. Excellent period detail.
VHS: S06993. $19.98.
Laser: Widescreen. **LD75924. $39.99.**
Michael Crichton, Great Britain, 1979, 111 mins.

Gulliver in Lilliput
Based on Jonathan Swift's famous satire, this clever BBC production recounts the adventures of Lemuel Gulliver in the land of the Lilliputians. With Andrew Burt, Elisabeth Sladen, Linda Polan.
VHS: S07179. $19.98.
Barry Letts, Great Britain, 1986, 107 mins.

A Handful of Dust
Evelyn Waugh's satiric novel on the decline of the British empire has been filmed in a very civilized manner. When the decent but very dull James Wilby finds out that his beautiful but cool wife (Kristin Scott Thomas) is having a serious affair with the dashing but penniless Rupert Graves, he goes exploring in South America. With Anjelica Huston and Alec Guinness.
VHS: S08351. $19.98.
Charles Sturridge, Great Britain, 1988, 117 mins.

Handmaid's Tale
Natasha Richardson, Robert Duvall, Faye Dunaway and Elizabeth McGovern star in Volker Schlondorff's stylish adaptation of Margaret Atwood's novel of the not-so-distant future. A fertile woman is forced by her country's government to serve as a Handmaid to the "Commander" and his wife, who has been made sterile by ecological disasters.
VHS: S12766. $19.98.
Volker Schlondorff, Great Britain/USA, 1990, 109 mins.

Harnessing Peacocks
Based on the best-selling novel by English author Mary Wesley, *Harnessing Peacocks* is the story of Hebe (Serena Scott Thomas), a young girl who is rejected by her family because of an illegitimate pregnancy. Forced to make it on her own, she creates an idyllic life for herself and her son in a seaside town while working as a cook and a courtesan, until one day when a stranger arrives in town who changes her life forever. 108 mins.
VHS: S30006. $14.98.

Hear My Song
A delightful romantic comic adventure based on the exploits of famed Irish tenor Josef Locke. Ned Beatty plays the cautious Irish tax exile being sought by a conniving but well meaning talent booker for a nightclub on the west coast of England. Adrian Dunbar, who co-wrote the script, plays the unemployed club manager, who must redeem himself in the eyes of the woman he loves as well as the community that trusted his judgement.
VHS: S16634. $19.95.
Laser: LD75205. $34.98.
Peter Chelsom, Great Britain, 1991, 104 mins.

Heat of the Day
Master playwright Harold Pinter's adaptation of the famous suspense novel by Elizabeth Bowen is given a full tilt treatment in this PBS production starring Michael York. England, 120 mins.
VHS: S15109. $19.98.

Hedd Wyn
This true story confronts the heedless human loss occasioned by World War I. A young poet is mortally wounded, and as he lies dying, he recalls not only his memories but his hopes and ambitions for the future. Nominated for an Academy Award for Best Foreign Language Film. Welsh with English subtitles.
VHS: S28393. $19.98.
Paul Turner, Wales, 1996, 123 mins.

Her Majesty Mrs. Brown
Judi Dench gives an exquisite performance as Queen Victoria in this true story of the relationship that scandalized a country. Deeply depressed after the death of her beloved husband, Prince Albert, the Queen disappeared from public life for two years, until her servant John Brown (Billy Connolly), a Highlander who tended the Queen's horse stable, brought her back to life with his love and admiration. The passionate friendship put the monarchy in crisis as it transformed an empire.
VHS: S33342. $103.99.
Laser: LD76818. $39.99.
John Madden, Great Britain, 1997, 105 mins.

Hitler: The Last Ten Days
Alec Guinness interprets the role of the Fuehrer whose Reich didn't quite last a thousand years. With Berlin in ruins, he gathers his top leaders around him in the bunker and rants a lot. Some days, world domination is not all it is cracked up to be. With Simon Ward, Aldofo Celli, Diane Cilento and Eric Porter.
VHS: S10825. $49.95.
Ennio de Concine, Great Britain/Italy, 1973, 108 mins.

How Many Miles to Babylon
A powerful drama about friendship and loyalty set against the havoc of World War I. Daniel Day-Lewis comes from a wealthy Irish family whose friendship with Christopher Fairbank, a kindred spirit from a lower economic class, ends both of them up in the Army during World War I. Despite their differences in rank, they remain close friends, both become disillusioned with the war, and in an odd twist of irony, one is court-martialed for desertion, the other put in charge of the firing squad. Produced by the BBC.
VHS: S03525. $19.98.
Moira Armstrong, Great Britain, 1986, 106 mins.

Ice House
From the best-selling novel by award-winning writer Minette Walters, a tangled web of secrets and murder as chief Inspector Walsh (Corin Redgrave) and Sergeant McLoughlin (Daniel Craig) investigate a dead body found in the ice house. With Penny Downie, Kitty Aldridge and Frances Barber.
VHS: S34414. $29.98.
Tim Fywell, Great Britain, 1997, 180 mins.

Into the Blue
Harry Barnett (John Thaw, TV's *Inspector Morse*), once married and successful, is now single, bankrupt and working as a caretaker at a villa on the Greek island of Rhodes. He finds himself mixed up in blackmail, deceit and murder when he has a fling with a woman (Abigail Cruttenden) he met in a bar.
VHS: S32690. $19.98.
Jack Gold, Great Britain, 1997, 120 mins.

Jane Austen's Persuasion
Jane Austen's last novel is superbly realized in this well-acted costume drama. After the end of the Napoleonic Wars, Captain Frederick Wentworth and his former fiance slowly but surely find themselves drawn to each other once again. Set amidst the luxurious trappings of the English upper class, this tale of true love is simply irresistible.
VHS: S27350. $19.95.
Laser: LD75498. $34.95.
Roger Michell, Great Britain, 1995, 104 mins.

Joseph Andrews
Director Tony Richardson *(Hotel New Hampshire)* adapts another of Henry Fielding's *(Tom Jones)* attacks on Victorian morals and their inherent hypocrisy. Peter Firth stars as a lowly functionary to Lady Booby (Ann-Margret), whose advances and seductions are rejected in favor of a simple peasant girl. Fielding's novel is purportedly based on Samuel Richardson's *Pamela*.
VHS: S02538. $49.95.
Tony Richardson, Great Britain, 1977, 99 mins.

Jude
Kate Winslet *(Sense and Sensibility)* and Christopher Eccleston *(Shallow Grave)* bring exquisite performances to this haunting adaptation of Thomas Hardy's *Jude the Obscure*, the story of an idealistic stonemason's obsession with the perfect woman: his headstrong cousin. "A sweeping film of power, passion and greatness" (Rex Reed).
VHS: S30896. $19.95.
Laser: LD76081. $49.99.
Michael Winterbottom, Great Britain, 1996, 122 mins.

Kitchen Toto
A moving drama about racial tensions and growing up in Kenya in the 1950's. The title refers to a term for a houseboy. A 12-year-old black child is placed with a white family to help around the house. He befriends the 11-year-old son of the white policeman as the Mau Mau's are preparing a violent uprising. With Edwin Mahinda, Bob Peck, Phyllis Logan and Robert Urquhart. A first film written and directed by Kenyan resident Harry Hook.
VHS: S09800. $19.98.
Harry Hook, Kenya/Great Britain, 1987, 95 mins.

The Krays
The fascinating, true story of Ronnie and Reggie Kray, England's most famous gangsters, *The Krays* chronicles the surprising success of the twin "brothers grim" who shared a terrifying taste for blood. Their rise to power and eventual fall from grace is both compelling and horrifying; a chilling portrait of brutal beauty. Starring Gary and Martin Kemp—founding members of the rock group *Spandau Ballet*.
VHS: S13828. $19.95.
Laser: Chapter stops, digital master, 3 sides. **LD75052. $39.95.**
Peter Medak, Great Britain, 1990, 119 mins.

Lady Jane
An historical recreation of the nine-day rule of a very minor and very young English monarch. Helena Bonham Carter is impressive in the title role. Cary Elwes is her carefully selected consort. Their romance holds little historical accuracy but it breaks up the parts where one has to wait to hear how the battles came out. With John Wood, Michael Hordern, and many other members of the Royal Shakespeare Company.
VHS: S10829. $79.95.
Laser: LD75301. $39.98.
Trevor Nunn, Great Britain, 1985, 140 mins.

The Lady's Not for Burning
Kenneth Branagh stars in this mystery tale beset by superstition. Branagh is a discharged soldier who must solve the murder of man in order to protect a beautiful woman. She stands accused of witchcraft. The murdered man's body is missing and the townspeople suspect that she has turned him into a dog. Based on the play by respected playwright Christopher Fry, this passionate love story is set in a time ruled by irrational fears. With Bernard Hepton and Cherie Lunghi.
VHS: S26776. $19.95.
Julian Aymes, Great Britain, 1995, 90 mins.

Lamb
Liam Neeson stars as Michael Lamb, a Catholic Brother working at an institution for troubled boys. There he meets 10-year-old Owen Kane, a boy with a series of problems relating both to his disadvantaged past and to the cruel treatment he receives at the hands of the other Brothers at the Home. When Michael Lamb receives an inheritance, he acts on the growing doubts he feels regarding both his faith and the mission of the school where he works. He decides to take Owen to London, setting off a chain of events that leads to tragedy.
VHS: S27055. $39.95.
Colin Gregg, Great Britain, 1995, 110 mins.

The Leading Man
Jon Bon Jovi stars in this Hitchcockian thriller as Robin, a Hollywood sex symbol who offers to seduce Elena (Anna Galiena), the wife of successful, middle-aged playwright Felix Webb (Lambert Wilson), so that Felix will be free to be with his mistress, Hilary (Thandie Newton, *Flirting*). Things get complicated when Robin stars in a play starring both Hilary and Elena and finds himself getting involved with both women.
VHS: S34906. $97.99.
John Duggan, Great Britain, 1996, 96 mins.

Let Him Have It
In 1953, Chris Craig, 17, and Derek Bentley, 16, were accused of murdering a South London policeman. The title of the film recalls the fateful words spoken by the unarmed Bentley just prior to a shot fired by his mate in the direction of the police. Director Peter Medak contends the lad was encouraging his friend to surrender the weapon, as this story re-examines a miscarriage of justice. With Christopher Eccleston, Paul Reynolds and Tom Courtenay as the father of the accused.
VHS: S16415. $19.95.
Peter Medak, Great Britain, 1991, 102 mins.

Lifeforce
Patrick Stuart is featured in this genuinely creepy sci-fi horror film about a female vampire. She was dozing in Halley's comet, but once brought back to Earth she awakens to a whole new world of vampiric exploits so vast that the entire planet could be sucked dry.
VHS: S27750. $14.95.
DVD: DV60325. $24.98.
Tobe Hooper, Great Britain, 1985, 101 mins.

Little Dorrit
Christine Edzard's film is a brilliant reworking of the Charles Dickens classic. Brilliant camerawork by Bruno De Keyzer and immaculate sets of John McMillan produce the flavor of Victorian England. Edzard goes to the heart of the novel and makes it new in the story of the pinch-faced, hard-nosed survivor whose belief in herself and in the redemption of humanity forces those about her to survive as well. With an all-star British cast including Alec Guiness, Derek Jacobi, and Sarah Pickering in a brilliant performance as Little Dorrit.
Little Dorrit Part One. *Nobody's Fault*. The first part is told from Arthur Clenman's point of view.
VHS: S09595. $24.98.
Little Dorrit Part Two. *Dorritt's Story*. The story is told from Little Dorrit's point of view.
VHS: S09596. $24.98.
Christine Edzard, Great Britain, 1988, 369 mins.

Little Lord Fauntleroy
Frances Hodgson Burnett's classic tale of innocence and unconditional goodness. Young Cedric Erroll's life changes forever when a lawyer from England arrives in New York City with the news that Cedric is the grandson of the Earl of Dorincourt and the only heir to his vast fortune.
VHS: S32522. $14.98.
Andrew Morgan, Great Britain, 1995, 100 mins.

Living Free
The sequel to *Born Free* continues the story of the Adamsons and their close relationship with Elsa the lioness. Nigel Davenport and Susan Hampshire are the Kenya game wardens who are trusted with the upbringing of three small cubs. Based on the book by Joy Adamson. With Geoffrey Keen.
VHS: S06179. $12.95.
Jack Couffer, Great Britain, 1972, 91 mins.

London Kills Me
The first film by Hanif Kureishi *(My Beautiful Laundrette, Sammy and Rosie Get Laid)* concerns a renegade group of drug dealers and the efforts of its confused protagonist to go straight after he's been humiliated. There's a vibrant sexual triangle played out among the three leads, along with a shaded, interesting portrait of atmosphere and local color.
Laser: LD75129. $24.98.
Hanif Kureishi, Great Britain, 1991, 107 mins.

The Lonely Passion of Judith Hearne
Judith Hearne (Maggie Smith) is a lonely woman in reduced circumstances but is determined to make a fresh start in life. Despite the dreariness of her surroundings, she believes her optimism is rewarded when she meets James Madden (Bob Hoskins). Judith, who craves romance, is flattered by his attention and does not recognize that his main interest in her is as an ideal business partner. When Judith is forced to confront reality she turns to the bottle for consolation and is propelled along a course of self-destruction.
VHS: S32498. $14.98.
Jack Clayton, Great Britain, 1987, 116 mins.

The Long Day Closes
Condensed childhood memories of 1940's England are related through elegiac and anecdotal episodes. Like the earlier *Distant Voices/Still Lives*, this film employs similar techniques but focuses on the mother instead of the father, resulting in a view infiltrated by gentle humor.
VHS: S20710. $19.95.
Terence Davies, Great Britain, 1993, 84 mins.

The Long Good Friday
Bob Hoskins and Helen Mirren star in this gritty but updated gangster film set in London's East End. Hoskins is a cockney hood with big plans. He hopes to enlist foreign help, both underworld and legit, in order to develop the docklands. Of course, his plans can't proceed without a little mob rivalry. Overall, it's a tough, hip thriller.
VHS: S27721. $14.95.
Laser: Letterboxed. **LD76183. $49.98.**
John MacKenzie, Great Britain, 1979, 114 mins.

The Looking Glass War
There may be allusions to Lewis Carroll, but this film is based on John Le Carre's best selling novel of cold war espionage, where Christopher Jones risks all to photograph a rocket in East Berlin. With Ralph Richardson, Anthony Hopkins, Susan George and Pia Degermark.
VHS: S03883. $19.98.
Frank Pierson, Great Britain, 1970, 108 mins.

Lorna Doone
Classic romantic drama set in 17th-century England. A woman named Lorna Doone (Polly Walker), of the bandit Doone family, falls in love with a man from a rival family (Sean Bean), who blames her family for the death of his parents. Love conquers all. Made for British television.
VHS: S20608. $79.98.
Andrew Grieve, Great Britain, 1990, 90 mins.

The Lost Language of the Cranes
A moody BBC adaptation of David Leavitt's novel about family secrets and sexual identity. The film centers on a young man's sexual declaration and its volatile and revealing consequences on the rest of the family. "Graced with subtle, intense performances" *(Time Magazine)*. With Corey Parker, Brian Cox, Eileen Atkins and Angus MacFadyen.
VHS: S18604. $19.98.
Nigel Finch, Great Britain, 1992, 84 mins.

Madame Sousatzka
Shirley MacLaine is magnificent as an aging, highly disciplined London concert piano teacher who resents having her best pupils snatched by greedy musical promoters. Beautiful music and brilliant acting. With Navin Chowdhry, Twiggy, Shabana Azmi and Peggy Ashcroft. Adapted from the novel by Bernice Rubens.
VHS: S09108. $19.95.
John Schlesinger, Great Britain, 1988, 121 mins.

The Madness of King George
Nigel Hawthorne plays the last king ever to rule the North American colonies. He is joined by Helen Mirren (winner of Best Actress Award at Cannes) as the queen and Ian Holm as the Prince of Wales, in this film based on a true story. King George went mad and a variety of cures were brought to bear on this once imposing figure. The result is a tale of maddening cures, political intrigue and overall decline with a touch of British humor. Based on Alan Bennett's play.
VHS: S26268. $19.98.
Laser: LD75069. $39.99.
Nicholas Hytner, Great Britain, 1995, 110 mins.

A Man of No Importance
Albert Finney leads a cast of fine performers in this entertaining and touching story about the conductor of a double decker bus in Ireland. The conductor is fascinated by two things, directing plays (he attempts Oscar Wilde's *Salome*) and his co-worker, the bus driver.
VHS: S26209. $19.95.
Laser: LD75040. $34.95.
Suri Krishnama, Great Britain, 1994, 98 mins.

Meetings with Remarkable Men
Peter Brook directed this unique search through the Middle East, Central Asia for answers to the question of the meaning of life, based on Gurdijeff's search for hidden knowledge. As a boy, Gurdijeff is influenced by his father, a man of remarkable character, who nurtures his thirst for knowledge while preparing him for a career in medicine and priesthood. But a brush with death and other extraordinary, inexplicable events heighten his sense of wonder about the meaning of man's life, and in hidden ruins, he and his comrades discover ancient scrolls which confirm the existence of a brotherhood with ancient knowledge passed orally from generation to generation. Among those appearing in this extraordinary film are Athol Fugard, Colin Blakely, Terence Stamp.
VHS: S06033. $69.95.
Peter Brook, Great Britain, 1979, 108 mins.

A Midwinter's Tale
Written and directed by Kenneth Branagh, this biting comedy takes a satirical look at show business. Celebrating the acting profession, with all its passion, humor, drama and naivete, Branagh is supported by a top-notch cast including Joan Collins, John Sessions and *Absolutely Fabulous'* Julia Sawalha.
VHS: S28621. $96.99.
Laser: LD75957. $34.95.
Kenneth Branagh, Great Britain, 1996, 99 mins.

A Mind to Kill
Tension invades a small English seaside town when a brutally murdered girl is found. Police link her body to a previous murder and decide to call in a brilliant university professor for help. The professor also becomes subject to this killer's terror as another fresh body surfaces which turns out to be someone he knew well. Finally, even the police detective in charge of the case finds that someone he loves could suffer if the madman is not caught soon. With Hywel Bennett, Philip Madoc, Sue Jones-Davies and Nicola Beddoe.
VHS: S26777. $19.98.
Peter Edwards, Great Britain, 1995, 95 mins.

Mirror Crack'd
Agatha Christie's beloved Miss Marple tackles an assembly of all-star suspects in this film version of one of her favorite mystery novels. Angela Lansbury, Elizabeth Taylor and Tony Curtis star.
VHS: S04543. $19.99.
Guy Hamilton, Great Britain, 1980, 105 mins.

Mona Lisa
A moody, expressionist and haunting work by Irish novelist Neil Jordan stars Bob Hoskins as a low-level underground figure caught in a dangerous and intricate game of saving the life of a beautiful prostitute (Cathy Tyson). With Michael Caine, Robbie Coltrane and Clarke Peters.
VHS: S03294. $14.95.
Neil Jordan, Great Britain, 1986, 104 mins.

Monsignor Quixote
Sir Alec Guinness stars as Father Quixote, a parish priest and ancestor of the legendary Don Quixote. It is only a matter of time before he assumes the courage and fury of his demented namesake to "tilt at the windmills" and do battle with evil. England, 118 mins.
VHS: S14627. $19.98.

The Moth
Set in 1913, this classic from Catherine Cookson tells the story of carpenter Robert Bradley, who leaves the shipyards for a job in his uncle's furniture business, then finds work as a servant in the dysfunctional Thorman household where an attraction develops between Robert and the aristocratic young Sarah Thorman. With Juliet Aubrey, David Bradley, Jeremy Clyde, Janet Dale and Jack Davenport. 1997 British TV mini-series. 150 mins.
VHS: S34107. $34.98.

Mrs. 'Arris Goes to Paris
Angela Lansbury stars, while Omar Sharif makes a special appearance in this adaptation of the Paul Gallico novel. Mrs. 'Arris sees a Dior gown in one of the homes she cleans for a living. This inspires her to save for a visit to Paris and the fabled House of Dior. It's a light, frothy comedy with terrific acting and a fairy tale feel.
VHS: S29979. $14.95.
Anthony Shaw, Great Britain, 1992, 90 mins.

Mrs. Dalloway
Vanessa Redgrave gives an exquisite performance in Marlene Gorris' *(Antonia's Line)* adaptation of Virginia Woolf's 1923 novel which follows a day in the life of Clarissa Dalloway, a respectable, 60ish wife of a London cabinet official, as she prepares for and gives a party. During the course of the day she is visited by Peter, an old suitor, and Sally, with whom she had a flirtation as a young woman. Through flashbacks we learn about the choices Clarissa made during her life as she wonders about what might have been. With Natascha McElhone, Rupert Graves, Michael Kitchen, Lena Headey and Alan Cox.
VHS: S35020. $97.99.
Marleen Gorris, Great Britain, 1997, 97 mins.

Murder on The Orient Express
A classic whodunit on a very stylish mode of transportation. Richard Widmark is the type of guy everyone would like to kill and it is up to Albert Finney, as Hercule Poirot, to figure out who did it and why. One of the best Agatha Christie adaptations. Suspects include Lauren Bacall, Sean Connery, Jacqueline Bisset, Anthony Perkins, Vanessa Redgrave, Wendy Hiller, Michael York and Ingrid Bergman—who won an Oscar for her speech about "the little brown babies".
VHS: S10832. $29.95.
Sidney Lumet, Great Britain, 1974, 128 mins.

Naked Civil Servant
John Hurt delivers a compelling performance in the role of Quentin Crisp, based on Crisp's autobiography as a witty homosexual growing up in England of the 30's and 40's through years of intolerance, ostracism and violence. Hurt's tour-de-force performance brings to life Crisp's unique and often sharp wit at once critical of the society as well as of himself.
VHS: S00914. $19.99.
Jack Gold, Great Britain, 1980, 80 mins.

The Neon Bible
Based on an early novel by John Kennedy Toole, the posthumous Pulitzer Prize-winning author of *A Confederacy of Dunces*, *The Neon Bible* is the bittersweet story of David, a sensitive but conflicted young man (Jacob Tierney) growing up in the American South of the 1940s, who turns to his flamboyant Aunt Mae (Gena Rowlands, *A Woman Under the Influence*) for salvation from his troubled home life with his brutal father (Denis Leary, *The Ref*) and emotionally fragile mother (Diana Scarwid, *Silkwood*). From the acclaimed director of *The Long Day Closes*.
VHS: S30048. $19.95.
Terence Davies, Great Britain/USA, 1996, 92 mins.

Nicholas and Alexandra
Expensive epic about the final years of the Russian Tsar Nicholas II and Empress Alexandra and their children. Their lavish lifestyle comes to a halt with the rise of Lenin's power, leading to imprisonment and eventual execution. Lavish costume design and beautiful decor in this version based on the biography by Robert Massie. With Tom Baker as Rasputin and Michael Jayson as Nicholas II.
VHS: S03880. $29.95.
Laser: Widescreen. **LD75492. $39.95.**
Franklin J. Schaffner, Great Britain, 1971, 183 mins.

The Night and the Moment
An erotic look at a legendary playboy's countless seductions as he searches for his one true desire. With Willem Dafoe, Lena Olin and Miranda Richardson.
VHS: S33357. $103.99.
Anna Maria Tato, Great Britain/France/Italy, 1994, 90 mins.

Nil by Mouth
Gary Oldman's directorial debut is a powerfully raw and harrowing drama about a violent and alcoholic family living in South London. Stars Kathy Burke *(Absolutely Fabulous)* and Ray Winstone *(Quadrophenia)*. Original musical score by Eric Clapton. "The most intense film of the year" *(New York Times)*.
VHS: S34584. $98.99.
Gary Oldman, Great Britain, 1997, 128 mins.

Nothing Personal
It's Ireland 1975. A civil war explodes when an I.R.A. bomb destroys a crowded pub and divides the city of Belfast in fear. On one side is Kenny (James Frain, *Shadowlands*), the popular leader of a gang of Loyalists assassins. Before he can control the city, Kenny must control his men, especially Ginger (Ian Hart, *Michael Collins*), a hot-headed hit man who kills on contact. Caught in the middle is Liam (John Lynch, *Moll Flanders*), a single father determined to raise his two children in a safer world. When Kenny's crew kidnap Liam and beat him as a suspected I.R.A. member, Kenny must come to grips with the meaning of loyalty and the wisdom of war.
VHS: S32024. $99.99.
Thaddeus O'Sullivan, Great Britain, 1996, 85 mins.

O Lucky Man!
Developed from an original treatment by Malcolm McDowell, based on his experiences as a coffee salesman before he became an actor. The subject of the eternal, sometimes very funny, sometimes surreal, circle of human experience—aspiration, energy, wickedness, humor and folly. With Ralph Richardson, Rachel Roberts, Malcolm McDowell.
VHS: S00945. $24.98.
Lindsay Anderson, Great Britain, 1972, 165 mins.

The Object of Beauty
Jake and Tina (played by John Malkovich and Andie MacDowell) are a sexy, jet-setting couple, madly in love and living far beyond their means in a posh London hotel. Confronting a lifestyle-or-death situation, the two plot to collect an insurance payoff after staging the phony theft of Tina's prize sculpture. Unfortunately, Jake and Tina aren't the only crooks in London.
VHS: S14995. $19.98.
Michael Lindsay-Hogg, Great Britain, 1991, 105 mins.

Odessa File
Jon Voight plays an extremely dedicated German journalist out to uncover the whereabouts of ex-Nazis living in comfort 20 years after the war. Based on the bestseller by Frederick Forsyth. With Maximillian Schell, Maria Schell, Mary Tamm, Derek Jacobi and Klaus Lowitsch. As usual with Forsyth, prepare for the surprise ending.
VHS: S10381. $19.95.
Ronald Neame, Great Britain, 1974, 128 mins.

The Old Curiosity Shop
Sir Peter Ustinov, Tom Courtenay and James Fox head a superb cast in this film adaptation of a Charles Dickens classic. Young Nell Trent and her grandfather must escape the evil landlord, Quilp. Together they encounter a colorful range of characters that could only be found in 19th-century England.
VHS: S25903. $19.98.
Laser: LD75059. $49.95.
Kevin Connor, Great Britain, 1995, 190 mins.

The Old Man and the Sea

Anthony Quinn stars in this screen adaptation of the Ernest Hemingway classic novel. It is an epic battle of man against nature as waged by a simple but noble fisherman and the young boy who believes in him.

VHS: S24849. $19.98.
Jud Taylor, Great Britain, 1990, 97 mins.

One Russian Summer

John McEnery, as Vadim, holds a grudge against sadistic landowner Oliver Reed. Czarist Russia is on the brink of revolution but the war going on at the Palizyn estate is strictly personal. With Claudia Cardinale and some fancy camerawork. Based on the Lermontov novel.

VHS: S04623. $59.95.
Antonio Calenda, Great Britain/Italy, 1973, 112 mins.

Orlando

Virginia Woolf's ground-breaking novel about a transsexual from the time of Renaissance England has been transformed into a beautiful film. Tilda Swinton stars with Billy Zane as her romantic American lover while Quentin Crisp reigns as Queen Elizabeth the First.

VHS: S20829. $19.95.
Laser: LD74471. $34.95.
Sally Potter, Great Britain, 1993, 93 mins.

Othello

Laurence Olivier is the noble Moor with an unstoppable passion inflamed by jealousy. Frank Finlay is the cunning Iago, the man responsible for the horrible fate suffered by virtuous Desdemona, Maggie Smith. This legendary National Theater of Great Britain production garnered four Academy Award nominations.

VHS: S27838. $19.98.
Stuart Burge, Great Britain, 1965, 167 mins.

Out of Season

Cliff Robertson and Vanessa Redgrave star in this moody drama about a stranger who returns after twenty years to an English seaside resort and meets a former lover, who now has a daughter almost as old as the number of years he has stayed away. Susan George provides the friction.

VHS: S04667. $19.95.
Alan Bridges, Great Britain, 1975, 90 mins.

The Pale Horse

Jean Marsh stars in this chilling tale adapted from Agatha Christie's bestseller. When a priest called to attend to a dying woman is murdered on the way home, the only clue is a scrap of paper with eight seemingly unrelated names on it. Accused of the crime by an uncomprising police inspector, the young writer Mark Easterbrook and his girlfriend Kate set out to unravel the connection among the names and prove Mark's innocence.

VHS: S33192. $19.95.
Charles Beeson, Great Britain, 1997, 100 mins.

Pascali's Island

Ben Kingsley presents another riveting character in this dramatic tale of a Turkish spy on a pre-World War I Greek island. Written and directed by the author of *Fatal Attraction*, this beautifully photographed period piece was shot on location. With Charles Dance and Helen Mirren. A literate and satisfying entertainment. Based on the novel by Barry Unsworth.

VHS: S08934. $19.95.
James Dearden, Great Britain, 1988, 106 mins.

Picture of Dorian Gray

Shane Briant stars in this compelling version of Oscar Wilde's famous story of the young English aristocrat who sinks into the hedonism of London and finds his portrait aging.

VHS: S22986. $29.98.
Glenn Jordan, Great Britain, 1974, 130 mins.

The Playboys

In this small gem set in an isolated Irish village in the '50s, Robin Wright stars as Tara Maquire, a beautiful, free spirited young woman who steadfastly refuses to name the father of her young child. She's drawn to an itinerant, charming actor (Aidan Quinn), a member of a traveling theater company called The Playboys. Their romance incurs the jealous rage of a drunken police sergeant (Albert Finney) who's obsessed with Tara.
With Milo O'Shea.

VHS: S17027. $19.95.
Laser: LD71554. $29.98.
Gilles MacKinnon, Great Britain, 1992, 113 mins.

Plenty

Meryl Streep stars in this David Hare screenplay filmed by Fred Schepisi. Streep is intelligent and sexy in her role as a World War II resistance fighter returning to postwar Britain.

VHS: S01039. $14.95.
Fred Schepisi, Great Britain, 1985, 119 mins.

Priest

Controversial and powerful, this film concerns a young priest overcome by a daunting problem. He must reconcile the contradiction between the tenets of his faith and the desires of his own body. The film is made all the more riveting by its refusal of simple answers. Though spurred by events beyond his control, this priest must ultimately confront the intractable hypocrisy that shrouds homosexuality in the Catholic Church.

VHS: S26884. $19.99.
Laser: LD75445. $39.99.
Antonia Bird, Great Britain, 1995, 98 mins.

Prince Valiant

Valiant, a courageous young squire, is sent to escort the beautiful and headstrong Princess Ilene to her home. When their caravan is ambushed by bloodthirsty Vikings and an evil, power-hungry sorceress, Valiant learns their captors plan to take control of the kingdom, plunging it into a reign of terror. With Stephen Moyer, Katherine Heigl, Edward Fox, Ron Perlman, Warwick Davis, and Joanna Lumley.

VHS: S34572. $69.95.
Anthony Hickox, Germany/Great Britain/Ireland, 1997, 100 mins.

Rasputin: Dark Servant of Destiny

In this critically acclaimed HBO original movie, Alan Rickman *(Sense and Sensibility, Die Hard)* stars as Rasputin, the man/madman who turns the head of Russia's royal family and the world against him. Also stars Ian McKellen *(Richard III)* as the Tsar and Greta Scacchi *(Presumed Innocent, ThePlayer)* as the Tsarina who falls under Rasputin's spell.

VHS: S28497. $19.98.
Uli Edel, Great Britain, 1996, 104 mins.

Rebecca

Daphne du Maurier's classic tale of romance, suspense and jealousy, set in Monte Carlo and Cornwall in the 1930s, stars Charles Dance as the sophisticated Maxim de Winter and Emilia Fox as the young woman who becomes the second Mrs. de Winter and is haunted by the shadow of the first Mrs. de Winter, Rebecca. With Diana Rigg as the sinister, gothic housekeeper, Mrs. Danvers, and Faye Dunaway as Mrs. Van Hopper.

VHS: S31198. $29.98.
Jim O'Brien, Great Britain, 1996, 176 mins.

The Return of the Native

Joan Plowright and Catherine Zeta Jones are featured in this first-rate adaptation of Thomas Hardy's romantic classic. A young woman is torn between her love for two men and the vagaries of fate.

VHS: S24392. $14.98.
Jack Gold, Great Britain, 1994, 99 mins.

Richard III

Sir Ian McKellen leads an all-star cast including Annette Bening, Robert Downey, Jr., Nigel Hawthorne, Maggie Smith and more, in this updated film adaptation of the Shakespeare play. Visually stunning, it was nominated for Academy Awards for art direction and costume design. This film places the story in a fictional but loosely veiled representation of England in the 1930s, where pomp and fascism seem eerily well matched.

VHS: S27707. $19.98.
Laser: LD75566. $34.98.
Richard Loncraine, Great Britain, 1995, 104 mins.

Robin and Marian

Richard Lester continues the high-spirited Robin Hood adventure as Robin regroups the members of his Sherwood Forest band when King John assumes the throne. Sean Connery is Robin Hood, Audrey Hepburn is Marian.

VHS: S03694. $19.95.
Laser: LD75904. $34.95.
Richard Lester, Great Britain, 1976, 112 mins.

Sailor Who Fell from Grace with the Sea

Hauntingly erotic film based on a novel by Yukio Mishima, starring Kris Kristofferson as an American seaman whose love affair with Sarah Miles is disturbed by Miles' troubled young son.

VHS: S03449. $14.98.
Lewis John Carlino, Great Britain, 1976, 105 mins.

Saint-Ex

Bruno Ganz and Miranda Richardson star in this amazing film profiling the legendary French author/aviator Antoine de Saint-Exupery *(The Little Prince)*. Filled with mystery and metaphor, this freely inspired tale will haunt viewers with its beauty.

VHS: S32439. $89.95.
Anand Tucker, Great Britain, 1996, 90 mins.

The Sculptress

Olive Martin (Pauline Quike), a convicted murderess serving a life prison sentence, earned her nickname, "The Sculptress," because of the gruesome way she killed and dismembered her mother and sister. Writer Rosalind Lee (Caroline Goodall) is asked to write a book about the story, but is hesitant until she meets Olive. Now, the more she learns about the case, the more she is beginning to believe that Olive is hiding something. Did Olive really kill her loved ones or is she trying to protect someone else? Based on the award-winning novel by Minette Walters. Two-tape set.

VHS: S32961. $29.98.
Stuart Orme, Great Britain, 1996, 180 mins.

The Sea Wolves

British intelligence officers Col. Lewis Pugh (Gregory Peck) and Capt. Gavin Steward (Roger Moore) lead a top-secret British military mission to destroy Nazi radio ships in a neutral harbor during WWII. Based on a true story. With David Niven.

VHS: S33908. $14.95.
Andrew V. McLaglen, Great Britain, 1980, 120 mins.

The Secret Agent

Bob Hoskins, Patricia Arquette and Gerard Depardieu star in this first-rate adaptation of Joseph Conrad's chilling novel of political intrigue. Hoskins plays the quiet English shopkeeper who is actually a spy for the Russian embassy, and who faces an unexpected test of allegiance when he's ordered to plant a bomb that will wreak havoc on the British public. "High intensity... dense, faithful and absorbing" *(Los Angeles Times)*.

VHS: S31029. $99.99.
Laser: LD76143. $39.98.
Christopher Hampton, Great Britain, 1996, 95 mins.

Secret Places

Set in an English girls' boarding school during WW II, this is a sensitive film about growing up—four girls, their first loves, first sex, first discussions, first cigarettes, discussions of life, philosophy, and patriotism—and their "secret places."

VHS: S01173. $79.98.
Zelda Barron, Great Britain, 1985, 98 mins.

Sense and Sensibility

Emma Thompson and Hugh Grant are terrific as the central couple in this Oscar-winning adaptation of the Jane Austen classic. Two sisters fall in love, and their engaging romances play out in completely opposite ways. The settings and costumes are perfect without being overpowering. This film may well be the best adaptation of an Austen novel ever made. VHS letterboxed.

VHS: S27828. $19.95.
Laser: LD75582. $39.99.
Ang Lee, Great Britain, 1995, 136 mins.

Shades of Fear

Vanessa Redgrave, John Hurt and Jonathan Pryce star in this tale of an ocean voyage, a dark secret and a deadly betrayal. The journey begins when a young woman finds romance in the arms of a dashing stranger (Pryce) who could be a dangerous criminal with a passion for murder. An intricate web of lies is revealed on the last night at sea, erupting into a chilling confrontation.

VHS: S32603. $103.99.
Laser: LD76397. $39.99.
Beeban Kidron, Great Britain, 1997, 93 mins.

Shadey

A comedy-fantasy-thriller about a man who can read the minds of others and is able to transfer these images to film. He wants to use this gift to finance a sex change operation for himself. With Anthony Sher, Patrick Macnee and Katharine Helmond.

VHS: S04768. $79.98.
Philip Saville, Great Britain, 1985, 106 mins.

Shadowlands

This adaptation of an episode from C.S. Lewis' life stars Anthony Hopkins as the writer, who becomes infatuated with an American woman, Debra Winger. When this author and notorious loner discovers a hitherto unknown quality within himself, the capacity for love, it alters him forever.

VHS: S21137. $19.98.
Richard Attenborough, Great Britain, 1993, 133 mins.

Shallow Grave

Evil yuppie roommates get the chance to have it all because of a peculiar incident. Three flatmates seek a fourth, and when the new fellow dies they decide to keep his death a secret for their own greedy ends. Naturally their innate distrust of each other begins to surface, resulting in bizarre and at times sick actions. It's dark and by turns wickedly funny.

VHS: S29550. $19.95.
Danny Boyle, Great Britain, 1994, 91 mins.

Shirley Valentine

Pauline Collins repeats her award-winning stage role as a dissatisfied British housewife who finds some contentment from an impromptu vacation to Greece. With Tom Conti, Bernard Hill, Joanna Lumley and Julia McKenzie.

VHS: S11736. $14.95.
Laser: LD75256. $34.98.
Lewis Gilbert, Great Britain, 1989, 108 mins.

Shopping

Sadie Frost *(Bram Stoker's Dracula* and Jude Law (TV's *Families*) star as British juvenile delinquents who spend their time "shopping"—driving stolen cars through store windows and looting. Directed by Paul Anderson *(Mortal Kombat)*, this festival favorite features MTV machine gun-style editing, a loud soundtrack and hip cameo appearances by Marianne Faithfull, Jonathan Pryce and Sean Bean.

VHS: S28518. $92.99.
Laser: LD75982. $39.99.
Paul Anderson III, Great Britain, 1993, 87 mins.

Singleton's Pluck
A funny, inventive, bright film—Ian Holm is the single-minded farmer who, frustrated by a British trucking shortage, decides to walk his geese to England. What's funny is that the film is done entirely as a Western, and is full of scathing satire.
VHS: S01208. $19.95.
Richard Eyre, Great Britain, 1984, 89 mins.

Sister My Sister
Two sisters, Julie Walters and Jodhi May, are maids in a small provincial French town in the 1930's. They develop an incestuous passion that grows until it ends in the cold-blooded murder of their mistress and her daughter. The shocking true story is based on real events which inspired Jean Genet's *The Maids*.
VHS: S26287. $19.95.
Laser: LD75414. $39.99.
Nancy Meckler, Great Britain, 1995, 89 mins.

Small Faces
Before there was *Trainspotting*, there was *Small Faces*. This gritty and raw film is set in Glasgow in 1968, where respect and fear go hand in hand as the city's working-class Mod youth find escalating gang violence their only escape valve. Constantly looking over his shoulder, 13-year-old Lex MacLean spends each day in torment, not knowing whether or not he'll make it home without being harassed, beaten or shot. Torn between his two older brothers' lifestyles, young Lex faces life as a gang member or life running away from gangs. His tumultuous exploration is explosive, dramatic and brutally honest, as he discovers that manhood comes with a heavy price. "Surges with adrenaline" (Jay Carr, *Boston Globe*).
VHS: S30949. $99.99.
Laser: LD76161. $39.98.
Gilles MacKinnon, Great Britain, 1995, 109 mins.

Some Mother's Son
A mother (Helen Mirren, *Prime Suspect*) who's tried to stay clear of the conflict in Northern Ireland shifts from isolation to commitment when her son is jailed. With Fionnula Flanagan and Aidan Gillen. Co-written by Jim Sheridan *(My Left Foot, In the Name of the Father)*. "Terrific, riveting, passionate, unforgettable" (Jan Wahl, KRON-TV/San Francisco).
VHS: S32023. $19.98.
Terry George, Great Britain, 1997, 111 mins.

The Spy with the Cold Nose
A British espionage comedy that uses an English bulldog, that has been selected as a good-will gift for the Soviet prime minister, as a method of obtaining secret information. Lionel Jeffries is the British agent with the plan that will work with the cooperation of veterinarian Laurence Harvey. With Daliah Lavi, Denholm Elliott and Paul Ford.
VHS: S06192. $59.95.
Daniel Petrie, Great Britain, 1966, 93 mins.

Stormy Monday
The grimy industrial town of Newcastle has a chance for civic improvement if they play ball with American gangster/businessman Tommy Lee Jones. Only jazz club owner Sting and his new handy man Sean Bean don't much care for the Yank's methods. A raw and romantic thriller also starring Melanie Griffith as the very interesting romantic interest.
VHS: S07912. $14.95.
Mike Figgis, Great Britain, 1988, 93 mins.

Strapless
Blair Brown stars as a workaholic doctor whose sister, Bridget Fonda, forces her to reexamine her life. The sister has not only shown the doctor the importance of romance, but also displays to the doctor a new outlook that courts both spontaneity and danger. Featuring Bruno Ganz *(Wings of Desire)*.
VHS: S26286. $19.95.
David Hare, Great Britain, 1990, 99 mins.

Sunday Bloody Sunday
Nominated for four Academy Awards, *Sunday Bloody Sunday* stars Glenda Jackson, Peter Finch and Murray Head in an unusual love triangle on the rocks. Head plays the enigmatic bisexual involved with both a man and a woman.
VHS: S01283. $19.95.
Laser: LD71182. $49.95.
John Schlesinger, Great Britain, 1971, 110 mins.

Swept from the Sea
Vincent Perez *(The Crow: City of Angels)* and Rachel Weisz *(Stealing Beauty)* are star-crossed lovers in this haunting tale of love and loss. With Kathy Bates and Ian McKellen.
VHS: S34548. $104.99.
DVD: DV60258. $29.95.
Beeban Kidron, Great Britain, 1997, 115 mins.

The Tango Lesson
Sally Potter *(Orlando)* plays Sally, a middle-aged director who falls in love with Pablo (played by the great tango dancer Pablo Veron). Sally tells Pablo that if he gives her tango lessons, she will put him in a movie. Is this film blatant narcissism, an act of wild hubris, or mere self-indulgence, as critics have asserted? You decide—and be prepared to be entertained by truly virtuoso dance sequences and a beautifully seductive soundtrack along the way.
VHS: S34241. $98.99.
Sally Potter, Great Britain/France/Argentina, 1997, 101 mins.

The Tenant of Wildfell Hall
The story by Anne Bronte that shocked the Victorian world in 1848. Tara Fitzgerald *(Brassed Off)*, Rupert Graves and Toby Stephens star in this story of sensuality and indulgence, of a marriage gone bad and a woman's right to be free and independent, set in a romantic world of wind-swept moors and mysterious manors.
VHS: S32523. $29.98.
Mike Barker, Great Britain, 1997, 160 mins.

Terence Davies Trilogy
These magical films by Terence Davies, director of *The Long Day Closes* and *The Neon Bible*, are set against the background of industrial Liverpool and follow the main character, Robert Tucker, from his Catholic childhood to being bullied at school, dealing with a violent and sick father at home and struggling with his view of his own sexuality. The three films include *Children, Madonna & Child* and *Death & Transfiguration*.
VHS: S31107. $39.99.
Terence Davies, Great Britain, 1996, 101 mins.

Thicker Than Water
Theresa Russell and Jonathan Pryce star in this story of murder and psychological terror. A pregnant woman is killed in a car accident. As the husband tries to rebuild his life, he is hampered by the efforts of his deceased wife's identical twin. She is desperate to get her way, using every means at her disposal, including suicide and murder.
VHS: S22870. $19.95.
Marc Evans, Great Britain, 1993, 150 mins.

Tom & Viv
Willem Dafoe plays T.S. Eliot with Miranda Richardson as his first wife. Despite his brilliance as a poet, Eliot could not find personal happiness in his marriage because of an unspeakable secret that ultimately divided these two lovers. This riveting, true story is superbly acted. Richardson was nominated for an Oscar (Best Actress), along with Rosemary Harris (Best Supporting Actress).
VHS: S26035. $19.95.
Laser: LD75064. $39.99.
Brian Gilbert, USA, 1994, 115 mins.

Trainspotting
One of the most talked-about films of the year, *Trainspotting* is the wickedly witty story of the frustrations, aspirations and antics of a group of working class Scottish youths: unlikely hero Mark Renton (Ewan McGregor) and his so-called friends, unlucky but amiable "Spud," short-fused, knife-wielding "Begbie" and narcissistic, Sean Connery-idolizing "Sick Boy." As the foursome plans a risky scam, Renton ultimately must decide to follow his reckless pals or "choose life" and sell out his friends in the process. "Electrifying and hilarious" *(Rolling Stone)*.
VHS: S30637. $19.95.
Laser: Widescreen. **LD76092. $49.98.**
Danny Boyle, Great Britain, 1996, 94 mins.

The Trial
Kyle MacLachlan stars as K, the man who unexpectedly finds himself on trial for unnamed crimes. Though confused and unnerved, he resolves to fight an arbitrary and incompetent legal system, resulting in even more troubles, until his life seems hopelessly and irrevocably destroyed. Adapted from Kafka's original book, with Anthony Hopkins and Jason Robards. Screenplay by Harold Pinter.
VHS: S21116. $19.98.
David Jones, Great Britain, 1993, 120 mins.

Trojan Eddie
Eddie (Stephen Rea) is a hustling ex-con lackey to a larcenous, brutal mobster (Richard Harris) who rules a group of gypsy travelers. Unlucky in love and life, Eddie comes alive only when he's selling his boss' contraband. Fate throws Eddie a curve when the aging kingpin takes a child bride, with Eddie acting as the hapless go-between. Not surprisingly, the wife-to-be has a few ideas of her own which set off a chain of betrayal, infidelity and murder. With Sean McGinley and Brendan Gleeson.
VHS: S34516. $69.95.
Gillies MacKinnon, Great Britain/Ireland, 1996, 105 mins.

Truly, Madly, Deeply
A young woman is consumed by grief because of the death of her young lover (Alan Rickman). Just as her despair and anger seem overwhelming, the dead young man shows up on her doorstep. This unique film combines a love story with a decidedly supernatural angle.
VHS: S25516. $19.99.
Anthony Minghella, Great Britain, 1991, 107 mins.

Turtle Diary
An overlooked film when released, *Turtle Diary* is a romantic comedy starring Glenda Jackson as a children's novelist who seeks inspiration from the beauty and grace of the sea turtle, and Ben Kingsley, who shares her interest in the turtles.
VHS: S01378. $14.98.
John Irvin, Great Britain, 1985, 96 mins.

The Twelfth Night
Ben Kingsley, Helena Bonham Carter, Nigel Hawthorne and Richard E. Grant brings William Shakespeare's best-loved comedy to life. The outlandish, gender-bending tale of troublesome twins who win the hearts of an entire kingdom is as relevant and funny today as it was when it was first performed almost 400 years ago.
VHS: S31352. $19.98.
Laser: LD76283. $49.95.
Trevor Nunn, Great Britain, 1996, 133 mins.

Twin Town
Produced by Danny Boyle and Andrew MacDonald, this "*Trainspotting* with a twist," set in Swansea, Wales, is the story of two clans involved in an ugly feud after the father of one family falls off a ladder while working on contractor, developer and drug dealer Bryn Cartwright's roof. The injured party's grandsons try to reach an out-of-court settlement with Cartwright but he won't pay up, leading to an undeclared war between the families. Pathos, comedy, cursing and gore galore.
VHS: S32616. $19.95.
Kevin Allen, Great Britain, 1997, 101 mins.

Unnatural Pursuits
Alan Bates stars as a hilarious, booze-ridden, chain-smoking British playwright in this BBC production. In an all-out effort for success he tours the country with his latest work, experiencing the ignoble process of Americanization at the hands of an L.A. producer (Bob Balaban) and a New York impressario (John Mahoney).
VHS: S22871. $19.95.
Christopher Morahan, Great Britain, 1991, 143 mins.

Utz
George Sluizer's adaptation of Bruce Chatwin's novel about the eccentric passions of Baron Kaspar Joachim von Utz (Armin Mueller-Stahl), who collects decorative Meissen porcelain figures. Set in post-communist Prague, the story follows Marius Fischer (Peter Riegert), a New York-based art dealer, who visits the Baron and discovers that both the porcelain and Utz's housekeeper (Brenda Fricker) have vanished. Fischer and Dr. Vaclav Orlik (Paul Scofield) investigate the disappearance. With Miriam Karlin, Christian Rabe and Jakub Zdenek.
VHS: S19559. $29.95.
George Sluizer, Great Britain/Germany/Italy, 1992, 95 mins.

The Vacillations of Poppy Carew
While planning her father's funeral, Poppy Carew (Tara Fitzerald, *Sirens*) becomes involved with four men. Based on the best-selling novel by English author Mary Wesley, this film is a rollicking good time as we watch Poppy navigate her way through affairs of the heart. Also stars Sian Phillips *(Age of Innocence)* and Charlotte Coleman *(Four Weddings and a Funeral)*.
VHS: S30005. $14.98.
James Cellan Jones, 1995, Great Britain, 108 mins.

The Wedding Gift
Jim Broadbent and Julie Walters star as Deric and Diana in this dramatic film about a married couple who overcome tragedy through their devotion to one another. As Diana's health fails she orchestrates a gift of love, a new female companion for her soon-to-be-single husband.
VHS: S22878. $19.95.
Richard Loncraine, Great Britain, 1993, 87 mins.

The Whales of August
Bette Davis and Lilian Gish play aging sisters spending their twilight years in an island cottage on the New England coast. They comb hair, pick berries and chat with visitors Vincent Price, Ann Sothern and Harry Carey Jr. Gish is the sweet sister, Davis the sour and sightless sibling.
Laser: LD72316. $29.99.
Lindsay Anderson, USA, 1987, 91 mins.

Where Angels Fear to Tread
Helena Bonham Carter, Judy Davis and Rupert Graves are featured in this lavish adaptation of E.M. Forster's first novel. A British widow falls in love with a young Tuscan man while on vacation in Italy. Unleashed passion leads to heartache for all concerned.
VHS: S21221. $19.95.
Charles Sturridge, Great Britain, 1991, 112 mins.

Wild Little Bunch
Based on a true story, this moving film is based on a London slum where a mother struggles to raise 11 children. Beset by pains, she fears her end is near and makes her eldest boy (Jack Wild) promise to take care of his younger brothers. He keeps his promise in the face of many obstacles, and the young boys struggle in an uncaring society.
VHS: S10932. $49.95.
David Hemmings, Great Britain, 1972, 90 mins.

Wings of Fame
A surreal parody on the nature of celebrity. Otakar Votocek's film constructs a strange parallel universe where the afterlife is a hellish sanatorium in which the famous walking dead cavort. Peter O'Toole stars as a pretentious actor who confronts the anonymous, diabolical fan (Colin Firth) who killed him in his bid for recognition and fame.
VHS: S19938. $89.95.
Otakar Votocek, Great Britain/Czechoslovakia, 1990, 109 mins.

The Wings of the Dove
In this story based on the novel by Henry James, Helena Bonham Carter stars as Kate Croy, an impoverished British woman who is trapped by and dependent upon her wealthy Aunt Maude (Charlotte Rampling), who wants to marry Kate off to Lord Mark (Alex Jennings), even though Kate loves journalist Merton Densher (Linus Roache). When Kate befriends Millie Theale (Alison Elliott), a rich, but gravely ill young American woman who falls in love with Merton, Kate hatches a plan to be together with Merton while breaking free of her aunt and poverty.
VHS: S34402. $103.99.
Laser: LD76950. $39.99.
Iain Softley, Great Britain/USA, 1997, 102 mins.

The Winter Guest
Emma Thompson and her real-life mother, Phyllida Law, star in this absorbing drama about a grieving widow who unwittingly finds support from her very independent mother.
VHS: S34536. $100.99.
Laser: LD76973. $39.99.
Alan Rickman, Great Britain, 1998, 110 mins.

A Woman's Guide to Adultery
Rose disapproves of adulterous affairs, and with good reason. Her friends are all entangled in such liaisons, and predictably, the women suffer most. All this foresight fails Rose when she meets a handsome University lecturer. Now she too is trapped by passion that will inevitably lead to great pain for one of the unlucky parties concerned. With Sean Bean, Theresa Russell, Amanda Donohoe and Adrian Dunbar.
VHS: S26774. $24.98.
David Hayman, Great Britain, 1995, 145 mins.

Wonderland
A first-rate British thriller about two gay teens in Liverpool who witness a gangland murder and are forced to flee for their lives. Gritty Liverpool settings and a nuanced script by Frank Clarke *(Letter to Brezhnev)* distinguish this British gem.
VHS: S23343. $79.95.
Philip Saville, Great Britain, 1988, 103 mins.

The Young Poisoner's Handbook
Graham is a good student in a London suburb who becomes intrigued by the possibilities of his chemistry set and the mysteries of toxicology. He begins to experiment, but is soon sent off to a mental hospital for murder. After his release, it doesn't take him long to jumpstart the career that was so brutally cut off eight years ago. This film is especially violent and horrific, though it is a solid and suspenseful work.
VHS: S28405. $89.95.
Laser: LD76392. $39.99.
Benjamin Ross, Great Britain, 1996, 93 mins.

Young Winston
Director Richard Attenborough chronicles the tumultuous rise of one of this century's greatest public figures, and one of its most complex, private men: Winston Churchill, as played by Simon Ward. Also featuring Anne Bancroft and Robert Shaw, *Young Winston* presents a memorable testament to the man and his career.
VHS: S12998. $19.95.
Richard Attenborough, Great Britain, 1972, 157 mins.

Zeppelin
Germany's most dreaded World War I aerial weapon takes to the skies. The mission—bomb England! Interesting special effects highlight this entertaining story of a German-born British aviator emotionally torn by duty and homeland during the war. Starring Michael York and Elke Sommer.
VHS: S13622. $19.98.
Etienne Perier, Great Britain, 1971, 101 mins.

PETER GREENAWAY

26 Bathrooms
The British structuralist Peter Greenaway *(Prospero's Books)* is best known for his pattern-obsessive, symmetrical, intellectual, playful and visually flamboyant features on the nature of the body and art. This short is a brief, comic essay on his larger themes, in short a work about bathrooms and the activities and people inhabiting them.
VHS: S18203. $19.95.
Peter Greenaway, Great Britain, 1993, 30 mins.

The Cook, The Thief, His Wife and Her Lover
Few contemporary filmmakers rival director Peter Greenaway's visual complexity and elaboration. In this style he creates a graphic and layered fable that casts a cynical eye on man's most primal urges: food, lust and violence. A brutal satire on capitalism set predominantly in an exclusive restaurant called "Le Hollandais".
VHS: S13017. $19.95.
Laser: LD75309. $39.98.
Peter Greenaway, Great Britain, 1990, 123 mins.

Death in the Seine
Peter Greenaway's fascinating essay on death and revolution is set in a period between April 1795 and September 1801, when over 300 bodies were pulled from the River Seine in Paris. Two mortuary attendants dutifully noted the condition of each body in great detail, including their clothing, possessions and wounds. This bounty of information is the basis for Greenaway's structuralist speculation on the lives of these corpses and their relationship to the French Revolution.
VHS: S27254. $29.95.
Peter Greenaway, Great Britain, 1994, 44 mins.

Drowning by Numbers
Three generations of women with the same name have rid themselves of their unwanted husbands in the same manner—they drown them. The local coroner, Madgett, agrees to declare the deaths accidental in return for sexual favors. But when things don't go exactly as planned, he devises a final game that could result in the undoing of them all. Another romp through the gutter with writer/director Peter Greenaway *(The Thief, The Cook, His Wife & Her Lover)*, characterized by the same sterile beauty that can be found in nearly all of his work.
VHS: S15584. $19.98.
Peter Greenaway, Great Britain, 1991, 121 mins.

The Pillow Book
Peter Greenaway's bold, stylistic experiment has, as its theme, the "correspondence" between the daughter of a famous writer and a publisher, written on the bodies of their lovers. With a bravura use of video technology, this erotic, visually beautiful film is a powerful treatise on signs, silence, communication and desire. With Ewan McGregor, Vivian Yu, Ken Ogata, Yoshi Oida, Hideko Yoshida and Judy Ongg. Japanese and Mandarin with English subtitles.
VHS: S33013. $104.95.
Peter Greenaway, France/Great Britain/Netherlands, 1996, 126 mins.

Prospero's Books
Peter Greenaway's pattern-obsessed reworking of Shakespeare's *The Tempest* furthers his thematic obsession with numbers and order. Sir John Gielgud is Prospero, the former Duke of Milan who's banished on a magical, isolated island, where he plots his revenge against the men who dethroned him, engages in magic and spectacle, and seeks solace in his collection of extravagantly illustrated books. With Michael Clark, Isabelle Pasco, Erland Josephson and Michael Gambon.
VHS: S17065. $19.95.
Peter Greenaway, Great Britain, 1991, 126 mins.

MIKE LEIGH

Abigail's Party
Mike Leigh's brilliant satire about middle-class English consumerism and appearances, with Alison Steadman's frightening performance as a frantic woman trying to orchestrate an important dinner party, which is interrupted by her husband's untimely heart attack. In this situation, the "unbearable and hopeless fuse to create an explosion of incredible hilarity."
VHS: S17604. $29.95.
Mike Leigh, Great Britain, 1977, 105 mins.

Bleak Moments
This breakthrough film from Leigh is the shrewdly observed and brilliantly understated portrait of London's offbeat residents and the fleeting but significant moments which define their lives. Sylvia (Anne Raitt), a clever but bored secretary, desperately seeks to escape from the bleak moments of her life, first in an awkward flirtation with a sexually repressed schoolteacher (Eric Allan), and then with the eccentric, guitar-playing hippie tenant living in her garage (Mike Bradwell).
VHS: S31636. $59.95.
Mike Leigh, Great Britain, 1971, 110 mins.

Career Girls
Mike Leigh's *(Secrets and Lies)* intelligent, poignant comedy about the reunion of two very different 30-ish women who were battling college roomates in London six years ago. Over the course of their brief reunion, Hannah and Annie (Katrin Cartlidge, *Naked* and *Breaking the Waves*, and Lynda Steadman, in stand-out performances) reveal the present while they talk about the past, in jittery flashbacks that match their emotions. As we watch these two progress from black leather to discreet beige, we also watch the growth that has carried them beyond the shared, angry turmoil of their college years.
VHS: S32797. $99.99.
Laser: LD76422. $39.98.
Mike Leigh, Great Britain, 1997, 87 mins.

Four Days in July
Mike Leigh's humanism is the hallmark of this BBC television film about the opposite fortunes of two couples in Northern Ireland, one Catholic and one Protestant, both of whom are expecting children. With Brid Brennan, Desmond McAleer, Charles Lawson and Paula Hamilton.
VHS: S17602. $29.95.
Mike Leigh, Great Britain, 1984, 99 mins.

Grown Ups
Mike Leigh's working class comedy about a recently wed couple who must deal with the wife's idiosyncratic sister and their next door neighbor, who was a high school instructor. With Philip Davis, Leslie Manville, Sam Kelly, Lindsay Duncan and Brenda Blethyn.
VHS: S19404. $29.95.
Mike Leigh, Great Britain, 1980, 95 mins.

Hard Labor
This emotionally horrific and yet oddly amusing film is a scathing indictment of classicism and sexism. The grinding daily abuse suffered by a poor elderly woman at the hands of her husband, her children and even her employer illustrate the nature of oppression. Ben Kingsley appears as a hairy but friendly cab driver.
VHS: S21507. $29.95.
Mike Leigh, Great Britain, 1973, 70 mins.

Home Sweet Home
This, the story of three not terribly jolly postmen, centers on Stan, a would-be ladies' man whose wife has left him. Insightful comedy results when Stan compensates for his loneliness by seducing his co-workers' wives. In this unusual film, England emerges as a land of bitter, isolated individuals unconsoled by marriage and pigeonholed by the state.
VHS: S21509. $29.95.
Mike Leigh, Great Britain, 1982, 90 mins.

Kiss of Death
Trevor is a quiet undertaker's assistant. His attempts at romance give shape to a plot characterized by whimsy and a puckish sense of humor. The courtship attempts of this strange misfit must rank among cinema's most funny and awkward expressions of tortured love.
VHS: S21508. $29.95.
Mike Leigh, Great Britain, 1977, 80 mins.

Life Is Sweet
Satirist Mike Leigh is at it again in the London south side with this decidedly bittersweet comedy about the members of a dysfunctional family and their oddball friends. It seems everyone in this film is striving for change. The family tries to balance their differences with alcoholic friends and their short fuses proves a challenge, but they don't forget to laugh a lot along the way.
VHS: S16628. $14.98.
Laser: LD71503. $29.98.
Mike Leigh, Great Britain, 1992, 103 mins.

Meantime
An early work by Mike Leigh, this wry and amusing working-class comedy is the story of Frank and his two unemployed, deadbeat sons, Mark and Colin (Phil Daniels and Tim Roth), who live in a cramped apartment in London's East End. Wanting to escape the doldrums of his mediocre world, Colin starts hanging out with Coxy (Gary Oldman), a reckless skinhead. The new friendship sparks fear in Colin's family, whose overzealous attempts to direct Colin on a straight path prove futile.
VHS: S32361. $79.98.
Mike Leigh, Great Britain, 1983, 103 mins.

Naked
This film won in both the Best Film and Best Actor category at the Cannes Film Festival. David Thewlis stars in this funny, erotic and bizarre odyssey, set in the streets of London, that explores the seamy side of desire and longing of post-Thatcherite England.
VHS: S21119. $19.95.
Laser: Includes director's commentary, still photo gallery, trailers and short films. **LD74468. $69.95.**
Mike Leigh, Great Britain, 1993, 131 mins.

Nuts in May

British filmmaker Mike Leigh has a wonderful sense of rhythms and improvisational textures, and this film recounts the weird adventures of a fierce young couple trying to abide to their strict vegetarian diet, with dangerous repercussions. "Hilarious and appalling" (Vincent Canby). With Roger Sloman, Alison Steadman and Anthony O'Donnell.

VHS: S17603. $29.95.

Mike Leigh, Great Britain, 1976, 84 mins.

Secrets and Lies

Mike Leigh's heartwarming comedy of a young black woman (Marianne Jean-Baptiste) searching for her natural birth mother only to discover that her mom (the magnificent Brenda Blethyn) is white, makes for a film with "rare heart and soul" (Janet Maslin, The New York Times), from Britain's master of improvisational, working-class social comedies. With Timothy Spall. Winner of the Palm d'Or at Cannes Film Festival.

VHS: S31027. $103.99.
Laser: LD76141. $49.95.

Mike Leigh, Great Britain, 1996, 114 mins.

Who's Who

Set in a brokerage firm, the movie charts the greed and avarice of some ambitious young traders, each trying to step on top of the other. "In each of [Leigh's] films there comes a transforming moment when the unbearable and the hopeless fuse to create an explosion of recognition of high, incredible hilarity" (Vincent Canby). With Bridget Kane, Simon Chandler, Adam Norton, Philip Davis and Joolia Cappleman.

VHS: S19402. $29.95.

Mike Leigh, Great Britain, 1978, 75 mins.

KEN LOACH

Family Life

Ken Loach's stirring indictment of the generation gap, the mental health care system and society at large. Janice Baildon is a girl with an identity crisis. When she becomes pregnant, her parents force her to get an abortion, then take her to a psychiatric hospital where she undergoes nightmarish and brutal electroshock therapy and is left as little more than a shell of a human. "A haunting film...tender, touching and true" *(The New York Daily News)*.

VHS: S33352. $79.98.

Ken Loach, Great Britain, 1972, 108 mins.

Hidden Agenda

Based loosely on the notorious Stalker case of 1982, involving a British officer who discovered a massive government cover-up, *Hidden Agenda* begins when Kerrigan, the Stalker-like protagonist, travels to Belfast to investigate the killing of an American lawyer who is also an IRA sympathizer. He discovers the murder was committed by the Royal Ulster Constabulary and exposes the cover-up. With Frances McDormand, Brad Dourif and Brian Cox.

VHS: S14295. $19.98.

Ken Loach, Great Britain, 1990, 108 mins.

Ladybird Ladybird

A simply wonderful film from the talented Ken Loach. A small-time singer finds her tough, mostly uneventful life ripped apart by tragedy. A fire destroys her home and severely hurts one of her kids. This incident and a series of problems lead her to lose her children as an unfit mother. Loach's riveting drama is a powerful look at the machinery of the welfare state.

VHS: S26269. $19.98.

Ken Loach, Great Britain, 1994, 102 mins.

Land and Freedom

Ken Loach's moving love story set against the complex political background of the early days of the Spanish Civil War is brilliant, engaged cinema. A young lad from Liverpool, smitten by the idealism of the Republican cause, fights for land and freedom along with his multi-national comrades and a beautiful, fiery woman (Rosana Pastor) with whom he eventually falls in love. An epic film of war, hope and dissillusionment—uncompromising and powerful.

VHS: S28396. $14.95.
Laser: LD76082. $39.99.

Ken Loach, Great Britain, 1996, 109 mins.

Raining Stones

Ken Loach's funny social comedy is set in the British town of Middleton where Bob Williams, survivor, first has his van stolen and then learns the outfit for his daughter Coleen's first communion is going to cost 100 pounds. Among Loach's most accessible films, *Raining Stones* is a bitingly funny comedy that shows the downside to contemporary Britain even as it cleverly reveals the simple humor and tenacity that inspires the average bloke.

VHS: S24861. $19.98.

Ken Loach, Great Britain, 1994, 90 mins.

Riff Raff

Ken Loach directed this first-rate look at the British class system from the bottom up. Stevie is a construction worker whose luck can only improve. His colorful co-workers help keep him from any serious hard labor while Stevie's humor attracts many friends, including an aspiring singer who melts his heart. This down-to-earth comedy shows that being Riff Raff is not so bad.

VHS: S26338. $19.98.

Ken Loach, Great Britain, 1993, 96 mins.

STEPHEN FREARS

Dangerous Liaisons

Nominated for seven Academy Awards, the hottest love affair of 1782 is notable for its sense of style and decor, and strong performances from Glenn Close, John Malkovich and Michele Pfeiffer. A couple of nasty members of 18th century nobility enjoy manipulating the lives and loves of those around them through all kinds of mean-spiritedness. There are three versions of this story available, including Valmont and Liaisons Dangereuses.

VHS: S09449. $19.98.
Laser: LD70550. $29.98.

Stephen Frears, Great Britain, 1989, 120 mins.

The Grifters

Jim Thompson's novel of love, money and betrayal stars John Cusack as a master of the short con. He must gamble on trusting his dishonest mother or putting his faith in a greedy girlfriend who plays for bigger stakes. Anjelica Huston and Annette Bening were nominated for Oscars for their work, as was director Stephen Frears and scriptwriter Donald E. Westlake. Filmed in the seedier sections of Los Angeles. Don't rent this film for Mother's Day.

VHS: S13830. $19.98.
DVD: DV60317. $24.95.

Stephen Frears, USA, 1990, 114 mins.

Gumshoe

This satire of American film noir detective films from director Frears is filled with adventure, intrigue and laughs. Albert Finney plays a regular schmoe in a London nightclub who decides to become a detective like his movie idols.

VHS: S00535. $69.95.

Stephen Frears, Great Britain, 1971, 85 mins.

Hero

An entertaining movie with equal doses of Preston Sturges and Frank Capra. The story concerns an itinerant, small-time thief (Dustin Hoffman) who saves a group of passengers after a plane crashlands and watches an imposter (Andy Garcia) receive the credit. Geena Davis plays a sharp, ambitious television journalist trying to sort out the confusion.

VHS: S18249. $19.95.

Stephen Frears, USA, 1992, 116 mins.

Mary Reilly

Julia Roberts and John Malkovich star in this adaptation of the Dr. Jekyll and Mr. Hyde story. Roberts portrays Mary Reilly, the gentle doctor's maid, who witnesses all the horrors and contradictions of his work, and as a result, experiences all the terror firsthand.

VHS: S29823. $19.95.
Laser: LD75901. $34.95.

Stephen Frears, Great Britain, 1996, 108 mins.

My Beautiful Laundrette

The breakthrough film for director Stephen Frears and novelist/filmmaker Hanif Kureishi, about the relationship between a Pakistani innocent (Saeed Jaffrey) and the leader (Daniel Day-Lewis) of a neo-Nazi movement in East London. The first-rate cast includes Roshan Seth, Derrick Branche and Shirley Anne Field.

VHS: Out of print. For rental only.
Laser: CLV, widescreen. **LD75107. $39.95.**

Stephen Frears, Great Britain, 1986, 97 mins.

Saigon: Year of the Cat

Stephen Frears directed this tale of diplomatic failure and political blindness; playwright David Hare wrote the script. Set in Saigon, Frederic Forrest stars as a man who cannot convince his superiors of the imminent invasion of the Vietcong. As the Vietcong reach Saigon, Forrest and his girlfriend are forced to find their way out before their world goes up in flames.

VHS: S11006. $19.98.

Stephen Frears, Great Britain, 1989, 106 mins.

Sammy and Rosie Get Laid

A subversive comedy set in London revolving around the lives of immigrants, radicals and punks. From the director of *My Beautiful Laundrette*, with Claire Bloom.

VHS: S07290. $14.98.

Stephen Frears, Great Britain, 1987, 97 mins.

The Snapper

Stephen Frears' small-town comedy stars Tina Kellegher as the oldest daughter of a close-knit family, who, when she gets pregnant, refuses to name the father and insists on having the baby. The secret she carries throws the town into turmoil.

VHS: S21886. $96.99.
Laser: LD74531. $39.99.

Stephen Frears, Ireland, 1993, 90 mins.

The Van

The final chapter in the acclaimed Barrytown trilogy. In this comedy of errors, two partners in a mobile fast-food van business—Colm Meaney *(The Snapper, The Commitments)* and Donal O'Kelly *(Hard Shoulder)*—discover that their longtime friendship is challenged by their eccentric families, hair-raising encounters with rowdy customers and a few culinary disasters.

VHS: S32238. $99.99.
Laser: LD76348. $39.98.

Stephen Frears, Ireland, 1997, 96 mins.

NICOLAS ROEG

Castaway

Nicolas Roeg directed this sexy, stimulating, often brilliant story of a middle-aged Londoner who advertises for a "wife" to spend a year with him in a remote paradise. But life with the beautiful blonde (Amanda Donohoe) in the idyllic south seas turns out to be a bare-it-all battle of the sexes. With Oliver Reed.

VHS: S05925. $19.98.

Nicolas Roeg, USA, 1987, 118 mins.

Don't Look Now

Julie Christie and Donald Sutherland star in this beautiful, spellbinding mystery that'll have you on the edge of your seat. When their child drowns in a sudden rainstorm, Sutherland decides to go to Venice for an architectural job and Christie follows. While in Italy, Christie becomes convinced that a mysterious figure in a red raincoat is their beloved child returned from the dead. As the true character of the figure in the red raincoat is revealed, the film creates an atmosphere of terror, fear and ultimate tragedy in a knockout ending. Based on the novel by Daphne du Maurier.

VHS: S00358. $49.95.

Nicolas Roeg, Great Britain, 1974, 110 mins.

Eureka

Another visually stunning film from the director of *Walkabout* and *Don't Look Now*. Gene Hackman stars as a man who has made his fortune in the Canadian wilderness and has retired to a Caribbean island. With Theresa Russell and Mickey Rourke.

VHS: S00418. $14.95.

Nicolas Roeg, Great Britain, 1983, 130 mins.

Full Body Massage

Mimi Rogers and Bryan Brown star in this haunting and erotic tale. She is an art gallery owner who thrives on the finer things in life. One especially indulgent treat she grants herself is a weekly massage with a masseuse named Douglas. When Douglas can't make it one week, Fitch steps in, and suddenly once a week doesn't seem often enough.

VHS: S27428. $89.95.

Nicolas Roeg, USA, 1995, 93 mins.

Heart of Darkness

Based on Joseph Conrad's novel, this film casts John Malkovich in the lead as a character who ends up exploring the edges of his own moral universe in the jungles of Africa. Filmed on location in Belize, with co-stars Tim Roth and James Fox.

VHS: S20776. $92.98.
Laser: LD74489. $39.99.

Nicolas Roeg, USA, 1993, 105 mins.

The Man Who Fell to Earth

Nicolas Roeg's stylish classic stars David Bowie as a cosmic visitor to the planet, overwhelmed by capitalist society, human technology and earthly love. This video has now been re-issued with the twenty minutes cut from the original theatrical version fully restored. One of the most mysterious and visually intriguing science fiction films ever made.

VHS: S00815. $69.95.
Laser: LD76803. $99.95.

Nicolas Roeg, Great Britain, 1976, 140 mins.

Performance

Mick Jagger is Turner, a burnt-out rock star, in Roeg's mind-boggling study of consciousness and identity where nothing is true and everything is permitted. Edward Cox co-stars as Chas, a gangster on the run who takes shelter in Turner's home. *Performance* was years ahead of its time, and today remains an audacious and stunning achievement.

VHS: S01009. $19.98.
Laser: LD70652. $29.98.
Nicolas Roeg, Great Britain, 1968, 110 mins.

Sweet Bird of Youth

British stylist Nicolas Roeg *(The Man Who Fell to Earth)* directed this made-for-television adaptation of Tennessee Williams' play about the obsessive relationship between a fading moving star (Elizabeth Taylor) and her ambitious, handsome lover (Mark Harmon). With Rip Torn, Valerie Perrine, Ruta Lee, Kevin Geer and Michael Wilding.

VHS: S20184. $89.95.
Nicolas Roeg, USA, 1989, 95 mins.

Track 29

Theresa Russell stars in another film directed by her much older husband Nicolas Roeg. She plays a bored alcoholic wife of a much older man who is mainly interested in his train set and being spanked by his nurse. She is also visited by a young man who may be the son she gave away before marriage. With Gary Oldman, Christopher Lloyd, Collen Camp, and Sandra Bernhard as the spanking nurse. A bizarre, emotionally charged piece of work.

VHS: S09805. $14.98.
Nicolas Roeg, USA, 1988, 90 mins.

Two Deaths

Nicolas Roeg's lively tale of power, passion and obsession is set in a politically torn Eastern European country. Dr. Daniel Pavenic (Michael Gambon, *The Cook, The Thief, His Wife and Her Lover*) hosts a lavish banquet for three school chums. When he introduces a mysterious servant (Sonia Braga) to his guests, his revelation of how he ruined the life of this beautiful and strong woman becomes a confessional for Pavenic and his guests which changes their lives.

VHS: S30046. $19.98.
Nicolas Roeg, Great Britain, 1995, 102 mins.

Walkabout

Nicolas Roeg's solo directorial debut, based on the novel by James Vance Marshall, is the story of two British children lost in the Australian desert and rescued by an Aborigine boy. It is also a mystical, lyrical story of three children enjoying life in a free, uncomplicated, unspoiled, primitive world. With Jenny Agutter, Lucien John, David Gumpilil and John Meillon. "A movie that celebrates life—full of lovely things" (Vincent Canby, *The New York Times*).

VHS: S28614. $29.95.
Laser: Letterboxed. **LD76326. $49.95.**
DVD: DV60352. $29.99.
Nicolas Roeg, Australia, 1970, 100 mins.

Witches

When young Luke (Jasen Fisher of Parenthood) discovers who Miss Ernst (Academy Award winner Anjelica Huston of Prizzi's Honor) and her cackling cohorts really are, the adventure of a thousand lifetimes begins. Nicolas Roeg directed this modern fairy tale from a screenplay based on the book by Roald Dahl. It is also one of the last works from the late great Jim Henson (Sesame Street, The Muppet Movie), who served as executive producer.

VHS: S13440. $19.98.
Laser: LD70708. $24.98.
Nicolas Roeg, USA, 1990, 92 mins.

KEN RUSSELL

Altered States

William Hurt in a dazzling debut as a research scientist on an incredible journey into the inner space of the mind. With Blair Brown and spectacular special effects by Bran Ferren.

VHS: S00038. $14.95.
Laser: LD70501. $29.98.
Ken Russell, Great Britain, 1980, 103 mins.

Boyfriend

Ken Russell adapts the play by Sandy Wilson into an extravagant tribute to Hollywood musicals of the 1930's. Supermodel Twiggy stars as an assistant stage manager who gets her big break when leading lady Glenda Jackson hurts her ankle. With Christopher Gable, Max Adrian, Murray Melvin and Tommy Tune. The show must go on.

VHS: S12232. $19.95.
Laser: LD70532. $39.98.
Ken Russell, Great Britain, 1971, 108 mins.

Crimes of Passion

"You can be as violent as you want in this country, but you talk about sex and everyone reaches for their chastity belts. This picture is about sex and frankness" (Ken Russell). With Kathleen Turner and Anthony Perkins, music by Rick Wakeman.

VHS: S00283. $19.95.
Laser: CLV, widescreen, with original theatrical trailer. **LD70930. $49.95.**
DVD: DV60225. $24.99.
Ken Russell, Great Britain, 1984, 107 mins.

Dante's Inferno

A neglected film by Kenneth Russell, *Dante's Inferno* stars Oliver Reed, Judith Paris, and Gala Mitchell. Reed plays the morose and brilliant Dante Gabriel Rosetti. Sensual, prankish, and often drunk, Dante was a gifted poet and painter more concerned with his flamboyant life style than with his literary and artistic output. He drew into his pre-Raphaelite circle some of the most eminent figures of his time; William Morris and his wife Jane, the poet Swinburne, his poetess sister Christina Rosetti, and their critic and champion, John Rustin.

VHS: S11150. $39.95.
Ken Russell, Great Britain, 1968, 90 mins.

The Devils

Oliver Reed is Father Grandier, accused of sorcery by the half-mad nuns of the fortified city of Loudun; Vanessa Redgrave is Sister Jeanne of the Angels, whose own sexual obsession triggers the ferocious events that follow. Based on Aldous Huxley's book.

VHS: S00334. $19.98.
Ken Russell, Great Britain, 1971, 105 mins.

Gothic

Ken Russell recreates a bizarre night at a chateau in Switzerland where Lord Byron, Mary Shelley, Percy Bysshe Shelley and a few friends told scary stories that would later affect their lives. Cast includes Gabriel Byrne, Natasha Richardson and Julian Sands.

VHS: S04624. $14.98.
Ken Russell, Great Britain, 1987, 90 mins.

Isadora

One of Kenneth Russell's achievements has been the popularization of the term "biopic" and indeed, much of Russell's career as the *enfant terrible* of the British cinema has dealt with films of famous people—Elgar, Liszt, Tchaikovsky, Mahler, among others. This early bio-pic by Russell is an interesting attempt to depict the personality of Isadora Duncan; the film stars Vivien Pickles and Alexei Jawdokimow.

VHS: S07504. $39.95.
Ken Russell, Great Britain, 1966, 67 mins.

The Lair of the White Worm

Ken Russell unearths a tale written by Bram Stoker *(Dracula)* about an ancient pagan snake cult flourishing in the modern English countryside, and adds his own touches of excess and depravity and fun. Can the dashing lord save the beautiful virgin from the unholy clutches of a fiendish but fashionably dressed cult priestess? With Hugh Grant, Catherine Oxenberg, Peter Capaldi and Amanda Donohoe as Lady Sylvia. A forked-tongue-in-cheek horror spoof.

VHS: S09140. $14.98.
Ken Russell, Great Britain, 1988, 90 mins.

Lisztomania

The classical composer as rock superstar, this wild spectacle blends musical genres and cuts across historical generations. Starring Roger Daltry as Franz Liszt, with a guest appearance by Ringo Starr as the Pope. Lots of FUN!

VHS: S00759. $19.98.
Laser: Letterboxed. **LD71674. $34.98.**
Ken Russell, Great Britain, 1975, 105 mins.

Mahler

A dazzling evocation of the moods, loves and music of one of the foremost composers—Gustav Mahler. By means of flashbacks and dream imagery, the film focuses on the turbulent relationship Mahler had with his beautiful wife. Starring Robert Powell and Georgina Hale, with Mahler's symphonies played by the Concertgebouw Orchestra of Amsterdam.

VHS: S00807. $19.95.
Ken Russell, Great Britain, 1976, 110 mins.

The Music Lovers

Ken Russell's account of the life of Peter Tchaikovsky, a homosexual who sought "salvation" by marrying a persistent admirer who turned out to be a nymphomaniac, shocked many-including the Russian government, which put out its own cleaned-up "official" movie about the man who wrote the *1812 Overture*. Russell's film, however, is a sharp and satirical attack on society's hypocrisy and homophobia. Starring Richard Chamberlain and Glenda Jackson.

VHS: S14809. $19.99.
Ken Russell, Great Britain, 1971, 122 mins.

Prisoner of Honor

Richard Dreyfuss stars in this historical reexamination of the infamous "Dreyfus Affair" that kept France in an uproar for over ten years. With Oliver Reed, Jeremy Kemp, Brian Blessed and Peter Vaughn.

VHS: S15605. $89.99.
Ken Russell, USA, 1991, 88 mins.

Valentino

Ken Russell's flamboyant biography of Rudolph Valentino. His masterstroke was the casting of Russian ballet star Rudolf Nureyev in the title role. The screenplay by Russell and Mardik Martin was adapted from the book by Brad Steiger and Chaw Mank. With Leslie Caron, Michelle Phillips, Carol Kane, Felicity Kendal, Huntz Hall and Alfred Marks.

VHS: S20407. $19.98.
Ken Russell, Great Britain, 1977, 127 mins.

Whore

Theresa Russell has the title role in this film about a day in the life of a veteran street prostitute. This raw and raunchy drama seems to exist only to protest the fairy tale presentation of the world's oldest profession in *Pretty Woman*. With Antonio Fargas, Sanjay, Benjamin Monmouth and Elizabeth Morehead. Crude, lewd and in your face. The star and director are not related.

VHS: S15410. $19.98.
Ken Russell, USA, 1991, 85 minutes

Women in Love

Two sisters, sexually mature and intellectually active, struggle against the confines of a rural English mining town and its rigidly classed layers of society, in this adaptation of D.H. Lawrence's study of sexual uneasiness and doubt. With Alan Bates, Oliver Reed, Glenda Jackson, Jennie Linden.

VHS: S01479. $19.98.
Ken Russell, Great Britain, 1970, 129 mins.

DEREK JARMAN

The Angelic Conversation

Derek Jarman's apocalyptic visualization of 14 Shakespeare sonnets read by actress Judi Dench, capturing the director's characteristic themes: desire, longing, homoeroticism and mysticism. With Paul Reynolds and Phillip Williamson. Music by Coil. "A hypnotically beautiful film" *(Time Out)*.

VHS: S12677. $29.95.
Derek Jarman, Great Britain, 1985, 80 mins.

Blue

Faced by a worsening prognosis, Jarman confronts impending blindness and his own death in this moving and highly unusual work. Conceived as an homage to Yves Klein, its only visual component is a blue screen. The lush narration and beautifully composed sound environment, featuring Fisher Turner's score, chart an emotional landscape transformed by the brutally short life span afforded Jarman because of AIDS.

VHS: S26598. $24.95.
Derek Jarman, Great Britain, 1993, 76 mins.

Caravaggio

Derek Jarman's elegant and extraordinary film on the life of Caravaggio. "Set in a milieu of gamblers and prostitutes, the film evokes the fantasies of rough trade to which the artist supposedly subscribes and then transcends. Jarman's Carravaggio (Nigel Terry) is a cheeky Cockney—but he's ultimately less a character than a vehicle for a series of extraordinary tableaux that reconstruct the original paintings using the dramatic chiaroscuro that Caravaggio pioneered" (J. Hoberman, *The Village Voice*). With Sean Bean, Garry Cooper and Tilda Swinton.

VHS: S06024. $79.95.
Derek Jarman, Great Britain, 1986, 93 mins.

Edward II

Derek Jarman's adaptation of Christopher Marlowe's 16th century play about Edward II (Steven Waddington), who neglected his beautiful, ambitious wife (Tilda Swinton) to carry out an obsessive, homoerotic relationship with his military lieutenant (Andrew Tiernan). Annie Lennox sings "Every Time We Say Goodbye".

VHS: S17626. $19.95.
Laser: LD76784. $49.95.
Derek Jarman, Great Britain, 1991, 91 mins.

The Garden

Derek Jarman's haunting memoir of his anguish and struggle with AIDS. An examination of his own mortality and the repression of homosexuality, *The Garden* shifts from the coastal Kent landscapes to the urban decay of contemporary London. The film was shot alternately in Super-8, 16- and 35mm. With Kevin Colins, Roger Cook, Jody Graber and Tilda Swinton.

VHS: S18975. $19.98.
Derek Jarman, Great Britain, 1990, 90 mins.

Jubilee

An angel transports Queen Elizabeth I from the year 1578 to a post-punk, post-Thatcher wasteland where civilization has come to a halt, where bands of teenage girl punks and fascistic police roam the streets; Buckingham Palace is a recording studio, the center of an entertainment empire controlled by media czar Borgia Ginz, who owns everything. The anti-heroes of the film are led by Elizabeth's mirror image, Bod, the murderous leader of a mad household that includes the historian Amyl Nitrate, the pyromaniac Mad, the sex-obsessed actress Crabs, loving brothers Sphinx and Angel, the artist Viv and their French *au pair*, Chaos. With Jenny Runacre, Jordan, Little Nell, Toyah Wilcox, music by Brian Eno, Adam and the Ants, Sixousix and the Banshees, Wayne County. "One of the most original, bold and exciting features to have come out of Britain" *(Variety)*.

VHS: S12676. $29.95.
Derek Jarman, Great Britain, 1978, 105 mins.

Last of England

"Wrenchingly beautiful…the film is one of the few commanding works of personal cinema in the late 80's—a call to open our eyes to a world violated by greed and repression, to see what irrevocable damage has been wrought on city, countryside and soul, how our skies, our bodies, have turned poisonous," wrote *The Village Voice* of Derek Jarman's beautiful film. Synthesizing rock 'n roll, Super-8, gay erotica, old home movies, anti-totalitarian paranoia, Jarman "superimposes an incandescent Belfast over contemporary London …The doomsday rubble landscape…[is] rendered with the imagistic panache of Kenneth Anger and pulverized a la Brakhage. *The Last of England* is sinister and gorgeous" (J. Hoberman).

VHS: S09555. $29.95.

Derek Jarman, Great Britain, 1987, 87 mins.

Sebastiane

Sebastiane caused riots at the 1977 Locarno Film Festival and became a runaway hit in London. It has "a pretention and perversity about it that are surprisingly appealing in the long run" (Rob Baker, *Soho Weekly News*).The film tells the highly charged homoerotic story of St. Sebastian. Sebastian spends most of the film tied to the stake, haunted by sexual advances of his commander Severus, and tortured when he refuses him. Newly remastered. Latin with English subtitles.

VHS: S25523. $39.95.

Derek Jarman, Great Britain, 1976, 86 mins.

War Requiem

Derek Jarman's cinematic visualization of Benjamin Britten's celebrated oratorio uses live action and documentary footage from the whole range of 20th century wars.Told as the rueful remembrance of an old soldier, the film is a both faithful and exhilarating visual manifestation of Britten's work."Complex, beautiful, harrowing and utterly demanding" *(Los Angeles Times)*.

VHS: S13410. $29.95.

Derek Jarman, Great Britain, 1988, 92 mins.

Wittgenstein

Born into the same stressful Central European world which generated Freud, Schoenberg and Hitler, *Wittgenstein* emerged from Vienna to transform contemporary philosophy. His eccentricity only sharpened his critique of the absurdities of language and other aspects of Western culture.This experimental biographical film shows the stresses which afflicted this closeted homosexual man as he propounded a new philosophical tradition.

VHS: S26599. $79.95.

Derek Jarman, Great Britain, 1993, 75 mins.

TERRY GILLIAM

12 Monkeys

Bruce Willis, Brad Pitt and Madeline Stowe are at the center of this elaborate sci-fi drama where mankind faces near extinction. Inspired by Chris Marker's classic *La Jetee*, it follows the travails of a man sent back through time. His mission is to find an answer that may somehow stave off the certain destruction of most of humanity. Unfortunately, he lands in a mental hospital. VHS letterboxed.

VHS: S28391. $19.98.
Laser: LD75702. $49.95.
DVD: DV60217. $34.98.

Terry Gilliam, USA, 1995, 130 mins.

The Adventures of Baron Munchhausen

Terry Gilliam revives the tall tales of the 17th century German adventurer. John Neville has the title role and little Sarah Polley is his brave assistant as he travels to the Moon and back to save a besieged city. With Eric Idle, Oliver Reed, Uma Thurman, Jonathan Pryce and Robin Williams as the King of the Moon.

VHS: S10978. $19.95.
Laser: CAV. Director's cut. **LD71558. $134.95.**

Terry Gilliam, Great Britain/Germany, 1989, 126 mins.

Brazil

Terry Gilliam's acclaimed, surrealistic, nightmare vision of a "perfect" future where technology reigns supreme. Spectacular set design, this wildly visual treat stars Jonathan Pryce (as the "Everyman"), with a supporting cast of Robert De Niro and Michael Palin. A chilling black comedy, where *1984* meets *A Clockwork Orange*, with a script by Tom Stoppard.

VHS: S00177. $19.95.
Laser: LD70018. $124.95.
DVD: DV60219. $24.98.

Terry Gilliam, Great Britain/USA, 1986, 131 mins.

The Fisher King

Terry Gilliam blends romantic comedy with urban angst in this ambitious epic that includes a firebreathing medieval knight running amok in Manhattan. Jeff Bridges stars as a top radio shock jock who loses his job and his self-respect when a faithful listener shotguns a popular yuppie dining spot. Enter Robin Williams as a charming but mentally unstrung, homeless ex-professor of medieval history who sincerely believes the Holy Grail is in New York and needs to be rescued. With Mercedes Ruehl and Amanda Plummer.

VHS: S15711. $19.95.
Laser: LD71180. $99.95.

Terry Gilliam, USA, 1991, 137 mins.

Monty Python and the Holy Grail

The legend of King Arthur as interpreted by Monty Python in this irreverent, insanely funny film. Graham Chapman as Arthur convenes the knights to seek the Holy Grail, but things go awry amid medieval pageantry, religious sentiment, transvestism and a man-eating rabbit.

VHS: S00878. $19.95.
Laser: CLV. **LD74617. $34.95.**

Terry Gilliam, Great Britain, 1974, 95 mins.

Time Bandits

John Cleese, Sean Connery, Shelley Duvall and Michael Palin are among the stars who keep popping up in the strangest of places throughout human history. It seems there are mysterious connections and the Time Bandits are able to jump around. The result is a wild, extravagant adventure that, though quite dark in places, delights everyone.

VHS: S01344. $14.95.
Laser: LD76741. $49.95.

Terry Gilliam, Great Britain, 1981, 110 mins.

PETER WATKINS

Battle of Culloden

A great film by Peter Watkins, based on a re-staging of the 18th century battle in which Bonnie Prince Charlie was defeated. Realistic beyond imagination, despite its historical, epic quality, the film acts as one of the greatest pacifist films ever made.

VHS: S01429. $79.95.

Peter Watkins, Great Britain, 1965, 75 mins.

Edvard Munch

Considered by some the greatest film about an artist ever made, Peter Watkins' feature focuses on Munch's formative years, a life marked by the absence of intimacy. "A long, abortive affair with an older woman joins the ubiquitous ghosts of a childhood scarred by sickness and death. In the end, it's the paintings which do Munch's talking for him…. A remarkable film" (Giovanni Dadomo). With Geir Westby, Gro Fraas and Iselin von Hanno Bart. Norwegian with English subtitles.

VHS: S20594. $29.95.

Peter Watkins, Norway/Sweden, 1976, 167 mins.

The Journey

Years in the making, filmed in 14 countries, and with a running time of slightly over 14 hours, *The Journey*, from director Peter Watkins *(The War Game, Battle of Culloden)*, is the most powerful and definitive film to date on the nuclear arms race and the threat of nuclear war. At the heart of this epic, seven-part documentary are Watkins' extended conversations with family groups and cultures around the world: the gripping, personal recollections of survivors of the bombing of Hiroshima and Hamburg during World War II, and the dramatizations of evacuation scenarios by community groups in Norway, the USA, Scotland and Australia. With *The Journey* Watkins was determined to break down the wall we commonly place between ourselves and the suffering of others; the result is a truly remarkable and uncompromising film. It is composed of seven volumes, which may be purchased individually or as a set.

Volume 1. Includes parts 1, 2 and 3: Citizens in Scotland discuss military expansion in their neighborhood. A Hiroshima survivor begins her recollection of the aftermath of the bombing…. 141 mins.

VHS: S14296. $29.95.

Volume 2. Includes parts 4, 5 and 6: Families from around the world respond to photographic images of Hiroshima. A Norwegian community dramatization of evacuation begins…. 134 mins.

VHS: S14297. $29.95.

Volume 3. Includes parts 7, 8 and 9: Recollections of the bombing of Hamburg during World War II. A woman describes her evacuation of Leningrad during the war…. 128 mins.

VHS: S14298. $29.95.

Volume 4. Includes parts 10, 11 and 12: Women of a Mozambique farming collective discuss the war in their country and its effects on their ability to produce food. Watkins details the amount the U.S. government pays American colleges and universities for their part in nuclear weapons design and production…. 136 mins.

VHS: S14299. $29.95.

Volume 5. Includes parts 13 and 14: An Australian family discusses local media coverage of the nuclear industry in Australia and the protest against it. The New York State evacuation dramatization culminates…. 87 mins.

VHS: S14300. $29.95.

Volume 6. Includes parts 15 and 16: A Korean man describes Japanese treatment of Koreans during World War II. A family demonstrates the personal cost of the MX missile, in bags of groceries…. 104 mins.

VHS: S14301. $29.95.

Volume 7. Includes parts 17, 18 and 19: The Australian community group discusses their experiences, dramatizing life in a bomb shelter. The Norwegian group discusses their experiences as "evacuees." The hundreds of people involved in the production of *The Journey* are acknowledged in an ingenious, entertaining, 30-minute credit sequence. 138 mins.

VHS: S14302. $29.95.

Complete seven-volume set: 870 mins.

VHS: S16588. $179.85.

Peter Watkins, Sweden/Canada, 1987, 870 mins.

WORLD OF JAMES BOND

Bond 007 Gift Set Volume 1

Sean Connery is featured in all three classic spy thrillers featuring the agent with a license to kill. In *Dr. No* (1962), 007 must travel to Jamaica to confront a diabolical fiend and beautiful women in swimwear. Then Bond must fight to stay alive as he spirits away key Russian technology in *From Russia with Love* (1963). Finally, gold represents an evil worth fighting for in *Goldfinger*. This volume includes *Behind-the-Scenes with Goldfinger*.

VHS: S26408. $44.92.

Bond 007 Gift Set Volume 2

This volume combines three of the best Sean Connery James Bond films, including *Thunderball* (1965), where Bond tries to prevent a nuclear explosion in Miami, *You Only Live Twice* (1967), the story of a mysterious plot to provoke World War III, and *Diamonds Are Forever* (1971), which is about smuggling from South Africa. This volume also contains *Behind-the-Scenes with Thunderball*.

VHS: S26409. $44.92.

Diamonds Are Forever

This seventh episode of the James Bond series, from the director of *Goldfinger*, stars Sean Connery, Jill St. John and Lana Wood as Plenty O'Toole. The action goes from an L.A. crematorium to the glitter of Las Vegas casinos. VHS letterboxed.

VHS: S00337. $14.98.
Laser: LD70555. $39.98.

Guy Hamilton, USA, 1971, 119 mins.

Dr. No

The first of the phenomenally successful James Bond movies: Sean Connery foils the master criminal Dr. No in the West Indies; Ursula Andress stars. VHS letterboxed.

VHS: S00365. $14.98.
Laser: CLV, 1 disc, Criterion. **LD70359. $79.95.**
Laser: CLV, MGM. **LD72186. $34.98.**
DVD: DV60179. $24.98.

Terence Young, Great Britain, 1962, 111 mins.

For Your Eyes Only

The twelfth James Bond adventure, this one starring Roger Moore and an array of gorgeous women. Action-packed, stunt-filled entertainment! VHS letterboxed.

VHS: S00456. $19.98.
Laser: LD70573. $49.95.

John Glen, USA, 1981, 128 mins.

From Russia with Love

The second James Bond film is one of the best, with Lotte Lenya playing the sinister Russian spy, and Sean Connery as Agent 007.

VHS: S05015. $14.98.
Laser: LD70367. $79.95.
Laser: LD72264. $34.98.
DVD: DV60180. $24.98.

Terence Young, Great Britain, 1963, 118 mins.

Goldeneye

Pierce Brosnan is Ian Fleming's James Bond, Agent 007, and he must save the world from disaster yet again. This time the secret code to Goldeneye, a space weapon capable of mass destruction, is about to fall into the wrong hands. Bond must resist the lure of beautiful women, battle amidst outrageous gadgets, and exercise his own license to kill, or the world will be lost. Bono, The Edge and Tina Turner are responsible for the theme song. VHS letterboxed.

VHS: S27651. $19.98.
Laser: LD75558. $44.98.
DVD: DV60046. $24.98.

Martin Campbell, USA, 1995, 130 mins.

Goldfinger

The third of the James Bond films, with Sean Connery as the sophisticated Agent 007 pursuing the ruthless Auric Goldfinger. With Gert Frobe and Honor Blackman as Pussy Galore. Letterboxed.

VHS: S00513. $14.95.
Laser: CLV, MGM. **LD70584. $98.99.**
DVD: DV60181. $24.98.

Guy Hamilton, USA, 1964, 108 mins.

License to Kill

James Bond is in Florida for his friend Felix Leiter's marriage, and on the eve of the wedding he and Felix capture South America's most ruthless drug lord. But after a two-million dollar bribe, Sanchez is a free man, and murders the new Mrs. Leifer and feeds Felix to the sharks. The usually cool Bond is beside himself with rage. Letterboxed.

VHS: S11265. $19.98.
Laser: THX. LD76229. $49.98.

John Glen, USA, 1989, 135 mins.

Live and Let Die

James Bond pursues the head of a giant heroin operation from harlem to exotic locales in New Orleans and the Caribbean. Moore's first appearance as 007; song by Paul McCartney. Letterboxed.

VHS: S07310. $14.95.

Guy Hamilton, Great Britain, 1973, 121 mins.

The Living Daylights

Timothy Dalton's debut as James Bond announced a darker, more introspective agent haunted by failure and the violent necessities of his job. In this sweeping, action packed work, Bond travels through Britain, Eastern Europe, and Afghanistan to track a double dealing Russian general. With Maryan d'Abo as the love interest, Jeroen Krabbe, Joe Don Baker, John Rhys-Davies and Art Malik. VHS letterboxed.
VHS: S27706. $19.95.
Laser: LD70159. $39.98.
John Glen, Great Britain, 1987, 130 mins.

Man with the Golden Gun

Bond plays a deadly game of cat and mouse in the exotic far East, with Roger Moore, Maud Adams, Christopher Lee, Herve Villechaize. VHS letterboxed.
VHS: S07311. $19.95.
Laser: LD70623. $39.98.
Guy Hamilton, Great Britain, 1974, 125 mins.

Moonraker

The world's foremost Special Agent blasts into space as Roger Moore stars in the film that took Agent 007 beyond the stratosphere. Letterboxed.
VHS: S07312. $19.95.
DVD: DV60148. $24.98.
Lewis Gilbert, USA, 1979, 126 mins.

Never Say Never Again

Although this is essentially a remake of *Thunderball*, this is a fine film in its own right featuring Sean Connery as James Bond with an all-star cast including Klaus Maria Brandauer, Max von Sydow and Kim Basinger.
VHS: S04389. $14.95.
Laser: LD70638. $39.98.
Irvin Kershner, Great Britain, 1983, 134 mins.

Octopussy

Agent 009 has been killed over an art object stolen from Moscow, and 007 must investigate. His hunt leads him across Cuba, India and Germany, to the secluded palace of the queen of the octopus cult (Maud Adams).
VHS: S07313. $19.95.
Laser: LD70648. $49.98.
John Glen, USA, 1983, 130 mins.

On Her Majesty's Secret Service

Bond's romance, marriage and nonstop action make up the combination of this 6th Bond film starring George Lazenby as Bond, and Diana Rigg and Telly Savalas.
VHS: S07314. $14.95.
Laser: LD70649. $39.98.
Peter Hunt, USA, 1969, 144 mins.

The Sean Connery Collection

The elegant wit, style and grace of Sean Connery, moving from rugged action to romantic appeal, is revealed in this collection of the first three James Bond films, with Terence Young's *Dr. No* and *From Russia with Love* and Guy Hamilton's *Goldfinger*.
Laser: LD71170. $79.98.

The Spy Who Loved Me

007 does battle against the arch villain Stromberg and his plans for world destruction. Teaming with a seductive Russian agent, Bond slyly overcomes a persistent, 7-foot-plus, steel-dentured thug played by Richard Kiel to foil the sinister plans of his nemesis. With Roger Moore, Barbara Bach and Curt Jurgens.
VHS: S05659. $19.98.
DVD: DV60154. $24.98.
Lewis Gilbert, Great Britain/USA, 1977, 125 mins.

Thunderball

Sean Connery stars as 007, the secret agent with clever gadgets and a license to kill. He must thwart SPECTRE, a group which is threatening to destroy Miami by an atomic bomb unless a ransom of 100 million pounds is paid. Tom Jones sings the title song. Letterboxed.
VHS: S26364. $14.98.
Terence Young, USA, 1965, 125 mins.

Tomorrow Never Dies

Pierce Brosnan is 007 in this Bond adventure in which mad media mogul Elliot Carver (Jonathan Pryce) attempts to start World War III between Britain and China. M (Judi Dench, *Mrs. Brown*) orders Bond to use his relationship with Carver's wife (Teri Hatcher) as a way of infiltrating his organization, but Carver soon realizes Bond's game. With the help of Chinese Army intelligence agent and karate expert Wai Lin (Michelle Yeoh), Bond tries to stop Carver from directing a UK missile at Beijing.
VHS: S34401. $104.99.
Laser: DTS. **LD76954. $39.99.**
DVD: DV60255. $24.90.
Roger Spottiswode, USA/Great Britain, 1997, 217 mins.

You Only Live Twice

The talented novelist Roald Dahl adapted the Ian Fleming original in this expansive and colorful James Bond entry starring Sean Connery as the British spy working undercover in Japan. With Tetsuro Tamba, Akiko Wakabayashi, and Mie Hama.
VHS: S26363. $14.98.
Laser: LD70719. $39.98.
Lewis Gilbert, Great Britain, 1967, 118 mins.

BRITISH CULTURE

Ballad to Scotland

This musical journey follows the unmistakable strains of Scottish bagpipes through the glorious panorama of the misty isle. It includes "A Scottish Welcome", "Dance in the Heather" and more. 50 mins.
VHS: S23141. $19.95.

British Military Pageantry

The spectacle of the Royal Tournament and the ceremony of the Changing of the Guard are traditions which lie at the heart of the illustrious British military heritage. 60 mins.
VHS: S23121. $19.95.

The British Way of Life

Geography and historical achievements helped shape the nature of the British people. These elements are explored and interviews from people across Britain help to give context to the endurance of British ways. 23 mins.
VHS: S23707. $99.95.
Laser: LD74789. $149.95.

Castle Ghosts of England

The Discovery Channel brings the most terrifying stories featuring ghostly presences which are known to linger in some of England's most historically important castles. At Muncaster Castle a murderous court jester is responsible for the headless man who searches for his lover, while in Sudeley Castle King Henry VII's last wife still searches for her dead infant. Even the Tower of London has its share of spirit visitors. 50 mins.
VHS: S27822. $19.95.

Chalk-Stream Trout

Trout fishing in the rivers of England and Scotland, including sequences on the raising and stocking of trout, tips on fly fishing and choosing the right fly. 33 mins.
VHS: S15537. $35.00.

Charles & Diana: For Better or Worse

This special BBC program reviews the royal tours, responsibilites and strains that marked the marriage of Prince Charles and Princess Diana, from their first meeting through their first 10 years together. 60 mins.
VHS: S33688. $14.98.

The Charm of London

Tour London with Susannah York, and see all the famous and picturesque sights of this historic city. Visit Parliament, St. Paul's, Buckingham Palace, the Tower of London, Harrod's, Piccadilly Circus, and many other interesting spots. 26 mins.
VHS: S05787. $24.95.

Chatsworth

Home to the Duke and Duchess of Devonshire, this stately home also houses a staff of 150 and over 100 pensioners. 500,000 visitors tour its 35,000 acres every year. In this three-part video, the story behind this historic manor is revealed in amazing detail.
VHS: S27104. $69.95.

Churchill and the Cabinet War Rooms

Stand with Sir Winston Churchill at Britain's finest hour in the Cabinet War Rooms, an underground headquarters so highly classified that few knew of its existence until years later. Rare, never-before-seen archival footage from the Imperial War Museum and special reconstructions evoke the drama of World War II in this fascinating video from The History Channel.
VHS: S30150. $19.95.
Andrew Johnston, USA, 1991, 50 mins.

Commando's Tale

On April 2, 1982, Argentine forces invaded the Falkland Islands in the South Atlantic. Three days later, a British task force set in, putting into motion Britain's biggest military operation since World War II. This program looks at the conflict from the Royal Marines' point of view, using footage and interviews. 82 mins.
VHS: S13129. $29.98.

Dragonquest: Sacred Sites of Britain

From neolithic Stone circles and ruins of early Christian churches to contemporary pilgrimage centers, people have been drawn to erect monuments to their beliefs. This documentary explores the mysteries of these monuments, and includes visits to Stonehenge, Avebury, Glastonbury, Iona, Lindisfarne and other sacred centers. 42 mins.
VHS: S07730. $39.95.

Edinburgh Military Tattoo 1987

Music, color, splendor and pageantry are the hallmarks of the Edinburgh Military Tatoo, the world's best-loved military spectacle and the main attraction of Edinburgh, Scotland's annual festival. Set against the atmospheric backdrop of an illuminated Edinburgh Castle, this stirring program provides dazzling displays of military and bagpipe bands. BBC Enterprises. 73 mins.
VHS: S05230. $19.94.

Edward and Mrs. Simpson

This Emmy-Award-winning series is about the king who gave up his throne for the love of a woman, a fairytale all the more romantic because it's true. On two 135-minute cassettes. Total running time: 270 minutes.
VHS: S04540. $29.95.

England's Historic Treasures

This three-volume boxed set includes *Treasures of the Trust*, a private viewing of the rooms and gardens of eight jewels in the crown of England's National Trust; *A Celebration of Roses*, a tribute to the beauty and history of the Old Rose and *The Spirit of England*, a spectacular tour of famous historic sights showcasing the legacy of England's past, including Stonehenge and Dover Castle. Three 60-minute programs.
VHS: S31364. $59.95.

England, Land of Splendor

The august House of Lords on the Thames in the heart of London, the great cathedrals at Salisbury and Winchester, and great country houses like Blenheim Palace are shown on this video. The Henley Regatta and even views from the Magnificent Lake District are included. 86 mins.
VHS: S21518. $29.95.

An Englishman's Home

This ten-volume series tells the stories of ten historic English houses, and the influential families who built, re-built, preserved and left them as a record of their lives.

Arundel Castle. Home of the Dukes of Norfolk since 1556. The present Duke shows the castle's splendor and explains the family "aura of fatal glory."
VHS: S05551. $29.95.

Breakmore House. A great house filled with exotic treasures, acquired through propitious marriages and licensed privateering.
VHS: S05552. $29.95.

Broadlands. The magnificent house of Lord Mountbatten, where Prince Charles and Diana honeymooned.
VHS: S05558. $29.95.

Chartwell. Winston Churchill's house, filled with history; his daughter, Mary, is the guide.
VHS: S05557. $29.95.

Goodwood House. Still occupied by the descendants of Charles II, this stately home is associated with the famous racecourse.
VHS: S05559. $29.95.

Penshurst Palace. A house with many wings, built at different times with different styles, filled with history dating back to Henry VIII.
VHS: S05560. $29.95.

Stratfield Saye. Filled with mementos of Waterloo, this house was England's gift to the Duke of Wellington after the defeat of Napoleon.
VHS: S05553. $29.95.

Sutton Place. The Tudor mansion occupied by Paul Getty, filled with superb art from ancient Greece to Miro.
VHS: S05555. $29.95.

Uppark. A house of history and legend, a time-capsule of the 18th century, preserved upstairs and downstairs as it was.
VHS: S05554. $29.95.

Wilton. Henry VIII gave Wilton to the first Early of Pembroke; the present Earl shows the magnificent Inigo Jones apartments, paintings by Van Dyck and Rembrandt and other treasures.
VHS: S05556. $29.95.

An Englishman's Home, Set. The complete ten-volume set of *An Englishman's Home* at a package price.
VHS: S05561. $269.95.

Forever and a Day

A tribute to the people of England during World War II. Nearly 80 stars, and virtually every Hollywood actor with English roots of the time, are featured in this collection of comic bits and dramatic episodes. Featuring Charles Laughton, Buster Keaton, Ray Milland, Claude Rains, Elsa Lanchester, and Merle Oberon.

VHS: S34138. $19.95.

Rene Clair/Edmund Goulding/Cedric Hardwicke/Frank Lloyd/Victor Saville/Robert Stevenson/Herbert Wilcox USA, USA, 1943, 104 mins.

The Heritage of England

This overview of English culture and life examines the influence of English language, law and literature on the shaping of America, from its colonial origins to the present. 28 mins.

VHS: S20273. $29.95.

King Arthur

This *A & E Biography* video explores the life and legend of King Arthur, the ruler of Camelot, who fought to save England, inspired the Knights of the Round Table, but was ultimately undone by his devotion to Guinevere. 50 mins.

VHS: S28495. $19.95.

King Arthur and His Country—Southern England

Learn the story of King Arthur and explore his kingdom-Southern England—as it is today. 25 mins.

VHS: S06694. $29.95.

Legacy of a Princess

Offers a retrospective of the Princess of Wales' often troubled life from the time she became a Windsor until her untimely death, including footage of the royal wedding, the young princes, official appearances and excerpts from *Diary of a Princess*, a short film made on Diana's trip to land-mine-ravaged Angola. 60 mins.

VHS: S33687. $14.98.

Legends of the Isles

Spans the history, myths and legends of the British Isles from pre-Christian times to the dawn of America, spotlighting such figures as Robin Hood, King Arthur, Grace O'Malley, Maeve the Warrior Queen, Merlin the Wizard and leprechauns. Volumes include *Saint Patrick/Brendan the Navigator, The Holy Grail/Stonehenge, Merlin the Wizard/Fairies and Leprechauns, Robin Hood/King Arthur, The Warrior Queen/The Pirate Queen* and *Richard the Lionheart/Bonnie Prince Charlie*. Six tapes, 52 mins. each.

VHS: S33391. $79.95.

London: City of Majesty

This program studies London's vast cultural outreach, providing an immediate view of the neighborhood and the communities, the Barbican Theatre, Lloyd's of London, Tower of London, Fleet Street, Sloane Square and the National Portrait Gallery. "When a man is tired of London, he is tired of life, for there is in London all that life can afford" (Samuel Johnson). 48 mins.

VHS: S19171. $19.98.

London: Flower of Cities Allo

The capitol of Britain in a tour of traditional and historic London: St. Paul's Cathedral, the Tower, Buckingham Palace, the House of Parliament, and the museums, theaters, concert halls, shops, restaurants, with spectacular aerial photography of the Thames, Royal Parks, Hampstead Heath and Kew Gardens. 20 mins.

VHS: S07090. $19.95.

Majesty: The History of the British Monarchy

Period images, recreated eyewitness accounts and reenactments shows the remarkable royal history of Great Britain through the centuries. This two-volume set features *The Anglo-Saxons to Elizabeth I* and *16th Century to the House of Windsor*, which offer a complete overview of the triumphs and tribulations of English royalty. 104 mins.

VHS: S27103. $39.95.

Malt Whisky Trail

A tour of the eight Speyside distilleries that make up the world's only malt whisky trail brings to life intriguing tales of whisky's illicit past and examines the modern-day art of distillation, while showcasing Scotland's most dramatic and wild scenery. 55 mins.

VHS: S31365. $19.95.

Mountbatten: The Last Viceroy

In the grand tradition of *Lawrence of Arabia* and *Ghandi*, this grandly staged, $15-million epic tells the story of India's struggle for independence in 1947. With sweeping cinematography and a cast of thousands, including Nicol Williamson, Dame Wendy Hiller and Janet Suzman. "Impressive, richly produced and a major contribution to dramatizing history" *(Variety)*.

VHS: S31763. $89.95.

Tom Clegg, Great Britain, 1987, 107 mins.

Peter Reading

This brilliant English poet's first American reading included selections from *Evagatory* and *Diplopic*. It took place on April 21, 1992, in Los Angeles. He then spoke with Christopher Hitchens and Michael Silverblatt. From the *Lannan Literary Videos* series. 90 mins.

VHS: S27135. $19.95.

Poetry of Landscape: Great Britain

Savor the Wordsworth's beloved Lake District, the Yorkshire moors of the Bronte sisters and Thomas Hardy's old Dorset, immortalized under the name of Wessex. 57 mins.

VHS: S31477. $14.99.

Portrait of England: Treasure Houses and Gardens

Stately homes and glorious gardens, and the sounds of Wynton Marsalis in his debut video album as the sole featured artist in this portrait that captures the pastoral vistas, stately homes, castles and gardens that crown Great Britain. 55 mins.

VHS: S11195. $29.95.

Prince Charles

This A & E Biography takes a look at Prince Charles: the private man and his public role. As the man who would be king, he is heir to the throne of the British Empire and unequaled privilege, as well as unequaled duty and scrutiny. 100 mins.

VHS: S30100. $19.95.

Queen Elizabeth II: 60 Glorious Years

For anyone interested in royalty, this documentary captures the high points of Queen Elizabeth II, as she marries, goes through coronation, and reigns as England's monarch, in this production authorized by Buckingham Palace. 55 mins.

VHS: S05175. $29.95.

Queen Mother

This fascinating retrospective celebrates the ninetieth birthday of one of Great Britain's favorite royal figures—the Queen Mum. From the BBC.

VHS: S12391. $19.94.

The Queen Mother's New Garden

Four centuries of kings and queens, castles and gardens, and rare archival footage of the many hallmarks of the life of Her Majesty Queen Elizabeth, the Queen Mother, surround the creation of a new garden presented to her on her 95th birthday. World-renowned garden designer Penelope Hobhouse shares her expertise and the adventure of bringing the royal garden to life. 26 mins.

VHS: S32730. $24.95.

The Royal Collection Set

An intimate look at more than 500 years of the British monarchy. The program features sweeping pageantry and spectacle. Christopher Lloyd, the Surveyor of the Queen's Pictures, hosts the program. 180 mins.

VHS: S19365. $99.95.

Royal Family at War

This revealing look at the British Royal family shows how they survived World War II. Group Captain Peter Townsend, the chaperon to both Princess Margaret and Princess Elizabeth, reveals all about these two. He was later involved in a scandal with Princess Margaret. Also includes footage of King George VI's wartime diary. 90 mins.

VHS: S25843. $19.95.

Royal Wedding: H.R.H. the Prince Andrew and Miss Sarah Ferguson

Drawing on the BBC's coverage of the ceremony and procession, an evocation of the color, pageantry and emotion of the Royal wedding, including the full Westminster Abbey service. Produced by the BBC. 100 mins.

VHS: S03387. $19.94.

Royal Windsor and Eton

Windsor Castle has long been a summer residence for the Royal family of Great Britain. In this video you will see it before the disastrous fire of 1992, on the occasion of a royal wedding. Then across the Thames, founding day at Eton, the venerable boy's school, is a chance to witness still more pomp and circumstance. 55 mins.

VHS: S21516. $24.95.

The Royal Windsor Style

This ABC News presentation explores the history of England's monarchy, from Edward VIII and his abdication to the youngest heir to the throne, Prince William. A look at the various attendant royal ceremonies provides a fascinating insight into the world's most publicly viewed family and its changes over the last 60 years. 60 mins.

VHS: S33689. $19.98.

Saraband

A lavish and tearful romance of a woman torn between royal responsibility and love for a young rogue. With Joan Greenwood, Stewart Granger and Anthony Quayle.

VHS: S35245. $19.95.

Basil Dearden, Great Britain, 1948, 95 mins.

Scotland the Brave

Prince Charles, Colonel in Chief of Scotland's legendary 51st Highland Brigade, leads the Gordon Highlanders as they make their farewell parade appearance in Aberdeen. Highlights of this occasion include crack military precision and patriotic pipe and drum music, the Highlanders' final inspection and their last royal salute. The regimental band also stages a farewell concert to the "Fighting 51st" as well as to the people of Scotland. 1995, 50 mins.

VHS: S27342. $19.95.

Scotland Yard

An inside look at the legendary crime-fighting institution, Scotland Yard, hosted by David Niven.

VHS: S02154. $24.95.

Frank Cvitanovich, USA, 1971, 60 mins.

Scotland Yard's Chamber of Crime

An eerie combination of docudrama and stylized re-enactments that investigates some notorious detective stories and unsolved mysteries, this collection of stories is set in the "The Black Museum," Scotland Yard's official crime museum, and includes Jack the Ripper, the Great Train Robbery and Ruth Ellis, the last woman hanged in Britain. 55 mins.

VHS: S18157. $19.95.

Scotland: World of Difference

Travel "North of the Border" and enter the world of the islands and the beautiful Border country; learn some of the history and legends, visit the people at work and play—fishing, playing golf, playing bagpipes, tossing cabers, making whisky. 25 mins.

VHS: S07088. $19.95.

Touring England

Experience England's rich history and heritage in this acclaimed travel tape which explores London, Windsor Castle, Stonehenge, Bath, Oxford and Cambridge, Warwick, Leeds, Liverpool, Wales and more. 65 mins.

VHS: S11515. $29.95.

Tower of London: The Official Guide

The Tower of London is an infamous Royal palace, fortress and prison, where many a royal prisoner was kept until they were forced to lose their head. Now it houses the unrivaled collection that comprises the Crown Jewels. All of it is magically accessible to the viewer through this video. 45 mins.

VHS: S21517. $24.95.

Treasure Houses of Britain

John Julius Norwich, The Viscount Norwich, explores some of Great Britain's most magnificent estates in this special series of one-hour films. Each program provides the viewer with unprecedented access to these stately homes and takes the time to explore the history, the collections and their architecture, as well as to introduce them to the current owners, who discuss both the privileges and problems of living in a historic house.

Building for Eternity. Explores the Church of St. Mary the Virgin in Bottesford, Hardwick Hall, Burghley House, Wilton House and Chatsworth. 58 mins.

VHS: S08489. $29.95.

Palaces of Reason and Delight. Features Blenheim Palace, Houghton Hall, Bowhill, Newmark Castle, Drumlanrig Castle, Boughton House, West Wycombe Park, St. Lawrence church in West Wycombe and Syo House. 58 mins.

VHS: S08490. $29.95.

Recapturing the Past. Features Belvoir Castle, Plas Newydd, Penrhyn Castle, Wightwick Manor, Haddon Hall, Lindisfarne Castle. 58 mins.

VHS: S08491. $29.95.

Video Visits: Discovering Wales

Shoot the rapids of wild rivers in North Wales, climb the slopes of the Snowdonia by steam train, explore the stone ruins of Chepstow Castle and Tintern Abbey, and attend the Eisteddfod celebration. 55 mins.

VHS: S31466. $24.99.

The Windsors: A Royal Family

A groundbreaking documentary examining the British royal family through five generations, from the crisis of 1917 through the "annus horribilus" of 1992. The four parts of the film are: *I'm Damned If I'm an Alien, Brothers at War, The Image of a Queen* and *Family Affairs*. Four-volume boxed set. 228 mins.

VHS: S23575. $79.98.

british classics

1984
Edmond O'Brien defies Big Brother in this effective adaptation of George Orwell's classic novel warning of the dangers of a totalitarian state. Michael Redgrave, Jan Sterling and Donald Pleasance complete the first-rate cast.
VHS: S01520. $29.95.
Michael Anderson, Great Britain, 1956, 88 mins.

21 Days
Graham Greene wrote the adaptation of John Galsworthy's play about a pair of lovers (Laurence Olivier and Vivien Leigh) who share a brief time together before Oliver goes on trial for murder. With Leslie Banks, Hay Petrie, Francis L. Sullivan and Robert Newton.
VHS: S19875. $29.95.
Basil Dean, Great Britain, 1937, 75 mins.

90 Degrees South: With Scott to the Antarctic
Herbert G. Ponting's chronicle of Captain Robert Scott's heroic and ultimately tragic race for the South Pole was originally released in 1913. Ponting, a renowned still photographer, dedicated his life to the memory of Scott, who died with his entire team on the return trip from the pole after losing the race to Amundsen. Twenty years after his friend's death, Ponting added narration to the film, drawing from Scott's diary entries. This is the deeply personal tribute to the heartbreaking last days of the doomed expedition.
VHS: S16434. $39.95.
Laser: CLV/CAV. **LD71592. $29.95.**
Herbert G. Ponting, Great Britain, 1933, 72 mins.

Action for Slander
The British drama concerns the honor of a valiant cavalry officer falsely accused of cheating at cards. When a whisper campaign sullies his good reputation, he goes to court to clear his name. With Clive Brook, Ann Todd, Francis Sullavan and Googie Withers.
VHS: S05704. $29.95.
Tim Whelan, Great Britain, 1938, 84 mins.

Adventures of Tartu
Robert Donat stars in this Secret Service drama as Captain Terence Stevenson, who is sent to get the formula for a new poison gas being invented by the Nazis in Czechoslovakia and to blow up the factory that's making it. Donat impersonates Captain Jan Tartu, a member of the Romanian Iron Guard. A first-rate British wartime drama. With Valerie Hobson.
VHS: S26391. $29.95.
Harold S. Bucquet, Great Britain, 1943, 103 mins.

After the Ball
An entertaining and informative biography of the English music hall star, Vesta Tilley, who became the toast of two continents. With Laurence Harvey and Pat Kirkwood.
VHS: S34184. $19.95.
Compton Bennett, Great Britain, 1953, 89 mins.

Against the Wind
A high school in World War II-era London is actually a training facility for British spies. When student Andrew (Peter Illing) is kidnapped by the Nazis, the rest of the students come to his rescue. With Robert Beatty, Jack Warner and Simone Signoret in her British film debut.
VHS: S27383. $19.95.
Charles Crichton, Great Britain, 1947, 96 mins.

Alphabet Murders
Agatha Christie's famous detective, Hercule Poirot, pursues a lunatic murderer who is choosing his victims in alphabetical order. This curious film from director Frank Tashlin offers an interesting combination of slapstick and whodunit suspense. Starring Tony Randall, Anita Ekberg and Robert Morley.
VHS: S13760. $19.98.
Frank Tashlin, Great Britain, 1965, 90 mins.

Anna Karenina
Vivien Leigh plays the title role of Anna, the married woman who gives up everything when she falls in love with the handsome young military officer in this British version of Tolstoy's classic tragedy. With magnificent costumes and sets and support from Ralph Richardson as the cold Karenin.
VHS: S07067. $39.95.
Julien Duvivier, Great Britain, 1948, 110 mins.

Anne of the Thousand Days
Richard Burton and Genevieve Bujold star as King Henry VIII of England and Anne Boleyn in the emotionally charged drama about one of history's most tragic love affairs.
VHS: S04860. $49.95.
Laser: Letterboxed. **LD74921. $39.99.**
Richard Jarrott, Great Britain, 1969, 146 mins.

The Anniversary
Bette Davis does it again as she creates a memorable screen monster in this adaptation of a play by Bill McIllwraith. The atmosphere is claustrophobic as a demanding mother terrorizes her three grown sons. The three are forced to return home on their parents' wedding anniversary despite the fact that their father is dead. Though they are determined to defy the one-eyed Bette, she has a different scenario in mind.
VHS: S27439. $19.98.
Roy Ward Baker, Great Britain, 1967, 95 mins.

Beat Girl
An expose-style melodrama about an architect's teenage daughter, who ends up becoming a big disappointment to her family. With Christopher Lee, Gillian Hills, and Noelle Adam.
VHS: S14654. $24.95.
Edmond T. Greville, Great Britain, 1960, 92 mins.

Beau Brummel
A lavish biography of Napoleon's contemporary George Bryan Brummel (Stewart Granger). A peasant who uses bravery, wit and skill to align himself with the Prince of Wales, Brummel simultaneously seduces a powerful noblewoman (Elizabeth Taylor) engaged to a dull fiance. With Peter Ustinov and Robert Morley.
VHS: S18527. $19.98.
Curtis Bernhardt, Great Britain/USA, 1954, 114 mins.

Beckett
Richard Burton and Peter O'Toole star in this grand historical drama adapted from the Jean Anouilh play about the tumultuous relationship of an archbishop and a royal monarch in the 12th century. Superb cast includes John Gielgud, Marita Hunt and Felix Aylmer.
VHS: S02638. $59.95.
Peter Glenville, Great Britain, 1964, 148 mins.

The Bells Go Down
Tommy Trinder and James Mason star in this tragic but good-humored account of fire fighters in London during the Second World War. Set in the East End, the film also includes on-screen appearances by genuine volunteer members of the Auxiliary Fire Service.
VHS: S23781. $24.95.
Basil Dearden, Great Britain, 1943, 89 mins.

Beware of Pity
Lilli Palmer portrays a crippled young woman who finds romance and meaning in her life. Based on the novel by Stefan Zweig. With Albert Lieven, Cedric Harwicke and Gladys Cooper.
VHS: S30429. $14.98.
Maurice Elvey, Great Britain, 1946, 102 mins.

Big Fella
Virtually unseen in the United States, *Big Fella* is a lively British musical based on the 1929 novel *Banjo*, by Claude McKay. Paul Robeson stars as Joe, a Marseilles dockworker who is asked by police to help find a young boy missing from an ocean liner. When Joe finally discovers the child (Eldon Grant), he learns that the boy escaped of his own will, and takes him to stay with a local cafe singer, Miranda (Elisabeth Welch). Joe and Miranda become surrogate parents to the boy, offering a welcome change from his wealthy and repressed white parents.
VHS: S33167. $24.95.
J. Elder Wills, Great Britain, 1937, 73 mins.

Bitter Sweet
Noel Coward story about an elderly woman's memories of a romance with an orchestra leader. With Anna Neagle, Fernand Gravet.
VHS: S02577. $24.95.
Herbert Wilcox, Great Britain, 1933, 76 mins.

Black Roses
Near the end of her life, Lilian Harvey asked to see only one of her films, *Black Roses*. A search of the major archives turned up nothing, and she was never again to see her favorite work. Set in 1900's Russia, Harvey (a ballerina) must sleep with the Tsarist governor in order to save the life of her true love. Dennis Hoey also stars. Mastered from the only known nitrate print. Produced in Germany in 1935, and then remade in Germany and Great Britain in 1936.
VHS: S10964. $29.95.
Paul Martin, Germany/Great Britain, 1936, 79 mins.

Blanche Fury
In this striking melodrama, Stewart Granger stars as a disinherited bastard who is the object of desire of a governess (Valerie Hobson) who is married to her widowed cousin.
VHS: S31141. $14.98.
Marc Allegret, Great Britain, 1948, 95 mins.

The Blue Lamp
An important British detective film which spawned many imitators, *The Blue Lamp* tells the tale of a young police officer who must capture the criminal who gunned down his older partner. Starring Dirk Bogarde.
VHS: S14660. $29.95.
Basil Dearden, Great Britain, 1949, 84 mins.

Bonnie Prince Charlie
David Niven and Margaret Leighton star in this costume drama about the legendary 16th-century Prince of Scotland. Beginning in Rome, this film charts the Stuart attempt to wrest control back from the Hanoverian regime.
VHS: S23798. $14.98.
Anthony Kimmins, Great Britain, 1948, 118 mins.

Break in the Circle
A political thriller about an unassuming boat owner who's enlisted by mysterious agents to help a brilliant young scientist escape from communist East Germany. With Forrest Tucker, Eva Bartok, Marius Goring and Guy Middleton.
VHS: S18937. $19.95.
Val Guest, Great Britain, 1957, 69 mins.

Breakthrough
Richard Burton stars as a German sergeant who gets involved in an anti-Hitler conspiracy and saves the life of an American colonel. With Rod Steiger and Robert Mitchum.
VHS: S34927. $14.95.
Andrew V. McLaglen, Great Britain/Germany, 1978, 115 mins.

Brighton Rock
John Boulting's first-rate postwar gangster drama is set in Brighton and stars Richard Attenborough as Pinkie Brown. The script was written by Terrence Rattigan and Graham Greene and based on Greene's novel. Also known as *The Young Scarface*.
VHS: S26067. $29.95.
John Boulting, Great Britain, 1947, 92 mins.

Broken Melody
Merle Oberon and John Garrick star in this romantic drama about a successful opera singer who is mistakenly imprisoned and must escape to get back to the woman he loves.
VHS: S14662. $29.95.
Bernard Vorhaus, Great Britain, 1934, 62 mins.

The Browning Version

Superb acting and an incisive screenplay bring to life the story of an aging and embittered boarding schoolteacher's painful last day of lessons. Once a brilliant scholar, he is now the target of his pupils' ridicule. His cruel wife's affair with a younger colleague only adds to his agony as he awaits a new—albeit undesirable—teaching position.

VHS: S16594. $19.95.
Anthony Asquith, Great Britain, 1951, 90 mins.

Bulldog Drummond at Bay

Hugh Drummond searches for international gun runners who are themselves searching for the secret plans of a remote-controlled British warplane. With John Lodge, Dorothy Mackaill and Victor Jory.

VHS: S33723. $24.95.
Norman Lee, Great Britain, 1937, 63 mins.

Captain Boycott

A spirited and intelligent drama about the man who led the peaceful battles between Irish landowners in the 19th century whose name became a synonym for ostracism. Fine period reconstruction and classy performances by a standout cast which includes Stewart Granger, Kathleen Ryan, Cecil Parker, Mervyn Johns, Noel Purcell, Niall MacGinnis, Alastair Sim and Robert Donat.

VHS: S30430. $14.98.
Frank Launder, Great Britain, 1947, 93 mins.

Captive Heart

An archetypal World War II POW drama with a poetic treatment laced with humor and melodrama. The story focuses on a Czech POW who has stolen the papers of a dead British officer and begins to assume the dead officer's identity.

VHS: S01944. $29.95.
Basil Dearden, Great Britain, 1948, 86 mins.

Cast a Dark Shadow

Lewis Gilbert's adaptation of Janet Green's melodrama about a sly charmer (Dirk Bogarde) who murders women for their inheritance. He finds his match when he marries and plots to kill a former barmaid (Margaret Lockwood). With Kay Walsh, Kathleen Harrison, Robert Flemyng and Mona Washbourne.

VHS: S19861. $29.95.
Lewis Gilbert, Great Britain, 1955, 82 mins.

Catherine the Great

The story of Catherine the Great's turbulent rise to power as a ruler of her empire and her many romances, in a lavish production starring Douglas Fairbanks Jr. and Elizabeth Bergner.

VHS: S03331. $19.95.
Paul Czinner, Great Britain, 1934, 100 mins.

Challenge

Breathtaking photography in the film about the conquest of the Matterhorn co-directed by Luis Trenker, who had worked as a mountain guide until being hired in 1921 to act in the film *Marvels of Ski*.

VHS: S02244. $29.95.
Luis Trenker/Vincent Korda, Great Britain, 1938, 77 mins.

The Charge of the Light Brigade

Tony Richardson's historical epic, based in part on Tennyson's poem, about the events that led to British involvement in the Crimean War. Richardson's playfulness and mock grandeur about the horrors of war—highlighted by Richard Williams' animation—are "extravagantly pretty...and some of it is very funny (especially John Gielgud as the whimsical, doddering supreme commander of the British forces, and an undressing sequence with Trevor Howard and Jill Bennett). With David Hemmings, Vanessa Redgrave and Harry Andrews.

VHS: S20388. $19.98.
Laser: Letterboxed. **LD76175. $49.98.**
Tony Richardson, Great Britain, 1968, 130 mins.

Children of the Damned

An accomplished sequel to *Village of the Damned*, about brilliant and misguided young children and their methodical and ruthless quest for power and control. With Ian Hendry, Alan Badel and Barbara Ferris.

VHS: S17534. $19.98.
Anton Leader, Great Britain, 1964, 90 mins.

A Christmas Carol

Alastair Sim is Scrooge in this wonderful adaptation of Charles Dickens' great story.

VHS: S02660. $19.95.
Brian Desmond Hurst, Great Britain, 1951, 86 mins.

Christopher Columbus

Frederic March is the intrepid Italian explorer who opened up a whole new world to the modern age. After convincing Queen Isabella of Spain to supply patronage, Columbus must brave the uncharted seas in search of his dream—a shorter, more direct route to Asia.

VHS: S21994. $14.98.
David MacDonald, Great Britain, 1949, 104 mins.

Circle of Danger

Ray Milland and Naughton Wayne star in this suspense-filled film about a man who must journey to Britain in order to uncover the mystery surrounding his brother's death. The dead man was part of a special combat unit in World War II.

VHS: S23887. $29.95.
Jacques Tourneur, Great Britain, 1955, 86 mins.

Circus of Fear

Christopher Lee stars in this outstanding psychological drama, released in its uncut 91-minute British release version. Based on an Edgar Wallace story of a murderer amidst the odd people who work in the circus. Re-released as *Psycho-Circus*.

VHS: S08416. $29.95.
John Moxey, Great Britain, 1967, 65 mins.

Citadel

Powerful film about a young idealistic doctor who loses his humanitarian goals and takes up a wealthy practice treating rich hypochondriacs, neglecting his wife and friends in the process. With Ralph Richardson, Rex Harrison and Robert Donat.

VHS: S03452. $24.95.
King Vidor, Great Britain, 1938, 114 mins.

The Clairvoyant

In this classic thriller Claude Rains stars as a phony clairvoyant who discovers his predictions come true in the presence of a girl (Jane Baxter). Despite his wife's (Fay Wray) disapproval of his involvement, he predicts a tunnel disaster which comes true and authorities blame him for causing it.

VHS: S31140. $14.98.
Maurice Elvey, Great Britain, 1935, 80 mins.

The Clouded Yellow

Trevor Howard stars as a leading British agent opposite a beautiful suspect played by Jean Simmons. Howard's character is fired and tries to get away from his dangerous work, only to find himself embroiled in danger once again by the mysterious beauty. They make a wonderfully glamorous pair of fugitives.

VHS: S24866. $39.95.
Ralph Thomas, Great Britain, 1951, 96 mins.

Clouds over Europe

Laurence Olivier stars as the pilot who helps inspector Ralph Richardson outwit a German spy ring intent on sabotaging Britain's airforce. These two stars bring their wit and charm to a story set in front of an ominous backdrop, Europe poised on the brink of war.

VHS: S21029. $19.98.
Laser: LD75171. $34.98.
Tim Whelan, Great Britain, 1939, 78 mins.

The Colditz Story

Allied prisoners who tried to escape from the Nazis were sent to Colditz, castle turned into an escape-proof fortress by the Third Reich. This film, based on P.C. Reid's book, tells the story of a group of prisoners who tried to escape despite seemingly insurmountable barriers.

VHS: S26481. $14.98.
Guy Hamilton, Great Britain, 1954, 93 mins.

Conspirator

The idyllic marriage of a beautiful and privileged, young American woman (Elizabeth Taylor) is shattered by the devastating admission that her husband (Robert Taylor), an officer in the British Army, is a communist agent. With Honor Blackman and Wilfrid Hyde-White.

VHS: S18521. $19.98.
Victor Saville, Great Britain, 1949, 85 mins.

Contraband Spain

Richard Greene is an American agent who rounds up a pack of smugglers and counterfeiters on the French-Spanish border after his brother is murdered, with the help of singer Anouk Aimee.

VHS: S21563. $24.95.
Philip Gartside, Great Britain, 1955, 82 mins.

Convoy

A chilling World War II film produced by Ealing Studios about the intricate games played out between a German pocket battleship and a British convoy. The only significant film of Pen Tennyson, who was subsequently killed in the war. With Clive Brook, John Clements and Edward Chapman.

VHS: S07070. $19.95.
Pen Tennyson, Great Britain, 1941, 90 mins.

Corridor of Mirrors

Eric Portman, Edna Romney and Christopher Lee are featured in this surreal drama about two soul-crossed lovers. A man fixated on the past falls in love with a woman who resembles one of his Renaissance portraits. Deeply hidden secrets, vengeance and even murder pepper this story of a strange obsession.

VHS: S24006. $24.95.
Terence Young, Great Britain, 1948, 94 mins.

Courageous Mr. Penn

Clifford Evans and Deborah Kerr star in this biography about the original Quaker, William Penn. He valiantly fought British persecution until he was permitted to go to America. There he struggled and eventually founded the City of Brotherly Love, Philadelphia. Kerr is magnificent as his converted wife.

VHS: S24005. $24.95.
Lance Comfort, Great Britain, 1941, 88 mins.

The Courtneys of Curzon Street

A multilayered melodrama that covers the years 1900-45 as a charismatic, wealthy, young financier upsets the social balance by falling in love with his housemaid. Also known as *The Courtney Affair*. With Anna Neagle, Michael Wilding, Gladys Young and Coral Browne.

VHS: S18939. $19.95.
Herbert Wilcox, Great Britain, 1947, 112 mins.

Crimes of Stephen Hawke

Tod Slaughter is the title character in this film treatment of one of his Grand Guignol theatrical melodramas. He plays a royal money lender who enjoys breaking the spines of strangers in his off hours. With Eric Portman, Marjorie Taylor and Gerald Berry as Miles Archer. What, no Sam Spade?

VHS: S04043. $29.95.
George King, Great Britain, 1936, 70 mins.

The Cruel Sea

One of the great war films, full of atmospheric detailing which captures the essence of the Battle of the Atlantic.

VHS: S04283. $39.95.
Charles Frend, Great Britain, 1953, 121 mins.

A Cry from the Streets

Max Bygraves stars in this semi-documentary style drama about orphan children in England. Also starring Barbara Murray and Colin Petersen.

VHS: S14668. $29.95.
Lewis Gilbert, Great Britain, 1957, 100 mins.

Cry, The Beloved Country

Based on Alan Paton's excellent novel about the poverty and abuses of the Apartheid Policy in South Africa, this poignant film features powerful performances from Canada Lee, Sidney Poitier and Geoffrey Keen.

VHS: S14783. $69.95.
Zoltan Korda, Great Britain, 1951, 111 mins.

The Dam Busters

Michael Redgrave, Richard Todd and Ursula Jeans are featured in this thrilling World War II yarn. It revolves around an ingenious British plot to sabotage a strategic dam. Suspense, spies and confounding plot twists make this well-crafted film a true crowd-pleaser.

VHS: S23005. $14.95.
Michael Anderson, Great Britain, 1954, 119 mins.

Damn the Defiant!

The commander of a British warship must battle Napoleon's fleet and his own mutinous crew in this thrilling historical adventure. The production, as a whole, shows fine attention to historic detail and stars Alec Guiness and Dirk Bogarde.

VHS: S13573. $14.95.
Lewis Gilbert, Great Britain, 1962, 101 mins.

Dance Little Lady

The moving drama of a prima ballerina whose career was cut short in a car accident, and as a result, her heel of a husband abandoned her. Her daughter becomes her whole life as she develops the talent she inherited from her mother. A moving story with good ballet sequences. With Mai Zetterling, Guy Rolfe, Terence Morgan, and Mandy Miller.

VHS: S34185. $19.95.
Val Guest, Great Britain, 1955, 87 mins.

Dark Journey
Vivien Leigh stars as a double agent during World War I in Stockholm, who becomes involved with the head of German Intelligence, Conrad Veidt.
VHS: S03591. $19.95.
Victor Saville, Great Britain, 1937, 82 mins.

Dark of the Sun
Ruthless mercenaries (Rod Taylor and Jim Brown) venture into the Congo to save refugees trapped by war and upheaval. They also have a reward for this selfless behavior in mind, the recovery of some valuable diamonds. It's a tense drama where the basic human impulses, greed and altruism, come into direct conflict.
VHS: S21016. $19.98.
Jack Cardiff, Great Britain, 1968, 101 mins.

Darling
Landmark British film made during the Kitchen Sink Drama period features Julie Christie as a woman who becomes a prisoner of her own modeling success, leaves her husband for a sexy TV commentator (Laurence Harvey), until she falls restless and falls in love with a jet setter.
Laser: LD70358. $69.95.
John Schlesinger, Great Britain, 1965, 122 mins.

David Copperfield
Robin Phillips, Susan Hampshire, Edith Evans, Michael Redgrave, Laurence Olivier and Richard Attenborough are among the first-rate cast in this adaptation of Charles Dickens' classic tale of a re-discovered orphan. This fine tale is full of more heartrending twists than anything written in our own time.
VHS: S23104. $19.95.
Delbert Mann, Great Britain, 1970, 110 mins.

The Day Will Dawn
Ralph Richardson and Deborah Kerr star in this saga about a reckless foreign correspondent. World War II is fast becoming a worldwide disaster when this journalist must decide to act courageously. He finally resolves to help the Norwegians in their hopeless struggle against the Nazis.
VHS: S27890. $19.98.
Harold French, Great Britain, 1942, 105 mins.

Dead Lucky
Martin's stab at gambling wins him a fortune—and traps him between a con artist, an assassin, and a mysterious seductress. In gripping conclusion, he becomes both victim and killer. Adapted from the award-winning novel *Lake of Darkness*.
VHS: S14327. $49.95.
Montgomery Tully, Great Britain, 1960, 91 mins.

Dead of Night
Michael Redgrave stars in this spine-tingling suspense classic featuring dreams, premonitions, hallucinations and some well-timed comic breathers. Redgrave is feverishly convincing in the role of the ventriloquist who achieves the ultimate in schizophrenia.
VHS: S00314. $14.95.
Charles Crichton/Alberto Cavalcanti/Basil Dearden, Great Britain, 1955, 104 mins.

Decameron Nights
Joan Fontaine, Joan Collins and Louis Jourdan star in this film adaptation of Boccaccio's classic work, *The Decameron*. Jordan is the author trying to woo Fontaine, who plays a young widow. This is the backdrop for three rather bawdy stories set in a lushly costumed and photographed film.
VHS: S23772. $24.95.
Hugo Fregonese, Great Britain, 1953, 87 mins.

Detective (aka Father Brown)
Alec Guiness is Father Brown in this film adaptation of the beloved character created in G.K. Chesterton's popular mysteries. The eccentric priest has a valuable cross stolen by Peter Finch on a journey from London to Rome. With Joan Greenwood and Bernard Lee. A gem of a mystery, not to be confused with the Frank Sinatra film.
VHS: S07584. $19.95.
Robert Hamer, Great Britain, 1954, 91 mins.

Devil's Sleep
A sordid little crime drama that deals with a slimeball drug dealer who pushes pills at a health spa, then tries to blackmail a female juvenile judge on his trail by threatening to sell nude photos of her teenage daughter. From the producer of *Glen or Glenda*. With Lita Grey Chaplin and Timothy Farrell.
VHS: S34207. $19.95.
W. Merle Connell, Great Britain, 1951, 73 mins.

Dinner at the Ritz
The hotel, not the cracker. David Niven has his first starring role in this murder mystery about the death of a French banker. The daughter of the banker (Annabella) seeks to clear the family name. The dashing Niven is only too happy to be of assistance. With Paul Lukas and Romney Brent.
VHS: S09830. $19.95.
Harold Schuster, Great Britain, 1937, 77 mins.

Dreaming Lips
Elisabeth Bergner gives an enchanting performance as Gaby, married to an orchestra conductor, who falls in love with a world-famous violinist (the young Raymond Massey). A witty, sophisticated tale of illicit romance.
VHS: S05603. $29.95.
Paul Czinner, Great Britain, 1937, 69 mins.

East Meets West
A Sultan from a small country is courted by the British and a competing Eastern power for the use of a strategically vital harbor. This scenario breeds intrigues, though a love interest with a rum-running beauty is added just in case. George Arliss and Godfrey Tearle are featured.
VHS: S27891. $19.98.

Elephant Boy
An early docu-drama about a young boy—the first screen appearance of Sabu—who knows the location of an elephant burial ground.
VHS: S04323. $19.98.
Laser: LD75188. $34.98.
Robert Flaherty/Zoltan Korda, Great Britain, 1937, 80 mins.

Endless Night
Agatha Christie's inimitable style is brought to the screen in this adaptation of her chilling novel, with Hywell Bennett the chauffer who marries a rich American girl (Hayley Mills) and moves into a dream house which turns out to be a nightmare.
VHS: S04544. $14.95.
Bruce Brown, Great Britain, 1966, 96 mins.

Evergreen
Unseen in the United States for 30 years, *Evergreen* is an enchanting film and remains one of the most fondly remembered musicals of the 1930s. Stunning Jessie Matthews became internationally famous for her role in this classic show business tale about a young girl who becomes a stage sensation when she begins masquerading as her long-retired mother. Music and lyrics by Rodgers and Hart.
VHS: S06133. $39.95.
Victor Saville, Great Britain, 1934, 91 mins.

Evil Under the Sun
Peter Ustinov is a delight as Hercule Poirot, Agatha Christie's detective hero. With James Mason and Diana Rigg.
VHS: S04545. $19.99.
Guy Hamilton, Great Britain, 1982, 112 mins.

Expresso Bongo
Johnny Jackson (Laurence Harvey), a sly, sleazy and unscrupulous music agent, discovers a Presleyesque, bongo-playing rebel (Cliff Richard) singing in a SoHo coffeehouse. He renames him "Bongo" Herbert and, with the help of his stripper girlfriend (Sylvia Syms), guides the potential teen idol along the rocky path to fame. Reminiscent of *The Sweet Smell of Success* in its savvy critique of the corruptive values of showbiz, *Expresso Bongo* is a witty, smart, entertaining exploration of one facet of the Brit Beat phenomenon.
VHS: S33010. $24.95.
Val Guest, Great Britain, 1959, 111 mins.

Faces in the Dark
In this taut psychological thriller, a blind man begins to fear for his sanity. A series of events seems to conspire against him, but he cannot be certain, at least not in the beginning. All at once it becomes clear that his life is in serious danger.
VHS: S27899. $19.98.
David Eady, Great Britain, 1960, 80 mins.

The Fallen Idol
In one of his finest performances, Ralph Richardson plays a butler who is idolized by eight-year-old Bobby Henrey. Drawn into the butler's tangled personal life during a weekend when his parents are away, the boy learns that Richardson is accused of having murdered his wife. Screenplay by Graham Greene from his story *The Basement Room*.
VHS: S00426. $29.95.
Laser: LD76979. $29.99.
Carol Reed, Great Britain, 1948, 92 mins.

Fanny by Gaslight
This romantic melodrama, set in the Victorian era, tells the story of the comely and illegitimate Fanny, who must somehow be saved from the lustful advances of a lascivious Lord. With James Mason.
VHS: S14659. $29.95.
Anthony Asquith, Great Britain, 1944, 108 mins.

Far from the Madding Crowd
John Schlesinger directed this first-rate adaptation of the novel by Thomas Hardy about a tempestuous Dorset girl and her profound influence on three different men—a young cavalry officer, a wealthy landowner and a herdsman. With brilliant performances from Julie Christie, Peter Finch, Terence Stamp, and Alan Bates.
VHS: S11551. $24.98.
Laser: LD70567. $39.98.
John Schlesinger, Great Britain, 1967, 169 mins.

Fighting Pilot
Richard Talmadge and Victor Mace star in this classic adventure film made at a time when talkies were still a novelty. Talmadge is a true warrior who must rescue plans for a secret military aircraft.
VHS: S23774. $24.95.
Noel Mason Smith, Great Britain, 1933, 62 mins.

Fire Down Below
Rita Hayworth declares that "armies have marched over me" but that doesn't deter Robert Mitchum and Jack Lemmon from putting on their hiking boots. Tempers flare in the Caribbean as two smugglers do more than arm wrestle for Rita's company. With Anthony Newley. Filmed in Tobago and London.
VHS: S04748. $19.95.
Robert Parrish, Great Britain, 1957, 116 mins.

Fire over England
Splendid historical spectacle set during the reign of Queen Elizabeth I; dashing young Laurence Olivier plays a daring Englishman who thwarts a Spanish plot against the Queen. Vivien Leigh, Flora Robson and Raymond Massey co-star.
VHS: S00442. $19.95.
Laser: Side 1 CLV. Side 2 CAV. **LD71590. $39.95.**
William K. Howard, Great Britain, 1937, 89 mins.

Flame over India
When a Moslem insurgency topples a British fortress in rural India, it's up to a few dignitaries to speed the Maharaja's son to safety. Escaping the fort in a rusty old train, the motley crew faces suspense and adventure, including a traitor in their midst. With Kenneth More, Lauren Bacall and Herbert Lom.
VHS: S16103. $29.95.
J. Lee Thompson, Great Britain, 1959, 130 mins.

Four Sided Triangle
Barbara Payton, once *The Bride of the Gorilla*, finds herself in another fine mess. Two clever scientists are in love with her but she loves only one of them so they make two of her. Two Barbaras should be enough to go around but will they?
VHS: S04091. $29.95.
Laser: Includes pressbook. **LD76823. $49.95.**
Terence Fisher, Great Britain, 1953, 81 mins.

Frieda
One of the gems of post-war British filmmaking, an unusually unsentimental drama that makes use of newsreel footage and explores the bitterness of the English people against the Germans within the context of a love story.
VHS: S02171. $29.95.
Basil Dearden, Great Britain, 1947, 98 mins.

The Frightened City
A ruthless crime syndicate holds London in its terrifying grip—and there is only one man who can stop them—in this hard-boiled tale of tough guys, tough broads and tough luck. With Sean Connery, Herbert Lom and John Gregson.
VHS: S31020. $14.98.
John Lemont, Great Britain, 1961, 91 mins.

Funeral in Berlin
Michael Caine stars as British espionage agent Harry Palmer in the second of three films based on the books by Len Deighton. His mission is to assist a Russian defector in the title city. He isn't pleased when the plans change without his knowledge. With Oscar Homolka, Paul Hubschmid and Eva Renzi.
VHS: S10835. $14.95.
Laser: LD75197. $34.98.
Guy Hamilton, Great Britain, 1966, 102 mins.

Gaslight
The first version of Patrick Hamilton's play about an insane criminal who drives his wife crazy in order to find the hidden jewels. Despite its low budget, the film succinctly conveys a sense of madness and evil. MGM supposedly tried to destroy the negative of this original when they made the remake. With Anton Walbrook, Diana Wynyard, Frank Pettingell and Cathleen Cordell.
VHS: S16270. $29.95.
Thorold Dickinson, Great Britain, 1939, 84 mins.

Get Carter

Michael Caine, Britt Ekland and Ian Hendry star in this widely acclaimed white-knuckler about a mobster who single-handedly, and with extreme precision, tears into a local crime syndicate after his brother is killed.

VHS: S30538. $19.98.

Mike Hodges, Great Britain, 1971, 111 mins.

Glory at Sea

Trevor Howard plays the demanding and unpopular commanding officer of a broken-down battleship. The hostile attitudes on deck take a turnabout after a conflict with the Germans proves the ancient battleship is still able to perform. With Richard Attenborough and Sonny Tufts.

VHS: S16107. $29.95.

Compton Bennett, Great Britain, 1952, 90 mins.

The Golden Salamander

Based on the suspenseful adventure novel by Victor Canning, this spirited version is also big on mystery and intrigue. Shot on location in Tunis, it also stars Trevor Howard at his peak as a romantic leading man and then new French star Anouk Aimee.

VHS: S14636. $29.95.

Ronald Neame, Great Britain, 1950, 96 mins.

Gorgo

A volcanic eruption in the North Atlantic brings to the surface a 65-foot prehistoric monster. Two treasure divers capture the creature and take him to London where he is put on display in a circus. But the creature is only an infant, and soon his mother comes thundering ashore to reclaim her offspring, trashing a generous portion of London in the process. A fun sci-fi story with exciting special effects.

VHS: S09519. $19.95.

Eugene Lourie, Great Britain, 1961, 76 mins.

The Great British Documentary Movement

This comprehensive boxed set features 20 films (1929-1948) presented with the aid of the British Documentary Film Movement, including *Drifters, Family Portrait, Coalface* and *North Sea*. 619 mins.

Laser: LD76752. $199.99.

Great Day

Flora Robson heads a stellar British cast as one of the heroic women who worked day and night for victory in wartime England.

VHS: S12376. $19.98.

Lance Comfort, USA, 1946, 62 mins.

Greek Street

An entertaining story of London's Italian quarter by Robert Stevenson. Starring Sari Marizia and Arthur Hambling.

VHS: S15177. $29.95.

Sinclair Hill, Great Britain, 1930, 51 mins.

Green for Danger

A puzzler for both Scotland Yard and the audience as Inspector Cockrill (Alastair Sim) is called in to investigate a murder in a hospital filled with suspicious doctors and staff. Cockrill's interrogation brings them all into question concerning both motive and opportunity and places Cockrill high in the cinema tradition of the droll Yard detective who always gets his man.

VHS: S12955. $39.95.

Sidney Gilliat, Great Britain, 1947, 91 mins.

The Guinea Pig

Richard Attenborough, Bernard Miles and Joan Hickson are featured in this dramatic look at changing educational ideals. A tobacconist's son is admitted to a posh public school as an experiment. The reactions of the staff and the other boys could not have been predicted. Bernard Miles wrote the screenplay.

VHS: S25015. $19.95.

John Boulting, Great Britain, 1948, 97 mins.

The Hasty Heart

Ronald Reagan and Patricia Neal star in this stirring World War II drama about wounded soldiers in a hospital in Burma. They are forced to question many deeply held beliefs when an embittered Scotsman with a few weeks left to live enters their compound.

VHS: S24727. $19.98.

Vincent Sherman, Great Britain, 1949, 101 mins.

The Haunted Strangler

Boris Karloff stars as a novelist who ends up investigating the haunted graves of a prison cemetery when he sets out to prove that the wrong man died for a crime committed 20 years ago.

VHS: S22987. $19.98.

DVD: DV60326. $24.99.

Robert Day, Great Britain, 1958, 81 mins.

The Headless Ghost

Three young exchange students on holiday in Britain take a tour of the famous Ambrose Castle, reputedly haunted by a headless ghost named Malcom who lost his head leading a rebellion against King Edward. When a portrait of the 4th Earl of Ambrose leaps from the wall asking for their help, the three students try to end Malcom's reign of terror. Letterboxed.

VHS: S34291. $19.99.

Peter Graham Scott, Great Britain, 1959, 63 mins.

The Hill

Sean Connery stars in this tense, unforgiving drama. During World War II, a British stockade in the African desert has a unique torture device. It is a hill over 60 feet high and 210 feet long. Prisoners are forced to climb its steep sides under an unrelenting sun. Rarely has the sadistic nature of the all-male military world been so startlingly captured on celluloid.

VHS: S27573. $19.98.

Sidney Lumet, Great Britain, 1965, 122 mins.

Horrors of the Black Museum

A mystery writer uses his hypnotized assistant to commit a series of killings that baffle Scotland Yard. Features a classic eyeball-gouging binoculars scene. With Michael Gough, June Cunningham, Graham Curnow, Geoffrey Keen.

VHS: S34211. $19.95.

Arthur Crabtree, Great Britain, 1959, 94 mins.

Hungry Hill

Margaret Lockwood, Dennis Price, Jean Simmons and Cecil Parker star in this costume drama about a wealthy Victorian era family. Despite appearances, the greatness of this Irish family dynasty is built upon generations of treachery. Based on Daphne du Maurier's novel.

VHS: S23894. $29.95.

Brian Desmond Hurst, Great Britain, 1947, 108 mins.

I Am a Camera

An earlier non-musical adaptation of the Christopher Isherwood stories that inspired *Cabaret*, starring Julie Harris as the outrageous Sally Bowles (Shall we have a drink first or shall we go right to bed?) and Laurence Harvey as Isherwood in pre-Nazi Berlin.

VHS: S00593. $24.95.

Henry Cornelius, Great Britain, 1955, 99 mins.

I Stand Condemned

Laurence Olivier plays a young Russian officer who falls in love with a Russian society girl in 1916. She is engaged to a wealthy contractor who trumps up espionage charges against his younger rival. Olivier looks quite dashing in his uniform and moustache.

VHS: S05068. $29.95.

Anthony Asquith, Great Britain, 1936, 71 mins.

If I Were Rich

A clever, witty, Depression-era British drama with Robert Donat as the man who goes through life avoiding paying his bills while waiting for prosperity to return.

VHS: S09213. $29.95.

Zoltan Korda, Great Britain, 1933, 63 mins.

If...

A sometimes shocking portrait of life in a repressive English boarding school. Three non-conforming senior schoolboys revolt against practically everything. Anderson skillfully employs both professional and non-professional actors in building to a shattering, violent climax.

VHS: S00606. $49.95.

Lindsay Anderson, Great Britain, 1969, 111 mins.

The Immortal Battalion (The Way Ahead)

Based on a script by Eric Ambler, with a foreword by Quentin Reynolds, a rousing drama of War—the story of newly recruited civilians who are molded into a hardened battalion of fighting men. With David Niven, Stanley Holloway, Reginald Tate, Peter Ustinov.

VHS: S03058. $19.95.

Carol Reed, Great Britain, 1944, 89 mins.

Impulse

A young married man gets mixed up with gangsters and an illicit love affair when his wife goes to visit her mother. Starring Arthur Kennedy and Constance Smith.

VHS: S14673. $29.95.

Charles De Latour, Great Britain, 1956, 81 mins.

The Informer

Lars Hanson stars as a man desperate to flee the poverty of Ireland. He turns in an IRA man for cash and runs off to America, but he is haunted by guilt. Based on a novel by Liam O'Flaherty, this film captures the tormented soul of traitor.

VHS: S26987. $24.95.

Arthur Robinson, Great Britain, 1929, 83 mins.

The Inheritance (Uncle Silas)

Jean Simmons and Derrick DeMarney are featured in this suspense-laden thriller. A Victorian girl is sent to her uncle's home after the death of her father. Unfortunately her uncle is more interested in her inheritance than her well-being and she finds herself locked in a desperate struggle to remain alive.

VHS: S23895. $29.95.

Charles Frank, Great Britain, 1947, 90 mins.

The Inn of the Sixth Happiness

A simple English servant girl, played by Ingrid Bergman, travels to China to become a missionary. Based on the true life story of Gladice Alyward, this biography reveals the difficulties she encounterd while pursuing the daunting task of founding an orphanage in the 1930's. Her goal was well within reach when political turmoil forced her into an even more heroic role.

VHS: S20705. $19.98.

Laser: LD75379. $49.98.

Mark Robson, Great Britain, 1958, 158 mins.

The Innocents

Deborah Kerr stars as a governess who comes to suspect something is terribly wrong with her seemingly innocent charges. Based on Henry James' *The Turn of the Screw*, this cinematic adaptation manages to enliven the original story with sinister film effects. It's a successful suspense-filled thriller.

VHS: S29985. $19.95.

Jack Clayton, Great Britain, 1961, 99 mins.

Interrupted Journey

Richard Todd and Valerie Harper play an indecisive couple running away together. Suddenly Todd's character gets cold feet and backs out to return to his wife. Unfortunately, the train he is on with his would-be lover crashes shortly thereafter and she dies. The plot contains an even graver twist, transforming this film into a compelling murder mystery.

VHS: S24009. $24.95.

Daniel Birt, Great Britain, 1949, 82 mins.

The Iron Duke

Not a statue of John Wayne but the historical film biography of the Duke of Wellington, Arthur Wellesley, who defeated Napoleon's army at Waterloo. The film deals with the years 1815-16 and stars George Arliss as the Iron Duke. With Gladys Cooper, Emlyn Williams, Franklin Dyall and Ellaline Terriss as Duchess Kitty. B&W.

VHS: S07072. $39.95.

Victor Saville, Great Britain, 1935, 80 mins.

Isadora

A terrific portrait of the eccentric, tempestuous American dancer who lived by her own rules, featuring an exceptional performance by Vanessa Redgrave, and co-starring Jason Robards and James Fox as Isadora's famous lovers.

VHS: S00638. $29.95.

Karel Reisz, Great Britain, 1969, 168 mins.

Jason and the Argonauts

Special effects wizard Ray Harryhausen provided the effects for this mythological adventure, which stars Todd Armstrong as the sailor and explorer who returns to the kingdom of Thessaly after a 20-year voyage, to make his rightful claim to the throne, but who must first find the magical fleece. Bernard Herrmann wrote the score.

VHS: S08522. $14.95.

Laser: CAV. LD71557. $99.95.

Don Chaffey, Great Britain, 1963, 104 mins.

Java Head

Gerrit, the son of a fair-minded seafaring man, is driven from the community by the stern family of the girl he wants to marry, and he's forced to set off on a long sea voyage. With Anna May Wong, Ralph Richardson.

VHS: S09232. $29.95.

J. Walter Ruben, Great Britain, 1934, 82 mins.

Journey for Margaret
A heartbreaking tale about orphaned children trying to survive in a ravaged, bombed out London, based on W.L. White's book as an American correspondent. Robert Young is an American journalist whose life is caught in the crossfire. With Laraine Day, Fay Bainter and Nigel Bruce).
VHS: S17338. $19.98.
W.S. Van Dyke, Great Britain, 1942, 81 mins.

Journey Together
Richard Attenborough and Edward G. Robinson star in this realistic portrayal of American fliers in England during World War II.
VHS: S09532. $29.95.
John Boulting, Great Britain, 1946, 80 mins.

The Jungle Book (Sabu)
Sabu stars as the boy who grew up among the animals and learned to speak their languages in this film based on Rudyard Kipling's tales.
VHS: S01900. $19.95.
Zoltan Korda, USA, 1942, 109 mins.

Khartoum
Charlton Heston vs. Laurence Olivier. Chuck plays British General Charles "Chinese" Gordon. Lord Larry is the Mahdi, the leader of thousands of angry Sudanese tribesmen who would like to remove the colonial influence from their little town. The epic 317 day siege, set in 1885, is well told, with a cast of thousands, some of which include Nigel Green, Alexander Knox, Johnny Sekka and Ralph Richardson as Mr. Gladstone. Narration provided by Leo Genn.
VHS: S12531. $19.98.
Basil Dearden, Great Britain, 1966, 134 mins.

A Kid for Two Farthings
Never underestimate the power of a child's imagination, especially if it's the charming Jonathan Ashmore, who plays Joe in this heartwarming sentimental fantasy from England—the story of a young boy who is convinced that through the powers of a unicorn he can grant the wishes of his mother and friends, who live in a poor part of London.
VHS: S14695. $29.95.
Carol Reed, Great Britain, 1955, 96 mins.

King and Country
In this reworking of *The Servant* as a war story, Tom Courtenay stars as a young, working-class, World War II deserter who is court-martialed, found wanting, and shot. Dirk Bogarde is the liberal middle-class officer assigned to defend him at his court-martial.
VHS: S30663. $39.95.
Joseph Losey, Great Britain, 1964, 86 mins.

King Solomon's Mines
The original exciting adventure adapted from H. Rider Haggard's famous story of the search for legendary diamond mines in the heart of Africa. Paul Robeson, Cedric Hardwicke and Roland Young star.
VHS: S00682. $39.95.
Robert Stevenson, Great Britain, 1937, 80 mins.

The King's Rhapsody
And exiled king leaves his lover in order to return home to a cold, politically arranged marriage. A classic treatment of the love versus duty theme starring the incomparable Errol Flynn.
VHS: S14658. $29.95.
Herbert Wilcox, Great Britain, 1955, 93 mins.

Lady in Distress
Also known as *A Window in London*, the intriguing story of a struggling couple who get caught up in an entertaining murder drama. Paul Lukas, Sally Gray and Michael Redgrave star.
VHS: S05383. $24.95.
Herbert Mason, Great Britain, 1939, 59 mins.

Land of Fury
Jack Hawkins, Glynis Johns and Noel Purcell are confronted with the beauty and dangers of pioneer life in the wilds of New Zealand. The land and the people who have always lived there, the Native Maoris, offer stiff resistance to the settlers' dreams.
VHS: S23896. $29.95.
Ken Annakin, Great Britain, 1954, 82 mins.

Last Days of Dolwyn
A dowager is called upon for help when her Welsh village is slated for extinction as part of a reservoir project. Richard Burtons's first film.
VHS: S14657. $29.95.
Emlyn Williams, Great Britain, 1949, 95 mins.

Last Holiday
Alec Guiness portrays a shy and friendless man who learns he has a fatal illness and vows to enjoy his final days to the fullest. He quits his job, withdraws his savings from the bank, and sets off for a fashionable seaside resort where his life takes an unexpected turn.
VHS: S16593. $39.95.
Henry Cass, Great Britain, 1950, 88 mins.

The Last Reunion
Members of a British bomber crew meet each year at the last request of their dying captain. Eric Portman and Michael Gough lead a fine cast in this eerie, atmospheric ghost story.
VHS: S04068. $29.95.
Leonard Brett, Great Britain, 1955

Late Extra
James Mason's first movie. Alastair Sim, Michael Wilding and Clifford McLaglen also star in this 1935 newspaper drama. Fine acting and tight direction.
VHS: S07397. $29.95.
Albert Parker, Great Britain, 1935, 69 mins.

League of Gentlemen
Eight former soldiers find themselves desperately in need now that the war is over. When they get together it's not to reminisce but to hatch a plan more in keeping with their shady leanings. Robbing a bank seems the perfect solution.
VHS: S14696. $39.95.
Laser: Widescreen. **LD76053. $49.95.**
Basil Dearden, Great Britain, 1960, 115 mins.

The Legend of the Seven Golden Vampires
Professor Van Helsing (Peter Cushing) and Count Dracula (John Forbes-Robinson) meet again in this kung-fu horror spectacular set in the village of Ping Kuei. After learning about the Seven Golden Vampires of the village, Van Hesling, his son, and three guides set out to free the village from the curse of Count Dracula.
VHS: S34421. $14.98.
Roy Ward Baker, Great Britain, 1974, 164 mins.

Let's Make Up
A film that combines gritty naturalism with epic spectacle. Set during the London Blitz, a young actress (Anna Neagle) is knocked unconscious during an air raid. She imagines herself as Nell Gwyn, Queen Victoria and her mother. But when she awakens, Neagle must confront the realities of her marriage to a mediocre vaudevillian (Errol Flynn). With Peter Graves, David Farrar and Kathleen Harrison. Alternate title is *Lilacs of the Spring*.
VHS: S19866. $29.95.
Herbert Wilcox, Great Britain, 1954, 94 mins.

The Lion in Winter
Peter O'Toole and Katharine Hepburn star in this costume drama concerning royal succession at the English court of Henry II. Based on the successful play, this sumptuous screen version is now transferred to video in a letterbox format, to capture its stunning visual impact, on the occasion of its 25th anniversary.
Laser: LD72304. $49.95.
Anthony Harvey, Great Britain, 1968, 134 mins.

The Living Dead
George Curzon devises a scheme to murder heavily insured people and then bring them back to life. Gerald Du Maurier, the inspector from the Yard, is baffled. Leslie Perrins, his potential son-in-law and a doctor working for the insurance company, helps find the solution.
VHS: S04056. $29.95.
Thomas Bentley, Great Britain, 1936, 63 mins.

Lloyd's of London
A young messenger boy (Freddie Bartholomew) grows up to rise in the ranks of a British insurance company, thanks to his friendship with lifelong buddy Lord Horatio Nelson (John Burton). With George Sanders and Madeleine Carroll. "If you wonder how the story of a British insurance company can be exciting, just watch this lavish spectacle" *(VideoHound's Golden Movie Retriever)*.
VHS: S28481. $19.98.
Henry King, Great Britain, 1936, 115 mins.

Loneliness of the Long Distance Runner
The engrossing story of a rebellious young man chosen to represent his reform school in a track race. A superbly acted film, it also confronts the rigidity of society's mores and institutions. This is a key British film from the 60s directed by Tony Richardson. Starring Tom Courtenay and Michael Redgrave.
VHS: S15359. $19.98.
Laser: LD71675. $34.98.
Tony Richardson, Great Britain, 1962, 103 mins.

Long Haul
Victor Mature stars as an honest American veteran trying to support his English wife in postwar Liverpool. When he stops a phony robbery, he loses his trucking job and falls in with a bad crowd. Not only is he now on the wrong side of the law, he is also on the wrong side of the road. With Gene Anderson, Patrick Allen and British bombshell Diana Dors.
VHS: S15896. $19.95.
Ken Hughes, Great Britain, 1957, 100 mins.

The Long Ships
Viking Rolfe (Richard Widmark), shipwrecked during a raid on the Barbary Coast, learns of a legendary gold bell made many years ago by monks. He is tortured by Islamic ruler Aly Mansuh (Sidney Poitier), who is obsessed with finding the bell. Rolfe escapes and returns home and steals King Harald's (Clifford Evans) ship to search for the bell, but is pursued by King Harald and again captured by the Moors.
VHS: S34114. $19.95.
Jack Cardiff, Great Britain/Yugoslavia, 1963, 124 mins.

Lord Jim
Lavish adaptation of Joseph Conrad's novel, the existential tale of a seaman in the Far East. With Peter O'Toole, Eli Wallach, James Mason.
VHS: S01711. $19.95.
Laser: Widescreen. **LD75903. $39.95.**
Richard Brooks, Great Britain, 1965, 154 mins.

Lord of the Flies
Peter Brook's classic adaptation of William Golding's novel about a group of English schoolboys stranded on a desolate island in the aftermath of a nuclear holocaust. Tensions and warfare break out over class grievances and social distinctions. Shot on location in Puerto Rico with nonprofessional actors, Brook images the work as a neo-realistic documentary. With James Aubrey, Tom Chapin and Hugh Edwards.
VHS: S18755. $29.95.
Laser: CLV. **LD72099. $49.95.**
Peter Brook, Great Britain, 1963, 91 mins.

Lorna Doone
Victoria Hopper, John Loder and Margaret Lockwood are featured in this tale of love set in rural Exmoor. An English farmer falls in love with the daughter of outlaws. Their passion places two very different families into conflict.
VHS: S25700. $19.95.
Basil Dean, Great Britain, 1934, 90 mins.

The Lost Continent
The nightmare begins when Captain Lansen (Eric Porter) attempts to transport illegal explosives and a motley group of passengers on a rusty tramp steamer that becomes stranded in the vast floating swamp of the mysterious Sargasso Sea. Under cover of night, the terrified travelers encounter unspeakable monsters, man-eating seaweed, vicious mutant pirates and stupendously endowed women. A Hammer Films classic.
VHS: S32497. $14.98.
Laser: Letterboxed. **LD76437. $39.95.**
Michael Carreras, Great Britain, 1968, 97 mins.

Love from a Stranger
Basil Rathbone plays a smooth, murdering conman who romances a vacationing American lottery winner to the altar. Ann Harding plays the unsuspecting damsel in distress who learns from a stranger that her hubby is a Bluebeard. Based on Agatha Christie's short story *Philomel Cottage*. A tension-filled game of nerves turns into a deadly game of who's got the poisoned coffee? With Jean Cadell and Bruce Seton. Remade in 1947.
VHS: S09134. $29.95.
Rowland V. Lee, Great Britain, 1937, 86 mins.

Love on the Dole
Deborah Kerr and Clifford Evans star in this story of a British slum family during the Great Depression of the 30s. Based on the novel and play by Walter Greenwood.
VHS: S09531. $29.95.
John Baxter, Great Britain, 1941, 89 mins.

The Magic Bow
Stewart Granger stars along with Phyllis Calvert, Cecil Parker and Dennis Price in this biographical film about the youthful violinist and composer Paganini. Roland Pertwee and Norman Ginsbury wrote the screenplay while Yehudi Menuhin provides the violin solos.
VHS: S23897. $14.98.
Bernard Knowles, Great Britain, 1946, 106 mins.

Malta Story
Alec Guinness and Jack Hawkins star in this unique combination of actual wartime footage and reenacted material. The subject is the heroic efforts of the Allied Forces to protect the tiny island of Malta in the Mediterranean.
VHS: S26958. $14.98.
Brian Desmond Hurst, Great Britain, 1953, 98 mins.

A Man for All Seasons
Literate, penetrating treatment of the conflict between Thomas More (Paul Scofield) and King Henry VIII (Robert Shaw). Director Zinnemann concentrates on characterization rather than spectacle with superior results. With Orson Welles, Susannah York and Vanessa Redgrave.
VHS: S02639. $19.95.
Laser: Widescreen. **LD75496. $44.95.**
Fred Zinnemann, Great Britain, 1966, 120 mins.

Man Who Could Work Miracles
An enjoyable and imaginative fantasy scripted by H.G. Wells, starring Roland Young as a recipient of a gift of great powers given by a bored group of aliens who decide to give the power to work miracles to an ordinary fellow to see what happens.
VHS: Out of print. For rental only.
Laser: LD75226. $34.98.
Lothar Mendes, Great Britain, 1937, 82 mins.

The Man Who Haunted Himself
The ordered life of a conservative businessman (Roger Moore) is shattered when he finds his every move shadowed by a mysterious, sinister doppelganger, in this psychological thriller. 90 mins.
VHS: S31023. $14.98.
Basil Dearden, Great Britain, 1970, 94 mins.

The Man Who Never Was
Clifton Webb, Gloria Grahame and Robert Flemyng star in this true and intriguing account of World War II espionage in which the British were able to dupe the Germans into believing that a Mediterranean invasion would take place in Greece instead of Sicily.
VHS: S14135. $19.98.
Ronald Neame, Great Britain, 1955, 102 mins.

Mayerling
Omar Sharif and Catherine Deneuve are doomed to a tragic love affair that ends at Mayerling. It is based on the true story of the Austro-Hungarian Crown Prince Rudolph and his lover, Maria Vetsera. This intriguing costume drama captures the romance and despair of two young people who were certain to gain everything but each other. James Mason and Ava Gardner portray the Emperor Franz Josef and the Empress Elizabeth.
VHS: S28050. $19.98.
Terence Young, Great Britain, 1968, 140 mins.

The Mill on the Floss
James Mason stars in this adaptation of George Eliot's novel of the scandal that erupts when a young woman spends the night with an engaged man.
VHS: S00856. $19.95.
Tim Whelan, Great Britain, 1936, 80 mins.

Millions Like Us
Patricia Roc, Moore Marriot and Eric Portman are featured in this drama about the impact of war on a family. The title is especially evocative of a situation common in World War II. Even as the hardships piled up at home, everyone was forced to concentrate on the problems afflicting millions more.
VHS: S23806. $24.95.
Sidney Gilliat, Great Britain, 1943, 103 mins.

Mimi
A liberal adaptation of Puccini's *La Boheme*, set in Paris' Latin Quarter, with Gertrude Lawrence as the heroine. Douglas Fairbanks Jr. is the dashing hero. Puccini's melodies are presented in synchronized accompaniment and heard throughout this romantic drama.
VHS: S14642. $29.95.
Paul L. Stein, Great Britain, 1935, 98 mins.

Mine Own Executioner
Burgess Meredith and Kieron Moore star in this tense psychological thriller. An ex-POW is haunted by fears and obsessions that could have deadly consequences. Either the psychiatrist can cure this man or he will kill someone.
VHS: S25016. $19.95.
Anthony Kimmins, Great Britain, 1947, 103 mins.

Moonlight Sonata
Featured appearance by one of the most famous concert pianists of the day, Ignace Jan Paderewski, in this romance set in the household of a Swedish baroness.
VHS: S03752. $34.95.
Lothar Mendes, Great Britain, 1938, 80 mins.

Moonraker
The year is 1651. George Baker and Sylvia Syms star in this historical drama concerning the escape of Charles Stuart during the time of Oliver Cromwell and his "Roundhead" followers. Based on Arthur Watkyn's play.
VHS: S23899. $29.95.
David MacDonald, Great Britain, 1957, 82 mins.

Murder Ahoy
In this Agatha Christie classic Miss Marple investigates a series of murders aboard a naval cadet training ship. With Margaret Rutherford, Lionel Jeffries, and Stringer Davis.
VHS: S13761. $19.98.
George Pollock, Great Britain, 1964, 74 mins.

Mutiny of the Elsinore
An intrepid reporter boards a ship in search of a story and he gets more than he could possibly have hoped for. Mutiny soon turns this trip into an adventure in which there's little room for objectivity. Starring Paul Lukas and Lyn Harding.
VHS: S21564. $24.95.
Roy Lockwood, Great Britain, 1937, 79 mins.

The Mysterious Island
A rousing adventure adapted from Jules Verne's sequel to *20,000 Leagues under the Sea*. The film charts the strange experiences of a group of escaped Union soldiers marooned on a fantastic island populated by outsized animals. With Michael Craig, Joan Greenwood, Michael Callan and Herbert Lom as Captain Nemo. Special visual effects by Ray Harryhausen.
VHS: S18605. $14.95.
Cy Endfield, Great Britain, 1961, 101 mins.

The Nanny
Bette Davis fans will love this taut thriller featuring Davis as a nanny with a murderous bent. A young boy has been accused of drowning his sister, but he insists he is innocent. As he makes his suspicions about the nanny public, murderous schemes develop. This film has terrific suspense and an overall macabre atmosphere.
VHS: S27438. $19.98.
Seth Holt, Great Britain, 1965, 93 mins.

Never Too Late to Mend
Tod Slaughter, the horror man of Europe, plays Squire Meadows, a good church goer and a very strict prison administrator. Based on Charles Reade's 1856 novel about the abominable conditions in English prisons that led Queen Victoria to start penal reforms. With Marjorie Taylor and Jack Livesay. B&W.
VHS: S04042. $29.95.
David MacDonald, Great Britain, 1937

The Night Has Eyes (Terror House)
James Mason stars as a moody music composer living a reclusive life on the Yorkshire Moors. His solitude is interrupted by a curious young woman (Joyce Howard) who suspects Mason of murdering her best friend a year before. Naturally, they fall in love and solve the mystery. B&W.
VHS: S04063. $29.95.
Leslie Arliss, Great Britain, 1942, 79 mins.

Night of the Generals
A World War II whodunit. As Germany is battling on two fronts for world domination, Omar Sharif is ordered to conduct an investigation into the allegation that one of the Fuehrer's finest officers might be a murdering sex criminal. The irony of the situation is fully explored. Suspects include Peter O'Toole, Tom Courtenay, Donald Pleasance, Christopher Plummer and John Gregson.
VHS: S10383. $19.95.
Anatole Litvak, Great Britain, 1967, 148 mins.

A Night to Remember
The maiden voyage of the Titanic is meticulously detailed in this remarkable black and white recreation. Based on the best seller by Walter Lord. Great special effects. A memorable ensemble including Kenneth More, Honor Blackman, David McCallum, George Rose and Laurence Naismith as the Captain.
VHS: S06231. $14.98.
Laser: LD74946. $99.95.
DVD: DV60176. $39.95.
Roy Ward Baker, Great Britain, 1958, 123 mins.

Night Train to Munich
British filmmaker Carol Reed's adaptation of Gordon Wellesley's novel *Report on a Fugitive* is a comic suspense thriller about a British intelligence officer (Rex Harrison) who impersonates a Nazi in order to rescue a Czech inventor and scientist who is being detained in Berlin. With Margaret Lockwood, Basil Radford, Naunton Wayne and Paul Henreid.
VHS: S19870. $24.95.
Laser: LD74932. $39.95.
Carol Reed, Great Britain, 1940, 93 mins.

Nightmare
A young woman continually relives the childhood terror of her insane mother stabbing her father to death, in her dreams. At her guardian's home, everything appears normal by day, but come nightfall this past event haunts her. Perhaps the startling vividness of this nightmare is due to more than mere memory. With David Knight, Moira Redmond, Jennie Linden and Brenda Bruce.
VHS: S25570. $14.98.
Freddie Francis, Great Britain, 1963, 83 mins.

Non Stop—New York
Anna Lee and John Loder star in this complex and fascinating 1937 mystery which uses a trans-Atlantic air plane ride in a climactic escape from England, three years before such flights existed. Wonderful, tongue-in-cheek mystery about a woman who can provide an alibi for an innocent man who stands accused of murder, but no one will believe her.
VHS: S07399. $29.95.
Robert Stevenson, Great Britain, 1937, 71 mins.

Norman Conquest
Tom Conway, Eva Bartok, Joy Shelton and Ian Fleming are cast in this elaborately plotted thriller. A famed private eye finds himself unwittingly framed by a blond bombshell in a hotel room. Scotland Yard doesn't believe it, even though there is a Nazi smuggler afoot.
VHS: S24017. $24.95.
Bernard Knowles, Great Britain, 1953, 78 mins.

The October Man
John Mills and Joan Greenwood are paired in this psychological whodunit. A man finds himself trapped in a deep depression brought on by a head injury. Before he can recover, he is suspected of murdering a girl.
VHS: S25708. $19.95.
Roy Ward Baker, Great Britain, 1948, 91 mins.

Odd Man Out
James Mason is Johnny McQueen, a wounded Irish revolutionary on the run in an unnamed northern Irish city. A classic thriller from filmmaker Carol Reed and an artistic exploration of lower class Gaelic life. The memorable cast includes Robert Newton, Kathleen Ryan, Cyril Cusack and Dan O'Herlihy.
VHS: Out of print. For rental only.
Laser: LD75376. $49.98.
Carol Reed, Great Britain, 1947, 113 mins.

Oh, Mr. Porter!
A stationmaster renovates an obscure railway post. There's trouble when a special train to transport the local soccer team is hijacked by gun runners. With Will Hay, Moore Marriott, and Frederick Piper.
VHS: S34500. $24.95.
Marcel Varnel, Great Britain, 1937, 85 mins.

Oscar Wilde
Robert Morley, Ralph Richardson and John Neville star in this recreation of the trial where the great Irish-born author was officially disgraced because he desired his own sex. Morley plays Wilde.
VHS: S23807. $24.95.
Gregory Ratoff, Great Britain, 1959, 96 mins.

The Outsider
George Sanders is a young medical scientist whose only medical background comes from his study of cattle at the Chicago Stockyards. When he devises a treatment to cure crippled patients, his advances are ignored by a doctors' committee until he cures the daughter of one of the doctors—and falls in love with her. With Mary Maguire, Barbara Blair and Peter Murray Hill.
VHS: S32945. $19.95.
Paul L. Stein, Great Britain, 1940, 90 mins.

Paranoiac
Oliver Reed and Janette Scott *(The Day of the Triffids)* star in this murky thriller from Hammer Films. A young heiress is dramatically saved from suicide by a man who claims to be her long lost brother. The two quickly bond, but the woman's other brother, a cruel sadist, remains skeptical, presuming that this newcomer is probably only interested in the vast family fortune. With Sheila Burrell, Alexander Davion and Liliane Brousse.
VHS: S25571. $14.98.
Freddie Francis, Great Britain, 1962, 80 mins.

Passing of the Third Floor Back

A wonderful, ultra-rare, British fantasy. The setting is an old boarding house filled with a variety of people, all with different problems. They're lorded over by an evil, mephisto-like slum lord. The tenants are changed forever by the arrival of a Christ-like stranger who aids them with their problems. A well-thought-out and meaningful storyline looks at many of the good and bad aspects of life. Veidt turns in a strong performance as the mysterious stranger in this top-notch British Gaumont production.

VHS: S12327. $29.95.
Berthold Viertel, Great Britain, 1935, 90 mins.

Personal Affair

Gene Tierney, Leo Genn and Glynis Johns star in this drama about an apparently harmless school girl infatuation. A popular high school teacher ignores the advances of a student, but her sudden disappearance sows suspicion around the helpless teacher. As he struggles to clear his name and save his marriage, passions of all sorts rage out of control.

VHS: S27907. $14.98.
Anthony Plissier, Great Britain, 1953, 119 mins.

Petulia

Julie Christie is the title character in this film about the idle rich in San Francisco in the mid-60's. She's a lovely kook who is very attracted to a prominent doctor, played by George C. Scott. A terrific film. With Richard Chamberlain, Shirley Knight and Joseph Cotten.

VHS: S06102. $19.98.
Richard Lester, Great Britain, 1968, 105 mins.

Phantom Fiend

A remake of Alfred Hitchcock's silent classic *The Lodger*, with Ivor Novello recreating his role as a lodger suspected of being Jack the Ripper. England, 70 mins.

VHS: S14675. $29.95.
Maurice Elvey, Great Britain, 1932, 85 mins.

Phantom Ship (Mystery of the Mary Celeste)

Bela Lugosi plays a one-armed seaman with homicidal tendencies who books passage on the ill-fated American sailing vessel *Mary Celeste*. This speculative tale of murder and mayhem was the second production of the newly formed English film company, Hammer Films.

VHS: S03337. $29.95.
Denison Clift, Great Britain, 1935, 80 mins.

The Pickwick Papers

A classic adaptation of Charles Dickens' masterpiece about the members of a fictional English social club, the Pickwick Club, featuring a distinguished English cast including James Hayter, Nigel Patrick.

VHS: S05221. $19.95.
Noel Langley, Great Britain, 1952, 109 mins.

Pimpernel Smith

On the eve of World War II, the most prominent artists and intellectuals are escaping from Germany, aided by a mysterious man who comes out of the shadows, performs his daring and clever rescues, and then vanishes. Filled with many twists, this enjoyable update of the Scarlet Pimpernel character features a charming performance by Leslie Howard.

VHS: S04347. $29.95.
Leslie Howard, Great Britain, 1941, 120 mins.

Police Dog

Joan Rice and Tim Turner star in this film about police dogs. These well-trained but tenaciously brutal working animals are instrumental in helping to catch criminals.

VHS: S27902. $19.98.
Derek Twist, Great Britain, 1955, 68 mins.

The Prime Minister

John Gielgud portrays Disraeli, the great British Prime Minister from Victorian times. Despite a lifetime of political successes, he suffered through many personal instances of turmoil and grief. Diana Wynyard and Owen Nares also star.

VHS: S23808. $24.95.
Thorold Dickinson, Great Britain, 1941, 109 mins.

The Prime of Miss Jean Brodie

Maggie Smith, in her Oscar-winning performance, is top-notch as the unconventional, eccentric teacher in an all-girls school in Edinburgh during the 1930s. Miss Brodie's students, the "creme de la creme," adore their teacher, but when they try to shape their lives after Miss Brodie's, disaster ensues. Based on Muriel Spark's novel.

VHS: S10746. $19.98.
Ronald Neame, Great Britain, 1969, 116 mins.

The Prisoner

The original movie-length version of what later became the famous television series. Alec Guinness and Jack Hawkins give superb performances, with Guinness as a cardinal who is arrested and mentally tortured into making a phony confession.

VHS: S09394. $69.95.
Peter Glenville, Great Britain, 1955, 91 mins.

The Prisoner of Corbal

Nils Asther, Hugh Sinclair and Hazel Terry star in this costume drama set during the French Revolution. A lovely young aristocrat escapes Paris disguised as the nephew of a citizen deputy. Corbal seems like the perfect place to hide until the young aristocratic woman is attracted to the local Marquis, forgetting the revolutionary who spirited her to safety.

VHS: S24010. $24.95.
Karl Grune, Great Britain, 1936, 72 mins.

The Private Life of Henry VIII

Charles Laughton gives a tour-de-force performance as the infamous British King Henry, a fat, strutting, arrogant, yet tender, vulnerable and loving man. Politics, statesmanship and international intrigue are just background for the lusty life of the king and his six wives. Also starring Merle Oberon, Robert Donat, and Elsa Lanchester. Digitally remastered.

VHS: S01062. $19.98.
Alexander Korda, Great Britain, 1933, 97 mins.

Private's Progress

Stanley Windrush (Ian Carmichael) must interrupt his college education when he is called to war, but is unfit for army life and passed over for a commission. Private Cox (Richard Attenborogh) fills Stanley in on all the scams in the world of the British Army, something Stanley's shady brigadier War office uncle seems acquainted with. With Terry-Thomas.

VHS: S33711. $29.99.
John Boulting, Great Britain, 1956, 102 mins.

The Pumpkin Eater

Harold Pinter wrote the script for this fabulous film based on Penelope Mortimer's novel about a woman (Anne Bancroft) whose middle-class marriage to an unfaithful screenwriter (Peter Finch) spins out of control. With a famous scene of Bancroft having a nervous breakdown in the midst of the Harrods Department Store. James Mason, Cedric Hardwicke and Maggie Smith also star.

VHS: S26447. $19.95.
Jack Clayton, Great Britain, 1964, 118 mins.

Pygmalion

Superlative version of George Bernard Shaw's play, later made as *My Fair Lady*. Leslie Howard excels as the professor, with Wendy Hiller as the Cockney-speaking pupil.

VHS: S01973. $24.95.
Laser: LD71283. $39.95.
Anthony Asquith, Great Britain, 1938, 90 mins.

Rhodes of Africa

Walter Huston, Oscar Homolka and Basil Sydney are featured in this recounting of the famed founder of the Rhodes scholarship fund. In life he was a much-feared representative of the British Empire. This film biography is based on Sarah Gertrude's novel.

VHS: S23809. $24.95.
Berthold Viertel, Great Britain, 1936, 91 mins.

The Rise of Catherine the Great

Alexander Korda returns to his themes of unrequited love and romantic shallowness in this tale of the Empress of Russia and her failing marriage to the Grand Duke (Douglas Fairbanks), while her obsession for an apparently royal madman is vanquished by society and royal indifference.

VHS: S02599. $19.98.
Laser: LD71304. $19.98.
Paul Czinner, Great Britain, 1934, 88 mins.

River of Unrest Ourselves Alone)

A wily rebel leader leads daring rescues of captured comrades and in general confounds the military might of Great Britain on his home sod of the Emerald Isle. Set before the establishment of the Irish Free State. Cast includes John Loder, John Lodge and Antoinette Cellier. B&W.

VHS: S06187. $29.95.
Brian Desmond Hurst, Great Britain, 1937, 69 mins.

Rogue Male

Peter O'Toole stars as an aristocrat with an heroic if dangerous idea: he plans to assassinate Hitler before the world is at war. Despite the failure of his plot, this man is hunted by both the Gestapo and the British police. This thrilling adventure also features Alastair Sim.

VHS: S25522. $19.95.
Clive Donner, Great Britain, 1976

The Romantic Age

Mai Zetterling stars as an art student infatuated with her teacher, who is played by Hugh Williams. This master finds himself hard pressed to resist the charms of his precocious French student.

VHS: S23789. $24.95.
Edmond T. Greville, Great Britain, 1949, 86 mins.

Room at the Top

Joe Lampton (Laurence Harvey) works in a dreary English factory town by day; at night he performs in a theatrical group. Also in the group is Joe's boss' daughter, Susan (Heather Sears), who plays the ingenue on stage and in real life and hatches a plan to get Joe, telling him he'll get ahead faster by being the boss' son-in-law. However, Joe is attracted to an older, unhappily married French woman who's also in the group (Simone Signoret), and Joe tries to get away with seeing both women. With Hermione Baddely.

VHS: S33712. $29.99.
Jack Clayton, Great Britain, 1959, 115 mins.

The Rough and the Smooth (Portrait of a Sinner)

A German nymphomaniac corrupts all that cross her path. She deftly lures an archeologist away from a newspaper heiress. Based on the Robert Maugham story. With Nadja Tiller, Tony Britton, William Bendix, and Donald Wolfit.

VHS: S34187. $19.95.
Robert Siodmak, Great Britain, 1959, 96 mins.

The Runaway Bus

A group of disgruntled passengers, among them several incognito thieves and police detectives, are stranded at the London Airport, and a relief bus driver takes them for an interesting ride. With Margaret Rutherford and Petula Clark. Written and directed by Val Guest.

VHS: S14646. $29.95.
Val Guest, Great Britain, 1954, 78 mins.

The Saint

George Sanders, Louis Hayward and Hugh Sinclair all portray Leslie Charteris' debonair detective in the original RKO film series that spawned the popular British TV series and 1997 theatrical remake with Val Kilmer. Includes introductions by Robert Osborne, host of TCM Network, exclusive star interviews, behind-the-scenes documentaries, collectable insert booklets and original theatrical trailers and lobby card art.

The Saint Volume I: Film Series 1938-1939. Includes *The Saint in New York* with Louis Hayward as the Saint and *The Saint Strikes Back* with George Sanders in the title role.

VHS: S30977. $19.98.

The Saint Volume II: Film Series 1939-1940. Includes *The Saint in London* and *The Saint's Double Trouble* with George Sanders.

VHS: S30978. $19.98.

The Saint Volume III: Film Series 1940-1941. Includes *The Saint Takes Over* with George Sanders and *The Saint's Vacation* with Hugh Sinclair.

VHS: S30979. $19.98.

The Saint Volume IV: Film Series 1941-1943. Includes *The Saint in Palm Springs* with George Sanders and *The Saint Meets the Tiger* with Hugh Sinclair.

VHS: S30980. $19.98.

The Satanic Rites of Dracula

Christopher Lee made his last appearance as the Count, which Lee described as "a cross between Fu Manchu and Howard Hughes" in this original uncut Hammer film. Dracula returns as the mysterious D.D. Denham, a reclusive billionaire who is never seen in daylight. Professor Van Helsing is called upon to challenge Dracula and save his granddaughter Jessica (a young and *Absolutely Fabulous* Joanna Lumley!). Includes theatrical trailers. Widescreen.

VHS: S34422. $14.98.
Alan Gibson, Great Britain, 1973, 87 mins.

Saturday Night and Sunday Morning

Angry young man Albert Finney became a star and made this British New Wave film—Reisz' first feature—a box office hit with the defiant phrase, "Don't let the bastards grind you down." Finney's brooding performance as the young Nottingham factory worker lashing out at the working class and his "dead from the neck up" parents is still fresh today. With Shirley Anne Field, Bryan Pringle, Hylda Baker, Norman Rossington, Colin Blakely and Rachel Roberts as his sad-sack mistress.

VHS: S30432. $14.98.
Laser: LD76030. $39.99.
Karel Reisz, Great Britain, 1960, 89 mins.

The Scamp (Strange Affection)
A confused young boy has been accused of murdering his abusive and drunken father and seeks the aid and consolation of a teacher. With Richard Attenborough, Colin Petersen, Jill Adams, and Terence Morgan.
VHS: S34188. $19.95.
Wolf Rilla, Great Britain, 1957, 84 mins.

Scott of the Antarctic
Dramatic rendition of the fateful British expedition to be the first to the South Pole. John Mills is Robert Falcon Scott, English explorer and naval officer, the leader of the 1910 drive, whose heroism has inspired many an English schoolboy. With Christopher Lee, Kenneth More and James Robertson Justice.
VHS: S04052. $14.98.
Charles Frend, Great Britain, 1948, 110 mins.

Scrooge
Sir Seymour Hicks stars as Ebenezer Scrooge in this charming and rather faithful adaptation of Charles Dickens' *A Christmas Carol*. The strength of this tale is in its ability to combine frightening elements like the ghosts with sincere sentiments of goodwill. B&W.
VHS: S27336. $19.95.
Henry Edwards, Great Britain, 1935, 60 mins.

Sea of Sand
Richard Attenborough stars as the commander of a key desert patrol set to sabotage Rommel's fuel supply. Their success could impact the outcome of the historic battle of El Alamein. On the way back to headquarters, their heroism is tested once again by an unforseen Nazi patrol.
VHS: S26959. $14.98.
Guy Green, Great Britain, 1958, 97 mins.

The Sea Shall Not Have Them
A tense British drama about rescuers who try to save the crew of a downed plane, which is hanging on to life by a thread on a rubber raft in the stormy North Seas. With Dirk Bogarde, Michael Redgrave.
VHS: S03720. $39.95.
Lewis Gilbert, Great Britain, 1957, 91 mins.

Seance on a Wet Afternoon
Novelist Bryan Forbes' eerie psychological thriller about a demented woman (Kim Stanley) trapped in a suffocating, childless marriage, who kidnaps a child and devises a scheme to "rescue" the child and claim the ransom. "Consistently intelligent and exciting, the film unerringly illuminates the dangerous areas between private fantasy and public madness" (British Film Institute). With Richard Attenborough, Mark Eden and Patrick Magee.
VHS: S01764. $29.95.
Bryan Forbes, Great Britain, 1964, 116 mins.

Secret Mission
James Mason appears in this early World War II thriller. Four British intelligence officers infiltrate Nazi-occupied France. Their mission is to evaluate German defenses, but their salvation is their cover as champagne merchants.
VHS: S26957. $14.98.
Harold French, Great Britain, 1942, 94 mins.

Seven Sinners (Doomed Cargo)
Also known as *Doomed Cargo*, this comedy-suspense is reminiscent of Alfred Hitchcock, and in particular, *The 39 Steps*. The film stars Edmund Lowe and Constance Cummings, in the story of gunrunners who wreck trains in order to cover up the traces of murder.
VHS: S06856. $14.98.
Michael Balcon, Great Britain, 1936, 70 mins.

Seven Years in Tibet
The film upon which the Brad Pitt Hollywood movie was based has been rediscovered. In this semi-documentary drama, Heinrich Hanner reenacts his escape from a P.O.W. camp and his journey into the Himalayas. The film presents the actual color footage Hanner shot of the Forbidden City, its amazing architecture and pageantry and the Dalai Lama himself as he and his people prepare for the Chinese invasion.
VHS: S34308. $24.95.
Hans Neiter, Great Britain, 1957, 76 mins.

The Seventh Veil
The line between music and madness is thin for the talented concert pianist whose abused childhood created a phobia that threatened her art, love and life in this superb psychological drama that won an Oscar for best screenplay. Features terrific performances from Ann Todd and James Mason. One of the best British films of the '40s.
VHS: S06428. $14.98.
Laser: LD76132. $39.99.
Compton Bennett, Great Britain, 1945, 95 mins.

The Shadow
A super-rare old dark house thriller. A mysterious figure in black, known only as the shadow, is responsible for a series of blackmailings and cold-blooded murders. The only clue to his identity is a strange oriental gem found in the hand of a dead police inspector. Terrific British chiller. With Henry Kendal, Elizabeth Allan, Sam Livesey.
VHS: S10001. $29.95.
George Cooper, Great Britain, 1936, 63 mins.

Shatter
In the bustling international port of Hong Kong, Shatter (Stuart Whitman), a tough American assassin, gets tricked into accepting an assignment that turns out to be a deadly trap set by an international drug cartel. Shatter is wanted by British Agent Rattwood (Peter Cushing) and the drug syndicate boss (Anton Diffring) for the drug smuggling info he possesses. Teamed with a martial arts instructor (Kung Fu star Ti-Lung), Shatter battles the drug syndicate goons. Letterboxed.
VHS: S34423. $14.98.
Monte Hellman/Michael Carreras, Great Britain, 1974, 90 mins.

She
Ursula Andress stars in the title role in this fantastic tale of immortal love. Three soldiers of fortune discover the legendary city of Kura, where She, a statuesque, 2000-year-old queen resides. She immediately falls in love with the leader of the three soldiers (John Richardson) and offers him a harrowing choice between a pact of eternal love or the full extent of her vengeful wrath. Peter Cushing is also featured in this Hammer Film Production.
VHS: S29502. $19.98.
Laser: LD76094. $39.98.
Robert Day, Great Britain, 1965, 107 mins.

Ships with Wings
This World War II film examines the crisis faced by a group of British naval officers who are locked in a struggle with German U-boats for strategic control in the Atlantic. With John Clements, Ann Todd, Leslie Banks and Hugh Williams.
VHS: S18934. $19.95.
Sergei Nolbandov, Great Britain, 1942, 89 mins.

Sidewalks of London
Charles Laughton puts on quite a show as a busker, or street entertainer, who takes young Vivien Leigh under his wing. Not content with small change from passersby, she dumps her mentor for the stage. With Rex Harrison, Tyrone Guthrie and Larry "Mr. Harmonica" Adler. B&W.
VHS: S05076. $29.95.
Tim Whelan, Great Britain, 1938, 84 mins.

Sleeping Car to Trieste
The terrific spy thriller set on the Orient Express stars Jean Kent, Albert Lieven, Derrick de Marney and Paul Dupuis competing in a cat-and-mouse game to find a political diary.
VHS: S31142. $14.98.
John Paddy Carstairs, Great Britain, 1948, 95 mins.

South Riding
Alexander Korda produced this superb melodrama based on Winifred Holtby's famous novel. Like many British films of the era, *South Riding* addresses social changes brought on by war and progress in England. The lives of six members of a country council are intertwined through life, love and work, with Ralph Richardson as the councilman who romances an idealistic young teacher (Edna Best).
VHS: S30753. $24.95.
Victor Saville, Great Britain, 1937, 85 mins.

Spitfire
Leslie Howard and David Niven star in this biographical story tracking the development of the famous Spitfire aircraft.
VHS: S03110. $19.98.
Laser: LD75261. $34.98.
Leslie Howard, Great Britain, 1942, 88 mins.

A Spy of Napoleon
Historical drama about the conflict between Emperor Napoleon III and Bismarck of Prussia. Featured is Richard Barthelmess, famous actor during the American silent era in his only British film.
VHS: S02246. $29.95.
Maurice Elvey, Great Britain, 1936, 101 mins.

St. Martin's Lane
Originally released as *Sidewalks of London*, Charles Laughton is the London street entertainer who picks up a waif (Vivien Leigh) and sees her go to stardom, sacrificing his love for her to do so.
VHS: S01555. $24.95.
Tim Whelan, Great Britain, 1938, 84 mins.

Stalag Luft
Stephen Fry stars in this rowdy comic adventure about a prison break at a Nazi P.O.W. camp. His character has an interesting past, 23 escapes and 23 recaptures. Despite these failures, escape is an intriguing possibility, one that could succeed if only he doesn't bungle this one last opportunity. Nicholas Lyndhurst and Geoffrey Palmer also star. 103 mins.
VHS: S24782. $24.95.

The Stars Look Down
Michael Redgrave tries to bring reform to the coal mining industry in Wales. A tough, gripping drama from the novel by A.J. Cronin. With Margaret Lockwood, Evelyn Williams and Cecil Parker. Dangerous working conditions bring real tragedy to light. B&W.
VHS: S02243. $29.95.
Carol Reed, Great Britain, 1939, 104 mins.

Stolen Hours
A stylish remake of *Dark Victory*, about a beautiful, precocious, oil heiress (Susan Hayward) whose decadent lifestyle in the English countryside takes a dramatic turn when she falls in love with a sympathetic doctor (Michael Craig). Cinematography by Harry Waxman. With Diane Baker, Edward Judd and Paul Rogers.
VHS: S19573. $19.98.
Daniel Petrie, Great Britain, 1963, 97 mins.

Sword of Lancelot
Cornel Wilde directs himself as the brave and noble Sir Lancelot in this action-packed return to the days when knights were bold. Brian Aherne is King Arthur and Jean Wallace (Mrs. Wilde) is the beautiful and bewitching Guinevere. How they carry on in Camelot and more.
VHS: S07777. $19.98.
Cornel Wilde, Great Britain, 1963, 116 mins.

A Tale of Two Cities
A richly detailed adaptation of the Charles Dickens novel of turmoil during the French Revolution. Dirk Bogarde, Donald Pleasance, Christopher Lee and Dorothy Tutin star in this epic of the storming of the Bastille, the uncountable deaths by guillotine.
VHS: S12345. $29.98.
Ralph Thomas, Great Britain, 1967, 113 mins.

Tam Lin
Ava Gardner stars as a sinister seductress who cajoles an impulsive Ian McShane into discovering that being the life of the party could have murderous consequences. With Cyrus Cusack and Sinead Cusack. With an introduction by the film's director, Roddy McDowell.
VHS: S33925. $14.98.
Roddy McDowell, Great Britain, 1971, 106 mins.

Taste of Honey
Tony Richardson's landmark British film heralded in so-called "kitchen sink realism" of British films in the 60's. Richardson adapted Shelagh Delaney's play about a young girl who gets pregnant after she leaves home, has an affair with a black sailor, and is cared for by a homosexual friend. Rita Tushingham, Robert Stephens and Dora Bryan star.
VHS: S01302. $19.95.
Tony Richardson, Great Britain, 1961, 100 mins.

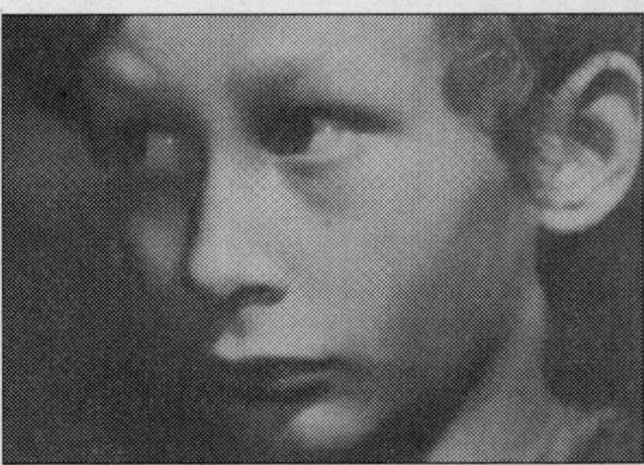

They Who Dare
Dirk Bogarde, Denholm Elliott and Akim Tamiroff portray a group of soldiers working to thwart the Germans in the Aegean. Robert Westerby wrote the screenplay for this tense and engaging wartime thriller.
VHS: S23812. $24.95.
Lewis Milestone, Great Britain, 1954, 100 mins.

The Third Key
Jack Hawkins and Geoffrey Keen star in this exciting mystery about Scotland Yard investigators. A former employee of a safe manufacturer is now a master thief, using his workaday knowledge to gain illicit booty.
VHS: S23905. $29.95.
Charles Frend, Great Britain, 1955, 94 mins.

The Third Man

Graham Greene wrote the script for Carol Reed's film about an American pulp fiction writer's search for the mysterious and enigmatic war profiteer Harry Lime (a wonderful Orson Welles) in post-war Vienna. The film welds German expressionism, British classicism and American B-movie energy and motion. Anton Karas's haunting zither score is nearly as well known as Welles's extraordinary entrance. With Joseph Cotton, Trevor Howard and Bernard Lee. Awardwinning cinematography by Robert Krasker.

VHS: S01327. $24.95.
Laser: LD71366. $39.95.
Carol Reed, Great Britain, 1949, 104 mins.

This England

John Clements and Greta Gynt are at the center of this historical feature about an enduring English village. A journalist learns about five distinct historical periods and the effects of each on this country hamlet, through the contrasting views of both landowner and laborer.

VHS: S25706. $19.95.
David MacDonald, Great Britain, 1942, 84 mins.

This Sporting Life

Richard Harris stars as Yorkshire coal miner who turns in his pick and helmet for a rugby uniform. A grueling sport is presented in an intense drama about the price of success and the meaning of love. With Rachel Roberts, Alan Badel, Colin Blakely and Arthur Lowe. B&W.

VHS: Out of print. For rental only.
Laser: Widescreen. **LD75934. $69.95.**
Lindsay Anderson, Great Britain, 1963, 129 mins.

Three Cases of Murder

One of the classic omnibus films, *Three Cases of Murder* combines a fantasy, a mystery and a psychological thriller. *In the Picture* is the story of an artist whose spirit resides in a macabre painting; in *You Killed Elizabeth*, two friends are in love with the same woman, one of whom turns up dead; and *Lord Mountdrago* features a stunning performance by Orson Welles as a statesman who is consumed with guilt over the ruin of his opponent.

VHS: S24933. $39.95.
Laser: LD75057. $49.95.
Wendy Toye/David Eady/George Moore O'Ferrall, Great Britain, 1955, 99 mins.

Three Weird Sisters

A terrific Gothic mystery combining the tension of Hitchcock with the color of Dylan Thomas, who wrote the screenplay. Set in Wales, the film concerns a younger brother who returns to his home town, summoned by his sisters, after a mine collapses. The sisters demand he pay for the repairs of the house, he refuses, and the sisters determine to eliminate him. Rich dialog by Thomas, with wonderful performances from Nancy Price, Nova Pilbeam, Raymond Lovell.

VHS: S07480. $34.95.
Daniel Birt, Great Britain, 1948, 83 mins.

Thursday's Child

Stewart Granger and Sally Ann Howes are joined in this saga about a precocious child star. The result is a disaster for the entire family of the young film actress, at least until she is sent away to boarding school.

VHS: S25701. $19.95.
Rodney Ackland, Great Britain, 1943, 95 mins.

To Sir, With Love

Sidney Poitier is Mark Thackery, a novice teacher assigned to a slum school in London's East End. Faced with tough opposition from the disinterested students and the remote school staff, he strives to teach his class what is important to really know in life. With Judy Geeson, Christian Roberts, and Lulu (who sings the title song).

VHS: S01355. $19.95.
Laser: LD75531. $34.95.
James Clavell, Great Britain, 1967, 105 mins.

Tom Brown's Schooldays

A man with revolutionary ideas becomes the headmaster of an exclusive boys' school in England.

VHS: S08364. $29.95.
Robert Stevenson, Great Britain, 1940, 81 mins.

Tomorrow We Live

John Clements and Greta Gynt star in this engaging drama set in occupied France. Villagers unite to help a spy escape the Nazis so that he can reach Britain.

VHS: S23813. $24.95.
George King, Great Britain, 1942, 85 mins.

Tony Draws a Horse

Cecil Parker and Anne Crawford star in this family-centered farce about a doctor, his wife and their free-spirited young son. While they fight over their son's expressive ability, or lack of discipline, the whole family weighs in with their unsolicited opinions. Meanwhile the boy continues to draw anatomically correct animals.

VHS: S23986. $24.95.
John Paddy Carstairs, Great Britain, 1950, 90 mins.

Tough Guy

Joan Collins stars as the girl friend of an underage hoodlum in London in this violent and controversial film. After Collins gets raped, she is driven to suicide.

VHS: S11110. $19.95.
Lewis Gilbert, Great Britain, 1953, 73 mins.

A Town Like Alice

Virginia McKenna, Peter Finch, Maureen Swanson and Vincent Ball star in this well-acted World War II story based on Nevil Shute's novel about Japanese oppression of female British POWs in Malaysia.

VHS: S27805. $19.95.
Jack Lee, Great Britain, 1956, 107 mins.

Train of Events

An ominous grouping of ghastly stories all linked by a terrible train disaster. With Valerie Hobson, John Clements and Peter Finch.

VHS: S14667. $29.95.
Basil Dearden, Great Britain, 1949, 89 mins.

Trans-Atlantic Tunnel

A favorite 1930's disaster movie as Richard Dix fights against human and natural odds to construct an undersea tunnel between Europe and America. Futuristic art deco sets and a top cast including Walter Huston as the U.S. president.

VHS: S01946. $29.95.
Maurice Elvey, Great Britain, 1935, 94 mins.

Treasure Island

Orson Welles and Walter Slezak lend their weight to this retelling of the Robert Louis Stevenson classic tale of sailors, pirates and buried treasure. Welles is great as the gamey eccentric, Long John Silver. It's a great tale for the kid in everyone.

VHS: S23103. $19.95.
John Hough, Great Britain, 1972, 94 mins.

The Trials of Oscar Wilde

Peter Finch and John Fraser star in this story based on the loving relationship between Oscar Wilde and Lord Alfred Douglas. John Furnell's *The Stringed Lute* and Montgomery Hyde's *Trials of Oscar Wilde* provide the literary sources for this intriguing film. Also known as *The Man with the Green Carnation*. With Yvonne Mitchell, Lionel Jeffries and Ian Fleming.

VHS: S26878. $24.95.
Ken Hughes, Great Britain, 1960, 123 mins.

Triple Cross

Christopher Plummer stars as the real-life safe cracker whose skills gave him a second chance. During World War II this skill was so useful that he earned the Triple Cross. Yul Brenner and Romy Schneider also star in this story of spies and betrayal.

VHS: S21012. $19.98.
Terence Young, Great Britain/France, 1967, 126 mins.

Trouble in the Glen

Orson Welles inherits some land in Scotland and does not get on very well with his new neighbors. When he closes a road, displaces some tinkers and upsets a crippled girl, they steal his cow and burn him in effigy. Forrest Tucker, as U.S. Major Lance Lansing, is asked to calm the situation. With Margaret Lockwood and Victor McLaglen. From the writer of *The Quiet Man*.

VHS: S07416. $19.98.
Herbert Wilcox, Great Britain, 1954, 91 mins.

Truth About Women

Laurence Harvey, Julie Harris, Eva Gabor and Wilfrid Hyde-White star in this British soaper about playboy Harvey's endless love affairs.

VHS: S03464. $24.95.
Muriel Box, Great Britain, 1958, 98 mins.

Tunes of Glory

Brilliant performances by Alec Guinness and John Mills as two rival colonels, one replacing the other in the Switzerland regiment. Winner of an Academy Award for Best Screenplay, this is a powerful and moving drama uncovering a clash of wills and ambition.

VHS: S01376. $29.95.
Laser: LD71380. $39.95.
Ronald Neame, Great Britain, 1960, 106 mins.

Undercover

Tom Walls and Michael Wilding star in this compelling drama about Yugoslav partisans. Brothers take different approaches to the Nazi occupation of their country, leading to tension, violence and finally even death.

VHS: S23815. $24.95.
Sergei Nolbandov, Great Britain, 1943, 80 mins.

Victim

Dirk Bogarde stars in this brooding drama with homosexual implications as a defense lawyer with a secret past. Approached by a man he suspects of blackmail, he refuses to help. Only when that same man is dead and it is made clear that he saved Bogarde from certain ruin, does the lawyer risk everything to make the senseless death mean something. Letterboxed.

VHS: S03489. $29.95.
Laser: Letterboxed. **LD76406. $49.95.**
Basil Dearden, Great Britain, 1961, 100 mins.

The VIP's

A glossy account of a group of privileged travelers and interlopers who are stranded in a London airport by fog. The characters include a flamboyant movie producer, a failed businessman, his dedicated secretary and a young woman about to run away with an aging lothario. With Elizabeth Taylor, Richard Burton, Louis Jourdan, Elsa Martinelli and Orson Welles.

VHS: S18526. $19.98.
Anthony Asquith, Great Britain, 1963, 119 mins.

The Way Ahead

David Niven, Peter Ustinov and Trevor Howard bring great intensity to this World War II drama. Seven civilians are called to serve their country. Niven must get them into shape for the grueling North African invasion.

VHS: S23956. $19.95.
Carol Reed, Great Britain, 1944, 110 mins.

We Dive at Dawn

John Mills and Eric Portman star in this first-rate World War II submarine saga. Unique for its unusually sensitive characterization of the men on the submarine.

VHS: S10581. $19.95.
Anthony Asquith, Great Britain, 1943, 98 mins.

The Weaker Sex

Ursula Jeans, Cecil Parker and Derek Bond bring realistic portrayals to this fictional account of a widow at home during the trauma of the Second World War. She manages to keep everything running even on the eve of D-Day.

VHS: S25707. $19.95.
Roy Ward Baker, Great Britain, 1949, 89 mins.

Windom's Way

Peter Finch plays an idealistic doctor stationed on a Far Eastern island that's seething with riots and political unrest, trying to encourage resistance to Communist takeover. One of Finch's most memorable and strongest performances.

VHS: S06431. $29.98.
Ronald Neame, Great Britain, 1958, 108 mins.

The Winslow Boy

Based on the play by Terrence Rattigan, a brilliantly acted courtroom drama with Robert Donat as the barrister who is defending Ronnie Winslow (Neil North) after he has been expelled from school.

VHS: S04559. $19.98.
Anthony Asquith, Great Britain, 1950, 117 mins.

The Woman in Question

Dirk Bogarde, Jean Kent and Hermione Baddeley star in this twisting murder mystery. A fortune-teller is killed, but on the fairground where she worked there are widely varying accounts detailing the nature of this dead person. This film offers a dark vision of the thoughts of a killer.

VHS: S29797. $29.95.
Anthony Asquith, Great Britain, 1950, 88 mins.

The Years Between

A poignant adaptation of Daphne du Maurier's play about a member of Parliament (Michael Redgrave) who was presumed killed in the war. He turns up unexpectedly in London and discovers his wife (Valerie Hobson) has been elected to replace him and is about to remarry. With Flora Robson, Felix Aylmer and James McKechnie.

VHS: S19878. $29.95.
Compton Bennett, Great Britain, 1946, 100 mins.

The Young Mr. Pitt

Robert Donat and Robert Morley are cast in this historical drama about the young Prime Minister who staved off the Continental forces marshalled by Napoleon. Made during World War II, it had a special resonance for the Allied forces, who were then facing a daunting Nazi threat.
VHS: S27893. $19.98.
Carol Reed, Great Britain, 1942, 115 mins.

Zulu

Michael Caine is featured in this version of British colonial troops under seige by thousands of Zulu warriors, based on a true incident from 1879.
VHS: S01740. $19.95.
Laser: Widescreen. **LD70491. $59.95.**
Cy Endfield, Great Britain, 1963, 130 mins.

DAVID LEAN

Blithe Spirit

Rex Harrison, Constance Cummings and Margaret Rutherford are brilliantly funny in this Noel Coward inspired romantic comedy about an interfering soul from beyond. When a novelist (Harrison) invites a spiritualist over for inspiration, she unexpectedly summons his deceased first wife, who then proceeds to make trouble for him and his new wife (Cummings). The special effects won an Oscar. In color.
VHS: S21995. $14.98.
David Lean, Great Britain, 1945, 96 mins.

The Bridge on the River Kwai

Epic story of British prisoners of war held by the Japanese combines psychological battles of will with gripping action. Winner of seven Oscars including Best Picture and Director. The Oscar for Screenplay went to Pierre Boulle, the novelist who spoke no English, because screenwriters Carl Foreman and Michael Wilson were blacklisted. With William Holden and Alec Guinness. Letterboxed.
VHS: S01785. $19.95.
Laser: LD72066. $49.95.
David Lean, Great Britain, 1957, 161 mins.

Doctor Zhivago

Lavish Hollywood adaptation of the epic love story set against the Russian Revolution, winner of six Academy Awards. A Russian poet and physician, who wishes to live a quiet, normal life, bears witness to a society in chaos as it struggles to bring forth a new world free from stagnation and oppression. Based on the novel by Boris Pasternak. Sweeping, majestic cinematography on a grand scale. 30th anniversary edition, with 60-minute documentary, trailer and introduction by Omar Sharif. VHS letterboxed.
VHS: S04332. $24.98.
Laser: LD70561. $49.95.
David Lean, USA/Great Britain, 1965, 176 mins.

Great Expectations

Charles Dickens' classic tale of young Pip and his rise in society is masterfully told by filmmaker David Lean. Oscars were given for cinematography and art direction. The cast includes John Mills, Alec Guinness, Marita Hunt, Jean Simmons, Valerie Hobson and Bernard Miles. B&W.
VHS: S06232. $14.95.
David Lean, Great Britain, 1946, 118 mins.

Hobson's Choice

Charles Laughton stars in this comedy as a boot shop owner whose despotic manner is challenged when his hot tempered daughter (Brenda de Banzie) decides to marry a meek boot maker played by John Mills. David Lean adapted this farce from one of Britain's most popular plays.
VHS: S02032. $29.95.
Laser: LD75382. $49.98.
David Lean, Great Britain, 1953, 107 mins.

In Which We Serve

Noel Coward stars in this World War II era drama. It follows the life on board a British destroyer as it faces the daily routine of boredom and the constant danger of Nazi U-boats.
VHS: S26960. $14.98.
Laser: LD76798. $49.95.
David Lean, Great Britain, 1942, 115 mins.

Lawrence of Arabia

Winner of seven Academy Awards, nominated by the American Film Institute as one of the top 400 American films of all time, this widescreen director's cut is presented in its original theatrical aspect ratio, brilliantly capturing the stunning beauty of the film's desert locations and honoring its Oscar-winning cinematography. Includes original theatrical trailer and historic, "making of" film short with interviews and behind-the-scenes footage. All-star cast includes Peter O'Toole, Sir Alec Guiness, Anthony Quinn, Omar Sharif, Jose Ferrer and Claude Rains.
VHS: S17926. $24.95.
David Lean, Great Britain, 1961, 228 mins.

Lawrence of Arabia (Criterion)

A labor of love by Robert A. Harris and Jim Painten and their team of restorers, who have returned nearly 35 minutes to the edited version of the David Lean epic of the exploits of T.E. Lawrence, adventurer and soldier. Peter O'Toole makes a striking impression in his first starring role. The film won seven Oscars. With Alec Guinness, Omar Sharif, Anthony Quinn and Jose Ferrer as the evil Turkish Colonel. Presented in the letterbox format which preserves the wide screen image.
Laser: CAV. **LD70413. $124.95.**
Laser: CLV. **LD70414. $69.95.**
David Lean, Great Britain, 1962, 216 mins.

Oliver Twist

There have been at least a dozen film versions of this classic tale from Charles Dickens of making the best of a bad situation. This one stars Alec Guiness as Fagin, the ruthless head of a crime school for underprivileged British riffraff. John Howard Davies is Oliver. Little Anthony Newley is his best friend Dodger. With Robert Newton, Kay Walsh and Diana Dors. B&W. A terrific film.
VHS: S06236. $19.98.
Laser: LD75410. $49.95.
David Lean, Great Britain, 1948, 116 mins.

A Passage to India

Judy Davis, Peggy Ashcroft and Victor Banerjee star in this adaptation of E.M. Forster's celebrated novel about the clash of Indian and British cultures and classes in 1920's colonial India.
VHS: S00996. $19.95.
Laser: CLV, widescreen. **LD74889. $39.95.**
David Lean, Great Britain, 1984, 163 mins.

The Passionate Friends (One Woman's Story)

Claude Rains, Trevor Howard and Ann Todd are superbly cast in this adaptation of an H.G. Wells novel. It all concerns a spurned marriage proposal. After many years the woman who married for money and not for love begins to consider her choice all over again when she meets her old beau.
VHS: S23957. $19.95.
David Lean, Great Britain, 1948, 86 mins.

Ryan's Daughter

Robert Bolt *(A Man for All Seasons, The Mission)* wrote the screenplay of this long but rewarding study by David Lean about a rich, unsatisfied, married woman (Sarah Miles) who falls for a British soldier (Christopher Jones) during British colonial rule of Ireland. Robert Mitchum is cast as Miles' British school teacher; John Mills is excellent as a crippled mute. VHS letterboxed.
VHS: S02570. $24.98.
Laser: LD70185. $59.95.
David Lean, Great Britain, 1970, 192 mins.

Summertime (Summer Madness)

Katharine Hepburn is a lonely American spinster vacationing in Venice who is swept into a mercurial romance with a charismatic though married local (Rossano Brazzi). "As an aging virgin, [Hepburn is] the archetype of a Henry James heroine grown old" (Pauline Kael). With Isa Miranda, Darren McGavin, Mari Aldon and Andre Morell.
VHS: S05632. $24.95.
Laser: LD70763. $39.95.
David Lean, Great Britain/USA, 1955, 99 mins.

This Happy Breed

David Lean's version of Noel Coward's play is a cavalcade about an ordinary family living in a suburban house over the course of several decades and generations. Filled with imaginative camera work and color, the film is both beautiful to look at and beautifully played by a winning cast. "It should be gratifying entertainment for those who put their faith in the human heart" (Bosley Crowther).
VHS: S13737. $39.95.
David Lean, Great Britain, 1944, 114 mins.

POWELL / PRESSBURGER

The 49th Parallel

Laurence Olivier heads the cast of this superior World War II movie commissioned by the Ministry of Information in 1940. When six Nazis are separated from their U-Boat in Northern Canada, it's up to the average citizens to stop them from reaching safety. With Eric Portman, Raymond Massey, Leslie Howard, Anton Walbrook and Glynis Johns. B&W.
Laser: LD70366. $39.95.
Michael Powell, Great Britain, 1941, 107 mins.

Black Narcissus

Considered one of the most beautiful films ever produced, Black Narcissus is set amidst the awesome grandeur of the Himalayas. Starring Deborah Kerr, this is a haunting emotional film about isolation, spiritual failure and sexual frustration in a convent.
VHS: S00137. $14.98.
Laser: LD70345. $79.95.
Laser: LD70347. $49.95.
Michael Powell/Emeric Pressburger, Great Britain, 1947, 100 mins.

A Canterbury Tale

A modern parallel to Chaucer's noted report is the story of the effects of that story's countryside on an American G.I. and three Britishers who find themselves en route to the hallowed cathedral on the same Pilgrims Way taken by travelers some 600 years ago. This rare Michael Powell and Emeric Pressburger film says simple, direct, unaffected and charming things about the venerated traditions of Canterbury, the English and the American Army which "invaded" the area in 1944.
VHS: S12960. $29.95.
Michael Powell/Emeric Pressburger, Great Britain, 1948, 97 mins.

Edge of the World

A fascinating early work from British stylist Michael Powell has the visual intensity and gothic romanticism of the Murnau/Flaherty masterpiece Tabu. Shot on the picturesque North Sea isle of Foula, the film centers on a torrid love affair which is disrupted by the harsh disapproval of the woman's father. "Rare for its time, this vigorous location drama in the Flaherty tradition [is]...usually exhilarating" (Leslie Halliwell). With Niall MacGinnis, Belle Chrystal, John Laurie and Finlay Currie.
VHS: S19863. $29.95.
Michael Powell, Great Britain, 1937, 80 mins.

The Elusive Pimpernel

David Niven plays Sir Percy Blakeney, the indolent dandy in London, who is also Pimpernel, the leader of a league of young men out to rescue the French aristocrats from the 1792 Terror of Paris. Based on Baroness Orczy's The Scarlet Pimpernel.
VHS: S13736. $29.95.
Michael Powell/Emeric Pressburger, Great Britain, 1950, 109 mins.

I Know Where I'm Going

A delightfully unpretentious romantic comedy about a girl who is going to marry for money and who finds her ideas challenged. She runs away and finds true love on a scenic island off the coast of Scotland. With an award-winning performance from Wendy Hiller.
VHS: S12958. $39.95.
Laser: LD76804. $69.95.
Michael Powell, Great Britain, 1946, 91 mins.

Life and Death of Colonel Blimp

From the creators of Red Shoes, this is the drastically cut version of the Powell-Pressburger classic about a pompous British officer who slowly recognizes the limitations of the Empire on the eve of World War II. As social history and satire, this is a brilliant glimpse of the rise and fall of the British monarchy-its antiquated systems personified by Clive Candy (Roger Livesey) as he moves from its imperial past (the Boer War) to its destructive future (Suez Canal, India). Deborah Kerr is excellent in three separate roles.
VHS: Out of print. For rental only.
Laser: CLV, 2 discs, Criterion. **LD70415. $69.95.**
Michael Powell/Emeric Pressburger, Great Britain, 1943, 115 mins.

The Lion Has Wings

Michael Powell was one of the three directors of Alexander Korda's documentary exploration of the political, social and military roots which occasioned the outbreak of the second World War. The film focuses on the professionalism and courage of the Royal Air Force. The other directors were Brian Desmond Hurst and Adrian Brunel. With Merle Oberon, Ralph Richardson, June Duprez, Robert Douglas, Anthony Bushell and Brian Worth.
VHS: S19867. $29.95.
Michael Powell/Brian Hurst/Adrian Brunel/Alexander Kord, Great Britain, 1939, 76 mins.

One of Our Aircraft Is Missing

Excellent war melodrama in which the crew of a downed bomber tries to get back to England from its landing place in Holland. From the director of Peeping Tom and Black Narcissus.
VHS: S02590. $39.95.
Michael Powell, Great Britain, 1941, 106 mins.

Peeping Tom
From the director of Red Shoes and Black Narcissus, a classic psychological study of a voyeuristic maniac who murders women while filming them with his 16mm camera. A riveting film in the tradition of Hitchcock. Rarely seen; recommended.
VHS: S01006. $29.95.
Laser: LD72275. $49.95.
Michael Powell, Great Britain, 1960, 88 mins.

Red Shoes
Michael Powell and Emeric Pressburger's classic, beautiful film about a young ballerina (Moira Shearer) and the young composer (Marius Goring) who are taken under the wing of impressario Anton Walbrook.
VHS: S01655. $14.98.
Michael Powell/Emeric Pressburger, Great Britain, 1948, 133 mins.

The Small Back Room
The mature and powerful story of crippled munitions expert David Farrar, who is frustrated by his infirmity and the mindless government bureaucracy he must repeatedly contend with during World War II.
VHS: S14529. $39.95.
Michael Powell/Emeric Pressburger, Great Britain, 1949, 106 mins.

Stairway to Heaven
Returning home from a bombing mission over Germany, RAF squadron leader Peter Carter (David Niven) survives a jump from his burning plane without a parachute. Due to the incompetence of an angel (Marius Goring), Carter escapes his appointment with death, which causes great consternation in Heaven. To further complicate matters, Carter falls in love with an American radio operator (Kim Hunter). With Raymond Massey.
VHS: S32201. $19.95.
Michael Powell/Emeric Pressburger, Great Britain, 1946, 104 mins.

Tales of Hoffman
Michael Powell and Emeric Pressburger's splendid tale of a poet's amorous adventures. Offenbach's magnificent score and impressive dancing by Moira Shearer and others highlight the pursuit of three women: Olympia is a puppet passed off as a real woman to Hoffman, who sees her torn to pieces before his eyes; a Venetian courtesan, Giulietta, captures Hoffman's mirror image, and his soul; a beautiful singer must remain silent lest she suffer the fate of her mother, who died of consumption.
VHS: S16211. $39.95.
Laser: 2 discs: CAV/CLV. LD71523. $99.95.
Michael Powell, Great Britain, 1951, 124 mins.

BRITISH COMEDY

Adventures of Sadie
In this hilarious British satire, three love-hungry men are shipwrecked on a deserted island with a very young and voluptuous Joan Collins. Originally titled *Our Girl Friday*, this film is adapted from a novel by Ernest K. Gann. With George Cole, Kenneth More, Robertson Hare and Hattie Jacques.
VHS: S16225. $19.95.
Noel Langley, Great Britain, 1955, 88 mins.

Alfie
Michael Caine stars as Alfie, a wonderfully shallow womanizer who is desperately trying to figure out what life is all about, in this five-time Oscar nominee satirizing the new British generation.
VHS: S00028. $14.95.
Laser: Letterboxed. **LD76037. $39.98.**
Lewis Gilbert, Great Britain, 1965, 99 mins.

Amazing Adventure
Cary Grant inherits two million pounds sterling (English money) but wagers he can live on what he earns by his own toil. Poor guy is suffering from underwork. Employment among the 1937 masses teaches valuable lessons and he meets a nice girl. With Mary Brian.
VHS: S05062. $29.95.
Alfred Zeisler, Great Britain, 1937, 61 mins.

The Amorous Adventures of Moll Flanders
Kim Novak is an ambitious servant girl who loses her virtue to a succession of rich gentlemen, but finally settles for a highwayman. A fine cast romps through 18th century England from bedroom to boudoir, including former Novak spouse Richard Johnson, in this adaptation of the Daniel Defoe novel.
VHS: S16623. $19.95.
Terence Young, Great Britain, 1965, 126 mins.

Antonia and Jane
Imelda Staunton and Saskia Reeves star as two grown women who unknowingly envy the lives of each other, in this charming English comedy. With Billy Nighy, Brenda Bruce and Richard Hope.
VHS: S16857. $89.95.
Laser: LD75147. $34.98.
Beeban Kidron, Great Britain, 1990, 75 mins.

August
In this hilarious love story based on the Chekhov classic *Uncle Vanya*, Anthony Hopkins stars as Ieuan, a country gentleman who is unsettled by some startling news. His ex-brother-in-law hopes to sell the family estate where he and the rest of the idiosyncratic household traditionally summer. The new wife of the ex-brother-in-law throws a twist into these proceedings, however, as Ieuan falls madly in love with her.
VHS: S29782. $99.99.
Laser: LD75915. $39.99.
Anthony Hopkins, Great Britain, 1995, 99 mins.

Bachelor of Hearts
Hardy Kruger is a German exchange student at Cambridge with Sylvia Syms and Ronald Lewis in this hysterical comedy. Kruger's character has troubles both with the English language and the English women around him. There is a great sequence where he tries to date two women at the same time.
VHS: S23780. $24.95.
Wolf Rilla, Great Britain, 1958, 94 mins.

Bad Behavior
Les Blair's spirited comedy about a couple whose marriage is fraying around the edges as they prepare to remodel their home. Ellie McAllister (Sinead Cusack) is turning away from her domestic responsibilities and dreams about independence while her husband Gerry (Stephen Rea) is a Walter Mitty-like dreamer who imagines himself as a superhero.
VHS: S20187. $94.95.
Laser: LD75153. $34.98.
Les Blair, Great Britain, 1993, 103 mins.

Battle of the Sexes
Mild-mannered Mr. Martin (Peter Sellers) tries to prevent a business takeover when British businessman Robert MacPherson (Robert Morley) enlists the aid of man-eating American businesswoman Angela Barrows (Constance Cummings) to bring his company into the 20th century in this sophisticated British comedy based on a short story by James Thurber.
VHS: S33714. $29.95.
Charles Crichton, Great Britain, 1959, 88 mins.

Beachcomber
Charles Laughton and Elsa Lanchester in this adaptation of a Somerset Maugham story about an intelligent but drunken Englishman living in the Dutch East Indies.
VHS: S01878. $29.95.
Erich Pommer, Great Britain, 1938, 87 mins.

Beastly Behavior
The wild but true sexual antics and bizarre mating rituals of more than 30 animals, insects, birds and sea creatures are hilariously animated and explained. Uproariously funny, often dangerous, always fascinating. With sidesplitting narration and special insights by the British "Professor" Roger Knightly, *Beastly Behavior* will have you roaring with laughter as all the shocking, intimate details unfold.
VHS: S30481. $19.95.
Andy Wyatt, Great Britain, 1996, 45 mins.

Belles of St. Trinians
The wild and funny students of St. Trinians engage in a hilarious caper. Alastair Sim is in the dual role of the prim headmistress and her slick bookmaker brother.
VHS: S03782. $19.98.
Frank Launder, Great Britain, 1955, 86 mins.

Bhaji on the Beach
In this warm but hip comedy, a group of women gather for a carefree day on the beach. By nightfall, gossiping, giggling, and arguing over things like battered wives, male strippers, race and sex have brought them closer together. With Peter Cellier, Zohra Segal and Jimmi Harkishin.
VHS: S26920. $96.99.
Gurinder Chadha, Great Britain, 1994, 100 mins.

Blue Murder at St. Trinian's
Terry Thomas and Alastair Sim star in this continuation of the antic adventures of England's most troublesome girls' school. Sim is once again the headmistress in drag, and this time he is also in jail. That gives Thomas the chance to lead the girls through misadventures on the continent.
VHS: S23782. $24.95.
Frank Launder, Great Britain, 1958, 86 mins.

The Bobo
Peter Sellers is a matador of little professional accomplishment who exists on cheese sandwiches. He makes a bet to romance a highly sought-after courtesan in order to achieve his dream of singing professionally while bullfighting. Britt Ekland is the object of his desires. She was also Mrs. Sellers at the time. With Rossano Brazzi.
VHS: S14567. $19.98.
Robert Parrish, Great Britain, 1967, 103 mins.

Brassed Off!
When a small Yorkshire mining town's pit is about to be closed, putting the town out of work, the miners vote to strike at the same time the town's brass band practices for an upcoming competition. Ewan McGregor *(Trainspotting)* and Tara Fitzgerald *(Sirens)* shine as two old friends and ex-lovers whose surprise reunion turns everything upside down. With Pete Postlethwaite as the band conductor.
VHS: S32929. $103.95.
Mark Herman, Great Britain, 1997, 101 mins.

Brothers-in-Law
A zany British comedy starring Ian Carmichael, Terry Thomas and Richard Attenborough in the story of two lawyers who share affections for the same girl, but who both lose out to a third guy.
VHS: S09527. $29.95.
Roy Boulting, Great Britain, 1957, 97 mins.

Bullshot
Zany English satire sends up the legendary Bulldog Drummond in this outrageous comedy set in the 1930s, when all Germans were devilish Huns, and lantern-jawed heroes were fighting for England and the Empire. In the face of mad professors, stolen formulas, helpless heroines and deadly enemies, our intrepid hero, Captain Hugh "Bullshot" Drummond, manages to remain distinctly British.
VHS: S31483. $14.98.
Dick Clement, Great Britain, 1989, 84 mins.

The Canterville Ghost
Sir John Gielgud stars as the title spirit in this update of a tale of a cowardly knight who was walled up in the castle and forced to haunt the place until an ancestor would perform a brave deed. Well, the ghost has been waiting for 300 years and his hopes rest on an American cousin played by Ted Wass. Good luck.
VHS: S04383. $19.95.
Paul Bogart, Great Britain, 1986, 96 mins.

The Caretaker's Daughter
Hugh Wakefield and Derek Bond are featured in this farce. A jealous wife is deceived by the convoluted stories her husband invents with the help of his friends. The gags that prove he is innocent of infidelity are hilarious.
VHS: S23886. $29.95.
Francis Searle, Great Britain, 1953, 83 mins.

Carry On Admiral
Impersonations and shenanigans abound in this riotous comedy portraying hi-jinx in the Royal Navy. A precursor to the "Carry On" series, the film was originally titled *The Ship Was Loaded*. With David Tomlinson, Peggy Cummins, Alfie Bass and Ronald Shiner.
VHS: S16226. $19.95.
Val Guest, Great Britain, 1957, 81 mins.

Carry On Nurse
Another hilarious spoof from the "Carry On" masters of comedy, this uproarious sendup of hospital people broke boxoffice records in England. Hilarious madcap comedy.
VHS: S04538. $24.95.
Gerald Thomas, Great Britain, 1960

The Case of the Mukkinese Battle Horn
Before there was "Monty Python" there was "The Goon Show" and England roared with laughter. Now you can too. Peter Sellers and Spike Milligan, two thirds of the BBC radio's resident comic madmen, join together in this free form featurette concerning the disappearance of a prize 9th Century relic and Scotland Yard's attempts to retrieve said item.
VHS: S03652. $19.95.
Joseph Sterling, Great Britain, 1956, 27 mins.

Cash (For Love or Money)
An excellent British comedy about a young man (Robert Donat) who suddenly discovers $100,000 in a sack. Before the film is over Donat learns that money can't buy him peace of mind.
VHS: S14633. $29.95.
Zoltan Korda, Great Britain, 1934, 63 mins.

Checking Out
Ray Macklin (Jeff Daniels) experiences shortness of breath, bloodshot eyes and a slight heart abnormality and has convinced himself that he's going to die any day now. He buys medical equipment, gets drunk and jogs, but his symptoms only worsen. He's driving his wife (Melanie Mayron) crazy. Jeff Daniels will keep you laughing with his hysterical portrait of this man who sees death at every turn. Also stars Michael Tucker.
VHS: S30494. $14.98.
David Leland, Great Britain, 1989, 93 mins.

Climbing High
Jessie Matthews, Michael Redgrave and Alistair Sim star in this frothy romantic comedy. Money, position and power are all in play as a trio of lovers vie for affection. The eternal question raised by this scenario concerns the respective merits of love or or money as the basis for a solid marriage.
VHS: S27894. $19.98.
Carol Reed, Great Britain, 1939, 76 mins.

Comfort and Joy
Bill Forsyth's hilarious, off-beat look at human nature. Bill Paterson plays Alan Bird, a Glasgow radio personality who gets embroiled in a cold war between two feuding Italian ice cream families. Original soundtrack by Mark Knopfler of Dire Straits.
VHS: S00260. $69.95.
Bill Forsyth, Scotland, 1984, 93 mins.

Cotton Queen
Jowly, rotund Will Fyffe, the popular Scottish comedian, and lanky Stanley Holloway, the equally popular British performer, headline this snappy comedy which offers an amusing glimpse of English music-hall style entertainment. Highlights include their drunken shenanigans in an amusement park and an odyssey in an inadvertently stolen police car.
VHS: S13516. $29.95.
Joe Rock, Great Britain, 1937, 80 mins.

Day in the Death of Joe Egg
Director Peter Medak *(The Ruling Class)* offers a well-done black comedy on the subject of mercy killing. Alan Bates and Janet Suzman are an English couple faced with what to do with their spastic daughter, Jo (Elizabeth Robillard). With Peter Bowles and Sheila Gish. Provocative comedy from playwright Peter Nichols.
VHS: S07583. $69.95.
Peter Medak, Great Britain, 1972, 106 mins.

The Demi-Paradise
Laurence Olivier stars as a Russian engineer whose preconceived notions about England are changed when he encounters friendship, love and support for his war-torn country. A satirical comedy populated by eccentrics.
VHS: S01626. $14.98.
Laser: LD75976. $39.99.
Anthony Asquith, Great Britain, 1943, 112 mins.

Dentist in the Chair
A mischievous dental student spends more time dodging the dean's eagle eye than he does with his studies. The trouble intensifies when the new girl on campus he's hitting on turns out to be the dean's niece.
VHS: S34186. $19.95.
Don Chaffey, Great Britain, 1960, 87 mins.

The Devil's Disciple
An adaptation of George Bernard Shaw's satire about the Revolutionary War, with Laurence Olivier as a British officer whose arrival in New England sets off the patriotic fervor of Burt Lancaster and Kirk Douglas.
VHS: S17986. $19.98.
Guy Hamilton, Great Britain, 1959, 83 mins.

Divorce of Lady X
Merle Oberon, Laurence Olivier and Ralph Richardson star in this sophisticated English comedy in which a London barrister allows a pretty lady to spend an "innocent night" in his flat, and finds out that he may be named as a correspondent in a divorce suit.
VHS: S02522. $19.95.
Laser: LD75181. $34.98.
Alexander Korda, Great Britain, 1938, 90 mins.

Doctor at Large
Dirk Bogarde stars as Dr. Sparrow, an intern who finds himself trapped in a series of hysterical situations. Between the neurotic women patients of the doctor he interns with and the seductive young wife of another miserly doctor, Dr. Sparrow has his hands full. With Muriel Pavlow, Donald Sinden, James Robertson Justice and Shirley Eaton.
VHS: S06432. $14.98.
Ralph Thomas, Great Britain, 1957, 104 mins.

Doctor at Sea
Sex kitten Brigitte Bardot cruises the high seas as Dirk Bogarde signs on as the ship's doctor, determined to remain a bachelor. Second in the series.
VHS: S06433. $19.98.
Ralph Thomas, Great Britain, 1956, 93 mins.

Don't Hang Up
Roseanna Arquette and David Suchet play a couple separated by 5000 miles in this comedy featuring the telephone. She's an intense and passionate actress, while he's a tormented but very British playwright. Together they're the phone company's dream couple, in touch only over the wires.
VHS: S20953. $29.95.
Barry Davis, Great Britain, 1990, 84 mins.

Eat the Rich
In direct opposition to the advice of Jonathan Swift, an anarchistic black comedy of questionable taste from the Comic Strip Troupe of Great Britain. The jet-set are in big trouble when a motley group of the less-privileged get hungry for the good life. With cameos from Paul McCartney and Koo Stark, music by Motorhead. Cast includes Jimmy Fagg, Lanah Pellay and Nosher Powell.
VHS: S08037. $19.98.
Peter Richardson, Great Britain, 1987, 100 mins.

Educating Rita
Successful comedy about a working-class hairdresser (Julie Walters) who enrolls in literature classes taught by Michael Caine. From the veteran director of *Alfie*.
VHS: S02002. $19.95.
Lewis Gilbert, Great Britain, 1983, 110 mins.

The Englishman Who Went up a Hill But Came down a Mountain
Hugh Grant stars as an upstanding surveyor on a mission in this warm comedy. He is sent to an Irish locale to survey the landscape and he makes a startling discovery. Though a certain promontory is a major landmark, it is not, as locally believed, a mountain. It may not be much, but to the local Irish population it is a mountain and they set about making sure it remains classified as such.
VHS: S26709. $19.98.
Laser: LD75321. $39.98.
Christopher Monger, Great Britain, 1995, 96 mins.

The Favor, The Watch and the Very Big Fish
A small-time photographer (Bob Hoskins) stages an elaborate icon portrait, and the ex-con pianist (Jeff Goldblum) he hires as Christ starts to believe in his own divinity in this whacky comedy. With Natasha Richardson, Michel Blanc and Jean-Pierre Cassel.
VHS: S17342. $92.95.
Laser: LD75194. $34.98.
Ben Lewin, Great Britain/France, 1991, 92 mins.

Ferry to Hong Kong
Orson Welles plays the straight-laced ferry boat skipper and Curt Jurgens is the drunken Austrian who are on their way to Macao in this classic comedy.
VHS: S10007. $14.98.
Lewis Gilbert, Great Britain, 1961, 103 mins.

Fierce Creatures
Jamie Lee Curtis, John Cleese, Michael Palin and Kevin Kline star in this funny, farcical follow-up to *A Fish Called Wanda*, about a zoo director who decides to do away with cute, cuddly animals and display only "fierce creatures," leading the outraged zookeepers to launch a revolt to save their furry friends.
VHS: S31533. $19.95.
Laser: LD76240. $34.99.
DVD: DV60146. $24.98.
Robert Young/Fred Schepisi, Great Britain, 1997, 94 mins.

A Fish Called Wanda
John Cleese wrote and stars in this hilarious crime caper film set in England. He plays a barrister called Archibald Leach who is seduced by a scheming American seductress (Jamie Lee Curtis) for the whereabouts of the missing loot. Kevin Kline and Michael Palin are also interested. And yes there is a fish named Wanda as well as a woman named Wanda. Not recommended for the owners of small noisy dogs.
VHS: S08234. $14.95.
Laser: LD74666. $34.98.
Charles Crichton, Great Britain, 1988, 108 mins.

Five Golden Hours
Ernie Kovacs is cast as Aldo Bondi, a professional mourner who lives off the generosity of grieving widows. He meets his match when he sincerely falls for broke Italian baroness Cyd Charisse, who has her own ideas about love and money. With Dennis Price, John Le Mesurier, Kay Hammond, Ron Moody and George Sanders as Mr. Bing, the fake lunatic.
VHS: S15897. $19.95.
Mario Zampi, Great Britain/Italy, 1961, 89 mins.

The Four Musketeers
Richard Chamberlain, Frank Finlay, Oliver Reed and Michael York are back as the musketeers in this film Lester made from leftover footage from *The Three Musketeers*. The result is another piece of fine, offbeat entertainment. With Raquel Welch, Charlton Heston, Faye Dunaway, Christopher Lee and Geraldine Chaplin.
VHS: S32794. $24.98.
Richard Lester, USA, 1975, 108 mins.

Four Weddings and a Funeral
Hugh Grant and Andie MacDowell star in this brightly entertaining romantic comedy. The family gatherings of the title offer more than ample opportunity for this unlikely pair, a handsome Brit and a lovely Yank who is already engaged, to slowly get acquainted. After so many weddings what else could they do?
VHS: S21506. $19.95.
Laser: LD74527. $39.95.
DVD: DV60007. $29.95.
Mike Newell, Great Britain, 1994, 117 mins.

Frozen Limits
The best of the films made by the Crazy Gang, a group of three English music hall duos. When the sextet orders fish and chips, it comes wrapped in a 40-year-old newspaper which hawked the discovery of gold in Alaska. The group leaves the big city and heads north, where they find an old prospector who can't quite find his gold mine. A fast-paced comedy.
VHS: S04483. $19.95.
Edward Black, Great Britain, 1939

The Full Monty
Six unemployed men, inspired by a troupe of male strippers, decide they can make a small fortune by putting on a show of their own, but with one difference: they intend to go the "full monty" and strip completely naked. With Robert Carlyle *(Trainspotting)*, Tom Wilkinson, Mark Addy, Steve Huison, Paul Barber, Hugo Speer and William Snape. "Irresistible… [and] hilarious" *(The New York Times)*.
VHS: S33262. $103.99.
Peter Cattaneo, Great Britain, 1997, 95 mins.

The Galloping Major
Basil Radford has a scheme to get rich using race horses. Naturally it all goes wrong at first, but after some great laughs the mistaken horse proves its mettle and brings in a happy ending. Includes a cast of great British comics and character actors.
VHS: S23982. $24.95.
Henry Cornelius, Great Britain, 1951, 82 mins.

The Gasbags
The Crazy Gang, a troupe of Brit funnymen, balloons over into enemy territory during World War II. Misadventure follows upon hilarious misadventure, including an attempt by one of the troupe to pass as Hitler. Despite it all, they return home heroes with a secret surprise.
VHS: S23783. $24.95.
Marcel Varnel, Great Britain, 1940, 77 mins.

Georgy Girl
An offbeat English comedy of modern day morals, with Lynn Redgrave as the ugly-duckling, and James Mason as the wealthy married man who wants her for his mistress. With a terrific performance from Charlotte Rampling as the violinist-roommate.
VHS: S03299. $19.95.
Silvio Narizzano, Great Britain, 1966, 100 mins.

Girls at Sea
Three young women are stranded on a battleship following a raucous shipboard party, with hilarious consequences. With Guy Rolfe, Ronald Shiner, Alan White and Anne Kimbell.
VHS: S18949. $19.95.
Gilbert Gunn, Great Britain, 1958, 80 mins.

Gospel According to Vic
Tom Conti and Helen Mirren star in this irreverent Scottish comedy about a very reluctant "miracle man", which was influenced by the films of Bill *(Local Hero)* Forsyth. "A heaven-sent comedy from Scotland with a delicious performance by Tom Conti," wrote Bob Thomas in *Associated Press*.
VHS: S03295. $79.98.
Charles Gormley, Great Britain, 1986, 91 mins.

The Great McGonagall
Unemployed Scotsman William McGonagall (Spike Milligan, who also co-wrote the script) aspires to become England's Poet Laureate. The only problem: his poetry stinks. With Peter Sellers.
VHS: S34941. $19.95.
Joseph McGrath, Great Britain, 1975, 95 mins.

Green Grow the Rushes
Honor Blackman and Richard Burton star in this knowing comedy about an isolated coastal community addicted to smuggling. Meddlesome government bureaucrats are set on ending this local custom but encounter stiff and humorous resistance from the natives. Burton leads the rebellion and even manages to win over a reporter (Blackman) with a nose for muckraking.
VHS: S27833. $39.95.
Derek Twist, Great Britain, 1951, 78 mins.

Gregory's Girl
A very funny film from the director of *Local Hero* and *Comfort and Joy*; centered on the lives of Glasgow teenagers, specifically Gregory and his girlfriend, Dorothy, who is the new teammate on the soccer team. Quirky, charming, and often very funny, the film is notable for Forsyth's great dialog and ensemble acting.
VHS: S00530. $19.95.
Bill Forsyth, Scotland, 1982, 91 mins.

Half a Sixpence
Musical based on an H.G. Wells story about a draper's assistant who suddenly inherits a fortune and attempts to move up in society. Starring Tommy Steele and Julia Foster.
VHS: S13785. $24.95.
George Sidney, Great Britain, 1967, 148 mins.

The Happiest Days of Your Life
Alastair Sim and Margaret Rutherford star in this madcap comedy about a group of girls accidentally billeted at a boys school. As the headmaster and headmistress join forces to fend off school inspectors, parents and kids, they find they are well in control of inspired anarchy.
VHS: S20854. $39.95.
Frank Lauder, USA, 1950, 83 mins.

Harassed Hero
Guy Middleton stars with Evelyn Brook Jones in this comedy about a hapless bachelor who finds himself mixed in with an unsavory lot of counterfeiters. Seriously funny trouble ensues for all concerned.
VHS: S23892. $29.95.
Maurice Elvey, Great Britain, 1954, 72 mins.

Head over Heels
A musical revue about a complicated romantic triangle as a career singer can't distinguish between the two men who are attracted to her. With Jessie Matthews, Robert Flemyng, Louis Borell and Romney Brent.
VHS: S18950. $19.95.
Sonnie Hale, Great Britain, 1937, 81 mins.

Heavens Above
Peter Sellers, Cecil Parker and Ian Carmichael star in this gentle satire about mixed up vicars. Sellers is mistakenly appointed to a rich parish, which is quite a contrast to his last job as a prison minister. The man who didn't get the cushy job, Carmichael, is Sellers' exact opposite. It's a great set-up for humor handled with delicacy.
VHS: S23784. $24.95.
John Boulting, Great Britain, 1963, 105 mins.

Help!
Richard Lester's follow-up to *A Hard Day's Night* doesn't try to assess the power and impact of the Beatles on popular culture, but creates as many chances and thin narrative lines for the brilliant group to reveal their power. Digitally encoded on Hi-fi, heightening the sharpness of the Beatles' work: "Help," "You're Gonna Lose That Girl," "You've Got to Hide Your Love Away" and "Ticket to Ride." Special Edition contains eight minutes of rare bonus footage.
VHS: S02013. $19.98.
Laser: CAV. **LD70376. $79.95.**
Laser: CLV. **LD70377. $39.95.**
DVD: DV60123. $24.98.
Richard Lester, Great Britain, 1965, 98 mins.

Hi-Di-Hi
A holiday camp in the late 50s is the setting for romance, adventure and, most of all, hysterical hijinks. Featuring a lively assortment of original characters, *Hi-Di-Hi* has been called Britain's answer to *Dirty Dancing!* From the BBC.
VHS: S11214. $39.98.

High Spirits
Peter O'Toole stars as an Irish nobleman who schemes to turn his ancestral castle into a popular tourist spot by claiming that it is haunted. Imagine his surprise when he and his guests discover that the castle really is haunted, by quarreling ghosts.
VHS: S08890. $19.95.
Neil Jordan, Great Britain, 1988, 96 mins.

The Horse's Mouth
Alec Guinness delivers a classic performance in this wonderful British comedy based on the novel by Joyce Cary about a non-conformist painter who seeks out bizarre surfaces for his work. Digitally remastered and letterboxed.
VHS: S04319. $24.95.
Laser: LD70382. $39.95.
Ronald Neame, Great Britain, 1958, 93 mins.

How I Won the War
John Lennon stars in his first solo film performance. A hilarious, surreal collage of battle footage and fast-moving comedy lampooning the absurdity of war. The tenuous plot concerns a troop of British soldiers with a mission to set up a cricket match behind enemy lines in order to impress a visiting V.I.P. Sheer, brilliant lunacy. With Jack MacDowran, Roy Kinnear and Lee Montague.
VHS: S00588. $59.95.
Richard Lester, Great Britain, 1967, 111 mins.

How to Get Ahead in Advertising
From the director of *Withnail and I* comes this eccentric comedy about life in not-so-jolly old England. Dennis Bagley is an advertising executive with a problem. During the anxiety of developing a pimple cream campaign, he notices a monstrous zit growing on his neck. The growth not only is getting bigger, but it also talks and has plans to take over his job, his wife and his life. With Richard E. Grant as Bagley and Rachel Ward as the worried spouse.
VHS: S11202. $14.98.
Laser: Letterboxed. **LD76182. $49.98.**
Bruce Robinson, Great Britain, 1989, 94 mins.

Hue and Cry
An outrageous romp of a movie with Alastair Sim having a field day as he plays a meek detective-story writer who, together with a group of kids, crack a gang of thieves. Terrific British comedy from the same team who made *The Lavender Hill Mob*.
VHS: S09526. $29.95.
Charles Crichton, Great Britain, 1947, 82 mins.

I Love You, Alice B. Toklas
Corporate lifer Peter Sellers tunes in and drops out in this landmark sixties comedy. "Sellers has never been better" (Leonard Maltin).
VHS: S14569. $19.98.
Laser: LD71474. $34.98.
Hy Averback, USA, 1968, 93 mins.

An Ideal Husband
Crafty young adventuress Mrs. Cheveley (Paulette Godard) tries to blackmail the politically ambitious Sir Robert Chiltern (Hugh Williams) when she discovers that he sold a cabinet secret in his youth regarding the Suez Canal. She threatens to expose him unless he supports a phony Parliament Argentine canal scheme, but the Lady Chiltern (Diana Wynyard) talks him out of it. With Michael Wildin, C. Aubrey Smith and Glynis Johns. Based on Oscar Wilde's play.
VHS: S32947. $19.95.
Alexander Korda, Great Britain, 1948, 96 mins.

Innocents in Paris
Alastair Sim, Margaret Rutherford and Christopher Lee are just some of the British stars loaded into this delightful comic romp. Seven different eccentrics are off to France. Crossing the channel, each has a wacky adventure made all the funnier by a stiff upper lip.
VHS: S23112. $24.95.
Gordon Perry, Great Britain, 1953, 60 mins.

Intimate Relations
This outrageous, dark comedy of seduction tells the true story of a handsome lodger caught in a tangled web of passion with his sexually frustrated landlady and her precocious teenage daughter. With Julie Walters *(Educating Rita)*, Rupert Graves and Laura Sadler. "A perfectly realized comedy" *(Variety)*.
VHS: S33032. $69.99.
Philip Goodhew, Great Britain, 1997, 105 mins.

The Italian Job
A British comedy set in Turin about a plan orchestrated by Michael Caine and playwright Noel Coward to steal $4 million in gold bullion pivots on diverting authorities with a complex and unruly "traffic jam." Some delirious action, chase scenes and set pieces and charming, local color.
VHS: S16895. $19.95.
Peter Collinson, Great Britain, 1969, 99 mins.

John & Julie
A gentle, eccentric, neglected British comedy set during the summer of 1953 in which two English children (Constance Cummings and Patric Doonan) run away to London to see the coronation of Queen Elizabeth II. They hope John's uncle, a guard in the royal escort, will help them. Contains actual scenes from the royal coronation. With Peter Sellers. "Colorful, memorable, cheerful entertainment!" *(The New York Times)*.
VHS: S34727. $24.95.
William Fairchild, Great Britain, 1955, 82 mins.

Just Like a Woman
Julia Walters and Adrian Pasdar star in this unlikely, comic romance between a suburban housewife and an investment banker who likes to dress in women's clothing. It may be hard to swallow but this charming farce is actually based on a true story. Pasdar does his best to pass as a woman and a charming male lead.
Laser: LD75061. $39.99.
Christopher Monger, Great Britain, 1995, 102 mins.

Kiepura in My Song for You
This slight but delightful comedy features Jan Kiepura as an opera singer who sets to work wooing a lovely young woman.
VHS: S24851. $34.95.
Maurice Elvey, Great Britain, 1934, 89 mins.

Kind Hearts and Coronets
A perennial favorite featuring Alec Guinness' famous performance in which he plays eight separate roles in the black comedy of a castoff member of an aristocratic family who sets out to eliminate them all. The sardonic script was written by director Robert Hamer, one of Ealing Studios best writer/directors.
VHS: S00676. $14.98.
Robert Hamer, Great Britain, 1949, 104 mins.

Kipps
Based on H.G. Wells' satirical comedy about a shopkeeper who inherits a fortune and tries to enter high society. With Michael Redgrave, Diana Wynyard.
VHS: S00683. $29.95.
Carol Reed, Great Britain, 1941, 112 mins.

The Knack...and How to Get It
Richard Lester's chic film set in swinging 60s London about three men (Michael Crawford, Ray Brooks and Donal Donnelly) who occupy the same London house, and a beautiful country girl (Rita Tushingham) who moves in with them. Sexual hijinks abound as the three angle to seduce women, with the charismatic Brooks in the lead as a master of killer charm.
VHS: S20400. $19.98.
Laser: LD76359. $39.99.
Richard Lester, Great Britain, 1965, 84 mins.

Ladies Who Do
In this madcap comedy, a group of cleaning ladies face off against a real estate robber baron who wants to tear down their homes for an office tower complex. Joining forces with a retired colonel, played by Robert Morley, they use stock market secrets from the waste paper baskets they empty to gain some vital economic clout. Peggy Mount also stars.
VHS: S22472. $29.95.
C.M. Pennington Richards, Great Britain, 1963, 90 mins.

Lady L
Peter Ustinov's stylish comedy is adapted from Romain Gary's popular novel, which chronicles the seedy characters and dangerous romantics who inhabit an atmospheric turn-of-the-century Europe. A "film of great wit, urbane elegance, and fast-paced nuttiness" *(The New York Times)*. With Paul Newman, David Niven, Sophia Loren and Philippe Noiret.
VHS: S19489. $19.98.
Peter Ustinov, Great Britain, 1965, 107 mins.

Ladykillers
Another wonderfully bizarre comedy from England's Ealing Studios, this starring Alec Guiness as the slightly demented leader of a group of thieves planning their heist in a boarding house while pretending to be a chamber orchestra.
VHS: S00719. $14.98.
Alexander Mackendrick, Great Britain, 1955, 87 mins.

The Lavender Hill Mob
Alec Guinness in one of his most memorable roles, as a shy bank clerk who conspires to steal a million pounds in gold bars from the Bank of England. His plan is to melt down the gold and mold it in the shape of tiny Eiffel Tower souvenirs for resale. Things appear to go well until… Zany, witty and very British, a beloved and classic British comedy.
VHS: S00732. $14.98.
Charles Crichton, Great Britain, 1951, 78 mins.

Leon the Pig Farmer
Leon, a nice Jewish boy in London, accidentally discovers that he is the product of artificial insemination. Thrown into doubt about his identity, he seeks out his biological father and discovers him to be a Yorkshire pig farmer. After teaching his new family some Yiddish phrases, he is overcome with Jewish guilt (what else!). Starring Mark Frankel, Connie Booth and Janet Suzman.
VHS: S21093. $19.98.
Vadim Jean/Gary Sinyor, Great Britain, 1993, 102 mins.

A Life Less Ordinary
From the director of *Trainspotting* comes this offbeat love story in which beautiful, spoiled Celine (Cameron Diaz) is kidnapped by the irresistibly inept Robert (Ewan McGregor). The foiled plan is kept strangely on course with a little help from a couple of celestial cops (Holly Hunter and Delroy Lind). "A profanely funny romance…a valentine spiked with mirth and malice" (Peter Travers, *Rolling Stone*).
VHS: S33228. $103.99.
Laser: LD76817. $39.99.
Danny Boyle, Great Britain, 1997, 96 mins.

Lilacs in the Spring
Anna Neagle, Errol Flynn and Peter Graves are featured in this musical comedy fantasy based on the play *The Glorious Days*, by Henry Purcell. A young woman is knocked out during the London blitz. While asleep she dreams of herself as Nell Gwynn, Queen Victoria and even as her own mother.
VHS: S23785. $24.95.
Herbert Wilcox, Great Britain, 1954, 94 mins.

Local Hero
The delicate ecological balance of a small unspoiled Scottish village is threatened by the plans of a wealthy oilman. *Local Hero* is a tender, very funny movie about astronomy, a mermaid, a village that wants to get rich and an old man who doesn't. With Burt Lancaster, Peter Riegert.
VHS: S00763. $19.98.
Laser: LD70617. $34.98.
Bill Forsyth, Great Britain, 1983, 111 mins.

London Town
Sid Field and Gretta Gynt play a comedian and his daughter in this humorous and warm film. Though the comedian seems eternally destined to play small venues, he has finally secured a role in a major London show. Schemes set in play by the daughter, and not his talent, may well be behind this unexpected turn in his luck.
VHS: S27895. $19.98.
Wesley Ruggles, Great Britain, 1946, 93 mins.

Lucky Jim
Ian Carmichael, Hugh Griffith and Terry Thomas star in this zany comedy about a university professor and a junior lecturer at a British University. Great gags and a keen cast keep this comedy moving.
VHS: S23786. $24.95.
John Boulting, Great Britain, 1957, 95 mins.

The Magic Christian
Peter Sellers tries to teach adopted son Ringo Starr about the power and abuses of vast wealth. He will go to outrageous lengths to prove that everyone has their price. With guest stars Raquel Welch, Christopher Lee, John Cleese, Spike Milligan, and Yul Brynner in drag. From the novel by Terry Southern.
VHS: S04244. $14.98.
Laser: CLV. **LD72006. $29.98.**
Joseph McGrath, Great Britain, 1970, 88 mins.

Man in the White Suit
Alec Guiness plays an unassuming lab assistant who invents a miracle fabric that can be woven into indestructible cloth. Few films have chastized industry so wittily and incisively as this great comedy. There is a Chaplin-like flavor to absurdist scenes pitting a captain of industry against his stubborn young employee.
VHS: S00812. $14.98.
Alexander Mackendrick, Great Britain, 1951, 82 mins.

Maytime in Mayfair
Anna Neagle and Michael Wilding are featured in this delightful musical comedy about dress designers. In the fashion salons of London intrigues abound, and one of these almost drives the pair apart for good. Fortunately, good spirits prevail.
VHS: S23898. $29.95.
Herbert Wilcox, Great Britain, 1949, 110 mins.

The Millionairess
Sophia Loren and Peter Sellers star in this comic drama based on a George Bernard Shaw play. Loren is a beautiful heiress used to getting her way because she can usually pay her way. Everything in this plush, orderly world is upset when an Indian doctor, brilliantly portrayed by Sellers, upsets her world view by sticking to his principles.
VHS: S28996. $19.98.
Anthony Asquith, Great Britain, 1960, 90 mins.

The Mouse That Roared
An inventive satire about the Duchy of Grand Fenwick and its mischievous duchess (Peter Sellers) that boldly declares war against America to boost its economy. Anticipating *Dr. Strangelove*, Sellers also appears as the prime minister and war minister. With Jean Seberg, David Kossoff and William Hartnell.
VHS: S01841. $19.95.
Jack Arnold, Great Britain, 1959, 90 mins.

The Naked Truth
Peter Sellers is a master of disguise in this outrageous comedy. As Nigel Dennis he decides to print a scandalous magazine that reveals the true secrets of several prominent people. They respond to this blackmail with a plot to eliminate this scabrous journalist, but when it fails there is only more scandal to print.
VHS: S21996. $19.95.
Mario Zampi, Great Britain, 1957, 90 mins.

Nino Martini in One Night with You
Patricia Roc, Irene Worth and Stanley Holloway join Martini for this madcap comic film about a tenor stranded without identity papers. In this rare treat the wildly flamboyant Italian film world is seen through droll English eyes.
VHS: S24561. $34.95.
Terence Young, Great Britain, 1948, 92 mins.

Nuns on the Run
Eric Idle and Robbie Coltrane decide to leave a life of crime and join a religious order to elude their unsavory pursuers. Sister Superior Janet Suzman thinks the new sisters a bit on the odd side but she does need the help. The disguised crooks also need some help in leaving the country with a bit of cash. Who says comedies about men in women's clothing have to be a drag?
VHS: S12604. $19.95.
Jonathan Lynn, Great Britain, 1990, 92 mins.

O-Kay for Sound
This Crazy Gang revue comedy of street musicians who are given parts in a drill dressed as city financiers and are then mistaken for the real thing stars Fred Duprez, Enid Taylor and Jimmy Gold.
VHS: S26068. $29.95.
Marcel Varnel, Great Britain, 1937, 86 mins.

On Approval
Highly amusing, often ingenious comedy starring Clive Brook and Beatrice Lillie, in which two couples spend a holiday on a deserted island home to see if they are suited for each other.
VHS: S00957. $24.95.
Laser: LD76087. $39.99.
Clive Brook, Great Britain, 1944, 80 mins.

On the Fiddle
Sean Connery and Alfred Lynch are a pair of lovable cons out to make fun, not war, as they take the Royal Air Force on the ride of its life.
VHS: S31019. $14.98.
Cyril Frankel, 1961, Great Britain, 93 mins.

Only Two Can Play
Peter Sellers stars as an ambitious librarian who is willing to seduce the wife of a prominent library board member in order to secure a promotion. Imagine his surprise when he finds that his wife is spending time with a local poet. With Richard Attenborough, Mai Zetterling, Kenneth Griffith and Virginia Maskell. B&W.
VHS: S06072. $69.95.
Sidney Gilliat, Great Britain, 1962, 106 mins.

Passport to Pimlico
Wry satire from the Golden Age of British comedy. A group of residents in Pimlico, a London suburb, discover an ancient treaty that ceded their land to the Duke of Burgundy, a discovery that leads to delightful mayhem.
VHS: S01000. $19.98.
Henry Cornelius, Great Britain, 1949, 85 mins.

Peter's Friends
Kenneth Branagh's witty comedy uses the structure of John Sayles' *Return of the Secaucus Seven* as six friends, members of an anarchic university theater collective, reunite for a ten-year anniversary over New Year's Eve in the inherited estate of Peter (Stephen Fry) to assess their personal and public successes, failures, family tragedies, heartbreak and romantic and professional disappointments. Sharp performances from Branagh, Emma Thompson and Alphonsia Emmanuel.
VHS: S18725. $19.98.
Kenneth Branagh, Great Britain, 1992, 102 mins.

The Private Secretary
Edward Everett Horton and Alastair Sim star in this amusing comedy set during the Victorian era. Horton is in disguise as a minister hiding from debt collectors. The Church of England is a great place to hide and find laughs as well.
VHS: S23788. $24.95.
Henry Edwards, Great Britain, 1935, 70 mins.

The Promoter
A low-key Ealing comedy adapted from Arnold Bennett's story *The Card*, about a young man's transformation from penniless hustler to provincial power. With his skills for self-promotion, he quickly assumes power and credentials in class-conscious England, though he loses his identity and soul. With Alec Guinness, Glynis Johns, Valerie Hobston and Petula Clark.
VHS: S01978. $39.95.
Ronald Neame, Great Britain, 1952, 88 mins.

The Return of the Musketeers
Richard Lester's boisterous continuation of the popular saga, adapted from Alexandre Dumas' novel *Twenty Years Later*, finds D'Artagnan (Michael York) enlisting the former crew to help save Queen Anne (Geraldine Chaplin) from the evil clutches of Justine (Kim Cattrall)—daughter of the mischievous Milady de Winter. With Oliver Reed, Frank Finlay, C. Thomas Howell, Philippe Noiret and Geraldine Chaplin.
VHS: S19580. $89.98.
Laser: LD71924. $34.98.
Richard Lester, Great Britain/France/Spain, 1989, 101 mins.

The Ruling Class
Peter O'Toole stars as the 14th Earl of Gurney, who happens to believe he is Jesus Christ. An irreverent comedy, *The Ruling Class* is filled with insane ideas and boisterously funny characters. This is the original, uncut version.
VHS: S01137. $39.95.
Peter Medak, Great Britain, 1972, 154 mins.

Sailing Along
A romantic British musical about a pretty and talented young woman working on a barge who meets the right man and ends up becoming a dancing star. Starring Jessie Matthews and Roland Young.
VHS: S14647. $29.95.
Sonnie Hale, Great Britain, 1938, 90 mins.

School for Scoundrels
Alastair Sim and Terry Thomas are joined by Ian Carmichael in this hysterical spoof of self-improvement techniques. Carmichael goes through a number of Sim's workshops to better himself in a variety of ways. Surprisingly enough these schemes work and Carmichael goes back to show up the ridiculously snooty Thomas.
VHS: S24051. $24.95.
Robert Hamer, Great Britain, 1960, 94 mins.

Smallest Show on Earth
A wonderful comedy starring Peter Sellers, Bill Travers, Virginia McKenna, and Margaret Rutherford, about a young couple who inherit an old movie house—and a couple of strange movie attendants (Sellers and Rutherford) in the process.
VHS: S07468. $19.95.
Basil Dearden, Great Britain, 1957, 80 mins.

Special British Comedy Boxed Set
Alastair Sim and Trevor Howard star in the comedy thriller *Green for Danger*, about a rash of mysterious deaths at a hospital. In *The Happiest Days of Your Life*, Alastair Sim and Margaret Rutherford try their best to control anarchy in a boy's school accidentally filled with girls. In the third tape, Wendy Hiller and Rex Harrison star in the ironic screen adaptation of George Bernard Shaw's *Major Barbara*. 401 mins.
VHS: S24796. $79.95.

Storm in a Teacup
A very witty social comedy with Vivien Leigh and Rex Harrison barbing over words, loves and politics in the case of an old lady who refuses to pay for a license for her dog. With Cecil Parker, Ivor Barnard.
VHS: S05177. $19.95.
Victor Saville, Great Britain, 1937, 87 mins.

Summer House
Jeanne Moreau, Joan Plowright and Julie Walters star in this serious comedy about love, marriage and friendship. A troubled young woman is about to engage in a loveless marriage with an older man. Only one strong, wise woman has the courage to save her from a sad fate. The end is a shocker.
VHS: S25101. $99.95.
Laser: LD75019. $39.99.
Waris Hussein, Great Britain, 1994, 93 mins.

The Tall Guy
Jeff Goldblum has the title role as an American actor eking out a living by performing in London. His luck changes when he loses his job as a second banana and falls in love with Kate Lemon, a nurse whose favorite color is orange. With Emma Thompson as the feisty angel of mercy, and Rowan Atkinson as England's most conceited actor.
VHS: S13580. $19.95.
Mel Smith, Great Britain, 1989, 92 mins.

That Sinking Feeling
A preposterous comedy set in Scotland, from the director of *Local Hero* and *Gregory's Girl*. A gang of teenagers invent a hilarious cure for boredom by stealing 100 sinks from a local plumbing warehouse. Forsyth's gift for dialog combined with outstanding performances make this an unforgettable story.
VHS: Out of print. For rental only.
Laser: LD75272. $34.98.
Bill Forsyth, Scotland, 1979, 82 mins.

Three Men in a Boat
Laurence Harvey, Jimmy Edwards and David Thomlinson are featured in this light comedy about three men in search of a vacation from the women in their lives. In search of tranquility they set sail on the Thames, where it becomes clear they won't be able to avoid female company at all. Jill Ireland is also featured.
VHS: S23984. $24.95.
Ken Annakin, Great Britain, 1956, 85 mins.

The Three Musketeers
Michael York stars as D'Artagnan, the musketeer who arrives in Paris, duels, and eventually joins forces with musketeers Athos, Porthos and Aramis (Oliver Reed, Frank Findlay and Richard Chamberlain) in their efforts to oppose Cardinal Richelieu, who's trying to increase his power over the king.
VHS: S32793. $24.98.
Richard Lester, Spain/Great Britain/Panama, 1974, 105 mins.

Thunder in the City
A smart-mouthed, fast-talking Yankee businessman confronts the very proper but relentlessly shrewd English method of high finance. A sophisticated British satire starring famous American "bad guy" Edward G. Robinson in his first comedy role. With Nigel Bruce.
VHS: S13862. $19.95.
Marion Gering, Great Britain, 1937, 86 mins.

To Paris with Love
Alec Guinness stars as a rich father who takes his unwordly son across the Channel to the City of Lights to learn about life and love and people who live in a different country. A comedy. With Odile Versois, Vernon Gray and Austin Trevor. On your right is the Eiffel Tower.
VHS: S04909. $14.98.
Robert Hamer, Great Britain, 1955, 78 mins.

Tom Jones
Winner of 4 Academy Awards, including Best Picture, *Tom Jones* is Tony Richardson's adaptation of Henry Fielding's famous novel about a mysteriously abandoned orphan who is adopted by the fussy Squire Allworthy, and thus begins a life of bawdy adventure. An outrageous and lusty comedy of 18th-century English life starring the sexy young Albert Finney. Screenplay by John Osborne.
VHS: S15548. $19.98.
Laser: LD71435. $29.98.
Tony Richardson, Great Britain, 1963, 129 mins.

Trial and Error (The Dock Brief)
An aging, incompetent barrister (Peter Sellers) represents an accused killer (Richard Attenborough) with strange and comic results in this satire.
VHS: S28403. $19.98.
James Hill, Great Britain, 1962, 88 mins.

Up the Creek
Peter Sellers plays an Irish petty officer in the British navy in this service comedy. Made in Hammarscope and black and white. Other distinguished members of the cast include David Tomlinson, Lionel Jeffries and Wilfrid Hyde-White as the Admiral. Not to be confused with the college rafting movie comedy of the same title.
VHS: S06098. $39.95.
Val Guest, Great Britain, 1958, 83 mins.

Waltz of the Toreadors
In this robust adaptation of the Jean Anouilh play, Peter Sellers is General Fitzjohn, whose pursuit of a sexy Parisian is thwarted by his put upon wife (Margaret Leighton) and a lecherous doctor. A breezy and tasteful comedy of sexual and social morals.
Laser: Widescreen. **LD75518. $49.95.**
John Guillermin, Great Britain, 1962, 100 mins.

War of the Buttons
Teen-age boys in two Irish villages engage in an all-out war over common buttons. It's all in play, as the kids will have to be home for supper. *Chariots of Fire* producer David Puttnam and writer Colin Welland are at the helm of this engaging family comedy.
VHS: S27280. $19.98.
John Roberts, Great Britain/Japan, 1995, 95 mins.

Water
Michael Caine follows up his success of *Hannah and Her Sisters* and *Half Moon Street* in this congenial comedy about the commercial and social exploitation of a small Caribbean outpost governed by Caine upon the discovery of a pure mineral water source. With Valerie Perrine, the film is a small satire of economic imperialism, bureaucracy and chic revolutionaries. With appearances by musicians Ringo Starr, George Harrison and Eric Clapton.
VHS: S02632. $29.95.
Dick Clement, Great Britain, 1986, 89 mins.

When Knights Were Bold
Fay Wray and Jack Buchanan star in this farce about a British nobleman who is having trouble at the manor. Accidentally hit in the head by a suit of armor, he dreams about his illustrious ancestors and learns how to act in a truly noble fashion.
VHS: S23791. $24.95.
Jack Raymond, Great Britain, 1936, 55 mins.

Whiskey Galore
One of the drollest, most amusing British films ever made. Scottish islanders take drastic measures when a cargo of whiskey is marooned off their shore. Also known by the title *Tight Little Island*.
VHS: S02030. $29.95.
Alexander Mackendrick, Great Britain, 1958, 80 mins.

Who Done It?
Benny Hill stars as Hugo Dill in this hilarious farce about a defective detective who stumbles upon a plot to take over the world. 79 mins.
VHS: S31024. $14.98.
Basil Dearden/Michael Relph, Great Britain, 1956, 85 mins.

Whoops Apocalypse
A black comedy starring Peter Cook, Loretta Swit, Michael Richards and Herbert Lom. Swit plays the first female President of the United States caught in a dispute over an island in the Caribbean. Targets for ridicule include the CIA, the British Royal Family, and atomic bomb misuse. With Rik Mayll and Alexei Sayle.
VHS: S08315. $14.95.
Tom Bussman, USA/Great Britain, 1988

Wicked Lady
Unsatisfied by carnal conquests, her passions drew her into a secret life of crime until she finally took one step too far. With Margaret Lockwood.
VHS: S06543. $19.98.
Leslie Arliss, Great Britain, 1945, 100 mins.

Withnail and I
The sixties are ending and two London actors down on their luck seek solace at a relative's summer place in the country. The rustic cottage is less than they expected. A frantic adult comedy starring Richard E. Grant, Paul McGann and Richard Griffiths as odd Uncle Monty. Based on the life of the actor-writer-director Bruce Robinson *(The Killing Fields)*.
VHS: S07577. $14.95.
Laser: LD71214. $49.95.
Bruce Robinson, Great Britain, 1988, 108 mins.

Without a Clue
Michael Caine and Ben Kingsley star in this revisionist comedy about what they claim is the true story of Sherlock Holmes and Dr. Watson. According to Watson, he was the brains that solved all those baffling cases. Holmes was actually a hired actor and a complete fool. With Jeffrey Jones, Lysette Anthony and Paul Freeman as Moriarty. Elementary good fun.
VHS: S09145. $19.98.
Thom Eberhardt, Great Britain, 1988, 108 mins.

Woman Hater
A battle of wits between a misogynist confirmed bachelor (Stewart Granger) and a misanthropic single girl (French star Edwige Feuillere) leads to romance in this light-hearted farce. With Terence Young, Ronald Squire and Mary Jerrold.
VHS: S30431. $14.98.
Terence Young, Great Britain, 1948, 105 mins.

Wrong Arm of the Law
Peter Sellers stars in this funny movie: a trio of cockney men have both the police and the crooks after them because they've been dressing as cops, and confiscating loot from apprehended robbers. With Lionel Jeffries, Bernard Cribbins.
VHS: S04788. $39.95.
Cliff Owen, Great Britain, 1963, 91 mins.

The Wrong Box
Ralph Richardson and John Mills star as two elderly brothers seeking the family inheritance in a film littered with comic talent. Among the the cast are Michael Caine, Dudley Moore, Peter Cook and a particularly outrageous Peter Sellers. This black comedy is based on a Robert Louis Stevenson story set during the Victorian era. Mills brings new and unforseen depths of humor and sinister delight to plans for becoming the sole heir at the age of 80.
Laser: LD75809. $34.95.
Bryan Forbes, Great Britain, 1966, 105 mins.

Young Wives' Tale
A British social comedy centered around post-war housing shortages. Adapted from the play by Ronald Jeans, the story concerns a playwright and his exuberant wife who are forced to share living quarters with a refined couple. With Joan Greenwood, Nigel Patrick, Derek Farr, Guy Middleton and Audrey Hepburn.
VHS: S19879. $29.95.
Henry Cass, Great Britain, 1951, 79 mins.

SHERLOCK HOLMES MYSTERIES

The Abbey Grange
A burnt dog collar provides the clue needed to solve the mysterious murder of Sir Eustace Brackenstall. Starring Jeremy Brett. Granada TV, 55 mins.
VHS: S11703. $24.95.

The Blue Carbuncle
While Holmes tries to discover the secret behind a precious stone, a man's life hangs in balance. Starring Jeremy Brett. 52 mins.
VHS: S24401. $19.98.

The Boscombe Valley Mystery
The stories of Arthur Conan Doyle are transposed to a contemporary setting, as Watson's fishing holiday is ruined by the shocking declaration of his son's arrest in the murder of a local farmer. With Jeremy Brett as Holmes, Edward Hardwicke as Watson, James Purefoy and Joanna Roth. 50 mins.
VHS: S18154. $24.98.

The Bruce Partington Plans
A young man is found brutally murdered. Starring Jeremy Brett. Granada TV, 55 mins.
VHS: S11713. $24.95.

The Cardboard Box
Susan Cushing needs Sherlock Holmes (Jeremy Brett) to find her missing sister. A grisly Christmas gift finally convinces Holmes that he must indeed take on this investigation. 50 mins.
VHS: S27447. $19.98.

The Copper Beeches
Why does Violet Hunter's prospective employer insist that she cut off her hair to take a position at The Copper Beeches as governess? Before too long, Holmes receives a panicked message from the girl. Jeremy Brett plays Holmes. From the new Granada TV series. 55 mins.
VHS: S11134. $24.95.

The Creeping Man
A dark, hunched silhouette at her bedroom window and the howling of the family's pet dog has terrified the daughter of an eminent professor. Holmes advises Miss Presbury to keep her door locked as he continues his investigations: "The prowler who looked in on you is no ordinary creature..." Starring Jeremy Brett and Edward Hardwicke. Granada TV, 50 mins.
VHS: S16015. $24.98.

The Crooked Man
Arguing is heard coming from the villa of Colonel James Barclay and his wife Nancy. Then, bloodsucking screams lead the servants to where the colonel lies dead. What happened to the Barclays? With Jeremy Brett as Holmes. From the new Granada TV series. 55 mins.
VHS: S11133. $24.95.

The Crucifer of Blood

Charlton Heston. You loved him as Moses. You cheered him as Ben Hur. Now you can enjoy the way his mind works as Sherlock Holmes, master detective. The case at hand: a 30-year blood oath which is behind a current crop of ghastly murders. Based on the characters created by A. Conan Doyle and the play by Paul Giovanni. With Richard Johnson as Dr. Watson and Simon Callow as Inspector Lestrade. Also in the cast are Clive Wood, Edward Fox and Susannah Harker as the mysterious Irene St. Claire.

VHS: S15616. $19.98.

Fraser C. Heston, USA/Great Britain, 1991, 105 mins.

The Dancing Men

It seemed like an innocent child's game, but in truth, it may lead to murder. From the acclaimed BBC series starring the incomparable Jeremy Brett as the world's greatest detective. 52 mins.

VHS: S24402. $19.98.

The Devil's Foot

A young woman is found dead, possibly murdered, but there is no trace of injury, sickness or violence. Starring Jeremy Brett. Granada TV, 55 mins.

VHS: S11711. $24.95.

The Disappearance of Lady Frances Carfax

A series of letters from Doctor Watson to Holmes about the enigmatic and mysterious Lady Frances elicits his curiosity, especially when she disappears and Holmes is called in to investigate. 50 mins.

VHS: S18156. $24.98.

Dressed to Kill

One of the more baffling of the classic Rathbone-Bruce "Holmes" films. Three music boxes, sold at auction, hold the secret to the location of banknote plates stolen from the Bank of England. Expert detection by Holmes solves the almost impossible cipher with the help of bumbling Dr. Watson. USA, 1946, 72 mins.

VHS: S01141. $19.95.

The Dying Detective

Adelaide Savage beseeches Sherlock Holmes (Jeremy Brett) to investigate her husband's cousin, Culverton Smith. Her fears of disaster are confirmed when Victor Savage dies of a rare parasitic fever. This type of illness, oddly enough, happens to be the specialty of the suspicious cousin. 50 mins.

VHS: S27445. $19.98.

The Eligible Bachelor

Jeremy Brett and David Burke star as Holmes and Watson in this story about a missing bride. A young American bride disappears at her wedding breakfast, but Holmes is plagued by nightmares that force him to consider the consequences of any action he might take to solve the mystery of this disappearance. 105 mins.

VHS: S24397. $19.95.

The Empty House

In this companion tape to The Final Problem, Holmes' confrontation with Professor Moriarty may be his last. Starring Jeremy Brett. Granada TV, 55 mins.

VHS: S11706. $24.95.

The Final Problem

When the Mona Lisa is stolen from the Louvre in Paris, the French government calls in Holmes to investigate, pitting him against the "Napoleon" of crime, arch criminal Professor Moriarty. With Jeremy Brett as Holmes; from Granada TV. 55 mins.

VHS: S11139. $24.95.

The Golden Pince-Nez

Scotland Yard seeks the help of Sherlock Holmes (Jeremy Brett) for a baffling case. The only clue is a golden pince-nez found in the clutches of a murdered young man. It's a mystery that stretches all the way to war-torn St. Petersburg. 50 mins.

VHS: S27443. $19.98.

The Greek Interpreter

Sherlock Holmes' brother Mycroft asks for assistance when Mr. Melas relays to him a mysterious story about a late night visitor. Who was the foreign young man who adamantly refused when Mr. Melas asked him to sign an unknown document? With Jeremy Brett. Granada Television. 55 mins.

VHS: S11135. $24.95.

Hands of a Murderer

Sherlock Holmes (Edward Woodward) and his trusted friend Dr. Watson (John Hillerman) appear to have finally tracked down and captured the devilish Moriarty (Anthony Andrews). A bungling constable lets the fiend escape the gallows and now Holmes and Watson find themselves enmeshed in a series of intrigues and double bluffs that place the fate of England at risk.

VHS: S26775. $24.98.

Stuart Orme, Great Britain, 1995, 97 mins.

The Hound of the Baskervilles (Brett)

What is the weird curse of the Baskerville family? Sir Charles Baskerville is found dead and when Sir Henry Baskerville arrives from America, he finds a death threat waiting for him at his hotel. An escaped killer roams the moors....A woman cries...A dog howls through the night...And Sherlock Holmes is called in to investigate. With Jeremy Brett as Holmes; Granada TV. Please specify Granada TV version. 120 mins.

VHS: S11141. $39.95.
Laser: LD71469. $29.98.

The Hound of the Baskervilles (Cushing)

An eerie rendering of Sir Arthur Conan Doyle's tale made by the Hammer studio. Director Terence Fisher interprets the Baskerville legend, the notorious "hound for hell" that stalks the gilded, secretive family. With Peter Cushing as Holmes, Andre Morell as Watson and Christopher Lee. "The best Sherlock Holmes movie ever made" (Time Out).

VHS: S18479. $19.98.

The Hound of the Baskervilles (Rathbone)

The first of the Basil Rathbone series of Sherlock Holmes films finds Britain's favorite sleuth afoot on the moors of Dartmoor in Devonshire. It seems the Baskerville family is laboring under the curse of a gigantic hound and seeks assistance. Holmes and Watson do their best. With Nigel Bruce, Richard Greene and Chief, a 140-pound Great Dane, as the title character. B&W.

VHS: S06078. $19.98.

Sidney Lanfield, USA, 1939, 80 mins.

The Hound of the Baskervilles (Richardson)

A stylish, well-acted adaptation of Sir Arthur Conan Doyle's story about Sherlock Holmes' investigation of an eerie string of unsolved murders at a gothic mansion, that's wonderfully photographed. With Donald Churchill, Martin Shaw, Denholm Elliott and Ian Richardson as Holmes.

VHS: S18071. $59.95.

Douglas Hickox, Great Britain, 1983, 100 mins.

The Illustrious Client

Holmes risks his life when he becomes involved with a murdering Austrian baron and the young, wealthy woman who wants to marry him. Can Holmes withstand the evil forces at the baron's command? Starring Jeremy Brett and Edward Hardwicke. Granada TV, 50 mins.

VHS: S16016. $24.98.

The Last Vampyre

Jeremy Brett and David Burke star as the peerless investigators created by Sir Arthur Conan Doyle. In this film villagers begin to suspect that a returned descendant of a family exterminated as vampires is once again causing trouble in their village. 105 mins.

VHS: S24396. $19.95.

The Man with the Twisted Lip

A worried wife consults Sherlock Holmes about her missing husband. Starring Jeremy Brett. Granada TV, 55 mins.

VHS: S11707. $24.95.

The Master Blackmailer

The brilliant Sherlock Holmes (Jeremy Brett) and Doctor Watson (Edward Hardwicke) are enlisted to capture a diabolical blackmailer who has been victimizing a group of Londoners. 120 mins.

VHS: S19930. $24.98.

The Mazarin Stone

Sherlock Holmes (Jeremy Brett) is not at home, so Watson must find the missing Garrideb family member. This person must be found to resolve the last will and testament of the deceased and formerly very wealthy Nathan Garrideb. Coincidentally, or so it seems, someone has stolen the Mazarin Stone, a valuable crown jewel. 50 mins.

VHS: S27444. $19.98.

The Musgrave Ritual

The butler didn't do it—he's dead, and nobody is quite sure why. Starring Jeremy Brett. Granada TV, 55 mins.

VHS: S11704. $24.95.

The Naval Treaty

A secret document disappears and the fate of the future of Europe depends on its retrieval by Sherlock Holmes. Starring Jeremy Brett. 52 mins.

VHS: S24400. $19.98.

The Norwood Builder

Is the young solicitor John McFarlane responsible for the death of the Norwood builder? Why did the builder, until a day before a virtual stranger to McFarlane, want his will suddenly changed to leave everything to McFarlane? From Granada TV; with Jeremy Brett as Holmes. 55 mins.

VHS: S11136. $24.95.

The Priory School

The Duke of Holdernesse's son is kidnapped from his prestigious preparatory school. Starring Jeremy Brett. Granada TV, 55 mins.

VHS: S11708. $24.95.

The Problem of Thor Bridge

An American gold magnate's governess is being held on charges of shooting his wife, and Holmes is invited to help in the matter. When the American makes an untimely and noisy departure, Holmes is perplexed until Watson suggests a visit to the governess. Starring Jeremy Brett and Edward Hardwicke. Granada TV, 50 mins.

VHS: S16017. $24.98.

The Red Circle

Mrs. Warren asks for Sherlock Holmes (Jeremy Brett) to investigate a strange lodger in her home, a man who never leaves his room. While searching for clues, Holmes finds a former lodger of Mrs. Warren's is dead. An American helps Holmes draw a connection between these two strange occurrences. 50 mins.

VHS: S27446. $19.98.

The Red-Headed League

A mysterious ad calls for all red-headed men to join a league that would pay handsomely for rather nominal services. Pawnbroker Jabez Wilson applies and thinks himself fortunate to get the job until two months later when the league is mysteriously dissolved. With Jeremy Brett as Sherlock Holmes; from the recent Granada TV production. 55 mins.

VHS: S11138. $24.95.

The Resident Patient

After a corpulent Mr. Blessington sets up doctor Percy Trevelyan in a fashionable practice, his benefactor installs himself at the house as the Resident Patient. When a Russian father and son disappear during a consultation, Holmes and Watson are called in to find out why Mr. Blessington is the most frightened man in town. With Jeremy Brett as Holmes. From Granada TV. 55 mins.

VHS: S11137. $24.95.

A Scandal in Bohemia

Starring Jeremy Brett and David Burke, this episode features a distressed King of Bohemia. Naturally the King needs Sherlock Holmes to help him. It seems some indiscretion with a lady could damage the reputation of royalty in Europe. 50 mins.

VHS: S24403. $19.98.

The Second Stain

A secret document is stolen from the house of The Secretary for European Affairs. Starring Jeremy Brett. Granada TV, 55 mins.

VHS: S11705. $24.95.

Sherlock Holmes and the Deadly Necklace

Christopher Lee stars as Sherlock Holmes as he and Dr. Watson again battle the evil Moriarty who's after a valuable necklace.

VHS: S09533. $29.95.

Terence Fisher, Great Britain, 1964, 85 mins.

Sherlock Holmes and the Incident at Victoria Falls

Called upon to transport the world's most valuable diamond from Africa to London, the great Sherlock Holmes finds himself in the middle of a murky new mystery that will bring him out of retirement. Romance, murder and mystery in the African jungle, starring Christopher Lee and Patrick Macnee.

VHS: S15583. $89.98.

Bill Corcoran, Great Britain, 1991, 120 mins.

Sherlock Holmes and the Secret Weapon

Dr. Tobel, a Swiss scientist, has invented a new bombsight, and is kidnapped by Holmes' old enemy, Dr. Moriarty. But Dr. Tobel left behind a strange cipher which Holmes will now uncover in a battle of wits. With Basil Rathbone, Nigel Bruce, Lionel Atwill. USA, 1942, 68 mins.

VHS: S01140. $19.95.

Sherlock Holmes and the Spider Woman

This was the first Sherlock Holmes film from Universal with the detective's name out of the title. Gale Sondergaard is the sinister title character who proves a worthy nemesis for Rathbone and Bruce by driving men to commit suicide in their pajamas. With Dennis Hoey as Lestrade. B&W.

VHS: S06085. $19.98.

Roy William Neill, USA, 1944, 62 mins.

Shoscombe Old Place

Holmes is enlisted to investigate the strange relationship of a brother and sister, a missing creditor and an intricate puzzle whose only clue is a human bone found in a furnace. With Jeremy Brett as Holmes, Edward Hardwicke as Watson and Robin Ellis. 50 mins.

VHS: S18155. $24.98.

The Sign of Four (Brett)

Why after the mysterious disappearance of her father does the beautiful Miss Morstan start receiving each year a present of a rare and lustrous pearl? Who is her mysterious benefactor? Why does this person all of a sudden want to meet her? The mystery builds as Holmes and Watson pursue a priceless hoard of Indian treasure and a murderer. With Jeremy Brett as Holmes. Please specify Granada TV version. 120 mins.
VHS: S11140. $39.95.

The Sign of Four (Richardson)

A superior adaptation of Sir Arthur Conan Doyle's Sherlock Holmes novel about the brilliant detective's face-off with a sinister, one-legged villain and dwarf. Ian Richardson stars as Holmes. With David Healy, Cherie Lunghi, Terence Rigby and Thorley Walters.
VHS: S18070. $59.95.
Desmond Davis, Great Britain, 1983, 100 mins.

The "Silent" Mr. Sherlock Holmes

Two early appearances of Sir Arthur Conan Doyle's immortal creation, Sherlock Holmes. The first, The Copper Beeches (1912), was produced under the personal supervision of Doyle. The Man with the Twisted Lip is one of the few Eille Norwood Holmes silents to survive. Hubert Willis is his Watson. B&W. Silent. USA/Great Britain, 1912-22, 68 mins.
VHS: S05448. $29.95.

Silver Blaze

A highly prized racehorse is abducted, and the horse's trainer is dead. Starring Jeremy Brett. Granada TV, 55 mins.
VHS: S11710. $24.95.

The Six Napoleons

Statues and busts of Napoleon are being smashed all over the London streets. Starring Jeremy Brett. Granada TV, 55 mins.
VHS: S11709. $24.95.

The Solitary Cyclist

A female client of Holmes is kidnapped and he must find her before it's too late. Starring Jeremy Brett. 52 mins.
VHS: S24398. $19.95.

The Speckled Band (Brett)

Holmes must discover a murder weapon that leaves no trace. The survival of a family depends on it. Starring Jeremy Brett. 52 mins.
VHS: S24399. $19.98.

The Speckled Band (Massey)

Raymond Massey in his first film as Sherlock Holmes.
VHS: S03784. $34.95.
Jack Raymond, Great Britain, 1931, 80 mins.

A Study in Scarlet

Reginald Owen stars as Sherlock Holmes in this film based on the A. Conan Doyle story.
VHS: S02591. $34.95.
Edwin L. Marin, USA, 1933

Terror by Night

Sherlock Holmes and the reliable Dr. Watson are engaged to protect the Star of Rhodesia on a train trip to Scotland. Murder and the disappearance of the huge diamond sets Holmes to work. The solution to the railroad robbery and the end of the mayhem is eventual. With Rathbone, Bruce, Alan Mowbray. USA, 1946, 72 mins.
VHS: S01142. $19.95.

The Three Gables

Mary Maberley is grieving the loss of her grandson when a realtor arrives and makes a strange offer to buy her house. A condition of the sale is that she cannot take any of her belongings out of the house. Her lawyer advises her to proceed with care, but it is Sherlock Holmes (Jeremy Brett) who finally unravels the origins of this mysterious offer. 50 mins.
VHS: S27442. $19.98.

The Triumph of Sherlock Holmes

The best of the five Arthur Wontner Holmes films is based on Doyle's Valley of Fear. Wontner looked like the spitting image of Holmes as originally drawn. His Watson was played by Ian Fleming. Not that Ian Fleming. Holmes battles Dr. Moriarty at Birlstone Castle. B&W.
VHS: S05449. $29.95.
Leslie S. Hiscott, Great Britain, 1935, 83 mins.

The Wisteria Lodge

After a murder, Holmes and Watson arrive at the Wisteria Lodge to try and uncover its secret. Starring Jeremy Brett. Granada TV, 55 mins.
VHS: S11712. $24.95.

Woman in Green

Holmes and Watson are up against the most atrocious crimes since Jack the Ripper. Scotland Yard is baffled, and so is Holmes, until he discovers that behind these crimes is his old nemesis, Dr. Moriarty. With Basil Rathbone, Nigel Bruce, Hillary Brooke. USA, 1945, 68 mins.
VHS: S01143. $19.95.

Young Sherlock Holmes

Story that speculates about the boyhood adventures of the Conan Doyle master sleuth. Includes his introduction to Watson and first case.
VHS: S06298. $19.95.
Laser: Letterboxed. **LD76099. $39.98.**
Barry Levinson, USA, 1985, 109 mins.

british television

AbFab Moments

Jennifer Saunders and Joanna Lumley are back as Edina and Patsy in a collection of outrageous outtakes, bloopers, lowdown moments and never-before-aired footage from the original series. Hosted by June Whitfield (who stars as Edina's mother). 94 mins.
VHS: S34658. $19.98.

Absolutely Fabulous Collection

Jennifer Saunders and Joanna Lumley made this irreverent BBC comedy series a smash hit with their scathingly funny impersonations of bored, dumb, wealthy London women. Edina and Patsy bring excess to new levels of absurdity. This set includes all 18 episodes and a 30-minute behind-the-scenes look at the show hosted by Saunders which also features priceless outtakes.
VHS: S29989. $99.98.

Absolutely Fabulous Volume One, Part 1

From the BBC, Jennifer Saunders and Joanna Lumley play Edina and Patsy in the biggest British comedy hit since *Fawlty Towers*. They are two 40ish fashionophiles who are out to prove they'll do anything in the name of fun. In this volume they battle with *Fashion, Fat, and France*. 90 mins.
VHS: S25661. $19.98.

Absolutely Fabulous Volume One, Part 2

Edina and Patsy, Jennifer Saunders and Joanna Lumley, are back with mindless over the top and wickedly rich humor in *ISO Tank, Birthday, and Magazine*. 90 mins.
VHS: S25662. $19.98.

Absolutely Fabulous Volume Two, Part 1

Too dumb to know any better and too rich to care, Edina and Patsy, Jennifer Saunders and Joanna Lumley, wend their way through *Hospital, Health, and Morocco*.
VHS: S25663. $19.98.

Absolutely Fabulous Volume Two, Part 2

Even if they could only sober up (or is it settle down?), Edina and Patsy (Jennifer Saunders and Joanna Lumley) would still be the most frighteningly dressed residents of Mayfair. *New Best Friend, Poor and Birth*.
VHS: S25664. $19.98.

Absolutely Fabulous Volume Three, Part 1

Edina and Patsy's comic misadventures are featured in this collection of three episodes. They represent the final season for this outrageous pair of dimwitted, fast-living, Eurotrash fashion victims. Included are the episodes *Doorhandle, Happy New Year* and *Sex*. Great Britain, 90 mins.
VHS: S27051. $19.98.

Absolutely Fabulous Volume Three, Part 2

These are the final three episodes of Edina and Patsy's adventures living larger than they should. The episodes *Jealous, Fear* and *The End* are the last words in comic excess. Great Britain, 90 mins.
VHS: S27052. $19.98.

Absolutely Fabulous: The Last Shout

This made-for-TV film, based on the popular British sitcom *Absolutely Fabulous*, has Edina (Jennifer Saunders) selling her fashion public relations business and going on the road with her pal Patsy (Joanna Lumley). Count on plenty of shopping and champagne swilling in their last adventure. Features a cameo appearance by Marianne Faithful. 90 mins.
VHS: S30043. $19.95.
Laser: LD76084. $39.99.

Agatha Christie's Miss Marple

100 minutes each.
4:50 from Paddington. When a friend decides to visit Miss Marple she has the disagreeable experience of seeing a man strangling a woman in a passing train. Miss Marple sets out to decipher this strange mystery.
VHS: S21162. $19.95.
A Caribbean Mystery. The unflappable Miss Marple goes off to an exclusive resort for a vacation. Just when she is about to become bored among the idle rich, someone is murdered. Now she can do what she does best: outwit the perpetrators of this terrible crime and best the local police.
VHS: S21159. $19.95.
Sleeping Murder. Giles and Gwenda Reed move into their dream house, but this idyll is destroyed by a strange apparition. When Miss Marple discovers the identity of this visitor, she unwittingly provokes the original murderer, placing new victims in danger.
VHS: S21161. $19.95.
The Mirror Cracked from Side to Side. An American movie star goes to the quiet hamlet St. Mary Mead in order to film a new movie. At a party she hosts for the entire village a woman is accidentally poisoned, but it was a mistake. Miss Marple must now investigate the invasion of intrigue from Hollywood that has followed this poor actress.
VHS: S21160. $19.95.
Collector's 4-Video Boxed Set.
VHS: S21163. $59.95.

Agatha Christie's Miss Marple II

Joan Hickson stars as the knitting heroine of this second series of Agatha Christie mysteries.
Agatha Christie's Miss Marple: Murder at the Vicarage. Joan Hickson is Miss Marple, a rather dry old woman with an uncanny sense of justice and a macabre taste for solving crimes. Her investigative powers are suddenly needed in the sleepy country village of St. Mary Mead when a much disliked man is found dead. 100 mins.
VHS: S24232. $19.95.
Agatha Christie's Miss Marple: The Moving Finger. Once again Joan Hickson plays Miss Marple on the trail of murderous intrigue. A rash of poison pen letters is stirring up not only fear but memories of a long forgotten incident many hoped was firmly buried in the past. 100 mins.
VHS: S24233. $19.95.
Agatha Christie's Miss Marple: They Do It with Mirrors. At a rambling country mansion Joan Hickson, as Miss Marple, must contend with a number of off-color incidents. Not only do these events reflect badly on the residents of this great house, but they represent a deadly malice. Only Miss Marple can solve the mystery of the murderer's identity. 100 mins.
VHS: S24234. $19.95.
Agatha Christie's Miss Marple: Nemesis. A cryptic letter sends Miss Marple (Joan Hickson) on a deadly itinerary. Amidst the glorious historic homes she visits there lurks a devious plot fixed on murder. Miss Marple must solve this mystery. 100 mins.
VHS: S24235. $19.95.
Agatha Christie's Miss Marple: At Bertram Hotel. Miss Marple (Joan Hickson) visits her favorite London hotel. Many might find this august setting quite stuffy, but it is just perfect for this sleuth, especially when a murder turns Miss Marple's trip to London into a working vacation. 100 mins.
VHS: S24236. $19.95.
Agatha Christie's Miss Marple II: Collector's Boxed Set. All five videos, each 100 mins.
VHS: S24237. $69.95.

Agatha Christie's Poirot

This witty, imaginative and well acted 10-part series focuses on a string of crimes and murders requiring the attention of Agatha Christie's brilliant detective, the Belgian sleuth Hercule Poirot, brought to vivid, immaculate life by the excellent British actor David Suchet *(The Falcon and the Snowman)*.
Four and Twenty Blackbirds.
VHS: S17461. $24.95.
Murder in the Mews.
VHS: S17459. $24.95.
Problem at Sea.
VHS: S17464. $24.95.
The Adventures of the Clapham Cook.
VHS: S17458. $24.95.
The Adventure of Johnnie Waverly.
VHS: S17460. $24.95.
The Dream.
VHS: S17467. $24.95.
The Incredible Theft.
VHS: S17465. $24.95.
The King of Clubs.
VHS: S17466. $24.95.
The Third Floor Flat.
VHS: S17462. $24.95.
Triangle at Rhodes.
VHS: S17463. $24.95.

All Creatures Great & Small (1 tape)

James Herriot's story of a British rural veterinarian, starring Christopher Timothy in a BBC production.
VHS: S01921. $19.98.
Claude Whatham, Great Britain, 1986, 94 mins.

All Creatures Great & Small (8 tapes)

The complete collection of the popular BBC and PBS favorite, based on the best-selling novels by James Herriot, following the true-life adventures of the veterinarian. Set in the serene beauty of the English countryside in the late 1930s, this is a time when animal medicine is as much folklore as science. With courage and humor, Herriot earns the trust of the local farmers and experiences all the joys and heartaches that go along with caring for all creatures great and small. Six-volume set includes *Horse Sense, Dog Days, It Takes All Kinds, Calf Love, Out of Practice, Nothing Like Experience, Golden Lads & Girls, Advice & Consent, The Last Furlong, Sleeping Partners, Bulldog Breed, Practice Makes Perfect,* and *Breath of Life*. 630 mins.
VHS: S34570. $99.98.

Arch of Triumph

A television remake of Lewis Milestone's adaptation of Erich Maria Remarque's novel. Anthony Hopkins returns to World War II era Paris to exact his revenge on a man who tormented him and the woman he loved. With Leslie-Anne Down and Donald Pleasance.
VHS: S17166. $19.95.
Waris Hussein, Great Britain, 1985, 95 mins.

Archie

The pilot episode of the irreverent and hilarious British comedy program, with John Simpson and Roland Winters. Not the comic strip. On the same program is *The Alan Young Show*.
VHS: S18958. $19.95.

Are You Being Served?

Step into Grace Brothers Department Store and enjoy seasonal cheer in hilarious fashion with one of the BBC's most successful comedies ever. This special holiday-themed collection includes two Christmas programs and the long-lost *Top Hat and Tails* episode.
VHS: S32535. $14.98.

Are You Being Served?

A cast of unbelievably colorful characters make shopping at Grace Brothers a true comic adventure. Their quirky behavior, hilarious banter, and all-round bad manners are on display in these three-episode collections from the BBC. Starring John Inman and Mollie Sugden.
Are You Being Served?: Volume 1. Episodes include 'Dear Sexy Knickers,' 'Our Figures Are Slipping' and 'Camping In.'
VHS: S15978. $14.98.
Are You Being Served?: Volume 2. Episodes include 'Big Brother,' His and Hers' and 'Cold Comfort.'
VHS: S15979. $14.98.
Are You Being Served?: Volume 3. Episodes include "German Week," "New Look" and "No Sale."
VHS: S30647. $14.98.
Are You Being Served?: Volume 4. Episodes include "Wedding Bells," "Do You Take This Man" and "The Erotic Dreams of Mrs. Slocumbe."
VHS: S30648. $14.98.
Are You Being Served?: Volume 5. Episodes include "Fifty Years On," "Oh What a Tangled Web" and "Forward Mr. Grainger."
VHS: S30649. $14.98.
Are You Being Served?: Volume 6.
VHS: S33016. $14.98.
Are You Being Served?: Volume 7.
VHS: S33017. $14.98.

Auf Wiedersehen Pet

In the belief that there will be a more rewarding life for them in Germany, three British bricklayers join up with other "down-to-earth" types and set off to find their fortunes. Perhaps the funniest comedy series of the 80's, *Auf Wiedersehen Pet* was hailed by critics and public alike when it premiered on British Television.
Auf Wiedersehen Pet: If I Were a Carpenter...101 mins.
VHS: S16130. $24.98.
Auf Wiedersehen Pet: The Fugitive...101 mins.
VHS: S16131. $24.98.

The Avengers

The British cult TV classic starring the exquisite Diana Rigg as Mrs. Emma Peel and the dashing Patrick Macnee as John Steed, digitally remastered. Each three-tape set contains six episodes.
The Avengers, 1967 Set 1. Includes *From Venus with Love, The Fear Merchants, Escape in Time, The See-Through Man, The Bird Who Knew Too Much* and *The Winged Avenger*. 312 mins.
VHS: S34663. $29.95.

The Avengers, 1967 Set 2. *The Living Dead; The Hidden Tiger; The Correct Way to Kill; Never, Never Say Die; Epic* and *The Superlative Seven*. 312 mins.
VHS: S34664. $29.95.

Benny Hill

The British clown prince of comedy in a series of madcap skits and hilarious sketches. Each tape is 55 mins.
Benny Hill's Crazy World!.
VHS: S10345. $19.99.
Benny Hill's Home Video Drive-In.
VHS: S10350. $19.99.
Benny Hill's One Night Video Stand.
VHS: S10349. $19.99.
Benny Hill's Video Follies.
VHS: S10351. $19.99.
Benny Hill's Video Revue.
VHS: S10348. $19.99.
Benny Hill's Video Sideshow.
VHS: S10347. $19.99.
Benny Hill's Video Spotlight.
VHS: S10346. $19.99.

Benny Hill's World: New York

Hill is all over New York, bringing his racy British humor to sites like Central Park, Times Square and the South Street Seaport. He impersonates a rapper and shares that quintessential New York experience, a cab ride. 60 mins.
VHS: S26038. $19.95.

The Best of British Film Comedy

A collection of the greatest moments from the golden age of British film comedy, with Benny Hill, Peter Sellers, Marty Feldman, Eric Idle, Alec Guiness, Margaret Rutherford, Tony Hancock, Spike Milligan and more. 91 mins.
VHS: S31818. $29.95.

The Best of Cracker Mysteries

Three films from this award-winning, hard-edged British mystery series which aired on A & E are included in this collector's boxed set. Robbie Coltrane stars as the volatile and enigmatic Dr. Eddie Fitzgerald, a boozing but brilliant forensic psychologist who tests his wits against cunning murderous minds in *The Mad Woman in the Attic* (100 mins.), *To Say I Love You* (150 mins.) and *One Day a Lemming Will Fly* (100 mins.). 350 mins.
VHS: S28503. $59.95.

The Best of the Lenny Henry Show

Thrill to revolution, romance, drama and sport with comprehensive comedian Lenny Henry—master of mimicry, devil of disguise. Also starring Frank Bruno, Robbie Coltrane *(Nuns on the Run)* and Dawn French.
VHS: S14514. $19.98.

The Best of the Lovejoy Mysteries

Ian McShane stars as Lovejoy, a charming, handsome, brilliant and thoroughly untrustworthy scoundrel. This disreputable antiques dealer can spot a fake in seconds but he is even more likely to find trouble. The enjoyable British series from A&E includes four episodes, 50 minutes each.
Friends in High Places. Lovejoy agrees to sell an Incan ring for Lady Jane's friend. The question is, which intrigues him more, the ring or its owner?
VHS: S25838. $14.95.
Loveknots. A seemingly ordinary Berber rug is bought for an inflated price at auction. Later this same rug is stolen, leading Lovejoy to suspect something sinister is afoot.
VHS: S25840. $14.95.
Scotch on the Rocks. Lovejoy purchases an 18th-century Scottish commemorative sword from his daughter. Unfortunately, someone else wants it and will do anything to possess it.
VHS: S25839. $14.95.
The Ring. An elaborate scheme should supply Lovejoy with desperately needed cash, except things don't go as planned. Lady Jane finds herself drawn into a game of deception and doesn't even realize it.
VHS: S25841. $14.95.
The Best of the Lovejoy Mysteries, Collector's Boxed Set.
VHS: S25842. $59.95.

The Best of the Two Ronnies

Ronnie Corbett and Ronnie Barker are the Two Ronnies. One is short and dark and the other is taller, whiter and a few pounds larger. They have kept England laughing for years, as well as those who watch public television. Now they are on video and ready to entertain anyone with the price of the rental. England, 1983.
VHS: S05613. $29.98.

The Best of What's Left... Not Only...But Also...

Written by and starring Peter Cook and Dudley Moore, the show is comprised of the best comedy sketches from this famous duo who were an inseparable act during the 60's and 70's. This is their reunion tape.
VHS: S14513. $19.98.

A Bit of Fry and Laurie

Irreverent and sly humor BBC style, literate and self-reflexive, with Stephen Fry and Hugh Laurie *(Jeeves and Wooster)* that's provocative and witty. 89 mins.
VHS: S18876. $19.98.

Black Adder Goes Forth: The Western Front of WWII, 1917

Rowan Atkinson, Tony Robinson, Brian Blessed, Tim McInnerny, Elspet Gray and Peter Cook take the Western Front by storm. Is the 20th Century ready for Black Adder's impudent brand of satire? In two relentless volumes.
Black Adder Goes Forth, Part 1. 100 mins.
VHS: S15974. $14.98.
Black Adder Goes Forth, Part 2. 100 mins.
VHS: S15975. $14.98.

The Black Adder I, Part I

Rowan Atkinson, Tony Robinson, Brian Blessed, Tim McInnerny, Elspet Gray and Peter Cook star in this very popular comedy series. Includes "The Foretelling", "Born to Be King" and "The Archbishop."
VHS: S14511. $14.98.

The Black Adder I, Part II

This irreverent British satire stars Rowan Atkinson, Tony Robinson, Brian Blessed, Tim McInnerny, Elspet Gray and Peter Cook. Includes "The Queen of Spain's Beard", "Witchsmeller Pursuivant" and "The Black Seal."
VHS: S14512. $14.98.

Black Adder II: The 16th Century

Being a Renaissance man is no reason to stop mucking up the pages of history. Edmund is at it again, with his incorrigible exploits tainting two darkly funny volumes. Rowan Atkinson, Tony Robinson, Brian Blessed, Tim McInnerny, Elspet Gray and Peter Cook star in Part 1. Part 2 features Miranda Richardson and Rowan Atkinson.
Black Adder II, Part 1. 100 mins.
VHS: S15972. $14.98.
Black Adder II, Part 2. 100 mins.
VHS: S15973. $14.98.

Black Adder the Third, Part I

Rowan Atkinson stars in this outrageously witty and popular satire, the Blackadder series. In three brilliantly funny episodes set in Regency England, Edmund Blackadder, valet and butler to the phenomenally "mini-brained" Prince Regent, sends up everything from the French Revolution to the British nobility. From the BBC.
VHS: S11212. $14.98.

Black Adder the Third, Part II

This successful series from Britain features three episodes from the scrolls of Blackadder, an English family of cowards and cads, who never seem to get a solid grip on life.
VHS: S12585. $14.98.

Black Adder's Christmas Carol

Rowan Atkinson, Robbie Coltrane and Miranda Richardson star in this farcical adaptation of Dickens's immortal *A Christmas Carol*.
VHS: S17373. $19.98.

The Black Candle & The Black Velvet Gown

Originally shown on Masterpiece Theater, this tape presents two British-made stories of passion and tragedy featuring well-drawn characters in class-divided Victorian England. Each tape is 105 mins.
VHS: S30035. $39.99.

Blakes 7

Intergalactic adventure follows an interplanetary resistance group battling for survival against a totalitarian superpower. Roaming a universe of boundless space and restrictive discipline, freedom-fighter Blake and the crew of spaceship *Liberator* lock in combat with the all-powerful forces of the Federation.
Blakes 7, Volume 1. *The Way Back/Space Fall*. 105 mins.
VHS: S16137. $19.98.
Blakes 7, Volume 2. *Cygnus Alpha/Time Squad*. 105 mins.
VHS: S16138. $19.98.
Blakes 7, Volume 3. *The Web/Seek, Locate, Destroy*. 105 mins.
VHS: S16139. $19.98.
Blakes 7, Volume 4. *Mission to Destiny/Duel*. 105 mins.
VHS: S16140. $19.98.
Blakes 7, Volume 5. *Project Avalon/Breakdown*. 105 mins.
VHS: S16141. $19.98.
Blakes 7, Volume 6. *Bounty/Deliverance*. 105 mins.
VHS: S16142. $19.98.
Blakes 7, Volume 7. *Orac/Redemption*.
VHS: S19267. $19.98.
Blakes 7, Volume 8. *Shadow/Weapon*.
VHS: S19268. $19.98.
Blakes 7, Volume 9. *Horizon/Pressure Point*.
VHS: S19269. $19.98.
Blakes 7, Volume 10. *Trial/Killer*.
VHS: S19270. $19.98.
Blakes 7, Volume 11. *Hostage/Countdown*.
VHS: S19271. $19.98.
Blakes 7, Volume 12. *Voices from Past/Gambit*.
VHS: S19272. $19.98.
Blakes 7, Volume 13. *Keeper/Star One*.
VHS: S19273. $19.98.
Blakes 7, Volume 14. *Aftermath/Powerplay*.
VHS: S19274. $19.98.
Blakes 7, Volume 15. *Volcano/Dawn of Gods*.
VHS: S19275. $19.98.
Blakes 7, Volume 16. *Harvest of Kairos/City at Edge of the World*.
VHS: S19276. $19.98.
Blakes 7, Volume 17. *Children of Auron/Rumors of Death*.
VHS: S19277. $19.98.
Blakes 7, Volume 18. *Sarcophagus/Ultraworld*.
VHS: S19278. $19.98.
Blakes 7, Volume 19. *Moloch/Death-Watch*.
VHS: S19279. $19.98.
Blakes 7, Volume 20. *Terminal/Rescue*.
VHS: S19280. $19.98.
Blakes 7, Volume 21. *Power/Traitor*.
VHS: S19281. $19.98.
Blakes 7, Volume 22. *Stardrive/Animals*.
VHS: S19282. $19.98.
Blakes 7, Volume 23. *Headhunter/Assassin*.
VHS: S19283. $19.98.
Blakes 7, Volume 24. *Games/Sand*.
VHS: S19284. $19.98.
Blakes 7, Volume 25. *Gold/Orbit*.
VHS: S19285. $19.98.
Blakes 7, Volume 26. *Warlord/Blake*.
VHS: S19286. $19.98.

Blat

The Russian *Sting*. This cross-cultural comedy pits an Italian-Russian gangster against the British financial establishment, with hilarious results. Robert Hardy stars. Great Britain, 90 mins.
VHS: S14326. $49.95.

Bleak House

Denholm Elliott and Diana Rigg star in Charles Dickens' biting social commentary on 19th century English justice. John Jarndyce (Elliott) rises above a notorious law suit that has devastated others. But tragedy ensues when his young ward becomes obsessed with the labyrinthine case and the intrigue surrounding it. Produced by the BBC.
VHS: S07176. $39.98.
Ross Devenish, Great Britain, 1985, 391 mins.

Body and Soul

This award-winning six-hour mini-series is the story of a young nun (Kristin Scott Thomas) who, after 16 years in a secluded convent in Wales, is forced to choose between two conflicting worlds when she must take charge of her deceased brother's young family and his bankrupt yarn-spinning mill. Three tapes. 5 hours, 12 mins.
VHS: S30907. $69.95.

The Body in the Library

From the BBC Miss Marple series comes another challenging murder mystery from the mind of Agatha Christie. Miss Marple (Joan Hickson) is asked to defend Colonel Bantry's reputation and find someone else responsible for leaving a corpse in a certain room in his country estate.
VHS: S06532. $19.98.
Silvio Narizzano, Great Britain, 1987, 151 mins.

Bramwell, Series 1

Jemma Redgrave stars as a determined young woman in this Victorian era mini-series from England. Bramwell has set herself an ambitious goal at odds with the Victorian era. She wants to be a leading surgeon. Against all convention, she pursues her goal with a single minded tenacity which can only be admired by even her most doubtful contemporaries. 4 volumes. 360 mins.
VHS: S29526. $89.95.

Bramwell, Series 3

The spirited young doctor Eleanor Bramwell (Jemma Redgrave) shakes up the Victorian medical world in four episodes. Each is a sensational journey through life in 1896 London. From an elegant gala in the Bramwell family home to the turbulence of life on the streets, we follow Eleanor as she struggles to sustain her small, charitable infirmary.
VHS: S32995. $29.98.
David Tucker/Paul Unwin, Great Britain, 1996, 240 mins.

Bread
A BBC comedy regarding the usual things: religion, baby christenings, unrequited love, sexual exploits and prowess. A classic dose of the Liverpool family's trials and tribulations. 85 mins.
VHS: S12631. $29.95.

The Bretts
The Bretts are a fiercely competitive family whose wit and charm have captivated audiences for the entire run of this series. They are the center of London's theater world at a time of unmatched glamour and excitement, the 1920s. Their public triumphs and private traumas, from the star couple at the center of the family to the younger, newer luminaries, offer endless riveting drama. Each set contains 6 episodes of 50 minutes for a total of 5 hours.
Collection 1.
VHS: S22938. $99.98.
Collection 2.
VHS: S22939. $99.98.

Brides of Christ
Brenda Fricker *(My Left Foot)* stars in a searing, award-winning, British drama that captures the restless desperation of a reclusive society and its encounters with the outside world. From student Rosemary's rejection of rigid sexual moral codes to Sister Paul's decision to leave the convent for a radical priest, this is a critically-acclaimed, riveting production. Three tapes in a boxed set. Total length: 300 mins.
VHS: S21903. $59.95.

Brideshead Revisited
The acclaimed BBC series, based on the novel by Evelyn Waugh, in videocassette in 6 volumes. 98 minutes each.
Book I: Chapter 1: Nostalgia for a Vanished Past. Charles meets flamboyant Sebastian Flyte. As the youngest son of the aristocratic Marchmain family, he introduces Charles to a charmed life.
VHS: S06621. $19.98.
Book II: Chapter 2: Home and Abroad. Chapter 3: Shadows Close In. Charles and Sebastian visit the self-exiled Lord Marchmain and his mistress in Venice. Then Charles finally meets the compelling Marchmains. Charles is mesmerized.
VHS: S06622. $19.98.
Book III: Chapter 4: Sebastian Against the World. Chapter 5: Julia Blossoms. Sebastian recognizes that his family is stealing Charles, his only friend. Despairing, he becomes a drunkard and runs away. Meanwhile, his sister Julia blossoms into full womanhood and captivates all.
VHS: S06623. $19.98.
Book IV: Chapter 6: Julia's Marriage. Chapter 7: The Unseen Hook. Julia and Rex Mottram marry despite family disapproval. Lady Marchmain falls ill. Julia asks Charles to find Sebastian and bring him back before his mother dies. Charles finds Sebastian in Morocco, but is shocked at what he finds.
VHS: S06624. $19.98.
Book V: Chapter 8: Brideshead Deserted. Chapter 9: Orphans of the Storm. Charles' and Julia's respective marriages begin to fail. Unexpectedly, they meet again. A torrid love affair ensues. Once again Charles returns to Brideshead Castle—this time as Julia's lover.
VHS: S06625. $19.98.
Book VI: Chapter 10: A Twitch upon the Thread. Chapter 11: Brideshead Revisited. Lord Marchmain returns to Brideshead Castle to die. Displeased with his eldest son, he decides to rewrite his will. A chapter of aristocratic tradition comes to a close.
VHS: S06626. $19.98.
Brideshead Revisited, Giftpack: All six books with a giftpack for storage.
VHS: S06627. $119.88.

Brother Cadfael
Medieval England provides the perfect gloomy setting for this engaging series of murder mysteries starring acclaimed British actor Sir Derek Jacobi. Jacobi brings the same intensity to this series that he demonstrated in *I, Claudius*. 75 mins. each.
Monk's Hood. The Abbey comes into a great inheritance just as a landowner decides to favor the church, because this patron dies from poison at the abbey itself. In addition to this crime, Cadfael must deal with another problem: the landowner's widow is his childhood sweetheart.
VHS: S23636. $19.95.
One Corpse Too Many. Cadfael has just settled into a new and apparently peaceful existence when he stumbles across a brutal murder. In a city at war, he sets out to find the killer.
VHS: S23633. $19.95.
The Leper of St. Giles. A great wedding is to be held at the abbey but the groom is absent. This powerful Baron mysteriously rode into the night and disappeared. Cadfael must find out who harmed the Baron.
VHS: S23635. $19.95.
The Sanctuary Sparrow. The town's goldsmith is robbed and left for dead, leading Cadfael to set off on a trail cloaked in treachery and murder. Can he succeed in finding the perpetrator before a local witch-hunt turns deadly?
VHS: S23634. $19.95.
Complete Set.
VHS: S23637. $79.80.

Brother Cadfael II
Sir Derek Jacobi stars as a monk with a past who has a passion for solving crimes, in this second series. Once a Crusader, he now uses his skills in botany and medicine to find a host of devilish wrongdoers. Each episode is approximately 75 minutes.
St. Peter's Fair. A disagreeable merchant is murdered, but Cadfael suspects that greed is not the motive for this death. Instead, his worst fears are confirmed as another merchant turns up dead. Cadfael becomes embroiled in a wild chase where his very life is at stake.
VHS: S27393. $19.95.
The Devil's Novice. Though a young man confesses to the murder of a cleric, his admission of guilt is nothing but a lie. He is hiding a family story of cowardice and treachery. Cadfael must uncover this torturous legacy.
VHS: S27394. $19.95.
The Virgin in the Ice. Cadfael's clumsy but much-loved Novice stands accused of murder and rape. In the desperate search for clues that could save this Novice, Cadfael discovers a renegade band of former Crusaders and a young squire who turns out to be a son he knew nothing about.
VHS: S27392. $19.95.
Brother Cadfael II: Boxed Set. The complete three-volume set.
VHS: S27395. $59.95.

Brother Cadfael III
In this three-volume set Sir Derek Jacobi *(I, Claudius)* returns as the sleuthing 12th-century monk with an affinity for solving crimes. Includes *The Raven in the Forgate, A Morbid Taste for Bones* and *The Rose Rent*. Based on the highly acclaimed books by Ellis Peters. Each tape is 85 mins.
VHS: S32608. $59.95.

The Buccaneers
Edith Wharton's book of the same name was adapted for this enthralling BBC mini-series. A group of rich American women find love, romance and marriage amidst English high society. New World charms delight the English at first, but a clash of cultures leads to a variety of troubles. This is a heartrending, beautifully staged and costumed production. 288 mins.
VHS: S27064. $59.95.

The Buddha of Suburbia
One of the larger artistic achievements of British television: Brenda Blethyn *(Secrets and Lies)*, Narveen Andrews *(The English Patient)* and Roshan Seth *(Indiana Jones and the Temple of Doom)* star in this acclaimed drama, based on the best-selling novel by Hanif Kureishi *(My Beautiful Laundrette)*, of Karim, a young schoolboy living in the suburbs, whose life changes when his Zen-obsessed father becomes a guru in the '70s Buddhist scene and leaves his suburban home for London. With original music by David Bowie.
VHS: S31262. $29.98.
Roger Michell, Great Britain, 1993, 220 mins.

Butterflies
A BBC comedy about a suburban housewife named Ria with two oafish but lovable sons. Although she's happily married, Ria experiences panic when she looks in the mirror: There's so much left to experience! Enter recent divorcee Leonard, lonely and romantic. 60 mins.
VHS: S12632. $29.95.

Catherine Cookson Collection Set 1
Includes *The Fifteen Streets, The Dwelling Place, The Cinder Path* and *The Man Who Cried*. Four tapes. Nine hours.
VHS: S34105. $89.95.

Catherine Cookson Collection Set 2
Includes *The Gambling Man* and *The Glass Virgin*. Two tapes. Five hours.
VHS: S34106. $69.95.

Catherine Cookson Collection Set 3
Two stories from popular British author Dame Catherine Cookson. In *The Moth* (150 mins.), set in 1913, carpenter Robert Bradley leaves the shipyards for a job in his uncle's furniture business, then finds work as a servant in the dysfunctional Thorman household, where an attraction develops between Robert and the aristocratic young Sarah Thorman. In *The Rag Nymph* (150 mins.), Aggie Winkowski takes in abandoned 10-year-old Millie Forrester to protect her from the rough streets. Four-tape set. Five hours.
VHS: S33021. $69.98.

Catherine Cookson: The Glass Virgin
This is a wonderful costume drama about a woman and her adventures. At age 10, Annabella Lagrange lives a life of luxury. Unfortunately, she is innocent of the shame which afflicts her family. All that changes at 17 when she ventures beyond her own doorstep and discovers the love and laughter she has always longed for. 150 mins.
VHS: S27835. $34.98.

Caught in the Act
In Britain this collection of surveillance camera video clips caused a sensation. Armed robbery, assaults, car thefts, drug deals and intimate sexual acts are all shown on this astonishing video. Included is a segment that has become known as "The Princess Di-Spy Story." 50 mins.
VHS: S29506. $14.95.

Chef!
Comedian Lenny Harry stars as Gareth Blackstock, the temperamental Chef de Cuisine at the prestigious Le Chateau Anglais restaurant. With one uncompromising chef, a loyal but loopy staff, and a two-Michelin-starred restaurant in constant financial distress, it's a guaranteed recipe for hilarity. Each three-episode tape is 87 mins.
Chef!
VHS: S31688. $19.98.
Chef!: A Second Helping.
VHS: S31687. $19.98.

Chiller: "Here Comes the Mirror Man"
Gary is a reclusive squatter living in a run down church that is painted entirely black inside. His social worker, Wendy, can't seem to leave him alone and wants to know if Michael was the reason he left the hostel and moved into the church. Oddly, though Gary likes to be alone, he is often seen with Michael. When Wendy is replaced by Anna, Michael's true identity is revealed and the revelation leads to unforeseen terrors.
VHS: S26782. $19.98.
Lawrence Gordon Clark, Great Britain, 50 mins.

Chiller: "Number Six"
Five children have fallen prey to a serial killer influenced by Celtic myth. After butchering each with a Druidic knife, he places the victims behind an old oak tree during a full moon. Now, as another full moon approaches, the only clues are the vestiges of a Celtic settlement and a child's drawing containing a shadowy figure.
VHS: S26784. $19.98.
Lawrence G. Clark/Peter Lover, Great Britain, 50 mins.

Chiller: "Prophecy"
A group of students hold a seance in a dark basement just for kicks. Everyone gets a message "from the Great Beyond," but one, addressed to Frannie, is in Latin. "Non Omnis Moriar" means "I shall not die," and one by one all the participants of the seance die except for Frannie. The mystery deepens when she stays with a family whose motto is "Non Omnis Moriar." It seems they are related to an infamous Satanist who died in the very basementwhere Frannie first heard this prophetic motto.
VHS: S26780. $19.98.
Lawrence Gordon Clark, Great Britain, 50 mins.

Chiller: "The Man Who Didn't Believe in Ghosts"
A young family move into a Victorian castle in Yorkshire. Mysterious events force the wife to conclude there is a paranormal presence at work in her new home. She flees to London with her son and leaves her doubting husband behind. He has made a career debunking stories of the supernatural. One night, all alone at home, he is forced to confront a mysterious figure who disturbs his sleep.
VHS: S26783. $19.98.
Bob Mahoney, Great Britain, 50 mins.

Chiller: "Toby"
When a young woman's pregnancy fails, she and her husband move to a new home in order to begin again. Just as they seem overwhelmed by the prospect of what might have been, the woman finds that she is pregnant again. Everything seems quite normal, except that the doctors can find no fetus in the woman's swelling body. Madness, or worse still, a manifestation of an otherworldly force, offers the only possible explanation.
VHS: S26781. $19.98.
Bob Mahoney, Great Britain, 50 mins.

Christabel

The acclaimed BBC series written by award-winning playwright Dennis Potter stars Elizabeth Hurley as a beautiful young Englishwoman, married to a young German national. Forced into politics by the events of the rising Nazism around her, *Christabel* is a moving, beautifully produced program about love, hardship, survival and the strength of the individual. Great Britain, 1989, 149 mins.

VHS: S10438. $19.98.

The Cinder Path

Lloyd Owen is Charlie MacFell, a man who despises the rough cinder path outside his bleak farmhouse home, as it was there that his brutal father handed out vicious beatings and crushed his confidence with taunts that he was a born loser. With Catherine Zeta Jones and Maria Miles. Based on the best-selling novel by Catherine Cookson. 145 mins.

VHS: S31111. $26.98.

Class Act

Joanna Lumley, of the hit British TV series *Absolutely Fabulous*, stars in this four-video collection of another hilarious British TV serial. It's liberally spiked with the vulgar amorality of the English upper class. Sex, theft, wit, and gut instinct drive a widow desperately searching for the lost fortune of her deceased husband. All she wants is enough champagne to stay wet, but avoiding jail becomes another passion by necessity. 6 hours.

VHS: S27834. $79.98.

The Complete Black Adder

Finally, all 24 episodes of the hilarious BBC series are available, with new outrageous footage that has never been seen before. Rowan Atkinson's historical and hysterical adventures span the ages for a good laugh.

VHS: S26416. $99.98.

Cool It—Phil Cool

Now meet Phil Cool. The remarkable talent of this new British TV comedian brings you some of the funniest sketches ever. Called "the most flexible face in the business"—watch impressions of the Pope in a fish and chip shop, and Prince Charles interviewing Mick Jagger. 59 mins.

VHS: S10634. $29.95.

The Country Diary of an Edwardian Lady

Pippa Guard stars as Edith Holden, the author who wrote the autobiographical best-seller on which this film is based. Beginning with her idyllic childhood in the British countryside, the film follows Edith through her marriage and her mysterious demise.

VHS: S20809. $26.98.

Dirk Campbell, Great Britain, 90 mins.

Cracker

Robbie Coltrane returns to his celebrated role as the brilliant, vice-ridden forensic psychologist Dr. Eddie "Fitz" Fitzgerald in this collector's set of three *Cracker Mysteries* from the award-winning British TV series. In *The Big Crunch*, a bizarre case draws Fitz into the secretive world of a fundamentalist Christian cult; in *Men Should Weep*, Fitz unwittingly helps a serial rapist avoid the law and turns him into a murderer; in *Brotherly Love*, a delicate murder investigation is upset by allegations of rape within the police department. Each video is 150 mins.

VHS: S34425. $59.95.

Dad's Army

An all-time classic! Join Captain Mainwaring and his bumbling group of British Home Guard at their incompetent best. This cowardly "force of ruthless killers" are always ready to strike terror into the heart of the Wehrmacht. Find them at the Walmington-On-Sea. Includes six volumes: *The Day the Balloon Went Up* (87 mins.), *Asleep in the Deep* (83 mins.), *The Two and a Half Feathers* (87 mins.), *The Deadly Attachment* (87 mins.), *Big Guns* (87 mins.) and *Mum's Army* (87 mins.). 8 hours total.

VHS: S31258. $89.98.

The Dangerous Brothers: World of Danger

Fractured, free spirited and volatile comedy from two of England's most versatile performers, R. Mayall and Adrian Edmondson *(Drop Dead Fred)*. 77 mins.

VHS: S18877. $19.98.

A Dark Adapted Eye

The BBC produced this adaptation of a Ruth Rendell, aka Barbara Vine, murder mystery. Two sisters are engaged in a bitter rivalry. Ultimately their competition ends in murder and execution. This story is adapted from the case of Vera Hillyard, one of the last women to hang in Britain. 150 mins.

VHS: S27745. $19.98.

The Darling Buds of May—Collection Set 1: The The Darling Buds of May

This series, filmed in rural England, is based on H.E. Bates' best-selling novels. Set in 1958, the stories are a nostalgic celebration of a flamboyant loving family. Includes *The Darling Buds of May*, in which an unsuspecting tax inspector named Cedric Charlton invades the private space of the Larkins' Kent farm to inquire about Pop's nonexistent accounts; *When the Green Woods Laugh*, in which Pop turns to developing properties for additional income, while the rest of the family is preparing for Charley and Mariette's extravagant wedding; and *A Breath of French Air*, in which Pop is reluctant to travel to foreign lands for the family's much desired vacation, though Charley convinces everyone France is their ideal destination. With their French primer and the smallest child in tow, everyone loads up the Rolls Royce for a surreal and hilarious road trip to "exotic" locales. Starring David Jason, Pam Ferris, Philip Franks, and Catherine Zeta Jones. 5 hours.

VHS: S19191. $74.98.

The Darling Buds of May—Collection Set 2: Oh! To Be in England

An exuberant look at the Larkin family. They're a large, boisterous Kent farmer family with a peculiar tendency to find adventure. With David Jason, Pam Ferris, Philip Franks and Catherine Zeta Jones. Includes *Oh! To Be in England*, in which, on the eve of the birth of the first grandchild, Pop is considering new lines of business and Charley is trying to forge his way as the family wage earner and provider; *Stranger at the Gates*, in which a young charismatic stranger arrives seeking work and insinuates himself into the Larkins' home, enchanting the kids with magic tricks; and *A Season of Heavenly Gifts*, in which Pop witnesses a plane crash in an adjoining field, agrees to transport the cargo, and unwittingly becomes involved in a complex smuggling operation. 5 hours.

VHS: S19192. $74.98.

The Darling Buds of May—Collection Set 3: The Happiest Days of Your Life

This series, filmed in rural England, is based on H.E. Bates' best-selling novels. Set in 1958, the stories are a nostalgic celebration of a flamboyant loving family. Includes *The Happiest Days of Your Life*, *Cast Not Your Pearls Before Swine* and *Climb the Greasy Pole*, in which Mariette and Charlie are making dough, Pop goes to the pigs and then makes political hay. Starring David Jason, Pam Ferris, Philip Franks, and Catherine Zeta Jones. Five hours.

VHS: S34410. $59.98.

The Darling Buds of May—Holiday Special Collection Set

Two videos from the British TV series based on the nostalgic novels of H.E. Bates, which look back to the 1950s. *Christmas Is Coming*: Christmas is a time of anticipation and joy. In the case of the Darling Buds, Marriette's pregnancy only adds to the holiday spirit. In fact there is so much good cheer in this household that the Bud family decide to share their joy with a family that has less to be thankful for. 50 mins. *Le Grand Weekend*: In this episode, the family wins a holiday in Paris. Preparations throw the household into chaos and just as things are bubbling along nicely a hurricane ambles into view. 50 mins.

VHS: S34109. $34.98.

Dennis Potter's Lipstick on Your Collar

Dennis Potter's last television series is still too hot for American television. His previous works for British TV, *The Singing Detective* and *Pennies from Heaven*, were critical and popular triumphs. In this series Potter combines rock 'n' roll daydreams with a story about the Suez crisis. As the War Office agonizes over waning British power, two clerks dream of sexual conquest to the driving new rhythms emanating from America. 120 mins.

VHS: S26696. $59.95.

Dennis Potter: The Last Interview

Potter transformed serious television drama with his insightful works for British TV. *The Singing Detective* and *Pennies from Heaven* were hailed as breakthroughs combining challenging themes with complex characters. Potter's stories went well beyond the usual manipulations found in standard psychological dramas. This interview with Potter, shot shortly before he died, finds him reflecting on both his work and his life. 70 mins.

VHS: S26634. $19.95.

Doctor Who

Fans of the world's most popular sci-fi star, the time-travelling Doctor Who, will enjoy this legendary "E-Space Trilogy," a trio of the Doctor's most-requested unreleased adventures. Starring the most popular Doctor Who, Tom Baker. Includes 4½ hours of programming.

VHS: S32536. $49.98.

The Duchess of Duke Street

One of the BBC's most acclaimed productions. Created by John Hawksworth *(Upstairs, Downstairs)*, this romantic, captivating and lavish drama is set in turn-of-the century London and is based on the life of Rosa Lewis (Gemma Jones), a lowly cook who rises to the pinnacle of English society.

VHS: S32028. $119.98.

The Dwelling Place

Based on the best-selling novel by Catherine Cookson, this is the story of a fiercely defiant 16-year-old girl (Tracy Whitwell), who struggles to hold her family together following the death of their parents, turning a hillside cave into a home for her younger brothers and sisters. She is raped and left pregnant by a drunken young aristocrat, then finds herself involved with Lord Fischel (James Fox), and is forced to make a heartbreaking decision between the two men who profoundly influence her life. 145 mins.

VHS: S31112. $26.98.

Edward the King

This sweeping 13-part saga based on the life of Great Britain's Edward VII covers 70 of the most tumultuous years of Britain at the height of her power. The story begins with the rebellion of a boy pampered beyond endurance, and continues through his mother's distrust and jealousy, his marriage and scandalous affairs, his most delicate international negotiations and his behind-the-throne carousing. With Sir John Gielgud as Disraeli, Timothy West as Edward VII, Helen Ryan as Alexandra, and Robert Hardy as Prince Albert.

VHS: S33142. $149.95.

Great Britain, 1985, 780 mins.

Elizabeth R.

Glenda Jackson stars in this Emmy-Award winning television series, first screened on *Masterpiece Theater*. Jackson plays Elizabeth, who became Elizabeth I, one of England's most venerable monarchs. The story begins during the reign of Henry VIII, when he turns from the Catholic Church in search of a male heir through a variety of wives. Despite the arrival of a male heir, it is Elizabeth who triumphs as Queen. 540 mins.

VHS: S25908. $149.98.

The Fall and Rise of Reginald Perrin

Distinguished actor Leonard Rossiter stars as Reginald E. Perrin, a man on the run from both success and the rat race in this smash hit BBC comedy. Two-video set.

VHS: S31260. $59.98.

Far from the Madding Crowd

Paloma Baeza *(The Odyssey)* stars as Bathsheba Everdene, a beautiful and proud young woman with a fiercely independent spirit who ensnares—and almost destroys—three men.

VHS: S34665. $29.98.

Nicholas Renton, Great Britain, 1998, 208 mins.

A Fatal Inversion

In this BBC-produced murder mystery a youthful summer vacation takes a deadly turn. Based on a Ruth Rendell story written under the name of Barbara Vine, it charts the realization among a group of friends that something terribly wrong happened at Wyvis Hall over 12 years ago. 150 mins.

VHS: S27746. $19.98.

Fawlty Towers

John Cleese and Connie Booth wrote and starred in this hilarious television series about a hotel plagued by crisis, chaos and bizarre characters. Each tape has three episodes.

Fawlty Towers

Enjoy the complete set of riotously bizarre episodes from the bonkers BBC comedy series, starring Monty Python's John Cleese as the owner of a disaster-prone English hotel. One of the most outrageous and original creations ever to escape onto the airwaves. 368 mins.

Laser: LD76748. $119.98.

Basil and the Rat. Although Manuel the waiter insists his pet is a Siberian hamster, the health inspector does not agree. Basil vows to solve the problem. With *Communications Problems* and *The Anniversary*. Directed by Douglas Argent. 94 minutes.

VHS: S01892. $14.98.

Kipper and the Corpse. When a guest dies in his sleep, everyone assumes he was killed by the kippers served at breakfast. Basil is concerned with hiding the body so the other guests won't panic. With *Gourmet Night* and *Waldorf Salad*. Directed by J.H. Davies. 90 minutes.

VHS: S01891. $14.98.

The Germans. With Sybil in the hospital, Basil is knocked in the head by a falling moose head and proceeds to tell his German guests the "truth" about their Fatherland. With *Hotel Inspectors* and *A Touch of Class*. Directed by J.H. Davies. 90 minutes.

VHS: S01894. $14.98.

The Psychiatrist. A visiting psychiatrist encounters Basil trying to prove a guest is smuggling women up to his room. With *The Builders* and *The Wedding Party*. Directed by J.H. Davies. 98 minutes.

VHS: S01893. $14.98.

Fawlty Towers: The Complete Set.

VHS: S17378. $54.98.

The Fifteen Streets

This International Emmy Award-nominated adaptation of Catherine Cookson's bestseller is the story of two brawling brothers, John O'Brien (Owen Teale) and Dominic (Sean Bean), who work on the docks at the shipyard. John meets and falls in love with the daughter (Clare Holman) of the local shipbuilder, but can their love survive the bigotry of *The Fifteen Streets*? 108 mins.

VHS: S31114. $24.98.

The Final Cut
Ian Richardson reprises his role as an unflappable British politician in this final part of the deviously funny *House of Cards/To Play the King* series. Richardson stars as Urquhart, a master of manipulation who furthers his own interests with frighteningly adroit abilities. It's a dark comedy that may well explain why politics leads many to despair. 200 mins.
VHS: S27063. $39.98.

Flambards
Early in this century, the young Christina is sent to live with her domineering but disabled Uncle Russel and her cousins Mark and William. They all share Flambards, a decaying but still grand mansion. As the world continues to change around them, these men try to preserve their traditional privileges as best they can, but Christina presents them an irresistible challenge. Six episodes. 105 minutes each.
VHS: S20798. $99.98.

Fortunes of War
This BBC mini-series launched the working relationship of Kenneth Branagh and Emma Thompson. He plays Guy Pringle, an English university professor who moves to Romania in 1939 with his bride (Emma Thompson). Their academic life in the Balkans brings them in touch with radical anti-fascist movements, the British Secret Service, as well as deposed European royalty on the run.
VHS: S16808. $29.98.
James Cellon-Jones, Great Britain, 1987, 160 mins.

French & Saunders
From the creators of the hit TV series *Absolutely Fabulous* come Dawn French and Jennifer Saunders with a series of sketches, spoofs and mayhem from their riotous BBC show.
French & Saunders Go to the Movies. 100 mins.
VHS: S31685. $19.98.
French & Saunders: Gentleman Prefer French & Saunders. 100 mins.
VHS: S31686. $19.98.
French & Saunders: Living in a Material World. Includes sketches from the last two seasons. 110 mins.
VHS: S34660. $19.98.
French & Saunders: The Ingenue Years. Includes sketches from the first two seasons. 85 mins.
VHS: S34659. $19.98.

Gallowglass
Ruth Rendell wrote this murder mystery under the pen name Barbara Vine. This BBC adaptation pits two men against each other in a plot centered on a kidnapped Italian princess. One of these men is good, while the other is evil. Their rivalry generates suspense and intrigue. 150 mins.
VHS: S27747. $19.98.

The Gambling Man
Rory O'Connor leaves behind his working class roots for a life of gambling. His flair and style make him a natural as an entrepenuerial spirit. Despite these advantages he cannot escape the reach of the law or the misadventures of fate. This is an engrossing costume drama filled with unexpected reversals tempered by moments of happiness. 150 mins.
VHS: S27836. $34.98.

Genghis Cohn
Robert Lindsay, Diana Rigg and Anthony Sher star in this strange comedy about a haunted ex-Nazi. After the war a Nazi concentration commandant seeks refuge in a small Bavarian town as a respectable chief of police. There he finds passion in the arms of a kinky widowed baroness, even as he is reminded of his crimes by the apparition of a Jewish comic whom he ordered killed. This comic, "Genghis Cohn," manages to extract a bizarre revenge.
VHS: S26400. $24.95.
Elijah Moshinsky, Great Britain, 1993, 100 mins.

The Girl
To Matthew Thornton, Hannah Boyle is a beloved daughter, but to his wife, Anne, she would always be "the Girl," a bitterly resented, tangible reminder of her husband's infidelity. A family tragedy gives Anne the perfect opportunity to get revenge for her years of humiliation in being forced to raise her illegitimate stepdaughter. Based on the novel by Catherine Cookson.
156 mins.
VHS: S31749. $29.95.

Girls on Top
Sharing a flat is never easy, especially when the people concerned are from vastly different backgrounds. Yet it provides the perfect setting for some of the most respected comediennes to showcase their comic talents. Tracey Ullman, Dawn French, Jennifer Saunders and Ruby Wax play a group of flatmates who don't always see eye-to-eye. 50 mins.
VHS: S16129. $59.98.

Good Neighbors Vol. 1
This special Christmas edition from the award-winning BBC comedy series features three short skits: "Backs to the Wall," "The Wind-Break War" and "Silly, But It's Fun." 83 mins.
VHS: S31228. $19.98.

Goon Show Movie
The only feature film made by the fabulously funny Goons: Peter Sellers, Spike Milligan and Harry Secombe. This is their version of *Down Among The Z-Men* (also known as *Stand Easy*). England, 1953, 75 mins.
VHS: S00517. $34.95.

Great Expectations
A splendid BBC production of Dickens' famous novel with Gerry Sundquist portraying Pip, the orphan who is smitten by the rich, spoiled Estella. With Stratford Johns, Joan Hickson, Phillip Joseph. 2 parts (5 hours total).
VHS: S07177. $39.98.
Julian Aymes, Great Britain, 1981, 300 mins.

The Green Man
This BBC production stars Albert Finney as the alcoholic owner of a countryside inn whose sinister, ghostly tales he conjures up to seduce his female guests turn on him when spirits and apparitions begin to haunt his every move. "Finney pounces with unflagging energy" *(The New York Times)*. With Sarah Berger, Linda Marlowe and Michael Hordern.
VHS: S16860. $24.95.
Laser: CLV. **LD72076. $49.95.**
Elijah Moshinsky, Great Britain, 1991, 150 mins.

Hancock Set
Tony Hancock stars and Sid James is featured in this hilarious British television series. Includes six volumes: *The Blood Donor* (90 mins.), *The Lift* (90 mins.), *The Bowmans* (85 mins.), *Radio Ham, The Bedsitter* (including "The New Nose") and *Poison Pen Letters* (90 mins.). 8 hours total.
VHS: S31257. $89.98.

Henry Fielding's Tom Jones
Sexy BBC adaptation stars engaging newcomer Max Beesley as Tom Jones, who, cast from his home and forbidden his true love, must overcome the charms of an older seductress and the sinister plots of a jealous rival to win his inheritance. With Samantha Morton as Sophia, Benjamin Whitrow as the virtuous Squire Allworthy, and Brian Blessed as the crass Squire Western.
VHS: S33426. $99.95.
Metin Huseyin, Great Britain, 1997, 50 mins.

The Hitchhiker's Guide to the Galaxy
A BBC-television adaptation of Douglas Adams' cult classic about Arthur Dent, a mild-mannered man snatched from Earth prior to its demolition, who takes part in a hyperspace bypass and engages in a journey through space and time with his rescuer and traveling researcher Ford Perfect.
VHS: S18076. $19.98.
Laser: Contains exclusive, unseen material. **LD72434. $59.98.**

Hotel Dulac
Anita Brookner's best-selling novel features Anna Massey as the London romance writer whose friends find her guilty of a "serious breach of etiquette," and who is sentenced to a lakefront Swiss hotel during off-season until "she regains her senses." Produced by the BBC.
VHS: S03524. $19.98.
Giles Foster, Great Britain, 1986, 75 mins.

House of Cards
Ian Richardson stars in this British production about corruption among the highest levels of her Majesty's government. Greed and intrigue set the stage for a chilling, puzzling and sinister drama that will delight all thriller fans. Richardson is terrific.
VHS: S26032. $39.98.

The House of Elliot
The BBC devised this charming period television series full of romance, adventure and stunning detail. Two sisters, Beatrice and Evangeline Elliot, struggle to regain the wealth and privilege they were born to but lost. Fashion provides them the opportunity to parlay good taste into wealth and influence, even as British society is transformed around them. Each of the 12 episodes is 50 minutes in length. Six-videotape set.
VHS: S23871. $99.95.

I, Claudius
This famous Masterpiece Theatre series, based on the novel by Robert Graves, has everything: sex, decadence, ambition, insatiable greed, and the fall of the Roman empire.
Complete Set. 7 cassettes.
VHS: S14130. $129.98.

Inspector Morse
A brilliantly acted series that subverts the standard television detective show. Oxford inspector Morse is an eccentric thinker with a keen ability to ferret out clues and signals. "One of the classiest things on television. John Thaw is irresistible as the magnetic but solitary Morse, an Oxford detective with an ear for music, a taste for beer and a nose for sordid crimes" *(The Wall Street Journal)*. With Kevin Whately as Sgt. Lewis.
Absolute Conviction.
VHS: S22070. $19.98.
Cherubim & Seraphim. 105 mins.
VHS: S29871. $19.95.
Day of the Devil. 105 mins.
VHS: S29874. $19.95.
Dead on Time.
VHS: S22066. $19.98.
Deadly Slumber. 105 mins.
VHS: S29873. $19.95.
Death of Self.
VHS: S22069. $19.98.
Deceived by Flight.
VHS: S19148. $19.98.
Driven to Distraction.
VHS: S19154. $19.98.
Fat Chance.
VHS: S19155. $19.98.
Greeks.
VHS: S22067. $19.98.
Happy Families.
VHS: S22065. $19.98.
Harry Field.
VHS: S22068. $19.98.
Infernal Serpent.
VHS: S19150. $19.98.
Last Bus to Woodstock.
VHS: S19144. $19.98.
Last Seen Wearing.
VHS: S19143. $19.98.
Masonic Mysteries.
VHS: S19152. $19.98.
Mystery of Morse. 50 mins.
VHS: S29876. $19.95.
Promised Land.
VHS: S19153. $19.98.
Second Time Around.
VHS: S19156. $19.98.
Service of All the Dead.
VHS: S19142. $19.98.
Sins of the Fathers.
VHS: S19151. $19.98.
The Dead of Jericho. 105 min.
VHS: S16133. $19.98.
The Ghost in the Machine.
VHS: S19146. $19.98.
The Last Enemy.
VHS: S19147. $19.98.
The Secret of Bay 5B.
VHS: S19149. $19.98.
The Settling of the Sun.
VHS: S19145. $19.98.
The Silent World of Nicholas Quinn. 101 mins.
VHS: S16134. $19.98.
The Way Through the Woods. 105 mins.
VHS: S29875. $19.95.
The Wolvercote Tongue.
VHS: S19141. $19.98.
Twilight of the Gods. 105 mins.
VHS: S29872. $19.95.

The Invisible Man
Based on H.G. Wells' novel, *The Invisible Man*, which aired in Britain 1958-60, was one of the most popular television series of its time. Peter Brady, a brilliant scientist, accidentally makes himself invisible and volunteers for British Intelligence, all the while working on an antidote. Six half-hour episodes.
VHS: S34903. $19.95.

The Irish R.M.

Follows the hilarious escapades of a retired English army officer who is appointed Resident Magistrate of the West of Ireland before Irish independence. Surrounded by a community of eccentric townspeople, the Major is confronted with a curious blend of affection and mutual misunderstanding that exists between the Irish and their English neighbors. Starring Peter Bowles. Based on the classic Anglo-Irish stories by Sommerville and Ross; written by Rosemary Anne Sisson *(Upstairs, Downstairs)*. Six-volume set. 325 mins.
VHS: S35128. $79.95.

It Ain't Half Hot Mum

From the land of hope and glory! Fall in for a feast of fun as Gloria and the boys in the concert party parade their special brand of army camp in three hilarious episodes. Includes *The Jungle Patrol, The Road to Bannu* and *The Night of the Thugs*. 91 mins.
VHS: S16132. $24.98.

Ivanhoe

Steven Waddington *(The Last of the Mohicans)*, Susan Lynch *(The Secret of Roan Inish)* and James Cosmo *(Braveheart)* star in this A&E/BBC production of Sir Walter Scott's tale of magnificent pageantry of knightly tournaments and whispered meetings of courtly lovers. Filmed on location in England. Six volumes, 50 minutes each.
VHS: S31271. $99.95.
Stuart Orme, Great Britain, 1996, 300 mins.

Jamaica Inn

Made-for-TV mini-series based on the Daphne DuMaurier story about an inn which stood on the Cornish moors in 19th-century England, where thieves and murderers plotted and celebrated their dastardly deeds. Remake of the 1939 Hitchcock film. Stars Patrick McGoohan and Jane Seymour.
VHS: S30657. $19.95.
Lawrence Gordon Clark, Great Britain, 1982, 192 mins.

Jane Austen's Emma

The BBC produced this adaptation of Austen's wry and insightful novel. Emma Wodehouse is an incorrigible matchmaker who presides over the small, provincial world of Highbury. But her deeds blur the line between good intentions and selfish gratification. Only Jane Austen could render this character's foibles with such perfect grace and agility. 257 mins.
VHS: S28044. $29.98.

Jane Austen's Persuasion

In this BBC adaptation of Austen's novel, all the charm and feeling of a lost era are successfully captured on film. Anne Elliot once spurned Captain Wentworth because of her snobby family. Ten years later the tables have turned but has Wentworth changed his mind? 225 mins.
VHS: S28045. $29.98.

Jane Austen's Pride and Prejudice

A first-rate BBC adaptation of the classic Jane Austen comedy of manners. Filmed on the occasion of the 200th anniversary of the novel's writing, this lavishly produced, five-hour, six-cassette production follows the elite of 19th-century English society through games of love and negotiations of marriage. Mrs. Bennet (Alison Steadman) is deeply worried about the fact that all five of her daughters, including the lively Elizabeth (Jennifer Ehle), are as yet unmarried. She plans to convince wealthy neighbor William Collins to marry one of her daughters, but his mischievous friend Fitzwilliam Darcy (Colin Firth) arrives to foul things up. Directed by Simon Langton *(Upstairs Downstairs)*. Featuring a superb soundtrack from composer Carl Davis.
VHS: S27206. $99.95.
Laser: LD75564. $99.99.
Simon Langton, Great Britain, 1995, 300 mins.

Jane Eyre (BBC)

Bronte's famous novel in a remarkable adaptation featuring Timothy Dalton as the mysterious Mr. Rochester, and London stage star Zelah Clarke as the mistreated woman who learns to survive by relying on her independence and intelligence.
VHS: S03527. $24.98.
Julian Aymes, Great Britain, 239 mins.

Jeeves & Wooster

P.G. Wodehouse's classic British farce gets three new volumes in the adventures of the bumbling, lovable Bertie Wooster and his elegant, unflappable valet, Jeeves. Starring Hugh Laurie and Stephen Fry. "The funniest set piece in the Wodehouse repertory" *(New York Times)*. Available individually or as a boxed set.
Golf Tournament/Gambling Event. In *Golf Tournament*, while in the heat of golf competition with pal Barmy Fotheringay-Phipps, Bertie inadvertently misplaces McIntosh, his Aunt Agatha's priceless pup. 120 mins. In *Gambling Event*, Bertie and his pal Bingo Little get into a sticky situation when they begin gambling on sporting events like the Boys and Girls Mixed Animal Potato Race. Only the ever-resourceful Jeeves can save the day.
VHS: S31006. $14.98.
Hunger Strike/The Matchmaker. In *The Hunger Strike*, Bertie launches a clever scheme to impress his uncle into investing in yet another trite diversion, only to be rescued by the ever-resourceful Jeeves. In *The Matchmaker*, the boys try their hand at matchmaking and find themselves tangled in a very difficult situation. 120 mins.
VHS: S31005. $14.98.
Jeeves' Arrival. When they first meet, Jeeves arrives on the scene just in time to witness Bertie's bachelorhood being threatened by awful Aunt Agatha, who has decided that her frivolous nephew should marry the highbred Honoria Glossop, the horror of Ditteridge Hall. 60 mins.
VHS: S31004. $14.98.
Three-Tape Set.
VHS: S31007. $39.98.

Jude the Obscure

Thomas Hardy's scathing indictment of Victorian society in a first-rate BBC adaptation. Jude Fawley is a working-class stonemason who aspires to the priesthood, but the tragedy of his unrealized ambition is compounded by his tempestuous relationship with Sue Bridehead, herself an outcast for daring to express her sexuality.
VHS: S19090. $29.98.
Hugh David, Great Britain, 1971, 262 mins.

Kavanagh Q.C.

John Thaw dons the silk once again and returns as James Kavanagh in this superlative British courtroom drama. *Kavanagh Q.C.* takes you beyond the traditional courtroom and uncovers the pressures of legal battles and the problems of defining the truth. It provides a compelling representation of the euphoric ups and downs of success and failure in the law.
Kavanagh Q.C. Collection Set 1. Includes *Nothing But the Truth, Heartland, A Family Affair* and *The Sweetest Thing*. Five hours, 30 minutes on four videocassettes.
VHS: S30940. $89.98.
Kavanagh Q.C. Collection Set 2. Includes *True Commitment, The Burning Deck* and *Men of Substance*. Four hours on three videocassettes.
VHS: S32975. $69.98.
Kavanagh Q.C. Collection Set 3. Includes *Sense of Loss, Stranger in the Family* and *Job Satisfaction*. Four hours on three videocassettes.
VHS: S32976. $69.98.

Keeping Up Appearances

Roy Clarke's BBC comedy hit starring award-winner Patricia Routledge in the misadventures of the socially conscious housewife Hyacinth "Bouquet."
Keeping Up Appearances: Angel Gabriel Blue. Special double episode with *Hyacinth is Alarmed*. 48 mins.
VHS: S34124. $19.98.
How to Enhance Your Husband's Retirement. Hyacinth is determined to help her husband have a fulfilling retirement in this collection from the outrageous BBC sitcom series. He doesn't stand a chance against Hyacinth's iron will and gift, or is it a curse, for perfecting all social exchange. 87 mins.
VHS: S28039. $19.98.
I'm Often Mistaken for Aristocracy. 87 mins.
VHS: S31225. $19.98.
Keeping Up Appearances: My Family in Broad Daylight. Episodes: *Golfing with the Major, Three-Piece Suite, Picnic for Daddy*. 89 mins.
VHS: S34125. $19.98.
Rural Retreat. Hyacinth Bucket—that's pronounced "Bouquet"—does her best to fit in with the landed gentry on a jaunt to the country. It shouldn't be much trouble, except that she gets so wound up keeping up appearances. This hilarious BBC sitcom is already a favorite throughout the U.S. 87 mins.
VHS: S28038. $19.98.
Sea Fever. 87 mins.
VHS: S31227. $19.98.
The Memoirs of Hyacinth Bucket. 60 mins.
VHS: S31226. $19.98.

Kevin Turvey Investigates

If one man can be hailed as the jewel among journalists, it must surely be the charismatic Kevin Turvey. He's an ace investigative reporter whose perceptive powers are so limited he backs quite unwittingly—into genius. Don't miss his exposes on the supernatural, death sex, nasty little sticky things and much, much more. The master of comic digression is played by Rik Mayall of *The Young Ones*. 44 mins.
VHS: S16126. $24.98.

The Last Place on Earth, Collection Set

This epic race to the South Pole between rival explorers Captain Robert Falcon Scott and Norwegian Roald Amundsen is one of the greatest adventures of the 20th century. In 1911 they crossed over 1500 miles of desolate, frozen waste for different reasons but with the same goal in mind. Both hoped to be the first man at the South Pole. 390 mins.
VHS: S22937. $129.98.

Lillie

A *Masterpiece Theater* adaptation of the scandalous times of Lillie Langtry, the independent, witty raconteur who upset Edwardian conventions as the first publicly acknowledged mistress of the Prince of Wales and for her flamboyant, active lifestyle and behavior. With Francesca Annis (as Lillie) and Anton Rodgers. A seven-box collector's set running nearly 700 mins.
VHS: S15799. $199.95.

Little Women (BBC)

An enchanting British adaptation of Louisa May Alcott's novel, set during the Civil War, as the four sisters of the March family struggle to grow up without the guiding hand of their loving father.
VHS: S19092. $29.95.
Paddy Russell, Great Britain, 1970, 205 mins.

Love for Lydia

Based on the 1952 novel by H.E. Bates, this enthralling Masterpiece Theater mini-series chronicles the final years of Britain's high-spirited "Careless Twenties" and is an unforgettable portrait of a beautiful and tempestuous woman who personifies the era. Mel Martin gives an exquisite performance as Lydia, who is transformed from a drab and awkward girl into a stunning woman. Seven cassette boxed set, 657 mins.
VHS: S15800. $199.95.

Magic Momen ts

Jenny Seagrove and John Shea star in the this dramatic battle of wills. She is an executive who convinces Shea to recreate his death-defying act on TV. He agrees as long as she will produce the show herself. This tense and romantic thriller is laced with occult touches and the magic of love. Great Britain, 103 mins.
VHS: S22668. $19.98.

Maid Marian and Her Merry Men

A hip, hilarious retelling of the Robin Hood legend from Maid Marian's point-of-view. She casts quite a different light on the story by showing that Robin Hood was really a wimp who stole all her glory! Kate Lonergan, Wayne Morris and Tony Robinson star in this irreverent spoof with great music—including a reggae theme song. Two episodes.
How the Band Got Together.
VHS: S14264. $14.98.
The Miracle of St. Charlene.
VHS: S14265. $14.95.

The Making of The Hitchhiker's Guide to the Galaxy

A behind-the-scenes on the filmmakers, performers and technicians involved in the filming of *The Hitchhiker's Guide to the Galaxy*, Douglas Adams' cult novel about an anonymous man marked for interplanetary travel. The program includes an interview with Adams and previously unseen archival footage.
VHS: S19091. $14.98.

The Man from the Pru

Jonathan Pryce and Susannah York star in this murder mystery based on a true story from 1931. Julia Wallace was brutally murdered in her Liverpool home. The public suspected her husband but the courts believed him innocent. Now this beautifully detailed film investigates the lonely, hard world that spawned this as-yet-unsolved mystery.
VHS: S26399. $24.95.
Bob Rohrer, Great Britain, 1989, 90 mins.

The Man Who Cried

Spanning the turbulent years between the Depression and World War II, this Writers' Guild-nominated story based on Catherine Cookson's bestseller is the powerful drama of an unhappily married man (Ciaran Hinds) who goes to deperate lengths to provide his young son with a virtuous life. He enters into a bigamous marriage with a young widow (Amanda Root), but risks losing it all when he falls in love with her sister (Kate Buffery). 156 mins.
VHS: S31113. $26.98.

Mansfield Park

A lavish treatment of one of the works of Jane Austen by the BBC is now available in this country. In 18th century England an impoverished woman arrives at the estate of her rich uncle, where she is badly treated. Young Fanny Price knows that quality does not come from wealth. She sets out to convince others of that fact. Great Britain, 1986, 261 mins.
VHS: S04671. $24.98.

Mapp & Lucia

This British television comedy series, based on the novels of E.F. Benson, has enjoyed a cult following in Britain and America since it aired on PBS in 1985. Set in 1930 in the fictional seaside village of Tilling, this quirky satire boasts an all-star cast, including Prunella Scales *(Fawlty Towers)*, Geraldine McEwan *(Barchester Chronicles)* and Nigel Hawthorne *(The Madness of King George)*. Packaged in a five-volume, 52-minute program box set.
VHS: S28482. $89.95.

Mapp & Lucia II

The second installment of *Mapp & Lucia*, one of the most sought-after PBS comedies of all time, carries on E.F. Benson's tale in five volumes, starring Prunella Scales, Geraldine McEwan and Nigel Hawthorne. 52 mins.
VHS: S31819. $89.95.

Martin Chuzzlewit

Perhaps Charles Dickens' most complex tale, this brilliant BBC adaptation has been hailed as one of the best. Martin Chuzzlewit is a wealthy old man. But who will inherit his riches? Paul Scofield, Sir John Mills, Pete Postlethwaite, Tom Wilkinson and Julia Sawalha star in this detailed, rich story of greed. Released in a three-tape set.
VHS: S31063. $59.98.
Pedr James, Great Britain, 1994, 288 mins.

Mastermind: Great Motor Race

Sam Waterston as an American scientist in London, experimenting with rocket propulsion in 1912. England, 1982, 50 mins.
VHS: S03872. $39.98.

Mastermind: Infernal Device

Sam Waterston, as Professor Quentin E. Deverill, is working on a remote control device and trying to prevent his invention from being used by terrorists plotting to blow up Britain. England, 1982, 49 mins.
VHS: S03873. $39.98.

Merlin of the Crystal Cave

Adapted from Mary Stewart's best-selling novel *The Crystal Cave*, this swashbuckling adventure and coming-of-age tale is set during the time of King Arthur and focuses on the life and times of Merlin, a young wizard whose mystical powers profoundly impact a kingdom. Great Britain, 1991, 160 mins.
VHS: S20172. $19.98.

Middlemarch

This BBC production of George Elliot's classic tale captures all the passion and disillusionment of the novel. It's an unforgettable tale of blackmail set in a small, 19th-century English village. Stars Rufus Sewell and Juliet Aubrey. 360 mins.
VHS: S26034. $59.98.

The Mill on the Floss

George Eliot's story of Maggie Tulliver and her brother Tom, their life at the mill and Maggie's love for two men. Stars Emily Watson *(Breaking the Waves)*, Cheryl Campbell, James Frain and Bernard Hill.
VHS: S32038. $19.98.

The Mixer

One of Britain's wittiest and most popular television dramas, based on the character of the same name by Edgar Wallace, *The Mixer* is the story of Sir Anthony Rose (Simon Williams), a cultured member of the idle rich, who, in private, becomes The Mixer, a fascinating cross between the Scarlet Pimpernel and Robin Hood. Catch him as he hands out his unique brand of justice in this stylish and sophisticated series. 10 hours on six videocassettes.
VHS: S30961. $99.98.

Moll Flanders

In this Masterpiece Theater production, Alex Kingston stars as Moll Flanders, Britain's most wanted woman, who was married five times, once to her own brother. "One of the year's most unexpected, riveting romps…a startlingly bawdy and immediately captivating adaptation of Daniel Defoe's still shocking classic of one woman's survive-at-all-costs life…unconventionally alluring and unblushingly brazen" *(U.S. Today)*. "*Moll Flanders* arrives like a firecracker tossed into a tea party" *(The New York Times)*.
VHS: S30610. $29.95.
DVD: DV60228. $29.95.

Monte Carlo

Entertaining made-for-TV production stars Joan Collins as a seductive Russian woman who aids the Allies by relaying messages during World War II. With George Hamilton, Lisa Eilbacher, Lauren Hutton, Robert Carradine and Malcolm McDowell.
VHS: S30658. $19.95.
Anthony Page, Great Britain, 1986, 200 mins.

The Moonstone

A sumptuous adaptation of Wilkie Collins' classic mystery story, the first detective novel ever written. Stars Greg Wise, Patricia Hodge, Keeley Hawes, Anthony Sher and Peter Vaughan.
VHS: S32039. $19.98.

More Jeeves & Wooster

Stephen Fry *(A Fish Called Wanda)* and Hugh Laurie *(Sense and Sensibility)* return to their acclaimed roles as the resourceful valet Jeeves and his well-meaning but dim-witted master, Bertie Wooster. In this series, Bertie sets sail for Manhattan, where troubles appear from his new apartment to a Broadway theater. It's up to Jeeves to see Bertie through his American sojourn and return him safely to England. Six videos, 50 minutes each.
VHS: S31781. $79.95.

Morecambe & Wise Musical Extravaganzas

A host of Britain's best, including Glenda Jackson, Vanessa Redgrave, Cliff Richard and Diana Rigg, join Morecambe and Wise in music and comedy series from their classic BBC comedy series. 60 mins.
VHS: S10012. $19.98.

Morecambe & Wise: Lots and Lots

The TV shows from Eric Morecambe and Ernie Wise are legendary. This collection of their most famous skits features comic delights and special appearances by Glenda Jackson and Eamonn Andrews. 45 mins.
VHS: S22683. $22.98.

Morecambe & Wise: Lots More

A collection of sketches from the British TV series starring Eric Morecambe and Ernie Wise. Celebrity guests include Peter Barkworth, Alec Guinness, Glenda Jackson, Peter Vaughan, Gemma Craven, Jill Gascoine and Mick McManus. 50 mins.
VHS: S14496. $22.98.

Mr. Bean

Rowan Atkinson, a.k.a. Mr. Bean, is everyone's favorite British clown. Children and adults alike find the antics of the funniest man in town irresistibly fun to watch again and again.
Volume 1: The Amazing Adventures of Mr. Bean. Rowan Atkinson is featured in two episodes from his original British comedy series. This video includes both the pilot episode, *Mr. Bean*, and the episodes *The Return of Mr. Bean* and *The Library*. In these shows, Mr. Bean tries to change on the beach, uses his first credit card and even meets the Royal Family.
VHS: S27053. $19.95.
Volume 2: The Exciting Escapades of Mr. Bean. Rowan Atkinson inspires more lunatic laughter as Mr. Bean. In *The Curse of Mr. Bean, Mr. Bean Goes to Town* and *The Bus Stop*, Atkinson's comic invention attempts to drive a car, dance at disco and swim at a public pool, as well as much more.
VHS: S27054. $19.95.
Volume 3: The Terrible Tales of Mr. Bean. Rowan Atkinson brings his absurd antics to two episodes of his hit series in this video. In *The Trouble with Mr. Bean* it all starts at the dentist. Then in *Mr. Bean Rides Again* Atkinson takes off on a bumpy and hilarious flight. 50 mins.
VHS: S28389. $19.95.
Volume 4: The Perilous Pursuits of Mr. Bean. This video contains two more episodes of the delightful Mr. Bean series. Rowan Atkinson is confounded by an infant in *Mind the Baby Mr. Bean*, while in *Do-It-Yourself Mr. Bean* Atkinson makes his room over and over again. 50 mins.
VHS: S28390. $19.95.
Volume 5: The Merry Mishaps of Mr. Bean. PBS's Mr. Bean (Rowan Atkinson) speaks the universal language of laughter in two Christmas episodes. In "Merry Christmas Mr. Bean," Mr. Bean shares his special recipe for turkey dressing on his head. In "Mr. Bean in Room 426," he makes alterations to his hotel room. 52 mins.
VHS: S28507. $19.95.
Volume 6: The Final Frolics of Mr. Bean. Rowan Atkinson displays his visual comedy as Mr. Bean in two adventures. He takes to the green in "Tee Off Mr. Bean," and adventures from the hospital to Windsor Castle in "Good Night Mr. Bean."
VHS: S28508. $19.95.
Volume 7: Unseen Bean. Thirty-minute episode never aired on TV.
VHS: S30749. $19.95.
Volume 8: The Best Bits of Mr. Bean. One-hour special highlighting Bean's most popular sketches.
VHS: S30750. $19.95.

A Murder Is Announced

Joan Hickson stars as Agatha Christie's crafty detective, Miss Marple, in the BBC presentation. When a hotel waiter is found shot during the playing of a party game of "murder", Marple suspects the death is not the suicide it appears to be. The movie that answers the question, "who killed Rudi Scherz?"
VHS: S06530. $19.98.
David Giles, Great Britain, 1987, 155 mins.

Murder of a Moderate Man

Denis Quilley stars as an Interpol agent investigating a rash of vicious assassinations set off by the killing of a moderate political leader. Brimming with excitement and foreign intrigue, the chase goes all the way to the Italian Alps. England, 165 mins.
VHS: S14331. $49.95.

The Mystery of Edwin Drood

Based on Charles Dickens' last, unfinished novel, this mystery film shows a corrupt Victorian world dominated by injustice and the resentment it breeds. Edwin Drood vanishes one stormy Christmas Eve. His betrothed, a chaste orphan, joins a choirmaster and a dark young stranger to find the missing man. In this battle between good and evil, passion, lust and intrigue become the weapons of choice.
VHS: S26401. $24.95.
Timothy Forder, Great Britain, 1993, 98 mins.

The New Statesman

A social satire about the unaccountable rise of Alan B'Stard (Rick Mayall), a highly ambitious, conservative MP elected to Parliament when all the opposing candidates mysteriously disappear.
The New Statesman, Collection.
VHS: S19051. $59.98.

Noble House

Based on James Clavell's novel, *Noble House* is an intriguing mini-series saga set in the panoramic backdrop of exotic Hong Kong. Pierce Brosnan stars as Ian Dunross, the all-powerful leader of Hong Kong's most influential international trading organization, Noble House, as he confronts takeover attempts, interlocking intrigues and ancient obligations. "Extravagantly romantic…not only is it as long as life, it's also rich with possibilities" *(The New York Times)*. With Deborah Raffin, Ben Masters, John Houseman and Denholm Elliott.
VHS: S32389. $39.98.
Gary Nelson, Great Britain/USA, 1988, 355 mins.

Northanger Abbey

A BBC adaptation of Jane Austen's novel of erotic attraction, danger and intrigue set in 18th century Bath, a morally decadent society that captures the fancy of Catherine Morland. She's invited by Henry Tilney for a romantic weekend at his estate, Northanger Abbey, where mystery and blood-curdling horror rule the moment. With Peter Finch, Googie Withers, Robert Hardy and Katherine Schlesinger. 90 mins.
VHS: S19180. $19.98.

Nostromo

One of the largest productions in the history of public television, this spectacular, three-volume BBC mini-series is based on Joseph Conrad's sprawling masterpiece of the quest for wealth and power in a backward South American country in the 1880s. When a revolution breaks out, one man is fated to determine the future-Nostromo. With Colin Firth, Brian Dennehy, Serena Scott Thomas, Joaquim DeAlmeida and Albert Finney.
VHS: S30472. $59.98.
Alastair Reid, Great Britain, 1996, 6 hrs.

Oliver Twist

Charles Dickens' classic tale of a young boy's triumph with Ben Rodska as Oliver Twist. A first-rate BBC production. 2 parts (333 minutes total).
VHS: S07178. $39.98.
Gareth Davies, Great Britain, 1985, 333 mins.

One Foot in the Grave: In Lutton Airport No-One Can Hear You Scream

Veteran complainer Victor and his long-suffering wife Margaret return from holiday to find their suburban home trashed—and decide to throw a housewarming party. 89 mins.
VHS: S20502. $19.98.

One Foot in the Grave: Who Will Buy?

A benefit concert gives retired suburbanite Victor Meldrew a chance to warm up his old ventriloquist act, and proves to his wife, Margaret, that whatever can go wrong always does, in this BBC-TV comedy. 89 mins.
VHS: S20501. $19.98.

Open All Hours

One of the last of the corner grocery stores that carry just about everything where you'll find Arkwright, the grasping grocer, and his brow-beaten nephew Granville, who dreams of discovering a world beyond his delivery route. It's also the place where the most amusing neighborhood scandals, romances and adventures are turned into inspired slice-of-life comedy. Stars Ronnie Barker, one half of Britain's internationally popular comedy team, *The Two Ronnies*.
VHS: S11213. $39.98.

Oranges Are Not the Only Fruit

This critically acclaimed film, set in '60s northern England, is the tale of Jess, a 16-year-old girl (Geraldine McEwan of BBC-TV's *Mapp and Lucia*) raised to be a missionary, who falls in love for the first time—with another girl. When Jess' strict Evangelist mother (Charlotte Coleman, *Four Weddings and a Funeral*) finds out, she determines to make her daughter renounce her sin, resulting in disaster. Based on Jeanette Winterson's autobiographical prize-winning novel.
VHS: S31261. $29.98.
Beeban Kidron, Great Britain, 1990, 165 mins.

P.D. James: A Mind to Murder

Roy Marsden returns to the role of the poetry-writing Commander Dalgliesh in this brilliant screen adaptation of P.D. James' bestselling classic. In an exclusive English psychiatric clinic, it is up to Commander Dalgliesh to solve the case of a macabre murder.
VHS: S30947. $19.95.
Gareth Davies, USA, 1994, 100 mins.

P.D. James: Devices and Desires

Author James has personally endorsed this film adaptation of her best-selling novel. This six-series mystery/drama is set on the east coast of England, where a serial killer is terrorizing the landscape. When an unpopular administrator of the local nuclear power plant is found dead, the death is attributed to the serial killer still at large. The real story is far more involved and disturbing than even this alleged scenario, as Commander Adam Dalgliesh of Scotland Yard sets out to prove. Each episode is 50 minutes long.
VHS: S29411. $79.95.

P.G. Wodehouse's Jeeves and Wooster

Wodehouse's comic stories, featuring a stunningly imbecilic British aristocrat and his cooly capable butler, are well realized in this film series. Their adventures among the horsey set spoof a world usually evoked in more reverent tones. Hugh Laurie and Stephen Fry star in six episodes, each 50 mins.
Jeeves Saves the Cow Creamer.
VHS: S29381. $19.95.
A Plan for Gussie.
VHS: S29382. $19.95.
Pearls Mean Tears.
VHS: S29383. $19.95.
Jeeves in the Country.
VHS: S29384. $19.95.
Kidnapped!
VHS: S29385. $19.95.
Jeeves the Matchmaker.
VHS: S29386. $19.95.
Jeeves and Wooster Set.
VHS: S29189. $99.95.

Painted Lady

Emmy winner Helen Mirren *(Prime Suspect)* turns in a first-rate performance as a former blues singer forced to uncover the truth about the murder of her protector, the key to which lies in a famous 16th-century painting.
VHS: S34666. $29.98.
Julian Jarrold, Great Britain, 1998, 204 mins.

Partners in Crime

This exciting mystery series stars Francesca Annis and James Warwick as Tuppence and Tommy Beresford, two of Agatha Christie's most elegant detectives.
The Ambassador's Boots/The Man in the Mist. In *The Ambassador's Boots* Tommy and Tuppence delve into diplomatic intrigue as they help an American ambassador unravel a curious incident. In *The Man in the Mist*, when a famous actress on the eve of marriage draws Tommy and Tuppence into a murder case, it takes them from the high style of a grand hotel to the trail of a policeman's ghost.
Laser: LD70818. $39.95.
The House of Lurking Death/Finessing the King. In *The House of Lurking Death* chocolates laced with arsenic are a recipe for murder at the grim country mansion of Thurnley Grange. In *Finessing the King* a cryptic newspaper notice leads to a lovers' rendezvous at a costume ball where the last whispered words of a slain socialite are clues to a deadly puzzle. Tommy and Tuppence investigate.
Laser: LD70816. $39.95.
The Sunningdale Mystery/The Clergyman's Daughter. In *The Sunningdale Mystery* golf becomes a deadly game when a victim is found on the links, stabbed by a woman's hat pin. In *The Clergyman's Daughter* Tommy and Tuppence investigate a poltergeist that seems to haunt the house of a cleric's daughter.
Laser: LD70817. $39.95.
The Unbreakable Alibi/The Case of the Missing Lady. *In The Unbreakable Alibi* love at first sight sparks a strange wager for two ardent detective fans, but their bet soon takes a sinister turn. In *The Case of the Missing Lady* Tommy and Tuppence help an acclaimed Arctic explorer in his most dangerous search, to find his beautiful fiance, who has disappeared under suspicious circumstances.
Laser: LD70819. $39.95.

A Perfect Spy

From the author of *The Russia House*, John Le Carre's intricate espionage work is an imaginative thriller about the response of British intelligence when a top member of British Secret Service inexplicably disappears. Peter Egan stars as master spy Magnus Pym, who is enlisted to track down the missing diplomat. "Gripping, sardonic and haunted, the film has the piercing chill of a cloudy autumn day" *(The Washington Post)*. With Dame Peggy Ashcroft. A three-tape set. 376 mins.
VHS: S19913. $79.98.

Pictures

This series is set during the exciting era of silent films. Peter McEnery plays a script writer inspired by the youthful ambitions of an aspiring actress, Wendy Morgan. They are thrown together by a big project but they can't anticipate the ambitions of those around them and their plans for love are threatened by the incessant wheeling and dealing of that bygone era. Four episodes.
VHS: S20803. $99.98.

Piece of Cake: Complete Set

During World War II, an RAF Hornet Squadron must undergo the rites of passage that will make them seasoned fighter pilots. Their aristocratic CO is arrogant and overconfident. Eventually the concerns of his squadron overtake his attitude as adventure and heartache build toward the climactic battle.
VHS: S21689. $99.98.
Ian Toynton, Great Britain, 1994, 650 mins.

A Pocketful of Rye

Another Agatha Christie BBC production featuring the aging but ever alert Miss Marple. When a London financier is poisoned, the maid seeks out the assistance of Joan Hickson, as the prim and proper sleuth Miss Marple. More bodies are found before the killer is revealed.
VHS: S06531. $19.98.
Guy Slater, Great Britain, 1987, 101 mins.

Poldark

A romance/adventure/epic set in the late 1770s in Cornwall, this film features the beautiful landscapes and historic buildings of old England. It is based on the best-selling book by Winston Graham and tells the story of a man with an iron will whose life shaped the lives of thousands. 12 hours on six cassettes.
VHS: S20626. $99.98.

Porridge

A madcap British comedy based on a highly-regarded television series that stars Ronnie Barker as habitual criminal Norman Stanley Fletcher who miraculously escapes from prison, and the repercussions when he demands to be placed back in. With Richard Beckinsale, Fulton Mackay, Brian Wilde and Peter Vaughan. Also known as *Doing Time*.
VHS: S14495. $29.95.
Dick Clement, Great Britain, 1979, 95 mins.

Portrait of a Lady

The story of a spirited young American woman searching for truth. Determined to choose her own destiny, she is brought to England by her Aunt and given every chance to better herself. While seeking freedom, however, she makes some disastrous choices. Richard Chamberlain stars in this classic BBC mini-series based on the Henry James novel. 240 mins.
VHS: S16135. $34.98.

Pride and Prejudice

This BBC production of another popular novel of Jane Austen was filmed on location in the scenic English countryside. The romantic novel of a young woman's adventures and frustrations in acquiring a suitable marriage partner is brought to life by a talented and diverse cast of British actors.
VHS: S04670. $24.98.
Cyril Coke, Great Britain, 1985, 226 mins.

Prime Suspect

In this Emmy Award-winning series, Helen Mirren plays a woman inspector eager to prove that she is as capable as any male police detective. When a young prostitute's body is found, she gets a chance to convince her colleagues of her abilities as she stalks the brutal serial killer responsible. Two cassettes, 230 mins.
VHS: S20827. $39.95.

Prime Suspect 2

In this sequel, Helen Mirren reprises her role as Jane Tennison, a woman detective fighting for respect in a male-dominated police force. As she investigates the murder of a young woman, she faces both community and police pressure to quickly resolve the case because of its racial overtones. Instead, she draws on her ability to solve this daunting case. Two cassettes, 230 mins.
VHS: S20828. $39.95.

Prime Suspect 3

Helen Mirren returns as Detective Jane Tennison, the thoughtful and tenacious woman detective who manages to solve the most complex and troubling cases. In this two tape set, she unravels the mystery surrounding a young boy burned alive. The child was somehow mixed up in a flesh-peddling ring. Now Detective Tennison must confront not only police department rigidity but a seamy underworld as well. Her own personal demons are summoned by this grisly and baffling case.
VHS: S26929. $39.98.
David Drury, Great Britain, 1995, 205 mins.

Prime Suspect 4

Three more episodes in the British TV series. Sold individually or as a set.
Inner Circles. Detective Superintendent Jane Tennison (Helen Mirren) finds herself at odds with police and the members of an affluent community when kids from a housing development are accused of murder. 102 mins.
VHS: S28633. $19.98.
The Lost Child. Newly promoted Detective Superintendent Jane Tennison (Helen Mirren) is assigned a case involving the disappearance of a young child. 102 mins.
VHS: S28634. $19.98.
The Scent of Darkness. Jane Tennison, a tough British investigator played superbly by Helen Mirren, is called in to solve the mystery behind the murder of two women. She has seen a similar pattern before. That case became known as the George Marlow serial killings. In this taut thriller, the original assumptions behind that earlier case come into question as Tennison digs for facts. 102 mins.
VHS: S29703. $19.98.
Set of Three Episodes.
VHS: S27356. $39.95.

Prime Suspect 5: Errors of Judgment

Transferred to Manchester, Detective Superintendent Jane Tennison (Helen Mirren) finds herself dealing with the murder of a drug dealer. A 14-year-old boy confesses to the killing, but Tennison has no evidence to connect him to the crime and she suspects a powerful and dangerous drug baron. Tennison also has her personal problems when she starts an affair with her married boss. She soon finds herself trapped in a world she does not know, surrounded by people she can't trust. Just when she thinks it cannot get any worse—it does. Four hours on two videocassettes.
VHS: S30883. $29.95.

Raffles

Raffles and Bunny Manders may seem like an unlikely pair of criminals. Bunny sought out his boyhood hero Raffles, an elegant man at home amidst the turn-of-the-century English aristocracy, precisely because of his sophisticated veneer. It makes the perfect cover that enables them to achieve their wildest criminal fantasies. Each of the six episodes is 52 minutes in length.
VHS: S23754. $99.98.

The Rag Nymph

In this classic tale by Catherine Cookson, Aggie Winkowski takes in abandoned 10-year-old Millie Forrester to protect her from the rough streets. 1997 British TV mini-series. 150 mins.
VHS: S34108. $34.98.

The Real Charlotte

Filmed against the breathtaking backdrop of Ireland, this is the Victorian story of two cousins—the young and irresistable Francie Fitzpatrick and the plain, pragmatic and middle-aged Charlotte—doomed to love the same man (Patrick Bergin), a fate that leads to heartache and tragedy for both. With Jeananne Crowley and Joanna Roth.
VHS: S31875. $29.98.
Tony Barry, Great Britain, 1991, 240 mins.

Reckless

In this six-hour British miniseries, Dr. Owen Springer (British TV heartthrob Robson Green), an infatuated young surgeon, falls for a glamorous older woman, Anna Fairley (Francesca Annis). Initially, she shuns his advances, but he is determined to win her over. Just when it seems love is on the horizon, an unexpected complication arises when Dr. Springer finds out Anna is the wife of his tyrannical and vindictive boss. Three-tape set.
VHS: S33866. $39.98.
David Richards/Sarah Harding, Great Britain, 1997, 312 mins.

The Rector's Wife

Set in England's picturesque Cotswald Villages and based on Joanna Trollope's bestseller, this Masterpiece Theater series is the story of Anna Bouverie, a spirited woman struggling to remain dutiful to her family as a life of independence beckons. When she incurs the wrath of the parishioners and her husband, Anna embarks on an intense journey of self-discovery. With Lindsay Duncan, Prunella Scales, Ronald Pickup and Stephen Dillane. 208 mins.
VHS: S23568. $59.95.

Red Dwarf

Described as a "cataclysmic comedy," this critically acclaimed BBC series has gained cult status for its inventive and merciless satire of *Dr. Who* and other postmodern futuristic programs, combining and merging various genres and situations to create an off-center, sublime comedy of manners.

Red Dwarf I, Part 1: The End. The cataclysmic space comedy saga, winner of the British Science Fiction Award, begins as a radiation leak aboard the space ship *Red Dwarf* leaves only one apparent survivor, the Chicken Soup Machine Repair Man, Lister. 87 mins.
VHS: S20497. $19.98.

Red Dwarf I, Part 2: Confidence & Paranoia. Lister endures hilarious hallucinations from a space virus. Personifications of his confidence and paranoia begin to battle amidst a rain of herring and exploding mayors. 87 mins.
VHS: S20498. $19.98.

Red Dwarf II, Part 1: Kryten. The crew of the *Red Dwarf* comes to the rescue of three damsels and an asteroid in distress, then experiences the new game sensation sweeping the solar system. 87 mins.
VHS: S20499. $19.98.

Red Dwarf II, Part 2: Statis Leak. The *Red Dwarf* goes back in time three million years and revisits the loves of Lister's life, then faces a revolt from the ship's backup computer, Queg 500. 89 mins.
VHS: S20500. $19.98.

Red Dwarf III, Part 1: Marooned & Polymorph. When the *Red Dwarf* returns to Earth, the crew discovers that time is running backwards. Then two crew members find themselves marooned. Finally, Polymorph is loose on the ship, subjecting everyone to a terrifying and gruesome bloodfest.
VHS: S18872. $19.98.

Red Dwarf III, Part 2: Time Slides, Bodyswap & The Last Day. In *Time Slides* mutated developing liquid allows the crew to step into photographs where they can alter their past. Then in *Bodyswap*, switched circuits in the ship foment an emergency that can only be solved by the crew switching bodies and genders. In *The Last Day*, a mechanoid realizes he must face the end of his programmed life and promptly sets off to experience all the pleasures this world has to offer.
VHS: S18873. $19.98.

Red Dwarf IV, Part 1: Camille, DNA & Justice. The mining vessel *Red Dwarf* contains a sloppy, whacked-out crew among whom lovesick androids are just part of the problem, in the episode *Camille*. Later, while floating about in space, they latch on to a vessel that can change the DNA of any living thing, resulting in some very strange creatures. Then in *Justice*, world criminals suffer the consequences of their crime, giving the crew cause for concern because of their own hidden histories.
VHS: S18874. $19.98.

Red Dwarf IV, Part 2: White Hole, Dimension Jump & Meltdown. When one of the crew regains her genius level IQ, she powers down the ship and places everyone in danger of disappearing down a White Hole. Then a parallel universe yields a double of the leading crew member via a dimension jump. And in *Meltdown*, wax figures of famous Earth people have broken free of their programming and are running amok.
VHS: S18875. $19.98.

Reilly: The Ace of Spies

Simply terrific—one of the grandest spy stories ever produced. Based on a true story, Reilly's exploits (which reportedly were the inspiration for James Bond), shook Europe as Reilly—scoundrel, womanizer, legend—uncovers startling information about Russian oil explorations. Sam Neill and Sebastian Shaw star. 80 mins.
VHS: S11007. $19.98.
Laser: LD71298. $39.95.

Reilly: The Ace of Spies Series

Scoundrel. Womanizer. Legend. Sydney Reilly lived by his wits and lived on danger. Now Reilly's escapades are compiled in this special series from the explosive BBC television drama starring Sam Neill as the world's first superspy.

Vol I. It is the early 1900s. Reilly takes on three of his most dangerous and challenging assignments. First he poses as a shipping agent in Manchuria to obtain vital information for the Imperial Japanese Navy, enabling them to sink the entire Russian Pacific Squadron and invade China. A year later, he infiltrates a German shipyard to steal the plans for the deadly new Krupps naval gun. Finally, disguised as a priest, he lies his way aboard a private yacht in Antibes to prevent the French government from taking control of vast oil deposits recently discovered in British territory. 154 mins.
VHS: S16018. $19.95.

Vol II. 1910. The Czar has ordered the construction of a new Russian fleet, and Reilly hopes to win the contract for his client, a German shipbuilder. Not only will he make a huge personal profit by negotiating the deal, he'll be able to intercept and photograph the drawings of every Russian warship for Britain. Eight years later, Reilly returns to post-Revolutionary Moscow with a daring plan to overthrow Lenin—and install himself as the new leader of the Russian government.
VHS: S16019. $19.95.

Vol III. The 1920s. The Russian Secret Police discover that Reilly is planning to overthrow the Bolsheviks. He narrowly escapes a hail of Bullets and returns to London. There, Reilly and co-conspirator Savinkov join The Trust, a secret organization desperately working to overthrow the Russians. Reilly moves to New York and raises money to support The Trust—until the treachery of one of his employees reveals the group's true nature and evil purpose.
VHS: S16020. $19.95.

Vol IV. Reilly marries Pepita, a beautiful showgirl, but their time together is brief. When Savinkov is killed, Reilly must return to Russia—a dangerous decision that pits him against Stalin. Knowing The Trust is a fraud, he challenges its leaders to prove to the world that they are truly anti-Bolshevik. Stalin learns of the plot, and has Reilly arrested before he can leave the country. Facing imprisonment, torture and certain death, Reilly must rely on the British government in this thrilling conclusion.
VHS: S16021. $19.95.

Rhodes

The 1996 British TV miniseries. From the excitement of the diamond rush to the tragic birth of apartheid, from the intrigues of a Russian princess to dangerous confrontations with local kings, this is the life and legend of Cecil Rhodes (Martin Shaw), the man who changed the face of Africa. By the time he was 40, the country of Rhodesia was named after him. Three-volume set. 336 mins.
VHS: S32796. $59.98.

Rising Damp, Collection Set 1

A Dickensian black comedy set in a crumbling boarding house. The landlord, Rigsby, fashions himself an aristocrat, though his manner is mean-spirited, miserly, self-absorbed and prejudiced. Episodes include *Rooksby, Black Magic, Night Out, Charisma, All Our Yesterdays* and *Prowler*. With Leonard Rossiter. 150 mins.
VHS: S19184. $59.98.

Rising Damp, Collection Set 2

British TV's comedy set in a down-and-out boarding house features some of the most hilarious antics ever located amid English squalor. Leonard Rossiter stars as the landlord in this comedy of gloom. Three volumes of two episodes each. *A Body Like Mine/Moonlight and Roses*: When the fitness craze hits Rigsby's home, he is set off balance by everyone's eager embrace of the "body beautiful aesthetic." Then Ruth's new love inspires Rigsby to declare his love for Miss Jones, but it's too little, too late. 50 mins. *Perfect Gentleman/Last of the Big Spenders*: Rigsby's well-concealed aristocratic demeanor is fully unleashed by the appearance of the courtly Seymour. In the consecutive episode, Rigsby's similarly buried free-spending ways are set loose by the presence of Brenda. This model just happens to like men that aren't afraid to part with their cash. *Permissive Society/Food Glorious Food*: When one of Rigsby's boarders, Allen, goes on a blind date, Rigsby betrays a little envy in his criticism. He gets all excited and blames Allan's faltering moral standing on his other boarder Phillip. In the next episode, Rigsby is set off by Ruth's zeal when she starts collecting for famine relief. Despite his worst intentions, Rigsby still manages to contribute something. 50 mins.
VHS: S20807. $59.98.

Root into Europe

This five-part British TV satire lampoons contemporary European politics and culture. It all begins when Root, a retired wet fish merchant, determines to fight for the survival of British culture against a threatening and expanding Europe. Root and his poor wife do battle across the continent from a topless beach in Spain to a hash bar in Amsterdam. Each episode is 52 mins.
VHS: S29531. $89.95.

Rowan Atkinson Live

Experience Rowan Atkinson, TV's *Mr. Bean*, as never before, in this hilarious stand-up comedy special filmed live in Boston in 1991, featuring a wide variety of sketch work and routines compiled by Atkinson.
VHS: S31205. $19.95.

A Royal Scandal

This BBC production is the witty, irreverent and true account of the unhappy marriage of England's King George IV and Queen Caroline. George married Caroline to please his father and clear his debts, but unbeknownst to Caroline, George was already secretly married to someone else when he married her. The historical events depicted cover a 25-year span ending with Caroline's trial, where she is accused of committing adultery with an Italian servant. With Richard Grant and Susan Lynch. Narrated by Ian Richardson.
VHS: S30473. $24.98.

Rumpole of the Bailey

Part lawyer, part detective, Horace Rumpole is one of the most colorful characters to approach the bench. With his brilliant mind and sly sense of humor, Rumpole's adventures behind the scenes and center stage in the British legal system are a delightful mix of comedy, mystery and courtroom drama. "Uproarious" *(Wall Street Journal)*. Each tape is 104 mins.

Rumpole of the Bailey, Vol. 1. Episodes 1 & 2. *Rumpole and the Genuine Article*. Has an art collector purchased a recently discovered masterpiece or a convincing fake? An embittered artist's jealousy erupts when Rumpole is called to defend him in a celebrated forgery case. *Rumpole and the Old Boy Network*. The discovery of a brothel in an otherwise respectable London neighborhood draws Rumpole into a web of blackmail and deceit.
VHS: S16028. $19.98.

Rumpole of the Bailey, Vol. 2. Episodes 3 & 4. *Rumpole and the Sporting Life*: Despite her tearful confession, Rumpole believes the unfaithful wife of a murdered barrister is not the perpetrator, and sets off to find the real killer. *Rumpole and the Blind Tasting*: The petty jealousies and bits of gossip Rumpole overhears at a high-brow wine tasting party proves useful as he prepares for a case of insurance fraud.
VHS: S16029. $19.98.

Rumpole of the Bailey, Vol. 3. Episodes 5 & 6. *Rumpole and the Old, Old Story*: Was the partner of a murdered property owner after his valuable land or his wife? *Rumpole and Portia*: While defending an antique shop owner accused of smuggling illegal weapons, Rumpole discovers a police plot to trap a terrorist.
VHS: S16030. $19.98.

Rumpole of the Bailey, Vol. 4. Episodes 7 & 8. *Rumpole's Last Case*: With a sure bet about to pay off, Rumpole agrees to what will undoubtedly be his last case: defending two criminals charged with bank robbery. *Rumpole and the Judge's Elbow*: In defending a man accused of running a massage parlor, Rumpole is offered judgeship if he promises to handle the case "discreetly."
VHS: S16031. $19.98.

Rumpole of the Bailey, Vol. 5. Episodes include *Rumpole and the Female of the Species* and *Rumpole and the Official Secret*.
VHS: S31927. $19.98.

Rumpole of the Bailey, Vol. 6. Episodes include *Rumpole and the Golden Thread* and *Rumpole and the Last Resort*.
VHS: S31928. $19.98.

Rumpole of the Bailey, Vol. 7. Episodes include *Rumpole and the Bubble Reputation* and *Rumpole and the Age of Miracles*.
VHS: S31929. $19.98.

Rumpole of the Bailey, Vol. 8. Episodes include *Rumpole and the Tap End* and *Rumpole and the Quality of Life*.
VHS: S31930. $19.98.

Rumpole of the Bailey, Vol. 9. Episodes include *Rumpole a la Carte* and *Rumpole and the Summer of Discontent*.
VHS: S31931. $19.98.

Rumpole of the Bailey, Vol. 10. Episodes include *Rumpole at Sea* and *Rumpole and the Right to Silence*.
VHS: S31932. $19.98.

The Saint

Roger Moore stars as Simon Templar in the TV action/adventure series, his precursor to James Bond. Each of four tapes contains two 50-minute episodes.

Volume 1: The Russian Prisoner/The Man Who Loved Lions.
VHS: S30745. $14.95.

Volume 2: Locate & Destroy/Queens Ransom.
VHS: S30746. $14.95.

Volume 3: Reluctant Revolution/Helpful Pirate.
VHS: S30747. $14.95.

Volume 4: The Angel's Eye/The Interlude with Venus.
VHS: S30748. $14.95.

The Sandbaggers

Britain's Secret Intelligence Service is often nicknamed The Sandbaggers. Neil Burnside (Roy Marsden) is the Director of Operations for SIS. This former Royal Marine and Sandbagger is dedicated to the service leading him to clash with the powers of the Foreign Office, Westminster and even Downing Street. The entire series is included. 300 mins.
VHS: S21157. $99.98.

Scotch & Wry

Rikki Fulton is Scotland's King of Comedy. These hilarious videos portray many of the popular Fulton characters including Reverend I.M. Jolly, Dirty Dickie Dandruff, the famous missionary Mrs. Ida Closehave and Supercop. Four-video collection set includes *Scotch & Wry, Double Scotch & Wry, Triple Scotch & Wry*, and *Scotch & Wry 4*. 350 mins.
VHS: S31379. $74.98.

Screening Middlemarch

The BBC and the British Film Institute produced this insightful documentary about the adaptation of a 19th century literary classic for television in the 1990's. Conceptualization, packaging and distribution are explored as George Elliot's work is prepared for new audiences. 90 mins.
VHS: S24904. $179.00.

Secret Agent Man

Enjoy the collectible episodes of the British hit spy series starring Patrick McGoohan as British spy John Drake. The entertaining and intelligent scripts developed a cult following, both in Britain and America. 55 minutes each.
Volume 4:
VHS: Out of print. For rental only.
Volume 5.
VHS: Out of print. For rental only.
Volume 7: The Man on the Beach.
VHS: S11127. $19.95.

Shadow on the Sun

Stefanie Powers is cast in this made-for-TV biography as the adventurous and celebrated Beryl Markham, aviator, author, and woman extraordinaire. She lived life as she pleased, much to the dismay of English society. She romanced royalty, screenwriters and famous African pilots. With Frederic Forrest, James Fox, John Rubinstein, Jack Thompson and Claire Bloom.
VHS: S10983. $29.95.
Tony Richardson, USA/Great Britain, 1988, 192 mins.

Sharpe's Collection I

Sean Bean stars in this acclaimed British TV series about the desperate battles fought during the Napoleonic wars in 19th-century Spain. Beans's character, Richard Sharpe, works under Lord Wellington with a group of men who fight behind enemy lines. Four episodes. *Sharpe's Rifles*: Based on Bernard Cornwall's best-selling novel, Bean is a maverick British officer who has risen in the ranks of Wellington's army because of his bravery. Assumpta Serna plays his lover, the sultry leader of a guerrilla troupe. Filmed on location in England, Portugal and Spain. *Sharpe's Eagles*: In this episode Sharpe seeks revenge for a fallen friend. He sets out to capture the French mascot, a carved golden eagle. *Sharpe's Company*: Sharpe discovers that he is a father. Now he must save his lover and daughter from the approaching French. *Sharpe's Enemy*. A gang of deserters have taken hold of hostages and demand a hefty ransom. Sharpe is sent with the money only to encounter an old enemy and a dirty trick. Each episode is 100 mins.
VHS: S24779. $89.98.

Sharpe's Collection II

The British hero of the Napoleonic Wars, Richard Sharpe (Sean Bean), returns for this second installment of dramatic episodes. Once again he leads his men behind enemy lines, fighting the French as well as battling the intrigues spawned by rivalry between men ostensibly on the same side. Based on Bernard Cornwell's best-selling novels. Four episodes. *Sharpe's Honor*: Romance adds to the sense of danger in this episode. Sharpe is unwittingly drawn to a pawn of a French spy, the alluring Marquesa Dorada. As a result, Sharpe is drawn into a French plot. Shot on location in the Crimea, Portugal and England. *Sharpe's Gold*: Aztec gold is at the center of this rollicking episode. Sharpe is detoured by the luster of this treasure and finds that he is not alone. Many are seeking this mythical cache. In the end, complications emanating from a deadly trade of guns for deserters overwhelms key players, including the lovely Ellie, daughter of Admiral Wellington. *Sharpe's Battle*: Sharpe must transform the Royal Irish Company, a ceremonial force, into a fighting regiment. The difficulty of this task is deepened by Lord Kiely's wife, a woman who needs help for a personal matter. Meanwhile, false reports of an English massacre in Ireland lead to even more unforeseen troubles. *Sharpe's Sword*: Sharpe is given a new, dangerous mission. He must protect the trusted spy El Mirador. Unfortunately, Colonel Leroux, an unmatched swordsman, is trying to capture this same spy. When Sharpe is hurt, a lovely, mute woman from a local convent offers Sharpe his only chance for survival. Each video is approximately 100 mins.
VHS: S27582. $89.98.

Sharpe's Collection III

The action and adventure continue in this adventure series based on Bernard Cornwell's best-selling novels. Sean Bean reprises his role as the daring British officer Richard Sharpe, Wellington's key subordinate in the battle against Napoleon. As Wellington prepares to invade France in 1813, Sharpe discovers corruption in the highest ranks of the British army. A secret mission in the Pyrenees takes the newlywed Sharpe away from his wife (Abigail Cruttenden)—who succumbs to a deadly fever. She survives, but in the final days of the war their marriage will face its most critical challenge. Five hours on three videocassettes.
VHS: S30882. $69.98.

Sharpe's Collection IV

Sean Beam returns as maverick British officer Richard Sharpe in the fourth and final entry in this award-winning series based on Bernard Cornwell's best-selling novels. Episodes include *Sharpe's Revenge, Sharpe's Justice* and *Sharpe's Waterloo*. 5 hours.
VHS: S32977. $69.98.

Sharpe: The Legend

Sean Bean stars in this action-packed account of Officer Richard Sharpe's most important battle, set several years after the Battle of Waterloo. 90 mins.
VHS: S34142. $19.98.

Silas Marner

Ben Kingsley leads a stellar cast including Jenny Agutter in a beautiful evocation of George Eliot's famous novel, shot in the Cotswold Hills of England. Produced by the BBC.
VHS: S03526. $29.98.
Giles Foster, Great Britain, 1986, 92 mins.

The Singing Detective

Dennis Potter's musically driven murder mystery masterpiece stars Michael Gambon *(Betrayal)* as cynical thriller writer Philip Marlow, recovering in a hospital while working through the plot of his greatest detective story, starring himself as a handsome, crooning '40s detective. Perhaps the greatest work ever written for television; a truly original masterpiece. With Janet Suzman *(Nicholas and Alexandra)*. Eight hours on cassette in slipcase.
VHS: S32414. $99.98.
Jon Amiel, Great Britain, 1986, 480 mins.

Sister Wendy's Story of Painting

This acclaimed BBC production takes viewers on a unique journey through art and history with best-selling author Sister Wendy. Filmed on location, the five-volume collection covers the history of art down through the ages, sweeping from cave paintings through the Renaissance, and on to the modern art scene in New York's SoHo scene. Volumes include *Early Art, The Renaissance, Baroque to Modernism, The Age of Revolution* and *Modernism*. 60 mins each.
VHS: S32093. $99.98.

Six Wives of Henry VIII

Few television series have attracted as much critical and public acclaim as these six triumphant plays, now preserved on video. Written by six different authors, each play is a lavish and authentic dramatization, produced with style and quality. Binding them together with his magnetic and dignified performance as the mighty monarch is Keith Michell—the definitive Henry VIII. This six-tape collector's set features the stories of Catherine of Aragon, Anne Boleyn, Jane Seymour, Anne of Cleves, Catherine Howard and Catherine Parr.
VHS: S20667. $99.98.

So You Wanna Get Laid

Everything is up for grabs in this hilarious, unrated English comedy made in the Monty Python tradition. Tony Slatterly's team of sexperts are more than able to coach the shy through a host of sexuations. It's a bizarre, raucous, sexucational whirl. 48 mins.
VHS: S28404. $24.95.

Some Mothers Do 'Ave 'Em!

Michael Crawford *(Phantom of the Opera)* stars as the well-meaning but inept and injury-prone Frank Spencer, in this BBC comedy series. Collection set includes *Have a Break, Take a Husband, Cliffhanger, The RAF Reunion, King of the Road, The Job Interview, The Psychiatrist, George's House, Love Thy Neighbor, The Hospital Visit, Father's Clinic* and *Moving House*. Four videos, 5½ hours.
VHS: S33683. $74.98.

Steptoe and Son

Wilfred Brambell (who played Paul McCartney's grandfather in *A Hard Day's Night*) stars as Albert and Harry H. Corbett as Harold in the classic British series that inspired *Sanford and Son*. The world's most famous rag and bone men clean up in four volumes. *Volume One* includes "Divided We Stand," "The Desperate Hours" and "Porn Yesterday." *Volume Two* includes "Men of Letters," "Live Now P.A.Y.E. Later" and "Christmas Special 1973." *Volume Three* is called *A Star Is Born*. And *Volume Four—Oh, What a Beautiful Morning*—includes "Loathe Story" and "And So to Bed." 6 hours, 20 minutes total.
VHS: S31259. $89.98.

The Strange Case of the End of Civilization as We Know It

John Cleese utilizes his comic skills in this contemporary detective thriller. Cleese plays the grandson of Sherlock Holmes, an unskilled plotter with an unrivaled reputation for making a mockery of various criminal investigations. The commissioner of police summons him to capture the diabolical genius criminal Professor Moriarty. With Arthur Lowe, Stratford Johns and Connie Booth. 55 mins.
VHS: S19738. $19.95.

Summer Wine

From award-winning comedy writer Roy Clarke *(Keeping Up Appearances)*. Three elderly, unemployed delinquents are outstanding examples of the positive benefits of being out of work in this comedy series. Free to wonder, wander and talk together for the first time since schooldays, our redundant heroes drift contentedly through the gainfully employed world of a small Yorkshire wool town. Four-volume set contains nine episodes. Volumes include: *Last of the Summer Wine, Forked Lightning, Spring Fever,* plus the full-length film *Getting Sam Home*. Six hours.
VHS: S31381. $74.98.

Sykes

Eric Sykes and the inhabitants of Sebastopol Terrace appear in three episodes from this insanely popular, long-running British television show. Peter Sellers appears as a guest. 88 mins.
VHS: S10623. $29.95.

Take a Letter Mr. Jones

Rula Lenska is a harried executive in this witty British television series. It centers on an unflappable male secretary who manages to keep the office running smoothly for his female boss. He has to, as she has a seven-year-old daughter depending on her. Two volumes; each contains three episodes, and is 75 mins.
VHS: S25063. $39.95.

The Thin Blue Line

Not your typical cop show, this PBS comedy series stars British funnyman Rowan Atkinson *(Mr. Bean)* as Inspector Fowler and David Haig as Detective Inspector Grim, who oversee a cramped police station in Grantly, a fictitious suburb of London.
Volume 1.
VHS: S31207. $19.95.
Volume 2.
VHS: S31208. $19.95.
Volume 3. 50 mins.
VHS: S33679. $19.95.
Volume 4. 70 mins.
VHS: S33680. $19.95.

Thomas Hardy's Tess of the D'Urbervilles

One of the most memorable heroines in literature comes to life in a stunning new screen adaptation of Thomas Hardy's most passionate work. Justine Waddell stars as the innocent farm girl seduced by her young aristocrat employer, but in love with a man of her own class. Boxed set includes two videos.
VHS: S34857. $29.95.
Ian Sharp, Great Britain, 1998, 180 mins.

Three of a Kind

A triple threat comedy team in a BBC presentation that boasts the talents of Lenny Henry, Tracey Ullman and David Copperfield. Copperfield is no relation to the magician or the fictional character. See a collection of skits, sketches and musical parodies that kept Tracey Ullman employed before her US comedy show. England, 1984, 84 mins.
VHS: S05620. $29.98.

The Tide of Life

Sixteen-year-old Emily Kennedy loves her job at the McGilby's. But when the invalid Mrs. McGilby dies, and Sep McGilby is killed in a car accident soon after, she rapidly grows from girl to woman. Based on the novel by Catherine Cookson. 156 mins.
VHS: S31750. $29.95.

To Play the King

This sequel to *House of Cards* features Ian Richardson once again lurking about at the highest levels of her Majesty's government. The difference is that this time the stakes are even higher. A magnificent BBC production, 200 mins.
VHS: S26031. $39.98.

To the Lighthouse

Kenneth Branagh and Rosemary Harris star in the BBC production of Virginia Woolf's most popular novel, about family life as friends settle in to enjoy a warm Edwardian summer at the beach, and romance and conflicting dreams simultaneously draw the family together and pull it apart.
VHS: S32021. $19.95.
Colin Gregg, Great Britain, 1983, 115 mins.

To the Manor Born

The first seven episodes of the popular BBC comedy series. Penelope Keith and Peter Bowles star as the upper crust but impoverished Audrey Forbes-Hamilton, once Lady of Grantly Manor, and Richard DeVere, the mysterious millionaire who buys her ancestral estate.
To the Manor Born—Vol. 1. Includes bonus episode.
VHS: S33014. $19.98.
To the Manor Born—Vol. 2.
VHS: S33015. $19.98.

A Touch of Frost

David Jason is Inspector Jack Frost, a cop who has no time for legal niceties or delicate sensibilities. Instinct drives this cop to seek justice as best he can. He knows his maverick ways mean he will never advance beyond the rank of detective. But that is a price he is willing to pay. Respect is his ultimate reward. This British television series consists of three tapes, each 102 mins. in length.
VHS: S23755. $59.98.

Two Ronnies

Two volumes. *By the Sea/Picnic*: Enjoy a double helping of delightful farce in these two irresistible "silent" films from that award-winning British TV comedy team, the Two Ronnies. 80 mins. *In a Packed Program Tonight*: Comedy and musical routines from Ronnie Barker and Ronnie Corbett. A humorous mix of music, quick fire news items and skits and sketches. 59 mins.
VHS: S31380. $34.98.

An Unsuitable Job for a Woman

This Masterpiece Theatre murder mystery is based on the novel by P.D. James and stars Helen Baxendale as private detective Cordelia Gray. Inheriting a ramshackle detective agency from her eccentric ex-policeman boss, Cordelia is thrown into a world of excitement and danger as she quickly learns the ropes of being a private detective. Three-tape set.

VHS: S34667. $39.98.

Ben Bolt, Great Britain, 1998, 330 mins.

Up Pompeii

Includes two episodes. *The Legacy*: Before Christ there was Senator Ludicrus Sextus, a philandering roue, and his wife Ammonia. Uncle Lucre's legacy seems a gift of the gods. But is Ludicrus man enough to meet the curious conditions attached to the inheritance? *Vestal Virgins*: It's Vestal Virgin time in Pompeii…Virgins! In Pompeii?! Can Lurcio the slave find an untouched, fair-skinned maiden or will soothsaying Senna's prophesy of doom come true? Stars Frankie Howerd. 3 hours on 2 videocassettes.

VHS: S31382. $34.98.

Upstairs Downstairs

A classic series from the BBC, *Upstairs Downstairs* follows the travails of the aristocratic Bellamy Family in Edwardian England. Just as important are the servants who live upstairs. Together they live through the conflicts and traumas of a changing world. This series offers a chance to see how society and the rigid hierarchies of class must evolve as England emerges into a new century where she is no longer preeminent.

Vol. 1: On Trial/For Love of Love.
VHS: S23262. $24.95.
Vol. 2: I Dies from Love/Why Is Her Door Locked.
VHS: S23263. $24.95.
Vol. 3: Guest of Honor/A Special Mischief.
VHS: S23264. $24.95.
Vol. 4: A Change of Scene/Desirous of Change.
VHS: S23265. $24.95.
Vol. 5: The Bolter/A Perfect Stranger.
VHS: S23266. $24.95.
Vol. 6: The Glorious Dead/Facing Fearful Odds.
VHS: S23267. $24.95.
Vol. 7: Wanted, A Good Home/An Old Flame.
VHS: S23268. $24.95.
Collector's Boxed Set.
VHS: S23269. $149.95.

Vanity Fair

The classic BBC adaptation of William Makepeace Thackeray's novel, a satire of the weaknesses and folly of human nature in early 19th-century England. The viewer is treated to the machinations of anti-heroine Becky Sharp (Susan Hampshire in an Emmy Award-winning performance), whom Alistair Cooke once called "one of the most accomplished bitches known to fact or fiction between the fall of Rome and the rise of Las Vegas."

VHS: S31357. $39.98.

David Giles, Great Britain, 1967, 250 mins.

Vendetta for the Saint

Roger Moore is Simon Templar in this televised series based on the character created by Leslie Charteris. A wealthy Robin Hood criminal with oodles of charm and class, he helps out the authorities against the really bad bad guys—like the Italian Mafia, for instance. England, 1968, 98 mins.

VHS: S06097. $59.98.

Vicar of Dibley

The popular BBC comedy stars Dawn French as the new vicar in the sleepy little town of Dibley. Three episodes per tape.

Vicar of Dibley, Volume 1: The New Girl in Town. Episodes include *Arrival, Songs of Praise* and *Community Spirit*. 86 mins.
VHS: S34661. $19.98.
Vicar of Dibley, Volume 2: My Congregation and Other Animals. Episodes include *The Window and the Weather, Electron* and *Animals*. 88 mins.
VHS: S34662. $19.98.

Victoria Wood: As Seen on TV

Starring and written by the reigning queen of British comedy, Victoria Wood, this tape promises to break new ground in humor in the United Kingdom. With guest stars Julie *(Educating Rita)* Walters, Duncan Preston, Susie Blake, Celia Immie, and Patricia Routledge.

VHS: S05614. $29.98.

Geoffrey Posner, Great Britain, 1986, 93 mins.

A Village Affair

Alice Jordan (Sophie Ward) appears to have the perfect life: a handsome, loyal husband, three healthy children, and a beautiful home. But when she meets Clodagh, the aristocratic daughter of the lord of the local manor, a scandalous relationship blossoms between the women which threatens to destroy her perfect life. Originally shown on *Masterpiece Theater*. Based on the best-selling novel by English author Joanna Trollope. 108 mins.

VHS: S30004. $14.98.

Voyage Round My Father

Laurence Olivier and Alan Bates star in this British television production. Olivier is an eccentric and successful lawyer who goes blind in middle age. Bates is his concerned and baffled son. The script is by John Mortime. With Jane Asher and Elizabeth Sellars.

VHS: S10613. $19.98.

Alvin Rakoff, Great Britain, 1983, 85 mins.

Waiting for God I

There are three episodes from the hit BBC comedy on this video. Whether confronting *The Funeral, The Hip Operation* or *The Boring Son*, the residents of Bevy Retirement Village manage to expose the humorous side of senior citizen living. 85 mins.

VHS: S28040. $19.98.

Waiting for God II

Among the three episodes from the BBC comedy collected on this video are *Cheering Tom Up, Fraulein Mueller* and *Power of Attorney*. 86 mins.

VHS: S28041. $19.98.

War and Peace

Anthony Hopkins stars as Pierre in this faithful BBC adaptation of Leo Tolstoy's classic 19th-century novel. It tells of the turmoil brought on by the Napoleonic Wars as experienced by two families, the Rostovs and Bolkonskys. This stunning, historically detailed six-volume work is filled with passion, spectacle and action. Also features Rupert Davies, Hugh Cross and Colin Baker. 751 mins.

VHS: S28394. $149.98.

The Wingless Bird

This captivating story set in 1913 finds an unlikely link between the fortunes of three very different families in this adaptation of the tale by beloved British author Catherine Cookson.

VHS: S34413. $29.98.

David Wheatley, Great Britain, 1997, 156 mins.

The Woman in Black

This Victorian-era story, starring Adrian Rawlins as a young solicitor, turns deadly with the sighting of a strange woman's apparition. The solicitor must settle the estate of his dead client but this task places him in grave danger as an old curse threatens his sanity.

VHS: S20810. $19.98.

Herbert Wise, Great Britain, 1993, 100 mins.

The Woman in White

Based on the Wilkie Collins detective novel. A mysterious woman haunts a country house as another young woman is held by her husband.

VHS: S32040. $19.98.

Yes, Minister

The prequel to the popular *Yes, Prime Minister*, this biting BBC comedy of political power and uncivil servants stars Oscar nominee Nigel Hawthorne, Paul Eddington *(Good Neighbors)*, and Derek Fowlds.

Yes, Minister—Volume 1. Episodes include *Open Government, The Official Visit, The Economy Drive,* and *Big Brother*. 115 mins.
VHS: S34126. $19.98.
Yes, Minister—Volume 2. Episodes include *The Writing on the Wall, The Right to Know, Jobs for the Boys*. 86 mins.
VHS: S34127. $19.98.

Yes, Prime Minister: Official Secrets

Three episodes from the BBC comedy series: "Official Secrets," "A Diplomatic Incident" and "A Conflict of Interest."

VHS: S15977. $19.98.

Yes, Prime Minister: Power to the People

A dead-on satire of English political power, class consciousness and cultural hegemony in this popular BBC production. Created by Anthony Jay and Jonathan Lynn. With Paul Eddington, Nigel Hawthorne and Derek Fowlds. 117 mins.

VHS: S18878. $19.98.

Yes, Prime Minister: The Bishop's Gambit

Three episodes form the BBC comedy series: "The Bishop's Gambit," "One of Us" and "Man Overboard."

VHS: S15976. $19.98.

Yes, Prime Minister: The Grand Design/The Ministerial Broadcast/ The Smoke Screen

Paul Eddington, Nigel Hawthorne and Derek Fowlds star in this very popular political comedy series from England, currently playing on PBS in all markets. Includes three episodes.

VHS: S14509. $19.98.

Yes, Prime Minister: The Key/A Real Partnership/A Victory for Democracy

This popular spoof of British Government stars Paul Eddington, Nigel Hawthorne, and Derek Fowlds. Includes three episodes.

VHS: S14510. $19.98.

The Young Ones: Bambi, Nasty, Time

The Young Ones represent their college at University Challenge. At home, videos and dating bring even more humorous possibilities to the fore. Three episodes of the BBC comedy series featuring these manic English students are collected on this video. 101 mins.

VHS: S29804. $14.98.

The Young Ones: Cash, Interesting, Summer Holiday

Money, parties and summer vacation are the primary concerns of The Young Ones in the three episodes on this video. This BBC comedy series reveals the laughable base reality of student life. 101 mins.

VHS: S29805. $14.98.

The Young Ones: Demolition, Bomb, Sick

Demolition threatens their home, a bomb could be in their future, and history's most congested sinuses portend a massive disaster, and yet the English college students from this hit BBC comedy series bumble onward. Three episodes are joined on this video. 104 mins.

VHS: S29803. $14.98.

The Young Ones: Oil, Boring, Flood

Three episodes of the '80s BBC comedy series featuring demented English students are joined on this video. An in-house revolution, manic self-destructive impulses, and a flood drive them to ever greater comic perils. 96 mins.

VHS: S12584. $14.98.

The Zero Imperative

This supernatural thriller is the latest thing from the creators of *Dr. Who, The Stranger* and *The Airzone Solution*. Colin Baker, Jon Pertwee, Caroline John and others from the original *Dr. Who* series are featured in this gruesome tale. A psychiatric hospital is suddenly at the center of a mysterious rash of murders. A patient known as Zero is involved, but how? 60 mins.

VHS: S24907. $24.99.

MONTY PYTHON

And Now for Something Completely Different

The first feature film by the Monty Python gang, featuring some of their funniest skits from their TV show, *Monty Python's Flying Circus*.

VHS: S00048. $19.95.
Laser: Widescreen. **LD74614. $34.95.**

Ian Macnaughton, Great Britain, 1971

Clockwise

John Cleese is the English head teacher, obsessed with punctuality, as he frantically races to the most important occasion of his life—a meeting of the National Headmaster's Conference. Needless to say, his best laid plans quickly dissolve into a series of epic disasters. Very funny.

VHS: S02973. $14.98.

Christopher Morahan, Great Britain, 1986, 96 mins.

How to Irritate People

Performed before a live audience, John Cleese demonstrates how to bother people so as to unnerve them. "Find out how to pay back job interviewers, movie chatterboxes, garage staff, even bank clerks in the only way they deserve." With support provided by Michael Palin, Graham Chapman, Connie Booth, Gillian Lind and Tim Brooke-Taylor. 65 mins.

VHS: S18133. $19.95.

Life of Brian

Oops, wrong manger! The story of Bethlehem's lesser-known son is a non-stop orgy of assaults, not on anyone's virtue, but on the funny bone. Rich ensemble acting, and animation by Terry Gilliam.

VHS: S00752. $19.98.
Laser: Letterboxed. **LD76408. $59.95.**

Terry Jones, Great Britain, 1979, 94 mins.

Life of Python

A madcap compilation of the remarkable 20-year history of the anarchic and revolutionary British comedy group Monty Python, framed in the voices, anecdotes, personal tales, words, actions and movements of its principal performers. 56 mins.

VHS: S17227. $19.95.

The Missionary
Monty Python performer Michael Palin wrote, co-produced and stars in this ribald comedy about a preacher who's returned from Africa and enlisted to supervise a home for fallen women ("You mean, women who've tripped?"), and becomes entangled in a series of delicate situations. With Maggie Smith, Trevor Howard, Denholm Elliott, Michael Hordern, Graham Crowden and Phoebe Nicholls.
VHS: S02034. $19.95.
Richard Loncraine, Great Britain, 1982, 86 mins.

Monty Python Live at the Hollywood Bowl
The anarchic wit of the British troupe is brought home with a vengeance in this performance film shot in Los Angeles, featuring a series of sketches, improvisations and routines performed by Graham Chapman, John Cleese, Terry Gilliam, Eric Idle, Michael Palin and others.
VHS: S02551. $19.95.
Terry Hughes, Great Britain, 1982, 81 mins.

Monty Python's Meaning of Life
This savagely satirical film is quite possibly the best of the Monty Python films with its balance of dark, subversive humor and light parodies of God, death, the Empire, Catholicism and gluttony. The film features animation sequences and a short film by Python member Terry Gilliam that bears strong thematic resemblance to his great film, *Brazil*.
VHS: S02550. $19.95.
Laser: LD70058. $34.95.
Terry Jones, Great Britain, 1983, 107 mins.

Parrot Sketch Not Included
Occasioned by its 20th anniversary of Monty Python, this clever program offers a kaleidoscopic look at the sketches, improvs, ramblings, bits and gags of "Python foolery." 75 mins.
VHS: S17228. $19.95.

Personal Services
Julie Walters *(Educating Rita)* winningly plays an English waitress-turned-madam in this fictionalized account of the life of the notorious brothel keeper, Cynthia Payne. She cheerfully caters to the bizarre tastes of the older gents. Ex-Python Terry Jones directs this naughty but nice comedy-drama about sexual attitudes in England.
VHS: S05172. $79.98.
Terry Jones, Great Britain, 1987, 104 mins.

Pole to Pole
Monty Python regular Michael Palin stars in this madcap adventure about one man's globe-trotting adventures, taken to every corner of the earth, though with a strict caveat: he's forbidden from using any modern means of travel. So he moves around in dog sleds, camels and canoes, with frightening and unpredictable results. Four volumes. 100 mins.
VHS: S17920. $49.95.
Laser: CLV. **LD72077. $129.95.**

Ripping Yarns
A collection from the BBC series that turns English legends, culture and society inside out. Written by Monty Python's Michael Palin and Terry Jones, starring Palin. Each tape has three episodes.
Ripping Yarns: *Tomkinson's Schooldays* is a satire on the stuffy, traditional English boarding school complete with bizarre headmaster and cruel school bully. With *Escape from Stalag Luft 112B* and *Golden Gordon*. 90 minutes.
VHS: S01895. $19.98.
More Ripping Yarns: Includes *The Testing of Eric Olthwaite*, about a boy from a mining town in the Depression who gets involved with a seasoned criminal, *Whinfrey's Last Case*, and *Curse of the Claw*. 92 minutes.
VHS: S01896. $19.98.
Even More Ripping Yarns: *Roger of the Raj* shows how Roger, son of wealthy parents, is posted in India during World War I and grows from a boy to an older boy. With *Murder at Moorstone Manor* and *Across the Andes by Frog*. 90 minutes.
VHS: S01897. $19.98.

Romance with a Double Bass
John Cleese (Monty Python) stars as a bass player scheduled to play in the orchestra at the royal wedding. Arriving early, he takes a quick skinny-dip only to find that the Princess (Connie Booth) has done the same. Hilarious adventure and romance follow.
VHS: S01128. $19.95.
Robert Young, Great Britain, 1974, 40 mins.

The Rutles: All You Need Is Cash
Eric Idle had the brilliant idea to parody the Beatles by creating a story about four young men who get a recording contract because they wear tight pants. Originally filmed as a *Saturday Night Live* skit, the audience response was so positive that Idle and *SNL* producer Lorne Michaels decided to create a full-length production. George Harrison, Mick Jagger, Paul Simon, John Belushi, Dan Aykroyd, Gilda Radner and Bill Murray are among the musical and comic greats that add to the inspired lunacy. *Sgt. Rutter's Only Darts Club Band* is a highlight that is not to be missed.
VHS: S27693. $19.98.
Laser: LD76228. $39.98.
Eric Idle, Great Britain, 70 mins.

DR. WHO

The Airzone Solution
Colin Baker is joined by three other former *Dr. Who* actors-Peter Davison, Sylvester McCoy and Jon Pertwee—in this feature created by Billy Bags, the producer of *The Stranger*. 65 mins.
VHS: S20912. $24.99.

The Android Invasion
When the TARDIS materializes just outside a sleepy English village, it appears the Doctor and Sarah Jane are nearly home at last. But all is not as it seems in this rural paradise. The Doctor must solve the mystery of the Thraals quickly, for the future of mankind hangs in the balance. Starring Tom Baker and Elizabeth Sladen.
VHS: S27161. $19.98.
Berry Letts, Great Britain, 1975, 96 mins.

The Androids of Tara
After the TARDIS lands on Tara, Romana locates the Fourth Segment and the time-travellers are drawn into the planet's complex political intrigues. The Doctor is unwillingly thrust into the roles of android repairman, king-maker and swashbucking hero, when he finds himself duelling with the wicked swordsman Count Grendel. Starring Tom Baker as the Doctor.
VHS: S27159. $19.98.
Michael Hayes, Great Britain, 1978, 98 mins.

Arc of Infinity
The Doctor is threatened with certain destruction. This threat also could bring doom to the entire universe. An anti-matter alien wants to bond with the Doctor. All known dimensions could be annihilated as a result. 98 mins.
VHS: S26435. $19.98.

The Ark in Space
In this feature-length space adventure, the Doctor (Tom Baker), Harry and Sarah accidentally arrive on an artificial satellite where the survivors of earth lie in cryogenic suspension waiting to begin life anew. Great Britain, 1975, 90 mins.
VHS: S13727. $19.98.

The Armageddon Factor
The Doctor (Tom Baker) is embroiled in a war between worlds while hunting for the Key to Time. Despite the terrors of this conflict the Doctor must worry about an even greater threat: the nefarious Shadow is in hiding, and he also covets the Key to Time. 148 mins.
VHS: S29790. $19.98.

The Awakening & Frontios
Double cassette. A peaceful English village hides an ancient alien curse in *Awakenings*. In *Fronticos*, the Tardis is stranded on a hostile planet, home to humanity's last survivors. With Sylvester McCoy as Doctor Who.
VHS: S33730. $29.98.

The Aztecs
The original Doctor, William Hartnell, finds himself in mortal danger when he unexpectedly materializes the TARDIS within an ancient but very much used Aztec temple. Though he and his companions are venerated as gods, they find that they may succumb to temple etiquette and be sacrificed to even more powerful gods. Great Britain, 1964, 100 mins.
VHS: S20783. $19.98.

Battlefield
Was the Doctor the legendary Merlin of King Arthur's Court? Old enemies Mordred and Morgaine vie with the Doctor and his old friend the Brigadier. With Sylvester McCoy as Doctor Who.
VHS: S33733. $19.98.

The Brain of Morbius (Collector's Edition)
On the desolate planet Karn, the Doctor discovers a scheme to resurrect the exiled Time Lord Moribus, the greatest criminal mind in the galaxy. Starring Tom Baker. Unedited.
VHS: S30644. $19.98.
Christopher Barry, Great Britain, 1976, 100 mins.

Carnival of Monsters
The BBC's best-selling sci-fi series comes to video! The Doctor has promised Jo Grant a holiday on Metebelis III, but instead of the famous blue planet, the TARDIS materializes on board the SS Bernice, sailing to India in 1926. Starring Jon Pertwee.
VHS: S27162. $19.98.
Barry Letts, Great Britain, 1973, 101 mins.

Castrovalva
In an epic battle with his arch nemesis, the Master, Doctor Who relies on his powers and gifts to gain an advantage, though he's mysteriously unable to conjure up his capacity for regeneration. With Peter Davidson. Great Britain, 1982, 97 mins.
VHS: S19302. $19.98.

The Caves of Androzani
The Doctor's life is saved by the masked Sharaz Jek, who controls all of the precious spectrox on Androzani. But is Jek really his savior? Great Britain, 1984, 101 mins.
VHS: S17377. $19.98.

City of Death
While on vacation in Paris, the Doctor (Tom Baker) is forced to battle a new and unforseen danger. Cracks have begun to tear at the fabric of time itself. The Doctor's nemesis, the sinister Count, is undoubtedly involved. Great Britain, 1979, 100 mins.
VHS: S20781. $19.98.

The Claws of Axos
The Doctor, Jon Pertwee, is on the earth to experience the arriving of the Axons. They come bearing a spectacular gift, but it may be a ruse or, even worse, a trap. 98 mins.
VHS: S27773. $19.98.

The Colin Baker Years
Colin Baker represents the oldest but most youthful appearing Dr. Who because as the Doctor grows older he is reincarnated in ever-younger bodies. This retrospective is filled with interviews and clips that recall Baker's most cherished moments as the sixth Doctor, including his historic debut in Great Britain, 1994, 88 mins.
VHS: S21553. $19.98.

The Curse of Fenric
Transported to Second World War England, Doctor Who battles a curse that summons the wolves of Fenric to usher in a reign of evil. Great Britain, 1991, 104 mins.
VHS: S15350. $19.98.

Curse of Peladon
A secret and indescribably malevolent force is careening along a predetermined course which threatens catastrophe. The entire Galactic Federation could be plunged into a bloody war unless the Doctor can discover the secret behind this mysterious force. 97 mins.
VHS: S26434. $19.98.

Cybermen—The Early Years
These ruthless, cold robots were favorite villains from their very first appearance in 1968. Four full episodes are included: numbers 2 and 4 from *The Moonbase* and numbers 3 and 6 from *The Wheel in Space*. With an introduction by Colin Baker; interviews with Morris Barry, director of many *Doctor Who* episodes; and testimonies from some of the actors who portrayed the evil Cybermen. Great Britain, 1992, 120 mins.
VHS: S18077. $19.98.

The Daemons
Doctor Who investigates the mystery of the Devil's Hump burial mound and discovers a fiendish plot set in motion by his nemesis, the Master. With Jon Pertwee. Great Britain, 1971, 123 mins.
VHS: S19301. $19.98.

The Dalek Invasion of Earth Parts 1 & 2
After the TARDIS sets down in a decaying London of the next century, the Doctor confronts an enemy he thought he vanquished, the Daleks, who currently dominate the Earth. With William Hartnell as the Doctor. Great Britain, 1964, 150 mins.
VHS: S20265. $29.98.

The Daleks
The Doctor has his first terrifying encounter with those mechanized monsters, the Daleks. This original, unedited, two-part classic stars William Hartnell and includes both *The Dead Planet* and *The Expedition* episodes. Great Britain, 174 mins.
VHS: S25750. $29.98.

The Daleks Boxed Set
In this limited edition collection, Doctor Who squares off with his most gifted adversaries, the diabolical Daleks, in a series of programs showcasing the talents and eccentric characterizations of the two actors portraying Doctor Who—William Hartnell and Sylvester McCoy. Great Britain, 1965, 248 mins.
VHS: S19298. $39.98.

Daleks Invasion Earth 2150 AD
Peter Cushing as Doctor Who ends up in London over 200 years in the future where a handful of resistance fighters are waging a guerrilla war against the Daleks. Dr. Who applies his brilliant brain to discovering what the Daleks need from the Earth. Available only in EP mode. Great Britain, 1968, 81 mins.
VHS: S01774. $14.98.

Daleks—The Early Years
A history of the Daleks includes two classic episodes encompassing the Hartnell and Troughton periods. Introduction by Peter Davidson. Great Britain, 1993, 106 mins.
VHS: S19299. $19.98.

The Day of the Daleks
One of the strangest and most intellectually challenging chapters in the Doctor's 25-year history—a classic in its time. Great Britain, 1972, 90 mins.
VHS: S09962. $19.98.

The Deadly Assassin
Doctor Who's arch enemy, The Master, is more deadly than ever in this ultimate showdown. Great Britain, 1976, 90 mins.
VHS: S09963. $19.95.

Death to the Daleks
As a plague spreads throughout the galaxy, a power loss strands Doctor Who (John Pertwee) on Exxilon, the only planet where the antidote to the plague is found. Unfortunately the planet is home to a savagely hostile and degenerate race and the Doctor and Sarah are caught in a struggle between humans, Daleks and Exxilens. Great Britain, 1987, 90 mins.
VHS: S11741. $19.98.

Destiny of the Daleks
The future of the universe itself may be at stake as the Doctor's old enemies, the Daleks, are now battling the Movellans for their own survival. Should he help destroy them? Starring Tom Baker as Doctor Who. 99 mins.
VHS: S31233. $19.98.

Doctor Who and the Daleks
Pure fun! While Doctor Who (Peter Cushing) is explaining the workings of T.A.R.D.I.S. to his granddaughter, their clumsy friend Ian falls onto the controls, sending them all tumbling through space and time and ending up on the planet of the Daleks. The Daleks hide their bodies in cone-shaped metal encasements and hunt down the peaceful Thals—humans. Doctor Who's mission is to save himself and the Thals from the Daleks. Available only in EP mode.
VHS: S00370. $14.98.
Gordon Flemyng, Great Britain, 1965, 78 mins.

Doctor Who and the Silurians
The Doctor, played by John Pertwee, uncovers more than anyone expected below a top secret atomic research installation. Deep within the shadowy depths lies an unforseen terror. A prehistoric monster threatens to wreak havoc if disturbed in its mysterious lair. 167 mins.
VHS: S25748. $29.98.

The Dominators
Doctor Who joins a handful of desperate Dulcians as they fight an invasion of ruthless Dominators, a battle that threatens even the Earth. This video includes original, unedited black and white footage. Starring Patrick Troughton as the Doctor. Great Britain, 1968, 121 mins.
VHS: S21550. $19.98.

Dragonfire
The 150th episode includes the introduction of the Doctor's Companion, Ace. On the trail of the legendary Dragonfire on the Ice World, the Doctor finds a frozen core of corruption ruled by the megalomaniac Kane. Starring Sylvester McCoy.
VHS: S30641. $19.98.
Chris Clough, Great Britain, 1987, 73 mins.

Earthshock
The 1980's brought the universe Peter Davison, the fifth Doctor. In this episode, 26th century Earth hides a system of subterranean caves where a group of geologists has recently been murdered. Androids are guarding the site, but who controls them? Soon the Cybermen make a much feared re-emergence into the light of day. Great Britain, 1982, 99 mins.
VHS: S18078. $19.98.

Enlightenment
The White Guardian's cryptic warning of imminent danger draws Doctor Who into a puzzling contest. Peter Davison is the Doctor who finds himself ensnared in a deadly trap set by the Black Guardian. Great Britain, 1983, 97 mins.
VHS: S21554. $19.98.

The Five Doctors
The legendary 90-minute special is a grand one-time-only union of the first Five Doctors as well as a reunion of all of their famous friends, foes and monsters. Great Britain, 1983, 90 mins.
VHS: S09961. $19.98.
Laser: LD74637. $39.98.

Frontier in Space
It is the 26th century and space is divided between the great empires of Earth and Draconia. When the TARDIS accidentally brings the Doctor and Jo aboard Earth cargo ship C982, they find it under attack. The Doctor discovers that the Orgons are employed by his sworn enemy, the Master, but discovers an even deadlier foe waiting in the wings. Starring Jon Pertwee.
VHS: S27163. $29.98.
Paul Bernard, Great Britain, 1973, 144 mins.

Ghost Light
Sylvester McCoy is the time-traveling Doctor in this suspense-filled episode from the long-running BBC television series. An alien ship holds a strange and malevolent cargo. Only the Doctor and his companion can solve the mystery of this dangerous force. 72 mins.
VHS: S27769. $19.98.

The Green Death
A special tribute to Jon Pertwee. A horrible terror at the bottom of a mine shaft spells doom for the earth's inhabitants. Double cassette.
VHS: S30646. $29.98.
Michael Briant, Great Britain, 1973, 154 mins.

The Hand of Fear
The Doctor's companion, Sarah, becomes possessed by the spirit of a murderous alien dictator millions of years old. Starring Tom Baker.
VHS: S30643. $19.98.
Lennie Moyne, Great Britain, 1976, 98 mins.

The Happiness Patrol
Doctor Who probes the dark secret of the planet Terra Alpha, where malevolent forces compel inhabitants to put on a happy face or die. With Sylvester McCoy as Doctor Who.
VHS: S33732. $19.98.

The Hartnell Years
Doctor Who's seventh being journeys back in time to glimpse his first incarnation as the anti-hero William Hartnell. Great Britain, 1991, 88 mins.
VHS: S15349. $19.98.

Image of the Fendahl
Tom Baker, as the Doctor, finds himself enmeshed in a fairytale world. Unfortunately the fairytale creature which holds sway in this world is capable of tremendous powers, and that could lead to an ending where everyone does not exactly live happily ever after. 95 mins.
VHS: S27772. $19.98.

Inferno
A top-secret drilling operation has put the entire planet Earth at risk. For the Doctor this operation becomes an unforseen path to a parallel universe. 167 mins.
VHS: S26436. $29.98.

The Invasion
Patrick Troughton stars as the eccentric but fearless space and time traveler. In this episode the disappearance of an eminent scientist draws the Doctor, along with Zoe and Jamie, into a sinister plot. Tobias Vaughn is afoot. 146 mins.
VHS: S25745. $19.98.

The Keeper of Traken
The once solid empire of the Traken begins to disintegrate when the evil Melkur invade their space. With Tom Baker as the Doctor. Great Britain, 1981, 98 mins.
VHS: S20267. $19.98.

Kinda
Peter Davison is the youngest appearing Doctor, which conversely means that he is the oldest. Despite his advancing age he continues to take on troubling forces wherever he goes. In this episode he finds that a planet seemingly like paradise actually contains a deadly, unknown power. 72 mins.
VHS: S27771. $19.98.

The King's Demons/The Five Doctors
In "The King's Demons" the Doctor confronts his oldest and deadliest enemy. State-of-the-art technology has been used to create one of the greatest Doctor Who adventures ever in "The Five Doctors," the famed 20th century episode in which the Doctor's incarnations meet in the Death Zone. Starring Peter Davison, Jon Pertwee and Patrick Troughton with Richard Hurndall, Tom Baker and William Hartnell.
VHS: S30645. $29.98.
Tony Virgoer/Peter Moffatt, Great Britain, 1983, 150 mins.

The Krotons
Once again with Patrick Troughton portraying Doctor Who, trouble in the Universe threatens another unsuspecting population. The Doctor and Zoe must help the Gonds escape enslavement from the merciless Krotons. But first they must discover the secret behind the mysterious teaching machines. Great Britain, 1969, 91 mins.
VHS: S21552. $19.98.

The Leisure Hive
A 20-minute war has reduced the planet Argolis to a cinder. When Doctor Who arrives, he's swept into a megalomaniacal plan to restore the planet's war-hungry heritage. Starring Tom Baker as Doctor Who. 87 mins.
VHS: S31232. $19.98.

Logopolis
In this eerie showdown of master intellects, Doctor Who tries to alter the Master's sinister theory to interrupt the causal nexus, destroying the universe's foundation. With Tom Baker. Great Britain, 1981, 99 mins.
VHS: S19300. $19.98.

The Mark of the Rani
A renegade Time Lord, the Rani, and the Doctor's old adversary, the Master, stir up widespread social disorder in 19th century England. The role of the Rani is played by Kate O'Mara of *Dynasty*. Starring Colin Baker.
VHS: S30642. $19.98.
Sara Hellings, Great Britain, 1985, 89 mins.

The Masque of Mandragora
Set in the 15th century, the Doctor (Tom Baker) must conjure up all of his peculiar talents and intuitive skills when he's locked in mortal combat with the mysterious, ancient cult of Demnos. Great Britain, 1976, 99 mins.
VHS: S20268. $19.98.

Mawdryn Undead
The Doctor's capacity for regeneration is put under strain when the Black Guardian earmarks him for assassination. With Peter Davidson as the Doctor. Great Britain, 1983, 99 mins.
VHS: S20269. $19.98.

The Mind Robber
The Doctor and his irreverent crew materialize in a surreal fantasy world overtaken by white robots and fictional monsters that assume staggeringly real proportions. With Patrick Troughton as the Doctor. Great Britain, 1968, 100 mins.
VHS: S20266. $19.98.

The Monster of Peladon
On the planet of Peladon, a revolt has erupted, jeopardizing the Galactic Federation's war with Galaxy 5, and thrusting the Doctor into the mystery behind the spirit of Aggedor. Starring Jon Pertwee as Doctor Who. 146 mins.
VHS: S31235. $29.98.

More Than 30 Years in the TARDIS
All seven doctors are featured in this informative documentary. The entire history of the series is detailed in a fascinating combination of clips and interviews. 87 mins.
VHS: S26431. $19.98.

Paradise Towers
Something is turning a high-tech housing complex into a deadly, filthy slum. Doctor Who must discover the secret of the terrible, mysterious force that dwells in the basement. Starring Sylvester McCoy. 98 mins.
VHS: S31231. $19.98.

The Pertwee Years

John Pertwee portrayed the Doctor in his third incarnation, from 1970 to 1974. This particular form had an inclination for gadgetry and a love for old cars. Pertwee himself narrates this collection, which looks back on scenes from some of his most popular episodes. Included are a behind-the-scenes look at BBC special effects, Pertwee's first appearance as the Doctor, an excerpt from *The Five Doctors*, episode seven from the series *Inferno* and the final episode of *The Daemons*. Great Britain, 1992, 88 mins.
VHS: S17376. $19.98.

The Pirate Planet

The hunt for segments of the Key to Time continues as the Doctor (Tom Baker) travels to Zanak. There a cruel cyborg plots mayhem for the planet Earth. 101 mins.
VHS: S29788. $19.98.

Planet of Evil

Tom Baker, one of the most popular Doctors, answers a distress call. Valiant as ever, he responds, though he may regret landing on the Planet of Evil. 94 mins.
VHS: S27770. $19.98.

Planet of the Spiders

Jon Pertwee's final and most suspenseful episode pits him against the deadly spiders from the planet Metebelis. It ultimately boils down to a perilous battle of wits. Fortunately Pertwee is among the most witty of the Doctor's incarnations, who proves more than capable of matching his evil foes. Great Britain, 1974, 150 mins.
VHS: S20779. $19.98.

The Power of Kroll

While searching for a segment to the Key to Time, the Doctor (Tom Baker) discovers he must go to the third moon of Delta Magna. This satellite is the home of the currently dormant but previously much-feared god, Kroll. 91 mins.
VHS: S29787. $19.98.

Pyramids of Mars

Doctor Who and his companion Sara find themselves in 1911 where they meet a professor possessed by an ancient Egyptian god of darkness. He is willing to use robot mummies to help release his controlling master. The Doctor doesn't cooperate with the plot. Great Britain, 1985, 91 mins.
VHS: S03871. $19.98.

The Rescue/The Romans

In "The Rescue," having left Susan on Earth, the Doctor, Ian and Barbara land the TARDIS on the planet Dido in the year 2493. There they discover two humans, Bennett and Vicki, trapped in their spaceship: the only crew to survive death at the hands of the hostile Didonians. In "The Romans," it is Italy 64 A.D. and the Doctor leaves for Rome with Vicki and is mistaken for a murdered musician, Maximus Petullian—an enemy of Nero. Will the doctor meet the same terrible fate? Starring William Hartnell.
VHS: S27164. $29.98.
Christopher Barry, Great Britain, 1965, 146 mins.

Resurrection of the Daleks

The Doctor—in his youthful incarnation, Peter Davison—is trapped with his companions in a time corridor by his most feared enemy, the Daleks. 20th century Earth is the unfortunate setting for the inevitable showdown between these inhuman creatures and the Doctor. Great Britain, 1984, 97 mins.
VHS: S20778. $19.98.

Revenge of the Cybermen

The Doctor (played by Tom Baker) returns to Space Station Nerva to find that his ship, TARDIS, has drifted back a few thousand years in time. The Cybermen attempt to take over TARDIS in order to destroy the planet Voga, where there are extensive gold mines. Great Britain, 1983, 92 mins.
VHS: S00354. $19.98.
Michael Briant, Great Britain, 1983, 92 mins.

The Ribos Operation

Tom Baker, as the Doctor, heeds the call of the White Guardian. It seems the Doctor must assemble the Key to Time. This quest sends him off to the Planet of Ribos and into a deep space con scheme. 99 mins.
VHS: S29786. $19.98.

Robot

Once again the Earth is under threat, and it's not only a dangerous alien who is to blame. The Doctor, Tom Baker, must fight the hijacker robot threatening the earth with atomic war, if only earthbound humans will let him. Great Britain, 1975, 99 mins.
VHS: S20780. $19.98.

The Robots of Death

Tom Baker, the most popular of all the doctors on this British tv speculative series, lands on a desert planet loaded with the valuable ore lucanol. The miners are now being killed by formerly friendly robots as they have a new, greedy master. This doesn't sit right with the Doctor. Great Britain, 1986, 91 mins.
VHS: S03870. $19.98.

The Sea Devils

The Doctor's old enemy, the Master, is imprisoned on a remote island. But his links to the remnants of an evil Silurian race, the Sea Devils, could spell doom for the Earth. Starring Jon Pertwee as Doctor Who. 149 mins.
VHS: S31236. $29.98.

The Seeds of Death

Patrick Troughton stars as the Doctor in the 21st century and Earth is totally dependent on T-Mat, a revolutionary form of instant travel. When the system breaks down, the Doctor makes a hazardous journey to the relay station only to find it's in the hands of Ice Warriors who plan to invade earth using T-Mat. Great Britain, 1985, 137 mins.
VHS: S11740. $19.98.

Seeds of Doom, Parts 1 & 2

The Krynoid are an alien plant species with a very aggressive sense for violence. They will take over the Earth unless the Doctor can arrest their luxurious but deadly growth. 144 mins.
VHS: S26433. $19.98.

Shada

Originally this 6-part series was not to be completed until Tom Baker, the fourth Doctor Who, stepped in. Now the entire story of the evil Shada is complete. When an artifact from Gallifrey dating back to the time of Rasillon goes missing, retired Timelord Dr. Chronotis calls on the Doctor and Romana to make sure this powerful relic does not fall into the wrong hands. Great Britain, 1979, 110 mins.
VHS: S17374. $19.98.

Silver Nemesis

Go behind the scenes to see how the fascinating episode "Silver Nemesis," from the *Dr. Who* series, was made. Sylvester McCoy is the star of this episode and he will lead fans on this much awaited tour inside one of television's most popular sci-fi series. Great Britain, 1988, 139 mins.
VHS: S21555. $19.98.

Snakedance

A simple navigational error lands the Doctor (Peter Davison) in the midst of a dastardly takeover scheme. The Mara have designs on the planet Manussa. 98 mins.
VHS: S29789. $19.98.

The Sontaran Experiment/ The Genesis of the Daleks

The Doctor is jettisoned 10,000 years into the future, where he is subjected to a horrifying experiment. In the follow-up *The Genesis of the Daleks*, the Doctor gets involved in a mission from the Timelords. With Tom Baker as the Doctor. Great Britain, 1975, 193 mins.
VHS: S20264. $29.98.

Spearhead from Space

Forbidden to continue his travels through time and space by his fellow time lords, the newly regenerated Doctor (Jon Pertwee) begins his exile on earth and finds himself hurled into one of his most exciting and terrifying adventures. Great Britain, 1970, 92 mins.
VHS: S13728. $19.98.

The Stones of Blood

The TARDIS lands on Earth close to the Nine Travellers, an ancient stone circle. Also interested in the circle are a group of druids-dedicated followers of the Cailleach, the Celtic goddess of war, death and magic. The Doctor must travel into hyperspace to solve the mystery of the Nine Travellers and save his companion from those blood-hungry alien life-forms, the Ogri. Starring Tom Baker.
VHS: S27160. $19.98.
Joel Blake, Great Britain, 1978, 96 mins.

The Stranger Double Feature: Summoned by Shadows/More Than a Messiah

This science fiction adventure stars Colin Baker and Nicola Bryant from the popular BBC English television series *Dr. Who*. Only this video represents a wholly original concept and story line, based on a project initiated by fans, called "The Stranger and Mrs. Brown." 75 mins.
VHS: S20910. $24.99.

The Stranger: Eye of the Beholder, Part 2

The Stranger revives the tradition of the BBC's greatest science fiction series, *Doctor Who*. Colin Baker, one of the more successful Doctors, is back. In this episode, Solomon Egan and Saul, the materialized terrorists from the Dimensional Web, stumble on a top secret research project called Metaphysic. It promises to open a few minds and no one can be sure of the outcome. 60 mins.
VHS: S26301. $24.99.

The Stranger: In Memory Alone

Colin Baker and Nicola Bryant reprise their roles from *The Stranger*. They are originally famous for their performances as the Doctor and his companion in the wildly popular BBC series, *Dr. Who*. 45 mins.
VHS: S20911. $19.99.

Survival

Sylvester McCoy is the Doctor, who appears back in London. Unfortunately, his sojourn in the Earth-bound capital is disturbed by the arrival of the Cheetah people. They are intergalactic hunters in search of human prey. 72 mins.
VHS: S29785. $19.98.

The Talons of Weng-Chiang

Tom Baker is Doctor Who in the heart of Victorian London where they are confronted by a series of bizarre and horrific events. The Doctor not only finds himself battling for his life against the hideously deformed Magnus Greel but also must deal with two other villains. Great Britain, 1988, 141 mins.
VHS: S11742. $19.98.

Terminus

The Black Guardian sabotages the doctor's most valuable asset, the TARDIS. The Doctor, played by Peter Davison, has one last hope. He must rescue a vessel carrying a human cargo of plague victims to ensure he will remain the universe's most respected time traveler. Great Britain, 1983, 99 mins.
VHS: S20782. $19.98.

Terror of the Autons

The Doctor (John Pertwee) finds the Earth in danger. Naturally, it is his most feared enemy, the Master, who is to blame. This fiend has a scheme to destroy humanity. As if that were not enough he also hopes to silence the Doctor forever. 95 mins.
VHS: S25747. $19.98.

Terror of the Zygons

In this thrilling adventure the Doctor (Tom Baker) defends earth from invasion by horrific, transforming aliens. He must vanquish the invading hordes before their reign of terror begins. Great Britain, 1975, 92 mins.
VHS: S13729. $19.98.

The Three Doctors

The three Doctor Whos unite to save the Timelords from an old arch enemy. Great Britain, 1973, 99 mins.
VHS: S15351. $19.98.

Time and the Rani

Unwittingly, the Doctor becomes part of Rani's master plan. She intends to build a time manipulator which will grant her nearly unfathomable powers. 89 mins.
VHS: S26432. $19.98.

The Time Warrior

A terrifying combination of past and future threatens the entire human race and plunges the Doctor (Jon Pertwee) and Sarah into a chilling race against time. Great Britain, 1973, 90 mins.
VHS: S13730. $19.98.

Doctor Who: Timelash

On the planet Karfel, the Doctor must plunge through a time tunnel on a dangerous search for a lost girl and a precious amulet. With Colin Baker as Doctor Who.
VHS: S33734. $19.98.

The Tom Baker Years

In late 1974, Tom Baker assumed the character of the Doctor, a role he would maintain for seven years. All his episodes remain in BBC archives, permitting this special collection of excerpted highlights from his most popular adventures to appear together. Double cassette. Great Britain, 1992, 170 mins.
VHS: S18080. $29.98.

The Tomb of the Cybermen

Patrick Troughton portrayed the Doctor's second incarnation in the late 1960's. In this episode, he is joined by his popular assistants Jamie and Victoria as they seek to prevent the re-emergence of the Cybermen, his age-old enemies. They lie harmlessly frozen, but a group of archeologists is poking around and one of them has treacherous plans that could endanger the Universe. Great Britain, 1967, 100 mins.
VHS: S17375. $19.98.

The Trial of the Timelord Boxed Set

A rare edition of the cult British science fiction show, featuring one of the best sagas, as Doctor Who must summon all of his intellectual skills and cunning to defeat a tribunal of timelords accusing him of cosmic interference. Great Britain, 1986, 350 mins.
VHS: S19297. $49.98.

The Troughton Years

A collector's edition of vintage *Doctor Who*. Three rare episodes featuring the Doctor's second incarnation, Patrick Troughton, presented by his successor, Jon Pertwee. Great Britain, 1991, 84 mins.
VHS: S15348. $19.98.

The Twin Dilemma

Is the Doctor's fifth incarnation going to be his last? He no longer seems in control of his powerful mental faculties and has nearly strangled his friend and helper, Peri. The Doctor decides to become a hermit under a dome on a lonely asteroid, but its strange inhabitants don't give him much peace of mind. Where are the original inhabitants, the Gastropods? Great Britain, 1984, 99 mins.
VHS: S18079. $19.98.

The Two Doctors

Colin Baker is now The Doctor, or at least he appears to be, until an earlier incarnation appears, that is Patrick Thornton. As the Doctor follows this image of his past, danger lurks in the shape of the Sontarans. It could mean death for both of them. 132 mins.
VHS: S25749. $19.98.

An Unearthly Child

The first ever televised Doctor Who adventure! The Doctor leads his young granddaughter and a pair of teachers on a quest for fire. Great Britain, 1963, 98 mins.
VHS: S15347. $19.98.

Vengeance on Varos

Colin Baker, the parodoxically younger-looking Doctor, must battle to save the TARDIS. Together with Peri, he journeys to a planet ruled by fear. At the heart of its capital lies the terrifying Punishment Dome. 89 mins.
VHS: S25746. $19.98.

The Visitation/Black Orchid

Once again the Doctor, played by Peter Davison, is enmeshed in a strange and murderous intrigue. Seventeenth-century England is being terrorized by an alien life force, so the Doctor does what is expected. He accepts an invitation to a masked ball knowing that it will lead to danger. 146 mins.
VHS: S27774. $29.95.

The War Games (Parts 1 & 2)

The Aliens have staged a horrifying combat game, pitting soldiers from throughout history against each other. Only the good Doctor can stop the slaughter. Double cassette. Great Britain, 1969, 243 mins.
VHS: S15346. $29.98.

The War Machines

Doctor Who battles an evil super-computer and deadly robots determined to destroy London. Includes restored footage not seen since 1966. With William Hartnell as Doctor Who.
VHS: S33731. $19.98.

Warriors of the Deep

In the year 2084, two power blocks are poised for war. On Sea Base Four, the Doctor finds a web of intrigue, nuclear missiles and sea monsters that could end the human race. Starring Peter Davison as Doctor Who. 97 mins.
VHS: S31234. $19.98.

The Web Planet

The deadly Zarbis ensnare the TARDIS, the vehicle key to Doctor Who's time traveling abilities. The Zarbis' hypnotic power has the Doctor trapped in an eerie alien world that he cannot escape. William Hartnell is the Doctor. Great Britain, 1965, 148 mins.
VHS: S21551. $19.98.

IRISH FEATURES

The Boxer

Daniel Day Lewis *(My Left Foot)* and Emily Watson *(Breaking the Waves)* star in this tense drama as fresh-out-of-prison Lewis fights to reclaim the woman he left behind, but the past keeps getting in the way.
VHS: S34546. $106.99.
DVD: DV60257. $34.95.
Jim Sheridan, USA/Ireland, 1997, 113 mins.

Broth of a Boy

A witty social comedy about an aggressive television producer (Tony Wright) who covers the village's celebration of the world's oldest living man (Barry Fitzgerald). The comic tension springs from Wright's desperate efforts to persuade Fitzgerald to appear on his program. With June Thorburn, Harry Brogan, Eddie Golden and Godfrey Quigley.
VHS: S19860. $29.95.
George Pollock, Ireland, 1958, 77 mins.

Cal

Helen Mirren stars in a performance that earned her the Best Actress Award in Cannes in 1984, in this sensitive love story set in war-torn Northern Ireland. Music score by Dire Straits' Mark Knopler enshrouds this stark drama haunted by Ulster's numbing violence.
VHS: S00205. $19.98.
Pat O'Connor, Ireland, 1984, 104 mins.

The Crying Game

Irish filmmaker Neil Jordan's film charts a fractured world of deception, abandon and terror. Stephen Rea becomes a reluctant IRA terrorist in exile who ends up protecting a beautiful, mysterious London woman. With Miranda Richardson, Forest Whitaker and the amazing Jaye Davidson. Academy award for best original screenplay (Jordan).
VHS: S18749. $19.98.
Laser: Widescreen. **LD75178. $34.99.**
Neil Jordan, Great Britain, 1992, 112 mins.

December Bride

In turn-of-the-century Ireland, a woman was expected to live with a stifling sense of decorum. This film concerns a strong-minded woman who went her own way. She has two lovers, brothers who both love her, and this unconventional triangle sets her at odds with the strict, unbending community where she lives because she chose them both. This unconventional film is an acclaimed feature from the Irish film renaissance.
VHS: S26280. $19.98.
Thaddeus O'Sullivan, Ireland, 1993, 90 mins.

The Field

Richard Harris makes his long-awaited return to the screen in this Oscar-nominated portrayal of a man fighting to preserve everything he believes in. Tradition-bound Irishman "Bull" McCabe (Harris) has devoted his life to cultivating a field. When it's put up for auction and might be bought by a wealthy American for development, the resulting conflict has a devastating effect on an entire village. A story of immense power and passion from the writer/director of *My Left Foot*. Also starring Brenda Fricker, Tom Berenger and John Hurt.
VHS: S14975. $19.98.
Jim Sheridan, Ireland, 1990, 113 mins.

In the Name of the Father

Over seven Academy Award nominations testify to the power of this film. Accused of an act of terrorism, a young man finds that not only his whole life is destroyed, but also the lives of those he loves most. From the streets of Belfast to the most hellish British prisons, this film recounts the true story of a man caught in the struggle for Irish independence. With Daniel Day-Lewis and Emma Thompson.
VHS: S21158. $19.98.
Laser: LD72420. $39.98.
Jim Sheridan, Great Britain, 1993, 133 mins.

James Joyce's Women

Fionnula Flanagan stars in episodes of the six women in the literary and personal life of James Joyce. Set at the turn of the century, and based on some of Joyce's writings and diaries, the film has been acknowledged as an erotic investigation of the life of the great writer.
VHS: S00652. $69.95.
Fionnula Flanagan, USA, 1985, 91 mins.

Michael Collins

Neil Jordan's underrated epic stars Liam Neeson, Julia Roberts, Aidan Quinn and Stephen Rea in the story of Ireland's legendary freedom-fighter who fought the British empire and changed the course of Irish history. "A passionate epic. Collins is played with thunder and grace by Liam Neeson" (Peter Travers, *Rolling Stone*).
VHS: S31009. $19.98.
Laser: LD76139. $39.99.
DVD: DV60089. $24.98.
Neil Jordan, USA/Great Britain, 1996, 133 mins.

My Left Foot

Distinguished by a brilliant performance from Daniel Day-Lewis, this is a true story about life, laughter and the occasional miracle. Day-Lewis plays Christy Brown, who has cerebral palsy, and whose mother's faith prompts him to paint and write. Nominated for five Academy Awards.
VHS: S12199. $19.98.
Jim Sheridan, Great Britain, 1989, 103 mins.

The Run of the Country

Albert Finney stars in this film about an unlikely romance. A young man escapes his overbearing father and the trauma of his mother's death through an adventurous affair with a spirited woman. Though she appears carefree, her advice finally helps the father and son reconcile.
VHS: S27187. $98.99.
Laser: LD75468. $34.95.
Peter Yates, Ireland, 1995, 116 mins.

Widow's Peak

Mia Farrow, Joan Plowright and Natasha Richardson star in this mysterious comedy about a sexy stranger. The stranger turns an Irish town upside down with her scandalous lies and devious secrets. She must be hiding something, and it could be murder.
VHS: S22665. $19.95.
John Irvin, Ireland/USA, 1994, 98 mins.

IRISH PERSPECTIVES

1641 and the Curse of Cromwell

Tens of thousands of Irish people were mercilessly forced from their lands or massacred at the hands of one of the most hated men in Irish history. These campaigns and the Catholic rebellion of 1641 are sifted through in order to separate myth from the truth. 60 mins.
VHS: S24898. $19.95.

Anna Livia, Dublin: A City of Splendor

Ireland's eastern landscape and long history come together in this splendidly scenic and exceptionally well-researched video narrated by *Late, Late Show* host Gay Byrne. This documentary shows seldom-seen footage of 1916-21 Dublin, along with a wealth of archival images and photographs that trace Dublin from medieval settlement to a modern, vibrant city. Anna Livia is the history of Dublin elegantly traced through the ages and is a must-see for anyone with an interest in Irish history or a love for the fair city. 73 mins.
VHS: S30634. $29.95.

Behind the Mask

A documentary on the Irish Republican Army (IRA) as seen through the eyes of its leading veterans. The documentary examines the personal motivations and actions behind the events of the IRA, the guerilla army, as members speak openly of saturation surveillance, silence, invisibility and anonymity as the IRA's weapons of survival.
VHS: S11599. $29.95.
Frank Martin, USA, 1988, 65 mins.

Broken Harvest

A lyrical look at the tensions that beset Ireland after the Civil War, focusing on a rivalry between two men who fell out over a woman and political differences. With Colin Lane, Marian Quinn, Niall O'Brien and Darren McHugh.
VHS: S30662. $89.95.
Maurice O'Callaghan, Ireland, 1994, 97 mins.

Celtic Feet

Colin Dunne, star of the hit show *Riverdance* and nine-time world dance champion, teaches you step-by-step how to learn the basics of Irish dance, in this spectacular music and dance-filled video. 55 mins.
VHS: S31543. $19.95.

Celtic Monasteries

A beautiful documentary on Ireland's Celtic Monasteries, built between the 6th and 12th centuries. Known as the universities of Ireland, they attracted students from all over Europe. Sites visited include Glendalough, Clonmacnoise, the Blasket Islands, Kells and Lismore. 104 mins.
VHS: S34837. $24.95.

The Celts: Rich Traditions and Ancient Myths

This three-tape set explores the bold approach to life, richly evocative music, poetry, art, tradition and ancient mythology of the Celts. Features the music of Enya. Over 300 minutes of programming.
VHS: S33236. $49.98.

Charles Haughey's Ireland

Ireland's Prime Minister leads this tour of Ireland, from the Walls of Derry to the charms of County Kerry, to Yeats Country, and Galway of James Joyce, Lady Gregory, W.B. Yeats. Features an open-air concert with Kris Kristofferson, Gaelic football. 60 mins.
VHS: S06656. $29.95.

The Clancy Brothers and Tommy Makem Reunion Concert

The Ulster Hall concert of the Clancy Brothers and Tommy Makem, the rousing Irish acts who strike the perfect balance of traditional folk and highly personal technicians. 60 mins.
VHS: S19207. $24.95.

Curious Journey: The Fight for Irish Freedom

The story of nine veterans of the 1916 Rising and the War of Independence. Dynamic and personal accounts capture the great awakening of Irish nationalism and the fight for Irish freedom. 70 mins.
VHS: S34833. $19.95.

The Day Before Yesterday

The Treaty, The Hungry '30s, The Emergency and Emigration during the 1950s are visually chronicled by world-renowned photographer Fr. Browne. His pictures and this production draw a picture of the Irish guerilla fighters who fought and wrestled independence from Britain. 180 mins.
VHS: S34835. $39.95.

A Day in the Life of Ireland

This video tells the story of one day during which legions of photographers went forth throughout Ireland to capture images of the many faces of modern Ireland. The resulting book has become a perennial favorite, and now this video tells the story of how the project came to be. Filled with revealing portraits of Irish life and breathtaking views of the Irish landscape, *A Day in the Life* vividly paints a lasting portrait of the traditional Ireland that remains today, alongside the new Ireland that is confidently emerging. 57 mins.
VHS: S30632. $29.95.

Derek Mahon

This Irish poet has won a Lannan Literary Fellowship for his verse. On March 8, 1994, he read from his *Selected Poems* and spoke to Michael Silverblatt. From the *Lannan Literary Videos* series. 45 mins.
VHS: S27145. $19.95.

Dubliners Live

Recorded live at the National Concert Hall in London, an evening of magic and excitement by Ireland's most celebrated folk group, as they are joined by two of the country's best ballad singers, Paddy Reilly and Jim McCann. 75 mins.
VHS: S06650. $29.95.

Eavan Boland

A major Irish poet, Eavan Boland explores the relationship between gender, art and national identity. She read from *In a Time of Violence* and *Outside History* on November 16, 1994, in Los Angeles. She also spoke with poet Eloise Klein Healy, author of *Artemis in Echo Park*. From the *Lannan Literary Videos* series. 60 mins.
VHS: S27149. $19.95.

Far Away from the Shamrock Shore: A History of Irish Music in America

Influences from Irish music and culture have had a lasting impact on American culture. Medieval Ireland and contemporary America share common roots. This moving document reveals the continuity of the Irish tradition. Music by the Clancy Brothers & Tommy Makem and Cherish the Ladies is featured. 53 mins.
VHS: S26002. $24.95.

Frank Patterson: Ireland's Golden Voice

Irish music and Ireland's greatest tenor provide the perfect excuse to visit a number of beautiful sights on the Emerald Isle. From Tipperary to Galway, with stops in Dublin and Mayo and views of many locales, this musical adventure is a great way to experience the best of Irish music. 60 mins.
VHS: S23063. $14.95.

Grosse Isle

The Canadian quarantine island of Grosse Isle on the St. Lawrence River became the largest mass grave of immigrant Irish famine victims in North America. This video is a journey into the depths of Ireland's great tragedy. 30 mins.
VHS: S31202. $14.95.

Hang Up Your Brightest Colors: The Life and Death of Michael Collins

After a 25-year suppresion, the definitive portrait of Michael Collins, tracing his life from his childhood in County Cork to his involvement in the Easter Rising of 1916, imprisonment, his revolutionary leadership in the War of Independence, the Treaty and finally his untimely death. Shot on location with archival footage and old newsreels. Kenneth Griffith, renowned actor, narrates. 90 mins.
VHS: S34834. $24.95.

Harp of My Country

The original music of Ireland's greatest national poet, Thomas Moore, recaptured with a 250-piece orchestra and the Ambrosia Chorus Choir, including *Last Rose of Summer, The Harp That Once Through Tara's Halls, Minstal Boy,* and others. 72 mins.
VHS: S06658. $29.95.

History of Ireland

A unique souvenir of history, scenery and people, bringing together various stages of Irish history starting with ancient Ireland and Newgrange, on through to the Celts, St. Patrick, the Vikings, and more. Shot on location and presented by Brian Munn. 58 mins.
VHS: S09163. $29.95.

Home Away from Home: The Yanks in Ireland

300,000 American servicemen trained and lived in Northern Ireland preparing for battle in World War II. This film documents veterans going back to their "home away from home." Old loves and closely guarded secrets are revealed through interviews and archival footage. 58 mins.
VHS: S26001. $24.95.

Ireland's Emerald Treasures

Journey through gorgeous Ireland and see all the elements of this "Emerald Isle." Begin in Dublin, then on to County Wicklow, Kilkenny, kiss the Blarney Stone, and watch the sun set over Galway Bay. 50 mins.
VHS: S05777. $24.95.

Ireland: The Isle of Memories

A visual journey of Ireland, visiting all 32 counties, including Galway, the Aran Islands (where Gaelic is still spoken), Ireland's Holy Mountains, Knock Shrine, Donegal's rugged coastline, Waterford (where the famous crystal is made), and a visit with one of Ireland's best ballad groups, The Barleycorn. 50 mins.
VHS: S06649. $29.95.

An Irish Country Calendar

The four seasons of the year are the focus for this set of videos which reveal eight of Ireland's most gracious country homes. From the misty bogs of County Sligo to the Galty Mountains of Tipperary, this series traces the gentle landscape and climate of the Emerald Isle. Each of the four videos is approximately 50 mins.
VHS: S27427. $59.95.

The Irish Country House

Homes at over 40 locations across Ireland reveal the important history preserved in these magnificent buildings. Whether cherished and preserved or decaying and forlorn, they reveal much about modern Ireland. 58 mins.
VHS: S26000. $24.95.

Irish Dance

Meet the people who keep the Irish dance, culture and tradition alive in this exciting two-tape set, as future Irish dance stars practice for competition and experience the rich history and beauty that has propelled Irish dance into the international spotlight with such hit shows as *Riverdance* and *Lord of the Dance*. Shot on location in Cork, Limerick and Dublin, Ireland; London, England; Queensland, Australia; and North America. 60 mins.
VHS: S31152. $12.99.

Irish Homecoming

Irish Americans are shown in this film as they return to Ireland in search of their roots. It is a moving document that reveals the strength of this people's traditions. Music by Clannad, Maura O'Connell and Brian Kennedy is featured. 58 mins.
VHS: S25999. $24.95.

The Irish Humor of Noel V. Ginnity

Paddy McGinty—or Noel V. Ginnity as he is known in Ireland-has been treading the boards for over 20 years now, during which time he has toured the U.S. and Canada and made countless appearances at London's Royal Albert Hall. Now you can enjoy this "leprechaun of Irish laughter" as he visits you in your own home, live from Ireland. "McGinty is more important to Ireland than the Blarney Stone" *(Irish Press)*. 60 mins.
VHS: S30631. $29.95.

The Irish in America: From the Emerald Isle to the Promised Land

Follow America's first immigrant group in their epic adventure to find the American Dream. From war hero Andrew Jackson to self-made tycoon Diamond Jim Brady, from boxer John L. Sullivan to union organizer "Mother" Jones, you'll meet colorful Irish Americans who fought and worked their way past oppression and into history. 2 cassettes, 50 minutes each.
VHS: S32665. $29.95.

The Irish in America: Long Journey Home

An historic, sweeping film event that chronicles the Irish experience in America. The four-volume set traces the Irish from early immigration through Ireland's infamous potato famine in *The Great Hunger*, examines how the Irish contributed to the building of a young America in *All Across America*, rose to new heights in big-city politics in *Up from City Streets* and became one of the most successful ethnic groups in the United States in *Succcess*. Six hours.
VHS: S33694. $79.95.

Irish Magic: Irish Music

The roots of the magic of Ireland are found in Irish music, and in this tribute, hosted by actor Sean McGraw and filmed on location in Ireland, appear such performers as The Chieftains, James Galway and Louis Browne, talented performers of the Ileann pipes, Irish harp, accordion and fiddle, as well as tributes to Irish music by Senator Ted Kennedy, novelist Mary Higgins Clark and Michael Burke. 50 mins.
VHS: S06648. $29.95.

Irish Waterways

This three-part series looks at the landscape of Ireland as a rumination on the country's history, culture and national wonder. 180 mins.
Tape 1: Forgotten Locks/Christian Crossing.
VHS: S19550. $19.95.
Tape 2: Viking Invasion/Yesterday's Journey.
VHS: S19551. $19.95.
Tape 3: The Great Race/Endless Road.
VHS: S19552. $19.95.

Island Soldiers: The History of the Celtic Saints

In this two-part series Anglican Canon Martin Shaw traces the roots of Celtic Christianity through the lives of the men and women who kindled its fire in the British Isles during the Dark Ages. Shaw explores the length and breadth of the ancient land to uncover the source of today's renewed interest in the Celtic spiritual traditions-meditation, prayer and music rooted in the ministries of the Celtic saints. Each tape is 60 mins.
VHS: S31214. $39.95.

J.P. Donleavy's Ireland

The witty novelist J.P. Donleavy captures the heart and soul of Ireland. This Discovery Channel video is a cinematic feast which joins the author's words with imagery of enchanting landscapes from the Emerald Isle. 60 mins.
VHS: S25078. $19.95.

Jig Don't Jog

Get fit the Irish way with this safe and easy-to-follow aerobic video incorporating elements of celtic dance. Filmed in Ireland with 24 favorite Irish songs. Get a great workout and enjoy the scenery and energetic Irish music at the same time. With Cahal Dunne. 45 mins.
VHS: S30628. $24.95.

Journey Back to Ireland

Katie Couric, joined by Bryant Gumbel, meets the people, sees the sights and explores some of the Ireland's ancient and modern treasures, including Connemara, the Aran Islands, the Book of Kells, the Blarney Stone, the pubs, and St. Patrick.
VHS: S34148. $19.95.

Kerry

The Kingdom of Kerry shows an Irish county full of contrasts and color, its craggy coastline fringed by a necklace of sandy beaches and washed by the warm waters of Atlantic's Gulf Stream. 56 mins.
VHS: S11997. $29.95.

Legends of Ireland

Shares five compelling and delightful stories of Ireland's most celebrated figures. From the tale of the world-renowned saint, to Ireland's oldest myth, to the truth about the magical beings known as leprechauns, this lavishly produced series travels through the Irish countryside, exploring the stuff of legend. Three volumes include *St. Patrick, Brendan the Navigator, The Warrior Queen, The Pirate Queen* and *Fairies and Leprechauns*. 130 mins.
VHS: S34894. $39.95.

Let's Have an Irish Party

Carmel Quinn, Paddy Noonan, Richie O'Shea and John Scott Trotter join in an hour-long of Irish song and dancing. 60 mins.
VHS: S06657. $29.95.

The Little Horse That Could

Children and adults alike will enjoy listening to and watching Erin Go Braugh, a Connemara Irish stallion, as he and his trainer, Carol Kozlowski, take you behind the scenes to see all that is involved in the caring for and training of a champion. Lilting Irish music accompanies Erin Go Braugh's narrative, delivered in a delightful Irish brogue. 60 mins.
VHS: S30120. $12.95.
Stirlin Harris, USA, 1996, 60 mins.

Little Ireland

Ireland's 6000 years of archeological heritage, the range and standards of places to stay, the quality of the food, the festive sounds of Irish music, its unique shopping possibilities, golf courses, and other sporting opportunities, are just some of the experiences that are covered in this program. 60 mins.

VHS: S23064. $14.95.

Man of Aran

One of the masterworks of Robert Flaherty, in which Flaherty's "passionate devotion to the portrayal of human gesture and of a man's fight for his family makes the film an incomparable account of human dignity" (Georges Sadoul). Filmed on the island of Inishmore, it depicts the daily life of people on this isolated island off the coast of Ireland, fishing in their tiny curraghs, the difficulty of their existence, the hunting of a basking shark. A masterpiece.

VHS: S09417. $29.95.

Robert Flaherty, Great Britain, 1934, 76 mins.

Men of Ireland

Set amid the wild Blasket Islands, this film combines ethnographic footage with a story about a medical student who has had too much of life. He finds in the harsh, simple ways of these remote islands a paradise removed from the cares of the modern world.

VHS: S23999. $19.95.

Richard Bird, Ireland, 1938, 62 mins.

Michael Collins: The Shadow of Bealnablath

Beginning with the death of this famous politician and rebel, this documentary traces the role Collins played in Irish history. Dramatic reenactments, photos, old newsreels and interviews explain his role in the great struggle for independence all the way through the civil war that plagued the young republic. 120 mins.

VHS: S21194. $29.95.

Mother Ireland

With historical photographs, political drawings, cartoons and music, this video discovers the unrecorded role of women in Irish history. Censored in Britain, the program features many of Ireland's most prominent women, including the late Mairead Farrell, before she was shot in Gibraltar in 1988. 50 mins.

VHS: S12001. $29.95.

National Geographic Video: Ballad of the Irish Horse

A romantic and moving portrait of the Irish people, and their attachment to the horses on the Emerald Isle.

VHS: S05887. $19.95.

Nova—Bomb Squad

In Northern Ireland and Great Britain, a quarter-century's worth of technological advances in terrorist bombs have led to a deadly game of cat and mouse. A former IRA member reveals some of the organization's most chilling tactics as *Nova* looks at the British Army's latest countermeasures, in which science and ingenuity are the only key to survival. 60 mins.

VHS: S33074. $19.95.

Off Our Knees

1988 marked the 20th anniversary of the continuous mass struggle in the North since the formation of the Civil Rights Movement in Ireland. *Off Our Knees* celebrates the stories and aspirations of the people involved, political activists, working people and human rights campaigners, and demonstrates how and why the basic demands of the Civil Rights Movement have developed into a demand for a United Ireland. 55 mins.

VHS: S11998. $29.95.

The Origins: The Two Traditions in Ireland

The Nationalist and the Unionist traditions are examined from an historic perspective in this intriguing documentary. Myths, fears and beliefs are central to the continuity of both traditions. 30 mins.

VHS: S24896. $14.95.

Out of Ireland

This documentary traces the dramatic sweep of Irish emigration brought on by 19th-century famine. The emigres helped build America. By focusing on ordinary people and their troubled lives this film makes history come alive. 111 mins.

VHS: S26358. $19.95.

Pack Up the Troubles

Can the British government find a solution to the Northern Ireland impasse? In this documentary, extensive interviews with politicians from both sides of this dispute, as well as the relatives of British soldiers who have died there, make a powerful case against continued British involvement. 60 mins.

VHS: S21195. $24.95.

Paddy Reilly Live

An intimate evening of music and song with Ireland's best-loved balladeer, with such favorites as *Spancil Hill, Carrickfergus, The Town I Loved So Well, Fields of Athenry*. 50 mins.

VHS: S06655. $29.95.

Patrick

This animated video brings to life a long-lost world of Druids, warriors and kings, blending historical facts with beloved traditions to tell the story of St. Patrick, the brave shepherd of the Emerald Isle, who was kidnapped by raiders from his parents' seaside villa and taken to Ireland. Patrick turned to God to save himself and with new strength and inner freedom, began an incredible saga of faith against which no enemy could prevail. 30 mins.

VHS: S30635. $19.95.

The Penal Days

The Penal Laws of post-Cromwellian Ireland were enacted to prevent the legal existence of Irish Catholics. A French Jurist described the Penal Laws as, "… conceived by demons, written in blood, and registered in Hell." 30 mins.

VHS: S24897. $14.95.

Phil Coulter—The Live Experience

Ireland's ambassador of music performs some of his best-known songs in this 90-minute 1995 concert at the University of Limerick. Includes Coulter compositions "Steal Away" and "The Old Man," as well as interpretations of music by Aaron Copland, Henry Mancini and Mark Knofler. Special guests Peadar O'Riada and the Coolea Choir. 90 mins.

VHS: S30580. $19.95.

Ramble to Cashel: Celtic Fingerstyle Guitar

Pierre Bensusan, Martin Simpson, Duck Baker, Pat Kirtley, El McMeen, Tom Long and Steve Baughman bring their own approach, style, technique and feel to Celtic fingerstyle guitar solos. Includes 72-page booklet. 62 mins.

VHS: S33374. $29.95.

Riverdance—The Show

American dancers Michael Flatley and Jean Butler are at the center of this thrilling dance experience. It joins traditional Irish dance and music with the passion of more recent American styles. It is as if a mixture of *Dirty Dancing* with the chemistry of Torvill and Dean were added to Irish folk ways.

VHS: S27643. $24.95.

Riverdance: A Journey

The story behind the creation of *Riverdance*, from its beginnings in Dublin to hit shows in London and New York. 76 mins.

VHS: S31199. $24.95.

Robin Williamson in Concert

Robin Williamson is a musician, poet, author, actor, storyteller, raconteur, composer and humanitarian. His String Band, founded in 1965, has had a vital influence on Celtic culture. This concert performance video captures the complete scope of his musical experience.

VHS: S27316. $29.95.

Seamus Heaney

Ireland's complex, violent past informs Seamus Heaney's poetry. He reads from *Selected Poems 1966-1987* and also speaks with Michael Silverblatt for this video. It was recorded on October 15, 1991, in Los Angeles. From the *Lannan Literary Videos* series. 60 mins.

VHS: S27134. $19.95.

The Secret Gardens of Ireland

Though nearly as far north as Moscow, County Kerry, at the western tip of Ireland, contains a treasure of a garden. Established in the late 19th century, it functions as a veritable museum of rare and unique plants. As revealed in this video, it is also a place of great natural beauty. 50 mins.

VHS: S26628. $29.95.

Song for Ireland

A showcase of the very best in Irish entertainment, filmed on location, featuring Phil Coulter, Mary Black with De Danann, Foster & Allen, the Fureys and Irish mist, hosted by Bryan Murray, and featuring such classics as "The Town I Love So Well," "Sweet Sixteen," "A Song for Ireland." 60 mins.

VHS: S06654. $29.95.

St. Patrick's Cathedral, Dublin

Over 800 years old, the Cathedral named for the patron saint of Ireland stands as a testament to the faith of the Irish people. It has stood witness over the tumultuous history of Ireland. Now this story is revealed by the natural raconteurs who have always flourished in its shadows. 35 mins.

VHS: S26627. $19.95.

St. Patrick: The Living Legend

As the patron saint of Ireland, the man credited with bringing Catholicism to his country, St. Patrick is revered by Irish people the world over. In this documentary, the various traditions and celebrations held in his honor on his day are shown and explained. 52 mins.

VHS: S26626. $19.95.

Stories from Ireland

Eamon Kelly, one of Ireland's most respected actors and master Seanachie (storyteller), draws on the rich Irish storytelling tradition with traditional dancing set to the music of Tony McMahon, Kevin Glackin and Paul McGrattan. Kelly, often seen at the Abbey Theatre in Dublin, embellishes old Irish stories with tricks of speech and gesture, in a delightful return to tradition. 60 mins.

VHS: S06652. $29.95.

The Story of the Clancy Brothers and Tommy Makem

The jubilant New York concert by the Clancy Brothers and Tommy Makem offers telling insight into their behavior and performing rituals. The documentary mixes concert material and interviews with Bob Dylan, Mary Travers and Tom Paxton. 60 mins.

VHS: S19208. $24.95.

Tony Kenny's Ireland, The Green Island

Tony Kenny stars in the world-famous Jurys Irish Cabaret in Dublin, entertaining countless thousands every year with his professional performances and his way with an audience. Special guests Hal Roach and Irish storyteller Eamon Kelly. Performances include "The Isle of Inishfree," "Danny Boy," "Green Island," "The Rare Ould Times," "Fields of Athenry," "Song for Ireland" and "Irish Wedding Song." 53 mins.

VHS: S30629. $24.95.

The Treaty

Set in Dublin and London, *The Treaty* is a tense, intriguing drama about a pivotal moment in history. Michael Collins led the Irish delegation to London to negotiate the end of 700 years of occupation. Knowing that force could not prevail, he ultimately signed a treaty that would deliver not freedom but the freedom to achieve it.

VHS: S30633. $29.95.

Jonathan Lewis, Great Britain, 109 mins.

Tribute to Noel V. Ginnity

This tribute to Paddy McGinty includes footage from *The Late Late Show* and *Doyle's Irish Cabaret*. Features special guests The Dubliners, Danny Doyle, Tony Kenny, Sonny Knowles, Deidre O' Callaghan and Twink.

VHS: S30630. $29.95.

Uncensored Voices: War of Peace in Ireland

From the 1969 Civil Rights marches, this documentary offers an insight into the people who remain under British rule in the North of Ireland. *Part I* is by award-winning Rights and Wrongs team with Charlayne Hunter-Gault; *Part II* features footage of the early civil rights marches, hunger strikes and Gerry Adam's first visit to the U.S. Two-tape boxed set. 70 mins.

VHS: S34836. $24.95.

When Ireland Starved

This extensive documentary charts the most horrific event of modern Ireland's history, the Great Famine in the middle of the 19th century. The effects of this catastrophe have left an indelible mark on this country. Now using archival sketches, many from *The London News*, the scope of this disaster is captured on film. 120 mins.

VHS: S21193. $29.95.

Wolfe Tones On the One Road

The long-awaited, on-location video of these veterans of Irish music at their best. The songs are a compilation of all their hits, including "Boston Rose," "The West's Awake," "The Foggy Dew," "The Zoological Gardens," "On the One Road" and others. 60 mins.

VHS: S12002. $29.95.

australian cinema

The Adventures of Priscilla, Queen of the Desert
Terence Stamp returns to the screen in this unlikely farce about three drag queens racing across the Australian outback in order to put on a show. Of course there is more to this film than unbelievably elaborate costumes, campily choreographed lip sync numbers and gay humor. It also tries to say something about love. Great disco numbers from ABBA, Gloria Gaynor, The Village People and Peaches and Herb.
VHS: S24030. $19.95.
DVD: DV60010. $29.95.
Stephen Elliott, Australia, 1994, 102 mins.

Alice to Nowhere
An Australian drama about murder, kidnapping and survival, starring Rosey Jones and John Waters *(Breaker Morant, Getting of Wisdom)* as Waters sets off on a 350-mile life-or-death trek through the harsh Australian outback. Based on the novel by Evan Green.
VHS: S03754. $59.95.
John Power, Australia, 1986, 210 mins.

All the Rivers Run
Sigrid Thornton and John Waters star in this two-volume blend of adventure, romance and drama about a gutsy, independent woman who forges her own place in the male-dominated society of nineteenth century Australia.
VHS: S04304. $79.95.
George Miller/Pino Amenta, Australia, 1984, 274 mins.

Beyond Innocence
Raymond Radiguet's novel *Devil in the Flesh* is the inspiration for yet another film treatment of a sensuous young woman who attracts the carnal attention of a younger schoolboy. Katia Caballero is Marthe, whose husband is a prisoner-of-war. Keith Smith is Paul, the 17-year-old looking to get beyond innocence. Lots of burning passion is promised.
VHS: S08027. $79.95.
Scott Murray, Australia, 1988, 90 mins.

Bliss
Winner of Australia's Best Picture Award, *Bliss* is an outrageous, surreal comedy about a successful ad executive who suffers a fatal heart attack and returns to view modern life in a new way. He sees how out of touch his family and friends are with nature and each other.
VHS: S00145. $19.95.
Ray Lawrence, Australia, 1985, 112 mins.

Breaker Morant
Edward Woodward is the legendary horsebreaker brought to court martial with two fellow soldiers for a murder committed during the 1901 Boer War. Winner of 10 Australian Awards, and one of the breakthrough Australian films in America.
VHS: S00178. $19.95.
Laser: Letterboxed. **LD76402. $49.95.**
DVD: DV60127. $29.98.
Bruce Beresford, Australia, 1979, 107 mins.

Cane Toads: An Unnatural History
A fat, ugly creature whose sole purpose in life is the pursuit of sexual gratification is rapidly taking over Australia. No, we're not talking about Paul Hogan. The cane toad—*Bufo marinus*-was imported to Australia in 1935 in an attempt to rid the country of the Greyback beetle, which was devouring the sugarcane crop. Problem was, the beetle could fly, and the cane toad couldn't. What the cane toad was unusually proficient at, however, was making more cane toads. A very humorous look at a serious problem.
VHS: S14731. $29.95.
Mark Lewis, Australia, 1987, 48 mins.

Cosi
Based on the experiences of the film's screenwriter, Louis Nowra, who also wrote the original play, *Cosi* is the story of Lewis (Ben Mendelsohn), a young man searching for direction in life. After a prolonged state of unemployment, Lewis accepts a position as a drama therapist in a psychiatric hospital. While he plans to produce a simple variety show, the patients rally around their ringleader (Barry Otto), who has decreed that they should launch a full-blown production of Mozart's opera *Cosi Fan Tutte*. With Toni Collette and Rachel Griffiths.
VHS: S32673. $103.99.
Mark Joffe, Australia, 1997, 100 mins.

Country Life
Sam Neill and Greta Scacchi star in this humorous love story. An older man returns to his hometown for a vacation with his young bride. Spring fever takes hold as one by one the men of the small town fall in love with this charming woman. The woman soon realizes she's developed feelings for a young doctor (Neill) that she can't ignore. It's a story where much of the best action happens behind closed doors. With Kerry Fox, John Hargreaves.
VHS: S27302. $99.98.
Laser: LD75475. $39.99.
Michael Blakemore, Australia, 1995, 107 mins.

Crocodile Dundee
The surprise hit of 1986 from Down Under. Paul Hogan plays the Outback's answer to Tarzan but just try to take him to a big city like New York. Lots of wholesome laughs. A "reel" crowd pleaser. With Linda Kozlowski as the American reporter.
Laser: LD75177. $34.98.
Peter Faiman, Australia, 1986, 98 mins.

Crocodile Dundee II
Paul Hogan returns in the role of "Crocodile" Mick Dundee, the Australian hero who speaks politely but carries a big knife. When his American love interest (Linda Kozlowski) is kidnapped by South American drug dealers he rescues her and returns to the land of koalas. The foolish villains track him down on his home turf and learn to regret the decision. Action with a smile.
VHS: S08352. $19.95.
John Cornell, Australia, 1988, 110 mins.

A Cry in the Dark
A riveting, true life human drama from Australia. Meryl Streep and Sam Neill play the parents accused of murdering their infant daughter while on vacation. They claim the baby was snatched from the tent by a dingo, a wild dog native to the continent. Streep has a new look and a new accent and another Oscar nomination.
VHS: S09308. $19.98.
Laser: LD70547. $29.98.
Fred Schepisi, Australia, 1988, 120 mins.

Dead Calm
An Australian thriller that combines murder and mayhem on the high seas. Sam Neill and Nicole Kidman are recovering from a private tragedy by taking a long ocean vacation. They encounter a crazed American and a sinking ship and learn that keeping a lunatic at bay is great therapy for some couples. With Billy Zane as the wacko. Originally a project unfinished by Orson Welles.
VHS: S10612. $19.98.
Laser: Letterboxed. **LD74693. $24.98.**
Phillip Noyce, Australia, 1989, 97 mins.

Dead Heart
Brian Brown *(Breaker Morant)* stars in this provocative thriller wrapped in a racially charged murder mystery: an illicit love affair between an Aborigine bootlegger and a schoolteacher's white wife is discovered. A murder leads to a tense investigation and an unsettling climax. "A thoughtful, exotic sizzler" *(Playboy)*.
VHS: S34538. $89.98.
Nick Parsons, Australia, 1996, 106 mins.

Death in Brunswick
Sam Neill stars as an ordinary short order cook who has some serious troubles. He's trying to clean up his act, but first he has to get rid of a body. The problems he encounters along the way are as annoying as they are hilarious. Somehow he manages to come out on top and even meet the girl of his dreams. It's how he gets there that makes all the difference.
VHS: S25567. $96.95.
John Ruane, Australia, 1990, 106 mins.

Death of a Soldier
Based on a true incident during World War II, James Coburn stars as a military lawyer reluctantly defending a confessed psychotic killer of three women in Melbourne.
VHS: S01906. $79.98.
Philippe Mora, Australia/USA, 1985, 93 mins.

Dingo
In this film by one of Australia's most challenging young filmmakers, Rolf de Heer *(Bay Boy Bubby)*, Colin Friels portrays a young man who contemplates giving up everything to follow his idol, a legendary jazz musician (played by real-life legend Miles Davis). He gets his chance to see if he will be a great musician when a trip to Paris comes along. Davis and Michel Legrand composed the score.
VHS: S29848. $89.95.
Rolf de Heer, Australia, 1990, 108 mins.

Dogs in Space
Michael Hutchence, the lead singer of INXS, heads a cast of youthful performers in this Australian counterculture drama. Alienated youth hang out in a rundown working class neighborhood in Melbourne circa 1978. A provocative look at being down and out down under.
VHS: S06612. $79.98.
Richard Lowenstein, Australia, 1987, 109 mins.

Don's Party
A riotous comedy by the director of *Breaker Morant* and *Tender Mercies*. Don and his wife plan an election night party. As the liquor starts to flow the party starts to go hysterically askew. All intellectual interest in politics goes down the drain as guests begin concentrating on drinking, brawling, flirting and sex. Not what Don had in mind, but definitely the party of the year!
VHS: S00356. $19.98.
Bruce Beresford, Australia, 1976, 90 mins.

Down Under
Patrick Macnee hosts this adventurous Australian comedy as two Americans find themselves amidst a vast continent they know little about, search for raw gold, and are adopted as sons amongst the aborigines. 1986, 90 mins.
VHS: S10027. $79.95.

Dusty
Bill Kerr stars in this heartwarming Australian story for all ages about the relationship between an old man and a champion sheepdog which is part dingo, part kelpie. Filmed in the Australian bush, this subtle tale of love and companionship is based on a popular children's book written by Frank Dalby Davison. With Carol Burns, Nicolas Holland, Kate Edwards, John Stanton and Noel Trevarthen.
VHS: S15900. $19.95.
John Richardson, Australia, 1982, 88 mins.

The Efficiency Expert
Originally titled *Spottiswoode*, this Australian film is reminiscent of BillForsyth's comedies about cultural and social dislocation. Anthony Hopkins, a demanding efficiency expert, is enlisted to rescue a struggling, family-operated footwear factory, run by a collection of oddballs and eccentrics. With Ben Mendelsohn, Alwyn Kurts and Bruno Lawrence.
VHS: S18765. $19.95.
Laser: LD75187. $34.98.
Mark Joffe, Australia, 1991, 97 mins.

The Everlasting Secret Family
A bizarre and brilliant Australian film that takes us into a fantasy universe of sex and politics. In public the Senator is a popular and powerful politician, happily married with a young son. In private he is a senior member of the "secret family", which controls a world of corruption and sexual manipulation at the highest levels of Australian society.
VHS: S14293. $79.95.
Michael Thornhill, Australia, 1988, 93 mins.

Father
Max Von Sydow is featured in this melodrama about a woman forced to question the very humanity of her father. It begins when she learns of an accusation against him on TV. He is suspected of being a Nazi war criminal. Though she remains convinced her father is innocent, doubts begin to grow.
VHS: S25969. $19.98.
John Power, Australia, 1990, 106 mins.

Flirting
The second part of John Duigan's *(The Year My Voice Broke)* autobiographical trilogy about growing up in the 60s. Danny Embling (Noah Taylor) falls for a beautiful and brilliant young Ugandan woman, Thandiwe Adjewa (Thandie Newton) at a gilded Australian boarding school. "This perceptive and gorgeously acted memory piece may even surpass [the first one] in subtlety, feeling and depth of characterization" (Jonathan Rosenbaum, *Chicago Reader*). With Nicole Kidman.
VHS: S18608. $19.95.
Laser: LD75196. $34.98.
John Duigan, Australia, 1991, 99 mins.

For Love Alone

The sensual story of a young woman's quest for love and creative fulfillment in 1930's Australia, from the producer of *My Brilliant Career*. Tess is the feisty romantic who follows her yearnings to despair and passion.

VHS: S05375. $69.95.
Stephen Wallace, Australia, 1986, 102 mins.

Forty Thousand Horsemen

An Australian World War II movie starring Chips Rafferty, Grant Taylor and Betty Bryant, "the breathtaking beauty from Australia." The fighting Anzacs battle the evil German war machine in the deserts of North Africa. Includes cavalry charges, romance, and lots of horses. Watch where you step.

VHS: S05478. $29.95.
Charles Chauvel, Australia, 1941, 84 mins.

Georgia

In this psychological thriller actress Judy Davis portrays two characters, a woman named Georgia, who died under strange circumstances, and her daughter Nina Bailey. Nina, a tough young lawyer, is intrigued when the strange facts surrounding her mother's death suddenly come to light. As Nina digs into the past, similar dangers emerge to threaten her life as well.

VHS: S20646. $19.98.
Ben Lewin, Australia, 1988, 90 mins.

The Getting of Wisdom

This "portrait of the artist as a young woman" is a sumptuous, Victorian, coming-of-age tale of a gifted young girl who is sent from the Australian bush to a proper Victorian ladies' school. Her personality and wisdom triumph over the school's conformity, resulting in a winning tale of adolescence. "Incomparably moving and powerful" *(Newhouse Newspapers)*.

VHS: S31115. $19.98.
Bruce Beresford, Australia, 1977, 100 mins.

Ground Zero

An Australian thriller about the secret results of British atomic tests down under in the early 1950's. Colin Friels (Malcolm) is an inquisitive photographer who learns that his father's death was no accident. Jack Thompson is the security man assigned to keep him in line. With Donald Pleasence as a crazy desert hermit with all the answers. Thought provoking and great scenery.

VHS: S09851. $19.95.
Michael Pattison/Bruce Myles, Australia, 1988, 99 mins.

Heaven's Burning

While honeymooning in Australia, Midori (Youki Kudoh, *Picture Bride*) deserts her husband to run off with her lover. When he gets cold feet, she's left alone and bewildered in a strange country. A trip to the bank to exchange money results in her being taken hostage, only to be saved by Colin (Russell Crowe, *L.A. Confidential*), the getaway driver. On the run, with Midori's jilted husband and the authorities in hot pursuit, the pair set off on a wild ride across the Australian outback, falling in love along the way.

VHS: S33425. $96.99.
Craig Lahiff, Australia, 1993, 99 mins.

I Live with Me Dad

A homeless father and son who have nothing but each other fight desperately to remain a family in this Australian drama of love, courage, devotion and hope.

VHS: S05896. $79.98.
Paul Maloney, Australia, 1986, 86 mins.

In the Wake of the Bounty

Errol Flynn's first film! A rollicking, swashbuckler of an adventure which has never before been available on video.

VHS: S15285. $24.95.
Charles Chanuel, Australia, 1933, 66 mins.

Joey

Billy McGregor, a 12-year-old boy living on a ranch in the Australian outback, sets out on a hilarious adventure as he tries to reunite a baby kangaroo with his abducted parents. Along the way he recruits the daughter of the local Ambassador (Ed Begley, Jr.) and together they create an international incident, capture news headlines and expose an evil ring of wrong-doers.

VHS: S33943. $14.95.
Ian Berry, Australia, 1997, 97 mins.

Kangaroo

A critically-acclaimed adaptation of D.H. Lawrence's semi-autobiographical novel follows an idealistic English writer and his wife to Australia, where they hope to find a more tolerant world in which to rebuild their lives. Judy Davis and Colin Friels star.

VHS: S04523. $79.95.
Tim Burstall, Australia, 1985, 110 mins.

Kiss or Kill

Nikki (Frances O'Connor) and Al (Matt Day) are a pair of sexy con artists who earn their living by ripping off businessmen until one of their targets ends up dead. When everyone they encounter dies, the lovers, with a pair of detectives on their trail, take to the road. Things get even hotter when the desperate pair have no choice but to suspect each other.

VHS: S33874. $99.99.
Bill Bennett, Australia, 1997, 97 mins.

The Last Days of Chez Nous

Australian director Gillian Armstrong's film about the multilayered relations between men and women in a rambunctious, crowded Sydney flat. A young woman (Kerry Fox), recovering from an unplanned pregnancy and a failed relationship, moves in with her sister (Lisa Harrow), a gifted novelist, who is trying to salvage her relationship with her French husband (Bruno Ganz). The underlying sexual tension erupts when Fox and Ganz eventually give in to their mutual attraction. With Miranda Otto, Kiri Paramore and Bill Hunter.

VHS: S19506. $19.95.
Gillian Armstrong, Australia, 1991, 96 mins.

The Lighthorsemen

An Australian action adventure based on a World War I attack of 800 mounted troops who charged overwhelming forces dug in the desert town of Beersheba in the Middle East. From the director of *Phar Lap*, a different approach to the special relationship some Australian men have with their horses. Improbable but true. With Anthony Andrews, Bill Kerr, Peter Phelps, Jon Blake and Sigrid Thornton.

VHS: S08235. $14.98.
Laser: Widescreen Special Edition, CAV. **LD75470. $59.95.**
Simon Wincer, Australia, 1988, 115 mins.

Lion's Den

This early film, written by, directed by and featuring Bryan Singer *(The Usual Suspects)*, is the story of a local restaurant which serves as the meeting place for a group of five passionate youths. Like young lions they meet and spar, learning the comfort of this den is but a memory. With David Leslie Conhaim, Ethan Hawke, Brandon Keith, Dylan Kussman and Susan Kussman. Also includes the short *Gothcha!*, a Special Broadcasting Service Children's Production of a prankster who gets his just desserts (24 mins.).

VHS: S32964. $29.95.
Bryan Singer/Howard Rubie, USA/Australia, 1990/1992, 48 mins.

Love Serenade

A wickedly funny story of two wacky sisters who are both on the lookout for love. When a slick, smooth-talking radio DJ from the big city blows into town, it sets off a hilarious battle for his affections.

VHS: S33040. $103.99.
Shirley Barrett, Australia, 1997, 101 mins.

Mad Dog Morgan

Dennis Hopper is great as the legendary outlaw roaming 19th-century Australia's outback in this very violent, moody and well-made film based on a true story. With Jack Thompson and David Gulpili *(Walkabout)*.

VHS: S34068. $19.95.
Philippe Mora, Australia, 1976, 93 mins.

Mad Max Beyond Thunderdome

"A series of films that just keeps getting better and better" (Gene Siskel). Mel Gibson is back as Mad Max, with Tina Turner as the deadly Auntie Entity, the Queen of Bartertown.

VHS: S00793. $14.95.
Laser: LD70619. $34.98.
DVD: DV60050. $24.98.
George Miller, Australia, 1985, 107 mins.

Man from Snowy River

A thrilling adventure story set in the Australian frontier of the 1880's, starring Kirk Douglas in a dual role, and highlighted by a climactic chase involving 40 horsemen and over 90 wild stallions.

VHS: S00811. $14.98.
George Miller, Australia, 1982, 104 mins.

Miracle Down Under

Filmed entirely on location in the breathtaking wilds of southern Australia, this feature captures the adventures and conflicts of a rugged group of settlers in the remote bush country during the 1890's. Visions of taming the frontier quickly fade one in summer's drought, until a series of miraculous events rekindles the pioneers' hope.

VHS: S05377. $29.95.
George Miller, Australia, 1987, 101 mins.

Muriel's Wedding

Life is one big comic adventure for Muriel. She leaves Porpoise Spit, her small town home, and her cruel, blonde friends in hopes of finding a new identity in the big city. She changes her name to Mariel, and, along with her best friend Rhonda, discovers eager young men and exciting adventures. Before long Muriel is engaged to be married to a handsome celebrity athlete, but ultimately she must learn that even a dream wedding can't make her a different person.

VHS: S27219. $19.95.
P.J. Hogan, Australia, 1994, 105 mins.

Only the Brave

Two wild teenage girls named Vicki and Alex experiment with everything from drugs and sex to violence and just hanging out. Alex wants to write and finds encouragement, along with a little erotic attention, from her English teacher Kate. Vicki wants to sing like Alex's mother did before she disappeared. Together, these girls explore new boundaries in their friendship until events spiral out of their control. Winner of the Best Feature Film award at the 1994 San Francisco Lesbian and Gay Film Festival.

VHS: S26918. $29.95.
Ana Kokkinos, Australia, 1994, 62 mins.

Oscar and Lucinda

Ralph Fiennes stars as a priest and Cate Blanchett stars as an independent businesswoman whose shared passion for gambling leads them down a road of romance, chance and fate.

VHS: S34086. $103.99.
Laser: LD76840. $39.98.
Gillian Armstrong, Australia, 1997, 130 mins.

Patrick

A chilling horror story about a 24-year-old patient in a small hospital who has been in a coma for four years and begins to play psychokinetic games with the staff of the hospital.

VHS: S03721. $29.95.
Richard Franklin, Australia, 1978, 96 mins.

Phar Lap

A beautiful and suspenseful movie about adversity, endurance, and the drive to win. *Phar Lap* tells the story of a champion race horse that won 37 races three years capturing the imagination of all of Australia in 1932.

VHS: S01021. $14.98.
Simon Wincer, Australia, 1984, 107 mins.

Prisoners of the Sun

Where does war end and murder begin? That is just one of the questions asked by Australian attorney Bryan Brown at a post-World War II war crimes trial. George Takei (Sulu on *Star Trek*) is cast as the Japanese general under indictment. With Terry O'Quinn as the American political officer who stands between them. It has been called a gripping military drama along the lines of *Breaker Morant*.

VHS: S15099. $89.95.
Laser: LD75242. $34.98.
Stephen Wallace, Australia/USA, 1991, 109 mins.

Proof

Jocelyn Moorhouse's debut film is a psychologically compelling work about a sinister three-way love relationship between a repressed blind photographer (Hugo Weaving), his friend (Russell Crowe) who describes the contents of the photographs, and the photographer's intensely jealous housekeeper (Genevieve Picot). Moorhouse has a brilliant facility for images, rhythms and texture.

VHS: S17710. $19.95.
Jocelyn Moorhouse, Australia, 1991, 90 mins.

The Quiet Room

A unique exploration into the inner thoughts of a seven-year-old girl. It is a world in which she has very little control, for her parents' marriage is disintegrating. Through her silence, the child attempts to influence her parents' behavior and force them to communicate properly with each other and with her. With the marriage speeding toward total collapse, the child finds ways to make her actions speak even louder and finds the means to reconcile herself with the world.

VHS: S32153. $19.98.
Laser: LD76354. $39.99.
Rolf de Heer, Australia, 1996, 91 mins.

Resistance

The cities have collapsed, driving the poor and desperate into the countryside, where they eke out a meager living as farmhands for a huge corporation. Now, trouble is brewing in a remote shanty town, and anti-terrorist squads are sent in to restore order among the rowdy workers and to get the crops harvested before food shortages panic the cities. Two women, a runaway tribal girl and a truckstop waitress forge a common bond in the tragedy they suffer and lead a bloody rebellion against the occupying forces. "An epic vision" (Stephen Holden, *The New York Times*).

VHS: S32933. $89.95.
Paul Elliott/Hugh Keays-Byrne, Australia, 1997, 100 mins.

Return to Snowy River
The Australian scenery and a magnificent herd of horses are once again the focus of this beautifully photographed adventure film. Tom Burlinson and Sigrid Thornton reprise their roles of the daring young horseman and his lady love, but Kirk Douglas, as the disapproving father, has been replaced by Brian Dennehy. Based on a the poem by Banjo Paterson.
VHS: S07919. $19.95.
Geoff Burrowes, Australia, 1987, 99 mins.

Road Warrior
Called by Andrew Sarris a "post-apocalyptic adventure yarn of such breathtaking velocity that it would have spun hopelessly out of control without the charismatic hero of Mel Gibson's *Mad Max* at its core," *The Road Warrior* features Gibson as the ultimate anti-hero, battling a gang at the last outpost of civilization. Hair-raising stunts and spectacular chase scenes.
VHS: S01801. $14.95.
Laser: LD70739. $29.98.
DVD: DV60054. $24.98.
George Miller, Australia, 1983, 94 mins.

Romper Stomper
Geoffrey Wright's chilling debut film is a harrowing examination of violence and terror among neo-Nazi skinheads in contemporary Australia. Gabe (Jacqueline McKenzie) escapes her sexually abusive father and falls in with a perverse band of racist skinheads. Initially she's drawn to the group's leader (Russell Crowe). They wreak havoc on Melbourne's Vietnamese community. "Complex and controversial in its politics, this is an expose from the inside" *(Toronto Festival of Festivals)*. With Alex Scott.
VHS: S20210. $19.98.
Geoffrey Wright, Australia, 1992, 85 mins.

Shine
Geoffrey Rush gives an Academy Award-winning performance as pianist David Helfgott in this extraordinary, true story of a young man who defies his father's wishes in order to pursue his dreams. Both thought-provoking and powerful, it tells a tale of rebellion and individuality through the eyes of an artist whose only form of self-expression is found in the keys of his instruments. With Lynn Redgrave, Armin Mueller-Stahl, Sir John Gielgud and Noah Taylor. VHS letterboxed.
VHS: S31545. $19.98.
Laser: LD76252. $39.99.
DVD: DV60098. $24.98.
Scott Hicks, Australia, 1996, 105 mins.

Sirens
Hugh Grant, Sam Neill and Elle MacPherson star in this erotic comedy about a painter, his model and the young vicar who is disturbed by the work they produce together. Though the vicar (Grant) hopes to change this couple, he finds himself seduced by their erotic relationship.
VHS: S22158. $19.95.
John Duigan, Australia, 1994, 102 mins.

Sky Pirates
An Australian fantasy adventure about a daredevil WWII pilot who crashes through a time warp and joins a search for a special stone. John Hargreaves stars as the daring adventurer. Lots of action from Down Under and beyond. With Max Phipps, Meredith Phillips and Bill Hunter.
VHS: S06613. $79.98.
Colin Eggleston, Australia, 1986, 88 mins.

Something to Sing About
The 100-member Sydney Gay and Lesbian Choir is the pride of Australia's vibrant gay and lesbian community. Decked in purple waistcoats with the odd touch of chain and leather, the Choir sings everything from Gershwin to Madrigals, spirituals to ABBA, as it takes its audiences on a rich, emotional journey across the continent of Australia to defend its title in the National Choral Competition. "A standing ovation" *(The Australian)*.
VHS: S30245. $29.95.
Martin Daley, Australia, 1995, 55 mins.

Starstruck
A wacky Australian musical comedy from the director of *My Brilliant Career*, Gillian Armstrong. Jo Kennedy stars as a teenage singing sensation who just knows she has what it takes to be a star if she can just reach the right people. With Ross O'Donovan as her energetic cousin and manager.
VHS: S06193. $19.98.
Gillian Armstrong, Australia, 1982, 95 mins.

Strictly Ballroom
The hit of film festivals in Cannes and Toronto, Baz Luhrmann's Australian film about the subculture of ballroom dancing competitions centers on a 21-year-old maverick dancer who refuses to comply with the rigid rules of the Dance Federation and gets dropped by his partner on the eve of an important dance. Luhrmann's film is an anthropological examination of a vanishing world, a funny and thrilling demystification of backdoor politics and small-scale intrigue. With Paul Mercurio, Tara Morice, Bill Hunter and Pat Thompson.
VHS: S20376. $19.95.
Laser: LD72422. $39.99.
Baz Luhrmann, Australia, 1992, 92 mins.

The Sum of Us
In this gay romantic comedy a young man finds the search for Mr. Right troubled by his busy-body father. Dad is just concerned for a son who seems unable to find that special someone. Altogether it's a light, amiable tale that is darkened by unexpected misfortune. In sunny Australia, however, things always get bright again. Based on David Stevens' play.
Laser: LD75085. $39.99.
Kevin Dowling/Geoff Burton, Australia, 1995, 99 mins.

Summer City
Mel *(Mad Max)* Gibson and his wild young friends descend upon a seaside resort for a weekend of surfing and adventure, but when a local girl is seduced she becomes a catalyst in a bizarre chain of events.
VHS: S01279. $19.95.
Christopher Fraser, Australia, 1976, 83 mins.

Sweet Talker
Bryan Brown, the genial star of *FX*, is cast as an ex-con with a bold scheme to raise money from a distressed seaside community by attracting interest in a legendary buried treasure ship. Complications ensue when he becomes emotionally involved with a young boy and his attractive mother, played by Karen Allen. Filmed on location in Australia. To scam or not to be scam, that is the question.
VHS: S15408. $89.98.
Michael Jenkins, Australia, 1991, 91 minutes

Sweetie
A true original—this breakthrough film from Australia's Jane Campion is "as disturbing as *Blue Velvet*", "an original." Bizarre, often hilarious, *Sweetie* is the story of two very different sisters, the guarded and repressed Kay and the overweight and spontaneous Sweetie.
VHS: S12478. $14.98.
Jane Campion, Australia, 1989, 97 mins.

Test of Love
Based on a true story of a highly intelligent disabled teen who had been misdiagnosed and institutionalized since the age of three in a home for the severely retarded.
VHS: S01505. $69.95.
Gil Brealey, Australia, 1984, 93 mins.

Tim
An engrossing love story; Piper Laurie is the woman who is physically attracted to her gardener who, though handsome, is also slightly retarded. With a great performance from Mel Gibson as the gardener.
VHS: S01736. $19.95.
Michael Pate, Australia, 1979, 108 mins.

A Town Like Alice
Based on Neville Shute's internationally best-selling novel, *A Town Like Alice* follows the lives of Jean Paget and Joe Harman. Meeting in Malaya—she is is an young English captive and he is a cheerful Australian POW—they are separated by their captors, and then, by the distance of passing years, finally reunited in the rugged outback of Australia. Starring Bryan Brown and Helen Morse.
VHS: S03463. $29.95.
Laser: LD72256. $69.95.
David Stevens, Australia, 1980, 301 mins.

Vincent
A box office smash, "the most profound exploration of an artist's soul ever to be put on film. In an aesthetic experience verging on an epiphany, [Paul] Cox has sketched from Van Gogh's voluminous letters the portrait of his illustrious countryman and fellow exile not as a mad artist but as an articulate intellectual. Many of the early Van Gogh drawings filmed in Vincent have been generally inaccessible until now and many of the letters were translated from the original Dutch by the director. Hence there are many new facets to the Van Gogh legend that come to life in *Vincent* for the first time" *(Village Voice)*. John Hurt is the voice of Van Gogh.
VHS: S12951. $89.95.
Paul Cox, Australia/Netherlands, 1989, 90 mins.

Violet's Visit
After running away from home, Violet searches for her biological father, and finds him, living with his longtime boyfriend. While initially stunned, the three negotiate this *La Cage aux Folles* existence with humor and sensitivity.
VHS: S34873. $59.95.
Richard Turner, Australia, 1995, 83 mins.

Waterfront
The sexy Greta Scacchi stars as an Italian immigrant in Australia thrown into a bitter dock workers dispute. Against the odds of language barriers and racial attitudes toward Italians, Greta and union leader Jack Thompson fall in love in a tragic love story.
VHS: S05843. $29.95.
Edward McQ Mason, Australia, 1987, 284 mins.

We of the Never Never
The true account of life on the Australian frontier based on the journals of a woman pioneer. A moving account of courage, hardship, conflicts, and eventually conquest of the beautiful land of the "never never" of the Aborigines through the power of love.
VHS: S01436. $59.95.
Igor Auzins, Australia, 1982, 90 mins.

Who Killed Baby Azaria
Another version of the story of Lindy Chamberlain and her missing baby Azaria, this was made before *A Cry in the Dark*. She claimed it was taken away by a wild dingo. This mystery-suspense film claims to contain the truth of Australia's most controversial murder trial. As details of the case were still enfolding in 1988, it obviously doesn't tell the whole story. With Elain Hudson, John Hamblin and Max Phipps.
VHS: S09920. $59.95.
Judy Rymer, Australia, 1983, 96 mins.

Wide Sargasso Sea
Talented Australian director John Duigan *(Flirting)* adapted Jean Rhys' sensual novel about the first marriage of Rochester (Nathaniel Parker), the brooding English romantic of Charlotte Bronte's *Jane Eyre*, to a beautiful Creole named Antoinette (Karina Lombard). Set in Jamaica during the 1840s, the film pivots on erotic obsession and sexual delusion. "Infinitely romantic, the film's eroticism is real" (Vincent Canby). With Rachel Ward as Antoinette's mentally unbalanced mother, Michael York, Martine Beswicke and Claudia Robinson.
VHS: S19936. $19.95.
John Duigan, USA/Australian, 1992, 100 mins.

A Woman's Tale
A haunting work about the demands of a bright, challenging 78-year-old woman (Sheila Florance, in her final performance) to find a grace and dignity in her life, carried out by her relationship with a sympathetic and equally tough nurse (Cox regular Gosia Dobrowlolska). With Norman Kaye, Chris Haywood and Ernest Gray.
VHS: S17882. $19.98.
Paul Cox, Australia, 1991, 93 mins.

Young Einstein
An intellectually serious slapstick comedy from Australia. Yahoo Serious (born Greg Pead) wrote, directed, produced and stars as the title character in this fictional biography of one of the world's greatest thinkers, had Einstein been born in Tasmania on a little apple farm instead of in Europe. Enjoy his comic exploits as he splits the atom, invents rock and roll and dates Marie Curie. Funny stuff from Down Under. With Jon Howard, Pee Wee Wilson and Odile Le Clezio.
VHS: S11577. $19.98.
Yahoo Serious, Australia, 1989, 90 mins.

PETER WEIR

The Cars That Ate Paris
Australian director Peter Weir's first feature is a delightful black comedy about a small Aussie town that makes its living solely on the visitors they ambush. Inspired, in part, by the driving conditions in Paris, France, Weir's gleefully murderous community is now available in its original uncut version.
VHS: S06069. $19.98.
Peter Weir, Australia, 1974, 91 mins.

Dead Poets Society
Robin Williams gets semi-serious about the written word as he shapes and guides young minds at an Eastern seaboard prep school in the late '50's. The title refers to a secret society of students designed to promote imagination and cultural exchange. With Ethan Hawke, Josh Charles, Sean Leonard, Norman Lloyd and Kurtwood Smith as a disapproving parent.
VHS: S11992. $29.95.
Laser: LD70943. $44.99.
Peter Weir, USA, 1989, 128 mins.

Fearless

Jeff Bridges, Isabella Rossellini and Rosie Perez (in an Oscar-nominated performance) star in this overlooked drama about life-altering experiences. The survivors of a plane crash reach out to each other in an effort to cope with the horrors of death and the accompanying guilt. Also featuring Tom Hulce as a sleazy personal injuries lawyer, and John Turturro.

VHS: S20720. $19.98.
Laser: LD72386. $39.98.
Peter Weir, USA, 1993, 122 mins.

Gallipoli

Adventure story that brings two young men together in the Australian army in 1915, leading to the legendary confrontation between the Australians and Turks at Gallipoli during World War I. From the director of *Last Wave* and *Picnic at Hanging Rock*. Letterboxed.

VHS: S00477. $19.95.
Peter Weir, Australia, 1981, 111 mins.

Green Card

The English-speaking debut of French actor Gerard Depardieu, *Green Card* is a sharp comedy of manners, about a repressed horticulturist (Andie MacDowell) who agrees to marry a French musician (Depardieu) and is forced to live with him when immigration authorities check out their backgrounds. They promptly fall in love.

Laser: LD71022. $39.99.
Peter Weir, USA, 1990, 107 mins.

Last Wave

Peter Weir's fourth feature is a visually compelling portrayal of inner hysteria and apocalyptic vision. David Burton (Richard Chamberlain), a Sydney corporate lawyer, is sucked into the whirlpool of events surrounding the mysterious death of an Australian Aborigine when he volunteers to defend those accused of the murder. During the course of the trial, Burton's abstracted dream images begin to reveal strange water-related events in the weather, and concern one of the four Aborigines he is defending.

VHS: S00729. $19.95.
Peter Weir, Australia, 1977, 109 mins.

The Mosquito Coast

Director Peter Weir re-teams with Harrison Ford as they tackle Paul Theroux's novel of an obsessive American inventor who transplants his family to a fictional Central American country which he hopes will welcome a jungle based ice factory. With River Phoenix as the long suffering son and Helen Mirren as the even longer suffering wife.

Laser: Letterboxed. **LD74481. $34.98.**
Peter Weir, USA, 1986, 119 mins.

Picnic at Hanging Rock

Digitally remastered, letterboxed, director's cut of Peter Weir's *(The Truman Show)* masterpiece. Set in 1900, this sensuous mystery dramatizes the disappearance of three Australian girls on a school picnic. Falling under nature's spell, the group climbs a tower of rocks, as if called away from their repressive boarding school life. Ravishing cinematography of the sun-drenched outback suggests the unfulfilled desires held beneath their Victorian linens and lace.

VHS: S33997. $79.95.
Peter Weir, Australia, 1975, 107 mins.

Witness

Harrison Ford is the cop who runs head-on into the non-violent world of the Amish community in this Academy Award-winning struggle of life and death in which a young Amish woman and her son are caught up in the murder of an undercover narcotics agent.

VHS: S01472. $14.95.
Peter Weir, USA, 1985, 112 mins.

Year of Living Dangerously

Mel Gibson and Sigourney Weaver begin an impassioned love affair intensified by the uncertainties of life in Indonesia on the eve of revolution. Linda Hunt stars as Billy Kwan, a Eurasian cameraman who befriends Gibson.

VHS: S01486. $19.98.
Laser: LD70715. $34.98.
DVD: DV60101. $24.98.
Peter Weir, Australia/USA, 1982, 115 mins.

NEW ZEALAND CINEMA

An Angel at My Table

The true story of one of our century's most gifted writers, *An Angel at My Table* chronicles the life and extraordinary times of Janet Frame. Born in the 1920s, Janet's early years of fairy tales and schoolgirl pranks were tempered by family tragedy. She retreated to her beloved books and began to write poetry and stories. As the years passed her talent grew and so did the challenges to her unique and inspired vision.

VHS: S15620. $19.98.
Jane Campion, New Zealand, 1991, 157 mins.

Broken English

Two beautiful lovers from very different worlds ignite racial and sexual tensions with their intensely passionate affair. Stars Julian Arahanga *(Once Were Warriors)*, Rade Serbedzua *(Before the Saint)* and Aleksandra Vujcic in her film debut.

VHS: S32974. $19.95.
Gregor Nicholas, New Zealand, 1997, 92 mins.

Crush

Lane (Marcia Gay Harden) is a reckless driver who inadvertently leaves her friend Christina hospitalized with severe injuries. Fleeing the scene of the crime, she crashes into the lives of a novelist and his teenage daughter Angela. At first she befriends the girl, only to betray this trust by seducing the father. Angela seeks revenge by helping and manipulating Christina to reveal Lane's guilt.

VHS: S21092. $19.98.
Alison MacLean, New Zealand, 1993, 100 mins.

Dead Alive

A strange creature, the Sumatran rat monkey, has bitten an old woman and thereby transformed her into a ghoulish, dead monster who sucks the life out of the living. Her son tries to live a normal life but mom's victims keep on multiplying and, even worse, go on living themselves. Soon a crowd of flesh-hungry monsters is menacing this once-peaceful small town.

VHS: S19240. $14.99.
Laser: LD75180. $34.98.
Peter Jackson, New Zealand, 1992, 85 mins.

The End of the Golden Weather

In this family drama set in New Zealand, young Geoff Crome immerses himself in his own private fantasy in which he meets Firpo, a strange being who dreams of being an Olympic athlete. As the two forge a friendship, it is not long before the adult world begins to put a damper on their dreams. With Stephen Fulford, Stephen Papps and Lucy Lawless (TV's *Xena: Warrior Princess*).

VHS: S34095. $19.95.
Ian Mune, New Zealand, 1992, 100 mins.

Forgotten Silver

In this insidiously funny yet utterly believable mockumentary, director Peter Jackson *(Heavenly Creatures)* discovers a cache of ancient nitrate in a neighbor's shed and realizes it is an extraordinary collection of films directed by Colin McKenzie, film pioneer and inventor extraordinaire in early 1900s New Zealand. Combining interviews with real people like actor Sam Neill, film critic Leonard Maltin and Miramax Chairman Harvey Weinstein, *Forgotten Silver* is "a gleeful, charming, tongue-in-cheek jest that is cleverly conceived and exceptionally well executed" (Kenneth Turan, *Los Angeles Times*).

VHS: S34418. $59.95.
Peter Jackson/Costa Botes, New Zealand, 1996, 70 mins.

Heart of the Stag

Bruno Lawrence *(Smash Palace)* stars as a farmhand who signs on with an isolated sheep ranch and disrupts an incestuous relationship in this offbeat, rather bizarre story. From the director of *Sylvia*.

VHS: S03462. $19.95.
Michael Firth, New Zealand, 1984, 94 mins.

Heavenly Creatures

Peter Jackson's chilling account of two teenage girls who develop an intense emotional and physical relationship, dominated by fantasy, which ultimately leads them to murder, is a stylistically original work. It is remarkable for its insights into the girls' adolescent world of make-believe, as well as the bland suburban world of 1950's New Zealand.

VHS: S24774. $19.95.
Laser: Widescreen. **LD74976. $39.99.**
Peter Jackson, New Zealand, 1994, 99 mins.

Jack Be Nimble

Alexis Arquette and Sarah Kennedy Smuts are featured in this supernatural thriller about a brother and sister who are split up when their parents abandon them. The brother, Jack, is trapped with a sadistic family. Luckily his sister Dora develops extra-sensory powers that warn her of the dangers faced by her brother.

VHS: S24381. $94.95.
Garth Maxwell, New Zealand, 1994, mins.

The Last Stand

A young Maori woman finds her loyalties torn between the people who raised her and the people who gave her life. When she stands with the Maori against the British, tragedy ensues and she is captured despite the best efforts of her beloved.

VHS: S27892. $19.98.
Rudall C. Hayward, New Zealand, 1933, 60 mins.

Loaded

In this critically acclaimed thriller inspired by a true story, a group of young adults spend a weekend together making their own low-budget horror film, and end up experimenting with seduction, jealousy and danger. When the night turns to getting loaded on LSD, the weekend becomes more terrifying than they ever could have imagined. With Catherine McCormack *(Braveheart)* and Thandie Newton.

VHS: S30453. $19.95.
Laser: LD76034. $39.99.
Anna Campion, New Zealand, 1996, 96 mins.

Map of the Human Heart

An epic love story between Avik (Jason Scott Lee), an Eskimo, and Albertine (French actress Anne Parillaud), a half-breed, that unfolds in the years 1931-1965. When the lovers are reunited, Avik, a World War II bomber pilot, discovers Albertine is married to Walter Scott (Patrick Bergin), his former protector who saved his life. "A sweeping romance, grand, noble and boldly imaginative" (Jay Carr, *Boston Globe*). With John Cusack, Ben Mendelsohn, Annie Galipeau and Jeanne Moreau.

VHS: S19060. $19.98.
Laser: LD75227. $34.98.
Vincent Ward, New Zealand, 1992, 109 mins.

Meet the Feebles

An adult fantasy film, *Meet the Feebles* relates the events that led up to the infamous "Feebles Variety Massacre," the day that rocked the puppet world. The film, directed by Peter Jackson *(Dead Alive, Heavenly Creatures)*, who describes it as "a kind of *Roger Rabbit* meets *Brazil*," is set in a contemporary world like ours, with one major difference: there are no human beings. The Feebles' world is entirely populated by puppets-living, breathing, eating puppets with larger-than-life human characteristics and weaknesses... *Meet the Feebles* is a darkly comic satire on greed, lust and jealousy... part satire/soap opera/ musical that is a wildly original feature" (Charles Coleman).

VHS: S26868. $89.95.
Peter Jackson, New Zealand, 1988, 97 mins.

The Mighty Civic

Blending history, fantasy and truth, New Zealand filmmaker Peter Wells weaves a magical spell over the history of old movie palaces. Within this world, showgirls reminisce about their experiences and an usher leads a tour into the secrets of Auckland's Xanadu. The program moves briskly through time, moving from Auckland in the 20s to World War II-era days when American soldiers confronted Kiwi women at the Civic's midnight roof.

VHS: S20216. $29.95.
Peter Wells, New Zealand, 62 mins.

Navigator: A Time Travel Adventure

A highly imaginative epic as a group of medieval villagers, on the verge of being decimated by the bubonic plague, are lead by a visionary boy through the bowels of the earth and end up in 20th-century New Zealand. Called "electrifying....a spellbinder" by *Rolling Stone*.

VHS: S10721. $24.95.
Vincent Ward, New Zealand, 1988, 101 mins.

Once Were Warriors

The title of Lee Tamahori's breakthrough feature refers to the Maori people and their proud history. Set in an apocalyptic suburban New Zealand landscape, the film focuses on a dysfunctional family. The abused wife struggles to keep her family together despite the brutish and violent ways of her alcoholic husband, which, the filmmaker suggests, is a result of alienation from the authentic (Maori) culture.

VHS: S26282. $19.98.
Laser: LD75060. $49.95.
Lee Tamahori, New Zealand, 1995, 102 mins.

The Piano

Holly Hunter's Oscar-winning performance as a mute woman dedicated to her music takes center stage in this lush drama set in 19th century New Zealand. Harvey Keitel co-stars as the brutish but sensitive man who gives her back what seemed irrevocably lost. A young Anna Paquin more than holds her own with a performance that garnered this new star an Oscar for Best Supporting Actress.

VHS: S20871. $19.98.
Jane Campion, Australia/New Zealand, 1993, 121 mins.

Starlight Hotel

A New Zealand road movie set in the Depression era of 1932. A 13-year-old girl disguises herself as a boy and runs away to find her father. She is assisted by a good looking, socially minded fugitive from justice. The title refers to sleeping out under the open sky. Fine performances by Greer Robson and Peter Phelps.
VHS: S08321. $79.95.
Laser: CLV. **LD72034. $29.98.**
Sam Pillsbury, New Zealand, 1987, 95 mins.

Strange Behavior

Teenage students become mindless killers after volunteering for an experimental college program. Michael Murphy stars as the police chief father looking for answers. With Fiona Lewis, Louise Fletcher, Dan Shor, Arthur Digham, Dey Young and Scott Brady as a Chicago cop. Set in Galesburg, Illinois but filmed, strangely enough, in New Zealand. Another original thriller from the director of *Strange Invaders*.
VHS: S15493. $19.95.
Michael Laughlin, New Zealand, 1981, 98 minutes.

Two Friends

Lost for over 10 years, Jane Campion's *(The Piano)* debut feature is the story of Louise and Kelly, once inseparable girlfriends, who grow apart as their friendship falls prey to the typical teenage problems of boys, sex and drugs. The story of their heartbreaking rush toward adulthood is told with the humor, honesty and passion that are the hallmarks of Campion's work. "The rarely seen first feature from Jane Campion is still her best" (Paul Sherman, *Boston Herald*). Letterboxed.
VHS: S31410. $89.95.
Jane Campion, New Zealand, 1986, 76 mins.

Utu: The Director's Cut

Fourteen minutes of footage of brutal warfare have been restored to Geoff Murphy's 1983 masterpiece of war, colonialism and cultural survival in New Zealand. Set in the 1870s, *Utu* chronicles the violent endgame between English colonial settlers of New Zealand and the Maori people they displaced and conquered. Having witnessed the massacre of his village by colonial troops, a Maori chieftain vows *utu*, or ritualized revenge, against the well-armed white settlers. "The ferocity of the skirmishes and the raids is played off against an arcadian beauty that makes your head swim" (Pauline Kael, *The New Yorker*).
VHS: S02011. $39.95.
Geoff Murphy, New Zealand, 1983, 118 mins.

Vigil

A mysterious, haunting and daring film by New Zealand's Vincent Ward, set in a remote valley in New Zealand. In a remote farm valley, a farmer is killed as his young daughter watches. In his wake, a hunter appears whom the daughter must expel from her valley. An extraordinary visual and psychological experience, mystical and eerie.
VHS: S10246. $19.98.
Vincent Ward, New Zealand, 1984, 90 mins.

AUSTRALIAN & NEW ZEALAND ISSUES

Aboriginal Art: Past, Present and Future

An exploration of the art of the Aboriginal people of Australia, from prehistoric cave art to contemporary artists. 13 mins.
VHS: S31765. $29.95.

Australia: Secrets of the Land Down Under

Sample the delights of Sydney, then continue on to Canberra, the Outback of New South Wales, Ayer's Rock, Melbourne, Perth, and the awesome Gold Coast. Australia—the land down under-is a unique and exciting continent; see it all here! 50 mins.
VHS: S05785. $24.95.

The Australian Way of Life

Australians are a largely urban people who paradoxically have access to great, unspoiled wilderness areas. They also enjoy free education and health care in a country that reflects a variety of international influences. 21 mins.
VHS: S23708. $129.95.

Cry of the Forgotten Land

This moving video profiles the endangered Moi people of New Guinea, the second-largest island on Earth, and examines the serious threats to the greatest remaining rainforest in Asia and the Pacific, in which they have lived for thousands of years. Winner of the Gold Cindy, 35th Annual Cindy Competition, and Silver Award, Houston International Film Festival. 26 mins.
VHS: S30091. $89.00.

The Dreaming Universe

Physicist Fred Wolf maintains that the world of dreams is ontologically real. This entertaining meditation on the nature of human consciousness explores the concept of "dreamtime" originated by Australian Aborigines. 60 mins.
VHS: S23623. $34.95.

Experience Pacific Islands—Fiji, Vanuatu and the Solomon Islands

Scuba dive among sunken warships, gallop down the beach on a runaway horse, walk through cannibal country, feed sharks and climb an active volcano on this extreme adventure to the Pacific Islands. 47 mins.
VHS: S31473. $19.99.

Great Train Journeys of Australia

This five-volume set showcases Australia, from its sacred aboriginal sites to spectacular rainforests to isolated ghost towns of the outback. Tapes include *The Queenslander, The Ghan-Adelaide to Alice Springs, Brisbane to Sydney on the XPT, Melbourne to Sydney on the XPT* and *Three Trains North*. 52 mins. each.
VHS: S31366. $69.95.

National Geographic Video: Australia's Aborigines

Travel to a distant land for a moving and memorable portrait of Australia's aborigines. Meet what may be the last generation of a noble culture that has endured for over 40,000 years. 60 mins.
VHS: S11409. $19.95.

New Zealand Coast to Coast

Explore spectacular New Zealand and see Auckland, Wellington, Christchurch, Queensland, and the amazing beaches, volcanoes, and dense forests that characterize this jewel of the South Pacific. 30 mins.
VHS: S05774. $24.95.

Touring Australia

This tour covers the cities of Melbourne, Sydney and Perth as well as the Kakadu National Park with its Aboriginal art, the inland sea of Lake Eyre, and the Great Barrier Reef. Various, USA, 1987, 48 mins.
VHS: S03327. $29.95.

Touring New Zealand

A land of awesome beauty, this island country with just three million people, 1,200 miles from Australia, is fast becoming one of the most visited destinations in the South Pacific. This fascinating video tour covers over 100 historic, scenic and cultural sites on both of the North and South Islands, including insightful visits to the center of the Maori culture. 70 mins.
VHS: S12293. $29.95.

canadian cinema

90 Days
Filmed and acted in almost documentary style, *90 Days* shows the attempt by two men to handle the absurd complications of modern life.
VHS: S04197. $79.98.
Giles Walker, Canada, 1986, 100 mins.

And Hope to Die
Rene Clement *(Purple Noon, Rider on the Rain)* directed this interesting thriller in Canada. Robert Ryan and Jean-Louis Trintignant star in the story of a freelance gangster who has an ingenious plan to steal the sexy and simple-minded kingpin's moll from police custody for a $1 million ransom before she can testify against the Mob. Very stylish. In English.
VHS: S08024. $49.95.
Rene Clement, Canada, 1972, 95 mins.

The Apprenticeship of Duddy Kravitz
Richard Dreyfuss stars as an ambitious Canadian Jew determined to become a success at any price. Based on Mordecai Richler's novel, this powerful comic-drama features an equally able supporting cast. With Jack Warden, Denholm Elliott, Joe Silver, Joseph Wiseman and Micheline Lanctot.
VHS: S06341. $19.95.
Ted Kotcheff, Canada, 1974, 121 mins.

Bay Boy
An autobiographical drama from writer-director Daniel Petrie. Keifer Sutherland stars as an impressionable young man growing up in a tiny Canadian community. Liv Ullmann is cast as his hardworking mother. The time is the 1930s, and local mischief abounds. Cast includes Robert Donat, Matthieu Carriere and Isabelle Mejias. Made on location in Nova Scotia.
VHS: S10468. $79.95.
Daniel Petrie, Canada, 1984, 107 mins.

Black Robe
1634 began the French colonization of Canada through Catholic missions. *Black Robe* tells the story of an extraordinary priest who braved the North American wilderness and extreme cultural difference to carry his message from Europe. An important indictment of the Church's refusal to assimilate other cultures, and the tragic corruption of Native American societies by the West. From the director of *Driving Miss Daisy* and *Breaker Morant*.
VHS: S15868. $19.95.
Laser: LD75159. $34.98.
DVD: DV60309. $24.99.
Bruce Beresford, Canada, 1991, 101 mins.

The Boys of St. Vincent
A sensitively told story of child molestation within the confines of a Catholic orphanage and the resulting massive cover-up by the Church. Henry Czerny is superb as the tortured Brother Peter Lavin, the stern and difficult guardian who secretly molests his favorite boys. Conspiring to save the reputation of the Catholic-run orphanage, the concerned authorities decide to keep Brother Lavin's actions a secret and bury the case. Now, 15 years later, the victims refuse to remain silent. With Johnny Morina and Brian Dooley.
VHS: S27432. $89.95.
John N. Smith, Canada, 1994, 186 mins.

Bullet to Beijing
Michael Caine is back as Harry Palmer, the unconventional British superspy of *The Ipcress File* and *Funeral in Berlin*. On a desperate mission to prevent the sale of an apocalyptic new genetic weapon, Harry embarks on a continent-spanning thrill ride into seductive adventure and explosive espionage action. With Jason Connery, Mia Sara, Michael Sarrazin and Michael Gambon.
VHS: S32631. $92.99.
George Mihalka, Canada, 1995, 105 mins.

Candy Mountain
Kevin O'Connor plays an ambitious young musician who goes off on a quest to find the legendary guitar maker Elmore Silk (Harris Yulin). He travels from New York to the wilds of Canada and encounters Tom Waits, David Johansen, Bulle Ogier, Dr. John, Leon Redbone, and many others in cameo roles in this entertaining and very odd road movie. Co-directed by Robert *(Pull My Daisy)* Frank and screenwriter Rudy Wurlitzer *(Walker)*.
VHS: S08063. $14.98.
Robert Frank/Rudy Wurlitzer, Canada/France/Switzerland, 1987, 90 mins.

Careful
From internationally acclaimed cult director Guy Maddin *(Tales from the Gimli Hospital, Archangel)* comes this Freudian parody of 1920's German mountain and expressionist films about the repressed people of the Alpine village of Tolzbad who must never utter a sound lest they cause an avalanche. When one man's incestuous dream triggers an emotional avalanche, the town is revealed as a hotbed of repressed desires, Oedipal angst and sibling rivalry. Stars Gosnia Dobrowolska, Kyle McCullough and Brent Neale.
VHS: S27593. $79.95.
Guy Maddin, Canada, 1992, 96 mins.

Carry On Sergeant
Not to be confused with the British *Carry On* series, which has the same title. This Canadian silent drama concerns a Man of Far North who leaves his wife to fight in World War I. Said to be a controversial and costly film. B&W.
VHS: S04814. $24.95.
Bruce Bairnsfather, Canada, 1928, 09 mins.

Clearcut
When Peter, a white lawyer (Ron Lea), loses an appeal to stop a paper mill from destroying Native American land, Indian militant Arthur (Graham Greene) drags the lawyer and the mill's manager (Michael Hogan) into the woods where Arthur tortures the manager in allegorical ways to mimick what companies do to the forest. Based on the novel by M.T. Kelly. "As radical in its message as any picture you're likely to see" *(Washington Post)*. With Floyd Red Crow and Raoul Trujillo.
VHS: S34477. $19.95.
Ryszard Bugajski, Canada, 1992, 102 mins.

Cold Journey
A feature drama about a young Canadian Indian's attempt to find a place for himself. It tells of the cultural shock of an educational system that teaches him to be a white man, and of his attempts to discover a way of life more meaningful to his Indian culture and ancestry. It is a tragic story of unexpected pitfalls and disillusionment that are as cruel as the bitter wind that greets him on his cold and lonely journey. Shot on location with the people of Indian reserves in Saskatchewan and Manitoba.
VHS: S07665. $69.95.
Martin Defalco, Canada, 76 mins.

The Darling Family
In this unconventional feature the glaring inconsistencies and deadening misunderstandings that govern heterosexual intimacy are openly aired. Despite this intense focus, the film has an immediacy that is hard to resist. A young woman who is mystical, emotional and angry confronts the man who made her pregnant. He, by contrast, is practical, reserved and witty. Not surprisingly, the pregnancy is not a disaster for her, but for him it is coming at the worst time. The results are anything but predictable. Linda Griffith wrote the original play and stars opposite Alan Williams in the film.
VHS: S26479. $59.95.
Alan Zweig, Canada, 1994, 85 mins.

The Disappearance
Donald Sutherland is a skilled, remorseless contract killer whose difficult assignment is complicated by the unsolved disappearance of his wife. With Francine Racette, David Hemmings and David Warner.
VHS: S18141. $9.95.
Stuart Cooper, Canada, 1977, 88 mins.

Double Happiness
This warm comedy by Canada's Mina Shum is a witty and charming cross between *The Joy Luck Club* and *The Hollywood Shuffle*. Sandra Oh stars as Jade, a young Chinese woman trying to balance her modern dreams of being an actress with living with her traditionally minded Chinese parents. Jade's parents set themselves on a mission to fix her up with a nice Chinese man, but Jade is already involved in a secret romance with a Caucasian man.
VHS: S27089. $19.95.
Laser: LD75449. $39.99.
Mina Shum, Canada, 1995, 87 mins.

Dr. Bethune
Donald Sutherland stars in this Canadian homage to Dr. Norman Bethune, who fought for medical progress and political justice on three continents, including China. With Helen Mirren and Helen Shaver.
VHS: S20573. $19.98.
Phillip Borsos, Canada, 1992, 115 mins.

Eclipse
Directed by Jeremy Podeswa, the producer for Canadian icon Atom Egoyan, this offbeat feature is set the week before a total solar eclipse which will plunge the city into total darkness. As the countdown continues, people come together in love, desire and need.
VHS: S31106. $39.99.
Jeremy Podeswa, Canada/Germany, 1994, 96 mins.

Fire
In modern New Delhi, the beautiful and intelligent young Sita lives with her extended family and is stuck in an arranged, loveless marriage to her cheating husband, Jatin. When her sister-in-law Radha is unable to conceive, Radha's husband Ashok becomes celibate and takes off with a swami. Soon Sita and Radha develop an intimate relationship more emotionally satisfying than with their husbands.
VHS: S34738. $94.98.
Deepa Mehta, Canada, 1996, 104 mins.

For the Moment
Russell Crowe is a cocky fighter pilot-in-training stationed in Canada. There he falls in love with a married woman. Forgetting his bravado and any sense of caution, he plunges headlong into an intoxicating affair that will certainly have no future.
VHS: S29799. $95.99.
Aaron Kim Johnston, Canada, 1996, 120 mins.

Going Home
A story suppressed for over 70 years; set in North Wales in 1919, thousands of Canadian infantrymen awaited the arrival of homeward bound ships. But they are passed over to accommodate grain shipments, and mutiny mounts among the rank and file.
VHS: S07321. $79.95.
Terry Ryan, Canada, 1986, 100 mins.

Highway 61
This off-center comedy is the second feature by the talented young Canadian independent Bruce McDonald *(Roadkill)*. Ostensibly a road movie which takes its title from the mythic Bob Dylan song, the film is about the unlikely adventures of a small-town barber (Don McKellar) who agrees to drive a beautiful, unconventional roadie (Valerie Buhagiar) from Ontario to New Orleans, carrying a corpse she claims is her brother.
VHS: S17071. $89.95.
Bruce McDonald, Canada, 1991, 103 mins.

The Housekeeper
Rita Tushingham plays a murdering illiterate who is unstable enough to do it again to protect her secret. She gets a job with a well-to-do Canadian family that eventually gets on her nerves. With great supporting work by Jackie Burroughs. From a novel by Ruth Rendell.
VHS: S04988. $19.98.
Ousama Rawi, Canada, 1986, 102 mins.

I Worship His Shadow
This interplanetary action film tells the story of the conflict between the dark forces of "His Shadow" and a daredevil band of intergalactic rebels. What begins as a simple act of defiance soon ignites into the ultimate sci-fi battle with the fate of the galaxy hanging in the balance. With Barry Bostwick and Michael McManus.
VHS: S32630. $92.99.
Paul Donovan, Canada, 1995, 94 mins.

Johnny Mnemonic
Keanu Reeves stars as a sci-fi courier with a difference. In the future they no longer handcuff couriers to the goods, they plant it in their heads. Reeves is set off on a chase not to protect the goods, but to save his life. It's an overload of suspense. Friends and foes played by Ice-T and Dolph Lundgren are also featured in this debut feature by 1980's art star Robert Longo.
VHS: S26611. $19.95.
Laser: LD75100. $39.99.
DVD: DV60038. $24.95.
Robert Longo, Canada, 1995, 98 mins.

Joshua Then and Now

Based on Mordecai *(Apprenticeship of Duddy Kravitz)* Richler's autobiographical novel, the film stars James Woods as Jewish writer Joshua Shapiro at a crucial stage in his life. The film is a realistic depiction of his growing up in the Jewish section of Montreal, with a gangster father (Alan Arkin) and a would-be entertainer mother (Linda Sorensen), who, as a special treat, does stripteases for his bar mitzvah. *Joshua* is an often funny and poignant portrait.
VHS: S10760. $79.98.
Ted Kotcheff, Canada, 1985, 118 mins.

The Last Winter

This beautiful, highly acclaimed film concerns a young boy who lives in a wonderful undisturbed country idyll. All his fantasy world, not to mention the world of his everyday life, is set in crisis by his family's impending move to the city. It's a film about learning to accept change that is great for kids and grown-ups alike.
VHS: S26389. $95.99.
Aaron Kim Johnston, Canada, 1989, 103 mins.

The Lotus Eaters

This coming-of-age film is set on an island off Canada's western coast, a place known for its dreamy, eccentric atmosphere, and a perfect place for Lotus eaters. It brings a ten-year-old sorceress, a teenage love story, two pigs called Mortimer and Ogilvy and a fabled Beatles concert together into a charming, romantic comedy.
VHS: S25951. $79.95.
Paul Shapiro, Canada, 1994, 101 mins.

Loyalties

A marriage is put to the test in a remote village in northern Alberta in this compelling Canadian drama about honesty and human weakness. Kenneth Welsh, Tantoo Cardinal and Susan Wooldridge head a superb cast that finds there is no place far enough to hide from the truth. Strong and memorable performances.
VHS: S06062. $19.95.
Anne Wheeler, Canada, 1986, 98 mins.

Margaret's Museum

In this gothic and poetic story set in a small, coal pit-reliant Nova Scotia town, Helena Bonham Carter is a woman who swears she'll never marry a miner, but her husband has other ideas, as things become stranger and stranger. With Kate Nelligan, Kenneth Welsh and Clive Russell.
VHS: S31677. $94.99.
Mort Ransen, Canada, 1996, 118 mins.

Masala

Srinivas Krishna's colorful, independent feature is set in the East Indian community in Toronto. Krishna (played by the director) is traumatized by his parents' deaths and believes he won't live long. "A brash and sprightly Canadian comedy about Indian emigres in Toronto, with musical numbers, erotic dream sequences, exploding airplanes, a blue-skinned Hindu deity who exists mainly on video, a fair amount of farce, and a great deal of satire" (Jonathan Rosenbaum, *Chicago Reader*). With Saeed Jaffrey, Zohra Segal, Sakina Jaffrey and Heri Johal.
VHS: S19728. $19.98.
Srinivas Krishna, Canada, 1991, 105 mins.

Masculine Mystique

What do "real men" think about Feminism? Can they ever learn to adjust to life with a modern woman? This docudrama of four men and their relationships is interwoven in a funny and revealing film. Blue, in his mid-thirties, has spent his adult years searching for the perfect woman, without any luck. Alex, the same age, is married with two children, but says he needs freedom. So he's having an affair. Mort has found someone new but she doesn't want a permanent relationship. And Ashley, devastated by divorce, doesn't want to risk a new commitment. Produced by the National Film Board of Canada.
VHS: S07671. $69.95.
John N. Smith/Giles Walker, Canada, 1984, 87 mins.

Obsessed

Kerrie Keane plays a distraught, divorced mother whose young son is struck by a hit and run driver. When the businessman responsible flees from Canada for the safety of the U.S., she starts making the life of Saul Rubinek miserable. Based on the book *Hit and Run* by Tom Alderman. With Alan Thicke, Daniel Pilon and Colleen Dewhurst. A drama with plenty of emotion.
VHS: S10985. $89.95.
Robin Spry, Canada, 1988, 100 mins.

Odyssey of the Pacific (The Emperor of Peru)

Mickey Rooney stars in this children's adventure of a retired railway engineer who is befriended by a trio of youngsters, including a Cambodian refugee who wants to go home by train. A heart warming tale with Monique Mercure, Jean-Louis Roux and Guy Hoffman.
VHS: S07776. $39.95.
Fernando Arrabal, Canada, 1981, 100 mins.

Oh, What a Night

A valentine to 50s romance, freedom and innocence, about two young friends and their first encounters with women, fast cars and music. With Corey Haim, Barbara Williams, Keir Dullea and Robbie Coltrane. A wonderfully evocative soundtrack of Bill Haley, the Penguins, The Monotones and The Dells.
VHS: S17788. $89.95.
Eric Till, Canada, 1992, 90 mins.

On My Own

Judy Davis is featured in this troubling drama about a struggling young man. Davis plays his mother, a woman who suffers from a nervous breakdown. Her son tries to cope as best he can by making new friends at school. Just as he begins to feel the sexual tension of a teenager, his mother makes an unexpected visit and reveals the source of her anguish.
VHS: S28067. $79.95.
Antonio Tibaldi, Canada, 1995, 130 mins.

Ordinary Magic

A funny adaptation of Malcolm Bosse's novel about Jeffrey (David Fox), an eccentric young dreamer who grew up in India and returns to America to live with his aunt (Glenne Headly) following the death of his parents. With Heath Lamberts, Paul Anka and Ryan Reynolds.
VHS: S20209. $89.95.
Giles Walker, Canada, 1993, 96 mins.

Paddle to the Sea

This Academy Award-nominated live-action film is based on the Caldecott Honor children's picture book from Holling C. Holling. A young Native American boy carves a boat with a passenger. He sets it in a small stream with hopes that his toy will reach the sea. Along the way it encounters numerous possible obstructions, from industrious beavers to Niagara Falls.
VHS: S29959. $12.95.
William Mason, Canada, 1966, 30 mins.

Paris, France

"Feverish eroticism...hot & kinky...goes gleefully over the top" *(The New York Times)*. Leslie Hope *(Talk Radio)* stars in this highly erotic film *The New York Post* calls, "a dizzying display of grappling bodies and sizzling hot sex."
VHS: S23862. $14.98.
Gerard Ciccoritti, Canada, 1993, 111 mins.

Pictures Don't Tell You Anything: Selected Films of Ann Marie Fleming

A compilation of 12 award-winning short films spanning 1987-1995 by Canadian filmmaker Ann Marie Fleming, including documentaries, narratives, experimental, music videos and animation: *Waving, You Take Care Now, Drumstix, New Shoes: An Interview in Exactly 5 Minutes, Pioneers of X-Ray Technology: A Film About Grandpa, Buckingham Palace, So Far So..., My Boyfriend Gave Me Peaches, I Love My Work, Jale's Not Happy, Pleasure Film (Ambed's Story)* and *It's Me Again*. "Her powerful, immediate short films display an extremely rare and sometimes acutely troubling honesty and focus. She is without doubt one of the most talented and under-appreciated Canadian filmmakers working today" (Mary Brennan, 5th International Festival of Films by Women Directors). "Fresh, funny, and completely unique" (Atom Egoyan).
VHS: S30439. $39.95.
Anne Marie Fleming, Canada, 106 mins.

The Pyx (The Hooker Cult Murders)

Karen Black stars in this compelling Canadian horror-mystery as a hooker who, after participating in a Black Mass, is found murdered, her hand clutching a host container. Christopher Plummer is the tough detective who investigates this conspiracy of Satanists in some surprisingly high places. Black wrote and sang three songs for the film.
VHS: S32950. $19.95.
Harvey Hart, Canada, 1973, 111 mins.

The Quarrel

Set in Montreal in 1948, this critically acclaimed film is the story of the reunion of two Holocaust survivors: one has become deeply religious; the other has turned his back on God. They have but one afternoon to reconcile their differences, renew their faith and friendship, or remain prisoners to the painful past. Stars Saul Rubinek.
VHS: S29811. $19.98.
Laser: LD75981. $39.99.
Eli Cohen, Canada, 1996, 90 mins.

Rude

Three black characters are the interwoven strands of this unique, stylized film. The action takes place over Easter weekend and follows the complex stories of a former drug dealer, a promising boxer who is also a closeted gay man, and a woman who chooses an abortion, though it could end her current romance. It's all held together by Rude, a pirate disc jockey who forces her way onto the airwaves and acts as the film's voice of reason.
VHS: S28407. $19.95.
Clement Vigo, Canada, 1995, 89 mins.

The Savage Woman

Lea Pool's drama about the shifting relationship of a battered woman and a sympathetic engineer who befriends and shelters her from the authorities. As the completion of his water project nears, she must confront the dark and frenzied horror of her past. Named the most popular film at the Montreal World Film Festival. With Patricia Tulasne and Matthias Habich. "A steamy sexual odyssey" *(Toronto Globe and Mail)*.
VHS: S18407. $39.95.
Lea Pool, Canada, 1991, 100 mins.

September 1939

A Canadian documentary on the Nazi invasion of Poland in September, 1939. Combining Polish newsreels, German propaganda and other rare archival footage, the Blitzkreig (Lightning War) is examined in great detail. Narrated by Frank Willis. See Warsaw reduced to rubble. Canada, 1961, 60 mins.
VHS: S05440. $24.95.

The Silent Enemy

Based on a 72-volume history of New France written by Jesuit missionaries between 1610 and 1791, this magical reconstruction of Ojibwa life tells of the time before white man settled the Hudson Bay region. The "silent enemy" is hunger that threatens the tribe as they desperately track thunderous caribou herds. Boasting an all-Native cast, the film begins with a moving narrative from Chief Yellow Robe: "This is the story of my people ...look not upon us as actors. We are Indians living once more our old life. Soon we will be gone. Your civilization will destroy us. But by your magic we will live forever." Newly restored from the 35mm nitrate original, with a music score by Massard Kur Zhene.
VHS: S16432. $39.95.
Laser: CLV/CAV. **LD72072. $39.95.**
H.P. Carver, Canada/USA, 1930, 87 mins.

The Silent Partner

Elliot Gould, Christopher Plummer and Suzannah York star in this terrifying thriller that pits a mild-mannered bank clerk against an evil and sadistic bank robber. When the former unexpectedly robs the latter, he doesn't realize he's made a psychotic killer very angry, until it's too late. With an early cinematic performance by John Candy.
VHS: S31290. $14.98.
Daryl Duke, Canada, 1978, 105 mins.

Some Letters to a Young Poet

This simple drama of friendship, courtship, solitude and tender beginnings was inspired by the writings of Austrian poet Rainer Maria Rilke. The rugged landscape of British Columbia provides the backdrop for this independent feature about a stonemason who lives the stripped-down lifestyle of a Zen poet and the lives that intersect his own. A very interesting debut feature from director Story.
VHS: S28513. $39.95.
Richard Story, Canada, 1994, 90 mins.

Souvenir

In 1944, a dashing German soldier and a beautiful French girl fall deeply in love. Now, more than 40 years later, Ernst Kestner (Christopher Plummer), retired and recently widowed, leaves his adopted home in New York and returns to France with his headstrong, estranged daughter (Catherine Hicks) and the fleeting hope of finding the love he left behind. But what they encounter in the French countryside is completely unexpected.
VHS: S09493. $79.95.
Geoffrey Reeve, Canada, 1988, 93 mins.

Special of the Day

Two Canadian chefs prepare a special meal together. Through their collaboration and friendship a special atmosphere arises as they express themselves in the kitchen. Ultimately an entire approach to life is revealed through their work. 24 mins.
VHS: S25049. $19.95.

Straight for the Heart

Lea Pool's erotic feature about a cynical photojournalist who returns to Montreal caught in a lurid sex triangle. After he's simultaneously abandoned by his two lovers, he embarks on a dangerous inner voyage, compensating for his loneliness and despair by photographing the streets, architecture and textures of Montreal. He eventually falls into a tentative and eerie friendship with Quentin, a deaf window washer. "A film filled with visual poetry, a compelling drama [that's] stunningly filmed" *(New York Times)*.
VHS: S18408. $39.95.
Lea Pool, Canada, 1988, 92 mins.

Strangers in Good Company

A comedy about eight radically different women in their '70s who are stranded in the Quebec countryside when their bus breaks down. The first feature by the talented documentarian Cynthia Scott, who skillfully depicts these women, a Mohawk, a nonconventional free thinker, a literary lesbian, a nun who's mechanically skilled, and a prodigiously talented blues singer. With Alice Diabo, Constance Garneau, Cissy Meddings and Mary Meigs.
VHS: S16902. $19.95.
Cynthia Scott, Canada, 1990, 101 mins.

Super 8½

Bruce La Bruce is back as a tired porn director with a decided lack of lust. With his career in shambles, a documentary about his former glory days offers him the only respite from his currently bleak and empty life. In this campy send-up of art, porn and rip-offs of classic films, queer icons Vaginal Creme Davis and comic Scott Thompson evoke a world grown weary of intimacy. It's rude and funny.

VHS: S26697. $39.95.
Bruce La Bruce, Canada, 1994, 106 mins.

Tales from the Gimli Hospital

The surreal first feature from Canadian independent Guy Maddin is set in the isolated village of Gimli, Manitoba, at the beginning of the century. Jealousy and madness overtake two men who share a hospital room. In chilling though mocking vignettes, they exchange wild, inventive tales involving pestilence, reckless envy and necrophilia. With Kyle McCullogh, Michael Gottli and Angela Heck.

VHS: S19409. $29.95.
Guy Maddin, Canada, 1987, 72 mins.

Termini Station

Alan King's independent Canadian feature examines the deep emotional bonds between a mother (Colleen Dewhurst) and daughter (the highly accomplished Megan Follows) as they try to cope with family secrets, the father's unexplained death, the mother's alcoholism and the young woman's prostitution. With Gordon Clapp, Debra McGrath, Leon Pownall, Elliott Smith and Norma Dell'Agnese.

VHS: S25970. $19.98.
Allen King, Canada, 1989, 105 mins.

Thirty-Two Short Films About Glenn Gould

In this inventive film, the unique genius of musician Glenn Gould is revealed in a series of dramatic re-enactments, archival footage and film interviews. It rises above the usual biographic movie formulas to capture intimate and revealing details about its elusive subject, who avoided public scrutiny by playing largely in his studio. Colm Feore stars.

VHS: S23677. $19.95.
Laser: LD74759. $34.95.
Francois Girard, Canada, 1993, 94 mins.

Tribute

Heartwarming joy as life-of-the-party Jack Lemmon tries to win back his estranged wife and son. A moving drama which also stars Robbie Benson and Lee Remick.

VHS: S14566. $19.98.
Bob Clark, Canada, 1980, 125 mins.

When Night Is Falling

Two women find one another in this sensitive love story. Camille is a repressed Catholic professor currently involved with a man. Her whole life changes, however, when she meets Petra, an enigmatic performer from a visiting circus. Before long, the two women embark on a romance that startles everyone, including themselves, with an unforseen passion.

VHS: S27541. $89.95.
Laser: LD75925. $39.99.
Patricia Rozema, Canada, 1995, 90 mins.

Who Is Killing the Great Chefs of Europe?

A sharp satire with a self-evident plot, with George Segal and Jacqueline Bisset thrown into the mix as travelers trying to solve the string of murders. With a delicious turn by Robert Morley. Also with Jean-Pierre Cassel, Philippe Noiret and Joss Ackland.

VHS: S17380. $19.98.
Ted Kotcheff, Canada, 1978, 112 mins.

Why Shoot the Teacher?

Bud Cort in a warm, amusing story of life on the Canadian prairie during the Depression. Cort plays a shy, awkward teacher from the city who has taken a job in the aptly named town of Bleke, Saskatchewan. With Samantha Eggar.

VHS: S01456. $29.95.
Silvio Narizzano, Canada, 1980, 101 mins.

Winter People

An acclaimed Canadian film by Ted Kotcheff, starring Kelly McGillis, Kurt Russell and Lloyd Bridges, which focuses on an unwed mother who must make a difficult decision when she falls in love with a stranger who's accidentally killed the father of her child.

VHS: S10901. $19.95.
Ted Kotcheff, Canada, 1989, 109 mins.

Wisecracks

Phyllis Diller, Carol Burnett, Whoopi Goldberg, Jenny Jones and other women comics are featured in this behind-the-scenes look at the gritty world of comedy. Women face a tough audience, one filled with unfair and even bigoted expectations, but somehow these woman manage to break the mold and make people laugh at the same time.

VHS: S24564. $19.95.
Gail Singer, Canada, 1994, 93 mins.

Zero Patience

An outrageous movie musical, this films depicts an imaginary love story between 19th-century Victorian writer and explorer Sir Richard Francis Burton and "Patient Zero", the Canadian flight attendant accused by the media of being the man who brought AIDS to North America.

VHS: S22669. $39.95.
John Greyson, Canada, 1993, 100 mins.

ATOM EGOYAN

The Adjuster

Atom Egoyan's fourth feature deals with his recurrent themes of the omnipresence of video, voyeurism, fractured nuclear families and sexual control and domination. Three stories are intercut: Noah is an insurance adjuster who manipulates and controls the clients who've lost their property; his wife Hera is a government film censor who surreptitiously records the objectionable material on video; and an ex-football player and his twisted wife play out elaborate sexual games on the unsuspecting. With Elias Koteas, Arsinee Khanjian and Maury Chaykin.

VHS: S18458. $19.98.
Atom Egoyan, Canada, 1991, 102 mins.

Calendar

Atom Egoyan directs and appears as a photographer in this disturbingly funny film. The photographer is sent to Armenia to take pictures of historic churches. He takes his wife along as a translator but she is sidelined by the depth of her heritage and the charms of her handsome guide.

VHS: S25992. $24.95.
Atom Egoyan, Armenia/Canada, 1993, 75 mins.

Exotica

Atom Egoyan's most accessible film is also one of his best: an obsessive and dangerous love story set in a seedy Toronto night club. An exotic dancer meets a man strangely obsessed with her, especially when she wears a girl's school uniform. Egoyan's complicated plot reveals layer after layer of lust, perversion, sexual abuse and violence in an original vision of the darker side.

VHS: S26373. $19.95.
Laser: Letterboxed. **LD75077. $39.99.**
Atom Egoyan, Canada, 1995, 103 mins.

Family Viewing

Atom Egoyan's second feature observes a contemporary Canadian family in the crisis mode. Van is upset when he discovers that his childhood movie memories on videotape are being erased to make room for his father's bedroom activities. This prompts him to leave and kidnap his maternal grandmother from the old age home and set up housekeeping in an unused wing of a downtown hotel. A fascinating and very funny study of alienation in a high tech society. With David Hemblen, Aidan Tierney, Gabrielle Rose, Arsinee Khanjian and Selma Kekikian.

VHS: S13268. $19.98.
Atom Egoyan, Canada, 1987, 86 mins.

Next of Kin

Profoundly unhappy with his family life, a young man named Peter (Patrick Tierney) undergoes video therapy with his parents. One day, while at the hospital studying the tapes, he sees the videos of an Armenian family who feel guilty about surrendering their own son, while still an infant, to a foster home. Peter decides to present himself to this family as their long lost son, to finally act out a role different from the one assigned to him in his own life. Filled with haunting images of travel and displacement, *Next of Kin* reveals both a young WASP's response to working class Armenian culture and discourses on the range of roles that life allows us to play.

VHS: S13587. $29.95.
Atom Egoyan, Canada, 1984, 72 mins.

Speaking Parts

A brilliant cinematic jigsaw puzzle. A handsome hotel housekeeper is willing to do anything to advance his film career. Luckily for him, he bears a strong resemblance to a lonely screenwriter's dead brother. A chilly film of obsession, ambition and advances in video technology. With Michael McManus, Arsinee Khanjian.

VHS: S13269. $19.98.
Atom Egoyan, Canada, 1989, 92 mins.

The Sweet Hereafter

Following a tragic schoolbus accident, high-profile lawyer Mitchell Stephens (Ian Holm) descends upon a small town, with promises of retribution and a class-action lawsuit filed on behalf of the community. But as his investigation into the quiet town begins, Stephens uncovers a tangled web of lies, deceit and forbidden desires that mirrors his own troubled personal life. Gradually, we learn that Stephens has his own agenda, and that everyone has secrets to keep.

VHS: S34412. $100.99.
Laser: LD76993. $29.99.
DVD: DV60324. $24.98.
Atom Egoyan, Canada, 1997, 112 mins.

DAVID CRONENBERG

Crash

Fasten your seatbelt (or not!) for Cronenberg's controversial, graphic and unconventional story of a man and woman who, after their cars collide, are lured into a mysterious world of sexually obsessed car crash enthusiasts. Winner of a special prize for originality and "audacity" at the Cannes Film Festival. With David Spader, Holly Hunter, Rosanna Arquette, Elias Koteas and Deborah Kara Unger. "Love it or hate it, David Cronenberg's *Crash* will be a film to live and contend with for a long time" (F.X. Feeney, *LA Weekly*).

VHS: S31676. $19.98.
Laser: Letterboxed. **LD76336. $49.95.**
David Cronenberg, Canada, 1996, 90 mins.

Dead Ringers

David Cronenberg does it again in this psychological horror film starring Jeremy Irons as a pair of disturbed, identical twin gynecologists. A technical and emotional masterpiece that subtly and quite creepily delves into what makes the Mantle brothers tick. With excellent supporting work by Genevieve Bujold. Based loosely on a true story.

VHS: S09841. $19.98.
Laser: LD75933. $124.95.
David Cronenberg, Canada, 1988, 113 mins.

The Dead Zone

Christopher Walken stars in this David Cronenberg film of a Stephen King novel about a man with the ability to read the thoughts of others. This gift is more a curse than a blessing. With Brooke Adams, Tom Skerritt, Herbert Lom and Martin Sheen as a very dangerous political candidate.

VHS: S06130. $19.95.
Laser: LD75359. $29.98.
David Cronenberg, USA, 1983, 104 mins.

The Fly

Cronenberg's *The Fly* is less a remake of the original film than a remake of the original short story about a brilliant scientist who develops a system to transport objects over space and reassemble the molecules in seconds. When an accident fuses his structure with that of a fly, the initial excitement turns to horror as the insect nature begins to exert itself. With an outstanding performance by Jeff Goldblum.

VHS: S02908. $29.98.
Laser: LD70984. $24.98.
David Cronenberg, USA, 1986, 96 mins.

M. Butterfly

Jeremy Irons stars as the French diplomatic functionary seduced by an illusionist from the Beijing Opera. Set in Maoist China and inspired by a true story of espionage, this tale of romance and reversal will surprise even the most jaded viewer. Previously a Broadway hit, the film convincingly portrays the unbelievable facts behind a startling and deceptive facade.

VHS: S20712. $19.98.
Laser: LD72383. $34.98.
David Cronenberg, USA, 1993, 101 mins.

Naked Lunch

David Cronenberg succeeds in filming what many considered unfilmable. He creates a bizarre, drug inspired world based on the once-banned 1959 underground novel by William Burroughs. Peter Weller couldn't be better as a Burroughs-like novelist/junkie who is sent to Interzone on a secret mission by a talking typewriter that transmutes to a roach. With Judy Davis, Julian Sands, Ian Holm and Roy Scheider as Dr. Benway. "A thrilling, astounding, devastating piece of work" (Dave Kehr, *Chicago Tribune*).

VHS: S16382. $94.98.
Laser: LD71581. $39.98.
David Cronenberg, USA, 1991, 117 mins.

Scanners

An explosive tale of mind control and the powers that exist to govern and observe its application. Patrick McGoohan *(The Prisoner)* is the manipulative head of a scientific corporate research facility. His character is called Dr. Ruth. With Stephen Lack and Michael Ironside as the telepathic scanners and Jennifer O'Neill as decoration.

VHS: S06189. $14.98.
David Cronenberg, Canada, 1981, 104 mins.

Shivers

This early, low-budget, "paranoid, prurient sexual nightmare" from kinky horror freak David Cronenberg takes place in a high-rise apartment building where pesky little parasites sneak inside resident's bodies and turn them into sex maniacs. "Horror movies don't come any cooler than *Shivers*…It's a timeless take on sexual terror" (Mick LaSalle, *San Francisco Chronicle*). With Paul Hampton, Joe Silver, Lynn Lowry and Barbara Steele. Special director's cut collector's edition includes never-before-seen interview with Cronenberg.

VHS: S33930. $89.95.
David Cronenberg, Canada, 1975, 89 mins.

Videodrome

Videodrome is a pulsating sci-fi nightmare from macabre master David Cronenberg *(Scanners)* about a world where video can control and alter human life. Featuring a wonderfully sleazy James Woods, and Deborah Harry as a kinky talk-show hostess.
VHS: S01414. $14.98.
David Cronenberg, Canada, 1982, 87 mins.

QUEBECOIS CINEMA

Being at Home with Claude

French-Canadian director Jean Beaudin's film centers on the violent relationship between two radically different men: Yves, a casual thrill seeker and prostitute, and Claude, a writer and student from a socially prominent family. Yves kills Claude in a fit of passion. "The film succeeds in bringing us all to a universal precipice and invites us to peer momentarily into the lonely void of an unimaginable future" *(Toronto Film Festival Program)*. Cinematography by Thomas Vamos. With Roy Dupuis, Jacques Godin, Jean-Francois Pichette and Gaston Lepage. French with English subtitles.
VHS: S19441. $19.98.
Jean Beaudin, Canada, 1991, 85 mins.

Blind Trust

A gripping thriller from French Canada concerning the robbery of an armored car. In the tradition of *The Asphalt Jungle*, a small gang of criminals meticulously plan a major heist. An intelligent and well acted crime story with Marie Tifo, Pierre Curzi, Yvan Ponton and Jean-Louis Millette. English dubbed.
VHS: S05892. $79.98.
Yves Simoneau, Canada, 1986, 86 mins.

Blood of the Hunter

Michael Biehn, Gabriel Arcand and Alexandra Vandernoot star in this icy thriller set in the era of the Canadian frontier. A postman sets off across the wilderness, leaving his wife alone. She soon is trapped by a killer tied mysteriously to her husband. Suspense mounts as the postman's mysterious past slowly unravels and the danger to his wife grows.
VHS: S25564. $92.99.
Gilles Carle, Canada, 1994, 92 mins.

Decline of the American Empire

Denys Arcand's critically acclaimed film of sex talk explores the complex and comic relationships between eight Quebec intellectuals who are brought together for a Sunday dinner. Funny, Quebecois drama that was a huge hit on its home ground, a portrait of the Big Chill generation from the perspective of sex. French with English subtitles.
VHS: S03312. $79.95.
Denys Arcand, Canada, 1986, 101 mins.

In Trouble

Julie LaChapelle plays an unhappy woman who finds herself seduced and abandoned and very pregnant. To explain her condition to her three overprotective brothers she invents an imaginary rapist, whom they locate after a diligent manhunt. This leaves Julie in trouble in more ways than the obvious. With Daniel and Donald Pilon.
VHS: S06166. $59.95.
Gilles Carle, Canada, 1967, 82 mins.

Jesus of Montreal

A charismatic actor is hired to punch up the annual Montreal Passion play and discovers he is beginning to take his work far more seriously than he intended. Lothaire Bluteau is truly inspirational in the title role of this award-winning film by Denys Arcand. With Catherine Wilkening, Johanne-Marie Tremblay, Remy Girard and Yves Jacques. French with English subtitles.
VHS: S13674. $19.98.
Denys Arcand, Canada/France, 1989, 118 mins.

Le Quebec

This documentary offers several views of Quebec, detailing the considerable contrast in daily life, from the frenetic pace of Montreal to the reflective and serene forest world of the rural settings. The images and commentaries are meant to spur class discussions. 55 mins.
English Narration.
VHS: S19778. $35.00.
French Narration.
VHS: S19777. $35.00.

Leolo

A French-Canadian coming-of-age film about a boy convinced he was fathered by a tomato. This strange premise sets the mood for a darkly comic fantasy/nightmare with mystical and sexual overtones. French with English subtitles.
VHS: S20579. $19.95.
Laser: LD74454. $49.99.
Jean-Claude Lauzon, Canada, 1992, 107 mins.

Love and Human Remains

Thomas Gibson and Mia Kirshner are at the center of this dazzling and twisted thriller. David and Candy were lovers; now they're roommates in search of thrills. Their restless and relentless hunt for new excitement eventually leads them into dangerous waters. Without limits, someone is bound to get hurt. With Matthew Ferguson and Ruth Marshall.
VHS: S26954. $19.95.
Laser: LD75427. $34.95.
Denys Arcand, Canada, 1993, 100 mins.

Mon Oncle Antoine

Director Claude Jutra's acclaimed, sensitive, breakthrough film of a young boy coming of age in the Canadian backwoods swept the Canadian Academy Awards. Young Benoit slowly becomes aware of the affinities between love, life and death as he works as a stock boy in his uncle Antoine's general store. Since Antoine serves as everything from notary to shopkeeper to undertaker, it is no wonder that Benoit learns about life quickly. French with English subtitles.
VHS: S12954. $39.95.
Claude Jutra, Canada, 1971, 104 mins.

Night Zoo

A French-Canadian crime thriller that won 13 Genie Awards, the equivalent of the U.S. Oscar. Set in Montreal, an ex-con returns to the free world to find his father is dying, his girlfriend is a little crazy and a couple of crooked cops are after the money he has hidden away. Brutal and sensitive. With Gilles Maheu, Roger Le Bel and Lynne Adams. The debut film of Jean-Claude Lauzon.
VHS: S07964. $19.95.
Jean-Claude Lauzon, Canada, 1987, 116 mins.

Paper Wedding

This emotionally honest and fiercely intelligent Canadian drama is the movie that *Green Card* should have been. Genevieve Bujold gives one of her best performances as a disillusioned single woman who agrees to marry, in name only, a Chilean political refugee to prevent his deportation. Chilean born actor Manuel Arranguiz is perfectly cast as the grateful husband. The relationship takes an unexpected turn when Canadian immigration officials take an active interest in the case. Shot on location in Quebec. With Dorothe Berryman, Gilbert Sicotte, Jean Mathieu, Monique Lepage and Teo Spychalski as Bujold's married former lover Milosh.
VHS: S15683. $79.95.
Laser: LD71487. $39.95.
Michel Brault, Canada, 1990, 90 mins.

The Sex of the Stars

This charming and lovely film recounts the painful growth experienced by a French Canadian family impacted by divorce and transsexualism. A 12-year-old girl seeks solace in star gazing when her parents divorce and her father becomes a woman. Though the girl tries to recreate the past she finds that her future lies in reconciliation. French with English subtitles.
VHS: S25035. $59.95.
Paule Baillargeon, Canada, 1994, 104 mins.

AMERICAN film

recent american cinema

12 Angry Men

As tempers rise and tensions mount, 12 jurors wrestle with the facts and each other in this powerful courtoom drama boasting a sensational cast including Courtney B. Vance, Ossie Davis, George C. Scott, Armin Mueller-Stahl, Dorian Harewood, James Gandolfini, Tony Danza, Jack Lemmon, Hume Cronyn, Mykelti Williamson, Edward James Olmos, William Peterson and Mary McDonnell.

VHS: S33749. $59.99.
Laser: LD76990. $29.99.
William Friedkin, USA, 1997, 96 mins.

1492: Conquest of Paradise

Ridley Scott's film is considered the definitive historical account of Christopher Columbus' voyages to North America. The film considers Columbus' legacy of colonialism, racism and genocide in the New World. Columbus (French actor Gerard Depardieu) is presented as a visionary scientist with boundless ambitions. With Armand Assante and Sigourney Weaver. Music by Vangelis. The film is letterboxed.

VHS: S18748. $29.95.
Ridley Scott, USA, 1992, 142 mins.

187

Fifteen months after being stabbed by one of his students in a Bed-Stuy high school, Trevor Garfield (Samuel L. Jackson) moves from New York to Los Angeles to work as a substitute teacher. There, a predatory high school student is found murdered. Was it a gang hit? An act of sudden rage? Or did this once-idealistic teacher finally snap? The tension hits home in this unflinching tale of when dangerous minds turn deadly. Written by former teacher Scott Yageman.

VHS: S32662. $19.98.
Laser: LD76418. $34.98.
Kevin Reynolds, USA, 1997, 199 mins.

9½ Weeks

Mickey Rourke as an advertising man and Kim Basinger as art gallery employee star in a saga of a sexually obsessive relationship with a decided edge toward light sado-masochism. Video contains scenes which are more explicit than the theatrical release.

VHS: S05868. $19.95.
Laser: Letterboxed. **LD72335. $34.98.**
DVD: DV60280. $24.98.
Adrian Lyne, USA, 1986, 117 mins.

"About Last Night..."

Loosely based on the one-act play by David Mamet, "Sexual Perversity in Chicago," Edward Zwick's film is less a quest for cultural identity than individual choice. Rob Lowe and Demi Moore's apparently innocent liaison becomes a love affair shuttered by convenience and necessity. The film's real power emerges in the performances of Chicagoans James Belushi and Elizabeth Perkins, whose hard-edged cynicism questions the durability of the affair. Co-written by Second City alumnus Tim Kazurinski.

VHS: S02512. $14.95.
Laser: LD75808. $34.95.
Edward Zwick, USA, 1986, 113 mins.

Absence of Malice

Sally Field plays a Miami journalist who writes a story that maligns an innocent man. Paul Newman is the injured party. An intriguing study into the power and privileges of the press written by former reporter Kurt Luedtke. Filmed on location. Strong supporting cast includes Barry Primus, Melinda Dillon, Bob Balaban, Josef Sommer and Wilford Brimley.

VHS: S10373. $19.95.
DVD: DV60239. $24.95.
Sydney Pollack, USA, 1981, 116 mins.

The Accidental Tourist

William Hurt is a travel writer who hates to travel. He also isn't willing to open himself up to what life has to offer until he splits with his wife Kathleen Turner and starts seeing a kookie dog trainer played by Geena Davis. Davis won an Oscar for her performance as Muriel in this film adaptation of the novel by Anne Tyler. Film was also nominated as Best Picture. With Amy Wright and Ed Begley Jr.

VHS: S09412. $19.98.
Laser: LD70495. $29.98.
Lawrence Kasdan, USA, 1988, 125 mins.

The Accused

A stern public prosecutor (Kelly McGillis) takes on a gang-rape case and tries to go simply by the book. But the victim, played powerfully by Jodie Foster (in a performance that earned her an Academy Award), refuses to make things easy, requiring full retribution for what she has suffered. Eventually, they begin to trust one another, and work together to put those responsible behind bars. Based on a notorious real-life case.

VHS: S13708. $19.95.
Laser: LD75116. $24.98.
Jonathan Kaplan, USA, 1988, 110 mins.

The Affair

A black G.I. in England during World War II becomes involved with a confused and lonely married woman. Their affair leads to tragedy when her husband discovers them in the act of love. Now this woman must decide if she can betray everything she has known for a young man from across the ocean. Courtney B. Vance, Ned Beatty and Kerry Fox *(An Angel at My Table, Friends)* are featured.

VHS: S27150. $19.95.
Paul Seed, USA/Great Britain, 1995, 104 mins.

After the Promise

Mark Harmon stars as an uneducated laborer who loses his four sons to the courts and state authority after his wife dies. Diana Scarwid plays his second wife, who assists him in his struggle to reunite his family. A study in courage and bureaucracy. With Rosemary Dunsmore and Donnelly Rhodes as Dr. Northfield.

VHS: S10618. $19.95.
David Greene, USA, 1987, 93 mins.

Afterburn

An excellent made-for-cable movie stars Laura Dern as the widow of a young fighter pilot who charges the Air Force with initiating a cover up when her husband's plane crashes in Korea, and claims his death was caused by "pilot error." With the help of a craggy, crusading attorney (Robert Loggia), she takes on the military establishment to resurrect her husband's reputation. Based on a true story. With Vincent Spano and Michael Rooker. Music by former Police member Stewart Copeland.

VHS: S17034. $19.98.
Laser: LD75117. $24.98.
Robert Markowitz, USA, 1992, 103 mins.

Against All Odds

Taylor Hackford's stylish remake of the film noir classic *Out of the Past* stars Jeff Bridges as a former football player sent to a remote Caribbean island to locate the daughter (Rachel Ward) of the team's owner. Ward is enserfed to a sleazy gambler/businessman (James Woods, in a great performance) who's also Bridges' closest friend. A solid cast includes a sinister Richard Widmark, Saul Rubinek and Jane Greer (the female lead in *Past*) as Ward's mother. Solid title track from Genesis' Phil Collins.

VHS: S022922. $14.98.
Taylor Hackford, USA, 1984, 122 mins.

Against the Wall

Attica is infamous for being the site of a prison uprising where guards were held hostage. While the nation watched, a gripping and deadly drama unfolded, revealing a savage institution that pushed men to the edge. This thriller tells the story of that place and time. Starring Kyle MacLachlan and Samuel L. Jackson, with Harry Dean Stanton.

VHS: S21741. $19.98.
Laser: LD75141. $34.98.
John Frankenheimer, USA, 1993, 115 mins.

Air Force One

Harrison Ford stars as U.S. President James Marshall, a Vietnam vet who finds himself using his military training to outwit crazed Russian neo-nationalist terrorist Korshunov (Gary Oldman) after he hijacks Air Force One. With Glenn Close, Dean Stockwell, William Macy and Philip Baker Hall. VHS letterboxed.

VHS: S32746. $24.95.
Laser: LD76420. $39.98.
DVD: DV60139. $24.95.
Wolfgang Petersen, USA, 1997, 124 mins.

An Alan Smithee Film: Burn Hollywood Burn

Eric Idle stars as fledgling director Alan Smithee, who comes to Hollywood to make a movie with Sylvester Stallone, Whoopi Goldberg and Jackie Chan (all in cameos as themselves). He soon realizes he has no creative control and is merely a puppet in the hands of the studio execs. When the movie turns into a monster, he wants to disown it and have his name disguised by a pseudonym in the credits. The only problem is that the Director's Guild requires that if a director disowns a movie, he must use the official pseudonym of...Alan Smithee. Written by Joe Eszterhas, the mockumentary is ironic in that its director, Arthur Hiller, hated the film's editing so much that he found himself in an "Alan Smithee" situation. With Ryan O'Neal, Coolio and Chuck D.

VHS: S34930. $103.99.
Laser: LD77006. $39.99.
Alan Smithee (Arthur Hiller), USA, 1997, 86 mins.

Alaska

In this "*Cliffhanger* for kids" *(Premier)* two teens (Thora Birch, *Now and Then*, and Vincent Kartheiser, *The Indian in the Closet*) set out to find their father (Dirk Benedict) after his plane crashes in the Alaskan mountains. Along the way they rescue a friendly polar bear cub from a poacher (Charlton Heston) and challenge both nature and themselves on a death-defying mission through the arctic wilderness, in this "lavish outdoor adventure that families will love" (Jeffrey Lyons, Lyons Den Radio).

VHS: S30597. $22.99.
Laser: LD76074. $34.95.
Fraser C. Heston, USA, 1996, 109 mins.

Albino Alligator

Kevin Spacey's directorial debut. After a robbery goes wrong, a gang of criminals take everyone in a local bar hostage. With nowhere to run and time running out, it's a deadly situation where every second counts. With Matt Dillon, Faye Dunaway and Gary Sinise.

VHS: S31530. $103.99.
Laser: LD76259. $39.99.
Kevin Spacey, USA, 1997, 94 mins.

Alex in Wonderland

Paul Mazursky's second feature is a surreal merging of Fellini's *8½* and Jim McBride's *David Holtzman's Diary*. The film is an ironic piece about the travails of a young filmmaker (Donald Sutherland) caught in the grip of burnout and artistic frustration. Ellen Burstyn plays Sutherland's long-suffering wife. With Viola Spolin and Jeanne Moreau. Fellini appears briefly.

VHS: S19496. $19.98.
Paul Mazursky, USA, 1970, 110 mins.

Alice in Wonderland

An all-star adaptation of Lewis Carroll's enchanting tale. Cinematography by Fred J. Koenenkamp. Special visual effects by John Dykstra. With Red Buttons, Anthony Newley, Ringo Starr, Telly Savalas, Robert Morley, Sammy Davis Jr., Steve Allen, Steve Lawrence and Edie Gorme.

VHS: S18999. $19.98.
Harry Harris, USA, 1985, 90 mins.

Alice in Wonderland Set

A two-video package containing *Alice in Wonderland* and *Alice Through the Looking Glass*.

VHS: S19001. $29.98.
Harry Harris, USA, 1985, 180 mins.

Alice Through the Looking Glass

A continuation of the theme of *Alice in Wonderland* in a fantasia about life on the reverse side of the mirror, where the plucky, indomitable Alice must stay away from the Jabberwocky. In her quest to return home, Alice runs into a host of eccentric and frightening figures. It's a visually extravagant, feverish ride of fancy and delight. With Ringo Starr, Sally Struthers, Jack Warden, Jonathan Winters, Steve Lawrence, Karl Malden, Beau Bridges and Lloyd Bridges.

VHS: S19000. $19.98.
Harry Harris, USA, 1985, 90 mins.

Alice, Sweet Alice

Brooke Shields makes her film debut in this thriller as a sweet 12-year-old girl suspected of killing her young sister minutes before she will receive her first holy communion. "Sole has a nice touch for the macabre—and there are some splendidly chilling scenes" (Roger Ebert).

VHS: S31678. $14.98.
Alfred Sole, USA, 1976, 111 mins.

Alien Nation
A few hundred thousand aliens from another planet are the Earth's new minority group. One of their members (Mandy Patinkin) is teamed with a hardboiled, jaded and bigoted cop (James Caan) to help him solve an important case. An entertaining twist on the cop/buddy movie.
VHS: S22657. $19.95.
Robert Cooney, USA, 1979, 28 mins.

Alien Resurrection
Sigourney Weaver is back as Ellen Ripley, who died 200 years ago but is brought back by a renegade team of military scientists who hope to breed the ultimate killing machine with the alien queen inside Ripley. With Winona Ryder. Contains bonus behind-the-scenes footage and interviews with Weaver, Ryder and Ron Perlman. VHS letterboxed.
VHS: S33696. $106.99.
Laser: LD76779. $39.98.
Jean-Pierre Jeunet, USA, 1997, 108 mins.

All Quiet on the Western Front
A television adaptation of Erich Maria Remarque's novel about a group of German soldiers engaged in trench warfare during World War I (first made by Lewis Milestone in 1930). Ernest Borgnine is the determined career soldier responsible for shaping them into fighting men. With Richard Thomas, Patricia Neal, Ian Holm and Donald Pleasance. Contains newly restored footage.
VHS: S07774. $19.95.
Delbert Mann, USA, 1979, 105 mins.

All the President's Men
Superb adaptation of the Woodward-Bernstein book about the events leading to the resignation of Richard Nixon. Quality performances by Dustin Hoffman, Robert Redford and Jason Robards, with Jane Alexander, Martin Balsam, Jack Warden.
VHS: S03362. $19.98.
Alan J. Pakula, USA, 1976, 139 mins.

Always
Critically acclaimed look at marriage, written, directed and featuring Henry Jaglom, about his failed marriage on screen and in real life with ex-wife and co-star Patrice Townsend.
Laser: LD70012. $39.98.
Henry Jaglom, USA, 1985, 105 mins.

American Buffalo
In this edgy, electrifying story by Pulitzer Prize-winning writer David Mamet, two-time Emmy Award-winner Dennis Franz stars as a down-and-out junk dealer who discovers that the rare, buffalo head nickel he sold for $90 is worth ten times as much. He enlists a young protege (Sean Nelson, *Fresh*) in a scheme to steal the coin back. But their plans are altered by the intrusion of an aggressive would-be-thief (two-time Oscar-winner Dustin Hoffman) who badgers the junk dealer into cutting him in on the heist. Mamet's screenplay is the "groundbreaking forerunner to the genre that reached its pinnacle with *Pulp Fiction*" (Stephen Holden, *New York Times*).
VHS: S30769. $14.95.
Laser: LD76108. $39.99.
Michael Corrente, USA, 1996, 87 mins.

American Fabulous
A highly regarded, independent work about the strange and hypnotic odyssey of its young hero. A nomadic, itinerant writer reflects on his midwestern origins and his travels from New York to Los Angeles. It's a "tour of a wild, low-life gay existence [that's] captivating, hilarious, yet touching. Jeffrey Strouth displays a wit that might conceivably amuse Oscar Wilde" (Kevin Thomas, *Los Angeles Times*).
VHS: S18413. $29.95.
Reno Dakota, USA, 1992, 105 mins.

American Gigolo
International model Lauren Hutton plays the dutiful, decent wife of a state senator with whom Julian (Richard Gere) falls in love. But when a murder is committed and missing jewels are placed in his car, someone is trying to frame him. The film which made a star of Richard Gere.
VHS: S10017. $14.95.
Laser: LD75360. $29.98.
Paul Schrader, USA, 1980, 117 mins.

American Graffiti
A new American classic, which single-handedly started the 60's nostalgia craze. A coming-of-age film that details the lives of several high school teenagers the summer after graduation. Launched the careers of Richard Dreyfuss, Harrison Ford and Suzanne Sommers and established George Lucas as an important new American filmmaker. A perceptive, sweet look at a more innocent time.
VHS: S00044. $14.95.
Laser: LD70013. $34.98.
George Lucas, USA, 1973, 112 mins.

American Me
Edward James Olmos' directorial debut is an ambitious attempt to convey the social, political and personal history of the Mexican Mafia, captured in the expansive life of a ruthless crime lord (Olmos) from his extensive prison stay to his power and influence in the Southwestern Hispanic barrios. It's a well-made, grim and fatalistic account about the allure of crime and the building of community and culture. With William Forsythe, Pepe Serna and Danny De La Paz.
VHS: S18500. $19.98.
Edward James Olmos, USA, 1992, 126 mins.

The American President
Michael Douglas and Annette Bening star in this winning romance set in the White House. President Andrew Shepard (Douglas) is the most popular President in decades. A widower, he is devoted to his daughter, as well as to gun control. Sydney Ellen Wade (Bening) is an environmental lobbyist who can hardly believe her luck when she realizes she is being courted by the number one lobbyist target inside the beltway. Soon, word leaks out and the couple find themselves in the center of a media feeding frenzy where the only thing standing between them and happiness is the approval of the American public. Martin Sheen and Michael J. Fox are featured. VHS letterboxed.
VHS: S27598. $19.95.
Laser: LD75533. $34.95.
Rob Reiner, USA, 1995, 114 mins.

An American Story
Five WWII vets, led by their former commanding officer (Brad Johnson), attempt to unseat a corrupt mayor and brutal sheriff and restore law and order to their Texas home town, but meet with resistance from those who wish to preserve the status quo. With Kathleen Quinlan and Tom Sizemore.
VHS: S31179. $14.98.
John Gray, USA, 1992, 97 mins.

An American Werewolf in Paris
A trio of young American tourists in Paris stop Serafine (Julie Delpy) from jumping off the Eiffel Tower. It turns out that Serafine, the daughter of the werewolf from *An American Werewolf in London* is involved in a secret society which uses a drug enabling its members to change into a werewolf at any time. With Tom Everett Scott (*That Thing You Do*).
VHS: S33950. $103.99.
Laser: LD76831. $39.99.
Anthony Miller, USA/Great Britain/Netherlands/Luxembourg/France, 1997, 98 mins.

Amongst Friends
The debut film of Rob Weiss charts the complicated relationships of three Jewish friends growing up in the affluent Five Towns section of Long Island, where, as the narrator notes, judges and wiseguys are neighbors. The film is about affluent kids who reject their privileged backgrounds and drift into drugs, graft and robbery. The action follows what happens when one of the friends, following a prison sentence, returns to his neighborhood to discover his friends are beholden to a local gangster. His girlfriend (Mira Sorvino) has patiently awaited his return. With Steve Parlavecchio, Joseph Lindsey and Patrick McGaw.
Laser: LD72427. $39.99.
Rob Weiss, USA, 1993, 90 mins.

Anastasia: The Mystery of Anna
Amy Irving stars in this TV-movie about the search for a living Romanov heir. Is Anna Anderson really the daughter of Czar Nicolas II or just an incredibly gifted pretender to the throne? Winner of two Emmy Awards and two Golden Globes. The international cast includes Omar Sharif, Olivia de Havilland, Rex Harrison, Claire Bloom, Edward Fox, Elke Sommer and Susan Lucci. Script by Oscar winner James Goldman (*A Lion In Winter*) is based on the Peter Knuth book *Anastasia: The Riddle of Anna Anderson*.
Laser: LD74639. $49.99.
Marvin J. Chomsky, USA, 1986, 200 mins.

And God Created Woman
Rebecca De Mornay stars in Roger Vadim's remake of his own classic tale of the dangers of being born beautiful. Echoing faintly the Bardot version, Vadim transplanted his story to the American Southwest where a sexy ex-con vixen causes trouble for her carpenter husband and her politician lover. With Victor Spano.
VHS: S06864. $14.98.
Roger Vadim, USA, 1988, 98 mins.

Andersonville
Andersonville was the site of a confederate prison for 30,000 union soldiers. This film captures the horrors of this place, where disease, overcrowding, starvation and violence took their toll on demoralized veterans. Friendship became the key to survival for these men.
VHS: S29475. $19.98.
Laser: LD75822. $59.98.
John Frankenheimer, USA, 1996, 168 mins.

Angel City
This powerful piece about social protest and worker exploitation follows the difficulties of migrant workers who are trapped in Angel City, a labor camp where kidnapping and extortion are used to coerce workers. Adapted from the book by Patricia Smith. With Paul Winfield, Jennifer Jason Leigh and Ralph Waite.
VHS: S18812. $19.95.
Philip Leacock, USA, 1980, 100 mins.

Angel Heart
Exotic journey into voodoo, cults, sex and death. A journey of violence and darkness that moves from the streets of New York to the swamps of Louisiana featuring Mickey Rourke, Lisa Bonet, Robert de Niro and Charlotte Rampling.
VHS: S04382. $14.95.
Alan Parker, USA, 1987, 112 mins.

Anguish
Zelda Rubinstein, the diminutive psychic of *Poltergeist I, II & III*, plays the concerned mother of a disturbed serial killer who removes the eyes of his victims. Michael Lerner is the murderer and Talia Paul, Angel Jove, Cala Pastor and Isabel Garcia-Lorca are some of his potential victims.
VHS: S07098. $79.98.
Bigas Luna, USA, 1988, 89 mins.

Anna Karenina
A recent version of the great Tolstoy novel with Jacqueline Bisset playing Anna, the married wife who sacrifices all for forbidden love. With Christopher Reeve as Count Vronsky and Paul Scofield as Anna's husband, Karenin.
VHS: S12417. $14.95.
Simon Langton, USA, 1985, 96 mins.

Anna Karenina
Tolstoy's classic story of a woman of wealth and privilege (Sophie Marceau, *Braveheart*) whose love for a soldier (Sean Bean, *Goldeneye*) causes scandal and tragedy. Filmed entirely in Russia and scored with the music of Tchaikovsky, Rachmaninoff and Prokofiev performed the St. Petersburg Philharmonic Orchestra conducted by Grammy Award winner Sir Georg Solti. "A pulsating update of the classic love story" (Dr. Joy Browne, WOR-Radio/New York).
VHS: S31728. $19.98.
Laser: LD76295. $34.99.
Bernard Rose, USA, 1996, 108 mins.

Annie O
Fifteen-year-old Annie is the first girl to play on her high school basketball team. Annie is an excellent player (the title of the film comes from her nickname, "Sure Shot Annie", a takeoff on Annie Oakley), rumored to never miss a shot. Annie is elated to be asked to join the varsity team, but her joy is quickly overshadowed by the jealousy her success inspires among her male team players, her brother, her friends, and even her boyfriend. In the end, Annie discovers who her real friends are and learns the power of believing in yourself. With Coco Yares, Chad Willett and Rob Stewart.
VHS: S27303. $19.98.
Laser: LD75476. $39.99.
J. Michael McClary, USA, 1995, 93 mins.

Another 48 Hours
After seven years, Eddie Murphy is released from jail in order to help San Francisco cop Nick Nolte solve a case and to save himself from a manslaughter charge. Lots of action in this sequel that also stars Brion James and Kevin Tighe.
VHS: S21476. $19.95.
Walter Hill, USA, 1990, 96 mins.

Any Wednesday
Jane Fonda is the mistress of Jason Robards and she isn't happy about turning 30 without a band of gold on her finger. She spends a lot of time getting hysterical and all teary in an apartment where the closets are filled with balloons. With Dean Jones and Rosemary Murphy. From the stage play.
VHS: S06101. $19.98.
Robert Ellis Miller, USA, 1966, 109 mins.

Any Which Way You Can
Clint Eastwood stars in this sequel to *Every Which Way But Loose*, about the comic adventures, fights and romantic pursuits of a Los Angeles trucker who inherits an orangutan. Nominally directed by Eastwood, though actual credit is given to his former stunt advisor, Buddy Van Horn. With Ruth Gordon, Sondra Locke, Geoffrey Lewis, and William Smith.
Laser: LD70505. $29.98.
Buddy Van Horn, USA, 1980, 116 mins.

Apartment Zero
A marvelously creepy and involved study of interpersonal relationships and murder in Buenos Aires. Colin Firth stars as a jittery, movie-mad proprietor of a failing art house cinema who is forced to take in a boarder to meet expenses. With Hart Bochner as Jack, the handsome American who is looking for a quiet room while the rest of the city is looking for a killer. Often grimly funny in its Hitchcockian tone and style.
VHS: S11690. $19.98.
Martin Donovan, USA, 1988, 124 mins.

Apollo 13
Tom Hanks, Kevin Bacon, Gary Sinise, Ed Harris and Bill Paxton are just some of the big stars featured in this entertaining but restrained film which examines the declining fortunes of America's space program. Just as everything about outer space appears to be routine, an unforseen accident rivets the entire planet's attention on the actions of three men. Based on actual events, it builds tension with great precision and power.
VHS letterboxed.
VHS: S26693. $22.98.
Laser: LD75111. $44.98.
Ron Howard, USA, 1995, 140 mins.

Appointment with Death
A posh 1973 tour of the Holy Land turns murderous when a malicious and wealthy dowager is mysteriously poisoned. Each of her fellow high-living tourists had the means to kill her-and a motive. Peter Ustinov stars as Hercule Poirot in this Agatha Christie whodunit. With Lauren Bacall, Carrie Fisher, John Gielgud, Piper Laurie, Hayley Mills.
VHS: S07775. $19.98.
Laser: LD74699. $34.98.
Michael Winner, USA, 1988, 103 mins.

April Morning
Howard Fast's novel is adapted for film in this gripping drama about the causes of the American Revolution. A New England farming family and their friends experience the tyranny of British rule until they finally revolt against the redcoats quartered in their midst.
VHS: S26512. $9.98.
Delbert Mann, USA, 1988, 99 mins.

Arctic Blue
Rutger Hauer stars as a viscious killer in this action-packed drama set in the Alaskan wilderness. A plane crash lands, forcing both a lawman (Dylan Walsh) and the accused killer whom he is accompanying to fight for survival together. The elements are fierce, but the adversarial relationship between these men is even more destructive.
VHS: S26208. $96.98.
Laser: LD75039. $34.95.
Peter Masterson, USA, 1995, 95 mins.

Around the World in 80 Days
Pierce Brosnan stars as Victorian gentleman Phileas Fogg, the man who bet his entire fortune that he could travel around the world in 80 days in this "star-studded, grand-scale entertainment extravaganza" mini-series based on the Jules Verne classic. With Eric Idle, Peter Ustinov, Julia Nickson, Jack Klugman, Lee Remick, John Hillerman, Darren McGavin, Jill St. John, Roddy McDowall, James B. Sikking, Pernell Roberts, Henry Gibson, Robert Morley, Simon Ward, Stephen Nichols, Patrick MacNee, and Christopher Lee. Two cassettes.
VHS: S34460. $29.95.
Buzz Kulik, USA, 1989, 270 mins.

Ash Wednesday
Elizabeth Taylor and Henry Fonda star in this film about an aging beauty who tries to rejuvenate her life by changing her looks through plastic surgery.
VHS: S13781. $19.95.
Larry Peerce, USA, 1973, 99 mins.

Assault at West Point
Sam Waterston, Samuel L. Jackson and John Glover star in this costume drama about racial exclusion at the nation's most prestigious military academy. It's a powerful and insightful look at the traditions which still shape our institutions.
VHS: S21141. $92.98.
Harry Moses, USA, 1993, 98 mins.

Assault on Precinct 13
John Carpenter's early, and arguably his best film: a tense police drama in which a nearly deserted police station is under siege by a violent street gang. An early urban horror film, notable for its atmosphere and unrelenting tension. Letterboxed.
VHS: S09611. $29.95.
Laser: LD74530. $39.99.
John Carpenter, USA, 1976, 90 mins.

The Assignment
For 20 years, Carlos the Jackal led a reign of terror so brutal, his capture was an international obsession. The world's deadliest terrorist and a devoted family man have nothing in common—except the mirror's reflection. With Aidan Quinn, Donald Sutherland and Ben Kingsley.
VHS: S33399. $83.99.
Laser: LD76764. $34.95.
DVD: DV60236. $24.95.
Christian Duguay, USA, 1997, 119 mins.

At Play in the Fields of The Lord
A cautionary epic adventure filmed on location in the rainforest jungles of Brazil. This exquisitely photographed drama about tests of faith and cultural interference puts the fate of an entire native Indian tribe in the hands of a few American missionaries. Tom Berenger stars as a Cheyenne-American mercenary who decides to join the isolated tribe he has been ordered to destroy. With John Lithgow, Aidan Quinn, Kathy Bates, Daryl Hannah and Tom Waits. Based on the novel by Peter Matthiessen.
VHS: S16033. $14.98.
Laser: LD70291. $44.98.
Hector Babenco, USA, 1991, 186 mins.

Attic
Ray Milland and Carrie Snodgrass star in this superior thriller about a sheltered spinster who revolts against her father, kills him, and escapes to the attic where the door slams shut and she is locked in the attic forever.
VHS: S08025. $14.98.
George Edwards, USA, 1979, 97 mins.

Avalanche Express
Lee Marvin, Maximilian Schell, Robert Shaw and Linda Evans star in this spy thriller in which the terrors of biological warfare underlie every move. A scientist is lured away to a train ride and his death. All bets are off when the snow begins to fall and these characters find themselves trapped.
VHS: S22509. $19.98.
Mark Robson, USA, 1979, 89 mins.

Avalon
Filmmaker Barry Levinson returns to his home town of Baltimore to tell the fictionalized story of how his family came to America and settled in a section of the city known as Avalon. This multigenerational, episodic drama features strong performances by Armin Mueller-Stahl, Aidan Quinn, Elizabeth Perkins, Joan Plowright and Lou Jacobi as the brother who was gravely insulted when the family didn't wait to cut the Thanksgiving turkey. An affectionate salute to the American immigrant.
VHS: S13754. $19.95.
Barry Levinson, USA, 1990, 126 mins.

Avenging Angel
Sequel to *Angel* starring Betsy Russell as a teenage ex-prostitute now in college working as an undercover cop.
VHS: S03909. $19.95.
Robert Vincent O'Neil, USA, 1985, 93 mins.

Awakenings
The title gives away a few major developments but this Penny Marshall drama still holds a few surprises. Robin Williams stars as a dedicated but painfully reserved research doctor who uncovers a radical form of treatment for a small group of comatose post-encephalitic patients which includes Robert De Niro. Based on the non-fiction account by Dr. Oliver Sacks. With John Heard and Julie Kavner.
VHS: S14479. $19.95.
Laser: LD75528. $39.95.
DVD: DV60029. $24.95.
Penny Marshall, USA, 1990, 121 mins.

The Babe
Arthur Hiller's biography of Babe Ruth chronicles his rise from a Baltimore orphanage, his herculean exploits, his aggressively, child-like behavior, his two radically different marriages, and his sudden flameout as a ballplayer who never realized his dream to manage the Yankees. John Goodman plays the Sultan of Swat, with Kelly McGillis, Trini Alvarado, and Bruce Boxleitner. Written by John Fusco *(Crossroads, Thunderheart)* with cinematography by Haskell Wexler.
VHS: S17340. $14.95.
Laser: LD71672. $34.98.
Arthur Hiller, USA, 1992, 115 mins.

Babyfever
Gina (Victoria Foyt) questions the merits of her current safe and secure boyfriend when her dynamic ex returns with an interesting proposition. Thinking she could be pregnant, Gina attends the baby shower of a friend where the women present debate the pros and cons of love, relationships and parenthood in the 1990s.
VHS: S27626. $19.98.
Henry Jaglom, USA, 1995, 110 mins.

The Bachelor
A drama about a shy physician forced to re-examine his life and values in the aftermath of a family tragedy, who opens himself up to new experiences that crystallize in his first significant relationship. With Miranda Richardson, Keith Carradine, Kristin Scott-Thomas, Sarah-Jane Fenton and Max von Sydow. Cinematography by Giuseppe Rotunno. Music by Ennio Morricone.
VHS: S18894. $89.95.
Roberto Faenza, USA/Great Britain, 1992, 105 mins.

Back in the USSR
A romantic glasnost thriller filmed on many locations in Moscow that are not usually featured on the standard Intourist Bus route. Frank Whaley stars as Archer, a naive American tourist who becomes involved with the Russian criminal underworld through his relationship with Natalya Negoda, the personable star of *Little Vera*. Director Roman Polanski plays Kurilov, the villainous owner of a seedy Soviet nightclub. With Dey Young, Andrew Divof and Brian Blessed as Chazon.
VHS: S16715. $94.98.
Deran Sarafian, USA/USSR, 1991, 89 mins.

Backdraft
This widescreen edition of Ron Howard's 1991 drama about Chicago firefighters preserves the correct aspect ratio of Mikael Solomon's images. Two brothers (Kurt Russell, William Baldwin) must deal with the psychological fallout of their father's death and deal with the women in their lives (Rebecca De Mornay and Jennifer Jason Leigh). Robert De Niro co-stars as a fire inspector tracking down a vicious arsonist. Some wonderful visual effects from George Lucas's Industrial Light and Magic (ILM). With Scott Glenn, Jason Gedrick, and J.T. Walsh. Letterboxed.
VHS: S17438. $19.98.
Laser: LD71580. $39.98.
DVD: DV60144. $24.98.
Ron Howard, USA, 1991, 135 mins.

Backtrack
When murder is your business, don't fall in love with your work. Milo (Hopper) is an eccentric mob hitman who becomes romantically obsessed with his latest assignment. Jodie Foster is Anne Benton, a successful modern artist who suddenly leaves L.A. for a new life after she witnesses a gangland murder. Some of the other familiar faces in this decidedly offbeat road movie romance include Dean Stockwell, John Turturro, Joe Pesci, Charlie Sheen, Vincent Price and Fred Ward. This is the director's cut and should not be confused with the botched studio version, which Hopper disowns.
VHS: S15693. $19.98.
Dennis Hopper, USA, 1991, 102 mins.

Bad Boys
Sean Penn stars as a Chicago kid in trouble who finds that life in a juvenile detention facility is even harder than life on the streets. His Hispanic arch enemy (Esai Morales) adds more tension to an already unpleasant situation. With Reni Santoni, Ally Sheedy and Eric Gurry.
VHS: S05396. $19.95.
Rick Rosenthal, USA, 1983, 123 mins.

Bad Company
Laurence Fishburne is a CIA operative who must contend with the seductive Ellen Barkin. In this political thriller, Fishburne goes undercover to infiltrate an industrial espionage group. Soon he is confounded by a deadly mix of passion, intrigue and murder.
VHS: S25634. $19.95.
Laser: LD75014. $39.99.
Damian Harris, USA, 1994, 108 mins.

Badlands
Martin Sheen and Sissy Spacek star in a story based on the 1950's murder spree across the Midwestern plains by Charlie Starkweather and his 15-year-old girlfriend, Carol Fugate. A chilling insight into the cold-hearted mind of the sociopath in one of the most stunning directorial debuts in the American cinema. The film, writes British critic Robin Wood, "produces a subtle, idiosyncratic balance between engagement and detachment, complicity and horror."
VHS: S00086. $19.98.
Laser: LD70513. $34.98.
Terence Malick, USA, 1973, 95 mins.

Bail Jumper
Joe is a small town thug and Elaine an ex-con; together they flee Murky Springs, Missouri, in search of an idyllic life in New York City. On the way they're delayed by a series of minor obstacles, including a tornado and a swarm of locusts. But the plagues don't end once they reach their destination. With everything around them falling apart will romance still prevail? "Hip and amusing… a hilarious, nervous odyssey across a vibrant but damaged landscape, something like a traveling *Mystery Train*" *(The Film Journal)*.
VHS: S14998. $19.98.
Christian Faber, USA, 1989, 96 mins.

Ballad of the Sad Cafe
Vanessa Redgrave stars in this adaptation of Carson McCullers' novella and the play by Edward Albee. She plays Miss Amelia, a strong-willed and short-haired woman who runs a profitable moonshine business in a small Southern town. When her ex-husband Keith Carradine returns—up to no good—they settle their differences in a most impressive boxing match. With Rod Steiger, Austin Pendleton and Cork Hubbert as Cousin Lymon.
VHS: S16471. $89.95.
Simon Callow, USA/Great Britain, 1991, 100 mins.

Bang the Drum Slowly
Robert De Niro stars in this perennial favorite about a simple baseball catcher who discovers he is dying. Michael Moriarty, as the pitcher, lends emotional support. A great sports movie and a real tearjerker with a touching performance that signalled the rise of a great actor in De Niro.
VHS: S04325. $14.95.
John Hancock, USA, 1973, 97 mins.

Barnum
Burt Lancaster is cast as Phineas T. Barnum, the illustrious American showman who invented ballyhoo and introduced the word "jumbo" into the American vernacular. In this made-for-tv spectacular the career of the founder of the Greatest Show on Earth is colorfully presented. With Hanna Schygulla as singer Jenny Lind and Sandor Raski as General Tom Thumb.
VHS: Out of print. For rental only.
Laser: LD70856. $39.95.
Lee Phillips, USA, 1988, 100 mins.

Basic Instinct
Paul Verhoeven's highly controversial film about a burnt out homicide detective (Michael Douglas) investigating a string of ice pick murders. Falling for the prime suspect, a smart, beautiful and wealthy bi-sexual novelist (Sharon Stone) could prove fatal. Screenplay by Joe Eszterhas.
VHS: S17400. $19.98.
Paul Verhoeven, USA, 1992, 124 mins.

Basic Instinct (Director's Cut)
Retains the excised footage that received an NC-17 rating and premiered at the 1992 Cannes Film Festival. The special edition features interviews with Verhoeven, Douglas and Stone and a theatrical trailer that was never shown. Shown in the widescreen letterbox format, preserving its original aspect ratio.
VHS: S18251. $24.98.
Paul Verhoeven, USA, 1992, 150 mins.

The Basketball Diaries
Jim Carroll's renowned autobiography about high school, heroin, sex, writing and, of course, basketball stars Leonardo DiCaprio as the brooding young Catholic boy struggling to find his voice. Featuring music and a rather amusing cameo by author Jim Carroll. With Bruno Kirby, Lorraine Bracco and "Marky" Mark Wahlberg.
VHS: S25953. $19.95.
DVD: DV60307. $29.95.
Scott Kalvert, USA, 1995, 102 mins.

Batman & Robin
Mr. Freeze (Arnold Schwarzenegger) aims to put the world on ice and only Batman (George Clooney) can stop him. Irritating Poison Ivy also gets under Batman's skin. But Batman has more than Gotham City to protect: the youthful eagerness of crime-fighting comrades Robin (Chris O'Donnell) and Batgirl (Alicia Silverstone) puts them frequently in harm's way.
VHS: S32239. $22.98.
Laser: LD76349. $39.98.
DVD: DV60019. $24.98.
Joel Schumacher, USA, 1997, 125 mins.

Batman Forever
Val Kilmer and Chris O'Donnell star as the crime-fighting duo of Gotham City. They are joined by Tommy Lee Jones, Jim Carrey and Drew Barrymore, who all play unforgettable villains. In this latest Batman film, the Riddler appears with a new invention that steals the very thoughts of its victims. Of course, only Batman and Robin can withstand his fiendish onslaught. Nicole Kidman plays the psychiatrist who tries to get under Batman's skin in a more conventional, romantic way.
VHS: S26486. $19.95.
Laser: LD75097. $39.98.
DVD: DV60041. $24.98.
Taylor Hackford, USA, 1995, 131 mins.

Beaches
Bittersweet story of the 30-year friendship between two women, Bette Midler and Barbara Hershey, one of whom is dying of a fatal disease. Above average soaper with several opportunities for Midler to sing; includes her top single, "Wind Beneath My Wings."
VHS: S09790. $19.95.
Garry Marshall, USA, 1988, 123 mins.

Beautiful Girls
Matt Dillon, Timothy Hutton and Michael Rapaport star as three buddies who get together just before their ten-year high school anniversary. Among the women who try to coach these perpetual adolescents towards adulthood are Mira Sorvino, Uma Thurman and a wisecracking Rosie O'Donnell. It's a good-natured comedy about guys and their fears.
VHS: S29967. $99.99.
Ted Demme, USA, 1996, 110 mins.

The Bedroom Window
Steve Guttenberg learns his affair with Isabelle Huppert, as the boss's wife, can cost him more than his present job, when he volunteers to be a proxy witness against a very disturbed misogynist. Elizabeth McGovern also stars as a spunky crime victim in this lively Hitchcock-like thriller filmed in Baltimore.
VHS: S03683. $14.98.
Curtis Hanson, USA, 1987, 113 mins.

The Beguiled
Don Siegel's offbeat story is set during the Civil War, and stars Clint Eastwood as a man brought to a girls school to recuperate. At the school, Eastwood only succeeds at stirring up jealousy and hatred. With Geraldine Page.
VHS: S06821. $14.98.
Don Siegel, USA, 1971, 109 mins.

Being Human
Robin Williams stars as a man who has experienced many lifetimes spanning from the Stone Age to the present. This series of vignettes gives Williams the chance to portray characters using his entire range as an actor. History has a way of repeating itself; all we have to do is learn from the past.
VHS: S21682. $19.98.
Laser: LD74493. $39.98.
Bill Forsyth, USA, 1994, 122 mins.

Bella Mafia
Call it *The Godmother*. When the favorite son of Don Luciano (Dennis Farina) and wife Graziella (Vanessa Redgrave) is kidnapped and murdered, the family suspect Mafia rival Peter Carolla (Tony Lo Bianco) and vow revenge. The bloodshed continues when the Luciano men are murdered at a family gathering. The Luciano women band together to avenge their husband's deaths, travelling from Sicily to New York where they befriend the charming Mafiosa Luka (James Marsden). With Jennifer Tilly, Illeana Douglas, and Nastassia Kinski.
VHS: S33952. $99.99.
David Greene, USA, 1997, 117 mins.

Berlin Conspiracy
It's 1989, the Berlin Wall is about to come down, and a battle of wills becomes a battle of survival when two men get caught in a deadly game of betrayal and deceit. With Marc Singer, Mary Crosby and Stephen Davies.
VHS: S31524. $19.95.
Terence H. Winkless, USA, 1991, 83 mins.

Beulah Land
Lesley Ann Warren and Michael Sarrazin star in this TV movie about life in the deep south at the time of the American Civil War. Neighborhood antebellum mansions are also occupied by Eddie Albert, Hope Lange, Paul Rudd and Don Johnson. Based on the novel by Lonnie Coleman.
VHS: S12844. $29.95.
Virgil W. Vogel, USA, 1980, 267 mins.

Beyond Rangoon
Patricia Arquette stars as an American doctor who inadvertently gets caught up in the troubled political intrigues of Myanmar, formerly known as Burma. John Boorman paints this epic drama with broad strokes as he reveals the tragedy of a land in turmoil.
VHS: S27065. $98.99.
Laser: LD75440. $34.95.
John Boorman, USA, 1995, 100 mins.

Beyond the Call
Sissy Spacek and David Stathairn star in this story of a woman who risks destroying her marriage and comfortable life to save a death row inmate whom she once loved. Directed by Academy Award winner Tony Bill (*Untamed Heart, A Home of Our Own*).
VHS: S28511. $99.95.
Laser: LD75972. $39.99.
Tony Bill, USA, 1996, 101 mins.

Big Chill
College friends from the 1960s are re-united at the funeral of a mutual friend who committed suicide, and have to re-examine the twenty years that have passed since the 1960's. Kasdan leads the film to a bittersweet but uplifting conclusion. With Glenn Close, Kevin Kline, Mary Kay Place, Tom Berenger, JoBeth Williams, William Hurt.
VHS: S00129. $19.95.
Laser: Widescreen. **LD70344. $49.95.**
Lawrence Kasdan, USA, 1983, 105 mins.

Birdy
A spellbinding, captivating movie about a Vietnam vet (Matthew Modine) who has come to believe he is a bird, and the efforts of his best friend (Nicolas Cage) to break him out of his silence. Part comedy, part drama, totally unlike any movie before.
VHS: S00132. $19.95.
Alan Parker, USA, 1985, 120 mins.

Black and White
Nick Furris and Kim Delgado star in this story of a close friendship between a black man and white man, from their childhood in Newark, through the Korean War and beyond. In the backwoods of the South, kinship turns to horror and forever changes the lives of these two men. Also known as *Lou, Pat and Joe D.*
VHS: S23328. $29.95.
Stephen Vittoria, USA, 1988, 104 mins.

Black Widow
Debra Winger and Theresa Russell star in this stylish story about an obsessive investigation of a young woman who seduces, marries and murders wealthy men. With Dennis Hopper, Mary Woronov and a cameo by David Mamet.
Laser: CLV. **LD72104. $24.98.**
Bob Rafelson, USA, 1986, 103 mins.

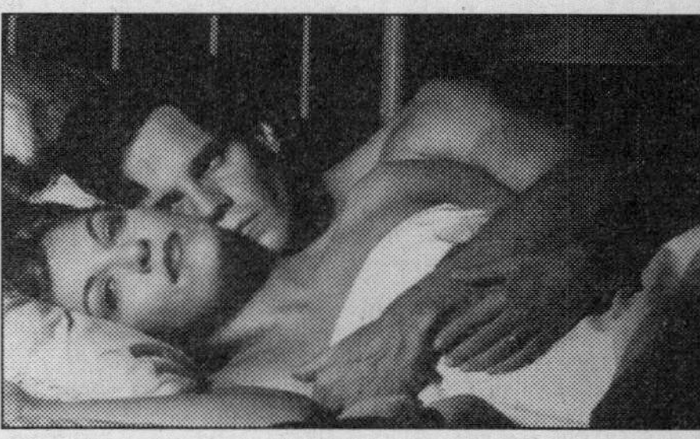

Bless the Beasts and Children
Six teenage boys at summer camp attempt to save a herd of buffalo from slaughter at a national preserve. Based on the novel by Glendon Swarthout. With Billy Mumy, Barty Robins, Miles Chapin, Darel Glaser, Bob Kramer, Ken Swofford, and Jesse White. The title song was nominated for an Oscar.
VHS: S34117. $19.95.
Stanley Kramer, USA, 1972, 109 mins.

Blessing
Twenty-three-year-old Randi (Melora Griffis) is desperate to escape the prison her family has made of her life on their Wisconsin dairy farm. When handsome young Lyle (Gareth Williams) comes rambling across the country in his Winnebago to seduce Randi with his wild dreams, she ultimately must decide between her loyalties to her family and herself. "An eloquent film" (*Hollywood Reporter*).
VHS: S31010. $59.95.
Paul Zehrer, USA, 1994, 95 mins.

Blind Fury
Rutger Hauer stars as a blind Vietnam veteran who keeps the son of an old way buddy safe from pursuing mobsters on a cross-country adventure. The ads read "He's lucky he can't see what he is up against." Slapstick humor mixes with graphic violence. Inspired by the Japanese blind swordsman, Zaitochi. With Terry O'Quinn, Lisa Blount, Randall "Tex" Cobb and Meg Foster.
VHS: S14000. $14.95.
Phillip Noyce, USA, 1990, 86 mins.

Blind Justice
Gripping drama about an innocent man tangled in the mechanics of the judicial system. Tim Matheson plays the family man arrested, identified, and jailed for a heinous crime. Based on a true story. With Tim Matheson, Lisa Eichhorn and Mimi Kuzyk.
VHS: S06615. $59.98.
Laser: LD75160. $34.98.
Rod Holcomb, USA, 1986, 94 mins.

Blind Spot
Academy Award winner Joanne Woodward stars with Laura Linney in a film about a seemingly close mother/daughter relationship. Sometimes the intimacy between a mother and her child can obscure the truth, a possibility discovered by Woodward's character in this deeply felt drama.
VHS: S20654. $19.98.
Michael Toshiyuki Uno, USA, 1993, 99 mins.

Blink
Madeleine Stowe and Aidan Quinn are the stars in this sexy thriller centered on a blind musician who regains her sight only to witness a brutal murder. Determined to find the psychotic serial killer who has invaded her dream world, she tracks him down in order to end the hallucinations that now plague her.
VHS: S21139. $19.95.
Michael Apted, USA, 1993, 106 mins.

Bliss
A daringly honest look at sexual intimacy and emotional risk, *Bliss* is the story of a young man who embarks on a sexual odyssey with his troubled wife. A passionate, compassionate film highlighted by three extraordinary performances by Craig Sheffer, Sheryl Lee and Terence Stamp. "Original and daring" *(Playboy)*.
VHS: S32687. $104.99.
Lance Young, USA, 1997, 103 mins.

Blood & Wine
Jack Nicholson is reunited with director Bob Rafelson *(Five Easy Pieces)* in this gritty drama of the perfect crime gone awry. Alex Gates (Nicholson) is a prominent wine merchant in Miami. With the aid of his partner, Victor (Michael Caine, in his darkest role to date), the two plan to steal a million-dollar necklace. When Alex's stepson falls for his mistress, the result could blow the whole plan apart. With Judy Davis, Stephen Dorff and Jennifer Lopez.
VHS: S31389. $103.99.
Laser: LD76231. $39.98.
Bob Rafelson, USA, 1997, 100 mins.

Blown Away
When an explosion rocks Boston, bomb squad expert Jimmy Dove (Jeff Bridges) dives into action. The evidence points to a bomber more menacing and skilled than any he's ever faced-except one. The possibility that his former mentor, Tommy Lee Jones, is the culprit, sets in motion a plot of revenge and betrayal leading to an explosive confrontation.
VHS: S22903. $19.98.
Laser: LD74622. $44.98.
DVD: DV60043. $24.98.
Stephen Hawkins, USA, 1994, 121 mins.

Blue Chips
Nick Nolte and Shaquille O'Neal combine on-court action with off-court drama to offer a behind-the-scenes look at professional basketball. These two stars from the world of sports and Hollywood bring gritty realism to this story of a coach whose principals are put to the test.
VHS: S21381. $19.95.
Laser: Widescreen. **LD75294. $39.98.**
William Friedkin, USA, 1994, 108 mins.

Blue River
Sam Elliott and Susan Dey are at the heart of this odd dramatic film. Henry Howland (Elliott) is a despotic small town high school principal. He first seduces and then abandons a single mother (Dey), leaving her son hungry for revenge. Howland's hypocritical stance toward the morality of those who look up to him is slowly destroyed by this young man, who cleverly exposes all the secrets hidden away in the village of Blue River.
VHS: S27263. $89.98.
Larry Elikann, USA, 1995, 90 mins.

Blue Sky
Tony Richardson's final film received a belated release despite Jessica Lange's Oscar-winning performance as Carly, which also won her a Golden Globe. Carly is a sultry woman who dreams of glamour. Tommy Lee Jones plays Army Major Hank Marshall. Together they share a passionate roller-coaster marriage. When Hank is thrust into the center of a high level military cover-up, the only person who can save him is Carly.
VHS: S24407. $14.98.
Laser: LD74918. $39.99.
Tony Richardson, USA, 1994, 88 mins.

Blue Steel
Jamie Lee Curtis plays a rookie New York City cop who gets suspended from the force and attracts the romantic attention of a psychotic killer on her first day of work. That's life in the big city for you. With Ron Silver as the nutty stockbroker Eugene. Also in the cast, Clancy Brown, Elizabeth Pena and Louise Fletcher. The look of the film by Kathryn Bigelow *(Near Dark)* is fabulous but don't start counting the number of bullets fired between reloadings.
VHS: S12549. $14.95.
Kathryn Bigelow, USA, 1990, 102 mins.

Blue Thunder
Roy Scheider stars in this action thriller as L.A. police pilot Frank Murphy, who is being trained to fly Blue Thunder, a specially modified helicopter. A conflict between Murphy and the project pilot heats up as Murphy begins to suspect that Blue Thunder is more than has been disclosed.
VHS: S34115. $19.95.
John Badham, USA, 1983, 108 mins.

Body and Soul
Corruption threatens an honorable young black boxer, played by Leon Isaac Kennedy, at every turn in this dramatic tale. The central question becomes can he resist the destructive influences of the professional boxing world and triumph on the strengths of his own formidable abilities? Muhammad Ali has a cameo.
VHS: S26871. $14.95.
George Bowers, USA, 1981, 100 mins.

Body Double
Brian De Palma once again pays tribute to Alfred Hitchcock in this tale of an actor involved in a murder where he is the prime witness. Craig Wasson is the voyeuristic thespian. Deborah Shelton is who he likes to watch. But Melanie Griffith, as porn actress Holly Body, is the real star of this twisted thriller.
VHS: S02862. $14.95.
Laser: Letterboxed, Dolby, chapter stops. **LD74477. $34.95.**
Brian DePalma, USA, 1984, 109 mins.

Body Heat
A sexy, haunting film that echoes the film noir dramas of the 1940's with a flare of irony and passion. Starring William Hurt and Kathleen Turner, it is the directorial debut of Kasdan, who went on to *Big Chill* and *Silverado*.
VHS: S00166. $14.95.
Laser: LD70530. $34.98.
DVD: DV60196. $24.98.
Lawrence Kasdan, USA, 1981, 113 mins.

Bonfire of the Vanities
When a Wall Street tycoon takes the wrong exit in a bad neighborhood in the Bronx he becomes the target for scandal and receives a mandatory invitation to appear in court. Tom Hanks stars in this Brian De Palma adaptation of the bestselling Tom Wolfe satire on life in the Big Apple during the 1980's. The all-star cast includes Melanie Griffith, Morgan Freeman, Kim Cattrall, Alan King, F. Murray Abraham, and Bruce Willis as the reporter responsible for the whole mess.
VHS: S13721. $19.98.
Brian DePalma, USA, 1990, 126 mins.

The Border
Between the US and Mexico lies a line crossed every day by countless immigrants seeking a better life. It is Jack Nicholson's job to see that they don't cross the border—that is, until he gives into pressure from his wife, Valerie Perrine. Also features Harvey Keitel.
VHS: S21281. $14.98.
Tony Richardson, USA, 1982, 107 mins.

Born on the 4th of July
Tom Cruise performs the true Vietnam experience of Ron Kovic, following his development as an eager, young war volunteer to a paralyzed, embittered veteran. As a youth, and representative of the nation in general, Kovic was inspired by Kennedy's "Ask not what your country can do for you..." speech, but returned from the war to a changed nation and became a vehement and outspoken anti-war demonstrator. With Kyra Sedgwick and Willem Dafoe.
VHS: S12464. $19.95.
Laser: LD70017. $39.98.
DVD: DV60241. $26.98.
Oliver Stone, USA, 1989, 145 mins.

Born to Be Wild
Rick Heller has troubles until he meets a new friend, Katie, a playful 400-pound gorilla. She knows her own mind and even communicates through sign language. Trouble sets in when Katie's owner puts her on display. Now she sorely needs her friend's help.
VHS: S25628. $19.99.
Laser: LD74986. $34.98.
John Gray, USA, 1995, 99 mins.

Born to Win
The unfairly neglected, American debut film of Czech emigre Ivan Passer *(Cutter's Way)* about the seamy underside of urban American life centers on two small-time hustlers, one of whom is a hairdresser suffering from heroin withdrawal. With terrific performances from Robert De Niro and George Segal, Paula Prentiss, Karen Black and Hector Elizondo.
VHS: S17644. $19.99.
Ivan Passer, USA, 1971, 90 mins.

Bound for Glory
The story of Woody Guthrie, America's great folk musician and poet, featuring David Carradine. Winner of two Academy Awards including Best Cinematography by Haskell Wexler, with many of Guthrie's songs, including "This Land Is Your Land" and "Roll On Columbia."
VHS: S00174. $19.98.
Hal Ashby, USA, 1976, 149 mins.

The Boy in the Plastic Bubble
John Travolta stars as a boy whose immune system cannot withstand the normal contagions of everyday life. He inhabits a plastic bubble which saves his life but cuts him off from even the most basic forms of human contact. This is a sensitive film that offers a chance to see a young but capable Travolta in action.
VHS: S28070. $14.98.
Randall Kleiser, USA, 1976, 100 mins.

Boys
Winona Ryder stars as a young woman on the run from a terrible secret. After she has a horse-riding accident, she is rescued by prep-school senior John Baker (Lukas Haas, *Witness*). As mutual attraction turns to romance, he sheds some of his boyhood innocence as this mysterious "older" woman moves toward reconciliation with the dark choices of her past. Soundtrack features Stewart Copeland (The Police).
VHS: S30465. $99.99.
Stacy Cochran, USA, 1996, 86 mins.

Boys on the Side
Whoopi Goldberg, Mary-Louise Parker and Drew Barrymore go on a road trip that careens through a gamut of adventure, but ends in lasting friendship. Though only Whoopi is a lesbian, issues like AIDS and boyfriend hardship make this melodrama a perfect fit for all kinds of girls.
VHS: S25572. $19.98.
Herbert Ross, USA, 1995, 117 mins.

Brainstorm
Directed by special effects wizard Douglas Trumbull, this high-tech movie, with state-of-the-art visual effects, stars Christopher Walken, Louise Fletcher and Natalie Wood (in her last film) in a story about research scientists who perfect a sensory experience device—in the form of a headset—with explosive results.
VHS: S14962. $14.95.
DVD: DV60320. $24.98.
Douglas Trumbull, USA, 1983, 106 mins.

Braveheart
Mel Gibson is Braveheart, the legendary Scottish warrior who battled the English in the 13th century. In this epic film, the very story of independence which still fires the Scottish imagination is brought alive. It's a tale of fierce determination and unforgettable courage with superb battle sequences and a touching love story. Letterboxed.
VHS: S27169. $24.95.
Laser: THX. **LD75536. $49.95.**
Mel Gibson, USA, 1995, 177 mins.

The Breakfast Club
Five teenagers on detention in a suburban school spend a Saturday in the school library and learn to get along. Cheerleader, jock, nerd, street punk and the super shy find harmony after smoking marijuana. The brat pack's finest hour and a half. With Molly Ringwald, Judd Nelson, Emilio Estevez, Anthony Michael Hall and Ally Sheedy.
VHS: S01985. $19.95.
DVD: DV60243. $24.98.
John Hughes, USA, 1985, 97 mins.

Breaking Away
Four college-age friends in Bloomington, Indiana, find some meaning in life when they enter a bicycle race. Script by Steve Tesich won an Oscar. Starring Dennis Christopher, Dennis Quaid, Daniel Stern and Jackie Earle Haley as the "cutters." With Paul Dooley and Barbara Barrie as Christopher's parents.
VHS: S04881. $19.95.
Peter Yates, USA, 1979, 100 mins.

Breast Men
In this entertaining little gem based on a true story, David Schwimmer and Chris Cooper star as two surgeons who embark on a partnership in the breast enhancement business. From the hip '60s to the excessive '80s they watch their business, bank accounts, and clients grow. But a rift in their relationship and the silicone scare threatens to destroy their reputation and their business. With Emily Procter and Louise Fletcher.
VHS: S34356. $71.99.
Lawrence O'Neil, USA, 1995, 95 mins.

Breathing Lessons
James Garner and Joanne Woodward star in this heartfelt chronicle of an older couple on a short trip. Though they are an odd match—he's a pragmatist and she's inspired if flighty—the road offers them the perfect opportunity to renew their love and commitment for one another. Based on the Pulitzer Prize-winning novel by Anne Tyler.
VHS: S21872. $19.98.
John Erman, USA, 1994, 98 mins.

Bright Angel
Dermot Mulroney embarks on a road trip he will never forget when he offers Lili Taylor a ride from Montana to Wyoming to bail her brother out of jail. This bold, quirky drama features a top notch, eclectic cast that includes Sam Shepard, Valerie Perrine, Burt Young, Sheila McCarthy, Mary Kay Place, Bill Pullman and Delroy Lindo. Based on the short stories by Richard Ford. A real sleeper.
VHS: S15441. $19.98.
Laser: Widescreen. **LD75165. $34.98.**
Michael Fields, USA, 1991, 94 mins.

Broken Arrow
John Travolta and Christian Slater star as two fighter pilots with an apparently solid working relationship, a relationship cemented by friendship. Money has the power to upset this balance of trust and the friends find themselves on opposite sides of a dangerous equation battling over two stolen nuclear warheads. Tense and action-filled, this drama offers non-stop adventure. VHS letterboxed.
VHS: S28055. $19.95.
Laser: LD75609. $39.98.
John Woo, USA, 1996, 108 mins.

The Broken Chain
During the Revolutionary War two Iroquois brothers fight to keep their land safe from encroaching European settlers. Pierce Brosnan, Eric Scwheig, Wes Studi and Graham Green form the cast for this moving drama about change and survival in colonial America.
VHS: S21122. $92.98.
Laser: LD74448. $39.99.
Lamont Johnson, USA, 1993, 93 mins.

A Bronx Tale
Robert De Niro is the father of an impressionable boy who is in danger of being seduced by the easy life and fast money he sees on the streets of the Bronx. Sonny, the local mob boss, would find in this youngster a willing accomplice in crime.
VHS: S20655. $19.98.
Laser: Widescreen. **LD75295. $39.98.**
DVD: DV60321. $24.98.
Robert De Niro, USA, 1993, 122 mins.

Brother John
Sidney Poitier stars as Brother John in a compelling drama set in a small Alabama town. Poitier is the Messiah come back to Earth—except that no one knows that he's come, and that he's black. Wonderful supporting performances by Will Geer, Bradford Dillman and Paul Winfield.
VHS: S06711. $14.95.
James Goldstone, USA, 1972, 94 mins.

Brother's Kiss
The harrowing urban drama of two brothers who grew up in Harlem—one a cop (Michael Raynor), one a crackhead (Nick Chinlund)—on a collision course, and how they got where they are. As a youth, Mick (Joshua Danowsky) is sexually assaulted by an off-duty cop; Lex (Justin Pierce) stabs the cop and this act sets the course for both of their lives. With strong performances across the board. With Cathy Moriarty, Marisa Tomei, Rosie Perez and John Leguizamo.
VHS: S34428. $97.99.
Seth Zvi Rosenfeld, USA, 1997, 93 mins.

Buddy
An animal-loving heiress (Rene Russo) adopts a baby gorilla, Buddy, into her thriving menagerie of pets and into her heart. A spirited adventure based on a remarkable, true story. Starring Robbie Coltrane, Alan Cummings and Paul Reubens (Pee-Wee Herman). With creature effects from Jim Henson Pictures; Francis Ford Coppola, Executive Producer. "Buddy is a beaut" (Gene Shalit, *Today*).
VHS: S32671. $22.99.
Laser: LD76419. $39.95.
Caroline Thompson, USA, 1997, 97 mins.

The Buddy Holly Story
Gary Busey puts in an electrifying, Oscar-nominated performance as the early rock legend, from his beginnings in Lubbock, Texas, to his meteoric rise, marriage, breakup with the Crickets, and untimely death in a plane crash in 1959. With Busey performing all the Holly hits. Academy Award winner for Best Adapted Score.
VHS: S34118. $19.95.
Steve Rash, USA, 1978, 113 mins.

Buffalo Soldiers
Danny Glover, Mykelty Williamson and Michael Warren star in this spirited salute to the famed African-American U.S. Cavalry corps whose fighting bravery in the West helped carve out a nation and the cavalrymen's rightful place in it.
VHS: S33684. $71.99.
Charles Haid, USA, 1997, 95 mins.

Bugsy
Warren Beatty's attempt to attach Hollywood glamour to the notorious American criminal was nominated for 11 Oscars and took home awards for art direction and best costume design. Beatty imbues East Coast mobster Benjamin "Bugsy" Siegel with an altruistic, pioneer spirit in the building of a casino empire in Las Vegas. Annette Bening is cast as the hard-nosed cutie Virginia Hill. Harvey Keitel and Ben Kingsley were nominated for Oscars, along with Beatty, for their sharp portrayals of famous gangsters. With Elliot Gould, Bebe Neuwirth, Wendy Phillips and Joe Mantegna as George Raft. Script by James Toback.
VHS: S16714. $19.95.
Laser: LD71572. $39.95.
Barry Levinson, USA, 1991, 135 mins.

Bulletproof Heart
Anthony LaPaglia and Mimi Rogers star in this film noir-style love story. A hit man (LaPaglia) sets out to kill his mark, a beautiful socialite who is actually eager to die. Though he is warned that he should steel himself for this assignment (as other men have tried and failed), his own self-doubts and her overwhelming beauty lead to the inevitable—he falls for her in a big way.
VHS: S26370. $19.95.
Mark Malone, USA, 1995, 95 mins.

The Bunker
Anthony Hopkins portrays Adolf Hitler, for which he won an Emmy, in this look at the last days of the Third Reich, based on the book by James P. O'Donnel. Piper Laurie is also featured as Madga Goebbels. Her vital performance was recognized with an Emmy nomination.
VHS: S21030. $19.95.
George Schaefer, USA, 1981, 150 mins.

The Burning Season
Raul Julia stars in this, his final film, as Chico Mendes. He is matched in this gripping biographical film with a supporting cast composed of Edward J. Olmos, Sonia Braga and Nigel Havers. Mendes fought to save the Amazon rain forest with firm conviction. Ultimately his struggle was an inspiration to the entire world.
VHS: S24058. $19.98.
John Frankenheimer, USA, 1994, 123 mins.

Cadillac Ranch
Christopher Lloyd stars in this drama of three estranged sisters in search of their father's hidden legacy. They find themselves pursued by their father's nemesis during a wild, 48-hour road trip that brings love and adventure. With Suzy Amis. "A kinder, gentler *Thelma & Louise (Reel Views)*". 95 mins.
VHS: S31362. $19.95.
Laser: LD76275. $39.99.
Lisa Gottlieb, USA, 1997, 100 mins.

Caligula: The Untold Story
Another adaptation chronicling the lurid spectacle of the notorious Roman emperor (played by David Cain Haugton). Directed by David Hills. With Joan McCoy and Laura Gemser.
VHS: S14156. $79.95.

Call of the Wild (1972)
Shot in the striking scenery of Finland, and featuring a cast including Charlton Heston and Michele Mercier, this is an epic adaptation of the classic Jack London adventure classic.
VHS: S09165. $19.95.
Ken Annakin, USA, 1972, 100 mins.

Call of the Wild (1997)
Richard Dreyfuss narrates and Rutger Hauer stars in Jack London's classic tale of love, loyalty and survival of the fittest. When a sled dog named Buck is sold to a miner, they travel the Great North together in search of gold. When Buck gets older, he must decide whether to stay with the master he loves or follow his instincts and join a pack of wolves.
VHS: S33159. $69.99.
Laser: LD76432. $39.98.
Peter Svatek, USA, 1997, 91 mins.

Calm at Sunset
In young James' (Peter Facinelli) pursuit to become a fisherman like his father and grandfather before him, he uncovers a dark secret that forces him to question the depth of his love for his father (Michael Moriarty) and the life he has chosen. From award-winning director Dan Petrie *(A Raisin in the Sun)*. With Kevin Conway and Kate Nelligan.
VHS: S31295. $99.99.
Laser: LD76218. $39.99.
Daniel Petrie, USA, 1996, 98 mins.

Camilla
Jessica Tandy and Bridget Fonda bring their undeniable star power to this warm, funny road movie. They play two strangers who find friendship and fun together despite their differences. It's a comic adventure perfect for all kinds of audiences.
VHS: S25052. $19.95.
Laser: LD74954. $39.99.
Deepa Mehta, USA, 1995, 91 mins.

Candidate
A still refreshing satire based on an original screenplay that grew out of Jeremy Larner's experience in the Eugene McCarthy campaign, with Robert Redford as an idealistic lawyer seeking a Senate seat in California, and Allen Garfield as the sleazy advertising man.
VHS: S01750. $19.98.
Laser: LD71409. $34.98.
Michael Ritchie, USA, 1972, 111 mins.

Cannery Row
Adaptation of John Steinbeck stars Nick Nolte as an ex-baseball player turned marine biologist and Debra Winger as a young runaway. Narration by John Huston, photography by Sven Nykvist, music by Jack Nitzsche.
VHS: S02988. $19.98.
Laser: Letterboxed. **LD76184. $49.98.**
David Ward, USA, 1982, 120 mins.

Captain America
The eponymous hero returns from the past and gets caught in a superhuman war with his archnemesis, the Red Skull, over control of the planet and the future in this live action adaptation of the popular cartoon hero created by Joe Simon and Jack Kirby.
VHS: S16909. $19.95.
Laser: LD71530. $34.95.
Albert Pyun, USA, 1990

Captains Courageous
Robert Urich *(Lonesome Dove)* stars in this high-seas adventure based on the Rudyard Kipling classic.
VHS: S30020. $79.98.
Michael Anderson, USA, 1995, 93 mins.

Captives
Tim Roth *(Pulp Fiction)* and Julia Ormond *(Sabrina)* star in this critically acclaimed, erotic thriller of passion run amok when an illicit affair turns deadly. While working as a dental assistant in a prison, a woman becomes sexually involved with an inmate. Soon, she is caught in a deadly web of deception and blackmail. "A riveting thriller!" *(Cover Magazine)*.
VHS: S30454. $19.95.
Laser: LD76035. $39.99.
Angela Pope, USA, 1996, 100 mins.

Carlito's Way
Al Pacino, the star of *Scarface*, is cast as a ruthless Cuban immigrant who finds that the world of 1990's America is still the toughest school of hard knocks. Penelope Ann Miller and Sean Penn also star in this acclaimed film. Letterboxed.
VHS: S20692. $19.98.
Laser: LD72380. $49.95.
DVD: DV60290. $26.98.
Brian DePalma, USA, 1993, 145 mins.

Carnal Knowledge
Jack Nicholson, Ann-Margret, Art Garfunkel and Candice Bergen star in this shattering, bitterly humorous film examining the sexual triumphs and disasters of two American men from college days into their 40's. Written by Jules Feiffer, directed by Mike Nichols.
Laser: CLV. **LD70126. $49.95.**
Mike Nichols, USA, 1971, 96 mins.

Caroline?
Stephanie Zimbalist once solved mysteries on a weekly basis as a television detective on "Remington Steele." Now she plays a very mysterious character in this outstanding Hall of Fame presentation about a young woman who turns up at her wealthy father's mansion 15 years after she was thought to have died in a plane crash. With George Grizzard, Pamela Reed, Patricia Neal, Dorothy McGuire, Shawn Phelan and Jenny Jacobs.
VHS: S16505. $89.98.
Laser: LD71455. $29.98.
Joseph Sargent, USA, 1990, 100 mins.

Carried Away
Dennis Hopper, Amy Irving, Gary Busey and Amy Locane star in this drama about passion and forbidden love. Hopper's character, Joseph, falls hard for a 17-year-old girl (Locane). Joseph must then contend with both her father (Busey) and his wife, Rosalee (Irving). In his passion, the middle-aged Joseph must uncover a newfound strength.
VHS: S29924. $19.98.
Bruno Barreto, USA, 1996, 108 mins.

Casualties of War
Michael J. Fox stars as a new recruit in Vietnam assigned to veteran Sgt. Sean Penn's squad. When Fox objects to having a little fun with a captured South Vietnamese woman, his fellow grunts get ugly. With John C. Reilly, Don Harvey, John Leguizamo, Thuy Thu Le and Sam Robards as Chaplain Kirk. Based on a real incident written by Daniel Lang for *New Yorker Magazine*. Script by playwright David Rabe *(Streamers)*.
VHS: S16602. $14.95.
Brian DePalma, USA, 1989, 113 mins.

Caught

A mysterious drifter lands in a Jersey City fish shop and changes its owners' lives forever in this steamy thriller starring Edward James Olmos and Maria Conchita Alonso. "A convincing portrait of obsessive sex and a poignant story of love and dreams" (Roger Ebert, *Chicago Sun Times*).

VHS: S31273. $98.99.
Laser: LD76203. $39.98.
Robert M. Young, USA, 1996, 109 mins.

Chapter Two

James Caan stars as George Schneider, a grief-striken writer whose wife has died. Classic witty Neil Simon dialogue as the widower meets wife number two (Marsha Mason, Simon's real-life wife). With Joseph Bolgna and Valerie Harper. Based on Simon's semi-autobiographical Broadway play.

VHS: S34120. $19.95.
Robert Moore, USA, 1979, 124 mins.

Chasers

Tom Berenger and William McNamara play Navy shore patrol officers who must transfer a dangerous prisoner, the beautiful Erika Eleniak. This comic look at today's coed navy combines great star power and road movie action. Also features Gary Busey.

VHS: S21356. $19.98.
Laser: LD74474. $34.98.
Dennis Hopper, USA, 1994, 102 mins.

Chattahoochee

Gary Oldman is cast as Emmett Foley, a Korean war veteran who was sent to a Florida state mental facility after he shot up his neighborhood for no apparent reason. This grim true story tells the tale of the man responsible for major changes in the care and treatment of the mentally ill. Excellent supporting cast includes Dennis Hopper, Frances McDormand, Pamela Reed, Ned Beatty and M. Emmet Walsh.

VHS: S14001. $19.98.
Mick Jackson, USA, 1989, 97 mins.

Children of a Lesser God

William Hurt, Marlee Matlin, Piper Laurie and Philip Bosco star in this Academy-Award nominated film, the screen version of a successful Broadway play, with Hurt the special education teacher who falls in love with a troubled deaf woman.

VHS: S03303. $19.95.
Randa Haines, USA, 1986, 119 mins.

China Moon

Ed Harris is Kyle Bodine, a detective who must investigate a murder involving beautiful Rachel Munro (Madeleine Stowe). This sexy and steamy thriller builds an atmosphere of eroticism and danger that threatens to draw in everyone entranced by the allure of *China Moon*.

VHS: S21827. $14.98.
John Bailey, USA, 1994, 99 mins.

China Syndrome

Things really start to rumble when a TV news crew stumbles over an accident at a California nuclear plant. Tempers flare and tensions rise when the piece is pulled and embarrassing questions are asked. With Jane Fonda, Michael Douglas, Jack Lemmon, Wilford Brimley, James Hampton, Peter Donat and James Karen. The title infers a total atomic meltdown that would bore a hole through the Earth all the way to China. A timely and taunt piece of work.

VHS: S10379. $19.95.
Laser: LD75529. $39.95.
James Bridges, USA, 1979, 123 mins.

Christmas Coal Mine Miracle

Made-for-tv story based on a true incident of miners trapped by an underground explosion on Christmas Eve. With Kurt Russell.

VHS: S05315. $59.95.
Jud Taylor, USA, 1977, 100 mins.

Christmas Lilies of the Field

Billy Dee Williams stars in this charming sequel to the Academy Award winning *Lilies of the Field*, a sensitive account of a mission's struggle to give a group of orphans a home.

VHS: S09246. $29.95.
Ralph Nelson, USA, 1984, 98 mins.

Christmas Wife

Jason Robards and Julie Harris star in a heartwarming film. Robards plays John Tanner, recently widowed, as he faces his first Christmas alone. He goes to an agency to find someone with whom to share Christmas and meets the shy Iris, who is happy to join him; but there's a secret which, when revealed, changes both their lives forever.

VHS: S11005. $79.99.
David Jones, USA, 1988, 73 mins.

Christopher Columbus: The Discovery

John Glen directs an all-star cast (Marlon Brando, Tom Selleck and Rachel Ward) in a massive international co-production from a story by *Godfather* author Mario Puzo.

VHS: S17707. $19.98.
Laser: LD71800. $39.98.
John Glen, USA, 1992, 121 mins.

Citizen Cohn

A complex and powerful, made-for-cable biography of lawyer and conservative activist Roy Cohn, energetically performed by James Woods. Adapted from Nicholas von Hoffman's biography, the film uses an intricate structure, as Cohn, dying from AIDS and denying his homosexuality, details his ambition and lust for power. In the hospital, he's visited by the ghosts of his past: his prosecution of the Rosenbergs, the communist witch hunts in conjunction with Joseph McCarthy, his fierce political battles with the Kennedys and the attempted destabilization of the civil rights movement. With Joe Don Baker, Joseph Bologna, Ed Flanders and Frederic Forrest.

VHS: S18790. $19.98.
Laser: LD75170. $34.98.
Frank Pierson, USA, 1992, 112 mins.

Citizen Ruth

Laura Dern stars as a dim-witted drifter who unwittingly finds herself the center of attention in a media circus after getting in trouble with the law. With Swoosie Kurtz, Kelly Preston and Burt Reynolds.

VHS: S31527. $103.99.
Laser: LD76258. $39.99.
Alexander Payne, USA, 1997, 105 mins.

Citizen X

Stephen Rea, Donald Sutherland and Max Von Sydow star in this dramatic HBO production about the most prolific serial killer of all time. It's a chilling, true story of the bungled investigative process that finally pieced together the identity of the dreaded Citizen X. He managed to kill 52 people before he was captured.

VHS: S25053. $19.98.
Chris Gerolmo, USA, 1995, 102 mins.

City Hall

Al Pacino, John Cusack, Bridget Fonda and Danny Aiello make up the cast for this tense political drama. Beyond corruption and scandal at New York's city hall is a classic cover-up and murder. In the city that never sleeps, somehow this story escaped everyone's intention, and that is the plan of the powerful interests involved.

VHS: S29456. $19.95.
Laser: LD75821. $39.95.
Harold Becker, USA, 1996, 112 mins.

City of Industry

In this hard-driven, modern film noir, small-time thief Lee Egan (Timothy Hutton) wants to pull off one big heist, leave L.A. and start a new life. With help from his brother Roy (Harvey Keitel) and a small crew (Stephen Dorff and Wade Dominguez), Lee plans to rob a jewelry store. But the perfect heist ends in a way only one of them could have known. Now Roy must right a wrong, for his brother and the beautiful widow (Famke Janssen) of a man he hardly knows.

VHS: S32022. $99.99.
Laser: LD76394. $39.99.
John Irvin, USA, 1997, 97 mins.

Clara's Heart

Whoopi Goldberg is cast as a caring Jamaican housekeeper who fascinates and inspires young Neil Patrick Harris to improve his attitude and enjoy life. With Kathleen Quinlan, Michael Ontkean, Beverley Todd and Spalding Gray. A sensitive drama with lots of Jamaican music.

VHS: S09167. $14.95.
Laser: LD74690. $24.98.
Robert Mulligan, USA, 1988, 108 mins.

Clean and Sober

Michael Keaton gets serious as an options trader with substance abuse and personality problems. He joins a de-tox program to hide out from his boss and the police when his life goes into the dumper. Excellent supporting work by Morgan Freeman and Kathy Baker. From the creator of "Moonlighting" TV show, Glenn Gordon Caron.

VHS: S09923. $19.98.
Glenn Gordon Caron, USA, 1988, 124 mins.

Clear and Present Danger

Harrison Ford returns as the CIA agent dedicated to the American way. After the cold war, the enemy is closer to home than before. A presidential advisor is linked to a South American drug cartel. Ford's discovery of this connection sends him into an action adventure/drama where truth must win out over injustice. Anne Archer, Willem Dafoe and James Earl Jones are also featured.

VHS: S23219. $19.98.
Laser: Widescreen. **LD75368. $44.98.**
Phillip Noyce, USA, 1994, 141 mins.

The Client

Susan Sarandon and Tommy Lee Jones star in this chilling thriller based on the John Grisham novel. When a rookie lawyer (Sarandon) takes on an overzealous prosecutor (Jones) to protect a young boy, a deadly chain of events is set in play. Soon it's a matter of life and death for everyone involved.

VHS: S22538. $19.98.
Laser: LD74613. $39.98.
Joel Schumacher, USA, 1994, 120 mins.

Cliffhanger

Renny Harlin's vertigo-inducing thriller is set in the Colorado Mountains. The ingenious opening—a group of terrorists hijack a treasury plane in midair but lose $100 million when the plane crashlands in the Rockies—builds up to a wonderfully tense and exciting action pretense. Sylvester Stallone and Michael Rooker play mountain rescue experts who are psychologically scarred by the death of a woman climber. John Lithgow plays the sinister terrorist. With Janine Turner, Paul Winfield, Ralph Waite, Rex Linn, Caroline Goodall, Leon and Michelle Joyner.

VHS: S19873. $19.95.
DVD: DV60023. $24.95.
Renny Harlin, USA, 1993, 118 mins.

Closet Land

Radha Bharadwaj's timely and harrowing drama stars Madeleine Stowe as a children's book author who becomes a political prisoner after a book she writes is deemed subversive. Alan Rickman co-stars.

VHS: S15096. $19.98.
Radha Bharadwaj, USA, 1991, 95 mins.

Cobb

Tommy Lee Jones is Ty Cobb, perhaps the most disliked baseball hero of all time. Robert Wuhl plays the writer who must try to tell this legend's story, but obnoxious behavior and plain ego stand in the way. Despite it all, the two manage to connect and have some wild times.

VHS: S25654. $19.98.
Ron Shelton, USA, 1994, 129 mins.

Cocktail

Tom Cruise and Bryan Brown are a pair of wild and crazy Manhattan bartenders who rise to the top of their profession. Cruise is young and cocky and Brown is older and sometimes wiser. Elisabeth Shue is the waitress with the trust fund. For those who like a production number with their mixed drinks. Based on the book by Heywood Gould.

VHS: S09154. $19.95.
Roger Donaldson, USA, 1988, 103 mins.

Cold Sassy Tree

Faye Dunaway and Richard Widmark star in this story of a May-December romance that scandalizes the quiet Southern town of Cold Sassy, Georgia, at the turn of the century. Based on the book by Olive Ann Burns.

VHS: S11613. $14.98.
Joan Tewkesbury, USA, 1989, 97 mins.

Color of Night (Director's Cut)

Bruce Willis stars in this super erotic thriller featuring the beautiful Jane March. Willis is a psychologist haunted by his friend and colleague's unexplained murder. Unable to control himself, he is led through passionate intrigues as he tries to find the killer. Includes an extra 15 minutes of controversial, erotic footage. Ruben Blades and Lesley Ann Warren also star.

VHS: S23668. $19.95.
Laser: Letterboxed. **LD74808. $39.99.**
Richard Rush, USA, 1994, 140 mins.

Colors

Dennis Hopper directs this controversial police story about two partners on an anti-gang patrol in the Los Angeles area. Robert Duvall is the seasoned pro and Sean Penn is cast as the cocky rookie. With Maria Conchita Alonso, Trinidad Silva and many actual members of L.A. street gangs in extra roles.

VHS: S07786. $19.98.
Dennis Hopper, USA, 1988, 120 mins.

Come Along with Me
An adaptation of Shirley Jackson's unfinished novel, starring Estelle Parsons and Silvia Sidney, directed by Joanne Woodward. The plot concerns Mabel Lederer, whose husband, Hughie, passed on. Mabel decides to re-invent herself with a new name and new town, and undertakes a slightly off-center profession: "I dabble in the supernatural."
VHS: S07540. $24.95.
Joanne Woodward, USA, 1986, 60 mins.

Come See the Paradise
Alan Parker turns his camera on another infamous American chapter in race relations. The story of the World War II imprisonment of thousands of American citizens with Japanese ancestry is told through the perspective of an Irish-American labor organizer who marries into a Little Tokyo family in Los Angeles. With Dennis Quaid, Tamlyn Tomita, Sab Shimono and Shizu-ko Hoshi. Compelling and questionable.
VHS: S13920. $19.98.
Alan Parker, USA, 1990, 135 mins.

The Comfort of Strangers
Director Paul Schrader returns to the screen with a lurid tale of innocents in jeopardy. English tourists Rupert Everett and Natasha Richardson accept the hospitality of Christopher Walken and Helen Mirren in Venice and hope they live to regret it. A stylish exercise written by Harold Pinter.
VHS: S14459. $79.95.
Laser: LD75172. $34.98.
Paul Schrader, USA/Great Britain, 1991, 102 mins.

Coming Home
Jane Fonda, Jon Voight and Bruce Dern star in a powerful drama about the effects of the Vietnam War on the home front. Fonda falls in love with a disabled vet (Voight) while husband Dern is fighting overseas. Good supporting work by Penelope Milford and Robert Carradine.
VHS: S04718. $19.98.
Laser: Chapter search. Includes original trailer. **LD71636. $39.98.**
Hal Ashby, USA, 1978, 127 mins.

The Competition
Pianist Paul (Richard Dreyfuss) is assured of success in his final competition. But his competitor, newcomer Heidi (Amy Irving), may prove a better pianist. As romance buds between them, Heidi must decide whether to take a dive, despite her teacher Greta's pressure to win, or condemn her new love to obscurity.
VHS: S34121. $19.95.
Joel Oliansky, USA, 1980, 125 mins.

Compromising Positions
Susan Sarandon and Raul Julia are the stars of this amusing thriller about murder in suburbia. A one-time journalist looks into the death of a seductive dentist. Before long this simple obsession leads to unsuspected perils and quite a few good laughs.
VHS: S23954. $14.95.
Laser: LD75362. $29.98.
Frank Perry, USA, 1985, 99 mins.

Con Air
U.S. ranger Cameron Poe (Nicolas Cage) is convicted of murder after killing a drunk man while protecting his wife. After eight years he is paroled and flown home aboard the Jailbird, which also transports society's most dangerous convicts to a maximum-security prison in Louisiana. A surprise escape is made under the direction of Cyrus "The Virus" (John Malkovich), who leads the plane's takeover. U.S. Marshall Vince Larkin (John Cusack) works with Poe on board and Poe's wife and daughter on the ground to get the plane under control before it is blown out of the sky by officials. With Steve Buscemi, Ving Rhames, Colm Meaney and Mykelti Williamson. Letterboxed.
VHS: S32658. $19.95.
Simon West, USA, 1997, 115 mins.

Conrack
Jon Voight stars as a teacher doing his best to educate a group of underachieving black children who live on an island off the coast of South Carolina. Based on the true story of Pat Conroy and his book *The Water Is Wide*. With Paul Winfield, Madge Sinclair and Hume Cronyn.
VHS: S01856. $59.98.
Martin Ritt, USA, 1974, 107 mins.

Consenting Adults
A seductive murder mystery about an unholy linking between two yuppie couples. A composer and his young wife attempt to inject some life into their dull marriage by experimenting with their beautiful, dangerous neighbors, with catastrophic results. With Kevin Kline, Mary Elizabeth Mastrantonio, Kevin Spacey and Rebecca Miller.
VHS: S18494. $94.95.
Alan J. Pakula, USA, 1992, 109 mins.

Conspiracy Theory
Jerry Fletcher (Mel Gibson) is a sometime New York cabbie and full-time conspiracy buff. Julia Roberts is a federal attorney who refused to believe him. Now they're scrambling for their lives because one of his wild-eyed theories just happens to be right. With Patrick Stewart. "Speedy, well-acted, smart" (Mike Clark, *USA Today*).
VHS: S32711. $19.98.
Laser: LD76740. $39.98.
Richard Donner, USA, 1997, 129 mins.

Convicts
Robert Duvall, James Earl Jones and Lukas Haas star in this film set on a plantation staffed by convict labor. The owner is violently unpredictable and paranoid, forcing all those around him to confront not only difficult conditions but their own sense of humanity.
VHS: S21149. $29.98.
Peter Materson, USA, 1991, 93 mins.

Cop Land
A small-town sheriff (Sylvester Stallone) has long idolized the big-city cops who live in his peaceful neighborhood, until he uncovers a potentially explosive conspiracy among them. With Harvey Keitel, Ray Liotta and Robert DeNiro.
VHS: S33395. $106.99.
Laser: LD76821. $39.99.
DVD: DV60310. $29.99.
James Mangold, USA, 1997, 105 mins.

Copycat
Sigourney Weaver and Holly Hunter star, while Harry Connick, Jr., makes his feature-length film debut. A serial killer attempts to destroy a psychiatrist (Weaver) who studies serial killers. Unnerved by this effort, Weaver's character finds that the plot against her is even more insidious than she suspected; it involves an ingenious use of her own research material.
VHS: S27168. $19.98.
Laser: LD75466. $39.98.
DVD: DV60304. $24.98.
Jon Amiel, USA, 1995, 123 mins.

Cornbread, Earl and Me
Called the original *Boyz N the Hood*, this story follows the life of a black youth on his way out of the ghetto on a basketball scholarship only to be gunned down by police, who try to squelch the truth with an elaborate cover-up. Features fine performances by Moses Gunn, Bernie Casie, Rosalind Cash, Madge Sinclair, NBA star Keith Wilkes, Tierre Turner, and Laurence Fishburne in his first starring role.
VHS: S30010. $14.98.
Joseph Manduke, USA, 1975, 95 mins.

Corrina, Corrina
Whoopi Goldberg and Ray Liotta star in this touching tale of two families joined by love. Ray is a widower in the 1950's who hires a new servant, played by Whoopi. Before long her charm and grace transform this rigid relationship into something that no one had expected. This film contains Don Ameche's last screen appearance.
VHS: S23879. $19.98.
Jessie Nelson, USA, 1994, 115 mins.

The Count of Monte Cristo
An adaptation of Dumas' novel about the charismatic swashbuckler Edmond Dantes (Richard Chamberlain), who was unjustly imprisoned. He assumes a new identity and seeks vengeance on the ruthless man who tried to destroy him. With Tony Curtis, Trevor Howard, Louis Jourdan and Kate Nelligan.
VHS: S18485. $19.98.
David Greene, USA, 1975, 100 mins.

Courtship—An American Romance
Horton Foote's first part of the trilogy of small town love and life that is continued in *One Valentine's Day* and *1918*. Hallie Foote, the author's daughter, heads a cast that includes Amanda Plummer, Steven Hill and William Converse-Roberts. The story is largely autobiographical based on Foote's parents.
VHS: S03602. $79.95.
Howard Cummings, USA, 1986-7, 85 mins.

Crazy Horse
The action-packed, true story of the Native American legend Crazy Horse, who led a band of 1,200 Oglala Sioux at the battle of Little Bighorn, where they defeated General Custer and the Seventh Cavalry. With Peter Horton *(Singles)*, Michael Greyeyes *(Geronimo)* and Wes Studi *(Dances with Wolves)*.
VHS: S30445. $49.98.
John Irvin, USA, 1996, 94 mins.

Crime of the Century
The kidnapping of the Lindbergh baby was a crime, but so was the miscarriage of justice that followed. After two years of failure, the investigation, headed by Colonel Schwartzkopf (J.T. Walsh), finds an almost perfect suspect—Bruno Richard Hauptmann (Stephen Rea). Now all they have to find is the evidence to execute him—whether it exists or not. With Isabella Rossellini and David Paymer. "Mesmerizing and provocative" *(Variety)*.
VHS: S30951. $19.98.
Mark Rydell, USA, 1996, 116 mins.

Crimson Tide
Denzel Washington and Gene Hackman star in this thriller set aboard a submarine armed with nuclear warheads. An unconfirmed order to launch these weapons sets off a battle for control of the ship. Ultimately, control over the warheads will determine if a battle that could provoke the third world war actually begins.
VHS: S26612. $19.99.
Laser: Widescreen, THX. **LD75370. $44.98.**
Tony Scott, USA, 1995, 116 mins.

Crisis at Central High
Joanne Woodward stars as teacher Elizabeth Huckaby in this vivid recreation of history: the 1957 integration of Little Rock's Central High. A brilliant performance by Woodward; based on Huckaby's own journals. Woodward won an Emmy for her performance.
VHS: S23443. $19.98.
Lamont Johnson, USA, 1981, 125 mins.

Critical Care
An idealistic and ambitious young doctor (James Spader) on the brink of a fabulous career becomes entangled in a web of ethical doubt and erotic treachery when he gets involved with the daughter (Kyra Sedgwick) of one his comatose patients, who is being kept alive through artificial means. With Helen Mirren, Anne Bancroft and Albert Brooks.
VHS: S33393. $99.99.
Sidney Lumet, USA, 1997, 103 mins.

Critical Choices
Dr. Ludlow's clinic is a haven for women needing safe, legal abortions, until a power-hungry evangelist incites its adversaries to violence that will change the lives of all involved. With Betty Buckley, Pamela Reed, Diana Scarwid, Lusa Repo-Martell and Brian Kerwin.
VHS: S32688. $92.99.
Claudia Weill, USA, 1996, 88 mins.

Cromwell
Richard Harris plays the fiery Oliver Cromwell in this Hollywood story of the 17th century Englishman determined to get England rid of tyrannical rule. Alec Guiness stars as King Charles I.
VHS: S04219. $19.95.
Laser: Widescreen. **LD75493. $39.95.**
Ken Hughes, USA, 1970, 145 mins.

Crooked Hearts
Based on Robert Boswell's critically acclaimed 1987 novel, *Crooked Hearts* is an endearing, insightful look at one family's struggle to come to terms with each other as they start to grow apart. A family secret surfaces in the midst of their seemingly happy environment, and results in tragedy—ultimately forcing them to face each other and the circumstances of their lives with a newfound independence and maturity. Starring Peter Coyote, Cindy Pickett and Jennifer Jason Leigh.
VHS: S14997. $14.95.
Michael Bortman, USA, 1991, 113 mins.

Cross Creek
The story of author Marjorie Kinnan Rawlings *(The Yearling)*, who left behind her husband and financial security to seek a new life for herself in the Florida Everglades. Superbly acted by Mary Steenburgen, with support from Rip Torn and Peter Coyote.
VHS: S02033. $14.98.
Martin Ritt, USA, 1983, 115 mins.

The Crossing Guard
Jack Nicholson and Anjelica Huston star in this dark play on death, revenge and murder. Nicholson aches for the release of a man who killed his daughter while driving under the influence. With his empty life and ruined wife, he has only one goal in mind—making this guy pay.
VHS: S27688. $19.95.
Laser: LD75574. $39.99.
Sean Penn, USA, 1995, 111 mins.

The Crow
Brandon Lee stars in this exciting and mysterious thriller about a man with strange powers. After a terrible crime, only revenge and justice can drive a man to the extremes that define *The Crow*. Brandon Lee, the son of Bruce Lee, is astounding in this, his last film.
VHS: S22157. $19.95.
Alex Proyas, USA, 1993, 100 mins.

The Crow: City of Angels
Vincent Perez takes over the role created by the late Brandon Lee in this action-packed sequel to the popular goth-comics film derived from *The Crow*. After a man is brutally murdered by an evil drug cartel, a mysterious crow brings him back from the dead to seek revenge against his killers. With Mia Kirshner *(Exotica)*, Richard Brooks and Iggy Pop. Features music by Hole, Filter, Bush, White Zombie, Seven Mary Three, PJ Harvey and Above the Law.
VHS: S30463. $19.95.
Laser: LD76057. $39.99.
Tim Pope, USA, 1996, 86 mins.

Cruising
Al Pacino and Karen Allen star in this controversial tale of an undercover cop who finds himself fatally attracted to his prey, a killer of gay men in New York's leather scene. Gritty New York locations offer a realistic backdrop to this strange S/M fantasy. Pacino gets his man, only he's no longer sure of what he wants.
VHS: S19447. $19.98.
William Friedkin, USA, 1980, 106 mins.

Cuba
Sean Connery plays a disinterested mercenary who falls for the beautiful Brooke Adams during the defeat of Batista in 1959. With Jack Weston, Hector Elizondo and Chris Sarandon.
VHS: S00286. $14.95.
Richard Lester, USA, 1979, 121 mins.

Cuba Crossing
Stuart Whitman, Robert Vaughn and Raymond St. Jacques are cast in this political thriller about a plot aimed at Fidel Castro. Said to be based on a true story, the film centers on a barkeep/ soldier of fortune who is drawn into an assassination for hire scheme.
VHS: S25695. $19.95.
Chuck Workman, USA, 1980, 90 mins.

Curdled
William Baldwin and Angela Jones star in this chilling story in the traditon of *Pulp Fiction* about a serial killer who shadows the sexy young woman who's assigned to clean up his latest murder site. With an introduction by Quentin Tarantino.
VHS: S31289. $103.99.
Reb Braddock, USA, 1996, 87 mins.

The Cure
Joseph Mazzello and Brad Renfo are featured in this heartfelt story of a summer filled with a special friendship. They had a dream, but their time together ultimately becomes a treasure which offers more than they had ever hoped for.
VHS: S26465. $98.99.
Laser: LD75092. $34.98.
Peter Horton, USA, 1995, 99 mins.

Cutter's Way
One of the most original American films of the last decade. Alex Cutter (John Heard) is the Vietnam veteran disfigured in the war. When his best friend Richard Bone (Jeff Bridges) is accused of the murder of a teenage girl, Cutter wants to set off after the real murderer with a vengeance. "A hauntingly powerful work," said *New York Magazine*.
VHS: S00290. $14.98.
Laser: LD76361. $39.99.
Ivan Passer, USA, 1982, 90 mins.

Cutthroat Island
Geena Davis and Matthew Modine star in this high seas action adventure film. Morgan Adams (Davis) is a pirate who has purchased the handsome, Harvard-educated William Shaw (Modine) to be her slave. Together they try to unravel the secrets of a buried treasure. In their path stands the vicious pirate Dawg Brown (Frank Langella), who forces them into a furious race for the disputed riches of jewels and gold. Letterboxed.
VHS: S27548. $19.98.
Renny Harlin, USA, 1995, 118 mins.

D.O.A.
Dennis Quaid is a college professor of literature who finds he has been poisoned, in this remake of the classic Edmond O'Brien film. As there is no antidote he does what he can to find out who has killed him and why. With Meg Ryan, Daniel Stern and Charlotte Rampling. Lots of action and a new use for superglue.
VHS: S07172. $19.95.
Rocky Morton/Annabel Jankel, USA, 1988, 98 mins.

Dad
Ted Danson takes a break from the business world where his mother, Olympia Dukakis, is hospitalized, and he finds his dad Jack Lemmon unable to care for himself. From Gary David Goldberg, the creator of TV's *Family Ties*, a sentimental family drama that goes for heart and funny bone with equal success. With Kathy Baker, Kevin Spacey and Ethan Hawke as the son Danson barely knows.
VHS: S12146. $19.95.
Gary David Goldberg, USA, 1989, 117 mins.

The Dain Curse
James Coburn stars as Hamilton Nash in this riveting miniseries set in 1928. When the jewel robbery he was assigned to solve was closed, private Nash's investigation was just beginning. Prompted by the beautiful Gabrielle (Nancy Addison), he challenges what appears to be true and goes on to solve a millionaire's suicide and dissolve the Dain family curse without getting himself killed in the process. Described by *The Los Angeles Times* as the most bizarre, exotic and complex of all Dashiell Hammett's novels. With Hector Elizondo, Jason Miller and Jean Simmons. "Absolutely first rate" *(The New York Post)*.
VHS: S32639. $39.98.
E.W. Swackhammer, USA, 1978, 192 mins.

Daisy Miller
Cybill Shepherd is over her head in this screen version of the classic short story by Henry James about an American girl who finds love and tragedy as a tourist in Europe in the 19th century.
VHS: S04317. $14.95.
Peter Bogdanovich, USA, 1974, 92 mins.

Dandy in Aspic
Laurence Harvey plays a Russian double agent posing as a British spy for the past 18 years, who finds his request to return home denied. His life is further complicated when British intelligence assigns him to eliminate his Russian counterpart and friend. With Tom Courtenay, Mia Farrow.
VHS: S09625. $69.95.
Anthony Mann, USA, 1968, 107 mins.

A Dangerous Woman
Debra Winger stars as a mentally disabled woman who becomes attached to Gabriel Byrne. This relationship is doomed when Barbara Hershey enters the picture. A powerful drama that gives Winger plenty of opportunity to display her skills as an actress, particularly when her character violently acts out her deepest feelings.
VHS: S20935. $19.98.
Laser: LD72401. $34.98.
Stephen Gyllenhaal, USA, 1993, 93 mins.

Daniel
Timothy Hutton has the title role in this Sidney Lumet adaptation of the book by E.L. Doctorow concerning a fictionalized account of the infamous Rosenberg executions and the consequences on their children. Mandy Patinkin and Lindsay Crouse star as the parents, Amanda Plummer as Daniel's sister. With Ed Asner and Ellen Barkin.
VHS: S06129. $59.95.
Sidney Lumet, USA, 1983, 130 mins.

Dark Horse
A sensitive story about families directed by David Hemmings focuses on Allie (Ari Meyers), a troubled young woman distraught over her forced relocation after her mother's death. Sentenced to community service on a horse farm, Allie's life is rejuvenated by her friendship with a prize winning horse.
VHS: S16862. $14.98.
David Hemmings, USA, 1992, 98 mins.

Dark Secret of Harvest Home
From the novel *Harvest Home* by Thomas Tryon *(The Other)* comes this made-for-tv gothic horror story set in New England. An innocent family moves into a small village and doesn't receive the welcome they deserve. With Bette Davis, Rosanna Arquette, Norman Lloyd, Rene Auberjonois, and David Ackroyd. Originally 200 mins.
VHS: S07799. $59.95.
Leonard Penn, USA, 1978, 118 mins.

The Day Lincoln Was Shot
Rob Morrow *(Quiz Show)* stars as John Wilkes Booth and Lance Henriksen *(Dog Day Afternoon)* stars as Abraham Lincoln in this gripping, minute-by-minute account told from the perspectives of both Lincoln and Booth, chronicling the hours leading up to the assassination of Lincoln, Booth's dash for freedom and the showdown that ended in his death.
VHS: S35124. $71.99.
John Gray, USA, 1998, 95 mins.

Day of the Locust
Nathaniel West's powerful novel about Hollywood in the '30's is faithfully transferred to the big screen. William Atherton is the naive artist who learns that Tinseltown has a heart of tin. With Karen Black, Burgess Meredith, Bo Hopkins, Geraldine Page, Richard A. Dysart, Jackie Earle Haley and Donald Sutherland as the unfortunate Homer.
VHS: S10824. $14.95.
Laser: LD75297. $39.98.
John Schlesinger, USA, 1975, 140 mins.

Days of Heaven
An Award winner both at Cannes and in Hollywood, this story follows a trio composed of a fugitive from the Chicago slums (Richard Gere), a shy, rich Texan (Sam Shepard) and a woman (Brooke Adams) caught in a love triangle. Set against the Midwestern wheat fields at the turn of the century, this film is often cited by cinematographers as being one of the most beautifully shot films ever made. Won the Best Oscar for Cinematography. VHS letterboxed.
VHS: S00313. $14.95.
Laser: LD75358. $29.98.
Terence Malick, USA, 1980, 95 mins.

Dead Again
Kenneth Branagh proves he can do more than just Shakespeare in his second film behind the camera. He stars as Mike Church, a cynical, American private detective whose latest missing person case is a real doozy. Emma Thompson co-stars as an amnesiac who is tormented by dreams about a murder that occurred before she was born. A stylish whodunit graced by terrific acting, a very smart script and impeccable camerawork. With Derek Jacobi, Andy Garcia, Hanna Schygulla and a very special cameo by Robin Williams.
VHS: S15675. $19.95.
Laser: LD75124. $24.99.
Kenneth Branagh, USA, 1991, 107 mins.

Dead Man Walking
Sean Penn is an unrepentant killer who is ministered to by a strong-willed nun (Susan Sarandon). This film is unique for staying so firmly glued to the harder issues and emotions that surround hardened killers and the state's use of the death penalty. Penn gives an especially brilliant performance in a film dominated by great acting.
VHS: S28059. $19.98.
Laser: LD75802. $44.95.
DVD: DV60004. $29.95.
Tim Robbins, USA, 1995, 122 mins.

The Dead Pool
Clint Eastwood returns as San Francisco Police Inspector Harry Callahan, for the fifth time. Some deranged person is killing celebrities whose names were listed in a macabre dead pool. When Harry's name is added to the list, he works even harder to catch the killer. With Liam Neeson, Patricia Clarkson and Evan Kim as the latest minority partner of Dirty Harry hoping to stay in one piece until the end of the film.
VHS: S08356. $19.98.
Laser: LD74694. $24.98.
Buddy Van Horn, USA, 1988, 91 mins.

Dead Presidents
A disaffected Vietnam vet turns to crime and finally hits upon a scheme that can change the demeanor of his entire life. Together with his war buddies, he plans to rob an armored car full of "Dead Presidents" (money, that is). In this tightly plotted action film the only color that matters is green.
VHS: S27603. $19.98.
Laser: LD75555. $99.95.
DVD: DV60312. $29.99.
The Hughes Brothers, USA, 1995, 119 mins.

Death Trap
Based on Ira Levin's Broadway hit about a playwright who, after a series of flops, might kill young author Christopher Reeve. A terrific mystery.
VHS: S04333. $69.95.
Sidney Lumet, USA, 1976, 116 mins.

Deceiver
Tim Roth and Renee Zellweger star in this psychological thriller about an unusual murder suspect who manages to turn the tables on a pair of detectives, played by Chris Penn and Michael Rooker, igniting a powder keg of shocking revelations. With Ellen Burstyn and Rosanna Arquette.
VHS: S34919. $99.99.
Jonas Pate/Joshua Pate, USA, 1997, 102 mins.

Decoration Day
As a retired Southern judge (James Garner) helps a disgruntled childhood friend who has refused his Medal of Honor, a decades-old mystery unravels, affecting all with its tragic secret. With Bill Cobbs, Laurence Fishburne, Ruby Dee and Judith Ivey.
VHS: S31181. $14.98.
Robert Markowitz, USA, 1990, 99 mins.

The Deer Hunter
Powerful drama that follows a group of friends from a steel town in Pennsylvania through their Vietnam experiences with fine ensemble work from Robert De Niro, Christopher Walken, John Savage, John Cazale and Meryl Streep.
VHS: S02738. $29.95.
Laser: LD70022. $44.98.
DVD: DV60223. $26.98.
Michael Cimino, USA, 1978, 183 mins.

Deliverance
Jon Voight, Burt Reynolds, Ronny Cox and Ned Beatty spend a weekend in the wilds canoeing and trying to avoid inbred, hostile mountain folk in Georgia. Based on the novel by James Dickey, this wilderness nightmare chills to the bone. With Bill McKinney and Herbert Coward. Letterboxed.
VHS: S00320. $19.98.
Laser: LD71676. $34.98.
John Boorman, USA, 1972, 109 mins.

Deranged
When Joyce's husband leaves for a month of business in London, she starts hearing voices—and seeing things. When a masked intruder attacks her, he unleashes in her a frightened little girl tormented by her "special" relationship with Daddy, and a crazed madwoman hungry for revenge.
VHS: S06367. $14.98.
Chuck Vincent, USA, 1987, 85 mins.

Destiny Turns on the Radio
James LeGros, Dylan McDermott, Nancy Travis, James Belushi and Quentin Tarantino are featured in this wide-ranging tale that turns on luck. Destiny brings an ex-con, his ex-girlfriend, his superstitious partner and a casino owner together. Destiny, by the way, is a character who turns up in a Las Vegas swimming pool to gamble with all these character's lives.
VHS: S26371. $19.95.
Jack Baran, USA, 1995, 102 mins.

Detonator
Pierce Brosnan, Patrick Stewart and Ted Levine star in this action-packed thriller about a renegade Russian general. The general has threatened the West with a nuclear weapon. Only a special mission led by Brosnan can stop this plot to reignite the cold war. Based on Alistair MacLean's novel.
VHS: S22421. $19.95.
David S. Jackson, USA, 1993, 98 mins.

The Devil's Own
Harrison Ford teams up with Brad Pitt, an IRA assassin who brings an innocent American family into the center of a deadly conspiracy. With Treat Williams, Margaret Colin, Ruben Blades and George Hearn. "A thrill to watch. Tense, exciting and slickly directed" (Rex Reed, *The New York Observer*).
VHS: S31719. $19.95.
Laser: LD76303. $39.99.
DVD: DV60233. $24.95.
Alan J. Pakula, USA, 1997, 111 mins.

Diabolique
Sharon Stone, Isabelle Adjani, Chazz Palminteri and Kathy Bates are featured in this remake of the suspense-laden classic. Two women love and hate the same man. Their odd friendship leads them to commit a crime of passion. Unfortunately, the crime they committed together does not end as they had both hoped.
VHS: S29489. $19.98.
Laser: LD75823. $34.98.
Jeremiah Chechik, USA, 1996, 107 mins.

Dick Tracy
Chester Gould's favorite crime fighter is the subject for a color coded, big budget extravaganza directed by and starring Warren Beatty in the title role. The guy in the bright yellow hat and overcoat is supported by Glenne Headly, Charlie Korsmo and Madonna as the slinky songstress Breathless Mahoney. The forces of evil can be found under pounds of latex and include Dustin Hoffman as Mumbles, William Forsythe as Flattop and Al Pacino as a cross between Richard III and Al Capone.
VHS: S13319. $92.95.
Warren Beatty, USA, 1990, 105 mins.

Diner
Nostalgic, funny, personal memoir of a group of young men in their early 20's, hanging out at their favorite diner in Baltimore, 1959. This was the time of innocence, when sex was something to giggle about but never get, and friendship and loyalty crucial. Mickey Rourke and Daniel Stern are featured.
VHS: S00341. $19.98.
Laser: LD70203. $34.95.
Barry Levinson, USA, 1982, 110 mins.

Dirty Dancing
At a Catskill Mountain resort in 1963 a young woman discovers her hidden talents for moving to the music. Her inspiration is her instructor, the poor and streetwise Johnny Castle. Young Baby (Jennifer Grey) also learns other physical moves with her sensitive hunk, played by Patrick Swayze. A real charmer. With Cynthia Rhodes and Jerry Orbach. Letterboxed.
VHS: S06043. $14.98.
Emile Ardolino, USA, 1987, 105 mins.

Dirty Harry
Clint Eastwood introduces his most popular character, San Francisco Police Inspector Harry Callahan. He's a tough cop who gets all the dirty jobs. His primary assignment in this film is to stop a psychotic killer named Scorpio. He does. With Andy Robinson, Reni Santoni and John Vernon. VHS letterboxed.
VHS: S00344. $14.95.
Laser: LD71806. $34.98.
DVD: DV60184. $24.98.
Don Siegel, USA, 1971, 102 mins.

The Disappearance of Garcia Lorca
Haunted by boyhood memories of the great poet Federico Garcia Lorca, a young journalist living in Puerto Rico returns to his Spanish home in search of the truth. With Esai Morales, Edward James Olmos, and Andy Garcia as Federico Garcia Lorca. In English.
VHS: S33018. $104.99.
Marcos Zurinaga, USA, 1996, 114 mins.

The Disappearance of Kevin Johnson
An edgy documentary-style lends a sense of streetwise authenticity to this dramatic piece about Hollywood, where sex sells and money talks. Starring Pierce Brosnan, James Coburn, Dudley Moore, and Kari Wuhrer.
VHS: S34357. $98.99.
Francis Megahy, USA, 1996, 105 mins.

Disclosure
Michael Douglas and Demi Moore portray two characters engaged in a deadly battle over sex, power and money. Tom Sanders (Douglas) is married and works for a large corporation. It's a comfortable position until his new boss (Moore) decides he's not giving his all. Soon accusations of sexual harassment and even more dire threats drive this thriller into ever graver danger and desperation. Based on the novel by Michael Crichton.
VHS: S24816. $19.98.
Laser: Widescreen. **LD74960. $39.99.**
DVD: DV60086. $24.98.
Barry Levinson, USA, 1994, 129 mins.

Diving In
An heroic film touching on themes of personal struggle and triumph, *Diving In* is the story of a talented springboard diver with Olympic dreams who must battle himself to overcome a paralyzing fear of heights. Featuring hot young stars Matt Lattanzi, Matt Adler (*Teen Wolf*) and Kristy Swanson (*Mannequin II*).
VHS: S13723. $89.95.
Strathford Hamilton, USA, 1990, 92 mins.

Dog Day Afternoon
This fantastic thriller centers on a bisexual and his buddy, who rob a bank in order to get the cash for a sex change operation for the ring leader's lover. With a first-rate performance by Al Pacino.
VHS: S21858. $19.98.
Laser: LD74523. $39.98.
Sidney Lumet, USA, 1975, 124 mins.

Dogfight
River Phoenix and Lili Taylor star in this poignant, offbeat romance set in the early 1960's. Just prior to shipping out to Vietnam, four Marine buddies try to find the ugliest women in San Francisco to win a bar bet. After Taylor catches on, Phoenix tries to take her out on a real date to apologize. With Richard Panebianco and a heavily disguised E.G. Dailey as the toothless winner of the dogfight.
VHS: S15529. $19.98.
Nancy Savoca, USA, 1991, 95 mins.

Dolores Claiborne
Kathy Bates and Jennifer Jason Leigh bring star power to this highly successful adaptation of a Stephen King bestseller. In a small New England town a woman is widely believed to have killed her husband. When her aged and mean-spirited employer has a mysterious accident, this woman must face renewed scrutiny and censure. Through it all her love for her only daughter carries her along. This suspenseful melodrama is filled with surprising insights. VHS letterboxed.
VHS: S26519. $19.95.
Laser: LD75098. $39.95.
Taylor Hackford, USA, 1995, 131 mins.

Dominick and Eugene
A touching story of twin brothers living in Pittsburgh. Ray Liotta is Eugene, the hard working medical student. Tom Hulce is his good natured, mentally slower and older brother Dominick. He works on a garbage truck and gets to find a lot of neat junk. The med student is afraid to leave his brother on his own and take a job in California. Fine performances from both leads. With Jamie Lee Curtis.
VHS: S09822. $19.98.
Robert M. Young, USA, 1988, 96 mins.

Don King: Only in America
From running numbers to "The Rumble in the Jungle," from Muhammad Ali to Mike Tyson, boxing promoter Don King made millions, and made millionaires, making himself the biggest name in boxing since boxing began. But how he got there—making and breaking the law and anyone who got in his way—is the kind of story that could happen only in America. With a knockout Golden Globe-winning lead performance by Ving Rhames (*Pulp Fiction*). Also with Vondie Curtis-Hall, Jeremy Piven and Loretta Devine.
VHS: S33890. $79.95.
John Herzfeld, USA, 1997, 112 mins,

Donnie Brasco
Posing as jewel broker Donnie Brasco, FBI agent Joe Pistone (Johnny Depp) is granted entrance into the violent mob family of aging hitman Lefty Ruggiero (Al Pacino). When his personal and professional lives collide, Pistone jeopardizes his marriage, his job, his life and ultimately the gangster mentor he has come to respect and admire. "A killer gangster picture" (Gene Shalit, *Today Show*) based on a true story.
VHS: S31768. $19.95.
Laser: LD76304. $39.99.
Mike Newell, USA, 1997, 127 mins.

Double Crossed
Dennis Hopper stars in this HBO movie about the life and death of Drug Enforcement Agency operative Barry Seal. Can a man who plays both sides of the law be safe on either one? In this case the question is probably moot. With Robert Carradine, Richard Jenkins, G.W. Bailey and Adrienne Barbeau. This true-life drama was awarded two 1991 Ace Awards for best movie/mini-series and best editing in a movie/mini-series.
VHS: S16568. $79.99.
Roger Young, USA, 1991, 111 mins.

Double Edge
Faye Dunaway stars as an ambitious New York journalist given her first international assignment, reporting on the Israeli/ Palestinian tensions, and the ensuing moral and ethical consequences of being involved with two men on opposite sides of the political spectrum. "A tough and provocative drama. It's suspenseful, intelligent and emotional" (William Wolf).
VHS: S17889. $19.98.
Amos Kollek, USA, 1991, 85 mins.

Down Came a Blackbird
Raul Julia's final performance is captured in this film which also stars Laura Dern and Vanessa Redgrave. Dern goes undercover at a sanctuary for political prisoners and finds herself kidnapped by military terrorists. Now Julia's character, a professor with a secret past, holds the key to her future.
VHS: S26952. $95.99.
Laser: LD75425. $34.98.
Jonathan Sanger, USA, 1995, 112 mins.

Dragonheart
The action-adventure story of a valiant knight (Dennis Quaid) and the last dragon, who join forces to free a kingdom enslaved by tyranny. Family entertainment with fantasy, humor, romance and dazzling special effects from Industrial Light & Magic. With Julie Christie, Pete Postlethwaite, David Thewlis and Sean Connery as the voice of Draco. Contains special behind-the-scenes footage and interviews. VHS letterboxed.
VHS: S31070. $19.98.
Laser: LD76145. $39.98.
Rob Cohen, USA, 1996, 103 mins.

Dream Lover
In this sensual thriller, James Spader plays Ray Reardon, an architect who has just met the woman of his dreams, Madchen Amick. Soon this dream becomes a nightmare as this woman's smiling seductive ways are revealed as the means to a horrible end. Unfortunately this is no dream, but a terrifying tale of love gone wrong.
VHS: S22888. $19.95.
Laser: LD74757. $34.95.
Nicholas Kazan, USA, 1993, 103 mins.

Dreamchild
The enchanting, critically-acclaimed story of Alice Hargreaves, the inspiration for Lewis Carroll's *Alice in Wonderland*. On a visit to New York in the 1930's, Alice, now 80 years old, has her early memories brought to life. With Coral Browne and Peter Gallagher.
VHS: S00372. $14.98.
Gavin Millar, USA, 1985, 90 mins.

Driving Miss Daisy
The Pulitzer prizewinning play of Alfred Uhry walked off with four Oscars, including Best Picture and Best Actress. The story concerns the long-term relationship between a strong-willed, elderly, Jewish Southern matron and her accommodating Black chauffeur. Jessica Tandy and Morgan Freeman star in this genteel comedy of bigotry and friendship. With Patti Lupone, Esther Rolle and Dan Aykroyd as Tandy's son, Boolie.
VHS: S12524. $19.98.
Laser: LD70562. $24.98.
DVD: DV60087. $24.98.
Bruce Beresford, USA, 1989, 99 mins.

Drop Squad
Eriq La Salle and Vondi Curtis Hall star in this unique thriller about a radical terrorist group. They abduct a black ad executive who sells out his race in a bid for success. Then they apply powerful and sometimes brutal persuasion to win him over to the community's cause. Produced by Spike Lee.
VHS: S24335. $19.98.
Laser: Letterboxed. **LD74924. $34.98.**
David Johnson, USA, 1994, 88 mins.

Drop Zone
Wesley Snipes stars in this action-packed adventure as a sky diving marshall. His quarry is Gary Busey, a gang leader for a band of techno-terrorists. The story sizzles as Snipes tries to head off this band of violent crazies so they don't succeed in hitting their next target.
VHS: S24873. $19.95.
Laser: LD75369. $44.98.
John Badham, USA, 1994, 101 mins.

Echo Park
This offbeat sleeper comedy follows the trials and tribulations of three roommates—a poet/pizza delivery man (Tom Hulce), a single-mother/waitress (Susan Dey) and an Austrian bodybuilder who hopes to become the next Arnold Schwarzenegger (Michael Bowen)—living in Los Angeles' Echo Park. With Richard "Cheech" Marin.
VHS: S30897. $14.95.
Robert Dornhelm, Austria/USA, 1986, 93 mins.

Eddie and the Cruisers
In 1963, Eddie's car plunged from a Jersey bridge. He was a rock revisionary who died before his time—or did he? Soundtrack by John Cafferty. With Tom Berenger, Michael Pare, and Ellen Barkin.
VHS: S33983. $14.98.
Martin Davidson, USA, 1983, 92 mins.

The Edge
A "nerve-racking adventure" (Janet Maslin, *New York Times*), written by David Mamet, in which a plane crash in the freezing Alaskan wilderness pits intellectual billionaire Charles Morse (Anthony Hopkins) against self-satisfied fashion photographer Robert Green (Alec Baldwin) in a brutal struggle for survival. Each will soon discover that the greatest danger comes not from nature, but from fear, treachery and, quite possibly, murder.
VHS: S33033. $103.99.
Laser: LD76431. $39.98.
Lee Tamahori, USA, 1997, 120 mins.

The Education of Little Tree
James Cromwell *(Babe)* stars in this heartwarming adaptation of the acclaimed bestseller about an orphaned eight-year-old Cherokee boy sent to live with his grandparents in Tennessee's Smoky Mountains during the 1930s.
VHS: S34277. $92.99.
Richard Friedenberg, USA, 1997, 117 mins.

Electra Glide in Blue
Robert Blake stars in this hard edged, well acted story of a pint-sized highway motorcycle patrolman who tries too hard to do the right thing. He finds himself at odds with his superiors, his partner and a van load of roadway hooligans. With Billy Green Bush, Mitchell Ryan, Jeannine Riley and Elisha Cook Jr. Title refers to a motorcycle.
VHS: S06058. $14.95.
Laser: LD76364. $39.99.
James W. Guercio, USA, 1973, 106 mins.

The Electric Horseman
A $12 million thoroughbred horse is missing and Robert Redford, playing a derelict, is riding high. Jane Fonda is strangely attracted to this man on a horse, even if it's not really his mount. Valerie Perrine is also featured in this contemporary film set in Las Vegas.
VHS: S21277. $14.98.
Sydney Pollack, USA, 1979, 120 mins.

Emerald Forest
Story of an American businessman who spends 10 years searching for his son who was captured by a primitive Amazon tribe. A fascinating look at primitive but unique civilization.
Laser: LD74464. $39.99.
John Boorman, USA, 1985, 113 mins.

Emma
A fun and lighthearted comedy based on Jane Austen's story about a mischievous young woman (Gwyneth Paltrow) who tries to play matchmaker and makes a tangled mess of everyone's lives, particularly that of friend Harriet Smith (Toni Collette, *Muriel's Wedding*). When Emma ultimately falls in love, everyone becomes free from her matchmaking escapades. "Devilishly funny" *(Rolling Stone)*.
VHS: S30967. $19.99.
Laser: LD76157. $39.98.
Douglas McGrath, USA, 1996, 121 mins.

End of Innocence
Dyan Cannon wrote, directed and stars in the story of a woman trying to survive dealing with her family, her friends and herself. A nervous breakdown triggers a lengthy stay in an expensive rehabilitation center where she meets a variety of supportive patients and learns to cope. With John Heard, George Coe, Lola Mason and the late Rebecca Schaeffer as Cannon at 18.
VHS: S13780. $89.95.
Dyan Cannon, USA, 1990, 102 mins.

The Endless Game
Albert Finney stars as Alec Hillsden, a British intelligence agent, who is determined to discover the truth behind the death of a former colleague, Caroline (Kristin Scott Thomas). They had been lovers once, until she was captured by the KGB, tortured, released and then murdered. George Segal plays a corrupt American agent who is ready to sell his secrets to the highest bidder. But in the world of espionage, facts don't come cheap, and Alec may have to turn traitor to get at the truth. This spy thriller, filmed entirely on location in England, Austria and Finland, was written and directed by Bryan Forbes *(King Rat, International Velvet)* from his best-selling novel.
VHS: S13523. $89.95.
Bryan Forbes, USA, 1989, 123 mins.

The English Patient
A stellar cast, meticulous attention to detail, first-rate cinematography, and a tragic love story combine for an irresistible package of a movie, the winner of nine Academy Awards, including Best Picture. When a mysterious stranger is rescued from a plane, his identity is gradually revealed and the secrets and passions of war are unlocked. With Ralph Fiennes, Kristin Scott-Thomas, Willem Dafoe, and Juliette Binoche in an Academy Award-winning role. Letterboxed.
VHS: S31822. $19.95.
Laser: LD76338. $99.95.
Anthony Minghella, USA, 1996, 162 mins.

Entertaining Angels: The Dorothy Day Story
Moira Kelly stars as Dorothy Day, the firebrand woman who brought food, shelter and hope to New York's downtrodden in the Depression, founded the nationwide Catholic Worker movement and became one of the era's leading human rights activists. With Martin Sheen, Brian Keith and Melinda Dillon.
VHS: S32067. $19.98.
Michael Ray Rhodes, USA, 1996, 112 mins.

Eraser
Arnold Schwarzenegger, Vanessa Williams, James Caan, James Coburn and Robert Pastorelli star in this effects-filled action film about a U.S. marshall protecting a federal witness from government turncoats selling an advanced super-gun to terrorists. VHS letterboxed.
VHS: S28487. $19.98.
Laser: LD75947. $44.95.
DVD: DV60044. $24.98.
Charles Russell, USA, 1996, 115 mins.

Erik the Viking
Gordon Mitchell stars in this drama of the Norse warrior and his battle-hardened men as they make it to North America and battle the elements, Indians and each other. 1972, 95 mins.
VHS: S11009. $59.95.

Escape from L.A.
Kurt Russell is back as Snake Plissken in John Carpenter's follow-up to his 1981 cult hit, *Escape from New York*. Snake is sent on a mission to a futuristic Los Angeles, an anarchist state left surrounded by water after a massive earthquake. Peter Fonda, Steve Buscemi and Pam Grier also star in a post-Apocalyptic Los Angeles.
VHS: S30586. $14.95.
John Carpenter, USA, 1996, 101 mins.

Escape from Sobibor
Richard Rashke's compelling book about the largest escape from a Nazi prison camp is successfully adapted by Reginald Rose in this nail-biting thriller. Stars Alan Arkin, Joanna Pacula and Rutger Hauer.
VHS: S22022. $19.98.
Laser: LD75190. $34.98.
Jack Gold, USA, 1987, 120 mins.

Everybody Wins
Nick Nolte and Debra Winger star in a complicated tale involving murder, blackmail, political corruption and the worship of a dead Civil War officer. Set in a small New England town, Nolte plays a highly principled private investigator who has trouble believing his client, who is a known prostitute and a suspected flake. With Jack Warden, Judith Ivey and Will Patton. The script is by Arthur Miller, his first since *The Misfits*.
VHS: S12422. $89.95.
Karel Reisz, USA, 1990, 97 mins.

Excalibur
A serious retelling of the King Arthur legend, visually brilliant. "The imagery is impassioned and has a hypnotic quality. The film is like Flaubert's more exotic fantasies—one lush, enraptured scene after another" (Pauline Kael).
VHS: S01754. $19.98.
John Boorman, USA, 1981, 140 mins.

Excess Baggage
Poor little rich girl Emily Hope (Alicia Silverstone) stages her own kidnapping to capture her father's attention. While she is waiting for her BMW to get de-booted, it's stolen by car thief Vincent Roche (Benicio del Toro, *The Usual Suspects*). But it is Emily who steals the thief's heart. Christopher Walken stars as hitman Uncle Ray. With Harry Connick, Jr.
VHS: S33034. $104.99.
Laser: LD76428. $34.95.
Marco Bambilla, USA, 1997, 101 mins.

Execution of Private Slovik
Martin Sheen delivers a powerful performance in the title role of the first American soldier to be sentenced to death for desertion since the Civil War. This true-life World War II drama examines the man and his motives to flee under fire. With Ned Beatty, Mariclare Costello, Matt Clark, Charles Haid and Gary Busey. The script based on the book by William Bradford Huie is written by Richard Levinson and William Link, the creators of *Columbo*.
VHS: S14944. $79.95.
Lamont Johnson, USA, 1974, 120 mins.

Executive Action
While Oliver Stone was making cheap horror movies in Canada, other filmmakers were hard at work debunking the Warren Commission's opinion on the assassination of JFK. Burt Lancaster stars as the disgruntled intelligence agent given the green light to silence the Commander in Chief in Dallas. Robert Ryan and Will Geer play right-wing businessmen who lend their support to the plan. The script by Dalton Trumbo is based on the book by conspiracy theorists Mark Lane and Donald Freed. A low-budget and leisurely effort, but occasionally blood curdling and certainly thought-provoking.
VHS: S15825. $19.98.
David Miller, USA, 1973, 91 mins.

Exposure
Peter Coyote plays an American photographer in Brazil who becomes involved in a murder. When he and his girlfriend Amanda Pays have been attacked, he takes knife-fighting lessons from a professional hitman. With Tcheky Karyo, Raul Cortez, Guila Gam and Cassia Kiss.
VHS: S16224. $19.95.
Laser: LD75192. $34.98.
Walter Salles Jr., USA/Brazil, 1991, 105 mins.

Extreme Measures
Emergency room physician Dr. Guy Luthan (Hugh Grant) discovers that not all surgery is intended to cure when he confronts a mystery that seems beyond his skills. His search for answers surrounding the bizarre death of a homeless man takes him into the dark frontiers of medical research and to a confrontation with Dr. Lawrence Myrick (Gene Hackman), one of the country's most revered medical figures. Now, his credibility, career and life are all at risk as he forces everyone to take "extreme measures." Produced by Elizabeth Hurley. "Compelling! It grabs you and won't let you go" (Susan Granger, *American Movie Classics*).
VHS: S30966. $19.98.
Laser: LD76138. $34.95.
Michael Apted, USA, 1996, 118 mins.

Eye for an Eye
Sally Field stars in this nerve-shattering suspense drama about a woman who finds that the justice system has failed after her daughter has been murdered. The police know who did it and have the killer (Kiefer Sutherland) in custody, but despite overwhelming evidence they have to let him go on a technicality. Empowered by her rage, she seeks out the killer to make him pay for his crime. Directed by Oscar winner John Schlesinger *(Midnight Cowboy)*. With Ed Harris.
VHS: S30953. $14.95.
John Schlesinger, USA, 1996, 102 mins.

Eye of God
In this "haunting debut" *(Boston Herald)* by Tim Blake Nelson, a young boy is discovered wandering aimlessly, blood on his head, along a country road. Stunned by what he has witnessed, the boy is interrogated by the town's Sheriff (Hal Holbrook). In a series of intermittent flashbacks beginning six months earier, the story of the doomed marriage between Ainsley Dupree (Martha Plimpton) and Jack Stillings (Kevin Anderson) unfolds. "The performances are a reminder of the illuminating power of exquisitely meticulous acting. Every detail feels absolutely right" *(The New York Times)*.
VHS: S34612. $69.95.
Tim Blake Nelson, USA, 1996, 88 mins.

Eye of the Needle
Donald Sutherland stars as a steely Nazi assassin on assignment in England during World War II, who finds his mission is complicated by the attentions of a frustrated married woman. With Kate Nelligan and Ian Bannen. From the best-seller by Ken Follett. Tension-filled performances.
VHS: S06059. $14.95.
Laser: LD76069. $39.98.
Richard Marquand, USA, 1981, 112 mins.

Eye on the Sparrow
Mare Winningham and Keith Carradine deliver strong performances in this inspirational true story. They play Ethel and James Lee, a blind-from-birth couple, who must fight the state bureaucracy for the right to legally adopt a child. With Conchata Ferrell, Sandy McPeak, Kaaren Lee and Bianca Rose.
VHS: S15916. $89.98.
John Korty, USA, 1987, 94 mins.

The Eyes of Amaryllis
An adventure tale adapted from Natalie Babbitt's engrossing tale about a young woman who is sent to visit her eccentric grandmother at her coastal beach home as she awaits her husband, lost at sea 30 years earlier. With Ruth Ford, Martha Byrne, and Jonathan Bolt.
VHS: S18513. $14.98.
Frederick King Keller, USA, 1982, 84 mins.

Fabulous Baker Boys
Michelle Pfeiffer, Jeff and Beau Bridges star in this Oscar-nominated film about two cocktail lounge piano players whose career has hit a sour note until they meet chain-smoking Susie Diamond, whose voice and sexy stage presence revitalize the Baker Boys' career as well as cause them to reevaluate their relationships with each other and their music.
VHS: S12004. $14.98.
Steven Kloves, USA, 1989, 116 mins.

Face/Off
John Woo's over-the-top thrill ride is an absurd, action-packed, scene-chewing competition between John Travolta, an FBI agent, and his worst enemy, Nicolas Cage, a psychopathic terrorist who killed his son. The FBI assigns Travolta to undergo plastic surgery to borrow the face of the captured, comatose Cage in order to play him and gather information from the terrorist's crime ring to find and dismantle a bomb that Cage set. When Cage awakes without his face, he must find revenge wearing Travolta's. Explosive fun as Travolta and Cage play each other and take turns wearing the black and white hats. With Joan Allen and Gina Gershon. Letterboxed.
VHS: S32517. $19.95.
John Woo, USA, 1997, 140 mins.

The Falcon and the Snowman
Timothy Hutton and Sean Penn are two typical American young men who are willing to sell U.S. government secrets to the Soviets in Mexico in this intriguing account of a true life story. Based on the book by Robert Lindsay. With Lori Singer, Pat Hingle and Dorian Harewood.
VHS: Out of print. For rental only.
Laser: Widescreen. **LD74832. $49.99.**
John Schlesinger, USA, 1985, 131 mins.

Falling Down
Michael Douglas plays the unemployed defense worker who goes on a one-man rampage in Los Angeles. "A wickedly mischievous, entertaining suspense thriller" (Vincent Canby). With Barbara Hershey, Robert Duvall and Tuesday Weld.
VHS: S19206. $19.98.
Laser: LD71897. $34.98.
Joel Schumacher, USA, 1993, 113 mins.

Falling from Grace
John Mellencamp's film about a famous singer who returns to his hometown for his grandfather's 80th birthday and to his past and the woman he left behind. "A funny and touching film" *(Rolling Stone)*.
VHS: S17069. $19.95.
John Cougar Mellencamp, USA, 1992, 102 mins.

A Family Thing
Robert Duvall and James Earl Jones star as two long-lost brothers, one white and one black, who unite in an uplifting and humorous journey of self-discovery. "Honest, brutal and beautiful. *A Family Thing* is simply astonishing" (*Interview* Magazine). VHS letterboxed.
VHS: S30448. $19.98.
Laser: LD76060. $39.98.
Richard Pearce, USA, 1996, 109 mins.

The Fan
When baseball's highest-paid star (Wesley Snipes) goes into a batting slump, his number-one fan (Robert De Niro) will stop at nothing—including murder—to get him back on track. With John Leguizamo, Benicio del Toro and Ellen Barkin. "Rarely has the allure and thrill of any sport been captured so vividly on screen!" (Alan Silverman, Voice of America).
VHS: S30596. $19.95.
Tony Scott, USA, 1996, 116 mins.

Far and Away
Ron Howard's epic vision of late 19th century Irish immigrants, with Tom Cruise as an indentured servant to Nicole Kidman, an aristocratic heiress fleeing her rigid, authoritarian father. The couple turns up in Boston, and moves west to take part in the Oklahoma land rush.
VHS: S17737. $19.98.
Ron Howard, USA, 1992, 140 mins.

Fast Forward
Follows eight talented teenagers from a small town to New York City for a one-in-a-million shot at stardom in a national dance competition. In the process, the teens get a crash course in self-sufficiency in a city that challenges them to survive, compete and grow.
VHS: S32924. $14.95.
Sidney Poitier, USA, 1985, 113 mins.

Fat Man and Little Boy
The story behind the making of the world's first atomic bombs. Paul Newman is cast as the general in charge of completing the project. Dwight Schultz from the A-Team is J. Robert Oppenheimer, the physicist in charge of making the project work. The title refers to the names of the bombs that were dropped on Japan. This historical drama also features John Cusack, Laura Dern and Bonnie Bedelia.
VHS: S11735. $14.95.
Laser: LD75350. $29.98.
Roland Joffe, USA, 1989, 127 mins.

Fatal Attraction (Director's Cut)
The controversial ending the public refused is restored in this widescreen format presentation with an introduction by the director, including personal insights and rehearsal footage. When Anne Archer goes out of town for the weekend, husband Michael Douglas involves himself in what he thinks is a harmless affair. Partner Glenn Close misinterprets their casual sex, and reacts by infiltrating the perfect family and trying to break them apart. Letterboxed.
VHS: S15709. $29.95.
Adrian Lyne, USA, 1987, 159 mins.

Fatherland
Rutger Hauer and Miranda Richardson star in this chilling thriller, packed with action, set in a world where Hitler triumphed. Together they may uncover the secret that allowed the Third Reich to win the war and prosper in a terrible peace. Based on the bestseller by Robert Harris.
VHS: S24567. $19.98.
Christopher Menaul, USA, 1994, 106 mins.

Fear
Mark Wahlberg stars as a seemingly ordinary young man whose obsession with a 16-year-old girl (Alyssa Milano) takes a frightening turn. Soon this young man's charisma and ingenuity take on a sinister character as he insists on the validity of his singular fascination.
VHS: S29921. $19.98.
Laser: LD75909. $34.98.
James Foley, USA, 1996, 119 mins.

Federal Hill
Nicholas Turturro is at the center of a young, talented cast in this powerful crime drama. Five reckless friends struggle with the hopelessness of an inner city Italian neighborhood in Providence, Rhode Island. An alluring college student, Libby Langdon, comes between two fast friends even as she leads her lover away from a life dominated by gangs. But before he can get away, there is one last scam.
VHS: S25902. $94.99.
Michael Corrente, USA, 1994, 100 mins.

A Few Good Men
Tom Cruise plays a Harvard-educated lawyer assigned to defend two Marines charged with killing another soldier. Jack Nicholson is a career officer with political ambitions whose actions precipitated the crime. With Demi Moore, Kevin Pollak and Kevin Bacon. Letterboxed.
VHS: S18764. $19.95.
DVD: DV60022. $24.95.
Rob Reiner, USA, 1992, 137 mins.

Field of Dreams
Kevin Costner stars as a struggling Iowa farmer who builds a baseball diamond in his corn field so that the ghosts of old players will have somewhere to play ball. This powerful movie fantasy is based on the novel *Shoeless Joe* by W.P. Kinsella and is dedicated to any kid who ever tossed a ball around with his dad. With Amy Madigan, James Earl Jones, Ray Liotta and Burt Lancaster.
VHS: S11694. $14.98.
Laser: LD70030. $89.95.
DVD: DV60216. $34.98.
Phil Alden Robinson, USA, 1989, 106 mins.

The Fifth Monkey
On a journey to sell four mischievous chimps, a simple peasant (played by Ben Kingsley) shares laughter, danger and heartbreak with the animals...eventually realizing that their friendship is worth more than money. Set in the lush Brazilian tropics, *The Fifth Monkey* is an inspiring and heart-warming tale, brimming with adventure. Great family entertainment.
VHS: S13829. $89.95.
Eric Rochant, USA, 1990, 93 mins.

Finish Line
James Brolin and his son Josh star in this drama about a track coach whose obsession with winning drives his son to take steroids.
VHS: S09876. $79.95.
John Nicolella, USA, 1988, 96 mins.

The Firm
Sydney Pollack's adaptation of John Grisham's best seller stars Tom Cruise as a Harvard-educated tax specialist who joins an impeccable Memphis law firm only to discover it's an elaborate front for the Chicago mob.
VHS: S19512. $19.95.
Laser: Widescreen. **LD75310. $39.98.**
Sydney Pollack, USA, 1993, 154 mins.

First Do No Harm
Meryl Streep is Lori, a determined mother who refuses to allow her happy, tight-knit family to unravel when her youngest son, Robbie (Seth Adkins), becomes ill. As the situation worsens and the family becomes emotionally and financially desperate, Lori struggles to keep them all afloat. Just when things appear to be at their darkest, a miraculous turn of events occurs that brings Robbie and the entire family back together.
VHS: S32750. $103.99.
Jim Abrahams, USA, 1997, 94 mins.

First Knight
Sean Connery, Richard Gere and Julia Ormond star in this costume epic based on the legend of King Arthur. Love and chivalry set the stage for a tempestuous tale. War is very nearly overpowered by the personal traumas of the fabled royal love triangle composed of King Arthur, Sir Lancelot and the Lady Guinevere. Featuring Ben Cross and the legendary Sir John Gielgud.
VHS: S26773. $19.95.
Laser: LD75114. $44.95.
DVD: DV60024. $24.95.
Jerry Zucker, USA, 1995, 133 mins.

Five Easy Pieces
A classic performance by Jack Nicholson as a classical pianist who has given up his musical career to work in the oil fields. Great supporting work by Karen Black, Susan Anspach, Billy Green Bush and Helena Kallianiotes as a complaining hitchhiker. Classic scene in which Jack finally figures out how to get a simple order of toast.
VHS: S07789. $14.95.
Laser: Widescreen. **LD70981. $34.95.**
Bob Rafelson, USA, 1970, 96 mins.

Flashdance
Jennifer Beals stars as a welder by day and interpretive dancer by night, who lives in a huge warehouse and really wants to be a member of the Pittsburgh Ballet company. Light on logic but heavy on hot numbers and popular music that started the torn sweatshirt trend of the day. With Michael Nouri, Sunny Johnson and Lilia Skala.
VHS: S01883. $19.95.
Laser: LD75195. $34.98.
Adrian Lyne, USA, 1983, 96 mins.

Flesh and Blood
Rutger Hauer stars in Paul Verhoeven's medieval tale about a mercenary soldier who kidnaps princess Jennifer Jason Leigh away from her husband in this adventure of intrigue and romance. With Tom Burlinson.
VHS: S06822. $14.98.
Paul Verhoeven, USA, 1985, 126 mins.

Flesh and Bone
Dennis Quaid and Meg Ryan star as lovers whose passion may lead to untold dangers. In their ignorance, they unknowingly share a common danger spawned by a deadly secret from the past. James Caan also stars in this romantic thriller.
VHS: S20718. $19.95.
Steven Kloves, USA, 1993, 127 mins.

Fly Away Home
One of the most critically acclaimed films of the year, *Fly Away Home* is the adventure of a teenage girl and her estranged father, who learn about family when they take in a flock of orphaned geese and find that they must teach them how to fly. Starring Academy Award-winner Anna Paquin *(The Piano)* and Jeff Daniels. "Soaring! A hymn to the human spirit!" (Richard Schickel, *Time*).
VHS: S30576. $24.99.
Laser: LD76073. $34.95.
DVD: DV60025. $24.95.
Carroll Ballard, USA, 1996, 107 mins.

Fools of Fortune
Set against the turbulent years of the Irish rebellion, *Fools of Fortune* is a compelling drama of one woman's struggle for survival against incredible odds. Starring Mary Elizabeth Mastrantonio, Iain Glen, and Julie Christie. "It is lush and absorbing with superb performances. One of Julie Christie's best performances" (Jeffrey Lyons).
VHS: S14258. $89.95.
Pat O'Connor, USA, 1991, 104 mins.

For Roseanna
In this charming, offbeat comedy, Jean Reno *(The Professional)* stars as Marcello, the most romantic man in the Italian village of Travento. He will do anything to please his beautiful, ailing wife, Roseanna (Mercedes Ruhl). What she desires most is to secure a family plot in the local cemetery. But when the church allows no reservations, and the last three spaces are going fast, the adventure begins. With Polly Walker and Mark Frankel.
VHS: S32689. $19.95.
Paul Weiland, USA/Italy, 1997, 95 mins.

Forced March
Chris Sarandon plays an actor hired to play a concentration camp inmate for a contemporary film about the Holocaust. He finds his life changed by the experience in ways that surprise him. With Renee Soutendijk, Josef Sommer, Rosalind Cash and Viveca Lindfors. Filmed in Budapest.
VHS: S11725. $89.95.
Rick King, USA, 1989, 104 mins.

Foreign Student
Robin Givens stars in this tale of obsessive love. A young French student finds himself transferred to a small Southern college in the 1950's. There he is befriended by a star quarterback, and falls in love with a young teacher (Givens). Soon their romance breaks all the rules and taboos.
VHS: S22887. $19.95.
Laser: Wide screen. **LD74830. $34.98.**
Eva Sereny, USA, 1994, 96 mins.

Forever Lulu
Hanna Schygulla stars as Elaine Hines, a struggling writer whose search for fame and fortune leads to a wacky misadventure of murder and mistaken identity in this offbeat comedy of errors. With Deborah Harry, Alec Baldwin.
VHS: S07318. $79.95.
Amos Kollek, USA, 1987, 100 mins.

Forgotten Prisoners
A look at the terrifying truth that lies behind the blood-stained walls of a Turkish prison. Ron Silver is Jordan Ford, an American expert in international law who is sent to Turkey by Amnesty International's head of research (Robert Daltrey) to investigate the horrifying stories of brutality in their prisons. What he discovers is that shocking and inhuman torture is routinely practiced on the innocent in the dark, secret underworld of Turkish "justice." USA, 1990, 92 mins.
VHS: S14161. $79.98.
Robert Greenwald, USA, 1990, 92 mins.

The Formula
Police detective George C. Scott investigates the murder of an old friend which leads him to billionaire oil magnate Marlon Brando and a secret Nazi formula for synthetic fuel.
VHS: S16444. $19.98.
Laser: LD76270. $39.99.
John G. Avildsen, USA, 1980, 117 mins.

Forrest Gump
Tom Hanks stars as the endearing, naive hero of this unlikely historical film that was nominated for 14 Oscars and won the Academy Awards for Best Picture, Best Actor and Best Director. Through the magic of trick photography, Gump encounters several important figures and plays a hitherto unknown role in the unfolding of current events. Gary Sinise and Sally Field also star. Letterboxed.
VHS: S24309. $19.95.
Laser: THX. **LD75300. $49.98.**
Robert Zemeckis, USA, 1994, 142 mins.

Fort Apache, the Bronx
This tough-talking street melodrama takes a disturbing look at New York's South Bronx at its down and dirty worst. The fine cast includes Paul Newman, Ken Wahl, Ed Asner, Pam Grier and Danny Aiello. It all adds up to an exciting urban nightmare story.
VHS: S07722. $19.98.
Daniel Petrie, USA, 1981, 123 mins.

The Fortune
During the 1920s, the "Mann Act" prohibited transporting a woman across state lines for "immoral purposes." So Nick (Warren Beatty), eager to run off to California with his wealthy sweetheart Freddie (Stockard Channing), arranges for her to marry his friend Oscar (Jack Nicholson) until his divorce is final. But love and lust turn this simple business arrangement into a confused lover's triangle. The idea strikes them to kill Freddie and split her inheritance—if they don't kill each other first.
VHS: S33945. $19.95.
Mike Nichols, USA, 1975, 88 mins.

The Fourth Wise Man
Martin Sheen, Alan Arkin and Eileen Brennan star in this drama about one man's search for the Messiah. With Lance Kerwin and Harold Gould.
VHS: S17911. $19.98.
Michael Rhodes, USA, 1979, 72 mins.

Foxes
Jodie Foster, Cherie Currie (from legendary '70s all-girl punk band, The Runaways), Marilyn Kagan and Kandice Stroh star as four troubled teens coping with divorce, drugs and alcohol abuse in L.A.'s fast lane. With Scott Baio, Sally Kellerman and Randy Quaid.
VHS: S33984. $14.98.
Adrian Lyne, USA, 1980, 106 mins.

Foxfire
This "rebelina without a cause" (Dennis Dermody, *The Paper*), based on the best-selling book by Joyce Carol Oates, is the story of four high school girls united by a mysterious stranger on a quest for revenge. With Angelina Jolie *(Hackers)*, Hedy Burress (TV's *Boston Common*), Cathy Moriarty *(Casper)* and Calvin Klein model Jenny Shimuzu. "Not since *Thelma & Louise* has a film captured the essence of female rebellion" (Pat Kramer, *Boxoffice*).
VHS: S30916. $97.99.
Laser: LD76133. $34.99.
Annette Haywood-Carter, USA, 1996, 102 mins.

Foxfire
Jessica Tandy won Tony and Emmy Awards for her portrayal of Annie Nations, a Blue Ridge Mountain widow who cannot forget her husband (Hume Cronyn) and is torn between living her life in the past or moving from her home and changing her future, as her son (John Denver) urges her to do.
VHS: S31180. $14.98.
Judson Taylor, USA, 1987, 118 mins.

Frances
Jessica Lange received an Oscar nomination for her portrayal of Frances Farmer, the intelligent Hollywood actress who was involuntarily committed to a mental institution.
VHS: S04335. $19.95.
Graeme Clifford, USA, 1982, 113 mins.

Frankie Starlight
Matt Dillon, Gabriel Byrne and Anne Parillaud star in this magical story of a young boy growing up with his beautiful mother (Parillaud) and the two men who love her. As a result, he finds himself pulled between their desires. Travelling from Ireland to Texas and back again, this film has a beautiful, sweeping quality that resolves toward a warm and humorous conclusion.
VHS: S27599. $19.98.
Laser: LD75552. $39.99.
Michael Lindsay-Hogg, USA/Ireland, 1995, 100 mins.

Freeway
All she wanted to do was get to Grandma's. But her life was no fairy tale. Kiefer Sutherland and Reese Witherspoon star in this hip road trip story which "gives Little Red Riding Hood a retrofit" (Michael Sagrow, *San Francisco Weekly*). With Brooke Shields, Amanda Plummer, Dan Hedaya, Bokeem Woodbine and Michael T. Weiss. "It's a revelation to discover *Freeway*... so shocking and fresh it defies description" (Rex Reed, *The New York Observer*). Letterboxed.
VHS: S30616. $14.98.
DVD: DV60018. $24.98.
Matthew Bright, USA, 1996, 102 mins.

The French Connection
William Friedkin's edge-of-the-seat thriller about two hard-nosed New York detectives who stumble into an international narcotics smuggling ring. Contains probably the most exciting car chase ever filmed. With an exceptional performance by the always good Gene Hackman, as well as Roy Scheider and Fernando Rey.
VHS: S21861. $14.98.
Laser: LD75484. $39.98.
William Friedkin, USA, 1971, 102 mins.

French Connection 2
New York detective Popeye Doyle goes to Marseilles to crack the heroin ring headed by Frog One. Gene Hackman delivers a first-rate performance. With Fernando Rey and Bernard Fresson.
VHS: S21862. $19.98.
John Frankenheimer, USA, 1975, 118 mins.

French Exit
A sharply funny, hip, insider's view of Hollywood starring Jonathan Silverman (TV's *The Single Guy*) and Madchen Amick *(Twin Peaks)* as dueling screenwriters who repel, then attract one another.
VHS: S34613. $98.99.
Daphna Kastner, USA, 1996, 88 mins.

Fresh Horses
Adapted from the Broadway play by Larry Ketron, a rough and tumble romance between a college student in Cincinnati and a young, rural Kentucky woman who is already married to a yahoo who collects guns. With Andrew McCarthy, Molly Ringwald, Ben Stiller, Patti D'Arbanville and author Ketron as an unruly party goer. The title refers to finding new women to replace the ones that don't work out.
VHS: S09141. $89.95.
David Anspaugh, USA, 1988, 105 mins.

Fried Green Tomatoes
A fresh, sentimental adaptation of comedienne Fannie Flagg's novel, which juxtaposes two distinct narratives. The first is a contemporary work about the relationship of an abused, self-loathing woman (Kathy Bates) and a fiercely independent, sharp octogenarian (Jessica Tandy). Tandy interweaves stories of her friendship with a young woman in the pre-World War II South, with intense, heartfelt performances from Mary Stuart Masterson and Mary-Louise Parker.
VHS: S17015. $19.98.
Laser: LD71538. $39.98.
Jon Avnet, USA, 1991, 130 mins.

The Frighteners
This wickedly funny suspense thriller stars Michael J. Fox as Frank Bannister, a psychic swindler with the perfect business partners: they work cheap, they're dedicated, and they're...dead! But a series of inexplicable deaths have diverted Frank and his ghostly entourage from their "spirit clearance" scams. With Trini Alvarado, Jeffrey Combs and John Astin. "A ghost story with attitude" (Michael Wilmington, *The Chicago Tribune*). VHS letterboxed.
VHS: S30455. $19.98.
Laser: LD76036. $39.95.
Peter Jackson, USA, 1996, 110 mins.

The Frisco Kid
Gene Wilder is an inexperienced Polish rabbi traveling West in the America of the 1850's to join a waiting congregation in San Francisco. Harrison Ford is the reluctant gunslinger who assists the calamity-prone teacher from the Old Country adjust and survive in the New World.
VHS: S06138. $14.95.
Robert Aldrich, USA, 1979, 119 mins.

From Here to Eternity

Enjoy the steamy remake of this classic love story. Into the cold, controlled, unyielding world of military life comes a story of forbidden sex, unbridled passion and sudden violence. A riveting romance set against the backdrop of World War II. With an all-star cast featuring Natalie Wood, William Devane, Kim Basinger and Steve Railsback.

VHS: S13722. $19.95.
Buzz Kulik, USA, 1979, 110 mins.

The Fugitive

Harrison Ford stars in this action adventure film about a doctor wrongly accused of a terrible crime. His adversary, played by Tommy Lee Jones, must track this man through a series of incredible settings to uncover the truth behind *The Fugitive*. Letterboxed.

VHS: S20604. $19.98.
Laser: LD72369. $39.98.
DVD: DV60045. $24.98.
Andrew Davis, USA, 1993, 131 mins.

The Fury

Kirk Douglas is engaged in top-secret psychic research when his son is snatched away. Fearing that terrorists have him, he uses a girl with psychic powers to find his missing son. The results are bloody and surprising as both the son and this girl grow stronger throughout the film.

VHS: S29793. $19.98.
Brian DePalma, USA, 1978, 117 mins.

Gaby—A True Story

The courageous story of Gabriella Brimmer, a poet and author who overcomes great odds to insure her full rights as a creative human being. Rachel Levin is Gaby. Liv Ullmann is her mother and Norma Aleandro, an Oscar winner for *Official Story*, is her Mexican nanny. A moving tale of love and determination and cerebral palsy.

VHS: S07132. $79.95.
Luis Mandoki, USA, 1987, 94 mins.

The Gambler

James Caan is a college professor with a compulsive bad habit that is mentioned in the title. He not only puts his money on the line but ultimately his life, his future and his family and friends. The script is by James Toback. With Lauren Hutton, Paul Sorvino, Burt Young and Morris Carnovsky.

VHS: S06140. $19.95.
Karel Reisz, USA, 1974, 114 mins.

Garbo Talks

While Gilbert Rolfe drudges away in an accountant's cubicle, his eccentric mother Estelle joins picket lines on behalf of good causes. But Gilbert rises to the challenge of his life when he learns his mother is dying and wants to meet her idol, Greta Garbo.

VHS: S15250. $19.98.
Sidney Lumet, USA, 1985, 104 mins.

George Wallace

John Frankenheimer's *(The Manchurian Candidate)* hard-hitting, true story of the rise, fall and redemption of the controversial governor of Alabama who supported segregration in the '60s and motivated such civil rights leaders as Martin Luther King to change the course of history. With a riveting performance by Gary Sinise in the title role. With Dennis Quaid, Tom Berenger and Tom Selleck.

VHS: S32988. $19.98.
Laser: LD76434. $49.98.
John Frankenheimer, USA, 1997, 180 mins.

The Getaway

Together in life, Kim Basinger and Alec Baldwin now bring the emotional intensity and sexual heat of their union to this exciting thriller. It involves a dangerous deal, a double cross and the ultimate set-up. James Woods also stars.

VHS: S21140. $19.98.
Laser: LD72418. $34.98.
Roger Donaldson, USA, 1993, 115 mins.

The Ghost and the Darkness

Michael Douglas and Val Kilmer electrify this tense, terrific and true story about two lions whose man-eating rampage shuts down the construction of a railway in 1896 East Africa. "A heart-pounding, white-knuckle adventure" (Bonnie Churchill, *National News Syndicate*). Letterboxed.

VHS: S30952. $14.95.
Stephen Hopkins, USA, 1996, 110 mins.

Ghosts of Mississippi

Based on the true story of civil rights leader Medgar Evers, who was murdered in 1963 in his driveway in front of his wife and children, this powerful drama stars Whoopi Goldberg as a widow fighting for justice and Alec Baldwin as the courageous attorney who helped her find it. With James Woods and William H. Macy.

VHS: S31643. $19.95.
Laser: LD76250. $39.95.
Rob Reiner, USA, 1996, 131 mins.

Gia

Based on a true story, this HBO movie follows the life of Gia Marie Carangi, America's first supermodel, from her beginnings as a 17-year-old Philadelphia dropout working in her father's diner, to her '70s superstardom as a model, and death in 1986 at age 26 from AIDS—one of the first women in America whose death was attributed to the disease. In between, Gia followed a downward spiral of drug abuse and failed relationships. With Faye Dunaway and Mercedes Ruehl.

VHS: S34702. $79.99.
Michael Cristofer, USA, 1998, 126 mins.

Gift of Love

An adaptation of O. Henry's classic short story *The Gift of the Magi*. Set in early 1900's New York, Marie Osmond stars as a wealthy orphan dutifully resigned to an arranged marriage to "socially acceptable" James Woods. Swiss immigrant Timothy Bottoms captures her heart, however, and she must struggle to please her relatives and herself.

VHS: S13010. $24.95.
Don Chaffey, USA, 1978, 96 mins.

Girl Friends

Claudia Weill's breakthrough feature, a bittersweet, true-to-life tale of a young woman learning to make it on her own, and coming to terms with the marriage of her best friend. With Eli Wallach, Melanie Mayron.

VHS: S03714. $19.95.
Claudia Weill, USA, 1978, 88 mins.

The Girl with the Crazy Brother

In this Emmy-nominated drama directed by Diane Keaton, 16-year-old Dana MacCallister (Patricia Arquette) notices her brother Bill (William Jane) is acting strangely shortly after the family moves to California. After Bill has an outburst that leads to his hospitalization, Dana begins to feel ignored as her parents devote all their time and energy to her brother. Preoccupied with the stress of starting at a new school, dating and the other travails of a teen, Dana is torn between her love for her brother and her desire to be normal and not "the girl with the crazy brother."

VHS: S34097. $19.95.
Diane Keaton, USA, 1990, 44 mins.

Girls Town

Lili Taylor *(I Shot Andy Warhol)* heads an impressive ensemble cast in this gritty coming-of-age tale of four tough inner-city high school friends and the unexpected forces that tear them apart. Only weeks from graduation, an unforseen tragedy shatters their already fragile world, forcing them into a soul-wrenching struggle over loyalty, love, betrayal and identity in this funny, raw, exciting slice of real life. Winner of the Filmmakers Trophy and Special Jury Prize at the Sundance Film Festival.

VHS: S30581. $19.98.
Jim McKay, USA, 1996, 90 mins.

The Glitter Dome

A Hollywood mogul turns up dead—and leaves behind a sordid trail of sex, lies and revenge—in this gritty police thriller based on a novel by best-selling author Joseph Wambaugh. With John Lithgow, James Garner and Margot Kidder.

VHS: S31022. $14.98.
Stuart Margolin, USA, 1984, 91 mins.

Glory & Honor

Based on the stunning, true story of African-American explorer Matthew Henson (Delroy Lindo, *Get Shorty*), who, along with Commander Robert E. Peary (Henry Czerny, *The Boys of St. Vincent, Clear and Present Danger*), conquered the North Pole but did not receive the recognition he deserved because of his race.

VHS: S35125. $71.99.
Kevin Hooks, USA, 1998, 94 mins.

The Glory Boys

Rod Steiger and Anthony Perkins star in this thriller about contemporary terrorism. Steiger is an Israeli scientist who is the target of a fanatical group. Perkins is the broken down agent assigned to help him. Together they must fight the assassins known as The Glory Boys.

VHS: S24780. $19.98.
Michael Ferguson, USA, 1984, 78 mins.

Go Tell the Spartans

Burt Lancaster stars as a worried major in charge of a small outpost in Vietnam back when we were there in just an advisory capacity. One of the earliest films about our involvement in Southeast Asia. With Craig Wasson, Marc Singer, Evan Kim, David Clennon, Dolph Sweet and Jonathan Goldsmith. Based on Daniel Ford's novel *Incident at Muc Wa*.

VHS: S00507. $19.95.
Ted Post, USA, 1977, 114 mins.

Good Morning Vietnam

Robin Williams won an Oscar nomination for Best Actor for the role of the wacky, motor-mouth, military disk jockey Adrian Cronauer. It's 1965 in Saigon and the Armed Forces Radio waves are getting a new sound. With Bruno Kirby and Forest Whitaker. The flip side of war and peace.

VHS: S07165. $14.98.
Laser: LD71011. $44.99.
Barry Levinson, USA, 1987, 121 mins.

Good Mother

Diane Keaton is the title character in this involving story of a divorced woman taken to court in a child custody battle. It seems that her sleep-over boyfriend (Liam Neeson) was a little too free in providing sexual information to her young daughter. With Jason Robards as the stuffy lawyer and Ralph Bellamy and Teresa Wright as the grandparents. Based on the novel by Sue Miller.

VHS: S09925. $19.95.
Leonard Nimoy, USA, 1988, 104 mins.

Goodbye, Norma Jean

A young Norma Jean Mortenson struggles to find her identity in marriage, pin-up photography, and, finally, stardom as Marilyn Monroe. This is her story as she lived it: the life she dreamed of having and the life she really found. With Misty Rowe as Marilyn.

VHS: S34942. $19.95.
Larry Buchanan, USA, 1976, 91 mins.

Gorillas in the Mist

Based on the true story of anthropologist Dian Fossey (Sigourney Weaver), who travels to the African mountains to study gorillas. In this paradise which she describes as "being as close to God as you can get," her interest in gorillas turns into a passion and finally into obsession; trying to save her animals from extinction, she turns to justice and finally revenge.

VHS: S10112. $19.95.
Laser: LD70035. $39.98.
Michael Apted, USA, 1988, 129 mins.

Grand Canyon

Lawrence Kasdan looks at the problems of living in Los Angeles in the '90s and offers a variety of possible alternatives to urban angst. Among them, an uplifting trip to the Grand Canyon. The all-star cast includes Danny Glover, Kevin Kline, Steve Martin, Mary McDonnell, Mary-Louise Parker and Alfre Woodard.

VHS: S16330. $19.98.
Lawrence Kasdan, USA, 1991, 134 mins.

Grand Theft Auto

No car goes unwrecked in Howard's directorial debut, which has been described as "an automobile snuff film." Howard also stars in this film, along with *Happy Days* co-star Marion Ross, Nancy Morgan, Peter Isackson and Barry Cahill.

VHS: S28611. $14.98.
Laser: LD76191. $39.98.
Ron Howard, USA, 1977, 85 mins.

The Grass Harp

Walter Matthau, Jack Lemmon, Sissy Spacek, Piper Laurie, Mary Steenburgen, Charles Durning and Edward Furlong star in this acclaimed film from the novel by Truman Capote about a young boy who learns about life by watching the eccentric grown-ups in a small town. "A sweet, wise, funny film" (Lawrence Van Gelder, *New York Times*).

VHS: S30867. $19.98.
Laser: LD76105. $39.99.
Charles Matthau, USA, 1996, 107 mins.

Gray Lady Down

After a collision, an American nuclear submarine lodges in the neck of an underwater canyon. This rescue film brandishes impressive special effects, with performances from Charlton Heston as the captain, and David Carradine as the designer of as experimental diving craft.

VHS: S16300. $14.95.
David Greene, USA, 1978, 111 mins.

Great Expectations

Gwyneth Paltrow, Ethan Hawke, Robert De Niro, Anne Bancroft and Hank Azaria star in this modern adaptation of Charles Dickens' timeless novel directed by Alfonso Cuaron *(A Little Princess)*. Desire gives way to passion for two people from different worlds, linked by destiny and fated to touch each other's souls.

VHS: S34571. $103.99.
Laser: LD76948. $39.95.
Alfonso Cuaron, USA, 1998, 122 mins.

Great Gatsby
Robert Redford and Mia Farrow star in a script by Francis F. Coppola, adapted from the book by F. Scott Fitzgerald about a mysterious man who crashes Long Island society in the 1920's, and the long-lost love he left behind.
VHS: S02652. $14.95.
Laser: LD75384. $35.98.
Jack Clayton, USA, 1974, 144 mins.

Great Santini
Critically acclaimed sleeper, with a standout performance by Robert Duvall as a career Marine who can only show love "through discipline." Great touches of pathos and humor, with outstanding supporting acting by Blythe Danner and Lisa Jane Persky.
VHS: S07283. $19.98.
Lewis John Carlino, USA, 1979, 116 mins.

The Great White Hype
A wicked satire on boxing, starring Samuel L. Jackson as top professional boxing promoter Rev. Fred Sultan, who sets up a publicity stunt match between the heavyweight champ, James "The Grim Reaper" Roper (Damon Wayans) and the only man to ever beat the champ, Terry Conklin (Peter Berg), now a grunge musician. The over-confident champ falls out of shape as Sultan gets the great white "hype" back into training. With Jeff Goldblum.
VHS: S33986. $14.95.
Reginald Hudlin, USA, 1996, 91 mins.

Gremlins
Director Joe Dante provides the Grinch's version of *It's a Wonderful Life* as an unusual Christmas present multiplies and turns nasty. Filled with cinematic in-jokes and cameo appearances. A young man tries to save his town from complete destruction before his father gets home. With Zack Galligan, Phoebe Cates and Hoyt Axton.
VHS: S01833. $19.98.
Laser: Letterboxed. **LD74695. $24.98.**
Joe Dante, USA, 1984, 111 mins.

Grim Prairie Tales
City slicker Brad Dourif and bounty hunter James Earl Jones sit around a campfire in the wide open spaces and keep each other up telling tall tales of violence and revenge. Topics include violating Indian burial grounds, bizarre sexual encounters and finding out who is the fastest gun alive.
VHS: S13290. $19.98.
Wayne Coe, USA, 1989, 90 mins.

A Guide for the Married Woman
Cybill Shepherd stars in this made-for-tv movie about an unsatisfied married woman looking to step out of the relationship for some change-of-pace romance. A light comedy follow up to writer Frank Tarloff's *Guide to the Married Man*. With Barbara Feldon, Eve Arden, Charles Frank, John Hillerman and George Gobel.
VHS: S10034. $59.98.
Hy Averback, USA, 1987, 96 mins.

Guilty by Suspicion
The Hollywood hysteria over the infamous House on Unamerican Activities Committee hearings in the 1950's is grippingly captured in this uncompromising drama. Robert De Niro stars as a successful director whose professional career takes a downward turn when he refuses to name names. The strong supporting cast includes Annette Bening, George Wendt, Patricia Wettig and Martin Scorsese. Sam Wanamaker, a real victim of the blacklist, appears as De Niro's legal advisor.
VHS: S15008. $19.98.
Irwin Winkler, USA, 1991, 105 mins.

Gulliver's Travels
Ted Danson and Mary Steenburgen are at the center of this film, based on the Swift classic. An amazing supporting cast is included for the smaller roles, among whom are: Ned Beatty, Geraldine Chaplin, Omar Sharif, Peter O'Toole and Sir John Gielgud. This film is different from most film versions based on Swift's work because it uses the entirety of the novels. As a result, Gulliver travels to all the strange lands Swift imagined.
VHS: S29399. $24.98.
Laser: LD75810. $49.99.
Charles Sturridge, USA, 1996, 179 mins.

Gumshoe Kid
A young man foregoes higher education at Harvard to join the family private detective business. Jeff's first big case is to keep a close watch on a mobster's fiance. Complications ensue. With Jay Underwood (*The Boy Who Could Fly*) as the intrepid Jeff and *Dynasty*'s Tracy Scoggins as his first big case. Also Vince Edwards, Arlene Golonka and Pamela Springsteen.
VHS: Out of print. For rental only.
Laser: CLV. **LD71723. $19.98.**
Joseph Manduke, USA, 1989, 98 mins.

Gunfighters of the West
Meet Wild Bill Hickock, Jesse James, Billy the Kid, John Wesley Hardin and the Earp Brothers, fearless outlaws who sparred with lawmen, leaving a trail of bloody bodies in their wake. Narrated by Brian Dennehy, this five-volume set combines stunning visuals with compelling narratives to explore the truth behind the myths. Each volume is 50 mins.
VHS: S34336. $79.98.
Kevin McCarey, USA, 1998, 250 mins.

The Habitation of Dragons
Academy Award winner Horton Foote wrote the screenplay for this surprising drama featuring Brad Davis. Two lawyer brothers have always found themselves engaged in rivalry. Now, just as one's success seems assured, everything that they always relied upon is about to come undone.
VHS: S24732. $49.98.
Michael Lindsay-Hogg, USA, 1992, 94 mins.

Hanoi Hilton
Michael Moriarty and Paul LeMat as American POW's during Vietnam in a brutal, compelling re-telling of the horrors of prison camps.
VHS: S05971. $14.95.
Laser: Hi-fi, digital. **LD74730. $39.98.**
Lionel Chetwynd, USA, 1987, 130 mins.

Hanover Street
Lt. David Halloran (Harrison Ford), a courageous American bomber pilot, and a British nurse (Lesley-Anne Down), accidentally meet during an air-raid and fall instantly in love. Committed to an assignment, David asks her to meet him two weeks later, in spite of the fact that she is married. Her husband, Paul Sellinger (Christopher Plummer), is a British intelligence officer in charge of a special, dangerous mission behind enemy lines. Halloran is chosen to fly Sellinger on the task. It is only when their plane is shot down that Halloran discovers who Sellinger is.
VHS: S32233. $14.95.
Peter Hyams, USA, 1979, 108 mins.

Happy New Year
Peter Falk has a field day in this English language remake of the Claude Lelouch film about a meticulous jewel thief who tries to court a beautiful woman while pulling off the biggest caper of his career. Virtually identical to the earlier 1973 film. Lelouch has a cameo as a train passenger. With Wendy Hughes and Charles Durning.
VHS: S04976. $79.95.
John G. Avildsen, USA, 1987, 86 mins.

Hard Choices
Highly original film that was overlooked upon its release and features an amazing performance by Margaret Klenck as a social worker who gets too close to a juvenile imprisoned and sentenced as an adult. With an appearance by director John Sayles.
VHS: S01860. $19.98.
Rick King, USA, 1984, 90 mins.

Hard Eight
Philip Baker Hall *(Secret Honor)* is a poker-faced professional gambler with a dark past, whose life is knocked off balance by a sad, simple-minded waitress (Gwyneth Paltrow, *Emma*) and a young loser (John C. Reilly, *Days of Thunder*). With Samuel L. Jackson.
VHS: S31789. $19.95.
Laser: LD76308. $34.95.
Paul Thomas Anderson, USA, 1997, 101 mins.

Hardware
Dylan McDermott, Stacy Travis, John Lynch and Iggy Pop star in this post-apocalyptic adventure. McDermott lives from trash cans. That's also where he finds his android girlfriend, Travis. She is part of a program that would control population growth by destroying prospective mates.
VHS: S22911. $19.98.
Richard Stanley, USA, 1990, 94 mins.

Harry and Tonto
Paul Mazursky's poignant drama about an elderly man's cross-country odyssey, featuring remarkable performances by Art Carney and Ellen Burstyn.
VHS: S04337. $19.98.
Paul Mazursky, USA, 1974, 115 mins.

Harvest of Fire
In this Emmy Award-nominated Hallmark Hall of Fame production, Lolita Davidovich *(Intersection)* stars as an FBI agent who must gain the trust of an Amish widow (Academy Award-winner Patty Duke) in order to catch an arsonist and bring him to justice. As the mystery unravels a new friendship is formed. "A bountiful drama" (Lou Grahnke, *Chicago Sun-Times*). "Gorgeous photography…atmospheric music…eloquent direction" (Laurence Vittes, *The Hollywood Reporter*).
VHS: S30157. $99.98.
Laser: LD76011. $39.99.
Arthur Allan Seidelman, USA, 1996, 99 mins.

Havana
The capital city of Cuba is the setting for romance and revolution as well as a loose remake of *Casablanca*. Before you can say "Here's looking at you, muchacho", gambler Robert Redford will have to decide whether to get on that boat with Lena Olin or see if her freedom-fighting husband Raul Julia would rather make the trip. With Alan Arkin, Thomas Milian, Tony Plana and an enticing musical score by Dave Grusin.
VHS: S13769. $19.98.
Sydney Pollack, USA, 1990, 145 mins.

Heart Beat
John Heard is Jack Kerouac, the acclaimed author and icon of the Beat Generation, in this narrative film based on Carolyn Cassady's memoirs. Sissy Spacek and Nick Nolte star as Kerouac's California companions Carolyn and Neal Cassady. Together they took chances and struck out toward new frontiers. With Steve Allen and John Larroquette.
VHS: S25871. $19.98.
John Byrum, USA, 1980, 105 mins.

Heartburn
Dismissed by many critics, Mike Nichols adapted Nora Ephron's meditation on her brief marriage to Watergate journalist Carl Bernstein by linking the film to questions of love, family and breakdown. Meryl Streep is excellent as Rachel, a magazine journalist whose marriage to Jack Nicholson, a powerful political columnist, is shattered upon revelations of his affair with a diplomat's wife. Ephron adapted her own screenplay. Cast includes Jeff Daniels, Stockard Channing, Maureen Stapleton and John Wood.
VHS: S02628. $19.95.
Mike Nichols, USA, 1986, 109 mins.

Hearts of Fire
From the director of *Jagged Edge* and *Return of the Jedi* comes this rock and roll drama about a rising young singer and her involvement with success and famous musicians. Fiona is the eager young performer who shares a bed with Englishman Rupert Everett and American Bob Dylan. The last film of Richard Marquand.
VHS: S07705. $14.95.
Richard Marquand, USA, 1988, 90 mins.

Heat
Al Pacino and Robert DeNiro are on opposite sides of the law in this searing, blood-spattered film from the originator of *Miami Vice*. Even as Pacino finds his personal life crumbling, he can't control his obsession with an ingenious criminal (DeNiro). Both men find love, only to question its value in the world of guns and honor they both inhabit. Despite these concerns, the film is tense and loaded with action. With Val Kilmer, Tom Sizemore, Diane Venora, Amy Brenneman, Natalie Portman and Jon Voight.
VHS: S27708. $19.98.
Laser: LD75567. $39.98.
Michael Mann, USA, 1995, 172 mins.

Heaven and Earth
Tommy Lee Jones and Joan Chen portray a man and a woman who come together despite their divided loyalties during the Vietnam War. He is a vet who can never forget, while she has seen her country ravaged by a brutal conflict whose effects are still painfully evident today.
VHS: S21086. $19.98.
Laser: LD72413. $39.98.
Oliver Stone, USA, 1993, 142 mins.

Heaven Is a Playground
The game of basketball is showcased in this independent film treatment of the non-fiction book by sportswriter Rick Telander. D.B. Sweeney stars as a white, small town lawyer who moves to Chicago to spend the summer playing basketball with inner city youth. Local talent scout Michael Warren lets him stick around on the condition he help coach a beginning team and handle the legal affairs of a young rising star. With Victor Love, Richard Jordan, Janet Julian and L.A. Clipper star Bo Kimble.
VHS: S15926. $19.95.
Randall Fried, USA, 1991, 111 mins.

Heaven's Prisoners
Sexy, intense mystery thriller as an ex-cop (Alec Baldwin) is pitted between the DEA, his childhood buddy—now a ruthless ringleader (Eric Roberts), and his sultry wife (Teri Hatcher). Every move he makes becomes a life and death decision, and every clue brings him one step closer to a killer. Great supporting cast includes Kelly Lynch and Mary Stuart Masterson.
VHS: S28636. $19.98.
Laser: LD75983. $49.99.
Phil Joanou, USA, 1996, 135 mins.

Henry & June
The story of controversial novelist Henry Miller as seen through the eyes of his lover Anais Nin. Director Philip Kaufman *(The Unbearable Lightness of Being)* once again explores the relationship between the erotic and the literate. With Fred Ward, Maria de Medeiros, and Uma Thurman as June Miller. Richard E. Grant and Kevin Spacey are also to be found hanging around Paris. The first film to receive the NC-17 rating due to its adult nature.
VHS: S13578. $19.98.
Philip Kaufman, USA, 1990, 136 mins.

A Hero Ain't Nothin' but a Sandwich
It takes a real hero to keep a family together. A timely and moving story of an intelligent but alienated ghetto youth's battle with drugs. Based on the popular children's book by Alice Childress. Starring Cicely Tyson, Paul Winfield and impressive young Larry B. Scott.
VHS: S14280. $19.95.
Laser: LD75126. $24.98.
Ralph Nelson, USA, 1978, 107 mins.

Hester Street
Set on the Lower East Side of New York in 1896, Gitl and her son reunite with husband Jake, who had previously immigrated from Russia. Jake has completely embraced America by shedding his ethnic heritage, and is embarrassed when Gitl clings to her old country ways. But in this charming and humorous portrait of the Jewish immigrant experience, Gitl finds a way to become victor instead of victim. Carol Kane was nominated for an Oscar for her portrayal of Gitl. With Stephen Keats.
VHS: S00564. $29.95.
Joan Micklin Silver, USA, 1974, 89 mins.

Hi, Mom!
Robert De Niro returns as Vietnam vet John Rubin, in this award-winning sequel to *Greetings*. Once again under the direction of a young Brian De Palma, DeNiro continues his adventures as an amateur filmmaker in Greenwich Village—this time as "Peeping John", an erotic artist who focuses his camera on four windows in a local high-rise apartment building: three gorgeous secretaries, a hippie couple, a playboy, and a housewife. This film laid the foundation for *Body Double*.
VHS: S13883. $14.95.
Brian DePalma, USA, 1970, 87 mins.

Hidden in America
Beau Bridges stars as Bill Januson, a laid-off factory worker who suddenly finds himself with no job, no wife, and no way to feed his young children. A sympathetic doctor (Bruce Davison) offers to help, but Bill's pride keeps him from accepting. When Bill's 11-year-old son tries to take on the role of bread-winner, the near-tragic result compels Bill to reach out for the compassion his family needs to survive. With Jeff Bridges, Frances McDormand, Jena Malone and Shelton Dane.
VHS: S31823. $90.99.
Laser: LD76335. $39.99.
Martin Bell, USA, 1996, 96 mins.

Hiding Place
Julie Harris stars in this true-life account of a heroic family's imprisonment in a World War II concentration camp for sheltering Jews in Nazi-occupied Holland. Produced by Billy Graham's Evangelistic Foundation.
VHS: S09665. $19.95.
James F. Collier, USA, 1975, 145 mins.

Highlander: The Director's Cut
Christopher Lambert stars as the immortal Scot from the 16th century while Sean Connery is his tutor, in this original, uncut version of the highly popular film. After spinning off a few sequels and a television series, it's finally available on the 10th anniversary of its release. Fans worldwide love its supernatural mixture of ancient warrior ways and contemporary, even futuristic, possibilities. VHS letterboxed.
VHS: S29802. $19.98.
Laser: LD75900. $69.98.
DVD: DV60009. $29.95.
Russell Mulcahy, USA, 1986, 116 mins.

Hindsight
In this erotic thriller, aspiring actor Jason Andrews becomes involved with Joanne, the wife of a studio executive. But he didn't plan on crossing paths with the gorgeous and sexually unrestrained Cassandra. It doesn't take much time for his affair with Joanne to take the back seat. With Ken Steadman, Cyndi Pass, Kathy Shower and Robert Forster.
VHS: S34923. $49.95.
John T. Bone, USA, 1996, 93 mins.

Hiroshima
This historical feature recreates the situations and decision-making moments that led up to the devastating nuclear blast over Hiroshima. Between Churchill, Truman and Hirohito, a drama of unimaginable proportions unfolds. This film tells the story behind the headlines, where ordinary people find themselves involved in events, the implications of which remain difficult to fathom.
VHS: S26460. $19.98.
Laser: LD75373. $49.98.
Roger Spottiswode/Koreyoshi Kurahara, USA, 1995, 165 mins.

Hobo's Christmas
Barnard Hughes, William Hickey and Gerald McRaney star in this emotional drama of a father's homecoming. After leaving his family to live a hobo's life for 25 years, Chance Grosvenor decides it's time to come home. His best traveling companion, Cincinnati Harold, warns him that his son and the past are memories best left behind. But Chance has to find out for himself.
VHS: S11238. $79.95.
Will MacKenzie, USA, 1987, 94 mins.

Hoffa
Director Danny DeVito, writer David Mamet and actor Jack Nicholson collaborated on this biography of James R. Hoffa. Mamet's screenplay is constructed in a series of flashbacks, built around the mysterious events of Hoffa's 1975 disappearance. The movie is an account of the labor movement, the unholy unions between Hoffa and the Mafia, and his epic battles with former Attorney General Robert Kennedy. The film is held together by Jack Nicholson's brave, gripping performance. With DeVito in a composite role of Hoffa's most loyal lieutenant, Armand Assante and Kevin Anderson.
VHS: S18601. $19.98.
Laser: LD72432. $49.98.
Danny DeVito, USA, 1992, 140 mins.

Hollow Reed
From the producers of *The Crying Game* comes this "*Kramer vs. Kramer* for the '90s." Martyn, a divorced father, is subjected to harsh scrutiny by the courts as he risks everything in a custody battle to protect his son Oliver from his ex-wife's boyfriend, Frank, whom he suspects is the cause of his son's strange injuries. With Martin Donovan *(Amateur)*, Joely Richardson, Ian Hart, Jason Flemyng and Sam Bould. "Wrenching and hypnotic" (Rex Reed, *The New York Observer*).
VHS: S33111. $98.99.
Angela Pope, USA, 1997, 105 mins.

Home for Christmas
The magic of Christmas is rediscovered by a well-to-do family when an elderly homeless man named Elmer (Mickey Rooney) enters their lives.
VHS: S15089. $79.95.
Peter McCubbin, USA, 1991, 96 mins.

Homecoming (Bancroft)
Abandoned by their mentally ill mother, the four Tillerman children, with nowhere to turn, travel across the country to find the reclusive grandmother they've never known. A bitter, lonely old woman, Abigail (Academy Award-winner Anne Bancroft) agrees to let the children into her house, and finally, into her heart, as they enjoy their new beginning together. "...a genuinely emotional and engrossing heart-warmer" *(USA Today)*. "Bancroft gives a powerful character performance" *(Hollywood Reporter)*.
VHS: S30156. $99.98.
Laser: LD76012. $39.99.
Mark Jean, USA, 1996, 105 mins.

Homecoming (Neal)
Made-for-television movie based on characters by Earl Hammer that became the series *The Waltons*. Starring Patricia Neal, Edgar Bergen and Richard Thomas, with a special appearance by Cleavon Little.
VHS: S01922. $59.98.
Fielder Cook, USA, 1971, 98 mins.

Homework
At the end of his senior year of high school, Tommy finds his education in the form of Diana, a mature woman. His friend Ralph learns the lessons of life from Ms. Jackson. Without knowing what will come of their relationships with these older women, the boys form a rock band as a means to unlimited sexual opportunity. Stars Joan Collins, Michael Morgan, Wings Hauser, Carrie Snodgrass and Betty Thomas.
VHS: S16075. $19.95.
James Beshears, USA, 1982, 90 mins.

Homicide
David Mamet's third feature stars Joe Mantegna as a hardened Baltimore detective whose investigation of a cop-killing drug runner is accidentally interrupted by an anti-Semitic slaying. Confronted by his Jewish heritage, Montegna must choose between his oath to the police force and his sudden affiliation with the Jewish Mafia. A powerful film which links racism toward Blacks and the still evident hatred of Jews.
VHS: S15928. $19.95.
David Mamet, USA, 1991, 102 mins.

Honor Amo ng Thieves
A tense thriller featuring Charles Bronson as a mercenary locked in a French bank over a weekend with Alain Delon, a doctor. While Bronson's in the bank to rob it, Delon is there to replace misappropriated securities. Both are in constant conflict, and both are ultimately betrayed. In English.
VHS: S04785. $59.95.
Jean Herman, France/USA, 1983, 93 mins.

Hoodlum
In this gangster crime thriller, complete with spectacular gun battles and brutal action, Bumby Johnson (Laurence Fishburne) is the kingpin who rules the numbers racket in 1930s Harlem. Drawn into a deadly face-off with Dutch Schultz (Tim Roth), Bumby is about to lose it all until he hooks up with Lucky Luciano (Andy Garcia), the nation's most feared gangster. With Vanessa Williams and Cicely Tyson. "Rich, handsomely crafted, grand and stunning" *(Boston Globe)*. Letterboxed.
VHS: S32710. $19.95.
DVD: DV60151. $24.98.
Bill Duke, USA, 1997, 130 mins.

Hoosiers
Gene Hackman stars as an aging basketball coach who finds a job molding a competitive high school team in a very small town in Indiana in the 1950's. He may be gruff and living under the shadow of a past mistake, but he knows how to produce a winning team. With Barbara Hershey, Sheb Wooley and Dennis Hopper as the town drunk.
VHS: S04526. $14.98.
Laser: LD71046. $19.98.
David Anspaugh, USA, 1986, 114 mins.

Hope
Goldie Hawn makes her directorial debut with this film about the October 1962 Cuban missile crisis. While the world is facing the threat of a nuclear attack, in a small southern town long-simmering racial tensions erupt, and one 13-year-old girl can save the town, if she reveals a terrible family secret. With Catherine O'Hara, Christine Lahti, Jena Malone, Jeffrey D. Sams and J.T. Walsh.
VHS: S33398. $71.99.
Laser: LD76996. $34.98.
Goldie Hawn, USA, 1997, 95 mins.

Hot Shot
Pele is the main reason to see this lets-go-for-it sports picture that *Soccer Match Magazine* calls "soccer's answer to *The Karate Kid*." The Brazilian world champion player is always amazing to watch in action. With Jim Youngs, Mario Van Peebles, David Groh and Billy Warlock.
VHS: S05308. $19.98.
Rick King, USA, 1986, 90 mins.

Hot Spot
Don Johnson drifts into a small Texas town that has two good-looking women and one frequently unattended bank. With Virginia Madsen and Jennifer Connelly as Taylor, Texas' alternatives to watching television. Based on the 1952 novel *Hell Hath No Fury* by Charles Williams. Steamy stuff indeed.
VHS: S13657. $99.95.
Dennis Hopper, USA, 1990, 120 mins.

House of Cards
In Michael Lessac's debut film, a widowed architect (Kathleen Turner) and her two children return to the United States following an expedition to Central America, where they studied Mayan ruins. The daughter suddenly becomes withdrawn and refuses to speak. Turner tries to discover the roots of her daughter's disorder. She argues with a prominent child psychologist (Tommy Lee Jones)—who diagnoses the girl's condition as a form of autism—over the exact nature of the illness and the correct treatment. With Park Overall, Shiloh Strong, Asha Menina and Michael Horse.
VHS: S19604. $19.98.
Laser: LD75207. $34.98.
Michael Lessac, USA, 1993, 109 mins.

The House of the Spirits
Isabel Allende's magically realist, best-selling novel about an aristocratic Argentinean family is now a lavish film with Meryl Streep, Glenn Close, Jeremy Irons, Winona Ryder and Antonio Banderas. This beautiful epic follows a tempestuous family driven by the conflict between tradition and passion. Ryder is in love but her desires are not fundamental to the family's interest. Only a series of small miracles can solve this impasse.
VHS: S21498. $19.98.
Laser: Widescreen. **LD75208. $34.98.**
Bille August, USA, 1993, 109 mins.

A House Without a Christmas Tree
Brighten up the holiday season with a tender, uplifting story of a father and daughter who discover that love and understanding are the greatest gifts of all. Jason Robards stars.
VHS: S14788. $14.98.
Paul Bogart, USA, 1972, 90 mins.

Housekeeping
Scottish director Bill Forsyth adapts the novel of Marilynne Robinson about two sisters left in the hands of various relatives after their mother's suicide. Christine Lahti shines as their eccentric Aunt Sylvie. With Sara Walker and Andrea Burchill and the great scenery of the Pacific Northwest. A touching lyrical tale.
VHS: S06998. $79.95.
Bill Forsyth, USA, 1987, 117 mins.

How to Make an American Quilt

An all-star cast, featuring Winona Ryder, Anne Bancroft, Ellen Burstyn, Kate Nelligan, Kate Capshaw, Samantha Mathis, Jean Simmons, Alfre Woodard and Maya Angelou, gives this romantic comedy heart and verve. A young woman (Ryder) learns about life, love and the power of choices as she hears the life stories of the women in her grandmother's quilting circle and reconsiders her own forthcoming marriage.

VHS: S27522. $19.98.
Laser: LD75524. $39.99.
Jocelyn Moorhouse, USA, 1995, 117 mins.

Hugo Pool

From acclaimed director Robert Downey, Sr. *(Putney Swope)* comes this quirky story, occurring over the course of one day, in the life of Hugo (Alyssa Milano), a young pool cleaner in Los Angeles who must clean 44 pools, deal with her eccentric clients and help her parents (Malcolm McDowell and Cathy Moriarty) sort out their own lives. During this chaos she meets a new client and falls in love. With Patrick Dempsey, Robert Downey, Jr., Richard Lewis and Sean Penn.

VHS: S34082. $97.99.
Laser: LD76984. $39.99.
Robert Downey Sr., USA, 1997, 93 mins.

The Human Factor

A British double agent, Nicol Williamson, faces a dilemma: either he defects to Russia or he dies. Tom Stoppard adapted Graham Greene's acclaimed novel for this stellar cast which includes Robert Morley, Richard Attenborough, Iman, Derek Jacobi and John Gielgud.

VHS: S21165. $19.98.
Otto Preminger, USA, 1979, 115 mins.

Hunchback (1982)

Anthony Hopkins, Derek Jacobi and Sir John Gielgud star in this film adaptation of Victor Hugo's masterwork, *The Hunchback of Notre Dame*. The story is heartrending. An evil arch deacon seeks control over a beautiful gypsy woman. Failing to possess her, he calls Quasimodo into action, and Quasimodo is publicly humiliated. A bond emerges between the *Hunchback* and the gypsy that is touching and ultimately tragic.

VHS: S22761. $19.98.
Michael Tuchner, USA, 1982, 102 mins.

The Hunchback (1997)

A vivid and thrilling retelling of Victor Hugo's classic tale of a deformed cathedral bell ringer, a compassionate gypsy woman, a minister's obsession and the redemptive power of love. With Mandy Patinkin, Richard Harris and Salma Hayek.

VHS: S33715. $19.98.
Peter Medak, USA/Hungary, 1997, 98 mins.

The Hunt for Red October

Set before Glastnost, a Soviet sub commander takes a prototype out for a test drive and panics both of the super-powers. With Sean Connery as Captain Marko Ramius and Alec Baldwin as CIA analyst Jack Ryan. With Scott Glenn, Sam Neill, Peter Firth and James Earl Jones. Underwater Cat and Mouse.

VHS: S12854. $14.95.
Laser: Letterboxed. **LD75311. $39.98.**
John McTiernan, USA, 1990, 135 mins.

I Know What You Did Last Summer

Four teens make a fatal mistake when trying to hide the body of an accident victim. They make a pact to keep it a secret; but now the secret's out and the horror begins. With Jennifer Love Hewitt *(Party of Five)*, Sarah Michelle Gellar *(Buffy the Vampire Slayer)*, Freddie Prinze, Jr., Ryan Phillippe, Anne Heche and Johnny Galecki.

VHS: S33350. $105.99.
Laser: LD76763. $34.95.
DVD: DV60199. $24.95.
Jim Gillespie, USA, 1997, 101 mins.

I Love You, I Love You Not

Claire Danes stars as Daisy, a painfully shy young woman uncomfortable with herself, who feels like a complete outsider at her stuffy New York prep school. When she catches the eye of the coolest guy in class, Daisy is overjoyed, but afraid that revealing too much will ruin her chances for acceptance. With Jude Law and Jeanne Moreau.

VHS: S34921. $103.99.
Billy Hopkins, France/Germany/USA, 1996, 92 mins.

I Never Sang for My Father

Gene Hackman and Melvyn Douglas star as son and aging father in this sensitive and soul-searching drama. Adapted for the screen from the Robert Anderson play, the subject of responsibility makes for very serious viewing. With Estelle Parsons and Lovelady Powell.

VHS: S04714. $69.95.
Gilbert Cates, USA, 1970, 93 mins.

The Ice Storm

Kevin Kline, Joan Allen and Sigourney Weaver turn in crystalline performances as two dysfunctional families learn to cope with the unyielding forces of nature and human nature, in this emotionally charged tale of suburban life in the '70s. When a self-centered husband's relationships with his wife and mistress grow cold, it takes a wife-swapping "key party" and a freak ice storm to clear the air and change their lives. With Christina Ricci, Elijah Wood, Adam Hann-Byrd, Tobey Maguire and Jamey Sheridan.

VHS: S33695. $103.99.
Laser: LD76778. $39.98.
Ang Lee, USA, 1997, 113 mins.

Iceman

From the director of *Chant of Jimmie Blacksmith*, Timothy Hutton stars in this drama about a team of researchers in the Artic who find a 40,000 year old man frozen in the ice and bring him back to life.

VHS: S00605. $19.95.
Laser: LD70040. $34.98.
Fred Schepisi, USA, 1984, 101 mins.

If I Ever See You Again

"You Light Up My Life" composer Joseph Brooks directs and stars in this story of a young composer who vows to win the heart of a woman who spurned him years ago. With Joseph Brooks, Shelly Hack and Jimmy Breslin.

VHS: S06713. $69.95.
Joseph Brooks, USA, 1978, 105 mins.

If These Walls Could Talk

In this intimate portrait of how times and freedoms have changed, Demi Moore, Sissy Spacek and Cher star as women living in the same house at different times—the '50s, '70s and '90s—who share one thing in common: the decision they must come to in dealing with an unplanned pregancy. With Anne Heche, Jada Pinkett, Lindsay Crouse and Craig T. Nelson. "The impressive lineup delivers" *(Chicago Tribune)*.

VHS: S30781. $19.95.
Nancy Savoca/Cher, USA, 1996, 97 mins.

Imaginary Crimes

Harvey Keitel stars in this emotional family drama about a troubled relationship between a man and his daughter. When the man does not live up to the expectations of his maturing child, conflict erupts between the two. Ultimately the woman must stand up for her own dreams.

VHS: S24057. $19.98.
Laser: LD74804. $34.98.
Anthony Drazan, USA, 1994, 106 mins.

Immediate Family

James Woods and Glenn Close are a nice married couple from Seattle who want a baby to call their own. Mary Stuart Masterson is a young, unwed, teenage mother-to-be from the Midwest who wants the best for her unborn child. Jonathan Kaplan *(Over the Edge)* directs this sensitive and fertile drama about the fears and responsibilities of parenting. With Kevin Dillon as the biological father who makes James Woods nervous. Don't let the soap to get in your eyes.

VHS: S12125. $19.95.
Jonathan Kaplan, USA, 1989, 94 mins.

Immortal Beloved

Gary Oldman, Jeroen Krabbe and Isabella Rossellini star in this drama about the secret love of composer Ludwig van Beethoven. Unashamedly lush and romantic, though the film rests on scant historic fact, the music and the passion make for a sumptuous entertainment in this grand and beautiful production. The soundtrack is directed by Sir Georg Solti.

VHS: S25540. $19.95.
Laser: LD74952. $39.95.
Bernard Rose, USA, 1994, 121 mins.

The Imported Bridegroom

Pamela Berger adapts Abraham Cahan's novella about a turn-of-the-century, widowed landlord who returns to the old country and becomes involved in the bidding war of a local scholar, with intentions of bringing him back to America to marry his daughter. With Eugene Troobnick, Avi Hoffman, Greta Cowan and Annette Miller. "An endearing film about the immigrant experience" *(Boston Globe)*.

VHS: S17929. $39.95.
Pamela Berger, USA, 1989, 93 mins.

The Impossible Spy

A polished, made-for-cable, spy thriller which chronicles the dramatic split in the life of Eli Cohen (John Shea), an Egyptian-born Jew who built an elaborate cover as a father, husband and businessman. In fact Cohen was a brilliant Israeli agent who infiltrated the top echelon of the Syrian government and secured vital information during the 1967 Six Day War. "A portrait of spies and spying that is as chilling as it is complete" *(The New York Times)*. With Eli Wallach, Michal Bat-Adam, Rami Danon, Sasson Gabray and Chaim Girafi.

Laser: LD71957. $39.95.
Jim Goddard, USA/Great Britain, 1987, 98 mins.

In and Out

Kevin Kline delivers a hilarious performance as Howard Brackett, a small-town teacher who becomes big news when a former student (Matt Dillon) announces on television that Howard is gay. With Joan Cusack, Tom Selleck, Debbie Reynolds and Bob Newhart.

VHS: S33389. $104.99.
Frank Oz, USA, 1997, 92 mins.

In Cold Blood

ER's Anthony Edwards and Eric Roberts star as Dick Hickock and Perry Smith, whose senseless slaughter of a Holcomb, Kansas, family in 1959 was examined in Truman Capote's famous book. Sam Neill is Detective Alvin Dewey, who breaks the case as the killers flee to Mexico in this psychologically riveting, true story.

VHS: S31740. $69.98.
Laser: LD76407. $49.95.
Jonathan Kaplan, USA, 1996, 180 mins.

In the Gloaming

Christopher Reeve's directorial debut is a moving family drama about a young man in his late '20s with AIDS (Robert Sean Leonard), long estranged from his family, who has returned home to be with them in the end. Features interviews with Christopher Reeve and the cast members and behind-the-scenes footage. With Glenn Close, Bridget Fonda, David Strathairn and Whoopi Goldberg.

VHS: S34559. $19.95.
Christopher Reeve, USA, 1997, 70 mins.

In the Line of Fire

Clint Eastwood stars as a maverick Secret Service agent haunted by his failure to protect John F. Kennedy in Dallas. John Malkovich is a CIA-trained professional assassin whose anger and resentment at American policies results in his chilling determination to kill the President. "This is easily the best American thriller since *The Silence of the Lambs*" (David Denby). With Rene Russo, Dylan McDermott and Gary Cole. Letterboxed.

VHS: S20328. $19.95.
Laser: LD72332. $39.95.
Wolfgang Petersen, USA, 1993, 127 mins.

In the Name of Brotherhood

Inspired by actual events, this film tells an unbelievable story about friends who possess a burning desire to pledge the glorified fraternity, Beta Phi Phi. It's an untold story about pledging, hazing, friendship, betrayal and survival. With Byron Daniel Bishop, Walter "Big Walt" Anderson, Laperrion Breedlove and Amir Ali.

VHS: S33311. $19.95.
Walter Anderson, USA, 1996, 85 mins.

In the Presence of Mine Enemies

Armin Mueller-Stahl *(Shine)* stars in Rod Serling's powerful story of courage and compassion. In the Warsaw ghetto of 1943 amidst the methodic cruelty of the occupying Germans and growing rumors of revolt, Rabbi Adam Heller (Mueller-Stahl) works to maintain calm within his community while wrestling reappearance of his son and a miraculous chance at survival for his daughter, leading him to confront the ultimate crisis of faith and one final shot at redemption. With Charles Dance and Elina Lowensohn.

VHS: S31730. $90.99.
Laser: LD76297. $39.99.
Joan Micklin Silver, USA, 1997, 96 mins.

Independence Day

From the director of *F/X*, Robert Mandel's neglected first film is an unsparing and moving profile of an isolated Southwestern town. Mandel counterpoints the drama with his two leads: Kathleen Quinlan, a talented photographer shuttered by provincial custom, and David Keith, an auto racing enthusiast who welcomes the slower lifestyle. In her first film role, Diane Wiest gives a haunting performance as a brutalized wife.

VHS: S04535. $19.98.
Robert Mandel, USA, 1983, 110 mins.

The Indian Runner

Sean Penn's directorial debut is a psychological drama about two brothers in 1968 Nebraska. Joe is a cop who settled down with wife and child; Frank, a recovering Vietnam veteran, lives his life breaking the laws his brother has vowed to uphold. With David Morse, Viggo Mortensen, Dennis Hopper, Charles Bronson and Sandy Dennis.

VHS: S16154. $14.95.
Laser: LD71417. $39.98.
Sean Penn, USA, 1991, 127 mins.

The Infiltrator

Oliver Platt stars in this gripping thriller based on a true story. An American journalist investigates young German skinheads and uncovers a link between these thugs and surviving Nazis. The extent of their evil influence is surprising. This is a dangerous enterprise that places not only his cover at risk, but also his life.

VHS: S26525. $19.95.
John MacKenzie, USA, 1995, 102 mins.

Infinity
In his critically acclaimed directorial debut, Matthew Broderick stars in the true-life story of Richard Feynman, the brilliant physicist who worked on the development of the A-Bomb, and his passionate love affair with a beautiful young woman (Patricia Arquette) who contracts Hodgkin's Disease. "An engaging, unexpected love story" *(Playboy)*.
VHS: S30872. $19.95.
Matthew Broderick, USA, 1996, 120 mins.

The Innocent
Campbell Scott, Isabella Rossellini and Anthony Hopkins star in this sexy thriller. An aggressive CIA man is forced to confront his young partner when he learns that the younger man has been seduced by a mysterious but beautiful woman. The choice placed before this couple is between deadly secrets and forbidden passions.
VHS: S27413. $19.95.
Laser: LD75507. $39.99.
John Schlesinger, USA, 1995, 119 mins.

Innocent Blood
John Landis balances the gangster movie with black humor. The talented French actress Anne Parillaud stars as a modern day vampire threatening the brutal reign of the local mob, knocking off its members serial style. With Robert Loggia, Anthony LaPaglia and Don Rickles.
VHS: S18222. $19.98.
John Landis, USA, 1992, 113 mins.

Interns
Cliff Robertson and Nick Adams star in this microcosm look at the life and conditions in a big city hospital.
VHS: S05013. $59.95.
David Swift, USA, 1962, 121 mins.

Intersection
Richard Gere is a successful architect whose personal life is on shaky ground. Between his beautiful but aloof wife, played by Sharon Stone, and his sexy, passionate lover, Lolita Davidovich, this man is forced to confront his true feelings when he must cross the intersection.
VHS: S21349. $19.95.
Laser: LD75313. $39.98.
Mark Rydell, USA, 1994, 98 mins.

Interview with the Vampire
Tom Cruise, Brad Pitt, Antonio Banderas, Stephen Rea and Christian Slater are all featured in this stylish adaptation of Anne Rice's runaway bestseller. Lestat is a charming fiend loose in old New Orleans. His hunger sets off a chain of events that span two continents and the gap between the living and the dead.
VHS: S24817. $19.98.
Laser: LD74904. $39.95.
DVD: DV60110. $24.98.
Neil Jordan, USA, 1994, 123 mins.

Intimate Deception
Charles Michaels is an artist whose marriage begins to crumble when he dreams about a killing that took place in his past. Into his life comes Tina, a beautiful model, and John, a new neighbor. But John isn't the innocent neighbor he appears to be. And Tina's appearance is also no coincidence. With Lisa Boyle.
VHS: S34631. $29.95.
George Saunders, USA, 1996, 96 mins.

Invasion of the Space Preachers
The extraterrestrial evangelist, Reverend Lash, has come to Earth to pick the minds and pockets of America on his quest for the ultimate religious experience—Network Television! Brought to you by the Troma Team, the people who brought you *The Toxic Avenger*.
VHS: S14938. $79.95.
Daniel Boyd, USA, 1990, 100 mins.

Inventing the Abbotts
Forbidden love and impossible dreams intertwine when the handsome working class Holt brothers are drawn to the beautiful and wealthy Abbott sisters in this powerful, critically acclaimed film about the coming of age in a time of innocence, directed by Pat O'Connor *(A Circle of Friends)* and produced by Ron Howard. With Liv Tyler, Joaquin Phoenix, Billy Crudup, Jennifer Connelly and Kathy Baker.
VHS: S32054. $99.99.
Laser: LD76313. $39.95.
Pat O'Connor, USA, 1996, 116 mins.

Ironweed
Based on the novel by William Kennedy, Hector Babenco's film stars Jack Nicholson and Meryl Streep and is set in 1938 Albany, New York. Francis Phelan, a drifter, returns to Albany to settle matters of conscience after staying away from his family for 22 years, and is haunted by visions from his past—his former love Helen, who is a failed singer now living as a bum.
VHS: S06865. $19.98.
Hector Babenco, USA, 1987, 98 mins.

Islander
A coming-of-age tale from the northern waters of the Great Lakes. Inga is an attractive girl of 16 who has grown up in the rough world of commercial fishing on Lake Michigan. Faster than it takes to catch a Coho, she finds childhood a distant memory. A sensitive drama personally recommended by Liv Ullmann. With Kit Wholihan, Jeff Weborg, Julie Johnson and Michael Rock.
VHS: S09871. $79.95.
Nancy Thurow, USA, 1988, 99 mins.

Islands
When Lacey, a punk teenager, is forced to spend the summer with a strange woman (Louise Fletcher), their worlds immediately collide. Unaware that the woman is her real mother, Lacey sees the remote island as a prison. But abrupt and shared dangers suddenly bring Lacey and her mother together, to a new understanding that changes both their lives. 1987, 55 mins.
VHS: S06446. $19.95.

Islands in the Stream
The primary collaborators of *Patton* re-unite for this adaptation of an unfinished Hemingway novel. George C. Scott is an alienated and isolated artist who lives in solitude on an island, his fragile paradise shattered by the arrival of three sons—one of whom is subsequently killed in battle.
VHS: S02537. $19.95.
Laser: LD75317. $39.98.
Franklin J. Schaffner, USA, 1977, 110 mins.

Istanbul
Brad Dourif portrays a man cast out from society and haunted by his past, in search of redemption—in an intriguing portrayal of two men playing the game of truth, where one man's adventure is another man's salvation.
VHS: S04346. $59.98.
Marc Didden, USA, 1986, 90 mins.

It's My Party
Eric Roberts stars as a young man diagnosed with AIDS who decides to throw a blow-out farewell party for himself in this inspirational celebration of love, life and friendship. All-star cast includes Margaret Cho, Lee Grant, Gregory Harrison, Marlee Matlin, Olivia Newton-John, Bronson Pinchot and George Segal.
VHS: S28498. $19.98.
Randal Kleiser, USA, 1995, 109 mins.

Jack and His Friends
A satire about Jack (Allen Garfield), a shoe salesman who is thrown out by his unfaithful wife. Jack is promptly kidnapped by a young outlaw couple (Judy Reyes and Sam Rockwell) on the run, who take refuge in Jack's deserted island home. Over a long, decadent weekend, the nature of their relationship subtly changes.
VHS: S19721. $79.95.
Bruce Ornstein, USA, 1992, 93 mins.

Jacknife
Delayed stress syndrome among Vietnam veterans is explored in this heartfelt drama starring Robert De Niro, Kathy Baker and Ed Harris. Based on the play *Strange Snow* by Stephen Metcalfe. DeNiro and Harris were best buddies until one fateful mission. Now the emotionally crippled Harris doesn't want his war buddy hanging around with his lonely schoolteacher sister. The performances are top notch.
VHS: S10336. $19.98.
David Jones, USA, 1989, 102 mins.

Jackson County Jail
Yvette Mimieux picks up the wrong hitchhiker and lands in the local slammer without identification. When she kills a horny guard she becomes a fugitive with a real desperado played by Tommy Lee Jones. Car chases and gunfire follow. A well-made, hard-edged action picture. With Mary Woronov and Robert Carradine.
VHS: S03715. $14.98.
Michael Miller, USA, 1976, 89 mins.

Jacob's Ladder
Don't let the biblical references scare you away. This beautifully photographed metaphysical thriller is more *Twilight Zone* than Old Testament. Tim Robbins stars as a Vietnam veteran with a serious case of post traumatic stress syndrome. He believes demons are out to get him and the surviving members of his old platoon. With Elizabeth Pena, Matt Craven, Macaulay Culkin, and Danny Aiello as the world's friendliest chiropractor.
VHS: S13717. $19.98.
Adrian Lyne, USA, 1990, 115 mins.

Jade
David Caruso and Linda Fiorentino star in this highly erotic thriller about jealousy, passion and murder. Any man would be furious if he found out his wife was cheating. This film stands out for the gruesome act a cuckolded man performs in his search for vengeance.
VHS: S26988. $14.98.
William Friedkin, USA, 1995, 94 mins.

Jagged Edge
In this tightly wound thriller, Glenn Close stars as lawyer Teddy Barnes, who defends powerful San Francisco publisher Jack Forrester (Jeff Bridges) against charges that he murdered his heiress wife. A chemistry develops between them and Teddy finds herself defending the man she loves.
VHS: S34123. $19.95.
Richard Marquand, USA, 1985, 108 mins.

James A. Michener's Texas
Pulitzer Prize-winner James A. Michener wrote the novel on which this historical drama is based. Maria Conchita Alonso, Patrick Duffy and Stacy Keach are just some of the stars featured in this sweeping epic. It charts the birth of the Lone Star State, where everything—including adventure—is bigger.
VHS: S22423. $19.98.
Laser: LD74831. $39.98.
Richard Lang, USA, 1994, 180 mins.

Jane Eyre
William Hurt heads an award-winning cast in this critically acclaimed production of Charlotte Bronte's classic story of a young woman who triumphs over fate and long hidden secrets to experience passion and romance. Also stars Charlotte Gainsbourg, Joan Plowright *(The Scarlet Letter)*, Anna Paquin *(The Piano)* and supermodel Elle McPherson *(Batman and Robin)*.
VHS: S28664. $19.95.
Laser: LD75964. $39.99.
Franco Zeffirelli, USA, 1995, 116 mins.

Jennifer 8
Bruce Robinson's film stars Andy Garcia as a disillusioned cop pursuing a serial killer who preys on blind women. Uma Thurman plays the love interest, a beautiful though emotionally wounded blind woman who is the key to unraveling the killer's identity.
VHS: S18679. $19.95.
Laser: Widescreen. **LD75318. $39.98.**
Bruce Robinson, USA, 1992, 127 mins.

Jeremiah Johnson
Beautifully shot story of a mountain man surviving winters and learning to live in harmony with Indians features Robert Redford and Will Geer.
VHS: S07495. $19.98.
Laser: LD74705. $34.98.
Sydney Pollack, USA, 1972, 107 mins.

JFK (Director's Cut)
The issues opened up by Oliver Stone's award-winning, politically incendiary and audacious reworking of the events, personalities, and alleged government conspiracy in the assassination of President John F. Kennedy are reconsidered with the "director's cut," featuring 17 minutes of additional footage cut from the theatrical release.
VHS: S17877. $24.98.
Laser: Letterboxed. **LD71468. $39.98.**
DVD: DV60088. $24.98.
Oliver Stone, USA, 1991, 206 mins.

Joe
Peter Boyle is a bigoted hardhat who overreacts to daughter Susan Sarandon's hippie lifestyle. A raw and emotional drama directed by John G. Avildsen *(Rocky, The Karate Kid)*. Think of Archie Bunker with a hunting rifle. With Dennis Patrick, K. Callan and Audrey Caire. America, love it or shoot it.
VHS: S08270. $14.98.
John G. Avildsen, USA, 1970, 107 mins.

Johnny Handsome
A small time criminal gets a new face and a fresh start but how can he forget the crooks who put him in jail and killed his best friend? Mickey Rourke stars in this Walter Hill drama set way down yonder in New Orleans. He goes from looking like the Elephant Man's brother to the spitting image of Mickey Rourke. Great atmosphere and excellent supporting work from Ellen Barkin, Lance Henriksen, Elizabeth McGovern, Forest Whitaker and Morgan Freeman.
VHS: S11766. $14.98.
Walter Hill, USA, 1989, 96 mins.

Journey
Jason Robards, Brenda Fricker, Max Pomeranc and Meg Tilly are all featured in this heartwarming drama about the troubles of creating a family. When a young mother leaves her children with her parents there is resentment all around. Slowly, an 11-year-old boy grows towards love and forgiveness through a friendship he develops with his grandfather. Produced by Glenn Close.
VHS: S29464. $90.99.
Laser: LD75936. $39.95.
Tom McLoughlin, USA, 1995, 99 mins.

The Journey of August King
Jason Patric stars as young widower who is brought out of the pain of mourning by the appearance of a beautiful runaway. Though it is illegal to help her, he cannot return her to the obsessed and dangerous Olaf. At great risk to himself he leads her North to freedom.
VHS: S29530. $99.99.
Laser: LD75827. $39.99.
John Duigan, USA, 1996, 92 mins.

Judgment in Berlin
In 1978, an East German seeking asylum in the West hijacked a Polish airliner. Martin Sheen plays Judge Herbert Stern, who wrote a book about this volatile and politically sensitive case. With Max Gail, Sean Penn.
VHS: S08133. $29.95.
Leonard Penn, USA, 1988, 92 mins.

Julia
Fred Zinnemann's film adaptation stars Jane Fonda as playwright and author Lillian Hellman and chronicles her deep and involving friendship with Julia (Vanessa Redgrave), a childhood friend. Zinnemann focuses on their intense relationship, which Julia forces by enlisting Hellman's aid to fund an anti-fascist Resistance. Redgrave won a best supporting Oscar. Jason Robards is brilliant in an extended cameo as Dashiell Hammett, Hellman's long-time lover. Film buffs will note a small role by Meryl Streep.
VHS: S02539. $19.98.
Fred Zinnemann, USA, 1977, 118 mins.

K2
Franc Roddam *(Quadrophenia)* adapts Patrick Meyers' play about a selfish Seattle lawyer (Michael Biehn) and a physicist (Matt Craven) and their struggle to scale the world's most difficult mountain, K2, in northern Pakistan. The stunning location photography is by Gabriel Beristain.
VHS: S17636. $19.95.
Laser: LD75216. $34.98.
Franc Roddam, USA, 1992, 104 mins.

Kalifornia
Dominic Sena's stylish road movie is an unsentimental depiction of madness. A writer (David Duchovny) and his photographer girlfriend (Michele Forbes), are preparing a road trip to research a book about mass murder sites. In order to finance the trip, they reluctantly enlist a white-trash couple (Brad Pitt and Juliette Lewis) to share the expenses. Unbeknownst to them, Pitt is a brutal killer who traps them in a nightmarish journey of dementia, abuse and sexual domination. Letterboxed, unrated.
VHS: S20219. $19.95.
Dominic Sena, USA, 1993, 116 mins.

The Keeper
Paul Lamont (Giancarlo Esposito) is a disillusioned corrections officer at the King's County House of Detention in Brooklyn, whose life changes when he meets Jean-Baptiste (Isaach De Bankole), a Haitian immigrant imprisoned for a rape he swears he did not commit. Moved by the young man's plight, Paul helps Jean-Baptiste with his bail and opens his home to him. Paul and his wife (Regina Taylor) soon find themselves under the spell of this charming stranger.
VHS: S33011. $79.95.
Joe Brewster, USA, 1997, 89 mins.

Keeping the Promise
A compelling story of the survival of a boy, alone in the wilderness, and the survival of a family threatened by separation, epidemic fever and other hardships in the wilds of Maine during the early 1700s. With Keith Carradine and Annette O'Toole. Based on the best-selling novel *The Sign of the Beaver*.
VHS: S32916. $29.95.
Sheldon Larry, USA, 1997, 93 mins.

Kelly's Heroes
An entertaining World War II movie about a weird collection of misfits and unconventional American soldiers who penetrate German lines to pull off a complicated gold heist. With Clint Eastwood, Telly Savalas, Don Rickles, Donald Sutherland, Carroll O'Connor and Harry Dean Stanton.
VHS: S27497. $19.95.
Laser: LD70606. $39.98.
Brian G. Hutton, USA, 1970, 145 mins,

Keys to Tulsa
In this deliciously steamy thriller laced with a Southern flavor, family black sheep Richter Boudreau (Eric Stoltz) is back home in Tulsa, looking to start fresh. When his ex-girlfriend Vicky (Deborah Kara Unger) and her sleazy husband, Ronnie (James Spader), approach him with a dangerous proposition, the trio may be in over their heads. With Mary Tyler Moore, Joanna Going, James Coburn, Peter Strauss, Michael Rooker and Cameron Diaz.
VHS: S32340. $19.95.
Laser: LD76351. $39.99.
Leslie Greif, USA, 1997, 119 mins.

The Kill-Off
Jim Thompson, author of *The Grifters, After Dark, My Sweet* and *The Getaway*, also wrote the novel behind this dark film. In a resort town, vicious gossip finds the bits of dirty information which have all the makings of a successful extortion ploy. Pushed too far, the principals in this story may find murder an unforseen addition to this bag of nasty tricks.
VHS: S29515. $69.95.
Maggie Greenwald, USA, 1990, 100 mins.

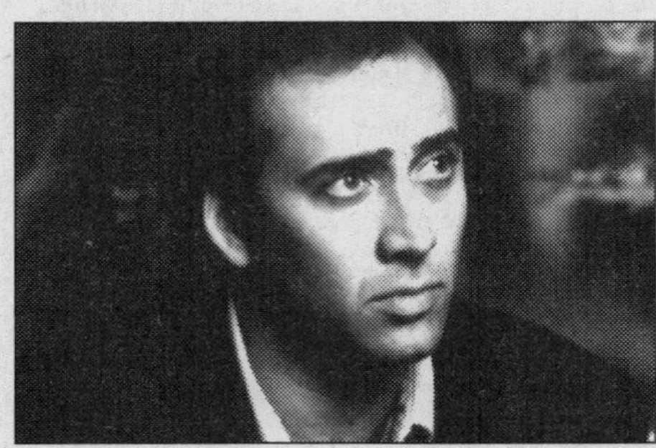

Killing Affair
Peter Weller and Kathy Baker star in the tension filled drama about a deadly feud in Appalachia in 1943. Weller shows up at Baker's isolated backwoods home and claims he killed her husband for crimes against Weller's family. With John Glover, Bill Smitrovich and Rhetta Hughes.
VHS: S02935. $79.95.
David Saperstein, USA, 1985, 100 mins.

Killing Fields
An epic story of friendship, combat and survival set within war-torn Cambodia after the victory of the Khmer Rouge. Winner of three Academy Awards, *Killing Fields* stars Dr. Haing S. Ngor, Sam Waterston and John Malkovich, with music by Mike Oldfield.
VHS: S00674. $19.98.
Laser: LD70607. $29.98.
Roland Joffe, USA, 1984, 142 mins.

Killing Zoe
In the bloody tradition of *Reservoir Dogs*, this thriller tells a tale of criminals gone worse than bad. An American safecracker goes to Paris to help a buddy with a Bastille Day bank heist. Naturally it goes awry in a totally unexpected way. With Eric Stoltz and Julie Delpy.
VHS: S23117. $14.98.
Laser: LD75215. $34.98.
Roger Avary, USA, 1994, 96 mins.

Kim
Peter O'Toole and Bryan Brown star in this recent adaptation of Rudyard Kipling's adventure novel. An orphan living on his wits in India is befriended by two radically different men. One is a Buddhist monk, while the other is a spy. The only thing these two can agree on is that they both want the boy to follow in their footsteps. John Rhys-Davies is also featured.
VHS: S27621. $19.95.
John Davies, USA, 1984, 150 mins.

King of Marvin Gardens
One of the most unaccountable films of the 70s, Bob Rafelson's feature stars Jack Nicholson and Bruce Dern as two brothers wounded by past failures. Set in Atlantic City, the plot charts their divergent paths to redemption and self-definition. Nicholson retreats into a protective job as a radio performer and Dern pursues a series of get-rich-quick schemes. With Ellen Burstyn and Scatman Crothers.
VHS: S18706. $19.95.
Laser: Chapter stops, digital master. **LD75090. $34.95.**
Bob Rafelson, USA, 1972, 104 mins.

King of the Gypsies
When Gypsy chief Sterling Hayden is near death he summons his grandson Eric Roberts to lead the tribe. Son Judd Hirsch is annoyed. With Shelley Winters, Annie Potts, and Michael V. Gazzo as part of the clan. Also Susan Sarandon and Brooke Shields, who repeat as mother and daughter. Based on the non-fiction book by Peter Maas. This was Roberts' film debut.
VHS: S10827. $14.95.
Frank Pierson, USA, 1978, 112 mins.

Kingfish: A Story of Huey P. Long
John Goodman is the crooked but charismatic Louisiana politician from the Depression era. To many he was a hero, but to others he was a frightening demagogue. Goodman superbly captures the larger than life quality of this colorful figure.
VHS: S25526. $14.95.
Laser: LD75018. $39.99.
Thomas Schlamme, USA, 1995, 96 mins.

Kiss of the Spider Woman
One of the finest films of 1985, from the director of *Pixote*. Featuring an Academy Award winning performance by William Hurt as Molina, and Raul Julia as Valentin, the political prisoner. With the incredible Sonia Braga. Based on the novel by Manuel Puig.
VHS: S00686. $14.98.
Hector Babenco, USA, 1985, 119 mins.

Kiss the Girls
Morgan Freeman and Ashley Judd race against time to capture a killer who collects beautiful women. With Cary Elwes.
VHS: S33400. $104.99.
Gary Fielder, USA, 1997, 117 mins.

Kisses in the Dark
An award-winning collection of short films starring Jennifer Rubin *(The Crush)*, James Wilder *(Melrose Place)*, Dana Ashbrook *(Twin Peaks)*, Corinne Bobrer *(ER)* and Quentin Tarantino. Includes Venice Film Festival winner *Coriolis Effect*, Academy Award nominee *Solly's Diner*, New York Film Expo *Looping*, and official Cannes Film Festival entry *Joe*. "Mordantly funny and sharp" *(The New York Times)*. 75 mins.
VHS: S34321. $29.95.

Klute
Jane Fonda stars as the high-priced call girl used as a bait to lure a killer in this suspense-filled mystery. She won the Best Actress Oscar for her compelling character study. With Donald Sutherland and Roy Scheider.
VHS: S11618. $19.98.
Alan J. Pakula, USA, 1971, 114 mins.

Kramer vs. Kramer
Dustin Hoffman must become a single parent when Meryl Streep walks out on their marriage and their young son. A terrific male weepie where Hoffman learns how to make French toast and lots of important parent stuff. With Justin Henry, Jane Alexander. Several Oscars, including Best Picture.
VHS: S03905. $19.95.
Laser: LD72188. $34.95.
Robert Benton, USA, 1979, 104 mins.

Kull the Conqueror
Action superstar Kevin Sorbo (TV's *Hercules: The Legendary Journeys*) slams evil as Kull, the Conqueror, a barbarian warrior turned king, who risks all to save the kingdom and his love in this fun adventure fantasy. With Tia Carrere and Karina Lombard. "You can keep your dinosaur romps and your cartoon fairy tales; this is the kind of kids' movie I treasured in my own youth, sexy, pictorial, and unfathomable…this one's a campy hoot" (Jonathan Rosenbaum, *Chicago Reader*).
VHS: S33261. $103.99.
John Nicolella, USA, 1997, 96 mins.

Kung Fu the Movie
A feature-length translation of the cult 1970s program about the mysterious, Zen-like actions of Kwai Chang Caine, who gets drawn into an opium plot with an evil warlord (Mako) during the gold rush fever of 1880s California. Brandon Lee, the son of Bruce Lee, co-stars as Caine's adversary. The late Keye Luke appears in flashback as Master Po, Caine's blind instructor.
VHS: S17922. $19.98.
Richard Lang, USA, 1986, 100 mins.

L.A. Confidential
"The best crime thriller since *Chinatown*" (Rex Reed, *New York Observer*), based on the book by James Ellroy. Six people are dead; one of them is a cop. But there's more to the grim discovery at the Nite Owl Cafe than a murder case. Three of the LAPD's finest (Kevin Spacey, Russell Crowe, Guy Pearce) uncover a scandal that goes to the heart of the sun-soaked paradise of '50s L.A. With Kim Basinger and Danny DeVito.
VHS: S33889. $106.99.
Laser: LD76781. $39.95.
DVD: DV60206. $24.95.
Curtis Hanson, USA, 1997, 138 mins.

The Labyrinth
Sarah (Jennifer Connelly) wished her baby brother would be taken away by goblins, and her wish came true. The Goblin King has taken the boy off to his castle to be goblinized, and Sarah must now rescue him and face the Wizard-King. Jim Henson's journey into enchantment.
VHS: Out of print. For rental only.
Laser: LD72303. $34.99.
Jim Henson, USA, 1986, 102 mins.

Ladyhawke
Matthew Broderick plays an unwilling and unlikely squire to Rutger Hauer's master knight, who labors under a dandy of a curse. He spends his nights as a ferocious beast while his lady love spends her days as a ferocious bird. And you thought the Middle Ages were uncomplicated.
VHS: S04178. $19.98.
Laser: LD74731. $39.98.
Richard Donner, USA, 1985, 121 mins.

Last Exit to Brooklyn
Hubert Selby Jr.'s controversial novel is now a visually arresting and powerfully performed motion picture. The depressed dock area of Brooklyn in the early 1950's serves as a background for anger, violence and forbidden emotions among hookers, drag queens, juvenile delinquents and union organizers. With Stephan Lang, Jerry Orbach, Burt Young, Peter Dobson and Jennifer Jason Leigh as the cold-hearted hooker Tralala.
VHS: S13289. $89.95.
Uli Edel, Germany, 1990, 102 mins.

The Last Good Time
Armin Mueller-Stahl stars with young Maureen Stapleton and Olivia d'Abo in this unusual love story. Stahl is an aging violinist who finds himself alone with dreams of the past. He happens to meet a young woman, d'Abo, who desperately needs to get away from the streets. Danger, desire and finally even love drive this film toward an unexpected climax.
Laser: LD75378. $49.98.
Bob Balaban, USA, 1994, 137 mins.

Last of the Dogmen
Sociologists Lewis Gates (Tom Berenger) and Lillian Sloan (Barbara Hershey) discover a Native American tribe that history believed had been massacred. For over 100 years, the last surviving Cheyenne Dog Soldiers escaped detection and preserved their culture by hiding out in the wilderness of Montana. Their discovery could spell the end of their way of life. It's a suspense-laden film with an updated Western flavor.
VHS: S27273. $19.95.
Tab Murphy, USA, 1995, 118 mins.

The Last of the Mobile Hot-Shots
James Coburn, Lynn Redgrave and Robert Hooks star in this tense drama filled with racial and sexual animosities. Three people are stranded by a never-ending rainstorm, in a dilapidated mansion set in the muggy, close atmosphere of the Louisiana Bayou.
VHS: S21147. $19.98.
Sidney Lumet, USA, 1970, 108 mins.

The Last of the Mohicans (1985)
James Fenimore Cooper's classic tale of friendship and adventure during the French and Indian War is given a sturdy re-telling in an above average made-for-tv version. It stars Steve Forrest as Hawkeye and features Andrew Prine, Ned Romero and Robert Tessier in this rousing tale of Colonial America.
VHS: S03639. $19.95.
James L. Conway, USA, 1985, 100 mins.

The Last of the Mohicans (1992)
Michael Mann's impassioned adaptation of James Fenimore Cooper's novel about the French-Indian War stars Daniel Day-Lewis as Hawkeye, the adopted son of the Mohicans; Madeleine Stowe is the beautiful daughter of a British colonel. Letterboxed.
VHS: S18115. $14.98.
Michael Mann, USA, 1992, 112 mins.

The Last Outlaw
Mickey Rourke is the ringleader of a gang of desperate bank-robbing outlaws. When they shoot him and leave him for dead it's their first mistake, and maybe their last. The undead desperado is slowly and calculatingly hunting down his old gang, one by one. Dermot Mulroney and Steve Buscemi also star.
VHS: S21714. $19.98.
Geoff Murphy, USA, 1994, 90 mins.

The Last Picture Show
Peter Bogdanovich's masterpiece about life in a small Texas town in the early 1950's received six Oscar nominations and swept the supporting actor and actress category. Based on the novel by Larry McMurtry. The all-star cast includes Jeff Bridges, Cybill Shepherd, Timothy Bottoms, Cloris Leachman, Ben Johnson, Ellen Burstyn, Randy Quaid and Eileen Brennan. The town of Anarene was never quite the same after they shut down the Royal theatre.
VHS: S13579. $19.95.
Laser: LD70758. $124.95.
Peter Bogdanovich, USA, 1971, 118 mins.

Last Prostitute
"It was her last chance for innocence, and his first chance for love." Brazilian bombshell Sonia Braga has the title role in this tender coming-of-age story. Co-starring Wil Wheaton, best known for his performance in *Stand by Me*. With David Kaufman, Woody Watson, Dennis Letts and Cotter Smith as Joe. Carmen Culver *(The Thorn Birds)* wrote the script based on the play by William Borden Chase.
VHS: S16025. $89.95.
Lou Antonio, USA, 1991, 93 mins.

The Last Seduction
Linda Fiorentino is a winning temptress who manages to bring ruin to all the men in her life. A scam goes all wrong, but not for Linda, who manages to move on to the next man—or is it victim? Beauty is all the more appealing in an ugly world centered on money and betrayal.
VHS: S24955. $19.95.
John Dahl, USA, 1994, 110 mins.

Last Summer in the Hamptons
Jaglom's star-studded story of three generations of a large and brilliant theatrical family spending the last weekend of their last summer together at the decades-old family retreat which economic circumstances have forced them to sell. In the course of a very unusual weekend, a Hollywood movie star surprises the family by moving in and manipulating everyone, and a series of comic and serious situations arise, as the family's secrets slowly begin to unravel. "Wry, witty and sophisticated" (Kevin Thomas, *Los Angeles Times*).
VHS: S32053. $94.99.
Henry Jaglom, USA, 1996, 108 mins.

The Last Time I Committed Suicide
Follow the adventures of Kerouac's beat buddy Neal Cassady in this jazzy, sexy, hip love story starring Keanu Reeves, Thomas Jane, Adrien Brody and Claire Forlani.
VHS: S32025. $19.95.
Laser: LD76390. $39.95.
Stephen Kay, USA, 1997, 93 mins.

Last Tycoon
Based on the last F. Scott Fitzgerald novel, an intimate look at the inner workings of a Hollywood studio. Robert De Niro stars as an Irving Thalberg-type producer who wants to accomplish great things and make wonderful pictures. Heavy-weight cast includes Tony Curtis, Robert Mitchum, Jeanne Moreau, Jack Nicholson, Ray Milland, Peter Strauss, Ingrid Boulting and Theresa Russell.
VHS: S10830. $19.95.
Laser: LD75326. $29.98.
Elia Kazan, USA, 1977, 123 mins.

Last Way Out
Kurt Johnson *(Mad City)* stars in this modern film noir about a one-time criminal trying to escape his deadly past. For two years, Frank White has kept himself hidden from his former partners in crime. But when an unexpected turn of events thrusts them together again, Frank's new life is turned upside down. Caught in the collision of past and present, Frank is forced to choose between one last heist and the last way out. "Epic...Daring." *(New York Times)*.
VHS: S34682. $24.95.
Mark Steensland, USA, 1996, 88 mins.

Latino
Wexler's *(Medium Cool)* drama set and shot in Nicaragua. Robert Beltran plays the Chicano Green Beret who is now in the jungles of South America fighting a war that includes innocent civilians among its victims. Slowly, Eddie begins to question what he's doing and why.
VHS: Out of print. For rental only.
Laser: LD71095. $34.98.
Haskell Wexler, USA, 1985, 108 mins.

Le Mans
Steve McQueen shows his skill behind the wheel of automobiles designed to compete in the world-famous, French, 24-hour endurance road race. He plays Michael Delaney, a top driver for the Gulf/Porsche team on the Grand Prix circuit, troubled by the death of a close friend and his own near-fatal accident. Superior racing footage. With Elga Andersen, Siegfried Rauch, Ronald Leigh-Hunt, Jean-Claude Bercq.
VHS: S13299. $39.99.
Lee Katzin, USA, 1971, 106 mins.

Lean on Me
The story of New Jersey educator Joe Clark. He kicked out the troublemakers in his inner city high school and locked the doors to prevent the drug dealers from coming back in. Morgan Freeman stars as the principal with the baseball bat who made the cover of Time Magazine. With Beverly Todd, Robert Guillaume, and Lynne Thigpen as the disgruntled parent. Another educational miracle film in the tradition of *Stand and Deliver*.
VHS: S10436. $14.95.
John G. Avildsen, USA, 1989, 109 mins.

Leap of Faith
This 90s version of *Elmer Gantry* stars Steve Martin as Jonas Nightengale, a charismatic con man whose traveling ministry conjures up DeMille-like religious spectacles and salvation as an elaborate sting operation co-planned with Debra Winger. Stranded in a Southwestern farming community, their ideas and principles are tested by actual hardship and pain. With Lolita Davidovich, Lukas Haas and Liam Neeson as a pessimistic sheriff in love with Winger.
VHS: S18766. $19.95.
Laser: Widescreen. **LD75219. $34.98.**
Richard Pearce, USA, 1992, 110 mins.

Leaving Las Vegas
Nicolas Cage and Elisabeth Shue star in this tender love story of two people living on the far side of hope. Ben Sanderson (Cage) is an alcoholic Los Angeles screenwriter who decides to move to Las Vegas to die. There he meets a prostitute (Shue), equally unapologetic about her own life choices, and together they fall in love. Cage won the Academy Award for his role in this engrossing, complex and beautiful film. VHS letterboxed.
VHS: S27709. $19.98.
Laser: LD75568. $34.98.
DVD: DV60150. $24.98.
Mike Figgis, USA, 1995, 113 mins.

Legends of the Fall
Brad Pitt, Anthony Hopkins and Aidan Quinn star in this beautifully filmed tale about a family in Montana. Tragedy strikes when three brothers find themselves locked in a bitter rivalry over a beautiful woman (Julia Ormond). Based on the novella by Jim Harrison, this film is an elemental tale of family ties, betrayal and love. VHS letterboxed.
VHS: S24815. $19.95.
Laser: LD74905. $39.95.
Edward Zwick, USA, 1994, 133 mins.

Legends of the North
Based on a Jack London classic, this story is set in the frozen north at the end of the 19th century. Randy Quaid stars a deceptive guide who teams up with a man he believes knows the site of a secret lake filled with gold. Tragedy intervenes and the search for Lake Esperanza must continue blindly.
VHS: S24334. $92.99.
Laser: LD75220. $34.98.
Rene Manzor, USA, 1994, 95 mins.

Lemon Sisters
Diane Keaton, Carol Kane and Kathryn Grody star as three childhood friends who find that Atlantic City is not what it used to be. Their hopes of making it big as professional singers is interrupted by healthy doses of reality. With Elliot Gould, Ruben Blades, Aidan Quinn and Matthew Modine.
VHS: S13702. $19.98.
Joyce Chopra, USA, 1990, 93 mins.

Lenny
Bob Fosse brilliantly directs this stark biography of self-destructive, controversial, persecuted comic talent Lenny Bruce. Dustin Hoffman captures all of these contrary emotions in his portrayal of the late 1950's and '60's stand-up comedian. Valerie Perrine stars in the low-key role as Bruce's stripper wife.
VHS: S00743. $19.95.
Bob Fosse, USA, 1974, 112 mins.

Les Miserables
A first-rate adaptation of Victor Hugo's monumental novel about Jean Valjean (Richard Jordan), a low-level thief trying to conceal his past and achieve respectable status despite the hostility and determination of the police chief, Javert (Anthony Perkins), to reveal his full identity. With Cyril Cusack, Claude Dauphin, Sir John Gielgud and Flora Robson.
VHS: S19030. $19.98.
Glenn Jordan, USA, 1978, 123 mins.

Less Than Zero
Bret Easton Ellis' novel of the poverty of spirit and common sense among the children of the rich in the posher areas of Southern California stars Andrew McCarthy, Jami Gertz and Robert Downey Jr. Sex, drugs, music and fashion are touched upon when a college student returns for the holidays to find all his friends have changed.
VHS: S06620. $19.98.
Marek Kanievska, USA, 1987, 100 mins.

Let It Rock
Dennis Hopper, in an effort to upgrade his screen image of playing psychos, drug dealers and alcoholics, is cast as a Hollywood agent/rock promoter who will do anything to make his client a star—including trying to have him killed. With Terrance Robay and Romana Sweeny. Written, produced and directed by Roland Klick.
VHS: S08297. $79.95.
Roland Klick, USA, 1988, 75 mins.

Lethal Weapon
Buddy film featuring Mel Gibson as a borderline psychopath cop and Danny Glover as his family man partner on the trail of a drug ring.
VHS: S05970. $19.98.
DVD: DV60048. $24.98.
Richard Donner, USA, 1987, 110 mins.

Lethal Weapon 2
Mel Gibson and Danny Glover are back as Riggs and Murtaugh, L.A.'s most action-oriented cops. This time the suicidal hunk and the Cosby-clone family man are up against a brutal gang of South African drug smugglers with diplomatic immunity. With Joss Ackland as the smarmy villain. Also Patsy Kensit, Darleen Love and Joe Pesci as a talkative witness in protective custody.
VHS: S11576. $19.98.
DVD: DV60049. $24.98.
Richard Donner, USA, 1989, 113 mins.

Lethal Weapon 3
As could be expected, Murtaugh's (Danny Glover) last week on the police force does not end with only a gold watch. He and partner Riggs (Mel Gibson) uncover a crooked ex-cop who is selling confiscated firearms. The film is non-stop action from beginning to end with comic relief provided by Joe Pesci, who reprises his role from *Lethal Weapon II*.
VHS: S21402. $19.98.
Richard Donner, USA, 1992, 118 mins.

Lewis & Clark & George
In this "darkly comic *Treasure of the Sierra Madre* homage" (Russell Smith, *Austin Chronicle*) for the '90s, two escaped convicts (Dan Gunther, *Denise Calls Up*, and Salvador Xuereb, *Doom Generation*) join forces with a seductive femme fatale (Rose McGowan, *Doom Generation, Scream*) on the trail of a long-forgotten gold mine. Cameos by Paul Bartel and James Brolin.
VHS: S34264. $69.99.
Rod McCall, USA, 1995, 84 mins.

Light of Day
Paul Schrader directed this story of a brother and sister trying to make a go of it at a Cleveland bar, an observant look at ordinary Americans trying to take control of their lives. With Michael J. Fox, Joan Jett, Gena Rowlands.
VHS: S04694. $19.98.
Paul Schrader, USA, 1987, 108 mins.

Light Sleeper
Paul Schrader's film is an investigation of a middle-level drug courier's disintegration. At the center is Willem Dafoe's performance as a former addict who runs drugs for Susan Sarandon. Dafoe attempts to regain his moral balance when he encounters his former girlfriend (Dana Delaney). Ed Lachman was the cinematographer. With David Clennon and Mary Beth Hurt.
VHS: S17969. $19.98.
Paul Schrader, USA, 1992, 103 mins.

Lily Dale
A spoiled teenage flirt harbors a deep, dark secret. She is threatened by the reappearance of her estranged brother who hints that he may expose the hidden truth to their mother (Stockard Channing) and stepfather (Sam Shepard). This riveting drama of a family about to be torn apart was written by Horton Foote *(Tender Mercies, To Kill a Mockingbird)*.
VHS: S28510. $99.99.
Laser: LD75973. $39.99.
Peter Masterson, USA, 1996, 98 mins.

Lincoln
Based on the famous historical novel by Gore Vidal, this film stars Sam Waterston as Lincoln and Mary Tyler Moore as his wife. The nation was divided by Lincoln's policies, but his dogged commitment to principle ultimately held the union together. Two-tape set.
VHS: S20638. $19.95.
Peter W. Kunhardt, USA, 1992, 190 mins.

The Lindbergh Kidnapping Case
Anthony Hopkins and Joseph Cotten star in the controversial account of the kidnapping of the Lindbergh baby. Hopkins, as the kidnapper, Bruno Hauptmann, gives a strong performance.
VHS: S10042. $69.95.
Buzz Kulik, USA, 1976, 105 mins.

Linguini Incident
Rosanna Arquette stars as a kooky but inept escape artist, who waits tables in a trendy NYC nightspot in hopes of making enough money to buy the wedding ring of Mrs. Houdini. When Rosanna decides to rob the eatery she works for, she is joined by her friend, lingerie designer Eszter Balint and bartender David Bowie, who for some reason has to get married before the week is up. With Marlee Matlin, Viveca Lindfors and Buck Henry and Andre Gregory as the restaurant owners who would not rather not pay off a million dollar bet.
Laser: LD72194. $34.95.
Richard Shepard, USA, 1991, 98 mins.

Little Man Tate
The emotional well being of a child prodigy is the subject of Jodie Foster's accomplished directorial debut. Newcomer Adam Hann-Byrd stars as seven-year-old Fred Tate, an artistic, musical and mathematical genius who worries a lot. Fred would rather have a friend than the correct answer. When his achievements attract the attention of noted educator Diane Wiest, Fred's waitress mom (played by Foster) has to make some hard choices. With Debi Mazar, George Plimpton and Harry Connick Jr.
VHS: S15823. $14.95.
Jodie Foster, USA, 1991, 110 mins.

Little Nikita
River Phoenix stars as Jeff Grant, a typical California teen who's recently applied to the Air Force Academy. During a routine investigation, veteran FBI agent Roy Parmenter (Sidney Poitier) discovers that Jeff's parents are deep-cover Russian spies planted in the U.S. for eventual call to duty. After 20 years, the day of reckoning has arrived for the Grants, who have been enlisted by master KGB agent Karpov (Richard Bradford) to deal with a renegade Soviet spy.
VHS: S32925. $14.95.
Richard Benjamin, USA, 1988, 98 mins.

Little Odessa
Two brothers, Tim Roth and Edward Furlong, star in this criminal drama about danger, deceit and family passions. Set amidst the Russian emigre underworld of Queens in New York known as "Little Odessa," this film captures the gritty urban experience of another new criminal syndicate in the making. Also features Moira Kelly, Vanessa Redgrave and Maximilian Schell.
VHS: S26283. $19.95.
William K. Howard, USA, 1995, 98 mins.

Little Romance
Charming romance about a young American girl living in Paris and running off with a French boy while chaperoned by Laurence Olivier.
VHS: S01820. $14.95.
George Roy Hill, USA, 1979, 108 mins.

Little Women
Louisa May Alcott's classic American novel comes to the screen for the fourth time in a lush production depicting the coming of age of four young women led by a strong matriarch. Set in the 19th century with lavish period costumes and sets, the film stars Academy Award nominee Winona Ryder, Susan Sarandon and Gabriel Byrne.
VHS: S24952. $19.95.
Laser: LD74910. $34.95.
DVD: DV60013. $29.95.
Gillian Armstrong, USA, 1994, 118 mins.

Little Women Gift Set
Louisa May Alcott's classic story, set in the late 19th century, depicts the coming-of-age of four young women led by a strong matriarch. Stars Winona Ryder, Susan Sarandon, Eric Stoltz and Gabriel Byrne. This special gift set includes a sterling silver locket in an enchanting keepsake case and a *Little Women* novelette.
VHS: S26622. $29.95.
Gillian Armstrong, USA, 1994, 118 mins.

The Long Hot Summer
A made-for-tv remake of the William Faulkner story of sexual frustration, greed, and the importance of having a good reputation in the Deep South. It stars Don Johnson, Cybill Shepherd, Judith Ivey, Ava Gardner, William Russ and Jason Robards in an emotional and well-acted drama that features barn burning and unbridled passion.
VHS: S06103. $79.98.
Laser: LD72253. $59.98.
Stuart Cooper, USA, 1985, 200 mins.

Looking for Mr. Goodbar
Diane Keaton stars as an idealistic young teacher caught up in the casual sex atmosphere of the 1970s. Based on the novel by Judith Rossner, this film follows Keaton's aimless exploration of singles bars and the various men that she meets in these quintessentially '70s locales. Of course she regrets it all, but not before she meets a young Richard Gere. Tuesday Weld and Tom Berenger are also featured.
VHS: S22511. $19.95.
Richard Brooks, USA, 1977, 136 mins.

Lord of the Flies
Sir William Golding's Pulitzer Prize-winning classic is updated, Americanized and presented in living color. Director Harry Hook *(The Kitchen Toto)* guides 25 novice, young performers through a compelling and dehumanizing adventure. Golding's message of the thin veneer of civilization remains relatively intact despite references to "Alf" and "Miss Piggy". With Bathazar Getty, Chris Furrh and Daniel Pipoly.
Laser: LD72305. $49.95.
Harry Hook, USA, 1990, 90 mins.

Lorenzo's Oil
George Miller's film is based on a true story. Nick Nolte and Susan Sarandon portray an economist and a linguist who take on the medical and scientific establishments in their desperate search to find a cure for their son (Zack O'Malley Greenberg), stricken with ALD, a rare, fatal, degenerative brain disorder.
VHS: S18763. $19.98.
Laser: LD71882. $39.98.
George Miller, USA, 1992, 136 mins.

Losing Chase
Helen Mirren gives a moving performance as the eccentric and disturbed Chase, a wife and mother recovering from a nervous breakdown at Martha's Vineyard. Elizabeth (Kyra Sedgwick), a young au pair who has lost her mother to suicide and her sister to mental illness, is hired to care for Chase, and the women develop an intimate bond. But the women's relationship is threatened when it is discovered by Chase's long-suffering husband (Beau Bridges). A strong directorial debut by Kevin Bacon.
VHS: S30950. $99.99.
Laser: LD76201. $39.98.
Kevin Bacon, USA, 1996, 93 mins.

Losing Isaiah
Jessica Lange and Halle Berry star in this wrenching drama about two women locked in a struggle over the same child. It poses tough questions about the most important elements of parenthood. Also featuring Samuel L. Jackson, David Strathairn and Cuba Gooding, Jr.
VHS: S26160. $19.95.
Stephen Gyllenhaal, USA, 1994, 108 mins.

Lost Angels
Hugh Hudson directed this recent feature which stars Donald Sutherland and Adam Horovitz. Set in the suburbs of Los Angeles, the film stars Horovitz as Tim, a high school student who's getting into trouble more than this parents can handle. Unwittingly admitted to a psychiatric hospital for wayward teens, he meets a doctor who sees Tim's bitterness as due to lack of family concern and tries to help him change and move ahead. Featured at the 1989 Cannes Film Festival.
VHS: S10899. $99.95.
Hugh Hudson, USA, 1989, 116 mins.

The Lost Boys
A divorced mother (Dianne Wiest) and her two sons Mike and Sam (Jason Patric and Corey Haim) move to a small town in California plagued by bikers and some mysterious deaths. Sam befriends the Frog Brothers, who claim to be vampire hunters, while the older Mike is drawn by a beautiful girl (Jami Gertz) to the gang of bikers, led by David (Kiefer Sutherland), who turn out to be teenage vampires. With Corey Feldman, Barnard Hughes, and Edward Herrmann.
VHS: S34607. $14.95.
Laser: LD76960. $29.98.
Joel Schumaker, USA, 1987, 98 mins.

Lost in Yonkers
Martha Coolidge's evocative adaptation of Neil Simon's Pulitzer Prize-winning play is a war-era tale of two young brothers left in the care of their German grandmother (Irene Worth). The boys fall under the spell of their eccentric, good-natured aunt (Mercedes Ruehl) and their gangster uncle (Richard Dreyfuss).
VHS: S19529. $19.95.
Laser: LD71923. $34.95.
Martha Coolidge, USA, 1993, 112 mins.

Louisa May Alcott's Little Men
Jo (Mariel Hemingway) the heroine from *Little Women* and her husband (Chris Sarandon), take Nat, an orphaned runaway into their country school for young boys. But when Nat's streetwise friend Dan shows up, what begins as harmless adventures soon turns the school upside down.
VHS: S34354. $19.95.
Rodney Gibbons, USA, 1997, 98 mins.

Love Affair
Warren Beatty and Annette Bening star in this remake of *An Affair to Remember* as two lovers who, despite their immediate connection, must face the problems of their other romantic attachments. Katharine Hepburn is featured along with Gary Shandling and Pierce Brosnan.
VHS: S24260. $19.98.
Laser: LD74842. $34.98.
Glenn Gordon Caron, USA, 1994, 108 mins.

Love Jones
In this hip *When Harry Met Sally*, a beautiful photographer (Nia Long, *Boyz 'N the Hood*) and a struggling writer (Larenz Tate, *Menace II Society*) are two star-crossed lovers caught in the ups and downs of modern-day romance. "Glamorous, romantic fun" *(Los Angeles Times)*.
VHS: S31729. $19.98.
Laser: LD76296. $39.99.
Theodore Witcher, USA, 1996, 110 mins.

Love Story
Ryan O'Neal and Ali MacGraw star in this melodramatic feast about young students in love who are thwarted by the travails of life. O'Neal's aristocratic heritage is just one of the hardships that almost come between him and his bride. Just when this pair seem to have defied all the odds against them an unforseen complication threatens to destroy everything. It received Oscar nominations for Best Actor, Best Actress, Best Director, Best Picture, and Best Story and Screenplay, and the Oscar for Best Original Score.
Laser: LD75345. $29.98.
Arthur Hiller, USA, 1970, 100 mins.

Lucas
In this humorous and thoughtful coming-of-age film, brainy 14-year-old Lucas (Corey Haim) falls in love for the first time and tries to win the heart of the new girl in town (Kerri Green) by trying out for the high school football team. With Charlie Sheen and Winona Ryder.
VHS: S31068. $14.98.
David Seltzer, USA, 1986, 100 mins.

Lush Life
Forest Whitaker gives a tour-de-force performance as an inspired jazz musician who introduces his best friend, Jeff Goldblum, to the jazz highlife. Wine, women and song make for a heady mix and a powerful film that shows how life and art are connected.
VHS: S21832. $94.95.
Michael Elias, USA, 1993, 106 mins.

Mad Dog and Glory
John McNaughton's drama forges a complicated relationship among three lost souls. A shy Chicago forensics cop (Robert De Niro) derisively named "Mad Dog" inadvertently saves the life of a sullen mobster and loan shark (Bill Murray). His reward is the ambiguous one-week services of Glory (Uma Thurman), a beautiful bartender indentured to the gangster. With David Caruso, Kathy Baker and McNaughton regular Tom Towles.
VHS: S18995. $19.98.
Laser: Letterboxed. **LD71890. $34.98.**
John McNaughton, USA, 1993, 99 mins.

Mad Love
The ultimate romantic couple, Chris O'Donnell and Drew Barrymore, are featured in this dark and disturbing road movie. Their love seems to make all the sense in the world, but it seems that everyone is against them. Slowly it becomes clear that they have an insurmountable problem, and they learn the hard way that the right choice is rarely the easiest choice, and that sometimes even love is not enough.
VHS: S26614. $99.99.
Laser: LD75319. $39.98.
Antonia Bird, USA, 1995, 96 mins.

Madame Sin
A made for television work about a diabolical genius (Bette Davis) who carefully manipulates a retired CIA agent (Robert Wagner) to gain control of the high-tech Polaris Submarine. With Roy Kinnear, Denholm Elliott, and Paul Maxwell.
VHS: S03913. $19.95.
David Greene, USA, 1972, 72 mins.

Malice
Alec Baldwin stars in this sexy thriller featuring deception, betrayal and murder. As a gynecologist he reveals a less-than-caring attitude toward a former patient, setting in motion this tense tale of obsessive violence.
VHS: S20719. $19.95.
Laser: LD74458. $39.99.
Harold Becker, USA, 1993, 106 mins.

A Man for All Seasons
Charlton Heston directs and stars in this remake of Robert Bolt's historical play about the moral battle between Sir Thomas More and King Henry VIII over the formation of the Church of England. A sweeping epic with Vanessa Redgrave and Sir John Gielgud as Cardinal Wolsey.
VHS: S08228. $79.98.
Charlton Heston, USA, 1988, 120 mins.

The Man in the Iron Mask (1997)
Playing both the evil King Louis XIV and his imprisoned twin, Philippe, Leonardo DiCaprio heads an all-star cast including Jeremy Irons, John Malkovich, Gerard Depardieu and Gabriel Byrne in this rousing adventure of honor, treachery, romance and intrigue based on the novel by Alexandre Dumas.
VHS: S34912. $103.99.
DVD: Widescreen, 5.1 surround, French & Spanish subtitles. **DV60372. $24.98.**
Randall Wallace, USA, 1997, 132 mins.

The Man in the Iron Mask (1998)
Timothy Bottoms, Meg Foster, and Edward Albert star in Alexandre Dumas' classic surrounding the Court of France where a dark secret of an imprisoned twin brother hovers over the cruel monarchy.
VHS: S34258. $49.95.
William Richert, USA, 1998, 85 mins.

Man in the Moon
An emotionally rewarding, coming-of-age story set in the deep South during the 1950's. Reese Witherspoon makes a memorable debut as 14-year-old Dani, an energetic Louisiana tomboy who suddenly discovers the wonder of the boy next door. Unfortunately for her, he also has eyes for her older sister. With Jason London, Emily Warfield, Gail Strickland, Sam Waterston and Tess Harper.
VHS: S16435. $19.98.
Laser: LD71453. $29.98.
Robert Mulligan, USA, 1991, 99 mins.

Man in the Wilderness
This true account concerns a man attacked by a savage grizzly who's left for dead by his cruel superiors during a fur trading expedition in the 1820s. With Richard Harris, John Huston and Percy Herbert.
VHS: S18610. $19.98.
Richard C. Sarafian, USA, 1971, 105 mins.

The Man Who Captured Eichmann
Fifteen years after World War II, Israeli agents track down and capture the elusive Nazi who sent millions of Jews to Hitler's death camps. With Robert Duvall and Arliss Howard.
VHS: S31288. $19.98.
William A. Graham, USA, 1996, 96 mins.

The Man Without a Face
In his debut film as a director, Mel Gibson adapts the novel by Isabelle Holland and plays the role of a disfigured loner who reluctantly agrees to tutor a fatherless boy (Nick Stahl) so the boy will be admitted into a military prep academy. The two develop an honest and deep relationship which becomes an invaluable lesson in the boy's search for identity, meaning and significance. With Margaret Whitton, Fay Masterson, Gaby Hoffmann, Geoffrey Lewis and Richard Masur.
VHS: S20375. $19.98.
Mel Gibson, USA, 1993, 115 mins.

Marvin's Room
A fiercely independent woman (Meryl Streep) and her rebellious son (Leonardo DiCaprio) return home after 17 years, and together they turn the family she left upside down. Based on Scott McPherson's play.
VHS: S31531. $103.99.
Laser: LD76273. $39.99.
Jerry Zaks, USA, 1996, 98 mins.

Mask
Based on a true story, Bogdanovich's account of a courageous teenager who suffers from a disease that enlarged his head, and who searches for love and tries to get his mother (Cher) off drugs.
VHS: S24563. $14.98.
Laser: LD70055. $39.95.
Peter Bogdanovich, USA, 1985, 120 mins.

Matinee
Joe Dante's unjustly neglected feature is a brilliant investigation of Cold War paranoia. Set in a coastal Florida town, John Goodman stars as a William Castle prototype 50s shock producer mounting his fiendish, low grade science fiction classic *Mant!* ("Half man, Half ant, All terror!") during the intense political tension of the Cuban Missile Crisis. The large ensemble cast (including Cathy Moriarty, John Sayles, Dick Miller and some engaging teenage performers) is excellent.
VHS: S18714. $19.98.
Laser: Letterboxed. **LD71879. $39.98.**
Joe Dante, USA, 1992, 98 mins.

The Member of the Wedding
Carson McCullers' touching 1940s Southern drama stars Anna Paquin *(The Piano)* as Frankie, a girl who daydreams of escaping her small town life. When her brother comes home for his wedding, Frankie hopes he will take her with him, but her nanny (Alfre Woodard) sees through her fantasies and must help the young girl face the truth.
VHS: S32108. $90.99.
Laser: Letterboxed. **LD76341. $39.99.**
Fielder Cook, USA, 1997, 93 mins.

Memphis
Cybill Shepherd stars as Reeny Purdew, one of three low-down Mississippi Delta drifters with a plan to kidnap the young grandson of a successful black Memphis businessman in 1957. Based on the novel *September September* by Civil War buff Shelby Foote. With John Laughlin, J.E. Freeman, Richard Brooks, Vanessa Bell Calloway, Martin C. Gardner and Moses Gunn. Script by Larry McMurtry, Cybill Shepherd and Susan Rhinehart. From the Canadian director of the riveting armored car heist film, *Pouvoir Intime*.
VHS: S15944. $89.98.
Yves Simoneau, USA, 1992, 92 mins.

Memphis Belle
They've flown 24 missions in their B-17 "Flying Fortress" called the *Memphis Belle*. Now there's just one thing keeping the flyboys from going home to a hero's welcome—mission #25, their most dangerous raid ever. Mathew Modine heads a popular young cast, including Eric Stoltz, Billy Zane, D.B. Sweeney and singer Harry Connick Jr., in this exciting World War II adventure based on a true story. Produced by David Puttnam and Catherine Wyler (whose father William Wyler first told the story of the *Memphis Belle* in a 1944 documentary).
VHS: S13581. $19.98.
DVD: DV60322. $24.98.
Michael Caton-Jones, USA, 1990, 107 mins.

Men Don't Leave
A warmly comic drama from the director of *Risky Business*. Jessica Lange is Beth, totally unprepared for life without her husband. Charming and unpredictable, Beth copes with teenage sons, a new job, and going out on her own.
VHS: S12920. $19.98.
Paul Brickman, USA, 1989, 115 mins.

Merlin
Sam Neill, Helena Bonham Carter, Isabella Rossellini, Miranda Richardson, Rutger Hauer, John Gielgud and Martin Short star in this acclaimed TV mini-series about the adventures of the mythical sorcerer in the mists of Avalon. With dazzling special effects. "Irresistible" *(New York Times)*.
VHS: S34861. $19.98.
Laser: LD77015. $29.99.
Steve Barron, USA/Great Britain, 1998, 140 mins.

Michael
John Travolta is a shabby but charming angel on the run with a pack of tabloid journalists eager to get a page-one story about him. With Bob Hoskins, William Hurt and Andie MacDowell.
VHS: S31390. $19.98.
Laser: LD76232. $34.98.
DVD: DV60068. $24.98.
Nora Ephron, USA, 1996, 106 mins.

A Midnight Clear
Keith Gordon improves on the promise of *The Chocolate War* with this naturalistic and intelligently made World War II film about a reconnaissance unit, made up of intellectually gifted soldiers, enlisted for a dangerous mission inside the German front near the end of the war. With Kevin Dillon, Gary Sinise, Peter Berg, Ethan Hawke, Frank Whaley and Arye Gross.
VHS: S17624. $19.95.
Laser: LD71775. $34.95.
Keith Gordon, USA, 1991, 107 mins.

Midnight Express
From the director of *Birdy* and *Pink Floyd's The Wall*, Alan Parker's hyper violent and grim portrait of American student Billy Hayes, who was sentenced to 30 years in a Turkish prison for attempting to smuggle hashish into the West. Brad Davis is riveting in the lead role as the frightened Hayes; Paul Smith is memorably brutish as the perversely sadistic chief guard. The Oscar-winning screenplay is by Oliver Stone.
VHS: S02549. $69.95.
Laser: Letterboxed, chapter stops, 3 sides. **LD74476. $39.95.**
Alan Parker, USA, 1978, 123 mins.

Midnight Run
Robert De Niro plays a bounty hunter assigned to find and return Charles Grodin to a sleazy L.A. bail bondsman. Grodin embezzled millions from the Mob, which he donated to charity, and they want him dead. An entertaining, action-packed, cross-country, serious comedy with Yaphet Kotto, John Ashton, Dennis Farina and the person who wrote this description as an extra in an airport scene. From the Director of *Beverly Hills Cop*.
VHS: S08325. $19.95.
Martin Brest, USA, 1988, 125 mins.

Midway
The tides turned for the Americans when the Japanese attacked the Pacific Island of Midway in 1942. Integrating antique Japanese war films and actual newsreel footage, *Midway* portrays this decisive battle as played out by the familiar faces of Charlton Heston, Henry Fonda, Robert Mitchum, Glenn Ford, James Coburn, Hal Holbrook and Robert Wagner, with Tom Selleck, Pat Morita and Erik Estrada.
VHS: S16302. $19.95.
DVD: DV60347. $24.99.
Jack Smight, USA, 1976, 131 mins.

The Mighty Quinn

Denzel Washington has the title role of a local police chief in Jamaica caught between doing his job and preserving a boyhood friendship. Robert Townsend is Maubee, a petty criminal and island legend who stumbles into an international situation that involves murder and large sums of money. A comic thriller loaded with lots of good music. With James Fox, Sheryl Lee Ralph and M. Emmet Walsh.

VHS: S11203. $89.98.
Carl Schenkel, USA, 1989, 98 mins.

The Migrants

Cloris Leachman, Ron Howard and Sissy Spacek star in this adaptation of Tennessee Williams' great drama. It's a story of a family working hard to achieve the ever-receding American dream. All their hopes come to reside in the fortunes of their son. Sadly, he may not be able to live up to all their expectations. Nominated for six Emmy Awards. 83 mins.

VHS: S21542. $89.95.
Tom Gries, USA, 1974, 83 mins.

Miles from Home

Richard Gere and Kevin Anderson play two Iowa farming brothers who would rather burn their debt-ridden property than turn it meekly over to the bank that eagerly gave them the loans in the first place. This act makes them folk heroes and wanted outlaws. Feature film directing debut of Gary Sinise, a member of the Steppenwolf Theatre Company, as are most of the cast. With John Malkovich, Terry Kinney, Laurie Metcalf, Judith Ivey and Brian Dennehy. A timely contemporary drama.

VHS: S09109. $19.98.
Gary Sinise, USA, 1988, 112 mins.

Mimic

An experiment to stop a deadly disease goes terribly wrong… and now threatens the entire city. With Mira Sorvino, Jeremy Northam, Josh Brolin, F. Murray Abraham and Charles S. Dutton.

VHS: S33396. $103.99.
Laser: DTS. **LD76825. $49.95.**
Guillermo Del Toro, USA, 1997, 105 mins.

Mindwalk

Bernt Capra's literate and often provocative meditation on ecology and self-preservation. A chance encounter with three distinct professionals (a poet, a physicist and a politician) leads to a lucid and often fascinating conversation about the fate of the earth. With Liv Ullmann, Sam Waterston, John Heard and Ione Skye. Based on Fritjof Capra's book, *The Turning Point*. Music by Philip Glass.

VHS: S18119. $19.95.
Bernt Capra, USA, 1990, 110 mins.

Miracle of the Heart: A Boy's Town Story

Art Carney stars in this made-for-tv movie about an aging priest fighting against forced retirement. The setting is the familiar stomping grounds of Father Flanagan. Mickey Rooney may be gone but kids like Casey Siemaszko are still acting up.

VHS: S04975. $19.95.
Georg Stanford Brown, USA, 1986, 96 mins.

The Mirror Has Two Faces

Barbra Streisand directed and stars in this romantic comedy that explores the modern myths of beauty and sex and how they complicate relationships. Rose Morgan (Streisand) teaches a course in romantic literature at Columbia University but doesn't have any romance in her own life. Love-burned Gregory Larkin (Jeff Bridges) teaches mathematics at the same university and seeks a relationship based on respect with someone he's not attracted to. The two meet and decide to marry while remaining celibate, leading to confusion and chaos. With Pierce Brosnan, George Segal, Brenda Vaccaro, Elle MacPherson and Oscar-nominated Lauren Bacall.

VHS: S31283. $19.95.
Laser: LD76205. $39.95.
Barbra Streisand, USA, 1996, 127 mins.

Misery

Academy Award winner for Best Actress Kathy Bates stars as a devoted and deranged fan of unsuspecting author Paul Sheldon (James Caan) in this thriller. From the novel by Stephen King.

Laser: LD72450. $39.99.
Rob Reiner, USA, 1990, 107 mins.

Mishima: A Life in Four Chapters

A bold, dramatic film, filmed in three visual styles shifting from the quasi-documentary view of Mishima, Japan's finest postwar author, to black and white flashbacks and highly stylized excerpts from his novels. Fascinating, ambitious, lyrical. English and Japanese with English subtitles.

VHS: S00861. $79.95.
Laser: LD76981. $39.99.
Paul Schrader, USA, 1985, 121 mins.

Miss Evers' Boys

Alfre Woodward stars as Eunice Evers, a nurse who was witness to and participant in the deaths of patients and friends in this powerful and provocative, true story of the Tuskegee Experiment, a government cause which sacrificed the lives of African American men. With Laurence Fishburne, Craig Sheffer and Joe Morton.

VHS: S31770. $19.98.
Joseph Sargent, USA, 1997, 118 mins.

Miss Rose White

American-as-apple-pie Rose White (Kyra Sedgwick) appears to be a modern young career woman in post-WWII New York, but she lives another life: she is actually a Polish Jew who emigrated as a young girl to the U.S. with her father, before the holocaust claimed her family. When her older brother, thought dead, comes to America after the war, she becomes haunted by her past. With Amanda Plummer, Maximillian Schell and Maureen Stapleton.

VHS: S31182. $14.98.
Joseph Sargent, USA, 1992, 95 mins.

Missiles of October

A gripping, true drama about the dark days of the 1960s Cuban missile crisis. Starring Martin Sheen, William Devane.

VHS: S03693. $19.98.
Anthony Page, USA, 1974, 150 mins.

The Mission

Two renegade Jesuit priests force the ruling European landowners to climb up a very tall mountain and massacre innocent South American indians. Robert De Niro and Jeremy Irons star in this beautifully photographed, historical drama. With Aidan Quinn.

VHS: S04306. $19.98.
Laser: Letterboxed. **LD71201. $39.98.**
Roland Joffe, USA, 1986, 126 mins.

Mission: Impossible

Tom Cruise stars in this blockbuster hit, a Cold War thriller involving double- and triple-crosses in undercover missions. Fantastic special effects and fine acting support by Vanessa Redgrave, Henry Czerny, Ving Rhames and Jon Voight make this enjoyable and fun video viewing.

VHS: S28640. $19.98.
Brian DePalma, USA, 1996, 110 mins.

Mississippi Burning

Gene Hackman and Willem Dafoe head an FBI investigative team looking to uncover the circumstances surrounding three missing civil rights workers. A powerfully acted and photographed film that blurs historic fact for dramatic effect. With Frances McDormand and Brad Dourif.

VHS: S09573. $19.98.
Alan Parker, USA, 1988, 127 mins.

Mister Johnson

Bruce Beresford directs this thoughtful and strongly performed study of British colonialism and human relations in Africa. Set in 1923, Pierce Brosnan stars as a district officer assigned to build a road through the bush. The task is accomplished with the help and creative financial calculations of his chief clerk, Mister Johnson. Maynard Eziashi is memorable as the ambitious and unlucky native. With Edward Woodward and Denis Quilley. Based on the novel by Joyce Cary.

VHS: S15407. $19.98.
DVD: DV60273. $19.95.
Bruce Beresford, USA, 1991, 105 mins.

Mistrial

When a cop-killer walks free and the cop that caught him is put on trial, the cop (Bill Pullman), rather than face the possibility that the verdict could destroy his career, takes the law into his own hands. Drawing a gun on the courtroom, the cop declares a mistrial and takes the accused, the judge and jury hostage. A new trial is about to begin, but this time justice isn't blind—it's armed. With Robert Loggia and Blair Underwood. "Explosive. Bill Pullman gives a blistering perfomance" *(Chicago Sun Times)*.

VHS: S30954. $19.98.
Heywood Gould, USA, 1996, 89 mins.

Moby Dick

Patrick Stewart stars as vengeful sea Captain Ahab, who seeks to kill the great white whale who took his leg, in Herman Melville's classic 1851 sea tale. With Gregory Peck as Father Mapple, Henry Thomas as Ishmael, and Pripi Waretin as Queequeg.

VHS: S34226. $19.98.
Franc Roddam, USA/Great Britain/Australia, 1998, 145 mins.

Mommie Dearest

The outrageous cult movie of the legendary star Joan Crawford, based upon the bestselling book by her adopted daughter Christina Crawford. Faye Dunaway plays Crawford struggling against her inner demons, desperate to be a mother, descending into alcoholism.

VHS: S00869. $19.95.
Laser: LD75385. $35.98.
Frank Perry, USA, 1981, 129 mins.

Money Train

Wesley Snipes and Woody Harrelson are two undercover cops who guard the New York City subway train known as the "Money Train." This action-comedy takes a strange twist when they realize that their work has prepared them for a unique career in crime. Hip, funny and violent, this is a gripping thriller.

VHS: S27507. $19.95.
Laser: LD75522. $34.95.
Joseph Ruben, USA, 1995, 110 mins.

Monkey Trouble

Thora Birch and Harvey Keitel star in this family film about a slightly neglected young girl who befriends a pickpocket monkey. Keitel is the monkey's trainer and owner, who just happens to need his partner for a big heist.

VHS: S22973. $19.95.
Franco Amurri, USA, 1994, 93 mins.

A Month by the Lake

A superb showcase for Vanessa Redgrave as Miss Bentley, an Englishwoman who travels to Italy's Lake Como as she had done for years with her late father before his death. On this particular trip, The Major (Edward Fox), a newcomer to lake Como, appears, and Miss Bentley has a chance at love. Unfortunately, the Major keeps getting distracted by a sexy, young, flirtatious woman (Uma Thurman). Many wonderful repartees result as the two women vie for the attentions of this wealthy bachelor against the backdrop of a luxurious resort. Based on a novel by H.E. Bates.

VHS: S27524. $99.99.
Laser: LD75547. $39.99.
John Irvin, USA, 1995, 91 mins.

Moonlight and Valentino

Elizabeth Perkins stars as Rebecca, a woman who turns to a support network which comprises of her best friend Sylvie (Whoopi Goldberg), her stepmother Alberta (Kathleen Turner), and her sister Lucie (Gwyneth Paltrow) when her husband dies suddenly. Neil Simon's daughter Ellen wrote this serious but humor-filled study of four women responding to grief. Their different approaches are exacerbated when the widow falls for her sexy house painter (played by rock star Jon Bon Jovi).

VHS: S27530. $19.95.
Laser: LD75526. $34.95.
David Anspaugh, USA, 1995, 104 mins.

Morning After

Jane Fonda stars as a struggling alcoholic who awakens in a strange bed next to a murdered man, with Jeff Bridges and Raul Julia.

VHS: S03437. $19.98.
Sidney Lumet, USA, 1986, 103 mins.

Moscow on the Hudson

Paul Mazursky *(Unmarried Woman, Blume in Love)* limits the abrupt improvisations that marred Robin Williams' other work, guiding the comedian to his best work as Vladimir, a Russian saxophonist in the Soviet Circus who defects to the West while visiting Bloomingdale's during a New York tour. Maria Conchita Alonso stars as Williams' love interest.

VHS: S02552. $14.95.
Laser: LD75803. $34.95.
Paul Mazursky, USA, 1984, 107 mins.

Mother Night

Adapted from the novel by Kurt Vonnegut. American playwright Howard W. Campbell Jr. (Nick Nolte) and his beautiful German wife (Sheryl Lee) are living in pre-World War II Berlin. A mysterious American (John Goodman) seduces him into becoming an allied spy within the Nazi Party. Campbell becomes a notorious spokesman for the Nazis' anti-American and anti-Semitic agenda, gaining celebrity in Germany and infamy in the U.S. With Alan Arkin and Kirsten Dunst. "Stylish and witty…Perfectly captures Vonnegut's tone" *(LA Weekly)*.

VHS: S31013. $101.95.
Laser: LD76159. $39.98.
Keith Gordon, USA, 1996, 113 mins.

Mountains of the Moon

Bob Rafelson directed this epic about finding the source of the mysterious River Nile during Victorian England, based on the novel by William Harrison. In an 1854 expedition, two remarkable men, Capt. Richard Burton and Lt. John Speke, embark upon a journey through the wilderness dangerous to both body and soul. The perils of the quest forge a strong bond between the men that one man honors and the other will eventually betray. A powerful adventure.

VHS: S12479. $14.98.

Bob Rafelson, USA, 1990, 140 mins.

Mr. and Mrs. Loving

Timothy Hutton and Lela Rochon star in this HBO adaptation of a story about an interracial couple from the 1960's. This true story shows that despite the couple's storybook romance, their lives were forever altered by exile from their home at the hands of the law. Nothing, however, could make them give up their rights as Americans or their love for each other.

VHS: S28046. $99.99.

Laser: LD75607. $39.99.

Richard Friedenberg, USA, 1995, 95 mins.

Mr. Corbett's Ghost

Circa 1767, New Year's Eve, in a small English town, and Ben Corbett (Paul Scofield) is kept late working by his boss at the apothecary. Ben wishes death upon his employer, and after a mysterious visit from a man who claims to bargain with souls (John Huston), his wish is granted. Now Ben is uncertain about to whom he really belongs, the ghost of his boss or his new master, the Collector of Souls. 1990, 60 mins.

VHS: S13011. $24.95.

Mr. Frost

He hasn't spoken in two years. No one knows his identity. Officially he doesn't exist…but 24 corpses do. Based on a true story, *Mr. Frost* tests the waters between good and evil, tempting human nature with one irreparable act. With an all-star cast featuring Jeff Goldblum, Alan Bates and Kathy Baker, this eerie thriller exposes the menacing power beneath the surface of a seemingly charming and civilized individual.

VHS: S13537. $89.95.

Phillip Setbon, USA, 1989, 92 mins.

Mr. Holland's Opus

Richard Dreyfuss is a composer turned teacher in a role nominated for an Academy Award. Though teaching is only meant to be a day job as Mr. Holland pursues a career in performance and composition, Holland's students soon become the focus of all his energy. Before long his desire to inspire these kids results in an unstoppable synergystic juggernaut joining his love for music to his new found love for teaching.

VHS: S29408. $19.98.

Laser: LD75817. $39.99.

Stephen Herek, USA, 1995, 143 mins.

Mr. Jones

Lena Olin plays a successful psychiatrist who gives in to an unprofessional impulse and starts an affair with the charismatic Mr. Jones, played by Richard Gere. This sexy drama tests the limits of professional standards and the irresistible needs of love.

VHS: S20739. $19.95.

Laser: LD72388. $34.95.

Mike Figgis, USA, 1993, 110 mins.

Mr. North

The directorial debut of Danny Huston, son of legendary director John Huston. A Yale graduate's life is suddenly transformed when word gets out that he has miraculous curative powers. Not everyone in the top drawer world of wealthy Rhode Islanders is pleased, however. While some admire him, others want nothing to do with this pleasant faith healer. Set during the 1920s, this film fable is adapted from *Theophilus North* by Thornton Wilder. With Anthony Edwards, Lauren Bacall, Anjelica Huston and Mary Stuart Masterson.

VHS: S26156. $14.98.

Danny Huston, USA, 1988, 90 mins.

Mr. Wonderful

Matt Dillon, Annabella Sciorra, Mary-Louise Parker and William Hurt star in this bittersweet love story about a divorced man who is trying to marry off his ex-wife so he can use her alimony money to start a bowling alley with his buddies.

VHS: S23441. $19.98.

Anthony Minghella, USA, 1993, 99 mins.

Mrs. Soffel

Diane Keaton is a prison warden's wife who falls under the spell of a condemned murderer and aids in his and his brother's dramatic escape. Mel Gibson is the clever and not-so-bad-looking criminal and Matthew Modine is the tag-along brother. Based on a true story set in 1901. With Edward Herrmann and Trini Alvarado. Well directed by Gillian Armstrong *(My Brilliant Career)*. VHS letterboxed.

VHS: S06152. $19.99.

Laser: LD72147. $34.98.

Gillian Armstrong, USA, 1984, 113 mins.

Mulholland Falls

Nick Nolte, Melanie Griffith, Chazz Palminteri, Michael Madsen, Chris Penn and John Malkovich make up the cast of this murder mystery/conspiracy film. Mulholland Falls is a mythical place where an elite and shadowy L.A. police unit metes out justice. Ironically, this group of cops find their own downfall in the very real place where America's nuclear weapons are made and tested.

VHS: S29810. $19.95.

Laser: LD75986. $34.95.

Lee Tamahori, USA, 1996, 106 mins.

Murder in the First

Christian Slater, Kevin Bacon and Gary Oldman star in this courtroom drama. An idealistic lawyer (Slater) takes on the case of a condemned man in Alcatraz (Bacon) and points out the unfair nature of his incarceration. As the story unfolds, their friendship becomes the sole means of keeping their hopes alive.

VHS: S24854. $19.98.

Marc Rocco, USA, 1994, 123 mins.

Murder One

The recreation of a murderous real life crime spree by three escaped prisoners and the younger brother of one of the convicts. Henry Thomas as the little brother tries to phone home for help but the law enforcement officers in Georgia don't take kindly to Yankees murdering the locals. With James Wilder, Stephen Shellen and Errol Slue. A gritty, realistic drama.

VHS: S07917. $79.98.

Graeme Campbell, USA, 1988, 83 mins.

My Antonia

Willa Cather's book has been adapted for the screen in this sensitive film starring Jason Robards, Eva Marie Saint and Neil Patrick Harris. An orphaned boy discovers the mysteries of life and love with a poor immigrant girl.

VHS: S24384. $79.95.

Joseph Sargent, USA, 1994, 92 mins.

My Little Girl

Mary Stuart Masterson stars as Franny, an affluent teen who volunteers to work in a city shelter for disadvantaged girls in Philadelphia. Her enthusiasm is met with scorn but she perseveres to make a difference. With James Earl Jones, Anne Meara and Geraldine Page, in her last role.

VHS: S07139. $79.95.

Connie Kaiserman, USA, 1987, 118 mins.

My Wicked Wicked Ways

Based on the best-selling autobiography of swashbuckling screen idol Errol Flynn, one of Hollywood's all-time most romantic and controversial figures. Duncan Regehr stars as Flynn, along with a supporting cast including Barbara Hershey and Darren McGavin.

VHS: S09933. $59.98.

Don Taylor, USA, 1984, 95 mins.

The Myth of Fingerprints

An ensemble cast featuring Blythe Danner, James LeGros, Julianne Moore, Roy Scheider and Noah Wyle stars in Bart Freundlich's debut film, in which a family, separated for three years, shares a secret at Thanksgiving in New England. "A fascinating portrait of modern American gothic angst" (Bruce Williamson, *Playboy*).

VHS: S33139. $98.99.

Bart Freundlich, USA, 1997, 91 mins.

Naked Lies

Shannon Tweed stars in this suspense thriller as Cara Landry, an FBI agent who is suspended from her duties after accidentally killing an innocent child during a drug bust. Her supervisor, Kevin Dowd (Steven Bauer), gives her the opportunity torepair her career by working undercover with her former lover, agent Mitch Campbell (Jay Baker), to capture international counterfeiter, Damian Medina (Fernando Allende).

VHS: S34743. $101.99.

Ralph Portillo, USA, 1997, 93 mins.

Nell

Jodie Foster and Liam Neeson star in this bizarre tale about a woman who inhabits her own world. A doctor discovers an isolated woman with a unique pattern of speech. Soon he must fight to keep her free from legal encroachment and the demands of research scientists. Foster won an Academy Award nomination for her role. Natasha Richardson is also featured.

VHS: S25615. $19.98.

Laser: Widescreen. **LD74978. $39.99.**

Michael Apted, USA, 1995, 113 mins.

The Net

Sandra Bullock stars as a nerdy computer consultant who finds herself trapped in an overwhelming conspiracy. Before she realizes what is happening, she becomes a woman without an identity, fighting villains and battling to save the country. Featuring Dennis Miller and Jeremy Northam.

VHS: S26921. $19.95.

Laser: LD75403. $39.95.

DVD: DV60135. $24.98.

Irwin Winkler, USA, 1995, 114 mins.

Network

A savage satire written by Paddy Chayefsky, looking at the powers behind television programming. With a sizzling performance by Peter Finch (I'm mad as hell and I'm not going to take it anymore) as newscaster Howard Beale, with Faye Dunaway and William Holden.

VHS: S01817. $14.95.

Laser: Letterboxed. **LD76399. $39.99.**

DVD: DV60153. $24.98.

Sidney Lumet, USA, 1976, 116 mins.

Never Talk to Strangers

Antonio Banderas, Rebecca De Mornay, Dennis Miller and Harry Dean Stanton all star in this erotic thriller. DeMornay's character, an aloof psychologist, unexpectedly falls for an odd stranger (Banderas). Though their sexual chemistry seems the prelude to a deeper understanding, it actually leads to danger and death.

VHS: S27307. $19.95.

Laser: LD75480. $34.95.

Peter Hall, USA, 1995, 86 mins.

The New Age

Peter Weller and Judy Davis play a married couple who quit their jobs to open their own boutique. Despite their best efforts, it never really succeeds. The story of their failure provides an amusing and engaging view of the feel-good precepts of "The New Age". Samuel Jackson and Adam West are also featured.

VHS: S23860. $19.98.

Laser: Widescreen. **LD74923. $34.98.**

Michael Tolkin, USA, 1994, 106 mins.

The New Centurions

An all-star cast in a brilliant episodic adaptation of Joseph Wambaugh's best seller about two rookie cops in Los Angeles who are addicted to danger. Cynical film with good performances and solid storytelling. Starring George C. Scott and Stacy Keach.

VHS: S13574. $14.95.

Richard Fleischer, USA, 1972, 103 mins.

New Jersey Drive

This tough urban tale follows a crew of homeys that live for the thrill of stealing cars. They ride them and sell them to chopshops for cash. A policeman takes a personal interest in stopping their game and the chase turns violent. The odds against survival are great but there's a chance they can get out alive. Music by Queen Latifah, Blak Panta, Heavy D, Naughty by Nature and others.

VHS: S26345. $19.98.

Laser: LD75056. $34.98.

Nick Gomez, USA, 1995, 98 mins.

New Year's Day...Time to Move On

Henry Jaglom once again attempts to examine the nature of contemporary relationships between men and women. He stars as a man in the middle of a mid-life crisis who takes possession of his new apartment only to find the previous tenants—three women—haven't quite moved out. With Gwen Welles, Maggie Jackson, Melanie Winter and Milos Forman.

VHS: S13199. $79.98.

Henry Jaglom, USA, 1989, 90 mins.

New York Nights

Three young and alluring women (Marilyn Chambers, Julia Parton and Susan Napoli), join forces in their quest for the good life in the Big Apple. One is a former model, one is just starting out as an actress, and the third is simply looking for gold. Together they share notes on life, love and the pursuit of happiness through financial security.

VHS: S22539. $89.95.

D. Gary Phelps, USA, 1994, 90 mins.

Niagara Niagara

Benny & Joon meets *Bonnie & Clyde* in this story of a couple of off-beat teenagers who discover just how odd the world really is when they go looking for the American dream and find more than they bargained for. With Venice Film Festival Winner Robin Tunney and Henry Thomas *(Suicide Kings)*.

VHS: S34839. $82.95.

Bob Gosse, USA, 1997, 93 mins.

Nick of Time

Johnny Depp faces off against Christopher Walken in this tense thriller. Walken has kidnapped Depp's young daughter, forcing Depp to comply with a political assassination plot for the ransom. It's a tense standoff where a taut sense of time racing by gives this dilemma added weight.

VHS: S27635. $19.95.

John Badham, USA, 1995, 89 mins.

Night and the City

Irwin Winkler's remake of Jules Dassin's classic 1950 noir stars Robert De Niro as Harry Fabian, a small-time, ambulance-chasing lawyer trying to escape his bleak, anonymous life as a fight promoter in the mob-influenced local boxing circuit. Jessica Lange stars as a bar maid caught in a violent marriage with a dangerous attraction to Fabian. With Cliff Gorman, Alan King, Jack Warden and Eli Wallach.

VHS: S18247. $19.98.

Irwin Winkler, USA, 1992, 104 mins.

Night Falls on Manhattan

Andy Garcia stars as a young assistant D.A., a second-generation Irish-Latino cop whose father (Ian Holm) is wounded in a bloody stakeout. An opportunist D.A. (Ron Leibman) sees the perfect public relations gimmick: Garcia will prosecute the case and avenge his father. Richard Dreyfuss defends the seemingly indefensible drug-dealing cop killer. After Garcia wins his case, he experiences a crisis of faith. Laser disc includes audio-commentary with Lumet, cast and producers. With Lena Olin.
VHS: S32199. $19.95.
Laser: LD76344. $34.98.
Sidney Lumet, USA, 1996, 114 mins.

The Night Flier

From Stephen King comes this relentlessly terrifying story of a beast untamed by human nature that flies by night in a dark-winged Cessna, lands at secluded airports, and brutally murders residents. For an inquisitive reporter, this story of a lifetime may be his last. With Miguel Ferrer.
VHS: S34088. $99.95.
DVD: DV60323. $24.98.
Mark Pavia, USA, 1997, 97 mins.

Night Owl

John Leguizamo, Caroline Munro, James Raferty and Holly Woodlawn are featured in this urban vampire story. Leguizamo is Jake, a man searching NYC because his sister has vanished. Soon he encounters a vampire who haunts the clubs in search of nightlife and victims. This is a classic creepy film set in the early 1980's.
VHS: S24823. $19.95.
Jeffrey Arsenault, USA, 1993, 77 mins.

Night Shade

Scott Travers is still grieving months after the death of his young, beautiful wife. Persuaded to start dating again, he goes to a club where he imagines that he sees her. Soon he discovers the mysterious woman really is his wife—but she's now a vampire. Scott knows he shouldn't return, but he can't control his own desire. With Tane McClure and Tim Abell.
VHS: S34630. $29.95.
Fred Olen Ray, USA, 1997, 90 mins.

The Night Visitor

An ingenious tale of Gothic horror and murderous revenge in which a man escapes from an asylum, night after night, to wreak vengeance on his accusers. With Max Von Sydow, Trevor Howard and Liv Ulmann. In English.
VHS: S34215. $19.95.
Laszlo Benedek, USA, 1971, 106 mins.

Nightbreaker

Martin Sheen and Emilio Estevez star in this examination of the U.S. Army's atomic testing of the 1950s, uncovering, in the process, a nuclear nightmare.
VHS: S09599. $79.98.
Peter Markle, USA, 1989, 100 mins.

Nightmare Years

Based on the memoirs of American writer William L. Shirer, and adapted for the screen by Bob Woodward. Sam Waterston and Marthe Keller star in this production shot in Europe detailing the battle to stop Hitler.
VHS: S12191. $89.98.
Anthony Page, USA, 1989, 237 mins.

Nina Takes a Lover

Laura San Giacomo stars as Nina, a young married woman itching for excitement. Her best friend has a lover and seeing them together plants the idea of taking a lover in Nina's head. All it takes is an exciting young British photographer and a series of interviews with a reporter about marriage and infidelity to get Nina going.
VHS: S26800. $95.95.
Alan Jacobs, USA, 1995, 100 mins.

Nixon

Anthony Hopkins is Nixon, while Joan Allen portrays his wife, Pat. Their performances were nominated for Oscars. This film, while vilified for its fanciful recreation of some key historical events, remains a compelling drama that captures the tortured soul of America's most reviled recent president.
VHS: S27845. $19.98.
Laser: LD75926. $69.99.
Oliver Stone, USA, 1995, 191 mins.

No Drums, No Bugles

A finely wrought drama adapted from a West Virginia story concerning moral convictions and political beliefs. Martin Sheen plays a conscientious objector who avoids military service during the Civil War by hiding in a cave for three years.
VHS: S05173. $19.95.
Clyde Ware, USA, 1971, 85 mins.

Nobody's Fool

Paul Newman, Jessica Tandy and Melanie Griffith are featured in this acclaimed film. It received Academy Award nominations for Best Actor and Best Screenplay. The story follows an older small town scamp leading a comfortable but irresponsible life. Everything changes with the arrival of his estranged son.
VHS: S25719. $19.95.
Robert Benton, USA, 1994, 110 mins.

Nobody's Girls

Cloris Leachman, Esther Rolle and Tanto Cardinal star in this collection of true stories from the Old West about women who used their talents to pioneer long and turbulent lives, from the dry Southwest to the colder climes of Alaska. Whether fighting political battles or simply engaged in making a living, the grit and tenacity of these women is inspiring.
VHS: S25743. $29.95.
Mirra Bank, USA, 1995, 90 mins.

Norma Rae

Sally Field in her Oscar-winning performance as a spunky Southern mill worker gradually won over to unionization by Ron Leibman as a New York organizer. With Beau Bridges.
VHS: S02343. $19.98.
Laser: LD71257. $34.98.
Martin Ritt, USA, 1979, 117 mins.

Normal Life

Natural Born Killers meets *True Romance* in this sexy, psychological thriller from acclaimed director John McNaughton *(Henry: Portrait of a Serial Killer)*, based on actual events. Luke Perry and Ashley Judd are Chris and Pam Anderson, a married couple who live a fairly normal life until Chris loses his job on the police force and secretly turns to robbing banks to make his wife's dreams come true. Upon discovering his secret, Pam joins his deadly crime wave as they terrorize a quiet Illinois town. "A gutsy little gem" *(Chicago Tribune)*.
VHS: S30784. $14.98.
John McNaughton, USA, 1996, 108 mins.

North Shore Fish

From the playwright Israel Horovitz comes this look at the workers of North Shore Fish, revealing a group of men and women fighting to keep their heads above water. With Tony Danza, Mercedes Ruehl, Peter Riegert and Wendi Malick. 94 mins.
VHS: S34672. $89.98.
Steve Zuckerman, USA, 1996, 94 mins.

Nostradamus

Tcheky Caryo, Rutger Hauer, F. Murray Abraham and Amanda Plummer star in this lavish film about the Western world's most visionary prophet. This monk from the 16th century committed his hellish visions of the future to paper and they have continued to haunt the world with their vividness and their accuracy.
VHS: S24387. $19.98.
Laser: LD74942. $39.99.
Roger Christian, USA, 1994, 118 mins.

Not Without My Daughter

Sally Field stars in the story of a woman, alone with her daughter, who must escape from her husband (Alfred Molina), and from a land where thousands of years of Islamic law makes women a man's personal property. Based on a true story of terror in the volatile Middle East.
VHS: S14101. $14.95.
Brian Gilbert, USA, 1990, 107 mins.

Now and Then

Rosie O'Donnell, Demi Moore, Melanie Griffith and Rita Wilson star in this coming-of-age story. Four women reunite as one of them prepares to give birth, and together they relive the most important summer of their youth. The lessons they learned and the friendships they forged back then have had the strength to carry them through the troubles they've faced in their adult lives. This light comedy has an upbeat and affirming core.
VHS: S27412. $19.98.
Laser: LD75510. $39.99.
Lesli Linka Glatter, USA, 1995, 102 mins.

Nuts

Barbra Streisand is a high priced prostitute arrested for murder. Richard Dreyfuss is the lawyer appointed to defend her. Her wealthy parents, Karl Malden and Maureen Stapleton, would rather have her locked away for mental illness. Will Dreyfuss be able to convince Judge James Whitmore otherwise? A courtroom drama with Eli Wallach as the shrink.
VHS: S06813. $19.98.
Martin Ritt, USA, 1987, 116 mins.

O Pioneers!

The astonishing Jessica Lange stars in this handsome and impeccable adaptation of Willa Cather's turn-of-the-century novel about a fiercely independent young woman who inherits her father's land, earns her family a fortune, though must confront her deep feelings for the visionary and dreamer who's returned with his own demands and ambitions. With John Sayles' regular David Strathairn, Tom Aldredge, Reed Diamond, Heather Graham, and Josh Hamilton.
Laser: LD71539. $29.98.
Glenn Jordan, USA, 1991, 100 mins.

Obsession

Cliff Robertson loses his wife and daughter to kidnappers. Years later, on a trip to Florence, he discovers a look-alike of his lost love restoring a church. His interest in life is also restored in this Brian de Palma hommage to Hitchcock. Music by Bernard Herrmann.
VHS: S04660. $14.98.
Brian DePalma, USA, 1976, 98 mins.

Odile & Yvette at the Edge of the World

Two sisters discover the power to live in a world of their own making in this family drama. With Noah Fisher, Kim Mundy, Heather Roheim and Karen Skloss.
VHS: S34096. $19.95.
Andrew Burke, USA, 1993, 95 mins.

Of Mice and Men

In this adaptation of John Steinbeck's novel, set in Depression-era California, John Malkovich and Gary Sinise star as childlike Lennie and his guardian George, who desperately attempt to hold on to a prominent piece of land. With Ray Walston, Casey Siemaszko and Sherilyn Fenn.
VHS: S17923. $19.98.
Laser: LD71839. $34.98.
Gary Sinise, USA, 1992, 114 mins.

Old Man

Adaptation of William Faulkner's compassionate story set during the great Mississippi flood of 1927 stars Arliss Howard as J.J. Taylor, a prisoner dispatched to rescue Addie (Jeanne Tripplehorn), a pregnant woman clinging to a tree above the raging river. When Addie gives birth after drifting off course on the Bayou, J.J.'s tenderness toward her newborn touches Addie, and their journey stirs a current in their hearts. Screenplay by Horton Foote *(To Kill a Mockingbird)*.
VHS: S31746. $90.99.
Laser: LD76300. $39.99.
John Kent Harrison, USA, 1997, 98 mins.

Oliver Twist

George C. Scott portrays Charles Dickens' most enduring villain in this film adaptation of the famous novel. Oliver suffers all the trepidations of a 19th-century English orphan. His courage and fortitude make him an unforgettable icon of the resiliency of the human spirit. Tim Curry is also featured.
VHS: S21008. $14.98.
Clive Donner, USA, 1982, 88 mins.

Olly Olly Oxen Free

Katharine Hepburn stars as a kooky but kindhearted junkyard merchant who help two young boys live their dream of sailing aloft in a hot-air balloon.
VHS: S31168. $14.95.
Richard A. Colla, USA, 1978, 83 mins.

On Golden Pond

Henry Fonda and Katharine Hepburn play an aging married couple, Norman and Ethel Thayer, spending a dramatic summer in the woods. Their estranged daughter (Jane Fonda) drops by to clear the air and leave Doug McKeon for them to watch. Three Oscars. Henry Fonda's last film.
VHS: S03479. $14.98.
Mark Rydell, USA, 1981, 110 mins.

Once Around

Richard Dreyfuss and Holly Hunter lead an all-star cast in this critically acclaimed tale of life, love and chance, which examines the way a close-knit Italian-American family is thrown into turmoil when the oldest daughter (Hunter) falls in love with an abrasive and forcefully charming businessman (Dreyfuss). Also starring Gena Rowlands, Laura San Giacomo and Danny Aiello.
VHS: S14256. $19.98.
Lasse Hallstrom, USA, 1991, 114 mins.

Once Upon a Time When We Were Colored

Al Freeman Jr., Phylicia Rashad and Leon star in this screen adaptation of Clifton L. Taubert's memoir. It depicts the land of cotton after slavery, but before the civil rights movement. Told through the eyes of a young boy, this story tells how people nurtured themselves through tough times with a spirit that cannot be forgotten.
VHS: S29791. $14.98.
Tim Reid, USA, 1996, 113 mins.

One Against the Wind

Set in Nazi-occupied France, Judy Davis plays Mark Lidell, a gilded British aristocrat who risks her standing, family's reputation and life to orchestrate a daring freedom movement for Allied soldiers in this true account. With Sam Neill, Denholm Elliott and Anthony Higgins.
VHS: S18001. $14.98.
Larry Elikann, USA, 1991, 100 mins.

One Good Turn

When successful executive Matt Forrest (Lenny Von Dohlen) accidently bumps into a man who saved his life 12 years ago (James Remar), gives him a job and lets him live at his home—despite the reluctance of his wife (Suzy Amis)—a detective (John Savage) discovers this meeting may not have been so accidental.
VHS: S28586. $19.95.
Laser: LD75979. $39.99.
Tony Randel, USA, 1995, 90 mins.

One Night Stand (Figgis)

Mike Figgis' *(Leaving Las Vegas)* erotically charged love story explores the passion and betrayal of a one-night stand. With Wesley Snipes, Nastassja Kinski, Kyle MacLachlan, Ming-Na Wen and Robert Downey, Jr.
VHS: S33348. $103.99.
Laser: Audio commentary by Mike Figgis. **LD76813. $39.99.**
DVD: DV60208. $24.98.
Mike Figgis, USA, 1997, 104 mins.

One Night Stand (Shire)

Ally Sheedy portrays a gutsy yet lonely woman in this bizarre and chilling tale. Even though she seems to know exactly what she desires in a man and how to get it, it may not actually be enough. Her story may well prove the inadequacy of one look, one line, and one night.
VHS: S27252. $92.99.
Talia Shire, USA, 1995

One Trick Pony

A rock-solid songfest of the music world's ups and downs, written by and starring Paul Simon, 1987 Best Album Award winner for his double-platinum album, "Graceland."
VHS: S03496. $14.95.
Laser: LD76963. $34.98.
Robert M. Young, USA, 1980, 98 mins.

Operation Daybreak

Reinhard "Hangman" Heydrich was Hitler's trusted right-hand man. In Prague during the war, the Czech underground tried to assassinate him. This heroic tale of Czech resistance is the focus of a gripping drama starring Timothy Bottoms, Anthony Andrews and Nicola Pagett.
VHS: S21011. $19.98.
Lewis Gilbert, USA, 1976, 102 mins.

Ordinary People

An intense examination of a family being torn apart by tragedy and tension, *Ordinary People* won four Academy Awards including Best Picture and Director. Featuring Donald Sutherland, Mary Tyler Moore and Timothy Hutton.
VHS: S03261. $19.95.
Robert Redford, USA, 1980, 124 mins.

Orphan Train

In 1854 New York City there were over 10,000 orphaned children living on the streets. After seeing a child hanged for stealing, Children's Rescue Mission worker Emma Simms (Jill Eikenberry), with help from newspaper man Frank Carlin (Kevin Dobson), decides to carry on her deceased uncle's work with the Orphan Train to place children with families out West. With Glenn Close.
VHS: S31218. $14.99.
William A. Graham, USA, 1980, 138 mins.

Orphans

Albert Finney stars in this acclaimed film adaptation of the New York play as Harold, a slick gangster who enters the bleak world of two teenaged orphans to become their unlikely "parent" and change their lives forever. With Matthew Mordine, Kevin Anderson.
VHS: S06607. $79.95.
Alan J. Pakula, USA, 1987, 101 mins.

Orpheus Descending

Based on the Tennessee Williams' classic, Vanessa Redgrave stars as Lady Torrance, a bored housewife rutted in a loveless marriage. Enter handsome young stranger Kevin Anderson, who evokes her long-neglected passion. While they submit to their attraction, Lady's dying husband, too weak himself, enlists the help of his klan to punish the lovers.
VHS: S13263. $79.98.
Peter Hall, USA, 1991, 117 mins.

Other People's Money

Danny DeVito is perfectly cast as Larry the Liquidator, a Wall Street shark who likes nothing better than to buy up small companies and sell them for a healthy profit. Gregory Peck, the highly principled owner of New England Wire and Cable, doesn't want to sell the family business. It is up to the crafty legal mind of Penelope Ann Miller to thwart the corporate takeover. Piper Laurie and Dean Jones are longtime NEW&C employees with agendas of their own. From the long-running play by Jerry Sterner.
VHS: S15724. $19.98.
Norman Jewison, USA, 1991, 101 mins.

The Other Side of the Mountain

Jill Kinmont was an Olympic hopeful until she suffered a skiing accident that left her paralyzed. Marilyn Hassett stars in this true life story of courage and recovery. With Beau Bridges, Dabney Coleman and Belinda J. Montgomery.
VHS: S07806. $59.95.
Larry Peerce, USA, 1975, 101 mins.

The Other Side of the Mountain, Part 2

Jill Kinmont was a shoo-in for the Olympics in downhill skiing until a sporting accident occurred. In Part 2 of her true-life story, she must overcome depression and the death of the man who helped her recover. Features Marilyn Hasset and Timothy Bottoms.
VHS: S21766. $19.98.
Larry Peerce, USA, 1978, 99 mins.

Out of Africa

The autobiographical story of Karen Blixen (pen name Isak Dinesen) and her life on a coffee plantation in Kenya around 1914. Winner of seven Academy Awards, starring Robert Redford, Meryl Streep and Klaus Maria Brandauer.
VHS: S00981. $19.95.
Laser: LD70063. $39.98.
Sydney Pollack, USA, 1985, 161 mins.

Out of the Blue

A stark and realistic portrayal of a young girl, Linda Manz, experiencing the frustrations of small town living and thinking. Her response: rebellion. With Raymond Burr and Dennis Hopper; theme song by Neil Young.
VHS: S00982. $59.95.
Dennis Hopper, USA, 1984, 94 mins.

Outbreak

Imagine a deadly virus is killing American citizens. Dustin Hoffman and Rene Russo play government scientists sent to prevent a deadly plague. Sadly, personal crises and governmental indifference (or is it intrigue?) combine to hinder their progress. Ultimately, the fear of contagion cannot match the terror unleashed by sheer murderous desire. Also features Donald Sutherland and Morgan Freeman.
VHS: S26159. $19.98.
Laser: LD75037. $39.98.
DVD: DV60051. $24.98.
Wolfgang Petersen, USA, 1995, 128 mins.

The Outfit

Robert Duvall and Karen Black star in this gripping film of revenge. A poignant look at life in crime. With Joe Don Baker, Robert Ryan and Timothy Carey. Based on a novel by Donald E. Westlake.
VHS: S30540. $19.98.
John Flynn, USA, 1974, 101 mins.

Over the Edge

A disturbing teen drama based on a true incident where alienated suburban youth go on a rampage after being pushed too far by insensitive police and out-of-touch educators. The film debut of Matt Dillon. Other solid performances by Vincent Spano, Pamela Ludwig and Michael Kramer. Co-written by Tim Hunter *(River's Edge)*.
VHS: S06162. $14.95.
Jonathan Kaplan, USA, 1979, 91 mins.

The Pallbearer

David Schwimmer *(Friends)* and Gwyneth Paltrow *(Seven, Emma)* star in this cute comedy about finding love where you least expect it. A down-on-his-luck college grad (Schwimmer) who lives at home with mom summons up the nerve to ask out the girl of his dreams—at the funeral of a classmate he never knew. Barbara Hershey rounds out this winning cast.
VHS: S28638. $99.99.
Laser: LD75965. $39.99.
Matt Reeves, USA, 1996, 98 mins.

The Paper

Michael Keaton, Glenn Close, Randy Quaid and Robert Duvall make up the cast of this fast-paced comedy. The world of newspaper journalism is a place where laughs must be had, even as the truth about the seamier realities of life must be uncovered and delivered to a waiting public.
VHS: S22037. $19.98.
Laser: Widescreen. **LD74630. $34.98.**
DVD: DV60156. $24.98.
Ron Howard, USA, 1994, 112 mins.

The Paper Chase

The popular drama about a freshman at Harvard Law School who realizes the biggest obstacle to his getting good grades is the brilliant but tough Professor Kingsfield (John Houseman). His problems become intensified when he falls in love with the professor's daughter.
VHS: S07369. $19.98.
James Bridges, USA, 1973, 111 mins.

Paper Moon

Ryan O'Neal stars with his young daughter Tatum in this Oscar-nominated adaptation of Joe David Brown's novel, *Addie Pray*. Ryan poses as a man of God, but he really is on the take. He inadvertently hooks up with an orphan who manages to outdo him in the cons he works for cash. Together they create quite a criminal team. Includes introductory segment with Peter Bogdanovich. Letterboxed.
VHS: S25683. $29.95.
Peter Bogdanovich, USA, 1973, 114 mins.

Papillon

The epic film version of the best-selling book by Henri Charriere, who escaped from Devil's Island and several other hellhole prisons in South America. Steve McQueen has the title role—which means butterfly in French. Dustin Hoffman is cast as his nearsighted friend and fellow convict. Watch for the scene in which they have to move logs in an alligator-infested swamp. With Victor Jory, Don Gordon. Letterboxed.
VHS: S10936. $19.98.
Franklin J. Schaffner, USA, 1973, 150 mins.

Paradise Road

Based on real events, *Paradise Road* is the powerful story of a group of women who find a way to survive imprisonment by the Japanese during World War II. These diverse women from different countries, speaking different languages, unite to form a vocal orchestra, creating an inspiring symphony of human voices. With Glenn Close, Frances McDormand *(Fargo)*, Julianna Margulies *(ER)* and Pauline Collins.
VHS: S32237. $99.99.
Laser: LD76347. $39.98.
Bruce Beresford, USA, 1997, 120 mins.

Paris Trout

Dennis Hopper has the title role in this dramatic tale of crime and prejudice in a small Southern town. With Barbara Hershey as his more liberal wife and Ed Harris as the man looking for the truth. Based on the National Book Award winning novel by Pete Dexter. "Truly powerful" *(New York Post)*.
VHS: S14503. $19.98.
Stephen Gyllenhaal, USA, 1991, 98 mins.

Passenger 57

Wesley Snipes portrays John Cutter, an ex-government agent, who is coincidentally on the same plane as an evil apprehended terrorist (Bruce Payne) headed to trial in L.A. Unfortunately, some of the terrorist's thugs have also sneaked aboard with plans to hijack the plane. Music by Stanley Clarke.
VHS: S21406. $19.98.
Laser: LD74740. $29.98.
DVD: DV60319. $24.98.
Kevin Hooks, USA, 1992, 84 mins.

Pastime
A classic drama about the game of baseball. William Russ gives an exceptional performance as Roy Dean Bream, an aging relief pitcher playing Class D ball in Central California in the late 1950's. With Glenn Plummer, Noble Willingham, Jeffrey Tambor, Scott Plank and Deirdre O'Connell. Watch for cameos by baseball greats Ernie Banks, Bob Feller, Harmon Killebrew, Bill Mazeroski, Don Newcombe and Duke Snider.
VHS: S16041. $19.95.
Robin Armstrong, USA, 1991, 95 mins.

Pathfinder
In this rousing final chapter of James Fennimore Cooper's *The Last of the Mohicans*, Mabel Dunham and the legendary woodsman known as the Pathfinder (Kevin Dillon, *Platoon*) find themselves plunged into the battle for America's far frontier in the war-torn colonial wilderness. Along with his adoptive Indian father (Graham Greene, *Dances with Wolves*), the Pathfinder and Mabel are swept up in a race to rescue a British fort besieged by hostile French forces and a deadly, unknown traitor. With Laurie Holden, Stephen Russell, Jaimz Woolvett and Russell Means.
VHS: S30768. $99.99.
Laser: LD76107. $39.99.
Donald Shebib, USA, 1996, 104 mins.

Patriot Games
Harrison Ford stars in this taut Tom Clancy thriller about a retired CIA analyst who saves his family and an English ambassador from an assassination attempt orchestrated by a rogue faction of the IRA. Ford incurs the vengeance of the lead terrorist when he kills the man's younger brother. With Anne Archer, James Earl Jones, Sean Bean, Samuel L. Jackson, Patrick Bergin, Polly Walker and Richard Harris.
VHS: S17772. $19.95.
Laser: Widescreen. **LD75236. $34.98.**
Phillip Noyce, USA, 1992, 117 mins.

The Peacemaker
George Clooney and Nicole Kidman strike sparks when they join forces to stop a political terrorist from detonating a nuclear weapon. Letterboxed.
VHS: S33349. $106.99.
Mimi Leder, USA, 1997, 124 mins.

Pelican Brief
Julia Roberts and Denzel Washington star in this fast-paced thriller adapted from John Grisham's novel about a law student (Roberts) who uncovers a conspiracy that puts her in grave danger. Only one journalist (Washington) has the ability and guts to help her expose this plot. Together they must outwit some of the most powerful men in Washington.
VHS: S21079. $19.98.
Laser: LD72411. $39.98.
DVD: DV60093. $24.98.
Alan J. Pakula, USA, 1993, 141 mins.

Penalty Phase
Peter Strauss stars as a respected judge in this above average tv movie who is faced with releasing a violent killer whose civil rights may have been violated. His decision could affect his upcoming re-election. With Melissa Gilbert, Jane Badler, Milly Perkins and Mitchell Ryan. A riveting drama.
VHS: S07343. $19.95.
Tony Richardson, USA, 1986, 90 mins.

Perfect
Rolling Stone investigative reporter John Travolta on the health club scene with Jamie Lee Curtis. From the director of *Mike's Murder*, with Laraine Newman.
VHS: S01008. $14.95.
James Bridges, USA, 1985, 120 mins.

Perfume
A study of passion, betrayal, rivalries and ambition as five beautiful women struggle to form an international cosmetics company and compete in the marketplace.
VHS: S18829. $79.95.
Roland S. Jefferson, USA, 1991, 98 mins.

Permanent Record
When a popular, talented, good looking student jumps off a cliff, he leaves behind a bunch of angry and confused friends. Hardest hit is his best friend, played by Keanu Reeves *(River's Edge)*, who wants to hold a memorial service at the high school. With Michelle Meyrink, Pamela Gidley and Alan Boyce as the Jumper.
VHS: S07819. $89.95.
Laser: LD75237. $34.98.
Marisa Silver, USA, 1988, 92 mins.

The Personals
A delightfully fresh film about contemporary relationships in a demanding society. The *L.A. Times* said, "*The Personals* has everything going for it...amid much humor and not a little anguish, there emerges an acute portrait of modern romance."
VHS: S01014. $24.95.
Laser: LD75238. $34.98.
Peter Markle, USA, 1983, 90 mins.

The Phantom
In one of the better comic-strip film adaptations of late, Billy Zane *(Tales from the Crypt)* dons purple tights to become the 1930s comic-strip superhero, The Phantom. Dad Patrick McGoohan *(Braveheart)*, Kristy Swanson *(Buffy the Vampire Slayer)*, and millionaire scoundrel Treat Williams *(Things to Do in Denver When You're Dead)* work wonderfully with Jeffrey Boams' clever script. "A great family picture! I really loved this movie" (Roger Ebert, *Siskel & Ebert*).
VHS: S30153. $19.95.
Simon Wincer, USA, 1996, 100 mins.

Phenomenon
On the night of his 37th birthday, a small-town California car mechanic (John Travolta) experiences a mysterious and blinding light from the sky which transforms him from an ordinary man into someone with extraordinary mental powers. While the people who surround him are fascinated and then alienated from him, he must find his new path in life with the help of the woman he loves (Kyra Sedgwick). "The must-see movie of the year" (National New Syndicate). With Robert Duvall and Forest Whittaker.
VHS: S30466. $19.95.
Laser: LD76063. $39.99.
Jon Turteltaub, USA, 1996, 100 mins.

A Piano for Mrs. Cimino
Widow Cimino (Bette Davis) is a former pianist and music store owner who has retreated into her own world since the death of her husband. Her sons wish to put her away in a home, but with the love and support of her granddaughter, she goes to a hospital, where she is able to regain her sanity and return to a normal life—only to discover that her home and belongings have been sold and that a complete stranger is in charge of her life savings.
VHS: S31220. $14.99.
George Schafer, USA, 1981, 92 mins.

Picture Windows
This omnibus film is a trilogy of heartrending stories directed by three of Hollywood's most highly acclaimed directors. Alan Arkin stars in *Soir Bleu*, the story of a circus clown in love with his boss' troubled but beautiful wife. The second story, *Song of Songs*, stars Sally Kirkland, Brooke Adams and George Segal in the tale of a baker and the women he loves. Finally, *Language of the Heart* is the story of a young ballerina and her street musician beau. This is an intelligent and highly watchable collection of stories that defy simple formulas and easy solutions.
VHS: S27258. $89.98.
Laser: LD75474. $39.99.
Norman Jewison/Peter Bogdanovich/Jonathan Kaplan, USA, 1995, 95 mins.

Pink Cadillac
Clint Eastwood is a skip tracer named Tommy Novak assigned to bring in Bernadette Peters for jumping bail. This modern day bounty hunter hadn't planned on falling in love with his spunky quarry or attracting the attention of a nasty white supremacist organization on the West Coast, but stuff happens. With Timothy Carhart, Bill McKinney, and Michael Des Barres as the deadly Alex.
VHS: S11412. $19.98.
Buddy Van Horn, USA, 1989, 121 mins.

A Place for Annie
Sissy Spacek, Joan Plowright and Mary-Louise Parker star in this story of courage, compassion and forgiveness. These women are competing to give a home to an abandoned baby. Along the way they learn the true meaning of family as they learn to reconcile their desires with the needs of the baby.
VHS: S22892. $19.98.
John Gray, USA, 1994, 98 mins.

Places in the Heart
Against a Depression-torn background in Waxahachi, Texas, Sally Field plays a Sheriff's widow who struggles against incredible hardships. With fine performances by John Malkovich, Danny Glover, Ed Harris and Amy Madigan.
Laser: LD71276. $34.98.
Robert Benton, USA, 1984, 113 mins.

Platoon
Charlie Sheen goes to Southeast Asia and finds out that war is a very traumatic experience. Giant leeches, killer dope and better-prepared opponents are almost as dangerous to his existance as the other members of his platoon. With Tom Berenger and Willem Dafoe. Oscar for Best Picture.
VHS: S04752. $19.98.
Oliver Stone, USA, 1986, 120 mins.

Playing God
Dr. Eugene Sands (David Duchovny) is an ex-surgeon who gets lured into the mob by Raymond Blossom (Timothy Hutton), who hires him to illegally practice on his "associates." Dragged deeper and deeper into the dangerous underworld, and growing too close to Raymond's seductive girlfriend (Angelina Jolie), Eugene wants out, but it may be too late.
VHS: S33948. $103.99.
Laser: LD76830. $39.99.
DVD: DV60314. $29.99.
Andy Wilson, USA, 1997, 94 mins.

Portrait in Red
When attractive young men begin disappearing from a downtown nightclub scene, Detective Wilder (Jim Hanks, *Night Skies*) begins searching for answers. The trail of clues leads him to the seductive artist Rebecca Barlow (Lisa Comshaw, *Scanner Cop*). With Clayton Norcross *(Defending Your Life)* and martial artist Cynthia Rothrock.
VHS: S32706. $89.95.
Gib T. Oidi, USA, 1997, 89 mins.

Portrait of an Artist as a Young Man
This beautiful adaptation of Joyce's autobiographical novel is a faithful portrait of the young author and his coming of age. It portrays Stephen Daedalus and his Irish Catholic upbringing-his confrontation with the tyranny of the church, his sexual guilt and frustration—which start him on the path of rebellion. "Packed with great passages of the Joycean language, and the cast is superb." With Bosco Hogan, T.P. McKenna, John Gielgud.
VHS: S09553. $29.95.
Joseph Strick, USA, 1977, 93 mins.

The Poseidon Adventure
The original Academy Award-winning, big, all-star-cast disaster movie that spawned an entire genre. Gene Hackman *(Independence Day)*, Ernest Borgnine, Red Buttons, Jack Albertson, Carol Lynley, Roddy McDowall and the unsinkable Shelley Winters (in a Golden Globe-winning performance) ring in the New Year struggling for their lives as survivors on the capsized cruise ship *Poseidon*. VHS letterboxed.
VHS: S30987. $19.98.
Laser: LD76166. $49.98.
Ronald Neame, USA, 1972, 117 mins.

Positive I.D.
When a woman learns that her brutal rapist is about to be paroled she sets in motion a complicated scheme of retribution. Unable to continue her life as a traumatized housewife whose husband is fooling around, she establishes a new identity. An intelligent and well acted thriller. With Stephanie Rascoe, John Davies, Laura Lane and Steve Fromholtz.
VHS: S07100. $79.90.
Andy Anderson, USA, 1986, 96 mins.

The Postman Always Rings Twice
Adaptation of the James M. Cain novel and remake of the John Garfield/Lana Turner original, about the perfect crime and how the criminals are punished. Jack Nicholson stars as the aimless drifter and Jessica Lange as the hot young wife with the tired old husband.
VHS: S05927. $19.98.
Laser: LD70657. $34.98.
DVD: DV60094. $24.98.
Bob Rafelson, USA, 1981, 123 mins.

Powder
Sean Patrick Flanery stars in this allegory-like tale of an astonishingly pale young man with unusual powers. Though this oddly beautiful young man is taunted by classmates for his startling appearance, he forever transforms the lives of those around him in wholly unexpected and magical ways. With Jeff Goldblum and Mary Steenburgen.
VHS: S27604. $19.98.
Laser: LD75549. $39.99.
Victor Salva, USA, 1995, 112 mins.

Powwow Highway
Philbert Bono (Gary Farmer) is a political renegade; Buddy Red Bows (A. Martinez) is a mammoth Cheyenne. With nothing in common but their Indian heritage and a beat-up '64 Buick Wildcat, the two set out on a cross-country adventure filled with comedic and dramatic detours and discover the lingering spirit of their people despite government injustice. With Amanda Wyss and songs by Robbie Robertson, John Fogarty and Rachel Sweet.
VHS: S30826. $14.98.
Jonathan Wacks, USA, 1989, 91 mins.

Prayer for the Dying
Mickey Rourke, Alan Bates, Bob Hoskins and Liam Neeson bring star power to this thriller. A priest accidentally witnesses an IRA hit, carried out by a man who was fulfilling his last assignment. Now this ordinary bit of everyday violence binds these men in a troubling quandary.
VHS: S26155. $9.99.
Mike Hodges, USA, 1987, 104 mins.

Presumed Innocent
Harrison Ford stars as a prosecuting attorney in Scott Turow's best-selling novel. Charged with the murder of his former mistress and fellow colleague, the circumstantial evidence looks damaging. With Brian Dennehy, Raul Julia, Bonnie Bedelia, Paul Winfield and Greta Scacchi as the victim. A finely crafted whodunit.
VHS: S13656. $14.95.
Laser: LD70658. $29.98.
Alan J. Pakula, USA, 1990, 127 mins.

Pretty Maids All in a Row
Rock Hudson, Angie Dickinson, Telly Savalas and Roddy McDowall are all featured in this film's stellar cast. Oceanfront High is the site of several murders of beautiful young women. Tiger (Hudson) is one of the school's most popular instructors and he has his suspicions about the identity of the murderer, but he may not be the most trustworthy detective given his extracurricular interests in the student body. This darkly comic film joins sexual tension with a rather light-hearted look at murder.
VHS: S29500. $19.98.
Roger Vadim, USA, 1971, 95 mins.

Primal Fear
Richard Gere thinks he has all the answers as a cocky attorney in this compelling thriller. He sets out to defend his client, a young man accused of murder, but that encompasses complications of a deadly sort. Corruption soon places more people in harm's way.
VHS: S29964. $19.95.
Gregory Hoblit, USA, 1996, 130 mins.

Primal Secrets
Meg Tilly and Ellen Burstyn are superb in this strange psychological thriller. A young artist is engaged by a wealthy socialite to paint a portrait. The artist soon finds herself caught in manipulative machinations behind which murder lurks.
VHS: S25100. $94.95.
Laser: LD75020. $39.99.
Ed Kaplan, USA, 1994, 93 mins.

The Prince of Tides
Barbra Streisand adapts Pat Conroy's expansive novel about Tom Wingo (Nick Nolte), an unemployed Southern football coach and English teacher who goes to New York to care for his suicidal twin sister and becomes involved with Dr. Lowenstein (Streisand), his sister's psychiatrist. Exceptionally well-acted, particularly by Nolte, Kate Nelligan (as Wingo's mother), and Blythe Danner (as Wingo's wife). With Jeroen Krabbe, Melinda Dillon and Jason Gould.
VHS: S17456. $14.95.
Laser: Criterion. **LD71520. $99.95.**
Barbra Streisand, USA, 1991, 135 mins.

The Prodigal
No one knows when the Stuart family started drifting apart. But their American dream has become a nightmare of broken relationships, a conflict of differing goals. When 21-year old Greg returns home from his island hideaway, the conflicts become even more obvious and stressful. With a special appearance by Rev. Billy Graham.
VHS: S09286. $19.98.
Laser: LD70138. $34.98.
James F. Collier, USA, 1983, 109 mins.

The Prophecy
A Los Angeles cop (Elias Koteas) is joined by an elementary school teacher (Virginia Madsen) for a thrilling showdown with the forces of evil. Christopher Walken is the fallen Gabriel, and he leads his troops into a deadly and mysterious battle that places the fate of the entire planet at his mercy.
VHS: S27498. $99.99.
Laser: LD75520. $39.99.
Gregory Widen, USA, 1995, 97 mins.

The Proposition
In this thriller set in 1935 on Boston's Beacon Hill, wealthy and influential socialite Arthur Barret (William Hurt) agrees to have law student Roger Martin (Neil Patrick Harris) sire a child with his wife, Eleanor (Madeleine Stowe). When Roger finds himself in love with Eleanor, the threat of an impending scandal leads to murder. Things get even more complicated when the priest (Kenneth Branagh) Eleanor turns to for solace also falls in love with her. With Robert Loggia.
VHS: S34700. $101.99.
Laser: LD77010. $39.99.
Leslie Linka Glatter, USA, 1998, 110 mins.

The Proprietor
Jeanne Moreau is a famous author living in New York who returns to her Paris home to discover secrets hidden from her for decades: the truth about her family's fate during Nazi occupation. With Sam Waterston, Sean Young and Nell Carter. "A film of admirable elegance and civility as beguiling as Jeanne Moreau herself" (Kevin Thomas, *Los Angeles Times*).
VHS: S31060. $19.98.
Ismail Merchant, USA, 1996, 114 mins.

The Proud and the Damned
Chuck Connors, Jose Greco and Cesar Romero star in this story of mercenaries and Civil War veterans caught up in a revolution in Latin America.
VHS: S10588. $24.95.
Ferde Grofe Jr., USA, 1973, 95 mins.

Pump Up the Volume
An alienated and politically disaffected teenager (Christian Slater) in an Arizona suburb makes pirate radio broadcasts venting his spleen and his libido. He eventually finds himself heading a student revolution in this exciting and affecting comedy-drama with a genuine lift. Written and directed by Canadian independent filmmaker Allan Moyle (*Montreal Main, The Rubber Gun*). "*Pump Up the Volume* qualifies as a generational statement in the same way *Rebel without a Cause* did 35 years ago, but without any of the defeatism or masochism of that earlier picture. Don't miss it (Jonathan Rosenbaum)."
VHS: S13554. $19.95.
Allan Moyle, USA, 1990, 105 mins.

Q & A
Sidney Lumet once again finds corruption in the New York police department. This time Nick Nolte is abusing his power by using his badge to cover up a deliberate murder. Can rookie D.A. Tim Hutton gather all the testimony needed to bring Nolte to justice? With Patrick O'Neal, Armand Assante and Jenny Lumet.
VHS: S12847. $19.98.
Sidney Lumet, USA, 1990, 132 mins.

Queen of the Stardust Ballroom
An enchanting and heartwarming story about the rediscovery of love. When Bea Asher (Academy Award winner Maureen Stapleton) is suddenly widowed, her comfortable life is shattered and all that lies ahead of her is a future of lonely independence. But this all changes when she meets Charles Durning at the Stardust Ballroom where he teaches her not only how to dance but how to love again.
VHS: S34205. $19.95.
Sam O'Steen, USA, 1975, 97 mins.

Quicksilver Highway
Terror titans Stephen King and Clive Barker team up for this frightfest starring Christopher Lloyd as Aaron Quicksilver, a mysterious storyteller whose listeners invariably end up as the subjects of his gruesome, grisly tales. With Matt Frewer and cameo appearances by Clive Barker and John Landis.
VHS: S34741. $69.99.
Mick Garris, USA, 1997, 87 mins.

Quiz Show
Rob Murrow and John Turturro star in this fascinating film based on the real life scandal caused by a television quiz show. A disgruntled ex-champ (Turturro) tells exactly how the show was contrived to make a telegenic newcomer (Ralph Fiennes) the reigning champ of daytime television.
VHS: S24320. $19.95.
Laser: Letterboxed. **LD74912. $39.99.**
Robert Redford, USA, 1994, 133 mins.

Radio Flyer
Set in the '60s, two young brothers (Elijah Wood and Joseph Mazzello) who've just arrived in an anonymous California town with their single mother (Lorraine Bracco) transform their ordinary red wagon into a fantastic machine to escape the rages of their stepfather. With John Heard and Adam Baldwin.
VHS: S16908. $19.95.
Laser: LD71529. $34.95.
Richard Donner, USA, 1992, 114 mins.

Radioland Murders
Director and innovator George Lucas conceived the story for this comic murder mystery starring Mary Stuart Masterson and Brian Benben. When radio station WBN makes its broadcasting debut something goes terribly wrong. As Masterson and Benben team up to find the killer, suspense builds around the possibility of their becoming romantically linked.
VHS: S24323. $19.98.
Mel Slater, USA, 1994, 108 mins.

The Railway Station Man
Adapted from Irish author Julie Johnston's novel, this film is set against a backdrop of violence and terrorism. A woman reeling from the murder of her husband flees to an Irish coastal village and falls in love with an eccentric American builder with a shadowy past. With Julie Christie, Donald Sutherland and John Lynch.
VHS: S18492. $19.95.
Michael Whyte, USA, 1992, 93 mins.

Rain Man
Four Oscars including Best Picture went to this road movie about two brothers who didn't know the other existed until fate tosses them together. The plot may be very similar to the movie comedy *Twins* starring Danny DeVito and Arnold Schwarzenegger but Tom Cruise and Dustin Hoffman look spiffier in their matching outfits. A sensitive and strongly performed film. VHS letterboxed.
VHS: S09575. $19.98.
Laser: LD70662. $29.98.
DVD: DV60095. $24.98.
Barry Levinson, USA, 1988, 120 mins.

Rambling Rose
A rare and intelligent film about sexual attitudes, enlightened behavior and family ties. Laura Dern is inspired as the title character, a beguiling free spirit with a soiled reputation. She finds understanding and a real home while working as a domestic for the Hillyer family in '30s Georgia. With fine performances from Robert Duvall, Diane Ladd, John Heard, David Ogden Stiers and Lukas Haas. Ladd and Dern made Oscar history as the first mother and daughter to be nominated in the same year for acting awards. Based on the novel by Calder Willingham.
VHS: S15692. $14.98.
Laser: LD75131. $24.98.
Martha Coolidge, USA, 1991, 115 mins.

Rampage
William Friedkin's documentary-like exploration of a serial killer's demented psychological condition and the profound moral crisis of an ambitious district attorney personally opposed to capital punishment who's ordered by his superiors to seek the death penalty. Inspired by a California case and the book by William P. Wood. With Michael Biehn, Alex McArthur and Nicholas Campbell.
VHS: S18681. $14.95.
Laser: LD75244. $34.98.
William Friedkin, USA, 1987, 92 mins.

Ransom
Mel Gibson and Rene Russo are millionaire parents whose son is kidnapped in this "deftly woven" (*Chicago Reader*) story. Gibson's manic, moody airline mogul goes nuts in pursuit of the kidnappers (Gary Sinise and Lili Taylor) with the help of a kind FBI agent (Delroy Lindo).
VHS: S31287. $106.99.
Laser: LD76216. $39.99.
Ron Howard, USA, 1996, 121 mins.

The Rapture
There are six definitions of "rapture" in the dictionary. This provocative thriller, written and directed by Michael Tolkin, tries to encompass them all. Mimi Rogers stars in this unusual drama that tests the religious faith of a born again Los Angeles telephone operator. She embarks on a sensual and spiritual odyssey that culminates in a cataclysm of Biblical proportions. With David Duchovny, Patrick Bauchau, Kimberly Cullum and Will Patton. Letterboxed.
VHS: S15925. $19.95.
Michael Tolkin, USA, 1991, 100 mins.

Ratboy
Sondra Locke, who co-starred in six Clint Eastwood films, makes her directorial debut with a curious tale of an odd looking human who is happy to live in a garbage dump. A bittersweet modern fairy tale features Locke, Robert Townsend, Louie Anderson, and Gerrit Graham as the exploiters of the Ratboy.
VHS: S05216. $19.98.
Sondra Locke, USA, 1987, 104 mins.

The Razor's Edge
Bill Murray makes his dramatic debut in this adaptation of W. Somerset Maugham's stirring novel. A returning soldier is disillusioned with Jazz age life and sets off to find the truth in the Himalayas. Home once again, he learns that enlightenment is a difficult passage, particularly when you love someone.
VHS: S24865. $14.95.
John Byrum, USA, 1984, 128 mins.

Real Men
James Belushi is Nick Pirandello, one of the best secret agents in the business. He is assigned to protect a wimpy civilian (John Ritter) who is being used by the government as a decoy in a very important mission concerning extraterrestrials. Lots of action and snappy patter in this spy spoof.
VHS: S06872. $79.98.
Dennis Feldman, USA, 1987, 86 mins.

A Reason to Believe
Allison Smith and Jay Underwood star in this college drama. Charlotte Byrne (Smith) is a sorority girl who has everything—looks, popularity, and the perfect boyfriend (Underwood). She suddenly loses all the things she thought were important when she attends a frat party where one man refuses to take no for an answer. This is the story of how she found the courage to speak out against a system that didn't want to know anything of her pain.
VHS: S27514. $92.99.
Douglas Tirola, USA, 1995, 108 mins.

Red Corner

In this suspense thriller set in modern-day China, Richard Gere is Jack Moore, an American attorney involved in talks about founding the first satellite TV joint venture. While in Beijing, he has a one-night stand with a Chinese woman who ends up dead in his bed. The law immediately accuses Jack of the murder and he is arrested. Jack and his young, female, Chinese, court-appointed attorney, Shen Yuelin (Bai Ling), must face China's corrupt and unfair system to prove Jack is the victim of a frame-up.

VHS: S33888. $103.99.
DVD: DV60298. $24.98.
Jon Avnet, USA, 1997, 122 mins.

Red Rock West

Nicolas Cage is just an average guy mistaken for a hit man. It's the perfect premise for a film noir thriller. Cage has just blown a chance for a high-paying oil rig job when this mistake occurs. Before he can decide what to do, his supposed target, Lara Flynn Boyle, doubles the offer made on her life by husband J.T. Walsh. Then the real killer, Dennis Hopper, appears.

VHS: S23356. $19.95.
John Dahl, USA, 1993, 98 mins.

Reds

A great American film. At its center, *Reds* is the passionate love affair of legendary journalist and American socialist John Reed (Warren Beatty) and feminist author Louise Bryant (Diane Keaton). Beatty, who co-wrote, produced and directed the film, also crisscrosses the emotional undercurrents with social history: exploring the birth of the American labor movement; the emergence of socialism; the bohemian Greenwich Village innergroup that included playwright Eugene O'Neill and anarchist Emma Goldman. A long, beguiling film of exquisite taste and intelligence. The extraordinary cast includes Jack Nicholson as O'Neill, Maureen Stapleton as Goldman, Edward Herrmann as editor Max Eastman and *Being There* author Jerzy Kosinski as bolshevik leader Gregory Zinoviev. Cinematography by the great Vittorio Storaro.

VHS: S02566. $29.95.
Warren Beatty, USA, 1981, 195 mins.

Redwood Curtain

A young woman seems to have set all the trauma of her origins in war-ravaged Saigon behind her. Even so, she yearns to discover the truth about her Vietnamese mother and American GI father. They abandoned her before. Can she bear the painful truth she must face in her search for answers?

VHS: S26610. $14.98.
John Korty, USA, 1995, 99 mins.

Reflecting Skin

For seven-year-old Seth Dove, the world is a very terrifying place. Writer-director Philip Ridley has created a strange and chilling universe on the plains of '50s Idaho where children disappear and death is always in the wind. Jeremy Duncan is unforgettable as the impressionable Seth. Viggo Mortensen co-stars as his older brother Cameron and Lindsay Duncan appears as the mysterious Dolphin Blue, the pale English neighbor widow who may just be a vampire. With David Longworth, Duncan Fraser, Evan Hall and Sherry Bie. This is a powerful film of particular visual splendor and impact.

VHS: S15707. $19.98.
Philip Ridley, USA, 1990, 93 mins.

Reflections in the Dark

Mimi Rogers gives an award-winning performance as a convicted killer in this original psychological thriller. A lone guard becomes privy to her chilling secret and this confidence is so unsettling that it haunts him indefinitely. Billy Zane also stars and John Terry is featured as the husband.

VHS: S26149. $92.98.
Laser: LD75070. $39.99.
Jon Purdy, USA, 1995, 123 mins.

Regarding Henry

Harrison Ford plays a despicable New York lawyer who radically changes his outlook on life after surviving a bullet to the head. This "Capra-esque" formula is not guaranteed so please refrain from trying this technique on any lawyers you may know. With Annette Bening and Miki Allen as the wife and young daughter thankful for the second chance and Bill Nunn as the patient and wise physical therapist.

VHS: S15471. $19.95.
Laser: Widescreen. **LD75246. $34.98.**
Mike Nichols, USA, 1991, 107 mins.

Regina

Anthony Quinn and Ava Gardner return to the screen in this shocking drama of family secrets and personal obsessions. An aging married couple uneasily awaits the homecoming of their only son and his new fiancee. With Ray Sharkey and Anna Karina, in what promises to be a harrowing evening of dinner and discovery.

VHS: S05930. $69.95.
Jean-Yves Prate, USA, 1983, 86 mins.

The Replacement Killers

After he betrays a ruthless crime boss, a professional hit man becomes the target of an army of killers and fights to survive the most violent shoot-out of his career. With Chow Yun-Fat and Mira Sorvino.

VHS: S34328. $104.99.
Laser: LD76947. $39.95.
DVD: DV60253. $24.95.
Antoine Fuqua, 1998, USA, 88 mins.

Report to the Commissioner

Rookie cop Michael Moriarty shoots the wrong person and ends up in a stalled elevator with a dangerous criminal. This is the movie that defines sweating it out. A police melodrama with Richard Gere, Susan Blakely, Vic Taybeck, Tony King, William Devane and Yaphet Kotto.

VHS: S06065. $29.95.
Milton Katselas, USA, 1975, 112 mins.

Restoration

The star-studded cast of this sumptuous film, set after the Restoration, comprises Robert Downey Jr., Meg Ryan, Sam Neill and Hugh Grant. Downey becomes a doctor at the court of King Charles II, and as such, he witnesses not only a host of personal successes and reversals, but also great historic events like the Plague of 1665 and the Great Fire of London in 1666.

VHS: S29401. $19.98.
Laser: LD75812. $39.99.
Michael Hoffman, USA, 1996, 118 mins.

Resurrection

Edna McCauley experienced clinical death, a journey toward a brightly lit place and then returned to her body with the amazing power of healing. Ellen Burstyn stars as Edna in this touching and unusual drama of faith and the hereafter. With Sam Shepard.

VHS: S03925. $59.95.
Daniel Petrie, USA, 1980, 102 mins.

Rich in Love

The collaborators of *Driving Miss Daisy*, director Bruce Beresford and writer Alfred Uhry, are reunited in this tender, Southern, coming-of-age tale about a man (Albert Finney) trying to put together his life when his wife (Jill Clayburgh) unexpectedly leaves him. The story is held together by Kathryn Erbe's tough, tender performance as their confused high school daughter trying to deal with her emerging sexuality. With Piper Laurie, Ethan Hawke and Alfre Woodard.

VHS: S19330. $19.98.
Laser: Letterboxed. **LD71917. $34.98.**
Bruce Beresford, USA, 1992, 105 mins.

Ricochet

Denzel Washington plays a cop who becomes a hero when he gets the bad guy (John Lithgow). Lithgow is a psycho who spends his time in prison plotting his sick revenge.

VHS: S21489. $19.98.
DVD: DV60212. $24.98.
Russell Mulcahy, USA, 1991, 97 mins.

Rift

As his friend's marriage begins to crumble, Tom becomes excited about the potential of finally becoming involved with Lisa, over whom he has obsessed for years. Overcome by the guilt and plagued by a recurring nightmare in which he is murdered by his friend, Tom goes to a psychiatrist, who may be driving him even further into insanity. Set in Manhattan, the movie really takes place in a triangle below reality, where one's fantasy can lead to murder. "Turns the conventions of the psychological thriller inside-out" *(Daily Variety)*.

VHS: S31011. $59.95.
Edward S. Barkin, USA, 1996, 92 mins.

The Right Stuff

Long but exhilarating adaptation of Tom Wolfe's account of the U.S. manned space program, with emphasis on test pilot Chuck Yeager, played by Sam Shepard. A contemplation of male mystique, and wonderful observations of the role of the press. With Ed Harris, Dennis Quaid.

VHS: S01116. $29.98.
Laser: LD70665. $39.98.
DVD: DV60052. $24.98.
Philip Kaufman, USA, 1983, 193 mins.

Ripe

In this wonderfully, dreadfully pretentious, low-budget suspense drama, teenage twin sisters Violet and Rosie (Monica Keena and Daisy Egan) run away to Kentucky after their abusive parents are killed in a car accident. When they hook up with a drifter who takes them in at an army base their childhood bond is tested as they learn about the dangerous repercussions of their sexual awakening.

VHS: S34929. $14.98.
Mo Ogrodnik, USA, 1996, 93 mins.

Rising Sun

Philip Kaufman's adaptation of Michael Crichton's novel about two Los Angeles cops, special liaisons to the Japanese, who are investigating the murder of a party girl in the American headquarters of a Japanese conglomerate. Sean Connery plays a mysterious, enigmatic expert on Japan who counsels junior partner Wesley Snipes in the art, skill and traditions of the notoriously insular Japanese society.

VHS: S19605. $19.95.
Laser: Letterboxed. **LD72338. $49.98.**
Philip Kaufman, USA, 1993, 126 mins.

The River

Australian Mel Gibson *(Mad Max)* and Sissy Spacek provide the emotional force behind this film about a young rural couple's struggle to make a go of it on an impoverished farm. Music by John Williams.

VHS: S01120. $19.95.
Laser: LD70071. $39.98.
Mark Rydell, USA, 1984, 124 mins.

A River Runs Through It

Robert Redford's adaptation of Norman MacLean's autobiographical novella about the tragic lives of two brothers, sons of a Presbyterian minister, and their personal, poetic and scientific fascination with the art of fly fishing. With Craig Sheffer, Brad Pitt, Tom Skerritt and Emily Lloyd.

VHS: S18451. $19.95.
Laser: Letterboxed. **LD71866. $39.95.**
Robert Redford, USA, 1992, 123 mins.

The River Wild

Meryl Streep stars opposite Kevin Bacon in this suspense-laden adventure film. While on a white-water rafting trip, a family is hijacked by three strangers. Soon Streep is put to the test trying to save her family. David Strathairn is also featured.

VHS: S23927. $19.98.
Laser: THX, Widescreen. **LD74920. $39.99.**
DVD: DV60142. $24.98.
Curtis Hanson, USA, 1994, 112 mins.

Rob Roy

Liam Neeson and Jessica Lange are at the center of this historical drama with a liberal dose of sex and romance about the legendary Scottish warrior Robert Roy McGregor. He fought off the English and was ultimately destroyed by the force of history, but his story lives on. Tim Roth is terrific as a foppish aristocratic fiend and Jessica Lange gives an outstanding performance.

VHS: S26284. $19.98.
DVD: DV60053. $24.98.
Michael Caton Jones, USA, 1995, 139 mins.

Robin Hood, Prince of Thieves

For the good of all men and the love of one woman Kevin Costner fights to uphold justice by breaking the law. The classic tale of the upstart aristocratic Saxon lord who matches wits and weapons with the debauched and greedy Norman rulers gets a vigorous and liberal retelling for the 90's. With Mary Elizabeth Mastrantonio, Morgan Freeman, Christian Slater and Alan Rickman as the scene stealing Sheriff of Nottingham. Film note: The Merry Men now live in treehouses that look suspiciously like an Ewok village. Letterboxed.

VHS: S15011. $24.98.
Kevin Reynolds, USA, 1991, 141 mins.

Robin Hood: The Movie

The swashbuckling legend of Robin Hood unfolds in the 12th century when the mighty Normans ruled England with an iron fist. Robert Hode is a Saxon nobleman who insults the evil knight Folcanet and is branded an outlaw. Clever and quick witted, he changes his name to Robin Hood and a legend is born. With Uma Thurman.

VHS: S14229. $19.95.
John Irvin, USA, 1991, 116 mins.

The Rock

In this action-packed thriller a disgruntled General (Ed Harris) and a team of crack commandos seize control of Alcatraz Island and threaten to launch rockets containing a deadly poison into the heart of San Francisco if their demands are not met. With tourists held hostage and the lives of thousands of innocent people at stake, a young FBI chemical weapons expert (Nicolas Cage) and a top secret federal prisoner (Sean Connery) provide the only hope for averting disaster. "A slam-bang thriller!" (Roger Ebert, *Chicago Sun-Times*).

VHS: S30452. $19.99.
Laser: LD76033. $124.95.
Michael Bay, USA, 1996, 136 mins.

Rocket Gibraltar
Burt Lancaster stars as Levi Rockwell, a writer, professor, comic and lover of the sea who is about to turn 77. In celebration of the event, Levi's four children and eight grandchildren return to his Long Island home. But what begins as a joyful day turns into a surprisingly ironic and moving event as the grandchildren honor Levi's most cherished gift.
VHS: S09984. $14.95.
Daniel Petrie, USA, 1988, 101 mins.

Romeo Is Bleeding
Gary Oldman plays a corrupt cop at the center of a complex tale of love and murder involving three beautiful women, played by Lena Olin, Annabella Sciorra and Juliette Lewis. When he is told to carry out one more criminal task, he chooses the ultimate betrayal and finds that his life is now, more than ever, in grave danger.
VHS: S21142. $19.95.
Peter Medak, USA, 1993, 110 mins.

The Rose
Bette Midler makes her starring debut an event as she lights up the screen in a familiar tale of an entertainer on her way down from the heights of stardom. With Alan Bates, Frederic Forrest and David Keith as the men in her drug- and booze-ridden life. Echoes of Janis Joplin, but the magic is all Midler.
VHS: S05622. $19.98.
Laser: Widescreen. **LD74821. $59.98.**
Mark Rydell, USA, 1979, 134 mins.

Rosebud
Peter O'Toole and Richard Attenborough star in this adventure-filled thriller, in which a group of Middle-Eastern terrorists hijack a yacht filled with young, rich women. Former New York Mayor John Lindsay is also featured in this film that captures headline topicality in a taut plot.
VHS: S21164. $19.98.
Otto Preminger, USA, 1975, 126 mins.

Rough Magic
Bridget Fonda and Russell Crowe star in this mix of romantic adventure, screwball comedy and mystery thriller set in a mystical, exotic world where illusion and reality play tricks on unsuspecting lovers. Set in 1952, it follows magician's assistant Myra (Fonda) as she flees an L.A. murder scene, and her Howard Hughes-like fiance (D.W. Moffett), who sends a private eye (Crowe) after her, with whom she falls in love. When she falls into the clutches of a quack doctor (Jim Broadbent), she also discovers that she has magical powers. With Paul Rodriguez.
VHS: S32629. $98.99.
Clare Peploe, USA, 1997, 104 mins.

Rough Riders
Based on events of the Spanish-American War, this critically acclaimed epic drama follows the experiences of a young Teddy Roosevelt (Tom Berenger) and his eclectic group of U.S. Calvary soldiers, called the Rough Riders. Roosevelt led this diverse mix of men through one of the most famous episodes in American military history, the charge on San Juan Hill. With Sam Elliott and Gary Busey. "Perhaps the best war movie ever made" (Vernon Scott, UPI). Two-tape set.
VHS: S32516. $19.98.
John Milius, USA, 1997, 187 mins.

Royal Deceit
A young prince, after discovering that his father has been murdered, vows to avenge the death and regain the crown. With Gabriel Byrne, Helen Mirren and Christian Bale.
VHS: S33112. $103.99.
Gabriel Axel, USA, 1997, 85 mins.

Rubin & Ed
This off-beat, dark and unsettling road movie stars the talented though truly bizarre Crispin Glover with Howard Hesseman as two unruly souls traveling through the desolate Southwest, attempting to bury a cat and make a killing in the real estate market. The other cast members are Karen Black and Michael Green.
VHS: S17020. $89.95.
Trent Harris, USA, 1991, 82 mins.

Run for the Dream: The Gail Devers Story
Academy Award-winner Louis Gossett Jr. stars in this remarkable true story of three-time Olympic gold-winning track star Gail Devers (Charlayne Woodard) and the extraordinary journey of faith and courage that took her from a wheelchair to become the "fastest woman on earth." With Robert Guillaume. Also includes an interview with Gail Devers and her coach Bob Kersee. "Classy performances make this a standout" *(People)*. "Inspiring" (Renee Graham, *Boston Globe*).
VHS: S30595. $19.95.
Laser: LD76106. $39.99.
Neema Barnette, USA, 1996, 99 mins.

Running on Empty
A superior family drama about a pair of 60s radicals, still on the run from the FBI, trying to raise a family. Christine Lahti and Judd Hirsch are the concerned parents. River Phoenix is the caring son who dreams of living a life free of constant changes in identity. With Martha Plimpton as the wise and rebellious love interest and Steven Hill as the establishment grandfather. Terrific acting all around.
VHS: S09840. $19.98.
Laser: LD74697. $24.98.
Sidney Lumet, USA, 1988, 116 mins.

Running Scared
Gregory Hines stars with Billy Crystal in this police buddy film set in Chicago. The two begin pursuit of a drug lord just days before they are to retire to Key West.
VHS: S21396. $14.95.
Laser: Letterboxed. **LD74681. $34.98.**
Peter Hyams, USA, 1986, 106 mins.

Rush
Jennifer Jason Leigh and Jason Patric burn up the screen as a pair of undercover Texas law enforcement officers and lovers who cross way over the line of self-control in pursuit of drug dealers. With Sam Elliott as their wise control officer, Max Perlich as a tormented small-time dealer and rocker Gregg Allman as the wily target of a major investigation.
VHS: S16629. $19.98.
Laser: LD71504. $39.98.
Lili Fini Zanuck, USA, 1991, 120 mins.

The Russia House
Sean Connery plays a cynical and lonely book publisher living in London, who is coerced by the CIA to aid them in a plot to smuggle out of the Soviet Union a book written by a Russian scientist (Klaus Maria Brandauer) which reveals numerous secrets about the Soviet Defense Program. Along the way he meets and falls in love with the book's Russian editor (Michelle Pfeiffer), who unwittingly becomes a pawn in the dangerous game. Intelligently scripted by Tom Stoppard, from the John le Carre novel.
VHS: S14243. $14.95.
Fred Schepisi, USA, 1990, 122 mins.

Sacred Cargo
Chris Penn and Martin Sheen are in the middle of it all as a dangerous smuggling ring works to deliver over $200 million in jewels. Though Penn's character is a former marine, he and Sheen need help. Anna Karin stars as the mysterious beauty who helps Penn discover the importance of love in a place where freedom has its price.
VHS: S29813. $89.95.
Alexander Buravsky, USA, 1996, 93 mins.

Safe Passage
Susan Sarandon and Sam Shepard are paired in this heartrending drama. Mag Singer (Sarandon) is about to start a new life, but an unforseen danger throws her off course. One of her seven sons is at risk, forcing this woman to re-examine all she holds dear.
VHS: S25656. $19.95.
Robert Allen Ackerman, USA, 1994, 98 mins.

The Saint of Fort Washington
Two homeless men, played by Matt Dillon and Danny Glover, grow together in friendship. This compelling drama shows a way of life often ignored by the rest of society. Its warm humor and superb performances challenge stereotypes about the least fortunate among us.
VHS: S20954. $19.98.
Laser: LD72417. $34.98.
Tim Hunter, USA, 1993, 104 mins.

Salvador
"A film that sings and screams...broils, snaps and explodes with energy" *(L.A. Times)*. James Woods as a photojournalist sent to El Salvador in 1980 to expose that government's use of death squads. With Michael Murphy, Jim Belushi and John Savage.
VHS: S01152. $14.95.
Oliver Stone, USA, 1985, 122 mins.

Satan's Harvest
An American detective claiming his inheritance discovers that the deed to the estate has been falsified by a ruthless group of cut-throat criminals who are using it as a front to run dope. His valiant attempt to regain control of the property leads him to an abandoned warehouse where he is forced to engage in a deadly game of wits and weapons against the outlaws.
VHS: S34182. $19.95.
George Montgomery, South Africa/USA, 1970, 104 mins.

Saturday Night Fever
John Travolta, in his best screen role, is Tony Manero, a paint store employee by day and a disco dancing legend by night. However, the streets of Brooklyn confine this street kid with a dream to better himself. With Karen Lynn Gorney, Donna Pescow and Julie Bocasso. Music by the Bee Gees.
VHS: S02865. $29.95.
Laser: LD75252. $34.98.
John Badham, USA, 1977, 118 mins.

Save the Tiger
Almost 20 years before *Glengarry Glen Ross*, Jack Lemmon won an Academy Award for his portrayal in this film of a decent but desperate middle-aged man who commits arson for the insurance money in order to save his business. Thayer David and Jack Gilford are excellent as the arsonist and Lemmon's business partner.
VHS: S30985. $19.98.
John G. Avildsen, USA, 1973, 100 mins.

Scarecrow
Gene Hackman and Al Pacino star as a pair of drifters on the run from impossible dreams and ex-wives. From the director of *Panic in Needle Park*, Jerry Schatzberg, this is an oddball drama about friendship and survival. With Eileen Brennan, Ann Wedgeworth, Dorothy Tristan and Richard Lynch as a prison bully. Terrific photography by Vilmos Zsigmond.
VHS: S08720. $19.98.
Laser: LD76995. $29.99.
Jerry Schatzberg, USA, 1973, 115 mins.

The Scarlet and the Black
An excellent made for television adaptation of J.P. Gallagher's book, *The Scarlet Pimpernel of the Vatican*, stars Gregory Peck in this fact-based account of a priest who provided sanctuary for escaped allied POWs in Nazi-occupied Rome, pursued by the maniacal Christopher Plummer. Sir John Gielgud is Pope Pius XII. With Barbara Bouchet, Olga Karlatos and Bill Berger.
VHS: S17284. $14.98.
Jerry London, USA, 1983, 156 mins.

The Scarlet Pimpernel
A flamboyant adaptation of two of Baroness Orczy's novels, *The Scarlet Pimpernel* and *Eldorado*, set during the French Revolution. A nobleman conceals his identity to prevent the decadent aristocracy from killing innocent people. With Anthony Andrews, Jane Seymour and Ian McKellen.
VHS: S18487. $19.98.
Clive Donner, USA, 1982, 150 mins.

Scent of a Woman
Martin Brest's entertainment about the curious friendship between a retired, disillusioned, career officer (Al Pacino), who accidentally blinded himself, and a working-class student (Chris O'Donnell) who's hired to care for him during a long weekend holiday. Gabrielle Anwar turns in a stunning performance as a mysterious object of Pacino's affection.
VHS: S19008. $19.98.
Laser: Letterboxed. **LD71891. $39.98.**
DVD: DV60242. $26.98.
Martin Brest, USA, 1992, 157 mins.

Schindler's List
This Academy Award-winning film tells the story of Oskar Schindler, who saved hundreds of Jews from certain death in Nazi-dominated Europe. Adapted from Thomas Keneally's novel and starring Ben Kingsley, Liam Neeson and Ralph Fiennes. The Collector's Edition includes the novel, a compact disc of the Academy Award-winning score by John Williams and a booklet with an introduction by Steven Spielberg. Letterboxed.
Collector's Edition.
VHS: S21540. $79.95.
Laser: Collector's Edition. Includes soundtrack, CD and book. **LD74526. $139.98.**
Standard Edition.
VHS: S21539. $29.95.
Laser: LD74525. $49.98.
Steven Spielberg, USA, 1993, 197 mins.

School Ties
A prep school tale of deception and anti-semitism, this story confronts bigotry among America's youth. Set in the Eisenhower era, it tells the story of a boy who would like to get an education through a football scholarship but finds his dream in jeopardy because he is Jewish.
VHS: S20660. $19.95.
Robert Mandel, USA, 1992, 107 mins.

Sea of Love
Someone is killing upscale yuppie males who use the personals to get dates in New York city. Detective Al Pacino is assigned to find the perpetrator even if he has to date some very dangerous women in the interim. With Ellen Barkin as a very likely suspect and John Goodman as Pacino's partner in crime control.
VHS: S11787. $19.95.
Laser: LD70075. $34.95.
DVD: DV60291. $24.98.
Harold Becker, USA, 1989, 113 mins.

Sea Wolf
Jack London's classic. Thrown overboard while unsuccessfully investigating a smuggling ring, Humphrey Van Weyden (Jason Simmons) is saved from a watery grave by the crew of *The Ghost*. The ship's formidable captain, Wolf Larsen (Stacy Keach), sees a challenge in Humphrey to turn this overeducated idealist into a man. He puts Humphrey through a series of violent tests, but nothing can prepare Van Weyden for the final confrontation with Larsen himself.
VHS: S33692. $59.98.
Gary McDonald, USA, 1997, 85 mins.

Search and Destroy

Dennis Hopper, Christopher Walken, John Turturro, Rosanna Arquette, Griffin Dunne, Illeana Douglas and Ethan Hawke are all featured in this strange story directed by the 1980's art star David Salle. A man with a disastrous life becomes convinced that the answer to all his trouble lies in making a screen epic on a grand scale. It must be fate when he meets a screenwriting receptionist, a karaoke-crazed businessman, and a quick talking street king who all encourage him.

VHS: S26458. $19.98.
Laser: LD75314. $39.98.
David Salle, USA, 1995, 91 mins.

Searching for Bobby Fischer

Joe Mantegna, Laurence Fishburne and Ben Kingsley star in this story about a childhood chess prodigy. In the cutthroat world of professional chess a father and son discover they must learn all the tricks, but only one skill can really help them—their love for one another.

VHS: S21138. $19.98.
Laser: Widescreen. **LD75254. $34.98.**
Steven Zallman, USA, 1993, 111 mins.

Season of Fear

For the purpose of this film that season is summer. A young man returns to his estranged father's ranch where he engages in a passionate romance with a beguiling woman he later discovers to be his new stepmother. He is drawn into a series of lies and danger. With Michael Bowen, Ray Wise, Clancy Brown, Michael J. Pollard.

VHS: S11204. $79.98.
Douglas Campbell, USA, 1989, 90 mins.

Secrets

Julie Harris stars with Veronica Hamel and Richard Kiley in this stylish, turn-of-the-century, coming-of-age story. Anna Berter is a 14-year-old girl who inhabits a well-ordered world, but behind her family's prosperous and gracious facade lies a scandalous and carefully guarded secret. The secrets of their scandalous past begin to unravel when Halius, a handsome young gentleman, arrives on the scene.

VHS: S27304. $79.98.
Laser: LD75477. $39.99.
Jud Taylor, USA, 1995, 92 mins.

Seize the Day

Robin Williams plays Tommy Wilhelm in this faithful adaptation of the great Saul Bellow novel of the same title. Nearing 40, a failure, desperately alone and much abused by the society at large, Tommy befriends a shyster, who finds him ripe for the picking. A melancholy tale well told through a weave of past and present. With Robin Williams, Joseph Wiseman, Jerry Stiller, Glenne Headly and Tony Roberts.

VHS: S05714. $29.95.
Laser: LD75563. $39.95.
Fielder Cook, USA, 1986, 93 mins.

Separate Peace

Adaptation of John Knowles novel about two school chums during World War II facing adult emotions and motivations.

VHS: S05003. $49.95.
Larry Peerce, USA, 1973, 104 mins.

September 30, 1995

Dennis Quaid made his screen debut in this drama about troubled teens. In a small Arkansas town, college student Jimmy gathers his friends together on the occasion of James Dean's death. Drinking, trouble with the law, and finally tragedy complete this oddly appropriate response to the death of the ultimate teen icon. Featuring Tom Hulce, Lisa Blount and Richard Thomas as Jimmy.

VHS: S26922. $14.98.
James Bridges, USA, 1977, 107 mins.

Serpico

Al Pacino stars in this adaptation of Peter Maas' book about Frank Serpico, the New York cop who exposed corruption within the Department. With John Randolph, Jack Kehoe and F. Murray Abraham.

VHS: S21860. $14.95.
Sidney Lumet, USA, 1973, 130 mins.

Set It Off

Jada Pinkett, Queen Latifah, Vivica A. Fox and Kimberly Elise star as four New York City women who take the law into their own hands and try to get some payback by robbing the city's biggest banks. Like *Mean Streets* and *Menace II Society*, this riveting, critically acclaimed drama isn't a story about right and wrong—but survival. "*Thelma and Louise* times two" (Kenneth Turan, *Los Angeles Times*).

VHS: S31031. $19.98.
Laser: LD76167. $49.98.
F. Gary Gray, USA, 1996, 123 mins.

Seven

Morgan Freeman and Brad Pitt are two police officers set to work on a baffling, gruesome collection of serial killings. Pitt is new to the big city, while Freeman is getting ready to retire from his hellish occupation. As they track down the murderer they descend into an arena of moral mayhem where the ultimate victim is innocence. VHS letterboxed.

VHS: S27256. $19.98.
Laser: LD75472. $124.95.
DVD: DV60096. $24.98.
David Fincher, USA, 1995, 127 mins.

Shattered

Tom Berenger stars as an amnesia victim who survived driving his Mercedes 560 SL off a California coastline road. Greta Scacchi is the woman who claims to be his wife in this complex thriller from director Wolfgang Petersen. With Joanne Whalley-Kilmer, Corbin Bernsen and Bob Hoskins as the colorful private detective who prefers animals to people. Based on the novel *The Plastic Nightmare* by Richard Neely.

VHS: S15712. $19.98.
Wolfgang Petersen, USA, 1991, 95 mins.

The Shawshank Redemption

Tim Robbins and Morgan Freeman star in this compelling prison drama. A banker who murdered his wife finds himself locked up with hardened criminals. The whole prison suspects he can't last. To everyone's surprise however, he makes common cause with a tough convict resulting in an enduring friendship.

VHS: S24132. $19.95.
Laser: LD74816. $39.95.
Frank Darabont, USA, 1994, 143 mins.

The Shell Seekers

A poignant adaptation of Rosamunde Pilcher's novel about an idiosyncratic widow (Angela Landsbury) who tries to claim some independence from her children after suffering a heart attack. "Lovely, graceful and eloquent" *(Boston Herald)*. Screenplay adaptation by playwright James Di Pasquale. With Sam Wannamaker, Christopher Bowen, Anna Carteret, Michael Gough, Patricia Hodge, Denis Quilley, Sophie Ward and Irene Worth.

VHS: S19940. $19.98.
Waris Hussein, USA/Great Britain, 1989, 100 mins.

Shoot the Moon

A thoroughly modern vision of marriage featuring Diane Keaton and Albert Finney as a couple whose 15 year marriage is coming apart.

VHS: S01191. $19.99.
Laser: LD72155. $39.98.
Alan Parker, USA, 1981, 124 mins.

Show of Force

Amy Irving stars as a Puerto Rico-based American TV reporter caught up in a government conspiracy that involves the murder of two suspected terrorists. Based on a true incident that occurred in 1978. With Andy Garcia, Robert Duvall and Lou Diamond Phillips as a really creepy police informant.

VHS: S12841. $19.95.
Laser: LD75257. $34.98.
Bruno Barreto, USA, 1990, 93 mins.

Showgirls

Elizabeth Berkley stars as a young girl who goes off to Las Vegas with a dream. She hopes to be a dancer, but instead finds herself sidetracked into the world of lap-dancing. This film's steamy demeanor reveals Las Vegas as a true oasis in the American desert, wholly void of puritanical mores.

VHS: S26951. $19.98.
Laser: LD75424. $49.99.
Paul Verhoeven, USA, 1995, 131 mins.

The Sicilian

Michael Cimino's film of the life and times of a popular Sicilian bandit and folk hero is available only on home video. Will it make more sense? Add a bit more flesh to the many minor characters? Or just show more European extras in vintage clothing? With Christopher Lambert as Guiliano, the title character, Terence Stamp, Joss Ackland and John Turturro. Based on the novel of Mario Puzo.

VHS: S06961. $14.98.
Michael Cimino, USA, 1987, 146 mins.

Siesta

Often compared to David Lynch's *Blue Velvet*, *Siesta* features Ellen Barkin, Martin Sheen, Jodie Foster, Isabella Rossellini and Grace Jones, with a hot soundtrack from Miles Davis. The film is an erotic thriller which journeys into the mind of Claire, a professional stunt woman, whose rendezvous with her Spanish lover becomes a nightmare of madness and violence.

VHS: S06860. $19.98.
Mary Lambert, USA, 1987, 97 mins.

Signs of Life

Beau Bridges, Vincent D'Onofrio and Arthur Kennedy star in a touching film about unique characters in a small town in Maine who face the closing of a boat yard that's been in existence for over a century.

VHS: S11556. $19.95.
John David Coles, USA, 1989, 95 mins.

Silence of the North

Oscar-winner Ellen Burstyn stars as the alter ego of Olive Fredrickson, whose autobiographical work was the story of courage and legend, a young widow and her three small children who braved the frontier conditions of Alberta in northern Canada from the early 1900's to the Depression.

VHS: S02602. $59.95.
Laser: Widescreen. **LD74948. $34.98.**
Allan Winton King, USA, 1981, 94 mins.

Silkwood

Meryl Streep plays Karen Silkwood in this true account of the mysterious circumstances under which Silkwood died while exposing the dangers of plutonium contamination. With Kurt Russell and a wonderful performance by Cher.

Laser: LD74833. $49.99.
Mike Nichols, USA, 1983, 131 mins.

Sister, Sister

A southern gothic drama from the writer of *Strange Behavior*, Bill Condon, who makes his directorial debut. Judith Ivey and Jennifer Jason Leigh are two very close siblings who live in a dilapidated Louisiana mansion and harbor a dark secret. Eric Stoltz is the young man with a lot of curiosity.

VHS: S06919. $14.95.
Bill Condon, USA, 1987, 91 mins.

Six Degrees of Separation

Stockard Channing, Will Smith and Donald Sutherland star in this unusual drama. John Guare adapted his hit Broadway play about a man pretending to be Sidney Poitier's son who works his way into the lives of a pair of rich Manhattanites. It's a witty and compelling scenario brought convincingly to the screen.

VHS: S21032. $19.98.
Laser: LD72407. $34.98.
Fred Schepisi, USA, 1993, 112 mins.

Slaughterhouse Five

Adaptation of Kurt Vonnegut's bizarre fantasy novel follows the story of Billy Pilgrim, who becomes unstuck in time and jumps back and forth in his life with no control. With Michael Sacks and Valerie Perrine. And so it goes.

VHS: S01903. $19.95.
Laser: LD70080. $34.95.
George Roy Hill, USA, 1972, 104 mins.

Sleepers

Robert DeNiro, Dustin Hoffman, Brad Pitt, Kevin Bacon and Jason Patric star in this story of four friends growing up in New York's Hell's Kitchen in the 1960s. Fifteen years after terrible events scar their lives, they're ready to even the score. Based on the controversial bestseller by Lorenzo Carcaterra. "A moviegoer's dream. Steamy, suspenseful, powerful and gripping" (Rex Reed, *New York Observer*).

VHS: S31056. $19.98.
Laser: LD76144. $39.95.
DVD: DV60099. $24.98.
Barry Levinson, USA, 1996, 148 mins.

Sleeping with the Enemy

For Laura (Julia Roberts), Martin Burney appeared to be the man of her dreams. He was handsome, successful and seductively attentive. It wasn't until they were married that she discovered Martin's dark side-compulsive, controlling and dangerously violent. She fakes drowning in a boating accident and relocates to a small midwestern town where she tries to rebuild her life. But Martin soon discovers that Laura is still alive, and he is determined to make her pay for her deceit. Also starring Patrick Bergin *(Mountains of the Moon)* and Kevin Anderson *(In Country)*.

VHS: S14228. $19.98.
Joseph Ruben, USA, 1991, 99 mins.

Slither

An ex-con (James Caan), a small-time bandleader (Peter Boyle), his doting wife (Louise Lasser) and a kooky drifter (Sally Kellerman) find themselves being followed while trying to locate a small fortune in embezzled money. They then embark on a chase through a surreal world of trailer camps, bingo halls and laundromats.

VHS: S15247. $19.98.
Howard Zieff, USA, 1973, 92 mins.

A Small Circle of Friends
A Harvard *menage a trois* struggles to make it through college in the '60s. With Brad Davis, Jameson Parker, Karen Allen and Shelley Long.
VHS: Out of print. For rental only.
Laser: LD76193. $39.98.
Rob Cohen, USA, 1980, 112 mins.

Smile
In this terrifically performed and insightfully observed slice of Americana, Michael Ritchie turns his camera on a teen beauty pageant in Santa Rosa, California. Among the contestants are such stars of the future as Melanie Griffith, Annette O'Toole, Collen Camp and Joan Prather. Contest officials include Bruce Dern, Barbara Feldon, Geoffrey Lewis and choreographer Michael Kidd. Title song by Charlie Chaplin. To keep the reactions real, the winner wasn't announced until the camera was rolling.
VHS: S12236. $19.95.
Laser: LD72132. $34.98.
Michael Ritchie, USA, 1975, 113 mins.

Smoke
A young and lonely bathroom attendant searches for solace in all the wrong places. The film is filled with memories of loves that might have been, from a distant family priest to an absent father.
VHS: S20580. $29.95.
Mark D'Aruia, USA, 1993, 90 mins.

Soldier's Tale
Gabriel Byrne and Judge Reinhold star in this tense World War II drama as Allied rivals for the romantic attentions of a French woman of questionable loyalties. Marianne Basler plays Belle, a beautiful woman accused of treason by the French Resistance. Will desire conquer all? Based on the novel by M.K. Joseph.
VHS: S15924. $89.98.
Laser: LD71501. $29.98.
Larry Parr, USA/France, 1991, 96 mins.

Some Kind of Hero
Richard Pryor is cast as a former P.O.W. returning from Vietnam. The world is no longer the place he remembers. His performance as a man dealing with newfound freedom is the saving grace in anotherwise undistinguished film.
VHS: S21450. $14.95.
Laser: LD75334. $29.98.
Michael Pressman, USA, 1982, 97 mins.

Some Kind of Wonderful
Another teenage exploration of alienation and current fashion sense from the John Hughes movie machine. He's farmed out the direction and recycles the plot of *Pretty in Pink* and the result is that it is better the second time around. With Eric Stoltz and Mary Stuart Masterson.
VHS: S04712. $19.95.
Laser: LD75335. $29.98.
Howard Deutch, USA, 1987, 95 mins.

Someone to Love
Orson Welles makes his farewell screen appearance as a one-man Greek chorus in this Henry Jaglom film that takes place in an old theatre on Valentine's Day. A personal comedy about modern relationships finds the director on camera once again asking about commitment and finding the right partner. With Sally Kellerman, Andrea Marcovicci and Jaglom's brother Michael Emil.
VHS: S08236. $79.95.
Laser: LD75259. $34.98.
Henry Jaglom, USA, 1987, 109 mins.

Someone to Watch over Me
When an attractive Manhattan socialite witnesses a brutal murder she is put in the protective custody of a married, good looking cop from another Borough. Sexual tension competes with a maniac killer for screen time. With Tom Berenger, Mimi Rogers and Lorraine Bracco as the cop's wife. A stylish thriller.
VHS: S06996. $14.95.
Ridley Scott, USA, 1987, 106 mins.

Something to Talk About
Julia Roberts stars opposite Dennis Quaid in this comedy about a woman who finds out her husband is playing around. Everything seemed perfect until she discovered he was being unfaithful. Now nothing in the small town where they live will ever be the same again as she goes on a personal rampage to root out the hypocrisy of infidelity. Robert Duvall, Kyra Sedgwick and Gena Rowlands are also featured.
VHS: S26930. $19.98.
Laser: LD75404. $34.98.
Lasse Hallstrom, USA, 1995, 105 mins.

Sometimes a Great Notion
Ken Kesey's powerful dramatic novel of the same name is realized with the help of some great star power, including Paul Newman, Lee Remick, Henry Fonda and Michael Sarrazin. The Northwest is home to the logging industry and the determined people who wrest resources directly from the some of the earth's most beautiful forests.
VHS: S21279. $14.98.
Laser: Widescreen. **LD74922. $34.98.**
Paul Newman, USA, 1971, 114 mins.

Sommersby
Jon Amiel's remake of Daniel Vigne's *The Return of Martin Guerre* transfers the action from a 16th century French village to post-Civil War American South. Richard Gere is the enigmatic lead figure, a former prisoner of war who turns up following a seven-year absence. With Jodie Foster, Bill Pullman, James Earl Jones and Lee Ermey.
VHS: S19331. $19.98.
Laser: LD71918. $34.98.
Jon Amiel, USA, 1993, 115 mins.

Sophie's Choice
Meryl Streep received an Oscar for her depiction of a Polish Catholic mother who survives the death camp at Auschwitz but not the memories that haunt her in her new life in the United States. Based on the William Styron novel. With Kevin Kline and Peter MacNicol.
VHS: S04600. $14.98.
Alan J. Pakula, USA, 1982, 150 mins.

Sorcerer
William Friedkin's American remake of Henri-Georges Clouzot's classic *The Wages of Fear* concerns four fugitives trapped in a nightmarish Latin American town who agree on a suicidal mission, transporting trucks filled with nitroglycerine, to gain their freedom. With Roy Scheider, Francisco Rabal, Ramon Bieri and Amidou.
VHS: S18998. $19.98.
William Friedkin, USA, 1977, 122 mins.

Soul Food
Sunday dinner at Mother Joe's is a mouth-watering, 40-year tradition, but the good times suddenly stop when bickering tears the family apart. Now it's up to Mother's young grandson to bring everyone back together and teach everyone the true meaning of soul food. With Vanessa Williams, Vivica Fox, Nia Long, Brandon Hammond and Michael Beach.
VHS: S33031. $19.98.
Laser: LD76430. $39.98.
George Tillman Jr., USA, 1997, 114 mins.

Soul Survivor
In the tradition of *Menace II Society, Fresh* and *Gridlock'd* comes this story of Tyrone, an idealistic Jamaican immigrant (Peter Williams), who, seduced by an opportunity for quick wealth, takes a job with a powerful local entrepreneur (George Harris). But when Tyrone finds that he is assigned the task of collecting an old debt from his irresponsible cousin (David Smith), his loyalties and career ambitions are tested.
VHS: S32512. $79.95.
Stephen Williams, USA, 1995, 89 mins.

The Sound and the Silence
Alexander Graham Bell (played by John Bach) was born in Scotland, where his nearly deaf mother (Brenda Fricker) inspired the course of his life's work. This biographical film continues through his greatest creative moments, including the invention of the telephone, the telegraph, and the iron lung.
VHS: S20628. $92.98.
Laser: LD72436. $49.99.
John Kent Harrison, USA, 1993, 93 mins.

Sparkle
Three sisters form a singing group and try to make it big. One of the women, "Sister" (Lonette McKee) falls for a lowlife named "Satin" (Tony King) while the youngest sister, "Sparkle" (Irene Cara) falls for a well-meaning young man, "Stix" (Philip Michael Thomas). Most of the film deals with "Stix" trying to make "Sparkle" a star and with the destructive relationship between "Sister" and "Satin". Also stars Dwan Smith, Mary Alice and Dorian Harewood.
VHS: S21436. $19.98.
Sam O'Steen, USA, 1976, 98 mins.

Speed
Keanu Reeves makes his first appearance as an action hero character in this breakneck adventure film. As a member of an elite swat team, his successes come back to haunt him as a bus is hijacked by a crazed and greedy technical wizard, Dennis Hopper. Sandra Bullock co-stars as the woman who inadvertently gets drawn into the bus ride of her life. VHS letterboxed.
VHS: S22529. $19.98.
Laser: THX sound. **LD74611. $34.95.**
Jan De Bont, USA, 1994, 115 mins.

Sphere
Dustin Hoffman, Sharon Stone and Samuel L. Jackson star in Michael Crichton's deep-water, deep-suspense sci-fi adventure centered on a spacecraft that plunged into the Pacific 300 years ago.
VHS: S34701. $106.99.
DVD: Behind the scenes, filmographies, widescreen, Spanish & French subtitles. **DV60363. $24.98.**
Barry Levinson, USA, 1998, 134 mins.

Spirit Lost
Leon *(Cool Runnings)*, Regina Taylor *(Courage Under Fire)* and Cynda Williams *(The Tie That Binds)* star in this story of an aspiring painter and his beautiful wife who discover they are not alone in their quaint new seaside home. Built by a philandering sea captain 200 years ago, the house now harbors the seductive, lustful and wickedly jealous spirit of one of his abandoned lovers, in this steamy, supernatural tale of obsession and possession.
VHS: S30975. $94.98.
Neema Barnette, USA, 1996, 90 mins.

St. Elmo's Fire
The new Brat Pack are featured as college kids having their problems. With Demi Moore, Rob Lowe and Emilio Estevez.
VHS: S07433. $19.95.
Joel Schumacher, USA, 1985, 108 mins.

The Stand
Stephen King's epic novel is now an epic film that tells the story of a world devastated by plague. The sad survivors of this catastrophe must face an even greater challenge. Mysteriously they all are drawn together. They find strength in a new community that must make a stand. Gary Sinise, Rob Lowe and Molly Ringwald star.
VHS: S21515. $102.95.
Laser: LD74491. $69.98.
Mick Garris, USA, 1994

Stand by Me
Rob Reiner's skillful adaptation of Stephen King's novella *The Body* is an odyssey of exploration and self-identity as four boys endure a difficult two-day trip to find the body of a dead youth. The film moves freely from adolescent reminiscence to male bonding. The performances by the young actors are uniformly fine—especially Wil Wheaton and River Phoenix; Kiefer Sutherland turns in a scruffy, horrifying caricature of teenage nihilism. Richard Dreyfuss and Evanston's John Cusack turn in cameo roles.
VHS: S02909. $19.95.
Laser: LD75530. $39.95.
DVD: DV60028. $24.95.
Rob Reiner, USA, 1986, 89 mins.

Stanley and Iris
Two-time Academy Award winners Jane Fonda and Robert De Niro triumph in this warm and wonderful romance. Forty-year-old Stanley can neither read nor write. Co-worker Iris learns his secret and becomes his teacher, but when romance unexpectedly blooms they find that love isn't so easy to read. From the director and writers (Harriet Frank Jr. and Irving Ravetch) who teamed on *Hud* and *Norma Rae*.
VHS: S13971. $19.99.
Martin Ritt, USA, 1990, 107 mins.

Star 80
The story of Playmate of the Year Dorothy Stratten and her tragic murder is brought to the screen in a mesmerizing, no holds barred manner. Yet the real focus is on her snake oil husband, played by Eric Roberts (who was robbed of a deserved Oscar nomination). Mariel Hemingway (with breast implants) is the unfortunate Dorothy.
VHS: S04181. $19.98.
Laser: LD74716. $34.98.
Bob Fosse, USA, 1983, 104 mins.

Stars and Bars
This isn't about celebrities with a drinking problem. The title refers to the flag of the Confederate States of America. Daniel Day-Lewis plays an English art expert who journeys to modern day Georgia to buy a Renoir from eccentric Harry Dean Stanton. The trip is complicated by gangsters, natural disasters and the flower of Southern womanhood. With Laurie Metcalf, Glenne Headly, Keith David, Joan Cusack and Spalding Gray. From the novel by William Boyd.
VHS: S07707. $19.95.
Pat O'Connor, USA, 1988, 95 mins.

The Stars Fell on Henrietta

Robert Duvall stars with Aidan Quinn, Frances Fisher and Brian Dennehy in this inspiring drama. A stranger stumbles across a family trapped on a bleak Texas farm during the Depression. Somehow, through his own self-confidence, he turns their lives around and gives them hope.

VHS: S27190. $19.98.
Laser: LD75469. $34.98.
James Keach, USA, 1995, 110 mins.

State of Grace

Sean Penn stars as an Irish tough, who together with his mob buddies Ed Harris and Gary Oldman, falls on hard times. This forces them to work as contract killers for the Italians. Between this comedown and the shrinking of their home turf, an intense urban story of desperation and violence emerges.

VHS: S22510. $14.98.
Phil Joanou, USA, 1990, 134 mins.

Stealing Home

Mark Harmon takes a sentimental journey in this nostalgic drama about a minor league baseball player who is summoned home to dispose of the ashes of his former free-spirited baby sitter with whom he shared a life-long bittersweet friendship. With Jodie Foster, William McNamara.

VHS: S09488. $19.98.
Laser: LD74698. $24.98.
Steven Kampmann, USA, 1988, 98 mins.

Steel Magnolias

In a small town in Louisiana, a local beauty parlor serves as the center for good times and gossip for six Southern women. A showcase for Hollywood actresses Sally Field, Shirley MacLaine, Dolly Parton, Olympia Dukakis, Julie Roberts and Daryl Hannah. Can you find the real daughters of the South in this picture? The title refers to the character of these fine examples of Southern womanhood. Based on the popular autobiographical play by Robert Harling.

VHS: S12420. $19.95.
Herbert Ross, USA, 1989, 118 mins.

Stella

Bette Midler is the latest actress to take on the role of the Olive Higgins Prouty heroine who sacrifices her own happiness in order that her daughter will have a better life. The contemporary setting detracts from the plausibility of the circumstances, but Midler is a wow as the barmaid who did it her way. With Stephen Collins, John Goodman and Marsha Mason.

VHS: S12852. $89.98.
John Erman, USA, 1990, 109 mins.

The Stepfather

This may look like your average mad slasher movie, but don't be misled by the packaging. This exploration of a deranged man just trying to find and maintain the perfect American family is several cuts above the usual shlock. Terry O'Quinn is mesmerizing in the title role. Script by Donald Westlake. A real chiller.

VHS: Out of print. For rental only.
Laser: LD72312. $29.99.
Joseph Ruben, USA, 1987, 89 mins.

Steppenwolf

Max von Sydow and Dominique Sanda star in this adaptation of Herman Hesse's classic novel about a man's internal struggle to find peace within himself. "A lush cinematic landscape, engagingly real yet properly symbolic" (Anne Hanley).

VHS: S02979. $59.95.
Fred Haines, USA, 1974, 105 mins.

Sterile Cuckoo

Offbeat tale of awakening love with Liza Minnelli and Wendell Burton. A "surprisingly gentle, surprisingly good film" (Pauline Kael). Based on the novel by John Nichols.

VHS: S02609. $49.95.
Laser: LD75337. $29.98.
Alan J. Pakula, USA, 1970, 107 mins.

The Sting

The Academy Award-winning classic starring Paul Newman and Robert Redford as a pair of con artists in 1930s Chicago who set out to rip off a big-time racketeer. With Robert Shaw, Charles Durning, Eileen Brennan and wonderful vintage ragtime music by Scott Joplin adapted by Marvin Hamlisch.

VHS: S30984. $19.98.
DVD: DV60221. $24.98.
George Roy Hill, USA, 1973, 129 mins.

The Stoned Age

In this 1970's party film, two dudes go cruisin' for hot babes and find them as well as a whole lot more. Before long they are at the jammingest party ever. The soundtrack includes Blue Oyster Cult, Black Sabbath, Ted Nugent, Foghat and Deep Purple. Michael Kopelow, China Kantner and Renee Griffen star.

VHS: S22866. $94.99.
Laser: LD75264. $34.98.
James Melkonian, USA, 1993, 90 mins.

The Story Lady

Jessica Tandy stars as a woman with an amazing ability to tell stories. When big business tries to commercialize her talents, she reveals an unsuspected strength and fights back. With Ed Begley Jr.

VHS: S20652. $89.95.
Larry Elikann, USA, 1993, 93 mins.

Straight Time

Dustin Hoffman gives a fine, demanding performance as a paroled robber, a man with psycho-sexual relationships with people from the prison world but seemingly unable to maintain relationships with outsiders. Based on the novel *No Beast So Fierce* by Edward Bunker, an ex-convict. With Harry Dean Stanton, Gary Busey and Theresa Russell.

VHS: S02610. $19.98.
Ulu Grosbard, USA, 1978, 114 mins.

Stranger

Adolfo Aristarain, one of Argentina's best filmmakers, directed this U.S. thriller about an amnesia patient and her doctor who are caught in a deadly race against time. With Bonnie Bedelia and Peter Riegert.

VHS: S07327. $79.95.
Adolfo Aristarain, USA, 1987, 100 mins.

A Stranger Among Us

Veteran director Sidney Lumet welds together the themes of police procedure and issues of Jewish identity, in this film about a beautiful, though emotionally troubled, New York detective (Melanie Griffith) who goes undercover in a Hassidic community to solve a young man's brutal murder. Complications ensue when she falls for a brilliant, though unavailable, rabbinical student (Eric Thall). With Mia Sara, Jamey Sheridan and John Pankow.

VHS: S18137. $19.95.
Sidney Lumet, USA, 1992, 117 mins.

The Substance of Fire

In the high-stakes world of publishing, a businessman puts his company on the brink of bankruptcy and threatens to destroy his family and their fortune by doing the right thing. With Sarah Jessica Parker, Timothy Hutton, Ron Rifkin and Tony Goldwyn.

VHS: S31528. $103.99.
Laser: LD76256. $39.99.
Daniel Sullivan, USA, 1996, 101 mins.

Subway Stories

Jonathan Demme, Ted Demme, Abel Ferrara and Craig McKay direct 10 stories capturing the laughter, fear, sexiness, money—or lack or it—and strangeness that shapes the lives of those who ride the subways of New York. With Christine Lahti, Denis Leary, Bonnie Hunt, Lili Taylor, Mercedes Ruehl, Rosie Perez and Gregory Hines.

VHS: S33158. $109.73.
Jonathan Demme/Ted Demme/Abel Ferrara/Craig McKay, USA, 1997, 81 mins.

Sugar Hill

Wesley Snipes stars as a hardened drug dealer who made it big through crime and drugs. Now he wants a new life with a respectable woman, away from Sugar Hill, where he rules with his brother, Michael Wright. As pressures mount he finds that he cannot simply abandon his past or his kin.

VHS: S21256. $19.95.
Leon Ichaso, USA, 1994, 123 mins.

The Summer of Ben Tyler

James Woods is Temple Rayburn, a family man and honest Southern lawyer challenging the conventional wisdom of the world around him with courage and integrity. As the defense on a local murder trial, he discovers shocking evience that could have serious repercussions. With his values on trial, Temple must find the courage to face his toughest challenge. "Fine cast and top-notch direction" (*The New York Times*).

VHS: S31540. $99.99.
Laser: Letterboxed. **LD76254. $39.99.**
Arthur Allan Seidelman, USA, 1996, 134 mins.

Summer to Remember

A deaf boy and a runaway orangutan learn to communicate and enjoy each other's company. The special relationship is jeopardized when the hairier friend is captured by a traveling circus. Can little Toby save his buddy Casey from the cruel circus trainer? With James Farentino, Tess Harper, Bridgette Andersen, Sean Justin Gerlis and C.J. the Orangutan, who is not to be confused with fellow cast member Burt Young. Made-for-TV.

VHS: S08505. $39.95.
Robert Lewis, USA, 1985, 98 mins.

Summer Wishes, Winter Dreams

Joanne Woodward won the New York Critics Award for Best Actress for her portrayal of a woman coming to grips with a mid-life crisis. With Martin Balsam. Music by Johnny Mandel.

VHS: S01281. $19.95.
Gilbert Cates, USA, 1973, 95 mins.

Sunshine's on the Way

Amy Wright and Scatman Crothers star in this uplifting tale of a dedicated young woman and her dream to rekindle the music in the lives of the folks in the Sugar Hill nursing home. Wright organizes a band of senior citizens including Crothers, as a cranky jazz trombonist, and draws national attention. With Theresa Merritt, Susan Kingsley and Doc Severinsen as himself.

VHS: S10616. $19.95.
Robert Mandel, USA, 1980, 46 mins.

Superman II

Richard Lester directs this fun-filled sequel that features three escapees from the Phantom Zone who have equal powers with the Man of Steel but not an ounce of his moral fiber. Lex Luthor is eager to be of assistance. With Terence Stamp, Valerie Perrine, Sarah Douglas and of course, Christopher Reeve.

VHS: S04004. $19.98.
Laser: LD74744. $29.98.
Richard Lester, USA, 1980, 127 mins.

Superman: The Movie

Christopher Reeve is the Man of Steel in this epic adventure of the famed hero of comic books, tv and the Broadway stage, as well as the big screen. From exploding planet to writing for the Daily Planet, the story is told. Special Oscar for special effects. With Margot Kidder, Jackie Cooper, Marlon Brando and Gene Hackman as super villain Lex Luthor.

VHS: S01286. $19.98.
Laser: LD74743. $29.98.
Richard Donner, USA, 1978, 143 mins.

Suspect

Cher stars as an attorney who becomes involved in a case that takes her outside of the law when juror Dennis Quaid provides information about drug trafficking.

VHS: S08225. $14.95.
Peter Yates, USA, 1988, 101 mins.

Sweet Lies

Sometimes the only way to win the man of your dreams is to cheat. Treat Williams is the romantic quarry of Joanna Pacula and Julianne Phillips. Williams plays an insurance investigator on a case in France. The title song of this comedy about fraud and deception is composed and sung by Robert Palmer.

VHS: S11165. $79.98.
Nathalie Delon, USA, 1987, 101 mins.

Sweet Lorraine

Maureen Stapleton is the proprietress of a run-down Catskill resort hotel called The Lorraine. Her concerned granddaughter is played by Trini Alvarado. A sweet and sentimental comedy-drama heavy on atmosphere and characterization. With Edith Falco and Todd Graff.

VHS: S05312. $79.95.
Steve Gomer, USA, 1987, 91 mins.

Sweet Nothing

Their wedding vows said "for better or for worse." A middle-class couple (Mira Sorvino and Michael Imperioli) copes with the worse and struggles to recapture the better in this taut, terrific tale of crack addiction, inspired by a real-life diary found in a Bronx apartment. "Mesmerizing. It grips you like a vise. Not to be missed" (Rex Reed, *New York Observer*).

VHS: S30934. $19.98.
Gary Winick, USA, 1996, 89 mins.

T Bone n Weasel

The talented B-movie director Lewis Teague (*Piranha*) directs this engrossing road movie about the reluctant pairing of a former convict (Gregory Hines) and a mentally unbalanced hustler (Christopher Lloyd). With Ned Beatty and Rip Torn.

VHS: S18318. $89.98.
Lewis Teague, USA, 1992, 94 mins.

The Taking of Pelham 1 2 3

A sharp thriller about a group of terrorists who commander a New York City subway car and threaten to kill the hostages unless the bankrupt city agrees to pay them $1 million in one hour. Walter Matthau plays a security transit cop tracking their moves. The cast includes Robert Shaw as the head villain, Martin Balsam, Hector Elizondo and Jerry Stiller.

VHS: S17974. $14.95.
Laser: LD71177. $34.98.
Joseph Sargent, USA, 1974, 104 mins.

A Tale of Two Cities

A reworking of Dickens' novel about the French Revolution. Chris Sarandon stars in the dual role of a lawyer (and French nobleman) who sacrifices himself to save another man. With Alice Krige, Peter Cushing and Kenneth More.

VHS: S18486. $19.98.
Jim Goddard, USA, 1980, 156 mins.

Tales of Erotica
The directors of *Desperately Seeking Susan, The Postman Always Rings Twice, Sweet Sweetback's Badasss Song* and *Women in Love* bring their uninhibited erotic fantasies to the screen in this joint project. In all four stories, desire unleashes unforseen consequences. This film also offers a chance to see Academy Award winner Mira Sorvino in a frank new light.
VHS: S29000. $14.95.
Ken Russell/Susan Seidelman/Melvin Van Peebles/Bob Rafelson, USA, 1996, 103 mins.

Talk Radio
Oliver Stone directed this adaptation of Eric Bogosian's hit stage play, which is loosely based on the murder of Denver talk show host Alan Berg by a neo-Nazi group. Stone transplants the setting to Texas, and weaves in a more intricate subplot involving the talk show host's estranged wife.
VHS: S09456. $19.95.
Laser: LD70086. $34.98.
Oliver Stone, USA, 1988, 103 mins.

Tank Girl
Lori Petty is Tank Girl, an armed and well made-up vigilante justice machine for the future. Her goal is to defeat Water and Power, an evil syndicate controlling the world's supply of water. Ice-T and Malcolm McDowell are also featured.
VHS: S25627. $19.98.
Laser: LD74985. $34.98.
Rachel Talalay, USA, 1995, 106 mins.

Tap
Gregory Hines dances up a storm as Max Washington, ex-con and tap dancer extraordinaire. Max must decide between a life of crime or using his talents for the betterment of mankind. With Sammy Davis, Jr. as Little Mo and an aging but very active collection of tap legends like Sandman Simms and Harold Nicolaus. Also the performing talents of Suzanne Douglas and Savion Glover. A movie with a lot of heart and a lot of history.
VHS: S08701. $14.95.
Nick Castle Jr., USA, 1989, 111 mins.

The Teacher
A lurid thriller about a repressed man drawn into a madly passionate affair with an older, experienced woman at the moment a psychopathic killer trails both of them. With Angel Tompkins, Jay North, and Anthony James.
Laser: LD71360. $39.95.
Hikmet Avedis, USA, 1974, 98 mins.

Telefon
Charles Bronson is a KGB agent sent from Moscow to the U.S.A. to prevent a renegade Russian general from starting WWIII by activating sleeper agents all over America. Lots of explosions and an astute use of rattlesnakes in this Don Siegel thriller. With Lee Remick, Donald Pleasance, Tyne Daley and Sheree North.
VHS: S06197. $69.95.
Don Siegel, USA, 1977, 102 mins.

Tell Me a Riddle
Melvyn Douglas and Lila Kedrova play a happily aging couple who have been married for forty years and now she is dying. This sensitive and touching drama is based on the novella by Tillie Olsen. With Brooke Adams, Zalman King, Dolores Dorn and Joan Harris. Lee Grant's feature film debut as a director.
VHS: S06020. $79.95.
Lee Grant, USA, 1980, 94 mins.

Telling Lies in America
Based on the memories of top American screenwriter, Joe Eszterhas *(Basic Instinct)*. Brad Renfro is Karchy, a high school student from Hungary who moves to Cleveland in the 1960s. While struggling at school and trying to adjust to American culture, he hears about a DJ named Billy Magic (Kevin Bacon, in one of his best performances). After cheating to win a radio contest Karchy starts hanging out with Billy Magic to become cool and begins telling lies to impress people. Both Karchy and Billy eventually learn a lesson about the damage done by lying. With Maximilian Schell.
VHS: S34099. $97.99.
Guy Ferland, USA, 1997, 101 mins.

Tender Mercies
A gentle film starring Robert Duvall as a hard-luck country singer trying to get his life together with the support of a new family. Written by Horton Foote, directed by the Australian director of *Breaker Morant*.
VHS: S01309. $19.98.
Bruce Beresford, USA, 1982, 93 mins.

The Tenth Man
A fascinating adaptation of Graham Greene's novella. A wealthy French lawyer surrenders his possessions to avoid the Nazi firing squad. The lawyer gets entangled with the dead man's beautiful, heartbroken sister. With Anthony Hopkins, Derek Jacobi, Kristin Scott Thomas and Cyril Cusack.
VHS: S18488. $19.98.
Laser: LD71868. $34.98.
Jack Gold, USA, 1988, 100 mins.

Terms of Endearment
Winner of five Oscars including Best Picture, the story of the changing relationship between a mother and daughter over the years mixes humor and heartache. A tear-jerker. With Shirley MacLaine, Jack Nicholson and Debra Winger.
VHS: S03916. $19.95.
James L. Brooks, USA, 1983, 132 mins.

That Was Then...This Is Now
S.E. Hinton's novel achieves a sensitive adaptation in this story of two boys raised as brothers who take on the challenges of growing up, and of the street, at the same time. With Emilio Estevez, Craig Sheffer.
VHS: S03619. $79.95.
Laser: LD75327. $29.98.
Christopher Cain, USA, 1985, 102 mins.

Thelma and Louise
An unhappy housewife named Thelma (Geena Davis) and her wisecracking waitress friend Louise (Susan Sarandon) embark on a short trip to escape some of the boredom and dissatisfaction they feel in their daily lives. But a twist of fate turns their weekend "getaway" into just that, and they soon find themselves fleeing across the American southwest with the police only two steps behind. This "feminist"/ buddy/road/adventure movie created quite a sensation when it was first released in 1991, and, surprisingly, it lives up to most of the hype. The excellent cast also includes Harvey Keitel, Michael Madsen, Christopher MacDonald and newcomer Brad Pitt.
VHS: S15283. $19.98.
Laser: Audio commentary by Ridley Scott. **LD76327. $49.95.**
DVD: DV60197. $24.98.
Ridley Scott, USA, 1991, 127 mins.

They Only Kill Their Masters
A thriller about the chief of an idyllic coastal California community who tries to piece together the details of a strange murder, the death of a young pregnant woman who may have been attacked by her Doberman. With James Garner, Katharine Ross, Hal Holbrook and Peter Lawford.
VHS: S18481. $19.98.
James Goldstone, USA, 1972, 97 mins.

A Thing Called Love
Peter Bogdanovich's underrated drama is set in Nashville and stars River Phoenix, Samantha Mathis, Dermot Mulroney and Sandra Bullock in the story of four singer/songwriters who chase fame and fortune and find "The Thing Called Love." First-rate performances are supported by an all-country soundtrack.
VHS: S20490. $19.95.
Laser: LD75273. $34.98.
Peter Bogdanovich, USA, 1993, 116 mins.

The Third Solution
If you feel you missed the first two solutions, join the club. Treat Williams stars as a man who uncovers a secret pact between Moscow and the Vatican and is willing to expose the story to the world. This causes a certain level of tension in the international community. Whatever the Kremlin and the Pope had to discuss in private also interests F. Murray Abraham and Danny Aiello.
VHS: S11687. $79.95.
Pasquale Squitieri, USA/Italy, 1989, 113 mins.

This Boy's Life
Scottish director Michael Caton-Jones' somber adaptation of Tobias Wolff's memoirs about growing up in the Pacific Northwest in the 50s. The film is a collection of painful vignettes about the author as a young boy. Toby (Leonardo DiCaprio) and his mother Caroline (Ellen Barkin) stake out a forlorn, nomadic existence as they move from town to anonymous town without desires or expectations. With Robert De Niro and Jonah Blechman.
VHS: S19239. $19.98.
Laser: LD71916. $34.98.
Michael Caton-Jones, USA, 1993, 115 mins.

This World, Then the Fireworks
In this seductive film noir, Billy Zane *(Titanic)* and Gina Gershon *(Face/Off)* are Marty and Carol, a pair of twisted twins, beautiful on the outside, bad on the inside. Ruthless grifters, driven by greed and enslaved by desire, they discover a beautiful woman (Sheryl Lee), whom they intend to make their next victim. As murderous clues start criss-crossing, the police begin to connect the dots. With Rue McClanahan and Will Patton.
VHS: S34547. $99.99.
Laser: LD76974. $39.99.
Michael Oblowitz, USA, 1996, 100 mins.

A Thousand Acres
Through an explosive series of events, a generous gift from a father to his three daughters reveals long-guarded secrets, unspoken rivalries and hidden desires. With Michelle Pfeiffer, Jessica Lange, Jason Robards and Jennifer Jason Leigh.
VHS: S33397. $103.99.
Laser: LD76820. $39.99.
Jocelyn Moorhouse, USA, 1997, 105 mins.

Threesome
John Charles, Lara Flynn Boyle and Stephen Baldwin star in this bittersweet reminiscence about dorm life. Once everything seemed fluid and possibilities just presented themselves. This celebrated, sexually adventurous movie shows what happens when three roommates just go with the flow.
VHS: S21681. $19.95.
Laser: LD74492. $34.95.
Andrew Fleming, USA, 1994, 93 mins.

Til Death Us Do Part
Treat Williams proves to be menacing in this true crime thriller based on one of the more difficult cases of Los Angeles District Attorney Vincent Bugliosi, the man who prosecuted Charles Manson. Williams is suspected of several murders, including that of the husband of his flashy blonde lover but the evidence is only circumstantial. Contains deleted footage not shown in the original television movie.
VHS: S16702. $89.95.
Yves Simoneau, USA, 1991, 93 mins.

A Time to Kill
This controversial film, based on the novel by John Grisham, is the story of a revenge killing in a small Mississippi town and the young lawyer who wages a battle for courtroom justice, igniting a firestorm of racial tension, Klan terror and media madness. With Sandra Bullock, Samuel L. Jackson, Matthew McConaughey, Kevin Spacey, Donald Sutherland, Ashley Judd and Patrick McGoohan. "The best version of a John Grisham novel" (Roger Ebert). VHS letterboxed.
VHS: S30447. $19.98.
Laser: LD76031. $39.98.
DVD: DV60100. $24.98.
Joel Schumacher, USA, 1996, 150 mins.

Titanic (1996)
George C. Scott, Peter Gallagher, Eva Marie Saint, Tim Curry and Marilu Henner star in this stunning recreation of the famous luxury ship's maiden voyage and its collision course with destiny on April 14, 1912, in which 1,523 passengers died and 705 survived, their lives, loves and fortunes irrevocably changed forever.
VHS: S31255. $9.95.
Laser: LD76219. $49.99.
Robert Lieberman, USA, 1996, 165 mins.

Titanic (1997)
The blockbuster and Academy Award winner of titanic proportions and running time from the self-proclaimed "King of the World." With a script that would win D.W. Griffith's heart, the film stars Leonardo DiCaprio as Jack, an artist who wins a ticket in a card game for a trip aboard the ill-fated ship, where he falls in love with the upper-class Rose (Kate Winslet), unhappily engaged to the dastardly Cal (Billy Zane). Though the great ship goes down, their hearts will go on.... With Bill Paxton, Frances Fisher and Kathy Bates as Molly Brown. Widescreen.
VHS: S34911. $29.99.
James Cameron, USA, 1997, 195 mins.

Tomorrow's Child
A fictional drama about the world's first test-tube baby conceived and grown to full term in the laboratory. William Atherton and Stephanie Zimbalist are the concerned parents in this made-for-tv look at modern science at work. With James Shigeta, Ed Flanders, Salome Jens and Bruce Davison.
VHS: S08039. $59.98.
Joseph Sargent, USA, 1982, 100 minus.

Top Gun
Tom Cruise plays a cocky jet pilot in this unabashed recruitment promo for the U.S. Air Force. At a special combat training school he learns new moves and tries them out on a civilian instructor. With Kelly McGillis, Anthony Edwards, Val Kilmer and Tom Skerritt. Into the air junior birdman!
VHS: S04003. $14.95.
Tony Scott, USA, 1986, 110 mins.

Tora! Tora! Tora!

An expensively mounted battle sequence of the bombing of Pearl Harbor takes up half of this super war drama, which re-creates the events leading up to and following the "day of infamy." With Jason Robards, Martin Balsam, Joseph Cotten. Letterboxed.
VHS: S09452. $19.98.
Richard Fleischer/Toshio Masuda/Kinji Fukusaku, USA, 1970, 142 min.

Tough Guys

Burt Lancaster and Kirk Douglas are two old-time master criminals who pulled off the last great train robbery, are released from prison, and face difficulties adjusting to outside life. With Charles Durning, Dana Carvey and Eli Wallach.
Laser: LD71374. $36.99.
Jeff Kanew, USA, 1986, 104 mins.

Tough Guys Don't Dance

Ryan O'Neal and Isabella Rossellini star in this tongue-in-cheek sendup of film noir written and directed by Norman Mailer. Taken from his novel about greed, lust, ambition, and corpses without heads in Provincetown. With Wings Hauser, Debra Sandlund and Lawrence Tierney. The title is a quote from a real life mobster.
VHS: S06061. $19.98.
Norman Mailer, USA, 1987, 110 mins.

The Towering Inferno

Big cast! Big thrills! Widescreen! It's the classic Oscar-winning follow-up to Irwin Allen's *Poseidon Adventure*, about a fire that engulfs the world's tallest skyscraper on the night of its dedication ceremony. Starring Steve McQueen, Paul Newman, William Holden, Faye Dunaway, Fred Astaire, Jennifer Jones, Richard Chamberlain, Susan Blakely, Robert Vaughn, Robert Wagner and O.J. Simpson in happier times. Letterboxed.
VHS: S30986. $19.98.
John Guillermin/Irwin Allen, USA, 1974, 165 mins.

Tracks

Dennis Hopper delivers an impressive performance as the decorated, disoriented Vietnam Vet soldier who is escorting home the body of a friend killed in Nam. On the way he encounters a relentless parade of American caricatures.
VHS: S01366. $19.95.
Henry Jaglom, USA, 1974, 90 mins.

Trading Hearts

Raul Julia is an ex-baseball giant who falls head over heels in love with a minor league singer, played by Beverly D'Angelo. Set in the fabulous 50's, this is a timeless tale of shattered dreams and newfound love.
VHS: S09284. $14.95.
Laser: LD75136. $24.98.
Neil Leifer, USA, 1988, 88 mins.

Train Robbers

John Wayne agrees to help widow Ann-Margret retrieve a half-million dollar treasure in stolen gold bullion buried somewhere in the Mexican desert. He enlists the help of saddle buddies Rod Taylor, Ben Johnson, Bobby Vinton, Jerry Gatlin and Christopher George. Together they must face the mysterious Ricardo Montalban and twenty nameless riders who are also intrigued by the expedition.
VHS: S16293. $19.98.
Laser: Letterboxed. **LD71807. $34.98.**
Burt Kennedy, USA, 1973, 92 mins.

Traveller

Bill Paxton and Mark Wahlberg are Bokky and his apprentice, Pat, a pair of modern-day gypsy con-artists known as Travellers, who carve a path of riotous larceny and trouble-bound romance until they fall under the spell of outlaw Traveller Double D (James Gammon). "A hot little sleeper...made with a sharp, appealing simplicity that has all but gone out of style" (Janet Maslin, *The New York Times*). With Julianna Margulies *(ER)*.
VHS: S32192. $98.99.
Laser: LD76395. $39.99.
Jack Green, USA, 1997, 101 mins.

Treasure Island

An all-new production of Robert Louis Stevenson's timeless classic, with Charlton Heston as the infamous pirate captain Long John Silver, Christian Bale as the cabin boy Jim Hawkins, Oliver Reed as Capt. Billy Bones and Christopher Lee as Blind Pew.
VHS: S12299. $79.98.
Fraser C. Heston, USA, 1990, 132 mins.

Trespass

Bill Paxton and William Sadler try to escape from a black drug gang in an East St. Louis factory. Crack kingpin Ice-T faces off against Ice Cube in a complicated plot that uses a rap soundtrack, video, and much gratuitous violence.
VHS: S21490. $19.95.
Walter Hill, USA, 1992, 101 mins.

Tribes

An intense and occasionally humorous tv-movie about a group of young marine recruits going through basic training. Darren McGavin is the tough-as-leather Drill Instructor. Jan Michael Vincent is the hippie who was drafted. This Emmy award winning script is set in the late '60's. Cast includes Earl Holliman Jr., Danny Goldman and Richard Yniguez.
VHS: S08038. $59.98.
Joseph Sargent, USA, 1970, 74 mins.

The Trigger Effect

Elisabeth Shue *(Leaving Las Vegas)*, Kyle MacLachlan *(Twin Peaks)* and Dermot Mulroney *(How to Make an American Quilt)* star in this intense story of a mysterious power failure that leads to the social breakdown of a major city as all forms of communication are wiped out. Now that everything that society has taken for granted no longer works, ordinary rules no longer apply. Directorial debut by David Koepp.
VHS: S30783. $96.99.
David Koepp, USA, 1996, 95 mins.

The Trip to Bountiful

Geraldine Page won the Oscar for Best Actress in this story of an old woman returning to her childhood home in order to embrace memories. But she is trapped inside an apartment and treated like a child by her son, and ultimately escapes and gets a chance to revive her dreams.
VHS: S01811. $14.98.
Laser: LD72314. $29.99.
Peter Masterson, USA, 1985, 105 mins.

Triumph of the Spirit

Willem Dafoe is cast as Salamo Arouch, a Greek Jew who survived the concentration camp at Auschwitz by boxing for the entertainment of the German officers. His true story is designed to be even more poignant by the fact that the movie was made on location in the former death camp. With Robert Loggia, Wendy Gazelle and Edward James Olmos as a wily Gypsy kapo.
VHS: S12212. $89.95.
Robert M. Young, USA, 1989, 115 mins.

Tropic of Cancer

Joseph Strick's rendering of Henry Miller's autobiographical novel. Set in 30s Paris cafe society, Rip Torn is a disaffected American expatriate novelist searching for meaning and purpose and drifting into a succession of erotic adventures. With James Callahan, David Bauer and Laurence Ligneres. Ellen Burstyn gives a small, remarkable performance as Henry's wife June.
VHS: S19025. $19.95.
Joseph Strick, USA, 1970, 87 mins.

True Confessions

Robert De Niro and Robert Duvall star as conscientious brothers, whose chosen professions—the priesthood and law enforcement—collide in Los Angeles circa 1948. Based on the popular novel by John Gregory Dunne, this underrated crime drama combines corruption within the Catholic Church with a sensational murder mystery. The sturdy supporting cast includes Charles Durning, Ed Flanders, Burgess Meredith, Kenneth McMillan, Rose Gregorio, Dan Hedaya, Louisa Moritz and Cyril Cusack as Cardinal Danaher. Letterboxed.
VHS: S16445. $19.98.
Ulu Grosbard, USA, 1981, 108 mins.

True Women

In this true-life epic set on the rugged West Texas plains during the Civil War, Sarah Ashby McClure (Dana Delany) and her younger sister Euphemia (Annabeth Gish) are two fearless women determined to find their place in a male-dominated world. When Mexican forces threaten their homeland and Indians raid the plains, the sisters defy the odds to lead their family and friends to safety.
VHS: S32917. $19.95.
Karen Arthur, USA, 1997, 170 mins.

Trusting Beatrice

Irene Jacob *(Double Life of Veronique)* is the star of this quirky romantic comedy about a mysterious French woman and her adopted Cambodian child. One day they find themselves homeless because their desperate neighbor has burned down their apartment building. As a result they all move in together with the arsonist's odd family. Love somehow also finds a home in these strange, secret-laden surroundings. Also features Steve Buscemi and Mark Evan Jacobs.
VHS: S24210. $59.95.
Cindy Lou Johnson, USA, 1994, 86 mins.

Truth or Consequences N.M.

A simple robbery goes wrong when an undercover cop is shot. Now four luckless bandits are on the run with two hostages and a suitcase full of drugs. With Kiefer Sutherland, Vincent Gallo, Mykelti Williamson, Kevin Pollack and Rod Steiger.
VHS: S32359. $104.99.
Kiefer Sutherland, USA, 1997, 101 mins.

The Turn of the Screw

Lynn Redgrave portrays a young governess who must protect her charges from the menacing spirits of their former governess and her evil lover.
VHS: S02624. $29.98.
Dan Curtis, USA, 1974, 120 mins.

Turning Point

Anne Bancroft and Shirley MacLaine star as two friends and rivals reunited after a number of years apart, Bancroft as the aging ballerina, MacLaine as the one who abandoned her career to raise a family. Superb dance sequences featuring Mikhail Baryshnikov.
VHS: S01828. $19.98.
Herbert Ross, USA, 1977, 119 mins.

The Tuskegee Airmen

Laurence Fishburne stars along with John Lithgow and Cuba Gooding, Jr., in this tale of heroic African-American World War II fighter pilots. Four new recruits are given the mission to help defend American troops from the air, but their mission also has another important goal. Their success could prove that the courage and skills of African-Americans are equal to those of their countrymen.
VHS: S27725. $19.98.
Robert Markowitz, USA, 1994, 52 mins.

Twilight of the Golds

With loving parents, a handsome son and an expectant daughter married to a doctor, the Golds make a picture-perfect family. But a revelation about the pregnancy turns the blessed event into a trial of values and ideals that challenges both the family and the marriage. With Brendan Fraser, Jennifer Beals, Garry Marshall, Jon Tenney, Rosie O'Donnell and Jack Klugman. Based on the off-Broadway play.
VHS: S33240. $98.99.
Laser: LD76806. $39.99.
Ross Marks, USA, 1996, 90 mins.

Twisted Obsession

A screenwriter is uninspired by his current project and decides to back out—that is, until he meets the director's younger sister. An affair ensues in which the writer learns of the unnaturally domineering relationship the director holds with his sibling. Why, and who is dominating whom, becomes the man's obsession. With Jeff Goldblum and Miranda Richardson.
VHS: S12743. $89.95.
Fernando Trueba, USA, 1990, 109 mins.

Twister

Helen Hunt and Bill Paxton star as scientists in search of answers. They hope to plant a special device in a twister. Together they must face not only the terrific force of these weather systems, but also competing scientists funded by corporate money. The awesome special effects are reason enough to see this film. VHS letterboxed.
VHS: S29966. $19.98.
Laser: THX, CLV. **LD76070. $34.98.**
DVD: DV60056. $24.98.
Jan De Bont, USA, 1996, 113 mins.

Two Bits

Al Pacino stars in this heartwarming coming-of-age story that revolves around a lucky quarterhorse. A young boy discovers the special Two Bits and through the magic that only a child can muster, he finds himself drawn closer to his grandfather (Pacino). Philadelphia offers the perfect backdrop to this engaging story.
VHS: S27850. $99.99.
Laser: LD75930. $39.99.
James Foley, USA, 1995, 84 mins.

Two Days in the Valley

Danny Aiello, Jeff Daniels, Teri Hatcher, Glenne Headly, Peter Horton, Marsha Mason, Paul Mazursky, James Spader, Eric Stoltz and Charlize Theron star in this "sleek, amusingly nasty" *(The New York Times)*, "violent, funny crime caper" *(Philadelphia Inquirer)* about ten people who have two things in common: murder and two days to get out of the valley. "The talent-crammed cast make sure *Two Days* never runs out of gas" *(L.A. Daily News)*.
VHS: S30782. $19.98.
John Herzfeld, USA, 1996, 105 mins.

The Two Jakes
The long awaited sequel to *Chinatown*. Much has changed since Jake's last adventure in sunburnt Los Angeles. The war has come and gone. The city teems with optimism and fast bucks. But the more things change, the more they stay the same. Especially when a routine marital snoop job explodes into a murder that's tied to a grab for oil—and to Jake's own *Chinatown* past. Two-time Academy Award winner Jack Nicholson stars and directs from a script by renowned screenwriter Robert Towne (*Chinatown, Tequila Sunrise*).
VHS: S13433. $14.95.
Laser: Widescreen. **LD75329. $29.98.**
Jack Nicholson, USA, 1990, 137 mins.

Two Kinds of Love
Ricky Schroder, Lindsay Wagner and Peter Weller star in this drama of a father seeking reconciliation with his son in the face of the mother's death. Based on the novel *There Are Two Kinds of Terrible* by Peggy Mann.
VHS: S06358. $59.98.
Jack Bender, USA, 1983, 100 mins.

U-Turn
When a broken radiator hose strands a small-time gambler (Sean Penn) in Superior, Arizona, a desert mining town, a treacherous couple draws him into a twisted game with deadly stakes. With Nick Nolte, Powers Boothe, Claire Danes, Joaquin Phoenix, Billy Bob Thornton, Jon Voight and Jennifer Lopez. "*U-Turn* paints a funny, hellish, mean little picture of a man on the run" (*Chicago Tribune*).
VHS: S33343. $104.99.
Laser: LD76762. $34.95.
DVD: DV60237. $24.95.
Oliver Stone, USA, 1997, 125 mins.

Unbearable Lightness of Being
Czech author Milan Kundera's novel has been transferred to film by director Philip Kaufman (*The Right Stuff*). The emphasis is less on the philosophic debates of love and life and more on epic visualization of passion and revolution. With Englishman Daniel Day-Lewis as the doctor with two life long loves to choose from—French actress Juliette Binoche and Swedish actress Lena Olin. This polyglot cast is supposed to be all Czechs in this English language version that uses hats and mirrors as sexual aides.
VHS: S07757. $19.98.
Laser: LD71386. $49.95.
Philip Kaufman, USA, 1988, 156 mins.

Under Suspicion
Liam Neeson and Laura San Giacomo star in this thriller that meshes two unsavory characters in an unforseen murder. Neeson's character uses his own wife to set up phony adultery charges. When she and a prospective mark are murdered, he comes under suspicion. There is, however, another suspect, the beautiful mistress of the dead man. Soon she has trapped Neeson's character in another plot.
VHS: S26285. $19.95.
Simon Moore, USA, 1991, 100 mins.

Undercover Blues
What's a family to do when confronted by international arms thieves, local New Orleans hoods and a distinct dearth of affordable child care? In this movie Dennis Quaid and Kathleen Turner have fun fighting crime and simultaneously raising a family.
VHS: S20716. $19.95.
Laser: LD72385. $34.98.
Herbert Ross, USA, 1993, 90 mins.

Unforgettable
Ray Liotta and Linda Fiorentino star in this thriller that plunges into the mind of a murdered woman. Fiorentino is a doctor who has discovered a drug that allows the user to relive the memories of another person. In order to prove he did not murder his wife, Liotta's character takes this drug and falls into a desperate battle filled with physical and psychic danger.
VHS: S29404. $19.98.
Laser: LD75815. $34.98.
John Dahl, USA, 1996, 116 mins.

An Unmarried Woman
A compassionate story in which Jill Clayburgh delivers an unsparing self-examination of a woman's individuality, as she attempts to survive alone. With Alan Bates, Michael Murphy.
VHS: S04590. $69.98.
Paul Mazursky, USA, 1978, 122 mins.

Unremarkable Life
Patricia Neal and Shelley Winters co-star in this story of love, life and emotional rebirth. For the past 15 years, Frances (Neal), carefree but obediently naive, has shared her house with her sister Evelyn (Winters), a stern matriarch who finds comfort in her sister's misery. The two women go about their household duties, never changing their routines, until Frances meets a charming widower and a relationship develops.
VHS: S12280. $14.95.
Amin Q. Chaudhri, USA, 1989, 111 mins.

The Untouchables
Eliot Ness versus Al Capone, and the battlefield is Chicago. Historically flawed and often physically impossible, this film delivers lots of action, fine performances and snappy one-liners. Kevin Costner is Ness, Robert De Niro is Capone and Sean Connery is the Irish beat cop with a plan to make the Windy City a decent place to live. Watch for the *Potemkin* tribute at Union Station. Letterboxed.
VHS: S06241. $19.95.
Brian DePalma, USA, 1987, 119 mins.

Urban Cowboy
John Travolta is a Houston oil refinery worker by day and a honky-tonk cowpoke at night who rides a mechanical bull at Gilley's. His biggest competition is a little old gal played by Debra Winger.
VHS: S32667. $14.95.
James Bridges, USA, 1980, 135 mins.

The Usual Suspects
Stephen Baldwin, Gabriel Byrne, Benicio del Toro, Kevin Pollak and Kevin Spacey star in this inventive crime story as a bunch of guys brought together for a police line-up. Finding themselves alone together after the cops are through with them, they decide to plan a crime. This plot about a multi-million dollar drug deal gets even stranger because somehow, amidst all the intricately placed flashbacks, these eccentric criminals end up causing a catastrophic explosion. Featuring Chazz Palminteri, Pete Postlethwaite and Suzy Amis. VHS letterboxed.
VHS: S27071. $19.95.
Laser: LD75442. $39.95.
DVD: DV60008. $29.95.
Bryan Singer, USA, 1995, 106 mins.

Valley Girl
Solid acting by Nicholas Cage in this funny, appealing film about a romance between a Hollywood punker and a San Francisco Valley girl.
VHS: S01768. $14.98.
Martha Coolidge, USA, 1982, 95 mins.

Vamping
Fantasy, remembrance and murder combine in this story about a jazz musician who burglarizes a rich widow to get his saxophone out of the pawn shop, only to fall in love with the widow.
VHS: S10098. $59.98.
Frederick King Keller, USA, 1984, 110 mins.

Venice/Venice
Henry Jaglom stars as a director who is slightly bemused when his film is sent to compete at the Venice Film Festival. There, amid the mad comings and goings of an international festival, a beautiful French journalist (Nelly Alard) interviews the director and discovers the unending stream of appearances behind the silver screen. David Duchovny is also featured.
VHS: S28395. $19.98.
Henry Jaglom, USA, 1996, 108 mins.

The Verdict
Paul Newman stars as the aging attorney who overcomes his personal failure by taking on a case of medical malpractice and suing a hospital in a tense courtroom examination of medical and legal ethics. Screenplay by David Mamet, based on the novel by Barry Reed. With Charlotte Rampling, James Mason.
VHS: S02344. $19.98.
Laser: LD71392. $44.98.
Sidney Lumet, USA, 1982, 128 mins.

Victory at Entebbe
Helmut Berger, Linda Blair, Kirk Douglas, Richard Dreyfuss, Anthony Hopkins, Helen Hayes, Burt Lancaster, Jessica Walter and Elizabeth Taylor are among the stars featured in this big-cast disaster film about an airplane full of Israeli and Jewish passengers that is hijacked by the PLO. While the hostages cope with confinement and death threats, the Israeli cabinet and military struggle to avert disaster.
VHS: S33910. $14.95.
Marvin J. Chomsky, USA, 1976, 119 mins.

Vigilante
When an honest cop becomes the victim of a ruthless gang of street punks, he is forced to take the law into his own hands. With Robert Forster and Fred Williamson.
VHS: S34618. $14.95.
DVD: DV60256. $29.95.
William Lustig, USA, 1982, 90 mins.

The Visitors
James Woods makes his cinematic debut in this tough, suspenseful drama about a Vietnam veteran who cannot escape his past. On his Connecticut farm all appears peaceful until two friends from his soldier days arrive, bringing with them the unburied memories of difficult times.
VHS: S21148. $19.98.
Elia Kazan, USA, 1972, 88 mins.

Wait Until Spring Bandini
Joe Mantegna stars as the philandering head of an immigrant Italian family in Colorado in the 1920s. Ornella Muti is the faithful wife who must compete with stylish Faye Dunaway as the rich Mrs. Hildegarde. With Michael Bacall, Daniel Wilson, Alex Vincent and Burt Young as Rocco. Based on the novel by John Fante with music composed by Angelo Badalamenti (*Twin Peaks*). Presented by Francis Ford Coppola.
VHS: S14996. $19.98.
Dominique Dereddere, USA, 1990, 104 mins.

A Walk in the Clouds
Keanu Reeves stars in this openly sentimental love story. The story unfolds at a family-run vineyard in the 1940s. Two people meet on a bus and accidentally end up posing as a married couple. This scenario is meant to fool the young woman's traditionally-minded Mexican parents. Naturally, there are suspicions, but in the end, the charade succeeds. With Anthony Quinn, Aitana Sanchez-Gijon and Giancarlo Giannini.
VHS: S27209. $19.95.
Laser: LD75481. $39.98.
Alfonso Arau, USA, 1995, 102 mins.

Walker
Ed Harris inhabits the role of the political adventurer William Walker, an American who invaded Nicaragua in 1855 with 58 men and won a dubious place in history. Director Alex Cox (*Sid and Nancy*) plays the story for political irony and bizarre humor. With Peter Boyle, Rene Auberjonois and Marlee Matlin as Ellen Martin.
VHS: S06922. $79.95.
Alex Cox, USA, 1987, 95 mins.

Walking Tall: The Trilogy
This ultra-violent '70s classic is based on real life folk hero Buford Pusser. Joe Don Baker (*Mars Attacks*) stars in *Walking Tall* (126 mins.) as the original Sheriff Buford Pusser, a former wrestler and man of action bent on ridding his small Tennessee town of corruption and debauchery. In *Walking Tall, Part 2* (113 mins.), Bo Svenson (*Heartbreak Ridge*) takes over the role of Sheriff Pusser, who's now out to avenge his wife's death at the hands of the mob. Svenson returns as the small-town American hero in the last, action-packed chapter of the trilogy, *Walking Tall: The Final Chapter* (116 mins.). With Noah Beery, Jr., Forrest Tucker, Red West and Leif Garrett.
VHS: S32615. $19.95.
Phil Karlson/Earl Bellamy/Jack Starrett, USA, 1973/1975/1977, 355 mins.

Wall Street
Oliver Stone invades the stone canyons of the stock market battle zone with the story of a young broker who is willing to do most anything to land the big account. Michael Douglas won an Oscar for his greed is good philosophy. With Charlie Sheen, Martin Sheen, Hal Holbrook, Sean Young and Daryl Hannah.
VHS: Out of print. For rental only.
Laser: CLV. **LD72105. $39.98.**
Oliver Stone, USA, 1987, 128 mins.

The War at Home
Emilio Estevez stars with and directs father Martin Sheen, along with Kathy Bates, in this "beautifully acted" (*The New York Times*) story about a young war hero haunted by his past who returns home only to face an explosive situation.
VHS: S32062. $19.95.
Laser: LD76333. $39.99.
Emilio Estevez, USA, 1997, 123 mins.

Wargames
Computer kid whiz taps into the Defense Department's master war computer and nearly starts World War III. Slick feature with Matthew Broderick, Dabney Coleman and Ally Sheedy.
VHS: S03494. $19.95.
Laser: Letterboxed. **LD74591. $34.98.**
DVD: DV60299. $24.98.
John Badham, USA, 1983, 114 mins.

Warriors
Inventive comic book style story of a gang crossing rivals' turf in a neon underworld New York. Upon its release this film caused a furor because it supposedly started riots in and around theatres where it played. Creative use of color and action, music by Joe Walsh.
VHS: S07497. $19.95.
Walter Hill, USA, 1979, 90 mins.

The Waterdance
This autobiographical work by Neal Jimenez (*River's Edge*) is a tragicomedy about the recovery of a talented young novelist (Eric Stoltz) paralyzed in a mountain climbing accident, and his time in a paraplegic ward at a local hospital. With Wesley Snipes and William Forsythe as two embittered antagonists, Elizabeth Pena, and Helen Hunt as Stoltz's married lover.
VHS: S18116. $19.95.
Laser: LD71843. $34.95.
Neal Jimenez/Michael Steinberg, USA, 1991, 110 mins.

Waterland

In this age of cynicism and despair, history teacher Tom Crick, played by Academy Award winner Jeremy Irons, inspires his students to embrace the past. Ethan Hawke is the student who learns to see the marvels and mysteries that life holds.

VHS: S21089. $19.98.

Stephen Gyllenhaal, USA, 1992, 94 mins.

The Way We Were

Sydney Pollack directed this poignant and beguiling love story about two hopelessly opposite people who fall in love, are married and subsequently divorce over the contradictions of their clashing worlds. As he proved with *Out of Africa*, Pollack handles actors exceptionally well. Robert Redford is a conservative screenwriter at the height of the McCarthy paranoia. Barbra Streisand is a left-wing, Jewish radical unable to embrace the social and political privileges of Redford's past. A stunning score from Marvin Hamlisch, as well as a nicely rendered title track from Streisand.

VHS: S02921. $19.95.

Laser: Chapter stops, 2 sides, theatrical trailer. **LD75053. $34.95.**

Sydney Pollack, USA, 1973, 118 mins.

Welcome to Sarajevo

Based on a true story of dangerous risks and courage, this explosive film follows a group of journalists covering a war head on. With Woody Harrelson, Marisa Tomei, and Stephen Dillane.

VHS: S34289. $103.99.

Laser: LD76951. $39.99.

Michael Winterbottom, USA/Great Britain, 102 mins.

What Can I Do?

This highly innovative film follows the fascinating dinner conversation between an elderly, affluent woman and her five dinner guests. It offers a daring exploration of the relationship between viewers, the screen image and a performer.

VHS: S21863. $19.95.

Wheeler Winston Dixon, USA, 1993, 80 mins.

What's Eating Gilbert Grape

Trapped in a small town, Johnny Depp supports his eccentric family, which includes a 500-pound mother, a mentally disabled brother and two problematic sisters. All this is put in jeopardy when he finds new hope in the outsider Juliette Lewis. Co-stars Leonardo Di Caprio and Mary Steenburgen.

VHS: S21210. $19.95.

Lasse Hallstrom, USA, 1993, 118 mins.

When a Man Loves a Woman

Meg Ryan and Andy Garcia star in this drama about a couple facing alcoholism. Through tears and laughter they overcome this challenge to their marriage and their family. Ultimately it brings them closer to each other by forcing them to concentrate on the most important element in their lives, their enduring love.

VHS: S22711. $19.95.

Luis Mandoki, USA, 1993, 126 mins.

When the Whales Came

A highly acclaimed family film with Paul Scofield starring in a poignant drama about co-existing with the whales. It has been 70 years since the people of Samson Island preyed upon a school of narwhal whales, only to be destroyed by a mysterious curse. The last survivor—an enigmatic mystic known only as the Birdman, lives on Bryher, a neighboring island that is about to be visited by those very same whales. If Bryher is to be spared the deadly curse of Samson, it will be up to two trusting children, Daniel and Gracie, to befriend the deaf bird sculptor and learn his ancient secrets. "A whale of a childhood fable" *(New York Post)*. Close-captioned.

VHS: S12185. $89.98.

Clive Rees, USA, 1989, 100 mins.

White Dawn

Based on James Houston's true story of three sailors separated from their ship in the Arctic during a hunt for polar bear and walrus. Magnificent scenery and intense drama combine for an intriguing film. With Warren Oates, Timothy Bottoms, Lou Gossett, Jr.

VHS: S01450. $19.95.

Laser: LD75330. $29.98.

Philip Kaufman, USA, 1975, 110 mins.

White Man's Burden

This is the film that takes as its premise the idea that everyone hates John Travolta because he is white. Harry Belafonte stars as Travolta's blithely unconcerned and bigoted boss. In this drama/thriller, all race relations are reversed, with blacks dominating an unequal society where whites do the hardest and most punishing work. Travolta revolts when he loses his job, and forces everyone to reconsider the price of the "White Man's Burden."

VHS: S27525. $19.98.

Desmond Nakano, USA, 1995, 89 mins.

White Nights

Mikhail Baryshnikov stars as a Russian ballet defector who finds himself back in the USSR. Interesting primarily for the excellent dance sequences. With Gregory Hines and Isabella Rossellini.

VHS: S05333. $19.95.

Laser: Widescreen. **LD75494. $39.95.**

Taylor Hackford, USA, 1985, 135 mins.

White Palace

James Spader and Susan Sarandon star in this contemporary love story about a younger man and a bolder woman. She's a waitress in a fast food burger joint; he's a rising ad executive. About all they have in common is that they both live in St. Louis and enjoy great sex. Lasting relationships have been built on less. Based on the novel by Glenn Savan.

VHS: S13585. $19.95.

Luis Mandoki, USA, 1990, 103 mins.

White Sands

An invigorating thriller about a small-town sheriff (Willem Dafoe) who impersonates a dead man and becomes entangled in a complex web of FBI sting operations, black market gun runners, Third World guerrillas, and a wealthy socialite drawn to dangerous causes. With Mickey Rourke, Mary Elizabeth Mastrantonio, M. Emmet Walsh, Samuel L. Jackson and an uncredited Mimi Rogers.

VHS: S17036. $19.98.

Roger Donaldson, USA, 1992, 101 mins.

White Squall

Jeff Bridges leads a group of young men on a sailing adventure in the Caribbean. After an unexpected, ferocious storm at sea, Bridges' character and his stern demands no longer go casually unheeded by the young crew. Set during the 1960s, the lessons in survival these benighted young men learn intimates something almost intangible about an era now tinged with nostalgia because of a loss of leadership.

VHS: S29400. $19.95.

Laser: LD75811. $39.99.

Ridley Scott, USA, 1995, 129 mins.

Who'll Stop the Rain

Nick Nolte is the Vietnam vet who can save Tuesday Weld and her husband Michael Moriarty from their own stupidity and the viciousness of Richard Masur, Ray Sharkey and Anthony Zerbe. A thriller about drug smuggling and much more. From Robert Stone's novel *Dog Soldiers*.

VHS: S06992. $14.95.

Laser: LD76367. $49.98.

Karel Reisz, USA, 1978, 126 mins.

The Whole Wide World

The acclaimed true story of the star-crossed love between a small-town schoolteacher and the writer who was the passionate creator of *Conan the Barbarian* and *Red Sonja*. With Renee Zellweger *(Jerry Maguire)*, Vincent D'Onofrio, Ann Wedgeworth and Harve Presnell. "One of the most endearingly human, romantic films ever made" (David Elliot, *San Diego Union-Tribune*).

VHS: S32235. $98.99.

Laser: LD76345. $39.95.

Dan Ireland, USA, 1996, 111 mins.

Whose Life Is It Anyway?

Richard Dreyfuss, John Cassavetes and Christine Lahti deliver outstanding performances in this adaptation of the Broadway hit with Dreyfuss as the sculptor paralyzed in an accident, who argues for his right to die. 1981, 118 mins.

VHS: S02863. $79.95.

John Badham, USA, 1981, 118 mins.

Wide Sargasso Sea

Talented Australian director John Duigan *(Flirting)* adapted Jean Rhys' sensual novel about the first marriage of Rochester (Nathaniel Parker), the brooding English romantic of Charlotte Bronte's *Jane Eyre*, to a beautiful Creole named Antoinette (Karina Lombard). Set in Jamaica during the 1840s, the film pivots on erotic obsession and sexual delusion. "Infinitely romantic, the film's eroticism is real" (Vincent Canby). With Rachel Ward as Antoinette's mentally unbalanced mother, Michael York, Martine Beswicke and Claudia Robinson.

VHS: S19936. $19.95.

John Duigan, USA/Australian, 1992, 100 mins.

Wild Side

Christopher Walken, Joan Chen and Anne Heche star in this steamy, erotic thriller. Heche is a bank executive with a profitable sideline in prostitution. It all seems as safe as money in the bank until she meets a millionaire and his wife (Walken and Chen). Then things devolve into a kinky mess where the most important desire may well be the desire for cold, hard cash. USA, 1995, 96 mins.

VHS: S27511. $14.98.

Wild Things

A steamy, suspenseful Florida noir from the director of *Henry: Portrait of a Serial Killer*. Well-respected high school teacher Sam Lombardo's (Matt Dillon) structured life begins to unravel when he is accused of raping wealthy, popular student Kelly Van Ryan (Denise Richards). Outcast student Suzie Toller (Neve Campbell) testifies, claiming she was also raped by the teacher, but may also have information to free Sam. Detective Ray Duquette (Kevin Bacon) begins to suspect that something devious may be going on in this story where nothing is as it seems. "Lurid trash…like a three-way collision between a softcore sex film, a soap opera and a B-grade noir. I liked it" (Roger Ebert, *Chicago Sun-Times*).

VHS: S34744. $104.99.

John McNaughton, USA, 1998, 107 mins.

Wild Women

Hugh O'Brian leads a group of army engineers who recruit female convicts to pose as their spouses on a secret government mission. The wagon train in this made-for-tv western includes Anne Francis, Marie Windsor, Marilyn Maxwell, Sherry Jackson and Cynthia Hull. Head 'em up and move 'em out.

VHS: S08298. $19.98.

Don Taylor, USA, 1980, 90 mins.

Wind

A film about the quest for the America's Cup and the intrigue surrounding a brilliant though reluctant sailor's (Matthew Modine) determination to reclaim the honor and respect of a brilliant tactician (Jennifer Grey). With Stallan Skarsgard and Cliff Robertson.

VHS: S18158. $94.95.

Carroll Ballard, USA, 1992, 115 mins.

The Wind and the Lion

When Arab chieftain Sean Connery kidnaps American beauty Candice Bergen and her two small children, President Teddy Roosevelt (Brian Keith) sends in the Marines. Based extremely loosely on a true incident, but filled with bluster, spectacle and romantic horseback rides. Keith is "bully" as the U.S. prez with the big stick.

VHS: S06205. $19.98.

Laser: LD70182. $34.98.

John Milius, USA, 1975, 120 mins.

The Windy City

Four friends gather for a 10-year high school reunion. Anthony Griffith *(Tales from the Hood)* is Adam, a successful lawyer and the leader of the pack. James Black *(The Don King Story)* is Marco, the ladies man with a secret. Ted Lyde (writer and director) is the emotionally unstable cop Vic. New York stage actor Victor Mack is Trip, the recently gunned down comic book writer and narrator of the story. After 10 years apart these men reunite and discover their friendship has a price tag they can no longer afford.

VHS: S34079. $69.95.

Ted Lyde, USA, 1997, 97 mins.

The Winner

Rebecca DeMornay, Vincent D'Onofrio, Delroy Lindo, Michael Madsen, Frank Whaley and Billy Bob Thornton prove a fool and his money are soon parted, in this arresting action-thriller from the director of *Highway Patrolman* and *Sid and Nancy*. The Winner has the Midas touch when it comes to gambling, and no one knows why. He's on top of the world, and much to his chagrin, everyone around him—particularly a vicious loan shark, a seductive showgirl, a trio of hustlers and a desperate ex-con—wants a piece of the action.

VHS: S32301. $96.99.

Alex Cox, USA, 1997, 83 mins.

Wired

The life and times of comic performer John Belushi as seen through the eyes of reporter Bob Woodward. You may not have realized what a big fan Belushi was of the guy who helped crack the Watergate scandal. With Michael Chiklis and Gary Groomes as Saturday Night Live stars Belushi and Ackroyd. The resemblance is physically good but the story seems written under the influence. With J.T. Walsh as Woodward and Ray Sharkey as a Puerto Rican guardian angel. Includes a powerful anti-drug message.

VHS: S11530. $89.95.

Larry Peerce, USA, 1989, 112 mins.

Witch Hunt

Dennis Hopper, Penelope Ann Miller and Julian Sands bring strange intensity to their roles in this macabre thriller. Hopper is a private eye looking into the death of a murdered movie mogul. But an evil old as time, not to mention a beautiful woman, eliminate any chance that this case will be solved easily.

VHS: S24393. $19.95.

Laser: LD75287. $34.98.

Paul Schrader, USA, 1994, 100 mins.

The Witches of Eastwick

Jack Nicholson, Susan Sarandon, Michelle Pfeiffer and Cher star in this loose adaptation of the John Updike novel about three New England women who summon the Devil to spice up their drab small-town lives. Nicholson has the time of his life as the horny Prince of Darkness. With Veronica Cartwright and lots of cherry pits and balloons.

VHS: S06548. $19.98.

Laser: LD74745. $29.98.

DVD: DV60082. $24.98.

George Miller, USA, 1987, 118 mins.

Without Warning: The James Brady Story

The affecting story of James Brady, the second victim of John Hinkley Jr.'s failed assasination attempt of then president Ronald Reagan. It is also the story behind the major national move towards gun control in the United States. USA, 120 mins.

VHS: S15275. $89.95.

Laser: LD75288. $34.98.

Michael Toshiyuki Uno, USA, 1991, 120 mins.

A Woman at War

Martha Plimpton and Eric Stoltz star in this unnerving, suspense-laden drama about one woman's effort to save the lives of Jews in occupied Belgium. She finds herself alone after her parents are killed by the Gestapo. Now she infiltrates this very organization in order to combat its horrific goals.

VHS: S23861. $92.98.

Edward Bennett, USA, 1994, 115 mins.

Woman of the Wolf

This fairy tale-like drama, based on a 1904 short story by American poet and feminist author Renee Vivien, tells two opposing versions of the same narrative: one told verbally by Pierre Lenoir at a Victorian dinner party; the other told visually through the behavior of a woman who meets him on a fantasy cargo boat. The intercutting of the two stories creates a tension between the woman and the man.

VHS: S34433. $59.95.

Wendy Surinsky, USA, 1997, 40 mins.

Word's Up

In this Emmy Award-nominated drama, Henry Brooks (Kadeem Hardison, *A Different World*), a 25-year-old dropout is rejected again and again for jobs because he doesn't know how to read. Frustration begins to mount when his illiteracy keeps affecting his everyday life. In an attempt to learn to read, Henry decides to sneak back into high school, returning to the teen world of football practice, dating, and school lunch. With David Faustino *(Married with Children)*, Vanna White *(Wheel of Fortune)* and Richard Moll *(Night Court)*. 48 mins.

VHS: S34098. $19.95.

The World According to Garp

Robin Williams is writer, wrestler and family man T.S. Garp in this George Roy Hill adaptation of the John Irving bestseller. With Glenn Close as his mother, Mary Beth Hurt as his wife and John Lithgow as his transsexual friend who used to play professional football.

VHS: S04472. $19.98.
Laser: LD74738. $39.98.

George Roy Hill, USA, 1982, 136 mins.

Wrestling Ernest Hemingway

Robert Duvall and Richard Harris appear to be complete opposites. One is a reserved, retired Cuban barber, while the other is a salty, Irish ex-sea captain. Also features Academy-Award winning actress Shirley MacLaine.

VHS: S21088. $19.98.
Laser: LD72415. $39.98.

Randa Haines, USA, 1993, 123 mins.

The Wrong Man

Jim McBride *(Big Easy)* directs this taut thriller set in steamy Mexico, with John Lithgow as the innocent bystander caught in a web of murder and obsession for the sultry, mysterious Rosanna Arquette. With Kevin Anderson.

VHS: S20523. $19.95.
Laser: LD72359. $34.98.

Jim McBride, USA, 1993, 98 mins.

Yanks

Richard Gere, Vanessa Redgrave, William Devane and Lisa Eichhorn are all featured in this lavish World War II drama about romance between American soldiers and English women. It's a bittersweet tale of hopeless love. During wartime, the threat of eminent death make every moment precious.

VHS: S21276. $14.98.

John Schlesinger, USA, 1979, 139 mins.

You Light Up My Life

In the process of putting her life back in order, a young woman sets out to fulfill elusive dreams of acting and songwriting. Moving performances from Didi Conn and Joe Silver, with Michael Zaslow, Stephen Nathan and Melanie Mayron. Features the familiar Oscar-winning title song.

VHS: S16413. $19.95.

Joseph Brooks, USA, 1977, 90 mins.

Zelly and Me

The story of a young orphan girl and her foreign nanny. Isabella Rossellini is Mademoiselle, or "Zelly", and Alexandra Jones is the child who falls under her spell. A drama of love and growth with Glynis Johns and director David Lynch in an acting role.

VHS: S07679. $79.95.

Tina Rathborne, USA, 1988, 87 mins.

Zorro: A Conspiracy of Blood

The legend continues as Zorro (Duncan Regehr), his father, Don Alejandro de la Vega (Henry Darow), and the entire village of Los Angeles wage war against a Spanish Emissary (James Horan) who has come to claim the wealth of the land in the name of the King.

VHS: S34890. $9.99.

Ray Austin, USA, 1992, 97 mins.

Zorro: The Legend Begins

Duncan Regehr *(The Last Samurai)* stars in this version of the Zorro legend. In the days of yore, Los Angeles is but a small desert village governed by the corrupt Alcalde. Only the masked rider can make him change his ways. With Efrem Zimbalist Jr. as Don Alejandro.

VHS: S34889. $9.99.

USA, 1990, 120 mins.

MARTIN SCORSESE

After Hours

An inventive dark comedy, in which all reality seems to be turned upside-down, peopled by a cast including Rosanna Arquette, Teri Garr, Griffin Dunne and Cheech & Chong. Scorsese received Best Director honors at the 1986 Cannes Film Festival for this. Written by Joseph Minion.

VHS: S00021. $19.98.
Laser: LD70497. $34.98.
Laser: Letterboxed, widescreen. **LD70498. $34.98.**

Martin Scorsese, USA, 1985, 97 mins.

The Age of Innocence

Edith Wharton's Pulitzer Prize-winning novel, set in 1870's New York, is brought to the screen with lavish sets, costumes, and the star power of Daniel Day-Lewis, Michelle Pfeiffer, and Winona Ryder. It is a tale from a time ruled by rigid conventions and moral standards, but love cannot and should not be denied.

VHS: S20666. $19.95.
Laser: LD72377. $39.95.

Martin Scorsese, USA, 1993, 138 mins.

Alice Doesn't Live Here Anymore

A subtle masterpiece that transforms the struggle of one woman into a memorable symbol of liberation and courage. Stars Ellen Burstyn in an Academy Award winning performance, with Kris Kristofferson and Diane Ladd.

VHS: S03481. $19.98.
Laser: LD70500. $34.98.

Martin Scorsese, USA, 1974, 105 mins.

Cape Fear

Robert De Niro was nominated for an Oscar for his role as Max Cady, a vengeful ex-con on the trail of lawyer Nick Nolte, his wife Jessica Lange and their rebellious teenage daughter Juliette Lewis. Based on the John D. MacDonald novel *The Executioners*, and a remake of the 1962 thriller. Letterboxed.

VHS: S16329. $19.98.
Laser: LD71437. $39.98.

Martin Scorsese, USA, 1991, 127 mins.

Casino

Robert DeNiro, Sharon Stone and Joe Pesci are at the center of this glamorous but hard-hitting film about the Mob in Las Vegas. DeNiro stars as Ace Rothstein (based on the life of Frank Rosenthal), a long-suffering professional gambler who is saved from destruction by his childhood pal Nicky Santoro (Joe Pesci). Rothstein marries Ginger McKenna (Stone), a chip hustler and con artist who very nearly destroys Rothstein's friendship with Santori. Despite this film's excesses (or perhaps because of them), the old Mob-dominated gambling town emerges as a twisted but exciting and seductive pleasure ground where a tangible, tense uncertainty underlays all the hype. Based on Nicholas Pileggi's book *Casino: Love and Honor in Las Vegas*. VHS letterboxed.

VHS: S27631. $19.98.
Laser: LD75538. $44.99.

Martin Scorsese, USA, 1995, 179 mins.

The Color of Money

Martin Scorsese's acclaimed update of *The Hustler*. Paul Newman returns as the pool-hall wizard Fast Eddie, who pursues his belief that "money won is twice as sweet as money earned." With Tom Cruise and Mary Elizabeth Mastrantonio.

VHS: S03470. $19.95.
Laser: LD70924. $44.99.

Martin Scorsese, USA, 1986, 119 mins.

Goodfellas

Scorsese once again demonstrates his formal brilliance in this impeccably constructed film about three decades of life with the mob. Based on Nicholas Pileggi's best seller *Wiseguy, Goodfellas* displays a stunning narrative virtuosity from its first shot to its last. And the actors, especially Joe Pesci and Lorraine Bracco, all give powerful, passionate performances. Don't miss this. Also starring Robert De Niro, Ray Liotta, and Paul Sorvino. Photographed by Michael Ballhaus. VHS letterboxed.

VHS: S14085. $19.98.
Laser: LD70589. $29.98.
DVD: DV60047. $24.98.

Martin Scorsese, USA, 1990, 148 mins.

Italian American/The Big Shave

Two short films from Martin Scorsese. *Italian American* (starring Charles and Catherine Scorsese), shot on location in his parents' little Italy apartment among plastic sofa covers, fancy picture frames, and assorted lamps and figurines, is a funny look at one family's ancestry, their arrival in America, and the successes that followed. In *The Big Shave* a young man nicks himself shaving and a frightening religious experience suddenly develops. It features Scorsese's black humor at an early age, highlighting his preoccupation with religion, suffering and blood (i.e., Catholicism).

VHS: S14497. $24.95.

Martin Scorsese, USA, 1974/1967, 54 mins.

King of Comedy

Robert De Niro is an obsessive stand-up comic performing in front of cardboard cutouts of his idols. Jerry Lewis is a host of a talk show that De Niro desperately wants to be on. Incredibly funny, true-to-life film by Martin Scorsese.

VHS: S00679. $19.95.

Martin Scorsese, USA, 1982, 101 mins.

Kundun

Set in 1937 Tibet, four years after the death of the 13th Dalai Lama, Scorsese's visually elegant film tells the story of the 14th Dalai Lama, from his discovery at age two by monks who sensed he may be their reincarnated leader, to his escape when Communist China invaded Tibet, to his exile in India. With music by Philip Glass.

VHS: S34924. $103.99.

Martin Scorsese, USA, 1997, 114 mins.

Last Temptation of Christ

Martin Scorsese's powerful adaptation of the novel by Nikos Kazantzakis. Particularly notable is Willem Dafoe's performance as Christ.

VHS: S09455. $19.95.
Laser: LD70050. $99.95.

Martin Scorsese, USA, 1988, 131 mins.

Last Waltz

One of the greatest concert movies ever made, *Last Waltz* documents the 1976 Thanksgiving night farewell concert given by The Band at the Winterland in San Francisco. With appearances by Bob Dylan, Eric Clapton, Neil Young, Van Morrison and many more!

VHS: S00728. $19.95.

Martin Scorsese, USA, 1978, 117 mins.

Mean Streets

Set in New York's Little Italy, *Mean Streets* follows Harvey Keitel as he slowly climbs into the hierarchy of a local Mafia family. Keenly observed, gritty and violent, this early film by Scorsese clearly foreshadows his later work, and established him as a major American talent. With Robert De Niro, Cesare Danova, Amy Robinson.

VHS: S00840. $19.98.
Laser: LD70626. $34.98.

Martin Scorsese, USA, 1973, 112 mins.

New York, New York

A celebration of the Big Band Era, starring Robert De Niro and Liza Minnelli, as well as Diahnne Abbott, Mary Kay Place and Lionel Stander. Cinematography by Laszlo Kovacs. This is the long version with the intact Minnelli number, "Happy Endings", restored. VHS letterboxed.

VHS: S00927. $24.98.

Martin Scorsese, USA, 1977, 163 mins.

Raging Bull

Robert De Niro gives an incredible performance as Jake LaMotta, the controversial middleweight fighter of the 1940's. *Raging Bull* shows how LaMotta turned his fears into the physical energy needed to become a champion, while destroying his private life. Breathtaking cinematography!

VHS: S01084. $19.95.
Laser: Letterboxed, chapter search. Includes original theatrical trailer. **LD71669. $39.98.**
DVD: DV60092. $24.98.

Martin Scorsese, USA, 1980, 127 mins.

Taxi Driver

Scorsese's now-classic film with Robert De Niro as the psychotic cabbie driven to violence in an attempt to "rescue" a teenage prostitute (Jodie Foster). With Albert Brooks, Harvey Keitel, Leonard Harris, Peter Boyle and Cybill Shepherd.
VHS: S01303. $14.95.
Laser: CAV, widescreen. **LD70470. $99.95.**
Laser: CLV, widescreen. **LD70471. $49.95.**
DVD: DV60027. $24.95.
Martin Scorsese, USA, 1975, 114 mins.

Who's That Knocking at My Door?

Martin Scorsese's directorial debut (made when he was only 25 years old) is a fascinating, autobiographical story about the relationship between a young, Catholic kid (Harvey Keitel) who still has a lot of ties to the old neighborhood, and the independent college student (Zina Bethune) he falls for. Featuring a strong performance from Keitel in his screen debut.
VHS: S14082. $59.99.
Martin Scorsese, USA, 1968, 90 mins.

ROBERT ALTMAN

Beyond Therapy

Christopher Durang's play about neurotic New Yorkers and their even crazier shrinks is translated to film by Robert Altman. Julie Hagerty and Jeff Goldblum are the patients. Tom Conti and Glenda Jackson are the therapists. With Christopher Guest as Jeff's boyfriend. A movie that needs professional help.
VHS: S05215. $19.95.
Robert Altman, USA, 1987, 93 mins.

Brewster McCloud

Robert Altman's moody parable is virtually unclassifiable. The anti-hero is the virginal young man, Brewster (Bud Cort), who is building a set of wings in order to take flight in the Houston Astrodome. Altman equates flight with freedom, which he renders through a skillful use of aerial photography. "The first American film to apply an appropriate tone and style to the absurdist follies of our time" (Andrew Sarris). With Sally Kellerman, Michael Murphy, William Windom, Shelley Duvall, Rene Auberjonois and Stacy Keach.
VHS: S20408. $19.98.
Laser: LD74669. $34.98.
Robert Altman, USA, 1970, 105 mins.

Buffalo Bill and the Indians or Sitting Bull's History Lesson

From director Robert Altman comes this uproarious, high-spirited look at "Buffalo Bill" Cody (Paul Newman), the legendary Western adventurer. Although Bill has fought Indians and Civil War battles, nothing can prepare him for his newest challenge: show business. His popular "Wild West Show" features stunt-riders, battle recreations and Annie Oakley (Geraldine Chaplin), the beautiful sharpshooter. But when Bill signs Chief Sitting Bull for a featured role in the show, a hilarious clash of cultures ensues. With Burt Lancaster, Harvey Keitel, Joel Grey and Shelley Duvall.
VHS: S31367. $19.95.
Laser: LD76130. $49.98.
Robert Altman, USA, 1976, 123 mins.

Caine Mutiny Court-Martial

Robert Altman directs this made-for-TV version of the classic drama based on Herman Wouk's Pulitzer Prize-winning novel. Brad Davis stars as Lt. Cmdr. Phillip Queeg, who lost the command of his Navy vessel during a severe typhoon due to his overt concern for missing strawberries. Eric Bogosian plays the sharp military lawyer trying to defend Jeff Daniels from charges of mutiny. With Peter Gallagher, Michael Murphy, Kevin J. O'Connor and Daniel Jenkins.
VHS: S16472. $19.95.
Robert Altman, USA, 1988, 100 mins.

Countdown

James Caan and Robert Duvall landed on the Moon one year before Neil Armstrong with the help of director Robert Altman. In this effective ensemble performance the lives of the astronauts, their families and their co-workers are realistically portrayed. Only the technology is dated.
VHS: S04183. $19.98.
Robert Altman, USA, 1968, 101 mins.

Fool for Love

The minimalist, barren landscapes energize the smothering, claustrophobic interiors of Sam Shepard's play in this Robert Altman adaptation that stars Shepard and Kim Basinger as formerly obsessive lovers whose fragmented, scarred past is mysteriously connected to an old man (Harry Dean Stanton), who hides out in an abandoned motel. Randy Quaid has a small but quietly effective role as Basinger's befuddled gentleman caller.
VHS: S02261. $14.95.
Robert Altman, USA, 1985, 108 mins.

The Gingerbread Man

In this thriller written by John Grisham and directed by Robert Altman, Kenneth Branagh stars as a lawyer whose obsession with a mysterious and beautiful client leads him into a world of terrifying intrigue and deadly deceit. With Robert Duvall, Robert Downey, Jr., Daryl Hannah, Tom Berrenger and Embeth Davidtz.
VHS: S34699. $101.99.
Laser: Audio commentary by Robert Altman. **LD77011. $39.99.**
Robert Altman, USA, 1998, 114 mins.

James Dean Story

Robert Altman co-directed with G.W. George in 1957, the film explores Dean's personal life through interviews with family and friends, as well as Dean's short career. Contains footage from *East of Eden*, a TV public service message, and more.
VHS: S00651. $9.99.
Robert Altman/George W. George, USA, 1957, 80 mins.

Kansas City

Master filmmaker Robert Altman returns to the city of his youth. Kansas City, 1934: the jazz was cool, the action was hot and nobody messed with the mob. But when a small-time hood knocks over the buddy of the city's top gangster, a club owner named Seldom Seen (Harry Belafonte), he finds himself in deep trouble. His tough-talking girlfriend, Blondie O'Hara (Jennifer Jason Leigh), comes to his rescue when she kidnaps a wealthy presidential advisor's wife (Miranda Richardson) and swaps her for her boyfriend.
VHS: S30575. $19.98.
Robert Altman, USA, 1996, 115 mins.

Long Goodbye

A revisionist updating of Raymond Chandler's well-respected novel. Elliott Gould stars as a shabby, unkempt Philip Marlowe helping out an eccentric friend who is accused of murdering his own wife. Altman's strange film continuously borders on parody of the genre. Also starring Sterling Hayden, Mark Rydell, Henry Gibson, Jim Bouton, and Arnold Schwarzenegger and David Carradine in small, cameo roles.
VHS: S13758. $19.98.
Laser: LD70139. $34.98.
Robert Altman, USA, 1973, 112 mins.

M*A*S*H

Donald Sutherland, Elliott Gould and Robert Duvall in the original, superb, classic dark comedy directed with verve by Robert Altman, juxtaposing the horrors of war with the resiliency of the human spirit. Written by Ring Lardner, Jr.
VHS: S02643. $14.98.
Laser: Letterboxed. **LD76743. $24.98.**
Robert Altman, USA, 1970, 116 mins.

McCabe and Mrs. Miller

A brilliant, offbeat drama of frontier life starring Warren Beatty and Julie Christie. This is Altman's personal and poetic interpretation of an American myth, resulting in a truly original Western. Also appearing are Shelley Duvall, Keith Carradine, Michael Murphy and William Devane.
VHS: S00839. $14.95.
Laser: LD74710. $39.98.
Robert Altman, USA, 1971, 120 mins.

Nashville

The recipient of five Academy Award nominations, Robert Altman's *Nashville* is an explosive drama and human comedy that interweaves the lives of 24 major characters during a five day period in the country music capital. A penetrating and multi-level portrait of America starring Keith Carradine, Karen Black, Geraldine Chaplin, Ronee Blakley, Lily Tomlin and Henry Gibson.
VHS: S00919. $29.95.
Robert Altman, USA, 1975, 159 mins.

The Player

Robert Altman's dark valentine to the American movie industry. The plot is absurdly comic, with Tim Robbins as an icy studio executive who receives a series of threatening, anonymous postcards from a screenwriter he abused, setting in motion a murder and seduction. With Greta Scacchi, Whoopi Goldberg, Fred Ward, Peter Gallagher and 59 actors, directors and stars appearing as themselves.
VHS: S18263. $19.98.
Laser: Audio commentary by Robert Altman. **LD76269. $39.99.**
DVD: DV60078. $24.98.
Robert Altman, USA, 1992, 123 mins.

Popeye

The legendary anvil-armed sailor is brought to life in this musical version directed by Robert Altman and starring Robin Williams and Shelley Duvall.
VHS: S04703. $14.95.
Robert Altman, USA, 1980, 114 mins.

Quintet

A stark film of survivors during the final ice age, beautifully photographed in wintry Canada, starring Paul Newman, Bibi Andersson and Fernando Rey. A meditation on life and death from Robert Altman *(Nashville, Three Women)*.
VHS: S01083. $19.98.
Robert Altman, USA, 1979, 118 mins.

Ready to Wear (Pret-a-Porter)

Marcello Mastroianni, Julia Roberts, Tim Robbins, Kim Basinger, Sophia Loren, Forest Whitaker, Danny Aiello and other stars, including walk-ons like Cher, make this look at the fashion industry a truly unique enterprise. Funny, irreverent and odd, when Aiello donned drag and high-fashion models appeared naked, this film created havoc in the sensitive world of fashion.
VHS: S25115. $19.95.
Laser: LD74953. $39.99.
Robert Altman, USA, 1995, 133 mins.

The Room

Robert Altman directed this drama, which stars Linda Hunt, Julian Sands, and Donald Pleasance. A woman dreams and schemes in a small room while her husband ominously creates scenes in glass bottles. When their sinister landlord plots to rent their space to two mysterious visitors, the room becomes a death trap.
VHS: S10900. $79.95.
Robert Altman, USA, 1987, 48 mins.

Secret Honor

Philip Baker Hall's one-man performance of a fictional meditation/monologue by Richard Nixon. "One of the most scathing, lacerating, and brilliant movies… Nixon is portrayed…with such savage intensity, such passion, such scandal, that we cannot turn away" (Roger Ebert).
VHS: Out of print. For rental only.
Laser: CLV. **LD71802. $49.95.**
Robert Altman, USA, 1984, 85 mins.

Short Cuts

Raymond Carver's short stories are brought to the screen in this Golden Globe winner, employing some of Hollywood's biggest stars. Jack Lemmon, Lyle Lovett, Matthew Modine, Lily Tomlin and Jennifer Jason Leigh are just some of the big names seen in this harrowing portrayal of everyday people living extraordinary lives.
VHS: S20889. $19.95.
Laser: LD74462. $124.95.
Robert Altman, USA, 1993, 189 mins.

Streamers

Based on the controversial play by David Rabe, the film focuses on the lives of 3 young recruits waiting to receive orders to go to Vietnam. They develop close bonds which are shattered when an aggressive and confused inner city black enters their lives, igniting the underlying racial tension and strain of homosexuality that are the volatile undercurrents in the men's relationships.
VHS: S01267. $29.95.
Robert Altman, USA, 1983, 118 mins.

Tanner '88

A collaboration between Robert Altman and writer and cartoonist Gary Trudeau in their demystification of presidential politics and the television-dominated process. The eponymous character (Michael Murphy) is a liberal Senator running for president who embarks on this surreal odyssey through the political landscape. With Gary Hart, Pat Robertson, Bruce Babbitt and Bob Dole.
Tanner, Part I.
Laser: LD71803. $49.95.
Tanner, Part II.
Laser: LD71804. $49.95.
Tanner, Part III.
Laser: LD71805. $49.95.
Robert Altman, USA, 1988, 360 mins.

That Cold Day in the Park

A 32-year-old Canadian spinster (Sandy Dennis) sees a young man (Michael Burns) as a symbol of the freedom and youth denied her by the Establishment and entices him into her home. They do not speak and she assumes he is mute. Soon, her compassion becomes a dangerous compulsion and she decides to keep him as her own possession. As he fights to keep her fantasy from becoming his reality, the situation becomes nightmarish, in this chilling, early feature by Robert Altman.
VHS: S13250. $14.98.
Robert Altman, USA, 1969, 91 mins.

Thieves Like Us

Robert Altman's colorful adaptation of Edward Anderson's 1937 novel is set in rural Mississippi during the Depression. The story follows a Southern boy (Keith Carradine) who takes part in a prison breakout with two bank robbers (John Schuck and Bert Remsen) and falls in love with the tough Keechie (Shelley Duvall). "Altman finds a sure, soft tone and never loses it. His account of Coca-Cola-swigging young lovers is the most quietly poetic of his films; it's sensuous right from the first pearly-green long shot, and it seems to achieve beauty without artifice" (Pauline Kael, *The New Yorker*). With Louise Fletcher and Tom Skerritt.
VHS: S20406. $19.98.
Robert Altman, USA, 1974, 123 mins.

Wedding

A freewheeling satire on marriage, with a large cast, in the same vein as *Nashville*, although more defined. With Lillian Gish, Carol Burnett, Lauren Hutton, Mia Farrow and Geraldine Chaplin, shot largely in Lake Forest, Illinois.
VHS: S01440. $59.98.
Robert Altman, USA, 1978, 125 mins.

JONATHAN DEMME

Caged Heat

Jonathan Demme wrote and directed this story about a beautiful petty criminal (Barbara Steele) who is thrown into the penal hell of Connorville. Here she must fight against ruthless inmates and even more cruel, corrupt and depraved officials to survive. When she makes friends with two hardened inmates, they set out on a sexy and violent adventure looking for money, power and revenge.

VHS: S32033. $14.98.

Jonathan Demme, USA, 1974, 83 mins.

Citizen's Band

Originally made to cash in on the CB radio craze, Jonathan Demme's ensemble comedy-drama is a funny, charming film that portrays Paul "Spider" Le Mat as a small-town CB maniac who stages a one-man crusade to clean up the cluttered air waves. In his way is a thoroughly senile father, gorgeous Candy "Electra" Clark, and the evil, menacing, unknown "Blood." There's also a hilarious subplot which involves an over-eager trucker whose two wives from different cities accidentally meet and discover his bigamist schemes.

VHS: S06846. $59.95.

Jonathan Demme, USA, 1977, 98 mins.

Cousin Bobby

Jonathan Demme's documentary about the Rev. Robert Castle, the director's distant cousin, is an audacious home movie that considers the fiery minister's political and religious convictions, his liberation theology, and estrangement from top church leaders as it shows his work and activism in a poverty-stricken, crime-ridden Harlem neighborhood. It's a "lovely, amiably persuasive demonstration of the personal sources of political conviction. That's entertainment" *(The New Yorker)*.

VHS: S17495. $19.95.

Jonathan Demme, USA, 1991, 70 mins.

Married to the Mob

Michelle Pfeiffer shines as the recent widow of a Mob hit man who just wants to live a normal non-criminal existence. Matthew Modine is the youthful FBI agent following her every move. A comedy with heart and bullets from Jonathan Demme. With Dean Stockwell, Mercedes Ruehl, Alec Baldwin and Tony Fitzpatrick as the surly immigration officer.

VHS: S08350. $19.98.

Jonathan Demme, USA, 1988, 104 mins.

Philadelphia

Winner of two Academy Awards, Tom Hanks for Best Actor and Bruce Springsteen for Best Song, this film tells the moving story of a man who must fight not only AIDS but an ignorant and bigoted society. Denzel Washington plays the lawyer who must struggle with his own unfounded fears to fight for justice on behalf of his colleague, Tom Hanks. With Jason Robards, Mary Steenburgen, Antonio Banderas and Joanne Woodward.

VHS: S21120. $19.95.
Laser: LD72416. $39.95.
DVD: DV60030. $24.95.

Jonathan Demme, USA, 1993, 125 mins.

The Silence of the Lambs

Jonathan Demme's impressive entry into the thriller/ slasher genre has more than a few interesting things to say about the way many of this country's most brutal mass murderers end up becoming something akin to minor celebrities (with their own television shows, books, newspaper profiles, movies and talk show appearances). In the film's final scene the audience is implicated most directly, as we are prompted to laugh at the gruesome prospect of another impending murder. Pretty dark and unsavory stuff, but along the way Demme manages to orchestrate several brilliant sequences in the midst of his well-structured narrative; and the performances, led by Jodie Foster and Anthony Hopkins, are uniformly excellent.

VHS: S14730. $19.98.
Laser: CLV. **LD72108. $99.98.**
DVD: DV60360. $39.95.

Jonathan Demme, USA, 1991, 118 mins.

Subway Stories

Jonathan Demme, Ted Demme, Abel Ferrara and Craig McKay direct 10 stories capturing the laughter, fear, sexiness, money—or lack or it—and strangeness that shapes the lives of those who ride the subways of New York. With Christine Lahti, Denis Leary, Bonnie Hunt, Lili Taylor, Mercedes Ruehl, Rosie Perez and Gregory Hines.

VHS: S33158. $109.73.

Jonathan Demme/Ted Demme/Abel Ferrara/Craig McKay, USA, 1997, 81 mins.

Swimming to Cambodia

Called "hilarious," "audacious," "amazing," *Swimming to Cambodia* is Jonathan Demme's concert film of Spalding Gray's highly successful one-man show. "No contemporary American artist tells better stories than Gray...a very funny, off-the-wall performance," wrote the *Los Angeles Reader*.

VHS: S04740. $14.98.
Laser: Remastered, widescreen, digital transfer. **LD75395. $39.95.**

Jonathan Demme, USA, 1986, 85 mins.

Swing Shift

Goldie Hawn and Kurt Russell star in this Jonathan Demme film about the rise of the American woman in the war workforce during World War II. While most of the men are at war, the women are at work in the factory building the planes and equipment needed for the war effort. With Christine Lahti, Holly Hunter, Patty Maloney, Susie Bond, Fred Ward, and Ed Harris as Goldie's husband in the Navy.

VHS: S09315. $19.98.
Laser: LD74718. $34.98.

Jonathan Demme, USA, 1984, 100 mins.

Who Am I This Time?

A shorter work from the director of *Melvin and Howard* and *Silence of the Lambs*. Christopher Walken and Susan Sarandon portray the relationship of two actors in a local theater company. Based on a story by Kurt Vonnegut, Jr. with music by John Cale.

VHS: S01455. $24.95.

Jonathan Demme, USA, 1982, 60 mins.

TIM BURTON

Batman

A wealthy, embittered orphan grows up to make the lives of criminals miserable in this big budget boxoffice extravaganza. Michael Keaton is the muscular caped Crusader, Jack Nicholson is his evil and goofily deranged nemesis, the Joker. Gotham City is the place they meet for fun and games. With Kim Basinger as frosting on the cake and Michael Gough as Alfred the butler. The comic book character is not just for kids anymore.

VHS: S10949. $19.98.
Laser: LD70519. $39.98.
DVD: DV60040. $24.98.

Tim Burton, USA, 1989, 130 mins.

Batman Returns

Tim Burton's brooding sequel is notable for Michael Keaton's warrior/hero, Danny DeVito's perverse charm as the nefarious Penguin, and best of all, Michelle Pfeiffer's coiled, pent-up aggression and sexuality as the Catwoman. Daniel Waters wrote the screenplay. Cinematography by Stefan Czapsky and art design by Bo Welch.

VHS: S17494. $19.98.
Laser: LD71768. $39.98.
DVD: DV60042. $24.98.

Tim Burton, USA, 1992, 126 mins.

Beetlejuice

Michael Keaton stars as the title character, a wacko freelance bio-exorcist who removes humans from the homes of troubled ghosts. A peculiar and energetic comedy with Geena Davis and Alec Baldwin as the nice dead people and Jeffrey Jones, Catherine O'Hara and Winona Ryder as the living family that irks them. Cameos by Dick Cavett and Robert Goulet.

VHS: S01824. $14.95.
Laser: LD76728. $29.98.
DVD: DV60070. $24.98.

Tim Burton, USA, 1988, 92 mins.

Ed Wood

Johnny Depp portrays the nearly inconceivable cult film director/cross-dresser Ed Wood in this imaginative biographical film that won an Academy Award for Martin Landau in the role of actor Bela Lugosi, who (in real life) died during the making of one of Wood's notorious films. A truly singular Hollywood achievement about a stranger-than-fiction filmmaker whose atrocious films, like *Plan 9 from Outer Space* and *Glen or Glenda*, have become cult classics. With Patricia Arquette and Bill Murray.

VHS: S24321. $19.98.
Laser: Letterboxed. **LD74914. $39.99.**

Tim Burton, USA, 1994, 127 mins.

Edward Scissorhands

This touching fable about a quiet boy with sharp, metal shears for hands manages to entertain and amuse while making some sensitive observations about adolescent loneliness and emotional estrangement. With especially poignant performances from Diane Wiest and Johnny Depp. Also starring Winona Ryder, Alan Arkin, Kathy Baker, Anthony Michael Hall, and Vincent Price as Edward's inventor.

VHS: S13922. $19.98.

Tim Burton, USA, 1990, 100 mins.

Frankenweenie

Young Victor Frankenstein has lost his dog Sparky to a car accident. When his biology teacher makes a dead frog move with electricity, Victor is inspired as only a mad scientist can be. A hilarious satire, evoking the original 1931 *Frankenstein*, from bolts in the sides of Sparky's neck to the "burning castle" scene—here transported to a miniature golf course windmill. The short that launched Tim Burton's career when Paul Reubens enlisted him to direct *Pee Wee's Big Adventure*, Burton moved on to create *Beetlejuice* and *Edward Scissorhands*.

VHS: S16034. $14.99.

Tim Burton, USA, 1984, 28 mins.

Mars Attacks

In this star-studded sci-fi comedy based on the comic book of the same name, Jack Nicholson stars in dual roles as President of the United States and a slimy Vegas entrepreneur as the world is invaded by pesky little green Martians. But their insta-fry ray guns are no match when the Earth fights back with an unexpected weapon. With Glenn Close, Pierce Brosnan, Danny DeVito, Annette Bening, Martin Short, Michael J. Fox, Sarah Jessica Parker, Rod Steiger and Tom Jones.

VHS: S31402. $19.98.
Laser: LD76235. $34.98.
DVD: DV60071. $24.98.

Tim Burton, USA, 1997, 106 mins.

Pee-Wee's Big Adventure

Paul Reubens star as Pee-Wee in a comedy he also helped co-write. The basic premise has Pee-Wee looking for his lost bike, but it's really just a good reason to see this brilliant comic display his virtuosity in some now classic sequences.

VHS: S24845. $19.98.

Tim Burton, USA, 1985, 92 mins.

STANLEY KUBRICK

2001: A Space Odyssey

Light years ahead of its time, 2001: A Space Odyssey is a spectacular movie that looks even more wondrous as time passes. This 1968 masterpiece reaches the outer limits of interplanetary space while penetrating the depths of man's inner destiny. Based on the novel by Arthur C. Clarke, featuring the music of Richard Strauss. This version is the result of a new digital video transfer and is presented in widescreen letterbox format.

VHS: Out of print. For rental only.
Laser: CAV, Criterion. **LD70481. $124.95.**
Laser: Deluxe letterboxed, chapter search, MGM. **LD70164. $39.98.**
Laser: CLV, Criterion. **LD70482. $59.95.**

Stanley Kubrick, USA, 1968, 139 mins.

2001: A Space Odyssey (25th Anniversary Edition)

Stanley Kubrick's landmark film traces the three stages of man, from evolutionary, predatory animals to futuristic space travelers, astronauts on a mission to Jupiter sabotaged by a malfunctioning computer known as HAL. "A uniquely poetic piece of science fiction that's hypnotically entertaining" *(The New Yorker)*. Adapted from Arthur C. Clarke's story *The Sentinel*. With Keir Dullea, Gary Lockwood and William Sylvester. Special visual effects by Douglas Trumbull. Letterboxed.

VHS: S18674. $19.98.
Laser: CAV, 3 discs, with 4-page insert. **LD71876. $69.98.**

Stanley Kubrick, USA, 1968, 141 mins.

Barry Lyndon

Kubrick's tenth feature film is a lavish treatment of Thackeray's 18th century novel and features Ryan O'Neal as a conniving rogue and Marisa Berenson as the widowed Lady Lyndon. Kubrick used antique clothes instead of costumes, and all shooting was on authentic locations.

VHS: S01689. $29.98.
Laser: Letterboxed. **LD74726. $39.98.**

Stanley Kubrick, USA, 1975, 184 mins.

A Clockwork Orange
An exploration of Stanley Kubrick's award-winning film with film historian William Everson, Anthony Burgess, the novel's author, and Malcolm McDowell, star of the film, examining the future-oriented story's mix of brutality and humor, its made-up language of Russian and English, its synthesized classical score, and its sex scenes, which almost threatened it with an "X" rating. 1972, 28 mins.
VHS: S31606. $59.95.

A Clockwork Orange
One of the most audaciously conceived films of recent decades, a merciless vision of the near-future based on Anthony Burgess' chilling novel. The New York Times called it a "brilliant, tour-de-force of extraordinary images, music, words and feelings…so beautiful to look at and to hear that it dazzles the senses and the mind."
VHS: S00251. $19.98.
Stanley Kubrick, USA, 1971, 137 mins.

Conversation with Arthur C. Clarke About "2001: A Space Odyssey"
Two years after the premiere of *2001: A Space Odyssey*, Arthur C. Clarke, co-author with Stanley Kubrick of the book and the film, agreed to be interviewed by film critic Joe Gelmis (who originally gave the film a poor review and later recanted, along with other critics) on how this masterpiece was created. Here Clarke reveals many fascinating details about choosing the basic plot, how he and Kubrick worked together, early title ideas, early shapes and materials for the monoliths and more.
VHS: S30990. $89.95.
1970, 27 mins.

Dr. Strangelove
This great black comedy stars Peter Sellers as the wheelchair-bound nuclear scientist plotting a scheme to attack Russia's nuclear targets with nuclear bombs. Very funny and very frightening, *Dr. Strangelove or: How I Learned to Stop Worrying and Love the Bomb* also stars Sterling Hayden as U.S. Air Force Commander Jack D. Ripper, and George C. Scott as Joint Chief of Staff "Buck" Turgidson. VHS letterboxed.
VHS: S00367. $19.95.
Laser: LD70750. $99.95.
DVD: DV60026. $24.95.
Stanley Kubrick, USA, 1963, 93 mins.

Full Metal Jacket
Stanley Kubrick visits Vietnam. Based on the short but powerful novel, *The Short Timers*, by Gustav Hasford. Follow a few Marines from training on Parris Island to fighting in the Tet Offensive. With Matthew Modine, Adam Baldwin, Dorian Harewood, Lee Ermey and Vincent D'Onofrio. War is hell even when filmed in England.
VHS: S07003. $19.98.
Laser: LD70577. $24.98.
Stanley Kubrick, USA, 1987, 116 mins.

Killer's Kiss
A prizefighter rescues a young woman from her gangster lover and, as a result, is marked for death. An intense film-noir thriller that first brought Stanley Kubrick to the world's attention—he not only wrote and directed this independent production, but also photographed it. Starring Frank Silvera and Irene Kane. "Her soft mouth was the road to sin-smeared violence!"
VHS: S14515. $19.98.
Stanley Kubrick, USA, 1955, 67 mins.

The Killing
Stanley Kubrick directed this classic caper film that concerns illegally removing large amounts of cash from a busy racetrack. Sterling Hayden leads his gang of five on a successful heist but then problems occur for which he hadn't planned. Kubrick uses an elaborate and unusual structure of flashbacks to tell his story. With Vince Edwards, Jay C. Flippan, Marie Windsor, Colleen Gray, Elisha Cook Jr., and Timothy Carey as the grinning sharpshooter, Nikki Arane.
VHS: S11223. $19.95.
Laser: LD71075. $39.95.
Stanley Kubrick, USA, 1956, 83 mins.

The Killing/Killer's Kiss
Two early works from Stanley Kubrick that share a great many of the stylistic and thematic concerns of his later work. The first is a brilliant noir about the planning, execution and aftermath of a daring racetrack heist. *Killer's Kiss* is a dark piece about the relationship of a boxer and a working class woman and the deadly implications of obsession.
Laser: LD71857. $39.98.

Lolita
Kubrick's adaptation of Vladimir Nabokov's classic novel captures the author's black humor with ghoulish understatement. James Mason plays the college professor who marries the lonely widow Shelley Winters purely out of lust for her adolescent daughter. With Peter Sellers playing several characters—all delightfully sinister.
VHS: S02545. $19.98.
Laser: LD70760. $59.95.
Stanley Kubrick, USA, 1961, 150 mins.

Paths of Glory
A shattering film from Stanley Kubrick, bringing into focus the insanity of war in the story of French General Macready, who, during World War I, orders his men into a futile mission. When the men fail, Macready selects three soldiers for trial and execution for cowardice. With incredible performances from Kirk Douglas, Ralph Meeker, Adolphe Menjou, George Macready, Wayne Morris, Richard Anderson. One of the high points of the American cinema.
VHS: S11433. $19.97.
Laser: LD70433. $49.95.
Stanley Kubrick, USA, 1957, 86 mins.

A Primer for 2001: "A Space Odyssey"
This television documentary, made two years after the premiere of Stanley Kubrick's masterpiece, offers a clear explanation of the film's epic perspective, its themes, how the plot unfolds, the monoliths, the music, the "star child," the literary sources in the works of Arthur C. Clarke, and many other topics. Narrated by *2001*'s Keir Dullea.
VHS: S30991. $89.95.
1970, 27 mins.

The Shining
A real thriller based on a Stephen King novel, with Jack Nicholson going slowly mad and terrorizing his wife Shelley Duvall and their little boy, who has strange powers of ESP. With Scatman Crothers.
VHS: S01189. $19.98.
Laser: LD74736. $39.98.
Stanley Kubrick, USA, 1980, 146 mins.

Spartacus
This edition of Stanley Kubrick's epic classic features additional footage cut from the film's initial release print, plus the complete original overture and extended soundtrack. Kirk Douglas stars as the leader of slaves rebelling against their Roman masters. With Jean Simmons, Laurence Olivier, Tony Curtis, Charles Laughton and Peter Ustinov. The screenplay was written by the legendary Dalton Trumbo, based on a book by Howard Fast. The restored version of this historical spectacle is presented in widescreen letterboxed format.
VHS: S15075. $19.95.
Laser: 3 discs: CLV/CAV. Second soundtrack commentary by Kirk Douglas, Peter Ustinov and others. Includes original storyboards and titles as well as newsreel footage of the film's London premiere. **LD70082. $124.95.**
DVD: DV60222. $26.98.
Stanley Kubrick, USA, 1960, 196 mins.

CLINT EASTWOOD

Absolute Power
Clint Eastwood starred in and directed this "wickedly entertaining spine-tingler" (Peter Travers, *Rolling Stone*) about a career thief and ex-con (Eastwood) who says a woman's death was caused by the President of the United States (Gene Hackman). With Ed Harris, Judy Davis, Scott Glenn, Dennis Haysbert and E.G. Marshall.
VHS: S31610. $19.98.
Laser: LD76246. $39.95.
DVD: DV60039. $24.98.
Clint Eastwood, USA, 1996, 121 mins.

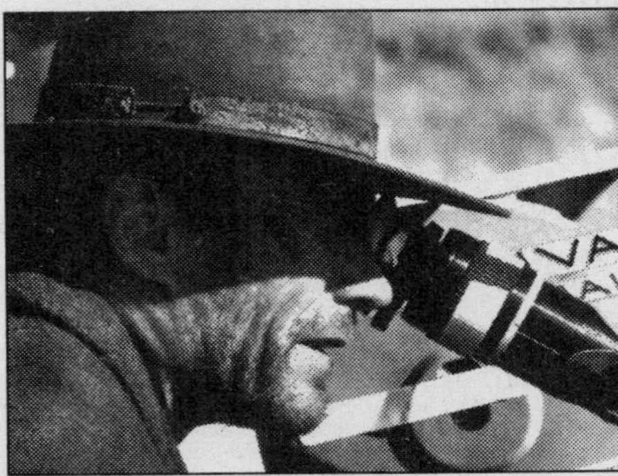

Bird
The film biography of Charlie "Bird" Parker. This legend of modern jazz has his life transformed into a cinematic masterpiece under the direction of Clint Eastwood. Forest Whitaker is Charlie. Diane Venora plays Chan, his loving and long-suffering wife. An epic-length salute to the man, the myths and the music.
VHS: S09321. $19.98.
Laser: LD70526. $29.98.
Clint Eastwood, USA, 1988, 160 mins.

Breezy
Despite their age difference, a jaded divorcee begins an affair with the free-sprited young woman he finds sleeping on his doorstep. With William Holden and Kay Lenz.
VHS: S33716. $19.95.
Clint Eastwood, USA, 1973, 106 mins.

The Bridges of Madison County
Clint Eastwood and Meryl Streep are perfectly matched as a mature couple who only late in life discover each other. Based on the best-selling novel from Robert James Waller, it begins with a photo of a covered bridge and blossoms into the romance of a lifetime.
VHS: S27504. $19.98.
Laser: LD75521. $39.98.
DVD: DV60083. $24.98.
Clint Eastwood, USA, 1995, 135 mins.

Bronco Billy
Traces the exploits and fantasy adventures of a shoe salesman as he leads a star-crossed group of disparate hustlers and dreamers on the road in pursuit of a traveling show. "Eastwood manages to both undermine and celebrate his character's fantasy life, while offering a few gentle swipes at contemporary America" (*Time Out*). With Sandra Locke, Scatman Crothers and Geoffrey Lewis.
VHS: S18613. $19.98.
Laser: LD74688. $24.98.
Clint Eastwood, USA, 1980, 119 mins.

Clint Eastwood Western Box Set
Clint Eastwood's Western trilogy—the Academy Award-winning *Unforgiven* (1992), *Pale Rider* (1985) and *The Outlaw Josey Wales* (1976)—are available in digitally remastered, letterboxed versions.
Laser: LD71881. $119.98.

The Eiger Sanction
An interesting if flawed Clint Eastwood film about an art history professor and CIA professional assassin who tracks down spies in the Andes.
Laser: Letterboxed. **LD70292. $39.98.**
Clint Eastwood, USA, 1975, 125 mins.

Heartbreak Ridge
Clint Eastwood produced, directed and stars in this film, as Sargeant Tom "Gunney" Highway, a combat-hardened Korean and Vietnam War veteran and hard-drinking loser who returns to the U.S. for his last tour of duty with the Marine Corps, where he is assigned to train a recon unit. The invasion of Grenada tests the usefulness of "anachronism" Gunney, as well as the skill of his platoon of hippy recruits. With Marsha Mason, Everett McGill, Moses Gunn, Eileen Heckart, Bo Svenson and Mario Van Peebles. "Eastwood…caresses the material as if he didn't know B movies have gone out of style" (Roger Ebert, *Chicago Sun-Times*).
VHS: S33911. $14.95.
Clint Eastwood, USA, 1986, 114 mins.

High Plains Drifter
Clint Eastwood's western about an enigmatic drifter enlisted by a frontier community to protect them from newly released prisoners. Kind of a vigilante force on the prairie type situation, influenced by the Sergio Leone films that came before it. With Verna Bloom and Marianna Hill.
VHS: S20530. $19.98.
Laser: LD71404. $34.98.
Clint Eastwood, USA, 1973, 105 mins.

Midnight in the Garden of Good and Evil
Eastwood directed this "smoky Southern murder mystery, packed with wit, old secrets and incredible characters" (Pat Collins, WWOR-TV), from John Berendt's best-seller based on the real-life murder trial of Savannah antiques dealer Jim Williams. Starring Kevin Spacey and John Cusack.
VHS: S34259. $104.99.
Laser: LD76944. $39.95.
DVD: DV60251. $24.98.
Clint Eastwood, USA, 1997, 155 mins.

Outlaw Josey Wales
Clint Eastwood plays a peaceful farmer turned vigilante during the period after the Civil war. Eastwood took over directing from Philip Kaufman who co-scripted.
VHS: S07496. $19.98.
Laser: LD70650. $39.98.
Clint Eastwood, USA, 1976, 135 mins.

Pale Rider
A film in which Eastwood explores the state of the Western film genre and his own screen image, mixing action and humor. Eastwood stars as a mysterious avenger aiding gold prospectors. With Michael Moriarty and Carrie Snodgrass.
VHS: S02916. $19.98.
Laser: LD74696. $24.98.
DVD: DV60186. $24.98.
Clint Eastwood, USA, 1985, 116 mins.

A Perfect World
Kevin Costner and Clint Eastwood star in this tale of kidnapping gone awry. Costner plays the would-be kidnapper who is set upon by Eastwood, a determined lawman. With Laura Dern. It's a gripping suspense story with emotional depth.
VHS: S20888. $19.98.
Laser: LD72391. $39.98.
Clint Eastwood, USA, 1993, 138 mins.

Play Misty for Me
Clint Eastwood self-directs in his directorial debut. He plays a late-night radio disc jockey who is haunted by the ultimate obsessive, "will-not-be-ignored," fatal attraction-type groupie Jessica Walter, who is just as scary as can be. A very competent thriller that still delivers lots of surprises and chills.
VHS: S06818. $19.95.
Clint Eastwood, USA, 1971, 102 mins.

The Rookie
Clint Eastwood's inversion of the buddy film; Eastwood plays a craggy police officer paired with an inexperienced rookie (Charlie Sheen), a wealthy kid with a dark past, investigating a pair of flamboyant German car thieves (Raul Julia and Sonia Braga) responsible in the death of his former partner. With Lara Flynn Boyle and Tom Skerritt.
Laser: LD70729. $29.98.
Clint Eastwood, USA, 1990, 121 mins.

Unforgiven
Clint Eastwood's brilliant reconsideration of the American western. Set in the 1880s, a reformed gunman and failed farmer (Eastwood) reluctantly agrees to collect the bounty on two cowboys who slashed a prostitute's face, setting in motion a mythic confrontation with a corrupt sheriff (Gene Hackman), a hired English assassin (Richard Harris) and a dime novelist (Saul Rubinek). With Morgan Freeman and Frances Fisher. Winner of four Academy Awards.
VHS: S18724. $19.98.
DVD: DV60120. $24.98.
Clint Eastwood, USA, 1992, 131 mins.

White Hunter, Black Heart
An adaptation of Peter Viertel's roman a clef about the making of *The African Queen*. Clint Eastwood directs this intelligent and challenging film about obsession, among other things, and also stars in a highly stylized portrayal of John Huston (the director of *The African Queen*). "The year's most masterful and suggestive Hollywood movie" (Jonathan Rosenbaum).
VHS: S13488. $19.98.
Laser: LD70704. $29.98.
Clint Eastwood, USA, 1990, 112 mins.

DAVID LYNCH

Blue Velvet
David Lynch's demystification of American normalcy. Pitched between '40s camp and '80s post-modernism, Lynch alter ego Kyle McLachlan stars as a college student who discovers a severed ear, leading to a strange and perverse odyssey. He alternates between the innocent (Laura Dern) and the mysterious (Isabella Rossellini). Dennis Hopper stars as the creepy and dangerous, oxygen-sniffing outlaw Frank Booth. With Dean Stockwell.
VHS: S02778. $14.98.
David Lynch, USA, 1986, 120 mins.

Dune
A monumental film by the director of *Eraserhead* featuring Max Von Sydow, Linda Hunt and Sting. The saga of an intergalactic warrior and his rise to leadership, based on the book by Frank Herbert. Music by Toto; music for the Prophecy Theme by Brian Eno. VHS letterboxed.
VHS: S00381. $14.98.
Laser: AG3 Dolby Digital, widescreen. **LD70025. $39.98.**
DVD: DV60220. $24.98.
David Lynch, USA, 1984, 137 mins.

Lost Highway
Lynch's sexy, eerie thriller is a blend of horrifying violence and dark mysterious characters in which a man's (Bill Pullman) feelings for his wife (Patricia Arquette) lead him to the edge of madness. A romantic tragedy fantasy nightmare in true Lynchian tradition. With Robert Loggia, Gary Busey, Robert Blake and Richard Pryor. "Transfixing, seriously spooky" (*The New York Times*). VHS letterboxed.
VHS: S31739. $19.95.
Laser: LD76298. $49.99.
David Lynch, USA, 1997, 135 mins.

Pretty as a Picture: The Art of David Lynch
A rare and personal look at one of the most prolific directors of our time, what inspired him as a youth, his comments on his first films and his life-long quest for creative expression. 80 mins.
VHS: S32179. $19.98.

Twin Peaks
The original seven episodes of the cult television series by filmmakers David Lynch and Mark Frost about the surreal, depraved acts unfolding under the small-town textures of the eponymous community. Lynch alter ego Kyle MacLachlan stars as a quirky federal agent investigating the disappearance and murder of a beautiful, popular, high school woman. The eccentric ensemble includes Joan Chen, Ray Wise, Lara Flynn Boyle, Sherilyn Fenn, James Marshall and Piper Laurie.
Twin Peaks, Vol. 1.
VHS: S17547. $14.95.
Twin Peaks, Vol. 2.
VHS: S17548. $14.95.
Laser: LD72276. $124.99.
Twin Peaks, Vol. 3.
VHS: S17549. $14.95.
Twin Peaks, Vol. 4.
VHS: S17550. $14.95.
Twin Peaks, Vol. 5.
VHS: S17551. $14.95.
Twin Peaks, Vol. 6.
VHS: S17552. $14.95.
Twin Peaks, Vol. 7.
VHS: S17553. $14.95.
Twin Peaks Collector's Series #1. Seven videocassettes.
VHS: S15304. $99.95.
David Lynch

Twin Peaks Pilot
See the Peabody Award-winning series pilot of the cult favorite that the entire country was talking about. Plus, witness exclusive, never-before-broadcast sequences solving Laura Palmer's killing. Created by David Lynch and Mark Frost.
VHS: S14532. $14.95.
David Lynch, USA, 1990, 113 mins.

Twin Peaks: Fire Walk with Me
David Lynch's study of the American Dream in this surreal evocation of small-town America. The plot covers the week leading up to the death of Laura Palmer, the beautiful, emotionally scarred woman whose brutal murder set in motion the plot of the television series. With Sheryl Lee, Moira Kelly, David Bowie, Harry Dean Stanton, Ray Wise, James Marshall, Madchen Amick and Kyle MacLachlan.
VHS: S17866. $19.95.
David Lynch, USA, 1992, 135 mins.

Wild at Heart
Based on Barry Gifford's novel about two southern lovers on the run, this film is director David Lynch's *(Blue Velvet, Eraserhead)* campiest feature to date. Despite the loopy subtext of references (mostly to Elvis and *The Wizard of Oz*), Lynch manages to present some powerful visual compositions here and gets all-out performances from stars Nicolas Cage and Laura Dern. Also starring Willem Dafoe, Crispin Glover, Diane Ladd, Isabella Rossellini and Harry Dean Stanton. Winner of the Cannes Film Festival's 1990 Palme d'Or.
VHS: S13515. $19.98.
Laser: LD71210. $49.95.
David Lynch, USA, 1990, 125 mins.

ALAN RUDOLPH

Afterglow
Rudolph's "doozy of digression and tonal shifts" (Ray Pride, *New City*) about four characters in four different emotional time zones. A fable about two married couples whose lives intersect in contemporary Montreal, *Afterglow* stars Nick Nolte as Lucky Mann, a Mr. Fix-It who knows most of the married women on his side of town, and Julie Christie, in an Oscar-nominated performance, as his former B-actress wife, who mourns the past as she watches old tapes of herself. With Lara Flynn Boyle and Jonny Lee Miller.
VHS: S34240. $104.99.
Alan Rudolph, USA, 1997, 114 mins.

Choose Me
Keith Carradine, Genevieve Bujold and Lesley Ann Warren star in this stylish and sexy romance that explores the quirky, ambiguous truths of heterosexual relationships. A cult favorite for its off-enter, eccentric look at contemporary love.
VHS: S00237. $14.95.
Alan Rudolph, USA, 1984, 106 mins.

Equinox
Alan Rudolph's film is about the intersecting fates of twins—an introverted auto mechanic and an underworld gangster, both played by Matthew Modine—who were separated at birth. Lara Flynn Boyle plays a fragile young woman whom the good twin is trying to protect. With Tyra Ferrell, Marisa Tomei as a frightened prostitute, and Kevin J. O'Connor.
VHS: S19731. $19.95.
Laser: Letterboxed. **LD72440. $34.95.**
Alan Rudolph, USA, 1992, 115 mins.

Love at Large
"A pleasingly complex, often comic tale of love as seen through the filter of a detective film noir. A beautiful woman offers private detective Harry (Tom Berenger) a lot of money to tail her lover, but the description she gives of him is vague (tall, blonde hair, smells good). Harry ends up tailing the wrong guy, and now someone is tailing him. Rudolph's highly stylized sets create an 'alternate' world for his action to take place, focusing on his large cast of characters" (Edwin Jahiel). With Annette O'Toole, Kate Capshaw, Elizabeth Perkins and Ann Magneson.
VHS: S12978. $89.95.
Alan Rudolph, USA, 1990, 97 mins.

The Moderns
Alan Rudolph recreates the cafe society of Paris in 1926. Hemingway, Gertrude Stein, and Marcel Duchamp are background figures in this intriguing tale of art forgery and complicated human relationships. With Keith Carradine, Linda Fiorentino, Genevieve Bujold, Wallace Shawn, Geraldine Chaplin and John Lone as the ruthless art collector.
VHS: S07790. $19.98.
Alan Rudolph, USA, 1988, 126 mins.

Mortal Thoughts
Alan Rudolph's characteristically hypnotic thriller in the form of a police interrogation, with Demi Moore playing a New Jersey housewife drawn into events around the murder of her best friend's (Glenne Headly) abusive husband (Bruce Willis). The intricate flashback structure, Elliot Davis's dazzling camera work and fluid ensemble work create a haunting work. With Harvey Keitel as the homicide detective.
VHS: S15113. $19.95.
Alan Rudolph, USA, 1991, 104 mins.

Mrs. Parker and the Vicious Circle
Jennifer Jason Leigh is Dorothy Parker, the legendary, witty writer and Algonquin Roundtable member. Leigh delivers a dazzling—if controversial—performance that captures something of Parker's razor-sharp tongue, romantic escapades, alcoholism and chronic unhappiness. The film is also a unique portrait of a flamboyant literary era. Matthew Broderick and Stephen Baldwin star; produced by Robert Altman.
VHS: S24568. $19.98.
Laser: LD74916. $39.99.
Alan Rudolph, USA, 1994, 124 mins.

Songwriter
Willie Nelson and Kris Kristofferson team up as two country/western singers who band together to outwit a greedy backer. Plenty of good music and good feeling, with Lesley Ann Warren, Rip Torn and Melinda Dillon.
VHS: S01765. $79.95.
Alan Rudolph, USA, 1984, 94 mins.

Trouble in Mind
Kris Kristofferson, Keith Carradine and Genevieve Bujold star in a passionate, highly stylized love triangle in Rain City, a steamy, unlikely place. Haunting score by Mark Isham, sung by Marianne Faithful.
VHS: Out of print. For rental only.
Laser: LD72315. $29.99.
Alan Rudolph, USA, 1986, 111 mins.

ARTHUR PENN

Alice's Restaurant
You can get anything you want in this Arthur Penn film of the song by Arlo Guthrie which was inspired by his arrest for littering in a small New England town. Relive the late sixties where love was free and some churches were used creatively. With Arlo Guthrie, James Broderick and Pat Quinn as Alice.
VHS: S06228. $14.95.
Arthur Penn, USA, 1969, 111 mins.

Bonnie and Clyde
Bank robbers Bonnie Parker and Clyde Barrow probably didn't deserve the cinematic immortality guaranteed by this masterwork directed by Arthur Penn, but I'm sure they wouldn't object to being played by Faye Dunaway and Warren Beatty. Also along for the ride on this Depression era crime spree are Gene Hackman, Estelle Parsons and Michael J. Pollard.
VHS: S00168. $19.98.
Laser: LD70531. $34.98.
DVD: DV60058. $24.98.
Arthur Penn, USA, 1967, 111 mins.

The Chase
Marlon Brando and Robert Redford are on opposite ends of the law in this complex film featuring an all star cast. E.G. Marshall, Angie Dickinson, Jane Fonda, and Robert Duvall all play a role in this screen adaptation of Horton Foote's play, penned by Foote and Lillian Hellman. A prisoner (Redford) escapes and is rumored to be back in his hometown, setting everyone on edge. Brando is the sheriff who must make the best of this peculiar set-up.
Laser: LD75534. $39.95.
Arthur Penn, USA, 1966, 135 mins.

Dead of Winter
Mary Steenburgen stars in multiple roles in this old-fashioned thriller about a naive New York actress who has put her life on the line for a starring role in a very independent feature. Roddy McDowall provides just the right tone as a sinister servant and former mental patient.
VHS: S04666. $14.95.
Arthur Penn, USA, 1987, 100 mins.

Inside

When Marty Strydom (Eric Stoltz), an idealistic university professor, is arrested for conspiring to overthrow the racist government in South Africa, he comes under the control of Police Colonel Kruger (Nigel Hawthorne), who is determined to destroy Marty and all those like him. Kruger ruthlessly interrogates Marty during brutal solitary confinement and finally breaks him, with disastrous consequences. Ten years later, another political prisoner (Louis Gossett, Jr.) who witnessed the whole event has become an investigator of crimes of physical and mental abuse by the previous regime. Will justice finally be served when he confonts Kruger? "A story of visceral and visual power" *(The New York Times)*.

VHS: S30955. $99.99.
Laser: LD76160. $39.98.
Arthur Penn, USA, 1996, 94 mins.

Left-Handed Gun

Arthur Penn's first film, a psychological Western starring Paul Newman as Billy the Kid. Penn explores the theme he would frequently return to: the alienated outsider confronted by a hostile society.

VHS: S03435. $14.95.
Arthur Penn, USA, 1957, 102 mins.

Mickey One

A groundbreaking film with Warren Beatty as a pretty tough comic with a nasty problem. He is convinced that the mob is after him, so he hides out in Chicago. Nightclub life has led to some major disappointments so Mickey is desperately searching for some new leads on a different kind of existence. This gritty and absorbing film was shot on location in Chicago. Written by Alan Surgal, with improvised music from Stan Getz.

Laser: LD75093. $39.95.
Arthur Penn, USA, 1965, 93 mins.

The Miracle Worker

Anne Bancroft and Patty Duke both won Oscars for their roles in Arthur Penn's version of Annie Sullivan and her pupil, Helen Keller. The dramatic force of the battle between the strong willed Annie and the animal-willed Helen carries this extraordinary film.

VHS: S00860. $24.95.
Laser: LD71175. $34.98.
Arthur Penn, USA, 1962, 107 mins.

The Missouri Breaks

In 1880's Montana, ranchers and cattle rustlers fight over land and livestock. Interesting for the head-to-head meeting of two great big talents, Jack Nicholson and Marlon Brando. From a screenplay by Thomas McGuane. Letterboxed.

VHS: S03622. $19.98.
Laser: LD74970. $49.99.
Arthur Penn, USA, 1976, 127 mins.

Penn and Teller Get Killed

A virtually unclassifiable gem from Arthur Penn about postmodern magicians/comedians Penn and Teller, who announce on national television their desire to be killed, and spend the rest of the film avoiding dire fate. Bleak, funny and nihilistic, the movie was permanently shelved and then turned up in a few film festivals. With Penn Jillette, Teller, Caitlin Clarke, Christopher Durang and David Patrick Kelly.

Laser: LD70651. $24.98.
Arthur Penn, USA, 1989, 90 mins.

STEVEN SPIELBERG

Always

A supernatural romance-adventure involving forest firefighting pilots and strong attachments. Richard Dreyfuss, a cocky pilot in love with Holly Hunter, is reluctant to say the words until after he is dead and assigned to act as guardian angel for a rookie flyer. Based on the 1943 romantic fantasy war movie *A Guy Named Joe*. With John Goodman, Brad Johnson and Audrey Hepburn.

VHS: S12230. $19.95.
Steven Spielberg, USA, 1989

Amistad

Spielberg's Oscar-nominated epic starring Morgan Freeman, Nigel Hawthorne, Anthony Hopkins, Djimon Hounsou, Matthew McConaughey, David Paymer, Pete Postlethwaite, and Stellan Skarsgard. In the summer of 1839, 53 Africans held captive in the cramped cargo holds of the Spanish slave ship *La Amistad* break free of their shackles, arm themselves, take control of the ship and reclaim their freedom as they try to return to Africa. The two surviving members of the crew trick them and they are captured by an American naval ship and put on trial for the murder of the crew. Letterboxed.

VHS: S34573. $106.99.
Steven Spielberg, USA, 1997, 155 mins.

Close Encounters of the Third Kind (Director's Cut)

Richard Dreyfuss, Teri Garr, Melinda Dillon and Francois Truffaut star in this director's cut of Spielberg's alien sci-fi masterpiece. Includes a 15-minute *Making Of* featurette containing new interviews with Spielberg, the cast and crew, and exclusive behind-the-scenes footage from the film. Digitally remastered from newly restored film elements. VHS letterboxed.

VHS: S03482. $19.99.
Laser: Re-edited and expanded special edition. Dolby.
LD74543. $39.95.
Steven Spielberg, USA, 1977, 152 mins.

The Color Purple

Steven Spielberg's magnum opus, with Whoopi Goldberg and Danny Glover, in an adaptation of Alice Walker's seminal book about a poor black woman who overcomes horrible conditions in her life and finally comes out on top. Excellent performances by all make this a better-than-average story with drama, humor and gentleness shining through.

VHS: S03551. $19.98.
Laser: CAV. **LD70545. $59.98.**
Laser: CLV. **LD70546. $29.98.**
DVD: DV60084. $24.98.
Steven Spielberg, USA, 1985, 154 mins.

Duel

Dennis Weaver is a traveling businessman who provokes the wrath of a nameless, faceless driver of a diesel truck in the American Southwest. Directed by Steven Spielberg for television, the script is by Richard Matheson. A wild, nerve-crunching ride. Footage added for theatrical release.

VHS: S07809. $14.98.
Laser: LD72297. $34.98.
Steven Spielberg, USA, 1971, 90 mins.

E.T.

Steven Spielberg's magnum opus—finally on video. An endearing alien, stranded on Earth, befriends a sweet young boy and his lovable siblings, who all help him to find his way back home. One of the most popular and highest grossing movies in history and quickly becoming a children's classic in the league of *The Wizard of Oz*. Letterboxed.

VHS: S07032. $19.95.
Laser: THX, CAV. **LD76047. $149.98.**
Steven Spielberg, USA, 1985, 101 mins.

Empire of the Sun

Andrew Sarris thought Spielberg's story of 11-year-old Jim Graham fighting for survival in Shanghai while it was being invaded by the Japanese army was one of the year's best films.

VHS: S07306. $19.95.
Steven Spielberg, USA, 1987, 153 mins.

Hook

The classic J.M. Barrie story of *Peter Pan* is updated and given the Steven Spielberg treatment. Dustin Hoffman has the title role as the most feared pirate captain in Never Never Land. Robin Williams is the grown-up Pan and Maggie Smith is Granny Wendy. With Bob Hoskins, Julia Roberts and Glenn Close.

VHS: S16626. $19.95.
Laser: LD71571. $39.95.
Steven Spielberg, USA, 1991, 144 mins.

Indiana Jones and the Last Crusade

Everyone's favorite archeologist adventurer is back in action as Harrison Ford seeks the Holy Grail and the whereabouts of his scholar father Sean Connery. Can he find both and ride off into the sunset before the nasty Nazis cause him wear and tear on another set of clothes? With Julian Glover, Alison Doody, Denholm Elliott, John Rhys-Davies and River Phoenix as young Indiana Jones.

VHS: S11479. $14.95.
Steven Spielberg, USA, 1989, 126 mins.

Indiana Jones and the Temple of Doom

Action-packed, stunt-infested, and with loads of special effects, the long-awaited release of this boxoffice smash (the second in the series) stars Harrison Ford, this time with Kate Capshaw as the female interest, who ended up the new Mrs. Steven Spielberg after the filming. Booming score by John Williams keeps the activity at a fever pitch.

VHS: S01804. $14.95.
Laser: Widescreen. **LD75312. $39.98.**
Steven Spielberg, USA, 1984, 118 mins.

Jaws

The original is a chilling movie about a New England shore community terrorized by shark attacks. Three Oscars including music score and editing. Cameo by Peter Benchley, who wrote the novel upon which film was based. Special collector's edition, letterboxed, featuring interviews with Steven Spielberg. Letterboxed.

VHS: S03692. $19.98.
Laser: LD71438. $149.98.
Steven Spielberg, USA, 1975, 125 mins.

Jurassic Park

Sam Neil, Laura Dern, Jeff Goldblum, and Richard Attenborough star in this sci-fi adventure blockbuster. The recreation of dinosaurs is the concept behind a theme park. Everything seems fine until the science behind this revivifying scheme goes haywire. Life is a dangerous and unpredictable force. Letterboxed.

VHS: S21499. $19.98.
Laser: CLV. **LD74528. $49.98.**
Laser: CAV. **LD74529. $74.98.**
Steven Spielberg, USA, 1993, 126 mins.

The Lost World

Spielberg returns to the land of scary dinosaurs in a film based on Michael Crichton's best seller. Six years ago a bio-engineer (Richard Attenborough) created a theme park filled with dinosaurs. Now he secretly breeds dinosaurs to roam free on an island. But can man co-exist with these powerful critters? That's what Jeff Goldblum and Julianne Moore are bound to discover. Includes a seven-minute featurette with a behind-the-scenes look at the film. VHS letterboxed.

VHS: S32542. $22.98.
Laser: LD76376. $39.98.
Steven Spielberg, USA, 1997, 129 mins.

Poltergeist

When you build a community over a graveyard and don't move the bodies, expect the kind of problems that plague this typically American suburban family. Moving furniture and floating toys lead to alternative dimensions and the lowering of real estate values. With Craig T. Nelson, JoBeth Williams and Heather O'Rourke. Great special effects. Co-written and produced by Steven Spielberg. VHS letterboxed.

VHS: S04502. $19.95.
Laser: CAV, special collector's edition. **LD74490. $39.98.**
DVD: DV60111. $24.98.
Tobe Hooper, USA, 1982, 114 mins.

Raiders of the Lost Ark

Harrison Ford is an adventure-seeking archeologist after rare and well-guarded ancient artifacts. The entertaining Indiana Jones battles Nazi hordes for the sacred Ark of the Covenant and the company of a spunky Karen Allen. Whiz bang thrills and special effects.

VHS: S01882. $14.95.
Steven Spielberg, USA, 1981, 115 mins.

Schindler's List

This Academy Award-winning film tells the story of Oskar Schindler, who saved hundreds of Jews from certain death in Nazi-dominated Europe. Adapted from Thomas Keneally's novel and starring Ben Kingsley, Liam Neeson and Ralph Fiennes. The Collector's Edition includes the novel, a compact disc of the Academy Award-winning score by John Williams and a booklet with an introduction by Steven Spielberg. Letterboxed.

Collector's Edition.
VHS: S21540. $79.95.
Laser: Collector's Edition. Includes soundtrack, CD and book.
LD74526. $139.98.
Standard Edition.
VHS: S21539. $29.95.
Laser: LD74525. $49.98.
Steven Spielberg, USA, 1993, 197 mins.

Twilight Zone—The Movie

Four segments, directed by four different directors in the spirit of the original Rod Serling TV series, including "Kick the Can," "It's a Good Life," "Nighmare at 20,000 Feet," remakes of original episodes and one new episode. Starring Dan Aykroyd, Albert Brooks, John Lithgow, Burgess Meredith, John Larroquette, Scatman Crothers, Selma Diamond, Kathleen Quinlan, Nancy Cartwright, Bill Mumy, Cherie Currie, and Vic Morrow (who died in a helicopter accident while filming).

VHS: S34608. $14.95.
Joe Dante/John Landis/George Miller/Steven Spielberg, USA, 1983, 101 mins.

JAMES IVORY

Autobiography of a Princess

An East Indian princess, long divorced and living in self-enforced exile in London, invites her father's ex-tutor to an annual tea party, where they watch old movie footage of Royal India. In this tightly written character study, James Mason and Madhur Jaffrey celebrate a happier past, conveying among the finest of their performances. From the renowned filmmaking team of James Ivory and Ismail Merchant.

VHS: S15670. $29.95.
Laser: CAV. LD71587. $39.95.
James Ivory, India, 1975, 59 mins.

The Bostonians

A Merchant/Ivory literary adaptation of Henry James' novel. The plot concerns an intriguing sexual triangle. A beautiful though innocent orator (Madeleine Potter) is caught between a stern suffragette (Vanessa Redgrave) and a repressed, upper class lawyer (Christopher Reeve). With Jessica Tandy, Linda Hunt and Wallace Shawn. Adaptation by Ruth Prawer Jhabvala.

VHS: S00171. $19.95.
James Ivory, USA, 1984, 120 mins.

The Europeans

An European aristocrat and her brash younger brother upset the lives of their Boston cousins upon their arrival, in Merchant/Ivory's adaptation of Henry James' novel. Screenplay by Ruth Prawer Jhabvala. With Lee Remick, Robin Ellis, Tim Woodward, Wesley Addy and Lisa Eichhorn.
VHS: S00419. $59.95.
Laser: LD71593. $39.95.
James Ivory, USA, 1979, 90 mins.

The Householder

The first collaboration of producer Ismail Merchant, director James Ivory and novelist and screenwriter Ruth Prawer Jhabvala *(A Room with a View, Howards End)* is this perceptive comedy about the difficulties of a young Indian man trying to adapt to his arranged marriage. It "tells us some eternal truths about the maturity pains a young husband undergoes but also paints a fresh, vivid and pointed picture of an emerging society" (Judith Crist). With Shashi Kapoor, Leela Naidu and Durga Khote.
VHS: S17631. $29.95.
Laser: CLV. **LD72067. $39.95.**
James Ivory, Great Britain, 1962, 101 mins.

Howards End

Merchant/Ivory's wonderfully acted, beautifully constructed adaptation of E.M. Forster's novel about the unconventional love, class struggle and hypocrisy of upper class Edwardian England. The film concerns two sisters (Academy Award winner Emma Thompson and Helena Bonham Carter) and their romantic and personal entanglements with aristocratic, wealthy landowners (Anthony Hopkins and Vanessa Redgrave). Cinematography is by Tony Pierce-Roberts. Academy Award-winning screenplay by Ruth Prawer Jhabvala. With James Wilby, Samuel West and Prunella Scales.
VHS: S18519. $19.95.
Laser: LD71869. $39.95.
James Ivory, Great Britain, 1992, 143 mins.

Jefferson in Paris

Nick Nolte and Greta Scacchi star in this detailed period piece. Thomas Jefferson, one of the United States' founding fathers, had a rather impetuous youthful sojourn in Paris, the City of Light. This fact is the basis for a dramatic recreation of his stay there. A mysterious and worldly woman leads him into a steamy love affair, one that forces him to question old allegiances.
VHS: S26204. $19.95.
Laser: LD75063. $39.99.
James Ivory, USA, 1995, 139 mins.

Maurice

James Ivory directs this sensitive film about the love relationship between two men who meet studying at Cambridge in 1910. Based on the novel by E.M. Forster which was published after his death. That love that dare not speak its name is now a movie. With James Wilby, Hugh Grant, Rupert Graves, Denholm Elliott and Ben Kingsley.
VHS: S06208. $19.98.
Laser: CAV, widescreen. **LD75106. $59.95.**
James Ivory, Great Britain, 1987, 135 mins.

Mr. and Mrs. Bridge

Paul Newman and Joanne Woodward are cast as a conservative Kansas City couple whose marriage comes under close scrutiny as the years go past. Based on two novels by Evan S. Connell, this finely etched family drama spends its time and energies on life's quieter moments. With Blythe Danner, Simon Callow and Kyra Sedgwick. Woodward was nominated for an Oscar.
VHS: S13876. $19.98.
James Ivory, USA, 1990, 127 mins.

Noon Wine

Katherine Ann Porter's short story about a Swedish immigrant who finds work on a small Texas farm, and through no fault of his own, becomes the focal point of strife. Starring Fred Ward *(Remo Williams)* and produced by Ismail Merchant and James Ivory *(Room with a View)*.
VHS: S05320. $24.95.
James Ivory, USA, 1984, 60 mins.

Quartet

A James Ivory film based on the book by Jean Rhys, which stars Maggie Smith, Alan Bates, Isabelle Adjani and Anthony Higgins. These fine performers are involved in a 1920's Bohemian drama set in Paris, wherein seduction and decadence are the name of the game. Not to be confused with the film of the same name based on the writing of Somerset Maugham.
VHS: S06184. $19.98.
James Ivory, Great Britain/France, 1981, 101 mins.

Remains of the Day

In this drama, the relationship between a butler and a housekeeper, played by Anthony Hopkins and Emma Thompson, is stifled by the demands of conflicting duties. The household they manage plays host to important political gatherings attended by fascist leaders. Their roles may very well hasten the demise of their country, not to mention their growing affection for one another. Based on the novel by Kazuo Ishiguri.
VHS: S20777. $19.95.
Laser: LD72389. $39.95.
James Ivory, Great Britain, 1993, 134 mins.

Room with a View

Maggie Smith stars in this acclaimed film, based on the E.M. Forster novel, which evokes the manners and mores of an era. A witty, lush film with Denholm Elliott, Judi Dench and Simon Callow.
VHS: S02767. $19.98.
Laser: LD71312. $34.98.
James Ivory, Great Britain, 1986, 117 mins.

Roseland

This Merchant/Ivory trilogy centers on romance in the famous New York dance hall, the Roseland Ballroom, and is a gentle, spirited work redolent in the memories, ambitions and idealized preoccupations of the forlorn souls who inhabit its room. With Christopher Walken, Geraldine Chaplin, Teresa Wright and Lilia Skala. Written by Ruth Prawer Jhabvala.
VHS: S01134. $29.95.
Laser: CLV. **LD72068. $39.95.**
James Ivory, USA, 1977, 104 mins.

Savages

James Ivory's offbeat look at society, in which a naked band of primitives, disturbed from their sacrifices by a croquet ball, discover a deserted mansion, and begin to "get civilized." But the line between savages and civilization is not that strong.
VHS: S01160. $29.95.
Laser: CLV. **LD72069. $39.95.**
James Ivory, USA, 1973, 108 mins.

Slaves of New York

The Tama Janowitz novel of the young and terminally trendy in the Big Apple art community stars Bernadette Peters as a funky hat designer who lives with an up and coming artist who mistreats her. Author Janowitz plays her best friend in a few scenes. Cast includes Madeleine Potter, Mary Beth Hurt, Nick Corri, Chris Sarandon and Adam Coleman Howard as Stash Stotz.
VHS: S10611. $89.95.
James Ivory, USA, 1989, 115 mins.

Surviving Picasso

The premier artist of our century, played by one of the finest actors of our time. Academy Award winner Anthony Hopkins gives a towering performance, as Pablo Picasso, focusing on the charismatic painter's other great passion: romancing women spellbound by his genius. "Anthony Hopkins' most vital performance since *The Silence of the Lambs*" (Janet Maslin, *The New York Times*).
VHS: S30606. $19.98.
Laser: LD76136. $39.98.
James Ivory, USA, 1996, 126 mins.

FRANCIS F. COPPOLA

Apocalypse Now (Remastered)

Francis Ford Coppola's Vietnam War epic conveys a madness with parallels to Joseph Conrad's *Heart of Darkness*. Lieutenant Willard receives orders to seek out a renegade military outpost led by errant officer Colonel Kurtz, and to "terminate his command with extreme prejudice." This newly enhanced version features a remastered soundtrack in Dolby surround stereo.
VHS: S00066. $29.95.
Francis F. Coppola, USA, 1979, 153 mins.

Bram Stoker's Dracula

Francis Ford Coppola's adaptation of Stoker's novel emphasizes sexual undertones. Gary Oldman's Dracula is unhinged as he tries to seduce the beautiful Winona Ryder and destroy his rivals. Anthony Hopkins is Van Helsing, the determined doctor obsessed with the count's destruction. With Keanu Reeves, Sadie Frost and Tom Waits. VHS letterboxed.
VHS: S18655. $19.95.
Laser: Features documentary *The Making of Bram Stoker's Dracula*. **LD71875. $49.95.**
DVD: DV60021. $24.95.
Francis F. Coppola, USA, 1992, 126 mins.

The Conversation

Gene Hackman is brilliant as Harry Caul, the surveillance man who becomes the object of surveillance himself. Coppola's great achievement is in evoking an obsessive sense of paranoia as Hackman struggles to free himself from the maze of secrecy and murder. With Cindy Williams, Harrison Ford, Frederic Forrest.
Laser: LD75356. $29.98.
Francis F. Coppola, USA, 1974, 113 mins.

Dementia 13

Coppola's second film, produced by Roger Corman, is the eerie story of a greedy woman who sets out to gain control of a fortune. Her actions trigger a series of brutal and gory axe murders. The psychological makeup of each suspect is explored in this chilling cult classic filmed in the Republic of Ireland. With William Campell, Luana Anders and Patrick Magee.
VHS: S18175. $19.95.
Laser: LD75940. $49.95.
Francis F. Coppola, USA, 1963, 75 mins.

Finian's Rainbow

A wily Irishman, his beautiful daughter and a feisty leprechaun come to a magical valley where anything can happen—and does—in this film version of the famous Broadway classic. Fred Astaire and Petula Clark star.
VHS: S04974. $19.98.
Laser: Letterboxed. **LD71141. $39.98.**
Francis F. Coppola, USA, 1968, 142 mins.

The Godfather

An epic featuring Marlon Brando as the patriarch of the Corleone family, masterfully balanced between the story of family life and the family crime business. With Al Pacino, James Caan, Robert Duvall, Diane Keaton. Based on Mario Puzo's novel. Music by Nino Rota. Letterboxed.
VHS: S00509. $24.95.
Francis F. Coppola, USA, 1972, 171 mins.

The Godfather Part II

A companion piece to the original *Godfather*, this continues the saga of two generations of successive power in the Corleone family. Coppola tells the story of the rise of a young Don Vito, played by Robert De Niro, and the ascension of the new Don Michael, played by Al Pacino. Letterboxed.
VHS: S00510. $24.95.
Francis F. Coppola, USA, 1974, 200 mins.

The Godfather Part III

The saga of the Corleone family is continued under the direction of Francis Ford Coppola. This video release contains the director's cut with additional footage not included in its theatrical release. Al Pacino returns in the title role as an aging Italian-American trying very hard to be legit, without success. The plot involves banking with the Vatican, pursuing a career in opera, and killing your enemies. With Diane Keaton, Talia Shire, Andy Garcia, Eli Wallach, Joe Mantegna, Sophia Coppola, Bridget Fonda and George Hamilton in the role for which Robert Duvall asked for too much money. Letterboxed.
VHS: S14795. $24.95.
Francis F. Coppola, USA, 1990, 170 mins.

The Godfather Collection

Contains the individual videotapes of *The Godfather, The Godfather Part II* and *The Godfather Part III*, packaged together in a special gift box. Letterboxed.
VHS: S12851. $64.95.
Francis F. Coppola, USA, 1972-1990, 541 mins.

The Godfather Trilogy: 1901-1980

Director Francis Ford Coppola supervised the re-editing of *The Godfather, The Godfather Part II* and *The Godfather Part III* into one continuous film. Spanning nearly eight decades, *The Godfather Trilogy: 1901-1980* is the chronological telling of the legacy of the Corleone family. As a special bonus, this package also contains *The Godfather Family: A Look Inside*, a 73-minute program which goes behind the scenes of the epic saga, and a comprehensive 28-page companion booklet as well. Packaged in an elegant, all-leather deluxe gift box. Six-tape set.
VHS: S13534. $149.95.

Hearts of Darkness: A Filmmaker's Apocalypse

A riveting behind-the-scenes look at the making of Francis Ford Coppola's *Apocalypse Now*. The film combines interviews with documentary footage shot on location in the Philippines by Eleanor Coppola. This is a must-see for anyone with the slightest interest in how Hollywood movies get made. With Martin Sheen, Dennis Hopper, Larry Fishburne, Robert Duvall, Sam Bottoms, Frederic Forrest, George Lucas, John Milius and Francis Ford Coppola. Watch Marlon Brando improvise his lines and eat a bug.
VHS: S16459. $19.95.
Fax Bahr/George Hickenlooper/Eleanor Coppola, USA, 1991, 96 mins.

New York Stories

Three major directors, one city. Martin Scorsese, Francis Ford Coppola and Woody Allen offer an omnibus of short films based on life in the Big Apple. Scorsese leads off with *Life Lessons*, in which master painter Nick Nolte puts the moves on art student Rosanna Arquette. *Life with Zoe* is written by Coppola and his daughter Sofia. It tells the story of a precocious little girl who lives in a fancy hotel. Allen tops off the trio with *Oedipus Wrecks*, a comedy about an unmarried middle aged man whose problems with his pushy mother suddenly involve the entire city. With Woody Allen, Mia Farrow, Julie Kavner and Mae Questel, the voice of Betty Boop, as Woody's mom.

Laser: LD71255. $39.99.

Martin Scorsese/Francis F. Coppola/Woody Allen, USA, 1988, 123 mins

Outsiders

A powerful film based on a classic S.E. Hinton novel about teen hopes, fears and rebellion. Coppola has brought together an ensemble of young actors including Matt Dillon, Emilio Estevez, Tom Cruise and Ralph Macchio.

VHS: S00984. $19.98.

Laser: Letterboxed. **LD74713. $34.98.**

Francis F. Coppola, USA, 1983, 91 mins.

Peggy Sue Got Married

Francis Ford Coppola returned to the screen in triumphant form in this drama starring Kathleen Turner, who gets the chance to change her life. The mother of two coping with impending divorce, a freak mishap at her high school reunion sends her back in time, giving her a chance to create an entirely new future for herself.

VHS: Out of print. For rental only.

Laser: LD71274. $34.98.

Francis F. Coppola, USA, 1986, 103 mins.

The Rain People

Pregnant Long Island housewife (Shirley Knight) leaves home and goes traveling across America. Along the way in this strongly acted, sensitive drama she meets James Caan, Robert Duvall and some lesser known American actors, one of whom owns a pistol.

VHS: S04179. $19.98.

Francis F. Coppola, USA, 1969, 102 mins.

The Rainmaker

Matt Damon *(Good Will Hunting)* stars as an inexperienced attorney who, together with his crafty sidekick (Danny DeVito), challenges corporate America in this compelling John Grisham tale of legal intrigue and moral bankruptcy. With Jon Voight, Mickey Rourke and Claire Danes.

VHS: S34260. $104.99.

Francis F. Coppola, USA, 1997, 137 mins.

Rumble Fish

In black and white with color sequences, *Rumble Fish* is a visually stunning adaptation of S.E. Hinton's novel, starring Matt Dillon and Mickey Rourke as brothers trying to break out of their urban trap. With Dennis Hopper. Music by Stewart Copeland (Police).

VHS: S01138. $19.95.

Laser: Letterboxed. **LD74470. $34.98.**

Francis F. Coppola, USA, 1983, 94 mins.

Tonight for Sure

Francis Coppola's first film, an exploitation comedy, done while he was attending UCLA. The story centers on two gentlemen trying to stamp out indecency, which gives Coppola the excuse to show a bevy of naked women running through the desert.

VHS: S01359. $29.95.

Francis F. Coppola, USA, 1961, 66 mins.

Tucker: The Man and His Dream

Jeff Bridges is Preston Tucker, American inventor and the designer of an automobile too many years ahead of its time to succeed against the major car makers in Michigan. A brilliant, touching family drama about a visionary individual whose life director Coppola has been trying to film for years. With Martin Landau, Joan Allen, Frederic Forrest, Mako, Lloyd Bridges and Jay O. Sanders as William Kirby, Tucker's lawyer.

VHS: S08354. $19.95.

Laser: Widescreen. **LD75137. $24.99.**

Francis F. Coppola, USA, 1988, 111 mins.

You're a Big Boy Now

Francis Ford Coppola's second feature film deals with the problems of surviving a sheltered childhood in a large and inviting city like New York. Peter Kastner is the innocent willing to be corrupted by Elizabeth Hartman. Cast includes Karen Black, Julie Harris, Rip Torn, Geraldine Page and Dolph Sweet as a tough cop.

VHS: S06207. $19.98.

Laser: LD76962. $34.98.

Francis F. Coppola, USA, 1966, 98 mins.

SAM SHEPARD

Far North

Sam Shepard makes his feature film directorial debut with the story of an eccentric Minnesota farming family. Charles Durning is the opinionated patriarch who wants oldest daughter Jessica Lange to shoot the family horse. To shoot or not to shoot, that is but one of the questions raised in this quirk-ridden drama. With Tess Harper, Patricia Arquette, Donald Moffat and Ann Wedgeworth.

VHS: S09144. $79.98.

Sam Shepard, USA, 1988, 90 mins.

Silent Tongue

River Phoenix in his final screen appearance is joined by Richard Harris, Dermot Mulroney and Alan Bates in this western about honor and love. A young woman, who is half Native American, is kidnapped, setting off a desperate struggle to set her free. Justice can never be silenced.

VHS: S21104. $19.95.

Sam Shepard, USA, 1993, 101 mins.

american comedy

100 Years of Comedy

Journey on a rip-roaring trip through the world of cinema comedy with the funniest moments in the history of Hollywood, from the slapstick of the silents through the screwball comedies of the '30s and '40s, to Hollywood's most recent comedies. 120 mins.
VHS: S32420. $19.99.

48 Hours

Street-weary cop Nick Nolte springs smart-aleck convict Eddie Murphy for two days in order to capture a mad dog killer. James Remar is the dangerous quarry and Murphy's ex-partner in crime. A violent, comic thriller from Walter Hill. With David Patrick Kelly and Sonny Landham. The redneck bar scene is a classic.
VHS: S02354. $19.95.
Walter Hill, USA, 1982, 97 mins.

60 Years with Bob Hope

This documentary takes a rare look at the life of the remarkable performer. Includes some exclusive, never-before-seen footage. USA, 56 mins.
VHS: S15028. $19.95.

Abbott and Costello

Nine feature films showing the zany duo at their wackiest.
Abbott and Costello Meet Dr. Jekyll and Mr. Hyde. You'll laugh your way through the foggy London street as Abbott and Costello take on Boris Karloff in a hilarious spoof of the famed horror classic. Directed by Charles Lamont, USA, 1952, 77 mins.
VHS: S10443. $14.95.
Abbott and Costello Meet Frankenstein. As railroad baggage clerks, Abbott and Costello receive a strange shipment—the not-so-dead remains of Dracula and Frankenstein's monster. Directed by Charles T. Barton, USA, 1948, 83 mins.
VHS: S10440. $14.95.
Laser: LD70010. $34.98.
Abbott and Costello: Buck Privates. Abbott and Costello play two dim-witted salesmen who accidentally enlist in the Army and turn it upside down in this hilarious WWII comedy. Directed by Arthur Lubin, USA, 1941, 84 mins.
VHS: S10441. $14.95.
Abbott and Costello: Hit the Ice. Abbott and Costello get mixed up with gangsters, gun molls and gumshoes in one of their funniest, zaniest comedies. Directed by Charles Lamont, USA, 1943, 89 mins.
VHS: S10445. $14.95.
Abbott and Costello: Hold That Ghost. Bud and Lou inherit an abandoned roadhouse belonging to a rubbed-out monster, in one of the funniest Abbott and Costello movies of all time. Directed by Arthur Lubin, USA, 1941, 86 mins.
VHS: S10442. $14.95.
Abbott and Costello: Naughty Nineties. Abbott and Costello keep the laughs flowing on a Mississippi showboat, performing many of their most famous hits, including the hysterical "Who's On First?" dialog that has become one of the most popular comedy routines ever captured on film. Directed by Jean Yarborough, USA, 1945, 72 mins.
VHS: S10447. $14.95.
Abbott and Costello: Time of Their Lives. Alternate title: *The Ghost Steps Out.* A ghostly Lou Costello haunts a nervous Bud Abbott in a mansion built during the Revolutionary War. Directed by Charles T. Barton, USA, 1946, 82 mins.
VHS: S10446. $14.95.
Abbott and Costello: Who Done It? Abbott and Costello are would-be radio writers who find themselves involved in real murder during the recording of a "whodunit" play. Directed by Erle C. Kenton, USA, 1942, 77 mins.
VHS: S10444. $14.95.

The Abbott and Costello Collection

The comic misadventures of Abbott & Costello in three of their hits: S. Sylvan Simon's 1942 musical *Rio Rito* and the 1945 *Abbott & Costello in Hollywood*, and Charles Riesner's *Lost in a Harem*.
VHS: S17326. $49.92.

Abbott and Costello Comin' Round the Mountain

Together the famed comic duo are off for the hills, where their antics make them stand out even more. This pair of not very slick city slickers need to do more than don a coonskin cap to fit in. Maybe they should just give up and laugh along with everyone else.
VHS: S21315. $14.98.
Charles Lamont, USA, 1951, 77 mins.

Abbott and Costello Go to Mars

Only the presence of this pair could explain the mix-up. Though they are supposed to be off to Mars according to the title, they actually end up on Venus, where there is a brief appearance by Anita Ekberg. Maybe the escaped gangster on board is to blame.
VHS: S21314. $14.98.
Charles Lamont, USA, 1953, 77 mins.

Abbott and Costello in Hollywood

Here our two zany friends play a pair of barbers who want their own Hollywood barber shop—and to get it, they find themselves in the middle of numerous close shaves. With cameo appearances by Lucille Ball, Rags Ragland and Preston Foster. Look for a young Dean Stockwell in the supporting cast. USA, 1945, 83 mins.
VHS: S15425. $19.98.

Abbott and Costello in the Foreign Legion

Walter Slezak is the tough sergeant who must whip these two comic mishaps into fighting shape. Can his tough ways succeed against the bumbling antics of these hopelessly funny ne'er-do-wells? With the desert sun beating down on them all, someone has got to give in.
VHS: S21313. $14.98.
Charles Lamont, USA, 1950, 80 mins.

Abbott and Costello Meet the Invisible Man

One of the duo's best works has them playing private detectives who use an invisible potion to help a boxer framed by a notorious mobster. With Nancy Guild, Arthur Franz, and Sheldon Leonard.
VHS: S17260. $14.98.
Charles Lamont, USA, 1951, 82 mins.

Abbott and Costello Meet the Keystone Kops

In this period piece, the famed comic duo confronts one of silent film's most enduring legendary institutions, the Keystone Kops. Fred Clark is great as a conniving producer, proving that Hollywood's evil ways started early. It's a laugh-filled adventure into entertainment history.
VHS: S21312. $14.98.
Charles Lamont, USA, 1955, 75 mins.

Abbott and Costello Meet the Mummy

The two comics are caught in a thick web of intrigue and adventure as they pursue a beautiful villain, a highly valuable tomb and a fiendish mummy that haunts the entire proceedings. With Marie Windsor, Michael Ansara and Dan Seymour.
VHS: S19070. $14.98.
Charles Lamont, USA, 1955, 79 mins.

Abbott and Costello Vol. I Who's on First

What's on second, I don't know...third base. One of this country's classic comedy routines is now available on video. The version presented here is the one perfected on the comedy team's famous television series. Featuring the manager of the *St. Louis Wolves* and much, much more. USA, 60 mins.
VHS: S15027. $19.95.

Abbott and Costello: Mexican Hayride

Adapted from an original Cole Porter musical without the songs, this Abbott and Costello vehicle unfolds south of the border, with the boys desperately tracking down an old mine deed. With John Hubbard, Pedro de Cordoba, and Fritz Field.
VHS: S17259. $14.98.
Charles Barton, USA, 1947, 77 mins.

Ace Ventura: When Nature Calls

Animal sleuth and hair style freak Ace Ventura returns in this outrageous sequel. Ace and his companion, the monkey Spike, go to Africa to rescue a sacred bat that's been kidnapped. There they manage to baffle an entire continent with their absurd but eminently watchable antics. Starring Jim Carrey as Ace Ventura.
VHS: S27306. $19.98.
Laser: LD75479. $34.98.
Steve Oedekerk, USA, 1995, 94 mins.

Addams Family

Raul Julia, Anjelica Huston, Christopher Lloyd and Christina Ricci head a lively cast of macabre but upbeat characters created by the late cartoonist Charles Addams. The plot concerns foisting a phony Fester on the family in order to find the fabulous hidden Addams fortune. Ace cinematographer Barry Sonnenfeld *(Raising Arizona)* makes his directorial debut. Nominated for an Oscar for Best Costume Design.
VHS: Out of print. For rental only.
Laser: Widescreen. **LD75140. $34.98.**
Barry Sonnenfeld, USA, 1991, 102 mins.

Addams Family Values

It is always refreshing to get a new perspective on the endlessly dreary debate of family values. Gomez and Morticia (Raul Julia and Anjelica Huston) have their own contribution to make on this subject. It may disturb or frighten some, but then again what could be more horrible than a close look at someone else's family?
VHS: S20874. $14.95.
Laser: Widescreen. **LD75139. $34.98.**
Barry Sonnenfeld, USA, 1993, 90 mins.

Adventures in Babysitting

Elizabeth Shue stars as babysitter Chris Parker in this comic nightmare in which a normal suburban babysitter and her three young charges find themselves swept up in a series of outrageous events.
VHS: S06369. $19.95.
Chris Columbus, USA, 1987, 102 mins.

Affairs of Annabel

One of Lucy's funniest comedies. Ball plays a nutty actress kept in line by her scheming press agent.
VHS: S10646. $19.98.
Ben Stoloff, USA, 1938, 68 mins.

Africa Screams

Abbott & Costello turn up on expedition in Africa. They are after a giant gorilla, but nothing is as simple or organized as it would seem. With Bud Abbott, Lou Costello, Hillary Brooke, Max Baer, and Clyde Beatty.
VHS: S34191. $14.95.
Charles Barton, USA, 1949, 80 mins.

After the Thin Man

William Powell and Myrna Loy recreate their famous roles as Nick and Nora Charles in an adaptation of a Dashiell Hammett story set on Nob Hill in San Francisco. With assists from their faithful dog Asta, and James Stewart.
VHS: S00023. $24.95.
W.S. Van Dyke, USA, 1936, 113 mins.

Aggie Appleby, Maker of Men

An early film from the director of *Top Hat* and *Shall We Dance*. A comedy of errors occurs when a wimpy society type must take the place of the title character's macho boyfriend. Wynne Gibson stars as Aggie. Charles Farrell is Adoniram Schlump and William Gargan is the brawny Red Branahan. Based on a play by Joseph O. Kesserling. Also known as *Cupid in the Rough*.
VHS: S15773. $19.98.
Mark Sandrich, USA, 1933, 73 mins.

Air Raid Wardens

A late period Laurel and Hardy World War II comedy. Laurel and Hardy are rejected from the armed services, and get entangled in a German spy ring which is trying to destroy a large munitions factory. With Edgar Kennedy, Jacqueline White, and Donald Meek.
VHS: S17892. $19.98.
Edward Sedgwick, USA, 1943, 67 mins.

Airplane!

A very funny spoof of the airport pictures of the 70's, with a nonstop stream of gags from beginning to end. With Robert Hays, Peter Graves, Robert Stack, Lloyd Bridges, Julie Hagerty.
VHS: S09565. $14.95.
Laser: Remastered. **LD75142. $34.98.**
Jerry Zucker/Jim Abrahams/David Zucker, USA, 1980, 88 mins.

Alias Jesse James
An insurance salesman (Bob Hope) is assigned to keep the deadliest outlaw in history alive in this "downright hilarious" *(Time)* wild west farce featuring hysterical cameos from Western stars. With Rhonda Fleming.
VHS: S31516. $14.95.
Norman Z. McLeod, USA, 1959, 92 mins.

All Night Long
Gene Hackman stars in this comedy about middle-age crises. He is a recently demoted drugstore executive who responds by rebelling. He divorces his wife and gets involved with a distant relative while hoping to invent something miraculous. This new career and life lead him into contact with all kinds of creatures of the night. Barbra Streisand, Diane Ladd and Dennis Quaid also star.
VHS: S22031. $7.95.
Jean-Claude Tramont, USA, 1981, 100 mins.

Amazon Women on the Moon
A comedy compilation from five filmmakers of short skits and spoofs on a variety of topics including modern dating, personalized video adult selections, the dangers of social diseases, modern technology and landing on a planet with hostile armed women in charge. With Arsenio Hall, Rosanna Arquette, Carrie Fisher, Griffin Dunne, Steve Forrest and Sybil Danning.
VHS: S05928. $79.95.
John Landis/Joe Dante/Peter Horton/Carl Gottlieb, USA, 1987, 85 mins.

Americathon
The future seems bleak in 1998 America when the entire country teeters on the edge of financial ruin. George Carlin narrates this hilarious yarn about a motley group of public figures who organize a telethon to get Uncle Sam out of debt. Stars a host of familiar faces, including Harvey Korman, John Ritter, Fred Willard, Jay Leno, Zane Buzby, Elvis Costello and Meatloaf.
VHS: S16277. $19.98.
Neal Israel, USA, 1979, 84 mins.

And God Spoke
This hilarious mockumentary continues in the tradition of *Spinal Tap*. It shows the crazy antics that go on behind the scenes during the filming of a movie based on the Bible. Troubles of all sorts crop up, particularly financial ones. The first commandment of movie-making must be, "Don't Go Over Budget."
VHS: S23114. $92.98.
Laser: LD75146. $34.98.
Arthur Borman, USA, 1994, 82 mins.

And Justice for All
Al Pacino stars as an angry lawyer in a sharply critical black comedy about the contemporary legal system. Written by Barry Levinson and Valerie Curtin. Jack Warden stars as a crazy judge. John Forsythe plays a sadistic member of the bench. With Craig T. Nelson, Christine Lahti, Jeffrey Tambor and Sam Levene. A film that reinforces the notion that Shakespeare had the right idea of what to do with lawyers.
VHS: S10375. $19.95.
Laser: LD75527. $39.95.
Norman Jewison, USA, 1979, 117 mins.

Angel on My Shoulder
Paul Muni is a murdered convict given a chance to do even worse when the Devil offers to return him to the land of the living to tarnish the reputation of an honorable judge. A sweet fantasy also starring Claude Rains, Anne Baxter and George Cleveland.
VHS: S09829. $19.95.
Archie Mayo, USA, 1946, 101 mins.

Angels in the Outfield
Danny Glover, Tony Danza and Christopher Lloyd star in this sentimental remake of the story of a preteen boy who prays that the team can win so that he can be reunited with his father.
VHS: S23226. $19.99.
Laser: Letterboxed. **LD74809. $39.99.**
William Dear, USA, 1994, 105 mins.

Angels over Broadway
Written and directed by Ben Hecht at his usual breakneck pace, this black comedy tells of a con man (Douglas Fairbanks, Jr.) who undergoes a change of heart and who, with the assistance of a call-girl (Rita Hayworth), helps turn around the life of his mark. An offbeat morality play.
VHS: S01588. $19.95.
Ben Hecht, USA, 1940, 80 mins.

Angie
Academy-Award winner Geena Davis is the perfect comedienne for this humorous look at impending motherhood. Her predicament drives friends and family crazy, but she manages to find her way through this situation with laughter and verve, in New York City, no less.
VHS: S21361. $96.98.
Martha Coolidge, USA, 1994, 108 mins.

Angus
In this comic coming-of-age story, Angus is a teen terror who cuts up on the football field but still can't manage to fit in at high school. Luckily, his geeky friend Troy and his chess-playing grandfather are there to help Angus turn a practical joke into an evening of magic. With Kathy Bates, George C. Scott and Rita Moreno, and introducing Charlie Talbert as Angus.
VHS: S27213. $19.98.
Laser: LD75483. $39.98.
Patrick Read Johnson, USA, 1995, 87 mins.

Animal Crackers
The four Marx Brothers in the uproariously funny film based on the George S. Kaufman musical. Groucho introduced the character of Captain Spaulding, whose song became the theme song of "You Bet Your Life."
VHS: S00053. $19.95.
Laser: LD70096. $34.98.
Victor Heerman, USA, 1930, 98 mins.

Animal House
Tasteless but extremely funny, thanks to John Belushi's rowdy depiction of Bluto Blutarsky, chief animal of the Delta fraternity.
VHS: S00055. $19.95.
John Landis, USA, 1978, 109 mins.

Annabel Takes a Tour/Maid's Night Out
A comedy double feature. Lucy plays the wacky Annabel. Then a rich man's son becomes a milkman (also with Lucille Ball).
VHS: S10647. $19.98.
Lew Landers, USA, 1938, 131 mins.

Another Thin Man
William Powell and Myrna Loy re-team for the third screen adventure of Nick and Nora Charles. They are joined by Nick Jr. Will parenthood deter the solving of society murders? Don't be silly. Asta can always babysit. Script by Dashiell Hammett. B&W.
VHS: S03552. $24.95.
W.S. Van Dyke, USA, 1939, 102 mins.

Another You
Richard Pryor and Gene Wilder are paired in this comedy in which Pryor has to do community service after being paroled by caring for Wilder who has just been released from a sanitarium. The two immediately get mixed up in a scam.
VHS: S21477. $19.95.
Maurice Phillips, USA, 1991, 98 mins.

Arthur
Arthur, played by actor Dudley Moore, has $750 million in the bank and yet he's drunk and unhappy almost every waking hour of his life. Enter Liza Minnelli. Boy meets girl; boy loses girl; will boy get girl back? Also starring John Gielgud.
VHS: S14564. $19.95.
Laser: Digital. **LD74686. $24.98.**
DVD: DV60069. $24.98.
Steve Gordon, USA, 1981, 97 mins.

Arthur 2: On the Rocks
Dudley Moore recreates his Oscar-nominated role as tipsy millionaire Arthur Bach, who is swindled out of his fortune by the father of his ex-fiance. Liza Minnelli returns as the devoted ex-wife who must teach Arthur how to be poor. Very funny. 113 mins.
VHS: S08463. $19.98.
Laser: LD70508. $24.98.

As Good As It Gets
Jack Nicholson and Helen Hunt star in Oscar-winning performances in James L. Brooks' hit comedy. Nicholson is the Scrooge-like Melvin Udall, a cranky, bigoted, obsessive-compulsive writer whose life is turned upside down when single mom/waitress Carol (Hunt), the only waitress who will tolerate Melvin, must leave her job to care for her sick son, making it impossivle for Melvin to eat breakfast. In addition, when Melvin's gay artist neighbor Simon (Greg Kinnear) is injured in a robbery, Melvin gets stuck taking care of Simon's dog. The dog warms Melvin's heart, and an unlikely friendship develops between Melvin, Carol and Simon. Letterboxed.
VHS: S34261. $22.99.
Laser: LD76945. $39.98.
DVD: DV60252. $24.98.
James L. Brooks, USA, 1997, 138 mins.

At the Circus
The Marx Brothers try to save Wilson's Wonder Circus from a loan shark, a strongman and a midget and find themselves with Margaret Dumont and a gorilla swinging from a trapeze. With Eve Arden.
VHS: S01826. $19.95.
Laser: LD70156. $39.98.
Edward Buzzell, USA, 1939, 87 mins.

At War with the Army
Dean Martin and Jerry Lewis in their first starring vehicle follow in the tradition of previous comedic greats and attempt a service comedy. The title tells all. With Polly Bergen, Mike Kellin and Angela Greene. Watch for the soda machine gag. B&W.
VHS: S05060. $29.95.
Hal Walker, USA, 1950, 93 mins.

Austin Powers: International Man of Mystery
Frozen in the '60s, swinging London secret agent Austin Powers (Mike Myers, *Wayne's World*) is thawed back into action to once again battle his enemy, Dr. Evil (also played by Myers). With his sexy sidekick Ms. Kensington (Elizabeth Hurley, *Dangerous Ground*), the time-warped swinger must stop Dr. Evil's outrageous plot to control the world—and get hip to the fact that there's no free love in the '90s. With Michael York, Robert Wagner, Mimi Rogers and Carrie Fisher.
VHS: S32236. $19.98.
Jay Roach, USA, 1997, 90 mins.

The Awful Truth
Wildly funny romp which won the Academy Award opens when a battling couple files for divorce. The only hitch seems to be who will get custody of their beloved terrier, Mr. Smith. Cary Grant and Irene Dunne co-star in this very wacky comedy.
VHS: S00083. $19.95.
Leo McCarey, USA, 1937, 92 mins.

Baby Boom
Diane Keaton is J.C. Wiatt, a Harvard MBA grad and a corporate executive known as the Dragon Lady. Her business and personal life are turned upside down when she inherits an infant girl from a deceased cousin she hasn't seen in years. Eventually she moves to Vermont and meets Sam Shepard and starts a business marketing gourmet baby food. With Harold Ramis and Michelle and Kristina Kennedy as Elizabeth.
VHS: S29396. $19.95.
Laser: Chapter search. Includes original theatrical trailer. **LD71638. $29.98.**
Charles Shyer, USA, 1987, 103 mins.

Bachelor Apartment
Lowell Sherman stars, along with a cast of beautiful women (Irene Dunne, Mae Murray, Claudia Dell, Bess Flowers), in the story of a certified ladies man who shuffles his girlfriends back and forth.
VHS: S13360. $19.98.
Lowell Sherman, USA, 1931, 77 mins.

Bachelor Mother
A department store employee, played buoyantly by Ginger Rogers, discovers an abandoned baby and is quickly mistaken for its mother; the misunderstandings continue as the store owner's son is then thought to be the baby's father. A delightful comedy, also starring David Niven, Charles Coburn and Frank Albertson.
VHS: S02150. $19.95.
Garson Kanin, USA, 1939, 82 mins.

Back to the Future
Michael J. Fox is a teenager of the 80's who must travel back in time to make sure his parents meet. One problem is that Mom thinks the son is a lot cuter than his future Dad. Christopher Lloyd is a standout as the scientist who made this all possible. With Lea Thompson and Crispin Glover. Primo frantic entertainment.
Laser: Letterboxed. **LD74947. $34.98.**
Robert Zemeckis, USA, 1985, 116 mins.

Back to the Future II
Michael J. Fox and Christopher Lloyd reprise their roles as Marty McFly and Doc Brown in this new adventure. An exhilarating visit by Marty and the Doc to the year 2015 seemingly resolves a few problems with the future McFly family. But when the two return home, they soon discover someone has tampered with time to produce a nightmarish Hill Valley, 1985. Their only hope is to once again get back to 1955 and save the future.
VHS: S12283. $19.95.
Robert Zemeckis, USA, 1989, 104 mins.

The Bank Dick
As a reward for capturing a robber, W.C. Fields is given the job as a bank security guard. A wonderfully funny romp in what is often considered Fields' best film.
VHS: S03323. $29.95.
Laser: LD70014. $34.98.
Eddie Cline, USA, 1940, 74 mins.

Barbarians at the Gate
A hilarious satire about the go go 80s, as greed and narcissism ruled American big business, encompassing a surreal landscape of junk bonds, high rollers and corporate raiders. Based on the book by Bryan Burrough and John Helyar, this HBO film is a witty examination of the personalties, behind-the-scenes intrigue and power plays to acquire RJ Nabisco. "A sharp-toothed satire and there's a smart, sassy cast to bring it to life" *(Houston Post)*. Screenplay by Larry Gelbart *(Tootsie)*. With James Garner, Jonathan Pryce, Peter Riegert and Joanna Cassidy.
VHS: S19238. $19.98.
Laser: LD75156. $34.98.
Glenn Jordan, USA, 1993, 107 mins.

Barefoot in the Park
Jane Fonda and Robert Redford star in this breezy film adaptation of the Neil Simon comedy about newly weds living in a five-story walk-up apartment. Charles Boyer plays Victor Velasco, their Greenwich Village neighbor and bon vivant. With Mildred Natwick as Fonda's mother.
VHS: S02084. $19.95.
Laser: LD75361. $29.98.
Gene Saks, USA, 1967, 106 mins.

Bathing Beauty
Red Skelton enrolls in a girl's college to be near his swimming-coach wife Esther Williams. A lavish piece of escapist entertainment filled with South American music and spectacular water ballet sequences.
VHS: S14163. $19.98.
Laser: LD72118. $34.98.
George Sidney, USA, 1944, 101 mins.

Batteries Not Included
When an unscrupulous real estate developer sends thugs into a deteriorating tenement to get rid of the last five residents, they need nothing short of a miracle to stay where they are. A delightful fantasy starring Jessica Tandy and Hume Cronyn.
VHS: S07294. $19.95.
Matthew Robbins, USA, 1987, 107 mins.

Bedtime for Bonzo
It's Ronald Reagan proving that environment, not heredity, determines a youngster's future. RR decides to bring up a chimpanzee as a human baby in order to prove his theory. A classic in a league all by itself.
VHS: S00114. $14.95.
Fred De Cordova, USA, 1951, 83 mins.

Bedtime Story
In his first comedic role, Marlon Brando joins David Niven to portray two charming scoundrels who prey on wealthy single women, in this lighthearted romantic comedy set on the Riviera. While masquerading as a deposed Middle European prince, Niven's plans to oust his competitor backfires when the brash Brando portrays Niven's dim-witted brother.
VHS: S10449. $14.98.
Ralph Levy, USA, 1963, 99 mins.

Beethoven
Ivan Reitman produced this appealing family comedy that stars the talented deadpan wit Charles Grodin as the father of a family that welcomes the 185-pound dog who slowly asserts his authority and control over the rest of the family. With Bonnie Hunt and Dean Jones. Written by Edmond Dantes and Amy Holden Jones.
VHS: S17341. $24.98.
DVD: DV60157. $24.98.
Brian Levant, USA, 1992, 95 mins.

Being There
Sublimely funny and bitingly satiric comedy featuring Peter Sellers as a simple-minded gardener who knows only what he watches on television. With Shirley MacLaine and Melvyn Douglas.
VHS: S02823. $19.98.
Laser: LD70522. $29.98.
Hal Ashby, USA, 1979, 130 mins.

Bell, Book and Candle
An attractive young witch (Kim Novak) vows not to use her magic powers but can't help throwing a love spell when she eyes the new man in her building, James Stewart. This screen version of the Broadway play by John Van Druten also features Jack Lemmon and Ernie Kovacs.
VHS: S03903. $19.95.
Laser: LD75805. $34.95.
Richard Quine, USA, 1959, 106 mins.

The Bellboy
Miami Beach's fabled Fountainbleau has a select group of bellboys, including one monumental klutz, Jerry Lewis. No matter how hard he tries, the results are disastrous and ridiculous, whether he's catering to mafiosi or celebrities like Milton Berle.
VHS: S21740. $14.98.
Jerry Lewis, USA, 1960, 72 mins.

Belle of the Nineties
The talented Leo McCarey directs Mae West in this shrewd comedy about a nightclub singer who makes a valiant play for a prize fighter. Music by Duke Ellington Orchestra. West performs "My Old Flame". With Roger Pryor, Johnny Mack Brown and Warren Hymer.
VHS: S18864. $14.98.
Leo McCarey, USA, 1934, 73 mins.

Benny & Joon
Funny, heartwarming and full of romance, *Benny & Joon* tells the story of two quirky misfits whose chance meeting sends their hearts soaring—despite an overprotective brother who wants to keep their feet on the ground. With Johnny Depp, Mary Stuart Masterson and Aidan Quinn.
VHS: S31164. $14.98.
Jeremiah Chechik, USA, 1992, 99 mins.

Best of Andy Hardy
One of the most popular movie series of all time, with Mickey Rooney, Judy Garland, Kathryn Grayson and Ann Rutherford. Rooney is the typical American teenager, Lewis Stone his stern father, Fay Holden his "swell" mother, Cecilia Parker his older sister Marian. Sara Haden is Aunt Millie and Ann Rutherford is Polly, the girlfriend to whom Andy always returns. Winner of a special Oscar for "its achievement in representing the American Way of Life," this MGM series introduced many starlets-later-to-be-stars. Films from a nostalgic era of Hollywood unlikely to return.
Andy Hardy Gets Spring Fever. With Mickey Rooney and Ann Rutherford. Directed by Woodbridge S. Van Dyke, USA, 1939, 88 mins.
VHS: S11441. $19.95.
Andy Hardy Meets Debutante. With Mickey Rooney and Judy Garland. Directed by George B. Seitz, USA, 1940, 86 mins.
VHS: S11439. $19.95.
Laser: LD70198. $49.98.
Andy Hardy's Double Life. With Mickey Rooney and Esther Williams. Directed by George B. Seitz, USA, 1942, 91 mins.
VHS: S11442. $19.95.
Andy Hardy's Private Secretary. With Mickey Rooney and Kathryn Grayson. Directed by George B. Seitz, USA, 1941, 101 mins.
VHS: S11440. $19.95.
Life Begins for Andy Hardy. With Mickey Rooney and Judy Garland.
VHS: S11437. $19.95.
Love Finds Andy Hardy. With Mickey Rooney and Judy Garland.
VHS: S11438. $19.95.

Beverly Hills Cop
The breakthrough film for Eddie Murphy as the Detroit cop who hits L.A. to track down the killers of an old friend. A very clever blend of comedy and action. With Judge Reinhold, Lisa Eilbacher.
VHS: S01839. $19.95.
Laser: LD75158. $34.98.
Martin Brest, USA, 1984, 105 mins.

Beverly Hills Cop 2
Eddie Murphy is back to help out his L.A. buddies and is fast on the track of an illegal arms dealer (Juergen Prochnow) and his hitlady (Brigitte Nielsen) in this sequel.
VHS: S21478. $19.95.
Tony Scott, USA, 1987, 102 mins.

Beware Spooks!
Joe E. Brown is a cop afraid of his own shadow who gets mixed up with a haunted house, a pretty girl (Mary Carlisle) and some thugs. An outrageous vehicle for Brown's unique comical style. USA, 76 mins.
VHS: S15381. $24.95.

Big
Tom Hanks stars in this fantasy comedy directed by Penny Marshall about a young boy who makes a magic wish and wakes up looking like Tom Hanks. Be careful of what you ask of a carnival mechanical genie. From 12 to 35 overnight, Josh Baskin now gets to play in the adult world and does pretty well for someone without a high school diploma. With Elizabeth Perkins, John Heard and Robert Loggia. This is a fun movie.
VHS: S09821. $14.98.
Laser: Widescreen. **LD74820. $49.98.**
Penny Marshall, USA, 1988

The Big Broadcast of 1938
Bob Hope stars in this classic early musical farce set on a ship. While the boat races across the Atlantic, Hope sings and laughs it up with an all star cast which includes W.C. Fields, Martha Raye and Dorothy Lamour. The song "Thanks for the Memories" became Hope's signature tune and won an Oscar.
VHS: S25527. $14.98.
Mitchell Leisen, USA, 1938, 91 mins.

Big Girls Don't Cry
Also known as *Step Kids*, this hilarious comedy by Joan Micklin Silver concerns the complications of a young girl's new and eccentric stepfamily. With Hillary Wolf, Griffin Dunne, Margaret Whitton, Adrienne Shelley and David Strathairn.
VHS: S17767. $9.98.
Joan Micklin Silver, USA, 1991, 98 mins.

Big Mouth
An appropriate title; Jerry Lewis, in this self-directed effort, makes waves as an eccentric fisherman who dives for sunken treasure but winds up being chased by thugs.
VHS: S07340. $19.95.
Jerry Lewis, USA, 1967, 107 mins.

The Big Picture
Today's Hollywood scene is hilariously lampooned in this behind-the-scenes look at costs of making it in show business. Kevin Bacon stars as a naive kid from Ohio who wins a best student film award from the prestigious National Film Institute and suddenly ends up in the Hollywood fast lane, where he sells out. With Jennifer Jason Leigh, Michael McKeon and J.T. Walsh, as well as appearances by Eddie Albert, Richard Belzer, John Cleese, Stephen Collins, June Lockhart and Roddy McDowell.
VHS: S31143. $14.95.
Christopher Guest, USA, 1988, 102 mins.

The Big Store
The three Marx brothers disrupt the peace and quiet of a large department store where pilfering causes Margaret Dumont to hire Groucho (as Wolf J. Flywheel) to investigate. With Virginia Grey and Douglas Dumbrille. B&W.
VHS: S06976. $19.95.
Charles Riesner, USA, 1941, 80 mins.

The Big Store/ Abbott and Costello in Hollywood
A zany double feature from two of Hollywood's greatest comedy teams. The first stars the Marx Brothers as bumbling detectives who nearly demolish a department store while trying to prevent a murder. The second follows Abbott and Costello as they try to open a barber shop in Tinsel Town.
Laser: LD71662. $44.98.

Billie
Patty Duke plays a girl who has it all: talent, charm and "the Beat"—the rock 'n' roll rhythm in her head that has her out-running every boy on the high school track team. Also starring Jim Backus.
VHS: S15241. $19.98.
Laser: LD72260. $34.98.
Don Weis, USA, 1965, 86 mins.

Bing at Sennett Vol. 2
These Mack Sennett shorts feature Bing Crosby in *I Surrender Dear, One More Chance* and *Sing, Bing, Sing*, all from 1931. Bob DeFlores' collection is the source for these beautifully mastered, musical comedy films.
VHS: S29465. $24.95.

Bingo Long Traveling All-Stars and Motor Kings
Comedy-adventure story of a group of barnstorming players in the 1930's Negro Baseball League stars Richard Pryor, Billy Dee Williams and James Earl Jones. Based on the novel by Chicago author William Brashler.
VHS: S05370. $14.98.
John Badham, USA, 1976, 111 mins.

The Birdcage
Robin Williams and Nathan Lane star as the gay couple in this readaptation of the classic French farce *La Cage aux Folles*. They camp it up big to impress their son's prospective in-laws, played by Gene Hackman and Dianne Wiest. Of course, it all goes wrong, but not before some big laughs emerge, and there is the rare opportunity to see Hackman in drag. VHS letterboxed.
VHS: S29827. $19.98.
Laser: LD75987. $49.98.
DVD: DV60072. $24.98.
Mike Nichols, USA, 1996, 119 mins.

The Bishop's Wife
Romance, laughter and fantasy abound when Cary Grant appears as a blithe spirit in answer to a Bishop's prayers (David Niven). Niven is in desperate need of funds for a new cathedral, and solutions to an array of other problems including his own marital ones. Grant takes over in a supernatural way, restoring faith, hope and love. Teresa Wright was originally cast in the title role but left to have a baby and was replaced by Loretta Young. Digitally remastered.
VHS: S03118. $19.98.
DVD: DV60191. $24.98.
Henry Koster, USA, 1947, 109 mins.

Blank Check
Every kid's fantasy comes true in this Disney comedy. Brian Bonsall is riding his bike when a crook accidentally runs over it. The crook writes a check to cover the damages but forgets to fill in the amount. Would $1 million be enough?
VHS: S21866. $96.98.
Rupert Wainwright, USA, 1993, 93 mins.

Blazing Saddles
Lunatic humor nominally about the "Old West" stars Cleavon Little as the new sheriff in town, Gene Wilder as the Waco Kid, Slim Pickens, Madeline Kahn and Harvey Korman. The gags never stop.
VHS: S01692. $14.95.
Laser: LD74687. $24.98.
DVD: DV60073. $24.98.
Mel Brooks, USA, 1974, 90 mins.

Blessed Event
A penetrating account of a Walter Winchell-type newspaper columnist (Lee Tracy) whose restless probing of Broadway and Hollywood personalities threatens his own welfare in this sharp comedy. With Dick Powell, Ned Sparks, Mary Brian and Ruth Donnelly.
VHS: S18124. $19.98.
Roy Del Ruth, USA, 1932, 78 mins.

Blonde Crazy
James Cagney stars in this "chipper, hardboiled, amusing essay on petty thievery" *(Time)*. He plays a likable Depression Era con-man who teams up with Joan Blondell to make sure suckers and their money are soon parted. They pull off a series of daring and often hilariously funny scams...until Blondell marries a society boy. Also starring Ray Milland.
VHS: S15012. $19.98.
Laser: LD71162. $39.98.
Roy Del Ruth, USA, 1931, 79 mins.

Blondie
The first of 28 feature films adapted from Chic Young's popular comic strip. The films used small, comic episodes to play out the social and family dynamics of the Bumstead clan. On the eve of their fifth anniversary, Dagwood (Arthur Lake) is fired from his job, and his strange behavior has Blondie (Penny Singleton) thinking he's romantically involved with other women. With Jonathan Hale, Larry Simms, Gene Lockhart, Ann Doran and Danny Mummert.
VHS: S20173. $14.95.
Frank Strayer, USA, 1938, 68 mins.

Blondie Has Trouble
Also known as *Blondie Has Servant Trouble*, this witty farce finds the Bumsteads occupying a haunted house rife with supernatural forces and domestic incompetence. With Penny Singleton, Arthur Lake, Larry Simms, Danny Mummert, Jonathan Hale and Arthur Hohl.
VHS: S20178. $14.95.
Frank Strayer, USA, 1940, 70 mins.

Blondie Hits the Jackpot
Blondie wins a killing on a quiz show sponsored by the local radio station, saving Dagwood from having to perform menial labor at a construction site. With Penny Singleton, Arthur Lake, Larry Simms, Danny Mummert, Jonathan Hale and Arthur Hohl.
VHS: S20174. $14.95.
Edward Bernds, USA, 1949, 66 mins.

Blondie in Society
Blondie enters a prize-winning Great Dane in a dog show, which causes problems for Dagwood—whose important business client also has a dog in competition. With Penny Singleton, Arthur Lake, Larry Simms, Jonathan Hale, Danny Mummert, William Frawley and Edgar Kennedy.
VHS: S20176. $14.95.
Frank Strayer, USA, 1941, 75 mins.

Blondie Knows Best
Dagwood causes a lot of problems when he momentarily pretends to be his boss, J.C. Dithers (Jonathan Hale). One of the Three Stooges, Shemp Howard, turns in a hilarious cameo as an eccentric process server. With Penny Singleton, Arthur Lake, Larry Simms, Marjorie Kent, Steven Geray and Jerome Cowan.
VHS: S20175. $14.95.
Abby Berlin, USA, 1946, 69 mins.

Blondie's Blessed Event
Biology and madcap farce intersect as Dagwood inadvertently causes a minor sensation during an important convention while Blondie awaits the arrival of a beautiful, bouncing girl. With Penny Singleton, Arthur Lake, Larry Simms, Marjorie Kent, William Frawley and Danny Mummert.
VHS: S20179. $14.95.
Frank Strayer, USA, 1942, 69 mins.

The Blues Brothers
Jake and Elwood, that is, John Belushi and Dan Aykroyd, bring the characters first seen on *Saturday Night Live* to the streets of Chicago. The plot is a great excuse for fun musical numbers, cop car chases and even the occasional shootout. Carrie Fisher plays a jilted girlfriend packing a big gun. Blues and soul performers Aretha Franklin, Ray Charles, James Brown and Cab Calloway make memorable appearances. Letterboxed.
VHS: S22405. $19.95.
John Landis, USA, 1980, 130 mins.

Blues Busters
Huntz Hall stars as Sach Debussy Jones in this tuneful Bowery Boys comedy. Louie's Sweet Shop is turned into a popular night spot when a tonsillectomy makes a surprise singing star out of Hall. This riles local nightclub owner Craig Stevens who sends Adele Jergens to distract the man with the golden throat. With Leo Gorcey, Billy Benedict, Gabriel Dell, and Phyllis Coats.
VHS: S15828. $14.98.
William Beaudine, USA, 1950, 67 mins.

Bob Hope: America's Ambassador of Comedy
Having entertained U.S. troops for more than 50 years, Bob Hope has become the country's most beloved good-will ambassador. This glorious profile spans the highlights of his career, starting with his early days in vaudeville, to the "Road" films, to his pioneering variety specials for television. Packed with one-liners, world leaders, and history-breaking moments. 40 mins.
VHS: S15842. $14.99.

Boeing Boeing
Tony Curtis is paired opposite a toned-down Jerry Lewis in this elegant farce about an American journalist in Paris juggling multiple relationships, with frantic, madcap results. With Thelma Ritter, Dany Saval and Christine Schmidtmer.
VHS: S17977. $14.95.
Laser: LD75289. $34.98.
John Rich, USA, 1965, 102 mins.

The Bohemian Girl
Laurel and Hardy team up for this monumental comic effort as gypsies who find themselves trapped with a wholly unexpected responsibility. They must raise a young girl despite their limited means. A whimsical short, *Below Zero*, is also included.
VHS: S21534. $19.95.
James W. Horne, USA, 1936, 90 mins.

Bonnie Scotland
Laurel and Hardy in a spoof of the Gary Cooper film *Lives of a Bengal Lancer*.
VHS: S03451. $19.98.
James W. Horne, USA, 1935, 81 mins.

Bonnie Scotland/Pick a Star
The jovial wit and physical humor of Laurel and Hardy are represented in two of their signature works, James Horne's 1935 *Bonnie Scotland*, about their adventures in a Scottish military regiment stationed in India. Edward Sedgwick's (1937) puts the two in the background, focusing on an aspiring young actress (Rosina Lawrence) in search of fame. Includes the theatrical trailers for both films. 157 mins.
Laser: LD71658. $39.98.

Booty Call
A young man's plans for romance are hilariously foiled by his crude best friend, his safe-sex obsessed girlfriend and her voluptuous neighbor. With Jamie Foxx *(The Truth About Cats & Dogs)*, Tommy Davidson, Viveca A. Fox *(Independence Day)*, Tamala Jones, Gedde Watanabe *(That Thing You Do)*, Art Malik *(True Lies)* and Bernie Mac. "Sassy, brassy and full of mischief. Down-dirty hilarious" (Bob Strauss, *Los Angeles Daily News*).
VHS: S31769. $101.99.
Laser: LD76305. $39.99.
Jeff Pollack, USA, 1997, 79 mins.

Bowery Buckaroos
The Bowery Boys go west prospecting for gold. Along the way they raise a ruckus in Hangman's Hollow which leads to Leo Gorcey being charged with murder. They also see what they can do to help a nice girl get back her stolen mine. With Huntz Hall, Bobby Jordan, Gabriel Dell, David Gorcey, Jack Norman, Julie Briggs, Iron Eyes Cody and Chief Yowlachi as Chief Hi-Octane.
VHS: S15827. $14.98.
William Beaudine, USA, 1947, 66 mins.

Boy Did I Get a Wrong Number
Would Bob Hope lie? A comical farce made by Mr. Ski Nose late in his career that places him between Elke Sommer and Phyllis Diller. Remember this is Phyllis Diller prior to plastic surgery. Who do you think Bob is going to want to get chummy with? Billed as "the picture that gets you where you laugh."
VHS: S11270. $19.95.
George Marshall, USA, 1966, 99 mins.

Boy Meets Girl
A comically inspired satire of Hollywood artifice stars James Cagney and Pat O'Brien as screenwriters who concoct an elaborate scheme to build up the talent and skills of an unborn child whose mother is a commissary waitress. With Marie Wilson, Ralph Bellamy and Ronald Reagan. "It bounces from one hilarious absurdity to another with all the resilience of a rubber ball" *(Monthly Film Bulletin)*.
VHS: S19037. $19.98.
Lloyd Bacon, USA, 1938, 86 mins.

The Brady Bunch
Here's the story of a 70's television show that found new life as a camp cult hit in the 1990's. Shelley Long leads an eerie cast of credible facsimiles in this spoof on the long-running series that mesmerized a nation of vidiots. When the home of the Bradys is threatened by greedy developers, their inane, cheerful attitude comes shining through.
VHS: S25632. $14.95.
Betty Thomas, USA, 1994, 88 mins.

Brain Candy
The cast of the ***Kids in the Hall***, the over-the-top Canadian comedy show, appeared together for the last time in this, their first feature film. A happiness drug threatens to consume the nation. This plot gives the Kids plenty of excuses to trot out their best characterization skills, especially their terrific drag. Bruce McCulloch, Kevin McDonald, Mark McKinney and Scott Thompson star.
VHS: S29866. $14.95.
Kelly Makin, USA, 1996, 89 mins.

Bride Came C.O.D.
Bette Davis, James Cagney, Harry Davenport star in this comedy about a charter pilot who kidnaps an heiress and then crash lands with her in the desert.
VHS: S13393. $19.98.
William Keighley, USA, 1941, 92 mins.

Brighton Beach Memoirs
Neil Simon's semi-autobiographical trilogy, transitioned from Broadway to the screen, with Jonathan Silverman as Eugene, the adolescent Simon, growing up in Brooklyn of the 30's, dreaming of girls and writing.
VHS: S03951. $19.95.
Gene Saks, USA, 1986, 108 mins.

Broadcast News
William Hurt, Holly Hunter and Albert Brooks play a TV news reporter, producer and writer in this involving and very funny inside look at the high pressure world of electronic journalism. The recipient of seven Oscar nominations including Best Picture, it also features Robert Prosky, Joan Cusack and Lois Chiles. Written, produced and directed by James L. Brooks *(Terms of Endearment)*.
VHS: S07382. $19.95.
James L. Brooks, USA, 1987, 132 mins.

Broadway Bound
Neil Simon wrote this film as the final installment of his trilogy, featuring his alter ego, aspiring writer Eugene Morris Jerome. In this film he tries to leave Brooklyn for good in order to be a comedy writer for a radio show. When left alone, his mother finally decides to do something about his unfaithful father. This touching comic tale is also a moving chronicle of a family in transition.
Laser: LD74813. $39.99.
Paul Bogart, USA, 1992, 90 mins.

Brother Rat
Ronald Reagan, Wayne Morris and Eddie Albert (in his film debut from a role he played on stage) are teamed up in this wholesome comedy drama as military academy cadets who must keep a secret for ten troublesome weeks or risk not graduating. With Jane Wyman, Priscilla Lane, Johnnie Davis, Jane Bryan and William Tracy.
VHS: S30541. $19.98.
William Keighley, USA, 1983, 89 mins.

Buck Privates
Abbott and Costello turn the U.S. Army upside down in this hilarious World War II comedy that made them stars. The Andrews Sisters sing "Boogie Woogie Bugle Boy."
VHS: S05924. $14.95.
Arthur Lubin, USA, 1941, 84 mins.

Buck Privates Come Home
This engaging movie has Abbott and Costello returning home, adjusting to civilian life, and caught in a plan to smuggle a young European child into the country. With Tom Brown, Joan Fulton, Nat Pendleton and Beverly Simmons.
VHS: S17262. $14.98.
Charles Barton, USA, 1947, 77 mins.

Bud Abbott and Lou Costello Meet Jerry Seinfeld
Television star Jerry Seinfeld hosts this look at the comic duo famous for skits like "Who's on First?" There are clips, behind-the-scenes footage and interviews with friends and family of these two stars. 46 mins.
VHS: S24390. $14.98.

Bud Abbott and Lou Costello Meet the Killer
The comic duo reveal their sleuthing side in this thriller that features Boris Karloff as a strange hypnotist. Lou is a bellboy who happens upon a corpse. Fortunately, Bud is there to help him through the ensuing wacky hysteria.
VHS: S24389. $14.98.
Charles Barton, USA, 1949, 84 mins.

The Bullfighters
When Laurel and Hardy go South, everyone goes into hysterics over America's favorite pair of stumblebums. USA, 1945, 61 mins.
VHS: S04606. $29.98.

Buona Sera, Mrs. Campbell
It's the eve of a 20th anniversary reunion of an American World War II squadron. A beautiful Italian woman (Gina Lollobrigida), who's collected money from three flyers, each of whom believes he's the father of her child, is thrown into a panic when her daughter insists on her meeting her actual father. With Phil Silvers, Peter Lawford and Telly Savalas.
VHS: S18010. $19.98.
Laser: LD72166. $34.95.
Melvin Frank, USA, 1968, 113 mins.

The 'Burbs
Joe Dante presents a darkly humorous look at suburban living. Neighbors Tom Hanks, Rick Ducommun and Bruce Dern think there is something very odd about the Klopeks, the latest addition to their cul-de-sac community. After all, folks that don't keep up with their yard work might be guilty of devil worship, human sacrifice and lowering property values. With Henry Gibson, Carrie Fisher and Brother Theodore.
VHS: S08710. $14.95.
Joe Dante, USA, 1989, 102 mins.

A Business Affair
Christopher Walken, Carole Bouquet and Jonathan Pryce star in this charming romantic comedy set in contemporary Manhattan. An egotistical writer (Pryce) feels jealous when his young wife (Bouquet) writes a book and is pursued by an American publisher (Walken).
VHS: S29547. $93.99.
Charlotte Brandstrom, USA, 1995, 105 mins.

The Cable Guy
Jim Carrey is frighteningly funny as a psychotic cable installer who will do anything to make a friend in this dark, comic thriller. Also stars Matthew Broderick, Leslie Mann, George Segal, Janeane Garofalo and Ben Stiller, who also directed this box office hit.
VHS: S30152. $19.95.
Laser: LD75996. $34.95.
DVD: DV60020. $24.95.
Ben Stiller, USA, 1996, 96 mins.

Cactus Flower
Goldie Hawn won an Oscar for her role as the ditzy salesgirl pursuing philandering dentist Walter Matthau. Based on the Broadway play. Ingrid Bergman plays Matthau's repressed nurse. With Jack Weston, Rick Lenz and Vito Scotti. A comical romp about acting your age and finding someone to love in your own age bracket.
VHS: S10376. $19.95.
Laser: LD75495. $34.95.
Gene Saks, USA, 1969, 103 mins.

The Caddy
Jerry Lewis is a very shy golfer who pretends to be a caddy because he can't play the game before a crowd. He tries to coach Dean Martin to play as his championship proxy. Expect a lot of dropped clubs. Dino sings "That's Amore". With Donna Reed, Fred Clark and Barbara Bates. B&W.
VHS: S06989. $19.95.
Norman Taurog, USA, 1953, 95 mins.

California Suite
Neil Simon adapts his Broadway play for the movies as he presents four short stories of guests at the Beverly Hills Hotel. Highlight is Maggie Smith and Michael Caine as a bickering British couple in town for the Academy Awards. Other guests include Jane Fonda, Alan Alda, Elaine May, Walter Matthau, Bill Cosby and Richard Pryor. Smith won a best supporting Oscar for her part.
VHS: S10374. $19.95.
Herbert Ross, USA, 1978, 103 mins.

Call Me Bwana
Passing himself off as an expert on African affairs, Bob Hope is unwittingly exploited by the CIA to recover a strategically important space capsule. Edie Adams goes along for the ride, and they encounter a mysterious couple played by Anita Ekberg and Lionel Davies.
VHS: S19561. $19.98.
Laser: LD76271. $39.99.
Gordon Douglas, USA, 1963, 103 mins.

Cancel My Reservation
Bob Hope is a New York talk show host who is so stressed out his doctor tells him to take a vacation. Leaving his wife home, he heads to a ranch in Arizona, where he is implicated in a murder he did not commit.
VHS: S09396. $14.95.
Paul Bogart, USA, 1972, 99 mins.

The Canterville Ghost
Charles Laughton is trapped as a fearful ghost for 300 years, awaiting a brave deed that will set him free, in the classic tale loosely adapted from Oscar Wilde. A charmer for the whole family. With Margaret O'Brien and Robert Young.
VHS: S13062. $19.98.
Jules Dassin, USA, 1943, 95 mins.

The Canterville Ghost (Stewart)
Patrick Stewart is the Oscar Wilde character the Canterville Ghost. Neve Campbell plays the young woman who moves into the Ghost's 400-year-old home and disturbs his sanctuary. Despite this conflict the two team up for laughs and drama, finally dispelling the curse that looms over the ancient pile of Canterville.
Laser: LD75550. $39.99.
Syd Macartney, USA, 1995, 91 mins.

Casanova Brown
A hilarious social comedy about an estranged couple (Gary Cooper and Teresa Wright) who discover that she is pregnant. Cooper orchestrates an elaborate scheme to steal the baby upon learning she wants to put it up for adoption. With Frank Morgan, Anita Louise and Isobel Olsom.
VHS: S19490. $19.98.
Sam Wood, USA, 1944, 94 mins.

Casanova's Big Night
Bob Hope at his funniest, as a timid tailor who impersonates the great lover Casanova. With Joan Fontaine, Audrey Dalton, Basil Rathbone, Raymond Burr.
VHS: S04427. $14.95.
Norman Z. McLeod, USA, 1954, 86 mins.

Catch-22
Joseph Heller's modern classic novel about war and its absurdity for the common man stars Alan Arkin, Martin Balsam, Richard Benjamin, Art Garfunkel.
VHS: S01751. $19.95.
Laser: LD75332. $29.99.
Mike Nichols, USA, 1970, 121 mins.

Catered Affair
Gore Vidal's adaptation of a Paddy Chayefsky comedy about the daughter of a New York taxicab driver whose mother insists on a bigger wedding than the family can afford. Bette Davis stars with Ernest Borgnine and Debbie Reynolds.
VHS: S13394. $19.98.
Richard Brooks, USA, 1956, 93 mins.

Caught in the Draft
This Bob Hope vehicle casts the comedian as a gilded movie star trying desperately to avoid national service. Hope inadvertently enlists himself, with some peculiar and funny consequences. With Dorothy Lamour, Lynne Overman and Eddie Bracken.
VHS: S18548. $14.98.
David Butler, USA, 1941, 82 mins.

Chances Are
When Cybil Shepherd's murdered husband is reincarnated as Robert Downey Jr., she finds herself falling for a mysterious younger man. Downey has little recollection of his past life but he is willing to see what the future will bring. A romantic comedy with a twist set in Washington, D.C. With Ryan O'Neal and Mary Stuart Masterson as the lovelorn best friend and the attractive daughter Downey never had.
VHS: S11167. $14.95.
Emile Ardolino, USA, 1989, 108 mins.

Chasing Laughter
Three Hal Roach comic shorts, featuring Charley Chase, showcase his frenetic, fast-paced style, in *Mum's the Word*, *Tell 'Em Nothing* and *Mama Behave*. With an organ soundtrack by David Knudtsen.
VHS: S19597. $29.95.
Hal Roach, USA, 1926, 60 mins.

Chasing Those Depression Blues
Four comic shorts that must have made them laugh in the '30's. They include *Dental Follies* with Pinky Lee, *Any Day in Hollywood* with Ben Turpin, *Money on Your Life* with Danny Kaye, and *Art in the Raw*, that teams Edgar Kennedy with Franklin Pangborn. B&W. USA, 1933-38, 58 mins.
VHS: S05454. $24.95.

The Cheap Detective
Peter Falk, Ann-Margret, Eileen Brennan, Sid Caesar, Stockard Channing, James Coco, Dom DeLuise, Louise Fletcher, John Houseman, Madeline Kahn and Fernando Lamas are just some of the stars featured in this madcap spoof of 40's style detective stories. A private dick investigates a strange case littered with molls, mysterious women and double-crossing eccentrics. Written by Neil Simon.
Laser: LD75006. $39.95.
Robert Moore, USA, 1978, 92 mins.

Chilly Scenes of Winter
An affectionate, off-beat comedy from director Joan Micklin Silver featuring early film performances by John Heard and Mary Beth Hurt. Based on the novel by Ann Beattie, the film is populated by memorable characters.
VHS: S00234. $19.98.
Joan Micklin Silver, USA, 1979, 96 mins.

Christmas in Connecticut
Barbara Stanwyck, an unmarried recipe-writer, must whip up a phony family to attend a holiday dinner that is designed to impress her tradition-minded boss (Sidney Greenstreet). Guests at the table include Dennis Morgan, S.Z. "Cuddles" Sakall and Una O'Connor. B&W.
VHS: S04978. $14.98.
Laser: LD70184. $34.98.
Peter Godfrey, USA, 1945, 101 mins.

A Chump at Oxford
Laurel and Hardy earn the opportunity to receive "the finest education money can buy" at Oxford University. They end up getting more than they bargained for as hilarious predicaments ensue.
VHS: S13864. $14.98.
Alfred Goulding, USA, 1940, 63 mins.

Cinderfella
Jerry Lewis transforms the old fable by becoming Cinderfella. In his Bel Air home an evil stepmother and two scheming stepbrothers keep Lewis occupied with housework. Suddenly his life is transformed by the magical appearance of a Fairy Godfather. Can a princess be far behind? This comedy shows Lewis at his best.
VHS: S21738. $14.98.
Jerry Lewis, USA, 1960, 85 mins.

Circle of Friends
Chris O'Donnell and Minnie Driver are at the center of this romantic comedy. Bernadette, Eve and Nan are three girlhood friends reunited at college. They all set off on romantic adventures. Bernadette (Driver) falls for the most unlikely candidate: Jack Foley, the big man on campus. As Bernadette's relationship with Jack intensifies, the three women learn some valuable and troublesome lessons about the nature of friendship.
VHS: S25885. $19.98.
DVD: DV60209. $24.98.
Pat O'Connor, USA, 1994, 112 mins.

City Slickers
Billy Crystal, Bruno Kirby and Daniel Stern play three buddies from the Big Apple who each year try to find something new and different to road test their testosterone levels. This vacation it's a cattle drive in the still wild American West. Jack Palance is along for the ride as a trail boss who makes the Marlboro Man look like a wimp. A comic adventure with the emphasis on cute. With Helen Slater, Josh Mostel and Patricia Wettig. Yee hah, little dogies.
VHS: S15173. $19.95.
Laser: Letterboxed. **LD74488. $39.99.**
Ron Underwood, USA, 1991, 114 mins.

Clarence
Being an angel isn't easy…especially when your name is Clarence Oddbody (Robert Carradine, *Revenge of the Nerds*). The delightfully dizzy guardian angel who saved Jimmy Stewart in *It's a Wonderful Life* is back. And this time he's got the modern world to contend with. An inspiring fantasy for the whole family, *Clarence* proves that with the right spirit, everyone can have a wonderful life.
VHS: S15136. $79.98.
Eric Till, USA, 1990, 92 mins.

Clean Slate
Dana Carvey stars as M.L. Pogue, a witness to a crime. The problem is he can't remember the details. With his eye-patched pooch and the beautiful femme fatale Valeria Golina, he tries to uncover the forgotten facts that will solve this crime. This fun-filled comedy shows Carvey at his antic best.
VHS: S22126. $19.95.
Mick Jackson, USA, 1994, 107 mins.

Clipped Wings
The Bowery Boys unknowingly enlist in the Army Air Corps while visiting a chum and discover the women's barracks are off limits. They also discover a nest of Nazi spies much to the FBI's delight. With Leo Gorcey, Huntz Hall, Philip Van Zandt, Todd Karns, Lyle Talbot and June Vincent.
VHS: S15829. $14.98.
Edward Bernds, USA, 1953, 62 mins.

Clueless
Alicia Silverstone is perfect as Cher, the *Clueless* Beverly Hills teenager who can shop with the best. Longing for something deeper, and a boyfriend as well, Cher manages to skate through a variety of off-putting situations. Though transformed, she manages to come out of it all with her wit and superficiality largely intact.
VHS: S26715. $19.95.
Amy Heckerling, USA, 1995, 97 mins.

The Cocoanuts
The hilarious, never-before-released first film of the Marx Brothers, shot on a New York sound stage, with some terrific scenes, including the "Why a duck?" routine, a hilarious auction, and a wonderful classic "viaduct" routine. With Groucho, Harpo, Chico and Zeppo.
VHS: S09458. $19.95.
DVD: DV60329. $29.99.
Joseph Santley/Robert Florey, USA, 1929, 96 mins.

Cocoon
Ron Howard directs a fine batch of Hollywood's senior citizens, who find that the Fountain of Youth is located not far from their Florida retirement community. This new lease on life is provided unintentionally by space aliens led by Brian Dennehy. With Jack Gilford, Hume Cronyn, Jessica Tandy, and Don Ameche as the break-dancing winner of a Best Supporting Actor award.
VHS: S04773. $14.98.
Ron Howard, USA, 1985, 117 mins.

Cold Comfort Farm
A witty film starring Kate Beckinsdale as Flora Poste, a recently orphaned London society girl who ignores the advice of her friend and mentor, Mrs. Smiley, and moves to the country to live with her eccentric relatives on a decrepit farm. Stars Rufus Sewell, Ian McKellen, Stephen Fry *(Peter's Friends)* and Eileen Atkins.
VHS: S30045. $14.98.
Laser: LD75993. $39.95.
John Schlesinger, USA, 1995, 94 mins.

Cold Dog Soup
Michael Latchmer (Frank Whaley), crazed cabby Jack Cloud (Randy Quaid) and Sarah Hughes (Christine Harnos) are three adults whose lives are turned upside-down during a bizarre, all-night quest to bury Jasper, Sarah's late dog. The comedic attempt to find the proper burial place for Jasper creates the backdrop for Jack to explore the value of life with Michael, who had hoped for an evening of passion with Sarah, but instead experiences several strange series of exploits with the cabby, resulting in an odyssey of events.
VHS: S30827. $14.98.
Alan Metter, USA, 1989, 85 mins.

Coming to America
Eddie Murphy is a spoiled African prince in search of a suitable mate. He begins his search in New York City in the section known as Queens. Where better to find a royal partner? He poses as a poor student and tries to win the heart of a fast food manager's daughter, with comic results. With John Amos, Arsenio Hall and James Earl Jones. Murphy plays several roles in special makeup. How many can you spot?
VHS: S08353. $14.95.
Laser: LD75173. $34.98.
John Landis, USA, 1988, 116 mins.

Cookie
Susan Seidelman looks for the lighter side of organized crime in the New York City area with a family comedy where most of the characters are members of the Family. Peter Falk plays reformed racketeer Dino Capisco. Emily Lloyd is cast as his spunky teenage daughter Cookie, a love-child of Dino's faithful mistress, played by Diane Wiest. Can father and daughter do business? With Jerry Lewis, Adrian Pasdar and Brenda Vaccaro, script by Nora Ephron and Alice Arden.
VHS: S11663. $14.95.
Susan Seidelman, USA, 1989, 93 mins.

Copacabana
Groucho Marx and Carmen Miranda! What more needs to be said?
VHS: S00269. $19.98.
Laser: CLV. **LD71978. $29.98.**
Alfred E. Green, USA, 1947, 91 mins.

Court Jester
Danny Kaye finds himself impersonating a medieval fool in this complicated comedy classic. A plot is afoot to kill the king and that's no joke to a loyal subject. If you were wondering which brew is true, the pellet with the poison is in the vessel with the pestle. Cast includes Glynis Johns, Basil Rathbone, Angela Lansbury, Cecil Parker, Mildred Natwick and John Carradine.
VHS: S10811. $14.95.
Laser: LD75357. $29.98.
Norman Panama/Melvin Frank, USA, 1956, 101 mins.

Courting Courtney
A hilarious and award-winning look at sex and singles in the '90s, Courtney (Eliza Cole, *Mighty Ducks 3*) allows old boyfriend and amateur documentary filmmaker Dick (Dana Gould, *Working* and TV's *Ellen*) to film the traumas of her dating life as she approaches the big three-oh. With Taylor Negron, Kathy Griffin, Ryan Stiles, Julia Sweeney and Chris Hardwick.
VHS: S34466. $89.95.
Paul Tarantino, USA, 1997, 87 mins.

The Courtship of Eddie's Father
Little Ronny Howard plays Eddie, the son of widower Glenn Ford, who is determined to find a suitable wife for his dad and a wonderful mother for himself. Shirley Jones, Stella Stevens and Dina Merrill play the blonde, redhead and brunette respectively as they each fall prey to Eddie's pint-sized precocity.
VHS: S14556. $19.98.
Laser: LD76263. $39.99.
Vincente Minnelli, USA, 1962, 117 mins.

Cousins
The American version of the 1975 French film *Cousin, Cousine* from director Jean-Charles Tacchella that proved to be a big hit in the U.S. Ted Danson and Isabella Rossellini play nice people married to mates Sean Young and William Peterson, who are involved in an affair. To get even, they pretend to become involved physically and find much to their surprise they are truly falling in love. A robust family comedy about fidelity. With Lloyd Bridges and Norma Aleandro.
VHS: S10355. $19.95.
Laser: LD75175. $34.98.
Joel Schumacker, USA, 1989, 110 mins.

Cracking Up
This Jerry Lewis comedy is also known as *Smorgasbord*, the Swedish word that loosely translates as "more food than you should eat at one sitting." Lewis plays Warren Nefron, a most unlucky person when it comes being employed. In a series of flashback sketches he informs his psychiatrist Herb Edelman why he can't hold on to a job. With Foster Brooks, Buddy Lester, Zane Buzby. Dick Butkus, Sammy Davis Jr. and Milton Berle as a female patient.
VHS: S16460. $19.98.
Jerry Lewis, USA, 1983, 91 mins.

Critical Condition
Richard Pryor stars in this comedy that also features Ruben Blades, Joe Dallesandro and Sylvia Miles. Pryor tries to escape the Mafia by pleading insanity. Soon he's longing for the safety of the mental ward after he escapes and is mistaken for a doctor.
VHS: S23953. $14.95.
Laser: LD75296. $29.98.
Michael Apted, USA, 1987, 99 mins.

The Crooked Circle
A comic mystery about a secret agent who goes undercover as a swami to get the goods on the Crooked Circle. Hocus pocus and spirits from beyond are up to no good. With Ben Lyons, ZaSu Pitts, Roscoe Karns, and C. Henry Gordon as Yoganda. James Gleason is a comic cop.
VHS: S04078. $29.95.
H. Bruce Humberstone, USA, 1932, 68 mins.

Cross My Heart
Martin Short and Annette O'Toole star as two modern singles trying desperately not to screw up what seems like a possible perfect relationship. They are about to embark on the critical third date and each has a pile of personal secrets that include a seven-year-old child and being fired. A very funny comedy with lots of charm.
VHS: S07143. $14.98.
Armyan Bernstein, USA, 1987, 91 mins.

Crossing Delancey
A warm and genuinely witty modern romance. Amy Irving is a bright, single Jewish woman living in New York who is infatuated with a notorious writer (Jeroen Krabbe) and fears she may be settling for less if she becomes involved with a nice man who sells pickles (Peter Riegert). With Sylvia Miles as the matchmaker.
VHS: S09804. $19.98.
Laser: LD74692. $24.98.
Joan Micklin Silver, USA, 1988, 97 mins.

Dance with Me, Henry
In their final film together, Abbott & Costello star in this comedy about an amusement park owner (Costello) who tends to adopt strays—children, animals, and even Uncle Bud, a conniving gambler (Abbott) with some rather substantial racing debts that manage to pull the two of them into the rough realm of gangsters, corruption and gangland murder. USA, 1956, 80 mins.
VHS: S15423. $19.98.

The Daring Young Man
Joe E. Brown stars as a meek weakling who tries to enlist in the armed forces. He soon becomes mixed up with foreign spies and a radio controlled bowling ball that could affect the security of our nation. Silly and great fun. With Marguerite Chapman, William Wright, Roger Clark. USA, 74 mins.
VHS: S15382. $24.95.

Dave
Ivan Reitman's engaging political satire about Dave Kovic (Kevin Kline), the owner of an employment agency, who bears an uncanny resemblance to the president. When the president is felled by a massive stroke, two Machiavellian political players install Kovic as the president's stand-in. With Sigourney Weaver, Frank Langella, Kevin Dunn, Ving Rhames, and Ben Kingsley as the vice president. Capra-esque.
VHS: S19528. $19.98.
Laser: LD71922. $34.98.
DVD: DV60305. $24.98.
Ivan Reitman, USA, 1993, 107 mins.

A Day at the Races
Those zany boys are at it again! Groucho is Dr. Hugo Z. Hackenbush, a veterinarian put in charge of a sanitarium for wealthy hypochondriacs. He gets involved with two from the racetrack: Harpo the jockey and Chico, a vendor of bad racing tips.
VHS: S02594. $19.95.
Laser: LD70553. $25.98.
Sam Wood, USA, 1937, 111 mins.

The Daytrippers
A suspicious love note sends a dysfunctional Long Island family on a scavenger hunt of the heart in this romantic comedy starring Hope Davis, Pat McNamara, Parker Posey, Anne Meara, Liev Schreiber, Campbell Scott and Stanley Tucci.
VHS: S32029. $98.99.
Greg Mottola, USA, 1997, 87 mins.

Dead Heat on a Merry-Go-Round

James Coburn stars as Eli Kotch, a captivating rogue and full-time con man, in this comical crime caper. In prison, Coburn cleverly seduces an attractive psychologist to win parole.

VHS: S09393. $69.95.
Bernard Girard, USA, 1966, 107 mins.

Dead Men Don't Wear Plaid

Steve Martin stars in this Carl Reiner comic salute to the detective movies of the 1940's. As Rigby Reardon, private eye, he is hired to solve a perplexing mystery that holds the fate of Terre Haute, Indiana, in the balance. Martin interacts with old film clips. A great gimmick and fun for film buffs. With Rachel Ward and Carl Reiner.

VHS: S05542. $19.95.
Carl Reiner, USA, 1982, 89 mins.

Dean Martin & Jerry Lewis Comedy Collection

A collection of three Martin & Lewis films: *My Friend Irma* (1949), *Jumping Jacks* (1952) and *Scared Stiff* (1953).

VHS: S18678. $59.85.

Defending Your Life

Yet another masterpiece from America's finest comedic filmmaker, Albert Brooks *(Real Life, Modern Romance, Lost in America)*. Meryl Streep, Lee Grant, Rip Torn and Buck Henry co-star in this hilarious romantic fantasy about judgment in the afterlife. A funny, beautifully conceived and often quite touching film.

VHS: S15052. $19.98.
Albert Brooks, USA, 1991, 112 mins.

Denise Calls Up

This comedy for the electronic age is the story of six young New Yorkers who fall in and out of love, give birth, and die without ever getting off the phone, until a seventh member (Alanna Ubach) joins the party line and forces the group to try to make real contact. Also starring Tim Daly, Dana Wheeler Nicholson, Aida Turturro and Sylvia Miles, this romantic, oddball satire received a Cannes Film Festival Camera d'Or Special Mention and was hailed by the *New York Post* as "the funniest film of the year."

VHS: S28512. $19.95.
Laser: LD75949. $34.95.
Hal Salwen, USA, 1995, 80 mins.

Dental Follies

Sure to be a laughing gas, this collection has extracted the most hilarious and recognizable dental hijinx ever captured on film. Short films include: Abbott & Costello in *Oh, My Achin' Tooth*, The Little Rascals in *Awful Tooth*, Charlie Chaplin in *Laughing Gas*, W.C. Fields in *The Dentist* and The Three Stooges in *I Can Hardly Wait*. Their pain is sure to bring you pleasure. 60 mins.

VHS: S31264. $19.95.

Desk Set

One of the true wonders of Hollywood—a top notch comedy with sparks between Spencer Tracy as the efficiency expert and Katharine Hepburn as the intelligent researcher in a TV network. Sparks fly as Tracy and Hepburn mix business with pleasure.

VHS: S11561. $19.98.
Laser: LD70945. $59.99.
Walter Lang, USA, 1957, 103 mins.

Desperately Seeking Susan

Director Seidelman's move toward the mainstream after *Smithereens*. With Rosanna Arquette, Madonna as Susan, and Aidan Quinn.

VHS: Out of print. For rental only.
Laser: Widescreen. **LD76179. $49.99.**
Susan Seidelman, USA, 1985, 104 mins.

Devil Dogs of the Air

A screen comedy about the rivalry of two legendary pilots. James Cagney is an irreverent, selfish pilot interested in the Marines who receives instructions from his idol (Pat O'Brien). Both are drawn to the same carefree woman (Margaret Lindsay). "A loud and roughneck screen comedy, both amusing and exciting" (Andre Sennwald).

VHS: S19040. $19.98.
Lloyd Bacon, USA, 1935, 86 mins.

The Devil's Brother

Laurel and Hardy star as bandits who try to rob the most notorious highwayman of them all: Fra Diavolo, the Devil's Brother! Brilliant gags, lavish sets, and sublime music from Auber's operetta. Co-starring Thelma Todd. USA, 1933, 90 mins.

VHS: S15419. $19.98.

Dirty Rotten Scoundrels

Steve Martin and Michael Caine occupy the roles played by Marlon Brando and David Niven in this very faithful and very comic remake of the 1964 comical farce, *Bedtime Story*. They play a pair of con men on the French Riviera battling to see who can first swindle money from an American soap queen. With Glenne Headly in the Shirley Jones role. Also Barbara Harris as Lady Fanny of Omaha.

VHS: S09400. $19.98.
Laser: CLV. **LD71715. $29.95.**
Frank Oz, USA, 1988, 110 mins.

Disorderly Orderly

A crazy Frank Tashlin comedy with Jerry Lewis as an orderly who nearly destroys a nursing home. With Glenda Farrell, Susan Oliver, Everett Sloane.

VHS: S04429. $14.95.
Frank Tashlin, USA, 1964, 90 mins.

Divorce American Style

Dick Van Dyke and Debbie Reynolds are the central couple in this manic comedy featuring Lee Grant, Jason Robards, Van Johnson and Jean Simmons. When a couple opt for divorce, they don't contemplate all the hassles which the single life entails. In the end, after watching the farcical mismatches that unfold around them, they both pick the most unlikely way out.

VHS: S27186. $19.95.
Bud Yorkin, USA, 1967, 109 mins.

Doc Hollywood

Michael J. Fox stars as Dr. Ben Stone, a self-centered, ambitious physician who was on his way to interview for a staff position in the office of a Beverly Hills plastic surgeon until a car accident stranded him in the very small town of Grady, South Carolina. With Julie Warner, Woody Harrelson, David Ogden Stiers and Bridget Fonda.

VHS: S15701. $19.98.
Michael Caton-Jones, USA, 1991, 104 mins.

Don Juan DeMarco

Marlon Brando, Johnny Depp and Faye Dunaway star in this comedy about a man who is either the greatest lover the world has ever known or just a kook. Depp is great as the would be Don Juan, while Brando and Dunaway make a great pair, who are touched by the ravings of this romantic obsessive.

VHS: S26278. $19.98.
Laser: LD75068. $39.99.
DVD: DV60226. $24.98.
Jeremy Leven, USA, 1995, 92 mins.

Don't Go Near the Water

The Navy establishes a public relations unit on a South Sea island to increase recruitment and promote the glamour and wonder of national service. But the men are terrified of the water and spend their time pursuing women, fun and romance. With Glenn Ford, Fred Clark and Gia Scala.

VHS: S20201. $19.98.
Charles Walters, USA, 1957, 107 mins.

Don't Raise the Bridge, Lower the River

Jerry Lewis is George Lester, an American in London, whose grandiose schemes constantly get him in trouble. With the help of his friend Willy Homer (Terry-Thomas), he unveils a scheme to sell stolen plans for an electronic oil drill to the Arabs, then learns that the plans are phony.

VHS: S33358. $19.95.
Jerry Paris, USA, 1967, 99 mins.

Dragnet

Dan Aykroyd in the Jack Webb role provides comic parody, featuring Tom Hanks in the Henry Morgan role of side-kick.

VHS: S06037. $14.95.
Tom Mankiewicz, USA, 1987, 106 mins.

Dream a Little Dream

Another body switching comedy. This time golden agers Jason Robards and Piper Laurie are transported by a mystical ceremony into the bodies of two unaware 15-year-olds played by Corey Feldman and Meredith Salenger. Only Feldman knows the truth of the situation. With Harry Dean Stanton, Susan Blakely and Corey Haim as a few of the folks trying to figure out the change in behavior.

VHS: S10339. $89.95.
Marc Rocco, USA, 1989, 99 mins.

Dream Team

Michael Keaton heads an all-star cast in this comedy about four mental patients who are separated from their therapist on the way to a baseball game. A chronic liar with a violent streak, Billy (Michael Keaton) finds himself on the loose in New York City with his fellow group therapy patients Christopher Lloyd (a clean freak), Peter Boyle (a former advertising executive with a Christ complex), and Stephen Furst (a near-catatonic couch potato).

VHS: S10451. $19.95.
Howard Zieff, USA, 1989, 113 mins.

Dream Wife

East meets West in this hilariously entertaining film by the director of *The Bachelor and the Bobby-Soxer*, starring Cary Grant as Clemson Reade, an American businessman who forsakes his career-girl fiancee, Effie, (Deborah Kerr) for an Eastern princess (Betta St. John) for reasons of goodwill. The phony affair soon turns into an affair of State presided over by Effie. With Walter Pigeon. "Filled with inventive incident... directed and acted with zing...[and] studded with laughs from beginning to end" *(Cue)*.

VHS: S30546. $19.98.
Sidney Sheldon, USA, 1953, 99 mins.

Duchess and the Dirtwater Fox

Goldie Hawn plays a hooker called Duchess and George Segal is a saddle tramp named Fox. Together they romp through the Old West in search of a dollar. A comedy/western for serious followers only.

VHS: S13018. $19.98.
Laser: LD72219. $59.98.
Melvin Frank, USA, 1976, 104 mins.

Duck Soup

The most immortal film of the Marx Brothers! About the small nation of Fredonia, which has given Groucho complete power to restore order. Political satire and madness both. With Margaret Dumont and Louis Calhern.

VHS: S02018. $19.95.
Leo McCarey, USA, 1933, 70 mins.

Dumb and Dumber

It's a real toss up as to whose character, Jim Carrey or Jeff Daniels, is actually dumber. But it's great fun watching this battle for the last place on the evolutionary ladder. These dimwitted pals travel cross-country to return a suitcase full of cash and somehow manage to outwit everyone who tries to stop them.

VHS: S25655. $14.98.
Laser: Letterboxed. **LD76268. $39.99.**
DVD: DV60074. $24.98.
Peter Farrelly, USA, 1994, 110 mins.

Dutchess of Idaho

Slipping a fur-lined parka over her trademark bathing suit, Hollywood's favorite mermaid, Esther Williams, hits the snowy slopes of Idaho's famous Sun Valley in this charming light comedy. Along with Van Johnson, Paula Raymond and John Lund, Esther swims and skis her way into romance.

VHS: S16604. $19.98.
Robert Z. Leonard, USA, 1950, 98 mins.

Earthworm Tractors

In this ground-shaking comedy Joe E. Brown stars as an ambitious salesman who learns that his fiancee (Carol Hughes) will not marry him unless he sells a big, important product. He contacts the Earthworm Tractor Company, determined to sell tractors. Impressed by his initiative, the company head hires him, hoping that he'll be able to close a big sale with a difficult client.

VHS: S30406. $19.95.
Ray Enright, USA, 1936, 69 mins.

Easy Living

When a sable coat lands on secretary Jean Arthur's head, it kicks off a series of madcap misadventures in this stylish, screwball, romantic comedy by Preston Sturges. With Edward Arnold and Ray Milland.

VHS: S04142. $14.98.
Mitchell Leisen, USA, 1937, 88 mins.

Eating Raoul

Characterized as a "dextrous, beautifully timed, macabre comedy of manners which tackles kinky sex, economics, gourmet cooking, modern marriage, and even cannibalism," by David Chute in *Film Comment*, *Eating Raoul* features a married couple who, poor but proud, are bent on destroying the evil that surrounds them in the swinging singles complex in which they live.

VHS: S00392. $19.98.
Paul Bartel, USA, 1981, 90 mins.

Edgar Kennedy Slow Burn Festival

Three gems selected from the many two-reelers of this master of the slow burn. They include *Poisoned Ivory, Edgar Hamlet*, and A Clean Sweep. Edgar is aggravated by doctors, in-laws and vacuum cleaners in this trio of time-tested laugh-getters. USA, 1934-37, 59 mins.

VHS: S05460. $24.95.

The Egg and I

This movie may have starred Fred MacMurray and Claudette Colbert as a young couple trying to make a living from a chicken farm, but it will always be remembered as the film debut of Ma and Pa Kettle. Marjorie Main and Percy Kilbride kept up the corn pone act for a total of ten films. Amusing comedy based on the bestselling book by Betty MacDonald.

VHS: S03625. $14.98.
Laser: LD70027. $34.98.
Chester Erskine, USA, 1947, 108 mins.

Eight on the Lam
A father of seven just found $10,000 and a whole lot of trouble in this riotously funny comedy of errors starring Bob Hope, Phyllis Diller and Jonathan Winters.
VHS: S31517. $14.95.
Laser: LD76253. $39.99.
George Marshall, USA, 1966, 107 mins.

Employees' Entrance
A quick-witted comedy about a destitute young woman (Loretta Young) who's forced to take a job at a sprawling, emotionally cold department store run by a vindictive and authoritarian executive (Warren William).
VHS: S18125. $19.98.
Roy Del Ruth, USA, 1933, 75 mins.

Ensign Pulver
Wiseacre gob Jack Nicholson trades gags aboard the U.S.S. *Reluctant* with Walter Matthau, Larry Hagman, Burl Ives and more in this zany sequel to *Mister Roberts*.
VHS: S12588. $19.98.
Joshua Logan, USA, 1964, 105 mins.

The Errand Boy
Jerry Lewis stars in this madcap comedy about an errand boy who is actually a spy, watching his fellow employees to gauge their efficiency. The only problem is this spy can't do anything without setting off wild mishaps. Even the simplest of tasks, like getting the car washed or eating lunch, leads to disaster.
VHS: S21737. $14.98.
Jerry Lewis, USA, 1961, 95 mins.

Every Day's a Holiday
Mae West stars as a flamboyant confidence woman trapped in the Bowery, who fools a group of suitors into purchasing sections of the Brooklyn Bridge. With Edmund Lowe, Charles Butterworth and Charles Winninger.
VHS: S18866. $14.98.
A. Edward Sutherland, USA, 1937, 79 mins.

The Facts of Life
Bob Hope and Lucille Ball star as a couple deeply in love—and in deep trouble with their spouses—in this hilarious look at romance, marriage and other of life's calamities.
VHS: S31518. $14.95.
Melvin Frank, USA, 1960, 103 mins.

Faithful
Cher, Ryan O'Neal and Chazz Palminteri star in this black comedy about love, marriage and the death of a relationship. In this threesome, the third party is not brought in for an affair, he is brought in to murder one of the spouses. Unexpectedly, he is forced to try and figure out which one.
VHS: S29488. $19.98.
Laser: LD75916. $39.99.
Paul Mazursky, USA, 1996, 91 mins.

Family Business
Sean Connery, Dustin Hoffman and Matthew Broderick play three generations of a family of small time New York crooks. When the first caper they pull together goes sour, hard choices must be made concerning blood ties and prison time. Based on the novel by Vincent Patrick. With Rosana DeSoto.
VHS: S12853. $14.95.
Sidney Lumet, USA, 1989, 114 mins.

The Family Jewels
Jerry Lewis plays seven (count 'em, seven) different roles in this comedy about a little girl with a big inheritance. Donna Butterworth is the little charmer who needs seven Jerry's to act as her guardians. With Sebastian Cabot, Robert Strauss and Anne Baxter.
VHS: S06988. $19.95.
Jerry Lewis, USA, 1965, 100 mins.

Fancy Pants
Bob Hope convinces Lucille Ball that he is a real British lord and she invites him back to New Mexico to meet the locals. A musical comedy remake of *Ruggles of Red Gap*. With Bruce Cabot, Eric Blore and John Alexander as Teddy Roosevelt. Songs include "Home Cookin'" and the title song.
VHS: S12849. $19.95.
Laser: LD75193. $34.98.
George Marshall, USA, 1950, 92 mins.

Father Goose
Cary Grant and Leslie Caron in a comedy of wits which has Grant protecting Caron and seven schoolgirls on a South Seas island from the Japanese during World War II. Letterboxed.
VHS: S02978. $19.95.
Ralph Nelson, USA, 1964, 116 mins.

Father of the Bride
Spencer Tracy is the title character, a successful lawyer who is totally unprepared for the aggravation of a big wedding. Elizabeth Taylor is the apple of his eye scheduled to marry Don Taylor. A perceptive comedy with Joan Bennett, Billie Burke and Leo G. Carroll. B&W.
VHS: S07009. $19.95.
Laser: LD70195. $34.98.
Vincente Minnelli, USA, 1950, 93 mins.

Father Was a Fullback
Fred MacMurray, Maureen O'Hara, Rudy Vallee and Natalie Wood star in this family comedy about a football coach with plenty of worries. Whether on the gridiron, or at home, he needs all his strategic capabilities just to stay ahead of either game.
VHS: S25975. $14.98.
John M. Stahl, USA, 1949, 99 mins.

Father's Little Dividend
The gruff but lovable Spencer Tracy stars in this delightful comedy about the true-to-life family foibles which accompany the birth of a first grandchild. Featuring the same cast as *Father of the Bride*, one of MGM's most popular films of 1950.
VHS: S15024. $19.98.
Vincente Minnelli, USA, 1951, 83 mins.

Female
This invigorating comedy was ahead of its time. It portrays the life of the strong-willed, feminist president (Ruth Chatterton) of a car company whose life is jolted by the appearance of a brash, independent nonconformist (George Brent). With Ruth Donnelly, Ferdinand Gottschalk and Douglas Dumbrille.
VHS: S18126. $19.98.
Michael Curtiz, USA, 1933, 60 mins.

A Few Moments with Buster Keaton and Laurel & Hardy
Laurel and Hardy are featured in a color short produced by the Department of Agriculture Forest Service. They are reminded by an off-screen voice how important wood is to the war effort. The other two segments feature Buster Keaton doing commercials for "Simon Pure Beer" and performing a silent routine on the Ed Sullivan Show. USA, 1943-63, 17 mins.
VHS: S05432. $9.95.

Fifth Avenue Girl
A "social comedy" with Ginger Rogers as a homeless girl taken in by a disconcerted millionaire, disrupting his entire household. With Franklin Pangborn.
VHS: S10654. $19.98.
Gregory La Cava, USA, 1939, 83 mins.

First Wives Club
Bette Midler, Goldie Hawn and Diane Keaton portray mid-life Manhattanites who have helped their husbands climb the ladder of success only to be dumped by their hubbies for younger models. They come up with a cleverly devious plan to hit their exes where it really hurts: in the wallet. With Maggie Smith, Dan Hedaya, Bronson Pinchot and Marcia Gay Harden. "A comedy dream team. It's irresistible fun" (Peter Travers, *Rolling Stone*).
VHS: S30895. $14.95.
Hugh Wilson, USA, 1996, 104 mins.

Fitzwilly
This spirited comedy stars Dick Van Dyke as Fitzwilliam, a dutiful servant to an eccentric philanthropist who has become penniless. Fitzwilliam resorts to thievery in order to keep his employer living in style. With Barbara Feldon and Sam Waterston (in their screen debuts), Edith Evans, John McGiver, Harry Townes, John Fiedler, Norman Fell and Cecil Kellaway.
VHS: S30542. $19.98.
Delbert Mann, USA, 1967, 102 mins.

Five Corners
An endearing, offbeat black comedy set in the Bronx in 1962, featuring a top notch ensemble cast including Jodie Foster, Todd Graff, Tim Robbins and John Turturro as Heinz, the ex-con nutcase. This film does show scenes of violence to penguins and math teachers as well as the entertainment possibilities of an elevator shaft.
VHS: S07913. $14.98.
Laser: Letterboxed. **LD76357. $49.95.**
Tony Bill, USA, 1987, 94 mins.

Flirting with Disaster
"Hang on and prepare to laugh" *(USA Today)* with this all-star comedy voted one of the year's ten best by *Time Magazine*. Mel Coplin (Ben Stiller) and his wife Nancy (Patricia Arquette) are led by a wacky adoption counselor (Tea Leone) on a wild cross-country search to find his birth parents (Alan Alda and Lily Tomlin). Hilarious and unpredictable situations complicate the trip as Mel searches for his roots. By the time Mel's adoptive parents (Mary Tyler Moore and George Segal) show up to crash the reunion, everyone seems to be "flirting with disaster."
VHS: S30829. $19.95.
Laser: LD76100. $39.99.
David O. Russell, USA, 1996, 92 mins.

Flying Deuces
Some of Laurel and Hardy's best routines. They vacation in Paris, where Ollie falls in love, and finding out his girlfriend is the wife of a legionnaire, they join the Foreign Legion. The result? Total mayhem.
VHS: S00453. $19.95.
A. Edward Sutherland, USA, 1939, 67 mins.

Fools Rush In
Matthew Perry *(Friends)* and Salma Hayek *(Desperado)* star in this culture-colliding romantic comedy about a one-night stand that becomes the love of a lifetime.
VHS: S31611. $103.99.
Laser: LD76247. $34.95.
DVD: DV60234. $24.95.
Andy Tennant, USA, 1996, 109 mins.

Footsteps in the Dark
Errol Flynn shows his comic flair as a high society investment banker who secretly moonlights as a mystery writer and amateur sleuth in this tongue-in-cheek whodunit. Maintaining a suave wordly exterior while investigating the seamier side of life inevitably leads to some ridiculous juxtapositions.
VHS: S22897. $19.98.
Lloyd Bacon, USA, 1941, 96 mins.

For Auld Lang Syne
Four comic shorts from the '30's featuring four differing views of humor. The Marx Brothers preview *Monkey Business* for theatre owners. Jacques Tati teams with Rhum in *Gai Dimanche (Jolly Sunday)*, as pickpockets on an outing. Harry Langdon gets in trouble in a seedy bar when he orders milk. And to conclude, a star-studded tribute to Will Rogers. USA/France, 1932-37, 46 mins.
VHS: S05434. $24.95.

For Pete's Sake
A Brahma bull is not the only one chasing Henrietta (Barbra Streisand) after she convinces husband Michael Sarrazin that the 3,000 dollars she invested in stock was a gift from a rich Texan uncle. When the stock doesn't rise, the loan sharks do. Estelle Parsons and Molly Picon co-star.
VHS: S13000. $9.95.
Peter Yates, USA, 1974, 90 mins.

Foreign Affairs
A romantic comedy about two trans-Atlantic travelers—a refined, New England teacher (Joanne Woodward) and a gruff, unapologetically persistent suitor (Brian Dennehy)—whose paths repeatedly cross in London. With Stephanie Beacham, Eric Stoltz and Ian Richardson.
VHS: S18786. $19.95.
Jim O'Brien, USA, 1992, 100 mins.

Forever, Darling
One of America's favorite comedic couples, Lucille Ball and Desi Arnaz, star in this enchanting story of a pair whose marriage gets into trouble. They find some help when her Guardian Angel (James Mason) steps in.
VHS: S15243. $19.98.
Alexander Hall, USA, 1955, 91 mins.

Forget Paris
Billy Crystal and Debra Winger star in this charming romantic comedy. Surprisingly, the story gets underway with Crystal searching for his father's body. It seems the corpse was misplaced. Fortunately, this all happens in Paris and as a result it does not take long for a romantic struggle to start between an aggravated son and the airline representative who relays the bad news.
VHS: S26526. $19.95.
Laser: LD75099. $39.95.
Billy Crystal, USA, 1995, 101 mins.

Forsaking All Others
Clark Gable is quietly in love with Joan Crawford, even though she is engaged to Robert Montgomery. When her intended leaves her at the altar to marry someone else, Clark makes his move. With Billie Burke, Charles Butterworth, Frances Drake, Rosalind Russell and Arthur Treacher.
VHS: S16449. $19.98.
W.S. Van Dyke, USA, 1934, 83 mins.

Francis Goes to the Races
Francis the talking mule and Peter, played by Donald O'Connor, visit a breeding ranch where love and the good life are found for both these heros. But the ranch is terribly in debt, and only Francis and Peter can raise the money. Fortunately Francis has the inside scoop at the local racetrack.
VHS: S20943. $14.98.
Arthur Lubin, USA, 1951, 91 mins.

Francis in the Navy
This is Donald O'Connor's last appearance as the sidekick of a talking mule and he makes the best of it, appearing in two roles. The problem occurs when he tries to save Francis from being sold off as surplus. Also features a young Clint Eastwood.
VHS: S20945. $14.98.
Arthur Lubin, USA, 1955, 80 mins.

Francis Joins the WACS
Donald O'Connor (Peter) and Francis the talking mule find themselves transferred to a WAC base. This mix-up leads to all kinds of mayhem when the women of the WAC suspect this mistake is actually part of a plot. Oddly enough though, these two turn out to be good for morale in a funny sort of way.
VHS: S20944. $14.98.
Arthur Lubin, USA, 1954, 95 mins.

Francis the Talking Mule
This is the original movie, featuring Hollywood's first talking pack animal—sorry Mr. Ed. In this comedy Francis rescues his buddy, a private in the army, from behind enemy lines, proving that heroics are not the sole preserve of the two-legged species.
VHS: S20942. $14.98.
Arthur Lubin, USA, 1949, 91 mins.

Frankie and Johnny
Al Pacino and Michelle Pfeiffer star in the comic film adaptation of the 1987 hit stage play *Frankie and Johnny in the Clair de Lune*. Author Terrence McNally opens up his play to include a vast array of supporting characters, but centers on a very persistent short order cook and a world-weary waitress who has heard it all before. With Hector Elizondo, Kate Nelligan, Nathan Lane and Jane Morris.
VHS: S15952. $19.95.
Laser: Widescreen. **LD75351. $29.98.**
Garry Marshall, USA, 1991, 117 mins.

Freaked
At the center of this black comedy is a child with unusually large ears. Branded a freak, he manages to get the best of all the kids and adults who would make fun of his unfortunate looks. With a face like his, laughing proves to be the only option. With Randy Quaid, Alex Winter and an uncredited appearance by Keanu Reeves.
VHS: S20714. $96.98.
Laser: LD74453. $39.98.
Tom Stern/Alex Winter, USA, 1993, 90 mins.

French Kiss
Kevin Kline and Meg Ryan star in this light, frothy romantic comedy set in Paris. Ryan is Kate, a woman determined to win back her fiance, who has fallen for someone else. She flies to Paris to find him and instead meets a cunning French con man, Kevin Kline. There is, it seems, a unique magic specific to a genuine French kiss.
VHS: S26388. $19.95.
Laser: LD75079. $39.98.
Lawrence Kasdan, USA, 1995, 111 mins.

French Postcards
Calm down. This feature film chronicles the mostly comical adventures of a small group of American exchange students learning about life and love in Paris. The expatriates for one school year include Blanche Baker, Miles Chapin, David Arshall Grant and Debra Winger. They encounter foreigners like Marie-France Pisier, Mandy Patinkin, Valerie Quennessen and Jean Rochefort. From the writers of *American Graffiti*.
VHS: S10813. $59.95.
Willard Huyck, USA, 1979, 95 mins.

Freshman
An unexpectedly wonderful comedy from Andrew Bergman *(The In-Laws)* that concerns the extracurricular and probably illegal education of a young film student played by Matthew Broderick. Marlon Brando steals the movie with a comic send-up of his role in *The Godfather*. He even ice-skates. Also making a good impression are Bruno Kirby, Penelope Ann Miller, Maximilian Schell and Bert Parks. Yes, Bert Parks. One of the few movies daring enough to co-star a komodo dragon.
VHS: S13317. $14.95.
Andrew Bergman, USA, 1990, 102 mins.

Fuller Brush Girl
A reworking of 1948 Red Skelton vehicle tailored for Lucille Ball's frantic gifts about an ambitious saleswoman inadvertently mixed with some thieves. With Eddie Albert, Jeff Donnell and Jerome Cowan.
VHS: S18857. $19.95.
Lloyd Bacon, USA, 1950, 93 mins.

Fuller Brush Man
Red Skelton is cast as a struggling door-to-door salesman caught in an intricate murder mystery. With Janet Blair, Don McGuire and Adele Jergens.
VHS: S18858. $14.95.
Frank Tashlin, USA, 1948, 93 mins.

The Fuller Brush Man/ The Fuller Brush Girl
Frank Tashlin penned the screenplays for this pair of wacky films. First Red Skeleton stars as a door-to-door salesman who is accused of murdering his ex-boss. Then Lucille Ball takes her turn going house to house selling cosmetics and finds herself entangled in a double murder. Also features Eddie Albert.
Laser: LD75005. $49.95.
S. Sylvan Simon/Lloyd Bacon, USA, 1948/1950, 178 mins.

Funny Bones
Jerry Lewis is the famous father of a man (Oliver Platt) struggling to get out from under his parent's shadow. This scenario makes for a great comedy full of slapstick and warm humor. It all begins when the younger man makes the mistake of going back to his small hometown for inspiration.
VHS: S26205. $19.95.
Laser: LD75066. $39.99.
Peter Chelsom, USA, 1995, 128 mins.

Funny Guys and Gals of the Talkies
Four shorts: *Golf Specialist* starring W.C. Fields, *Pardon My Pups* with Shirley Temple, *Girls Will Be Boys* with Charlotte Greenwood; and *Groucho Marx, Carole Landis*, which is footage from a radio broadcast during which the two sing.
VHS: S04103. $29.95.

The Gazebo
When a television writer (Glenn Ford) is blackmailed by a mysterious figure with compromising photographs of his Broadway star wife (Debbie Reynolds), he kills the man and disposes of the body under his backyard gazebo. Unfortunately, the body refuses to stay dead. With Carl Reiner, John McGiver, Mabel Albertson, Doro Merande and ZaSu Pitts.
VHS: S20203. $19.98.
George Marshall, USA, 1959, 102 mins.

The Geisha Boy
Jerry Lewis is the Great Wooley, a traveling magician entertaining soldiers in the Far East. Along the way he adopts an orphaned Japanese boy and falls in love with a lovely woman. This warm comedy is a great treat.
VHS: S25834. $14.95.
Frank Tashlin, USA, 1958, 98 mins.

General Spanky
Comedy runs wild when Our Gang's Spanky runs his own ragamuffin Civil War Army. Alfalfa and Buckwheat are among the recruits who use clowning tactics instead of military tactics when Union troops approach.
VHS: S14559. $19.98.
Laser: LD74671. $34.98.
Fred Newmeyer, USA, 1936, 73 mins.

George Washington Slept Here
An adaptation of the George S. Kaufman/Moss Hart play about the ramifications of an urban couple who flee to the country to rehabilitate a run down house. With Jack Benny, Ann Sheridan, Charles Coburn, Hattie McDaniel and Percy Kilbride.
VHS: S17658. $19.98.
William Keighley, USA, 1942, 93 mins.

Get Shorty
John Travolta won a Golden Globe for starring in this superbly cast, dark comedy. Gene Hackman, Rene Russo and Danny De Vito round out the crew of Hollywood creatures who surround a Las Vegas hitman. Though this guy is only out to collect on a loan, he fits right in and becomes Hollywood's hottest producer. Even his black gangster clothes mesh perfectly with the L.A. scene.
VHS: S27762. $19.98.
Laser: LD75580. $39.98.
DVD: DV60075. $24.98.
Barry Sonnenfeld, USA, 1995, 105 mins.

Ghost
A romantic-supernatural-fantasy-thriller that seems to have caught on with the movie-going public. Patrick Swayze is murdered but hangs around his old girlfriend to try to warn her that she could be next. With Whoopi Goldberg as the phony spiritualist who finally makes real contact with the other side, and Demi Moore as the lady in danger. Watch for Tony Goldwyn, Rick Aviles, and Vincent Schiavelli as a cranky subway spirit.
VHS: S13653. $14.95.
Jerry Zucker, USA, 1990, 127 mins.

The Ghost and Mr. Chicken
Don Knotts spends a night in a haunted house in this comedy. Though he's terrified, the ordeal gives him the chance to get out of the business of typsetting newsprint and into the job of writing copy while solving the mystery of the haunted mansion.
VHS: S29992. $14.98.
Alan Rafkin, USA, 1966, 90 mins.

The Ghost Breakers
Bob Hope is a radio commentator who inadvertently becomes part of a gothic murder investigation, set in an atmospheric Cuban mansion Paulette Goddard has inherited. With Richard Carlson, Paul Lukas and Anthony Quinn.
VHS: S18546. $14.98.
George Marshall, USA, 1940, 85 mins.

Ghost Chasers
The Bowery Boys break up a phony seance racket. Huntz Hall is helped in this endeavor by a real ghost that only he can see. Spooky stuff, starring Leo Gorcey, David Gorcey, Bernard Gorcey, Billy Benedict and Lela Bliss as Margo the Medium.
VHS: S15832. $14.98.
William Beaudine, USA, 1951, 67 mins.

Ghostbusters
Dan Aykroyd and Harold Ramis wrote and star in this wild flick about a manic band of parapsychologists ridding Manhattan of bizarre apparitions. Bill Murray steals the show, Sigourney Weaver goes along for the ride. Cinematography by Laszlo Kovacs.
VHS: S00498. $19.95.
Laser: CAV. **LD70368. $99.95.**
Laser: CLV. **LD70369. $49.95.**
Ivan Reitman, USA, 1984, 105 mins.

Girl Can't Help It
Raucous comedy with Jayne Mansfield as the "dumb bombshell" and Edmond O'Brien as her retired racketeer boyfriend. Jayne is trying to get into show biz, Tom Ewell is the comic talent agent helping out. With Fats Domino, The Platters, Gene Vincent.
VHS: S00503. $59.98.
Frank Tashlin, USA, 1956, 99 mins.

Give Me a Sailor
Bob Hope, Betty Grable and Martha Raye are at the center of this complicated romantic farce. Hope loves Grable but needs to enlist the aid of Raye to get Grable's attention. Unfortunately, Hope must agree to help Raye woo his brother, Jack Whiting.
VHS: S25529. $14.98.
Elliott Nugent, USA, 1938, 78 mins.

Gladiator
Mild-mannered Joe E. Brown takes serum which turns him into a major he-man. Full of comic turns with lots of Brown's physical humor and slapstick.
VHS: S08880. $29.95.
Edward Sedgwick, USA, 1938, 65 mins.

The Glass Bottom Boat
Doris Day gets reeled in by handsome fisherman Rod Taylor while moonlighting as a mermaid on Catalina Island. Also starring Dom DeLuise and Paul Lynde.
VHS: S15244. $19.98.
Laser: LD72175. $34.98.
Frank Tashlin, USA, 1966, 110 mins.

A Global Affair
Bob Hope is hilarious as a United Nations official who is saddled with an abandoned child and is promptly seduced by an international bevy of beautiful women who want the child for themselves. With Yvonne DeCarlo, Robert Sterling and John McGiver.
VHS: S19562. $19.98.
Jack Arnold, USA, 1964, 84 mins.

Go West
The Marx Brothers clown around the sagebrush circuit and ride a train where no iron horse has gone before. Groucho is S. Quentin Quale, a con man trying to flimflam the Panello brothers, Rusty (Harpo) and Joe (Chico). With John Carroll and Diana Lewis. B&W.
VHS: S06979. $19.95.
Edward Buzzell, USA, 1940, 81 mins.

Go West, Young Man
Mae West is a privileged movie queen stranded in a desolate farm community who gets entangled with a local (Randolph Scott), despite a film contract that prohibits such a relationship. With Warren William, Alice Brady and Elizabeth Patterson.
VHS: S18867. $14.98.
Henry Hathaway, USA, 1936, 82 mins.

Goin' to Town
A screwball farce with Mae West as an ambitious dance hall girl who wins a husband playing dice and tries to insinuate herself into upper-class society. Features a hilarious rendition of "Samson and Delilah". With Paul Cavanagh, Ivan Lebedeff and Marjorie Gateson.
VHS: S18868. $14.98.
Alexander Hall, USA, 1935, 74 mins.

Going Bananas
David Mendenhall *(Over the Top)* is adopted by a talking chimp (midget-actor Deep Roy) and enlists the aid of Dom DeLuise and Jimmie Walker when his friend is sold to the circus. Filmed in Kenya with some live animals like boa constrictors. With Warren Berlinger and Herbert Lom. Said to be a slapstick safari.
VHS: S09514. $19.95.
Boaz Davidson, USA, 1988, 95 mins.

The Golden Child

In many ways this is Murphy's remake of Chaplin's *The Kid*, except that instead of rescuing a child from the authorities he must rescue a child from the powers of hell. A detective/kung-fu comedy reviled by some as a throw away. However, it's full of action and humor and features an excellent villain in Charles Dance. Murphy's interracial romance in the picture is not exploitative but is shown as perfectly natural.

VHS: S21394. $14.95.
Michael Ritchie, USA, 1986, 96 mins.

Good Night, Michelangelo

A charming, sexy comedy about a family of Italian immigrants living under one roof and trying to pursue their loves and ambitions in a strange environment. Eight-year-old Michelangelo learns important lessons about life and growing up by watching his family's hilarious adventures. Starring Kim Cattrall (*Bonfire of the Vanities*) and Giancarlo Giannini (*New York Stories*). Winner—Best Comedy at the Greater Fort Lauderdale Film Festival 1990.

VHS: S13540. $89.98.
Carlo Liconti, USA, 1989, 91 mins.

The Goodbye Girl

Richard Dreyfuss won an Oscar for his role in this Neil Simon comedy about an egotistical looking-for-work actor and the opinionated divorcee with whom he shares an apartment. Marsha Mason is his unwilling roommate. Quinn Cummings is the child who is wise beyond her years. Funny and tender and set in New York City. With Paul Benedict and Barbara Rhoades.

VHS: S08296. $19.98.
Laser: LD70144. $34.98.
Herbert Ross, USA, 1977, 110 mins.

Goodbye Love

Charlie Ruggles and Sidney Blackmer headline this comedy about a group of henpecked husbands who refuse to pay their alimony and end up in the city jail.

VHS: S14663. $29.95.
H. Bruce Humberstone, USA, 1934, 65 mins.

Goonies

When a band of misfit youngsters find a 17th century pirate map, they begin an adventure in a fabulous subterranean world filled with caverns, crooks, skeletons and booby-traps.

VHS: S04390. $19.98.
Laser: LD71142. $34.98.
Richard Donner, USA, 1986, 114 mins.

The Gorilla

Bela Lugosi replaced Peter Lorre in the role of Peters the sinister butler, in this Ritz Brothers comedy about a trio of klutzy private detectives out to capture a killer gorilla who escaped from a circus. Cast includes Patsy Kelly, Anita Louise and Lionel Atwill. B&W.

VHS: S04005. $29.95.
Allan Dwan, USA, 1939, 65 mins.

The Grass Is Greener

Robert Mitchum shakes up the proper English marriage of Cary Grant and Deborah Kerr in this drawing-room comedy of manners and mores. Jean Simmons offers Cary solace. In other words, it's highbrow hanky panky. From the play by Hugh and Margaret Williams. VHS letterboxed.

VHS: S04241. $19.95.
Laser: LD71859. $34.98.
Stanley Donen, USA, 1960, 105 mins.

Great Guns

Laurel and Hardy get ready for war as they mobilize for merry madness. USA, 1941, 74 mins.

VHS: S04607. $29.98.

The Great Lover

Bob Hope is a reporter assigned to escort a troop of Boy Rangers on an ocean liner to Europe. Aboard are Rhonda Fleming, her dad the Grand Duke, and a murderer who Bob insists is not him. With Roland Young as the card shark and Jim Backus as the detective. A sea worthy comedy. B&W. 80 mins.

VHS: S07585. $14.95.
Alexander Hall, USA, 1949, 80 mins.

Greedy

Michael J. Fox, Kirk Douglas and Nancy Travis star in this riotously funny comedy about the perils of inheritance. All kinds of wacky cousins crawl out in search of the millions sure to be left behind when an old uncle appears to be on the verge of passing on. The uncle, Kirk Douglas, finds that he's not a forgotten old man but the very heart of a loving and Greedy clan.

VHS: S22075. $19.98.
Laser: LD74549. $34.98.
Jonathan Lynn, USA, 1994, 113 mins.

Grosse Pointe Blank

A black comedy co-written by and starring John Cusack as a hitman returning to Michigan for his 10th high school reunion. With Dan Ackroyd as a burly hitman competitor and Minnie Driver as his spurned high school sweetheart. Also with Alan Arkin.

VHS: S32198. $19.95.
Laser: LD76387. $39.99.
DVD: DV60313. $29.99.
George Armitage, USA, 1997, 107 mins.

Groucho Marx—Classic Television

Groucho Marx hosts the 1950 television pilot of *You Bet Your Life*, recorded live with all the bloopers left in. A rare TV document. 60 mins.

VHS: S10593. $29.95.

Groundhog Day

Bill Murray stars as an obnoxious television weatherman caught in a time warp that forces him to relive the day he's stranded in a small Pennsylvania town. Andie MacDowell is Murray's romantic interest, an independent producer. Chris Elliott is a deadpan camera operator.

VHS: S19047. $19.95.
Harold Ramis, USA, 1993, 101 mins.

Grumpier Old Men

Walter Matthau and Jack Lemmon are even more prickly and funny in this comic sequel. This time they fight over another woman, Sophia Loren, and contend with unthinkable change, as their bait shop becomes a fashionable restaurant. Ann-Margret also manages to invade the fracas.

VHS: S27763. $19.98.
Laser: LD75581. $39.98.
DVD: DV60189. $24.98.
Howard Deutch, USA, 1995, 101 mins.

Grumpy Old Men

Walter Matthau and Jack Lemmon have been a film comedy team since their portrayal of two zany, mismatched friends in the *Odd Couple*. In this film their age-old enmity is put to the test by renewed rivalry over an attractive young widow, Daryl Hannah. Also features Burgess Meredith, Ann-Margret and Buck Henry.

VHS: S21084. $19.98.
Laser: LD72412. $34.98.
DVD: DV60076. $24.98.
Donald Petrie, USA, 1993, 104 mins.

The Guardsman

An adaptation of Molnar's comedy about a jealous husband who tests his wife's fidelity. The film stars the real-life married couple, Alfred Lunt and Lynn Fontanne. With Roland Young, ZaSu Pitts and Herman Bing.

VHS: S17659. $19.98.
Sidney Franklin, USA, 1931, 89 mins.

Guest Wife

Determined to impress his sentimental boss, a quick-thinking bachelor (Don Ameche) talks his best friend's bride (Claudette Colbert) into posing as his own wife. When the hoax gets hopelessly out of hand, he nearly ruins the couple's honeymoon and their marriage.

VHS: S12446. $19.98.
Laser: CLV. **LD71987. $29.98.**
Sam Wood, USA, 1945, 90 mins.

Half Shot at Sunrise

Max Steiner received his first credit as musical director for this classic comedy featuring vaudeville comedians Wheeler and Woolsey. Plenty of slapstick, one-liners and sight gags.

VHS: S04495. $29.95.
Paul Sloane, USA, 1930, 78 mins.

Half-Baked

When pothead Kenny gets arrested for accidentally killing a New York City police horse, his stoner crew try to raise the bail by selling pot stolen from a pharmaceutical company. Fun, politically incorrect "high"-jinks. With Dave Chappelle (*The Nutty Professor*), Jim Breuer (*Saturday Night Live*), Guillermo Diaz (*Girls Town*), Harland Williams (*Rocket Man*), Rachel True, Laura Silverman, Clarence Williams III, Stephen Wright and Tommy Chong, and cameos by Janeane Garofalo, Snoop Doggy Dogg, Willie Nelson, Stephen Baldwin, Bob Saget, and Jon Stewart.

VHS: S34575. $106.99.
DVD: DV60259. $29.95.
Dave Chappelle/Neal Brennan, USA, 1998, 73 mins.

Hands Across the Table

Carole Lombard is a delight opposite Fred MacMurray in this effervescent comedy. It's a charming tale about a manicurist in search of a husband, ideally a rich husband. There are all the usual deceptions of romance and some rather novel ones that keep this film light and amusing.

VHS: S26224. $19.98.
Mitchell Leisen, USA, 1935, 80 mins.

Hardboiled Mahoney

Terence "Slip" Mahoney (Leo Gorcey) is mistaken for a detective in this Bowery Boys comedy from Monogram Pictures. An inquiry on behalf of a mysterious woman uncovers a phony medium and a blackmailing scam. With Huntz Hall, Gabriel Dell, Betty Compson, Teala Loring and Byron Foulger. This was the last Bowery Boys movie for Bobby Jordan.

VHS: S15830. $14.98.
William Beaudine, USA, 1947, 63 mins.

Harold and Maude

Bud Cort is Harold, an introverted suicidal 19 year old; Ruth Gordon is Maude, a spunky 79 year old. They fall in love in this witty romantic comedy. The early scenes in which Harold tries out suicide methods are outstanding. Music by Cat Stevens.

VHS: S00543. $19.95.
Laser: LD75352. $29.98.
Hal Ashby, USA, 1971, 92 mins.

Harry and the Hendersons

A comic fantasy starring John Lithgow as George Henderson, an easy-going father whose life is suddenly turned upside down when his car hits a real-life Bigfoot at the tail end of a camping trip. Thinking the beast is dead, they take it home, but soon find out the lovable creature is alive and well, and life at the Hendersons becomes a whirlwind of bizarre adventures. With Don Ameche.

VHS: S05248. $89.95.
William Dear, USA, 1987, 111 mins.

Harvey

James Stewart is Elwood P. Dowd, a gentle alcoholic whose best friend is an invisible six foot rabbit. Stewart was nominated for an Oscar for his performance in the screen adaptation of the Pulitzer Prize winning play by Mary Chase. Cast includes Josephine Hull, Peggy Dow, Jesse White, Charles Drake, and Cecil Kellaway as Dr. Chumley of the Chumley Rest Home. See for yourself how an invisible rabbit can add something special to your life.

VHS: S12131. $19.95.
Laser: LD70037. $34.98.
Henry Koster, USA, 1951, 104 mins.

Heartbreak Kid

A wonderful Neil Simon comedy based on an idea by Bruce Jay Friedman, directed by Elaine May. Charles Grodin is the Jewish boy who gets married to Jeannie Berlin but meets Cybill Shepherd on their honeymoon, and decides to have it both ways. Both hilarious and poignant.

VHS: S10008. $14.98.
Elaine May, USA, 1972, 104 mins.

Heathers

This wicked satire, from first-time screenwriter Daniel Waters, takes on high school, adolescent angst, the ironic glorification of teen suicide, homophobia, popularity, football players, funerals, croquet, and just about anything else you can think of. With Winona Ryder and Christian Slater. Quite dark and funny. Letterboxed.

VHS: S13691. $19.95.
Laser: CLV, with cast interviews. **LD75009. $49.95.**
Michael Lehmann, USA, 1989, 102 mins.

Her Favorite Patient (aka Bedside Manner)

A romantic comedy with John Carroll as a pilot whose doctor, played by Ruth Hussey, gives him some extra special tender lovin' care.

VHS: S14672. $29.95.
Andrew L. Stone, USA, 1946, 72 mins.

Her First Romance

This delightful romantic comedy features a confusing mix-up involving two sisters, an attractive cousin and her fiance, played by Alan Ladd. Fortunately it ends as a good comedy should, with everyone finding the right mate. Edith Fellows, Wilbur Evans, Judith Linden and Jacqueline Wells are also featured.

VHS: S22600. $19.95.
George Dmytryk, USA, 1940, 77 mins.

Here Come the Co-Eds

Abbott and Costello play two wacky caretakers whose zany antics inject some life and personality into a boring and repressed girls school. With Peggy Ryan, Martha O'Driscoll, June Vincent and Lon Chaney.

VHS: S19072. $14.98.
Jean Yarbrough, USA, 1945, 87 mins.

Here Come the Girls

Bob Hope is the show biz impresario who tries to ward off a deranged killer. With Arlene Dahl, Rosemary Clooney and Tony Martin. Entertainment from the Four Step Brothers.
VHS: S17978. $14.95.
Claude Binyon, USA, 1953, 100 mins.

Here Come the WAVES

This is a wartime comedy that pairs Bing Crosby and Betty Hutton with the U.S. Navy. Together they sing and dance through just about everything, with Bing even using blackface make-up to perform the superhit that became one of his signature tunes, "Accentuate the Positive."
VHS: S21200. $14.98.
Mark Sandrich, USA, 1944, 99 mins.

Here Comes Cookie

Gracie Allen stars as a wealthy girl who has some fun by cutting off her dad and sister's allowances and converting their mansion into a shelter for indigent vaudevillians with trained dogs and performing seals.
VHS: S28592. $14.98.
Norman Z. McLeod, USA, 1935, 63 mins.

Here Comes Mr. Jordan

A prizefighter who is also an amateur saxophonist crashes in his private plane and goes to heaven by mistake—this is the setup of the classic fantasy, as when he goes back to Earth, he has to find another body. With Robert Montgomery, Evelyn Keyes, Claude Rains, James Gleason.
VHS: Out of print. For rental only.
Laser: LD71040. $49.95.
Alexander Hall, USA, 1941, 94 mins.

Hey Abbott!

Abbott and Costello were the definitive burlesque comedy team. This retrospective of their work together, hosted by Milton Berle, contains the most famous routines, including *Who's on First*, *Oyster Stew* and *Floogle Street*. Steve Allen and Phil Silvers tell all through hilarious interviews and reminiscences about this legendary pair. 76 mins.
VHS: S15999. $19.98.

High Anxiety

Mel Brooks takes on Alfred Hitchcock in this funny spoof of some of the Master of Suspense's greatest moments. With Brooks, Madeline Kahn, Harvey Korman.
VHS: S04318. $19.98.
Laser: LD76331. $39.99.
Mel Brooks, USA, 1977, 94 mins.

The History of the World, Part One

Mel Brooks turns his special brand of humor on various periods of history including the Stone Age, Biblical times, the Spanish Inquisition and the French Revolution. Cast includes Dom DeLuise, Gregory Hines, Madeline Kahn, Harvey Korman, Cloris Leachman and Brooks himself. Orson Welles narrates. Guaranteed to be funnier than the Black Plague.
VHS: S06147. $14.98.
Mel Brooks, USA, 1981, 92 mins.

Hold Me Thrill Me Kiss Me

Joel Hershman's outlandish comedy features Max Parrish as the handsome drifter Eli fleeing his spurned fiance (a hilarious Sean Young). He falls under the hypnotic spell of a dominatrix stripper (former porn star Andrea Naschak) who imprisons him in a sleazy trailer park, where he promptly falls for the woman's virginal, beautiful sister (Adrienne Shelly). With Diane Ladd, Dr. Timothy Leary and Bela Lehoczky. The eclectic soundtrack features Poi Dog Pondering, The Violent Femmes, Fred Schneider, The Pixies, The Cramps, King Missile and Jazz Butcher.
VHS: S20197. $92.98.
Joel Hershman, USA, 1992, 92 mins.

Hold Your Man

A brisk comedy of manners about the affair between Jean Harlow and Clark Gable, low-rent grifters whose lifestyle and career choices can't diminish their love. With Stuart Erwin and Elizabeth Patterson.
VHS: S17779. $19.98.
Sam Wood, USA, 1933, 87 mins

Hollywood Hot Tubs

When your parents and your probation officer make you get a job…why not work where everybody plays? This highly original cult comedy is an all time favorite. Getting into hot water has never been so much fun!
VHS: S15033. $19.95.
Chck Vincent, USA, 1984, 105 mins.

Hollywood or Bust

Dean Martin and Jerry Lewis in their last film together, with Jerry playing an obsessed fan who heads West determined to meet his idol. With Anita Ekberg and Pat Crowley.
VHS: S04428. $14.95.
Frank Tashlin, USA, 1956, 95 mins.

Hollywood Revels

From the Follies Theatre in Los Angeles, welcome to the wonderful world of Burlesque. Baggy pants comedians, candy butchers, and of course, a bevy of beautiful gals all eager to disrobe. With Aleene Dupree, Mickey Lotus Wing and Hillary Dawn. Music written and conducted by Billy Rose. USA, 1947, 58 mins.
VHS: S05476. $24.95.

Home for the Holidays

Holly Hunter, Robert Downey, Jr., Dylan McDermott, Anne Bancroft, Claire Danes, Charles Durning, Geraldine Chaplin and Steve Guttenberg are the all-star cast of this family comedy. Hunter was laid off from work, made a pass at her boss, and her daughter's planning to lose her virginity. Just when it seems things can't get any worse for this Chicago art restoration expert, she heads to her parents' house for Thanksgiving. Her brother's gay, her sister and her husband are uptight, her aunt's a drunk and her parents are crazy, but at least it's home.
VHS: S27515. $19.95.
Laser: LD75523. $34.95.
Jodie Foster, USA, 1995, 103 mins.

The Honeymoon Machine

Steve McQueen and Jim Hutton star as two American sailors in Venice, Italy, who try to access a Navy computer and electronically manipulate the roulette tables. With Paula Prentiss, Jack Mullaney and Dean Jagger. "A series of laugh explosions that recur with happy frequency" (*The Hollywood Reporter*).
VHS: S18011. $19.98.
Richard Thorpe, USA, 1961, 87 mins.

Honky Tonk

Con artist Candy Johnson (Clark Gable) had been run out of town after town. Then he got wise, went out and got a town of his own: Yellow Creek, Nevada. A lively, lusty, comic-western co-starring sassy Lana Turner.
VHS: S15259. $19.98.
Jack Conway, USA, 1941, 105 mins.

Honolulu

Comic repercussions, confusion and intrigue abound when a matinee idol movie star exchanges identities with a Hawaiian plantation owner. With Eleanor Powell, Robert Young, George Burns and Gracie Allen.
VHS: S18554. $19.98.
Edward Buzzell, USA, 1939, 84 mins.

The Horn Blows at Midnight

A rip-roaring comedy starring Jack Benny as Athaniel, an angel sent from Heaven to destroy Earth, where persecution and hatred have soared out of control. Well-cast fantasy that is highly enjoyable.
VHS: S14562. $19.98.
Raoul Walsh, USA, 1945, 78 mins.

Horse Feathers

The four Marx Brothers go to college in this classic comedy written by humorist S.J. Perelman. The new president of Huxley College is Professor Wagstaff (Groucho), and he needs better football players to have a winning team. He can find them in a speakeasy if only he can guess the password. I'll give you a clue. It isn't horsefeathers. B&W.
VHS: S08323. $19.95.
Laser: LD70039. $34.98.
DVD: DV60344. $24.99.
Norman Z. McLeod, USA, 1932, 67 mins.

The Hospital

Paddy Chayefsky wrote this biting black comedy about a modern mega-hospital that strangles its patients—and doctors—in red tape. George C. Scott stars in a ferocious, Oscar-nominated performance.
VHS: S15251. $19.98.
Laser: LD76414. $34.98.
Arthur Hiller, USA, 1971, 102 mins.

Hot Millions

Peter Ustinov is a shrewd hustler and trickster who manipulates a computer to devise a fake company and embezzle millions, in this engaging comedy. With Maggie Smith, Bob Newhart, Karl Malden, Robert Morley and Cesar Romero.
VHS: S20206. $19.98.
Eric Till, USA, 1968, 106 mins.

Hotel Paradiso

In this boulevard farce, Alec Guinness and Gina Lollobrigida are neighbors trying to carry off an improbable affair in a sleazy hotel. The arrival of an eccentric group of fellow guests leads to a series of zany adventures and mixed up identities. Written by Peter Glenville and Jean-Claude Carriere, from the play by Georges Feydeau. Cinematography by Henri Decae. With Robert Morley, Peggy Mount, Douglas Byng, Akim Tamiroff and Robertson Hare.
VHS: S20205. $19.98.
Peter Glenville, USA, 1966, 99 mins.

The House of Yes

Existing "somewhere between *Long Day's Journey into Night* and *The Addams Family*" (Roger Ebert, *Chicago Sun-Times*), *The House of Yes* is an offbeat comedy about Marty Pascal (Josh Hamilton), who brings his fiance, Lesly (Tori Spelling), home for Thanksgiving in 1983 to meet his dysfunctional family. It soon becomes clear that Marty's jealous twin sister (Parker Posey)—who calls herself Jackie-O—is a little too close to her twin. But Jackie isn't the only family member with problems in this house where the word "no" is never heard. With Freddie Prinze, Jr., and Genevieve Bujold.
VHS: S33697. $103.99.
Laser: LD76814. $39.99.
Mark Waters, USA, 1997, 87 mins.

Houseboat

Cary Grant and Sophia Loren are teamed in this Oscar-nominated romantic comedy about a widower who hires a governess to look after his three unruly children.
VHS: S04430. $19.95.
Laser: LD75353. $29.98.
Melville Shavelson, USA, 1958, 110 mins.

Household Saints

When the Santangelos, an Italian-American couple, pray for a miracle, their wish is granted, or so they originally think, in the form of a daughter they call Teresa. Tracey Ullman, Vincent D'Onofrio, Lili Taylor and Judith Malina star in this humorous fable of faith, sainthood and sausage.
VHS: S21095. $94.95.
Nancy Savoca, USA, 1993, 124 mins.

How to Commit Marriage

A strange Bob Hope/Jackie Gleason comedy about a divorcing couple who are shaken by their daughter's announcement she's about to marry a raffish musician. Gleason is the father of the groom with a bizarre plan to exploit the situation to create a hip new band. With Jane Wyman, Tim Matthieson, Joanna Cameron and Tina Louise.
VHS: S18444. $14.95.
Norman Panama, USA, 1969, 95 mins.

How to Frame a Figg

Don Knotts stars as an accountant who happens upon a discrepancy in the books of Dalton Township. Soon this mild-mannered character is the toast of the town as government officials curry his favor in this comedy of cover-ups.
VHS: S29998. $14.98.
Edward J. Montagne, USA, 1971, 103 mins.

How to Marry a Millionaire

Post World War II comedy in which Marilyn Monroe, Betty Grable and Lauren Bacall try to attract rich men to marry, but discover that love is preferable to money.
VHS: S04202. $19.98.
Laser: LD71059. $69.98.
Jean Negulesco, USA, 1953, 96 mins.

How to Murder Your Wife

Jack Lemmon marries Virna Lisi while under the influence and begins to regret the decision. Is it his fault the blonde Italian who popped out of a bachelor party cake was so alluring, at the time, to this famous cartoonist for a man's adventure strip? With Terry-Thomas as his disapproving manservant and Eddie Mayerhof as his henpecked lawyer. A hilarious comedy about mixing marriage with an active imagination.
VHS: S11220. $19.95.
Laser: LD72266. $39.98.
Richard Quine, USA, 1965, 118 mins.

I'll Do Anything

Nick Nolte, Albert Brooks, Julie Kavner and Tracey Ullman are all featured in this romantic comedy about a father who unexpectedly gains custody of his six-year-old daughter. Nolte is the actor and father whose life is thrown completely out of kilter when Hollywood comes knocking, forcing him to be both a good parent and a star.
VHS: S21382. $19.95.
Laser: LD74475. $34.95.
James L. Brooks, USA, 1994, 116 mins.

I'll Take Sweden

In this madcap comedy, Bob Hope prevents his daughter's (Tuesday Weld) marriage to her uncouth boyfriend (Frankie Avalon) by moving the family to Sweden. Hope's plans for domestic tranquility are shattered when Weld falls for a charismatic and devilish Swedish playboy.
VHS: S19563. $19.98.
Fred De Cordova, USA, 1965, 96 mins.

I'm from Hollywood: Andy Kaufman

This program examines the peculiar genius of the late comedian Andy Kaufman, the brilliant, nervous, sometimes unstable actor and comedian whose signature work came on the NBC program *Taxi*. Features interviews with Marilu Henner, Tony Danza and Kaufman's stand up contemporaries, and footage from Kaufman's television appearances, particularly *Late Night with David Letterman*. 60 mins.
VHS: S17347. $19.95.

I'm No Angel

A comedy set against a strange backdrop of carnivals and freak shows, about a beautiful lion tamer (Mae West) who pursues a charismatic playboy (Cary Grant). With Edward Arnold, Gertrude Michael and Kent Taylor.
VHS: S18869. $14.98.
Wesley Ruggles, USA, 1933, 87 mins.

I'm Not Rappaport

Walter Matthau and Ossie Davis star in this adaptation of Herb Gardner's Tony Award-winning play, the humorous and charming story of two lively old-timers who form an unlikely bond within the colorful confines of Central Park. With Craig T. Nelson, Amy Irving and Martha Plimpton.
VHS: S31400. $19.95.
Laser: LD76233. $34.95.
Herb Gardner, USA, 1996, 137 mins.

I.Q.

Meg Ryan, Tim Robbins and Walter Matthau are joined in this unlikely romantic comedy in which Albert Einstein plays cupid. Matthau is great as the genius matchmaker whose classic formula (one plus one equals two), generates some real chemistry.
VHS: S25653. $19.95.
Fred Schepisi, USA, 1994, 95 mins.

Iceland

A high-style romantic comedy about a Norwegian beauty (Sonja Henie) who becomes the fixation of an American marine (John Payne). Music by Sammy Kaye and his orchestra, featuring the hit song, "There Will Never Be Another You." With Jack Oakie, Sterling Holloway and Osa Massen.
VHS: S20263. $19.98.
H. Bruce Humberstone, USA, 1942, 79 mins.

If I Were King

Black humor abounds in this spectacular romantic adventure when roguish poet Ronald Colman matches wits with sly French monarch Basil Rathbone in 15th-century Paris. With Frances Dee. Includes original theatrical trailer.
VHS: S34680. $14.98.
Frank Lloyd, USA, 1938, 102 mins.

If It's Tuesday, This Must Be Belgium

A comedy about cultural displacement and Americans abroad. A group of Americans travel through Europe in a series of comic adventures. With Suzanne Pleshette, Norman Fell, Michael Constantine and Peggy Cass.
VHS: S18017. $19.98.
Laser: LD72178. $34.98.
Mel Stuart, USA, 1969, 99 mins.

The Impossible Years

David Niven plays a university psychiatrist writing a book about controlling adolescent difficulties and encountering insurmountable problems trying to contain the sexual curiosity of his beautiful 17-year-old daughter. "A comedy of the generation gap which didn't bridge it but fell right into it" (Gerald Garrett). With Lola Albright, Chad Everett and Ozzie Nelson.
VHS: S20202. $19.98.
Michael Gordon, USA, 1968, 98 mins.

In Like Flint

Flint returns. This time the super secret agent fights a group of wealthy and powerful female tycoons who have developed a way of brainwashing women through beauty salon hair dryers! With all the women in the world enslaved, they commandeer the first U.S. space platform and then replace the President with their own surgically reproduced clone.
VHS: S11264. $19.98.
Gordon Douglas, USA, 1967, 114 mins.

In Society

Abbott and Costello play two down-on-their-luck plumbers who are mistaken for gilded aristocrats. With Marion Hutton, Arthur Treacher and Thomas Gomez.
VHS: S19068. $14.98.
Jean Yarbrough, USA, 1944, 75 mins.

In the Navy

In this rollicking nautical musical-comedy, Abbott and Costello are two sailors bound for duty on the high seas. They befriend a singing star and must help him evade an ambitious reporter. Includes musical numbers by The Andrews Sisters.
VHS: S14903. $14.95.
Laser: LD71406. $34.98.
Arthur Lubin, USA, 1941, 85 mins.

The In-Laws

This wild comedy stars Peter Falk as a CIA agent, or at least he claims to be one. Alan Arkin is really a dentist whose daughter is marrying Falk's son. Somehow the comic relationship between these future in-laws leads them into a plot that foils a South American dictator and his counterfeiting schemes.
VHS: S22865. $19.98.
Laser: LD74704. $34.98.
Arthur Hiller, USA, 1979, 103 mins.

The Incredible Shrinking Woman

Lily Tomlin stars in this spoof of the original 50's film *The Incredible Shrinking Man*. She shrinks as a result of chemical pollution in the home and becomes an instant celebrity, only to find herself the target of a large corporation. Also features Charles Grodin and Ned Beatty.
VHS: S21765. $14.98.
Joel Schumacher, USA, 1981, 88 mins.

Indian Summer

Mike Binder's autobiographical comedy reworks the *Secaucus 7/Big Chill* genre for Generation X. Eight childhood friends in their 30s return to their idyllic summer camp to rekindle the protective innocence and joy of their post-adolescence, though the messy complications of real life intrude. With Alan Arkin, Diane Lane, Matt Craven and Elizabeth Perkins.
VHS: S19435. $94.95.
Mike Binder, USA, 1993, 97 mins.

Indiscreet

Singin' in the Rain co-director Stanley Donen produced and directed this elegantly sophisticated comedy about a secret love affair between a beautiful actress and a NATO diplomat. The leads are brilliant: Cary Grant is charming, aloof and funny; Ingrid Bergman alluring, mysterious and quixotic. Letterboxed.
VHS: S02641. $19.95.
Stanley Donen, USA, 1958, 100 mins.

International House

W.C. Fields, George Burns and Gracie Allen romp through China where a scientist has created the first television. With Rudy Vallee, Bela Lugosi and Sterling Holloway, and a special appearance by Cab Calloway singing "Reefer Man."
VHS: S01991. $29.95.
A. Edward Sutherland, USA, 1933, 72 mins.

Is There Sex After Death?

Buck Henry takes a wacky look at the ins and outs of the sexual revolution, with his journey beginning at the Bureau of Sexological Investigation, where researchers are grappling with the most difficult of questions. An outrageous and often funny satire.
VHS: S03483. $29.95.
Alan and Jeanne Abel, USA, 1971, 97 mins.

It Could Happen to You

Nicolas Cage, Bridget Fonda and Rosie Perez star in this screwball comedy about the travails of winning big. A cop (Cage) promises a waitress (Fonda) part of his winnings from a lottery ticket when he doesn't have enough cash for a tip. Though she doesn't believe him, he wins and actually makes good on his promise. Perez is great as the wife who can't understand his generosity.
VHS: S23298. $19.95.
Andrew Bergman, USA, 1994, 101 mins.

It Happens Every Spring

A wacky comedy featuring a mild-mannered academic who accidentally uncovers a wood repellent. From this chance discovery he manages to find a career as an unstoppable pitcher. This charming classic laughs at America's favorite springtime preoccupation. With Ray Milland and Ed Begley.
VHS: S20704. $19.98.
Lloyd Bacon, USA, 1949, 87 mins.

It Started in Naples

Clark Gable travels to Italy to bring home his recently orphaned nephew and runs up against the boy's fiery guardian, Sophia Loren. Mama mia, What fun! USA, 1960, 100 mins.
VHS: S15160. $19.95.

It Started with a Kiss

A clear-eyed comedy about romance and class. An Air Force sergeant (Glenn Ford) is transferred to Spain and has to deal with his wife (Debbie Reynolds) and the car he won in a lottery. With Eva Gabor, Harry Morgan and Fred Clark.
VHS: S18018. $19.98.
Melville Shavelson, USA, 1959, 104 mins.

It Started with Eve

Charles Laughton stars with Deanna Durbin in this hilarious misadventure of love and romance. Laughton plays a grumpy old millionaire whose dying wish is to meet the young lady who is engaged to marry his son. Unfortunately, the bride in question is unavailable. Believing his father is not long for this world, the son finds a quick replacement, a hat check girl (Durbin).
VHS: S23282. $19.98.
Henry Koster, USA, 1941, 90 mins.

It's a Great Life

Dagwood is dispatched to buy a house, returns as the owner of a prize-winning horse, and gets involved in an epic fox hunt. With Penny Singleton, Arthur Lake and Larry Simms.
VHS: S20180. $14.95.
Frank Strayer, USA, 1943, 75 mins.

It's a Joke, Son!

A folksy, down-home comedy that brought radio's popular "Senator Claghorn" (from the Fred Allen Show) to the screen. Starring Kenny Delmar, Una Merkel, June Lockhart and Douglass Dumbrille.
VHS: S14324. $19.98.
Ben Stoloff, USA, 1947, 67 mins.

It's a Mad, Mad, Mad, Mad World

Forty stars and a million laughs in this wild romp featuring a cast of some of America's greatest funnymen: Jimmy Durante, Milton Berle, Spencer Tracy, Sid Caesar, Buddy Hackett, Ethel Merman, Mickey Rooney, Phil Silvers, Jonathan Winters, the Three Stooges and more. A cult classic!
VHS: S02327. $29.98.
Laser: LD70602. $69.98.
Stanley Kramer, USA, 1963, 155 mins.

It's in the Bag

This outrageous comedy-mystery has Fred Allen inheriting five seemingly worthless chairs from his recently-deceased, rich uncle. But once he sells them for much needed cash, Fred discovers his uncle hid a huge fortune in the missing furniture. And so, he's off on a hilarious treasure hunt that leads to laughter and lunacy. With Jack Benny.
VHS: S09496. $19.95.
Richard Wallace, USA, 1945, 87 mins.

Jack and the Beanstalk

A comic adventure in Never-Never Land in which Lou Costello falls asleep while babysitting and dreams that he is Jack from the famous fairy tale *Jack and the Beanstalk*.
VHS: S34192. $14.95.
Jean Yarbrough, USA, 1952, 78 mins.

The Jackpot

In this classic comedy, Jimmy Stewart and Barbara Hale are a couple whose lives are transformed when they win a jackpot from a radio giveaway show. Though Stewart's character tries to help others by shedding his prizes, the beneficiaries of his generosity experience unforseen complications. Natalie Wood also appears.
VHS: S29801. $19.98.
Walter Lang, USA, 1950, 87 mins.

The Jerky Boys: The Movie

One day a couple of losers from Queens make the wrong prank call. Before they know what to do, the mob is after them. Along the way they encounter a number of hilarious adventures. Alan Arkin is great as the mob hitman with the perfect demeanor but lousy aim.
VHS: S26288. $19.95.
Laser: LD75067. $39.99.
James Melkonian, USA, 1995, 81 mins.

Jerry Maguire

From *Mission Impossible* to mission statement? In this romantic story, Tom Cruise stars as a sports agent who is all business until an inspiration strikes which changes his life. With Oscar-winner Cuba Gooding Jr. and Renee Zellweger.
VHS: S31293. $14.95.
Laser: LD76207. $39.95.
DVD: DV60015. $29.95.
Cameron Crowe, USA, 1996, 139 mins.

Joe Versus the Volcano

In this well received Hollywood comedy, Tom Hanks stars as a terminally ill man who sets forth on one final tour of the globe. What he finds is mystical adventure and an odd, romantic companion with the island-bound Meg Ryan.
VHS: S12666. $14.95.
John Patrick Shanley, USA, 1990, 106 mins.

Joe's Apartment

With a little help from David Geffen and MTV, John Payson has expanded his "sex, bugs and rock 'n' roll" short film about cockroaches who take over the apartment of a hapless new tenant into a live-action/animated musical comedy. Filmmaker Reginald Hudlin offers his vocal talents as a roach and Don Ho makes an appearance as an evil landlord. "The *Citizen Kane* of cockroach movies. Should do for roaches what *Babe* did for pigs!" (Larry Worth, *New York Post*).
VHS: S30444. $19.98.
Laser: LD76029. $34.98.
John Payson, USA, 1996, 82 mins.

Joey Breaker

A hilarious Hollywood movie starring Richard Edson as a smooth-talking agent on the fast track whose priorities are radically altered when he's drawn to a beautiful and mysterious young Jamaican woman (Cedella Marley). Winner of top prize at the Santa Barbara International Film Festival. Cinematography by Joe DeSalvo. With Erik King, Gina Gershon, Phillip Seymour Hoffman and Fred Fondren.
VHS: S19204. $92.95.
Steven Starr, USA, 1993, 92 mins.

Joy of Sex

Martha Coolidge *(Real Genius)* takes the title of a popular sex manual and uses it to front a high school teenage sex comedy. She populates the film with some supporting performers from *Valley Girl*, like Cameron Dye, Michelle Meyrink and Colleen Camp. Plot concerns a teen virgin who would like to alter that situation before she dies of a fatal disease.

VHS: S06172. $79.95.
Martha Coolidge, USA, 1984, 93 mins.

Julia Misbehaves

Elegant farce and unruly, slapstick energy carry this light and charming work about a divorced couple (Greer Garson and Walter Pidgeon) who are reunited on the eve of their daughter's (Elizabeth Taylor) wedding. With Peter Lawford, Cesar Romero and Lucile Watson.

VHS: S18523. $19.98.
Jack Conway, USA, 1949, 99 mins.

Jumping Jacks

Screwball farce and manic comedy in this Dean Martin and Jerry Lewis comedy detailing their destruction of military order and authoritarian rules when they're enlisted into a military paratroop division. With Mona Freeman, Don DeFore and Robert Strauss.

VHS: S18676. $19.95.
Laser: LD75213. $34.98.
Norman Taurog, USA, 1952, 96 mins.

June Bride

Bretaigne Windust directs this sly farce about the romantic dynamics of two young magazine journalists (Bette Davis and Robert Montgomery) sent to cover a traditional wedding to research an article about June Brides. With Fay Bainter, Tom Tully, Barbara Bates, Jerome Cowan, and Debbie Reynolds's film debut.

VHS: S17333. $19.98.
Bretaigne Windust, USA, 1948, 97 mins.

Keep 'Em Flying

This wacky escapade takes Abbott and Costello on a high-flying adventure as new recruits in the Army Air Corps. Loaded with wonderful music, daring stunts and great comic routines.

VHS: S14904. $14.95.
Laser: LD71407. $34.98.
Arthur Lubin, USA, 1941, 86 mins.

The Kettles in the Ozarks

It starts as just a simple visit to some kin folk in Mournful Hollow. Uncle Sedge however needs help from Ma Kettle and all her kids with his housekeeper/fiance and the evil scientists that have just bought his entire corn crop. Great laughs and a twisted plot make this another winner in the series with Marjorie Main.

VHS: S24331. $14.98.
Charles Lamont, USA, 1955, 81 mins.

The Kettles on Old MacDonald's Farm

Marjorie Main stars with Parker Fenelly in this the last of the Kettle films. Ma and Pa offer marriage advice to a young couple, a lumber man and the pampered daughter of his boss, John Smith and Gloria Talbott.

VHS: S24333. $14.98.
Virgil W. Vogel, USA, 1957, 82 mins.

Kid from Brooklyn

Remake of Harold Lloyd's *The Milky Way* works very well for Danny Kaye as a milkman accidentally turned into a prizefighter.

VHS: S03124. $19.98.
Norman Z. McLeod, USA, 1946, 113 mins.

Kid from Spain

In this comedy, Eddie Cantor is a man who unwittingly finds himself involved in a bank robbery, poses as a bullfighter, and is forced to really fight a bull to avoid a detective. With Lyda Roberti, Robert Young, Ruth Hall and Sydney Franklin.

VHS: S31810. $14.95.
Leo McCarey, USA, 1933, 98 mins.

Kin Folks

A humorous look at one South Central clan from the eyes of the youngest son, Sean Green (Casey Lee, *Don't Be a Menace*), an aspiring rapper, who's afraid to invite his girlfriend Lissa (Maia Campbel, *In the House*) over for Christmas because he's embarrassed by his family. A heartwarming and flavorful story about love and family and the drama that comes with it.

VHS: S34080. $69.95.
Karl P. Epps II, USA, 1997, 98 mins.

Kingpin

"From the idiots who brung you *Dumb and Dumber*" comes this wild and crazy tale of a washed-up bowler (Woody Harrelson) who recruits an Amish man (Randy Quaid) to compete in a million-dollar bowling tournament with the help of a brainy babe (Vanessa Angel). With Bill Murray. "*Kingpin* is just too funny" *(Los Angeles Times)*.

VHS: S30464. $19.98.
Laser: LD76059. $39.98.
Peter Farrelly/Bobby Farrelly, USA, 1996, 107 mins.

Kisses for My President

Polly Bergen is hailed as the chief in this comic "what if?" about the first female president. Fred MacMurray catches plenty of flak as the first Hubby. With Arlene Dahl, Eli Wallach and Edward Andrews.

VHS: S16275. $19.98.
Laser: LD70047. $34.98.
Curtis Bernhardt, USA, 1964, 113 mins.

Ladies' Man

The adventures of an accident-prone confirmed bachelor who gets a job in a women's boarding house for aspiring actresses. He starts out as the handyman but ends up as the ladies' man. Jerry Lewis, Helen Traubel star.

VHS: S12571. $19.95.
Jerry Lewis, USA, 1961, 106 mins.

The Lady Is Willing

A screwball farce with serious overtones about a musical comedy performer (Marlene Dietrich) who adopts a young baby and falls for her simple though charming pediatrician. With Fred MacMurray, Aline MacMahon and Stanley Ridges.

VHS: S19022. $19.95.
Mitchell Leisen, USA, 1942, 91 mins.

Lady on a Train

Ralph Bellamy joins Deanna Durbin for this murder mystery with a comic twist. It all begins when a girl sees a violent murder aboard a train. Initially no one believes her, so she must set out to solve the case herself. Fortunately, she has been mistaken for an heiress, which makes this task a little easier, even as it leads to interesting misunderstandings.

VHS: S27013. $19.98.
Charles David, USA, 1945, 95 mins.

The Lady Says No

A delightful comedy about fickle Joan Caulfield who just can't decide if marriage is right for her. Also starring David Niven.

VHS: S14674. $29.95.
Frank Ross, USA, 1951, 80 mins.

Lady Takes a Chance

John Wayne and Jean Arthur star in a hilarious romantic comedy about a New York girl with matrimonial ideas and a rope-shy rodeo rider who yearns for the wide-open spaces.

VHS: S06414. $14.98.
William A. Seiter, USA, 1943, 86 mins.

The Landlord

Beau Bridges is a rich young man who buys a tenement in Brooklyn. Originally, he intended to renovate it for himself but the current tenants have other ideas. Pearl Bailey, Douglas Grant and Louis Gossett Jr. play some of the characters whom Bridges encounters. In the end the landlord learns to appreciate the diversity of Brooklyn. This is a warm comedy with heart.

VHS: S28051. $19.98.
Hal Ashby, USA, 1970, 114 mins.

Larger Than Life

In this comedy "for children of all ages" (Gene Siskel, *Chicago Tribune*), Bill Murray stars as a successful businessman who inherits an elephant from his circus clown father. He decides to unload the lovable elephant, Vera, to the highest bidder, who is 3,000 miles away. So begins an outrageous cross-country journey complete with crazed truck drivers, eccentric circus veterans, mystifying miracles and hilarious run-ins with the law

VHS: S31151. $19.98.
Laser: LD76196. $39.98.
Howard Franklin, USA, 1996, 93 mins.

The Last Detail

Comedy drama about two career sailors escorting a sailor to the brig, who decide to show the young sailor a good time before he begins his prison sentence. Jack Nicholson is simply marvelous, with Otis Young, Randy Quaid, Michael Moriarty. Screenplay by Robert Towne.

VHS: S02173. $14.95.
Laser: Chapter stops, digital master. **LD75089. $34.95.**
Hal Ashby, USA, 1973, 105 mins.

Last of the Red Hot Lovers

This is not a salute to a frankfurter aficionado but another Neil Simon stage comedy being filmed for the movies. Alan Arkin is a restaurateur who seeks the romantic company of three different women, played by Sally Kellerman, Paula Prentiss and Renee Taylor. His biggest fear is that he smells of fish.

VHS: S10819. $19.95.
Gene Saks, USA, 1972, 98 mins.

The Last Remake of Beau Geste

Director, co-screenwriter and performer Marty Feldman may not have made the last version of the classic P.C. Wren novel of life in the Foreign Legion, but he certainly is responsible for the goofiest. Feldman and Michael York play identical twin brothers who join the Legion on a point of honor. With Ann-Margret as the sexy stepmother and Peter Ustinov as the villainous sergeant.

VHS: S06175. $14.95.
Marty Feldman, USA, 1977, 83 mins.

The Last Supper

In this critically acclaimed *Big Chill*-style comedy, five liberal Iowa graduate students serve up serial murder when a redneck guest comes to dinner. Stars Jason Alexander, Cameron Diaz, Nora Dunn, Charles Durning, Ron Eldard, Annabeth Gish, Mark Harmon, Bill Paxton, Jonathan Penner, Ron Perlman and Courtney B. Vance.

VHS: S28516. $19.95.
Laser: LD75950. $34.95.
Stacy Title, USA, 1995, 94 mins.

The Late Shift

Kathy Bates stars along with Daniel Roebuck, John Michael Higgins and Treat Williams in this rollicking farce about Jay Leno and David Letterman's fight for Johnny Carson's late night spot. It shows the hard feelings and harder tactics that gave America a new man to go to sleep with nightly.

VHS: S28063. $19.98.
Betty Thomas, USA, 1995, 95 mins.

Latin Lovers

A romantic comedy about a wealthy heiress and businesswoman (Lana Turner) searching for authentic romance. With John Lund, Ricardo Montalban, Jean Hagen and Rita Moreno.

VHS: S18660. $19.98.
Mervyn LeRoy, USA, 1953, 104 mins.

Laurel & Hardy in Spanish

NOT dubbed, NOT subtitled, this series of Laurel & Hardy classics feature "El Gordo y El Flaco"—as they are known to the Spanish-speaking world—actually speaking Spanish! These are separate films with different, supporting players than in the American releases; some of these films feature additional gags and even different resolutions to stories in certain cases. This series of films is of special interest because it gives us a rare example of Hollywood's early attempt at internationalizing the talking picture. Completely digitally remastered.

El Gordo y El Flaco: La Vida Nocturna. This expanded version of *Blotto* features some interesting variations on Laurel & Hardy's drunk routine in the nightclub. There are some additional variety acts not seen in the American release version as well. As an additional bonus, Stan Laurel narrates a brief segment about how the foreign versions were made. Included in this tape is an excerpt from the Spanish version of *Pardon Us (De Botte y de Botte)*, with the missing fire-rescue scene restored. 55 mins.

VHS: S29858. $24.98.

El Gordo y El Flaco: Politiquerias. This Spanish version of *Chickens Come Home* is one of the most interesting of the Spanish series. While the basic story is the same, the addition of vaudeville acts to the party scene are something unique—one of the performers, Hadji Ali, has to be seen to be believed! As an added bonus, a short newsreel clip is included featuring Hadji Ali performing his water routine and Stan Laurel at a swimming contest. 60 mins.

VHS: S29859. $24.98.

El Gordo y El Flaco: Noche de Duendes. The "Laurel-Hardy Murder Case" is combined with "Berth Marks" to form a feature-length scare comedy. When Hardy reads that Ebeneezer Laurel has died and they are looking for the heirs to the multi-million-dollar estate, he and Stan Laurel show up at the old mansion to collect. Locked in by the police, they must stay there overnight with a murderer loose in the house. 51 mins.

VHS: S29860. $24.98.

El Gordo y El Flaco: Los Calaveras. In this offering, *Be Big* is combined with *Laughing Gravy* to form a feature-length comedy. When Stan and Ollie try to sneak out of their homes to attend a lodge meeting, the wives catch them. After the divorce, they are living in a boarding house with a small dog and a landlord who doesn't allow pets. Full of great sight gags, this adaptation is among the most true to the original versions of both films. Still there are a few new gags sprinkled in for good measure. 63 mins.

VHS: S29861. $24.98.

El Gordo y El Flaco: Ladrones. New gags abound, as well as a completely different ending in this expanded Spanish version of *Night Owls*. Also included is *Tiemblea y Titubuea (Below Zero)*, which contains new footage as well. 63 mins.

VHS: S29862. $24.98.

El Gordo y El Flaco: De Botte en de Botte. Laurel & Hardy's first feature-length movie, *Pardon Us*, was the only one filmed in foreign language editions. Of them, only this Spanish-language re-issue seems to have survived. When Laurel & Hardy try to make their own beer they get arrested and put in prison, where they encounter all sorts of adventures. They finally get pardoned when they save the warden's daughter from the clutches of The Tiger, a ruthless convict bent on escape. 65 mins.
VHS: S29863. $24.98.

Laurel and Hardy and the Family

Four classic comedies explore the joys, frustrations and obligations of family life. Features *Brats, Their First Mistake, Twice Two* and *Perfect Day*. 85 mins.
VHS: S14698. $14.98.

Laurel and Hardy at Work

In this collection of short subjects, the boys are engaged in three different lines of work and fail at all of them. Featuring *Towed in a Hole, Busy Bodies* and *The Music Box*. USA, 1932/1933, 70 mins.
VHS: S13867. $14.98.

Laurel and Hardy on the Lam

In this quartet of classic comedies, Stan and Ollie try to flee their troubles, but the trouble always seems to catch up to them-hilariously. Featuring *Scram!, Another Fine Mess, One Good Turn* and *Going Bye-Bye!* USA, 1930-1934, 90 mins.
VHS: S13868. $14.98.

Laurel and Hardy Spooktacular

There are screams galore in these four hilarious comedies from Laurel and Hardy. Includes *The Live Ghost, Oliver the Eighth, Laurel and Hardy Murder Case* and *Dirty Work*. 95 mins.
VHS: S14697. $14.98.

Laurel and Hardy's Laughing '20s

This affectionate compilation of the most hilarious highlights from their classic comedy shorts includes perhaps the greatest pie-throwing melee of the silent era. A must for buffs. USA, 1965, 90 mins.
Laser: LD70197. $39.98.

Laurel and Hardy: Rare Home Movies

The comedy team visits the homeland of Stan Laurel in this two-part cinema verite. In the first, the pair visits Tynemouth, England, where they amuse the crowd and sightsee. Ollie is shown wearing his glasses. Part 2 finds them in Edinburgh, Scotland, where they visit a castle and a movie theatre. A rare, behind-the-scenes look. 1932, 25 mins.
VHS: S05712. $19.95.

Laurel and Hardy: Stan "Helps" Ollie

Disaster always strikes in these four hysterical shorts when Stan tries to help Ollie. Includes *County Hospital, Me and My Pal, Hogwild* and *Helpmates*. 85 mins.
VHS: S14699. $14.98.

Leader of the Band

"Barney Miller's" Steve Landesburg orchestrates this offbeat comedy in which he plays a big city musician who struggles to turn the world's worst high school band into a first-class combo.
VHS: S09285. $14.95.
Nessa Hyams, USA, 1987, 90 mins.

Legends of Comedy

The greatest comedic legends from Hollywood are seen in this series. Early silent films, the movies and radio shows of the 30's and 40's, even the best gags of TV's golden era, are included in this collection of classic antics. It's a history lesson in humor. Three volumes, each 55 minutes long.

Volume I: The Golden Age of Comedy. The keystone cops, Charlie Chaplin and Buster Keaton set a high standard for film comedy during the silent era. With the coming of sound, W.C. Fields, Laurel and Hardy and even the kids from Our Gang continued this tradition in their best works. *Volume I* contains the most memorable gags ever unleashed by these comic entertainers. 55 mins.
VHS: S20860. $24.95.

Volume II: Great Stars of Film and Radio. From the Broadway stage, great stars of slapstick invaded the developing world of film and broadcasting. Mae West, The Marx Brothers, even Jimmy Durante all brought skills honed in front of live audiences to the cinema and radio broadcasts, thereby reaching homes all across America. 55 mins.
VHS: S20861. $24.95.

Volume III: TV Comedy Classics. With the birth of television, live performances could be heard and seen electronically for the first time. Comic pioneers like Burns and Allen, Jackie Gleason and Art Carney, Red Skelton, Sid Caesar and Imogene Coca realized the potential of TV from the start. Their best efforts are collected on this tape. 55 mins.
VHS: S20862. $24.95.

Legends of Comedy, Three-Volume Set.
VHS: S20863. $59.95.

The Lemon Drop Kid

The Lemon Drop Kid is a racetrack con-man who gets in big trouble when he gives a bad tip to a local gangster. Given until Christmas to make up for a $10,000 loss, he hits on a brilliant and ultimately hilarious scheme. He opens an old folks' home as a ruse to license phony Santa Clauses. Bob Hope stars.
VHS: S22762. $14.98.
Sidney Lanfield, USA, 1951, 91 mins.

Let's Make It Legal

An attractive grandmother falls back in love with an old flame, and casually divorces her gambler husband. A comedy where friendship and love aren't always found in the same man. Stars Claudette Colbert, MacDonald Carey, Zachary Scott, Robert Wagner and Marilyn Monroe.
VHS: S16398. $19.98.
Richard Sale, USA, 1951, 77 mins.

Liar Liar

Jim Carrey is Fletcher Reede, a fast-talking attorney and habitual liar. When his son, Max (Justin Cooper), blows out the birthday candles on his fifth birthday cake, he has just one wish—that his dad will stop lying for 24 hours. When Max's wish miraculously comes true, Fletcher discovers that his biggest asset—his mouth—has suddenly become his biggest liability. Hilarious havoc ensues as Fletcher tries to keep his practice afloat and his ex-wife Audrey (Maura Tierney) from taking their son and moving to Boston. With Jennifer Tilly, Swoosie Kurtz, Amanda Donohoe and Cary Elwes.
VHS: S32055. $22.98.
Laser: LD76339. $44.98.
DVD: DV60145. $24.98.
Tom Shadyac, USA, 1997, 87 mins.

Libeled Lady

A crackerjack comedy starring four of Hollywood's finest. Spencer Tracy is a newspaper editor without scruples. Myrna Loy is the society dame he'd like to keep in the headlines. Add in William Powell and Jean Harlow as Tracy's somewhat reluctant accomplices and wait for the fun to begin. A delight in black and white; remade in 1946 as *Easy to Wed*.
VHS: S11728. $19.98.
Jack Conway, USA, 1936, 98 mins.

Life Begins for Andy Hardy/ Andy Hardy's Private Secretary

This double-feature disc offers two of the best works from the Andy Hardy series, George B. Seitz's 1941 *Life Begins for Andy Hardy*, about Andy's cruel lesson when he travels to New York in search of a job, with Mickey Rooney and Judy Garland (her last appearance in the series). The second program is Seitz's *Andy Hardy's Private Secretary*, about Andy's tutorship with Kathryn Grayson (her debut) and the consequences of his failed English test. Features the original theatrical trailer from each film.
Laser: LD71650. $44.98.

Life Stinks

Only Mel Brooks could find laughs in a comedy about the homeless. He directs, co-writes and stars as a greedy billionaire who pretends to be down and out in order to win a bet and acquire the land needed for a new building complex. Lesley Ann Warren is sensational as the streetwise bag lady who helps Brooks with some long overdue attitude adjustment. With Jeffrey Tambor, Rudy De Luca, Stuart Pankin and Howard Morris as Sailor.
VHS: S15433. $14.95.
Laser: LD74676. $34.98.
Mel Brooks, USA, 1991, 93 mins.

Life with Father

Based on the hit Broadway play by Lindsay and Crouse, music by Max Steiner, with William Powell, Irene Dunne and Elizabeth Taylor, set in 1880's New York.
VHS: S00754. $19.95.
Michael Curtiz, USA, 1947, 118 mins.

Like Father Like Son

Dudley Moore and Kirk Cameron are father and son until by an odd set of events they become son and father. Imagine the fun when a teenager switches bodies with his shorter father who is a respected heart surgeon. Will the son get to operate? Will the father pass the biology final?
VHS: S06920. $14.95.
Rod Daniel, USA, 1987, 101 mins.

Lip Service

It's bad news for veteran reporter Gil Hutchinson (Paul Dooley) when newcomer Len Burdette (Griffin Dunne) turns his staid morning TV show into a circus. Len's irreverent antics cost Gil his job, but he returns to have his first—and last—laugh.
VHS: S09607. $79.95.
William H. Macy, USA, 1988, 67 mins.

Little Giant

A rare Bud Abbott and Lou Costello work features the comic duo playing separate roles rather than being paired together. The frantic plot charts the misadventures of Costello as a harried door-to-door vacuum cleaner salesman. Also known as *On the Carpet*. With Brenda Joyce, George Cleveland and Elena Verdugo.
VHS: S19071. $14.98.
William A. Seiter, USA, 1946, 91 mins.

Little Miss Marker

A remake of the Damon Runyan story that once starred Shirley Temple as the darling child who is left as collateral on a debt that is never going to be paid. With Walter Matthau as the disgruntled bookie, Sara Stimson as the kid and Julie Andrews as the bookie's dame. This fourth telling of the story also features Tony Curtis and Bob Newhart.
VHS: S07802. $49.95.
Walter Bernstein, USA, 1980, 103 mins.

Little Murders

Elliot Gould is the meek photographer roped into marriage with the overly aggressive Marcia Rodd in this hilarious black comedy about modern relationships, urban living and sniping as a form of therapy. With Vincent Gardenia, Elizabeth Wilson, Donald Sutherland and Alan Arkin, who also makes his film debut as a director. A sure fire hit from the pen of Jules Feiffer.
VHS: S07969. $59.98.
Alan Arkin, USA, 1971, 107 mins.

Lonely Guy

Steve Martin stars as a lonely guy in N.Y.C who seeks the advice of fellow lonely guy Charles Grodin. "Get a dog" is usually a good suggestion. Life size cardboard cut-outs of popular celebrities will also brighten up an empty apartment. One day Steve discovers he doesn't have to eat alone, if he can only find what he did with Judith Ivey's phone number. With Robin Douglass, Steve Lawrence, Merv Griffin and Dr. Joyce Brothers. Based on Bruce Jay Friedman's humorous self-help book *The Lonely Guy's Book of Life*.
VHS: S15771. $19.95.
Arthur Hiller, USA, 1984, 91 mins.

Long, Long Trailer

Lucille Ball, Desi Arnaz and Marjorie Main star in this riotous comedy in which a cumbersome travel trailer creates havoc for a newlywed couple (Ball and Arnaz) on their honeymoon.
VHS: S13355. $19.98.
Vincente Minnelli, USA, 1954, 97 mins.

Look Who's Talking

A surprise boxoffice hit about an unwed mother looking for the perfect father to help raise little Mikey. The gimmick here is that the baby has help from Bruce Willis to voice his opinions from the first charge of conception all the way through toddlerhood. Kirstie Alley is the mom with a mission. John Travolta is the irresponsible cabdriver who could be Mr. Right. With Olympia Dukakis, Abe Vigoda and George Segal as the biological father.
VHS: S12124. $14.95.
DVD: DV60230. $24.95.
Amy Heckerling, USA, 1989, 96 mins.

Lord Love a Duck

Roddy McDowall, Tuesday Weld and Ruth Gordon star in this offbeat comedy which parodies the 1960s Southern California teen scene. McDowall plays a high school senior with psychic powers; when he develops a crush on Weld, a beautiful but hopelessly self-absorbed co-ed, he sets out to make her every dream come true.
VHS: S28493. $19.98.
George Axelrod, USA, 1966, 105 mins.

Lost in a Harem

This timeless Abbott & Costello comedy is embellished with lavish production numbers, the Big Band swing of Jimmy Dorsey's Orchestra, gorgeous gal-pal Marilyn Maxwell and hit tunes of the time. A hilarious takeoff on the "sons of the desert" genre.
VHS: S15424. $19.98.
Charles Riesner, USA, 1944, 89 mins.

Lost in Alaska

Bud Abbott and Lou Costello are 19th century prospect hunters in Alaska who are supposed to be helping out a friend but end up getting in more trouble. With Mitzi Green, Tom Ewell and Bruce Cabot.
VHS: S19073. $14.98.
Jean Yarbrough, USA, 1952, 76 mins.

Lost in America
Albert Brooks' masterpiece, an existential road film about an obsessive Yuppie couple (Brooks and Julie Hagerty) who drop out when Brooks' character is denied a promotion in an advertising job. Their dreams of absolute freedom are soon shattered when Hagerty loses their life's fortune during a bad run at the Vegas tables.
VHS: S02546. $19.98.
Laser: Letterboxed. **LD74708. $34.98.**
Albert Brooks, USA, 1985, 91 mins.

Lotto Land
Two growing romances are at the center of this fresh comedy set in a down-home and diverse section of Brooklyn. A fun-loving teenager and his college-bound girlfriend discover they have their differences, while their older relatives learn to bridge theirs. When a winning lottery ticket lands in their midst it sets off a host of further complications with both serious and humorous results.
VHS: S29812. $19.98.
Laser: LD75978. $39.99.
John Rubino, USA, 1996, 90 mins.

Love and Other Catastrophes
A wild and wacky romp through the land of romance with five friends whose lives intersect and collide in unexpected and comical ways. A refreshing look at the often hilarious catastrophes of love and dating in the '90s.
VHS: S31838. $69.98.
Laser: LD76312. $39.98.
Emma-Kate Croghan, USA, 1997, 76 mins.

The Love God
A con man convinces Don Knotts to sell his failing bird watcher publication. The result is an hilarious trial for obscenity as the new owner brings the fusty old nature publication into the swinging sixties as a pornographic enterprise. Anne Francis also stars.
VHS: S29994. $14.98.
Nat Hiken, USA, 1969, 103 mins.

Love Happy
Harpo, Chico and Groucho Marx find themselves in a fine mess involving stolen gems hidden in tins of fish. Femme fatale Ilona Massey wants them back and Raymond Burr is willing to do nasty things to see she gets what she wants. Marilyn Monroe has a bit part as a woman who thinks she is being followed. B&W.
VHS: S04249. $19.95.
David Miller, USA, 1949, 85 mins.

Love in Bloom
George Burns, Gracie Allen and Dixie Lee (Mrs. Bing Crosby) star in this story of a girl with a past and a penniless songwriter who try to make a go of life together. In spite of her love for him, rather than ruin his life, she runs away.
VHS: S28591. $14.98.
Elliott Nugent, USA, 1935, 62 mins.

Love Is Better Than Ever
Stanley Donen's shrewd romantic comedy about a small-town dance contest winner (Elizabeth Taylor) who visits New York City and falls for a big city lady killer (Larry Parks). With Tom Tully, Josephine Hutchinson and Ann Doran. Cameo by Gene Kelly.
VHS: S18524. $19.98.
Stanley Donen, USA, 1952, 81 mins.

Loved One
Welcome to the lighter side of death, American style. Based on the novel by Evelyn Waugh, Robert Morse plays a naive British writer who takes a crash course in the California funeral industry that includes both human and animal customers. The all-star cast includes Liberace, James Coburn, Milton Berle, Tab Hunter, Robert Morley, Rod Steiger and Jonathan Winters. Written by Christopher Isherwood and Terry Southern.
Laser: LD72141. $39.95.
Tony Richardson, USA, 1965, 116 mins.

Lucille Ball Redhead Set
Three of Lucy's earliest and funniest comedies: *The Affairs of Annabel, Too Many Girls,* and *You Can't Fool Your Wife.*
VHS: S10690. $59.98.

Lucky Ghost
Black star Mantan Moreland does a crazy, bug-eyed bit in this 1941 comedy successor to *Mr. Washington Goes to Town.*
VHS: S15481. $29.95.
Jed Buell, USA, 1941

Lust in the Dust
Tab Hunter and Divine. California magazine said: "Raunchy but irresistible. It would have made John Wayne lose his lunch." Divine's first film away from director John Waters—still decidedly distasteful.
VHS: S00785. $19.95.
Paul Bartel, USA, 1984, 85 mins.

Luv
A neurotic comedy about a romantic triangle involving Jack Lemmon, Elaine May and Peter Falk. Murray Schisgal's three-character hit play has been expanded to include roles for Eddie Mayehoff, Paul Hartman, Severn Darden and a young Harrison Ford. Lots of talk and double-talk and threatening to jump off bridges in the New York City area.
VHS: S10384. $19.95.
Clive Donner, USA, 1967, 95 mins.

Ma and Pa Kettle
Marjorie Main and Percy Kilbride are the original Ma and Pa Kettle. After appearing as ancillary characters with Fred MacMurray and Claudette Colbert in the The Egg and I, this hilarious comic duo spawned a whole series of films. This is the first film starring the famous hillbilly pair who, together with their enormous family, face eviction with humor.
VHS: S21306. $14.98.
Charles Lamont, USA, 1949, 75 mins.

Ma and Pa Kettle at Home
Marjorie Main and Percy Kilbride are back in their roles as a hilarious backwoods couple. In this film they try to fix up their run-down shack of a home in order to convince an editor that they deserve a scholarship for their eldest son (Brett Halsey). Naturally there are plenty of gags in this over-the-top comedy.
VHS: S23876. $14.98.
Charles Lamont, USA, 1952, 82 mins.

Ma and Pa Kettle at the Fair
Sending one of their children to college presents a huge problem for Ma and Pa Kettle, whose modest means will need to be augmented for this ambitious plan. So they decide to enter a number of contests at the State Fair with Ma cooking up a storm and Pa trying his hand at horse-racing.
VHS: S21309. $14.98.
Charles Barton, USA, 1952, 78 mins.

Ma and Pa Kettle at Waikiki
Percy Kilbride makes his final appearance as Pa Kettle in this wacky tropical adventure. The Kettles visit an ailing relative's pineapple factory and Pa has a great idea which inadvertently increases production. This happy accident leads to a plot against the Kettles waged by unscrupulous competitors.
VHS: S24332. $14.98.
Lee Sholem, USA, 1952, 79 mins.

Ma and Pa Kettle Back on the Farm
Majorie Main and Percy Kilbride fight with crooks again, but this time it's because the crooks believe there are uranium deposits buried on their apparently worthless farm. Ma and Pa Kettle manage somehow to save the homestead in this hilarious film.
VHS: S21308. $14.98.
Edward Sedgwick, USA, 1951, 80 mins.

Ma and Pa Kettle Go to Town
In this Ma and Pa Kettle film, Majorie Main and Percy Kilbride get mixed up with some slick city crooks in New York City. Of course, with their country smarts the duo outwits these know-it-all thieves, resulting in one of the best films in this series.
VHS: S21307. $14.98.
Charles Lamont, USA, 1949, 75 mins.

Ma and Pa Kettle on Vacation
On their way to Paris, Ma and Pa (Marjorie Main and Percy Kilbride) are a backwoods couple who find themselves nearly cheated out of a vacation by a spy scheme. Pa unwittingly agreed to deliver a letter, but after getting them into trouble he seems more interested in Paris nightlife than in helping Ma fix this mess.
VHS: S23875. $14.98.
Charles Lamont, USA, 1953, 76 mins.

Mad Miss Manton
Barbara Stanwyck as a screwball socialite who fancies solving murder mysteries. She eventually involves Henry Fonda in a trail of clues combining sleuth and slapstick from start to finish.
Laser: CLV. **LD71728. $19.98.**
Leigh Jason, USA, 1938, 80 mins.

Made in America
Ted Danson and Whoopi Goldberg star in this comedy about a mix-up at a sperm bank. When Goldberg's artificially inseminated child wants to know who her father is, she finds that he's an uncouth used car salesman.
VHS: S21399. $19.98.
Richard Benjamin, USA, 1993, 109 mins.

Mae West Collection: Special Edition Boxed Set
The flamboyance, spectacle and wit of Mae West are showcased in four different films: Archie Mayo's 1932 Night after Night, West's debut work; Wesley Ruggles' 1933 I'm No Angel; Leo McCarey's 1934 Belle of the Nineties and Raoul Walsh's 1936 Klondike Annie. Includes liner notes.
Laser: LD71887. $99.98.

Magic Town
James Stewart and Jane Wyman star in this comedy with Stewart as a pollster who finds the perfect average American town and ruins it when the people of the town find out about Stewart's discovery.
VHS: S09146. $19.95.
Laser: CLV. **LD72007. $34.98.**
William Wellman, USA, 1947, 103 mins.

The Main Event
Barbra Streisand is a wacky but bankrupt cosmetics executive who finds her finances are dependent upon an over-the-hill boxer played by Ryan O'Neal. The chemistry is apparent from the beginning as Barbra badgers and cajoles the demoralized fighter to perform in the ring. Streisand sings the title song.
VHS: S21929. $14.95.
Howard Zieff, USA, 1979, 105 mins.

The Male Animal
Henry Fonda is a distracted college professor at risk of losing his wife (Olivia de Havilland) to her old college flame (Jack Carson). This trio brings fine comic performances to an intelligent comedy that pits a seemingly weak liberal against a backdrop of overbearing right wing virility. Elliot Nugent and James Thurber wrote the screenplay.
VHS: S28053. $19.98.
Elliot Nugent, USA, 1942, 101 mins.

Man Trouble
Director Bob Rafelson, writer Carol Eastman and actor Jack Nicholson are reunited in this absurd comedy about a misogynist owner (Nicholson) of a dog guard agency who's hired by a beautiful woman (Ellen Barkin) for protection. The two become inadvertent pawns of a nasty underworld crime figure.
VHS: S17921. $19.98.
Bob Rafelson, USA, 1992, 100 mins.

The Man Who Came to Dinner
Based on the play by George Kaufman and Moss Hart, this delightful film is a caricature of Alexander Wolcott and is the story of an acid-tongued radio celebrity who breaks his hip on a lecture tour. Hilarity ensues as he terrorizes the suburban home where he recuperates. With Bette Davis, Monty Woolley, Ann Sheridan, Jimmy Durante (in a spoof of Harpo Marx) and Reginald Gardiner (in a spoof of Noel Coward).
VHS: S11626. $19.95.
Laser: LD74677. $34.98.
William Keighley, USA, 1941, 112 mins.

March of the Wooden Soldiers
Victor Herbert's operetta Babes in Toyland gets the full Laurel and Hardy treatment. This early feature is one of the great comic pair's first successes.
VHS: S23787. $24.95.
Charles Rogers, USA, 1934, 73 mins.

Marriage on the Rocks
Frank Sinatra stars in this comedy as advertising executive Dan Edwards, who finds himself divorced from his wife (Deborah Kerr) by a clever Mexican lawyer (Cesar Romero). Then his wife somehow winds up married to his best friend (Dean Martin). With Hermione Baddeley, Nancy Sinatra and DeForest Kelly.
VHS: S34689. $19.98.
Jack Donohue, USA, 1965, 109 mins.

The Mask
Jim Carrey breaks into the bigtime with this major comic role. When a bank clerk finds an ancient mask it changes his life, turning him into a super-hero character with unbelievable plastic abilities. It's a great chance for Carrey to use his antic abilities to their fullest advantage, with amazing computer effects that extend his reach even further.
VHS: S23054. $19.98.
Laser: Widescreen, THX sound. **LD74807. $39.99.**
DVD: DV60077. $24.98.
Chuck Russell, USA, 1994, 100 mins.

Mastermind
Zero Mostel stars as Inspector Hoku in this comic spoof of the Charlie Chan detective movies. His assignment is to protect a robot from various foreign agents. Lots of slapstick and comic car chases. With Bradford Dillman, Jules Munshen and Sorel Brook.
VHS: S12839. $29.95.
Alex March, USA, 1976, 131 mins.

The Matchmaker
Thornton Wilder's classic romp set in turn-of-the-century New York stars Shirley Booth, Shirley MacLaine, Anthony Perkins, and Robert Morse. This highly amusing farce about a middle-aged widower deciding to re-wed is brought off at breakneck speed, with plenty of laughs.
VHS: S13790. $19.95.
Joseph Anthony, USA, 1958, 101 mins.

The Mating Game

A lyrical, funny, no-holds-barred comedy of manners about class and society. Tony Randall plays a repressed IRS agent who descends on a sleepy, backwater farm house to learn about a family's failure to report their taxes. He quickly falls for the eager, seductive daughter (Debbie Reynolds).
VHS: S18019. $19.98.
George Marshall, USA, 1959, 96 mins.

McHale's Navy

Determined to save a struggling orphanage, McHale recreates the Australian Derby on a South Pacific isle. When the plan backfires, he and the crew of the PT-73 find Captain Binghampton hot on their trail. With Ernest Borgnine, Joe Flynn and Tim Conway.
VHS: S33709. $14.98.
Edward Montagne, USA, 1964, 93 mins.

McHale's Navy Joins the Air Force

When Ensign Parker (Tim Conway) is mistaken for a hotshot pilot, he is quickly promoted, but soon finds himself in big trouble up in the air. With Joe Flynn.
VHS: S33710. $14.98.
Edward Montagne, USA, 1965, 91 mins.

Me and the Colonel

Danny Kaye and Curt Jurgens star in this unique blend of comedy and suspense. On the eve of the Nazi takeover of Paris, an anti-Semitic Polish colonel (Jurgens) is forced to flee in the company of a Jewish refugee (Kaye). Though their interactions are strained at first, under the threat of discovery they learn to rely upon and trust each other.
VHS: S27185. $19.95.
Peter Glenville, USA, 1958, 110 mins.

Meet the Applegates

From the director of Heathers comes an environmental black comedy about intelligent insects from the Amazon rain forest who disguise themselves as a typical sit-com family from the 1950s and invade Ohio in the 1990s. The cast includes Ed Begley Jr., Stockard Channing, Glenn Shadix and Dabney Coleman as Aunt Bea.
VHS: S13921. $92.98.
Michael Lehmann, USA, 1991, 90 mins.

Mel Brooks Collector's Set

This specially priced seven-volume Mel Brooks collector's set includes Brooks' first feature—The Twelve Chairs, starring Dom DeLuise, Frank Langella and Ron Moody as three men hunting for jewels sewn into one of 12 scattered chairs in pre-Revolutionary Russia—as well as Brooks classics Young Frankenstein, Robin Hood: Men in Tights, Silent Movie, History of the World: Part I and To Be or Not to Be.
VHS: S31416. $59.98.

Memoirs of an Invisible Man

A special effects bonanza starring funnyman Chevy Chase as a San Francisco stock analyst who takes a nap too close to a secret, off-limits, government-sponsored laboratory.
VHS: S16735. $19.98.
Laser: Letterboxed. **LD71810. $29.98.**
John Carpenter, USA, 1992, 99 mins.

Men in Black

In this hip, hilarious sci-fi comedy, Tommy Lee Jones and Will Smith are the best-kept secret in the universe. Their mission: to monitor extra-terrestrial activity on earth. They are the best, last and only line of defense. They work in secret. They exist in shadow. And, of course, they dress in black. With Linda Fiorentino, Vincent D'Onfrio and Rip Torn and a gallery of creepy aliens, courtesy of Industrial Light & Magic.
VHS: S32519. $24.99.
Laser: LD76375. $39.95.
DVD: DV60037. $24.95.
Barry Sonnenfeld, USA, 1997, 97 mins.

Merton of the Movies

An adaptation of George S. Kaufman and Marc Connelly's comedy about the early days of Hollywood. The plot concerns a sweet, naive dreamer (Red Skelton) who arrives in Hollywood and is befriended by a stunt double (Virginia O'Brien). She helps him land his first break. With Gloria Grahame, Alan Mowbray and Hugo Haas.
VHS: S19564. $19.98.
Robert Alton, USA, 1947, 83 mins.

MGM's Big Parade of Comedy

An anthology of more than 50 Hollywood actors, directors and stars performing their magic. The compilation encompasses the silent era through the 1940s, and features Laurel and Hardy, the Marx Brothers, W.C. Fields and Abbott and Costello, as well as Greta Garbo, Clark Gable, Katharine Hepburn and Jean Harlow. "A delight" (Hollywood Reporter). 100 mins.
VHS: S17895. $19.98.

Miami Rhapsody

Sarah Jessica Parker, Antonio Banderas and Mia Farrow are at their best in this light-hearted romantic comedy set in a very contemporary Miami. Parker thinks she is happily engaged until she finds out that every member of her family is involved in an outrageous affair.
VHS: S25633. $19.95.
Laser: LD75013. $39.99.
David Frankel, USA, 1994, 95 mins.

Mikey and Nicky

On the run from the mob, Nicky (John Cassavetes) turns to his old friend Mikey (Peter Falk) for help. Throughout the night they roam the streets of Philadelphia, hiding out and reminiscing about old times, as their stormy past comes to light and the mob closes in. With Ned Beatty. "A gangster film like no other" (Michael Ventura, LA Weekly).
VHS: S31557. $29.95.
Elaine May, USA, 1976, 106 mins.

The Milky Way

Long unseen screwball comedy with Harold Lloyd playing a mild-mannered milkman who accidentally knocks out the middleweight boxing champion and through a wild chain of events, becomes the champion of the world himself. With Adolphe Menjou, Verree Teasdale, and Lionel Stander.
VHS: S34189. $19.95.
Leo McCarey, USA, 1936, 89 mins.

Miss Firecracker

Holly Hunter is great as a young woman with a questionable reputation who decides to enter a beauty contest. Tim Robbins, Scott Glenn and Mary Steenburgen are just some of the other talented people involved in this fun film. Though it seems hokey at first, a beauty pageant is absolutely the right path to love and popularity available to this woman in her conservative, Southern hometown.
VHS: S26334. $19.98.
Thomas Schlamme, USA, 1988, 102 mins.

Miss Grant Takes Richmond

Lucille Ball stars in this dizzy comedy about a screwball secretary who innocently gets involved with a gang of crooks…and unwittingly reforms them. Co-starring William Holden.
VHS: S14089. $19.95.
Lloyd Bacon, USA, 1949, 87 mins.

Miss Right

William Tepper (Drive, He Said) stars in and wrote this sexual comedy about a modern guy looking for Miss Right in Rome. He has to choose from Karen Black, Virna Lisi, Marie-France Pisier, Margot Kidder, Dalilia Di Lazzaro and Clio Goldsmith. Music by Art Garfunkel. Directed by songwriter-performer Paul Williams.
VHS: S06850. $79.95.
Paul Williams, USA, 1988, 98 mins.

Mistress

A hilarious satire about the lower fringes of the film industry, settling on a failed director's (Robert Wuhl) last chance at redemption when his script about a tormented, self-destructive painter is bought by a fading producer (Martin Landau). The problems ensue when each of the ego-driven financiers demands his respective girlfriend be cast in the lead. With Danny Aiello, Robert De Niro, Sheryl Lee Ralph, Laurie Metcalf and in a wonderful cameo, Christopher Walken.
VHS: S18197. $19.98.
Barry Primus, USA, 1992, 109 mins.

Mo' Money

Daman Wayans stars in this comedy about a con man who goes straight—for a while. When he begins work at a credit card company he reverts to his old ways. He then gets sucked into more dangerous scams. This comedy also stars Marlon Wayans and Stacey Dash.
VHS: S21442. $19.95.
Peter MacDonald, USA, 1992, 97 mins.

Modern Romance

Albert Brooks' second feature film as director is a hilarious look at filmmaking, neurotic behavior and preserving a love relationship. Film editor Brooks is crazy about Katharine Harrold—perhaps too crazy. Sometimes stuffed animals as presents work, sometimes they don't. With Bruno Kirby, George Kennedy and Bob Einstein (Albert's real brother).
VHS: S06151. $14.95.
Albert Brooks, USA, 1981, 93 mins.

Monkey Business

The Marx Brothers are stowaways on the high seas who become bodyguards to rival gangsters with the usual hilarious results, courtesy of an S.J. Perelman script and an unending number of Maurice Chevalier impersonations.
VHS: S03322. $19.95.
Laser: LD70057. $34.95.
DVD: DV60357. $29.99.
Norman Z. McLeod, USA, 1931, 77 mins.

Monsieur Beaucaire

A pleasant satire of the French aristocracy and ancien regime with Bob Hope as a court barber sent on a suicidal mission, with strange and unexpected pleasures. With Joan Caulfield, Patric Knowles and Marjorie Reynolds.
VHS: S18550. $14.98.
George Marshall, USA, 1946, 83 mins.

The Moon Is Blue

Hugh Herbert adapted his stage hit, a sexy comedy about a proud, virginal woman. Striking the right pose, actors William Holden and David Niven bring real charm to this light, romantic comedy. Their perfect foil is Academy Award nominee Maggie McNamara.
VHS: S21166. $19.98.
Otto Preminger, USA, 1953, 95 mins.

Moon over Parador

Richard Dreyfuss plays an American actor asked to impersonate an unexpectedly dead Caribbean dictator. On the plus side is the company of the dictator's mistress (Sonia Braga) and the fact that chief of security (Raul Julia) will not kill him if he says yes. Decisions. Decisions. With Jonathan Winters, Dick Cavett, Charo, Sammy Davis, Jr. and director Paul Mazursky as the dictator's mother.
VHS: S08503. $19.95.
Paul Mazursky, USA, 1988, 103 mins.

Moonstruck

The winner of three Oscars, this charming, romantic, ethnic comedy involves a somewhat dowdy Cher involved with two brothers. She's engaged to Danny Aiello but in love with Nicolas Cage. Her parents, Olympia Dukakis and Vincent Gardenia, have their own problems, but wish her the best. Screenplay by John Patrick Shanley (Five Corners). Set in Brooklyn.
VHS: S07105. $19.98.
Laser: LD76278. $39.99.
DVD: DV60279. $24.98.
Norman Jewison, USA, 1987, 103 mins.

Mother

After his second divorce, John Henderson (Albert Brooks) realizes that his unsuccessful relationships with women date back to the first woman in his life—his mother (Debbie Reynolds). In a hilarious attempt to figure out why, John moves back home. With Rob Morrow.
VHS: S31721. $19.95.
Albert Brooks, USA, 1996, 104 mins.

Mother, Jugs and Speed

A funny comedy-thriller about an L.A. ambulance service that's in hot competition with a rival company. Bill Cosby gets some funny lines. With Harvey Keitel, Raquel Welch, Larry Hagman.
VHS: S21487. $14.98.
Peter Yates, USA, 1976, 98 mins.

Moving

Richard Pryor has just lost his engineering job but has the chance of a lifetime if he can just move 2,000 miles to Boise, Idaho. Predictably, the move is full of comic obstacles. With Beverly Todd and Randy Quaid.
VHS: S21452. $19.98.
Alan Metter, USA, 1988, 89 mins.

Mr. Blandings Builds His Dream House

Classic screwball comedy stars Cary Grant and Myrna Loy as a couple who retreat from the city to the country to settle into a serene lifestyle. Of course reality conflicts with their fantasies.
VHS: S03265. $14.98.
H.C. Potter, USA, 1948, 93 mins.

Mr. Hobbs Takes a Vacation

James Stewart and Maureen O'Hara take the family to a seashore summer house. Good-natured fun with idealized parents trying their best to make things right for their children.
VHS: S06528. $19.98.
Henry Koster, USA, 1962, 116 mins.

Mr. Peabody and the Mermaid

William Powell stars in this comical fantasy about a man who catches a blonde Ann Blyth while fishing for something other than a mermaid. He brings his catch of the day home and hides her in the pond at his villa. Lucky Mr. Peabody is rich—she could have ended up in the bathtub. B&W.
VHS: S04243. $19.95.
Irving Pichel, USA, 1948, 89 mins.

Mr. Saturday Night

Billy Crystal stars as a self-destructive comedian whose entire career is chronicled in this compelling drama/comedy. The biting humor is wickedly satisfying. Significantly this is also a poignant portrayal of a rich and complex life. David Paymar plays the manager/brother and Jerry Lewis makes a surprise cameo appearance. Outtakes hosted by Crystal are also included.
VHS: S22030. $14.95.
Billy Crystal, USA, 1992, 118 mins.

Mr. Wrong
Ellen DeGeneres, of the popular TV Sitcom Ellen, plays a very unlikely bride-to-be in this outrageous comedy. Bill Pullman is the suitor who can't take a hint. Together the pair show how a relationship can deteriorate from a dream date to a nightmare featuring Mr. Wrong. Joan Cusack, Dean Stockwell and Joan Plowright are also featured.
VHS: S29406. $19.95.
Laser: LD75816. $39.99.
Nick Castle, USA, 1996, 97 mins.

Mrs. Doubtfire
Robin Williams camps it up as a cross-dressing nanny when he finds that it's the only way he can continue to see his children every day. His wife, Sally Fields, has thrown him out for his childish behavior, a trait he comes to understand as a failing when seen from the standpoint of a stern old woman.
VHS: S20784. $19.98.
Chris Columbus, USA, 1993, 120 mins.

Mrs. Wiggs of the Cabbage Patch
W.C. Fields romances ZaSu Pitts, the neighbor of the title character. Pauline Lord is the long suffering Mrs. Wiggs, who must deal with calamity on a regular basis. A melodrama made hilarious with the courting scenes of Fields and Pitts. B&W.
VHS: S05527. $19.95.
Norman Taurog, USA, 1934, 80 mins.

Mrs. Winterbourne
Shirley MacLaine, Ricki Lake and Brendan Fraser star in this modern-day Cinderella story about a poor, unwed mother who is mistaken for the widow of a millionaire's son, leading to hilarious and heartwarming results.
VHS: S28639. $19.95.
Laser: LD75959. $34.95.
Richard Benjamin, USA, 1996, 106 mins.

Multiplicity
From Harold Ramis (Groundhog Day, Ghostbusters, Stripes) comes this tale of an overworked contractor (Michael Keaton) who has himself cloned so that he can spend more time with his neglected family. Instead of helping, the unpredictable clones make life hilariously complicated. A sweet and funny film, Andie MacDowell co-stars as his bewildered wife.
VHS: S28641. $19.95.
Laser: LD75960. $39.95.
Harold Ramis, USA, 1996, 110 mins.

Murder by Death
Truman Capote is at the center of this film featuring a great comic cast. Peter Falk, Alec Guinness, David Niven, Dame Maggie Smith, Peter Sellers, Eileen Brennan, Nancy Walker, James Coco and Elsa Lanchester star as just a few of the detectives put in an untenable situation by an eccentric millionaire. He has invited the world's best sleuths to solve a murder for one million dollars. It's a great spoof of over-complicated murder mysteries. Written by Neil Simon.
VHS: S26474. $19.95.
Laser: LD74618. $34.95.
Robert Moore, USA, 1976, 95 mins.

Murphy's Romance
A divorced young mother (Sally Field) and a charming pharmacist (James Garner) spar and fall in love in Martin Ritt's comic love story.
VHS: S00900. $14.95.
Martin Ritt, USA, 1985, 107 mins.

My Best Friend's Wedding
Julia Roberts and Dermot Mulroney are long-time pals who make a pact to marry each other if neither is hitched by the time they are 29. When he introduces his fiance (Cameron Diaz) to her, she is set on sabotaging the engaged couple's relationship. With Rupert Everett.
VHS: S32515. $22.99.
Laser: LD76374. $39.95.
DVD: DV60036. $24.95.
P.J. Hogan, USA, 1997, 105 mins.

My Breakfast with Blassie
This hysterical sendup of My Dinner with Andre has received unanimously rave reviews. Exclusively shot for video, it stars the most famous professional wrestler of all time, Fred Blassie, and comedian Andy Kaufman in his final role. 60 mins.
VHS: S05190. $19.95.

My Cousin Vinny
This inventive comedy of manners and class conflicts stars Joe Pesci as a Brooklyn-trained lawyer whose first assignment is going to Alabama to defend his cousin, mistakenly charged with the murder of a convenience store clerk. With some hilarious Oscar-winning work by Marisa Tomei as Pesci's gum-popping, leather clad girlfriend and Fred Gwynne as the presiding judge. With Ralph Macchio and Mitchell Whitfield.
VHS: S17229. $19.95.
Laser: LD72192. $39.98.
Jonathan Lynn, USA, 1992, 120 mins.

My Dear Secretary
Kirk Douglas stars as a writer who can't separate business from pleasure. His latest secretary agrees to marry him despite his irresponsible ways, and they elope to the mountains with hilarious results. Also starring Laraine Day.
VHS: S13845. $19.95.
Charles Martin, USA, 1949, 94 mins.

My Father the Hero
Gerard Depardieu is the father and hero of the title who brings a Gallic charm to this hilarious comedy. A beautiful and sunny resort is the location for this story of love, relationships and the wackier side of family interaction, where a daughter tests the limits of fraternal devotion. Lauren Hutton is also featured.
VHS: S21310. $19.98.
Steve Miner, France/USA, 1993, 90 mins.

My Favorite Blonde
Bob Hope plays a vaudeville performer with his loyal penguin who is manipulated by a beautiful woman into a dangerous and very funny chess game of espionage and intrigue. With Madeleine Carroll, Gale Sondergaard and George Zucco.
VHS: S18549. $14.98.
Sidney Lanfield, USA, 1942, 78 mins.

My Favorite Brunette
A spoof of hard-boiled detective stories as baby photographer Bob Hope is involved with Dorothy Lamour in espionage doings, with Peter Lorre the hit-man.
VHS: S03340. $19.95.
Elliott Nugent, USA, 1947, 87 mins.

My Favorite Year
Peter O'Toole delivers a wonderful performance in this story of a young writer who discovers that his favorite swashbuckling hero is actually a womanizing alcoholic who has trouble living up to his image. With Lainie Kazan, Bill Macy, Lou Jacobi.
Laser: LD74522. $34.98.
Richard Benjamin, USA, 1983, 92 mins.

My Friend Irma
Adapted from the popular radio series, this is the film debut of Dean Martin and Jerry Lewis, as juice-bar operators on the show business fringe encountering vivacious blonde Marie Wilson and John Lund. With Diana Lynn, Don DeFore and Hans Conried.
VHS: S18675. $19.95.
George Marshall, USA, 1949, 103 mins.

My Geisha
Shirley MacLaine disguises herself as a geisha to win a role in her husband's new film. This delightful comedy was filmed on location in Japan and features an all-star cast, including Yves Montand, Robert Cummings and Edward G. Robinson.
VHS: S14281. $14.95.
Jack Cardiff, USA, 1962, 120 mins.

My Life's in Turnaround
Phoebe Cates, John Sayles and Martha Plimpton are featured in cameos along with Eric Schaeffer and Donald Lardner Ward in this hilarious behind-the-scenes look at movie making. This hit from the San Francisco Film Festival shows how a guy with nothing can come out on top.
VHS: S25846. $89.95.
Eric Schaeffer, USA, 1994, 84 mins.

My Little Chickadee
W.C. Fields meets his match in Mae West in this rollicking, double entendre comedy Western. When Cuthbert J. Twillie takes a gander at Flora Belle Lee, it's lust at first sight. Greasewood City may not survive the barrage of one-liners penned by the stars. With Margaret Hamilton and Joseph Calleia. B&W.
VHS: S03073. $14.98.
Eddie Cline, USA, 1940, 83 mins.

My Man Godfrey
Carole Lombard is the madcap heiress who finds a gentleman-bum (William Powell) on a garbage heap, brings him home to become the butler. The result is a wonderful, eccentric satire of the idle rich as Godfrey tries to bring sanity into their lives.
VHS: S18178. $19.95.
Gregory La Cava, USA, 1936, 93 mins.

My Stepmother Is an Alien
A comedy in which the title character hails from another planet, where it is not considered odd to chew cigarette butts and swill car battery fluid. Kim Basinger is the alien sent by her planet to undo the harm caused by widowed Earth scientist Dan Aykroyd. With Allyson Hannigan and Jon Lovitz and a special tribute to the song stylings of Jimmy Durante.
VHS: S09392. $14.95.
Richard Benjamin, USA, 1988, 94 mins.

Mystery Science Theater 3000: The Movie
Finally the hit cable TV show has been turned into that which it has always lampooned, a feature-length movie. It all begins when a young man is kidnapped by an evil scientist and forced to watch a B-movie. Junk-made sidekick puppets Tom Servo, Gypsy and Crow help to transform a terrible film into an hilarious participatory experience, at least for them. Don't try this at the local cineplex. 100 mins.
VHS: S29920. $19.95.
Laser: LD75908. $34.98.

Mystic Pizza
The comedy that takes a bite out of the seaside resort of Mystic, Connecticut, home to three young waitresses who decide their futures look as appetizing as yesterday's pizza and decide an overhaul is in order. Feisty Jojo, sexy Daisy and bookworm Kat discover that life has a secret ingredient, that friendship is a spice worth savoring and that romance can be a slice of heaven. With Julia Roberts, LiliTaylor and Annabeth Gish.
VHS: S24739. $14.98.
Donald Petrie, USA, 1988, 100 mins.

Naked Gun
A short-lived tv series is the inspiration for this boxoffice bonanza from the same guys who gave the world Airplane. Leslie Nielsen reprises his role as Lt. Frank Drebin, a dim witted but very successful L.A. cop. His latest assignment is to safeguard the Queen of England, but that is not as important as the non-stop puns, in-jokes, rude noises, and just plain silliness that fill the screen. With O.J. Simpson, Priscilla Presley, Ricardo Montalban and a host of cameo appearances.
VHS: S08714. $14.95.
Laser: LD75233. $34.98.
David Zucker, USA, 1988, 125 mins.

Nasty Habits
If Watergate had taken place in a Philadelphia convent instead of the White House is the premise of this satiric black comedy. Glenda Jackson has the Nixon role. Sandy Dennis is perfect as scapegoat Joan Dean. With Geraldine Page, Melina Mercouri, Anne Jackson, Anne Meara, Jerry Stiller, Rip Torn and Eli Wallach as other religious members involved in scandal and coverup. Buying this video is not a mortal sin, but taking pleasure from watching it is.
VHS: S10736. $19.95.
Michael Lindsay-Hogg, USA, 1977, 97 mins.

National Lampoon's Class of '86
Satiric musical comedy revue.
VHS: S03467. $29.95.
Jerry Adler, USA, 1986, 86 mins.

National Lampoon's Class Reunion
An outrageous band of party-ready alumni return to the scene of past crimes, prepared for some rah-rah nostalgia and revenge. An innocent prank played on one of the former students has made the entire class a target for his revenge, and the reunion turns into a hilarious homicidal homecoming for the wacky psychopath. With Gerrit Graham, Fred McCarren, Miriam Flynn, Stephen Furst, Shelley Smith, Zane Buzby, and Michael Lerner.
VHS: S34078. $14.95.
Michael Miller, USA, 1982, 85 mins.

National Lampoon's European Vacation
The sequel to Vacation also stars Chevy Chase as the head of the Griswald family, which wreaks havoc wherever it goes. With Eric Idle.
VHS: S10051. $19.98.
Laser: LD74711. $34.98.
Amy Heckerling, USA, 1985, 94 mins.

Never a Dull Moment
When a New York songwriter (Irene Dunne) marries a rodeo star (played by Fred MacMurray), she finds life on his rustic Wyoming ranch more of a challenge than she bargained for. But there's never a dull moment and plenty of good-natured fun.
VHS: S13996. $19.98.
George Marshall, USA, 1950, 89 mins.

Never Give a Sucker an Even Break
W.C. Fields' last starring role finds him in his prime, playing himself making a movie. It's a collection of song, slapstick and sketches that defy description. Filled with famous lines. ("She drove me to drink, the one thing I'm indebted to her for.")
VHS: Out of print. For rental only.
Laser: LD70062. $34.95.
Eddie Cline, USA, 1941, 71 mins.

Never Say Die
When millionaire Bob Hope mistakenly thinks he has only a month to live, he marries Martha Raye with hilarious results, in this classic comedy of matrimonial mayhem. Includes original theatrical trailer.
VHS: S34681. $14.98.
Elliott Nugent, USA, 1939, 82 mins.

Never Say Goodbye
Errol Flynn and Eleanor Parker are delightful in this comedy about a young girl's attempts to reunite her divorced parents. Flynn turns on all his most polished charms in order to convince Parker that he truly has changed.
VHS: S22896. $19.98.
James V. Kern, USA, 1946, 97 mins.

Never Too Late
In this classic comedy, Paul Ford and Maureen O'Sullivan recreate their stage roles from the Broadway smash as a near-retirement couple who find they are expecting a child. With Connie Stevens and Jim Hutton. In Panavision.
VHS: S31157. $19.98.
Bud Yorkin, USA, 1965, 105 mins.

Never Wave at a WAC
An over-indulged, wise-cracking Senator's daughter enters the Women's Army Core to be with her soldier beau, but she can't get above the rank of private. Stars Rosalind Russell, Marie Wilson, Paul Douglas, Arleen Whelan and Hillary Brooke. Alternatively titled *The Private Wore Skirts.*
VHS: S16553. $19.95.
Norman Z. McLeod, USA, 1952, 87 mins.

A New Leaf
Elaine May at her funniest—she wrote, directed and stars in this now classic comedy about a penniless playboy (Walter Matthau) who plots to marry and then murder the klutzy botanist (May).
VHS: S04432. $34.95.
Elaine May, USA, 1971, 102 mins.

Next Stop, Greenwich Village
Larry Lapinsky is a young man seeking fame and discovering independence in this bittersweet comedy set in 1950s New York. His mother, deftly played by Shelley Winters, is distraught when he leaves his traditional family home in Brooklyn and moves to bohemian Greenwich Village.
VHS: S16686. $59.98.
Paul Mazursky, USA, 1976, 109 mins.

Next Time I Marry
In this excellent comedy, Lucille Ball is heir to a $20 million fortune but is forced to marry a poor ditch digger in order to get it. Worse than that, she must travel cross-country with him in a tiny trailer—a situation loaded with laughs and surprises.
VHS: S13997. $19.98.
Garson Kanin, USA, 1938, 65 mins.

Nice Girl?
To shed her "nice girl" image, Deanna Durbin snubs her boyfriend (Robert Stack) and bungles a play for an older man (Franchot Tone). Includes alternative ending.
VHS: S30622. $19.98.
William A. Seiter, USA, 1941, 96 mins.

A Night at the Opera
Along with Duck Soup, the funniest of the Marx Brothers films, featuring the boys amidst high society. The five minutes in Groucho's stateroom is one of the funniest continuous laugh inducers on film.
VHS: S02365. $19.95.
Laser: CAV, 2 discs, Criterion. **LD70424. $79.95.**
Laser: CLV, 1 disc, Criterion. **LD70425. $39.95.**
Laser: CLV, MGM. LD70643. **$43.98.**
Sam Wood, USA, 1935, 90 mins.

Nine Months
Hugh Grant is at the lead of an exciting cast in this delightful comedy. Julianne Moore, Joan Cusack, Jeff Goldblum and Robin Williams are all featured. Grant plays a young man who has the best in life. He thinks he has everything until his girlfriend discovers she is pregnant and Grant is forced to consider how his life will change when he becomes a father.
VHS: S26996. $19.95.
Laser: LD75436. $39.98.
Chris Columbus, USA, 1995, 103 mins.

No Man of Her Own
The only film to star legendary lovers Clark Gable and Carole Lombard is a light and funny meditation on avarice and gambling. Gable is a card shark with little conscience, toward neither the men whose money he takes nor the women whose commitment he cannot abide…until he meets the dangerously alluring Lombard.
VHS: S02788. $19.95.
Wesley Ruggles, USA, 1932, 81 mins.

The Noose Hangs High
Working with long-time collaborator Charles Barton, Bud Abbott and Lou Costello play low level window washers mistaken for mob functionaries who are entrusted with $50,000 and given 36 hours to repay the note when the money is inadvertently spent. Features the notorious routine, "Are You There?" With Cathy Downs, Joseph Calleia and Leon Errol.
VHS: S17896. $19.98.
Charles Barton, USA, 1948, 77 mins.

Norman…Is That You?
A comedy of race, class, sex and duplicity. Redd Foxx is heartbroken when his wife flees to Mexico with his brother, turns to his son for comfort and solace, and discovers the young man is homosexual. He is determined to "convert" his son's sexual orientation, or die trying. With Pearl Bailey and Dennis Dugan.
VHS: S20207. $19.98.
George Schlatter, USA, 1976, 92 mins.

Nothing But Trouble
In their last film made for MGM, set during World War II, Laurel and Hardy are household servants who unexpectedly befriend a gilded child king and stand guard when his life is endangered. With Mary Boland and Henry O'Neill. Directed by Sam Taylor, a frequent collaborator of Harold Lloyd.
VHS: S17897. $19.98.
Sam Taylor, USA, 1944, 79 mins.

Nothing Sacred
One of the funniest movies ever made; Carole Lombard is the small-town girl who thinks she is dying until she is turned into the sweetheart of New York City as a newspaper publicity stunt. Fredric March is the reporter who falls in love with Lombard. When he discovers Carole is not dying after all, it's up to him to get her out of the predicament.
VHS: S18188. $24.95.
Laser: CLV. **LD72064. $39.95.**
DVD: DV60131. $24.95.
William Wellman, USA, 1937, 71 mins.

The Nutty Professor (1963)
Jerry Lewis is a mild mannered chemistry professor who follows in the footsteps of Dr. Jekyll and becomes Buddy Love, a heartless lounge lizard and heartbreaker. Considered to be Jerry's best comedy and worthy of the adoration of the French. With Stella Stevens, Howard Morris, Kathleen Freeman and Henry Gibson.
VHS: S06990. $19.95.
Jerry Lewis, USA, 1963, 108 mins.

The Nutty Professor (1996)
Eddie Murphy gives the "performances of his career" in no less than seven roles in this remake of the Jerry Lewis classic. (Lewis was one of the film's executive producers.) When shy Dr. Sherman Klump, a kind, brilliant, "calorically challenged" genetics professor, falls hard for beautiful faculty member Carla Purty (Jada Pinkett), he concocts an experimental fat-reducing serum that transforms him into "Buddy Love," a buff and handsome but conniving and fast-talking Don Juan. With James Coburn, Larry Miller, Dave Chappelle and John Ales.
VHS: S30053. $22.98.
Laser: LD75994. $34.98.
DVD: DV60147. $24.98.
Tom Shadyac, USA, 1996, 96 mins.

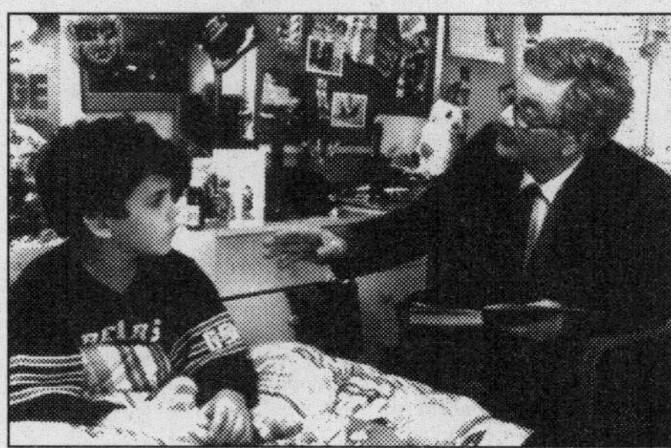

Odd Couple
Jack Lemmon and Walter Matthau are two divorced buddies who decide to be roommates in this film adaptation of the Neil Simon smash hit play. Felix is neat and Oscar is a slob but you probably already knew that. With Hohn Fiedler, Herb Edelman, Monica Evans and Carole Shelley as the Pigeon Sisters.
VHS: S10820. $19.95.
Gene Saks, USA, 1968, 105 mins.

Off Limits
A small and wispy Bob Hope vehicle about a charming and cunning fight manager (Hope) unexpectedly drafted into the Army. When his prize recruit is denied entrance into the war, Hope reluctantly backs Mickey Rooney, whose greatest asset may be his beautiful aunt, Marilyn Maxwell.
VHS: S02780. $19.95.
George Marshall, USA, 1953, 89 mins.

Once Bitten
Jim Carrey and Lauren Hutton team up in this vampire spoof. Lauren is an unaging member of the living dead who needs fresh, virginal blood to keep young and beautiful. The only problem is that she lives in L.A. It's a good thing that Carrey happens to come along to help her find the only hold-outs in La La land.
VHS: S26276. $14.98.
Dimitri Villard, USA, 1985, 93 mins.

One Fine Day
Michelle Pfeiffer is juggling single parenthood with a career as an architect; George Clooney is a commitment-shy newspaper columnist who sees his young daughter every other weekend. When their kids miss a school field trip, they agree to take shifts babysitting for the day, resulting in funny misadventures and romance.
VHS: S31401. $19.98.
Laser: LD76234. $39.98.
Michael Hoffman, USA, 1996, 109 mins.

Only You
Robert Downey, Jr., and Marisa Tomei are a dream couple in this Cinderella story for the 1990's. Tomei's character believes in the old fashioned ideals of romantic love, and on a trip to Europe this dream is fulfilled beyond her wildest expectations.
VHS: S23926. $19.95.
Laser: LD74800. $34.95.
DVD: DV60238. $24.95.
Norman Jewison, USA, 1994, 109 mins.

Our Man Flint
On his first cinematic secret mission, Secret Agent Flint (James Coburn) faces off against the most dangerous weapon of all, the weather. An evil organization called Galaxy has learned how to send icebergs crashing into the Mediterranean to flood whole valleys.
VHS: S11263. $19.98.
Laser: LD71264. $59.98.
Daniel Mann, USA, 1966, 103 mins.

Our Miss Brooks
Eve Arden is a wise-cracking English teacher trying to snag her colleague Mr. Boynton, played by Robert Rockwell. The film is based on the popular TV series, with veteran actors Gale Gordon and Richard Crenna also featured. Crenna singing "It's Magic" is a high point.
VHS: S21344. $37.95.
Al Lewis, USA, 1956, 85 mins.

The Out-of-Towners
Jack Lemmon and Sandy Dennis are having the time of their lives in New York City. Unfortunately that time is nothing like the one they expected, where the plane would land on time, their hotel reservations would be held, their luggage would be found and no one would walk off with their money. A New York nightmare disguised as a frantic comedy from Neil Simon. Cast includes Sandy Baron, Anne Meara, Billy Dee Williams and Paul Dooley.
VHS: S10821. $19.95.
Arthur Hiller, USA, 1970, 98 mins.

Pack Up Your Troubles
When one of their World War I soldier buddies is killed, Laurel and Hardy resolve to take care of his orphaned little girl. Good fun.
VHS: S13866. $14.98.
George Marshall, USA, 1932, 68 mins.

Paleface
Bob Hope is Painless Potter, a timid dentist on his way west with his bride Jane Russell, who is an undercover government agent out to discover who is selling guns to the Indians. This movie won an Oscar for Best Song and spawned a sequel and a remake with Don Knotts. With Robert Armstrong, Iris Adrian and Jack Searle. In color.
VHS: S07804. $59.95.
Laser: LD70064. $34.98.
Norman Z. McLeod, USA, 1948, 91 mins.

Palooka
Jimmy Durante stars as a hard-nosed fight manager determined to make a champion out of Palooka, a hapless country bumpkin, in this delightful comedy. The fine cast includes James Cagney's look-alike brother, William.
VHS: S13857. $19.95.
Ben Stoloff, USA, 1934, 86 mins.

Pardners
Dean Martin and Jerry Lewis formed one of the zaniest comedy teams ever to come out of Hollywood. In this team effort they take on the Western, with its gunslingers, prospectors and, most importantly, its fast women. It's among these unlikely characters that they intend to regain the lost family seat.
VHS: S21135. $14.95.
Norman Taurog, USA, 1956, 90 mins.

Pardon My Sarong—Abbott and Costello
An Abbott and Costello feature set in the South Seas, about two bus drivers marooned on a tropical island, and the confusion that results when Lou is mistaken for a god, and the two get entangled with jewel thieves. With Lionel Atwill, Virginia Bruce, Robert Paige and William Demarest.
VHS: S17257. $14.98.
Erle C. Kenton, USA, 1942, 84 mins.

Parents
A very black comedy about growing up in 1958. Randy Quaid and Mary Beth Hurt play suburban Indiana cannibals trying to teach little Brian Madorsky traditional family values. Sandy Dennis plays the concerned school guidance counselor. Actor Bob Balaban serves up an arty and odd little shocker in his directorial debut.
VHS: S09534. $19.98.
Bob Balaban, USA, 1989, 81 mins.

Paris Holiday
This comedy farce brings together Bob Hope and the great Fernandel as they live for the affections of a beautiful spy, Anita Ekberg. Filmmaker Preston Sturges appears in a cameo role.
VHS: S11113. $19.95.
Gerd Oswald, USA, 1957, 100 mins.

Paris When It Sizzles
A screenwriter on deadline (William Holden) has his secretary act out the various plot ideas in an engaging comedy starring Audrey Hepburn and Noel Coward.
VHS: S04433. $29.95.
Richard Quine, USA, 1964, 110 mins.

Party Girl
Parker Posey is a fresh presence in this new film about a girl living in a non-stop party called her life. This club kid must tone it down if she is to keep her exciting new job and her prospective mate. Inevitably, her formerly wild ways keep intruding into her more sober lifestyle. The result is a comedy for today.
VHS: S27175. $19.95.
Laser: LD75467. $34.95.
Daisy Von Scherler Mayer, USA, 1995, 98 mins.

The Patsy
When a well-known entertainer dies, his management company will do anything to continue, even drafting a bellhop (Jerry Lewis) to become his replacement. It doesn't matter that the patsy has no talent; he is positively hilarious and ultimately becomes the toast of Hollywood.
VHS: S21739. $14.98.
Jerry Lewis, USA, 1964, 106 mins.

People Are Funny
And kids say the darndest things, too. Yes, friends, Art Linkletter is part of the cast in this salute to big-time radio. Also adding music and laughs are Ozzie Nelson, Jack Haley, Rudy Vallee and Frances Langford. Performances by the Vagabonds.
VHS: S05467. $29.95.
Sam White, USA, 1946, 94 mins.

The Perez Family
Alfred Molina, Anjelica Huston, Marisa Tomei and Chazz Palminteri star in this super sexy comedy about family, emigration and love, set amidst the Cuban community in Miami. Molina is finally leaving Cuba after 20 years to join his wife, Huston, but a beautiful woman, Tomei, leads him astray. Twenty years of pent-up passion make this diversion an explosive proposition.
VHS: S26442. $19.98.
Laser: LD75086. $39.99.
Mira Nair, USA, 1995, 135 mins.

The Perfect Marriage
A screwball farce about the marriage of airplane factory executive David Niven and fashion editor Loretta Young. On their tenth anniversary, a minor argument escalates into a severe misunderstanding and the two promptly initiate divorce proceedings. Their precocious nine-year-old daughter (Nina Griffith), caught in the middle, tries to bring about a reconciliation. With Eddie Albert, Virginia Field, Jerome Cowan and Rita Johnson.
VHS: S19903. $19.98.
Lewis Allen, USA, 1946, 88 mins.

The Perils of Pauline
Hold tight for this one! It's one harrowing escape after another. Betty Hutton comes on like fireworks in this witty comedy about the former star of the famous 1914 serials. Great songs, a host of comedy superstars, and incredible stunt scenes.
VHS: S13858. $19.95.
George Marshall, USA, 1947, 96 mins.

Pete 'n' Tillie
Walter Matthau and Carol Burnett are cast as the title couple who meet, marry and manage not to kill each other when the going gets rough. Geraldine Page and the script were nominated for an Oscar. With Rene Auberjonois and Henry Jones. Adapted from Witch's Milk by Peter de Vries. Warning: this film does contain nude piano playing.
VHS: S10799. $19.98.
Martin Ritt, USA, 1972, 100 mins.

Pick a Star
A Hal Roach production frequently mistaken for a Laurel and Hardy effort actually centers on a small-town girl (Rosina Lawrence) and her extravagant ambition to become a Hollywood star. The film features some highly stylized musical numbers and two brief though funny interludes with Laurel and Hardy. With Mischa Auer and Patsy Kelly.
VHS: S17898. $19.98.
Edward Sedgwick, USA, 1937, 70 mins.

Pigskin Parade
This enchanting comedy marks the film debut of 15-year-old Judy Garland and also features Betty Grable long before she became a Hollywood legend. Jack Haley and Patsy Kelly co-star as married football coaches who turn a hillbilly farmhand (Stuart Erwin) into a star passing ace.
VHS: S31369. $19.98.
David Butler, USA, 1936, 90 mins.

Pillow Talk
Rock Hudson and Doris Day at their best. Doris is a pert interior decorator. Together they share a party line, and a lot more.... Tony Randall is very funny, and the dialog is witty—if you find it funny.
VHS: S04840. $14.95.
Michael Gordon, USA, 1959, 102 mins.

Pin-Up Girl
Betty Grable stars as the leggy girl who is in love with a sailor in this wartime vehicle loaded with songs and specialty numbers.
VHS: S09444. $19.98.
H. Bruce Humberstone, USA, 1944, 83 mins.

Plain Clothes
A high school comedy from Martha Coolidge (Valley Girl) about a tough cop who goes undercover. Arliss Howard stars as Nick Dunbar, the cop trying to solve the murder of a teacher. With Abe Vigoda, George Wendt, Seymour Cassel, Diane Ladd, Suzy Amis and Robert Stack.
VHS: S07818. $89.95.
Martha Coolidge, USA, 1988, 98 mins.

Planes, Trains and Automobiles
Steve Martin is an uptight ad exec trying to get home to Chicago for Thanksgiving with his family. His flight from New York City is detoured to Wichita and he finds himself saddled with John Candy, a well meaning but very annoying shower curtain salesman. A traveler's nightmare filled with slapstick, intolerance and more modes of transportation than are mentioned in the title.
VHS: S06243. $19.95.
Laser: LD75240. $34.98.
John Hughes, USA, 1987, 93 mins.

Plaza Suite
Walter Matthau is cast in three separate roles in this Neil Simon comedy centered in a New York hotel. He plays a father of the bride, a film producer and a philanderer opposite Lee Grant, Barbara Harris and Maureen Stapleton. All the stories take place in the same room. With Louise Latham as the bride.
VHS: S10823. $19.95.
Laser: LD75339. $29.98.
Arthur Hiller, USA, 1971, 114 mins.

Please Don't Eat My Mother
A sexy remake of the cult classic Little Shop of Horrors. This time around, our nerdy hero winds up feeding his plant the bodies of dead lovers. Starring Rene Bond and Buck Kartalian.
VHS: S12314. $24.95.
Carl Monson, USA, 1971, 95 mins.

Please Don't Eat the Daisies
A successful drama critic moves his family to the country in this film which inspired the later television series. A family comedy with amusing and mischievous children, and Doris Day singing the title song. Starring David Niven, Doris Day, Janis Paige, and Spring Byington.
VHS: S13645. $19.98.
Laser: LD72129. $34.98.
Charles Walters, USA, 1960, 111 mins.

Police Academy
A very silly comedy about a bunch of misfits who are allowed to train as law enforcement officers when a woman becomes mayor of a nameless metropolitan city. Filmed in Toronto. A huge financial success that has spawned three sequels, so far. With Steve Guttenberg, Bubba Smith, Michael Winslow, David Graf and Kim Cattrall.
VHS: S05094. $14.95.
Hugh Wilson, USA, 1984, 95 mins.

The Pope of Greenwich Village
Two small-time hustlers find big-time trouble when they steal from the Mafia in this "explosively funny, tautly dangerous and absolutely irresistible" (Los Angeles Times) modern classic. With Eric Roberts, Mickey Rourke, Daryl Hannah and Geraldine Page.
VHS: S33985. $14.98.
Stuart Rosenberg, USA, 1984, 122 mins.

Portnoy's Complaint
Philip Roth's sexual novel of frustration and self-abuse is now a movie starring Dick Benjamin as Alexander Portnoy. Lee Grant is his Jewish mother and Karen Black is Monkey, his sexual fantasy playmate. Not recommended for the visually impaired—it could give them ideas.
VHS: S04176. $19.98.
Ernest Lehman, USA, 1972, 101 mins.

Portrait of a White Marriage
Martin Mull is back in another acerbic satire made for cable TV. As the host of a small town talk show he becomes involved with a local married housewife and is asked to participate in the Founder's Day Parade. With longtime sidekick Fred Willard and "Mary Hartman" co-star Mary Kay Place. Also Jack Riley, Michael McKean, Harry Shearer and Conchata Ferrell. Co-written and co-produced by Mull.
VHS: S08324. $39.95.
Harry Shearer, USA, 1988, 101 mins.

The Positively True Adventures of the Alleged Texas Cheerleader-Murdering Mom
Michael Ritchie's HBO film returns to the themes and style of his 1975 Smile in an audacious satire based on actual events. Holly Hunter is Wanda Holloway, a devoted mother who will stop at nothing to ensure her daughter's placement on the cheerleading squad. She contracts the services of her former brother-in-law (Beau Bridges) to murder the mother of a rival cheerleader. With Swoosie Kurtz.
VHS: S19237. $19.95.
Michael Ritchie, USA, 1993, 100 mins.

Postcards from the Edge
Meryl Streep and Shirley MacLaine star as a disturbed daughter and her overbearing Hollywood mother in this adaptation of the Carrie Fisher novel. Please do not think this is about Carrie Fisher and her mother Debbie Reynolds; that would be jumping to conclusions. This is a fictional work that also includes the talents of Dennis Quaid, Gene Hackman and Richard Dreyfuss. See Tinseltown through the eyes of an insider.
VHS: S13875. $14.95.
Mike Nichols, USA, 1990, 101 mins.

The Preacher's Wife
In this romantic comedy—a remake of *The Bishop's Wife*—an angel (Denzel Washington) accidentally falls in love with a young woman (Whitney Houston) even though he is assigned to rekindle her marriage with her pastor husband (Courtney B. Vance). With Gregory Hines.
VHS: S31030. $19.95.
Laser: LD76195. $39.98.
Penny Marshall, USA, 1996, 124 mins.

Prelude to a Kiss
Playwright Craig Lucas adapts his prize-winning work about a beautiful, ethereal woman (Meg Ryan) who exchanges souls with a crusty, 80-year-old man (Sydney Walker) on the afternoon of her wedding to a charismatic young editor (Alec Baldwin). A devastating and sharply observed parable about AIDS. With Kathy Bates, Ned Beatty and Patty Duke.
VHS: Out of print. For rental only.
Laser: LD71825. $39.98.
Norman Rene, USA, 1992, 109 mins.

Pretty in Pink
Molly Ringwald is the school girl from the wrong side of town, Andrew McCarthy the wealthy heartthrob who asks her to the prom. A bittersweet, critically acclaimed love story with an upbeat ending.
VHS: S01523. $19.95.
Laser: LD75342. $29.98.
John Hughes, USA, 1986, 96 mins.

Pride of the Bowery
The East Side Kids swagger off to a Civilian Conservation Corps camp where they predictably get into all sorts of trouble. With Leo Gorcey and, of course, the East Side Kids.
VHS: S13859. $19.95.
Joseph H. Lewis, USA, 1941, 60 mins.

Primary Colors
John Travolta fits the bill as Jack Stanton, a virtually unknownSouthern governor on a hilarious, heart-wrenching roller-coaster ride to the presidency. With the help of his equally ambitious wife, Susan (Emma Thompson), and his colorful political team, Stanton defies all odds and makes history along the way in this savagely funny satire. With Billy Bob Thornton, Kathy Bates, Adrian Lester, Larry Hagman, Paul Guilfoyle and Maura Tierney.
VHS: S35014. $106.99.
DVD: DV60381. $29.95.
Mike Nichols, USA, 1998, 104 mins.

Prime Time
A funny satire of television and television commercials comprised of black out sketches, like Grove Tube, the targets are politics, airline spots, sports programming, with titles such as The Charles Whitman Invitational and The Sexual Deviation Telethon. With Warren Oates, Kinky Friedman, Harry Shearer, Harris Yulin, George Furth and Fred Dryer. 1980, 75 mins.
VHS: S17446. $19.95.

The Prince and the Showgirl
A romantic comedy pairing Laurence Olivier (who also directed) and Marilyn Monroe. The title pretty much explains it all.
VHS: S03561. $19.98.
Laser: LD72151. $34.98.
Laurence Olivier, USA, 1957, 117 mins.

Princess and the Pirate
Bob Hope in a hilarious send up of swashbuckling. Hope is the egotistical vaudevillian who gets shanghaied by pirates, gets involved with a lovely princess, and ends up leading a band of cutthroats.
VHS: S03126. $19.98.
David Butler, USA, 1944, 94 mins.

The Princess Bride
A fractured fairy tale from director Rob Reiner which includes a kidnapped beautiful princess, a mysterious pirate, a swordsman with a quest, a lovable giant, comic wizards, and some really nasty villains. With Cary Elwes, Mandy Patinkin, Chris Sarandon, Andre the Giant and Robin Wright as the princess bride.
VHS: S05932. $19.95.
Laser: CAV. **LD70434. $99.98.**
Laser: CLV. **LD70435. $39.95.**
Rob Reiner, USA, 1987, 101 mins.

Princess Caraboo
Phoebe Cates stars as a charming, exotic princess who transforms the stuffy English aristocracy. Kevin Kline, John Lithgow and Stephen Rea are also featured in this irresistible and romantic live-action fairy tale. It is like a dream come true.
VHS: S24314. $19.95.
Michael Austin, USA, 1994, 96 mins.

Princess Comes Across
Carole Lombard is once again deceiving an attractive young man, Fred MacMurray. Lombard is putting on airs on board a ship and passing as a princess. She is actually hoping for an acting career, but a murder mystery, not to mention a romance, inflect her desires into a wholly unexpected sphere.
VHS: S26225. $19.98.
William K. Howard, USA, 1936, 77 mins.

The Prisoner of Second Avenue
Jack Lemmon and Anne Bancroft star in this film version of the Neil Simon play about an unemployed executive going through a nervous breakdown. Bancroft is the supporting wife. A comedy with bite. With F. Murray Abraham and Sylvester Stallone in small roles, and Gene Saks, Elizabeth Wilson and Florence Stanley in larger ones.
VHS: S06183. $19.98.
Melvin Frank, USA, 1975, 98 mins.

Private Benjamin
Goldie Hawn is a pampered, rich young woman who decides to take control of her life by joining the army after being widowed. It's a long way from the mall to bootcamp as the young novice soon discovers. Eileen Brennan is great as the tough-as-nails sarge. Also features Albert Brooks.
VHS: S22028. $14.95.
Laser: LD74741. $29.98.
Howard Zieff, USA, 1980, 110 mins.

The Private Navy of Sgt. O'Farrel
Bob Hope stars in this zany comedy as a serviceman who tries to lay his hands on some beer for his men. When that fails and Phyllis Diller turns up instead, Hope sets off to recover the missing alcohol. Heroism is the last thing any one would expect to find in this antic plot, but heroism and lots of laughs are there in the end. Gina Lollobrigida is also featured.
VHS: S23962. $14.98.
Frank Tashlin, USA, 1968, 92 mins.

Private Parts
Legendary cult director Paul Bartel *(Eating Raoul)* delivers his first feature with all the dark comedy and fantastic situations that have turned his films into underground sensations. Private Parts plunges us into the foreboding world of a young girl whose adolescent passion for a strange photographer leads her toward a secret that a series of ghastly murders has tried to silence.
VHS: S14960. $19.98.
Paul Bartel, USA, 1972, 86 mins.

Private Parts
Shock jock and self-proclaimed "king of all media" Howard Stern gets the last laugh with this hit film version of his best-selling autobiography of the same name. "A comic firecracker. Explosive laughs" (Peter Travers, *Rolling Stone*). With Howard Stern Show stars Robin Quivers, Fred Norris, Jackie Martling and Gary "Baba Booey" Dell'abate, and a hit soundtrack featuring Porno for Pyros and Rob Zombie.
VHS: S31645. $103.99.
Betty Thomas, USA, 1997, 108 mins.

The Producers
Mel Brooks' hilarious hit about the plot to produce a Broadway bomb titled "Springtime for Hitler." Unfortunately, the play is a smash…so is this film. With Zero Mostel and Gene Wilder.
VHS: Out of print. For rental only.
Laser: LD70436. $39.95.
Mel Brooks, USA, 1968, 88 mins.

Promise Her Anything
Written by William Peter Blatty, this comedy tells of a different sort of possession, namely that of a trouble-making baby. Warren Beatty stars as a "blue film" director who falls for young French widow Leslie Caron in the next flat.
VHS: S16625. $14.95.
Arthur Hiller, USA, 1966, 98 mins.

Quackser Fortune Has a Cousin in the Bronx
An insightful comedy filmed in Ireland stars Gene Wilder as an independent-minded Irishman who triumphs over conformity, and Margot Kidder as an American exchange student. Funny, sad and wonderful!
VHS: S02724. $19.95.
Waris Hussein, USA, 1970, 88 mins.

Real Life
Albert Brooks' highly underrated film about a documentary filmmaker (Brooks) whose invasion of a "typically American family" to record their lives tears apart the nuclear family, exposing deeper and darker truths about contemporary America. Brooks' film is raw in its visual patterns, yet the long, uninterrupted takes established him as a filmmaker of flair and talent. Co-written by Harry Shearer and produced by Penelope Spheeris, whose directing career has recently flourished (Suburbia, The Boys Next Door).
VHS: S02565. $19.95.
Albert Brooks, USA, 1978, 99 mins.

Reality Bites
Winona Ryder stars in this romantic comedy that looks at the dazed confusion of the generation lost between The Brady Bunch and Melrose Place. Gainful employment seems to elude everyone trapped here. Ethan Hawke and Ben Stiller also star.
VHS: S21205. $19.98.
Ben Stiller, USA, 1994, 98 mins.

Reckless
Mia Farrow and Scott Glenn head a cast featuring Mary-Louise Parker, Tony Goldwyn and Stephen Dorff in this surprising Christmastime comedy. Farrow is a woman who cherishes Christmas at home with her family until her husband arranges a deadly surprise. He has hired someone to do her in. Now she must question everything she held dear about family, the holidays and canned mirth.
VHS: S27608. $99.98.
Laser: LD75551. $39.99.
Norman Rene, USA, 1995, 91 mins.

Red Headed Woman
A sexy shopgirl (Jean Harlow) sets her sights on marrying the boss. She succeeds on that count but finds that she still isn't welcome in his social circles. Written by Anita Loos and also starring Lewis Stone and Charles Boyer.
VHS: S13648. $29.98.
Jack Conway, USA, 1932, 79 mins.

The Ref
Criminal Dennis Leary has a problem. The couple he has taken hostage, Judy Davis and Kevin Spacey, are driving him nuts. It began as a simple burglary but before it's all over jail would be the best thing that could happen to this thief-turned-victim, as the whole bickering family nags him on to justice.
VHS: S21360. $19.99.
Ted Demme, USA, 1994, 97 mins.

The Reluctant Astronaut
Though afraid of heights, Don Knotts is forced into outer space because he continually brags about his heroic deeds and actions in World War I. Leslie Nielsen is also featured in this sci-fi comedy.
VHS: S29993. $14.98.
Edward J. Montagne, USA, 1967, 103 mins.

The Reluctant Debutante
Real-life marriage partners Rex Harrison and Kay Kendall team up as a pair of British high society members in this sophisticated comedy about a young American girl who comes for a visit only to find she must make her debut to the blue-blood set.
VHS: S15246. $19.98.
Laser: LD72152. $34.98.
Vincente Minnelli, USA, 1958, 97 mins.

Remember the Night
Once again Barbara Stanwyck plays a woman in trouble with the law. Fortunately, the man prosecuting her for a shoplifting offense, Fred MacMurray, decides to take her home over the Christmas holiday. It offers the kind of family experience Stanwyck's character never had before. When the holiday is over, however, there is still the small matter of the trial. Preston Sturges wrote the script for this romantic comedy.
VHS: S26228. $19.98.
Mitchell Leisen, USA, 1940, 94 mins.

Rented Lips
Martin Mull and Dick Shawn are two documentary filmmakers hired to complete a low budget porn film when the first director died under kinky circumstances. Using the same cast they decide to make a musical movie extravaganza instead. With Jennifer Tilly, Robert Downey Jr., Kenneth Mars, Edy Williams and June Lockhart. Script by Martin Mull. From the director of Greaser's Palace.
VHS: S07778. $79.95.
Robert Downey, USA, 1988, 82 mins.

Rich Kids
Robert Altman produced this witty and touching comedy which views divorce from the perspective of children. Trini Alvarado and Jeremy Levy star as the two bright New York adolescents who escape the trauma of their parents' divorces in a puppy-love relationship.
VHS: S08132. $59.95.
Robert M. Young, USA, 1979, 97 mins.

Ride 'Em Cowboy—Abbott and Costello
In this blithe, funny merging of musical, comedy and western formats, Abbott and Costello are hot dog vendors traveling the American West, with Ella Fitzgerald and the Merry Macs performing, "A Tisket, A Tasket." With Dick Foran, Anne Gwynne, and Johnny Mack Brown.
VHS: S17261. $14.98.
Arthur Lubin, USA, 1942, 81 mins.

Riding on Air
Joe E. Brown stars as Elmer, a bungling small town newspaper reporter with a knack for doing the wrong thing…and having it turn out right. A delightful comedy based on the Elmer Lane stories by Richard Macaulay.
VHS: S13860. $19.95.
Edward Sedgwick, USA, 1937, 58 mins.

The Right to Remain Silent
Lea Thompson and Robert Loggia star in this edgy comedy featuring appearances by Amanda Plummer, LL Cool J, Laura San Giacomo, Carl Reiner and Christopher Lloyd. Thompson is a rookie cop who processes incoming suspects. All the world in its overwhelming oddness parades before her in this kaleidoscopic view of the human condition.
VHS: S27512. $95.99.
Hubert de la Bouillerie, USA, 1995, 96 mins.

Rio Rita
Abbott & Costello are at their funniest as two city-bound guys who end up in a small Texas town where they are chased by Nazi spies as they try to do a little matchmaking for a new friend. Kathryn Grayson and John Carroll. Songs co-written by Harold Arlen. USA, 1942, 91 mins.
VHS: S15422. $19.98.

Risky Business
An original comedy abut the wild teenager who goes wilder while his parents are out of town. Established Tom Cruise as a star and re-introduced Ray-Bans as cool. With Rebecca De Mornay and Curtis Armstrong.
VHS: S02176. $14.95.
DVD: DV60079. $24.98.
Paul Brickman, USA, 1983, 96 mins.

Ritz
Director Richard Lester *(A Hard Day's Night, Three Musketeers)* keeps the pace fast and furious in this crisp farce about Gaetano Proclo hiding out in a men's bathhouse in New York. With Jack Weston, Rita Moreno, Jerry Stiller and F. Murray Abraham.
VHS: S01118. $19.98.
Laser: LD71475. $34.98.
Richard Lester, USA, 1976, 91 mins.

The Road to Bali

The only color road film of Bing Crosby and Bob Hope, with many guest stars. Hope and Crosby save Dorothy Lamour from an evil princess and the dangers of the jungle. 91 mins.
VHS: S11112. $29.95.
Hal Walker, USA, 1952, 90 mins.

The Road to Hong Kong

The last of the Road movies for Bob Hope and Bing Crosby takes them to the Far East. They play con men who share a rickshaw with Joan Collins. Watch for Peter Sellers and Dorothy Lamour. Also Robert Morley when Bob and Bing get involved in the space program. Color.
VHS: S13216. $19.98.
Laser: LD74483. $34.98.
Norman Panama, USA, 1962, 91 mins.

The Road to Morocco

One of the funniest Hope/Crosby road pictures has Crosby selling Hope to a charismatic, devilish sheik played by Anthony Quinn, as they both pursue the beautiful princess Dorothy Lamour. With Dona Drake, Vladimir Sokoloff, Monte Blue and Yvonne De Carlo.
VHS: S17245. $14.98.
DVD: DV60358. $29.99.
David Butler, USA, 1942, 83 mins.

The Road to Rio

Bob Hope and Bing Crosby are a zany and trouble-prone pair of musicians who stow away on a Brazil-bound liner that includes Dorothy Lamour on its passenger list. She is under the evil hypnotic spell of her evil aunt Gale Sondergaard. Leave it to Bob and Bing to open those eyes to romance and one liners. B&W.
VHS: S06068. $19.95.
Norman Z. McLeod, USA, 1947, 100 mins.

The Road to Singapore

The debut road picture has Crosby and Hope as a couple of frustrated men holding out in Singapore, who've given up women, and then vie for the affections of Dorothy Lamour. With Charles Coburn, Judith Barrett and Anthony Quinn.
VHS: S17247. $14.98.
Victor Schertzinger, USA, 1940, 84 mins.

The Road to Utopia

The best of Bob Hope-Bing Crosby-Dorothy Lamour road movies, and also the funniest. The plot finds the duo posing as a pair of escaped killers in an attempt to find an Alaskan gold mine, with Lamour on board the laugh-packed trek across the Yukon as the rightful heiress to the gold claim. With Robert Benchley as the narrator.
VHS: S06555. $14.98.
DVD: DV60333. $29.99.
Hal Walker, USA, 1946, 90 mins.

The Road to Wellville

Anthony Hopkins is a quack of a doctor who runs a health spa where the likes of Bridget Fonda, Matthew Broderick, John Cusack and Dana Carvey all cross paths. Aside from the wacky cures and contraptions on offer at this turn of the century spa, there are plenty of laughs and romance in this charming film.
VHS: S24327. $19.95.
Laser: Letterboxed. **LD74893. $39.95.**
Alan Parker, USA, 1994, 120 mins.

The Road to Zanzibar

A charming road picture with intimations of cannibalism and anarchy has Hope and Crosby portraying carnival performers crossing the African jungle with Dorothy Lamour in search of a diamond mine. With Una Merkel and Eric Blore.
VHS: S17246. $14.98.
Victor Schertzinger, USA, 1941, 92 mins.

The Road 3to Collector's Set

Bob Hope is joined by his regular companions, Bing Crosby and Dorothy Lamour, in this series of road comedies. *The Road to Morocco, The Road to Singapore, The Road to Utopia* and *The Road to Zanzibar* are joined in this boxed set.
VHS: S25530. $49.98.

Rockin' Ronnie

America's leading man and our most colorful president to date is the subject of this hilarious, tongue-in-cheek scrapbook, prepared by the creators of the Nightflight program. The off-the-wall comic collection includes such bits as *The Pilot, The Detergent Salesmen, The Conductor, The Gangster, The Ballroom Dancer, The Actor*. 45 mins.
VHS: S06590. $29.95.

Roommates

Peter Falk, D.B. Sweeney and Ellen Burstyn are featured in this comedy arising from cramped conditions. Falk plays a gruff old man who comes to stay in his grandson's one-room apartment. Together they explore all the adventures that roommates can, and often must, experience.
VHS: S26203. $19.95.
Laser: LD75065. $39.99.
Peter Yates, USA, 1995, 109 mins.

The Ropin' Fool, With Will Rogers

American humorist Will Rogers demonstrates the grace and skill required for roping, assembled in extracts and never-before-seen outtakes from his 1921 film *The Ropin' Fool*, which has been restored and reedited by his family's estate. Narrated by his son, Will Rogers, Jr. 28 mins.
VHS: S18788. $9.99.

Roxanne

Steve Martin successfully updates the story of Cyrano de Bergerac as he plays a soulful small-town fire chief with a big heart and an even larger nose. He falls for Roxanne (Daryl Hannah) but she has eyes only for hunk Rick Rossovich. With Michael J. Pollard, Shelley Duvall and Fred Willard.
VHS: S05318. $14.95.
Laser: LD75804. $34.95.
Fred Schepisi, USA, 1987, 107 mins.

Ruggles of Red Gap

A simply wonderful film, with Charles Laughton as a British butler who is "lost" in a poker game by his master, the Duke of Burnstead (Roland Young) to a rough-and-tumble American rancher. Arriving in the U.S., Laughton's stiff upper lip begins to quiver as he is introduced by his new employer as Colonel Ruggles and soon has such notable grand dames of cinematic comedy as Mary Boland, ZaSu Pitts and Maude Eburne vying for his attention.
VHS: S05995. $14.98.
Laser: LD71570. $34.98.
Leo McCarey, USA, 1935, 90 mins.

Sabrina

Harrison Ford, Julia Ormand and Greg Kinnear make the perfect love triangle in this updated version of a classic Hollywood romantic comedy. Two rich brothers, one a scion of respectability, the other a playboy, rival each other for the attentions of their servant's daughter, the surprisingly transformed Sabrina.
VHS: S27761. $19.95.
Sydney Pollack, USA, 1995, 127 mins.

Saps at Sea

Stan and Ollie find themselves adrift on the high seas along with an escaped killer in this Laurel and Hardy comedy vehicle made in 1940. Harry Langdon was one of the writers.
VHS: S13865. $14.98.
Gordon Douglas, USA, 1940, 57 mins.

Saratoga

In her final film Jean Harlow stars as a determined woman dueling a charismatic gambler over the deed on her family's thoroughbred farm. With Walter Pidgeon, Lionel Barrymore and Hattie McDaniel.
VHS: S17783. $19.98.
Jack Conway, USA, 1937, 92 mins.

Say Anything...

A wonderfully evocative portrait of a tender and sensitive relationship between a 19-year-old army brat (John Cusack) who loves the class brain (Ione Skye), trying to deal with a very complicated relationship with her father (John Mahoney). A wonderful supporting cast includes Lili Taylor, Amy Brooks and Jason Gould and a great soundtrack.
VHS: S10609. $19.98.
Cameron Crowe, USA, 1989, 100 mins.

Scared Stiff

Dean Martin and Jerry Lewis remake Bob Hope's Ghost Breakers, stationed on an eerie Caribbean island inhabited by supernatural forces. With Lizabeth Scott, Carmen Miranda and Dorothy Malone.
VHS: S18677. $19.95.
George Marshall, USA, 1953, 108 mins.

Scenes from the Class Struggle in Beverly Hills

Paul Bartel, the man who gave the world Death Race 2000, Private Parts and Eating Raoul, now turns his attention to the filthy rich. Jacqueline Bisset heads a cast of unhappy, sex-starved people with money. Can servants Robert Beltran and Ray Sharkey alleviate the problems of Bisset, Mary Woronov and Ed Begley Jr.? With Bartel as a plump diet doctor and Paul Mazursky as a randy ghost.
VHS: S10994. $19.95.
Paul Bartel, USA, 1989, 103 mins.

Scrooged

Bill Murray is a modern TV executive who is mocking Christmas and finds himself reliving the life of Ebenezer Scrooge. With John Forsythe, Carol Kane and David Johansen as the ghosts of his life who provide him with real holiday spirit. Watch for Buddy Hackett and Mary Lou Retton as Scrooge and Tiny Tim in the TV-show-within-the movie production.
Laser: LD75343. $29.98.
Richard Donner, USA, 1988, 101 mins.

Secret Diary of Sigmund Freud

Offbeat, hilarious spoof of the life and times of the father of modern psychiatry. Bud Cort (Harold and Maude) stars as Freud, Carroll Baker as the young Freud's mother, and Klaus Kinski as her lover. With Carol Kane, Marisa Berenson and Dick Shawn.
VHS: S02325. $79.98.
Danford Greene, USA, 1984, 129 mins.

The Secret Life of Walter Mitty

The irrepressible Danny Kaye stars as a mild-mannered mouse who imagines himself as a number of daredevil heroes, including a gunslinger in the Old West and a Mississippi riverboat gambler. It's the ultimate daydreamer's film based on a story by James Thurber. Cut from the final film was one of Walter's fantasies in which he's a gunman involved with the Irish Republican Army! Also starring Virginia Mayo, Ann Rutherford and Boris Karloff. "Danny Kaye's funniest" *(Time)*. Digitally remastered.
VHS: S02179. $19.98.
Norman Z. McLeod, USA, 1947, 110 mins.

The Secret of My Success

Michael J. Fox takes the New York business world by storm in this breezy comedy of corporate confusion. By taking full advantage of his uncle's company inefficiency and by being lucky, he works both in the mailroom and the exec boardroom. With Helen Slater, Richard Jordan and John Pankow.
VHS: S05316. $19.95.
Herbert Ross, USA, 1987, 110 mins.

The Secret War of Harry Frigg

In 1943, a private engineers the escape of five captured generals. A slick war comedy, starring Paul Newman, John Williams, Sylva Koscina, Andrew Duggan and Tom Bosley.
VHS: S16303. $14.95.
Jack Smight, USA, 1967, 109 mins.

See No Evil, Hear No Evil

The third pairing of Richard Pryor and Gene Wilder has Pryor cast as a deaf man and Wilder as a blind man. The two are being sought by the police and most of the plot revolves around their slapstick attempts to escape. Not up to their previous efforts but the chemistry between the two is still there.
VHS: S21441. $14.95.
Arthur Hiller, USA, 1989, 103 mins.

Semi-Tough

Burt Reynolds, Kris Kristofferson and Jill Clayburgh star in Michael Ritchie's modern screwball comedy, which deftly links the bone-crunching world of pro football with the psyche-jarring "consciousness" movement.
VHS: S15253. $14.95.
Michael Ritchie, USA, 1977, 108 mins.

The Senator Was Indiscreet

William Powell wants to be President of the United States. The only thing that may stop him is his own diary, filled with years of political deals and shenanigans. George S. Kaufman's only shot at directing a movie proves to be a success. With Peter Lind Hayes and Ella Raines.
VHS: S04245. $19.95.
George S. Kaufman, USA, 1947, 81 mins.

Send Me No Flowers

Hypochondriac Rock Hudson sincerely believes he's dying so he asks his best friend Tony Randall to help find his wife, Doris Day, a second husband. This third pairing of Hudson, Day and Randall is a breezy farce that includes Paul Lynde as a cemetery plot salesman—"When you're ready, we're ready."
VHS: S03680. $14.95.
Norman Jewison, USA, 1964, 100 mins.

Seven Days Ashore/Hurry, Charlie, Hurry

Comedy double feature. A sailor has three girls in one port. A husband tries to sneak away on a fishing trip. A fish in the bush is worth three birds in the hand. USA, 1944, 140 mins.
VHS: S10637. $19.98.

Seven Little Foys
Bob Hope's perennial favorite, with Hope playing famous vaudevillian Eddie Foy, with the seven little Foys filling in the action. James Cagney is terrific as George M. Cohan.
VHS: S07013. $14.95.
Melville Shavelson, USA, 1955, 93 mins.

Seven Thieves
Comic caper story of an elderly crook who conceives one last plan to rob a Monte Carlo casino. With Edward G. Robinson, Rod Steiger, Joan Collins and Eli Wallach.
VHS: S13202. $39.98.
Henry Hathaway, USA, 1960, 102 mins.

Sex and the Single Girl
Helen Gurley Brown's phenomenal best seller was translated into a battle of wills between the sexes, with soft core pornographer Tony Curtis attempting to seduce the brilliant and beautiful psychologist Natalie Wood. With Henry Fonda, Mel Ferrer, Fran Jeffries, and Stubby Kaye.
VHS: S15936. $19.98.
Laser: LD71188. $34.98.
Richard Quine, USA, 1964, 114 mins.

Sextette
Mae West came out of retirement to do this campy comedy based on her own life with support from Timothy Dalton, Ringo Starr, Alice Cooper and Dom DeLuise.
VHS: S02572. $19.95.
Ken Hughes, USA, 1977, 91 mins.

Sgt. Bilko
Steve Martin was born to play the wacky military man from the classic early television sitcom. Dan Ackroyd and Phil Hartman are also featured in this over-the-top comedy. Bilko's beloved Fort Baxter is threatened, along with his reputation. As a result, he must find a way to save his neck and his livelihood without betraying too much competence or too keen a love for work.
VHS: S29916. $19.95.
Laser: LD75907. $34.98.
DVD: DV60302. $24.98.
Jonathan Lynn, USA, 1996, 95 mins.

Shadow of the Thin Man
The fourth Thin Man finds Nick and Nora working on the murder of a racetrack jockey. The suspects include Barry Nelson, Donna Reed, Alan Baxter and Henry O'Neill. San Levene is the official cop on duty. Dickie Hall plays the growing Nick Jr. William Powell and Myrna Loy are the proud parents.
VHS: S05609. $24.95.
W.S. Van Dyke, USA, 1941, 97 mins.

The Shakiest Gun in the West
Don Knotts stars as a dentist in this remake of Bob Hope's 1948 The Paleface. Setting out from Philadelphia, Knotts resolves to bring good dental health to the frontier. But the rough-and-ready West soon has him brandishing a gun.
VHS: S29997. $14.98.
Alan Rafkin, USA, 1967, 101 mins.

Shampoo
Warren Beatty stars as a Beverly Hills hairdresser in this satiric comic drama of life in Southern California in the late 60's. Beatty has success in his career and all the women he can handle, but he feels there is more to life than cutting heads. With Julie Christie, Goldie Hawn, Lee Grant and Jack Warden.
VHS: S01885. $14.95.
Laser: CLV, Criterion. **LD70762. $34.95.**
Hal Ashby, USA, 1975, 109 mins.

She Done Him Wrong
Mae West in a terrific spoof of the gay 1890's, with Mae repeating her stage success in the role of Diamond Lil, and Cary Grant the guy who gets asked to come up and see her sometime-which he does, with volatile results.
VHS: S04521. $14.98.
Lowell Sherman, USA, 1933, 66 mins.

Shirley Temple and Friends
Three classic two-reelers starring Shirley Temple, including Merrily Yours, What's to Do and Dora's Dunkin Donuts. 90 mins.
VHS: S08446. $29.95.

Shirley Temple's Baby Burlesks
The curly-topped cutie stars at the age of four in five parodies of popular films, with an all-kid cast. Kid in Africa finds Shirley as Madam Cradlebait the Missionary, who is saved from the cannibals by Diaperzan. Other titles include The Pie-Covered Wagon, Polly-Tix in Washington and Glad Rags to Riches, where she sings her first on-screen song. B&W.
VHS: S05438. $24.95.
Charles Lamont, USA, 1934-33, 50 mins.

Shut My Big Mouth
Joe E. Brown is mistaken for a wealthy businessman, foils a stagecoach holdup, is elected Marshall and tries to win a woman's hand by rescuing her father from a band of evil kidnappers. Hilarious fun with Victory Jory, Fritz Feld and Adele Mara. USA, 80 mins.
VHS: S15383. $24.95.

Silent Movie
Mel Brooks' romp about director Mel Funn, a washed-up alcoholic whose comeback is hinged on his ability to solicit stars Paul Newman, Liza Minnelli and Burt Reynolds to appear in a blockbuster silent film. Brooks' alternate send-up/homage of the silent film generation is embellished with comedic undercurrents from his regulars Dom Deluise and Marty Feldman.
VHS: S02603. $19.98.
Laser: LD76330. $39.99.
Mel Brooks, USA, 1976, 88 mins.

Silver Streak
Richard Pryor teams up with Gene Wilder in this story of a white executive on vacation who winds up involved in a murder. Pryor portrays "Grover", who assists Wilder in evading the police and ultimately in catching the bad guys. The film contains the classic scene where Pryor teaches Wilder to be "Black".
Laser: Widescreen. **LD75485. $39.98.**
Arthur Hiller, USA, 1976, 113 mins.

Singles
Set in the world of Seattle's music scene, this romantic comedy features Matt Dillon and Bridget Fonda. Together they and a charming cast explore the trials and tribulations of young love accompanied by the music of bands like Pearl Jam, Soundgarden and Mudhoney.
VHS: S22602. $19.98.
Cameron Crowe, USA, 1992, 99 mins.

Sister Act
Whoopi Goldberg plays a second rate Reno lounge performer whose connections to her mob-tied boyfriend (Harvey Keitel) force her into the rigid authoritarianism of a local convent and its Mother Superior (Maggie Smith). Nothing is ever the same. With Bill Nunn, Kathy Najimy and scene-stealer Mary Wickes.
VHS: S17635. $19.99.
Laser: Letterboxed. **LD71824. $29.99.**
Emile Ardolino, USA, 1992, 100 mins.

Sister Act II: Back in the Habit
Whoopi Goldberg received the largest paycheck ever for an actress to reprise her role as a nightclub singer and undercover nun in this sequel to the blockbuster Sister Act. Most of her supporting cast including Maggie Smith and scene-stealing Kathy Najimy are back as well.
VHS: S21432. $19.95.
Bill Duke, USA, 1993, 107 mins.

Six of a Kind
Burns and Allen star in this madcap story of alarming events on a cross-country auto trip. Just as J. Pinkham Winney and his wife set out on their second honeymoon, they discover they have to take George, Gracie and their impossibly large Great Dane.
VHS: S28593. $14.98.
Leo McCarey, USA, 1934, 62 mins.

Sleep with Me
Eric Stoltz, Craig Sheffer and Meg Tilly wind up exploring sex, relationships and each other in this offbeat romantic comedy. Six social events provide the backdrop for this unfolding love triangle between a man, his wife and his best friend. Featuring Quentin Tarantino in a truly silly cameo role.
VHS: S23749. $94.99.
Rory Kelly, USA, 1994, 87 mins.

Sleepless in Seattle
Nora Ephron's second film features Tom Hanks as a Seattle architect who grieves over the death of his beautiful wife. His son calls up a national radio show, and prevails on its listeners to help him find a new wife for his father. With Meg Ryan as the new love interest. VHS letterboxed.
VHS: S19513. $19.95.
Laser: LD71921. $34.95.
DVD: DV60017. $29.95.
Nora Ephron, USA, 1993, 104 mins.

Snow White and the Three Stooges
Champion figure skater Carol Heiss makes her film debut in this silly version of the classic fairy tale, enlivened by the ridiculous antics of Moe, Larry and Curly.
VHS: S10741. $14.98.
Walter Lang, USA, 1961, 107 mins.

Son of Paleface
A return of the hit comedy Paleface in which Bob Hope embarks on an hysterical venture West to claim an inheritance and crosses the paths of Jane Russell, Roy Rogers and Trigger.
VHS: S07765. $14.95.
Frank Tashlin, USA, 1952, 95 mins.

Song of the Thin Man
The sixth and last of the Thin Man movies with Powell and Loy concerns the murder of a bandleader on a gambling ship. The supporting cast includes Gloria Grahame, Keenan Wynn, Jayne Meadows, Ralph Morgan and Dean Stockwell as Nick, Jr. Asta Jr. plays the role of Asta.
VHS: S05611. $24.95.
Edward Buzzell, USA, 1947, 86 mins.

Sons of the Desert
Laurel and Hardy attend a convention of the fraternal order of the Sons of the Desert without letting their wives know the real reason for their absence from home and hearth. Said to be their best feature. With Charley Chase, Mae Busch and Dorothy Christy. B&W.
VHS: S01904. $14.98.
William A. Seiter, USA, 1933, 69 mins.

Sorrowful Jones
Bob Hope and Lucille Ball star in this comedy based on a Damon Runyan tale about a penny-pinching Broadway bookmaker who "inherits" a five-year-old girl when her father puts the mopper up as a collateral for a bet and never comes back. Easing Hope's entry into reluctant fatherhood is old flame Lucy, a nightclub singer who just happens to be the personal property of gangster Bruce Cabot, who'll do anything to make sure his horse wins a big race.
VHS: S05997. $14.98.
Sidney Lanfield, USA, 1949, 88 mins.

A Southern Yankee
Red Skelton is delightful as Aubrey Filmore, a featherbrained but loveable bellboy who dreams of becoming an agent for the Union Forces' Secret Service during the Civil War. Buster Keaton devised many of the gags in the film.
VHS: S15248. $19.98.
Edward Sedgwick, USA, 1948, 90 mins.

Spook Busters
Long before the Ghostbusters were organized, the Bowery Boys learned how to exterminate supernatural pests. In addition to dehaunting an old house, Leo Gorcey and his pals must deal with Douglas Dumbrille as Dr. Coslow, the mad scientist who wants to put the brain of Huntz Hall inside the body of a gorilla. With Charles Middleton, Bobby Jordan, Gabriel Dell, Billy Benedict and Vera Lewis. The first of 25 Bowery Boys movies from director William Beaudine.
VHS: S15831. $14.98.
William Beaudine, USA, 1946, 68 mins.

Spooks Run Wild
Bela Lugosi meets the East End Kids during a holiday in the country. Leo Gorcey, Huntz Hall and Co. believe the creepy guy in the cape and evening clothes is the notorious Monster, and boy, are they scared. Lugosi's midget assistant is played by Angelo Rossitto (Mad Max beyond Thunderdome). B&W.
VHS: S04006. $29.95.
Phil Rosen, USA, 1941, 69 mins.

Squeal of Death
Cast somewhere between Monty Python and MAD, from the criminally funny minds of young filmmakers Tom Stern and Alex Winter, this program contains three short comedies, including Aisles of Doom and Cherub.
VHS: S17165. $14.95.

Star Shorts
A six-part dose of comedy vignettes starring Bill Murray, his brother Brian Doyle-Murray, Bobcat Goldthwait, Griffin Dunne and Dom DeLuise. 60 mins.
VHS: S13096. $59.98.

Start the Revolution Without Me
Gene Wilder and Donald Sutherland play two sets of twins mixed up at birth who grow to manhood during the French Revolution on opposite sides of the economic spectrum. With Hugh Griffith and Billie Whitelaw as the King and Queen of France. A historical comedy of considerable hilarity. Orson Welles narrates.
VHS: S06194. $19.98.
Bud Yorkin, USA, 1970, 91 mins.

Steal Big, Steal Little
Andy Garcia appears as twin brothers in this comedy. Ruben and Robby were adopted by a rich woman in Santa Barbara. When she dies, the brothers learn that she designated only Ruben as her heir. As a result, legal battles, mayhem and even murder could result from their brotherly rivalry. Alan Arkin also stars.
VHS: S27486. $19.98.
Andrew Davis, USA, 1995, 134 mins.

The Stooge
Dean Martin and Jerry Lewis are a musical comedy team on the stage with a fair amount of success, only the singer doesn't realize that it is really the Stooge, and not him, that everyone is interested in. In the end they manage to laugh and sing through it all, with scarcely a blip.
VHS: S21136. $14.95.
Hal B. Wallis, USA, 1951, 100 mins.

The Stoogephile Trivia Movie
Stooge appearances from the stage, screen and television, never before released. This tape "answers all the questions about the world's funniest comedy team." 55 mins.
VHS: S09248. $19.95.

Strawberry Blonde
James Cagney stars as a good-hearted dentist who carries a torch for the vacuous Rita Hayworth, not fully appreciating the great wife Olivia de Havilland is.
VHS: S02611. $19.98.
Raoul Walsh, USA, 1941, 97 mins.

Strictly Business
Tommy Davidson from In Living Color stars as Bobby Johnson, a streetsmart mailroom employee with a strong desire to better himself. Enter Joseph C. Phillips as Wayman Tinsdale III, a love smitten buppie executive who wishes to meet Halle Berry, a tantalizing nightclub hostess. With David Marshall Grant, Jon Cypher, Anne Marie Johnson and Sam Jackson.
VHS: S15987. $19.98.
Kevin Hooks, USA, 1991, 84 mins.

Striptease
In the most revealing and provocative performance of her career, Demi Moore stars in this bold comedy as housewife Erin Grant, who has lost her job and her daughter in a custody battle with her lunatic ex-husband, Darrell. To get the money for an appeal, Erin takes a job at the Eager Beaver, a Miami strip club with clientele as colorful as the dancers. When Erin attracts the lustful attention of a deranged U.S. Congressman (Burt Reynolds), she finds that he'll stop at nothing—even murder—to possess her. Also stars Armand Assante and Ving Rhames. Special unrated version with additional footage not seen in theaters.
VHS: S30155. $19.95.
Laser: LD75997. $39.95.
Andrew Bergman, USA, 1996, 115 mins.

Stuart Saves His Family
Al Franken is Stuart Smalley, the cable-access affirmation expert with firsthand knowledge of a variety of twelve-step programs. In this feature film comedy he must confront the sense of rejection and negative feelings occasioned by the cancellation of his show. His good friend (Laura San Giacomo) helps him through the dysfunctional morass that threatens his life and family.
VHS: S26394. $19.95.
Harold Ramis, USA, 1994, 95 mins.

Summer Fling
It's June and 17-year-old Frankie (Jared Leto) is sure he's completely blown his end-of-school exams, along with his one shot at getting into college. But before the test results hit in August, he's determined to have a wild time pursing this summer's major goals: planning the ultimate beach bash and getting better acquainted with the bikini babes he's been checking out. Along the way we also get to meet his wacky, offbeat family, in this comedy starring Gabriel Byrne, Catherine O'Hara and Christina Ricci.
VHS: S34920. $103.99.
David Keating, USA, 1997, 103 mins.

The Sunshine Boys
Neil Simon adapts his own play about two former vaudeville performers who are reluctantly pressed into service for a special television program. A sharp, observant comedy of manners, with superb performances by Walter Matthau and Oscar-winner George Burns.
VHS: S20504. $14.95.
Laser: LD70145. $34.98.
Herbert Ross, USA, 1975, 111 mins.

Swimming with Sharks
Kevin Spacey and Frank Whaley star in this dazzling, wicked comedy. The vile fun begins as Whaley's character is humiliated, kicked and even spit on all before ten in the morning. It's enough to make a man take up a gun in self-defense.
VHS: S26660. $14.99.
George Huang, USA, 1995, 93 mins.

Swingers
This competent comedy about contemporary dating as encountered by two lounge lizards is "a scrupulously detailed little sociological treatise…a delicate little scalpel job, slivering away at the sorry sadisms and masochisms of a microcosm of dating rituals" (New City).
VHS: S31286. $103.99.
Laser: LD76215. $39.99.
Doug Liman, USA, 1996, 96 mins.

Teacher's Pet
George Seaton directs this quick paced comedy/drama about a cynical, hardboiled newsroom editor (Clark Gable) whose distrust of journalism schools brings considerable consternation to journalism teacher Doris Day. Gig Young received an Oscar nomination for his role as Day's drunken playboy boyfriend.
VHS: S02786. $14.95.
Laser: LD75390. $39.98.
George Seaton, USA, 1958, 120 mins.

Teachers
A black comedy about the state of inner city high schools. The film is grounded in Nick Nolte's brave performance as a brilliant though burnt out history teacher and JoBeth Williams as his former student, now a lawyer, who brings suit on behalf of an exploited student. With Judd Hirsch, Ralph Macchio, Laura Dern, Lee Grant and Allen Garfield.
VHS: S17975. $14.95.
Arthur Hiller, USA, 1984, 106 mins.

Ted & Venus
A quirky comedy directed by and starring Bud Cort as a loopy, cult poet whose erotic obsession leads him on a complicated and strange odyssey. With Carol Kane, James Brolin, Martin Mull, Woody Harrelson and Dr. Timothy Leary.
VHS: S18442. $89.95.
Bud Cort, USA, 1992, 100 mins.

Teresa's Tattoo
In this goofy comedy, two thugs accidentally kill the girl they're holding for ransom and must find a replacement for her quickly. The only catch: the dead redhead had a large tattoo on her chest. With cameos by Melissa Ethridge and k.d. lang.
VHS: S28517. $19.95.
D. Julie Cypher, USA, 1995, 95 mins.

That Thing You Do!
Two-time Oscar-winner Tom Hanks wrote, directed and stars in this "irresistably catchy…lovingly crafted pop fable" (Owen Gleiberman, Entertainment Weekly) about an American rock band, the Wonders, and their overnight triumph when their hit song skyrockets to the top of the charts. With original music evoking the glory days of rock 'n' roll. With Liv Tyler, Tom Everett Scott, Johnathon Schaech, Steve Zahn and Ethan Embry.
VHS: S30868. $19.98.
Laser: LD76104. $39.99.
Tom Hanks, USA, 1996, 108 mins.

That Touch of Mink
Cary Grant's Rolls Royce splashes water all over Doris Day, a small-town girl alone in the big city. Naturally, they are mutually attracted. He wants to fool around. She wants a ring, first. Can a honeymoon in Bermuda be far behind? With Gig Young, Audrey Meadows and Mickey Mantle. VHS letterboxed.
VHS: S04248. $19.95.
Laser: LD71860. $34.98.
Delbert Mann, USA, 1962, 99 mins.

Theodora Goes Wild
Irene Dunne deviated from her melodramatic roles to star in this comedy opposite Melvyn Douglas. Dunne appears to be an ordinary small town woman with no outward signs that indicate she is in fact the author of a torrid and sexy romance novel. All that changes when her identity is revealed to the priggish townsfolk. Her New York illustrator (Douglas), a suave New Yorker from a prominent family, comes calling. Together they throw aside convention to have the time of their lives.
VHS: S27182. $19.95.
Richard Boleslawski, USA, 1936, 93 mins.

They All Kissed the Bride
Joan Crawford (in a role originally intended for Carole Lombard before her death in a plane crash) stars in this witty and wonderful, screwball comedy as an icy businesswoman—"a machine, not a woman"—thawed by muckraking journalist Melvyn Douglas. With Billie Burke, Allen Jenkins and Helen Parrish.
VHS: S30778. $19.95.
Alexander Hall, USA, 1942, 87 mins.

They All Laughed
Ben Gazzara stars in this madcap private detective chase around New York City, as he and partner John Ritter follow and are followed by Audrey Hepburn, Patti Hansen and Dorothy Stratten in her last film role. A hilarious romantic comedy!
VHS: S01321. $19.95.
Peter Bogdanovich, USA, 1981, 115 mins.

They Got Me Covered
In "one of the funniest movies Bob Hope has ever made" (New York Mirror), Hope springs eternal in the role of an eager but not-too-bright newspaper correspondent who seeks to expose the activities of foreign spies in Washington D.C. The lovely Dorothy Lamour just happens to be the head of the news bureau office there too.
VHS: S31809. $14.95.
David Butler, USA, 1942, 95 mins.

They Might Be Giants
A funny movie; George C. Scott is the gentleman who believes himself to be Sherlock Homes, and his psychiatrist companion whose real name is Dr. Watson. With Joanne Woodward, Jack Gifford.
VHS: S04966. $59.95.
Anthony Harvey, USA, 1971, 98 mins.

The Thin Man
Dashiell Hammett's 1932 crime thriller-comedy stars William Powell, Myrna Loy, and Asta, the terrier, in the now-classic plot in which the daughter of an inventor hires private eye Nick Charles to get to the bottom of a case.
VHS: S01324. $19.98.
Laser: LD70694. $34.98.
W.S. Van Dyke, USA, 1934, 90 mins.

The Thin Man Goes Home
Nick goes home to Sycamore Springs to visit his parents and wouldn't you know it, a murder occurs. The fifth entry in the film series finds that small towns can be just as deadly as the big city. With Anne Revere as Crazy Mary. Also Donald Meek and Leon Ames and, of course, Myrna Loy as sophisticated Nora Charles.
VHS: S05610. $24.95.
Richard Thorpe, USA, 1944, 100 mins.

The Thin Man Collection
William Powell and Myrna Loy symbolized the witty discourse, light entertainment and wisecracking repartee in the The Thin Man. In addition to the title entry, there's After the Thin Man, Another Thin Man, Shadow of the Thin Man, The Thin Man Goes Home and Song of the Thin Man.
Laser: LD70172. $124.98.

Things Change
A hilariously funny black comedy about the Mafia and mistaken identity from David Mamet. Joe Mantegna is assigned to deliver Mob witness Don Ameche to court to take a phony rap for a bigshot hoodlum. He decides to give the old man a weekend vacation in Lake Tahoe for being such a stand-up guy. Problems occur when Ameche is mistaken for a bigshot hoodlum. With Robert Prosky. Great Fun.
VHS: S09834. $14.95.
David Mamet, USA, 1988, 114 mins.

This Could Be the Night
Robert Wise's comedy about a beautiful schoolteacher (Jean Simmons) who goes to work at a nightclub, and sets off a volatile sexual triangle with the club's two mercurial owners (Paul Douglas and Anthony Franciosa). With Joan Blondell, Julie Wilson and ZaSu Pitts.
VHS: S18013. $19.98.
Laser: LD74684. $34.98.
Robert Wise, USA, 1957, 105 mins.

Those Magnificent Men in Their Flying Machines
From the opening prologue by Red Skeleton, who gives a hysterical aviatic history lesson, this comic feature will delight audiences with its story of a gag-filled international airplane race. Sarah Miles, Terry Thomas, Benny Hill and Sam Wanamaker are just some of the comic stars included in this fun-filled movie.
VHS: S21025. $14.98.
Ken Annakin, USA, 1965, 132 mins.

Three Broadway Girls
This vintage comedy about three gold-diggers stars Joan Blondell, Madge Evans and Ina Claire. Big spenders in the Big Apple had better watch their p's and q's when these husband hunters are on the loose. With David Manners and Lowell Sherman (who also directed). B&W.
VHS: S05061. $29.95.
Lowell Sherman, USA, 1932, 78 mins.

Three Coins in the Fountain
In this "ingenious and funny fifties comedy classic" (Newsweek), three American roommates (Dorothy McGuire, Jean Peters and Maggie McNamara) working in Italy throw coins into Rome's Trevi Fountain and wish for the man of their dreams. Before long they've set their sights on Clifton Webb, Rossano Brazzi and Louis Jourdan. Featuring the legendary Sammy Cahn/Jules Styne title song.
VHS: S31684. $19.98.
Jean Negulesco, USA, 1954, 102 mins.

Three Men and a Baby
Leonard Nimoy directs Tom Selleck, Ted Danson and Steve Guttenberg as a trio of fun loving single guys who find a baby on the doorstep of their swinging bachelor apartment, in this box office hit based on the French film Three Men and a Cradle. The six-month-old Blair twins, Lisa and Michelle of Kitchener, Ontario, play the baby.
VHS: S07914. $19.95.
Leonard Nimoy, USA, 1987, 102 mins.

Three Men on a Horse
A spirited and reflective comedy about a shy, passive young man with an uncanny ability for picking race horse winners. With Frank McHugh, Sam Levene, Joan Blondell and Teddy Hart. Adapted from the play by George Abbott and John Cecil Holm.
VHS: S17664. $19.98.
Mervyn Le Roy, USA, 1936, 88 mins.

The Three Musketeers
Charlie Sheen, Kiefer Sutherland, Chris O'Donnell, Oliver Platt, Tim Curry, Rebecca De Mornay and Gabrielle Anwar star in this new, classic version based on the original tale of chivalrous love and camaraderie. It's a swashbuckling, action-packed romp with the immortal honor guard known as The Three Musketeers.
VHS: S21143. $96.98.
Stephen Herek, USA, 1993, 105 mins.

The Three Stooges
The Stooges made over 200 short comedies from 1934 to 1958. Included here are three of the funniest: Disorder in the Court (1936), Sing a Song of Six Pants (1947) and Malice in the Palace (1949). Wonderful madness. USA, 50 mins.
VHS: S02235. $24.95.

Three Stooges
Six more collections of priceless moments from the career of the Stooges.
All the World's a Stooge and Other Nyuks.
VHS: S11541. $14.95.
Hold That Lion and Other Nyuks.
VHS: S11536. $14.95.
Studio Stoops and Other Nyuks.
VHS: S11540. $14.95.
The Hot Scots and Other Nyuks.
VHS: S11538. $14.95.
The Uncivil War Birds and Other Nyuks.
VHS: S11537. $14.95.
Three Smart Saps and Other Nyuks.
VHS: S11539. $14.95.

The Three Stooges Go Around the World in a Daze
Jules Verne's classic tale of exploration and adventure takes a wacky turn when the Three Stooges team up with the grandson of the original hero. This has some of the best sight gags dreamed up by the Three Stooges.
VHS: S26507. $14.95.
Norman Maurer, USA, 1963, 94 mins.

Three Stooges Hit Home
New-to-video episodes of Larry, Moe and Curly.
A Ducking They Will Go and Other Nyuks.
VHS: S07999. $14.95.
Ants in the Pantry and Other Nyuks.
VHS: S07998. $14.95.
In the Sweet Pie and Pie and Other Nyuks.
VHS: S08000. $14.95.
Phony Express and Other Nyuks.
VHS: S08001. $14.95.
Playing the Ponies and Other Nyuks.
VHS: S08002. $14.95.
Three Little Twerps and Other Nyuks.
VHS: S07997. $14.95.

The Three Stooges in Orbit
Despotic television producers exhort the Three Stooges to formulate a new concept for a cartoon. Along the way they accidentally launch a scientist's new invention, a rocket that brings them into contact with Martian invaders. Now they must brainstorm to save their TV careers and the world.
VHS: S26510. $14.95.
Edward Bernds, USA, 1962, 87 mins.

The Three Stooges Meet Hercules
A time machine places the comic antics of the Three Stooges into the ancient era. There, they encounter a villainous Hercules but transform him into the hero of myth and legend. This is the film that mixes Hollywood historical epics and zany Stooges magic.
VHS: S26509. $14.95.
Edward Bernds, USA, 1961, 89 mins.

Three Stooges—More Nyuks
Six more volumes of the uncensored bits of the Three Stooges.
Cookoo Cavaliers and Other Nyuks.
VHS: S09407. $14.95.
From Nurse to Worse and Other Nyuks.
VHS: S09408. $14.95.
Half-Wit's Holiday and Other Nyuks.
VHS: S09409. $14.95.
Idiots Deluxe and Other Nyuks.
VHS: S09410. $14.95.
Nutty But Nice and Other Nyuks.
VHS: S09411. $14.95.
They Stooge to Conga and Other Nyuks.
VHS: S09406. $14.95.

The Three Stooges: A Pain in the Pullman
Get your Curly fix with these three Stooges episodes. In A Pain in the Pullman (1936), The Stooges and their pet monkey join a travelling vaudeville troupe, making for non-stop hilarity. In Gents Without Cents (1944), Moe, Larry and Curly team up with acrobatic beauties Flo, Mary and Shirley for a lively song and dance revue at a local shipyard. In Termites of 1938 (1938), The Stooges, as Acme Exterminators, are mistakenly invited to a swanky party and teach the society pests a thing or two about bad manners. 56 mins.
VHS: S30972. $14.95.

The Three Stooges: Corny Casanovas
Moe, Larry and Shemp star in this 1952 classic directed by Edward Bernds, in which these three laughable Lotharios all romance the same gold-digging gal with hilarious results. Also includes A Missed Fortune (1951), in which Shemp wins $50,000 in a radio contest and three larcenous lovelies try to swindle The Stooges out of their fortune; and He Cooked His Goose (1952), in which Larry is caught cheating with both Moe's wife and Shemp's fiancee. 48 mins.
VHS: S30968. $14.95.

The Three Stooges: Dizzy Doctors
Three episodes—Dizzy Doctors, Goofs and Saddles and Three Little Sew and Sews—show Moe, Larry and Curly in a series of outrageous situations. As salesmen, cowboys and sailors, this triumvirate of slapstick mastery makes nonstop zaniness an unforgettable event. 51 mins.
VHS: S29438. $14.95.

The Three Stooges: Dopey Dicks
Moe, Larry and Shemp are featured in three episodes on this video: Dopey Dicks, The Tooth Will Out and Scrambled Brains. Confronting a mad scientist and his headless robot, an outlaw with a toothache, or Shemp's approaching marriage drives the Stooges to comic heights. 48 mins.
VHS: S29433. $14.95.

The Three Stooges: False Alarms
The threesome of dopes, Moe, Larry and Curly, are featured in three of their best episodes on this video. False Alarms, Three Pests in a Mess and Flat Foot Stooges find the trio fighting fires, winning a sweepstakes, confronting an explosive duck and murdering a mannequin. 48 mins.
VHS: S29434. $14.95.

The Three Stooges: Have Rocket Will Travel
This is the very first Three Stooges feature film. It's a hilarious romp through outer space that all begins when the three find themselves accidentally aboard a rocket. Though disaster looms, laughs carry the day, and the Three Stooges become national heroes.
VHS: S26506. $14.95.
David Lowell Rich, USA, 1959, 76 mins.

The Three Stooges: Heavenly Daze
On this tape, Moe, Larry and Shemp star in the comedy classic Heavenly Daze (1948), in which Shemp goes to heaven but isn't allowed to go through the Pearly Gates until he can reform his bad-boy buddies Moe and Larry. On The Ghost Talks (1949), The Stooges scare up some laughs as movers hired to clear out a haunted castle, who come face-to-face with poltergeists. Under the spell of the hypnotist Svengarlic, The Stooges become flagpole walkers and foil an insurance scam in the process on Hokus Pokus (1949). 49 mins.
VHS: S30970. $14.95.

The Three Stooges: Hoi Polloi
In Hoi Polloi, A Gem of a Jam and Half-Shot Shooters, Moe, Larry and Curly make the best out of a series of mistaken identities and mismatched career choices. Posing as gentlemen or doctors, or even mistakenly given weapons by the army, these comic buffoons deliver big laughs. 53 mins.
VHS: S29437. $14.95.

The Three Stooges: Listen Judge
Three episodes show Moe, Larry and Shemp at their wacky best. The boys mix with the law, dabble in science and get caught up in espionage in these episodes. Contains Listen Judge, Bubble Trouble and Dunked in the Deep. 51 mins.
VHS: S29435. $14.95.

The Three Stooges: Out West
Moe, Larry and Shemp turn the Wild West upside down in these three episodes: Out West, Punchy Cowpunchers and Merry Mavericks. Whether with the calvary or as marshalls, these guys make the frontier safe for laughs. 51 mins.
VHS: S29436. $14.95.

The Three Stooges: Stop! Look! and Laugh!
This film brings together episodes from earlier Three Stooges shorts. Ventriloquist Paul Winchell and his dummy Jerry Mahoney are featured as the originators of these classic comic bits.
VHS: S26508. $14.95.
Jules White, USA, 1960, 78 mins.

The Three Stooges: The Outlaws
Adam West co-stars in this final Three Stooges feature. It's a broad parody of that great American film genre, the Western. Nothing holds the comic threesome back as they lampoon everything held sacred the world over by John Wayne and Clint Eastwood fans.
VHS: S26511. $14.95.
Norman Maurer, USA, 1964, 88 mins.

The Three Stooges: Vagabond Loafers
On this tape, The Stooges (with Shemp) first unleash a flood of laughter as plumbers hired to fix the leaky pipes during a pompous high society party in Vagabond Loafers (1949). Then, on the Pest Man Wins (1951), The Stooges are exterminators who wreak havoc on a society matron's lavish dessert party, complete with a classic pie-throwing finale. On Three Dark Horses (1952), The Stooges are delegates to the Presidential convention and get involved with crooked politics. 48 mins.
VHS: S30969. $14.95.

The Three Stooges: Wee Wee Monsieur
In Wee Wee Monsieur (1937), laughter is international when Larry, Moe and Curly accidently enlist in the French Legion. Disguised as Santa Claus and harem girls, The Stooges must rescue their general or face the firing squad. In Pardon My Clutch (1947), Moe and Larry plan a restful camping holiday to calm Shemp's tattered nerves. But car trouble makes their travel plans go amuck. In Fiddlers Three (1947), Zaniness rules in the land of Coleslaw-vania, as Old King Cole's fiddlers, Larry, Moe and Shemp, come to the aid of their monarchy when the princess is kidnapped. 50 mins.
VHS: S30973. $14.95.

The Three Stooges: Whoops I'm an Indian
Three more Curlys! When their crooked gambling scheme is exposed, The Stooges disguise themselves as Indians to escape the posse in the uproarious comedy classic Whoops I'm an Indian (1936). In Rockin' Thru the Rockies (1940), The Stooges are hired as travel guides for Nelle's Belles, and mayhem follows them along their way out west. With Linda Winters (who later changed her name to Dorothy Comingore, and starred in Citizen Kane). In Cactus Makes Perfect (1942) Curly's new gold-seeking adventure makes prosperous prospectors out of the trio. 72 mins.
VHS: S30971. $14.95.

Three Wishes
Patrick Swayze and Mary Elizabeth Mastrantonio star in this tender romantic comedy. Mastrantonio plays a woman with two sons who has been left alone because her husband is missing in the Korean War. She and her sons open their home to a scruffy man with an even scruffier dog and unexpectedly find their lives changed forever.
VHS: S27499. $19.98.
Martha Coolidge, USA, 1995, 115 mins.

Thrill of a Romance
A 22-year-old Esther Williams reaches Hollywood stardom in this light romantic comedy. Thrill of a Romance also marks the first leading role for Van Johnson whose boyish charm made him the heartthrob of a wholesome '40s America, and secured four more film roles that he would star in with Williams.
VHS: S16611. $19.98.
Richard Thorpe, USA, 1945, 104 mins.

The Thrill of It All!
This early work by Norman Jewison (Moonstruck) is a hilarious satire of American normalcy and the plastic tendencies of suburbia, soap operas and television commercials. An average woman (Doris Day) becomes an overnight television celebrity despite her husband's (James Garner) objections. The screenplay is by Carl Reiner and Larry Gelbart (Tootsie). With Edward Andrews, Elliott Reid, Reginald Owen and ZaSu Pitts.
VHS: S17946. $14.98.
Norman Jewison, USA, 1963, 108 mins.

Throw Momma from the Train
Billy Crystal has two major problems in this slightly black comedy. One is a severe case of writer's block and the other is Owen, who wants his writing instructor to kill his overbearing mother. Danny DeVito is Owen. Oscar nominee Anne Ramsey is the target for termination. Loosely based on Hitchcock's Strangers on a Train, only funnier.
VHS: S06448. $19.98.
Danny DeVito, USA, 1987, 88 mins.

'Til There Was You

Jeanne Tripplehorn, Dylan McDermott, Sarah Jessica Parker and Jennifer Aniston star in this romantic comedy about two mismatched strangers who, after a lifetime of chance encounters, find love and laughs together.
VHS: S32713. $101.99.
Scott Winant, USA, 1997, 114 mins.

Tin Cup

In this critically acclaimed hit, Kevin Costner stars as a middle-aged golf pro who prefers to stay on his own West Texas desert golf range rather than compromise his standards on a golf tour. Rene Russo is the goofball shrink who's taking lessons from him while sleeping with his old rival, a slick ultraconservative ultraprofessional (Don Johnson). Sidekick Cheech Marin adds to the comic fun. "Clever, sexy, funny. Full of surprises and charm. A winner all the way" (Henry Cabor Beck, Newhouse News Service). VHS letterboxed.
VHS: S30449. $19.98.
Laser: LD76032. $39.98.
DVD: DV60081. $24.98.
Ron Shelton, USA, 1996, 133 mins.

To Be or Not to Be

This remake of the 1942 comedy features Mel Brooks and Anne Bancroft as stars of a Polish theater who become involved with invading Nazis.
VHS: S20445. $14.98.
Laser: LD71370. $34.98.
Alan Johnson, USA, 1983, 108 mins.

To Wong Foo, Thanks for Everything! Julie Newmar

Patrick Swayze, Wesley Snipes and John Leguizamo star as beautiful young drag queens out for a jaunt across America. Along the way, they break some hearts, deepen their sense of fashion and even throw a party. This warm comedy is a perfect gender-bending confection. Stockard Channing and Blythe Danner are both featured.
VHS: S27180. $19.95.
Laser: LD75465. $39.98.
Beeban Kidron, USA, 1995, 109 mins.

Tom, Dick and Harry

Academy-Award nominee for best screenplay, this classic comedy tells the delightful tale of a daydreaming girl who can't decide which beau she likes best. Ginger Rogers, Burgess Meredith, Alan Marshall, George Murphy star.
VHS: S05665. $19.98.
Garson Kanin, USA, 1941, 86 mins.

Too Far to Go

Michael Moriarty, Blythe Danner and Glenn Close star in this eccentric comedy about a couple who can't resist being cruel to one another. It has all the insight and wit one would expect from a film based on the stories of Pulitzer Prize-winner John Updike. USA, 1995, 98 mins.
VHS: S27500. $89.95.

Tootsie

Dustin Hoffman plays an unemployed actor who dons women's clothing and becomes a great success in a popular TV soap opera. He also falls in love with a female co-star and learns that he has become a better man by pretending to be a woman. With Jessica Lange, Geena Davis, Dabney Coleman and Bill Murray as his amused roommate.
VHS: S04218. $14.95.
Laser: LD70765. $124.95.
Sydney Pollack, USA, 1982, 116 mins.

Top Banana

Phil Silvers brings his stage role to the screen as "the funniest man on television," who meddles once too often and gets outsmarted himself, in this adaptation of the smash Broadway production. With Rose Marie, Danny Scholl, Judy Lynn, Jack Albertson and Herbie Faye. Filmed in 3-D. With a Johnny Mercer score.
VHS: S30544. $19.98.
Alfred E. Green, USA, 1954, 84 mins.

Topper Returns

A ghoulish romp in a sinister house of thrills. A funny, spooky mystery with Roland Young, Joan Blondell and Carole Landis.
VHS: S03339. $19.95.
Roy Del Ruth, USA, 1941, 87 mins.

The Toy

A flat-broke reporter must resort to becoming the "toy" of a rich millionaire's son. Richard Pryor portrays the "Toy" while Jackie Gleason is cast as the millionaire. Both turn in good performances but there is something offensive about the whole idea. It would have been more interesting had the two comedians switched roles.
VHS: S21474. $14.95.
Richard Donner, USA, 1982, 99 mins.

Toys

A black comedy about the military industrial complex. A general (Michael Gambon) assumes control of a family toy manufacturer and tries to convert the vast, surreal plant into a state-of-the-art munitions factory. Robin Williams stars as the general's nephew, a dreamy, lost romantic who leads the counterattack against the general to regain control of the family business. With Joan Cusack, Robin Wright and rapper LL Cool J.
VHS: S18602. $19.98.
Barry Levinson, USA, 1992, 121 mins.

Trading Places

Eddie Murphy is the street hustler, Dan Aykroyd the preppie in this blockbuster comedy of manners where the two leads switch lives and see how they adapt. Very funny. Also stars Don Ameche, Ralph Bellamy and Denholm Elliott.
VHS: S02175. $19.95.
John Landis, USA, 1983, 106 mins.

Trial and Error

Jeff Daniels stars as a legal eagle who becomes a lame duck when his best friend, an out-of-work actor (Michael Richards, TV's Seinfeld), steps into a small-town courtroom pretending he's the attorney. In no time these clowns turn the courtroom into a circus, and while the actor delivers the performance of his career, the lawyer finds true love with Charlize Theron. With Rip Torn.
VHS: S32518. $19.98.
Laser: LD76384. $29.99.
Jonathan Lynn, USA, 1997, 98 mins.

Trouble Along the Way

The Quiet Man has a "new kind of dame to tame" in this riotous and moving comedy about a hopeless college football team that coopts a famous coach to lead their school out of financial straits. The plan works, but the new coach's methods are not quite above board. John Wayne, Donna Reed and Charles Coburn star.
VHS: S15989. $19.98.
Laser: LD74721. $34.98.
Michael Curtiz, USA, 1953, 110 mins.

The Trouble with Angels

The authority of the church and adolescent rebellion meet head on in Ida Lupino's film about two young thrill seekers (Hayley Mills and June Harding) who continually test the will and fortitude of their Mother Superior, Rosalind Russell, during their stay in a Pennsylvania convent school.
VHS: S16912. $14.95.
Ida Lupino, USA, 1966, 112 mins.

The Trouble with Spies

Donald Sutherland stars as Appleton Porter, a secret agent in her Majesty's Secret Service and Britain's least capable investigator since Inspector Clouseau assisted Scotland Yard. An action adventure with comedy and romance with Robert Morley, Ned Beatty, and Lucy Gutteridge as an attractive Soviet agent.
VHS: S06395. $79.99.
Burt Kennedy, USA, 1987, 91 mins.

True Stories

David Byrne stars in this wacky view of the people and events of Virgil, Texas, population 40,000 and growing, a gleeful glimpse of Americana where the social fabric might be polyester but the hearts are pure gold…and the good times never end. Featuring a cast of unforgettable characters including John Goodman, who has a flashing "Wife Wanted" sign on his front lawn, and a dancin' faith healer. With Annie McEnroe, Swoosie Kurtz and Spalding Gray.
VHS: S03107. $19.98.
Laser: LD74722. $34.98.
David Byrne, USA, 1986, 89 mins.

The Truth About Cats and Dogs

Uma Thurman, Janeane Garofalo and Ben Chaplin star in this three-way comic love story of mistaken identity. Garofalo is a veterinarian on a call-in radio show. When one of her callers asks her out for a date, the short brunette describes herself as tall and blond. This is where Thurman comes in as Garofalo's stand-in to mix everything up, with outrageous results.
VHS: S29798. $19.95.
Laser: LD75899. $39.98.
Michael Lehmann, USA, 1996, 97 mins.

The Tunnel of Love

An adult comedy of manners directed by Gene Kelly, adapted from the long-running play by Joseph Fields and Peter De Vries. A young couple (Doris Day and Richard Widmark) resorts to desperate measures when they're unable to conceive, and encounter bureaucratic confusion when they decide to adopt. With Gig Young and Gia Scala.
VHS: S18014. $19.98.
Gene Kelly, USA, 1958, 98 mins.

The Twelve Chairs

Set in Russia against the backdrop of post-revolutionary chaos, Twelve Chairs is a satirical madcap adventure about Russian life, revolving around a zany quest for a fortune in jewels hidden in the upholstery of twelve chairs. With Dom DeLuise, Ron Moody.
VHS: S01380. $9.98.
Laser: LD76329. $39.99.
Mel Brooks, USA, 1970, 94 mins.

Twenty Bucks

This comic portrayal of contemporary America follows the path of a twenty dollar bill as it crosses the divides of race and class which separate the strata of big city life. Linda Hunt, Steve Buscemi and Gladys Knight portray some of the quirky characters encountered on this cash-driven journey.
VHS: S20887. $19.95.
Keva Rosenfeld, USA, 1992, 91 mins.

Two Much

Two Antonio Banderases may seem like a dream-like proposition, but in this comedy it becomes something of a madcap nightmare. Melanie Griffith and Daryl Hannah are both dating the Spanish star, who has cleverly decided to pose as twins. This zany comedy is just "Two Much" of a good thing. From the director of Belle Epoque.
VHS: S29947. $19.98.
Laser: LD75911. $39.99.
Fernando Trueba, USA, 1996, 118 mins.

Unaccustomed As We Are

Stan Laurel and Oliver Hardy join Thelma Todd and Mae Busch for their very first talkie. It has a simple but brilliant premise. Babe (Hardy) brings his friend home for dinner completely unannounced. This sets off a domestic spat rife with comic possibilities. Both the sound version and the simultaneously released, silent intertitled version are included on this video.
VHS: S26812. $16.95.
Lewis R. Foster, USA, 1929, 39 mins.

Under the Yum-Yum Tree

In this uproarious swinging singles sex comedy in the tradition of Pillow Talk, a "wonderfully comical" (Bosley Crowther, The New York Times) Jack Lemmon stars as a libidinous landlord intent on bedding all his female tenants, including his newest renter: a sexy, virginal coed (Carol Lynley). With Edie Adams, Dean Jones, Paul Lynde, Imogene Coca and Robert Lansing.
VHS: S30777. $19.95.
David Swift, USA, 1963, 110 mins.

Unfaithfully Yours

Remake of the Preston Sturges film, featuring Dudley Moore and Nastassia Kinski, in a story of a conductor who plans to murder his wife.
VHS: S01403. $79.98.
Howard Zieff, USA, 1984, 96 mins.

The Unknown Marx Brothers

This extraordinary program focuses on the Marx Brothers everyone knows and loves while showing a side of Groucho, Chico and Harpo rarely seen by the public. Host Leslie Nielsen leads a journey through rare home movies, insightful interviews with family members, never-before-seen outtakes and hilarious film clips to paint an intimate portrait of the influential American comedy troupe.
VHS: S32502. $19.98.
David Leaf/John Scheinfeld, USA, 1997, 126 mins.

The Unofficial Dan Quayle Video

A highly unauthorized and naturally funny collection of Quayle's speeches, non sequiturs, misstatements, press conferences and interviews. 27 minutes.
VHS: S16901. $9.99.

Unstrung Heroes

Andie MacDowell, John Turturro and Michael Richards star in this family comedy. A young man with a rambunctious sense of life is drawn to the very pair of uncles which the entire family finds crazy. It's a film which proves that heroes can be found in even the most unlikely places.
VHS: S27411. $19.98.
Laser: LD75508. $39.99.
Diane Keaton, USA, 1995, 93 mins.

Up Close & Personal

Robert Redford and Michelle Pfeiffer star as glamorous news anchors in this dramatic film. Redford mentors Pfeiffer, leading her from a role as a weathergirl toward a position of respect and fame as an anchor for a national show. Along the way, they fall in love. Only success can overwhelm their passion.
VHS: S29825. $19.95.
Laser: LD75968. $39.99.
Jon Avnet, USA, 1996, 124 mins.

Up the Academy (Mad Magazine Presents Up the Academy)

A raunchy comedy about a tenth rate military school where scholarship and discipline are just two of the words that the cadets would have great difficulty spelling. Lead Ron Leibman had his name removed from the film and from all advertising. Barbara Bach and Ralph Macchio didn't.
VHS: S04177. $59.95.
Robert Downey, USA, 1980, 88 mins.

Up the Sandbox

Barbra Streisand stars as a discontented Manhattan housewife and mother of two small children. She's married to professor David Selby and escapes frequently into dreams of Fidel Castro, bombing the Statue of Liberty and traveling to Africa. With Jane Hoffman, Anne Ramsey and Stockard Channing. Filmed in New York and Kenya.
VHS: S07007. $19.98.
Laser: LD71472. $34.98.
Irvin Kershner, USA, 1972, 97 mins.

Used Cars

"A classic screwball fantasy—a neglected modern comedy that's like a more restless and visually high-spirited version of the W.C. Fields pictures" (Pauline Kael). Hilarious, energetic! With Kurt Russell and Jack Warden in a brilliant double role.
VHS: S01406. $19.95.
Laser: CLV, chapter stops. **LD74995. $34.95.**
Robert Zemeckis, USA, 1980, 95 mins.

Used People

This dark-edged comedy is set in Queens, 1969. The film's comic premise considers the aftermath when a Jewish woman (Shirley MacLaine) is courted by an Italian lothario (Marcello Mastroianni) on the afternoon of her husband's funeral. The movie also deals with MacLaine's relationships with her two monstrously unhappy adult daughters, Bibby (Kathy Bates) and Norma (Marcia Gay Harden). With Jessica Tandy and Sylvia Sidney.
VHS: S18603. $19.98.
Beeban Kidron, USA, 1992, 116 mins.

Utopia

The final film of Laurel and Hardy, a French-Italian co-production also known as Atoll K or Robinson Crusoe-Land. Laurel and Hardy inherit an island which turns out to be valuable as a source of uranium.
VHS: S02236. $29.95.
Leo Joannon, France/USA, 1952, 83 mins.

A Very Brady Sequel

The Bradys' anniversary party gets a surprise guest when Mrs. Brady's first husband shows up—and tears the family in two! When he kidnaps her and heads for Hawaii, the Bradys put on their paisley shorts and polka-dot bikinis and head for fun, sun and the grooviest adventure of their lives. Starring Shelley Long, Gary Cole and Tim Matheson, with cameos by Zsa Zsa Gabor, Barbara Eden and others. "A genuine movie rarity—a sequel better than the original!" (Gene Siskel, Chicago Tribune).
VHS: S30636. $14.98.
Arlene Sanford, USA, 1996, 90 mins.

Vibes

Cyndi Lauper teams up with Jeff Goldblum and Peter Falk in this supernatural South American treasure hunt comedy. Lauper and Goldblum have psychic abilities that con man Falk thinks he can put to good use in Ecuador. With Julian Sands and Googy Gress. Cindy sings "Hole in My Heart" in her feature film debut.
VHS: S10099. $89.95.
Ken Kwapis, USA, 1988, 99 mins.

Viva Max

Peter Ustinov plays a Mexican general who invades Texas and retakes the Alamo from a crowd of surprised tourists. This contemporary comedy boasts a fine supporting cast which includes John Astin, Pamela Tiffin, Jonathan Winters and Keenan Wynn. Remember the Alamo, once again.
VHS: S04247. $14.98.
Jerry Paris, USA, 1969, 93 mins.

Volunteers

When a spoiled playboy fleeing from a gambling debt joins the Peace Corps, Thailand is not the better for it. Tom Hanks is the jaded American who finds the jungle too primitive and the local bandits a bit on the aggressive side. With Rita Wilson (now Mrs. Tom Hanks), Tim Thomerson and John Candy as a running dog lacky of an imperialist regime. Ask not what this movie can do for you.
VHS: S09517. $19.95.
Nicholas Meyer, USA, 1985, 107 mins.

W.C. Fields: 6 Short Films

A wonderful compilation tape that pays homage to one of America's most beloved film comedians. Includes Fields' first film (Pool Sharks 1915), a silent version of his famous pool routine, and his first sound film (The Golf Specialist 1930). Four Mack Sennett comedy classics featuring Fields round out the tape: The Dentist (1932), The Pharmacist (1933), The Barber Shop (1933) and The Fatal Glass of Beer (1933). 12 mins.
VHS: S28617. $19.95.
Laser: LD76792. $49.95.

W.C. Fields: On Stage, on Screen, on the Air

W.C. Fields at his cynical best in a classic radio rivalry with Charlie McCarthy and later on the golf course. 60 mins.
VHS: S07025. $19.95.

Wag the Dog

The wickedly funny and timely political satire written by David Mamet. When the President is caught in a sex scandal less than two weeks before the election, White House spinmaster Conrad Brean (Robert De Niro) creates a phony war with the help of Hollywood producer Stanley Motss (Dustin Hoffman). "Swift, hilarious, and impossible to resist" (Janet Maslin, New York Times). With Ann Heche, William H. Macy, Denis Leary and William H. Macy.
VHS: S34398. $104.99.
Laser: LD76953. $39.99.
DVD: DV60254. $24.98.
Barry Levinson, USA, 1997, 96 mins.

Waiting for Guffman

A sort of Spinal Tap for community theater, this hilarious mockumentary stars Tap alumnus Christopher Guest as Corky St. Clair, a flamboyant and desperate Broadway wannabe who directs an ambitious, hapless and unintentionally hilarious musical celebrating Blaine, Missouri's 150th anniversary. Fred Willard, Parker Posey, Bob Balaban and SCTV alumni Eugene Levy and Catherine O'Hara costar as stage-struck residents hoping to be discovered when they hear reports that big-time talent scout Mort Guffman will be in the audience.
VHS: S31683. $19.95.
Christopher Guest, USA, 1997, 84 mins.

Walk, Don't Run

Cary Grant's last feature film is a briskly moving comedy of manners set against the Tokyo Olympics of 1964. He's a British industrialist with a housing problem both solved and complicated when he moves in with an American athlete and a proper young English woman. A remake of The More the Merrier. With Jim Hutton and Samantha Eggar.
VHS: S06070. $19.95.
Laser: CLV, letterboxed, chapter stops. **LD74996. $34.95.**
Charles Walters, USA, 1966, 114 mins.

Walking and Talking

This "wildly funny" (CBS Radio, Los Angeles) comedy for everyone who wants to get married and stay single at the same time follows the antics of four friends as they search for true love, from bad dates to long-distance phone sex. With Anne Heche, Todd Field, Liev Schreiber and Catherine Keener.
VHS: S30830. $19.95.
Laser: LD76101. $39.99.
Nicole Holofcener, USA, 1996, 85 mins.

War of the Roses

Those looking for an historical drama about a bitter civil war in England are going to be disappointed. This conflict is an all-American marital struggle over division of community property. Danny DeVito directs his pal Michael Douglas and Kathleen Turner in a brutal story of a disintegrating marriage. DeVito also takes the part of a lawyer who cautions others not to follow the example of Oliver and Barbara Rose.
VHS: S12347. $14.98.
Laser: LD72433. $99.98.
Danny DeVito, USA, 1989, 116 mins.

Watch the Birdie

Red Skelton plays three roles (father, son, grandfather) in this madcap adventure involving three beautiful women and two suave crooks. Co-starring Ann Miller.
VHS: S15249. $19.98.
Jack Donohue, USA, 1950, 71 mins.

Wayne's World

Penelope Spheeris directs the feature-length adaptation of the Saturday Night Live sketch program detailing the comic adventures of two young hipsters who host a postmodern television show on cable-access from their parents' basement in Aurora, Illinois. Mike Myers and Dana Carvey are the ubiquitous Wayne and Garth. Rob Lowe is a sleazy television programmer and Tia Carrere plays the love interest, a gilded rock goddess.
VHS: S17422. $14.95.
Penelope Spheeris, USA, 1992, 95 mins.

We're No Angels

Humphrey Bogart, Peter Ustinov and Aldo Ray star as three escaped convicts from Devil's Island, who come to the aid of a shopkeeper and his family.
VHS: S04322. $19.95.
Michael Curtiz, USA, 1955, 106 mins.

We're No Angels

Robert De Niro and Sean Penn star as a couple of affable convicts who disguise themselves as priests in order to escape into the safety of Canada during the Depression. Based very loosely on the 1955 escaped convict comedy starring Humphrey Bogart, Aldo Ray and Peter Ustinov. The remake also features Demi Moore, Wallace Shawn and James Russo. Excellent period detail.
VHS: S12238. $19.95.
Neil Jordan, USA, 1989, 110 mins.

We're Not Married

Six couples find that they were never legally married in this smartly played comedy. Stars Ginger Rogers, Fred Allen, Victor Moore, Paul Douglas, Eve Arden, Marilyn Monroe, David Wayne, Louis Calhern, Zsa Zsa Gabor, Mitzi Gaynor, Eddie Bracken, James Gleason and Jane Darwell.
VHS: S16399. $19.98.
Edmund Goulding, USA, 1952, 85 mins.

Weapons of Mass Destraction

In this outrageous comedy, Gabriel Byrne and Ben Kingsley are two competitive media moguls who will stop at nothing to gain ownership of a pro football team. Their weapons: the newspapers, magazines and television stations they own. Their ammunition: blackmail, bribery, sexual manipulation and revelation. With Illeana Douglas, Jeffrey Tambor and Mimi Rogers.
VHS: S32609. $19.98.
Stephen Surjik, USA, 1997, 96 mins.

The Wedding Singer

It's 1985 and Robbie Hart (Adam Sandler) is the ultimate master of ceremonies, until he is left at the altar at his own widding. Devastated, he becomes a newlywed's worst nightmare, an entertainer who can do nothing but destroy other people's weddings. It's not until he meets a warm-hearted waitress named Julia (Drew Barrymore) that he starts to pick up the pieces of his heart. With Steve Buscemi, Jon Lovitz, Billy Idol and rapping grandma Ellen Dow.
VHS: S34913. $106.99.
Laser: DTS. **LD77018. $39.99.**
DVD: DV60373. $24.98.
Frank Coraci, USA, 1998, 93 mins.

Weekend at the Waldorf

A glossy American remake of Grand Hotel, this episodic collection of vignettes mixes drawing room comedy with slapstick farce. Lana Turner and Ginger Rodgers are pursued by Van Johnson and Walter Pidgeon. With Edward Arnold, Phyllis Thaxter and Keenan Wynn.
VHS: S18664. $19.98.
Robert Z. Leonard, USA, 1945, 130 mins.

A Weekend in the Country

Faith Ford, Christine Lahti, Jack Lemmon, Richard Lewis, Dudley Moore, Rita Rudner and Betty White star in this city-meets-country comedy about old flames, new flings and last chances.
VHS: S28514. $99.99.
Laser: LD75974. $39.99.
Martin Bergman, USA, 1995, 94 mins.

Welcome Home, Roxy Carmichael

A gentle satire about celebrity and small-town life. An Ohio community anticipates the return of a reclusive star, while a moody, brilliant, though alienated young hipster (Winona Ryder) secretly fantasizes the mysterious woman is her long-lost natural mother. With Jeff Daniels, Laila Robbins, Dinah Manoff and Thomas Wilson Brown.
VHS: S17981. $14.95.
Jim Abrahams, USA, 1990, 98 mins.

Welcome Stranger

Bing Crosby and Joan Caulfield are joined in this romantic comedy about a young doctor. Old doctor Barry Fitzgerald goes on vacation and a brash young upstart is the surprising substitute who takes over his practice.
VHS: S25013. $14.98.
Elliott Nugent, USA, 1947, 107 mins.

What About Bob?

Bill Murray is unforgettable as a wacky patient who drives his psychiatrist, Richard Dreyfuss, to madness. It all begins innocently enough when Murray arrives unannounced at Dreyfuss' peaceful country home. The family immediately takes to the incurable neurotic and thereby drives the doctor to commit cruel acts notable for their obsessiveness and their humor.
VHS: S27888. $19.95.
Frank Oz, USA, 1991, 99 mins.

What's New Pussycat

Peter O'Toole visits Parisian psychiatrist Peter Sellers for advice on his love life, but soon learns he is dealing with a quack. With Romy Schneider, Capucine, Paula Prentiss and Woody Allen (the scriptwriter) as Victor Shakadopoulos. Title song by Burt Bacharach and Hal David sung by Tom Jones. Watch for chess games by the Seine, comic bed-hopping and go-kart races.
VHS: S13217. $19.95.
Laser: LD72134. $34.98.
Clive Donner, USA, 1965, 108 mins.

What's Up Doc

Barbra Streisand and Ryan O'Neal star in this Peter Bogdanovich salute to the screwball comedy. She's a nutcase and he's a very absent-minded musicologist. Together they upset quite a few people in San Francisco. With Madeline Kahn, Kenneth Mars and Liam Dunn.
VHS: S04657. $19.98.
Laser: Includes theatrical trailer. **LD71471. $34.98.**
Peter Bogdanovich, USA, 1972, 94 mins.

The Wheeler Dealers

A comedy of cultural and social observation about a sardonic Texas oilman (James Garner) who tries his luck in the hostile environs of Wall Street and captures the attention of stock analyst Lee Remick. With Phil Harris, Chill Wils and Jim Backus.
VHS: S18669. $19.98.
Arthur Hiller, USA, 1963, 100 mins.

When Harry Met Sally

Billy Crystal and Meg Ryan are unforgettable as the pair of would be former lovers who simply can't pull away from one another. It's a romantic comedy about two people who have trouble admitting their own feelings, even if it's plain to everyone else that they were made for each other.
VHS: S22603. $14.95.
Rob Reiner, USA, 1989, 96 mins.

When's Your Birthday?

Astrology mixes with prizefighting in this comedy starring Joe E. Brown as a boxer who can only win when the stars are in the proper conjunction. His star studies also help pick winning horses at the track. With Edgar Kennedy, Marian Marsh and Fred Keating.
VHS: S10101. $29.95.
Harry Beaumont, USA, 1937, 76 mins.

Where the Boys Are

A witty comedy about four beautiful young college students in Fort Lauderdale who share a hotel room and are on the make for male companionship. Connie Francis stars and performs the title song. With Paula Prentiss, Yvette Mimieux, George Hamilton and Jim Hutton.
VHS: S18016. $19.98.
Henry Levin, USA, 1960, 100 mins.

Where the Girls Are

This military short humorously exposes the dangers of VD in an unwittingly campy fashion. A young soldier off to Vietnam tries to heed his C.O.'s warning about the dangers of massage parlors, but when letters from his girl back home are interrupted, he succumbs to temptation with disastrous consequences. 23 mins.
VHS: S24007. $14.95.

Where There's Life

Bob Hope is a hapless and previously unkown heir to a small kingdom. The life of this former dog food peddler is hilariously turned around by court intrigues, kidnapping plots and romance. With Signe Hasso and William Bendix.
VHS: S25528. $14.98.
Sidney Lanfield, USA, 1947, 75 mins.

Where Were You When the Lights Went Out?

A comedy about the personal, romantic and social complications of a Hollywood starlet (Doris Day), known for her virtue, who deals with her straying husband and unnerved producer, and the ensuing mayhem during a massive power blackout in Manhattan. With Robert Morse, Terry-Thomas and Patrick O'Neal.
VHS: S18015. $19.98.
Hy Averback, USA, 1968, 94 mins.

Where's Poppa?

Carl Reiner directs this very black comedy about an uptight New York attorney whose social life is constantly being ruined by his senile mother. George Segal is the lawyer at his wits end. Ruth Gordon is the albatross around his neck. With Trish Van Devere as the new girlfriend and Ron Leibman as Segal's brother Sidney who finds Central Park a place of peril and romance while dressed in a gorilla suit. Script by Robert Klane from his novel.
VHS: S01448. $19.95.
Laser: LD71144. $34.98.
Carl Reiner, USA, 1970, 83 mins.

While You Were Sleeping

Sandra Bullock, Bill Pullman and Peter Gallagher star in this film that offers a strange twist on an old comic theme of romantic rivalry. Bullock is a public transportation worker in Chicago who secretly longs for a stranger. One day he is mugged and falls into a coma. By chance Bullock is mistaken as the man's fiance. As she spins stories about their affair the man's brother comes to figure in her actual erotic life. Of course everything changes when the man in the coma wakes up.
VHS: S26397. $19.98.
Laser: LD75081. $39.99.
Jon Turteltaub, USA, 1995, 103 mins.

Whistling in Brooklyn

Red Skelton appears as the popular radio criminologist code-named "The Fox" whose efforts to solve a string of bizarre murders involves various forms of deception and his getting entangled with the Brooklyn Dodgers baseball team. With Ann Rutherford, Polly Benedict, Ray Collins and William Frawley.
VHS: S18482. $19.98.
S. Sylvan Simon, USA, 1943, 87 mins.

Whistling in Dixie

Red Skelton is cast as radio sleuth Wally "The Fox" Benton, whose honeymoon with Ann Rutherford is interrupted by the usual murder and mayhem. With George Bancroft and Guy Kibbee.
VHS: S19567. $19.98.
S. Sylvan Simon, USA, 1942, 73 mins.

Whistling in the Dark

The popular radio sleuth self-named "The Fox" is kidnapped by a cult and ordered by their leader to execute the perfect murder to remove the heir who's blocking the cult's receipt of a vast inheritance. With Red Skelton, Conrad Veidt, Ann Rutherford and Virginia Grey.
VHS: S18483. $19.98.
S. Sylvan Simon, USA, 1941, 78 mins.

White Men Can't Jump

Wesley Snipes and Woody Harrelson team up as a couple of hustlers who prey on pick-up basketball players who assume that white men can't jump. The film is a fast paced comedy with fine performances from Snipes and Rosie Perez as Harrelson's girlfriend. Features Tyra Ferrell, Cylk Cozart and Kadeem Hardison.
VHS: S21443. $19.98.
Ron Shelton, USA, 1992, 115 mins.

Who Killed "Doc" Robbin? (Curley and His Gang in the Haunted Mansion)

An Our Gang comedy, of sorts, in color, starring George Zucco as a mad scientist involved with an atomic firing chamber. It explodes and "Fix-It" Dan and Nurse Ann are both suspects. With Virginia Grey and the successors to the Our Gang Kids.
VHS: S10104. $24.95.
Bernard Carr, USA, 1948, 50 mins.

Who's Harry Crumb?

The real question should be why is Harry Crumb so good at coming up with the right answers to all the wrong questions, but that would be too much to put on a movie marquee. John Candy plays a bumbling private detective who has a yen to dress up in various disguises. His current case involves a kidnap and murder plot. With Jeffrey Jones, Barry Corbin and Annie Potts. Pick a suspect.
VHS: S09509. $14.95.
Paul Flaherty, USA, 1989, 89 mins.

Wicked Stepmother

Bette Davis and Barbara Carrera star in this black comedy about witchcraft. When Davis quit production, Carrera was hired by cult director Larry Cohen (It's Alive) to complete the film. The plot concerns shrinking victims of a bizarre cult. The cast includes Colleen Camp, David Rasche, Tom Bosley, Richard Moll, Evelyn Keyes and Lionel Stander.
VHS: S11164. $14.95.
Larry Cohen, USA, 1988, 95 mins.

Wilder Napalm

This quirky romantic comedy stars Dennis Quaid and Debra Winger. Two brothers fight fires together but battle each other through their innate telekinetic powers over the love of the same woman. The results of this incendiary mix are passionate, and even fiery.
VHS: S20715. $95.95.
Laser: LD72384. $34.95.
Glenn Gordon Caron, USA, 1993, 109 mins.

Will Success Spoil Rock Hunter

Tony Randall stars opposite the unforgettable bombshell Jayne Mansfield in this clever but wacky satire of the 1950's. Randall must convince Mansfield to endorse his company's product, but she will only agree to the job if Randall helps her make her lover jealous. From this premise a whole chain of outlandish mishaps evolve, one of which features Groucho Marx. Joan Blondell also appears.
VHS: S28066. $19.98.
Laser: LD75611. $39.98.
Frank Tashlin, USA, 1957, 94 mins.

Willie and Phil

The year was 1970. Willie and Phil met quite accidentally, coming out of an art house in Greenwich Village. They soon became great friends—sharing the same sense of humor, protesting the war in Vietnam, enjoying the films of Francois Truffaut; they were inseparable. Then one day Willie and Phil met Jeanette. Willie and Phil is an insightful comedy about three loving people growing together and apart in the midst of a decade of change. Starring Michael Ontkean, Margot Kidder and Ray Sharkey.
VHS: S15070. $59.98.
Paul Mazursky, USA, 1980, 115 mins.

Wise Guys

A comedy from director Brian De Palma. After trying to hoodwink their mob boss, Harry (Danny DeVito) and Moe (Joe Piscopo) go on the run together. The problem is that each has been secretly assigned to rub out the other. "An abundant movie, filled with ideas and gags and great characters. It never runs dry" (Roger Ebert).
VHS: S13973. $19.99.
Brian DePalma, USA, 1986, 100 mins.

The Wistful Widow of Wagon Gap-Abbott and Costello

Abbott and Costello star in this western parody set in the frontier community of Wagon Gap, Montana. Lou accidentally kills a man and is legally obligated to care for his wife and seven children, rising to become sheriff of the town. With Marjorie Main, George Cleveland, Gordon Jones and William Ching.
VHS: S17258. $14.98.
Charles Barton, USA, 1947, 78 mins.

Without Love

In Hepburn and Tracy's third film together, Hepburn plays a Washington D.C. widow who allows scientist Tracy to set up a laboratory in her basement to conduct secret war-time experiments. Both disillusioned with love, they agree to a marriage strictly for convenience. But can romance be far behind? A witty and winning farce. Lucille Ball co-stars as Hepburn's wise-cracking friend.
VHS: S15023. $19.98.
Laser: Chapter search. Includes original theatrical trailer.
LD71665. $34.98.
Harold S. Bucquet, USA, 1945, 103 mins.

Woman of Distinction

Rosalind Russell is a leading figure in the community as well as Dean of Benton College. She has no time for romance until she meets Ray Milland, a handsome British astronomer. A captivating comedy!
VHS: S01911. $69.95.
Edward Buzzell, USA, 1950, 85 mins.

Woman's World

This terrific 50's comedy/drama features an all star cast. Clifton Webb, Lauren Bacall, Fred MacMurray, Arlene Dahl, Cornel Wilde and June Allyson star as three couples all set in a highly competitive world of corporate advancement. Three men could become general manager, but this promotion is dependent upon which woman is the perfect wife for the job.
VHS: S24577. $19.98.
Jean Negulesco, USA, 1954, 94 mins.

Wonder Man

Danny Kaye plays the dual role of a scholarly bookworm and his twin brother, a song-and-dance man with gangster troubles. When the latter meets up with a fatal bullet, the bookworm takes his place in a nightclub, resulting in hilarious complications. This entertaining film romp won an Academy Award for Best Special Effects in 1945. Digitally remastered.
VHS: S03487. $19.98.
H. Bruce Humberstone, USA, 1945, 97 mins.

Working Girl
Mike Nichols' insightful romantic comedy has an ebullient spirit, carried by Melanie Griffith's hard-edged portrait of an ambitious secretary caught in corporate games with her vengeful boss (Sigourney Weaver) and the attractive, charismatic lawyer (Harrison Ford) they're both in love with. With strong supporting work from Alec Baldwin and Joan Cusack. Carly Simon performs the Academy Award winning song, "Let the River Run."
VHS: Out of print. For rental only.
Laser: LD71218. $44.98.
Mike Nichols, USA, 1988, 113 mins.

The World of Abbott and Costello
Over 18 films have been mined to compile this video featuring the humor of Abbott and Costello. This is a great introduction to the entire range of their comic work. 75 mins.
VHS: S24391. $14.98.

The World of Henry Orient
George Roy Hill's mischievous comedy about a brilliant, nonconformist pianist (Peter Sellers) whose strange world is turned out of control by two young girls' dangerous infatuation with him. They follow him around New York City, charting his every move and gesture. With Tippy Walker, Merrie Spaeth, Paula Prentiss and Tom Bosley.
VHS: S19568. $19.98.
Laser: Letterboxed. **LD72208. $34.98.**
George Roy Hill, USA, 1964, 106 mins.

Yankee Zulu
Two childhood friends meet 25 years after parting and are forced to "switch" races. From this premise, a hilarious comedy develops that is perfect family viewing. One catastrophe leads to another until a full-fledged farce emerges from the chaos.
VHS: S27508. $95.99.
Gray Hofmeyr, USA/South Africa, 1995, 90 mins.

The Yellow Cab Man
This very funny comedy stars Red Skelton as an accident-prone inventor of safety gadgets forced by economic necessity into driving a cab, with bizarre and unpredictable consequences. With Gloria De Haven, Walter Slezak, Edward Arnold and James Gleason.
VHS: S17900. $19.98.
Jack Donohue, USA, 1950, 85 mins.

Young Frankenstein
Both a spoof of the original and an affectionate tribute to all the horror films of the 1930's. With Gene Wilder as the young Dr. Frankenstein, Marty Feldman as his bizarre laboratory assistant and Peter Boyle as the scatter-brained monster.
VHS: S01495. $19.98.
Laser: LD71223. $89.95.
Mel Brooks, USA, 1974, 106 mins.

Younger and Younger
Donald Sutherland, Lolita Davidovich, Sally Kellerman, Julie Delpy and Linda Hunt star in this offbeat romantic comedy. At the center of the film is a marriage from hell that is transformed into a match made in heaven.
Laser: LD74981. $39.99.
Percy Adlon, USA, 1994, 97 mins.

Yours, Mine and Ours
Lucille Ball plays a widow with eight kids who marries Henry Fonda—and his ten kids. The result is unbelievable bedlam, needless to say. With Van Johnson, Tom Bosley.
VHS: S11158. $14.95.
Melville Shavelson, USA, 1968, 111 mins.

Zenobia
Oliver Hardy played in a number of films as a solo comic act. In this classic film he plays Dr. Tibbit, an animal-loving physician who wins the heart of a carnival elephant. Laughing Gravy, a hilarious short starring both Laurel and Hardy, is also included. 93 mins.
VHS: S21533. $19.95.

Zero Effect
The funny, moving and clever story of a genius gumshoe who can barely function in the real world. Starring Bill Pullman in a great performance.
VHS: S34637. $103.99.
Laser: Dolby Digital. **LD77007. $34.98.**
DVD: Widescreen, director commentary, filmographies, French subtitles. **DV60401. $24.98.**
Jake Kasdan, USA, 1998, 116 mins.

WOODY ALLEN

Alice
Mia Farrow plays an upscale housewife and lapsed Catholic who visits an old Chinese herbalist for treatment of her bad back and ends up, as the result of a potion, invisible, whereupon she embarks on a series of magical and romantic adventures. With Joe Mantegna and Blythe Danner.
VHS: S14259. $94.98.
Woody Allen, USA, 1990, 106 mins.

Annie Hall
One of Woody Allen's best and funniest films, with Diane Keaton as the sometime object of Woody Allen's affections and expressions of his neurosis. Winner of many Academy Awards. With Paul Simon and Carol Kane.
VHS: S00059. $19.95.
Laser: CLV, Criterion. **LD70339. $49.95.**
Laser: Deluxe, letterboxed edition. Includes original theatrical trailer. **LD71506. $34.98.**
DVD: DV60296. $24.98.
Woody Allen, USA, 1977, 94 mins.

Another Woman
Gena Rowlands stars in this Woody Allen drama as an accomplished philosophy professor who eventually realizes she has no friends and not much of a personal life. By listening through a vent to the problems of Mia Farrow she regains her humanity. A distinguished cast includes Gene Hackman, Ian Holm, Sandy Dennis, Martha Plimpton, John Houseman, Blythe Danner and Harris Yulin.
VHS: S09156. $19.95.
Woody Allen, USA, 1988, 81 mins.

Bananas
Woody Allen stars as Fielding Mellish, a New York City products tester who finds himself appointed the president of a Latin American country after a revolution. With Louise Lasser, Charlotte Rae, Conrad Bain, and Howard Cosell as himself. Watch for Sylvester Stallone as a subway hoodlum. Music by Marvin Hamlisch.
VHS: S00092. $19.98.
Laser: LD70191. $44.98.
Woody Allen, USA, 1971, 82 mins.

Bullets over Broadway
Woody Allen cast Jim Broadbent, John Cusack, Harvey Fierstein, Mary Louise Parker, Rob Reiner, Tracey Ullman and other great actors in this comedy where gangsters collide with Broadway. A young playwright is desperate to get his play produced and goes to the mob for backing. Like any producer, they do whatever they can to preserve and promote their investment, with hilarious results.
VHS: S23963. $19.95.
Laser: Letterboxed. **LD74938. $39.99.**
Woody Allen, USA, 1994, 95 mins.

Crimes and Misdemeanors
Woody Allen presents two interlocking stories set in New York. One comic, one serious, but both thoughtful. Martin Landau is a prominent, married eye surgeon troubled by the demands of his mistress Anjelica Huston. Woody Allen is a talented but struggling documentary filmmaker in love with co-worker Mia Farrow but saddled with a dead relationship to wife Joanna Gleason. With Alan Alda, Jerry Orbach and Claire Bloom in a strong supporting role.
VHS: S12157. $14.98.
Laser: Widescreen. **LD76090. $49.95.**
Woody Allen, USA, 1989, 107 mins.

Deconstructing Harry
Woody Allen stars as Harry Block, a writer who's gone through six psychiatrists and dozens of girlfriends in his long literary career. But when Harry writes a bestseller about his best friends, they become his worst enemies. Now, instead of going back to his old school to be honored for his literary achievements, Harry's going straight to hell. With Judy Davis, Kirstie Alley, Demi Moore, Billy Crystal, Robin Williams, Elisabeth Shue, Julia Louis-Dreyfuss, Richard Benjamin, Eric Bogosian, Amy Irving, Julie Kavner, Stanley Tucci and Mariel Hemingway.
VHS: S34081. $104.99.
Laser: LD76994. $29.99.
DVD: DV60249. $24.98.
Woody Allen, USA, 1997, 96 mins.

Everyone Says I Love You
Woody Allen's musical celebration of an eccentric family from New York City follows a father (Allen), a mother (Goldie Hawn), a daughter (Natasha Lyonne), a sister (Drew Barrymore), an ex-con (Tim Roth), a fiancee (Ed Norton) and two half-sisters (Natalie Portman and Gaby Hoffman) as they move from New York to Paris to Venice in search of love.
VHS: S31718. $19.99.
Laser: LD76291. $39.99.
Woody Allen, USA, 1996, 106 mins.

Everything You Always Wanted to Know About Sex (But Were Afraid to Ask)
Maybe not everything, but Woody Allen does offer a generous selection of topics that include bestiality, transvestism, chastity belts, abnormal sexual research, exhibitionism, and the life of a sperm. With Gene Wilder, Lynn Redgrave, Burt Reynolds, Lou Jacobi, John Carradine, Tony Randall and Louise Lasser. Very loosely based on the best-selling book by Dr. David Reuben.
VHS: S03426. $19.98.
Laser: LD70165. $44.98.
Woody Allen, USA, 1972, 87 mins.

The Front
Woody Allen, in a non-Allen vehicle, stars as Howard Prince, a cashier who is persuaded to "front" for a writer friend who has been blacklisted during the McCarthy-era witch-hunts. With Zero Mostel, Herschel Bernardi and Michael Murphy.
VHS: S02021. $19.98.
Martin Ritt, USA, 1976, 94 mins.

Husbands and Wives
Woody Allen's savagely funny comedy traces the opposite fortunes of two parallel marriages through their extended stages of collapse and rejuvenation. A major subplot concerns Allen, playing a novelist and literature professor, getting emotionally involved with a brilliant 20-year-old student (Juliette Lewis). The movie is shot in the form of a cinema verite documentary. With Judy Davis, Mia Farrow, Liam Neeson and Sydney Pollack.
VHS: S18196. $19.95.
Laser: LD71844. $34.95.
Woody Allen, USA, 1992, 107 mins.

Interiors
Diane Keaton, Marybeth Hurt and Kristin Griffith are sisters who try to come to terms with themselves when their parents undergo divorce. Called Woody Allen's masterpiece by many critics, *Interiors* features brilliant performances from Maureen Stapleton, Geraldine Page and E.G. Marshall.
VHS: S00629. $14.95.
Laser: LD70599. $34.98.
Woody Allen, USA, 1978, 92 mins.

Love and Death
The films of Ingmar Bergman and the literature of 19th century Russian authors take a good-natured, comic drubbing at the hands of filmmaker Woody Allen. He plays a nebbish in love with a distant cousin who only agrees to marry him on the condition that he is reasonably sure he will be killed in battle fighting Napoleon. To Diane Keaton's immediate shock, Woody survives by hiding in a loaded cannon. Duels, herring and walks with the Grim Reaper are also featured.
VHS: S01713. $19.98.
Woody Allen, USA, 1975, 82 mins.

Manhattan
Woody Allen's valentine to his favorite city. Vincent Canby called it "the only truly great American film of the 1970's." Middle-aged writer falls in love with high school senior and trouble ensues. Sound familiar? With a fabulous soundtrack of George and Ira Gershwin classics and the contributed talents of Meryl Streep, Diane Keaton, Mariel Hemingway, Michael Murphy and, of course, Woody Allen. Wonderful black and white photography by Gordon Willis.
VHS: S00822. $19.98.
Laser: Deluxe letterboxed, MGM. **LD70175. $34.98.**
Woody Allen, USA, 1979, 96 mins.

Manhattan Murder Mystery
Woody Allen and Diane Keaton reunited in a wacky mystery about a bored housewife who enlists her skeptical husband in a dangerous murder investigation. With Alan Alda and Anjelica Huston. "What a treat to see Diane Keaton and Woody Allen together again" (Joel Siegel, *Good Morning America*).
VHS: S20546. $19.95.
Laser: LD72363. $34.95.
Woody Allen, USA, 1993, 107 mins.

Mighty Aphrodite
Miro Sorvino rightly won an Oscar for her portrayal of a prostitute in this warm and comic love story between two unlikely people. Woody Allen is a bumbling sportswriter who searches for the real mother of his adopted son and happens upon an unusual but hilarious set of gags. Helena Bonham Carter is also featured.
VHS: S27689. $19.98.
Laser: LD75575. $39.99.
Woody Allen, USA, 1995, 99 mins.

New York Stories
Three major directors, one city. Martin Scorsese, Francis Ford Coppola and Woody Allen offer an omnibus of short films based on life in the Big Apple. Scorsese leads off with *Life Lessons*, in which master painter Nick Nolte puts the moves on art student Rosanna Arquette. *Life with Zoe* is written by Coppola and his daughter Sofia. It tells the story of a precocious little girl who lives in a fancy hotel. Allen tops off the trio with *Oedipus Wrecks*, a comedy about an unmarried middle aged man whose problems with his pushy mother suddenly involve the entire city. With Woody Allen, Mia Farrow, Julie Kavner and Mae Questel, the voice of Betty Boop, as Woody's mom.
Laser: LD71255. $39.99.
Martin Scorsese/Francis F. Coppola/Woody Allen, USA, 1988, 123 mins

Play It Again, Sam

Woody Allen's first film with Diane Keaton. Allen plays Allen, a fanatical movie buff with an outrageous recurring hallucination: Humphrey Bogart offering tips on how to make it with the ladies. Eventually Allen discovers that there is one woman with whom he can be himself: his best friend's wife. The final scene is a terrific take-off on *Casablanca*, with roaring plane propellers, heavy fog, and Bogart-style trench coats.

VHS: S01037. $19.95.
Laser: LD75349. $29.98.
Herbert Ross, USA, 1972, 86 mins.

Purple Rose of Cairo

Woody Allen at his best, combining tenderly poignant moments with subtle touches of humor, artfully playing fiction against reality to create superb entertainment. A waitress, bored by her drab life, seeks escape in the movies, where the hero of the film, bored with the monotony of playing the same role over and over, jumps from the screen to join her in the real world. With Mia Farrow and Jeff Daniels. Photographed by Gordon Willis.

VHS: S01074. $14.98.
Woody Allen, USA, 1985, 82 mins.

Radio Days

Woody Allen's wonderful period comedy returning to the nostalgia of the days of radio, with Julie Kavner, Michael Tucker, Mia Farrow, Diane Wiest and Diane Keaton, mixing humor with pathos in one of Allen's best.

VHS: Out of print. For rental only.
Laser: Widescreen. **LD76010. $39.99.**
Woody Allen, USA, 1987, 89 mins.

September

Woody Allen's intimate drama set in the last days of summer in a Vermont country house. Starring Mia Farrow, Denholm Elliott and Sam Waterston, the film focuses on the life, relationships, trials and tribulations, mothers and daughters, and what it's like to survive in a complex world of difficult relationships.

VHS: S07341. $99.95.
Woody Allen, USA, 1987, 82 mins.

Shadows and Fog

Woody Allen's adaptation of his unproduced, one-act, 1977 play *Death* grafts the compulsive tendencies of his own persona to the psychological intensity of German expressionism. Shot in a highly textured, black and white photography by Carlo Di Palma and set in a vaguely middle European village against the surreal backdrop of local circus performers, Allen stars as a clerk caught up in the paranoia and hysteria to capture a depraved serial killer. With Kathy Bates, John Cusack, Mia Farrow, Jodie Foster, Julie Kavner, John Malkovich, Kate Nelligan and Lily Tomlin. Madonna has a cameo as a trapeze artist.

VHS: S17630. $89.98.
Woody Allen, USA, 1991, 89 mins.

Sleeper

Sleeper is loaded with hilarious sight gags and brilliant wit as Woody pokes fun at everything from sex to politics to health foods in this look at the future through the eyes of Woody waking up from 200 years of suspended animation. With Diane Keaton.

VHS: S01213. $19.98.
Woody Allen, USA, 1973, 88 mins.

Stardust Memories

Woody Allen plays a troubled filmmaker attending a film seminar weekend where space aliens confide that they enjoyed his earlier funnier movies. He also has to contend with autograph hounds and several neurotic women. Allen indulges himself in his Fellini period. B&W.

VHS: S03885. $14.98.
Woody Allen, USA, 1980, 91 mins.

What's Up Tiger Lily?

Woody Allen provides the dubbed dialog for a chopped up Japanese sexy-spy thriller where the object of international intrigue is a recipe for egg salad. The results are wild, sophomoric, and hilarious. With music by the Lovin' Spoonful.

VHS: S01445. $14.98.
Woody Allen, USA, 1966, 80 mins.

Zelig

Woody Allen's side-splitting comic documentary and a scathing attack on the shallowness of American culture. Allen plays Leonard Zelig, a man famous for being famous, who has found a way to be the ultimate conformist: he transforms himself into a likeness of whomever he is with. With Mia Farrow, Saul Bellow, Susan Sontag and Bruno Bettelheim.

VHS: S01499. $19.98.
Laser: LD70722. $34.98.
Woody Allen, USA, 1983, 84 mins.

american westerns

8 Seconds
Luke Perry stars as the rodeo celebrity Lane Frost. This world champion was killed in 1990 at the age of 25. In his short lifetime, Frost managed to find a successful career, fame and most importantly, a strong marriage that endured all the trials of the professional rodeo circuit.
VHS: S22159. $19.95.
John G. Avildsen, USA, 1994, 104 mins.

Ace High
Eli Wallach holds the winning hand in this rambunctious spaghetti western about honor (and double dealing) among thieves. Also starring Kevin McCarthy and Terence Hill (playing a character named Cat Stevens).
VHS: S13713. $19.95.
Giuseppe Colizzi, Italy, 1968, 120 mins.

The Alamo (Original)
A big movie spectacle about the defense of the Alamo was directed by (and stars) John Wayne as Davy Crockett, Richard Widmark as Jim Bowie and Laurence Harvey as Will Travis, in a flag-waving, super production aided with a first-rate musical score by Dmitri Tiomkin.
VHS: S04884. $29.98.
Laser: LD70499. $69.95.
John Wayne, USA, 1960, 161 mins.

The Alamo (Restored)
John Wayne produced, directed and starred in this much underrated historical epic now restored with over half an hour of footage unseen since the film's 1960 premiere. With an Academy-Award nominated score by Dimitri Tiomkin, the film chronicles how 185 men banded together in a crumbling adobe mission and held off an army of 7,000 to ensure the ultimate independence of Texas. Stars Richard Widmark, Laurence Harvey, Richard Boone, and the "Duke" as Davy Crockett.
VHS: S16589. $29.98.
John Wayne, USA, 1960, 202 mins.

Along Came Jones
This Western parody stars Gary Cooper (who performs a couple of musical numbers) as the eccentric cowboy Melody Jones, who gets mistaken for a ruthless killer. Cinematography by Milton Krasner. Music by Charles Maxwell, Arthur Lange and Hugo Friedhofer. With Loretta Young, William Demarest, Dan Duryea and Frank Sully.
VHS: S01866. $19.98.
Stuart Heisler, USA, 1945, 90 mins.

Along the Great Divide
Spectacular scenery highlights this Western featuring Kirk Douglas as a marshall who rescues accused murderer Walter Brennan from a mob and then escorts him to trial.
VHS: S03433. $14.95.
Raoul Walsh, USA, 1951, 88 mins.

Alvarez Kelly
William Holden stars as the cattle driver who sells cattle to the Union army, and is kidnapped by southern rebel Richard Widmark who wants him to steal cattle for the southern cause.
VHS: S03884. $19.95.
Laser: CLV, letterboxed, chapter stops. **LD74907. $39.95.**
Edward Dmytryk, USA, 1966, 116 mins.

The Americano
Glenn Ford goes South of the Border all the way to Brazil in this western, or is it a southern? He's delivering a shipment of prize bulls under less than friendly circumstances. With Cesar Romero, Abbe Lane, Frank Lovejoy and Ursula Thiess. In color.
VHS: S04220. $19.95.
William Castle, USA, 1955, 85 mins.

Angel and the Badman
One of the best westerns, with Gail Russell trying to make a human being out of gunslinger John Wayne after he is shot and nursed back to health by her pacifist family. With Bruce Cabot and Harry Carey, Sr.
VHS: S15909. $14.98.
Laser: 45th Anniversary edition. **LD71498. $34.98.**
James Edward Grant, USA, 1947, 100 mins.

Apache
After the surrender of Geronimo, one Apache leader remains unconquered. This pacifist Indian (played by, of all people, Burt Lancaster) learns from the U.S. Cavalry that sometimes fighting is the only way. But his one man fighting crusade for his tribe's rights ends rather surprisingly. Also starring Charles Bronson.
VHS: S13634. $19.98.
Robert Aldrich, USA, 1954, 91 mins.

Apaches Last Battle (Old Shatterhand)
A boundary scout discovers the ward of an Apache chief has been framed for murder by a shifty army officer who wants to start an Indian war. With Lex Barker, Guy Madison and Pierre Brice. Dubbed in English.
VHS: S32591. $24.95.
Hugo Fregonese, Germany/France/Italy/Yugoslavia, 1964, 122 mins.

The Appaloosa
Marlon Brando stars as Matt Fletcher, a man who has tasted all the vice the Wild West has to offer. Seeking a new life, he returns to his quiet border hometown with his prize possession, a beautiful Appaloosa stallion. When this horse is stolen by the ruthless Mexican bandit Chuy (John Saxon), Matt is forced to return to his bloodthirsty ways in order to regain his property and his honor. Also known as *Southwest to Sonora*.
VHS: S27670. $14.98.
Sidney J. Furie, USA, 1966, 99 mins.

Arizona
This classic Western stars Jean Arthur as a tenacious frontierswoman opposed to corruption and greed in the Wild West. William Holden also stars as the man who falls for this determined woman. It's a big story shot on some of the most elaborate sets ever built for a Hollywood western.
VHS: S20987. $14.95.
Wesley Ruggles, USA, 1940, 121 mins.

Arrowhead
Charlton Heston, Jack Palance and Katy Jurado star in this story about enmity between an army scout and an Indian chief, which is resolved in a dramatic combat. Based on the novel by W.R. Burnett.
VHS: S10433. $19.95.
Laser: LD75149. $34.98.
Charles Marquis Warren, USA, 1953, 105 mins.

The Badlanders
W.R. Burnett's classic story of urban crime and punishment, *The Asphalt Jungle* is transferred to the Arizona Old West. Ex-cons Alan Ladd and Ernest Borgnine team up with buddy Nehemiah Persoff to rob crooked land baron Kent Smith's gold mine with unexpected results. With Katy Jurado and Claire Kelly as the women who wait for their men to come home rich and alive.
VHS: S16439. $19.98.
Delmer Daves, USA, 1958, 85 mins.

Badman's Territory
Western veteran Randolph Scott plays a U.S. Marshall who goes up against the James brothers and the Daltons. USA, 1946, 79 mins.
VHS: S10666. $19.98.

The Ballad of Little Jo
Suzy Amis is the original cross-dressing cowboy in this new western. She finds that the old West is not a hospitable place for a woman unless she can prove she is as good as any man. Under the circumstances, she more than rises to the occasion.
VHS: S20717. $19.95.
Laser: LD74459. $54.95.
Maggie Greenwald, USA, 1993, 124 mins.

Bandolero!
Personalities clash and sparks fly when the Bishop brothers hit Val Verde, Texas. They fought on opposite sides of the Civil War, now they are on opposite sides of the law. James Stewart is the honest brother, Dean Martin is the bank-robber brother, sentenced to die. With Raquel Welch.
VHS: S06529. $19.98.
Andrew V. McLaglen, USA, 1968, 106 mins.

Battles with Chief Pontiac
Lon Chaney, Jr., Lex Barker and Helen Westcott star in this frontier film about conflicts between the British and Native Americans. Peace talks are sabotaged through the efforts of a colonel leading German troops.
VHS: S23803. $24.95.
Felix E. Feist, USA, 1953, 75 mins.

Behind Two Guns
One of J.B. Warner's excellent surviving works, *Behind Two Guns* is a delightful, lighthearted western comedy. Carter (Warner) and his partner Slowfoot (Calles) are on the trail of a mysterious stage robber who can make funds disappear while the stage is en route. With Hazel Newman, Marin Sais, Jay Morley, Jim Welch, Otto Lederer, William Calles, Jack Waltemeyer, Emily Gerdes, Bartlett A. Carre and Robert N. Bradbury. Silent with orchestra score.
VHS: S32047. $19.95.
Robert N. Bradbury, USA, 1924, 58 mins.

Bend of the River
Set in 1840s Oregon, with James Stewart as the outlaw who now works as a wagon train scout, and his conflict with Arthur Kennedy, his one-time friend who now hijacks the supplies of the settlers in order to turn profit. With Julia Adams and Rock Hudson.
VHS: S06814. $19.95.
Anthony Mann, USA, 1952, 91 mins.

Big Hand for the Little Lady
A high stakes game of poker is the subject of this tantalizing western adventure that takes place almost entirely in the backroom of a Texas saloon circa 1896. Joanne Woodward is the little lady who sits in when husband Henry Fonda falls ill. Other players include Jason Robards Jr., Charles Bickford, Kevin McCarthy and John Qualen.
VHS: S16288. $19.98.
Fielder Cook, USA, 1966, 94 mins.

Big Jake
An elderly Texas cattleman swings into action when his grandson is kidnapped by bandits. Violent action sequences distinguish this film from others of John Wayne's later period. With Richard Boone and Maureen O'Hara.
VHS: S15984. $14.98.
George Sherman, USA, 1975, 110 mins.

The Big Stampede
When John Wayne was only 25 years old he already possessed a career as an actor inseparable from the history of the western. In this action-packed feature a cattle stampede becomes the dramatic focus for a hard-riding, gun-obsessed cadre of cowboys.
VHS: S20948. $19.98.
Tenny Wright, USA, 1932, 63 mins.

Billy Two Hats
When their robbery turns deadly, an elderly bandit and his young partner struggle to escape the ruthless lawman on their trail in this gripping, imaginative western. With Gregory Peck and Desi Arnaz, Jr.
VHS: S31221. $14.95.
Ted Kotcheff, Great Britain, 1973, 99 mins.

Blue
An intriguing cast of B-players enlivens this Western about a quintessential outsider, an American-born, Mexican-raised gunfighter (Terence Stamp) who falls in love and must deal with his past, in the form of the gang controlled by his adoptive father (Ricardo Montalban). With Joanna Pettet, Karl Malden, Joe De Santis and Sally Kirkland.
VHS: S16887. $19.95.
Silvio Narizzano, Italy/USA, 1968, 113 mins.

Blue Steel
John Wayne has to convince a town to stay and fight for their land when a mean bunch of outlaws try to muscle their way in. The bad guys know there is gold to be mined under Main Street but the Duke is willing to offer them blue steel and hot lead for their trouble. B&W.
VHS: S04081. $19.99.
Robert North Bradbury, USA, 1934, 59 mins.

Born in America
A dark western about an undertaker who finds business slow, so he goes into town and instigates a gun brawl to create a few bodies to bury. Starring James Westerfield and Glen Lee.
VHS: S13881. $59.95.
Jose Antonio Bolanos, USA, 1990, 90 mins.

Branded
Alan Ladd goes along with an outlaw's scheme to impersonate the long lost son of wealthy rancher Charles Bickford until he finds he really enjoys being part of the family. Some desperados don't like being double-crossed. With Mona Freeman, Milburn Stone and Joseph Calleia. One of Ladd's better roles.
VHS: S12240. $19.95.
Laser: LD75163. $34.98.
Rudolph Mate, USA, 1951, 103 mins.

Bravados
A first-rate Western with Gregory Peck starring as a man in search for four men who raped and killed his wife, and, in the process, discovering the evils inherent in seeking revenge. With Joan Collins, Stephen Boyd.
VHS: S11190. $39.98.
Henry King, USA, 1958, 98 mins.

Breakheart Pass
Charles Bronson plays an undercover Federal agent investigating a murder on a train in the Old West. Based on the novel by Alistair MacLean, who also wrote the script, which features Ben Johnson, Richard Crenna, Jill Ireland, Charles Durning, Ed Lauter and ex-boxer Archie Moore. Avalanches, Indians and lots of red herrings.
VHS: S09158. $19.95.
Tom Gries, USA, 1976, 95 mins.

Broken Arrow
Delmer Daves' melodramatic western is based on a historical incident—the elaborate efforts of a tribe leader and a former military official attempting to broker peace accords between warring Army and Native American factions. Strong acting, location photography and distinct, colorful acting. With James Stewart, Jeff Chandler and Debra Paget.
VHS: S06527. $14.98.
Delmer Daves, USA, 1950, 93 mins.

Broken Lance
A fascinating remake of Joseph Mankiewicz's *House of Strangers*, about a patriarchal rancher's dissolution of his empire, which opens up deep family resentments and tensions. With Spencer Tracy, Robert Wagner and Jean Peters.
VHS: S11191. $14.98.
Edward Dmytryk, USA, 1954, 96 mins.

Buffalo Bill
A wonderfully colorful biography of the famous Man of the West, with a top-notch cast including Maureen O'Hara, Joel McCrea, Linda Darnell, Anthony Quinn.
VHS: S11189. $39.98.
William Wellman, USA, 1944, 90 mins.

Bugles in the Afternoon
Ray Milland stars as an officer of the Seventh Cavalry stripped of his rank over a mysterious feud with a fellow officer. Years later they meet at Little Big Horn. With Forrest Tucker, George Reeves, Helena Carter and Hugh Marlowe, as Milland's nemesis.
VHS: S04293. $14.95.
Roy Rowland, USA, 1952, 85 mins.

The Burning Hills
Half-breed and social outcast Natalie Wood offers a desperate Tab Hunter a hiding place when this cowboy finds himself on the run from a group of notorious gunmen hot on his trail. Together this couple face the unrelenting danger until they can't run anymore.
VHS: S21001. $19.98.
Stuart Heisler, USA, 1956, 94 mins.

Butch and Sundance: The Early Days
A prequel to *Butch Cassidy and the Sundance Kid* finds Tom Berenger and William Katt as the look-alikes for the Newman/Redford roles. Great scenery and pleasant performances. Our heroes deliver needed medical supplies to a mining camp cut off by snow. With Brian Dennehy, Jeff Corey, John Schuck and Jill Eikenberry.
VHS: S07149. $19.98.
Richard Lester, USA, 1979, 111 mins.

Butch Cassidy and the Sundance Kid
A first-rate Western comedy/drama with Paul Newman and Robert Redford playing the two bank robbers who stay one step ahead of the law and are finally tracked down in Bolivia. Screenplay by William Goldman.
VHS: S00196. $14.98.
George Roy Hill, USA, 1969, 110 mins.

Cahill—U.S. Marshall
A late period John Wayne (1973) western casts the Duke as a frontier lawman whose life is unnerved by his son's descent into a life of crime and depravity. With George Kennedy, Gary Grimes, and Neville Brand.
VHS: S16292. $19.98.
Laser: LD74701. $34.98.
Andrew V. McLaglen, USA, 1973, 103 mins.

Canyon of the Missing Men and Wolfheart's Revenge
Canyon is apparently the only Tom Tyler Western which has survived; *Wolfheart* is an enjoyable, breezy western with the dog star and Guinn "Big Boy" Williams. USA, 1930.
VHS: S05979. $49.95.

Canyon Passage
Susan Hayward, Dana Andrews, and Brian Donlevy star in this rough-and-ready Western about pioneers in 1856 Oregon.
VHS: S34579. $14.98.
Jacques Tourneur, USA, 1946, 92 mins.

The Capture
A reformed gunslinger turned detective investigates an episode from his past, to determine if he shot an innocent man. Breathtaking scenery and landscapes with a terrific Mexican shoot-out finale. With Lew Ayres, Teresa Wright, Victor Jory and Duncan Renaldo.
VHS: S17450. $19.95.
John Sturges, USA, 1950, 90 mins.

Cat Ballou
Jane Fonda is the title character in this satirical western with music, that won Lee Marvin an Oscar for riding a drunken horse. She plays a school teacher turned outlaw in a just cause. Nat King Cole and Stubby Kaye are the strolling minstrels and Cat's gang includes Dwayne Hickman, Michael Callan, Tom Nardidi, and of course, Marvin Lee as Kid Shelleen and his evil no-nosed brother. Great fun.
VHS: S10977. $19.95.
Elliot Silverstein, USA, 1965, 96 mins.

Catlow
Louis L'Amour's Western comedy about the opposite fates of two friends: a good-natured marshall (Richard Crenna) with a penchant for trouble and an amoral thief (Yul Brynner) who orchestrates a $2 million gold robbery. "Relaxing, lighthearted entertainment" *(Los Angeles Times)*. With Leonard Nimoy, Jo Ann Pflug and Jeff Corey.
VHS: S18670. $19.98.
Sam Wanamaker, USA, 1971, 103 mins.

Chato's Land
Charles Bronson is cast as Pardon Chato, a peaceable half-breed Apache rancher until he is riled by a boorish posse that molests his woman after Chato accidentally shot the local sheriff. With Jack Palance, Richard Basehart, James Whitmore, Simon Oakland, Richard Jordan. Bronson has only 15 lines in this violent western and 13 of them are in Apache. Filmed in Spain but set in New Mexico.
VHS: S12533. $19.98.
Michael Winner, USA, 1972, 100 mins.

Cheyenne Social Club
Gene Kelly directs this bawdy western adventure about an old cowpoke who inherits a brothel in Wyoming and can't decide whether to enjoy himself or close the place down. James Stewart stars as John O'Hanlon, the uncomfortable new owner of the Cheyenne Social Club. Henry Fonda tags along as his talkative saddle buddy Harley Sullivan. With Shirley Jones, Sue Ann Langdon, Jackie Russell and Elaine Devry.
VHS: S16285. $19.98.
Gene Kelly, USA, 1970, 103 mins.

Chisum
The Lincoln County War is restaged, this time with John Wayne as John Simpson Chisum, one of the primary historical figures in the conflict. No need to guess which side wins. With Forrest Tucker, Ben Johnson, Andrew Prine, Christopher George and Geoffrey Deuel as Billy the Kid, another historical figure you might have heard about.
VHS: S04972. $14.95.
Laser: Letterboxed. **LD74482. $34.98.**
Andrew V. McLaglen, USA, 1970, 110 mins.

Chuka
Rod Taylor straps on his six-gun in this hard-hitting tale of a heroic gunslinger trying to make peace between Indians and the soldiers at a nearby fort. An excellent supporting cast featuring Ernest Borgnine, John Mills and James Whitmore.
VHS: S13709. $19.95.
Gordon Douglas, USA, 1967, 105 mins.

Cimarron
The first Western to win an Oscar for Best Picture (the second being Eastwood's *Unforgiven*) stars Richard Dix and Irene Dunne. Based on the popular novel by Edna Ferber, it chronicles the life of a homesteading family from the Oklahoma Land Rush until 1915. Oscar also went for screenplay. With Estelle Taylor and Nance O'Neil.
VHS: S08338. $19.95.
Laser: LD76186. $49.98.
Wesley Ruggles, USA, 1930, 124 mins.

Circus World
John Wayne stars as Matt Masters, the owner of a Wild West Show on a European tour. He is plagued by personal and natural disasters but never gives up. Rita Hayworth and Claudia Cardinale provide some comfort and some pain. With Lloyd Nolan.
VHS: S04515. $29.95.
Laser: LD76009. $59.95.
Henry Hathaway, USA, 1964, 131 mins.

Cold Feet
A goofy contemporary Western about love, revenge and high fashion footwear, scripted by Tom McGuane and Jim Harrison. When the roguish Keith Carradine double-crosses his partners in crime over a horse in Mexico, he finds that the great state of Montana isn't big enough to hide him from their wrath. With Sally Kirkland and Tom Waits as the injured parties and Rip Torn as the curious local lawman. Watch for Jeff Bridges in an unbilled cameo role.
VHS: S11723. $19.95.
Laser: LD70922. $39.95.
Robert Dornhelm, USA, 1989, 94 mins.

Comanche Territory
Maureen O'Hara stars as a conniving frontierswoman who seeks to cheat the Comanche out of land deeded to them by the government. She's only after silver until she meets James Bowie (Carey MacDonald) and his friend the local government official (Will Geer). Before long, her love of Bowie makes her a new woman.
VHS: S23675. $14.98.
Leonard Goldstein, USA, 1950, 76 mins.

Comancheros
Big scale Western about a member of the Texas Rangers who works undercover to foil a notorious gang of outlaws. With Lee Marvin, John Wayne, Stuart Whitman. Last film of Michael Curtiz.
VHS: S05911. $19.98.
Laser: CLV. **LD72115. $49.98.**
Michael Curtiz, USA, 1961, 107 mins.

Comes a Horseman
In this landmark western of "uncomon sensibility and extraordinary action" *(Los Angeles Times)*, steadfast ranchers pledge their lives to protect the beauty and bounty of their land. With James Caan, Jason Robards, Jane Fonda and Richard Farnsworth. VHS letterboxed.
VHS: S31222. $14.95.
Laser: LD76280. $49.98.
Alan J. Pakula, USA, 1978, 118 mins.

Companeros
Jack Palance, Fernando Rey, Franco Nero and Tomas Milian star in this politically-minded Western. A mercenary helps a revolutionary to rescue a pacifist professor and his followers. Palance is great as a wooden-handed killer who lost his hand when he was nailed to a cross—his pet hawk ate it off to save him.
VHS: S23322. $24.95.
Sergio Corbucci, Italy/Spain/Germany, 1970, 105 mins.

Conagher
A moody western adapted from Louis L'Amour's novel about the relationship between a hardened loner and a fiercely independent frontier woman. With Sam Elliott, Katharine Ross and Barry Corbin. Directed by the talented cinematographer Reynaldo Villalobos.
VHS: S18498. $14.98.
Reynaldo Villalobos, USA, 1991, 94 mins.

Copper Canyon
A vaudeville marksman does some fancy shootin' to protect ex-Confederate miners from their harsh Yankee bosses. Starring Ray Milland and Hedy Lamarr in colorful, change-of-pace roles.
VHS: S13710. $19.95.
Laser: LD75174. $34.98.
John Farrow, USA, 1950, 84 mins.

Coroner Creek
Western superstar Randolph Scott is a loner out to avenge the death of his fiancee in this significant, suspense-packed adventure that many film scholars agree marks the shift from simplistic horse operas of the 1930s and '40s to the later adult themes and sensibilities of the Western genre. With Marguerite Chapman, George Macready, Sally Eilers and Edgar Buchanan.
VHS: S30775. $19.95.
Ray Enright, USA, 1948, 90 mins.

The Cowboys
John Wayne leads a cattle drive with 11 youngsters and one black cook. He makes the mistake of insulting Bruce Dern, an unemployed psycho riding the range and up to no good. The boys must learn to grow up in a hurry. With Robert Carradine, Roscoe Lee Browne and Colleen Dewhurst.
VHS: S04973. $14.95.
Laser: Letterboxed. **LD74485. $39.98.**
Mark Rydell, USA, 1972, 128 mins.

Custer of the West
Robert Shaw stars as Custer, from his service in the Civil War, his takeover of the 7th Cavalry and testimony before Congress to reveal the corruption of President Grant, to his expedition to Little Big Horn. With Jeffrey Hunter, Ty Hardin and Lawrence Tierney. Letterboxed.
VHS: S34263. $14.98.
Robert Siodmak, USA/Spain, 1968, 143 mins.

Dakota
John Wayne becomes involved with a land war in Fargo, North Dakota. He sides with the wheat farmers against a gang of greedy opportunists, headed by Ward Bond and Mike Mazurki. Lots of two-fisted action before the cavalry shows up. With Vera Ralston and Walter Brennan as Capt. Bounce. B&W.
VHS: S04891. $19.95.
Laser: LD71576. $34.98.
Joseph Kane, USA, 1945, 82 mins.

Dances with Wolves (Deluxe Collector's Set)
This winner of seven Oscars is now available in a deluxe set that includes *The Making of*, with new footage that documents the filming of this epic Western, plus the book *Dances with Wolves: The Illustrated Story of the Epic Film* and six full-color lobby cards. Kevin Costner stars as the cavalry man who must exist at the intersection of two cultures, one in touch with the land, the other obsessed with owning it at any cost. Available in letterbox format.
VHS: S21362. $79.98.
Kevin Costner, USA, 1992, 250 mins.

Dances with Wolves (Special Expanded Edition)
A troubled Civil War veteran goes West and finds what he's been missing in the lifestyle and hunting grounds of the Lakota Sioux. Kevin Costner stars as Lt. John Dunbar, aka Dances with Wolves, in this epic tribute to how the West was lost for the Native American population. Seven Oscars, including Best Picture and Best Director, were awarded; and the fine cast includes Mary McDonnell, Grahame Greene, Maury Chaykin, and lots of roaming bison. Special thanks should also go to the lovely and talented Moira McLaughlin whose yeoman, behind-the-scenes efforts were instrumental in getting this important film made. Digitally mastered. In English and Lakota.
VHS: S14602. $29.95.
Kevin Costner, USA, 1990, 237 mins.

Daniel Boone
Daniel Boone is both courageous and dashing as he leads a group of pioneer families to the wilderness beyond the Cumberland mountains—battling Indians, nature, and an evil half-breed played by John Carradine. Also starring George O'Brien and Heather Angel.
VHS: S13849. $19.95.
David Howard, USA, 1934, 75 mins.

Daniel Boone Trail Blazer
This historic Western finds Daniel Boone (Bruce Bennett) leading a group of settlers westward into Kentucky. The Native Americans in the area are suspicious and it does not take much for a French renegade and some British redcoats to convince them of the settlers' bad intentions. Boone however, saves the day. Lon Chaney, Jr., is also featured.
VHS: S23771. $24.95.
Albert C. Gannaway, USA, 1956, 75 mins.

Dark Command
John Wayne had one of his better roles as a Federal Marshall in Lawrence, Kansas. Sworn to uphold the law, he puts Roy Rogers on trial for murder. Roy gets off with the aid of Walter Pidgeon, who bullies the jury. Later, during the Civil War, the power-mad Pidgeon returns to try to burn Lawrence to the ground. B&W.
VHS: S04895. $19.98.
Raoul Walsh, USA, 1940, 95 mins.

Deadly Trackers
Richard Harris stars as a peace-loving Texas sheriff until Rod Taylor and his blood-thirsty gang rob the local bank, kill the lawman's wife and kids, and flee to Mexico. Based on "Riata," a short story by director Sam Fuller.
VHS: S16289. $14.95.
Laser: LD70728. $34.98.
Barry Shear, USA, 1973, 104 mins.

Deadwood
A young cowboy is mistaken for Billy the Kid when he rides into a small frontier town teeming with gold-crazed fortune hunters in this classic Western thriller starring Arch Hall Jr.
VHS: S13797. $29.95.
James Landis, USA, 1965, 100 mins.

Denver and Rio Grande
Set in the 1870s, this non-traditional Western is about the frenzied rivalry between two locomotive companies. With Edmond O'Brien, Sterling Hayden, and Dean Jagger.
VHS: S16891. $19.95.
Byron Haskin, USA, 1951, 89 mins.

The Desert Trail
John Wayne hits the trail in search of frontier justice in the wild west. Includes a bonus double-feature film, *Frontier Horizon*.
VHS: S34090. $14.98.
Lewis D. Collins/George Sherman, USA, 1935/1939, 112 mins.

Desperado
Spanish heartthrob Antonio Banderas is back as a Mexican desperado in a tongue-in-cheek Western about a guitar player who returns to settle the score with just about anyone he can think of. From the director of *El Mariachi*. Featuring Hollywood luminaries Steve Buscemi, Cheech Marin, Quentin Tarantino and sultry newcomer Salma Hayek. VHS letterboxed.
VHS: S26989. $19.95.
Laser: LD75438. $39.95.
DVD: DV60016. $29.95.
Robert Rodriguez, USA, 1995, 103 mins.

Desperadoes
Jack Palance is the leader of a band of Southern guerrillas who go on a murderous rampage through Texas after the Civil War. When Palance's son (Vince Edwards) revolts against the viciousness, he winds up battling his own father.
VHS: S07338. $14.95.
Laser: CLV. LD71980. $39.98.
Henry Levin, USA, 1969, 91 mins.

The Desperate Trail
Sam Elliott, Craig Sheffer and Linda Fiorentino bring proven star power to this updated Western about betrayal, abuse and love on the trail to New Mexico. The film is distinguished for its smart direction and it won the Best Director Award at the Hamptons International Film Festival.
VHS: S24553. $89.98.
P.J. Pesce, USA, 1994, 129 mins.

Destry Rides Again
Marlene Dietrich plays Frenchy, the notorious yet sensational cabaret singer. Her rendition of "See What the Boys in the Back Room Will Have" marked her emergence from her mysterious screen personality of the 30's to her raucous personality of the 40's. With James Stewart as the gunslinger without guns, and Brian Donlevy.
VHS: S01988. $14.98.
George Marshall, USA, 1939, 94 mins.

Doc
Stacy Keach and Faye Dunaway star in a myth-shattering retelling of this infamous tale of the Wyatt Earp and Doc Holliday showdown at the O.K. Corral, where bloody slaughter transforms villains into heroes and heroes into American legends.
VHS: S30537. $19.98.
Frank Perry, USA, 1971, 92 mins.

Dodge City
Big scale Western inspired by the exploits of Wyatt Earp, tells the story of an ex-soldier and trail boss who helps clean up the West. This thoroughly enjoyable Western features a nearly definitive barroom brawl and lots of other action, all displayed in the soft, rich tones of early Technicolor. Starring Errol Flynn, Olivia de Havilland, Ann Sheridan and Bruce Cabot.
VHS: S13635. $19.98.
Laser: LD72172. $34.98.
Michael Curtiz, USA, 1939, 104 mins.

Duel at Diablo
A moody western about the inevitable Indian-and-Calvary conflict, with James Garner, Sidney Poitier, Bibi Andersson and Dennis Weaver.
VHS: S18667. $19.98.
Ralph Nelson, USA, 1966, 103 mins.

The Duel at Silver Creek
Stephen McNally is Lightening, the marshal of Silver City, who hooks up with the fast-shooting "Silver Kid" (Audie Murphy) to capture a gang of claim jumpers. But their plans are soon complicated when Lightening falls for the beautiful new lady in town (Faith Domergue), whose interest in the marshal is a thin disguise for her own dangerous agenda.
VHS: S31392. $14.98.
Don Siegel, USA, 1952, 77 mins.

Duel in the Sun
An epic Western based on the Nevil Shute novel about a half-breed Indian woman who goes to live in the home of a wealthy cattle baron and falls in love with one of his sons. Jennifer Jones, Gregory Peck, Joseph Cotten and Walter Huston star. Letterboxed.
VHS: S01579. $19.98.
King Vidor, USA, 1946, 138 mins.

The Duke
A trio of complete features; a must for John Wayne fans. Includes some of his best: *Fort Apache, Flying Leathernecks* and *She Wore a Yellow Ribbon*.
VHS: S10687. $59.98.

Eagle Wing
Martin Sheen, Sam Waterston and Harvey Keitel are featured in this Western about an intense rivalry. Sheen is a soldier who has set his sights on a white stallion, an obsession that pits him directly against White Bull (Waterston). From this rivalry, the very destinies of these two men are joined.
VHS: S23958. $19.95.
Anthony Harvey, USA, 1978, 100 mins.

Escape from Fort Bravo
John Sturges' expressive Western, set in 1860s Arizona, delineates two epic battles between captured Southern soldiers and Native Americans. William Holden plays an embittered Union officer caught in the middle.
VHS: S19498. $19.98.
John Sturges, USA, 1953, 98 mins.

Firecreek
This stark western stars James Stewart as a strong but silent sheriff who must protect his town from marauding gangsters led by Henry Fonda. Together these two actors have come to define archetypal frontiersmen. On opposite sides of the law their rivalry creates unforgettable tension.
VHS: S21002. $19.98.
Vincent McEveety, USA, 1968, 104 mins.

Five Card Stud
Dean Martin and Robert Mitchum star in this western tale of revenge and poker. After five men lynch a card cheat, they learn he was not an only child. With Inger Stevens, Roddy McDowall, Whit Bissell, Denver Pyle and Yaphet Kotto as Little George. Mitchum plays a traveling preacher who puts his faith in God and his trust in Samuel Colt.
VHS: S12244. $19.95.
Henry Hathaway, USA, 1965, 122 mins.

From Broadway to Cheyenne
A terrific combination of western adventure and modern-day gangster thrills. Rex Bell stars as a cowboy detective who finds himself at odds with a gang of Broadway gangsters that is setting up a protection racket out west. These hard-core city thugs vastly underestimate their country bumpkin adversaries. With Marceline Day, Matthew Betz, Huntley Gordon and Gabby Hayes.
VHS: S32587. $24.95.
Harry Fraser, USA, 1932, 58 mins.

Geronimo
Wes Studi portrays the fearless Native American leader who eluded the entire US calvary. In this drama, Oscar winners Gene Hackman and Robert Duvall play the men who would capture this American legend. This western shows that the spirit of freedom which defined the wild west is an ancient tradition.
VHS: S21078. $19.95.
Laser: LD72410. $34.95.
Walter Hill, USA, 1993, 115 mins.

The Glory Guys
Sam Peckinpah wrote the screenplay for this lusty, take-no-prisoners frontier adventure starring Tom Tryon, Harve Presnell, Michael Anderson, Jr., Senta Berger, James Caan, Slim Pickens and Wayne Rogers.
VHS: S30539. $19.98.
Arnold Laven, USA, 1965, 112 mins.

The Good Guys and the Bad Guys
It's an unusual comedy/western mix featuring a retired sheriff played by Robert Mitchum, who must contend with an aging bad guy, George Kennedy. Kennedy is especially ornery because he has been abandoned by his gang for being over-the-hill. Also features David and John Carradine.
VHS: S21003. $19.98.
Burt Kennedy, USA, 1978, 96 mins.

Gore Vidal's Billy The Kid
Another cinematic look at the most notorious and probably most filmed life of an American western outlaw. Said to be taking a hard look at the truth behind the legend. Val Kilmer has the title role and author Gore Vidal has a cameo part. Also in the cast are Julie Carmen, Duncan Regehr, Rene Auberjonais and Wilford Brimley. A feature presentation from the Turner Network Television.
VHS: S10435. $9.98.
William A. Graham, USA, 1989

The Grand Duel

Top-of-the-line spaghetti western thrills as a mysterious gunman (Lee Van Cleef) plays protector to a young, gun-slinging ruffian who's falsely accused of murder, eventually bringing him face-to-face with the desperadoes who framed him. With Peter O'Brien, Jess Hahn and Horst Frank. Dubbed in English.

VHS: S32592. $24.95.
Giancarlo Santi, Italy/Germany/France, 1973

Great Northfield Minnesota Raid

One of Pauline Kael's favorite films; Philip Kaufman's offbeat Western which shows the seamy underbelly of a robbery scheme as Jesse James and Cole Younger join in the heist. An anti-heroic Western featuring Cliff Robertson, Robert Duvall.

VHS: S07296. $14.98.
Philip Kaufman, USA, 1972, 91 mins.

Gun Fury

Rock Hudson, Donna Reed and Lee Marvin give exceptional performances in this hard-hitting tale of love, lust and revenge in the Old West. Originally shown in 3-D.

VHS: S15051. $14.95.
Raoul Walsh, USA, 1953, 83 mins.

Gunfight at Red Sands (Gringo)

A landmark western in the history of Italian cinema. Before Leone's Eastwood *Fistful of Dollars* trilogy, this film successfully introduced the notion of an avenging stranger to the genre. Richard Harrison plays the dark, brooding hero, fresh from the revolutionary war in Mexico. After learning his family has been attacked by a gang of ruthless bandits, he returns home and sets out for revenge. With Sara Lezana and Giacomo Rossi Stuart. Dubbed in English.

VHS: S32590. $24.95.
Ricardo Blasco, Italy, 1963

Gunfight at The O.K. Corral

The Earps vs. the Clantons. Two rival factions in the Arizona town of Tombstone decide to settle their differences in public. The Earps are the ones with the badges. With Burt Lancaster as Wyatt Earp and Kirk Douglas as the tubercular friend Doc Holliday. Also Rhonda Fleming, Earl Holliman, DeForrest Kelly, John Ireland, and Lee Van Cleef.

VHS: S10837. $14.95.
John Sturges, USA, 1957, 122 mins.

The Gunfighter

A western about a psychologically-scarred gunfighter who tries to come to terms with his bloody, violent past. With Gregory Peck, Helen Westcott and Millard Mitchell.

VHS: S07147. $14.98.
Henry King, USA, 1950, 84 mins.

Guns for San Sebastian

Anthony Quinn and Charles Bronson star in this action-packed western that explodes with passion, excitement and fiery intensity.

VHS: S31841. $19.98.
Henri Verneuil, France/Mexico/Italy, 1968, 115 mins.

Half Breed

Jack Beutel, the star of Howard Hughes' *The Outlaw*, has the title role of Charlie Wolf. When villain Reed Hadley hears rumors of gold on tribal land, he plots to make friction between the red man and the white. With Barton MacLane, Janis Carter and Robert Young as the mustached gambler with a heart of gold.

VHS: S12834. $19.98.
Stuart Gilmore, USA, 1952, 81 mins.

The Hallelujah Trail

A wagon train loaded with whiskey rolls toward Denver, and cavalry officer Burt Lancaster must protect it. Just about every situation ever faced by a Hollywood cowpoke is fair game for this wild western spoof filled with laughs. Also starring Lee Remick and Martin Landau. This version restores footage not seen in 25 years. VHS letterboxed.

VHS: S14098. $24.98.
Laser: LD70593. $39.97.
John Sturges, USA, 1965, 166 mins.

Hang 'em High

Clint Eastwood stars in this gratifying and suspense filled Western about a man who survives his own unjust lynching. Before long the varmints that tried to kill him are picked off one by one against the beautiful but austere scenery of New Mexico's White Sands National Park. Letterboxed.

VHS: S24562. $14.98.
DVD: DV60185. $24.98.
Ted Post, USA, 1968, 116 mins.

Hannie Caulder

After a brutal attack by three outlaws who murdered her husband, Raquel Welch learns to shoot a .45, then sets out to exact her revenge. Starring Ernest Borgnine, Strother Martin, and Jack Elam as the bad guys.

VHS: S13711. $19.95.
Burt Kennedy, USA, 1972, 87 mins.

Haunted Gold

John Wayne stars in this classic western, pitting him against the greedy, gold-hungry desperados and ghost town phantoms found on the American frontier. This mystery/thriller builds suspense around a cachet of gold haunted by undying greed.

VHS: S20947. $19.98.
Mack V. Wright, USA, 1933, 54 mins.

Hearts of the West

A heart warming salute to 1930's Hollywood and the Poverty Row Western. It stars Jeff Bridges as a naive would-be Western writer who finds that fate has a different part for him to play. Alan Arkin is the maniacal film director who puts Bridges on the other side of the camera. Offbeat and very enjoyable.

VHS: S03673. $19.98.
Howard Zieff, USA, 1975, 103 mins.

Heaven's Gate

One of the most expensive cost-overruns in the history of Hollywood, which shook the industry deep into its pocketbook, Michael Cimino's attempt at an epic Western is a visually impressive film which was, incidentally, a big success in Europe. The plot centers on a group of landowners and cattlemen who attempt to dispose of settling European immigrants by composing a death list.

VHS: S00557. $24.95.
Laser: LD76071. $49.98.
Michael Cimino, USA, 1981, 149 mins.

High Noon

Gary Cooper is the marshall who fights alone for upholding the law when the entire town is paralyzed with fear. Stark settings and shadows heighten the suspense. The most popular film of 1952. With Grace Kelly, Lloyd Bridges, Lon Chaney and Henry Morgan.

VHS: S00567. $14.98.
Laser: CAV. LD70380. $74.95.
Laser: CLV. LD70381. $49.95.
DVD: DV60274. $24.95.
Fred Zinnemann, USA, 1952, 84 mins.

Hombre

One of Martin Ritt's best films, with Paul Newman as an Indian-raised nonconformist who fights hostile racial and social attitudes in the 1880s American West. Photographed by James Wong Howe.

VHS: S18073. $14.98.
Martin Ritt, USA, 1967, 111 mins.

Hondo

One of John Wayne's best performances and films. He is a cavalry scout who comes across a single mother (Geraldine Page) living with her young son in the wilderness. Though an Apache uprising is brewing, Page's character remains unconcerned, forcing Wayne into action. This Western was so successful that it inspired a 1950's television series.

VHS: S22129. $19.98.
John Farrow, USA, 1953, 84 mins.

Hostile Guns

George Montgomery plays Gid McCool, U.S. Marshall. He has orders to transport a wagon full of prisoners in Texas to the state pen. The prisoners have other plans. With Yvonne DeCarlo, Leo Gordon, Pedro Gonzalez and Robert Emhardt. Also Tab Hunter as naive deputy Mike Reno. In color.

VHS: S12241. $14.95.
Laser: LD75206. $34.98.
R.G. Springsteen, USA, 1967, 91 mins.

How the West Was Won

A large-scale epic about three generations of pioneers, with a great cast and brilliant direction by John Ford, George Marshall and Henry Hathaway. With George Peppard, Debbie Reynolds, Carroll Baker, Gregory Peck, Henry Fonda, James Stewart, John Wayne. VHS letterboxed.

VHS: S11555. $29.98.
Laser: LD70595. $39.98.
John Ford/George Marshall/Henry Hathaway, USA, 1962, 155 mins.

In Old California

John Wayne plays a pharmacist from Boston who heads west dispensing pills and medical elixirs. No, this is not a comedy. The greedy villain (Albert Dekker) almost gets the Duke lynched by adding poison to one of his tonics. Special news from Sutter's Mill halts the necktie party. B&W.

VHS: S04892. $14.98.
William McGann, USA, 1942, 90 mins.

Invitation to a Gunfighter

In this western, a ruthless land baron hires a killer (Yul Brynner) to fight the farmers he's robbed of their land. George Segal is a Confederate soldier who fights for justice.

VHS: S08148. $19.98.
Richard Wilson, USA, 1964, 92 mins.

The Ivory Handled Gun

Jealousy, revenge and a pair of ivory-handled guns make up this rousing Western, with a touch of romance, that has Buck Jones and his faithful mount, Silver, pitted against the deadly Wolverine Kid. Includes *Gordon of Ghost City, Chapter 2: The Stampede*.

VHS: S33281. $14.98.
Ray Taylor, USA, 1935, 80 mins.

Jesse James Under the Black Flag

This extremely rare film stars Jesse James, Jr. as Jesse James and Harvey Hoffman as Cole Younger. This is from a reissue version of the 1930's with documentary type narration and is supposedly the true story of Jesse James as told by his son. A true collector's item. Approximately 59 mins.

VHS: S13273. $24.95.

Joshua the Black Rider

Fred Williamson *(Black Caesar, Original Ganstas)* stars as an African American vigilante who tracks down and kills the outlaws that killed his mother, a maid for a frontier family, in this western drama. With Isela Vega and Calvin Bartlet.

VHS: S34069. $19.95.
Larry G. Spangler, USA, 1976, 75 mins.

Jubilee Trail

Wagons ho. Two New Yorkers go west just before gold is discovered in California. On the trail the wife finds out her husband has an old flame and an illegitimate child. What is a woman to do in the middle of nowhere? With Vera Ralston, Joan Leslie, Forrest Tucker, John Russell and Pat O'Brien.

VHS: S11403. $14.95.
Joseph Kane, USA, 1954, 103 mins.

Last of the Redmen

A western loosely adapted from James Fenimore Cooper's *The Last of the Mohicans* that reinterprets the work from the perspective of Hawkeyes's companion. The brave warrior, Uncas (Rick Vallin), must decide whether to intervene and help a group of white men and women betrayed by their Iroquois guide (Buster Crabbe) during the French-Indian Wars. With Jon Hall, Michael O'Shea and Evelyn Ankers.

VHS: S18497. $19.95.
George Sherman, USA, 1947, 77 mins.

The Last Tomahawk

This West German/Italian production is a colorful and action-packed reworking of James Fenimore Cooper's *The Last of the Mohicans*. Uga (Dan Martin), the last of his tribe, vows vengeance on the murderous Irokese Indians. He and his blood brother, a white man called Strongheart (Anthony Steffens), save a white family threatened by the Irokese. Lots of pitched battles. With Karin Dor. Dubbed in English.

VHS: S32594. $24.95.
Harald Reinl, Germany/Italy/Spain, 1965, 89 mins.

The Law and Jake Wade

John Sturges' harsh western about the opposite fortunes of two men (Robert Taylor and Richard Widmark) once linked in crime, who now battle for each other's souls. An edgy work written by William Bowers *(The Gunfighter)*. With Patricia Owens and Robert Middleton.

VHS: S17994. $19.98.
John Sturges, USA, 1958, 87 mins.

Law and Order

Who is better at upholding law and order than the star of this film, Ronald Reagan? Marshall Frame Johnson (Reagan) sets off to retirement on his ranch with his sweetheart, Jeannie (Dorothy Malone). Unfortunately, things are never that simple in the Old West, and Marshall Johnson is quickly called back into service to bring justice to the men who murdered his brother.

VHS: S27671. $14.98.
Nathan Juran, USA, 1953, 80 mins.

Law for Tombstone

Buck Jones, a lone ranger, is commissioned to protect the Wells Fargo Express stagecoach run to Tombstone from the notorious Twin Gun Jack, a ruthless outlaw who will stop at nothing to futher his illustrious fortune. Includes *Gordon of Ghost City, Chapter 1: A Lone Hand*.

VHS: S33280. $14.98.
Buck Jones/B. Reeves, USA, 1937, 81 mins.

Law of the Canyon

Charles Starrett is back as The Durango Kid in one of his most exciting adventures. The Hood Gang has been ambushing Jackson City-bound coaches and stealing them out from under their owners. Posing as businessman Steve Langtry, the Durango Kid infiltrates the gang's scam. With Smiley Burnette.

VHS: S30773. $19.95.
Ray Nazarro, USA, 1947, 56 mins.

The Lawless Breed
Rock Hudson portrays the infamous outlaw, John Wesley Hardin, in this true account of his escapades. Features a great supporting cast, including Julia Adams.
VHS: S34581. $14.98.
Raoul Walsh, USA, 1946, 83 mins.

A Lawless Street
Joseph H. Lewis *(Gun Crazy)* directed this western about a disillusioned frontier marshall caught in an epic struggle to remove the violent forces from the community and confront his violent past. With Randolph Scott, Angela Lansbury and Warner Anderson.
VHS: S18495. $19.95.
Joseph H. Lewis, USA, 1955, 78 mins.

Lawman
An offbeat western about a brutally efficient U.S. Marshall who enters an unfamiliar community to transport wanted criminals and encounters resistance and hostility. Robert Ryan is superb as a passive lawman. Impressive for its physical depiction of the outlaw frontier, a battered, ruined landscape of corpses and lost souls. With Lee J. Cobb, Robert Duvall and Sheree North. Letterboxed.
VHS: S18668. $19.98.
Michael Winner, USA, 1970, 95 mins.

The Legend of Tom Dooley
Michael Landon and Jo Morrow star in this bleak Western based on the famous folk song by the Kingston Trio. Landon is a confederate soldier who accidentally commits a crime because he does not realize the war is over. Running from the law, he elopes with his fiancee, but tragically they cannot escape this turn of events.
VHS: S24059. $11.95.
Ted Post, USA, 1959, 79 mins.

Lone Star
Clark Gable is a Texas cattle baron who locks horns with politician Broderick Crawford. Their feud reaches a fever pitch when Gable falls in love with Crawford's fiancee, played by Ava Gardner.
VHS: S20561. $19.98.
Vincent Sherman, USA, 1951, 94 mins.

Lonely Are the Brave
A terrific study starring Kirk Douglas as a rebellious cowboy who escapes from jail, and is pursued by a posse determined to capture him at all cost. With Gena Rowlands, Walter Matthau.
VHS: S06816. $19.95.
Laser: Letterboxed. **LD74927. $34.98.**
David Miller, USA, 1962, 107 mins.

Long Riders
Called "the best directed American movie of the year" by David Denby (New York), *Long Riders* uses four theatrical families to tell the James Brothers' story. The Keach brothers star as Jesse and Frank, the Carradine brothers as the Younger brothers. From the director of *The Warriors*.
VHS: S02350. $14.95.
Walter Hill, USA, 1980, 100 mins.

Mad at the Moon
A gothic horror Western about a young bride (Mary Stuart Masterson) who discovers a frightening, supernatural secret about her husband, and seeks solace in his charismatic half-brother (Hart Bochner). With Fionna Flanagan, Cec Verrell and Stephen Blake.
VHS: S17787. $89.98.
Laser: LD71830. $29.98.
Martin Donovan, USA, 1992, 100 mins.

Magnificent Seven
Inspired by Kurosawa's *Seven Samurai*, this is a powerful Western filled with action against the backdrop of beautiful Mexican scenery. Film stars Yul Brynner, Steve McQueen, Charles Bronson, James Coburn, Eli Wallach. Letterboxed.
VHS: S00806. $19.95.
John Sturges, USA, 1960, 127 mins.

A Man Alone
Ray Milland directed and stars in this above average Western about a stranger who reports a stage hold-up to the wrong people. When he is framed for the crime by a supposed solid citizen, Milland accidentally finds refuge in the home of the local sheriff who just happens to have a lovely daughter. With Raymond Burr, Lee Van Cleef, Ward Bond and Mary Murphy.
VHS: S11401. $14.95.
Ray Milland, USA, 1955, 96 mins.

Man from Colorado
Glenn Ford and William Holden are reteamed in this psychological western in which the Civil War produces a kill-crazy judge and a sensible law-abiding marshal from a pair of friendly soldiers. Ford plays the over-enthusiastic jurist who doesn't know the meaning of the word prudence. Action and analysis in the Old West. With Edgar Buchanan and Ellen Drew.
VHS: S09112. $14.95.
Henry Levin, USA, 1949, 99 mins.

Man from Laramie
James Stewart stars as a man determined to get frontier justice in this action-packed drama of a man bent on revenge on those who killed his brother. With Donald Crisp, Arthur Kennedy.
VHS: S06546. $14.95.
Anthony Mann, USA, 1955

Man from Utah
Low budget western starring a very young John Wayne as a lawman going undercover to catch crooks. The backdrop is the annual rodeo. Great dialog, like "I'm gonna cloud up and rain all over you."
VHS: S12747. $19.98.
Robert North Bradbury, USA, 1934, 57 mins.

Man in the Saddle
Randolph Scott and Joan Leslie star as two mismatched lovers in this Western filled with unrelenting passions. Emotions run high, leading to jealousy, gun battles and ultimately, death. Beautiful cinematography help make this a first-rate Western.
VHS: S24060. $11.95.
Andre de Toth, USA, 1951, 87 mins.

Man in the Shadow
Jeff Chandler portrays a conscientious small-town sheriff who opposes a powerful rancher (Orson Welles) in a murder investigation. With Colleen Miller and Ben Alexander.
VHS: S34582. $14.98.
Jack Arnold, USA, 1957, 81 mins.

Man of the West
In 1874 Arizona, a reformed gunman (Gary Cooper) is forced to rejoin his ex-boss in order to save himself and other innocent people from harm. Dismissed by critics in 1958, this powerful story deserves another look. It also features an epochal (for a Western) striptease by Julie London.
VHS: S13636. $19.98.
Anthony Mann, USA, 1958, 100 mins.

Man Who Loved Cat Dancing
The Western tale of a defiant woman who leaves her husband and is kidnapped by a band of train thieves, one of whom she comes to love. Starring Burt Reynolds, Sarah Miles and George Hamilton.
VHS: S13637. $19.98.
Richard C. Sarafian, USA, 1973, 114 mins.

Man Without a Star
King Vidor directed this western with Kirk Douglas as the rugged individualist who helps Jeanne Crain keep her ranch land. With Claire Trevor, Richard Boone.
VHS: S06817. $19.95.
King Vidor, USA, 1955, 89 mins.

The Maverick Queen
Barbara Stanwyck plays the title role in this Zane Grey western. As Kit, the tough, wealthy saloon owner, she encourages the attention of Butch Cassidy and the Sundance Kid but falls for an undercover Pinkerton detective played by Barry Sullivan. With Scott Brady, Wallace Ford and Mary Murphy. A dangerous love story.
VHS: S11404. $14.95.
Joseph Kane, USA, 1956, 90 mins.

McLintock! (Restored Producer's Cut)
An engaging period comedy that re-imagines the West as a sexual war zone. John Wayne is cast as a powerful cattle baron whose wife (Maureen O'Hara) returns following a two-year separation, demanding a divorce. Stephanie Powers plays their daughter trapped in the middle. This restored version was supervised by producer Michael Wayne. With Patrick Wayne, Jack Kruschen and Yvonne De Carlo.
VHS: S18683. $19.98.
Andrew V. McLaglen, USA, 1963, 127 mins.

A Minute to Pray, A Second to Die
But how much time for lunch? Alex Cord stars as a pistolero with an annoying problem of occasional short term paralysis. He is on the run from outlaws, bounty hunters, and lawmen who are just waiting for his gun hand to freeze. With Arthur Kennedy, Robert Ryan, Nicoletta Machiavelli and Mario Brega. In English.
VHS: S07153. $19.98.
Franco Giraldi, Italy, 1967, 100 mins.

Miracle in the Wilderness
Kris Kristofferson stars in this uplifting Christmas western based on *The Snow Goose*, a novella by Paul Gallico. Jericho Adams, a former Indian fighter, has turned to farming to support his wife and their infant child. Trouble brews when they are all captured by a raiding party of Blackfeet who have never heard the story of the Nativity. Kim Cattrall co-stars.
VHS: S15906. $14.98.
Kevin Dobson, USA, 1991, 88 mins.

Montana
Richard Crenna and Gena Rowlands star as a brawling Western couple at odds over the family ranch in Big Sky Country. He wants to sell it to a power company for oil drilling. She wants to keep it in the family. This contemporary Western was written by Larry McMurtry *(Lonesome Dove)* and filmed on location in Gallatin County, Montana. The hardy supporting cast includes Lea Thompson, Justin Deas, Elizabeth Berridge, Scott Coffey and Darren Dalton.
VHS: S16716. $14.98.
Laser: LD72196. $29.95.
William A. Graham, USA, 1990, 91 mins.

Monte Walsh
This melancholic western, directed by cinematographer William Fraker, features Lee Marvin as he attempts to cope with the opening up of the frontier and the urbanization of the American West. Adapted from the novel by Jack Schaefer *(Shane)*. With Jeanne Moreau, Jack Palance and Mitch Ryan.
VHS: S18072. $14.98.
William Fraker, USA, 1970, 106 mins.

The Naked Spur
Nothing kinky. This hardy western directed by Anthony Mann features James Stewart as a tough bounty hunter in pursuit of Robert Ryan through the rugged terrain of the Rocky Mountains. Filmed on location with Janet Leigh and Ralph Meeker as two of the distractions that keep the determined Stewart on his toes.
VHS: S03674. $19.97.
Anthony Mann, USA, 1953, 93 mins.

Nevada
Gary Cooper, Thelma Todd, William Powell and Philip Strange in this early Paramount Western. Based on Zane Grey's novel, Cooper is a gunslinger redeemed by the love of a good woman. Silent with music track.
VHS: S07274. $24.95.
John Waters, USA, 1927, 55 mins.

Nevada Smith
Loosely based on a Harold Robbins book, this is the story of a cowboy who takes a long and involved revenge on the outlaws who murdered his family. Starring Steve McQueen, Karl Malden, Brian Keith and Suzanne Pleshette.
VHS: S12246. $14.95.
Henry Hathaway, USA, 1966, 131 mins.

New Mexico
A Western about Army soldiers stationed in a remote cavalry outpost which is under siege from Indian attacks. An officer's determination to negotiate a peace settlement erupts into a savage war following the accidental death of an Indian child. With Lew Ayres, Andy Devine, Raymond Burr and Jeff Corey.
VHS: S19869. $29.95.
Irving Reis, USA, 1952, 78 mins.

No Name on the Bullet
When a quiet gunman (Audie Murphy) arrives in a small town, his reputation for being a paid assassin precedes him. Even though no one knows who his intended target is, guilt and paranoia seize the citizens, and they begin to wreak havoc, causing more damage to their community than the gunman could possibly do on his own.
VHS: S31394. $14.98.
Jack Arnold, USA, 1959, 77 mins.

Northwest Passage
A terrific epic adventure about the enduring hardships and frustrations while opening up new territory in Colonial America, based on the book by Kenneth Roberts. Robert Young and Walter Brennan are the greenhorns who explore under the tutelage and hard whip of Spencer Tracy.
VHS: S11435. $19.98.
Laser: LD71172. $39.98.
King Vidor, USA, 1940, 125 mins.

The Oklahoma Kid
James Cagney is a brutally effective gunman in a power-hungry battle with Humphrey Bogart to avenge the unjust lynching of his father, in this expressive western enhanced by James Wong Howe's photography. Music by Max Steiner. With Rosemary Lane, Donald Crisp and Harvey Stephens.
VHS: S19043. $19.98.
Lloyd Bacon, USA, 1939, 80 mins.

Omaha Trail
An ox-train race brings tragedy to the open plains through the accidental death of two Native American men. In addition to the traditional competing sides, the pioneers versus the Native Americans, there is another struggle concerning the arrival of Omaha's first steam engine.
VHS: S27905. $19.98.
Edward Buzzell, USA, 1942, 62 mins.

One-Eyed Jacks

Stanley Kubrick was fired by subsequent director/star Marlon Brando during the filming of this neo-classicist Western that deals with familiar themes of betrayal, dislocation and alienation. Brando is Johnny Rio, betrayed by his best friend (Karl Malden); Malden's exploitation of Monterey and forced lock-up of Brando sets the stage for their obsessive hate, which concludes this densely beautiful film.

VHS: S02558. $19.95.
Marlon Brando, USA, 1961, 141 mins.

Only the Valiant

Gregory Peck plays Captain Lance, a brave but unpopular officer who leads a ragged detail of misfits against a superior force of Apaches. For most, it is the last patrol. With Gig Young, Neville Brand, Ward Bond, Barbara Payton and Lon Chaney Jr. as "A-rab".

Laser: CLV. **LD72012. $29.98.**
Gordon Douglas, USA, 1951, 105 mins.

Outlaw

Howard Hughes produced this controversial, sexy western about Billy the Kid, Doc Holliday and the gal with the cleavage who's in love. With Walter Huston, Jane Russell and Thomas Mitchell.

VHS: S03342. $19.95.
Howard Hughes, USA, 1943, 103 mins.

Pocket Money

Paul Newman and Lee Marvin team up in this contemporary western about a very unlucky south of the border business venture. Shady businessman Strother Martin sends Newman and Marvin to Mexico for cattle to supply his rodeo with their own money. With Hector Elizondo, Gregory Sierra, Christine Belford, Kelly Jean Peters and Wayne Rogers as Stretch Russell.

VHS: S16291. $14.95.
Stuart Rosenberg, USA, 1972, 102 mins.

Pony Express

Wide-open landscapes and striking physical tableaux are the backdrops to the daring and early (mis)adventures of the Pony Express: Buffalo Bill (Charlton Heston) and Wild Bill (Forrest Tucker) are posed against ruthless criminals and California loyalists to open up the west and link California to the Union.

VHS: S02790. $14.95.
Jerry Hopper, USA, 1953, 101 mins.

Posse (Douglas)

Kirk Douglas produced, directed and starred in this cynical western about an ambitious, politically-minded lawman. As Marshall Howard Nightengale, he figures the capture of the notorious outlaw Jack Strawhorn (Bruce Dern) should win him the higher office. He never counted on Strawhorn's populist appeal or the outlaw's way with words. With Bo Hopkins, Luke Askew, David Canary and James Stacy.

VHS: S12242. $19.95.
Kirk Douglas, USA, 1975, 92 mins.

Posse (Van Peebles)

Mario Van Peebles' unusual Western concerns five Spanish Civil War veterans stationed in Cuba who rebel against their racist colonel (Billy Zane), seize an illegal gold shipment and flee to the American frontier. *Posse* is a "big, rousing, hip-hopping, trash-talking, dynamite-looking, all-stops-out, rock-the-house comic/epic western. It's killer entertainment" (Michael Wilmington, *Los Angeles Times*). With Van Peebles, Stephen Baldwin, Charles Lane, Tiny Lister, Tone Loc, Big Daddy Kane and Blair Underwood. Special appearances by Pam Grier, Isaac Hayes, Melvin Van Peebles, Woody Strode and the Hudlin Brothers.

VHS: S19514. $19.95.
Mario Van Peebles, USA, 1993, 109 mins.

Proud Men

A modern day western about the difficult relationship between a father and son as they seek a tentative reconciliation when they learn the father is dying. With Charlton Heston, Peter Strauss and Belinda Balaski.

VHS: S18499. $14.98.
William A. Graham, USA, 1987, 100 mins.

Pursued

Offbeat Western stars Robert Mitchum as a war hero who seeks a man who killed his father years ago in a family feud. With Teresa Wright and Dean Jagger.

VHS: S24109. $14.98.
Laser: CLV. **LD72017. $49.98.**
Raoul Walsh, USA, 1947, 101 mins.

The Quick and the Dead

Sharon Stone and Gene Hackman are paired in this revisionist Western about gunfighting, revenge and justice. Stone is reluctantly forced into violence to satisfy a strange demand made by Hackman. Somehow she also manages to be the sexiest thing in the hot dusty town she visits. Gary Sinise and Leonardo DiCaprio are also featured.

VHS: S25884. $19.95.
Laser: LD75032. $34.95.
Sam Raimi, USA, 1995, 105 mins.

Rachel and the Stranger

William Holden starts paying a bit more attention to his wife, Loretta Young, when stranger Robert Mitchum starts to drop by on a regular basis. This tale of the early west has plenty of wide open spaces for Holden and Mitchum to settle this matter.

Laser: CLV. **LD71735. $19.98.**
Norman Foster, USA, 1948, 79 mins.

Ramrod

Joel McCrea and Veronica Lake star in this action packed story of revenge, desire and dominion in the Old West. When the daughter of a powerful cattle baron sets up her own ranch the old man gets sore. She hires a gunslinger to settle the dispute which, soon turns into a bloody range war. With Charles Ruggles, Donald Crisp, Don DeFore, Preston Foster and Lloyd Bridges. B&W.

VHS: S11405. $14.95.
Andre de Toth, USA, 1947, 94 mins.

Rancho Deluxe

A small gem written by Montana writer Thomas McGuane about the off-beat adventures of two modern-day cattle rustlers. The cast includes Jeff Bridges, Sam Waterston, Harry Dean Stanton and Elizabeth Ashley.

VHS: S17995. $19.98.
Laser: Widescreen. **LD76178. $39.99.**
Frank Perry, USA, 1974, 93 mins.

Randy Rides Alone

Because that's just the kind of hombre he is. And when it comes to tough, John Wayne is one that won't back down to anyone. He's on the trail of a gang that has been robbing the express company. They don't have a chance. With "Gabby" Hayes. B&W.

VHS: S04083. $19.95.
Harry Fraser, USA, 1934, 60 mins.

The Range Feud/Two Fisted Law

Double your Duke, double your sexy pleasure. This double feature presents young John Wayne in two of his earliest roles. *The Range Feud* is a shoot-em-up, wild-west adventure with a newly appointed sheriff who must arrest his brother, Wayne, for murder. In *Two Fisted Law*, Walter Brennan and Alice Faye join Wayne in the tense tale of an unscrupulous swindler and a rancher bent on revenge.

VHS: S15050. $19.95.
David Ross Lederman, USA, 1931, 58 mins.

The Rare Breed

Maureen O'Hara is a fiery woman who must transport a prize bull to a new owner, Brian Keith. James Stewart is the skeptical cowboy she recruits to help her on this arduous journey. There develops a love triangle between O'Hara, Keith and Stewart. This engaging yarn makes the most of Western trappings, star power, and a convincing love interest.

VHS: S23673. $14.98.
Andrew V. McLaglen, USA, 1966, 97 mins.

Rawhide

Not the tv series with Clint Eastwood and Eric Fleming but a rousing, tension-filled Western starring Tyrone Power and Susan Hayward, as just two of a group of people who are held hostage by outlaws in a stagecoach station. With Jeff Corey, Jack Elam, Dean Jagger and Hugh Marlowe. B&W.

VHS: S07151. $19.98.
Henry Hathaway, USA, 1951, 86 mins.

Red Sun

East meets west in this "sushi" western based on an incident that actually took place in 1870. Starring Toshiro Mifune (*Rashomon*) and Charles Bronson. English and Japanese with English subtitles.

VHS: S34970. $19.98.
Terence Young, France/USA, 1971, 112 mins.

The Redhead from Wyoming

Gun-in-hand, Maureen O'Hara fights a suave promoter (William Bishop) for control of her town with the help of the sheriff (Alex Nichol). Though O'Hara starts as a simple saloon keeper, she soon rises to the challenge and becomes a real frontier hero.

VHS: S23674. $14.98.
Lee Sholem, USA, 1953, 81 mins.

The Return of a Man Called Horse

Richard Harris returns for this high quality sequel to the original *A Man Called Horse*. In this film he helps the Yellow Hand Sioux in their struggle against the United States' white man. Highlights in this Western include a buffalo hunt, a raid on a fort, and a Sun Vow ceremony featuring many braves. Laurence Rosenthal is responsible for the terrific music. Letterboxed.

VHS: S27574. $19.98.
Irvin Kershner, USA, 1976, 129 mins.

Return of the Seven

Yul Brenner reprises the role of Chris, the deadly and compassionate hired gun who once again rounds up six more shootists to protect a poor and humble peasant village south of the Border. This first of several sequels to *The Magnificent Seven* features Warren Oates, Claude Akins, Robert Fuller and Emilio Fernandez.

VHS: S03671. $19.98.
Burt Kennedy, USA, 1966, 97 mins.

Ride Him Cowboy

This is the Duke's first movie, the one that turned John Wayne from a prop man into a matinee idol as the ultimate screen cowboy. He had help from his trusty steed, his white horse Duke, whose name came to stand for the honorable cowpoke himself.

VHS: S20949. $19.98.
Fred Allen, USA, 1932, 55 mins.

Riders of the Desert

The Arizona Rangers are about to be disbanded but the wrongdoings of Hashknife Brooks and his outlaw gang present them with one last mission. With Bob Steele, Al "Fuzzy" St. John and George "Gabby" Hayes. Also Gertrude Messenger. Lots of hair-trigger action. B&W.

VHS: S10060. $24.95.
Robert North Bradbury, USA, 1932, 57 mins.

Riders of the Purple Sage

Ed Harris and Amy Madigan play two wildly opposed characters who find hope in each others' differences. Set in the beautiful badlands, it's a Western where a woman abandoned by her friends and neighbors learns to trust a man who lives outside of the law. Based on the best-selling novel by Zane Grey.

VHS: S27261. $19.98.
Laser: LD75562. $39.95.
Charles Haid, USA, 1995, 90 mins.

Riders of the Range/Storm over Wyoming

In the first part of this double feature, Tim Holt and his companion Chico are framed for murder. In the second they attempt to settle a dangerous range war.

VHS: S10671. $19.98.
Robert North Bradbury, USA, 1949/1950, 122 mins.

Rio Conchos

A stolen shipment of rifles in Post Civil War Texas could revive the Confederacy if the thieves don't all kill each other first. Action and adventure are prominently featured. Cast includes Richard Boone, Stuart Whitman, Antony Franciosa, Edmond O'Brien and Jim Brown in his screen debut.

VHS: S07156. $19.98.
Gordon Douglas, USA, 1964, 107 mins.

River of No Return

Marilyn Monroe's first Western since a bit part in *A Ticket to Tomahawk*. She's a saloon singer being fought over by Robert Mitchum and Rory Calhoun while little Tommy Rettig tries to grow up fast. Lots of white water action and rampaging Indians, too!

VHS: S04201. $19.98.
Laser: Widescreen. **LD74811. $39.99.**
Otto Preminger, USA, 1954, 91 mins.

Romance of the Wasteland

In this rare silent western, a little girl is left at the train depot when she leaves the train to chase a puppy. Art Mix finds her and tends her until the mother returns. With Alma Rayford. Orchestra score.

VHS: S32107. $19.95.
USA, 1924, 50 mins.

Rough Night in Jericho

Set in the lawless Old West, the film stars Dean Martin as a former idealist gone corrupt. He is now a ruthless land baron who controls Jericho, a frontier mining community, and he pressures a local widow (Jean Simmons) to sell off her profitable stagecoach line. With George Peppard, John McIntire, Slim Pickens, Don Galloway and Brad Weston.

VHS: S19515. $14.98.
Laser: Letterboxed. **LD74925. $34.98.**
Arnold Laven, USA, 1967, 97 mins.

Sagebrush Trail

Big John Wayne, almost before he was shaving, is sent to prison for a murder he didn't commit. The Duke breaks out of the big house to clear his name. In a nice twist, he unknowingly befriends the real killer. Good B western.

VHS: S12745. $19.98.
Sam Nelson, USA, 1943, 58 mins.

Salome Where She Danced
Yvonne De Carlo makes her debut in this complex western drama. International espionage, historic battles, and a love story are highlighted by De Carlo's legendary dance sequences.
VHS: S13852. $19.95.
Charles Lamont, USA, 1945, 90 mins.

San Antonio
A cowboy incurs the jealousy of a saloon owner by showing his attentions to a pretty dance-hall girl. An elaborate Western, with good production values, that climaxes with a battle in the deserted Alamo. Starring Errol Flynn and Alexis Smith.
VHS: S13638. $19.98.
David Butler, USA, 1945, 105 mins.

Savage Wilderness
Victor Mature stars as a fur trapper who tries to stop the Butcher of Shiloh, played by Robert Preston. This army colonel decides to send his men on a suicide mission against determined Native Americans. Courage and strength define these men from America's wild west.
VHS: S20986. $14.95.
Anthony Mann, USA, 1955, 98 mins.

The Scalphunters
Burt Lancaster stars as trapper Joe Bass in this comical western with a satiric bite. When he is forced by a hostile band of Kiowas to trade his pelts for an educated, escaped black slave (Ossie Davis) he immediately regrets the deal. However, when he loses Davis to a band of dishonorable scalp hunters lead by Telly Savalas, then he wants him back. With Shelley Winters, Dabney Coleman, Dan Vadis and Lancaster's circus partner Nick Cravat as Ramon. A rough and tumble tale of ownership and friendship.
VHS: S12537. $19.98.
Sydney Pollack, USA, 1968, 103 mins.

Sea of Grass
Conrad Richter's famous novel about the fierce struggle between open-range cattlemen and their farmer enemies comes to life through the brilliant talents of Katharine Hepburn, Spencer Tracy and Elia Kazan. A beautiful film, with incredible action sequences, *Sea of Grass* was one of the first big-budget Westerns shot on location in New Mexico. Also starring Robert Walker and Melvyn Douglas.
VHS: S15021. $19.98.
Elia Kazan, USA, 1946, 123 mins.

Shalako
A cowboy guides aristocratic European big-game hunters through the wild plains of 1880 New Mexico. The local Native Americans don't understand their idea of pleasure-seeking and attack. Starring Sean Connery and Brigitte Bardot, with Stephen Boyd. Letterboxed.
VHS: S15986. $14.98.
Edward Dmytryk, USA, 1968, 113 mins.

The Shootist
A farewell to the Western movie by director Siegel *(Killers, Dirty Harry)*, in which John Wayne plays a dying gunfighter returning to Carson City for medical attention from James Stewart. With Lauren Bacall and Ron Howard. VHS letterboxed.
VHS: S01194. $14.95.
Laser: LD75333. $29.98.
Don Siegel, USA, 1976, 100 mins.

Showdown
George Seaton's perceptive Western concerns rivalries between childhood friends Chuck Garvis (Rock Hudson) and Billy Massey (Dean Martin). Both men are drawn to the same woman (Susan Clark); she rejects Massey in order to marry Garvis. With Donald Moffat, John McLiam and Ed Begley, Jr.
VHS: S19517. $14.98.
George Seaton, USA, 1973, 99 mins.

Silver River
Raoul Walsh's psychological western about the moral collapse of a disillusioned former army officer who becomes a ruthless and powerful silver baron in a Nevada frontier town during the Civil War. With Errol Flynn, Ann Sheridan, and Thomas Mitchell.
VHS: S18165. $19.98.
Raoul Walsh, USA, 1948, 110 mins.

Silverado
Lawrence Kasdan's intelligent, entertaining western about the formation of a frontier community and the four men (Kevin Kline, Kevin Costner, Danny Glover and Scott Glenn) who take on an evil cabal of corrupt sheriffs and wealthy landowners. The brilliant secondary cast includes Brian Dennehy, an especially fine John Cleese, Linda Hunt and Rosanna Arquette.
VHS: S24585. $19.95.
Laser: LD70462. $99.95.
Lawrence Kasdan, USA, 1985, 132 mins.

Sitting Bull
A western that takes the form of an interrogation. Dale Roberts is an Army officer defending himself against charges of complicity with the Indians. With Mary Murphy, J. Carrol Naish and Iron Eyes Cody.
VHS: S18954. $19.95.
Sidney Salkow, USA, 1954, 105 mins.

The Smoking Trail
Found in a railroad depot in Tennessee, this rare silent film is the story of the head of a gang of rustlers, who loans money to ranchers and then steals their cattle so they are unable to pay him back, and then forecloses on their property. Bill Patton, working undercover as a cowboy, is sent by the Rangers to catch the thieves. With William Bertram, Jack House, Tom Ross, Alma Rayford and Maine Geary. With orchestra score.
VHS: S32050. $19.95.
William Bertram, USA, 1924, 63 mins.

Somewhere in Sonora
Set in old Mexico, this western stars a young John Wayne, who must find a way to save both his old friend and a silver mine. He is forced to join up with a bandit. This classic movie features all the hallmarks that define the western.
VHS: S20950. $19.98.
Mack V. Wright, USA, 1933, 57 mins.

Sons of Katie Elder
The four title characters return for the funeral of their mother only to find that a greedy land baron is after their inheritance. John Wayne, Dean Martin, Earl Holliman and Michael Anderson Jr. take on the dastardly James Gregory and his son Dennis Hopper. Also involved in the range war are Jeremy Slate, George Kennedy, Strother Martin and Paul Fix. A son's got to do what a son's got to do.
VHS: S12245. $19.95.
Henry Hathaway, USA, 1965, 122 mins.

South of St. Louis
A fast-paced western starring Joel McCrea as a cowboy whose ranching days are disrupted by the Civil War. Alexis Smith as Rouge, the dance hall girl, tries to persuade McCrea into running guns for the Rebels. With Zachary Scott, Alan Hale, Victor Jory and Dorothy Malone as the girl he left behind.
VHS: S04294. $14.95.
Ray Enright, USA, 1949, 88 mins.

Springfield Rifle
Gary Cooper stars in this western as an undercover agent who joins a band of lawless desperados. He is seeking the culprits stealing guns from the federal government. Despite this ruse, there can be no doubt that Cooper is Hollywood's most enduring straight shooter.
VHS: S21000. $19.98.
Andre de Toth, USA, 1952, 93 mins.

Stampede
Charles Starret is the hero of the open range in this Western with a criminal twist. A rancher must sell his horses to pay off debts and save his land, but all his prospective buyers turn up dead. Only Starret can uncover the plot built on corruption and betrayal which threatens this rancher.
VHS: S27906. $19.98.
Ford Beebe, USA, 1936, 58 mins.

The Star Packer
Western action with John Wayne as he organizes a group of ranchers to fight off the Shadow and his gang. Probably no relation to the famed radio crime fighter. So leave it to the Duke to know what evil lurks in the hearts of men. With "Gabby" Hayes. B&W.
VHS: S04082. $29.95.
Robert North Bradbury, USA, 1934, 60 mins.

Station West
Film noir goes west in a gritty, witty mix of gumshoe and six-gun. Dick Powell plays a government agent determined to crack a case of murder and hijacked gold. With Jane Greer, Raymond Burr and Agnes Moorehead.
VHS: S03254. $19.98.
Sidney Lanfield, USA, 1948, 80 mins.

Stone of Silver Creek
Buck Jones takes his turn as dance emporium/gambling saloon owner T. William Stone, who becomes co-owner of a profitable mine after its owner is cheated by two no-good gamblers who continue to make trouble in Silver Creek. Includes *Gordon of Ghost City, Chapter 3: Trapped.*
VHS: S33282. $14.98.
Nick Grinde, USA, 1935, 83 mins.

The Stranger Wore a Gun
Shot in 3-D, this western stars Randolph Scott, who is in the service of a cold-blooded bandit and must take part in a hold up before returning to his former life. The great secondary cast includes Ernest Borgnine, Lee Marvin, Claire Trevor and Joan Weldon.
VHS: S17031. $19.95.
Andre de Toth, USA, 1953, 83 mins.

Sunset Range
Hoot Gibson stars as a foreman on a beautiful ranch known as Sunset Range. He and his longtime cowboy buddy raise money so they can buy the ranch but are shocked to find out it's been sold to another party—who happens to be a woman. Gibson's humorous western persona and an exciting climax make this one of the best "B" westerns. With Mary Doran, James Eagles, Walter McGrail and John Elliot.
VHS: S32589. $24.95.
Ray McCarey, USA, 1935, 53 mins.

Support Your Local Gunfighter
Talented genre director Burt Kennedy directs this amiable and shrewd western about an amoral con man (James Garner) who manipulates a mining dispute by passing off a crazed reprobate (Jack Elman) as a notorious killer. The rogues list of character actors includes Joan Blondell, Harry Morgan, Marie Windsor and Dub Taylor.
VHS: S18671. $19.98.
Burt Kennedy, USA, 1971, 92 mins.

The Tall Men
Clark Gable and Cameron Mitchell sign on to drive cattle for Robert Ryan not knowing how much trouble is waiting for them along the trail. Bad weather, unfriendly native Americans and the presence of Jane Russell, in color, make for an increase of stress in the Old West.
VHS: S06196. $19.98.
Raoul Walsh, USA, 1955, 122 mins.

The Telegraph Trail
As a heroic government scout, a young John Wayne and his valued steed, the white miracle horse Duke, must combat crooked traders and Native Americans in this early classic western. Movies like these turned the young actor into an international star.
VHS: S20952. $19.98.
Tenny Wright, USA, 1933, 54 mins.

Ten Wanted Men
Not to be confused with *Ten Tall Men* or *Ten Little Indians*, this is a Randolph Scott western. He plays a rancher who has built a vast empire in Arizona and doesn't want trouble. Villain Richard Boone doesn't have the same notions. With Jocelyn Brando, Skip Homeier, Alfonso Bedoya and Leo Gordon. In color.
VHS: S08705. $14.97.
H. Bruce Humberstone, USA, 1955, 80 mins.

Terror in a Texas Town
Sterling Hayden turns in a brilliant performance as a Swedish seaman determined to hunt down the man who murdered his father in this compelling and powerful western.
VHS: S31223. $14.95.
Joseph H. Lewis, USA, 1958, 80 mins.

Texas Across the River
A genre-defying Western about the epic adventures of three outsiders. A Southern aristocrat (Rosemary Forsyth) on the run from the law crosses paths with two hip "revolutionaries," Sam Hollis (Dean Martin) and his Indian guide (Joey Bishop), as they try to provide safe passage for guns through rugged Comanche territory. With Alain Delon, Rina Marquand, Peter Graves and Andrew Prine.
VHS: S19516. $14.98.
Laser: Letterboxed. LD74928. $34.98.
Michael Gordon, USA, 1966, 101 mins.

Texas Cyclone
An early John Wayne effort casts the Duke as a quiet loner who teams with a mysterious figure to restore peace and order in a frontier community where a widow is besieged by a ruthless gang. With Tim McCoy, Shirley Grey and Wheeler Oakman.
VHS: S18496. $14.95.
David Ross Lederman, USA, 1932, 58 mins.

There Was a Crooked Man

Kirk Douglas and Henry Fonda star in this comic western adventure about hidden treasure and life in an 1880 territorial prison. Prisoner Douglas was used to running things until Fonda, the strict new warden arrived. Douglas then decides the time is right to plan an escape. Fellow prisoners include Warren Oates, Hume Cronyn, John Randolph, Michael Blodgett, C.K. Yang and Burgess Meredith as the Missouri Kid.
VHS: S16286. $14.95.
Laser: Letterboxed. **LD71808. $39.98.**
Joseph L. Mankiewicz, USA, 1970, 126 mins.

They Came to Cordura

Gary Cooper is assigned to find some heroes in a raid on Pancho Villa that will be given medals in Washington. He selects Van Heflin, Richard Conte, Michael Callan, Dick York and Tab Hunter to be decorated. Rita Hayworth is along to be decorative.
Laser: CLV. **LD71752. $29.98.**
Robert Rossen, USA, 1959, 123 mins.

They Died with Their Boots On

Errol Flynn is a natural choice for the role of the flamboyant George Armstrong Custer, whose military career came to an abrupt halt during the Battle of Little Big Horn in 1876. The Hollywood version may be historically dubious but it does nothing to tarnish the Custer legend. Olivia de Havilland makes her eighth and final screen appearance with Flynn, as Custer's devoted wife Libbie. With Arthur Kennedy, Charley Grapewin, Gene Lockhart and Anthony Quinn as Chief Crazy Horse.
VHS: S01867. $19.95.
Laser: LD71692. $39.98.
Raoul Walsh, USA, 1942, 140 mins.

The Tin Star

Anthony Perkins plays an inexperienced sheriff, a bit too young, who is assisted in taming a wild town by veteran lawman-turned-bounty hunter Henry Fonda.
VHS: S02791. $14.95.
Laser: LD75275. $34.98.
Anthony Mann, USA, 1957, 93 mins.

To the Last Man

A "B" movie classic. A longstanding feud between two frontier families heats up when one clan undertakes cattle rustling. With a host of talent: Randolph Scott, Shirley Temple, Noah Beery Sr., Buster Crabbe and Barton MacLane.
VHS: S04117. $29.95.
Henry Hathaway, USA, 1933, 70 mins.

The Tollgate

When Black Deering (William S. Hart) and his gang are ambushed during a daring train holdup, he learns his betrayer was one of his own men, Jordan (Joseph Singleton), whose blood money has bought him a parlor of gambling and prostitution. Upon escaping from the authorities, Deering flees into the wilderness and finds shelter in the home of an abandoned woman (Anna Q. Nilsson). There, the vengeful gunfighter finds the possibility of redemption, but his happiness is short-lived when two posses—one led by the murderous Jordan, the other by a local sheriff—converge upon the isolated cabin. With *His Bitter Pill* (1916, 20 mins), Mack Sennett's famous parody of Hart in which the noble cowboy is viciously lampooned by Mack Swain *(The Gold Rush)*.
VHS: S34317. $24.95.
Lambert Hillyer, USA, 1920, 73 mins.

Tomahawk

This Western adventure stars Van Heflin as legendary Indian sympathizer, Jim Bridger. Features strong action and first-rate acting. With Yvonne DeCarlo and Alex Nicol.
VHS: S34580. $14.98.
George Sherman, USA, 1951, 82 mins.

Tombstone

Kurt Russell, Charlton Heston and Val Kilmer are just some of the stars featured in this blockbuster Western. Its a classic tale of good guys and bad guys fighting it out on the lonely American frontier. Justice must be defended at all costs.
VHS: S21106. $19.95.
Laser: Widescreen. **LD74634. $49.99.**
George P. Kosmatis, USA, 1993, 130 mins.

True Grit

John Wayne won an Oscar for his portrayal of a one-eyed, overweight lawman named Rooster Cogburn. He is recruited by a tenacious teenage girl to find the killer of her father. Glen Campbell is the handsome Texas Ranger after the same gang. With Robert Duvall, Dennis Hopper, Jeff Corey and Kim Darby as Mattie Ross.
VHS: S05097. $14.95.
Laser: LD75393. $35.98.
Henry Hathaway, USA, 1969, 128 mins.

Tumbleweeds

One of the screen's most famous Westerns, in which William S. Hart plays a rancher who decides to try his luck when the Cherokee strip opens in 1889. He would like to take along the beautiful Barbara Bedford, if she were willing to settle down and become his wife. This version includes an eight-minute introduction by Hart that was added to the film with its reissue in 1939.
VHS: S16503. $24.95.
King Baggot, USA, 1925, 81 mins.

Under California Stars

Roy Rogers and Trigger star in this color Western with music and action. A group of horse thieves figure they can make more money by stealing one horse if his name is Trigger. Roy and the rest of the folks at the Double R Ranch disagree. With Andy Devine and Jane Frazee.
VHS: S05490. $19.95.
William Witney, USA, 1948, 71 mins.

Utah

Ranch foreman Roy Rogers and neighbor rancher George "Gabby" Hayes try to convince Dale Evans to keep the Utah ranch she inherited. But Dale wants to sell the ranch in order to get the money she needs to keep her musical comedy show open in Chicago. Rare uncut version.
VHS: S34169. $19.95.
John English, USA, 1945, 78 mins.

Valdez Is Coming

A moody western shot in Spain with Burt Lancaster as a victimized Mexican-American lawman who stages a violent crusade against the dictatorial land baron and gunrunner (Jon Cypher) in his quest for justice and redemption. With Susan Clark, Barton Heyman and Richard Jordan.
VHS: S18672. $19.98.
Edwin Sherin, USA, 1971, 90 mins.

Vengeance Valley

Burt Lancaster and Robert Walker are rivals who can't get along in the open spaces of the Old West. They fight indoors as well. Joanne Dru and Sally Forrest are their womenfolk. Hugh O'Brian and John Ireland play supporting hombres. Bring bullets.
VHS: S05071. $29.95.
Richard Thorpe, USA, 1951, 83 mins.

Vera Cruz

This exciting Western, set in 1860 Mexico, features Gary Cooper and Burt Lancaster involved in a plot to overthrow Emperor Maximilian. A lively and entertaining melodrama, *Vera Cruz* is highlighted by the use of many unusual locations, and its alternating touches of comedy and suspense. Also starring Cesar Romero, Ernest Borgnine, and Charles Bronson. VHS letterboxed.
VHS: S01870. $19.98.
Laser: LD72158. $34.98.
Robert Aldrich, USA, 1953, 94 mins.

The Villain

In this Road Runner-like western, Kirk Douglas is an incompetent outlaw impersonating the human form of Wile E. Coyote, as director Hal Needham attempts to transform the hapless cartoon figure into the stylized landscapes of the American West. With Ann-Margret, Arnold Schwarzenegger, Paul Lynde, Ruth Buzzi and Strother Martin.
VHS: S17032. $19.95.
Hal Needham, USA, 1979, 89 mins.

The Violent Men

Adapted from Donald Hamilton's novel, this dark Western pits evil land baron Edward G. Robinson against the innocent settlers. An excellent cast includes Barbara Stanwyck, Glenn Ford and Brian Keith.
VHS: S17030. $19.95.
Rudolph Mate, USA, 1955, 96 mins.

Virginia City

Hollywood's greatest stars headline this epic Civil War Western. Based on the true story about a group of Southern sympathizers out to smuggle five million dollars in gold from Nevada and bring the loot to Virginia, this swiftly paced yarn boasts spectacular action sequences, sweeping panoramas and a rousing Max Steiner score. Miriam Hopkins is the dance hall girl who helps the rebels set up her Yankee boyfriend. This was Humphrey Bogart and Errol Flynn's only film together. Also stars Randolph Scott.
VHS: S16099. $19.98.
Michael Curtiz, USA, 1940, 121 mins.

The Virginian

Joel McCrea, Brian Donlevy and Sonny Tufts star in this remake of a classic silent-era Western. A Wild West cowboy (McCrea) marries a Wyoming schoolteacher he has rescued from a villainous cattle rustler. When the cowboy is confronted by thieves and finds that he has been betrayed by his closest friend, he knows he must fight for his honor, even if it means losing his new bride. Based on the novel by Owen Wister.
VHS: S27672. $14.98.
Stuart Gilmore, USA, 1946, 90 mins.

Walk the Proud Land

Audie Murphy stars as an Indian agent sent to an Apache reservation in Arizona in 1874 to take over the Army's position. He tries to install self-government for the Apaches and eventually becomes the first white man to persuade Geromino to surrender. Co-starring Anne Bancroft, Pat Crowley, Charles Drake and Jay Silverheels.
VHS: S31393. $14.98.
Jesse Hibbs, USA, 1956, 88 mins.

Wanda Nevada

Brooke Shields stars as a young, precocious and beautiful orphan who sets her sights on a gambler (Peter Fonda) and a fortune in gold. Features a cameo appearance by Henry Fonda in his only screen pairing with his son. Letterboxed.
VHS: S32678. $14.95.
Peter Fonda, USA, 1979, 105 mins.

War Arrow

Jeff Chandler must end the Kiowa uprisings in Texas, placing him in direct conflict with the officer in charge, John McIntire. There is another element to this rivalry. Maureen O'Hara's husband is a missing cavalry officer, whose absence ultimately places her in a love triangle between these two. It's a western based on an actual historical incident.
VHS: S23676. $14.98.
George Sherman, USA, 1953, 79 mins.

War Wagon

Plenty of action and laughs as John Wayne and Kirk Douglas team up to capture a stagecoach loaded with gold bullion.
VHS: S03535. $14.98.
Burt Kennedy, USA, 1967, 101 mins.

Warlock

Well-paced Western features Richard Widmark, Henry Fonda and Anthony Quinn. A marshal cleans up a town in this unusual turn by Edward Dmytryk.
VHS: S06519. $19.98.
Laser: LD75281. $34.98.
Edward Dmytryk, USA, 1959, 121 mins.

West of the Divide

John Wayne is on the trail of his father's murderer. This time the Duke also searches for his baby brother, who has been missing since dad took the fatal bullet.
VHS: S12748. $19.98.
Robert North Bradbury, USA, 1934, 54 mins.

Western Classics Collection: Vengeance Valley and The Big Trees

Burt Lancaster stars as a heroic man who atones for all the wrongs committed by his brother, in *Vengeance Valley*. Robert Walker and Joanne Dru are also featured in this adult melodrama. In *The Big Trees*, Kirk Douglas is determined to make a killing by cutting the trees on land settled by Quakers. Though they object, he schemes to cheat them of their home. Patrice Wymore and Edgar Buchanan also star.
Laser: LD75938. $69.95.
Richard Thorpe/Felix E. Feist, USA, 1952/1951, 83/89 mins.

Wheel of Fortune

Before there was Vanna White, John Wayne took a spin at being a lawyer who gambled he could uncover the killer of a good friend and put an end to political corruption in Temple City. All the Duke needed was 83 minutes. With Frances Dee, Ward Bond and Wallace Ford. B&W.
VHS: S04893. $19.95.
John H. Auer, USA, 1941, 83 mins.

When the Legends Die

A powerful contemporary Western drama about an aging rodeo cowboy (Richard Widmark) training a young American Indian protege (Frederic Forrest). Excellent performances and exciting rodeo action. With Luana Anders, Vito Scotti and Herbert Nelson. An impressive debut by director Stuart Miller.
VHS: S07148. $19.98.
Stuart Millar, USA, 1972, 105 mins.

Whirlwind Raiders

Highlighted by spectacular horse stunts, singing and dancing cowboys and blazing six-shooter action, *Whirlwind Raiders* is a winning installment from one of the most popular and longest-running Western series ever. Matinee idol Charles Starrett stars as masked avenger The Durango Kid and his alter-ego Steve Lanning, a former Texas Ranger who comes to the aid of the citizens of Indian Springs when they are harrassed by a group calling themselves the "Texas State Police." With Smiley Burnette.
VHS: S30772. $19.95.
Vernon Keays, USA, 1948, 54 mins.

White Buffalo

Charles Bronson stars as Wild Bill Hickok in this western adventure about an arduous hunt for a great white buffalo. Will Sampson co-stars as Chief Crazy Horse—or is it Capt. Ahab, as there are certain similarities to a certain novel by Herman Melville. With Kim Novak, Jack Warden, Slim Pickens, Clint Walker and John Carradine. Buffalo designed by the same guy who built King Kong, in the remake.
VHS: S12529. $19.98.
J. Lee Thompson, USA, 1977, 97 mins.

White Commanche

A pre-Kirk William Shatner delights us in this spaghetti western with a wonderful dual role as half-breed brothers (one good, one bad) who are mixed up in a love triangle. With Joseph Cotten and Perla Cristal. Dubbed in English.
VHS: S32593. $24.95.
Joseph Briz/Gilbert L. Kay, Spain/USA, 1967, 92 mins.

Wild Bill

Jeff Bridges and Ellen Barkin star in this Western based on the legendary Wild Bill Hickok. It's a tale of an unmatched gunfighter who singlehandedly stood for justice in a lawless landscape. John Hurt and Keith Carradine are also featured. VHS letterboxed.
VHS: S27690. $14.95.
Laser: LD75565. $34.99.
Walter Hill, USA, 1995, 98 mins.

Wild West

This offbeat comedy follows an urban cowboy and his crew on the perilous road to country and western stardom. They meet a smart, sultry singer with a past. Suddenly, success seems within their grasp. There may even be a romance in the works. Songs from Garth Brooks and Dwight Yokum are included.
VHS: S24957. $92.99.
Laser: LD75285. $34.98.
David Attwood, USA, 1994, 85 mins.

Will Penny

One of the last great Westerns, with unusually deep characterization. Charlton Heston is the tired cowboy who is staked out to die in the desert by a gang of outlaws. Moments before death, he is taken in by a young frontier woman (Joan Hackett) who is heading west with her young son to join her husband. As she nurses him back to health, he has two problems to deal with: he is madly in love with another man's wife and the outlaw gang is on its way to finish him off. With Donald Pleasence, Lee Majors, Bruce Dern.
VHS: S09569. $19.95.
Laser: LD75286. $34.98.
Tom Gries, USA, 1968, 109 mins.

Winchester '73

A major western with James Stewart involved in hunting down a man and his stolen gun through a series of inter-related episodes. With a great shootout among the hills at the end, Leonard Maltin credits this film with reviving the popularity of Westerns during the 1950's. With Shelley Winters, Dan Duryea.
VHS: S06819. $14.98.
Anthony Mann, USA, 1950, 92 mins.

Winds of the Wasteland

John Wayne appears in this early Western, which was made before he became one of the most popular screen cowboys ever known. 1936, 54 mins.
VHS: S26685. $19.95.

Woman of the Town

Sheriff Bat Masterson cleans up Dodge City with his toughness and grit. The only crime he can't stop is letting dance hall belle Dora Hand steal his heart. With Claire Trevor and Barry Sullivan.
VHS: S14754. $19.95.
George Archainbaud, USA, 1943, 90 mins.

Wyatt Earp

Kevin Costner is the law man who tamed the West, with Dennis Quaid as the cadaverous Doc Holliday. This film offers a dark view of the most metaphysical of American landscapes, the enduring frontier. There men must rely on their own inner strength to define what's right and wrong before they fight for it. Gene Hackman co-stars.
VHS: S22528. $24.98.
Laser: LD74610. $44.98.
Lawrence Kasdan, USA, 1994, 191 mins.

Young Guns

The legend of William H. Bonney, alias Billy the Kid, notorious back-shooter and cult western figure, gets still another shot at cinematic immortality. Emilio Estevez may just be the definitive Billy the Kid. The Lincoln County War is re-fought by juvenile delinquents with guns. With Charlie Sheen, Keifer Sutherland, Lou Diamond Phillips and Brian Keith.
VHS: S10082. $19.95.
Christopher Cain, USA, 1988, 102 mins.

The Young Land

Pat Wayne, Yvonne Craig, Dan O'Herlihy, Ken Curtis and a young Dennis Hopper are all featured in this western about a racist town. Hopper is a young bully who murders a Mexican. Now a sheriff and a judge must convince opposing sides that they will both be served justly by the American legal system.
VHS: S23907. $19.95.
Ted Tetzlaff, USA, 1959, 89 mins.

Yuma

Clint Walker stars in this made-for-TV western as an honest sheriff whose reputation is tarnished by unknown plotters. The always tall-in-the-saddle Walker fights to restore law and order and his good name. With Barry Sullivan, Edgar Buchanan, Kathryn Hays and Morgan Woodward.
VHS: S08299. $19.98.
Ted Post, USA, 1970, 73 mins.

THE AMERICAN WEST

Adventures of the Old West

This six-volume series, hosted by Kris Kristofferson, tells the story of the frontier through archival footage, rare photos, personal diaries, letters, official documents and first hand accounts. Original songs by Kristofferson enliven this engaging exploration of America's past. Each title is 50 mins.
Frontier Justice the Law and the Lawless.
VHS: S22524. $19.98.
Great Chiefs at the Crossroads.
VHS: S22526. $19.98.
Pioneers and the Promised Land.
VHS: S22525. $19.98.
Scouts in the Wilderness.
VHS: S22521. $19.98.
Texas Cowboys and the Trail Drives.
VHS: S22522. $19.98.
The 49ers and the California Gold Rush.
VHS: S22523. $19.98.
Gift Box Set.
VHS: S22527. $99.98.

The Best of the Real West Complete Set

Kenny Rogers is host for this documentary series that combines original footage, authentic diaries, paintings, photos, and expert commentary to reawaken the adventure of that fabled landscape. *Wild Bill, The Alamo, Texas Rangers, Wild Women* and *Sitting Bull* are the five topics covered in depth by this collection. Each video is 50 mins.
VHS: S22535. $59.95.

Centennial

A stunning panorama of the great saga of the American West based on the novel by James A. Michener. Spanning 200 years, this acclaimed 1978 mini-series features vivid, unforgettable characters-Native Americans, traders, trappers, gold seekers, homesteaders, ranchers, hunters, soldiers, lawmen, outlaws, politicians and conservationists—all caught up in the dramatic events and violent conflicts that shaped the destiny of the West. Starring Richard Chamberlain, Robert Conrad, Raymond Burr and Sally Kellerman. 12 tapes. 20 hours, 58 mins.
VHS: S32397. $129.98.

Custer's Last Trooper

This documentary depicts the drama of the Battle of Little Big Horn and the life of General Armstrong Custer. Authentic artifacts, photos and diary excerpts punctuate this historical essay. 1990, 47 mins.
VHS: S16325. $24.95.

Donner Pass: The Road to Survival

A dramatic re-creation of one of the most horrifying episodes from the American frontier: In 1846, a party of American settlers moving from Illinois to California are reduced to cannibalism when they're decimated by blinding snow storms and other natural disasters. With Robert Fuller, Andrew Prine, Michael Callan and John Anderson.
VHS: S17967. $19.95.
James L. Conway, USA, 1978, 100 mins.

Elko: The Cowboy Gathering

Baxter Black, Waddy Mitchell, Riders in the Sky…they're all here to share their love of the cowboy lifestyle. Music and cowboy poetry make this an enjoyable video with great laughs. 60 mins.
VHS: S23124. $19.95.

A Few MenF Well-Conducted: The George Rogers Clark Story

This is the story of George Rogers Clark and his courageous frontiersmen, who fought on the Kentucky and Illinois frontier during the American Revolution. 23 mins.
VHS: S06676. $29.95.

Frontier Heritage

James Whitmore narrates this journey through the wilderness telling the story of the people who conquered America's wild frontiers and started to create a new life in these challenging times.
VHS: S05246. $39.95.

Frontier Progress

James Whitmore is the narrator for this second in a two-part look at the building of America in the great western wilderness, a fascinating look at the courage, strength and perseverance of the people who built a nation.
VHS: S05247. $39.95.

Goldrush Country

Hugh O'Brian narrates this documentary about the lure of gold in the American frontier. Period drawings and engravings help illustrate this historical account of the westward expansion of the nation. 18 mins.
VHS: S23730. $49.95.

The Great West Collection

From Texas to Hawaii, Arizona to Canada, the five-part *Great West Collection* explores a prominent American tradition.
Great Ranches of the West. Join Michael Martin Murphey for a visit to four of the largest and oldest family-owned ranches in America. Includes a stop at *Eaton's Dude Ranch*, the original 1879 "Dude ranch". 60 mins.
VHS: S16479. $19.95.
My Heroes Have Always Been Cowboys. Working cattle by day and singing around a campfire at night, Waylon Jennings leads this old fashioned roundup in West Texas. A look at the rugged life of real cowboys on a modern ranch against the background of great songs, including *Sweet Mother Texas, A Long Time Ago, I've Always Been Crazy* and *Last Cowboy Song*. 60 mins.
VHS: S16478. $19.95.
Ranch Album. Portraying a way of life that is rooted in hard work, family, a love of nature and a hunger for independence, the *Ranch Album* celebrates the demanding world of ranching—season by season, and generation by generation. 60 mins.
VHS: S16477. $19.95.
The Last Cowboys. Journey to the ranges of Utah and Nevada to discover the true-life legend of the cowboy. At a modern rodeo, the vital skills of yesterday's cowboys are transformed into a popular sport. Includes a visit to Robbers Roost Ranch, where Butch Cassidy, the Sundance Kid and the Hole in the Wall Gang all laid their hats.
VHS: S16476. $19.95.
The Working Cowboy—In Search of the Cowboy Song. Country musician, cowboy poet and rancher Ian Tyson has always found inspiration in the cowboy's life. His search for the cowboy song drives him to many of Canada's great ranches, underscoring the powerful link between true country living and Western music. 60 mins.
VHS: S16480. $19.95.

How the West Was Lost

This compelling documentary series tells the epic story of the struggle over the American West. Witness the tragic plight of five Native American nations: The Navajo, Nez Perce, Apache, Cheyenne and Lakota. 60-100 mins.
Vol. 1: Clash of Cultures/I Will Fight No More Forever.
VHS: S21801. $29.95.
Vol. 2: Always the Enemy/The Only Good Indian Is a Dead Indian.
VHS: S21802. $29.95.
Vol. 3: A Good Day to Die/Kill the Indian, Save the Man.
VHS: S21803. $29.95.
How the West Was Lost, Set.
VHS: S22002. $79.96.

How The West Was Lost II

The story of the American West is compellingly told in this continuation of the documentary series from the *Discovery Channel*. Two distinct cultures fought for more than just territory. For Native Americans it was a struggle to survive. Four-volume set, each 90 mins.

VHS: S26048. $79.95.

Life and Times of Wyatt Earp

This documentary tells the story of the gambler, bounty hunter, lawman, and Indian fighter who became an American folk hero. 52 mins.

VHS: S20488. $9.95.

Opening the West (1860-1900)

Reconstruction and *Westward Expansion* are the themes here following President Lincoln's courageous efforts to reunite the nation after the bloody fratricide of the Civil War. With the settlement of the lands beyond the Mississippi, the young nation is well on its way toward maturity and a place among the leading countries of the world.

VHS: S03974. $64.95.

Outlaws: The Ten Most Wanted

Featured in the program *The Real West*, this documentary looks at the myth and culture of the outlaw. Jesse James, Cole Younger and the rest of the villains are examined, with a special interest in explaining their hold on popular American culture. 60 mins.

VHS: S19724. $19.95.

The Real West

An impressionistic look at the life, times and landscape of the American west, examining the intertwining myths, language, culture and texture of the American frontier. Narrated by Gary Cooper. "A fascinatingly authentic look at the West" (*New York Times*). 60 mins.

VHS: S19247. $19.95.

The Untold West

The Wild West is a source of enduring myths and legends that go to the heart of what it is to be an American. But it was also a place where real people, with all their weaknesses and foibles, lived and died. In this series the truth about a number of formerly taboo topics finally comes to light.

Hot on the Trail. The Wild West was home to innumerable tales of passion and desire. Tobacco was packaged with "girlie cards" to use a vice to sell another vice. Even the infamous Calamity Jane had her weaknesses, blazing a trail across 12 husbands. 60 mins.

VHS: S20955. $14.98.

Outlaws, Rebels and Rogues. Were the West's most notorious bad guys really as tough as they seemed? Or were these desperados just desperate for attention, especially from the press? This humorous look at outlaws includes a close look at the most famous of them all, Billy the Kid. 60 mins.

VHS: S20956. $14.98.

The Black West. It's a little known fact, but Afro-American pioneers, farmers, entrepeneurs, cowboys and even outlaws all played a part in the exploration of the Wild West. Will Rogers and Teddy Roosevelt are just some of the white Americans who learned from these nearly forgotten settlers. 60 mins.

VHS: S20957. $14.98.

The Complete Set.

VHS: S20958. $19.98.

The Way West

Ric Burns crafted this six-hour series that chronicles the story of the West from the San Francisco Gold Rush to the Battle of Wounded Knee. Stunning photos, along with paintings, maps and motion pictures, enliven this historic series. Russell Baker narrates and a host of other voices are featured, including F. Murray Abraham, Graham Greene, Wes Studi, Eli Wallach and many others. Four 90-minute videocassettes.

VHS: S24493. $69.95.

The West

Ken Burns' 12½ hour epic saga of the personal triumphs and tragedies involved in the expansion of the U.S. West. This nine-volume set, narrated by Peter Coyote, begins before European settlement and continues into the 20th century, overturning old stereotypes and discovering new personalities. Individual episodes include *The People* (82 mins.), *Empire upon the Trails* (84 mins.), *The Speck of the Future* (84 mins.), *Death Runes Riot* (84 mins.), *The Grandest Enterprise Under God* (84 mins), *Fight No More* (85 mins.), *The Geography of Hope* (84 mins.), *Ghost Dance* (58 mins.) and *One Sky Above Us* (62 mins.).

VHS: S28618. $149.98.

Stephen Ives, USA, 1996

West of the Imagination

The West of awesome landscape and fearsome dangers, of Indians, pioneers, outlaws, cowboys, tradesmen, explorers…this six-volume set explores the sweeping story of the American West as seen through the eyes of its mythmakers and mythologizers—the West of the historians with paintbrush, explorers with camera.

Enduring Dreams. The West of our own century, of Grant Wood, Thomas Hart Benton, and the Dust Bowl.

VHS: S05567. $29.95.

Images of Glory. Nature's grandeur, a thirst for adventure, the last Indian wars—the West continued to beckon.

VHS: S05564. $29.95.

Play the Legend. The West of the cowboy stars and circus barkers, of songsmiths and rodeo artists.

VHS: S05566. $29.95.

The Romantic Horizon. The magical landscapes, noble savages and half-wild mountain men of the new continent.

VHS: S05562. $29.95.

The Wild Riders. The working cowboy and how he became a hero of American folklore.

VHS: S05565. $29.95.

West of the Imagination, Complete. The complete six-volume set of *West of the Imagination*.

VHS: S05568. $169.00.

Wyatt Earp: Justice at the OK Corral

The myths, legends and realities of the Old West come alive in the Real West with Kenny Rogers as the narrator. Through original footage, authentic diaries, paintings, photos and expert commentary, this video will breathe new life into the legend of Wyatt Earp. The two-tape set also includes the documentary *Dodge City*. Both tapes are 50 mins.

VHS: S21547. $19.95.

literature on screen

1984
An extraordinary film version of George Orwell's masterpiece starring John Hurt and Richard Burton. A story of impossible love and tragic betrayal set in the twisted world of *Nineteen Eighty-Four*. Music by Dominic Muldowney and the Eurythmics.
VHS: S00002. $14.95.
Michael Radford, Great Britain, 1984, 115 mins.

Almos' a Man
Based on the short story by Richard Wright, and starring LeVar Burton, Madge Sinclair, Robert Dogui. From American Short Story Series.
VHS: S01956. $24.95.
Stan Lathan, USA, 52 mins.

Anais Observed
Anais Nin's surrealistic novels, extensive diaries and deep friendships were all formed at the heart of a developing modern consciousness. Her distinct female persona is especially noteworthy for its overall embrace of human diversity. This portrait captures her life and philosophy. D.H. Lawrence, Otto Rank, Henry Miller, Kenneth Anger and Maya Deren are just some of the personalities captured alongside this singular literary artist.
VHS: S26714. $29.95.

Anna Karenina
Based on Tolstoy's beloved 1870 novel, this Russian production of the classic tale of tragic passion and human morality traces the paths chosen by two different people, Anna and Vronsky. Letterboxed. With Tatyana Samoylova, Nikolai Gritsenko and Vasili Lanovoi. Russian with English subtitles.
VHS: S31780. $19.98.
Alexander Zarkhi, Russia, 1967, 103 mins.

The Ballads of Madison County
Robert James Waller's best-selling book, *The Bridges of Madison County*, was the inspiration for this romantic journey. The author introduces you to the landscape and the people of Madison County in both word and song, while interviews reveal the man behind the writer.
VHS: S20838. $14.98.

Barn Burning
Based on the short story by William Faulkner, with a script by Horton Foote, and starring Tommy Lee Jones and Diane Kagan. From American Short Story Series.
VHS: S02133. $24.95.
Peter Werner, USA, 52 mins.

Bernice Bobs Her Hair
Based on the short story by F. Scott Fitzgerald, and featuring Shelley Duvall, Veronica Cartwright and Bud Cort. From American Short Story Series.
VHS: S02065. $24.95.
Joan Micklin Silver, USA, 52 mins.

The Black Unicorn: Dudley Randall and the Broadside Press
Documentary chronicles the life and literary career of a major black American poet, Dudley Randall, the poet laureate of Detroit and publisher/editor of Broadside Press. Interviews with other black poets reveal the extent of Randall's influence on the development of African-American literature. Public performance rights included.
VHS: S33384. $99.95.
Melba Joyce Boyd, USA, 1996, 54 mins.

The Blue Men
Adapted from the short story by Joy Williams, this haunting tale of adolescent isolation features a young boy's experiences while staying with his grandmother on a small summer island. The narrative touches on the need for the boy and his grandmother to come to terms with their past and deal with tragedy. With Estelle Parsons. 45 mins.
VHS: S20387. $24.95.

A Brighter Garden
Emily Dickinson's poems for each of Nature's seasons are read by actress Frances Sternhagen. "Summer" includes the famed "I'm Nobody! Who are you?" Tasha Tudor's cameo watercolor paintings reflect her deep appreciation of Dickinson's 19th century New England. A mutual love of nature is perfectly reflected in Tudor's snowy winter landscapes, the brighter shades of spring and fall, and even moonlit nights.
VHS: S16336. $44.95.

The Cask of Amontillado
Insults between Italian noblemen lead into this charming tale. Montresor seeks revenge on Fortunato by playing on his friend's vanity and love of wine. Soon Fortunato finds himself deep underground in Montresor's cellar in search of the prized amontillado wine. Based on the story by Edgar Allan Poe. 18 mins.
VHS: S23496. $79.95.

Classic Books on Video
A series of introductions to great works of literature. Each tape contains a dramatization of key scenes from the novel, followed by an on-screen discussion and analysis of the meaning and context of the entire work. Each tape is 40 mins.
Crime and Punishment.
VHS: S06276. $19.99.
Hamlet.
VHS: S06280. $19.99.
The Iliad.
VHS: S06278. $19.99.
The Scarlet Letter.
VHS: S06277. $19.99.
Thomas Jefferson.
VHS: S06281. $19.99.

Classic Literary Stories, Vol. 1
All The Troubles of the World, from a story by Isaac Asimov, exploring the implications of a world served by an all-knowing, benevolent computer, and *The Bear*, from a story by William Faulkner, based on the second of his short story versions in which a boy confronts the legend and finds the truth of an old bear. 37 mins.
VHS: S05813. $19.95.

Classic Literary Stories, Vol. 2
The Cask of Amontillado, based on a story by Edgar Allan Poe, one of the masterpieces of horror fiction, and *The Necklace*, based on a story by Guy de Maupassant, in which the borrowed necklace is lost, and the couple must mortgage the last ten years of their life. 40 mins.
VHS: S05814. $19.95.

Classic Literary Stories, Vol. 3
The Coup de Grace, based on a short story by Ambrose Bierce, as a Union soldier searches for his childhood friend amid the scattered dead and wounded, and Bierce's *An Occurrance at Owl Creek Bridge*, the great brooding story of a man's life going before him shortly before his execution. 19 mins.,
VHS: S05815. $19.95.

D.P.
Kurt Vonnegut Jr.'s short story is magically transformed in this Emmy Award-winning production starring Stan Shaw, Rosemary Leach and Julius Gordon. In the barren wasteland of post WW II Germany, a lonely black orphan discovers the only other black he has ever seen—the soldier—and dubs him "Papa." 60 mins.
VHS: S05321. $24.95.

Displaced Person
Based on the short story by Flannery O'Connor, with a script by Horton Foote. With Irene Worth, John Houseman, Shirley Stoler. From American Short Story Series.
VHS: S01958. $24.95.
Glenn Jordan, USA, 52 mins.

Ethan Frome
This adaptation of Edith Wharton's 1911 novel is set in the wintry landscapes of New England. Liam Neeson plays the simple farmer trapped in an emotionless marriage with a hypochondriac (Joan Allen). With Patricia Arquette, Tate Donovan as a sympathetic minister, and Katharine Houghton.
VHS: S19287. $19.95.
John Madden, USA, 1992, 99 mins.

The Glorious Romantics
British actress Jean Marsh (*Upstairs, Downstairs*) complements a wonderful ensemble of actors who portray the great poets Keats, Shelley and Byron, as well as other figures from the Romantic period. Excerpts from the poems "Ode on a Grecian Urn", "Love's Philosophy", "Ozymandias" and more are recited in this charming film. Great Britain, 90 mins.
VHS: S23605. $24.95.

Golden Honeymoon
Based on the short story by Ring Lardner, and starring James Whitmore, Teresa Wright and Stephen Elliot. From American Short Story Series.
VHS: S01959. $24.95.
Noel Black, USA, 52 mins.

Great Expectations
Dickens' novel about the powerful benefactor and the poor man whom he transforms into a respected London businessman is realized with a top cast including Michael York, Sarah Miles, James Mason, Anthony Quayle and Robert Morley.
VHS: S19029. $19.98.
Joseph Hardy, USA/Great Britain, 1974, 124 mins.

Greatest Man in the World
From the American Short Story Collection, an adaptation of James Thurber's story about a flyer who bests Lindbergh's non-stop flying record only to have the glory withheld until he can be transformed into the right kind of hero. With Brad Davis and Carol Kane.
VHS: S00528. $24.95.
Ralph Rosenblum, USA, 1980, 51 mins.

The Hitchhikers
An low-key adaptation of Eudora Welty's tale of the strange happenings in a gothic Southern town when the body of a hitchhiker is discovered brutally murdered on an isolated country road. "A gem of a film" (*Los Angeles Times*). With Richard Hatch and Patty Duke. 30 mins.
VHS: S20386. $24.95.

The Hollow Boy
American Playhouse's *American Short Story Collection* offers this story by Hortense Calisher. It's set in New York City during 1936. A young German immigrant and a Jewish neighbor attempt an uneasy friendship that is further complicated by the troubles of this time. 60 mins.
VHS: S21245. $24.95.

Hooray for Abbie!
This video tribute to Abbie Hoffman features the Abbie memorials from the Summer of 1989—The Palladium New York—plus the picnic at Washington's Crossing. There are fond remembrances by many friends, including Peter Yarrow, Paul Krassner, Allen Ginsberg, Norman Mailer, Jerry Rubin, The Fugs, Bobby Seale, Dave Dellinger, David Amram, Richie Havens and William Kunstler. Also features brother Jack Hoffman and his wife, Anita. 76 mins.
VHS: S21846. $39.95.

Horse Dealer's Daughter
A haunting film, based on the D.H. Lawrence short story, about a young woman's search for identity. Taken for granted by her brothers after the death of her father, she struggles with an uncertain future—discovering her own self worth through the eyes of the young town doctor. 30 mins.
VHS: S14261. $24.95.

I'm a Fool
Based on a short story by Sherwood Anderson, and starring Ron Howard, Santiago Gonzalez, Amy Irving. From American Short Story series.
VHS: S02134. $24.95.
Noel Black, USA, 52 mins.

Ishmael Reed
Mixing comic fantasy and social commentary, this novelist, poet, dramatist and publisher has broken new literary ground. Works from his *New and Selected Poems* and *The Terrible Threes* were read by him in Venice, California, on May 26, 1989. Lewis MacAdams conducted the interview. From the *Lannan Literary Videos* series. 60 mins.
VHS: S27122. $19.95.

Jilting of Granny Weatherall

Based on the short story by Katherine Anne Porter, and starring Geraldine Fitzgerald and Lois Smith. From American Short Story series.
VHS: S02003. $24.95.
Randa Haines, USA, 52 mins.

Jolly Corner

From the American Short Story collection: Henry James-based story concerns a haunted house where a man obsessed by his past is able to see what he might have been like had circumstances been different. With Salome Jens and Fritz Weaver.
VHS: S01538. $24.95.
Arthur Barron, USA, 1977, 43 mins.

Lawrenceville Stories: Prodigious Hickey

An adaptation of Owen Johnson's stories set in the Lawrence Prep School, originally published in *Saturday Evening Post*, centers on a charismatic young man, William Hicks, "The Prodigious Hickey," who devises a plan to restore the reputation of his undistinguished roommate. 60 mins.
VHS: S17168. $24.95.

Lawrenceville Stories: The Return of Hickey

The continuation of Owen Johnson's *Saturday Evening Post* stories set in the Lawrence Prep School finds Hickey returning to school following a suspension, where he's promptly entangled with a polished newcomer who threatens his reign as the local powerbroker. 60 mins.
VHS: S17169. $24.95.

Lawrenceville Stories: Beginning of the Firm

In this concluding episode of Owen Johnson's lyrical stories, Hickey reluctantly joins wits with his rival, "The Tennessee Shad," to impart lessons on humility and order to an insufferably wealthy freshman. "A beguiling, winsome exercise in nostalgic Americana" (*Washington Post*). 60 mins.
VHS: S17170. $24.95.

Lawrenceville Stories: 3-Pack Miniseries

All three stories, *Prodigious Hickey*, *Return of Hickey*, and *Beginning of the Firm*, collected in one package. 180 mins.
VHS: S17171. $64.95.

Love and OtherSorrows

Harold Brodkey's story is adapted for film with actors Christopher Collet and Elizabeth Franz in this episode from the American Playhouse American Short Story Collection. It's about a 16-year-old boy who, over the course of a summer in St. Louis, learns about love and life. This gentle film is entertaining for all ages. 60 mins.
VHS: S21244. $24.95.

The Man and the Snake/The Return

Two tales by Ambrose Bierce from the American Short Story collection which capture the mystery and mood of Bierce's writing. Oscar-winning cinematographer Sture Rydman shot both of the tales, which star John Fraser and Andre Morrell, and Peter Vaughan and Rosalie Crutchley. 60 mins.
VHS: S08791. $24.95.

The Mystery of Edwin Drood

Based on Charles Dickens' last, unfinished novel, this mystery film shows a corrupt Victorian world dominated by injustice and the resentment it breeds. Edwin Drood vanishes one stormy Christmas Eve. His betrothed, a chaste orphan, joins a choirmaster and a dark young stranger to find the missing man. In this battle between good and evil, passion, lust and intrigue become the weapons of choice.
VHS: S26401. $24.95.
Timothy Forder, Great Britain, 1993, 98 mins.

Norman and the Killer

Adapted from a short story by the American novelist, essayist and playwright Joyce Carol Oates, *Norman and the Killer* concerns the psychological and emotional trauma inflicted upon a young man and his efforts to reconcile his trauma and guilt when he confronts the man responsible for the crime against him. 30 mins.
VHS: S17023. $24.95.

Notes from a Lady at a Dinner Party

Based on a short story by the great American writer Bernard Malamud (*The Fixer*), David Angsten directed this elegant, sordid tale about the casual flirtation and deceptive planning when a young architect carries out his seduction of his mentor's wife at a dinner party. With Yvonne Suhor, Tim Gregory and John Kirk.
VHS: S16193. $29.95.
David Angsten, USA, 25 mins.

An Occurrence at Owl Creek Bridge

Award winning short film based on a story by Ambrose Bierce about the final moments of a man about to be hung for sabotage during the Civil War. Highly recommended.
VHS: S02247. $19.95.
Robert Enrico, France, 1962, 29 mins.

The Odyssey

This ambitious adaptation of Homer's epic is a four-hour mini-series produced by Francis Ford Coppola and Robert Halmi Sr. and starring Armand Assante, Greta Scacchi, Isabella Rossellini, Vanessa Williams, Eric Roberts, Christopher Lee, Geraldine Chaplin, Jeroen Krabbe and Bernadette Peters, complete with slick special effects by Jim Henson's Creature Shop and colossal props, including a to-scale Trojan horse. "A major entertainment event" (*The New York Times*).
VHS: S31747. $19.95.
Laser: LD76301. $49.98.
Andrei Konchalovsky, USA, 1997, 165 mins.

The Old Forest

A fascinating short film set in 1937 Memphis, *The Old Forest* focuses on the dilemma faced by a young gentleman when his engagement to a wealthy lady is threatened by the disappearance of a working class woman. A brilliant adaptation of author Peter Taylor's acclaimed short story. USA, 60 mins.
VHS: S15002. $29.95.

Open Window/Child's Play (Two from Saki)

Hector Hugh Munro was an imaginative writer who wrote some of our most moving and studied short stories under the pen name Saki. Film versions of two of his most famous stories are included in this collection: *The Open Window* and *Child's Play*. Combined running time 39 mins.
VHS: S14262. $24.95.

An Outpost of Progress

Joseph Conrad's short story is wonderfully adapted in this film version starring Simon MacCorkindale and Thomas Hellberg. From an African outpost, in a land still relatively untouched by Western ideals of civilization, a man must struggle with his own sense of morality and search for personal honor. 45 mins.
VHS: S29462. $24.95.

Parker Adderson Philosopher and The Music School

Based on short stories by Ambrose Bierce and John Updike; *Parker Adderson* stars Harris Yulin and was directed by Arthur Barron; *The Music School* stars Ron Weyand and was directed by John Korty. 52 mins. From American Short Story series.
VHS: S01539. $24.95.

Paul's Case

Based on the short story by Willa Cather, and starring Eric Roberts and Lindsay Crouse. From American Short Story series.
VHS: S01961. $24.95.
Lamont Johnson, USA, 52 mins.

Pigeon Feathers

From the pen of Pulitzer Prize-winning author John Updike comes the story of a young man's search through the questions of life and death, and the discovery of living. Christopher Collet and Carole McWilliams star as the mother and son returning to life on a farm and finding some answers to the paradox of living. From the American Short Story Collection. 55 mins.
VHS: S07539. $24.95.

Rappaccini's Daughter

Based on the short story by Nathaniel Hawthorne and starring Kristoffer Tabori and Kathleen Beller. From The American Short Story series.
VHS: S02004. $24.95.
Dezso Magyar, USA, 52 mins.

Revolt of Mother

Based on a short story by Mary E. Wilkins Freeman, the story of two hard-working people of the land, portrayed by Amy Madigan and Jay O. Sanders. While father is going to build a new barn, mother wants a new house—a simple story, set against the rustic backdrop of farming life in New England 1890, the story reveals much about love and respect and the often difficult times between those who strive to build a life together. From the American Short Story Collection. 55 mins.
VHS: S07538. $24.95.

A Rose for Emily

A sensitive treatment of William Faulkner's short story about a gilded, repressed young Southern woman, whose strict, suffocating father drove her into an ill-suited relationship with a Northern laborer. Narrated by John Houseman. With Anjelica Huston, John Randolph and John Carradine.
VHS: S14449. $29.95.

Rosencrantz & Guildenstern Are Dead

Two minor characters in Shakespeare's *Hamlet* are elevated to star status in the hilarious adaptation of Tom Stoppard's 1967 hit play. Stoppard makes his debut behind the camera directing a cast that includes Gary Oldman and Tim Roth in the title roles and Richard Dreyfuss as the Player King. Only 250 lines belong to the Bard; the rest is all Stoppard.
VHS: S14533. $19.99.
Tom Stoppard, Great Britain, 1990, 118 mins.

The Scarlet Letter

Nathanial Hawthorne's novel brings to life the attitudes and passions of 17th-century New England. His central character, Hester Prynne (Meg Foster), overcomes the stigma of adultery to emerge as the first great heroine in American literature. Hawthorne's themes—the nature of sin, social hypocrisy and community repression—still reverberate through American society. With John Heard and Kevin Conway. A PBS WGBH Boston Special. Two videos.
VHS: S33102. $39.95.
Rick Hauser, USA, 1982, 480 mins.

Sense and Sensibility

The literary inspiration of Jane Austen's first novel comes to the screen in this BBC adaptation. Elinor and Marianne are two sisters out to catch a husband. One is restrained and the other impetuous, yet both find that finding a suitable mate is not such an easy task to complete.
VHS: S04669. $24.98.
Rodney Bennett, Great Britain, 1986, 174 mins.

Soldier's Home

From the American Short Story Collection, an adaptation of Ernest Hemingway's story of a young man's return from World War I finding that one of the hardest parts of war is the coming home. With Richard Backus and Nancy Marchand.
VHS: S01227. $24.95.
Robert Young, USA, 1976, 41 mins.

Soldier's Story

A spellbinding mystery and drama about a black army attorney, sent to investigate a murder on a black army base. Starring Howard E. Rollins, music by Herbie Hancock, based on the play by Charles Fuller.
VHS: S01229. $14.95.
Norman Jewison, USA, 1984, 102 mins.

A Tale of Two Cities (Masterpiece Theatre)

A four-hour Masterpiece Theatre adaptation of Charles Dickens' novel about the events leading to the storming of the Bastille and the birth of the French Revolution. "The love is red hot, and the guillotine works" (*London Daily Mail*). With Sir John Mills.
VHS: S15107. $29.98.

To Build a Fire

Jack London's short story is brought to life as narrated by Orson Welles. A lone man travels through the wilderness in -75° weather. The stark realism of the images combines with the power of Orson Welles' reading. 56 mins.
VHS: S09399. $29.95.

Two Soldiers

Taken from *Arts and Entertainment Short Story Collection II*, this free spirited adaptation of a William Faulkner story concerns a naive, determined farm boy who leaves his rural surroundings to find the older brother who abandoned him to fight in World War II. "A rural view of American patriotism (that) provides entertaining viewing for general library audiences" (*Book List*). 30 mins.
VHS: S17024. $24.95.

Uncle Tom's Cabin

An exceptional cast highlights this television interpretation of Harriet Beecher Stowe's incendiary novel about pre-Civil War relations between blacks and whites, epitomized in the brutally racist actions of landowner Simon Legree (Edward Woodward). With Avery Brooks, Phylicia Rashad, Bruce Dern, Kate Burton, Paula Kelly and Kathryn Walker.
VHS: S19683. $9.98.
Stan Lathan, USA, 1987, 110 mins.

Under the Biltmore Clock

An American Playhouse presentation of the F. Scott Fitzgerald short story Myra Meets His Family. Sean Young plays a social-climbing flapper who is interested in a wealthy young man played by Lenny Von Dohlen. She is thrilled at his invitation to meet his family at the family estate until she meets his family. How she will react to this eccentric bunch could preclude her joining them on a regular basis.
VHS: S10991. $19.95.
Neal Miller, USA, 1985, 90 mins.

Women & Men—Stories of Seduction

Six big name Hollywood performers star in three separate stories of interaction between the sexes in this made-for-HBO anthology. Adapted from the works of Mary McCarthy, Ernest Hemingway, and Dorothy Parker and directed by Ken Russell, Tony Richardson, and Frederic Raphael. Cast includes James Woods, Melanie Griffith, Beau Bridges, Elizabeth McGovern, Molly Ringwald and Peter Weller. Music by Marvin Hamlisch. USA, 1990, 90 mins.

VHS: S13300. $19.95.

Wuthering Heights

The tempestuous romance of Heathcliff and Cathy on the Yorkshire landscape is once again the subject for a filmed adaptation of the Emily Bronte novel. Timothy Dalton and Anna Calder-Marshall are the ill-fated lovers. Filmed on location with a cast that includes Harry Andrews, Ian Ogilvy, Hugh Griffith and Julian Glover.

VHS: S03002. $19.99.

Robert Fuest, Great Britain, 1970, 105 mins.

A Year in Provence

Adapted from Peter Mayle's international best seller, the video recounts the first year of Mayle's stay in rustic Provence. Mayle and his wife Annie have abandoned the London rat race to savor the small pleasures and grace of the French way of life, a world characterized by great food, fine wines and a seductive climate. The Mayles explore the charm of the region and meet a group of unconventional characters who complicate their lives with intrigue and misadventures. Four-cassette deluxe boxed set.

VHS: S18970. $59.95.

David Tucker, Great Britain, 1989, 360 mins.

WRITERS & THEIR WORKS

A.M. Klein: The Poet as Landscape

The personality of the century's leading Anglo-Jewish poet, A.M. Klein, is revealed through interviews, selections from his writing, film footage and historical stills. This is the biography of a fascinating but little understood poet; it touches on everything from his lyrical childhood memories to the tragic silence that overtook Klein in his later years. 58 mins.

VHS: S12867. $39.95.

ABC No Rio, Open Mike

Document of young poets and musicians reading at New York Lower East Side gallery's open mike. Matthew Courtney is MC. 1985, 20 mins.

VHS: S10195. $19.95.

Adrienne Rich

This poet has revolutionized poetry and the cause of woman-centered culture. She reads from *An Atlas of the Difficult World, Diving into the Wreck* and *The Fact of a Doorframe* and speaks with Michael Silverblatt in Los Angeles on May 14, 1992. From the *Lannan Literary Videos* series. 60 mins.

VHS: S27136. $19.95.

Allen Ginsberg

As the bard of the Beat Generation, Allen Ginsberg helped revive American poetry in the 1950s. In this video, his reading and musical performance of poems from *Collected Poems 1947-1980* is captured as it was experienced on February 25, 1989. Lewis MacAdams conducted the interview. From the *Lannan Literary Videos* series. 90 mins.

VHS: S27116. $19.95.

Allen Ginsberg Meets Nanao Sakaki

In a quaint East Village poetry performance space called The Gas Station, internationally renowned poets Allen Ginsberg and Nanao Sakaki gathered. There in the winter of 1988 they made great personal and humanistic music. Since the end of World War II, Nanao Sakaki has lived the life of a wandering poet-storyteller.

VHS: S21845. $29.95.

The Amazing Art of Beauford Delaney: From David Leming's Reading from his Biography of James Baldwin

David Lemming, author of *James Baldwin, A Biography*, narrates an incident involving the African American painter Beauford Delaney and James Baldwin. Stills of the artwork of this little-known painter are interspersed throughout.

VHS: S33820. $24.95.

Claire Burch, USA, 1993, 20 mins.

America in Portrait

Selections from the acclaimed PBS series, "Anyone for Tennyson?" Henry Fonda, William Shatner and James Whitmore are featured in readings of great poetry, often on location, including Frost, Sandburg, Holmes, Edgar Lee Masters (*Spoon River Anthology*), Edgar Allan Poe, Emerson and T.S. Eliot. 45 mins.

VHS: S08792. $24.95.

American Lifestyle Series: Writers

This series offers a view of truly great Americans. These lives stand as testament to the virtues and values of individuality, creativity, and leadership. This collection of four videos profiles some of the greatest U.S. writers.

Helen Keller: Voices and Vision in the Soul. Hugh Downs narrates this program celebrating the accomplishments of the deaf, blind, mute woman who dedicated her life to helping those who were, in her words, "less fortunate than myself." 24 mins.

VHS: S23547. $49.95.

Laser: LD74777. $99.95.

Mark Twain's Hartford Home. E.G. Marshall narrates this tour through Twain's Victorian home in Hartford, where he lived for 20 happy and productive years. 24 mins.

VHS: S23548. $49.95.

Laser: LD74778. $99.95.

Carl Sandburg: Poet of the People. Hugh Downs narrates the story of Sandburg's life. He was born to hardworking immigrants and grew up to be a formidable literary figure. His passion for democracy and the wisdom of the people remains vital through his work. 24 mins.

VHS: S23549. $49.95.

Pearl Buck: The Woman, the World, and Two Good Earths. This visit to the home of the Nobel Prize-winning author is hosted and narrated by Hugh Downs. Buck is a sculptor, a pianist, a philanthropist and a mother to nine adopted children. 24 mins.

VHS: S23550. $49.95.

Laser: LD74779. $99.95.

Angel Rama

The peripatetic critic and editor, whom some would describe as the "Edmund Wilson" of Latin America, converses with novelist Mario Szichman about the state of letters in Latin America, the role of Brazil, and the phenomenon of the so-called "boom" of the novel. He analyses the key works and touches on the work of the youngest writers in the post-boom era. Spanish *without* English subtitles.

Home Video.

VHS: S06945. $59.95.

Public Performance.

VHS: S08834. $100.00.

Anne Rice: Birth of the Vampire

Rice is the author and creator of the most popular contemporary fiction series about vampires. Her central character, the vampire Lestat, has become known to millions of readers. In this profile, the story behind the series is revealed through Anne Rice herself. 50 mins.

VHS: S22533. $14.98.

Anne Waldman

Two-time World Heavyweight Poetry Bout champion, Anne Waldman has a reputation as both a poet and consummate performer. In this video she reads from *Helping the Dreamer* and *New and Selected Poems* and also recites from unpublished work. This video was recorded on March 11, 1991, in Los Angeles, and the interview was conducted by Lewis MacAdams. From the *Lannan Literary Videos* series. 60 mins.

VHS: S27131. $19.95.

Anthony Burgess on D.H. Lawrence

This film, commissioned to mark the 1985 centennary of Lawrence's birth, uses both modern and archival footage to evoke the world of one of Britain's most famous writers. Burgess presents his own appraisal of the man whose explicit views on sex made him a controversial figure in his own time and long beyond. 55 mins.

VHS: S02398. $19.95.

Author to Author Video Series

George Garrett discusses literature with a panel of authors and poets. Series guide included.

Contemporary Poets. Rita Dove, Elizabeth Spire and Henry Taylor discuss American poetry. This panel of poets is particularly insightful about the process of creative writing. 40 mins.

VHS: S24110. $240.00.

Contemporary Short Story Writers. Richard Bausch, Madison Smartt Bell and Alan Cheuse comprise a panel of short story writers. They examine their motivations and explain their decision to concentrate on this literary form. 40 mins.

VHS: S24111. $240.00.

First Novelists. Sydney Blair, Cathryn Hankla and Darcey Steinke expound upon their initial writing experiences, particularly their apprenticeships. 40 mins.

VHS: S24113. $240.00.

The Fiction of Mary Lee Settle. Settle explains the background of her novel *Blood Tie*, and discusses her long career as an author. 40 mins.

VHS: S24112. $240.00.

The Modernist Movement in Poetry. James Dickey and R.W.B. Lewis counter recent arguments put forth against both Modernism and T.S. Eliot. 40 mins.

VHS: S24114. $240.00.

The Beat Generation Show

In May 1994, the first Beat Generation Conference took place in New York City. Participants included Ann Charters, Ray Manzarek (Doors keyboard player), Michael McClure, Allen Ginsberg, Gregory Corso, Lawrence Ferlinghetti, Hettie Jones, Ed Sanders (of Fugs fame), Dr. Hunter S. Thompson and many others. Discussions, performances, poetry and music are all featured. 60 mins.

VHS: S23287. $29.95.

Beat Generation: An American Dream

A look at the small group of writers and artists of the early 1950s that voiced their concerns over America's post-WWII euphoria and values in a manner so raucous and colorful that the media dubbed them the Beat Generation. 86 mins.

VHS: S34968. $19.98.

Beat Legends: Allen Ginsberg

Ginsberg unleashes a storm of dream visions and poetic polemics, sometimes accompanied by a mini-pump organ, and bracketed with historical background information. He reads *Western Ballad* (the first song he ever wrote), *The Fifth Internationale, CIA Dope Calypso, Why I Meditate, Plutonium Ode* and *Broken Bone Blues*. A series of poems from 1984-1990 is also shown, which includes the work *Dreamed a Long Walk with Henry Kissinger*. 92 mins.

VHS: S21842. $24.95.

Beat Legends: Gregory Corso

Hypnotic, hyperbolic and trigger-happy, the charismatic Corso rolls and flows at the trip of the tongue, here in a historic reading in Greenwich Village, New York, 1991. Corso reads *Flu Ramblings, Wreck of the Nordling, Amnesia in Memphis, Prophesy 1958, The Whole Mess, Almost* and much more.

VHS: S21840. $24.95.

The Beats: An Existential Comedy

Focusing on the beat poetry scene of the late '50s, this video is not a conventional documentary, but a film poem which celebrates a colorful generation of American artists, including Stuart Perkoff, Aya, Jack Hirschman, Lawrence Ferlinghetti and Allen Ginsberg, who read their poems and discuss what it means to be a poet in America. Public performance.

VHS: S32117. $79.95.

Philomene Long, USA, 1980, 60 mins.

Bukowski at Bellevue

In the spring of 1970, Charles Bukowski, then little known, packed his overnight bag, locked the door of his tumbledown East Hollywood apartment behind him, and took his first plane ride to the state of Washington to read at Bellevue Community College. This pioneer reading, his fourth ever, was videotaped in black and white. While the technical aspects of the film are shaky, here is Bukowski at the beginning of a great career, reading powerfully and with grit and humor. 60 mins.

VHS: S06897. $45.00.

Burroughs

Brilliant documentary about William S. Burroughs—writer, homosexual, iconoclast. The film examines both Burroughs' career as a foremost 20th century writer, and his personal life including his relationship with his brother, his killing of his wife.

VHS: S00193. $39.95.

Howard Brookner, USA, 1984, 90 mins.

Carolyn Forche (2/12/90)

Reading from *Gathering the Tribes* and *The Country Between Us* along with works in progress, Forche underscores her interest in the brutal events of the 20th century. Recorded in Los Angeles on February 12, 1990, this video includes an interview with this Lannan Literary Fellowship winner, conducted by Lewis MacAdams. From the *Lannan Literary Videos* series. 65 mins.

VHS: S27125. $19.95.

Carolyn Forche (5/24/94)

This Lannan Literary Fellowship-winner reads the entire text of her work *The Angel of History*. It occurred on May 24, 1994, in Los Angeles. In addition, she spoke to Michael Silverblatt about her enduring concerns with the traumatic events of our time. From the *Lannan Literary Videos* series. 94 mins.

VHS: S27147. $19.95.

Caryl Phillips

West Indian-born Caryl Phillips has published six works of fiction including *Cambridge* and *Higher Ground*. He explores provocatively different perspectives of the African diaspora as well as the anatomy of slavery with stylistic virtuosity. On March 7, 1995, Phillips read from *Crossing the River*, a Booker Prize finalist, and spoke with novelist and essayist Pico Iyer in Los Angeles. From the *Lannan Literary Videos* series. 60 mins.
VHS: S32428. $19.95.

Charles Dickens

Born to a life of obscurity and despair, his genius made him one of the most beloved and influential writers of all time. An *A & E Biography*.
VHS: S30841. $19.95.

The Circle of the Hills

A biography on the life, art and times of Alfred Lord Tennyson, the brilliant Victorian poet whose odyssey—from one of the 11 children born to a poor country cleric to poet laureate—is beautifully rendered. The program features extracts from Tennyson's best works, including his masterpiece, *The Charge of the Light Brigade*. 61 mins.
VHS: S19686. $29.95.

Cittee Cittee Cittee: The Poetry of Herschel Silverman with the Music of Perry Robinson

Herschel Silverman was there at the beginning in the Village. He always hung with the best of the Beat poets. Now he is back with his Beat jazz poems accompanied by jazz clarinetist Perry Robinson. USA, 1995, 45 mins.
VHS: S26943. $29.95.

The Coney Island of Lawrence Ferlinghetti

Beat mythology from the legendary San Francisco poet with appearances by Allen Ginsberg and Gregory Corso. 30 mins.
VHS: S31852. $29.95.

Conversation with Richard Wilbur

Richard Wilbur, Pulitzer Prize-winning poet, reads some of his favorite poems and reminiscences about his life and work with Grace Cavalieri, poet and host of the national radio series, *The Poet and the Poem*. Produced by the Library of Congress. 28 mins.
VHS: S08131. $49.95.

Denise Levertov

Denise Levertov, though born in England, has become an important American poet, essayist, editor and teacher. In this video she reads from *Evening Train* and from some of her unpublished works. The reading took place in Los Angeles on December 7, 1993. From the *Lannan Literary Videos* series. 60 mins.
VHS: S27144. $19.95.

Destroy All Rational Thought

A documentary of the *Here to Go* event in Ireland: a one-time celebration of the lives of literary outlaw William S. Burroughs and Brion Gysin, celebrated painter and inventor of the cut-up method. Watch the fascinating proceedings, with one of Burrough's last interviews, plus his '60s black-and-white films. With appearances by Moroccan national treasure Hamri and the Master Musicians of Joujouka.
VHS: S34128. $19.98.
Joe Ambrose/Frank Rynne, Great Britain, 1992, 45 mins.

Diane DiPrima: Recollections of My Life as a Woman

Writer-poet-healer Diane DiPrima reads from her autobiography at the New York Open Center, touching on issues of family, womanhood, aging, anarchy and The Bomb, which fell on her 11th birthday. 100 mins.
VHS: S30798. $24.95.

Echoes Without Saying

The Coach House is an innovative Toronto-based publishing house. Since 1965 it has produced distinctive and experimental books of fiction, poetry and visual art. Through interviews with editors, writers and staff the work of this unique institution is captured on film. 28 mins.
VHS: S25050. $19.95.

Ed McBain

A portrait of the famous novelist of *The Blackboard Jungle* and of the immensely popular series of thrillers about the 87th Precinct detective squad. Follows McBain on a nighttime journey through McBain's world, and dramatizes sequences from his novels. 55 mins.
VHS: S02272. $39.95.

Edgar Allan Poe

He is the uncontested master of the macabre, a man whose melancholy nature made his own life as tragic as one of his dark tales. An *A & E Biography*.
VHS: S30839. $19.95.

Edgar Allan Poe: Architect of Dreams

Poet, short-story writer and critic, Edgar Allan Poe mastered all of these areas, but is perhaps best known for his macabre sensibility. In works like *The Murders in the Rue Morgue* and *The Tell-Tale Heart*, he showed the world a new and strange literary universe. Dave Smith hosts this documentary which looks at Poe's unhappy life and his literary legacy. From the *About the Authors...* series. USA, 1991, 30 mins.
VHS: S27043. $24.95.

Eduardo Galeano

Eduardo Galeano, born in Montevideo, Uruguay, is a journalist, historian, caricaturist and political activist best-known for his *Memory of Fire*, a poetic historical trilogy of the Americas from the native creation myths to modern time. The trilogy is a brilliant collage that strives to restore the cultural heritage of Latin America. Mr. Galeano read from *Walking Words*, *The Book of Embraces*, and spoke with Michael Silverblatt, the host of the radio interview program *Bookworm*. From the *Lannan Literary Videos* series. 60 mins.
VHS: S32431. $19.95.

Elmore Leonard

We follow Leonard on his travels as he revisits some of the inspirations for his best-selling books. Throughout the film, excerpts from his novels are read by people who have, in one way or another, helped shape his work—a police officer, a bomb disposal expert, a Hollywood producer and his wife. 61 min.
VHS: S18389. $19.95.

Emily Dickinson: "A Certain Slant of Light"

Julie Harris hosts this documentary exploration of the unique American Poet Emily Dickinson. Though she inhabited a rather small town in New England, Dickinson managed to touch an astonishing range of human experience in her poetry. This video shows where and how Dickinson lived, and reveals the astonishing power of her poetry. From the *About the Authors...* series.
VHS: S27042. $24.95.
Jean Mudge, USA, 1977, 30 mins.

Eminent Scholars Series

Distinguished educators and critics in an organized syllabus of documented lectures on modern American literature. Comes complete with study guide. Each tape is 45 minutes.

American Literature of the Thirties. Leslie Fiedler surveys the major and popular writers of the decade, as well as three writers whose works have been unjustly neglected by critics: Henry Roth, Dashiell Hammett and Margaret Mitchell.
VHS: S08196. $240.00.

American Literature of World War II. Prof. George Garrett explains the differences between the world wars which account for the literature they produced and examines the various responses to the harshness of the war in poets and writers such as Randall Jarrell, James Gould Cozzens, James Jones and Norman Mailer.
VHS: S08197. $240.00.

American Literature and Politics. Critic Leslie Fiedler explores the political dimensions of works as diverse as *Huckleberry Finn* and *Gone with the Wind* in this discussion of the relationship of writing and politics in American culture.
VHS: S08200. $240.00.

American Literature of the Twenties. North Carolina State Professor Michael Reynolds discusses the American writers who came of age during the Roaring Twenties: T.S. Eliot, William Faulkner, Ernest Hemingway and F. Scott Fitzgerald.
VHS: S08394. $240.00.

Black American Literature. Professor Valerie Smith surveys the development of Black American literature from the 1890s to the 1930s, examining the achievements of the authors who consolidated the Afro-American literary tradition at the turn of the century, and the poets and novelists of the Harlem Renaissance.
VHS: S08201. $240.00.

Introduction to John Dos Passos' Fiction. Prof. Townsend Luddington explores the cultural and personal causes for Dos Passos' literary and political radicalism, describes his decline as a writer from the 1940s onwards, and his concurrent move toward increasing political conservatism.
VHS: S08174. $240.00.

Introduction to Theodore Dreiser's Fiction. Warner Bertoff surveys Dreiser's six most important novels, from *Sister Carrie* to *An American Tragedy*, distinguishing between the realist and naturalist world views in the fiction.
VHS: S08175. $240.00.

Introduction to William Faulkner's Fiction. Professor Cleanth Brooks examines the society, culture, geography and history of northern Mississippi and how Faulkner incorporated it into his fiction.
VHS: S08176. $240.00.

Introduction to F. Scott Fitzgerald's Fiction. University of South Carolina professor Matthew Bruccoli presents an overview of Fitzgerald's life and work and identifies the chief themes and techniques of Fitzgerald's fiction.
VHS: S08177. $240.00.

Introduction to Ernest Hemingway's Fiction. Noted literary scholar Alfred Kazin describes Hemingway's transformation of the English language into something immediate and direct.
VHS: S08178. $240.00.

Introduction to John Steinbeck's Fiction. Steinbeck biographer Jackson Benson provides an informative and detailed discussion of the author's life, career and views.
VHS: S08179. $240.00.

Introduction to Edith Wharton's Fiction. Wharton's biographer, R.W.B. Lewis, surveys her major works of fiction and her chief theme—the oppression of the individual by society.
VHS: S08181. $240.00.

Introduction to Thomas Wolfe's Fiction. University of North Carolina Professor Louis D. Rubin Jr. discusses how Thomas Wolfe's personality dominates his art of recreated memory.
VHS: S08182. $240.00.

Introduction to Richard Wright's Fiction. Prof. Valerie Smith describes Wright's childhood experiences of poverty and oppression which he transmuted into art, particularly his landmark novel, *Native Son*.
VHS: S08183. $240.00.

Introduction to Robert Frost's Poetry. Harvard Professor Helen Vendler shows how Frost's poetry expresses underlying ambiguity and pain.
VHS: S08184. $240.00.

Introduction to T.S. Eliot's Poetry. Princeton Professor A. Walton Liz traces Eliot's career and surveys the early poetry that culminated in *The Wasteland* and *The Four Quartets*.
VHS: S08185. $240.00.

Modern American Novel. Prof. George Garrett provides an informative overview of American fiction from 1910 to 1950, identifying over 60 prominent novelists and commenting on their work.
VHS: S08198. $240.00.

Modern American Poetry. Professor Helen Vendler surveys the ideas and explicates representative poems of the American internationalists (Eliot and Pound), nationalists (Crane, Cullen, Frost, Hughes, Moore and Williams) and Wallace Stevens.
VHS: S08199. $240.00.

Profession of Authorship in America. Prof. Matthew J. Bruccoli corrects the misapprehension that writing books is the way to fame and fortune, in his detailed account of the business of publishing, stressing the effects of marketing considerations, competing media and financial arrangements, and the influence they've had on the course of 20th century American literature.
VHS: S08203. $240.00.

Realism and Naturalism in American Literature. Prof. Michael S. Reynolds explores the influences of modern art, technology and ideas on American culture of the 20's including the contributions made by the new generation of writers—T.S. Eliot, William Faulkner, Fitzgerald, Hemingway.
VHS: S07732. $240.00.

Southern Literary Renaissance. Professor Louis D. Rubin Jr. contends that the defining characteristic of the 20th century South American writers was their sense of history.
VHS: S08202. $240.00.

Understanding Faulkner's As I Lay Dying. Yale Professor Cleanth Brooks explains how Faulkner surprises and challenges the reader by his multiple use of view and unusual mixture of styles.
VHS: S08186. $240.00.

Understanding Hemingway's A Farewell to Arms. Prof. Michael S. Reynolds separates the autobiographical from the fictional in his analysis of the novel's backgrounds and composition.
VHS: S08187. $240.00.

Understanding Steinbeck's Grapes of Wrath. Prof. Jackson Benson clarifies the ideological backgrounds, composition and literary merits of Steinbeck's masterpiece.
VHS: S08188. $240.00.

Understanding Fitzgerald's The Great Gatsby. F. Scott Fitzgerald biographer Matthew Bruccoli explicates Fitzgerald's solution to the problems of fiction structure by means of first-person, secondary character as the narrator.
VHS: S08189. $240.00.

Understanding Wharton's House of Mirth. Yale Professor R.W.B. Lewis examines the composition and themes of Wharton's devastating critique of shallow, hypocritical and materialistic high society of New York during the Gilded Age.
VHS: S08190. $240.00.

Understanding Wolfe's Look Homeward Angel. Professor Louis D. Rubin Jr. describes Wolfe's first novel as autobiographical, not merely told, but imbued with the emotional fervor of a rhetorical high style.
VHS: S08191. $240.00.

Understanding Dreiser's Sister Carrie. Critic Alfred Kazin calls Dreiser the most enduring of American naturalists, and explains the viewpoints that environment and heredity determined human conduct, as exemplified in *Sister Carrie*.
VHS: S08192. $240.00.

Understanding Dos Passos' U.S.A. Prof. Townsend Luddington explains the political thesis and technical innovations, the prophetic and satiric vision of American culture in Dos Passos' trilogy.
VHS: S08193. $240.00.

Understanding Eliot's The Wasteland. Professor A. Walton Liz focuses on Ezra Pound's role as a virtual collaborator in the making of the poem and explores its methods through an examination of key motifs and passages.
VHS: S09904. $240.00.

Eugene O'Neill, Journey into Genius

This episode from the PBS series *American Masters* stars Matthew Modine as the young Pulitzer Prize winning author. O'Neill's plays, *Mourning Becomes Electra, The Iceman Cometh* and *Long Day's Journey into Night*, are unmatched achievements in American drama. This film explores the obsessions and demons of the brilliant dramatist. 60 mins.
VHS: S23606. $24.95.

An Evening with Ed Sanders and the Fugs

Poet, publisher, Woodstock freelance writer and musician Ed Sanders performs on this video at St. Marks Poetry Project and Town Hall, New York City, in 1994. Ed accompanies himself on the dulcimer and his electronic tie. A 1989 Fugs tribute to Abbie Hoffman with Sanders, Tull Kupferberg and Steven Taylor is also included.
VHS: S26944. $24.95.

Fried Shoes, Cooked Diamonds

A joyous reunion of the Beat poets at the Jack Kerouac School of Disembodied Poetics at Naropa Institute in Boulder. With a special narration by Allen Ginsberg, the film shows the warmth and ease of interchange between the poets, as they read their poetry to each other and discuss their thoughts on writing, politics, religion, and the adventure of consciousness. With William Burroughs, Timothy Leary, Allen Ginsberg, Gregory Corso, Diane di Prima, Peter Orlovsky, Meredith Monk, Amiri Baraka, Anne Waldman, Miguel Pinero, Miguel Algarin and Chogyam Trungpa Rinopche.
VHS: S04537. $29.95.
Costanzo Allione, USA, 1978, 55 mins.

Galway Kinnell

Galway Kinnell is a winner of the Pulitzer Prize and of a 1983 American Book Award. In this video, he reads from his books *What a Kingdom It Was, Body Rags, The Book of Nightmares, Mortal Acts, Mortal Wounds, The Past and Selected Poems* in Los Angeles on April 18, 1988. Lewis MacAdams conducts the interview. From the *Lannan Literary Videos* series. 60 mins.
VHS: S27109. $19.95.

Gang of Souls

Maria Beatty rediscovers the Beat Generation in this fascinating documentary featuring appearances and reminiscences by William S. Burroughs, Allen Ginsberg, Marianne Faithful, John Giorno, Henry Rollins, Lydia Lunch, Jim Carroll, Gregory Corso, Diane DiPrima, Ed Sanders, Anne Waldman and Richard Hell. 60 mins.
VHS: S11995. $29.95.

Gary Snyder, Vols. 1 & 2

Influenced by Zen and other elements of Eastern culture, this winner of the Pulitzer Prize is one of the United States' most highly regarded poets. He read from *Axe Handles, Left Out in the Rain* and unpublished manuscripts on December 12, 1988. Lewis MacAdams conducted the interview. From the *Lannan Literary Videos* series. Two volumes. 60 minutes each.
VHS: S27115. $39.95.

Gary Soto

Chicano poet, essayist and children's book writer Gary Soto was born and raised in Fresno, California. Mr. Soto has published six poetry collections, including *Home Course in Religion, The Elements of San Joaquin* and *Who Will Know Us?* He read from his *New and Selected Poems* on May 2, 1995, and talked with novelist Alejandro Morales, whose books include *The Brick People* and *Death of an Anglo*. From the *Lannan Literary Videos* series. 60 mins.
VHS: S32430. $19.95.

Gertrude Stein: When This You See, Remember Me

This portrait of the famous American writer shows Stein in Paris from 1905 through the 1930's. Her creativity was expressed not only in writing but in influential friendships with a host of major artists. Picasso, T.S. Eliot, Thorton Wilder, James Joyce, Ernest Hemingway and many more relied on her companionship, criticism and support. Home movies of Stein and her longtime lover, Alice B. Toklas, a rare radio interview, and footage of Stein's art collection round out this exciting documentary. 89 mins.
VHS: S26648. $59.95.
Perry Miller Adato, USA, 1970, 89 mins.

The Ghost of James Baldwin at Glide Memorial

A touching reminder of poverty in San Francisco. Across from the church dispensing free Christmas dinners, a homeless break-in is taking place.
VHS: S33792. $24.95.
Claire Burch, USA, 1995, 30 mins.

Ghost of the San Francisco Oracle Meets Timothy Leary

Partly surreal documentation of a book-signing of *Chaos and Cyberculture* by Timothy Leary at Cody's Bookstore in Berkeley. The "Ghost" consists of images from the Facsimile Edition of the old Haight Ashbury *San Francisco Oracle*. Contains *Ghost of the "Others" Meets Timothy Leary* and *The "Naked People" of Berkeley*.
VHS: S33806. $24.95.
Claire Burch, USA, 1996, 75 mins.

Gielgud's Chekhov

Sir John Gielgud hosts and narrates these dramatizations of some of Chekhov's greatest works. 50 minutes each.
Volume 1: *The Fugitive, Desire for Sleep*, and *Rothschild's Violin*.
VHS: S02214. $74.95.
Volume 2: *Volodya* and *The Boarding House*.
VHS: S02215. $74.95.
Volume 3: *The Wallet* and *Revenge*.
VHS: S02216. $74.95.

Gilbert Sorrentino

This innovative and darkly humorous writer has written over 20 books. On this video he reads from his book of stories, *Under the Shadow*. The reading was recorded on March 2, 1993, in Los Angeles. Michael Silverblatt then talked with Sorrentino about his work. From the *Lannan Literary Videos* series. 60 mins.
VHS: S27139. $19.95.

Gore Vidal

Politician, novelist, playwright, moviemaker, society's observer. Vidal talks about his relatives-in-law, the Kennedys, his fellow writers, Hemingway, Capote, Mailer, in Vidal's usual, acerbic candidness, as well as excerpts from his movies, *The Best Man* and *Myra Breckenridge*. 58 mins.
VHS: S06972. $19.95.

Great Books

Donald Sutherland narrates this 10-volume set from The Learning Channel which explores the themes, characters and authors of single masterpieces: *Huck Finn, Le Morte D'Arthur, The Art of War, The War of the Worlds, Moby Dick, The Origin of Species, The Scarlet Letter, Alice in Wonderland and Gulliver's Travels*. Each tape is 50 mins.
VHS: S31946. $99.95.

Great Books: Frankenstein: The Making of the Monster

This work examines the issues brought out with the publication of Mary Shelley's *Frankenstein*, and the source of the novel's power and durability. 50 mins.
VHS: S20080. $19.95.

Great Books: Le Morte d'Arthur: The Legend of the King

This program suggests a possible location of Camelot and explores the connection between Sir Thomas Malory's 15th-century masterpiece, *Le Morte d'Arthur* and George Lucas' ki netic and hair-raising *Star Wars* film trilogy. 50 mins.
VHS: S20078. $19.95.

Great Books: Origin of Species: Beyond Genesis

A mythic journey with Charles Darwin on the H.M.S. *Beagle*, during which Darwin developed the theory of the natural selection of the species. 50 mins.
VHS: S20079. $19.95.

Halfmoon

Three of legendary writer Paul Bowles' greatest and strangest stories are presented in this winner of the Critic's Prize (1995 Berlin Film Festival). *Merkala Beach* tells the story of two young Moroccan men whose friendship is tested by the appearance of a beautiful temptress; *Call at Corazon* joins a honeymooning couple as they travel the Amazon; *Allal* is a supernatural, surreal exchange between a young orphan and a poisonous cobra. In English and Arabic with English subtitles.
VHS: S28616. $29.95.
Frieder Schlaich/Irene von Alberti, Germany, 1995, 90 mins.

Hayden Carruth

Hayden Carruth, a winner of a National Book Critics Circle Award, read from his *Collected Shorter Poems, 1946-1991* on November 9, 1993, in Los Angeles. Carruth spoke about his poetry with Michael Silverblatt. From the *Lannan Literary Videos* series. 60 mins.
VHS: S27143. $19.95.

Hemingway in Cuba

The American author Ernest Hemingway is revealed in all his complexity in this detailed portrait. For over 30 years he inhabited an island paradise, eschewing both the public life that often dominates literary figures and his native land. As Hemingway himself wrote, "The country that a novelist writes about is the country he knows, and the country he knows is in his heart." 30 mins.
VHS: S27565. $19.95.

Hemingway...In the Autumn

This video memoir features rare archival footage and photos, plus interviews with Hemingway's son, Jack, as well as numerous friends and associates, and Hemingway biographers and scholars. Public performance.
VHS: S32116. $79.95.
David Butterfield, USA, 1996, 51 mins.

Henry Miller Odyssey

Miller describes how he saw his era, his peers and himself. Whether at Big Sur, or on jaunts to old hangouts in Brooklyn and Paris, Miller shares his life in this film. Along the way he describes his painful youth and his art. Lawrence Durrell, Anais Nin, Jakov Gimpel and others appear, adding depth to this intriguing portrait.
VHS: S26713. $29.95.

Herman Hesse's Long Summer

Takes account of the external circumstances of the writer of *Siddhartha* and *Steppenwolf* while focusing on the soul of one of the most original thinkers of this century. 60 mins.
VHS: S32081. $29.95.

Herman Melville: Consider the Sea

At the age of 20, Herman Melville set sail for the first time. It was a fateful step that ultimately led him to write such nautically inspired works as *Moby Dick* and *Billy Budd*. Richard Wilbur hosts this incisive documentary which looks at both Melville's life and his life work. From the *About the Authors...* series.
VHS: S27045. $24.95.
Jean Mudge, USA, 1981, 30 mins.

Interview & Reading: Kenward Elmslie

The high-wire energy of Kenward Elmslie's poems, tales and songs is captured on this compilation of readings and interviews. Readings include "Pulmonette," "Bimbo Dirt," "Brazil," "Media Madelaine," "TV-Lunch-VT," "Upscale," "Six Vermont Haikus," "Original Parkway," "And I Was There" and "Schlock and Sleaze." "His work is characterized by bizarre imagery...suggestion, on the tangential, the put-on—they're his forte. This kind of writing yields the maximum possibilities of meaning" (Sanford Dorbin, *Library Journal*). 60 mins.
VHS: S30804. $24.95.

Interview & Reading: Ron Padgett

In a revealing interview, poet Ron Padgett, director of publications for the Teachers and Writers Collaborative, tackles the prose poem vs. free verse debate and brings insight into the arts of translation and collaboration. Readings include "High Heels," "Oklahoma Dawn," "To Woody Woodpecker," "Love Poem," "Snowman," "Polish Star," "Igor Sikorsky," "Be Glad," "Doing Something," "Shave," "Medieval Yawn," "The Morning Coffee," "Essay on Imagination," "Flowers Escape" and "Black-Topped Highway." 60 mins.
VHS: S30803. $24.95.

Jack London

An episodic biography of the famed writer produced during World War II. Susan Hayward and Michael O'Shea star.
VHS: S10589. $24.95.
Alfred Santell, USA, 1943, 94 mins.

The James Baldwin Anthology

A celebration of the ideas of James Baldwin, punctuated by original music and a ride through the city of Oakland during one of his visits. Also includes additional excerpts from his work, read by Professor Erskine Peters of Notre Dame University, and an illuminating speech by Baldwin.
VHS: S33840. $24.95.
Claire Burch, USA, 1990, 90 mins.

James Fenimore Cooper's Leatherstocking Tales: I & II

"The true American myth"—D.H. Lawrence. PBS's authentic adaptation of *Leatherstocking Tales* (I & II): *Deerslayer, Pathfinder, Last of the Mobicans, Pioneers*, and *Prairie*. Natty Bumpo (Hawkeye) and Chingachgook, Delaware chief, bring alive the early 1700s, when Americans, French and Huron were fighting for the vast, uncharted wilderness.
Part I.
VHS: S03959. $19.95.
Part II.
VHS: S03960. $19.95.

James Schuyler: Interview/Reading

In this rare interview with the late Pulitzer-Prize-winning poet, Schuyler elegantly discusses his poetic technique. He also muses on the place of the natural world in poetry. A full-length reading is included.
VHS: S22625. $24.95.
Mitch Corber, USA, 1990, 75 mins.

Joseph Heller

Shows the famous American writer at home and on Coney Island, where he grew up, and captures the vitality of his latest novel, *God Knows*, with cleverly dramatized excerpts. 55 mins.
VHS: S02249. $19.95.

Katherine Anne Porter: The Eye of Memory

Joanne Woodward hosts this episode from the PBS series *American Masters*. Porter was one of America's most intriguing authors. Now the unique perspective of this Pulitzer Prize winner is revealed through an in-depth show highlighted by memories from authors Eudora Welty and Robert Penn Warren. 60 mins.
VHS: S23607. $24.95.

Kay Boyle

Reading from *This Is Not a Letter and Other Poems* and *Testament for My Students* in Los Angeles on September 11, 1989, poet Kay Boyle revealed her interest in human rights. Shawn Wong interviews this author of over 30 books. From the *Lannan Literary Videos* series. 60 mins.
VHS: S27120. $19.95.

Kazuo Ishiguro

Kazuo Ishiguro, born in Nagasaki, Japan, and raised in England, is the author of *View of the Hills, An Artist of the Floating World* and *Remains of the Day*, which received the prestigious Booker Prize. Mr. Ishiguro read from his fourth novel, *The Unconsoled*, on October 19, 1995. Pico Iyer, essayist and novelist (*Falling Off the Map*), talked with Mr. Ishiguro following the reading. From the *Lannan Literary Videos* series. 60 mins.
VHS: S32432. $19.95.

Kerouac

An award winning docu-drama about the King of the Beat Generation, Jack Kerouac. Rare footage featuring Allen Ginsberg, Lawrence Ferlinghetti, William Burroughs with music by Charles Mingus, Duke Ellington, Zoot Sims.
VHS: S00671. $29.95.
John Antonelli, USA, 1985, 73 mins.

The Language of Life: A Festival of Poets with Bill Moyers

For Bill Moyers, poetry is news of the mind and the heart. This series features a number of poets whose work have hastened a resurgent interest in this literary tradition. Today poetry is often read, sung, and even performed before large and appreciative audiences. Eighteen poets from an array of cultural traditions are represented in this series.

Come Celebrate with Me. Lucille Clifton and David Mara are two poets who reflect on their respective cultural legacies. Together these authors effectively employ humor while offering insightful observations on the past and the present. 58 mins.
VHS: S26588. $24.95.

Here in the Mind. Gary Snyder and Daisy Zamora have forged a weapon for battle from the same powerful force: eloquent and inspiring language. Snyder defends the natural world from shortsighted onslaughts while Zamora speaks to the causes and passions of the Nicaraguan civil war. 58 mins.
VHS: S26591. $19.95.

Love's Confusing Joy. Coleman Barks has dedicated his efforts to the translation of poems by 13th-century Islamic mystic Jelahudden Rumi. These works are alternately ecstatic, wise and hilarious. Surprisingly, Rumi has much to say to a contemporary American audience. 58 mins.
VHS: S26594. $19.95.

Some Can Sing. Robert Hass, Claribel Alegria, and Carolyn Forche are three poets whose works bridge gaps and cross boundaries. Representing a diverse blend of charisma, background and style, these poets transport audiences to new places. 58 mins.
VHS: S26592. $19.95.

Swirl Like a Leaf. Jimmy Santiago, Robert Bly and Marilyn Chin have all pioneered the use of poetry toward greater understanding of the self. Through the exploration of motivations and fears, these writers have found routes to self discovery and personal reconciliation. 58 mins.
VHS: S26590. $19.95.

The Field of Time. Sandra McPherson and Linda McCarriston are courageous artists who have turned potential tragedy into triumph. Both revel in the beauty of love, family and nature through the use of wondrous and passionate words. 58 mins.
VHS: S26593. $19.95.

The Heart of Things. Adrienne Rich, Victor Hernandez Cruz, and Michael S. Harper join Bill Moyers for this discussion about language. All three writers revel in the ability of language to reveal history and culture even as they change the way poetry is heard, read and absorbed. 58 mins.
VHS: S26589. $19.95.

Welcome to the Mainland. African-American poet Sekou Sundiata is joined by Palestinian born Naomi Shihab Nye in this video. Both celebrate vibrant cultural traditions that have contributed mightily to the contemporary American mosaic. This is the opening program of the series and helps sets a tone of openness and diversity. 58 mins.
VHS: S26595. $19.95.

The Language of Life: A Festival of Poets with Bill Moyers Series.
VHS: S26596. $179.95.

Larry Heinemann

Radicalized by a stint in Vietnam, Heinemann went on to write *Paco's Story*. It garnered him a National Book Award. He read from this book on March 12, 1990, in Los Angeles. Ken Lincoln then interviewed this highly regarded author. From the *Lannan Literary Videos* series. 60 mins.
VHS: S27127. $19.95.

The Last Time I Committed Suicide

Follow the adventures of Kerouac's beat buddy Neal Cassady in this jazzy, sexy, hip love story starring Keanu Reeves, Thomas Jane, Adrien Brody and Claire Forlani.
VHS: S32025. $19.95.
Laser: LD76390. $39.95.
Stephen Kay, USA, 1997, 93 mins.

The Lectures: Volumes 1-3

Poets who are also critics share their state of the art.

Volume 1. Ron Padgett, Alice Notley, Ron Silliman and Bernadette Mayer examine the terrain of Poetry of Everyday Life. 1988.
VHS: S31084. $24.95.

Volume 2. Marjorie Perloff, Hugh Kenner, Allen Ginsberg and Houston A. Baker look ahead to Poetry for the Next Society. 1989.
VHS: S31082. $29.95.

Volume 3. Charles Bernstein, Kenneth Koch and Amiri Baraka set forth the State of the Art. 1990.
VHS: S31083. $29.95.

Li-Young Lee

Li-Young Lee has published two books of poetry, *Rose* and *The City in Which I Love You*. Mr. Lee crafts haunting poetry that weaves cultural politics with personal desire and loss. On April 18, 1995, in Los Angeles, Mr. Lee read from his two poetry collections and from *The Winged Seed*, his memoirs of his family's journey from the political turmoil of Indonesia to a small Pennsylvania town. Novelist and editor Shawn Wong talked with Mr. Lee. From the *Lannan Literary Videos* series. 60 mins.
VHS: S32429. $19.95.

The Life and Times of Allen Ginsberg

William S. Burroughs, Ken Kesey, Abbie Hoffman, Jack Kerouac, Norman Mailer, Joan Baez, Amiri Baraka, Dick Cavett, Timothy Leary and William F. Buckley, Jr., are among the luminaries who provide perspective on Ginsberg, the poet, pacifist and sexual outlaw who collaborated with the filmmaker to provide this compelling scrapbook of a remarkable life.
VHS: S21887. $29.95.
Jerry Aronson, USA, 1993, 82 mins.

Linda Hogan

A member of the Chickasaw Nation, Hogan is a poet, novelist, playwright and teacher who inspires hope and healing from the human and global community. On February 7, 1995, she read from *The Book of Medicines* in Los Angeles and spoke with poet Wendy Rose (*The Halfbreed Chronicles*). From the *Lannan Literary Videos* series. 60 mins.
VHS: S32427. $19.95.

Lost Man's River

Peter Matthiessen, naturalist, author and student of Zen, journeys through the wilderness of the Everglades' Ten Thousand Islands. A last frontier, this labyrinth of islands has always been a natural haven for smugglers, gator poachers and notorious characters such as Edgar "Bloody" Watson, the inspiration for Matthiessen's latest novel, *Killing Mister Watson*. Matthiessen returns to the Everglades, where he reflects on the islands that have occupied him for decades.
Laser: LD71115. $29.95.

Louise Gluck

Louise Gluck, winner of the 1985 National Book Critics Circle Award, reads excerpts from her books *Firstborn, Descending Figure, The House on Marshland* and *The Triumph of Achilles* in Los Angeles on April 4, 1988. Lewis MacAdams interviews her. From the *Lannan Literary Videos* series. 60 mins.
VHS: S27108. $19.95.

Lucille Clifton

Lucille Clifton read from *Good Woman: Poems and a Memoir* and *Next: New Poems*, in Los Angeles on June 16, 1988. Lewis MacAdams conducted the interview with the former Poet Laureate of Maryland. From the *Lannan Literary Videos* series. 60 mins.
VHS: S27111. $19.95.

M.F.K.

Mary Frances Kennedy Fisher was America's premier gastronomical writer, a woman whose distinctive gift for the free expression of sensual pleasures defined her life and her art. Combines interviews, excerpts from Fisher's works, and footage shot both in the U.S. and France to tell the story of this most independent and passionate woman. With Julia Child, Jacques Pepin, editor Judith Jones and many other friends and colleagues.
VHS: S31884. $34.95.
Barbara Wornum, USA, 1992, 44 mins.

The Master Poets Collection I

Claire Bloom, Richard Kiley, William Shatner and other performers bring to life the words of Dickinson, Frost, Whitman, Plath, the Brontes, e.e. cummings, the Brownings, Wordsworth and other poets. Each tape is 30 mins.

Robert Frost: New England in Autumn.
VHS: S32939. $24.95.

Spoon River Anthology & A Poetic Portrait Gallery.
VHS: S32938. $24.95.

The World of Emily Dickinson.
VHS: S32936. $24.95.

William Shakespeare: A Poet for All Time.
VHS: S32937. $24.95.

Master Poets Collection Boxed Set 1.
VHS: S32940. $89.95.

The Master Poets Collection II

Four-tape boxed set includes *The Brontes of Haworth, Robert & Elizabeth Browning, Wordsworth & Coleridge: The Lake Poets and Scott, Tennyson & Kipling: The Heroic Traditions*. Performed by distinguished actor Jack Gwillim and The First Poetry Quartet. 120 mins.
VHS: S34892. $89.95.

Maxwell Anderson: Lost in the Stars

Robert Lansing hosts this look at one of America's most acclaimed dramatists. Maxwell Anderson penned both dramas and comedies, including *What Price Glory?, Key Largo, The Bad Seed* and more. His works capture the essence of the theater. Featuring Helen Hayes and Burgess Meredith. From the*About the Authors...* series. USA, 1990, 60 mins.
VHS: S27044. $24.95.

The Modern World: Ten Great Writers

A ground-breaking series of profiles of ten great 20th-century writers who helped shape literature. Each program examines the author's experiences and includes commentary by noted scholars as well as dramatized excerpts performed by actors from Great Britain's National Theatre and the Royal Shakespeare Company, including David Suchet, Eileen Atkins, Patrick Malahide, Tim McInnerny, Tim Roth, Brian Glover, Michael Gough and Edward Fox.

Vol. 1: Fyodor Mikhailovich Dostoyevsky. Dostoyevsky ushered in modern literature with his novels *Crime and Punishment, Brothers Karamazov* and *The Idiot*. 58 mins.
VHS: S21906. $24.95.

Vol. 2: Henrik Ibsen. Far ahead of his time, Ibsen outraged audiences by stripping away hypocrisy and convention in his plays *Hedda Gabler, A Doll's House* and *Wild Duck*. 58 mins.
VHS: S21907. $24.95.

Vol. 3: Joseph Conrad. The author of *Lord Jim* and *Heart of Darkness* explored political and existential themes. 58 mins.
VHS: S21908. $24.95.

Vol. 4: Luigi Pirandello. In landmark plays like *Enrico IV* and *Six Characters in Search of an Author*, and in a novel and short stories, Pirandello explored the relationship between outward experience and inward reality. 58 mins.
VHS: S21909. $24.95.

Vol. 5: Marcel Proust. Proust's *Remembrance of Things Past* has rightly taken its place as one of the world's literary masterworks. 58 mins.
VHS: S21910. $24.95.

Vol. 6: Thomas Mann. With *Buddenbrooks, The Magic Mountain, Doctor Faustus* and the novella *Death in Venice*, Mann became the leading German author who confronted the spiritual controversies of 20th-century human experience. 58 mins.
VHS: S21911. $24.95.

Vol. 7: James Joyce. Joyce took stream of consciousness to its extremes in *Finnegan's Wake*. David Suchet stars as Leopold Bloom in scenes from Joyce's *Ulysses*. 58 mins.
VHS: S21912. $24.95.

Vol. 8: Virginia Woolf. Woolf's innovative narrative method in *Orlando, To the Lighthouse* and *The Waves* established her as a leading 20th-century novelist. 58 mins.
VHS: S21913. $24.95.

Vol. 9: Thomas Stearns Eliot. In *Prufrock and Other Observations, The Waste Land* and *The Murder in the Cathedral*, Eliot consciously devised a new idiom of expression. Edward Fox, Eileen Atkins and Michael Gough read excerpts from some of Eliot's most famous poems. 58 mins.
VHS: S21914. $24.95.

Vol. 10: Franz Kafka. With such disturbing works as *The Metamorphosis* and *The Trial*, Kafka's name has become synonymous with the sense of alienation when individuals are confronted by faceless and nameless authority. Tim Roth appears as Kafka and as the character Joseph K. from Kafka's *The Trial*. 58 mins.
VHS: S21915. $24.95.

Modern World: Ten Great Writers, Complete Set. The ten-volume set at a reduced price.
VHS: S21916. $199.95.

Moll Flanders

Inspired by one of literature's most passionate and spirited heroines, *Moll Flanders* tells the story of a poor, 18th-century London girl who struggles to hold on to her dreams of a better life. A dramatic twist of fate could ultimately lead her to the happiness she deserves. A lavish costume drama with glorious cinematography and top-notch acting (Robin Wright, Morgan Freeman and Stockard Channing) make this a memorable telling of a classic story.
VHS: S28635. $19.98.
Pen Densham, USA, 1994, 123 mins.

A Moveable Feast: Profiles of Contemporary American Authors

An enlightened series profiling contemporary American authors and their work in the environments that most influenced them. From the beaches of Hawaii to the streets of New York, this unique collection presents interviews with, readings by, and documentary segments about some of the most vibrant voices in modern American literature—a true banquet of ideas, identities and intelligence. Eight volumes.
Allen Ginsberg: When the Muse Calls, Answer! 30 mins.
VHS: S14765. $19.95.
Joyce Carol Oates: American Appetites. 30 mins.
VHS: S14768. $19.95.
Li-Young Lee: Always a Rose. 30 mins.
VHS: S14766. $19.95.
Sonia Sanchez: Wear the New Day Well. 30 mins.
VHS: S14770. $19.95.
T. Corraghessan Boyle: World's End. 30 mins.
VHS: S14763. $19.95.
T.R. Pearson: A Short History of a Small Place. 30 mins.
VHS: S14769. $19.95.
Trey Ellis: Platitudes. 30 mins.
VHS: S14764. $19.95.
W.S. Merwin: The Rain in the Trees. 30 mins.
VHS: S14767. $19.95.

The Mystery Writer Series—Aaron Elkins

A fascinating hour of dialogue with the award-winning creator of Gideon Oliver and Chris Norgren. Elkins weaves artful tapestries of bone fragments, centuries-old masterpieces and murder, leaving his readers begging for more. He also reveals how he sold his first book to the very first publisher who looked at it, methods he uses that he doesn't recommend for others, how he deals with plot, setting, transitions, maguffins, and more. 57 mins.
VHS: S34454. $19.95.

The Mystery Writer Series—Earl Emerson

Earl Emerson, firefighter/mystery author of the Mac Fontana and Thomas Black series reveals the real-life, fatal fire that inspired *Black Hearts and Slow Dancing*, his personal techniques for overcoming writer's block and enduring 14 years of publisher rejection. 57 mins.
VHS: S34455. $19.95.

The Mystery Writer Series—J.A. Jance

The creator of the J.P. Beaumont and Janna Brady series and the suspense novel *Hour of the Hunter* reveals how a single mother of two children made "dreaming the dream" pay big, how it takes more than a formula to write so-called "formula fiction," how her characters even surprise her, and how to get away with murder. 57 mins.
VHS: S34457. $19.95.

The Mystery Writer Series—Jane Yolen

The author of more than 120 children's books, spinner of yarns, and teller of award-winning tales opens this program with a dramatic reading from *Tam Lin*. The author shares how she coaxes her characters onto the printed page, uses actual illustrations from dozens of her stories to help visualize, and shares her best thoughts on writing good stories for young people. 54 mins.
VHS: S34458. $19.95.

The Mystery Writer Series—Tony Hillerman

Creator of the Lt. Joseph Leaphorn and Officer Jim Chee series, Hillerman tells how he decided to become a journalist, and what influenced him to try writing mysteries. He tells how he gets inside the minds of his Navajo characters and shares tips on how he gets his story on the page. Also see a traditional brush arbor, hogans, Turquoise Mountain, the Chaco Canyon ruins, 200-year-old Hubbell Trading Post and more. 54 mins.
VHS: S34456. $19.95.

Nathalie Sarraute

An insightful portrait of the great French novelist, including discussions of her novels, *Portrait d'un inconnu* and *L'ere du soupcon*. 50 mins. French *without* English subtitles.
Home Video.
VHS: S06953. $59.95.
Public Performance.
VHS: S09501. $100.00.

Norman Mailer

A self-portrait which includes interviews with Mailer's family, and clips from his films, as well as extensive commentary by Mailer about his generation, drugs, power, boxing, and his view of immortality in light of his book about Gary Gilmore, *The Executioner's Song*. 57 mins.
VHS: S02303. $39.95.

Oz: The American Fairyland

A documentary exploring Oz, from its creator, L. Frank Baum, to interviews with literary authorities and artists, to discover how Oz, over the course of a century, has entered the American popular imagination to become a shared myth. 115 mins.
VHS: S31830. $49.95.

Patricia Highsmith

A portrait of the first lady of crime, famous for her creation Tom Ripley, amoral crook and killer. Conversations with Highsmith are combined with dramatizations showing Ripley in a chilling game of fraud, impersonation, murder. 55 mins.
VHS: S02271. $39.95.

Pattiann Rogers

Biological, botanical and zoological details give Pattiann Rogers' poetry an intense, sensual and spiritual quality. Works from *Geocentric, The Tattooed Lady in the Garden* and *Splitting and Binding*, as well as unpublished works, were read by Rogers on May 4, 1993, in Los Angeles. Michael Silverblatt also spoke with Rogers about her work. From the *Lannan Literary Videos* series. 90 mins.
VHS: S27140. $19.95.

Paul Bowles in Morocco

Highly acclaimed composer and writer Paul Bowles has lived in Tangier since the 1940s. Conklin "captures some of the ominous tone so brilliantly manipulated by the author…crowded bazaars, snake charmers, religious ecstatics, camel caravans, magnificent oases."
VHS: S01002. $29.95.
Gary Conklin, USA, 1970, 57 mins.

Paul Bowles: The Complete Outsider

Author of the *The Sheltering Sky*, Paul Bowles reveals all in this intimate portrait. Though he was married to the acclaimed writer Jane Bowles, both he and his wife had numerous homosexual affairs. An icon of the Beat Generation, Paul Bowles has inspired many with his disregard for conventional morality, including William Burroughs, who is said to have based *The Naked Lunch* on this iconoclastic inhabitant of Morocco.
VHS: S25720. $29.95.
Catherine Warnow/Regina Weinreich, 1993, 57 mins.

Paul West

Paul West read his work in Los Angeles on September 21, 1993. He read excerpts from *Tenement of Clay, Out of My Depths, Rat Man of Paris* and *Love's Mansion*. In addition, Michael Silverblatt spoke with this winner of a Lannan Literary Award. From the *Lannan Literary Videos* series. 60 mins.
VHS: S27142. $19.95.

Paule Marshall

A MacArthur Fellowship was awarded to this writer from Brooklyn. Her work reflects the West Indian voices she heard as a child. Excerpts from *Daughters* and a discussion with Michael Silverblatt were recorded on April 12, 1994, in Los Angeles. From the *Lannan Literary Videos* series. 60 mins.
VHS: S27146. $19.95.

Philip Levine

Philip Levine is a winner of a 1991 National Book Award. In this video he reads excerpts from his poetry books *Selected Poems, Sweet Will* and *A Walk with Tom Jefferson*. The reading took place in Los Angeles on June 20, 1988. Lewis MacAdams interviewed him. From the *Lannan Literary Videos* series. 60 mins.
VHS: S27112. $19.95.

Poetry by Americans Series

Biographical sketches of four great American poets are collected in this series. Each short also includes a dramatic reading of one of their best regarded poems.
Poetry by Americans: Edgar Allan Poe. Lorne Greene reads "Annabel Lee." 9 mins.
VHS: S23466. $49.95.
Poetry by Americans: James Weldon Johnson. Raymond St. John reads "The Creation." 12 mins.
VHS: S23468. $49.95.
Poetry by Americans: Robert Frost. "Mending Wall" is read by Leonard Nimoy. 10 mins.
VHS: S23467. $49.95.
Poetry by Americans: Walt Whitman. "O Captain! My Captain!" is read by Efram Zimbalist, Jr. 10 mins.
VHS: S23469. $49.95.

The Poetry Hall of Fame

An incredible collection of great writers, great poems and the best of the human spirit.
The Poetry Hall of Fame: Volume One. William Shatner, Vincent Price, LeVar Burton and Valerie Harper join to recite poetry by some of the greatest English language poets. Shakespeare, Marlow, Whitman, Milton, Wadsworth, Longfellow, Coleridge and Frost are just some of the poets included in this video. 58 mins.
VHS: S23600. $24.95.
The Poetry Hall of Fame: Volume Two. Claire Bloom, Henry Fonda, Irene Worth and Jack Lemmon are featured in this video dedicated to poetry. They recite classics from English and American literature by poets Spencer, Keats, Pope, Blake, Yeats, Dickinson and Plath, among many more. 58 mins.
VHS: S23601. $24.95.
The Poetry Hall of Fame: Volume Three. Vincent Price, Henry Fonda, Robert Culp and Ruby Dee recite a collection of enduring poems that span the gamut from Shakespeare to Eliot. Dryden, Bronte, Burns, Tennyson and Dorothy Parker are among the many poets included. 58 mins.
VHS: S23602. $24.95.
The Poetry Hall of Fame: Volume Four. Ruby Dee, Jack Lemmon, Will Geer and Fred Gwynne recite from a large assortment of classic poems. Works by Poe, Swift, Auden, Longfellow and many more are included. 58 mins.
VHS: S23603. $24.95.
The Poetry Hall of Fame Four-Volume Set.
VHS: S23604. $91.80.

Poetry in Motion

Experience the power and passion as poets perform their own work in this film of electrifying energy. Performances by Jim Carroll, Amiri Baraka, William Burroughs, Ted Berrigan, John Cage, Ed Sanders, Ntozake Shange, Allen Ginsberg.
VHS: S01042. $59.95.
Laser: LD70319. $39.95.
Ron Mann, USA, 1985, 90 mins.

Poetry in Times of War

This is a discussion sparked by the sudden onslaught of the Gulf War. Allen Ginsberg, Anne Waldman, Douglas Oliver, Tuli Kupferberg and D.H. Mellon all participated in this forum held at St. Mark's Poetry Project, New York City, May 1991. 105 mins.
VHS: S21843. $29.95.

Poetry on Telegraph Avenue

Poetry Flash sponsors a street reading, featuring such stirring poets as Diane DiPrima, adjunct to the annual Telegraph Avenue Bookfair.
VHS: S33841. $24.95.
Claire Burch, USA, 1996, 90 mins.

Quip with Yip and Friends

A collection of poetry, limericks and light verse as read by Jack Lemmon and Fred Gwynne. The verse is provided by such greats as Ogden Nash, Dorothy Parker, Phyllis McGinley, e.e. cummings, Edgar "Yip" Harburg and others. 45 mins.
VHS: S12819. $24.95.

Ralph Ellison: The Self-Taught Writer

Ralph Ellison's struggle with poverty and segregation as a child shaped his character. Ultimately he rose to world fame with his most popular and insightful novel, *The Invisible Man*. 30 mins.
VHS: S26769. $49.95.

Ray Bradbury: An American Icon

This definitive biography, through personal anecdotes, interviews with friends and associates, clips from the exceptional television series *The Ray Bradbury Theatre* and footage at home, at rehearsals of his plays and on the lecture circuit, captures the essence of this truly gifted writer. Narrated by Rod Steiger. 47 mins.
VHS: S32104. $24.95.

Ray Bremser: The Jazz Poems

Ray Bremser was one of Jack Kerouac's and Bob Dylan's favorite Beat poets. In this rare appearance from 1995, Bremser puts forth one of the best readings of his life. This is a candid documentary that captures the feel of the moment. USA, 1995.
VHS: S26942. $24.95.

Recent Readings/NY

This series has been launched to make accessible significant poetry readings which have taken place in New York City from 1988 to the present.

Recent Readings/NY—Volume 1: John Ashbery/ Barbara Guest.
VHS: S30805. $24.95.
Recent Readings/NY—Volume 2: Anne Waldman/ Cecilia Vicuna.
VHS: S30806. $24.95.
Recent Readings/NY—Volume 3: Kenneth Koch/ Joel Oppenheimer.
VHS: S30807. $24.95.
Recent Readings/NY—Volume 4: Mei-Mei Berssenbrugge/Barbara Einzig.
VHS: S30808. $24.95.
Recent Readings/NY—Volume 5: Amiri Baraka/ Kofi Natambu.
VHS: S30809. $24.95.
Recent Readings/NY—Volume 6: Alice Notley/Tom Mandel.
VHS: S30810. $24.95.
Recent Readings/NY—Volume 7: Jackson Mac Low/ Charles Bernstein.
VHS: S30811. $24.95.
Recent Readings/NY—Volume 8: M.L. Liebler/Todd Colby.
VHS: S30812. $24.95.
Recent Readings/NY—Volume 9: Clark Coolidge/ John Giorno.
VHS: S30813. $24.95.
Recent Readings/NY—Volume 10: Maureen Owen/ Paul Violi.
VHS: S30814. $24.95.
Recent Readings/NY—Volume 11: Clayton Eshleman/ Keith Waldrop.
VHS: S30815. $24.95.
Recent Readings/NY—Volume 12: Charlotte Carter/ Akua Lezli Hope.
VHS: S30816. $24.95.
Recent Readings/NY—Volume 13: Philip Whalen /John Godfrey.
VHS: S30817. $24.95.
Recent Readings/NY—Volume 14: Jack Micheline/ Andy Clausen.
VHS: S30818. $24.95.
Recent Readings/NY—Volume 15: Lewis Warsh /Leslie Scalapino.
VHS: S30819. $24.95.
Recent Readings/NY—Volume 16: David Trinidad/ Sharon Mesmer.
VHS: S30820. $24.95.

Richard Wilbur

A poet, teacher, critic, lyricist and editor, Richard Wilbur was also the second Poet Laureate of the United States. In this video filmed on April 16, 1990, he reads works from *New and Collected Poems* and unpublished manuscripts, at the University of Southern California. David St. John interviews the two-time Pulitzer Prize winner. From the *Lannan Literary Videos* series. 60 mins.
VHS: S27123. $19.95.

Richard Wright: Writing Is His Weapon

Born in poverty, Richard Wright rose to become one of the United States' most respected authors. His prolific output was just one of many things that helped him become successful. 30 mins.
VHS: S26768. $49.95.

Robert Creeley

This co-founder of the Black Mountain poetry movement reads poems from his *Collected Poems, 1945-1975* and *Mirrors, Windows*, as well as work in progress in this video. Recorded on April 16, 1990, this tape also includes an interview of the poet conducted by Lewis MacAdams. From the *Lannan Literary Videos* series. 60 mins.
VHS: S27126. $19.95.

Robert Creeley: 70th Birthday Reading

Influential poet, essayist, novelist, short story writer, editor and teacher Robert Creeley treats audiences to a landmark 70th Birthday Reading, in which he recites selected poems from various stages of his career. 55 mins.
VHS: S30799. $24.95.

Scott Russell Sanders: Lannan Literary Video No. 63

Essayist Scott Russell Sanders reads from *Writing from the Center, In Limestone Country, Staying Put* and new work in Los Angeles in May 1997. He also speaks to novelist Bernard Cooper, author of *Maps to Anywhere*. 90 mins.
VHS: S34472. $19.95.

Sharon Olds

Sharon Olds' first book, *Satan Says*, won the inaugural San Francisco Poetry Center Award, while her next book, *The Dead and the Living*, won a National Book Critics Circle Award. Ms. Olds read from the latter book and from *The Gold Cell* on April 8, 1991, in Los Angeles. Lewis MacAdams conducted the interview. From the *Lannan Literary Videos* series. 60 mins.
VHS: S27132. $19.95.

Spymaker: The Secret Life of Ian Fleming

An action-packed adventure based on the real life of the man who created James Bond, with Jason Connery, Kristin Scott Thomas and Joss Ackland. Fleming, born into an aristocratic English family, single-handedly outwits Soviet intelligence, foils an S.S. monster at a glamorous casino, steals the secrets of the German high command, storms an enemy stronghold at impossible odds and still has time for the fastest cars and the most desirable women.
VHS: S12370. $79.98.
Ferdinand Fairfax, USA, 1990, 96 mins.

A Talk with Ann McGovern

The author of *Shark Lady* not only describes her book, she actually goes underwater and explores the sea. From *The "Good Conversation!" Video Series*. 24 mins.
VHS: S27038. $49.98.

A Talk with Avi

The Newbery Award-winner and author of *Nothing But the Truth* and *The True Confessions of Charlotte Doyle* speaks about his life as a writer. From *The "Good Conversation!" Video Series*. 22 mins.
VHS: S27024. $49.98.

A Talk with Betsy Byars

Betsy Byars, author of the Newbery Award-winning *Summer of the Swans*, describes how she came to write this book. She also has many hobbies which she discusses, including her love of aviation. From *The "Good Conversation!" Video Series*. 18 mins.
VHS: S27027. $49.98.

A Talk with Bruce Coville

My Teacher Is an Alien sold over one million copies. Bruce Coville talks about this comic book and his hilarious twin brother "Igor." From *The "Good Conversation!" Video Series*. 22 mins.
VHS: S27029. $49.98.

A Talk with E.L. Konigsburg

The author of the Newbery Award-winning *From the Mixed Up Files of Mrs. Basil E. Frankweiler* is revealed in this candid discussion of reading and writing. From *The "Good Conversation!" Video Series*. 22 mins.
VHS: S27035. $49.98.

A Talk with Jean Craighead George

The author of *Julie of the Wolves* shares her writing techniques. In a rare personal moment, this Newbery Award-winner even talks with her dog, Kimiq. From *The "Good Conversation!" Video Series*. 26 mins.
VHS: S27032. $49.98.

A Talk with Jean Fritz

Homesick: My Own Story, a Newbery honor book, describes the travels and experiences of author Jean Fritz, who grew up in China. From *The "Good Conversation!" Video Series*. 20 mins.
VHS: S27031. $49.98.

A Talk with Jerry Spinelli

The Newbery Award-winning book *Maniac Magee* is discussed by its author, Jerry Spinelli, who also introduces viewers to his pet rat, Daisy. From *The "Good Conversation!" Video Series*. 20 mins.
VHS: S27040. $49.98.

A Talk with Karla Kuskin

Karla Kuskin explains how she combatted adolescent loneliness with a passion for writing and poetry. From *The "Good Conversation!" Video Series*. 25 mins.
VHS: S27036. $49.98.

A Talk with Lee Bennett Hopkins

This noted author and poet describes how he used reading to help him overcome an impoverished childhood. From *The "Good Conversation!" Video Series*. 18 mins.
VHS: S27033. $49.98.

A Talk with Lynne Reid Banks

The author of *The Indian in the Cupboard* hosts an English tea party and discusses her life and her work. From *The "Good Conversation!" Video Series*. 22 mins.
VHS: S27026. $49.98.

A Talk with M.E. Kerr

This popular young author discusses her book *Gentlehands* and explains why she writes under pseudonyms. From *The "Good Conversation!" Video Series*. 24 mins.
VHS: S27034. $49.98.

A Talk with Madeleine L'Engle

In addition to giving young authors useful tips, this Newbery Award-winning author answers questions about her book *A Wrinkle in Time*. From *The "Good Conversation!" Video Series*. 22 mins.
VHS: S27037. $49.98.

A Talk with Matt Christopher

This former semi-pro ball player has written over one hundred popular sports books. In this video he talks about his writing, his family and his days in sports. From *The "Good Conversation!" Video Series*. 18 mins.
VHS: S27028. $49.98.

A Talk with Nancy Willard

Nancy Willard reads aloud from her Newbery Award-winning book *A Visit to William Blake's Inn: Poems for Innocent and Experienced Travelers*. From *The "Good Conversation!" Video Series*. 18 mins.
VHS: S27041. $49.98.

A Talk with Natalie Babbitt

Natalie Babbitt discusses her modern children's classic *Tuck*. In addition, she gives a guided tour through the miniature house she constructed together with her husband. From *The "Good Conversation!" Video Series*. 20 mins.
VHS: S27025. $49.98.

A Talk with Paula Fox

The Slave Dancer won a Newbery Award. In this video, children's author Paula Fox describes the importance of imagination for her work. From *The "Good Conversation!" Video Series*. 24 mins.
VHS: S27030. $49.98.

A Talk with Phyllis Reynolds Naylor

This Newbery Award-winning author reads from her novel *Shiloh* and gives the behind-the-scenes story which describes how it came to be written. From *The "Good Conversation!" Video Series*. 25 mins.
VHS: S27039. $49.98.

Thom Gunn

Born in England, Thom Gunn has lived in northern California since 1954. His austere poems of love and death testify to his mastery as a poet. In this video he reads from his *Collected Poems* and talks with Wendy Lesser, the founding editor of *The Threepenny Review*. The interview and reading took place on October 18, 1994, in Los Angeles. From the *Lannan Literary Videos* series. 60 mins.
VHS: S27148. $19.95.

To Save Jack Kerouac's Daughter

Archival documentation, including surreal visual material, of a benefit to save Jan Kerouac, daughter of Jack, by raising money for her kidney transplant. Ken Kesey, Paul Krassner, Allen Cohen, editor of the old *Oracle*, Ramblin' Jack Elliot and others present tributes to Jack Kerouac, and poet Gerald Nicosia describes the controversy about a "conspiracy" involving Kerouac's will.
VHS: S33817. $24.95.
Claire Burch, USA, 1995, 58 mins.

To the Lighthouse

Kenneth Branagh and Rosemary Harris star in the BBC production of Virginia Woolf's most popular novel, about family life as friends settle in to enjoy a warm Edwardian summer at the beach, and romance and conflicting dreams simultaneously draw the family together and pull it apart.
VHS: S32021. $19.95.
Colin Gregg, Great Britain, 1983, 115 mins.

Toni Morrison

Toni Morrison has established herself as the leading chronicler of the black experience in America and as one of America's finest novelists. This program focuses on Morrison on the eve of publication of her new novel, *Beloved*, which already won the Pulitzer Prize for fiction. Morrison talks about the problems of dealing with painful material, and of writing about ordinary people whose experiences seem monumentally larger than life. 55 mins.
VHS: S07599. $19.95.

The Unbearables: Brooklyn Bridge Readings 1995/1996

The Unbearables are some 30-odd highly talented "outcast" poets (including Ron Kolm, Sharon Mesmer, Hal Sirowitz, Sparrow, Carl Watson, Michael Carter, Tsaurah Litzky, Peter Lamborn Wilson and Jill Rapaport) who have gathered together to create their own movement. The well-published group gives collective readings every September 13 on the Brooklyn Bridge. "The Unbearables…are conscience-angels with pitchforks ready to prod and poke…these poets are for real" (Taproots Reviews).
VHS: S30802. $24.95.

Uncle Tom's Cabin

An adaptation of Harriet Beecher Stowe's controversial novel about social and racial conditions and black enfranchisement in the pre-Civil War South. When Abraham Lincoln met Stowe, he reportedly told her, "So, you're the little lady who started this big war." With Herbert Lom as the nefarious Simon Legree.
VHS: S18836. $19.95.
Geza von Radvanyi, France/Germany/Yugoslavia/Italy, 1969, 113 mins.

United States of Poetry

Over two hours of recent poems are joined on this two-tape video set. Produced by KQED, Public Television New York, it includes some of the most exciting young poets around. They are placed in a quick-paced and hip format that suits the excitement of the work. Over 50 poets are included, past and present, from writers as diverse as Lord Buckley, Czeslaw Milosz, Amiri Baraka, Jenny Holzer and Elizabeth Barrett Browning. 150 mins.
VHS: S27700. $29.95.

Voices and Visions

This remarkable video series traces the development of the American poetry tradition. Both the life story and the work of major poets are covered in each video. Perfect for the serious student and those who simply love poetry.
Voices and Visions Volume I: Hart Crane, Walt Whitman, Ezra Pound, William Carlos Williams. A look at poet-physician William Carlos Williams, who established a distinctly American poem; at Hart Crane's preoccupation with technology and its human impact; at the controversial Ezra Pound, who became a leader of the Modernist movement and became enmeshed in economic and political ideals during World War II; and at the remarkable Whitman, including the eclectic sources of his poetry. 240 minutes.
VHS: S24315. $69.95.
Voices and Visions Volume II: Emily Dickinson, Marianne Moore, Elizabeth Bishop, Sylvia Plath. Four unique, American women poets are covered in this four-volume set. Period dramatic recreations evoke the domestic context in which Emily Dickinson wrote her metaphysical poetry. Poets and critics explain the "wild decorum" of Marianne Moore's unique style. Exotic documentary footage heightens the magical realism of Elizabeth Bishop's poems and explores her preoccupation with perception and the boundaries of consciousness. And archival footage of the 1950s pop culture chronicles Sylvia Plath's historical environments and the complex relationship between her troubled life and work. 240 minutes.
VHS: S24316. $69.95.
Voices and Visions Volume III: T.S. Eliot, Robert Lowell, Langston Hughes, Robert Frost, Wallace Stevens. Five videos explore these major poets. They trace the career of T.S. Eliot from the bold originality of *Prufrock* to the meditative style of *Four Quartets*. They contain footage of Robert Lowell in his apartment and on anti-war protest marches, intercut with interviews that discuss his use of autobiography as subject matter for poetry. On-location footage in Senegal, France, Kansas and Harlem chronicles the life of Langston Hughes. Through his lyric poems and dramatic narratives, Robert Frost asserts that nature is the clearest window into the human personality. And presentations of the works of Wallace Stevens reveal his sense of imagination as a journey to a new reality. 300 minutes.
VHS: S24317. $89.95.

Voices and Visions: Elizabeth Bishop

Bishop's fanciful but accessible poems betray her interest with perception and the boundaries of consciousness. Exotic documentary footage extends the magical realism of her work. Mary McCarthy and Octavio Paz are among the commentators included in this video. 60 mins.
VHS: S26318. $19.95.

Voices and Visions: Emily Dickinson

Expressing both doubt and joy, Dickinson's poems are compressed and urgent. At times they reflect lucidity and wit or despair and death-obsession. Adrienne Rich, Joyce Carol Oates and others comment on the legacy of this 19th-century female poet who lived largely as a recluse. 60 mins.
VHS: S26317. $19.95.

Voices and Visions: Ezra Pound

Though a driving force of the Modernist movement, Pound's classically poetic voice recalls ancient and medieval sources. His social and political views led to controversy through accusations of treason and the suspicion of madness. Hugh Kenner, Alfred Kazin and Pound himself are seen in this video, discussing the poet and his work. 60 mins.
VHS: S26314. $19.95.

Voices and Visions: Hart Crane

Advanced technology spurred Crane into lyrical language and a literature of ecstasy. This disorderly and lusty poet's frenzy of illumination had a darker, debauched side. His deterioration and suicide could be traced to this conflicted life. Derek Wolcott, Malcolm Cowley and Richard Howard provide commentary. 60 mins.
VHS: S26315. $19.95.

Voices and Visions: Langston Hughes

Scenes of Hughes' travels in Europe and film of him reading his own work make this video an especially personal view of this great African-American writer. He was active in the black artistic and political movements of his time, a fact attested to by James Baldwin, Gwendolyn Brooks and others. 60 mins.
VHS: S26322. $19.95.

Voices and Visions: Marianne Moore

Witty, subversive and precise, Moore's poems evince remarkable clarity of observation. This film traces her life, times and friendships. Her unusual sources and idiosyncratic work depended on both natural science and her vivid imagination. Grace Schulman, Charles Tomlinson and Kenneth Burkes discuss this poet and her work. 60 mins.
VHS: S26319. $19.95.

Voices and Visions: Robert Frost

Though Frost presented a harsh vision of the world, his work achieved startling popularity. This film mixes interviews with Frost, dramatizations of his work, and commentary by Seamus Heaney, Alfred Edwards and Richard Wilbur. 60 mins.
VHS: S26323. $19.95.

Voices and Visions: Robert Lowell

Interviews with Lowell betray his keen interest in contemporary issues, such as racial injustice, cultural decline and nuclear war. This film examines Lowell's autobiographical and historical concerns as well as his mental anguish. Robert Giroux, Robert Hass and novelist Elizabeth Hardwick, Lowell's second wife, speak about the poet and his work. 60 mins.
VHS: S26325. $19.95.

Voices and Visions: Sylvia Plath

Rage, grief and anger mark the poems of this tragic figure's work. Archival footage, including a long interview with Plath herself, helps to explain some of the power and misery which afflicted the young poet. She committed suicide at 30. 60 mins.
VHS: S26320. $19.95.

Voices and Visions: T.S. Eliot

This poet and philosopher lived in London most of his life. There he worked as a publisher and dramatist whose poems confronted the spiritual uncertainty of his generation. Though Stephen Spender, Quentin Bell, Frank Kermode and others speak about his work, Eliot himself reads his own poems in this video. 60 mins.
VHS: S26321. $19.95.

Voices and Visions: Wallace Stevens

This melancholy existentialist was also an insurance executive. His comic and meditative poems elicit meaning and solace from the landscapes he visited, the weather and the conditions of the soul. Harold Bloom, Joan Richardson and James Merrill address the power of Stevens' work. 60 mins.
VHS: S26324. $19.95.

Voices and Visions: Walt Whitman

Walt Whitman pioneered a new American style of poetry that remains highly influential. This tape recreates the sights and sounds that inspired him. Whitman's idealism continues to inspire new generations of writers from the Beat movement onwards. Allen Ginsberg, Galway Kinnell and Donald Hall comment on this democratic, homosexual lover of the human voice. 60 mins.
VHS: S26313. $19.95.

Voices and Visions: William Carlos Williams

Williams' penetrating work betrays a clean and insightful style focused on concrete particulars. This style reflects his other concerns as a small town pediatrician. Allen Ginsberg, Marjorie Perloff and Hugh Kenner discuss Williams the man and the poet. 60 mins.
VHS: S26316. $19.95.

W.S. Merwin

This winner of the Pulitzer Prize is a poet, playwright, translator and activist. He read from *Selected Poems* and *Rain in the Trees* in Los Angeles on May 16, 1988. Lewis MacAdams conducted the interview. From the *Lannan Literary Videos* series. 60 mins.
VHS: S27110. $19.95.

Walt Whitman and the Civil War

At the age of 42, Walt Whitman began service on the battlefields of the Civil War as a nurse. The experience profoundly changed his life. This video explores the personal transformation he underwent tending the wounded and the dying and its effect on his poetry. Excerpts of some of his greatest works are included. 28 mins.
VHS: S26532. $29.95.

What Happened to Kerouac? (1985)

A lively homage to and biography of a difficult and vulnerable individual who happened to be one of the most influential writers of recent history, Jack Kerouac. Contains footage of Kerouac as well as Allen Ginsberg, William Burroughs, Gregory Corso and Lawrence Ferlinghetti.
VHS: S04513. $69.95.
Lewis MacAdams/Richard Lerner, USA, 1985, 96 mins.

What Happened to Kerouac? (1996)

A lively and revealing investigation into the personal history and creative process of Jack Kerouac, father of the Beat Generation. Features Beat luminaries Steve Allen, William Burroughs, Neal Cassady, Allen Ginsberg and many more. "Brings us closer to Jack Kerouac than any other film" (*Los Angeles Times*). 96 mins.
VHS: S34969. $19.98.

Whispers on the Wind

Focusing on the distinct voices of our poetic heritage, this is a collection of verse as read by LeVar Burton, Ruby Dee and Cameron Mitchell. Included are works by D.H. Lawrence, Alexander Pope, DeBose Heyward, Tennessee Williams and James Dickey. 45 mins.
VHS: S12818. $24.95.

Whodunnit: The Art of the Detective Story

This program takes a look at the popular, perennial art form from its evolution to its history, heroes, characters and conventions. Viewers learn how authors build suspense and clues, present evidence and hold viewer interest. 36 mins.
VHS: S12277. $174.00.

William S. Burroughs: Commissioner of the Sewers

A portrait of the author who created *Naked Lunch*. With his characteristically dry wit and subtle humor, Burroughs talks about language and other weapons, about the word as a virus, about death and dreams, about travel in time and space. Burroughs also reads from his own work to the visual accompaniment of his paintings and films.
VHS: S16621. $29.95.
Klaus Maeck, USA, 1986, 60 mins.

William Shakespeare

He is the most influential and admired writer—a man whose imaginative genius still moves us, nearly four centuries after his death. An *A & E Biography*.
VHS: S30838. $19.95.

With a Feminine Touch

Selections from the acclaimed PBS series, "Anyone for Tennyson?" focusing on the work of women poets, including Edna St. Vincent Millay, Emily Dickinson, the Brontes and Sylvia Plath. Valerie Harper, Claire Bloom and Ruby Dee are captured in some of the most memorable poems, often on location. 45 mins.
VHS: S08793. $24.95.

Women and the Beats: The Beat Generation Show, Volume II

Anne Waldman, Joyce Johnson and Jan Kerouac are just some of the women who helped shape this important literary movement. Readings, interviews and lectures help clarify the value of the contributions made by these women.
VHS: S24312. $39.95.

MARK TWAIN ADAPTATIONS

The Adventures of Huck Finn (Disney)

Stephen Sommers wrote and directed this Disney adaptation of Mark Twain's classic novel about the shifting friendship between Huck Finn (Elijah Wood), an energetic, go-for-broke kid, and Jim (Courtney B. Vance), a runaway slave who is desperately trying to secure his freedom. With Robbie Coltrane, Jason Robards, Ron Perlman and Dana Ivey.
VHS: S19726. $19.95.
Laser: Letterboxed. **LD72340. $39.99.**
Stephen Sommers, USA, 1993, 108 mins.

The Adventures of Huckleberry Finn (Hodges/Moore)

A good screen version of the Mark Twain classic, with an engaging Huck Finn (Eddie Hodges) and an excellent Jim (Archie Moore). Other assorted characters are played by Buster Keaton, Tony Randall, John Carradine, and Sterling Holloway.
VHS: S13639. $19.98.
Michael Curtiz, USA, 1960, 107 mins.

The Adventures of Huckleberry Finn (Rooney)

Mickey Rooney stars as Mark Twain's Huckleberry Finn, with William Frawley and Walter Connolly.
VHS: S03532. $24.95.
Richard Thorpe, USA, 1939, 88 mins.

The Adventures of Mark Twain: Fredric March

An eccentric biography of the life and art of the American writer and humorist. Fredric March imbues Twain with wit and invention, perfectly appropriating Twain's gestures and rhythms. With Alexis Smith, Donald Crisp, George Barbier and Binnie Barnes.
VHS: S19466. $19.98.
Irving Rapper, USA, 1944, 130 mins.

The Adventures of Tom Sawyer (Kelly/Brennan)

Tommy Kelly stars as Tom Sawyer in this excellent David O. Selznick production of the classic Mark Twain story. Co-starring Walter Brennan and May Robson; photographed by James Wong Howe.
VHS: S14224. $14.98.
Laser: LD70812. $39.98.
Norman Taurog, USA, 1938, 91 mins.

A Connecticut Yankee (Will Rogers)

Will Rogers is a radio expert who travels back in time to the court of King Arthur and changes medieval life by introducing telephones, automobiles, hotdogs and advertising. Maureen O'Sullivan and Myrna Loy co-star in this adaptation of Mark Twain's classic. For a scene in which the queen expresses her affection, Will's face was hand-tinted, frame by frame, to show him "blushing."
VHS: S13493. $19.98.
David Butler, USA, 1931, 96 mins.

A Connecticut Yankee in King Arthur's Court (Bing Crosby)

Bing Crosby is a modern American chap, circa 1949, who loses consciousness and awakes in the Sixth Century with a lot of explaining to do. This third screen version of the Samuel Clemens cautionary tale is an elaborate musical which features the talents of William Bendix, Sir Cedric Hardwicke and Rhonda Fleming in living color.
VHS: S03492. $14.98.
Tay Garnett, USA, 1949, 107 mins.

A Connecticut Yankee in King Arthur's Court (Westinghouse Studio One)

Boris Karloff plays King Arthur in this live tv adaptation of the Mark Twain classic about a modern New Englander who finds himself back in the days of Camelot. Also in the cast are Thomas Mitchell and Berry Kroeger. Program opening and commercials deleted. USA, 1952, 51 mins.
VHS: S05442. $24.95.

Huckleberry Finn (1974/Musical)

A colorful musical interpretation of Mark Twain's classic text. Jeff East plays Huck, with Paul Winfield as runaway slave Jim.
VHS: S19031. $14.95.
Laser: LD72123. $34.98.
J. Lee Thompson, USA, 1972, 118 mins.

Huckleberry Finn (1975/Howard)

Ron Howard is Huckleberry Finn in this folksy, homespun version of Mark Twain's eternal tale about Huck and Jim's misadventures on the mighty Mississippi. An enjoyable treatment which nonetheless sacrifices the social criticism and darker elements of the classic novel for simple, straightforward storytelling.
VHS: S03556. $14.98.
Robert Totten, USA, 1975, 74 mins.

Innocents Abroad

Mark Twain on his grand tour of the continents, joined by Brooke Adams and David Ogden Stiers. 116 mins.
VHS: S06393. $19.95.

Life on the Mississippi

A film commissioned for public television, another adaptation of an episode from Mark Twain's boyhood collections of growing up in pre-Civil War Missouri. Robert Lansing is a river boat pilot named Horace Bixby who allows young Sam (David Knell) a chance to test his manhood as an apprentice on an arduous journey up the Mississippi River.
VHS: S02544. $19.95.
Peter Hunt, USA, 1980, 115 mins.

Man That Corrupted Hadleyburg

Based on the short story by Mark Twain, and starring Robert Preston, Fred Gwynne and Tom Aldredge. From American Short Story series.
VHS: S01716. $24.95.
Ralph Rosenblum, USA, 52 mins.

Mark Twain's America

This documentary examines the cultural, artistic, political and social transformation in American society captured through the work and art of Mark Twain. Twain's metamorphosis from droll, regional writer to revolutionary literary figure is paralleled by America's rise from frontier society to world power. Narrated by Howard Lindsay. 60 mins.
VHS: S19248. $19.95.

Mark Twain's Connecticut Yankee

A Connecticut Yankee in King Arthur's Court. What does an innocent young citizen of Hartford, Connecticut do when he's plucked up from the 19th Century and plunked down into King Arthur's medieval court? Mark Twain's tale of American ingenuity in Camelot stars Richard Basehart, Roscoe Lee Browne and Paul Rudd in a satirical spectacular.
VHS: S03958. $19.95.

Mark Twain: A Musical Biography

A biography of Mark Twain framed by the tenets of the roadway musical. "An original biographical tribute to Twain, an extravaganza of singing, dancing and acting" (*The New York Times*). 87 mins.
VHS: S17022. $24.95.

Mysterious Stranger

Mark Twain's irreverent fantasy focuses on a printer's apprentice from Missouri who daydreams himself into a medieval European castle and meets a mysterious, magical youth with formidable powers. 89 mins.
VHS: S06154. $19.95.

The Notorious Jumping Frog of Calaveras County

Based on the classic story by Mark Twain. Jim Smiley would bet on anything, and his frog, Dan'l Webster, was his favorite betting animal. Dan'l Webster could jump farther than any other frog alive. Smiley never lost a bet with Dan'l until the stranger came to town. 24 mins.
VHS: S30727. $19.95.

The Prince and the Pauper

An all-star cast including Errol Flynn, Claude Rains and Barton MacLane was assembled for this story of the young Prince of England who trades places with his look-alike, a street beggar. Based on the story by Mark Twain.
VHS: S01871. $19.98.
Laser: LD72130. $39.98.
William Keighley, USA, 1937, 120 mins.

Private History of a Campaign That Failed

Mark Twain's fictionalized reminiscences of his brief, inglorious career in the Confederate militia. Pat Hingle stars as the leader of a troop of rangers who panic and react disgracefully when confronted with the realities of battle. 89 mins.
VHS: S10058. $19.95.

Pudd'nhead Wilson

Ken Howard stars as Pudd'nhead Wilson, a lawyer whose humor no one understands, in this adaptation of Mark Twain's classic story that explores the issues of slavery, justice, and mother/son relationships. Filmed in historic Harper's Ferry, West Virginia.
VHS: S01070. $19.95.
Alan Bridges, USA, 1983, 87 mins.

Rascals and Robbers—The Secret Adventures of Tom Sawyer and Huck Finn

Patrick Creadon and Anthony Michael Hall are Tom and Huck in this made-for-tv accounting of their lives that Mark Twain did not write. They join a circus, help free a slave and try to stop a con artist named Scree (Anthony James) from bilking their neighbors. Life on the Mississippi just never slows down.
VHS: S04379. $59.98.
Dick Lowery, USA, 1982, 100 mins.

Tom Sawyer

The Mark Twain novel in a musical adaptation features Johnnie Whitaker, Celeste Holmes, Warren Oates and Jodie Foster, set in real Mississippi locations, and with musical direction by John Williams.
VHS: S12430. $19.98.
Don Taylor, USA, 1973, 103 mins.

A Young Connecticut Yankee in King Arthur's Court

A modern, action-packed twist on the classic Mark Twain tale of knighthood and sorcery in King Arthur's Camelot. An all-star cast features Michael York, Theresa Russell and Nick Mancuso.
VHS: S30021. $79.98.
Ralph L. Thomas, USA, 1995, 93 mins.

theatre on screen

Actors on Acting
A discussion program in which actors Murray Hamilton, James Earl Jones, Jack Klugman and Rip Torn give advice to young and would-be actors. Themes: the lack of good roles, the incursions of TV, Hollywood vs. Broadway, the importance of regional theater, the necessary mobility of an actor, and why these stars went into acting themselves. 1966, 27 mins.
VHS: S32329. $89.95.

Agnes of God
Meg Tilly stars in the film adaptation of the John Pielmeyer play as a young nun who conceived, delivered and may have murdered a baby within the confines of the convent. Jane Fonda is the sensitive, chain-smoking court appointed psychiatrist sent to find out the truth. Anne Bancroft is the disapproving Mother Superior. A disturbing drama with no easy answers. Sven Nykvist shot the film in Canada.
VHS: S10377. $19.95.
Norman Jewison, USA, 1985, 98 mins.

Ah, Wilderness
A poignant adaptation of Eugene O'Neill's play about early 20th century small-town life, focusing on the confusion and difficulty confronting a young man's leap into adulthood. With Wallace Beery, Lionel Barrymore and Mickey Rooney. Screenplay by Albert Hackett and Francis Goodrich.
VHS: S17656. $19.98.
Clarence Brown, USA, 1935, 101 mins.

All My Sons
A superb cast brings Arthur Miller's critically-acclaimed play of human frailty and guilt to life. Originally produced in the 1940's, this all-new production remains a moving theatrical experience. Joan Allen, Michael Learned, James Whitmore and Aidan Quinn star.
VHS: S04524. $39.95.
John Power, USA, 1986, 122 mins.

American Theater Conversations: The Actors Studio
Frank Cosaro, Paul Newman, Geraldine Page, Fred Stewart, Rip Torn and Michael Wager discuss The Actors Studio, its origins, its goals and the influence of "Method" acting. The conversation was filmed at the time of the first Broadway success of The Actors Studio Theater, Eugene O'Neill's *Strange Interlude*, in which Miss Page had a starring role.
VHS: S30996. $89.95.
1963, 28 mins.

Andre Serban: Experimental Theater
A profile of the experimental theater director, including conversation with critic Margaret Croyden and reflections by director and theater producer Joseph Papp and Ellen Stewart, owner of Cafe La Mama in New York City. With excerpts from Serban's workshop production of *The Master and the Margarita* and auditions for a forthcoming production of *The Umbrellas of Cherbourg*. Serban is seen working with actors and commenting on the values in the plays. 1978, 27 mins.
VHS: S32317. $89.95.

Andre Serban: The Greek Trilogy
Performance of excerpts from off-Broadway experimental productions of Andrei Serban's flamboyant interpretations of classic Greek theater pieces: Euripides' *Electra, Medea* and *The Trojan Women*. Margaret Croyden provides introductions and commentary. With music by Elizabeth Swados. 1974, 54 mins.
VHS: S32318. $89.95.

Anthony and Cleopatra (Dalton/Redgrave)
Shakespeare's most popular tale of love, war and political intrigues is realized with the star power of Timothy Dalton, Lynn Redgrave, John Carradine and Anthony Geary. History's most famous lovers are magnificently portrayed, bringing their passion and their ultimate dilemma into sharp focus.
VHS: S19414. $59.95.

Antigone
Irene Papas stars in this faithful adaptation of Sophocles' classic tragedy about the descendants of Oedipus. Greek with English subtitles.
VHS: S09874. $39.95.

Antony and Cleopatra (Royal Shakespeare Company/Patrick Stewart)
Patrick Stewart stars in this Royal Shakespeare Company production of Shakespeare's play. 160 mins.
VHS: S19027. $19.98.

As You Like It
Laurence Olivier and Elisabeth Bergner star in this handsome and fairly faithful translation of the Shakespeare comedy, in which Rosalind (Bergner) and her love Orlando (Olivier) withstand the brutal tactics of her uncle Frederick to secure the throne for her deposed father, Duke Senior.
VHS: S18173. $24.95.
Paul Czinner, Great Britain, 1936, 96 mins.

Athol Fugard: Blood Knot
South African playwright, director and actor Athol Fugard has been writing for several decades about the lives of blacks and poor whites in South Africa. *Blood Knot*, Fugard's first important play, was the first performed in South Africa with an interracial cast. This rare filmed recording features excerpts from the original New York production with James Earl Jones and J.D. Cannon.
VHS: S30992. $89.95.
1964, 28 mins.

Bacchantes
Euripides' famous Greek play, a provocative look at the turmoil of a dancer's professional and private life, performed by a cast including Tiana Ela, Pierre Brice, Akim Tamiroff. In English.
VHS: S07461. $19.95.
Giorgio Ferroni, Italy/USA, 100 mins.

The Balcony
In a brothel of illusion the customers take over real power during a revolution. Madame Irma (Shelley Winters) runs the house of illusion where ordinary people play out their dreams. Outside, a revolution is in progress. For the Police Chief (Peter Falk), the brothel is the rallying point from which he can suppress the revolution. Roger (Leonard Nimoy), leader of the revolution, seeks refuge in the brothel where he poses as his opponent. Based on the play by Jean Genet.
VHS: S09554. $29.95.
Joseph Strick, USA, 1963, 87 mins.

Barnum
A filmed performance of the London production of the international stage hit starring Broadway sensation Michael Crawford. The show traces the legendary P.T. Barnum's career from his humble beginnings as a promoter of side shows to his eventual triumph as the co-founder of the Barnum and Bailey Circus.
VHS: S14294. $29.95.
Terry Hughes, Great Britain, 1990, 113 mins.

Beckett Directs Beckett: Endgame
Samuel Beckett's favorite play was reportedly *Endgame*, his portrait of modern alienation and despair, set in a dystopic, underground universe where nothing makes sense. Made in collaboration with the San Quentin Drama Workshop. With Bud Thorpe, Rick Cluchey and Teresito Garcia Suro. 96 mins.
VHS: S18456. $29.95.

Beckett Directs Beckett: Krapp's Last Tape
A presentation of the San Quentin Drama Workshop, this play about a retired civil servant reviewing his life by listening to reel to reel tapes features Rick Cluchey in the title role. "This is the essential addition; for those meeting him [Beckett] for the first time, there could be no better way to start" (Australian press). 46 mins.
VHS: S18455. $29.95.

Beckett Directs Beckett: Waiting for Godot
In collaboration with the San Quentin Drama Workshop, Samuel Beckett directs his existential parable about two lost souls awaiting a rendezvous that may or may not be imaginary. With Bud Thorpe, Rick Cluchey, Lawrence Held and Alan Mandell. The play has never been "more human, more accessible or more beautiful" *(Newsweek)*. In two acts running 77 and 60 mins.
VHS: S18454. $39.95.

Beckett Directs Beckett Collection
The three-tape set.
VHS: S18143. $89.95.

The Belle of Amherst
Julie Harris stars as the most famous 19th century American woman poet, Emily Dickinson. In this dramatization, her life as a recluse and spinster is recreated to reveal the sources of her poetry. Dickinson was inspired by the humble everyday occurences found in rural America.
VHS: S22940. $59.95.

Ben Jonson: The Alchemist
Excerpts from Jonson's 17th-century "comedy of humors," in which a con man with a "philosopher's stone" dupes respectable but greedy members of the establishment. With the cast of the 1964 off-Broadway production. 1964, 27 mins.
VHS: S32322. $89.95.

Bertolt Brecht Practice Pieces
Lotte Lenya, Roscoe Lee Browne, Micki Grant and Oliver Clark are shown rehearsing two of Bertolt Brecht's largely unknown and seldom performed "Ubungstucke fur Schauspieler" (Practice Pieces for Actors). Brecht wrote these scenes to train actors in his own method for doing classical drama. Contains scenes from *Romeo and Juliet* and *Hamlet* and a brief discussion of the theater of Brecht with Lenya and translator Michael Lebeck.
VHS: S30994. $89.95.
1964, 28 mins.

Blithe Spirit
Rex Harrison, Constance Cummings and Margaret Rutherford are brilliantly funny in this Noel Coward inspired romantic comedy about an interfering soul from beyond. When a novelist (Harrison) invites a spiritualist over for inspiration, she unexpectedly summons his deceased first wife, who then proceeds to make trouble for him and his new wife (Cummings). The special effects won an Oscar. In color.
VHS: S21995. $14.98.
David Lean, Great Britain, 1945, 96 mins.

Breaking the Code
Mathematical genius Alan Turing (Derek Jacobi) designed the computer that cracked the German Enigma code and, quite possibly, won World War II. His admittance to homosexuality, however, at a time when it was illegal, created problems for him, his colleagues and national security. "A riveting, intelligent, provocative play" (Susan Granger, WMVA Radio). 90 mins.
VHS: S31008. $19.98.

British Theater in the United States: Backstage with Richardson and Gielgud
A discussion of theater, acting, British versus American audiences and schools of acting, with Alexander Cohen, producer of the David Storey play *Home*, and its two stars, Sir John Gielgud and Sir Ralph Richardson. 1970, 27 mins.
VHS: S32327. $89.95.

Building a Character
Creating a foundation for character development can be made simple using this basic formulated approach. Learn to analyze character, discover emotions, and use your body to become a better, more convincing actor. 86 mins.
VHS: S15917. $59.95.

Bunraku
Bunraku, the classical Japanese puppet art, uses three-quarter-life-sized figures, handled by black-clothed manipulators who remain in plain view of the audience. Includes performances from two traditional Bunraku dramas and filmed scenes showing how the puppets are made and articulated. Commentary by Faubion Bowers, expert on dance and Asian arts. 1973, 27 mins.
VHS: S32333. $89.95.

Caesar and Cleopatra
Based on the play by George Bernard Shaw and full of Shaw's indomitable wit; with Claude Rains, Vivien Leigh, Stewart Granger.
VHS: S08268. $14.98.
Gabriel Pascal, Great Britain, 1948, 134 mins.

Cat on a Hot Tin Roof (1958)
Paul Newman and Elizabeth Taylor star in this steamy screen version of Tennessee Williams' famous play about a rich plantation owner, dying of cancer, who finds most of his family fawning all over him for his money. Fine performances from a cast that includes Burl Ives, Madeleine Sherwood and Larry Gates.
VHS: S13776. $19.98.
Laser: LD76807. $39.99.
DVD: DV60059. $24.98.
Richard Brooks, USA, 1958, 108 mins.

Cat on a Hot Tin Roof (1984)

Jessica Lange is Maggie in Tennessee Williams' sexually obsessed melodrama, with Tommy Lee Jones as Brick and Rip Torn as Big Daddy. Made for American Playhouse television.
VHS: Out of print. For rental only.
Laser: LD70541. $34.98.
Jack Hofsiss, USA, 1984, 122 mins.

Chalk Garden

A moving, beautifully acted drama about a teenager (Hayley Mills) who is set on the right path by her governess (Deborah Kerr). With John Mills, Edith Evans.
VHS: S04522. $14.98.
Ronald Neame, Great Britain, 1964, 106 mins.

The Circle in the Square: The First Twenty-Five Years

Commemorating the first quarter century of the group that put Off-Broadway on the map, Dustin Hoffman, Colleen Dewhurst, George C. Scott, James Earl Jones, Paul Rudd and Vanessa Redgrave discuss acting, ambition and their life with The Circle in the Square. In this review of its origins and successes, theater critic Margaret Croyden talks to some of The Circle's leading lights. Includes interviews with founder Ted Mann and his associate Paul Libin and performance excerpts with some of The Circle's celebrated actors.
VHS: S30998. $89.95.
1977, 85 mins.

Clarence Darrow

Henry Fonda in a command performance as the famous Clarence Darrow, the legendary attorney who fought for the rights of individuals. "I urge every man, woman and child interested in justice and America to see this…As for Mr. Fonda, it would be difficult to think of praise too high…It is just plain wonderful," wrote Clive Barnes in *The New York Times*.
VHS: S06091. $39.95.
John Houseman, USA, 1980, 81 mins.

The Connection

The Living Theatre's production of the play by Jack Gelber: a quintessential work of theatre of the 60's, a harrowing depiction of the dope peddling milieu, as the characters wait for the arrival of Cowboy with the heroin. Critics Prize, Cannes.
VHS: S00265. $29.95.
Shirley Clarke, USA, 1961, 105 mins.

Conversations with Playwrights: Arthur Miller and Israel Horovitz

Conversations between Pulitzer Prize-winning author Miller and writer Israel Horovitz. They talk about theater, the writer, playwriting and politics, and the playwright's responsibility to society. 1970, 27 mins.
VHS: S32328. $89.95.

Coriolanus—Westinghouse Studio One

A modern dress update of Shakespeare's Roman play that moves the action to Fascist Italy. Written by Worthington Minor, who introduces the play. With Richard Greene, Judith Evelyn, Richard Purdy and Tom Poston of the *Newhart* show. Betty Furness does the commercials. USA, 1951, 60 mins.
VHS: S05435. $24.95.

Creative Drama & Improvisation

The imagination is the most powerful tool accessible to the actor. It enables the actor and comedian to create situations and background information on a character that might not be drawn from life experience otherwise. These exercises and improvisations will assist you in exploring your imagination.
VHS: S15919. $59.95.

The Crucible

Arthur Miller's dramatic masterpiece; the screenplay and dialogue were written by Jean-Paul Sartre and this French film stars Simone Signoret, Yves Montand and Mylene Demongeot. Set in Salem, Massachusetts, in 1692, the film dramatizes the persecution of witches and serves as a powerful allegory for the anti-communist hysteria of America in the 1950s. French with English subtitles.
VHS: S23571. $39.95.
Raymond Rouleau, France, 1957, 108 mins.

The Crucible

Nicholas Hytner's intelligent adaptation of Arthur Miller's quintessential American play ***The Crucible*** stars Daniel Day-Lewis and Winona Ryder in this moving story set during the Salem witch trials.
VHS: S31520. $103.99.
Laser: LD76238. $49.98.
Nicholas Hytner, USA, 1996, 123 mins.

Curse of the Starving Class

James Woods, Kathy Bates, Randy Quaid and Louis Gossett, Jr. star in this strange film based on Sam Shepard's acclaimed play. A farm family is in trouble and in debt. In addition, they are fully dysfunctional and seemingly good targets for villains like a shady real estate dealer, a slick bar keep and a motorcycle gang. Somehow though, their humanity and humor make it all work.
VHS: S24566. $19.95.
Laser: LD75179. $34.98.
J. Michael McClary, USA, 1994, 102 mins.

Cyrano de Bergerac (Ferrer)

Jose Ferrer won an Academy Award for his role as the classic soldier of fortune with the oversize nose. With Mala Powers.
VHS: S18180. $19.95.
Michael Gordon, USA, 1950, 112 mins.

Da

Hugh Leonard's autobiographical play of growing up adopted in a small seacoast town in Ireland. The film version is directed by character actor Matt Clark. Barnard Hughes is the lovable and crusty title character with whom son Martin Sheen has many mixed emotions. A ghost story. A comedy. A celebration of life. With William Hickey.
VHS: S07581. $19.95.
Matt Clark, Ireland/USA, 1988, 102 mins.

David Mamet: The Playwright as Director

Playwright David Mamet rehearses Lindsay Crouse and Michael Higgins in scenes from two of his plays, *Dark Pony* and *Reunion*. Discussion of the art of directing and the Stanislavsky method. 1979, 27 mins.
VHS: S32326. $89.95.

Days of Wine and Roses

Piper Laurie and Cliff Robertson star in the Playhouse 90 production of the J.P. Miller play about a couple facing alcoholism.
VHS: S05014. $24.95.
Laser: Letterboxed. **LD71200. $34.98.**
John Frankenheimer, USA, 1958, 89 mins.

Death of a Salesman

CBS theatrical production of Arthur Miller's dark and surrealistic parable on the fallout of the American dream. Dustin Hoffman stars as Miller's anti-hero, Willy Loman, whose obsessive regard to be well-liked prompts the indifference and betrayal of his family. An extraordinary cast includes Kate Reid as Loman's long-suffering wife, and John Malkovich and Stephen Lang as Loman's failed sons, Biff and Happy.
VHS: S02113. $29.95.
Volker Schlondorff, USA, 1986, 135 mins.

Desire Under the Elms

In Eugene O'Neill's play adapted by Irwin Shaw, a 19th century New England family is beset by greed, lust and family hatred. With Anthony Perkins, Sophia Loren, Burl Ives and Pernell Roberts.
VHS: S00322. $19.95.
Delbert Mann, USA, 1958, 114 mins.

Don't Start Me to Talking...

This adaptation of John O'Neal's one-man play features Junebug, a mythic folk storyteller born out of the civil rights movement of the 60s. Junebug reveals the wisdom of the common people, who, through great ingenuity and resourcefulness, overcome tremendous adversities in order to survive. 45 mins.
VHS: S23301. $29.95.

The Empty Space

Gerald Feil's film documents a 1970 visit by Peter Brook and his Parisian experimental theater group at the Brooklyn Academy of music. It reveals the exercises and techniques used by this acclaimed director which challenge distinctions between actors and the audience. 60 mins.
VHS: S21192. $29.95.

The Entertainer

Playwright John Osborne assisted Tony Richardson in the adaptation of his play in this brilliant depiction of the moral, spiritual and professional decline of a bogus entertainer, Archie Rice. Set against the background of the noisy holiday makers pushing past the placard proclaiming the Suez crisis in which Archie's only contact with real life, his son Mick, is to die. "Richardson used large, oppressive close-ups and shock cutting to the point of technical arrogance, but he brought the audience relentlessly face to face with the failure of the sad characters of Archie and his debilitated alcoholic wife, beautifully played by Brenda de Banzie" (Roger Manvell).
VHS: S08261. $19.95.
Laser: Widescreen. **LD75918. $49.95.**
Tony Richardson, Great Britain, 1960, 97 mins.

Equus

Richard Burton and Peter Firth in the film version of Peter Shaffer's play about a part-time stableboy who has blinded six horses. Burton as the psychiatrist discovers that the boy comes from a repressive family background.
VHS: S00411. $14.95.
Laser: LD70967. $39.98.
Sidney Lumet, USA, 1977, 145 mins.

Fortune and Men's Eyes

A realistic adaptation of John Herbert's play about homosexual life inside a prison cell. Brutal and uncompromising. "A powerful and often shocking film" *(Newsweek)*. With Wendell Burton, Michael Greer and Zooey (David) Hall.
VHS: S17657. $19.98.
Harvey Hart, Canada, 1971, 102 mins.

Futz

One of the legendary theatre productions of the 1960s, La Mama Troupe presents the story of Cyrus Futz, a farmer in love with his pig. With references to transvestism, pyromania, sex, murder and incest, the film opened to critical shouts of "Bravo!" "Brilliant!" and, "You can't make a slick farce from a sow's rear!"—or can you?! Not for the faint of heart. From the director of the original stage version of *Hair*. "*Futz* is a witty, harsh, farcical, and touching dramatic poem about the love—romantic, domestic and sexual—of a farmer for his pig…I'd suggest that you watch out for *Futz*" *(The New Yorker)*.
VHS: S30731. $29.95.
Tom O'Horgan, USA, 1969, 92 mins.

The Glass Menagerie

Set in depression-era St. Louis, Tennessee Williams' first play is a hallmark of American theatre, and receives a loving production at the hands of director Paul Newman. The familial, tension-ridden triangle receives brilliant performances from Joanne Woodward, John Malkovich, Karen Allen and James Naughton.
VHS: S07142. $19.98.
Laser: LD70032. $39.98.
Paul Newman, USA, 1987, 134 mins.

Glengarry Glen Ross

James Foley's adaptation of David Mamet's Pulitzer prize-winning play about the confidence games and male bravado of a group of Chicago real estate salesmen. The performances are first-rate, with Al Pacino as the silver-tongued, shrewd operator, Jack Lemmon as the one-time kingpin who's fallen on hard times and Ed Harris as an anonymous, grubby loser. Alec Baldwin turns in a terrifying cameo.
VHS: S18465. $19.98.
Laser: Widescreen. **LD75198. $34.98.**
James Foley, USA, 1992, 100 mins.

Globalstage

Globalstage travels the world to select the best live, professional theatre productions for kids ages 7 to 14. Creatively filmed and edited by the BBC, each program is hosted by Professor Elizabeth McNamer, a dynamic guide who explores the cultural, literary, and historical significance of the plays with her 11-year-old sidekick, Preston. Both kids and parents will be delighted with the thought-provoking subjects, creative staging, and entertaining stories that these videos capture.

Globalstage—Cyrano. The exquisite avant-garde adaptation of Rostrand's French classic about the power of the written word, and the speciousness of ephemeral beauty. The internationally acclaimed theater company Blauw Vier of Antwerp, Belgium portrays this poetic comedy of a mismatched love triangle. Filmed on location in Antwerp. Directed by Jo Roets, Great Britain/Belgium, 1998, 100 mins.
VHS: S34554. $24.95.

Globalstage—Frankenstein. Masterful direction combines with vivid costumes and sets in this Stage One production of Mary Shelley's classic tale. Professor Elizabeth McNamer provides background on Mary Shelley and the 19th-century Romantic movement and comments on the story's key themes. Filmed on location in Louisville. Directed by J. Clements, Great Britain/USA, 1997, 90 mins.
VHS: S34555. $24.95.

Globalstage—Pinocchio. A live Stage One performance musical of the classic story about the wooden puppet who struggles to become real, but disobeys his father's wishes to go to school. Examines the themes of unconditional love, the importance of education to our success in life, and how we determine what is right and wrong. Performed in the style of the commedia dell'arte, the colorful set and costumes take the viewer back to Renaissance Florence with original songs, dancing, and creative staging. Includes a behind-the-scenes interview with writer and lyricist Moses Goldberg and composer Scott Kasbaum. Filmed on location in Louisville. Directed by J. Clements, Great Britain, 1997, 90 mins.
VHS: S34553. $24.95.

Gogol: Diary of a Madman
An adaptation of the off-Broadway production of the celebrated story by Nicolai Gogol (1809-1852), about a clerk's disintegration into complete madness. Performed by actor and drama teacher William Hickey in a one-man tour-de-force. 1964, 27 mins.
VHS: S32321. $89.95.

Hamlet (1948/Olivier)
Laurence Olivier produces, directs and interprets the title character, a melancholy Dane dealing with a range of feelings for his stepfather, the new King of Denmark. The film won four Oscars and Olivier received his knighthood. Based on a play by William Shakespeare. Cast includes Jean Simmons, Felix Aylmer and Peter Cushing. Don't look for Rosencrantz and Guildenstern. Filmed in glorious black and white.
VHS: S06230. $19.98.
Laser: LD75461. $69.95.
Laurence Olivier, Great Britain, 1948, 153 mins.

Hamlet (1969/Williamson)
A brilliant, Tony Richardson-directed version of Shakespeare's *Hamlet*, starring Nicol Williamson, Gordon Jackson, Anthony Hopkins, Judy Parfitt.
VHS: S07033. $29.95.
Tony Richardson, Great Britain, 1969, 114 mins.

Hamlet (1990/Gibson)
Mel Gibson stars as the melancholy Dane in this film adaptation of the Shakespeare classic, directed by Franco Zeffirelli. The distinguished supporting cast includes Glenn Close, Alan Bates, Paul Scofield, Helena Bonham Carter and Ian Holm.
VHS: S14279. $19.98.
Franco Zeffirelli, USA, 1990, 135 mins.

Hamlet (1996/Branagh)
Kenneth Branagh does Shakespeare again in this virtuoso performance as the Great Dane, featuring a stellar cast including Julie Christie, Billy Crystal, Gerard Depardieu, Charlton Heston, Derek Jacobi, Jack Lemmon, Rufus Sewell, Robin Williams and Kate Winslet.
VHS: S31644. $29.95.
Laser: LD76251. $69.95.
Kenneth Branagh, Great Britain, 1996, 242 mins.

Harold Clurman
A celebration of the art and life of Harold Clurman, producer, director and critic who was a vital force in American theater for 50 years. Introduced and narrated by Meryl Streep, the film contains impassioned and heartfelt remembrances from Roy Scheider, Arthur Miller, Lee Strasberg, Stella Adler, Julie Harris, Elia Kazan and Karl Malden. 55 mins.
VHS: S18732. $39.95.

The Heidi Chronicles
Jamie Lee Curtis and Tom Hulce star in this screen adaptation of the highly regarded stage play. Penned by Wendy Wasserstein, this play won both the Pulitzer Prize and a Tony Award. The film is the story of Heidi Holland (Curtis), a woman determined to experience life and all its possibilities. Over the course of three decades she fights for the political goals she believes in and manages to develop a successful career. It's a success story with real feminist ideals.
VHS: S27262. $19.98.
Laser: LD75561. $39.95.
Paul Bogart, USA, 1995

Henry V (Branagh)
Kenneth Branagh makes his astounding directorial debut and stars in this critically acclaimed adaptation of Shakespeare's rousing play. With Derek Jacobi, Ian Holm, Judi Dench and Paul Scofield. "...a depth and authority seldom encountered these days on stage or in film" (Dave Kehr, *Chicago Tribune*).
VHS: S12590. $29.98.
Kenneth Branagh, Great Britain, 1990, 138 mins.

Henry V (Olivier)
Laurence Olivier won a special Oscar for outstanding achievement as an actor, producer and director in bringing this work of Shakespeare to the screen. A colorful historical spectacle that includes the battle of Agincourt and serves as a stirring patriotic metaphor for England's survival in WWII. With Robert Newton, Leslie Banks, Renee Asherson and Leo Genn.
VHS: S06237. $19.98.
Laser: LD75076. $69.95.
Laurence Olivier, Great Britain, 1944, 137 mins.

Hobson's Choice
Not the English film, but an American adaptation of the classic stage comedy, based on the plight of three young sisters in desperate need of dowries. With Richard Thomas, Lillian Gish and Jack Warden.
VHS: S06359. $59.98.
Gilbert Cates, USA, 1983, 100 mins.

The Importance of Being Earnest
Oscar Wilde's play took over 57 years to reach the big screen but it was worth the wait. A colorful theatrical film about mating rituals in Great Britain before the turn of the century, when manners and background were more important than the truth. A grand cast includes Michael Redgrave, Joan Greenwood, Margaret Rutherford, Michael Dennison and Edith Evans as Lady Bracknell. VHS: Out of print. For rental only.
Laser: LD76787. $49.95.
Anthony Asquith, Great Britain, 1952, 95 mins.

Inspector General
Danny Kaye pulls the wool over the eyes of the town elders when he pretends to be the important Inspector General whom this Russian village anxiously awaits to impress. Based on a story by Gogol. With music. Cast includes Walter Slezak, Elsa Lancaster and Alan Hale.
VHS: S18186. $19.98.
Henry Koster, USA, 1949, 102 mins.

Jerzy Grotowski
The director of the Polish Lab Theater talks with theater critic Margaret Croyden (translated by Jacques Chwat, theater director). Grotowski discusses the relationship between director and actor, a playwright's function, and the idea of his "poor" theater that renounces everything not essential to the work. 1970, 55 mins.
VHS: S32314. $89.95.

Joseph Chaikin and the Open Theater
The group in its last performance before disbanding. *Nightwalk* is a collective theater piece, the work of writers Jean-Claude van Itallie, Sam Shepard, Megan Terry and Open Theater director Joseph Chaikin, as well as the actors. *Nightwalk* is a montage of surreal situations that examine the human condition in worlds both real and fantastic, presenting exaggerations of human pretensions. Human and birdlike creatures weave in and out; the "plot" is a journey, liberated from convention. 1947, 55 mins.
VHS: S32316. $89.95.

Joseph Papp and the Public Theater: American Playwrights 1976
This program explores the goals and techniques of Joe Papp's famous enterprise in New York City, The Public Theater. Several plays are seen in excerpt form as finished productions or works in progress. Theater critic Margaret Croyden interviews Papp and the playwrights whose work is seen. Plays highlighted include David Freeman's *Jessie and the Bandit Queen*, John Guare's *Rich and Famous* and Myrna Lamb's *Apple Pie*. 1976, 54 mins.
VHS: S32319. $89.95.

Julius Caesar (Heston/Gielgud)
John Gielgud gives a superior performance as Julius Caesar in this adaptation of Shakespeare's play, also featuring Charlton Heston, Richard Chamberlain, Robert Vaughn and Diana Rigg.
VHS: S01677. $19.95.
Stuart Burge, Great Britain, 1970, 116 mins.

Julius Caesar (MGM/Brando)
Friends, Romans, countrymen—before Marlon Brando wore a motorcycle jacket, he proved to be quite impressive decked out in a toga. Brando plays Mark Antony in this lavish production of the Shakespeare play. The film won an Oscar for set decoration and art direction, and includes such fine actors as James Mason, John Gielgud, Louis Calhern, Edmond O'Brien, Greer Garson, Deborah Kerr and George Macready. The producer was John Houseman.
VHS: S11222. $19.95.
Joseph L. Mankiewicz, USA, 1953, 120 mins.

Kabuki Classics: Onoe Baiko VII in The Salt Gatherer
Performance by "living national treasure" Kabuki actor Baiko VII of a famous 18th-century Kabuki dance based on a Noh drama about a simple girl who loves a court noble, a poet, during his exile to a remote island, and her subsequent abandonment. Baiko also grants a rare interview, explains his art and the origin of the dance he performs, and gives notes on technique to his son, also an actor in Kabuki theater. 1972, 27 mins.
VHS: S32332. $89.95.

Kabuki Techniques
Two of the greatest stars of Japan's Kabuki theater reveal the acting techniques used in this most difficult of theater forms. Onoe Shoroku II and Onoe Baiko VII discuss and demonstrate their craft in conversation with Asian art commentator Faubion Bowers. Includes film of great Kabuki performances of the past. 1969, 27 mins.
VHS: S32331. $99.00.

King Lear (Laurence Olivier)
Critically acclaimed as "a performance as great as anything he has ever done in his illustrious acting career", *King Lear* proved to be Laurence Olivier's final major screen role. The all-star Shakespearean cast includes Diana Rigg as Lear's daughter Regan. Olivier's monumental portrayal of Shakespeare's embittered King Lear is truly a performance for the ages.
VHS: S10709. $29.95.

King Lear (Orson Welles)
A legendary production of Shakespeare's masterpiece, directed by the acclaimed British stage and film director Peter Brook, and starring Orson Welles. Virtually unseen since its broadcast in the mid-1950's, this is a treasure of a lifetime for fans of film, Shakespeare, Welles, theatre.
VHS: S11175. $39.95.

The Lady's Not for Burning
Kenneth Branagh stars in this mystery tale beset by superstition. Branagh is a discharged soldier who must solve the murder of man in order to protect a beautiful woman. She stands accused of witchcraft. The murdered man's body is missing and the townspeople suspect that she has turned him into a dog. Based on the play by respected playwright Christopher Fry, this passionate love story is set in a time ruled by irrational fears. With Bernard Hepton and Cherie Lunghi.
VHS: S26776. $19.95.
Julian Aymes, Great Britain, 1995, 90 mins.

Laurence Olivier: A Life
Famed for being camera shy, this legend of film and theater appears for the first time in a comprehensive, candid interview. Key partnerships, both on and offstage, are recalled by Olivier and by his many friends and colleagues. Features Sir John Gielgud, Sir Ralph Richardson, Douglas Fairbanks, Jr., Dame Peggy Ashcroft and Olivier's wife, actress Joan Plowright. 159 mins.
VHS: S16597. $29.95.

Les Miserables
On October 8, 1995, many members of the most widely respected cast from this musical were gathered for a 10-year anniversary concert performance at the Royal Albert Hall in London. The Royal Philharmonic Orchestra provided the musical accompaniment for this event. 160 mins.
VHS: S29957. $24.95.
Laser: LD75945. $49.99.

The Life and Adventures of Nicholas Nickleby
Thirty-nine actors from the Royal Shakespeare Company are presented in this dramatization of Charles Dickens' masterful tale. From Wackford Squeer's Dotheboys to the itinerant theater troupe of Mr. Vincent Crummies, this set of videos offers nine hours of engrossing viewing pleasure.
VHS: S23877. $99.95.
Laser: LD75935. $149.95.

A Life in the Theater
Jack Lemmon stars as an aging theater actor who finds himself living in an increasingly artificial dream world, in David Mamet's drama of theater, life, age and experience. Matthew Broderick co-stars. Powerful performances highlight this riveting drama.
VHS: S21514. $94.95.
Gregory Mosher, USA, 1993, 78 mins.

Long Day's Journey into Night
Eugene O'Neill's drama of a problem-prone Tyrone family is faithfully brought to the big screen with all the vices and vitriol intact. Ralph Richardson heads a cast that includes Katharine Hepburn, Jason Robards, Jr. and Dean Stockwell.
VHS: S02576. $19.98.
Laser: LD71550. $39.98.
Sidney Lumet, USA, 1962, 170 mins.

Look Back in Anger—Kenneth Branagh
John Osborne's play has had many successful productions featuring great British actors, including Richard Burton and Malcolm McDowell. Now Kenneth Branagh and Emma Thompson are featured in a convincing production that brings alive the fury which inspired a generation of angry young men.
VHS: S24665. $29.98.
David Jones, Great Britain, 1989, 114 mins.

Looking for Richard
Al Pacino's critically acclaimed tribute to Shakespeare features Winona Ryder, Kevin Spacey, Alec Baldwin, Estelle Parsons and Aidan Quinn in rehearsals and meetings, allowing the audience to eavesdrop on the behind-the-scenes process that goes into creating characters and mounting a production. In this case, the production is Shakespeare's gripping drama of power and betrayal, *Richard III*. With Sir John Gielgud, Kenneth Branagh, Vanessa Redgrave, James Earl Jones and Kevin Kline.
VHS: S31028. $103.99.
Laser: LD76142. $49.95.
Al Pacino, 1996, USA, 112 mins.

Lysistrata

Aristophanes' ancient Greek play is brought to life in this new adaptation starring Jenny Karezi and Costas Kazakos. Lysistrata is the Athenian woman disgusted by the way men have ruined the country with their endless war. Rallying other women, she proposes that they impose an embargo on sexual relations with men as long as the war lasts. The film liberates the action from the stage, places it on location in the acropolis, and renders Aristophanes' plea in a forceful manner. Contains nudity and strong language. Greek with English subtitles.
VHS: S11718. $39.95.
Yiannis Negrepontis, Greece, 1987, 97 mins.

Macbeth (Evans)

Sir Maurice Evans and Dame Judith Anderson star in Shakespeare's turbulent drama, produced for television. Great Britain, 1954, 103 mins.
VHS: S01650. $19.95.

Macbeth (Jayson)

Thames Television produced this brilliant adaptation of Shakespeare's play with the cast including Michael Jayson, Barbara Lee Hunt, Ralph Nosseck, Richard Warner.
VHS: S12738. $39.99.

Mack the Knife

Raul Julia returns to the role that made him a star on the Broadway stage. He plays Mac Heath, the suave London master criminal and womanizer, in this film adaption of the Bertolt Brecht and Kurt Weill musical *Threepenny Opera*. Cast includes Richard Harris, Julia Migenes, Julie Walters, Clive Revill and Rachel Robertson. Roger Daltry sings the familiar title tune. Filmed in Yugoslavia to save money.
VHS: S12419. $89.95.
Menahem Golan, USA, 1989, 122 mins.

The Madwoman of Chaillot

British filmmaker Bryan Forbes *(The Stepford Wives)* adapts Jean Giradoux's play about an eccentric and possibly demented woman (Katharine Hepburn) who's convinced the world is no longer worthy of her attention. The all-star cast includes Charles Boyer, Claude Dauphin, Paul Henreid, Giulietta Masina, Richard Chamberlain and Yul Brynner.
VHS: S15934. $19.98.
Laser: LD71187. $39.98.
Bryan Forbes, Great Britain, 1969, 132 mins.

The Mahabharata (1989/166 mins.)

The ground-breaking theatrical experience by Peter Brook based on the ancient Sanskrit story of two families whose warring feud brings civilization to the brink of doom. With a script written by Jean-Claude Carriere and a cast of multi-ethnic and talented actors, this milestone of theatrical performance, according to one reviewer, "accomplishes the seemingly impossible…in terms of modern cinema, it is somewhat of a miracle."
VHS: S20825. $49.95.
Peter Brook, Great Britain, 1989, 166 mins.

The Mahabharata (1992/318 mins.)

Adapted from the sacred 2000-year-old Sanskrit poem *The Great Story of Mankind*, this full-length film adaptation of the milestone theatre piece by an international company directed by Peter Brook captures the epic sweep of an entire world view. 318 mins.
VHS: S13333. $99.95.
Peter Brook, France/Great Britain, 1992, 318 mins.

Maidsplay and Dreiske Discipline Lecture Demonstration

One of the best realizations of theatre on film, this 1983 Hungarian production documents Nicole Dreiske's production of *Maidsplay*, an original theatre piece inspired by Jean Genet's *The Maids* in Budapest. The production utilizes actual information about the two sisters whose extraordinary crime inspired Genet to write *The Maids* and highlights the themes of violence, sex, drugs, jealousy and incest in the story of the two sisters who, employed as maids in the same house, take turns playing the role of their mistress in a secret and bizarre ritual. The second part of the tape illustrates the basic techniques of The Dreiske Discipline as led by Nicole Dreiske in actor workshops in Budapest. Produced by Judit Koszanyi, directed by Ildiko Szabo. A BBS/Mafilm production. In English. Color, 80 mins.
VHS: S03474. $60.00.

Major Barbara

Filmed in war-torn England, Gabriel Pascal's screen version of George Bernard Shaw's famous play is a memorial to the artists who made it and proof that it takes more than bombs to subdue the English wit. The story of a Salvation Army girl, her munitions manufacturing father and her pragmatic scholar fiance, this film version is a triumph—demonstrating Shaw's own words that "the greatest of our evils and the worst of our crimes is poverty." With Rex Harrison and Deborah Kerr.
VHS: S13734. $39.95.
Gabriel Pascal, Great Britain, 1940, 90 mins.

The Making of Miss Saigon

All the drama, tension and excitement surrounding the creation of this major musical is captured here, from the nervous excitement of the first read-through to the triumphant first night. Features the producer, the authors, the stars. 75 mins.
VHS: S34611. $19.98.

Making Theatre: Rashomon

Alternating between rehearsals and performances of Rashomon, the classic Japanese "I-Dunnit," this film is at once the portrait and the agent of a revelation. As the actors, under the benevolent dictatorship of master-director, Niel Munro, come to understand their roles and thus become the characters they portray, the viewer comes to appreciate the intricate, mysterious and laborious creative process at the end of which a play is born. 96 mins.
VHS: S34384. $19.98.

Mambo Mouth

This funny program captures the essence of writer-comedian-actor John Leguizamo's off-Broadway hit. Performing six monologues that illustrate Latin stereotypes, Leguizamo transforms from Loco Louie, a sex crazed 14-year-old, to Manny the Fanny, a female prostitute, to Angel, the epitome of angry Latin machismo, to other poignant characters. The play won both an Obie and an Outer Critics Circle Award.
VHS: S16157. $19.95.
Thomas Schlamme, USA, 1991, 60 mins.

Marat/Sade (The Persecution and Assassination of Jean-Paul Marat as Performed by the Inmates of the Asylum of Charenton Under the Direction of Marquis de Sade)

Peter Weiss' monumental play, in a mesmerizing adaptation directed by the world-famous stage director Peter Brook, in its original production by the Royal Shakespeare Company. The play features Glenda Jackson as a nutcase in the role of Charlotte Chorday, the assassin of Marat. With Ian Richardson, Patrick Magee, Ruth Baker and Freddie Jones. Terrifying and intense.
VHS: S09855. $29.95.
Laser: LD70264. $39.95.
DVD: DV60343. $24.99.
Peter Brook, Great Britain, 1967, 115 mins.

Marc Blitzstein: The Cradle Will Rock

Excerpts from the musical work *The Cradle Will Rock* performed by a very young Jerry Orbach and Nancy Andrews, Hal Buckley, Clifford David and Micki Grant. Howard da Silva, who had been in the original 1937 cast, is director. Also, a profile of the life, work and influence of Mark Blitzstein, bringing together comrades and admirers Aaron Copeland, Arvin Brown and John Houseman. 1964/1976, 85 mins.
VHS: S32320. $89.95.

The Marquise

Noel Coward's drawing room comedy unfolds in the mad opulence of the Compte Raoul De Vriac's spacious chateau outside Paris. Set in 1735, the Compte's former mistress, the Marquise Eloise De Kertournel, floors everybody with her announcement she's staying permanently. With Diana Rigg, Richard Johnson and James Villiers. 55 mins.
VHS: S19179. $24.98.

Marty—Goodyear TV Playhouse

Two years before Ernest Borgnine made the movie, Rod Steiger won praise for his portrayal of the lonely, overweight butcher from the Bronx. The live tv drama featured Nancy Marchand, Betsy Palmer and Nehemiah Persoff. From the Golden Age of tv. Commercials deleted. USA, 1953, 51 mins.
VHS: S05517. $19.95.

Master Harold and the Boys

The Broadway hit play by South Africa's eminent playwright Athol Fugard stars Matthew Broderick. USA, 1986, 90 mins.
VHS: S01528. $19.98.

Masters of the French Stage: Jean-Louis Barrault and Madeline Renaud

Leading figures on the French stage since World War II, director/actor Jean-Louis Barrault and his wife, actress Madeleine Renaud, present the jealousy scene from Moliere's *Le Misanthrope* and recitations from other works of French drama and poetry, including Jacques Prevert's *Bird*, Paul Valois' *Liberte* and a charming fable about animal intelligence. Barrault performs his famous circus horse-riding pantomime and discusses the importance of state subsidies to the theater for the good of the country's intellectual life. Some French dialog.
VHS: S30997. $89.95.
1969, 28 mins.

Max Frisch

Performance of scenes from Max Frisch's off-Broadway plays *Andorra* and *I'm Not Stiller*. Interview with the celebrated Swiss novelist and playwright. 1963, 27 mins.
VHS: S32323. $89.95.

Medea

An intense rendering of Euripides' masterpiece in this famous production which features Dame Judith Anderson, reprising her role from Broadway. With Colleen Dewhurst.
VHS: S18027. $29.95.

Meet Marcel Marceau

Don't expect an opening monologue. The famed French mime lets his body and his features do all the talking he needs. This one-man show consists of nine parts including a special tribute to Harpo Marx, Buster Keaton, Stan Laurel and Charlie Chaplin. Marceau is said to do a voice-over narration to some skits, but hearing is believing. USA, 1965, 52 mins.
VHS: S05518. $24.95.

The Merchant of Venice

Sir Laurence Olivier and Joan Plowright star in Shakespeare's complex tale of jealousy and greed. 131 mins.
VHS: S19028. $19.98.

The Merry Wives of Windsor (Esquire 4+4)

Shakespeare's play about a lover wooing a potentially unfaithful wife. Starring Leon Charles and Gloria Grahame. 160 mins. Two videocassettes.
VHS: S15187. $59.95.

A Midsummer Night's Dream (BBC)

A live BBC production of Shakespeare's play of star-crossed lovers and the influence of supernatural creatures. Benny Hill appears in the role of Bottom. Also in the cast are Anna Massey, Jill Bennett, Cyril Luckham, Patrick Allen and Peter Wyngarde. A comical fantasy. England, 1960's, 111 mins.
VHS: S05520. $29.95.

A Midsummer Night's Dream (Peter Hall)

Peter Hall's delicate and merry adaptation of Shakespeare's enchanting farce about the shifting loyalties and evolving relationships among two pairs of lovers. Their romantic affection is manipulated with the help of Puck, a magic fairy. With Diana Rigg as Helena, David Warner as Lysander, Ian Richardson as Oberon, King of the Fairies, Judi Dench as Tatania, Queen of the Fairies and Ian Holm as Puck.
VHS: S06074. $24.95.
Peter Hall, Great Britain, 1968, 124 mins.

A Midsummer Night's Dream (Reinhardt)

The brilliant German theater director Max Reinhardt adapts his Broadway production of Shakespeare's enchanting and lyrical play about love, companionship, fate and star-crossed affairs. Two opposite pairs of lovers ward off extravagant spells and the supernatural to consummate their transcendent passion. The film is visually intoxicating and dramatically powerful, retaining Shakespeare's words though finding a sublime grace and subtlety to the moods and rhythms. Music by Mendelssohn. Choreography by Bronislawa Nijinska and Anton Grot. With James Cagney, Dick Powell, Olivia de Havilland and Joe E. Brown.
VHS: S01679. $19.98.
Laser: LD71150. $39.98.
Max Reinhardt, USA, 1935, 135 mins.

Miracle in the Rain—Westinghouse Studio One

The love story written by Ben Hecht is slightly marred by noisy stagehands and sloppy camerawork. The writing is said to overcome any defects of live TV. With Jeffrey Lynn and Joy Geffen in a story of a lonely girl and the soldier who went away. USA, 1950, 56 mins.
VHS: S05452. $24.95.

Monster in a Box

This film version of Spalding Gray's acclaimed stage hit follows an hilarious and insightful tale about a writer with a block. Writer's block metamorphoses into a behemoth document that won't go back in the box. Gray is thus set off on an itinerary that includes stops in an Eastern haunted writer's retreat, an L.A. where screenwriters don't write, and a movie set in Nicaragua where he plays a spy.
VHS: S26337. $19.98.
Nick Broomfield, USA, 1992, 90 mins.

Much Ado About Nothing

Kenneth Branagh's energetic, highly cinematic adaptation of Shakespeare's comedy of love is notable for its beautiful Italian locations and first-rate performances from Branagh, Emma Thompson, Michael Keaton, Robert Sean Leonard, Keanu Reeves and Denzel Washington. "Ravishing entertainment" (Vincent Canby, *The New York Times*).
VHS: S20528. $19.95.
Laser: LD72362. $34.95.
Kenneth Branagh, Great Britain, 1993, 110 mins.

'Night Mother

Adaptation of the Pulitzer Prize winning play stars Sissy Spacek and Anne Bancroft as a mother and daughter whose psyches are slowly unveiled to expose their real feelings about the events of their lives together.
VHS: S03466. $79.95.
Tom Moore, USA, 1986, 96 mins.

The Norman Conquests: Table Manners

HBO continues the story of Norman and his way with impressing three sisters. Based on the work by British playwright Alan Ayckbourn, the same story is told in the living room, the garden and the dining room. With Lucie Arnaz, Ken Howard, Craig Wasson, Leonard Rossiter and Malcolm McDowell. 108 mins.
VHS: S06159. $59.95.

Oedipus Rex

A landmark production of Sophocles' great tragedy, as directed and filmed by Sir Tyrone Guthrie; performed in masks, as in original Greece; a play and film which retain the primal emotional power of the original.
VHS: S00947. $59.95.
Tyrone Guthrie, Canada, 1956, 90 mins.

Oh Calcutta!

Video taped telecast of the long-running theatrical revue spoofing modern ideas of sex and sensuality, famous primarily for its nudity.
VHS: S02556. $29.95.
G.M. Aucion, USA, 1980, 120 mins.

Oleanna

David Mamet adapted his own provocative and acclaimed stage play that brilliantly explores the issues of sexual harassment. William H. Macy stars as the college professor who is forced to confront the moral and political implications of power, blackmail and revenge on a contemporary college campus when he is accused of sexual harassment.
Laser: LD74958. $39.99.
David Mamet, USA, 1994, 90 mins.

On Borrowed Time

A witty adaptation of Lawrence Edward Watkin's dark fable about death. A middle-aged man is trapped in a tree built by his father and son. The cast includes Lionel Barrymore, Cedric Hardwicke and Una Merkel.
VHS: S17660. $19.98.
Harold S. Bucquet, USA, 1939, 99 mins.

The Open Theater: Terminal

Performance of several experimental pieces by the Open Theater Ensemble. Includes portions of the ensemble's 1971 off-Broadway production *Terminal*, written by Susan Yankowitz and directed by Joseph Chaikin and Roberta Sklar. *Terminal* holds an unflinching mirror up to contemporary values and theater conventions. The metaphor through which this is focused is the "terminal" experience: dying, death and afterdeath. With the original New York company.
VHS: S34000. $89.95.
Joseph Chaikin/Roberta Sklar, USA, 1971, 27 mins.

Othello (1922/Silent)

A remarkably successful silent transposition of Shakespeare's great play, featuring great performances from some of German Expressionism's best actors: Emil Jannings, Werner Kraus, Lya de Putti. Moody, elaborate costumes and sets and first-class acting. Silent with English subtitles.
VHS: S00978. $29.95.
Dimitri Buchowetzki, Germany, 1922, 81 mins.

Othello (1996/Parker)

Laurence Fishburne stars along with Irene Jacob and Kenneth Branagh in this recent screen adaptation of the Shakespeare play. His tale of passion, intrigue, jealousy and murder has fascinated audiences for centuries. This version is both entertaining and accessible to today's audience.
VHS: S29441. $19.95.
Laser: LD75819. $39.98.
Oliver Parker, USA, 1996, 124 mins.

Our Town (1940)

Thornton Wilder's classic American play about life, marriage and death in a small town is transposed to film with William Holden as the boy-next-door George Gibbs, while Oscar nominee Martha Scott and Frank Craven re-create their original Broadway cast roles.
VHS: S00980. $19.95.
Sam Wood, USA, 1940, 89 mins.

Our Town (1977)

Thorton Wilder's Pulitzer prize- and Emmy Award-winning play is brought to the screen by Hal Holbrook, Barbara Bel Geddes, John Houseman, Robby Benson, Ronny Cox and Sada Thompson. Here is the full poignant portrayal of love, life and death in a small American town that has brought pleasure to millions.
VHS: S05624. $74.95.
Franklin J. Schnaffner, USA, 1977, 120 mins.

Our Town (1988)

Thornton Wilder's classic play about life in a small town brings Yankee simplicity to new depths. In this version Eric Stoltz, Penelope Ann Miller, Peter Maloney, Roberta Maxwell, Frances Conroy, James Reborn and Spalding Gray, the noted monologist, portray the rural characters that epitomize the best of rural America. Produced at Lincoln Center for PBS's Great Performances series.
VHS: S24020. $74.95.
Gregory Mosher, USA, 1988

Paradise Now

Shot during the last presentation of *Paradise Now* by The Living Theatre in Brussels, and before 7,000 spectators in Berlin, made on videotape with expressionist coloring, a unique record of this famous play by The Living Theatre, capturing the frenzy of the original.
VHS: S00991. $29.95.
Sheldon Rochlin, USA, 1970, 95 mins.

Paul Robeson

James Earl Jones delivers a powerful performance as Paul Robeson, the legendary actor, singer, and early champion of human rights, a man of peace, whose career was destroyed by the zealots of the Cold War. "Americans need to see this, not because an actor rises to superlative heights…which Jones does, but because it reintroduces Paul Robeson to the American public."
VHS: S06092. $49.95.
Lloyd Richards, USA, 1980, 118 mins.

Peter Brook

An interview with the great director just after he returned from Africa with his Center of Research, his group of young actors based in Paris. Brook explains his views on theater, cross-cultural performances, improvisation, Shakespeare and working with young actors. 1973, 27 mins.
VHS: S32315. $89.95.

The Piano Lesson

Charles Dutton and Alfre Woodard star in this film adaptation of August Wilson's Pulitzer Prize-winning play. A brother and sister fight over differing visions of their future. If they sell a piano they could buy a farm, but this piano represents more than money. It is a link to a vibrant tradition. With Courtney Vance, Carl Gordon, Tommy Hollis and Zelda Harris.
VHS: S26143. $14.98.
Lloyd Richards, USA, 1995, 99 mins.

Playhouse 90: Requiem for a Heavyweight

Famous live television drama version of the classic Clifford Odets play with Jack Palance, Ed and Keenan Wynn in feature roles.
VHS: S09547. $29.95.

Playwrights '56

Paul Newman stars in this early television adaptation of Ernest Hemingway's story *The Butler*.
VHS: S10596. $29.95.

Porgy: A Gullah Version

The classic Dubose Heyward play gains authenticity in this version with African-American characters speaking Gullah, an English-based creole language spoken along the South Atlantic coast. This tape captures the world premiere of *Porgy: A Gullah Version*, performed in Charleston, South Carolina. 120 mins.
VHS: S31704. $19.95.

Private Lives

A witty adaptation of Noel Coward's play about a high-society, rancorous couple who can neither stay apart nor together, beautifully acted by Norma Shearer, Robert Montgomery and Una Merkel.
VHS: S17662. $19.98.
Laser: LD72337. $34.98.
Sidney Franklin, USA, 1931, 84 mins.

Ran

Kurosawa's masterpiece is a decade-in-the-making version of *King Lear* that brilliantly blends Japanese history with Shakespeare's themes. A triumphant film about ruthless ambition, evil plots and "Chaos"—the meaning of the title in Japanese. Japanese with English subtitles. VHS letterboxed.
VHS: S02012. $29.95.
Akira Kurosawa, Japan, 1985, 160 mins.

Richard Burton's Hamlet

Sir John Gielgud directed this legendary 1964 live performance of Shakespeare's play on Broadway starring Richard Burton. The video is made from an original 35mm negative restored by the British Film Institute, with a digitally remastered soundtrack.
VHS: S34668. $89.95.
John Gielgud, Great Britain, 1964, 206 mins.

Richard III

Laurence Olivier's third Shakespeare adaptation moves away from the brooding, austere staging of the early works to a delirious Technicolor treatment of the ruthless tyrant who seizes his throne and wages war at Bosworth. With Olivier, Claire Bloom, Ralph Richardson, John Gielgud and Stanley Baker. Remastered. Letterboxed.
VHS: S01680. $24.95.
Laser: LD72285. $99.95.
Laurence Olivier, Great Britain, 1956, 161 mins.

Rime of the Ancient Mariner

Coleridge's epic poem is brought to life in a recital featuring Sir Michael Redgrave, accompanied by images both real and animated. 60 mins.
VHS: S03158. $59.95.

Robbie Burkett: A Line of Balance

A look at the remarkable career of puppeteer Robbie Burkett as he prepares his production of the Gothic musical thriller *Awful Manors*. A behind-the-scenes look at a man who manipulates over 40 marionettes, speaks and sings in 22 different voices, operates special effects all in one spectacular production and still keeps his strings attached.
VHS: S21958. $24.95.
Margaret Mardirossian, Canada, 1992, 58 mins.

Romeo and Juliet (Laurence Harvey)

Laurence Harvey stars in this commanding interpretation of Shakespeare's great tale of star-crossed lovers. Stunningly photographed on location in Italy, Renato Castellani's version stars Susan Shentall and Flora Robson, and the transitions are narrated by Sir John Gielgud.
VHS: S12346. $29.98.
Laser: LD76131. $49.95.
Renato Castellani, Great Britain, 1964, 135 mins.

Romeo and Juliet (Zeffirelli)

One of the most popular film adaptations of Shakespeare's classic, the recipient of international acclaim and four Academy Award nominations. Starring Olivia Hussey, Leonard Whiting and Michael York, this modern version brings new vitality and fresh insight to the world's most durable love story. English dialog. Letterboxed.
VHS: S01130. $24.95.
Laser: LD76048. $44.98.
Franco Zeffirelli, USA/Italy, 1968, 138 mins.

The Rose Tattoo

A happy-go-lucky trucker awakens a widow to life's joys in this flavorful adaptation of a Tennessee Williams play. Starring Burt Lancaster and the brilliant Anna Magnani. Photographed by James Wong Howe.
VHS: S13787. $19.95.
Daniel Mann, USA, 1955, 117 mins.

School for Scandal

A live television adaptation of the classic satire of the morals and manners of 18th century England by Richard Sheridan. Featuring Joan Plowright as Lady Oliver and Felix Aylmer. England, 1965, 100 mins.
VHS: S01168. $29.95.

Shakespeare by the English Theater Company

Richard II, Henry IV parts 1 and 2 and *Henry the V* follow the story of two powerful dynasties. In this video collection the legendary conflicts of Agincourt and Tewkesbury are rendered into living history.
VHS: S24890. $129.95.

Shakespeare's Globe Theater Restored: Much Ado About Something

Documents 18 months of planning, rehearsal, location work and post-production by the Shakespeare Program of the University of California at Berkeley, culminating in the first recorded Elizabethan production of Shakespeare's *Much Ado About Nothing* on the newly rebuilt Globe stage in London. 30 mins.
VHS: S33766. $39.95.

Sidney Lumet: From Theater to Film

This 1962 program is an illustrated exploration of how stage plays can be translated to the screen, with particular attention to the work of stage, film and television director Sidney Lumet and discussion with Yale University literature professor John Gassner and film commentator Peretz Johnnes. Among the themes discussed in this energetic roundtable are how film can reveal more of the playwright's intentions than the theater, how the camera becomes a leading actor, how film time differs from stage time, and the way that the theater audience's focus is flexible whereas on screen the focus is controlled by the director. 60 mins.
VHS: S31577. $59.95.

Signals Through the Flames

The Odyssey of the Living Theatre, the courageous, audacious American theatre company which for 35 years occupied the stages and jails of the world. The film gives a unique sense of a company that, said *Newsweek*, "produced more guts, passion and controversy than any other."
VHS: S01199. $29.95.
Sheldon Rochlin, USA, 1983, 97 mins.

Sleuth

Mystery tour-de-force based on Anthony Schaffer's play starring Laurence Olivier as an eccentric writer of detective novels coercing his neighbor Michael Caine into a series of well-planned capers.
VHS: S02605. $14.98.
Joseph L. Mankiewicz, USA, 1972, 139 mins.

Strange Interlude (1932)

A polished adaptation of Eugene O'Neill's Pulitzer prize-winning play about a brilliant young woman's affair with her husband's best friend. With Clark Gable, Norma Shearer and Maureen O'Sullivan.
VHS: S17663. $19.98.
Robert Z. Leonard, USA, 1932, 110 mins.

Strasberg on Acting

Author/theater critic Margaret Croyden talks with Lee Strasberg, director of The Actors Studio in New York City, considered the foremost training ground for actors in the United States. The father of "Method" acting discusses his career and ideas, reminisces about actors and the craft of acting and is shown lecturing and working with actors in scenes from *Uncle Vanya* at his Lee Strasberg Acting Institute.
VHS: S30995. $89.95.
1975, 28 mins.

A Streetcar Named Desire (1984)

A made-for-television adaptation of Tennessee Williams' play about Blanche du Bois (Ann-Margret), the fading descendant of the once prominent Southern aristocracy, who gets entangled in the lives of her sister (Beverly D'Angelo) and her brutal husband, Stanley Kowalski (Treat Williams). With Randy Quaid, Rafael Campos and Erica Yohn.
VHS: S19684. $9.98.
John Erman, USA, 1984, 94 mins.

A Streetcar Named Desire (1995)

Jessica Lange is Blanche DuBois to Alec Baldwin's Stanley Kowalski in this uncut film version of Tennessee Williams' immortal play. Lange won a Golden Globe for her portrayal of the delicate and mad woman who relies "on the kindness of strangers." John Goodman and Diane Lane also star.
VHS: S27744. $79.95.
Laser: LD75932. $49.95.
Glenn Jordan, USA, 1995, 156 mins.

A Streetcar Named Desire: Director's Cut (1951)

Tennessee Williams' notorious play was censored when adapted for the screen. Now four minutes of the originally cut material have been found and restored to this "director's cut". Marlon Brando, Kim Hunter and Vivien Leigh star in this drama of betrayal, madness and rape.
VHS: S21085. $19.98.
Laser: LD70687. $39.98.
DVD: DV60067. $24.98.
Elia Kazan, USA, 1951, 125 mins.

Strindberg and His Women: 3 One-Act Dramas

In the three mini-dramas presented here, love, ambition, and friendship are brought within range of the great modernist Swedish playwright August Strindberg's uncompromising glare. Revealing and sometimes painful, the works are fired with an intensity whose destructive power is rivaled only by its cathartic potential. 76 mins.
VHS: S34385. $19.98.

Strindberg's Miss Julie: Royal Shakespeare Company

August Strindberg, "...one of the prime innovators of our time...the impact of his dramatic method reflected in his Miss Julie is probably greater and less acknowledged than any other modern writer. Strindberg struck strongly into O'Neill, Becket and Tennessee Williams...entering the subconscious where sexual encounter has a fight to the death..." (Arthur Miller, *N.Y. Times*).
VHS: S02006. $74.95.

Summer and Smoke

This vivid adaptation of a Tennessee Williams play tells the story of a spinster who is tortured by her unrequited love for the town's handsome young doctor. Good performances from Geraldine Page, Laurence Harvey, and Rita Moreno. Musical score by Elmer Bernstein.
VHS: S13786. $19.95.
Laser: Widescreen. **LD75267. $34.98.**
Peter Glenville, USA, 1961, 118 mins.

The Taming of the Shrew (Esquire 4+4)

Shakespeare's story of two sisters, Katherina and Bianca, and their suitors. Starring Franklin Seales and Karen Austin. 117 mins. Two videocassettes.
VHS: S15189. $59.95.

The Taming of the Shrew (Westinghouse Studio)

Seen on live television, and part of the Westinghouse Studio television program. Charlton Heston and Lisa Kirk star in this 1950 modern dress version with Heston wearing sunglasses and downing beer with the boys while Lisa Kirk appears in tight slacks and with a riding whip. Broadcast June 5, 1950. USA, 1950, 60 mins.
VHS: S06987. $24.95.

The Taming of the Shrew (Zeffirelli)

An exquisite mounting of Shakespeare's comic look at male-female relationships stars Richard Burton as Petruchio, the wily gentleman from Verona who travels to Padua to wed Elizabeth Taylor as the fiery Katharina.
VHS: S01681. $19.95.
Franco Zeffirelli, USA/Italy, 1967, 127 mins.

Tea & Sympathy

Deborah Kerr, John Kerr and Leif Erickson recreate their Broadway roles in this glossy Vincente Minnelli adaptation of the Robert Anderson play. A sensitive prep school student finds his extracurricular activity with a teacher's wife quite educational. With Edward Andrews, Dean Jones and Darryl Hickman.
VHS: S13190. $19.98.
Vincente Minnelli, USA, 1956, 122 mins.

The Tempest (Mazursky)

Paul Mazursky's soaring imagination combined with a fine cast make for a real treat. John Cassavetes, Gena Rowlands, Susan Sarandon and Raul Julia are featured in this story loosely based on Shakespeare's play. Set in Greece, the photography is superb.
VHS: S01682. $19.95.
Paul Mazursky, USA, 1982, 140 mins.

The Tempest (Woodman)

Shakespeare's classic tale of the fantasy world of spirits, sorcery, monsters, and shipwrecked scheming noblemen is brought to life in a stunning production featuring Efrem Zimbalist Jr., William H. Bassett, Ted Sorel.
VHS: S04203. $59.95.
William Woodman, USA, 127 mins.

That Championship Season

Jason Miller's play, first presented by the New York Shakespeare Festival, takes place at the 24th reunion of the Scranton High School basketball team. Featuring Robert Mitchum, Bruce Dern, Martin Sheen, Stacy Keach and Paul Sorvino.
VHS: S02367. $79.95.
Jason Miller, USA, 1982, 108 mins.

The Theatre of Tadeusz Kantor

A unique documentary on the work of a legendary genius of theatre, Tadeusz Kantor. Filmmaker Denis Bablet traces Kantor's roots as a visual artist in Poland and explores his ingenious methods of designing the props which become living sculptures in his extraordinary theatre productions. The program features rare scenes of Kantor at work with the dedicated actors in his troupe, Cricot 2. In a unique scene, Kantor is on-stage and "conducts" the actors much as a symphony conductor leads an orchestra. Extensive segments from some of Kantor's most famous works, *Wielopole, Wielopole* and *The Dead Class*, are also included. Narrated in English. 144 mins.
VHS: S14812. $59.95.

Theatre of the Iron Curtain

This film provides a behind-the-scenes look at legitimate theatre in the Soviet Union, and gives a concise history to the art. The camera goes inside theatre schools where actors, directors and producers are trained for a life in the theatre. 55 mins.
VHS: S12723. $19.98.

The Three Sisters

Shelley Winters, Sandy Dennis, Geraldine Page and Kevin McCarthy star in this famed Actor's Studio production of the equally famous Chekhov play.
VHS: S14677. $59.95.
Paul Bogart, USA, 1965, 167 mins.

Torch Song Trilogy

Harvey Fierstein adapted his Broadway hit play about the trials and tribulations of being a sexually active gay urban male in the 1970's for the big screen. He repeats the role of Arnold Beckoff, a drag artiste looking for love. He finds it with Brian Kerwin and Matthew Broderick. Anne Bancroft is Arnold's very Jewish mother and a prime cause of Arnold's frustrated anger.
VHS: S09390. $19.95.
Paul Bogart, USA, 1988, 126 mins.

Toys in the Attic

George Roy Hill's fluent adaptation of Lillian Hellman's Southern gothic play about a repressed young man's return to his New Orleans home town with a child-like wife. Geraldine Page and Wendy Hiller contribute two horrifying performances as the man's overprotective sisters. With Dean Martin and Yvette Mimieux.
VHS: S17665. $19.98.
George Roy Hill, USA, 1963, 90 mins.

Tragedy of Antony and Cleopatra

Shakespeare's most popular tale of two of history's most famous personages. Starring Lynn Redgrave, John Carradine, Timothy Dalton and Anthony Geary.
VHS: S02373. $59.95.
Lawrence Carra, USA, 183 mins.

The Tragedy of King Lear

Shakespeare's tragedy about an aging king who has chosen to lay aside the care of his kingship and divide his kingdom among his three daughters. Starring Mike Kellen and Darryl Hickman. 182 mins. Two videocassettes.
VHS: S15188. $89.95.
Laser: LD71376. $69.95.

Tragedy of King Richard II

Shakespeare's drama of the self-centered, weak kind. Starring David Birney, Paul Shenar, John Devlin and William Bassett.
VHS: S03011. $59.95.
William Woodman, USA, 172 mins.

Tragedy of Macbeth

Shakespeare's story of murder, greed and untimely death. Starring Jeremy Brett, Piper Laurie, Simon MacCorkindale and Barry Primus.
VHS: S02222. $59.95.
Arthur Allan Seidelman, USA, 151 mins.

Tragedy of Othello the Moor of Venice

Shakespeare's keen understanding of jealousy in love results in perhaps his greatest triumph as a stage play, and his prime example of the tragic hero, Othello. With William Marshall, Ron Moody and Jenny Agutter. With meticulously constructed costumes and an artist's reproduction of the Globe Theater stage. 159 mins.
VHS: S02987. $59.95.

The Tragedy of Romeo and Juliet

Shakespeare's play of star-crossed young love, feuding families and death. Starring Alex Hyde-White and Blanche Baker. 165 mins. Two videocassettes.
VHS: S15186. $59.95.
Laser: LD71377. $69.95.

The Twelfth Night

Ben Kingsley, Helena Bonham Carter, Nigel Hawthorne and Richard E. Grant brings William Shakespeare's best-loved comedy to life. The outlandish, gender-bending tale of troublesome twins who win the hearts of an entire kingdom is as relevant and funny today as it was when it was first performed almost 400 years ago.
VHS: S31352. $19.98.
Laser: LD76283. $49.95.
Trevor Nunn, Great Britain, 1996, 133 mins.

Two for the Seesaw

Robert Wise's eccentric comedy about the off-beat romantic flourishes and consequences of an unlikely romance between lawyer Robert Mitchum and free spirit Shirley MacLaine. With Edmund Ryan and Elisabeth Fraser.
VHS: S17666. $19.98.
Laser: LD72157. $39.98.
Robert Wise, USA, 1962, 120 mins.

Uncovering Shakespeare: An Update

William F. Buckley, Jr., moderates this panel discussion featuring a wide range of experts who examine the centuries-old question about Shakespeare's authorship. This documentary was awarded the CINE Golden Eagle Award. 161 mins.
VHS: S21927. $149.95.

Understanding Shakespeare

Easy-to-follow dramatic interpretations cut through the 16th-century language barrier to deliver a fuller understanding of the beauty and magnificence of Shakespeare's plays. Features renowned Shakespearean actors in key scenes from each play. Noted Shakespearean scholars comment, interpret and explain the action. Each title is 90 mins.
Understanding Shakespeare: Hamlet.
VHS: S37081. $49.95.
Understanding Shakespeare: MacBeth.
VHS: S37082. $49.95.
Understanding Shakespeare: Othello.
VHS: S37080. $49.95.
Understanding Shakespeare: Romeo & Juliet.
VHS: S37083. $49.95.
Understanding Shakespeare: Complete 4-Tape Set.
VHS: S37084. $159.95.

Vaudeville Videos

Comics, jugglers, animal acts, skaters, famous names and forgotten names, in a nostalgic look at entertainment from the early years of the century. Includes Weber and Fields, George and Gracie, Jack Smith, Smith and Dale. 60 mins.
VHS: S08013. $29.95.

Vincent

On July 29, 1890, Vincent Van Gogh died in his brother Theo's arms. Devastated, Theo was unable to speak at his brother's funeral. One week later, Theo invited an audience of artists and friends to a Paris lecture hall. In this acclaimed one-man drama presented at the Guthrie Theater, Leonard Nimoy portrays the stricken Theo as he finds the words to honor his late brother's memory.
VHS: S16577. $59.95.
Leonard Nimoy/Bonnie Burns, USA, 1981, 88 mins.

Walls in the City

Paula Killen stars in this independent video directed by Jim Sikora and featuring Tony Fitzpatrick, David Yow, Bill Cusak and original music by the Denison-Kimble Trio.
VHS: S21207. $19.98.

The Water Engine

David Mamet wrote this strange exercise about the deceptions of success. Charles Lang (William H. Macy) is a factory worker who invents an engine that runs on water. He expects this device will save him and his sister (Patti Lupone) from poverty. But Lang never understood that betrayal is just another game in the world of business.
VHS: S24733. $49.98.
Steven Schachter, USA, 1995, 89 mins.

William Shakespeare Series

These five 45-minute lectures explore key issues in the works of this great author, including his comedies, tragedies and historical dramas.
Death in Victory: Shakespeare's Tragic Reconciliations. Fresden Bowers.
VHS: S24115. $240.00.
Feuding and Loving in Shakespeare's Romeo and Juliet. George Walton Williams.
VHS: S24116. $240.00.
Hamlet as Minister and Scourge. Fredson Bowers.
VHS: S24117. $240.00.
The Staging of Shakespeare's Plays. George Walton Williams.
VHS: S24118. $240.00.
The Why and How of Poisoning in Shakespeare's Othello. George Walton Williams.
VHS: S24119. $240.00.

William Shakespeare's Romeo & Juliet

Baz Luhrmann's justifiably acclaimed, truly original, modern-day updating of William Shakespeare's great play stars Claire Danes, Leonardo DiCaprio, John Leguizamo, Brian Dennehy, Pete Postlethwaite and Paul Sorvino. "Enough positive energy and dizzying high spirits to make it irresistible…not your father's Shakespeare" (Kenneth Turan, *Los Angeles Times*).
VHS: S31026. $14.98.
Laser: LD76140. $49.95.
Baz Luhrmann, USA, 1996, 120 mins.

Winterset

Burgess Meredith, Eduardo Ciannelli and John Carradine star in this adaptation of a play by Maxwell Anderson, based on the trial of Sacco and Vanzetti. 1936.
VHS: S08424. $29.95.

Without You I'm Nothing

Sandra Bernhard's adaptation of her off-Broadway show is a documentary-like examination of the nature of performance, identity and the culture of celebrity. In a brilliant dialectic on the relationship of performer and audience, Bernhard inhabits various roles and personalities to make hilarious comments about music, art, fashion, politics and sex. With John Doe, Steve Antin and Cynthia Bailey, a beautiful black woman who's Bernhard's alter ego.
Laser: CLV. LD72096. $29.98.
John Boskovich, USA, 1990, 90 mins.

PERFORMING ARTS INSTRUCTION

The 16mm Camera

The complete overview of the 12 major 16mm camera systems, including detailed examinations of viewing systems, motor types, running speeds, magazine types, camera loading technique, turret types, lenses and lens mounts, camera noise and baffling, claw mechanisms, metering systems, and more. Two-tape set, 195 mins.
VHS: S22754. $299.00.

Advanced Television Lighting: A Seminar with Bill Millar, BBC-TV

The unedited classroom lectures of Bill Millar, full of invaluable information for students of television lighting.
Introduction to Drama. Preplanning, special lighting problems, extreme low light situations, lighting for a desert scene, and lighting for a moonlight scene are all discussed. 35 mins.
VHS: S22770. $149.00.
A Question of Quality. An examination of the lighting techniques used in several BBC productions, including the creation of a sunset and lighting to mimic the lighting of Rembrandt and Vermeer. 45 mins.
VHS: S22771. $149.00.
Complete Set. The two-volume series.
VHS: S22769. $249.00.

Advanced Voice Workout for the Actor

Voice expert Susan Leigh focuses on the mechanics of breathing and vocal projection for the theater, leading the viewer through a series of simple stretching, yoga and rib awareness exercises in this sequel to *Voice Workout for the Actor*. 40 mins.
VHS: S22843. $99.00.

Animation Games

Award-winning video exploring alternatives to the traditional method of photographing painted, registered cels. Composed of four sections, the first details an overview of animation techniques, followed by segments on puppet, cutout and pixilation animation. 51 mins.
VHS: S22864. $149.00.

The Art of Radio Advertising

An approach to concept development, copywriting, and directing radio ads by two of the medium's most successful producers. Humor and team work are emphasized. 20 mins.
VHS: S22814. $119.00.

Auditioning for the Actor

How to evaluate your own strengths as an actor and how to select material that supports these strengths, pre-audition skills and strategies, performance critiques and more. 46 mins.
VHS: S22839. $119.00.

The Basic Costumer

An introduction to costume research, taking measurements, costume acquisition and maintenance, and approaches to pattern making. Includes a teacher's guide. 73 mins.
VHS: S22852. $119.00.

Basic Field Production: Lighting

An introduction to effective lighting choices for a basic interview shoot, including balancing mixed light sources, setting exposure, monitoring, and more. 24 mins.
VHS: S22751. $149.00.

Basic Field Production: Sound Recording

A step-by-step demonstration of the necessary planning, equipment selection, mixing strategies, test recording and session procedure for an interview shoot. 32 mins.
VHS: S22730. $149.00.

Basic Radio Skills Series

A comprehensive introduction to both the technical and creative aspects of the radio environment.
Basic Radio Skills: Announcing and Presentation. A typical radio day with six announcers on talk, news and music shows providing insights into their formats and their own personal approaches to their shows. 28 mins.
VHS: S22821. $149.00.
Basic Radio Skills: Editing. A presentation of the two audiotape editing techniques: splice editing and dub editing. Examples of voice edits and music dubbing are included. 16 mins.
VHS: S22820. $119.00.
Basic Radio Skills: Radio News. An in-depth view of radio news at work. Topics include news sources, item selection and scripting, preparation for broadcast and much more. 38 mins.
VHS: S22818. $149.00.
Basic Radio Skills: Radio Talkback. Styles and approaches for the live call-in show. A special instructional segment deals with phone operation, delay systems and call dumping. 35 mins.
VHS: S22819. $149.00.
Basic Radio Skills: Radio Writing. Writing for news and current affairs, commercial copywriting and radio comedy writing are covered in detail. Specialists in each area offer their insights. 47 mins.
VHS: S22822. $149.00.
Basic Radio Skills: The Radio Interview. Basic technical skills of the audio interview are covered, emphasizing content, interaction, preparation of the interviewee. By acting out problem situations (often to humorous results) the viewer learns first hand how to handle effective strategies for dealing with them. 20 mins.
VHS: S22823. $149.00.
Basic Radio Skills: The Radio Studio. Introduction to the hardware of the radio studio: the console, microphones, telephone talkback, turntables and CDs, cart players, etc. Cueing, labeling, cleaning and machine care are emphasized. 31 mins.
VHS: S22817. $149.00.
Complete Set. The seven-volume series. 215 mins.
VHS: S22816. $695.00.

Basic Shooting

This video takes the viewer through all the steps needed in order to produce a videotape. From shopping for a camcorder through all the basics, everything is here, including lighting, microphones, lenses and composition. 47 mins.
VHS: S23951. $19.95.

Being on TV: The Crash Course

Gwenn Kelly teaches what to expect when you go on TV, how to handle yourself in front of the camera, and how to dress and shape your message for a television audience. 30 mins.
VHS: S22803. $275.00.

Blocking a Scene: Basic Staging with Actors

The basic steps in blocking a scene, from script analysis to dividing the scene into working units to developing a floor plan. Includes an exercise from the play *Candida*. 70 mins.
VHS: S22847. $175.00.

Chroma Key Techniques

An introduction to a wide range of chroma key techniques, including interiors, exteriors, and such refinements as casting shadows and reflections onto chroma keyed backgrounds. 30 mins.
VHS: S22739. $149.00.

Combat for the Stage

There is much more to realistic sword and fist fighting than meets the eye. This exciting and safely illustrated lesson provides all the skills needed to understand sword, fist and firearm combat techniques, as well as choreography for stage falls. 96 mins.
VHS: S15920. $59.95.

Combat for the Stage and Screen

David Boushey, founder of the Society of American Fight Directors and the United Stuntmen's Association, presents a three-part guide to producing a dramatically effective fight scene.
Elizabethan Weaponry. Techniques for the rapier, dagger and rapier, courtsword and single dagger, including slow motion analysis of selected fight sequences. 90 mins.
VHS: S22857. $275.00.

Medieval Weaponry. Moves and safe techniques for broadsword, sword and shield, and quarterstaff fighting, including an orientation to the military technology and technique of the period. 90 mins.
VHS: S22856. $275.00.
Unarmed Combat. Techniques for punching, slapping, hair pulling, kneeing, kicking, gouging and head-bashing are all included in this lively and informative tape. 90 mins.
VHS: S22855. $275.00.
Complete Set. The three-tape set. 270 mins.
VHS: S22854. $700.00.

The Complete Camera Clinic

A complete guide to proper adjustment of all of the internal controls of modern three chip or tube video cameras. Included is a 30-page manual and guide. 60 mins.
VHS: S22756. $179.00.

Creative Drama and Improvisation

Rives Collins leads students through theater games and improvisational exercises, giving them invaluable tools for warm-up, rehearsal, self-exploration and character development. 110 mins.
VHS: S22848. $119.00.

A Creative Partnership: The Actor and Director

A guide through the development of the actor/director relationship in the feature film process, from the auditions and screen tests through the rehearsal process and the shoot. 37 mins.
VHS: S22837. $149.00.

Creative Video Techniques

Harry Mathias, author of *Electronic Cinematography*, give an overview of commercial and feature film technique.
The Art of Using Filters. How to select the right filter to create a mood, the use of polarizers, grads, contrast control filters, color filters, and more. 46 mins.
VHS: S22743. $149.00.
Controlling the Image. Alternatives for determining correct exposure, high key, low key and backlighting tips, the value of waveform monitors, and more. 40 mins.
VHS: S22742. $149.00.
Complete Set. The two-volume set.
VHS: S22741. $249.00.

Design—An Introduction

An introduction to scene and prop design and costume and makeup selection for film and video. 18 mins.
VHS: S22731. $119.00.

Designing and Building Your Desktop Video System

A guide to the many options available through desktop video, including selection of a computer platform, peripherals, software, graphics, paint, animation, special effects, video format, video post-production equipment, system configuration, and design. 45 mins.
VHS: S22789. $149.00.

The Directing Process

If you are planning to direct your first play, or wish to expand what you already know, this video supplies all the organizational tools. An all-encompassing overview that furnishes methods from analyzing the script, selecting a successful production and arranging auditions, to staging the action, coordinating designers and directing rehearsals.
VHS: S15918. $59.95.

The Drama Training Videos I and II

This is a great resource for grade school teachers. It explains useful ways to instruct students in drama within the outlines set up in the Goals 2000 movement. Originally broadcast on PBS, this series is the culmination of the Model Program in Drama Education. Each video is 26 mins.
Video I. This tape presents an overview of important goals and includes a variety of ways to integrate drama into grade levels kindergarten through eight.
VHS: S27829. $19.95.
Video II. Successful techniques and methods are detailed in this second video. In addition, objectives and assessment standards are explained.
VHS: S27830. $19.95.

The Dub

A program covering the breakdown of location sounds, dialogue replacement, track building, the preparation of tracks for a mixing session, and the actual mix itself. 18 mins.
VHS: S22784. $119.00.

An Editing Exercise

An introduction to film and video editing that uses shots from a sequence of a historical drama as its example. Included are a complete shot list and marked script. 15 mins.
VHS: S22786. $149.00.

Editing Techniques: Reducing Time

An introduction to basic time reduction techniques for shooting and editing, including camera movement, jump cuts, exits and entrances, cut-ins, cutaways, parallel action, and visual effects. 10 mins.
VHS: S22785. $149.00.

The Essentials—4000 Series

In-depth instruction in the use of the Toaster 4000 and Toaster System 3.0 from Lee Stranahan, "the world's smartest Toaster Guy".
Toaster CG Essentials. A look at the Toaster CG's text capabilities, including font sizing, color brush loading, and layer options.
VHS: S22794. $59.95.
Video Toaster Essentials. A guide through the Toaster's switcher, digital video effects, set-up functions, chroma FX and luminance keyer. 90 mins.
VHS: S22793. $59.95.

Feature Film Lighting

In a program designed for professionals and students alike, professional D.P. Russell Boyd discusses lighting in technical terms and touches on many common lighting problems, such as lighting for rain and the use of nets. 56 mins.
VHS: S22757. $149.00.

Film Graphics

A classic of film analysis, this tape demonstrates the structural principles inherent in all art forms and features an in-depth, shot-by-shot analysis of a sequence from Sergei Eisenstein's *Potemkin*. 15 mins.
VHS: S22729. $119.00.

Firearm Safety Onstage

This video dispels the myth that just because you're not using live ammunition, you're safe. A must for all administrators, directors, stage managers, actors and students. 45 mins.
VHS: S22851. $119.00.

Fundamentals of Scenic Painting

A look at the basic components of paint, the characteristics and uses of various media, and a wide range of tools and application techniques. Includes five elevations with overlay grids for student projects as well as an eight-page manual and guide. 81 mins.
VHS: S22860. $249.00.

Great Screenwriting

John Truby (Truby's Writers Studio) provides a four-hour video workshop for would-be writers, covering how to make scripts more powerful and commercially viable. Charting, shaping a script and analyzing story structure are demonstrated through examples by legendary screenwriters. 480 mins.
VHS: S22835. $295.00.

The Hold Up: An Editing Exercise

Roger Ebert guides students through the editing process of a bank robbery scene, from the rushes through the fine cut, and demonstrates how different approaches to editing can result in entirely different films. 20 mins.
VHS: S22781. $119.00.

Hollywood Directors and Their Craft

Top male directors John Badham, Clint Eastwood, John Flynn, Delbert Mann, Michael Schultz, Abraham Polonsky and Robert Wise examine their craft and analyze their working methods. 80 mins.
VHS: S22838. $149.00.

How to Use a C-Stand

A quick guide to the proper use of Century Stands, or "C-Stands" as they're called in the industry. 6 mins.
VHS: S22752. $89.00.

Interview Techniques

The development of an interview is developed, from putting the subject at ease to obtaining all the information you need. Also included is the approach for a current affairs interview. 25 mins.
VHS: S22811. $149.00.

Introduction to Floor Managing

An overview of the duties of the floor manager in a multi-camera studio, including the role of the floor manager in establishing mood, cueing, time signals, and more. 25 mins.
VHS: S22737. $149.00.

Introduction to Television Lighting

Bob Forster demonstrates how to model three dimensional objects with light, how to create day and evening lighting, color correction alternatives, and more. 20 mins.
VHS: S22753. $149.00.

Kodak Cinematography Master Class Series

Five of the world's finest cinematographers share lighting tips and techniques in a workshop setting.
Lighting Dances with Wolves with Dean Semler. A demonstration of the techniques that won Dean Semler an Academy Award for the cinematography of *Dances with Wolves*. 29 mins.
VHS: S22773. $89.95.
Lighting Dead Poets Society with John Seale. John Seale guides students through the lighting setups he used to create the feel of different times and seasons in *Dead Poets Society*. 28 mins.
VHS: S22774. $89.95.
Location Lighting with Geoff Burton. Geoff Burton emphasizes making the most of natural lighting, and using tungsten lights to imitate nature. 29 mins.
VHS: S22775. $89.95.
Studio Lighting: A Comparative Workshop with Donald McAlpine and Denis Lenoir. Donald McAlpine and Denis Lenoir go back-to-back to show how creative differences in lighting style can change the feel of a scene. 59 mins.
VHS: S22776. $89.95.
Complete Set. The complete 4-program series.
VHS: S22772. $579.00.

Lessons in Visual Language

Peter Thompson narrates this ten-volume series dealing with the language of moving images.
Editing. A lesson in the creative ways in which editing can be used to reconstruct or rearrange spaces and events. 10 mins.
VHS: S22725. $99.00.
Framing. Tips on how the framing of the screen can convey emotion, define relationships, tell a story, and allude to off-screen surroundings. 10 mins.
VHS: S22718. $99.00.
Image and Screen. A discussion of luminosity, definition, grain, and other sensory qualities of the filmed image. 14 mins.
VHS: S22720. $99.00.
Lenses and Perspective. A lesson in how the position of the viewer of the camera is the central factor in the perception of spacial relationships. 9 mins.
VHS: S22722. $99.00.
Movement and Moving the Camera. A discussion of how camera movement should accommodate (but not duplicate) the natural way the human eye moves as it interacts with visual scenes. 11 mins.
VHS: S22723. $99.00.
Music. A look at the evocative and emotive power of music in film, as well as the structure and purpose of the musical score. 16 mins.
VHS: S22727. $99.00.
Orientation of the Camera. How to use the moving image to either orient the viewer to a space or to deliberately disturb and challenge the viewer's senses. 11 mins.
VHS: S22724. $99.00.
Rhythm. A look at natural and mechanical rhythms and how a sense of rhythm can be achieved through editing. 10 mins.
VHS: S22726. $99.00.
Shot Sizes and Framing Faults. This tape defines the basic types of shots and offers suggestions on how to build a sequence using different types of shots. In addition, common framing errors and their psychological impacts are discussed. 9 mins.
VHS: S22719. $99.00.
The Third Dimension. How to use visual cues to define spacial relationships, construct three-dimensional space, and fool the eye, including a number of startling optical illusions. 7 mins.
VHS: S22721. $99.00.
Complete Set. The complete ten-volume set.
VHS: S22728. $795.00.

Lighting in the Real World

An introduction to how lighting gels and diffusion can solve common lighting problems as demonstrated with several carefully produced sample lighting exercises. 65 mins.
VHS: S22755. $119.00.

LightWave 3D—4000 Series

In-depth instruction in the use of LightWave 3D for animation work. Four tapes.
LightWave 3D Camera & Lighting Techniques. Learn about camera and lighting tips, camera motion paths, animating lights, motion envelopes, lens flare tips, and more. 120 mins.
VHS: S22796. $59.95.
LightWave 3D Displacement Mapping, Morphing & Bones. A guide to using LightWave to twist, bend, deform and animate objects in layout. 100 mins.
VHS: S22797. $59.95.
LightWave 3D Essentials. Learn how to create animations, designs and screens and do key framing using LightWave 3D. 120 mins.
VHS: S22795. $59.95.
LightWave 3D Surfaces & Textures. An exploration of LightWave 3D's surface and texture techniques and how to increase your speed by selecting the proper surfaces for your objects. 115 mins.
VHS: S22798. $59.95.
Complete Set. The four-program series.
VHS: S22800. $239.80.

Location Sound Recording

An introduction to various microphone types and pickup patterns, mic selection and operating technique, the special problems of lavaliere mics, and more. 37 mins.
VHS: S22732. $149.00.

Make-Up for Theatre with Ellen Dennis

Taught by Ellen Dennis, professor of Make-Up and Costume Design at Southern Oregon State College; emphasis on how light and shadow work on the facial structure, use of hairpieces, wigs, period make-up, old-age, hair pieces, and fantasy make-up. 2 complete tapes.
Make-Up for Theatre, Part 1. 60 mins.
VHS: S12862. $39.95.
Make-Up for Theatre, Part 2. 60 mins.
VHS: S12863. $39.95.

The Make-Up Workshop

Learn to age an actor's face 40 years, build mustaches and beards, or change facial features entirely. With some practice and a little creativity, this step-by-step instruction on make-up design and application can turn anyone into an expert make-up artist. 104 min.
VHS: S15921. $59.95.

Making a Video Program

A comprehensive overview of the process involved in video production, from scriptwriting to shooting to editing and titling. 49 mins.
VHS: S22734. $149.00.

Making Grimm Movies

In this series of three tapes, the secrets of motion pictures are clearly demonstrated using outtakes from *The Brothers Grimm*. It shows how you can make your own movies using limited resources available locally. Each tape is 20 minutes long and the set comes with the book *The Guide to Making Grimm Movies*.
Part 1: Scriptwriting, Casting, Makeup. In this first tape viewers learn how to write a script and plan their shoot, as well as how to cast actors and dress them appropriately.
VHS: S21215. $19.95.
Part 2: Locations, Set Design, Sound. Scouting locations and making sets are key to filmmaking. Storyboards are one tool that can help achieve the desired look. Sound is another important technical consideration covered in this part.
VHS: S21216. $19.95.
Part 3: Cinematography, Editing, Acting. Cinematography and editing are demystified in this final tape in the set. Directing and acting, originally theatrical techniques, are very different in filmmaking and are fully explained.
VHS: S21217. $19.95.
Complete Set with Study Guide.
VHS: S21218. $89.95.

Mime over Matter

This complete course in Mime offers the knowledge to unravel the mysteries of one of the world's oldest art forms. Entertain your friends and family in no time following the carefully demonstrated instructions. 101 mins.
VHS: S15922. $59.95.

Movement for the Actor

Northwestern University professor Dawn Maura and her students lead you through a series of movement exercises, including stretching, warmups, and dynamic activity keyed to emotion and memory. 20 mins.
VHS: S22844. $119.00.

Multicamera Direction Planning

The planning and production of a multi-camera video shoot, including read-throughs, design, rehearsals, camera planning, camera scripting, technical run-through, and shooting. 30 mins.
VHS: S22738. $149.00.

Multimedia in Education

New uses for multimedia in fields ranging from business to engineering to psychology to interior design, exploring new ways of teaching and learning. 30 mins.
VHS: S22792. $149.00.

Music for Film

A guide to film music production procedures, including timing, synchronization, and click tracks. Hosted by British composer Ron Goodwin. 55 mins.
VHS: S22787. $149.00.

The New Digital Imaging

An examination of new photographic technologies, including computer manipulation of digital images, digital still cameras, use of scanners, new printing systems, and disc-based storage of photographic images. 20 mins.
VHS: S22788. $149.00.

Off-Line Editing

This two-part series offers a thorough introduction to the strategies and techniques for off-line editing.
Off-Line Editing: An Introduction. An introduction to both linear and non-linear editing, control track, time code, blacking, window dubbing, logging, both assembly and insert editing, straight cuts, split ends, and more. 45 mins.
VHS: S22779. $149.00.
Off-Line Editing: Working with Edit Decision Lists. A guide to the EDL, or Edit Decision List, including how to read an EDL, linear and non-linear formats, editing tips, cleaning, tracing, and more. 27 mins.
VHS: S22780. $149.00.
Complete Set. The two-volume set.
VHS: S22778. $249.00.

The Painters Forum Scene Painting Library

Master painter and teacher Lester Polakov hosts this two-part guide to scene painting.
Volume 1: Introduction. A discussion of the tools of scene painting, including customized implements, priming and lining techniques. Includes a 10-page viewer's guide. 18 mins.
VHS: S22862. $59.95.
Volume 2: Trompe L'Oeil. A guide to the mathematically precise "trompe l'oeil" ("fool the eye") technique used to give two-dimensional surfaces the illusion of being three-dimensional. Includes an 18-page viewer's guide. 41 mins.
VHS: S22863.$175.00.

The Pattern Development Video

A must for cutters and drapers. Author and costumer Rosemary Ingham presents the basics of measuring an actor, analyzing the costume sketch, developing a paper pattern and making and fitting a design mock-up. 75 mins.
VHS: S22853. $149.00.

Performing Shakespeare

Expert Kathleen Conlin leads you through a highly physical series of exercises designed to move you from the exploration of specific words and phrases through the development of complete Shakespearean scenes. 75 mins.
VHS: S22840. $186.00.

Personal Performance Techniques

This video shows how to make a more effective presentation by use of visual cues and performance techniques, and how personal appearance, clothing and hairstyle affect your audience. "Show and tell" techniques are demonstrated and stand up examples are included to provide highly useful tips for TV reporters or anyone involved in presenting information. 20 mins.
VHS: S22810. $149.00.

Post Synchronization: The Editor's Role

A guide through dialogue replacement procedures: the original method, the "rock and roll" method, and ADR, or Automatic Dialogue Replacement. 28 mins.
VHS: S22783. $149.00.

Radio Drama

The rehearsal and recording processes of drama for radio are shown in this first-rate production. Valuable for anyone in the dramatic arts. 55 mins.
VHS: S22815. $149.00.

Radio Production: Making a Radio Commercial

The production process of a commercial is amusingly depicted, from working with the client to recording, through the editing process and up to the final mix. 43 mins.
VHS: S22813. $149.00.

The Role of the Assistant Editor

An introduction to basic procedures of the film editing suite, including logging, edge numbers, syncing, coding, shot breakdown, preparation of a cut work print, and more. 45 mins.
VHS: S22782. $149.00.

The Role of the Script Supervisor

A look at the duties of the script supervisor, including both visual and narrative continuity, script timing and script breakdown, notes, and more. 28 mins.
VHS: S22735. $149.00.

Script to Screen

An overview of the differences between scripting for the stage and screenwriting, including an in-depth look at the work in the studio. 30 mins.
VHS: S22733. $149.00.

Setting the Stage

A companion to *The Fundamentals of Scenic Painting*, this three-tape set gives alternate approaches to common scene painting problems and emphasizes specific paint mixing formulas. 48 mins.
VHS: S22861. $119.00.

Shedding Some Light

An overview of common types of lighting units, gels, light boards and accessories, the basic principles of electricity, lighting safety, hanging, focusing, circuiting, and how to lay out and read a light plot. 95 mins.
VHS: S22858. $119.00.

Shurtleff on Acting

Michael Shurtleff, noted casting director and author of the bestselling *Audition*, teaches for the first time on video in a film that speaks to the heart of what it means to be an actor. 60 mins.
VHS: S22849. $149.00.

The Sitcom Seminars

Three U.S. comedy writers and producers *(Roseanne, Designing Women, The Wonder Years, Murphy Brown, Married... With Children)* provide an in-depth course covering every aspect of the sitcom craft.
Dramatic Structure and Comic Development. The comic possibilities of a premise are explored by John Vorhaus from the hero's goals, the rewards of victory and the escalating jeopardy of failure. 29 mins.
VHS: S22830. $79.00.
Sitcom Rules and Forms. The rules for eight different types of sitcoms are mapped out in this informative video hosted by John Vorhaus. 30 mins.
VHS: S22828. $79.00.
Sitcom Story Structure. From introduction to complication to consequence to relevance, the substructure of every successful comedy television program is demonstrated. 21 mins.
VHS: S22829. $59.00.
A Survival Guide for Sitcom Writers. Hosted by Russ Woody *(Murphy Brown)*, this informative video provides guides on getting an agent, the art of pitching your ideas, and the shaping of a writer's career. 23 mins.
VHS: S22834. $59.00.
The Production Process: Part 1. Beginning with the dynamics of the writer's and actor's table, rehearsal, through recording and editing of the program, an inside look at early production is explored. 30 mins.
VHS: S22831. $79.00.
The Production Process: Part 2. Norma S. Vela *(Roseanne, Designing Women)* discusses the role of a sitcom's showrunner. A showrunner is responsible for juggling the demands of writers, actors, directors and the network. 23 mins.
VHS: S22832. $59.00.
The Sitcom Writer's Comic Toolbox. John Vorhaus (*The Wonder Years* and *Married... With Children*) defines the characteristics of a good comic premise, the importance of a central character with a comic perspective on the world, and how to balance endearing traits with exaggerated flaws. 36 mins.
VHS: S22826. $79.00.
The Sitcom Writer's Craft. John Vorhaus approaches the mechanics of sitcom writing, the application of the three-act comic structure and the levels of comic conflict. 29 mins.
VHS: S22827. $79.00.
Three In-Depth Case Studies. Three writers provide an inside look at writing for a specific sitcom. The process of writing for *Roseanne, Murphy Brown* and *Married... With Children* is discussed by their writers. 30 mins.
VHS: S22833. $59.00.
What Is Sitcom? Details the necessary ingredients for a good situation comedy. One essential element is emotional truth and honesty. The writers from *Roseanne* and *Murphy Brown* host. 19 mins.
VHS: S22825. $59.00.
Complete Set. 10 program series.
VHS: S22824. $449.00.

So You Want to Be An Actor

Hosted by Jerry Stiller and Anne Meara, this informational program offers telling insights from leading industry professionals and performers on the techniques aspiring actors can utilize to further their professional ambitions. The video treats such important subjects as locating the right theater schools, finding a photographer for the proper portfolio, preparing the right resume and finding an agent to represent you. It offers insights into casting agents, auditions and how to enter the lucrative arena of commercials and soap operas. With appearances by Christopher Walken, Roscoe Lee Browne, Uta Hagen and Michael Storm. 75 mins.
VHS: S19526. $29.95.

Speak for Yourself: A Dynamic Vocal Workout

Voice expert Susan Leigh offers a series of voice and body warm-ups to help build a strong voice, establish focus and concentration while speaking, and expand your vocal capacity and skills. 26 mins.
VHS: S22805. $99.00.

The Stage Fight Director

Master combat choreographer David Boushey leads you through the many combat scenes in a production of *Romeo and Juliet*. Fascinating for drama students and professionals alike. 30 mins.
VHS: S22859. $119.00.

Stella Adler: Awake and Dream
A documentary portrait of Stella Adler, the influential acting teacher and Method guru whose students included Marlon Brando, Robert De Niro, Warren Beatty and Candice Bergen. Narrated by Frank Langella. 56 mins.
VHS: S18730. $39.95.

Studio Seconds: The Assistant Sound Engineer Video
A lively dramatization of the duties of the assistant sound engineer in a beautifully produced program designed for people planning a career in the recording field. 80 mins.
VHS: S22812. $159.00.

The Subject Is Light
Charles Potts demonstrates the "laws of light" that apply to photography and cinematography while using the fundamental shapes found in nature. 44 mins.
VHS: S22750. $149.00.

Teaching Shakespeare: New Approaches from the Folger Shakespeare Library
This videotape, featuring lively and successful ways to teach Shakespeare, draws on Folger's outstanding Shakespearean resources. The production emphasizes language, improvisation, paraphrasing, performance directing and scholarship, and provides an introduction to Shakespeare's world and Elizabethan music. The central idea is that Shakespeare's words were meant to be heard, that understanding comes through performance. 75 mins. Includes Public Performance Rights.
VHS: S09264. $95.00.

Techniques of TV Interviewing
The elements of a successful television interview and what makes an exciting television story are explored. The program is full of cautionary tales and role models, including an entertaining exchange involving Margaret Thatcher trapping an ill-prepared journalist and turning the tables on him. 20 mins.
VHS: S22808. $149.00.

TV Current Affairs Reporting
What makes an exciting television story? Producers of four Australian current affairs programs discuss their views and stress the importance of building stories around visuals. 48 mins.
VHS: S22809. $149.00.

TV Makeup: The Basics
The basics of materials for a makeup kit, makeup technique for both men and women, makeup removal, "quick fix" techniques, makeup hygiene, and more. 30 mins.
VHS: S22736. $149.00.

TV Newsroom: News Gathering
The interlocking roles of the staff of the WHDH newsroom, including assignment editor, producers, news directors, reporters, writers and photographers. Learn how these professionals work against the clock to produce the newsbreaking stories of today. 12 mins.
VHS: S22806. $119.00.

TV Newsroom: News Production
Follows a real day of news gathering and production at a Boston affiliate. Dozens of employees work together to shape the evening newscast. 10 mins.
VHS: S22807. $119.00.

Video Dance/The Video Dance Lectures
In *Video Dance*, we see the end result of a two-week workshop with seven choreographers and six video directors creating "choreography for the camera". *The Video Dance Lectures* traces the path from choreographer to final shooting script and looks at how the viewer's eye experiences dance. 79 mins.
VHS: S22740. $249.00.

Video Editing
This is a step-by-step guide to the techniques and equipment of video editing. Titles, sound and special effects are all explored. In addition this video covers the basics of edit controllers and discusses the future of nonlinear editing possibilities. 42 mins.
VHS: S23952. $19.95.

Video Post Production
An introduction to pre-production planning, time code and user bits use, structuring the off-line edit, digital effects, audio sweetening, digital audio, and more. 28 mins.
VHS: S22777. $149.00.

Video Scriptwriting for Success and Profit
Stewart Jacoby leads you step-by-step through the stages of scriptwriting, including communicating to the client, script development, the treatment, writing and formatting of your script and storyboarding. 45 mins.
VHS: S22836. $99.00.

Voice Workout for the Actor
Voice expert Susan Leigh leads you through full-body relaxation and stretching, and exercises for pitch and resonance, clarity and dynamic control, resulting in a complete voice and body warm-up. 33 mins.
VHS: S22842. $99.00.

What Is Multimedia?
An examination of hardware, software, scripting, interactivity, robotics, and the latest developments in the field of multimedia. 20 mins.
VHS: S22791. $149.00.

"What's the Score?"— Text Analysis for the Actor
Arthur Wagner teaches his method of examining each action of a script in terms of immediate and overall objectives, and then relating these objectives to personal experience. Also, a guide to examining character dynamics and interactions. 85 mins.
VHS: S22841. $179.00.

Where Do I Start: Basic Set Construction
Basic set construction from start to finish, including building supplies and tools, the construction of flats and platforms, assembly of window and door frames, adding hinges, stiffeners, jacks and moldings, and the transport and assembly of the finished set. 72 mins.
VHS: S22850. $119.00.

The Working Actor: Actors on Acting
Four professional actors talk about techniques for making a character come alive, approaches to body movement, methods of research, ways to work with the script, rehearsal techniques and more. 27 mins.
VHS: S22845. $149.00.

The Working Actor: Teachers on Acting
Three acting teachers discuss assisting natural talent to full expression, the power of live performance versus film and television work, and more. 21 mins.
VHS: S22846. $149.00.

Writing for Film
Four top screen writers, including Oscar winner Frank Pierson *(Cool Hand Luke, Dog Day Afternoon)* and David Williamson *(Gallipoli, The Year of Living Dangerously)*, discuss the nuts and bolts of their craft. Topics include finding a story, research techniques, character development, dialog, the three act script structure, plot and subplot, formula scripts, and much more. 52 mins.
VHS: S16542. $149.00.

Writing for Radio
Four expert radio writers talk about their craft, with an emphasis on the writing of radio drama. All participants emphasize the unlimited potential of radio as a medium of the imagination. Topics include the characteristics of a good radio writer; how to work within the limitations of time slots and tight budgets; plot development; the proper use of stage directions in a radio script; the use of music and sound effects, and more. 44 mins.
VHS: S16544. $149.00.

Writing for Television
Four veteran TV writers discuss the components of a successful television script and reveal their own working methods. Topics include telling a story with pictures; creating a character; generating dialog; collaboration and roleplaying; the rewrite process; adapting a novel; researching and developing a major miniseries. 48 mins.
VHS: S16543. $149.00.

AMERICAN MUSICALS

1776
The hit Broadway musical focuses on the efforts of the Founding Fathers to have the Declaration of Independence ratified. With Ken Howard, William Daniels and Blythe Danner.
VHS: S05859. $19.95.
Laser: Widescreen. **LD74898. $44.95.**
Peter Hunt, USA, 1972, 150 mins.

42nd Street
The archetypal backstage musical given depth, life and power by the extravagant touch of Busby Berkeley. Warner Baxter is Julian Marsh, the musical-comedy director, who inserts unknown Ruby Keeler into the lead role when star Bebe Daniels suffers a sprained ankle. The first of Berkeley's musicals that established a populist escapism in American entertainment.
VHS: S02326. $19.98.
Laser: LD70493. $34.98.
Lloyd Bacon, USA, 1933, 89 mins.

The Affairs of Dobie Gillis
An exuberant musical comedy graced by big-band music, inventive dance numbers and the romantic difficulties of Dobie Gillis (Bobby Van), an inveterate girlwatcher in search of love on his idyllic campus setting. With Debbie Reynolds, Hans Conried, Barbara Ruick and Bob Fosse.
VHS: S20199. $19.98.
Don Weis, USA, 1953, 74 mins.

The Al Jolson Collection
The wit and grand style of master showman Al Jolson is recollected in this collection of eight of his films, from the landmark *The Jazz Singer* to *The Singing Fool, Say It with Songs, Mammy, Big Boy, Wonder Bar, Go Into Your Dance* and *The Singing Kid*.
Laser: LD70143. $149.98.

Alexander's Ragtime Band
In this exuberant musical, with a score by Irving Berlin, Tyrone Power plays an aristocrat who turns his back on his powerful family business to pursue a career as the leader of a ragtime band. Alice Faye plays a singer and Don Ameche is a virtuoso pianist. The numbers include the title track, "Now It Can Be Told," "My Walking Stick" and "I'm Marching Along with Time." With Ethel Merman, Jean Hersholt and Jack Haley.
VHS: S20255. $19.98.
Laser: LD74822. $124.99.
Henry King, USA, 1938, 105 mins.

All That Jazz
Bob Fosse casts Roy Scheider as basically himself in this semi-autobiographical musical extravaganza. He's a talented director-choreographer who loves show business, cigarettes and too many other women to keep his marriage intact. With Ann Reinking, Ben Vereen, Leland Palmer and Jessica Lange as the Angel of Death. A prophetic and dazzling film.
VHS: S07558. $19.98.
Bob Fosse, USA, 1979, 123 mins.

An American in Paris
No film can match *An American in Paris* for all the joy, all the songs, and all the romance in music and dance. Gene Kelly and Leslie Caron star in this movie set to the glorious melodies of George Gershwin, including: "Embraceable You," "Love Is Here to Stay," "I Got Rhythm" and more.
VHS: S00045. $19.95.
Vincente Minnelli, USA, 1951, 102 mins.

Anchors Aweigh
Gene Kelly and Frank Sinatra play two sailors on leave in Hollywood. While setting up his shy friend Clarence (Sinatra), Gene Kelly, as Joe, falls for Kathryn Grayson and also dances with MGM star Jerry the Mouse. Pamela Britton is the girl from Brooklyn. This musical is recommended by Louella Parsons.
VHS: Out of print. For rental only.
Laser: LD70503. $39.98.
George Sidney, USA, 1945, 146 mins.

Andrew Lloyd Webber: The Premiere Collection Encore
A spirited video collection of some of the best known production numbers and scenes from the hit musicals of Andrew Lloyd Webber, including excerpts from *Phantom of the Opera, Aspects of Love, Song and Dance, Evita* and *Requiem*. With Sarah Brightman, Jose Carreras, Cliff Richard, Michael Ball and David Essex. 58 mins.
VHS: S18320. $19.95.

Another Evening with Fred Astaire
Fred Astaire joins Barrie Chase for an unforgettable hour of dancing. This is a rare television appearance by America's most suave dancer ever.
VHS: S23883. $29.95.

April in Paris

Doris Day stars as Ethel "Dynamite" Jackson, an energetic singer who is mistakenly invited to participate in a State Department sponsored theatre festival in the City of Lights. Would you believe they were expecting Ethel Barrymore? Stuffy bureaucrat Ray Bolger is assigned to keep a lid on her exuberance. Naturally they fall in love. With Claude Dauphin, Eve Miller and Paul Harvey. Songs include "I'm Going to Rock the Boat", "I'm Gonna Ring the Bell Tonight" and "Give Me Your Lips".

VHS: S15781. $19.98.
David Butler, USA, 1952, 101 mins.

Athena

A romantic musical comedy about the parallel fortunes of two couples. A repressed lawyer leaves his snobbish girlfriend to romance an eccentric health fanatic while his best friend, a television singer, attempts to court the woman's equally quirky sister. With Jane Powell, Debbie Reynolds, Edmund Purdom and Vic Damone.

VHS: S18557. $19.98.
Richard Thorpe, USA, 1954, 96 mins.

Babes in Arms

The original "hey gang, let's put on a show" musical with Mickey Rooney and Judy Garland. Based loosely on a Rodgers and Hart musical, these energetic youngsters follow in their vaudeville parents' footsteps. Songs include "Good Morning", "Where and When" and title tune. With Guy Kibbee and Margaret Hamilton. B&W.

VHS: S06116. $19.98.
Laser: LD70510. $34.98.
Busby Berkeley, USA, 1939, 91 mins.

Babes on Broadway

A terrific showcase for the talents of Judy Garland and Mickey Rooney, with Judy's famous "F.D.R. Jones." The story of young hopefuls on Broadway, Mickey and Judy do everything from Carmen Miranda to Sarah Bernhardt imitations. With Donna Reed and Margaret O'Brien.

VHS: S11159. $19.98.
Laser: LD70511. $39.98.
Busby Berkeley, USA, 1941, 118 mins.

Balalaika

This musical comedy romance finds Nelson Eddy at the head of a Cossack regiment pursuing a young Bolshevik (Ilona Massey). Some of the songs that pepper this delightful MGM operetta, set during the Russian Revolution, are "Ride, Cossack, Ride"; "Tanya"; "Beneath the Winter Snows" and " Soldiers of the Czar".

VHS: S20786. $19.98.
Reinhold Schnuzel, USA, 1939, 102 mins.

The Band Wagon

Delightful musical featuring Fred Astaire and Cyd Charisse in a story line that revolves around the difficulties of putting up a Broadway show. Astaire is in top form!

VHS: Out of print. For rental only.
Laser: CLV. **LD70516. $34.98.**
Vincente Minnelli, USA, 1953, 112 mins.

Barkleys of Broadway

Astaire and Rogers were re-united after a ten-year separation in this tune-filled musical, with dances ranging from ballroom to swing. Songs include "You'd Be Hard to Replace" and "They Can't Take That Away from Me."

VHS: S05384. $19.98.
Laser: LD70518. $34.98.
Charles Walters, USA, 1949, 109 mins.

Because You're Mine

A farce about opera star Mario Lanza, who's drafted and promptly falls in love with the sister (Doretta Morrow) of his commanding officer (James Whitmore). Features the song "The Lord's Prayer." With Jeff Donnell, Spring Byington and Don Porter.

VHS: S17650. $19.98.
Alexander Hall, USA, 1952, 103 mins.

Belle of New York

Fred Astaire is a rich playboy chasing Vera-Ellen, a Bowery mission worker, in this musical. The numbers include "Let a Little Love Come In" and "Naughty But Nice."

VHS: S05385. $19.98.
Laser: LD72201. $39.98.
Charles Walters, USA, 1952, 82 mins.

Belle of New York/I Love Melvin

Two delightful comedies. The first stars Fred Astaire as a fancy-free playboy and Vera-Ellen as a Bowery mission worker set on reforming him. Directed by Charles Walters, USA, 1952, 82 mins. The second stars Debbie Reynolds and Donald O'Connor in a joyous boy-meets-girl musical. Directed by Don Weis, USA, 1953, 77 mins.

Laser: LD71661. $39.98.

Belle of the Yukon

Randolph Scott must choose between his love for gold and his love for Gypsy Rose Lee in this Technicolor musical comedy, co-starring Dinah Shore, about a clever con man who falls for an honest dance hall girl.

VHS: S30533. $19.98.
William A. Seiter, USA, 1944, 84 mins.

Bells Are Ringing

A cheerful musical featuring Judy Holliday in her last film role as the operator at an answering service who gets involved in the lives of her clients. With Dean Martin, Fred Clark.

VHS: S04400. $19.98.
Laser: LD70523. $39.98.
Vincente Minnelli, USA, 1960, 127 mins.

The Bells of St. Mary's

The sequel to *Going My Way* finds Bing Crosby as Father O'Malley, with a new assignment at a run-down parish. He finds his methods at odds with those of Sister Superior Ingrid Bergman. Good wholesome fun with a song or two, and a tug at the heart.

VHS: S04224. $19.95.
Laser: CLV. **LD71970. $39.98.**
Leo McCarey, USA, 1945, 126 mins.

The Benny Goodman Story

Bandleader Benny Goodman gets the Hollywood treatment in this glossy and tune-filled, semi-factual biography. It stars the multi-talented and somewhat look-alike Steve Allen as the bandleader and Donna Reed as the love interest. Goodman himself provides the music for Allen's fingering on the clarinet.

VHS: S03678. $19.95.
Valentine Davies, USA, 1955, 116 mins.

Bert Rigby You're a Fool

A contemporary light musical comedy from Carl Reiner that celebrates the kind of movies Hollywood used to make. Robert Lindsay (the star of Broadway's *You're My Girl*) has the title role of an English coal miner with a talent for entertaining in the manner of Astaire, Buster Keaton and other greats. He is discovered and sent to be a star in Hollywood and then reality sets in. A gentle and whimsical film. With Anne Bancroft, Jackie Gayle, Robbie Coltrane and Corbin Bernsen.

VHS: S08719. $19.98.
Carl Reiner, USA, 1989, 94 mins.

Best Foot Forward

Lucille Ball invades a military school in this happy-go-lucky Technicolor musical. Non-stop fun and plenty of trouble, along with many lively tunes. With June Allyson and Nancy Walker.

VHS: S15431. $19.98.
Laser: LD71173. $39.98.
Edward Buzzell, USA, 1943, 95 mins.

The Best Little Whorehouse in Texas

Burt Reynolds and Dolly Parton star in this musical version of *Chicken Ranch*. Music and lyrics by Carol Hall, choreography by Tony Stevens. With Jim Nabors, Dom Deluise and Charles Durning.

VHS: S02739. $19.95.
Colin Higgins, USA, 1982, 115 mins.

Bing—The Sennett Shorts

Bing Crosby became a film star because of his beautiful crooning singing style. This video contains three shorts from 1932-33, which show the young Crosby to great advantage. It includes a version of Crosby's hit "I Surrender Dear."

VHS: S26799. $24.95.
Mack Sennett, USA, 1932-1933, 60 mins.

Birth of the Blues

Bing Crosby and Mary Martin star in this musical about the origins of the actual Original Dixieland Jazz Group. It starts as a simple gig at a nightclub arranged by a wealthy young man and soon leads to massive fame. Jack Teagarden, the trombonist from the actual jazz group, is featured.

VHS: S25010. $14.98.
Victor Schertzinger, USA, 1941, 76 mins.

Bitter Sweet

This Jeanette MacDonald/Nelson Eddy vehicle was a remake of a 1933 British film. A sentimental operetta from MGM set in 1880 Vienna written by Noel Coward. Songs include "I'll See You Again" and "Tokay". With George Sanders, Herman Bing, Ian Hunter and Sig Ruman.

VHS: S09845. $29.95.
W.S. Van Dyke, USA, 1940, 92 mins.

Bizet's Dream

Young Michelle is inspired by the newest operatic work written by her piano teacher, Georges Bizet. The plot of *Carmen* leads her to imagine a scenario involving her parents in a love scandal. This delightful story mixes fact and fiction to offer an intriguing portrait of the great composer Bizet. 53 mins.

VHS: S26213. $19.98.

Blue Skies

Over 30 Irving Berlin songs blanket this musical comedy with Fred Astaire and Bing Crosby. Astaire plays a radio personality who relates the story of his rivalry with friend Crosby for the affections of beautiful young lady played by Joan Caulfield.

VHS: S21204. $19.98.
Stuart Heisler, USA, 1946, 104 mins.

Born to Dance

A classic Eleanor Powell musical about a sailor who meets a girl in New York, with songs by Cole Porter, musical direction by Alfred Newman, and terrific performances from Powell, James Stewart, Virginia Bruce, Reginald Gardiner. Oscar nomination for "I've Got You under My Skin".

VHS: S12145. $19.95.
Laser: LD70131. $34.98.
Roy Del Ruth, USA, 1936, 108 mins.

Brigadoon

Gene Kelly and Van Johnson are two Americans afoot and lost in the Scottish highlands when they discover the charming village of Brigadoon and the charms of Cyd Charisse as Fiona Campbell. This endearing Lerner-Loewe musical is directed by Vincente Minnelli and features Barry Jones and Elaine Stewart.

VHS: S07158. $19.95.
Laser: Letterboxed. **LD74670. $34.98.**
DVD: DV60117. $24.98.
Vincente Minnelli, USA, 1954, 108 mins.

Bright Eyes

Shirley Temple is a young orphan at the center of a custody battle and a sensation when she sings "On the Good Ship Lollipop." With James Dunn and Jane Darwell.

VHS: S09990. $19.98.
David Butler, USA, 1934, 90 mins.

Broadway Melody

This early talkie was the first musical to win a Best Picture Oscar. Score by Arthur Freed and Herb Brown. Bessie Love and Anita Page are two sisters dazzled by the lights of the Great White Way. Tunes include "You Were Meant for Me" and "The Wedding of the Painted Doll." With Charles King, Jed Prouty and Mary Doran.

VHS: S08337. $19.98.
Harry Beaumont, USA, 1929, 104 mins.

Broadway Melody of 1936

This engaging musical about a small-town girl with the gifts to match her big-time dreams featured the spectacular talents of Eleanor Powell, and made her an overnight star. Jack Benny also stars. Winner of the 1935 Oscar for Best Dance Direction.

VHS: S15426. $19.98.
Roy Del Ruth, USA, 1935, 110 mins.

Broadway Melody of 1938

An appearance by a youthful Judy Garland singing "Dear Mr. Gable" highlights this big production musical which also features Robert Taylor, Sophie Tucker and Eleanor Powell.

VHS: S02255. $19.98.
Roy Del Ruth, USA, 1937, 113 mins.

Broadway Melody of 1940

Eleanor Powell and Fred Astaire team up in a sparkling musical treasure as the two dancers (Astaire and George Murphy) compete for a job as well as for a beautiful Broadway star. Cole Porter wrote the score.

VHS: S03103. $19.98.
Laser: LD70533. $34.98.
Norman Taurog, USA, 1940, 103 mins.

Broadway Rhythm

This MGM musical is about a young producer trying to woo a beautiful movie star for his new production. He's rejected in favor of a show produced by his father, setting off some fierce rivalries. With George Murphy, Ginny Simms, Lena Horne, Nancy Walker and the three singing contortionists, the Ross Sisters. Music by Tommy Dorsey and his Orchestra and the pianist Hazel Scott.

VHS: S18558. $19.98.
Roy Del Ruth, USA, 1944, 114 mins.

Broadway Serenade
A period musical about the difficulties and tensions in the marriage of a singer (Jeannette MacDonald) and a songwriter (Lew Ayres). With Ian Hunter, Frank Morgan and Rita Johnson.
VHS: S17651. $19.98.
Robert Z. Leonard, USA, 1939, 114 mins.

The Bronze Venus
Lena Horne and Ralph Cooper star in this groundbreaking musical about a singer on her way to the top, and her boyfriend's willingness to sacrifice his ambition for hers.
VHS: S33255. $19.98.
William L. Nolte, USA, 1938, 80 mins.

Bugsy Malone
A musical unlike any other! *Bugsy Malone* is a gangster musical set in 1929 New York City, a city populated by hoodlums, showgirls and dreamers. The cast has an average age of 12, led by Jodie Foster as Tallulah. Music by Paul Williams, a pint-size himself.
VHS: S00187. $14.95.
Laser: LD75331. $29.98.
Alan Parker, USA, 1976, 94 mins.

Bundle of Joy
Made when they were America's favorite couple, Debbie Reynolds and Eddie Fisher (in his starring debut) star in this musical comedy remake of *The Bachelor Mother*, about a salesgirl who takes custody of a baby, causing a scandal that her boyfriend is the baby's father.
VHS: S30956. $19.98.
Norman Taurog, USA, 1956, 98 mins.

By the Light of the Silvery Moon
The sequel to *On Moonlight Bay*, from the original story by Booth Tarkington, sets the action in the aftermath of World War I, with the young lovers trying to adjust to civilian life. With Doris Day, Gordon MacRae and Mary Wickes.
VHS: S18461. $19.98.
Laser: LD72167. $34.95.
David Butler, USA, 1953, 102 mins.

Bye Bye Birdie
Dick Van Dyke, Ann-Margret and Janet Leigh star in this energetic musical comedy. Conrad Birdie, an Elvis-like entertainer (Jesse Pearson), is going to be drafted into the Armed Forces. Ann-Margret is the small-town Ohio girl chosen to receive one last kiss live on the Ed Sullivan Show. Paul Lynde is the disapproving father.
VHS: S05338. $19.95.
George Sidney, USA, 1963, 112 mins.

Cabaret
Liza Minnelli and Joel Grey give extraordinary performances in Bob Fosse's musical drama that mirrors the decay and decadence of Germany on the eve of Hitler's rise to power. With Marisa Berenson and Michael York.
VHS: S01837. $19.98.
Laser: LD72168. $39.98.
DVD: DV60190. $24.98.
Bob Fosse, USA, 1972, 119 mins.

Cairo
Jeanette MacDonald stars as mysterious actress and singer who manages to confuse a very interested Robert Young. Though Young is working for the U.S. war effort, this film remains a campy romp. After all, this is an MGM musical comedy, where romance is inspired by the exotic backdrop of Cairo.
VHS: S20789. $19.98.
John McClain, USA, 1942, 100 mins.

Calamity Jane
Sassy, entertaining musical featuring Doris Day, Howard Keel and Phil Carey. Day shines as the gun-slingin', dirty, tough and ragged Jane in a cute story with a lively score. The song "Secret Love" was a big hit and won an Oscar.
VHS: S06123. $19.98.
Laser: LD70290. $34.98.
David Butler, USA, 1953, 101 mins.

Calendar Girl
A delightful, turn-of-the-century musical romp about a boarding house and its collection of characters. Jane Frazee is the girl who posed for a calendar and Victor McLaglen is an Irish fireman.
VHS: S34943. $19.95.
Allan Dwan, USA, 1947, 80 mins.

Camelot
The epic Broadway hit comes alive with stunning performances by Richard Harris and Vanessa Redgrave as King Arthur and Lady Guinevere. Music by Frederick Loewe, lyrics by Alan Jay Lerner, based on the novel by T.H. White. With Franco Nero, David Hemmings. Letterboxed.
VHS: S01749. $24.98.
Laser: LD71408. $39.98.
Joshua Logan, USA, 1967, 173 mins.

Can't Help Singing
A senator's (Ray Collins) spirited daughter (Deanna Durbin) leaves Washington pursuing a cavalry officer (David Bruce). In Technicolor. Music by Jerome Kern. Includes original theatrical trailer.
VHS: S30621. $19.98.
Frank Ryan, USA, 1944, 90 mins.

Can't Stop the Music
A lavish, gay-themed musical that looks at corruption inside the music-publishing industry. The topliners are the 70s act the Village People, each of whom falls madly in love with Valerie Perrine. "It follows that most of the dialogue is gay in-jokes, with the odd music business joke for variety" *(Time Out)*. "YMCA" and "Macho Man" are highlights. With Steve Guttenberg, Tammy Grimes, June Havoc and Barbara Rush.
VHS: S20417. $14.98.
Nancy Walker, USA, 1980, 119 mins.

Can-Can
Frank Sinatra is a roguish lawyer in Paris trying to keep his cafe owner and performer sweetheart (Shirley MacLaine) from being jailed for doing a forbidden dance. Maurice Chevalier approves but the younger judge Louis Jourdan is not as gallant. With Juliet Prowse and songs by Cole Porter. Based on the Abe Burrows musical. Ooh-la-la. 130 mins.
Laser: LD70899. $49.98.
Walter Lang, USA, 1960, 130 mins.

Captain January
Shirley Temple is a happy tot being raised by a lighthouse keeper until a prissy truant officer insists she have a proper home. Shirley sings "The Right Somebody to Love," and "At the Codfish Ball."
VHS: S09992. $19.98.
David Butler, USA, 1936, 76 mins.

Carnegie Hall
This 1947 feature film, starring Marsha Hunt, is the story of a Carnegie Hall employee who wants her son to be a musician and raises him in the Hall, where they attend performances by many greats of the day. Features performances by Walter Damrosch, Jascha Heifetz, Harry James, Vaughn Monroe, Jan Peerce, Gregor Piatigorsky, Ezio Pinza, Lily Pons, Fritz Reiner, Artur Rodzinski, Artur Rubinstein, Rise Stevens, Leopold Stokowski, Bruno Walter and the New York Philharmonic.
VHS: S28421. $34.95.
Edgar G. Ulmer, USA, 1947, 144 mins.

The Chocolate Soldier
Nelson Eddy starred with Metropolitan Opera star and movie novice Riise Stevens in this MGM musical that mated Oscar Strauss's title and music to the play *The Guardsman*, by Ferenc Molnar. They play opera stars. To test his wife's fidelity he romances her in the guise of a Cossack. With Nigel Bruce and Florence Bates. Remade as *Lilly in Love*.
VHS: S09869. $19.98.
Roy Del Ruth, USA, 1941, 102 mins.

A Christmas Carol
Fredric March stars as Scrooge in this musical adaptation of the Dickens classic with the long-suffering, good-hearted Bob Cratchit and his ever-optimistic family converting the miserly ways of the miserable Scrooge. With Basil Rathbone. USA, 1954, 54 mins.
VHS: S00239. $29.95.
Laser: LD70543. $34.98.

Cinderella
Lesley Ann Warren stars in the Rodgers and Hammerstein musical version of the classic. With Ginger Rogers as the Queen, Walter Pidgeon as the fairy godmother, Jo Ann Fleet, and dozens of sparkling musical numbers.
VHS: S01923. $19.98.
Charles Dubin, USA, 1964, 83 mins.

The Clock
Judy Garland and Robert Walker star in this classic Minnelli musical about a soldier and an office worker who meet in New York, fall in love and marry, all on his 48-hour furlough. First rate performances from Garland, Walker, James Gleason and Keenan Wynn.
VHS: S13356. $19.98.
Laser: LD70544. $34.97.
Vincente Minnelli, USA, 1945, 91 mins.

Coal Miner's Daughter
The film biography of country-western superstar Loretta Lynn. Sissy Spacek won an Academy Award for her performance as the little kid from Butcher's Hollow who grew up to entertain millions. With excellent supporting work by Tommy Lee Jones, Levon Helm and Beverly D'Angelo as Patsy Cline.
VHS: S07805. $19.95.
Michael Apted, USA, 1980, 125 mins.

College Swing
This strange musical features a top-heavy cast with George Burns and Gracie Allen, Bob Hope and Jackie Coogan in the light and charming story about Gracie's exhaustive attempts to graduate college. With Martha Raye and Betty Grable.
VHS: S18547. $14.98.
Raoul Walsh, USA, 1938, 86 mins.

The Commitments
Alan Parker directs this joyful musical drama about a talented young group of Dublin musicians from the gritty North Side who try to make good playing American soul music. Robert Arkins stars as the band's resourceful manager Jimmy Rabbitte. He and the rest of The Commitments were chosen from open auditions in Dublin. With Maria Doyle, Dave Finnegan, Johnny Murphy, Dick Massey, Angeline Ball, Bronagh Gallagher, Michael Aherne, Glen Hansard, Felim Gormley, Kenneth McCluskey and Andrew Strong as lead singer Deco Cuffe. Songs include "Mustang Sally", "Try a Little Tenderness" and "In the Midnight Hour". A major delight.
VHS: S15776. $19.98.
Alan Parker, USA/Ireland, 1991, 116 mins.

Cover Girl
A Jerome Kern/Ira Gershwin musical that traces the rise of a chorus girl to stardom as a cover girl, with classic songs, including "Long Ago and Far Away." With Rita Hayworth, Gene Kelly, Phil Silvers, and Eve Arden.
VHS: S11631. $19.95.
Laser: LD74896. $34.95.
Charles Vidor, USA, 1944, 107 mins.

Daddy Long Legs
Fred Astaire and Leslie Caron dance together and fall in love in this sentimental tale of a globe-trotting playboy who anonymously adopts a French orphan. Thelma Ritter and Fred Clark co-star.
VHS: S14505. $19.98.
Jean Negulesco, USA, 1955, 126 mins.

Dames
Joan Blondell, Ruby Keeler, Dick Powell, ZaSu Pitts and Hugh Herbert star in this classic Warner Brothers musical, distinguished for its Busby Berkeley dance numbers, including "When You Were a Smile on Mother's Lips and a Twinkle in Your Daddy's Eye." The plot (about the backing of a Broadway musical) is almost incidental to the lavish costumes and first-rate production ensembles.
VHS: S07373. $19.98.
Laser: LD70548. $34.98.
Ray Enright, USA, 1934, 90 mins.

Damn Yankees
A baseball fan sells his soul to the Devil for the chance at rejuvenation and the opportunity to play major league ball. The old geezer becomes Tab Hunter and starts winning games for his team. With Ray Walston as the Prince of Darkness and Gwen Verdon as the tantalizing Lola, who we all know gets whatever Lola wants. Adapted and restaged from the Broadway musical; the choreography is by Bob Fosse.
VHS: S11661. $19.98.
Laser: LD70549. $24.98.
George Abbott/Stanley Donen, USA, 1958, 110 mins.

Dancing Lady
Joan Crawford gives her all as a young burlesque dancer seeking Broadway fame, romanced along the Great White Way by one-time real life flame Clark Gable and her future husband (Franchot Tone). Fred Astaire is featured in his screen debut.
VHS: S03105. $19.98.
Laser: LD70732. $39.98.
Robert Z. Leonard, USA, 1933, 93 mins.

The Dancing Pirate
The second feature to ever be shot in 3-strip Technicolor, with songs by Rodgers and Hart, and starring Frank Morgan and Rita Hayworth in the swashbuckling story of a dance teacher who is shanghaied by pirates.
VHS: S05052. $34.95.
Lloyd Corrigan, USA, 1936, 83 mins.

A Date with Judy
I'll bet she has a wonderful personality. Spunky Jane Powell has the title role with Elizabeth Taylor as her best friend in this MGM technicolor musical. Wallace Beery is Judy's dad, who later dances with Carmen Miranda. Powell is hoping to date Robert Stack and Xavier Cugat plays himself. Songs include "I'm Strictly on the Corny Side" and "It's a Most Unusual Day."
VHS: S08521. $19.95.
Laser: LD74665. $34.98.
Richard Thorpe, USA, 1948, 113 mins.

The Dawn of Sound
Three musicals trace the evolution of the form, capturing its exuberance and style: Charles Riesner's *The Broadway Revue of 1929*, Harry Beaumont's *The Broadway Melody* and *Show of Shows*.
Laser: LD70285. $99.98.

Deep in My Heart
Jose Ferrer leads a galaxy of stars in a spectacular celebration of musical magic in this exuberant rendition of the life and times of Sigmund Romberg. Also starring Gene Kelly, Ann Miller and Cyd Charisse.
VHS: S15430. $19.98.
Laser: LD71155. $39.98.
Stanley Donen, USA, 1954, 132 mins.

The Desert Song
This beautifully staged and produced version of the Broadway musical stars Gordon MacRae and Kathryn Grayson. The entire uncut score of this Sigmund Romberg/Oscar Hammerstein show is sung and danced with all the customary panache from the golden age of the American musical.
VHS: S20658. $19.98.
H. Bruce Humberstone, USA, 1953, 96 mins.

Dimples
Shirley Temple stars with Frank *(Wizard of Oz)* Morgan and the legendary Stepin Fetchit in this heartwarming period musical.
VHS: S05900. $19.98.
William A. Seiter, USA, 1936, 78 mins.

Disney Presents the Best of Broadway Musicals
John Raitt narrates this exciting compilation of excerpts from some of Hollywood's most popular musicals. Performances by Ethel Merman, Florence Henderson, Carol Channing, Julie Andrews, Pearl Bailey and many more are included from such shows as *Hello Dolly, Camelot* and *My Fair Lady*.
Laser: LD74636. $24.99.

Dixie Jamboree
Francis Langford, Guy Kibbee and Charles Butterworth star in this musical comedy about life on the last great Mississippi showboat. The free and easy life aboard offers the perfect cover for a gangster on the lam.
VHS: S23818. $24.95.
Christy Cabanne, USA, 1945, 69 mins.

Doctor Dolittle
Rex Harrison is the man who can talk to the animals in this epic musical entertainment for children of all ages. Based on the stories of Hugh Lofting. Oscars went to best Song and Special Visual Effects. With Samantha Eggar, Anthony Newley, Geoffrey Holder and the Pushme-Pullyou llamas.
VHS: S07559. $19.98.
Richard Fleischer, USA, 1967, 144 mins.

Doll Face
Vivian Blaine plays a burlesque dancer out to make it big in show business. The musical featured the performing talents of such diverse individuals as Carmen Miranda and Perry Como. Mr. Relaxation sings "Hubba Hubba Hubba". Dennis O'Keefe was the male lead. B&W.
VHS: S05067. $29.95.
Lewis Seiler, USA, 1945, 80 mins.

The Dolly Sisters
Betty Grable and June Haver star as vaudeville sensations who must balance glamorous careers with the demands of romance. After arriving as refugees from Hungary, they quickly begin singing and dancing their way to the top. The Oscar nominated song "I Can't Begin to Tell You" is just one of the many great tunes featured in this film's lavish production numbers. With John Payne.
VHS: S26923. $19.98.
Laser: LD75455. $39.95.
Irving Cummings, USA, 1945, 114 mins.

Down Argentine Way
A fun musical about an American heiress (Betty Grable) and a South American cowboy (Don Ameche), with a big horse race finale—with Carmen Miranda.
VHS: S09445. $19.98.
Irving Cummings, USA, 1940, 94 mins.

Du Barry Was a Lady
Red Skelton imagines himself in the court of King Louis XIV in this entertaining musical which features Lucille Ball, Zero Mostel and Gene Kelly. Music by the Tommy Dorsey Orchestra.
VHS: S01594. $19.98.
Roy Del Ruth, USA, 1943, 101 mins.

Easter Parade
Judy Garland and Fred Astaire team up in an exuberant film featuring the music and lyrics of Irving Berlin. With Ann Miller and Peter Lawford.
VHS: Out of print. For rental only.
Laser: Remastered, MGM. **LD70129. $34.98.**
Charles Walters, USA, 1948, 103 mins.

Easy to Love
Busby Berkeley staged the lavish water sequence in this aqua-musical set against picture postcard perfect Cypress Gardens, Florida. As a hardworking water queen, Esther Williams swims, dives and water-skis her way through a series of romantic entanglements with Van Johnson, Tony Martin and John Bromfield.
VHS: S16605. $19.98.
Charles Walters, USA, 1953, 97 mins.

Easy to Wed
A smooth-talking Romeo is hired to frame a snobby heiress in this brisk, laugh-packed musical comedy classic featuring the comic, singing and dancing, and aquatic talents of Lucille Ball, Van Johnson and Esther Williams, respectively.
VHS: S31075. $19.98.
Edward Buzzell, USA, 1946, 111 mins.

The Eddy Duchin Story
Scored to the golden oldies of Cole Porter, George and Ira Gershwin, and Hammerstein, this film biography covers the career of the pianist and bandleader of the '30s and '40s. Tyrone Powers stars as Duchin. With Kim Novak, Victoria Shaw and James Whitmore.
VHS: S16412. $19.95.
George Sidney, USA, 1956, 123 mins.

Everybody Sing
A musical extravaganza featuring the talents of 15-year-old Judy Garland one year before she appeared in *The Wizard of Oz*. Teamed up with "funny girl" Fanny Brice, Billie Burke and Allen Jones, Judy turns this lighthearted story about a stage family into a zany, unforgettable masterpiece.
VHS: S15853. $19.98.
Edwin L. Marin, USA, 1938, 91 mins.

Evita
The much-anticipated, Golden Globe-winning film version of the hit musical starring Antonio Banderas, Jonathan Pryce and Madonna as Evita. Music and lyrics by Tim Rice and Andrew Lloyd Webber. VHS letterboxed.
VHS: S31699. $19.95.
Laser: LD76292. $124.95.
Alan Parker, USA, 1996, 135 mins.

The Fabulous Dorseys
A Big Band biography of sorts with the famous musical brothers playing themselves. They argue a lot but the tunes are what's really happening. With Paul Whiteman, Janet Blair, and a jam session with Art Tatum, Ziggy Elman and Charlie Barnet. B&W.
VHS: S18184. $19.95.
Alfred E. Green, USA, 1947, 91 mins.

Fame
A cross-section of young performers at New York's High School for the Performing Arts. With Irene Cara and Anne Meara.
VHS: S05952. $19.98.
Laser: LD76980. $49.98.
Alan Parker, USA, 1980, 133 mins.

Fashions
A snappy comedy with musical numbers directed by Busby Berkeley. William Powell is a con man and Bette Davis is his girlfriend, who aids him in stealing the latest Paris creations.
VHS: S12317. $24.95.
William Dieterle, USA, 1934, 78 mins.

Fiddler on the Roof
The long-running Broadway musical based on the stories of Sholom Aleichem. Starring Topol, Molly Picon, Norman Crane and Leonard Frey. Music by Jerry Bock adapted for the film by John Williams. VHS letterboxed.
VHS: S01702. $29.95.
Laser: LD70568. $39.98.
DVD: DV60278. $24.98.
Norman Jewison, USA, 1971, 169 mins.

The Firefly
The adventures of a Spanish spy during the Napoleonic war are the setting for this extravagant operetta. With Jeannette MacDonald, Allan Jones, Warren William and Billy Gilbert.
VHS: S17653. $19.98.
Robert Z. Leonard, USA, 1937, 131 mins.

First Love
Robert Stack joins Deanna Durbin for her first on-screen kiss in this fairy tale-like movie. It's an update of the *Cinderella* story set in a 1930's musical comedy, only in this instance, Durbin is an orphan who goes to live with an uncle.
VHS: S27011. $19.98.
Henry Koster, USA, 1939, 85 mins.

Flirtation Walk
Frank Borzage directs an engaging musical about a complicated romance between an ambitious Army private (Dick Powell) and a general's daughter (Ruby Keeler) determined to win him. Best number is "Mr. and Mrs. Is the Name." With Pat O'Brien, Ross Alexander and Guinn Williams.
VHS: S18804. $19.98.
Frank Borzage, USA, 1934, 98 mins.

Flower Drum Song
An outstanding cast stars in this screen adaptation of the famous Rodgers and Hammerstein musical about life and love in San Francisco's Chinatown, with Nancy Kwan, James Shigeta.
VHS: S04401. $19.95.
Henry Koster, USA, 1961, 133 mins.

Footlight Parade
James Cagney plays a stage director who tries to outdo himself with lavish musical numbers. Joan Blondell, Dick Powell, Guy Kibbee and Ruth Donnelly star in this first-rate Warner Brothers musical which features three Busby Berkeley numbers back-to-back: "Honeymoon Hotel," "By a Waterfall" and "Shanghai Lil."
Laser: LD70572. $34.98.
Lloyd Bacon, USA, 1933, 104 mins.

Footlight Serenade
A champion heavyweight fighter takes a role in a Broadway show and makes a play for one of the dancers (Betty Grable) who, for career reasons, doesn't want it known that she's married. But her husband is also an actor in the show, and watching the lady-killer champ going after his wife leads to some terrific moments.
VHS: S09331. $19.98.
Gregory Ratoff, USA, 1942, 81 mins.

Footloose
Kevin Bacon is tops in this musical about a city kid who moves to a small town where dancing has been banned, and battles with the fire-and-brimstone minister in an effort to bring it back. With Lori Singer, John Lithgow.
VHS: S09567. $19.95.
Laser: Widescreen. **LD75299. $39.98.**
Herbert Ross, USA, 1984, 107 mins.

For Me and My Gal
Gene Kelly teams up with Judy Garland in his first film, as a pair of vaudeville entertainers working the small towns on their way to the glamour and rewards of Broadway. Kelly is an opportunist who really pushes the limits of Garland's affection in this Busby Berkeley musical. With George Murphy and Ben Blue.
VHS: S07161. $19.95.
Busby Berkeley, USA, 1942, 100 mins.

ForFbidden Music
A rare film: Jimmy Durante and Richard Tauber star in this original film version of the satirical operetta written for the screen by Oscar Strauss.
VHS: S05178. $29.95.

Funny Face
Fred Astaire and Audrey Hepburn star in this appealing musical from director Stanley Donen. Fred is a fashion photographer who sees Audrey as star material. Set in Paris with music by George and Ira Gershwin. Songs include "How Long Has This Been Going On". With Suzy Parker, Ruta Lee and Kay Thompson.
VHS: S06139. $14.95.
Laser: Widescreen. **LD75364. $44.98.**
Stanley Donen, USA, 1957, 103 mins.

Funny Lady
The sequel to *Funny Girl*. Barbra Streisand continues the show biz bio of Fanny Brice as she becomes a bigger star and meets and marries showman Billy Rose (James Caan). Lots of big production numbers. With Roddy McDowall, Ben Vereen and Omar Sharif as Nicky Arnstein.
VHS: S05095. $14.95.
Herbert Ross, USA, 1975, 137 mins.

A Funny Thing Happened on the Way to the Forum
Richard Lester's fractured adaptation of the Broadway musical hit about a conniving slave in ancient Rome. Featuring comedy legends Zero Mostel (recreating his Tony award-winning role), Phil Silvers, and the great Buster Keaton. Plenty of bawdy fun, with music and lyrics by Stephen Sondheim. Letterboxed.
VHS: S02336. $19.99.
Laser: Chapter search. Includes original trailer. **LD71644. $34.98.**
Richard Lester, USA, 1966, 100 mins.

Gay Divorcee
One of Astaire and Rogers' best-loved song-and-dance comedies. Astaire is caught in a case of mistaken identity when Rogers fakes a love affair to win a divorce.
VHS: S03268. $19.98.
Mark Sandrich, USA, 1934, 107 mins.

The Gene Kelly Collection
This collection features three restored and remastered Gene Kelly films: *Brigadoon, It's Always Fair Weather* and *On The Town*, along with their original trailers. Also includes outtakes, re-recordings and stills. 308 mins.
Laser: LD76751. $124.98.

Gigi
Leslie Caron is the bewitching title character in this dazzling musical that won nine Oscars including Best Picture. Maurice Chevalier sings "Thank Heaven for Little Girls" and doesn't get arrested. Based on a story by Colette, a young girl at the turn of the century is trained in Paris to be a courtesan. With Hermione Gingold and Louis Jourdan. VHS letterboxed.
VHS: S07159. $19.95.
Laser: LD70582. $39.99.
Vincente Minnelli, USA, 1958, 116 mins.

Girl Crazy
Mickey Rooney is sent to a small Southwestern school to forget girls, but he meets Judy Garland, and the experiment's over. A great score by George Gershwin, with Judy Garland, Tommy Dorsey and June Allyson.
VHS: S04402. $19.98.
Laser: LD74672. $34.98.
Norman Taurog, USA, 1943, 99 mins.

Girl of the Golden West
Jeanette MacDonald and Nelson Eddy go west in this MGM musical about a singing saloon owner and a dashing bandit who can harmonize. Based on the old stage melodrama by David Belasco. Cast includes Walter Pidgeon, Leo Carillo, Buddy Ebsen, Monty Woolley and Noah Beery. Music by Sigmund Romberg and Gus Kahn. Meet you at the pass for a duet.
VHS: S09847. $19.98.
Robert Z. Leonard, USA, 1938, 120 mins.

Give a Girl a Break
Burton Lane and Ira Gershwin wrote the songs for this sprightly tale of three young hopefuls looking for stardom. It's tough to get a break…until the leading lady walks out and someone has to step in and take her place. Who will it be? Starring Debbie Reynolds, Marge and Gower Champion, and Bob Fosse.
VHS: S14164. $19.98.
Stanley Donen, USA, 1953, 84 mins.

Glenn Miller Story
Jimmy Stewart and June Allyson star as the popular band leader and his wife in this Anthony Mann film bio loaded with swinging music and fine musicians. Performers include Louis Armstrong, Gene Krupa, Frances Langford and members of the original Glenn Miller orchestra. Tunes include "Chattanooga Choo Choo" and "Pennsylvania 6-5000."
VHS: S07810. $19.95.
Laser: LD70033. $34.98.
Anthony Mann, USA, 1954, 116 mins.

Glorifying the American Girl
An early technicolor musical—the only film produced by Florenz Ziegfeld—with Mary Eaton, Eddie Cantor, Helen Morgan, Rudy Vallee and "famous beauties." Numerous production numbers.
VHS: S06226. $49.95.
Millard Webb, USA, 1929, 96 mins.

Godspell
The international hit musical sensation in the tradition of *Hair, Tommy* and *Jesus Christ Superstar*. A 1970s interpretation of the Gospel's teachings filled with spectacular song and dance. With Victor Garber, Lynne Thigpen and Katie Hanley. "Funny and beautiful…incomparably romantic" *(New York Times)*.
VHS: S34872. $19.95.
David Greene, USA, 1973, 101 mins.

Godspell and the Filming of Godspell
Taking the hit off-Broadway musical to the screen. Features on-location scenes, rehearsals and reflections by director David Greene, composer/lyricist Stephen Schwartz and writer John-Michael Tebelak. 1973, 28 mins.
VHS: S31585. $59.95.

Going Hollywood
Raoul Walsh's charming musical about a Hollywood love triangle in which a disaffected school teacher (Marion Davies) falls for a young crooner (Bing Crosby). With Fifi D'Orsay, Stuart Erwin and Ned Sparks.
VHS: S18552. $19.98.
Raoul Walsh, USA, 1933, 78 mins.

Going My Way
Irving Berlin's hit with Bing Crosby as the unconventional singing priest who tries to save a poor parish presided over by the gruff-but-lovable Barry Fitzgerald. Winner of seven Academy Awards. Fred Astaire co-stars.
VHS: S01534. $19.98.
Laser: LD70034. $34.98.
Leo McCarey, USA, 1944, 101 mins.

Gold Diggers of 1933
A Busby Berkeley extravaganza that is pure entertainment. In addition to Berkeley's chorus girls, there's Joan Blondell, Ginger Rogers (singing "We're in the Money" in pig Latin), Ruby Keeler and Dick Powell. The original and most famous of the "gold digger" films.
Laser: LD70583. $34.98.
Mervyn Le Roy, USA, 1933, 98 mins.

Gold Diggers of 1935
A big-scale Busby Berkeley musical that features Dick Powell, Adolphe Menjou, Gloria Stuart, Alice Brady and Glenda Farrell. Notable for its precision numbers, including such classic numbers as "The Words Are in My Heart" and the Oscar-winner "Lullaby of Broadway."
VHS: S11162. $29.95.
Busby Berkeley, USA, 1935, 95 mins.

The Goldyn Follies
The music of George Gershwin and lyrics of Ira Gershwin, combined with a lavish production, in a romantic musical comedy extravaganza about Hollywood. The many featured stars include Edgar Bergen, Charlie McCarthy, Adolphe Menjou, George Balanchine American Ballet, Zorina, Phil Baker, Bobby Clark and the Goldwyn Girls.
VHS: S03122. $19.98.
DVD: DV60210. $24.98.
George Marshall, USA, 1938, 115 mins.

Good News
June Allyson and Peter Lawford star as college students in the Roaring Twenties. This remake of the 1930 musical finds a student librarian involved with tutoring a football hero who has eyes for the campus sexpot. With Patricia Marshall, Joan McCracken, and Mel Torme. The script is by Betty Comden and Adolph Green. Songs include "The Varsity Drag" and "The French Lesson".
VHS: S13306. $19.98.
Charles Walters, USA, 1947, 92 mins.

Goodbye, Mr. Chips
A remake of the 1939 film tracing the life of a shy schoolteacher, adapted from James Hilton's novel. With lyrics and music by Leslie Bricusse. With Peter O'Toole, Petula Clark, Michael Bryant and Michael Redgrave.
Laser: LD70588. $39.97.
Herbert Ross, Great Britain, 1969, 151 mins.

Graffiti Bridge
Prince returns as "The Kid" to face his old nemesis from *Purple Rain*, Morris Day. Once again the two battle over a woman. The focus of the film is the music.
VHS: S21437. $14.95.
Prince, USA, 1990, 90 mins.

Grease
The movie version of a play that got its start in a bus barn in Chicago stars John Travolta and Olivia Newton-John as California high schoolers addicted to being cool. A high energy, tune-filled romp that features such quasi-teens (at the time) as Stockard Channing, Jeff Conaway and Didi Conn. Eve Arden, Sid Caesar and Edd "Kookie" Byrnes play the bona fide adults. "Grease" is the word and the word is fun. Letterboxed.
VHS: S08292. $19.95.
Randal Kleiser, USA, 1978, 110 mins.

The Great Rupert
A funny musical-fantasy about a trained squirrel who discovers a suitcase full of money and gives it to the down-and-out Jimmy Durante, who's at his comic best.
VHS: S14671. $29.95.
Irving Pichel, USA, 1950, 86 mins.

The Great Waltz
This cinematic rhapsody captures the spirit of Johann Strauss' music with spirited inventiveness. Splendid back lot recreations of Vienna, inspiring musical arrangements and bravura camerawork shape this overlooked gem. Joseph Ruttenberg's lovely cinematography earned him an Oscar.
VHS: S14312. $19.98.
Laser: LD74486. $34.98.
Julien Duvivier, USA, 1938, 102 mins.

The Great Ziegfeld
William Powell plays the title character, Broadway showman Florenz Ziegfeld (1867-1932), in a film that won three Oscars, including Best Picture. The ads read "50 Stars" and "300 Girls" in this nearly three-hour biography packed with some of the stars that Ziegfeld made possible. Fanny Brice, Ann Pennington and Ray Bolger play themselves. Will Rogers and Eddie Cantor were doubled. With Myrna Loy and Luise Rainer as Ziegfeld's wives.
VHS: S08339. $29.95.
Laser: LD70134. $39.98.
Robert Z. Leonard, USA, 1936, 176 mins.

Guys and Dolls
Marlon Brando, Frank Sinatra and Jean Simmons star in Joseph Mankiewicz's quality adaptation of the Broadway hit about the gamblers, missionaries and underworld sinners that populate writer Damon Runyon's cityscapes. Despite the heavyweight top billing, the best performance is Stubby Kaye's Nicely-Nicely and his brilliant rendition of "Sit Down, You're Rocking the Boat."
VHS: S02529. $19.98.
Joseph L. Mankiewicz, USA, 1955, 150 mins.

Gypsy (1962/Wood)
Everything is coming up roses in the big screen biography of egendary entertainer Gypsy Rose Lee. Natalie Wood stars as the child vaudeville performer who finds stardom as the classiest striptease artist on the runway. Rosalind Russell plays the ultimate show biz mom who has difficultly letting her daughters grow up. With Karl Malden, Harvey Korman and Faith Dane. Songs include "You Gotta Have a Gimmick" and "Let Me Entertain You." Music by Julie Styne. Lyrics by Stephen Sondheim. Based on the play by Arthur Laurents and the book *Gypsy: A Memoir by Gypsy Rose Lee aka Rose Louise Hovick*.
VHS: S15840. $19.98.
Mervyn Le Roy, USA, 1962, 149 mins.

Gypsy (1993/Midler)
Unbeatable Bette Midler recreates the infamous backstage mother as Mama Rose, the original driving force behind famous striptease artiste, Gypsy. This film features the original Broadway choreography by Jerome Robbins with music by Jule Styne and Stephen Sondheim.
VHS: S20650. $14.98.
Emile Ardolino, USA, 1993, 150 mins.

Hallelujah!
King Vidor's vibrant, colorful musical depicts the hardship and difficulties of daily black life. The film focuses on a poor Southern farmer who becomes a preacher, on his powerful temptations and fate and on the problems of reconciling these two radically different worlds. The work balances traditional black spirituals with numbers by Irving Berlin ("Waiting at the End of the Road" and "Swanee Shuffle". With Daniel L. Haynes, Nina Mae McKinney and William Fontaine.
VHS: S18504. $19.98.
King Vidor, USA, 1929, 90 mins.

Hallelujah, I'm a Bum
S.N. Berman and Ben Hecht wrote the screenplay for this musical entertainment starring Al Jolson. A tramp meets a woman suffering from temporary amnesia. Soon he falls in love with her and resolves to reform his easy-going ways.
VHS: S23819. $19.98.
Laser: LD76067. $39.99.
Lewis Milestone, USA, 1933, 83 mins.

Hank Williams: "The Show He Never Gave"
A speculative biography of Hank Williams. The filmmakers showcase the definitive Hank Williams concert performance, with country singer "Sneezy" Waters impersonating Williams playing an intimate concert at a roadside bar. 86 mins.
VHS: S17318. $24.95.

Hans Christian Andersen
The incredibly talented Danny Kaye stars as Hans Christian Andersen, a young cobbler with a special gift for storytelling. A wonderful musical tale that will teach and delight both young and old. "A magnificent production that is sheer poetry on film" *(Hollywood Reporter)*. Digitally remastered.
VHS: S02530. $19.98.
Charles Vidor, USA, 1951, 112 mins.

A Hard Day's Night
Richard Lester meets John, Paul, George and Ringo in this exuberant film following an average day in the life of the Beatles as they take under their wing Paul's grandfather while they prepare for a television special in London. Along the way there are 15 now classic songs and a non-stop barrage of verbal and visual gags. Special Edition contains over 15 minutes of bonus footage.
VHS: S00540. $19.98.
Laser: CAV. LD70374. $79.95.
Laser: CLV. LD70375. $49.97.
DVD: DV60122. $24.98.
Richard Lester, Great Britain, 1969, 108 mins.

The Harvey Girls
Judy Garland goes West to work as a waitress in a Fred Harvey railroad restaurant. When she is not serving grub to prominent westerners like John Hodiak, Ray Bolger and Preston Foster, she is probably singing or setting a good example. With Angela Lansbury, Cyd Charisse.
VHS: S04985. $19.95.
George Sidney, USA, 1946, 102 mins.

Hear My Song

A delightful romantic comic adventure based on the exploits of famed Irish tenor Josef Locke. Ned Beatty plays the cautious Irish tax exile being sought by a conniving but well meaning talent booker for a nightclub on the west coast of England. Adrian Dunbar, who co-wrote the script, plays the unemployed club manager, who must redeem himself in the eyes of the woman he loves as well as the community that trusted his judgement.

VHS: S16634. $19.95.
Laser: LD75205. $34.98.
Peter Chelsom, Great Britain, 1991, 104 mins.

The Heat's On

Mae West stars as a fading Broadway performer who tries to convince an aging financier to bankroll her bawdy new musical, despite the objections of the man's sister, who runs the Legion of Purity. With Victor Moore, William Gaxton and Almira Sessions.

VHS: S19021. $19.95.
Gregory Ratoff, USA, 1943, 79 mins.

Hello, Dolly!

Barbra Streisand is Dolly Levi, matchmaker extraordinaire, in this Gene Kelly film of the Broadway hit musical. Walter Matthau is Horace Vandergelder, a wealthy, unmarried businessman. Set at the turn of this century, schemes will be hatched and songs will be sung. With Louis Armstrong.

VHS: S02927. $19.98.
Laser: LD71037. $79.95.
Gene Kelly, USA, 1969, 146 mins.

Hello, Frisco, Hello

Alice Faye stars as singer who rises to fame after her saloon-owner boyfriend (John Payne) leaves her for a socialite. As luck would have it, in the world of musical comedies at least, his marriage crumbles, leaving him destitute, until Faye returns to see if he still loves her.

VHS: S21304. $19.98.
H. Bruce Humberstone, USA, 1943, 98 mins.

Help!

Richard Lester's follow-up to *A Hard Day's Night* doesn't try to assess the power and impact of the Beatles on popular culture, but creates as many chances and thin narrative lines for the brilliant group to reveal their power. Digitally encoded on Hi-fi, heightening the sharpness of the Beatles' work: "Help," "You're Gonna Lose That Girl," "You've Got to Hide Your Love Away" and "Ticket to Ride." Special Edition contains eight minutes of rare bonus footage.

VHS: S02013. $19.98.
Laser: CAV. **LD70376. $79.95.**
Laser: CLV. **LD70377. $39.95.**
DVD: DV60123. $24.98.
Richard Lester, Great Britain, 1965, 98 mins.

High Society

One of the best musicals of the fifties! With Bing Crosby, Frank Sinatra, and Grace Kelly, the score written by Cole Porter and played by Louis Armstrong and his Band. *High Society* is highly entertaining and highly recommended!

VHS: S00570. $19.95.
Charles Walters, USA, 1956, 112 mins.

Higher and Higher

Frank Sinatra is the crooning victim of a crazy plot: a bankrupt millionaire tries to pass off his maid as a debutante in order to marry rich boy next door: Frankie! With the beautiful Michele Morgan.

VHS: S11605. $19.98.
Tim Whelan, USA, 1943, 90 mins.

His Butler's Sister

Deanna Durbin goes off to visit her brother (Pat O'Brien) and finds that he is a butler to a Broadway composer (Franchot Tone). Durbin becomes smitten with the handsome composer and takes up residence with the two, posing as a maid. It's a delightful musical comedy. Charles Previn acted as the music director.

VHS: S27012. $19.98.
Frank Borzage, USA, 1943, 94 mins.

Hit the Deck

The Broadway hit of 1927 was filmed twice before this 1955 MGM set sail. Nine major characters mix the ship-shape world of the Navy with other shapes in a Broadway show. Jane Powell is Admiral Walter Pidgeon's daughter, who wants to be in show business like stage starlet Debbie Reynolds. You can be sure the shore patrol will be involved somewhere. With Vic Damone, Ann Miller, Russ Tamblyn, Tony Martin and Alan King.

VHS: S08520. $19.95.
Laser: Letterboxed. **LD74673. $34.98.**
Roy Rowland, USA, 1955, 112 mins.

Hollywood Canteen

Will a GI on leave meet his dream girl at the Hollywood Canteen? You bet—especially when Bette Davis, John Garfield, Barbara Stanwyck, Peter Lorre, Ida Lupino, Joan Crawford and over 30 more Hollywood luminaries give him a helping hand. Vibrant wartime entertainment.

VHS: S14316. $29.98.
Laser: Chapter Search. Includes original theatrical trailer. **LD71671. $39.98.**
Delmer Daves, USA, 1944, 124 mins.

Hollywood Musicals of the '50s

All the music, dancing, exotic locales, comedy and drama of the greatest musicals of the 1950s are presented in this program. With clips and revealing interviews with such stars as Shirley Jones, Ann Miller and Debbie Reynolds. 60 mins.

VHS: S32421. $19.99.

Hollywood Party

It's party time in Tinsel Town and look who's invited! Laurel and Hardy, The Three Stooges, Jimmy Durante, Mickey Mouse, plus a host of Hollywood's top stars of the '30s and a bevy of beautiful dancing girls! Filled with gags, popular songs, and lavish production numbers. USA, 1934, 69 mins.

VHS: S15420. $19.98.

Hollywood Rhythm

Four volumes of over 30 all-star musical shorts from the Golden Age of Hollywood and Paramount Studio Vaults.

Blue Melodies. With Billie Holiday, Duke Ellington, Bessie Smith, Ethel Merman, George Dewey Washington and Vincent Lopez. USA, 1929-35, 83 mins.
VHS: S31815. $24.95.

Jazz Cocktails. With Ginger Rogers, Duke Ellington, Cab Calloway, Artie Shaw, Rodgers and Hart, Fats Waller and Fredi Washington. USA, 1929-41, 78 mins.
VHS: S31814. $24.95.

Radio Rhythms. With Bing Crosby, Hoagy Carmichael, Rudy Vallee, Ruth Etting, Lillian Roth, Mae Questel and Helen Kane. USA, 1929-39, 86 mins.
VHS: S31813. $24.95.

Rhapsodies in Black and Blue. With Cary Grant, Eddie Cantor, Ethel Merman, Anna Chang, Louis Armstrong, Nino Martini and Mae Questel. Directed by Aubrey Scotto, USA, 1930-32, 78 mins.
VHS: S31816. $24.95.

Complete Set.
VHS: S31817. $89.95.
Laser: LD76416. $99.98.

How to Succeed in Business Without Really Trying

Robert Morse is an ambitious window washer who has dreams of climbing the corporate ladder from inside a building for a change. This Broadway musical transfers entertainingly to film form. Songs by Frank Losesser include "The Brotherhood of Man" and "I Believe in You". With Michelle Lee, Anthony Teague, Maureen Arthur and Rudy Vallee as the head of the Worldwide Wicket Company. VHS letterboxed.

VHS: S11733. $19.95.
Laser: LD70596. $39.98.
David Swift, USA, 1967, 121 mins.

I Could Go on Singing

Judy Garland's last motion picture. She plays an American singing star visiting London to top the bill at the London Palladium, where she meets old flame Dirk Bogarde, who is raising the son they had out of wedlock. Will Judy admit to motherhood and rekindle the old emotions, or just find a bottle to crawl inside? With Gregory Phillips as little Matt and Jack Klugman as her manager.

VHS: S09149. $19.98.
Laser: LD74674. $34.98.
Ronald Neame, Great Britain, 1963, 99 mins.

I Dood It

The timeless comedy of Red Skelton is backed by Eleanor Powell's splendid dancing and the Big Band jazz of Jimmy Dorsey and his Orchestra in this madcap tale of a lovesick stage-door Johnny who finds out that masquerades can backfire—spectacularly. Includes a performance by Lena Horne.

VHS: S15429. $19.98.
Vincente Minnelli, USA, 1943, 102 mins.

I Dream of Jeannie

Ray Middleton and Bill Shirley are featured in this fictional biography of the tin pan alley composer Stephen Foster. Though this Irish-American died at a relatively young age, his songs remain standards that everyone knows. "I Dream of Jeannie" is just one of his many lasting works.

VHS: S23820. $24.95.
Allan Dwan, USA, 1952, 90 mins.

I Love Melvin

Donald O'Connor's just a gofer for *Look* magazine. But he promises chorus girl Debbie Reynolds her face will get onto the cover. Seven songs and a million complications later, it all comes true.

VHS: S14165. $19.98.
Don Weis, USA, 1953, 77 mins.

I Married an Angel

Nelson Eddy and Jeanette MacDonald in their last film together. He plays a playboy who sings and is smitten by a heavenly visitor. Based on a Rodgers and Hart musical which was based on a piece by Hungarian Vaszary Janos. Script for the MGM film by Anita Loos. With Janis Carter, Inez Cooper, Edward Everett Horton and Binnie Barnes.

VHS: S09846. $19.98.
W.S. Van Dyke, USA, 1942, 84 mins.

I Wanna Hold Your Hand

Exhilarating comedy on Beatlemania from Robert Zemeckis. Seven teenagers will do anything to see the Fab Four on the Ed Sullivan Show. Will Jordan accurately impersonates Sullivan. With Nancy Allen, Bobby DiCicco, Marc McClure, Susan Kendall Newman, Theresa Saldana, Wendie Jo Sperber and the undefinable Eddie Deezen as the crazy kids. Featuring 17 songs by John, Paul, George and Ringo.

VHS: S08499. $19.98.
Robert Zemeckis, USA, 1978, 104 mins.

I'll See You in My Dreams

Michael Curtiz's biographical retelling of the amazing career of lyricist Gus Kahn, who wrote more than 800 tunes, including the memorable pop tunes "Makin' Whoopee", "Ain't We Got Fun", "Toot Tootsie", "It Had to Be You" and "Pretty Baby". With Doris Day, Danny Thomas and Frank Lovejoy.

VHS: S18462. $19.98.
Michael Curtiz, USA, 1951, 110 mins.

In the Good Old Summertime

Judy Garland and Van Johnson are feuding shop clerks who unknowingly exchange romantic pen pal letters in this musical adaptation of *Shop Around the Corner*. The score includes "I Don't Care" and "Wait Til the Sun Shines."

VHS: S09940. $29.95.
Robert Z. Leonard, USA, 1949, 102 mins.

Interrupted Melody

Eleanor Parker portrays famed Australian opera singer Marjorie Lawrence in this Oscar-winning film (Best Screenplay). Lawrence made a heroic comeback after being stricken by polio. Glenn Ford and Roger Moore co-star, with Eileen Farrell providing the singing voice of the diva.

VHS: S21170. $19.98.
Laser: LD76264. $39.99.
Curtis Bernhardt, USA, 1955, 106 mins.

It Happened in Brooklyn

Frank Sinatra plays a singing ex-GI back in Brooklyn and ready for love and success. He finds himself sharing an apartment with high school janitor Jimmy Durante instead. Enter snobby Peter Lawford with a song to sell and no voice to sing it. With Kathryn Grayson and Gloria Grahame. Songs include "Time After Time", "Whose Baby Are You?" and "The Song's Gotta Have Heart".

VHS: S13305. $19.98.
Laser: Chapter search. Includes original theatrical trailer. **LD71637. $34.98.**
Richard Whorf, USA, 1947, 104 mins.

It's a Date

Following her latest stage triumph, Broadway star Kay Francis decides to vacation in Hawaii before tackling her new role. While she's away her daughter (Deanna Durbin) is offered a part in a prize-winning play—which just happens to be the same part her mother is planning to do in the coming season. A charming musical comedy. With S.Z. Sakall and Walter Pidgeon.

VHS: S14317. $29.98.
William A. Seiter, USA, 1940, 103 mins.

t's a Great Feeling

This breezy musical comedy stars Dennis Morgan and Jack Carson as two Hollywood actors about to begin work on a new movie. The problem is finding a director and a leading lady to work with Carson, who has a reputation as a "ham" and "wolf." Enter Doris Day as a young hopeful from the studio commissary whom Carson attempts to turn into a star.

VHS: S14311. $29.98.
David Butler, USA, 1949, 85 mins.

It's a Great Feeling/ Thank Your Lucky Stars

Two classical all-star Hollywood romps, the first is an ensemble comedy about the crazed efforts of Dennis Morgan, Doris Day and Jack Carson to break an unknown into show business. David Butler's *Thank Your Lucky Stars* is a buoyant and expansive musical with Bette Davis, Humphrey Bogart, Eddie Cantor, Errol Flynn, Ann Sheridan and John Garfield.
Laser: LD70170. $44.98.

It's Always Fair Weather

Gene Kelly and Cyd Charisse star in this fast-tempoed, toe-tapping musical featuring three WW II buddies who are re-united ten years after their discharge to find they have nothing in common and dislike one another.
VHS: S03600. $19.98.
Gene Kelly/Stanley Donen, USA, 1955, 109 mins.

The Jazz Singer (Crosland)

It's more than a movie; it's history—the first feature-length film with spoken dialog. Audiences at the October 6, 1927 premiere were electrified by what they could now see *and* hear when star Al Jolson, in the film's best-remembered line, proclaimed: "Wait a minute, you ain't heard nothing yet!" Includes Jolson's famous renditions of "Toot Toot Tootsie Goodbye" and "Mammy."
VHS: S04338. $29.98.
Alan Crosland, USA, 1927, 89 mins.

The Jazz Singer (Curtiz)

Danny Thomas and Peggy Lee star in this version of the musical made famous by both Broadway and Hollywood. You'll be touched by the story of a cantor's son who rejects his father's hopes that he will continue the family tradition, to become a show biz performer. "If I Could Be with You" and "Just One of Those Things" are among the memorable songs contained in this musical drama.
VHS: S20657. $19.98.
Michael Curtiz, USA, 1953, 107 mins.

The Jazz Singer (Fleischer)

Neil Diamond is the son of a Cantor (Laurence Olivier), who rejects family tradition in order to pursue a career as a popular singer. Of course, this secular lifestyle creates a clash with his father that is only resolved after a great deal of angst. Based on the early successful sound film from the late 1920's.
VHS: S22032. $14.98.
Richard Fleischer, USA, 1980, 115 mins.

Jesus Christ Superstar

The words and music of Tim Rice and Andrew Lloyd Webber find a home on film in this innovative retelling of the life of Christ. This modern approach to the events of 2000 years ago will not please everyone, but what can? With Ted Neeley, Carl Anderson, Josh Mostel and Yvonne Elliman as Mary Magdalene. Letterboxed.
VHS: S04920. $19.98.
Laser: Chapter search. **LD71579. $34.98.**
Norman Jewison, USA, 1973, 103 mins.

Jolson Sings Again

Vibrant and joyous sequel to *The Jolson Story* has Larry Parks reprising his role as Al Jolson at the decline of his film career. He returns to Broadway to discover the minstrel "blackface" phenomenon that created his popularity has lost its appeal. His manager persuades him to perform for GI's overseas—where he falls passionately in love with Army nurse Barbara Hale. With William Demarest.
VHS: S02918. $19.95.
Harry Levin, USA, 1949, 96 mins.

Jolson Story

A sprawling, big musical that records the life of Al Jolson, the controversial entertainer who played to almost exclusively white audiences, in black face, as the lead in "minstrel jazz productions." The film traces the origins of Jolson's entry into show business and the effects of his enormous popularity. Larry Parks received an Academy Award nomination for his work as Jolson, elevating the standard biopic conventions through excellent use of Jolson's music, including "My Mammy" and "You Made Me Love You."
VHS: S02917. $19.95.
Alfred E. Green, USA, 1946, 129 mins.

Julie Andrews—Broadway: The Making of Broadway, The Music of Richard Rodgers

From the beginning, Richard Rodgers had Julie Andrews in mind for his blockbuster musical *The Sound of Music*. In this video, Andrews sings songs from this Broadway success, as well as works from the later Andrews hit *Victor/Victoria—The Musical*. 50 mins.
VHS: S26490. $29.95.

Jumbo

A razzle-dazzle circus epic starring Doris Day and Stephen Boyd as the romantic duo who sing the sublime music of Rodgers and Hart. Also starring Jimmy Durante and Martha Raye. Busby Berkeley directed the lavish and breathtaking circus scenes.
VHS: S15432. $19.98.
Laser: LD74667. $39.98.
Charles Walters, USA, 1962, 125 mins.

Kid Millions

Eddie Cantor stars in this early color musical comedy. A large inheritance dislodges a rather unimpressive Brooklyn boy by promising him the hope of great wealth. Before long, Cantor is off on an adventure to Egypt in order to collect. Great songs and an early appearance by Lucille Ball make this a must for fans of classic films.
VHS: S24206. $19.98.
Roy Del Ruth, USA, 1934, 90 mins.

The King and I

Stern Siamese monarch Brynner is softened by the influence of English governess Kerr as their clashing cultures and personalities give way to an unspoken love. Magnificent performance by Brynner (who won an Oscar) in this sumptuously produced and moving adaptation of the Broadway musical. "Shall We Dance" highlights the Rogers and Hammerstein score.
VHS: S02541. $19.98.
Laser: THX. **LD75920. $124.98.**
Walter Lang, USA, 1956, 133 mins.

King of Jazz

This vibrant, sparkling piece of celluloid nostalgia takes the form of a lavish jazz revue with music by American giants such as George Gershwin played out against dazzling production numbers featuring Bing Crosby, Paul Whiteman, and John Boles. This was Universal Pictures' first all-Technicolor feature length musical film, and contains the first sound cartoon sequence as well.
VHS: S00681. $19.98.
John M. Anderson, USA, 1930, 93 mins.

Kismet

The perennial fable of poets, lovers and the Arabian nights, based on the Broadway success featuring Howard Keel, Sebastian Cabot, Vic Damone and Ann Blyth. Music adapted from themes by Alexander Borodin.
VHS: S02259. $19.95.
Laser: LD70609. $34.97.
Vincente Minnelli, USA, 1955, 113 mins.

Kissin' Cousins

Elvis Presley is in the air force and finds himself stationed at a base in the South. There he quickly discovers a hillbilly double. This farcical plot offers plenty of good laughs and functions as a sturdy vehicle for songs like "Smokey Mountain Boy" and "Barefoot Ballad," as well as the title song.
VHS: S23004. $19.95.
Gene Nelson, USA, 1964, 96 mins.

La Cucaracha

The first three-color, live-action production was this Oscar-winning comic short about a hot-tempered cantina girl out to regain the lost love of a fellow dancer. Lots of music and dancing with Steffi Dunn, Paul Porcasi and Don Alvarado. The triumph of Technicolor. USA, 1934, 21 mins.
VHS: S05698. $19.95.

Ladies of the Chorus

Marilyn Monroe's first sizable role pairs her with Adele Jergens as a mother/daughter burlesque team in this lively film. Differences arise between them when the budding Monroe takes interest in a wealthy young bachelor, and seems headed for the same romantic blunder that mom made.
VHS: S16592. $19.95.
Phil Karlson, USA, 1949, 61 mins.

Lady Be Good

Husband and wife songwriting team Robert Young and Ann Sothern find a love song's a great way to patch up a marital spat, in this musical with Red Skelton and Eleanor Powell. With music by the Gershwins, Oscar Hammerstein and Jerome Kern. That's one talented couple!
VHS: S14166. $19.98.
Norman Z. McLeod, USA, 1941, 111 mins.

Lady Be Good/Ship Ahoy

Two romantic comedies starring comedian Red Skelton and dancer Eleanor Powell. Norman Z. McLeod's 1941 *Lady Be Good* concerns a husband and wife songwriting team (played by Robert Young and Ann Sothern). Edward Buzzell's 1942 *Ship Ahoy* has the two caught up in international intrigue on a Naval ship. Includes the theatrical trailers for both films. 207 mins.
Laser: LD71657. $44.98.

Lady Sings the Blues

Diana Ross makes her screen debut as Lady Day, the legendary jazz singer Billie Holiday. More soap opera and fine songs than accurate biography but fans of Miss Ross and Billie Holiday will be happy. With Billy Dee Williams, Sid Melton and Richard Pryor as Piano Man. Film received five Oscar nominations.
VHS: S10836. $29.95.
Laser: LD75302. $39.98.
Sidney J. Furie, USA, 1972, 144 mins.

Let Freedom Ring

Ben Hecht wrote the screenplay for this Western starring Nelson Eddy. When he returns to his hometown, Eddy finds it overrun with corruption and promptly sets out to reclaim this frontier outpost. It's an action-filled patriotic film that includes a particularly noteworthy musical number, Eddy singing "The Star Spangled Banner".
VHS: S20791. $19.98.
Jack Conway, USA, 1939, 100 mins.

Let's Dance

Terrific dance numbers by Fred Astaire distinguish this drama as Betty Hutton tries to win her son back from her Back Bay in-laws. With Roland Young, Ruth Warrick.
VHS: S10434. $19.95.
Laser: LD75221. $34.98.
Norman Z. McLeod, USA, 1950, 112 mins.

Li'l Abner

A colorful and fast-paced romp based on the hit Broadway version of Al Capp's beloved cartoon strip. This musical comedy features Julie Newmar, Stella Stevens, and Robert Strauss.
VHS: S13705. $19.95.
Laser: LD75222. $34.98.
Melvin Frank, USA, 1959, 114 mins.

Lili

Leslie Caron is Lili Daurier, a 16-year-old orphan who finds a home with a traveling carnival and befriends a crippled puppeteer. A charming MGM musical based on a story by Paul Gallico. Cast includes Zsa Zsa Gabor, Amanda Blake, Jean-Pierre Aumont and Mel Ferrer as the puppeteer. Bronislau Kaper's score won an Oscar.
VHS: S06178. $19.98.
Laser: LD76272. $39.99.
Charles Walters, USA, 1953, 81 mins.

Listen, Darling

Unwilling to let her widowed mother marry just anyone, Pinky Wingate and her pal Buzz take matters into their own hands. They kidnap Dottie and take her for what becomes a cross-country husband hunt. Walter Pidgeon becomes the affable victim of everyone's affections. Starring Judy Garland and Mary Astor.
VHS: S15854. $19.98.
Edwin L. Marin, USA, 1938, 75 mins.

Lisztomania

The classical composer as rock superstar, this wild spectacle blends musical genres and cuts across historical generations. Starring Roger Daltry as Franz Liszt, with a guest appearance by Ringo Starr as the Pope. Lots of FUN!
VHS: S00759. $19.98.
Laser: Letterboxed. **LD71674. $34.98.**
Ken Russell, Great Britain, 1975, 105 mins.

The Little Colonel

Shirley Temple, Lionel Barrymore and Bill "Bojangles" Robinson star in this toe-tapping musical set in the Old South.
VHS: S05903. $19.98.
David Butler, USA, 1935, 80 mins.

Little Miss Broadway

Shirley Temple, George Murphy and Jimmy Durante star in this very amusing backstage musical that includes Shirley's classic "Be Optimistic."
VHS: S05904. $19.98.
Irving Cummings, USA, 1938, 71 mins.

Little Nelly Kelly

The first film to feature Judy Garland as a "solo" actress, *Little Nelly Kelly* follows the daughter of an Irish cop who struggles to maintain family unity while making good on the stage. Garland plays both mother and daughter in this heartfelt musical adapted from George M. Cohan's play about Irish pride. With George Murphy and Charles Winninger.
VHS: S15852. $19.98.
Norman Taurog, USA, 1940, 99 mins.

The Little Prince

Antoine de Saint-Exupery's wonderful book is transformed into a musical with songs written by Alan Jay Lerner and Frederick Loewe. 89 mins.
VHS: S06113. $19.95.
Stanley Donen, USA, 1974, 88 mins.

Little Shop of Horrors

The recent re-make of Roger Corman's classic film, adapted from the smash hit Broadway musical, stars Steve Martin, Christopher Guest and Ellen Greene. With a fabulous Bill Murray performance as the masochistic dental patient.
VHS: S03865. $19.98.
Frank Oz, USA, 1986, 88 mins.

Littlest Rebel

Shirley Temple sings "Polly Wolly Doodle" and taps her way in and out of Civil War trouble with Bill "Bojangles" Robinson.
VHS: S05902. $19.98.
David Butler, USA, 1935, 70 mins.

Look for the Silver Lining

This visually opulent biography of Broadway star Marilyn Miller (June Haver) interweaves stylish vaudeville numbers and engaging musical routines in a look at her life and work. With Ray Bolger, Rosemary DeCamp and Gordon MacRae.
VHS: S19470. $19.98.
David Butler, USA, 1949, 100 mins.

Louisiana Purchase

Irving Berlin's elegant and witty music sets the tone of this funny and lyrical political satire about the legislative process, with Bob Hope as a shrewd Congressman. With Vera Zorina, Victor Moore and Irene Bordoni.
VHS: S18545. $14.98.
Irving Cummings, USA, 1941, 98 mins.

Love Me or Leave Me

Doris Day stars as singer Ruth Etting in the best performance of her career. A serious show biz bio has Doris sing 12 songs and act up a storm opposite James Cagney as her gimpy, overbearing mentor. Day even got top billing. With Cameron Mitchell. Numbers include "You Made Me Love You" and "Ten Cents a Dance".
VHS: S07160. $19.95.
Charles Vidor, USA, 1955, 122 mins.

Lovely to Look At

Red is the color this season. When Red Skelton inherits a Paris fashion house, he and his buddies turn haute couture inside out. This comic musical also stars Kathryn Grayson, Howard Keel and Ann Miller.
VHS: S14167. $19.98.
Mervyn Le Roy, USA, 1952, 105 mins.

The Loves of Carmen

Rita Hayworth and Glenn Ford are re-teamed in living color as the popular Bizet opera gets the Hollywood treatment. Only the plot remains as Rita's sultry charms turn honest men into sunbaked jellyfish. With Victor Jory, Ron Randell and Luther Adler.
VHS: S04675. $19.95.
Laser: LD74895. $34.95.
Charles Vidor, USA, 1948, 99 mins.

Lucky Me

Doris Day stars in this energetic musical set in Miami about an ambitious performer stuck in a third-rate revue show who unexpectedly gets the notice of a Broadway songwriter. With Robert Cummings, Phil Silvers, and Eddie Foy.
VHS: S15783. $19.98.
Jack Donohue, USA, 1952, 100 mins.

Lullaby of Broadway

A bright Warner Bros. melodrama and musical stars Doris Day as a prominent Broadway star who returns to New York and discovers her mother destitute. A sharp cast includes Gene Nelson, Gladys George, Billy de Wolfe and Florence Bates.
VHS: S15722. $19.98.
Laser: LD74709. $34.98.
David Butler, USA, 1951, 92 mins.

Mad About Music

Deanna Durbin stars as a lonely schoolgirl in Switzerland who feels rejected by her movie star father. At first she invents a father to impress her friends and then actually finds a handsome composer to play the part. In the end, despite these problems, Durbin finds even more family than she could have hoped for.
VHS: S27010. $19.98.
Norman Taurog, USA, 1938, 96 mins.

Make a Wish

Basil Rathbone stars as a charming composer who lives across the lake from a boys' camp. He befriends singing prodigy Bobby Breen and finds inspiration for a new operetta when he meets the boy's mother. With Marion Clare, Leon Errol, Donald Meek and Henry Armetta. B&W.
VHS: S06148. $29.95.
Kurt Neumann, USA, 1937, 77 mins.

The Making of a Musical

Discussion of the premiere production of the Richard Rodgers musical *Do I Hear a Waltz?* With the author of the book for the show, Arthur Laurents, set designer Beni Montresor and lyricist Stephen Sondheim. 1965, 27 mins.
VHS: S32324. $89.95.

Mame

America's comedienne, Lucille Ball, as one of the stage and screen's most enduring dames—Auntie Mame. With a musical score by Jerry Herman.
VHS: S03954. $19.98.
Laser: LD70622. $39.98.
Gene Saks, USA, 1974, 132 mins.

Man of La Mancha

The film version of this popular stage musical stars Peter O'Toole as Don Quixote, James Coco as the faithful Sancho Panza and Sophia Loren as Dulcinea. As if that isn't enough, the soaring musical score includes one of the finest songs ever written-"The Impossible Dream." Enjoy!
VHS: S01715. $19.99.
Laser: LD72125. $39.98.
Arthur Hiller, USA, 1972, 129 mins.

Manhattan Merry-Go-Round

Phil Regan, Ann Dvorak and Cab Calloway star in this melodrama in which a gangster takes over a record company and uses his coercive methods on musical groups. Despite his ruthless ways, the gangster is undone by a temperamental opera singer.
VHS: S23821. $24.95.
Charles F. Reisner, USA, 1937, 89 mins.

Maytime

John Barrymore stands between a romance between an opera star and a poverty ridden singer in Paris. He plays the husband/mentor of Jeanette MacDonald, who is fonder of Nelson Eddy. One of their better vehicles. With Sig Ruman, Herman Bing and Rafaela Ottiano. B&W.
VHS: S06978. $19.95.
Laser: LD72143. $39.98.
Robert Z. Leonard, USA, 1937, 132 mins.

Meet Danny Wilson

Frank Sinatra and Shelley Winters star in this romantic musical drama about a singer who becomes involved in backstage intrigues. A roguish success in New York, his move to Hollywood and ever greater success is tarnished by racketeers. Sinatra is eminently believable in the part.
VHS: S21497. $14.98.
Joseph Pevney, USA, 1951, 86 mins.

Meet Me in Las Vegas

Cowpoke Dan Dailey can't lose in Vegas as long as he holds hands with lovely Cyd Charisse. Big, splashy entertainment loaded with guest stars and Vegas glamour. Cameos by Frank Sinatra, Lena Horne, and Debbie Reynolds.
VHS: S14168. $19.98.
Laser: LD72144. $34.98.
Roy Rowland, USA, 1956, 112 mins.

Meet Me in St. Louis

Judy Garland is the classic American teenager in love, in song, in one of the brightest hours of her career. *Meet Me in St. Louis* is a charming turn-of-the-century album full of magic and memories. 50th Anniversary edition. Newly remastered. Includes a "making of" documentary, interviews with cast and team, a trailer from 1955, and a recreation of a deleted musical number.
VHS: S00845. $19.95.
Laser: LD70627. $29.95.
Vincente Minnelli, USA, 1944, 114 mins.

Melody Cruise

Step aboard a luxury ocean liner with millionaires Charlie Ruggles, Phil Harris and a cargo of laughs as they try to outsmart the fair sex in a rollicking musical comedy.
VHS: S11608. $19.98.
Mark Sandrich, USA, 1932, 75 mins.

The Merry Widow

A classic adaptation of Franz Lehar's opera, with Lana Turner as an attractive, eligible widow courted by the king of Marshovia (Fernando Lamas), who has designs on her vast wealth, though she foils his schemes.
VHS: S18556. $19.98.
Curtis Bernhardt, USA, 1952, 105 mins.

Million-Dollar Mermaid

One of Esther Williams' best—Williams is the leggy swim star, while Annette Kellerman switches between swimming and romancing Victor Mature. Busby Berkeley produced some of the most spectacular dance numbers for this musical.
VHS: S11160. $29.95.
Laser: LD71153. $34.98.
Mervyn LeRoy, USA, 1952, 115 mins.

Minstrel Man

A rare musical showing a side of American entertainment never shown. Benny Fields is a minstrel performer who gives his daughter over to friends to raise after the death of his wife.
VHS: S09581. $29.95.

Moon over Miami

An entertaining musical romance with Betty Grable, her sister Carole Landis and Charlotte Greenwood going fortune hunting in Miami and coming up with more than they bargained for. Includes the title song, "You Started Something."
VHS: S09448. $19.98.
Walter Lang, USA, 1941, 91 mins.

Moonlight Sonata

Polish composer and patriot Paderewski portrays himself in this 1937 film which features a 21-minute recital of Chopin's "Heroic Polonaise," Liszt's "Hungarian Rhapsody," Beethoven's "Moonlight," and Padrewski's "Minuet in G." With Marie Tempest and Eric Portman. "[Paderewski] casts his spell directly, and the shifting camera never once discovers a flaw in the expression of his face and body or in the behavior of his hands. He is completedly absorbed in his own playing and so is the audience" (Samuel Chotzinoff, *New York Post*, 1937). 87 mins.
VHS: S28432. $34.95.

Movie Struck (Pick a Star)

Laurel and Hardy guest star in this Hollywood musical as themselves. They appear in two long sequences which add up to one reel out of the eight. The story concerns a young girl who wants to be in the movies with the help of publicity man Jack Haley. With Rosina Lawrence and Patsy Kelly. B&W.
VHS: S05065. $29.95.
Edward Sedgwick, USA, 1937, 69 mins.

Mr. Music

A remake of *Accent on Youth*. Bing Crosby stars as a Broadway songwriter who tries to rejuvenate his life, reclaim his youth and use his music as a means of overcoming personal obstacles and career setbacks. With Nancy Olson, Charles Coburn and Ruth Hussey. Cameos by Groucho Marx and Peggy Lee.
VHS: S17980. $14.95.
Richard Hadyn, USA, 1950, 113 mins.

The Music Man

If you are looking for a movie with 76 trombones and trouble in River City, have I got a musical for you. Robert Preston stars as the energetic Professor Harold Hill, a silver-tongued conman willing to separate a small town of Iowans from their money. With Buddy Hackett, Ronny Howard and Shirley Jones as Marian the Librarian.
VHS: S03264. $19.98.
Morton Da Costa, USA, 1962, 151 mins.

My Dream Is Yours

Doris Day sings her way to the top of the charts in this buoyant Technicolor musical comedy set in the days of live radio variety shows. Jack Carson plays her hard-working agent, and a live-action/animated sequence features a very special superstar: Bugs Bunny.
VHS: S14318. $29.98.
Michael Curtiz, USA, 1949, 101 mins.

My Sister Eileen

This exuberant musical remake of the 1942 social comedy is a succession of funny vignettes about two young Ohio women adjusting to the severe culture shock of Greenwich Village and trying to retain their innocence. With Betty Garrett, Janet Leigh, Jack Lemmon, Bob Fosse and Kurt Kasznar.
VHS: S18418. $19.95.
Richard Quine, USA, 1955, 108 mins.

Nancy Goes to Rio

A veteran Broadway actress (Ann Sothern) and her talented, stage-struck daughter (Jane Powell) are chasing the same role and the same man—but neither knows what the other is up to. Includes several Gershwin tunes and a stunning performance by Carmen Miranda.
VHS: S15427. $19.98.
Robert Z. Leonard, USA, 1950, 99 mins.

Naughty Marietta (1935)

Jeanette MacDonald and Nelson Eddy appeared together for the first time in this favorite operetta about a princess who runs away to America and falls in love with an Indian scout.
VHS: S00920. $19.95.
Laser: LD70637. $34.98.
W.S. Van Dyke, USA, 1935, 106 mins.

Naughty Marietta (1955)

Patrice Munsel, as Marietta d'Altena, and Alfred Drake, as Captain Warrington, star in this 1955 adaptation of Victor Herbert's operetta *Naughty Marietta*. The work includes such popular melodies as "Ah!, Sweet Mystery of Life," "Italian Street Song," "I'm Falling in Love with Someone" and "Tramp! Tramp! Tramp!" 78 mins.
VHS: S20374. $39.95.

Neptune's Daughter

Esther Williams and Ricardo Montalban demonstrate there is more to do in a swimming pool than laps, in the MGM aquatic spectacular. They also sing the Oscar winning song "Baby, It's Cold Outside." With Red Skelton and Betty Garnett as the comic relief. Also Xavier Cugat, Keenan Wynn and Mel Blanc. The last one in the pool has to do a car commercial.
VHS: S08519. $19.95.
Laser: LD72148. $34.98.
Edward Buzzell, USA, 1949, 93 mins.

New Faces

A famous Broadway hit which established the careers of Eartha Kitt, Ronny Graham, Alice Ghostley, Robert Clary, June Carroll, Paul Lynde, Carol Lawrence and Mel Brooks. Eartha Kitt sings the songs that made her famous: "Monotonous," "C'est Si Bon," and "Santa Baby." Alice Ghostley sings "Boston Beguine," and the entire company romps through "Lizzie Borden."
VHS: S04700. $49.95.
Henry Horner, USA, 1954, 98 mins.

New Moon

Jeanette MacDonald and Nelson Eddy meet in the Bayou State, sing some songs and fall in love. The Oscar Hammerstein/Sigmund Romberg score includes "One Kiss," "Stout-Hearted Men" and "Lover Come Back to Me." With Mary Boland, George Zucco and H.B. Warner. Remake of 1930 film.
VHS: S06975. $19.95.
Laser: LD75541. $39.98.
Robert Z. Leonard, USA, 1940, 105 mins.

New York, New York

A celebration of the Big Band Era, starring Robert De Niro and Liza Minnelli, as well as Diahnne Abbott, Mary Kay Place and Lionel Stander. Cinematography by Laszlo Kovacs. This is the long version with the intact Minnelli number, "Happy Endings", restored. VHS letterboxed.
VHS: S00927. $24.98.
Martin Scorsese, USA, 1977, 163 mins.

Night and Day

Cary Grant plays Cole Porter, the composer who thrilled the world for 40 years with his witty, dramatic and memorable songs. Grant and the rest of the cast sing over twenty Porter classics in this Technicolor film that follows Porter from his undergraduate days at Yale to international acclaim.
VHS: S14315. $19.98.
Laser: LD72351. $39.98.
Michael Curtiz, USA, 1946, 128 mins.

No No Nanette

Anne Neagle, Victor Mature, Richard Carlson, Roland Young and ZaSu Pitts star in this second of three versions of the 1925 Broadway musical.
VHS: S08457. $29.95.
Herbert Wilcox, USA, 1940, 96 mins.

Nunsense

Emmy Award-winner Rue McClanahan stars in the long-running madcap musical about the trials and tribulations of the Little Sisters of Hoboken, who display their divine talents in benefit revues. Two-tape set includes *Nunsense* and *Nunsense 2: The Sequel*. 220 mins.
VHS: S31820. $29.95.

Oliver!—30th Anniversary Edition

The memorable musical version of Dickens' classic tale of the young orphan Oliver Twist and The Artful Dodger seeking their fortune on the streets of London. Winner of six Academy Awards, including Best Picture. With Mark Lester, Jack Wild, Ron Moody and Oliver Reed. Digitally remastered and restored.
VHS: S00952. $19.95.
Laser: Letterboxed. **LD72187. $39.95.**
DVD: Letterboxed, DD5.1, Spanish & French subtitles. **DV60420. $24.95.**
Carol Reed, Great Britain, 1968, 146 mins.

On a Clear Day You Can See Forever

Barbra Streisand and Yves Montand star in this cheerful musical about past lives. A girl visits a psychiatrist to stop smoking but learns that she has had a series of exciting identities in the past. One of these identities becomes a magnet for the psychiatrist's amorous attentions. Alan Jay Lerner wrote the lyrics and the book, while the film is based on the Lerner and Burton Lane musical.
VHS: S22027. $14.95.
Vincente Minnelli, USA, 1970, 129 mins.

On an Island with You

Esther Williams and Peter Lawford travel from shimmering swimming pools to shiny dance floors to remote blue lagoons in this South Seas musical romance.
VHS: S16607. $19.98.
Richard Thorpe, USA, 1948, 117 mins.

On Moonlight Bay

A musical essay about turn-of-the-century innocence and joy. This early Doris Day vehicle is taken from Booth Tarkington's *Penrod* series about the relationship of two brash young innocents. With Gordon MacRae, Billy Gray and Mary Wickes. Songs include "I'm Forever Blowing Bubbles", "Till We Meet Again", and "Cuddle Up a Little Closer".
VHS: S18460. $19.98.
Laser: LD72149. $34.98.
Roy Del Ruth, USA, 1951, 95 mins.

On the Avenue

Dick Powell stars as a producer of a satiric musical show featuring Alice Faye. Faye is impersonating the well-known socialite and heiress, played by Madeleine Carrol. This scenario spawns a romantic plot perfect for musical comedy, with an engaging score provided by Irving Berlin.
VHS: S21301. $19.98.
Roy Del Ruth, USA, 1937, 89 mins.

On the Town

Leonard Bernstein's Broadway musical, a war-era tale about three soldiers searching for the magical Miss Turnstiles in New York City, has been restaged as a concert at London's Barbican Centre. Conducted by Michael Tilson Thomas, this production includes numbers never performed in the show. Based on an idea by Jerome Robbins, the book and lyrics were composed by Betty Comden and Adolph Green. With Tyne Daly, Thomas Hampson, Frederica von Stade and David Garrison.
VHS: S19709. $29.95.
Laser: LD71932. $34.95.

One Hundred Men and a Girl

Deanna Durbin, the daughter of an unemployed musician, decides to persuade the famous conductor Leopold Stokowski to help her launch an orchestra that will employ her widowed father and another 99 out-of-work musicians. Charles Previn's score won an Oscar for his work on this comedy.
VHS: S23281. $19.98.
Henry Koster, USA, 1937, 84 mins.

One Night in the Tropics

A musical interpretation of Earl Derr Biggers' story *Love Insurance*, with songs by Jerome Kern, Oscar Hammerstein and Dorothy Fields. In their debut roles, Bud Abbott and Lou Costello are peripheral players to a complicated love triangle of Allan Jones, Nancy Kelly and Robert Cummings. The lunatic pair perform some of their "Who's on First?" routine.
VHS: S19069. $14.98.
A. Edward Sutherland, USA, 1940, 82 mins.

One Night of Love

Louis Silver won an Oscar for his score of this big box office success musical about an opera star who revolts against her tough teacher; it solidified the Hollywood careers of its stars, including Lily Pons, Gladys Swarthout, Miliza Korjus.
VHS: S11632. $19.95.
Victor Schertzinger, USA, 1934, 95 mins.

One Touch of Venus

Ava Gardner brightens up the life of Robert Walker, a window dresser, when his statue of the goddess of love becomes flesh. With Eve Arden, Dick Haymes and a few songs.
VHS: S04221. $19.95.
Laser: CLV. **LD72011. $34.98.**
William A. Seiter, USA, 1948, 82 mins.

Opposite Sex

The musical version of Clare Booth Luce's popular 1936 play *The Women* adds men and musical numbers. June Allyson is the good wife who may lose hubby Leslie Nielsen to temptress Joan Collins if she doesn't wise up. Those available with advice include Ann Sheridan, Dolores Gray, Ann Miller, Agnes Moorehead, Carolyn Jones and Joan Blondell. The guys include Dick Shawn, Dean Jones, Jim Backus and bandleader Harry James himself.
VHS: S13308. $19.98.
Laser: LD70730. $34.98.
David Miller, USA, 1956, 115 mins.

Orchestra Wives

George Montgomery and Ann Rutherford are newlyweds coping with the strain of life on the road in this big band film that's one of two Glenn Miller musicals from Fox. With Cesar Romero and Jackie Gleason.
VHS: S14507. $19.98.
Archie Mayo, USA, 1942, 98 mins.

Pagan Love Song

Clad in a sarong, her long hair bleached by the sun and skin the color of bronze, Esther Williams plays a half-American, half-Tahitian girl in this lavish island musical from producer Arthur Freed.
VHS: S16608. $19.98.
Robert Alton, USA, 1950, 76 mins.

Paint Your Wagon

Musical set during the gold rush days in California features Lee Marvin and Clint Eastwood as prospectors who share wife Jean Seberg, whom they purchased at an auction.
VHS: S06474. $29.95.
Joshua Logan, USA, 1969, 166 mins.

Pal Joey

One of the great Rodgers and Hart musicals about the fast-talking, womanizing nightclub entertainer who falls in love with one woman while another, richer one, woos him with the lure of his own night club. The songs include "Bewitched, Bothered and Bewildered," "My Funny Valentine," and "The Lady Is a Tramp." With Frank Sinatra, Kim Novak, Rita Hayworth.
VHS: S11630. $19.95.
Laser: LD74894. $34.95.
George Sidney, USA, 1957, 111 mins.

Palmy Days

Eddie Cantor stars in this musical comedy set in a bakery. With Charlotte Greenwood and George Raft.
VHS: S31811. $14.95.
A. Edward Sutherland, USA, 1931, 77 mins.

Panama Hattie

Ann Sothern is Panama Hattie, a salt-of-the-earth nightclub singer in love with a pedigreed officer in Canal Zone, Panama. A spirited WWII montage sparkling with the music of Cole Porter and the classic slapstick of Red Skelton.
VHS: S15428. $19.98.
Norman Z. McLeod, USA, 1942, 79 mins.

Passion

The Tony award-winning musical from Stephen Sondheim and James Lapine, set in romantic 19th-century Italy, about one woman's overwhelming love for a handsome, young army captain. With Donna Murphy, Jere Shea and Marin Mazzie.
VHS: S32219. $19.98.
James Lapine, USA, 1994, 105 mins.

Pennies from Heaven

Based on Dennis Potter's British television series, *Pennies from Heaven* is the unique and stylish story of a Depression-era sheet music salesman, played by Steve Martin, whose own dreary, joyless life is contrasted with the cloying optimism of Tin Pan Alley songs from the period. The stunning, escapist splendor of the 1930's-style musical numbers (set to the original recordings) repeatedly clashes with the bleak circumstances of Martin's real-life existence in this dazzling and intellectually provocative musical—beautifully photographed by Gordon Willis. Newly remastered for video.
VHS: S13970. $19.99.
Herbert Ross, USA, 1981, 108 mins.

Peter Pan

This is the 30th anniversary edition of the classic story of eternal youth, starring Mary Martin as Peter, Cyril Ritchard as Hook, and Sondra Lee as Tiger Lily. The original, uncut family musical.
VHS: S12665. $24.95.
Vincent J. Donehue, USA, 1960, 100 mins.

The Phantom of the Opera

Gaston Leroux's 1911 novel is beautifully translated by the Hirshfeld Theater Company in this gothic work about the sinister composer (David Staller) who hides out in the catacombs of a Paris opera house. Raged with guilt, he kidnaps the beautiful and soulful Christine (Elizabeth Walsh). The evocative sets and baroque production establish an eerie mood and discord. "Staller is as impressive as Michael Crawford and... Elizabeth Walsh is warmer, both vocally and emotionally, than Sarah Brightman was on Broadway" (Stephen Holden, *The New York Times*). Music and lyrics by Lawrence Rosen and Paul Schierhorn. Book and adaptation by Bruce Falstein.
VHS: S19748. $24.95.
Ken Kurtz, USA, 1990, 93 mins.

Pippin

Ben Vereen and William Katt star in this filmed account of the Broadway smash, a colorful, bright pastiche of the fable and romantic epic, designed and choreographed by the brilliant Bob Fosse *(Cabaret, All That Jazz)*. "An eye-popping extravaganza" *(L.A. Herald Examiner)*.
VHS: S04867. $29.95.

Pirates of Penzance

Linda Ronstadt stars in this modern adaptation of the Gilbert and Sullivan musical, as originally produced by Joseph Papp. With Angela Lansbury, George Rose.
VHS: S04839. $19.98.
Wilford Leach, USA, 1983, 112 mins.

Poor Little Rich Girl

One of Shirley Temple's best films finds Temple running away from home to join a vaudeville team. Wonderful musical numbers include "Military Man". With Jack Haley and Alice Faye.
VHS: S07360. $19.98.
Irving Cummings, USA, 1936, 72 mins.

Presenting Lily Mars
Judy Garland as a small town girl who dreams of fame in this adaptation of the Booth Tarkington novel, featuring Tommy Dorsey and His Orchestra, as well as the Bob Crosby Orchestra.
VHS: S03454. $19.98.
Laser: LD71146. $34.98.
Norman Taurog, USA, 1943, 105 mins.

Private Buckaroo
Sparkling entertainment featuring comedy, song, and the sensational trumpet of Harry James. Nostalgic showcase set during World Wor II, with America's favorite singing siblings, The Andrew Sisters, putting on a show for the soldiers.
VHS: S13863. $19.95.
Eddie Cline, USA, 1942, 70 mins.

Purple Rain
Prince's film debut is a semi-autobiographical account of an up-and-coming musician. Tormented by family problems, he takes his frustrations out on those around him, risking his career and relationships. One of these relationships is with a young woman (Apollonia Kotero) who has her own musical ambitions. A subplot involves a bitter rivalry with another musician played humorously by Morris Day. Also features Olga Karlatos, Clarence Williams III and Jerome Benton.
VHS: S21473. $19.95.
Laser: LD70660. $24.98.
DVD: DV60115. $24.98.
Albert Magnoli, USA, 1984, 111 mins.

Rappin'
Mario Van Peebles *(Posse, New Jack City)* stars in this action-musical as an ex-con trying to stay straight. He winds up in conflict with both his landlord and a gang leader. The music is the real focus of this film. Songs include "Snack Attack" and "FU 12".
VHS: S21401. $14.95.
Joel Silberg, USA, 1985, 92 mins.

Rebecca of Sunnybrook Farm
A heartwarming study and a dozen musical numbers including "On the Good Ship Lollipop" in this Shirley Temple favorite.
VHS: S06338. $19.98.
Laser: CLV. **LD71737. $19.98.**
Allan Dwan, USA, 1938, 80 mins.

Rhapsody in Blue
The life of George Gershwin, perhaps the greatest composer in American history, is depicted in this lavish motion picture. Robert Alda portrays the gifted musician torn between his love for American popular music and his reverence for the great classics.
VHS: S14314. $19.98.
Laser: Two-disc set. **LD70199. $39.88.**
Irving Rapper, USA, 1945, 139 mins.

Rhythm on the Range
Cowboy Bing Crosby meets an heiress played by Frances Farmer. She is out to lose her fiance, an arranged match. It is a simple, engaging love story with plenty of singing from the crooning cowpoke Crosby. Johnny Mercer, Martha Raye and Bob Burns also star.
VHS: S25012. $14.98.
Norman Taurog, USA, 1936, 68 mins.

Rhythm on the River
Bing Crosby and Mary Martin star as struggling songwriters ghostwriting for the evil Basil Rathbone. In this light romantic comedy, their struggle to be recognized takes them through several funny episodes. Billy Wilder had a hand in the script.
VHS: S21199. $14.98.
Victor Schertzinger, USA, 1940, 92 mins.

Rich, Young and Pretty
An opulent MGM musical coming-of-age story about a sheltered young woman (Jane Powell) who experiences freedom and excitement in Paris. Her hopes of a dashing romance with a charismatic Parisian are stifled by her mother (Danielle Darrieux). With Wendell Corey, Vic Damone and Fernando Lamas.
VHS: S18559. $19.98.
Laser: LD71659. $39.98.
Norman Taurog, USA, 1951, 95 mins.

Robin and the 7 Hoods
Frank Sinatra stars as the lead criminal in this gangland musical comedy featuring Bing Crosby, Dean Martin, Sammy Davis, Jr. and Peter Falk. These criminals are trapped in the usual murderous competition, only they manage to make everyone laugh and dance in the process.
VHS: S26865. $14.95.
Gordon Douglas, USA, 1964, 124 mins.

Rock 'n' Roll High School
The Ramones provide the high-energy music that drives this cult classic reworking of the rock 'n' roll teen movie format of the '50s. Stars P.J. Soles, Vincent Van Patten, Paul Bartel, Don Steele, Clint Howard, Dey Young, Mary Woronov, Dick Miller and Grady Sutton.
VHS: S28610. $14.98.
Laser: Widescreen, CLV. **LD76026. $49.95.**
DVD: DV60293. $29.95.
Allan Arkush, USA, 1979, 93 mins.

Roman Scandals
Comedian Eddie Cantor leaves behind the realities of the Depression for a fantasy trip to Ancient Rome. Lots of fun and plenty of musical numbers. With Gloria Stuart, Ruth Etting, Edward Arnold and Verree Teasdale. Watch closely for Lucille Ball in the chorus of one of the Busby Berkeley production numbers.
VHS: S15490. $19.98.
Laser: LD75250. $34.98.
Frank Tuttle, USA, 1933, 93 mins.

Romance on the High Seas
This romantic musical comedy introduced the dazzling Doris Day in her first feature role. Playing a talented but unfulfilled nightclub singer, she agrees to take a cruise posing as a wealthy socialite who'd rather stay home and spy on her husband. But it's all spoiled when the private dick (Jack Carson) hired to spy on the vacationing wife falls in love with the beautiful impostor. The musical numbers were directed by the legendary Busby Berkeley.
VHS: S14313. $29.98.
Laser: LD70173. $39.98.
Michael Curtiz, USA, 1948, 99 mins.

Rosalie
Big MGM musical starring Eleanor Powell as a princess involved with a West Point cadet. Cole Porter supplied the tunes, including "In the Still of the Night". With Nelson Eddy, Frank Morgan, Ray Bolger, Billy Gilbert and Edna May Oliver. Filmed in glorious black and white.
VHS: S08093. $19.98.
W.S. Van Dyke, USA, 1937, 122 mins.

Rose Marie (1936)
Jeanette MacDonald is the opera star searching for her fugitive brother (James Stewart), as Royal Canadian Mountie Nelson Eddy is searching for the same man, and the two fall in love. "Indian Call" is one of the great songs in this musical.
VHS: S04403. $19.95.
Laser: LD70668. $34.98.
W.S. Van Dyke II, USA, 1936, 110 mins.

Rose Marie (1954)
Mervyn Le Roy's widescreen remake of W.S. Van Dyke II's 1936 filmed operetta, with choreography by Busby Berkeley. The story concerns a Canadian mountie who falls in love with the woman he's supposed to educate. With Howard Keel, Ann Blyth, Fernando Lamas, Bert Lahr and Marjorie Main. Letterboxed edition.
Laser: LD70168. $34.98.
Mervyn Le Roy, USA, 1954, 115 mins.

Rose of Washington Square
Al Jolson provides a number of his legendary hit songs for this musical set during Prohibition. Alice Faye is a Ziegfeld star and Tyrone Power plays her crooked husband, leading ultimately to a showdown with the law. When he hits the skids, Faye must decide what to do.
VHS: S21305. $19.98.
Gregory Ratoff, USA, 1939, 86 mins.

Rossini
Nino Besozzi stars as Rossini in this 1943 account of the composer's career from 1815 to 1829. The meeting of Rossini and Beethoven in Vienna in 1822 is the most memorable scene in this well-photographed and directed production. Features Gianna Pederzini, Tancredi Pasero, Gabriella Gatti, Mariano Stabile, Enzo De Muro Lomanto, Piero Pauli, De Taranto and Vittorio Gui in performances of *Otello*, *Barbiere*, *Mose* and *Tell*. "The only footage of some of these artists. An engrossing, accurate dramatization of the composer's life from *Otello* to *Tell*. Includes the booing of *Barbiere*. Pasero's 'Calunnia' is the film's highlight" (Stefan Zucker, *Opera Fanatic*). Italian with English subtitles.
94 mins.
VHS: S28431. $34.95.

Royal Wedding
Fred Astaire stars as the brother of Jane Powell, both of them in England to perform for Queen Elizabeth's wedding, and each of them finds their true love. Contains one of the most famous of Astaire's dance sequences—the dance on the ceiling and walls. Songs by Alan Jay Lerner.
VHS: S07366. $19.95.
Laser: LD74680. $34.98.
DVD: DV60270. $19.95.
Stanley Donen, USA, 1951, 93 mins.

Second Chorus
Fred Astaire and Burgess Meredith vie for the attention of Paulette Goddard in this musical which co-stars Artie Shaw. Includes "Sweet Sue" and "Swing Concerto."
VHS: S01941. $19.95.
Laser: CLV. **LD72028. $29.98.**
H.C. Potter, USA, 1940, 83 mins.

Second Fiddle
An ambitious Hollywood publicist (Tyrone Power) stages a romance between a skating instructor (Sonja Henie) and a romantic Hollywood star (Rudy Vallee), and slowly falls in love with the breathtaking skater. Irving Berlin wrote the music. With Edna May Oliver and Lyle Talbot.
VHS: S20254. $19.98.
Sidney Lanfield, USA, 1939, 86 mins.

Selena
A music sensation by the age of 23, this young performer's star was rising fast when she was killed by the president of her fan club. Jennifer Lopez and Edward James Olmos star in the true-life drama that charts the musical rise of Selena from Texas barrio to stardom.
VHS: S32066. $19.95.
Laser: LD76314. $39.98.
Gregory Nava, USA, 1997, 128 mins.

Sensations
An all-star musical comedy extravaganza starring Eleanor Powell, W.C. Fields, Cab Calloway, Woody Herman, and Sophie Tucker. Powell plays a publicity agent out to book the best acts of the year.
VHS: S12319. $24.95.
Chuck Vincent, USA, 1945, 85 mins.

Serenade
Mario Lanza stars as a fruit picker who sings his way to a better life as a world-renowned opera singer. Complications arise when two women try to claim his affections. Joan Fontaine and Vincent Price co-star.
VHS: S20659. $19.98.
Anthony Mann, USA, 1956, 121 mins.

Seven Brides for Seven Brothers
When outdoorsman Howard Keel decides to get married, his six younger brothers also get the urge. The musical movie inspiration for the tv series contains many toe-tapping numbers, including Russ Tamblyn dancing with an axe. With Jane Powell, Julie Newmar and Ruta Lee. VHS letterboxed.
VHS: S05096. $19.95.
Laser: LD70673. $34.98.
Stanley Donen, USA, 1954, 103 mins.

Seven Hills of Rome
Out and about among the seven hills, Mario Lanza is a popular American singer at the center of a musical romantic comedy involving a classic switch of affections. When he can't find his jet-setting fiance, he turns to a local girl for comfort. With Peggy Castle and Marisa Allasio.
VHS: S20787. $19.98.
Roy Rowland, USA, 1957, 104 mins.

Sgt. Pepper's Lonely Heart's Club Band
The Brothers Gibb invade the sacred territory of Beatlemania for this all star musical romp. When the Bee Gees are not singing, guest performers include George Burns, Steve Martin, Billy Preston and Peter Frampton. Comedy provided by Frankie Howerd and Donald Pleasance.
VHS: S07811. $19.98.
Michael Schultz, USA, 1978, 111 mins.

Shall We Dance
One of the best of the Fred Astaire and Ginger Rogers films, in this one the pair star as a dance team who pose as husband and wife in order to achieve stardom. With a hummable score by George Gershwin.
VHS: S01881. $19.98.
Mark Sandrich, USA, 1937, 116 mins.

Ship Ahoy
A romantic comedy musical about a beautiful dancer on a cruise ship who is enlisted to transport a dangerous package, completely unaware she's duped by foreign agents. With Eleanor Powell, Red Skelton, Bert Lahr and Frank Sinatra in a supporting performance as a shipmate.
VHS: S18555. $19.98.
Edward Buzzell, USA, 1942, 95 mins.

Show Boat (1936)
This musical collaboration of Jerome Kern and Oscar Hammerstein captures the heartbreak, excitement and romantic preoccupations on an old line Mississippi show boat. Hammerstein wrote the screenplay, adapted from Edna Ferber's novel. With Irene Dunne, Allan Jones, Helen Morgan, Paul Robeson (who performs "Old Man River") and Charles Winninger. "Sentimental, literary, but oddly appealing" (Graham Greene). Available in two versions, a three-disc collection or a single disc.
Laser: CAV, 3 discs, Criterion. **LD70459. $124.95.**
Laser: CLV, 1 disc, Criterion. **LD70460. $49.95.**
James Whale, USA, 1936, 110 mins.

Show Boat (1951)
George Sidney supplies movement and grace to the great Jerome Kern score that colors the lives of misfits and losers in a musical that deftly moves from love story to musical melodrama. Complete with great music (the spiritually haunting "Ol' Man River") and good performances from Kathryn Grayson, Ava Gardner and Howard Keel.
VHS: S02257. $19.95.
DVD: DV60116. $24.98.
George Sidney, USA, 1951, 107 mins.

Silk Stockings
Cole Porter wrote the lyrics for this funny and energetic musical version of *Ninotchka*. Cyd Charisse is a KGB agent sent to Paris to kidnap a defecting composer. Fred Astaire is the playboy who shows her the charmed side of life in the West. Director Mamoulian's last film.
VHS: S04405. $19.98.
Laser: LD70678. $34.98.
Rouben Mamoulian, USA, 1957, 117 mins.

Singin' in the Rain
Deservedly one of the best-loved movies of all time! An exhilarating and fast-moving musical comedy that traces the transition from silent films to "talkies," starring dancing Gene Kelly and Debbie Reynolds, with Donald O'Connor, Jean Hagen and Rita Moreno.
VHS: S15851. $19.98.
Laser: CAV, 2 discs, Criterion. **LD70463. $89.95.**
Laser: CLV, 1 disc, Criterion. **LD70464. $39.95.**
Laser: CLV, MGM. **LD70679. $24.98.**
Laser: CAV, MGM. **LD70680. $89.95.**
DVD: DV60118. $24.98.
Gene Kelly/Stanley Donen, USA, 1951, 103 mins.

The Singing Fool
Al Jolson stars as a struggling hopeful singer in this delightful blend of schmaltz and showbiz.
VHS: S31844. $19.98.
Lloyd Bacon, USA, 1928, 102 mins.

The Singing Nun
Debbie Reynolds, Greer Garson, Katharine Ross and Agnes Moorehead appear in this comedic tale of a starkly unconventional Belgian nun (Reynolds) trying to reconcile her musical ambitions with her religious calling.
VHS: S17339. $19.98.
Henry Koster, USA, 1966, 97 mins.

Skirts Ahoy!
Esther Williams joins Vivian Blaine and Joan Evans as a trio of Navy Waves on the lookout for love in this frothy musical comedy. Williams sings, dances and sidestrokes her way through ten weeks of boot camp training.
VHS: S16609. $19.98.
Sidney Lanfield, USA, 1952, 109 mins.

Small Town Girl
A romantic comedy about a handsome stranger who's trapped into a marriage proposal when he's drunk, starring Jane Powell, Farley Granger, Bobby Van, Ann Miller, Nat King Cole. Oscar nomination for the song "My Flaming Heart". Busby Berkeley choreographed the numbers.
VHS: S12144. $19.95.
Laser: Chapter search. Includes original theatrical trailer.
LD71666. $34.98.
Leslie Kardos, USA, 1953, 93 mins.

Smilin' Through
Jeanette MacDonald stars in this second remake of the 1922 Norma Talmadge vehicle about a man who loses his fiancee on his wedding day and then raises a niece who grows to look exactly like his long-lost love. With Gene Raymond and Brian Aherne. In color and filled with songs like "A Little Love, A Little Kiss" and "Land of Hope and Glory."
VHS: S08095. $19.98.
Frank Borzage, USA, 1941, 100 mins.

Something to Sing About
James Cagney is the two-fisted band leader in this musical melodrama about Hollywood studio life. With William Frawley and Evelyn Daw.
VHS: S03259. $39.95.
Victor Schertzinger, USA, 1937, 94 mins.

Song of the Islands
Victor Mature is the new arrival to the Pacific Island paradise, Betty Grable the local girl whom he fights with and romances.
VHS: S09446. $19.98.
Walter Lang, USA, 1942, 75 mins.

A Song to Remember
An almost campy portrait of Frederic Chopin, which inspired many remakes, starring Paul Muni, Cornel Wilde and Merle Oberon. A colorful biography which portrays his flight from Poland and liaison with George Sand.
VHS: S01232. $19.95.
Charles Vidor, USA, 1945, 112 mins.

The Sound of Music
The hills are alive with the sounds of the Von Trapp family in this beloved Rodgers and Hammerstein epic musical. Julie Andrews and Christopher Plummer lead a cast of wholesome warblers through some terrific scenery and memorable songs. Five Oscars including Best Picture. Letterboxed.
VHS: S04772. $19.98.
Robert Wise, USA, 1965, 172 mins.

South Pacific
An enchanting adaptation of the Rodgers and Hammerstein musical, based on James Michener's *Tales of the South Pacific*. A young Navy man falls in love with an Island girl while stationed in the South Pacific. With Mitzi Gaynor and Rossano Brazzi.
VHS: S04406. $19.98.
Joshua Logan, USA, 1957, 150 mins.

Spotlight Scandals
Frank Fay, Billy Gilbert and Harry Langdon join forces for this inspiring film about fame and the power of the proverbial comeback. Scandal destroys a vaudevillian, but he teams up with a new partner and creates a Broadway smash. Bonnie Baker and Radio Rogues provide some great musical numbers.
VHS: S23904. $29.95.
William Beaudine, USA, 1943, 69 mins.

Springtime in the Rockies
A musical comedy from Twentieth Century-Fox with an all star cast that includes Betty Grable, John Payne, Carmen Miranda, Jackie Gleason, Cesar Romero, Charlotte Greenwood and Edward Everett Horton. In Technicolor with Harry James and his band. Miranda sings "Chattanooga Choo Choo". Lots of laughs and musical numbers when a Broadway couple go West.
VHS: S09833. $19.95.
Irving Cummings, USA, 1942, 91 mins.

Stand Up and Cheer
Shirley Temple does her best to help cure America's Depression-era blues in this upbeat musical comedy that suggests laughter is the best remedy for despair. James Dunn co-stars and Shirley sings, "Baby, Take a Bow."
VHS: S09995. $19.98.
Hamilton McFadden, USA, 1934, 69 mins.

A Star Is Born
Barbra Streisand and Kris Kristofferson are the leads in this third version. A talented wife whose star is on the rise quickly overshadows her husband as his career fades. Streisand sings "Evergreen," which won an Oscar for Best Song. With Gary Busey, Oliver Clark and Paul Mazursky.
VHS: S07006. $19.98.
Laser: Letterboxed. **LD71470. $39.98.**
Frank Pierson, USA, 1976, 140 mins.

Star Spangled Rhythm
In this WWII extravaganza Bing Crosby is crowded by a host of famous MGM stars, including Bob Hope, Ray Milland, Veronica Lake, Susan Hayward, Dick Powell, Mary Martin, Cecil B. De Mille and many others. It includes that favorite hit, "That Old Black Magic."
VHS: S21203. $14.98.
George Marshall, USA, 1942, 99 mins.

Star!
Robert Wise's ambitious musical biography of Gertrude Lawrence was a box office failure when first released. The studio cut nearly an hour from its running time and re-released the film under the title *Those Were the Happy Times*. This expressive work, buttressed by 17 songs from Cole Porter, Kurt Weill and George and Ira Gershwin, dramatizes Lawrence's (Julie Andrews) spectacular rise from seedy London vaudeville halls to West End superstar. The emotional focus is played out through her two principal relationships, her friendship with playwright Noel Coward (Daniel Massey) and her marriage to banker Richard Aldrich (Richard Crenna). With John Collin, Robert Reed, Bruce Forsyth, Beryl Reid and Jenny Agutter.
VHS: S19485. $89.98.
Robert Wise, USA, 1968, 175 mins.

Starlight—A Musical Movie
The talented campers at an upstate New York summer camp for the performing arts must put on a show that will raise enough money to head off the impending sale to a villainous real estate developer (William Hickey). Sounds like "Fame" meets "Meatballs". With the talents of Ricki Lake, Victor Cook, Danny Gerard and Tichina Arnold. Winner of the 1988 Ruby Slipper Award for Best Feature. USA, 1988, 78 mins.
VHS: S10069. $79.95.

Stars and Stripes Forever
Clifton Webb is a pure delight as "March King" John Philip Sousa in this entertaining biography of the man who gave the world some of its most stirring music. Co-stars Robert Wagner, Debra Paget and Ruth Hussey.
VHS: S14506. $19.98.
Henry Koster, USA, 1952, 89 mins.

Step Lively
A musical version of *Room Service* with Frank Sinatra and George Murphy. Scored by Cahn and Styne. A young playwright is forced to become the lead in his own play.
VHS: S10641. $19.98.
Tim Whelan, USA, 1944, 89 mins.

Stop the World I Want to Get Off
This hit from the stages of London and Broadway features the well-known musical songs "What Kind of Fool Am I?", "Once in a Lifetime" and "Gonna Build a Mountain". Shot from a live performance.
VHS: S20656. $19.98.

Stormy Weather
Following the revisionist success of *Cabin in the Sky*, the few black entertainers allowed to work consistently were enlisted for this all-black musical that features Lena Horne, Cab Calloway, Fats Waller and Bill Robinson. The affairs and times of some talented war-era entertainers are loosely connected as a storyline to the powerful music, including Waller's "Ain't Misbehavin'" and Horne's title rendition, which provide depth and resonance. Featuring *Casablanca*'s Dooley Wilson.
VHS: S02828. $19.98.
Andrew L. Stone, USA, 1943, 78 mins.

Stowaway
Shirley Temple, Alice Faye, Robert Young star in this musical adventure of a young orphan in China adopted by a bickering young couple. Shirley smooths things over.
VHS: S05901. $19.98.
William A. Seiter, USA, 1936, 86 mins.

Strike Me Pink
Eddie Cantor is Eddie Pink, a shy tailor who becomes a bigshot around town after reading a book, *A Man or Mouse: What Are You?* He takes over the running of the amusement park—but the mob wants part of the action. With Ethel Merman.
VHS: S31812. $14.95.
Norman Taurog, USA, 1936, 100 mins.

Strike Up the Band
Busby Berkeley directs Mickey Rooney and Judy Garland in this lively musical about Mickey trying to get a job with the Paul Whiteman orchestra. Music by the Gershwin brothers, Alan Arthur Freed and Roger Edens. Tunes include the title song and "La Conga." With Larry Nunn, William Tracy and Paul Whiteman.
VHS: S08096. $19.98.
Laser: LD70688. $39.98.
Busby Berkeley, USA, 1940, 120 mins.

The Student Prince
Sigmund Romberg's opera is the basis for this romantic drama about the heir to the throne (Edmund Purdom) given one last fling in Heidelberg, where he falls madly in love with a forlorn barmaid played by Ann Blyth. With John Ericson, Louis Calhern and Edmund Gwenn. Mario Lanza's singing voice is substituted for Purdom's voice.
VHS: S17654. $19.98.
Richard Thorpe, USA, 1954, 107 mins.

Summer Holiday
Warm and winning Americana from Eugene O'Neill's *Ah, Wilderness*. Mickey Rooney plays an eager lad coming of age in an era of Stanley Steamers and nickel beer. This delightful musical also features excellent supporting performances from Walter Huston and Agnes Moorehead.
VHS: S14169. $19.98.
Laser: LD71167. $39.98.
Rouben Mamoulian, USA, 1948, 92 mins.

Summer Stock
A theater troupe lead by Gene Kelly takes over a farm owned by Judy Garland, and Judy falls in love with show business. With Eddie Bracken, Marjorie Main, Phil Silvers.
VHS: S04983. $19.98.
Laser: LD74683. $34.98.
Charles Waters, USA, 1950, 100 mins.

Sun Valley Serenade
Milton Berle and friends hit the slopes of Sun Valley in this lighthearted romance about a musician who adopts a beautiful Norwegian war refugee. The second of two Fox musicals about the great Glenn Miller.
VHS: S14508. $19.98.
H. Bruce Humberstone, USA, 1941, 86 mins.

Sweet Charity

Shirley MacLaine has the title role in director Bob Fosse's debut musical about the dime-a-dance girl with the heart of gold. This uncut version is based on the Neil Simon play based on Fellini's *Nights of Cabiria*. Highlights of the Cy Coleman-Dorothy Fields score include "If My Friends Could See Me Now" and "Big Spender."
VHS: S03493. $19.95.
Laser: LD70085. $44.98.
Bob Fosse, USA, 1969, 148 mins.

Sweethearts

Jeanette MacDonald and Nelson Eddy play a temperamental couple of theatre stars currently performing a Victor Herbert operetta. Frank Morgan is their manipulating manager. With Ray Bolger, Florence Rice, and Mischa Auer. Script by Dorothy Parker and husband Alan Campbell. An Oscar for cinematography.
VHS: S09870. $19.98.
Laser: LD71691. $34.98.
W.S. Van Dyke, USA, 1938, 120 mins.

Swing High, Swing Low

Carole Lombard and Fred MacMurray star as two entertainers who meet aboard a cruise ship bound for Panama. Musical comedy that includes Dorothy Lamour and Anthony Quinn.
VHS: S01291. $29.95.
Mitchell Leisen, USA, 1937, 95 mins.

Swing It Professor

Pinky Tomlin and Milburn Stone star in this delightful musical comedy. Tomlin is a college music professor who will not permit jazz in his classroom.
VHS: S09583. $29.95.
Marshall Neilan, USA, 1937, 62 mins.

Take Me Out to the Ball Game

Gene Kelly, Frank Sinatra and Jules Munshin are star players for the Wolves. Esther Williams is the new manager of this turn-of-the-century team. The drive for the pennant has never included so many musical numbers. Including "O'Brien to Ryan to Goldberg".
VHS: S04986. $19.95.
Laser: LD70162. $34.98.
Busby Berkeley, USA, 1949, 90 mins.

Tales from Vienna Woods

Magda Schneider, Wolf Albach-Retty and Walter Slezak star in this musical romance featuring music by Johann Strauss. A singing auto mechanic inherits a castle that fails to live up to his initial high expectations. Fortunately there are two women competing for his attention to liven things up. The Vienna Philharmonic Orchestra provides the music for this film set in a Vienna still unharmed by war. German with English subtitles.
VHS: S23987. $24.95.
George Jacoby, Austria, 1937, 82 mins.

Tauber in Blossom Time

Tauber stars as composer Franz Schubert in this musical set in early 19th-century Vienna. He loves a woman who loves someone else and despite these feelings, he helps her win the affections of this other man. Among the great songs used in this film are "Love Lost for Evermore," "Serenade," "Impatience" and "Faith in Spring," all by Schubert.
VHS: S24035. $34.95.
Paul L. Stein, Great Britain, 1934, 87 mins.

Tea for Two

Doris Day is cast as Nanette Carter, an heiress who invests $25,000 in a 1926 Broadway show not knowing that once she has the lead, she doesn't have the money to spend after all, due to a stock market crash. To secure the promised funds, she must say no to every question for the next 48 hours to win a bet. With Gordon MacRae, Gene Nelson, Eve Arden and Billy DeWolfe. Based loosely on the popular musical *No, No Nanette*. Songs include "I Only Have Eyes for You", "Oh Me, Oh My", "I Know That You Know" and "I Want to Be Happy".
VHS: S15782. $19.98.
David Butler, USA, 1950, 98 mins.

The Tender Trap

Julius Jay Epstein *(Casablanca)* adapted the play by Max Schulman and Robert Paul Smith about a shrewd New York agent and notorious lothario (Frank Sinatra) who meets his match in an intelligent and gritty young actress (Debbie Reynolds). Shot in widescreen by Paul Vogel, with a sharp title song by James Van Heusen and lyrics by Sammy Cahn. With David Wayne and Celeste Holm.
VHS: S18012. $19.98.
Laser: LD70147. $34.98.
Charles Walters, USA, 1955, 111 mins.

Thank Your Lucky Stars

Warner Brothers' wartime effort features cameos by many of the studio stars, including Bette Davis singing, Humphrey Bogart, Errol Flynn, Olivia de Havilland and Spike Jones and his City Slickers.
VHS: S02258. $29.98.
David Butler, USA, 1943, 130 mins.

That Certain Age

Deanna Durbin experiences the turbulence of a first crush for an a older man (Melvyn Douglas), to the chagrin of her young and loyal admirer (Jackie Cooper). Includes original theatrical trailer.
VHS: S30623. $19.98.
Edward Ludwig, USA, 1938, 101 mins.

That Midnight Kiss

Mario Lanza's first screen appearance in this biography of an unknown who gets his first break and enters into a tentative affair. With Kathryn Grayson, Ethel Barrymore, Jose Turbi and Keenan Wynn.
VHS: S17655. $19.98.
Norman Taurog, USA, 1949, 98 mins.

That's Dancing

Gene Kelly, Liza Minnelli, Baryshnikov and Ray Bolger host a look at some of the great dance scenes in Hollywood musicals from Fred Astaire films through *West Side Story*.
VHS: S03365. $29.98.
Laser: LD71154. $39.98.
Jack Haley Jr., USA, 1985, 105 mins.

That's Entertainment

A cavalcade of stars host scenes from over 100 MGM musicals, with many cherished moments. Including Fred Astaire, Peter Lawford, Bing Crosby, Gene Kelly, Liza Minnelli, Debbie Reynolds, Frank Sinatra and many others.
Laser: CAV. LD70691. $69.98.
Jack Haley Jr., USA, 1974, 132 mins.

That's Entertainment II

A spectacular sequel that interweaves footage from 75 films featuring some of the best examples of song and dance in the American cinema. Includes sequences of Gene Kelly and Fred Astaire dancing together for the first time in 30 years.
VHS: S01598. $19.95.
Laser: LD70693. $39.98.
Laser: LD71152. $69.98.
Gene Kelly, USA, 1976, 133 mins.

That's Entertainment III

This collection of clips from classic MGM musicals features elaborate production numbers and outtakes of never-before-seen footage. June Allyson, Cyd Charisse, Lena Horne, Gene Kelly, Ann Miller, Debbie Reynolds, Mickey Rooney and Esther Williams are just some of the stars featured in this exciting new collection.
VHS: S22188. $19.98.
Bud Friedgen/Michael J. Sheridan, USA, 1993, 113 mins.

That's Singing

The Best of Broadway—a celebration of American musical comedy, a star-studded Broadway event! USA, 1986, 120 mins.
VHS: S01530. $19.98.

There's No Business Like Show Business

Dan Dailey and Ethel Merman head a performing family that includes Donald O'Connor, Mitzi Gaynor and Johnny Ray. They all like to sing songs by Irving Berlin, and Marilyn Monroe raises everyone's temperature with a sizzling version of "Heat Wave." The script was nominated for an Oscar and the musical numbers are quite energetic. See for yourself why it's like no business you know.
VHS: S07681. $19.98.
Walter Lang, USA, 1954, 117 mins.

They Shall Have Music

Master violinist Jascha Heifetz plays himself in this sincere melodrama about poor kids and classical music. When the inner city music school run by Walter Brennan faces a financial crisis, his students organize a benefit concert. With Joel McCrea, Andrea Leeds, Marjorie Main, Porter Hall and Gene Reynolds. Watch for Diana Lynn as the little girl at the piano.
VHS: S15841. $19.98.
Archie Mayo, USA, 1939, 105 mins.

This Is the Army

George Murphy plays Ronald Reagan's father is this topical melange of songs and skits. Also with Joe Louis, Kate Smith and a host of others.
VHS: S02957. $19.95.
Michael Curtiz, USA, 1943, 121 mins.

A Thousand and One Nights

Cornel Wilde stars as Aladdin with Adele Jergens as his love interest. Aladdin is just a poor boy who loves a princess. All that changes when he becomes the owner of a lamp inhabited by a beautiful genie. Despite the genie's own designs on her master she helps reunite Aladdin and the princess. Along the way there is adventure and intrigue in this delightful musical from the golden era of Hollywood.
VHS: S27181. $19.95.
Alfred E. Green, USA, 1945, 92 mins.

Thousands Cheer

All-star World War II musical featuring Gene Kelly, Kathryn Grayson, Judy Garland, Mickey Rooney and a host of others. Glossy, snappy and designed to inspire.
VHS: S01595. $19.98.
Laser: LD70160. $39.98.
George Sidney, USA, 1943, 126 mins.

Three Daring Daughters

When Jeanette MacDonald decides to marry again, Jose Iturbi is not welcomed with open arms by her three daughters, Jane Powell, Anne Todd and Mary Elinor Donahue. But with a little romance, some songs and a cheerful attitude, no problem is insurmountable.
VHS: S20790. $19.98.
Fred M. Wilcox, USA, 1948, 115 mins.

Three for the Show

Fall under Betty Grable's spell in this deliciously racy musical comedy about a woman who finds herself legally married to two men. Also starring Gower Champion and Jack Lemmon. "Grable plays the queen in a giddy double checkmate!" *(Time Magazine)*.
VHS: S34871. $19.95.
H.C. Potter, USA, 1954, 89 mins.

Three Little Words

Famous songwriters Harry Ruby and Bert Kalmar on their climb to fame, with Fred Astaire, Vera-Ellen, Red Skelton, Debbie Reynolds. Songs include "Who's Sorry Now?" and "Thinking of You."
VHS: S05386. $19.98.
Laser: LD71168. $34.98.
Richard Thorpe, USA, 1950, 102 mins.

The Three Musketeers

A spirited musical adaptation of Alexandre Dumas' popular novel combines slapstick farce (with the appearance of the Ritz Brothers), madcap action and romance. Don Ameche plays D'Artagnan and Binnie Barnes is Lady DeWinter. With Lionel Atwill, Miles Mander, Gloria Stuart and Pauline Moore.
VHS: S20253. $19.98.
Allan Dwan, USA, 1939, 73 mins.

Three Smart Girls

Deanna Durbin was introduced as "Universal's new discovery" in this delightful debut that launched her film career. The adventure begins when three lovely, high spirited girls attempt to reunite their mother and father, who divorced a decade ago. Also features Ray Milland.
VHS: S23279. $19.98.
Henry Koster, USA, 1936, 84 mins.

Three Smart Girls Grow Up

This sequel to *Three Smart Girls* finds Deanna Durbin reprising her role as Penny, the youngest of three sisters. This time she is determined to marry off her two older sisters. Robert Cummings and William Lundigan are the lucky fellas subjected to the affections and schemes of the charming sisters.
VHS: S23280. $19.98.
Henry Koster, USA, 1939, 90 mins.

Till the Clouds Roll By

Musical biography of Jerome Kern, the celebrated composer of stage musicals, including *Show Boat* and screenplays such as *Swing Time* and *Lady Be Good*. Starring Robert Walker as Kern, with Judy Garland, Van Johnson and Lena Horne.
VHS: S01597. $19.95.
Richard Whorf, USA, 1946, 137 mins.

The Toast of New Orleans

If you guessed raisin, you're wrong. Mario Lanza sings "Be My Love" and selections from several popular operas as he plays a Cajun fisherman attracted to a society opera star. Kathryn Grayson also lends her voice to the love story of a woman torn between a spectacular voice and the charm of David Niven. With Rita Moreno.
VHS: S04984. $19.98.
Norman Taurog, USA, 1950, 98 mins.

Tonight and Every Night

Rita Hayworth and Janet Blair star in living color as a pair of London musical entertainers who never miss a performance during World War II. Heartaches and the Heinie's bombs will not deter the spirit of these troupers. With Shelley Winters, Lee Bowman.
VHS: S04674. $29.95.
Victor Saville, USA, 1945, 92 mins.

Top Hat

A Fred Astaire and Ginger Rogers classic! A knockout musical featuring a great score by Irving Berlin.
VHS: S01362. $14.98.
Laser: LD76046. $39.98.
Mark Sandrich, USA, 1935, 97 mins.

Two Girls and a Sailor
Terrific musical entertainment set during the war. June Allyson, Gloria de Haven, Van Johnson, Xavier Cugat and his Orchestra, Jimmy Durante, Tom Drake, Lena Horne, Carlos Ramirez, Harry James and his Orchestra, Jose Iturbi, Gracie Allen, Virginia O'Brien star.
VHS: S12143. $19.95.
Laser: LD70154. $39.98.
Richard Thorpe, USA, 1944, 124 mins.

Two Sisters from Boston
Kathryn Grayson and June Allyson are the toast of the New York nightlife scene in this fun turn-of-the-century musical classic. Grayson must pretend to be an opera singer to impress her very proper Boston family when they come to visit her.
VHS: S28490. $19.98.
Henry Koster, USA, 1946, 112 mins.

Two Weeks with Love
But how much time for lunch? Long before *Dirty Dancing*, other families with eligible daughters found romance on vacations to the Catskills. Jane Powell and Debbie Reynolds are the Robinson sisters, Patti and Melba. With Ricardo Montalban and Carleton Carpenter as the men they attract and Louis Calhern and Ann Harding as the concerned parents. Songs include "Abba Dabba Honeymoon", "Row, Row, Row" and "By the Light of the Silvery Moon".
VHS: S13307. $19.98.
Roy Rowland, USA, 1950, 92 mins.

Ultimate Oz (Collector's Edition)
This commemorative, two-video edition offers a digitally remastered, visually restored version of Victor Fleming's 1939 classic, *The Wizard of Oz*, adapted from Frank Baum's classic tale about the Kansas girl (Judy Garland) who is projected into a surreal landscape of magical characters. The film is complemented by a behind-the-scenes documentary, *The Wonderful Wizard of Oz: The Making of a Movie Classic*, that combines interviews, archival footage, outtakes, a reproduction of the original script, the theatrical trailer and the notes. The documentary, directed by Jack Haley, Jr., features interviews with Ray Bolger, Garland, Jack Haley, Margaret Hamilton, King Vidor and Robert Young.
VHS: S19475. $99.98.
Laser: LD71920. $99.98.
Victor Fleming, USA, 1939, 52 mins.

Under the Cherry Moon
Prince stars as Christopher Tracy, an American musician on the French Riviera, living off the bank accounts of rich, bored divorcees. But he didn't count either on confronting the heiress' enraged father, or on falling in love.
VHS: S01816. $19.98.
Laser: LD74723. $34.98.
Prince, USA, 1986, 80 mins.

The Unsinkable Molly Brown
Debbie Reynolds is the feisty title character who earns her moniker by surviving a trip on the *Titanic*. Based on the true story of the wealthiest woman in Denver in the late 1800's. Meredith Willson's score includes "Belly up to the Bar, Boys". With Ed Begley and Harve Presnell.
VHS: S07157. $19.95.
Charles Walters, USA, 1964, 128 mins.

Up in Arms
In a splashy, Goldwyn musical, Danny Kaye makes his feature debut as a hypochondriac drafted into the army, who is subsequently captured by the Japanese and becomes a highly decorated hero. Dinah Shore co-stars as Kaye's love interest. The cast also includes Dana Andrews and the Goldwyn Girls.
VHS: S02597. $14.95.
Elliott Nugent, USA, 1944, 105 mins.

The Vagabond Lover
Rudy Vallee is suddenly thrust into the limelight when he impersonates a famous band leader while conducting his college orchestra. Soon the whole world is clamoring for them. Marie Dressler is also featured in this light musical entertainment.
VHS: S23822. $24.95.
Marshall Neilan, USA, 1929, 66 mins.

Waikiki Wedding
Bing Crosby stars in this delightful musical comedy set in Hawaii. Bing is a press agent who has designs on a beautiful young woman, Shirley Ross, the Miss Pineapple Girl. The song "Sweet Leilani" won an Oscar. Martha Raye is also featured.
VHS: S25011. $14.98.
Frank Tuttle, USA, 1937, 99 mins.

Week-End in Havana
Alice Faye finds herself torn between John Payne and Cesar Romero in beautiful old Havana. Faye is stranded there when a cruise ship runs aground and Payne shows up to smooth things over, but it gets a little more serious than that during the warm Caribbean nights. Carmen Miranda brings her exciting nightlife personality to this charming musical comedy.
VHS: S21303. $19.98.
Walter Lang, USA, 1941, 80 mins.

The West Point Story
Doris Day, Gordon MacRae and James Cagney form an unholy union to stage an ambitious musical at West Point. With music and lyrics by Jule Styne and Sammy Cahn. With Gene Nelson and Alan Hale, Jr.
VHS: S18463. $59.99.
Roy Del Ruth, USA, 1950, 107 mins.

West Side Story
An extravaganza acclaimed for its musical and choreographic expertise. Score by Leonard Bernstein, lyrics by Stephen Sondheim, choreography by Jerome Robbins, starring Natalie Wood (her songs were dubbed by Marni Nixon) and Rita Moreno. Letterboxed.
VHS: S01444. $19.95.
Laser: CAV. **LD70485. $124.95.**
Laser: CLV, widescreen. **LD70486. $69.95.**
Robert Wise/Jerome Robbins, USA, 1961, 152 mins.

What's Love Got to Do with It
Based on the autobiography of pop diva Tina Turner, this film follows her rise to stardom. It includes the controversial realization of her tempestuous marriage to abusive Ike Turner, and her remarkable comeback.
VHS: S20607. $96.95.
Laser: LD74456. $39.99.
Brian Gibson, USA, 1993, 118 mins.

White Christmas
Bing Crosby and Danny Kaye team up as a show biz act, are joined by Rosemary Clooney and Vera-Ellen, and trek off to Vermont for a Christmas holiday. With a classic score by Irving Berlin that includes "Count Your Blessings Instead of Sheep" and, of course, "White Christmas."
VHS: S01585. $14.95.
Michael Curtiz, USA, 1954, 120 mins.

Whoopee
Eddie Cantor became a star in his screen debut in this comedy about a hypochondriac who goes west for his health. Cantor sings "Making Whoopee" and "My Baby Just Cares for Me." With Eleanor Hunt, Paul Gregory, John Rutherford and Ethel Shutta. Musical numbers by Busby Berkeley. Watch for a young Betty Grable in the chorus. Filmed in early Technicolor.
VHS: S03130. $19.98.
Thornton Freeland, USA, 1930, 93 mins.

Wiz
The smash Broadway musical based on the L. Frank Baum book features Diana Ross as Dorothy, with a pre-surgical Michael Jackson, Nipsey Russell and Lena Horne.
VHS: S05098. $19.98.
Sidney Lumet, USA, 1978, 133 mins.

The Wizard of Oz
Judy Garland, Ray Bolger, Jack Haley, Bert Lahr, Frank Morgan, Margaret Hamilton, Billie Burke and Toto in the land of Oz, in MGM's great, Technicolor fantasy where Judy follows the Yellow Brick Road.
VHS: S09609. $19.95.
Laser: CLV, MGM. **LD70709. $34.95.**
Laser: CAV, Criterion. **LD71215. $99.95.**
DVD: DV60104. $24.98.
Victor Fleming, USA, 1939, 101 mins.

Words and Music
This film bio of Richard Rodgers and Lorenz Hart is highlighted by the likes of Judy Garland, Lena Horne, Gene Kelly, Perry Como and Mel Torme performing a treasure-trove of lavish production numbers and show-stopping solos. Don't miss Judy Garland and Mickey Rooney's duet of *I Wish I Were in Love Again*. Starring Tom Drake and Mickey Rooney.
VHS: S15855. $19.98.
Norman Taurog, USA, 1948, 122 mins.

Xanadu
Olivia Newton-John is a muse to a young roller-boogie artist in this contemporary musical. Music by John Ferrar and the Electric Light Orchestra is featured. Gene Kelly is also present but it really is a chance for Olivia to sing and dance amid wild, futuristic sets.
VHS: S21857. $14.98.
Robert Greenwald, USA, 1980, 88 mins.

Yankee Doodle Dandy
James Cagney won a richly deserved Oscar for his red, white an' blue account of the life of George M. Cohan. He sings, he dances, he talks to the president of the United States. Filmed in B&W though two colorized versions exist. With Walter Huston, Joan Leslie, Jeanne Cagney, S.Z. Sakall and Rosemary DeCamp.
VHS: S01835. $14.95.
Laser: LD70714. $39.98.
Michael Curtiz, USA, 1942, 126 mins.

Yentl
Barbra Streisand directs herself in a sweeping entertainment based on the Isaac Bashevis Singer short story about a young woman who disguises herself as a young man in order to study the Talmud. With Amy Irving and Mandy Patinkin.
VHS: S03476. $19.95.
Barbra Streisand, USA, 1983, 134 mins.

Yolanda and the Thief
Fred Astaire dances and romances with Lucille Bremer in this classical musical fantasy. Astaire is a slick con man out to swindle heiress Yolanda by posing as her guardian angel, but his plans go awry when she steals his heart instead.
VHS: S03102. $19.98.
Laser: LD71174. $34.98.
Vincente Minnelli, USA, 1945, 109 mins.

You Were Never Lovelier
Fred Astaire romances the beautiful Rita Hayworth to a Jerome Kern-Johnny Mercer score in this musical classic set in Buenos Aires. Featured songs include "I'm Old Fashioned" and the title song. Great dance numbers.
VHS: S04750. $19.95.
William A. Seiter, USA, 1942, 92 mins.

You'll Never Get Rich
Robert Benchley is the lecherous stage producer with an eye for chorus girl Sheila Winthrop (Rita Hayworth), while his friend Fred Astaire becomes a suitor for Sheila's affections. A musical comedy.
VHS: S04751. $19.95.
Sidney Lanfield, USA, 1941, 88 mins.

Young at Heart
Frank Sinatra steals Doris Day's heart from Gig Young. Both of the young lovers sing. Songs included are "One for My Baby" and "Someone to Watch over Me". 40th anniversary edition. Digitally remastered. Includes original trailer.
VHS: S04514. $19.95.
Gordon Douglas, USA, 1954, 117 mins.

Ziegfeld Follies
Notable for Fred Astaire's only dance with Gene Kelly, this all-star vehicle also features great performances from William Powell, Judy Garland, Lucille Ball, Lena Horne, Fanny Brice, Red Skelton, Cyd Charisse, Edward Arnold, Esther Williams and Virginia O'Brien. Collector's edition. New digital transfer. Includes original theatrical trailer, original overture and exit music.
VHS: S04407. $19.95.
Vincente Minnelli, USA, 1946, 110 mins.

Ziegfeld Girl
One of Hollywood's great, lavish musicals, with James Stewart, Hedy Lamarr, Lana Turner and Judy Garland. The subject is Ziegfeld's girls as Turner, Lamarr and Garland are recruited by him with their lives changed forever. Contains Busby Berkeley's famous number, "You Stepped out of a Dream," and Judy Garland singing "I'm Always Chasing Rainbows."
VHS: S11161. $19.98.
Laser: LD70724. $39.98.
Robert Z. Leonard, USA, 1941, 131 mins.

Zoot Suit
A stylized musical about the arrest of Chicano gang members in Los Angeles in 1942 and the resulting controversial trial. Written and directed by Luis Valdez, based on his own play. Starring Daniel Valdez, Tyne Daly, Mike Gomez, Abel Franco and Edward James Olmos as El Pachuco, the spirit of the Zoot Suit experience.
VHS: S14453. $14.98.
Luis Valdez, USA, 1981, 103 mins.

movies about movies

100 Years of Comedy
Journey on a rip-roaring trip through the world of cinema comedy with the funniest moments in the history of Hollywood, from the slapstick of the silents through the screwball comedies of the '30s and '40s, to Hollywood's most recent comedies. 120 mins.
VHS: S32420. $19.99.

100 Years of Horror
Christopher Lee hosts this two-hour program chronicling the history of movie horror from the earliest experimental chillers through the unforgettable "golden age of movie monsters" and on to today's horrifying fright films. 120 mins.
VHS: S32419. $19.99.

20th Century Fox: The First 50 Years
James Coburn hosts this chronicle filled with clips from over 120 unforgettable films, plus revealing interviews, rare archival footage and fascinating film outtakes. 129 mins.
VHS: S33238. $19.98.
Laser: LD76992. $39.99.

75 Years of Award Winners
A chronicle of award-winning films throughout Warner Bros. history, with backstage stories behind the triumphs. 50 mins.
VHS: S33686. $19.98.

A&E Biography: The Three Stooges
Slapstick masters for four decades, the Three Stooges made physical humor their own with a wide array of choreographed slaps, kicks, jabs and silly noises. Rare recordings, interviews and outtakes tell the story behind these consummate pranksters. 50 mins.
VHS: S29419. $19.95.

Abu Simbel
Documenting the threat to the temple of Ramses by the building of the Aswan Dam and the rising Nile waters, and a solution in the cutting up and transportation of the entire site to high ground. Filmmaker William MacQuitty discusses his years of work on the film. 1966, 28 mins.
VHS: S31586. $59.95.

The AFI Life Achievement Awards
The American Film Institute's star-studded tributes to movie greats for a lifetime of achievement.
The AFI Life Achievement Awards: Alfred Hitchcock. 72 mins.
VHS: S29006. $14.98.
The AFI Life Achievement Awards: Billy Wilder. 72 mins.
VHS: S29010. $14.98.
The AFI Life Achievement Awards: Clint Eastwood. 90 mins.
VHS: S33148. $14.98.
The AFI Life Achievement Awards: Frank Capra. 71 mins.
VHS: S29002. $14.95.
The AFI Life Achievement Awards: Henry Fonda. 97 mins.
VHS: S29003. $14.98.
The AFI Life Achievement Awards: Jack Lemmon. 70 mins.
VHS: S29007. $14.98.
The AFI Life Achievement Awards: Jack Nicholson. 92 mins.
VHS: S33145. $14.98.
The AFI Life Achievement Awards: Jimmy Stewart. 71 mins.
VHS: S29008. $14.98.
The AFI Life Achievement Awards: John Ford. 75 mins.
VHS: S29004. $14.98.
The AFI Life Achievement Awards: Lillian Gish. 72 mins.
VHS: S29005. $14.98.
The AFI Life Achievement Awards: Martin Scorsese. 90 mins.
VHS: S33146. $14.98.
The AFI Life Achievement Awards: Orson Welles. 75 mins.
VHS: S29009. $14.98.
The AFI Life Achievement Awards: Steven Spielberg. 93 mins.
VHS: S33147. $14.98.

After Sunset: The Life & Times of the Drive-In Theater
Once an integral part of America's classic pop culture, drive-in theaters are nearly gone today. Using existing drive-ins as their map, filmmaker Jon Bokencamp leads his ragtag crew across the American West to discover what the era of the outdoor movie was all about, searching out the people who've built and LIVED these theaters. "A wonderful evocation of a distinct piece of Americana" (Leonard Maltin).
VHS: S30937. $24.95.
Jon Bokenkamp, USA, 1995, 45 mins.

Alfred Hitchcock: Master of Suspense
Presents the master of suspense in a rare discussion of his filmmaking techniques and his illustrious 50-year career as director. Filled with classic film clips from *Psycho, North by Northwest, The Birds, Frenzy, Rear Window* and *Shadow of a Doubt*. Narrated by Cliff Robertson.
VHS: S33436. $19.95.
Richard Schickel, USA, 1973, 58 mins.

American Cinema
PBS compiled this 10-part series about American film. Clips from great movies and interviews with some of the most important figures in front of and behind the camera today make this a vital resource for any cineaste. Martin Scorsese, Clint Eastwood, Steven Spielberg, Harrison Ford, Sidney Lumet and Quentin Tarantino are just some of the popular figures who explain the magic of movies. Each of these five videos is 120 mins.
The Film School Generation/The Edge of Hollywood. Out of the tumult of the 1960's a new generation of young filmmakers emerged, who enlivened Hollywood traditions. Today that transformation continues with the growing influence of independent producers.
VHS: S24139. $29.98.
The Hollywood Style/The Star. Production methods magically transform the world in front of the camera. And the star system is a key element of the way films develop and maintain their mesmerizing appeal.
VHS: S24137. $29.98.
Romantic Comedy/Film Noir. These distinctive Hollywood genres present opposing world views. One is light and optimistic while the other sees the darker aspects governing our emotions and actions.
VHS: S24135. $29.98.
The Studio System/Film in the Television Age. This insightful examination of the two critical institutions shaping American film sheds new light on the formation of this popular art form.
VHS: S24136. $29.98.
The Western/The Combat Film. Masculinity has been defined by the movies centered on the iconic West and the enduring experience of Americans at war.
VHS: S24138. $29.98.
American Cinema, Gift Set. The complete ten-episode, five-tape set.
VHS: S24140. $124.98.

Anatomy of a Filmmaker
The great director Otto Preminger is the subject of this documentary featuring interviews with some of the famous stars he worked with, including Frank Sinatra, Vincent Price, James Stewart, Michael Caine, Deborah Kerr and Burgess Meredith. 119 mins.
VHS: S21167. $19.98.

Anthony Quinn: An Original
This is the incredible odyssey of a man who worked at a "thousand jobs" before appearing in a film by Cecil B. De Mille and marrying the director's daughter. Includes numerous clips from his films and interviews with friends like Julie Harris and Tony Franciosa. Narrated by Anthony Quinn. 60 mins.
VHS: S14624. $19.98.

The Art of Illusion—One Hundred Years of Hollywood Special Effects
From the earliest films onwards, special effects have mesmerized audiences. Now some of the best effects are shown and explained in this informative video. Towering infernos, intergalactic battles, the Apollo 13 blastoff, gremlins, and even dinosaurs from *Jurassic Park* are among the illusions found in this video. 50 mins.
VHS: S26455. $14.98.

Audrey Hepburn
Chronicles Audrey Hepburn's life of stunning achievement and generosity. An *A & E Biography*. 50 mins.
VHS: S34709. $19.95.

Audrey Hepburn Remembered
A nostalgic look at Audrey Hepburn, her career as a star and her role as an ambassador for UNICEF is offered in this documentary. Clips from some of her more popular films are included and a glimpse of her more intimate life is evoked by her family and friends. 66 mins.
VHS: S21519. $19.98.

Bacall on Bogart
Lauren Bacall hosts this loving look at the man behind the reel image. Includes outtakes, home movies, film clips and revealing recollections, with guests including Katharine Hepburn and John Huston. 60 mins.
VHS: S09803. $59.98.

Behind the Scenes with King Kong in Special Effects
NOVA goes behind the scenes as effects experts bring a legend to life in this exclusive look at how King Kong was created for the Oscar-nominated IMAX film *Special Effects*. 60 mins.
VHS: S31428. $12.95.

Bela Lugosi: The Forgotten King
Examines the man who became Dracula, through footage from some of his famous films and also outtakes, trailers and stills; from his childhood days in Hungary, career on Broadway and the Hollywood era. 55 mins.
VHS: S09423. $19.95.

Best of Nightline
Lucille Ball Dies. 30 mins.
VHS: S14058. $14.98.
Sir Laurence Olivier Dies. 30 mins.
VHS: S14060. $14.98.

Bette Davis (A & E Biography)
Fasten your seatbelts as *A & E Biography* looks at the life of Bette Davis, a liberated woman in a world dominated by men, who rose to become "the first lady of the American screen." 50 mins.
VHS: S30103. $19.95.

Bette Davis: The Bumpy Road to Stardom
A portrait of the star who was once billed as "the woman who was loved when she should have been whipped." 22 mins.
VHS: S06419. $14.98.

Bing Crosby
A & E Biography looks at one of the most popular and successful entertainers in history—and one his fans knew least. 50 mins.
VHS: S30102. $19.95.

Breaking into Hollywood
Fifteen crucial steps outlined by Hollywood insiders detail a blueprint for a successful acting career. A producer, an editor and a casting director explain such basic first steps as joining the actors union. USA, 1995, 42 mins.
VHS: S26873. $29.95.

Cameramen at War
The story of the British Film Unit newsreel cameramen during both world wars, produced by the British Ministry of Information and compiled by Len Lye. Special highlights include sensational footage from campaigns in France, Norway, and North Africa, as well as over the skies of England. 26 mins.
VHS: S03346. $29.95.

Cameramen Who Dared
Go behind the lens with the incredible documentary filmmakers who risk their lives to get the perfect shot. Discover what drives these professionals to pioneer their cameras where limits are unknown. 60 mins.
VHS: S11410. $19.95.

Cary Grant: A Celebration
Michael Caine hosts this glamorous and loving retrospective of the more than 30-year career of one of America's most beloved screen personalities. Includes clips from his almost 100 films, family photographs and home movies. 56 mins.
VHS: S31886. $29.95.

Cary Grant: The Leading Man
Cary Grant was the very essence of a movie star. His deft comic style merged easily with his strength as a leading man. This documentary portrait goes behind the scenes with clips from his greatest films and interviews with friends and associates like Stanley Donen and Deborah Kerr. Narrated by Richard Kiley. 60 mins.
VHS: S14622. $19.98.

Cavalcade of MGM Shorts
At its height, Metro-Goldwyn-Mayer was not only the preeminent producer of feature films, but also one of the finest creators of short subjects. This box set contains 34 of the most beloved MGM shorts from the '30s and '40s, including gems from Pete Smith, Robert Benchley, John Nesbitt and The Three Stooges. Vol. 1, 460 mins.
Laser: LD76746. $99.99.

Celebrity Propaganda
The Hollywood effort for World War II as many top stars come out for the war effort. Features Frank Sinatra, James Cagney, Bob Hope, and many more.
VHS: S10580. $19.95.

The Celluloid Closet
Lily Tomlin, Shirley MacLaine, Tony Curtis, Susan Sarandon, Tom Hanks, Whoopi Goldberg and others provide the commentary to entertaining clips from over 120 films as we learn all the secrets and hear all the stories in this compilation of the history of homosexuality in Hollywood movies. A fun romp with some amazing pre-Breen-code early footage. "An indispensable addition to the history of Hollywood, with the popular appeal of *That's Entertainment*" (Janet Maslin, *New York Times*).
VHS: S30403. $19.95.
Laser: LD76027. $39.95.
Rob Epstein/Jeffrey Friedman, USA, 1996, 102 mins.

A Century of Black Cinema
A celebration of the finest African-American entertainers to grace the silver screen. With rare film footage ranging from pioneer director Oscar Micheaux to Spike Lee. With behind-the-scenes takes with Richard Pryor, Sidney Poitier and James Earl Jones, and interviews with Eddie Murphy, Whoopi Goldberg, Denzel Washington, Laurence Fishburne, Danny Glover and Fayard Nicholas. 90 mins.
VHS: S32422. $19.99.

A Century of Science-Fiction
Christopher Lee hosts this two-hour, star-studded program tracing the roots of science-fiction movies from marvelous trick films like *A Trip to the Moon* to mega-hits such as *The Day the Earth Stood Still, The Terminator, The Island of Dr. Moreau* and *Independence Day*. 120 mins.
VHS: S32418. $19.99.

Century of the Cinema: Journey
Martin Scorsese directed this engrossing installment of the British Film Institute's prestigious and global *Century of the Cinema* series. His *Journey* charts the history of American cinema as he talks about the influences of his career and introduces hundreds of extensive, rare clips. Warm, funny and astute, this is film school with America's most celebrated director. A must-have for any laserdisc collection. 3 hours.
VHS: S33356. $59.95.
Laser: LD76097. $99.95.

Cinema Europe: The Other Hollywood
Created by award-winning Photoplay Productions team Kevin Brownlow and David Gill, this extraordinary three-part documentary explores the birth and early development of cinema in Europe. Includes rarely seen footage from early movies and interviews with some of the film industry's pioneers. Narrated by Kenneth Branagh. Each volume contains two programs.
Cinema Europe: The Other Hollywood—Volume I: Where It All Began & Art's Promised Land (Sweden). The introductory episode, *Where It All Began* covers Paris, the first performance of films; comedies by Max Linder; Abel Gance's *J'Accuse*; and the onset of World War I. *Art's Promised Land (Sweden)* includes *Ingeborg Holm* by Victor Sjostrom and Mauritz Stiller and *Gosta Berling's Saga*, starring Greta Garbo. Two hours.
VHS: S34885. $29.95.
Cinema Europe: The Other Hollywood—Volume II: The Unchained Camera & The Music of Light (France). *The Unchained Camera* includes *The Battleship Potemkin*, by Eisenstein; *Metropolis*, by Fritz Lang; *Joyless Street*, starring Greta Garbo; *The White Hell of Pitz Palu*, featuring Leni Riefenstahl; and *Pandora's Box*, starring Louise Brooks. *The Music of Light (France)* includes *Napoleon*, by Abel Gance. Two hours.
VHS: S34886. $29.95.
Cinema Europe: The Other Hollywood—Volume III: Opportunity Lost (Britain) & End of an Era. In *Opportunity Lost (Britain)* Alfred Hitchcock embarks on his stellar career. *End of an Era* covers the debut of films with soun,; the release of *The Jazz Singer*, and the onset of World War II. Two hours.
VHS: S34887. $29.95.
Three-Volume Set. Six hours.
VHS: S34884. $74.95.

Clark Gable
He was the screen's ultimate romantic lead, a man's man and every woman's desire. Meet the undisputed King of Hollywood, Clark Gable, in this *A & E Biography*. 50 mins.
VHS: S30106. $19.95.

Conversation with Arthur C. Clarke About "2001: A Space Odyssey"
Two years after the premiere of *2001: A Space Odyssey*, Arthur C. Clarke, co-author with Stanley Kubrick of the book and the film, agreed to be interviewed by film critic Joe Gelmis (who originally gave the film a poor review and later recanted, along with other critics) on how this masterpiece was created. Here Clarke reveals many fascinating details about choosing the basic plot, how he and Kubrick worked together, early title ideas, early shapes and materials for the monoliths and more.
VHS: S30990. $89.95.
1970, 27 mins.

Cowboys of the Saturday Matinee
James Coburn narrates this fond look at Hollywood's best-loved Western heroes, including all the film elements that make Westerns an enduring art form. Classic clips highlight this light-hearted tribute. 75 minutes.
VHS: S02472. $14.95.

The Craft of Acting: Auditioning
Allan Miller is a successful actor and teacher. Some of his pupils, including Dustin Hoffman and Meryl Streep, have become huge stars. Here Miller offers useful advice for a variety of auditioning situations both warm and cold, as well as a prepared monologue and even a call back. 43 mins.
VHS: S24899. $119.00.

Dean Martin
A & E Biography traces the life of the famous singer and performer. Discovered by Jerry Lewis at Atlantic City, Martin went on to have a career spanning 50 years. His work with Lewis and the original "Rat Pack" were just the high points of a stellar career. 50 mins.
VHS: S29910. $19.95.

Dear Mr. Gable
This MGM documentary presents the fascinating life story of the man who became *the* symbol of rugged American masculinity. Narrated by Burgess Meredith and featuring remembrances from friends and peers, as well as a parade of film clips and home movies.
VHS: S15257. $14.95.
Nicolas L. Noxon, USA, 1968, 52 mins.

The Divine Garbo
To many she was a goddess: the most glamorous and mysterious movie star the world has ever known. Greta Garbo arrived in Hollywood in 1924 as a frightened 19-year-old Swedish girl and vanished from the screen 16 years later. In that brief period, she made motion picture history. Loaded with film clips from her greatest performances, this documentary is hosted by Glenn Close. USA, 1990, 47 mins.
VHS: S14934. $19.98.

Dragon and the Cobra: The Collector's Edition
Martial artists from around the world gather for a violent, no-holds-barred competition in Madison Square Garden. The reason: to find a successor to the title of World Karate Champion. Fred Williamson and Ron Van Clief, along with rare footage of Bruce Lee, lend excitement to the story. Adolph Caeser chronicles the events leading to the showdown and solicits insights and comments from famous martial arts greats regarding Bruce Lee's mysterious death. Includes *Dragon and the Cobra* along with an additional 30 minutes of dynamic, rare footage of Bruce Lee one on one.
VHS: S33996. $14.95.
Matthew Mallinson, USA, 110 mins.

East Side Story
A unique documentary about the world of Communist musicals—a world unknown in the West. Hearty peasants and workers sing and dance their way through fields and factories in films which border on campiness, in this unorthodox view of socialist propaganda. "Bright as a spangled sputnik. Don't dream of missing *East Side Story*, with its beach blanket bingo, Bulgarian-style" (Janet Maslin, *New York Times*).
VHS: S33314. $59.95.
Dana Ranga, Germany, 1997, 77 mins.

Elia Kazan: A Director's Journey
A revealing documentary of the director of *On the Waterfront* and *A Streetcar Named Desire*, whose work with Marlon Brando and James Dean brought him adulation, but whose testimony in front of the House of Unamerican Activities caused Hollywood to regard him as a turncoat. Narrated by Eli Wallach.
VHS: S34131. $29.95.
Richard Schickel, USA, 1995, 75 mins.

Epic That Never Was
An examination of the story behind why the adaptation of the epic novel *I Claudius*, begun in 1937 by Josef von Sternberg, was never completed. *Epic That Never Was* includes footage shot by von Sternberg, as well as interviews with Robert Graves, Merle Oberon, and Eileen Corbett. England, 80 mins.
VHS: S02811. $39.95.

Errol Flynn: Portrait of a Swashbuckler
The life and art of Errol Flynn is explored in this uncensored documentary that studies his Hollywood work, drawing on footage and interviews with his former wives, friends, children, collaborators and close friends. 50 mins.
VHS: S18134. $19.95.

Evening with Marlene Dietrich
A live stage performance which recreates the finest musical sequences from Dietrich's films, including songs like *Lili Marlene, I Wish You Love, Honeysuckle Rose*. 60 mins.
VHS: S07026. $29.98.

Face to Face
A tribute to the two most eminent martial arts experts in cinematic history: Jackie Chan and Bruce Lee. Contains rare archival footage. 50 mins.
VHS: S33995. $14.95.

Film Parade
An extremely rare and priceless film record of the history of motion pictures, produced by film pioneer J. Stuart Blackton. Utilizing rare film footage, including sequences from *The Big Parade* and *Steamboat Willie*, this first compilation history of the motion picture includes glimpses of many who played an important part in Blackton's life and career, including Theodore Roosevelt, Mary Pickford, Blanche Sweet, Harold Lloyd and John Lowell.
VHS: S09524. $39.95.
J. Stuart Blackton, USA, 1933

Film Reality and Film Fantasy
Linwood Dunn, a Hollywood special effects master from the glory days of Hollywood, and Robert Abel, a member of the following generation, each discuss the making of film illusions. Dunn, of the post-*King Kong* era, shows how the "optical printer" can combine separately recorded images on one strand of film, while Abel, of the "post-*2001*" special effects era, explains how he looks for illusions that don't exist at all in real life. 1975.
VHS: S31580. $59.95.

Filming Ballet
Techniques of filming classic dance. Interview of director Herbert Ross and his wife, the former ballerina Nora Kaye, who together made the film *The Turning Point*, starring Baryshnikov and Leslie Browne. With journalist Cliff Jahr. Many clips illustrate the discussion points about angles, pacing, lighting and costume. 1978, 28 mins.
VHS: S31602. $59.95.

The Filming of the Leopard Son
Observe the complexities of wildlife filmmaking as you go behind the scenes of Discovery Channel Pictures' first wildlife feature film, *The Leopard Son*, and follow renowned filmmaker and naturalist Hugo van Lawick and his crew as they devote two years to tracking and filming the adventures of a young leopard growing up on the Serengeti Plain. Witness Stewart Copeland's (The Police) creation of the musical score, then listen as a 60-piece orchestra brings the music to life.
VHS: S30590. $14.95.
Holly Barden Stadtler, USA, 1996, 50 mins.

Filmmakers on Their Craft
Burt Lancaster. Beginning with his early days as a circus performer, Lancaster discusses his work with Kirk Douglas on *Gunfight at the OK Corral*, with Alexander MacKendrick on *The Sweet Smell of Success* and with Luchino Visconti on *The Leopard*. 60 mins.
VHS: S16537. $79.00.
Freddie Young. Young talks in technical terms about his work as director of photography on such films as *Dr. Zhivago, Ryan's Daughter, Lord Jim* and *Lawrence of Arabia*. He also reflects on the changes in film technology during his long career. 61 mins.
VHS: S16538. $79.00.
James Stewart. The veteran actor discusses his work with such directors as Frank Capra, John Ford and Alfred Hitchcock. 40 mins.
VHS: S16539. $79.00.
Milos Forman. The Czech director of *Amadeus* and *One Flew Over the Cuckoo's Nest* discusses his approach to filmmaking with Peter Thompson. He compares his working in Eastern Europe under Communism to his work with the Hollywood studio system, and draws some surprising conclusions. 32 mins.
VHS: S16534. $79.00.
Nicholas Roeg. Peter Thompson interviews the director of *Performance, Walkabout* and *The Man Who Fell to Earth* about his role as a visionary filmmaker operating, for the most part, outside the mainstream. 34 mins.
VHS: S16535. $79.00.
Peter Weir. Weir, director of *Witness* and *Picnic at Hanging Rock*, is interviewed by Peter Thompson in 1982, shortly after making *The Year of Living Dangerously*. He talks about his working methods, and about the dark element in his films. 45 mins.
VHS: S16536. $79.00.
Ronald Neame. This program reveals technique and insight into the filmmaking process as understood by legendary director Ronald Neame, who began his career at the end of the silent era with Alfred Hitchcock's *Blackmail*. 105 mins.
VHS: S16540. $179.00.

First Works

This two-volume series focuses on some of today's hottest directors. They include interviews with these famous filmmakers, their first films, and clips from their blockbuster movies. *Volume One* contains segments from Taylor Hackford's *Teenage Father*, Spike Lee's *The Answer*, Oliver Stone's *Last Year in Vietnam* and Robert Zemeckis's *Field of Honor*. Roger Corman and Paul Mazursky are also featured. *Volume Two* features clips from John Carpenter's *Dark Star*, Martin Scorsese's *What's a Nice Girl Like You Doing in a Place Like This?* and *It's Just Not You, Murray*, Susan Seidelman's *And You Act Like One, Too* and John Milius's *Marcello, I'm So Bored*. Richard Donner and Ron Howard are also profiled.

First Works Volume One. 122 mins.
VHS: S26349. $39.95.
First Works Volume Two. 120 mins.
VHS: S26350. $39.95.
Marva Nabili, USA, 1984, 116 mins.

Flying Saucers over Hollywood

A documentary video on the making of Ed Wood's landmark 1959 disaster movie, *Plan 9 from Outer Space*. The program studies the film's contribution to the genre, with commentary by Sam Raimi, Valda Hansen, Harry Medved and Joe Dante. Narrated by Lee Harris.

VHS: S18258. $24.95.
Mark Patrick Carducci, USA, 1992

Fonda on Fonda

Who else but Jane Fonda, one of the biggest stars in films today, could show her father, Henry Fonda, with such warmth and insight? Henry Fonda's career as an actor spanned decades of motion picture history, from *The Grapes of Wrath* to *On Golden Pond*. Seeing these two stars together sheds light on an important and vital Hollywood family. 47 mins.

VHS: S20877. $14.98.

Forever James Dean

This documentary is part of the 35th Anniversary salute to the star of *East of Eden, Rebel Without a Cause* and *Giant*. It features never-before-seen material, including Dean's soft-drink T.V. commercial. Visit his Indiana hometown and listen to his high school dramatics teacher, friends and associates reminisce about him. Not to be confused with anyone who sells pork sausage.

VHS: S14007. $19.98.
Ara Chekmayan, USA, 1988, 69 mins.

Francois Truffaut: Stolen Portraits

A brilliant documentary which provides new insights and revelations. Full of extensive clips and in-depth interviews with dozens of Truffaut's collaborators and friends, including Gerard Depardieu, Eric Rohmer, Marcel Ophuls, Claude Chabrol, Jacques Rivette, Truffaut's daughter and Truffaut's former wife, Madeleine Morgenstern, this remarkable film shines new light on the psychological motivations of Truffaut's life and on his filmmaking career. French with English subtitles.

VHS: S26965. $19.98.
Serge Toubiana/Michel Pascal, France, 1993, 93 mins.

Gary Cooper

An honest and insightful look at "the cowboy" and "womanizer" images of the two-time Oscar winner as best actor. 22 mins.

VHS: S06418. $14.98.

Gary Cooper: American Life, American Legend

Superstar and super Gary Cooper fan Clint Eastwood hosts a fascinating tribute to the man who, more than any other screen great, represented the character of America at its best. For over 35 years, the legendary "Coop" lit up the screen with our hopes, our fears, our doubts and our dreams. USA, 1989, 47 mins.

VHS: S14935. $19.98.

Gene Autry

This *A & E Biography* tells the story of the man who left Oklahoma with an eight-dollar guitar and a dream of singing on the radio. By the time he rode out of Hollywood, Gene Autry was one of the most powerful men in show business. 50 mins.

VHS: S30096. $19.95.

George Romero: Document of the Dead

No, this isn't a last will and testament but a documentary on the life and films of George Romero. Graphic scenes of horror from such films as *Night of the Living Dead, Martin* and *Monkey Shines* are included as well as footage from *Two Evil Eyes*, Romero's current work-in-progress. Lots of behind the scenes peeks and rare glimpses at unseen special effects.

VHS: S10987. $19.95.
DVD: DV60353. $29.95.
Roy Frumkes, USA, 1989, 90 mins.

Getting the Message Across

In this video about making videos, videomakers Carlos Fontes, Justin Lewis and Amy Loomis use simple techniques and non-professional, community access equipment to demonstrate how to produce an effective video without expensive equipment. 26 mins.

VHS: S28446. $100.00.

Godspell and the Filming of Godspell

Taking the hit off-Broadway musical to the screen. Features on-location scenes, rehearsals and reflections by director David Greene, composer/lyricist Stephen Schwartz and writer John-Michael Tebelak. 1973, 28 mins.

VHS: S31585. $59.95.

Going Hollywood: The War Years

Van Johnson hosts this nostalgic documentary that spotlights Hollywood's on-and-off the screen efforts during World War II. Includes scenes from such films as *To Be or Not to Be, Guadalcanal Diary* and *The More the Merrier* with reminiscences by actors who lived through the era, including Douglas Fairbanks Jr. and Tony Randall. 76 mins.

VHS: S08169. $19.98.

Grace Kelly—The American Princess

Using home movies and moments from her finest films (like *High Noon* and *Dial M for Murder*), and conversations with Jimmy Stewart, Louis Jourdan and Alec Guiness, this is the story of the American movie star who gave up her career to become Her Serene Highness Princess Grace of Monaco. 60 mins.

VHS: S05953. $19.98.

Great Actors of the 20th Century: Vol. 1

Three different movie stars are profiled. James Cagney plays a sensitive professor whose dissatisfaction about his career is altered when he encounters a box of memorabilia. Errol Flynn is a debt-laden gambler who, in order to marry a reluctant heiress, must defeat an expert young marksman in a duel. David Niven is a mad genius who has devoted the last 15 years to writing a book that he believes will transform their lives. 75 mins.

VHS: S19165. $19.95.

Great Actors of the 20th Century: Vol. 2

Three illustrious horror figures display their gifts for fright and mayhem. Boris Karloff takes form as an apparition and communicates a strange message to a sea captain's wife whose determination to solve a puzzle drives her mad. Vincent Price is under siege from Chinese communists trying to brainwash him. Lon Chaney Jr. is a prosperous junkman who teaches his sons about pride, commitment and honor. 75 mins.

VHS: S19166. $19.95.

Great Actors of the 20th Century: Vol. 3

Three matinee idols are faced with agonizing decisions. Douglas Fairbanks antagonizes a mob boss when he tries to transform a thoroughbred into a champion race horse. Ronald Reagan wants to disavow his troubled past, until he encounters the judge whom he regards as responsible for his brother's death. Charles Boyer takes a bleak outlook on Christmas until his relationship with his wife (Maureen O'Sullivan) alters his perspective. 75 mins.

VHS: S19167. $19.95.

Great Actresses of the 20th Century: Vol. 1

Three actresses take a stand and declare their ambitions. Bette Davis must act decisively to save herself and a band of children from a violent blizzard. Joan Fontaine is a cautious observer who awaits meeting her friend's enigmatic groom. Gloria Swanson must decide to sacrifice her career to prolong her life. 75 mins.

VHS: S19168. $19.95.

Great Actresses of the 20th Century: Vol. 2

This program looks at three young actresses on the eve of their breakthrough. Natalie Wood and her siblings find respect and awe for their new father-figure (Charles Boyer) through a complex reign of errors. Joanne Woodward is a disillusioned high school outcast until a mysterious older man (Dick Powell) orchestrates her personal transformation. Angela Lansbury devises an elaborate plan to withhold information about her troubled past. 75 mins.

VHS: S19169. $19.95.

Great Actresses of the 20th Century: Vol. 3

Three actresses at the peak of their craft highlight this video collection. Greer Garson pursues the vicious killer who murdered her fiance. Loretta Young reunites with her estranged son. Ida Lupino is confined to a penthouse with virtually no food and must decipher the contents of a tape recording in order to escape. 75 mins.

VHS: S19170. $19.95.

Great Hollywood Memories: Volume I

Host Gene Kelly takes us on a history tour of motion pictures from the turn of the century until the beginning of sound. USA, 60 mins.

VHS: S15227. $19.95.

Great Hollywood Memories: Volume II

Host Henry Fonda continues the history of motion pictures from the beginning of sound through the fabulous years of the 30s, 40s, 50s and early 60s. USA, 60 mins.

VHS: S15228. $19.95.

Gregory Peck: His Own Man

This tape tells the story of Gregory Peck, a shy and inarticulate boy from a broken family who eventually rose to superstardom. With clips from *To Kill a Mockingbird, MacArthur* and *The Guns of Navarone*. Narrated by Peck himself. 60 mins.

VHS: S14621. $19.98.

The Haunted World of Edward D. Wood, Jr.

The first feature-length documentary of the Orson Welles of low-budget pictures, Ed Wood, produced by Wood's first partner, Crawford John Thompson. See clips from Wood's first, inept attempt at filmmaking, *Crossroads of Laredo*, and hear him comment about his "craft." Bela Lugosi, Jr. discusses his father's unusual relationship with Wood. Also featuring Bela Lugosi, Maila Nurmi, Delores Fuller, Paul Marco, Conrad Brooks, Gregory Walcott and rare appearances by Loretta King, Lyle Talbot, Mona McKinnon and Norma McCarty-Wood.

VHS: S32302. $19.95.
Brett Thompson, USA, 1997, 110 mins.

Hearts of Darkness: A Filmmaker's Apocalypse

A riveting behind-the-scenes look at the making of Francis Ford Coppola's *Apocalypse Now*. The film combines interviews with documentary footage shot on location in the Philippines by Eleanor Coppola. This is a must-see for anyone with the slightest interest in how Hollywood movies get made. With Martin Sheen, Dennis Hopper, Larry Fishburne, Robert Duvall, Sam Bottoms, Frederic Forrest, George Lucas, John Milius and Francis Ford Coppola. Watch Marlon Brando improvise his lines and eat a bug.

VHS: S16459. $19.95.
Fax Bahr/George Hickenlooper/Eleanor Coppola, USA, 1991, 96 mins.

Hedda Hopper's Hollywood

Join Hollywood's most renowned entertainment reporter for an intimate behind-the-scenes visit with the screen's greatest stars as seen in rare film footage. Bob Hope, Gary Cooper, Betty Grable, Ernest Hemingway and many more stars come out to play in their favorite playgrounds. 58 mins.

VHS: S09495. $19.95.

Here's Looking at You, Warner Bros.

An in-house documentary about the origins, growth and glamour of Warner Bros. Narrated by Clint Eastwood, Barbra Streisand, Goldie Hawn, Steven Spielberg and Chevy Chase.

VHS: S18450. $19.95.
Laser: LD71865. $29.98.
Robert Guenette, USA, 1992, 108 mins.

Hollywood Babylon

Past the studio gates, in the Hollywood backlots and behind the scenes are some of Tinsel Town's most desperately held secrets. In this series the lives of 13 highly acclaimed stars are revealed. Witness the shocking truths and the real life costs that fame and fortune bring to those in the limelight. Each tape is 55 mins.

Volume 1: Grace Kelly/Howard Hughes/Marilyn Monroe/William Holden.
VHS: S21876. $24.95.
Volume 2: John Lennon/Errol Flynn/Vivien Leigh/ John Belushi.
VHS: S21877. $24.95.
Volume 3: James Dean/Joseph Kennedy & Gloria Swanson/Alfred Hitchcock/Sophia Loren.
VHS: S21878. $24.95.
Complete Set.
VHS: S22001. $59.95.

Hollywood Chronicles: Censorship—The Unseen Cinema/Sex in the Movies

Censorship—The Unseen Cinema examines the struggle for artistic freedom in Hollywood. From sex to drugs to propaganda, Hollywood has always been under fire from those who wish to control the content of films. *Sex in the Movies* looks at the role of sex and sexual innuendo in motion pictures. Sex symbols Theda Bara, Clara Bow, Marilyn Monroe and others helped to fuel the controversy but did not stop Hollywood's portrayal of sex on film. Hosted by Jackie Cooper. USA, 1991, 50 mins.

VHS: S14839. $19.98.

Hollywood Chronicles: In the Beginning/The Studio System Takes Over

In the Beginning is a story as dramatic as the films themselves, an overview of the earliest years of film: meet film mavericks like Carl Laemmle and D.W. Griffith; track the move of motion picture studios from the East Coast to Hollywood. *The Studio System Takes Over* looks at the founding of the major studios-Paramount, 20th Century Fox, United Artists, and MGM. Tour the studios as you learn how smaller studios merged to become the powerhouses of Hollywood. Hosted by Jackie Cooper. USA, 1991, 50 mins.

VHS: S14837. $19.98.

Hollywood Chronicles: Pen & Ink Movies/The Evolution of Sound

Pen & Ink Movies looks at the development of animation in the 20 years before Walt Disney created Mickey Mouse, featuring an interview with Walter Lantz, the creator of Woody Woodpecker. *The Evolution of Sound* is an in-depth review of how the "talkies" came into Hollywood as the Warner Brothers studio revolutionized the industry and the ways in which sound engineering changed over the years. Hosted by Jackie Cooper. USA, 1991, 50 mins.
VHS: S14847. $19.98.

Hollywood Chronicles: Poverty Row/The New Rebels

Poverty Row is the story of the "B" movies, the low budget films and serials of yesteryear. These low budget pictures were the vehicles that launched many actors to stardom and the studios where they worked have a rich history that is unfolded here. *The New Rebels* looks at the maverick directors and producers of Hollywood. D.W. Griffith, Orson Welles, and others are the focus; and some of today's "rebels", like Stanley Kramer and Paul Bartel, are interviewed. Hosted by Jackie Cooper. USA, 1991, 50 mins.
VHS: S14842. $19.98.

Hollywood Chronicles: Publicity Stunts & Coming Attractions/ How Movies Are Made

Publicity Stunts & Coming Attractions reviews the outlandish stunts, publicity campaigns, and preview trailers that have been the cornerstone of Hollywood's publicity machine. *How Movies Are Made* explains the movie-making process. From the development of camera techniques to editing to props and costumes, see how the ideas are brought to life. Hosted by Jackie Cooper. USA, 1991, 50 mins.
VHS: S14841. $19.98.

Hollywood Chronicles: Riding into the Sunset/ The American Hero

Riding into the Sunset is the story of the most American genre in all the world—the Western. Join Gene Autry as he talks about the rich history of Westerns in Hollywood. *The American Hero* focuses on the actors that have become the "American Hero." The careers of Douglas Fairbanks, Gary Cooper, James Stewart, James Dean and more are examined for the values that they portrayed on the screen. Hosted by Jackie Cooper. USA, 1991, 50 mins.
VHS: S14838. $19.98.

Hollywood Chronicles: Scandal!/Mysteries & Secrets

Scandal! uncovers some of Hollywood's greatest scandals. The Roscoe "Fatty" Arbuckle case, the suicide of Jean Harlow's husband Paul Bern, Errol Flynn's arrest on rape charges, the Communist scare of the 1950's and more are investigated. *Mysteries & Secrets* explores some of Hollywood's still unsolved mysteries. The William Desmond Taylor murder, the murder of Thelma Todd, the death of "Superman" George Reeves, and more are recounted with rare footage and the headlines of the day. Hosted by Jackie Cooper. USA 1991, 50 mins.
VHS: S14835. $19.98.

Hollywood Chronicles: Stereotypes & Minorities/ Familiar Faces, Unknown Names

Stereotypes & Minorities is an overview of the treatment of black actors in Hollywood. Actors Della Reese and Nick Stewart offer their insights and reflect on the changing roles of blacks in films. *Familiar Faces, Unknown Names* features the character actors—those supporting players that we recognize but never know who they are. Hosted by Jackie Cooper. USA, 1991, 50 mins.
VHS: S14843. $19.98.

Hollywood Chronicles: The Depression Years/The Silent Witness

The Depression Years centers on the development of musicals, gangster films and the screwball comedy. Escaping the Depression was the theme of this era, and travelogs, cartoons, and newsreels were all staples of the cinematic entertainment of the time. *The Silent Witness* covers the newsreels and their role in bringing the news to the public. Beyond hard news, the newsreel also brought sports and entertainment news to the public. Hosted by Jackie Cooper. USA, 1991, 50 mins.
VHS: S14846. $19.98.

Hollywood Chronicles: The Futurists/ The Wizards of the EFX

The Futurists goes where no man has gone before—the realm of science fiction. From *Metropolis* to *Star Trek*, science fiction films have been the mirror of our future and a tantalizing peek into what that future may be. *The Wizards of EFX explains the mechanics of special effects, those dazzling moments in film that leave the audience asking, "How did they do that?" Learn how it was done with footage from King Kong, Ghostbusters II* and more. Hosted by Jackie Cooper. USA 1991, 50 mins.
VHS: S14836. $19.98.

Hollywood Chronicles: The Great Detectives/The Great Clowns

The Great Detectives does its own detective work as it looks at the famous sleuths of film. Dick Tracy, Bulldog Drummond, Charlie Chan, Sherlock Holmes and more are investigated. *The Great Clowns* will leave you laughing helplessly as Charlie Chaplin, Harold Lloyd, Buster Keaton, Laurel & Hardy, The Marx Brothers and W.C. Fields leave their vaudeville roots behind to come to Hollywood and create their special brands of comedy. Hosted by Jackie Cooper. USA, 1991, 50 mins.
VHS: S14840. $19.98.

Hollywood Chronicles: The Search for God, Grails & Profits/ The Nightmare Factory

The Search for God, Grails & Profits looks at the ties between religion and Hollywood, on film and behind-the-scenes. *The Nightmare Factory* creeps through the world of the horror movies and features interviews with Samuel Arkoff and Roger Corman. The careers of Lon Chaney, Bela Lugosi, and other greats are also included. Hosted by Jackie Cooper. USA, 1991, 50 mins.
VHS: S14845. $19.98.

Hollywood Chronicles: Women with Clout/Hollywood's Children

Women with Clout recaps the career of some of the most powerful women in Hollywood—actresses and directors who controlled their own careers. Mary Pickford, Joan Crawford, Lucille Ball and others are highlighted along with some of the most powerful women in Hollywood today. *Hollywood's Children* features the child stars of Hollywood, including host Jackie Cooper and interviews with Hal Roach and Spanky McFarland. Hosted by Jackie Cooper. USA, 1991, 50 mins.
VHS: S14844. $19.98.

Hollywood Dinosaurs

A program that looks at the creation and evolution of the dinosaur or monsters in early silents, cartoons and the science fiction films of the 50s and 60s, with scenes from *The Lost World, Godzilla, Gorgo* and *King Kong*. 60 mins.
VHS: S18789. $9.99.

Hollywood Goes to War

A collection of short subjects produced by the Office of War Information. *The All Star Bond Rally* features Bob Hope, Frank Sinatra, Harpo Marx and Betty Grable. *Hollywood Canteen Overseas Special* boasts Dinah Shore, Red Skelton, Eddie Cantor and Jimmy Durante. Also included are Kay Francis, Carole Landis, Martha Raye and Mitzi Mayfair, those "Four Jills in a Jeep." And much more. USA, 1945, 41 mins.
VHS: S05507. $24.95.

Hollywood Hookers

This documentary takes an in-depth look at the oldest profession in the world, Hollywood style, with interviews and famous scenes from more than 20 films, including *Irma La Douce, Midnight Cowboy, American Gigolo, Klute, Risky Business, Taxi Driver, Sweet Charity, Hustling, Miss Sadie Thompson, Belle de Jour, Crimes of Passion* and *Butterfield 8*. 60 mins.
VHS: S33333. $14.99.

Hollywood Mavericks

From Erich Von Stroheim to David Lynch, this portrait features rare interview footage with filmmakers, including Coppola, Hopper, Scorsese, Bogdanovich, Schrader, Rudolph and Lynch. 90 mins.
VHS: S34925. $14.95.
Laser: CLV(1), CAV(2). **LD71495. $39.95.**

Hollywood Musicals of the '50s

All the music, dancing, exotic locales, comedy and drama of the greatest musicals of the 1950s are presented in this program. With clips and revealing interviews with such stars as Shirley Jones, Ann Miller and Debbie Reynolds. 60 mins.
VHS: S32421. $19.99.

Hollywood on Trial

John Huston narrates this feature-length documentary about the Hollywood Ten who would not cooperate when accused by the House Committee on Un-American Activities of communist activities. Appearances by Ronald Reagan, Otto Preminger, Zero Mostel, and others. 1979, 90 mins.
VHS: S09422. $29.95.

Hollywood Scandals and Tragedies

A video scandal sheet of tantalizing truths filled with remembrances of those who fell from grace with the public, criminal trials of the stars, celebrity suicides, murders, Hollywood funerals, graveyards, and Hollywood myths. 90 mins.
VHS: S07473. $79.95.

Hollywood Screenwriters and Their Craft

Hollywood Screenwriters and Their Craft is presented in three separate programs which can be viewed independently. Program one focuses on the origin of ideas, theme and character. Program two addresses strategies for exposition, the point of attack for the individual scene, and the writing of dialog. Program three examines methodology, artistic preparation, and the place of personal philosophy and point of view in a screenwriter's work. Featuring seven top Hollywood screenwriters, including Julius Epstein *(Casablanca)*, Lawrence Kasdan *(Body Heat)* and Waldo Salt *(Midnight Cowboy)*.
VHS: S16545. $179.00.

Hollywood Without Make-Up

The home movies of Ken Murray contain dozens of the movie capitol's brightest stars. Thirty years of memories of the film greats at work and at play. Famous faces include Marilyn Monroe, Walt Disney, Clark Gable, Clara Bow, the Marx Brothers, Laurel and Hardy, Mae West, Charlie Chaplin, Humphrey Bogart and many, many more.
VHS: S10037. $24.95.
Ken Murray, USA, 1962, 51 mins.

Hollywood's Children

Roddy McDowall narrates this fascinating look at Hollywood and the child star—from Shirley Temple and Jackie Cooper to Deanna Durbin, Judy Garland and Mickey Rooney—their triumphs and growing up. 58 mins.
VHS: S06040. $19.98.

Hollywood—The Definitive Story

A 13-part series produced by England's Thames Television, narrated by James Mason, covering the stars, stories and scandals of early Hollywood's silent era.

Hollywood—Comedy—A Serious Business. Chaplin, Keaton and Lloyd. 52 mins.
VHS: S09012. $9.95.

Hollywood—Hollywood Goes to War. The war film is born. 52 mins.
VHS: S09008. $9.95.

Hollywood—Hazard of the Game. Stunt men and their greatest moments. 52 mins.
VHS: S09009. $9.95.

Hollywood—In the Beginning. Hollywood—from peaceful farmland to film capital. 52 mins.
VHS: S09006. $9.95.

Hollywood—Out West The Cowboy Movie—and the first Western stars. 52 mins.
VHS: S09013. $9.95.

Hollywood—Single Beds and Double Standards. The scandals and the stars. 52 mins.
VHS: S09007. $9.95.

Hollywood—Swanson and Valentino. Two greats who personified Hollywood. 52 mins.
VHS: S09010. $9.95.

Hollywood—Star Treatment. The star system—Clara Bow and John Gilbert. 52 mins.
VHS: S09016. $9.95.

Hollywood—The Pioneers. Movies come of age. 52 mins.
VHS: S09005. $9.95.

Hollywood—The Autocrats. On the set—De Mille and Von Stroheim. 52 mins.
VHS: S09011. $9.95.

Hollywood—The Man with the Megaphone. Early film directors create classics. 52 mins.
VHS: S09014. $9.95.

Hollywood—Trick of the Light. Brilliant work by early cameramen. 52 mins.
VHS: S09015. $9.95.

Hollywood—The End of an Era. Talking Pictures arrive. 52 mins.
VHS: S09017. $9.95.

Hollywood—Definitive Story, Giftpack. The complete set.
VHS: S09018. $120.92.

The House That Shadows Built

This early documentary is a history of Paramount Pictures from 1912 to the early sound years of 1932, with many interesting looks at the birth and growth of a major Hollywood studio. 60 mins.
VHS: S26069. $29.95.

How to See Hollywood

An affectionate look at Hollywood, from the silent screen to the Golden Era, for tourists from the movie buff to the cultivated museum-goer. You'll see the Walk of Fame, the Hollywood sign, the Chinese Theater, Sunset Strip, Rodeo Drive, Universal Studios, Venice, the Gene Autry Western Museum, the Hollywood Bowl, the Warner Bros. backlot, homes of the stars, the Tournament of Roses, Disneyland and more.

VHS: S32728. $19.95.

Clay Francisco, USA, 1993, 80 mins.

Howard Hawks: American Artist

Previously unseen home movies, out-takes, and interviews with James Caan, Angie Dickinson, Lauren Bacall, and Peter Bogdanovich trace the genius of the man who directed *Bringing Up Baby, His Girl Friday, To Have and Have Not,* and *Gentlemen Prefer Blondes*. 57 mins.

VHS: S34537. $19.98.

In the Grip of Evil

The true story behind *The Exorcist*. This in-depth look at exorcism, framed within the most famous and widely documented exorcism in history—the 1949 case of a 13-year-old-boy, on which William Peter Blaty based his novel *The Exorcist*—explores demonic possession as leading experts in the fields of psychology and theology face off in the battle of science vs. religion and good vs. evil. 50 mins.

VHS: S31658. $19.98.

Ingrid Bergman: Portrait of a Star

This widely praised video biography centers on the life and accomplishments of Ingrid Bergman, the actress and the woman. Featuring clips from 25 of her greatest films, rare Hollywood screen tests, home movies from the 1940s and much more. Narrated by Sir John Gielgud. 60 mins.

VHS: S14625. $19.98.

Interview with Jonas Mekas

The famed director of the Anthology Film Archives discusses his film work and his newly re-built institution.

VHS: S10205. $19.95.

Jordi Torrent, USA, 1986, 20 mins.

Jack L. Warner: The Last Mogul

Newly available photographs reveal the life story of one of Hollywood's most important producers. Bette Davis, Errol Flynn, James Cagney, Edward G. Robinson, Humphrey Bogart and Bugs Bunny are just some of the stars who called Warner boss. Clips from some of his most successful films are included. 104 mins.

VHS: S26375. $19.95.

James Cagney Scrapbook

James Cagney in his most memorable roles including "Blood on the Sun" and "Time of Our Lives." 60 mins.

VHS: S07024. $19.95.

James Cagney: Top of the World

Michael J. Fox hosts this tribute to one of Hollywood's most enduring legends. It is a documentary which includes scenes from some of Cagney's highly popular movies and interviews with the star himself. 60 mins.

VHS: S20876. $14.98.

James Dean and Me

An unforgettable look into the life of the modern age of Hollywood's first superstar, James Dean. This revealing program explores the myth and legend of one of film's most mysterious personalities. Includes rare film clips and photographs from the James Dean estate. Features Dennis Hopper, Eartha Kitt, Rod Steiger, Liz Sheridan and many others. 50 mins.

VHS: S31371. $19.95.

James Dean at High Speed\

The story of James Dean's love of racing is told through never-before-seen film clips of his auto-racing career. Includes interviews with drivers who raced against him. Features a breathtaking point-of-view ride in an exact replica of Dean's Porsche Spyder. 50 mins.

VHS: S31372. $19.95.

James Dean: A Portrait

This is the most comprehensive and revealing profile ever produced on the life of Hollywood legend James Dean. It presents a wealth of new material from the James Dean estate, including photos, film footage from Dean's early television dramas and commercials, as well as his own home movies. Also featured are rare screen tests and wardrobe tests from *Rebel Without a Cause, East of Eden* and *Giant*. Includes interviews with many actors who worked with Dean, including Dennis Hopper, Rod Steiger, Sal Mineo, Eli Wallach and others. 55 mins.

VHS: S30682. $19.95.

James Stewart: A Wonderful Life

Johnny Carson hosts this tribute to the life and art of James Stewart, whose essential goodness, honesty and simplicity shaped one indelible performance after another. The program weaves interviews and documentary footage on the set of Stewart's best films. USA, 1987, 111 mins.

VHS: S19472. $19.98.

Jean Gabin

The great French actor is remembered by some of the writers, directors and co-stars who worked with him through 50 years and 100 films, including Rene Clement, Jean Dellanoy, Denys de la Patelliere, Michel Audiard, Granier Deferre, Jean Desailly, Francois Arnoul, Lino Ventura, Danielle Darrieux and Madeleine Renaud. With clips from *Pepe le Moko, Grande Illusion, La Bete Humaine, Le Chat* and many others. Narrated by Nadia Gray. 1978, 60 mins.

VHS: S31572. $59.95.

Jeanette MacDonald

From the interview program *Person to Person*; Jeanette MacDonald is seen in prevues of many of her films, along with Nelson Eddy.

VHS: S10604. $29.95.

Jerry Lewis

The inspirational story of America's beloved clown, from his childhood in New Jersey to his legendary career as a film star, from his tumultuous 10-year partnership with Dean Martin to his commitment as spokesman for the Muscular Dystrophy Association. Rare archival footage and exclusive interviews with friends, collaborators and Lewis himself. 100 mins.

VHS: S32374. $19.95.

Jimmy Stewart

This *A & E Biography* celebrates the life of the all-American icon. 50 mins.

VHS: S34708. $19.95.

John Wayne: On Board with the Duke

Never-before-seen home movies, rare photographs and interviews present the off-screen life of the legendary Duke as the privateman-at play with family and friends, exploring ports-of-call from Alaska to Mexico, at home in Newport Beach and aboard the *Wild Goose*, a former U.S. Navy minesweeper.

VHS: S31766. $19.95.

Clark Sharon, USA, 1995, 68 mins.

Judy Garland Scrapbook

Judy's formative years through the premiere of her screen triumph, *A Star Is Born* 60 mins.

VHS: S07022. $19.95.

Katharine Hepburn

This *A&E Biography* examines the over-six-decade career of Academy Award-winning actress Katharine Hepburn. 50 mins.

VHS: S33193. $19.95.

Ken Russell

The celebrated, unconventional, British film director discusses his life and work with writer Colin Wilson. Russell talks of his attempts to break into filmmaking through acting and photography, his passion for music, and his first jobs in television. With clips from *Amelia and the Angel, Poet's London*, early music profiles for the BBC, *Billion Dollar Brain, The Devils, The Boy Friend* and *Savage Messiah*. 1973, 60 mins.

VHS: S31604. $59.95.

Kingdom of Shadows

The evolution of the horror film, from the turn of the century to the end of the silent era, is explored in this haunting, sometimes shocking documentary. Featuring scenes from more than 45 of cinema's best-known and most obscure thrillers, *Kingdom of Shadows* is a *danse macabre* of religion, science, shadows, monstrosity and death.

VHS: S34315. $24.95.

Bret Wood, USA, 1998, 85 mins.

Kisses

From the innocent puppy-love pecks of Mickey Rooney and Judy Garland in *Girl Crazy* to the steamy passion erupting between Ingrid Bergman and Humphrey Bogart in *Casablanca, Kisses* is an intimate look at the best kisses from nearly 100 years of the movies. Hosted by Lauren Bacall. 1991, 47 mins.

VHS: S15463. $14.98.

The Last Diva

Born in Florence in 1888, Francesca Bertini made her film debut in a 1907 short about a beauty contestant, *Goddess of the Sea*. Exactly 70 years later she starred in Bernardo Bertolucci's *1900* as Burt Lancaster's mother. Temperamental, capricious, willful, egocentric, amazingly elegant and beautiful, Francesca was one of the silver screen's last divas. In this touching, funny and wondrous portrait of a unique woman, scenes from many of her classic films are juxtaposed with interviews of the geniuses of Italian cinema—such as the late Sergio Leone, whose father, Roberto Roberti, directed some of Bertini's finest performances. Italian with English subtitles.

VHS: S14170. $29.95.

Gianfranco Mingozzi, Italy, 1982, 85 mins.

Lavender Limelight

This acclaimed film goes behind the scenes to reveal American's most successful lesbian directors, who enlighten and entertain as they explore their sexual identity, growing up gay, inspirations and techniques, Hollywood vs. Indie, and love and sex—on-screen and off. Featuring, and with scenes from Cheryl Dunye *(The Watermelon Woman)*, Rose Troche *(Go Fish)*, Jennie Livingston *(Paris is Burning)*, Monika Treut *(Virgin Machine)*, Maria Maggenti *(The Incredibly True Adventures of Two Girls in Love)*, Su Friedrick *(Hide and Seek)*, and Heather MacDonald *(Ballot Measure 9)*. 57 mins.

VHS: S34319. $29.95.

Leading Ladies

Bette Davis, Joan Crawford, Carole Lombard, Barbara Stanwyck are highlighted in this homage to the leading ladies of Hollywood's golden era. 55 mins.

VHS: S06628. $19.95.

Leading Men

Errol Flynn, Gary Cooper, James Stewart and Gary Cooper in a nostalgic re-examination of their screen careers. 55 mins.

VHS: S06629. $19.95.

Legends

A documentary about kitsch focusing on actors and performers who impersonate show business icons such as Marilyn Monroe, Judy Garland and Elvis Presley in their bid for legitimacy and acceptance. 54 mins.

VHS: S18742. $19.98.

Love Goddesses

A sixty year survey of women on the American screen, reflecting with extraordinary accuracy the customs, manners and mores of the times. Featured at the 1980 Cannes Film Festival's retrospective on "Women in American Cinema."

VHS: Out of print. For rental only.

Laser: LD70006. $49.95.

Saul Turell/Graeme Ferguson, USA, 1974, 83 mins.

Lumiere & Company

To commemorate the centennial of the Lumiere brothers' first "motion picture," David Lynch, Spike Lee, Wim Wenders, Zhang Yimou, John Boorman, Arthur Penn, Peter Greenaway, Claude LeLouch, Costa Gavras, James Ivory and a host of leading international filmmakers created their own one-minute Lumiere film. Using the restored original camera, each director offered his own signature style to the film. Sandwiched between these 40 exciting, eclectic shorts are intriguing interviews with the filmmakers. A must-see for all movie fans, *Lumiere & Company* speaks for the passion, beauty and visionary dream of this 100-year-old art form. English and French with English subtitles.

VHS: S30468. $19.98.

DVD: DV60162. $24.98.

Sarah Moon, France, 1996, 88 mins.

Mae West and the Men Who Knew Her

Dom DeLuise hosts this look at the life of America's legendary sex goddess. She appeared with the greatest stars, including Cary Grant and W.C. Fields. The video includes interviews with many who knew her work, from Anthony Quinn to Rex Reed and director Robert Wise. A fascinating exploration of one of the first blond bombshells. 57 mins.

VHS: S25997. $24.95.

Making of a Legend: Gone with the Wind

A feature-length documentary detailing the making of the classic Civil War drama, including rare footage of the screen tests, Clark Gable's explanation of why he originally didn't want the role of Rhett Butler and a demonstration of how special effects turned Los Angeles into Tara. Narrated by Christopher Plummer. 124 mins.

VHS: S09816. $29.95.

Laser: LD70585. $39.98.

The Making of Short Cuts (Luck, Trust & Ketchup)

Robert Altman's award winning film *Short Cuts* was based on the stories of Raymond Carver and featured a cast that included Anne Archer, Jennifer Jason Leigh, Jack Lemmon, Matthew Modine, Lily Tomlin and Tim Robbins. This documentary reveals the behind-the-scenes story of their interactions. 94 mins.

VHS: S24367. $19.98.

Maneaters of Tsavo

This documentary revisits Colonel John Patterson's spine-chilling account of the two lions responsible for the deaths of nearly 200 railway workers in Southern Kenya. Travel to Africa and uncover the incredible facts behind the hit film *The Ghost & The Darkness*, based on the same story. Features interviews with the film's stars, Michael Douglas and Val Kilmer, as well as director Stephen Hopkins.
VHS: S31178. $19.98.

The Marilyn Files

Former husband and close friend Robert Slatzer presents this dedication to Marilyn Monroe that uncovers the events leading to the tragic night of August 4, 1962. 55 mins.
VHS: S16603. $19.95.

Marilyn Monroe

She was Hollywood's quintessential sex symbol and ultimate glamour queen, a living legend trapped between public adulation and private torment. An *A & E Biography*. 50 mins.
VHS: S30111. $19.95.

Marilyn Monroe—Beyond the Legend

She scaled the heights few could even dream of—and was one of the loneliest stars. This portrait draws on some of her greatest moments in film, including *The Seven Year Itch* and *Gentlemen Prefer Blondes*, on archival footage, and conversations with some of those who knew her best, including Robert Mitchum, Celeste Holm and Shelley Winters. 60 mins.
VHS: S10046. $19.98.

The Maysles Brothers: Direct Cinema

In this 1969 documentary writer-editor Jack Kroll interviews filmmakers Albert and David Maysles about what they called a "new technique of natural movie making, Direct Cinema." Program includes excerpts from their feature-length film *The Salesman*, about door-to-door sales of *The Bible* to working people in Boston. The Maysles formed a two-man crew and followed the salesmen around in an early example of "cinema verite." They discuss their film techniques, the purpose of working in their verite style, getting the subjects to agree to being documented, and their rejection of the idea that they are reformers. 60 mins.
VHS: S31565. $59.95.

Memories of Hollywood, Vol. 1

Highlights from over 50 films set to the music of Academy Award-winning composers. Includes liner notes that list the stars, films and composers, some of whom include Gene Autry, Shirley Temple, Douglas Fairbanks, Errol Flynn, Olivia de Havilland, Buster Keaton and Bette Davis.
VHS: S14009. $19.95.
Dann Moss, USA, 1990, 47 mins.

MGM: When the Lion Roars

This six-decade chronicle of the great movie studio is loaded with film clips, rarely seen archival footage and fascinating commentary from the stars. A three-part documentary, available in individual volumes, or as a specially packaged deluxe set complete with companion booklet.

Part I: The Lion's Roar (1924-1936). Empire builders Louis B. Mayer and "Boy Wonder" Irving G. Thalberg mastermind the star-making machinery that made MGM the nation's foremost "Dream Factory." From the first film (*He Who Gets Slapped*, 1924) through the transition from silent to talkies, and ending with the death of Thalberg in 1936. 123 mins.
VHS: S16613. $19.98.

Part II: The Lion Reigns Supreme (1936-1946). The busiest years for MGM were the war years, a time of bright family-films that are still familiars. With L.B. Mayer as the sole head of the studio, an "MGM look" is created featuring magnificent costumes and sets. 121 mins.
VHS: S16614. $19.98.

Part III: The Lion in Winter (1946 and Beyond). The Golden Age of the MGM Musical sings, dances and swims up a storm. New Vice President Dore Schary turns out gritty, reality-based hits like *Battleground*, and the Mayer-Schary rift turns the boardroom into a different kind of battleground. 122 mins.
VHS: S16615. $19.98.

MGM: When the Lion Roars. Deluxe packaged set.
VHS: S16616. $59.98.
Laser: LD71502. $69.98.

Michael Caine: Breaking the Mold

Told in Michael Caine's own words, this biography relates the story of one of Britain's most well-respected actors. He rose from humble beginnings and overcame the stigma of his working class accent to become an international star. Clips from his most popular films and comments from fellow actors, friends and family complete this amazing story. 60 mins.
VHS: S21520. $19.98.

Milton Berle

This *A & E Biography* tells the story of "Uncle Miltie," television's first superstar. 50 mins.
VHS: S30097. $19.95.

Minnelli on Minnelli

Liza Minnelli hosts this impressionistic "home movie" about her father, MGM director Vincente Minnelli. From 1943 to 1963, Minnelli made 30 films, including *Yolanda and the Thief, Father of the Bride, An American in Paris, The Bandwagon* and *Some Came Running*. USA, 1987, 84 mins.
VHS: S19473. $19.98.

Moments: The Making of Claire of the Moon

A behind-the-scenes documentary about the production history and personal difficulties in the making of *Claire of the Moon*, independent filmmaker Nicole Conn's highly personal and erotically charged lesbian drama. The program looks at rehearsals, professional and creative relations between the primary collaborators and the shaping and cutting of the film. 1992.
VHS: S18773. $39.98.

Movie Magic: Disasters at Sea

See how big Oscar winner *Titanic* was brought to the screen; go on board a U.S. Navy submarine, 1,000 feet below sea level, in the underwater action-thriller *Crimson Tide*; and discover how new digital effects are utilized to create a prehistoric creature in the maritime cliff-hanger *Deep Rising*. 45 mins.
VHS: S33954. $14.98.
DVD: DV60351. $19.99.

Movies About Movies

A compilation of comedies about the movie industry: Oliver Hardy makes a rare appearance in a Sennett film, *Crazy to Act*. The great Mack Swain kids movie idols in *A Movie Star*. Sennett himself along with Andy Clude and Vernon Dent appear in *Hollywood Kid*, while Snub Pollard is a temperamental director in *The Dumbell*. 70 mins.
VHS: S08601. $34.95.

Movies of the '20s

An array of classic silents featuring Chaplin, Keaton, Fairbanks, Barrymore and Lon Chaney. 55 mins.
VHS: S06630. $19.95.

Movies of the '30s

Recalls the films of the Depression era, the horror classics, the award winners, and heroes and heroines of the thirties. 55 mins.
VHS: S06631. $19.95.

Movies of the '40s

Parades past Hollywood pre-war propaganda through "The War to End All Wars". This film subjects director Frank Capra's triumphs and the threat to Hollywood of a new medium: television. 55 mins.
VHS: S06632. $19.95.

Music for the Movies: Bernard Herrmann

This documentary was nominated for an Academy Award because it so successfully illustrates the importance of music to the movies. Herrmann worked on over 50 films during his career, including the legendary *Citizen Kane*. Though most widely known for his work with Hitchcock on films like *The Man Who Knew Too Much* and *Psycho*, he also collaborated with other great directors, such as Martin Scorsese on *Taxi Driver*. Includes clips from these and other films.
VHS: S26668. $24.98.
Laser: LD75108. $24.98.
Josh Waletzky, USA, 1992, 58 mins.

Music for the Movies: Georges Delerue

Though remembered for his work on French New Wave films like *Shoot the Piano Player* and *Jules and Jim*, Delerue also worked in Hollywood on films such as *Silkwood* and *Steel Magnolias*. This documentary charts Delerue's career with clips from these films and interviews with Oliver Stone and Ken Russell. 60 mins.
VHS: S26667. $24.98.
Laser: LD75110. $24.98.

Music for the Movies: The Hollywood Sound

During the golden age of Hollywood, from the 1930's to the 1950's, musical accompaniment in American film reached a high point. Based on the achievements of 19th century masters, these scores transformed films into overwhelming sensory experiences. This BBC documentary explains their evolution. Under the direction of John Mauceri, the BBC National Orchestra of Wales performs this tribute to Hollywood films like *Laura* and *Casablanca*.
VHS: S26917. $24.98.
Laser: LD75401. $29.98.
Josh Waletzky/Margaret Smilow, Great Britain, 86 mins.

Music for the Movies: Toru Takemitsu

Charlotte Zwerin directed this documentary about the master composer Takemitsu. In addition to his many concert hall works he has composed music for numerous classic Japanese films, including *Kwaidan, Double Suicide, Empire of Passion, Dodes'kaden, Ran, Black Rain* and many more. Interviews with directors Oshima, Kurosawa and Teshigahara are featured. 58 mins.
VHS: S26666. $24.98.
Laser: LD75109. $24.98.

Music of the West: A Tribute to the Singing Cowboys

This program honors the spirit and artistry of the classic Western movie stars, the singing cowboys of the 30s, 40s and 50s. Performers include Rex Allen, Gene Autry, Eddie Dean, Monte Hale, Herb Jeffries, Roy Rogers, Sons of the Pioneers and cowboy sex symbol Dwight Yoakam, Clint Black, Emmylou Harris, Ry Cooder, Dusty Rogers and Jane Withers.
VHS: S19685. $19.98.
Charles Gayton, USA, 1993, 70 mins.

Myrna Loy: So Nice to Come Home To

She wasn't a vamp, a vixen or a victim. She was a grown-up woman, the woman everyone fell in love with back in the 1930s and 40s. With priceless film clips and guest star reminiscences, Kathleen Turner hosts this joyful profile of Myrna Loy, the beloved star whose greatest weapon was a raised eyebrow. USA, 1990, 46 mins.
VHS: S14936. $19.98.
Laser: LD72199. $29.95.

The New Cinema

Robert Frank, Wim Wenders, Chantal Akerman, Emile de Antonio, Paul Morrissey, Midori Kurisaki and Michael Snow are all present in this documentary about independent film and video. Altogether 25 directors from around the world share their insights on this vital art practice. Topics range from personal and collective approaches to filmmaking, to the problems and practicalities involved in the process, to wiser attempts to define the very nature of film itself.
VHS: S25048. $59.95.
Peter Wintonick, Canada, 1983, 100 mins.

Origins of the Motion Picture

This collection contains three documentaries about the origins of film, including *Origins of the Motion Picture, Archaeology of the Cinema* and *Let's Go to the Movies*, as well as two films about editing, *Gunsmoke Editing Film* and *You Only Live Once Editing Film*. 100 mins.
VHS: S29894. $49.95.

Oscar's Greatest Moments: 1971-1991

The Academy of Motion Picture Arts and Sciences presents a compilation of memorable highlights from 21 years of televised Oscar presentations. Hollywood's biggest stars, funniest moments, famous speeches, outrageous fashions, lavish productions, sensational songs and most touching memories. Hosted by Karl Malden. 110 mins.
VHS: S16560. $14.95.
Laser: CLV, chapter stops. **LD74890. $29.95.**

Person to Person Interviews—Volume 1

A compilation of interviews with Marilyn Monroe, Bogart and Bacall, Bing Crosby, Eddie and Debbie, Louis Armstrong, W.C. Handy, Rube Goldberg and Ella Fitzgerald.
VHS: S10601. $29.95.

Person to Person Interviews—Volume 2

Groucho Marx, Harpo Marx, Dizzy Gillespie, Carol Channing, Fred Astaire, Janet Leigh and Tony Curtis, and Maria Callas are featured in this collection of interviews.
VHS: S10602. $29.95.

Peter Bogdanovich and Henry Jaglom: The Ninth New York Film Festival

A discussion of their experiences as directors with critic Molly Haskell and their films entered in the Ninth New York Film Festival. With clips from *The Last Picture Show* and *A Safe Place*. 1973, 28 mins.
VHS: S31607. $59.95.

Peter Ustinov

A two-time Oscar winner and notable raconteur, Ustinov appears in a one-man show that is an eye-opening experience. His humorous insights on the film industry and its biggest luminaries—including Elizabeth Taylor, Marlon Brando and Alfred Hitchcock— make for delightful viewing. 60 mins.
VHS: S29905. $19.95.

The Pin-Ups: A Picture History of America's Dream Girls

From French Can-Can dancers to today's supermodels, screen sirens to sex kittens, this encyclopedic look at the pin-up reveals the continuing allure of this sturdy tradition. Marilyn Monroe, Betty Grable, Sophia Loren and Brigitte Bardot are just a few of the unforgettable models included in this video. 60 mins.
VHS: S26154. $19.95.
Laser: CLV. **LD75101. $34.95.**
Jerome Camuzat, USA, 1994, 60 mins.

Premiere of "A Star Is Born"

A who's who of Hollywood is captured showing up for the premiere of the Judy Garland version of *A Star Is Born*. Jack Carson, George Jessel and others interview such luminaries as Tony Curtis, Lauren Bacall, Dean Martin, Hedda Hopper, Elizabeth Taylor, Liberace and his mother, Joan Crawford, Jack Palance, Cesar Romero, James Dean, Kim Novak and, of course, Judy Garland, and many, many others. USA, 1954, 30 mins.
VHS: S05711. $19.95.

A Primer for 2001: "A Space Odyssey"

This television documentary, made two years after the premiere of Stanley Kubrick's masterpiece, offers a clear explanation of the film's epic perspective, its themes, how the plot unfolds, the monoliths, the music, the "star child," the literary sources in the works of Arthur C. Clarke, and many other topics. Narrated by *2001*'s Keir Dullea.

VHS: S30901. $89.95.

1970, 27 mins.

Queenie

TV mini-series exploring the life and rise to stardom of actress Merle Oberon, based on the best-selling novel by her nephew, Michael Korda. A fascinating journey into the glamour of 1930s Hollywood and one woman's flight from a past she can't escape. With Kirk Douglas, Mia Sara, Martin Balsam, Claire Bloom, Chaim Topol, Joel Grey, Sarah Miles and Joss Ackland.

VHS: S30659. $19.95.

Larry Peerce, USA, 1987, 233 mins.

Remembering Marilyn

Lee Remick hosts this program about Hollywood's most public yet misunderstood celebrity, with rare footage of "Norma Jean Baker" from her teenage years, never-before-released films of her stormy marriages to Joe DiMaggio and Arthur Miller, and interviews with many who knew her, including Robert Wagner, Robert Mitchum and Gloria Steinem. 48 mins.

VHS: S09929. $14.98.

The Republic Pictures Story

Gene Autry, Roy Rogers and John Wayne headline this star-spangled tribute to the studio that brought America singing cowboys, action-packed cliffhanger serials and futuristic sci-fi fantasies. 114 mins.

Laser: LD71500. $29.98.

Richard Lester

The film director discusses his career, from early work in commercials to the experimental *Running, Jumping, Standing Still Film* with Peter Sellers and *The Goon Show* cast, through features, including the Beatles' film *A Hard Day's Night, The Knack and How to Get It, How I Won the War, The Bed Sitting Room, The Three Musketeers* and *The Four Musketeers*. Clips from all these works. Lester talks of "the benevolent dictatorship of being a director," his commitment to the subject of his films, his anti-war message and his desire to widen the understanding of the audience. 1973, 60 mins.

VHS: S31603. $59.95.

Rita Hayworth's Champagne Safari

A true rarity unseen for more than 40 years, this is the theatrically released account of the fabulous honeymoon of Rita Hayworth and husband Prince Aly Kahn. Hayworth, in her beautiful prime, travels by limo and private plane through Tanganyika, Uganda, the Congo and Kenya while waving to the natives and posing for the camera.

VHS: S34306. $24.95.

Jackson Leighter, USA, 1955, 60 mins.

Rivals: Karloff vs. Lugosi

When *Dracula* star Bela Lugosi got too big for his belfry, Hollywood turned to unknown actor Boris Karloff to play the title role in *Frankenstein*, and a monstrous rivalry was born. With interviews and rare footage. 46 mins.

VHS: S33166. $9.95.

Rivals: Monroe vs. Mansfield

Two blonde bombshells battle it out for the title of Hollywood's reigning screen queen in a revealing look at the star who wanted respect and the starlet who wanted fame. With interviews and rare footage. 46 mins.

VHS: S33165. $9.95.

Robe rt Mitchum: The Reluctant Star

At 12 he was riding box cars; by the time he was 15, he was sentenced to a Georgia chain gang. Robert Mitchum got his first acting job because he "looked mean around the eyes", and what followed was film history in the making. Includes film clips and discussions with friends such as Deborah Kerr and Jane Russell. 60 mins.

VHS: S14626. $19.98.

Rodgers and Hammerstein: The Sound of Movies

Shirley Jones hosts this look at the unique Rodgers and Hammerstein contribution to film music. Leading ladies Rita Moreno, Nancy Kwan and Julie Andrews also contribute to this behind-the-scenes view of the Rodgers and Hammerstein sound. Newly discovered footage from *Carousel* and *The King and I*, as well as Ann-Margret's screen test for *State Fair* and Frank Sinatra singing "If I Loved You," make this a must for musical fans. 100 mins.

VHS: S29897. $19.95.
DVD: DV60348. $24.99.

Roy Rogers

Roy Rogers' straightforward cowboy manner made him—and his horse, Trigger—American icons in a more innocent era. An *A & E Biography*.

VHS: S30112. $19.95.

Sammy Davis Jr.

"Mr. Entertainment"'s life and career are thoroughly documented in this *A & E Biography*. From vaudeville to Broadway and Vegas, Davis wowed audiences with both his singing and his dancing. He went on to Hollywood for a successful film career. 50 mins.

VHS: S29911. $19.95.

Scoring Films: Bernard Herrmann

A profile of composer Bernard Herrmann (1911-1975), whose scores set a new standard in American cinema. Includes selections from *Citizen Kane, Jane Eyre, The Ghost and Mrs Muir, Psycho, North by Northwest, Taxi Driver* and other films. Herrmann's early classical training, his techniques for matching music to mood, and his unconventional ideas are discussed. With commentary by friend and music professor David Raksin. 1976, 28 mins.

VHS: S31584. $59.95.

Scoring Films: Marvin Hamlisch

Marvin Hamlisch comments on difficulties in capturing the personality of a film, how music enhances film, writing to click-track and working with an orchestra to fit his music to scenes from *Starting Over*. Includes clips from several films that feature his music, and interviews with theater friend Joel Grey and others. 1979, 28 mins.

VHS: S31583. $59.95.

The Search for Haunted Hollywood

A chilling investigation into Hollywood's gothic past and surreal underside, as host John Davidson takes the viewer on a haunted tour of studio backlots, expressive mansions, and eerie grave sites, looking at Tom Mix's haunted house or Mary Pickford's strange dressing room. With Patrick Macnee, Harry Blackstone, Max Maven, Nonie Fagatt and Richard Senate. 90 mins.

VHS: S17982. $59.95.

Sex and Buttered Popcorn

An uncensored look at the era of movie making which had its roots in the tinsel of the carnival, flourishing throughout the twenties to the fifties. Candid looks at such films as: *She Should'a Said No, They Wear No Clothes* and *Child Bride*. Hosted by Ned Beatty. "Wild…funny stuff" (Leonard Maltin).

VHS: S14735. $29.95.

Shirley Temple Scrapbook

Shirley Temple's career on and off the screen from her only color film, *The Little Princess* and in "screen magazine" footage of her personal appearances and marriage. 60 mins.

VHS: S07023. $19.95.

Shirley Temple's Sing and Dance Along

The pint-sized pixie is at her perkiest and most precocious as she performs 11 of her most famous and memorable musical numbers, including "You Gotta Smile to Be Happy," "Animal Crackers in My Soup," "The Codfish Ball" and "Be Optimistic." 40 mins.

VHS: S33726. $14.98.

Shoot to Thrill

An action-packed portrait of Hollywood's leading aerial filmmaker, Marc Wolff, who risked his life creating stunts for some of cinema's most daring moments, as seen in *Superman, Star Wars, Full Metal Jacket, Cliffhanger* and most of the James Bond movies. 50 mins.

VHS: S34564. $19.98.

Shooting for Black and White with Allen Daviau and Denis Lenoir

Daviau is a Hollywood DP who shot *E.T., The Color Purple* and more, while *Monsieur Hire* and *Shuttlecock* are two of Lenoir's films. Here these cinematographers provide a storehouse of information by shooting black and white, exploring silent film techniques and the integration of color film with black and white film. 55 mins.

VHS: S24903. $89.95.

Shooting for Drama with Robby Muller and Peter James

Muller shot *Paris, Texas* and *To Live and Die in LA* among other films, while James is known for his work in *Alive* and *Driving Miss Daisy*. Together these pros provide great technical and aesthetic insights into the art of cinematography, by shooting the same script with startlingly different results. 55 mins.

VHS: S24900. $89.95.

Shooting for Fantasy with Sacha Vierny and Denis Lenoir

Monsieur Hire and *Shuttlecock* are two of Lenoir's films. Vierny is famed for his work on films like *Hiroshima, Mon Amour* and *The Cook, The Thief, His Wife and Her Lover*. In this video they shoot the same script but rely on differing special effects to create a fantasy world. 55 mins.

VHS: S24902. $89.95.

Shooting for Realism with Allen Daviau and Sacha Vierny

Daviau is a Hollywood DP who shot *E.T., The Color Purple* and more, while Vierny is a French cinematographer who shot *Hiroshima, Mon Amour* and *The Cook, The Thief, His Wife and Her Lover*. Given the same set-up, they create original images that are compared and explained to reveal cinematographic insights. 55 mins.

VHS: S24901. $89.95.

Sidney Lumet: From Theater to Film

This 1962 program is an illustrated exploration of how stage plays can be translated to the screen, with particular attention to the work of stage, film and television director Sidney Lumet and discussion with Yale University literature professor John Gassner and film commentator Peretz Johnnes. Among the themes discussed in this energetic roundtable are how film can reveal more of the playwright's intentions than the theater, how the camera becomes a leading actor, how film time differs from stage time, and the way that the theater audience's focus is flexible whereas on screen the focus is controlled by the director. 60 mins.

VHS: S31577. $59.95.

Small Steps, Big Strides: The Black Experience in Hollywood

A brilliant, fun and fast-paced tribute to the groundbreaking achievements of Hollywood's most renowned African-American actors from 1903-1970. 56 mins.

VHS: S33038. $19.98.

The Spencer Tracy Legacy

Hosted by Katharine Hepburn, his glamorous co-star and best friend of 25 years, this delightful film delivers a warm, engrossing, personal insight into the life of Hollywood legend Spencer Tracy. This documentary tribute features interviews with Frank Sinatra, Elizabeth Taylor and many more. USA, 1986, 88 mins.

VHS: S15020. $19.98.

Starring Bette Davis: The TV Years

Davis brings her big screen talent to this trio of TV films. She plays an interior designer, a nasty magazine publisher and a theatrical agent. All three roles give her the chance to be both naughty and nice, but the last is especially good. It will remind the devoted fan of *All About Eve*, and features Gary Merrill, Joi Lansing and Jack Albertson. 76 mins.

VHS: S25923. $24.95.

The Stars and Films That Made Hollywood the Film Capital of the World

Highlights over 100 stars and films that made Hollywood the film capital of the world. 90 mins.

VHS: S33905. $14.95.

Steve McQueen—Man on the Edge

The story of the reform school kid who became one of Hollywood's highest paid stars with roles in such films as *Magnificent Seven, The Great Escape* and *Bullitt*. Home movies, clips, actors Chuck Norris and Karl Malden recollect McQueen's career. Narrated by James Coburn. 60 mins.

VHS: S05954. $19.98.

Steve McQueen: Man Behind the Wheel

A documentary profile of Steve McQueen, created from behind-the-scenes interviews and production history on two of his films, Peter Yates' *Bullitt* (1968) and Lee H. Katzin's *Le Mans* (1971).

VHS: S18900. $19.95.

Strictly G.I.

A collection of wartime shorts featuring Judy Garland, Harpo Marx, Bob Hope, Frank Sinatra, Betty Grable, Bing Crosby, and many others.

VHS: S10579. $19.95.

Tribute to Dar Robinson

Dar Robinson was Hollywood's premier stuntman, who never broke a bone during his 19-year stunt career but lost his life in a freak motorcycle accident at the age of 39. Sylvester Stallone, Burt Reynolds, Clint Eastwood and others pay tribute to Robinson; the tape features stunts from *Lethal Weapon, Magnum Force, Papillon* and other films. 60 mins.

VHS: S12471. $19.98.

Tribute to Hollywood Stuntmen

Christopher Reeve hosts this special starring Mel Gibson, Tom Selleck, Arnold Schwarzenegger and thrilling stunt scenes from *Rambo, Red Heat, Running Man* and other films. 60 mins.

VHS: S12470. $19.98.

TVTV Looks at the Oscars

Lily Tomlin is your guide to this irreverent, backstage look at Hollywood's annual awards ceremony. Watch Steven Spielberg lose out in his first bid for best director. Join Lily as she buys her acceptance gown, Lee Grant rehearsing her "losing smile" and Michael Douglas planning his nominations sweep. 60 mins.

VHS: S15556. $24.95.

The Universal Story

Richard Dreyfuss leads viewers behind the scenes for a look at the history of one of Hollywood's greatest studios. From horror icons like Bela Lugosi and Boris Karloff to America's sweetheart, Deanna Durbin, to the thrillers of Alfred Hitchcock, Universal has orchestrated the best movie talents. Clips from the work of these earlier figures are joined with material from today. Sections of *E.T. the Extra-Terrestrial, Jurassic Park* and *Schindler's List* are featured.
VHS: S27531. $12.95.
Laser: LD75537. $34.98.
David Heeley, USA, 1995, 119 mins.

The Unknown Marx Brothers

This extraordinary program focuses on the Marx Brothers everyone knows and loves while showing a side of Groucho, Chico and Harpo rarely seen by the public. Host Leslie Nielsen leads a journey through rare home movies, insightful interviews with family members, never-before-seen outtakes and hilarious film clips to paint an intimate portrait of the influential American comedy troupe.
VHS: S32502. $19.98.
David Leaf/John Scheinfeld, USA, 1997, 126 mins.

Victor Sjostrom

Born and raised in Sweden, his movies are classics which influence filmmakers to this day. Chaplin called him "the greatest director in the world." In the States he directed Chaney, Gish and Garbo. Today most Americans only know him as the star of Ingmar Bergman's (his most famous pupil) 1957 *Wild Strawberries*. But his legacy remains—*The Phantom Carriage, He Who Gets Slapped* and *The Wind*, to name just a few of his many wonderful films—and this fascinating documentary tells the dramatic story of one of cinema's giants. Swedish with English subtitles.
VHS: S14171. $29.95.
Gosta Werner, Sweden, 1981, 65 mins.

Visions of Light

Cinematography is the art on which all motion pictures are based. In this documentary over 125 unforgettable films are used to tell the story of this evolving art form. This 1993 winner of the New York Film Critics Circle Award will transfix cinephiles with the glory of motion picture photography.
VHS: S20742. $94.98.
Laser: LD71986. $39.99.
Arnold Glassman, USA, 1993, 95 mins.

Vivien Leigh: Scarlett and Beyond

Vivien Leigh, so many years after her death, still remains elusive, never to be fully known; hosted by Jessica Lange and featuring numerous celebrity interview clips, this documentary tribute gives us new insights into the star who captured the greatest woman's role in the history of motion pictures: Scarlett O'Hara in *Gone with the Wind*. USA, 1990, 46 mins.
VHS: S14937. $19.98.

The Voice from the Screen

A look behind the scenes of the Vitaphone sound-film system. This curious demonstration film was made in 1926 and features the Executive Vice President of Bell Telephone Laboratories explaining just how the sound-on-disc system works. Two musicians play a guitar and ukelele duet for the audience one year before *The Jazz Singer*. USA, 1926, 34 mins.
VHS: S06475. $24.95.

We're Off to See the Munchkins

Follow the yellow brick road to Chesterton, Indiana, site of the annual *Wizard of Oz* festival. This documentary tells the history of the beloved film through the perspective of the little people who portrayed the Munchkins. They tell how they first came upon Oz and recall the past glory of MGM. 78 mins.
VHS: S21870. $39.95.

What Do Those Old Films Mean?

Noel Burch's remarkable Channel 4 series, discovering the world of silent cinema never before told.

Volume 1: Great Britain 1900-1912—Along the Great Divide. Using extremely rare films, newly scored music and a lively commentary, film historian Noel Burch explores the contradictions in early British cinema between the "gentlemen inventors of the cinema" and film as an entertainment for the poor. Early films in Britain, says Burch, either showed the poor what bright, happy lives their "betters" led, or held up to them their own, usually drunken, depravity. At the same time, the early filmmakers worked in a climate of fear in an era of panic that "the empire was in danger." By examining the earliest classics, like Cecil Hepworth's *Rescued by Rover* and other, much more obscure films, Burch documents the British filmmakers as the earliest pioneers in the techniques of film editing. 26 mins.
VHS: S08682. $29.95.

Volume 2: U.S.A. 1902-1914—Tomorrow the World. Film historian Noel Burch examines early filmmaking in America against the social background of the immigrant masses streaming into the slums, factories and sweatshops of an industrialized America. It was these immigrants who became the earliest patrons of the nickelodeons, in spite of the fact that many of the earliest films depicted non-Americans as ridiculous or loathsome. But when the middle class discovered the cinema, American movies changed—American film discovered narrative, and at the same time began to censor its own productions, depriving them of social content and criticism. Rare film footage provides the background for this fascinating cinematic and social analysis in this second volume in a remarkable series produced by Britain's Channel Four Television. 26 mins.
VHS: S08683. $29.95.

Volume 3: Denmark 1902-1914—She! Why was Copenhagen the undisputed birthplace of the mature cinema, of psychological realism on the screen, at a time when French or American films were no more than rudimentary melodramas? Film historian Noel Burch examines the Danish silent film phenomenon both from the standpoint of its key figures (the actors Asta Nielsen and Urban Gad, the powerful producer Ole Olsen), and from the social perspective of a Denmark in which women had an advanced position for the time, where feminism was prominent and attitudes toward sexuality liberal. The early Danish cinema was innovative, and in such techniques as lighting, camera angles or editing within one and the same scene, they adopted many techniques before the American directors. As the legendary actress Asta Nielsen wrote in her autobiography, "At a time when almost no one considered that films might be an art, I was determined to put all my energies into the artistic potentialities I had discovered in myself during that first film...If I had had a clear awareness of the terrifying world of unscrupulous businessmen who in those days ran the film industry—I would probably not have embarked on that adventure with such enthusiasm." 26 mins.
VHS: S08684. $29.95.

Volume 4: France 1904-1912—The Enemy Below. "One of the most remarkable features of the seventh art is its unanimous appeal to the masses, with none of the intellectual preparation needed for literature or music," wrote Louis Delluc, and in this fascinating program covering the early years of cinema in France, film historian and critic Noel Burch follows the thesis that the appeal of the silent French cinema was to the working class. "We were attracted to everything denied us by a moral code laid down by others: luxury, wild parties, the great brass band of vices and the image of woman too, but a woman heroized, elevated to adventuress...a generation of young men fell head over heels in love with Musidora in *Les Vampires*," wrote the poet Louis Aragon. 26 mins.
VHS: S08685. $29.95.

Volume 5: U.S.S.R. 1926-1930—Born Yesterday. Amid general poverty, social disorder, an exodus from the rural areas, and the sudden arrival of women in industry, post-Revolutionary Russia was also a period of extraordinary social and cultural experiment. The artists saw art as an instrument of social change, of encouraging new relationships between individuals. The filmmakers and filmmaking groups concentrated on social agitation, on new forms of newsreel, on incorporating into film the great formal experiments of the era. In this fascinating program, film historian Noel Burch focuses on the sexual politics of Soviet cinema—issues such as the collectivization of domestic tasks and child care and the abolition of sexual division of labor in the home. Using rare films which are virtually unknown in the West, Burch provides a unique perspective on this great era of cinema in a climate of virulent change. 26 mins.
VHS: S08686. $29.95.

Volume 6: Germany 1926-1932—Under Two Flags. This volume of *What Do Those Old Films Mean?* focuses on films produced in Germany in the '20s, rarely shown or discussed today. But influenced by the achievements of the young Soviet cinema, the German social workers' movements created the German Workers' Film. Among these early productions were such landmark films as *The Other Side of the Street, Our Daily Bread, Mother Krausen's Journey to Happiness* and *Kuhle Wampe*. This remarkable movement for a "populist" cinema in Germany of the Weimar Republic had much in common with similar efforts in other fields of the arts—for example, the art of Kathe Kollwitz. But it was ultimately replaced by the more palatable—and cheerful—films of Billy Wilder and Robert Siodmak, and, ultimately, by the victory of Nazism. 26 mins.
VHS: S08687. $29.95.

Complete Set. Available at a special price.
VHS: S08688. $149.75.

When Chicago Was Hollywood

An examination of Chicago's film culture during the silent era when Chicago was the center of the comedy film as well as the all-black-owned silent movie company at the birth of the form in the early 20th century.
VHS: S18901. $19.95.

Who Is Henry Jaglom?

The director of *Eating, Someone to Love, BabyFever, Tracks* and *Last Summer in the Hamptons* is the subject of this irreverent documentary. With Orson Welles, Candice Bergen, Louis Malle, Dennis Hopper and Karen Black. "A film that even Jaglom haters can love!" (*New York Post*).
VHS: S33320. $29.95.
Alex Rubin/Jeremy Workman, USA, 1997, 52 mins.

Wild Bill: Hollywood Maverick

This "fascinating, revealing film" (Caryn James, *The New York Times*) explores the life and times of William A. Wellman, the larger-than-life director of Hollywood classics, including *Public Enemy, A Star Is Born* and *The High and the Mighty*, and the first-ever winner of the Academy Award for Best Picture, *Wings*. Produced by William Wellman, Jr., narrated by Alec Baldwin and featuring commentary by Martin Scorsese, Clint Eastwood, Robert Redford, Robert Stack, Richard Widmark, Nancy Reagan, Jane Wyman and others. "An exceptional job of linking a colorful life story with a keen analysis of an immense body of work...A clear-eyed labor of love" (Betsy Sherman, *The Boston Globe*).
VHS: S31217. $29.95.
Todd Robinson, USA, 1996, 93 mins.

William Holden: The Golden Boy

This program reveals a charming and unconventional man with a "wild streak" and a compulsion to test himself at every turn. With clips from his best films, such as *Sunset Boulevard, Stalag 17* and *Sabrina*. Narrated by Richard Kiley. 60 mins.
VHS: S14623. $19.98.

Women Who Made the Movies

Little has been publicized about the many contributions women have made to the growth of the motion picture industry. This unique documentary uses rare film clips and stills to trace the careers and works of such filmmakers as Alice Guy-Blache, Ida Lupino, Ruth Ann Baldwin, Leni Riefenstahl, Lois Weber, Cleo Madison and many others who made a lasting contribution to cinema history. 56 mins.
VHS: S15694. $29.95.

Yul Brynner: The Man Who Was King

Eli Wallach, Rita Moreno and director John Frankenheimer are among the professionals who join Brynner's family to discuss the screen legend. Clips from his films *The King and I, The Ten Commandments, The Magnificent Seven* and *Westworld*, among others, show how this Oscar-winner managed to stay on top until the very end. 58 mins.
VHS: S26763. $24.95.

classic american cinema

JOHN FORD

Arrowsmith

Ronald Coleman stars as Martin Arrowsmith, a small town doctor and research scientist who goes to work in the West Indies with a serum to halt the plague. Tragedy forces a reevaluation of his career and personal life. Based on Sinclair Lewis' novel.
VHS: S00068. $19.98.
John Ford, USA, 1931, 95 mins.

Drums Along the Mohawk

Claudette Colbert and Henry Fonda are featured in this story of Colonial life in upstate New York during the Revolutionary War.
VHS: S06521. $19.98.
John Ford, USA, 1939, 103 mins.

Fort Apache

Henry Fonda stars as Col. Thursday, assigned to a remote southwestern garrison, determined to develop a reputation as an Indian fighter. John Wayne is the boot-strap veteran who sees folly in this dangerous scheme.
VHS: S03220. $19.95.
John Ford, USA, 1948, 127 mins.

The Grapes of Wrath

Certainly one of the all-time classics, this adaptation of the John Steinbeck novel of the dust bowl migration from Oklahoma to California stars Henry Fonda as Tom Joad, John Carradine as Casey. The film won the Academy Award for Best Director.
VHS: S00525. $19.98.
Laser: LD71013. $49.98.
John Ford, USA, 1940, 129 mins.

Hangman's House

Ford's last major silent film is an old-fashioned melodrama about an Irish girl who frustrates her father in his choice for her husband. This is a curious collection of various styles with a nod to Murnau's expressionism. Stars Victor McLaglen and June Collyer. Look for a very young John Wayne as an extra in several scenes.
VHS: S30204. $24.95.
John Ford, USA, 1928, 71 mins.

The History of World War II: Battle of Midway

John Ford's documentary on the Battle of Midway, the large-scale naval engagement that irrevocably changed the course of the war, giving the momentum to the American forces. Ford was hurt during the shooting.
VHS: S19677. $19.95.
John Ford, USA, 1943, 18 mins.

The History of World War II: December 7th

John Ford re-staged the Japanese attack on Pearl Harbor by using Hollywood sound stages to approximate the confusion, panic and disorder. Winner of the Academy Award for Best Documentary Production in 1943.
VHS: S19676. $19.95.
John Ford, USA, 1943, 34 mins.

The Horse Soldiers

John Wayne stars as Colonel Marlowe in this John Ford Civil War adventure. The year is 1863 and the war along the Mississippi River has bogged down. Wayne takes a brigade of Union cavalry on a 600-mile raid to stir things up. With William Holden as the pacifist surgeon and Constance Towers as a troublesome plantation owner. Also along for the ride are Hoot Gibson, Strother Martin, Ken Curtis and Denver Pyle.
VHS: S12138. $19.95.
Laser: Chapter search. Includes original theatrical trailer. **LD71664. $34.98.**
John Ford, USA, 1858, 119 mins.

How Green Was My Valley

An offscreen narrator reflects on his life and work in John Ford's poetic and beautiful rendering of Welsh village life. Based on the novel by Richard Llewellyn. With Walter Pidgeon, Maureen O'Hara and Roddy McDowall. Winner for Best Picture in 1941.
VHS: S18449. $19.98.
John Ford, USA, 1941, 118 mins.

How the West Was Won

A large-scale epic about three generations of pioneers, with a great cast and brilliant direction by John Ford, George Marshall and Henry Hathaway. With George Peppard, Debbie Reynolds, Carroll Baker, Gregory Peck, Henry Fonda, James Stewart, John Wayne. VHS letterboxed.
VHS: S11555. $29.98.
Laser: LD70595. $39.98.
John Ford/George Marshall/Henry Hathaway, USA, 1962, 155 mins.

Hurricane

John Ford directed Dorothy Lamour and Jon Hall as two people seeking to escape the vengeance of a relentless policeman on the island of Manikoora. The special storm effects have yet to be topped. With Raymond Massey, C. Aubrey Smith, Thomas Mitchell and John Carradine. Based by the novel by Charles Nordhoff and James Norman Hall.
VHS: S00592. $19.98.
John Ford, USA, 1937, 102 mins.

The Informer

Brilliant cinema from John Ford with Victor McLaglen starring as a traitor who turns in a compatriot and suffers the consequences. Script by Dudley Nichols, based on the novel by Liam O'Flaherty. A great American film.
VHS: S12022. $19.98.
John Ford, USA, 1935, 91 mins.

Judge Priest

John Ford's masterpiece of classic Americana, set in a small southern town in 1890. Will Rogers is funny and touching as the aging judge, and Stepin Fetchit is the original method actor.
VHS: S03012. $19.95.
John Ford, USA, 1934, 84 mins.

The Last Hurrah

John Ford directs Spencer Tracy as Frank Skeffington, an Irish-Catholic big city mayor running his toughest political race. Based on the Edwin O'Connor novel. Top notch cast includes Pat O'Brien, Basil Rathbone, Jeffrey Hunter, Jane Darwell, John Carradine, Donald Crisp and Dianne Foster. B&W.
VHS: S06827. $19.95.
John Ford, USA, 1958, 121 mins.

Long Grey Line

Tyrone Power stars in this sentimental John Ford salute to a cherished West Point athletic instructor. Power plays Maher, a rebellious cadet who finds discipline under athletic coach Ward Bond and responsibility by marrying Maureen O'Hara. With Donald Crisp, Robert Francis, Betsy Palmer, Phil Carey, Milburn Stone as John Pershing and Harry Carey Jr. as Dwight Eisenhower.
VHS: S16406. $19.95.
John Ford, USA, 1955, 138 mins.

Long Voyage Home

One of John Ford's most important films, loosely based on stories by Eugene O'Neill, the film focuses on a group of men at sea, set during World War II, and on their dreams and ambitions. With John Wayne, Thomas Mitchell.
VHS: S04415. $19.98.
John Ford, USA, 1940, 101 mins.

Man Who Shot Liberty Valance

Jimmy Stewart is the big-city bungling lawyer determined to rid the town of Shinbone of its Number One Nuisance: Liberty Valance (Lee Marvin). With John Wayne and Vera Miles. A culminating Ford western, debunking of western mythology.
VHS: S03891. $19.95.
John Ford, USA, 1962, 120 mins.

Mister Roberts

World War II comedy drama about a cargo ship and its crew restless for combat action, with Henry Fonda, James Cagney and Jack Lemmon in an Academy Award winning supporting role as Ensign Pulver.
VHS: S02172. $19.98.
John Ford, USA, 1955, 123 mins.

Mogambo

Clark Gable is cast as a great white hunter being pursued by two desirable women in the wilds of Africa. Grace Kelly and Ava Gardner supply Gable with a safari he will never forget. With Donald Sinden, Laurence Naismith and Philip Stainton. A lusty, full-color remake of *Red Dust*, which also starred Gable.
VHS: S13193. $19.98.
Laser: LD76413. $34.98.
John Ford, USA, 1953, 115 mins.

My Darling Clementine

A genuine American classic, with the climactic shoot-out at the O.K. Corral between Wyatt Earp, Doc Holliday and the vicious Clanton boys. With Henry Fonda, Victor Mature, Walter Brennan, Tim Holt and Linda Darnell.
VHS: S01784. $19.98.
John Ford, USA, 1946, 97 mins.

The Quiet Man

John Ford's lyrical portrait of Ireland revolves around an American prizefighter (John Wayne) who returns to his birthplace to buy back the family cottage and marry the temptress Maureen O'Hara. Just wonderful.
VHS: S15908. $19.98.
Laser: 40th Anniversary edition includes *The Making of the Quiet Man*. **LD71497. $59.98.**
John Ford, USA, 1952, 153 mins.

Rio Grande

John Wayne is Lt. Colonel Kirby Yorke in the third of the trilogy of John Ford's films on the U.S. Cavalry. His mission is to cross the Rio Grande into Mexico and put an end to an annoying band of Apaches. On another front he fights to regain the love of his southern wife who hasn't forgiven him for burning down her family plantation during the Civil War. With Maureen O'Hara, Ben Johnson and J. Carrol Naish. B&W. 45th Anniversary Edition; digitally remastered. Includes original trailer and "The Making of Rio Grande," hosted by Leonard Maltin.
VHS: S06186. $19.98.
Laser: CLV. **LD72023. $39.98.**
John Ford, USA, 1950, 105 mins.

The Searchers

Classic John Ford Western starring John Wayne as Ethan Edwards, a Civil War veteran intent on finding the daughters of his murdered brother, who have been captured by the Comanches. With Jeffrey Hunter, Ward Bond and Natalie Wood.
VHS: S01731. $19.98.
John Ford, USA, 1956, 119 mins.

Sergeant Rutledge

John Ford's post-Civil War courtroom drama about a highly decorated black cavalry officer (Woody Strode) on trial for allegedly raping a white woman. Ford employs highly cinematic devices, flashbacks and multiple perspectives to chronicle Strode's accomplishments. With Jeffrey Hunter, Constance Towers and Billie Burke.
VHS: S18609. $19.98.
John Ford, USA, 1960, 118 mins.

Seven Women

John Ford's last film is a stern melodrama about a group of American women operating a Chinese mission in 1935 under the threat of bandits trying to overrun them. The cast includes Anne Bancroft, Flora Robson, Margaret Leighton, Sue Lyon and Betty Field.
Laser: LD70149. $34.98.
John Ford, USA, 1966, 100 mins.

Stagecoach

John Ford at his greatest in a story of nine passengers on a Cheyenne-bound stagecoach, each with a singular reason for the journey, determined to live through the dangerous trip. With John Wayne, Claire Trevor, John Carradine, Andy Devine.
VHS: S01247. $19.98.
Laser: LD74715. $34.98.
John Ford, USA, 1939, 96 mins.

Straight Shooting

John Ford's first feature. A silent western starring Harry Carey as Cheyenne Harry, an outlaw hired by greedy ranchers to drive off the farmers. Harry has a change of heart and fights for the sodbusters. With Hoot Gibson, Vester Pegg and Molly Malone. Silent.
VHS: S04811. $24.95.
John Ford, USA, 1917, 57 mins.

Sun Shines Bright

It is four decades since General Lee surrendered, but Fairfield, Kentucky's proud Judge Priest (Charles Winninger) still has the Confederate spirit in his heart. Though he is up for reelection, his compassionate nature involves him in romantic and racial affairs that threaten his political career.
VHS: S12444. $19.98.
John Ford, USA, 92 mins.

They Were Expendable

So much for the surprise ending. John Wayne and Robert Montgomery star as P.T. boat commanders in the Philippines when the Japanese bomb Pearl Harbor. They battle enemy cruisers, planes and floating mine fields and still find time for romance with Army nurses like Donna Reed. A gutsy tribute to brave men from director John Ford. Cast includes Ward Bond, Jack Holt, Marshall Thompson and Cameron Mitchell.
VHS: S12141. $19.98.
Laser: LD71158. $39.98.
John Ford, USA, 1945, 136 mins.

Three Godfathers

Just before Christmas, John Wayne, Pedro Armendariz and Harry Carey Sr. rob a bank in Welcome, Arizona and head into the desert to avoid a posse lead by Ward Bond. They encounter an ailing, pregnant woman in a sandstorm and agree to take care of the child they deliver no matter what. The original "three men and a baby" wasn't directed for laughs. Adapted from the story by Peter B. Kyne.
VHS: S12136. $19.95.
Laser: LD71693. $34.98.
John Ford, USA, 1948, 106 mins.

Two by John Ford

James Stewart in *Flashing Spikes* and John Wayne in *Rookie of the Year*. Two baseball stories directed by John Ford.
VHS: S15223. $19.95.
John Ford, USA, 90 mins.

Two Rode Together

Jimmy Stewart is the cynical marshall who is hired to rescue pioneers of the west who are being held by the Comanches. With Richard Widmark.
VHS: S03866. $14.95.
John Ford, USA, 1961, 109 mins.

Wee Willie Winkie

Shirley Temple becomes a little soldier in this blend of comedy and adventure based on a story by Rudyard Kipling and directed by John Ford as she earns her stripes when she averts a bloody uprising. With Cesar Romero and Victor McLaglen.
VHS: S09991. $19.98.
John Ford, USA, 1937, 100 mins.

What Price Glory?

James Cagney and Dan Dailey star in John Ford's stirring film about rambunctious soldiers seeing combat in World War I France.
VHS: S14145. $19.98.
John Ford, USA, 1952, 111 mins.

The Whole Town's Talking

Edward G. Robinson is public enemy number one—and two—in a dual role as both a timid clerk and a notorious gangster in this screwball comedy co-starring Jean Arthur.
VHS: S33991. $19.95.
John Ford, USA, 1935, 92 mins.

Wings of Eagles

John Wayne stars in the film bio of Navy airman Frank "Spig" Wead, who turned to screenwriting after a serious accident. This John Ford film covers two World Wars and a rocky marriage to Maureen O'Hara. With Dan Dailey, Ken Curtis, Kenneth Tobey and Ward Bond as John Dodge, a film director comically modeled on John Ford.
VHS: S12135. $19.95.
John Ford, USA, 1957, 118 mins.

Young Mr. Lincoln

Henry Fonda stars as Abraham Lincoln during his years of struggle as a beginning lawyer. Considered an American masterpiece by French cinephiles.
VHS: S06523. $19.98.
Laser: LD71225. $39.98.
John Ford, USA, 1939, 100 mins.

SAM FULLER

Baron of Arizona

Vincent Price is a land office clerk who marries an orphan girl (Ellen Drew) after persuading the government that she is an Arizona heiress. With Beulah Bondi.
VHS: S31265. $24.95.
Sam Fuller, USA, 1950, 95 mins.

The Big Red One

Sam Fuller directs in his comeback film this epic story of five fighting men who cut a path from North Africa to Czechoslovakia, based on Fuller's own experiences as a rifleman with the Army's First Infantry Division. A rich, realistic and individual look at war. With Lee Marvin.
VHS: S03528. $19.98.
Laser: LD76975. $34.98.
Sam Fuller, USA, 1980, 114 mins.

China Gate

Sam Fuller's saga of war and romance set in Indochina. Gene Barry stars as part of a multi-national troop engaging in a deadly mission behind enemy lines; a true melodrama with Nat King Cole singing a couple of songs and playing a foreign legionnaire, and a co-starring performance by Angie Dickinson.
VHS: S09623. $19.95.
Sam Fuller, USA, 1957, 97 mins.

Dead Pigeon on Beethoven Street

A strange, very unique, paranoid thriller from Sam Fuller, with Glenn Corbett playing a government agent intent on digging up incriminating evidence that he can use to frame big-time politicians. The film managed to anticipate the murky feeling of the Nixon era with its credible depiction of a government intent on subverting justice.
VHS: S25924. $24.95.
Sam Fuller, USA, 1972, 92 mins.

Merrill's Marauders

In this World War II actioner set in the Pacific, Jeff Chandler stars as Brigadier General Frank D. Merrill, upon whose actual exploits the film is based. Merrill leads a war-weary battalion in the Burmese jungle on a trek through hostile terrain hiding deadly Japanese troops. With Ty Hardin, Claude Akins and Peter Brown.
VHS: S33913. $14.95.
Laser: LD76976. $34.98.
Samuel Fuller, USA, 1962, 99 mins.

The Naked Kiss

A reformed big city prostitute (ably played by Constance Towers) who tries to go the straight and narrow route in small town America finds that beneath the little town's squeaky clean veneer lies perversion and corruption of the highest order. Michael Dante plays her creepy new boyfriend. One of the best from Fuller and a cult classic.
VHS: S06479. $29.95.
Laser: LD70423. $44.95.
Sam Fuller, USA, 1964, 90 mins.

Pick Up on South Street

A pickpocket inadvertently acquires top-secret microfilm and becomes a target for espionage agents. Starring Richard Widmark and Thelma Ritter. "This lyrical skid-row noir is one of the great movies of the '50s. The Cold War plot pushes McCarthyism to the far side of the moon" (J. Hoberman). Written and directed by Sam Fuller.
VHS: S13608. $19.98.
Sam Fuller, USA, 1953, 80 mins.

Shock Corridor

To catch a killer and win a Pulitzer prize, reporter-hero Johnny Barrett has himself committed to a mental institution. He must find out who killed Sloan in the kitchen by questioning three inmates who witnessed the crime—men driven crazy by the hypocrisies of the American dream relating to racism, anti-communism and the bomb. A complex, wacky masterpiece by one of Hollywood's great directors, Sam Fuller.
VHS: S18328. $29.95.
Laser: LD70458. $49.95.
Sam Fuller, USA, 1963, 101 mins.

The Steel Helmet

Sam Fuller directed this gritty Korean War film which stars Gene Evans as a gritty sergeant who's seen it all and is determined that his men live to see it too. With Robert Hutton, Steve Brodie, James Edwards, Richard Loo.
VHS: S13060. $24.95.
Sam Fuller, USA, 1951, 84 mins.

Underworld, U.S.A.

Cliff Robertson stars in this Sam Fuller film about a young man who infiltrates a criminal organization to gain revenge for the death of his father. With Dolores Dorn, Beatrice Kay, and Robert Emhardt as a Mob boss. Crime doesn't pay as well as it used to when bullets were cheaper. B&W.
VHS: S06828. $69.95.
Sam Fuller, USA, 1961, 99 mins.

HOWARD HAWKS

Air Force

This is the daring story of a B-17 "flying fortress" and her tough, brave crew who, after setting out on a routine mission, end up becoming WWII heroes. Directed by the great Howard Hawks in the tradition of his own *The Dawn Patrol*.
VHS: S15130. $19.98.
Howard Hawks, USA, 1943, 119 mins.

Ball of Fire

Mild-mannered professor Gary Cooper is hard at work on a new encyclopedia. He finds the help of a brassy nightclub singer, played by Barbara Stanwyck, both invigorating and distracting. With S.Z. Sakall, Oscar Homolka and Leonid Kinskey as interested faculty members and Dan Duryea as trouble. Script by Billy Wilder and Charles Brackett. B&W.
VHS: S03115. $19.98.
Howard Hawks, USA, 1942, 111 mins.

Barbary Coast

Edward G. Robinson shines as a big shot San Francisco saloon owner during the Gold Rush days. Miriam Hopkins is the dance hall queen who attracts his attention. With Joel McCrea, Walter Brennan, Brian Donlevy and Donald Meek. A brawling action adventure from Howard Hawks. Script by Ben Hecht and Charles MacArthur.
VHS: S03116. $19.98.
Howard Hawks, USA, 1935, 91 mins.

The Big Sleep

Humphrey Bogart is Philip Marlowe in this entertaining adaptation of Raymond Chandler's novel. Blackmail, murder, sex and drugs all come into play as the ace detective tries to sort out the guilty parties. Even the author couldn't figure out who killed the chauffeur. With Lauren Bacall, Martha Vickers and Elisha Cook, Jr.
VHS: S09389. $19.95.
Laser: LD70174. $34.98.
Howard Hawks, USA, 1946, 114 mins.

Bringing Up Baby

One of the funniest movies from Hollywood, a classic screwball comedy. Katharine Hepburn is the madcap heiress with her pet leopard "Baby", who falls for an absent-minded zoologist (Cary Grant) and makes a shambles of his life. Briskly paced fun with May Robson, Charlie Ruggles and Barry Fitzgerald supporting the leads.
VHS: S09362. $19.98.
Howard Hawks, USA, 1938, 102 mins.

Ceiling Zero

Howard Hawks' treatment of professionalism and honor, about a brilliant through irresponsible civil airlines pilot (James Cagney) forced to re-evaluate his life when his self-absorption causes a friend's death. "Directed at a breakneck pace which emphasizes its lean fiber and its concentration on the essentials of its theme" (Andrew Sarris). With Pat O'Brien, June Travis, Stuart Erwin and Isabel Jewell.
VHS: S19039. $19.98.
Howard Hawks, USA, 1936, 95 mins.

Come and Get It

Frances Farmer is cast as a beautiful woman desired by both a father and his son in this drama set in the timber country of the Northwest. Walter Brennan made his mark in this film which was based on a novel by Edna Ferber. William Wyler took over direction from Howard Hawks.
VHS: S01537. $19.98.
William Wyler/Howard Hawks, USA, 1936, 99 mins.

Criminal Code

A young man's birthday party turns into a nightmare when he kills a man in self-defense. After a series of twists the D.A. who railroaded him into prison hires the convict years later to be his chauffeur, and through this he meets and falls in love with the D.A.'s daughter. A very well done, early Howard Hawks film. With Walter Huston, Phillip Holmes, Constance Cummings, and Boris Karloff.
VHS: S07759. $59.95.
Howard Hawks, USA, 1931, 98 mins.

El Dorado

Howard Hawks revisits and revises *Rio Bravo*, with John Wayne squaring off against numerically superior numbers of bad guys while depending on the help of a drunk, a kid and a fussy senior citizen. With Robert Mitchum, James Caan and Arthur Hemingway as the good guys and Ed Asner and Christopher George as the villains. Watch carefully for George Plimpton as one of the baddies Wayne ko's in a barroom brawl.
VHS: S12243. $19.95.
Howard Hawks, USA, 1967, 125 mins.

Gentlemen Prefer Blondes

Marilyn Monroe and Jane Russell form a unique duo in *Gentlemen Prefer Blondes*, one of the classic musicals of the 1950's. Two "little girls from Little Rock" seek their fortune in Paris in Anita Loos' story. Featuring Marilyn's rendition of "Diamonds Are a Girl's Best Friend."
VHS: S00487. $19.98.
Howard Hawks, USA, 1953, 92 mins.

A Girl in Every Port

In the film that influential Swiss writer Blaise Cendrars declared "definitely marked the first appearance of contemporary cinema," sailor Spike Madden (Victor McLaglen) discovers that he has competition for his girlfriends in various ports of call. He finally overtakes his rival, Salami (Robert Armstrong), another sailor, and after a fight they become fast friends. When Madden falls in love with gold digging vamp Marie (Louise Brooks), Salami must decide whether to tell his friend the truth about her. Orchestra score.

VHS: S31173. $24.95.

Howard Hawks, USA, 1928, 79 mins.

His Girl Friday

One of the wittiest Hollywood comedies: Rosalind Russell is the ace reporter ready to quit for marriage, Cary Grant, her editor trying to convince her to stay. An escaped murderer puts Russell's determination to test. Sophisticated comedy from Howard Hawks.

VHS: S00572. $14.95.

Laser: Chapter stops, restored, digital master, theatrical trailer. **LD75051. $39.95.**

Howard Hawks, USA, 1940, 95 mins.

Howard Hawks: American Artist

Previously unseen home movies, out-takes, and interviews with James Caan, Angie Dickinson, Lauren Bacall, and Peter Bogdanovich trace the genius of the man who directed *Bringing Up Baby, His Girl Friday, To Have and Have Not*, and *Gentlemen Prefer Blondes*. 57 mins.

VHS: S34537. $19.98.

I Was a Male War Bride

Ann Sheridan portrays a WAC in World War II who marries a French Army Officer (Cary Grant). Though it's a fairly routine scenario for returning American soldiers, this WAC's new spouse baffles the army bureaucracy, leading to a number of funny mishaps, including Grant appearing in drag.

VHS: S21331. $19.98.

Howard Hawks, USA, 1949, 105 mins.

Land of the Pharaohs

A strange work from Howard Hawks, based on a script by William Faulkner and Harry Kurnitz, about the epic construction of the Great Pyramid. With Jack Hawkins, James Robertson Justice, and a smarmy, dark turn by Joan Collins.

VHS: S15930. $19.98.

Laser: LD71186. $34.98.

Howard Hawks, USA, 1955, 106 mins.

Man's Favorite Sport

Rock Hudson is cast as a fishing supply salesman who doesn't know the first thing about what goes in a tackle box. When publicity agent Paula Prentiss enters the handsome phony in a big time fishing contest, he's hooked. With John McGiver, Maria Perschy, Charlene Holt, Roscoe Karns, Regis Toomey and Norman Alden as fishing guide John Screaming Eagle. Based on the story *The Girl That Almost Got Away*.

VHS: S15770. $14.95.

Howard Hawks, USA, 1964, 121 mins.

Only Angels Have Wings

Cary Grant takes center stage as the mail pilot, in Howard Hawks' two-fisted adventure tale set in South America during the 30's. Jean Arthur is the showgirl; with an outstanding performance from Rita Hayworth.

VHS: S07753. $19.95.

Howard Hawks, USA, 1939, 121 mins.

Red River

The classic cattle-drive movie, often cited as one of the best American westerns. John Wayne is Thomas Dunson, a tyrant of the trail who alienates his foster son (Montgomery Clift) and causes a sagebrush mutiny. Plenty of two-fisted Western action in this battle of the wills, and featuring a great supporting cast. With Walter Brennan, Joanne Dru, Harry Carey Jr. and Sr., John Ireland and Shelley Winters.

VHS: S01101. $19.95.

Howard Hawks, USA, 1948, 133 mins.

Rio Bravo

An American classic features John Wayne as a sheriff trying to prevent a killer from escaping or being captured by a group of men determined to handle him on their own terms. With Dean Martin, Angie Dickinson and Walter Brennan.

VHS: S03588. $19.98.

Laser: LD71679. $39.98.

Howard Hawks, USA, 1959, 141 mins.

Rio Lobo

John Wayne is cast as Union Col. Cord McNally, a tough soldier in the Civil War whose private battles continue when the larger contest is over. A story of revenge, settling scores after the War, this was Hawks' last film.

VHS: S04598. $19.98.

Howard Hawks, USA, 1970, 102 mins.

Scarface: The Shame of a Nation

Paul Muni plays Tony Carmonte, an ambitious hood fighting his way up to be the number one gang boss. Produced by Howard Hughes, *Scarface* is regarded as the best and most brutal of the classic gangster films.

VHS: S01163. $19.95.

Laser: LD70074. $34.95.

Howard Hawks, USA, 1932, 90 mins.

Sergeant York

Gary Cooper stars in an Oscar-winning role as Alvin York, a backwoods boy from Tennesee who overcomes his pacifist principles and decides to fight in World War I, with heroic results. Based on a true story, York worked as consultant on the film. An inspiration.

VHS: S01868. $19.98.

Laser: Chapter search. Includes theatrical trailer. **LD71642. $39.98.**

Howard Hawks, USA, 1941, 134 mins.

Song Is Born

Danny Kaye stars in this lively remake of *Ball of Fire*, once again directed by Howard Hawks. Kaye is cast as a shy professor who hides a gangster's moll wanted for questioning by the authorities. With Virginia Mayo livening up the study hall of fellow bookworm Hugh Herbert and away from tough guy Steve Cochran. With special musical guests Benny Goodman, Louis Armstrong, Lionel Hampton and Tommy Dorsey.

VHS: S15489. $19.98.

Howard Hawks, USA, 1948, 113 mins.

To Have and Have Not

Humphrey Bogart and 19-year old Lauren Bacall in this adaptation of Ernest Hemingway's wartime adventure. William Faulkner contributes to the screenplay. With Bacall's: "You know how to whistle, don't you Steve? You just put your lips together... and blow."

VHS: S01353. $19.95.

Laser: LD70697. $34.98.

Howard Hawks, USA, 1945, 101 mins.

Today We Live

A fascinating collaboration between Howard Hawks and novelist William Faulkner, who adapted his own semi-autobiographical novel about World War I aviation. Gary Cooper plays an American fighter pilot who is caught in battles with the Germans and is attracted to Joan Crawford. With Robert Young, Franchot Tone and Roscoe Karns.

VHS: S19494. $19.98.

Howard Hawks, USA, 1933, 113 mins.

Twentieth Century

Howard Hawks' classic with John Barrymore as the maniacal Broadway director who takes talented starlet Carole Lombard and transforms her into a smashing success adored by the public and press. But when Lombard tires of Barrymore's manic-excessive ways, she heads to Hollywood for even greater stardom, but possibly loses the one good thing in her life-Barrymore. A treasure.

VHS: S07752. $19.95.

Howard Hawks, USA, 1934, 91 mins.

DOUGLAS SIRK

All I Desire

Barbara Stanwyck is a woman of the theater who is driven from a small Wisconsin town by scandal. Now she hopes to return to her estranged family. Her husband (Richard Carlson) is now seeing a school teacher (Maureen O'Sullivan). Aside from this potential love triangle, there is plenty of drama in the form of her previous lover, the man who hastened her original departure from small town life.

VHS: S26227. $19.98.

Douglas Sirk, USA, 1953, 80 mins.

All That Heaven Allows

One of the best films from one of American cinema's most underrated directors, this never-before-available film is a scathing attack on the American Dream, in which a widow (Jane Wyman) faces the wrath of her friends and family when she becomes romantically involved with a younger man (Rock Hudson). Succumbing to the pressures of society, she stops seeing the man and settles back into her lonely life, but eventually rebels against her conformist surroundings and finds love with him again. "A stylized, beautifully photographed commentary on the emotional numbness of suburban life" (*The Motion Picture Guide*). Later remade by Fassbinder as *Ali: Fear Eats the Soul*. With Agnes Moorehead, Conrad Nagel, Virginia Grey and Charles Drake.

VHS: S30796. $19.95.

Douglas Sirk, USA, 1955, 89 mins.

Battle Hymn

Rock Hudson stars in this tale of courage and selflessness, inspired by the true story of an Ohio minister who became a World War II fighter pilot. During the war, U.S. Air Force Colonel Dean Hess (Hudson) accidentally killed 37 orphans in Germany. Rather than return to his ministry in Ohio, he decided to reenlist and ultimately quieted his guilty conscience by founding an orphanage in Korea. Anna Kashfi and Dan Duryea also star.

VHS: S27666. $14.98.

Douglas Sirk, USA, 1957, 108 mins.

Imitation of Life

A remake of the original (with Claudette Colbert), underrated director Douglas Sirk's last film draws the audience into an underworld of backstairs, neon gutters and assembly-line chorus-lines, and includes an exploited black maid with a vitally erotic daughter (Susan Kohner) trying to pass for white. With Lana Turner, John Gavin.

VHS: S00611. $14.95.

Douglas Sirk, USA, 1959, 124 mins.

Magnificent Obsession

Douglas Sirk's elegant transposition of Lloyd Douglas' best seller stars Rock Hudson as an irresponsible playboy who causes the widowhood and blindness of a beautiful woman (Jane Wyman). Lavish color photography and Sirk's brilliant mise-en-scene.

VHS: S00805. $14.95.

Douglas Sirk, USA, 1954, 108 mins.

The Tarnished Angels

Robert Stack, Dorothy Malone and Rock Hudson form a romantic triangle set amidst the tumultuous world of air circus performers. Roger Schulman (Stack) is a former World War I flying ace who is now a tormented and dedicated racing pilot. Schulman overlooks his trick parachutist wife Laverne (Malone) for his first love, flying. Burke Devlin (Hudson) is a reporter doing a story on the air circus who quickly becomes more fascinated with Laverne than with his story. This powerful drama, based on William Faulkner's novel *Pylon*, is a complicated exploration of desire and obsession. With Troy Donahue and Jack Carson.

VHS: S27669. $14.98.

Douglas Sirk, USA, 1957, 91 mins.

Written on the Wind

The lurid lifestyles of the very rich and famous are the subject of this box office champ of 1957 from director Douglas Sirk. Robert Stack is the irresponsible son of an oil magnate. Lauren Bacall is his suffering wife. Rock Hudson plays his best friend and Dorothy Malone won an Oscar for her role as the nymphomaniac sister. Classy trash.

VHS: S07144. $14.95.

Douglas Sirk, USA, 1956, 99 mins.

Zu Neuen Ufern

No less than Douglas Sirk directed this rare German feature set in colonial Australia. Zarah Leander plays a singer who is threatened with deportation for the sake of the man she loves, who has stolen money. With Willy Birgel and Viktor Staal; script by Sirk. German *without* English subtitles.

VHS: S24127. $29.95.

Douglas Sirk, Germany, 1937

GEORGE STEVENS

A Damsel in Distress

Fred Astaire has a terrific time dancing and clowning with Burns and Allen in this P.G. Wodehouse story. George and Ira Gershwin wrote the score, and the classics include "A Foggy Day in London Town" and "Nice Work If You Can Get It."

VHS: S03234. $19.95.

George Stevens, USA, 1937, 101 mins.

Diary of Anne Frank

One of literature's most powerful works is translated into a film which won eight Oscars, as it reenacts the harrowing experiences of the Frank family as they are forced to hide from the Nazis.

VHS: S04330. $24.98.

Laser: LD70946. $49.98.

George Stevens, USA, 1959, 151 mins.

George Stevens: A Filmmaker's Journey
An intimate documentary about the Hollywood director, the film weaves interviews, remembrances, on-camera interviews with his collaborators and colleagues, footage from his films and footage he shot during World War II. The interviews include Warren Beatty, Katharine Hepburn, Fred Astaire, Frank Capra and John Huston. "A wonderfully informative tribute, lit together with love, intelligence, wit and, most important of all, a knowledge of film history" (Vincent Canby).
Laser: LD71556. $49.95.
George Stevens Jr., USA, 1984, 111 mins.

George Stevens: D-Day to Berlin
Director George Stevens shot this documentary footage which depicts American efforts in Europe during World War II. It includes some of the most extensive color footage available of both the Normandy invasion and the fall of Berlin. This film won 3 Emmy Awards and was originally commissioned by Dwight D. Eisenhower. George Stevens, Jr. narrates. With William Saroyan, Irwin Shaw and Ivan Moffat.
VHS: S26760. $19.98.
George Stevens, USA, 50 mins.

Giant
A film of staggering scale and grandeur detailing the lives of cattleman Rock Hudson and his society wife Elizabeth Taylor and three generations of land-rich Texans. Featuring a stellar performance by James Dean in the last role of his career. VHS letterboxed.
VHS: S00499. $24.98.
Laser: LD70581. $39.98.
George Stevens, USA, 1956, 201 mins.

Greatest Story Ever Told
The ultimate Hollywood Christian epic, with spectacular scenes and cameo appearances by a stable of Hollywood stars, including John Wayne as the Roman officer during Christ's crucifixion, Charlton Heston, Carroll Baker, Max von Sydow, Angela Lansbury, Sidney Poitier, Shelley Winers, Claude Rains and others.
VHS: S11552. $24.98.
Laser: LD70200. $49.98.
George Stevens, USA, 1965, 141 mins.

I Remember Mama
Classic screen adaptation of the John Van Druten play stars the immensely talented Irene Dunne as the matriarch of a close-knit Norwegian family living in San Francisco at the turn of the century. The sterling cast of this heartfelt, sentimental drama also includes Barbara Bel Geddes, Oscar Homolka, Philip Dorn and Ellen Corby. B&W.
VHS: S03221. $19.98.
George Stevens, USA, 1948, 134 mins.

Kentucky Kernels
The great slapstick comedy team of Wheeler and Woolsey join forces with Our Gang's Spanky McFarland for a hilarious backwoods adventure in which the zany trio find themselves staring down the barrels of a hillbilly firing squad.
VHS: S13995. $19.98.
George Stevens, USA, 1934, 75 mins.

The More the Merrier
James Coburn won an Oscar for Best Supporting Actor in this hilarious comedy. Jean Arthur is the working-class girl who finds herself in the predicament of having to share an apartment in World War II-era Washington, D.C. with two men—Joel McCrea and Coburn.
VHS: S11744. $19.95.
Laser: CLV. **LD74891. $34.95.**
George Stevens, USA, 1943, 104 mins.

Penny Serenade
Romantic comedy starring Cary Grant and Irene Dunne as a couple which adopts a child but then encounters tragedy.
VHS: S01940. $19.95.
Laser: CLV. **LD72015. $29.98.**
George Stevens, USA, 1941, 125 mins.

A Place in the Sun
Based on Theodore Dreiser's *An American Tragedy*, and featuring strong performances from Montgomery Clift, Elizabeth Taylor and Shelley Winters. Monty Clift is the poor boy driven by the lure of wealth, with his success threatened by complications from his simultaneous affairs with factory girl Shelley Winters and socialite Liz Taylor.
VHS: S04663. $19.95.
George Stevens, USA, 1951, 122 mins

Shane
George Stevens' legendary rendition of the archetypal Western myth earned six Academy nominations. Alan Ladd stars as the retired gunfighter who comes to the aid of a frontier family and wins the adoration of the family's impressionable young son. With Jack Palance, Van Heflin and Jean Arthur.
VHS: S03316. $14.95.
Laser: LD75344. $29.98.
George Stevens, USA, 1953, 118 mins.

Swing Time
Fred Astaire and Ginger Rogers star in this nostalgic film about the high life in Manhattan during the Twenties, when fortunes were made and lost in an evening at the roulette tables. Music by Jerome Kern, lyrics by Dorothy Fields.
Laser: CAV. **LD70468. $74.95.**
Laser: CLV. **LD70469. $39.95.**
George Stevens, USA, 1936, 103 mins.

Talk of the Town
A wonderful comedy with an intelligent cast, including Jean Arthur, Cary Grant and Ronald Colman. Grant is a fugitive hiding out with unsuspecting professor Colman and landlady Arthur, who tries to convince the legal-minded Colman that there's a human side to all laws.
VHS: S03297. $19.95.
Laser: CLV, chapter stops. **LD74997. $39.95.**
George Stevens, USA, 1942, 118 mins.

Woman of the Year
Tracy and Hepburn's first film together; Hepburn is the political journalist much too serious about her work, Tracy the sports reporter who teaches her how to enjoy life. Simply terrific.
VHS: S04741. $19.98.
Laser: LD70710. $34.98.
DVD: DV60066. $24.98.
George Stevens, USA, 1942, 118 mins.

WILLIAM WYLER

Ben-Hur
Winner of 11 Oscars, including Charlton Heston for Best Actor, an epic spectacle concerning a prince of Judea who incurs the wrath of the Roman Empire. The famous chariot race required a year of film preparation and lasts nearly 20 minutes. VHS letterboxed.
VHS: S02517. $29.98.
Laser: LD70524. $49.98.
William Wyler, USA, 1959, 270 mins.

Ben-Hur (35th Anniversary Edition)
Celebrating the timelessness of this multi-academy award-winning film, this new Deluxe Collector's Edition of the classic starring Charlton Heston also includes the documentary *Ben Hur: The Making of an Epic*, narrated by Christopher Plummer, and the original theatrical trailer. VHS letterboxed.
Laser: 5-disc CAV boxed set. **LD72371. $99.98.**
William Wyler, 1959, USA, 204 mins.

The Best Years of Our Lives
This epic film focuses on the troubles of three World War II servicemen as they try to pick up the threads of their lives after returning home to the States. An insightful portrait of small-town American life and its values. Starring Myrna Loy, Frederic March, Dana Andrews, Virginia Mayo and Teresa Wright. *The Best Years of Our Lives* was named one of the 50 greatest motion pictures of all time by the members of The American Film Institute. Digitally remastered.
VHS: S03117. $19.98.
William Wyler, USA, 1946, 170 mins.

Big Country
Gregory Peck is the retired sea captain who comes to marry Carroll Baker, but is instead thrown into a battle against Burl Ives and his sons over water rights. Ives won an Oscar as the patriarch; Charlton Heston delivers a strong performance as the ranch foreman. A brilliant musical score by Jerome Moross. Letterboxed.
VHS: S11554. $24.98.
Laser: LD75030. $79.99.
William Wyler, USA, 1958, 166 mins.

Carrie
Based on Theodore Dreiser's famous satirical novel *Sister Carrie*, Laurence Olivier and Jennifer Jones star in this is story of a middle-aged man who risks his marriage and wealth for the love of young beauty. "Graced by one of Olivier's finest screen performances" (Pauline Kael).
VHS: S13791. $19.95.
William Wyler, USA, 1952, 118 mins.

The Children's Hour
Lillian Hellman's classic play about two teachers who are accused of lesbianism by a student receives powerful treatment from Shirley MacLaine, Audrey Hepburn and James Garner.
VHS: S13345. $19.98.
Laser: LD72169. $34.98.
William Wyler, USA, 1961, 107 mins.

Collector
An adaptation of the John Fowles novel by veteran director Wyler (*Jezebel, Dodsworth*) is an effective psychological thriller about a plan by a psychotic Terence Stamp to kidnap and keep an art student, played by Samantha Eggar.
VHS: S01697. $59.95.
William Wyler, USA, 1965, 119 mins.

Come and Get It
Frances Farmer is cast as a beautiful woman desired by both a father and his son in this drama set in the timber country of the Northwest. Walter Brennan made his mark in this film which was based on a novel by Edna Ferber. William Wyler took over direction from Howard Hawks.
VHS: S01537. $19.98.
William Wyler/Howard Hawks, USA, 1936, 99 mins.

Dead End
Humphrey Bogart is the young man who has grown up knowing only one kind of law—his own. Sylvia Sidney is the sensitive young woman who falls for touchy but tender Joel McCrea in this tense film, set on New York's turbulent Lower East Side.
VHS: S03119. $19.95.
William Wyler, USA, 1937, 92 mins.

Desperate Hours
Inspired by actual events, based on Joseph Hayes' novel and the Broadway play, an all-star cast including Humphrey Bogart, Frederic March, Arthur Kennedy, Martha Scott and Gig Young star in this tour-de-force. Bogart is the escaped con who has nothing to lose. March is a suburban Everyman who has everything to lose—his family is held hostage by Bogart. As *The Desperate Hours* tick by, the two men square off in a battle of wills and cunning that tightens into a fear-drenched finale.
VHS: S09566. $14.95.
William Wyler, USA, 1955, 112 mins.

Dodsworth
Sam Dodsworth, a recently retired industrialist, sets off to Europe with his young wife, Fran. In Paris, Fran's yearning for romance leads her into an open flirtation with an attractive gentleman. Tormented by his wife's actions, Dodsworth begins a search for the happiness which seems to have eluded him. With Walter Huston, Mary Astor, Ruth Chatterton and David Niven. Digitally remastered.
VHS: S00355. $19.98.
William Wyler, USA, 1936, 101 mins.

Funny Girl
Barbra Streisand made her Oscar-winning film debut in this epic screen biography of entertainer Fanny Brice. She sings, dances and roller-skates her way to the top of the show business ladder. There is no doubt about it, a star is born, so please don't rain on her parade. With Omar Sharif as gambler and first husband Nicky Arnstein, Anne Francis, Kay Medford, and Walter Pidgeon as Flo Ziegfeld.
VHS: S10976. $19.95.
William Wyler, USA, 1968, 155 mins.

The Heiress
William Wyler directed Olivia de Havilland and an all-star cast in this Oscar-winning classic. De Havilland is the homely, awkward girl who falls in love with the dashing fortune hunter. With brilliant performances by Montgomery Clift and Ralph Richardson, musical score by Aaron Copeland. Based on *Washington Square* by Henry James.
VHS: S03533. $14.95.
William Wyler, USA, 1949, 115 mins.

How to Steal a Million
Audrey Hepburn and Peter O'Toole look great in this comedy shot, in part, on location in Paris. Hepburn's dad is a forger of fine art and he is about to be unmasked by experts. To prevent this, Hepburn schemes to steal one of dad's phony works with O'Toole's help so that it will never be examined. Eli Wallach and Charles Boyer co-star.
VHS: S26406. $19.98.
William Wyler, USA, 1966, 127 mins.

Jezebel
Bette Davis won an Oscar for her performance as the tempestuous Southern belle who manipulates the men in her life. Her engagement to Henry Fonda is broken off due to her insensitivity, and when he returns married, her ruthless jealousy explodes.
VHS: S00654. $19.95.
Laser: LD70604. $34.98.
DVD: DV60062. $24.98.
William Wyler, USA, 1938, 105 mins.

The Letter
A masterpiece of suspense and sexual repression, largely due to the muted tension between Bette Davis and James Stephenson. When a woman is accused of murder, her husband and lawyer try to get her off on a self-defense plea, but was it really? Based on the novel by W. Somerset Maugham. Excellent film noir.
VHS: S01757. $19.95.
William Wyler, USA, 1940, 95 mins.

Little Foxes
Lillian Hellman's famous play about the intrigues of a Southern family features Bette Davis at her best as Regina, the bitchy but totally wonderful vixen presiding over the family's double-dealings. With Teresa Wright and Dan Duryea.
VHS: S03125. $19.98.
DVD: DV60318. $24.95.
William Wyler, USA, 1941, 116 mins.

The Love Trap

Laura La Plante stars in this light-hearted farce about a chorus girl determined to marry the nephew of a powerful and respected judge. Naturally, the entire family is against the young couple, but love will find a way, particularly when there is a good deal of money at stake. Neil Hamilton and Robert Ellis are featured.
VHS: S26770. $24.95.
William Wyler, USA, 1929, 71 mins.

Memphis Belle

World War II documentary produced by the U.S. War Department supervised by Lt. Col. William Wyler, director of *Dodsworth* and *Wuthering Heights*.
VHS: S02593. $19.95.
Laser: LD70628. $29.95.
William Wyler, USA, 1944

Mrs. Miniver

This winner of seven Oscars in 1942 was an effective morale boost for all the folks on the home front. Greer Garson and Walter Pidgeon head a middle-class English family under siege and worried about their son in the RAF. Garson later married the actor who played her son, Richard Ney. With Dame May Whitty, Reginald Owen and Teresa Wright.
VHS: S08341. $19.95.
William Wyler, USA, 1942, 134 mins.

Roman Holiday

Stylish production starring Gregory Peck and Audrey Hepburn about a rebellious princess who wishes to discover living on her own. With Eddie Albert as Peck's pal.
VHS: S01763. $19.95.
Laser: LD75249. $44.95.
William Wyler, USA, 1953, 118 mins.

These Three

Boarding school brat Bonita Granville spreads lies about officials Miriam Hopkins, Merle Oberon and Joel McCrea—the man they both love. Excellent acting and superb direction highlight this Lillian Hellman adaptation of her play *The Children's Hour*, re-made, by that name, by Wyler 25 years later.
VHS: S03128. $19.98.
William Wyler, USA, 1936, 93 mins.

Thunderbolt

William Wyler supervised the production. James Stewart introduces and Lloyd Bridges narrates the activities of the 57th fighter group during "Operation Strangle," which destroyed vital supply routes deep behind German lines. Color.
VHS: S03350. $39.95.
Laser: LD70169. $34.98.
William Wyler, USA, 1945, 45 mins.

The Westerner

Gary Cooper is a wandering saddle bum caught up in a range war between homesteaders and cattlemen who squares off with the legendary Judge Roy Bean (Walter Brennan) in West Texas of the 1880's. When the film was released in 1940 critics praised its realistic touches, especially the way it showed gunfighters stopping to reload their pistols in the middle of shootouts—something other westerns had never shown before.
Digitally remastered.
VHS: S03129. $19.98.
William Wyler, USA, 1940, 100 mins.

Wuthering Heights

A romantic film classic. Set against the desolation of the English moors, Laurence Olivier and Merle Oberon portray the tragic lovers, Heathcliff and Cathy. After Cathy's marriage to the wealthy Edgar (David Niven), Heathcliff bides his time before his savage retaliation upon the woman he loves. Academy Award-winning black & white cinematography by the legendary Gregg Toland. This digitally remastered video version includes the original theatrical trailer.
VHS: S01484. $19.98.
William Wyler, USA, 1939, 104 mins.

ORSON WELLES

Chimes at Midnight/Falstaff

The final masterpiece from Orson Welles, an austere, haunting work that reaches the greatness of *Kane, Ambersons* and *Touch of Evil*. Based on his 1938 Theater Guild Production, Welles has meticulously assembled the Falstaff parts from Shakespeare's history plays (including *Merry Wives of Windsor*) and thematically linked them with Holinshed's *Chronicles* to explore the full arc of Falstaff's relationship with Prince Hal—moving from grand affection to bitter disillusionment. Featuring the extraordinary montage sequence at the Battle of Shrewsbury. With Welles, John Gielgud and Ralph Richardson supplying Holinshed's narration.
VHS: S02950. $79.95.
Orson Welles, Italy/USA, 1967, 115 mins.

Citizen Kane (50th Anniversary Edition)

One of the greatest films ever made is now available in a version painstakingly restored to its original brilliance in honor of the film's 50th anniversary. With Orson Welles, Dorothy Comingore, Everett Sloane, Paul Stewart. Cinematography by Gregg Toland, script by Welles and Herman Mankiewicz.
Laser: CAV. **LD70745. $124.95.**
Laser: CLV. **LD70746. $39.95.**
Orson Welles, USA, 1941, 119 mins.

Citizen Kane

Turner Classic Movies' collector's edition of one of the greatest films includes highlights about the film, its stars and director Orson Welles; exclusive star interviews; "making of" documentary; original trailer and lobby card art; collectible inserts; and an introduction by Oscar historian, film critic and TCM host Robert Osborne. Original black-and-white format. With Dorothy Comingore, Everett Sloane and Paul Stewart, cinematography by Gregg Toland, and a script by Welles and Herman J. Mankiewicz.
VHS: S14599. $19.98.
Laser: CLV. **LD70356. $39.95.**
Orson Welles, USA, 1941, 119 mins.

F for Fake

Orson Welles's "magnificent confidence game, a trick, a seduction and a magic act: a buoyant film about forgery and fakery which, beneath our astonished gaze, explodes into wonderment and guilt" (Michael Wilmington, *Chicago Tribune*). Welles's theme of forgery in art focuses on the forger, Elmyr de Hory, as well as Clifford Irving, de Hory's biographer, Howard Hughes, Pablo Picasso and Welles himself. "Alternately superficial and profound, hollow and moving, simple and complex, this film also enlists the services of Oja Kodar, Welles's principal collaborator after the late 60s, as actor, erotic spectacle and co-writer" (Jonathan Rosenbaum, *Chicago Reader*).
VHS: S24864. $39.95.
Laser: Digital transfer. **LD75024. $49.95.**
Orson Welles/Francois Reichenbach, USA/France/Iran/Germany, 1976, 125 mins.

A Film Genius: Orson Welles Gift Pack

Includes three of Welles' greatest films: *Citizen Kane, Journey into Fear* and *The Magnificent Ambersons*. Also includes an 8" x 10" glossy still from each movie.
VHS: S14600. $59.98.

The Immortal Story

Orson Welles' baroque adaptation of Isak Dinesen's short story about a wealthy merchant (Welles) who hires a sailor to seduce his wife. With his first color film, Welles drew on a painterly mise-en-scene and gothic, deep focus compositions to evoke the characters' haunted psychological states. Music by Erik Satie. With Jeanne Moreau, Norman Eshley and Roger Coggio.
VHS: S18955. $29.95.
Orson Welles, USA, 1968, 63 mins.

It's All True

Orson Welles went to Brazil, where he hoped to make a film that captured the essence of that beautiful country. Because of disagreements with the studio over the amount of money he spent it was never completed. Now, using footage he shot and combining interviews with actual crew members, this unfinished work and its tale of lost opportunity can at last be told.
VHS: S21350. $92.98.
Orson Welles/Richard Wilson/Myron Meisel/Bill Krohn, USA, 1993, 85 mins.

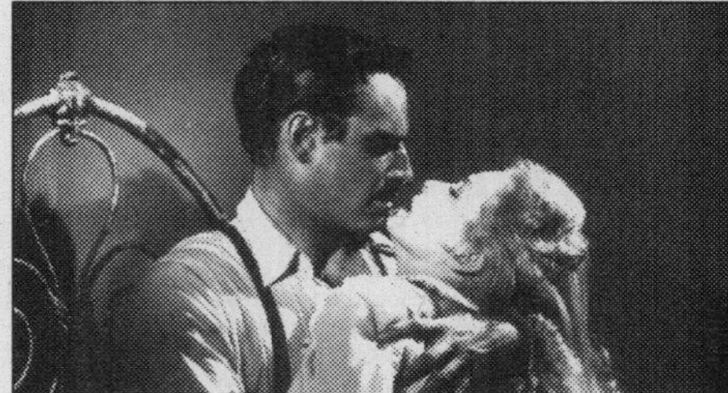

Journey into Fear

Orson Welles and the Mercury Theatre of the Air Players tackle foreign intrigue in this WWII spy drama set in Turkey. Joseph Cotten is the naive American targeted for death who is offered assistance by Turkish policeman Welles. With Agnes Moorehead, Ruth Warrick and Everett Sloane. Welles co-directed (with Norman Foster) and his scenes stand out. B&W.
Laser: LD76966. $24.99.
Orson Welles, USA, 1942, 68 mins.

Lady from Shanghai

Welles' great thriller stars Rita Hayworth as the millionairess in a web of intrigue which includes Welles being accused of murder, and concludes in the dazzling climax played out in a hall of mirrors.
VHS: S00715. $19.95.
Orson Welles, USA, 1948, 87 mins.

Macbeth

Orson Welles' *Macbeth* was shot in 23 days on an extremely low budget, yet is memorable for its rhythm, murky atmosphere of evil, and imaginative visualizations.
VHS: S00788. $19.95.
Orson Welles, USA, 1948, 89 mins.

Magnificent Ambersons

Produced, written and directed by Orson Welles, the follow-up film to *Citizen Kane*, and a work of depth and genius. Welles traces the details of a midwestern family's tragedy. From the novel by Booth Tarkington. With Tim Holt, Anne Baxter, Agnes Moorehead.
VHS: S00804. $19.95.
Laser: LD70417. $99.95.
Orson Welles, USA, 1942, 88 mins.

Mr. Arkadin (Confidential Report)

Orson Welles' mythical feature about a powerful financier who pays to reconstruct his forgotten past. Claiming to have amnesia, millionaire Arkadin (Welles) hires would-be blackmailer Guy Van Stratten to investigate his past. When Van Stratten's worldwide search reveals the sordid source of Arkadin's wealth, witnesses are ruthlessly murdered. With Robert Arden and Michael Redgrave. "A playfully eccentric display of egocentrism and a magician's perverse revelation of its own trickery…irresistible." This is the longer, 99-minute European release version, presented in a newly mastered print.
VHS: S33020. $29.95.
Laser: LD70125. $39.95.
Orson Welles, Spain/Switzerland, 1955, 99 mins.

Orson Welles

Welles was still alive and trying to get his stalled career going again when this 1967 documentary was produced. It traces his life and creativity, with emphasis on his high ideals, the literary influences on his enthusiasms, radio productions like *War of the Worlds*, his years with the Work Projects Administration and John Houseman, experiments for the theater with colleagues like Peter Brook, and his budget struggles to go his own way in an entertainment business grown steadily more wary of his unconventional methods. With a wealth of photographs, and clips from some of his less well-known films, including *A Man for All Seasons, Falstaff, The Trial* and *Touch of Evil*. 60 mins.
VHS: S31573. $59.95.

Orson Welles' Ghost Story

While on break from the shooting of *Othello*, Orson Welles starred in this short film. The plot focuses on a young man haunted by two mysterious women whom he drives home one night. Peter Bogdanovich introduces this newly restored version.
VHS: S22183. $19.98.

Othello

Orson Welles' 1952 film is one of the most important of his career. Shot over four years and made on the run, the images literally composed inside the director's head, Welles' virtuoso *Othello* unfolds in flashbacks, detailing the Moor's shifting relationships with Iago (Michael MacLiammoir) and his beautiful young wife, Desdemona (Suzanne Cloutier). With Robert Coote, Fay Compton and Michael Laurence. Art direction by Alexander Trauner. The film has undergone a significant restoration, cleaning up the images and digitally re-recording the soundtrack in stereo, with members of the Chicago Symphony Orchestra and Lyric Opera of Chicago. The voices were electronically isolated to improve the fidelity of the soundtrack.
VHS: Out of print. For rental only.
Laser: LD72284. $99.95.
Orson Welles, Italy/France/USA, 1952, 93 mins.

Scene of the Crime

Orson Welles hosts a trio of intricate and involving mysteries of murder and assorted crimes against humanity. Welles presents a rogue's gallery of celebrity suspects and then will ask the viewer to make their best case before revealing the culprit and the modus operandi. Culled from the television show, at least there shouldn't be any commercials. USA, 1984-85, 74 mins.
VHS: S10063. $19.98.

The Stranger

Orson Welles followed his production of *Citizen Kane* and *Magnificent Ambersons* with this thriller. Welles stars as an escaped Nazi war criminal, Loretta Young is his unsuspecting wife, and Edward G. Robinson is the War Crimes inspector who tracks him down.
VHS: S01262. $19.95.
Laser: LD76965. $24.99.
Orson Welles, USA, 1946, 95 mins.

Touch of Evil

A masterpiece! This is a complete, restored version. Welles plays a sleazy corrupt police official in a squalid town on the Mexican border, matching wits with Charlton Heston. With Janet Leigh, Marlene Dietrich and Zsa Zsa Gabor.
VHS: S01990. $19.98.
Laser: LD70091. $34.98.
Orson Welles, USA, 1958, 108 mins.

The Trial

A newly mastered version of Orson Welles' brilliant film (the one he considered his best), a masterful adaptation of Franz Kafka's novel. With Jeanne Moreau, Anthony Perkins, Romy Schneider, Orson Welles. Original English-language version.
VHS: S08696. $39.95.
Laser: Letterboxed. **LD76192. $69.95.**
Orson Welles, France, 1963, 118 mins.

Working with Orson Welles

A documentary of fascinating insights into the work of Orson Welles as captured by his longtime colleague and cinematographer Gary Graver. As Welles dreams of completing *The Other Side of the Wind*, Graver charts the frustration of this dream. Famous directors, actors, producers and friends of Welles, including Peter Bogdanovich, Stacy Keach and John Huston, describe both Welles and his work. With many rare, never-before-seen clips from Welles' unfinished work.
VHS: S26704. $29.95.
Laser: LD76969. $24.99.
Gary Graver, USA, 1994, 97 mins.

ERNST LUBITSCH

Angel

Lady Maria Barker (Marlene Dietrich) has the perfect life: a famous husband (Herbert Marshall), an English manor, and endless travel. But her husband's inattention forces her into a brief affair with a British stranger in Paris (Melvyn Douglas), who knows her only as *Angel*.
VHS: S22184. $14.98.
Ernst Lubitsch, USA, 1937, 91 mins.

Bluebeard' s Eighth Wife

Claudette Colbert is the daughter of a poor French aristocrat who attracts a young millionaire (Gary Cooper) on the French Riviera. The attraction is so obvious that they set a date before Colbert finds out that her fiance has been married seven times before. She decides to teach him a lesson in a series of comic situations that often run counter to her intentions. David Niven is also featured in this light-hearted comic romp.
VHS: S24027. $14.98.
Ernst Lubitsch, USA, 1938, 101 mins.

The Eyes of the Mummy

A very rare, early film by Ernst Lubitsch which integrates elements of the grotesque with a vast, historic theme. An Egyptian religious fanatic seeks revenge on a dancing girl who has deserted him. With Pola Negri and Emil Jannings. German with English intertitles.
VHS: S31267. $24.95.
Ernst Lubitsch, Germany, 1918, 60 mins.

Gypsy Blood

Ernst Lubitsch's first important film, and the second time he directed Pola Negri, who played a role that made her an international star. Notable for its beautiful sets, the story is tentatively based on Bizet's opera *Carmen*, though, as Georges Sadoul points out, it is closer to the original novella by Prosper Merrimee. Silent with music track. Best copy available.
VHS: S02095. $44.95.
Ernst Lubitsch, Germany, 1918, 104 mins.

Heaven Can Wait

Ernst Lubitsch at his best in this wonderful comedy-fantasy, with Don Ameche as the earthly sinner trying to get admitted to Hell by convincing the Devil that his busy love life has earned him damnation. Gene Tierney is beautiful, and the sparks fly. With Charles Coburn, Marjorie Main.
VHS: S11564. $19.98.
Ernst Lubitsch, USA, 1943, 112 mins

Lady Windermere's Fan

Oscar Wilde's comedy of manners, directed by a filmmaker who was a natural to translate its precise nuances to the screen. The scandalous Mrs. Erlynne returns to save her daughter from disgrace in London and sacrifices her own reputation by claiming the fan left by Lady Windermere in the apartment of Lord Darlington. With Ronald Colman, May McAvoy. Silent, B&W, music track.
VHS: S02087. $29.95.
Ernst Lubitsch, USA, 1925, 85 mins.

The Lubitsch Touch

This extraordinary collection highlights six films never before released on home video, from Lubitsch's most productive period: the opera-esque *The Love Parade* (1929), with Maurice Chevalier and Jeanette McDonald; *Monte Carlo* (1930), featuring the song "Beyond the Blue Horizon"; *The Smiling Lieutenant* (1931); *One Hour with You* (1932), starring Chevalier, MacDonald and Charles Ruggles; Lubitsch's signature work, the delicately balanced *Trouble in Paradise* (1932); *Design for Living* (1933), based on the Noel Coward play, starring Fredric March and Gary Cooper; and a Lubitsch-directed 10-minute segment from *If I Had a Million* (1932), featuring Charles Laughton.
Laser: LD76370. $189.99.
Ernst Lubitsch, USA, 1929-1933, 550 mins.

Marriage Circle

A delightful continental comedy with the visual wit that became known as the Lubitsch touch. Marie Prevost loves nothing more than to entice the husbands of others, while her husband, Adolphe Menjou, is left to his own devices. Silent.
VHS: S01942. $29.95.
Ernst Lubitsch, USA, 1924, 104 mins.

The Merry Widow

Maurice Chevalier must woo Jeanette MacDonald on the orders of the King of Marshovia in this MGM musical directed by Ernst Lubitsch. Based on the operetta by Franz Lehar, a wealthy woman leaves her small country to join the chorus line in Paris. A charming Prince must bring her back to save the economy. With Edward Everett Horton, Una Merkel and Akim Tamiroff.
VHS: S09868. $19.98.
Ernst Lubitsch, USA, 1934, 99 mins.

Meyer aus Berlin

Lubitsch starred in and directed this German comedy, in which he played a character named Meyer. It was believed to be lost but was rediscovered in the Netherlands' film archives. With Ethel Orff, Heinz Landsmann and Trude Troll. Silent with German and Swedish intertitles, music track.
VHS: S33054. $24.95.
Ernst Lubitsch, Germany, 1919, 58 mins.

Ninotchka

"Garbo laughs!"—and indeed, she does, in her first romantic comedy as the dour Soviet official who discovers the pleasures of Paris (and Melvyn Douglas) and must choose between romance and duty. Lubitsch at his best.
VHS: S00935. $19.98.
Ernst Lubitsch, USA, 1939, 108 mins.

One Arabian Night

Elaborate blend of romance, melodrama and comedy that established the reputation of director Lubitsch as well as the star actress Pola Negri, who plays an exotic dancer. Lubitsch himself appears in the film as a hunchback performer in the dancer's troupe. Silent.
VHS: S02169. $29.95.
Ernst Lubitsch, Germany, 1920, 85 mins.

Passion

Pola Negri stars as a young girl who forsakes a life with a man who loves her in order to enter high society, eventually becoming the mistress of King Louis. Silent with music soundtrack.
VHS: S02813. $39.95.
Ernst Lubitsch, USA, 1919, 133 mins.

The Shop Around the Corner

James Stewart and Margaret Sullavan are co-workers in a Budapest notions shop run by Frank Morgan. The employees are actively feuding, not realizing that each is the other's romantic pen-pal. A charming period comedy, later remade as *In the Good Old Summertime*.
VHS: S04977. $19.98.
Laser: LD70194. $34.98.
Ernst Lubitsch, USA, 1940, 97 mins.

So This Is Paris

A rare film by Ernst Lubitsch, a delightful tale of marital infidelity, starring Monte Blue, Myrna Roy, Ruth Miller. Silent with musical score.
VHS: S06445. $29.95.
Ernst Lubitsch, USA, 1926, 68 mins.

The Student Prince in Old Heidelberg

An extremely rare 1927 film by Ernst Lubitsch stars Ramon Novarro and Norma Shearer in this melodrama of the prince who woos a bar girl. Silent with music track.
VHS: S13400. $29.98.
Ernst Lubitsch, USA, 1927, 102 mins.

That Uncertain Feeling

Elegant, sophisticated comedy from a master, the director of *Ninotchka*. Starring Merle Oberon and Melvyn Douglas as a couple whose marriage has lost its excitement. Oberon's attempts to reawaken the attentions of Douglas are inspired.
VHS: S01316. $29.95.
Ernst Lubitsch, USA, 1941, 83 mins.

To Be or Not to Be

In what might be, in the hands of someone other than Ernest Lubitsch, a contradiction of terms—a witty, delightfully satirical comedy set in Nazi-occupied Warsaw—Jack Benny leads a troupe of ham actors in outsmarting the Gestapo and reducing them to ridiculous rubble. Benny gives an animated, beautifully-paced performance and Carole Lombard stars as his wife in her last screen performance.
VHS: S01350. $19.98.
Ernst Lubitsch, USA, 1942, 102 mins.

BILLY WILDER

The Apartment

Billy Wilder's great film of tears and laughter as Jack Lemmon and Shirley MacLaine wheel and deal over a New York apartment in a comedy of morality. Winner of five Oscars and worth at least 20 more. VHS letterboxed.
VHS: S05880. $19.95.
Laser: LD70506. $39.98.
Billy Wilder, USA, 1960, 125 mins.

Avanti!

Jack Lemmon stars in this romantic comedy about an American businessman who goes to Italy for a very special reason, to collect the body of his father. Oddly enough, murder and foul play also play a role in this well-crafted film, proving that love and justice are indeed blind.
VHS: S21022. $19.98.
Laser: LD76265. $39.99.
Billy Wilder, USA, 1972, 144 mins.

Buddy Buddy

Walter Matthau and Jack Lemmon have been famous as the ultimate pair of grumpy old men ever since *The Odd Couple*. Together they star in this black comedy about a hit man who runs into an unshakable stranger. Paula Prentiss and Klaus Kinski are also featured.
VHS: S21024. $19.98.
Billy Wilder, USA, 1982, 98 mins.

Double Indemnity

A great Billy Wilder film in which "every turn and twist is exactly calculated and achieves its effect with the simplest of means; this shrewd, smooth, tawdry thriller is one of the high points of 40s films" (Kael). Raymond Chandler collaborated on the screenplay in adapting James Cain's story. Barbara Stanwyck is the platinum blonde, Fred MacMurray the insurance salesman she ensnares in a plot to kill her businessman-husband and collect on the double-indemnity clause in his policy.
VHS: S02940. $19.95.
Laser: LD70024. $34.98.
Billy Wilder, USA, 1944, 107 mins.

The Emperor Waltz

In this lavish musical, Bing Crosby plays a salesman of record players to the royalty of the Austro-Hungarian empire. Vienna is magically recreated as only Hollywood could imagine it, and there is plenty of froth to go around.
VHS: S21202. $14.98.
Billy Wilder, USA, 1948, 106 mins.

Fedora

Billy Wilder's German-financed production, based on Thomas Tryon's short story about a charismatic producer who tries to lure an actress out of seclusion to star in the film he's preparing. With William Holden, Martha Keller, Henry Fonda and Jose Ferrer.
Laser: LD71184. $34.98.
Billy Wilder, Germany, 1978, 114 mins.

Five Graves to Cairo

Billy Wilder directed and Charles Bracket wrote this suspense-filled, often humorous, wartime thriller that stars Franchot Tone, Anne Baxter and Akim Tamiroff.
VHS: S31345. $14.98.
Billy Wilder, USA, 1943, 97 mins.

Fortune Cookie

When TV cameraman Jack Lemmon is knocked down at a football game, his shyster lawyer advises him to get all he can out of the fortuitous injury. Walter Matthau won an Oscar for his performance as the conniving legal counsel. With Ron Rich, Cliff Osmond, Judi West and Lurene Tuttle. Biting script by A.L. Diamond and the director. Letterboxed.
VHS: S13214. $19.98.
Billy Wilder, USA, 1966, 125 mins.

Irma La Douce

When French policeman Jack Lemmon becomes involved with street walker Shirley MacLaine, he finds his days on the beat coming to an end. The Broadway musical set in Paris is played as a straight comedy by Billy Wilder. Cast includes Lou Jacobi, Herschel Bernardi, Joan Shawlee, Hope Holiday and Bill Bixby. VHS letterboxed.
VHS: S02536. $19.98.
Laser: LD71062. $49.95.
Billy Wilder, USA, 1963, 142 mins.

Kiss Me, Stupid

Dean Martin stars as a famous singer who is duped into spending the night in a small town while on his way from Las Vegas to Hollywood by a couple of local hopefuls who want to sell him some of their songs. With Kim Novak.
VHS: S15245. $19.98.
Laser: LD71161. $39.98.
Billy Wilder, USA, 1964, 126 mins.

The Lost Weekend
Billy Wilder's classic drama stars Ray Milland in a sobering study of alcoholism. The winner of Oscars for Best Picture, Director, Actor and Screenplay in 1945. Cast includes Frank Faylen, Howard da Silva, Jane Wyman and Philip Terry. The D.T.'s are in glorious black and white.
VHS: S06869. $19.95.
Billy Wilder, USA, 1945, 100 mins.

Love in the Afternoon
A sophisticated romantic farce from Billy Wilder featuring Audrey Hepburn and Gary Cooper as an American playboy in Paris. Filled with bubbling champagne and gypsy musicians, as well as Maurice Chevalier.
Laser: LD72254. $49.98.
Billy Wilder, USA, 1957, 130 mins.

Mauvaise Graine
Wilder's first directoral effort is a unique comedy with a dramatic twist. A young dandy is cut off from his wealthy family and turns to crime in order to get by in style. He falls in with a gang of car thieves, among whom is a young, beautiful female decoy. In French with English subtitles.
VHS: S29870. $39.95.
Billy Wilder/Alexandre Esway, France, 1933, 76 mins.

One, Two, Three
James Cagney plays a Coca Cola executive stationed in West Berlin who finds himself in trouble when his boss's daughter marries a fierce young Communist. It's rowdy entertainment co-scripted and directed by Billy Wilder.
VHS: S15254. $19.98.
Laser: LD75971. $39.99.
Billy Wilder, USA, 1961, 110 mins.

The Private Life of Sherlock Holmes
How much would we know if Sherlock Holmes' devoted sidekick, Dr. Watson, actually kept a detailed diary of his times with the most famous detective ever produced within the English literary tradition? In this humorous mystery involving German spies and even the Loch Ness Monster, you'll find out.
VHS: S21023. $19.98.
Billy Wilder, Great Britain, 1970, 125 mins.

Sabrina
Audrey Hepburn is the title character, a chauffeur's daughter who captivates the hearts of two wealthy brothers. Humphrey Bogart and William Holden compete for her company. Based on the play by Samuel Taylor. With Francis X. Bushman, Martha Hyer and John Williams. B&W.
VHS: S06991. $14.95.
Laser: LD76040. $39.98.
Billy Wilder, USA, 1954, 113 mins.

Seven Year Itch
A very funny examination of modern sexual mores with Marilyn Monroe and Tom Ewell. *Seven Year Itch* added to the Monroe Mystique with the image of Marilyn standing over the sidewalk grating to catch the breeze of passing subway trains. Screenplay co-written by Billy Wilder.
VHS: S01183. $19.98.
Billy Wilder, USA, 1955, 105 mins.

Some Like It Hot
Perhaps the funniest American film of the 1950's, Tony Curtis and Jack Lemmon play two second rate musicians on the run from the Chicago mob, who take to dressing in drag. Marilyn Monroe plays Sugar, the singer in an all-female band, and Joe E. Brown is an eccentric millionaire in love with Lemmon in drag.
VHS: S01836. $19.98.
Laser: CAV, 3 discs, Criterion. **LD70466. $124.95.**
Laser: Remastered, MGM. **LD71169. $39.98.**
Billy Wilder, USA, 1959, 122 mins.

Spirit of St. Louis
James Stewart stars as Charles Lindbergh, hero of the first trans-Atlantic flight. Based on Lindbergh's Pulitzer winning autobiography. Letterboxed.
VHS: S02606. $19.98.
Laser: LD76738. $39.98.
Billy Wilder, USA, 1957, 137 mins.

Stalag 17
World War II POW drama stars William Holden in an Oscar performance as a soldier suspected of being a spy when two prisoners are killed trying to escape. Otto Preminger also appears.
VHS: S02608. $19.95.
Billy Wilder, USA, 1953, 120 mins.

Sunset Boulevard
Gloria Swanson is the aging silent film queen and William Holden the struggling writer in this bizarre, dark and desperate portrait of Hollywood. Winner of three Academy Awards, and one of the greatest American films.
VHS: S01285. $14.95.
Laser: LD75268. $34.98.
Billy Wilder, USA, 1950, 110 mins.

Witness for the Prosecution
Agatha Christie's play about a sensational London murder trial features great performances from Charles Laughton as the aging lawyer, and from Tyrone Power, Marlene Dietrich and Elsa Lanchester.
VHS: S01767. $19.98.
Laser: LD71148. $34.98.
Billy Wilder, USA, 1957, 116 mins.

PRESTON STURGES

Beautiful Blonde from Bashful Bend
Betty Grable is the Wild West girl who's an excellent marksman. When her boyfriend starts flirting with another girl, she takes a shot at him, and accidentally hits a judge in the rear end. Absurd predicaments, a brisk script, and terrific performances from Grable, Cesar Romero and Rudy Vallee.
VHS: S09329. $19.98.
Laser: LD72216. $49.98.
Preston Sturges, USA, 1949, 76 mins.

Christmas in July
Zany, madcap film about a clerk in a coffee company who mistakenly believes he has won a $25,000 prize for a new company slogan and begins a shopping orgy. With Dick Powell and Ellen Drew.
VHS: S01753. $29.95.
Preston Sturges, USA, 1940, 67 mins.

The Great McGinty
A tour-de-force which won Sturges an Oscar, this no-kickbacks-barred fable of grafting politicians stars Brian Donlevy as a down-and-out bartender in South America who tells the story of his rise to political power as the two-fisted crony of party leader Akim Tamiroff. Sturges' sharp-eyed dialog explains American politics as "You got to pay somebody to protect you from human greed."
VHS: S05996. $29.95.
Laser: LD70036. $34.98.
Preston Sturges, USA, 1940, 82 mins.

Hail the Conquering Hero
A brilliant comedy, the story of an army reject who is accidentally treated as a hero when he returns to his small-town home. "The energy, the verbal intensity, the rush of Americana and the congestion seen periodically in *Miracle of Morgan's Creek* stagger the senses." With Eddie Bracken, William Demarest, Ella Raines.
VHS: S13020. $29.95.
Preston Sturges, USA, 1944, 101 mins.

The Lady Eve
Barbara Stanwyck is the cardshark, Henry Fonda the millionaire scientist who knows more about snakes than about women. "Neither performer has ever been funnier. The film, based on a story by Monckton Hoffe, is full of classic moments and classic lines; it represents the dizzy high point of Sturges' comedy writing."
VHS: S02941. $19.98.
Laser: LD70044. $34.98.
Preston Sturges, USA, 1941, 97 mins.

Miracle of Morgan's Creek
A great—and very, very funny—American film, with Preston Sturges at his best. Betty Hutton plays the small-town girl who becomes pregnant, only she can't remember who the father is, and whether or not they are married. With Eddie Bracken and William Demarest.
VHS: S04431. $34.95.
Preston Sturges, USA, 1944, 98 mins.

Palm Beach Story
"One of the giddiest and most chaotic of Preston Sturges' satiric orgies. The romantic problems of the leads (Joel McCrea and Claudette Colbert) get shoved aside by the secondary characters. Colbert, travelling by train, gets involved with a bunch of drunken millionaires who....stage an informal skeet shoot in the club car and demolish the glassware. Sturges' comic invention soars..." (Pauline Kael).
VHS: S02942. $29.95.
Laser: LD70065. $34.98.
Preston Sturges, USA, 1942, 88 mins.

Sin of Harold Diddlebock
Harold Lloyd is the former football star who has spent 20 years in the bookkeeping department of an ad agency. Having lived a boring life, he goes to the other extreme, and goes on a wild binge of drinking and gambling—a riotous comedy from Sturges.
VHS: S01206. $19.95.
Preston Sturges, USA, 1946, 90 mins.

Sullivan's Travels
Preston Sturges directed this classic tale of a Hollywood director who is fed up with creating fluff and decides to find out what is really happening in America. To research a "serious" film he disguises himself as a bum and goes on the road. Along the way, Joel McCrea as John L. Sullivan (the director) meets Veronica Lake, William Demarest, Porter Hall, Eric Blore and Franklin Pangborn. Still relevant and profound.
VHS: S08507. $29.95.
Laser: LD70084. $34.98.
Preston Sturges, USA, 1941, 91 mins.

Unfaithfully Yours
Rex Harrison is a famous conductor blessed with both a brilliant career and a young wife. This sidesplitting classic comedy by Sturges follows Rex's downfall when his jealous spying on his wife leads him to believe she's having an affair.
VHS: S05019. $59.98.
Preston Sturges, USA, 1948, 105 mins.

NICHOLAS RAY

55 Days at Peking
Nicholas Ray's superb account of the Boxer Rebellion in 1900s China and the fate of the British caught amidst the fighting. Starring Ava Gardner, Charlton Heston, Flora Robson, David Niven and Paul Lukas.
VHS: S05016. $29.95.
Laser: LD76008. $59.95.
Nicholas Ray, USA, 1963, 150 mins.

Flying Leathernecks
The commander of a fighter squadron (John Wayne) has to sacrifice his men unmercifully, an attitude for which he is hated by the more sensitive executive officer, Robert Ryan. The day comes when the tables are turned and Mr. Sensitivity finds himself wearing John Wayne's shoes. Director Ray breathes new life into this old formula and the air-battle montages are terrific. Produced by Howard Hughes. An updating of *The Dawn Patrol* to the World War II action in the Pacific.
Laser: LD76042. $39.98.
Nicholas Ray, USA, 1951, 102 mins.

In a Lonely Place
Humphrey Bogart stars as Dixon Steele, an alcoholic Hollywood screenwriter who is prone to violence and accused of murder. Gloria Grahame provides him with an alibi and additional headaches. A hard hitting, cynical drama directed by Nicholas Ray from the novel by Dorothy B. Hughes. With Frank Lovejoy, Martha Stewart and Jeff Donnell. B&W.
VHS: S09110. $69.95.
Nicholas Ray, USA, 1950, 91 mins.

Johnny Guitar
A camp and cult favorite, and "the most baroque thing I ever attempted" (Ray), *Johnny Guitar* stars Joan Crawford and Sterling Hayden in an explosive film about two women fighting to control a frontier boomtown that is along the line of a new railroad. This film promotes all kinds of arguing among its fans: is it a comment on McCarthyism, a gender-bending satire, or a western parody? It's a fun watch, whatever it is. With a wild Mercedes McCambridge. Theme song sung by Peggy Lee.
VHS: S04474. $14.95.
Nicholas Ray, USA, 1954, 110 mins.

King of Kings
An excellent production of the life of Jesus Christ from the director of *Rebel Without a Cause*. Intelligently told, with many lavishly filmed and deeply moving scenes, including the Sermon on the Mount. Featuring Jeffrey Hunter, Harry Guardino, Rip Torn and Robert Ryan; narration by Orson Welles.
VHS: S02727. $24.98.
Laser: LD70608. $39.97.
Nicholas Ray, USA, 1961, 170 mins.

Knock on Any Door

Humphrey Bogart is the street-bred-kid-turned-lawyer who's defending Nick Romano, accused of killing a cop, in this gritty depiction of life in the 1930's Chicago stockyard district.
VHS: S04392. $19.95.
Nicholas Ray, USA, 1949, 101 mins.

Party Girl

Glamour mixes with gangland violence in 1930s Chicago! Robert Taylor and the sultry Cyd Charisse star in this absorbing melodrama. Great dance numbers by Ms. Charisse and weird Nick Ray touches.
VHS: S15525. $19.98.
Laser: LD70148. $34.98.
Nicholas Ray, USA, 1958, 99 mins.

Rebel Without a Cause

James Dean stars in this quintessential story of teenage angst and rebellion. The generation gap movie of the 1950's, with a mixture of innocence, hope, despair and disillusionment set against the injustice and insensitivity of the adult world. One of the greats. With supporting parts by Natalie Wood, Sal Mineo, Nick Adams and Dennis Hopper as Goon. VHS letterboxed.
VHS: S01097. $19.98.
Laser: LD70663. $24.98.
Nicholas Ray, USA, 1955, 111 mins.

SAM PECKINPAH

The Ballad of Cable Hogue

A magnificent tribute to the West that was. It stars Jason Robards, Jr., as an ornery cuss who runs a waterhole for profit and learns a valuable lesson. When progress approaches, get out of the way. With Stella Stevens, David Warner and L.Q. Jones.
VHS: S04194. $14.95.
Laser: LD70514. $39.98.
Sam Peckinpah, USA, 1970, 122 mins.

Bring Me the Head of Alfredo Garcia

Warren Oates stars in this underrated film by Sam Peckinpah, as a seedy piano player south of the border who knows the location of all of the title character, who deflowered the daughter of a wealthy patron. Expect a high body count and excellent character studies from a cast that includes Gig Young, Robert Webber, Isela Vega, Emilio Fernandez and Kris Kristofferson as a mean biker.
VHS: S06057. $19.98.
Laser: Letterboxed. **LD76044. $39.98.**
Sam Peckinpah, USA, 1974, 112 mins.

The Deadly Companions

Sam Peckinpah's first film is a western which stars Brian Keith as a revenge-bent ex-soldier out to find the man who scalped him during the Civil War. Along the way he meets Maureen O'Hara and becomes involved in a cross country funeral procession. With Chill Wills, Strother Martin and Steve Cochran.
VHS: S10025. $19.95.
Sam Peckinpah, USA, 1961, 90 mins.

The Getaway

Steve McQueen and Ali MacGraw star in this classic, action-packed thriller. Together they tear up the screen, stealing and shooting their way through a plot of intrigue and love. The chemistry between these two stars cannot be beaten in this, the original version of *The Getaway*.
VHS: S04173. $19.98.
Laser: Widescreen. **LD74987. $39.98.**
DVD: DV60188. $24.98.
Sam Peckinpah, USA, 1972, 123 mins.

Junior Bonner

Steve McQueen has one of his best roles as the title character in this contemporary Western about an ex-rodeo star still making the effort. An entertaining character study from Sam Peckinpah without massive bloodshed. With Robert Preston, Ida Lupino, Joe Don Baker and Ben Johnson. Letterboxed.
VHS: S07154. $19.98.
Sam Peckinpah, USA, 1972, 101 mins.

Major Dundee

Peckinpah's lavish Western features Charlton Heston and Richard Harris leading a band of rebel cavalry soldiers in pursuit of Apaches into Mexico. Peckinpah disowned the film, having had it taken away from him by the studio and re-cut by others, but it's still interesting.
VHS: S01714. $19.95.
Laser: Letterboxed, chapter stops. **LD74906. $39.95.**
Sam Peckinpah, USA, 1965, 134 mins.

Pat Garrett and Billy the Kid

Romantic mythic version of the changing West, James Coburn stars as Pat Garrett, the former outlaw who has put on a badge to work for the cattlemen and hunt down Kris Kristofferson as Billy. Original score by Bob Dylan, featuring support from Jason Robards, Rita Coolidge and Dylan.
VHS: S02366. $19.95.
Laser: LD70183. $39.98.
Sam Peckinpah, USA, 1973, 106 mins.

Ride the High Country

Two aging gunfighters embark on their last adventure, transporting a shipment of gold. Breathtaking photography by Lucien Ballard; with great performances from Randolph Scott and Joel McCrea.
VHS: S04409. $19.98.
Sam Peckinpah, USA, 1962, 94 mins.

Straw Dogs

Banned in the UK to this day, Peckinpah's classic film flawlessly "expresses the belief that manhood requires rites of violence" (*Newsweek*). A film of startling suspense and involvement wherein a young couple's idyllic life is disrupted. David (Dustin Hoffman) is a quiet young American mathematician who moves with his English wife (Susan George) to a farmhouse outside a seemingly peaceful Cornish village. But their life is changed forever when the savagery and violence they sought to escape suddenly engulfs them. Includes footage that was cut from the original American theatrical release. VHS letterboxed.
VHS: S01266. $14.98.
Laser: LD71344. $49.98.
Sam Peckinpah, USA, 1971, 118 mins.

The Wild Bunch (Boxed Set)

William Holden, Robert Ryan and Ernest Borgnine head up the cast of this classic Western full of unremitting action. Outlaws past their prime go on one last desperate spree. Renowned for its dialog, quick pace and beautiful slow-motion violence sequences, this unforgettable film is now available uncut. Also includes behind-the-scenes footage and interviews with the director and cast, as well as the original theatrical trailer.
Laser: LD74973. $129.98.
Sam Peckinpah, USA, 1969, 145 mins.

The Wild Bunch (Director's Cut)

An authentic American western classic and Peckinpah's best film. An aging group of outlaws decides to pull off one last heist, led by William Holden, who plays Pike Bishop, leader of The Wild Bunch, with Robert Ryan as Deke Thornton, who once rode with Pike and now faces return to prison. *The Wild Bunch* broke new ground in the realistic depiction of violence on the screen. Letterboxed.
VHS: S01459. $39.99.
Laser: CLV. LD70706. $129.98.
DVD: DV60121. $24.98.
Sam Peckinpah, USA, 1969, 127 mins.

JOSEF VON STERNBERG

Anatahan

Anatahan is the last fiercely independent gesture of the cinema's most uncompromising visionary. Von Sternberg narrates this true story of 12 Japanese sailors who, isolated on a jungle island, continue to believe for years that the war is not yet over. When a girl appears on the island, *Anatahan* becomes the spectacle of man's dignity and honor crumbling before the assault of desire. With Akemi Negishi, Tadashi Suganuma. 95 mins.
VHS: S06859. $29.95.
Josef von Sternberg, USA, 1953, 95 mins.

Blonde Venus

Von Sternberg's only Marlene Dietrich film set in the U.S., Dietrich plays an ex-actress who returns to the stage to raise money to treat her husband's rare illness. She meets wealthy playboy Cary Grant, who falls in love with her, complicating her life. Dietrich is the center of three elaborately staged songs including appearing in a gorilla suit for a rendition of "Hot Voodoo."
VHS: S01987. $14.98.
Josef von Sternberg, USA, 1932, 89 mins.

The Blue Angel (English)

The English-language version of Von Sternberg's classic which differs not only in language, but also in some plot variations from the original German version. Marlene Dietrich stars as the cabaret singer Lola Lola, who brings men to her knees. English dialog.
VHS: S00154. $29.95.
Josef von Sternberg, Germany/USA, 1930, 90 mins.

The Blue Angel (German)

Josef von Sternberg's adaptation of Heinrich Mann's novel about a repressed school teacher (Emil Jannings) who is seduced and destroyed by his demonic obsession for nightclub singer Lola Lola (Marlene Dietrich). "The film is striking for its creative use of sound and its impressive recreation of the sleazy atmosphere of cabaret life" (David Cook, *The History of Narrative Film*). With Kurt Gerron, Hans Albers and Eduard von Winterstein. German with English subtitles.
VHS: S10872. $24.95.
Josef von Sternberg, Germany, 1930, 108 mins.

Crime and Punishment

Made in 28 days and shot on the cheap, Josef von Sternberg's adaptation of Dostoyevsky's novel is a psychological potboiler about Raskolnikov (Peter Lorre), a criminal tortured over his murder of a pawnbroker. He is relentlessly pursued by an inventive detective (Edward Arnold). Full of von Sternberg's trademark visual motifs. With Marian Marsh, Tala Birell and Elizabeth Risdon.
VHS: S18856. $19.95.
Laser: LD71885. $34.95.
Josef von Sternberg, USA, 1935, 88 mins.

Dishonored

In this variation of the *Mata Hari* tale, Marlene Dietrich plays a whore who is recruited by a covert spy ring; she's given the code name "X 27" and falls for a rogue agent (McLaglen). "*Dishonored* is to the cinema what Ravel's *La Valse* is to music—the Viennese Waltz disintegrating into the First World War" (Herman G. Weinberg).
VHS: S19078. $14.98.
Josef von Sternberg, USA, 1931, 91 mins.

Docks of New York

George Bancroft stars in a story of a stocker on the docks whose life is changed by saving a suicidal woman. Released at the same time as *The Jazz Singer*, it unfortunately fell to obscurity. It is now recognized as a great, expressive silent film and considered by some film historians to be the greatest film von Sternberg ever made. Silent.
VHS: S03441. $29.95.
Josef von Sternberg, USA, 1928, 60 mins.

I Kiss Your Hand, Madame

An extremely rare, early, silent Marlene Dietrich film in which Dietrich displays her talents as a comedienne. Dietrich portrays a Parisian divorcee who loses her divorce papers with comical results. With Harry Liedtke, Pierre de Guingand and Karl Huszar-Puffy. Silent with German intertitles, music track.
VHS: S33048. $24.95.
Josef von Sternberg, Germany, 1929, 74 mins.

Jet Pilot

A curious collaboration between von Sternberg and Howard Hughes which reworks the themes of *Hell's Angels*. John Wayne plays an American pilot who falls for a beautiful Russian aviator (Janet Leigh). Shot in 1950, the film wasn't finished until 1957. Chuck Yeager performed some of the stunt flying.
VHS: S17256. $14.98.
Josef von Sternberg, USA, 1957, 112 mins.

Josef von Sternberg

The director talks with film critic Stanley Kaufmann about his early career in German films before World War II, the effect of film on popular culture, reminiscences of famous actor Emil Jannings, and of the young Marlene Dietrich, whose career von Sternberg influenced. Clips from *The Blue Angel*. 1965, 28 mins.
VHS: S31574. $59.95.

Last Command

Emil Jannings stars as an immigrant Czarist general reduced to working as a Hollywood film extra. Von Sternberg cuts back to the general's time of grandeur to show how far the mighty can fall, and to criticize the status of Hollywood's power hungry moguls. Preston Sturges considered this the only perfect film ever made. Silent.
VHS: S03442. $29.95.
Josef von Sternberg, USA, 1928, 88 mins.

Macao

Three strangers arrive on the infamous island off the south coast of China and are caught up in a web of intrigue and deception. Jane Russell and Robert Mitchum ignite the plot with their famous, passionate rapport. A modern tale of paradise regained and the magical power of love.
VHS: S02870. $19.98.
Josef von Sternberg, USA, 1952, 80 mins.

Morocco

Marlene Dietrich's American debut. Dietrich is an exotic cabaret singer who's stranded in Morocco and slays every man in her path until she's torn between a wealthy French industrialist (Adolphe Menjou) and an attractive American French Foreign Legion soldier (Gary Cooper). "A cinematic pattern, brilliant, profuse, subtle and at almost every turn inventive" (Wilton A. Barrett). With Ullrich Haupt, Juliette Compton and Francis McDonald.
VHS: S02285. $14.98.
Josef von Sternberg, USA, 1930, 97 mins.

Scarlet Empress

Josef von Sternberg's flamboyant biography on the life and reign of Catherine of Russia. The film chronicles her rise from provincial origins to a cold-hearted killer who used her sexuality to seduce, conquer and attain power. "With grotesque statues and gargoyles, Byzantinesque icons and portraits, impossibly magnificent costumes and perhaps the most lavish production ever undertaken, *Scarlet Empress* apotheosized Dietrich as the ultimate symbol of sexual domination and degradation" (David Cook, *The History of Narrative Film*). With John Lodge, Sam Jaffe and Louise Dresser.

VHS: S19077. $14.98.

Josef von Sternberg, USA, 1934, 109 mins.

Shanghai Express

Josef von Sternberg's spellbinding melodrama about a group of passengers on an express train from Peking to Shanghai who are hijacked by a Chinese warlord. The prostitute "Chinese Lily" (Marlene Dietrich) and the British officer (Clive Brook) she once abandoned are thrown together. "From the hypnotic chiaroscuro photography, the incredibly exotic costumes and the lavish production design, von Sternberg created a mythological China where 'dead space' is virtually absent" (David Cook). With Warner Oland, Anna May Wong and Eugene Pallette.

VHS: S19074. $14.98.

Josef von Sternberg, USA, 1932, 84 mins.

The Shanghai Gesture

The Shanghai Gesture has been called "a delirious melodrama of decadence and sexual guilt that uses its Oriental motifs as a cypher for all that is unknown and unknowable. The battle is waged between a Western hypocrite (Walter Huston) and an Eastern pleasure- queen (Ona Munson); the erotic skirmishes occur between the self-willed but helpless heroine (Gene Tierney) and the apathetic object of her passion (Victor Mature, amazing 'Doctor of Nothing,' poet of Shanghai and Gomorrha'); the chief arena is a casino built like a circle of hell, where nothing is left to change. Subversive cinema at its most sublime" (Tony Rayns, *London Time Out*).

VHS: S06319. $29.95.

Josef von Sternberg, USA, 1941, 97 mins.

Underworld

A gangster is rescued from prison by his moll and his right-hand man. But he soon realizes that the two of them are in love, and he must make a tough decision as the police close in. This melodrama, co-written by Ben Hecht and Joseph von Sternberg, was one of the first to look at crime from the gangster's point of view. With George Bancroft and Evelyn Brent. Silent.

VHS: S15286. $49.95.

Josef von Sternberg, USA, 1927, 82 mins.

ERICH VON STROHEIM

Blind Husbands

Stroheim's first film as a director, set in the Alps. Stroheim plays a handsome officer having an affair with the wife of a boring doctor. The world was shocked when the film was first released. Silent, with English subtitles.

VHS: S00144. $29.95.

Erich von Stroheim, USA, 1919, 98 mins.

Foolish Wives

Publicized as the first film to cost a million dollars, praised for its extravagant visual design and condemned for its portrayal of a rogue count's unbridled and often peculiar sexual obsessions. Characteristic of von Stroheim's greatest work, this newly mastered (from a 35mm print) version has been restored to its full 107 minutes by the American Film Institute.

VHS: S02090. $29.95.

Erich von Stroheim, USA, 1922, 107 mins.

Greed

One of the wonders of film, this miracle of filmmaking, made by Erich von Stroheim against the most impossible of odds, stars Gibson Gowland as McTeague, a San Francisco dentist, who marries ZaSu Pitts, the daughter of German immigrants. When Trina (Pitts) becomes greedy, McTeague becomes a drunken tramp and ends up killing her. A powerful, powerful masterpiece. This tape includes a prologue by film historian Kevin Brownlow, who describes the controversy surrounding the original cuts made to the film by the studio.

VHS: S09281. $29.95.

Laser: LD70592. $39.98.

Erich von Stroheim, USA, 1924, 133 mins.

The Man You Loved to Hate

This exciting and historically important look at the bizarre career of Erich von Stroheim features interviews of his wife, associates, and friends. Excerpts from *Blind Husbands, Foolish Wives* and many others help to provide a detailed study of a creative genius whose perverse aberrations regarding women, art and finances made him a Hollywood outcast. NOTE: Certain film clips used in the television version of this film have been omitted due to copyright restrictions.

VHS: S14172. $29.95.

Patrick Montgomery, USA, 1979, 70 mins.

The Merry Widow

Von Stroheim's stylish, witty and grotesque adaptation of Franz Lehar's operetta of sadism and fetishism, in which a prince (John Gilbert) is ordered to woo a wealthy American widow (Mae Murray). One of several films over which producer Irving Thalberg went to battle with the extravagant von Stroheim: his long scenes with shots of the contents of the Baron's wardrobe—boots, shoes, slippers, shoe trees—made Thalberg wonder who was the true foot fetishist. Look for a young Clark Gable as an extra.

VHS: S31170. $24.95.

Erich von Stroheim, USA, 1925, 113 mins.

The Merry Widow (German Version)

Von Stroheim's German version of this classic silent Hollywood film about two royal cousins, Prince Danilo and Crown Prince Mirko (John Gilbert and Roy D'Arcy), insatiable Don Juans in a showdown for the same girl, Sally O'Hara (Mae Murray), the premiere danseuse of The Manhattan Follies. "Make no mistake about it: *The Merry Widow* is loaded with sexual innuendo" (The Silent Majority). With English titles.

VHS: S33931. $24.95.

Erich von Stroheim, Germany, 1925, 110 mins.

Merry-Go-Round

Count von Hohenegg plans to marry the Minister of War's daughter, but he falls in love with the organ grinder for a merry-go-round. Forced into the original marriage, the Count is severed from his lover first by law, and then by war. The film was originally directed by Erich von Stroheim but he lost the project in a fight with producer Irving Thalberg. With Norman Kerry, Mary Philbin, Cesare Gravina and Dorothy Wallace. Silent with added music track.

VHS: S16109. $29.95.

Rupert Julian/Erich von Stroheim, USA, 1923, 110 mins.

Queen Kelly

With its restoration in 1985, Erich von Stroheim's eighth and final silent film emerged from over 50 years of obscurity to its first official release and worldwide acclaim. As such, it now ranks as one of the great treasures of film history. The collaboration of Gloria Swanson, then Hollywood's greatest star, and financier Joseph Kennedy, the film was near completion when, after three months of production, Swanson closed it down enraged by von Stroheim's excesses. The story, a gothic romance in which a convent girl is seduced by a Prince and inherits a brother in Africa, is told with stunning visual effect.

VHS: S08943. $39.95.

Erich von Stroheim, USA, 1929, 97 mins.

The Wedding March

Erich von Stroheim and Fay Wray in a story that proves that the greatest wealth of a marriage is love. Set in pre-World War I Vienna, a prince set to marry a wealthy princess falls in love with a poor woman. Written by von Stroheim. Silent.

VHS: S03443. $29.95.

Erich von Stroheim, USA, 1928, 113 mins.

JOHN HUSTON

Across the Pacific

The director (John Huston) and stars of *The Maltese Falcon* (Humphrey Bogart, Mary Astor, Sydney Greenstreet) are reunited in this brisk World War II adventure about Bogart's attempt to track down spies in Panama, seduce Astor and confront the elegantly vicious Greenstreet.

VHS: S14304. $19.98.

John Huston, USA, 1942, 97 mins.

The African Queen

Inspired casting teamed Bogart and Hepburn in this romantic adventure/comedy set in a war-torn African jungle. Surviving malaria, insects and persistent conflicts of their personalities, they share victory and tender romance.

VHS: S00020. $19.98.

John Huston, USA, 1951, 105 mins.

The African Queen (Commemorative Edition)

John Huston's adaptation of C.S. Forester's novel focuses on the spirited conflict of two resolute individualists, a drunken captain (Humphrey Bogart) and a repressed missionary (Katharine Hepburn), who undertake a dangerous river odyssey in East Africa against the elite German Navy during World War I. Cinematography by Jack Cardiff. Screenplay by James Agee and John Huston (and an uncredited Peter Viertel). With Robert Morley, Peter Bull, Theodore Bikel and Walter Gotell. The film has been digitally remastered and visually restored. The commemorative edition offers a hardcover edition of Hepburn's *The Making of The African Queen* and a copy of the original shooting script.

VHS: S19474. $59.98.

John Huston, USA, 1951, 105 mins.

Annie

Aileen Quinn, Carol Burnett and Albert Finney star in this adaptation of the Broadway hit based on the comic strip. With Tim Curry and Bernadette Peters.

VHS: S01884. $12.95.

John Huston, USA, 1981, 128 mins.

The Asphalt Jungle

John Huston directs this excellent underworld drama about crime and punishment. Five guys pull off a jewelry heist only to be double-crossed by their fence. With Sterling Hayden, Louis Calhern and Marilyn Monroe as Calhern's "niece."

VHS: S03458. $24.95.

Laser: LD70844. $39.95.

John Huston, USA, 1950, 112 mins.

Beat the Devil

An audacious, offbeat comedy with Humphrey Bogart, Gina Lollobrigida and Peter Lorre, and screenplay by Truman Capote, about a motley group of petty thieves and con artists hoping to grab some valuable uranium deposits. With Robert Morley and Jennifer Jones.

VHS: S00107. $24.95.

John Huston, USA, 1953, 92 mins.

The Bible

John Huston directs the first 22 chapters of Genesis and claims the title of the whole book. He also plays Noah. International cast includes Peter O'Toole, Ava Gardner, Franco Nero, Richard Harris and Michael Parks and Ully Bergryd as Adam and Eve. This is one situation where more people read the book and with good reason.

VHS: S04594. $19.98.

Laser: LD70880. $49.98.

John Huston, Italy, 1966, 155 mins.

Casino Royale

Sean Connery, Peter Sellers, David Niven, Woody Allen, Orson Welles and Ursula Andress star in the film based on the first Fleming 007 novel; the farce begins when Bond is persuaded to join the HMSS and take on a mission to stop Le Chiffre from his big winnings supporting the evil organization.

VHS: S00217. $14.95.

Laser: CAV, widescreen. LD74615. $39.95.

John Huston, USA, 1967, 130 mins.

The Dead

This swan song of the great American director is a faithful and artful adaptation of James Joyce's poignant story from *The Dubliners*, set in turn-of-the-century Dublin. During the revelry of a Christmas dinner party, a man rediscovers his wife's heart when a song reminds her of a lost love of her youth. With an exquisite preformance by Anjelica Huston. Also with Dan O'Herlihy, Donal McCann, Cathleen Delany, Marie Kern and Donal Donnelly.

VHS: S07921. $19.95.

John Huston, USA/Ireland, 1987, 95 mins.

The Dubliners

A very moving and uniquely privileged look at the making of the last film of the late, great John Huston—the making of *The Dead* in Ireland. Few filmmakers have had an opportunity to close their illustrious career as well as Huston, and Lillian Sievernich's film captures Huston, already ill, working to complete his dream project of adapting a story from James Joyce's *The Dubliners* as his film, *The Dead*.

VHS: S08947. $29.95.

Lillian Sievernich, USA, 1987, 83 mins.

Fat City

Stacy Keach and Jeff Bridges star in this brilliant John Huston drama about small time boxers. Move over, Rocky. This is the reality of what life is like for guys who punch each other for a living. With Susan Tyrell and Candy Clark. Based on the Leonard Gardner novel.

VHS: S06067. $19.95.

John Huston, USA, 1972, 100 mins.

Heaven Knows, Mr Allison

Set during World War II, John Huston's emotionally charged romantic drama stars Robert Mitchum as a heroic marine and Deborah Kerr as an Irish nun stranded together on a Pacific Island. Hiding from invading Japanese troops and living under perilous conditions, the two soon find themselves at odds over their increasing feelings for each other. In Cinemascope.

VHS: S31016. $19.98.

John Huston, USA, 1957, 107 mins.

In This Our Life

Bette Davis stars as a neurotic girl who steals her sister's husband, leaves him in the lurch, dominates her family and finally is killed as she runs from the police. A first-rate melodrama with Charles Coburn, Olivia de Havilland and Frank Craven.

VHS: S11627. $19.95.

John Huston, USA, 1942, 101 mins.

Independence

A short subject directed by John Huston that concerns the historical events that led to the writing and signing of the Declaration of Independence. E.G. Marshall provides the narration. Cast includes Eli Wallach, Anne Jackson and Patrick O'Neal. In color and with liberty and justice for all.
VHS: S06167. $19.95.
John Huston, USA, 1976, 30 mins.

John Huston: The Man, The Movies, The Maverick

Robert Mitchum hosts this special personal tribute to John Huston that is warm, funny, poignant and full of insights into the life of the man who lived life to the hilt. Joined by stars Paul Newman, Lauren Bacall, Michael Caine, Anjelica Huston, Arthur Miller and Evelyn Keyes, Mitchum shares a fond look at the man who made *The Maltese Falcon, African Queen, The Dead, The Misfits* and *Treasure of Sierra Madre*.
VHS: S10743. $29.98.

Juarez

John Huston at his best. Paul Muni is brilliant as the revolutionary Mexican leader who causes the downfall of Emperor Maximilian. With Bette Davis, Brian Aherne, Claude Rains, John Garfield.
VHS: S13395. $19.98.
John Huston, USA, 1939, 132 mins.

Key Largo

Humphrey Bogart goes to visit the widow of an old war buddy (played by Lauren Bacall), and finds himself in a confrontation with Edward G. Robinson. With an Oscar-winning performance from Claire Trevor.
VHS: S01708. $19.95.
Laser: LD70181. $34.39.
John Huston, USA, 1948, 101 mins.

Let There Be Light

Documentary commissioned by the U.S. War Department on the psychiatric treatment of shell-shocked World War II veterans. The film was confiscated upon completion and banned until 1980 in the fear that it would discourage recruitment. Deeply humanitarian and pacifist.
VHS: S00749. $29.95.
John Huston, USA, 1945, 60 mins.

The Life and Times of Judge Roy Bean

Paul Newman is the self-appointed hanging judge, the only law west of the Pecos. He's stern but he is fair. He's also in love with Lily Langtry (Ava Gardner). Watch for Stacy Keach as the Original Bad Bob, the albino gunman. With Roddy McDowall and Victoria Principal.
VHS: S04196. $14.95.
John Huston, USA, 1972, 124 mins.

List of Adrian Messenger

A witty thriller in which George C. Scott must uncover the identity of a murderer who is killing off the heirs to a family fortune. The audience gets in on the fun by trying to identify the stars who are playing disguised roles in the film: Sinatra, Mitchum, Kirk Douglas, Burt Lancaster and Tony Curtis.
VHS: S01710. $19.98.
John Huston, USA, 1963, 98 mins.

The Mackintosh Man

Paul Newman spends most of this film running for his life all over picturesque locations in Ireland. He has been sent to infiltrate a criminal organization headed by James Mason, a high government official. He doesn't seem amused. Screenplay by Walter Hill.
VHS: S04174. $19.98.
John Huston, USA, 1973, 100 mins.

The Maltese Falcon

Even if you've seen this film so often that you know all the dialog, it never ceases to amaze. A search for a priceless statuette provides the action in this classic, excellent film favorite. Noir at its best with great actors Humphrey Bogart, Mary Astor, Sydney Greenstreet and Peter Lorre, based on Dashiell Hammet's thriller.
VHS: S00810. $19.95.
Laser: LD70621. $34.98.
John Huston, USA, 1941, 101 mins.

The Man Who Would Be King

Grand telling of the Rudyard Kipling classic adventure story of two soldiers of fortune in 19th century India, who set out to conquer lands and make themselves king. Sean Connery and Michael Caine are brilliantly cast. VHS letterboxed.
VHS: S00819. $19.98.
Laser: LD76816. $39.99.
DVD: DV60182. $24.98.
John Huston, USA, 1975, 129 mins.

Misfits

The last film completed by both Marilyn Monroe and Clark Gable, scripted by Monroe's husband at the time, Arthur Miller. Young divorcee Marilyn settles in Reno, first in the boarding house of Thelma Ritter, then in the home and heart of grizzled cowboy Clark Gable. Her tender-hearted ways clash with the macho culture of rodeo, saloons, and wild horse wrangling—leading to a dramatic climax in the barren desert. Featuring fine supporting performances by Eli Wallach and Montgomery Clift.
VHS: S04198. $19.98.
Laser: LD70631. $39.98.
John Huston, USA, 1961, 124 mins.

Moby Dick

John Huston directs Herman Melville's classic tale of a large, albino, water-based mammal and the obsessive sea captain with one real leg. The script is by Ray Bradbury. Gregory Peck stars as Ahab, Richard Basehart is the lucky Ishmael. Other crew members of the Pequod include Leo Genn, Harry Andrews and Frederick Ledebur as Queequeg. Three white whales were used in the filming off the coast of Ireland; two were lost at sea and still frighten the locals.
VHS: S00865. $19.95.
Laser: LD72127. $34.98.
John Huston, USA/Great Britain, 1956, 116 mins.

Moulin Rouge

The colorful story of French painter Henri Toulouse-Lautrec as interpreted by director John Huston. Jose Ferrer is cast as the Parisian artist who may have been short of stature but never of talent. The film won Oscars for its art direction, set decoration and costumes. Return to the exciting and naughty world of Montmartre in the late 19th century. The cast includes Eric Pohlmann, Colette Marchant, Peter Cushing, Christopher Lee and Zsa Zsa Gabor, who was hot stuff in 1952.
VHS: S11216. $19.95.
Laser: LD72128. $39.98.
John Huston, USA, 1952, 123 mins.

Night of the Iguana

Richard Burton, Deborah Kerr and Ava Gardner star in this adaptation of Tennessee Williams' play about a fallen, alcoholic ex-minister, who is self-exiled to Mexico, where he works as a tour guide.
VHS: S04394. $19.98.
Laser: LD72352. $39.98.
John Huston, USA, 1964, 125 mins.

Phobia

A virtually unknown film by John Huston made in Canada, *Phobia* is a tense whodunit which takes place in a unique treatment center. First a bathtub drowning. Then a fatal elevator ride. A lethal snake bite. One by one, phobia-ridden patients are being murdered, and a patient, a jilted lover, or even their doctor (Paul Michael Glaser) could be the killer.
VHS: S09492. $79.95.
John Huston, Canada, 1980, 91 mins.

Red Badge of Courage

Huston's powerful adaptation of Stephen Crane's novel about the horrors of war. Set during the Civil War, the film features strong performances from Audie Murphy and Bill Mauldin.
VHS: S01762. $24.95.
John Huston, USA, 1951, 69 mins.

Reflections in a Golden Eye

Sexual tensions simmer in the heat of a Georgia army base. A sextet of characters, based on Carson McCullers' novel, try to come to grips with their desires. They include Marlon Brando, Elizabeth Taylor, Brian Keith, Julie Harris and Robert Forster as the soldier who likes to ride bareback.
VHS: S04180. $19.98.
John Huston, USA, 1967, 109 mins.

The Treasure of the Sierra Madre

Pauline Kael calls this "one of the strongest of all American movies." Three Americans strike it rich and greed takes over. With Humphrey Bogart, Walter Huston, Tim Holt and Robert Blake, based on the novel by B. Traven.
VHS: S01368. $19.95.
Laser: LD70699. $39.98.
John Huston, USA, 1948, 120 mins.

Under the Volcano

Malcolm Lowry's cult classic brought to life by the legendary director John Huston, starring Albert Finney and Jacqueline Bisset. Filmed on location in Mexico, this film has all the beauty and foreboding of the novel, which paints a vivid picture of alcoholism.
VHS: S01399. $79.95.
Laser: LD70093. $34.98.
John Huston, USA, 1984, 112 mins.

The Unforgiven

A powerful western drama about racism and family ties directed by John Huston. Set in Texas in the 1950's, a proud and strongwilled family discovers an adopted daughter might have Indian blood. The cast includes Burt Lancaster, Audrey Hepburn, Lillian Gish, Charles Bickford and Audie Murphy.
VHS: S03670. $19.98.
Laser: LD72271. $39.98.
John Huston, USA, 1960, 123 mins.

Victory (Escape to Victory)

Michael Caine, Sylvester Stallone, Max von Sydow and Pele star in this combination prisoner of war/sports drama set during World War II, in which a group of Nazi officers plan a progaganda soccer match pitting an all-star Nazi team against a team of allied prisoners of war. The POWs use the game to try to escape from the camp.
VHS: S33912. $14.95.
DVD: DV60227. $24.98.
John Huston, USA, 1981, 114 mins.

Wise Blood

Based on the powerful novel by Flannery O'Connor, *Wise Blood* traces the career of a religious fanatic who attempts to found a church without salvation. An offbeat masterpiece featuring superb performances by Ned Beatty and Harry Dean Stanton.
VHS: S01470. $59.95.
John Huston, USA, 1979, 106 mins.

GEORGE CUKOR

Adam's Rib

Spencer Tracy and Katharine Hepburn in one of their all-time great appearances as married attorneys who find themselves on opposite sides of a murder case in which Judy Holliday is the accused.
VHS: S03456. $19.95.
Laser: LD70202. $49.98.
Laser: LD70336. $39.95.
DVD: DV60057. $24.98.
George Cukor, USA, 1949, 101 mins.

Bhowani Junction

Earthy Ava Gardner is half-English, half-Indian and all woman in George Cukor's spectacular drama of chaos and revolt in post-colonial India. Shot by Frederick A. Young, who was also the cinematographer for *Lawrence of Arabia*.
VHS: S15115. $19.98.
Laser: LD72164. $34.95.
George Cukor, USA, 1956, 109 mins.

A Bill of Divorcement

Katharine Hepburn's screen debut, starring opposite the legendary John Barrymore. This is a charming and poignant romantic comedy about the unexpected homecoming of a former madman.
VHS: S12168. $39.98.
George Cukor, USA, 1932, 70 mins.

Born Yesterday

Judy Holliday won the Best Actress Oscar for her funny role as the dumb blond girlfriend of Broderick Crawford, a corrupt millionaire junk dealer. Brock, a man with social ambitions, is embarassed by Billie's crass behavior and hires a writer, William Holden, to smarten her up. A classic comedy.
VHS: S03863. $19.95.
George Cukor, USA, 1950, 103 mins.

Camille

Greta Garbo at the peak of her career, as the consumptive courtesan who falls in love with the young nobleman with tragic results. This adaptation of the Alexandre Dumas play and novel, with Lionel Barrymore and Robert Taylor, is beautiful to look at and clearly defines the Garbo magic.
VHS: S03453. $24.95.
George Cukor, USA, 1936, 110 mins.

The Corn Is Green
One of the George Cukor's parting glances was this seamless, old-fashioned and enjoyable remake of Irving Rapper's 1945 classic, about the intellectual passion and energy a spinster teacher (Katharine Hepburn) brings to a South Wales mining community.
VHS: S15933. $19.98.
George Cukor, USA, 1974, 100 mins.

David Copperfield
Director Cukor assembled a fine cast to portray the assortment of characters who populate Charles Dickens' epic novel. With W.C. Fields, Lionel Barrymore, Maureen O'Sullivan and Basil Rathbone.
VHS: S03003. $19.98.
Laser: LD70552. $39.98.
George Cukor, USA, 1935, 131 mins.

Dinner at Eight
Based on George S. Kaufman and Edna Ferber's Broadway hit, in which an elaborate dinner party reveals a web of intrigue and romance. A classic American comedy. With Marie Dressler, John Barrymore, Wallace Beery, an adorable Jean Harlow, Lionel Barrymore and Lee Tracy.
VHS: S00342. $19.95.
Laser: LD70556. $34.98.
George Cukor, USA, 1933, 111 mins.

A Double Life
Ronald Colman plays a brilliant actor whose stage roles are beginning to affect the rest of his life. In an Oscar winning performance Colman performs *Othello* once too often for his own good. With Signe Hasso, Edmond O'Brien and Shelley Winters.
VHS: S04228. $19.98.
George Cukor, USA, 1947, 103 mins.

Gaslight
Ingrid Bergman won her first Oscar for her stunning role as a susceptible young woman who marries the suave, romantic Charles Boyer, never suspecting he is involved in a murderous scandal in Cukor's electrifying mystery drama.
VHS: S00482. $19.98.
George Cukor, USA, 1944, 113 mins.

Holiday
Katharine Hepburn and Cary Grant are two kindred spirits trapped in a love triangle in this stylish, intelligent adaptation of the play by Philip Barry as Grant confronts the stuffy New York society. Very delightful.
VHS: S03867. $19.95.
Laser: CLV. **LD74616. $34.95.**
George Cukor, USA, 1938, 93 mins.

Justine
The mysterious wife of a well-to-do banker becomes involved in 1930's Middle East politics. Director Cukor gets fine performances from his cast, which includes Anouk Aimee, Dirk Bogarde, Philippe Noiret and Michael York.
VHS: S02324. $59.98.
George Cukor, USA, 1969, 115 mins.

Keeper of the Flame
Top-notch reporter Spencer Tracy has come to a small town to investigate the death of Robert Forrest, a national hero. He's determined to get a story, but things change when he falls in love with Forrest's beautiful widow (Katharine Hepburn).
VHS: S15022. $19.98.
George Cukor, USA, 1942, 100 mins.

Les Girls
A delightful romantic musical comedy with a Cole Porter score, starring Gene Kelly, Mitzi Gaynor, and Kay Kendall. A witty story, delightful musical numbers and a very talented cast.
VHS: S00747. $19.98.
Laser: LD70613. $34.97.
George Cukor, USA, 1957, 114 mins.

Let's Make Love
Marilyn Monroe sings "My Heart Belongs to Daddy" in this breezy comedy of billionaires, show business and the truth. Yves Montand, a very wealthy man, learns he is to be satirized in an off-Broadway revue and wants to close the show until he meets Marilyn.
VHS: S04199. $19.98.
George Cukor, USA, 1960, 118 mins.

A Life of Her Own
George Cukor's romantic triangle about a beautiful and ambitious Midwestern woman (Lana Turner) who arrives in New York with hopes of attaining top status as a model, encounters amazing success, and promptly falls for a charismatic married man (Ray Milland). With Tom Ewell, Louis Calhern and Ann Dvorak. Screenplay by Isabel Lennart.
VHS: S18662. $19.98.
George Cukor, USA, 1950, 108 mins.

Little Women
"Endless pleasure no matter how many times you've seen it" (Leonard Maltin). The Louisa May Alcott novel is portrayed on film featuring Katharine Hepburn, Joan Bennett, Frances Dee and Paul Lukas.
VHS: S03008. $19.95.
Laser: LD70137. $34.98.
George Cukor, USA, 1933, 116 mins.

The Marrying Kind
Judy Holliday stars in this groundbreaking blend of comedy, tragedy and fantasy, written by Ruth Gordon and Garson Kanin, which chronicles the relationship of a young couple on the verge of a divorce. With Aldo Ray and Madge Kennedy. "Genuinely and touchingly comic" (*Newstand*).
VHS: S30780. $19.95.
George Cukor, USA, 1952, 92 mins.

My Fair Lady
Alan Jay Lerner and Frederick Loewe's variation of Shaw's *Pygmalion* is turned into an intellectual comedy of manners by expert director George Cukor, who skillfully allows the byplay of co-star Stanley Holloway to co-exist with the primary storyline of Henry Higgins' schooling of Eliza Doolittle. Rex Harrison and Audrey Hepburn (songs dubbed by Marni Nixon) are the leads; Holloway's "Get Me to the Church on Time" steals the show. VHS letterboxed.
VHS: S02345. $24.95.
Laser: LD71247. $59.98.
George Cukor, USA, 1964, 170 mins.

Pat and Mike
Katharine Hepburn and Spencer Tracy team up for their seventh film, as a top female athlete and a shady sports promoter. Ruth Gordon and Garson Kanin supplied the script, which features many popular golf and tennis pros, like Babe Didrikson Zaharias and Gussie Moran, in bit parts. Watch for Charles Bronson as a judo trained thug.
VHS: S09151. $19.98.
George Cukor, USA, 1952, 95 mins.

The Philadelphia Story
One of the most hilarious and captivating romantic comedies ever to grace the screen. Katharine Hepburn is caught between her fiance and her charming ex-husband. With a splendid cast, including Cary Grant, James Stewart and Ruth Hussey.
VHS: S01023. $24.95.
Laser: LD70152. $39.98.
DVD: DV60063. $24.98.
George Cukor, USA, 1940, 118 mins.

Romeo and Juliet
Leslie Howard and Norma Shearer play the title roles in Shakespeare's immortal tale of star-crossed lovers. A fabulous production.
VHS: S15654. $19.98.
Laser: LD72153. $39.98.
George Cukor, USA, 1936, 126 mins.

Song Without End
Dirk Bogarde stars in this biographical drama about the tempestuous life and scandalous career of renowned Hungarian pianist Franz Liszt. With Capucine, Genevieve Page, Patricia Morison and Lou Jacobi.
VHS: S16635. $19.95.
King Vidor/George Cukor, USA, 1960, 141 mins.

A Star Is Born
The second version of the story of a young performer's rise to fame as her actor husband's star fades. Garland's genius makes the story effective, with help from a wonderful performance by James Mason.
VHS: S01734. $29.98.
Laser: LD71337. $39.95.
George Cukor, USA, 1954, 154 mins.

Susan and God
Joan Crawford is cast as a society matron who returns from Europe "aflame with the spirit of do-goodism." Her persistent attempts to convert her jaded society chums prove disruptive, but do cause her husband, Fredric March, to sober up. With Rita Hayworth, Ruth Hussey, John Carroll, Rita Quigley, Rose Hobart, Nigel Bruce and Bruce Cabot. Anita Loos wrote the screenplay.
VHS: S16455. $19.98.
George Cukor, USA, 1940, 117 mins.

Travels with My Aunt
Based on the Graham Greene novel of the same name, this film features an all-star cast. Maggie Smith, Alec McCowen, Lou Gossett, Jr., and Cindy Williams are all caught up in a European tour with a secret rationale. Though everything seems to be stylish and graceful, the plot centers on an unconventional lady smuggler who brings style and class to the world of hustling and swindling.
VHS: S27575. $19.98.
George Cukor, USA, 1972, 109 mins.

Two-Faced Woman
Greta Garbo stopped making movies after this comedy failed to generate much interest. She plays an insecure ski instructor who must invent and impersonate a vivacious sister to prevent her brand new husband from going back to his more sophisticated old flame. With Melvyn Douglas as the former playboy publisher who enjoys seeing double. Also with Constance Bennett, Roland Young and Ruth Gordon.
VHS: S11731. $19.98.
George Cukor, USA, 1941, 94 mins.

A Woman's Face
Joan Crawford stars as a professional blackmailer with a disfiguring scar whose life is changed by Melvyn Douglas' plastic surgery, which heals her features but not her scarred emotions. With Conrad Veidt.
VHS: S03455. $19.98.
George Cukor, USA, 1941, 107 mins.

The Women
Brilliant, witty comedy with a stellar cast of women: Norma Shearer, Joan Crawford, Rosalind Russell, Mary Boland, Paulette Goddard and Joan Fontaine. No men appear in the film, but men is what the film is all about. Superb American comedy, with perhaps the wittiest dialog ever put on screen. A must-see.
VHS: S01480. $19.95.
George Cukor, USA, 1939, 133 mins.

FRANK CAPRA

American Madness
A quintessential Capra film set in the midst of the Depression, in which an idealistic bank president (Walter Huston) goes against the cruelty of a conservative, impersonal board of bank directors, as a bank theft from an unscrupulous bank officer (Gavin Gordon) leads to a stampede of panicky depositors. With outstanding performances by Pat O'Brien, Constance Cummings and Kay Johnson.
VHS: S31514. $19.95.
Frank Capra, USA, 1932, 76 mins.

Arsenic and Old Lace
Cary Grant stars in this hilarious black comedy about two sweet old ladies who poison lonely old men with elderberry wine, as a kindness. Cary is the confused nephew who has to juggle dead bodies, escaped murderers and an uncle who thinks he's Teddy Roosevelt with a marriage announcement and the police. With Peter Lorre as Dr. Einstein.
VHS: S02351. $19.95.
Laser: CLV, 1 disc, Criterion. **LD70340. $39.95.**
Frank Capra, USA, 1944, 118 mins.

The Bitter Tea of General Yen
Frank Capra's film concerns an American missionary (Barbara Stanwyck) who is kidnapped by a powerful Chinese warlord and falls prey to his intoxicating spell. With Nils Asther, Toshia Mori and Walter Connolly.
VHS: S19023. $19.95.
Frank Capra, USA, 1932, 89 mins.

Broadway Bill
Lost for over 40 years, *Broadway Bill* is available for the first time on video. An heiress bets she'll find true love at the racetrack and saddles up to a cheery horse trainer. A romantic comedy in true Capra style. Margaret Hamilton and Jason Robards star.
VHS: S15866. $19.95.
Laser: LD75166. $34.98.
Frank Capra, USA, 1934, 100 mins.

Frank Capra's American Dream
Commemorating his centennial birthday, this definitive portrait illuminates the life and career of Frank Capra, from penniless immigrant to world-class Hollywood filmmaker. Produced in collaboration with the Capra family and narrated by Ron Howard.
VHS: S31512. $19.95.
Kenneth Bowser, USA, 1997, 105 mins.

Here Comes the Groom
A happy-go-lucky reporter plots and schemes to keep his former fiancee from marrying a millionaire. If he adopts war orphans, will this win her over? Bing Crosby and Jane Wyman star.
VHS: S12570. $19.95.
Frank Capra, USA, 1951, 114 mins.

A Hole in the Head
The last important film of Frank Capra's career, with Frank Sinatra playing a Miami hotel owner on the verge of bankruptcy, who's forced to scramble to raise funds in order to stay in business. With a terrific performance from Edward G. Robinson, Carolyn Jones, Keenan Wynn.
VHS: Out of print. For rental only.
Laser: LD72177. $39.98.
Frank Capra, USA, 1959, 120 mins.

It Happened One Night
Winner of five Academy Awards, this famous screwball comedy stars Clark Gable and Claudette Colbert as two mismatched lovers. Colbert escapes from her millionaire father, who wants to stop her from marrying a worthless playboy.
VHS: S00642. $19.95.
Laser: LD72146. $34.95.
Frank Capra, USA, 1934, 105 mins.

It's a Wonderful Life
James Stewart is George Bailey, trapped in Bedford Falls, until his faith in life is restored by his Guardian Angel in Frank Capra's delightful comedy, nominated for multiple Academy Awards. Donna Reed, Lionel Barrymore, Thomas Mitchell and Beulah Bondi also star.
VHS: S15106. $19.98.
Laser: CAV. **LD70387. $89.95.**
Laser: CLV. **LD71996. $59.98.**
Frank Capra, USA, 1946, 160 mins.

Ladies of Leisure
Early Frank Capra social comedy stars Barbara Stanwyck in her debut performance as an ambitious adventuress and careerist who falls for a roguish artist (Robert Graves) who wishes to make a portrait of her. "The climactic sequence is genuinely tense, exciting and visual in the manner of the best silents" (William K. Everson). With Lowell Sherman, Marie Prevost and George Fawcett.
VHS: S18948. $19.95.
Frank Capra, USA, 1930, 98 mins.

Lady for a Day
Frank Capra's romantic fable of a soft-hearted gangster who helps transform an old apple-seller into a perfect lady was nominated for four Academy Awards, and features wonderful performances from Warren William, May Robson, Guy Kibbee, Glenda Farrell. Adapted from a Damon Runyan story, and one of Capra's first great successes.
VHS: Out of print. For rental only.
Laser: CLV. **LD70757. $39.95.**
Frank Capra, USA, 1933, 88 mins.

Long Pants
One of Harry Langdon's best silent features, this twisted, coming-of-age, silent comedy directed by Frank Capra is the story of a simple man (Harry Langdon) who plots to kill his girlfriend (Priscilla Bonner) while under the influence of a drug-smuggling seductress (Alma Bennett). Includes the 1926 silent short *Saturday Afternoon*.
VHS: S30715. $29.95.
Frank Capra, USA, 1927, 88 mins.

Lost Horizon
Frank Capra's hypnotic and perversely appealing adaptation of James Hilton's novel featuring 22 minutes of restored footage that fully explores the psychological implications of Capra's "utopian paradise." Though the material seems foreign to Capra's style and sensibility, it is a work of lost innocence and spiritual redemption. A plane fleeing revolutionary China is highjacked to a mysterious valley in the Himalayas known as Shangri-La. Ronald Colman stars as a British diplomat who falls for Jane Wyatt. The expansive, post-modern sets and art direction were inspired by the architecture of Frank Lloyd Wright.
VHS: S02919. $19.95.
Frank Capra, USA, 1937, 132 mins.

Meet John Doe
Capra's classic ode to the common man: Gary Cooper is the unemployed worker built into a symbol by a newspaper publisher only to discover he's the object of political ambitions. With Barbara Stanwyck, Edward Arnold, Walter Brennan.
VHS: S00844. $19.95.
Frank Capra, USA, 1941, 123 mins.

The Miracle Woman
In one of her earliest starring roles, Barbara Stanwyck delivers a riveting performance as a crusading phoney evangelist who becomes wealthy, then undergoes a crisis of faith when her radio sermon saves a man from committing suicide. Extremely controversial for its time, *The Miracle Woman* was banned in the British Empire for its irreverence.
VHS: S31513. $19.95.
Frank Capra, USA, 1931, 90 mins.

Mr. Deeds Goes to Town
One of Frank Capra's best films, shot during the height of the Depression. Gary Cooper plays Longfellow Deeds, who inherits 20 million dollars and wants to spend it on people during the height of the Depression. Jean Arthur plays the city reporter who is captivated by the naive Deeds.
VHS: S11163. $19.95.
Frank Capra, USA, 1936, 115 mins.

Mr. Smith Goes to Washington
James Stewart stars in Frank Capra's famous film as the naive Jeff Smith, appointed a U.S. senator by a corrupt political party machine. Famous for its heroic one-man fillibuster, it is a moving vision of honor amid political squalor.
VHS: S00889. $19.95.
Laser: Restored, 3 sides, digital master, chapter stops. **LD75054. $44.95.**
Frank Capra, USA, 1939, 125 mins.

Negro Soldier
Frank Capra supervised this documentary focusing on black participation in World War II. Langston Hughes hailed it as the most remarkable Negro film ever flashed on the American screen.
VHS: S03347. $19.98.
Frank Capra, USA, 1944, 40 mins.

Platinum Blonde
Jean Harlow and Loretta Young face off in this raucous comedy of romance between the haves and have-nots. Robert Williams is a wise-cracking reporter married to the wealthy Harlow, but his distaste for the confinement of "high society" may just give Young a fighting chance.
VHS: S16591. $19.95.
Frank Capra, USA, 1931, 90 mins.

Pocketful of Miracles
Bette Davis stars as an aging apple-seller who poses as a wealthy grande dame in order to have her daughter marry into a legitimately rich family. Others in the talented cast include Glenn Ford, Hope Lange, Peter Falk, and, making her film debut, Ann-Margret. Letterboxed.
VHS: S01041. $14.95.
Laser: 2 discs. **LD74590. $49.98.**
Frank Capra, USA, 1961, 137 mins.

Riding High
Bing Crosby and Colleen Gray star in this entertaining musical comedy that has the special Capra touch. Crosby is a race horse owner just waiting for his horse to come in, but of course romance won't wait, especially when there's music in the air. This remake of the classic 30's musical *Broadway Bill* is a delightful update.
VHS: S21600. $19.95.
Laser: LD75247. $34.98.
Frank Capra, USA, 1950, 112 mins.

State of the Union
Spencer Tracy stars as an honest industrialist who finds himself in danger of losing his integrity when he is drafted to run for the presidency. With Katharine Hepburn as his steadfast wife, Angela Lansbury, and Van Johnson.
VHS: S01735. $19.98.
Laser: LD70083. $39.98.
Frank Capra, USA, 1948, 122 mins.

The Strong Man
Harry Langdon stars in this wonderful silent comedy, newly restored by Kevin Brownlow and David Gill. A World War I veteran comes to America with a travelling show, hoping to meet the girl whose letters gave him hope at the front. Musical score compiled by Harry Langdon. Arranged and performed by Eric Beheim. Includes a 20-minute short, *His Marriage Vow*.
VHS: S10917. $29.95.
Frank Capra, USA, 1926, 94 mins.

That Certain Thing
Frank Capra's first Columbia Picture. It tells the story of Molly Kelly, a hardworking young woman who marries a millionaire, only to be impoverished once again when his dad disinherits the son, thinking her to be a gold-digger. When she starts a successful box lunch business, dad comes around. With Viola Dana and Ralph Graves. Silent.
VHS: S04805. $24.95.
Frank Capra, USA, 1928, 70 mins.

You Can't Take It with You
James Stewart, Jean Arthur, Lionel Barrymore and Edward Arnold star in this 1938 Academy Award-winning, nutty comedy. Based on the play by George S. Kaufman and Moss Hart. The scenes in which Barrymore confronts an IRS man by refusing to pay taxes are among the funniest in film.
VHS: S11745. $19.95.
Frank Capra, USA, 1938, 126 mins.

ALFRED HITCHCOCK

Alfred Hitchcock
Two conversations with the director explore many of his ideas, career decisions, film aesthetic and techniques. Part 1 includes an interview by Hitchcock's daughter, Pia Lindstrom and Ingrid Bergman. Discussion topics include: what is fear?, method actingvs. film acting, the difference between the "Who Done It" and real suspense, choice of leading ladies and the use of humor as a release in a tense situation. Part 2 includes an interview by film historian William Everson, with emphasis on the beginning of Hitchcock's career, years in Britain, early films, Hitchcock in Hollywood, and film techniques, as well as a section on Hitchcock's trademark appearance in his own films. 1972, 60 mins.
VHS: S31571. $59.95.

Alfred Hitchcock TV
Two episodes of the infamous Alfred Hitchcock television series are included on this video. *The Chaney Vase* and *The Sorcerer's Apprentice* both have the master's touch. They are not only suspenseful, but they are both introduced by the rotund thriller king himself.
VHS: S27333. $19.95.
Alfred Hitchcock, USA, 52 mins.

Alfred Hitchcock: Master of Suspense
Presents the master of suspense in a rare discussion of his filmmaking techniques and his illustrious 50-year career as director. Filled with classic film clips from *Psycho, North by Northwest, The Birds, Frenzy, Rear Window* and *Shadow of a Doubt*. Narrated by Cliff Robertson.
VHS: S33436. $19.95.
Richard Schickel, USA, 1973, 58 mins.

The Birds
Sheer terror from the master. *The Birds* is based on a novella by Daphne Du Maurier and was accomplished by nearly 400 trick shots using thousands of birds. With Tippi Hedren, Rod Taylor, Jessica Tandy and Suzanne Pleshette.
VHS: S01845. $19.95.
Laser: LD70015. $39.98.
Alfred Hitchcock, USA, 1963, 119 mins.

Blackmail
Hitchcock's first sound picture, *Blackmail* is the story of a young girl who stabs an artist to death in defense of her honor. Her boyfriend, a Scotland Yard detective, puts the clues together and decides to protect her. But then an unknown blackmailer comes on the scene, and the film builds into a tense, exciting climax. With Anny Ondra, John Londgen, Cyril Ritchard.
VHS: S00141. $19.95.
Laser: LD71521. $49.95.
Alfred Hitchcock, Great Britain, 1929, 86 mins.

Bon Voyage & Aventure Malgache
Many great directors were drafted for the Allied effort in World War II. These two shorts were commissioned by the British Ministry of Information and meant to be screened in France upon liberation. Suspenseful dramas of betrayal and murder were not exactly what they had in mind at the ministry however, and these films were never used for their originally stated purpose. 27 and 31 minutes. French with English subtitles.
VHS: S20960. $24.95.
Alfred Hitchcock, Great Britain, 1944, 58 mins.

Champagne
A millionaire father objects to the man his daughter is in love with, and to teach her a lesson he allows his daughter to think he has become bankrupt. The young woman goes to work in a cabaret serving the same champagne the family fortune was based upon. Filled with sight gags. Silent.
VHS: S00225. $19.98.
Alfred Hitchcock, Great Britain, 1928

Dial M for Murder

Grace Kelly, Ray Milland and Robert Cummings star in Alfred Hitchcock's sophisticated study of the perfect crime. Suave (but rotten to the core) Milland frames his wife (icy beauty Grace Kelly) for murder in this twisting and turning, imaginative thriller from the master of suspense. One of the first 3-D feature films of 1954.
VHS: S00336. $19.98.
Laser: LD70554. $34.98.
Alfred Hitchcock, USA, 1954, 123 mins.

Easy Virtue

Alfred Hitchcock's early silent film about the destruction of a woman's life, in which a suicide leads to the heroine's divorce scandal and a sorry end. Silent with musical track.
VHS: S01640. $24.95.
Alfred Hitchcock, USA, 1927, 60 mins.

Family Plot

Hitchcock's last movie is a diabolically funny search for a missing heir, starring Bruce Dern, Barbara Harris, William Devane, and Karen Black.
VHS: S01853. $14.98.
Laser: LD70029. $39.98.
Alfred Hitchcock, USA, 1976, 120 mins.

The Farmer's Wife

A rustic silent comedy from Alfred Hitchcock. Farmer (Jameson Thomas) doesn't know his housekeeper (Lillian Hall-Davies) is willing to take on more responsibilities around the place. In his search for a bride he is overlooking his own backyard. Silent.
VHS: S04089. $19.98.
Alfred Hitchcock, Great Britain, 1928, 97 mins.

Foreign Correspondent

Hitchcock's second American film was a return to the flawless architecture of his best British thrillers. Set in London and Amsterdam during the war, the film is an entertaining blend of suspense and dark humor involving an American reporter sent to cover the European situation. Among the highlights are the attempted murder atop Westminster Cathedral, a brilliant sequence in an isolated Dutch windmill and an assassination scene in pouring rain. With Herbert Marshall, Joel McCrea, Laraine Day.
VHS: S02020. $19.98.
Laser: LD70575. $39.98.
Alfred Hitchcock, USA, 1940, 120 mins.

Frenzy

A great Hitchcock thriller: the wrong man is suspected when his wife is murdered. Full of Hitchcock's humor, the film stars Alec McCowen, Vivien Merchant, Jon Finch.
VHS: S01703. $19.95.
Laser: LD70031. $34.98.
Alfred Hitchcock, Great Britain, 1972, 116 mins.

I Confess

Montgomery Clift plays a priest who hears a murderer's confession and will not violate the sanctity of the confessional even to protect himself. With Anne Baxter and Karl Malden.
VHS: S01705. $19.98.
Laser: LD70597. $34.98.
Alfred Hitchcock, USA, 1953, 95 mins.

Inside Hitchcock

Enter the mind of Alfred Hitchcock, one of the cinema's greatest directors. See clips from his best films and listen to the Master himself discuss his techniques, his actors, his intentions. Notoriously spellbinding!
VHS: S01948. $39.95.
Richard Schickel, USA, 55 mins.

Jamaica Inn

Hitchcock's last film in England before moving to Hollywood. With Charles Laughton in a story set in the eighteenth century about a young Irish girl who moves to Cornwall, England, to set up an inn.
VHS: S18182. $24.95.
Laser: LD76400. $39.99.
Alfred Hitchcock, Great Britain, 1939, 98 mins.

Juno and the Paycock

This almost-never seen film by Alfred Hitchcock is based on the play by Sean O'Casey and the script was written by Hitchcock and his wife Alma Reville. Set in Ireland in the 1920's, the story revolves around the tragedies of a single, poor Dublin family. James Agee called it "a film which completely justifies the talkies." With Satra Allgood, Edward Chapman, Maire O'Neill. One of the very early sound efforts by Hitchcock.
VHS: S06388. $24.95.
Alfred Hitchcock, Great Britain, 1930, 85 mins.

The Lady Vanishes

One of Hitchcock's best British films; Dame May Whitty stars as the kindly old woman who befriends a young English girl on a European train, and then disappears. All her fellow travellers swear she never existed—only the hero, Michael Redgrave, and she together uncover the web of intrigue.
VHS: S23482. $24.95.
Laser: LD71091. $39.95.
DVD: DV60172. $39.95.
Alfred Hitchcock, Great Britain, 1938, 97 mins.

Lifeboat

Riveting war drama, written by John Steinbeck, starring William Bendix and Tallulah Bankhead as survivors of an American vessel torpedoed by a German sub during World War II. The eight are set adrift in a tiny lifeboat and the drama unfolds as they take aboard a stranded Nazi. Another gem from Alfred Hitchcock with his "appearance" coming in a most unusual way.
VHS: S01949. $19.98.
Laser: LD71107. $39.98.
Alfred Hitchcock, USA, 1944, 96 mins.

Lodger

Hitchcock's first major film, about a young tenant suspected by his landlady of being Jack the Ripper. A tense, imaginative thriller that features Hitchcock's first cameo appearance and first use of the innocent man falsely accused. Silent.
VHS: S00764. $14.98.
Alfred Hitchcock, Great Britain, 1926, 65 mins.

Man Who Knew Too Much (1934)

Hitchcock's first version of this film is the story of an ordinary family caught in a web of international intrigue. The film ends in a brilliant tour-de-force of suspense at the Royal Albert Hall in London. With Leslie Banks, Edna Best, Peter Lorre, Nova Pilbeam.
VHS: S18183. $19.95.
Alfred Hitchcock, Great Britain, 1934, 72 mins.

Man Who Knew Too Much (1955)

Hitchcock's brilliant remake of his own 1934 version features James Stewart and Doris Day as an innocent American couple caught up in a web of international intrigue, kidnapping and assassination.
VHS: S00817. $14.98.
Laser: LD70053. $34.95.
Alfred Hitchcock, USA, 1955, 120 mins.

Manxman

Hitchcock's last silent film was an ambitious film about a lovers' triangle in which some of his favorite themes, such as vertigo and moral conflict, begin to develop. Film was shot on the Isle of Man. Silent.
VHS: S00823. $19.98.
Alfred Hitchcock, Great Britain, 1929

Marnie

Sean Connery and Tippi Hendren star in Hitchcock's psychological thriller of a habitual thief (Hendren) and her employer (Connery), who is determined to help her. One of Hitchcock's most interesting films, with a symbolic use of color to represent emotional fears and reactions, with Hendren unable to help herself because of repressed memories and Connery obsessed with the idea of possessing a beautiful criminal.
VHS: S01770. $19.95.
Laser: LD70054. $39.95.
Alfred Hitchcock, USA, 1964, 130 mins.

Murder

Herbert Marshall is the actor who serves on a jury at a murder trial and believes the accused woman is innocent in one of Hitchcock's best early British films. With Norah Baring, Phyllis Konstam, Edward Chapman.
VHS: S00896. $19.98.
Alfred Hitchcock, Great Britain, 1930, 108 mins.

North by Northwest

One of Hitchcock's greatest films; Cary Grant plays Roger Thornhill, the suave ad man mistaken for a Federal agent, trapped in a web of intrigue that ends with the classic climax atop Mount Rushmore. Eva Marie Saint is the amorous spy, Leo G. Carroll the FBI man with double-edged tactics, and James Mason and Martin Landau the icily villainous traders in state secrets.
VHS: S00938. $19.98.
Laser: CAV, 3 discs, Criterion. **LD70427. $124.95.**
Laser: CLV, 2 discs, Criterion. **LD70428. $69.95.**
Alfred Hitchcock, USA, 1959, 136 mins.

Notorious

One of the greatest, if not the greatest, of Hitchcock's films. A conflict between love and duty pushes the action of this thriller set in Rio just after World War II. A beautiful party girl, the daughter of a Nazi traitor, is enlisted by the U.S. government to marry Nazi spy Claude Rains in order to infiltrate his ring. Cary Grant is the U.S. agent sent to aid her, and one of the great screen romances of all time develops. Beautifully shot, the work of the master at the top of his form.
VHS: S04454. $19.98.
Laser: CAV. **LD70429. $99.95.**
Laser: CLV. **LD70430. $49.95.**
Alfred Hitchcock, USA, 1946, 102 mins.

Number Seventeen

A dead body in a deserted house found with handcuffs and a gun in its pocket suddenly disappears. That's the beginning of Hitchcock's early thriller, shot almost entirely at night, providing a display of his early camera technique.
VHS: S00943. $19.98.
Alfred Hitchcock, Great Britain, 1932, 64 mins.

Paradine Case

A very little known, but very interesting Alfred Hitchcock film, based on a novel by Robert Hitchens. Gregory Peck is the lawyer who falls in love with the woman (Alida Valli) whom he's defending. With Ethel Barrymore, Charles Laughton.
VHS: S05908. $19.98.
Alfred Hitchcock, USA, 1948, 125 mins.

Psycho

The Classic! Anthony Perkins is Norman Bates and Janet Leigh is Marion Crane in this masterpiece of the macabre by Alfred Hitchcock.
VHS: S01068. $19.95.
Laser: LD70068. $34.98.
DVD: DV60289. $34.98.
Alfred Hitchcock, USA, 1960, 109 mins.

Rear Window

Injured magazine photographer, confined to his apartment because of a broken leg, suspects a murder has been committed in a neighboring flat. Confined to one set, *Rear Window* is a tour-de-force; James Stewart plays the photographer, Grace Kelly his New York girlfriend, and Raymond Burr the killer.
VHS: S01095. $19.95.
Alfred Hitchcock, USA, 1954, 101 mins.

Rebecca

Hitchcock's first American film, based on a Daphne du Maurier gothic romance. With Laurence Olivier and a fine performance by Joan Fontaine as a shy young woman who marries Olivier. Excellent supporting roles by Judith Anderson, George Sanders, Leo G. Carroll and Nigel Bruce.
VHS: S01096. $19.98.
Laser: CAV. **LD70441. $124.95.**
Laser: CLV. **LD70442. $69.95.**
Alfred Hitchcock, USA, 1940, 104 mins.

Rich and Strange

Regarded by many as the key film in Hitchcock's career with themes that foreshadow *39 Steps* and *North by Northwest, Rich and Strange* tells the story of a young couple on a world cruise that turns out catastrophically.
VHS: S01112. $19.98.
Alfred Hitchcock, Great Britain, 1932, 83 mins.

The Ring

A story of two prizefighters in love with the same woman, the title refers both to the boxing ring and a wedding band. Silent.
VHS: S01117. $19.98.
Alfred Hitchcock, Great Britain, 1927, 82 mins.

Rope

One of Hitchcock's most daring experiments in suspense and long takes. Farley Granger and John Dall are the two friends who strangle a classmate for intellectual thrills and then proceed to invite his family and mutual friends to dinner—with the body stuffed inside the trunk they use as a buffet table. James Stewart is the teacher who suspects his students. Inspired by the Leopold-Loeb case.
VHS: S01133. $19.95.
Laser: LD70072. $34.95.
Alfred Hitchcock, USA, 1948, 81 mins.

Sabotage

Based on Joseph Conrad's *Secret Agent*, in which Sylvia Sidney suspects her husband, a theater manager, is keeping something from her—he is a saboteur, planning to explode a bomb in a railroad station. Suspense from start to finish.
VHS: S01144. $19.95.
Laser: LD70447. $34.95.
Alfred Hitchcock, Great Britain, 1936, 76 mins.

Saboteur

Wartime thriller starring Robert Cummings as an aircraft factory worker who witnesses the firebombing of his plant by a Nazi agent, and finds himself accused of the crime. Hitchcock's first film with an entire cast from the U.S.
VHS: S01730. $19.95.
Laser: LD70073. $34.95.
Alfred Hitchcock, USA, 1942, 108 mins.

Secret Agent

Elsa and Dick are British espionage agents during World War I. Sent to Switzerland to find a German spy, they masquerade as husband and wife. The film ends in a climactic train wreck. Peter Lorre is brilliant as the General sent to assassinate the spy.
VHS: S01171. $24.95.
Laser: LD70450. $34.95.
Alfred Hitchcock, Great Britain, 1936, 84 mins.

Shadow of a Doubt

Hitchcock has said that this is his best American film. Joseph Cotten plays the widow-murderer Charley, who dodges the police and joins his relatives in a small California town. Although his niece (Teresa Wright) takes him to her heart, she eventually recognizes him as the murderer. Tense, subtle, brilliant Hitchcock.

VHS: S07295. $19.95.
Laser: LD70077. $34.95.
Alfred Hitchcock, USA, 1943, 108 mins.

Skin Game

Skillful adaptation of a stage play, the story is of a feud between the landed gentry and a rising mercantile family—one of Hitchcock's more successful social commentaries.

VHS: S01210. $19.98.
Alfred Hitchcock, Great Britain, 1931, 85 mins.

Stage Fright

Another Hitchcock film set within the confines of the theatre as were *Murder, 39 Steps* and *Sabotage*. Drama student Jane Wyman envisions the acting challenge of her life trying to prove the innocence of Richard Todd being framed by Marlene Dietrich.

VHS: S01246. $19.98.
Laser: LD74714. $34.98.
Alfred Hitchcock, USA, 1949, 110 mins.

Strangers on a Train (American Version)

A brilliantly plotted, diabolically humorous suspense thriller about two murders planned by strangers after an accidental meeting. Hitchcock's mise-en-scene is rich in detail and subtle in its insinuations of guilt and homosexuality. With Robert Walker, Farley Granger, Ruth Roman, based on the novel by Raymond Chandler.

VHS: S01265. $19.98.
Laser: LD70686. $24.98.
Alfred Hitchcock, USA, 1951, 101 mins.

Strangers on a Train (British Version)

Marking the 45th anniversary of this Hitchcock classic, this rediscovered British version sharpens the divide between two men (Robert Walker and Farley Granger) whose chance encounter on a train leads to a bizarre pact of exchanged murders. Includes two minutes of extra, never-before-seen footage, new digital transfer and the original theatrical trailer.

VHS: S30915. $19.98.
Alfred Hitchcock, Great Britain, 1951, 103 mins.

Suspicion

Cary Grant and Joan Fontaine in Hitchcock's thriller about a woman who gradually suspects her husband is a murderer. Fontaine won an Oscar for her performance.

VHS: S01287. $19.95.
Alfred Hitchcock, USA, 1941, 99 mins.

The Thirty-Nine Steps

A Canadian leaves London and goes to Scotland in order to find the spy ring that has stabbed a woman to death at his flat. What follows is Hitchcock's most popular British picture; there is suspense, humor, and great technical finesse.

VHS: S18181. $24.95.
Laser: LD70799. $39.95.
Alfred Hitchcock, Great Britain, 1935, 88 mins.

To Catch a Thief

Cary Grant and Grace Kelly star in this suspenseful thriller about an ex-jewel thief who is suspected of a string of new thefts. Set in the French Riviera, the film has spectacular scenery and won three Oscars, including Best Cinematography.

VHS: S01351. $14.95.
Laser: LD75328. $29.98.
Alfred Hitchcock, USA, 1955, 103 mins.

Topaz

Based on Leon Uris' spy novel, *Topaz* features John Forsythe as a CIA agent who learns of the Cuban missiles from a defecting Russian. He enlists the aid of a French agent to uncover the espionage in a tense Hitchcock thriller.

VHS: S01363. $19.95.
Alfred Hitchcock, USA, 1969, 126 mins.

Torn Curtain

Paul Newman is a famous scientist who goes to an international congress on physics in Copenhagen with his fiancee, Julie Andrews. While there, she mistakenly picks up a message meant for him and discovers that he's defecting to East Berlin.

VHS: S03324. $19.98.
Laser: LD70090. $39.98.
Alfred Hitchcock, USA, 1966, 128 mins.

The Trouble with Harry

Alfred Hitchcock's macabre comedy about the manic efforts of a group of Vermont residents to dispatch a dead body that refuses to stay buried. Framed by the director's usual preoccupation with sin, guilt and redemption, with some excellent performances by Edmund Gwenn, Shirley MacLaine and John Forsythe. Brilliantly photographed by Robert Burks, with an eerie, understated Bernard Herrmann score.

VHS: S01786. $14.98.
Laser: LD70092. $34.98.
Alfred Hitchcock, USA, 1955, 99 mins.

Vertigo

The elaborately constructed murder story in which an ex-cop who suffers from vertigo is the innocent pawn, is a masterful study of sexual obsession, and one of Hitchcock's best films. With James Stewart, Kim Novak, Barbara Bel Geddes. VHS fully restored, THX, letterboxed.

VHS: S01795. $19.95.
Laser: LD70094. $79.95.
DVD: DV60218. $34.98.
Alfred Hitchcock, USA, 1958, 95 mins.

The Wrong Man

The true story of a musician for whom a case of mistaken identity becomes a nightmare. With Henry Fonda and Vera Miles, musical score by Bernard Herrmann and screenplay by Maxwell Anderson.

VHS: S04182. $19.98.
Laser: LD70713. $34.98.
Alfred Hitchcock, USA, 1956, 126 mins.

Young and Innocent

Derrick de Marney is a young writer accused of murder. He escapes, meets a girl, and persuades her to help him find evidence that will prove his innocence. Spiced with Hitchcock's wry humor, the film follows the two of them through adventures with tramps, hotel lounges, lime pits, and a web of suspense.

VHS: S01493. $19.95.
Laser: LD71222. $34.95.
Alfred Hitchcock, Great Britain, 1937, 82 mins.

JOSEPH LOSEY

Blind Date

A Dutch painter finds romance with an intriguing woman, but it ends rather badly. She is found dead, and the painter, a man without any resources, could be the only suspect the police are likely to find.

VHS: S27896. $19.98.
Joseph Losey, Great Britain, 1959, 90 mins.

Don Giovanni

Finally on video, this sumptuous production of Mozart's great opera was shot on location in Venice, and is one of the great films of Joseph Losey. Ruggero Raimondi, Kiri Te Kanawa and Teresa Berganza are principal singers, with Lorin Maazel conducting the Paris Opera Orchestra. Sung in Italian with English subtitles.

VHS: S07688. $39.95.
Joseph Losey, Italy/France, 1972, 185 mins.

The Go-Between

Joseph Losey's tense, sexual class drama based on a brilliant script by Harold Pinter. Julie Christie is the upper-class beauty whose passionate, illicit affair with the groundskeeper (Alan Bates) is orchestrated through notes carried by a young boy, the go-between. The film, told largely in flashback through the boy's eyes, is full of nuance and innuendo; a brilliant dissection of sex and class.

VHS: S27183. $19.95.
Joseph Losey, Great Britain, 1971, 118 mins.

Joseph Losey and Adolfus Mekas: The First New York Film Festival

This 1963 program brings together film directors Joseph Losey and Adolfus Mekas and Festival organizers Richard Roud and Amos Vogel in 1963 to discuss the launching of what soon became one of the most important film festivals in the world. The program includes excerpts from the films *The Servant* (Losey) and *Hallelujah the Hills* (Mekas), both of which were screened at the Festival. Themes discussed on this program include: the importance of establishing an international film festival in New York City, Harold Pinter's script for Losey's *The Servant*, marketing films through the Festival, and the freedom and risks in independent film production. 28 mins.

VHS: S31576. $59.95.

Mr. Klein

Set in France during the 1942 occupation, Joseph Losey's French film stars Alain Delon as a cultivated and ruthless art dealer who discovers that someone is using his identity to cover their anti-Nazi resistance activities. As Mr. Klein becomes obsessed with the search for his imposter, he meets an elegant society lady (Jeanne Moreau), who leads him further into the trap. This existential period thriller was hailed by the *New York Times* as "seductive, splendidly visual, witty, cool, and elegant." French with English subtitles.

VHS: S32685. $29.95.
Joseph Losey, France/Italy, 1976, 123 mins.

Road to the South

Joseph Losey's second French film is the story of a screenplay writer who is the son of Spanish political refugees. He and his wife have long been settled in France, and, though he still keeps ties to his native land, he even writes in French. But his son seems to be growing in the opposite direction; he wants to go back to Spain and discover his roots. This politically charged drama deals with the collisions, rivalries and misunderstandings of one family against the backdrop of Spain's political struggles, especially the turbulence during the last year of the Franco dictatorship. Starring Yves Montand and Miou-Miou. French with English subtitles.

VHS: S13658. $29.95.
Laser: LD71627. $49.95.
Joseph Losey, France, 1978, 100 mins.

Sleeping Tiger

Joseph Losey directed this film noir under a pseudonym while in exile in England. The young Dirk Bogarde is a fifties hood with a "sleeping tiger"—desires that must be tamed before they explode into madness. A prominent psychiatrist (Alexander Knox) tries to help Bogarde as the charming delinquent seduces the doctor's wife. B&W.

VHS: S01214. $34.95.
Joseph Losey, Great Britain, 1954, 89 mins.

Time Without Pity

Director Joseph Losey, blacklisted in the United States during the reign of Joseph McCarthy, creates a tense and threatening atmosphere in this film noir thriller. Michael Redgrave stars as a guilt-ridden alcoholic who has 24 hours to prevent his son, wrongly accused of murder, from being executed. Featuring Peter Cushing and Joan Plowright.

VHS: S24932. $39.95.
Joseph Losey, Great Britain, 1957, 88 mins.

BLAKE EDWARDS

10

Dudley Moore is suffering a mid-life crises that he feels can be solved by a romantic interlude with Bo Derek. Julie Andrews, as the mature relationship in Moore's life, is not amused. The movie that made Ravel's *Bolero* a hit record. With Robert Webber, Brian Dennehy, Sam Jones and Dee Wallace.

VHS: S06198. $19.98.
DVD: DV60080. $24.98.
Blake Edwards, USA, 1979, 121 mins.

Blind Date

Bruce Willis makes his starring feature film debut as a serious, corporate-minded young man who makes the mistake of accepting a blind date with Kim Basinger (as a brunette). Under the influence of alcohol she destroys his life and they fall in love. It's a comedy.

VHS: S04672. $14.95.
Laser: LD75807. $34.95.
Blake Edwards, USA, 1987, 95 mins.

Breakfast at Tiffany's

Audrey Hepburn is superb in this dazzling romantic comedy based on Truman Capote's novella. Audrey is the New York playgirl with a secret, determined to marry a Brazilian millionaire, who falls in love with her next-door neighbor, George Peppard.

VHS: S03776. $14.95.
Laser: Widescreen. **LD75307. $39.98.**
Blake Edwards, USA, 1961, 114 mins.

Breakfast at Tiffany's: Collector's Edition

Audrey Hepburn and George Peppard star in this classic film based on a story by Truman Capote about love in Manhattan. Henry Mancini wrote the score that won an Oscar for this unforgettable comedy. Hepburn is magical as the young woman who achieves her wildest dreams. This version includes the original theatrical trailer.

VHS: S21768. $59.95.
Laser: Widescreen. **LD75392. $79.98.**
Blake Edwards, USA, 1961, 114 mins.

Curse of the Pink Panther

Shot simultaneously with *Trail of the Pink Panther*, Blake Edwards tries to preserve his popular series by installing Ted Wass, playing "the world's worst detective," to replace Clouseau, who has disappeared. With Joanna Lumley, Herbert Lom, David Niven, Robert Wagner, Capucine, Harvey Korman and Burt Kwouk.
VHS: S20409. $19.98.
Blake Edwards, USA, 1983, 110 mins.

Days of Wine and Roses

Jack Lemmon and Lee Remick star in this harrowing look at the lives of an alcoholic pair. Lemmon is an advertising executive who drags his wife into his hellish habit. Based on J.P. Miller's television play, this film received many Oscar nominations and won an Oscar for Henry Mancini's title song. Also featuring Jack Klugman and Charles Bickford. The video duplicates the experience of a night at the theater, with a Bugs Bunny cartoon (*Martian Through Georgia*), a newsreel, and previews for *Gypsy* and *Rome Adventure*.
VHS: S25896. $19.98.
Blake Edwards, USA, 1962, 138 mins.

The Great Race

1908's New York/Paris auto race zips along in one gear: hilarious! Join Jack Lemmon, Tony Curtis and Natalie Wood. 2,357 pies are thrown before the end credits.
VHS: S14565. $19.98.
Laser: Letterboxed. **LD74728. $39.98.**
Blake Edwards, USA, 1965, 160 mins.

The Man Who Loved Women

Remake of the Truffaut film features Burt Reynolds and Julie Andrews.
VHS: S05368. $79.95.
Blake Edwards, USA, 1983, 110 mins.

Micki and Maude

Dudley Moore stars in this hilarious comedy about a lovable bigamist. The fun really begins when both wives become pregnant and are delivering in adjoining rooms at the hospital. Several laugh-out-loud scenes.
VHS: S00852. $79.95.
Blake Edwards, Great Britain, 1984, 120 mins.

Operation Petticoat

Cary Grant commands the submarine *Sea Tiger* during WW II and the war is going fine until he meets military con artist Tony Curtis. Then he must rescue and house a detachment of nurses and meet the enemy in a pink painted sub. With Dina Merrill and Arthur O'Connell. Later a tv series. Letterboxed.
VHS: S04242. $19.95.
Blake Edwards, USA, 1959, 120 mins.

The Party

Peter Sellers teams up with Blake Edwards to make a film that does not include a certain French policeman but does provide plenty of comical embarrassments. Sellers is a bumbling Indian actor—the kind with the turbans—who finds his film career might be advanced by attending a posh Hollywood party—if he doesn't destroy his host's home in the process. With Claudine Longet, Denny Miller and Gavin McLeod.
VHS: S11734. $19.98.
Laser: LD71166. $34.98.
Blake Edwards, USA, 1968, 99 mins.

The Perfect Furlough

An early slapstick work from Blake Edwards (*10*) stars Tony Curtis as a smooth Lothario offered a "perfect furlough" from an Arctic outpost to romance a beautiful film star (Linda Cristal). But military psychiatrist Janet Leigh steps in to restore order following a disastrous publicity gimmick and woo Curtis' wavering affection.
VHS: S02787. $24.98.
Blake Edwards, USA, 1958, 93 mins.

The Pink Panther

The film that established director Blake Edwards' slightly subversive point of view and heightened the diversity of Peter Sellers. Sellers is Inspector Clouseau, the perpetually inept detective in pursuit of David Niven, the charming and brilliant cat burglar known as the Phantom. Robert Wagner, Capucine and Claudia Cardinale are along for the ride. Music by Henry Mancini. VHS letterboxed.
VHS: S02328. $14.95.
Laser: LD70655. $34.98.
Blake Edwards, Great Britain, 1964, 118 mins.

The Pink Panther Strikes Again

Inspector Clouseau is back on the job and before the case is solved, expect an avalanche of comic anarchy. The character created by Blake Edwards and brought to amazing life by Peter Sellers must now defeat his former boss, Herbert Lom, who has been driven mad by the luckiest klutz alive. Lom has a gaunt ray gun ready to pulverize the planet from a small castle in Bavaria if Clouseau is not assassinated by the security agents of the entire world. With Lesley-Anne Down, Omar Sharif, Colin Blakely and Burt Kwouk. VHS letterboxed.
VHS: S02329. $14.95.
Laser: LD71641. $34.98.
Blake Edwards, Great Britain, 1976, 103 mins.

Return of the Pink Panther

An assortment of props, including a steam bath, vacuum cleaner, waxed dance room floor and a deliriously deranged monkey are the comic springs for Peter Sellers' jagged rhythm and off-beat versatility. The story is fairly simple: a diamond is stolen and Clouseau is assigned to retrieve it.
VHS: S02331. $14.98.
Laser: Letterboxed. **LD76038. $39.98.**
Blake Edwards, USA, 1974, 113 mins.

Revenge of the Pink Panther

Peter Sellers and Herbert Lom return in the fifth installment of the popular spoof of mastermind police detectives. With the mafia gunning for Inspector Clouseau, he prefers to let them think he is deceased. Living undercover can have its drawbacks, particularly when your servant converts your apartment into a bordello. Watch for the fireworks when Sellers visits Hong Kong. With Dyan Cannon, Robert Loggia, Robert Webber and Burt Kwouk. VHS letterboxed.
VHS: S02333. $14.98.
Laser: LD70204. $34.98.
Blake Edwards, USA, 1978, 99 mins.

S.O.B.

William Holden made his last screen appearance in this film comedy alongside such Hollywood notables as Robert Preston, Shelley Winters, Larry Hagman and Julie Andrews. This bitter send-up of desperate film industry insiders concerns a director who decides to save a multi-million dollar flop by adding a little exposed flesh. In a startling reflection of real life, Andrews, the wife of the director, goes topless.
VHS: S26327. $19.95.
Blake Edwards, USA, 1981, 121 mins.

A Shot in the Dark

Inspector Clouseau has doubts about the guilt of the maid accused of murder in a French chateau. Peter Sellers and Elke Sommer star in this Blake Edwards classic farce co-written by William Peter Blatty. Top notch comedy with plenty of slapstick and fractured English. With George Sanders, Herbert Lom, Tracy Reed, Graham Stark and Burt Kwouk. VHS letterboxed.
VHS: S02330. $14.95.
Laser: LD70675. $34.98.
Blake Edwards, USA, 1964, 101 mins.

Sunset

Bruce Willis and James Garner play two real-life heroes who meet in a fictional setting in Hollywood in the late 1920s. Willis is Tom Mix, rodeo and movie star, and Garner is the legendary lawman Wyatt Earp. Together they team up to solve a murder in a brothel and swap tall tales. With Mariel Hemingway, Kathleen Quinlan, and Malcolm McDowell as the evil English clown prince of comedy.
VHS: S07980. $14.95.
Blake Edwards, USA, 1988, 107 mins.

Trail of the Pink Panther

Following the unexpected death of Peter Sellers, Blake Edwards responded by using the form and structure of Orson Welles' *Citizen Kane* for a new entry in the *Panther* series. When Inspector Clouseau turns up missing, an intrepid television reporter interviews the people from Clouseau's past to create a biographical portrait. Edwards incorporates previously unused material and outtakes. With David Niven, Herbert Lom, Richard Mulligan, Joanna Lumley, Robert Wagner, Capucine and Robert Loggia. Letterboxed.
VHS: S02332. $14.98.
Blake Edwards, USA, 1982, 97 mins.

Victor/Victoria

A very funny sexual comedy of errors. Julie Andrews portrays a gay female impersonator, with Robert Preston, James Garner and Lesley Ann Warren. Music by Henry Mancini.
VHS: S01412. $19.98.
Laser: LD70700. $59.95.
Blake Edwards, USA, 1982, 133 mins.

Wild Rovers

Blake Edwards takes a shot at doing a western. He pairs William Holden with Ryan O'Neal, as a couple of down-on-their-luck cowpokes who turn to bank robbing on a whim. They spend the rest of the movie being pursued by Joe Don Baker and Tom Skerritt. This version is nearly 30 minutes longer than the theatrical release.
VHS: S03669. $19.98.
Laser: LD72135. $39.98.
Blake Edwards, USA, 1971, 138 mins.

CECIL B. DEMILLE

Carmen (DeMille)

Cecil B. DeMille's much talked-about but seldom-seen version of *Carmen* has been superbly restored with a new soundtrack featuring the London Philharmonic Orchestra. Geraldine Farrar, the Metropolitan Opera's biggest box-office draw from 1906-1922, was engaged by DeMille to recreate one of her greatest roles for the silent screen. The film was rapturously received at its 1915 world premiere performance, with Farrar elevated to Hollywood stardom. Also includes passages of the opera sung by Farrar herself, taken from a recording of the period.
VHS: S30710. $29.95.
Cecil B. DeMille, USA, 1915, 75 mins.

Cecil B. DeMille: The Greatest Showman on Earth

This boxed set contains five outstanding films from DeMille's career in silent pictures: *Carmen* (1915), *Joan the Woman* (1916), *The Whispering Chorus* (1918), *Male and Female* (1919) and *The Volga Boatman* (1926). Features some of the most talented actors of the period, including Gloria Swanson, William Boyd, Geraldine Farrar and Wallace Reid. Each film has a new stereo music score and has been tinted to its original specifications.
Laser: LD76369. $159.99.
Cecil B. DeMille, USA, 1915-1926, 519 mins.

The Cheat

A very early film from Cecil B. De Mille; the story of a young society woman (Fanny Ward) who comes under the control of a scheming Asiatic when she is unable to repay the money she borrows from him. With Sessue Hayakawa.
VHS: S06907. $29.95.
Cecil B. DeMille, USA, 1915, 58 mins.

Cleopatra

Claudette Colbert portrays the infamous Queen of the Nile in this Cecil B. De Mille production. Naturally there is a cast of thousands including Warren William, C. Aubrey Smith, Henrey Wilcoxson, Joseph Schildkraut and Gertrude Michael. Opulence abounds. B&W.
VHS: S02669. $39.95.
Cecil B. DeMille, USA, 1934, 95 mins.

The Crusades

Loretta Young and Henry Wilcoxon are involved in a curious love affair at the heart of *The Crusades*. Wilcoxon is Richard the Lion-Hearted, a man forced to marry a woman he has never seen for political reasons, the beautiful Berengaria (Young). As they battle to save Jerusalem from the Saracens, their love falls victim to other threatening perils. The battle scenes are unmatched in their virtuosity.
VHS: S24024. $14.98.
Cecil B. DeMille, USA, 1935, 126 mins.

The Greatest Show on Earth

This Cecil B. De Mille production won best picture in 1952 and is a rousing tribute to life under the Big Top. Against a background of the Ringling Brothers circus, stars Charlton Heston, Cornel Wilde, Betty Hutton, Gloria Grahame, James Stewart and Dorothy Lamour combine to bring love, adventure, spectacle and suspense to the big screen.
VHS: S06146. $29.95.
Cecil B. DeMille, USA, 1952, 147 mins.

Joan the Woman

Geraldine Farrar portrays Joan of Arc in this beautifully restored silent film, enlivened by massive battle sequences, experimental camerawork and a hand-tinted color finale.
VHS: S30711. $29.95.
Cecil B. DeMille, USA, 1916, 127 mins.

King of Kings

Cecil B. De Mille's opulent Hollywoodization of the new testament, with casts of thousands, in its original silent (with music track) re-incarnation. Featured are H.B. Warner, Dorothy Cumming, Ernest Torrence, Joseph Schildkraut and William Boyd. B&W, with the Resurrection sequence in color.
VHS: S03368. $29.95.
Cecil B. DeMille, USA, 1927, 115 mins.

Little American

A super-rare Mary Pickford silent, with Pickford as an American sweetheart in Europe caught in the intrigues of the First World War. With Jack Holt.
VHS: S08335. $49.95.
Cecil B. DeMille, USA, 1917, 80 mins.

Madam Satan
A surreal musical extravaganza from Cecil B. De Mille about the efforts of a wealthy socialite to win back her husband's affection following his affair with a showgirl. The production numbers include a masquerade party atop a zeppelin. With Kay Johnson, Reginald Denny and Roland Young.
VHS: S18128. $19.98.
Cecil B. DeMille, USA, 1930, 116 mins.

Male and Female
Gloria Swanson plays a spoiled maiden who always gets her way until shipwrecked with her servants—then it's every man for himself! Silent.
VHS: S08331. $29.95.
Cecil B. DeMille, USA, 1919, 110 mins.

Manslaughter
Speed-crazy, thrill-seeking society girl Lydia (Leatrice Joy) causes the death of a motorcycle cop and is prosecuted by her fiance, Daniel (Thomas Meighan), who attempts to draw parallels between the destructive nature of speed and the collapse of Rome. While Lydia reforms in prison, Daniel becomes an alcoholic. With Spottiswode Aitken, William Boyd and J. Farrell MacDonald. Silent, music track.
VHS: S33049. $24.95.
Cecil B. DeMille, USA, 1922, 101 mins.

Plainsman
Cecil B. De Mille's massive Western with Gary Cooper as Wild Bill Hickok and Jean Arthur as Calamity Jane, full of terrific action and offbeat romance.
VHS: S04520. $14.98.
Laser: LD70067. $34.98.
Cecil B. DeMille, USA, 1936, 115 mins.

Reap the Wild Wind
This is a movie in which John Wayne takes on a giant squid. He plays Captain Jack Stuart, who battles Key West salvage pirates, hurricanes and the wrath of Paulette Goddard. Ray Milland is the sea lawyer trying to clear the Duke's good name. Raymond Massey is the villainous King Cutler. With Susan Hayward, Robert Preston and Hedda Hopper.
VHS: S08504. $14.98.
Cecil B. DeMille, USA, 1942, 123 mins.

Road to Yesterday
An early, silent production by Cecil B. De Mille, in which four train passengers are transported back to the 18th century into previous lives. Starring Joseph Schildkraut and William Boyd.
VHS: S07465. $49.95.
Cecil B. DeMille, USA, 1925, 136 mins.

Samson and Delilah
The unequalled epic style of Cecil B. De Mille in this story of the legendary strongman and the woman who seduces and then betrays him. With Hedy Lamarr and Victor Mature.
VHS: S04340. $29.95.
Cecil B. DeMille, USA, 1951, 127 mins.

Sign of the Cross
Charles Laughton plays a cruelly indifferent Nero, who burns Rome merely to blame the Christians. Meanwhile, Rome's Prefect (Fredric March) falls in love with a beautiful Christian (Claudette Colbert). This lavish costume drama was a sensation upon its release and continues to fascinate audiences with its intense performances and decadent eroticism.
VHS: S24023. $14.98.
Cecil B. DeMille, USA, 1932, 125 mins.

The Spoilers
The first film version of the classic story of gold hunters in the Alaskan wilderness, starring William Farnum and Tom Santschi. Included at the end are clips from *The Squaw Man*, directed by De Mille. Silent with music score.
VHS: S07488. $19.95.
Cecil B. DeMille, USA, 1914, 110 mins.

The Story of Dr. Wassell
Based on the actual experiences of Dr. Corydon M. Wassell, this film tells the true story of the country doctor who won the Navy Cross for humanitarianism. Dr. Wassell (Gary Cooper) and his love (Laraine Day) are tending to wounded American soldiers in Java. When the Japanese invade, Dr. Wassell learns that only those who can walk are going to be evacuated. Remaining behind with his patients, the doctor manages to save many more of his patients than the Navy thought possible.
VHS: S27668. $14.98.
Cecil B. DeMille, USA, 1944, 137 mins.

The Ten Commandments (1923)
Cecil B. De Mille's first treatment of this Biblical epic, with a cast of thousands and imaginative special effects. Follows Moses' life from birth to manhood to slavery to, finally, leading the Jews out of Egypt. Silent.
VHS: S03439. $29.95.
Cecil B. DeMille, USA, 1923, 146 mins.

The Ten Commandments (1956)
De Mille's extravagant spectacle remake of his own epic cost millions, and made Charlton Heston synonymous with Moses.
VHS: S05372. $29.95.
Cecil B. DeMille, USA, 1956, 210 mins.

The Ten Commandments: 40th Anniversary Collector's Edition
One of the most famous screen epics ever made is finally presented on video, fully restored to its original form. This 40th Anniversary edition of *The Ten Commandments* includes the original theatrical trailer (never before seen on video) and is presented uncut, in widescreen format with spectacular Dolby Surround stereo. Enjoy the gaudy, Technicolor splendor of a bearded Charlton Heston parting the Red Sea; see slaves whipped, pyramids built, false idols worshipped.
VHS: S15100. $35.00.
Cecil B. DeMille, USA, 1956, 245 mins.

The Unconquered
Gary Cooper and Paulette Goddard star in this historical epic set in the young English colonies of North America. Goddard is a convict/slave who is freed by Cooper. She is forced back into servitude, however, by an evil gun-runner (Howard Da Silva). War with the Native Americans is soon at hand and Cooper must decide how he feels about Goddard before it is too late. Boris Karloff is featured as Seneca Chief Guyasuta.
VHS: S24025. $14.98.
Cecil B. DeMille, USA, 1947, 127 mins.

Union Pacific
Barbara Stanwyck and Joel McCrea are joined by Robert Preston and Anthony Quinn in this Western about the first transcontinental rail link. The setting and plot provide more than enough justification for gun-toting action and melodramatic twists, making this a sweeping historical spectacle.
VHS: S24026. $14.98.
Cecil B. DeMille, USA, 1939, 136 mins.

The Volga Boatman
The Russian Revolution is given the DeMille treatment in this silent, apolitical spectacle of class, sex and emotional intrigue.
VHS: S30713. $29.95.
Cecil B. DeMille, USA, 1926, 118 mins.

The Whispering Chorus
In this moody and surreal psychological, silent drama, a fugitive assumes the identity of a dead man and is haunted by the voices of his conscience.
VHS: S30712. $29.95.
Cecil B. DeMille, USA, 1918, 89 mins.

Why Change Your Wife
Gloria Swanson, T. Meighan and Bebe Daniels star in this rare De Mille treasure, made before his "pseudo-epic" period. Silent.
VHS: S08332. $29.95.
Cecil B. DeMille, USA, 1920, 100 mins.

RELIGIOUS FEATURES & EPICS

Abraham
Richard Harris and Barbara Hershey star in this version of the timeless story of Abraham, the biblical patriarch. Abraham's love for his son Isaac is tested when his God demands the ultimate sacrifice. This feature-length drama recalls the struggle that faith represents for all people. With Maximillian Schell.
VHS: S22156. $19.98.
Joseph Sargent, USA/Italy, 1993

Barabbas
A stirring adaptation of Nobel prize-winner Par Lagerkvist's novel about the robber set free when Christ was crucified. With Anthony Quinn and Silvana Mangano.
VHS: S04326. $14.95.
Richard Fleischer, USA, 1962, 134 mins.

The Cardinal
Handsomely produced saga about the personal and religious life of a dedicated Catholic priest who rises to the position of Cardinal. Starring Tom Tryon, Romy Schneider, Ossie Davis and John Huston. VHS letterboxed.
VHS: S01996. $29.98.
Laser: LD70902. $59.95.
Otto Preminger, USA, 1963, 175 mins.

Catholics
Winner of the Peabody Award, a moving contemporary drama about the changing attitudes of the Church, adapted from Brian Moore's novel about simple worship in an ancient Irish monastery now threatened with the increasing permissiveness of the Church. With Trevor Howard and Martin Sheen.
VHS: S01607. $39.95.
Jack Gold, USA, 1973, 86 mins.

David and Bathsheba
Gregory Peck and Susan Hayward play the Biblical sinners who were the talk of Jerusalem a few years back. When the king of the Israelites becomes attracted to the red headed wife of one of his best officers, passion clouds the royal judgement and a valuable lesson is learned. With Kieron Moore, James Robertson Justice and Raymond Massey as a disapproving prophet.
VHS: S10325. $19.98.
Henry King, USA, 1951, 116 mins.

Demetrius and the Gladiators
This sword and sandal saga is the sequel to *The Robe* and features Victor Mature—who was Roman centurion Richard Burton's Christian slave in the original. While the Emperor Caligula (Jay Robinson) searches for the mystical robe of Christ, Demetrius endures a test of faith and goes to gladiator school. With Michael Renie. Susan Hayward, Richard Egan, Debra Paget, Anne Bancroft and Ernest Borgnine.
VHS: S10327. $19.98.
Delmer Daves, USA, 1954, 101 mins.

Esther and the King
Lots of action and court intrigue in this wonderful spectacle film about the King of Persia, who marries a Jewish woman. He eventually banishes her after discovering her unfaithfulness. He then falls in love with a Hebrew girl, Esther, but is plotted against by his evil prime minister. A terrific sword and sandal film. With Joan Collins, Richard Egan and cinematography by Mario Bava.
VHS: S32586. $24.95.
Raoul Walsh, USA, 1961, 109 mins.

Golgotha
Robert Levigan stars as Jesus in the first sound film made about the life of Jesus of Nazareth. Jean Gabin is Pontius Pilate, while Harry Bauer appears as King Herod in this early Biblical film. It's a moving and credible account of the story, and it tells this story without any undue flourishes. Dubbed in English.
VHS: S29448. $29.95.
Julien Duvivier, France, 1935, 95 mins.

Jacob
Matthew Modine, Lara Flynn Boyle, Irene Papas and Giancarlo Giannini star in this adaptation of the biblical story. In addition to its religious meaning, *Jacob* is a tale of brotherly rivalry, exile and deeply felt passions and emotions. This epic film was shot on location with advice from religious experts and historians.
94 mins.
VHS: S29819. $19.98.

Jesus of Nazareth
Italian director Franco Zeffirelli's impassioned interpretation of the life of Christ. British novelist Anthony Burgess (*A Clockwork Orange*) wrote the screenplay. With Anne Bancroft, Ernest Borgnine, Valentina Cortese, James Mason, Robert Powell and Olivia Hussey.
VHS: S17908. $69.98.
Franco Zeffirelli, USA, 1977, 279 mins.

John Hus
John Hus, a priest and scholar, was willing to pay the ultimate price for his faith. His relentless pursuit of God's truth planted the seeds for the Reformation. He refused to recant and was burned at the stake in 1415. He died singing. With Rod Collins, Regis Cordic, and Sandor Naszody. Best Film, Christian Cinemagraphic Arts.
VHS: S34519. $19.95.
Michael Economou, USA, 1977, 55 mins.

Joseph
Paul Mercurio stars as the youngest son of an Israelite patriarch who turns betrayal into good fortune. Ben Kingsley, Martin Landau and Lesley Ann Warren are featured in this film adaptation of a biblical story. Location shoots and input from respected religious leaders and historians add to the authenticity of this film. 185 mins.
VHS: S29820. $19.98.

Moses (Kingsley)

Ben Kingsley stars in this dramatic adaptation based on the biblical story of the great Israelite prophet. Seemingly an ordinary man, God chose Moses to lead his people out of slavery in Egypt and into the promised land. Shot on location, the scenario is informed by respected religious leaders and historians. 185 mins.

VHS: S29821. $19.98.

Moses (Lancaster)

An all-star cast including Burt Lancaster, Anthony Quayle, Ingrid Thulin, Irene Papas and Mariangela Melato, star in this epic theatrical adaptation with a screenplay by Anthony Burgess and Vittorio Bonicelli.

VHS: S04593. $19.98.
Gianfranco De Bosio, Great Britain/Italy, 1975, 141 mins.

The Prodigal

A lavish MGM production shot in Cinemascope. Set in 70 B.C., Edmund Purdom plays a gilded farmer who is obsessed with the beautiful Samarra (Lana Turner). Lavish production of the Biblical favorite. With James Mitchell, Louis Calhern and Audrey Dalton.

VHS: S18661. $19.98.
Richard Thorpe, USA, 1955, 115 mins.

Quo Vadis (1951)

"A super-spectacle in all its meaning" (*Variety*). Robert Taylor, Deborah Kerr and a cast of thousands in Rome in 64 A.D. under Nero the mad emperor, played by Peter Ustinov.

VHS: S02564. $24.98.
Laser: LD70161. $39.98.
Mervyn Le Roy, USA, 1951, 291 mins.

The Robe

Richard Burton won an Oscar nomination for his portrayal of a Roman soldier in charge of the crucifixion of Jesus Christ. The passionate spectacle about the birth of Christianity was the first film made in Cinemascope. Based on the Lloyd C. Douglas novel. With Jean Simmons and Victor Mature. Letterboxed.

VHS: S04595. $19.98.
Henry Koster, USA, 1953, 135 mins.

Shoes of the Fisherman

International cast in this adaptation of the Morris West novel about the election of the first Russian Pope includes Anthony Quinn as Pope Kiril I, plus John Gielgud, Vittorio De Sica, David Janssen and Oskar Werner. VHS letterboxed.

VHS: S02728. $24.98.
Laser: LD70180. $39.98.
Michael Anderson, USA, 1968, 152 mins.

Sodom and Gomorrah

Don't look for them on any recent maps. The twin cities of sin made so popular by the Bible can only be found in film form in this Robert Aldrich epic made in Europe. A cast of thousands, and some of them are name performers like Stewart Granger, Anouk Aimee, Pier Angeli, Stanley Baker and Rossana Podesta. Said to have vivid scenes of vice, gore and God's wrath.

VHS: S10324. $19.98.
Laser: LD72204. $69.98.
Robert Aldrich, Italy, 1963, 148 mins.

Song of Bernadette

Jennifer Jones received an Oscar for her performance as the 19th century French peasant girl who claimed to speak to the Virgin Mary near her village of Lourdes. Three other Oscars were awarded to this inspirational but lengthy account. With Vincent Price, Lee J. Cobb, Charles Bickford and Gladys Cooper. Linda Darnell appeared, unbilled, as the Blessed Virgin. B&W.

VHS: S15607. $19.98.
Henry King, USA, 1943, 156 mins.

Story of Ruth

Elana Eden stars as the Biblical Ruth, who renounces her beliefs when she discovers the true Christian faith. With Stuart Whitan, Tom Tryon.

VHS: S11738. $29.98.
Henry Koster, USA, 1960, 132 mins.

AMERICAN CLASSICS

12 O'Clock High

Gregory Peck is commander of a US bomber unit during World War II. As the number of missions flown accumulates, he begins to crack under the strain. Well-made character drama with some fine performances.

VHS: S14138. $19.98.
Laser: LD71381. $49.98.
Henry King, USA, 1949, 132 mins.

13 Rue Madeleine

A documentary-style narrative about the attempts of an O.S.S. agent to locate a secret German missile site in France during World War II. Featuring strong performances from James Cagney, Annabella, and Richard Conte. A rough-and-tumble spy adventure from director Henry Hathaway.

VHS: S03915. $19.98.
Henry Hathaway, USA, 1946, 95 mins.

24 Hours in a Woman's Life

Ingrid Bergman plays a bereaved widow trying to escape her sorrow while traveling. At Monte Carlo she meets a desperate young gambler (Rip Torn), rescues him from suicide, and all within the span of 24 hours falls in love, tries to change him and fails.

VHS: S13432. $29.95.
Silvio Narizzano, USA, 1961, 90 mins.

36 Hours

In this spine-tingling thriller, James Garner stars as an American intelligence officer who is brainwashed by the Nazis into revealing the secrets of the Normandy invasion on the eve of D-Day. Co-stars Rod Taylor and Eva Marie Saint.

VHS: S28472. $19.98.
George Seaton, USA, 1964, 115 mins.

40 Pounds of Trouble

Tony Curtis, Suzanne Pleshette and Phil Silvers star in this romantic comedy about a wild getaway. Curtis plays a recently divorced casino manager who becomes enmeshed with his latest headliner's niece (Pleshette) and a recently abandoned five-year-old. Together these three are off on an adventure as Curtis must avoid detectives sent by his ex-wife.

VHS: S22125. $14.98.
Norman Jewison, USA, 1962, 106 mins.

The 5000 Fingers of Dr. T

This neglected classic tells the fantastic tale of a young boy who so hates taking piano lessons that he dreams his teacher is a cruel genius ruling over a baroque castle where kidnapped boys are sadistically forced to practice the piano over and over again. Screenplay by Dr. Seuss (Theodore Geisel)—his only full-length, live-action feature. Produced by Stanley Kramer.

VHS: S13189. $19.95.
Roy Rowland, USA, 1953, 88 mins.

633 Squadron

Spectacular aerial photography and a pulse-pounding climactic sequence highlight this WWII drama in the air, starring Cliff Robertson as a combat-weary pilot who is sent on a suicide mission. Screenplay by James Clavell.

VHS: S15131. $19.98.
Walter Grauman, USA, 1964, 95 mins.

The 7th Voyage of Sinbad

Ray Harryhausen's special visual effects enliven this spirited fantasy/drama which pits Sinbad against a cruel and sadistic magician who's reduced the beautiful princess Parisa to microscopic size. Full of imagination and verve, with a musical score by Hitchcock's brilliant collaborator, Bernard Herrmann. With Kerwin Mathews, Kathryn Grant, Torin Thatcher and Richard Eyer.

VHS: S16683. $14.95.
Nathan Juran, USA, 1958, 87 mins.

Abandon Ship!

In this "thoughtful and often gripping drama that mirrors man at his best and worst" (A.H. Weiler, *The New York Times*), Tyrone Power stars as the man who must decide the fate of 27 survivors of a luxury ocean liner disaster after the ship hits a derelict mine. With Lloyd Nolan, Mai Zetterling and Stephen Boyd.

VHS: S30776. $19.95.
Richard Sale, USA, 1956, 97 mins.

Above and Beyond

This film focuses on the grueling training and personal motives which shaped the pilots who delivered the final blow to Japan by dropping the first atomic bomb. Starring Norman Panama, Robert Taylor and James Whitmore.

VHS: S21013. $19.98.
Melvin Frank, USA, 1952, 122 mins.

Above Suspicion

Fred MacMurray and Joan Crawford are American honeymooners in pre-war Europe who are asked to do British intelligence a favor and help track down a missing agent. Also starring Basil Rathbone as a Nazi agent—a role that shocked and surprised Sherlock Holmes fans.

VHS: S15114. $19.98.
Richard Thorpe, USA, 1943, 90 mins.

Ace of Aces

Richard Dix is an American artist who enlists in World War I against his inner feelings to prove to his girlfriend that he is a patriot and becomes a bloodthirsty fighter pilot in a high flying aerial combat. An early anti-war film.

VHS: S12371. $19.98.
J. Walter Ruben, USA, 1933, 77 mins.

Across the Wide Missouri

Clark Gable plays trapper and fighter Flint Mitchell, a man of action whose marriage to a woman of the Blackfoot tribe leads him to a profound respect for her people. A breathtakingly beautiful epic, filmed in the Colorado Rockies at elevations of 9,000 to 14,000 feet. With Ricardo Montalban, John Hodiak and Adolphe Menjou as a hooch-swigging Frenchman.

VHS: S15256. $19.98.
William Wellman, USA, 1951, 78 mins.

Action in Arabia

George Sanders is a newspaperman who finds himself in treacherous surroundings amid Nazis in Damascus as he seeks a fellow reporter's murder. Uses stock desert footage shot by Merian C. Cooper and Ernest B. Schoedsack for a film which was never made.

VHS: S10673. $19.98.
Leonide Moguy, USA, 1944, 76 mins.

Action in the North Atlantic

Humphrey Bogart and Raymond Massey head the crew of the S.S. *Seawitch* in this cinematic salute to the Merchant Marines of World War II. A tense and thrilling tribute to unsung sailors-based on a true story.

VHS: S14305. $19.98.
Lloyd Bacon, USA, 1943, 127 mins.

Actors and Sin

Two stories by Ben Hecht: *Actor's Blood*, with Edward G. Robinson as the father of a murdered actress, and *Woman of Sin*, a satire on Hollywood with Robinson playing the second-rate agent.

VHS: S05715. $19.95.
Lee Garmes/Ben Hecht, USA, 1952, 82 mins.

The Admiral Was a Lady

Edmond O'Brien, Wanda Hendrix and Rudy Vallee are featured in this romantic comedy, with some delightful songs. O'Brien and Hendrix are meant for each other but there is one problem: O'Brien and his veteran pals have vowed never to work again. Ex-WAVE Hendrix needs some convincing, leading to great visual gags. The songs "Once Over Lightly" and "Everything That's Wonderful" add to this upbeat story.

VHS: S23779. $24.95.
Albert S. Rogell, USA, 1950, 87 mins.

Adventure

Clark Gable plays the brawling sailor with a girl in every port who is reeled in by Greer Garson in a love story that "does the whole film industry proud" (*Hollywood Reporter*).

VHS: S20557. $19.98.
Victor Fleming, USA, 1946, 125 mins.

Adventure Girl

Joan Lowell's novel *Adventure Girl* was the basis for this early sound film. Lowell narrates this exciting story about her sea voyage and exploration of jungles in Central America.

VHS: S23881. $29.95.
Herman C. Raymaker, USA, 1931, 65 mins.

Adventures of Don Juan

This Errol Flynn swashbuckling vehicle won the Academy Award for costumes and features a score by Max Steiner.

VHS: S02513. $19.98.
Laser: LD70496. $34.97.
Vincent Sherman, USA, 1948, 110 mins.

The Adventures of Marco Polo

Gary Cooper stars as Marco Polo, the intrepid traveler from medieval times. He sets off for the distant Eastern kingdom, the lavish court of Kubla Khan, where intrigues and adventure abound. This is a classic realized with all the pomp and excess that only old Hollywood could muster.

VHS: S20671. $19.98.
Archie Mayo, USA, 1938, 100 mins.

The Adventures of Robin Hood

The most acclaimed screen version of the King of Sherwood Forest. Errol Flynn is Robin Hood to Olivia de Havilland's Maid Marion. Basil Rathbone and Claude Rains are the villains. Action, drama and romance that has satisfied audiences for years.

VHS: S00019. $19.98.
Laser: LD70731. $34.98.
Michael Curtiz, USA, 1938, 102 mins.

Advise and Consent

Political drama in which blackmail, suicide and scandal follow the President's appointment of an unpopular Secretary of State. Featuring Henry Fonda, Charles Laughton, Burgess Meredith and Peter Lawford.

VHS: S01994. $29.95.
Otto Preminger, USA, 1962, 142 mins.

Aerial Gunner

World War II action in the Pacific as Chester Morris and Richard Arlen take time out from fighting each other to battle the Japanese. They both love Lita Ward and feel responsible for her kid brother Jimmy Lydon. From training to fighting on enemy-filled islands, this actioner packs a wallop.

VHS: S07066. $39.95.
William H. Pine, USA, 1943, 78 mins.

Affair in Trinidad

Rita Hayworth sizzles in this romantic spy drama of international intrigue also featuring Glenn Ford and Alexander Scourby. Hayworth stars as Chris Emery, a sultry singer-dancer whose life is turned upside down when her husband is murdered by a globe trotting thief.

VHS: S12996. $19.95.
Vincent Sherman, USA, 1952, 98 mins.

An Affair to Remember

Cary Grant and Deborah Kerr star in Leo McCarey's own remake of *Love Affair*. Grant and Kerr are the shipboard lovers who decide to meet after an absence to see if it all still works.

VHS: S11562. $14.98.
Laser: LD70813. $59.98.
Leo McCarey, USA, 1957, 114 mins.

Agony and the Ecstasy

Based on Irving Stone's best-selling biography of Michelangelo, this mammoth Hollywood production starring Charlton Heston and Rex Harrison focuses on Michelangelo's painting of the Sistine Chapel.

VHS: S05926. $19.98.
Laser: LD70821. $69.98.
Carol Reed, USA, 1965, 140 mins.

Alexander the Great

Robert Rossen (*The Hustler*) wrote and directed this biography of the brilliant military strategist and warrior who conquered everything in his path before his death at 33. Photographed by Robert Krasker in Cinemascope, preserved in the letterbox presentation. With Richard Burton, Frederic March, Danielle Darrieux and Claire Bloom.

VHS: S20769. $19.98.
Laser: LD71648. $39.98.
Robert Rossen, USA, 1956, 135 mins.

Algiers

A classic love story that combines adventure and intrigue, starring Charles Boyer as Pepe le Moko, a crook who seeks refuge from the police in the casbah in North Africa. With Hedy Lamarr.

VHS: S00029. $19.95.
John Cromwell, USA, 1938, 95 mins.

Ali Baba and the Forty Thieves

In this colorful, stylized *Arabian Nights* tale, a deposed prince and his band of outlaws seek vengeance on the nefarious Hulagu Khan and the Mongol forces who murdered his father and seized the throne. Cinematography by George Robinson. With Jon Hall, Maria Montez, Scotty Beckett and Turhan Bey.

VHS: S19313. $14.98.
Arthur Lubin, USA, 1943, 87 mins.

All About Eve

Six Oscars were awarded this cynical and entertaining examination of life as it exists on the Broadway theatre scene. Bette Davis glows as the aging star being undermined by her protege Anne Baxter, as Eve Harrington. With George Sanders, Celeste Holm and Marilyn Monroe. A gem.

VHS: S03911. $19.98.
Laser: LD70823. $49.98.
Joseph L. Mankiewicz, USA, 1950, 138 mins.

All Fall Down

Warren Beatty plays the amoral ladies' man Berry-Berry Willant in this adaptation of the James Leo Herlihy novel by playwright William Inge. Eva Marie Saint is just one of the older women who fall for his soulless charm. With Brandon de Wilde as Beatty's admiring little brother. Karl Malden and Angela Lansbury play his alcoholic and possessive parents.

VHS: S16436. $19.98.
John Frankenheimer, USA, 1962, 111 mins.

All My Sons

A family torn apart by war is forced to come to grips with the aftereffects of a terrible tragedy, in this classic film based on the work of legendary playwright Arthur Miller. Starring Burt Lancaster and Edward G. Robinson. Includes original theatrical trailer.

VHS: S34626. $14.98.
Irving Reis, USA, 1948, 94 mins.

All Quiet on the Western Front

Classic adaptation of Erich Maria Remarque's anti-war novel has lost little of its impact over the years. The film follows a group of German recruits during World War I from their idealism to disillusionment.

VHS: S01686. $19.95.
Laser: LD70011. $39.98.
Lewis Milestone, USA, 1930, 103 mins.

All the Brothers Were Valiant

Robert Taylor and Stewart Granger are brothers who compete for Ann Blyth in this film adaptation of Ben Ames' novel about New England whalers. It's a romantic adventure set on the high seas, where trust is often a matter of life and death.

VHS: S21014. $19.98.
Richard Thorpe, USA, 1953, 101 mins.

All the King's Men

Broderick Crawford gives a legendary performance as the brawling, bull-headed Southern politician. A riveting thriller about corruption in the political arena, based on the novel by Robert Penn Warren.

VHS: S00033. $19.95.
Laser: LD72160. $34.95.
Robert Rossen, USA, 1949, 109 mins.

All This and Heaven Too

Charles Boyer and Bette Davis star in this story based upon Rachel Field's novel of a scandalous love affair between an aristocrat and servant, set in Paris of the 1840's.

VHS: S03457. $19.98.
Anatole Litvak, USA, 1940, 141 mins.

All Through the Night

Humphrey Bogart is Gloves Donahue, a Broadway big-shot who takes on a Nazi spy ring in this gangster spoof. When the German baker of his favorite cheesecakes is mysteriously murdered, Bogie sets out to find the killer and ends up in the middle of an international plot to blow up an American warship. With Conrad Veidt, Peter Lorre, Karen Verne and Jackie Gleason.

VHS: S16094. $19.98.
Vincent Sherman, USA, 1942, 107 mins.

The Amazing Mr. X (The Spiritualist)

Turhan Bey is a phony spiritualist who teams up with not-so-dead husband in order to deceive the wealthy widow. Lynn Bari is the bereaved young woman driven to seek the "help" of the mystic. This eerie film also includes Richard Carlson and Donald Curtis. B&W.

VHS: S04066. $29.95.
Laser: CLV/CAV. LD72060. $39.95.
Bernard Vorhaus, USA, 1948, 78 mins.

Ambassador Bill

When Will Rogers is appointed U.S. Ambassador to the revolutionary-plagued European kingdom of Sylvania, his down-to-earth ways and homespun wisdom endear him to the Queen and her son. Ray Milland co-stars in this political satire.

VHS: S13494. $19.98.
Sam Taylor, USA, 1931, 68 mins.

America America

This rarely screened classic was originally nominated for four Academy Awards. It's based on the story of acclaimed director Elia Kazan's uncle, who struggled mightily at the turn of the century in order to fulfill his dream of emigrating to America. A moving, powerful story of American immigration.

VHS: S21146. $19.98.
Elia Kazan, USA, 1963, 168 mins.

The Americanization of Emily

William Bradford Huie's novel is brought to the screen with the star power of Julie Andrews, James Garner and James Coburn. Andrews is a nurse in World War II who falls love in with the first victim of the Normandy landing. The only problem is that the victim, a cynical Garner, was set up by top brass in this role so that an American would be the first casualty. Even so, with these two a touching romance is unavoidable.

VHS: S12235. $19.98.
Laser: LD72116. $34.98.
Arthur Hiller, USA, 1964, 117 mins.

Anastasia

Yul Brynner and Ingrid Bergman star in this strange but engrossing story about Czar Nicholas' missing daughter, Anastasia. Brynner is a general who devises a scheme to collect the last Czar's money by coaching a young woman to pass as his sole surviving heir. As the training progresses, however, even he begins to wonder if this woman might actually be the Czarina Anastasia. Bergman won an Oscar for her performance as the confused young woman. Helen Hayes is also featured.

VHS: S26148. $19.98.
Anatole Litvak, USA, 1956, 105 mins.

Anatomy of a Murder

A riveting courtroom drama pitting small town lawyer James Stewart against big city prosecutor George C. Scott in a trial of Ben Gazzara, accused of murdering his wife's rapist. With a brilliant score by Duke Ellington.

VHS: S01525. $19.95.
Otto Preminger, USA, 1959, 160 mins.

Androcles and the Lion

In Chester Erskine's spirited adaptation of the George Bernard Shaw satire, Jean Simmons, Alan Young and Victor Mature star in a film that moves deftly from Shavian pungency and wit to mordant satire. Androcles volunteers to take on the deadly lion, who, it turns out, is indebted to Androcles for removing a thorn from its wounded paw.

VHS: S02598. $29.95.
Chester Erskine, USA, 1952, 98 mins.

Angels in the Outfield

Paul Douglas, Janet Leigh, and Keenan Wynn star in this tale of baseball fantasy. The Pittsburgh Pirates need a little celestial help to turn a losing season around. Divine intervention puts them on the path to an unforgettable pennant race.

VHS: S21521. $19.98.
Laser: LD75517. $39.98.
Clarence Brown, USA, 1951, 102 mins.

Angels with Dirty Faces

Rocky Sullivan and Jerry Connolly, two tough East Side kids, grow up to be James Cagney and Pat O'Brien, one a crook and the other a priest, but friends all the way to the electric chair and perhaps beyond. With Humphrey Bogart and the Dead End Kids. A top notch melodrama from Warner Brothers.

VHS: S03317. $19.95.
Laser: LD70146. $34.98.
Michael Curtiz, USA, 1938, 97 mins.

The Animal Kingdom

An intellectual publisher (Leslie Howard) suffers from a moral crisis as he tries to keep both a wife (middle-class Myrna Loy) and a mistress (free-spirited Ann Harding). Sophisticated comedy-drama adapted from a successful Broadway play by Philip Barry.

VHS: S13509. $29.95.
Edward H. Griffith, USA, 1932, 95 mins.

Ann Vickers

Sinclair Lewis' classic novel features Irene Dunne as the man-hating head of a detention home for women, with Walter Huston as the army officer who's also the reason why she hates men.

VHS: S03257. $39.95.
John Cromwell, USA, 1939, 76 mins.

Anna and the King of Siam

A lavish adaptation of Margaret Landon's book on Anna Leonowens (the source of the Rogers and Hammerstein musical, *The King and I*), detailing the experiences of an English governess (Irene Dunne) in 19th-century Thailand. The story examines her complicated relationship with the King of Siam. Oscar-winning cinematography by Arthur Miller. Screenplay by Talbot Jennings and Sally Benson. With Rex Harrison (his Hollywood debut), Lee J. Cobb, Linda Darnell, Gale Sondergaard and Mikhail Rasumny.

VHS: S20256. $19.98.
John Cromwell, USA, 1946, 128 mins.

Anna Christie

Garbo in a great role as a disillusioned prostitute, based on Eugene O'Neill's play, who returns to her father, a barge captain, and falls in love with a sailor, only to be rejected when her tarnished past is revealed.

VHS: S00057. $19.98.
Clarence Brown, USA, 1930, 89 mins.

Anna Karenina

Tolstoy's novel is skillfully brought to the screen for the second time with a melancholy Greta Garbo in her first "talkie." *Love*, her silent version, with John Gilbert as Vronsky, did not pay as much attention to authentic costumes and settings as this sound version. With Fredric March as Vronsky and Basil Rathbone as her unfeeling husband.

VHS: S04211. $24.95.
Clarence Brown, USA, 1935, 95 mins.

An Annapolis Story

This romantic drama set during the Korean War finds Kevin McCarthy and John Derek as brothers who are both naval cadets and happen to be after the same woman. With Diana Lynn as the object of their attentions.

VHS: S14144. $19.98.
Don Siegel, USA, 1955, 81 mins.

Another Time Another Place

Lana Turner is a U.S. correspondent in London who has a fling with a married man who then dies in a plane crash. When she recovers from a nervous breakdown, she decides to visit Sean Connery's wife and child. With Barry Sullivan, Glynis Johns and Terrence Longden. Based on the novel by Lenore Coffee.

VHS: S12850. $39.95.
Lewis Allen, USA, 1958, 95 mins.

Anthony Adverse

Magnificent entertainment from the Golden Years of Hollywood. Winner of Four Academy Awards in 1936, and nominated for Best Picture. Starring Fredric March, Olivia de Havilland, and Claude Rains. Film follows March through the time of Napoleon.
VHS: S00063. $19.98.
Mervyn LeRoy, USA, 1936, 135 mins.

Any Number Can Play

Clark Gable is an ailing casino owner who is used to 20-hour days and high-stakes games. But this time, the jackpot is his life. If he doesn't slow down, his enemies will deal him out—or they'll do him in.
VHS: S20558. $19.98.
VHS: S20558. $19.98.
Mervyn LeRoy, USA, 1949, 112 mins.

Anzio

A stellar cast and a large-scale action production distinguish this Hollywood re-telling of the battle of Anzio. Robert Mitchum, Peter Falk, Arthur Kennedy and Earl Holliman are among the stars.
VHS: S10019. $69.95.
Edward Dmytryk, USA/Italy, 1968, 117 mins.

Arabesque

Gregory Peck and Sophia Loren star in this modern tale of espionage and intrigue in the Middle East and fashionable London. Sophia gets to model many dazzling outfits as she and Peck are pursued by the bad guys. With Alan Badel, Kieron Moore and George Coulouris.
VHS: S07807. $14.95.
Stanley Donen, USA, 1966, 105 mins.

Arabian Nights

Two brothers fight over possession of the evil Caliph of Baghdad and the liberation of the enslaved Scheherazade. A film notable for its expressive use of color and decor. With Jon Hall, Maria Montez, Sabu, Leif Erickson and Turhan Bey.
VHS: S19311. $14.98.
John Rawlins, USA, 1942, 87 mins.

Arch of Triumph

Charles Boyer and Ingrid Bergman star in this adaptation of Erich Maria Remarque's novel about a refugee doctor and a girl with a past in Paris, just before the Nazi invasion.
VHS: S01687. $19.95.
Lewis Milestone, USA, 1948, 120 mins.

Archie Mayo Collection: Angel on My Shoulder and Svengali

Paul Muni, Claude Rains and Anne Baxter are an otherworldy but comic trio in *Angel on My Shoulder*. Muni is a gangster who plots to come back from the dead for revenge. He makes a pact with the devil (Rains) but fortunately, an angel and an earthbound love interest (both played by Baxter) intervene. This comedy offers a delightful contrast to the more somber tragedy of *Svengali*. John Barrymore, Marian Marsh and Bramwell Fletcher star. A young woman is lured away by a hypnotic character. Though she becomes a success, she is utterly dependent upon Svengali. Through it all her original love pursues her without fail. Based on the novel *Trilby* from George du Maurier.
Laser: LD75937. $69.95.
Archie Mayo, USA, 1946/1931, 102/80 mins.

Armored Command

Howard Keel, Tina Louise and Burt Reynolds star in this story of a beautiful Nazi spy who infiltrates an American Army base. An offbeat war drama.
VHS: S14143. $19.98.
Byron Haskin, USA, 1961, 105 mins.

Around the World in 80 Days

David Niven as Jules Verne's character Phineas Fogg makes a wager he can circumnavigate the globe in four score days. Along the way he meets 40 major stars in cameo appearances and saves Shirley MacLaine from being cooked on an Indian funeral pyre. Lots of Oscars, including Best Picture.
VHS: S06045. $29.98.
Laser: LD70507. $39.98.
Michael Anderson, USA, 1956, 167 mins.

The Arrangement

Kirk Douglas plays successful ad executive Eddie Anderson, a man with seemingly everything he needs except piece of mind. When he goes over the edge there is little his understanding wife Deborah Kerr or his classy mistress Faye Dunaway can do to reassemble the Eddie they both knew and loved. With Richard Boone and Hume Cronyn. Based on Elia Kazan's best-selling novel.
VHS: S06115. $19.98.
Elia Kazan, USA, 1969, 125 mins.

Artists and Models

Comic book artist Dean uses Jerry's dreams as inspiration, sparking one of the zaniest Martin & Lewis laugh fests you've ever seen. With Shirley MacLaine, Eva Gabor and Anita Ekberg joining the fun.
VHS: S15158. $19.95.
Frank Tashlin, USA, 1955, 109 mins.

As You Desire Me

Based on the play by Pirandello. Greta Garbo is married to Erich von Stroheim but she doesn't actually remember marrying the man. Amnesia is not the only problem they have. With Melvyn Douglas, Hedda Hopper and Owen Moore. B&W.
VHS: S13196. $19.98.
George Fitzmaurice, USA, 1932, 71 mins.

As Young As You Feel

An elderly man, resenting retirement at age 65, is determined to alter corporate policy. He impersonates the company president, and saves the firm from bankruptcy. Based on a story by Paddy Chayefsky. Stars Monty Woolley, with a marvelous cast including Marilyn Monroe, Constance Bennett, Thelma Ritter, David Wayne and Jean Peters.
VHS: S16397. $19.98.
Harmon Jones, USA, 1951, 77 mins.

Ask Any Girl

Charles Walters' elegant, witty comedy about an ambitious young advertising executive (Shirley MacLaine) and her determination to find the right man. When everything else fails, she turns to the brilliant older brother (David Niven) of the man she's attempting to seduce, with unpredictable, funny results. With Rod Taylor and Jim Backus.
VHS: S18009. $19.98.
Charles Walters, USA, 1959, 101 mins.

Assault on a Queen

Crooks dredge up a submarine and use it to hi-jack the vault aboard *H.M.S. Queen Mary*. Rod Serling scripted the film from a novel by Jack Finney. Stars Frank Sinatra, Verna Lisi, Tony Franciosa, Richard Conte and Reginald Denny.
VHS: S16458. $14.95.
Jack Donohue, USA, 1966, 106 mins.

Attack

The Battle of the Bulge is under way. Jack Palance stars as a heroic soldier fighting against two fronts—the Nazi armored units and his own incompetent captain.
VHS: S31840. $19.98.
Robert Aldrich, USA, 1956, 107 mins.

Auntie Mame

Morton Da Costa's film adaptation of the play by Jerome Lawrence and Robert E. Lee about an abandoned child whose cruel world is awakened to flamboyant dreams and fantasy when he's adopted by an extravagant, unconventional woman. With Rosalind Russell, Forrest Tucker, Fred Clark and Coral Browne.
VHS: S18895. $19.98.
Laser: LD70509. $29.98.
Morton Da Costa, USA, 1958, 144 mins.

Autumn Leaves

Joan Crawford is cast as a lonely New England spinster who travels to California and becomes involved with a man half her age. Cliff Robertson is the new love in her life. When he begins to show signs of mental instability and violence, she is distressed but decides to stand by her man. With Vera Miles and Lorne "Pa Cartwright" Greene as an abusive father. B&W.
VHS: S10382. $19.95.
Robert Aldrich, USA, 1956, 102 mins.

Baby Doll

Karl Malden, Eli Wallach and Carroll Baker star in this explosive, provocative drama written by Tennessee Williams. Condemned by the Legion of Decency as well as Time and Variety, *Baby Doll* is not only a work of smoldering screen history, but also artistry.
VHS: S00085. $19.98.
Elia Kazan, USA, 1956, 115 mins.

Baby Face

The amorous adventures of an ambitious working girl who tries to sleep her way to the top. This obviously pre-Production Code melodrama is generally fast-paced and features some good performances. Starring Barbara Stanwyck, George Brent, and John Wayne in a coat and tie.
VHS: S13646. $19.98.
Alfred E. Green, USA, 1933, 70 mins.

Baby, The Rain Must Fall

Steve McQueen is Henry Thomas, out on parole in a small Texas town, where he spends his nights singing in a band, against the wishes of his foster mother, who wants him to go back to school. His wife Georgette (Lee Remick) and daughter unexpectedly come to live with him. His parole is jeopardized when his temper gets him into fights.
VHS: S34111. $19.95.
Robert Mulligan, USA, 1965, 100 mins.

Bachelor in Paradise

Bob Hope plays a writer who conceals his identity in order to collect data on the sexual activities of a California suburban community. Hope is the only bachelor in this antiseptic environment, a land populated by unhappy wives and distracted husbands. Lana Turner plays Hope's love interest. With Janis Paige, Jim Hutton and Paula Prentiss.
VHS: S19560. $19.98.
Jack Arnold, USA, 1961, 109 mins.

Back Door to Heaven

William K. Howard's potent social docu-drama stars Wallace Ford and Stuart Erwin. Ford turns to crime during the depression, and the well-off members of the community discover that it was their lack of concern that was responsible.
VHS: S06905. $29.95.
William K. Howard, USA, 1939, 85 mins.

Back Street

Susan Hayward plays a glamorous, lonely fashion designer who falls for a charismatic businessman (John Gavin), rejects his marriage overtures, and years later, attempts to resume the affair, despite his wife and children. A film notable for its symbolic use of color, European locations and striking musical score. With Charles Drake, Virginia Grey and Reginald Gardiner. Based on the novel by Fannie Hurst.
VHS: S17945. $14.98.
David Miller, USA, 1961, 107 mins.

Background to Danger

Raoul Walsh's gritty noir set in World War II Turkey stars George Raft as a cynical maverick who hires two colorful villains, Nazi Sidney Greenstreet and Turk Peter Lorre, in his efforts to prevent Turkey from aligning its military and political forces with Germany. With Brenda Marshall. WR Burnett adapted Eric Ambler's novel.
VHS: S18502. $19.98.
Raoul Walsh, USA, 1943, 80 mins.

Bad and the Beautiful

The winner of five Oscars captures the underbelly of life in Tinseltown. Kirk Douglas is an ambitious producer with few personal scruples. He manages to upset Lana Turner, Dick Powell, Barry Sullivan, Walter Pidgeon and Gloria Grahame. A powerful and revealing drama from Vincente Minnelli. B&W.
VHS: S07978. $19.95.
Laser: LD70512. $34.98.
Vincente Minnelli, USA, 1952, 118 mins.

Bad Day at Black Rock

Spencer Tracy stops off in a small town to award a medal and finds he is visiting a hotbed of racism and inhospitality. Even with one arm he manages to shake up this sleepy little burg. With Robert Ryan, Lee Marvin, Anne Francis, Ernest Borgnine, Dean Jagger and Walter Brennan.
VHS: S07977. $19.98.
Laser: Widescreen. **LD70855. $49.95.**
John Sturges, USA, 1954, 81 mins.

Bad Lord Byron

Lord Byron is seriously ill on a military campaign in Greece. He dreams of being judged a poet and soldier, and a seducer and libertine. As part of a mock trial we discover his transgressions in a series of flashbacks in which his wife, Annabella, and Lady Caroline Lamb are called as witnesses. With Dennis Price, Mai Zetterling and Joan Greenwood.
VHS: S34947. $19.95.
David MacDonald, Great Britain, 1949, 95 mins.

The Bad Seed

Patty McCormack is the darling, blonde, pigtailed little girl who simply can't keep herself from murdering her playmates. Nominated for four Academy Awards, this classic chiller also features Nancy Kelly, Eileen Heckart and William Hopper. B&W.
VHS: S02659. $19.98.
Laser: LD71681. $39.98.
Mervyn Le Roy, USA, 1956, 129 mins.

Bagdad

When the daughter (Maureen O'Hara) of an Arabian tribal chieftain learns her father has been killed, she is led to a band of suspected outlaws. It soon becomes clear that the Turkish ruler (Vincent Price) she has entrusted may be her real enemy.
VHS: S30890. $14.98.
Charles Lamont, USA, 1949, 83 mins.

Band of Angels
Based on the best seller by Pulitzer Prize winner Robert Penn Warren, this Civil War era film portrays the romance between a rich plantation owner and a half-caste woman. Clark Gable stars with Sydney Poitier.
VHS: S20686. $19.98.
Raoul Walsh, USA, 1957, 128 mins.

Barefoot Contessa
Ava Gardner stars as a fiery Latin dancer destined to be a major Hollywood star. Loosely based on the life of Rita Hayworth, this cynical drama uncovers the underbelly of show business and marriage to the upper crust. With Humphrey Bogart as her only true friend. Also starring Edmond O'Brien and Rossano Brazzi.
VHS: S03908. $19.98.
Laser: LD72117. $39.98.
Joseph L. Mankiewicz, USA, 1954, 128 mins.

The Barretts of Wimpole Street
Norma Shearer and Fredric March star as literary giants Elizabeth Barrett and Robert Browning. A delightful mix of romance and poetry.
VHS: S15656. $19.98.
Laser: LD72162. $34.98.
Sidney Franklin, USA, 1934, 110 mins.

Bataan
A picture of war in its true, ugly detail. The story focuses on 13 Americans of various races fighting a suicidal rearguard action to stave off the Japanese offensive in the Philippines in order to allow the retreating Allied forces to make their escape. Stars Robert Taylor, Thomas Mitchell, Robert Walker and Desi Arnaz.
VHS: S02861. $19.98.
Tay Garnett, USA, 1943, 114 mins.

Battle Circus
Humphrey Bogart is a hard-bitten Army surgeon with a weakness for women and strong liquor. June Allyson is the idealistic combat nurse who wins his love. A gritty and patriotic portrayal of the now familiar M.A.S.H. units, filmed while the war was still raging in Korea.
VHS: S16095. $19.98.
Richard Brooks, USA, 1953, 90 mins.

Battle Cry
Raoul Walsh's hard-hitting, realistic drama of Marine Corps heroism in the Pacific. Based on a novel and screenplay by Leon Uris.
VHS: S10020. $69.95.
Laser: LD70520. $39.98.
Raoul Walsh, USA, 1955, 169 mins.

Battle of the Bulge
An ambitious drama about the last major German counteroffensive for control of the Ardennes in late 1944, with German panzer division commander Robert Shaw engaged in a series of intricate land maneuvers with Allied forces. An excellent ensemble cast includes Henry Fonda, Dana Andrews, George Montgomery and Ty Hardin. The widescreen cinematography is by Jack Hildyard. Screenplay by Philip Yordan, Milton Sperling and John Melson.
VHS: S18606. $19.98.
Laser: LD70521. $39.98.
Ken Annakin, USA, 1965, 167 mins.

Battle Shock
When as artist on vacation is accused of murder in Acapulco, his wife must try to arrange his escape. Ralph Meeker is the suspect when they learn about his shell-shocked related violence. Janice Rule is his devoted wife. With Paul Henreid and Rosenda Monteros.
VHS: S04226. $39.95.
Paul Henreid, USA, 1956, 88 mins.

Battleground
The heroic American defense of a little Belgian town named Bastogne during the Battle of the Bulge. Van Johnson leads a cast of American fighting men in this World War II drama. They include John Hodiak, George Murphy, Marshall Thompson, Don Taylor, James Whitmore, Leon Ames, Richard Jaeckel and Ricardo Montalban as the Hispanic GI who has never seen snow before. Supporting the actors are actual members of the "Screaming Eagles" of the 101st Airborne Division.
VHS: S12536. $19.98.
Laser: LD72163. $34.95.
William Wellman, USA, 1949, 118 mins.

Beau Geste
William Wellman's spectacular version of his adventure classic stars Gary Cooper, Ray Milland, Robert Preston, as the most famous brothers ever to join the foreign legion. Full of wonderful character actors, this is a great adventure from the best of Hollywood.
VHS: S05998. $29.95.
Laser: Encore edition. **LD71439. $34.98.**
William Wellman, USA, 1939, 114 mins.

Becky Sharp
The first feature photographed in Technicolor, an adaptation of Thackeray's *Vanity Fair*, in which a hardened orphan wages war on English society as an ambitious social climber. Miriam Hopkins, Frances Dee, Sir Cedric Hardwicke star.
VHS: S00111. $19.95.
Rouben Mamoulian, USA, 1935, 83 mins.

The Bedford Incident
The tale of a U.S. Naval vessel on a routine NATO patrol which ends up in a freakish showdown with a German submarine. Richard Widmark is Capt. Eric Finlander, the near-maniacal commander who drives his tense crew to the brink of nervous exhaustion. Sidney Poitier is a photojournalist aboard, assigned to record a "typical" mission. With Eric Portman, Martin Balsam and Wally Cox.
VHS: S32926. $14.95.
James B. Harris, USA, 1965, 102 mins.

Beggars in Ermine
Lionel Atwill, Betty Furness and George Hayes star in this melodrama from Monogram Pictures. Atwill is the head of a steel mill with social leanings, who is betrayed, and begins to organize all of the beggars of the nation into a financial force. A very unusual social drama.
VHS: S06906. $29.95.
Phil Rosen, USA, 1934, 80 mins.

Beginning of the End
In this original "big bug" movie, Peggie Castle stars as journalist Audrey Ames, who winds up trying to save Chicago while getting the scoop on the military cover-up of giant grasshoppers accidentally created at the Illinois State experimental farm. With Peter Graves.
VHS: S33990. $14.95.
Bert I. Gordon, USA, 1957, 80 mins.

Behave Yourself
Farley Granger and Shelley Winters are cast as a couple who mistakenly get caught up in gang warfare. A dog follows Granger home and his wife (Winters) thinks it's a present for her. He readily agrees, but finds out this apparently innocent animal has been trained in gangland espionage. Lon Chaney, Jr., is featured as a gangster.
VHS: S23983. $24.95.
George Beck, USA, 1951, 81 mins.

Behind Office Doors
A "power behind the throne" theme is the essence of this story of the executive secretary who is taken for granted. Mary Astor and Ricardo Cortez star in a pre-code outing.
VHS: S04493. $29.95.
Melville Brown, USA, 1932, 82 mins.

Behold a Pale Horse
Civil War bandit Manuel Artiquez (Gregory Peck) has lived in exile in France for 20 years. He wishes to pay his dying mother a final visit in his Spanish hometown, but his old enemy, the Spanish officer Vinolas (Anthony Quinn) plans to use this visit to try to finally catch Artiquez.
VHS: S34112. $19.95.
Fred Zinnemann, USA/France, 1964, 118 mins.

Beloved Enemy
David Niven plays the male secretary to a top British civil servant trying to solve the Irish problem in 1921. Though it was a small part, Niven was noticed in a cast that top-billed Merle Oberon and Brian Aherne as lovers on opposing sides.
VHS: S05077. $14.95.
Laser: LD75157. $34.98.
H.C. Potter, USA, 1937, 90 mins.

Beloved Infidel
Gregory Peck is F. Scott Fitzgerald and Deborah Kerr is Hollywood columnist Sheila Graham. Their romance provides the rationale for this beautifully composed look at early Hollywood glamour. Originally in Cinemascope, it also features Eddie Albert.
VHS: S29461. $19.98.
Henry King, USA, 1959, 123 mins.

Beneath the 12-Mile Reef
Robert Webb's film follows two people caught up in the business rivalries of two sponge-diving families on Key West. It is best known for its pioneering use of Cinemascope and its experimental underwater footage. Cinematography by Edward Conjager. Music by Bernard Herrmann. With Robert Wagner, Terry Moore, Gilbert Roland, Peter Graves and J. Carrol Naish. Letterboxed.
VHS: S32230. $19.95.
Robert Webb, USA, 1953, 103 mins.

The Bermuda Affair
Kim Hunter stars with Gary Merill and Ron Randell in this tense melodrama. Two pilots are trapped in a failing plane with only one parachute. Suddenly they recount the complicated business dealings and romantic entanglements that governed their life up until this desperate moment.
VHS: S23884. $29.95.
A. Edward Sullivan, USA, 1956, 88 mins.

The Best Man
Based on Gore Vidal's play and screenplay; an incisive look at the American political process in the story of several presidential candidates who will do virtually anything to get endorsement; a sharp satire on political conventions with dynamite performances from Henry Fonda, Cliff Robertson, Edie Adams, and others.
VHS: S11434. $19.98.
Laser: LD76156. $39.98.
Franklin J. Schaffner, USA, 1964, 102 mins.

The Best of Everything
Joan Crawford, Hope Lange and Louis Jourdan star in this adaptation of Rona Jaffe's best-selling novel about the world of publishing. It is an engaging yarn mixing passion, ambition and power into an effective story. Crawford is great as the editor who can never seem to find love amidst the witty literary set.
VHS: S26488. $19.98.
Jean Negulesco, USA, 1959, 121 mins.

Best of the Badmen
Robert Ryan plays an ex-Quantrill Raider who would like to forget the Civil War, but devious Yankee detective Robert Preston won't let him in. Preston is after the rewards on Ryan and his friends (the James boys) and their cousins, the Younger brothers. With Lawrence Tierney, Bruce Cabot, Jack Beutel, Tom Tyler, Claire Trevor and Walter Brennan as Doc Butcher.
VHS: S12831. $19.98.
William D. Russell, USA, 1951, 84 mins.

The Bette Davis Collection
The wit and energy of Bette Davis are reflected in this collection of five of her finest works: Edmund Goulding's *The Old Maid*, William Wyler's *The Letter*, John Huston's *In This Our Life*, Irving Rapper's *Now, Voyager*, and Curtis Bernhardt's *A Stolen Life*. The original theatrical trailer is shown with each film.
Laser: LD70142. $99.98.

Between Heaven and Hell
Robert Wagner, Terry Moore and Buddy Ebsen star in this psychological drama about a self-centered, prejudiced young recruit who comes of age during WWII. Praise has been lavished on the performance of Buddy Ebsen. With Broderick Crawford as the psycho commander.
VHS: S15196. $14.95.
Richard Fleischer, USA, 1956, 94 mins.

Beware My Lovely
Widow Ida Lupino hires Robert Ryan as a handyman, then discovers he is a psychopath. (Don't you hate it when that happens?) A dark and atmospheric thriller that delivers chills and good performances from its talented leads.
VHS: S05670. $19.95.
Laser: LD71814. $29.98.
Harry Horner, USA, 1952, 77 mins.

Beyond the Forest
Bette Davis stars as the unhappy wife of a small-town doctor who has an affair with a wealthy man, murders a witness, attempts suicide, and dies of fever. With Davis' famous line, "If I don't get out of here, I'll just die!"
VHS: S13392. $19.98.
King Vidor, USA, 1949, 96 mins.

Beyond Tomorrow
Three spirits disguised as wealthy men spend Christmas with a down and out couple who deserve a little happiness. A sensitive drama with the obvious Biblical overtones. Richard Carlsona and Jean Parker are the couple. With Maria Ouspenskaya, Harry Carey and C. Aubrey Smith in support. B&W.
VHS: S04086. $29.95.
A. Edward Sutherland, USA, 1940, 84 mins.

Big Business Girl
A youthful Loretta Young plays a business-minded career girl on the way to the top, whose boyfriend must sing for his supper. But Loretta finds that the workaday world is not without hazards as she fends off a boss more interested in her time off. Joan Blondell is also featured in this film, made before the adoption of the censoring pre-Production Code.
VHS: S20830. $19.98.
William A. Seiter, USA, 1931, 75 mins.

The Big Chance
John Darrow and Mickey Rooney act in this early film about a crooked boxer. Suddenly the boxer decides he wants to play it straight, but his manager has other ideas. 1933, 60 mins.
VHS: S26678. $19.95.

The Big Clock
Ray Milland, Charles Laughton, Maureen O'Sullivan and George Macready star in this classic thriller. Laughton is the publisher of a crime magazine where Milland works as an editor. In a new story assigned by Laughton, the more Milland digs, the more he finds himself implicated in murder. Remade as *No Way Out* (1987).
VHS: S28400. $14.98.
John Farrow, USA, 1948, 95 mins.

The Big Hangover
Van Johnson is a talented lawyer with a troubled past and a hilariously fatal allergy to alcohol. Elizabeth Taylor is the object of his affection, the boss's daughter who helps him cope with his perilous condition. With Leon Ames, Edgar Buchanan and Rosemary DeCamp.
VHS: S18528. $19.98.
Norman Krasna, USA, 1950, 82 mins.

The Big House
Wallace Beery gives a great performance as the consummate tough guy in this classic prison drama. Rage and violence are inevitable when 3000 prisoners share a space built for only 1800. This movie stands the test of time, especially since it inspired so many lesser copies. Also features Robert Montgomery.
VHS: S21015. $19.98.
George W. Hill, USA, 1930, 86 mins.

Big Jim
A quick visit to Cora's grown son turns into an ordeal when Jim insists she stay for awhile. Although he loves his mother, her "business" becomes suspect, and he soon discovers what she *really* does for a living. With Loretta Young and Bobby Driscoll.
VHS: S16746. $14.95.
Richard Morris, USA, 1954, 30 mins.

Big Jim McLain
Trouble in paradise! John Wayne stars as a special agent for the House Un-American Activities Committee, who must ferret out a Hawaiian-based Communist spy ring. Another right-wing star vehicle for the Duke. This one also features James Arness (*Gunsmoke*) and some rather exotic locales in pre-statehood Hawaii.
VHS: S13490. $19.98.
Edward Ludwig, USA, 1952, 90 mins.

The Big Knife
Robert Aldrich's brilliant exploration of greed and desperation in Hollywood. The story of blackmail involves movie star Charlie Castle (Jack Palance), his estranged wife (Ida Lupino) and a sleazy, ruthless studio boss (Rod Steiger). Adapted by James Poe from Clifford Odets's play. With Everett Sloane, Jean Hagen, Shelley Winters and Wesley Addy.
Laser: LD71663. $34.98.
Robert Aldrich, USA, 1955, 113 mins.

The Big Lift
Montgomery Clift, Paul Douglas and Cornell Borchers star in this serious drama about the days of and immediately following the Berlin airlift. The concerted efforts of the U.S. Air Force helped stave off disaster when the Russians blocked passage to the Allied Forces' sectors of the divided German Capitol. Danny MacCullough (Clift) is an American GI in love with Frederica (Borchers), a German woman who turns out to be a villain. This film tells the story of GI pilots romancing German women and also dramatizes the tense effects on daily life that occurred as a result of the Soviet blockade.
VHS: S27332. $19.95.
George Seaton, USA, 1950, 120 mins.

Big News
This early sound film stars Robert Armstrong as an ambitious, no-nonsense reporter fired for antagonizing a gangster and subsequently drawn into a murder plot. With Carole Lombard, Tom Kennedy and Warner Richmond.
VHS: S04489. $19.95.
Gregory La Cava, USA, 1929, 75 mins.

The Bigamist
Edmond O'Brien plays a traveling salesman who gets bored in Los Angeles and picks up lonely greasy-spoon cook Ida Lupino. When she announces her pregnancy, they marry. The only problem is that O'Brien already has a wife in San Francisco (Joan Fontaine). This film is the only work in which Lupino directs herself.
VHS: S16102. $24.95.
Ida Lupino, USA, 1953, 79 mins.

Bill and Coo
Dean Riesner directed this imaginative, live-action fantasy film cast exclusively with trained birds in an amusing comedy story. Hollywood was so taken with the film they awarded it a special Oscar.
VHS: S01823. $29.95.
Dean Riesner, USA, 1947, 61 mins.

Bird of Paradise
Dolores del Rio is a beautiful native girl on a South Sea island rescued from a volcano by a man (Joel McCrea) aboard a yacht. He falls in love with her, wishing he could stay, but has to overcome many obstacles.
VHS: S00131. $19.99.
King Vidor, USA, 1932, 80 mins.

Birdman of Alcatraz
When is a man rehabilitated? And what determines the dignity of a human being? These are some of the issues raised in this stirring true story about Robert Stroud (brilliantly played by Burt Lancaster), who became one of the world's leading experts on birds while serving a life sentence for murder. Also starring Thelma Ritter, Telly Savalas and Karl Malden.
VHS: S14306. $19.98.
Laser: LD71689. $39.98.
John Frankenheimer, USA, 1962, 143 mins.

Bite the Bullet
An excellent cast—Gene Hackman, James Coburn, Candice Bergen, Dabney Coleman, Paul Michael Vincent, Ben Johnson, Paul Stewart and Sally Kirkland—stars in this epic western of a grueling 600-mile horse race in which the participants grudgingly develop mutual respect for one another.
VHS: S32960. $19.95.
Richard Brooks, USA, 1975, 131 mins.

Black Angel
A beautiful blackmailer is murdered and John Phillips, who's cheating on his wife with her, Dan Duryea and Peter Lorre are suspects.
VHS: S33915. $14.98.
Roy William Neill, USA, 1946, 81 mins.

Black Arrow
From the novel by Robert Louis Stevenson. The War of the Roses in England is refought by Louis Hayward and George MacReady with the lovely Janet Blair rooting for the heroic Mr. Hayward. Swashbuckling action and adventure set against an involved tale of revenge that produces a considerable number of bodies punctured by the title instrument of death. With Edgar Buchanan.
VHS: S09111. $19.95.
Gordon Douglas, USA, 1948, 76 mins.

Black Artists of the Silver Screen—Harlem Variety Review (Showtime at the Apollo)
With Duke Ellington, Nipsey Russell, Herb Jeffries, Nat "King" Cole, Mantan Moreland, Lionel Hampton and more. 80 mins.
VHS: S32152. $24.95.

Black Artists of the Silver Screen—Proud Valley
Paul Robeson and Edward Chapman star in this story of a Welsh coal-mining village beset by a mine shutdown.
VHS: S32151. $24.95.
Penrose Tennyson, Great Britain, 1940, 75 mins.

Black Book (Reign of Terror)
Robert Cummings, Richard Basehart, Arlene Dahl star in this vivid costume drama of the French Revolution. Cummings goes undercover with revolutionaries who plan to topple the reign of Robespierre.
VHS: S13049. $19.95.
Anthony Mann, USA, 1949, 89 mins.

Black Dragons
Bela Lugosi plays a Nazi plastic surgeon who transforms six Japanese agents into American industrialists. Inspired by an actual "Black Dragon" Japanese society, this is one of the first anti-Japanese WWII films released after Pearl Harbor. Clayton Moore co-stars without his Lone Ranger mask.
VHS: S04007. $19.98.
William Nigh, USA, 1942, 61 mins.

Black Like Me
James Whitmore stars in this classic and controversial drama about a white magazine reporter who changes the color of his skin so he can experience life as a black man.
VHS: S06585. $19.95.
Laser: LD75316. $39.98.
Carl Lerner, USA, 1964, 107 mins.

The Black Orch id
From the director of *Sounder* and *Norma Rae*, an early film from Martin Ritt stars Sophia Loren as a recently widowed wife, whose late gangster husband's sordid activities threaten the balanced family of her new lover, Anthony Quinn. An excellent performance from Ina Balin as a put-upon daughter.
VHS: S02794. $14.95.
Martin Ritt, USA, 1959, 96 mins.

Black Room
Boris Karloff has a dual role as a pair of aristocratic Czechoslavakian twins in the early 1800's. When the crippled but good brother returns home to take control of the de Berghmann family castle, the peasants are pleased, but the evil twin has a scheme that involves a secret torture chamber. With Marion Marsh, Thurston Hall, Robert Allen and Katharine De Mille as Mashka. B&W.
VHS: S10385. $19.95.
Roy William Neill, USA, 1935, 73 mins.

The Black Shield of Falworth
The swashbuckling story of a medieval knight who fights to quash a conspiracy against King Henry IV. Starring Tony Curtis and Janet Leigh. Based on Howard Pyles's *Men of Iron*.
VHS: S33719. $19.95.
Rudolph Mate, USA, 1954, 98 mins.

The Black Swan
Tyrone Power stars in the original pirate adventure, winner of the 1942 Oscar for color cinematography. The 17th-century pirate Jamie Waring (Power) is granted a pardon in exchange for clearing the Caribbean and stopping the high-sea piracy of the fighting ship *The Black Swan*. A former officer on the infamous ship, Power rescues the lovely Maureen O'Hara from the evil clutches of George Sanders and Anthony Quinn. Unfortunately, a traitor is undermining Power's work by giving away information of sailings and arrivals. This swashbuckling classic is based on the novel by Rafael Sabatini.
VHS: S27207. $19.98.
Henry King, USA, 1942, 82 mins.

Blackbeard the Pirate
Robert Newton is the evil captain, Linda Darnell the kidnapped noble lady, and Keith Andes the heroic doctor who rescues her. Filmed in three-strip technicolor.
VHS: S03227. $19.98.
Raoul Walsh, USA, 1952, 99 mins.

Blackboard Jungle
Based on the novel by Evan Hunter. Glenn Ford is a teacher trying to survive in the New York City Public School system. His class of juvenile delinquents includes Vic Morrow, Sidney Poitier, Jamie Farr and Paul Mazursky. A serious drama that also launched Bill Haley's "Rock around the Clock." With Anne Francis, John Hoyt, Louis Calhern and Richard Kiley.
VHS: S11215. $19.95.
Laser: LD74668. $34.98.
Richard Brooks, USA, 1955, 101 mins.

Blood Alley
Produced during the height of the Cold War, William Wellman's *Blood Alley* stars John Wayne as he and Lauren Bacall lead a group of Chinese refugees along a dangerous waterway.
VHS: S12497. $19.98.
Laser: Letterboxed. **LD74700. $34.98.**
William Wellman, USA, 1955, 115 mins.

Blood on the Sun
James Cagney plays a tough newspaper editor in Tokyo in the late 1920's. He learns of a secret Japanese invasion plan from reporters Wallace Ford and Rosemary DeCamp just before they are murdered. When Japanese agents charge him with the killings, Cagney really gets sore. Based on the 1927 Tanaka document scandal. With Robert Armstrong, Jack Holloran, John Emery and several other Caucasian actors in Japanese roles.
VHS: S12902. $19.98.
Laser: CLV. **LD71971. $29.98.**
Frank Lloyd, USA, 1945, 98 mins.

Blossoms in the Dust
Greer Garson adopts a family of 2000 with her boundless love in this Oscar-nominated Best Picture that's a classic tear jerker. An enormous success, Garson founds an orphanage after she loses her husband and child.
VHS: S13063. $19.98.
Mervyn Le Roy, USA, 1941, 99 mins.

Blowing Wild
Filmed in Mexico, this stars Gary Cooper as an oil man wildcatter pursued by Barbara Stanwyck, who happens to be married to Anthony Quinn. Greed, lust and vengeance in the early 30's.
VHS: S03503. $19.98.
Hugo Fregonese, USA, 1953, 92 mins.

Blue Bird
Shirley Temple searches for the Blue Bird of Happiness in various fantasy lands, only to find it at home, in this imaginative fantasy that was Twentieth Century Fox's answer to *The Wizard of Oz*. With Gale Sondergaard.
VHS: S09993. $19.98.
Walter Lang, USA, 1940, 83 mins.

Blue Dahlia
Alan Ladd and Veronica Lake made their movie careers in film noirs like this. Raymond Chandler's first original screenplay is classic in its simplicity. Johnny Morrison (Ladd) returns from Naval duty to discover his wife has been cheating on him. Soon she is murdered, leaving Johnny as the prime suspect. Now it's up to him—with the help of sultry vixen Joyce Harwood (Lake)—to clear his name. Includes the original theatrical trailer.
VHS: S27353. $14.98.
George Marshall, USA, 1945, 100 mins.

Blue Max
A German airman (George Peppard) becomes a national hero for his courage and skill in World War II dogfights in this spectacularly filmed adventure. James Mason also stars.
VHS: S12163. $19.98.
John Guillermin, USA, 1966, 152 mins.

Bluebeard
John Carradine, a clever puppeteer, has a way with women—he does away with them. His eventual downfall is a beautiful and smart dress shop owner (Jean Parker) who senses that something is not quite right about him. Very effective thriller from an often overlooked director.
VHS: S03006. $39.95.
Edgar G. Ulmer, USA, 1944, 74 mins.

Bob & Carol & Ted & Alice
Mazursky's directorial debut is the classic farce about spouse swapping in the swinging '60s. When filmmaker Bob (Robert Culp) and his wife Carol (Natalie Wood) attend a trendy California sex therapy group, their free thinking rubs off on their married friends Ted (Elliott Gould) and Alice (Dyan Cannon).
VHS: S34116. $19.95.
Paul Mazursky, USA, 1969, 104 mins.

The Bogart Collection
Four of Bogart's best works: Raoul Walsh's *High Sierra* (1941), John Huston's *The Maltese Falcon* (1941), Archie Mayo's *The Petrified Forest* (1936) and John Huston's *The Treasure of the Sierra Madre* (1948). The original theatrical trailer of each film is also presented. 476 mins.
Laser: LD71649. $99.98.

The Bold Caballero: A Zorro Adventure
Filled with action and adventure, this film marks the first sound and color feature for the dashing avenger known as Zorro. For the first time since its 1936 theatrical debut, experience *The Bold Caballero* the way it was originally shot: in color. With Robert Livingston as Zorro.
VHS: S33926. $14.98.
Wells Root, USA, 1936, 69 mins.

Bombardier
A World War II drama of the men being trained to drop, with accuracy, deadly bombs on the enemy. Constructed as a tribute to those men in uniform.
VHS: S10661. $19.98.
Richard Wallace, USA, 1943, 99 mins.

Bombers B-52
Karl Malden and Efrem Zimbalist Jr. star as airmen who were responsible for the backbone of America's cold war defense. When Zimbalist falls in love with a sergeant's daughter, played by Natalie Wood, this wartime story becomes even more tense.
VHS: S21009. $19.98.
Gordon Douglas, USA, 1957, 106 mins.

Bombshell
Jean Harlow stars in this satire on the 1930's Hollywood star machine. Harlow is the much-used star who tires of the games and quits, thoroughly frustrating an unscrupulous publicity agent. Her attempts to start a new life are continually thwarted by the studios and the Hollywood system. With Lee Tracy, Frank Morgan.
VHS: S13357. $19.98.
Victor Fleming, USA, 1933, 96 mins.

Bonjour Tristesse
Set on the beautiful French Riviera, and adapted from the best-selling book by Francoise Sagan. Deborah Kerr and David Niven star in a portrait of love, lust and tragedy as Kerr falls in love with a playboy (Niven), but is unable to cope with his constant philandering. Co-starring Jean Seberg.
VHS: S06999. $69.95.
Otto Preminger, USA, 1958, 94 mins.

Boom Town
Clark Gable plays Big John McMasters and Spencer Tracy is Square John Sand in this manly saga of oil fields and making lots of money. The women in their lives are Claudette Colbert and Hedy Lamarr. Friendships are strained and punches exchanged over the search for black gold and Texas tea. With Frank Morgan, Joe Yule and Chill Wills as Harmony Jones.
VHS: S12532. $19.98.
Jack Conway, USA, 1940, 117 mins.

Borderline
Fred MacMurray and Claire Trevor are drug agents fighting smugglers at the Mexican border and yet neither one is quite sure whether the other one is not a crook. With Raymond Burr and Roy Roberts.
VHS: S34217. $19.95.
William Seiter, USA, 1950, 88 mins.

Boys Town
Spencer Tracy won an Oscar for his role as Father Flanagan, the man who believed there is no such thing as a bad boy. Mickey Rooney is around to thoroughly test that theory. A heartwarming and heart-tugging film about the creation of the home for juvenile delinquents. With Addison Richards, Leslie Fenton, Henry Hull and Gene Reynolds. Oscars also went to the writers Dore Schary and Eleanor Griffin.
VHS: S11219. $19.95.
Laser: LD70153. $34.98.
Norman Taurog, USA, 1938, 96 mins.

Boys' Night Out
A group of married men and an independent friend (James Garner), impatient and tired of their dull, suburban comfort, set up a covert New York apartment for their beautiful, shared "mistress" (Kim Novak), unaware they're part of an elaborate social behavior experiment that has gone awry. With Tony Randall, Howard Duff and Janet Blair.
VHS: S20200. $19.98.
Michael Gordon, USA, 1962, 115 mins.

Boys' Reformatory
When two brothers are framed for a crime, the more responsible one (Frankie Darro) takes the rap, is imprisoned, escapes, and relentlessly pursues the criminals responsible for the acts. With Grant Withers, David Durand and Warren McCollum.
VHS: S18946. $19.95.
Howard Bretherton, USA, 1939, 62 mins.

The Bramble Bush
A gothic thriller about a charismatic New England doctor (Richard Burton) who returns to his small-town origins and gets entangled in the mysterious death of his lover's fatally ill husband. Milton Sperling and Philip Yordan adapted the novel by Charles Mergendahl. With Barbara Rush, Jack Carson and Angie Dickinson.
VHS: S20193. $19.98.
Daniel Petrie, USA, 1960, 105 mins.

The Brass Bottle
Harold (Tony Randall) buys an old Arabian lamp at an auction—and ends up freeing a genie (Burl Ives) imprisoned there for thousands of years. Forever indebted, the genie announces that every wish will be his command. But things go from bad to worse when his fiancee (Barbara Eden) discovers a herd of camels living in his garage and belly dancers in his house. Inspired the TV series *I Dream of Jeannie*.
VHS: S34364. $14.98.
Harry Keller, USA, 1964, 90 mins.

The Brave One
Written by Dalton Trumbo under a pseudonym after he was blacklisted by the HUAC committee, this rare classic of a boy's struggle to save the life of his pet bull is presented in a letter-box format.
VHS: S06005. $19.95.
Laser: CLV. LD74746. $39.95.
Irving Rapper, USA, 1956, 100 mins.

A Breath of Scandal
Casablanca director Michael Curtiz fashions this high-spirited costume period piece based on the celebrated Ferenc Molnar play, *Olympia*. Sophia Loren is a widowed, defiant young princess whose amorous plays for American John Gavin invalidate her supposed romantic arrangement with a not-too-bright prince. A good cast includes Maurice Chevalier and Angela Lansbury.
VHS: S02784. $19.95.
Michael Curtiz, USA, 1960, 98 mins.

Bride Wore Red
Joan Crawford is cast as a poor, embittered cabaret singer who accepts the offer of an all-expense paid holiday at a resort in the Tyrolian Alps. There she is wooed by Robert Young, a wealthy playboy and Franchot Tone, a poetic village postman. With Billie Burke, Reginald Owen and George Zucco as Joan's aristocratic benefactor.
VHS: S16447. $19.98.
Dorothy Arzner, USA, 1937, 103 mins.

The Bridge at Remagen
For the Americans, the bridge at Remagen is the link to the heart of the Third Reich; for the retreating Germans, it's the last hope. Starring Robert Vaughan, E.G. Marshall and Ben Gazzara.
VHS: S15127. $19.98.
John Guillermin, USA, 1969, 116 mins.

The Bridges at Toko-Ri
William Holden, Grace Kelly and Mickey Rooney head a fine cast that explores the lives and loves of Navy jet pilots in Korea. Based on the best seller by James Michener, the special effects earned an Oscar. Exciting action sequences. Also in the cast are Fredric March, Earl Holliman and Robert Strauss.
VHS: S06029. $19.95.
Laser: LD75164. $34.98.
Mark Robson, USA, 1954, 103 mins.

British Intelligence
Boris Karloff plays a German spy acting as a butler in the household of an important British war official. Margaret Lindsay is the double-agent out to expose his organization. This is the third film based on the play *Three Faces East*. A 1930 version featured Eric Von Stroheim and Constance Bennett in the same roles. B&W.
VHS: S04022. $29.95.
Terry Morse, USA, 1940, 62 mins.

Broadway Limited
Three aspiring actors head for Broadway with a baby to use as a prop. When the baby is thought to be kidnapped, the cops make things tough on the thespians. With Victor McLaglen, Dennis O'Keefe, Patsy Kelly, Marjorie Woodworth, and Zasu Pitts.
VHS: S34499. $24.95.
Gordon Douglas, USA, 1941, 75 mins.

Brother Orchid
Two of Hollywood's greatest gangsters (Edward G. Robinson and Humphrey Bogart) star in this fish-out-of-water story featuring bare knuckles, one-liners and a wild story twist. A mobster has to hide out in a monastery while he tries to dodge the enemy and regain control of his gang.
VHS: S15521. $19.98.
Lloyd Bacon, USA, 1940, 87 mins.

Brothers Karamazov
Lavish production of the Dostoevsky novel featuring Yul Brynner, Maria Schell, Claire Bloom and Lee J. Cobb. From the director of *Cat on a Hot Tin Roof* and *Lord Jim*.
VHS: S00186. $24.95.
Richard Brooks, USA, 1957, 147 mins.

The Buccaneer
A swashbuckling tale of adventures taking place during the battle of New Orleans, when Andrew Jackson relies on buccaneer Lafitte to help curb or stall the British invasion. Good cast includes Yul Brynner, Charlton Heston, Claire Bloom and Charles Boyer. This also happens to be the only film Anthony Quinn ever directed.
VHS: S13782. $14.95.
Laser: LD75168. $34.98.
Anthony Quinn, USA, 1958, 121 mins.

Bulldog Drummond
Ronald Colman appeared in his first speaking role as the classic adventurer Captain Hugh "Bulldog" Drummond. The ex-war hero is approached to rescue a young woman's uncle from a nursing home. With Joan Bennett, Montagu Love and Lilyan Tashman. The sets by William Cameron Menzies won an Oscar. B&W.
VHS: S00188. $19.98.
F. Richard Jones, USA, 1929, 90 mins.

Bulldog Drummond Series
Double features.
Volume 1: *Bulldog Drummond Escapes*. Bulldog's girl Phyllis has been made the pawn of an international spy ring and only a daring rescue attempt can save her. 1937. 67 mins. *Bulldog Drummond Comes Back*. An old enemy has kidnapped Bulldog's bride-to-be. Bulldog has little time to rescue her and gets involved in an exciting chase through the English countryside. With Ray Milland and John Barrymore. 1937. 59 mins.
VHS: S03080. $29.95.

Volume 2: *Bulldog Drummond's Revenge*. Bulldog's wife-to-be can't be—just yet. Our hero must investigate the mysterious disappearance of a powerful secret weapon. With John Barrymore, John Howard and Louise Campbell. 1937. 55 mins. *Bulldog Drummond's Peril*. The announcements are out, and our hero moves closer to marriage. Among the wedding gifts is a beautiful diamond, one created using a new synthetic process. When the gem is stolen, Bulldog sets off in hot pursuit! 1938. 66 mins.
VHS: S03081. $29.95.

Volume 3: *Bulldog Drummond's Secret Police*. The ultimate adventurer has been hit with some exciting news about a fabulous treasure hidden beneath a medieval castle guarded by a mad killer. John Howard, Heather Angel and H.B. Warner star. 1939. 54 mins. *Bulldog Drummond's Bride*. The big day has finally arrived. Bulldog shall wed the love of his life, putting an end to his rovings of bachelorhood forever. But just for old-times sake, he agrees to help his good friend solve a most difficult case. 1939. 56 mins.
VHS: S03082. $29.95.
Volume 4: *Bulldog Drummond in Africa*. The head of Scotland Yard has been abducted and threatened with certain death. But they didn't count on Bulldog Drummond leading the rescue operation. With John Howard and Heather Angel. 1938. 58 mins. *Arrest Bulldog Drummond*. Bulldog heads for yet another bachelor dinner to celebrate his ever-pending marriage when a villainous international spy confronts and detains him. 1937. 57 mins.
VHS: S03083. $29.95.
Bulldog Drummond, Set
VHS: S26955. $99.95.

Bullets or Ballots
In this colorful classic Edward G. Robinson stars as a tough New York cop who infiltrates the mob from within in order to break it up. Humphrey Bogart provides added interest and danger. Above average gangster yarn.
VHS: S15522. $19.98.
William Keighley, USA, 1938, 82 mins.

Bullfighter and the Lady
While vacationing in Mexico, Chuck Regan is fascinated by both the bullfights and a local beauty. Hoping to arouse her passion, he trains for the ring with a popular matador. But when Chuck's restlessness results in tragedy, his courage is tested in a brutal contest for love, honor and redemption. Budd Boetticher's great film has been restored to its original length, with unforgettable bullfighting sequences and terrific performances from Robert Stack, Joy Page and Gilbert Roland.
VHS: S09667. $19.95.
Laser: LD71577. $34.98.
Budd Boetticher, USA, 1951, 87 mins.

Bullitt
Cop Steve McQueen spins through San Francisco's streets in a chase that's one of the screen's all-time best. McQueen is the police detective who conceals the death of an underground witness and goes after the killers himself.
VHS: S11614. $19.95.
Laser: LD74689. $24.98.
DVD: DV60187. $24.98.
Peter Yates, USA, 1968, 113 mins.

Bureau of Missing Persons
A drama about the case loads from the bureau of missing people, with Lewis S. Stone as a powerful boss who determines everyone's fate, Pat O'Brien as a neurotic cop, and Bette Davis as an enigmatic woman drawn to him. With Allen Jenkins, Ruth Donnelly and Hugh Herbert.
VHS: S17330. $19.98.
Roy Del Ruth, USA, 1933, 73 mins.

But Not for Me
A theatrical manager, played by Clark Gable, must thwart the amorous advances of his young secretary in order to go after the sophisticated Lilli Palmer.
VHS: S13783. $14.95.
Walter Lang, USA, 1959, 105 mins.

Butterfield 8
Elizabeth Taylor won her first Oscar for her performance as call-girl Gloria Wandrous, a high class NYC tart who yearns to settle down and find Mr. Right. Based on the 1935 novel by John O'Hara. The title refers to a phone number. With Eddie Fisher, Dina Merrill, Mildred Dunnock, Susan Oliver, Kay Medford and Laurence Harvey as Weston Liggett.
VHS: S09148. $29.95.
Laser: LD70163. $34.98.
Daniel Mann, USA, 1960, 109 mins.

Butterflies Are Free
Don Baker (Edward Albert), blind since birth, moves to a Greenwich Village apartment to get away from his over-protective mother (Eileen Heckart in an Oscar-winning performance). There he meets his wacky neighbor, a liberated actress named Jill (Goldie Hawn). Don learns from Jill what his mother never taught him, and Jill learns from Don what freedom is all about. With Paul Michael Glaser.
VHS: S34119. $19.95.
Milton Katselas, USA, 1972, 109 mins.

By Love Possessed
Lana Turner is the center of attention in this glossy romantic vehicle. Based loosely on the novel by James Gould Cozzens. Sparks fly when Turner becomes involved with a prominent New England attorney played by Efrem Zimbalist Jr. Cast includes Jason Robards Jr., George Hamilton and Thomas Mitchell.
VHS: S11284. $14.95.
Laser: Chapter search. Includes original trailer. **LD71639. $34.98.**
John Sturges, USA, 1961, 115 mins.

C-Man
A hard-hitting 1949 crime drama told in a semi-documentary style, starring John Carradine and Dean Jagger. Jagger plays a customs agent on the trail of jewel smugglers.
VHS: S07396. $29.95.
Joseph Lerner, USA, 1949, 75 mins.

The Cabin in the Cotton
"I'd love to kiss ya, but I jest washt ma hair." Michael Curtiz's melodrama about Southern sharecroppers caught in a romantic tangle between the respectable Richard Barthelmess and sexy Southern seductress Bette Davis. With Dorothy Jordan, Henry B. Walthall and Tully Marshall.
VHS: S17331. $19.98.
Michael Curtiz, USA, 1932, 78 mins.

Cabin in the Sky
Minnelli's first chance to direct was by MGM starring an all-black cast. Eddie Anderson (Rochester on the Jack Benny Show) proves to be an outstanding actor, with Ethel Waters as the woman who saves his life, Lena Horne, and an appearance by Louis Armstrong.
VHS: S01747. $19.98.
Laser: LD70538. $34.98.
Vincente Minnelli, USA, 1943, 99 mins.

The Caine Mutiny
Humphrey Bogart, as Captain Philip Francis Queeg, provokes Van Johnson to seize his ship during a typhoon. Van and fellow officer Robert Francis go on trial defended by Jose Ferrer. A top notch cast in a great courtroom drama. Find out what really happened to the strawberries. With Fred MacMurray as a creep.
VHS: S01854. $19.95.
Laser: 3 sides. **LD72443. $39.95.**
Edward Dmytryk, USA, 1954, 125 mins.

Call It Murder
Originally released as *Midnight*, based on a novel by the same name. The foreman of a jury sends a young woman to the electric chair and pays with pangs of conscience. He is faced with a moral dilemma when his own daughter is arrested for the same crime. An early performance by Humphrey Bogart led to this film being reissued (after he became a star) under this new title.
VHS: S08415. $29.95.

Call Northside 777
James Stewart stars along with Richard Conte and E.G. Marshall in this absorbing, dramatic film. A reporter, going on his own hunch, investigates a murder where he remains convinced that the law has fingered the wrong man. The semi-documentary style employed in this film makes this tale even more compelling.
VHS: S22532. $19.98.
Laser: LD75931. $39.98.
Henry Hathaway, USA, 1948, 111 mins.

Call Out the Marines
Frank Ryan and William Hamilton directed this updating of the Lowe and McLaglen Flagg and Quint comedy; their last film together. It's the story of two marines fighting over seductress Binnie Barnes while trying to unmask a nest of spies.
VHS: S08879. $24.95.
Frank Ryan, USA, 1942, 67 mins.

Call Out the Marines/The Clay Pigeons
Call Out the Marines follows two marines forced by circumstance to become spies. Frank Ryan, USA, 1942, 67 mins. *The Clay Pigeons* has an honest seaman wrongly accused of treason. Richard Fleischer, USA, 1949, 63 mins.
VHS: S10662. $19.98.

Cape Fear
Robert Mitchum is a sadistic rapist seeking out the lawyer who put him behind bars (played by Gregory Peck). His search ends in a small North Carolina town where he commences a campaign of terror against Peck's family, which the police are powerless to stop. A tense and well-paced suspenser highlighted by Mitchum's riveting portrayal of a shrewd psychopath, and a terrific cat-and-mouse chase through the Southern bayous.
VHS: S14979. $19.95.
Laser: LD70293. $34.98.
J. Lee Thompson, USA, 1962, 106 mins.

Captain Blood
One of the great Hollywood swashbuckling sagas: Errol Flynn and Olivia de Havilland star in the story of a young doctor unjustly condemned to slavery. Bought from the slave ship by Arabella, he escapes and becomes a notorious pirate.
VHS: S01874. $19.98.
Laser: LD71690. $39.98.
Michael Curtiz, USA, 1935, 120 mins.

Captain from Castile
In this colorful, lavish production packed with action, romance and adventure, Tyrone Power stars as a dashing, swashbuckling captain who follows Herman Cortez (Cesar Romero) to the New World. Magnificent on-location photography by Charles Clarke and Arthur E. Arling and one of Hollywood's best scores by Alfred Newman. With Lee J. Cobb, John Sutton, Antonio Moreno and Jean Peters in her film debut. "Excellent entertainment" (*Hollywood Reporter*).
VHS: S30871. $19.98.
Laser: LD76110. $49.98.
Henry King, USA, 1947, 140 mins.

Captain Horatio Hornblower
Based on the adventure novels of C.S. Forester, Gregory Peck plays a fearless 19th-century sailor who outwits the Spaniards and the French, and marries his admiral's widow. With Virginia Mayo, Robert Beatty, James Robertson Justice and Terence Morgan. One of Peck's personal favorite roles.
VHS: S16734. $19.98.
Laser: LD71514. $34.98.
Raoul Walsh, USA, 1951, 117 mins.

Captain Kidd
Charles Laughton is the ruthless, greedy pirate in this great Hollywood swashbuckler set in the late 17th century. The action-packed plot on the high seas contains typical elements: buried treasure, double-crossing, and even romance. An outstanding pirate movie.
VHS: S00211. $19.95.
Rowland V. Lee, USA, 1945, 82 mins.

Captain Newman, M.D.
This provocative comedy-drama features Gregory Peck as a dedicated Army psychiatrist who battles the bureaucracy and the macho military mentality on a stateside air base during WWII. With a host of fine performances from Tony Curtis, Angie Dickinson, Bobby Darin, Jane Withers and Robert Duvall. Based on Leo Rosten's bestselling novel.
VHS: S16306. $19.95.
David Miller, USA, 1963, 126 mins.

Captain Sinbad
The romance, splendor and adventure of *The Arabian Nights* comes to life as Sinbad returns from his latest voyage and discovers that the kingdom of Baristan has been usurped by the evil despot El Kerim.
VHS: S16846. $19.98.
Byron Haskin, USA, 1963, 86 mins.

Captain Sirocco
Louis Hayward and Binnie Barnes star in this costume epic about a deceitful but dashing pirate. The fiend lives two lives, hiding his identity in order to play the fool and the queen's confidant.
VHS: S23885. $29.95.
Edgar G. Ulmer, USA, 1949, 93 mins.

Captains Courageous
Spencer Tracy won the Oscar for Best Actor for his portrayal of Manuel, the Portuguese fisherman who teaches a millionaire's spoiled son human values in this adaptation of Rudyard Kipling's popular story. With Lionel Barrymore, Melvyn Douglas and Mickey Rooney.
VHS: S01788. $19.98.
Laser: LD71159. $34.98.
Victor Fleming, USA, 1937, 118 mins.

Captains of the Clouds
James Cagney plays a daredevil Canadian bush pilot who longs for the chance to prove his valor and service in World War II. His superiors and the military hierarchy at the Royal Canadian Air Force doubt his prowess, though Cagney proves his skills under fire. Music by Max Steiner. With Dennis Morman, Brenda Marshall and George Tobias.
VHS: S19038. $19.98.
Michael Curtiz, USA, 1942, 113 mins.

Career
Nominated for three Academy awards, Joseph Anthony's caustic story of an ambitious young actor's (Tony Franciosa) fanatic quest for fame and celebrity as a Broadway actor. With Dean Martin, Shirley MacLaine, Joan Blackman, and Carolyn Jones in an expressive, startling performance as an alienated talent agent.
VHS: S16889. $19.95.
Laser: LD75169. $34.98.
Joseph Anthony, USA, 1959, 105 mins.

The Caretakers
Robert Stack and Joan Crawford are caretakers warring over the proper care and treatment of a mentally ill patient, played by Polly Bergen, in this flawless tale of chilling suspense. Only the caretakers can determine the ultimate fate for Polly—eventual release or permanent incarceration.
VHS: S31072. $19.98.
Hall Bartlett, USA, 1963, 98 mins.

Carnival Story
Anne Baxter stars as a scheming circus performer in Germany. She finds out her fooling with the affections of her fellow performers will affect the timing of a high wire act. With Steve Cochran, Lyle Bettger, George Nader, and Jay C. Flippan as the circus owner.
VHS: S05075. $29.95.
Kurt Newmann, USA, 1954, 95 mins.

Cary Grant (Boxed Set)
These three films demonstrate Mr. Sophistication's remarkable versatility. Includes *The Bachelor and the Bobby Soxer, Gunga Din* and *Suspicion*.
VHS: S10686. $59.98.

Casablanca
The ultimate in the Bogart myth: his Rick Blaine is cynical, tough, hardened by life's misfortunes, yet still sentimental and idealistic. The dialog is full of quotable Bogart lines, the camerawork by Arthur Edeson evocative, the casting inspired. With Ingrid Bergman, Paul Henreid, Claude Rains, Peter Lorre, Sydney Greenstreet.
Laser: CAV, 2 discs, Criterion. **LD70353. $99.95.**
Laser: CLV, 1 disc, MGM. **LD70540. $34.98.**
Michael Curtiz, USA, 1943, 102 mins.

Casablanca (50th Anniversary)
The high-water mark of classic American studio filmmaking, this special 50th anniversary edition has been digitally remastered and includes the original theatrical trailer and a documentary on the making of the film. With Humphrey Bogart, Ingrid Bergman, Paul Henreid, Claude Rains, Conrad Veidt, Sydney Greenstreet and Peter Lorre. Music by Max Steiner.
VHS: S17125. $19.98.
Michael Curtiz, USA, 1942, 102 mins.

Cash McCall
James Garner plays a ruthless futures analyst who is irrevocably altered by his attraction to a beautiful young woman (Natalie Wood). Based on the novel by Cameron Hawley. With Nina Foch, Dean Jagger and E.G. Marshall.
VHS: S20194. $19.98.
Joseph Pevney, USA, 1960, 102 mins.

Cass Timberlane
Sinclair Lewis' story of social and political regionalism deals with the marriage of a lonely judge (Spencer Tracy) and a younger woman (Lana Turner) with a troubling past that threatens the social fabric of a Minnesota town. With Zachary Scott, Tom Drake and Mary Astor.
VHS: S18658. $19.98.
George Sidney, USA, 1947, 119 mins.

Cast a Giant Shadow
Set against the backdrop of Israel's drive for an independent statehood, this absorbing historical document stars Kirk Douglas as David "Mickey" Marcus, an American Jew who helped transform the undisciplined Israeli army into an elite fighting force. The all-star cast includes Frank Sinatra, Yul Brynner, Senta Berger and Angie Dickinson.
VHS: S19491. $19.98.
Laser: LD76185. $49.98.
Melville Shavelson, USA, 1962, 142 mins.

The Castilian
Offbeat casting and historical opulence informs this curious piece about the extraordinary efforts of a Spanish nobleman to rally a gang of guerrilla fighters against invading Moorish armies. With Cesar Romero, Alida Valli, Frankie Avalon and Broderick Crawford.
VHS: S19006. $19.98.
Javier Seto, USA/Spain, 1963, 128 mins.

Castle Keep
An extraordinary melding of war drama, satiric comedy and heroic action adventure in which a group of infantrymen take refuge in a luxurious Belgian castle, defending it to the death when the allied retreat begins. With Burt Lancaster, Peter Falk and Bruce Dern.
VHS: S31523. $19.95.
Sidney Pollack, USA, 1969, 107 mins.

Cause for Alarm
This low-budget thriller features Loretta Young as a panic-stricken woman whose jealousy-crazed psychotic husband (Barry Sullivan) has made her appear to be his murderer. With music by Andre Previn.
VHS: S34216. $19.95.
Tay Garnett, USA, 1951, 74 min.

Cavalcade
This lavish Academy Award-winning adaptation of Noel Coward's hit play traces the ups and downs of the British Marryot family from the death of Queen Victoria through the Depression. With Diana Wynyard, Clive Brook, Herbert Mundin, Una O'Connor, Ursula Jeans, Beryl Mercer, Merle Tottenham, Frank Lawton, John Warburton, Margaret Lindsay and Billy Bevan. "Nostalgic, richly atmospheric, but also sharply critical of war and the aftershocks that brought an end to a wonderful way of life" (Leonard Maltin).
VHS: S30918. $19.98.
Frank Lloyd, USA, 1933, 110 mins.

Cavalry Charge
Ronald Reagan, Rhonda Fleming, Hugh Beaumont and Bruce Bennett star in this Civil War era drama. Reagan and Bennett are brothers divided by their allegiances to opposing sides in The War Between the States. They overcome these differences in order to fight off Native Americans from the Apache tribe enraged by a dishonest trader. Fleming complicates the story with her red hair and green eyes. Also known as *The Last Outpost*.
VHS: S26875. $29.95.
Lewis R. Foster, USA, 1951, 88 mins.

Chain Lightning
Bogie is a heroic barnstormer who made good during WWII in this romantic air show. Riding on his reputation, he must execute daredevil feats with an experimental ultra-high performance jet. Eleanor Parker gives a charmingly understated portrayal of his earth-bound romantic interest. Humphrey Bogart leads Raymond Massey, Richard Whorf and James Brown.
VHS: S16096. $19.98.
Laser: LD76983. $39.99.
Stuart Heisler, USA, 1950, 95 mins.

The Champ
Jackie Cooper has unflinching faith in his father, a washed-up prize boxer, in this melodrama that features a dynamite performance from Wallace Beery as the fighter.
VHS: S13387. $19.98.
Laser: LD72119. $34.98.
King Vidor, USA, 1931, 87 mins.

Champion
Kirk Douglas has the title role in this brutal film about a boxer with a goal and very little humanity. He thinks he doesn't need anybody, but the Syndicate thinks otherwise. With Arthur Kennedy, Marilyn Maxwell, Ruth Roman and Lola Albright. B&W.
VHS: S04227. $19.95.
Mark Robson, USA, 1949, 99 mins.

Charade
An elegant, sophisticated thriller featuring Audrey Hepburn as the widow of a swindler, Cary Grant as an undercover CIA agent, and a cast of bad guys that includes James Coburn, George Kennedy and Walter Matthau. With a score by Henry Mancini.
VHS: S01752. $19.98.
DVD: DV60272. $19.95.
Stanley Donen, USA, 1963, 113 mins.

The Charge of the Light Brigade
Errol Flynn and Olivia de Havilland star in this epic production about the British involvement in the Crimean War. Adapted from Alfred Tennyson's classic poem.
VHS: S01865. $19.98.
Laser: Chapter search. Includes original theatrical trailer.
LD71667. $34.98.
Michael Curtiz, USA, 1936, 115 mins.

Charlie Chan Collection
Seven of Charlie Chan's most intriguing cases, available for the first time on video.
Castle in the Desert. Directed by Harry Lachman, USA, 1942, 62 mins.
VHS: S09096. $19.98.
Charlie Chan at the Opera. Directed by H. Bruce Humberstone, USA, 1936, 66 mins.
VHS: S09090. $19.98.
Charlie Chan at the Wax Museum. Directed by Lynn Shores, USA, 1940, 63 mins.
VHS: S09091. $19.98.
Charlie Chan in Paris. Directed by Lewis Seller, USA, 1935, 72 mins.
VHS: S09092. $19.98.
Charlie Chan in Rio. Directed by Harry Lachman, USA, 1941, 60 mins.
VHS: S09093. $19.98.
Charlie Chan's Secret. Directed by Gordon Wiles, USA, 1936, 71 mins.
VHS: S09094. $19.98.
Murder over New York. Directed by Harry Lachman, USA, 1940, 65 mins.
VHS: S09095. $19.98.

Charli3e Chan: Meeting at Midnight
Charlie Chan (Sidney Toler) must summon all of his intuitive skills to solve a murder and absolve his daughter, a prime suspect in the crime. With Frances Chan, Mantan Moreland and Jacqueline de Wit. Originally released as *Black Magic*.
VHS: S18475. $14.98.
Phil Rosen, USA, 1944, 67 mins.

Charlie Chan: The Chinese Cat
A beautiful young woman requests Rommy Chan's help in finding her father's killer. The investigation leads Charlie (Sidney Toler) into a labyrinth of mazesin search of uncut diamonds. With Benson Fong, Joan Woodbury and Mantan Moreland.
VHS: S18473. $14.98.
Phil Rosen, USA, 1944, 65 mins.

Charlie Chan: The Jade Mask
Charlie Chan (Sidney Toler) examines the circumstances behind the death of a scientist. Together with Number Four Son and the world's laziest sheriff, Charlie must negotiate a minefield of traps and daggers in the dead man's contraption-filled mansion. With Mantan Moreland, Edwin Luke and Janet Warren.
VHS: S18474. $14.98.
Phil Rosen, USA, 1945, 66 mins.

Charlie Chan: The Scarlet Clue
This unusual movie identifies the killer early on. The story is a satire of 40s radio shows and sophisticated big city farce. With Sidney Toler (as Chan), Mantan Moreland, Benson Fong and Helen Deveraux.
VHS: S18476. $14.98.
Phil Rosen, USA, 1944, 75 mins.

Charlie Chan: The Secret Service
In this espionage thriller, Charlie Chan (Sidney Toler) pursues the killer of a brilliant inventor and the loss of a device instrumental in combating German U-boats. With Benson Fong. Screenplay by George Callahan (*The Babe Ruth Story*).
VHS: S18477. $14.98.
Phil Rosen, USA, 1944, 64 mins.

Charlie Chan: The Shanghai Cobra
Three men are found dead, victims of cobra venom. Charlie's investigation centers on a bank holding government radium enrichment deposits, a failing detective agency and a beautiful secretary. With Sidney Toler, Benson Fong, Mantan Moreland and Walter Fenner.
VHS: S18478. $14.98.
Phil Karlson, USA, 1945, 65 mins.

The Chase
Peter Lorre plays a bodyguard for a rich gangster whose wife is thinking about running away with Robert Cummings. Michele Morgan may love that Bob but racketeer Steve Cochran wants his newly hired chauffeur dead. Based on a Cornell Woolrich short story. B&W.
VHS: S04039. $29.95.
Arthur Ripley, USA, 1946, 86 mins.

Cheers for Miss Bishop
Midwestern schoolteacher Ella Bishop's (Martha Scott) fiancee runs off with her vixen cousin, Amy. After Amy dies in childbirth, Ella is left to care for Amy's daughter, Hope. Despite Ella's sad love life, her 50-year career as a schoolmistress is rich and rewarding with the love of family, friends and fellow teachers. With William Gargan and Edmund Gwenn.
VHS: S34944. $19.95.
Tay Garnett, USA, 1941, 95 mins.

China
China in 1941 is the setting for this engrossing tale about an American who secretly sells oil to the Japanese. With Alan Ladd and Loretta Young.
VHS: S31346. $14.98.
John Farrow, USA, 1943, 79 mins.

China Seas
Clark Gable is the skipper of a Hong Kong freighter that attracts the attention of Chinese pirates. Should he survive their attack, he must make up his mind on whether he loves his mistress or his fiancee more. With Jean Harlow as China Doll and Rosalind Russell as Sybil Barclay. Based on the novel by Crosbie Garstin.
VHS: S08094. $19.98.
Tay Garnett, USA, 1935, 90 mins.

A Christmas Carol
MGM version of the Charles Dickens' classic about a miser who learns to re-think his approach to life. Starring Reginald Owen as Scrooge. He replaced Lionel Barrymore, whose lameness prevented his participation. With Leo G. Carroll, Ann Rutherford and Gene Lockhart. B&W.
VHS: S04980. $19.95.
Edwin L. Marin, USA, 1938, 69 mins.

Cincinnati Kid
Steve McQueen is terrific in the title role as Eric Stoner, professional poker player. Talk has it, the Kid is the only one good enough to challenge the legendary gambler Edward G. Robinson and win. Place your bets. Among those interested in the results of a certain high stakes game in New Orleans are Karl Malden, Ann-Margret, Tuesday Weld, Rip Torn, Joan Blondell, Cab Calloway and Jack Weston. Directed by Norman Jewison, who replaced Sam Peckinpah after he wanted to use Sharon Tate in a nude scene.
VHS: S16443. $19.98.
Norman Jewison, USA, 1965, 104 mins.

City for Conquest

James Cagney and an all-star cast dazzle in this powerful film about a poor young boxer and his brother who dream of one day escaping the ghetto. Beautiful production also features a young Elia Kazan in an acting role as a neighborhood friend turned gangster.

VHS: S15523. $19.98.

Anatole Litvak, USA, 1940, 101 mins.

City That Never Sleeps

Gig Young is a Chicago cop involved in adultery, blackmail and murder and he is the good guy. William Talman is Young's buddy who is responsible for the death of several people and trespassing on CTA property. With Mala Powers, Edward Arnold, Marie Windsor and Chill Wills as Sgt. Joe, the Voice of Chicago. B&W.

VHS: S07134. $19.95.

John H. Auer, USA, 1953, 90 mins.

City Without Men

The personal struggles and social drama of a group of women stationed in a boarding house who tirelessly await the release from prison of their husbands. With Linda Darnell, Michael Duane, Sara Allgood and Edgar Buchanan. Screenplay by W.L. River, George Skier and Donald Davis.

VHS: S18951. $19.95.

Sidney Salkow, USA, 1943, 75 mins.

The Clark Gable Collection

Clark Gable's intelligence, vigor and stunning screen presence are the focus in this collection of three films: Frank Lloyd's original (and superior) 1937 *Mutiny on the Bounty*, W.S. Van Dyke's 1936 *San Francisco*, and Jack Conway's 1940 *Boom Town*.

VHS: S17328. $49.92.

Laser: LD71654. $99.98.

Cleopatra

Elizabeth Taylor and Richard Burton carry on as one of the most famous romantic couples of the ancient and modern ages. A truly mammoth production filled with spectacle and thousands of extras. With Rex Harrison as Caesar and Roddy McDowall.

VHS: S04586. $29.95.

Joseph L. Mankiewicz, USA, 1963, 251 mins.

Cobweb

A melancholic work by Vincente Minnelli about the painful disintegration of a psychologist operating a special clinic. With some terrifying performances from Gloria Grahame and Lauren Bacall. With Charles Boyer and Lillian Gish.

Laser: LD70155. $39.98.

Vincente Minnelli, USA, 1955, 124 mins.

Come Back, Little Sheba

Based on the William Inge play, which paints a gripping portrait of a marriage washed up by booze and alienation. Featuring Burt Lancaster and an Oscar and Tony Award-winning, gut-wrenching performance by Shirley Booth. The title refers to Booth's despairing search for her lost dog but, of course, it's symbolic of a whole lot more than that.

VHS: S13789. $19.95.

Daniel Mann, USA, 1952, 99 mins.

Command Decision

Clark Gable takes a lot of flak as the general in charge of Operation Stitch. Despite heavy losses over Germany he keeps sending more planes to take out a heavily defended jet fighter factory. With Walter Pidgeon, Brian Donlevy, John Hodiak. Bombs away.

VHS: S13311. $19.98.

Laser: Chapter search. Includes original trailer. **LD71668. $34.98.**

Sam Wood, USA, 1948, 112 mins.

Commandos Strike at Dawn

Paul Muni is dynamic as a simple fisherman living on the coast of Norway, who, after falling in love with Anna Lee, is forced to flee the Nazi invasion by escaping to England, and then returns to his home village as the leader of the British troops against the Germans.

VHS: S07339. $69.95.

John Farrow, USA, 1942, 96 mins.

Compulsion

Orson Welles stars as Clarence Darrow in this true story of the infamous 1924 Leopold-Loeb murder trial, the trial of two wealthy, intellectual, gay Jewish men who plotted and carried out what they thought would be the perfect crime—the kidnapping and murder of a young cousin. Featuring Dean Stockwell, Bradford Dillman and E.G. Marshall.

VHS: S25573. $19.98.

Laser: Widescreen. **LD74971. $39.98.**

Richard Fleischer, USA, 1959, 103 mins.

Comrade X

A *Ninotchka*-inspired satire with Clark Gable playing an American correspondent in Moscow who is blackmailed into marrying a die-hard Communist (Hedy Lamarr).

VHS: S20559. $19.98.

King Vidor, USA, 1940, 90 mins.

Conflict

In this taut psychological drama, a killer is brought to bay by a wily psychologist and a nagging conscience. Humphrey Bogart plays a man who plots to kill his wife because his affections have turned to her younger sister. Sydney Greenstreet is the psychiatrist and family friend who uses mind games to release the killer's remorse. Alexis Smith plays Bogart's femme fatale.

VHS: S16097. $19.98.

Curtis Bernhardt, USA, 1945, 86 mins.

Conqueror

John Wayne plays Genghis Khan in this seldom seen adventure produced by Howard Hughes and directed by Dick Powell in his debut behind the camera. Action, adventure and passion of Mongols on the move all filmed near a hot atomic testing site. Cast includes Susan Hayward, Thomas Gomez, Agnes Moorehead, and Pedro Armendariz Jr. In color.

VHS: S07795. $39.95.

Dick Powell, USA, 1956, 111 mins.

Conquest

Greta Garbo is cast as a married Polish countess who delays Napoleon on his march to conquer Russia. Charles Boyer is the Little Corporal who violates his vows of fidelity to Josephine. With Alan Marshall, Henry Stephenson, Leif Erickson and Dame May Whitty. A costume drama with historical relevance.

VHS: S13194. $19.98.

Clarence Brown, USA, 1937, 115 mins.

Consolation Marriage

Pat O'Brien and Irene Dunne are married after they've both been jilted by their spouses, but years later they face the decision of what to do when their former lovers return. Very charming.

VHS: S09459. $19.98.

Paul Sloane, USA, 1931, 82 mins.

Constantine and the Cross

In the year 303 A.D., Constantine declares the Edict of Tolerance when he becomes Emperor of Gaul. Rallying his forces, he defeats the Roman legions, assuring freedom of worship for Christians. With Cornel Wilde, Belinda Lee, Christine Kaufman, Elisa Cegani, and Massimo Serato. Filmed in Italy.

VHS: S34198. $19.95.

Lionello de Felice, USA, 1942, 120 mins.

Cool Hand Luke

Christ-figure Paul Newman won't let the yard boss crush him in this fine-spirited chain-gang film. Strother Martin, in a supporting role as the chain gang's boss, made the line "what we have here is a failure to communicate" a cultural catch-phrase of the 1960's. George Kennedy won the Best Supporting Actor Oscar as the leader of the chain gang. VHS letterboxed.

VHS: S11615. $19.98.

Laser: LD74727. $39.98.

DVD: DV60060. $24.98.

Stuart Rosenberg, USA, 1967, 126 mins.

Coquette

Mary Pickford's first sound film was adapted from the Broadway play by George Abbott and Ann Preston Bridges. Pickford plays a gilded Southern belle with an unconventional streak who defies her oppressive father by falling for a charismatic though poor man. With Johnny Mack Brown, Matt Moore and William Janney. Pickford won the 1929 Best Actress Academy Award.

VHS: S17924. $19.98.

Sam Taylor, USA, 1929, 75 mins.

The Corn Is Green

Bette Davis is an English school mistress who volunteers to teach the underprivileged young folks in a poor Welsh mining town. She meets with local opposition but is determined to bring the gift of education to her new home. With John Dall, Joan Lorring and Nigel Bruce.

VHS: S06315. $19.95.

Irving Rapper, USA, 1945, 115 mins.

The Country Girl

In this Academy Award-winning adaptation of Clifford Odets' play, Bing Crosby, in one of his finest roles, portrays an alcoholic singer trying to make a comeback with the help of his director (William Holden). Grace Kelly won an Oscar for her performance as the wife who may be driving her husband to drink.

VHS: S30964. $14.95.

George Seaton, USA, 1954, 104 mins.

Court-Martial of Billy Mitchell

In the early twenties, an American Army general was court-martialed for accusing the war department of criminal negligence. A dramatic recreation of historical fact is created by stars Gary Cooper, Rod Steiger, Ralph Bellamy and Elizabeth Montgomery.

Laser: CLV. LD71979. $29.98.

Otto Preminger, USA, 1955, 100 mins.

The Cowboy and the Lady

Merle Oberon is a bored aristocrat and daughter of a presidential hopeful. She goes to a rodeo for kicks and falls for bronco bustin' Gary Cooper, who's ignorant of her background. Comedy features script contributions from Dorothy Parker and Anita Loos.

VHS: S32351. $14.98.

H.C. Potter, USA, 1938, 91 mins.

Craig's Wife

The film that rocketed Rosalind Russell to stardom. The dramatic story of a heartless woman (Russell) who has married a kindly man (John Boles) who refuses to see her manipulations.

VHS: S02925. $19.95.

Dorothy Arzner, USA, 1936, 78 mins.

Crash Dive

Two navy men, Tyrone Power and Dana Andrews, find they are on the same side in the naval war against the Axis forces, but in love they must compete for the same woman, Anne Baxter. This drama of rivalry and love set against the backdrop of World War II won an Academy Award for special effects.

VHS: S21071. $19.98.

Archie Mayo, USA, 1943, 105 mins.

Crashout

Six hardened criminals escape from prison and attempt to remain at large. William Bendix heads this dangerous bunch of fugitives from justice. With William Talman, Luther Adler, and Arthur Kennedy as the humane gang member. See how many tough guys elude the intensive manhunt.

VHS: S07136. $19.95.

Lewis R. Foster, USA, 1955, 82 mins.

Crime of Passion

A pessimistic 50s film noir about a famous columnist (Barbara Stanwyck) whose melodramatic rise to the top is complicated by her affair with a detective (Sterling Hayden). With Raymond Burr, Fay Wray and Royal Dano.

VHS: S19571. $19.98.

Gerd Oswald, USA, 1956, 84 mins.

The Crimson Pirate

One of the great swashbuckler films, starring Burt Lancaster and Nick Cravat as buccaneers in the Mediterranean during the 18th century.

VHS: S03431. $19.98.

Laser: LD74691. $24.98.

Robert Siodmak, USA, 1952, 104 mins.

The Crimson Romance

Ben Lyon, Erich von Stroheim and Sari Maritza are featured in this intriguing saga set during World War I. Two American pilots decide to end their unemployment by joining forces with the Germans. Ultimately, a sadistic commanding officer convinces them to rejoin the Allies.

VHS: S23804. $19.95.

David Howard, USA, 1934, 70 mins.

Criss Cross

Interesting film noir study with Burt Lancaster as a petty crook, Yvonne DeCarlo as his ex-wife and Dan Duryea as her shady new boyfriend. With Tony Curtis in his film debut as DeCarlo's dance partner. One of the best sleazy underworld films of the 1940s and remade in 1995 by Steven Soderbergh as *The Underneath*.

VHS: S08222. $19.95.

Robert Siodmak, USA, 1949, 87 mins.

Crossfire

This tense thriller was shot entirely at night with a style reminiscent of expressionism. A Jew is murdered in a New York hotel, and three ex-soldiers are suspected. Hollywood's first strong statement against anti-Semitism, starring Robert Mitchum, Robert Young and Robert Ryan as the insane veteran with a rabid hatred of Jews. Based on the novel *The Brick Foxhole*, by Richard Brooks.

VHS: S03582. $19.98.

Edward Dmytryk, USA, 1947, 86 mins.

Crowded Paradise

Hume Cronyn, Frank Silvera and Nancy Kelly are featured in this insightful and unique social drama about Puerto Ricans living on New York's lower East Side. At first a man is happy about coming to New York to be reunited with his girl friend but bigotry and discrimination soon overtake his joy. A film quite daring for its time.

VHS: S23888. $29.95.

Fred Pressburger, USA, 1956, 94 mins.

Cry Danger

Dick Powell is an ex-con named Rocky fresh out of the joint and looking for the people who framed him and a buddy on a charge of murder and robbery. He touches base with Rhonda Fleming, his buddy's wife and Rocky's former girlfriend. He also looks up William Conrad as Castro, a racketeer he suspects of doing him wrong. A taut film noir.

VHS: S07133. $19.95.

Robert Parrish, USA, 1951, 80 mins.

Cry Vengeance
Mark Stevens is after the people responsible for his undeserved time spent in prison. The tough San Francisco detective takes on the gangsters who set him up. With Skip Homeier, Martha Hyer and Joan Vohs. No one kills this guy's wife and child and walks away clean. Directed by the star.
VHS: S07137. $19.95.
Mark Stevens, USA, 1954, 83 mins.

Cry Wolf
As a mysterious scientist, Errol Flynn matches wits with a determined young widow, played by Barbara Stanwyck, who tries to unravel family secrets. They trade insults but there is romance lurking somewhere just beneath all the hostility.
VHS: S22898. $19.98.
Peter Godfrey, USA, 1947, 83 mins.

D-Day, The Sixth of June
An American soldier has a love affair with a married Englishwoman (Dana Wynter) and weeks later finds himself in the uncomfortable position of fighting along side her husband. Robert Taylor and Richard Todd star as the two officers.
VHS: S09453. $19.98.
Henry Koster, USA, 1965, 106 mins.

D.O.A.
Noir classic (remade with Dennis Quaid and Meg Ryan in 1988) concerns an accountant (Edmond O'Brien) who has been poisoned, has only a few days to live, and must find out who poisoned him and why. Surprisingly effective thriller, with music by Dmitri Tiomkin.
VHS: S04664. $19.95.
Rudolph Mate, USA, 1949, 83 mins.

Dance Fools Dance
A lonely Joan Crawford proves her worth as a Chicago reporter by going after gangster Clark Gable in this brisk, dramatic thriller based on the Jake Lingle killing.
VHS: S13647. $19.98.
Harry Beaumont, USA, 1931, 82 mins.

Dangerous
Bette Davis won her first Oscar (and felt it was a belated award from her having lost the previous year) for her portrayal of an alcoholic, once-famous stage actress hell-bent on self-destruction. She undergoes a change of heart when she meets an admiring architect (Franchot Tone) but now has to get rid of an unwanted husband. She's dangerous!
VHS: S11621. $19.95.
Laser: LD70150. $39.98.
Alfred E. Green, USA, 1935, 78 mins.

Dangerous Paradise
William Wellman's adaptation of Joseph Conrad's *Victory*, about a man dissatisfied with society who retreats to a coastal island and is pursued by a band of criminals. With Nancy Carroll, Richard Arlen, Warner Oland and Gustav von Seyffertitz.
VHS: S18947. $19.95.
William Wellman, USA, 1930, 59 mins.

Dangerous When Wet
Esther Williams plays a farmer's daughter who travels to England to swim the English Channel and finds romance with dashing Frenchman Fernando Lamas. She also joins in a delightful water ballet with cartoon favorites Tom and Jerry.
VHS: S16612. $19.98.
Laser: LD71694. $34.98.
Charles Walters, USA, 1953, 96 mins.

Danny Boy
Robert "Buzz" Henry stars in this sentimental story about a Marine mascot's (Danny the Dog) return home after World War II. The famous dog is kidnapped but escapes; later he sees the crooks and attacks them. The crooks press charges, and Danny is sentenced to the gas chamber, but Henry argues that the sentence should be death by firing squad because he was a marine.
VHS: S04494. $29.95.
Terry Morse, USA, 1946, 67 mins.

Daring Game
Lloyd Bridges leads a group of skydiving frogmen on a mission to free the husband and daughter of his former girlfriend. Known as "The Flying Fish", these guys just love a good adventure. With Michael Ansara, Brock Peters and Joan Blackman. In color.
VHS: S04225. $39.95.
Laszlo Benedek, USA, 1968, 100 mins.

The Dark Angel
A man falls in love with a woman (Merle Oberon) who turns to him when she receives a report that her boyfriend (his cousin) is killed in the war. Things get complicated when it turns out that he's alive, but blind and living in hiding. With Fredric March and Herbert Marshall. Script by Lillian Hellman and slick photography by Gregg Toland.
VHS: S32352. $14.98.
Sidney Franklin, USA, 1935, 110 mins.

Dark Corner
When a suave detective is framed for murder for the second time, it's up to his loyal secretary (Lucille Ball) to help untangle the mystery. His best plans go awry when a sinister man in a white suit appears. A classic, intricate 40's film noir, with Mark Stevens, Clifton Webb and William Bendix.
VHS: S10745. $59.98.
Henry Hathaway, USA, 1947, 98 mins.

The Dark Mirror
Olivia De Havilland plays twin sisters, one of whom is probably a psychotic killer. Is it Ruth or is it Terry? Only their psychiatrist knows for sure, and Lew Ayres isn't talking until he's sure he is not in love with a murderer.
VHS: S04234. $19.95.
Robert Siodmak, USA, 1946, 85 mins.

Dark Passage
Humphrey Bogart plays an escaped San Quentin convict who thinks plastic surgery can be his ticket to a new life. While his face is healing he hides out in the San Francisco home of Lauren Bacall, who believes he is an innocent man. The early part of the film, shot from Bogart's point of view, makes for interesting camera work. With Agnes Moorehead, Bruce Bennett and Douglas Kennedy. Based on the novel by David Goodis.
VHS: S01698. $19.95.
Delmer Daves, USA, 1947, 106 mins.

The Dark Past
William Holden is an escaped convict holed up in the home of psychiatrist Lee J. Cobb with his girlfriend and two fellow inmates. Holden is a bit trigger happy and the doctor is willing to see him without an appointment. With Nina Foch, Adele Jergens and Stephen Dunne.
VHS: S06071. $69.95.
Rudolph Mate, USA, 1948, 75 mins.

Dark Victory
Bette Davis in a great role as a head-strong heiress who suddenly learns she has six months to live. After partying hard for a few months, she falls in love with her doctor. A tear-jerker. With Humphrey Bogart, George Brent and Ronald Reagan.
VHS: S00304. $19.95.
Laser: LD70551. $34.98.
DVD: DV60061. $24.98.
Edmund Goulding, USA, 1939, 106 mins.

The Dawn Patrol
Edmund Goulding's remake of Howard Hawks' 1930 film about the deep seated rivalries between World War I Royal Flying Corps pilots stationed in France in 1915. The cast includes Basil Rathbone as the officer and Errol Flynn and David Niven as brave, rugged recruits. With Donald Crisp and Melville Cooper.
VHS: S01873. $19.98.
Edmund Goulding, USA, 1938, 103 mins.

Dead Reckoning
Humphrey Bogart stars as a hard-boiled sleuth, a World War II veteran, who's out to solve the murder of his soldier-buddy, a fellow paratrooper who disappeared on his way to Washington to collect a medal. A must for Bogey fans. With Lizabeth Scott and Wallace Ford.
VHS: S06547. $19.95.
John Cromwell, USA, 1947, 100 mins.

Dead Ringer
A dark, grueling thriller stars Bette Davis as twin sisters who harbor deep resentments over a man who once humiliated them, and the efforts of the nefarious, nasty half to achieve vengeance. With Peter Lorre, Karl Malden and George Macready.
VHS: S15931. $19.98.
Laser: LD71183. $34.98.
Paul Henreid, USA, 1964, 115 mins.

Dear Brigitte
College professor James Stuart has a genius son who can not only work computers, but also calculate race track odds for enormous profit. But mature I.Q.'s lead to mature desires and the boy wants the woman of his dreams: Brigitte Bardot. With Glynis Johns, Fabian and Billy Mumy as the precocious son.
VHS: S06525. $19.98.
Henry Koster, USA, 1965, 100 mins.

Dear Wife
In this pleasant and dry sequel to *Dear Ruth*, William Holden and Joan Caulfield reprise their roles as newlyweds whose domestic life is clouded by Caulfield's younger sister (Mona Freeman) provoking Holden into a state senator's race—against his new wife's father.
VHS: S02785. $19.95.
Richard Haydn, USA, 1949, 88 mins.

Death Kiss
The cast of Dracula in an exciting murder mystery set in a movie studio, notable for its snappy dialog and clever plotting. With Bela Lugosi, Edward Van Sloan.
VHS: S03332. $29.95.
Edwin L. Marin, USA, 1933, 72 mins.

The Deep Six
Alan Ladd stars as a Naval officer whose wartime duty leads him to question the Quaker faith and its pacifist ethos. To prove his commitment and courage he leads a dangerous shore mission in the Pacific arena. This World War II drama also co-stars James Whitmore and William Bendix.
VHS: S21010. $19.98.
Rudolph Mate, USA, 1957, 105 mins.

Defiant Ones
Sidney Poitier and Tony Curtis were both nominated for Oscars for their controversial roles in this savvy study of racism. They play a pair of decidedly unfriendly convicts who escape shackled at the wrist in the Deep South. Oscars went for screenplay and cinematography. With Lon Chaney Jr., Theodore Bikel, Claude Akins and Cara Williams.
VHS: S09157. $19.95.
Laser: LD71687. $34.98.
Stanley Kramer, USA, 1958, 97 mins.

Della
An attorney is retained to negotiate the purchase of land for a new factory from a wealthy woman who has remained in seclusion with her daughter for 15 years. His probing into their lives brings tragedy to one and liberation to the other. With Joan Crawford, Paul Burke, Charles Bickford, Richard Carlson, and Diane Baker.
VHS: S34200. $19.95.
Robert Gist, USA, 1964, 70 mins.

Desert Rats
Richard Burton leads the hopelessly outnumbered, but stubbornly defiant, Australian 9th Division in their heroic stand against Rommel in North Africa. Directed by Robert Wise, this film co-stars James Mason as Rommel—recreating his role from *The Desert Fox*. Photographed by Lucien Ballard.
VHS: S14136. $19.98.
Robert Wise, USA, 1953, 88 mins.

Designing Woman
George Wells' Academy Award-winning script takes us through the whirlwind marriage of a rough-edged sportswriter and a chic fashion designer, deftly played by Gregory Peck and Lauren Bacall.
VHS: S15242. $19.98.
Laser: Deluxe letterboxed edition. LD70189. $34.98.
Vincente Minnelli, USA, 1957, 118 mins.

Desire
Marlene Dietrich is the "Countess" Madeline, an embezzler of a small fortune in pearls. Car trouble foils her getaway until a young tourist, played by Gary Cooper, helps her escape. Once safely away she promptly dumps him, only to realize he has something she desperately wants—the pearls.
VHS: S22185. $14.98.
Frank Borzage, USA, 1936, 96 mins.

Desiree
Marlon Brando stars as Napoleon, Jean Simmons as Desiree, his 17-year-old mistress and the woman he could not conquer, in this larger-than-life historical melodrama. Based on the novel by Anne-Marie Selinko.
VHS: S05913. $19.98.
Henry Koster, USA, 1954, 110 mins.

Desperate Cargo
Ralph Byrd rescues two show girls, Carol Hughes and Julie Duncan, stranded in a Latin American city. On the way home, pirates attack and once again the hero must find a way to save these women. Naturally there is a running love interest, given the exotic setting.
VHS: S23773. $24.95.
William Beaudine, USA, 1941, 69 mins.

Desperate Journey
Five Allied airmen downed in Germany fight and finagle their way back to England in this rousing WWII spirit-lifter starring Errol Flynn and Ronald Reagan. A film that is heavily laden with anti-German propaganda, which makes it interesting to watch today.
VHS: S15128. $19.98.
Raoul Walsh, USA, 1942, 119 mins.

Destination Tokyo
Cary Grant is the captain of the submarine *U.S.S. Copperfin*. His mission is to land a meteorologist in Tokyo Bay. Along the way he must watch out for submarine nets, floating mines and treacherous prisoners-of-war. With John Garfield and Alan Hale. Script by Albert Maltz, later one of the Hollywood Ten.
VHS: S12535. $19.98.
Delmer Daves, USA, 1944, 135 mins.

Detour
One of the great "B" classics: a masterwork by director Ulmer. A young pianist (Tom Neal) hitchhikes across the country and becomes involved in two murders he didn't commit. (He's not the smartest guy.) Femme fatale Ann Savage hops a ride with Neal and practically steals the film as what is surely one of the most unpleasant creatures that has ever graced the silver screen.
VHS: S00328. $19.95.
Edgar G. Ulmer, USA, 1946, 69 mins.

The Devil and Daniel Webster
A simple New England farmer contracts his soul to the devil and needs the intervention of Daniel Webster, a lawyer, to save the town's souls. With Edward Arnold, Walter Huston and Anne Shirley.
VHS: S04331. $24.95.
Laser: Restored version, CLV. **LD70127. $49.95.**
William Dieterle, USA, 1941, 86 mins.

The Devil and Miss Jones
Do not confuse this delightful comedy about working conditions in a big city department store with the adults-only feature starring Georgina Spelvin. Spunky Jean Arthur stars as the working girl who befriends Charles Coburn, a millionaire in disguise. Good fun. B&W.
VHS: S04256. $19.95.
Sam Wood, USA, 1941, 92 mins.

The Devil at 4 o'Clock
Spencer Tracy is a priest trying, with the aid of three convicts, to evacuate a children's leper hospital in the midst of a volcanic eruption. With Frank Sinatra, Kerwin Matthews.
VHS: S04329. $14.95.
Mervyn LeRoy, USA, 1961, 126 mins.

The Devil's Brigade
William Holden leads the way in an explosive, fact-based story of the formation, training and hell-in-battle exploits of WWII's renowned 1st Special Service Force. A *Dirty Dozen*-style film.
VHS: S15125. $19.98.
David L. Wolper, USA, 1968, 87 mins.

Devotion
The ever-suffering Ann Harding stars as a young woman who disguises herself as a middle-aged governess in order to be with the man she loves. Leslie Howard plays the heartthrob barrister. Based on the novel *A Little Flat in the Temple* by Pamela Wynne. With Robert Williams, O.P. Heggie, Louise Closser Hale and Dudley Digges. Bring your handkerchiefs.
VHS: S15464. $19.98.
Robert Milton, USA, 1931, 84 mins.

Diamond Head
Charlton Heston is the domineering head of a Hawaiian family ruining nearly everyone's life. With Yvette Mimieux and George Chakiris, based on a novel by Peter Gilman.
VHS: S04531. $69.95.
Guy Green, USA, 1962, 107 mins.

Diane
A costume drama set in 16th century France which stars Lana Turner and Roger Moore as the class-torn lovers whose relationships threaten the political divisions fighting for power. With Pedro Armendariz, Marisa Pavan and Sir Cedric Hardwicke.
VHS: S18665. $19.98.
Laser: LD72262. $34.98.
David Miller, USA, 1956, 110 mins.

Dillinger
The story of John Dillinger's notorious career, from street punk to public enemy number one. A slick, fast-paced gangster thriller featuring a fine performance by Lawrence Tierney in the title role. One of the best films to come out of the Monogram Studio.
VHS: S13618. $19.98.
Max Nosseck, USA, 1945, 70 mins.

Dirty Dozen
Very tough, very funny and ultimately very violent film featuring a great all-male cast which includes Lee Marvin, Charles Bronson, John Cassavetes and Robert Ryan as convicts offered amnesty if they go on a suicide mission behind enemy lines during World War II.
VHS: S02348. $19.98.
Laser: LD70557. $39.98.
DVD: DV60297. $24.98.
Robert Aldrich, USA, 1967, 149 mins.

Dishonored Lady
Hedy Lamarr plays a suicidal magazine editor who moves to Greenwich Village and takes up painting on the advice of her shrink. There she falls in love with a scientist who goes out of town for six months. In the meantime she is a chief suspect in the murder of a jeweler. Oh, those career women!
VHS: S05074. $29.95.
Robert Stevenson, USA, 1947, 86 mins.

Disraeli
An adaptation of the long-running play about the British prime minister, a colorful, bright and electric statesman who ruled during the reign of Queen Victoria. With George Arliss, Joan Bennett, Florence Arliss and Anthony Bushnell.
VHS: S17925. $19.98.
Alfred E. Green, USA, 1929, 87 mins.

Distant Drums
Gary Cooper heads a group of swamp fighters in this serio-comic adventure re-creation of the Seminole Indian War. Filmed on location in the Florida Everglades with Arthur Hunnicutt and Sheb Wooley, this is the last film Coop made before *High Noon*.
VHS: S03504. $19.98.
Laser: LD71457. $29.98.
Raoul Walsh, USA, 1951, 101 mins.

Dive Bomber
A fascinating World War II-era film about the experiments of military flight surgeons to correct pilot "blackout" during strategic flight missions. With Errol Flynn, Fred MacMurray, and Ralph Bellamy. The brilliant aerial photography is by Bert Glennon and Winton C. Hoch.
VHS: S18163. $19.98.
Michael Curtiz, USA, 1941, 133 mins.

Doctor Ehrlich's Magic Bullet
Edward G. Robinson gives a powerful performance as Dr. Paul Ehrlich, a German medical maverick who develops tuberculosis while trying to discover a diagnosis for the disease. He travels to Egypt with his wife (Ruth Gordon) in search of a cure and stumbles upon a theory of poison immunity which he hopes will eradicate diptheria and syphilis. When he returns to Germany he must brave prejudice, fascism, sickness and financial ruin in order to actualize his vision and further modern medicine.
VHS: S30545. $19.98.
William Dieterle, USA, 1940, 103 mins.

Doctor Takes a Wife
Loretta Young and Ray Milland are caught in a matrimonial mayhem when Young, an independent career woman and writer, is snagged into a major publicity snafu and forced to tie the knot with a brainy medical professor in this whimsical comedy.
VHS: S07002. $69.95.
Alexander Hall, USA, 1940, 89 mins.

Doomed to Die
Boris Karloff continues his role as Mr. Wong, who is called in to investigate the mysterious demise of a shipping magnate. He attracts a variety of suspects which include an ex-chauffeur, a blackmailing general manager and a supposedly drowned Chinese passenger.
VHS: S04020. $29.95.
William Nigh, USA, 1940, 68 mins.

Double Dynamite
Frank Sinatra is the bank clerk falsely accused of stealing when his racetrack winnings are confused with the money taken during a bank robbery. With Jane Russell and Groucho Marx. Also known as *It's Only Money*.
VHS: S09179. $19.98.
Irving Cummings, USA, 1951, 80 mins.

Double Wedding
A strange William Powell and Myrna Loy collaboration that casts them against type as, respectively, an aggressive off-beat, avant-garde artist and an eccentric art designer trying to marry off Loy's sistery. With Florence Rice, Edgar Kennedy and Sidney Toler.
VHS: S18802. $19.98.
Richard Thorpe, USA, 1937, 87 mins.

Doubting Thomas
As a traditional husband whose happy home is turned upside down by an amateur acting company, Will Rogers concocts an elaborate scheme to discourage his wife's theatrical ambitions. An appealing star vehicle.
VHS: S13496. $19.98.
David Butler, USA, 1935, 78 mins.

Down to Earth
Rita Hayworth stars as a goddess, a muse to be more precise, who comes to Broadway. She objects to the way the nine muses are portrayed in a play, but is derailed from her plan to halt the production when she falls for the producer. Also features Larry Parks and Edward Everett Horton. Later remade as *Xanadu*.
VHS: S15527. $19.95.
Laser: LD74007. $34.95.
Alexander Hall, USA, 1947, 101 mins.

Downhill Racer
Robert Redford stars as a go-for-it member of the U.S. Ski Team, with Gene Hackman as Redford's relentless coach in Michael Ritchie's ski-action picture shot in Europe's Alps.
VHS: S05888. $19.95.
Laser: LD75298. $29.98.
Michael Ritchie, USA, 1969, 102 mins.

Dr. Christian Meets the Women
An entry in the popular series based on the experiences of the Canadian doctor who delivered quintuplets in 1935. The doctor (Jean Hersholt) exposes the harmful practices of a sham doctor exploiting women with a diet and physical culture. With Dorothy Lovett, Edgar Kennedy and Rod La Rocque.
VHS: S18940. $19.95.
William McGann, USA, 1940, 68 mins.

Dr. Syn
A great pirate story, with George Arliss, Margaret Lockwood and John Loder in the film adaptation of Russell Thorndyke's novel about the smuggling vicar of Dymchurch.
VHS: S02994. $24.95.
Roy William Neill, USA, 1937, 90 mins.

The Drag-Net
Rod LaRoque stars as a lawyer who fails at his father's firm and becomes assistant D.A. While dining with a woman, a murder is committed, and he finds himself involved in a big case. With Marian Nixon and Betty Compson.
VHS: S32948. $19.95.
Vin Moore, USA, 1936, 67 mins.

Dragon Seed
Katharine Hepburn and Walter Huston star in this adaptation of the Pearl Buck novel set in China during the Japanese invasion in the 30s. Hepburn plays the part of a peasant woman who becomes a heroic guerilla fighter against the Japanese.
VHS: S04204. $19.98.
Jack Conway/Harold S. Bucquet, USA, 1944, 149 mins.

Dream of Kings
Anthony Quinn is a respected Greek-American, small-time gambler in Chicago who learns his 12-year-old son (Radames Pera) has a fatal disease. Contrary to his wife's (Irene Papas) constant nagging and disbelief he knows the boy will get better in Greece. From the novel by Harry Mark Petrakis. With Sam Levene, Val Avery and Inger Stevens in her last screen role before her suicide.
VHS: S08126. $59.95.
Daniel Mann, USA, 1969, 107 mins.

Dreaming Out Loud
The popular radio team Lum 'n Abner get involved in several capers in this short film. It all happens because they are trying to bring progress to their small hometown.
VHS: S26680. $19.95.
Harold Young, USA, 1940, 65 mins.

Drifting Souls
A young lady marries for money in order to save the life of her father. This early talkie stars Lois Wilson, Theodore Von Eltz and Shirley Grey.
VHS: S15231. $19.95.
Louis King, USA, 1932, 65 mins.

Driftwood

Natalie Wood plays a spirited eight-year-old in this funny and charming story of a lost orphan girl's effect on the townspeople who find her. With Ruth Warrick, Walter Brennan and Dean Jagger.

VHS: S34986. $19.95.
Alan Dwan, USA, 1947, 88 mins.

Drums in the Deep South

Guy Madison stars in this classic Civil War story of a group of desperate Confederates who try to blow up Sherman's trains from the top of a mountain. One of the first films to utilize Supercinecolor. With Barbara Payton.

VHS: S32229. $19.95.
William C. Menzies, USA, 1951, 87 mins.

The Duel

Lord Brandt is a ruthless overbearing gambler whose wagers have exceeded his modest pocketbook. To pay off his debts he attempts to blackmail Ann, heir to the Gainsby estate. With Errol Flynn and Ann Stephens.

VHS: S16747. $14.95.
John Lemont, USA, 1957, 30 mins.

Each Dawn I Die

James Cagney is framed and sent to prison, where he meets tough-guy George Raft. In spite of its contrived plot, the film is remarkable for strong performances by a trio of actors-Cagney, Raft and George Bancroft.

VHS: S09391. $19.95.
William Keighley, USA, 1939, 92 mins.

The Eagle and the Hawk

Fredric March, Cary Grant, Jack Oakie and Carole Lombard shine in this compelling action story centered around a division of the Royal Flying Corps.

VHS: S31348. $14.98.
Stuart Walker, USA, 1933, 73 mins.

East of Borneo

Rose Hobart stars as a housewife who braves the jungle to find her missing husband. She carefully contrives a plot to free him but meets resistance from the sinister Prince Hashin. A great adventure! With Charles Bickford.

VHS: S13850. $19.95.
George Melford, USA, 1931, 76 mins.

East of Eden

The film that catapulted James Dean to cult status! Adapted from the Steinbeck novel, *East of Eden* is a modern retelling of the Cain and Abel story. Dean shines in an emotionally charged performance as the lost innocent in search of love and acceptance. Also featuring excellent performances by Raymond Massey and Julie Harris.

VHS: S00390. $19.98.
Laser: LD70563. $24.98.
Elia Kazan, USA, 1954, 105 mins.

East Side, West Side

Gracious society matron Barbara Stanwyck wants to save her marriage, but ex-mistress Ava Gardner's back in town, claws unsheathed and ready for combat. Also starring James Mason.

VHS: S15116. $19.98.
Mervyn Le Roy, USA, 1949, 108 mins.

Edge of Darkness

Robert Rossen wrote this compelling World War II drama about the Norwegian resistance movement, centered on a small village's heroic opposition to the Nazi occupation. With Errol Flynn, Ann Sheridan, Walter Huston and Nancy Coleman.

VHS: S18162. $19.98.
Lewis Milestone, USA, 1943, 124 mins.

Edison, the Man

Spencer Tracy ignites the screen with a powerful and touching portrayal of America's most beloved scientific wonder, Thomas Edison. Written by Dore Schary and Hugo Butler, an Oscar-nominated script.

VHS: S15017. $19.98.
Clarence Brown, USA, 1940, 107 mins.

Egyptian

Lavish costumes and sets recreate ancient Egypt at the dawn of monotheism. The struggle for power in a very hot country is the subject of this epic length saga that stars Jean Simmons, Victor Mature and Gene Tierney. Also in the cast are Michael Wilding, Bella Darvi, Edmund Purdom and Peter Ustinov. Be prepared for treachery, outings on the Nile and visits to elaborate royal tombs.

VHS: S10326. $19.98.
Laser: LD72205. $69.98.
Michael Curtiz, USA, 1954, 139 mins.

El Cid

Charlton Heston plays El Cid, the legendary 11th century Spanish hero who drove the Moors from his country, in one of Hollywood's great spectacle epics. Here Mann's visual style has moved from the breathtaking landscapes of his earlier Westerns to a rich expression of decadence. Highly entertaining.

VHS: S04324. $29.95.
Anthony Mann, USA, 1961, 184 mins.

Elephant Walk

The owner of a tea plantation brings back his English wife, who finds the exotic atmosphere strange and turns to a friendly overseer for comfort. Starring Elizabeth Taylor, Peter Finch, and Dana Andrews.

VHS: S13784. $19.95.
William Dieterle, USA, 1954, 103 mins.

Elmer Gantry

Writer/director Richard Brooks' skillful adaptation of the Sinclair Lewis novel is an unsparing attack on a corrupt but charismatic evangelist named Elmer Gantry (Burt Lancaster), whose perverse pursuit of wealth and power tears apart the social and economic fabric of a small, midwestern town. Lancaster won an Oscar; Shirley Jones is brilliantly cast against type as a prostitute.

VHS: S02339. $19.98.
Laser: LD70193. $39.98.
Richard Brooks, USA, 1960, 146 mins.

Enchantment

David Niven and Teresa Wright star in this touching tale of an aging general who recalls the lost love of his life. Includes original theatrical trailer.

VHS: S23438. $19.98.
Irving Reis, USA, 1948, 102 mins.

Enemy Below

Considered one of the best naval war movies ever made, this suspense-packed film follows an American destroyer and a German U-boat in a deadly game of cat and mouse. Robert Mitchum and Curt Jurgens star as rival captains in two powerful performances.

VHS: S12176. $19.98.
Dick Powell, USA, 1957, 98 mis.

Enforcer

Humphrey Bogart is a district attorney up against a murder for profit mob. When his only witness plunges to his death, Bogart must find new evidence. With Zero Mostel.

Laser: CLV. LD71982. $29.98.
Bretaigne Windust, USA, 1951, 87 mins.

Escape Me Never

This melodramatic remake of the 1935 Elisabeth Bergner work, adapted from Margaret Kennedy's novel, details the confusion and resultant hysteria of two musician brothers and the diverse women —a small, anonymous waif and a wealthy heiress—with whom they become involved. With Errol Flynn, Ida Lupino and Gig Young.

VHS: S18164. $19.98.
Peter Godfrey, USA, 1947, 104 mins.

Eternally Yours

David Niven stars as "The Great Arturo"—hypnotist, daredevil, magician, and above all, ladies man. He is attracted to the attractive Loretta Young, who becomes his eager stage assistant and wedded wife. They quarrel. She considers marrying Broderick Crawford and then Niven drops back into her life from an airplane.

VHS: S05063. $29.95.
Tay Garnett, USA, 1939, 95 mins.

Evelyn Prentice

Myrna Loy plays the wife of a criminal defense attorney (William Powell). When her lover (Harvey Stephens), who is blackmailing her, turns up dead, Powell must defend his wife on charges of murder. With Una Merkel, Harvey Stephens, Isabel Jewell and Rosalind Russell.

VHS: S20410. $29.98.
William K. Howard, USA, 1934, 80 mins.

Everything Happens at Night

Ray Milland and Robert Cummings are rival American journalists who travel to Switzerland to verify a rumor about the death of a political commentator, and end up falling in love with and fighting over the affections of the man's daughter (Sonja Henie). With Alan Dinehart, Fritz Feld and Jody Gilbert.

VHS: S20260. $19.98.
Irving Cummings, USA, 1939, 77 mins.

Ex-Lady

Bette Davis stars as an unconventional young woman in love with Gene Raymond. "Provocative and sexy" (Leonard Maltin). With Frank McHugh, Claire Dodd and Ferdinand Gottschalk.

VHS: S17332. $19.98.
Robert Florey, USA, 1933, 67 mins.

Executive Suite

The corporate power struggle, circa 1954, in the big city. William Holden stars as a rising young exec. June Allyson is his supportive wife. Based on the novel by Cameron Hawley. Cast includes Fredric March, Barbara Stanwyck, Louis Calhern, Paul Douglas and Dean Jagger. This is the movie that explains why they call it a rat race. B&W.

VHS: S07976. $19.98.
Robert Wise, USA, 1954, 104 mins.

Exodus

Paul Newman stars as an idealistic freedom fighter in this sweeping saga depicting the struggle to establish the modern state of Israel. Based on the international bestseller by Leon Uris. Letterboxed.

VHS: S02338. $24.98.
Laser: LD71683. $49.98.
Otto Preminger, USA, 1960, 208 mins.

Eyes of the Night

Edward Arnold, Ann Harding and Donna Reed are at the center of an all-star cast in this murky thriller. Though blind and older, a detective is called upon by an old friend to solve the mystery surrounding the murder of an actor. This man was involved with a family which becomes trapped by internal suspicions and intrigues.

VHS: S27898. $19.98.
Fred Zinnemann, USA, 1942, 80 mins.

Face in the Crowd

Andy Griffith stars as the hobo who is discovered by Patricia Neal and turned into a TV star in Elia Kazan's perceptive comment on American values, aided by a strong script by Budd Schulberg, who also collaborated with Kazan in *On the Waterfront*.

VHS: S02825. $19.98.
Elia Kazan, USA, 1957, 125 mins.

Fail Safe

One of the what-if-nuclear-war classics, with President Henry Fonda trying to convince the Soviet Premier that the nuclear attack was a mistake.

VHS: S03778. $14.98.
Sidney Lumet, USA, 1964, 111 mins.

Fall of the Roman Empire

After poisoning the Emperor, his insane son succumbs to apathy and dissipation, allowing Rome to be overrun by pestilence and the Barbarians. An epic spectacle with several exciting action sequences, extremely high production values and some fine acting. The distinguished cast includes Alec Guinness, James Mason, Christopher Plummer, Sophia Loren, Mel Ferrer and Omar Sharif.

VHS: S09309. $29.95.
Laser: LD76007. $59.95.
Anthony Mann, USA, 1964, 187 mins.

Fanny

An American remake of the famous film by Marcel Pagnol is beautifully shot on the Marseilles waterfront in the story of a young girl left with a child by a sailor. With Leslie Caron, Maurice Chevalier, Charles Boyer and Horst Buchholz.

VHS: S23481. $19.95.
Joshua Logan, USA, 1961, 129 mins.

A Farewell to Arms

The first Hemingway novel to reach the screen, nominated for four Oscars, with riveting performances by Helen Hayes and Gary Cooper as the sweet English nurse and the cynical American ambulance driver who fall in love on the Italian front and are separated by combat and another man's jealousy.

VHS: S00433. $24.95.
Frank Borzage, USA, 1932, 79 mins.

Farmer Takes a Wife

Betty Grable is the girlfriend of the toughest captain on the Erie Canal, who falls in love with a young farmer hired as a boat hand. The farmer gradually brings Grable around to his love of the land in this fun-filled story. With John Carroll, Dale Robertson.

VHS: S09330. $19.98.
Henry Levin, USA, 1953, 80 mins.

The Fatal Hour

Boris Karloff, as that case-solving detective Mr. Wong, is asked by Capt. Street to look into the death of a personal friend. Three more deaths occur before the culprit is nabbed just before the final credits. Jewel smuggling is the motive. With Grant Withers as the Captain.

VHS: S04021. $19.95.
William Nigh, USA, 1940, 68 mins.

FBI Story
FBI career man Jimmy Stewart reflects on his life with the bureau. Machine Gun Kelly, the Ku Klux Klan, and even Nazi spy rings are among those who make the foolhardy mistake of tangling with one of J. Edgar Hoover's finest. Directed by Mervyn LeRoy (*I Am a Fugitive from a Chain Gang*).
VHS: S13491. $19.98.
Laser: LD70727. $39.95.
Mervyn LeRoy, USA, 1959, 149 mins.

Federal Agent
William Boyd interrupted his work in the Hopalong Cassidy series to make this clever and fresh work about a government police officer. Note:A short missing sequence has been bridged by
a title card.
VHS: S17491. $14.95.
Sam Newfield, USA, 1936, 53 mins.

Fight for the Title
World War II has just begun, and so has Benny Leonard's reign as lightweight boxing champion of the world. His manager's plea not to enlist falls upon deaf ears as the duty cry beckons the young fighter. Stars Michael Landon and George Brenlin.
VHS: S16740. $14.95.
Eric Kenton, USA, 1957, 30 mins.

Fighter
In revolution-torn Mexico of 1910, a young patriot offers his services as a boxer to raise money for the cause. A well-made and absorbing drama starring Richard Conte, Canessa Brown and Lee J. Cobb.
VHS: S35241. $19.95.
Herbert Kilne, USA, 1951, 78 mins.

Fighter Attack
In this World War II actioner set in Italy, Sterling Hayden stars as a fighter pilot on his last sortie who receives help from Italian partisans in an effort to complete it. With J. Carrol Nash and Joy Page.
VHS: S34928. $14.95.
Lesley Selander, USA, 1953, 80 mins.

The Fighting 69th
James Cagney plays the cocky Brooklyn kid who is a member of the legendary Irish-American unit caught in the apocalyptic battles in the European trenches in WW I. "Forget the plot and think of it instead as the human, amusing and frequently gripping record of a regiment marching off to war" (*New York Times*). With Pat O'Brien, George Brent, Jeffrey Lynn and Alan Hale.
VHS: S19041. $19.98.
William Keighley, USA, 1940, 89 mins.

The Fighting Kentuckian
John Wayne and Oliver Hardy battle land grabbers and river pirates in order to protect a small French settlement in Alabama in 1819. Before you start laughing too hard, there may be some historical facts to back up the scenario. With Vera Hruba Ralston and Paul Fix.
VHS: S04239. $19.95.
George Waggner, USA, 1949, 100 mins.

Fighting Seabees
John Wayne is construction chief Wedge Donovan, who helps create a new branch of military service with buddy Dennis O'Keefe. He uses guts and a bulldozer to stop a Japanese attack. With William Frawley, Paul Fix, Duncan Renaldo and Leonid Kinskey. B&W. With Susan Hayward as the love interest. Trivia note: Seabees stands for "construction battalion" and their motto is "Can Do."
VHS: S09843. $19.95.
Howard Lydecker/Edward Ludwig, USA, 1944, 100 mins.

The Fighting Sullivans
Taken from the true-life account of five brothers, the extraordinarily close-knit Sullivan family disregards military rules and order to ensure each other's safety and protection during the Battle of Guadalcanal. With Anne Baxter, Thomas Mitchell and Ward Bond.
VHS: S18025. $29.95.
Lloyd Bacon, USA, 1944, 110 mins.

Films of John Wayne
This collection of rare short films features Wayne in simple appearances and as a star. *Rookie of the Year* is an early television episode where the Duke plays a hard-hitting newsman. Wayne is also featured in a 1971 commercial and hosts *The Marguerite Piazza Story*. There's even a plug for the Will Rogers Institute. 59 mins.
VHS: S22436. $19.95.

The Films of Leo Maloney
Leo Maloney was born in 1888 and began his film career in the Hazard of Helen series in 1914 and continued making films until his death in 1929. This collection of rare silent shorts from the *Range Rider Series*, all directed by Ford Beebe includes *Unsuspecting Stranger* (1924, 24 mins.) with Josephine Hill, Tom London, Bob Clark, Clarence Severn, and Whitehorse; *100% Nerve* (1923, 25 mins.), with Pauline Curley, Ed Burns, Fred Burns, and Bud Osborne; *Double Cinched* (1923, 25 mins) with Pauline Curley, Whitehorse, Noah Hendricks, Bud Osborne, and Harry Belmore; and *Smoked Out* (1924, 21 mins.), with Ray Meyers, Pauline Curley, Bud Osborne, Pat Rooney, and Minna Ferry Redman.
VHS: S37088. $19.95.
Ford Beebe, USA, 1922-1924, 95 mins.

Finger Man
Federal agents persuade a convicted bootlegger to go undercover and blow the lid off the rackets of a top crime boss. Will he live to enjoy the official pardon or will this uneasy informer end up dead meat? With Frank Lovejoy, Forrest Tucker, Peggy Castle, Glenn Gordon and Evelynne Eaton.
VHS: S11398. $19.95.
Harold Schuster, USA, 1955, 82 mins.

First to Fight
Chad Everett stars and a young Gene Hackman ise featured in this gritty World War II movie. Marriage forces a soldier to reconsider his commitment to fighting. Ultimately the very heat of battle rekindles his courage.
VHS: S24729. $19.98.
Christian Nyby, USA, 1967, 92 mins.

Five Fingers
James Mason stars as a cool-headed supplier of secret information for the Germans during World War II. He manages to steal secrets from his British Government employers without their ever noticing exactly what he is up to. It's a fascinating and suspense-filled account of espionage superbly filmed.
VHS: S21330. $19.98.
Laser: LD75016. $39.99.
Joseph L. Mankiewicz, USA, 1952, 108 mins.

Five Miles to Midnight
Sophia Loren and Anthony Perkins star in this psychological suspense thriller about a poor Parisian couple who enter into a get-rich-quick scheme which leads them into desperation, deceit and madness.
VHS: S28470. $19.98.
Anatole Litvak, France/Italy, 1962, 108 mins.

Flame and the Arrow
Burt Lancaster leads the peasants in revolt against the vile Hessian warlord in medieval Lombardy. Colorful action film from the director of *Cat People* and *Curse of the Demon*.
VHS: S03430. $19.98.
Laser: LD70571. $29.98.
Jacques Tourneur, USA, 1950, 88 mins.

Flame of Araby
When her father is poisoned, the princess (Maureen O'Hara) finds herself in danger of losing the throne and being married off by her evil cousin. Her only hope for freedom is a Bedouin chief and a swift black stallion. This rousing action-adventure ignites the screen with smoldering sensuality and swashbuckling action.
VHS: S30891. $14.98.
Charles Lamont, USA, 1951, 78 mins.

Flame of the Barbary Coast
John Wayne plays Duke Fergus, a naive Montana cattleman visiting San Francisco, where he loses his money and his heart. Ann Dvorak is Flaxen Tarry, the flame of the Barbary Coast. She kinda likes the Duke but she likes money a lot better. The San Francisco earthquake also puts in an appearance.
VHS: S04894. $19.95.
Joseph Kane, USA, 1945, 92 mins.

Flames
Johnny Mack Brown, Noel Francis, George Cooper and Marjorie Beebe star in this touching drama. John and Noel find their love nearly destroyed by distrust. When Noel finds herself under distress because of an evil villain, John rescues her from a raging fire. This film depicted many new lifesaving techniques for its time and was made with the L.A. fire department's help.
VHS: S22435. $19.95.
Karl Brown, USA, 1932, 63 mins.

Flamingo Road
Passion and politics collide when a carnival dancer played by Joan Crawford is stranded in a small Southern town run by Sidney Greenstreet. When he frames her for prostitution, she returns to get revenge by any means possible. With Zachary Scott, David Brian and Virginia Huston.
VHS: S16448. $19.98.
Laser: LD72174. $34.98.
Michael Curtiz, USA, 1949, 94 mins.

Flat Top
Sterling Hayden stars in this WW II service drama about the lives and training of those who fly from aircraft carriers. Combat footage of the real thing is successfully integrated into the fictional story. With Richard Carlson, Keith Larson and Bill Phipps.
VHS: S04253. $19.98.
Leslie Selander, USA, 1952, 85 mins.

Flight of the Phoenix
Story of the trials and tensions facing a group of men stranded in the Arabian desert as a result of a plane crash. With James Stewart, Richard Attenborough and Peter Finch.
VHS: S06526. $19.98.
Robert Aldrich, USA, 1966, 147 mins.

Flying Tigers
John Wayne helps the people of China fight the Japanese in this rousing war movie set prior to the U.S. entry into World War II. He plays Squadron Leader Jim Gordon, who is at odds with his mercenary buddy (John Carroll) for stealing his Red Cross girlfriend. With Anna Lee, Gordon Jones and Mae Clarke. From Republic Pictures.
VHS: S15910. $19.95.
Laser: 50th Anniversary edition. **LD71499. $34.98.**
David Miller, USA, 1942, 101 mins.

Follow the Boys
Tony West (George Raft) is rejected for the war effort, but hides this news and opts to organize shows that will cheer the troops. Marlene Dietrich, Orson Welles, W.C. Fields, Dinah Shore, The Andrew Sisters, Sophie Tucker, Jeanette MacDonald and many more do their bit as World War II extras.
VHS: S22187. $14.98.
A. Edward Sutherland, USA, 1944, 111 mins.

The Fool Killer
Twelve-year old runaway George is on a carefree road to adventure when he meets up with an old hobo who tells him a tale of a mythical 8-foot murderer. But George's journey takes a dangerous detour when he suspects that his new-found friend, Milo, a Civil War vet with amnesia, is the real life-wielding killer. With Anthony Perkins, Edward Albert.
VHS: S09668. $19.95.
Servando Gonzalez, USA, 1965, 100 mins.

For the Love of Mary
Deanna Durbin, Edmond O'Brien, Don Taylor and Ray Collins star in this romantic comedy set in Washington, DC, in which Deanna portrays a White House operator who must delicately juggle the attentions of three suitors. Includes 8-minute extra ending and song.
VHS: S32971. $19.98.
Frederick De Cordova, USA, 1948, 99 mins.

For Whom the Bell Tolls
Gary Cooper, Ingrid Bergman and Katina Patinou all won Oscars for their work in this adaptation of the classic Ernest Hemingway novel. Overall, it won nine Academy Awards, including Best Picture. The story revolves around an American demolition expert who decides that he must fight against the fascists in Spain. Even as civil war rages, a romance grows between him and a beautiful Spanish woman. This restored version includes the original theatrical trailer and music cut from other released versions.
VHS: S26184. $19.98.
Laser: LD75038. $44.98.
Sam Wood, USA, 1943, 166 mins.

The Forbidden Hollywood
Six fascinating, pre-code, uncensored classics in a deluxe boxed set. Feature *Female, Blessed Event, Ladies They Talk About, Three on a Match, Skyscraper Souls* and *Employees Entrance*. Stars include Bette Davis and Barbara Stanwyck. 449 mins.
Laser: LD76750. $99.98.

Force of Arms
William Holden and Nancy Olson star in this film about a World War II soldier and his lovely young wife. While Holden struggles toward Rome, his wife desperately tries to find out if he is still alive.
VHS: S24730. $19.98.
Michael Curtiz, USA, 1952, 99 mins.

Force of Evil
Film noir featuring John Garfield as an attorney who works for a mobster and finds himself caught in a numbers racket scheme that could bankrupt New York's "numbers banks."
VHS: S04232. $14.95.
Laser: CLV. **LD71984. $29.98.**
Abraham Polonsky, USA, 1949, 80 mins.

Forever Amber
Linda Darnell, George Sanders and Cornel Wilde star in Darryl Zanuck's "lavish and beautiful" 17th-century swashbuckler. Darnell conquers the king but she can't have the man she really wants, in this opulent drama directed by Otto Preminger.
VHS: S21955. $19.98.
Laser: LD75460. $49.98.
Otto Preminger, USA, 1947, 140 mins.

The Forgotten Village
John Steinbeck wrote the story and script for this moving film about the ancient life of Mexico, the story of the little pueblo of Santiago on the skirts of a hill in the mountains. An extremely moving portrait of life in a Mexican village. Narrated by Burgess Meredith.
VHS: S08785. $39.95.
Herbert Kline, USA, 1941

Fountainhead
Based on Ayn Rand's bestseller, the story of a talented architect who is forced to compromise his talents for the woman he loves. With Gary Cooper, Patricia Neal, Raymond Massey.
VHS: S01869. $19.98.
Laser: Chapter search. Includes original trailer. **LD71643. $34.98.**
King Vidor, USA, 1949, 114 mins.

Four Daughters
Four sisters, four romances—a much-loved melodramatic treat starring Rosemary Lane, Priscilla Lane, Lola Lane and Gale Page. Claude Rains and John Garfield are in the supporting cast. "Sentimental, but it's grand cinema" (*New York Times*).
VHS: S15652. $19.98.
Michael Curtiz, USA, 1938, 90 mins.

Four for Texas
Rat Pack members Frank Sinatra and Dean Martin enjoy playing rival con-men competing for control of a profitable river-boat gambling palace anchored in 1870 Galveston. With Anita Ekberg, Ursula Andress, Charles Bronson and a special appearance by the Three Stooges.
VHS: S16290. $19.98.
Robert Aldrich, USA, 1963, 124 mins.

The Four Horsemen of the Apocalypse
The story of three generations of a wealthy Argentine family that is split by the rise of the Nazis in Europe. With Glenn Ford, Lee J. Cobb, Ingrid Thulin and Yvette Mimieux.
VHS: S04205. $19.98.
Laser: LD76091. $49.98.
Vincente Minnelli, USA, 1961, 154 mins.

A Free Soul
Lionel Barrymore won an Oscar for his famous courtroom scene in this story of a hard-drinking lawyer who successfully defends gangster Clark Gable on a murder rap and then discovers that his daughter has fallen in love with him. With Norma Shearer, Leslie Howard.
VHS: S13389. $19.98.
Clarence Brown, USA, 1931, 91 mins.

From Hell to Borneo
A soldier of fortune fights off pirates and an internationally known gangster in order to keep control of his privately owned island. With George Montgomery, Lisa Moreno, Torin Thatcher, and Julie Gregg.
VHS: S34181. $19.95.
George Montgomery, USA, 1964, 96 mins.

From Here to Eternity
The talented Fred Zinnemann (*Man for All Seasons, Julia*) perfectly captures the static isolation and boredom that envelops the military personnel in peacetime Hawaii on the eve of American participation in World War II. Zinnemann counterposes social history with riveting drama: Burt Lancaster is a career soldier who seduces a commander's unattended wife, Deborah Kerr. Montgomery Clift staggers social convention by falling for Donna Reed, a prostitute. Frank Sinatra and Ernest Borgnine add quality performances as bitter rivals. Winner of eight Academy Awards, including best picture and director.
VHS: S02923. $19.95.
Laser: LD72185. $39.98.
Fred Zinnemann, USA, 1953, 118 mins.

Front Page
Produced by Howard Hughes, the classic Ben Hecht/ Charles MacArthur story about the newspaper business. When a convict escapes, Hily Johnson (Pat O'Brien, in his film debut), a young reporter about to leave journalism and enter marriage, is drawn back to work. He and Walter Burns (Adolphe Menjou), the managing editor, hide the convict in a roll-top desk in the press room in their obsessive search for a sensational story.
VHS: S18174. $19.95.
Lewis Milestone, USA, 1931, 101 mins.

Fugitive Kind
Based on Tennessee Williams' play *Orpheus Descending*, Marlon Brando stars as Val Xavier, a drifter from New Orleans whose arrival in Two Rivers, Mississippi, leads to all sorts of commotion. Anna Magnani and Joanne Woodward are just two of the women who enjoy his company.
VHS: S03500. $19.98.
Sidney Lumet, USA, 1959, 119 mins.

Fugitive Road and Crime of Dr. Crespi
Two "B" movies starring Erich von Stroheim. *Fugitive Road* enabled von Stroheim to recreate his role in *Grand Illusion* in which he played a World War I Austrian officer. In *Crime of Dr. Crespi* he plays a mad scientist in a story loosely based on writings by Edgar Allan Poe.
VHS: S02321. $29.95.
John H. Auer, USA, 1935, 66 mins.

Full of Life
Judy Holliday stars in this charming dramatic comedy about a non-religious woman who marries into a strict, Catholic Italian-American family in New York. With a baby due in one month, her in-laws are still holding out hopes for a church wedding. With Richard Conte, Esther Minciotti, Joe De Santis and opera star Salvatore Baccaloni as Papa Rocco. Based on a novel by John Fante.
VHS: S15890. $19.95.
Richard Quine, USA, 1956, 91 mins.

"G" Men
Cast as a "good guy" for the first time in his career, tough-man James Cagney is a federal agent raised by a crime-boss, hot on the trail of America's Ten Most Wanted criminals. A tense, action-packed classic.
VHS: S15524. $19.98.
William Keighley, USA, 1935, 86 mins.

Gabriel over the White House
A Depression-era fable about a second-rate hustler who is elected president and becomes an uncompromising leader who tries to wipe out corruption and facilitate world peace. With Walter Huston, Karen Morley, Franchot Tone and Dickie Moore.
VHS: S18503. $19.98.
Laser: LD76322. $39.99.
Gregory La Cava, USA, 1933, 86 mins.

Gallant Hours
James Cagney plays Admiral William F. "Bull" Halsey. Robert Montgomery, who served under Halsey in the Pacific during World War II, directed this impressive war film without showing any scenes of combat. This semi-documentary approach concentrates on the command decisions of Halsey and his Japanese adversary Admiral Hamamoto during a five-week period in late 1942.
VHS: S16438. $19.98.
Robert Montgomery, USA, 1960, 116 mins.

Gambit
Michael Caine and Shirley MacLaine star in this classic. It's a film about a great heist scheme. Caine hires the mysterious Eurasian MacLaine to help him steal an invaluable piece of sculpture. His mastermind and her daring help pull off a great fun yarn.
VHS: S20486. $19.98.
Ronald Neame, USA, 1966, 109 mins.

The Gamblers
A team of professional card sharks set out to fleece an aristocrat of his savings and receive an I.O.U. in payment, which turns out to be worthless. An interesting international cast and a setting in the beautiful downtown Yugoslavian resort town of Dubrovnk makes for an enjoyable caper film. With Suzy Kendall, Don Gordon, and Stuart Margolin.
VHS: S34190. $19.95.
Ron Winston, USA, 1970, 93 mins.

Gangster Story
Walter Matthau directed and starred in this early gem about a Mob-connected bank robber who falls in love with a sympathetic woman (Carol Grace). Caught in a vortex of extremes, with both the police and the mob hunting him down, Matthau runs from his past and tries to live a straight, easy life. With Bruce McFarlan and Garrett Wallberg.
VHS: S19864. $29.95.
Walter Matthau, USA, 1960, 65 mins.

The Gene Krupa Story
Sal Mineo plays the great jazz drummer whose life and career were sidetracked by drugs and fast living. Krupa provides the drum solos himself. Special appearances by song stylist Anita O'Day and musician-band leader Red Nichols. With James Darren and Susan Oliver. B&W.
VHS: S03942. $19.95.
Laser: LD74897. $34.95.
Don Weis, USA, 1960, 101 mins.

General Died at Dawn
Clifford Odets supplied the screenplay for this Lewis Milestone action adventure set in Northern China during the turbulent 30's. Gary Cooper is the American soldier-of-fortune carrying money to buy arms for the peasants. He is captured by the powerful General Yang (Akim Tamiroff, who was nominated for an Oscar). A test of nerves and quick thinking follows. With William Frawley, Porter Hall and Madeleine Carroll as the beautiful spy.
VHS: S08506. $14.98.
Lewis Milestone, USA, 1936, 97 mins.

The Gentle Sex
Joan Gates, Joan Greenwood and Lilli Palmer join the ATS. Despite the variations in their backgrounds, they coalesce into a group at training camp. This is especially important when, after being separated, they find themselves posted together again.
VHS: S23805. $24.95.
Leslie Howard, USA, 1943, 92 mins.

Gentleman Jim
Raoul Walsh's biography of boxer Jim Corbett, who rose from an obscure bank clerk to champion fighter, features strong performances from Errol Flynn and Ward Bond as heavyweight champion John L. Sullivan. Entertaining fare.
VHS: S01876. $19.98.
Raoul Walsh, USA, 1942, 104 mins.

Gentleman's Agreement
Moss Hart adapted Laura Z. Hobson's prize-winning novel about a talented journalist (Gregory Peck) who poses as a Jew in order to research a series of articles about anti-Semitism and discovers a dark and disturbing backlash experienced by his family. With Celeste Holm, Dorothy McGuire and John Garfield.
VHS: S18448. $19.98.
Laser: LD72252. $39.98.
Elia Kazan, USA, 1947, 118 mins.

Ghost and Mrs. Muir
A truly charming, touching fantasy, with a great musical score from Bernard Herrmann. Gene Tierney, Rex Harrison, George Sanders, Edna Best, Vanessa Brown and Natalie Wood star in the story of a lonely widow who is romanced by the ghost of a sea captain in her haunted English cottage.
VHS: S11563. $39.98.
Joseph L. Mankiewicz, USA, 1947, 101 mins.

Ghost of Zorro
The *Lone Ranger*'s Clayton Moore stars as the mysterious, whip-wielding avenger of justice in this action-packed serial of sabotage, betrayal and murder.
VHS: S33928. $14.98.
Fred C. Bannon, USA, 1959, 69 mins.

Gigolettes of Paris
Madge Bellamy stars as a shop girl whose heart is broken by a shiftless gigolo (Theodore von Eltz). She later begins an affair with another man (Gilbert Roland) and the gigolo reforms after discovering true love.
VHS: S30554. $19.95.
Alphonse Martell, USA, 1933, 64 mins.

Gilda
Rita Hayworth has never been more alluring as the pampered wife of a casino owner in South America who has eyes for her husband's new assistant. The second teaming of Glenn Ford and the gorgeous Hayworth, who steams up the screen by removing just her gloves.
VHS: S02167. $19.95.
Charles Vidor, USA, 1946, 110 mins.

The Girl from Missouri
Jean Harlow plays a young non-conformist of questionable virtue who tries to charm a millionaire but falls for a playboy (Franchot Tone) who's on to her game. With Lionel Barrymore and Patsy Kelly.
VHS: S17781. $19.98.
Jack Conway, USA, 1934, 72 mins.

The Girl Who Had Everything
A melodramatic remake of the 1933 *A Free Soul*, about an innocent and beautiful young woman (Elizabeth Taylor) who falls in love with a sullen underground crime boss (Fernando Lamas) defended by her hard-drinking father (William Powell). With Gig Young and James Whitmore.
VHS: S18522. $19.98.
Richard Thorpe, USA, 1953, 69 mins.

The Glass Key
A pretty terrific, fast-moving thriller with Brian Donlevy accused of murder, henchman Alan Ladd trying to bail him out, and Veronica Lake as the mysterious love interest. Akira Kurosawa, according to one source, claims that this film was the inspiration for his *Yojimbo*. With William Bendix as the brutal bodyguard; based on a novel by Dashiell Hammett.
VHS: S09457. $14.98.
Stuart Heisler, USA, 1942, 85 mins.

Go for Broke!
When Pearl Harbor is attacked, resentment against the Japanese runs high, especially with Lt. Michael Grayson (Van Johnson), who is assigned to command a Japanese/American combat unit.
VHS: S15132. $19.98.
Robert Pirosh, USA, 1951, 91 mins.

God's Little Acre
Faithful, effective adaptation of Erskine Caldwell's novel about the lusty, violent aspects of life in rural Georgia. With Robert Ryan, Michael Landon and Buddy Hackett.
VHS: S03592. $19.95.
Anthony Mann, USA, 1958, 118 mins.

The Goddess
Based on Paddy Chayefsky's sordid story of an aspiring film actress who makes her body available to anyone who can help her career, leading to drugs, alcohol and tragedy. With Kim Stanley, Lloyd Bridges, and Patty Duke.
VHS: S34122. $69.95.
John Cromwell, USA, 1958, 104 mins.

Golden Boy
Based on the famous play by Clifford Odets, the story of a music-minded boy who becomes a prize fighter. The starring debut of William Holden; with Barbara Stanwyck, Adolphe Menjou.
VHS: S04336. $19.95.
Rouben Mamoulian, USA, 1939, 99 mins.

Golden Earrings
Abraham Polonsky contributed to the screenplay of this intriguing war-era espionage thriller. A British operative (Ray Milland) is aided by a mysterious gypsy (Marlene Dietrich) in a plot to steal a poison gas formula from Nazi Germany.
VHS: S19076. $14.98.
Mitchell Leisen, USA, 1947, 95 mins.

Gone with the Wind
A film beyond criticism, a work that welds together Hollywood classicism and literary adaptation with grace. Victor Fleming is the credited director, though at various times Howard Hawks, George Cukor and Sam Wood helped shape the narrative and rhythm. Ben Hecht worked on the screenplay. William Cameron Menzies was the production designer. With Clark Gable, Vivien Leigh, Leslie Howard, Olivia de Havilland and Hattie McDaniel.
VHS: S00515. $89.98.
Victor Fleming, USA, 1939, 222 mins.

The Good Earth
Pearl Buck's novel of famine and the fight for survival in pre-revolution China was transformed into one of Hollywood's greatest films, featuring excellent performances by Paul Muni and Oscar-winner Best Actress Luise Rainer. The locust plague sequences are still memorable examples of cinematography.
VHS: S02899. $19.98.
Sidney Franklin, USA, 1937, 138 mins.

Good Sam
Gary Cooper is Sam Clayton, an extremely nice guy who is always willing to help out in any way he can. From loaning his car to preventing a suicide, no one has a better friend, but the tables turn when he finds himself with money troubles. With Ann Sheridan, Ray Collins and Joan Lorring. Not to be confused with *Good Neighbor Sam*.
VHS: S06229. $19.95.
Leo McCarey, USA, 1948, 116 mins.

Good Times
In their only movie together, Sonny and Cher appear as themselves. Cher is content with their success, but Sonny insists on accepting a movie offer from Mr. Mordicus, a film tycoon. In a series of vignettes, Sonny daydreams of himself as Sheriff Irving Ringo, Jingle Morry and Johnny Pitzacotta. With George Sanders and original music by Sono Bono.
VHS: S34417. $14.98.
William Friedkin, USA, 1967, 91 mins.

Goodbye Again
Ingrid Bergman stars in this Parisian melodrama as a middle-aged woman caught in a web of desire. Based on the chic novel by Francoise Sagan. Can Bergman carry on an affair with both Anthony Perkins and Yves Montand and still respect herself? She loved two men but her heart had only room for one. Sounds like it's time to remodel or break out the hankies.
VHS: S11282. $19.95.
Anatole Litvak, USA, 1961, 120 mins.

Goodbye Columbus
Richard Benjamin and Ali MacGraw, in their first starring roles, deal with growing up in an affluent Jewish suburban environment. Based on a novella by Phillip Roth. Benjamin is a discontented Bronx librarian romancing a college girl from suburbia. Sexual politics, spiritual values and material success will be discussed.
VHS: S02852. $19.95.
Larry Peerce, USA, 1969, 105 mins.

Goodbye, Mr. Chips
Robert Donat (in an Oscar-winning performance) and Greer Garson (in her film debut) star in this adaptation of James Hinton's best seller. A shy English schoolmaster falls in love and becomes a better man and teacher for it. A classic from MGM and a nostalgic tribute to the English public school system, the story is set in 1870.
VHS: S00516. $19.98.
Laser: MGM, **1939. LD70166. $34.98.**
Sam Wood, USA, 1939, 115 mins.

Goodbye, My Lady
Brandon de Wilde, Walter Brennan and Sidney Poitier star in this unforgettable story of a backwoods boy and his new-found dog. A real tear-jerker.
VHS: S14570. $14.95.
William Wellman, USA, 1956, 95 mins.

Gorgeous Hussy
Joan Crawford stirs up Washington D.C.'s high society as an innkeeper's daughter who proves an inspiration to President Andrew Jackson. She also spices up the lives of a few senators. With Melvyn Douglas, Robert Taylor, Franchot Tone, James Stewart, and Lionel Barrymore as Old Hickory.
VHS: S16450. $19.98.
Clarence Brown, USA, 1936, 103 mins.

The Graduate
A modern classic! Dustin Hoffman as the young graduate trying not to get into plastics, and Anne Bancroft as Mrs. Robinson. With a great soundtrack by Simon and Garfunkel, directed by Mike Nichols.
VHS: S00522. $14.95.
Mike Nichols, USA, 1967, 105 mins.

The Graduate (25th Anniversary Edition)
Mike Nichols' film in a new, 25th anniversary edition. Dustin Hoffman stars as the naive college graduate who's seduced by the middle-aged Mrs. Robinson (Anne Bancroft) and promptly falls in love with her daughter (Katharine Ross). This special limited edition is presented in its original wide-screen format and features interviews with the original cast and crew.
Laser: CAV. LD70371. $99.95.
Mike Nichols, USA, 1967, 106 mins.

Grand Hotel
Greta Garbo's great role as the world-weary ballerina, John Barrymore as the elegant but broke Baron von Geiger, Lionel Barrymore as Otto Kringelein, a dying nobody, Joan Crawford as a stenographer, and Wallace Beery as General Director Preysing.
VHS: S00523. $19.95.
Edmund Goulding, USA, 1932, 112 mins.

Grand Prix
The famous auto-racing event is the backdrop for personal lives of four top drivers. Spectacular racing sequences are set against the soapsuds of fast cars and fast women. With James Garner, Toshiro Mifune, Yves Montand, Jessica Walter and Eva Marie Saint. Watch out for the curves. VHS letterboxed.
VHS: S03630. $24.98.
Laser: LD70591. $39.97.
John Frankenheimer, USA, 1966, 161 mins.

The Great Escape
John Sturges' film is based on a true story about the escape from the Stalag Luft North. With Steve McQueen, James Garner, Richard Attenborough, Charles Bronson, James Coburn and Donald Pleasance. VHS letterboxed.
VHS: S28449. $24.98.
Laser: LD70752. $89.95.
DVD: DV60214. $24.98.
John Sturges, USA, 1962, 173 mins.

Great Expectations
Raised together as playmates by the embittered Miss Havershim, a lonely spinster ruled by revenge, Pip and Estella ultimately find themselves at a crossroads between friendship and love. With Jane Wyatt and Alan Hale, Sr. Includes original theatrical trailer.
VHS: S34625. $14.98.
Stuart Walker, USA, 1934, 102 mins.

Great Flamarion
Dan Duryea co-stars in this outing as a drunken performer in Erich von Stroheim's stage act. The catch is that in the act von Stroheim uses guns and knives, while Duryea stands between him and the girl he loves.
VHS: S06009. $29.95.
Anthony Mann, USA, 1945, 72 mins.

The Great Gabbo
Erich Von Stroheim, complete with monocle, plays an egocentric ventriloquist in this backstage musical drama. His dummy Otto sings on stage and in restaurants. Based on a Ben Hecht story. Musical numbers include "Caught in the Web of Love," where chorus girls perform in a giant spider web. B&W.
VHS: S04090. $29.95.
James Cruze, USA, 1929, 89 mins.

Great Guy
James Cagney swings into action as a dedicated chief of the Bureau of Weights and Measures with an unbending determination to crusade against corruption in the meat business.
VHS: S02992. $29.95.
John G. Blystone, USA, 1936, 75 mins.

Great Imposter
The incredible but true story of the world's greatest masquerader, Ferdinand Waldo Demara, who succeeded in a variety of guises including college professor, Trappist monk and prison warden. Starring Tony Curtis.
VHS: S02939. $59.95.
Robert Mulligan, USA, 1960, 112 mins.

Great Kate
The indomitable brilliance of Katharine Hepburn in three of her most popular performances: *Bringing up Baby, Morning Glory,* and *Stage Door*.
VHS: S10689. $59.98.

The Great Lie
Bette Davis and Mary Astor are splendid as two bitchy women in this sparkling drama about a determined girl who loses the man she loves. Davis believes he's dead in a plane crash and takes over the baby which his selfish wife doesn't want. With George Brent, Lucille Watson.
VHS: S11625. $19.95.
Edmund Goulding, USA, 1941, 107 mins.

The Great Man's Lady
Barbara Stanwyck and Joel McCrea star in this melodrama about life in the old days. Stanwyck is the wife of a town founder and rather consciously decides to defer to this great man's glory. As an old widow, the actual story of her husband's life as a pioneer can be told. It seems she significantly influenced and shaped the town with her courage and ability.
VHS: S26229. $19.98.
William Wellman, USA, 1942, 91 mins.

The Great St. Louis Bank Robbery
Based on an actual sequence of events, this film is an intense psychological drama that boasts an early Steve McQueen performance. Four cons and "young turk" McQueen join to mastermind the perfect heist, but once inside the bank, it's every man for himself. Filmed in a semi-documentary style, there is a gritty, realistic feel, enhanced by casting not only real police, but customers who were in the bank at the time of the real robbery. With Molly McCarthy. "A razor-edged film noir...tense, riveting and way ahead of its time" (*The Phantom of the Movies*).
VHS: S30728. $29.95.
Laser: Letterboxed. LD76189. $49.98.
Charles Guggenheim/John Stix, USA, 1959, 88 mins.

The Great White Hope
James Earl Jones gives a powerful performance as boxer Jack Jefferson, a thinly disguised portrait of Jack Johnson, the first black heavyweight champion. Based on the play by Howard Sackler, the film follows his career up and down the ladder of success all the way to his Hungarian tour as the lead role in *Uncle Tom's Cabin*. With Jane Alexander as his faithful companion in exile. Also in the cast: Robert Webber, Hal Holbrook, R.G. Armstrong, Beah Richards, Moses Gunn, Marlene Whitfield and Chester Morris.
VHS: S12519. $19.98.
Martin Ritt, USA, 1970, 102 mins.

Green Berets
Cliched wartime propaganda with Wayne as a Special Forces Colonel out to wipe out the Viet Cong. The only American film in support of the U.S. involvement in the Vietnam War.
VHS: S06977. $19.98.
Laser: Letterboxed. **LD74729. $39.98.**
John Wayne, USA, 1968, 141 mins.

Green Dolphin Street
Lana Turner, Donna Reed and Van Heflin star in this adventurous story of two sisters in 19th century New Zealand who are both after the same man. Academy Award-winning special effects.
VHS: S15123. $19.98.
Laser: LD71695. $39.98.
Victor Saville, USA, 1947, 141 mins.

Green Fire
Grace Kelly stars in this melodramatic love story. The desires of an emerald prospector (Stewart Granger) conflict with his love for this alluring woman. Grace manages a coffee plantation in Colombia, giving this steamy film an exotic and romantic locale.
VHS: S21168. $19.98.
Andrew Marton, USA, 1954, 100 mins.

The Green Glove
Murder, love and mystery yield an entangled web of intrigue in this post-World War II drama. A jewel thief steals a valuable relic from a church and the church sends out a relentless tracker to find it. Starring Glenn Ford.
VHS: S14752. $19.95.
Rudolph Mate, USA, 1952, 88 mins.

Green Mansions
Anthony Perkins plays a young man who went in search of wealth in the jungle in order to fuel his plot for revenge. Once there, however, he discovers love in the shape of Audrey Hepburn. Forgetting his original goal, Perkins must now try to unravel the strange mystery that ensnares this couple.
VHS: S21173. $19.98.
Laser: LD76321. $39.99.
Mel Ferrer, USA, 1959, 104 mins.

The Green Pastures
A heavily criticized adaptation of Marc Connelly's Pulitzer prize-winning stage play that interprets African-American tales of spirituality and oral black storytelling through a collection of vignettes on various Biblical stories and figures. With Rex Ingram, Oscar Polk, Eddie Anderson and Frank Wilson.
VHS: S02528. $19.98.
William Keighley/Marc Connelly, USA, 1936, 90 mins.

The Greta Garbo Collection
The spirit of Greta Garbo animates four films in this four-disc boxed set of Clarence Brown's *Anna Christie, Anna Karenina* and *Flesh and the Devil*, and Ernst Lubitsch's *Camille*.
Laser: LD70192. $99.98.

The Group
Candace Bergen is at the center of this engrossing melodrama featuring James Congdon, Larry Hagman and Hal Holbrook. It follows the lives of eight graduates from an exclusive women's college. Bergen's character makes a particularly big splash compared to her classmates as a movie star, though all lead eventful lives. Based on Mary McCarthy's novel, the result is a soapy, enjoyable treat.
VHS: S28052. $19.98.
Sidney Lumet, USA, 1966, 150 mins.

Guerillas in Pink Lace
As the Japanese advance on Manila early in WWII, Brass Murphy, trying to escape, is given a military pass by a kindly priest. In cleric's disguise, Murphy finds himself the chaperone of a group of five showgirls. The plane in which they escape is shot down, and they land on an enemy-held, small island, leading to harrowing and hilarious misadventures. With George Montgomery and Valerie Varda.
VHS: S34180. $19.95.
George Montgomery, USA, 1954, 96 mins.

Guess Who's Coming to Dinner
Stanley Kramer directs this Oscar-winning movie about the reaction to an interracial relationship by the parents of both parties. Spencer Tracy and Katharine Hepburn make their last film together as the liberal but frazzled couple who are a bit uneasy about Katharine Houghton's fiance Sidney Poitier. With Beach Richards, Cecil Kellaway and Roy E. Glenn Sr. Oscars went to Hepburn and the script.
VHS: S13316. $14.98.
Stanley Kramer, USA, 1967, 108 mins.

Guest in the House
Anne Baxter is causing trouble again. This time she is a disturbed girl who upsets the household in which she plays the title character. With Ralph Bellamy, Ruth Warrick, Margaret Hamilton and Jerome Cowan. Said to be a grim melodrama, made even grimmer by being in black and white.
VHS: S05073. $29.95.
John Brahm, USA, 1944, 121 mins.

Guilty of Treason
One of the Cold War Iron Curtain films. Charles Bickford plays Cardinal Mindszenty of Hungary and of his trial after the communist take-over amid the communist state's mistreatment of enemies of the state.
VHS: S06908. $29.95.
Felix E. Feist, USA, 1949, 86 mins.

Gun Crazy
A femme fatale leads a gun-crazy man into a life of crime as they both set off on a spree of armed robbery and murder. A sort of updated Bonnie and Clyde story which has achieved minor cult status. Starring Peggy Cummins and John Dall. Dalton Trumbo wrote the screenplay.
VHS: S13609. $19.98.
Joseph H. Lewis, USA, 1950, 87 mins.

A Guy Named Joe
Spencer Tracy is a hot shot WWII pilot until he is killed in action. He is sent from Heaven to protect the surviving members of his squadron. In addition to military pointers, he also supplies advice to the lovelorn. With Van Johnson, Irene Dunne, Ward Bond and Lionel Barrymore as the General.
VHS: S07008. $19.98.
Laser: LD76221. $39.98.
Victor Fleming, USA, 1943, 120 mins.

Hairy Ape
William Bendix stars as the title character in this rarely-seen drama by Eugene O'Neill. Susan Hayward co-stars as the spoiled heiress forced to flee Lisbon on Bendix's tramp steamer.
VHS: S06004. $29.95.
Alfred Santell, USA, 1944, 90 mins.

The Happy Ending
Stunning performances from an all-star cast highlight this hard-hitting and deeply personal look at marriage from director Richard Brooks. Starring Jean Simmons as the disillusioned wife and John Forsythe as the preoccupied husband. Co-stars Shirley Jones, Lloyd Bridges, Tina Louise, Nanette Fabray and Bobby Darin.
VHS: S31073. $19.98.
Richard Brooks, USA, 1969, 113 mins.

Happy Landing
Sonja Henie plays a Norwegian figure skater who follows a charismatic band leader (Cesar Romero) to America. Once there, she falls in love with a pilot (Don Ameche). With Ethel Merman, Jean Hersholt and Billy Gilbert.
VHS: S20261. $19.98.
Roy Del Ruth, USA, 1938, 102 mins.

The Harder They Fall
One of Humphrey Bogart's most memorable performances as Eddie Willis, a sportswriter who joins forces with a corrupt boxing promoter and works to dupe the public into believing Toro Moreno (Mike Lane) has a chance at the heavyweight title. With Rod Steiger.
VHS: S05862. $19.95.
Mark Robson, USA, 1956, 109 mins.

Harmon of Michigan
Tom Harmon plays himself in this story about one of the all-time great and legendary football players. Football, American style, has been an obsession for much of this century. This film portrays a more innocent time, before big money and television had completely transformed the sport.
VHS: S20634. $19.95.
Charles Barton, USA, 1941, 65 mins.

Harriet Craig
Joan Crawford was born to play the part of this psychotic and manipulative homemaker. All the household help live in fear of her exacting ways. When the man of the house is set to make a career advancement which requires some major traveling, Crawford springs into action with meticulously planned ferocity. It's a melodrama featuring Joan at her monstrous best.
VHS: S27184. $19.95.
Vincent Sherman, USA, 1950, 94 mins.

Hat Box Mystery
Tom Neal stars as the proprietor of a struggling detective agency, and Pamela Blake is the beautiful, much-too-inquisitive secretary. While Neal is out of town, Blake is called on to gather incriminating evidence against a cheating wife, only to commit a murder herself.
VHS: S06930. $24.95.
Lambert Hillyer, USA, 1947, 44 mins.

Hawaii
Julie Andrews, Max von Sydow and Richard Harris star in this grand adventure of the Hawaiian islands in the 1800's, based on the best-selling book by James Michener. Letterboxed.
VHS: S12425. $24.98.
George Roy Hill, USA, 1966, 186 mins.

He Walked by Night
Called "a gritty masterpiece" by filmmaker Erroll Morris. Richard Basehart stars as a psychotic killer mercilessly tracked down by police detectives. Shot in a highly realistic manner with a fantastic final shoot-out in the L.A. drainage tunnel system. Largely directed by an uncredited Anthony Mann.
VHS: S05959. $29.95.
Laser: CLV/CAV. LD72062. $34.95.
Alfred Werker, USA, 1948, 78 mins.

The Heart Is a Lonely Hunter
Alan Arkin stars as John Singer, bringing resourcefulness and resonance to the film adaptation of Carson McCullers' well-received first novel. When his lone friend is institutionalized, Singer's enclosed world explodes in anger and newly-awakened confidence as he comes into contact with a town drunk (Stacy Keach), a young, black activist (Cicely Tyson) and Mick (Sondra Locke), a sympathetic young girl.
VHS: S02533. $19.98.
Robert Ellis Miller, USA, 1968, 124 mins.

Heartbeat
In this charming American remake of *Battement de Coeur*, Ginger Rogers is a French gamine reform school escapee who goes to a pickpocket academy in Paris. She is caught on her first attempt at stealing by an upper-class man. He recruits her to do him a favor at a society party, where she meets and falls in love with a young, handsome, rich diplomat (Jean-Pierre Aumont). With Adolphe Menjou and Basil Rathbone.
VHS: S33736. $9.95.
Sam Wood, USA, 1946, 102 mins.

Helen of Troy
Rossana Podesta is Helen, the face that launched a thousand ships. This lavish production, based on *The Iliad*, joins the best of the Hollywood costume epic tradition with Greek legend. Romance and brutal war sequences make this film a gripping experience. A 19-year-old Brigitte Bardot makes an appearance.
VHS: S27837. $19.98.
Laser: LD75584. $39.98.
Robert Wise, USA, 1955, 135 mins.

Hell Harbor
The beauty of '30s Tampa is captured in this early talkie about a grandson of a Caribbean pirate, who tries to force his daughter to marry a moneylender, and the American sailor who comes to her rescue. With Lupe Velez, Jean Hersholt, John Holland and Gibson Gowland.
VHS: S30556. $19.95.
Henry King, USA, 1930, 65 mins.

Hell Ship Mutiny
Two murderous smugglers are terrorizing the natives on a South Sea island. Jon Hall plays a noble sea captain who helps the lovely island princess Mareva to rid her domain of the evil criminals. With Peter Lorre, John Carradine, Roberta Haynes and Mike Mazurki.
VHS: S16112. $29.95.
Lee Sholem, USA, 1957, 66 mins.

Hell's Angels
Howard Hughes made his name in Hollywood as the producer-director of this World War I aviation film notable for incredible aerial action scenes and for launching the career of Jean (Do you mind if I change into something more comfortable?) Harlow.
VHS: S00561. $29.95.
Howard Hughes, USA, 1930, 113 mins.

Heroes Die Young
American soldiers go behind enemy lines to pave the way for a devastating air attack on Nazi-held oil fields. This fast-paced film is based on a true story. With Scott Borland and Krika Peters.
VHS: S14141. $19.98.
Gerald S. Shepard, USA, 1960, 76 mins.

Heroes for Sale
Addict, thief, Commie, bum. They called him everything but what he really was: a hero. Hollywood confronted the Depression head-on with this vivid slice-of-life melodrama. Richard Barthelmess stars as a wounded ex-doughboy who overcomes morphine addiction, joblessness and false imprisonment. A powerful, touching winner! Also starring Loretta Young. "A fascinating social document of the early 1930s" (Leonard Maltin).
VHS: S15013. $19.98.
William Wellman, USA, 1933, 71 mins.

High Sierra
Humphrey Bogart stars as Roy "Mad Dog" Earle, a kindhearted gangster from Indiana who runs into serious trouble in the scenic mountains of Northern California. With Ida Lupino, Arthur Kennedy, Henry Hull, Barton MacLane, Cornel Wilde and Joan Leslie as the young woman with the clubfoot. Script by John Huston and W.R. Burnett, based on Burnett's novel.
VHS: S00569. $19.95.
Raoul Walsh, USA, 1941, 100 mins.

His Double Life
A shy but famous artist finds life much easier once he assumes the role of his recently deceased butler. Based on the play "Buried Alive", this first sound version starred Roland Young. Lionel Barrymore did an earlier version and Monty Woolley had the most success ten years later in *Holy Matrimony*. With Lillian Gish.
VHS: S05064. $29.95.
Arthur Hopkins, USA, 1933, 67 mins.

His Majesty O'Keefe
Coconut oil is the precious lifeblood of 1870s South Seas traders and scalawags. Easy going mariner Burt Lancaster teaches Fiji Island natives how to exploit their natural resources and defend themselves against pirates. With Joan Rice, Andre Morell, Abraham Sofaer, Benson Fong and Archie Savage.
VHS: S16733. $19.98.
Laser: LD71513. $34.98.
Byron Haskin, USA, 1954, 92 mins.

His Private Secretary
In this early John Wayne film, Wayne is Dick Wallace, a jetsetting son of a successful businessman. Dick wants to marry Marion Hall (Evalyn Knapp), a minister's granddaughter, but his father is opposed and wants him to work at the company business. Marion proves herself by getting a job with the company. With Reginald Barlow, Alec B. Francis, Arthur Hoyt, Natalie Kingston, Patrick Cunning, Al St. John and Hugh Kidder.
VHS: S33701. $24.95.
Philip H. Whitman, USA, 1933, 60 mins.

History Is Made at Night
A story of jealousy, divorce, and true love discovered. It transcends all the cliches of its type. Andrew Sarris said, "Not only the most romantic title in the history of the cinema but a profound expression of Borzage's commitment to love over probability."
VHS: S00573. $19.98.
Frank Borzage, USA, 1937, 98 mins.

The Hitch-Hiker
Frank Lovejoy, Edmond O'Brien and William Talman star in a classic film noir directed by Ida Lupino. Talman is an ex-convict who hitches rides, and then robs and kills the driver. A fascinating psychological study, very rare.
VHS: S06909. $24.95.
Ida Lupino, USA, 1953, 71 mins.

Hitler Dead or Alive
A wealthy American doctor's brother is killed by the Nazis, and holds Hitler personally responsible. He offers a $1,000,000 reward for Hitler, dead or alive, and three American gangsters just out of prison take him up on it: Ward Bond, Paul Fix and Warren Hymer.
VHS: S06002. $29.95.
Nick Grinde, USA, 1942, 70 mins.

Holiday in Mexico
The privileged daughter of the Ambassador to Mexico objects to his relationship with a beautiful singer. With Walter Pidgeon, Jane Powell, Ilona Massey and Roddy McDowall.
VHS: S18553. $19.98.
George Sidney, USA, 1946, 127 mins.

Home from the Hill
George Peppard and George Hamilton receive their screen debuts in Vincente Minnelli's drama about a southern landowner and his conflicts with his sons and wife. With a terrific performance from Robert Mitchum.
VHS: S11436. $19.98.
Vincente Minnelli, USA, 1960, 150 mins.

Homecoming
In this World War II romance, Clark Gable plays an egocentric doctor who leaves his wife (Anne Baxter) to work in the European campaign, where he falls for the dedicated and selfless battlefield nurse Lana Turner. With John Hodiak, Ray Collins and Cameron Mitchell.
VHS: S18666. $19.98.
Mervyn LeRoy, USA, 1948, 113 mins.

Hoodlum Empire
When a Mob chieftain's top gun goes legit and threatens to testify, the streets of the big city fill with blood. Can a senate investigation turn up any evidence of criminal wrongdoing? Or have they been scared or bribed into playing ball with organized crime? With Brian Donlevy, Claire Trevor, Forrest Tucker, Vera Ralston and Luther Adler.
VHS: S11399. $19.95.
Joseph Kane, USA, 1952, 98 mins.

The Hoodlum Priest
Irvin Kershner's compelling drama is based on the story of the Rev. Charles Dismas Clark (Don Murray), a controversial Jesuit priest who pursued the rehabilitation of career criminals. The story focuses on his efforts to help a cynical young thief (Keir Dullea).
VHS: S19495. $19.98.
Irvin Kershner, USA, 1961, 102 mins.

Hoosier Schoolboy
Mickey Rooney and Anne Nagel star in this hard-hitting drama about life in a small town. Schockey (Rooney) is a boy from the wrong side of the tracks. His father is the town drunk despite his heroic World War I record. Fortunately a sympathetic young woman arrives who gives Schockey the will to overcome the odds against him.
VHS: S24008. $24.95.
William Nigh, USA, 1937, 63 mins.

Hoosier Schoolmaster
Norman Foster stars in this post-Civil War drama as an ex-Union soldier who becomes a small-town schoolmaster in Indiana. Conflicts arise when he finds out about the corrupt city council's plans to use federal land grants to benefit themselves, and he falls in love with the girlfriend of the school bully. With Charlotte Henry and Dorothy Libaire.
VHS: S32949. $19.95.
Lewis D. Collins, USA, 1935, 71 mins.

The Horizontal Lieutenant
Set during World War II, Jim Hutton plays an inept Army Intelligence officer stationed on a remote Hawaiian Army outpost, whose idyllic life is interrupted when he inadvertently captures a Japanese spy. With Paula Prentiss, Jim Backus, Miyoshi Umeki and Jack Carter.
VHS: S20204. $19.98.
Richard Thorpe, USA, 1962, 90 mins.

Houdini
Tony Curtis stars as the great Houdini, a struggling circus performer who emerges as the world's most captivating escape artist. Co-starring Janet Leigh.
VHS: S13704. $19.95.
George Marshall, USA, 1953, 107 mins.

House of Strangers
Edward G. Robinson stars in this thoughtful and well-performed melodrama about an Italian-American banker who has rigid control over his three sons until he is arrested for illegal practices. Susan Hayward is the wife who must keep the family together. With Richard Conte and Luther Adler.
VHS: S13200. $39.98.
Joseph L. Mankiewicz, USA, 1949, 101 mins.

The House of the Seven Gables
George Sanders, Margaret Lindsay and Vincent Price star in this classic story based on the novel by Nathaniel Hawthorne, of one family's fight to overcome its turbulent past.
VHS: S34624. $14.98.
Joe May, USA, 1940, 89 mins.

The House on 92nd Street
A super thriller, this film introduced a new feeling of realism to Hollywood films through documentary techniques. It uses actual FBI footage to tell a riveting story about the pursuit and capture of a German spy ring. A German-American is approached by the Gestapo but goes to work for the FBI instead. The screenplay won an Academy Award.
VHS: S25524. $19.98.
Henry Hathaway, USA, 1945, 88 mins.

Howards of Virginia
A historical account of the Revolutionary war, an epic production which features Cary Grant, Martha Scott, Cedric Hardwicke, Alan Marshall, Richard Karlson, and a cast of thousands.
VHS: S03651. $19.95.
Frank Lloyd, USA, 1940, 122 mins.

Hucksters
Clark Gable plays a Madison Avenue adman who gets his hands dirty trying to sell Beautee soap to the American public. Boss Adolphe Menjou encourages Clark to romance socialite Deborah Kerr to acquire her product endorsement. With Ava Gardner, Sydney Greenstreet, Keenan Wynn and Edward Arnold.
VHS: S13192. $19.98.
Laser: LD71688. $34.98.
Jack Conway, USA, 1947, 115 mins.

Hud
Paul Newman is Hud, a man at odds with his father, tradition and himself. Patricia Neal and Melvyn Douglas both won Academy Awards for their roles, as did James Wong for his brilliant cinematography.
VHS: S00590. $14.95.
Laser: Widescreen. **LD75305. $39.98.**
Martin Ritt, USA, 1963, 112 mins.

Human Comedy
Clarence Brown directed many quality films for MGM, excursions into rural Americana. *Human Comedy*, based on the story by William Saroyan, stars Mickey Rooney as a telegraph messenger in Ithaca, California, learning the lessons that come from the experience of separation and loss.
VHS: S04206. $24.95.
Laser: LD72267. $34.98.
Clarence Brown, USA, 1943, 117 mins.

Humoresque
An ambitious violinist finds a patron in a rich, unstable woman in this involving drama starring John Garfield, Joan Crawford and Oscar Levant.
VHS: S13346. $19.98.
Jean Negulesco, USA, 1946, 123 mins.

The Hunchback of Notre Dame
William Dieterle's remake of Lon Chaney's 1923 silent has an eerie feel suggested by Charles Laughton's complex rendering of the character of Quasimodo. With Sir Cedric Hardwicke, Thomas Mitchell and Maureen O'Hara.
VHS: S29455. $19.98.
William Dieterle, USA, 1939, 115 mins.

The Hurricane Express
John Wayne stars in this railroad serial, as a son out to avenge the death of his father at the hands of the evil fiend who calls himself the Wreaker. Plenty of action and thrills are provided as the Duke tracks down his chameleon-like foe. With Tully Marshall and Conway Tearle.
VHS: S05491. $24.95.
Armand Schaefer/J.P. McGowan, USA, 1932, 223 mins.

I Am a Fugitive from a Chain Gang
They put his feet and hands in irons, but they couldn't shackle his will. A gripping tale about an innocent man brutally victimized by the criminal justice system. Based on a true story, *Fugitive* stars the charismatic Paul Muni (*Scarface*) in the lead role.
VHS: S01706. $19.98.
Laser: Includes original theatrical trailer. **LD71508. $34.98.**
Mervyn Le Roy, USA, 1932, 93 mins.

I Am the Law
Edward G. Robinson plays dedicated law professor John Lindsay, who uses his students to ferret out corruption in big city politics. A courtroom drama based on a serial by Fred Allhoff in Liberty Magazine. Cast includes Barbara O'Neil, John Beal, Wendy Barrie, Fay Helm, Louis Jean Heydt and Otto Kruger.
VHS: S08703. $69.95.
Alexander Hall, USA, 1938, 83 mins.

I Conquer the Sea
Sexual and family rivalry are the dominant themes of this work about two brothers (Stanley Morner and Dennis Morgan) who work as whalers and who fall madly in love with the same woman (Steffi Duna). With Douglas Walton and George Cleveland.
VHS: S18942. $19.95.
Victor Halperin, USA, 1936, 68 mins.

I Died a Thousand Times
Time may have passed Mad Dog Earle by…but the law has yet to catch up with him. This gritty manhunt thriller is one of the lushest and most expensively mounted gangster movies of the '50s. A rousing color remake of *High Sierra*; written by W.R. Burnett, whose credits include *Little Caesar, High Sierra, The Asphalt Jungle*, and *The Great Escape*. Starring Jack Palance, Shelley Winters, Lon Chaney Jr. and Dennis Hopper.
VHS: S14083. $59.99.
Stuart Heisler, USA, 1955, 109 mins.

I Live My Life
Joan Crawford plays a bored New York society girl who travels to Greece and meets a young archeologist played by Brian Aherne. He follows her back to the Big Apple to persuade her to give up her cocktail parties and polo ponies and join him digging up old civilizations in the Aegean.
VHS: S16451. $19.98.
W.S. Van Dyke, USA, 1935, 97 mins.

I Love You Again
A quiet, dignified man (Dick Powell) is transformed by amnesia into a shrewd con man. His wife (Myrna Loy), preparing to divorce him, is drawn back into his life.
VHS: S18806. $19.98.
W.S. Van Dyke II, USA, 1940, 99 mins.

I Wake Up Screaming
An entertaining mystery with Betty Grable and Victor Mature implicated in the murder of Betty's sister (Carole Landis) and pursued by a determined cop (Laird Cregar); with a terrific twist ending.
VHS: S09447. $19.98.
H. Bruce Humberstone, USA, 1941, 82 mins.

I Want to Live
Susan Hayward won an Oscar for her portrayal of a prostitute framed for murder and sentenced to the gas chamber. Fine jazz score by Johnny Mandel, featuring Theodore Bikel.
VHS: S03459. $24.95.
Laser: LD72268. $39.98.
Robert Wise, USA, 1958, 122 mins.

I Want You
Dana Andrews is Martin Greer, returned from World War II to settle in the small town of Greenhill with his father, kid brother and loving wife Nancy. But dark clouds of war are gathering once again over Korea, and they soon cast their shadow over the Greer household.
VHS: S31805. $14.95.
Mark Robson, USA, 1951, 101 mins.

I'll Cry Tomorrow
Susan Hayward is superb in this screen bio of singer-actress Lillian Roth, who fought to overcome bad marriages and alcoholism. Based on Roth's autobiography written with Mike Connolly and Gerold Frank. Cast includes Eddie Albert, Ray Danton, Richard Conte, and Jo Van Fleet as Lillian's mother. Hayward sings "Happiness is a Thing Called Joe", "Sing You Sinners" and several other Roth tunes. The costumes won an Oscar.
VHS: S09150. $24.95.
Daniel Mann, USA, 1955, 117 mins.

I've Always Loved You
Frank Borzage's lavish 1946 romantic drama of love and jealousy is filled out with classical music and the talents of Artur Rubenstein. With Philip Dorn and Catherine McLeod.
VHS: S14322. $19.98.
Laser: CLV. LD71993. $29.98.
Frank Borzage, USA, 1946, 117 mins.

Illicit
A racy Barbara Stanwyck prefers her independence no matter how much she loves James Rennie, so she remains illicitly his. Her careless disregard of conventions comprises the kind of theme which could only be filmed in the early 30s, before the Motion Picture Code was enforced and more sensational topics were placed out of bounds. Joan Blondell also stars.
VHS: S20831. $19.98.
Archie Mayo, USA, 1931, 81 mins.

Imitation of Life
Claudette Colbert, a widow, and Louise Beavers, her maid, go into business together, finding wealth and heartache in Fannie Hurst's all-time tear-jerker. An early look at a young woman's struggle with her racial identity. Includes original theatrical trailer.
VHS: S34679. $14.98.
John M. Stahl, USA, 1934, 111 mins.

Impact
Leo Popkin produced and Arthur Lubin directed this complicated crime drama with Brian Donlevy as the target of a murder plot. The wrong man is killed but everyone believes it to be Donlevy, who is now hiding. Jason Robards, Charles Coburn, Mae Marsh appear in supporting roles.
VHS: S08418. $29.95.
Arthur Lubin, USA, 1949, 83 mins.

In Cold Blood
Based on Truman Capote's novel, which in turn is based on an historical incident: the account of a real-life crime in which an entire family was brutally murdered by wandering gunmen. With Robert Blake, Scott Wilson and John Forsythe.
VHS: S00615. $19.95.
Richard Brooks, USA, 1967, 134 mins.

In Harm's Way
Otto Preminger directed this star-studded World War II epic of naval warfare in the Pacific. John Wayne, Kirk Douglas, Henry Fonda, Dana Andrews, Patricia Neal, Tom Tryon, Larry Hagman, George Kennedy, Carroll O'Connor, Burgess Meredith, Franchot Tone, Slim Pickens and Patrick O'Neal wear uniforms and do brave and noble deeds. War is hell but it's easier to take when it is filmed in Hawaii. B&W. 165 mins.
VHS: S07521. $29.95.
Otto Preminger, USA, 1965, 165 mins.

In Old Chicago
This quasi-historical melodrama is centered on one of the most enduring urban legends, the cow that kicked over the lamp and started the great Chicago fire over 100 years ago. Alice Brady is Mrs. O'Leary, with Don Ameche as the good son and Tyrone Power as his villianous brother. It's a good thing Tyrone is so bad. We get a chance to follow this cad to all the dives that made old Chicago so interesting.
VHS: S20707. $19.98.
Henry King, USA, 1938, 115 mins.

In the Heat of the Night
Winner of five Oscars including Best Picture, Rod Steiger stars as a red neck sheriff who grudgingly accepts help from Sidney Poitier, a black big city detective. Music score by Quincy Jones. VHS letterboxed.
VHS: S03621. $19.95.
Laser: LD74675. $34.98.
Norman Jewison, USA, 1967, 110 mins.

Indiscreet
Gloria Swanson is surrounded by wonderful art deco scenery in this romantic comedy that has Swanson trying to hide her scarlet past from Ben Lyon.
VHS: S00620. $29.95.
Leo McCarey, USA, 1931, 81 mins.

The Indiscreet Mrs. Jarvis
The checkered past of Brenda Jarvis is conjured up when her husband wants to promote one of his employees and invites him over for dinner. Sam Weston and his wife Helen arrive, and Brenda is shocked to discover that she and Helen shared an apartment long ago, when Brenda was not so "refined." Stars Angela Lansbury.
VHS: S16741. $14.95.
Alan Smithee, USA, 1955, 30 mins.

Inherit the Wind
Social consciousness director Stanley Kramer choreographs this stark and minimalist examination of the famous Scopes Monkey Trial in which highly charged emotional warfare is staked out between science and fundamental religion. The cast is extraordinary: Spencer Tracy is the sly and spirited Darrow-like defense attorney and Frederic March plays the William Jennings Bryan role. The surprise performance is Gene Kelly as a journalist assigned to the case.
VHS: S02341. $19.98.
Laser: LD72122. $39.98.
Stanley Kramer, USA, 1960, 128 mins.

Inside Daisy Clover
Robert Mulligan (*To Kill a Mockingbird*) directed this sour adaptation of Gavin Lambert's novel about a Hollywood starlet's (Natalie Wood) rise and fall. With Robert Redford, Christopher Plummer, Ruth Gordon and Roddy McDowall.
VHS: S15935. $19.98.
Laser: LD71185. $39.98.
Robert Mulligan, USA, 1965, 128 mins.

Inspiration
A modern version of *Sappho*, the enigmatic Garbo is Yvonne, an alluring artist's model in Paris, whose misfortune is her imprudent past, which compels her to leave the man she loves. Starring Robert Montgomery and Lewis Stone.
VHS: S15117. $19.98.
Clarence Brown, USA, 1931, 76 mins.

Internes Can't Take Money
Barbara Stanwyck is the patient of a young doctor played by Joel McCrea. Though the doctor falls in love, his patient has other pressing needs. She must find her daughter. The child was hidden by her criminal husband before he died. Now she will use any means to find the lost girl, even the abilities of the intern.
VHS: S26230. $19.98.
Alfred Santell, USA, 1937, 79 mins.

Intruder in the Dust
A powerful adaptation of William Faulkner's novel about a proud, independent black man who is accused of shooting an unarmed white man in the back. The film concentrates on the search for the actual killer. It depicts the complex racial and class psychology of the South and presents its protagonist in a perspective that was quite rare for its time. Shot largely in Faulkner's home town of Oxford, Mississippi. With Claude Jarman, Jr., David Brian and Juano Hernandez.
VHS: S18505. $19.98.
Clarence Brown, USA, 1949, 87 mins.

Iron Major
Pat O'Brien is the rugged World War I officer in this biography of Frank Cavanaugh, football coach and war hero. A flag-waver to boost morale.
VHS: S12015. $19.98.
Ray Enright, USA, 1943, 82 mins.

Island in the Sun
In this steamy tale of an island paradise torn apart by passion and politics, Harry Belafonte is reunited with his *Carmen Jones* co-star, Dorothy Dandridge. With James Mason and Joan Fontaine.
VHS: S33036. $14.98.
Robert Rossen, USA, 1957, 119 mins.

Istanbul
Cornell Borchers and Errol Flynn bring sophisticated passion to this romantic thriller. Jim Brennan (Flynn) is a flyer who uncovers a smuggling ring's stash of diamonds. Now he and his fiancee (Borchers) must save themselves from the tense international intrigue their discovery unleashes. The on-screen romance between Flynn and Borchers brings added excitement to this tale of espionage. Nat "King" Cole is featured performing his hit single "When I Fall in Love." The film's original theatrical trailer is also included.
VHS: S27352. $14.98.
Joseph Pevney, USA, 1956, 86 mins.

It Means That to Me
Eddie Constantine, complete with trenchcoat, plays a down-on-his-luck reporter who's set up on espionage charges by the government, then hired to transport top secret micro film. Dubbed in English. Italy, 1963.
VHS: S15363. $29.95.

It's a Dog's Life
The surprise is that the hero and narrator of this story happens to be a dog! Dean Jagger and Edmund Gwenn star in this revealing look at the world of humans through the eyes of man's best friend. Based on the Richard Harding Davis short story, "The Bar Sinister."
VHS: S16843. $19.98.
Hermann Hoffman, USA, 1955, 87 mins.

It's a Pleasure
Sonja Henie stars as a professional ice skater who helps her fallen hockey pro husband by getting him a job in her new show. Gorgeous Marie McDonald is determined to cause trouble for the married couple, even if it means telling a few white lies along the way. Sumptuous sets, glittering costumes and fantastic skating from three-time Olympic champion Henie.
VHS: S28492. $19.98.
William A. Seiter, USA, 1945, 90 mins.

Ivanhoe
An elaborately staged costume drama based on the novel by Sir Walter Scott, with an all-star cast including Robert Taylor, Elizabeth Taylor, Joan Fontaine, Emlyn Williams and others.
VHS: S03858. $19.98.
Laser: LD72136. $34.98.
Richard Thorpe, USA, 1952, 106 mins.

The James Cagney Collection
James Cagney's best work is represented in three of his signature films: William Wellman's 1931 *Public Enemy*, Raoul Walsh's 1949 *White Heat* and Michael Curtiz's flamboyant musical biography, *Yankee Doodle Dandy*.
VHS: S17329. $49.92.

Jane Eyre (1934)
Colin Clive is Rochester in this early sound era (the first sound version of the story) Monogram Studio production of Charlotte Bronte's classic novel. Virginia Bruce plays the title role of the English orphan who grows up to be the governess in a moody, mysterious English manor, and her growing love for its equally curious owner.
VHS: S09579. $39.95.
Christy Cabanne, USA, 1934, 67 mins.

Jane Eyre (1944)
Beautiful adaptation of the Charlotte Bronte novel stars Joan Fontaine as the fragile and noble Jane, in love with the brooding, mysterious and tragic Rochester (Orson Welles in a memorable performance), and is set within a romantic, Gothic framework. With a delicious musical score by famed composer Bernard Herrmann. Also features Agnes Moorehead and a young Elizabeth Taylor.
VHS: S18101. $19.98.
Laser: CLV. LD72107. $59.98.

Japanese War Bride
A Korean War veteran falls in love with a Japanese nurse (Shirley Yamaguchi) and brings her back to his California home as his wife. The neighboring farmers still harbor anti-Japanese sentiment from WWII and try to break up their marriage. With Don Taylor, Cameron Mitchell and Marie Windsor.
VHS: S31864. $24.95.
King Vidor, USA, 1952, 91 mins.

Jayhawkers
In the maelstrom of pre-Civil War Kansas, a government agent infiltrates a vigilante group called the Jayhawks and a battle for power begins. Starring Jeff Chandler, Fess Parker, and Nicole Maurey.
VHS: S13712. $19.95.
Melvin Frank, USA, 1959, 100 mins.

The Joan Crawford Collection
Three films starring Joan Crawford: Michael Curtiz's 1945 *Mildred Pierce*, Jean Negulesco's *Humoresque*, and Curtis Bernhardt's 1947 remake of Crawford's earlier *Possessed*.
VHS: S17327. $49.92.

The Joan Crawford Collection
Deluxe boxed set includes five classic Joan Crawford films: *Ice Follies of 1939, Mannequin, A Woman's Face, When Ladies Meet and Sadie McKee*. 480 mins.
Laser: LD76753. $99.98.

Joan of Arc
Ingrid Bergman and Jose Ferrer star in this lavish Hollywood production based on the play by Maxwell Anderson. One of Bergman's most famous roles.
VHS: S04391. $19.98.
Victor Fleming, USA, 1948, 100 mins.

The Joe Louis Story
The classic true-life story of Joe Louis, the first great black boxer, who not only defeated his opponents in the ring but helped to battle racism outside the ring as well.
VHS: S06336. $19.95.
Robert Gordon, USA, 1953, 88 mins.

John Paul Jones
This famous Scotsman, when confronted with the prospect of Britons fighting on American soil, took the battle across the ocean to English coastal waters uttering the phrase, "I have not yet begun to fight." Robert Stack stars as the revolutionary hero with Bette Davis as Catherine the Great.
VHS: S20685. $19.98.
John Farrow, 1959, USA, 126 mins.

The John Wayne RKO Collection
Six classics from the Duke in one boxed set: *Allegheny Uprising, Tall in the Saddle, Back to Bataan, Fort Apache, She Wore a Yellow Ribbon* and *Flying Leathernecks*. 594 mins.
Laser: LD76754. $149.99.

Johnny Apollo
An impeccably executed crime melodrama about a powerful Wall Street broker who is convicted and jailed for embezzling, and his son, who resorts to crime to raise money to help his father get out of prison. Directed by Henry Hathaway, and starring Tyrone Power, Dorothy Lamour and Lloyd Nolan.
VHS: S13613. $19.98.
Henry Hathaway, USA, 1940, 93 mins.

Johnny Belinda
Sensitive story of a deaf mute in Nova Scotia and the gentle doctor who recognizes her intelligence and teaches her sign language. Jane Wyman won Best Actress Award for her performance, with Lew Ayres, Agnes Moorehead.
VHS: S03460. $24.95.
Jean Negulesco, USA, 1948, 103 mins.

Johnny Come Lately
James Cagney plays an itinerant reporter who is given a job on a small town newspaper run by Grace George. When he begins to expose graft and corruption, the crooks that run the town get sore. With Margaret Hamilton, Hattie McDaniel, Arthur Hunnicut and Margorie Lord. Music was nominated for an Oscar. George's only screen appearance.
VHS: S12900. $19.98.
Laser: LD71575. $34.98.
William K. Howard, USA, 1943, 97 mins.

Johnny Eager
This late studio gangster film concerns a brutal racketeer (Robert Taylor) who tries to consolidate his power on the local gambling fronts and on the beautiful society woman (Lana Turner) he manipulates in his bid for control. With Van Heflin, Robert Sterling and Edward Arnold.
VHS: S18659. $19.98.
Mervyn LeRoy, USA, 1941, 107 mins.

Johnny One-Eye
A highly unusual crime story based on a Damon Runyon tale about gangsters out to kill each other. Pat O'Brien plays a man desperate to escape his past, whose life is transformed by his emotional attachment to an abandoned young girl and her dog. With Wayne Morris, Dolores Moran and Gayle Reed.
VHS: S19865. $29.95.
Robert Florey, USA, 1950, 80 mins.

Judgment at Nuremberg
Spencer Tracy presides over the trials of German war criminals in this well scripted, star-spangled production. Both Maximillian Schell and writer Abbey Mann won Oscars for this film. With Richard Widmark, Marlene Dietrich, Judy Garland, Montgomery Clift and William Shatner.
VHS: S09918. $29.95.
Laser: LD70605. $39.98.
Stanley Kramer, USA, 1961, 178 mins.

Julie
The honeymoon is over and the terror is about to begin in this chilling thriller that stars Doris Day as a young widow who marries a psychotic new husband (Louis Jourdan).
VHS: S30534. $19.98.
Andrew L. Stone, USA, 1956, 97 mins.

Jungle Cavalcade
Jack Buck goes into the wilds once again. This time he brings back exciting footage of wild animals in conflict.
VHS: S23776. $24.95.
Clyde E. Elliot, USA, 1930, 80 mins.

The Jungle Trap
Living in Africa, Steve Davis thought he'd outrun his past, but when the judge who wrongly sentenced his brother to death and his wife arrive, he seizes the opportunity to take revenge. Stars Ronald Reagan and Barbara Billingsley.
VHS: S16745. $14.95.
Jus Addiss, USA, 1954, 30 mins.

Jupiter's Darling
In ancient Rome, the beautiful Amytis would rather race her chariot than listen to boring speeches from her fiance. But when the mighty general Hannibal and his army prepare to lay siege, she sneaks away to see the barbarian in person.
VHS: S16606. $19.98.
Laser: LD70158. $34.98.
George Sidney, USA, 1955, 96 mins.

Kansas City Confidential
Preston Foster, John Payne, Coleen Gray and Lee Van Cleef are featured in this exciting crime drama. Payne is accused of a crime he didn't commit and goes to excessive measures to prove it.
VHS: S08419. $29.95.
Phil Karlson, USA, 1952, 98 mins.

The Katharine Hepburn Collection
Three works from the four-time Oscar winning actress, two from her golden period, her remarkable collaboration with George Cukor, the 1939 *The Philadephia Story* and the 1933 adaptation of Louisa May Alcott's *Little Women*, and Jack Conway's reworking of Pearl Buck's novel, *Dragon Seed*.
VHS: S17307. $49.92.

Keep Punching
A fight film with the womanizing gambler and boxer Henry Armstrong almost seduced by the fast life, and an equally fast woman, played by Mae Johnson. An all-black-cast film also featuring an appearance by Canada Lee.
VHS: S06858. $34.95.
John Clein, USA, 1939, 80 mins.

Kennel Murder Case
Terrific mystery at a breathless pace; William Powell is S.S. Van Dyke's super-sleuth.
VHS: S03341. $19.95.
Michael Curtiz, USA, 1933, 73 mins.

The Kentuckian
Burt Lancaster stars in and directs this adaptation of Felix Holt's novel. The film concerns a father and son's odyssey from Kentucky to the wild frontier of Texas. With John Carradine, Una Merkel, John McIntire and Walter Matthau (in his debut).
VHS: S17993. $19.98.
Burt Lancaster, USA, 1955, 104 mins.

Kept Husbands
Sparks fly between a blue-collar man and the boss' daughter. Class conflict arises. This "study" of the "kept" society husbands of rich, shallow girls stars Joel McCrea and Dorothy Mackaill, and features Ned Sparks.
VHS: S06007. $29.95.
Lloyd Bacon, USA, 1931, 95 mins.

The Key
William Holden and Sophia Loren star in this wartime story, as Loren, in the relentless wartime struggle, falls into a series of unhappy relationships in which she passes her apartment key from man to man. When she meets Captain Ross, she learns to love and struggles to keep her promise to be true to him.
VHS: S09630. $19.95.
Carol Reed, USA, 1958, 134 mins.

Key to the City
Loretta Young plays the prim and proper Harvard graduate to Clark Gable's former longshoreman as both are arrested in a nightclub brawl and realize just how different they are—but that doesn't stop them from falling in love.
VHS: S20560. $19.98.
George Sidney, USA, 1950, 101 mins.

Keys of the Kingdom
Based on the novel by A.J. Cronin, with a terrific performance from Gregory Peck as the dedicated missionary spreading Christianity in 19th century China. Also starring Vincent Price, Edmund Gwenn and Roddy McDowall as the young missionary.
VHS: S11737. $19.98.
Laser: LD72206. $49.98.
John M. Stahl, USA, 1944, 137 mins.

Kid Galahad
Michael Curtiz (*Casablanca*) directs Bette Davis, Edward G. Robinson and Humphrey Bogart in this gritty film about a gangster's moll who falls for an innocent young heavyweight. With Wayne Morris, Harry Carey and Jane Bryan.
VHS: S17334. $19.98.
Michael Curtiz, USA, 1937, 101 mins.

Kiki
Mary Pickford and Reginald Denny star in this story of a French girl's efforts to secure her position in the forefront of the show and the affections of her manager. With a 15-year-old Betty Grable in her second film.
VHS: S30555. $19.95.
Sam Taylor, USA, 1931, 87 mins.

Killers
A thriller based on the Ernest Hemingway story, *Killers* stars Lee Marvin, John Cassavetes and Angie Dickinson, with Ronald Reagan as a wealthy, unscrupulous underworld character.
VHS: S00673. $19.98.
Don Siegel, USA, 1964, 95 mins.

The Killers
Ava Gardner and Burt Lancaster star in this expansion of Hemingway's short story. John Huston co-wrote the screenplay without credit.
VHS: S33918. $14.95.
Robert Siodmak, USA, 1946, 103 mins.

Kim
Rousing action and a terrific performance by Errol Flynn distinguish this adaptation of Rudyard Kipling's tale of 1880s colonialist India, with British soldiers battling the rebelling Indians.
VHS: S00675. $24.95.
Victor Saville, USA, 1950, 113 mins.

The King and Four Queens
Clark Gable is holed up in a desert ghost town whose only inhabitants are four comely young widows and their flinty mother-in-law. With Jo Van Fleet and Eleanor Parker.
VHS: S15260. $19.98.
Raoul Walsh, USA, 1956, 85 mins.

King Rat
George Segal stars as Corporal King in this adaptation of James Clavell's novel of existence on a Japanese-run POW camp in Singapore towards the close of World War II. Opportunistic King enlists the services of British prisoner Peter Marlowe (James Fox) after learning that he can speak Malay and a bond forms between the two. With Tom Courtenay, Patrick O'Neal, and Denholm Elliott.
VHS: S34113. $19.95.
Bryan Forbes, USA, 1965, 134 mins.

King Richard and the Crusaders
An ambitious, historical adaptation of Walter Scott's *The Talisman*, set during the Crusades. Richard Harrison is Saladin, a dreaded historical figure who arrives in England impersonating a nobleman and falls madly in love with Lady Edith (Virginia Mayo). With George Sanders, Laurence Harvey and Robert Douglas.
VHS: S19007. $19.98.
David Butler, USA, 1954, 113 mins.

King's Row
Ronald Reagan's performance and Erich Wolfgang Korngold's score highlight this powerful tale of small-town decadence. With Ann Sheridan and Robert Cummings.
VHS: S15657. $19.98.
Laser: LD71684. $39.98.
Sam Wood, USA, 1942, 127 mins.

The King's Thief

David Niven plays a noble scoundrel enmeshed in overlapping intrigues at the court of King Charles II. The costumes and sets recreate the pageantry of 17th-century England, giving Niven plenty of opportunity to display his swashbuckling talents. Ann Blyth, George Sanders and Roger Moore are also featured.

VHS: S21017. $19.98.
Robert Z. Leonard, USA, 1955, 78 mins.

Kings Go Forth

Frank Sinatra and Tony Curtis are battle-hardened GIs in France who fall for Natalie Wood, the half-black woman who causes them to confront their bigotry.

VHS: S15124. $19.98.
Laser: LD76360. $39.99.
Delmer Daves, USA, 1958, 110 mins.

Kismet

Laughter and lavish spectacle unfold in this Arabian Nights fantasy starring Ronald Colman and Marlene Dietrich.

VHS: S30535. $19.98.
William Dieterle, USA, 1944, 100 mins.

A Kiss Before Dying

Robert Wagner gambled with his clean-cut image to play a student who seduces a rich man's daughter, then kills her and turns his attention to her sister, in this unrelenting thriller which co-stars Joanne Woodward, Jeffrey Hunter and Mary Astor. Based on the novel by suspense master Ira Levin.

VHS: S31839. $19.98.
Gerd Oswald, USA, 1955, 94 mins.

Kiss Me Deadly

Private dick Mike Hammer foils the attempt of some crooks to steal a crate of radioactive materials but finds himself unable to protect the woman he originally signed on to help. "Art" meets pulp literature in this fast and violent thriller, filled with tilt shots and symbols, which had a major influence on the young directors of the French New Wave. With Ralph Meeker, Cloris Leachman, and Strother Martin. "I don't care what you do to me, Mike—just do it fast!"

VHS: S13756. $19.98.
Laser: LD72139. $39.95.
Robert Aldrich, USA, 1955, 105 mins.

Kiss Tomorrow Goodbye

No, this isn't about the last performance of *Annie*, but a Jimmy Cagney gangster picture. He's mean. He's tough. And he's very dangerous as Ralph Cotter, criminal and killer. With Ward Bond, Neville Brand, Luther Adler and Barbara Payton. This film was banned in Ohio for brutality.

VHS: S04711. $29.95.
Laser: CLV. LD72003. $29.98.
Gordon Douglas, USA, 1950, 102 mins.

Kitty Foyle

Ginger Rogers snared a Best Actress Oscar for her remarkable portrayal of a working girl who must choose between a life of upper-crust manners with a wealthy aristocrat, or a simple life with a nearly penniless intern.

VHS: S00688. $19.95.
Sam Wood, USA, 1940, 108 mins.

Klondike Annie

A sharp Mae West vehicle adapted from her play *Frisco Kate*. West is an unjustly accused woman hiding from the law, paired with Victor McLaglen and concealing her identity by living in the Yukon as a Salvation Army worker. With Philip Reed, Helen Jerome Eddy and Harry Beresford.

VHS: S18870. $14.98.
DVD: DV60330. $29.99.
Raoul Walsh, USA, 1936, 80 mins.

Knights of the Round Table

Robert Taylor, Ava Gardner and Mel Ferrer star as King Arthur, Guinevere and Lancelot in this film which was MGM's first production done in Cinemascope.

VHS: S04207. $19.95.
Laser: LD70611. $34.98.
Richard Thorpe, USA, 1953, 117 mins.

Knute Rockne, All American

Pat O'Brien delivers a winning performance as the legendary Notre Dame football coach Knute Rockne, whose all-star career came to a tragic end in a plane crash. Gale Page shines as the coach's supportive wife. With Donald Crisp, John Qualen, Albert Basserman and future president Ronald Reagan as the immortal Notre Dame star player George Gipp.

VHS: S15659. $19.98.
Lloyd Bacon, USA, 1940, 96 mins.

Krakatoa: East of Java

A group sets sail in search of a treasure believed to be located in a sunken ship off the island coast of Java. Waiting for them is the legendary volcano Krakatoa, and to their surprise, the largest tidal wave ever witnessed on film. With Maximillian Schell, Brian Keith, Diane Baker, Sal Mineo and J.D. Cannon.

VHS: S32696. $19.98.
Bernard L. Kowalski, USA, 1968, 128 mins.

Ladies They Talk About

Adapted from the play *Women in Prison*, this sharp, Depression-era work stars Barbara Stanwyck as an imprisoned bank robber and Preston Foster as a reformer who falls in love with her. A strong social and political critique of American life. With Lyle Talbot, Lillian Roth and Susan Hayward.

VHS: S18127. $19.98.
William Keighley, USA, 1933, 67 mins.

Lady by Choice

Carole Lombard plays an exotic fan dancer who takes in bag lady May Robson to clean up her show. She plans to turn the downtrodden into a proper lady and use her for a Mother's Day publicity stunt, but Robson has a few acts of her own. The lively sequel to *Lady for a Day*.

VHS: S16590. $19.95.
David Burton, USA, 1934, 78 mins.

Lady for a Night

Joan Blondell stars as the owner of a Mississippi gambling boat who is accused of murder; John Wayne is her saviour.

VHS: S10011. $14.95.
Leigh Jason, USA, 1941, 87 mins.

Lady from Louisiana

John Wayne fights city corruption that taints the local lottery in New Orleans. As a fearless lawyer he romances the daughter of General Mirbeau, the supposed head of a crooked machine, and works for reform in his spare time. With Ona Munson and Ray Middleton.

VHS: S04889. $19.95.
Bernard Vorhaus, USA, 1941, 85 mins.

Lady Godiva

When a Saxon nobleman (George Nader) takes Lady Godiva (Maureen O'Hara) as his bride, the scheming Normans attempt to increase their hold over King Edward. The couple's fight to thwart them leads to Lady Godiva taking her famous nude ride to prove her Saxon loyalty. Features an early screen appearance by Clint Eastwood. Includes original theatrical trailer.

VHS: S30892. $14.98.
Arthur Lubin, USA, 1955, 89 mins.

Lady Hamilton

A new version of the historical tragic love story of Lord Horatio Nelson and Lady Emma Hamilton. With John Mills, Richard Johnson, and Michele Merciere.

VHS: S34202. $19.95.
Christian-Jaque, USA/Germany/France/Italy, 1969, 87 mins.

Lady in a Cage

When wealthy widow Olivia de Havilland is trapped in a glass elevator in her mansion, uninvited guests come out of the woodwork. They include a wino, a prostitute and three hooligans—one of which is young James Caan. A very nasty thriller about faulty machinery and freaky people. With Jeff Corey, Ann Sothern, Rafael Campos and Scatman Crothers. B&W.

VHS: S10828. $49.95.
Walter Grauman, USA, 1964, 95 mins.

Lady in Cement

Frank Sinatra returns as Florida detective Tony Rome. When he finds a dead blonde underwater, ex-con Dan Blocker turns up on his doorstep in an unpleasant mood. Raquel Welch plays the pretty rich lady who may have all the answers. With Martin Gabel, Lainie Kazan, Pat Henry, Richard Deacon and Joe E. Lewis as himself.

VHS: S12522. $59.98.
Laser: LD71821. $59.98.
Gordon Douglas, USA, 1968, 93 mins.

The Lady in Question

Rita Hayworth plays the title character, who is on trial for murder in Paris. Brian Aherne is the kindly juror who believes in her innocence but begins to have his doubts when she falls in love with his son (Glenn Ford). A mixture of comedy, romance and drama that marked the first screen pairing of Hayworth and Ford.

VHS: S08704. $19.95.
Charles Vidor, USA, 1940, 81 mins.

Lady in the Lake

This Raymond Chandler mystery, in which a private eye searches for a man's missing wife, turns out to be an interesting experiment in subjective camera work. The camera takes the first-person point of view of detective Philip Marlowe (Robert Montgomery) throughout the film, only allowing us to see his face when he looks in a mirror. With Lloyd Nolan and Audrey Totter.

VHS: S13757. $19.98.
Laser: LD76223. $39.98.
Robert Montgomery, USA, 1946, 103 mins.

Lady Killer

James Cagney shows why he's one of the greats in this live-wire 1933 film that's "a kind of resume of everything he's done to date in the movies" (*New York Evening Post*). Cagney's a New York thug who stumbles into fame as a movie star in L.A. and then discovers his old gang has come to cash in on his celebrity status. "One of Cagney's best" (*Video Review*). Also starring Mae Clarke. (Cagney squashed a grapefruit in her kisser in *Public Enemy*.)

VHS: S15015. $19.98.
Roy Del Ruth, USA, 1933, 77 mins.

Lady of Burlesque

Based on Gypsy Rose Lee's *G String Murders*, an unusual and entertaining mystery-thriller with an unknown strangler at large in the backstage world of a burlesque opera house. With Barbara Stanwyck and Michael O'Shea.

VHS: S03214. $39.95.
William Wellman, USA, 1943, 92 mins.

The Lady Refuses

In this early melodrama, a young woman, destined to become a streetwalker, is recruited by a wealthy socialite to try and woo his son away from a golddigger. In the end, she accomplishes her mission and winds up with the son's father as her prize. With Betty Compson, John Darrow and Gilbert Emery.

VHS: S34176. $19.95.
George Archainbaud, USA, 1931, 72 mins.

Last Angry Man

The last film of Paul Muni casts him as an idealistic, aging physician who lives in the slums of Brooklyn. Adapted from the novel by Gerald Green with a script by the author; Muni delivers a powerful performance, sentimental and heartfelt. With David Wayne, Luther Adler, Betsy Palmer, Godfrey Cambridge and Billy Dee Williams.

VHS: S09113. $19.99.
Daniel Mann, USA, 1959, 100 mins.

The Last Mile

Preston Foster stars as "Killer" Mears in this prison drama based on the 1929 penal riots in New York. Clark Gable and Spencer Tracy played the same role on the stage. Prologue has a real prison warden speaking against capital punishment. A taunt, tension-filled drama. With Howard Phillips, Paul Fix and Albert J. Smith as the mean guard.

VHS: S05708. $29.95.
Sam Bischoff, USA, 1932, 69 mins.

Last of Mrs. Cheyney

Larceny among the English upper classes is the subject of this breezy Joan Crawford vehicle. She plays Fay Cheyney, a "respectable adventuress" who worms her way into aristocratic house parties in search of expensive jewels. William Powell plays Charles, her phony butler accomplice. With Robert Montgomery, Frank Morgan, Jessie Ralph, Colleen Clare and Nigel Bruce.

VHS: S16452. $19.98.
Richard Boleslawski, USA, 1937, 99 mins.

The Last of the Mohicans

In 1757, colonial America is being torn apart by the French and Indian War. When the daughter of a British General is captured, Hawkeye, played by Randolph Scott, is set in action by his desire to free the woman he loves. Based on James Fenimore Cooper's classic novel.

VHS: S21998. $19.95.
George B. Seitz, USA, 1936, 91 mins.

The Last Safari

A late effort from Western director Henry Hathaway (*True Grit*) about an embittered hunter coming to terms with his friend's death when a young couple hire him to guide a safari hunt. With Kaz Garas, Gabriella Licudi and Johnny Sekka.

VHS: S17979. $14.95.
Henry Hathaway, USA, 1967, 111 mins.

Last Time I Saw Paris

Van Johnson returns to the City of Lights right after World War II only to find that some things and people have changed. Loosely based on F. Scott Fitzgerald's *Babylon Revisited*. Among the disillusioned are Elizabeth Taylor, Donna Reed, Eva Gabor and Roger Moore, in his big screen debut.

VHS: S05070. $19.95.
Laser: LD72140. $34.98.
Richard Brooks, USA, 1954, 116 mins.

The Last Voyage

The harrowing events of a sinking ocean liner, with devastating psychological fallout for the captain (George Sanders), and the desperate attempts of a man (Robert Stack) to save his wife and child. With Edmond O'Brien and Dorothy Malone.

VHS: S17987. $19.98.
Laser: LD76319. $39.99.
Andrew L. Stone, USA, 1960, 87 mins.

Laughing Sinners

In this bleak Depression era work, Joan Crawford is a tense, insecure cafe entertainer in suicidal despair when her lover leaves her. She is saved by the romantic and selfless Salvation Army officer (Clark Gable). With Neil Hamilton, John Mack Brown and Marjorie Rambeau.

VHS: S18805. $19.98.
Harry Beaumont, USA, 1931, 72 mins.

Laura

Otto Preminger's 1944 film noir is a witty murder mystery with an elaborate cast of characters—detective, beautiful woman and cynical reporter-who get entangled in the plot. Joseph La Shelle won an Academy Award for cinematography. With Gene Tierney, Dana Andrews, Clifton Webb and Vincent Price.

VHS: S18074. $19.98.
Laser: LD71096. $39.98.
Otto Preminger, USA, 1944, 85 mins.

Leave Her to Heaven

Gene Tierney received a best actress nomination for her depiction of a jealous woman unable to control her possessive instincts. This film is a delightful, melodramatic wallow in one of nature's basest passions. Vincent Price and Jeanne Crain co-star.

VHS: S23757. $19.98.
Laser: LD74915. $39.99.
John M. Stahl, USA, 1945, 110 mins.

Legend of the Lost

John Wayne is cast as Joe January, the foremost guide to the Sahara desert. He is hired by Rossano Brazzi to lead him to the lost city of Timgad, said to be filled with gold and precious stones. Local slave girl Sophia Loren also wants to join the expedition. A sand dune saga of romance, betrayal, archeology and thirst.

VHS: S12140. $19.95.
Henry Hathaway, USA, 1957, 109 mins.

Les Miserables

A classy staging of Victor Hugo's novel about a small-time thief (Fredric March) fleeing his past. Charles Laughton plays the police chief. Written by W.P. Lipscomb. With Cedric Hardwicke, Rochelle Hudson and Frances Drake.

VHS: S05853. $59.98.
Richard Boleslawski, USA, 1935, 108 mins.

Let 'Em Have It

The newly formed FBI declares war on gangsters and public enemies. At the top of their list is Joe Keeper, an escaped convict. So begins a spectacular manhunt as the Keefer gang tries to stay one step ahead. With Richard Arlen, Virginia Bruce.

VHS: S09631. $14.95.
Sam Wood, USA, 1935, 96 mins.

Let's Sing Again

Henry Armetta delivers a sensitive performance as an opera star who's lost his voice and now works in a traveling show. He adopts Bobby Breen (in his first film) and together they search out the boy's real father.

VHS: S09580. $29.95.
Kurt Neumann, USA, 1936, 70 mins.

A Letter of Introduction

Adolphe Menjou stars as a famous father of a struggling actress who wants to make it on her own. Andrea Leeds is the determined daughter. Other personalities include Charlie McCarthy and Edgar Bergen, George Murphy, Eve Arden and Ann Sheridan.

VHS: S05072. $29.95.
John M. Stahl, USA, 1938, 104 mins.

Letter to Three Wives

Joseph L. Mankiewicz received an Oscar for his direction of three women reacting to a letter sent by the town flirt, who has run off with one of their husbands. With Jeanne Crain, Linda Darnell, Ann Sothern and Kirk Douglas.

VHS: S18097. $19.98.
Joseph L. Mankiewicz, USA, 1949, 103 mins.

License to Kill

Agent Nick Carter is called in when enemy agents attempt to steal a new secret weapon. Starring Eddie Consantine and Daphne Dayle.

VHS: S15362. $29.95.
Henri Decoin, USA, 1964, 100 mins.

A Life at Stake (aka Key Man)

Andes, a young building contractor, goes into partnership with a businessman (Douglas Dumbrille) and his sexy wife (Angela Lansbury). Although he becomes suspicious when the investors require him to take out a large insurance policy, he finds himself irresistibly attracted to the businessman's wife. Unable to stay away, he agrees to the deal but soon realizes this may be a deadly scheme.

VHS: S30408. $19.95.
Montgomery Tully, USA, 1954, 78 mins.

The Life of Emile Zola

A penetrating drama and social documentary starring Paul Muni as the famous author of *Nana*. The film documents Zola's struggle as a novelist, his long friendship with the painter Cezanne and his impassioned fight against bigotry as evidenced by his role in the Dreyfuss Case.

VHS: S01758. $19.95.
William Dieterle, USA, 1937, 110 mins.

Lights of New York

The underworld is running a bootlegging operation in this first Warner Bros. talkie. With Helene Costello, Cullen Landis, Gladys Brockwell, Mary Carr, Wheeler Oakman, Eugene Palette, Robert Elliott and Tom Dugan.

VHS: S33702. $24.95.
Bryan Foy, USA, 1928, 52 mins.

Lilies of the Field

Sidney Poitier won an Oscar for this earnest, well-meaning and quiet work about a black handyman who reluctantly agrees to help a group of emigre East German nuns build a chapel. The heart of the film is the tender and expressive relationship between Poitier and Lilia Skala, who plays the Mother Superior. With Lisa Mann, Isa Crino and Stanley Adams. Music by Jerry Goldsmith. Screenplay by James Poe.

VHS: S13390. $19.98.
Laser: LD72124. $34.98.
Ralph Nelson, USA, 1963, 93 mins.

Lilith

Warren Beatty and Jean Seberg co-star in this drama about the obsessive love between a therapist and his patient.

VHS: S04662. $59.95.
Robert Rossen, USA, 1964, 126 mins.

A Link in the Chain

On the eve of an awards banquet in his honor, Professor Graham's doubts about his illustrious career are put to rest when he opens a musty box of memorabilia. The three students he recalls—a handicapped artist, rebellious debutante and college hero—have learned about kindness and dignity from him, each in a special way. James Cagney stars in a performance both powerful and touching.

VHS: S16749. $14.95.
Larry Marcus, USA, 1955, 30 mins.

A Lion Is in the Streets

An itinerant confidence trickster becomes a self-titled defender of the people when James Cagney takes on "one of his most colorful and meaningful roles." This busy melodrama cleverly exposes the corruption of southern populist politics. Stars Barbara Hale, Anne Francis, Warner Anderson and Lon Chaney, Jr.

VHS: S16276. $19.98.
Laser: LD70048. $34.98.
Raoul Walsh, USA, 1953, 88 mins.

Little Big Horn

Lloyd Bridges, John Ireland and Marie Windsor star in this suspenseful, true story of a small band of cavalry men who try to warn General Custer of a probable Sioux ambush. Moving through enemy territory, the men are killed off by arrows until only Bridges and Ireland (in wonderfully nerve-wracking performances) are left. Warren's directorial debut.

VHS: S32956. $19.95.
Charles Marquis Warren, USA, 1951, 86 mins.

Little Caesar

This archetypal gangster film stars Edward G. Robinson as a small town thug who, along with his cohort, heads for the big city and ruthlessly pushes his way to the top of the mob. A landmark film, this action-packed melodrama ia also a probing social commentary on the criminal mind and Depression era America. Director Mervyn LeRoy had such a fascination for the subject that he went so far as to hire three mobsters from Chicago as advisors on the production.

VHS: S14307. $19.98.
Mervyn LeRoy, USA, 1930, 80 mins.

The Little Fugitive

Capturing the pleasures and pain of childhood as no film has before or since, this lyrical comedy/drama about a seven-year-old boy who runs away to Coney Island after being tricked into believing he's killed his older brother traverses all generational boundaries to remain a cherished and timeless American classic. "Our New Wave would never have come into being if it hadn't been for the young American Morris Engel, who showed us the way to independent production with his fine movie *The Little Fugitive*" (Francois Truffaut).

VHS: S30704. $24.95.
Morris Engel, USA, 1953, 80 mins.

Little Lord Fauntleroy

The enchanting story of a young boy, brought up in Brooklyn, who's discovered to be a long-lost heir and a British Lord. Fine performances by a superb cast, including Freddie Bartholomew, Mickey Rooney, and Delores Costello.

VHS: S13846. $14.98.
John Cromwell, USA, 1936, 102 mins.

Little Men

Cute adaptation of the Louisa May Alcott tale featuring Kay Francis, Jimmy Lydon and William Demarest. Jack Oakie steals the show as a wild con man.

VHS: S05635. $24.95.
Norman Z. McLeod, USA, 1940, 84 mins.

The Little Minister

Based on a play by Sir James Barrie. Katharine Hepburn is the gypsy girl who falls for the new cleric in a small Scottish village, with near-tragic results.

Laser: CLV. LD71727. $19.98.
Richard Wallace, USA, 1934, 101 mins.

Little Orphan Annie

Set in a blighted America beset at the height of the Depression, this is an early adaptation of the prize-winning comic strip about a charismatic, charming young orphan who falls into the warm embraces of a lonely, childless millionaire. With Mitzi Green, Edgar Kennedy, May Robson and Buster Phelps. Written by Wanda Tuchock and Tom McNamara.

VHS: S17445. $19.95.
John S. Robertson, USA, 1932, 60 mins.

The Little Princess

Shirley Temple is the pampered daughter of a British officer who's reported killed in action. Refusing to believe he's dead, she haunts army hospitals to find him. Based on the classic riches to rags story by Frances Hodgson Burnett.

VHS: S09996. $19.98.
Laser: CLV. LD72063. $39.95.
Walter Lang, USA, 1939, 93 mins.

Little Red Schoolhouse

Unprepared for the perils of city life, a rebellious young boy falls in with a gang of crooks after running away from home. This delightful adventure follows him through the consequences of his youthful folly.

VHS: S13847. $19.95.
Charles Lamont, USA, 1936, 64 mins.

Little Women

Four New England sisters wage a Civil War battle for a wealthy neighbor's grandson in this adaptation of Louisa May Alcott's story which stars Elizabeth Taylor, Janet Leigh, June Allyson and Margaret O'Brien.

VHS: S13066. $19.98.
Mervyn LeRoy, USA, 1949, 122 mins.

Lives of a Bengal Lancer

Adventure film set in India during the rule of the British, Gary Cooper stars as an officer of troops guarding the Kyber Pass on India's northern border. One of Hollywood's greatest adventure films.

VHS: S01989. $14.98.
Henry Hathaway, USA, 1935, 110 mins.

Lola (The Statutory Affair; Twinky)

The romantic story of a marriage between a 16-year-old nymphet (Susan George) and an aging 38-year-old American porno book writer (Charles Bronson) that doesn't work out because of a lack of communication—not to mention the meddling of family and friends. Letterboxed.

VHS: S34292. $19.99.
Richard Donner, USA, 1969, 88 mins.

Lonelyhearts
Montgomery Clift stars as the writer of an advice column who becomes too involved for his own good in the problems of his readers. Adapted from Nathanael West's *Miss Lonelyhearts*. The excellent cast includes Myrna Loy, Robert Ryan, Jackie Coogan and Maureen Stapleton.
VHS: S04212. $19.98.
Vincent J. Donehue, USA, 1958, 101 mins.

Longest Day
With an all-star cast that includes John Wayne, Robert Mitchum, Henry Fonda, Richard Burton and Sean Connery, this epic retelling of the events of D-Day is one of the greatest war films ever made.
VHS: S06537. $24.98.
Laser: LD71114. $69.98.
Ken Annakin, USA, 1962, 180 mins.

The Lost Moment
Robert Cummings is an ambitious publisher in Europe trying to locate the lost love letters of a famous writer. Susan Hayward claims she has access to them, and Bob believes her. With Agnes Moorehead, Eduardo Cianelli. Based on Henry James' *Aspern Papers*. B&W.
VHS: S04223. $19.98.
Laser: CLV. LD72005. $34.98.
Martin Gabel, USA, 1947, 89 mins.

Lost Zeppelin
Ricardo Cortez stars in this adventure tale of explorers in the Antarctic. Fine acting and (for 1930) great special effects highlight this Tiffany production.
VHS: S10963. $29.95.
Edward Sloman, USA, 1930, 73 mins.

Love Affair
This RKO classic stars Irene Dunne and Charles Boyer, and was later remade as *An Affair to Remember*. It received five Oscar nominations, and featured songs by Harold Arlen and Buddy De Sylva.
VHS: S04491. $29.95.
Leo McCarey, USA, 1939, 87 mins.

Love Crazy
William Powell and Myrna Loy, America's favorite screen couple, are at it again as an old flame appears on their anniversary and sets flames to the wedded bliss. A crazy love story also starring Jack Carson, Gail Patrick and Florence Bates as the classic, bothersome mother-in-law.
VHS: S15118. $19.98.
Jack Conway, USA, 1941, 99 mins.

Love Is a Many Splendored Thing
Set in Hong Kong during the Korean War, Jennifer Jones plays a Eurasian doctor who falls in love with war corespondent William Holden. With Murray Matheson, Torin Thatcher and Keye Luke.
VHS: S18100. $19.98.
Henry King, USA, 1955, 102 mins.

Love Letters
Jennifer Jones and Joseph Cotten star in this classic drama about a woman suffering from amnesia who starts to remember her identity when she falls in love. With Ann Richards, Cecil Kellaway, Gladys Cooper, Anita Louise and Reginald Denny.
VHS: S30797. $19.95.
William Dieterle, USA, 1945, 101 mins.

Love Nest
A writer returns from the Army and discovers that his wife has bought a broken-down brownstone apartment building. The couple finds their landlord responsibilities a consuming activity. Stars William Lundigan, June Haver, Frank Fay, Marilyn Monroe, Leatrice Joy, and future TV host Jack Paar.
VHS: S16400. $19.98.
Joseph M. Newman, USA, 1951, 84 mins.

Love on the Run
A romantic and cosmopolitan thriller about the intertwining fates and activities of a gilded heiress (Joan Crawford) in love with a carefree reporter (Clark Gable) who is pursued by spies. With Franchot Tone, William Demarest and Reginald Owen.
VHS: S18803. $19.98.
W.S. Van Dyke II, USA, 1936, 80 mins.

Love with a Proper Stranger
Natalie Wood is pregnant and Steve McQueen is responsible in this tough, urban love story set in New York City. Gritty locations enhance this study in neo-realism with laughs. It doesn't matter if you believe that McQueen is Italian; you will believe he could get Natalie pregnant. With Edie Adams, Herschel Bernardi, Vic Tayback and introducing Tom Bosley. B&W.
VHS: S08271. $19.95.
Laser: LD75224. $34.98.
Robert Mulligan, USA, 1963, 102 mins.

Lovers and Lollipops
This "miniature movie masterpiece" (*Cue*) centers around a seven-year-old girl's resentment toward the old friend who has been taking up too much of her mother's time. Engel's camera captures the utterly natural performances of the girl and the lovers as they linger with affection in such New York landmarks as Macy's toy department, Central Park and Chinatown.
VHS: S30705. $24.95.
Morris Engel, USA, 1955, 83 mins.

Lust for Life
Kirk Douglas is cast as the tormented genius Vincent Van Gogh in this Vincente Minnelli film in full color. Based on the best-selling biographical novel by Irving Stone. Douglas throws himself into the role, but Anthony Quinn walked away with the Oscar as his best friend Gauguin. A first-class production with James Donald, Pamela Brown and Everett Sloane.
VHS: S11218. $19.95.
Laser: LD70618. $39.98.
Vincente Minnelli, USA, 1956, 122 mins.

Lydia
Merle Oberon revisits her youthful loves in this sentimental adaptation of the French film *Carnet de Bal*. With Joseph Cotten and Edna May Oliver.
VHS: S23437. $19.98.
Julien Duvivier, USA, 1941, 104 mins.

Ma Barker's Killer Brood
The true adventures of America's most notorious mother begins in dust-bowl Oklahoma. Barker leads her sons astray and gives advice to such infamous names as Dillinger, Baby Face Nelson and Machine Gun Kelly. The law finally catches up with her at her plush Florida hideout in an action-packed shoot-out. Derived from the tele-series. With Lurene Tuttle, Tris Coffin, Paul Dubov, Nelson Leigh and Myrna Dell.
VHS: S16113. $29.95.
Bill Karn, USA, 1960, 82 mins.

Madame Bovary
Jennifer Jones stars as the Gustave Flaubert heroine who sacrifices her husband and security for love, with tragic consequences. Features the famous ball scene, which is one of the greatest set pieces ever filmed. With James Mason and Louis Jourdan.
VHS: S01847. $19.98.
Laser: LD71686. $34.98.
Vincente Minnelli, USA, 1949, 115 mins.

Madame Curie
The celebrated story of the discovery of radium reunites *Mrs. Miniver's* Greer Garson and Walter Pidgeon. An excellent screen biography in the lush Hollywood tradition.
VHS: S15653. $19.98.
Laser: LD72142. $34.98.
Mervyn LeRoy, USA, 1943, 124 mins.

Madame X (1937)
Gladys George is the woman who is forced by social customs and circumstances to abandon her son, in this adaptation of the novel by Alexandre Bisson. Years later, when Gladys stands trial for murder, she is defended by a son who is unaware of her actual identity. With John Beal, Warren William, Reginald Owen, William Henry and Henry Daniel.
VHS: S20411. $29.98.
Sam Wood, USA, 1937, 71 mins.

Madame X (1966)
Lana Turner stars in the sixth screen version of a fallen woman on trial for killing the blackmailer who would reveal her identity to the son who is unknowingly defending his mother. A time-proven soap opera with John Forsythe, Ricardo Montalban, Burgess Meredith, Keir Dullea and Constance Bennett in her final role.
VHS: S06182. $14.95.
David Lowell Rich, USA, 1966, 100 mins.

Made for Each Other
James Stewart and Carole Lombard star as an appealing married couple battling interfering in-laws, no money, and illness. With Charles Coburn and Louise Beavers.
VHS: S00795. $19.95.
John Cromwell, USA, 1939, 85 mins.

Mademoiselle Fifi
Simone Simon, the star of the original *Cat People*, is once again cast by producer Val Lewton. This time she plays Elizabeth Rousett, a valiant French laundress who stands up to the invading Prussian Army, circa 1870. Filmed in 1944 as an allegory of conditions in Nazi occupied France. With John Emery, Alan Napier, Helen Freeman, Jason Robards Sr. and Kurt Kreuger as the menacing Lt. Von Eyrick. Based on the stories by French novelist Guy de Maupassant.
Laser: CLV. LD71729. $19.98.
Robert Wise, USA, 1944, 69 mins.

Madigan
Richard Widmark plays Detective Madigan, who faces a plethora of problems and police commissioner Henry Fonda as well, in this feature film that later became the basis of a long-running TV series. Shot on location in New York and featuring Harry Guardino, Inger Stevens and James Whitmore.
VHS: S21917. $19.98.
Don Siegel, USA, 1968, 101 mins.

The Magic Sword
A rousing sword and sorcery adventure starring Basil Rathbone, Estelle Winwood and Gary Lockwood. Two-headed dragons, giant ogres and magic demons are all part of this epic tale based on the historic legend of Sir George and the Dragon. From the director of *Food of the Gods*.
VHS: S15267. $9.95.
Laser: LD76317. $39.99.
Bert I. Gordon, USA, 1962, 90 mins.

The Magnificent Yankee
John Sturges' biography of Supreme Court Justice Oliver Wendell Holmes (Louis Calhern) dramatizes his relationship with his devoted, independent wife (Ann Harding). With Eduard Franz, James Lydon and Philip Ober.
VHS: S19469. $19.98.
John Sturges, USA, 1950, 80 mins.

The Major and the Minor
Susan Applegate (Ginger Rogers) is broke and wants to get home, so she masquerades as a young schoolgirl on her train ride back. Hiding from the conductors she ends up in a cabin already occupied by Major Kirby (Ray Milland), a military academy instructor. The train stalls out, and the Major demands that she accompany him to the academy since she's without parental supervision. Now, she must remain in character as she finds herself falling for the Major, who is about to marry the wrong woman.
VHS: S34363. $14.98.
Billy Wilder, USA, 1948, 101 mins.

A Majority of One
Rosalind Russell plays a Jewish matron from Brooklyn who slowly but surely falls in love with a Japanese businessman and widower (Alec Guiness). It's a successful translation of the original Broadway play written by Leonard Spiegelgass.
VHS: S21324. $19.98.
Mervyn LeRoy, USA, 1962, 149 mins.

Make Haste to Live
Dorothy McGuire and Stephen McNally star. Crystal's new husband, Steve, is a handsome charmer, but what she doesn't know is that he's also a cold-blooded killer. She thinks her nightmare has ended when she runs away and starts a new life. But Steve is dead set on a touching reunion, and when he gets his hands on her, he'll love her to pieces.
VHS: S09669. $19.95.
William A. Seiter, USA, 1954, 90 mins.

Malaya
James Stewart and Spencer Tracy star in this World War II melodrama set in the Pacific. Smuggling rubber is a dangerous part of the Allied war effort, which requires the help of these two extraordinary characters.
VHS: S21018. $19.98.
Richard Thorpe, USA, 1949, 98 mins.

Mambo
A passion for dancing, a longing for fame, and a deep need for love—these are the powerful forces that flame within the heart of sultry Giovanna Masetti (Silvana Mangano), a beautiful young Venetian woman who resents her drab lot as a factory worker and fosters not-so-secret ambitions to be a great and famous dancer. Directed by Robert Rossen, and co-starring Michael Rennie and Shelley Winters.
VHS: S15174. $29.95.
Robert Rossen, USA/Italy, 1954, 94 mins.

A Man Called Peter
Richard Todd delivers a compelling performance as Peter Marshall, who emigrates to the U.S. from Scotland, becomes a pastor, and then the chaplain of the U.S. Senate. With Jean Peters, Marjorie Rambeau.
VHS: S11739. $19.98.
Henry Koster, USA, 1955, 119 mins.

The Man from Monterey
From the annals of early California history comes this tale of love and rivalry starring young John Wayne. This ornate production features elaborate Mexican-style costumes and Spanish-style colonial architecture.
VHS: S20951. $19.98.
Mack V. Wright, USA, 1933, 57 mins.

The Man I Love
Raoul Walsh's absorbing *noir* is set in a sinister Los Angeles nightclub populated by gangsters and hoods, where Ida Lupino is a beautiful seductress who gets caught up with a charismatic mobster (Robert Alda). With Andrea King, Martha Vickers, Bruce Bennett and Alan Hale.
VHS: S19570. $19.98.
Raoul Walsh, USA, 1946, 76 mins.

Man in the Attic
This remake of *The Lodger*, by Mary Belloc Lowndes, stars Jack Palance and Constance Smith. An actress rents out rooms, one of which is taken by a young medical student. At the very time when this man takes up residence, a series of gruesome murders begins. They were perpetrated by a madman who comes to be known as Jack the Ripper.
VHS: S27901. $19.98.
Hugo Fregonese, USA, 1954, 82 mins.

Man in the Gray Flannel Suit
Gregory Peck plays a Madison Avenue executive caught between his wife's nagging and the news from his wartime mistress back in Europe. Based on the popular novel by Sloan Wilson. The distinguished cast includes Fredric March, Jennifer Jones, Lee J. Cobb, Keenan Wynn and Marisa Pavan as Maria. Produced by Daryl F. Zanuck and written for the screen by Nunnally Johnson.
VHS: S12518. $19.98.
Laser: LD72220. $69.95.
Nunnally Johnson, USA, 1956, 152 mins.

Man of a Thousand Faces
James Cagney stars in this film biography of Lon Chaney, the "master of disguise" who overcame a traumatic childhood to use his skills in mime and impersonation to forge an astonishing film career. The film restages many of the actor's signature roles, including *The Hunchback of Notre Dame*, *The Miracle*, and *Phantom of the Opera*. With Roger Smith, Robert Evans, Jim Backus, and Marjorie Rambeau.
VHS: S17016. $14.98.
DVD: DV60331. $29.99.
Joseph Pevney, USA, 1957, 122 mins.

Man on the Eiffel Tower
The first directing effort of Burgess Meredith: a taut psychological thriller set in Paris centering on a battle of wits between a police investigator and a suspected murderer. With Charles Laughton, Burgess Meredith.
VHS: S03593. $19.95.
Burgess Meredith, USA, 1949, 97 mins.

The Man Who Cheated Himself
A film noir about a cynical detective (Lee J. Cobb) who falls for a beautiful femme fatale (Jane Wyatt). The woman kills her husband and convinces Cobb to shield her from the authorities and help cover up her crime. With John Dall and Terry Frost.
VHS: S19868. $29.95.
Felix E. Feist, USA, 1950, 81 mins.

Man with the Golden Arm
Otto Preminger's adaptation of Nelson Algren's psychological portrait of a drug addict trying to go straight stars Frank Sinatra (who received an Oscar nomination for his portrayal), Eleanor Parker, Kim Novak and Darren McGavin.
VHS: S04439. $19.98.
Otto Preminger, USA, 1955, 119 mins.

The Manchurian Candidate
A compelling thriller based on the Richard Condon novel about brainwashing American soldiers to serve as assassins in secret global domination. Starring Frank Sinatra, Janet Leigh, Angela Lansbury and Laurence Harvey as the walking time bomb. B&W.
VHS: S07005. $19.98.
Laser: This deluxe collector's edition is letterboxed, newly digitally remastered and features commentary by John Frankenheimer. **LD70624. $59.98.**
DVD: DV60152. $24.98.
John Frankenheimer, USA, 1962, 126 mins.

Mandarin Mystery
Last of the Republic Ellery Queen mysteries. Here Eddie Quillan, a star from his days of Pathe through the 1970's, portrays the great detective as he tries to recover the Chinese Mandarin stamp. 1936.
VHS: S08420. $29.95.

Manhattan Madness
When his friends stage mysterious events at a mansion outside New York, a Western clubman (Douglas Fairbanks) believes that Manhattan is a thrillride. With Jewel Carmen.
VHS: S32149. $24.95.
Allan Dwan, USA, 1916, 50 mins.

Manhattan Melodrama
A memorable tale of boyhood friends who end up on opposite sides of the law...and who both fall for the same mysterious woman. With Clark Gable, William Powell and Myrna Loy.
VHS: S15261. $19.98.
W.S. Van Dyke, USA, 1934, 91 mins.

Mannequin
Joan Crawford and Spencer Tracy star is this rags-to-riches soap opera in which a poor girl meets a rich man and does all right for herself. But first she has to dump the small-time chiseler she has already married and try her luck as a high fashion model.
VHS: S16453. $19.98.
Frank Borzage, USA, 1937, 95 mins.

Marie Antoinette
Norma Shearer is the Austrian princess who found being the queen of France had its down side as well. This lavish MGM production combines palace intrigues with political revolution. Robert Morley is a standout as King Louis XVI. Also in the cast: Tyrone Power, John Barrymore, Gladys George, Anita Louise and Joseph Schildkraut. Feel free to eat cake as you watch.
VHS: S11726. $19.98.
W.S. Van Dyke, USA, 1938, 149 mins.

Marie Galante
Spencer Tracy and Ketti Gallian in a story of international intrigue. Fine acting in a spy drama where the principals must stop the bombing of the Panama Canal.
VHS: S07758. $29.95.
Henry King, USA, 1934, 88 mins.

Marjorie Morningstar
Natalie Wood and Gene Kelly star in a drama about growing up Jewish and striving to find a place in the entertainment world. Wood gives perhaps the first glimpse of the modern Jewish American Princess. With Ed Wynn, Martin Milner and Carolyn Jones. From the novel by Herman Wouk.
VHS: S04897. $19.95.
Laser: LD71551. $49.98.
Irving Rapper, USA, 1958, 123 mins.

Mark of Zorro
Tyrone Power is fabulous as the son of a California aristocrat who masquerades as the swashbuckling hero who fights evil in this great Hollywood version. With Linda Darnell, Basil Rathbone and Gale Sondergaard. Famous for its incredible swashbuckling ending between Power and Rathbone. Music by Alfred Newman.
VHS: S01857. $19.98.
Rouben Mamoulian, USA, 1940, 93 mins.

Marked Woman
Bette Davis plays a hostess in a clip joint persuaded by special prosecutor Humphrey Bogart to spill the beans on her crooked employer. In the days before the witness relocation program, harsh rewards were often the price of conviction. With Mayo Methot, Lola Lane and Eduardo Ciannelli as Johnny Vanning. B&W.
VHS: S06351. $19.95.
Laser: LD74678. $34.98.
Lloyd Bacon, USA, 1937, 96 mins.

Marlowe
James Garner stars as Philip Marlowe in this slick update of Raymond Chandler's *The Little Sister*. Marlowe is hired by a nervous young girl to find her missing brother. With a sizzling performance by Rita Moreno as a stripper who helps Garner crack the case.
VHS: S13759. $19.98.
Paul Bogart, USA, 1969, 95 mins.

Maroc 7
Set in Morocco, structured around a robbery and murder tale, *Maroc 7* concerns a spy's operation to unmask the identity of thief with multiple personalities. With Gene Barry, Cyd Charisse, and Denholm Elliott.
VHS: S16896. $19.95.
Gerry O'Hara, USA, 1967, 92 mins.

Marty
Ernest Borgnine won a well-deserved Oscar for Best Actor as the shy Bronx butcher who finds love. Academy Awards also went for direction, screenplay and Best Picture. With Betsy Blair, Joe De Santis and Esther Minciotti. From the teleplay by Paddy Chayefsky.
Laser: Chapter Search. Includes original theatrical trailer. **LD71670. $34.98.**
Delbert Mann, USA, 1955, 91 mins.

Mask of Dimitrios
Sidney Greenstreet and Peter Lorre make a marvelous team in this exhilarating and atmospheric film noir the *Daily Variety* hailed as "one of the most brilliant crime dramas yet filmed." When the body of murderous sociopath Dimitrios Makropoulos (Zachary Scott) washes ashore in Istanbul, mystery writer Cornelius Leyden (Lorre), interested in chronicling his unscrupulous exploits, takes up the master criminal's trail, aided by a mysterious man named Peters (Greenstreet), who turns out to be as dangerous as Dimitrios himself. Based on the novel by Eric Ambler. "An exceptional picture—a highly intellectualized mystery thriller comparing with *The Maltese Falcon*" (*L.A. Times*).
VHS: S30547. $19.98.
Jean Negulesco, USA, 1944, 95 mins.

The Master of Ballantrae
Two brothers toss to decide who will join the 1745 rebellion to make Bonnie Prince Charles king of England. "Declare your allegiance—or answer to his blade!" Supreme swashbuckler Errol Flynn stars in this adaptation of the Robert Louis Stevenson novel, filmed on location in Scotland, England's Cornwall and Sicily. With Anthony Steel, Roger Livesey, Beatrice Campbell and Felix Aylmer.
VHS: S16732. $19.98.
Laser: LD71512. $34.98.
William Keighley, USA, 1953, 89 mins.

Mata Hari
Greta Garbo adds her glamour to the tale of the exotic World War I spy. She dances, she flirts, she gives comfort to wounded soldiers. With Ramon Navarro, Lionel Barrymore, Lewis Stone and Karen Morley.
VHS: S13197. $19.98.
George Fitzmaurice, USA, 1932, 90 mins.

The McConnell Story
Alan Ladd roars into combat in the exciting, true story of Captain Joseph McConnell Jr., America's first triple jet ace. Also starring "America's sweetheart," June Allyson, as the fiery test pilot's understanding wife. Newly restored in true surround stereo.
VHS: S13621. $19.98.
Gordon Douglas, USA, 1955, 107 mins.

Medium Cool
Playing on Marshall McLuhan's phrase, "the cool medium," director Wexler uses a TV cameraman as the eyes through which the 1968 Chicago Democratic convention riots are viewed. An idyllic romance is framed by the realities of death, political hypocrisy, race hatred and revolution.
VHS: S00843. $14.95.
Laser: Widescreen. **LD75228. $34.98.**
Haskell Wexler, USA, 1969, 110 mins.

Meeting at Midnight (aka Black Magic)
Charlie Chan is forced to solve a murder committed during a seance to clear his daughter, whom the police suspect to be the murderer! Starring Sidney Toler and Manton Moreland.
VHS: S13851. $19.95.
Phil Rosen, USA, 1944, 67 mins.

Melody for Three
Fay Wray is a music teacher and mother of a violin prodigy, who is divorced from orchestra conductor Schuyler Standish.
VHS: S05700. $29.95.
Erle C. Kenton, USA, 1941, 67 mins.

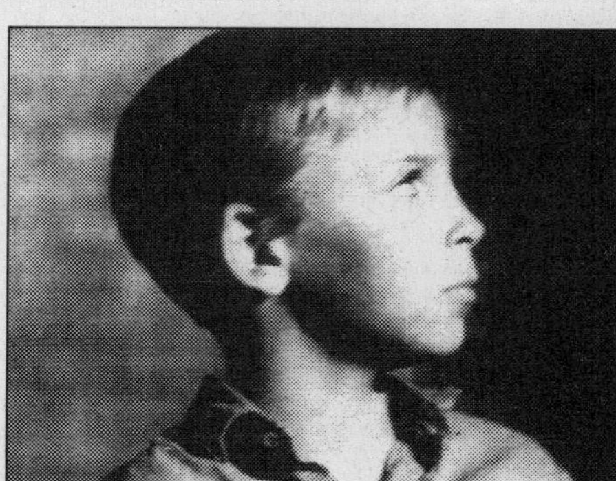

Member of the Wedding
Julie Harris gives an exceptional performance as a motherless, 12-year-old girl who is tormented by the awkwardness of adolescence and her struggle toward womanhood. With Ethel Waters and Brandon De Wilde.
VHS: S07001. $19.99.
Fred Zinnemann, USA, 1953, 91 mins.

Men
Marlon Brando gives a powerful screen debut performance as a World War II vet confined to a wheelchair who is embittered by his condition. With Teresa Wright and Jack Webb, produced by Stanley Kramer.
VHS: S01759. $19.95.
Laser: CLV. **LD72008. $34.98.**
Fred Zinnemann, USA, 1950, 85 mins.

Men of Boys Town
"There's no such thing as a bad boy," was the motto of Father Edward J. Flanagan, though his axiom was sometimes sorely tested. Spencer Tracy reprises his role as the benevolent priest who devoted his life to caring for abused and abandoned youths.
VHS: S14563. $19.98.
Norman Taurog, USA, 1941, 106 mins.

Men of the Fighting Lady
Jet pilot Van Johnson sling-shots from the deck of an aircraft carrier stationed off Korea in the Sea of Japan. Based on a thrilling true-life story.
VHS: S15126. $19.98.
Laser: LD76324. $39.99.
Andrew Marton, USA, 1954, 82 mins.

Mercy Plane
James Dunn, Frances Gifford, Matt Fain, William Pawley and Harry Harvey star in this action adventure film about a new rescue airplane. When it is stolen, all indications point to the aircraft's pilot, but he is saved by a young woman unknowingly connected to the thieves.
VHS: S24012. $24.95.
Richard Harlan, USA, 1940, 73 mins.

Midnight
Claudette Colbert, Don Ameche and John Barrymore star in this delightful comedy written by Billy Wilder and Charles Brackett. Colbert is a gold-digger unsatisfied with her cabbie boyfriend (Ameche). To her delight a French aristocrat asks her to pose as a Hungarian Countess in order to distract his wife's latest love interest.
VHS: S24029. $14.98.
Mitchell Leisen, USA, 1939, 94 mins.

Midnight Cowboy (25th Anniversary)
The shocking story of Cowboy Joe Buck, played by Jon Voight, made history when it was released 25 years ago. This naive country boy with a horrible secret moves to New York, where the streetwise Ratso Rizzo (Dustin Hoffman) becomes his guide to seamy city life. Together they explore the world of hustling and even visit Warhol's factory, developing a deep friendship in the process. This film won Oscars for Best Picture, Screenplay and Director. Also features Brenda Vaccaro. A 25th Anniversary re-release.
VHS: S21826. $19.98.
Laser: LD74499. $49.98.
DVD: DV60090. $24.98.
John Schlesinger, USA, 1969, 113 mins.

Midnight Lace
Doris Day is being driven mad and her rich industrialist husband, Rex Harrison, doesn't believe her. Suspects threatening Doris' well-being include Roddy McDowall, John Gavin and Herbert Marshall.
VHS: S03550. $19.95.
David Miller, USA, 1960, 108 mins.

Mighty Joe Young
A tongue-in-cheek sequel to *King Kong*, featuring special effects by Ray Harryhausen. Joe Young is a 10-foot-tall simian discovered in the African jungle and brought back to Hollywood, where Joe, drunk, goes on a rampage. Very funny.
VHS: Out of print. For rental only.
Laser: LD76978. $29.99.
Ernest B. Schoedsack, USA, 1949, 94 mins

Mildred Pierce
Michael Curtiz, who directed *Casablanca* and *Yankee Doodle Dandy*, elevates this Joan Crawford vehicle into a perverse and personal exploration of psychological disorder and collapse. Based on the novel by James M. Cain, Crawford won an Oscar as the hard-working mother with the world's most unpleasant, snobby, status-seeking and boyfriend-stealing daughter (Ann Blyth).
VHS: S02340. $19.98.
Laser: LD70630. $34.98.
Michael Curtiz, USA, 1945, 109 mins.

Millie
An adaptation of Donald Henderson's novel of sexual revenge and tragedy about a rejected man who pursues his disinterested lover's daughter, setting in motion a series of grave mishaps. With Helen Twelvetrees, Robert Ames, Lilyan Tashman and Joan Blondell.
VHS: S18941. $19.95.
John Francis Dillon, USA, 1931, 85 mins.

Min & Bill
Marie Dressler, Wallace Beery, Marjorie Rambeau and Dorothy Jordan star in this early talkie about two people living in a houseboat who struggle to keep their daughter from being taken from them.
VHS: S30920. $19.98.
George Roy Hill, USA, 1930, 66 mins.

The Miniver Story
This sequel to William Wyler's award-winning *Mrs. Miniver* confronts the emotional and psychological effects of World War II, as Greer Garson and Walter Pidgeon try to cope with the social and political fraying of their peculiar family dynamics. Toby dreams about America and Judy falls for a married officer as Mrs. Miniver tries to suppress a long suppressed secret. With John Hodiak, Leo Glenn and Cathy O'Donnell.
VHS: S18801. $19.98.
H.C. Potter, USA, 1950, 104 mins.

Miracle of Our Lady of Fatima
Gilbert Roland and Angela Clarke star in this account of the religious miracle witnessed by farm children in the 1910's, in an event that inspired the small community and the world.
VHS: S06535. $19.98.
Laser: LD74732. $34.98.
John Brahm, USA, 1952, 102 mins.

The Miracle of the Bells
Frank Sinatra and Fred MacMurray star as a priest and a press agent who move heaven and earth to get a movie released after the death of its star (Alida Valli). Lee J. Cobb is the stubborn studio exec who needs a miracle to convince him the picture will be accepted by the public. B&W.
VHS: S05217. $19.95.
Irving Pichel, USA, 1948, 120 mins.

Miracle on 34th Street
The transcendent fable about a young girl (Natalie Wood) who doesn't believe in the spirit of Santa Claus, and the kindly department store clerk (Edmund Gwenn) who goes on trial to prove his identity and validity. With Maureen O'Hara, John Payne, Gene Lockhart and Thelma Ritter. "A delightful comedy-fantasy" (Leonard Maltin).
VHS: S00859. $19.98.
George Seaton, USA, 1947, 96 mins.

Miss Sadie Thompson
Rita Hayworth is the bawdy nightclub entertainer stranded on a tropical island during World War II and loving every minute of it, until she encounters Reverend Davidson (Jose Ferrer).
VHS: S04536. $19.95.
Curtis Bernhardt, USA, 1952, 91 mins.

Mission in Morocco
Bruce Reynolds (Lex Barker), an oil firm executive, learns that an employee who discovered oil in the Sahara has been murdered. He sets off for Morocco with his fiancee (Juli Reding), determined to find the stolen microfilm that reveals the location of the precious oil. Their search puts them head to head with a ruthless gang of Middle Eastern thugs, equally determined to find the microfilm.
VHS: S12447. $19.98.
Anthony Squire, USA, 1959, 79 mins.

Molly Maguires
Sean Connery stars as a leader of the Molly Maguires, a secret society of Irish mine-workers in Pennsylvania in the 1870's who battle their exploitation by mine owners with violence. With Richard Harris and Samantha Eggar.
VHS: S02024. $29.95.
Martin Ritt, USA, 1969, 123 mins.

Moment to Moment
In this unusual love story by Mervyn LeRoy, the adulterous affair between a neglected young wife and a handsome naval officer takes a perilous turn when she accidently shoots him during a quarrel. With Jean Seberg, Arthur Hill and Sean Garrison.
VHS: S33717. $19.95.
Mervyn LeRoy, USA, 1966, 108 mins.

Monsoon
John Carradine stars as a deep sea diver hired to recover three million dollars in sunken treasure with his buddy, Frank Fenton. Problems arise when Sidney Toler, the ship's captain, wants a bigger cut and fewer partners. With Gale Sondergaard. Also known as *Isle of Forgotten Sins*.
VHS: S13318. $19.95.
Edgar G. Ulmer, USA, 1943, 77 mins.

The Moon and Sixpence
An adaptation of W. Somerset Maugham's fictional biography of post-impressionist painter Paul Gauguin shows him as he moves to Tahiti. Largely in black and white, with the paintings in color. With George Sanders, Herbert Marshall, Doris Dudley and Eric Blore.
VHS: S18029. $29.95.
Albert Lewin, USA, 1943, 89 mins.

Moonrise
Frank Borzage at his best; primal passions erupt in a small southern town when a handsome young man is branded the son of a killer and tormented by unforgiving townspeople who hung his father. Mercilessly goaded into committing murder himself, the wanted fugitive must confront the consequences of his actions or be condemned to relive his father's brutal fate. With Ethel Barrymore, Lloyd Bridges.
VHS: S09494. $19.95.
Laser: LD71812. $29.98.
Frank Borzage, USA, 1948, 90 mins.

Morituri
German filmmaker Bernhard Wicki (*The Bridge*) directed this story of a German employed by the British to undertake a dangerous mission aboard a Nazi ship. Marlon Brando and Yul Brynner star.
VHS: S05914. $19.98.
Bernhard Wicki, USA, 1965, 123 mins.

The Mortal Storm
Phyllis Bottom's moving novel, set in Nazi Germany, details the trauma faced by a family split over Hitler's rise. James Stewart is a student who falls in love with his professor's daughter, Margaret Sullavan. As the young couple faces the growing threat of Nazism, they decide to leave. Also includes Robert Young and Robert Stack.
VHS: S21171. $19.98.
Frank Borzage, USA, 1940, 100 mins.

The Most Dangerous Game
On a jungle island Zaroff, a mad nobleman, tires of hunting big game and stalks men instead. When Bob, Eve and Martin are shipwrecked there, he pursues them relentlessly. Hunter and prey match wits in this classic. Joel McCrea, Fay Wray, Leslie Banks star.
VHS: S00885. $19.95.
Laser: Collector's Edition. **LD75944. $49.95.**
Ernest B. Schoedsack/Irving Pichel, USA, 1932, 62 mins.

The Mountain
When a plane goes down in the Alps veteran mountain guide Spencer Tracy wants to see if there are any survivors. His younger brother Robert Wagner just wants to loot the remains of the passengers for valuables. With E.G. Marshall, Claire Trevor, and William Demarest. 105 mins.
VHS: S08171. $19.95.
Edward Dmytryk, USA, 1956, 105 mins.

Mr. Imperium
A beautiful singer/dancer-turned-actress and playboy crown prince-turned-monarch have their clandestine affair interfered with by their changing circumstances. With Lana Turner, Debbie Reynolds, Ezio Pinza, Barry Sullivan, Cedric Hardwicke and Keenan Wynn.
VHS: S33735. $9.95.
Don Hartman, USA, 1951, 87 mins.

Mr. Moto's Last Warning
Peter Lorre, as that super sleuth of Japanese ancestry, is called to Port Said near the Suez Canal. It seems that George Sanders and Richardo Cortez want to mine shipping lanes for nefarious purposes. Mr. Moto does not allow the plan to succeed. With John Carradine as the unfortunate British agent.
VHS: S18177. $19.95.
Norman Foster, USA, 1939, 71 mins.

Mr. Robinson Crusoe
Lively adventure story finds Douglas Fairbanks betting he can live on a deserted island for a year without any of the luxuries of the civilized world. Filmed in Tahiti.
VHS: S03786. $19.95.
A. Edward Sutherland, USA, 1932, 80 mins.

Mr. Skeffington
Bette Davis marries the title character to prevent him from having her brother prosecuted for embezzling. Claude Rains doesn't hold her to the marriage when the brother dies, and leaves for Europe. Years pass and Bette loses her hair to diphtheria while Mr. Skeffington has Nazi trouble. Lots of heartache in this soap opera.
VHS: S06352. $19.95.
Laser: LD70632. $39.98.
Vincent Sherman, USA, 1944, 145 mins.

Mr. Skitch
Will Rogers portrays a man fallen on hard times who must pack up his family and head for California. Good family entertainment which depicts life on the road during the Depression.
VHS: S13495. $19.98.
James Cruze, USA, 1933, 70 mins.

Mr. Wong in Chinatown
Boris Karloff's third entry in this detective series. A Chinese princess is murdered by a poisoned arrow and the only witness is a mute dwarf (an orientalized Angelo Rossitto) who disappears. Wong is assisted by Police Captain and his reporter-girlfriend.
VHS: S04018. $19.95.
William Nigh, USA, 1939, 70 mins.

Mr. Wong, Detective
Boris Karloff stars as the title character, a famous Oriental detective based in San Francisco. Chemical manufacturers are being killed by poison gas and James Lee Wong is on the case. This series was to challenge Charlie Chan films yet this story was later remade as *Docks of New Orleans*, a Charlie Chan 1948 release.
VHS: S04017. $19.95.
William Nigh, USA, 1938, 69 mins.

Mrs. Parkington
This lavish historical spectacle covers six decades of the personal fortune and dramatic self-destruction of an American dynasty. An ambitious woman (Greer Garson) marries a powerful though simple man (Walter Pidgeon) and immediately insinuates herself into his family. With Edward Arnold, Gladys Cooper and Agnes Moorehead.
VHS: S18807. $19.98.
Tay Garnett, USA, 1944, 124 mins.

Murder My Sweet
Dick Powell stars as Raymond Chandler's hard-boiled detective, Phillip Marlowe. A complex web of murder, blackmail and double-dealing make it one of the most exciting detective thrillers of the 40s. Also starring Claire Trevor.
VHS: S00898. $19.98.
Edward Dmytryk, USA, 1944, 95 mins.

Murders in the Zoo
Zoo animals become unlikely weapons in this chilling tale of love, betrayal and revenge. A zoologist resolves to end the outside romantic interests he suspects his wife pursues. His unique method of attack offers many useful advantages, particularly since he can rely on the instinct of wild creatures.
VHS: S29525. $14.98.
A. Edward Sutherland, USA, 1933, 62 mins.

Music in My Heart
The lovely Rita Hayworth cold-shoulders a millionaire in favor of a lowly nightclub singer. A light, fairy-tale romance. Tony Martin co-stars.
VHS: S15528. $19.95.
Joseph Santley, USA, 1940, 69 mins.

Mutiny on the Bounty (Brando)
Marlon Brando makes a foppish Fletcher Christian in this lavish MGM remake of the classic Nordhoff-Hall tale of rebellion in the South Seas. Trevor Howard is the hard-driving Captain Bligh. Other crew members include Richard Harris, Gordon Jackson, Hugh Griffith, Percy Herbert and Tarita as the daughter of the native chief. Filmed on location in Tahiti. VHS letterboxed.
VHS: S06153. $24.98.
Laser: LD70633. $49.98.
Lewis Milestone, USA, 1962, 177 mins.

Mutiny on the Bounty (Laughton)
The classic version, starring Charles Laughton in an unforgettable role as Captain Bligh and Clark Gable as Christian. The picture deservedly won the Oscar for the Best Movie of the Year.
VHS: S02714. $19.95.
Laser: LD70634. $39.98.
Frank Lloyd, USA, 1935, 133 mins.

My Foolish Heart
Dana Andrews is a soldier in love with Susan Hayward in this well-handled, sentimental WWII love story. Based on J.D. Salinger's story *Uncle Wiggly in Connecticut*. Theme by Victor Young.
VHS: S32353. $14.98.
Mark Robson, USA, 1949, 98 mins.

My Forbidden Past
In 1890s New Orleans, a woman with a tainted past falls in love with a Yankee doctor. Using her wealth in a cold-blooded scheme to win his affections from his wife, the plot explodes in fateful irony.
VHS: S02873. $19.98.
Robert Stevenson, USA, 1951, 72 mins.

My Girl Tisa
An immigrant girl (Lilli Palmer) is determined to save enough money to bring her father to America. When she falls for an aspiring lawyer (Sam Wanamaker), he begs her to let him use her savings for his education. Torn between her father and the man she loves, a series of comic misadventures leaves her on the verge of being deported.
VHS: S12445. $19.98.
Elliott Nugent, USA, 1948, 95 mins.

My Lucky Star
Sonja Henie plays a department store clerk who enrolls in a local college as a publicity stunt. She is promptly pursued by a group of love-obsessed suitors. The film's glorious climax is a stylized ice ballet from *Alice in Wonderland*. With Richard Greene, Buddy Ebsen, Arthur Treacher and Joan Davis.
VHS: S20262. $19.98.
Roy Del Ruth, USA, 1938, 84 mins.

Mysterious Lady
The magnificent Greta Garbo portrays a Russian spy as only she can. Set during World War I, Garbo vamps a handsome Austrian soldier while scheming to keep her occupation top secret. Directed with panache by Fred Niblo (*Ben Hur: A Tale of the Christ*). Silent film with synchronized musical score.
VHS: S13978. $29.99.
Fred Niblo, USA, 1928, 99 mins.

Mysterious Mr. Wong
Bela Lugosi plays the title character who will stop at nothing to obtain the twelve coins of Confucius. Set in New York's Chinatown, Wong is the first madman mandarin to sport a marked slavic accent—but he does have a way with instruments of torture.
VHS: S04000. $29.95.
William Nigh, USA, 1935, 60 mins.

The Mystery of Edwin Drood
Claude Rains and Heather Angel star in this early screen adaptation of the classic suspense story by Charles Dickens. An opium-addicted choirmaster stands accused of murdering his nephew, Edwin Drood. It seems to be a clear explanation for this crime, but many figures appear who also have a reason for wanting Drood dead.
VHS: S29519. $14.98.
Stuart Walker, USA, 1935, 86 mins.

Mystery of Marie Roget
Detective thriller based on a short story by Edgar Allan Poe, a medical examiner investigates the disappearance of a famous actress. With Maria Montez.
VHS: S03785. $34.95.
Phil Rosen, USA, 1942, 60 mins.

The Mystery of Mr. Wong
The largest star sapphire in the world is stolen during a game of charades when the host of a fancy party is shot dead. Boris Karloff, as the effective detective Mr. Wong, just happens to be one of the guests. After several more murders he solves the case.
VHS: S04019. $19.95.
William Nigh, USA, 1939, 68 mins.

The Naked City
Blacklisted filmmaker Jules Dassin directed this key film noir and achieved realistic settings by using actual New York locations. The plot concerns the police department's unrelenting search for the killer of a young girl. Famous for its astonishing denouement on the Williamsburg bridge. With Barry Fitzgerald, Howard Duff and Dorothy Hart.
VHS: S18239. $29.95.
Laser: Collector's Edition. **LD75943. $49.95.**
Jules Dassin, USA, 1948, 96 mins.

The Naked Edge
A taut suspense thriller about a woman (Deborah Kerr) who investigates the possibility that her husband (Gary Cooper) is a killer. With Eric Portman, Diane Cilento and Hermione Gingold.
VHS: S17985. $19.98.
Michael Anderson, USA, 1961, 97 mins.

The Naked Jungle
Charlton Heston is a proud and prosperous plantation owner in South America who thinks the time is right for a mail order bride. When Eleanor Parker arrives, he's not satisfied and prepares to ship her back up the Amazon until an army of soldier ants delays his decision. Great special effects by George Pal.
VHS: S06030. $19.95.
Laser: LD75234. $34.98.
Byron Haskin, USA, 1953, 94 mins.

The Naked Maja
A retelling of the torrid love affair between painter Francisco Goya (Anthony Franciosa) and the Duchess of Alba (Ava Gardner), who sponsored his work. With Amedeo Nzaarai, Gino Cervi and Lea Padovani.
VHS: S19569. $19.98.
Henry Koster, USA, 1959, 112 mins.

The Naked Runner
Frank Sinatra is Sam Laker, an American industrialist traveling in Europe with his 10-year-old son, who meets a British Intelligenceofficer who served with Sam in WWII and tries to coerce him into carrying out the assassination of a defected British agent.
VHS: S34690. $14.95.
Sidney J. Furie, Great Britain, 1967, 101 mins.

Nancy Drew Reporter
Bonita Granville stars as America's favorite teenage sleuth. When Nancy wins a newspaper contest, she gets a shot at the crime beat and discovers an innocent woman has been charged with murder. With John Litel as Carson Drew and Frank Thomas as Ned Nickerson, Jr. Based on the characters created by Carolyn Keene.
VHS: S15797. $19.95.
William Clemens/John Langan, USA, 1939, 65 mins.

Navy Blue and Gold
A colorful tale set at the U.S. Naval Academy. Three friends with distinct personalities (the wealthy innocent, the cynical outsider, and the mysterious figure with a complicated past) enter Annapolis and learn about tradition, discipline and honor. With Robert Young, James Stewart, Florence Rice, Billie Burke, Lionel Barrymore and Tom Brown.
VHS: S20415. $29.98.
Sam Wood, USA, 1937, 93 mins.

Never Let Me Go
Clark Gable is featured as a foreign correspondent whose passion leads him to kidnap his Russian bride (Gene Tierney) after she is denied an exit visa to the U.S.
VHS: S20562. $19.98.
Delmer Daves, USA, 1953, 94 mins.

Never Love a Stranger
John Drew Barrymore, the son of John, the father of Drew, stars in this Harold Robbins adaptation of a young hoodlum on the rise. Also in the cast is Steve McQueen, with fourth billing in his second feature film. McQueen had a bit part in *Somebody Up There Likes Me*. Apparently so, for he never had fourth billing again. B&W.
VHS: S04231. $19.95.
Robert Stevens, USA, 1958, 93 mins.

Never on Sunday
Melina Mercouri stars as Illia, the most popular whore on the Greek port city of Piraeus. Director Dassin (her real life husband) stars as Homer, an American self-styled philosopher who tries to raise her above streetwalking. Hilarious, carefree, with great Greek music throughout.
VHS: S01723. $19.98.
Laser: Letterboxed. **LD76045. $39.98.**
Jules Dassin, USA/Greece, 1960, 91 mins.

Next Voice You Hear
God works in mysterious ways. God speaks to mankind on the radio, and the life of Joe Smith American is changed in this Dore Schary MGM tenure film which stars James Whitmore and Nancy Davis in a story of frustrations and answered prayer.
VHS: S13064. $19.98.
William Wellman, USA, 1950, 83 mins.

Niagara
Marilyn Monroe in full Technicolor does her best to upstage one of the Natural Wonders of the World. All that rushing water just can't compete with a tight dress. The plot to drive Joseph Cotten crazy, however, could use a little work. With Jean Peters.
VHS: S04200. $19.98.
Henry Hathaway, USA, 1953, 89 mins.

Night After Night
A glossy melodrama about a worn-down fighter (George Raft) who buys a bar and tries to seduce a gilded society woman (Constance Cummings) but is upstaged by the flamboyant theatrics of Mae West, in her screen debut. Contains the memorable line, "Goodness had nothing to do with it." With Wynne Gibson and Alison Skipworth.
VHS: S18865. $14.98.
Archie Mayo, USA, 1932, 70 mins.

Night Must Fall
Robert Montgomery stars as a psychopathic page boy who seduces women with his boyish but deadly charm in this gripping study of homicide. Notable in its time for using a murder story not as a mystery but as a psychological study, this was one of the most daring thrillers to come out of Hollywood in the '30s. Co-stars Rosalind Russell and Dame May Whitty.
VHS: S28471. $19.98.
Richard Thorpe, USA, 1937, 105 min.

Night Nurse
Barbara Stanwyck, Joan Blondell and Clark Gable are delightfully entertaining in this Pre-Code film full of racy dialog, decadent settings and daring performances. Stanwyck is a private nurse who discovers quite unethical behavior going on at the residence where she and Blondell are employed. And Gable's intent on making sure she keeps her trap shut.
VHS: S15014. $19.98.
William Wellman, USA, 1931, 73 mins.

The Night of the Following Day
In this chilling adaptation of Lionel White's *The Snatches*, Marlon Brando, together with three associates, orchestrates a daring plan to kidnap a young girl (Pamela Franklin). The plan slowly unravels as each criminal goes slightly mad. "A keenly conducted seminar in the poetics of psychological terror, the film is one of the tensest, toughest thrillers in a long time" (*Time Magazine*). With Richard Boone, Rita Moreno and Jess Hahn.
VHS: S19575. $89.98.
Stuart Cornfield, USA, 1969, 93 mins.

The Night of the Hunter
Robert Mitchum gives one of his best performances as Harry Powell, a psychotic self-styled preacher who is after the stolen money of a hanged man. Set in a small West Virginia community during the Depression, this is Charles Laughton's only screen credit as a director. He makes the most of the opportunity.
VHS: S04213. $19.98.
Laser: LD70426. $39.95.
Charles Laughton, USA, 1955, 93 mins.

The Night They Raided Minsky's
Britt Ekland stars as a beautiful young Amish woman who leaves her strict family home and comes to New York to become a dancer. While she originally intends to interpret biblical scenes through dance, a series of mishaps lead her to invent another kind of dance—the striptease.
VHS: S15252. $19.98.
William Friedkin, USA, 1968, 99 mins.

No Highway in the Sky
James Stewart is an engineer fighting against imminent disaster in the air. Only fellow passenger Marlene Dietrich and a flight attendant played by Glynis Johns believe him. Together they must make sure the plane does not take off again. This thriller is based on the gripping novel by Nevil Shute.
VHS: S25909. $19.98.
Henry Koster, USA, 1951, 98 mins.

No Man Is an Island
A U.S. Navy radio operator, stationed in Guam during WWII, must make a daring escape into the jungle when the island is invaded by the Japanese. Based on a true story. With Jeffrey Hunter and Marshall Thompson.
VHS: S33718. $19.95.
Richard Goldstone/John Monks Jr., USA, 1962, 114 mins.

No Way Out
Sidney Poitier made his awesome screen debut in this controversial, Oscar-nominated action thriller about a young black doctor hounded by a psychotic gangster. With Richard Widmark, Ruby Dee and Ossie Davis.
VHS: S33037. $14.98.
Joseph L. Mankiewicz, USA, 1950, 106 mins.

The North Star
Ruth Gordon, Walter Huston and Anne Baxter star in this story about Russian peasants resisting Nazi invaders, based upon a Lillian Hellman script.
VHS: S02184. $24.95.
Lewis Milestone, USA, 1943, 105 mins.

North to Alaska
A couple of prospectors are the focus of this brawling adventure story set in the Klondike in the early 1900's. John Wayne, Stewart Granger, Ernie Kovacs, Capucine, Fabian star.
VHS: S05910. $19.98.
Henry Hathaway, USA, 1960, 117 mins.

Northern Pursuit
Set in the awesome snowbound wasteland of Canada, Errol Flynn is the mountie who is ordered to break up a ring of Nazi saboteurs.
VHS: S01875. $19.98.
Raoul Walsh, USA, 1943, 94 mins.

Northwest Outpost
The last film of Nelson Eddy. He plays a cavalry captain entranced by a married Russian aristocrat living in California. But that's okay, because the beautiful Ilona Massey was forced into marrying Count Igor and would welcome a change in men. With Joseph Schildkraut, Hugo Haas and Elsa Lanchester.
VHS: S12901. $19.98.
Allan Dwan, USA, 1947, 91 mins.

Not As a Stranger
Stanley Kramer's flamboyant melodrama about the strains of professional marriage between a doctor (Robert Mitchum) and the nurse (Olivia de Havilland) who supported him through medical school and his troubled past. With Frank Sinatra, Gloria Grahame, Lon Chaney and Harry Morgan.
VHS: S17996. $19.98.
Stanley Kramer, USA, 1955, 136 mins.

Not Wanted
Ida Lupino produced this story of an unwed mother who is turned out by her family. With Sally Forrest, Keefe Brasselle, Leo Penn, Dorothy Adams and Wheaton Chambers.
VHS: S32045. $24.95.
Elmer Clifton, USA, 1949, 94 mins.

Now Voyager
Bette Davis blossoms under the psychiatric care of Claude Rains, only to fall in love with a married man on a South American cruise. Paul Henreid is the romantic stranger who also has a daughter who could benefit from the care of Claude Rains. A first-rate tear-jerker.
VHS: S02900. $19.95.
Irving Rapper, USA, 1942, 117 mins.

Nun's Story
Adaptation of the book by Kathryn Hulme, with Audrey Hepburn cast as the nun who serves in the Belgian Congo and later decides to leave the convent. With Coleen Dewhurst as the maniacal patient, and a cast including Peter Finch, Edith Evans and Peggy Ashcroft.
VHS: Out of print. For rental only.
Laser: LD74735. $39.98.
Fred Zinnemann, USA, 1959, 149 mins.

O.S.S.
Actual secret files of the Office of Strategic Services were used to create the screenplay for this exciting war drama that features Alan Ladd and Geraldine Fitzgerald.
VHS: S31347. $14.98.
Irving Pichel, USA, 1946, 108 mins.

Objective, Burma!
A taut, thrilling blockbuster of a war melodrama about a group of tough, tight-lipped paratroopers who are dropped into the Burmese jungle to wipe out a Japanese radar station. Starring Errol Flynn.
VHS: S15129. $19.98.
Raoul Walsh, USA, 1945, 142 mins.

Ocean's 11
Frank Sinatra, Dean Martin, Sammy Davis, Jr., Peter Lawford and Angie Dickinson star in this criminal suspense yarn. A gang decides to cash in on five casinos all at once. The only way to do it is with a complicated and elegant scheme for robbery.
VHS: S26864. $14.95.
Lewis Milestone, USA, 1960, 148 mins.

Odds Against Tomorrow
Harry Belafonte, Robert Ryan, Shelley Winters, Ed Begley and Gloria Grahame make up the terrific cast in this taut crime story. An interracial pair of criminals find their robbery attempt foiled, which leads to unexpected consequences. Along the way there is plenty of action and tension. John Lewis wrote the cool jazz score.
VHS: S29472. $19.98.
Laser: LD75970. $39.99.
Robert Wise, USA, 1959, 95 mins.

Of Human Bondage
Based on the novel by W. Somerset Maugham, this is a poignant story of self-destructive love, starring Leslie Howard as a young clubfooted medical student, and Bette Davis as the low-class waitress with whom he falls disastrously in love.
VHS: S18176. $19.95.
John Cromwell, USA, 1934, 83 mins.

Of Human Hearts
Clarence Brown's film dramatizes the estrangement between a fervent, small-town preacher and his son. "A curious all-American fable [that is] splendidly made and acted" (Leslie Halliwell). With Walter Huston, James Stewart, Beulah Bondi, Gene Reynolds, Charles Coburn and Guy Kibbee.
VHS: S20413. $29.98.
Clarence Brown, USA, 1938, 100 mins.

Oklahoma Annie
Judy Canova (Queen of the Cowgirls), granddaughter of the first female sheriff, helps capture bank robbers and clean up a corrupt town. With John Russell, Grant Withers, Roy Barcroft, Emmett "Pappy" Lynn, Frank Ferguson, Minerva Urecal, Houseley Stevenson, Almira Session, Allen Jenkins, Maxine Gates, Denver Pyle, House Peters, Jr., Andrew Toms, Fuzzy Knight and Si Jenks.
VHS: S37091. $19.95.
R.G. Springsteen, USA, 1952, 90 mins.

The Old Maid
Bette Davis is in quite a fix when her intended is killed in the Civil War and leaves her expecting their child. When the war is over she opens a nursery school in Philadelphia for orphans and has her daughter adopted by a scheming cousin to insure a proper future. A real tear-jerker. With Miriam Hopkins, George Brent, and Donald Crisp. B&W.
VHS: S06316. $19.95.
Edmund Goulding, USA, 1939, 95 mins.

Old Man and the Sea
Spencer Tracy stars as the fisherman in this screen adaptation of Ernest Hemingway's brief novel of the same name. At the center of the story is a struggle between this old Mexican fisherman and a giant marlin. Their exchange sets the stage for ruminations on the heroics of even the most mundane of activities.
VHS: S27632. $19.98.
Laser: LD75824. $34.98.
John Sturges, USA, 1958, 86 mins.

The Old Swimmin' Hole
The joys of small town life are disrupted for young Chris when a lawyer, acting for his evil millionaire grandfather, wants to take him away to be brought up properly in the city. With Jackie Moran, Marcia Mae Jones and Theodore Von Eltz. Gosh, what's a kid to do?
VHS: S05477. $29.95.
Robert McGowan, USA, 1940, 78 mins.

Oliver Twist
Charles Dickens' great story of the workhouse orphan forced into the criminal world of London pickpockets is notable for its strong performances from Dickie Moore, Irvin Pichel and George Arthur.
VHS: S18189. $19.95.
William J. Cowan, USA, 1933, 71 mins.

Omar Khayyam
William Dieterle directs this large scale, medieval period biography of Persia's celebrated poet and patriot. The cast includes Cornel Wilde, Debra Paget, Raymond Massey and Sebastian Cabot.
VHS: S16897. $19.95.
William Dieterle, USA, 1957, 100 mins.

On the Beach
Powerful adaptation of Nevil Shute's novel about the last people on earth, who face certain death from radioactivity. This film became one of the most celebrated anti-nuclear movies of the Fifties. With Gregory Peck, Ava Gardner and Fred Astaire.
VHS: S02557. $19.98.
Stanley Kramer, USA, 1959, 135 mins.

On the Waterfront
Marlon Brando stars in the archetypal role as ex-fighter Terry Malloy, working for Boss Johnny Friendly (Lee J. Cobb) on the gang-ridden waterfront. The classic American movie of redemption, with a great script by Budd Schulberg.
VHS: S00960. $19.95.
Laser: LD72070. $34.95.
Elia Kazan, USA, 1954, 108 mins.

One in a Million
The debut film of Norwegian Olympic skating star Sonja Henie. The story follows the meteoric fortunes of a beautiful skater after her dazzling New York performance catapults her to the top. With Adolphe Menjou, Don Ameche and the Ritz Brothers.
VHS: S20257. $19.98.
Sidney Lanfield, USA, 1936, 94 mins.

One Man's Way
A low-key biography of controversial minister and proselytizer Norman Vincent Peale (Don Murray) examines his relationship with his wife (Diana Hyland), amid accusations of blasphemy because of his unconventional preaching methods. With Veronica Cartwright, Ian Wolfe and Virginia Christine.
VHS: S19471. $19.98.
Denis Sanders, USA, 1963, 105 mins.

One Minute to Zero
Tay Garnett directed this gritty melodrama starring Robert Mitchum, set during the Korean War. Mitchum is a colonel evacuating American civilians, while Ann Blyth, as a United Nations envoy, provides romance.
VHS: S09175. $19.95.
Tay Garnett, USA, 1952, 105 mins.

One Rainy Afternoon
An actor kisses a strange woman in a Parisian movie house and is put on trial as the Kissing Monster. When she pays his bail a scandal erupts and soon every woman in Paris wants to be kissed by a stranger. With Francis Lederer, Ida Lupino, Hugh Herbert and Donald Meek. B&W.
VHS: S08455. $29.95.
Rowland V. Lee, USA, 1936, 78 mins.

Operation Pacific
The Duke plays Duke Gifford, a submarine commander involved in a hazardous World War II mission against the Japanese while dealing with issues of guilt about the death of his former commanding officer, as well as about his failed marriage.
VHS: S33907. $14.95.
George Waggner, USA, 1951, 111 mins.

Our Daily Bread
An ordinary urban couple become farmers and, incidentally, host to a collection of drifters who join together and become a unified community. This tale of organic socialism was released independently because the major studios feared its political theme. An exclusive introduction from the director and two newsreels, *California Election News*, which were meant to hurt the socialist campaign of Upton Sinclair, are also included. This collector's version is mastered from the finest print available.
VHS: S00979. $59.95.
King Vidor, USA, 1934, 74 mins.

Our Very Own
Ann Blyth and Farley Granger star in a classic film that "makes going to the movies worthwhile" (*Milwaukee Sentinel*). A high school girl who learns that she is adopted is taunted by her sister into believing that she is not wanted by either her foster parents or her fiance.
VHS: S31806. $14.95.
David Miller, USA, 1950, 92 mins.

Our Vines Have Tender Grapes
A tender adaptation of George Victor Martin's novel (by blacklisted writer Dalton Trumbo) of an immigrant Scandinavian family and the difficulties of acceptance and assimilation they encounter when they resettle in a Wisconsin farm community. With Edward G. Robinson, Agnes Moorehead and Margaret O'Brien.
VHS: S18506. $19.98.
Roy Rowland, USA, 1945, 105 mins.

Outpost in Morocco
George Raft, Marie Windsor and Akim Tamiroff star in this drama about Arab rebellion. Raft is a legionnaire sent to quell the troubles in the desert, but he finds himself trapped in a dilemma when he falls for the rebel leader's daughter (Windsor).
VHS: S23777. $24.95.
Robert Florey, USA, 1949, 92 mins.

The Ox-Bow Incident
Superb drama illustrating the terror of mob rule based on the Walter Van Tilburg Clark novel. With Henry Fonda, Dana Andrews, Anthony Quinn.
VHS: S06524. $19.98.
William Wellman, USA, 1943, 75 mins.

Painted Veil
Greta Garbo has difficulties remaining faithful to her husband in this adaptation of the Somerset Maugham novel. Set in the Orient, George Brent plays her lover, Herbert Marshall is the supportive husband. With Keye Luke, Warner Oland and Jean Hersholt.
VHS: S13195. $19.98.
Richard Boleslawski, USA, 1934, 83 mins.

Pandora and the Flying Dutchman
Ava Gardner and James Mason star in this wildly ambitious interpretation of the legend of the Flying Dutchman. On the south coast of Spain, between cocktail parties and costume changes, Gardner vamps for exciting international playboys. Only the mysterious yachtsman Hendrick van der Zee (Mason), none other than the legendary Flying Dutchman, manages to capture her heart. As the legend goes, he is set to wander until he finds a woman willing to make the ultimate sacrifice for love.
VHS: S26992. $19.95.
Laser: LD75435. $49.99.
Albert Lewin, USA, 1950, 123 mins.

Panic in the Streets
Public health officials search for a carrier of the bubonic plague. An Oscar winner for Best Original Story, director Elia Kazan concocts a semi-documentary suspense story set on the New Orleans waterfront. Great location shooting. With Richard Widmark, Barbara Bel Geddes, Paul Douglas and Jack Palance.
VHS: S13203. $39.98.
Laser: LD72319. $39.98.
Elia Kazan, USA, 1950, 96 mins.

Papa's Delicate Condition
In turn of the century Grangeville, Texas, Jackie Gleason is a railroad supervisor whose "delicate condition," a drinking problem, threatens the stable environment of his family and deeply upsets his wife and eldest daughter. A small, likable film about morals and responsibility, as seen through the eyes of Gleason's six-year-old daughter.
VHS: S02781. $19.95.
Laser: LD75235. $34.98.
George Marshall, USA, 1963, 98 mins.

Paris Blues
Martin Ritt's highly personal essay on Americans abroad. The story concerns two expatriate jazz musicians (Paul Newman and Sidney Poitier) who are caught up in the transcendent energy of Paris' Left Bank. Joanne Woodward and Diahann Carroll play their respective romantic interests. The film features a moody, evocative Duke Ellington score. Special appearance by Louis Armstrong. With Serge Reggiani.
VHS: S19492. $19.98.
Martin Ritt, USA, 1961, 98 mins.

Park Avenue Logger
Lloyd Ingraham thinks his son is less than a man and sends him off to a lumber camp to prove his manhood, not knowing he is already a top wrestler. There he exposes some crooked foremen and wins the heart of a beautiful girl by saving her father's lumber operation.
VHS: S21561. $24.95.
David Howard, USA, 1937, 65 mins.

Parrish
Delmer Daves' bittersweet, operatic adaptation of Mildred Savage's novel set on Connecticut's tobacco farms. Troy Donahue plays an ambitious young man who lives with his mother (Claudette Colbert) on an aristocrat's plantation and falls in love with three different women. With Karl Malden, Dean Jagger, Connie Stevens, Diane McBain and Sharon Hugueny.
VHS: S20195. $19.98.
Delmer Daves, USA, 1961, 138 mins.

Passage to Marseilles
Humphrey Bogart dishes out plenty of excitement in this story of five Devil's Island escapees determined to join the fight against the Nazis. Also starring Claude Rains, Peter Lorre and Sydney Greenstreet.
VHS: S02559. $19.98.
Michael Curtiz, USA, 1944, 109 mins.

A Patch of Blue
Sidney Poitier befriends a reclusive blind girl in the park on her first day out of the house in 13 years. Elizabeth Hartman doesn't care what color Sidney is because he is just so nice. Shelley Winters won a best supporting Oscar for her role as the mean-spirited prostitute mother. With Ivan Dixon and Wallace Ford. Based on the story *Be Ready with Bells and Drums*, by Elizabeth Kata. VHS letterboxed.
VHS: S12530. $19.98.
Laser: LD76222. $39.98.
Guy Green, USA, 1965, 105 mins.

Patton
George C. Scott delivers a stirring performance in this classic screen biography of the charismatic and controversial General George S. Patton. Winner of six Academy Awards. VHS letterboxed.
VHS: S03475. $29.98.
Laser: THX. **LD76096. $89.98.**
Franklin J. Schaffner, USA, 1970, 176 mins.

The Pawnbroker
Rod Steiger won an Academy Award nomination for Best Actor for his performance as *The Pawnbroker*, Sidney Lumet's powerful film about a New York pawnbroker who has lost all faith in mankind as a result of his imprisonment in Nazi Germany.
VHS: S01004. $14.98.
Sidney Lumet, USA, 1965, 116 mins.

People Will Talk
Cary Grant and Jeanne Crain star as a doctor and patient in this absorbing comedy/drama. Eventually they get married, but not before everyone has had a chance to gossip—that is, discuss the merits and problems their earlier relationship is likely to bequeath on their matrimonial union.
VHS: S21332. $19.98.
Joseph L. Mankiewicz, USA, 1951, 110 mins.

Period of Adjustment
An early film from George Roy Hill about the difficulties and tensions of a young married couple whose life is thrown out of balance by their friends' unraveling marriage. With Jane Fonda, Tony Franciosa, Jim Hutton and Jack Albertson.
VHS: S17661. $19.98.
George Roy Hill, USA, 1962, 112 mins.

Personal Property
A stylish remake of *The Man in Possession*, about mistaken identities and poor assumptions, stars Jean Harlow as an impoverished American widow who falls for a poor though immaculate Englishman. Both are in for the ride of their lives. With Robert Taylor, Una O'Connor and Reginald Owen.
VHS: S17784. $19.98.
W.S. Van Dyke II, USA, 1937, 85 mins.

Petrified Forest
Bette Davis is teamed with Humphrey Bogart in this melodrama based on the play by Robert Sherwood, set in the Arizona desert. Bogart, in his first important screen role, holds a writer (Leslie Howard) and a waitress (Davis) hostage in a diner. Tense drama, with great ensemble acting.
VHS: S11624. $19.95.
Archie Mayo, USA, 1936, 83 mins.

Peyton Place
This long-awaited classic was nominated for nine Academy Awards in 1957 (including Best Picture) and has an all star cast that includes Lana Turner, Hope Lange, Arthur Kennedy, Lloyd Nolan and Lorne Greene. It is the soap opera story of life behind closed doors in a small New England town. The photography of the small town and its setting, and a touchingly sympathetic musical score by Franz Waxman, make this romantic melodrama a gem.
VHS: S13725. $39.98.
Mark Robson, USA, 1957, 157 mins.

Phantom Broadcast
A handsome crooner sings a sweet love song on a radio broadcast, in front of a live audience. He's a popular entertainer with a large, loyal following—particularly among the ladies. However, Grant Murdock is not what he seems. He's just a "splendid dummy": the stand-in for Norman Wilder, a hunchback who's fiercely dedicated to music, and who is actually the one with the velvet voice. The plot of this ironic, strikingly plotted drama starts rolling when an attractive, ambitious, but poor young woman, Laura Hamilton, enlists Murdock's advice regarding her fledgling singing career. It is Wilder who encourages her talent, and he becomes upset when he senses the egotistical, womanizing Murdock is about to seduce her. Featuring a soulful, memorable performance by Ralph Forbes and a ravishing Gail Patrick in one of her earliest screen roles.
VHS: S13604. $29.95.
Phil Rosen, USA, 1933, 63 mins.

Phantom Lady
Ella Raines stalks suspects to save the man she loves (Alan Curtis). She ultimately faces the psychopathic friend of her boss (Franchot Tone).
VHS: S33917. $14.98.
Robert Siodmak, USA, 1944, 87 mins.

Phantom of Chinatown
Keye Luke, Lotus Long and Grant Withers are featured in this clever mystery. An archeologist is just about to lecture on his newest discovery. Before he can begin, however, he chokes and dies. Ancient curses and more mundane criminal elements are bound up in this seemingly unsolvable crime.
VHS: S24015. $14.95.
Phil Rosen, USA, 1941, 61 mins.

Phone Call from a Stranger
A plane crash and phone call bring Bette Davis and Gary Merrill together for a moving encounter that spells both tragedy and hope.
VHS: S05915. $19.98.
Jean Negulesco, USA, 1952, 96 mins.

Picnic
A great adaptation of the play by William Inge about a drifter who captivates a beautiful young woman as he passes through town during a Labor Day weekend. With sizzling performances from William Holden, Kim Novak, Rosalind Russell and Arthur O'Connell.
VHS: S11743. $19.95.
Joshua Logan, USA, 1955, 115 mins.

Picture of Dorian Gray
A fabulously eerie film based on Oscar Wilde's famous tale of evil and madness in Victorian London. A vain and wealthy 19th-century Londoner, who values his looks above all else, admires his newly painted portrait so much that he wishes that he will never grow old. His wish is granted and he looks great, but don't check out the picture of him hidden in the attic. With George Sanders and Donna Reed. The picture was painted by famed artist Ivan Albright.
VHS: S01028. $19.98.
Laser: LD70656. $34.98.
Albert Lewin, USA, 1945, 110 mins.

The Pink Jungle
Ben Morris (James Garner) is a fashion photographer who has journeyed to a South American jungle for a photo shoot with a beautiful model (Eva Renzi). Their expedition turns into a fiasco when local officials are convinced that Garner is a CIA agent sent in to spy. They find themselves on the run and in despair, until they cross paths with an American con man (George Kennedy).
VHS: S34365. $14.98.
Delbert Mann, USA, 1968, 104 mins.

Pinky
Jeanne Crain stars in this powerful drama about a young woman who passes for white in Boston until she goes home to experience life as a black woman in the deep South. It's a compelling indictment of racism and bigotry. Co-starring Ethel Waters and Ethel Barrymore.
VHS: S21300. $19.98.
Elia Kazan, USA, 1949, 102 mins.

Pitfall
An intriguing film noir which stars Dick Powell as a bored husband whose philandering ways bring tragedy to himself and his family. Suspenseful and well acted. With Jane Wyatt, Lizabeth Scott and Raymond Burr.
VHS: S14321. $19.98.
Laser: CLV. **LD72016. $29.98.**
Andre de Toth, USA, 1948, 85 mins.

Pittsburgh
The beautiful Marlene Dietrich is courted by rivals John Wayne and Randolph Scott in this love triangle of class differences set in the coal and steel business world. With Frank Craven, Louise Allbritton and Shemp Howard.
VHS: S19075. $14.98.
Lewis Seiler, USA, 1942, 91 mins.

Plunder Road
Five guys knock off a train shipment of gold and try to elude capture by the law enforcement agencies in California. They divide the loot and go their separate ways. Some of the gold is actually melted down into car bumpers. A low budget thriller with Gene Raymond, Wayne Morris, Elisha Cook Jr., Staffor Repp, Steven Ritch and Jeanne Cooper.
VHS: S07135. $19.95.
Hubert Cornfield, USA, 1957, 76 mins.

Plymouth Adventure
Critics hailed this extravagant, Academy Award-winning retelling of the voyage of the *Mayflower* as "an inspiring bit of Americana" (*The Hollywood Reporter*) and "a film milepost" (*Variety*). Spencer Tracy is Christopher Jones, captain of the ship-for-hire *Mayflower*, who agrees to take 100 passengers across the Atlantic and into the New World. Although he planned to abandon them there and return to England immediately, he is moved by the tenacity of the pilgrims to rise up to the challenges of the rigorous voyage, and vows his support to their cause. With Gene Tierney, Van Johnson, Lloyd Bridges and Leo Genn.
VHS: S30548. $19.98.
Clarence Brown, USA, 1952, 104 mins.

Point Blank
A superior crime thriller starring Lee Marvin as a double-crossed professional criminal out to settle the score with everyone who sold him out and left him for dead. Based on the novel by Donald Westlake writing as Richard Stark. Cast includes Angie Dickinson, Carroll O'Connor, Keenan Wynn, John Vernon and Lloyd Bochner. Wait for the shootout at Alcatraz.
VHS: S08064. $19.98.
Laser: Letterboxed. **LD74679. $34.98.**
John Boorman, USA, 1967, 89 mins.

Pork Chop Hill
Gregory Peck is in charge of holding an elevated piece of Korean real estate against the onslaught of North Korean and Chinese Communist troops. A stirring tribute to the American fighting man from the director of *All Quiet on the Western Front*. The fine cast includes Rip Torn, Harry Guardino, Robert Blake, Woody Strode and George Peppard.
VHS: S06066. $19.95.
Laser: LD76412. $34.98.
Lewis Milestone, USA, 1959, 97 mins.

Port of New York
A G-man goes undercover to infiltrate drug smugglers and mobsters in New York. Yul Brynner's screen debut.
VHS: S05866. $29.95.
Laszlo Benedek, USA, 1949, 86 mins.

Portrait in Black
Lana Turner and Anthony Quinn star in this devilish murder mystery, which also features Sandra Dee and John Saxon in supporting roles. A woman married to a bedridden man falls in love with her husband's doctor. There seems to be only one resolution, a violent one.
VHS: S28399. $14.98.
Michael Gordon, USA, 1960, 113 mins.

Possessed (1931)
Joan Crawford plays a back street girl who rejects her small town job as box factory worker to become the mistress of big city lawyer Clark Gable. When he runs for governor, she becomes a topic of scandal. Based on the novel by Edgar Selwyn, *The Mirage*. Good soaper not to be confused with later Crawford picture of the same title.
VHS: S08097. $24.95.
Clarence Brown, USA, 1931, 76 mins.

Possessed (1947)
Joan Crawford gives a stunning performance as a woman driven mad by obsessive love; many critics at the time believed that her portrayal in this film topped her performance in *Mildred Pierce*. The outstanding supporting cast includes Van Heflin, Raymond Massey and Geraldine Brooks.
VHS: S15119. $19.98.
Laser: LD70141. $34.98.
Clarence Brown, USA, 1947, 108 mins.

The Postman Always Rings Twice
Lana Turner and John Garfield are the illicit lovers in this James M. Cain thriller, who plot to murder the husband who is standing in the way of a real good time. A classic film noir available in the original black and white. Cast includes Cecil Kellaway, Leon Ames and Hume Cronyn. Remade in 1981.
VHS: S09152. $19.98.
Tay Garnett, USA, 1946, 113 mins.

Pressure Point
Stanley Kramer's prison drama about a psychiatrist (Sidney Poitier) who tries to get inside the head of his most diabolical patient, an inveterate Nazi fascist (Bobby Darin). Intelligent, provocative and fascinating, taken from an actual case file reported in Dr. Robert Lindner's *The Fifty-Minute Hour*. With Peter Falk, Barry Gordon and Howard Caine.
VHS: S17990. $19.98.
Stanley Kramer, USA, 1962, 88 mins.

Pride and Prejudice
Outstanding adaptation of the Jane Austen novel with a fine cast including Greer Garson, Laurence Olivier and Maureen O'Sullivan.
VHS: S01880. $19.98.
Laser: LD72150. $34.98.
Robert Z. Leonard, USA, 1940, 118 mins.

The Pride and the Passion
A rousing adaptation of C.S. Forester's novel about the Spanish War of Independence (1810). The plot unfolds in the aftermath of Napoleon's invasion of Spain. Cary Grant, Frank Sinatra and Sophia Loren star as counterguerillas trying to transport a huge canon across the country in order to launch a surprise attack.
VHS: S17989. $19.98.
Laser: LD76163. $49.98.
Stanley Kramer, USA, 1957, 132 mins.

Pride of St. Louis
The life of baseball star Dizzy Dean, who injured himself and then became a sports commentator. With Dan Dailey, Joanne Dru, Richard Haydn, Richard Crenna.
VHS: S11620. $19.98.
Harmon Jones, USA, 1952, 93 mins.

Prince Valiant
Prince Valiant steps out of the Sunday comics and onto the screen, in this swashbuckling tale of royalty and rogues set in the time of King Arthur. Starring James Mason, Janet Leigh and Robert Wagner. Photographed by Lucien Ballard.
VHS: S14222. $14.98.
Henry Hathaway, USA, 1954, 100 mins.

Prisoner of Japan
Alan Baxter and Gertrude Michael star in this thought-provoking melodrama based on a story by Edgar G. Ulmer. David Bowman (Baxter) is a philosophical young astronomer who can't bring himself to thwart a Japanese offensive against American ships. This is a film that speaks to the isolationist sentiment prevalent before the bombing of Pearl Harbor.
VHS: S23989. $24.95.
Arthur Ripley, USA, 1942, 65 mins.

Prisoner of Zenda (1937)
The classic costume drama and among Hollywood's best swashbucklers. Ronald Colman is a commoner who is forced to substitute for his look-alike cousin and falls in love with Madeleine Carroll while Douglas Fairbanks, Jr. is Rupert of Hentzau.
VHS: S11444. $29.95.
John Cromwell, USA, 1937, 101 mins.

Prisoner of Zenda (1952)
The tale of the king's double, who is called on to impersonate the king in order to save the crown, features Stewart Granger in a dual role, with Deborah Kerr and James Mason.
VHS: S02561. $29.95.
Richard Thorpe, USA, 1952, 100 mins.

The Private Affairs of Bel Ami
A ruthless schemer (George Sanders) gets ahead by charming prominent women. Angela Lansbury (*Manchurian Candidate; Murder, She Wrote*) co-stars in this 1947 adaptation of Guy de Maupassant's famous story. "All women take to men who have the appearance of wickedness!"
VHS: S14319. $19.98.
Albert Lewin, USA, 1947, 112 mins.

Private Hell #36
Ida Lupino wrote, starred in and co-produced this taut dramatic tale of two cops who locate stolen money and keep some for themselves. The boys in blue must now face a heavy case of the guilts. With Howard Duff, Steve Cochran and Dean Jagger. B&W.
VHS: S04716. $19.95.
Laser: LD71813. $34.98.
Don Siegel, USA, 1954, 81 mins.

Private Life of Don Juan
Douglas Fairbanks stars in his final film, pursuing a string of beautiful women, including Merle Oberon.
VHS: S08888. $19.98.
Alexander Korda, USA, 1934, 80 mins.

Proud Rebel
A post-Civil War sentimental drama about a Confederate veteran searching for a doctor who can cure his mute son, with father and son playing father and son. The principles are great, the chemistry excellent and Alan Ladd's last film. Also featuring David Ladd and Olivia de Havilland.
VHS: S12567. $19.98.
Laser: LD75243. $34.98.
Michael Curtiz, USA, 1958, 103 mins.

Prize
This stylish thriller set in Stockholm stars Paul Newman as a Nobel Prize nominee for literature who becomes involved in international intrigue with physicist Edward G. Robinson just prior to the famous award ceremonies. Based on the novel by Irving Wallace. With Elke Sommer, Diane Baker, Kevin McCarthy and Leo G. Carroll. Watch for the scene where Newman eludes Communist agents by ducking into a nudist convention.
VHS: S16437. $19.98.
Mark Robson, USA, 1963, 135 mins.

Public Enemy
James Cagney explodes on the screen in one of his most famous roles as a notorious criminal. This is the film with the infamous "grapefruit scene"! With Jean Harlow and Joan Blondell, from the director of the initial version of *A Star Is Born* and *The Ox-Bow Incident*.
VHS: S01771. $19.95.
Laser: LD71179. $39.98.
William Wellman, USA, 1931, 83 mins.

The Purchase Price
Barbara Stanwyck is a torch singer who escapes from her racketeering boyfriend, played by Eddie Fields. She enters into a loveless, arranged marriage with a farmer played by Jim Gilson. Though it's quite a switch from her big city life, Stanwyck manages to wrest romance from even these extremely dire circumstances.
VHS: S20832. $19.98.
William Wellman, USA, 1932, 68 mins.

Queen Bee
Joan Crawford is at her evil best in this gothic southern melodrama. Crawford is married to a wealthy mill owner which gives her nearly unlimited power to manipulate and destroy the lives of those around her. The results are achingly tragic. Barry Sullivan and Betsy Palmer also star.
VHS: S26448. $19.95.
Ronald MacDougall, USA, 1955, 95 mins.

Queen Christina
Greta Garbo had one of her finest roles as the 17th century Swedish monarch who gave up her crown for the man she loved. John Gilbert, Garbo's real-life ex-lover and her frequent co-star in silent pictures, made a brief comeback as the dashing Don Antonio. With Ian Keith, C. Aubrey Smith and Lewis Stone. A classic that boasts more than a memorable last shot.
VHS: S11732. $19.98.
Laser: LD70661. $29.98.
Rouben Mamoulian, USA, 1933, 97 mins.

Quicksand
Mickey Rooney finds himself sinking into a mire of violence and criminal activity when he unofficially borrows twenty bucks from the till at the garage where he works. Peter Lorre is around to blackmail the kid into further trouble, all because he wanted to impress a date. B&W.
VHS: S04040. $19.95.
Irving Pichel, USA, 1950, 79 mins.

Racers
Kirk Douglas is in the driver's seat in this high speed drama about a cocky American trying to be number one in the European racing circuit. His attitude and skill may win him races but not very many friends. With Lee J. Cobb, Cesar Romero, Bella Darvi, Gilbert Roland, Katy Jurado. Filmed on location. Vroom. Vroom.
VHS: S13298. $39.98.
Henry Hathaway, USA, 1955, 112 mins.

Racing Luck
William Boyd stars in this film about a dashing young jockey (Boyd) who's framed into working for a rival horse stable. With Barbara Worth, George Ernest, Esther Muir and Dick Curtis.
VHS: S17490. $14.95.
Sam Newfield, USA, 1935, 56 mins.

The Racketeer
Carole Lombard and Robert Armstrong star in this romantic drama in which the heroine agrees to marry a racketeer in order for her true love to further his career as a violinist. Talk about your sacrifices for the sake of happiness. With Hedda Hopper and John Loder.
VHS: S04490. $19.95.
Howard Higgin, USA, 1929, 66 mins.

Raffles
Ronald Colman stars as the debonair amateur safe-cracker who can easily find the combination to any lock—or any woman's heart. Raffles has always managed to elude the law, but just when he decides to retire, he finds he must agree to one final robbery to save a suicidal schoolfriend from disgrace.
VHS: S31807. $14.95.
Harry d'Abbadie D'Arrast/George Fitzmaurice, USA, 1930, 71 mins.

Rage of Paris
Danielle Darrieux, star of *Mayerling* and *Club des Femmes*, was brought to Hollywood to star opposite Douglas Fairbanks, Jr. in this funny tale of a young French woman adrift in Manhattan.
VHS: S03788. $29.95.
Henry Koster, USA, 1938, 78 mins.

Railroaded
When a policeman is killed attempting to thwart a holdup, Detective Mickey Ferguson is assigned to the case. Just before he dies, one of the gang incriminates Steve Ryan, the kid brother of Mickey's girlfriend. Mickey is determined to prove Steve's innocence, especially when he discovers that a notorious gunman named Duke (John Ireland) is mixed up in the killing. With Sheila Ryan and Hugh Beaumont.
VHS: S33431. $24.95.
Anthony Mann, USA, 1947, 74 mins.

Rain
W. Somerset Maugham's story of Sadie Thompson, who became a classic of stage, screen and literature, with a brilliant performance from Joan Crawford as the cynical prostitute, and Walter Huston as the minister who tries to reform her.
VHS: S01086. $19.95.
Lewis Milestone, USA, 1932, 91 mins.

Rainmaker
Burt Lancaster and Katharine Hepburn star in this entertaining version of the play by N. Richard Nash. Lancaster is a slick talking con-man and Hepburn is the dubious spinster who doubts whether this Starbuck fellow can produce rain for the crops or sunshine for the heart of a tough single lady. With Earl Holliman, Lloyd Bridges and Wendell Corey.
VHS: S07519. $19.95.
Joseph Anthony, USA, 1956, 121 mins.

The Rains Came
Tyrone Power stars as a powerful man in India who falls for the alluring Myrna Loy in this costume melodrama based on the Louis Bromfield novel. It charts the sweeping events that overpower their attraction for one another, and won an Academy Award for special effects recreating an earthquake.
VHS: S21070. $19.98.
Clarence Brown, USA, 1939, 104 mins.

Raintree County
Elizabeth Taylor is the southern belle who gets the man she thinks she wants but then finds life as a schoolmaster's wife boring. A lush MGM production which features Montgomery Clift, Eva Marie Saint, Nigel Patrick, Rod Taylor, Agnes Moorhead, Walter Abel. VHS letterboxed.
VHS: S01087. $24.98.
Laser: LD70187. $39.98.
Edward Dmytryk, USA, 1958, 166 mins.

Random Harvest
Ronald Colman and Greer Garson star in this lavish MGM production of a James Hilton novel about an amnesiac soldier who leaves a mental hospital and is rescued by a music hall entertainer, whom he marries. A car accident restores his memory a few years later and he returns to the aristocratic life he once knew. The second wife (Garson) must bide her time and hope for a happy ending. With Philip Dorn and Susan Peters. B&W.
VHS: S09153. $19.98.
Laser: LD71171. $39.98.
Mervyn LeRoy, USA, 1942, 124 mins.

Rasputin and the Empress
Three members of the Barrymore family—John, Ethel and Lionel—enact the final days of the Czar's reign, when Rasputin (Lionel) cured the Czar's son of hemophilia and exerted tremendous influence over the family. Some impressive sets, decor and costumes. Prince Youssoupoff filed a suit against MGM claiming historical inaccuracies. With Diana Wynyard and Ralph Morgan.
VHS: S18507. $19.98.
Richard Boleslawski, USA, 1933, 133 mins.

Raw Deal
Film noir classic from Anthony Mann which weaves the ultimate story of murder, jailbreaks, and jealousy! A hostage (Marsha Hunt) finds herself pitted against her captor's tough-as-nails moll girlfriend (Claire Trevor), a situation where this demure young secretary will even commit murder to save the man she loves. Co-stars Raymond Burr and Dennis O'Keefe. Called "a pistol-powered crime melodrama" by the *New York Times*.
VHS: S28644. $29.95.
Anthony Mann, USA, 1948, 79 mins.

The Razor's Edge
W. Somerset Maugham's powerful novel about a flyer who returns from WWI seeking spiritual peace is given a great rendition with Tyrone Power as the flyer, Gene Tierney as his fiancee, and Anne Baxter.
VHS: S03557. $19.98.
Laser: LD72217. $49.98.
Edmund Goulding, USA, 1946, 146 mins.

Real Glory
The Moro Rebellion in the Philippines just after the Spanish-American War is the subject of this action adventure starring Gary Cooper as Doctor Bill Canavon. With the help of soldiers-of-fortune David Niven and Broderick Crawford, Cooper tries to make peace, combat a cholera epidemic, blow up a dam, defend a besieged fort and fall in love with nurse Andrea Leeds. With Reginald Owen, Kay Johnson, Tetsu Komai and Rudy Robles. Watch for Elmo Lincoln, the first screen Tarzan, as a U.S. captain.
VHS: S16446. $19.98.
Henry Hathaway, USA, 1939, 96 mins.

Reckless
Musical star Mona Leslie (Jean Harlow) goes on a bender with a confused aristocrat—and they wake up married. When he commits suicide, Mona is publicly blamed for his death and must fight her way back to Broadway. Also starring William Powell. The story of this film was written by David O. Selznick, under the pseudonym of Oliver Jeffries.
VHS: S15120. $19.98.
Victor Fleming, USA, 1935, 97 mins.

The Reckless Way
This story explores the ups and downs of a young lady trying to break into the movies. This early sound film stars Marion Nixon, Kane Richmond and Inez Courtney.
VHS: S15232. $19.95.
Raymond K. Johnson, USA, 1936, 72 mins.

Red Ball Express
Jeff Chandler, Alex Nicol and Sidney Poitier are soldiers running an emergency supply convoy to a group of Patton's tanks that are surrounded by the Nazis. Based on a true story, this film shows the unsung heroism that helped them overcome enemy bombardment and divisiveness in the ranks, caused, in part, by racism.
VHS: S27667. $14.98.
Budd Boetticher, USA, 1952, 84 mins.

Red Dust
Clark Gable runs a rubber plantation in Indochina and finds he is attracted to both of his female visitors. Will he stick with the brazen bad girl Jean Harlow or steal the refined Mary Astor from her ailing husband? Remade by Gable (with Ava Gardner) as *Mogambo* in 1953. Based on the play by William Collison. With Gene Raymond and Donald Crisp.
VHS: S08098. $19.98.
Victor Fleming, USA, 1932, 83 mins.

The Red Menace
Attempting to show the dangers of Communism, this 1949 film, deliberately made with unknown actors, caused quite a stir at the time of its release with its over-the-top McCarthyesque propaganda. Now it all just seems ridiculously funny, and more than a little sad.
VHS: S14320. $19.98.
Laser: CLV. **LD72021. $29.98.**
R.G. Springsteen, USA, 1949, 87 mins.

Red Pony
John Steinbeck's classic story is brought to life in this tasteful version. A boy escapes his unpleasant family life through his love of a horse. With Robert Mitchum and Myrna Loy. Music by Aaron Copeland.
VHS: S01100. $19.95.
Laser: CLV. **LD72022. $39.98.**
Lewis Milestone, USA, 1949, 89 mins.

The Reivers
Based upon William Faulkner's last novel, *The Reivers* is the story of a young man and two adults travelling from small town Mississippi to Memphis. Steve McQueen and Juano Hernandez *(Intruder in the Dust)* star.
VHS: S21403. $14.98.
Mark Rydell, USA, 1969, 107 mins.

Remedy for Riches
The fourth film in the Dr. Paul Christian series takes a lighter approach as the good doctor investigates a phony geologist and a troublesome chicken. Jean Hersholt also tries to get the town druggist and his nurse back together. Big doin's in River's End, Minnesota. With Warren Hull, Jed Pouty and Walter Catlett.
VHS: S05702. $29.95.
Erle C. Kenton, USA, 1940, 66 mins.

Requiem for a Heavyweight (1962)
The poignant pugilistic classic written by Rod Serling. After 17 years in the ring, it's the final bell for washed-up heavyweight Mountain Rivera (Anthony Quinn). A fight doctor confirms one more punch could permanently disable Mountain. With the support of his faithful trainer (Mickey Rooney), and a kindly employment counselor (Julie Harris), Rivera tries to land a job outside the ring. But as the mob closes in for payment of a huge gambling debt, Mountain is coerced by his calculating manager (Jackie Gleason) into a lucrative, yet humiliating career of staged wrestling.
VHS: S33992. $19.95.
Ralph Nelson, USA, 1962, 86 mins.

Retreat, Hell!
Frank Lovejoy stars in this Korean war drama. General O.P. Smith defies direct orders to retreat from enemy lines, and engages his troops in a bloody battle against the Communist troops in North Korea. With Richard Carlson, Russ Tamblyn, Anita Louise.
VHS: S09632. $19.95.
Joseph H. Lewis, USA, 1952, 95 mins.

The Return of Peter Grimm
The father of a close-knit family returns from the dead to make amends for all the things he did wrong in his lifetime. With good performances from Lionel Barrymore and a talented cast.
VHS: S14162. $19.98.
George Nicholls, USA, 1935, 82 mins.

Return to Paradise
A South Seas story about a wandering nonconformist (Gary Cooper) as he searches for excitement and meaning. When he turns up on an idyllic coastal island, he falls for a beautiful local (Roberta Haynes) and unwittingly gets entangled in a local rebellion. With Barry Jones and Moira MacDonald.
VHS: S19497. $19.98.
Mark Robson, USA, 1953, 100 mins.

Return to Peyton Place
This sizzling sequel picks up where the original all-star hit left off. It examines the impact the novel supposedly made on the small New England town it chose to uncover and in particular the reaction of several inhabitants who feel they have been maligned. The star-studded cast includes: Carol Lynley, Jeff Chandler, Eleanor Parker, Mary Astor, Robert Sterling, and Tuesday Weld. More closets are unlocked; more skeletons fall out—a must for fans of the original.
VHS: S13726. $39.98.
Jose Ferrer, USA, 1961, 122 mins.

Reunion in France
John Wayne is a wounded RAF pilot who seeks the help of Joan Crawford, a French aristocrat who's fallen on hard times. Her mansion has been turned into a coal allotment bureau by the Nazis and she is forced to find employment as a shop girl. She also believes her ex-boyfriend Philip Dorn is working for the enemy. Can she and the Yank flyer escape to England?
VHS: S12137. $19.95.
Jules Dassin, USA, 1942, 104 mins.

Rhapsody
A passionate three-way love triangle between a strong willed woman (Elizabeth Taylor) used to getting what she wants, a violinist (Vittorio Gassman) more interested in his career and a more appreciative and open pianist (John Ericson) who is drawn to her. With Louis Calhern and Michael Chekhov.
VHS: S18525. $19.98.
Charles Vidor, USA, 1954, 115 mins.

Riffraff
Another Jean Harlow vehicle on the war between the sexes, pitting the tough, no-nonsense Harlow as a cannery worker who falls for an alcoholic fisherman played by Spencer Tracy, a disillusioned drifter trying to find stability. With Joseph Calleia and Mickey Rooney.
VHS: S17780. $19.98.
J. Walter Ruben, USA, 1936, 94 mins.

Riot in Cell Block 11
Powerful prison drama filmed realistically. Some of those involved in disturbing the peace of this correctional facility include Neville Brand, Emile Meyer, Frank Faylen, Leo Gordon, and Robert Osterloh. Be advised, the media will be manipulated by hardened criminals.
VHS: S04222. $19.95.
Don Siegel, USA, 1954, 80 mins.

Riptide

A Manhattan chorus girl with a lively past enters into loveless marriage with a dour British diplomat. Matters are complicated when the woman's former lover re-emerges and demands her back. With Norma Shearer, Robert Montgomery, Herbert Marshall, Skeets Gallagher, Ralph Forbes and Lilyan Tashman.

VHS: S20414. $29.98.

Edmund Goulding, USA, 1934, 90 mins.

The Rise and Fall of Legs Diamond

The fast and impressive saga of the Roaring '20s crime lord called "Legs" because of his ability to escape law enforcers. Directed by one of the most fascinating unrecognized talents in the American cinema, Budd Boetticher—and featuring the outstanding photography of Lucien Ballard. "A minor classic" (Andrew Sarris).

VHS: S14084. $59.99.

Budd Boetticher, USA, 1960, 101 mins.

Road Agent

The hero and his friends discover a stolen consignment of gold and clear themselves of the charge of murder of the coach driver sheriff. With Dick Foran, Leo Carrillo, Andy Devine, Anne Gwynne, Richard Davies, Ann Nagel, Reed Hadley, Emmett Lynn and Ernie Adams.

VHS: S33703. $24.95.

Charles LaMont, USA, 1941, 60 mins.

Road House

A psychotic owner of a roadhouse becomes insanely jealous when his singer falls in love with his manager, so he decides to frame him for embezzlement. A 40's film noir with all the characters typically cynical or homicidal. Starring Richard Widmark and the luminous Ida Lupino.

VHS: S13615. $19.98.

Jean Negulesco, USA, 1948, 95 mins.

Roaring Twenties

James Cagney stars as a good man turned crook in this recreation of the world of bootleggers, speakeasies and violence; Humphrey Bogart is the gangster who won't let anything stand in his way.

VHS: S05356. $19.95.

Laser: LD70188. $34.98.

Raoul Walsh, USA, 1939, 106 mins.

Roman Spring of Mrs. Stone

A predatory gigolo preys upon a vulnerable middle-aged actress seeking love—and willing to pay for it. Vivien Leigh is powerful in this adaptation of Tennessee Williams' novel. With Warren Beatty and Lotte Lenya.

VHS: S05865. $19.98.

Jose Quintero, USA, 1961, 104 mins.

Romance

Greta Garbo stars as diva Madame Cavallini, a worldly woman who tries to transcend her colorful past in the arms of a devout young clergyman. Co-starring the young Gavin Gordon.

VHS: S15121. $19.98.

Clarence Brown, USA, 1930, 76 mins.

Rome Adventure

When in Rome, Troy Donahue gets romantic—and falls in love with *both* Angie Dickinson and Suzanne Pleshette. This splendidly scenic drama features breathtaking glimpses of Rome, Verona, Pisa and the Italian Alps, plus a luxuriant score by Max Steiner.

VHS: S13802. $19.98.

Laser: LD70735. $39.98.

Delmer Daves, USA, 1962, 119 mins.

The Rose Bowl Story

The heart of a football star and the beauty of a Rose Bowl Princess come together in this emotional love story set among the blooms of the California Rose Bowl. Starring Natalie Wood, Vera Miles and Marshall Thompson.

VHS: S34987. $19.95.

William Beaudine, USA, 1952, 73 mins.

Roseanna McCoy

Irving Reis, Farley Granger, Joan Evans, Charles Bickford and Raymond Massey star in this saga of the Hatfields and the McCoys, in which young lovers from the two feuding families reopen old wounds.

VHS: S32354. $14.98.

Irving Reis, USA, 1949, 100 mins.

The Rounders

An adaptation of Max Evans' novel with Henry Fonda and Glenn Ford as amiable bronco busters confronted with the challenge of breaking an ornery horse as they reflect on their life and times. With Edgar Buchanan, Sue Ane Langdon and Hope Holiday.

VHS: S18673. $19.98.

Burt Kennedy, USA, 1964, 85 mins.

Royal Bed

The king of a small island must call all the shots for the first time as his overbearing wife is away on holiday. Lowell Sherman, Mary Astor and Robert Warwick star.

VHS: S08456. $29.95.

Lowell Sherman, USA, 1931, 74 mins.

Run for Your Money

A political drama focusing on two Welsh miners who go off on a madcap and lavish spending spree in London. With Donald Houston, Meredith Edwards, Moira Lister and Alec Guinness.

VHS: S18944. $19.95.

Charles Frend, USA, 1949, 83 mins.

Saint Joan

Graham Greene wrote the screenplay based on George Bernard Shaw's drama, and Jean Seberg made her screen debut as Joan of Arc. With a superb performance by John Gielgud as the Earl of Warwick.

VHS: S01995. $19.98.

Otto Preminger, USA, 1957, 110 mins.

Salome

Rita Hayworth does the dance of the seven veils in order to keep the head of John the Baptist where it belongs. This novel interpretation of the court of King Herod also stars Charles Laughton, Judith Anderson, Stewart Granger, and Alan Badel as the unfortunate prophet. Historically dubious, but it is in Technicolor.

VHS: S04676. $19.95.

William Dieterle, USA, 1953, 105 mins.

Salt of the Earth

Blacklisted during the McCarthy Era, *Salt of the Earth* portrays the true events of Chicano zinc workers on strike in New Mexico. When the mine owners get a court injunction to forbid picketing, the wives of the strikers take up the battle. A classic.

VHS: S01151. $29.95.

Herbert J. Biberman, USA, 1954, 94 mins.

Samar

A strange and suspenseful story of a prisoner who arrives in a penal camp in Spain and attempts to alleviate the suffering of the prisoners.

VHS: S34179. $19.95.

George Montgomery, Panama/USA, 1962, 102 mins.

San Francisco

Clark Gable plays the owner of the saloon, Spencer Tracy is the priest, and Jeanette MacDonald the belle of San Francisco in this lavish production set against the climax of the San Francisco earthquake.

VHS: S04404. $19.98.

W.S. Van Dyke, USA, 1936, 115 mins.

Sand Pebbles

Steve McQueen is superb as a sailor on an American gunboat patrolling the Yangtze river in 1926 China. Explosive entertainment with Vietnam parallels for those who care to pick up on them. Two video cassettes.

VHS: S14139. $29.98.

Robert Wise, USA, 1966, 193 mins.

Santa Fe Trail

Young calvary officers Jeb Stuart (Errol Flynn) and George Armstrong (Ronald Reagan) duel militant abolitionist John Brown (Raymond Massey) and fight over the affections of Olivia de Havilland. The film was roundly condemned for its historical misunderstandings. With Alan Hale, Guinn Williams and William Lundigan.

VHS: S01159. $19.98.

Michael Curtiz, USA, 1940, 109 mins.

Saratoga Trunk

Ingrid Bergman is a Creole of unmatched beauty whose Parisian ways beguile all of New Orleans, especially a young Texan oil man played by Gary Cooper. Bergman is the perfect coquette in this beautiful costume drama about the joys and drawbacks of digging for gold. Based on Edna Ferber's novel, for the most part this film is a wonderfully realized work, but it also features Flora Robson as a maid in blackface.

VHS: S27748. $19.98.

Sam Wood, USA, 1945, 135 mins.

Satan Met a Lady

A fascinating rewrite of *The Maltese Falcon* with Bette Davis, Warren William and Alison Skipworth among the band of crooks and a private detective out to find a rare artifact.

VHS: S13396. $19.98.

William Dieterle, USA, 1936, 74 mins.

The Savage Eye

A cinema-verite documentary-style feature about a dissatisfied Los Angeles woman (Barbara Baxley) who undertakes an excursion into the city's eccentric haunts and nightspots. The film presents Los Angeles as a junk heap of faith healers, con men and social climbers. With Gary Merrill and Herschel Bernardi.

VHS: S19871. $29.95.

Ben Maddow/Joseph Strick/Sidney Meyers, USA, 1959, 68 mins.

Sayonara

Marlon Brando stars as a pilot in postwar Japan who falls in love with a Japanese entertainer in spite of directives to the contrary issued by Occupation Command. Fine supporting performances by Red Buttons, James Garner and Miyoshi Umeki, based on a novel by James Michener.

VHS: S03508. $19.98.

Joshua Logan, USA, 1957, 147 mins.

The Scar (Hollow Triumph)

Fugitive Paul Henreid kills a psychiatrist whom he physically resembles, and then, while impersonating him, finds out the good doctor has committed some crimes of his own. Also starring Joan Bennett and Eduard Franz.

VHS: S14323. $19.98.

Steve Sekely, USA, 1948, 83 mins.

Scaramouche

A Technicolor swashbuckler starring Stewart Granger, Mel Ferrer and Janet Leigh, and set in the French Revolution. Featuring "one of the finest sword battles in movie history" (*The Motion Picture Guide*).

VHS: S14555. $19.98.

Laser: CAV. LD70448. $89.95.

Laser: CLV. LD70449. $39.95.

George Sidney, USA, 1952, 111 mins.

Scarlet Dawn

Douglas Fairbanks Jr. stars as a Russian aristocrat who falls on hard times because of the Communist revolution. With the help of his former servant, Nancy Carroll, he begins a new life in exile, but treachery and politics intervene, leaving these two characters with nothing more certain than their love for each other.

VHS: S20833. $19.98.

William Dieterle, USA, 1932, 76 mins.

The Scarlet Letter

A story of adultery, Puritan attitudes and an unusual love triangle based upon the classic novel by Nathaniel Hawthorne.

VHS: S01164. $19.95.

Robert Vignola, USA, 1934, 69 mins.

The Scarlet Pimpernel

Leslie Howard is the dashing hero who masquerades as a foppish dandy in this entertaining adventure yarn set during the French Revolution. Raymond Massey and Merle Oberon co-star. A lavish production, and an entertaining script by S.N. Behrman and Robert Sherwood.

VHS: S01165. $19.98.

Harold Young, USA, 1934, 98 mins.

Sea Chase

Half of the navies of the world hunt for freighter captain John Wayne and passenger Lana Turner as the German freighter tries to make it back to Germany from Sydney harbor in 1939.

VHS: S12498. $19.98.

Laser: LD70671. $24.98.

John Farrow, USA, 1955, 117 mins.

Sea Fury

Victor McLaglen and Stanley Baker star as competing tugboat captains in this convincing seafaring yarn. Romance, adventure and treasure combine to heighten this rivalry. It makes a potent driving force at the center of an engaging melodrama.

VHS: S23955. $19.95.

Cy Endfield, USA, 1958, 97 mins.

Sea Hawk

Errol Flynn at his finest. He plays an English privateer making life miserable for Spanish galleons in the 16th century, under the authority of Queen Elizabeth I. In the course of his swashbuckling adventures he invades Panama, is captured, enslaved and then escapes to warn England of a secret Spanish Armada. He also finds time to fall in love with the beautiful niece of the Spanish ambassador. With Claude Rains, Brenda Marshall, Flora Robson, Donald Crisp and Alan Hale. Great swordplay and a memorable musical score by Erich Wolfgang Korngold.

VHS: S01863. $19.95.

Michael Curtiz, USA, 1940, 127 mins.

The Sea Wolf

An adaptation of Jack London's work about a fugitive couple (Ida Lupino and John Garfield) on a ship caught in the vice grip between a hardened though gifted sea captain (Edward G. Robinson) and a writer (Alexander Knox) trying to assert intellectual dominance and superiority.

VHS: S18508. $19.98.

Michael Cu·tiz, USA, 1941, 90 mins.

The Search for Bridey Murphy

A woman under hypnosis remembers a prior life…and death. Based on real-life events that had all of America talking, this mystery stars Teresa Wright and Louis Hayward.

VHS: S14458. $19.95.

Noel Langley, USA, 1956, 84 mins.

The Second Face

A strange film about the inner transformation of Ella Raines, a beautiful young woman who undergoes plastic surgery to repair her scarred face. With Bruce Bennett, Rita Johnson and Jane Darwell.

VHS: S18935. $19.95.

Jack Bernhard, USA, 1950, 77 mins.

Second Woman

A whole community suspects an architect to be responsible for the death of his fiancee. Robert Young stars in this stylish film noir as the young man who must face not only the wrath of his community, but that of his late fiancee's father as well. With his new love (Betsy Drake) he must prove his innocence.

VHS: S07482. $24.95.

James V. Kern, USA, 1951, 90 mins.

Seconds

Rock Hudson delivers a tour-de-force performance in director John Frankenheimer's (*The Manchurian Candidate*) critically acclaimed thriller about a man who buys a new identity and pays a terrifying price. John Randolph stars as a middle-aged banker, Arthur Hamilton, who, summoned by a mysterious corporation, undergoes plastic surgery and emerges as handsome bohemian artist Tony Wilson (Hudson). With nightmarish (Oscar-nominated) cinematography by James Wong Howe.

VHS: S31145. $79.95.

Laser: Letterboxed. **LD76340. $39.99.**

John Frankenheimer, USA, 1966, 107 mins.

The Secret of Santa Vittoria

Anthony Quinn and Anna Magnani star in this hectic comedy about the love of wine. A tiny Italian village does its best to hide its prized possession, a million bottles of wine, from the Nazis. This film has all the elements of a fast-paced farce with plenty of opportunity for a little alcoholic inspiration. Quinn is the central agent of this comic turn, beginning as little more than a helpless alcoholic and ending as hero.

VHS: S27577. $19.98.

Stanley Kramer, USA, 1969, 139 mins.

September Affair

Talk about your lucky breaks. When a married man and an unmarried female pianist discover they have been listed as dead in a plane crash, they decide to continue their romantic adventure in Florence, Italy. Joseph Cotten and Joan Fontaine are the forbidden lovers who enjoy classical music and each other. With Jessica Tandy and Francoise Rosay.

VHS: S08272. $24.95.

Laser: LD75255. $34.98.

William Dieterle, USA, 1959, 105 mins.

Seven Days in May

A chiller with its subject an attempt to overthrow the U.S. government by military coup. Kirk Douglas, Fredric March, Ava Gardner, Edmund O'Brien and Burt Lancaster star.

VHS: S04396. $19.98.

Laser: LD76997. $34.98.

John Frankenheimer, USA, 1964, 118 mins.

Seven Faces of Dr. Lao

Tony Randall plays six roles in this western fantasy about a traveling circus that has the power to alter lives. Randall plays the ancient Dr. Lao as well as Pan, Medusa, Merlin, Apolonius and the Abominable Snowman. Special effects won an Oscar. With Barbara Eden and Arthur O'Connell.

VHS: S03109. $19.98.

Laser: LD72154. $34.98.

George Pal, USA, 1964, 100 mins.

Seven Sinners

A sexy singer called Bijou Blanche (Marlene Dietrich) is also nicknamed the naval "Destroyer." She quickly seduces a young navy Lieutenant played by John Wayne. A jealous suitor would keep these young lovers apart, but Bijou Blanche proves her resolve by staying true to the man she loves.

VHS: S22186. $14.98.

Tay Garnett, USA, 1940, 87 mins.

The Seventh Cross

1936. Hitler's stormtroopers comb the countryside. George Heisler (Spencer Tracy) barely keeps one step ahead, running from town to town, escaping the fate that awaits him. He is finally aided by a friendly farmer (Hume Cronyn) and his gentle wife (Jessica Tandy). Fred Zinnemann's feature film directorial debut.

VHS: S15018. $19.98.

Fred Zinnemann, USA, 1944, 112 mins.

The Seventh Dawn

Action-packed adventure as an American guerrilla fighter (William Holden), now a wealthy plantation owner, tries to convince his former comrade to stop a terrorist attack on the British. When he cannot, the authorities arrest his beautiful mistress (Capucine) on a charge of high treason. He is offered
a deal he can't afford to resist. Susannah York is featured.

VHS: S28491. $19.98.

Lewis Gilbert, USA, 1964, 123 mins.

The Shadow of Silk Lennox

Lon Chaney, Jr., Dean Benton and Jack Mulhall star in this engaging story of a troubled nightclub owner. His world begins to crumble when he is fingered by an undercover G-man.

VHS: S26879. $24.95.

Ray Kirkwood, USA, 1935, 60 mins.

The Shadow of the Eagle

John Wayne stars as a daredevil pilot out to discover the identity of the criminal genius, the Eagle, who threatens corporation execs through skywriting. This 12-chapter serial has the background of a traveling carnival and lots of thrills. With Pat O'Malley and Little Billy the midget.

VHS: S06337. $24.95.

Ford Beebe, USA, 1932, 226 mins.

Shame (Not Wanted)

Ida Lupino produced and co-wrote the script for this film about the once taboo subject of unwed mothers. Ostracism and disillusionment still greet young women who face childbirth and parenthood alone. This earlier film is a revealing example of how things have changed and yet stayed the same.

VHS: S23903. $29.95.

Elmer Clifton, USA, 1949, 94 mins.

She

Lavish sets and a score by Max Steiner are two features that should have helped propel this film to success like that garnered by producer Merian C. Cooper's earlier film, *King Kong*. Two explorers, Randolph Scott and Nigel Bruce, find a goddess living beneath the frozen Arctic, She Who Must Be Obeyed. This adventure film has great 1930's style. Based on H. Rider Haggard's novel.

VHS: S26457. $24.95.

Irving Pichel/Lansing C. Holden, USA, 1935, 95 mins.

Shenandoah

James Stewart gives a great performance as a Virginia farmer during the Civil War who opposes both slavery and warfare until his son is captured and Stewart must act.

VHS: S02740. $19.95.

Laser: LD70078. $34.95.

Andrew V. McLaglen, USA, 1965, 106 mins.

Shining Hour

Director Frank Borzage directs this dramatic tale of four people caught in a web of frustrated passion and family discord. Joan Crawford stars as the night club dancer who marries one brother only to find out she may prefer his younger sibling. With Robert Young, Melvyn Douglas, Fay Bainter, Hattie McDaniel and Margaret Sullavan as the self-sacrificing Judy. Humorist Ogden Nash co-wrote the screenplay.

VHS: S16454. $19.98.

Frank Borzage, USA, 1938, 77 mins.

Ship of Fools

Based on Katherine Anne Porter's acclaimed novel, the interlocking stories tell of passengers on a ship sailing from Mexico to pre-Hitler Germany. With Simone Signoret, Michael Dunn, Vivien Leigh, Lee Marvin and others.

VHS: S07513. $19.95.

Stanley Kramer, USA, 1965, 149 mins.

Shock

Vincent Price stars in this thriller about a group of killers who have to silence a girl who witnessed one of their crimes. With Lynn Bari and Frank Latimore.

VHS: S07365. $19.95.

Alfred Werker, USA, 1946, 70 mins.

The Shopworn Angel

In this remake of the 1928 Richard Wallace film, Margaret Sullavan plays a beautiful showgirl who changes the life of an innocent young soldier (James Stewart) on his way to the war. Waldo Salt's screenplay is adapted from the play by Dana Burnet. With Walter Pidgeon, Hattie McDaniel and Sam Levene.

VHS: S20412. $29.98.

H.C. Potter, USA, 1938, 85 mins.

Show Them No Mercy

A young couple and their baby are kidnapped by thugs and eventually rescued by the FBI. A lively crime-thriller starring Cesar Romero, Rochelle Hudson and Bruce Cabot.

VHS: S13611. $19.98.

George Marshall, USA, 1935, 76 mins.

Shriek in the Night

An absorbing "B" picture starring Ginger Rogers before her roles with Fred Astaire. The story involves the mystery death of a respected philanthropist who plummets from his balcony.

VHS: S01877. $29.95.

Albert Ray, USA, 1933, 92 mins.

The Silver Horde

Jean Arthur, Joel McCrea and Evelyn Brent star in this classic film about a down-on-his-luck miner. He becomes involved in the salmon business, but his spoiled fiancee provides an unexpected complication—her father is an investor in a competing and crooked cannery.

VHS: S22599. $19.95.

George Archainbaud, USA, 1930, 80 mins.

The Sin of Madelon Claudet

A first-rate sobber about a mother who must give up everything so that her illegitimate son will have a good life. Helen Hayes won an Academy Award for her tragic portrayal of this woman who pays such a terrible price for the choices she is forced to make in her life.

VHS: S13568. $19.98.

Edgar Selwyn, USA, 1931, 74 mins.

Singapore

Fred MacMurray and Ava Gardner are the perfect pair for this melodramatic mix of an exotic smuggler and a seemingly hopeless love affair. MacMurray is a jewel smuggler who hid some contraband pearls in Singapore. He is also drawn to Singapore because it is where he left the memory of his beloved fiancee (Gardner), killed in an air raid. When he returns to collect his fortune, there is a startling surprise reunion when he discovers that Gardner is in fact alive, although she is afflicted by a loss of memory and married to another man (Roland Culver). Includes the original theatrical trailer.

VHS: S27354. $14.98.

John Brahm, USA, 1947, 79 mins.

Sins of the Children

Louis Mann, Robert Montgomery and Francis X. Bushman star in this early sound film. Mann and Bushman play a father and son team who go off for a two-year vacation. While they explore drier climes, the father's business partner writes the vacationing man off as a failure.

VHS: S27885. $19.98.

Sam Wood, USA, 1930, 86 mins.

Sirocco

Humphrey Bogart as a gun-runner in Damascus caught in a web of mystery, romance and intrigue. With Lee J. Cobb, Zero Mostel.

VHS: S02604. $19.95.

Curtis Bernhardt, USA, 1951, 98 mins.

The Sisters

Anatole Litvak's expansive tale crosscuts between three sisters, Bette Davis, Anita Louise, and Jane Bryan, and their various romantic entanglements, betrayals and difficulties. The primary story concerns Davis and her philandering husband, Errol Flynn, caught in San Francisco during the 1906 earthquake. With Ian Hunter, Donald Crisp and Beulah Bondi.

VHS: S17335. $19.98.

Anatole Litvak, USA, 1938, 99 mins.

Sixteen Fathoms Deep

Lon Chaney Jr. is billed under his real name, Creighton Chaney, in this early Monogram underwater saga. The dangers of the deep are pitted against those bold enough to discover its secrets. With Sally O'Neil and Maurice Black. Not to be confused with the 1948 remake that also featured Chaney in the cast.

VHS: S04032. $29.95.

Armand Schaefer, USA, 1933, 57 mins.

Skyjacked

Jet-propelled excitement powers this intense, riveting thriller that has drama, intrigue and an all-star cast, including Charlton Heston, Yvette Mimieux, James Brolin and Walter Pidgeon.

VHS: S31842. $19.98.

John Guillermin, USA, 1972, 102 mins.

Skyscraper Souls

A gritty melodrama about passion and greed concerns a ruthless real estate developer (Warren William) who manipulates markets and personalities in order to build a 100-story office building as he tries to balance his personal life, his wife, his lover and the young woman employed by his office. With Maureen O'Sullivan, Hedda Hopper and Anita Page.

VHS: S18130. $19.98.

Edgar Selwyn, USA, 1932, 99 mins.

The Slender Thread
Anne Bancroft takes an overdose of sleeping pills and phones the crisis clinic for help. It's up to volunteer Sidney Poitier to keep her on the line until the police can trace the call.
VHS: S16457. $14.95.
Sydney Pollack, USA, 1965, 98 mins.

Slightly Honorable
This murder mystery spoof weaves a funny and suspenseful tale around a tough young lawyer who steps up to put an end to Vincent Cushing (Edward Arnold) and his powerful political machine. With Pat O'Brien and Broderick Crawford.
VHS: S13853. $19.95.
Tay Garnett, USA, 1940, 75 mins.

Smash-Up: The Story of a Woman
This taut drama, with a script by John Howard Lawson, tells the story of a night club singer and her descent into the nightmare of alcoholism. With Susan Hayward in her first Oscar-nominated performance, Lee Bowman, Marsh Hunt, and Eddie Albert.
VHS: S34197. $14.95.
Stuart Heisler, USA, 1947, 103 mins.

Smilin' Through
A lavish romantic remake about the strange pattern of events that attends three generations of people caught up in the passion and murky circumstances behind the death of a Victorian woman on the afternoon of her wedding. With Norma Shearer, Leslie Howard, Fredric March and Ralph Forbes.
VHS: S19572. $19.98.
Sidney Franklin, USA, 1932, 97 mins.

Snake Pit
Olivia de Havilland is brilliant as a woman committed to a mental hospital who is pronounced fit to leave before her consultant thinks she's ready.
VHS: S18103. $19.98.
Laser: CLV. LD72113. $49.98.
Anatole Litvak, USA, 1948, 108 mins.

Snows of Kilimanjaro
Based on Ernest Hemingway's short story, Gregory Peck stars as Harry Street, a renowned writer who reflects on his life and loves while lying wounded on the slopes of the East African mountain Kilimanjaro. With Susan Hayward, Ava Gardner, Leo G. Carroll.
VHS: S01223. $19.95.
Henry King, USA, 1952, 109 mins.

So Ends Our Night
Set against the dark reign of Nazi oppression, John Cromwell's film is an excellent adaptation of Erich Maria Remarque's novel *Flotsam*, about a German refugee's escape and attempted flight. With Fredric March, Glenn Ford, Erich von Stroheim and Frances Dee.
VHS: S18032. $29.95.
John Cromwell, USA, 1941, 117 mins.

So Proudly We Hail
Claudette Colbert is joined by Paulette Goddard, Veronica Lake and Barbara Britton in this wartime drama about nurses in the Pacific. They suffer through the worst of the Second World War in order to help and comfort wounded soldiers, even as they combat their own demoralization and fear.
VHS: S24028. $14.98.
Mark Sandrich, USA, 1943, 126 mins.

Soldier of Fortune
When Susan Hayward's photographer husband disappears in Communist China, she turns to American smuggler Clark Gable to bring Gene Barry back alive. He agrees but demands her company as part of the payment. With Michael Rennie as a representative of the Hong Kong police department. Also Alex D'Arcy, Tom Tully, Richard Loo, Victor Sen Yung and Jack Kruschen as assorted Fragrent Harbor riffraff. A love story with a mercenary heart. Based on the novel by Ernest Gann.
VHS: S12520. $39.98.
Edward Dmytryk, USA, 1955, 96 mins.

The Solid Gold Cadillac
Judy Holliday sparkles in this romantic comedy about a seemingly innocent blond stockholder who uncovers corruption in the upper reaches of her company. Not only does she manage to save the firm, but she also catches the eye of a lonely but successful tycoon. Also features Paul Douglas and Fred Clark.
VHS: S26446. $19.95.
Richard Quine, USA, 1956, 99 mins.

Somebody up There Likes Me
Paul Newman stars in this film bio of boxer Rocky Graziano, from his youth as street hoodlum in NYC through his Army service to the height of this fighting career. A fine lead performance. Also in the cast are Pier Angeli, Eileen Heckart, Sal Mineo, Robert Loggia, and Steve McQueen in a bit part. B&W.
VHS: S07974. $19.98.
Robert Wise, USA, 1956, 113 mins.

Something in the Wind
Deanna Durbin stars in this comical story of a young girl trying to swindle her family's fortune—with good reason. Donald O'Connor is her singing and dancing ally, who helps her to realize that success can often be the best revenge. Includes theatrical trailer. With John Dall.
VHS: S32973. $19.98.
Irving Pichel, USA, 1947, 89 mins.

Somewhere I'll Find You
A romantic triangle set against a World War II backdrop. Clark Gable is a foreign correspondent pursued by ambitious journalist Lana Turner, who eventually settles for Gable's younger, more secure brother (Robert Sterling). With Van Johnson, Keenan Wynn and Frank Faylen.
VHS: S18663. $19.98.
Wesley Ruggles, USA, 1942, 117 mins.

Son of Ali Baba
In this *Arabian Nights* tale, Tony Curtis is a charismatic hero locked in a deadly confrontation with the evil Caliph, who exploits beautiful princess Piper Laurie to obtain Ali Baba's gold shipment. With Susan Cabot and Victor Joy.
VHS: S19312. $14.98.
Kurt Neumann, USA, 1952, 75 mins.

Son of Fury
Tyrone Power leads a stellar cast on an 18th-century adventure to the South Seas with Gene Tierney, Frances Farmer, Roddy McDowall and John Carradine. When Power is rejected by his rich uncle, he sets off to plot his revenge, in a beautiful tropical paradise.
VHS: S21069. $19.98.
John Cromwell, USA, 1942, 98 mins.

Son of Monte Cristo
A big-budget Hollywood production full of last-minute rescues, clashing sabres and beautifully detailed sets, featuring Clayton Moore, Louis Hayward, Joan Bennett and George Sanders.
VHS: S03078. $19.95.
Rowland V. Lee, USA, 1940, 105 mins.

Song of Love
Katharine Hepburn delivers an unforgettable performance as world-famous concert pianist Clara Wieck. A story of tragedy and eventual triumph, *Song of Love* includes Wieck's encounters with some of the greatest musicians and composers of her time—Franz Liszt, Johannes Brahms and Robert Schumann.
VHS: S15019. $19.98.
Clarence Brown, USA, 1947, 120 mins.

Sorry, Wrong Number
Barbara Stanwyck plays an invalid heiress whose husband is being blackmailed by William Conrad. One day she overhears a plot to murder a woman on a crossed-wire telephone connection. By the time she figures out she is the intended victim it could be too late. With Burt Lancaster, Wendell Corey and Ed Begley Sr. Based on the radio play by Lucille Fletcher.
VHS: S10833. $19.95.
Laser: LD75260. $34.98.
Anatole Litvak, USA, 1948, 89 mins.

Souls at Sea
Gary Cooper, George Raft and Frances Dee star in this seafaring drama about men who oppose slavery. Cooper and Raft become allies against this unjust practice and the result is a rare combination of pathos, humor and action.
VHS: S28402. $14.98.
Henry Hathaway, USA, 1964, 93 mins.

Spawn of the North
Henry Fonda is Jim Kimmerlee, an honest fisherman forced by Russian pirates to become a one-man vigilante fighting injustices inflicted upon the Alaskan wilderness, in this wild-eyed "western of the north." Academy Award winner for special photographic and sound effects. With Dorothy Lamour and George Raft.
VHS: S33708. $14.98.
Henry Hathaway, USA, 1938, 110 mins.

Speed Reporter
Richard Talmadge stars as a crackerjack reporter out to smash a bogus reform league. With Luana Walters and Richard Cramer.
VHS: S21556. $24.95.
Bernard B. Ray, USA, 1936, 58 mins.

The Spencer Tracy Collection
Three of Spencer Tracy's films are bound in one collection: John Sturges' offbeat 1955 western, *Bad Day at Black Rock*, his Oscar-winning performance in Victor Fleming's 1937 *Captains Courageous*, and his award-winning work in Norman Taurog's 1938 *Boys Town*.
VHS: S17305. $49.92.

The Sphinx
Lionel Atwill stars in a dual role in this Monogram murder mystery. He plays twin brothers, one a deaf mute, the other a criminal mastermind. When a hotshot reporter and a society editor see through the deception, the brothers are forced to act. With Paul Fix and "Gabby" Hayes.
VHS: S04030. $29.95.
Phil Rosen, USA, 1933, 64 mins.

Splendor
Miriam Hopkins, David Niven and Joel McCrea star in this powerful classic. High drama erupts when a spirited Southern beauty marries into one of New York's "first families" and is ruthlessly sacrificed in the battle to preserve their crumbling grandeur. "A major entertainment achievement...outstanding performances" (*Chicago Daily News*).
VHS: S31808. $14.95.
Elliott Nugent, USA, 1935, 76 mins.

Splendor in the Grass
Natalie Wood and Warren Beatty (in his screen debut) star as two teenage lovers ripped apart by the repressive mentality of their 1920s Kansas town.
VHS: S11617. $19.95.
Laser: LD71414. $39.98.
Elia Kazan, USA, 1961, 124 mins.

Split Second
Dick Powell's first effort as a director is a taut thriller about escaped convicts who overtake a nearly deserted town and hold its residents captive.
Laser: LD75262. $34.98.
Dick Powell, USA, 1953, 86 mins.

The Spoilers
The fourth version of the Rex Beach Klondike adventure about two roguish adventurers, Randolph Scott and John Wayne, fighting over Alaskan landscapes and a sexy, exotic saloon performer (Marlene Dietrich). "It's a well-packaged mixture of saloon brawls, romance and adventure; much [of the movie] was filmed as a silent" (Leslie Halliwell). With Margaret Lindsay, Harry Carey and Richard Barthelmess.
VHS: S19079. $14.98.
Ray Enright, USA, 1942, 87 mins.

Spy Who Came in from the Cold
Richard Burton is a disillusioned and weary secret agent in this serious espionage drama taken from the novel by John Le Carre. A fine cast under the direction of Martin Ritt includes Claire Bloom, Oskar Werner, Sam Wanamaker, Cyril Cusack, Peter Van Eyck and Michael Hordern. A gripping and realistic thriller. B&W.
VHS: S07520. $19.95.
Laser: LD75263. $34.98.
Martin Ritt, USA, 1966, 105 mins.

St. Benny the Dip
Comic drama about three con men hiding from the authorities by the director of numerous grade Z movies, Edgar G. Ulmer. Starring Dick Haymes and Roland Young.
VHS: S01245. $29.95.
Edgar G. Ulmer, USA, 1951, 81 mins.

Stage Door Canteen
An all-star cast including Tallulah Bankhead, Katharine Hepburn, George Raft, Ethel Merman, Merle Oberon, Harpo Marx and George Jessel in this romantic drama of a soldier boy and a canteen hostess.
VHS: S03260. $19.95.
Frank Borzage, USA, 1943, 135 mins.

Stanley and Livingstone
Spencer Tracy lends his abilities to this Hollywood version of the famous reporter sent to find a missing Scottish missionary in Africa. You don't have to presume with Sir Cedric Hardwicke as the latter half of the title role. A grand adventure film with Walter Brennan, Richard Greene, Charles Coburn, Henry Hull and Nancy Kelly as the invented romantic interest. Some of the footage was shot in Africa.
VHS: S12517. $39.98.
Henry King, USA, 1939, 101 mins.

The Star
An impulsive variation on Billy Wilder's *Sunset Boulevard* stars Bette Davis as a faded, one-time award winning actress who must confront the bitter truth her career is over and consider the implications of a new life and identity. With Sterling Hayden, Natalie Wood, and Warner Anderson.
VHS: S15932. $19.98.
Stuart Heisler, USA, 1952, 89 mins.

A Star Is Born
Janet Gaynor and Fredric March star in the first version of *A Star Is Born*, the story of a young girl whose career is on the rise while that of her husband is on the wane. Adolphe Menjou, May Robson and Andy Devine co-star.
VHS: S18187. $24.95.
Laser: LD70684. $39.98.
William Wellman, USA, 1937, 112 mins.

Steel Claw
A one-handed Marine captain leads a mission into the interior of the Philippines during early days of WWII to rescue an American general held captive there. Beset by jungle and the enemy, the group sets off on what becomes an amazing adventure. With George Montgomery and Charito Luna.
VHS: S34183. $19.95.
George Montgomery, USA, 1961, 96 mins.

Stella Dallas
Barbara Stanwyck has the title role in this moving soap opera about an unrefined but socially ambitious woman who sacrifices all so that her daughter can benefit from her mistakes. Anne Shirley is the perfect daughter with the great future. With John Boles, Alan Hale and Barbara O'Neil. Based on the novel by Olive Higgins Prouty. Remade in 1990 with Bette Midler.
VHS: S02928. $19.98.
King Vidor, USA, 1937, 105 mins.

A Stolen Life
A true showcase for the talents of Bette Davis as a woman living in New England, who deceives her husband by exchanging identities with her dead twin. Glenn Ford stars as the husband.
VHS: S11623. $19.95.
Curtis Bernhardt, USA, 1946, 107 mins.

The Story of Alexander Graham Bell
Don Ameche, Loretta Young and Henry Fonda star in this biographical blockbuster about the famous inventor. The sets and costumes make this a pretty lavish production, but the scene where Alexander and his assistant realize that the telephone works is the most unforgettable element of the film.
VHS: S28072. $19.98.
Irving Cummings, USA, 1939, 97 mins.

The Story of Esther Costello
A wealthy woman (Joan Crawford) rehabilitates a deaf-mute child (Heather Sears) and is swindled by her devious husband (Rossano Brazzi). Powerful melodrama featuring one of Crawford's finest-yet lesser-known—screen performances. Take it from Joan herself: "This was my last really top picture, and frankly, if I think I deserved an Oscar for *Mildred Pierce*, I deserved two for *Esther Costello*." With Lee Patterson, Ron Randell and Denis O'Dea.
VHS: S30779. $19.95.
David Miller, USA, 1957, 102 mins.

Story of Louis Pasteur
The life story and struggles of the legendary French scientist receive heroic treatment in this engrossing adaptation, which features a brilliant (and Oscar-winning) performance. Writers Sheridan Gibney and Pierre Collings also received an Oscar.
VHS: S11550. $19.98.
William Dieterle, USA, 1936, 85 mins.

Stranded
When a courageous teacher and her students are stranded in a blizzard, Miss Enter uses every bit of her skill to keep them alive. But as their food and firewood run out, it becomes apparent that the snowplow sent to rescue them may not arrive on time. Stars Bette Davis and Claudia Bryar.
VHS: S16743. $14.95.
Allen Miner, USA, 1957, 30 mins.

The Strange Affair of Uncle Harry
George Sanders takes drastic steps when his domineering sisters interfere with his romance in this engrossing and melodramatic film noir. With Geraldine Fitzgerald and Ella Raines.
VHS: S14325. $19.98.
Laser: CLV. **LD72035. $29.98.**
Robert Siodmak, USA, 1945, 80 mins.

Strange Cargo
Clark Gable and Joan Crawford star in this offbeat drama about a motley group of convicts who escape from Devil's Island. The catch in this allegorical tale is that one of the passengers is showing strong signs of being a Christ-like figure. With Ian Hunter, Paul Lukas, Albert Dekker and Peter Lorre as M'sier Pig. Condemned by the Catholic League of Decency upon release.
VHS: S11729. $19.98.
Frank Borzage, USA, 1940, 105 mins.

The Strange Door
Charles Laughton is a haughty and dangerous nobleman who, together with his servant, Boris Karloff, terrorizes his own family. While his brother is locked away, Laughton's character faces an unforseen threat from a prospective addition to the family, his niece's beloved. He may be the one who gets beyond the strange door.
VHS: S29520. $14.98.
Joseph Pevney, USA, 1951, 81 mins.

Strange Illusion
In this bizarre B-movie updating of *Hamlet* by poverty row director Edgar Ulmer, a boy (James Lyndon) dreams of his father's death and his widowed mother (Sally Eilers) being wooed by a fast-talking schemer (Warren William)—which all comes true.
VHS: S10962. $19.99.
Edgar G. Ulmer, USA, 1945, 80 mins.

Strange Love of Martha Ivers
A complex mystery featuring Van Heflin, Barbara Stanwyck, Kirk Douglas and Lizabeth Scott in which Stanwyck is tied to her husband through his knowledge of a crime she committed a long time ago.
VHS: S05999. $24.95.
Laser: CLV. **LD72065. $34.95.**
Lewis Milestone, USA, 1946, 117 mins.

The Strange Love of Molly Louvain
Ann Dvorak finds herself an unwed mother in trouble. Her charms lead her from one troublesome man to the next until finally the law must intervene. Even a cynical reporter, Lee Tracy, cannot resist her, though he knows the whole story of crime, infidelity and heartache behind this young woman. Only before the adoption of the pre-Production Code could a theme like this be explored in motion pictures.
VHS: S20834. $19.98.
Michael Curtiz, USA, 1932, 72 mins.

The Strange One
A gripping, suspenseful drama about life in a prestigious Southern military academy lorded over by a sadistic upperclassman, featuring the knock-out screen debuts of Ben Gazzara and George Peppard. With James Olson and Julie Wilson. Based on the novel by Calder Willingham. "A cleverly constructed thriller" (*Time Magazine*).
VHS: S32211. $19.95.
Jack Garfein, USA, 1957, 98 mins.

Strange Woman
Hedy Lamarr stars as a sultry and vicious man-killer in this thriller from that legendary master of B grade cinema, Edgar G. Ulmer. Also starring George Sanders, Louis Hayward and June Lockhart.
VHS: S14664. $29.95.
Edgar G. Ulmer, USA, 1946, 89 mins.

A Stranger in Town
Frank Morgan, Richard Carlson and Jean Rogers star in this dramatic film concerning a Supreme Court Justice. The judge decides he needs a vacation. Though His Honor expects to take it easy, he uncovers corruption in the small town where he sought only peace.
VHS: S27886. $19.98.
Roy Rowland, USA, 1943, 67 mins.

Strangers When We Meet
Kirk Douglas is a married architect involved with his beautiful married neighbor Kim Novak. Will this interfere with his building a hill-top home for writer Ernie Kovacs? A compelling and well acted drama of infidelity in California with Barbara Rush, Nancy Kovak and Walter Matthau. 117 mins.
VHS: S07675. $19.95.
Richard Quine, USA, 1960, 117 mins.

The Strangler
Victor Buono is a mama's boy living in Boston who goes off the deep end and starts strangling women all over the city. An atmospheric thriller starring David McLean and Ellen Corby.
VHS: S14792. $14.98.
Burt Topper, USA, 1964, 89 mins.

The Stratton Story
James Stewart plays the Chicago White Sox ace who refused to allow a tragic accident impair his prominent baseball career. The baseball scenes are remarkably authentic and exciting. Academy Award-winning screenplay by Douglas Morrow and Guy Trosper. With June Allyson, Frank Morgan, Agnes Moorehead and Bill Williams.
VHS: S19467. $19.98.
Sam Wood, USA, 1949, 106 mins.

Street Scene
Realistic account of life in NY tenements adapted from Elmer Rice's play with a score by Alfred Newman.
VHS: S02001. $24.95.
King Vidor, USA, 1931, 80 mins.

Street with No Name
Based on an actual FBI case of an agent uncovering the head of the city mob. Built around a psychopathic character similar to the one Richard Widmark created in *Kiss of Death*. Starring Widmark, Ed Begley, Mark Stevens and Lloyd Nolan.
VHS: S13614. $19.98.
William Keighley, USA, 1948, 93 mins.

Studs Lonigan
Gritty tale of life on Chicago's South Side in the 1920's features Frank Gorshin and an early appearance by Jack Nicholson.
VHS: S02115. $24.95.
Irving Lerner, USA, 1960, 96 mins.

The Subject Was Roses
Patricia Neal, Jack Alberston and Martin Sheen are superb as a family separated by a lifetime of domestic slights and grievances. Timmy (Sheen) gets out of the service after World War II and provokes a complex emotional response from his parents through a simple act of affection, one that could lead to reconciliation or destruction. Based on a Pulitzer-Prize winning play by Frank D. Gilroy.
VHS: S29501. $19.98.
Ulu Grosbard, USA, 1968, 107 mins.

Sudden Fear
Joan Crawford is an heiress, a successful playwright, and the toast of Broadway. Everything points to untold happiness when she meets the ideal man (Jack Palance). Things sour, however, when Crawford realizes that Palance is intent on murdering her and inheriting her fortune. Soon murder and revenge twist her perfect life into a nightmare. Gloria Grahame is also featured as the other woman.
VHS: S26993. $19.95.
Laser: LD75431. $39.99.
David Miller, USA, 1952, 111 mins.

Suddenly
Frank Sinatra heads a team of assassins who plan to gun down the President of the United States as he steps off the train in Suddenly, California, on his way to a fishing trip. It's up to local lawman Sterling Hayden to see that the Chief Exec has a pleasant vacation. Feature withdrawn for many years after JFK slaying.
VHS: S05078. $19.95.
Laser: Letterboxed. **LD75941. $34.95.**
Lewis Allen, USA, 1954, 77 mins.

Suddenly Last Summer
Elizabeth Taylor and Katharine Hepburn both won Oscars for their riveting performances in Tennessee Williams' classic story. When the beautiful Catherine (Taylor), committed to a mental institution, threatens to disrupt the eerily intimate relationship between her possessive Aunt Violet (Hepburn) and Violet's son, Sebastian, Violet tries to influence a young surgeon (Montgomery Clift) to lobotomize Catherine. Instead, the doctor helps Catherine uncover the truth about her cousin.
VHS: S01277. $19.95.
Joseph L. Mankiewicz, USA, 1959, 114 mins.

Suicide Battalion/Hell Squad
Two exciting WWII action films in one program! *Suicide Battalion*. American soldiers fighting behind enemy lines in the Philippines are ordered to destroy vital military documents left behind at an abandoned U.S. base. Stars Michael Connors, John Ashley, Jewell Lian and Russ Bender. Directed by Edward L Cahn. 1958, 64 mins. *Hell Squad*. Five American soldiers do their best to survive when they become lost in the Tunisian desert. It won't be easy with enemy patrols, planes and mine fields waiting around every sand dune. Stars Wally Campo, Brandon Carroll, Fred Galvin, Grey Stuart, Leon Schrier and Cecil Addis. Directed by Burt Topper. 1958, 79 mins.
VHS: S16407. $14.95.

Summer of '42
A young adolescent discovers love and sex by meeting a beautiful older war-bride in this light nostalgic film about pubescent boyhood. With Gary Grimes, Jerry Houser, and Jennifer O'Neill. Also, a beautiful Oscar-winning score by Michel Legrand.
VHS: S06309. $19.98.
Laser: LD74717. $34.98.
Robert Mulligan, USA, 1962, 102 mins.

A Summer Place
Romantic summer adventures of the idle rich on an island off the coast of Maine. Sandra Dee and Troy Donahue star in a story of "illicit" love that features "one of the best-known romantic songs in movie history." From the best-seller by Sloan Wilson and also starring Dorothy McGuire and Arthur Kennedy.
VHS: S12582. $19.98.
Laser: LD74742. $29.98.
Delmer Daves, USA, 1959, 130 mins.

Sunday in New York
Jane Fonda is a 22-year-old virgin lost in the wilds of the city that never sleeps—alone! With Cliff Robertson, Rod Taylor, Robert Culp, Jim Backus, and a score by Peter Nero.
VHS: S30536. $19.98.
Peter Tewksbury, USA, 1963, 105 mins.

Sundown
Gene Tierney stars as a native girl who uncovers a Nazi plot in Africa. To make sure the sun never sets on the British empire, Bruce Cabot, George Sanders, Harry Carey, Joseph Calleia and Reginald Gardner (one of whom is an enemy agent) try to keep a stiff upper lip and keep the region under control. Lots of action and tea.
VHS: S05069. $19.95.
Henry Hathaway, USA, 1941, 91 mins.

Sundowners
Robert Mitchum and Deborah Kerr as sheepherders in 1920's Australia. Attentive, beautiful care to pictorial detail, nominated for five Academy Awards. With Peter Ustinov and Glynis Johns.
VHS: S03010. $14.95.
Laser: LD74737. $39.98.
Fred Zinnemann, USA, 1960, 113 mins.

Sunrise at Campobello
This is a sincere look at the early life of Franklin Delano Roosevelt. His struggle against polio and return to politics is convincingly played by Ralph Bellamy from his Tony Award winning Broadway performance. Greer Garson stars as Eleanor, with Anne Shoemaker, Hume Cronyn and Jean Hagen. From the play by Dore Schary.
VHS: S16278. $19.98.
Laser: LD70049. $39.98.
Vincent J. Donehue, USA, 1960, 144 mins.

Supernatural
Carole Lombard stars along with Randolph Scott and Viviene Osborne in this engaging thriller about murder and possession. Lombard is an heiress who longs for contact with her dead brother. A spiritualist offers help but in fact has a completely different turn of events planned.
VHS: S26226. $19.98.
Victor Halperin, USA, 1933, 65 mins.

Surprise Package
When American gangster Yul Brenner is deported to Greece, he becomes attached to the crown jewels of a deposed king living in exile. With Mitzi Gaynor, George Coulouris, Eric Pohlmann, Warren Mitchell, Barry Foster and Noel Coward as King Pavel II. Coward also sings the title song in this caper comedy. Based on *A Gift from the Boys* by Art Buchwald.
VHS: S15891. $19.95.
Stanley Donen, USA/Great Britain, 1960, 100 mins.

Susan Lennox: Her Fall and Rise
Greta Garbo runs away from her brutal father, who wants to marry her off to farmer Alan Hale, only to find that handsome engineer Clark Gable rejects her love when he learns of her affair with a carnival owner. She then becomes a professional mistress while she waits for Clark to change his mind. Based on the novel by David Graham Phillips, who was later shot by a disgruntled reader for his depiction of women.
VHS: S13198. $19.98.
Robert Z. Leonard, USA, 1931, 84 mins.

Suzy
In their lone appearance together, Jean Harlow and Cary Grant star in this World War II-era tale about an American chorus girl marooned in London who turns up in Paris and falls for an enigmatic and charismatic playboy (Grant). With Franchot Tone, Lewis Stone and Benita Hume. Some startling aviation sequences, appropriated from the negative of the classic *Hell's Angels*. Written by Dorothy Parker.
VHS: S17782. $19.98.
George Fitzmaurice, USA, 1936, 93 mins.

Svengali
Although George Du Maurier's *Trilby* has been done several times, this 1931 version with John Barrymore stands as the classic against which the others are measured.
VHS: S01288. $24.95.
Archie Mayo, USA, 1931, 82 mins.

Swamp Fire
Johnny Weissmuller, the Olympic champion, is paired with Buster Crabbe in this heroic tale. When Weissmuller, a river boat captain, falls for a beautiful young woman, he must confront her wealthy and powerful father.
VHS: S25699. $19.95.
William H. Pine, USA, 1946, 69 mins.

The Swan
Charles Vidor's remake of *One Romantic Night* stars Grace Kelly as a mythical princess whose attraction to a charismatic crown prince (Alec Guinness) sets the dizzying, frantic plot of romance, fear and loss in motion. Based on the play by Ferenc Molnar. With Louis Jourdan, Agnes Moorehead, and Leo G. Carroll. This laser disc version also contains the short, *The Wedding in Monaco*.
Laser: LD71651. $39.98.
Charles Vidor, USA, 1956, 109 mins.

Sweet Bird of Youth
Paul Newman and Geraldine Page star in this Tennessee Williams drama of ambition, lust and faded glory. When a not-so-young stud hooks up with an aging movie star, he makes the mistake of revisiting his home town. The fine cast includes Shirley Knight, Rip Torn, Mildred Dunnock and Ed Begley, who won an Oscar for his role as the unforgiving town boss.
VHS: S11221. $19.95.
Laser: LD71178. $39.98.
Richard Brooks, USA, 1962, 120 mins.

Sweet Smell of Success
Burt Lancaster is J.J. Hunsecker, a ruthless and powerful New York columnist, and Tony Curtis is the press agent who will do anything to be in his good graces. Scripted by Clifford Odets and Ernest Lehman. A cult film that was quoted in *Diner*. With Martin Milner, Sam Levene and Barbara Nichols.
VHS: S07979. $19.98.
Laser: LD70689. $34.98.
Alexander Mackendrick, USA, 1957, 96 mins.

The Swimmer
Based on the short story by John Cheever, with Burt Lancaster as the middle-aged swimmer who hops from pool to pool on his way home during an afternoon and evokes the past at each pool.
VHS: S04398. $19.95.
Frank Perry, USA, 1968, 94 mins.

Sword of Venus
A splashy, swashbuckling film about the exploits of the son of the famous Monte Christo. Starring Robert Clarke and Dan O'Herlihy.
VHS: S14665. $29.95.
Harold Daniels, USA, 1953, 72 mins.

T-Men
Classic underworld thriller from director Anthony Mann. Centered around a sting operation run by the U.S. Treasury Department, T-men go undercover to infiltrate the inner workings of the Vantucci crime family's counterfeiting ring. A riveting, realistic and atmospheric portrait of the West Coast underworld of the 1940s.
VHS: S28643. $29.95.
Anthony Mann, USA, 1947, 92 mins.

A Tale of Two Cities
For those of you who didn't know, it was the best of times, it was the worst of times and *this* often filmed classic of Charles Dickens stars Ronald Colman. The two cities are Paris and London and the time is the French Revolution. Splendid MGM production. With Basil Rathbone, Elizabeth Allan and Edna May Oliver.
VHS: S02986. $24.95.
Laser: LD71682. $39.98.
Jack Conway, USA, 1935, 121 mins.

Tales of Manhattan
In addition to W.C. Fields, who appears in a hilarious, classic sequence, Ben Hecht's screenplay is brought to life in this episodic movie by a variety of movie idols, including Rita Hayworth, Ginger Rogers, Henry Fonda, Cesar Romero, Charles Laughton, Paul Robeson and more. It is built around a tailcoat that has unexpected effects on a series of different characters.
VHS: S27607. $19.98.
Laser: LD75921. $39.98.
Julien Duvivier, USA, 1942, 106 mins.

Tall Story
Anthony Perkins is a college basketball star who welcomes disaster when he marries a young coed. Don't miss Jane Fonda's hilarious film debut!
VHS: S15991. $19.98.
Joshua Logan, USA, 1960, 91 mins.

Tamango
American expatriate John Berry, a blacklisted director, spent much of the last five decades in Europe. In this frenetic melodrama, with a curious affinity for racial and class exploitation, Curt Jurgens is a sinister Dutch slave trader in love with a beautiful black woman (Dorothy Dandridge) who's trying to suppress a slave revolt led by Tamango (Alex Cressan). With Jean Servais, Roger Hanin and Guy Mairesse.
VHS: S18254. $29.95.
John Berry, USA, 1959, 98 mins.

Tammy and the Bachelor
Debbie Reynolds introduced the Mississippi riverboat girl in this Ross Hunter production about the headstrong woman who falls for a wealthy Southern aristocrat (Leslie Nielsen) and raises his consciousness about class and ideas. With Fay Wray, Sidney Blackmer, Mildred Natwick and Mala Powers.
VHS: S17947. $14.98.
Joseph Pevney, USA, 1957, 89 mins.

Tammy and the Doctor
Sandra Dee is a Southern charmer who makes the pilgrimage to a Los Angeles hospital to begin her training as a nurse, where she promptly unnerves a young intern (Peter Fonda) and throws medicine and hospital rules upside down. With MacDonald Carey, Beulah Bondi, Margaret Lindsay and Reginald Owen.
VHS: S17948. $14.98.
Harry Keller, USA, 1963, 88 mins.

Tango
Franklin Pangborn is featured in this melodrama starring Hermann Bing and Marie Prevost. A chorus girl falls for a rich guy, a setup certain to lead to heartache. Based on a novel by Vida Hurst, this film also features some interesting dance routines.
VHS: S23790. $24.95.
Phil Rosen, USA, 1936, 66 mins.

Taras Bulba
Yul Brenner and Tony Curtis star in this tale of 16th century Cossack life in the Ukraine. Shot on location in Argentina, this adventure of hard riding and mighty fighters is based on the novel by Nikolai Gogol. With Christine Kaufmann.
VHS: S04214. $19.98.
Laser: LD72133. $39.98.
J. Lee Thompson, USA, 1962, 122 mins.

Targets
The stunning film-making debut of critic-turned-director Peter Bogdanovich about a psychotic sniper and an aging horror movie star (Boris Karloff in his final film).
VHS: S03286. $49.95.
Peter Bogdanovich, USA, 1968, 92 mins.

Tarzan, The Ape Man
The first great Tarzan movie stars Johnny Weissmuller and Maureen O'Sullivan as the King of the Apes and Jane, the beautiful English girl who leaves civilization behind to become his lover. An exciting and romantic family classic.
VHS: S14308. $19.98.
W.S. Van Dyke, USA, 1932, 99 mins.

Task Force
Delmer Daves' well-made, compelling film balances personal drama, the struggles of Naval officer Gary Cooper, and, within a larger historical purpose, the evolution of the aircraft carrier. The narrative is buttressed with authentic combat footage. With Walter Brennan and Jane Wyatt.
VHS: S19493. $19.98.
Delmer Daves, USA, 1949, 116 mins.

Teahouse of the August Moon
Marlon Brando stars as Sakini, an Okinawan interpreter for the U.S. military in this postwar comedy about tradition, progress and red tape. Glen Ford is the officer in charge of building a schoolhouse but the villagers would really prefer a new teahouse instead. Based on the Broadway play by John Patrick. With Eddie Albert, Paul Ford, Harry Morgan, Machiko Kyo and Nijiko Kiyokawa as Miss Higa Jiga.
VHS: S12528. $19.98.
Laser: LD71145. $39.98.
Daniel Mann, USA, 1956, 123 mins.

Test Pilot
Clark Gable, Myrna Loy and Spencer Tracy headline this tense drama of the hazardous exploits of a test pilot and their effect on the lives of those who love him.
VHS: S15262. $19.98.
Victor Fleming, USA, 1938, 118 mins.

Texas Carnival
Esther Williams and Red Skelton play a carnival sideshow team mistaken for a pair of Texas multimillionaires at a swank resort hotel in this lively musical. Skelton proves his rank among the screens greatest clowns in an hilarious slapstick performance.
VHS: S16610. $19.98.
Charles Walters, USA, 1951, 97 mins.

That Brennan Girl
An unaccountable, Freudian thriller that examines the consequences of a mother's oppressive behavior on her daughter (Mona Freeman). The plot studies the woman's subsequent coldness and distrust, until her charismatic second husband (James Dunn) helps her recover. With William Marshall, June Duprez and Frank Jenks.
VHS: S18938. $19.95.
Alfred Santell, USA, 1946, 95 mins.

That Certain Woman
Edmund Goulding (*Dark Victory*) directs this fresh, operatic melodrama based on his earlier work *The Trespasser*, about a gangster's widow (Bette Davis) who falls in love with a socially prominent young man (Henry Fonda), while trying to conceal her past.
VHS: S17336. $19.98.
Edmund Goulding, USA, 1937, 96 mins.

That Forsyte Woman
Greer Garson and Errol Flynn in the sumptuous screen version of John Galsworthy's tale of moneyed elite in the Victorian Era.
VHS: S15655. $19.98.
Compton Bennett, USA, 1949, 114 mins.

There Goes Barder
Eddie Constantine plays a sleazy con-man who's hired by a shady ship owner to be a security agent. Suspenseful spy thriller co-starring May Britt. USA, 1964.
VHS: S15364. $29.95.

They Call It Sin
A young Kansas farm girl, Loretta Young, is a composer who finds herself bewildered by the big bad city. Her musical career is about to take off when an old lover re-emerges and destroys her big chance. Tragedy follows but ultimately true love wins out in this romantic melodrama filmed before the pre-Production Code went into effect.
VHS: S20835. $19.98.
Thornton Freeland, USA, 1932, 75 mins.

They Drive by Night
Humphrey Bogart in one of his finest roles! *They Drive by Night* is a riveting social drama about the trucking trade—fast, hard, bitter, and brilliantly realized. The stunning cast includes George Raft, Ann Sheridan and, of course, Ida Lupino.
VHS: S01322. $19.98.
Laser: LD71149. $34.98.
Raoul Walsh, USA, 1940, 97 mins.

They Made Me a Criminal
John Garfield gives a dynamic yet sensitive portrayal of a fugitive boxer who thinks he has murdered a man. Ann Sheridan is the woman who gives him a second chance. Also stars Claude Rains and the Dead End Kids.
VHS: S01637. $24.95.
Busby Berkeley, USA, 1939, 92 mins.

They Meet Again
A doctor attempts to vindicate a bank teller accused of filching $3,000 in this entry of Hersholt's *Dr. Christian* series. With Jean Hersholt, Dorothy Lovett, Robert Baldwin, Barton Yarborough, Anne Bennett and an entertaining jive number by Leon Tyler.
VHS: S05699. $29.95.
Erle C. Kenton, USA, 1941, 67 mins.

They Met in Bombay
Clark Gable and Rosalind Russell star as two thieves who steal each other's hearts in this sparkling international caper. A Japanese invasion gives Russell second thoughts about a life of crime—and gives Gable a chance to be a hero.
VHS: S20563. $19.98.
Clarence Brown, USA, 1941, 93 mins.

They Shoot Horses, Don't They?
Set in 1932, this film follows the heart-wrenching Depression-era story of desperate participants in a dance marathon. This unique digital version contains an image specific, two-hour audio commentary by director Sydney Pollack and interviews with Jane Fonda, producer Irwin Winkler, Red Buttons and others from behind the scenes of this production. The theatrical trailer, stills and assorted paraphernalia are also preserved on this laser disc. The 2,500 discs manufactured in this limited edition are signed by Sidney Pollack.
Laser: LD75912. $129.98.
Sydney Pollack, USA, 1969, 120 mins.

The Thief of Baghdad (Donner)
Prince Taj (Kabir Bedi) wants to marry Princess Jasmine (Paula Ustinov). But in order to win her he must bring her father "the most valuable thing in the world." With Roddy McDowall as Hasan, Peter Ustinov as Caliph, and Terence Stamp as Wazir Jaudur.
VHS: S32955. $19.95.
Clive Donner, Great Britain/France, 1978, 102 mins.

The Thief of Baghdad (Korda)
This sound version of *The Thief* is the winner of three Academy Awards. It stars Sabu as the mischievous Abu. When Abu helps the rightful King of Baghdad escape from prison, he finds himself involved in an incredible series of adventures.
VHS: S17379. $19.98.
Alexander Korda, USA, 1940, 106 mins.

Thin Ice
Olympic skating champion Sonja Henie plays a skating teacher at a Swiss Hotel whose relationship with a charming guest has wide-reaching repercussions when she discovers the mysterious man (Tyrone Power) is an internationally prominent prince. With Arthur Treacher, Joan Davis, Alan Hale, Raymond Walburn and Sig Ruman.
VHS: S20258. $19.98.
Sidney Lanfield, USA, 1937, 86 mins.

Thirteenth Guest
A rare example of output from Monogram Pictures, so admired by Godard: in this old house, a dead millionaire and a mystery are to be solved in this chiller starring Ginger Rogers and Lyle Talbot. Recently re-discovered print.
VHS: S02932. $19.95.
Albert Ray, USA, 1932, 70 mins.

Thirty Seconds over Tokyo
Van Johnson leads a valiant crew on an historic bombing raid over Japan just 131 days after Pearl Harbor. Spencer Tracy makes a cameo appearance as Lt. Col. Jimmy Doolittle, the mission's leader, but the real focus is on Johnson and his crew. With Robert Mitchum, Robert Walker, Don DeFore, and Benson Fong as Young Chung. The semi-documentary style script is by Dalton Trumbo. The special effects won an Oscar.
VHS: S13309. $19.98.
Mervyn Le Roy, USA, 1944, 138 mins.

This Gun for Hire
This uncharacteristically dark adaptation of Graham Greene's novel *A Gun for Sale* stars Alan Ladd as a brutally efficient gunman. He's caught in a complicated conspiracy plot involving an undercover agent (Veronica Lake) as he plots revenge against the man (Laird Cregar) who betrayed him. With Robert Preston and Tully Marshall.
VHS: S18997. $14.98.
Frank Tuttle, USA, 1942, 81 mins.

This Property Is Condemned
Natalie Wood, Robert Redford, Charles Bronson and Robert Blake star in this film adaptation of Tennessee Williams' one-act play, set in a Mississippi railroad town, with Wood falling for Redford, the out-of-towner staying in her mama's boarding house.
VHS: S04399. $19.95.
Laser: LD75274. $34.98.
Sydney Pollack, USA, 1966, 110 mins.

Thomas Crown Affair
A bored millionaire, played by Steve McQueen, masterminds the perfect bank robbery and is pursued by a lovely and dogged insurance investigator (Faye Dunaway) determined to catch him. The stylish photography by Haskell Wexler includes the clever use of multiple-image screens.
VHS: S13755. $19.98.
Laser: Letterboxed, chapter search. Includes original theatrical trailer. **LD71646. $34.98.**
Norman Jewison, USA, 1968, 102 mins.

The Thoroughbred
Once a respected horse trainer, Mr. Fitshue now earns a living as a horse consultant to an unscrupulous group of characters. But when his conscience finally catches up with him, Fairbanks runs into a beautiful victim of one of his scams. Stars Douglas Fairbanks, Jr.
VHS: S16744. $14.95.
Harold Huth, USA, 1954, 30 mins.

Those Daring Young Men in Their Jaunty Jalopies
Follows the numerous accidents and slapstick exploits of participants in a 1500 mile car race to Monte Carlo. It's "Monte Carlo or Bust" in this road rally set in the 1920's. Starring Tony Curtis and Dudley Moore.
VHS: S13538. $39.95.
Ken Annakin, USA, 1969, 125 mins.

A Thousand Clowns
Jason Robards is the voluntarily unemployed writer of the *Chuckles the Chipmunk Show*. He is equally devoted to raising his nephew and avoiding the rat race. But his defiance of the system is tested when social workers tell him to shape up and get a job…or the boy will be shipped to a foster home. Based on the Herb Gardner Broadway play.
VHS: S02342. $19.98.
Laser: LD76095. $39.98.
Fred Coe, USA, 1965, 114 mins.

Three Came Home
Claudette Colbert stars as a woman writer who is imprisoned in a Japanese camp during World War II. The deprivation suffered by the internees and the personal anguish experienced by the camp commander, torn between compassion and duty, is explored. With Sessue Hayakawa, Florence Desmond, Patrick Knowles. Based on the story of writer Agnes Newton Keith, with a script by Nunnaly Johnson.
VHS: S13050. $19.95.
Jean Negulesco, USA, 1950, 106 mins.

Three Comrades
F. Scott Fitzgerald adapted Erich Maria Remarque's novel about three German army officers (Robert Taylor, Robert Young and Franchot Tone) who attempt to rebuild their lives in the aftermath of the Armistice. They find meaning in their relationship with an impoverished English woman (Margaret Sullavan), who exercises a magnetic pull over their habits and lives.
VHS: S18509. $19.98.
Frank Borzage, USA, 1938, 98 mins.

The Three Faces of Eve
Tour de force by Joanne Woodward as a young woman with multiple personalities and three separate lives. Lee J. Cobb is the psychiatrist who tries to cure her.
VHS: S18098. $19.98.
Laser: Letterboxed. **LD72339. $59.98.**
Nunnally Johnson, USA, 1957, 91 mins.

Three Faces West
John Wayne leads a Dust Bowl community to workable land in Oregon in this contemporary (1940) drama that combines the New West and anti-Nazi sentiments. Wayne is in love with the daughter of a Viennese surgeon (Charles Coburn), who escaped from a concentration camp.
VHS: S10071. $19.95.
Bernard Vorhaus, USA, 1940, 80 mins.

Three Husbands
From the beyond, a playboy sends a letter to three husbands, hinting that one of their wives was a mistress. A haunting follow-up to the Oscar-winning "Letter to Three Wives." With Eve Arden, Ruth Warrick, Jane Darwell.
VHS: S04851. $29.95.
Irving Reis, USA, 1950, 78 mins.

The Three Musketeers (1933)
Three French Foreign Legionnaires, led by John Wayne, battle evil desert warriors under the blazing sun in this entertaining Saturday matinee serial. While tracking down the elusive El Shaitan, leader of the "Circle of Death", this cunning and resourceful team dodges bullets and bayonets, eventually uncovering the desert devil's maniacal plans and his true identity. Also featuring Lon Chaney Jr.
VHS: S13512. $24.95.
Colbert Clark/Armand Schaefer, USA, 1933, 215 mins.

The Three Musketeers (1948)
En Garde! Gene Kelly is a jaunty D'Artagnan in this funny and thrilling swashbuckler based on the classic Dumas story. With an all-star cast, including Lana Turner, June Allyson, and Van Heflin.
VHS: S15658. $19.98.
Laser: LD70695. $39.98.
George Sidney, USA, 1948, 125 mins.

Three on a Match
Three women who were childhood friends meet again in the big city, and the sad melodrama of their lives unfolds. Equal doses of suspense and tragedy are bolstered by good performances from Ann Dvorak, Bette Davis, and Joan Blondell.
VHS: S13649. $19.98.
Mervyn Le Roy, USA, 1932, 64 mins.

Three Secrets
Eleanor Parker, Patricia Neal and Ruth Roman are three women who each suspect that the foster five-year-old boy who survived a plane crash is the son they gave up for adoption. It's no secret that at least two of them must be wrong. With Frank Lovejoy, Leif Erickson and Duncan Richardson as Johnny. B&W.
VHS: S07415. $19.98.
Robert Wise, USA, 1950, 93 mins.

Thunder Road
Robert Mitchum stars as Lucas Doolin, the fastest and luckiest hauler of moonshine in Kentucky. Mitchum wrote the story and the hit song *Whippoorwill*, which is sung by Keely Smith. His 16-year-old son James plays his adoring kid brother. A cult film and the grand daddy of all those "moonshiner vs. revenooer" movies that followed. B&W.
VHS: S10072. $19.95.
Laser: LD76362. $39.99.
Arthur Ripley, USA, 1958, 92 mins.

Tight Spot
In this classic noir crime thriller based on Leonard Kantor's play (*Dead Pigeon*), Ginger Rogers is refreshingly cast against type as Sherry Conley, a wise-cracking blonde convict who is set up by a U.S. attorney (Edward G. Robinson) to play the patsy and testify against a powerful mobster (Lorne Greene). With Brian Keith.
VHS: S34710. $19.95.
Phil Karlson, USA, 1955, 97 mins.

A Time for Dying
"The indispensable last piece in an auteurist jigsaw puzzle…a haunting depiction of waste and futility of violence" (Sarris). Withheld from release for over ten years, the film stars Audie Murphy in a story of youthful innocence and foolish bravado. Boetticher's last film.
VHS: S01345. $34.95.
Budd Boetticher, USA, 1969, 73 mins.

The Tip Off
Ginger Rogers drew favorable notices for this early role as Baby Face, the spitfire girlfriend of boxer Robert Armstrong. Eddie Quillan stars as a radio mechanic whose innocent involvement with a gangster's girlfriend puts him a jam until he makes friends with a prizefighter. With Joan Peers and Ralf Harolde as Nick Vatelli.
VHS: S15468. $19.98.
Albert S. Rogell, USA, 1931, 71 mins.

Titanic
Clifton Webb, Barbara Stanwyck and Audrey Dalton star in this gripping re-enactment of the tragic sinking of the *Titanic*. Eyewitness accounts were used as the basis for the Academy Award-winning Best Story and Screenplay. Before this wholly unexpected accident the mammoth ship was set to revolutionize trans-Atlantic travel. Instead 1500 people drowned, celebrities and common folk alike.
VHS: S24133. $19.98.
Laser: LD74940. $39.99.
Jean Negulesco, USA, 1953, 98 mins.

To Each His Own
Olivia de Havilland won an Academy Award for her portrayal of an unwed mother who gives up her son, and then pretends to be his loving aunt in order to be near him, in this "well-turned soaper" (Leonard Maltin). With John Lund.
VHS: S30794. $19.95.
Mitchell Leisen, USA, 1946, 122 mins.

To Kill a Mockingbird
Gregory Peck won an Oscar for his role of Atticus Finch, the defense lawyer of a black man accused of rape in the American South. Script by Horton Foote from the novel by Harper Lee. A sensitive and powerful drama. Robert Duvall's film debut. Also Brock Peters, and Mary Badham as Scout. B&W. VHS letterboxed.
VHS: S02640. $19.95.
Laser: LD70089. $39.98.
DVD: DV60245. $34.98.
Robert Mulligan, USA, 1962, 129 mins.

To Please a Lady
She's an eat-'em-alive journalist; he's a ruthless racing driver—they're a perfect match! Clark Gable and Barbara Stanwyck star in this movie that's a "thriller from beginning to end" (*Hollywood Reporter*).
VHS: S20564. $19.98.
Clarence Brown, USA, 1950, 91 mins.

To the Shores of Tripoli
Produced during World War II, this memorable war film details the transformation of a spoiled rich boy into a tough and battle-wise Marine. With John Payne, Maureen O'Hara, Randolph Scott.
VHS: S12166. $19.98.
H. Bruce Humberstone, USA, 1942, 85 mins.

The Toast of New York
Edward Arnold is "Jubilee Jim" Fish in this historical drama about the rise to power of one of the tycoons who ruled Wall Street after the Civil War. Cary Grant starred as his friend and eventual rival for the affections of the legendary Frances Farmer.
Laser: CLV. LD71742. $19.98.
Rowland V. Lee, USA, 1939, 109 mins.

Tobruk
During the war in North Africa, a British major and some German Jews try to blow up Rommel's fuel supply. A tough and spectacular war adventure, starring Rock Hudson, George Peppard, Nigel Green, Guy Stockwell and Leo Gordon.
VHS: S16304. $14.95.
Arthur Hiller, USA, 1967, 110 mins.

Tokyo File
Florence Marly and Robert Peyton star in this post-World War II drama. Communist sabotage is an overwhelming danger. An intelligence operator must do everything he can to minimize the harm posed by the international communist conspiracy.
VHS: S27887. $19.98.
Dorrell McGowan/Stuart E. McGowan, USA, 1951, 84 mins.

Tokyo Joe
Humphrey Bogart plays an American war hero in post-war Japan who becomes involved in smuggling and blackmail to protect his wife and child. He flies planes of contraband goods, sits in a hot tub and gets to talk tough—though probably not all at the same time. With Alexander Knox, Florence Marley, Sessue Hayakawa and Jerome Courtland.
VHS: S08702. $69.95.
Stuart Heisler, USA, 1949, 88 mins.

Tomorrow Is Forever
Orson Welles and Claudette Colbert star in a fateful drama that bridges two World Wars. When Welles is wounded while fighting the Huns in the First World War, he decides to start over with a new name in a new country. Colbert, thinking herself a widow, marries George Brent and starts a new family that includes six year old Natalie Wood in her debut role.
VHS: S16441. $19.98.
Laser: LD76411. $34.98.
Irving Pichel, USA, 1946, 104 mins.

Tony Rome
Frank Sinatra plays the title character, a Miami-based private detective who becomes involved with blackmail, phony gems, and the unpleasant Kosterman family. The supporting players include Gena Rowlands, Sue Lyon, Simon Oakland, Jill St. John and Richard Conte as Lt. Santini. Watch for Rocky Graziano, Shecky Greene and Deanna Lund in small roles. Based on the novel *Miami Mayhem* by Marvin H. Albert.
VHS: S12521. $59.98.
Gordon Douglas, USA, 1967, 110 mins.

Too Hot to Handle
Rival newsreel cameramen Clark Gable and Walter Pidgeon are invited by aviatrix Myrna Loy to locate her missing brother in the wilds of the Amazon. Adventure, romance and comic quick thinking prevail. With Leo Carillo, Johnny Hinds and Marjorie Main. Not to be confused with movies of the same title starring Jayne Mansfield and Cherie Caffaro.
VHS: S13191. $19.98.
Jack Conway, USA, 1938, 105 mins.

Topkapi
Jules Dassin's imaginative adaptation of Eric Ambler's novel, *The Light of Day*, about a group of sophisticated thieves orchestrating the perfect heist, the gem-strewn dagger from the Topkapi Museum in Constantinople. Peter Ustinov won the 1964 Academy Award for his performance. With Melina Mercouri, Maximilian Schell and Robert Morley.
VHS: S27576. $19.98.
Laser: LD71652. $34.98.
Jules Dassin, USA, 1964, 120 mins.

The Torch
Paulette Goddard and Gilbert Roland are featured in this tale of love and war. A Mexican revolutionary restores the rule of law to a small town, but the love of a young, aristocratic woman threatens to break his concentration. With Pedro Armendariz and Antonio Kaneen. Cinematography by Gabriel Figueroa.
VHS: S25702. $19.95.
Emilio Fernandez, USA/Mexico, 1949, 83 mins.

Torch Song
Joan Crawford claws her way to the top of the Great White Way and likes the view. Broadway is her oyster until she meets a blind pianist who isn't exactly dazzled by her beauty and moves. With Michael Wilding, Gig Young, Harry Morgan, Marjorie Rambeau, and Nancy Gates. Watch for Crawford doing a number in black face.
VHS: S11727. $19.98.
Laser: LD70698. $34.98.
Charles Walters, USA, 1953, 90 mins.

Torpedo Alley
A WWII Navy pilot loses his plane and is rescued by a U.S. sub. Thepilot blames himself for the death of his crewmen, and he seeks redemption through a transfer to the silent service. With Warren Douglas, Dorothy Malone and Charles Winninger.
VHS: S34926. $14.95.
Lew Landers, USA, 1953, 84 mins.

Torpedo Run
Glenn Ford plays an obsessed U.S. submarine commander who is out to destroy a Japanese aircraft carrier that was indirectly responsible for the death of his wife and child. With Ernest Borgnine as his sensible second-in-command. Other crew members include Dean Jones, Fred Wayne and L.Q. Jones as Hash Benson. Originally in Cinemascope.
VHS: S12534. $19.98.
Joseph Penney, USA, 1958, 98 mins.

Tortilla Flat
Steinbeck's salty story about a California fishing community gets star treatment from Spencer Tracy, Hedy Lamarr, John Garfield, Akim Tamiroff and Sheldon Leonard, and a moving performance by Frank Morgan as a canine devotee.
VHS: S15651. $19.98.
Laser: LD76266. $39.99.
Victor Fleming, USA, 1942, 105 mins.

Tower of London
Many mistakenly assume this is a horror work, with the presence of Boris Karloff and Basil Rathbone, though it's actually an historical adaptation that recounts the relationship of the power-obsessed, ruthless Richard III (Rathbone) and his deranged executioner Mord (Karloff). With Barbara O'Neil, Ian Hunter and Vincent Price.
VHS: S17519. $14.98.
Rowland V. Lee, USA, 1939, 92 mins.

Town Without Pity
In this gripping drama, Kirk Douglas stars as Major Steve Garret, a compassionate but driven attorney who must struggle with his own moral fiber as he defends four soldiers accused of attacking a 16-year-old girl in an occupied German town. As timely today as it was shocking upon its original release.
VHS: S28473. $19.98.
Gottfried Reinhardt, USA/Germany/Switzerland, 1961, 103 mins.

The Tracy and Hepburn Collection
Sexual dynamics and role playing infuse the gentle, witty spirit of these three works with Spencer Tracy and Katharine Hepburn, two directed by George Cukor: *Adam's Rib* (1949) and *Pat and Mike* (1952), and George Stevens's 1952 film, *Woman of the Year*.
VHS: S17306. $49.92.

Trader Horn
An Ivory trader, played by Harry Carey, must find the lost daughter of a missionary. Myriad dangers, including inhospitable tribal peoples, stand in the way. Shot largely in the jungles of Africa, this film represents one of the earliest action adventures to use real locations.
VHS: S21019. $19.98.
W.S. Van Dyke II, USA, 1931, 120 mins.

The Trail of the Lonesome Pine
Henry Fonda and Sylvia Sydney star in this remake of a 1915 film about how the building of a railroad on the land of two feuding families wreaks havoc on their lives. The first outdoor film in full Technicolor, this classic is still remarkably strong today. With Fred MacMurray, Fred Stone, Fuzzy Knight, Beulah Bondi, Spanky McFarland and Nigel Bruce.
VHS: S30795. $19.95.
Henry Hathaway, USA, 1936, 102 mins.

Trapeze
This expressive work directed by Carol Reed (*The Third Man*) is centered around the high-wire Parisian circus. The drama unfolds in the professional and personal rivalry of a curious and intricate three-way love affair among Tony Curtis, Burt Lancaster and Gina Lollobrigida. Shot at the Cirque d'Hiver in Paris.
VHS: S17988. $19.98.
Laser: Letterboxed. **LD72354. $34.98.**
Carol Reed, USA, 1956, 106 mins.

Trapped by Television
A young television inventor seeks backing for his research. He ends up working with a fly-by-night promotions lady who tries to get him in with a big research development company. Unfortunately, someone within the company wants to see him dead. A gang of thugs attempt to sabotage his invention and lay him out in a coffin. With Mary Astor, Lyle Talbot, Nat Pendleton, Marc Lawrence and Joyce Compton.
VHS: S34478. $29.95.
Del Lord, USA, 1936, 64 mins.

Treasure Island
Wallace Beery stars as the dreaded pirate Long John Silver, whose love of a small boy, Jackie Cooper, takes the two on a mysterious journey. With John Barrymore as the wandering fugitive Billy Bones.
VHS: S04210. $24.95.
Victor Fleming, USA, 1934, 104 mins.

A Tree Grows in Brooklyn
Peggy Ann Gardner finds that life can be difficult if you are poor and live in Brooklyn at the turn of the century. Adapted from Betty Smith's novel, a fine drama with a splendid cast. With Dorothy McGuire, Joan Blondell, James Dunn, and Lloyd Nolan.
VHS: S05313. $14.98.
Laser: LD71378. $49.98.
Elia Kazan, USA, 1945, 128 mins.

Try and Get Me
Frank Lovejoy and Lloyd Bridges are two guys down on their luck when they decide to pull off a kidnapping to raise some money. Their victim dies by accident and they try to return to living a normal life. The community demands that the killers be caught and punished. With Richard Carlson, Dabbs Greer, Kathleen Ryan and Adele Jergens. Based on a factual case in California in 1933.
VHS: S07138. $19.95.
Cy Endfield, USA, 1950, 91 mins.

Tulsa
Oil woman Susan Hayward has to fight for her property while involved in wildcat drilling.
VHS: S05967. $19.95.
Stuart Heisler, USA, 1949, 90 mins.

Tundra
A "flying doctor" whose plane crashes near the Arctic Circle must cover over 400 miles with the help of only a knife and a lighter. Along the way spectacular scenery, unrivaled wild life footage and intimate scenes of Eskimo daily life turn this film into an unparalleled portrayal of this Northernmost region of the U.S.
VHS: S21609. $24.95.
Norman Dawn, USA, 1936, 72 mins.

Twelve Angry Men
A teenage boy is accused of killing his father, and between him and capital punishment stands just one man. A vivid, shocking courtroom drama with a powerful cast including Henry Fonda, Lee J. Cobb, E.G. Marshall and Jack Warden.
VHS: S11432. $29.95.
Laser: LD70478. $39.95.
Sidney Lumet, USA, 1957, 96 mins.

Two for the Road
Audrey Hepburn and Albert Finney star as a bickering couple travelling through France who stop to reminisce about their twelve years of marriage.
VHS: S18102. $19.98.
Stanley Donen, USA/Great Britain, 1967, 112 mins.

The Two Mrs. Carrolls
In one of his most off-beat film roles, Humphrey Bogart portrays a psychopathic artist who paints his wives as the Angel of Death, and then poisons them. Alexis Smith plays the iciest of femme fatales, and the first Mrs. Carroll to fall victim to his prey. Barbara Stanwyck co-stars as the second Mrs. Carroll, with Nigel Bruce as the bumbling doctor who both drinks and talks too much.
VHS: S16098. $19.98.
Peter Godfrey, USA, 1947, 99 mins.

Two Weeks in Another Town
Vincente Minnelli's imaginative translation of Irwin Shaw's novel about a Rome film production, using footage from Minnelli's *The Bad and the Beautiful*. With Kirk Douglas, Edward G. Robinson, Cyd Charisse and George Hamilton.
Laser: LD70733. $39.98.
Vincente Minnelli, USA, 1962, 107 mins.

Two Years Before the Mast
When the idealistic son (Alan Ladd) of a rich shipowner unwillingly takes a part in a voyage, he discovers the shameful brutality inflicted upon sailors, and is forced to mutiny both against a ruthless captain and his own past, in this glimpse into life at sea in the 1800s.
VHS: S33707. $14.98.
John Farrow, USA, 1946, 98 mins.

U-Boat Prisoner
An American sailor is captured by a Nazi U-Boat during World War II. This gripping tale of imprisonment during war time has the gritty feel of its time. The rousing spirit that helped the country endure the ravages of this war are convincingly portrayed.
VHS: S20635. $19.95.
Lew Landers, USA, 1944, 65 mins.

The Ugly American
Marlon Brando plays Harrison Carter MacWhite, the U.S. Ambassador to Sarkhan, a mythical Southeast Asian country fraught with factional disputes and growing Communist menace. His good intentions only increase the turmoil. Based on the book by Lederer and Burdick.
VHS: S03679. $59.95.
George H. Englund, USA, 1962, 120 mins.

Ulysses
Joseph Strick directed this daring stream-of-consciousness adaptation of James Joyce's great novel which follows Leopold Bloom through the streets and brothels of turn-of-the-century Dublin. The film culminates in the torrentially earthy monologue of his wife Molly. The intimacy of Joyce's language was without precedent in literature, and its flashbacks, dream episodes, sounds and visual montages translate freely into the language of the cinema. "Joyce's great novel becomes a movie masterpiece," said *Life Magazine*.
VHS: S09552. $29.95.
Joseph Strick, USA, 1967, 120 mins.

Uncertain Glory
Errol Flynn plays an escaped criminal whose fate changes at the hands of the Nazis. He is aboard a Paris-bound train that is suddenly derailed. Hostages are taken and amid the hostility Flynn's character must decide exactly what kind of man he is, given the life and death circumstances.
VHS: S22899. $19.98.
Raoul Walsh, USA, 1944, 102 mins.

The Undefeated
John Wayne and Rock Hudson star as Yankee and Rebel commanders learning to trust each other as they start new lives immediately after the Civil War. With beautiful views of the Rio Grande.
VHS: S15985. $14.98.
Laser: LD72221. $59.98.
Andrew V. McLaglen, USA, 1969, 119 mins.

Undercurrent
Departing from her more usual, lighthearted roles, Katharine Hepburn "gives a resounding portrayal" (*New York Herald Tribune*) as the unsuspecting wife of a man driven to madness by his thirst for power. A moody suspense thriller with Robert Taylor, Jayne Meadows (in her screen debut) and a young Robert Mitchum.
VHS: S15025. $19.98.
Vincente Minnelli, USA, 1946, 126 mins.

Until They Sail
Director Robert Wise and author James Michener paint an evocative and unsettling portrait of World War II New Zealand, with Paul Newman as an American soldier who gets involved in a murder case, insinuating himself into the lives of four sisters-Jean Simmons, Joan Fontaine, Piper Laurie and Sandra Dee.
VHS: S17991. $19.98.
Robert Wise, USA, 1957, 95 mins.

Up in Central Park
Deanna Durbin portrays a young Irish immigrant who comes to America with her father. Vincent Price is a crooked politician who tries to use the young talented beauty to further his political gain in this engrossing story, set in New York City, that features two lavish song-and-dance numbers. With Dick Haymes. Includes original theatrical trailer.
VHS: S32972. $19.98.
William A. Seiter, USA, 1948, 88 mins.

Up Periscope
Lieutenant Ken Braden (James Garner) is assigned to be smuggled into a Japanese-held island via submarine to photograph radio codes. In the meantime he discovers that his flame, Sally (Andrea Martin), is checking out his qualifications to be a U.S. Navy frogman. With Edmond O'Brien and Alan Hale, Jr.
VHS: S33909. $14.95.
Gordon Douglas, USA, 1959, 112 mins.

Up the Down Staircase
Academy Award winner Sandy Dennis stars in this compelling drama as a new teacher at an inner city school. Based on the bestseller by Bel Kaufman, it follows this teacher's struggle to make a difference against great odds. Jean Stapleton also makes an appearance.
VHS: S21345. $29.99.
Robert Mulligan, USA, 1967, 124 mins.

Uptown New York
Jack Oakie proves himself to be a dramatic actor of considerable effectiveness as Eddie Doyle, a man whose wife marries him on the rebound from an affair with another man.
VHS: S13848. $19.95.
Victor Schertzinger, USA, 1932, 81 mins.

The Valley of Decision
Set in the 1870's in Pittsburgh, this love story follows the trouble experienced by a young couple from opposite sides of the social spectrum. Gregory Peck is a mill owner who loves the family's maid, Greer Garson. It's adapted from Marcia Davenport's novel and includes Lionel Barrymore and Dean Stockwell.
VHS: S21172. $19.98.
Tay Garnett, USA, 1945, 111 mins.

Valley of the Kings
A hard-boiled archeologist and a red-headed beauty search for Egyptian treasure in this classic tale of high adventure starring Robert Taylor and Eleanor Parker. Complete with hidden tombs, poisonous scorpions and sinister villains, *Valley of the Kings* is a thriller in the *Indiana Jones* tradition.
VHS: S31074. $19.98.
Robert Pirosh, USA, 1954, 96 mins.

Vanity Fair
Myrna Loy stars as Becky Sharp in this modern dance version of the Thackeray novel. Billy Bevan and Montagu Love also star.
VHS: S07065. $39.95.
Chester M. Franklin, USA, 1932, 80 mins.

Vikings
Filmed on location in Norway, this rousing saga tells the story of a proud warrior and a stubborn slave who have the same father but completely opposite ways of approaching life. Kirk Douglas and Tony Curtis are the battling half-siblings fighting over the favors of kidnapped English princess Janet Leigh. With James Donald, Frank Thring and Ernest Borgnine as Ragnar, viking lord and wolf bait. Based on the novel by Edison Marshall.
VHS: S12237. $19.95.
Laser: Letterboxed. **LD72336. $34.98.**
Richard Fleischer, USA, 1958, 114 mins.

The Virgin Queen
Bette Davis is Queen Elizabeth I, jealously in love with Sir Walter Raleigh (Richard Todd) with Joan Collins her rival. Notable for a flamboyant performance by Davis.
VHS: S05916. $19.98.
Henry Koster, USA, 1955, 92 mins.

Viva Villa!
Ben Hecht wrote this biography of the revolutionary Mexican bandit Pancho Villa, whose guerrilla armies ended the bloody suppression of the governing elite. Wallace Beery plays Villa. With Leo Carrillo, Fay Wray and Donald Cook.
VHS: S18510. $19.98.
Laser: LD72159. $34.98.
Jack Conway, USA, 1934, 115 mins.

Von Ryan's Express
Frank Sinatra and Trevor Howard star in this suspenseful drama about a daring mass escape from a POW camp in World War II Italy. This straightforward adventure boasts a strong cast and impressive action sequences.
VHS: S14140. $19.98.
Laser: LD76968. $24.99.
Mark Robson, USA, 1965, 117 mins.

Wait Until Dark
Audrey Hepburn plays a blind woman who is left alone in her apartment, terrorized by a psychotic (Alan Arkin) and a group of men looking for a heroin stash they are sure is in there. A tense thriller, based on Frederick Knott's Broadway play.
VHS: S31511. $19.98.
Laser: LD72448. $34.98.
Terence Young, USA, 1967, 108 mins.

Wake Island
Award-winning Hollywood account of the Battle for Wake Island during World War II in which outnumbered Marines fought Japanese forces for over two weeks. With Brian Donlevy, Robert Preston and William Bendix.
VHS: S06390. $19.95.
John Farrow, USA, 1942, 88 mins.

Wake of the Red Witch

John Wayne finds high adventure, romance and danger in the South Seas as Captain Ralls. Luther Adler is Wayne's rival in love and commerce. Gail Russell, Adele Mara and Gig Young are on Wayne's side. This is the movie where he wrestles the giant octopus. B&W.
VHS: S04240. $19.95.
Edward Ludwig, USA, 1948, 106 mins.

Walk on the Wild Side

Laurence Harvey travels to Louisiana with runaway Jane Fonda, determined to find his long-lost love (Capucine). But he's devastated when he finds out that Capucine has been reduced to working in a brothel run by a ruthless madam (Barbara Stanwyck). Loosely based on a novel by Nelson Algren, with a terrific score by Elmer Bernstein.
VHS: S07337. $69.95.
Edward Dmytryk, USA, 1962, 114 mins.

Walk Softly, Stranger

Joseph Cotten takes on an unusual role as a two-timing crook laying low in a small Ohio town. Alida Valli, Jack Paar also star.
VHS: S12020. $19.98.
Robert Stevenson, USA, 1950, 81 mins.

War and Peace

This classic version of the Leo Tolstoy epic masterpiece following a Russian family at the time of Napoleon's invasion stars Audrey Hepburn, Henry Fonda, Mel Ferrer, John Mills, and is a mammoth, sumptuous production.
VHS: S01427. $29.95.
King Vidor, USA, 1956, 208 mins.

War of the Wildcats

This is the movie where the Indians ask John Wayne to take over the oil lease on their tribal land in Oklahoma so that the evil Albert Dekker won't steal the whole operation. The Duke takes on the extra responsibility and tries to win the girl as well. With Martha Scott and Gabby Hayes.
VHS: S04890. $19.95.
Albert S. Rogell, USA, 1943, 102 mins.

Watch on the Rhine

Outstanding performances by Paul Dukas, Bette Davis, Lucille Watson distinguish this adaptation of the famous Lillian Hellman play about a German refugee and his family, who are pursued by Nazi agents in Washington.
VHS: S13397. $19.98.
Herman Shumlin, USA, 1943, 114 mins.

Waterhole #3

James Coburn, Carroll O'Connor and Bruce Dern are the three Army buddies who rob a fortune in gold, bury it in the desert, and then have their hands full trying to recover it. With Joan Blondell and Margaret Blye.
VHS: S04435. $19.95.
Laser: Widescreen. **LD75304. $39.98.**
William A. Graham, USA, 1967, 95 mins.

Waterloo Bridge

Robert Taylor is the American soldier and Vivien Leigh the dancer who meet in war-torn London and fall in love in this well-acted, touching romance. Based on the play by Robert Sherwood.
VHS: S02625. $19.98.
Mervyn LeRoy, USA, 1940, 103 mins.

We're Not Dressing

When Bing is a shipwrecked sailor on a deserted island you can be sure plenty of other entertainers will show up to keep him company. Carole Lombard plays the romantic interest, with George Burns and Gracie Allen along as expeditionists, while Ethel Merman is the spurned suitor of a harried Bing Crosby.
VHS: S21201. $14.98.
Norman Taurog, USA, 1934, 77 mins.

The Wedding Night

New York writer Gary Cooper falls in love with a New England farm girl (Anna Sten) in this touching, sentimental romance which also stars Ralph Bellamy and Walter Brennan.
VHS: S23440. $19.98.
King Vidor, USA, 1953, 84 mins.

Weddings and Babies

Viveca Lindfors stars in this charming love story between a photographer who resists commitment and the model who yearns for a child of her own. Shot on location in New York's Little Italy. "Each successive [Engel] film is astonishing" (Saul Bellow, *Horizon Magazine*).
VHS: S30706. $24.95.
Morris Engel, USA, 1958, 81 mins.

When Gangland Strikes

Public Prosecutor Luke Ellis wants to put Mobster Duke Martella behind bars. The chances for conviction dim when Martella finds something scandalous in the crime fighter's past. A hard-boiled tale of a man driven to see justice done, one way or the other. With Raymond Greenleaf, Marie Millar, Anthony Caruso and John Hudson. The remake of *Main Street Lawyer* (1939). B&W.
VHS: S11400. $19.95.
R.G. Springsteen, USA, 1956, 70 mins.

When Ladies Meet

Sophisticated author Joan Crawford is romantically drawn to suave publisher Herbert Marshall even though the cad is a married man. Young hunk Robert Taylor tries to woo her anyway. With Spring Byington, Florence Shirley and Greer Garson. Anita Loos co-wrote the screenplay.
VHS: S16456. $19.98.
Robert Z. Leonard, USA, 1941, 105 mins.

Where Love Has Gone

A florid melodrama loosely based on the notorious Lana Turner affair about a young woman charged with killing her mother's abusive and tyrannical boyfriend. Joey Heatherton is the young woman; Susan Hayward plays her mother. Greer Garson is a trusting probation officer. Bette Davis camps it up as the matriarchal leader. Adapted from the novel by Harold Robbins.
VHS: S19026. $14.95.
Edward Dmytryk, USA, 1964, 114 mins.

Whistle Stop

Desperation turns passion's flame into deadly obsession when one man tries to piece back together the fragments of his shattered dreams. Ava Gardner and George Raft star.
VHS: S14753. $19.95.
Leonide Moguy, USA, 1946, 85 mins.

White Cargo

While on an expedition, Walter Pidgeon falls madly in love with a beautiful, sarong-clad girl played by Hedy Lamarr. Survival is a constant struggle at the remote jungle plantation where they meet. This steamy and exotic tale brings melodrama to the tropics.
VHS: S21020. $19.98.
Richard Thorpe, USA, 1942, 90 mins.

The White Cliffs of Dover

A visual interpretation of Alice Duer Miller's poem about an Englishman who seduces a beautiful young American woman, conceives a child and dies in combat during the First World War. Their child, a young man, enters the army on the eve of the Second World War. With Irene Dunne, Roddy McDowall, Van Johnson and Dame May Whitty. "A glorious emotional experience in the fine tradition of romantic theatre" (*Hollywood Reporter*).
VHS: S18511. $19.98.
Clarence Brown, USA, 1944, 126 mins.

White Heat

James Cagney gives a masterful performance as the mentally unhinged gangster Cody Jarrett. Edmond O'Brien is the undercover cop who infiltrates the gang, which includes Steve Cochran, Fred Clark, and Virginia Mayo as Cody's unfaithful wife. This is the movie where Cagney learns that bullets and gasoline storage tanks don't mix. A terrific film in black and white. As the ads say, "Cagney is Red Hot in White Heat."
VHS: S09852. $19.95.
Raoul Walsh, USA, 1949, 114 mins.

The White Orchid

American archeologists journey into the Mexican interior. With William Lundigan, Peggy Castle and Armando Silvestre.
VHS: S33737. $9.95.
Reginald LeBorg, USA/Mexico, 1954, 82 mins.

Who's Afraid of Virginia Woolf?

Based on Edward Albee's smash hit play; Elizabeth Taylor and Richard Burton star in the story of the love-hate relationship between a middle-aged professor and his vitriolic but seductive wife.
VHS: S01737. $19.98.
Laser: LD70705. $39.98.
Laser: Widescreen. **LD71415. $39.98.**
DVD: DV60065. $24.98.
Mike Nichols, USA, 1966, 129 mins.

Wife vs. Secretary

Clark Gable, Jean Harlow and Myrna Loy are drawn into a threatening love triangle when a wife's jealousies overpower her reason. Jimmy Stewart shines in an early supporting role as secretary Harlow's frustrated boyfriend.
VHS: S15122. $19.98.
Clarence Brown, USA, 1936, 88 mins.

The Wild Bunch

When newlywed George Burrel is left alone with his wife's three teenagers, he gains their love and respect through a comedy of errors. As a parent George has no experience, all he can offer is something that has been missing since their father died: guidance. With George Boyer and Natalie Wood. *Not to be confused with the Sam Peckinpah Western.*
VHS: S16748. $14.95.
William A. Seiter, USA, 1955, 30 mins.

The Wild One

Marlon Brando is Johnny, the leader of a vicious biker gang which invades a small, sleepy California town. The leather-jacketed biker seems bent on destruction until he falls for Kathie, a "good girl," whose father happens to be a cop.
VHS: S01460. $19.95.
Laser: Remastered, 2 sides, side 2 CAV. **LD74478. $34.95.**
Laszlo Benedek, USA, 1954, 79 mins.

Wilson

Winner of five Oscars, this is the brilliant biography of the World War I era President whose League of Nations idea became an obsession. With Alexander Knox, Charles Coburn and Geraldine Fitzgerald.
VHS: S18099. $19.98.
Henry King, USA, 1944, 145 mins.

Wing and a Prayer

Don Ameche and Dana Andrews star in this outstanding drama about newly-trained pilots aboard a Pacific-based aircraft carrier in the early days of the war. Featuring actual combat footage.
VHS: S15197. $14.98.
Henry Hathaway, USA, 1944, 97 mins.

Winning

Winning is everything for Paul Newman, a determined car racer. Nothing can get in his way, not Joanne Woodward, and certainly not his rival Robert Wagner. This film brings all the excitement and drama of professional racing to the screen.
VHS: S21278. $14.98.
James Goldstone, USA, 1969, 123 mins.

The Winning Team

Ronald Reagan and Doris Day catch baseball fever in this romantic true story. A telephone linesman turns out to become Hall of Fame pitcher Grover Cleveland.
VHS: S15990. $19.98.
Lewis Seiler, USA, 1952, 98 mins.

Winter Meeting

Bretaigne Windust's stylish melodrama about a disillusioned poet (Bette Davis) who falls for a dark, embittered war hero (Jim Davis), setting in motion a comically romantic love triangle and hidden revelations. With Janis Paige, John Hoyt and Florence Bates.
VHS: S17337. $19.98.
Bretaigne Windust, USA, 1948, 105 mins.

Wintertime

Sonja Henie plays a world-champion figure skater whose charisma and marquee value help stave off the closing of an eccentric hotel owned and operated by her uncle. Music by the Woody Herman Orchestra. With Jack Oakie, Cesar Romero, Carole Landis and Cornel Wilde.
VHS: S20259. $19.98.
John Brahm, USA, 1943, 82 mins.

The Witness

Accused of killing a bank guard and stealing $150,000, Frank Dana's only hope of avoiding death row relies on the testimony of a beautiful mystery woman. Wearing the judge's patience thin with his continued delays, lawyer Mike Donnegan's search for the key witness ends when she seeks him out and gives a surprising testimony. Stars Charles Bronson and Dick Powell.
VHS: S16742. $14.95.
Robert Aldrich, USA, 1953, 30 mins.

Wives Under Suspicion

James Whale's own remake of his *Kiss before the Mirror*, based on the novel by Ladislaus Fodor. A fine cast includes Warren William, Gail Patrick, Ralph Morgan.
VHS: S08425. $29.95.
James Whale, USA, 1938, 75 mins.

Wolf Call

A pleasing, diverting adventure yarn adapted from the Jack London novel. It stars suave John Carroll as a frivolous and wealthy playboy who arrives in Radium City with his trusty, heroic dog Smoky to determine the value of his father's pitchblende mine. Things become complicated as he must contend with a conniving mine manager and his cronies—who represent those who are aware of the property's true value.
VHS: S13603. $24.95.
George Waggner, USA, 1939, 60 mins.

World Gone Mad

Tall ships, rolling seas, buried treasures and treachery are all part of this old-fashioned pirate adventure starring Charles Laughton as Captain Kidd. With John Carradine, Randolph Scott and Reginald Owen. 1939, 85 mins.

VHS: S03001. $39.95.

The World in His Arms

Gregory Peck and Ann Blyth fall in love in this dramatic, adventurous story set in the mid-19th century. A Russian countess is desperate to escape the threat of marriage to a man she does not love. She finds both refuge and passion with a seal fisher in Alaska. Anthony Quinn is also featured.

VHS: S28401. $14.98.

Raoul Walsh, USA, 1952, 105 mins.

World of Suzie Wong

William Holden is the American artist in Hong Kong who falls heavily for Nancy Kwan, his prostitute model. East meets West and both meet a terrific mud slide. A technicolor romance in the infamous Wanchai district where all the B-girls are beautiful. With Sylvia Sims, Michael Wilding and Jacqueline Chan as Gwenny Lee.

VHS: S08273. $19.95.

Richard Quine, USA, 1960, 129 mins.

The Wreck of the Mary Deare

A rousing tale of mutiny, disorder and failed reputation. When the captain of the ship is charged with negligence, a sympathetic salvage boat skipper offers aid and comfort. With Gary Cooper, Charlton Heston and Michael Redgrave.

VHS: S17992. $19.98.

Laser: LD72161. $34.98.

Michael Anderson, USA/Great Britain, 1959, 100 mins.

A Yank in the RAF

Tyrone Power, Betty Grable, and actual air combat footage spark this romantic drama about a cocky American flier who joins the RAF to be near the woman he loves. With upbeat musical numbers, this 1941 Oscar-nominee for Special Effects was one of the most popular war movies of its day.

VHS: S14137. $19.98.

Henry King, USA, 1941, 98 mins.

Yellowneck

Lin McCarthy and Bill Mason are the individuals who star in this fascinating story about a group of Civil War deserters who end up stranded in the Florida Everglades and must face starvation and the elements in their efforts to survive. An insightful drama.

VHS: S14666. $29.95.

Robert Hossman, USA, 1955, 83 mins.

You Can't Fool Your Wife

Lucille Ball is a wife separated from her husband by a meddling mother in-law. They meet again at a bachelor, or rather, at a masked party.

VHS: S10640. $19.98.

Ray McCarey, USA, 1940, 69 mins.

You Gotta Stay Happy

Dee Dee (Joan Fontaine) is a wealthy heiress who has just made the mistake of her life by marrying the wrong man. Looking to get away she hooks up with failing airline entrepreneur Marvin Payne (James Stewart), who reluctantly agrees to let her hitch a ride across the country in his cargo plane. The crazy flight begins when the co-pilot (Eddie Albert) has illegally booked a group of wacky passengers, including a cigar-smoking chimp.

VHS: S34362. $14.98.

H.C. Potter, USA, 1948, 101 mins.

Young Bess

In this lavish historical costume drama a young Elizabeth I is played by Jean Simmons, while her real-life husband, Stewart Granger, plays her amorous would-be lover. Charles Laughton and Deborah Kerr co-star. Sparks fly in this tempestuous tale.

VHS: S21169. $19.98.

George Sidney, USA, 1953, 112 mins.

Young Billy Young

Robert Mitchum is superb in this western as Ben Kane, a peace-loving man who takes a job as deputy marshal of Lords because he has an old score to settle with the town's chief trouble-maker (John Anderson). Once on the job, Kane must also deal with a young fast-draw drifter, Billy Young (Robert Walker Jr.), and a sassy saloon dancer, Lily (Angie Dickinson). With David Carradine. Letterboxed.

VHS: S33720. $14.95.

Burt Kennedy, USA, 1969, 89 mins.

Young Man with a Horn

Kirk Douglas stars in this story based on the life of jazzman Bix Beiderbecke, with Harry James dubbing in the trumpet playing. With Hoagy Carmichael, Lauren Bacall and Doris Day.

VHS: S03432. $19.98.

Laser: LD70720. $34.98.

Michael Curtiz, USA, 1950, 112 mins.

Young Savages

Burt Lancaster gives a forceful performance as a prosecutor whose search for the truth puts his career in jeopardy in this tough, hard-hitting expose of juvenile crime. With Telly Savalas, Dina Merrill and Edward Andrews.

VHS: S31870. $19.98.

John Frankenheimer, USA, 1961, 103 mins.

Young Tom Edison

An earnest essay about the American dream in the story of Tom Edison (Mickey Rooney), the greatest American inventor of his era. Rooney's self-effacement, charm and understatement creates a vivid biographical portrait of Edison's early years. With Fay Bainter, George Bancroft, Virginia Weidler and Eugene Pallette.

VHS: S19468. $19.98.

Norman Taurog, USA, 1940, 82 mins.

Zorro Rides Again

In this feature-length version, the mysterious Zorro battles a group of bandits in a mighty mission fraught with a freight-load of perils.

VHS: S33929. $14.98.

John English/William Witney, USA, 1959, 68 mins.

silent american cinema

20,000 Leagues Under the Sea-
For the first time on video, the 1916 film version of the Jules Verne classic, newly remastered from an archive print. This landmark film was 1½ years in the making, and was one of the first great special effects spectaculars of the early cinema. The thrilling story of the renegade Captain Nemo and the sea monster he discovers from the submarine Nautilus is as impressive today as it was upon its initial release 75 years ago.
VHS: S15039. $29.95.
Stuart Paton, USA, 1916, 105 mins.

Adventures of Hairbreadth Harry
These rare silent films are fun-filled, short comedy spoofs of the early silent melodramas, produced by Chaplin imitator Billy West. The fast-paced romps are guaranteed to keep you laughing. Includes *Sawdust Baby, Fearless Harry* and *Rudolph's Revenge*. With orchestral music soundtrack. USA, 65 mins.
VHS: S15230. $19.95.

All Night
This delightful comedy-drama stars Rudolph Valentino as a lovesick young man trying to get up the courage to ask his long-time friend (Carmel Myers) for a date. A friend (Charles Dorian) invites both to dinner so Valentino can get her alone, romance her and possibly propose. When Dorian's help quits just before an important client is to be entertained, Valentino and Myers are forced to pretend to be husband and wife to impress his friend's client, as Dorian and his wife take over the servants' duties. Edith Mary Warren, William Dyer, Wadsworth Harris and Jack Hull. Silent with orchestra score.
VHS: S32052. $24.95.
Paul Powell, USA, 1918, 58 mins.

American Aristocracy
Douglas Fairbanks stars in this silent action comedy involving speeding cars, seaplanes and motor cruises.
VHS: S08886. $24.95.
Lloyd Ingraham, USA, 1917, 52 mins.

American Pluck
George Walsh, Wanda Hawley, Sidney De Grey, Frank Leigh, Leo White star.
VHS: S07217. $19.95.
Richard Stanton, USA, 1925, 64 mins.

Anna Christie
Adaptation of Eugene O'Neill's play about a world-weary prostitute's first encounter with her father, a sentimental old seaman. Blanche Sweet in the title role, this version was re-edited in the USSR.
VHS: S04810. $34.95.
John Griffith Wray, USA, 1923, 75 mins.

Annapolis
An early Pathe production about two Navy men who fall for the same girl. Featuring Johnny Mack Brown, Hugh Allan, Jeanette Loff and Maurice Ryan.
VHS: S07235. $19.95.
Christy Cabanne, USA, 1928, 63 mins.

April Fool
An out-of-work pants-presser makes a fortune in the umbrella business and has to give it all up for the happiness of his daughter. One of Baby Peggy Montgomery's few surviving silent films, it includes a piano score. Mary Alden, Raymond Keane and Snitz Edwards also star.
VHS: S22431. $19.95.
Nat Ross, USA, 1926, 63 mins.

Are Parents People?
Betty Bronson, Florence Vidor, Adolphe Menjou and Lawrence Gray star in this Famous Players-Lasky production. Silent with music track.
VHS: S07237. $19.95.
Malcolm St. Clair, USA, 1925, 63 mins.

Babes in the Woods
This intriguing silent film contains a story within a story. A number of fairy tales are joined to yield a lesson for a woman pining after her brother-in-law. This film includes a charming rendition of the *Hansel and Gretel tale*. Francis Parker and Virginia Lee Corbin star along with a cast of children who act out the fairy tales.
VHS: S23823. $24.95.
Charles Franklin, USA, 1917, 44 mins.

The Back Trail
Hoxie was one of the silent screen's most popular cowboy stars, who could ride and fight with the best of them. In this film he is a war veteran afflicted by amnesia. He is induced to break the law and take over his sister's estate, but his memory returns in time for him to foil the real crooks.
VHS: S18903. $19.95.
Clifford Smith, USA, 1924

Barbara Frietchie
Florence Vidor and Edmund Lowe star in what was originally described as "the drama of glorious American womanhood." Silent with music track.
VHS: S07251. $24.95.

Barbarian
The only surviving film of Monroe Salisbury. The drama is set in the north woods, and the film also stars Jane Novak. Decomposition of nitrate original in some scenes. USA, 1921, 52 mins.
VHS: S08854. $19.95.

Bare Knees
The quintessential '20s "flapper" movie about free spirited women, the story concerns Billie (Virginia Lee Corbin), whose arrival at her sister's birthday party unleashes a series of a strange and unsettling events. With a full orchestra score. With Donald Keith, Jane Winton, Johnnie Walker, Forest Stanley and Maude Fulton.
VHS: S17489. $19.95.
Erle C. Kenton, USA, 1928, 61 mins.

The Bat (1926)
One of the great silent horror films. A maniacal killer dressed in a weird bat-like costume terrorizes a group of people in a shuddery, spooky old house riddled with secret passageways. The use of miniatures and the overall cinematography is stunning for its day.
VHS: S15365. $19.95.
Roland West, USA, 1926, 81 mins.

Battling Bunyon
Wesley Barry, Molly Malone, Frank Campeau, Harry Mann and Chester Conklin star.
VHS: S07239. $19.95.
Paul Hurst, USA, 1925, 63 mins.

Battling Orioles
Glenn Tryon, Blanche Megaffey, Noah Young, Sam Lufkin, Robert Page star.
VHS: S07262. $19.95.
Ted Wilde/Fred Guiol, USA, 1924, 60 mins.

Beast of Babylon Against the Son of Hercules
Gordon Scott stars in this action film from the silent era. It has a wealth of imaginative detail that compensates for its lack of historical accuracy. 98 mins.
VHS: S23150. $24.95.

Beau Brummel
John Barrymore stars in this early silent version of the English dandy and ladies' man.
VHS: S02584. $34.95.
Harry Beaumont, USA, 1924, 80 mins.

Beau Ravel
Thomas Ince produced this story of aged love starring Lewis Stone, Florence Vidor, Lloyd Hughes and William Conklin. Jitter in two short parts of the film.
VHS: S08858. $24.95.
John Griffith Wray, USA, 1921, 70 mins.

Beggars of Life
The curious and melodramatic adventures of an everyday hobo. This rarely seen Wellman film stars Richard Arlen, Wallace Beery and young Louise Brooks in her finest early role outside of Hawks' *A Girl in Every Port*.
VHS: S15287. $49.95.
William Wellman, USA, 1928, 80 mins.

Behind the Front
Wallace Beery and Raymond Haton star in this drama which was the third highest grossing film of 1926.
VHS: S08847. $24.95.
A. Edward Sutherland, USA, 1926, 65 mins.

Behind Two Guns
One of J.B. Warner's excellent surviving works, *Behind Two Guns* is a delightful, lighthearted western comedy. Carter (Warner) and his partner Slowfoot (Calles) are on the trail of a mysterious stage robber who can make funds disappear while the stage is en route. With Hazel Newman, Marin Sais, Jay Morley, Jim Welch, Otto Lederer, William Calles, Jack Waltemeyer, Emily Gerdes, Bartlett A. Carre and Robert N. Bradbury. Silent with orchestra score.
VHS: S32047. $19.95.
Robert N. Bradbury, USA, 1924, 58 mins.

The Bellhop/The Noon Whistle
These two comic shorts are classics from the silent era. The first is directed by Larry Semon and Norman Taurog, and stars Semon opposite Oliver Hardy. Stan Laurel then gets his chance to amuse in *The Noon Whistle*.
VHS: S26689. $19.95.

The Bells
When a carnival hypnotist (Boris Karloff, bearing a striking resemblance to Dr. Caligari) arrives in a small town, the local lodge-keeper (Lionel Barrymore) is haunted by the spirit of the man he brutally murdered. Adapted from the story by Edgar Allen Poe. Silent.
VHS: S04084. $24.95.
James Young, USA, 1926, 70 mins.

Beloved Rogue
A beautiful silent epic romance of medieval France, notable for its art direction and massive sets. With John Barrymore, Conrad Veidt, Marceline Day.
VHS: S05978. $29.95.
Laser: LD70768. $39.95.
Alan Crosland, USA, 1927, 110 mins.

Ben-Hur
Ramon Novarro is the title character in the silent version known for its classic chariot race. Novarro races against Francis X. Bushman who plays his sworn enemy Messala. Truly a thrilling race on a colossal set staged by second unit director Reaves Eason. Based on the novel by Lew Wallace, the film also has a sea battle, lepers and a meeting with Jesus Christ.
VHS: S07791. $29.95.
Fred Niblo, USA, 1926, 116 mins.

Betsy Ross
This great historical silent film has a cast that includes Alice Brady, John Bowers, Lillian Cook, Victor Kennard, Eugenie Woodward and many others. It's based on the intriguing story of Quaker Betsy Griscom, who married John Ross and helped fashion the American flag. Orchestral score.
VHS: S22434. $19.95.
Travers Vale, USA, 1919, 58 mins.

Big Parade
John Gilbert learns that war is not a grand and glorious adventure when he barely survives the trenches of World War I. Produced and directed by King Vidor. With Renee Adoree as the French girl who Gilbert teaches how to chew gum. Also Karl Dane, Hobart Bosworth and Tom O'Brien as Bull. A realistic look at modern warfare.
VHS: S07792. $29.95.
Laser: LD70130. $39.98.
King Vidor, USA, 1925, 126 mins.

Bill Fields and Will Rogers
W.C. Fields stars in his first film as a suitor for the affections of a good-looking woman who is willing to settle his difference with a rival over a friendly game of pool. *Pool Sharks* (1915) recreated his famous vaudeville routine. *The Ropin' Fool* features Will Rogers slipping a lasso over anyone or thing within range. USA/Great Britain, 1915-21, 48 mins.
VHS: S05447. $24.95.

The Black Pirate
Now you can enjoy this Douglas Fairbanks, Sr. swashbuckler in the two-strip color process as it was originally shot. Taken from a rare French print, all of the titles have been replaced in English from the U.S. release. This is a true classic from the silent era and a must for every collection. Orchestra scored.
VHS: S05709. $24.95.
Laser: LD70394. $49.95.
Albert Parker, USA, 1926, 104 mins.

Blonde for a Night
Marie Prevost stars as a suspicious wife who tests her husband (Franklin Pangborn) while she's disguised as another woman. With Harrison Ford. Silent, music track.
VHS: S33059. $24.95.
E. Mason Hopper/F. McGrew Willis, USA, 1926, 55 mins.

Blood and Sand
In one of his most famous roles, Rudolph Valentino portrays a poor boy who works his way up to becoming a famous matador. In the process he marries his childhood sweetheart but falls into the clutches of a beautiful society woman (Nita Naldi). Shining through gloriously in every shot of the film is the astonishing grace that made Valentino one of the most popular stars in the history of the cinema. Also included is a rare Valentino short. Piano score.
VHS: S00147. $29.95.
Fred Niblo, USA, 1922, 87 mins.

Blood and Steel
William Desmond is out to destroy the railroad of his father's enemy in this silent railroad stunt drama.
VHS: S08876. $24.95.
J.P. McGowan, USA, 1925, 65 mins.

Blot
A carefully observed depiction of social values under pressure in small-town America, the story is of a teacher's wife who steals a chicken for her child.
VHS: S03710. $29.95.
Lois Weber, USA, 1921, 79 mins.

Brass
Monte Blue, Marie Prevost, Harry Myers, Irene Rich, Frank Keenan star.
VHS: S07230. $19.95.
Sidney Franklin, USA, 1923, 60 mins.

Braveheart
Silent film star Rod La Rocque is an Indian brave sent East to study law so that he can defend the tribe's fishing rights. At college, Braveheart becomes an outstanding scholar and an all-American football player. Trouble brews when Braveheart is accused of selling game signals to the opposing team. Orchestra score.
VHS: S22012. $19.95.
Alan Hale, USA, 1925, 62 mins.

Broken Hearts of Broadway
Colleen Moore, John Walker, Alice Lake, Tully Marshall, Kate Price star.
VHS: S07223. $24.95.
Irving Cummings, USA, 1923, 85 mins.

Broken Mask
Cullen Landis, Barbara Bedford, Wheeler Oakman star. Silent with music track.
VHS: S07225. $19.95.
James P. Hogan, USA, 1928, 60 mins.

Bronco Billy Anderson
Four short films from the silent Bronco Billy series: *The Making of Bronco Billy, Bronco Billy's Sentence, The Prisoner, Naked Hands*. 62 mins.
VHS: S08874. $24.95.

Brown of Harvard
Hailed as one of the best college pictures of the silent era, this film depicts college life seen through the eyes of a typical college freshman who dreams of being a football star. Many of the sport scenes were taken from footage shot at Harvard University. With William Haines, Mary Brian and an unbilled John Wayne in his first film appearance as an extra, portraying a football player.
VHS: S30791. $19.95.
Jack Conway, USA, 1926, 85 mins.

Burn 'em Up Barnes
Stars Johnny Hines as a car racer who leaves home to conquer the world but discovers freedom among a group of hobos instead. With Edmund Breese, George Fawcett and Betty Carpenter. Produced by Mastodon Films.
VHS: S07257. $24.95.
George Beranger/Johnny Hines, USA, 1921, 70 mins.

Burning Daylight
Milton Sills, Doris Kenyon, Arthur Stone and "Big Boy" Williams are just some of the silent stars featured in this gripping melodrama. It's based on Jack London's story of an Alaskan real estate mogul who loses everything to a group of San Francisco investment sharks. Silent, with orchestra score.
VHS: S26968. $24.95.
Richard A. Rowland, USA, 1928, 72 mins.

The Busher
Charles Ray stars in this Thomas Ince production which also features John Gilbert as a young baseball pitcher given a chance in the major leagues. With Margaret Livingston.
VHS: S07241. $19.95.
Jerome Storm, USA, 1919, 60 mins.

California in '49
Jacques Jaccard and Ben Wilson directed the feature version of this 15-chapter serial, *Days of '49*, starring Neva Gerber and Edmund Cobb. USA, 1925, 70 mins.
VHS: S08865. $24.95.

California Straight Ahead
A hilarious trip to California is the subject of this early comedy starring Reginald Denny, Gertrude Olmsted and Tom Wilson.
VHS: S07263. $24.95.
Harry Pollard, USA, 1925, 90 mins.

The Call of the Wilderness
Sandow the dog was one of the silent screen's greatest stars. In this nail-biting melodrama he helps his master fight off competing homesteaders. It's a film that brings the phrase "man's best friend" alive.
VHS: S24001. $19.95.
Jack Nelson, USA, 1926, 56 mins.

Camille
Rudolph Valentino is at his prime in this silent classic. It's based on a tale that has inspired stage plays, operas and other films. A dying courtesan falls for an innocent young man. Despite her life of ill repute, their love holds the promise of a better life, if only it weren't for that pesky cough.
VHS: S25696. $19.95.
Fred Niblo, USA, 1921, 55 mins.

Campus Nights
Albert Kelly, Raymond McKee, Shirley Palmer, Marie Quillen, Jean Laverty and J.C. Fowler star in this silent film.
VHS: S07268. $24.95.
Albert Kelly, USA, 1929, 70 mins.

Capital Punishment
Two wealthy men decide to test the system and make it look like one of them has been murdered. Clara Bow plays the wife of a young man who allows himself to be caught up in the "murder," but things become tense when the wealthy "victim" actually ends up dead. An interesting early drama and a great chance to see an early Bow performance. Very rare!
VHS: S30557. $19.95.
James P. Hogan, USA, 1925

The Cat and the Canary
A shadowy mansion provides the setting for chills, laughter and amazing Expressionist filmmaking when a family gathers for the reading of an eccentric relative's will. Combining masterful art direction, photography and pacing, Leni's film is the most famous of the classic *Old Dark House* story. Silent.
VHS: S00219. $29.95.
Laser: LD76290. $39.99.
Paul Leni, USA, 1927, 71 mins.

Chang
Chang is a revelation, a prototype for Cooper and Schoedsack's *King Kong*, and a terrifically entertaining film in its own right. Shot entirely in Siam, it tells the story of a farmer and his family, who have settled on a small patch of land at the edge of the jungle. They constantly struggle against the wild animals around them—bears, tigers, leopards, and even…changs! Silent, with a new score by Bangkok composer Bruce Gaston.
VHS: S16428. $39.95.
Laser: CLV/CAV. LD72071. $39.95.
Merian Cooper/Ernest Schoedsack, USA, 1927, 67 mins.

Chapter in Her Life
Rare film from one of the first women directors, Lois Weber, who began her directing career in 1913 after success as a concert pianist and actress. Weber specialized in the concerns of women, and *Chapter in Her Life* tells of the paralysis in the household of an embittered aging man and his widowed daughter-in-law who has no where to go.
VHS: S03711. $24.95.
Lois Weber, USA, 1923, 70 mins.

The Charlatan
A woman is poisoned while in a magician's cabinet. In this suspensful tale, the identity of the murderer and his motive drive an inspired plot. Transferred from the only known original print available. Margaret Livingston, Rockliffe Fellows, Philo McCullough and Anita Garvin are among the principal stars of this silent classic.
VHS: S23308. $24.95.
George Melford, USA, 1929, 63 mins.

Charley's Aunt
Sydney Chaplin portrays the aunt in this classic comedy. Silent with music track.
VHS: S07265. $24.95.
Scott Sidney, USA, 1925, 85 mins.

Cheerful Fraud
Reginald Denny, Gertrude Olmstead, Emily Fitzroy, Gertrude Astor star.
VHS: S07244. $24.95.
William A. Seiter, USA, 1927, 64 mins.

Chloe/Love Is Calling You/Sun
Terrific southern melodrama starring Olive Borden as a woman caught between two men. With Reed Howes. Silent, music track.
VHS: S33060. $24.95.
Mickey Neilan, USA, 1929, 70 mins.

Civilization
Known also as *He Who Returned*, this was one of three pacifist films made in 1916 on the eve of the US entry into World War I. Set in a mythical kingdom, a king declares war on his neighbors to satisfy a lust for power.
VHS: S00246. $29.95.
Thomas Ince, USA, 1916, 80 mins.

Classic Photoplays
Contains *Ben Hur* (1908, 11 mins); *She*, the first film version of the classic Rider Haggard story with Marguerite Snow and James Cruze; and *Two Orphans* (1911), produced by Carl Selig and released a reel at a time with T.J. Kerrigan, Charles Clory and Kathlyn Williams.
VHS: S05284. $19.95.

Claw
Norman Kerry, Claire Windsor and Helene Sullivan star in this film based on the novel by Cynthia Stockley.
VHS: S07205. $19.95.
Sidney Olcott, USA, 1927, 55 mins.

The Clodhopper
An early Charles Ray production. A boy from the sticks is lured by the Broadway footlights.
VHS: S07242. $19.95.
Victor Schertzinger, USA, 1917, 47 mins.

Coast Patrol
Kenneth McDonald, Claire De Lorez and Fay Wray star. Smugglers run into trouble with the Coast Guard. Grainy.
VHS: S07216. $19.95.
Bud Barsky, USA, 1925, 60 mins.

Cobra
Rudolph Valentino stars as a gambler trying to go straight, who messes around with one too many women and ends up involved in a murder. An early effort for Ritz-Carlton, with Nita Naldi, Casson Ferguson, Gertrude Olmsted and Ellen Percy.
VHS: S04799. $24.95.
Laser: LD76958. $39.99.
Joseph Henabery, USA, 1925, 70 mins.

Come Up Smiling
Tap dancer Will Mahoney plays a carnival worker trying to raise money for his girlfriend's operation. With the short *She's My Lilly*. Silent, music track.
VHS: S33061. $24.95.
USA, 1934, 70 mins.

The Comediennes, Volume 1
Delightful comedies by three ladies of the silent screen are joined in this video, including *The Detectress* (1919, Gale Henry), *Cinderella Cinders* (1924, Alice Howell) and *Spanking Breezes* (1926, Alice Day). 58 mins.
VHS: S23316. $19.95.

The Comediennes, Volume 2
Three more comedy shorts featuring the ladies of the silent screen make up this video. In *'Twas Henry's Fault* (1919) Elinor Field buys a flivver—not quite what her husband expected. In *A Roman Scandal* (1920) Colleen Moore joins a theatrical troupe over the protests of her boyfriend. In *Her First Flame* (1920) Gale Henry becomes a fireman as women take over men's jobs. 58 mins.
VHS: S23317. $19.95.

Comedy of Max Linder
These early, short, comic films capture the zany innovations of Max Linder, the comic who inspired Charlie Chaplin. Over a dozen shorts show Max fighting against a world heavy with comic possibilities. From ice skates to fly paper, Max struggles just to get a grip on things. Silent with orchestra score. USA, 1905-1913, 105 mins.
VHS: S27322. $24.95.

Coming of Amos
Rod La Rocque and Noah Beery star in this Cecil B. De Mille production. La Rocque is a vacationing Australian in France who rescues Jetta Goudal from the evil Beery.
VHS: S07207. $19.95.
Paul Sloane, USA, 1923, 58 mins.

Conductor
Charles Hines stars as an Irish street car conductor. USA, 1924, 85 mins.
VHS: S07259. $29.95.

Conquering Power
Rudolph Valentino is perfectly cast in this early silent adaptation of Balzac's *Eugenie Grandet*. It is a story of true love that conquers all, including the overreaching power of wealth.
VHS: S25697. $19.95.
Rex Ingram, USA, 1921, 60 mins.

Covered Wagon
An epic western of the silent screen. A cast of 3,000, including 1,000 Native Americans, was employed to bring the Emerson Hough novel to the big screen. Follow the adventures of the Wingate family as they cross the Platte River, witness cattle stampedes, buffalo hunts and Indian attacks. With J. Warren Kerrigan, Lois Wilson, Ernest Torrence and Alan Hale. Westward Ho!
VHS: S12239. $19.95.
Laser: LD75176. $34.98.
James Cruze, USA, 1923, 60 mins.

The Coward
Charles Ray and Frank Keenan star, with the young John Gilbert in a bit part.
VHS: S07234. $19.95.
Thomas H. Ince, USA, 1915, 60 mins.

The Crackerjack
Johnny Hines is a pickle salesman who ends up posing as a south-of-the-border dictator in this fast-paced, rare silent film. Music track.
VHS: S33062. $24.95.
Charles Hines, USA, 1936, 67 mins.

Cradle of Courage
In one of his few non-westerns, William S. Hart stars as a cop and reformed bad guy who gets caught up in the murder of his brother during post-World War I. Some interesting San Francisco locations provide novelty, as does an especially good fight with Tom Santschi. With short subject *Hell's Hinges* (26 mins.). Silent, music track.
VHS: S33046. $24.95.
Lambert Hillyer, USA, 1920, 80 mins.

Cricket on the Hearth
This silent film is based on Charles Dickens' story of young love. A newlywed couple discovers a sign of good luck as they enter their new home—a cricket on the hearth. Featuring Paul Gerson, Virginia Brown Faire, Paul Moore and Joan Standing. 1923, 68 mins.
VHS: S23109. $24.95.

The Crowd
An ordinary man struggles to maintain his individuality in a heartless city. Featuring James Murray as John, a store clerk, and Eleanor Boardman as his wife Mary. *The Crowd* is one of the most important films of the silent era; its visual innovations still astonish viewers, and the relevance of its theme has only increased over the years" *(Pacific Film Archive)*.
VHS: S09279. $29.95.
King Vidor, USA, 1928, 104 mins.

Cyclone Cavalier
Reed Howes stars as an irresponsible city boy who gets in over his head when he is sent to South America. Silent, music track.
VHS: S33063. $24.95.
Albert S. Rogell, USA, 1926, 55 mins.

D'Artagnan
A very early version of Dumas' *The Three Musketeers*, with Orrin Johnson and Dorothy Dalton.
VHS: S13320. $29.95.
Thomas Ince, USA, 1916, c. 65 mins.

Daddies
Mae Marsh, Harry Myers, Claire Adams star in this early William A. Seiter production for Warner Brothers.
VHS: S07240. $19.95.
William A. Seiter, USA, 1924, 60 mins.

Dames Ahoy
Glenn Tryon, Helen Wright, Otis Harlan, Eddie Gribon and Gertrude Astor star. Three sailors on shore leave try to find the blonde who tricked one into drawing half his pay. A silent classic with piano music.
VHS: S22428. $19.95.

Dancing Mothers
Alice Joyce, Norm Trevor and Clara Bow, the "It" girl, star in one of Clara Bow's best flapper roles. Silent with musical track.
VHS: S05599. $24.95.
Herbert Brenon, USA, 1926, 85 mins.

Dangerous Hours
One of the first anti-Communist films to be made in Hollywood, produced by Thomas Ince, and starring Lloyd Hughes.
VHS: S11458. $24.95.
Fred Niblo, USA, 1919, 84 mins.

The Deerslayer
Bela Lugosi is featured as a Native American in this silent adaptation of James Fenimore Cooper's novel *The Deerslayer*. It's an inspiring tale from a time when the promise of this continent seemed limitless. 1920, 60 mins.
VHS: S23826. $24.95.

The Devil's Circus
Norma Shearer is Mary, in love with handsome young pickpocket Richard Carlstop (Charles Emmet Mack). When Carlstop gets arrested, Mary, desperate for money, finds work with a circus in a dangerous aerialist act over a lion cage. While waiting for Carlstop to be released from prison, Mary bears the advances of Lieberkind (John Miljan), an infatuated lion tamer, and the jealousy of his mistress, Yonna (Carmel Myers), which causes Mary to be seriously injured. Silent, music track.
VHS: S33050. $24.95.
Benjamin Christensen, USA, 1926, 72 mins.

Devil's Island
This silent film tells of inhumanity set amidst the isolation of the legendary prison Devil's Island. Pauline Frederick and Marion Nixon star.
VHS: S23827. $24.95.
Frank O'Connor, USA, 1926, 73 mins.

Dick Turpin
Tom Mix portrays the famous English highwayman. Silent with music track.
VHS: S07222. $24.95.
John G. Blystone, USA, 1925, 70 mins.

The Disciple
William S. Hart's stirring saga of love, lust and conflicting emotions, with Hart as Jim Houston, the shootin' Iron Parson, out to rid a prairie town of corruption. Silent with music score.
VHS: S06929. $29.95.
William S. Hart, USA, 1915, 80 mins.

Don Juan
John Barrymore is stunning as the famous lover and adventurer in the court of Lucrezia Borgia in this top-notch swashbuckler. With Mary Astor, Warner Oland, Myrna Loy, Estelle Taylor. Newly mastered. Silent with music track.
VHS: S13399. $29.98.
Laser: LD70558. $39.98.
Alan Crosland, USA, 1926, 126 mins.

Don Q, Son of Zorro
Douglas Fairbanks swashbuckles his way through two roles as both Zorro and his lesser known son Don Q, also known as Cesar de Vega. This silent screen adventure is filled with action and swordplay. With Mary Astor, Donald Crisp, Warner Oland and Jean Hersholt.
VHS: S05479. $24.95.
Laser: CLV. **LD71714. $19.98.**
Donald Crisp, USA, 1925, 148 mins.

The Douglas Fairbanks Sr. Collection
Douglas Fairbanks Sr. quickly developed into one of the most sought-after silent film stars. Four of his classic works, all newly remastered, are joined on this laser disc, including *The Three Musketeers, Robin Hood, The Gaucho* and *The Thief of Bagdad*. 494 mins.
Laser: LD75914. $124.99.

Down to Earth
Douglas Fairbanks is a health nut who causes all kinds of problems. USA, 1917.
VHS: S08885. $19.95.

Down to the Sea in Ships
Curtis Pierce, Ada Laycock, Marguerite Courtot, Clara Bow, James Turfler star.
VHS: S07249. $24.95.
Elmer Clifton, USA, 1922, 100 mins.

Drake Case
This rare Universal courtroom drama was made at the very end of the silent era and stars Robert Frasier, Doris Lloyd and Gladys Brockwell. USA, 1929, 56 mins.
VHS: S11457. $19.95.

Drop Kick
A very rare Richard Barthelmess drama of a college football star, with a cameo appearance by John Wayne. USA, 1927, 62 mins.
VHS: S07762. $24.95.

The Duchess of Buffalo
Marian Duncan (Constance Talmadge) is an American dancer who climaxes her theatrical success in Russia by becoming the fiancee of Vladimir Orloff (Tullio Carminatii), a young army officer, unaware that the Grand Duke Alexandrovich (Edward Martindel) is also in love with her. Enraged over his rival, the Duke wants Orloff arrested. Marian flees with her lover to another city. There the citizens and soldiers believe Marian and Orloff to be a grand duchess and her adjutant. With Rose Done, Chester Conklin, Lawrence Grant, Martha Franklin and Jean De Briac. Silent with orchestra score.
VHS: S30677. $24.95.
Sidney Franklin, USA, 1926, 75 mins.

Dynamite Dan
Boris Karloff, Bruce Mitchell, Kenneth McDonald, Frank Rise star. Silent with music track. Grainy.
VHS: S07227. $19.95.
Bruce Mitchell, USA, 1924, 60 mins.

The Eagle
Rudolph Valentino and Vilma Banky star in this story of love and revenge set in old Russia. Valentino plays The Eagle—the leader of a gang of bandits who fight for the poor and oppressed. With brilliant art direction by William Cameron Menzies, directed by Clarence Brown. A new musical score by Carl Davis.
VHS: S10914. $39.99.
Clarence Brown, USA, 1925, 81 mins.

Eagle of the Night
This rare Pathe, ten-part silent film serial follows the diabolical plans of a group of villians who hope to steal the "Mystic Muffler." This device would render airplanes silent and thus have momentous implications to anyone possessing it. Elements of some of the serial are missing as this copy was made from the only known 35mm nitrate print. Orchestra score. 102 mins.
VHS: S29458. $29.95.

Early Silent Movie Prevues
This hour-long collection features those thrilling shorts always prefaced with the exciting words, "coming soon." Dozens of stars from the silent era can be seen in their most memorable screen moments.
VHS: S23149. $24.95.

Early Westerns #1
A collection of very early silent Westerns, including *Fatherhood of Buck McKee* (1912, released by Vitagraph), *Sherriff of Stone Gulch* (1918, with Ruth Roland), *The Man from Nowhere* (1914, with J. Warren Kerrigan, Vera Sussan, George Perilet), *Man from Tia Juana* (1917, Jack Hoxie), *Four Gun Bandit* (1919, with Pete Morrison), and *Fight It Out* (1920, with Hoot Gibson). Total length: 115 mins.
VHS: S08870. $24.95.

Early Westerns #2
Contains *Get Your Man* (Neal Hart, 23 mins), *Battling Travers* (Dick Hatton, 26 mins), *Extra Man and The Milk Fed Lion* (Art Accord, 27 mins), *The Man with a Punch* (Hoot Gibson, 18 mins), and *Bashful Whirlwind* (Edmund Cobb, 22 mins).
VHS: S08871. $24.95.

Ella Cinders
Colleen Moore stars as the would-be Cinderella who escapes her evil step-father and sisters by winning a contest to go to Hollywood—only to find it a scam; she nevertheless wins a role in the movies and finds true love. With Lloyd Hughes, Vera Lewis and Harry Langdon. Silent with music track.
VHS: S07281. $19.95.
Alfred E. Green, USA, 1926, 60 mins.

Ella Cinders and Mormon Maid
Two rare silents: Colleen Moore as Ella, a delightful Cinderella-goes-to-Hollywood theme; and Mae Murray, in one of her few extant films, is the maid, co-starring with Frank Borzage (!) and villainous Noah Beery. USA, 1925/1917.
VHS: S05981. $24.95.

Episodes of the Hazards of Helen
Produced by Kalem in 1914, this 119 chapter serial did not contain cliff hanger endings. Each episode is a complete story. The first three star Helen Holmes, the last Helen Gibson. Contains Episode #9, Leap from the Water Tower; #31, The Paytrain; #33, In Danger's Path and #63, The Open Track. 56 mins.
VHS: S11462. $19.95.

Evangeline
Delores Del Rio, Roland Drew and Alec B. Frances star in this silent film classic. The bittersweet love story of the title character is based on Henry Wadsworth Longfellow's tale of a woman in search of her lost love. This film's last reel is heavily damaged but the conclusion is intact. Piano score.
VHS: S22895. $14.95.
Edwin Carewe, USA, 1929, 72 mins.

Eve's Leaves
Leatrice Joy, William Boyd, Robert Edeson star in this early De Mille production.
VHS: S07247. $24.95.
Paul Sloane, USA, 1926, 80 mins.

Evolution
Live-action footage is combined with animation in this early silent drama. Produced by the great Max Fleischer.
VHS: S23828. $24.95.
Max Fleischer, USA, 1923, 75 mins.

The Extra Girl
Mabel Normand stars in a comedy about a young woman's attempts to break into the movies. Made after her involvement in the William Desmond Taylor scandal. Story by Mack Sennett. The scene where she unknowingly leads a lion through a movie lot is a classic. With Billy Bevan, Ralph Graves and Vernon Dent.
VHS: S04803. $24.95.
Laser: Extended play CLV. **LD71524. $49.95.**
F. Richard Jones, USA, 1923, 70 mins.

Eyes of Youth
Vitagraph star Clara Kimball Young at her peak in 1919 as a young girl with a golden heart who must choose between marrying a rich banker, waiting for assistant bank cashier Milton Sills to earn his fortune, pursuing an operatic career or marrying the man she truly loves. Allowed a glimpse into the future, she learns something very intriguing. At the end of the film, a small role is an actor, new to motion pictures in 1919, credited as "Rudolfo Valentino." 85 mins. 1919, silent with music score.
VHS: S06982. $29.95.

Eyes Right!
Francis X. Bushman stars in this drama about life at a military academy. With Fiobelle Fairbanks, Dora Dean and Larry Kent.
VHS: S08859. $19.95.
Louis Ghaudet, USA, 1926, 46 mins.

False Faces
Lon Chaney and Henry B. Walthall star in this silent spy thriller. Lone Wolf is working as a secret agent for the allies. Soon he is on a mission to the US to find a master German spy played by Chaney.
VHS: S25709. $29.95.
Irvin Willat, 1918, USA, 65 mins.

Fighting American
Pat O'Malley, Mary Astor, Raymond Hatton and Warner Oland star in this drama about an uprising in China that is thwarted by an enterprising American. Silent with music score.
VHS: S10363. $19.95.
Tom Forman, USA, 1924, 65 mins.

The Fighting Coward
A shrewd comedy of manners and observation about the emotional and physical transformation of an insecure young man who leaves home and returns as a brave individual. With Cullen Landis, Ernest Torrence, Mary Astor and Noah Beery. Silent with musical score.
VHS: S20052. $19.95.
James Cruze, USA, 1924, 66 mins.

Fighting Eagle
Rod La Rocque, Phyllis Haver, Sam De Grasse, Sally Rand and Clarence Burton star in this melodrama set during the Napoleonic Wars, in which a love-struck young man is arrested by the enemies of Napoleon. Silent with music track.
VHS: S07236. $19.95.
Donald Crisp, USA, 1927

The Fighting Legion
Ken assumes the identity of a murdered Texas Ranger in order to root out the killer and understand the killer's motives. The film was originally released in both silent and sound versions, though only the silent version survives. With Ken Maynard and Dorothy Dwan. Silent with musical score.
VHS: S20053. $19.95.
Harry J. Brown, USA, 1930, 69 mins.

Films of Edmund Cobb
Three complete films by Cobb were transferred from mint 9.5mm prints. The first two are from the Cobb Mountie series, *The Courage of Collier* and *Two Fister*. In the *Western Man Tamer*, Walter Brennan makes an appearance in a small role. These silent films include orchestral score. 55 mins.
VHS: S22433. $24.95.

Films of Thomas Ince
Five films by Thomas Ince: *The Invaders, The Struggle, Drummer of the Eighth, Silent Heroes* and *Last of the Line*, made in 1914 and starring Sessue Hayakawa.
VHS: S05413. $29.95.

The Final Extra
This silent drama tells the sordid tale of bootlegging, murder, show business and the cub reporter who is out to save the girl and get the scoop. With Marguerite De La Motte as Ruth, John Miljan as Mervyn LeRoy and Grant Withers as Pat Riley, the eager beaver reporter.
VHS: S05703. $29.95.
James P. Hogan, USA, 1927, 76 mins.

First American Features
This boxed set highlights some of the greatest accomplishments in American cinema, from its groundbreaking beginnings. Includes Cecil B. DeMille's *The Cheat*, Sidney Olcott's *From the Manger to the Cross*, Thomas Ince's *Civilization, Regeneration, Traffic in Souls* and *Young Romance*, and an abridgement of Maurice Tourneur's comedy *A Girl's Folly*, as well as the 1910 short *The Police Force of New York City*. 474 mins.
Laser: LD76749. $139.99.

Flesh and Blood
Lon Chaney stars as an escaped convict who swears revenge. With Edith Roberts and De Witt Jennings.
VHS: S03654. $29.95.
Irving Cummings, USA, 1922, 74 mins.

Flesh and the Devil
"The first of the Garbo-Gilbert romances, [this] was quite certainly a box office milestone—and it also represents something of a high-water mark in the sheer elegance and 'bigness' of movies in their most glamorous era…Honor, loyalty, love—strong emotions all of them, are given full expression in a story which permits no facile solutions" (*Classics of the Silent Screen*). Garbo is simply magnificent as the seductive temptress who drives a wedge between two old friends.
VHS: S09280. $29.95.
Clarence Brown, USA, 1927, 103 mins.

The Flying Fool
Pilot Bill returns from the First World War and finds that he must protect his little brother from a formidable new enemy, a woman. When Bill and his brother's girlfriend meet, his own desires enter the picture. She is a smalltown girl, decent and likable. Before long the brothers are engaged in duel in the air to see who wins her affections.
VHS: S18904. $19.95.
Tay Garnett, USA, 1929, 63 mins.

A Fool There Was
Theda Bara's first and most legendary film tells the story of a good man brought down by an irresistable vamp.
VHS: S05983. $19.95.
Frank Powell, USA, 1915

The Forbidden City
Norma Talmadge and Thomas Meigan are at the center of this early tear-jerker about love in a faraway land. A Chinese woman falls in love with a visiting American official, with disastrous consequences.
VHS: S23829. $24.95.
Sidney Franklin, USA, 1918, 55 mins.

Forty-Nine Seventeen
Joseph Girard, Leo Pierson and Jean Hersholt are featured in this silent film set in a Western ghost town. A retired judge sets out on a mission. He intends to restore this eerie remnant from frontier days.
VHS: S23314. $19.95.
Ruth Ann Baldwin, USA, 1917, 61 mins.

The Four Horsemen of the Apocalypse
Rudolph Valentino became a certified star for his work in this film, especially his notorious tango scene. Based on Blasco Ibanez' novel, this is a story of two brothers who end up on opposing sides in World War I. Stark imagery make this unforgettable anti-war film a silent classic.
VHS: S23111. $24.95.
Rex Ingram, USA, 1921, 114 mins.

Free to Love
A roaring twenties American classic, starring the great Clara Bow.
VHS: S06219. $49.95.
Frank O'Connor, USA, 1925, 61 mins.

From the Manger to the Cross
The Kalem Company reenacted their passion play for the camera, resulting in this, the first Biblical epic to be filmed in the Holy Land. In a straightfoward fashion it shows the life of Christ, beginning with the Nativity and ending with the Crucifixion. It includes footage of the Holy Family at the Sphinx and is tinted to match the release prints.
VHS: S25740. $29.95.
Sidney Olcott, USA, 1915, 71 mins.

The Fugitive (The Taking of Luke McVane)
William S. Hart shoots a man for cheating at cards and is pursued into the desert by a vigilant sheriff. There they meet a pack of bloodthirsty savages. A pretty busy day in the Old West. Hart's twelfth film. With Enid Markey.
VHS: S05488. $24.95.
William S. Hart, USA, 1915, 36 mins.

Garden of Eden
Naughty Lubitsch-like comedy with Corinne Griffith, Lowell Sherman, Louise Dresser.
VHS: S05984. $49.95.
Lewis Milestone, USA, 1928

The Gaucho
Against the peaks of the Andes, Douglas Fairbanks confounds corrupt government forces that would impinge on the romantic free lifestyles of the South American cowboys. This lavishly produced work from the early days of technicolor is an inspiring and exciting romp through the Pampas.
VHS: S27571. $24.95.
F. Richard Jones, USA, 1928, 103 mins.

Getting Gertie's Garter
Marie Prevost, Charles Ray and Franklin Pangborn star in this classic comedy from the golden age of silent film. Gertie's ex-fiance tries to recover an embarrassing token of his former love's affection. The trick is that he must do this without alerting either Gertie or his new love.
VHS: S23830. $24.95.
E. Mason Harper, USA, 1927, 74 mins.

The Ghost of Rosy Taylor
Mary Miles Minter stars in this silent about a dead housekeeper who has been cleaning the mansion of the DuVivier family each week, much to the current homeowner's surprise. With Alan Forrest, George Periolat, Helen Howard, Emma Kluge, Kate Price, and Ann Schaefer.
VHS: S37089. $19.95.
Edward S. Sloman, USA, 1918

The Girl in the Pullman

Marie Prevost and Harrison Ford (not the same guy) are paired in this romantic comedy. After divorcing her husband, a wife begins to reconsider her husband's worth. Then she sets out to regain his affection while he is on a honeymoon with his new wife.
VHS: S23831. $24.95.
Erle C. Kenton, USA, 1927, 65 mins.

A Girl's Folly

Doris Kenyon stars as a country girl captivated by the magic of moving pictures. When she can't make it as an actress the actor she adores, Robert Warwick, offers her another path to riches. Soon she is faced with a troubling situation when her mother decides to visit her "successful" daughter.
VHS: S23309. $24.95.
Maurice Tourneur, USA, 1917, 60 mins.

Going Straight

Former criminals John Remington and his wife Grace are now respected, affluent members of their community. A member of their old gang finds them and threatens to tell the police about their past if they refuse to help him pull one more heist. Silent with orchestra score.
VHS: S32051. $19.95.
Chester M. Franklin, USA, 1916, 60 mins.

Goose Woman

Based on a Rex Beach story about a goose woman who was once a famous opera singer. She accidentally involves her son in a murder just to see her name hit the headlines again. With a remarkable performance by Louise Dresser. Extremely rare silent film.
VHS: S06220. $49.95.
Clarence Brown, USA, 1925

Grand Duchess and the Waiter

Adolphe Menjou and Florence Vidor star in this light comic farce. A millionaire could not possibly attract the attentions of a grand duchess, so he must disguise himself as a waiter.
VHS: S23832. $24.95.
Malcolm St. Clair, USA, 1926, 55 mins.

Grass

In 1924, neophyte filmmakers Merian C. Cooper and Ernest Schoedsack joined forces with journalist and sometime spy Marguerite Harrison and set off to film an adventure. They found excitement, danger and unparalleled drama in the migration of the Bakhtiari tribe of Persia. Each year, more than 50 thousand people and half a million animals crossed the snow-covered mountain ranges and torrential rapids to take their herds to pasture. Few have seen *Grass* outside of archives. This issue is struck from the original negative, with an updated soundtrack by Iranian Gholam Hussein Janati Ataie.
VHS: S16429. $39.95.
Laser: CLV/CAV. Digitally mastered and transferred.
LD71815. $44.95.
Merian Cooper/Ernest Schoedsack, USA, 1925, 70 mins.

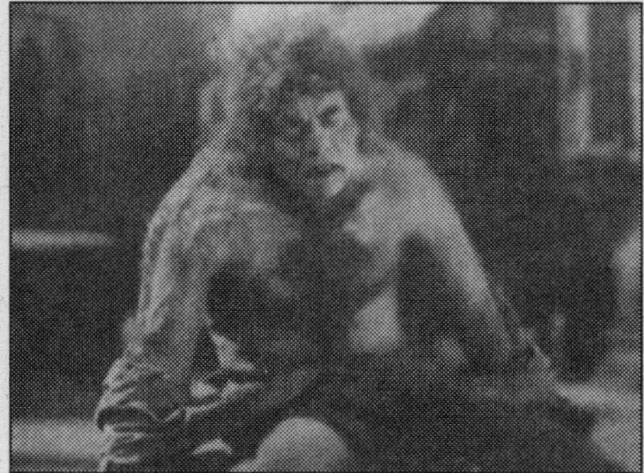

The Great Chase

This amazing look back at cinema's silent years reveals the roots of today's most popular comedies and thrillers and features some of the wildest stunts ever created for film. Includes clips from Buster Keaton's uproarious Civil War comedy *The General*; Pearl White's *The Perils of Pauline*; Douglas Fairbanks, Sr.'s first swashbuckler, *The Mark of Zorro*; Edwin S. Porter's *The Great Train Robbery*—regarded by many as the first film to tell a story; William S. Hart's western classic, *Tumbleweeds* and D.W. Griffith's *The Birth of a Nation*. Features narration explaining each film's cinematic significance and music by harmonica virtuoso Larry Adler. 81 mins.
VHS: S30029. $19.95.

Hail the Woman

A controlling father ruins the lives of those around him. With Florence Vidor, Lloyd Hughes, Theodore Roberts, Gertrude Claire, Madge Bellamy, Tully Marshall, Vernon Dent, Edward Martindel, Charles Meredith, Mathilde Brandage and Eugene Hoffman. Silent, music track.
VHS: S33698. $24.95.
John Griffith Wray, USA, 1921, 85 mins.

Hands Up

Raymond Griffith, to save the South, attempts to destroy and divert the gold from a northern mine.
VHS: S07256. $19.95.
Clarence Badger, USA, 1928, 58 mins.

Hawk of the Hills

Allene Ray, Walter Miller, Robert Chandler are featured in this feature version of the 1927 serial. Soft focus.
VHS: S07184. $19.95.
Spencer Gordon Bennett, USA, 1929, 58 mins.

Hawthorne of the USA

This is an amazing find, one of the rarest of the Wallace Reid films known. Lila Lee and Harrison Ford also appear in this story of an expatriate American in Europe. Reid's character wastes his fortune at the gaming tables of Monte Carlo. Then, in search of peace, he finds instead a princess to love and a communist coup. Transferred from a tinted 35mm nitrate print. Orchestra score.
VHS: S23310. $24.95.
James Cruze, USA, 1919, 55 mins.

Heading Home

Legendary baseball player Babe Ruth stars in this homespun version of his life story. Ruth Taylor, William Sheer, Margaret Sedden and many more star in this silent sports film classic. Orchestra score.
VHS: S23311. $24.95.
Lawrence Windom, USA, 1920, 56 mins.

Headless Horseman

Will Rogers is Ichabod Crane in Washington Irving's *Legend of Sleepy Hollow*. Silent with music track. USA, 1922, 68 mins.
VHS: S07245. $24.95.

Heart o' the Hills

Mary Pickford is beautiful and spunky 13-year-old Mavis Hawn, an uneducated Appalachian girl who promises to marry local boy Jason (Harold Goodwin), but her attention turns to sophisticated city boy Gray Pendleton (Jack Gilbert). Tragedy occurs when Mavis's father is thought to be killed by a stranger and her family life deteriorates as her widowed mother (Claire McDowell) takes up with slippery character Steve Honeycutt (Sam DeGrasse). Silent.
VHS: S34167. $19.95.
Sidney Franklin, USA, 1919, 55 mins.

Heart's Haven

A rare look at the work of actress Claire Adams. Robert McKim and Carl Gantvoort also star.
VHS: S08856. $24.95.
Benjamin B. Hampton, USA, 1922, 61 mins.

Hell Hounds of the Plains

A band of cattle thieves known as "The Hell Hounds" are stripping ranches of their cattle. Yakima Canutt is out to track down their leader and their hideout. Also with Neva Gerver, Lafe McKee, Al Ferguson and Lee Meechan. Transferred from an excellent original tinted print. Orchestra score.
VHS: S30680. $19.95.
USA, 1926, 58 mins.

Hell's Hinges

William S. Hart, the first great star of the Westerns, plays Blaze Tracy, a notorious outlaw in the town of Hell's Hinges. When a new minister pulls into town, Blaze is transformed by the sight of the minister's daughter. One of the great silent Westerns.
VHS: S01879. $29.95.
William S. Hart, USA, 1916, 65 mins.

Hero for a Night

This Universal print with original release tints is a real find. It's 1920s L.A., and Patsy Ruth Miller (Esmeralda in Lon Chaney's *Hunchback*) is a rich model who is wooed by taxi driver Glenn Tryon. This tape also includes a reel of silent trailers, including one for *Hot Heels* (1928), another Miller/Tryon film, and *Leather Pushers* (1922), an episode from a serial film with Reginald Denny.
VHS: S30123. $14.95.
William J. Craft, USA, 1927

Hidden Aces

Charles Hutchinson, Alice Calhoun, Barbara Tennant, James Bradbury Jr. star. Silent with music track.
VHS: S07232. $19.95.
Howard Mitchell, USA, 1927, 62 mins.

His First Command

William Boyd and Dorothy Sebastian star in this romance between a city slicker and the rugged daughter of a cavalryman. Boyd is sent out of Manhattan to manage a ranch in Kansas but he can't keep his mind on his work. He falls for a woman who only is interested in army men, so he enlists.
VHS: S24004. $19.95.
Gregory La Cava, USA, 1929, 60 mins.

His First Flame

They say love is the only fire against which there is no insurance. Hapless Harry Langdon is beset by two types of flames. He tries firefighting to take his mind off women and nearly burns down the fire station. With Vernon Dent and Natalie Kingston.
VHS: S05695. $24.95.
Harry Edwards, USA, 1926, 62 mins.

His Majesty, the American

Douglas Fairbanks arrives at the court of the Kingdom Alaine just in time to become involved in a plot. The king's minister wants to overthrow the king. Marjorie Daw, Frank Campeau and Sam Southern are just some of the silent era stars showcased in this first film from United Artists.
VHS: S23307. $29.95.
Joseph Henabery, USA, 1919, 100 mins.

The History of Chase in Film, Volume One: Comedy Chase

A wild and exciting compilation of chase sequences traces the early historical evolution of the film chase. Thrills, gags and suspense are studded throughout these clips, featuring cars, boats, trains and airplanes.
VHS: S27484. $19.95.

Hotel Imperial

Pola Negri and James Hall star in this lavish tale based in Hungary. In 1917, six Hussars find themselves in a frontier town occupied by Russians. Led by Hall, they take refuge in the beautifully appointed Hotel Imperial.
VHS: S23312. $24.95.
Mauritz Stiller, USA, 1927, 84 mins.

Hula

Clara Bow, Clive Brook and Patricia Dupont star in this delightful tale of love and adventure on a South Sea Island.
VHS: S08850. $24.95.
Victor Fleming, USA, 1928, 64 mins.

The Hunchback of Notre Dame

Filled with huge crowd scenes and massive sets recreating medieval Paris, *The Hunchback of Notre Dame* is one of the greatest spectacles of the silent era. Starring the legendary Lon Chaney as Quasimodo. Digitally remastered.
VHS: S14337. $19.98.
Laser: CLV. **LD71992. $39.95.**
Wallace Worsley, USA, 1923, 100 mins.

Hunted Men

Villainous Nate Spitzer (Lew Meehan) wants Dorothy Gordon's (Jean Reno) ranch; Dick Stockdale (Bob Steele) finds a blood-soaked money wrapper, a clue that will help him find the culprits at the last minute. With Mac V. Wright, Thomas G. Lingham and Clark Comstock. Silent, music track.
VHS: S33700. $24.95.
J.P. McGowan, USA, 1930, 57 mins.

In the Land of the War Canoes

Edward S. Curtis devoted his life to documenting the world of dwindling Native American cultures. In this film, Curtis told a story of love and revenge among the Kwakiutl Indians of Vancouver Island. Curtis spent three years with the Kwakiutl to meticulously recreate their way of life before the white man came. In addition to the magnificent painted war canoes, the film pictures authentic costumes, ceremonial dances and religious rituals. Silent with soundtrack from 1972 restoration.
VHS: S16431. $39.95.
Laser: LD71816. $34.95.
Edward S. Curtis, USA/Canada, 1914, 47 mins.

In the Tentacles of the North

An exciting tale about the extraordinary courage of a young girl who manages to survive when the ship she is traveling on is caught in the frozen Arctic ice. She battles vainly to preserve her sanity. With Caston Glass, Alice Calhoun and Al Roscoe. Silent with orchestral score.
VHS: S20051. $19.95.
Louis Chaudet, USA, 1926, 54 mins.

The Irish Cinderella

Emralila is a poor orphan girl much abused by an old biddy known as the Ulster Crag—half-man, half-bag and all witch. She has two equally abusive daughters. This silent feature with original organ score parallels the poor child with the struggle for Irish independence. A "reel" oddity. With Pattie MacNamara. 1920's, 72 mins.
VHS: S03659. $29.95.

Iron Mask

Alexandre Dumas' exciting novel of fights, spectacle and romance, in the great thrill show of 1929. With Douglas Fairbanks and Margaret de la Motte.
VHS: S03330. $24.95.
Laser: CLV. **LD71995. $29.98.**
Allan Dwan, USA, 1929

Is Life Worth Living?
Selznick Pictures produced this moral tale in 1921. It teaches about the value of life through a hard luck story concerning a young man wrongly accused of a crime. This copy was made from a beautiful 35mm print and scored with orchestra music of the period. 66 mins.
VHS: S20633. $19.95.
Alan Crosland, USA, 1921, 66 mins.

It
Clara Bow stars in the definitive flapper film as a store clerk infatuated with the store's heir (Antonio Moreno). Josef von Sternberg was the uncredited co-director. With Elinor Glyn and Gary Cooper in an uncredited role. Silent with music track.
VHS: S07279. $19.95.
Laser: LD70097. $39.95.
Clarence Badger, USA, 1927, 71 mins.

It's the Old Army Game
This rare Paramount release features the inimitable W.C. Fields as a small town druggist; lovely, young Louise Brooks co-stars as his beautiful daughter. An excellent print of a predominantly unseen film. Organ scored.
VHS: S15512. $29.95.
A. Edward Sutherland, USA, 1926, 75 mins.

The Italian
The story of Italian immigrants in the slums of New York, notable for its realism; produced by Thomas Ince, and starring George Beban. Silent with music score. USA, 1915, 78 mins.
VHS: S07487. $24.95.
Reginald Barker, USA, 1915, 78 mins.

Jack-Knife Man
This tear-jerker was one of King Vidor's early directorial efforts. A lonely old riverboat man is left a child by a dying mother. The old man carves many toys from wood for the boy and they grow to love one another. The village snoop feels the child would be better off in an orphanage rather than living on the river and the sheriff is sent to try to take the child away. Organ music track.
VHS: S13272. $24.95.
King Vidor, USA, 1920, 70 mins.

Jesus of Nazareth (The Story of the Saviour's Life)
A realistic, thoroughly detailed, dramatic recreation of the life of Christ, from the Anunciation through the Ascension. In between, we view episodes from his infancy and youth, his preachings and miracles and, finally, his betrayal by Judas Iscariot, his delivery before Pontius Pilate, and the Crucifixion. Silent film with an original organ score, shown at its correct projection speed. USA, 1928, 85 mins.
VHS: S13602. $29.95.

Jungle Princess
E.R. Martin directed this feature version of the 15-chapter 1920 serial *The Lost City*, which features Juanita Hansen, George Chesebro and Frank Clark.
VHS: S08866. $24.95.
E.R. Martin, USA, 1920, 68 mins.

Just Suppose
A prince pretends to be a pauper, but when love strikes and duty calls, complications arise. Richard Barthelmess, Lois Moran and Geoffrey Kerr star.
VHS: S07202. $24.95.
Kenneth Webb, USA, 1926, 90 mins.

King of the Wild Horses
Charley Chase plays the weak-willed brother of a girl whose new love saves the family from thieves. Starring Rex, the Wonder Horse. With the Will Rogers short *Two Wagons, Both Covered*. Music track.
VHS: S33064. $24.95.
Hal Roach, USA, 1924, 50 mins.

The Kiss
One of the very last silent films released by MGM, it was also Garbo's last venture before she "talked" in *Anna Christie*. *The Kiss* is a classy melodrama co-starring Garbo opposite a handsome and very young Lew Ayres (making his film debut for MGM). Silent film with synchronized musical score.
VHS: S13975. $29.99.
Laser: LD71081. $39.95.
Jacques Feyder, USA, 1929, 89 mins.

L. Frank Baum's Silent Film Collection of Oz
Fourteen years before Judy Garland's ruby slippers led her down the yellow brick road, "Oz" creator and author L. Frank Baum made the first feature films about the magical land we know and love. In 1914 Baum produced and directed three silent film classics: *His Majesty, The Scarecrow of Oz* (59 mins.), *The Patchwork Girl of Oz* (67 mins.) and *The Magic Cloak of Oz* (40 mins.). Also included is the original 1925 film version of *The Wizard of Oz* (40 mins.), produced and directed by, and starring silent film great Larry Semon as the scarecrow and film legend Oliver Hardy as the tin woodsman.
VHS: S30785. $34.95.
L. Frank Baum/Larry Semon, USA, 1914/1925

La Boheme
Lillian Gish stars as Mimi, a poor waif in 1830s Paris. Rodolphe (John Gilbert) falls in love with her, and Mimi works to support him as he works on his play. Count Paul (Roy D'Arcy) offers to help, but also has his lusting eye on Mimi. Silent, music track.
VHS: S33047. $24.95.
King Vidor, USA, 1926, 95 mins.

Lamb
The first feature starring Douglas Fairbanks, produced by Triangle Film Corporation. Fairbanks plays a man who proves he is not a "lamb" by being ultra-macho.
VHS: S08881. $24.95.
Christy Cabanne, USA, 1915, 60 mins.

The Last of the Mohicans
This silent adaptation of James Fenimore Cooper's novel is set in colonial America during the French and Indian Wars, and pits the fierce warrior Magua (Wallace Beery) against Hawkeye and his adopted brothers, Uncas and Chingachgook. With Barbara Bedford, Albert Roscoe, James Gordon and Boris Karloff.
VHS: S06225. $39.95.
Laser: CLV/CAV. **LD72046. $49.95.**
Maurice Tourneur/Clarence Brown, USA, 1920, 75 mins.

The Last Outlaw
Gary Cooper, Jack Luden, Betty Jewell and Flash, The Wonder Horse. Silent with music track, with lots of swell action shots on Flash.
VHS: S07275. $19.95.
Arthur Rosson, USA, 1927, 63 mins.

Leatherneck
William Boyd, Alan Hale and Diane Ellis star in this silent story of love and adventure. USA, 65 mins. 1928.
VHS: S08849. $24.95.

Leopard Woman
Louise Glaum, the most famous of the screen vamps, in an epic of passion, intrigue and espionage in the equatorial jungle. USA, 1920, 68 mins.
VHS: S07218. $19.95.

Let 'Er Go Gallegher
Junior Coghlan, Harrison Ford, Elinor Fair, Wade Boteler and Inan Lebedeff star in this adventure with a waif of the streets. Silent with music score.
VHS: S10360. $19.95.
Elmer Clifton, USA, 1928, 57 mins.

The Light of Faith
Lon Chaney and Hope Hampton star in this inspirational movie. In the 30s, the original 1922 silent film was cut down to be shown to Christians.
VHS: S23196. $29.95.
Clarence Brown, USA, 1922, 33 mins.

Lighting Brice
The complete, exciting 15-chapter serial starring Jack Hoxie and Ann Little. USA, 1919, orchestra music. 300 mins.
VHS: S08861. $49.95.

Lightning Hutch
After 60 years, all 10 chapters of this rare silent serial featuring the king of the stuntmen are finally available. With Charles Hutchison, Edith Thornton, Virginia Pearson, Sheldon Lewis, Eddie Phillips, Ben Walker and Violet Schram. Complete with the original opening credits and closing title cards. Orchestra score.
VHS: S31865. $39.95.
Charles Hutchison, USA, 1926, 230 mins.

Lilac Time
Gary Cooper and Colleen Moore star in this silent WWI aerial drama about the romance between an English flyer and a French farm girl, prompted by a British Airdrome built on her family's land.
VHS: S30793. $19.95.
George Fitzmaurice, USA, 1928, 90 mins.

Linda
A young mountain girl (Helen Foster) is forced to marry a much older man. Noah Beery plays the thoughtful husband who tries to cheer his unhappy young wife, while Warner Baxter portrays the dashing young doctor who becomes her lover. This classic silent melodrama is accompanied by a reconstructed orchestra score.
VHS: S22425. $24.95.
Dorothy Davenport Reid, USA, 1929, 75 mins.

Little Annie Rooney
A good Irish girl takes care of her dad and brother. Mary Pickford, William Heines and Walter James star.
VHS: S08852. $24.95.
William Beaudine, USA, 1925, 100 mins.

Little Orphan Annie
Colleen Moore, Thomas Santschi and Harry Lonsdale star in this early film about a delightful young girl who makes the most of being an orphan. Poet James Whitcomb Riley narrates the story to a group of children gathered about him.
VHS: S26771. $14.95.
Colin Campbell, USA, 1918, 57 mins.

Live Wire
Johnny Hines, part of a circus troupe, uses his skills to save a heroine.
VHS: S07260. $24.95.
Charles Hines, USA, 1925, 85 mins.

Lorna Doone
Madge Bellamy and John Bowers are featured together in this silent film about a young girl. She is kidnapped and taken from her rich parents and then must be raised by bandits in Scotland.
VHS: S23833. $24.95.
Maurice Tourneur, USA, 1922, 65 mins.

Lost Express
A complete steam locomotive and its cargo disappear without a trace in this early railroad drama that stars Helen Holmes and Henry Barrows. Silent with music score.
VHS: S10366. $19.95.
J.P. McGowan, USA, 1926, 48 mins.

The Lost World
Adapted from a short story by Sir Arthur Conan Doyle, this is the classic tale of prehistoric monsters running amok in contemporary London. The real star is special effects virtuoso Willis O'Brien, whose life-like monsters have an astounding authenticity. Wallace Beery plays Professor Challenger, who must devise a way to defeat the raging monsters. This 90-minute version includes the original trailer, O'Brien's earlier works, *Prehistoric Poultry, R.F.D. 10,000 B.C.* and *The Dinosaur and the Missing Link*, and a recreation of some of the long-lost footage.
VHS: S19673. $24.95.
Harry O. Hoyt, USA, 1925, 90 mins.

Love 'Em and Leave 'Em
Frank Tuttle directed this delightful and rambunctious story of the roaring Twenties, and Louise Brooks shines in one of her early film roles. Also starring Evelyn Brent and Lawrence Gray. Orchestra scored.
VHS: S15513. $29.95.
Frank Tuttle, USA, 1927, 70 mins.

Love Never Dies
Madge Bellamy and Lloyd Hughes are great in this dramatic silent film about love, revenge and the violence provoked by these two primal forces. Great action scenes and color tinted.
VHS: S23834. $24.95.
King Vidor, USA, 1922, 55 mins.

The Love of Sunya
Gloria Swanson and John Boies star in this silent film about a young woman who meets an Eastern yogi who believes that he wronged her in a past life. He tries to make amends by allowing her to see what her future would be like with each of her four suitors.
VHS: S30792. $19.95.
Albert Parker, USA, 1927, 80 mins.

The Lubin Studios
Lubin Studios, an early producer of silent shorts, gave figures like Pearl White and Oliver Hardy their start in the movies. This video shows works from as early as 1904 that reveal the influence of Edison's films. Perhaps more importantly, there are comic films included in this collection which reveal the developing comic abilities of Oliver Hardy. Music track added.
VHS: S27482. $19.95.

Lucky Devil
Richard Dix, Esther Ralston, Edna May Oliver, Tom Findley and Anthony Jowitt star. Silent with music track.
VHS: S07269. $19.95.
Frank Tuttle, USA, 1925, 63 mins.

Lure of the Range
Dick Hatton stars in this early silent Western filled with terrific comic gags. 1924, 56 mins.
VHS: S23835. $24.95.

Mad Whirl
Myrtle Stedman, Barbara Bedford, Alec B. Francis, Jack Mulhall and May McAvoy star in this William Seiter production. Silent with music track. USA, 1925, 80 mins.
VHS: S07238. $24.95.

Made for Love
A couple falls in love and fall into a tomb in Egypt. Edmund Burns, Paul Sloane and Leatrice Joy star.
VHS: S07226. $19.95.
Paul Sloane, USA, 1926, 65 mins.

Mademoiselle Midnight
This is one of Mae Murray's last surviving films, a melodrama set in Mexico during Emperor Maximilian's time.
VHS: S23836. $24.95.
Robert Z. Leonard, USA, 1924, 70 mins.

Man from Beyond
Harry Houdini, the celebrated escape artist, starred and produced this film in which Artic explorers discover a shipwreck from 1820 and a frozen sailor whom they revive.
VHS: S03787. $29.95.
Burton King, USA, 1922

The Man from Painted Post
A 1917 silent western starring Douglas Fairbanks Sr. who impersonates a sophisticated city man to tackle of a gang of horse rustlers and win the affections of a beautiful young woman.
VHS: S06224. $19.95.
Joseph Henabery, USA, 1917

Man Who Had Everything
Jack Pickford stars in this story of a young man who is given his every wish, and must decide whether it's a blessing or a curse. Silent with music track.
VHS: S07213. $24.95.
Alfred E. Green, USA, 1920, 60 mins.

The Man Who Laughs
Considered one of Leni's best films, this rare silent film is an excellent example of a UFA-inspired gothic drama. Based on the Victor Hugo novel *L'Homme qui rit*, this is the melodramatic tale of Gwynplaine, a boy whose features are surgically altered into a permanent grin by order of James II because his father was a political enemy. Gwynplaine becomes a famous clown and falls in love with a blind girl rescued from a snowstorm by his traveling circus, but is summoned back to England when he discovers he is heir to a peerage. Stars Conrad Veidt, Mary Philbin, Olga Baclanova and Josephine Crowell.
VHS: S30203. $24.95.
Paul Leni, USA, 1927, 110 mins.

Manhandled
An examination of a shop girl and her man-troubles in the big city. With Gloria Swanson, Tom Moore, Frank Morgan and Ann Pennington. Silent film with musical score.
VHS: S15384. $24.95.
Allan Dwan, USA, 1924

Mantrap
A Famous Players-Lasky production starring Clara Bow as a temptress, Ernest Torrence, Percy Marmont and Tom Kennedy. Silent with music track.
VHS: S07250. $24.95.
Victor Fleming, USA, 1926, 68 mins.

Mark of Zorro
Of the many films made about the legendary Zorro, most consider this to be the best, with its exciting duel sequences, romance and high adventure. Douglas Fairbanks, Marguerite de la Motte and Noah Beery star. Digitally remastered.
VHS: S14441. $24.95.
Laser: CLV. **LD71730. $19.98.**
Fred Niblo, USA, 1920, 80 mins.

Marked Money
The villains are after a chest with a secret in this Junior Coghlan drama which also stars George Duryea, Virginia Bradford, Tom Kennedy, Bert Woodruff and Jack Richardson. Silent with music score.
VHS: S10361. $19.95.
Spencer Gordon Bennett, USA, 1928, 61 mins.

Married?
Constance Bennett and Owen Moore star in this story of a couple who must marry for a year in order to inherit a large sum of money.
VHS: S07270. $24.95.
George Terwilliger, USA, 1926, 65 mins.

Mary Pickford—The Early Years
A collection of early films featuring the great Pickford, including *Sweet Memories* and clips from *On Account of Milk, Arcadian Maid, Never Again, The Unchanging Sea, Artful Kate* and *In Old Madrid*, which also stars Owen Moore. 65 mins.
VHS: S11454. $19.95.

Matinee Idols: The Gentlemen
A collection of short films from the years 1911-1914, illustrative of the early male stars of the era: Henry B. Walthall *(Love and Charity)*, *Every Inch a Man* (Wallace Reid), *Dawn and Twilight* (Francis X. Bushman), *Under Royal Patronage* (Francis X. Bushman).
VHS: S07586. $19.95.

Matinee Idols: The Ladies
Short films from the years 1912-1913, featuring early female leads: Clara Kimball Young and Helen Costello *(Lulu's Doctor)*; Mary Fuller (9th episode of *What Happened to Mary)*; Kathleen Williams, Vera Hamilton *(The Girl at the Cupola)*; Florence Lawrence *(Flo's Discipline)*; Edith Storey *(A Modern Atlanta)*; Kathleen Williams *(How They Stopped the Run on the Bank)*; Beverly Bayne and Eleanor Blanchard *(Teaching Hickville to Sing)*; Beverly Bayne *(Will-Be-Weds)*, and Pearl White *(The Paper Doll)*. 120 mins.
VHS: S07418. $29.95.

Matrimaniac
Douglas Fairbanks and Constance Talmadge star in this action-packed comedy about a man determined, against all odds and outside pressures, to marry the girl he wants. USA, 1918, 48 mins.
VHS: S08884. $24.95.

Menschen am Sontag (People on Sunday)
The relationships of two couples spending a lazy afternoon at the beach are explored as they veer from friendship to jealousy and hatred, and then return to normal, aided by surprisingly subtle acting performances by nonprofessionals. Noted as a seminal work in the careers of Robert Siodmak, Edgar G. Ulmer, Fred Zinnemann, Billy Wilder (who co-wrote the screenplay with the brothers Siodmak) and cinematographer Eugen Schufftan. Silent, music track.
VHS: S33053. $24.95.
Edgar G. Ulmer/Robert Siodmak/Curt Siodmak/Fred Zinnemann, USA, 1929, 58 mins.

Mickey
Mabel Normand brightens the silent screen in one of her most popular roles. She plays a Western girl sent East to live with unkind relations. They force her to become a domestic, with hilarious and heart-tugging results. With Lew Cody, Minta Durfee and Minnie Ha Ha. Produced by Mack Sennett.
VHS: S04804. $29.95.
F. Richard Jones, USA, 1919, 110 mins.

Midnight Faces
An eerie psychological thriller about a young woman (Francis X. Bushman) who inherits a beachhouse in the Florida everglades and is subjected to a series of unexplained incidents and events. With Rocky Aoki, Jack Perrin and Kathryn McGuire.
VHS: S18945. $19.95.
Bennett Cohn, USA, 1926, 72 mins.

Midnight Girl
Bela Lugosi, screen's elegant villain, in a rare silent role. Lugosi plays Nicholas Harmon, the immensely wealthy patron of music, in love with Mimi, an opera singer. Lugosi's seductive manner is countered by his son's indifference to an arranged marriage into a socially prominent family.
VHS: S04853. $29.95.
Wilfred Noy, USA, 1925, 61 mins.

Midnight Message
Wanda Hawley, Mary Carr, John Fox Jr., Stuart Holmes star. Grainy.
VHS: S07215. $19.95.
Paul Hurst, USA, 1926, 65 mins.

Mistaken Orders
Helen Holmes, Henry Barrows and Hal Waters star. The wrong orders send two trains dashing toward each other. Silent with music score. 1925. 52 mins.
VHS: S10365. $19.95.
J.P. McGowan, USA, 1925, 52 mins.

The Mollycoddle
Douglas Fairbanks and Wallace Beery are featured in this action-filled silent comedy. As a dashing playboy, Fairbanks steals the show and the girl. He vies with a rather distasteful diamond slugger, culminating in a bang-up climax.
VHS: S23838. $24.95.
Victor Fleming, USA, 1920, 63 mins.

Moran of the Lady Letty
A never-seen Valentino film, re-discovered overseas, and available with English titles. A dandy is kidnapped and taken hostage aboard a pirate ship.
VHS: S08333. $29.95.
George Melford, USA, 1922, 71 mins.

A Mormon Maid
Mae Murray, Frank Borzage and Noah Beery are cast in this silent tragic film. Polygamy drives a woman to suicide. Then her daughter is faced with the same marriage prospects. As a result, she is forced to flee to her true love.
VHS: S23839. $24.95.
Robert Z. Leonard, USA, 1917, 60 mins.

My Four Years in Germany
This World War I drama is based on the story of Ambassador James W. Gerard, who witnessed many instances of German intrigue and cruelty. With Halbert Brown, Willard Dashiel, Louis Dean, Earl Schenck and George Riddell. Orchestral score.
VHS: S22429. $24.95.
William Knight, USA, 1918, 122 mins.

My Lady of Whims
Clara Bow stars as a spoiled young lady who is constantly spied upon by her father. With Carmelita Geraghty, Betty Baker, Donald Keith. Silent with music score.
VHS: S07483. $19.95.
Dallas N. Fitzgerald, USA, 1925, 42 mins.

Mystery of the Double Cross
The complete, 15-chapter, 1917 Pathe serial with Molly King and Leon Barry. Not the ordinary cliff-hanger, this is presented as a mystery which it challenges you to solve. 6 hours on 3 video cassettes.
VHS: S11459. $49.95.

The Narrow Road/Alias Jimmy Valentine
Alias Jimmy Valentine (1915), by Maurice Tourneur, tells the story of a bank robber who ends up in the real Sing Sing prison. It's an incredibly realistic early feature that makes startling use of deep staging. *The Narrow Road* (1912) represents a rarely seen work by the master, D.W. Griffith, with Mary Pickford as a woman who must keep her husband from a life of crime. From the *Origins of American Films* series, a joint project of the Library of Congress and Smithsonian Video.
VHS: S21263. $34.95.

Nervous Wreck
A hilarious, silent version of *Whoopee*, with Harrison Ford, Phyllis Haver, in a rollicking comedy.
VHS: S05973. $49.95.
Scott Sidney, USA, 1926, 70 mins.

New School Teacher
Gregory La Cava directs this film based on the rustic humor of Irvin S. Cobb, the story of shy Professor Timmins (Chic Sale) and his adventures with young hooligans. When he isn't busy sitting on thumb tacks, and "keeping up with all the dead languages," he is courting the pretty sister of one of the little pranksters. Great vitality from La Cava, with an entertaining performance from Chic Sale. Silent with music score.
VHS: S06984. $29.95.
Gregory La Cava, USA, 1923, 75 mins.

The Nicklehopper
Mabel Normand and Boris Karloff are featured in this silent story about a dance hall hostess. 1926, 30 mins.
VHS: S23840. $24.95.

Night Bird
It's Reginald Denny to the rescue in this low-key comedy. Silent with music track.
VHS: S07264. $19.95.
Fred Newmeyer, USA, 1928, 76 mins.

Night Club
To prove his love for Vera Reynolds, Raymond Griffith hires Wallace Beery as an assassin. Silent with music track.
VHS: S07254. $19.95.
Frank Urson/Paul Iribe, USA, 1925, 62 mins.

No Man's Law
Oliver Hardy gets a rare chance to play a dramatic villain rather than the broad comic "heavy" he usually portrayed in this light, dramatic western featuring Rex, King of the Wild Horses, part of a rare series of non-comic ventures produced by Hal Roach during the silent era. 62 mins.
VHS: S33121. $24.95.

Nomads of the North

Lon Chaney Sr. stars as Raoul Challoner, an innocent man on the run from the mounted police in the Great White North. With Lewis Stone as the relentless Cpl. O'Connor and Betty Blythe as Nanette Roland, Raoul's secret love. This silent adventure also features several adorable animals and an impressive forest fire. Silent with music track.
VHS: S16179. $24.95.
David M. Hartford, USA, 1920, 120 mins.

Norma Talmadge Films

This collection includes five early films of the silent era's rough equivalent to Greer Garson. Talmadge made over 250 films in the silent era. Included in this introduction are *Father's Hatband* (1913), *Sawdust & Salome* (1914), *The Helpful Sisterhood* (1914), *John Rance, Gentleman* (1914), and the 51-minute feature *Children of the House*, made under the supervision of D.W. Griffith. USA, 1913-1916, 112 mins.
VHS: S04809. $29.95.

The Notorious Lady

Lewis Stone and Barbara Bedford star in this miraculously preserved print of an early film tragedy. Stone is a British officer who kills a man he finds in his wife's room. Although innocent of any wrong, his wife claims to be guilty in order to save him. Orchestra score.
VHS: S22013. $19.95.
King Baggot, USA, 1927, 79 mins.

Nurse Marjorie

The only surviving film of the four that director William Desmond Taylor and Mary Miles Minter collaborated on. (Taylor was found murdered at his Hollywood mansion in February 1922. The inquest which followed his still-unsolved murder case revealed his involvement with Minter—among others—and ended her career.) Also with Clyde Fillmore, George Periolt, Mollie MacConnell, Frank Leigh, Vera Lewis, Arthur Hoyt, Frankie Lee and Lydia Yeamans. Silent with orchestra score.
VHS: S31866. $29.95.
William Desmond Taylor, USA, 1925, 78 mins.

The Nut

Douglas Fairbanks is a wacky inventor who finds himself convinced of an interesting theory. His wealthy girlfriend believes he can be improved through contact with the better off.
VHS: S25710. $24.95.
Theodore Reed, USA, 1921, 61 mins.

Officer 444

Francis Ford directed this 10-chapter serial produced in 1926, starring Ben Wilson and Neva Gerber.
VHS: S08862. $39.95.
Francis Ford, USA, 1926, 200 mins.

Old Heidelberg

Dorothy Gish, Wallace Reid and Erich von Stroheim all are featured in this early version of an old story. Based on W. Meyer-Forster's novel and Richard Mansfield's play, this film follows the troubled love affair between a prince and a barmaid.
VHS: S25711. $19.95.
John Emerson, USA, 1915, 35 mins.

Old Ironsides

Adventure and action film set in the southern Mediterranean, based on the 1930 poem by Oliver Wendell Holmes. Wallace Beery and Boris Karloff are members of the merchant marine fighting pirates of Tripoli.
VHS: S03440. $29.95.
James Cruze, USA, 1926, 111 mins.

Oliver Twist

Lon Chaney as Fagin and Jackie Coogan as Oliver star in this Charles Dickens classic of a master criminal who teaches children to steal.
VHS: S11456. $24.95.
Frank Lloyd, USA, 1922, 80 mins.

One Punch O'Day

Billy Sullivan, Jack Herrick and Charlotte Merrian star in this boxing story.
VHS: S07267. $19.95.
Harry J. Brown, USA, 1926, 60 mins.

Open Switch

Helen Holmes, Jack Perrin, Charles Wittaker and Mack Wright star in this action railroad story of stolen express packages. 1925, 50 mins. Silent with music score.
VHS: S10367. $19.95.

Orchids and Ermine

Carey Wilson wrote the screenplay for this silent romantic comedy about a former telephone switchboard operator played by Colleen Moore. A millionaire could be the answer to all her woes if only she could find one suitably rich and handsome.
VHS: S23841. $24.95.
Alfred Santell, USA, 1926, 75 mins.

Our Dancing Daughters

It's Joan Crawford in the role that brought her true movie stardom. Joan portrays a free-spirited flapper with a penchant for dancing, sin, and bathtub gin. Anita Page co-stars as the society debutante forced to steal Joan's betrothed (Johnny Mack Brown). Silent film with synchronized music score and sound effects.
VHS: S13976. $29.99.
Harry Beaumont, USA, 1928, 98 mins.

Our Modern Maidens

This silent work about the opulence and energy of the Jazz Age pivots on the romantic and political entanglements of a group of twenties flappers and musicians. With Joan Crawford, Anita Page and Rod La Rocque.
VHS: S18129. $19.98.
Jack Conway, USA, 1929, 75 mins.

Outside the Law

Tod Browning wrote, produced and directed this silent criminal drama that features Lon Chaney in three roles. Chaney, as Black Mike, threatens the happiness of the daughter of a former underworld leader now reformed by a Chinese philosopher. With Priscilla Dean, Ralph Lewis and Wheeler Oakman.
VHS: S05705. $24.95.
Tod Browning, USA, 1921, 113 mins.

Pampered Youths

Cullen Landis and Alice Calhoun star in this silent adaptation of Booth Tarkington's *The Magnificent Ambersons*. It's a timeless story of the decline of a once mighty family. 1925, 35 mins.
VHS: S23842. $24.95.

Party Girl (Dangerous Business)

"An exploitive warning about those who would seek to enslave women as 'party girls.'" Starring Douglas Fairbanks, Jr., and Jeanette Loff.
VHS: S33065. $24.95.
Victor Halperin, USA, 1930, 60 mins.

The Patchwork Girl of Oz/ A Florida Enchantment

Novelist Frank Baum produced *The Patchwork Girl* (1914). It's a film about a journey to Oz in search of an antidote for a spell that turns innocent bystanders to stone. Hal Roach is featured as the cowardly lion while a young Frenchman plays the girl of the title. In *A Florida Enchantment* (1914), magic transforms men into women and women into men, resulting in a film that has an interesting modern edge, even though it was vilified in its time. From the *Origins of American Films* series, a joint project of the Library of Congress and Smithsonian Video.
VHS: S21265. $34.95.

Paths to Paradise

Raymond Griffith, an international jewel thief, attempts to steal a famous diamond. Silent with music track.
VHS: S07255. $19.95.
Clarence Badger, USA, 1925, 62 mins.

The Peacock Fan

Lucian Preval stars in this silent murder mystery about a peacock fan protected by a deadly curse which brings death to its possessor.
VHS: S33066. $24.95.
Lee Rosen, USA, 1929, 60 mins.

The Penalty

A young boy whose legs where amputated by an inept doctor grows up to carry out an elaborate and gruesome vengeance. One of Lon Chaney's most terrifying roles, it was rumored that he suffered permanent spinal damage from the contortions necessary to portray the legless "Blizzard." Silent.
VHS: S25698. $24.95.
Wallace Worsley, USA, 1920, 82 mins.

Perils of the Rails

One of the best silent action railroad films with many great stunts, featuring Helen Holmes, Edward Hearn and J.P. McGowan. USA, 1925, 61 mins.
VHS: S08875. $24.95.

Phantom Flyer

Al Wilson, Lillian Gilmore, Buck Connors and Billy Red Jones star. Silent with music track.
VHS: S07209. $19.95.
Bruce Mitchell, USA, 1928, 53 mins.

The Phantom of the Opera

Lon Chaney stars in the greatest role of his career as Erik, the love-torn resident of the hidden depths of the Opera House. This 70th anniversary edition has been completely remastered from a 35mm archive print and features the original 2-strip Technicolor masked ball sequence and fantastic score performed by a 60-piece orchestra.
VHS: S01019. $24.95.
DVD: DV60033. $29.95.
Rupert Julian, USA, 1925, 101 mins.

Pioneer's Gold

In this rare silent film, an old dying rancher wants to leave his wealth to his brother's children whom he has never met. The villain tries to send in substitutes to claim the inheritance. With Pete Morrison, Kathryn McGuire, Virginia Warwick, Spottiswood Aiken, Louis Emmons, Madge Lorese Bates, Merrill McCormick, Les Bates, George King and William McCormick.
VHS: S37087. $19.95.
Denver Dixon, USA, 1924, 62 mins.

The Plastic Age

Clara Bow is a knockout in this comedy about a college girl whose flirtation with a young football player (Donald Keith) causes him to fail at all he does. When she stops toying with his emotions he wins the big game, causing her to really fall in love with him. Look for Clark Gable in a bit part in a locker room scene—his first film appearance! Based on the novel by Percy Marks. Original organ score.
VHS: S30552. $19.95.
Wesley Ruggles, USA, 1925

Playing Dead

A Vitagraph production of a Sidney Drew film, in which he orchestrates his own death so that his wife can enter into a relationship with a man he believes she is in love with. With Donald Hall, Harry English, Isadore Marcil and Alice Lake. Silent with piano score.
VHS: S20025. $24.95.
Sidney Drew, USA, 1915, 58 mins.

Pollyanna

Mary Pickford, America's Sweetheart, stars in this silent slapstick comedy based on Eleanor Porter's book. The optimistic girl smiles at everything no matter how troubling it may be. When she is orphaned, a dour aunt takes her in and is soon transformed by the glad girl's good cheer.
VHS: S26688. $19.95.
Paul Powell, USA, 1920, 60 mins.

Poor Little Rich Girl

Mary Pickford in her first appearance as a child in a major film, an enchanting masterpiece of the early American cinema. Pickford, who was 24 at the time, plays Gwendolyn, a rich girl with everything except her parents' love and attention.
VHS: S01047. $29.95.
Maurice Tourneur, USA, 1917, 99 mins.

Power

William Boyd, Alan Hale, Jacqueline Logan, Carole Lombard and Joan Bennett star. Silent with music track.
VHS: S07212. $24.95.
Howard Hughes, USA, 1928, 74 mins.

Power God

Ben Wilson and Neva Gerber star in this complete 15-chapter serial. Silent with music track.
VHS: S07186. $49.95.
Francis Ford, USA, 1927, 330 mins.

Pride of the Clan

Extremely rare Mary Pickford film, directed by Maurice Tourneur, with Matt Moore.
VHS: S05974. $49.95.
Maurice Tourneur, USA, 1916, 80 mins.

Primitive Lover

Constance Talmadge, Harrison Ford and Kenneth Harlan star in this delightful silent comedy of a woman who wants more from her marriage.
VHS: S08846. $24.95.
Sidney Franklin, USA, 1916, 67 mins.

Q Ships
The story of a German submarine commander during World War I, and the conflicts he suffers over his morality and his loyalty to his country. Silent with music track.
VHS: S10585. $19.95.
Geoffrey Barkas, USA, 1928, 78 mins.

Queen of the Chorus
An early chorus line melodrama about a woman with a heart of gold who makes the ultimate sacrifice. With Rex Lease, Virginia Brown Faire and Crawford Kent. Silent film with musical score.
VHS: S15385. $24.95.
Charles J. Hunt, USA, 1929

Raffles, The Amateur Racksman
John Barrymore plays the debonair society burglar. Silent with music track.
VHS: S07253. $24.95.
George Irving, USA, 1917, 70 mins.

Raggedy Rose
Stan Laurel directed Mabel Normand in this touching Cinderella story.
VHS: S08848. $24.95.
Stan Laurel, USA, 1926, 56 mins.

Railroad Dramas
Three early short films featuring Helen Holmes and Helen Gibson, and featuring railroads: *The Wild Engine, Rival Railroad Plot* and *The Ghost of the Canyon*. 75 mins.
VHS: S08878. $24.95.

Ranson's Folly
A very rare Richard Barthelmess film, this is a period drama set during the Civil War.
VHS: S05975. $49.95.
Sidney Olcott, USA, 1926

The Raven
This rare feature opens with a history of Edgar Allan Poe's ancestors and follows his rise to maturity. Unable to integrate himself into society, Poe turns to alcohol. This crutch inspires his hallucinatory vision and throws him into the world of "The Raven." Although Poe was more accurately addicted to narcotics, this film remains one of the earliest and most eccentric biopics. With Henry B. Walthall and Wanda Howard. Silent with an added music track.
VHS: S15278. $19.95.
Charles J. Brabin, USA, 1915, 80 mins.

Reaching for the Moon
Douglas Fairbanks is a dreamer who becomes king of Vulgaria and discovers royalty can have its down side. As the constant target for assassins and the object of desire of a homely princess, he looks for a way out in this energetic comedic adventure. With Eileen Percy.
VHS: S05694. $29.95.
John Emerson, USA, 1917, 91 mins.

Red Kimono
A woman is forced into an immoral life, compelling her to take drastic measures. She succeeds but only in part and must soon support herself in the only way that she can, as a prostitute. This is a fascinating silent melodrama.
VHS: S23843. $24.95.
Walter Lang, USA, 1925, 70 mins.

Red Signals
Wallace MacDonald, Earle Williams, Eva Novak star. Silent with music track.
VHS: S07228. $24.95.
J.P. McGowan, USA, 1927, 70 mins.

Regeneration
The first feature by the remarkable Raoul Walsh *(High Sierra, The Big Trail), Regeneration* is an early look at the possibilities of filmmaking. Walsh used gritty New York locations to create a heightened sense of danger and excitement. With Rockliffe Fellows, John McCann, James Marcus and Maggie Weston. Silent with music track.
VHS: S17449. $29.95.
Raoul Walsh, USA, 1915

Reggie Mixes In
Douglas Fairbanks and Bessie Love star in this drama of intrigue set in the underworld.
VHS: S08883. $24.95.
Christy Cabanne, USA, 1916, 58 mins.

The Return of Boston Blackie
Corliss Palmer, Raymond Glenn, Rosemary Cooper and Strongheart the dog star in this silent melodrama. Boston Blackie tries to reform a pretty blonde thief with the help of Strongheart. Orchestral score.
VHS: S22430. $19.95.
Harry O. Hoyt, USA, 1927, 58 mins.

Riders of the Purple Sage
Zane Grey's novel is adapted for the screen in this silent film featuring Tom Mix. It's a tale of revenge sought by a man for the sake of his sister, who suffered under Mormonism.
VHS: S23844. $19.95.
Edfrid Bingham, USA, 1925, 63 mins.

Riding for Life
Bob Reeves stars as a cowboy who befriends a family beset by crooks. Gorgeous; restored from 35mm nitrate.
VHS: S33067. $24.95.
W. Ray Johnson, USA, 1925, 65 mins.

Rip Van Winkle
A silent adaptation of the classic tale about a somnambulent man awakened after a 20-year sleep. With Thomas Jefferson. 1914.
VHS: S18898. $19.95.

Risky Business
Vera Reynolds, a society girl, is shown the hardships of a doctor's life by her gold-digging mother in an attempt to stop the marriage. Also included is the great Snub Pollard short, *Sold at Auction*. With ZaSu Pitts, Ethel Clayton. Silent with music score.
VHS: S07484. $24.95.
Alan Hale, USA, 1928, 104 mins.

The Roaring Road
Darco Motor Company president J.D. "The Bear" Ward (Theodore Roberts), wants a Darco car to win the Santa Monica Grand Prize road race for the third time. Darco top salesman Walter Thomas "Toodles" Walden (Wallace Reid) wants to drive in the race, but J.D. wants no amateurs. The only thing Toodles wants more than racing is to marry The Bear's daughter Dorothy (Ann Little).
VHS: S34168. $19.95.
James Cruze, USA, 1919, 57 mins.

Robin Hood
In his *The Parade's GoneBy*, film critic Kevin Brownlow says, "*Robin Hood*, if not the most flamboyant of Fairbanks' swashbuckling, is certainly the most awe-inspiring. Its center piece is an enormous castle, said to be the largest set ever constructed in Hollywood. Purely on the level of art direction, *Robin Hood* is an unsurpassed and unsurpassable achievement." This full, almost three-hour version is the most complete available.
VHS: S06389. $24.95.
Allan Dwan, USA, 1922, 120 mins.

Robinson Crusoe
Tinted print of this silent version of the famous tale by an unknown director.
VHS: S33068. $24.95.
50 mins.

Romance of the Wasteland
In this rare silent western, a little girl is left at the train depot when she leaves the train to chase a puppy. Art Mix finds her and tends her until the mother returns. With Alma Rayford. Orchestra score.
VHS: S32107. $19.95.
USA, 1924, 50 mins.

Romola
This rarely-seen Gish film features both of the Gish sisters (Lillian and Dorothy), with Ronald Colman, William Powell, and a new piano score. Silent with musical score.
VHS: S05976. $24.95.
Henry King, USA, 1924, 120 mins.

Rubber Tires
A film that foreshadowed the Depression soon to come, a family moves to California to seek better fortunes, unaware that their car is unique and worth a great deal of money. USA, 1927.
VHS: S02582. $19.95.

Sadie Thompson
The first film version of Somerset Maugham's classic novella, with the creative talents of Raoul Walsh, Gloria Swanson, Lionel Barrymore and art director William Cameron Menzies.
A landmark of the silent era, the film's great achievement is the uncompromising translation of Maugham's controversial story of a San Francisco prostitute and a South Pacific reformer. The tragedy of the film is that, for many years, the last scenes were missing from the only existing print. In this version, the final minutes have been carefully restored and the result is one of the most important triumphs of the silent era. Restored by Dennis Doros. Silent with music score.
VHS: S08944. $29.95.
Laser: LD71315. $49.95.
Raoul Walsh, USA, 1928, 97 mins.

Salome
Alla Nazimova, the notorious wife of Rudolph Valentino, directed this controversial version of Salome with its highly stylized acting and sets.
VHS: S08851. $19.95.
Alla Nazimova, USA, 1922, 35 mins.

Salome and Queen Elizabeth
Two very rare silent films; *Salome* (1922) stars Alla Nazimova in a bold and bizarre adaptation of Oscar Wilde's play, with Azimova's famous "Dance of the Seven Veils" sequence; *Queen Elizabeth* features the famous Sarah Bernhardt when she was 56 years old. Silent films with music score, 91 mins. total.
VHS: S06932. $29.95.

The Saturday Night Kid
A curious silent work enlivened by the appearance of two skilled performers, Clara Bow and Jean Arthur. USA, 1929.
VHS: S18952. $19.95.

Scarlet Car
Lon Chaney, Franklyn Farnum and Edith Johnson star in this early Chaney film. Trying to hide the fact of embezzlement, Chaney, the teller in a bank, is left for dead. Silent with music score.
VHS: S10370. $24.95.
Joseph DeGrasse, USA, 1917, 70 mins.

Secrets of the Night
Hilarious turmoil ensues when a banker hosts a large party and stages his own murder to hide records from the bank examiner. Stars James Kirkwood, Madge Bellamy, ZaSu Pitts, Tom Ricketts, Tom S. Guise, Arthur Stuart Hull, Rosemary Theby, Tom Wilson, Joe Singleton, Bull Montana, Tyrone Brereton and Otto Hoffman. Silent with music track.
VHS: S30158. $19.95.
Herbert Blache, USA, 1928, 64 mins.

Selected Shorts #2
Family Life (1924, Mark June and Ruth Hatt); *Why Worry* (1926, George Bunny); *Be My King* (1928, Lupino Lane); *Idle Eyes*, (1928, Ben Turpin). Various, USA, 1924-28, 70 mins.
VHS: S04818. $19.95.

Seventh Heaven
"*Seventh Heaven* tracks the transformational love of Farrell and Gaynor from the sewers to the stars, across time and space, and beyond death itself, affirming triumphantly that melodrama can mean much more than just an excuse for a good weep" *(Time Out Film Guide)*. Janet Gaynor won an Oscar for her portrayal of a mistreated Paris street waif redeemed by cockney sewer man Charles Farrell.
VHS: S31171. $24.95.
Frank Borzage, USA, 1927, 119 mins.

Sex
The beautiful star of a Broadway show seduces a married man in this silent drama. His marriage collapses but the star finds someone else. Eventually all this fooling around brings personal tragedy. With Louise Glaum, William Conklin and Irving Cummings.
VHS: S05433. $29.95.
Fred Niblo, USA, 1920, 94 mins.

Shadows
Lon Chaney, Marguerite de la Motte, Harrison Ford and Walter Long star in this atmospheric and haunting drama set in Urkey, a small fishing village, with Chaney as a Chinaman barred from the village, whom the Reverend Malden (Harrison Ford, no relation) and his wife de la Motte try to convert to Christianity. Silent with music score.
VHS: S05605. $24.95.
Tom Forman, USA, 1922, 85 mins.

The Shamrock and the Rose
Mack Swain and Maurice Costello are cast in this story of feuding families. Even the priest cannot convince these warring clans to forget their differences. 1927, 60 mins.
VHS: S23845. $24.95.

She Goes to War
Humor, tragedy and romance are all part of this World War I tale directed by Henry King and starring Eleanor Boardman and Al St. John.
VHS: S10582. $19.95.
Henry King, USA, 1929, 50 mins.

The Sheik
The original famous version of Rudolph Valentino's romantic melodrama, as Valentino (Sheik Ahmed) rescues a proud English girl (Agnes Ayres) disguised as a slave. The film that made Valentino an international idol.
VHS: S09401. $19.98.
George Melford, USA, 1921, 80 mins.

Shifting Sands
Gloria Swanson appears in an off-beat role as a woman sent to jail for a crime she didn't commit; she is blackmailed by a ring of spies to obtain a set of secret plans.
VHS: S08855. $19.95.
Albert Parker, USA, 1918, 52 mins.

A Ship Comes In
Rudolph Schildkraut, Louise Dresser, Milton Holmes and Linda Landi star. Silent with music track.
VHS: S07219. $24.95.
William K. Howard, USA, 1928, 70 mins.

Ships of the Night
Frank Moran and Jacqueline Logan star in this tale of the south seas and the search for her fugitive brother. Silent with music score.
VHS: S10362. $19.95.
Duke Worne, USA, 1928, 63 mins.

Shock
Lambert Hillyer directed this early silent horror-thriller starring Lon Chaney, Virginia Valli and Christine Mayo.
VHS: S04798. $24.95.
Lambert Hillyer, USA, 1923, 85 mins.

Shore Leave
Richard Barthelmess is a reluctant seaman who has been spotted by Dorothy Mackaill, a dressmaker determined to be married. In this romantic comedy she gives her all to land Barthelmess. It's a scenario that always engages the romantically inclined.
VHS: S23148. $24.95.
John S. Robertson, USA, 1925, 90 mins.

The Short Films of Mary Pickford
America's silent sweetheart in several of her most endearing film shorts. Includes *In Old Madrid* (10 mins.), *Lonely Villa* (10 mins.), *Sweet Memories* (10 mins.), *Her First Biscuits* (5 mins.), *The Female of the Species* (10 mins.), *100% Canadian* (10 mins.), *The New York Hat* (10 mins.), *Violin Maker of Cremona* (10 mins) and *1776 or The Hessian Renegades*) (10 mins.).
VHS: S14929. $29.95.

Show People
"In this delightful satire on Hollywood in the twenties, Marion Davies plays a star-struck country girl who arrives in Hollywood seeking the glamour of the bright lights, only to find herself the lesser half of a slapstick team. Davies proves herself as the comedienne, whether as Peggy Pepper, baptized into show usiness with seltzer sprayed from a siphon bottle, or Peggy Pepoire, motion picture star. Intended as a gentle satire on the career of Gloria Swanson, it pokes fun at other Hollywood luminaries along the way" *(Pacific Film Archive)*.
VHS: S09282. $29.95.
Laser: LD76155. $39.98.
King Vidor, USA, 1928, 81 mins.

The Show-Off
Slapstick veteran Ford Sterling delivers the performance of his career as Aubrey Piper, an irresponsible blowhard whose incessant boasting wreaks havoc in the home of Amy, his gullible fiancee (Lois Wilson). When Amy marries Aubrey in spite of her family's objections, their lives spiral toward poverty, and it falls to the abrasive braggart to somehow save the day. Louise Brooks is a scene stealer as the fetching girl next door. Wittily directed by Malcolm St. Clair, the film makes outstanding use of actual Philadelphia locations.
VHS: S19565. $24.95.
Laser: LD76957. $39.99.
Malcolm St. Clair, USA, 1926, 82 mins.

Silk Husbands and Calico Wives
House Peters and Mary Alden are cast in this story about the ideal marriage, for a man that is. A wife is supposed to love, honor and obey her husband, at least in older silent movies.
VHS: S23847. $24.95.
Alfred E. Green, USA, 1920, 65 mins.

The Single Standard
It's the incomparable Greta Garbo breaking convention as a society girl with bohemian sensibilities, who has an affair with a local artist. An enjoyable melodrama with fine performances all around. See the radiant and scandalous Garbo in (gasp!) slacks for the first time on screen. Silent film with synchronized musical score.
VHS: S13979. $29.99.
John S. Robertson, USA, 1929, 93 mins.

The Sky Pilot
John Bowers, Colleen Moore, David Butler and Harry Todd star in this film set in the Canadian Northwest. Bowers is the preacher who fights the God-hating natives in the lawless territory for the salvation of their souls.
VHS: S03783. $29.95.
King Vidor, USA, 1921, 72 mins.

Skyscraper
Adapted from a story by Dudley Murphy by Elliott Clawson and Tay Garnett, and starring William Boyd. Nominated for an Oscar in 1930 for Best Script. A Pathe production by DeMille.
VHS: S07248. $24.95.
Howard Higgin, USA, 1928, 68 mins.

Smith Family Series
The 1920's version of the sit-com, in six short serials produced by Mack Sennett, called *The Smith Family Series: Smith's New Home, Smith's Fishing Trip, Smith's Picnic, Smith's Customer, Smith's Cook* and *Smith's Army Life*. USA, 118 mins.
VHS: S03172. $24.95.

The Smoking Trail
Found in a railroad depot in Tennessee, this rare silent film is the story of the head of a gang of rustlers, who loans money to ranchers and then steals their cattle so they are unable to pay him back, and then forecloses on their property. Bill Patton, working undercover as a cowboy, is sent by the Rangers to catch the thieves. With William Bertram, Jack House, Tom Ross, Alma Rayford and Maine Geary. With orchestra score.
VHS: S32050. $19.95.
William Bertram, USA, 1924, 63 mins.

Smouldering Fires
A very rare drama from Clarence Brown, this is a superbly directed triangle with Laura La Plante, Pauline Frederick. Tape comes from British print never seen in the U.S.
VHS: S05977. $24.95.
Clarence Brown, USA, 1924, 100 mins.

The Social Secretary
Norma Talmadge is Mayme, a good looking girl looking for a job without male interference. Disguised as a plain jane, she is hired by a wealthy woman for the title position. Mayme saves the lady's daughter from a villainous count. With Kate Lester, Gladden Jones and Erich von Stroheim as the Buzzard. A comedy.
VHS: S04808. $19.95.
John Emerson, USA, 1916, 56 mins.

Sold for Marriage
Lillian Gish and Walter Long star in this silent film about a young Russian women in distress. She believes her tormentor is dead and escapes to America.
VHS: S23848. $24.95.
William Christy Cabanne, USA, 1916, 43 mins.

Son of the Sheik
The last film of Rudolph Valentino, a sequel to his big hit, *The Sheik*. Valentino plays the son of the desert warrior and lover who is out to capture the bandits who wronged a poor dancing girl.
VHS: S03071. $24.95.
Laser: CLV. LD70769. $39.95.
George Fitzmaurice, USA, 1926, 68 mins.

Soul of the Beast
Madge Bellamy, Cullen Landis, Noah Beery and Vola Vale star. Madge and her only friend, a circus elephant, are runaways from an abusing stepfather. Silent with music score.
VHS: S10364. $19.95.
John Griffith Wray, USA, 1923, 65 mins.

Soul-Fire
Richard Barthelmess, Bessie Love, Walter Lang and Arthur Metcalf star in this inspirational drama.
VHS: S07201. $24.95.
John S. Robertson, USA, 1925, 100 mins.

The Spanish Dancer
The legendary Pola Negri plays a fiery gypsy who maneuvers the King (Wallace Beery) into restoring an impoverished nobleman's estates. With Anthony Moreno and Adolphe Menjou.
VHS: S03171. $18.95.
Herbert Brenon, USA, 1923, 55 mins.

Sparrows
Considered to be Mary Pickford's best feature and a super-production of its day, *Sparrows* is an expert blend of thrilling spectacle and hissable villainy. The story concerns a group of orphan children held in virtual slavery on a southern farm surrounded by a treacherous swamp. In the climax, Mollie (Pickford) leads the children to safety after a hair-raising chase through a wilderness filled with alligators and quicksand. Organ score.
VHS: S01744. $29.95.
William Beaudine, USA, 1926, 81 min.

Speed Spook
Auto racing is the theme of this early silent film starring Johnny Hines, Faire Binney.
VHS: S07258. $29.95.
Charles Hines, USA, 1924, 85 mins.

The Spieler
Renee Adoree and Alan Hale are cast in this silent dramatic film that reveals the seamier side of carnival life. Love, jealousy and murder all play a role in this frank tale.
VHS: S23849. $24.95.
Frank Lloyd, USA, 1928, 70 mins.

Square Shoulders
Junior Coghlan, Louis Wolheim, Anita Louis and Montague Shaw star in this drama set in a military academy. Silent with music score.
VHS: S10359. $19.95.
E. Mason Hopper, USA, 1929, 56 mins.

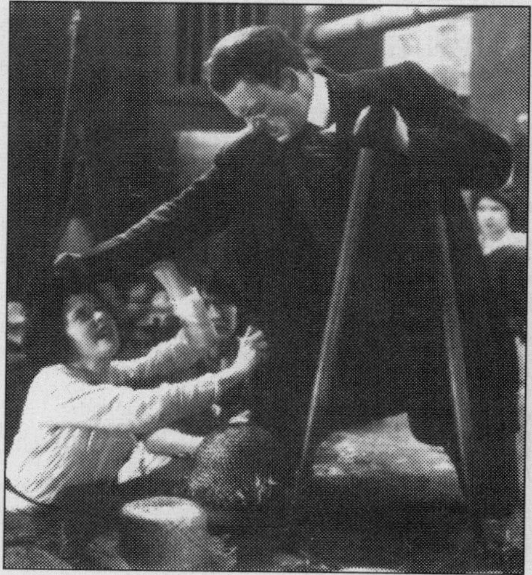

The Star Prince
The Star Prince falls to earth on a star and is found and reared by a woodcutter. The Prince sets out to find his real mother and survives several adventures involving the wicked witch and the little princess. This film is enacted by children from the Little Players Film Co. of Chicago.
VHS: S22883. $19.95.
Madeline Brandeis, USA, 1918, 54 mins.

Stella Maris
Mary Pickford stars in this melodrama about a rich, crippled girl and a poor orphan girl, both of whom fall in love with the same (married though separated) man. Silent with music track.
VHS: S07221. $24.95.
Marshall Neilan, USA, 1918, 70 mins.

Stop at Nothing
The only known surviving film of George Larkin, a very popular silent era actor. USA, 1922, 56 mins.
VHS: S08853. $19.95.

The Street of Forgotten Women
This exploitative look at prostitution was made after a number of scandals rocked the silent film world. It purports to be an expose, but actually manages to expose plenty of flesh instead. A young girl is seduced into a life of prostitution after being brutalized and even stripped of her underwear. 55 mins.
VHS: S24002. $19.95.
Donald Crisp, USA, 1926, 72 mins.

Suds
Mary Pickford, America's sweetheart during the silent era, stars in this charming tale of fantasy and young love. Pickford is a cockney laundress who dreams of a finer life until she finds true love with someone from her own station.
VHS: S23851. $24.95.
John Francis Dillon, USA, 1920, 75 mins.

Surrender
Mary Philbin and Ivan Mousjoukine star in this silent epic set in Russia during World War I. A small village is threatened with utter destruction by Russian generals.
VHS: S23852. $24.95.
Edward Sloan, USA, 1927, 75 mins.

Swan

A young woman of noble blood is encouraged by her mother to marry the older crown prince, but she falls in love with her handsome tutor instead. With Frances Howard, Adolphe Menjou, Richardo Cortez and Ida Waterman. Based on the 1922 Ferenc Molnar play about the Hapsburg royal family. Silent with music track.
VHS: S16177. $29.95.
Dimitri Buchowetzki, USA, 1925, 120 mins.

Sweet Adeline

Charles Ray stars. Silent with music track. Hick becomes a big musical star but loses his girlfriend to his brother.
VHS: S07243. $19.95.
Jerome Storm, USA, 1926, 60 mins.

A Tale of Two Cities/In the Switch Tower

Norma Talmadge was only 14 years old when she was cast as a lead in her first important film, the original screen version of *A Tale of Two Cities*, in 1911. With *In the Switch Tower* from 1915. Silent. USA, 70 mins.
VHS: S03655. $29.95.

A Tale of Two Worlds (Water Lily)

A young Caucasian girl is brought up by a Chinese servant as Chinese after the death of her parents. She is coveted by Ling Jo, a leader of the Boxer rebellion, in which her parents were killed. With J. Frank Glendon, Leatrice Joy, Wallace Beery, E.A. Warren, Margaret McWade, Togo Yamamoto, Jack Abbe, Louie Cheune, Chow Young and Etta Lee. Silent with piano score.
VHS: S30678. $19.95.
Frank Lloyd, USA, 1921, 74 mins.

Tarzan of the Apes

Elmo Lincoln and Enid Markey star in this first screen version of the classic story.
VHS: S11455. $19.95.
Scott Sidney, USA, 1918, 59 mins.

The Tempest

An officer in the army of the Czar finds his romance with a princess violently interrupted by the Russian revolutionaries. Featuring a brave—though very melodramatic—performance by John Barrymore. Silent, music track.
VHS: S02089. $29.95.
Sam Taylor, USA, 1928, 99 mins.

The Temptress

In her second American film, Greta Garbo stars as Elena, a wicked woman who drives men to death and destruction, only to have her own life ruined by falling in love with Robledo (Antonio Moreno). With Roy D'Arcy and Lionel Barrymore. Silent, music track.
VHS: S33055. $24.95.
Fred Niblo, USA, 1926, 115 mins.

Ten Nights in a Barroom

This classic film underscores the evil of drinking alcohol. Perhaps its most famous scene is the final fight sequence. William Farnum, Tom Santschi, Patty Lou Lynd, Robert Fraser and other luminaries of the early cinema are featured.
VHS: S23319. $19.95.
William O'Connor, USA, 1931, 72 mins.

Tess of the Storm Country

Mary Pickford stars in this silent revival of the story of a little girl in a fishing village. With Lloyd Hughes, Gloria Hope, David Torrence and Jean Hersholt. Original organ score.
VHS: S30553. $19.95.
John S. Robertson, USA, 1922, 137 mins.

Test of Donald Norton

George Walsh, Tyrone Power, Robert Graves and Eugenie Gilbert star. A man raised by Indians is troubled by fears of being half-Indian.
VHS: S07203. $24.95.
B. Reeves Eason, USA, 1926, 85 mins.

That Girl Montana

Blanche Sweet is the daughter of a crooked cardshark who must hide when her father is run out of town. She falls in love with a man and becomes part owner in a gold mine. Her father returns to insist he receive part of the claim. With Mahlon Hamilton, Frank Lanning, Edward Peil, Charles Edler, Claire de Brey, Kate Price and Jack Roseleigh. Silent with orchestra score.
VHS: S32048. $19.95.
Robert Thornby, USA, 1921, 67 mins.

These Girls Won't Talk

That's only because these are silent movies. Titles include *Her Bridal Nightmare* with Colleen Moore as a bride whose hubby has been arrested for losing his pants, *The Campus Carmen* with Daphne Pollard and Carole Lombard, and *As Luck Would Have It* with Betty Compson as a daffy dame who wants to be a nurse.
VHS: S05861. $29.95.
Harry Edwards et al., USA, 1918-28, 81 mins.

The Thief of Baghdad

Douglas Fairbanks on a marvelous quest in an Arabian Nights fantasy/adventure with the lovely Julanne Johnston as the princess who rides off with Fairbanks on his magic carpet. From Raoul Walsh, a dynamic, prolific director.
VHS: S01323. $24.95.
Raoul Walsh, USA, 1924, 132 mins.

The Three Musketeers

An early silent version of the famous novel starring Fairbanks with Leon Barry, Marguerite de la Motte, George Siegmann, Adolphe Menjou.
VHS: S08887. $24.95.
Fred Niblo, USA, 1921, 120 mins.

Three Pals

Marilyn Mills stars as a woman who raises horses and must prove her father innocent of murder. With Josef Swickard and Gary Cooper in an uncredited bit part.
VHS: S33069. $24.95.
Wilbur McGaugh, USA, 1926, 65 mins.

Through the Breakers

Margaret Livingston, Holmes Herbert, Clyde Cook, Natalie Joyce and Frank Hagney star in this tale of lost love on a South Sea Island. Silent with music score. 1928, 55 mins.
VHS: S10369. $19.95.

Tol'able David

In the Appalachian mountains three evil mountain men cause havoc in a small community. After they kill his dog, cripple his brother and cause the death of his father, little David is forced to deal with them when they try to rob the mail wagon. With Richard Barthelmess, Marion Abbott and Warner Richmond. One hand-tinted sequence.
VHS: S05481. $24.95.
Laser: LD76267. $39.99.
Henry King, USA, 1921, 106 mins.

Toll of the Sea

A poignant variation on the Madame Butterfly story, Anna May Wong stars as Lotus Flower, a young Chinese woman who rescues a man who washes up on the seashore. They fall in love and marry but heartache ensues when the young man returns to America. Notable because it was the first feature film to be shot in Technicolor, and one of the few films produced by the Technicolor Company. The film runs 41 minutes, and the final shot was reconstructed using the original two-strip color cameras to film the final sunset.
VHS: S06010. $29.95.
Chester M. Franklin, USA, 1922, 41 mins.

The Tollgate

When Black Deering (William S. Hart) and his gang are ambushed during a daring train holdup, he learns his betrayer was one of his own men, Jordan (Joseph Singleton), whose blood money has bought him a parlor of gambling and prostitution. Upon escaping from the authorities, Deering flees into the wilderness and finds shelter in the home of an abandoned woman (Anna Q. Nilsson). There, the vengeful gunfighter finds the possibility of redemption, but his happiness is short-lived when two posses—one led by the murderous Jordan, the other by a local sheriff—converge upon the isolated cabin. With *His Bitter Pill* (1916, 20 mins), Mack Sennett's famous parody of Hart in which the noble cowboy is viciously lampooned by Mack Swain (*The Gold Rush*).
VHS: S34317. $24.95.
Lambert Hillyer, USA, 1920, 73 mins.

Tom Mix Short Subjects

Five short films of Tom Mix produced by Carl Selig: *A Bear of a Story, The Stagecoach Driver and the Girl, How Weary Goes Wooing, Using His Brain, Sage Brush Tom*.
VHS: S08872. $24.95.

Tomboy

Lotta Williams, Herbert Rawliston, Harry Gibbon star.
VHS: S07231. $19.95.
David Kirkland, USA, 1924, 64 mins.

Tong Man

Sessue Hayakawa and Helen Eddy star in this rare film based on Clyde Westovers' novel *The Dragon's Daughter*. Silent with music track.
VHS: S07233. $19.95.
William Worthington, USA, 1919, 60 mins.

The Torrent

Greta Garbo, in her first American film, and Ricardo Cortez star as Spanish sweethearts who are parted by a domineering mother. The girl consoles herself by becoming a Paris prima donna. An emotional vehicle for its day. Silent.
VHS: S33933. $24.95.
Monta Bell, USA, 1926, 75 mins.

Touring the Silent Studios

Accompanied by an organ score, this collection contains five films which offer a view of early moviemaking. *Universal Studio Tour* (1916), *MGM Studio Tour* (1925), *Ghost Town: The Fort Lee Story, City of Stars* (1925 at Universal) and *A Girl's Folly* (1917) are all included. The last of these is about filmmaking at a New Jersey studio. 115 mins.
VHS: S29895. $39.95.

Tracy the Outlaw

This rare silent film details the true life story of Harry Tracy, one of the bad men of the old west, who escaped from a Texas gambling hall and was hunted by posses from state to state. With Jack Hoey and Dorris Chadwick.
VHS: S33070. $24.95.
Otis B. Thayer, USA, 1928, 70 mins.

Traffic in Souls

Unseen for many years, this rare classic tells the story of the turn-of-the-century white slave trade, running rampant in this country at the time. An early social-problem film, it attempted to make the general public aware of this rarely-talked-about problem. A beautiful condition print. Piano scored.
VHS: S15511. $29.95.
George Tucker, USA, 1913, 74 mins.

Trail of the Axe

Dustin Farnum stars in this story of love and adventure in a Northwoods logging camp. USA, 1919, silent with music track, 55 mins.
VHS: S07204. $24.95.

Tramp, Tramp, Tramp

Harry Langdon, in his first successful independent feature, co-stars with a young Joan Crawford in this silent romantic comedy about a man who enters a cross-country walkathon in order to win money, all leading up to a whirlwind finale. Includes the classic scene with Harry breaking rocks with a chain gang, "a masterpiece of careful timing" (Kevin Brownlow, *The Parade's Gone By*...). "This picture takes Langdon's doleful face and pathetic figure out of the two-reel class and into the Chaplin and Lloyd screen dimensions" (*Photoplay*, August 1926). Includes the 1924 short *All Night Long*.
VHS: S30714. $29.95.
Harry Edwards, USA, 1926, 84 mins.

Trilby

The first of many versions of the famous story by George Du Maurier about the mesmerizing Svengali and his beautiful victim. From a beautiful quality print.
VHS: S13274. $19.95.
Maurice Tourneur, USA, 1917, 59 mins.

Twelve Miles Out

In this rare silent, Jerry Fay (John Gilbert), a bootlegger pursued by the coast Guard, finds refuge in a seashore house owned by Jane (Joan Crawford). When she threatens to inform the authorities, he takes her aboard his boat. Red McGue (Ernest Torrence), a rival bootlegger, hijacks the boat and makes advances to Jane.
VHS: S37090. $19.95.
Jack Conway, USA, 1927, 61 mins.

Twinkletoes

Colleen Moore is Twinkletoes, a dancer from the London Limehouse district. She falls for a married boxer, and tries to hide her feelings for him, but when he saves her from an attack, she can resist him no longer. Also with Kenneth Harlan, Tully Marshall, Gladys Brockwell, Lucien Littlefield, Warner Oland, John Philip Kolb, Julianne Johnston and William McDonald. Silent with piano score.
VHS: S30681. $24.95.
Charles Babin, USA, 1926, 78 mins.

Unchastened Woman

Theda Bara stars in her comeback role as a pregnant wife who discovers her husband is cheating on her. With Wyndham Standing, Dale Fuller and Eileen Percy. Silent with music track.
VHS: S07224. $19.95.
James Young, USA, 1925, 52 mins.

Uncle Tom's Cabin (1903 & 1914)

This tape includes the two earliest film versions of Harriet Beecher Stowe's classic tale of slavery. The 1903 version was restored from Library of Congress paper prints. The 1914 version features Sam Lucas—the first black actor to star in a film.
VHS: S15482. $29.95.

Uncle Tom's Cabin (1914)

An early version of the Harriet Beecher Stowe novel of slavery stars Sam Lucas, who was said to be the first black man to have a leading role in films, as Tom, and also has some black stage actors in the cast.
VHS: S11452. $19.95.
William R. Daly, USA, 1914, 54 mins.

The Unholy Three

A ventriloquist, a dwarf and a strong man carry out a series of bizarre crimes which end in murder. The first in a series of off-kilter tales starring Lon Chaney under Browning's direction. With Harry Earles, Victor McLaglen, Mae Busch and Matt Moore. Silent with music track.
VHS: S16172. $29.95.
Tod Browning, USA, 1925, 76 mins.

The Unknown

One of the rare Lon Chaney films—located in France—now with English subtitles. Chaney plays a knife-thrower who falls in love with the star of a circus (Joan Crawford). He has his hands amputated when she rejects him. Bizarre. Silent with music score.
VHS: S10371. $24.95.
Tod Browning, USA, 1927, 60 mins.

The Untamable

Gladys Walton, Malcolm McGregor, John Sainpolis and Etta Lee star in this film about a woman with a split personality beautifully changing from an innocent lady to a lady who is cruel and campish. A truly unique film from the silent era. Silent with music score.
VHS: S10368. $19.95.
Herbert Blache, USA, 1923, 65 mins.

Until They Get Me

Pauline Atarke and Joe King star in this adventure in the north as a mountie searches for years to get his man.
VHS: S08857. $24.95.
Frank Borzage, USA, 1918, 58 mins.

The Valley of Hate

A wealthy young man (Raymond McKee) inherits property in a South Carolina valley he has never seen. When he goes to inspect his new holdings he is mistaken for a revenue officer by the native population. He then falls in love with a ward (Helen Ferguson) of one of the moonshiners and must fight to help her leave the valley. Excellent original print of this rare silent film.
VHS: S31172. $19.95.
Russell Allen, USA, 1924, 63 mins.

The Vanishing American

One of the great silent epics. Richard Dix stars in this Zane Grey tale about a modern American Indian who fights the Germans in WWI only to return to find his people being mistreated by a crooked Indian agent (Noah Beery). Filmed partly in Monument Valley. With Lois Wilson as the schoolmarm and plenty of native American history.
VHS: S05489. $49.95.
George B. Seitz, USA, 1915, 148 mins.

Venus of the South Seas

A girl raised on a lonely isle falls in love with a wealthy young man. Includes a beautiful, two-color, fantasy underwater ballet sequence filmed when Esther Williams was still in her water wings. With Annette Kellerman. Silent with organ score.
VHS: S32049. $19.95.
James R. Sullivan, USA, 1924, 55 mins.

The Virginian

An early, faithful adaptation of the famous book, with Kenneth Harlan, Florence Vidor and Raymond Hatton.
VHS: S08889. $24.95.
Tom Forman, USA, 1923, 74 mins.

Walking Back

Sue Carrol stars. Troubled teenagers go for a joyride and wind up involved in a robbery scheme. Silent with music track.
VHS: S07246. $19.95.
Rupert Julian, USA, 1926, 53 mins.

We're in the Navy Now

After the huge success of their *Behind the Front*, Wallace Beery and Raymond Hatton were teamed up again in another hilarious look at military life. Silent with music score.
VHS: S07485. $19.95.
A. Edward Sutherland, USA, 1927, 60 mins.

Webs of Steel

J.P. McGowan directed Helen Holmes and Andrew Waldro in this railroad action drama.
VHS: S08877. $24.95.
J.P. McGowan, USA, 1925, 55 mins.

West of Zanzibar/The Unholy Three

Two early silent collaborations between Tod Browning and Lon Chaney. *West of Zanzibar* (1928) deals with a man's determination to destroy the man who caused his crippling injury. *The Unholy Three* (1925) is about the underworld activities of a ventriloquist who forms an unholy trinity with a grotesque strongman and midget. Chaney remade the film in 1930, his only talkie.
Laser: LD71858. $39.98.

What Happened to Rosa?

In this great light comedy, a bumbling shopgirl (Mabel Normand) is told by a fortune teller that she is the reincarnation of a noble Spanish maiden. When she goes to a party aboard ship dressed as a highborn Spanish maiden, there is a row over her, and rather than reveal her identity, she discards her costume and swims ashore. Everyone wants to know *What Happened to Rosa*.
VHS: S30679. $19.95.
Victor Schertzinger, USA, 1921, 54 mins.

What Price Glory?

In this silent World War I drama, Victor McLaglen is Captain Flagg and Edmund Lowe is Sergeant Micky Quirt, U.S. Marine Corps friends battling for the affections of Frenchwoman, Charmaine de la Cognac (Dolores Del Rio) until the realities of war make them realize their true fight.
VHS: S30789. $19.95.
Raoul Walsh, USA, 1926, 120 mins.

Where the North Holds Sway

When a Northwest Mounted's (Jack Perrin) brother is murdered, he leaves the service to seek revenge. With Pauline Curley. Silent, music track.
VHS: S33699. $24.95.
Bennett Cohn, USA, 1927, 54 mins.

The Whip

Maurice Tourneur directed this rare early feature about a racehorse, the whip and the villains who try to keep its nobleman owner from racing him.
VHS: S04807. $24.95.
Maurice Tourneur, USA, 1917, 60 mins.

White Gold

William K. Howard directed this western which stars Jetta Goudal, Kenneth Thomson and George Bancroft. Tay Garnett worked on the script. Silent with music tack.
VHS: S07252. $24.95.
William K. Howard, USA, 1927, 70 mins.

White Sheep

Glen Tryon stars as the weakling of the family, who proves himself at the end.
VHS: S07261. $19.95.
Hal Roach, USA, 1924, 70 mins.

The White Sister

Lillian Gish plays an Italian aristocrat who is driven away from home when her nasty sister alters their father's will following his death. Gish falls in love with an Italian army officer, but when he is reported killed in the war, the broken-hearted girl decides to become a nun. With Ronald Colman and Gail Cane. Silent with music track.
VHS: S16110. $29.95.
Henry King, USA, 1923, 68 mins.

White Tiger

Three international crooks attempt the crime of the century. Hiding out together in a mountain cabin after the deed, their mutual distrust grows daily. With Priscilla Dean, Matt Moore, Raymond Griffith and Wallace Beery. Though rough, this video was transferred from the best print available. Organ score included.
VHS: S22426. $19.95.
Tod Browning, USA, 1923, 81 mins.

Wild and Woolly

Douglas Fairbanks stars in this comic Western as an overzealous aficionado of Western lore, who somehow manages to best both Native Americans and desperados. Eileen Percy, Walter Bytell, Joseph Singleton, Sam De Grasse and Tom Wilson are also featured.
VHS: S22983. $24.95.
John Emerson, USA, 1917, 58 mins.

Wild Orchids

Garbo is bewitching as a married woman caught in a steamy love triangle set in Java. Lewis Stone co-stars as her husband, and Nils Asther appears as the native prince who steals her heart. Silent film with synchronized music score and sound effects.
VHS: S13977. $29.99.
Sidney Franklin, USA, 1928, 119 mins.

Wings

One of the most exciting of the silent dramas, *Wings* was the first film to be awarded the Oscar for Best Picture. Featuring Clara Bow (The IT Girl) and a short appearance by Gary Cooper, the film has incredible aerial battle sequences. Director Wellman makes a humanistic statement as he explores the devastation of World War I.
VHS: S02831. $19.95.
William Wellman, USA, 1927, 139 mins.

Winning the Futurity

Cullen Landis, Clara Horton, Henry Kolker, Pat Harman star.
VHS: S07211. $19.95.
Scott Dunlap, USA, 1926, 70 mins.

Wishing Ring

An extremely rare film from Maurice Tourneur. A light and charming romance based on the play by Owen Davis.
VHS: S05986. $24.95.
Maurice Tourneur, USA, 1915, 50 mins.

With Byrd at the South Pole

Byrd's establishment of Little America and the spectacular first flight over the South Pole—part publicity stunt, part scientific milestone—marked the end of an era. This film is a remarkable document of courage and achievement. Byrd, his terrier Igloo, and his companions became legends as popular as Lindbergh, Babe Ruth and Valentino. Winner of the Academy Award for Best Cinematography. Silent with music track.
VHS: S16433. $39.95.
Laser: CLV/CAV. **LD72074. $39.95.**
Joseph Rucker, USA, 1930, 82 mins.

The Wizard of Oz

Not the Judy Garland version, but the original silent adaptation of Frank Baum's book, with Larry Semon as Scarecrow, Oliver Hardy as the Tin Man, and Dorothy Dwan as Dorothy, in this very ambitious slapstick comedy. Silent with music track.
VHS: S02097. $29.95.
Larry Semon, USA, 1925, 65 mins.

Wolf Blood

Marguerite Clayton, George Chesebro, Ray Hanford and Roy Watson star in this gothic tale. George is hurt in an accident and Dr. Horton must use a wolf's blood to save him. Unexplained deaths soon follow, leading George to fear that he is becoming a beast. This may well be the forerunner for the classic wolfman films of the 1930's. From a 35mm tinted print.
VHS: S23313. $19.95.
George Chesebro/George Mitchell, USA, 1925, 68 mins.

Wolves of Kultur

A seven chapter condensation of the great early Charles Hutchinson action serial about stolen plans that must be regained. 1918, 182 mins.
VHS: S11460. $39.95.

A Woman in Grey

This excellent, action-packed, 15-chapter, silent serial—considered to be one of the last true adult serials—is the story of a mysterious woman, hidden treasure and a map that changes hands many times. With superb cliff-hanging endings and a cast that includes Arline Pretty, Henry G. Sell, Fred Jones, Margaret Fielding, James A. Heenan, Ann Brodie, Violet de Bicari and Adelaine Fitzgallen. Orchestra score.
VHS: S31174. $24.95.
James Vincent, USA, 1920, 235 mins.

Woman of Affairs

Greta Garbo and John Gilbert star in this silent romance about a wild rich girl who goes from man to man until she finally kills herself in a car crash. With Lewis Stone, Douglas Fairbanks Jr. Silent with music track.
VHS: S13401. $29.98.
Laser: Chapter search. Includes original theatrical trailer.
LD71645. $34.98.
Clarence Brown, USA, 1928, 90 mins.

Won in the Clouds

Al Wilson, Helen Foster, Frank Rice, George French and Joe Bennett star in this adventure story. Silent with music track.
VHS: S07208. $19.95.
Bruce Mitchell, USA, 1928, 55 mins.

The Worldly Madonna

Clara Kimball Young has two roles in this rare silent film. As Janet, a convent novitiate, she agrees to exchange places with her sister Lucy, a cabaret dancer, who believes she has killed a man. Though shorter than the original version, the complete story has been preserved in this video version. Organ music accompaniment.
VHS: S22427. $19.95.
Harry Garson, USA, 1922, 47 mins.

Yankee Doodle in Berlin
An early Mack Sennett comedy, a spoof of the Kaiser, with Bothwell Browne, Ford Sterling, Mal St. Clair.
VHS: S07266. $19.95.
Richard Jones, USA, 1918, 60 mins.

The Young April
Bessie Love, Joseph and Rudolph Schildkraut and Bryant Washburn star in this silent comedy about a young orphan. Poor in America, a young woman inherits a great deal of money and a title back in her native Belgravia. There she is to wed the reluctant crown prince. While the prince is off on a last wild fling in Paris, he meets the woman he truly wants to marry, only she has a big surprise in store for the reckless prince.
VHS: S24000. $24.95.
Donald Crisp, USA, 1926, 72 mins.

CHARLES CHAPLIN

Burlesque of Carmen
Chaplin's parody of Cecil B. De Mille's 1915 high budget version of *Carmen*, with Edna Purviance and Ben Turpin.
VHS: S00191. $29.95.
Charles Chaplin, USA, 1916, 30 mins.

Chaplin
Starring Robert Downey Jr., this biography traces Charlie Chaplin's career, including his vaudeville beginnings, his complicated relationship with his mentally unbalanced mother (Geraldine Chaplin, playing her grandmother), his discovery by Mack Sennett (Dan Aykroyd), the birth of the one- and two-reel comedies, and his emergence as the popular artist. Cinematography by Sven Nykvist. Screenplay by novelist William Boyd, filmmaker Bryan Forbes and screenwriter William Goldman. With Milla Jovovich, Moira Kelly, Kevin Kline (as Douglas Fairbanks Jr.), Diane Lane (as Paula Goddard), Marisa Tomei (as Mabel Normand), Nancy Travis and James Woods.
VHS: S19052. $19.98.
Laser: Widescreen. **LD75308. $39.98.**
Richard Attenborough, USA, 1992, 142 mins.

Chaplin Revue
Three great Chaplin shorts: *A Dog's Life* is regarded by many as Chaplin's first masterpiece, in which the Little Tramp rescues a mutt from a dogfight; *Shoulder Arms* is a comedy about men at the front lines during World War I; and *The Pilgrim* centers on an ex-convict posing as a preacher.
VHS: S00227. $19.98.
Charles Chaplin, USA, 1918, 123 mins.

Charlie Chaplin
The film biography of the genius Chaplin features appearances by Stan Laurel and Oliver Hardy, Fatty Arbuckle and Ben Turpin. USA, 105 mins.
VHS: S02098. $29.95.

Charlie Chaplin Early Years I
Chaplin's early work, including *The Immigrant, The Count* and *Easy Street*, in a tape transferred from original nitrate prints.
VHS: S00383. $19.98.
Laser: CLV. **LD71973. $29.98.**
Charles Chaplin, USA, 1917, 62 mins.

Charlie Chaplin Early Years II
Three Chaplin classics: *The Pawnshop*, in which Charlie—janitor and clerk—causes pandemonium; *The Adventurer*, in which Chaplin is an escaped convict; and *One A.M.*, in which inanimate objects take on a life of their own to disturb Charlie's rest.
VHS: S00384. $19.98.
Laser: CLV. **LD71974. $29.98.**
Charles Chaplin, USA, 1916-17, 61 mins.

Charlie Chaplin Early Years III
In *The Cure*, Charlie is an alcohol-tippling man-about-town; in *The Floorwalker*, he runs afoul of a store detective on the escalator; in *The Vagabond*, Chaplin is a wandering violinist who rescues a young girl kidnapped by the gypsies.
VHS: S00385. $19.98.
Charles Chaplin, USA, 1916-17, 64 mins.

Charlie Chaplin Early Years IV
Behind the Screen is Chaplin's amusing satire on Keystone slapstick stars; in *The Fireman*, Chaplin gets involved in an arson plot; and in the famous *The Rink*, Chaplin is a waiter who serves a live cat to a restaurant patron.
VHS: S00386. $19.98.
Charles Chaplin, USA, 1916, 63 mins.

Charlie Chaplin's Keystone Comedies
Six one-reel comedies from the first year Chaplin appeared in films. In *Making a Living*, his first film, he plays a seedy Englishman. In *The Tramp*, his second, The Tramp is born. *A Busy Day* finds Charlie in drag. *Mabel's Married Life* he shares with Mabel Normand. In *Laughing Gas* he is a porter working for Dr. Pain, a dentist. In *The New Janitor* he prevents a hold-up.
VHS: S05463. $29.95.
Charles Chaplin, USA, 1914, 67 mins.

Circus/Day of Pleasure
Chaplin joins a traveling circus and falls in love with a bareback rider in one of his great comedies; presented with the short *Day of Pleasure*.
VHS: S02636. $19.98.
Charles Chaplin, USA, 1928, 105 mins.

City Lights
One of Chaplin's most highly acclaimed films, a silent film in the era of talkies that demonstrated Chaplin's genius. The Little Tramp falls in love with a beautiful, blind flower girl and sets out to raise money for an operation to cure her.
VHS: S00245. $19.98.
Laser: LD72318. $69.98.
Charles Chaplin, USA, 1931, 86 mins.

Classic Chaplin
An authoritative collection of Chaplin's early work, with each volume containing program notes that provide biographical information on Chaplin's early career. Available in individual volumes, or as a six-pack at a special price.
Charlie Chaplin at Keystone Studios. A side-splitting collection of Chaplin's first films—comedy classics that feature Chaplin's first-ever on-screen appearance as the legendary Little Tramp. Includes *Making a Living, Caught in a Cabaret, Mabel's Busy Day, The Masquerader, The Rounders*. 56 mins.
VHS: S12980. $19.98.
Charlie Chaplin at Essanay Studios I. His first films at Essanay Studios show Chaplin developing his legendary style, especially in the classic short *The Tramp*. Also includes *His New Job, The Champion, A Woman*. 83 mins.
VHS: S12981. $19.98.
Charlie Chaplin at Essanay Studios II. In this second collection from Essanay Studios, Chaplin continues to develop The Little Tramp character, adding more subtlety and pathos to his work. Includes *By the Sea, The Bank, Shanghaied, A Night in the Show*. 63 mins.
VHS: S12982. $19.98.
Charlie Chaplin at Mutual Studios I. Four delightful films from Chaplin's early period with Mutual Studios, these shorts showcase some of his best-loved work: *The Count, The Vagabond, The Fireman, Behind the Screen*. 100 mins.
VHS: S12983. $19.98.
Charlie Chaplin at Mutual Studios II. The second volume from Mutual Studios includes four tour-de-force comedy classics, including Chaplin in a rare solo performance in *One A.M.*. Also in this volume are *The Pawnshop, The Floorwalker, The Rink*. 97 mins.
VHS: S12984. $19.98.
Charlie Chaplin at Mutual Studios III. In the last volume of films from Mutual Studios, Chaplin gives a brilliant comedic performance as an immigrant, an escaped convict, and a former tramp turned policeman. Includes *The Immigrant, The Cure, The Adventurer, Easy Street*. 101 mins.
VHS: S12985. $19.98.
Charlie Chaplin at Mutual Studios I-III on Laser Disc.
Laser: LD76747. $99.99.
Charles Chaplin, USA, 1914-1917

The Count and the Adventurer
Charlie Chaplin stars in two two-reel silent comedies. *The Count* (or *The Phoney Nobleman*) finds out-of-work Charlie impersonating Count Broko, who makes a big hit in high society. *The Adventurer* finds Charlie as an escaped convict. With Edna Purviance.
VHS: S05464. $24.95.
Charles Chaplin, USA, 1916-17, 57 mins.

A Countess from Hong Kong
Marlon Brando and Sophia Loren bring glamour to Charlie Chaplin's final film. Loren stars as Natascha, a Russian countess who has lost her fortune and decides to stow away in the stateroom of Ogden, a wealthy American (Brando). Though Ogden resists, he is ultimately dazzled by Natascha, and the antic slapstick situations created by Harvey (Chaplin) only serve to confuse Ogden more. Includes the original theatrical trailer.
VHS: S27351. $14.98.
Charles Chaplin, USA, 1966, 120 mins.

Emerging Chaplin
Narrated by Douglas Fairbanks Jr., a roller coaster ride featuring Chaplin as the Little Tramp, from his early films to his stint at Mack Sennett's studios to the classics—*Kid Auto Races, The Bank, The Tramp, The Floorwalker, The Rink, Easy Street*. 30 mins.
VHS: S09424. $19.95.
Charles Chaplin, USA, 30 mins.

Essanay #1
Charles Chaplin at the Essanay Studios: *His New Job, A Night Out, The Champion, In the Park, A Jitney Elopement*.
VHS: S04820. $29.95.
Charles Chaplin, USA, 101 mins.

Essanay #2
The Tramp, By the Sea, Work, A Woman, The Bank.
VHS: S04821. $29.95.
Charles Chaplin, USA, 102 mins.

Essanay #3
Shanghaied, A Night in the Show, Burlesque on Carmen, Police, Triple Trouble (also known as *The Bond*).
VHS: S04822. $29.95.
Charles Chaplin, USA, 118 mins.

The Eternal Tramp
Charlie Chaplin's rise from the impoverished son of London vaudeville performers to acclaim as a pioneer director, actor, writer and comedian. Narrated by Gloria Swanson, with some footage from his rarely screened early works. 55 mins.
VHS: S17763. $14.98.

The Gold Rush
Charlie Chaplin's immortal, icon-making film, which pits Chaplin as the Little Tramp against the elements of the Yukon, ruthless prospectors and the affections of a dance hall girl. This is the film that includes the classic scene of Chaplin eating his leather shoe and shows his wooden cabin precariously balanced on the edge of a cliff. Silent with music track.
VHS: S26489. $19.95.
Laser: CLV. **LD70099. $39.95.**
Charles Chaplin, USA, 1925, 82 mins.

The Great Dictator
Chaplin's first film with dialog displays his boundless talent for both comedy and drama. Features Chaplin in two roles, one of a little Jewish barber facing the constant threat of religious persecution, the second a devastating lampoon of Hitler, because of which Hitler banned it in Germany.
VHS: S00527. $19.98.
Laser: LD76745. $49.95.
Charles Chaplin, USA, 1940, 126 mins.

Keystones #1
Charlie Chaplin in early Keystone comedies: *Making a Living, Kid's Auto Race, Mabel's Strange Predicament, Between Showers, A Film Johnny, Tango Tangles, His Favorite Pastime, The Star Border, Mabel at the Wheel*.
VHS: S04823. $29.95.
Charles Chaplin, USA, c. 1910

Keystones #2
Twenty Minutes of Love, Caught in a Cabaret, Caught in the Rain, A Busy Day, The Fatal Mallet, The Knockout, Mabel's Busy Day, Mabel's Married Life.
VHS: S04824. $29.95.
Charles Chaplin, USA, 107 mins.

Keystones #3
Laughing Gas, The Property Man, Face on the Barroom Floor, Recreation, The Masquerader, His New Profession, The Rounders, The New Janitor, Those Love Fangs, Dough and Dynamite.
VHS: S04825. $29.95.
Charles Chaplin, USA, 120 mins.

The Kid/The Idle Class
The Kid was Chaplin's first feature film and features The Tramp taking in an abandoned baby who grows into an impish urchin played by Jackie Coogan. On the same program is *The Idle Class*, a rare short in which The Tramp wreaks havoc on a golf course.
VHS: S00672. $19.98.
Charles Chaplin, USA, 1921, 85 mins.

King in New York

A satire starring Chaplin as a European monarch who flees to New York hoping to win support for his idealistic plans—an end to nuclear weapons and the creation of a utopian country. Unfortunately, he is met with a deaf ear.

VHS: S00677. $19.98.
Charles Chaplin, USA, 1957, 104 mins.

Limelight

Chaplin blends dark comedy and tragedy in the story of an aging music hall comic who's convinced he can no longer move people to laughter. With Chaplin, Claire Bloom, and the great Buster Keaton.

VHS: S00757. $19.98.
Charles Chaplin, USA, 1951, 120 mins.

Modern Times

Charlie Chaplin's silent homage to the human spirit, in which Chaplin is the victim of industrial boom. He plays the factory worker gone looney by the assembly line who falls in love with a down-and-out young lady and tries through various and eccentric means to find a bit of financial peace. A great comedy, and a great film.

VHS: S00866. $19.98.
Charles Chaplin, USA, 1936, 89 mins.

Monsieur Verdoux

Henri Verdoux is the bank teller who marries and subsequently murders wealthy women in order to support his own wife and child. Chaplin's dark comedy was a commercial failure, yet is an ingenious blend of dark comedy and philosophy.

VHS: S00873. $19.98.
Charles Chaplin, USA, 1947, 122 mins.

Rare Chaplin

Three classic Chaplin shorts, taken from original 35mm prints, of Chaplin during his Essanay period. *The Bank* (1915) features Charlie as a cleaner at the bank, struggling with broom and bucket. *Shanghaied* (1915) features Charlie tricked into service on an old tub about to leave port, ignorant that the owners are preparing to dynamite the boat and collect the insurance. And *A Night in the Show* (1915) features Charlie as a dapper gentleman attending the theatre, who romances the pretty girl in the next seat and in the process manages to get into a fight with a trombone. Silent with musical accompaniment.

VHS: S10761. $29.95.
Charles Chaplin, USA, 1915, 90 mins.

The Tramp and a Woman

Charlie Chapin stars in two short, silent comedies. *The Tramp* features Charlie in his best-known character saving a farmer's daughter from ruffians. Pathos mixes with slapstick for the first time. *A Woman* finds Charlie in women's clothes to escape angry suitors. With Billy Armstrong, Charles Insley and Edna Purviance.

VHS: S05469. $24.95.
Charles Chaplin, USA, 1915, 57 mins.

Unknown Chaplin

One of the wonders of television was this British-TV-financed, truly remarkable series, directed by Kevin Brownlow, in which, for the first time, a filmmaker was allowed access to the Chaplin family's private film vaults. The result is stunning: a beautifully produced exploration of the work and life of the great comic genius, using exquisitely restored film footage mixed together with interviews, insightful commentary and the Chaplin family's home movies. Not to be missed. 55 minutes each.

Hidden Treasures. The lost gems of a glittering career revealed for the first time include home movies, early gags that found their way into *The Great Dictator* and *Limelight*, and the rescued opening sequence from *City Lights*, presented with its original music score.

VHS: S12565. $19.99.

My Happiest Years. In his earliest films, Chaplin left no stone unturned—or tripped over—in his search for comic excellence. Included is lost footage, unseen for nearly 70 years, from *The Cure* and *The Immigrant*.

VHS: S12563. $19.99.

The Great Director. Producing his greatest work on a simple back lot and two stages, rare footage reveals Chaplin at work on his biggest career gambles. Lost footage from *The Kid, The Gold Rush* and *City Lights*.

VHS: S12564. $19.99.

Unknown Chaplin, 3-Pack.

VHS: S12566. $39.99.
Kevin Brownlow

A Woman of Paris

A Woman of Paris is a moving story of love gone awry in the life of a pretty country girl who winds up in Paris as a kept woman. Also contains the short comedy, *Sunnyside*.

VHS: S01478. $19.98.
Charles Chaplin, USA, 1919, 111 mins.

Work and Police

Two silent shorts by Charlie Chaplin. The first has Charlie as a paper-hanger, the second as Convict 999 returning to a life of crime.

VHS: S05465. $29.95.
Charles Chaplin, USA, 1915 & 1916, 81 mins.

BUSTER KEATON

Art of Buster Keaton—Box 1

A boxed set of four Keaton features: *The Saphead, Three Ages, Our Hospitality/Sherlock Jr.* and accompanying short films. Newly mastered.

VHS: S23125. $79.95.
Laser: LD74801. $99.99.

Art of Buster Keaton—Box 2

A boxed set of four Keaton features: *Navigator, Seven Chances, Go West, Battling Butler* and collected short films. Newly mastered.

VHS: S23126. $109.95.
Laser: LD74802. $139.00.

Art of Buster Keaton—Box 3

A boxed set of three Buster Keaton features: *The General, College and Steamboat Bill Jr.*, and assorted shorts. Newly mastered.

VHS: S23127. $79.95.
Laser: LD74803. $99.99.

Battling Butler

A brilliant Keaton comedy about a timid aristocrat who tries to impress his beloved's father by claiming that he is the famous boxer "Battling" Butler. Things are going well until the real Battling Butler shows up and challenges Keaton to a fight. Newly mastered; also contains the Keaton shorts *Haunted House* and *Frozen North*. Silent with music track.

VHS: S05598. $29.95.
Buster Keaton, USA, 1926, 78 mins.

Blacksmith and Balloonatic

Two Buster Keaton rarities: in *The Blacksmith*, Keaton is the local blacksmith apprentice who works the anvil and forge to fry his eggs at lunch; in *The Balloonatic*, Keaton is trapped in a lighter-than-air balloon at an amusement park with expectedly hilarious results. Silent with musical score. USA, c. 1922, 76 mins.

VHS: S01742. $29.95.

Bluebeard Goes to the Moon

A rare and bizarre Keaton film, in which he plays a World War II soldier who is marooned in Italy, where a scientist recruits him for a rocket ship trip to the moon. The special effects are as laughable as the plot, but this is a rare example of Keaton at the end of his career. 65 mins.

VHS: S05799. $39.95.

Boom in the Moon

Not a sequel to the Elizabeth Taylor and Richard Burton film *Boom*, but a comedy starring Buster Keaton in an adventure of lunar lunacy. The classic deadpan comedian could get a laugh just by standing in front of a camera. Discover how he convulsed millions in this little-known comedy that is literally out of this world.

VHS: S06120. $39.95.
Jaime Salvador, USA, 1946, 83 mins.

Buster and Fatty

Fatty Arbuckle, Buster Keaton and Al St. John are featured in all five of these beautifully preserved and rare short films. Included are *Coney Island* (1917), *Butcher Boy* (1917), *Good Night Nurse* (1918), *Out West* (1918) and *Back Stage* (1919). These comic films all have orchestra accompaniment and come from good to excellent prints. USA, 1917-1919, 94 mins.

VHS: S26852. $19.95.

Buster Keaton

Henry Morgan tells you the story of The Great Stone Face from his early childhood to his maturity as one of Hollywood's greatest comics. Included from the Rohauer Collection is seldom-seen footage from such classics as *Fatty at Coney Island, Cops, The Balloonatic, Day Dreams* and *The General*.

VHS: S03961. $29.95.

Buster Keaton (1917-22)

Four of Keaton's early great short films: *The Blacksmith, Playhouse, The Balloonatic, Cops,* and *The Garage*.

VHS: S04792. $24.95.
Buster Keaton, USA, 1917-22

Buster Keaton Festival Volume 1

Buster stars in three silent shorts: *The Blacksmith, The Paleface* and *Cops*. All silent with a newly added musical score. USA, c. 1921, 55 mins.

VHS: S01641. $19.95.

Buster Keaton Festival Volume 2

Three rare silent shorts starring Keaton: *The Boat, Frozen North* and *Electric Horse*. All are silent with newly added musical score. USA, c. 1921, 55 mins.

VHS: S01642. $19.95.

Buster Keaton Festival Volume 3

Three classic shorts: *Day Dreams, The Balloonatic* and *The Garage* (with Fatty Arbuckle). Silent with new music score. USA, c. 1921, 55 mins.

VHS: S01643. $19.95.

The Buster Keaton Show

Two shows in one! A rare glimpse of Keaton's television appearances in the '50s reveals his dedication in the gym, and his savoir-faire when he ends up in the boxing ring. In another episode, Buster makes an unlikely hero when he catches some crooks with taffy. Includes the original Studebaker commercials.

VHS: S15698. $29.95.

The Buster Keaton Show: Fishing Story & The Collapsible Clerk

The original nitrate prints of these hilarious "talkie" shorts have been locked away since the 50's. Now they are available, featuring Keaton at his best. His dead-pan style makes him a classic comic and one of America's most beloved humorists.

VHS: S21879. $19.95.

Buster Keaton Talkies, Vol. 1

Three films which star Buster Keaton in the sound era: *One Run Elmer, The Chemist,* and *Love Nest on Wheels*.

VHS: S05794. $29.95.
Buster Keaton, USA

Buster Keaton Talkies, Vol. 2

Three more short films featuring Keaton in the sound age: *Grand Slam Opera, Tars and Stripes*, and *Three on a Limb*.

VHS: S05795. $29.95.
Buster Keaton, USA

Buster Keaton Talkies, Vol. 3

Keaton stars in *Blue Blazes, Mixed Magic*, and the one-reeler *Allez Oop*.

VHS: S05796. $29.95.
Buster Keaton, USA

Buster Keaton Talkies, Vol. 6

Keaton stars in *Ditto, Jailbait,* and *Palooka from Paducha*.

VHS: S05797. $29.95.
Buster Keaton, USA

Buster Keaton Talkies, Vol. 7

Two films starring Keaton: *Timid Young Man* and *Hayseed Romance*.

VHS: S05798. $29.95.
Buster Keaton, USA

Buster Keaton: A Hard Act to Follow

A brilliant three-volume biography of the great Keaton, prepared by film historians Kevin Brownlow and David Gill. Interviews with Keaton and reminiscences of friends and associates, rare footage and clips from many Keaton films in a unique portrait of this great genius of the silent cinema. Available either separately, or as a set.

From Vaudeville to Movies.

VHS: S10248. $19.99.

Star Without a Studio.

VHS: S10249. $19.99.

A Genius Recognized.

VHS: S10250. $19.99.

Buster Keaton, Complete Set.

VHS: S10247. $39.99.

Buster Keaton: The Metaphysics of His Films

A 1970 exploration of the great film director-actor with some unusual perspectives on his goals and motivations. Illustrated with many film excerpts from his most creative period, the end of the silent film era, 1917 to 1928. Film critic Andrew Sarris and film archivist Raymond Rohauer focus on deeper intentions in Keaton's work, relationship of things to people, man's place in nature and humor in helplessness. 28 mins.

VHS: S31566. $59.95.

The Cameraman
Buster Keaton at his greatest as a street photographer, enamored of a movie star, who decides to become a newsreel cameraman. Hilarious. Silent with music track.
VHS: S13398. $29.98.
Clyde Bruckman, USA, 1928, 78 mins.

The Cameraman/Spite Marriage
Two Keaton classics on one laserdisc! Gatefold jacket.
Laser: LD71476. $39.98.
Buster Keaton

College
An incredible demonstration of Keaton's formidable athletic skills in this famous comedy in which he plays the bookish college student who is forced to prove himself a jock in order to get the girl. Famous sequences include Keaton in a decathlon knocking down every single hurdle with precision, being thrown by a hammer rather than throwing it, and finally catapulting himself through a window to save the heroine from her jock admirer. Includes the shorts *The Blacksmith, Electric House* and *Hard Luck*. Silent with music track.
VHS: S23034. $29.95.
James W. Horne, USA, 1927, 67 mins.

Doughboys
Buster Keaton re-teams with his collaborator from *The Cameraman*, Edward Sedgwick, in this military comedy about the reluctant army recruit who becomes a certified war hero and local treasure. With Sally Eilers, Cliff Edwards, and Edward Brophy.
VHS: S17893. $19.98.
Edward Sedgwick, USA, 1930, 79 mins.

Free and Easy
Buster Keaton's first sound movie shows Buster's phenomenal rise from a mechanic to iconic movie star. With cameos from Cecil B. De Mille, Lionel Barrymore, Jackie Coogan and Arthur Lange.
VHS: S17894. $19.98.
Edward Sedgwick, USA, 1930, 92 mins.

The General
Considered by many to be the last great comedy of the silent era, and consistently ranked as a masterpiece. Based on a true incident in the Civil War, the "General" is the railroad engine "engineered" by Confederate Army reject Keaton, who is also humiliated by his girlfriend (Marion Mack), who thinks him a coward. When a small company of Union soldiers penetrates behind Confederate lines, Keaton sets off in hot pursuit in one of the truly great chase scenes ever. The scenes were shot on the narrow gauge lines of Oregon and Keaton used less than 50 titles to explain the whole story. Also contains the shorts *The Playhouse* and *Cops* Newly mastered. Silent with music track.
VHS: S23033. $29.95.
Buster Keaton/Clyde Bruckman, USA, 1927, 76 mins.

Go West
Keaton leaves the Midwest for Arizona on his way to becoming a cowboy named Friendless. He removes a pebble from the foot of an injured cow, Brown Eyes, and they become inseparable. When Brown Eyes is shipped to Los Angeles, Friendless accompanies her with comic results: Keaton and Brown Eyes exploring department stores and beauty parlors. But this is "the most atypical and at the same time one of the most endearing of his [Keaton's] films. With acrobatics and gag comedy at a minimum, he experimented uncharacteristically with a quality of pathos in his depiction of Friendless and his comradeship with a gentle, sweet cow" (David Thomson). Includes the short films *The Scarecrow* and *The Paleface*. Newly mastered. Silent with music track.
VHS: S23032. $29.95.
Buster Keaton, USA, 1925, 72 mins.

Great Stone Face—Buster Keaton—Volume 1
Film clips of Keaton's career, three of his early comedies, *The Paleface, Day Dreams* and *The Blacksmith*, as well as, from the early days of television, a show titled *The Silent Partner*, with Keaton, Joe E. Brown and ZaSu Pitts.
VHS: S10606. $29.95.

Great Stone Face—Buster Keaton—Volume 2
One of Keaton's best comedies, *Cops*, plus his television show *Buster Keaton Detective*. In this episode, Keaton performs a classic spoof of Sam Spade in *The Maltese Falcon*.
VHS: S10603. $29.95.

Kovacs & Keaton
Two rare television appearances by master comedians—Kovacs is silent in *Eugene* (1960) as he mimes his way through life, while Keaton is *Wrestling with Trouble* as he and his buddy get tangled with two real-life wrestlers (1953). USA, 60 mins.
VHS: S01651. $24.95.

The Lovable Cheat
Based on a Balzac play, this independent film features the comic antics of Charlie Ruggles battling against his many creditors. With Fritz Feld and Buster Keaton.
VHS: S14676. $29.95.
Richard Oswald, USA, 1949, 75 mins.

The Misadventures of Buster Keaton
The wacky owner of a sporting goods store moonlights as the director/producer of a small theater. The hilarious Buster Keaton, with his brilliant flair for slapstick, shines in this comedy classic. USA, 65 mins.
VHS: S15032. $19.95.

The Navigator
One of the funniest of Keaton's comedies, in which he runs a deserted ocean liner single-handed. The original script was to have a penniless man and woman marooned on a dead ship in the middle of the Atlantic. But the question arose as to how two penniless people could afford to be on the ship in the first place, and so the screenwriter, Jean Havez, suggested, "I want a rich boy and a rich girl who never had to lift a finger. I put these two beautiful spoiled brats—the two most helpless people in the world—adrift on a ship, all alone. A dead ship. No lights, no steam." Also contains the shorts *The Boat* and *Love Nest*. Newly mastered. Silent with music track.
VHS: S08845. $29.95.
Donald Crisp, USA, 1924, 60 mins.

Old Spanish Custom
Rare sound film by Keaton in which he plays Leander Proudfoot, a sap who is the patsy in a torrid love triangle. Lupita Tovar is also featured.
VHS: S01644. $24.95.
Adrian Brunel, USA, 1936, 58 mins.

Our Hospitality/Sherlock Jr.
Keaton's hilarious satire on the Hatfield-McCoy family feud was his second feature. Brilliantly set against the backdrop of early rail travel in 1831, the film features Keaton as the scion of an old Southern family, who carelessly starts dating from a feuding family. In *Sherlock Jr.* Keaton plays a projectionist who is framed for theft by a jealous rival for the hand of a beautiful girl. Contains an astonishing sequence in which Keaton imagines himself to be a detective, and makes his way into the action of the movie he is projecting on screen. This sequence made Keaton an early favorite of the surrealists. Newly mastered. Silent with music track.
VHS: S23030. $29.95.
Buster Keaton, USA, 1923/1924

Parlor, Bedroom and Bath
A rare Keaton film of the sound era in which he proves he was as brilliant as ever; Keaton is a sign-tacker hit by a car outside a mansion, brought in to recover—a very complicated screwball comedy ensues. A rare glimpse of one of comedy's extraordinary talents.
VHS: S00994. $24.95.
Edward Sedgwick, USA, 1931, 73 mins.

The Saphead
Keaton plays the pampered son of "The Wolf of Wall Street," who shocks everyone by making a fortune on the stock market, thus winning the girl of his dreams. Keaton's first feature as a star is based on a play, *The New Henrietta*, and clearly foreshadows the comic mayhem in which Keaton's athletic prowess and impeccable timing would create timeless comedy—as he does here, when he creates total upheaval on the stock market trading floor. Includes the shorts *High Sign* and *One Week*. Silent with music track.
VHS: S23029. $29.95.
Herbert Blache, USA, 1920, 70 mins.

Seven Chances
On his 27th birthday lawyer Buster Keaton is told that he will inherit $7 million if he gets married by 7 p.m. that evening. But his own sweetheart rejects him when she discovers the true nature of his affection and he is driven to desperation, proposing to anyone in skirts, including a Scotsman. An ad in the paper saves the day and 500 prospective brides show up at the church. A very funny collection of gags culminating in a hilarious chase scene with the bachelor lawyer being pursued by 500 brides straight into a rock slide. Also includes two shorts: *Neighbors* and *The Balloonatic*. Newly mastered. Silent with music track.
VHS: S23031. $29.95.
Edward Sedgwick, USA, 1929, 77 mins.

Sidewalks of New York
A Buster Keaton talkie casts the virtuoso comedian as a lonely New York millionaire who falls for a poor street girl (Anita Page), and tries to prove his worth by reforming her younger brother and transforming their socially neglected neighborhood. With Cliff Edwards, Frank Rowan and Norman Phillips, Jr.
VHS: S19566. $19.98.
Jules White, USA, 1931, 70 mins.

Speak Easily
After his career as a director was destroyed, Buster Keaton played in a series of sound comedies. This is one of his later period works, about a wealthy college instructor who reluctantly bankrolls a third-rate theatrical troupe. With Jimmy Durante, Thelma Todd and Sidney Toler.
VHS: S17899. $19.98.
Edward Sedgwick, USA, 1932, 82 mins.

Spite Marriage
The great Stone Face himself, Buster Keaton, in his final silent film. This backstage comedy is about a tailor's assistant in love with a young actress (Dorothy Sebastian), who marries him to spite someone else. Here Keaton displays his comic genius in some truly inspired slapstick routines. Silent film with synchronized musical score.
VHS: S13974. $29.99.
Edward Sedgwick, USA, 1929, 82 mins.

Steamboat Bill Jr.
Buster Keaton's great comedy, his "most entertaining balance of the instinctual and the cerebral in a tale of father worship, young love, abject humiliation and heroic redemption" (J. Hoberman, *The Village Voice*). Set in the deep South, Buster plays the city-bred boy who returns to his steamboat captain father and reluctantly joins him in fighting off a rival trying to take over the river. The cyclone finale is as famous as it is hilarious. Newly mastered; also contains two Keaton shorts: *Convict 13* and *Day Dreams*. Silent with music track.
VHS: S23035. $29.95.
Charles F. Reisner, USA, 1928, 71 mins.

The Railrodder/Buster Keaton Rides Again
Made by the Canadian Film Board when Buster Keaton was 69, *The Railrodder*, Keaton's 87th film, is a jaunty and atmospheric journey across the Canadian landscape in a railway handcar. Showcasing Keaton's impeccable timing and vigorous physical comedy, *The Railrodder* is one of the only dialog-free films of the time (Gerald Potterton, Canada, 1965, 25 mins.). In *Buster Keaton Rides Again*, a freewheeling look at the making of *The Railrodder*, director John Spotten gives us a fresh look behind-the-scenes with Buster Keaton. Features candid footage of Keaton's everyday life, conversations with his wife, Eleanor, and his official designation by the townspeople of Manitoba as "Manitoba Voyageur." Also provides fascinating historical glimpses into Keaton's early life, highlights from his classic films, and archival photos from his vaudeville days (John Spotten, Canada, 1965, 56 mins.).
VHS: S30243. $29.95.

Three Ages
Keaton's first feature as a director is a spoof of Griffith's *Intolerance*. Keaton and Wallace Beery parody film cliches. In the Stone Age, Keaton arrives on a date on a dinosaur; in ancient Rome Buster is forced into a chariot race in a blizzard. Keaton pokes fun at the incongruity of cinematic history. Newly mastered. Contains the shorts *The Goat* and *My Wife's Relations*. Silent with music track.
VHS: S01335. $29.95.
Buster Keaton/Eddie Cline, USA, 1923

The Villain Still Pursued Her
Buster Keaton is part of the cast in this spoof of melodramas, complete with mustache twisting villain and an innocent harp-playing heroine. Title cards encourage audience participation. Keaton plays the hero's best friend. With Alan Mowbray, Anita Louise, Hugh Herbert and Margaret Hamilton.
VHS: S05459. $29.95.
Eddie Cline, USA, 1940, 68 mins.

What! No Beer?
In his final lead role in an American production, Buster Keaton is teamed with Jimmy Durante as hopeless Prohibition bootleggers drawn into a zany and crazed plot to make a fortune. With Roscoe Ates, Phyllis Barry and John Milijan.
VHS: S17901. $19.98.
Edward Sedgwick, USA, 1933, 66 mins.

HAROLD LLOYD

Films of Harold Lloyd—Volume 1
A collection of early Harold Lloyd shorts including *The Cinema Director* (1916), *Non-Stop Kid* (1918), *Why Pick on Me* (1918), *On the Fire* (1919); *Ring up the Curtain* (1919), *Just Neighbors* (1919) and *Haunted Spooks* (1920). 120 mins.
VHS: S02353. $29.95.

Films of Harold Lloyd—Volume 2
A selection of early work by Harold Lloyd; also featured are Bebe Daniels and Snub Pollard. Includes *All Aboard, Two Gun Gussie, The City Slicker, Why Pick on Me, Ask Father*, and *I'm on My Way*. 75 mins.
VHS: S13208. $24.95.

Films of Harold Lloyd—Volume 3

Films from the years 1919-1921: *Snob Fever, Don't Shove, Pay Your Dues* and *His Royal Slyness*, as well as a film by Harold's brother Gaylord Lloyd, *Dodge Your Debts*. With Bebe Daniels, Snub Pollard and Mildred Harris. 70 mins.
VHS: S13209. $24.95.

Films of Harold Lloyd—Volume 5

Three extremely rare Harold Lloyd shorts subjects on one video. *The Hairdresser* (1918), with Bebe Daniels and Snub Pollard; *From Hand to Mouth* (1921), with Mildred Harris; and *The Brat*, a rare three-reeler from a Spanish print. 62 mins.
VHS: S32708. $19.95.

Harold Lloyd Comedies Vol. 1

The famous comedian in *All Aboard, The Non-Stop Kid, Ring up the Curtain*, and *Haunted Spooks*. 60 mins.
VHS: S08016. $29.95.

Harold Lloyd Comedies Vol. 2

Harold Lloyd in *I'm on My Way, High and Dizzy, Bashful* and *Never Waken*. 60 mins.
VHS: S08017. $29.95.

Harold Lloyd Comedies Vol. 3

Includes *Spring Fever, Two Gun Gussie, Eastern Westerner*, and *His Royal Slyness*. 60 mins.
VHS: S08018. $29.95.

Harold Lloyd's Comedy Classics

Four greats from a master of the silent era. Lloyd is *The Chef* complete with Rube Goldberg contraptions; *Cinema Director* is influenced by Chaplin; *Two Gun Gussie* has mild mannered Lloyd mistaken as an outlaw; and *I'm on My Way* is a hilarious view of marriage! USA, 1919, 51 mins.
VHS: S00544. $24.95.

Harold Lloyd: Girl Shy

Harold Lloyd plays a small-town man who overcomes his fright of women by writing a controversial book about lovemaking. The film interweaves stylized physical humor with some hypnotic fantasy sequences of Lloyd's sexual experiences. With Jobyna Ralston, Richard Daniels and Carlton Griffin. Silent with musical score.
VHS: S19905. $24.95.
Fred Newmeyer/Sam Taylor, USA, 1924, 65 mins.

His Royal Slyness and Haunted Spooks

Harold Lloyd stars in a pair of two-reel silent comedies. The first is a send-up of *The Prisoner of Zenda* with Harold offered the throne of Thermosa. In *Haunted Spooks* the bespectacled nice guy helps a southern heiress acquire her inheritance by marrying her and spending the night in a haunted mansion.
VHS: S01743. $29.95.
Hal Roach/Alfred Goulding, USA, 1920, 72 mins.

A Sailor-Made Man

In his first feature, Harold Lloyd joins the navy so he can prove his worth to his girlfriend's father so he can marry her. He ends up rescuing her from the clutches of an evil maharajah in the Far East. With Noah Young and Dick Sutherland. Silent.
VHS: S33724. $24.95.
Fred C. Newmeyer, USA, 1921, 45 mins.

Sin of Harold Diddlebock

Harold Lloyd is the former football star who has spent 20 years in the bookkeeping department of an ad agency. Having lived a boring life, he goes to the other extreme, and goes on a wild binge of drinking and gambling—a riotous comedy from Sturges.
VHS: S01206. $19.95.
Preston Sturges, USA, 1946, 90 mins.

SILENT COMEDY

Airplane Comedies

A compilation of early silent comedies all including airplanes of a bygone era, notable for some of the incredible stunts. Includes *Air Pockets* with some rooftop to rooftop escapades, and Larry Semon, Laurel and Hardy, Little Rascals, Ben Turpin, Billy Bevan and Mack Sennett. Silent and sound.
VHS: S08012. $29.95.

All Night Long and Smile Please

Two comic gems produced by Mack Sennett and starring the extraordinary Harry Langdon: *All Night Long*, in which Langdon encounters a burly man leading a gang in a robbery, and *Smile Please*, in which Harry is a small-town photographer and sheriff. A tour-de-force of Sennett stunts and comic bits. USA, 1924, 66 mins.
VHS: S01741. $29.95.

Arbuckle Volume 3

Early Fatty Arbuckle comedies including *Fatty's New Role; Fatty and Mabel at San Diego; Fatty and Mabel's Simple Life; Fatty and Mabel's Smash Day; Mabel Lost; Mabel, Mabel; Fatty and the Law; and Fatty's Plucky Pup*. 120 mins.
VHS: S08604. $49.95.

Babe Hardy: Early Training

A young Oliver Hardy is seen in this collection of early silent comedies, which includes *Hungry Hearts* (1915), *One Too Many* (1915), Billy West's *Fiddlin' Around, The Best and The Villain*, a parody of *Tillie's Punctured Romance* in which Hardy is cast as a female character. 60 mins.
VHS: S33122. $24.95.

Baby Face Harry Langdon

Two short films which combine the talents of Harry Langdon with writer-gagman Frank Capra: *Sunday Afternoon*, which poses the question whether in 1864, when Lincoln declared all men free, did he or did he not include husbands; and *Lucky Stars*, in which Langdon is a trusting soul out to become a great physician and taken for a ride by a quack surgeon. 60 mins. total. Silent with music score.
VHS: S06928. $29.95.

Battling Fool

In this light-hearted look at the world of boxing, William Fairbanks enters the ring to restore his loved one's ability to walk. Golden-faced beauty Eve Novak stars as the broken flower. Silent with an added music track.
VHS: S16108. $29.95.
W.S. Van Dyke, USA, 1924, 56 mins.

Ben Turpin #1

A collection of short comedies starring Ben Turpin, including *A Clever Dummy, Cross-Eyed Love, Blondes Revenge, Jolly Jilter, Total Loss and Keystone Hotel*. USA, 95 mins.
VHS: S04794. $24.95.

Cannonball/Dizzy Heights

Two farces produced by Mack Sennett featuring the walrus-moustached Chester Conklin. In *Cannonball*, Conklin is an inspector at an explosives factory. *Dizzy Heights* features incredible aerial stunts. USA, 1915, 71 mins.
VHS: S02225. $29.95.

Charley Chase and Ben Turpin

Two silent comedies starring Charley Chase produced by Hal Roach: *All Wet* (1924) and *Publicity Pays* (1924), and a Ben Turpin comedy produced by Mack Sennett: *A Clever Dummy* (1917) with Chester Conklin and Wallace Beery. USA, 67 mins.
VHS: S02228. $29.95.

Charley Chase Jimmy Jump Series

Includes *All Wet, Powder and Smoke, Fighting Fluid, Fraidy Cat, Big Red Riding Hood, Rats Knuckles, Young Oldfield, Poor Fish, Ten Minute Egg* and *One of the Family* Silent with music track, 120 mins.
VHS: S07188. $24.95.

Charley Chase Vol. 1

Features *Stolen Goods, Publicity Pays, All Dolled Up, His Wooden Wedding, There Ain't No Santa Claus, Forgotten Sweeties*. Silent with music track, 120 mins.
VHS: S07189. $24.95.

Charley Chase Vol. 2

Features *Dog Shy, Mum's The Word, Looking for Sally, Crazy Like a Fox, Bromo and Juliet*. Silent with music track, 110 mins.
VHS: S07190. $24.95.

Comedy Classics of Mack Sennett and Hal Roach

Three silent gems: *Looking for Trouble, A Desperate Scoundrel* and *Love, Loot and Crash*. 74 minutes.
VHS: S02223. $29.95.

Comedy of Chester Conklin

Conklin had a successful career in silent comedy as both a Keystone Cop and a fellow performer in numerous early Charlie Chaplin films. These three shorts, *A One Night Stand* (1915), *Dizzy Heights and Daring Hearts* (1916) and *Lame Brains* (1920), capture his unique visual humor. In the first of these shorts he appears with Mae Bush, while in the second he is a Keystone Cop. 60 mins.
VHS: S29457. $19.95.

Comedy Shorts #4

Wine, Women and Sauerkraut—20 Legs Under the Sea, Caretaker's Daughter (Charley Chase), *Busy Buddies* (Neal Burns), *Kiddin Kate* (Dorothy Devore), *Eve's Love Letters* (Stan Laurel). Silent with music track, 110 mins.
VHS: S07194. $24.95.

Directed by Stan Laurel

Stan Laurel narrates the opening segment of this compilation describing how he switched from a silent film comedian to writer and director for the Hal Roach comedy studios. Photos and film clips detail the working atmosphere at the studio in the roaring '20s era. Mabel Norman and Anita Garvin star in *Raggety Rose* with James Finlayson. Ted Healy minus the Stooges stars in *Wise Guys Prefer Brunettes*. Oliver Hardy is directed by his future partner in Yes, Yes, Nanette. James Finlayson is a chronic woman chaser in *Chasing the Chaser*. Clyde Cook and Oliver Hardy appear in *Wandering Papas*. 120 mins.
VHS: S33126. $24.95.

Early Comedies Volume 1

Dash Through the Clouds (1912, Mabel Normand); *Barney Oldfield's Race for Life* (1913, Sennett); *Settled at the Seaside* (1914, Charlie Chase); *A Mud Bath* (1914, Mabel Normand); *Hogan Out West* (1915); *A Desperate Scoundrel* (1915, Ford Sterling); *Love, Loot and Crash* (1915, Chester Conklin); *Teddy at the Throttle* (1916, Gloria Swanson). Music track. 110 mins.
VHS: S07196. $24.95.

Early Comedies Volume 2

Midnight at the Old Mill (Ham and Bud), *Ring Up the Curtain* (Harold Lloyd), *At the Ringside* (Snub Pollard), *White Wings* (Stan Laurel), *Don't Shove—All Aboard* (Harold Lloyd), *Noon Whistle—Oranges and Lemons* (Stan Laurel). Silent with music track. 90 mins.
VHS: S07197. $24.95.

Eyes of Ben Turpin Are upon You!

Two of the best performances by the incomparable one-eyed clown, Ben Turpin. *Idle Eyes* (1918) has Ben working in a beauty parlor, making a hilarious mess out of cold-cream treatments and egg shampoos. In *Small Town Idol*, produced by Mack Sennett, Turpin is a small-town guy whose worship of movie actresses gets him into a lot of trouble. This is a condensation of the Mack Sennett feature. Silent with musical score. USA, 1918-21.
VHS: S02993. $24.95.

Fatty Arbuckle

A collection of short films starring Fatty Arbuckle including *Mabel and Fatty's Wash Day, Fatty and Mabel at the San Diego Exposition, Fatty and Mable's Simple Life, Fatty's New Role, Fatty's Faithful Fido, Miss Fatty's Seaside Lovers, Tintype Tangle*. All made in the year 1915. 118 mins.
VHS: S07200. $29.95.

Films of Harry Langdon Volume 1

Includes *Saturday Afternoon* and *Soldier Man*. Approximately 57 mins.
VHS: S10035. $24.95.

Films of Harry Langdon Volume 2

Includes *Boobs in the Woods, Feet of Mud* and *Lucky Stars*. Approximately 58 mins.
VHS: S07278. $24.95.

Films of Oliver Hardy

Oliver Hardy alone in a collection of comedies, including *Battle Royal, Stationmaster, Enough to Do, Paperhanger's Helper, Kid Speed, Hard Boiled Eggs* and *Along Came Auntie*. Various, USA, 1916-27, 110 mins.
VHS: S04790. $24.95.

Films of Stan Laurel Volume 1

Stan Laurel alone in a collection of short comedies, including *Greater Than Sherlock Holmes, Pick and Shovel, On the Job, Mixed Nuts, Roughest Africa, Half a Man, On the Front Page*, and *Should Tall Men Marry?* Various, USA, 1922-27, 110 mins.
VHS: S04791. $24.95.

Films of Stan Laurel Volume 2

Contains *Kill or Cure* (1915), *Oranges and Lemons* (1912), *Man About Town* (1923). 42 mins.
VHS: S11463. $19.95.

Films of Stan Laurel Volume 3

Contains *Roughest Africa* (1930), *House Boat* (1918), *The Soldiers* (1923). 54 mins.
VHS: S11464. $19.95.

Films of Stan Laurel Volume 4

Contains *Smithy* (1924), *Near Dublin* (1924), *Mixed Nuts* (1924). 50 mins.
VHS: S11465. $19.95.

Flying Elephants

Stan Laurel and Oliver Hardy go back to the Stone Age in this Hal Roach comedy. The head caveman decrees that everyone must marry or else. Hardy falls for the most beautiful girl around, and so does a surprisingly effeminate Stan. Before long, the two resort to the crudest and funniest he-man tactics to impress her and attack each other. Roach apparently directed this film but the credit was given to Butler.
VHS: S26811. $9.95.
Frank Butler, USA, 1928, 20 mins.

Forgotten Comedians
A collection of short films by some of silent comedy's very talented, and funny, but now unjustly neglected comedians. Eddie Quillan stars in *The Channel Swimmer,* Walter Heirs in *Wireless Lizzies,* Jack Richardson, Al Alt, and Dixie Lamont in *Show Business,* Mr. and Mrs. Carter De Haven in *Private, Keep Off,* Lionel Barrymore in *Wife Tamers,* and Monte Banks in *Be Reasonable.* Various, USA.
VHS: S04793. $24.95.

Hardy and Ray
In 1925 Oliver Hardy appeared in a series of silent comedies teamed with a small, slight comic named Bobby Ray. These films, filled with slapstick and sight-gags, are traditional, pre-Laurel and Hardy comedy team material. Includes *Hop to It, Stick Around, The Paperhanger's Helper* and *They All Fall.* 60 mins.
VHS: S33120. $24.95.

Heavy Hardy
As Hollywood's most sought-after comic, "heavy"—or villain-Oliver "Babe" Hardy worked nearly everywhere. He's seen here in three early silent comedies: *Her Boyfriend, The Bellhop* and *The Bakery.* 80 mins.
VHS: S33119. $24.95.

His Picture in the Papers
Douglas Fairbanks stars in this comedy about a non-conformist son of a health food tycoon.
VHS: S03653. $24.95.
John Emerson, USA, 1916, 68 mins.

Hollywood Spoofs
Featured are *Uncensored Movies* with Will Rogers, *When Quackle Did Hyde* with Charlie Jau, *Mud and Sand* with Stan Laurel, *Howling Hollywood* with Verna Dent, *Big Moments from Big Pictures* with Will Rogers. Silent with music track, 120 mins.
VHS: S07187. $24.95.

Langdon at Sennett
Veteran vaudeville comic Harry Langdon got his start in movies with Mack Sennett. Frank Capra and Harry Edwards wrote and directed Harry through these memorable early comedies, including *Remember When, Boobs in the Woods* and *Saturday Afternoon.* 55 mins.
VHS: S08602. $29.95.

Larry Semon #1
A collection of short comedies starring Larry Semon: *The Show, The Bellhop, The Sawmill, The Stuntman,* and *The Clodhopper.* Various, USA, 120 mins.
VHS: S04796. $24.95.

Larry Semon #2
A second volume of short comedies starring Larry Semon: *Risk and Roughnecks, Her Boyfriend, Dome Doctor, Sleuth, Well, I'll Be the Sportsman* and *The Clodhopper.* Various, USA, 118 mins.
VHS: S04797. $24.95.

Larry Semon #3
Includes the following shorts starring Larry Semon: *Frauds and Frenzies* (1918), *The Grocery Clerk* (1920), *The Bakery* (1921), *The Sportsman* (1925), and *A Simple Sap* (1928). 118 mins.
VHS: S08867. $24.95.

Laurel and Hardy Solo Flights
This compilation features silent solo efforts by both Stan Laurel and Oliver Hardy. Stan stars in *No Place Like Jail,* a 1918 blueprint for the Laurel and Hardy comedy 10 years later titled *The Second One Hundred Years,* and *Short Kilts.* Oliver Hardy is showcased in some early comedies, including *Something in Her Eye* and *Servant Girl's Legacy.* 60 mins.
VHS: S33123. $24.95.

Laurel and Hardy's Magic Lantern Show
This collection of Laurel and Hardy miscellany features a rare 1950 interview with Oliver Hardy, along with their only color short film, *Tree in a Test Tube.* Also included is an old-time lantern show of hand-tinted glass movie slides featuring coming attractions of silent Laurel and Hardy comedies, rarely seen live-action movie trailers from the talking era, and newsreel footage of their tours. 60 mins.
VHS: S33125. $24.95.

Laurel and Hardy: The Legend Begins
Stan Laurel narrates a montage of clips and rare photos telling how he and Hardy were teamed. The most complete version of the silent *Lucky Dog* (1917) available is highlighted, along with other clips from the career of Laurel and Hardy. 60 mins.
VHS: S33124. $24.95.

Leap Year
The only feature film of Roscoe "Fatty" Arbuckle to survive both time and scandal. This pleasant comedy was not available in the U.S. until the 1960's. It played Europe in 1921. A rare look at a master of slapstick in action. Give the big guy a chance.
VHS: S04802. $24.95.
James Cruze, USA, 1921, 60 mins.

Lloyd and Chase at Keystone
Harold Lloyd is prominently featured in two films, *Miss Fatty's Seaside Lovers* and *Courthouse Crooks.* Charley Chase stars in *Love, Loot and Crash* and Lloyd is featured in *Luke's Movie Muddle.* 60 mins. Silent with music track.
VHS: S08014. $29.95.

Mabel Normand Comedies, Vol. 1
Mabel Normand is teamed with Fatty Arbuckle in *Fatty and Mabel Adrift,* with Chaplin and Marie Dressler in *Tillie's Punctured Romance,* and in *The Nicklehopper.* Various, USA, 118 mins.
VHS: S04795. $24.95.

Mabel Normand Comedies, Vol. 2
Includes the following Mabel Normand shorts: *Troublesome Secretary* (1911), *Cohen Saves the Flag* (1913), *Barney Oldfield's Race for Life* (1913), *Mabel's New Hero* (1913), *A Muddy Romance* (1913). 55 mins.
VHS: S11461. $19.95.

Mabel Normand, Vol. 1
This collection, featuring the great comedienne from the silent era, shows the true extent of her talent. She was a worthy equal to the greats of that special time. Includes *The Water Nymph* (1912), *A Strong Revenge* (1913), *The Jazz Band* (1913), *Fatty and Mabel at San Francisco* (1915) and *Anything Goes* (1927). 64 mins.
VHS: S21082. $24.95.

Mack Sennett: The Biograph Years
The evolution of film comedy took a major step forward when part-time actor-director Mack Sennett started directing films at the Biograph Studio. This selection of six comedies shows how Sennett employed Griffith's "Biograph editing" technique and accelerated it for comic effect. Includes: *Happy Jack: A Hero, Turning the Tables, A Villain Foiled, The Baron, Dash Through the Clouds,* and *The Manicure Lady.* 60 mins.
VHS: S08603. $29.95.

Peck's Bad Boy
An early Jackie Coogan vehicle in which Jackie is always getting into trouble. With Wheeler, Oakman, Doris May.
VHS: S04789. $24.95.
Laser: LD70406. $29.95.
Sam Wood, USA, 1921, 60 mins.

Perfect Clown
Larry Semon, a forgotten comedy star of the 1920's, is in love with a stenographer named Rosie, and is entrusted with $10,000 in cash by his boss. When he arrives to make the deposit at the bank, it's closed, and he panics and ends up on a zany odyssey through the streets of his city. Oliver Hardy appears in a minor role. Silent with music score.
VHS: S06980. $29.95.
Fred Newmeyer, USA, 1925, 72 mins.

Sawmill and Dome Doctor
Two comedy shorts by Larry Semon, one of the most popular and highest paid comedians of the early 1920's. His screen character had a huge nose, saucer ears, white face with stupid grin and slicked down hair.
VHS: S02230. $29.95.
Larry Semon, USA, 1922, 71 mins.

Seven Years Bad Luck
A film filled with many classic comedy routines by French comedian Max Linder, called "my teacher" by Charles Chaplin. A broken mirror brings about the seven years of bad luck—all at the same time! Linder exhibits expert timing and physical grace.
VHS: S01184. $29.95.
Max Linder, USA, 1920, 85 mins.

Slapstick Encyclopedia
From the golden age of film, 1909-1927. Comedies that created a new visual vocabulary.

Slapstick Encyclopedia—Vol. 1: In the Beginning… Film Comedy Pioneers. Includes *One Two Many* (1916) with Oliver Hardy; *The Wrong Mr. Fox* (1917) with Victor Moore; *Mr. Flip* (1909) with Ben Turpin; *Mabel's Dramatic Career* (1913) with Mabel Normand and Mack Sennett; *Fox-Trot Finesse* (1915) with Mr. & Mrs. Sidney Drew; *A Cure for Pokeritis* (1912) with John Bunny and Flora Finch; *Alkali Ike's Auto* (1911) with Augustus Carney; *A Natural Born Gambler* (1916) with Bert Williams; and *Be My Wife* (1921) with Max Linder. 1909-1921, 126 mins.
VHS: S33977. $24.95.

Slapstick Encyclopedia—Vol. 2: Keystone Tonight! The Mack Sennett Comedies. Includes *Saturday Afternoon* (1926) with Harry Langdon; *Super-Hooper-Dyne Lizzies* (1925) with Billy Bevin and Andy Clyde; *Wandering Willies* (1926) with Billy Bevin and the Keystone Kops; *A Muddy Romance* (1913) with Mabel Normand and the Keystone Kops; *A Movie Star* (1916) with Mack Swain and Harry McCoy; and *Barney Oldfield's Race for a Life* (1913) with Mabel Normand, Mack Sennett, and Ford Sterling. 1913-1926, 121 mins.
VHS: S33978. $24.95.

Slapstick Encyclopedia—Vol. 3: Funny Girls. Includes *Mighty Like a Moose* (1926) with Charley Chase; *The Detectress* (1919) with Gale Henry; *One Wet Night* (1924) with Alice Howell; *Know Thy Wife* (1918) with Dorothy Devore; *Rowdy Ann* (1919) with Fay Tincher and Harry Depp; and *Hearts and Flowers* (1919) with Louise Fazenda and Ford Sterling. 1918-1926, 117 mins.
VHS: S33979. $24.95.

Slapstick Encyclopedia—Vol. 4: Keaton, Arbuckle & Al St. John. Includes *The Rounders* (1914) with Roscoe "Fatty" Arbuckle, Al St. John and Charles Chaplin; *Fatty and Mabel Adrift* (1916) with "Fatty" Arbuckle and Mabel Normand and Al St. John; *Oh, Doctor!* (1917) with Buster Keaton, "Fatty" Arbuckle, and Al St. John; *The Garage* (1920) with Buster Keaton and "Fatty" Arbuckle; *The Boat* (1921) with Buster Keaton; and *The Iron Mule* (1925) with Al St. John. 1914-1921, 135 mins.
VHS: S33980. $24.95.

Slapstick Encyclopedia—Vol. 5: Chaplin and Co.: The Music Hall Tradition. 1915-1929. With Charles Chaplin, Stan Laurel, Billy West, Billie Ritchie, Lupino Lane and Edna Purviance. Includes *A Night in the Show* (1915), *Rare Chaplin Snippet* (1916), *The Rink* (1916), *Live Wires and Love Sparks* (1916), *He's in Again* (1918), *Pie-Eyed* (1925) and *Only Me* (1929). 120 mins.
VHS: S34683. $89.95.

Slapstick Encyclopedia—Vol. 6: Hal Roach: The Lot of Fun. 1920-1927. With Roach team greats Laurel and Hardy, Harold Lloyd, Charley Chase, Snub Pollard, Will Rogers and Our Gang. Includes *Lafftoons* (featuring *Angora Love, You're Darn Tootin', Liberty* and *Battle of the Century*), *Get Out and Get Under* (1920), *Dogs of War* (1923), *Big Moments from Little Picture* (1924), *Fluttering Hearts* (1927) and *It's a Gift* (1923). Also with the the rare 1923 film *Oranges and Lemons,* starring Stan Laurel. 120 mins.
VHS: S34684. $89.95.

Slapstick Encyclopedia—Vol. 7: The Rage Is On. 1917-1927. With Gloria Swanson, Wallace Beery, Andy Clyde, Madeline Hurlock, Sid Smith, Billy Bevan, Monty Banks and Hairbreadth Harry. Includes *Teddy at the Throttle* (1917), *Circus Today* (1926), *Water Wagons* (1926), *Out of Bound* (1924), *Chasing Choo Choos* (1927) and *Danger Ahead* (1926). 120 mins.
VHS: S34685. $89.95.

Slapstick Encyclopedia—Vol. 8: Tons of Fun: Comedy's Anarchic Fringe. 1920-1926. With Charley Bowers, Billy Bletcher, LarrySemon, Ben Turpin, Frank Alexander, Hillard Karr and Kewpie Ross. Includes *Yukon Jake* (1924), *The Grocery Clerk* (1920), *Three of a Kind* (1926), *Dry and Thirsty* (1920), *Family Life* (1924) and *Now You Tell One* (1926). 120 mins.
VHS: S34686. $89.95.

Slapstick Encyclopedia—Slapstick Boxed Set 1. Includes all four volumes; eight tapes. 500 mins.
VHS: S33981. $89.95.

Snub Pollard...A Short But Funny Man
Australian-born Snub Pollard, one of the most prolific of slapstick comedians, in a trip of typically funny Pollard vehicles: *It's a Gift* (1923), in which Pollard plays a hilariously lazy inventor, *Looking for Trouble* in which he instigates a mud fight among a group of civilized gentlemen, and *Mitt the Prince,* in which he dusts a sidewalk which ends up filthier than when he began. 60 mins total, silent with music score.
VHS: S06981. $24.95.

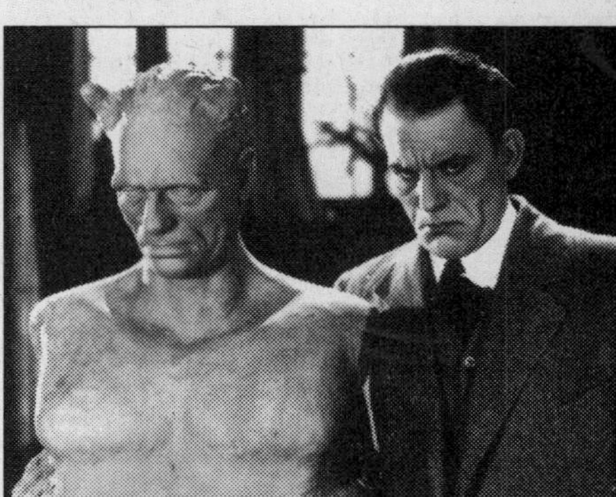

Stan "Tex" Laurel Rides Again
Stan parodies the western genre in this collection of silent comedies, which includes *West of Hot Dog* and *The Soilers,* Stan's take-off of Rex Beach's famous western novel about the Alaskan gold rush. 60 mins.
VHS: S33116. $24.95.

Stan About Town
Stan Laurel stars in four early, silent comedies set in the big city: *Man About Town, The Sleuth, Mandarin Mix-Up* and *White Wings.* 60 mins.
VHS: S33118. $24.95.

Stan Laurel: At the Beginning
Stan Laurel narrates his early life in Britain and his beginnings in the entertainment business. A montage of rare movie footage of Stan visiting his father and stepmother in England and photographs highlight this biographical introduction, followed by three early Laurel comedies: *Mixed Nuts, Just Rambling Along* (1918) and *Frauds & Frenzies* (1918). 60 mins.
VHS: S33117. $24.95.

Stanley on the Job
Stan Laurel uses the workplace as a setting in this brilliantly inventive collection of silent, fast-paced, comic shorts. Sight gags, pantomime and Rube-Goldberg gadgetry abound in *The Noon Whistle, Short Orders, Smithy, Oranges and Lemons* and *Pick and Shovel*. 60 mins.
VHS: S33115. $24.95.

Syd Chaplin at Keystone
Five comedies by Sydney Chaplin including *Gussle's Wayward Path, Gussle the Golfer, Gussle's Day of Rest, Gussle Tied to Trouble, Gus' Backward Way*. 60 mins.
VHS: S08015. $29.95.

Teddy at the Throttle
One of the most famous Mack Sennett comedies features Gloria Swanson and Wallace Beery near the start of their careers with Teddy, one of the screen's first animal stars. A superb parody of melodramas and Griffith-style last minute rescues. USA, 1917, 62 mins.
VHS: S02227. $29.95.

The Three Must-Get-Theirs
This rare spoof of the Fairbanks' *The Three Musketeers* is still a delight. It's presented with the original French subtitles, but they do not diminish the enjoyment value of this rare, orchestra-scored film.
VHS: S22432. $19.95.
Max Linder, USA, 1921, 47 mins.

Tillie Wakes Up
Marie Dressler stars in this sequel to Charlie Chaplin's comic feature-length film *Tillie's Punctured Romance*. Dressler reprises her role as a simple girl from the country bewildered by the complicated ways of the big city. 1917, 50 mins.
VHS: S23147. $24.95.

Tillie's Punctured Romance
Historically important as the first feature-length comedy ever produced, *Tillie's Punctured Romance* is perhaps more noteworthy for its teaming of the greatest silent comedians of the day: Charley Chase, Mabel Normand, the Keystone Kops, Marie Dressler and Charlie Chaplin appears in a rare departure from his Little Tramp characterizations. This version is entirely restored with all new intertitles. Includes the Chaplin short, *Mabel's Married Life*.
VHS: S16739. $19.95.
Laser: CLV. **LD72037. $29.98.**
Mack Sennett, USA, 1914, 73 mins.

Versatile Mr. Laurel
Stan Laurel plays a variety of roles in this collection of silent comedies, which includes *Kill or Cure, Save the Ship, Collars and Cuffs* and *Near Dublin*. 60 mins.
VHS: S33114. $24.95.

When Comedy Was King
A hilarious collection of silent comedians, including The Keystone Cops, Charlie Chaplin, Fatty Arbuckle, Laurel and Hardy, Buster Keaton and many, many more. Various, USA, 1987, 81 mins.
Laser: LD75282. $34.98.

When the Clouds Roll By
A hilarious spoof starring Douglas Fairbanks and Kathleen Clifford on the then-new science of psychoanalysis. Silent with music score.
VHS: S07489. $24.95.
Victor Fleming, USA, 1919, 77 mins.

The Wild Party
The funny story of a dishy new professor at an all-girls' school and his rocky relationship with a sexy student who thinks college is just a lark. Stars Clara Bow, Fredric March, Shirley O'Hara and Marceline Day.
VHS: S16175. $29.95.
Dorothy Arzner, USA, 1929, 76 mins.

D.W. GRIFFITH

Abraham Lincoln
Griffith's epic biography of Lincoln begins just prior to his ascent to the White House, and features a remarkable performance from Walter Huston as Lincoln. Griffith's remarkable handling of actors results in a believable portrait of the martyred president.
VHS: S00014. $19.95.
D.W. Griffith, USA, 1930, 84 mins.

America
Griffith's patriotic, historical spectacle about the American Revolution, which combines a love story with events from Virginia to New England. The film is notable for Griffith's recreation of many of the famous battles; with Neil Hamilton, Lionel Barrymore. Silent, music track.
VHS: S02094. $29.95.
D.W. Griffith, USA, 1924, 81 mins.

Avenging Conscience
Griffith's first elaborate feature is notable for its use of double exposures and masks which would later influence the German Expressionist cinema. With Henry B. Walthall, Blanche Sweet. Silent with music track.
VHS: S02091. $39.95.
D.W. Griffith, USA, 1914, 58 mins.

The Birth of a Nation
D.W. Griffith's debut feature is credited with revolutionizing form and content in the cinema. Its epic story assessed the political, social, racial and personal consequences of the Civil War on American life, from the perspective of two families, the Southern Stonemans and the Northern Camerons. The story intersects the personal with the historic and political, Lincoln's assassination, the Reconstruction and the rise of the Ku Klux Klan. This deluxe edition includes a 30-minute documentary on the making of the film, with interviews, archival footage and outtakes. Adapted from Thomas Dixon's novel and play *The Clansman*. With Lillian Gish, Mae Marsh, Miriam Cooper and filmmaker Raoul Walsh. Cinematography by Billy Bitzer and Karl Brown.
VHS: S18433. $39.95.
Laser: LD70883. $79.95.
D.W. Griffith, USA, 1914, 187 mins.

Broken Blossoms
D.W. Griffith's pastoral effort set in a Dickensian London about the oppression of a frail young street urchin desperate to escape her bleak circumstances. The young woman falls in love with a sympathetic Chinese missionary, who shields her from her tyrannical and abusive father. "There are stretches of Griffith poetry, a marvelous use of light and shadow in cameraman Billy Bitzer's evocation of foggy Limehouse, and a truly unforgettable performance from Lillian Gish" (*Time Out*). With Richard Barthelmess and Donald Crisp. Newly remastered print struck from an archival source.
VHS: S18434. $24.95.
D.W. Griffith, USA, 1919, 90 mins.

A Corner in Wheat and Selected Biograph Shorts
A collection of eight one- and two-reel works D.W. Griffith directed from 1909-1913 for the American Mutoscope and Biograph Company that highlighted Griffith's narrative inventions. The other works showcased are *Those Awful Hats, The Sealed Room, The Unchanging Sea, His Trust, The New York Hat, An Unseen Enemy* and *The Mothering Heart*. Featuring Mary Pickford and Lillian and Dorothy Gish. 118 mins.
VHS: S18431. $24.95.

D.W. Griffith Triple Feature
Mae Marsh, Lillian Gish, Mary Pickford and Blanche Sweet are among those featured in these three landmark Griffith westerns, including: *The Battle at Elderbush Gulch* (1913), *Lola's Promise* (1912) and *The Goddess of Sagebrush Gulch* (1912). *Elderbush* was considered by Griffith to be the third best film he ever made. It also marked the film debut of beautiful young Lillian Gish.
VHS: S00533. $19.95.
D.W. Griffith, USA, 1912-13, 50 mins.

D.W. Griffith's Years of Discovery
Twenty-two masterworks from D.W. Griffith are included in this special laserdisc collector's edition, each one speed corrected, with all but two featuring new digital scores by various composers. Includes *The Redman's View, In the Border States, What Shall We Do With Our Old?, For His Son, The Female of the Species, The House of Darkness, The Musketeers of Pig Alley, The Burglar's Dilemma, The Sunbeam, The Painted Lady, One Is Business, The Other Crime, Death's Marathon, The Battle at Elderbush Gulch, The Awful Hats, The Sealed Room, Corner in Wheat, The Unchanging Sea, His Trust, The New York Hat, An Unseen Enemy, The Mothering Heart* and *The Girl in Her Trust*.
Laser: LD76427. $99.99.
D.W. Griffith, USA, 1909-13, 450 mins.

D.W. Griffith: Biograph Years
Commentary on Griffith's life and work by film historian Ron Mottram and silent film star Blanche Sweet. With clips from *Death's Marathon, The Painted Lady, Feud in the Kentucky Hills, A Corner in Wheat, The Informer* and *Country Doctor*, made between 1908-1913 for the Biograph company. Sweet, who starred in many of these films, reminisces about the method of shooting in those days, including some of the first "pans," "zooms" or "close ups" ever used. 1975, 28 mins.
VHS: S31569. $59.95.

D.W. Griffith: Feature Film Years
Commentary on Griffith's life and work by film historian Ron Mottram with silent film star Lillian Gish. Film excerpts include portions of *Way Down East* (1920), *Intolerance* (1916), *True Heart Susie* (1919) and *Birth of a Nation*. Gish reminiscences about the long hours, dangerous situations, the presentation of character without recourse to spoken dialogue, and Griffith as creator of historical film with crowds of people. 1975, 28 mins.
VHS: S31570. $59.95.

Dream Street
A follow-up to *Broken Blossoms*, based on material by the same author, featuring Tyrone Power Sr., Ralph Graves and Carol Dempster. A story of two brothers, both in love with the same dancing girl, while a gambler plans to take her for his own.
VHS: S02245. $19.95.
D.W. Griffith, USA, 1921, 148 mins.

The Female of the Species & Selected Biograph Shorts (Volume III)
This collection of D.W. Griffith shorts produced between 1909 and 1913 and featuring Mary Pickford, Lillian Gish and Robert Harron, illustrates the filmmaker's craftsmanship and social concerns, including the plight of Native Americans (*The Redman's View*), mental illness (*The House of Darkness*), the Civil War (*In the Border States*), drug addiction (*For His Son*) and aging (*What Shall We Do with Our Old?*).
VHS: S28588. $29.95.
D.W. Griffith, USA, 1924, 100 mins.

Greatest Question
Josephine Crowell, George Nichols and Lillian Gish star. Gish witnessed a murder many years ago and finds it is still haunting her. Silent with music track.
VHS: S07277. $24.95.
D.W. Griffith, USA, 1919, 80 mins.

Griffith Shorts (1908-09)
Short films made by Griffith during 1908-1909: *Crossroads of Life, Adventures of Dolly, A Calamitous Elopement, The Curtain Pole, The Jones Have Amateur Theatricals, A Drunkard's Reformation, What Drink Did, Confidence, Resurrection, Her First Biscuits, Violin Maker of Cremona*.
VHS: S04827. $29.95.
D.W. Griffith, USA, 1909-09, 120 mins.

Griffith Shorts (1909)
Griffith films made in 1909: *The Country Doctor, The Renunciation, Sweet and Twenty, The Mended Lute-Sealed Room, 1776 or The Hessian Renegades, Pippa Passes, Lines of White on a Sullen Sea, The Gibson Goddess, The Light That Came*.
VHS: S04828. $29.95.
D.W. Griffith, USA, 1909, 110 mins.

Griffith Shorts (1909-1910)
Griffith films from 1909-1910: *A Corner in Wheat, Her Terrible Ordeal, The Last Deal, In the Border States, Mugzy's First Sweetheart, An Arcadian Maid, House with Closed Shutters, The Usurer, Modern Prodigal, The Rose*.
VHS: S04829. $29.95.
D.W. Griffith, USA, 1909-1910, 120 mins.

Griffith Shorts (1909-1911)

Those Awful Hats, The Son's Return, A Strange Meeting, Romance of Western Hills, Sorrows of the Unfaithful, What Shall We Do With Our Old, The Long Road, Love in the Hills, A Woman Scorned, With the Enemy's Help.
VHS: S04838. $29.95.
D.W. Griffith, USA, 1909-1911, 120 mins.

Griffith Shorts (1910-1911)

The Message of the Violin, The Fugitive, Sunshine Sue, Winning Back His Love, When a Man Loves, Two Paths, His Trust, Fates Turning, Fisher Folks, Lily of the Tenements.
VHS: S04830. $29.95.
D.W. Griffith, USA, 1910-1911, 120 mins.

Griffith Shorts (1911)

The Lonedale Operator, Enoch Arden (parts 1 and 2), *Primal Call, Fighting Blood, Bobby The Coward, Country Cupid, Last Drop of Water, As a Boy Dreams, The Revenue Man* and *His Girl.*
VHS: S04831. $29.95.
D.W. Griffith, USA, 1911, 120 mins.

Griffith Shorts (1911-1912)

A Squaw's Love, Adventures of Billy, The Battle, Through Darking Vales, The Miser's Heart, Failure, Saved from Himself, For His Son, The Transformation of Mike.
VHS: S04832. $29.95.
D.W. Griffith, USA, 1911-1912, 129 mins.

Griffith Shorts (1912, #1)

The Sunbeam, Iola's Promise, The Goddess of Sagebrush Gulch, A Girl and Her Trust, The Female of the Species, Lesser Evil, A Beast at Bay, Lena and the Geese, Man's Genesis, The Sands of Dee.
VHS: S04833. $29.95.
D.W. Griffith, USA, 1912, 120 mins.

Griffith Shorts (1912, #2)

The Narrow Road, Under Burning Skies, One Is Business the Other Crime, School Teacher and the Waif, A Change of Spirit, Unseen Enemy, Blind Love, Two Daughters of Eve, Friends, So Near Yet So Far.
VHS: S04834. $29.95.
D.W. Griffith, USA, 1912, 120 mins.

Griffith Shorts (1912, #3)

The Painted Lady, Musketeers of Pig Alley, Massacre, The New York Hat, The Burglar's Dilemma, The God Within, Telephone Girl and the Lady, Oil and Water.
VHS: S04835. $29.95.
D.W. Griffith, USA, 1912, 120 mins.

Griffith Shorts (1913)

The Unwelcome Guest, Near to the Earth, The Wanderer, House of Darkness, His Mother's Son, Timely Interception, Death's Marathon, Mothering Heart.
VHS: S04836. $29.95.
D.W. Griffith, USA, 1913, 120 mins.

Griffith Shorts (1913-1914)

The Switch Tower, Brute Force, The Reformers, The Battle at Elderbush Gulch, Pathways of Life.
VHS: S04837. $29.95.
D.W. Griffith, USA, 1913-1914, 120 mins.

Hearts of the World

Noel Coward made his first appearance in this story which takes place in a French village during World War I. The film espouses democracy and patriotism, and was a great commercial success. With Lillian Gish, Erich von Stroheim.
VHS: S00552. $24.95.
Laser: CLV. **LD71988. $29.98.**
D.W. Griffith, USA, 1918

Home Sweet Home

What started out as a one-reeler Griffith later expanded into a feature-length biography of John Howard Payne and his immortal song, "Home Sweet Home." Lillian Gish, Dorothy Gish, Mae Marsh, Blanche Sweet star in this series of vignettes, each illustrating a Payne song.
VHS: S01746. $29.95.
D.W. Griffith, USA, 1914, 62 mins.

Idol Dancer

A drunken Yankee beachcomber befriends a half-caste native girl scorned by the villagers in this Griffith epic set in the South Seas. Richard Barthelmess, Claire Seymour and Creighton Hale star in the film, which ends in a rousing climax. Silent, music track.
VHS: S02092. $29.95.
D.W. Griffith, USA, 1920, 76 mins.

Intolerance

Four separate stories are interwoven: the fall of Babylon, the death of Christ, the massacre of the Hugenots, and a modern drama—all cross-cut and building with enormous energy to a thrilling chase and finale. Far ahead of its time, Griffith created a spectacle which audiences of the day did not accept but which has become a classic of world cinema. This specially packaged double cassette edition of *Intolerance* has been remastered using variable speed projection and color tints to match the original release prints, making it the best version available anywhere. Tinted with organ score.
VHS: S13048. $29.95.
Laser: CAV. **LD71052. $69.95.**
D.W. Griffith, USA, 1919, 190 min.

Isn't Life Wonderful

Griffith's last independent production, shot on location in Germany. A compassionate, romantic drama of postwar deprivation that decried the evils that led to the War, and exalted the power of love.
VHS: S00641. $29.95.
Laser: LD76181. $49.98.
D.W. Griffith, USA, 1924

Judith of Bethula

The first four-reel film done in America (approximately 40 minutes), *Judith of Bethula* is a Biblical epic considered a stupendous production in its day. It was expanded to a longer version by Biograph Studios in 1917. Silent with music track.
VHS: S00662. $24.95.
D.W. Griffith, USA, 1914

Judith of Bethula/Home Sweet Home

D.W. Griffith's biblical epic anticipates the structural elements of *Intolerance* as it interweaves four contrapuntal tales about a beautiful Bethulian widow, Judith, who seduces the Assyrian conqueror Holofernes in order to assassinate him and preserve her city. The film is important for its sweep and technical innovations and dense storytelling. *Home Sweet Home* is considerably different, a fascinating musical biography of John Howard Payne. With Lillian and Dorothy Gish, Mae Marsh, Blanche Sweet and Henry B. Walthall.
VHS: S18436. $24.95.
D.W. Griffith, USA, 1913/14, 118 mins.

Love Flower

One of three pictures Griffith shot for First National, a melodrama about a man who, with his daughter, escapes to a tropical island to elude a police detective. Shot on location in Fort Lauderdale, Florida, and in the Bahamas.
VHS: S00775. $19.95.
D.W. Griffith, USA, 1920, 70 mins.

Mother and the Law

An extremely rare D.W. Griffith film, which was later incorporated into Griffith's famous *Intolerance*, with many of the scenes deleted.
VHS: S11451. $24.95.
D.W. Griffith, USA, 1914, 93 mins.

The Musketeers of Pig Alley and Selected Biograph Shorts

Seven key works from D.W. Griffith's Biograph period are represented, most of them dealing with social themes, class distinctions and pure action. Works include *The Burglar's Dilemma, The Sunbeam, The Painted Lady, One Is Business the Other Crime, Death's Marathon* and *The Battle at Elderbush Gulch*. With Lillian Gish, Mae Marsh, Blanche Sweet and Donald Crisp. 117 mins.
VHS: S18432. $24.95.

Orphans of the Storm

Two innocent orphans (Lillian and Dorothy Gish) arrive in Paris just prior to the French Revolution and are exploited, separated, and nearly find each other again—until they become involved in the Revolution themselves. A luxurious, large-scale Griffith spectacle. Digitally remastered.
VHS: S14444. $29.95.
Laser: CLV. **LD72013. $59.95.**
D.W. Griffith, USA, 1921, 190 mins.

Romance of Happy Valley

A country boy (Robert Harron) leaves his home and sweetheart to make his fortune in the city, returning years later to find those he loves suffering.
VHS: S31762. $19.95.
D.W. Griffith, USA, 1919, 60 mins.

Sally of the Sawdust

W.C. Fields' first major film, a classic of circus life, also starring Carol Dempster and Alfred Lunt. Music track.
VHS: S01150. $29.95.
Laser: LD76088. $39.99.
D.W. Griffith, USA, 1925, 124 mins.

The Short Films of D.W. Griffith—Volume 1

Includes four early works by Griffith: *The Battle* (10 mins.), *The Battle at Elderbush Gulch* (10 mins.), *His Trust and His Trust Fulfilled* (28 mins.) and *Her Terrible Ordeal* (10 mins.).
VHS: S14925. $29.95.
D.W. Griffith, USA

The Short Films of D.W. Griffith—Volume 2

Six more early films from the American master: *The Unseen Enemy* (15 mins.), *The Little Tease* (10 mins.), *Man's Genesis* (10 mins.), *Musketeers of Pig Alley* (10 mins.), *The Switch Tower* (10 mins.) and *The Lonedale Operator* (11 mins.).
VHS: S14926. $29.95.
D.W. Griffith, USA

The Short Films of D.W. Griffith—Volume 3

Two silent shorts by the legendary D.W. Griffith: *The Tunnel Workers* (23 mins.) and *The Girls and Daddy* (26 mins.).
VHS: S14927. $29.95.
D.W. Griffith, USA

The Short Films of D.W. Griffith—Volume 4

Includes three more early short films from Griffith: *Enoch Arden* (20 mins.), *The Transformation of Mike* (20 mins.) and *What Shall We Do with Our Old* (10 mins.).
VHS: S14928. $29.95.
D.W. Griffith, USA

Sorrows of Satan

The last major film by D.W. Griffith, in a lavish production originally intended for De Mille. With Carol Dempster, Adolphe Menjou, Ricardo Cortez and an exotic Lya de Putti.
VHS: S08334. $29.95.
D.W. Griffith, USA, 1926, 111 mins.

The Struggle

D.W. Griffith pulls no punches in this rarely seen last film, shot in 1931 on a tiny budget, which illustrates the destructive influence of alcohol. In this "talkie," Hal Skelly stars as a hardworking Everyman who falls victim to alcoholism and despair and makes his home a living hell for his trusting daughter. Also starring Zita Johann and Evelyn Baldwin.
VHS: S28589. $29.95.
D.W. Griffith, USA, 1931, 77 mins.

True Heart Susie

One of the lesser known great films by Griffith, director of *Birth of a Nation* and *Intolerance*, *True Heart Susie* features a superlative performance by Lillian Gish. The story of a childhood romance is told with simple charm and unpretentious style.
VHS: S01375. $29.95.
D.W. Griffith, USA, 1919, 62 mins.

Way Down East

D.W. Griffith's Victorian pastoral stars Lillian Gish as an eager though exploited young woman abandoned by her obsessive, cavalier husband when he learns she's pregnant, who finds temporary comfort and solace with a wealthy, passive, small-town lawyer. The film has two constructs, an evocative portrait of small-town Americana and a suspense melodrama about desire and attraction and despair that attains its climax in the famous ice floe sequence. With Richard Barthelmess, Lowell Sherman and Edgar Nelson.
VHS: S18435. $24.95.
D.W. Griffith, USA, 1920, 149 mins.

White Rose

A very rare D.W. Griffith film. Shot in the bayous of Louisiana, it's a simple, sentimental outlook on life. Mae Marsh and Ivor Novello star in the story of a minister who falls in love with an abandoned and outcast orphan girl.
VHS: S12151. $29.95.
D.W. Griffith, USA, 1923, 120 mins.

television shows

The Abbott and Costello Television Show

Abbott and Costello's television comedy series recaptures the vivid atmosphere of live television during the early 50s."The show pioneered the use of ensemble cast comedy sketches on live television and the intricate sense of timing reflects those vaudeville origins" (*Washington Post*).

Tape 1. This collection includes *Duck Dinner, Hillary's Birthday, Million Dollar Refund and Actors' Home*. 110 mins.
VHS: S19586. $19.95.

Tape 2. This collection includes *Lou's Birthday, Getting a Job, Uncle Bozzo* and *Stolen Skates*. 110 mins.
VHS: S19587. $19.95.

Tape 3. This collection includes *Lou Falls for Ruby, Hillary's Father, Uncle Ruppert* and *Bingo's Troubles*. 110 mins.
VHS: S19588. $19.95.

Tape 4. This collection includes *The Drugstore, Square Meal, $1,000 Prize* and *Wife Wanted*. 110 mins.
VHS: S19589. $19.95.

Tape 5. This collection includes *Police Academy, Charity Bazaar, Killer's Wife* and *Well Oiled*. 110 mins.
VHS: S19590. $19.95.

Tape 6. This collection includes *Wrestling Match, In Society, Lou's Marriage* and *Beauty Contest*. 110 mins.
VHS: S19591. $19.95.

ABC Stage 67: Truman Capote's A Christmas Memory

Geraldine Page and Donnie Melvin star in this dramatic television adaptation of Capote's autobiographical account of his youth during the depression in the South. Living on severely limited means with his dottie cousin, the 10-year-old Capote was enriched by singular experiences. In this film, the baking of Christmas fruitcakes for relatives becomes the center of a warm and involved undertaking. 51 mins.
VHS: S29527. $19.95.

Abraham Lincoln—Westinghouse Studio One

The life and death of the 16th President of the United States comes to live tv.The story by John Drinkwater covers Lincoln from his acceptance of the nomination to Ford's Theatre. With Robert Pastene, Judith Evelyn and a 21-year-old James Dean as a Union soldier sentenced to be shot for sleeping on guard duty. USA, 1952, 60 mins.
VHS: S05436. $24.95.

Absolutely the Best of the Soupy Sales Show

Before David Letterman there was Soupy Sales and his inventive and charged parody of the talk show format. This collection of his best work, culled from some of his television shows, features the work of his gang of outcasts—White Tooth, Black Fang and Pookie—as well as some of his strange songs, e.g., "Your Brains Fell Out." 60 mins.
VHS: S18138. $19.95.

All Color News—Sampler

A remarkable collection of clips from the New York City feature news program for cable TV. Hard and gritty, this is the early political and socially-oriented work by artists Scott & Beth B, Charlie Ahearn, John Ahearn, and Tom Otterness—now well-known for their other productions.
VHS: S07110. $29.95.
All Color News, USA, 1978, 28 mins.

All My Children: Behind the Scenes

If you have ever wondered what goes on beneath the sheets during those steamy love scenes, then this video offers an unbeatable opportunity. Walt Wiley hosts this candid view of the most famous daytime series. Not only are the workings of this show exposed, but Erica Kane's closet is thrown wide open.
VHS: S22545. $14.98.

Amazing Stories: Book 1

Two great episodes from executive producer Steven Spielberg's acclaimed television series: *The Wedding Ring*, directed by Danny DeVito, and *The Mission*, directed by Spielberg himself. Featuring Kevin Costner, Kiefer Sutherland, Danny DeVito and Rhea Perlman. USA, 70 mins.
VHS: S13827. $79.95.

Amazing Stories: Book 4

Explore the incredible in these three episodes from *Amazing Stories*, the popular series from executive producer Steven Spielberg. Includes *Mirror, Mirror*, directed by Martin Scorsese; *Blue Man Down*, directed by Paul Michael Glaser; and *Mr. Magic*, directed by Donald Petrie. USA, 71 mins.
VHS: S15582. $79.95.

America's Funniest Animal Foul-Ups

Outrageous animals steal the show in this menagerie of mayhem. From the makers of "Foul-Ups, Bleeps and Blunders." Hosted by funnyman and "Tonight Show" regular Kelly Monteith. 30 mins.
VHS: S16332. $9.95.

America's Funniest Kid Foul-Ups

Comedian Kelly Monteith, a frequent guest on *The Tonight Show*, hosts this candid collection of gags and blunders starring the youth of America. Or at least those youngsters whose parents own video camcorders. From the producer of the ABC network hit *Foul-Ups, Bleeps and Blunders* comes the real story about what kindergartners think of being on television. 30 mins.
VHS: S15496. $9.95.

America's Funniest TV Foul-Ups

Some of television's funniest moments have been hidden away...until now. See President Nixon as he attempts to throw out the season's first baseball, car dealer tycoon Cal Worthington being attacked by a two-ton truck, a cooking show that goes up in flames, and other hilarities. Hosted by comedian Kelly Monteith. 30 mins.
VHS: S16331. $9.95.

And a Nightingale Sang

A comedy/drama set in World War II England starring the great Joan Plowright. Originally broadcast on PBS. England, 90 mins.
VHS: S15110. $19.98.

The Andy Rooney Television Collection

The droll, idiosyncratic voice of Americana, humorist and essayist Andy Rooney offers his vignettes, anecdotes and quirky stories about man, nature, technology and contemporary life in three video programs: *His Minutes, Volumes 1 & 2* and *A Bird's Eye View of America*.
VHS: S19098. $39.98.

Andy Rooney: His Best Minutes, Vol. 1

Andy Rooney's deadpan observations on American institutions, humor, bureaucracy, culture, society, politics and the individual character are collected in this witty assemblage of his *60 Minutes* vignettes, *A Few Minutes with Andy Rooney*. 70 mins.
VHS: S19322. $19.98.

Andy Rooney: His Best Minutes, Vol. 2

A follow-up to the humorist's earlier collection of his *60 Minutes* pieces, quiet, reflective and droll reflections on the American character. 73 mins.
VHS: S19323. $19.98.

Bank on the Stars

Bill Cullen hosts this tv quiz show where contestants watch scenes from newly released films and must answer questions about what they have seen. Films on this program include *Apache* with Burt Lancaster, Jacques Tati's *Mr. Hulot's Holiday*, and *The Caine Mutiny*, with Humphrey Bogart and Van Johnson. Someone ought to bring this show back. USA, 1954, 30 mins.
VHS: S06477. $19.95.

The Bastard: Part I of the Kent Family Chronicles

Andrew Stevens leads an all-star cast in this exciting, sweeping adventure saga based on John Jakes' best-selling American Bicentennial series. Olivia Hussey and Kim Cattrall co-star in this fascinating and compelling drama set against one of the most exciting periods of American history.
VHS: S15277. $29.98.
Lee Katzin, USA, 1978, 189 mins.

Beauty and the Beast

This television series starring Linda Hamilton had a cult following. It placed the fairy tale of *Beauty and the Beast* right under contemporary Manhattan. Romance and fantasy take on a dark perspective, rendering this age-old tale suitable for our times. Each episode is approximately 49 minutes.

Episode 1: Once Upon a Time in New York.
VHS: S07437. $19.95.
Episode 2: Terrible Savior.
VHS: S23092. $14.98.
Episode 3: Siege.
VHS: S23093. $14.98.
Episode 4: No Way Down.
VHS: S23094. $14.98.
Episode 5: Masques.
VHS: S23095. $14.98.
Episode 6: The Beast Within.
VHS: S23096. $14.98.
Episode 7: Nor Iron Bars a Cage.
VHS: S23097. $14.98.
Episode 8: Song of Orpheus.
VHS: S23098. $14.98.
Episode 9: Dark Spirit.
VHS: S23099. $14.98.
Episode 10: A Children's Story.
VHS: S23100. $14.98.
Episode 11: An Impossible Silence.
VHS: S23101. $14.98.
Episode 12: Shades of Grey.
VHS: S23102. $14.98.

Beauty and the Beast: Above, Below and Beyond

A sequel to the tremendously popular television series which follows the adventures of Beauty and her Beast. 100 mins.
VHS: S09664. $19.95.

The Bells of Cockaigne & Broadway Trust

James Dean and Gene Lockhart star in *The Bells of Cockaigne* (30 mins.), an Armstrong Circle Theatre television production written by George Lawther. James Dean is a long-suffering dock worker struggling to save enough money to move his family to a warmer climate in the hopes that the dry air will improve his asthmatic son's health. His co-worker Pat (Gene Lockhart) dreams of winning a local newspaper contest and using the prize money to see his native Ireland one last time. *Broadway Trust* (25 mins.) stars Lloyd Bridges in a true story of embezzlement, faith and friendship from the *Crossroads* television series. *Crossroads* was a television series overseen by religious officials, which produced programs based on true stories of the decisions people made when they found themselves at moral crossroads in their lives. B&W. From *The James Dean Collection*.
VHS: S27328. $19.95.
James Sheldon, USA, 1952, 55 mins.

The Best of Ernie Kovacs

The work of the great Ernie Kovacs is now available for the first time on home video. His television career from 1950 to 1962 has been painstakingly researched and collected from over 100 hours of footage to create this series of his best comedy bits. Most of this rare film material has not been seen for decades. Five volumes.

Volume 1. Features classic bits from the early television shows, including the "crazy" 1812 Overture and the "Whom Dunnit" game show.
VHS: S14701. $19.95.

Volume 2. "The Music Show" features the gorilla *Swan Lake* ballet, and a street scene set to Bartok.
VHS: S14702. $19.95.

Volume 3. Featuring material from the final "Eugene" broadcast. Plus the comic Dutch Masters commercials.
VHS: S14703. $19.95.

Volume 4. Featuring Miklos Molnar making "Chicken Molnar" and the best of the oscilloscope gags.
VHS: S14704. $19.95.

Volume 5. Containing material broadcast in January 1962, just after Kovacs death.
VHS: S14705. $19.95.

The complete five-volume set.
VHS: S14706. $99.75.

Best of On the Road with Charles Kuralt

One of America's premier journalists, Charles Kuralt goes on the road and provides an epic vision of America, its people, cultures, landscapes and diversity in three separate videos: *American Heritage, Seasons of America* and *Unforgettable People*.
VHS: S19097. $49.98.

The Best of Red Green

The PBS cult comedy hit *The Red Green Show* features do-it-yourselfer Red Green (Steve Smith) and his nephew Harold as they host a hilarious round-up of memorable moments from Possum Lodge. Called "...the funniest thing to hit public television since *Monty Python's Flying Circus*" (*Milwaukee Journal*), *The Best of Red Green* features numerous episodes of *Adventures with Bill* and *Handyman Corner*. Includes the seven-minute documentary *The Making of Red Green*. With Pat McKenna and Rick Green.
VHS: S27198. $19.95.
Stephen Benedict/Steve Lambert/Andrew Robertson, USA, 1995, 67 mins.

The Best of Sex Bytes

This tape from HBO shows what people share in cyberspace, from the pleasures of food and sex, and artists who bodycast human sculptures, to the pleasures of public nudity. 60 mins.
VHS: S31617. $14.95.

Best of Spike Jones—Volume 1
An anthology of snippets from his popular TV show produced and edited under the personal supervision of Spike Jones, Jr. Enjoy once again the melodic sounds of cowbells, foghorns, slide whistles and various other musical paraphernalia that were standard issue for Spike and the City Slickers. B&W. 1952-57, 51 mins.
VHS: S10809. $29.95.
Laser: LD75120. $24.98.

Best of Spike Jones—Volume 2
More of the wacky and weird musical renditions of Spike Jones and his band of City Slickers. Ten popular songs are presented with the special Spike touch. See how many you can still identify. Feel free to ring your cowbell at home while you watch this unusual comedy-variety show. B&W. 1952-57, 53 mins.
VHS: S10810. $29.95.
Laser: LD75121. $24.98.

Best of Spike Jones—Volume 3
An all-new hilarious highlights from Spike Jones' popular 50's TV shows. 54 mins.
VHS: S08112. $29.95.

The Best of the 90's Home Video
This collection features some of the best moments from the first season of what is easily the most important and innovative news show on the air, a show that does all the things that television is supposed to do but never does. "The 90's" comes out of Chicago, appearing mainly on local PBS stations; part "60 Minutes," part counterculture documentary, part rock and roll, all experimental and groundbreaking, it presents a truly global and often radical view of world events.
VHS: S13773. $19.95.

The Beverly Hillbillies Go Hollywood
Four episodes of the popular television comedy are seamlessly woven together in this story detailing misadventures and crazy antics when Jed decides to buy a movie studio. Will American movies ever be the same? With Buddy Ebsen, Max Baer Jr. and Donna Douglas. 104 mins.
VHS: S19749. $19.98.

The Bill Dana Show
A classic television series. Dana is cast as Jose Jimenez, a Chaplinesque New York City bellman who represents the ambitions and desires of the American Dream he has turned upside down. He's an everyman with a burning desire to succeed but who has an inopportune tendency to screw up. With his friend Byron Glick (Don Adams), he experiences one strange encounter after another with heartbreaking and ironic consequences. "I rank Dana's Jose Jimenez among the true great original characters in the world scope of show business" (Ed Sullivan).
The Bill Dana Show: Vol. 1.
VHS: S19250. $14.95.
The Bill Dana Show: Vol. 2.
VHS: S19251. $14.95.
The Bill Dana Show: Vol. 3.
VHS: S19252. $14.95.
The Bill Dana Show: Vol. 4.
VHS: S19253. $14.95.
The Bill Dana Show: Vol. 5.
VHS: S19254. $14.95.
The Bill Dana Show: Vol. 6.
VHS: S19255. $14.95.
The Bill Dana Show: Vol. 7.
VHS: S19256. $14.95.
The Bill Dana Show: Vol. 8.
VHS: S19257. $14.95.
The Bill Dana Show: Vol. 9.
VHS: S19258. $14.95.
The Bill Dana Show: Vol. 10.
VHS: S19259. $14.95.
The Collectors Boxed Edition: Vol. 1-5.
VHS: S19260. $59.95.
The Collectors Boxed Edition: Vol. 6-10.
VHS: S19261. $59.95.

Bloopers: Vol. 2
A compilation of special screw-ups never before included in one video. Includes Robin Williams, Henry Winkler, Alan Alda, Elizabeth Taylor and many more. Parental discretion advised. USA, 55 mins.
VHS: S15029. $19.95.

A Bolt of Lightning
Charlton Heston and Romney Brent star in this 1951 Westinghouse Studio One production. 60 mins.
VHS: S32144. $24.95.

Bosom Buddies, Vol. 1
Tom Hanks was famous as a man in woman's clothing long before he played a gay man in *Philadelphia*. Together with Peter Scolari he waltzed through a number of strange, comic situations in which he and his friend had to explain their presence in drag despite their deeply ingrained heterosexual longings. They just happened to live in a "women only" hotel. Includes the pilot and the aptly titled "Macho Man." 51 mins.
VHS: S25959. $9.95.

Bosom Buddies, Vol. 2
Tom Hanks and Peter Scolari stayed true to form in these episodes that mix gender-bending with humor. Includes "Kip and Sonny's Date" and "Revenge." 51 mins.
VHS: S25960. $9.95.

Bosom Buddies, Vol. 3
Hanks and Scolari keep up the good ruse in "Kip Quits" and "The Hospital." 51 mins.
VHS: S25961. $9.95.

Bosom Buddies, Vol. 4
"There's No Business/Other Than That" and "She's a Wonderful Person" show Tom Hanks and Peter Scolari at their most beautifully comic. 51 mins.
VHS: S25962. $9.95.

The Bowery Boys
An intimate compilation work featuring the madcap charm and flair of *The Bowery Boys*, with interviews with the major players, hilarious outtakes and bloopers, rare archival still photographs and clips of the best programs. With Huntz Hall, Leo Gorcey and Robby Jordan.
VHS: S17554. $14.98.

The Brady Bunch, Vol. 1
It's the lovely story of a lovely lady who was bringing up three very lovely girls 'til one day... This is it—the original 1970's television series. Includes the first episode, "The Honeymoon," and "A Camping We Will Go." 51 mins.
VHS: S25955. $9.95.

The Brady Bunch, Vol. 2
This volume from the original 1970's television series includes the episodes "The Tattletale" and "Law and Disorder." 51 mins.
VHS: S25956. $9.95.

The Brady Bunch, Vol. 3
The episodes "Will the Real Jan Brady Please Stand Up" and "Her Sister's Shadow" effectively encapsulate 1970's sitcom wisdom on sibling rivalry. 51 mins.
VHS: S25957. $9.95.

The Brady Bunch, Vol. 4
"Getting Davy Jones" and "The Subject Was Noses" span the gamut of teenage angst from idol worship to the importance of appearance. 51 mins.
VHS: S25958. $9.95.

Bronco: Death of an Outlaw
This television western with Ty Hardin re-invents the western legend of Pat Garrett and Billy the Kid. The program paints Billy as a respectable family man unfairly prosecuted for past misdeeds by buffalo hunter and "opportunist" Pat Garrett. 1960, 60 mins.
VHS: S16283. $14.98.

Bronco: Shadow of Jesse James
Another piece that demythologizes the west, with its eponymous hero inadvertently crossing paths with the famed outlaws of the time, the vicious Jesse James (played by James Coburn), Cole Younger and Belle Starr. With Ty Hardin (as Bronco).
VHS: S16284. $14.98.

Bruce Lee and the Green Hornet
A rare screen test of the martial arts icon and charismatic figure Bruce Lee, on the making of the television series *The Green Hornet*, with three complete, uncut episodes and a short film on the making of Robert Clouzet's *Enter the Dragon*, the actor's fullest and most satisfying work. 90 mins.
VHS: S17577. $19.95.

Bumbledown/Sound of Maggie
A bitingly satirical puppet show on the life of Ronald Reagan from the people at *Spitting Image*. Directed by Graham C. Williams. Also on the cassette is *The Sound of Maggie*. 76 mins.
VHS: S15181. $24.98.

Bumbledown: The Life and Times of Ronald Reagan
The character assassinators known as "Spitting Image" target our 43rd President. This puppet show reveals the sometimes painful and always shameful truth, from the moment Ronald opened his mouth to the time he tried to say something that made sense. 38 mins.
VHS: S16115. $14.98.

A Candle for St. Jude
A Westinghouse Studio One presentation, this program tells the story of a ballet troupe in conflict. The prima ballerina is forcing Hilda to change her ballet. Choreography by Ruthanna Boris with Lili Darvas and Tanaquil LeClerq in the cast. Betty Furness hosts the program which is missing its opening and first commercial. USA, 1952, 56 mins.
VHS: S03657. $24.95.

Car 54: Where Are You?
The cult 60's television series, collected in two-episode packs which follow the original air dates.
Car 54: Volume 1. Contains *Who's for Swordfish?* and *Something Nice for Sol*. 50 mins.
VHS: S12126. $14.95.
Car 54: Volume 2. Contains *Home Sweet Sing Sing* and *Change Your Partner*. 50 mins.
VHS: S12127. $14.95.
Car 54: Volume 3. Contains *I Won't Go* and *Muldoon's Star*. 50 mins.
VHS: S12128. $14.95.
Car 54: Volume 4. Contains *Paint Job* and *Love Finds Muldoon*. 50 mins.
VHS: S12129. $14.95.
Car 54 Pre-Pack. Volumes 1-4 of *Car 54* at a special price.
VHS: S12130. $59.98.

Charles Kuralt: American Heritage
From Charles Kuralt's essay on Americana, *On the Road*, this program uses the openness and expanse of the road to look at the evolution of American traditions, culture and society from colonial settlers to the rugged individualists of the Wild West. 60 mins.
VHS: S19320. $19.98.

Charles Kuralt: Seasons of America
Collected from journalist Charles Kuralt's provocative *On the Road* series, this work looks at the year-long celebration of American spectacle and insight, of small-town festivals and social and community traditions. 60 mins.
VHS: S19321. $19.98.

Charles Kuralt: Unforgettable People
A portrait of eccentric and inspiring people discovered by journalist Charles Kuralt on his *On the Road* program. 55 mins.
VHS: S19319. $19.98.

Charlie's Angels
The big hair, bright teeth and bitchin' bods of that trio of gorgeous gal detectives known as *Charlie's Angels* return in this high-styling '70s series starring Kate Jackson, Farrah Fawcett-Majors and Jaclyn Smith.
Charlie's Angels—Angels in Chains. Two episodes. In *Angels in Chains* the Angels infiltrate a corrupt prison and are forced to join guest star Kim Basinger in the warden's bordello. In *Blue Angels*, the Angels rub a crooked cop the wrong way when they go undercover in a massage parlour. Dirk Benedict stars. 98 mins.
VHS: S32378. $9.95.
Charlie's Angels—Angels Under Covers. Two episodes. In *To Kill an Angel*, a trip to the carnival leads to a tunnel of horrors when Kelly gets caught in the crossfire between two paid killers and an autistic child. In *Night of the Strangler*, the Angels go undercover as fashion models while investigating a kinky case of multiple murders. 101 mins.
VHS: S32379. $9.95.

Cheyenne: The Iron Trail
Clint Walker stars as the cryptic drifter. *The Iron Trail* features Dennis Hopper as a ruthless outlaw planning a daring assassination attempt of President Ulysses S. Grant. 1957, 60 mins.
VHS: S16281. $14.98.

Cheyenne: White Warrior
Michael Landon guest starred in this episode of the '50s television western as a white youth brought up by Commanches who becomes the bargaining chip between Apache warriors and the wagon master Cheyene Bodie. 1958, 60 mins.
VHS: S16282. $14.98.

Chicago Television
A look at the world of live TV in Chicago through clips from Svengoolie, Kukla, Fran and Ollie, Dick Tracy Show, Chicago Cubs, White Sox, Bulls and Blackhawks, complete episodes from Frosty the Snowman to the Mighty Hercules and sights of Chicago including Riverview and the Beatles at Comiskey Park. 120 mins.
VHS: S26083. $29.95.

China Beach

The pilot episode for the popular TV dramatic series about medical care, music and moral dilemma in Southeast Asia. Emmy winning Dana Delaney as McMurphy leads a well chosen cast in this opening barrage of nostalgia that features Nan Woods, Michael Boatman, Robert Riccardo, Brian Wimmer and Chloe Webb. Written and produced by John Sacret Young.
VHS: S12859. $19.98.
Rod Holcomb, USA, 1988, 95 mins.

A Concert in Pantomime

An extremely rare performance featuring Red Skelton and Marcel Marceau. USA, 60 mins.
VHS: S15225. $19.95.

A Conversation with George Burns

An interview with George Burns, conducted by Monty Hall, that traces his Jewish roots and expounds on his philosophy. With selected clips from the Burns and Allen routine that made his reputation. 27 mins.
VHS: S17930. $29.95.

Cracker: To Be a Somebody

Robbie Coltrane stars as Dr. Eddie Fitzgerald, a combatative and enigmatic forensic psychologist who has a nose for crime solving. In this first of the series, an Asian shopkeeper is killed in an apparently racist attack. The killer breaks the pattern however, when one of the investigative team is murdered. Finally the police turn to Fitz for help. 150 mins.
VHS: S26665. $19.95.

Crosscurrents and C-Man

Two classic episodes from the 1950's are presented as prime examples of television film noir. First up, from *Crosscurrents*, is "The Case of the Forged Passports." Agent Christopher Storm (Gerald Mohr) battles beauties and shady characters in Vienna as he searches for stolen printing plates which are being used to produce forged American passports. Written and directed by Sheldon Reynolds. In the *C-Man* episode, "The Case of the Perfect Gentleman," a nightclub owner gets mixed up with a couple of gangsters, federal agents, the IRS and two women. Written and directed by Robert Sloane.
VHS: S13503. $24.95.

Dark Shadows 1: The Resurrection of Barnabas Collins

The popular Gothic TV show is now on video. The first collection includes the first year prelude and then episodes 1-5 of the saga of TV's favorite daytime drama vampire. In the New England community of Collinsport, a courtly bloodsucker really livens up the town. With Jonathan Frid, Joan Bennett, Lara Parker, Grayson Hall and John Carlen. 120 mins.
VHS: S10992. $29.95.

Dark Shadows 2: Three-Pack

The saga of the Collins family continues with episodes 6-20 in this three-pack set of home video gothic drama. Jonathan Frid stars as the tormented vampire revived two hundred years after falling ill to a witch's curse. With Lara Parker as the devilish Angelique. 360 mins.
VHS: S10993. $79.95.

Dark Shadows, Volumes 5-8

Twenty complete episodes from the late 1960's (five episodes per videocassette). Though susceptible to Barnabas' powers, Maggie becomes aware of Barnabas' vampirism and devises a plan to drive a stake through his heart.
VHS: S12694. $79.98.

Dark Shadows, Volumes 9-12

The plot begins to thicken. Maggie Evans has disappeared. Barnabas, still looking for a new lover, sets his evil eye on a new beauty, Victoria Winter. Twenty episodes.
VHS: S12695. $79.98.

Dark Shadows, Volumes 13-16

Twenty complete episodes from the original series, five episodes per volume.
VHS: S12696. $79.98.

Dark Shadows, Volumes 17-20

David Collins begins to understand his family secrets. Twenty episodes.
VHS: S12697. $79.98.

Dark Shadows, Volumes 25-28

Barnabas is determined to make Victoria his bride, and he enslaves Carolyn to assist him in his romantic plan. Volume 28 includes a flashback sequence; drama takes place in 1795. Twenty episodes.
VHS: S12698. $79.98.

Dark Shadows, Volumes 29-32

The 1795 flashback continues. Vicki is transported back to 1795, where she meets 18th century Collins family members. The 1795 Collinses are puzzled by Vicki's strange behavior and clothing. A youthful and human Barnabas Collins anxiously awaits his marriage to Josette DuPres. Josette's maidservant Angelique wants Barnabas for herself, and is determined to destroy Barnabas' and Josette's relationship through her black magic. 4 individually packaged tapes. Available only as a four-pack.
VHS: S12525. $79.98.

Dark Shadows, Volumes 45-48

The 1795 flashback continues. Victoria Winters is led to the gallows, convicted of witchcraft. After the noose is placed around her neck, she mysteriously reappears at Collinwood in the 20th century. 4 individually packaged tapes.
VHS: S13279. $79.98.

Dark Shadows, Volumes 49-52

Roger Collins marries a beautiful young lady named Cassandra, who is really Angelique in disguise. Julia Hoffman and Dr. Lang experiment to find a permanent cure for Barnabas' vampirism. Cassandra, however, is determined to make Barnabas a creature of the night once more, and she initiates a dream curse that affects everyone at Collinwood. Four individually packaged tapes in the set; five episodes per tape. 105 mins. each cassette.
VHS: S13533. $79.98.

Dark Shadows, Volumes 53-56

Hoping to free himself and the entire Collins family of Angelique's evil schemes, Barnabas Collins hires artist Sam Evans to age Angelique's portrait, causing her to turn into a 200-year-old woman. The man-made creature Adam kidnaps Carolyn Stoddard and hides her in an abandoned farm cellar. Willie Loomis becomes the next victim of Angelique's evil dream curse. The vengeful ghost of Reverend Trask appears at the Old House and bricks up the now-human Barnabas inside the basement wall to die. Four individually packaged tapes in the set; five episodes per tape. 105 mins. each cassette.
VHS: S13567. $79.98.

Dark Shadows, Volumes 57-60

Reverend Trask's ghost captures Cassandra Collins (alias Angelique) and tries to destroy her through an exorcism. Barnabas Collins fears Angelique will return and again curse him as a vampire. Warlock Nicholas Blair arrives at Collinwood, claiming to be Cassandra's brother. Through black magic he returns Angelique to Collinwood in the guise of Cassandra. Professor Stokes warns Victoria Winters that she is the next intended victim of the dream curse. He befriends Adam and learns of the man-made creature's hatred of Barnabas. Four individually packaged tapes in the set; five episodes per tape. 105 mins. each cassette.
VHS: S13536. $79.98.

Dark Shadows, Volumes 61-64

Fearing for Victoria Winter's safety, Barnabas Collins forces Vicki to reveal her nightmare resulting from Angelique's frightening dream curse. Warlock Nicholas Blair causes Angelique to age and vows to destroy her unless she returns the vampire curse to Barnabas. Angelique learns of the mysterious link between Barnabas and Adam. Four individually packaged tapes in the set, with five *Dark Shadows* episodes per tape. 105 mins. per tape.
VHS: S13681. $79.98.

Dark Shadows, Volumes 65-68

Warlock Nicholas Blair brings Angelique back from the dead as a vampire. After handyman Tom Jennings' death, Barnabas and Julia Hoffman seek the identity of the vampire responsible for his demise. Barnabas discovers fang marks on Julia's neck and realizes she is a victim of Tom, who has now risen as one of the living dead. 4 individually packaged tapes. 5 episodes per tape (105 mins. each tape).
VHS: S13840. $79.98.

Dark Shadows, Volumes 69-72

While being held captive in the mausoleum secret room, Maggie begins to remember how Barnabas kidnapped her months before and attempted to turn her into his vampire bride.... Four individually packaged tapes. Five *Dark Shadows* episodes per tape.
VHS: S14475. $79.98.

Dark Shadows, Volumes 73-76

Barnabas Collins and Julia Hoffman succeed in creating Eve, a mate for the man-made Adam, unaware they have reincarnated Danielle Roget, one of the 18th century's most evil women.... Four individually packaged tapes. Five *Dark Shadows* episodes per tape.
VHS: S14474. $79.98.

Dark Shadows, Volumes 81-84

After David and Amy discover Quentin's skeleton in a sealed-off room, the ghosts of Quentin and Beth Chavez appear to the children.... Four individually packaged tapes. Five *Dark Shadows* episodes per tape.
VHS: S14613. $79.98.

Dark Shadows, Volumes 85-88

Barnabas Collins summons the ghost of Peter Bradford to help Barnabas travel back to the 18th century in an attempt to prevent Victoria Winters from hanging as a witch.... Four individually packaged tapes. Five *Dark Shadows* episodes per tape. (105 mins. each tape)
VHS: S14980. $79.95.

Dark Shadows, Volumes 89-92

The mysterious ghost of Beth Chavez leads Chris Jennings to the unmarked grave of a child. Barnabas Collins and Chris discover a pentagram inside the child's coffin. As the ghost of Quentin Collins furthers his control of David Collins and Amy Jennings, the residents at Collinwood realize that the children are possessed by an evil spirit.... 4 videocassettes; 5 episodes per tape.
VHS: S14946. $79.95.

Dark Shadows, Volumes 93-96

In the year 1897, Barnabas finds himself a vampire once again as he is trapped inside his chained coffin after being unexpectedly transported back in time from the 20th century.... 4 individually packaged videos. 5 episodes per tape. Complete set only.
VHS: S15097. $79.98.

Dark Shadows, Volumes 97-100

In 1897, the insane Jenny Collins escapes from the tower room at Collinwood. Barnabas Collins is shocked to find Angelique, who advises him to return to the 20th century.... 4 individually packaged tapes. 5 episodes per tape. Complete set only.
VHS: S15270. $79.98.

Dark Shadows, Volumes 101-104

Quentin Collins and Magda the gypsy discover the mysterious urn which contains the flames of life for Laura Collins, who is a creature of the supernatural—an immortal Phoenix.... 4 individually packaged tapes; 5 episodes per tape (105 mins. each).
VHS: S15608. $79.98.

Dark Shadows, Volumes 105-108

The 1897 flashback continues with Barnabas, Quentin and the rest of the inhabitants of Collinwood. Four individually packaged tapes, five episodes per tape. 420 minutes.
VHS: S15870. $79.98.

Dark Shadows, Volumes 109-112

The Collins family discovers that Barnabas is a vampire as the 1897 flashback continues. Four individually packaged tapes, five episodes per tape. 420 mins.
VHS: S15888. $79.98.

Dark Shadows, Volumes 117-120

Julia travels back in time to 1897, and attempts to save Barnabas, who has been trapped in a basement cell in Collinwood. Four individually packaged cassettes, five episodes per tape. 420 mins.
VHS: S16530. $79.98.

Dark Shadows, Volumes 121-124

The 1897 flashback continues as Barnabas meets the reincarnation of Josette. Four individually packaged cassettes, five episodes per tape. 420 mins.
VHS: S16793. $79.98.

Dark Shadows: Behind the Scenes

This is a complete history of the legendary Gothic drama, tracing its beginnings, development into a national phenomenon, and its vibrant cult afterlife. A must-see for fans. 60 mins.
VHS: S15520. $19.98.

Dark Shadows: Music Videos

This specially compiled videocassette features musical highlights from the original soundtrack of *Dark Shadows* combined with memorable scenes from the classic series. Includes "Quentin's Theme"! 40 mins.
VHS: S15519. $19.98.

Dark Shadows: Vampires & Ghosts

This chilling compilation from the macabre daytime series brings the most frightening moments of that series together on one videotape. Barnabas Collins the vampire and other dark shadows from the Collinwood mansion are featured. 60 mins.
VHS: S26802. $19.98.

Dave Garroway's Wide Wide World

A special show from the '50s taped at Gene Autry's Melody Ranch. With John Wayne, Gary Cooper, Clayton Moore, John Ford and many more stars of the Hollywood Western. 75 mins.
VHS: S15697. $29.95.

Day One

A superb television docudrama about the personalities, history, politics and dramatic momentum of how the Manhattan Project—the American project to build the first atomic bomb-ended with the dropping of two bombs on Japan. The drama concentrates on the uneasy collaboration between Gen. Leslie R. Groves (Brian Dennehy), the nuts-and-bolts military commander who orchestrated the massive project, and visionary scientist J. Robert Oppenheimer (John Sayles regular David Stathairn). With Michael Tucker, Hume Cronyn, Richard Dysart, Barnard Hughes, Hal Holbrook and David Ogden Stiers.
VHS: S20285. $89.95.
Joseph Sargent, USA, 1989, 150 mins.

Daytime's Greatest Weddings: All My Children

Susan Lucci, known to millions as the complex and disturbing Erica Kane, hosts this collection of video memories that feature Pine Valley's most romantic couples. Of course, Erica Kane's own unforgettable marital merry-go-round is also featured. 45 mins.
VHS: S22548. $14.98.

Daytime's Greatest Weddings: General Hospital

This collection of nuptial bliss contains the most historic wedding from daytime television, the wedding of Luke and Laura. Their union even made the cover of Newsweek. Jackie Zeman and Brad Maule (Bobby and Tony Jones) act as hosts.
VHS: S22549. $14.98.

Daytime's Most Wanted

ABC's soap operas employ dynamic leading men who romance women for a living, at least on screen. In this video their personal lives are revealed as something completely different. Historical footage also shows the rich romantic evolution of these charismatic screen figures.
VHS: S22546. $14.98.

The Defender

Steve McQueen, Ralph Bellamy, William Shatner and Martin Balsam star in the pilot of this controversial TV series. These original live television broadcasts from 1957 pit attorney Bellamy, who is convinced his client McQueen is guilty, against his own son (Shatner), who believes him innocent. 112 mins.
VHS: S13431. $19.95.

Dennis the Movie Star

Now Dennis is menacing the movies in a hilarious collection of movie exclusives from the top-rated, animated TV series.
VHS: S10753. $19.98.

The Ed Sullivan Show

This two-tape set features performance highlights from some of Ed's best, "really big *shoos*," including Elvis Presley, The Beatles, The Rolling Stones, Louis Armstrong, Ella Fitzgerald, Judy Garland, The Supremes, The Jackson 5, The Beach Boys, The Doors, Lucille Ball and Desi Arnaz, Carol Burnett, Jackie Gleason, and of course, Topo Gigio. With new and never-before-seen footage and interviews. Each tape is 105 mins.
VHS: S31772. $34.95.

Edward R. Murrow: The Best of Person to Person

This video culls together the best of intimate, freewheeling conversations of legendary journalist Edward R. Murrow, with President and Mrs. Kennedy, Frank Sinatra, Marilyn Monroe and Marlon Brando. 90 mins.
VHS: S19318. $19.98.

Errol Flynn Theatre

Legendary screen swashbuckler Errol Flynn presents three episodes from his 1956-1957 television series. Besides acting as host, Flynn stars in two of the stories, while the third is a chilling tale of the supernatural. In "The Duel" Flynn is a villainous swordsman. In "The Strange Auction" Flynn co-stars with his wife, Patrice Wymore, and son, Sean Flynn; Patrice buys Errol at an auction. And in "The Sealed Room" a young lady is possessed by the spirit of a dead woman.
VHS: S13426. $29.95.

The Far Pavilions

Ben Cross and Amy Irving star in an eventful love story set against the backdrop of India during the British Raj. Treachery, intrigue and spectacular battles litter the landscape of this epic series based on M.M. Kaye's best-selling novel. Christopher Lee, Omar Sharif, Rossano Brazzi and Sir John Gielgud are featured.
4-tape boxed set, 320 mins.
VHS: S27397. $89.95.

First Draw Gift Set

The high point of American television westerns is presented in this impressive collection of *Gunsmoke, Rawhide* and *Wild, Wild West*.
VHS: S19101. $39.98.

Fishing Trip: I Love Lucy: Deep Sea Fishing and The Honeymooners: Something Fishy

A pair of hilarious fishing expeditions as two of TV's big clowns try to get the big one. 60 mins.
VHS: S12348. $14.98.

Flowers from a Stranger

Yul Brynner and Felicia Montealegre star in this 1949 Westinghouse Studio One production. 60 mins.
VHS: S32146. $24.95.

Ford Star Jubilee

Noel Coward and Mary Martin star in this live television production of *Together with Music*.
VHS: S10597. $29.95.

Ford Star Jubilee Salute to Cole Porter

A record of the live television salute to Cole Porter, featuring Louis Armstrong, Gordon MacRae, Shirley Jones and Bing Crosby, among others.
VHS: S10598. $29.95.

Four Star Playhouse

This classic television dramatic series was produced by the "Four Stars" who owned the company: Dick Powell, David Niven, Charles Boyer, and Ida Lupino. All of Hollywood's greatest stars appeared on this program, one of the best of television's *Golden Age*.

Volume 1: *The Test* stars Dick Powell and Francis Rafferty; *The Interlude*, Dick Powell and Joanne Woodward.
VHS: S09535. $29.95.

Volume 2: *The Lost Silk Hat* stars Ronald Colman; *Welcome Home*, Dick Powell and David Hart.
VHS: S09536. $29.95.

Volume 3: *The Listener* stars Ida Lupino and Richard Lupono; *The Devil to Pay* features Charles Boyer and Mary Field.
VHS: S09537. $29.95.

Volume 4: *Vote of Confidence* features David Niven, Amanda Blake and Chuck Connors; *Tusitala*, David Niven portraying Robert Louis Stevenson.
VHS: S09538. $29.95.

Volume 5: *Girl on the Bridge* features Dick Powell and Coleen Gray; *The Gift* is with Charles Boyer and Maureen O'Sullivan.
VHS: S09539. $29.95.

Volume 6: *Shadowed* stars Dick Powell and Francis Dee; Dick Powell and Barbara Billingsley are featured in *The Gun*.
VHS: S09540. $29.95.

Volume 7: *Girl on the Park Bench* stars Joan Fontaine with Craig Stevens; *A Place of His Own*, Charles Boyer and Stacy Harris.
VHS: S09541. $29.95.

Volume 8: *The Adolescent* stars Ida Lupino and Hugh Beaumont; *The Bomb* features David Niven and Margaret Sullavan.
VHS: S09542. $29.95.

Volume 9: *The Bad Streak* features Charles Boyer and Virginia Grey; Beverly Garland and David Niven are in *Touch and Go*.
VHS: S09543. $29.95.

Volume 10: Ida Lupino and George Macready are featured in *House for Sale*; Dick Powell stars in *To Die at Midnight*.
VHS: S09544. $29.95.

Volume 11: Dick Powell and Regis Toomey star in *The Squeeze*; Dick Powell and Dick Foran are in *Detective's Holiday*.
VHS: S09545. $29.95.

Volume 12: Dick Powell and Frances Bergen star in *High Stakes*; Dick Powell, Regis Toomey and Alan Mowbray are featured in *The Stacked Deck*.
VHS: S09546. $29.95.

The Fugitive

The television show starring David Janssen as a doctor falsely charged with killing his wife, who escapes police custody and relentlessly pursues a one-armed man responsible for the act. One of the hallmarks of television, this collection includes the famous final episode.

Brass Ring/In a Plain Paper Wrapper.
VHS: S17584. $24.95.

Cry Uncle/Flight from the Final Demon.
VHS: S17582. $24.95.

First Episode/Fear in a Desert City.
VHS: S17578. $24.95.

Nemesis/World's End.
VHS: S17581. $24.95.

Never Wave Goodbye Parts One & Two.
VHS: S17579. $24.95.

Stroke of Genius/Stranger in the Mirror.
VHS: S17583. $24.95.

Terror at High Point/Glass Tightrope.
VHS: S17580. $24.95.

The Judgment Parts One & Two.
VHS: S17585. $24.95.

G.E. Theatre

Ronald Reagan hosts and stars in *The Martyr*, a story of civil war in 1923 Ireland.
VHS: S10595. $29.95.

George Washington: The Forging of a Nation

In this sequel to *George Washington*, Barry Bostwick and Patty Duke Astin reprise their roles as Mr. and Mrs. George Washington. Washington's career was based on political acumen and charisma. In this film the story of this historic figure continues.
VHS: S20640. $29.98.
William A. Graham, USA, 1986, 190 mins.

Gidget

It's fun in the California sun with six episodes from the classic '60s comedy starring teenaged Sally Field as an adorable surfer girl.

Gidget—Beach Blanket Gidget. In *Dear Diary—Et Al*, the series pilot, Gidget's sister reads her diary and assumes Gidget's highly imaginative confessions are true; in *Is It Love or Symbiosis?*, Gidget's meddling big sister and brother-in-law convince her father that he should send Gidget away to a private girl's school in Paris; in *I Love You, I Think*, while Jeff is way at Princeton, Gidget dedicates herself to a life of loneliness, until she meets a tall, dark and handsome surfer. 78 mins.
VHS: S32381. $9.95.

Gidget-a-Go-Go!. In *My Ever Faithful Friend*, Gidget gives her best friend, LaRue, a makeover, then is outraged when LaRue seems to attract an older, more sophisticated admirer, Gidget's Dad; in *Ego-a-Go-Go*, Gidget's convinced that one date with her will transform "Derf the Nerf" into a big man on campus, but a little boost to the male ego goes a long way, as guest star Richard Dreyfuss proves; and in *The In and Out with the In-Laws*, when Gidget's boyfriend Jeff casually mentions that he wants her to meet his parents, Gidget hears wedding bells—and alarm bells. 75 mins.
VHS: S32380. $9.95.

Golden T.V. Memories of the 50's, Volume 1

A mishmash of programming from the 50's including dramas, westerns, comedy, talent and more. Includes Abbott and Costello, Jack Benny, Ed Wynn and excerpts from *Space Ranger, Fu Manchu and Arthur Godfrey.* 60 mins.
VHS: S13161. $19.98.

Golden T.V. Memories of the 50's, Volume 2

Includes Groucho Marx, Edward R. Murrow, Jack Lemmon, excerpts from *Robin Hood, Scarlet Pimpernel, Life with Luigi*, and more. 60 mins.
VHS: S13162. $19.98.

Golden T.V. Memories of the 50's, Volume 3

Includes Robert Shaw, Buster Crabbe, Alan Hale Jr., excerpts from *Howdy Doody, Winky Dink and Me, The Cisco Kid, Biff Baker U.S.A.*, and more. 60 mins.
VHS: S13163. $19.98.

Golf Classic: I Love Lucy: The Golf Game and The Honeymooners: The Golfer

Comedy that's way above par. Riotous "fore" play as TV's two top clowns try to get in the swing of things.
VHS: S12349. $14.98.

Good Night and Good Luck: The Edward R. Murrow Television Collection

Arguably the greatest journalist in the history of American media, Edward R. Murrow traces the social, political and personal tensions in post-war American life, in *The Best of Person to Person, The Best of See It Now, The McCarthy Years* and *Harvest of Shame*.
VHS: S19099. $69.98.

The Grace Kelly Story

Cheryl Ladd is the young star who becomes a princess. Lloyd Bridges and Diane Ladd are also featured in this dramatic version of the fairy tale life that captivated the entire world. 104 mins.
VHS: S25755. $19.95.

Harvest

James Dean, Dorothy Gish and Ed Begley star in this tragic story of a small town family and the hopes they pin on the coming harvest. From *The James Dean Collection*.
VHS: S27329. $19.95.
James Sheldon, USA, 1953, 53 mins.

Henry IV

Richard Purdy and Berry Kroeger star in this 1949 Westinghouse Studio One production. 60 mins.
VHS: S32145. $24.95.

Highlander: The Animated Series, The History Lesson

Two more new episodes, *The Cursed* and *The History Lesson*, follow the adventures of Quentin MacLeod in his epic pursuit of lost human knowledge. 44 mins.
VHS: S29480. $9.95.

Highlander: The Animated Series, The Suspended Village

Quentin MacLeod, the last Highlander, battled Lord Kortan for the lost knowledge of mankind in the original feature-length animated film. This video contains two new episodes from this ongoing mythic battle, *The Suspended Village* and *Exodus*. 44 mins.
VHS: S29479. $9.95.

Highlander: The Animated Series, The Valley of Thorn Pods

The Valley of Thorn Pods and *Fall Out* find Quentin MacLeod, the last Highlander, engaged in continuing struggles on behalf of mankind. 44 mins.
VHS: S29481. $9.95.

Hill Number One

A story of faith and inspiration. Originally broadcast on Easter Sunday in 1951, the enlightening program, about Christ's Passion, is as inspirational today as it was 40 years ago. Starring James Dean, Leif Erickson and Roddy McDowall. 57 mins.
VHS: S14091. $19.95.

The Honeymooners Hidden Episodes

Total mayhem starring Ralph Kramden, in these never-released episodes of *The Honeymooners* from the Fifties. Jackie Gleason, Art Carney, Audrey Meadows and Joyce Randolph star. Collect them all! 55 minutes each.
Volume 1: "Letter to the Boss," "Suspense," and "Dinner Guest".
VHS: S02853. $29.95.
Volume 10: "Cupid" and "Manager of a Baseball Team".
VHS: S02869. $29.95.
Volume 9: "Ralph's Sweet Tooth," "Cold," and "Pickles".
VHS: S08903. $29.95.
Volume 8: "My Fair Landlord" and "Income Tax".
VHS: S08905. $29.95.
Volume 7: "The Little Man Who Wasn't There" and "Goodnight Sweet Prince".
VHS: S08906. $29.95.
Volume 6: "Move Uptown" and "Lucky Number".
VHS: S08908. $29.95.
Volume 5: "The Next Champ" and "Expectant Father".
VHS: S08910. $29.95.
Volume 4: "New Year's Eve Party" and "Two-Family Car".
VHS: S08912. $29.95.
Volume 3: "Christmas Party" and "Forgot to Register".
VHS: S08914. $29.95.
Volume 2: "Songs and Witty Sayings" and "Norton Moves In".
VHS: S08915. $29.95.

The Honeymooners Lost Episodes

Celebrate the 40th Anniversary of the now legendary television comedy with the release of these remaining lost episodes. Volume 26. *Boxtop Kid*. Ralph becomes obsessed with entering contests after Alice's sister and brother-in-law win a trip to Europe. *Halloween Party for the Boss*. Ralph assumes that a party being thrown for his boss on Halloween is a costume party in this remake of an earlier skit. 1954, 50 mins.
VHS: S15885. $19.98.
Volume 27. *The People's Choice*. A pair of crooked politicians hand-pick Ralph as their candidate for a local election after he helps capture a notorious killer. *What's the Name*. Ralph and Alice sing in this skit about an actress' name that eludes the Kramdens and Nortons. The song "One of These Days" is featured in this remake of an earlier episode. 1954, 50 mins.
VHS: S15886. $19.98.
Volume 28. *Hero*. Ralph convinces a new kid in the building that he was a star athlete in school. *Manager of the Baseball Team*. Ralph thinks he's going to be manager of the bus company, but his boss has other ideas in this remake of a 1953 episode. 1955/1957, 50 mins.
VHS: S15887. $19.98.

The Honeymooners Lost Episodes: 12-Volume Set

This boxed set comprises 22 *Honeymooners* skits, in their uncut and original format, compiled on 11 cassettes. Also included is a bonus cassette, *History of the Lost Episodes: The First Season*, which examines the development of the characters Ralph, Alice, Ed and Trixie, starting with the earliest *Honeymooners* skits. B&W, approximately 10 hours.
VHS: S26531. $129.98.

The Honeymooners Valentine's Special

The Honeymooners make love, not war, in some of the most hilarious romantic scenes and sketches of Brooklyn's famous foursome. 30 mins.
VHS: S09806. $14.95.

The Honeymooners—Honeybloopers!

See the Great One's most riotous on-the-air mishaps—classic foul-ups, props that wouldn't work, scenery that falls down. 52 mins.
VHS: S11126. $19.95.

The Honeymooners: The Best of the Lost Episodes

Two years of the finest work of this groundbreaking, stylistically daring comedy that used a stripped down, psychologically dense naturalism to convey class, social and sexual tensions and make trenchant comments about the American dream is distilled into this single tape. These are works that were unearthed in Jackie Gleason's basement. The frenetic pace, existential wit and comic edge are on view. 30 mins.
VHS: S18597. $14.98.

I Love Lucy

Classic episodes which helped establish Lucy as the First Lady of Television.
I Love Lucy Volume 5. The love affair with Lucy continues with two episodes: *Lucy and Bob Hope* in which Lucy dons disguises to get Bob Hope to appear at the Club Babalu, and *Lucy and Superman* in which only the Man of Steel can save Lucy from the jam she's in. 53 mins.
VHS: S11266. $14.98.
I Love Lucy Volume 6. *Pioneer Women* features Lucy and Ethel as a bet leaves them without modern appliances and the apartment in shambles, and in *The Camping Trip*, Lucy and Ricky scheme against each other. 53 mins.
VHS: S11267. $14.98.
I Love Lucy Volume 7. An old washing machine comes between the Ricardos and the Mertzes in *Never Do Business with Friends* and a pair of trashed TV's gives the Ricardos and Mertzes their day in court— against each other—in *The Courtroom*. 53 mins.
VHS: S11268. $14.98.
I Love Lucy Volume 8. A botched magic trick makes Lucy and Ricky a hilariously inseparable couple in *The Handcuffs*, and a shot at show biz puts stars in Lucy's eyes and pie in Ricky's face in *The Ballet*. 53 mins.
VHS: S11269. $14.98.

I Love Lucy

This 90-minute compilation features the best of the *I Love Lucy* show from 1951 to 1952.
Laser: LD70121. $49.95.

I Love Lucy's Zany Road Trip

Struck from the original 35mm prints, this pristine collection of 27 *I Love Lucy* episodes features all of the "California Trip," taking the gang through Tennessee and New Mexico on their way to L.A. Almost 20 shows direct from La La Land feature an abundance of cameos, including John Wayne, Rock Hudson and Harpo Marx among many others. In two specially boxed volumes, with a collectible poster map of their trip inserted with Part 1.
I Love Lucy's Zany Road Trip, Part 1. 360 mins.
VHS: S15980. $49.98.
I Love Lucy's Zany Road Trip, Part 2. 330 mins.
VHS: S15981. $49.98.

I Love Lucy: Adventures in Europe

Seventeen episodes from the classic American sitcom have been seamlessly edited together, providing a marathon of viewing pleasure. Lucy, Ricky, Ethel and Fred inspire laughter throughout. This whirlwind tour follows the entire gang on vacation in Europe. 6½ hours are included on three tapes.
VHS: S21713. $69.98.

I Love Lucy: The Classics

Three classic Lucy favorites, two episodes per tape.
I Love Lucy: The Classics—Job Switching/Lucy Meets Bob Hope.
VHS: S33729. $9.95.
I Love Lucy: The Classics—Lucy and Harpo/Lucy Meets John Wayne.
VHS: S33728. $9.95.
I Love Lucy: The Classics—Lucy Meets Superman/ The Freezer.
VHS: S33727. $9.95.

I Love Lucy: The Very First Show

This pilot revolutionized the nascent television industry when it first appeared. Ever since, the succeeding episodes of this American original have never missed a broadcast day. Lucy and Ricky, not to mention Fred and Ethel, are part of TV history. 45 mins.
VHS: S21007. $12.98.

I Want My MTV

Among the most creative of MTV segments are the quick promos that use everything from live action spots featuring stars like Denis Leary, to the most imaginative, cutting edge animation. They are grouped on this tape so that now you can see favorites like Jimmy the Cab Driver, Toby (the Frank Sinatra impersonator) or Randee of the Redwoods any time. 45 mins.
VHS: S26305. $12.98.

I'm a Fool and The Wild Bunch

Ronald Reagan hosts *I'm a Fool* (26 mins.), a television production based on a Sherwood Anderson short story and starring James Dean, Natalie Wood and Eddie Albert. James Dean is a poor, young stable boy who lies about his position in life to impress Natalie Wood. When he realizes his lie will prevent her from ever being able to find him again he tries to recant, but it's too late. *The Wild Bunch* (31 mins.) stars Natalie Wood and Charles Boyer in a familial comedy of errors. When newlywed George Burrel (Boyer) is left alone with his wife's three teenage children, he's in for a crash course in parenting. Luckily, eldest daughter Louise (Wood) shows him that his love and guidance are both needed and appreciated. From *The James Dean Collection*.
VHS: S27330. $19.95.
Don Medford/William A. Seiter, USA, 1953-1955, 57 mins.

It's Hullabaloo!

Shows of the popular music show from 1965-66 are collected in this set of four volumes. Famous guest hosts like Frankie Avalon, Annette, Soupy Sales and Petula Clark will inspire uncontrollable outbreaks of nostalgia. But it's music from The Shangri-Las, Marianne Faithfull, Brenda Lee, The Rolling Stones, The Supremes, Lola Falana, The Everly Brothers and more that make this collection so worthwhile. Each video is approximately 60 mins.
VHS: S27638. $79.98.

Jack Benny Program

The funniest man who ever lived in Waukegan, Illinois, is remembered in this one hour, two episode B&W presentation from 1958. Joining Jack are Eddie "Rochester" Anderson, Don Wilson and Mel Blanc. If you are lucky Jack might also play his violin. USA, 1958, 60 mins.
VHS: S07801. $29.95.

The Jack Benny Program

Jack Benny was on television from the very beginning. His live variety show presented the perfect showcase for his comedic ability as well as the diverse talents of his assorted guests, many of whom were also legendary stars of film and television. This five-volume set joins some of his most memorable programs together for the first time.

1: Johnny Carson Guests/Jack Takes Boat to Hawaii. The *Tonight Show*'s Johnny Carson went on to become television's most famous late night television talk show host. In this installment of *The Jack Benny Program* Carson's youthful zany persona is seen at a crucial stage of development, while Jack is off to Hawaii in this famous comic take-off on the perils of travel. 60 mins.
VHS: S20842. $14.98.
2: The Peter Lorre—Joanie Sommers Show/The Smothers Brothers Show. Acclaimed entertainers Peter Lorre and Joanie Sommers star in this edition of the *The Jack Benny Program*, giving them a chance to showcase their comic abilities. The Smothers Brothers developed their own successful career in variety television after their appearance with Jack Benny. 60 mins.
VHS: S20843. $14.98.
3: The Income Tax Show/Jack Adopts a Son. Jack Benny spoofs the common man's gravest bane—income tax—and its hand servant, the tax man. Then he tackles the difficulties of adoption and the prospect of proving his suitability for fatherhood. 60 mins.
VHS: S20844. $14.98.
4: Jack on Trial for Murder/Jack Plays Tarzan. Jack Benny lampoons the legal system, finding laughs in court. When Jack makes fun of that mythic figure Tarzan, the sobriquet "king of the apes" gains unforseen dimensions. 60 mins.
VHS: S20845. $14.98.
5: Jack Is Kidnapped/The Lucille Ball Show. Only Jack Benny could have this much fun when captured and held against his will. Once again his quiet humor sneaks up on his adversaries and takes them completely by surprise. Lucille Ball and Jack Benny combine the best that early television has to offer in this installment of his show. 60 mins.
VHS: S20846. $14.98.

Jane Eyre

A Westinghouse Studio One Summer Theatre production of Charlotte Bronte's classic tale of a young governess in peril. This well-done tv version performed live includes Katharine Bard, Kevin McCarthy and Frances Starr in its distinguished cast. USA, 1952, 59 mins.
VHS: S03658. $24.95.

Johnny Carson: His Favorite Moments

Each tape comprises Johnny Carson's personally chosen moments of the decade, including rarely seen sketch bloopers collected from *The Tonite Show* archives.
60's & 70's: Heeere's Johnny! 52 mins.
VHS: S30603. $14.99.
70's & 80's: The Master of Laughs. 52 mins.
VHS: S30604. $14.99.
80's & 90's: The King of Late Night. 62 mins.
VHS: S30605. $14.99.
The Comedians: "Good Stuff!"—Stand-up Debuts from "The Tonite Show." Features the hilarious *Tonite Show* debuts of superstar comics, including Jerry Seinfeld, Garry Shandling, Roseanne, Drew Carey and others. 50 mins.
VHS: S30602. $14.99.

Judy Garland (General Electric Theatre)

Ronald Reagan hosts a musical half-hour with the talented and tragic Judy Garland. She starts off with "I Feel a Song Coming On" and then proceeds to sing as many as possible, time permitting. Joe Bushkin is on piano and Nelson Riddle and his Orchestra provide the rest of the musical accompaniment. USA, 1956, 30 mins.

VHS: S05516. $19.95.

L.A. Law

The feature length, made-for-tv pilot that introduced most of the characters of the popular tv series about the legal profession in Southern California. It all started with a senior partner found face down dead in a plate of beans. With Corbin Bernsen, Harry Hamlin, Susan Dey, Jill Eikenberry and Michael Tucker. USA, 1986, 100 mins.

VHS: S06534. $79.98.

The Legend of the Beverly Hillbillies

A collection of outtakes and comic highlights from the long-running television program. This tape also features interviews with series regulars Buddy Ebsen, Max Baer Jr. and Donna Douglas. 48 mins.

VHS: S19750. $12.98.

The Life of Riley: The Bendix Episodes

Veteran film star William Bendix takes on network television and the role of the ever-bumbling Chester A. Riley. The four episodes are *Riley Engages an Escort, Riley Executive Type, Riley Steps Out* and *Riley Camps Out*. Hilarious. 90 mins.

VHS: S21900. $14.99.

The Life of Riley: The Gleason Episodes

The TV series which introduced Jackie Gleason as the first Chester A. Riley, blue collar hero. With an incredible supporting cast. The four episodes in this two-volume set are: *Tonsils, Babs and Simon Step Out, Egbert's Chemistry Set* and *The French Professor*. All were originally broadcast in 1949. 90 mins.

VHS: S21899. $14.99.

Little Women

Nancy Marchand stars in this adaptation of Louisa May Alcott's classic tale. Directed by Lela Swift, 60 mins.

VHS: S27334. $19.95.

A Long Time Till Dawn

James Dean, Naomi Riordan and Robert Simon star in the Kraft Television Theatre production of Rod Serling's melodrama *A Long Time Till Dawn*. When juvenile delinquent Joe Harris (Dean) is released from prison, he returns home to find his wife, Barbie (Riordan), has left him. In a heartbroken rage he beats up "Pops," the mutual friend who told her to leave him, then flees New York for his father (Simon) and his small-town boyhood home. From *The James Dean Collection*.

VHS: S27331. $19.95.

Dick Dunlop, USA, 1953, 60 mins.

Lost in Space

The adventures of "the Swiss Family Robinson in Space" aired on TV from 1965-68. Relive the fun and adventure of this sci-fi classic starring Guy Williams, June Lockhart, Angela Cartwright, Billy Mumy and Jonathan Harris. This special selection of shows from the first season includes *The Reluctant Stowaway*, the show's pilot episode, *The Derelict*, and *Island in the Sky*. Three tapes. 156 mins.

VHS: S32642. $24.98.

The Lost Stooges

Just when you thought you've heard every nyuk, woop and Hey, Moe, a collection of rare, unbilled walk-ons by Larry, Moe and Curly in MGM feature films, including The Stooges with Clark Gable, Joan Crawford, Jimmy Durante and Robert Montgomery, and (!) their only appearance in Technicolor. 68 mins.

VHS: S12012. $14.98.

The Lou Gehrig Story—Climax

Wendell Corey stars as the Iron Man of the Yankees in this live tv drama from 1956. Documentary footage is integrated skillfully into the drama of a sportsman struck down by a fatal disease. With Jean Hagen, James Gregory and Harry Carey Jr. *Climax* is sponsored by Chrysler Corp. USA, 1956, 60 mins.

VHS: S05441. $24.95.

Lucy and Desi: A Home Movie

Television's most famous couple, Lucille Ball and Desi Arnaz, reveal their intimate family life in this touching documentary. It is a wonderful romance, told with the help of never-before-seen film clips. Lucie Arnaz, their only daughter, hosts this behind-the-scenes look at two of TV's first superstars. 111 mins.

VHS: S22935. $19.95.

The Man from U.N.C.L.E.

Espionage, Cold War politics and international intrigue defined this superb 60s television series starring Robert Vaughn and David McCallum as the bravura and intellectually daring spies. The show typically attracted leading actors and directors for their involvement. It was set apart by its location shooting, set pieces, writing and production qualities. For the first time, 22 volumes are available on cassette.

The Man from U.N.C.L.E., Vol. 1.
VHS: S17555. $14.98.
The Man from U.N.C.L.E., Vol. 2.
VHS: S17556. $14.98.
The Man from U.N.C.L.E., Vol. 3.
VHS: S17557. $14.98.
The Man from U.N.C.L.E., Vol. 4.
VHS: S17558. $14.98.
The Man from U.N.C.L.E., Vol. 5.
VHS: S17559. $14.98.
The Man from U.N.C.L.E., Vol. 6.
VHS: S17560. $14.98.
The Man from U.N.C.L.E., Vol. 7.
VHS: S17561. $14.98.
The Man from U.N.C.L.E., Vol. 8.
VHS: S17562. $14.98.
The Man from U.N.C.L.E., Vol. 9.
VHS: S17563. $14.98.
The Man from U.N.C.L.E., Vol. 10.
VHS: S17564. $14.98.
The Man from U.N.C.L.E., Vol. 11.
VHS: S17565. $14.98.
The Man from U.N.C.L.E., Vol. 12.
VHS: S17566. $14.98.
The Man from U.N.C.L.E., Vol. 13.
VHS: S17567. $14.98.
The Man from U.N.C.L.E., Vol. 14.
VHS: S17568. $14.98.
The Man from U.N.C.L.E., Vol. 15.
VHS: S17569. $14.98.
The Man from U.N.C.L.E., Vol. 16.
VHS: S17570. $14.98.
The Man from U.N.C.L.E., Vol. 17.
VHS: S17571. $14.98.
The Man from U.N.C.L.E., Vol. 18.
VHS: S17572. $14.98.
The Man from U.N.C.L.E., Vol. 19.
VHS: S17573. $14.98.
The Man from U.N.C.L.E., Vol. 20.
VHS: S17574. $14.98.
The Man from U.N.C.L.E., Vol. 21.
VHS: S17575. $14.98.
The Man from U.N.C.L.E., Vol. 22.
VHS: S17576. $14.98.

Mark of Cain—Westinghouse Studio One

A live tv drama about a young man on parole from Sing Sing who tries to start his life with a clean slate. After seven years in prison his mother and his girlfriend are glad to see him, but his brother is less than warm. With Warren Stevens, Everett Sloane and Mildred Dunnock. USA, 1953, 60 mins.

VHS: S05443. $24.95.

Maverick: Duel at Sundown

Squinting, itchy-trigger badman Clint Eastwood becomes Maverick's rival in romance. This is a glimpse of the stoic grit and wily charm that would become Eastwood's trademark in his later roles. James Garner stars as television's most infamous gambler of the Old West. 1959, 60 mins.

VHS: S16279. $79.95.

Maverick: Shady Deal at Sunny Acres

The con is on when Maverick bamboozles the banker who swindled him. A sparkling crew of rogues and rascals along with his brother all chip in to recover the lost loot. Stars James Garner, Efrem Zimbalist, Jr. and Diane Brewster. 1958, 60 mins.

VHS: S16280. $14.98.

Medusa: Dare to Be Truthful

A dead-on parody of Madonna's 1991 documentary *Truth or Dare*, written and performed by MTV comedian Julie Brown. Brown stars as Medusa, embarking on her *Blonde Leading the Blonde* tour. Featuring the videos "Vague," "Expose Yourself," and "Everybody, Be Excited." With cameos from Bobcat Goldthwait and Chris Elliott.

VHS: S17219. $14.95.

The Mike Douglas Show—John Lennon & Yoko Ono

The week that John Lennon and Yoko Ono hosted the Mike Douglas Show made for five strange days that changed the course of television. Guests included Chuck Berry, George Carlin, Black Panther leader Bobby Seale, consumer advocate Ralph Nader, Frank Gorshin and others. Includes 48-page hardcover book with new and rare interviews and previously unpublished photos. Five-tape box set. Each tape is 75 mins.

VHS: S34257. $99.95.

Milton Berle's Buick Hour Collector's Series

This six-volume, 12-episode set features Uncle Miltie at his comedic best, along with favorite recurring characters. *Volume 1: Broadway/Party Date* starring Frank Sinatra, Tallulah Bankhead, Martha Raye and John Payne; *Volume 2: How to Put on a Show/Art and Culture*, starring Vic Damone, Dagmar, Jackie Cooper and Denise Darcel; *Volume 3: What's My Racket/Sherlock Holmes*, starring Peter Lawford, Carol Channing, Maria Riva, Mickey Spillane and Walter Greaza; *Volume 4: Show Business/Night Club*, starring Robert Cummings, Gertrude Berg, Jane Froman, and Charlie Applewhite; *Volume 5: Music Man/Dragnet Investigation*, starring Judith Anderson, Cyril Ritchard, Georgia Gibbs, and Charlie Applewhite; *Volume 6: Fired/Champ*, starring Kay Thompson, Charlie Applewhite, Steve Allen, Janet Blair and Ezzard Charles. 12 one-hour tapes.

VHS: S34094. $69.99.

The Mod Squad Lost Pilot

The Teeth of the Barracuda was originally aired as a TV movie of the week in 1968. It explains how this trio of hip, young kids were formed into a police unit known as the Mod Squad. 76 mins.

VHS: S26200. $14.98.

The Mod Squad

Peggy Lipton, Michael Cole and Clarence Williams III are the hippest crime fighters from the 1960's. They bridged the generation gap with their up-to-date fashions, including bell bottom pants and hippie-inspired hairdos, but combined them with hard-edged law-and-order ways.

The Mod Squad, Volume 1. *The Teeth of the Barracuda* and *Mother of Sorrow*.
VHS: S26195. $19.99.
The Mod Squad, Volume 2. *Keep the Faith Baby* and *The Comeback*.
VHS: S26196. $19.99.
The Mod Squad, Volume 3. *A Run for the Money* and *To Linc—With Love*.
VHS: S26197. $19.99.
The Mod Squad, Volume 4. *The Guru* and *A Short Course in War*.
VHS: S26198. $19.99.
The Mod Squad, Volume 5. *The Connection (Part One)* and *The Connection (Part Two)*.
VHS: S26199. $19.99.
The Mod Squad Boxed Set—Volumes 1-5.
VHS: S26201. $88.75.

More! Police Squad!

The second collection of three more episodes of the inspired but short-lived tv police comedy. Titles include *Revenge and Remorse, The Butler Did It* and *Testimony of Evil*. Written and co-directed by ZAZ, Jim and David Zucker and pal Jim Abrahams, and starring Leslie Nielsen and Allan North, this is fun for the whole family if your whole family has a sense of humor.

VHS: S08716. $19.95.

David Zucker/Jim Abrahams/Jerry Zucker, USA, 1982, 75 mins.

Muhammad Ali vs. Zora Folley

From Madison Square Garden, a World Heavyweight Bout fought on March 22, 1967. Don Duphy reports the blow-by-blow. Win Elliot supplies the color commentary. Pre-fight training films and interviews are shown, as is a post-fight interview with Ali and his father. USA, 1967, 68 mins.

VHS: S05455. $29.95.

My Man Norton

From the producer-director of *The Great Gleason* comes this tribute to TV cult figure Ed Norton, the sewer worker who climbed out of a manhole and into the living rooms and hearts of millions of viewers. This compilation of some of the funniest routines performed by actor Art Carney on *The Honeymooners* is hosted by Joyce Randolph, who played Norton's wife, Trixie. With Jackie Gleason and Audrey Meadows, also a new Norton music video.

VHS: S08119. $29.95.

Jeff Forrester, USA, 1988, 50 mins.

My Name Is Bill W.

This Emmy Award-winning Hallmark Hall of Fame production stars James Woods as Bill Wilson, a reformed alcoholic. This maverick confounds the local chapter of Alcoholics Anonymous. Also features James Garner.

VHS: S21775. $19.98.

Mystery of the Riverboat

The Mississippi River and the swamps of Louisiana comprise the setting for mystery, murder and plenty of serial-style heroics. An unusually atmospheric and intelligent chapter play starring Robert Lowery, Eddie Quillan and Lyle Talbot. 13 episodes on two cassettes.
VHS: S13015. $24.95.

Mystery Science Theater 3000

Yuk it up with Mike Nelson, Joel Hodgson, Tom Servo and Crow as they make fun of cheesy B-movies (presented by Roger Corman) beamed aboard the Satellite of Love by Dr. Forrester and his assistant, Frank.

Mystery Science Theater 3000—Manos: Hands of Fate. A family falls victim to the undead and their slow-witted, disfigured caretaker, Torgo. With John Ireland and Beverly Garland. 97 mins.
VHS: S33243. $19.95.

Mystery Science Theater 3000—The Gunslinger. The wife of a murdered marshall carries on her husband's work, to the dismay of a small, lawless, western town. With John Ireland and Beverly Garland. 97 mins.
VHS: S33242. $19.95.

Mystery Science Theater 3000: I Accuse My Parents. With John Carradine, Allison Hayes, Myron Healy and Sally Todd. 97 mins.
VHS: S32654. $19.95.

Mystery Science Theater 3000: Red Zone Cuba. B-movie big man Coleman Francis and his buddies set out to stage their own Bay of Pigs. With John Carradine and Tony Cordoza. 97 mins.
VHS: S32653. $19.95.

Mystery Science Theater 3000: The Atomic Brain. An aging debutante's crazy doc transfers the brain of a cat into a European beauty. With Gerstie Frank, Judy Bamber, Marjorie Eaton and Frank Fowler. 97 mins.
VHS: S32652. $19.95.

The Nativity—Westinghouse Studio One

The story of the first Christmas is presented in a moving live tv musical based on English mystery plays of the 14th and 15th centuries. With Hurd Hatfield, Miriam Wolfe, Paul Tripp and The Robert Shaw Chorale. With Betty Furness as the spokeswoman. USA, 1952, 60 mins.
VHS: S05314. $59.95.

The Night Stalker

In the series that set TV ratings records when it first aired, Darren McGavin stars as former top reporter Carl Kolchak on a mission to solve a series of Las Vegas murders, apparently committed by the same killer: a modern-day vampire? The closer Kolchak gets to the truth, the less he is able to reveal and the more frightened he becomes.
VHS: S34419. $14.98.
John Llewelyn Moxey, USA, 1971, 74 mins.

The Night Strangler

Darren McGavin reprises his role as the crusading newsman Carl Kolchak. Now Kolchak is challenged by his old Las Vegas editor, Tony Vincenzo (Simon Oakland), with uncovering a 120-year-old Jekyll and Hyde killer in Seattle's eerie underground city. With Wally Cox, Jo Ann Pflug, Richard Anderson, Margaret Hamilton, John Carradine and Al Lewis.
VHS: S34420. $14.98.
Dan Curtis, USA, 1972, 90 mins.

No Time for Sergeants

The original classic stars Andy Griffith as Will Stockdale as he takes on his old sergeant and the practical jokers who share his barrack. From the original live television broadcast of 1955. 60 mins.
VHS: S20487. $19.95.
Laser: LD74712. $34.98.

Of Human Bondage

This Westinghouse Studio One version first played in 1949 and starred Charlton Heston one year prior to the release of his first film, *Dark City*. Heston plays the crippled med student in love with an uncaring waitress. Betty Furness hosts and program includes a commercial for a 12½ inch picture tube tv set. USA, 1949, 60 mins.
VHS: S03656. $24.95.

One for the Road

Morley Safer joins Charles Kuralt in this portrait of the beloved television journalist. The program includes some of the most memorable moments from Kuralt's *Sunday Morning* and *On the Road* reports. 46 mins.
VHS: S21716. $19.98.

One Step Beyond

From the dramatic 1959-61 TV anthology that explored true cases of the strange and supernatural. Featuring early performances by Warren Beatty, Charles Bronson, William Shatner, Elizabeth Montgomery and more. With host John Newland as your "guide into the world of the unknown." Set of three tapes contains 12 half-hour episodes. Two hours each.
VHS: S34671. $24.95.

The Outer Limits Series

Forty-eight episodes from the popular TV series of the '60s. Approximately 60 minutes each.

100 Days of the Dragon. Popular American President conceives of a plan to take over the United States. 52 mins.
VHS: S03319. $12.98.

A Feasibility Study. A six-block section of Beverly Hills is transported to an alien planet in a grotesque experiment.
VHS: S11244. $12.98.

Architects of dFear. An idealistic scientist is surgically transformed into a bizarre and frightening alien creature in the hope that fear of annihilation at the hands of this creature will bring the warring people of the world together. 52 mins.
VHS: S08059. $12.98.

Behold, Eck!. Peter Lind Hayes stars in a spine-tingling tale of a two-dimensional alien trapped in our three-dimensional world.
VHS: S12441. $12.98.

Cold Hands, Warm Heart. William Shatner stars as an astronaut who's gone where no man's gone before. 52 mins.
VHS: S13982. $12.99.

Controlled Experiment. Barry Morse plays Martian Inspector Phobos, whose friendship with his fieldman, Carroll O'Connor, leads him to interfere in a forthcoming murder.
VHS: S12434. $12.98.

Corpus Earthling. Robert Culp stars as a man with a metal plate in his head, which allows him to hear aliens plotting to take over the world.
VHS: S11242. $12.98.

Counterweight. Something goes wrong when six astronauts embark on a simulated training mission. 52 mins.
VHS: S13988. $12.99.

Cry of Silence. Eddie Albert and June Havoc portray a farm couple who encounter a nightmare of alien creatures. 52 mins.
VHS: S13985. $12.99.

Demon with a Glass Hand. Robert Culp is a mysterious visitor from Earth's future being pursued by a team of aliens called the Kyben in the Bradbury Building in present day (1964) Los Angeles. He holds the secret of human survival in the prosthetic computer that serves as his hand. Script by Harlan Ellison. Directed by Byron Haskin, USA, 1964, 60 mins.
VHS: S06054. $12.98.

Don't Open till Doomsday. Miriam Hopkins gives a show-stopping performance as an overly-ripe flapper who will stop at nothing to complete her long overdue wedding night scenario.
VHS: S11243. $12.98.

Expanding Human. James Doohan ("Scotty") stars as a scientist in this Jekyll-and-Hyde story tinged with *Outer Limits* touches. 52 mins.
VHS: S13983. $12.99.

Forms of Things Unknown. A stormy night, a secluded mansion, a mysterious inventor, two frightened women, and a murdered blackmailer who won't stay dead in one of the classic *Outer Limits* programs.
VHS: S04948. $12.98.

Fun and Games. Nick Adams (*The Rebel*) stars as an ex-boxer and small-time criminal who is transported with a divorced woman to a distant planet to participate in planetary survival games. If the Earth team loses, the rest of the human race is doomed. Go, Nick, Go. With Nancy Malone, the voice of Robert Johnson and Bill Hart as the alien with the saw-toothed boomerang. Directed by Gerd Oswald, USA, 1964, 60 mins.
VHS: S08343. $12.98.

Galaxy Being. Cliff Robertson in a story about a visitor from outer space. 53 mins.
VHS: S03318. $12.98.

I, Robot. Leonard Nimoy stars in this tale that finds a robot on trial for murdering his creator. 52 mins.
VHS: S13987. $12.99.

It Crawled Out of the Woodwork. With Ed Asner.
VHS: S11245. $12.98.

Keeper of the Purple Twilight. A distraught scientist is willing to swap his emotions with an alien creature in order to receive the missing equations that will make his antimagnetic disintegrator a reality. This leads to a possible invasion of Earth. With Warren Stevens, Robert Webber and Mike Lane as Ikar in his alien form. Directed by Charles Haas, USA, 1964, 60 mins.
VHS: S06055. $12.98.

Man Who Was Never Born. An astronaut travels through time far into the future where a bacteria invented by a crazed scientist has turned humans into mutants. The astronaut travels back in time to kill the scientist. 52 mins.
VHS: S07316. $12.98.

Man with the Power. Timid college professor invents a device giving him mental control over cosmic energy. 52 mins.
VHS: S03320. $12.98.

Moonstone. Ruth Roman stars in this story of mysterious anemone-like aliens found buried on the moon in a spheroid space ship.
VHS: S12435. $12.98.

Nightmare. A six-man multi-national task force is captured on the planet Ebon and made prisoners of war. Among them is a traitor who must be killed. But who? 52 mins.
VHS: S07317. $12.98.

O.B.I.T.. U.S. military security forces keep a special eye on the scientists at a Defense Department research center by using a secret electronic surveillance machine called OBIT. The Outer Band Individual Teletracer also allows one-eyed monsters from another world a free trip to Earth. With Peter Breck, Jeff Corey and Joanne Gilbert. Directed by Gerd Oswald, USA, 1963, 60 mins.
VHS: S08342. $12.98.

Second Chance. Seven people aboard a space ship ride are transported to another planet to participate in a desperate attempt to prevent a galactic catastrophe.
VHS: S12438. $12.98.

Soldier. A crossfire of death beams flings an alien foot soldier from the future back into our present. A man born and bred of violence, he refuses to pacify his warrior instincts in the face of our peaceful world. 52 mins.
VHS: S08061. $12.98.

Specimen: Unknown. A young scientist discovers spores clinging to the walls of his space lab and incubates them. When they mature, he is sprayed with a deadly poison and before anyone realizes it the deadly plants are on a shuttle bound for earth. 52 mins.
VHS: S08060. $12.98.

The Bellero Shield. An alien accidentally brought to earth by a scientist's malfunctioning invention confronts Martin Landau and Sally Kellerman.
VHS: S11241. $12.98.

The Borderland. Wealthy industrialist Barry Jones funds his own experiments to reach his dead son.
VHS: S12439. $12.98.

The Brain of Colonel Barham. A disembodied brain floating in a three gallon tank is the pivotal character in this keenly written episode. 52 mins.
VHS: S13984. $12.99.

The Chameleon. With Robert Duvall as a CIA hired assassin. Directed by Gerd Oswald, USA, 1964, 52 mins.
VHS: S13980. $12.99.

The Children of Spider County. A sensitive young man is wrongly accused of murder. 52 mins.
VHS: S13981. $12.99.

The Duplicate Man. A man clones himself in order to hunt down a "megasoid." 52 mins.
VHS: S13989. $12.99.

The Guests. A man wanders into an ominous-looking mansion looking for help following a roadside accident and confronts a pulsating brain in the attic.
VHS: S12431. $12.98.

The Human Factor. Sally Kellerman, Harry Guardino and Gary Merrill star in this chilling tale of a psychiatrist's efforts to help a twisted mental patient.
VHS: S12440. $12.98.

The Inheritors. Academy Award-winner Robert Duvall challenges four men controlled by one alien mind.
VHS: S04949. $12.98.

The Invisible Enemy. Two astronauts travel to Mars but never return home. A second expedition follows to find out why, and two crew members mysteriously disappear after arrival. Only the Mission Commander and his Captain are left, and realize their enemy are man-eating sand sharks. 52 mins.
VHS: S07315. $12.98.

The Invisibles. Alien parasites are gaining control of high-ranking individuals in government and industry. Don Gordon is an undercover agent for the Government Intelligence Agency sent to stop the Invisibles, which actually look like football-sized crab lice. Directed by Gerd Oswald, USA, 1964, 60 mins.
VHS: S08344. $12.98.

The Mice. Henry Silva has a choice: life in prison or be a guinea pig for a scientific "inhabitant exchange" with the planet Chromo.
VHS: S12437. $12.98.

The Mutant. Larry Pennell investigates an earth colony on "Annex One", where a hairless, bug-eyed human mutant (Warren Oates) dominates the colony.
VHS: S12432. $12.98.

The Premonition. A husband and wife are hurled into a limbo state at the moment of their deaths. 52 mins.
VHS: S13991. $12.99.

The Probe. A cargo plane en route to Japan lands on a strange land mass in the uncharted Pacific. 52 mins.
VHS: S13990. $12.99.

The Production and Decay of Strange Particles. Workers at a nuclear power plant are being turned into "force creatures", whose purpose is to create an atomic explosion that will blow a doorway into their dimension. 52 mins.
VHS: S12442. $12.98.

The Sixth Finger. A bitter young coal miner (David McCallum) is transformed into the all-knowing man of the future.
VHS: S04950. $12.98.

The Zanti Misfits. When the Earth is selected by the planet Zanti to serve as a penal colony for the unwanted members of their society, no one expected Bruce Dern to violate the restricted and heavily guarded area of a California ghost town. Leave it to Dern and his wild girlfriend (Olive Deering) to stir up intergalactic trouble. Directed by Leonard Horn, USA, 1963, 60 mins.
VHS: S06056. $12.98.

Tourist Attraction. Ralph Meeker wants to take back to America an enormous, prehistoric, amphibious monster discovered in a Central American country, but is thwarted by the country's dictator (Henry Silva).
VHS: S11246. $12.98.

Wolf 359. Dabney Coleman and Patrick O'Neal are scientists who are faced with the impressive task of cloning an entire planet. 52 mins.
VHS: S13986. $12.99.

ZZZZ. A queen bee (Joanna Frank) evolves into a beautiful, red-haired woman and sets her sights on an entomologist (Philip Abbott).
VHS: S12436. $12.98.

The Outer Limits

A compendium of eight of the finest episodes of this eerie and provocative science fiction television program that captured '50s paranoia and hysteria, featuring the work of young actors Martin Sheen, Vera Miles, Ed Asner, Martin Landau, Sally Kellerman and Bruce Dern. "The best program of its type ever to run on network TV" (Harlan Ellison).

Volume 1.
Laser: LD71841. $99.98.
Volume 2.
Laser: LD71164. $99.98.

The Ox-Bow Incident

Robert Wagner, Cameron Mitchell and Raymond Burr are featured in this classic early television adaptation of the Walter Van Tilburg Clark novel.
VHS: S10594. $29.95.

The Partridge Family

C'mon get happy with these six popular episodes from the sunny '70s sitcom starring Shirley Jones and teen hearthrob David Cassidy. Each tape features three episodes.

The Partridge Family—C'mon Get Happy. Includes the pilot episode, *What? And Get Out of Show Business?*, in which the young widow Shirley reluctantly joins her kids' band; *Old Scrapmouth*, in which Laurie's braces create a major kink in the band's performing (guest starring Mark Hamill of *Star Wars*); and *Anchors Away*, the last show of the series, in which Shirley's high school beau sails into town and Danny's convinced the officer is no gentleman.
VHS: S32377. $9.95.

The Partridge Family—Caution: Nervous Mother Driving. In *Knight in Shining Armor*, a talented intruder heartthrob (Bobby Sherman) takes over the Partridge's studio while they are away; in *But the Memory Lingers*, a smelly stowaway boards the bus and leaves a lasting impression on the group (features the hit song, "I Think I Love You"); and in *The Eleven Year Itch*, guest star Jodie Foster develops a crush on Danny. 75 mins.
VHS: S32376. $9.95.

Patterns

A live television production of Rod Serling's drama about corporate politics and the destruction of individuality. Told from the perspective of Fred Staples (Richard Kiley), a new executive, the plot details the public humiliation of a decent, sensitive man (Ed Begley Sr.) carried out by the ruthless company boss (Orson Welles regular Everett Sloane). With Elizabeth Montgomery. Program includes interviews with cast and crew technicians.
VHS: S18795. $19.95.
Fielder Cook, USA, 1955, 59 mins.

The Patty Duke Show

Eight hilarious shows about identity and confusion with Patty Duke essaying the dual roles of identical cousins.
Laser: LD71147. $49.98.

Pee-Wee's Collector's Gift Set

Eight volumes of the award-winning *Pee-Wee's Playhouse* 1986/87 television series are presented in this gift set. Episodes include "Open House," "Pee-Wee Catches a Cold," "I Remember Curtis," "Conky's Breakdown," "Store," "Playhouse in Outer Space," "Pajama Party" and "To Tell the Tooth." Stars Paul Reubens as Pee-Wee, Laurence Fishburne as Cowboy Curtis, and Phil Hartman as Captain Carl. 224 mins.
VHS: S28485. $99.92.

Pee-Wee's Collector's Gift Set: Vols. 9-16

The secret word is fun with these 14 episodes from the Emmy Award-winning series. Each tape includes two half-hour episodes. Volume 9 includes *Dr. Pee-Wee and the Del Rubios* and *Rebarella*; Volume 10 includes *Let's Play Office* and *Mystery*; Volume 11 includes *Front Page Pee-Wee* and *Tango Time*; Volume 12 includes *Playhouse Day* and *Accidental Playhouse*; Volume 13 includes *Ice Cream Soup* and *Puppy in the Playhouse*; Volume 14 includes *The Cowboy and the Countess* and *Reba Eats and Pterri Runs*; Volume 15 includes *Tons of Fun* and *School*; and Volume 16 includes *Why Wasn't I Invited?* and *Ants in Your Pants*.
VHS: S31519. $99.92.

Pee-Wee's Playhouse Christmas Special

From the award-winning series *Pee-Wee's Playhouse* comes this Christmas special which features an all star-cast, including Magic Johnson, Cher, Whoopi Goldberg, Oprah Winfrey, Frankie Avalon, Annette Funicello, Charo, Grace Jones, k.d. lang, Little Richard, Joan Rivers, Dinah Shore and Zsa Zsa Gabor. 48 mins.
VHS: S28486. $12.95.
Laser: LD75988. $29.95.

The Persuaders—London Conspiracy

Tony Curtis and Roger Moore are two playboy adventurers in the television series where they team up to right wrongs and live the good life. In this episode Moore, as Sir Brett Sinclair, must impersonate himself, with Curtis as his phony butler, to foil the London conspiracy. England, 1976, 102 mins.
VHS: S06093. $59.98.

The Persuaders—Mission: Monte Carlo

Tony Curtis and Roger Moore are the Persuaders, a pair of wealthy bon vivants who enjoy disrupting stylish criminal plots in scenic parts of the globe—like Monaco for instance. This British tv series promises action, beautiful women and smart remarks. England, 1975, 96 mins.
VHS: S06094. $59.98.

The Persuaders—Sporting Chance

Roger Moore teams up with Tony Curtis to fight crime and drive very fast sports cars in the television series from England. In this episode the well dressed good guys face sabotage and bribery on the race car circuit. Are the Persuaders up to the challenge? Are you kidding? England, 1976, 102 mins.
VHS: S06095. $59.98.

Peter Gunn

Before Bond, before the Saint, there was Peter Gunn, the original American private eye. Craig Stevens stars as the suave, handsome detective Peter Gunn, as experienced in charming the ladies as battling dangerous criminals. Features six classic episodes from the 1958 TV series, directed by Blake Edwards. With the hot jazz of Henry Mancini. The six half-hour episodes include *The Briefcase, Down the Drain, Sing a Song of Murder, The Jockey, Man with a Scar* and *The Murder Bond*. 180 mins.
VHS: S34670. $12.95.

Police Squad! Help Wanted!

A compilation of three episodes from the defunct but very funny tv series that inspired the hit movie. From the creative team of Jerry Zucker, Jim Abrahams and David Zucker, who wrote and directed *Airplane* and *Top Secret*, comes this terrific spoof on tv cop shows. With Leslie Nielsen and Allan North as a pair of deadpan L.A. cops. Special guests Florence Henderson and Lorne Greene are announced but never appear.
VHS: S08715. $19.95.
Laser: LD75340. $29.98.
David Zucker/Jim Abrahams/Jerry Zucker, USA, 1982, 75 mins.

Pontius Pilate— Westinghouse Studio One

Set 15 years after the Crucifixion, the story is told from the Roman governor's point of view. A moving drama that depicts Pilate as a victim of circumstances. With Cyril Ritchard, Geraldine Fitzgerald and Francis L. Sullivan. Performed live. B&W. USA, 1952, 59 mins.
VHS: S05451. $24.95.

Prairie Home Companion: Last Show

The final live performance of Garrison Keillor's unique radio program at the World Theatre in St. Paul, Minnesota from June 13, 1987. With Chet Atkins and Leo Kottke, and all the news from Lake Wobegon. USA, 1987, 114 mins.
VHS: S03756. $29.95.

Prairie Home Companion: The Second Annual Farewell Performance

Garrison Keillor and the APHC cast return for a "second farewell" performance at the Radio City Music Hall on June 4, 1988. Guests include Chet Atkins, Butch Thompson, Leo Kottke, The Everly Brothers and Vince Giordano and the Nighthawks. Also Robin and Linda Williams and the latest news from Lake Wobegon. More fun than an invitation to a hot dinner. 1988.
VHS: S08347. $29.95.

QB VII

An epic television adaptation of the novel by Leon Uris, the courtroom drama of two men and how they react to the memory of the Holocaust. With strong performances by Anthony Hopkins, Ben Gazzara, Leslie Caron.
VHS: S04395. $139.95.
Tom Gries, USA, 1974, 360 mins.

The Real World Reunion: Inside Out

Outtakes, excerpts from the original cast tryouts, and profiles of the most popular cast members make this reunion a must for all MTV *Real World* fans. Few know that the original pilot was never aired. This video has scenes from the show that started it all. USA, 1995, 75 mins.
VHS: S27189. $12.98.

The Real World: Vacations

MTV's fascinating at-home glimpse of today's generation pioneered a new documentary-type soap opera. On vacation in Jamaica, Mexico and Hawaii, the casts of some of the best series go all out to have a good time. Of course, there are problems like a bad date at a nude beach and even an unexpected pregnancy. Includes appearances by Heather B. Rachel Campos, Jon Brennan and more. 55 mins.
VHS: S26306. $14.98.

Red Green's of Cars and Men

A hilarious bumper-to-bumper trip down memory lane with PBS' Red Green, his nephew Harold and the Possum Lodge gang, lined with car lore and Red's own driving tips. 60 mins.
VHS: S34256. $19.95.

Rich Little's Robin Hood

It's Rich Little as Groucho Marx portraying Robin Hood in this hilarious romp through Sherwood Forest. Imagine Carol Channing as Maid Marion, John Wayne as Little John...you get the idea. Hilarious comedy from an international impersonator. 60 mins.
VHS: S13796. $14.95.

Ride the Wind

The Cartwright clan is back in action on video. Taken from episodes of the long running classic tv western *Bonanza*, the owners of the Ponderosa battle angry Paiutes and unscrupulous tycoons. Starring Lorne Greene, Dan Blocker and Michael Landon. When Little Joe joins the Pony Express, can his father Ben get him out of serious trouble? In color, 100 mins.
VHS: S11406. $14.95.

The Rifleman

The legendary television program is presented in a two-package, ten-volume series. Chuck Connors is cast as a widower farmer trying to raise his young son (Johnny Crawford) amid a world of bandits and desperados. Some of the actors appearing in guest spots include Dennis Hopper, Warren Oates, Robert Culp, Lee Van Cleef, Agnes Moorehead and James Coburn. Various directors, including Sam Peckinpah, Robert Altman, Arthur Hiller and Richard Donner contributed to the show.

Vol. 1-5.
VHS: S18266. $59.95.
Vol. 6-10
VHS: Out of print. For rental only.

Roe vs. Wade

Winner of multiple Emmys, based on the 1973 court case regarding abortion rights, with Holly Hunter and Amy Madigan. The powerful story concerns Ellen Campbell, desperate to terminate an unwanted pregnancy, who, together with a young attorney, is determined to prove the Texas law forbidding abortion is unconstitutional. Their struggle leads them to the U.S. Supreme Court, where Jane Roe's personal ordeal changes U.S. history.
VHS: S11602. $14.95.
Laser: LD75133. $24.98.
Gregory Hoblit, USA, 1989, 92 mins.

Roy Rogers Show, Vol. 2

Two episodes from the original television series: *Smoking Guns* (will happy trails become war paths? Devious prospectors take ore that belongs to a local tribe) and *Sheriff Missing* (meet Roy Rogers, thug; he masquerades as a criminal to outfox villains intent on setting up a gambling parlor). 46 mins.
VHS: S12555. $12.95.

Roy Rogers Show, Vol. 4

Two episodes from the original television series: *Head for Cover* (when revenge-minded robbers come looking for their double-crossing boss, Roy trails the thieves and nabs 'em all!) and *Paleface Justice* (they've readied the hangman's noose for an innocent Indian lad; can Roy come up with proof that will prevent the lynching?). 46 mins.
VHS: S12557. $12.95.

Roy Rogers Show, Vol. 5

Two episodes from the original television series: *Tossup* (the mine is worthless...but can two families come up with gold in their hearts? Roy is peacemaker when a mine dispute erupts into a bitter feud) and *Brady's Bonanza* (jumpin' Geiger Counter! Pat Brady unwittingly sells his claim to a uranium mine for two dollars). 46 mins.
VHS: S12558. $12.95.

Roy Rogers Show, Vol. 6

Two episodes from the original television series: *Fishing for Fingerprints* (it's no fish story; the one that got away will be the criminal himself if Roy and Bullet don't cast about for clues) and *Fighting Sire* (a boxing champ is ashamed of his timid son until Roy shows the champ that being a man doesn't mean being a bully). 46 mins.
VHS: S12559. $12.95.

The Scarlet Letter—Westinghouse Studio One

The classic tale of adultery and retribution in Colonial America is presented on live tv. The cast includes Mary Sinclair, John Baragrey and Richard Purdy. Nathanial Hawthorne's granddaughter is on hand to receive a plaque in his memory. Commercials deleted. USA, 1950, 52 mins.
VHS: S05450. $24.95.

Secrets of the Unknown

This series, produced by ABC News, explores some of the mysteries of our time: Was Jack the Ripper more than one person? Could Ninja warriors transform themselves into panthers and beasts of prey? Hosted by Edward Mulhare.
Dreams & Nightmares.
VHS: S09174. $14.95.
Jack the Ripper.
VHS: S09170. $14.95.
Ninja: Real Story.
VHS: S09172. $14.95.
Pyramids.
VHS: S09173. $14.95.
The Titanic.
VHS: S09169. $14.95.
UFOs.
VHS: S09171. $14.95.

Shogun

Richard Chamberlain stars in this unedited Emmy Award-winning TV mini-series. Packed with action, romance and adventure, this is the story of a British navigator shipwrecked off the coast of 17th-century feudal Japan. Four cassettes.
VHS: S32180. $249.95.
Jerry London, USA/Japan, 1980, 9 hours, 9 mins.

Silver Theatre

Chico Marx stars in a situation comedy called "Papa Romani" on *Silver Theatre* on CBS in 1950. The Romani family has a new telephone installed, which leads to comic complications. With Margaret Hamilton and William Frawley. You'll have to watch the tape to find out if the family is Italian or Gypsy. USA, 1950, 25 mins.
VHS: S10066. $19.95.

Son of the Morning Star

The rise and fall of George Armstrong Custer is ably retold in this epic made-for-tv movie. Gary Cole (*Midnight Caller*) is the brazen cavalry officer whose bid for the Presidency stopped on a grassy slope near the Little Big Horn. Based on the book by Evan S. Connell. With Rosanna Arquette and Dean Stockwell. The title refers to the Indian name given to this controversial boy general.
VHS: S14478. $19.98.
Mike Robe, USA, 1991, 186 mins.

South Park

Comedy Central's highest rated series follows the sick, twisted, and gaseous misadventures of third-grade classmates Kyle: the Smart One, Stan: The Cute One, Cartman: The Fat One, and Kenny: The Dead One. Each video contains two full-length episodes. Includes fireside chats with South Park creators and other Comedy Central featurettes. Each episode is 30 mins.
South Park—Volume 1. Includes *Cartman Gets an Anal Probe* and *Volcano*.
VHS: S34134. $14.95.
South Park—Volume 2. Includes *Weight Gain 4000* and *Big Gay Al's Big Gay Boat Ride* (featuring the voice of George Clooney as Sparky, Stan's gay dog).
VHS: S34135. $14.95.
South Park—Volume 3. Includes *An Elephant Makes Love to a Pig* and *Death*.
VHS: S34136. $14.95.

Spitting Image: The Music Video

A sensational and hilarious musical extravaganza with performances from today's top pop star latex look-alikes. Stars Sting, Michael Jackson, Imelda Marcos, Queen Elizabeth II and many more. Includes "The Chicken Song." 56 mins.
VHS: S16116. $19.98.

Stars in the Eye

The opening of Television City in Hollywood. With Jack Benny, Lucille Ball, Amos & Andy, George Burns and many more. USA, 1952, 60 mins.
VHS: S15224. $19.95.

The Story of Television

A number of interesting short segments reveal key elements of the history of the television medium. There is a 1950's film explaining how TV works, scenes from the first telecast of Roosevelt at the World's Fair of 1939, and even a conversation between General David Sarnoff (Chair of RCA) and Dr. Vladimir Zworykin, the father of television. 27 mins.
VHS: S24074. $14.95.

Super Heroes

1966 fall TV preview hosted by Batman and Robin. On the same program, *Stamp Day for Superman* with *George Reeves*.
VHS: S09549. $29.95.

Super TV Bloopers

Rare goofs and outtakes from *Mash, Happy Days, Laverne & Shirley, Peyton Place, The Dick Van Dyke Show* and *You Bet Your Life*.
VHS: S09548. $29.95.

T.V. Classics, Vol. 1: Hollywood Half Hour & Public Defender

Two early live television dramas from the golden age of T.V. broadcasting. This tape includes representative episodes from two of the most obscure series. In the first, Joan Leslie accepts a job with madman Vincent Price. In the latter, Public Defender Reed Hadley helps Charles Bronson in his scrape with the law. 52 mins.
VHS: S13151. $19.98.

T.V. Classics, Vol. 2: Howdy Doody & Art Linkletter and the Kids

Everyone's favorite freckled puppet from the 50's teams up with the young pals of Art Linkletter who are saying "the darndest" things. Two episodes. 52 mins.
VHS: S13152. $19.98.

T.V. Classics, Vol. 3: Colonel March of Scotland Yard & Sherlock Holmes

Very early Sherlock Holmes plus Boris Karloff as Inspector March of Scotland Yard. Two episodes from television's earliest crime shows. 52 mins.
VHS: S13153. $19.98.

T.V. Classics, Vol. 4: Arthur Godfrey's Talent Scouts & The Ed Wynn Show

Here, Arthur Godfrey introduces a young Rod McKuen to the public, and the goofy Ed Wynn hosts the Three Stooges. 52 mins.
VHS: S13154. $19.98.

T.V. Classics, Vol. 5: The Burns and Allen Show & Heaven for Betsy

The pilot episode of the long running interplay between George Burns and Gracie Allen. Also, an episode from a short-lived domestic comedy starring Jack Lemmon. 52 mins.
VHS: S13155. $19.98.

T.V. Classics, Vol. 6: Armchair Detective & Public Prosecutor

Two early "whodunit" mysteries designed to involve audience participation—the viewer is asked to solve the mystery. In *Public Prosecutor*, the guessing becomes a game show as a panel of experts offer their choices. 52 mins.
VHS: S13156. $19.98.

T.V. Classics, Vol. 7: Four Star Playhouse & The Stars and The Story

Two high quality mystery programs from the 50's. The first stars Dick Powell as Willie Dante, owner of the San Francisco gambling parlor Dante's Inferno. The second features Peter Lorre tracking down the perpetrator of an art theft. 52 mins.
VHS: S13157. $19.98.

T.V. Classics, Vol. 8: The Jack Benny Show

Two episodes from the stylish programming of Jack Benny featuring two of the 50's biggest stars: Humphrey Bogart and Jayne Mansfield. 52 mins.
VHS: S13158. $19.98.

T.V. Classics, Vol. 9: The Cisco Kid & The Roy Rogers Show

Episodes from the two most popular television westerns, featuring "the Robin Hood of the West" and the Singing Cowboy. 52 mins.
VHS: S13159. $19.98.

T.V. Party

The best of the long-running New York City cable TV show produced in the early 1980s, features as guests Deborah Harry, David Byrne, Jean-Michel Basquiat, and others—with the T.V. Party Orchestra including Walter Stedding, Chris Stein, Bob Fripp and others. Interview magazine columnist Glenn O'Brien hosted what was called "the tv show that's a cocktail party that is also a political party" with lively guests, great music, late-night behavior and adult situations.
VHS: S07123. $29.95.
Glenn O'Brien, USA, 1980-82, 30 mins.

Ten Little Indians

A live television version of the classic Agatha Christie novel where ten invited guests are systematically bumped off by an unseen hand. Each death corresponds to the circumstances described in a children's poem. With Nina Foch, Barry Jones, Romney Brent, Peter Bathhurst and Kenneth Haigh. And the killer is... 60 mins.
VHS: S04908. $24.95.

This Is Your Life

The story of Stan Laurel and Oliver Hardy as told by Ralph Edwards. 30 minutes.
VHS: S02648. $29.95.

The Thorn Birds

The epic story of Father Ralph and Meggie Cleary, and their forbidden romance. Told in only 486 minutes with a cast that includes Barbara Stanwyck, Jean Simmons, Bryan Brown, Mare Winningham, Earl Holliman, Philip Anglim, Richard Kiley, Christopher Plummer, Ken Howard, Piper Laurie, and of course Richard Chamberlain and the lovely Rachel Ward. Set in Australia and based on the bestselling novel by Colleen McCullough. This popular tv mini-series won six Emmys. Four volume set.
VHS: S14579. $119.99.
Daryl Duke, USA, 1983, 486 mins.

The Three Stooges Comedy Classics

Moe, Larry, Curly and Shemp are comic characters responsible for some of the best and funniest shorts ever made. Eighteen of their best, fifteen with Curly and three with Shemp, are brought together in this boxed set. Over 300 mins.
Laser: LD75083. $99.95.

Thriller

Boris Karloff hosts this collection of the best episodes from the classic 1960's television series, *Thriller*. Some of these creepy stories even include Karloff as an actor. Grim tales like these have an unnatural life all their own, which keeps this series entertaining and frightening.
Masquerade. Tom Poston and Elizabeth Montgomery are a newly wed couple who accept the hospitality of a fiendish family. But the honeymooners prove more than a match for their hapless hosts. Co-stars John Carradine. 50 mins.
VHS: S21491. $12.98.
The Grim Reaper. William Shatner is a greedy young man who discovers the truth behind the legend of the Grim Reaper. This fiend exacts a terrible revenge on the murderous young man. 50 mins.
VHS: S21493. $12.98.
The Prediction. Boris Karloff hosts and stars in this episode of *Thriller*. Karloff is a mentalist who can predict the deaths of people around him. Those who ignore his predictions must face the dire consequences. 50 mins.
VHS: S21494. $12.98.
The Premature Burial. In this episode a wealthy old man is accidentally buried alive. Karloff is the friend that saves him from this grisly fate. When the old man marries again, his new young wife plans to put him back just where Karloff found him. 51 mins.
VHS: S21495. $12.98.
The Terror in Teakwood. In this episode a wife faces a mortal terror when her musician husband desecrates the grave of his arch rival. Revenge and rivalry know no bounds between life and death. 49 mins.
VHS: S21492. $12.98.

Tracey Takes On...

The best of Tracey Ullman's Emmy Award-winning series, in which Tracey takes on different subjects as seen through the eyes and lives of her hilarious array of characters, from make-up artist-to-the-stars Ruby Romaine and faded star Linda Granger to Chic, the New York City cab driver, flight attendant Trevor Ayliss, and donut store owner Mrs. Noh Nang Ning. Features Tracey's behind-the-scenes look at her exotic and eccentric characters, and outtakes from the making of the show. With guest appearances by Julie Kavner, George Segal and John Stamos. Each tape is 80 mins.
Tracey Takes On...Movies Vanity Fame.
VHS: S32993. $19.98.
Tracey Takes On...Sex Romance Fantasy.
VHS: S32994. $19.98.

Treasures of the Twilight Zone

Six highly sought-after episodes and rare unavailable footage of the anthology show that used science fiction as a startling take off into humans' greatest fears, desires and weaknesses.
VHS: S19100. $29.98.

Trip to Christmas

A traditional look at American Christmas' through the years gleaned from the live Telephone Hour Christmas shows. Hosted by Jane Wyatt, the stars include Earl Wrightson, Lois Hunt, The Lennon Sisters, Lisa Della Casa, Phyllis Curtin and Violette Verdy and Edward Villela dancing the Nutcracker Pas de Deux. 45 mins.
VHS: S08471. $19.95.

TV Nation

From Michael Moore (*Roger & Me*) comes this acclaimed, irreverent "kamikaze *60 Minutes*," "that goes where no TV magazine has gone before" (*Newsday*). Armed with a TV crew and a wicked sense of humor, Moore and his correspondents expose the excesses of corporate America and examine the absurdity of modern politics and popular culture. Both volumes contain a segment considered too controversial for network TV.
TV Nation, Vol. 1. With guest star Steven Wright. Includes the premiere episode, featuring the segments *Free Trade in Mexico, Taxi!, Appleton Prison, Love Canal* and *Looking for Missiles*; and the year-end special episode, featuring the segments *Corp-Aid, White House Security Guard, Where to Send Our Boys in '95, Predictions for the New Year, Meet the Republicans* and the network TV-banned *Condoms*.
VHS: S32605. $14.95.

TV Nation, Vol. 2. With guest star Janeane Garafolo. Includes the second season premiere episode, featuring the segments *Bruno for President, Slaves, Beach Party, Crime Scene Clean-Up* and *Crackers, The Corporate Crime-Fighting Chicken*; and the "Love Night" Episode, featuring the segments *Love Night, Michigan Militia, America's Most Wanted, Aquariums of the Damned, KGB III, Meet the Republicans* and the network TV-banned *Extra Credit*.
VHS: S32606. $14.95.
Michael Moore, USA, 1994/1995, 116/120 mins.

TV's Best Adventures of Superman: Volume 1

Three super-classics: *Superman on Earth* (1951) traces the caped hero from his Krypton origins to his first adult adventures on earth. *All That Glitters* (1957) finds Lois Lane and Jimmy Olsen swallowing Kryptonite pills to become like Superman. *Superman* (1941), the first-ever cartoon, pits our hero against a mad scientist and his terrifying ray gun. 63 mins.
VHS: S06246. $29.98.

TV's Best Adventures of Superman: Volume 2

Another trio of stories: *Crime Wave* (1953) asks, "Who's the secret mastermind behind crime in Metropolis?" Superman discovers the incredible answer. In *The Perils of Superman* (1957), the Man of Steel takes on a legion of lead-masked criminals. Finally, in *The Mechanical Monsters* (1941), four decades before "transformers" became a household word, Superman battles an ingenious, rampaging robot army in a cartoon classic. 62 mins.
VHS: S06247. $29.98.

Twilight Zone

The ever-popular TV series with stars including Robert Redford, Agnes Moorehead, William Shatner, Lee Marvin, Burgess Meredith, Jack Klugman and Jonathan Winters.
Twilight Zone Vol. 1. Contains two episodes: *The Invaders* and *Nothing in the Dark*.
VHS: S11918. $14.98.
Laser: LD71382. $39.98.
Twilight Zone Vol. 2. Contains two episodes: *Time Enough at Last* and *The Monsters Are Due on Maple Street*.
VHS: S11919. $14.98.
Laser: LD71383. $39.98.
Twilight Zone Vol. 3. Contains two episodes: *Nightmare at 20,000 Feet* and *The Odyssey of Flight 33*.
VHS: S11920. $14.98.
Twilight Zone Vol. 4. Contains two episodes: *A Game of Pool* and *Steel*.
VHS: S11921. $14.98.
Twilight Zone Vol. 5. Contains two episodes: *Walking Distance*, about a high-pressured executive who travels back in time; and *Kick the Can*, the story of an old man who tries to convince the other residents of his rest home that they can be young again if they play children's games.
VHS: S14270. $14.98.
Twilight Zone Vol. 6. Contains two episodes: *Mr. Dingle, The Strong*, starring Burgess Meredith and Don Rickles; and *Two*, starring Elizabeth Montgomery and Charles Bronson.
VHS: S14271. $14.98.
Twilight Zone Vol. 7. Contains two eerie tales: *A Passage for Trumpet*, starring Jack Klugman as a loser whose suicide attempt has even failed…or has it? and *The Four of Us Are Dying*, about a man who can change his face to look like anyone he chooses.
VHS: S14272. $14.98.
Twilight Zone Vol. 8. Contains two episodes: *Long Distance Call*, in which a boy talks to his dead Grandma—who wants him to join her—using a toy telephone; and *I Sing the Body Electric*, in which Anne, resentful of her new robot grandma, runs away…straight into the path of an oncoming car.
VHS: S14273. $14.98.

Twin Peaks Collector's Series

Enjoy all 29 episodes of David Lynch's influential 1990 TV series in this special collector's set. With Kyle MacLachlan, Michael Ontkean, Peggy Lipton, Piper Laurie, Sherilyn Fenn, Lara Flynn Boyle, Billy Zane, Ray Wise and James Marshall. Six volumes, 180 mins.
VHS: S31510. $89.98.

War and Remembrance

Robert Mitchum and Jane Seymour star in this landmark television mini-series. Herman Wouk's epic novel about World War II was realized in 12 parts. There are few comparable adaptations in television history, and the list of cameo appearances, which include stars like Sharon Stone, is similarly impressive. Each volume is 120 minutes, for a total of 24 hours of viewing.
VHS: S08230. $239.98.
Dan Curtis, USA, 1989, 600 mins.

We Can't Help It—We're Men

Over an hour of previously undiscovered gems from the first six seasons of the popular PBS *Red Green Show*, featuring handyman Red Green, his techno-geek nephew Harold and all the guys from the Possum Lodge. 65 mins.
VHS: S31395. $19.95.

Weird TV Chunk 1

Originally airing on Fox TV, *Weird TV* is a rapid-fire, off-the-wall, segment-driven, episodic adventure with a radical comic twist. Hosted by Chuck Cirino and featuring radio and TV personality Shadoe Stevens, "Chunk 1" includes episodes: Scrapple, Reel Fall Out, and Net Escape. Each episode features a hot new music segment with appearances by major label artists such as Oasis, Whale and Korn.
VHS: S28521. $39.90.

Wild Palms

Oliver Stone produced this audacious six-hour television series adapted from Bruce Wagner's surreal comic strip. An ambitious senator (Robert Loggia) invents a holographic television channel to program virtual reality. A television executive (James Belushi) is drawn into a sadistic web of murder, intrigue and sexual power. As the principals fight over control of the holographic image, an underground war breaks out and the individuals try desperately to connect their crazed, hyper dreams to their real life experiences. With Dana Delaney, Kim Cattrall, Angie Dickinson and Ernie Hudson. Directed by Peter Hewitt, Keith Gordon, Phil Joanou and Kathryn Bigelow. Two-tape set.
Laser: LD74824. $89.99.

The Willow Cabin

Charlton Heston and Priscilla Gillette star in this 1950 Westinghouse Studio One production. 60 mins.
VHS: S32147. $24.95.

Winds of War

The best seller by Herman Wouk, adapted for television in a massive, epic production, starring Robert Mitchum, Ali MacGraw, Jan-Michael Vincent, John Houseman, and a cast of thousands. Complete 14-hour, 43-minute version, on seven cassettes, in boxed set.
VHS: S11193. $139.95.
Dan Curtis, USA, 1988, 883 mins.

Wrestling with Gorgeous George

There were other "sports" on early television, but, for many, television, wrestling and Gorgeous George were almost synonymous; George Raymond Wagner was wrestling's greatest showman during the Fifties. This tape also includes Woodrow Wilson "Woody" Strode (one of the first black wrestlers on television, who later turned to acting, landing roles in four John Ford features), and a "spectacular" all-girl wrestling match.
VHS: S13427. $39.95.

Wuthering Heights—Westinghouse Studio One

Charlton Heston stars as the moody Heathcliff in this live tv adaptation of the Emily Bronte novel. Passions and tempers flare on the English moors. With Mary Sinclair and Richard Waring. The commercials have been deleted but the story is complete. USA, 1950, 51 mins.
VHS: S05444. $24.95.

You Bet Your Life

Groucho Marx hosted this classic quiz show from October 1950 to June 1951 and September 1958 to 1961 with famous guests, humorless announcer George Fenneman and a Grouchoid boid bearing a secret woid for big bucks. Each two-episode tape is 120 mins.
You Bet Your Life, Volume 1. Guests include Jack LaLanne, Monty Montana & His Horse Rex.
VHS: S32299. $14.95.
You Bet Your Life, Volume 2. Guests include Don Drysdale, Edgar Bergen, Candice Bergen and Melinda Marx.
VHS: S32300. $14.95.

Your Show of Shows

The 50s comedy show that showcased leading writing, directing and comedic talents, including writers Woody Allen, Mel Brooks, Carl Reiner and Steve Martin, and performers Sid Caesar, Imogene Coca, Jack Benny and countless others.
Volume 1.
VHS: S16946. $19.95.
Volume 2.
VHS: S16947. $19.95.

independent

SPIRITS

independent american cinema

1988
Selected as an outstanding film of the year at the London Film Festival, *1988* "mixes deadly seriousness and high camp, avant-garde aesthetics and transsexual athletics with an atmosphere that is alternately sordid and seductive" (David Harris, *Boston Phoenix*).
VHS: S01625. $59.95.
Richard Schmidt, USA, 1977, 93 mins.

27 Pieces of Me
In this bold, independent feature, Tanya (Tina M. Henning), a lesbian sculptor, is forced to confront her sister Ramona (Angelique von Halle) when she arrives on her doorstep unannounced. Both women have been having relationship troubles. Fortunately, Tanya's roommate Bold (Jonathan Harris) helps the two women begin a rapprochement that they desperately need and want.
VHS: S27479. $39.95.
Gerald Donohoe, USA, 1995, 90 mins.

Acid Is Groovy Kill the Pigs
This title is the Manson-like scrawl left at the scene of the *Fatal Vision* murders of a policeman's wife and two kids. It formed the basis of the cop's alibi that crazed hippies had done this horrible crime. In this fantasy the hippie killers come to life.
VHS: S22504. $29.95.
Joe Christ, USA, 1993, 35 mins.

The Addiction
Christopher Walken, Annabella Sciorra and Lili Taylor star in this stylish, blood-sucking thriller. Taylor is a grad student in philosophy at NYU when she happens upon a world governed quite literally by bloodlust. It seems to offer all the answers she so desperately sought in the more sterile realm of academia, but the perverse pleasures of the night also have a dangerous and deadly side.
VHS: S27884. $19.95.
Laser: LD76083. $39.99.
Abel Ferrara, USA, 1995, 82 mins.

The Age of Insects
Jack Ramey plays a N.Y. doctor conducting mad hormone experiments. A wealthy lingerie manufacturer pays to have his fey son Lance rehabilitated. The doctor's East Indian assistant, Lisa Zane, falls for the young man as she rubs insect enzymes on him. Lance awakens transformed, but not as foreseen.
VHS: S22615. $49.95.
Eric Marano, USA, 1991, 75 mins.

Alan and Naomi
Based on the novel by Myron Levoy, and set in World War II-era Brooklyn, this sensitive film studies the friendship between a brash, young local boy and a troubled French girl traumatized by a dark, grisly experience.
VHS: S16910. $89.95.
Sterling VanWagenen, USA, 1991, 94 mins.

Alice Dropped the Mirror and It Broke
In this experimental narrative a woman filmmaker edits a documentary about four men: a leader, a cowboy, an anarchist and an artist. These superficial representations of male romantic power force Alice into her film. She uncovers their hidden artifice.
VHS: S22647. $39.95.
Penelope Wehrli, USA, 1989, 63 mins.

All Over Me
An edgy look at a relationship between Claude, a sensitive and vulnerable girl, and her beautiful, quick-witted friend, Ellen, who shares Ellen's dream of forming an all-girl rock band. But Claude is hurt as Ellen becomes focused on her boyfriend. Living on the edge in New York City, the girls discover there's only one thing they can rely on: each other. "It leaps off the screen. The performances are uniformly truthful" *(Los Angeles Times)*. With Alison Folland, Tara Subkoff and Cole Hauser.
VHS: S32159. $19.98.
Laser: LD76388. $39.99.
Alex Sichel, USA, 1997, 95 mins.

All the Love in the World
Oscar-winning cinematographer Janusz Kaminski *(Schindler's List)* shot this beautiful story of love and murder. Eddy Wluicki is a young man who loves being in love, in a world where such romantic notions fade when confronted by the brutal realities of life. He strikes back at the innocent victims whom he blames for the death of love.
VHS: S21129. $59.95.
Daniel Curran, USA, 1990, 90 mins.

America's Deadliest Home Video
An impressive formal exercise by Jack Perez that's a cross between *They Live by Night* and *Henry: Portrait of a Serial Killer*. A home video enthusiast (former child actor and radio D.J. Danny Bonaduce) abandons his wife after learning of her affair and is taken hostage by the brutal Clint Dryer gang. He is forced by his captors to film their increasingly bizarre, fiendish and sadomasochistic crime spree. "The most original independent film since *Slacker*" (Christian Gore, *Film Threat*). With Mick Wynhoff, Mollena Williams and Melora alters.
VHS: S18977. $29.95.
Jack Perez, USA, 1992

American Blue Note
A truly pleasant slice of life set in 1960. Peter MacNicol stars as Jack "The Sax" Solow, the optimistic leader of a New Jersey jazz quintet looking for fame and fortune but willing to settle for a paying gig. This wry, well played, independent romantic comedy hits all the right notes. With Trini Alvarado, Louis Guss, Carl Capotorto, Jonathan Walker, Bill Christopher and Tim Guinee.
VHS: S15708. $89.95.
Ralph Toporoff, USA, 1989, 96 mins.

American Heart
Martin Bell's *(Streetwise)* dramatic debut examines the lifestyles of the socially marginal. Jeff Bridges plays Jack, a convict whose plans of moving to Alaska are thwarted by the appearance of his 14-year-old son, Nick (Edward Furlong). The two settle into a difficult daily existence in a Seattle boarding room as Jack tries desperately to avoid the temptation of the grift, while Nick is attracted to the romantic allure of the streets. Lucinda Jenney contributes a remarkable turn as Jack's battle-scarred girlfriend.
Laser: LD75145. $34.98.
Martin Bell, USA, 1992, 113 mins.

American Orpheus
Rick Schmidt's variation of Jean Cocteau's *Orphee*, about the relationship between a young mother and daughter, shattered by the absence of husband and father who abandoned them. "Shot with a lean, composed style, what is particularly striking is its sense of intimacy and simple emotional honesty" *(Seattle International Film Festival)*. With Jody Esther, Karen Rodriguez, Curtis Imrie and Willie Boy Walker. Cinematography by Kyle Bergersen.
VHS: S17768. $39.95.
Richard Schmidt, USA, 1992, 93 mins.

American Taboo
Paul Wunderlich is a 30-year-old assistant to his arrogant photographer boss, Michael, whose sexually suggestive fashion photos have made him the buzz of the town. While Michael photographs provocative young women, Paul smolders with desire and contempt. Reacting to a lifetime of sexual repression, Paul takes up his own camera, releasing tightly sealed boxes of childhood memories that culminate in a taboo relationship with the teenaged girl next door. This Academy Award winning film evokes a dream world where fear and love are merged.
VHS: S16335. $49.95.
Steve Lustgarten, USA, 1983, 94 mins.

And Another Honky Tonk Girl Says She Will
A beautiful country girl leaves her family farm and baby behind to pursue a singing career in Nashville. Her naive dreams of stardom are swiftly smashed by her lecherous agent uncle, who books her into sleazy bars and takes more than his cut of the action. Public performance.
VHS: S32133. $59.95.
Michelle Paymar, USA, 1990, 30 mins.

And the Earth Did Not Swallow Him (...y no se lo trago la tierra)
Based on Tomas Rivera's classic novella, this is the beautiful and moving semi-autobiographical account of 12-year-old Marcos Gonzales (Jose Alcala), the son of Mexican-American migrant workers in the 1950s, and their annual ritual of leaving Crystal City, Texas, for the harvest season work that will take them throughout the midwest during summer and fall. Reminscent of *To Kill a Mockingbird* or *Catcher in the Rye*. "An epic story of survival...affecting and beautifully photographed" (Kevin Thomas, *The Los Angeles Times*).
VHS: S30709. $79.95.
Severo Perez, USA, 1994, 99 mins.

The Apostle
Robert Duvall wrote, directed, and gives a critically acclaimed tour-de-force performance in this film as Sonny, a gifted, charismatic Southern preacher loved by his community, yet secretly plagued by the darker side of human desire and rage. When he commits a crime of passion, he is forced to run from the law and set out on a new mission: to find the road to redemption. With Farrah Fawcett, Billy Bob Thornton, Miranda Richardson and June Carter Cash.
VHS: S34966. $106.99.
DVD: Director commentary, widescreen, deleted scenes.
DV60382. $29.99.
Robert Duvall, USA, 1997, 134 mins.

Approaching Omega
A back-packing expedition is the setting for what the *LA Reader* called "an entertaining and playful manipulation of the conventions of storytelling."
VHS: S01546. $49.95.
John Dorr, USA, 1983

Art for Teachers of Children
Jennifer Montgomery's controversial, bravely autobiographical film takes a disquietingly original slant on underage sex. A 14-year-old starts an affair with her dorm counselor, who's into photographing his students in the nude. It's a relationship that won't stand still for parental interference or even investigation by the FBI, some years later. The director's deadpan, seemingly objective style downplays the outre subject matter and leaves the viewer to decide what is meant by the age of consent. "Sexually frank...startling" (Janet Maslin, *The New York Times*).
VHS: S32959. $59.95.
Jennifer Montgomery, USA, 1995, 82 mins.

Assignment: Rescue
The dramatic story of Varian Fry, who died in 1967, an unknown American "Schindler" responsible for the rescue of over 2,000 anti-Nazis, including many of Europe's most distinguished artists, writers and scholars, including Andre Breton, Marc Chagall, Max Ernst and Hannah Arendt. Narrated by Meryl Streep.
VHS: S33387. $24.95.
Richard Kaplan, USA, 1997, 26 mins.

The Bad Lieutenant
Abel Ferrara's portrait of a corrupt, self-destructive New York vice lieutenant. In a great performance, Harvey Keitel plays a drug-addicted rogue cop trying to settle his gambling debts while investigating the violent rape of a beautiful young nun. Despite sequences of wrenching horror, especially the cop's verbal humiliation of two New Jersey teenagers, *Bad Lieutenant* achieves a grace and poetic intensity. Cinematography by Ken Kelsch. Screenplay by Abel Ferrara and Zoe Lund. With Victor Argo, Paul Calderone, Leonard Thomas and Frankie Thorn.
VHS: S18912. $19.98.
Laser: LD75154. $34.98.
Abel Ferrara, USA, 1992, 98 mins.

The Badge
At 29, Michael still lives at home with his parents. His many failed career efforts disgust his Italian-American father, who favors his successful eldest son, Tommy. Michael joins the Los Angeles Police Department in a last-ditch effort to win his father's respect, but, in the process, faces personal demons he never bargained for. Public performance.
VHS: S32131. $59.95.
Robert Spara, USA, 1990, 30 mins.

Ballyhoo Baby
While on vacation, an attractive couple pick up a teenage hitchhiker in the Mojave Desert. The woman, a well-known TV model, is progressively alienated by this turn of events since her advertising executive husband can't seem to stop encouraging a liaison with the drifter. Public performance.
VHS: S32136. $59.95.
Paul Young, USA, 1990, 30 mins.

Barcelona
Taylor Nichols is a sales rep in Barcelona who can't quite master the fast Barcelona scene. His cousin (Christopher Eigeman), however, is an obnoxious Navy man easily at home in this exciting city. That is, before they both become aware of a lingering anti-American sentiment that sends this comic, sexy film off on a violent tangent.
VHS: S23678. $19.98.
Laser: Widescreen. **LD74812. $39.99.**
Whit Stillman, USA, 1994, 102 mins.

Basement Tape
A series of humorous sketches by Larry Hankin, including his Academy Award nominee *Solly's Diner*.
VHS: S01544. $49.95.

Basquiat
The critically acclaimed film about the rise and fall of controversial 1980s Haitian-Puerto Rican graffiti artist-turned-Soho-supernova Jean-Michel Basquiat, who died of a heroin overdose in 1988. Starring Dennis Hopper, Gary Oldman, David Bowie as Andy Warhol, and Tony Award-winner Jeffrey Wright *(Angels in America)* as Basquiat. With Willem Dafoe, Courtney Love, Parker Posey and Tatum O'Neal and music by David Bowie, Van Morrison and Tom Waits. "One of the year's best" *(Siskel & Ebert)*.
VHS: S30822. $103.99.
Laser: LD76102. $39.99.
Julian Schnabel, USA, 1996, 111 mins.

Bastard Out of Carolina
Anjelica Huston's directorial debut, produced by the Turner Network and then banned when Ted Turner saw it, has been controversial from the start because of its graphic depiction of a rape scene. Jennifer Jason Leigh delivers a very strong performance in this true story of a dysfunctional South Carolina family, which ends with tragedy. With Ron Eldard, Glenne Headly, Lyle Lovett, Diana Scarwid and Christina Ricci. "Directed…with a fine eye and a strong will" *(The New York Times)*.
VHS: S31061. $19.95.
Laser: LD76202. $39.98.
Anjelica Huston, USA, 1996, 97 mins.

Becoming Colette
From the director of *Mr. North*, this is an erotic and flamboyant dramatization of the artistic and sexual life of French writer Colette (Mathilda May). With Klaus Maria Brandauer, Virginia Madsen and Paul Rhys. Cinematography by Wolfgang Treu.
VHS: S18751. $29.95.
Danny Huston, USA, 1992, 97 mins.

Before Sunrise
Ethan Hawke is a heartbroken young journalist from Texas who invites a beautiful young French student, Julie Delpy, to take a sojourn in Vienna. It leads to a wonderful adventure/romance where the thought that they may never be together again permeates every moment.
VHS: S25616. $19.95.
Laser: LD74972. $34.95.
Richard Linklater, USA, 1995, 101 mins.

Begotten
A nightmare classic, this film chronicles the strange fate of a godlike thing that dies when it gives birth to a messiah thing. ("Thing" is the only appropriate word that can describe this creature.) There are no names, no dialogue, and no compromises in this bleak tale.
VHS: S23753. $24.95.
E. Elias Merhage, USA, 1991, 78 mins.

Best of the New York Underground
This collection of extraordinary films is best for the adventurous. *Queen Mercy, Screaming Chigger Productions, Pleasant Hill USA* and *Rosa Mi Amour* are just four of the films here that focus on odd, even unsavory material. A peep show dancer, child beating, a small town killer, and a graveyard where all is not dead yet are some of the elements explored in these films. 1994, 90 mins.
VHS: S25609. $29.95.

The Big Dis
This highly-regarded first feature by Gordon Eriksen and John O'Brien is a funny and trenchant interracial comedy about a young black soldier on weekend leave determined to find easy, anonymous sex, though his world shattered when he's dissed (i.e., "disrespected") by 12 candidates. It's an ambitious first effort shot in textured black and white. "A disarming fast-talking comedy, spiked with street jargon and rap music…with the buzz of authenticity," the *Village Voice* wrote.
VHS: S17104. $59.95.
Gordon Eriksen/John O'Brien, USA, 1989, 88 mins.

Big Night
This charmer of a movie—a big winner at Sundance and with audiences, and a treat for movie and food lovers—is the story of two Italian brothers whose restaurant teeters on the brink of bankruptcy. With Minnie Driver, Ian Holm, Isabella Rossellini, Campbell Scott, Tony Shalhoub and Stanley Tucci. "A feast of a film" (Peter Travers, *Newsday*).
VHS: S31122. $19.95.
Laser: LD76173. $34.99.
DVD: DV60232. $24.95.
Stanley Tucci, USA, 1996, 109 mins.

Black Hearts Bleed Red
Subterranean art icon and social menace Joe Coleman stars in this hard-edged but moving and respectful adaptation of Flannery O'Connor's short story about why lonely women should never accept help on the road.
VHS: S22628. $19.95.
Jeri Cain Rossi, USA, 1990, 15 mins.

The Blind Lead
From up-and-coming Chicago filmmaker John Covert *(Waiting for the Man)* comes this raw and powerful film about a struggling playwright as he descends into insanity. Based on the short story *Snow Blind*, by John Harriman, who also plays Johnny Boy, the playwright, this shoestring budget film was called "one of the best 'little' films of the year" by *Film Threat* magazine. Don't miss the stunning debut by this young filmmaker who has been compared to Quentin Tarantino and Robert Rodriguez.
VHS: S30050. $19.95.
John Covert, USA, 1996, 90 mins.

Blood
"A film about desperation in the New York streets. A funny, bitter look at white, middle-class youth trying to be touch in the trappings of pornography, drugs and quick money. The first punk film. In its stream-of-consciousness way, *Blood* evokes Manhattan street life even more powerfully than Martin Scorsese's *Taxi Driver*. Ms. Krasilovsky brings into camera an array of furtive, frustrated people—e.g., hookers and juvenile delinquents—and allows them to talk about themselves as we watch them in action. As a depiction of contemporary urban despair, *Blood*, more specifically, is an angry, outraged protest of the exploitation of women by men" (Kevin Thomas, *Los Angeles Times*).
VHS: S07772. $29.95.
Alexis Krasilovsky, USA, 1975, 21 mins.

Bloodhounds of Broadway
The Roaring Twenties as interpreted by a cast of performers from the Eighties. Four short stories by Damon Runyan are combined in this comic musical salute produced, directed and co-written by the late Howard Brookner. The cast includes Madonna, who sings "The Mooch" and "I Surrender, Dear," Matt Dillon, Julie Hagerty, Jennifer Grey, Rutger Hauer, Esai Morales and Randy Quaid.
VHS: S11574. $14.95.
Howard Brookner, USA, 1989, 100 mins.

The Bloody Child
Maverick American independent filmmaker Nina Menkes' film was inspired by the true story of a young U.S. marine, just back from the Gulf War, who was arrested while digging a grave in the middle of the Mojave Desert for his murdered wife, whose bloodied body lay in the backseat of his car. Menkes turns the mundane realism of the marine's arrest into a haunting, hallucinatory journey, a jagged look back at the nature of violence. The filmmaker's sister and collaborator, Tinka Menkes, portrays a marine captain; all other cast members are actual Desert Storm veterans.
VHS: S32371. $79.95.
Nina Menkes, USA, 1996, 85 mins.

Blue in the Face
Roseanne, Michael J. Fox and Mira Sorvino are just some of the stars featured in this comic continuation of *Smoke*. A series of skits are set in a Brooklyn neighborhood cigar shop which is set to close. Amidst the wacky set-ups, Giancarlo Esposito, Jim Jarmusch, Harvey Keitel, Lou Reed, Lily Tomlin and other celebrities improvise with panache and wit.
VHS: S27691. $19.95.
Laser: LD75572. $39.99.
Wayne Wang/Paul Auster, USA, 1995, 84 mins.

The Boardwalk Club
This comic short features an elderly couple in New York who are embroiled in a longstanding dispute about where to spend their retirement years. Sadie wants to leave Brighton Beach and move to Florida. Max wants to stay and play cards with his buddies of 50 years. In their ongoing battle of wit and wiles, who will be able to out-guilt whom? Public performance.
VHS: S32128. $59.95.
Craig Shapiro, USA, 1992, 27 mins.

Bob Roberts
Tim Robbins' directorial debut stars Robbins as a right-wing folk singer and political activist who manipulates the media to camouflage a fascist veneer. Framed as a mock documentary covering Roberts' senatorial campaign, the film is a funny, often devastating critique of the political process, the selling out of the media, and the emergence of style over substance. With Giancarlo Esposito, Ray Wise, Gore Vidal and Alan Rickman. Special appearances by John Cusack, Peter Gallagher, Susan Sarandon and James Spader.
VHS: S18464. $19.98.
Tim Robbins, USA, 1992, 102 mins.

Bodies, Rest & Motion
Michael Steinberg adapts Roger Heden's play about the sexual and social languor of Generation X. Set in an anonymous Arizona wasteland of concrete slabs and decaying landscapes, the film is a chamber drama which follows the turbulent social and sexual relations among four lost souls. The cast of characters includes Nick (Tim Roth), a dissatisfied television salesman; his girlfriend Beth (Bridget Fonda); Carol (Phoebe Cates), Beth's neighbor and friend, and Nick's former lover; and Sid (Eric Stoltz), a casually hip housepainter who becomes infatuated with Beth.
VHS: S19574. $19.95.
Laser: LD76793. $49.95.
Michael Steinberg, USA, 1993, 94 mins.

Body Snatchers
Gabrielle Anwar, Meg Tilly and Forest Whitaker star in this third remake of *Invasion of the Body Snatchers*, the classic science fiction story of aliens who intend to take over the world. The pod people are back with their incredible talent to infiltrate society and pose as normal human beings.
VHS: S21087. $19.98.
Laser: LD72414. $39.98.
Abel Ferrara, USA, 1993, 87 mins.

Boogie Nights
Paul Thomas Anderson's *(Hard Eight)* outrageous epic about the ups and downs of an unusual "family" of filmmakers in the adult entertainment industry of the swinging '70s features dynamite performances by Mark Wahlberg as well-endowed porn star Dirk Diggler, Burt Reynolds as porn director Jack Horner, Julianne Moore as Amber Waves, and John C. Reilly as Reid Rothchild. With William H. Macy, Heather Graham and Don Cheadle.
VHS: S33424. $104.99.
Laser: Widescreen. **LD76826. $99.95.**
DVD: DV60303. $24.98.
Paul Thomas Anderson, USA, 1997, 155 mins.

Borders
A kaleidoscopic survey of the physical, political and moral borders that inhibit the free movement of people and ideas, *Borders* mixes commentary, computer graphics, dramatic fiction, live documentary footage and investigative journalism to present a tremendous range of information. *Borders* tempers its serious and sometimes infuriatingly ludicrous subject matter with the sardonic wit of its interviewees and comic computer art.
VHS: S13336. $29.95.
M. Aldighieri/J. Tripician, USA, 1989, 53 mins.

Born in Flames
A landmark in the independent film movement, Lizzie Borden's sci-fi/feminist/adventure story is set in America ten years after the Second American Revolution, a socialist rebellion that has redefined the roles of women and minorities. When Adelaide Norris, the black lesbian founder of the Woman's Army, is mysteriously killed, a coalition of women across all lines of race, class, and sexual preference emerges to blow the system apart. "Funny, gutsy and inspiring" *(Ms. Magazine)*.
VHS: S31350. $29.95.
Lizzie Borden, USA, 1984, 90 mins.

Bottle Rocket
James Caan stars as a tough crime boss who won't take no for an answer in this unusual comedy. It's part coming-of-age story and part gangster film, where the three central assailants aren't especially good at crime, resulting in hysterical mishaps all the way to the pay-off. Owen Wilson also appears.
VHS: S29865. $19.95.
Laser: LD75905. $34.95.
Wes Anderson, USA, 1996, 92 mins.

bottom land
Hailed as "blunt and uncompromising" *(Los Angeles Times)* and "deeply moving" *(Variety)*, this is the story of three men in crisis. Stephen Saunders returns home to the family farm and must overcome the doubt and lost love of his son. A powerful, uncompromising, emotionally-stirring, debut feature. Voted Best First Feature.
VHS: S21131. $59.95.
Edward Radtke, USA, 1991, 75 mins.

Bound
Pulp prince James M. Cain meets lesbian sexpert Susie Bright in this "sultry slice of noir gamesmanship that boasts clever twists, crackling flirtations, smart, assertive camerawork, and a believable, sensual, sexual relationship between two women" *(Chicago Reader)* by the Wachowski Brothers. A mobster (Joe Pantoliano), his mistress (Jennifer Tilly) and a tough, female ex-con (Tina Gershon) are caught in a dangerous plot starting with $2 million of the Mob's money and ending in seduction and betrayal. "Sleek!" (Janet Maslin, *New York Times*).
VHS: S30825. $14.95.
Laser: LD76078. $34.98.
Andy Wachowski/Larry Wachowski, USA, 1996, 108 mins.

Box of Moonlight

Uptight electrical engineer Al Fountain (John Turturro) is a man struggling with the monotony of everyday life and the threat of middle age, when a routine business trip turns into a life-altering experience. With the help of a few bizarre but sincere strangers—a free spirit called "the Kid" (Sam Rockwell), a phone sex operator (Catherine Keener) and a paranoid mechanic (Dermot Mulroney)—Al discovers something incredible: himself. "Sexy, seductive, amazingly fresh" (Janet Maslin, *New York Times*).
VHS: S32691. $99.99.
Laser: LD76440. $34.98.
Tom DiCillo, USA, 1997, 111 mins.

Boxing Helena

Julian Sands and Sherilyn Fenn star in this provocative fable of obsession and desire. Taking the title a little too literally, Sand's character tries to contain the object of his interests in a brutally simple way.
VHS: S20599. $19.98.
Laser: LD72428. $39.99.
Jennifer Chambers Lynch, USA, 1993, 107 mins.

Break of Dawn

Unsung hero Pedro J. Gonzalez was an immensely popular musician and radio personality in Los Angeles during the Depression. This is the true-life story of a man who lived comfortably until he challenged a powerful and corrupt political system bent on prejudice, and of his controversial trial, which exposed the paranoid hysteria of a city suddenly faced with economic ruin. Mexico's great singer and actor Oscar Chavez stars as Gonzalez. With Maria Rojo and Tony Plana.95
VHS: S12553. $69.95.
Isaac Artenstein, USA, 1988, 100 mins.

Bronx Cheers

Set in the Bronx, immediately after the end of WWII, this delightful, Academy Award-nominated period comedy tells the story of Danny DiPalma, a returning veteran of Italian-American descent. The aspiring songwriter comes under the unlikely wing of a high-strung, heavyweight championship contender who has been reduced to throwing fights for money. In comical fashion, Danny struggles to free himself from the fighter's misguided friendship and win a few of his own. Public performance.
VHS: S32132. $59.95.
Raymond DeFelitta, USA, 1989, 30 mins.

The Brothers McMullen

In this romantic comedy, the Best Picture at the 1995 Sundance Festival, three brothers from Long Island confront the unknown territory of love and marriage. After their father dies, their mother returns to Ireland to be with the man she really loves. The three Irish Catholic brothers are left to deal with varying stages of love and marriage, ranging from initial attraction to engagement to the prospect of an extramarital affair. With Edward Burns, Jack Mulcahy, Mike McGlone and Connie Britton.
VHS: S27210. $19.95.
Laser: LD75482. $39.98.
Edward Burns, USA, 1995, 98 mins.

Brunch/28

The first of these two shorts is a breezy, animated video of an early morning vignette that is both light and beautiful. It is produced by painter Jill and video artist Carole. *28* is a birthday video that offers a bright comic romp with piquant edges by Carole.
VHS: S22658. $29.95.
Fleischmann Sisters, USA, 1986-1987, 15 mins.

Caligari's Cure

Tom Palazzolo's first narrative feature film is a hilarious take-off of Robert Wiene's 1919 classic, *The Cabinet of Dr. Caligari*. The veteran Chicago filmmaker draws on his memories of Catholic school and adolescent sexual fantasies, reenacted by a zany cast.
VHS: S00207. $39.95.
Tom Palazzolo, USA, 1983, 80 mins.

Canadian Bacon

John Candy is joined by Dan Aykroyd, Rhea Perlman, Kevin Pollak and Bill Nunn in this outrageous comedy satire. Imagine that the U.S. is threatened by a very close, immense neighbor. The country would rally together to defeat the nefarious foe. This scenario is presented to the President of the United States and he decides that in order to ensure his re-election and get those wartime industries humming, he will invade that colossus of the North, Canada.
VHS: S26804. $19.95.
Laser: LD75407. $34.95.
Michael Moore, USA, 1994, 95 mins.

Candide in the Americas

A video sketch of chapters 10-20 of Voltaire's novel, in which Candide and his faithful servant Cacambo bomb around this best of all possible worlds in an old Chevy. Quiet, curious, this is the German filmmaker's sketch for a feature film.
VHS: S10187. $49.95.
Harold Vogl/Andrew Bergen, USA, 1986, 62 min.

Cannes Man

Sy Lerner is the quintessential con-man: a movie producer with no script or scruples about lying to get a picture made. To win a bet and secure financing for his next picture, Lerner takes an errand boy and passes him off as the greatest screenwriter since Faulkner and Hemingway. Set at the festival in Cannes, this street-smart comedy about the art of the deal has cameos by more than a dozen celebrities, including Johnny Depp, Treat Williams, Dennis Hopper and John Malkovich. With Seymour Cassel, Francesco Quinn and Rebecca Broussard.
VHS: S33363. $19.99.
Richard Martini, USA, 1996, 87 mins.

Casual Relations

Rappaport's dazzling and bizarre feature-length debut focuses on states of imaginative possession and dispossession, demonstrating that it is impossible to separate fantasies and dreams from realities. "A discovery, a surprise…indescribable. The film is tender and ironic, simple and controlled all the way through" *(International HAD)*.
VHS: S31127. $29.99.
Mark Rappaport, USA, 1973, 80 mins.

Chain Letters

Rappaport's "most deliciously lush and Byzantine work" (Ray Carney, Boston University) is one where strange puzzles, symmetries and coincidences abound and doppelgangers lurk around every corner. Can we connect the dots to unlock the mysteries of life, or, as one character in the film believes, is all of life a plot orchestrated by a vast government bureaucracy? "Vintage Rappaport. Original, eccentric and highly amusing" *(American Film)*.
VHS: S31137. $29.99.
Mark Rappaport, USA, 1985, 96 mins.

Chasing Amy

From the talented young writer and director of *Clerks* comes this wickedly witty and insightful story of hip young comics artist Holden (Ben Affleck), who, against the advice of his jealous collaborator Banky (Jason Lee), falls for Alyssa, a funny and sexy fellow comics artist—who happens to be a lesbian. "Ripe with Smith's trademark virtuosic verbosity, raunchy sexual discussions, intense dramatic confrontations" *(New City)*.
VHS: S32660. $103.99.
Laser: LD76438. $49.95.
Kevin Smith, USA, 1997, 105 mins.

Childhood's End

A character-driven tale of the intersecting lives of a group of whip-smart Minneapolis teens fresh out of high school seeking love and sex. With its arch humor and no-holds barred sexuality, the film takes an incisive and uncompromising look at what happens when suburban alienation meets desire, as driven Generation "Q" and Xers intersect with Baby Boomers in the throes of mid-life regrets.
VHS: S33868. $29.95.
Jeff Lipsky, USA, 1996, 115 mins.

Chip Lord: Selected Works

A collection of short films by Chip Lord: *Celebrity Author, Bi-Coastal and Executive Air Traveller, Get Ready to March, Abscam (Framed), Three Drugs*, and *AUTO FIRE LIFE*. All of the films deal with media identity and mass media imagery-for example, *Abscam (Framed)* utilized FBI Abscam footage in a tongue-in-cheek re-enactment at the scene of the crime.
VHS: S09576. $39.95.
Chip Lord, USA, 28 mins.

The Church of Shooting Yourself

Selected programs from the public access show *The Church of Shooting Yourself* are featured in this collection. The World Trade Center after the bombing, a Beat reunion at a William Burroughs book signing, a protest against Time-Warner's anti cable-access stance, and even a visit to Jim Morrison's grave are included.
VHS: S22616. $29.95.
Rik Little, USA, 1993, 120 mins.

CineBLAST! Vol. 3

A collection of the best short independent features by contemporary American filmmakers. Includes Tom Gilroy's *Touchbase*, starring Lili Taylor; Dan Wain's *Aisle Six*, about the joys of bathroom plumbing; Ethan Spigland's *The Strange Case of Balthazar*, which reinvents the history of cinema; Jadina Lilen's cinema verite documentary *Marie*; Billy Kent's *Egg Salad*, an expose of the clownish behavior of the West Coast dating scene; Matt Mennees' animated short *Fan-Tasy* and David Capurso's *Emily's Song*, a different take on homelessness. 92 mins.
VHS: S32501. $89.95.

Citizen Tanya

Raymond Pettibon and Dave Markey co-direct the SLA/Patty Hearst drama in a detonation of 60's counterculture. "A free, sexy, right-on Tanya is forged of the uptight, poor little rich girl Patty over the white hot flame of 400 Amerikan years of bottled up race/sex/black/white fury in the person of Field Marshall Cinque."
VHS: S20527. $19.95.

Clean, Shaven

Peter Greene stars as a man desperately hoping to find his lost daughter. Schizophrenic hallucinations and a rabid policeman complicate this overwhelming task. Detective McNally won't let up because he suspects this strange character is actually a serial killer stalking children. Winner of Best First Feature award at the 1993 Chicago International Film Festival.
VHS: S26938. $19.98.
Lodge Kerrigan, USA, 1993, 80 mins.

Clerks

For the slacker generation life seems to be just a series of dead-end jobs where catering to jerks is the only way to pay the bills. This great, independently made comedy follows a parade of annoying shoppers helped by two friends. One works at a convenience store and the other at a video shop next door.
VHS: S24576. $19.95.
Laser: Letterboxed. **LD74977. $39.99.**
Kevin Smith, USA, 1994, 92 mins.

The Closest Thing to Heaven

Five interwoven tales of love, death, hope, greed and lust that take place in one day in Charlotte, North Carolina. Featuring an outstanding ensemble cast, these stories take us from the comical to the poignant and back again. The characters' lives criss-cross and reflect each other, all held together for us by an amiable Southern gentleman angel named Howard, who interjects bits of Charlotte lore and history along the way.
VHS: S32215. $79.95.
Dorne Pentes, USA, 1996, 98 mins.

Committed

The striking story of film star/leftist/iconoclast Frances Farmer. In 1935 Farmer was an overnight Hollywood sensation; within ten years she was in a state mental hospital. From stardom to a locked ward to a lobotomy, the film reconstructs a compelling and many-layered look at the life and repression of this culturally defiant woman. "Superbly shot and acted…more subtle than the sledgehammer Hollywood feature—and no less mythic" (J. Hoberman).
VHS: S14154. $29.95.
Sheila McLaughlin/Lynn Tillman, USA, 1984, 77 mins.

Counterclockwise

This short drama describes the 20-year friendship of four lively but vastly different women who gather for a three-day reunion after having drifted apart over the years. As they drag their now middle-aged bodies up a mountain to disperse the ashes of the late husband of one of the women, the film reveals the complex nature of their friendship and their acceptance of the changes that time has imprinted on their lives. Public performance.
VHS: S32123. $59.95.
Kathleen McFall, USA, 1996, 26 mins.

Crude Oasis

A young Kansas housewife is plagued by recurring nightmares until she meets a young man she recognizes from her dreams. The result of their meeting is a seductive and shocking tale filled with mystery, suspense and terror.
VHS: S28047. $89.95.
Alex Graves, USA, 1995, 82 mins.

Dad's Last Flight

In this short drama, Eli, a young father, in the midst of a family crisis with his wife and son, begins to lose his grip on sanity just in time to greet the mysterious visit of Sam, his mentally ill father. Sam's delusions push Eli to examine his own mental health and reclaim the love of his family and the hope and imagination of his childhood. Public performance.
VHS: S32120. $99.95.
Sheldon Schiffer, USA, 1992, 51 mins.

Dance Hall Racket
"Scalley's Dance Emporium" is a place where anything goes. Busty women, knife fights, lascivious dancing, and even a diamond smuggling ring keep the joint jumping. Lenny Bruce plays Scalley's assistant, a man whose talents include planting blades in the bellies of men who get too fresh with the girls. Scripted by Bruce, the film contains many pearls of dialog, such as "If you've got the money, I've got the time." Features his wife Honey Harlow as a bimbo, along with Phil Tucker, Timothy Farreland Sally Marr.
VHS: S16106. $29.95.
Phil Tucker, USA, 1953, 60 mins.

Dangerous Game
Madonna is joined by James Russo and Harvey Keitel in this violent and intense psychodrama. Playing a film director, Keitel pushes his art to ever greater extremes until the violence he creates begins to seep into his real life. Madonna and Russo play the actors who come to embody his darkest visions.
VHS: S21033. $95.98.
Laser: LD72408. $34.98.
Abel Ferrara, USA, 1993, 108 mins.

Dazed and Confused
Cult director Richard Linklater *(Slacker)* takes a hilarious look at the last day of school—and one wild night—in the lives of a group of high school students in 1976 in this nutty return to bongs and bell bottoms, polyester and pukka shells, macrame and mood rings. Music by Aerosmith, Black Sabbath, Alice Cooper, Foghat. "The most slyly funny and dead-on portrait of American teenage life ever made" *(Entertainment Weekly)*.
VHS: S20496. $19.98.
Laser: Letterboxed. **LD72291. $34.98.**
DVD: DV60301. $24.98.
Richard Linklater, USA, 1993, 103 mins.

Dear Carry
This video is based on the travel films of Caroline Wagner, a New York jewelry designer and amateur filmmaker, who traveled around the world from the 1920s to the 1980s. In this personal and idiosyncratic essay, written as a letter which interweaves Carry's travel films and letters with the filmmaker's own from a 1995 trip to Zimbabwe, Carry's films become a point of departure for an examination of the act of filming on personal, psychological, and emotional levels.
VHS: S34407. $275.00.
Joel Katz, USA, 1997, 45 mins.

The Deli
Clerks meets *Smoke* in this ensemble cast slice-of-life urban fable about Johnny Amico (Mike Starr), a lovable but incorrigibly bad gambler who has a tough time paying the bills at his Italian-American delicatessen in New York City. In the course of one intense, hilarious week, Johnny must use all his wits and charms to pay off his debt in a comic roller coaster that reaches its climax at an outdoor party at a Westchester mansion. With Matt Keeslar, Judith Malina, Brian Vincent, Michael Badalucco, Heavy D, Ice T, Iman, Michael Imperioli, David Johansen, Joey Kola, Heather Matarazzo, Debi Mazar, William McNamara, Gretchen Mol, Chris Noth, Tony Sirico, Jerry Stiller, Shirley Stoler, Frank Vincent and Burt Young.
VHS: S32692. $99.95.
John Gallagher, USA, 1997, 98 mins.

Depth Charge
Two former childhood pals have hitchhiked from New York City to rally against chemical waste dumping at their longtime summer camp in Maine. En route, they meet another ex-camper, who raises questions about the mysterious drowning of two camp counselors ten years before. A film about fear, misperception and male bonding. Public performance.
VHS: S32137. $59.95.
Sean Travis, USA, 1989, 20 mins.

Desert Hearts
Wonderful love story between a repressed English professor who is waiting for a divorce at a dude ranch for women, and a beautiful casino worker in Reno who lives at the ranch with her mother. Adapted from the novel *Desert of the Heart*, by Jane Rule, with a fabulous soundtrack!
VHS: S01919. $19.98.
Laser: LD75919. $39.99.
Donna Deitch, USA, 1985, 96 mins.

Desert Spirits
In this experimental feature, two men find themselves stranded in the desert when their car breaks down. They take peyote to kill some time and find themselves in another world, where lizards talk, sensory perception expands and demonic spirits seek their prey.
VHS: S22422. $19.95.
Patrick McGuinn, USA, 1994, 35 mins.

Desolation Angels
An "utterly compelling" (Kevin Thomas, *Los Angeles Times*) film dealing with a young man's desperate attempt to avenge the rape of his girlfriend by a mutual acquaintance. But is it his girlfriend's honor or his own male pride that he's really trying to protect? Made on a shoestring budget of $27,000, this semi-autobiographical tale, set and shot in a working-class Brooklyn neighborhood, is a provocative, wrenching and bleakly funny debut film by the talented Tim McCann.
VHS: S31194. $19.98.
Tim McCann, USA, 1995, 90 mins.

Destroy All Blondes/ The Naked Hipstress/Sick Sick Sister
In the first of these shorts there is a comic account of the lives of the great poohbahs of the early 80's downtown New York scene. Turgid rivalries threaten the very core of hip existence. Then two gorgeous but politically opposed sisters catfight to the death in a shocking expose. This second short features a young David Byrne.
VHS: S22613. $49.95.
Mark Kehoe, USA, 1979-1990, 45 mins.

Dirty Money
In this skillfully paced Hitchcockian neo-noir, a simple act of kindness triggers an avalanche of events that turn an innocent man's life upside down, changing him into an accused killer with no friends to turn to. Alone, Sam is forced to survive until all the elements of the chase collide with a force that will decide his fate. "The feel and look of *Reservoir Dogs*. A working man's *Die Hard*" *(Film Threat Magazine)*.
VHS: S32171. $89.98.
James Bruce, USA, 1996, 82 mins.

Don from Lakewood/You Talk, I Buy
These two infamous phone-prank video shorts use puppets, cardboard dioramas and Fisher-Price black-and-white photography to investigate the relationship between salesman and customer, displaying a clear microcosm of the infinitely larger McCluhanesque, technologically induced, schizophrenic society in which we live. Includes the special bonus short *Hide*. "Wickedly funny…a *Death of a Salesman*-in-miniature" *(The Village Voice)*.
VHS: S32221. $29.95.
Pat Tierney/Eric Saks, USA, 1989/1990, 42 mins.

The Doom Generation
From the maker of *The Living End* comes another installment of violence and sex cooled by stereotypical generation X elan. Two kids meet up with a bleeding dude and set off to terrorize the motorized world. A stop at a convenience store leaves a talking head without its body and a bizarre family murder/suicide, so the three main characters go on the run and all have sex with each other. Can they evade the gang of skinheads?
VHS: S27521. $14.95.
Gregg Araki, USA, 1995, 83 mins.

Doomed Love
Widely-praised feature that won honors in Berlin, the film is a moving psychological drama of obsession—combining elements of romantic mythology and melodrama. Actor and painter Bill Rice stars as a frustrated professor of romantic literature who reaches the end of his rope and resolves to be reunited with his deceased true love.
VHS: S07117. $59.95.
Andrew Horn, USA, 1983, 75 mins.

Dorothy and Alan at Norma Place
A two-hour dramatized biography of literary wit Dorothy Parker; Strawn Bovee stars as Parker, whose private life is traced from her celebrated Algonquin circle heyday in 1920s New York through her alcoholic vegetation in West Hollywood of the 1960s.
VHS: S05873. $49.95.
John Dorr, USA, 1987, 120 mins.

Dr. Jekyll and Ms. Hyde
A myopic visionary, Dr. Jekyll pursues her need for change and power through a labyrinth of falls, fires, transformations and escapes. Hand painted sets and simple effects add to this work's power.
VHS: S22618. $29.95.
J. Kathleen White, USA, 1980, 34 mins.

Dream with the Fishes
A comically rendered, gravebound road movie of an unholy pact between two men, one who is dying and another who is learning to live. With David Arquette, Brad Hunt, Cathy Moriarty and Kathryn Erbe. "A buddy movie that keeps you guessing" *(Harpers Bazaar)*.
VHS: S32899. $19.95.
Finn Taylor, USA, 1997, 96 mins.

Duet for Spies/ Frankie Lymon's Nephew Story
Jim Neu's script helps create a symbolic enactment of the covert relationship between power and sex in the first of these two shorts. It's a dark, post-Cold War comedy equating individual and institutional delusions. Then, in the Lymon story, we learn of a young night club singer who just said yes. He lived fast but died slow. Now several of his wives are fighting over his estate.
VHS: S22502. $39.95.
Jacob Burckhardt, USA, 1990-1993, 61 mins.

Easy Rider
Counter-culture road movie as Dennis Hopper and Peter Fonda cycle across the Southwest on their way to New Orleans, confronted by violence and bigotry. This film defined an American generation and created a mega-star of Jack Nicholson. Letterboxed.
VHS: S01821. $19.95.
Laser: New digital master, audio commentary with Peter Fonda and Dennis Hopper. **LD75091. $59.95.**
Dennis Hopper, USA, 1969, 94 mins.

Eating
Henry Jaglom uses the occasion of a birthday celebration for a discussion about sex, love, relationships, men, politics and self-expression. "A provocative tribute to women—the ideal movie for friends, of whatever sex, to share" *(San Francisco Chronicle)*. With Nelly Alard, Frances Bergen, Mary Crosby and Gwen Welles.
VHS: S18437. $89.95.
Laser: LD75184. $34.98.
Henry Jaglom, USA, 1989, 110 mins.

Ed's Next Move
One of the best little comedies of the year, and a big hit at the Sundance Film Festival, this independent feature stars Matt Ross as Ed Brodsky, who leaves his secure life in Wisconsin to go to the Big Apple in a humorous and honest look at the ups and downs of building a life and finding love in the big city.
VHS: S31018. $95.99.
Laser: LD76162. $39.98.
John Walsh, USA, 1996, 88 mins.

El Mariachi
This film by 24-year-old director Robert Rodriquez was made for the unbelievable sum of $7,000. Rodriguez playfully evokes Peckinpah, noir westerns and Hitchcock. A maverick loner and mariachi player (Carlos Gallardo) enters a Mexican border town and is instantly confused with a stark, brutally efficient assassin (Reinol Martinez). Spanish with English subtitles.
VHS: S19057. $19.95.
Laser: Special Collector's Edition. **LD71892. $49.95.**
Robert Rodriguez, USA, 1992, 80 mins.

Emerald Cities
"The film juxtaposes the Santa Claus myth, nuclear war, punk rock, hypnotic self-analysis, psychedelic drugs and video manipulation—you know, all that stuff we usually think about. This is one of the best independent films we've seen all year" (B.D. Rhodewalt, *L.A. Dee Da*).
VHS: S00405. $59.95.
Richard Schmidt, USA, 77 mins.

Empire Records
Young, hip and about to be unemployed, the staff at Empire Records are facing all the hilarious travails confronting today's terminally cool. From waiting for stardom as the next best grunge band to shaving, it's all here, including the conundrum of virginity—should she or shouldn't she? This is what could happen if you gambled it all away. Liv Tyler stars. Music from Gin Blossoms, The Cranberries, Edwyn Collins and others.
VHS: S27191. $19.98.
Allan Moyle, USA, 1995, 91 mins.

Enormous Changes at the Last Minute
Based on the short stories of Grace Paley comes a truly touching trilogy of connecting episodes in the lives of three women and the people that come into their lives. The film celebrates real life in its problems and its joys. Top notch cast includes Kevin Bacon, Ellen Barkin and Maria Tucci. Script by John Sayles and Susan Rice.
VHS: S03667. $79.95.
Ellen Hovde/Mirra Bank/Muffie Meyer, USA, 1985, 115 min.

The Enquirers
A cheesy Elvis impersonator is losing his ability to perform and has evidence that he has encountered the real Elvis at a nearby laundromat. A mysterious talent promoter wants to take a standup comic on the road to Vegas, L.A., New York and other places, including destinations beyond our solar system. An intellectual barfly does a little freelance psychoanalysis. Their paths cross and tabloid headlines come to life, engulfing these characters in a situation that can only be resolved by looking toward the unbelievable.
VHS: S33427. $29.95.
Rick Barnes, USA, 1995, 100 mins.

Erotique

This critically acclaimed, highly charged anthology features erotic short films from the female point of view. Lizzie Borden's *Let's Talk About Sex* is an uncompromising look at an aspiring young actress working as a phone sex operator who dramatically redefines the powers of sexual dynamics when she gets a caller to listen to her fantasies. *Taboo Parlor*, by Monika Treut, is an outrageous story about a lesbian couple who decide to pick up a man, leading to a night of uncontrollable desires where only the strong survive. A young teacher attacked on a train begins a sexual relationship with her rescuer, allowing her hidden emotions to rise to a feverish frenzy in Ana Maria's Magalhaes's *Final Call*. Two college lovers reunite in Hong Kong, where they discover their different cultures have caused them to grow apart. Determined to prove these obstacles can be overcome, the boy prepares an evening of gourmet food and ancient Chinese sexual techniques in Clara Law's funny and bold *Wonton Soup*. "One of the most freshly comedic depictions of sex in cinematic history" *(Film Threat)*.

VHS: S30885. $19.95.
DVD: DV60166. $29.98.
Lizzie Borden/Monika Treut/Ana Maria Magalhaes/ Clara Law, Germany/USA, 1996, 120 mins.

Eve's Bayou

This assured film debut by Kasi Lemmons explores the secrets of a Louisiana family through the eyes of a 10-year-old girl. "In the way it examines a family's emotional life, it reminded me of the family dramas of Ingmar Bergman" (Roger Ebert, *Chicago Sun-Times*). With Samuel Jackson, Lynn Whitfield and Debbi Morgan.

VHS: S33312. $105.99.
DVD: DV60295. $24.99.
Kasi Lemmons, USA, 1997, 109 mins.

Experienced Movers

A video epic—the story of the robbery of an art museum in "Boraxville,"—*X-Movers* savors the interpersonal seaminess of a world of petty thugs and downwardly mobile youth. A story of love and deception, from a play by Evan McHale.

VHS: S07115. $69.96.
Larry Fessenden, USA, 1985, 140 mins.

Fairgrounds

David Wells' film debut is an excellent example of contemporary American cinema. Shot in beautiful black and white, over 11 days, the low-budget feature concerns two partners in a circus sideshow junk-eating act who start to go their separate ways as the apprentice strives to replace the master, and the master becomes distracted by a strange yet compelling woman with a bizarre definition of romance. The wonderful screenplay, which Wells adapted from his award-winning play of the same name, contains some of the wittiest dialogue in recent memory. As a friend of the filmmaker said, "If Jim Jarmusch and Samuel Beckett went to the carnival and ate a bad corndog, you would get *Fairgrounds*."

VHS: S30440. $39.95.
David Wells, USA, 1996, 90 mins.

Fat of the Land

In this first kitchen grease-powered road movie, five Bay Area women make their way from New York to San Francisco in an '84 Chevy diesel van powered by used vegetable oil. The "Greasy Riders" careen across the nation stopping at greasy spoons, asking for leftover frying oil to fuel their "Lard Car" in this wacky 3,000-mile cross-country adventure. Other pit stops in this documentary include interviews with biofuel engineers, a quick overview of how-to-do-it fuel mixing, and conversations with the American public about our petroleum dependence.

VHS: S32426. $34.95.
Niki Cousino/Sarah Lewison, USA, 1995, 55 mins.

Film Musicals

Two remarkable films by New York writer and Hollywood emigre Tina L'hotsky. *Barbie* is self-portrait as dark surrealism, with the artist playing a human Barbie who fully nude at home ritually cooks and eats a Barbie doll. *Snakewoman* stars Patti Astor as the woman who conquers Africa as the Snakewoman—shot in a 30's styled adventure story.

VHS: S07118. $39.95.
Tina L'hotsky, USA, 1977, 45 mins.

Floundering

James LeGros, John Cusack, Ethan Hawke, Steve Buscemi and Kim Wayans star in this witty satire about generation X layabouts. After college there is a world just waiting to be explored, and these characters let it wait. Great soundtrack includes Sebadoh, Red House Painters, Drunken Boat and more.

VHS: S24664. $29.95.
Kevin Smith, USA, 1994, 92 mins.

Flow

This mind-blowing exploration of culture, race and sexuality in the '90s is a stylish and energetic compilation of short stories, including a postmodern slasher flick with a knife-wielding drag queen, an impressionistic film noir about a young man who kills his mother on Christmas day, a surrealistic tale of a vampire couple and the story of the trials and errors in romance and relationships of two freshmen—one gay and one straight. Binding these shorts together is a witty mockumentary about the fictional filmmaker of these films, his struggles as an independent filmmaker and his love for rice and boys.

VHS: S31791. $39.95.
Quentin Lee, USA, 1995, 80 mins.

Force of Circumstance

A political thriller, this film follows a Moroccan human rights activist's attempt to thwart a royal envoy. The envoy would buy an historic Virginia estate for his boss, the king. Eric Mitchell, as Boris Major, stars in this film, set in both Casablanca and Washington, D.C. Steve Buscemi and Mark Boone Jr. are featured.

VHS: S22607. $59.95.
Liza Bear, USA, 1990, 89 mins.

Foreigner

Poe's punk thriller stars filmmaker Eric Mitchell as Max Menace, replete with platinum hair, a secret agent who arrives in New York to meet his contact. Patti Astor co-stars as a mysterious blonde in this gritty depiction of New York.

VHS: S00460. $59.95.
Amos Poe, USA, 1978, 90 mins.

Forevermore: Biography of a Leach Lord

This highly original "cutting attack on American greed from the '50s through the '80s and beyond" (Michael Wilmington, *LA Times*) is a chilling pseudo-documentary about the culture of toxic waste dumpers from "arguably the most cynical media-artist on the West (or any) Coast today" (Craig Baldwin).

VHS: S32241. $29.95.
Eric Saks, USA, 1989, 90 mins.

Four Rooms

A host of stars, from Madonna to Antonio Banderas, are featured in this madcap comedy centered around Tim Roth. Roth is a bellhop whose first day on the job is rife with chaos and humor because of the four rooms he services. Four different directors worked on the different sections of this unique film. Jennifer Beals, Paul Calderon, Lili Taylor, and Marisa Tomei are just some of the other stars seen in this film.

VHS: S27849. $99.99.
Laser: LD75927. $39.99.
Allison Anders/Alexandre Rockwell/Robert Rodriguez/Quentin Tarantino, USA, 1995, 98 mins.

Freefall

Yuppie corporate attorney Emily is dissatisfied with both her job and her man, a burned-out fellow attorney bucking for a partnership. All work and no play takes its toll on the couple until Emily's old flame from Israel shows up on her doorstep and makes her an offer she might not refuse. Public performance.

VHS: S32139. $59.95.
Liz Leshin, USA, 1990, 28 mins.

Fresh

An electrifying feature about a 12-year-old boy (Sean Nelson) who walks a fine line between attending school and carrying drugs in his drug-infested Brooklyn environment. After witnessing a murder, he must fight for his own survival. A film that's at once powerful and riveting, and one that refuses to make a judgment call on its young protagonist. With Samuel L. Jackson.

VHS: S23480. $19.95.
Laser: Letterboxed. **LD74939. $39.99.**
Boaz Yakin, USA, 1994, 114 mins.

Frisk

Based on the novel by Dennis Cooper, this controversial, sensual and suggestive work is about fantasy, sexuality and how violence and pornography shape the human psyche. Punctuated with strobe flashes of layered S & M images, it unfolds in an elliptical style. Stars Michael Gunther, Craig Chester, Parker Posey, Alexis Arquette, Raoul O'Connell, Jaie Laplante, James Lyons and Michael Stock. "...a serious and discreet work of considerable dark impact—and no little humor" (Kevin Thomas, *Los Angeles Times*).

VHS: S30136. $59.99.
Todd Verow, USA, 1996, 84 mins.

From Dusk till Dawn

Harvey Keitel, George Clooney, Quentin Tarantino and Juliette Lewis star in this bizarre film based on a Tarantino script. A pair of outlaws have to hide out for just one night, but they never expected a confrontation with forces more dark and evil than themselves. Another life may have to be sacrificed to secure their freedom, only it may involve the ritual murder of an age-old vampire.

VHS: S29402. $19.95.
Laser: LD75813. $39.99.
DVD: DV60315. $29.99.
Robert Rodriguez, USA, 1996, 108 mins.

From the Journals of Jean Seberg

The life of Jean Seberg, from her Cinderella-like rise to national celebrity in Otto Preminger's *Saint Joan* to her fall into obscurity and death in 1979, is entertainingly examined through clips from a wide range of Seberg's films and other films from the period. Immensely entertaining and challenging, this is a film about the entanglement of life and art. Starring Mary Beth Hurt as Jean Seberg. "One of the most thought-provoking movies I've seen about the mysteries of personal images on the screen" (Roger Ebert, *Siskel & Ebert*).

VHS: S31195. $59.95.
Mark Rappaport, USA, 1995, 97 mins.

Fun

In this "dazzling and disturbing" *(New Musical Express)* psychological thriller, two suburban teenaged girls meet and quickly become best friends. In the span of a single afternoon they share their most guarded secrets, and, in a rising frenzy, murder an elderly woman for "fun." A kind of *Heavenly Creatures* from Hell. With Alicia Witt and Renee Humphrey. A Sundance Film Festival winner.

VHS: S32154. $94.95.
Rafael Zelinsky, USA, 1994, 95 mins.

The Funeral

Abel Ferrara's *(Bad Lieutenant)* "hot-blooded, broodingly well-acted" *(New York Times)* film of underworld betrayal and explosive retribution set in 1930s New York stars Christopher Walken, Chris Penn, Isabella Rossellini and Annabella Sciorra. A powerful crime family's three street-hardened brothers and the women they love are about to be plunged into a deadly confrontation with their enemies, with each other and with their own dark heritage of violence, madness and murder.

VHS: S31109. $101.99.
Laser: LD76198. $39.98.
Abel Ferrara, USA, 1996, 101 mins.

Gas Food Lodging

Allison Anders' depiction of the difficult, complex relationship between a single mother and her two daughters has some graceful, liquid camera work and an excellent performance by Ione Skye as a distracted, promiscuous vixen. Set in a ragged New Mexico town, Anders maps out some tangled relationships while fully exploring post-adolescent and adult sexuality. Adapted from the novel by Richard Peck. Cinematography by Dean Lent. With Brooke Adams, Fairuza Balk and James Brolin.

VHS: S18346. $19.95.
Laser: LD71864. $34.95.
Allison Anders, USA, 1992, 94 mins.

Geek Maggot Bingo

Cookie Mueller called this story of a mad doctor and his hunchback assistant a "breath of fresh air, but infected with bats, flies and spawning maggots." Special effects by Ed French. Stars Brenda Bergman and Donna Death.

VHS: S10163. $39.95.
Nick Zedd, USA, 1983, 70 mins.

Georgia

Jennifer Jason Leigh and Mare Winningham star in this tale of a rising young rock star. Leigh is the younger sister of a successful folk singer (Winningham). The resultant sibling rivalry only intensifies the extreme behavior of Leigh's character as she struggles for success. It's a tough and unsentimental view of a world where self-indulgent emotional turmoil can mean big bucks.

VHS: S27847. $19.95.
Laser: LD75929. $39.99.
Ulu Grosbard, USA, 1995, 117 mins.

Gift

A feature co-directed by former Jane's Addiction lead singer Perry Farrell blurs the distinctions between drama and music video, in a film that combines live music with a loose storyline dealing with memory, drug abuse, sex, racism, the cops and the medical profession. The musical numbers include "Step," "Classic Girl," "Ain't No Right" and "Don't Call Me Nigger, Whitey," performed by Farrell and guest performer Ice-T.

VHS: S19725. $19.98.
Perry Farrell/Casey Niccoli, USA, 1992, 80 mins.

Go Fish

A beguiling and charming look at the lives and loves of a small group of lesbian women in Chicago. Friends play matchmaker to bring together two very different women: Max, a beautiful, gregarious writer, and Ely, a quiet, thoughtful and almost terminally shy woman. They are, of course, perfect for each other in this gentle and offbeat film.

VHS: S26147. $19.98.
Laser: LD75315. $39.98.
Rose Troche, USA, 1994, 83 mins.

God's Police

Australian artist Robert Cooney crafted this indictment of religious bigotry from super-8 footage depicting the Pope in NYC. With Janet Stein, Vivienne Dick and others.

VHS: S22656. $39.95.
Robert Cooney, USA, 1980, 60 mins.

Grace of My Heart

In this lyrical tale, said to be loosely modeled after the career of Carole King, Ileana Douglas stars as a songwriting sensation who struggles from the late 1950s doo-wop era to the psychedelic '70s to escape the shadow of pop music icons and ultimately emerge as a star in her own right. Matt Dillon, Eric Stoltz and John Turturro co-star as the men in her life. Soundtrack features 15 original songs, including "God Give Me Strength," written and performed by Burt Bacharach and Elvis Costello. "Big emotions! A great, authentic-sounding score and a cast that is perfection" *(USA Today)*.

VHS: S30741. $19.95.
Laser: LD76077. $34.98.
Allison Anders, USA, 1996, 116 mins.

Gravesend

This ultra-low-budget knock-out debut by teenage NYU Film School drop-out Salvatore Stabile is a darkly comic and edgy drama about four friends from an Italian neighborhood in Brooklyn whose Saturday night spins wildly out of control when an accidental shooting results in a corpse. Their frantic plight to unload the body leads them to petty theft, more bodies and a series of pointless mind games.

VHS: S33140. $19.95.
DVD: DV60316. $29.95.
Salvatore Stabile, USA, 1997, 85 mins.

Grind

In this slice of blue-collar life, Billy Crudup *(Inventing the Abbotts)* is Eddie, a handsome 20-something who has just been released from prison. Broke, Eddie shows up on the doorstep of his older brother Terry (Paul Shulze, *Laws of Gravity*) and his wife, Janey (Adrienne Shelly, *Trust*), where he is taken into their family. When Eddie switches to the night shift at the treadmill factory, he finds himself spending his days with Janey. They discover that they yearn for something other than the monotony that characterizes their lives, and the three find themselves in a final, shattering confrontation. With Frank Vincent. "A true sense of the blue-collar soul" *(Newsday)*.

VHS: S31801. $19.98.
Chris Kentis, USA, 1996, 96 mins.

Gummo

Through a collection of dreamlike and devastating images, *Kids* creator Harmony Korine offers a glimpse of the southern suburb of Xenia, Ohio, a world existing in the aftermath of a tornado that ravaged the community in the 1970s, populated by glue-sniffing, cat-killing teens, albinos, dwarfs and assorted other freaks. Perversely funny and disturbingly sad, "*Gummo* plays like a redneck *Kids*...[it] deserves to be seen" (V.A. Musetto, *New York Post*).

VHS: S33332. $100.99.
Laser: LD76815. $39.99.
Harmony Korine, USA, 1997, 95 mins.

Habit

Talented independent filmmaker Larry Fessenden's modern vampire story set in New York City. Fessenden stars as world-weary, alcoholic Sam, who's lost his father and broken up with his girlfriend. He finds solace in Anna, a mysterious woman who draws him into a world of addiction, dangerous eroticism and madness. "A sly exercise in ambiguity.... Of all the recent vampire movies, this is the only one to suggest that the powerful symbolism of vampirism could create results even in the absence of causes" (Roger Ebert, *Chicago Sun-Times*).

VHS: S34877. $89.95.
Larry Fessenden, USA, 1995, 100 mins.

Hallelujah the Hills

"Imagine a combination of Huckleberry Finn, *Pull My Daisy*, the Marx Brothers and the complete works of Douglas Fairbanks, Mary Pickford and D.W. Griffith, and you've got it:...A film which is both deliriously funny and ravishingly lyrical. It is a hymn to the joys of youth and friendship" (*The Guardian*, London).

VHS: S33290. $75.00.
Adolfas Mekas, USA, 1963, 82 mins.

Hearing Voices

An unconventional feature follows Erika (Erika Nagy), a beautiful though emotionally troubled fashion model, who repeatedly falls into abusive relationships. Troubled by a succession of difficult medical complications, she falls for Lee (Stephen Gatta), a sensitive young man who is her doctor's gay lover. The film is "beautiful and rigorous, taking us to places the movies rarely, if ever, have gone" (Kevin Thomas, *Los Angeles Times*).

VHS: S19324. $79.95.
Sharon Greytak, USA, 1989, 87 mins.

Heat and Sunlight

Jealousy and obsession overwhelm a photographer during the final 16 hours of his love affair with a dancer. This independent American film, which won the Grand Prize at the U.S. Film Festival, is an intense look at the darker side of human relationships. "Narratively wild and aesthetically risky, it's an emotionally gritty and raucously tender film, a remarkable feat" *(Hollywood Reporter)*. B&W.

VHS: S12822. $29.95.
Rob Nilsson, USA, 1987, 98 mins.

Heavy

The life of an overweight pizza chef (Pruitt Taylor Vince) changes dramatically when his mother (Shelley Winters) dies and a beautiful and kind waitress (Liv Tyler) opens his heart to love. With Deborah Harry (Blondie) and Evan Dando (The Lemonheads) and music by Sonic Youth's Thurston Moore. "Quietly earthshaking...eloquent, purposeful" (Janet Maslin, *New York Times*).

VHS: S31197. $98.99.
James Mangold, USA, 1995, 104 mins.

Henry (Portrait of a Serial Killer)

John McNaughton's *Henry*, shot in Chicago using local theatrical talent, places an emphasis on acting, rather than special effects, that's almost unheard of in the psycho-killer genre. As Henry, Michael Rooker "becomes a coarser, working-class James Dean; he has the same shyness, the same vulnerability, but lacks the verbal gifts to express himself even to Dean's degree" (Dave Kehr, *Film Comment*).

Laser: LD74643. $29.98.
John McNaughton, USA, 1989, 90 mins.

High Water

Based on the short story by Vermont native Howard Frank Mosher, this is the tale of one 21-year-old Vermont farm boy's stubborn determination to enter his first stock car race, circa 1959. With his supportive younger sister at his side, he braves the wrath of their irascible father and Mother Nature to get his spiffy yellow '37 hotrod to the race before start time. Public performance.

VHS: S32140. $59.95.
Jay Craven, USA, 1989, 36 mins.

Highway Patrolman

Part road movie, part western, this "gringo valentine" (J. Hoberman, *Village Voice*) by Alex Cox *(Repo Man)* is the gripping story of Pedro and Anibal, their coming of age, and their loves. When police academy grad Pedro gets a job working as a highway patrolman in Matimi, Durango, his wife complains about the low wages, leading him into a life of corruption. "Vibrantly alive...*Highway Patrolman*...recalls the westerns of John Ford and John Huston" (Kevin Thomas, *Los Angeles Times*). Spanish with English subtitles.

VHS: S31627. $89.95.
Alex Cox, Mexico/USA, 1992, 104 mins.

Hippie Porn

Underground legend Jon Moritsugu's *(Mod Fuck Explosion, Fame Whore, Der Elvis)* first feature, which he describes as "the French New Wave goes to hell," follows three disaffected teens as they wander through the streets of L.A. to the discordant rumblings of Medicine Ball, Unsane, Cop Shoot Cop, Railroad Jerk and Superchunk.

VHS: S35135. $39.95.
Jon Moritsugu, USA, 1991, 95 mins.

Hollow Venus: Diary of a Go-Go Dancer

This is the story of Coco Dupree, a young New York performance artist who dances topless in a bar called Paradise. There she meets a mob boss called God, a thug named Richie, and a kept woman known as Desiree. Heather Woodbury stars in this semi-autobiographical glimpse of a netherworld where porn and art mix.

VHS: S22505. $49.95.
Larry Fessenden, USA, 1989, 58 mins.

Home Free All!

A small, intimate film from independent director Stewart Bird about the renewal of a stagnant friendship between childhood friends: Barry is a vague "hippie radical" in search of structure, comfort and family; Al wants to break from the comfort zone of his suburban existence into free and wide open spaces. A quiet contemplation on the implications of choice.

VHS: S02766. $69.95.
Stewart Bird, USA, 1983, 92 mins.

Homegrown

A low-budget little caper starring Billy Bob Thornton, Frank Azaria and Ryan Phillippe as a bumbling trio of Northern California marijuana growers who find themselves in the world of high-stakes contraband when their boss is shot. Along the way they get stoned and shot at, and fall in love. With Kelly Lynch. Cameos by Jamie Lee Curtis, John Lithgow, Ted Danson, Judge Reinholt and Jon Bon Jovi.

VHS: S34891. $99.99.
Laser: LD77005. $39.95.
DVD: Letterboxed, DD5.1/DSS, French & Spanish subtitles.
DV60380. $24.95.
Stephen Gyllenhaal, USA, 1998, 95 mins.

The Hours and Times

Christopher Munch's feature debut focuses on the circumstances and possible sexual relationship that existed between John Lennon and the Beatles' manager Brian Epstein during a four-day holiday in Barcelona in Spring 1963. A work of delicacy and heartbreak, the film delves into the inner world of each man, depicting Epstein's erotic obsession and Lennon's confusion and pain as an emerging rock-and-roll icon. With David Angus, Ian Hart and Stephanie Pack.

VHS: S18741. $19.98.
Christopher Munch, USA, 1991, 60 mins.

How to Survive

A collection of humorous video sketches written, directed and performed by Larry Hankin. In *Solly's Diner*, Larry plays a down-on-his-luck, penniless drifter trying to get fed. *Time for a Beer* details ways to drink in a bar without money. Three other shorts included.

VHS: S01654. $49.95.
Larry Hankin, USA, 1986

I Am the Cheese

A captivating independent film about a young man's lonely search for his own identity, starring Robert Wagner, Robert MacNaughton and Hope Lange. "Absorbing, brilliant," wrote *The New York Times*.

VHS: S00596. $59.95.
Robert Jiras, USA, 1984, 96 mins.

I Don't Hate Las Vegas Anymore

A real-life filmmaker heads off to Las Vegas with assorted members of his family in search of either a new film or God. If the Almighty exists, this filmmaker may well create a new work, because only an all powerful entity can give him the events on the road that give form to a road movie. This warm mock documentary is hilarious and unpredictable.

VHS: S29514. $79.95.
Caveh Zahedi, USA, 1991, 74 mins.

I Shot Andy Warhol

Lili Taylor is Valerie Solanas, the eccentric writer of a play called *Up Your Ass* and the founder and sole member of the revolutionary group the Society for Cutting Up Men. This film shows Warhol's Factory through its heyday, until it all was radically changed by a furious, gun-toting Solanas. Her revenge against Warhol for refusing to produce her play sent shockwaves through the art world. Stephen Dorff is Candy Darling and Jared Harris is Warhol.

VHS: S29783. $19.98.
Laser: LD76039. $39.98.
Mary Harron, USA, 1996, 100 mins.

I'm Not Fascinating—The Movie!

This twisted rock 'n' roll anti-history chronicles the pointless shenanigans of San Francisco rock ne'er-do-wells The Icky Boyfriends and their futile request for rock stardom. Undaunted by the universal hatred of both their music and their look, the band perseveres, netting themselves a major label contract. But stardom proves elusive as they descend into a world of murder, intrigue, nepotism, consumer research groups, excessive use of caffeine-laden soda pop and death. "A weirdly beautiful spectacle of self-defeat. An instant classic" *(San Francisco Bay Guardian)*.

VHS: S30493. $19.99.
Danny Plotnick, USA, 1996, 50 mins.

Illtown

Michael Rappaport, Lili Taylor and Kevin Corrigan star in this acclaimed thriller from director Nick Gomez *(Laws of Gravity)* about rival Miami dope dealers who fight for control of the streets. "Powerful. A cool, dreamy gangster's paradise" *(The New York Times)*.

VHS: S34860. $59.99.
Nick Gomez, USA, 1996, 101 mins.

Imposters

This "insolent, high-camp comedy about magic, obsession, role-playing and love" (David Denby, *New York*) is "one of the wildest and wittiest American movies of the decade. A hysterically convoluted, elegantly mounted tale of wisecracks and woe" (Jonathan Rosenbaum, *Chicago Reader*). With avant-garde theater pioneer Charles Ludlam.

VHS: S31138. $29.99.
Mark Rappaport, USA, 1980, 110 mins.

In Between

A unique exploration of feminine isolation, celebrated at many international film festivals—made by California filmmaker Wade Novy. The subject of the film is an isolated woman (Maggie McOmie), who gets cut off from reality because of her emotional reactions. In a tense study worthy of Antonioni, Novy portrays the woman's increasing sense of withdrawal and anxiety. The film displays great originality in editing, skillfully depicting a shattering, internal emotional state of an individual.

VHS: S03722. $39.95.
Wade Novy, USA, 1980, 30 mins.

In the Company of Men

Neil LaBute's disturbing, controversial, intelligent film about the male prerogative—two executives who compete for the same woman, a pretty, deaf clerk, in a callous sexist game. With stunning performances by Aaron Eckhart, Stacy Edwards and Matt Malloy. "The kind of bold, uncompromising film that insists on being thought about afterward" (Roger Ebert, *Chicago Sun-Times*).

VHS: S33318. $105.99.
DVD: DV60235. $24.95.
Neil LaBute, Canada, 1997, 97 mins.

In the Land of the Owl Turds

In this off-beat, humorous, and often poignant drama, a lonely, self-absorbed young man attempts to overcome the difficulties often inherent in his search for the ideal woman. Written and directed by and starring Harrod Blank. Produced by Les Blank.
VHS: S02903. $39.95.
Harrod Blank, USA, 1987, 30 mins.

In the Soup

Winner of the Grand Jury Prize at the Sundance Film Festival, Alexandre Rockwell's film features Seymour Cassel as a mid-level New York mobster entangled with a struggling Lower East Side filmmaker (Steve Buscemi) who's trying to finance production on his 500-page script. Jennifer Beals is a waitress and the object of Buscemi's affection. With Will Patton, Steve Randazzo, Frank Messina and cameos by Jim Jarmusch and Carol Kane.
VHS: S18854. $19.95.
Alexandre Rockwell, USA, 1992, 96 mins.

Inside Monkey Zetterland

Los Angeles before the earthquake was already an upside down kind of town. This complicated melodrama/comedy features terrorist boarders, a biker dad, a dysfunctional family, and at the center of it all a neurotic screenwriter named Monkey Zetterland.
Laser: LD74452. $39.99.
Jeffery Levy, USA, 1992, 93 mins.

It Don't Pay To Be an Honest Citizen

A mugged filmmaker tries to recover his stolen film and is thereby plunged into the ambiguous currents of the criminal world. This first feature is wryly observed, in part, because of its documentary roots.
VHS: S22608. $39.95.
Jacob Burckhardt, USA, 1985, 85 mins.

Johnny Suede

The debut work of the talented Tom DiCillo, Jim Jarmusch's frequent collaborator *(Stranger Than Paradise)*. Brad Pitt stars as a playfully cool hipster living among the ruin and devastation of the Lower East Side. Johnny is trying to make a living as a musician and play out the complicated relationships in his life, in particular a beautiful and sympathetic teacher to whom he can't fully commit.
VHS: S18565. $94.95.
Laser: LD75209. $34.98.
Tom DiCillo, USA, 1991, 97 mins.

Judgment Day Theater: The Book of Manson

Raymond Pettibon recreates the big bang of End-of-the-World cult projections with Robert Hecker as Charlie Manson and other characters including Tex Watson, Norman Mailer, Jimi Hendrix, Roman Polanski and Leslie Van Houten.
VHS: S20525. $19.95.

Jurgen Reble—Passion

Jurgen Reble, former member of the German filmmaking group Schmelzdahin, focuses on exploring the film material through bacterial processes, weathering and chemical treatment during and after development. Includes *Passion* (1989/1990, 54 mins.) and *Rumpelstilzchen* (1989, 15 mins.).
VHS: S35150. $29.95.
Jurgen Reble, 1989/1990, 69 mins.

Just Another Weekend

Two sisters find more than they bargain for when their escape from December's shop-til-you-drop ritual lands them on the snow covered high country of Colorado. As if family tension weren't high enough with Lisa and Ginny's awkward love affairs in the way, uncovering a property development scam to build condos on a uranium dump sends this wry comedy over the edge. An irrepressible first feature starring the hilarious talents of Justine Madero, Mary Elizabeth Holmes, Rinde Eckert and Jo Harvey Allen.
VHS: S15769. $45.00.
Elizabeth Sher, USA, 1988

Karl Krogstad Films

"Karl Krogstad is the most wonderful and strange filmmaker on earth" (Peter Greenaway). Each tape is 60 mins.

Karl Krogstad: Black & Decker Hedgetrimmer Murders. The *Black & Decker Hedgetrimmer Murders* is an animated comedy in which a Teamster goes on a homicidal rampage and is chased by Porky Pig dolls representing policemen. The film, touching on issues ranging from necrophilia to premeditated murder, is Krogstad's protest against unions and the kind of inflation that threatens to drive him out of filmmaking. With Farrah Fawcett's animated debut. In *The Party Line* (1977, 30 mins.), an animated detective epic featuring G.I. Joe, Barbie and Porky Pig dolls, AT&T fears a competing company from China, headed by the dreaded Chang Chu, and calls in their ace hitman, The Shredder, to investigate. The dislocating *Palm Sunday* (1981, 12 mins.) features a narrative told completely in scraps of stock footage from old medical films and travelogs that had been thrown out by the University of Washington.
VHS: S35137. $24.95.

Karl Krogstad: Eggnog, Gazebo, Frescade. Includes Krogstad's apocalyptic, largely animated *Eggnog* (1973, 33 mins.), which attempts an epic history of the United States, the scope of which "is as awesome as its protest against contemporary life is fervent" (Kevin Thomas, *The Los Angeles Times*); the live-action, very abstract *Gazebo by the Sea* (1975, 14 mins.), which humorously celebrates the supernatural; *Frescade* (1970, 20 mins.), the ultimate light show, poetically driven statement; and *Wynken & Blynken & Nod* (1968, 7 mins.), "Krogstad's first film," so he claims (actually his third).
VHS: S35136. $24.95.

Karl Krogstad: Idiot Savant & Catharsis. *Idiot Savant* (1991, 12 mins.) is a surrealistic revelation of the human face hidden behind the mask of superficial social convention. *Catharsis* (1982, 30 mins.) is a fast-paced food chain drama which uses fictional people in fictional places, creating a floating backdrop of tortured, dream-like nights. The film uses no narrative, with continuity always being called into question. Also includes John Purdy's documentary *Wanted KK* (1974, 15 mins.).
VHS: S35139. $24.95.

Karl Krogstad: Music Videos 1985-1987. Between 1985 and 1987, Krogstad produced 17 music videos for the emerging MTV market. This rare collection of ten music videos contains some of the best. Includes a 5-minute collaboration with author Tom Robbins, starring Debra Winger as an all-American housewife married to an anal-retentive Republican lawyer (Kevin Tighe). She falls in love with a tiny, blue paper man, the soul of a very famous, dead Russian poet. "The work that had once seemed dispersed and facile now appears unified and coherent. Krogstad knows instinctively when he has reached his mark. I used to think he put too much into every film. Now I just wish he'd put in more" *(Rolling Stone)*. 40 mins.
VHS: S35138. $24.95.

Karl Krogstad: Surrealism. In 1924 the world's most expansive art movement began. It's taken Karl Krogstad all this time to explain what it means.
VHS: S35140. $24.95.

Karl Krogstad: Temple, Fork & Jack in the Fox. Karl Krogstad describes *Temple on a Stick* (1995, 22 mins.) and *Fork on a Filling* (1995, 14 mins.) as his autobiography. The fairly linear *Temple* is the story of a filmmaker making a film; the experimental *Fork*, a story of good, evil and funny hats, is the film she makes. The films star Imogen Love, Brandon Romans and Joanne Glant. Also includes *Jack in the Fox* (1972, 7 mins.).
VHS: S35141. $24.95.

Karl Krogstad: The Gigabyte Trilogy. A tour-de-force that redefines the meaning of autobiography, Karl Krogstad's *Gigabyte Trilogy* is one of those rare, precious works that saturates itself with meaning. It "is a collage because it is the story of my life, a patchwork with many puzzle pieces" (Krogstad). Included are *Critical Path, State of Grace* and *Peace of Mind*.
VHS: S35142. $24.95.

Karl Krogstad: Seven-Tape Boxed Set.
VHS: S35143. $140.00.
Karl Krogstad, USA, 1970-1998

Kicked in the Head

In this offbeat comedy, Kevin Corrigan *(Goodfellas)* stars as a downwardly mobile Manhattanite who encounters a strong dose of reality on a spiritual quest for truth. With James Woods, Linda Fiorentino, Lili Taylor and Michael Rapaport.
VHS: S33231. $99.99.
Matthew Harrison, USA, 1997, 86 mins.

Kicking and Screaming

Four young men in their 20s discover there's not much to life after college. It's a scenario rife with comic possibilities, where romance and the trauma of getting on with life seem overwhelming and all-encompassing. When Grover's (Josh Hamilton) retainer-wearing girlfriend Jane (Olivia d'Abo) is accepted at a writing program in Prague, Grover chickens out and stays home with his buddies instead. While his friend Otis (Carlos Jacott) tries and tries again to get on a plane for graduate school and his friend Skippy (Jason Wiles) misses his younger girlfriend Miami (Parker Posey) so much that he re-enrolls in college, Grover confides in perennial student and bartender Chet (Eric Stoltz) and struggles with the pain of love lost.
VHS: S27260. $19.95.
Noah Baumbach, USA, 1995, 96 mins.

Kidnapped

Mitchell's first feature is a stark unedited recreation of Warhol's *Vinyl*. This film purports to be the story of bored terrorists who kidnap a businessman, and shows off a cast and crowd of hip poseurs talking sex, manners and politics.
VHS: S07122. $59.95.
Eric Mitchell, USA, 1978, 60 mins.

Kids

Famed photographer Larry Clark makes his directorial debut with this sensational story of teenage life in Manhattan. Ignoring the challenge posed by AIDS, these kids pursue sex and drugs with no regard for the future in a world as violent as it is hopeless. Justifiably controversial, *Kids* was hailed as "very, very powerful" (Roger Ebert) and denounced as manipulative and exploitative. "The confident visual style and flat, elliptical, near-plotless storytelling are tremendously accomplished, yet the same elements…could be seen as a celebration of amorality, as a contrived, romanticized celebration of the death wish" (Ray Pride, *New City*).
VHS: S26956. $14.95.
Larry Clark, USA, 1995, 91 mins.

The Killing Floor

A very powerful, raw film produced for American Playhouse. Shot in Chicago and set against the backdrop of the Chicago stock yards, the film focuses on Frank, recently returned from World War I, who wants a better life and becomes involved in the labor movement. But the pressures of the recession mount, and the stock yards become filled with racial tension. Finally, bloodshed erupts on the streets with the Chicago race riot of 1919. The film has a remarkable documentary feel, and features strong performances from Damien Leake, Alfre Woodard, Moses Gunn, Clarence Felder and Bill Bremer.
VHS: S10894. $29.95.
Bill Duke, USA, 1984, 118 mins.

King Blank

A sour-spirited, foul-mouthed epic of ennui, this film is set in a motel room at NYC's Kennedy Airport. Over two days an obsessive husband lost in a web of psychotic delusion and his immigrant wife find themselves trapped in a psycho-drama of absurdity. It even features a scene where Ron Vawter forces Gary Indiana to perform fellatio.
VHS: S22627. $49.95.
Michael Oblowitz, USA, 1983, 90 mins.

Klip

Klip follows a few days in the lives of two men and two women whose paths intercept in the New Mexico desert. Shayna is a teen runaway who's hit the road to escape abusive parents and a seemingly pointless life. Along the way she joins Juliette, a French backpacker making her way to Colorado. The women hitch a ride with Tommy and Sparrow, whose pot-fueled banter on such subjects as geography, art and religion is turned up a few degrees when Sparrow finds a new sparring (and sexual) partner in Juliette. "This film is about betrayal, cultural conflict, sexual innuendo, the automobile dashboard as pop culture altar, domestic mind violence and camping, in no particular order" (Michael Koster, *The New Mexican*).
VHS: S32412. $39.95.
Mark Oliver, USA, 1997, 123 mins.

La Senorita Lee

In this award-winning dramatic short, Jeanie Lee, a young Korean-American woman pregnant by her recently departed Mexican boyfriend and about to be married to a dull, parentally-approved Korean doctor, is torn between conflicting cultural values. Her untimely pregnancy awakens powerful desires and memories, forcing her to choose between traditional family values and personal freedom. Public performance.
VHS: S32125. $59.95.
Hyun Mi Oh, USA, 1995, 25 mins.

Landlord Blues

In this quintessentially New York story it's tenant vs. landlord. A sleazy real estate owner is spurred on by the hopes of changing a neighborhood. Fortunately for the people who live there, he's not too clever. Richly ironic, this film maintains an even balance between sadness and humor.
VHS: S22501. $39.95.
Jacob Burckhardt, USA, 1988, 96 mins.

Larry Smith/Apollo Belvedere

Flashbacks and urban paranoia yield a fast-paced schizo portrait in the first of these two short films. In *Apollo*, a foppish, tormented filmmaker inhabits a mock melodrama with his absurdly devoted spouse. Glenn Branca did the audio and Jim Jarmusch was on the crew.
VHS: S22614. $29.95.
Rick Little, USA, 1976-1977, 45 mins.

Laughing Horse

A stranded traveller in the desert finds himself working for an unusual couple as their driver in a search for a mysterious mustang. The trio drive through the Southwest waiting for the unexpected.
VHS: S01543. $49.95.
Michael Blake, USA, 1986

Laws of Gravity

Nick Gomez's first feature was shot in 12 days and made for $38,000. It's a daring excursion into male bravado, the story of the small-time criminal activities of two Bensonhurst hustlers and their strong, determined girlfriends. The plot is motivated by the reappearance of a neighborhood criminal, who turns up with a bag full of handguns and an unexplained source of money. The real star is cinematographer Jean de Segonzac, who shot the entire movie with a hand-held camera. With Peter Greene, Edie Falco, Adam Trese and Arabella Field.
VHS: S18443. $89.95.
Laser: LD74455. $39.99.
Nick Gomez, USA, 1992, 100 mins.

Letterist Films—Woman, Women!

This collection of films focusing on women, compiled by Maurice Lemaitre, includes *The Witness or Timid Expectations* (Christiane Guymer, 1984, 9 mins.); *Blue Kisses and Marshmallows* (Helene Richol, 1983, 10 mins.); *All Women Are Joan of Arcs* (Suzanne Lemaitre, 1984, 81 mins.); *Woman Is Not What She Used to Be* (Helene Richol, 1978, 10 mins.); *End Memory* (Pip Chodorov, 1995, 5½ mins.); and *A Love Story* (Maurice Lemaitre, 1978, 8 mins.).
VHS: S35144. $29.95.

Lighthearted Nation

A video essay that is a delightful look at the Duplex Nursing Home and the contributors to the *Duplex Planet* magazine. The magazine was started by the activities director for the home, and the contributors offer interesting anecdotes and opinions on subjects ranging from their mothers, moon-walking and fortune tellers to having a good attitude in life.
VHS: S14819. $39.95.
Jim McKay, USA, 1989, 60 mins.

Lion's Den

This early film, written by, directed by and featuring Bryan Singer (*The Usual Suspects*), is the story of a local restaurant which serves as the meeting place for a group of five passionate youths. Like young lions they meet and spar, learning the comfort of this den is but a memory. With David Leslie Conhaim, Ethan Hawke, Brandon Keith, Dylan Kussman and Susan Kussman. Also includes the short *Gothcha!*, a Special Broadcasting Service Children's Production of a prankster who gets his just desserts (24 mins.).
VHS: S32964. $29.95.
Bryan Singer/Howard Rubie, USA/Australia, 1990/1992, 48 mins.

A Little Stiff

This delightful romantic comedy charts a film student's unrequited love for an art student. It's a subtle, witty and charming movie that explores a world of student-led Bohemian angst.
VHS: S21513. $24.95.
Caveh Zahedi/Greg Watkins, USA, 1991, 85 mins.

The Living End

Gregg Araki's breakthrough $20,000 feature is a reworking of Godard's *Breathless*, with a blunt, gay veneer. The film is about two young men, a film critic and a narcissistic drifter, both of them HIV-positive, who undertake a mythic road journey after one of them kills a police officer. With Mike Dytri, Craig Gilmore and Mark Finch.
VHS: S18692. $29.95.
Gregg Araki, USA, 1992, 93 mins.

Living in Oblivion

Steve Buscemi heads up an exciting cast featuring James LeGros, Catherine Keener and Dermot Mulroney. This wrenching but comic look at independent filmmaking shows a young filmmaker forced to ponder the inevitable question: Can anything be worth going through the hell of making a low-budget feature film? Winner of the Screenwriting Award at the 1995 Sundance Film Festival.
VHS: S27066. $96.99.
Laser: LD75441. $34.95.
Tom DiCillo, USA, 1995, 92 mins.

Local Color

"Reaches new heights of hysteria. Eight characters are drawn into almost every conceivable relationship (including shared dreams) to create a kind of modernist melodrama, complete with laugh track" (Ian Christie, *British Film Institute*). "A strange and wonderful movie...I've never seen anything quite like it before" (Roger Ebert, *Chicago Sun-Times*).
VHS: S31126. $29.99.
Mark Rappaport, USA, 1977, 115 mins.

The Long Island Four

Based on a true-life incident, the Super-8 feature by the late director was an underground hit. It tells the story of four Nazi saboteurs who landed in the U.S. in 1942 and were captivated by the decadent nightlife of New York City.
VHS: S07116. $59.95.
Anders Grafstrom, USA, 1980, 100 mins.

Loser

Kirk Harris' debut film is the tragic tale of good-looking young James Dean Ray (Kirk Harris), a small-town drug dealer bent on destroying himself. As he lays bleeding from a gunshot wound, Jimmy Ray thinks back on his last 24 hours, triggering memories that brought him to this fate. An impressive, low-budget *Rebel Without a Cause* for the '90s. Shot by *Mean Streets* cinematographer Kent Wakeford.
VHS: S31696. $59.95.
Kirk Harris, USA, 1996, 85 mins.

The Lost Films of Cassandra Stark

The work of Cassandra Stark is poetic and disturbing. This collection reveals the reverent quality of her evolved ritualistic films. She is a protege of Nick Zedd.
VHS: S22629. $29.95.

Love & a .45

Two friends accidentally murder a young girl during a routine robbery. Deciding that his friend is crazy and may kill him next, Watty (Gil Bellows) takes off with his girlfriend, Star (Renee Zellweger, *Jerry Maguire*). It's a honeymoon on the lam. They are in love, they have a .45, and it's too bad the town they live in is as tough and ruthless as they are. Soundtrack includes music by The Meat Puppets, The Butthole Surfers and The Jesus and Mary Chain.
VHS: S23994. $19.95.
Laser: LD75223. $34.98.
C.M. Talkington, USA, 1994, 102 mins.

Love Crimes

Patrick Bergin, who played Julia Roberts' sadistic husband in *Sleeping with the Enemy*, continues to abuse women on film, this time in the guise of a famous fashion photographer. Sean Young plays Dana Greenway, an aggressive Atlanta assistant district attorney who goes beyond the scope of her office to play detective. With Arnetia Walker and James Read. Story by Allan Moyle is based on a true-life case in which a man impersonated photographer Richard Avedon in the 1970's. This unrated video contains eight minutes not seen in the theatrical release.
VHS: S16806. $19.98.
Laser: LD71685. $29.98.
Lizzie Borden, USA, 1991, 85 mins.

Love Show

A live television production by the painter and writer Walter Robinson features painted titles, taped and live skits on the perennial theme: a gem of its kind.
VHS: S10180. $29.95.
Walter Robinson, USA, 1982, 28 mins.

The Low Life

This bittersweet, subtle and honest Generation X comedy manages to capture both the absurd despair and humor of this era's entropic youth. The group of friends at the center of this film are all too real.
VHS: S29986. $19.98.
Laser: LD76391. $39.99.
George Hickenlooper, USA, 1996, 96 mins.

Lydia Lunch: Malicious Intent

Why We Murder and *Universal Infiltrators* were shot at The Knitting Factory in New York by Richard Kern while *The Beast* was shot at L.A.C.E. in L.A. by Chris Iovenko. Together these works explore a world of anti-social rantings that may inspire anger, violence and more. 90 mins.
VHS: S25608. $29.95.
Richard Kern/Chris Iovenko, USA, 1994, 90 mins.

M/W/F Music Video One

This collection features *Sharp's Downtown NY; Space Party*, with John Sex and Ann Magnuson; *Film Spectators Are Quiet Vampires; Heterosexual Love; No Sell Out; Wedding Show; Concrete People; Rumble; Twenty-Eight; Metal Modern Romance; Human Waste* and *Cezanne*. 45 mins.
VHS: S22640. $39.95.

Mac

Actor John Turturro's directing debut. Turturro plays Niccolo Vitelli, a first-generation Italian builder whose uncompromising craftsmanship and insistence on perfection ruptures his friendship with his brothers (Michael Badalucco and Carl Capotorto). With Katherine Borowitz, Ellen Barkin and John Amos.
VHS: S19059. $19.95.
Laser: LD71893. $34.95.
John Turturro, USA, 1992, 117 mins.

Magdalena Viraga

This mysterious and imaginative experimental feature film by Nina Menkes concerns the inner life of a prostitute who is arrested as a murder suspect. Filmed in the bars, dance halls, and churches of east L.A., it is a compelling portrayal of the young woman's psychological journey from passivity to awareness. Menkes uses closeup shots and surreal details, and a text woven with poetry to suggest the emotional numbing and physical torment the woman endures and the effort required to confront the condition of her life.
VHS: S07376. $49.95.
Nina Menkes, USA, 1986, 90 mins.

A Man, a Woman and a Killer

In part a film about the making of a film, within the framework of a fictional plot involving a hired killer and his victim. A collaboration by Rick Schmidt (*Emerald Cities*) and Wayne Wang (*Chan Is Missing*).
VHS: S00011. $59.95.
Rick Schmidt/Wayne Wang, USA, 75 mins.

Manhattan Naturally and Stories from Brooklyn

A fanciful drama of the sale of Manhattan by naive Indians. *Stories* features painter Paula Collery talking about her native borough.
VHS: S10176. $29.95.
Brian Pierson, USA, 1983, 28 mins.

Manny & Lo

Eleven-year-old Manny (Scarlett Johansson, *If Lucy Fell*) and pregnant 16-year-old Lo (Aleksa Palladino in her debut) are two runaway sisters escaping from foster homes who kidnap a lonesome, middle-aged practical nurse (Mary Kay Place, *The Big Chill*) to teach them how to raise the baby in "the most original and unexpected family values film of the year" (Jay Carr, *The Boston Globe*).
VHS: S30587. $19.95.
Laser: LD76075. $39.95.
Lisa Krueger, USA, 1996, 89 mins.

Many Wonder

A madcap fairy tale about an overly generous New York woman pursued by three bachelors with different agendas. One wants her money. The second wants money and marriage. The third may be Mr. Right. Or is he? Public performance.
VHS: S32130. $59.95.
Craig Lowy, USA, 1989, 40 mins.

Master Misery

Based on short story by Truman Capote, this film involves a young woman named Sylvia who encounters Mr. Revercomb, a mysterious man who buys dreams from people. As she gradually falls under his spell, Sylvia finds she is unable to break away. Public performance.
VHS: S32129. $59.95.
Elizabeth Dimon, USA, 1989, 40 mins.

Matthias Muller—Selected Films

This first video edition assembles Matthias Muller's most prominent collaborations with composer and musican Dirk Schaefer. Muller's image-rich films deal with the intersection of the private and public spheres. His seamless collages of personal imagery and appropriated materials weave a kinetic spell of motion and vitality. Learned in the the tradition of Eisenstein, Genet, Anger and Jarman, these films range from tender, magical and melancholy love poems to sarcastic comments on gender entrapment in classic-era Hollywood. Includes *Aus der Ferne—The Memo Book* (1989, 27 mins.); *The Flamethrowers* (1990, 9 mins.); *Home Stories* (1990, 6 mins.); *Sleepy Haven* (1993, 15 mins.); and *Sternenschauer* (1994, 14 mins.).
VHS: S35149. $29.95.
Matthias Muller, 1989/1990/1993/1994, 73 mins.

Medusa Challenger

Joe Mantegna stars in this classic independent film about a mildly retarded young man who helps his uncle (Jack Wallace) sell roses to motorists at a traffic signal. "The clarity of narrative and bittersweet view of human nature of an O. Henry story" (Roger Ebert). ALA selection for young adults.
VHS: S11641. $29.95.
Steven Elkins, USA, 1977, 24 mins.

Metropolitan

Charlie loves Audrey. Audrey loves Tom. Tom loves Serena. Refreshingly original and funny, *Metropolitan* is a wry and witty look at the high-spirited escapades of high society's rich children. A stunning debut for first-time writer-director Whit Stillman and his talented assortment of young, unknown actors. "...ironic, touching, and wickedly funny" (M. McGrady, *News Day*).
VHS: S14278. $19.95.
Whit Stillman, USA, 1990, 98 mins.

Mi Vida Loca: My Crazy Life

Allison Anders' vibrant feature is set in Echo Park, Los Angeles, where best friends Sad Girl and Mousie are now enemies as they have both become pregnant by the same man, Ernesto, a local drug dealer. A gritty slice of life.
VHS: S23484. $19.95.
Laser: LD75229. $34.98.
Allison Anders, USA, 1994, 94 mins.

Mississippi Masala

Moving to the American South in her American debut, the Indian-born, Harvard-educated filmmaker Mira Nair (*Salaam Bombay!*) inverts the Romeo and Juliet story, concerning the forbidden love affair of an entrepreneurial black man (Denzel Washington) and a sheltered, young, Indian woman (the startling newcomer Sarita Choudhury), despite the objections of their respective families. Brilliantly shot by Ed Lachman, Nair has a marvelous and open way with actors. With Roshan Seth, Charles S. Dutton, and Joe Seneca.
VHS: S17070. $19.95.
Laser: LD72200. $34.95.
Mira Nair, USA, 1991, 110 mins.

Mod Fuck Explosion

Named Best Feature Film at The New York Underground Film Festival. A twisted underground masterpiece and a take-off on *West Side Story* from director Jon Moritsugu (*Hippy Porn* and *My Degeneration*). An ode to teenage angst, a dynamic punk odyssey, featuring a famous dream sequence in a meat garden constructed from 800 pounds of rotting flesh. Official selection at the Berlin Film Festival Music by Unrest, S.F. Seals, American Soul Spiders.

VHS: S34129. $39.99.

Jon Moritsugu, USA, 1994, 71 mins.

Mondo New York

Shot over 11 days in the Big Apple, this uncensored travelogue chronicles the weird and the bizarre. Cockfights, crack houses, S&M clubs and slam dancers join with performance artists, musicians and street hookers in an afterhours tour of NYC. Name performers include Lydia Lunch, Dean Johnson, Ann Magnuson and a guy who bites the heads off mice.

VHS: S04315. $14.95.

Laser: LD76226. $39.98.

Harvey Keith, USA, 1988, 83 mins.

Morgan's Cake

A film of irony and ribald humor that deals with the mysteries of growing up, *Morgan's Cake* is Rick Schmidt's fourth feature, and is in some ways an homage to Karel Reisz' wacky comedy, *Morgan*. The character in the film is, in fact, named after "Morgan," and confronts problems of absurdly comic proportions: a love affair, divorced parents, draft registration, car payments—as, cut adrift, he must learn to fend for himself.

VHS: S07536. $49.95.

Rick Schmidt, USA, 1987, 87 mins.

The Motorist

"This sad, funny, gorgeous-looking feature-length videotape tracks the end of an American dream," wrote the *East Bay Express* of Chip Lord's video feature. For Lord, the automobile has been an object of distracted desire and metaphorical charge since 1974. That year, with Ant Farm, he buried ten Cadillacs nose-down in a Texas wheat field and called the public sculpture "Cadillac Ranch." The star of *Motorist* is a gray 1962 Ford Thunderbird. Behind the wheel the Motorist (played with glib rawness by Richard Marcus) is heading for L.A. and reminiscing about the formative influence of the automobile. He's a third-generation Ford man who spews franchise history while he fills the tank with premium. His almost continuous narrative mixes with tabloid news radio as the Motorist gets lost in the Los Angeles of Repoman on his way to meet a Japanese importer of classic American cars.

VHS: S09578. $59.95.

Chip Lord, USA, 1989, 69 mins.

Mozart in Love

Scored wih the music of Mozart and loosely based on events in the composer's life, *Mozart in Love* is "a deadpan, lip-synch, parody opera....The movie plays with illusion and reality to the point of utter confusion" (Ray Carney, Boston University). "There emerges a new kind of music film about which it's hard to know which to admire more—Rappaport's artistry or his daring" (*Saarbrucker Zeitung*).

VHS: S31136. $29.99.

Mark Rappaport, USA, 1975, 100 mins.

Ms. 45

Abel Ferrara's feminist revenge movie about a mute garment worker (Zoe Tamerlis) who is raped twice in one day. She arms herself and seeks retribution against skid-row losers and lower-Manhattan denizens who antagonize her. "Ferrara directs with a wit, flair and pace that belie his low budget, using sleazy locations to evoke everyday violence in the Big Apple" *(Time Out)*. The film is also known as *Angel of Vengeance*. With Darlene Stuto, Helen McGara, Nike Zachmanoglou and Jimmy Laine.

VHS: S18913. $19.95.

Abel Ferrara, USA, 1980, 84 mins.

The Music of Chance

The feature debut of documentary filmmaker Philip Haas *(Money Man)* is an adaptation of Paul Auster's allegorical novel. Mandy Patinkin plays a drifter and failed fireman who stakes a gifted card player (James Spader) in a game with two cagey, eccentric millionaires (Charles Durning and Joel Grey). When they're unable to pay off their debts, Patinkin and Spader are forced to build a wall composed of 15th century stones across a decayed landscape. "This haunting and elegantly made [film has] a sustaining air of mystery" (Janet Maslin, *The New York Times*). With M. Emmet Walsh, Samantha Mathis and Christopher Penn.

VHS: S19939. $19.95.

Laser: LD72229. $34.95.

Philip Haas, USA, 1993, 98 mins.

My Family

A powerful, three-generation, epic saga of the Sanchez family as told by the eldest son (Edward James Olmos). From the very beginnings of his father's adventurous journey from Mexico to California in the 1920s, to his brother Chucho's (Esai Morales) tragic rebellion of the 1950s, to the stark realities of modern days, the struggle to live the American dream is sometimes darkened but never diminished. With an unforgettable performance by Jimmy Smits. Also features a behind-the-scenes look at the making of the film. "Ambitious and sweeping! A generational epic like *The Godfather*" (Roger Ebert, *Chicago Sun-Times*).

VHS: S31003. $14.98.

Gregory Nava, USA, 1995, 126 mins.

My Neighborhood

Offbeat, deadpan comedy which stars Kriegman as the owner of a local bar, who indiscriminately invites people he meets on the street in, offers them free drinks, and shows them bizarre videotapes he's made. Gradually, the mood of the film darkens.

VHS: S00909. $60.00.

Mitchell Kriegman, USA, 1982, 28 mins.

My New Gun

Stacy Cochran's colorful farce—set in a claustrophobic New Jersey suburb—details the comic misadventures and curious chain of events which result when a repressed doctor (Stephen Collins) buys his dissatisfied housewife (Diane Lane) a .38 revolver. The troubles start when her mysterious neighbor Skippy (James LeGros)—who harbors a great crush on her—asks to borrow the prized weapon. With Tess Harper, Bill Raymond, Bruce Altman and Maddie Corman.

VHS: S19576. $94.95.

Laser: Letterboxed. **LD72356. $34.95.**

Stacy Cochran, USA, 1992, 99 mins.

My Sheroes, My Sheroes

A video by filmmaker Larry Fessenden *(Habit)* and performance artist David Leslie in which 100 women discuss their childhood influences.

VHS: S32346. $49.95.

Larry Fessenden/David Leslie, USA, 1993, 20 mins.

Nadja

In this stylish, supernatural thriller, a pair of twin brother and sister vampires haunt contemporary New York. Their father is killed by the meddling Dr. Van Helsing, but they resolve to fight back. On the prowl amidst New York's extensive nightlife, they attempt to seduce Van Helsing's beloved niece and nephew. Featuring Peter Fonda, Elina Lowensohn, Martin Donovan, Suzy Amis and Galaxy Craze. B&W.

VHS: S27056. $14.98.

Laser: LD75457. $39.95.

Michael Almereyda, USA, 1995, 92 mins.

The Natural History of Parking Lots

What can a father do with a languorous teenage son who hot-wires antique cars even though they inhabit a world of money-choked splendor in L.A.? Dad pays his hot, sexy gun-running older brother $2000 a week to watch out for him. From this set-up it's only a matter of time before all the weird fauna of a hazy, whacked-out L.A. make an appearance.

VHS: S22507. $39.95.

Everett Lewis, USA, 1994, 92 mins.

News News

A lively feature news program based on producer/television pioneer Peter Fend's view of the world. 28 mins.

VHS: S10173. $29.95.

The Newton Boys

From the director of *Slacker*. Matthew McConaughey, Ethan Hawke, Skeet Ulrich, Vincent D'Onofrio, Juliana Margulies and Dwight Yoakum star in this action-packed, true-life adventure about America's most successful bank robbers.

VHS: S34697. $103.99.

Laser: LD76998. $39.95.

Richard Linklater, USA, 1998, 122 mins.

Nice Girls...Films by and About Women

This compilation of award-winning short films is a sometimes challenging, always entertaining look into the lives, and through the lenses, of women today. Whatever you do, don't miss *Nice Girls Don't Do It*—an explicit, celebratory analysis of female ejaculation. This collection includes *Emergence of Eunice, You Take Care Now, Urban Steal, Constant State of Departure, Broken Heart, Social Experiment, New Shoes, A Still Life of Postcards, Another Great Day!, Giving Away* and, of course, *Nice Girls Don't Do It*. USA, 90 mins.

VHS: S15541. $19.95.

Nick Zedd

This is a portrait of no-budget filmmaker and Lower East Side punk icon, Nick Zedd. He is seen popping in and out of some of the area's most historic protests and riots.

VHS: S22652. $49.95.

Clayton Patterson, USA, 1989, 29 mins.

Nick Zedd: Steal This Video

This collection shows why Zedd is one of the most notorious filmmakers around. For *Thrust in Me* Zedd claims he was banned from every screening room in the country. *The Bogus Man, Police State, Whoregasm* and *The Wild World of Lydia Lunch* are all equally outrageous. 90 mins.

VHS: S25607. $29.95.

Nick Zedd, USA, 1994, 90 mins.

Niggernight

Four misguided youths into heavy metal music go on a self-ordained moral crusade, the twisted brainchild of Steve, the group's guru of hate. Stars Brian Cullen, Steve Witting, filmed in Brooklyn.

VHS: S10189. $29.95.

Michael Wolfe, USA, 1981, 20 mins.

Night Tide

The inspiration for *Night Tide* is the last stanza of Poe's "Annabel Lee." A young sailor on leave (Dennis Hopper) falls in love with an orphan girl posing as a mermaid in a California seafront show. Because of childhood fears which remain in her subconscious, she believes that she really is a mermaid. Raymond Durgnat wrote, "A collector's piece for connoisseurs of the offbeat...One is strongly reminded of Fritz Lang, of Aldrich's *Kiss Me Deadly*, of Charles Laughton's *Night of the Hunter*....A classically beautiful example of screen expressionism reconciled with realistic locales." Dennis Hopper stars.

VHS: S07457. $19.95.

Curtis Harrington, USA, 1961, 82 mins.

Nightsongs

This controversial feature by Marva Nabili folllows a Chinese-Vietnamese immigrant who comes to New York to live with her already established family. She works in a sweat shop along with her relatives. At night she writes in a journal about her husband and sons, whom she left behind. This simple story evokes the alienated and difficult world of today's immigrant experience. English and Chinese with English subtitles.

VHS: S26347. $29.95.

Marva Nabili, USA, 1984, 116 mins.

Nitrate Kisses

Unlike any other documentary, this work combines Barbara Hammer's unique experimental film style with archival footage to yield a unique view of overlooked lesbian and gay history. From the era of Nazism to today's AIDS epidemic, this work forces everyone to remember the importance of queer lives without evading any aspect of love, from the physical to the sublime.

VHS: S24031. $39.95.

Barbara Hammer, USA, 1992, 67 mins.

No Looking Back

Claudia (Lauren Holly) is a small-town girl trapped in a small town. She has a man (Jon Bon Jovi) who loves her and a family who needs her. When ex-lover Charlie (Edward Burns, *The Brothers McMullen, She's the One*) comes back into town, Claudia is conflicted when she realizes she still has feelings for him. Written and directed by Burns.

VHS: S34712. $101.99.

Edward Burns, USA, 1998, 96 mins.

No Telling

When medical researcher Geoffrey (Stephen Ramsey) receives a summer grant to study "chemo-electric therapy," his artist wife Lillian (Miriam Healy-Louie), worried about infertility, hopes that the summer will offer a little romance in her faltering marriage. Instead, Geoffrey locks himself in the laboratory with his animal experiments. Completely oblivious to the true nature of her husband's work, Lillian paints and passes time with ecologist Alex Vine (David van Tieghem). Her feelings of loneliness, however, are nothing compared to her reaction when she and Alex discover what Geoffrey's really been up to all summer. "A smart, spare, skewed update of the Frankenstein story" (Amy Taubin, *The Village Voice*).

VHS: S32216. $79.95.

Larry Fessenden, USA, 1991, 93 mins.

Not Quite Love
Film featurette stars a 10-year-old ghetto waif and prophet seeking love in an alienated metropolis. Shot in the night club ambience, with lots of music, singing and dancing.
VHS: S10185. $29.95.
David Schmidlapp, USA, 1981-88, 30 mins.

Not Top Gun
Produced by Paper Tiger TV in 1987, this irreverent take-off is a critique of the blockbuster movie *Top Gun* and a satire on its attitudes of militarization and fetishization of high-tech technology.
VHS: S09577. $39.95.
Chip Lord, USA, 1987, 26 mins.

Nowhere
This darkly funny film by the acclaimed writer/director of *The Living End* and *The Doom Generation* takes on teen angst with a vengeance in this overtly sexual and achingly real look at an 18-year-old searching for love in a fractured world. A kind of *Beverly Hills 90210* on acid. With Tracy Lords, John Ritter, Shannen Doherty, Christina Applegate, Debi Mazar and Kathleen Robertson.
VHS: S32220. $19.98.
Laser: LD76409. $34.99.
Gregg Araki, USA, 1997, 85 mins.

Odd Birds
Jeanne Collachia's period film, set in 1965, is a sensitive study of Joy Chan (Donna Lai Ming Lew), a 15-year-old Chinese-American teenager with burning ambition to become an actress, despite her mother's strong objections. Joy is encouraged by her friend with Brother T.S. Murphy (Michael Moriarty), an idiosyncratic math teacher at a local boys' school. The film has "humanism, validity and compassion that are rare in any film" (Joe Leyden, *Houston Chronicle*). With Nancy Lee, Bruce Gray, Karen Maruyama and Scott Crawford.
VHS: S19746. $19.98.
Jeanne Collachia, USA, 1985, 90 mins.

omaha (the movie)
A typical dysfunctional American family from the heartland is more than the young man at the center of this film can take. In Nepal he finds new hope and a new religion before returning to his native U.S. Once back, he again rejects the suburban wasteland of his family and seeks answers in a roadtrip. This funny and irreverent look at the maddeningly absurd landscape of 90's America combines the quirky with the criminal.
VHS: S29513. $79.95.
Dan Mervish, USA, 1994, 85 mins.

Oued Nefifik: A Foreign Movie
This comedy of manners is set in a post-colonial setting. A tourist's holiday falls apart in the aftermath of bloody riots in Casablanca, Morocco. Film, TV news and text are mixed in this deconstructed narrative.
VHS: S22606. $29.95.
Liza Bear, USA, 1982, 28 mins.

Palmetto
In this hot and sexy film noir from Volker Schlondorff *(The Tin Drum)*, Woody Harrelson is Harry, a small-timer facing hard time if he can't untangle a mystery involving three women (Elisabeth Shue, Gina Gershon, Chloe Sevigny), false identities, cold corpses and a string of clues that point to him as the murderer.
VHS: S34704. $103.99.
Laser: Dolby Digital. **LD77008. $39.98.**
DVD: DV60364. $24.98.
Volker Schlondorff, USA/Germany, 1998, 113 mins.

Palookaville
A comical story about a trio of bumbling down-and-out buddies who make a hilariously inept foray into the world of crime. William Forsythe and Frances McDormand star in this story of two New Jersey chums whose accomplishments include chiseling their way into a bakery when they try to rob a jewelry store. Winner of the Best Film Award at the 1995 Venice Film Festival. With Vincent Gallo and Adam Trese.
Laser: LD76199. $39.98.
Alan Taylor, USA, 1995, 92 mins.

Panic in the City
A thoroughly strange film about 60s revolutionaries trying to unleash World War III by detonating a bomb in Los Angeles, and a hardened sheriff (Howard Duff) trying to prevent the catastrophe. With Stephen McNally, Nehemiah Persoff and Dennis Hopper.
VHS: S18943. $19.95.
Eddie Davis, USA, 1968, 97 mins.

Paul Bartel's Secret Cinema
Two short early films by the director of *Eating Raoul* and *Lust in the Dust*. The first, entitled *Secret Cinema*, tells the story of a woman who cannot decide whether her life is real or she is a filmed subject; the second is an eight minute short called *Naughty Nurse*.
VHS: S01506. $19.95.
Paul Bartel, USA, 1966, 37 mins.

Photo Album
An original, quirky remembrance of the filmmaker's experiences as a young immigrant from Cuba settling in Boston. This sometimes surreal autobiography stars his real family, and demonstrates Oliver's ability to distinguish between satire and parody. English and Spanish with English subtitles.
VHS: S02906. $29.95.
Enrique Oliver, USA, 1985, 14 mins.

Picture Bride
Tamlyn Tomita stars in this gripping drama based on one woman's journey to a new life spawned by a photograph. Tomita's character travels to Hawaii in order to marry a man whom she has never met, with only a picture to help her find him. Once there, the tropical splendor of Hawaii inspires her toward a passionate romance. Winner of Best Picture Award at Sundance Film Festival.
VHS: S26398. $19.95.
Laser: LD75082. $39.99.
Kayo Hatta, USA, 1995, 95 mins.

Pink Nights
Kevin Anderson is Danny, a shy Chicago high schooler who helps out three beautiful women with a place to live when his mother goes out of town. A wholesome comedy about a platonic menage a quatre. Filmed in Chicago with the music of Phil N the Blanks, Bohemia and Planet Street. With Peri Kaczmarek, Shaun Allen and Jessica Vitkus.
VHS: S07344. $14.95.
Philip Koch, USA, 1985, 87 mins.

Pipsqueak Pfollies
A twisted tale wherein lots of little kids with metal teeth and bad ideas terrorize an unsuspecting ne'er-do-well. Painstakingly detailing everything kids can get away with, it is young at heart and mean in spirit. A super-8, die-hard joy ride.
VHS: S28581. $39.95.
Danny Plotnick, USA

The Plot Against Harry
A sleeper of Rip van Winkle dimensions, Michael Roemer's subtly innovative ethnic comedy went over the heads of preview audiences in 1969, sat on a shelf for 20 years, then resurfaced in 1989 to triumphant festival screenings and rave reviews. The central character is Harry Plotnik, a sad-sack Jewish gangster who finds his numbers racket slipping away. Under pressure from well-meaning relatives, Harry makes an erratic effort to go straight, triggering a series of humiliations and small disasters. Rather than partitioning the film's humor into a series of self-enclosed gags, Roemer instead creates a constant and pervasive comic atmosphere, based on sharply observed details, slow build-ups, throw-aways, deadpan reactions, egg-on-face ironies, and a precise sense of anticlimax.
VHS: S13576. $29.95.
Michael Roemer, USA, 1969/89, 81 mins.

Poison
An interwoven trilogy, the film uses three distinct stylistic conventions to explore the writings of Jean Genet, arriving at a profound realization of poison in the human mind, body and soul: A gritty prison drama reveals a homosexual's despair at being constantly confronted by forbidden passions; a campy '50s horror film send-up portrays a scientist's search for the essence of sexuality, and draws a compelling parallel to the HIV crisis when things go awry; and a tabloid mystery criticizes religious sentimentality as it reveals the circumstances surrounding the murder of a wife-beater by his own child, who then flew out the window toward heaven. Winner of the Grand Jury Prize at the Sundance Film Festival.
VHS: S15839. $19.98.
Laser: LD72226. $34.95.
Todd Haynes, USA, 1991, 85 mins.

Poker
Four regular Joes show up for their weekly poker game at a remote wilderness cabin. But paranoia soon replaces camaraderie as fear of an alien encounter begins to quake their normally level heads. A kind of Rod-Serling-meets-Alfred-Hitchcock film with its ironic black humor. Public performance.
VHS: S32138. $59.95.
Gaspar Hernandez, USA, 1988, 21 mins.

Police State
The Lower East Side king of sleaze is arrested for being a junkie/faggot by Officer Krupke, Willoughby Sharp. Sadistic Rockets Redglare shows that local police brutality is on par with anything that the world has to offer. Charles Horatio Crowley is also featured.
VHS: S22632. $19.95.
Nick Zedd, USA, 1987, 19 mins.

Polly Perverse Strikes Again!
Subtitled *A Love Story with Sociopathic Tendencies*, Dan Sallitt's film is the campy story of Nick Huxley, out of whose past comes Theresa, "a social disease who sleeps with anything that moves and who has decided that she wants Nick back. Nick, a successful photographer with a stable relationship, is determined to banish Theresa and youthful folly from his life. But neither Nick's girlfriend Arliss, a modern spirit who believes in driving buried emotions out in the open, nor Theresa, who seems to have an unseen power on her side, is willing to let it go at that." With S.A. Griffin, Strawn Bovee, Dawn Wildsmith.
VHS: S04585. $49.95.
Dan Salitt, USA, 1986

The Pompatus of Love
"A better guy-talk comedy than *The Brothers McMullen*" *(The Chicago Tribune)*, this film tells the tale of three days in the life of four thirty-something friends trying to come to terms with romance in New York City. Stars Jon Cryer, Adrian Pasdar, Mia Sara and Kristin Scott Thomas. "A funny film about men, women and the many mysteries of love in the '90s. The cast is excellent, the actors are good company and so is *The Pompatus of Love*" *(The New York Times)*.
VHS: S30561. $14.95.
Laser: LD76176. $39.98.
Richard Schenkman, USA, 1996, 99 mins.

Potato Wolf Coleslaw
Extracts from Wolfgang Staehle's *After Art*, Christy Rupp's Urban *Wildlife*, Walter Robinson's *Love Show*, Sally White's varieties and Scott Miller's wrestling special. Produced by the group Potato Wolf. 1983, 58 mins.
VHS: S10178. $49.95.

Potato Wolf Showcase
A sampler of the first year of the artists' cable TV series in black and white features a live performance by Cara Perlman, Kiki Smith, Ellen Cooper, Mitch Corber, Alan Moore, Jim Sutcliffe and others. 58 mins.
VHS: S10177. $49.95.

Potato Wolf Spring 1984
Extracts from George Schifini's *Philosophy*, Albert Di Martino's *Tesla*, Bradley Eros and Aline Mare's *Erotic Psyche*, Corber and White's live wedding, Moore's nightmare theatre, and McFerran's *May 19th*. 1984, 28 mins.
VHS: S10179. $49.95.

Prefontaine
From Steve James *(Hoop Dreams)* comes the story of Steve Prefontaine, the controversial "James Dean of track," who defied the rules, challenged the limits and smashed records to become the nation's greatest distance runner. With Jared Leto (TV's *My So-Called Life*), Ed O'Neill and Lindsay Crouse.
VHS: S32417. $103.99.
Laser: LD76398. $39.99.
Steve James, USA, 1997, 107 mins.

Promised Land
Jason Gedrick is a small town basketball player who turns to law enforcement when college doesn't work out. The hopes and dreams of young Americans are tested in this unusual drama about living with less. With Tracy Pollan, Kiefer Sutherland and Meg Ryan, as the very wild, red-haired Bev. The talent shines in this offbeat independent film.
VHS: S07440. $89.98.
Michael Hoffman, USA, 1987, 110 mins.

Pull My Daisy (The Beat Generation)
Inducted in 1996 into the National Film Archives, this 1959 historic beat happening based on the third act of Jack Kerouac's *The Beat Generation* is the documentary comedy of an evening with a young man who is visited by some poet friends at his Greenwich Village pad. Co-directed by Robert Frank, written and narrated by Kerouac, and featuring Allen Ginsberg, Gregory Corso, Larry Rivers, Peter Orlovsky, Delphine Seyrig and David Amram, with original music by Amram. With *The Last Clean Shirt* (1964, 45 mins.), which, "in premise and design, and its concentration on issues of language and speech, repetition and duration beyond the threshold of boredom, anticipates later influential films in the international avant-garde" (Blaine Allen, *The New American Cinema*); and *Birth of a Nation, 1965* (1965, 29 mins.), "a tantalizing, juicy, provocative fragment not only of a legendary lost work but of the '60s themselves: goofy, funny, challenging and unruly in the best sense" (Jonathan Rosenbaum, *Chicago Reader*).
VHS: S34620. $79.95.
Alfred Leslie, USA, 1959/1964/1965, 104 mins.

Puppets & Demons: Films by Patrick McGuinn

This anthology of ten award-winning short films by the director of *Suroh:Alien Hitchhiker* and *Desert Spirits* blends folkloric icons and modern dilemmas to tell humorous, fresh and unique stories. The collection includes *Terrance Baum: Intergalactic Assassin*, about one night in the life of an "intergalactic parasite terminator" who must save innocent Doris from an oozing being from the Planet Saliva; *Stella!, Gran'ma* and *Say Thankyou, Please*, starring Vincent, an id-like puppet doppelganger; *Agnes Keedan's Secret Plan*, a Hansel and Gretal tale of a lonely suburban witch; *Evolution*, the claymation comedy about the food chain; *Satan's Game; When the Owling Has Come; The Resurrectors* and *So Many People*. "If Jim Henson and David Lynch were genetically melded…these films might be the result" *(GO! Magazine)*.

VHS: S31139. $19.95.

Patrick McGuinn, USA, 1997, 60 mins.

Putney Swope

A token black accidentally becomes chairman of a conservative ad agency, transforming the firm into "Truth and Soul, Inc." Classic satire from director Robert Downey, featuring Mel Brooks in one of his first film roles.

VHS: S01075. $19.95.

Laser: LD74962. $39.99.

Robert Downey, USA, 1969, 88 mins.

Queen of Diamonds

Nina Menkes' audacious feature is set in contemporary Las Vegas. Menkes' style suggests an American Chantal Akerman, with her painterly, evocative depiction of real time characterized by long takes, natural light and a documentary-style naturalism. Tinka Menkes plays a Vegas blackjack dealer abandoned by her husband. Her life is irrevocably altered by her friendship and caring for a dying old man. "Within this arid emotional landscape the protagonist stands, able to dish out what she receives—anger, boredom, contempt—but threatening to vanish if she is not soon loved. *Queen of Diamonds* is a powerful film which spurns resolution, daring its viewers instead to tune into the psychic frequencies of American alienation" (Jon Stout, Los Angeles Film Forum).

VHS: S18685. $59.95.

Nina Menkes, USA, 1991, 77 mins.

Ralph's Arm

When his left arm up and leaves him in disgust, a world famous pianist searches the wilds of Beverly Hills for the rogue limb, and finds it in hiding in the hacienda of a blase Yuppie couple. A dizzy black comedy about the rewards of listening to your hand, not your heart. Public performance.

VHS: S32134. $59.95.

Michelle Truffaut, USA, 1991, 30 mins.

Ramona

A low-key, fresh road movie about a quiet, reflective American (Jason Scott), a free-spirited Mexican woman and an ethereal doll maker named Ramona, who hides in the back of his trunk to get through customs. The three undertake a mythic road trip through the colorful American landscape. "*Ramona* is a blend of drama, sophisticated romance and quirky comedy" *(Cinema)*. With Heidi Von Palleske, Cain Devore and Michael David Lally.

VHS: S20378. $89.95.

Jonathan Sarno, USA, 1990, 90 mins.

Raptures of the Deep

A live TV black and white production spoofing Jacques Cousteau; the bathyscaphe discovers undersea psychiatry and merpeople. Includes an advertisement by Peter Fend, and a skit by performance artist and painter Ilona Granet.

VHS: S10174. $29.95.

Alan Moore, USA, 1981, 28 mins.

The Real Blonde

A sexy to-dye-for comedy from the director of *Living in Oblivion, Box of Moonlight* and *Johnny Suede*. Matthew Modine, Daryl Hannah and Elizabeth Berkley grapple with love, wrestle with temptation and search for the holy grail of "the real blonde" in this wickedly entertaining tale set in New York's fashion world. With Kathleen Turner, Christopher Lloyd, Catherine Keener, Maxwell Caulfield and Bridgette Wilson.

VHS: S34983. $99.99.

Tom DiCillo, USA, 1998, 107 mins.

Red Italy

Second feature by the French-born film director is a Bertolucci-style story of a bored, rich woman looking for romance and adventure. She meets an American G.I., dumps him, and then falls for a Communist worker. Cast includes John Lurie and Mitchell himself in a b/w evocation of the post-war nightclub scene.

VHS: S07121. $59.95.

Eric Mitchell, USA, 1979, 55 mins.

Redlands

A singer booked for an audition must take time out to visit her retarded adult sister and break the news of their mother's death. In the process, the singer is forced to rethink her self-centered priorities and make a commitment to her sister. Public performance.

VHS: S32135. $59.95.

Joan Taylor, USA, 1989, 28 mins.

Repo Man

First film from the director of *Sid and Nancy*, an outrageous comedy combining the seedy world of auto repossessors and nuclear madness. With Emilio Estevez, Harry Dean Stanton and title song by Iggy Pop. A sleeper.

VHS: S02737. $14.98.

Laser: LD70070. $34.98.

Alex Cox, USA, 1984, 93 mins.

Reptile Mind

Dramatization of an anarchist's nightmare—his friends run into lizards. With Bobby G., Kiki Smith, Ellen Cooper, Carol Parkinson and others.

VHS: S10175. $29.95.

Alan Moore, USA, 1982, 28 mins.

Resident Alien

Quentin Crisp, author and professional pansy, has always led a charming, if not charmed, life. While *The Naked Civil Servant* tells of his early and troubled life in Great Britain, this film shows how celebrity in America suited the grand old dame. Fran Lebowitz, Holly Woodlawn, Michael Musto, and other New York scenesters are featured.

VHS: S25103. $19.95.

Jonathan Nossiter, USA, 1990, 85 mins.

Revenge of the Amazons/Metal Madam

Intimate cult secrets and group therapy pseudo sects are featured in this unusual musical. Behind the scenes, a buxom and hysterical Sandy Karbinsky (Janice DeRosa) finds there are unforseen consequences to joining an all-woman encounter group. Could it be a twist on the world's oldest profession?

VHS: S22612. $39.95.

Mark Kehoe, USA, 1979, 40 mins.

Rhythm Thief

In this "lower East Side *Breathless*" (Jay Carr, *Boston Globe*), Simon (Jason Andrews) is a New York City bootlegger who sells stolen music on the Lower East Side, in between trysts with Cyd, a Ludlow Street chick (Kimberly Flynn), and Marty, a former lover (Eddie Daniels). Simon's bootleg activity kickstarts an all-out war with a militant all-girl punk band. Driven out of town to Far Rockaway, Simon and his buddy Fuller (Kevin Corrigan, *Walking and Talking*) are drawn into a classic showdown under the 105th Street boardwalk. "Inventive, exciting, original" (Martin Scorsese).

VHS: S32682. $39.99.

Matthew Harrison, USA, 1994, 88 mins.

Risk

Direct from its Sundance premiere, this sexy drama stars Karen Sillas as a striking New York City model who poses in the nude. A strange man with a sordid past falls in love with her and his obsession soon transforms her life into a whirlwind of passion, desire and danger.

VHS: S26027. $69.95.

D. Deirdre Fishel, USA, 1994, 94 mins.

River of Grass

In this "incisive and funny…simultaneously subversive and compassionate" (J. Carr, *Boston Globe*), sun-drunk road movie, a would-be Bonnie and Clyde never actually commit a crime, fall in love, or even hit the road. "Highly original and filmed with perfect assurance…one of the finest independent films of recent years" (Dave Kehr, *New York Daily News*).

VHS: S31409. $39.99.

Kelly Reichardt, USA, 1995, 77 mins.

Road to Ruin

An updated Sturges-like effort, this Paris-based romantic comedy features Peter Weller as a dashing playboy and international financier who pretends he's broke to determine whether the intentions of his girlfriend (Carey Lowell) are honorable.

VHS: S16863. $14.98.

Monique Annaud, USA, 1992, 94 mins.

Roadracers

Part of Showtime's *Rebel Highway* series, in which 10 top directors revisited the lurid teen dramas of '50s drive-ins, Robert Rodriguez' *(Desperado)* stylish film takes its title from a '50s B movie. David Arquette is Dude, a misunderstood rebel in a small town. Selma Hayek is his tough, sexy girlfriend, Donna. Dogged by a cop who is determined to put him behind bars, Dude takes on the world, including a rival drag racer who just won't settle for being the second fastest guy in town. Excellent performances and soundtrack. "May be the most over-the-top parody of '50s exploitation flicks ever made" *(Video Store Magazine)*.

VHS: S32934. $103.99.

Laser: LD76424. $39.99.

Robert Rodriguez, USA, 1994, 94 mins.

Roadside Prophets

This road movie begins when the star, John Doe (formerly of the rock group X), receives the cremated remains of an unknown man. The dead man also left behind an intriguing image of a mythical Nevada town, which inspires John to go off in search of this unlikely shangri-la. A strange kid joins John on his search through back roads, where even stranger people are encountered. Music by the Pogues, the Beastie Boys and John Doe, and an appearance by Timothy Leary are featured.

VHS: S20690. 19.95.

VHS: S20690. $19.95.

Abbe Wool, USA, 1992, 96 mins.

Roadsinger

Independent video work by Gary LeGault, starring the filmmaker as a washed-up entertainer on the come-back trail working small bars and clubs.

VHS: S01545. $49.95.

Gary LeGault, USA, 1986

Ruby in Paradise

Winner of the 1993 Grand Prize at the Sundance Film Festival, this film, starring the beautiful and accomplished Ashley Judd, charts the progress of a woman toward her own personal paradise. Visually stunning cinematography shows the Florida locations to great advantage in this story of one woman's quest for meaning.

VHS: S20711. $19.95.

Victor Nunez, USA, 1993, 115 mins.

Runnin' Kind

Independent filmmaker Max Tash directed this journey of an Ohio-born, middle-class kid who takes off for the underground rock scene of L.A. With David Packer, Pleasant Gehman, Brie Howard, Rosie Flores. Music by The Screaming Sirens.

VHS: S11585. $79.98.

Max Tash, USA, 1989, 100 mins.

Safe

Todd Haynes *(Poison)* directs this unusual, stylish film which stars Julianne Moore *(Vanya on 42nd Street)* as a California suburban housewife who suffers from an insidious modern dilemma. Everything she is surrounded by becomes toxic to her; she is made ill by the poisoned, chemically-laden environment. She seeks refuge in a holistic center in Albuquerque only to discover that the center's magnetic leader has his own personal agenda.

VHS: S26860. $96.99.

Laser: LD75396. $39.95.

Todd Haynes, USA, 1995, 119 mins.

Safety in Numbers

Allen, a writer who doesn't write, is in love with his former next door neighbor, Lori, who's dating Isaac, a popular musician in the local club scene. This drives Allen to deeply absorb himself into his screenplay and he finally gains some interest from a talent agency. Yet every day seems to be a struggle between staying true to himself and falling into the environment which surrounds him.

VHS: S33752. $19.95.

Evan Jacobs, USA, 1997, 80 mins.

The Scenic Route

From the acclaimed independent American director of *Rock Hudson's Home Movies* comes this tale of two New York sisters who share the same lover without realizing it. The film, through its baroque landscape of interiors and tableaux, opera and soap opera, is held together by an unerring sense of visual style and persistently wry humor. Winner of the British Film Institute Award for Most Original and Innovative Film of 1978. "A movie of great, grave, tightly controlled visual daring, and you have never seen anything like it before" (Roger Ebert).

VHS: S31124. $29.99.

Mark Rappaport, USA, 1978, 76 mins.

The Search for One-Eye Jimmy

This offbeat, low-budget comedy features an amazing cast and is the first effort from *Seinfeld* writer Sam Henry Kass. Holt McCallany, Nicholas Turturro, John Turturro, Steve Buscemi, Samuel L. Jackson and Jennifer Beals are just a few of the actors in this wide-ranging work. A young filmmaker returns to his old Brooklyn neighborhood to shoot a documentary. After getting his bearings he realizes One-Eye Jimmy is missing. This immediately becomes the focus of his film, and a host of eccentric neighborhood characters become involved in the search, along with the FBI, the Catholic Church and the Mob.

VHS: S28406. $19.95.

Sam Henry Kass, USA, 1996, 86 mins.

Sex Is Sex

This remarkable film containing frank and compelling conversations with male prostitutes breaks through common cliches about prostitution to reveal a world more complex and compelling than popular perception permits. Neither desperately tragic nor overly romanticized, this film presents young New York hustlers telling what they know, whether it be the secret to faking sex, the dangers of crazy tricks, or just the pleasure of easy money. "A remarkable look at a world unseen by the average person…not to be missed" *(The New York Times)*.

VHS: S30933. $39.95.

Jennifer Milici/Brian Bergen, USA, 1994, 50 mins.

Sex, Drugs and Democracy

This provocative, award-winning film explores the limits of personal freedom through an uncensored look at morality and politics in Holland's free society, which includes a legalized sex industry, the open sale of marijuana, total equality for gays, the distribution of sterile syringes and methadone to drug addicts, government-financed abortion and euthanasia and comprehensive sex education for schoolchildren. "Marshalls some impressive statistics to suggest that a climate of freedom and tolerance reduces crime and addiction" (Stephen Holden, *The New York Times*).

VHS: S32978. $24.95.

Jonathan Blank, USA, 1994, 87 mins.

Sex, Drugs, Rock & Roll

Famed actor/writer Eric Bogosian creates ten different characters set in as many vignettes. Aggressively realized, these raw, thought-provoking mini-dramas startle and surprise the viewer with their power.

VHS: S20688. $19.98.

John McNaughton, USA, 1991, 100 mins.

She Must Be Seeing Things

"A wryly sophisticated comedy...plays like a lesbian homage to *Unfaithfully Yours*," wrote Jay Carr in *The Boston Globe*. Agatha is an international lawyer, Jo a filmmaker. While Jo is on the road with her film, Agatha reads her diary and becomes insanely jealous to the point of dressing up as a man and "shadowing" her. "Groundbreaking in its understated portrayal of sophisticated urban lesbians exploring such dynamics as sex and sexuality, career and commitment, fidelity and companionship. The film gives us characters who are richly realistic and demonstrates that McLaughlin is a complex and refreshingly thoughtful talent..." *(New York Native)*.

VHS: S10941. $29.95.

Sheila McLaughlin, USA, 1988, 85 mins.

She's So Lovely

Sean Penn stars in a film written by the late great John Cassavetes and directed by Cassavetes' son, Nick. A modern fairy tale about Eddie (Penn) and Maureen (Penn's wife, Robin Wright Penn), a down-and-out married couple of misfits living on nothing but passion for one another. When their outrageous love drives Eddie off the deep end and Maureen into a rags-to-riches marriage to Joey (John Travolta), a wealthy contractor, nothing can keep Eddie out of her life. With Gena Rowlands.

VHS: S34102. $103.99.

Laser: LD76942. $39.95.

Nick Cassavetes, USA/France, 1997, 96 mins.

She's the One

In this follow-up to Edward Burns' low-budget hit, *The Brothers McMullen*, Burns stars as a New York City cab driver, underachiever and brother of a stockbroker (Mike McGlone). Burns is attached to girlfriend Maxine Bahns and McGlone is married to Jenifer Aniston, but Cameron Diaz, a call girl, former flame of Burns and mistress of McGlone, is "the one" who causes complications for the brothers. With John Mahoney *(Frazier)*. Featuring music by Tom Petty & The Heartbreakers.

VHS: S30460. $19.98.

Laser: LD76058. $39.98.

Edward Burns, USA, 1996, 97 mins.

Short Cinema Journal, Issue #3

A monthly DVD video magazine of award-winning films from around the world. Includes excerpt of *Visions of Light*, featuring Academy Award-winning films and cinematographers; *Night & Fog*, 1956 Grand Prix du cinema Francais; 1996 Festival International du Film Fantastique Brussels winner, *Dada; Flying over Mother*, 1997 ACS Silver Award winner, Australia; *Os Camaradas*, featured in 25th Latin American Film Festival & Manheim-Heidelberg Film Festival; official Cannes selection *Joe*, and Ryan Stiles from *The Drew Carey Show* and Sean Masterson.

DVD: DV60261. $19.95.

Short Personal Films by Seven West Coast Women

Includes excerpts from the films *Film Flyer* by Judith Wardwell, *Orange* by Karen Johnson, *Angel Blue Sweet Wings* by Chick Strand, *Marguerite* by Betty Chen, *My Name Is Una* by Gunvor Nelson, *Bird* by Sharon Hennessy and *Folly* by Freude Bartlett. *1974, 28 mins.*

VHS: S31587. $59.95.

Signal 7

Sensitive portrayal of two San Francisco cabbies about a long night's journey into self-discovery, following the interactions of two middle-aged taxi drivers cum actors. Title comes from the alert signal that a driver not responding may be in trouble. One of the first features to be shot on video and transferred to film, with interesting visual results.

VHS: S03438. $79.95.

Rob Nilsson, USA, 1985, 92 mins.

Sir Drone

Raymond Pettibon presents the early days of Los Angeles punk rock as an attempt "to break the organic human chain of metaphysical fate. There and then and forever after, music was to be no longer music. Hippies were to be no longer hippies. Everything was instead to be punk."

VHS: S20526. $19.95.

Six Shorts (Pam Payne)

A collection of video motion paintings/visual songs, featuring *Up on the Roof*, about flying lessons from a six-year-old; *Brief Undermode*, a cryptic triptych with Terry Moore; *What We Do*, which illustrates the creative mode; *Octobre*, feminine perception confliction; *Microwave*, in which a child tells how to properly misuse an oven; and *Mira*, a portrait of East 4th Street.

VHS: S22642. $29.95.

Pam Payne, USA, 1988-90, 30 mins.

Slacker

A true sleeper. Richard Linklater's first feature film is a wickedly funny social satire on a new American sub-culture that's inventive, quite bizarre and refreshingly offbeat. Filmed entirely in Austin, Texas, with a cast of hundreds of local residents. The film is a human chain letter: you meet one person and through that person you meet another person, and another ... The local characters voice their opinions on a variety of subjects including Madonna's pap smear, the sniper Charles Whitman, and the JFK assassination.

VHS: S16328. $19.98.

Richard Linklater, USA, 1991, 101 mins.

Sling Blade

Billy Bob Thornton stars in his Academy Award-winning screenplay as Karl, a quiet and simple man who is released from prison 25 years after killing his mother and her lover, and returns to the small Arkansas town of his youth. After he befriends a young boy (Lucas Black), his mother (Natalie Canerday) and her boss (John Ritter), Karl's new life is shattered when he finds himself in conflict with the woman's violent lover (Dwight Yokum), as he confronts his past. With J.T. Walsh, Robert Duvall, and a cameo by Jim Jarmusch.

VHS: S31532. $19.95.

Laser: LD76306. $59.95.

Billy Bob Thornton, USA, 1996, 135 mins.

Smithereens

This rock movie, capturing the desperation of life in the streets, has become a minor cult classic. Directed by Susan Seidelman *(Desperately Seeking Susan)*, *Smithereens* was made on a budget of only $80,000. It also features an appearance by Richard Hell.

VHS: S01220. $29.95.

Susan Seidelman, USA, 1984, 90 mins.

Solo

A wordless, hypnotic masterpiece that follows a climber from a predawn canyon floor to a breathtaking panorama of snow, sky and peaks. Winner of numerous festival awards, including Film Festivals in Moscow, Melbourne and Chicago.

VHS: S01230. $29.95.

Mike Hoover, USA, 1971, 30 mins.

Some Folks Call It a Sling Blade

A young reporter hopes to interview a man judged criminally insane for the murder of his own mother. The criminal is about to released after 25 years of incarceration. Between the reporter and this exciting story is a neurotic bureaucrat who tries to protect the strange madman. The film features Molly Ringwald, J.T. Walsh and Billy Bob Thornton. Also included is a behind-the-scenes look at the making of the film.

VHS: S27084. $24.95.

Laser: LD76435. $24.99.

George Hickenlooper, USA, 1995, 45 mins.

Soul in the Hole

This rhythmic, basketball-slinging, rap soundtrack documentary is a bird's eye view of a troubled kid with basketball skills and his surrogate father/coach. "The best film ever made about basketball-and about growing up black, male and street" *(The Village Voice)*.

VHS: S35013. $59.95.

Danielle Gardner, USA, 1997, 90 mins.

The Spanish Prisoner

In this suspenseful gem from Mamet, Joe Ross (Campbell Scott) has invented a process that will earn his company millions, but he's afraid his boss won't reward him for his invention. He enlists the help of the wealthy Jimmy Dell (Steve Martin), whom Joe learns isn't what he seems. Joe's assistant, Susan (Rebecca Pigeon), helps Joe contact an FBI agent, and he assists in trapping Jimmy in a sting, but soon Joe is the one who has been conned and framed for murder. With Ben Gazzara.

VHS: S34745. $103.99.

David Mamet, USA, 1997, 110 mins.

Spanking the Monkey

Jeremy Davies stars as a young man on his way to a prestigious summer internship in Washington, D.C., after finishing his first year of pre-med. He returns to his home town for a weekend visit, to find his mother confined to her bed with a broken leg and his father unwilling and unable to care for her. Forced to delay his internship, he attempts to deal with his incestuous relationship with his mother and the absenteeism of his controlling father.

VHS: S22891. $19.95.

David O. Russell, USA, 1994, 99 mins.

Speed Freaks with Guns

The unregenerate spawn of Nick Zedd, Richard Kern, Tommy Turner, *et al.*, this Texan-come-lately continues to push the borders of bad taste. Sometimes this is an all too real jump into the mind of a psycho killer. Bad humor scarcely affects the manifest atrocities put on the screen by this short feature.

VHS: S22503. $29.95.

Joe Christ, USA, 1991, 30 mins.

The Spitfire Grill

After her release from prison, the mysterious Percy (Alison Elliot, *The Underneath*) arrives in the small town of Gilead, Maine, on the run from her past. Working as a waitress at the Spitfire Grill, run by cantankerous Hannah (Ellen Burstyn) and Shelby (Marcia Gay Harden), Percy comes face-to-face with her future. A Sundance Film Festival hit and "one of the year's most compelling, haunting and beautifully acted films" (CBS Radio Los Angeles).

VHS: S30965. $19.95.

Laser: LD76137. $39.95.

Lee David Zlotoff, USA, 1996, 111 mins.

Squeeze

An edgy and intense look at the pressures and the choices three inner-city teens are forced to make in the dangerous streets surrounding them. With Tyrone Burton, Eddie Cutanda, Phuong Duong and Geoffrey Rhue. "Fresh, raw and vigorous" *(The Boston Globe)*.

VHS: S33113. $103.99.

Robert Patton-Spruill, USA, 1997, 96 mins.

Star Maps

In this impressive debut by California filmmaker Miguel Arteta, dreams of stardom have led Carlos to Los Angeles. A naive young man, he works selling maps which point the way to the homes of Hollywood's biggest stars. But his job is really a front for a prostitution ring, and in this city of illusions, Carlos' plan to use one of his customers to help him get a movie role may be the biggest illusion of all.

VHS: S32912. $99.99.

Laser: LD76423. $39.98.

Miguel Arteta, USA, 1997, 86 mins.

Stations of the Elevated

An astonishingly beautiful film about graffiti-covered trains hurtling through a strange urban landscape filled with the debris of a decaying civilization. The music of Charles Mingus counterpoints the recurring visual riffs of the tension-filled imagery.

VHS: S12342. $19.95.

Manfred Kirchheimer, USA, 1980, 45 mins.

Sticky Fingers

A silly and upbeat comedy about two New York female musicians who cannot resist spending a ton of money that is left in their apartment by a frightened drug dealer for safekeeping. Helen Slater and Melanie Mayron are the heavy spenders. With Eileen Brennan and Carol Kane as their neighbors and Danitra Vance and Christopher Guest as their amazed friends. Co-written by Mayron with director Catlin Adams.

VHS: S07793. $89.95.

Catlin Adams, USA, 1988, 89 mins.

The Stranger

Chris Frieri's *(The Orbitrons, I Was a Teenage Mummy)* third feature follows the adventures of a cynical New Jersey bar janitor (Mark Fucille, *I Was a Teenage Mummy, The Toxic Avenger*), as he takes LSD, has nightmares, rides subway cars, yells at his pregnant girlfriend, and kills people. The film also features a cigar-smoking dwarf bar owner and a chimp wandering through a graveyard.

VHS: S34250. $19.95.

Chris Frieri, USA, 1994, 60 mins.

Stream of Social Intercourse

Following his therapist's advice, an introverted but determined young college student faces a class party with high hopes for his new social skills. His therapy takes a comical turn when the counselor crashes the party with worse problems of his own. Public performance.

VHS: S32141. $59.95.

Serj Minassians, USA, 1990, 26 mins.

Strong Medicine

Internationally acclaimed theater director Richard Foreman's complex, surreal and alternately funny and frightening first feature is the Alice-in-Wonderland-like adventure of Rhoda, whose husband gives her a gift of a vacation for her birthday, hoping to get her out of his life. Stars American avant-garde theater legends Kate Manheim, Ron Vawter and David Warrilow, with cameos by Wallace Shawn, Carol Kane, Buck Henry and Raul Julia. "Richard Foreman's work gives resonance and a disturbance not felt from any other company. A pioneer in end-of-milennium controlled chaos" (David Bowie).

VHS: S30250. $34.95.

Richard Foreman, USA, 1980, 95 mins.

SubUrbia

Richard Linklater *(Dazed and Confused)* directed and Eric Bogosian *(Talk Radio)* wrote the screenplay for this "*American Graffiti* for the *Dazed and Confused* set" (Bob Healy, *Satellite News Network*) about a successful rock star who returns home to find his old high school friends doing the same old high school thing—hanging out in the parking lot of a local convenience store. With Jayce Bartok, Parker Posey, Giovanni Ribisi, Steve Zahn, Nicky Katt and Dina Spybey.

VHS: S31720. $19.95.

Richard Linklater, USA, 1997, 121 mins.

Sullivan's Last Call

An intimate peek into the sexual and psychological underpinnings of a modern relationship. Late one evening two former lovers reunite, but when the man declares he is celibate, sparks fly and the woman sets out to prove him wrong. Without profanity or nudity, this sexy film noir explores the emotional complexities of getting too close for comfort. Public performance rights included.

VHS: S33382. $59.95.

Fran Rizzo, USA, 1995, 18 mins.

Suture

Dennis Haybert, Mel Harris and Michael Harris star in this tense thriller which mixes treachery, passion and mistaken identity. An homage to Hitchcock, the central characters are two brothers. When one brother is set up to be mistaken for the other all the worst of one's deeds come back to haunt them both. "Daringly original! A mind-blowing journey to the outer limits" *(New York Post)*.

VHS: S25099. $19.98.
Laser: LD75021. $39.99.

Scott McGehee/David Siegel, USA, 1994, 96 mins.

Sweet Love, Bitter

In this thinly disguised account of the last years in the life of Charlie "Bird" Parker, comedian Dick Gregory produces a diverse performance as Richie "Eagle" Coles, a Jazz saxophonist with a genius for friendship and self-destruction. Artist Charles McPherson ghosts for Gregory on the gorgeous score by Billie Holiday's pianist, Mal Waldron.

VHS: S15796. $59.95.

Herbert Danska, USA, 1966, 92 mins.

Talking to Strangers

Jesse wants to be a writer. In nine 10-minute takes he speaks to the camera. The result is one of the most highly original and critically praised feature debuts in American independent cinema. It is distinguished by intriguing wide-screen compositions and complex camera movements, in a style comparable to Hitchcock's *Rope*.

VHS: S29477. $89.95.

Rob Tregenza, USA, 1988, 93 mins.

Televoid

This nontraditional, Orwellian social commentary on television and western society's obsession with sensationalism and violence integrates film clips to create a moody and funny film noir, as Skully, a living skeleton and channel-flipping couch potato with a short attention span is inundated and controlled by images on his TV.

VHS: S32089. $19.98.

Michael Boydstun, USA, 1997, 45 mins.

Testament

Jane Alexander and William Devane star in this dramatic story of a family caught in the aftermath of a nuclear attack. Powerfully yet sensitively written, and acted out in a manner that enables the audience to care for the characters.

VHS: S01312. $14.95.
Laser: LD75338. $29.98.

Lynne Littman, USA, 1983, 90 mins.

Thank You and Goodnight

A highly original film by Jan Oxenberg that uses memory, anecdote and avant-garde representations (such as cardboard cut-outs) to explore the tender, beautiful and emotionally devastating relationship between the filmmaker and her grandmother. "Wildly inventive and unique, it's a cosmic, cerebral comedy of a Woody Allenish sort" *(Toronto Globe)*.

VHS: S18269. $19.98.

Jan Oxenberg, USA, 1991, 82 mins.

They Eat Scum

John Waters liked this "disgusting outlay of cheapness, decadence, nihilism and everyday cannibalism. Nick Zedd's film must rank as something of an ultimate achievement of non-committal, unblinking savagery, a true expression of what used to be called the 'punk ethos'." Stars Donna Death.

VHS: S10162. $39.95.

Nick Zedd, USA, 1979, 70 mins.

Things to Do in Denver When You're Dead

Andy Garcia and Christopher Walken are old Mob business associates who end up on opposing sides in this knockout thriller. Garcia returns from retirement for one more job, but things go desperately wrong and he himself is marked for a new forced retirement. Gabrielle Anwar is featured.

VHS: S29410. $99.99.
Laser: LD75818. $39.99.

Three Films by Chris Frieri

Includes *Mojica No Mojo* (1994, 4 mins.) in which Brazilian filmmaker Jose Marion Mojica *(Coffin Joe)* makes an appearance at St. Marks Place in front of East Village's Mojo Guitar shop, June 1994; *The Window* a 17-minute slice-of-life in which a man contends with a large rat in his Lower East Side apartment; and *Hot Rod Hearse* (1996, 38 mins.) in which New Jersey garage band, Hearse, abducted by exraterrestrials, are returned to earth, granted a fantasy, a revenge and an audience, and are inducted into the Rock and Roll Hall of Fame. "Pretty amazing and with lots of drug-inspired FX" *(Psychotronic)*.

VHS: S34249. $19.95.

Chris Frieri, USA, 1996, 59 mins.

Three Short Films (Mark Rappaport)

Three films from the filmmaker who's been called "more hilarious than the Coen brothers, weirder than Hal Hartley, deeper than Woody Allen, and more deadpan than Stephen Wright" (Ray Carney, Boston University). Includes *Mark Rappaport: The TV Spinoff* (1980; 28 mins.), which the *Chicago Reader* called "the best possible introduction to Rappaport's film work;" the "deliciously ironic…amusing, biting" *(Los Angeles Times) Postcards* (1990; 26 mins.), a love story told through 1960s postcards; and "the inventive, gorgeous" *(LA Weekly) Exterior Night* (1993; 36 mins.). "Mark Rappaport makes movies that look, sound and feel like nobody else's movies. He's an original" (Roger Ebert, *Chicago Sun-Times*).

VHS: S31125. $29.99.

Mark Rappaport, USA, 1980/1990/1993, 90 mins.

Time Expired

A powerful independent short about a convict (Bob Gosse) about to be released from jail who faces choosing between the two loves of his life—his loyal, spirited wife (Edie Falco) or his extravagant transvestite lover (John Leguizamo).

VHS: S18969. $14.95.

Danny Leiner, USA, 1992, 30 mins.

The Toll Collector

Paul Worley is leaving to go away to school in San Francisco. The only problem is that he wants to drop out. Then he finds out his girlfriend has been cheating on him; also, he hasn't heard from his friend Scott in weeks. Told mostly in flashbacks, the film looks at self-reliance, society's standards and finding out what you're made of.

VHS: S33753. $19.95.

Evan Jacobs, USA, 1997, 90 mins.

Totally F***ed Up

Araki's follow-up to *The Living End*, this gay, "'90s version of *The Breakfast Club*" *(San Francisco Club)* is an honest, open-structured look into the lives of gay and lesbian teens struggling with their emergent identities in the homophobic '90s. With music by Ministry, This Mortal Coil, Unrest, Babyland, The Wolfgang Press, Coil and His Name Is Alive. "A breakthrough" *(San Francisco Chronicle)*.

VHS: S29856. $59.95.

Gregg Araki, USA, 1994, 85 mins.

Trees Lounge

Written, directed and starring actor Steve Buscemi, *Trees Lounge* is the humorous, semi-autobiographical story of Tommy Basilio, a 31-year-old barfly and unemployed auto mechanic with a quick wit and a chip on his shoulder who spends most nights at his favorite bar, Trees Lounge, in the pursuit of one-night stands. When he loses his pregnant girlfriend (Elizabeth Bracco) to his best friend and former boss (Anthony LaPaglia), he makes an attempt to put his life back together. He finds temporary salvation driving his deceased uncle's ice cream truck, but gets dangerously close to his 17-year-old helper, Debbie (Chloe Sevigny, *Kids*). Tommy discovers a disturbing truth about himself in the last place he expected. "*Trees Lounge* is a winner!" *(People Magazine)*.

VHS: S30614. $96.99.

Steve Buscemi, USA, 1996, 94 mins.

Twins

A comedy of fratricide, this film by the independent director best known for his 1982 graffiti-rap adventure *Wild Style* stars performance artist Michael Smith in a double role as the psychopath Sam seeking to destroy his twin Stan, the policeman. *Twins* is Ahearn's second feature, and he uses a deliberately structured and largely stationary camera technique as a throwback to the era of Keystone comedies and Buster Keaton films.

VHS: S07109. $59.95.

Charlie Ahearn, USA, 1980, 50 mins.

Two Small Bodies

Fred Ward and Suzi Amis star in this psychosexual battle of the sexes. Ward is Lieutenant Brown, a detective who believes Eileen (Amis) has murdered her children. Repulsion and attraction send them spinning in orbit around each other until the boundary between truth and illusion is dissolved.

VHS: S21790. $19.98.

Beth B, USA/Germany, 1994, 85 mins.

Uforia

A New York cult classic; the off-beat satire on evangelism and UFO hysteria. Fred Ward plays a Waylon Jennings look-alike who becomes partners with phony preacher Harry Dean Stanton, while Ward's wacky girlfriend (Cindy Williams) is convinced aliens are about to land and save the world.

VHS: S04859. $59.95.

John Binder, USA, 1986, 92 mins.

Ulee's Gold

Peter Fonda stars as Ulee Jackson, a beekeeper working in northwest Florida in a swamp on the Apalachicola River who struggles to keep his broken family—two granddaughters, a son in prison, a daughter-in-law with debts to drug dealers—together in whatever fashion he can. That struggle leads him on a revealing journey that takes him far from the depths of the swamps that surround him physically and engulf him emotionally. With Patricia Richardson.

VHS: S33323. $99.99.
Laser: LD76812. $39.99.

Victor Nunez, USA, 1997, 113 mins.

Unconditional Love

In the setting of the pristine beaches and rolling dunes of Cape Cod, Egeli paints a canvas of beauty and love and the forces that form an artist. Steve (Pablo Bryant) is a driven young painter on the verge of discovery. Three beautiful women vie for his attention—his model, the sensual Theresa (Jessica Flannery); Melissa, (Isabelle Dahlin), a young art student; and Mary, whose art and life are about passion and emotion. Steve finds himself on the brink of self-destruction, where he must find the true meaning of unconditional love. "Glows with an aura of emotional and intellectual authenticity" (Kevin Thomas, *L.A. Times*).

VHS: S32172. $89.98.

Arthur Bjorn Egeli, USA, 1995, 90 mins.

Unhook the Stars

In this "self-assured, sweet surprise" *(New City)* about the value of growing up around a variety of women, Nick Cassavetes directs mom, Gena Rowlands, as a widow coping with loneliness, whose life is complicated by her young next door neighbor (Marisa Tomei) when she asks her to take care of her young son for a few hours. Delightful performances by both Rowlands and Tomei; with Gerard Depardieu and Moira Kelly.

VHS: S31285. $103.99.
Laser: LD76214. $39.99.

Nick Cassavetes, USA, 1996, 105 mins.

Union City

Deborah Harry stars in this tale of murder and paranoia set in a large industrial city. With a guest appearance by Pat Benatar, music composed by Blondie's Chris Stein.

VHS: S01766. $19.98.

Mark Reichert, USA, 1981, 82 mins.

Variety

In this groundbreaking look at feminism and pornography, written by the late Kathy Acker, a New York woman, desperate for work, takes a job as a ticket seller at an adult movie theater.

VHS: S34313. $24.95.

Bette Gordon, USA, 1984, 97 mins.

Vermont Is for Lovers

This unusual feature has become a cult hit. It's a mix of documentary and romantic comedy about a pair of transplanted New Yorkers who are working out their pre-marital angst in the Vermont countryside. Though the surroundings seem to promise peace and tranquility (as well as long-lived marriages), this couple can't seem to make the final commitment. The result is a charming, funny film which is a razor-sharp look at relationships, the roles of men and women and the institution of marriage.

VHS: S26140. $59.95.

John O'Brien, USA, 1993, 88 mins.

Walking Between the Raindrops

Reminiscent of Woody Allen, this feature film debut by writer/director Evan Jacobs centers around Stanley, who is in love with Sarah. The only problem: Sarah has a boyfriend. Should Stanley tell Sarah his feelings? As Stanley confronts each situation, he looks for advice from friends John and Chris.

VHS: S33751. $19.95.

Evan Jacobs, USA, 1995, 75 mins.

War Dance

This collection of music videos features the San Francisco-based Video Band. "War Dance", "Reagan Commercials" and "California Zones" are just some of the pieces included. 1986, 30 mins.

VHS: S22660. $29.95.

War Is Menstrual Envy—Parts I, II and III

Annie Sprinkle, Kembra Phaler, Nick Zedd and Ari Roussimoff star in this singular work. Everything is so alien and yet it all rings true. It's a raw and emotional experience.

VHS: S22633. $39.95.

Nick Zedd, USA, 1991, 80 mins.

Water and Power

Pat O'Neill's striking independent feature deploys a series of technically sophisticated processes, time and multiple exposure photography, to present a kaleidoscopic and enthralling vision of contemporary Los Angeles that is at once surreal and poetic. "An astonishing evocation of Los Angeles. If it is not the greatest film ever made about Los Angeles, it is certainly the most poetic and most profound" *(USA Today Magazine)*. Winner of the Grand Prize at the 1989 Sundance Film Festival.

Laser: LD71954. $34.95.

Pat O'Neill, USA, 1989, 55 mins.

The Watermelon Woman

Prompting an infamous little ruckus at the NEA because of its interracial lesbian lovemaking scene, Cheryl Dunye's startlingly fresh debut is a film within a film. Dunye, playing herself, is a young black woman making a documentary about Fae Richards, an obscure black actress known as "the Watermelon Woman." As Cheryl doggedly researches Fae's life, she discovers that the actress had a romance with her white lesbian filmmaker. Like Fae, Cheryl has an affair with a white woman, Diana (Guinevere Turner, *Go Fish*) and both Fae and Cheryl question this attraction.

VHS: S33336. $79.95.

Cheryl Dunye, USA, 1997, 85 mins.

Waterworks

Water is a universal symbol. It touches us all on numerous levels from the physical to the unconscious. This tape presents eight California artists and their diverse perceptions of water. Artists featured include: Robbert Flick, Mineko Grimmer, Doug Hall, Michael C. McMillen, Richard Misrach, Nam June Paik with Paul Garriin, Lewis de Soto and Bill Viola. 11 mins.

VHS: S14586. $39.95.

Wax, or the Discovery of the Television Among the Bees

A surreal science fiction thriller and narrative video by David Blair about Jacob Maker, a weapons-guidance expert and beekeeper whose will is manipulated by supernatural images projected on a television inserted inside his head. The device enables Jacob to enter an alternative universe (created through a dazzling use of computer graphics) of A-bombs (the Trinity nuclear test site), the Gulf War, the desert near Alamorado, New Mexico, the Tower of Babel and the "Garden of Eden." Blair narrates the film in a deadpan manner. "The images obliquely illustrate the narrative, and the constant visual flux often suggests a graphic novel translated into MTV" (Jonathan Rosenbaum, *Chicago Reader*).

VHS: S20284. $29.95.

David Blair, USA, 1990, 85 mins.

The Wedding Show

Not since Miss Vicky and Tiny Tim tied the knot on Carson has the sacrament of marriage been opened up to live TV. But the bride and groom would have it no other way. This actual wedding features a variety of comic episodes.

VHS: S10170. $29.95.

Mitch Corber/Sally White, USA, 1984, 28 mins.

Welcome to the Dollhouse

Winner of the Grand Jury Prize at the 1996 Sundance Film Festival, a dark and very funny look at adolescence told through the eyes of an angry, young, geeky girl. The usual teen stuff is covered-school, grades, puppy love, sex and rock 'n' roll—but with an original and highly amusing take which "never loses its sense of compassion and respect for the underdog" *(New York Daily News)*. With Heather Matarazzo, Matthew Faber, Angela Pietropinto and Eric Mabius *(I Shot Andy Warhol)*.

VHS: S30422. $19.95.

Laser: LD76028. $39.95.

Todd Solondz, USA, 1996, 88 mins.

West Is West

A culture clash comedy in the spirit of *Stranger Than Paradise*. Fresh from Bombay, handsome and broke college student Vikram hits the streets of San Francisco and falls for Sue, a feisty Bohemian artist who works at a local movie theater. With his visa running out, Vikram resorts to desperate measures and finds himself involved in an hilariously bungled burglary and impromptu curbside wedding, complete with a happy ending dance number straight out of an Indian musical.

VHS: S34737. $89.98.

David Rathod, USA, 1987, 80 mins.

What About Me

Filmed in black and white on location in Tompkins Square Park and the Lower East Side, this gritty film portrays the gradual deterioration of Lisa Napolitano (Rachel Amodeo), a young woman forced to exist on the streets, intermingling with the outcasts of society. Along the way she encounters a shell-shocked Vietnam veteran, Nick (Richard Edson), a nihilistic East Villager, Tom (Nick Zed), and a sympathetic good samaritan, Paul (Richard Hell). With Gregory Corso, Judy Carne, Johnny Thunders, Jerry Nolan and Dee Dee Ramone. Music by Johnny Thunders. "Rachel Amodeo keeps the spirit of Lower East Side filmmaking alive with *What About Me*" (Jim Jarmusch).

VHS: S30744. $29.98.

Rachel Amodeo, USA, 1993, 87 mins.

What Happened Was...

Karen Sillas stars in this exciting film that won the Grand Jury Prize at the 1994 Sundance Film Festival. Dating is often an unnerving, albeit exciting and sexy, prospect. Two young office workers venture into the unknown territory of their dreams and desires, which results in a number of startling revelations. The journey into the uncharted territory of erotic fantasies and private thoughts makes for one highly unpredictable romantic encounter.

VHS: S27257. $14.98.

Laser: LD75473. $39.99.

Tom Noonan, USA, 1994, 90 mins.

When Things Get Rough on Easy Street, Ovid and Shorts

This video features dissolving slides of web-like, calligraphic imagery set to stormy music mixes. *Ovid* is made up of scenes from the opera *X-S*, with music by Rhys Chatham. True ambient art video.

VHS: S22641. $49.95.

Joseph Nechvatal, USA, 60 mins.

Where Evil Dwells (The Trailer)

This collaboration is based on the story of the infamous "Satan Teen," Ricky Kasso. He killed himself in jail after he and a friend had been accused of murdering another boy in a satanic ritual on Long Island. This trailer is all that remains of the feature, which was destroyed by fire.

VHS: S22631. $39.95.

Tommy Turner/David Wojnarowicz, USA, 1986, 34 mins.

White Trash at Heart

This is an uproarious romp through the twisted byways of Lydia Lynch-land. Shocking and funny, it offers a satire of breakneck pacing and unlimited boundaries.

VHS: S22611. $24.95.

Holly Hardman, USA, 1992, 33 mins.

The Whole World Is Watching-Weatherman '69

Raymond Pettibon, Los Angeles artist, re-captures the drama of the Weathermen as Kim Gordon, playing Bernadine Dohrn, "whip[s] a detention room full of bad boys into a fightin' killin' guerilla band of right-on Nixonslayers."

VHS: S20524. $19.95.

Wide World of Lydia Lunch

An intimate portrait of the hard-bitten no-wave rocker Lydia Lunch. Also contains the shorts *Thrust in Me*, featuring the filmmaker in both male and female roles in collaboration with the cinematographer Richard Kern, *Kiss Me Goodbye* and *Go to Hell*.

VHS: S10164. $39.95.

Nick Zedd, USA, 1983-86, 61 mins.

The Wife

In this "new age *Who's Afraid of Virginia Woolf*" (Amy Taubin, *Village Voice*), actor/writer/director Tom Noonan *(What Happened Was...)* and Julie Hagerty *(Airplane)* star as Jack and Rita, a couple trapped in a fragile marriage who share their lives and professions as psychotherapists in a remote Vermont farmhouse. When Jack's patient Cosmo (Wallace Shawn, *My Dinner with Andre*) drops in for an unexpected visit with his uninhibited wife Arlie (Karen Young, *9½ Weeks*), both couples are in for a delirious night of heavy drinking, pill popping, sexual flirtations, verbal assaults—and shattering revelations. "One of the most strangely funny films of the last few years" (Mick LaSalle, *San Francisco Chronicle*).

VHS: S30738. $19.95.

Tom Noonan, USA, 1996, 101 mins.

Wigstock: The Movie

It all began with a bunch of New York drag queens who didn't want to stop partying so they put on a show in Tomkins Square Park—in the daytime. Now it has grown into an annual celebration of queer crossdressers from all over. Underground stars The "Lady" Bunny, Jackie Beat, the Mistress Formica, Lypsinka and Joey Arias are joined by RuPaul, Crystal Waters, Alexis Arquette and Deee-Lite on a trip across a landscape of cosmetic wonders.

Laser: LD75417. $39.99.

Barry Shils, USA, 1995, 82 mins.

Wild Flower

Set in the Depression-era South, Diane Keaton directed this evocative piece about a beautiful young woman's emotional and personal awakening, brought out by music, literature, poetry and romance. With Patricia Arquette, Beau Bridges, Susan Blakely, Reese Witherspoon and William McNamara. "Touching and staggeringly beautiful" *(Variety)*.

VHS: S17785. $19.95.

Diane Keaton, USA, 1992, 94 mins.

Wild Style

This breakthrough musical feature with style and attitude to spare is a rumination on hip hop: street art, break dancing and rap music. The plot follows the romantic passion of Zoro (Lee Quinones), a South Bronx artist caught up in a turbulent romance with Pink (Sandra Fabara), the queen of the underground graffiti movement. Fab Five Freddy is a playfully hip impressario. "*Wild Style* is easily among the best film musicals of the past half decade" (J. Hoberman). With musical performances by D.J.'s Grand Master Flash, Grand Wizard Theodore, Grand Master Caz and The Cold Crush. The cast includes Patti Astor and Busy Bee.

VHS: S01463. $14.95.

Charlie Ahearn, USA, 1982, 82 mins.

The Wind Is Driving Him Towards the Open Sea

Filmmaker David Brooks summarized his film thusly: "a boy travels, while we search for a man, Chandler Moore. He is never found but we see the world he has made for himself." Brooks was one of the first film diarists, but also "one of the most prominent lyricists of the experimental cinema. His work was eclipsed by his early death at age 24...most of his films are preoccupied with the relationship between music and image" (J.J. Murphy). "...a fascinating melancholy...surrounds it. It's a narrative of moods, of reflection, of things lost, gone, like autumn leaves—no tragedy, really, only a mood of melancholy, of sadness—of friends, of ways of life, of cultures gone, of ages coming and going" (Jonas Mekas).

VHS: S30231. $40.00.

David Brooks, USA, 1968, 52 mins.

A Winter Tan

Jackie Burroughs stars in a shattering account of one woman's sexual odyssey while on an extended vacation in Mexico. Based on the posthumously published *Give Sorrow Words: Mayrse Holder's Letters from Mexico, A Winter Tan* is raunchy and confessional, depicting a woman hot in pursuit of euphoria, fueled by despair.

VHS: S34314. $24.95.

Jackie Burroughs/John Frizzel/Louise Clark/John Walker/Aerlyn Weissman, Canada, 1988, 103 mins.

X-Rated: Movieyeur

A movie-length salad with suspense, malice, comedy, screams, commercials, music—just like the real thing. Also includes *Faxion* (1984, 11 mins), a morals tape based on a painting by Balthus, and *Sex*, a vagina story co-starring fingers, nipples, buttocks and a few extras.

VHS: S10186. $49.95.

Franz Villa, USA, 1986, 68 mins.

Yellow Fever/La Fievre Jaune

During an epidemic at the end of the 19th century, soldiers guard a quarantined village. The father of a Cajun family has broken the quarantine to return to his family, soon falls sick with the fever. Hiding his boat, the family tries to keep his presence from quarantine officials. To the authorities, interning the victims means stopping the fever; to the family, it means death. A film from Glen Pitre *(Belizaire the Cajun)*. In Cajun French with English subtitles.

VHS: S06503. $89.95.
Glen Pitre, USA, 1979, 30 mins.

Zebrahead

Anthony Drazan's feature debut is a poetic reworking of *Romeo and Juliet*. The film depicts an unlikely romance between battle-scarred, high school teens: Zack (Michael Rappaport), a tough Jewish kid who falls for Nikki (N'Bushe Wright), an independent black woman. With De Shon Castle, Ron Johnson and Ray Sharkey. Cinematography by Maryse Albert. Music by Taj Mahal.

VHS: S18871. $19.95.
Anthony Drazan, USA, 1991, 100 mins.

JOHN CASSAVETES

Big Trouble

Alan Arkin and Peter Falk, the co-stars of The In-Laws, are reteamed in a wacky comedy about murder and insurance scams. Arkin is hired by Beverly D'Angelo to knock off her nutty husband Falk. With Paul Dooley, Robert Stack, Richard Libertini and Charles Durning. The last film directed by John Cassavetes.

VHS: S09312. $19.95.
John Cassavetes, USA, 1985, 93 mins.

A Child Is Waiting

John Cassavetes directed this sensitive drama about the care and treatment of special education youngsters. Burt Lancaster is the benevolent but sometimes brusque administrator of a facility for the retarded; Judy Garland wants to help make the lives of the children as full and fun-filled as possible. With Gena Rowlands, Stephen Hill and Bruce Ritchey.

VHS: S11730. $19.98.
Laser: Chapter search. Includes original trailer. **LD71640. $34.98.**
John Cassavetes, USA, 1963, 102 mins.

Faces

One of the foundation stones of independent American cinema, Faces features Gena Rowlands, John Marley, Lynn Carlin and Seymour Cassel in a riveting account of the events leading to the breakdown of a marriage. The performances are extraordinary in a film which is a legend.

VHS: S26961. $19.95.
John Cassavetes, USA, 1968, 130 mins.

Gloria

John Cassavetes creates a powerful, tension-filled story about an ex-gun moll and showgirl on the run from the mob protecting the son of neighbors who have already been killed by the mob. With Gena Rowlands in an Oscar-nominated performance.

VHS: S00506. $69.95.
John Cassavetes, USA, 1980, 121 mins.

The Killing of a Chinese Bookie

John Cassavetes' unusual gangster drama features Ben Gazzara as the owner of a lurid Los Angeles strip joint who is ordered by the mafia to execute a Chinese gangster to pay off his gambling debts. This is one of Cassavetes' most personal films; it can be read as a ferocious critique of American capitalism and racism. With Seymour Cassel, Timothy Carey, Azizi Johari, Virginia Carrington and Meade Roberts.

VHS: S19263. $19.95.
John Cassavetes, USA, 1976, 109 mins.

Opening Night

John Cassavetes' neglected masterpiece about the nature of performance, art and the complicity between performer and audience. Gena Rowlands is a bitter, insecure actress on the verge of a breakdown. In previews for a play, she is haunted by the accidental death of an obsessive fan. The film was never commercially released until 1991. With Cassavetes, Ben Gazzara, Joan Blondell and Zohra Lampert. Cinematography by Frederick Elmes.

VHS: S18720. $19.95.
John Cassavetes, USA, 1977, 144 mins.

Shadows

One of the foundation stones of independent American cinema, John Cassavetes' first film features two brothers and a sister who move jerkily through their lives as Cassavetes' free-wheeling camera, naturalistic dialog and jump cuts capture their arguments, sexual encounters and parties. With Lelia Goldoni, Ben Carruthers and Hugh Hurd.

VHS: S26962. $19.95.
John Cassavetes, USA, 1959, 87 mins.

A Woman Under the Influence

John Cassavetes' masterpiece centers on a dysfunctional Los Angeles family; in an astounding performance, Gena Rowlands stars as a tightly-wound woman who loves her children too much, withholds her affection from her husband (Peter Falk), and goes slowly insane by her unrealized expectations. A brilliant, uncompromising work, with strong secondary work by Katherine Cassavetes, Lady Rowlands and Fred Draper.

VHS: S17304. $19.95.
John Cassavetes, USA, 1974, 155 mins.

JOHN SAYLES

Baby, It's You

John Sayles wrote and directed this look back at high school life in New Jersey in the early 1960's. Rosanna Arquette is a bright, middle class Jewish girl who becomes involved with Vincent Spano, an Italian Catholic from a lower economical and social level, who calls himself The Sheik. When she goes off to a fancy college, the Sheik tries his luck in Miami imitating Frank Sinatra. With Matthew Modine, Tracy Pollan and Robert Downey Jr. in small roles.

VHS: S10356. $79.95.
Laser: LD75151. $34.98.
John Sayles, USA, 1983, 105 mins.

The Brother from Another Planet

From the director of *Return of the Secaucus Seven and Lianna* comes an off-beat, fresh sci-fantasy adventure about a different sort of visitor from outer space. No E.T.—he's black, has three toes on two huge feet, and can heal humans and video arcade machines with a touch.

VHS: S00185. $19.98.
John Sayles, USA, 1984, 109 mins.

City of Hope

John Sayles wrote, directed and played a major role in this provocative drama of political corruption and racial upheaval. Vincent Spano and Joe Morton head an impressive ensemble cast of 31 principal characters. With David Strathairn as Asteroid, the befuddled street person, and Sayles, himself, as the sleazy Carl.

VHS: S16087. $19.95.
Laser: LD71573. $39.95.
John Sayles, USA, 1991, 130 mins.

Eight Men Out

John Sayles brings the saga of the 1919 White Sox World Series scandal to the movie-going public. Based on the book by Eliot Asinof, this is a rich, finely detailed account of the eight players who agreed to throw the World Series for money. A fine cast includes John Cusack, D.B. Sweeney, David Strathairn, Christopher Lloyd, Clifton James, John Mahoney, John Sayles, and Studs Terkel as the reporter who broke the hearts of every kid in America.

VHS: S09820. $14.98.
John Sayles, USA, 1988, 121 mins.

Lone Star

The discovery of a human skull and a sheriff's badge buried on the outskirts of a small west Texas border town reveals a 40-year-old mystery that touches the past of nearly everyone in town—including the current sheriff. As the clues to solving the puzzle are discovered, past wounds are re-opened, old flames are reignited and secrets long-hidden are revealed, in this gripping, suspenseful tale. With Kris Kristofferson, Matthew McConaughey, Chris Cooper, Elizabeth Pena and Frances McDormand. "Sayles' best film so far…quietly stunning" (Janet Maslin, *New York Times*).

VHS: S30944. $19.95.
Laser: LD76135. $39.95.
John Sayles, USA, 1996, 138 mins.

Matewan

Writer-director John Sayles recreates the life and labor conditions that led to the infamous West Virginia shoot-out known as the Matewan Massacre. In a coal mining town in the 1920's union organizers come up against strong opposition from the mine owners and violence flares. With Chris Cooper, Mary McDonnell and James Earl Jones.

VHS: S06028. $14.98.
John Sayles, USA, 1987, 132 mins.

Men with Guns

John Sayles' searing odyssey is an allegory about a wealthy doctor (Federico Luppi) who, after his wife dies, visits former students working in impoverished Indian villages in Central America. The doctor's journey becomes a singular, personal, political quest when he learns that some of his students may have been killed by guerillas. With Mandy Patinkin. "Immensely moving and sad, and yet because it dares so much, it is an exhilarating film" (Roger Ebert, *Chicago Sun-Times*).

VHS: S34742. $99.99.
John Sayles, USA, 1997, 127 mins.

Passion Fish

John Sayles' perceptive and lyrical film unfolds in the atmospheric Louisiana bayou and charts the emotional relationship of two fiercely independent women—an acerbic, caustic actress (Mary McDonnell) paralyzed in an accident and her idiosyncratic caretaker (Alfre Woodard)—as one attempts to confront her vulnerable past. Sayles' regular David Strathairn contributes a stunning performance as a local who makes the tentative seduction of McDonnell. With Vondie Curtis-Hall and Nora Dunn.

VHS: S18746. $19.95.
John Sayles, USA, 1992, 137 mins.

The Secret of Roan Inish

Magical and unforgettable, this beautiful film, shot on location in Ireland, captures the grandeur of simple lives transformed by fantasy. A young girl must find her missing brother. This simple but vital task sparks a story which brings an Irish legend to life. It involves an enchanted isle inhabited by seals.

VHS: S26620. $19.98.
Laser: LD75113. $34.95.
John Sayles, USA, 1995, 102 mins.

GUS VAN SANT

Drugstore Cowboy

Matt Dillon gives the performance of his career as the drug-addicted criminal who masterminds a series of robberies in the Pacific Northwest. A harsh and decidedly unsentimental look at life on the fringe that deals honestly with the world of controlled substances. A top notch cast includes Kelly Lynch, James LeGros, Heather Graham, James Remar and William Burroughs as Father Tom, the junkie priest. Don't say "no" to this drug movie.

VHS: S11724. $14.98.
Laser: LD70955. $39.95.
Gus Van Sant, USA, 1989, 100 mins.

Even Cowgirls Get the Blues

Uma Thurman, Rain Phoenix, Lorraine Bracco and William Hurt star in this adaptation of Tom Robbins' best-selling novel. Gus Van Sant, director of *Drugstore Cowboy* and *My Own Private Idaho*, brings his remarkable visual style to this high camp road movie set in the early 1970's, about a hitchhiker, free love and lesbian passion. Also features Angie Dickinson, Keanu Reeves, Roseanne Arnold, Crispin Glover, Sean Young and Buck Henry. Music by k.d. lang.

VHS: S22383. $19.95.
Gus Van Sant, USA, 1994, 96 mins.

Good Will Hunting

Matt Damon and Ben Affleck starred in and won best original screenplay Oscars for this story about Will Hunting, a genius janitor (Damon) at MIT who likes to party and hang around with his neighborhood friends. When professor Lambeau (Stellan Skarsgard, *Breaking the Waves*) offers a prize to the student who can answer a difficult math problem and discovers that Will correctly solved the problem anonymously on the blackboard, Lambeau tries to help Will get into school. Will's also hauled back from the brink of self-destruction by gifted counselor Sean McGuire (Robin Williams, in an Oscar-winning performance), Skylar (Minnie Driver), a Harvard Student who falls in love with Will, and Will's childhood friend, Chuckie (Affleck).

VHS: S34400. $106.99.
Laser: LD76949. $39.99.
Gus Van Sant, USA, 1997, 126 mins.

My Own Private Idaho

In this modern restructuring of the '60s road movie, River Phoenix and Keanu Reeves hustle their way through Seattle, Portland, Idaho and Rome on a quest for River's missing mother. With a meticulous, lyric style, the film combines sprawling landscapes, scenes of passionless sexuality and allusions to Orson Welles' *Chimes at Midnight* as it addresses issues of love, family, politics and homosexuality. A work of great complexity and beauty from the director of *Mala Noche* and *Drugstore Cowboy*.

VHS: S15927. $19.95.
Gus Van Sant, USA, 1991, 102 mins.

To Die For

Nicole Kidman stars as Suzanne Stone, a beautiful but vacuous weather girl whose real talents lie in manipulation, treachery, and self-promotion. Matt Dillon plays the unsuspecting husband who becomes the target of her murder plot. She doesn't plan to do it alone but rather enlists a love-struck teen-ager to act as assassin. It's the perfect scenario for launching her career as a celebrity. With Joaquin Phoenix and Illeana Douglas.

VHS: S27526. $19.95.
Laser: LD75525. $34.95.
Gus Van Sant, USA, 1995, 107 mins.

COEN BROTHERS

Barton Fink

An inside look in the average life of a Hollywood screenwriter as interpreted by the brothers Coen. John Turturro and John Goodman star as fellow residents of the Hotel Earle, a very quiet California hotel where the most unusual things happen. Set in 1941, this truly bizarre and scathing period drama won three major awards at the Cannes Film Festival. With Judy Davis, Jon Polito, John Mahoney and Michael Lerner as studio boss Jack Lipnick. Have you got that Barton Fink feeling?

VHS: S15450. $19.98.
Laser: Letterboxed. **LD76152. $39.98.**
Joel Coen, USA, 1991, 116 minutes.

The Big Lebowski

Jeff Bridges and John Goodman star in this hilarious story by the brothers Coen about mistaken identity, mistaken thieves, bowling and a plot to blackmail one of L.A.'s richest philanthropists. With Julianne Moore, John Turturro, Sam Elliott and Steve Buscemi.

VHS: S34650. $106.99.
Laser: LD77012. $39.99.
Ethan Coen/Joel Coen, USA, 1998, 117 mins.

Blood Simple

The first film scripted by the talented Coen brothers. A critically acclaimed thriller set in rural Texas tells the old story of a man who hires a sleazy private eye to kill his wife and her boyfriend. Told in a very imaginative way, it combines chilling suspense with offbeat humor, with double and triple crosses building to a blood-curdling surprise climax. The most inventive and original thriller in years.

VHS: S00149. $14.98.
Laser: LD70016. $34.98.
Joel Coen, USA, 1983, 96 mins.

Fargo

Steve Buscemi, William Macy and Frances McDormand (in her Academy Award-winning role as a pregnant homicide detective) find thievery, treachery and murder out in the frozen upper Midwest. This seemingly straightforward morality tale is laced with wicked humor. The film's deadpan style mirrors the large, cold, empty spaces of the Minnesota landscape. VHS letterboxed.

VHS: S29808. $19.98.
Laser: LD75990. $34.95.
DVD: DV60003. $29.95.
Joel and Ethan Coen, USA, 1996, 98 mins.

Fargo Collectors Set

Pan-and-scan letterboxed edition of the Coen Brothers hit with behind-the-scenes footage and theatrical trailer, and limited edition, numbered *Fargo* snow globe. Steve Buscemi, William Macy and Frances McDormand in an Oscar-winning performance as a very pregnant homicide detective, find thievery, treachery and murder out in the frozen upper Midwest. This seemingly straightforward morality tale is laced with wicked humor. The film's deadpan style mirrors the large, cold, empty spaces of the Minnesota landscape.

VHS: S31156. $34.95.
Joel and Ethan Coen, USA, 1996, 98 mins.

Hudsucker Proxy

The Coen Brothers' inventive, dazzling (and misunderstood) "comedy of invention" features dynamite performances from Tim Robbins as the fall guy and Jennifer Jason Leigh as the persuasive reporter who falls in love with him in this funny, stylish homage to the movies.

VHS: S21897. $19.98.
Laser: Widescreen. **LD74524. $34.98.**
Joel Coen, USA, 1993, 112 mins.

Miller's Crossing

A strikingly stylish gangster film. Set in 1929, *Miller's Crossing* is the story of the friendship between Leo (Albert Finney), the city's Irish political boss, and Tom (Gabriel Byrne), Leo's cool, brainy aide. Their friendship is severed when Leo and Tom both fall in love with Verna (Marcia Gay Harden). Tom joins ranks with Leo's foremost enemy and rival for political power, and a bloody gang war erupts. Also starring John Turturro and J.E. Freeman.

VHS: S13607. $19.98.
Laser: LD71228. $39.98.
Joel Coen, USA, 1990, 115 mins.

Raising Arizona

A comedy about parental expectations and criminal activity. Nicolas Cage and Holly Hunter are a childless couple who need a little bundle of joy to make their lives complete. So they borrow one of a group of quintuplets, but complications ensue in this wacky, live-action, road-runner-like farce.

VHS: S04626. $19.95.
Laser: LD71291. $39.98.
Joel Coen, USA, 1987, 94 mins.

QUENTIN TARANTINO

Four Rooms

A host of stars, from Madonna to Antonio Banderas, are featured in this madcap comedy centered around Tim Roth. Roth is a bellhop whose first day on the job is rife with chaos and humor because of the four rooms he services. Four different directors worked on the different sections of this unique film. Jennifer Beals, Paul Calderon, Lili Taylor, and Marisa Tomei are just some of the other stars seen in this film.

VHS: S27849. $99.99.
Laser: LD75927. $39.99.
Allison Anders/Alexandre Rockwell/Robert Rodriguez/Quentin Tarantino, USA, 1995, 98 mins.

Jackie Brown

Tarantino has not lost his considerable gift for dialog in this gritty adaptation of Elmore Leonard's novel *Rum Punch*. Pam Grier stars as Jackie Brown, a stewardess who supplements her meager income by smuggling cash for a gunrunner (Samuel L. Jackson) until an ATF agent busts her at the airport. With Robert Forster, Bridget Fonda, Michael Keaton and Robert De Niro.

VHS: S34698. $106.99.
Laser: LD76952. $59.95.
Quentin Tarantino, USA, 1997, 154 mins.

Natural Born Killers

Quentin Tarantino provided the story that sets Woody Harrelson and Juliette Lewis as a deranged couple intently killing their way across the American landscape. It's a unique mix of comic book, sitcom and MTV style, with a deadly serious plot about the nature of crime and murder in an age of mass media and celebrity. VHS letterboxed.

VHS: S23220. $19.98.
Laser: LD74663. $39.98.
Oliver Stone, USA, 1994, 119 mins.

Pulp Fiction

John Travolta, Uma Thurman, Samuel Jackson, Bruce Willis, Harvey Keitel and Rosanna Arquette are all part of the stellar cast of this highly acclaimed film. Two hit men encounter a bizarre series of adventures in a seamy L.A. world of criminals and kooks. The Academy Award-winning screenplay by Quentin Tarantino can't be beat. Letterboxed.

VHS: S26211. $19.95.
Laser: CLV, THX. **LD75062. $39.99.**
DVD: DV60311. $29.99.
Quentin Tarantino, USA, 1994, 154 mins.

Reservoir Dogs

The debut of Quentin Tarantino employs a novelistic structure to evoke the aftermath of a failed jewelry heist. Lawrence Tierney plays an underworld figure who recruits five criminals to stage a daring mid-afternoon robbery, led by Harvey Keitel. Quickly becoming a cult classic. With Tim Roth, Chris Penn, Steve Buscemi and Michael Madsen as an effective, sadistic creep. Letterboxed.

VHS: S18195. $14.95.
Laser: LD75161. $39.95.
Quentin Tarantino, USA, 1992, 99 mins.

True Romance

Tony Scott's stylish variation of the lovers on the run theme, with Christian Slater as a lonely Detroit comic book store clerk who impulsively marries a call girl (Patricia Arquette). After Slater inadvertently steals a suitcase full of cocaine from a vicious pimp (Gary Oldman), he and Arquette travel to Los Angeles, with the mob in feverish pursuit. Screenplay by Quentin Tarantino (*Reservoir Dogs*). This director's cut features three minutes of footage that was excised in order to secure an R-rating for its theatrical release. With Dennis Hopper, Val Kilmer, Brad Pitt, Christopher Walken, Bronson Pinchot, Saul Rubinek and Michael Rappaport.

VHS: S19941. $19.98.
Laser: Widescreen. **LD72251. $39.98.**
Tony Scott, USA, 1993, 121 mins.

JON JOST

All the Vermeers in New York

From the tenacious American independent Jon Jost, this visually ravishing, precise and emotionally fluid piece tracks the romantic obsession, emotional desperation, individual expression and tension of a disparate group of New York artists and businessmen. Largely about the conflicts produced between commerce and art, the movie is less a narrative than a collection of vignettes about the textures and off-center rhythms of urban culture. Shot in widescreen, with some wonderfully executed tracking shots, Jost conceived, wrote, photographed and edited this audacious work. With Stephen Lack, French actress Emmanuelle Chaulet and Katherine Bean.

VHS: S17499. $24.98.
Jon Jost, USA, 1990, 87 mins.

Angel City

In a comic, hard-boiled, detective story form, this film by Jon Jost intermixes an examination of the nature of images and their supposed truth with an elaborately detailed social, political and economic critique of the Los Angeles-Hollywood scene.

VHS: S03762. $59.95.
Jon Jost, USA, 1981, 75 mins.

Bell Diamond

A formally exquisite and politically pointed study of an alienated Vietnam veteran set against the backdrop of a bankrupt mining town. Filmed in Butte, Montana, director Jost collaborated with a cast that not only acted improvisationally without written texts, but was largely composed of non-professionals.

VHS: S07368. $69.95.
Jon Jost, USA, 1987, 96 mins.

Chameleon

A day in the life of a Los Angeles drug pusher featuring Bob Glaudini (*Angel City*). *Chameleon* is a cautionary tale about the self-destructiveness of American opportunism.

VHS: S07367. $69.95.
Jon Jost, USA, 90 mins.

Jon Jost's Frameup

America's iconoclastic filmmaker, Jon Jost, turns his attention to two losers, one an ex-con, the other a dizzy waitress, who hit the road. In Jost's tragi-comic tale, they travel over great swaths of the West encountering a host of "all-American" characters in a trenchant and subtle analysis of bonding and loneliness. Howard Swain and Nancy Carlin are a real-life couple who bring these characters to life.

VHS: S23752. $24.98.
Jon Jost, USA, 1993, 91 mins.

Last Chants for a Slow Dance

A feature by Jon Jost which chronicles the aimless wandering of a man named Tom Bates who travels in his truck around Montana. The film weaves the story through his encounters with hitchhikers and people on the road.

VHS: S03763. $69.95.
Jon Jost, USA, 1983, 90 mins.

Plain Talk and Common Sense

A 110-minute essay on the State of the Nation by one of America's leading independent filmmakers—Jon Jost. "*Plain Talk and Common Sense* (uncommon senses) is Jost's most successful film yet—a movie of expansive negativity that, putting patriotism under erasure, proposes to represent America and then revels in its inability to do so" (J. Hoberman, *Village Voice*).

VHS: S15190. $69.95.
Jon Jost, USA, 1987, 110 mins.

Rembrandt Laughing

Focuses on a pair of ex-lovers five years after their break-up. In cinema verite fashion, the film follows their daily encounters with friends and associates.

VHS: S16151. $79.95.
Jon Jost, 1989, USA, 100 mins.

Slow Moves

Two drifters meet on the Golden Gate Bridge, start an affair, run into money trouble and drive across the country on a spree which ends when one's gunned down trying to rob a store, in this independent film noir by Jon Jost.

VHS: S03764. $69.95.
Jon Jost, USA, 1984, 93 mins.

Speaking Directly

A unique and powerful film essay mixing autobiography, socio-political observation and reflexive cinema. "In the history of the American avant-garde, *Speaking Directly* stands as a remarkable achievement: between the currents of pure cinema and committed documentary/fiction" (Ian Christie).

VHS: S06107. $69.95.
Jon Jost, USA, 110 mins.

Stagefright

The most experimental of Jon Jost's feature-length films, *Stagefright* was shot for German television, and is a daring meditation on cinema, theater, performance and politics. "As long as Jost goes on making more films just as truthful, I don't expect him to win any popularity contests" (Jonathan Rosenbaum).

VHS: S06295. $69.95.
Jon Jost, USA, 1981, 74 mins.

Sure Fire

Tom Blair stars as an aggressive entrepreneur who tries to make a killing in real estate in the small, depressed towns of South-Central Utah, until he finds himself losing his grip, in Jon Jost's acclaimed independent feature. "It's clearly an American masterpiece. Spare and disturbing, but with dark, comic touches..." (*Variety*). With Kate Dezina, Robert Ernst, Kristi Hager. Letterboxed.

VHS: S20515. $24.98.
Jon Jost, USA, 1993, 86 mins.

HAL HARTLEY

Amateur

Hal Hartley directed this offbeat comedy, which stars Martin Donovan, Isabelle Huppert and Elina Lowensohn as three individuals joined in a love triangle and trapped in a fight for survival. How can an amnesiac, a porn star and a nymphomaniac ex-nun escape ruthless, single-minded corporate killers? That's where the comedy of this stylish film comes in.

VHS: S26700. $96.99.
Laser: LD75112. $39.95.
Hal Hartley, USA/Great Britain/France, 1994, 105 mins.

Flirt

One script, three different stories. Ruminating on whether place and culture can affect the course of desire and trouble, Hartley employs different characters, actors, settings and situations, using the same dialog in three different cities: New York, Tokyo and Berlin. With Bill Sage, Martin Donovan, Parker Posey, Hal Hartley and Miho Nikaidoh. "The quintessential Hartley movie, a gorgeously mounted bauble, a post-Godardian sketchbook" (Ray Pride, *New City*).

VHS: S31269. $98.99.
Hal Hartley, USA, 1996, 85 mins.

Surviving Desire

Hal Hartley offers a one-hour program about the affair between an uptight English professor (Martin Donovan) and Sophie (Mary Ward), one of his students, who has a penchant for poetry. The film is quirky, fun and unsettling. On the same program are two Hartley shorts, *Theory of Achievement* and *Ambition*, both very funny, Godardian works about art, sex and money.

VHS: S17919. $19.98.
Hal Hartley, USA, 1991, 86 mins.

Trust

She's a smart-mouthed suburban brat. He's a disillusioned computer genius with a hand grenade. Together they embark on a very different, very modern romance in which they both learn a lot about each other, about acceptance, about love, and about trust. This is Hal Hartley's hilarious follow-up to his equally funny and intelligent debut feature, *The Unbelievable Truth*. "Entertaining! Genuinely eccentric! A Godardian mixture of ardent talk, deadpan hyperbole and unexpected action!" (J. Hoberman, *Village Voice*).

VHS: S15526. $19.98.
Laser: CLV. **LD72039. $29.98.**
Hal Hartley, USA/Great Britain, 1991, 107 mins.

The Unbelievable Truth

Robert Burke and Adrienne Shelly star in this twisted black comedy. Burke is an ex-con who falls for the boss's daughter, but she has troubles of her own. Shelley stars as the model whose thoughts continually turn to the coming Armageddon.

VHS: S26110. $19.95.
Laser: LD75138. $24.98.
Hal Hartley, USA, 1990, 100 mins.

JILL GODMILOW

Far from Poland

A brilliant film: denied a visa to shoot a film in Poland, director Godmilow constructs a film over the bare bones of documentary footage while in New York, resulting in a deft dismemberment of the myth of "documentary truth." The film portrays the birth of the Solidarity movement at the Gdansk shipyards through moving personal testimony and a chilling look at the psychology of a censor.

VHS: S02656. $69.95.
Jill Godmilow, USA, 1984, 106 mins.

The Popovich Brothers of South Chicago

This ground-breaking film from Jill Godmilow focuses on a musical group that has been keeping traditional Serbian music alive and well within Chicago's ethnic Serbian community for over 50 years. In this documentary, the importance of old world customs, invigorated by the American values of tolerance and diversity, are reflected in the unique, rousing music of the Popovich Brothers.

VHS: S21130. $29.95.
Jill Godmilow, USA, 1978, 60 mins.

Roy Cohn/Jack Smith

An intense cinematic translation of a theatre piece in which actor Ron Vawter interprets the dual roles of Roy Cohn—the racist, reactionary prosecutor of the Joe McCarthy era and beyond who battled civil rights for homosexuals though he was homosexual himself—and Jack Smith, the open, avant-garde filmmaker/ performance artist of *Flaming Creatures*. "These two men, who had nothing in common except their death from AIDS in the late '80s, are resurrected by Vawter and Godmilow in a constrast of stance, from which is born, little by little, a sensation of undoing, of sadness, of finitude" (*La Stampa*).

VHS: S35313. $39.95.
Jill Godmilow, USA, 1995, 88 mins.

What's Underground About Marshmallows: Ron Vawter Performs Jack Smith

The complete, extraordinary "reperformance" by Ron Vawter of Jack Smith's 1981 performance piece, "What's Underground About Marshmallows?," in which Jack, strongly against the commodification of art and fearful that people were making illegal copies of his films, accuses Jonas Mekas, the champion of avant-garde film in the early '60s, of this diabolical infringement. In "Marshmallows," Jack tells a funny, pathetic tale "on" himself—a nightmare of failing to catch Mekas—called variously "Uncle Artcrust," "Uncle Fishhook" and sometimes "Old Uncle Oldie"—in the act of duplication.

VHS: S35376. $39.95.
Jill Godmilow, USA, 1996, 60 mins.

JIM JARMUSCH

Dead Man

Johnny Depp stars as a wounded man on the run from both bounty hunters and the law in this incredibly beautiful-looking film from American independent Jim Jarmusch. Through an odd chain of events, Depp becomes a hunted murder suspect as he sets out on life's final journey, meeting an interesting cast of characters along the way. Funny and unpredictable, Depp is supported by an amazing array of talent, including Robert Mitchum, Gabriel Byrne, John Hurt, Lance Henriksen and Crispin Glover. With bravura black-and-white cinematography by Robby Muller. "A masterpiece!" (*The Chicago Reader*).

VHS: S30457. $19.98.
Laser: LD76064. $39.99.
Jim Jarmusch, USA, 1996, 121 mins.

Down by Law

Jim Jarmusch's third feature following his immensely successful *Stranger Than Paradise* stars Tom Waits, John Lurie—and in a treasure of a performance, Roberto Benigni—as a group of escaped convicts in the swamps of Louisiana. A funny, original film featuring brilliant cinematography by the great Robby Muller.

VHS: S03022. $14.98.
Laser: LD76225. $39.98.
Jim Jarmusch, USA, 1986, 95 mins.

Mystery Train

"Jim Jarmusch makes bizarre, minimalist and simpatico road movies, with characters on the edge of pop culture discovering a poetically shabby America. We see the land through the eyes of foreigners, unspoiled but prejudiced by American myths." Three separate but interwoven episodes centered in a rundown Memphis hotel reveal the experiences of non-Americans in America. Two young Japanese lovers travel through town on a rock 'n roll pilgrimage, a newly widowed Italian woman waits for a flight back to Rome while she is visited by the ghost of Elvis, a British man makes some friends, gets drunk and commits murder. "There is no real mystery in *Mystery Train*. It makes it points on Elvis-worship, restlessness and race relations out front. But there is a mystery about its construction. The leisurely, distancing pace works beautifully" (Edwin Jahiel). 1990, 110 mins.

VHS: S12988. $19.98.
Jim Jarmusch, USA, 1989, 113 mins.

Night on Earth

Jim Jarmusch's film is structured episodically, with the narrative simultaneously unfolding in Los Angeles, New York, Paris, Rome and Helsinki, and concerns the relationship of cab drivers and their passengers. The ensemble cast includes Gena Rowlands, Winona Ryder, Rosie Perez, Giancarlo Esposito, Armin Mueller-Stahl, Beatrice Dalle, Isaach de Bankole, Roberto Benigni, Matti Pellonpaa and Kari Vaananen. Tom Waits composed the music and performs two numbers. Letterboxed.

VHS: S17625. $19.95.
Jim Jarmusch, USA, 1991, 125 mins.

Stranger Than Paradise

A wonderful film, a witty, new wave comedy about the Old World meeting the new, as Eddie's (Richard Edson) life is suddenly invaded by his friend Willie's (John Lurie) young Hungarian cousin, Eva. A totally unlikely series of very funny situations ensues.

VHS: Out of print. For rental only.
Laser: Letterboxed. **LD75917. $49.95.**
Jim Jarmusch, USA, 1985, 90 mins.

JONAS MEKAS

cup/saucer/two dancers/radio

"[This recording of Kenneth King's] key postmodern dance, [*cup/saucer/two dancers/radio*], has translated it into an extraordinary film, with colors that progress from soft to bold, and with a focus that so tightly frames the objects and isolated body fragments that, fittingly for its theme of human alienation, the viewer is forced to understand the totality of the dance by putting together these scraps in the mind's eye" (Sally Banes, *The Village Voice, October 18, 1983*).

VHS: S30220. $75.00.
Jonas Mekas, USA, 1965/1983, 23 mins.

Dr. Carl G. Jung or Lapis Philosophorum

In the summer of 1950, Jerome Hill went to Zurich with the intention of making a film about Dr. Carl G. Jung. After following Jung for a few weeks with his camera, Hill decided that Jung was not a good subject for cinema and abandoned the film. Instead he went to Africa to film Dr. Albert Schweitzer, whom he found a more "photogentic" subject, and made a film which brought him an Academy Award. After Hill's death in 1972, the unfinished film was deposited with Anthology Film Archives. Filmmaker Jonas Mekas, a close friend of Hill, edited the Jung footage into a 29-minute film. The result is a collection of unique and revealing fragments of the daily life of one of the 20th century's key spiritual and intellectual figures.

VHS: S30219. $75.00.
Jerome Hill/Jonas Mekas, USA, 1950/1991, 29 mins.

Guns of the Trees

This film features poetry interludes written and spoken by Allen Ginsberg, music by Lucia Diugoszewski, and folk songs by Sara and Caither Wiley and Tom Sankey. With Ben Carruthers, Frances Stillman, Argus Speare Juillard, Adolfas Mekas, Frank Kuenstler, Leonard Hicks, Sudie Bond, Louis Brigante, Jewel Walker, Sterling Jenson, George Maciunas, and others. "It may be one of the most personal and revealing films of the intellectual, beat and hip fringe of society of America today" (Gene Moskowitz, *Cahiers du Cinema*, Paris).

VHS: S30221. $75.00.
Jonas Mekas, USA, 1962, 75 mins.

He Stands in a Desert Counting the Seconds of His Life

Shot in 1965, this is part of Mekas' diary films. It includes very little personal material and focuses on sketches of events and people largely outside Mekas' life. Roberto Rossellini, Ken Jacobs, Alberto Cavalcanti, Peter Kubelka, Kenneth Anger, Jackie Onassis, Lee Radziwill, Andy Warhol, P. Adams Sitney, Yoko Ono, Allen Ginsberg and John Lennon are among those seen.

VHS: S25797. $100.00.
Jonas Mekas, USA, 1969, 160 mins.

In Between

Footage from 1964-1968 that did not find its way into the *Walden* reels is joined in this classic period piece. Mostly centered in New York, it also includes travel footage and appearances by David Wise, Salvador Dali, Allen Ginsberg, Jack Smith, Shirley Clarke, Jane Holzer and more. Mel Lyman plays his banjo on the roof.

VHS: S25795. $75.00.
Jonas Mekas, USA, 1975, 52 mins.

Lost, Lost, Lost

These diary sequences come from 1949-1963. In them Mekas documents his arrival in Brooklyn from Lithuania, his struggle with the exile community, his move to Manhattan, and his involvement with the New York poetry and experimental film scene.

VHS: S25796. $100.00.
Jonas Mekas, USA, 1963, 158 mins.

Notes for Jerome

Footage from three distinct visits to the home of Jerome Hill make up this tribute to him. Mekas visited Hill in 1966 with P. Adams Sitney. He then returned briefly in 1967 and again after Hill's death in 1974. This elegy is dedicated to Hill, who may have felt as much an exile as Mekas did. Music performed by Hill, Taylor Mead, Charles Rydell and others makes up the soundtrack.

VHS: S25799. $75.00.
Jonas Mekas, USA, 1978, 45 mins.

Paradise Not Yet Lost (aka Oona's Third Year)

These scenes from Mekas' film diaries were shot in 1977. It includes many memorable sequences from New York, including a visit to the mother of Maya Deren (Marie Deren), Peter Kubelka's concert, and the St. Patrick's Day Parade. Other sections focus on travel to friends and relatives in Sweden, Lithuania and Austria, and concludes again in New York.

VHS: S25798. $75.00.
Jonas Mekas, USA, 1979, 160 mins.

Reminiscences of a Journey to Lithuania

This diary film begins with footage shot by Mekas in New York in the early 1950's. Then a trip back to his native Lithuanian village in 1971 shows his reaction to the changes experienced by his homeland. Finally a sequence shot at the camp where Mekas was interned during the war and a trip to Austria end this poetic film experience.
VHS: S25800. $100.00.
Jonas Mekas, USA/Great Britain/Germany, 1971, 82 mins.

Scenes from the Life of Andy Warhol

This collection of footage shot between 1965 and 1982 includes many notables from the factory and other celebrities basking in the glow of Warhol. Nico, Lou Reed, Edie Sedgwick, Peter Orlovsky, John Lennon, Henry Geldzhaler, Paul Morrissey, Caroline Kennedy and Mick Jagger are just some of those present in this work from the acclaimed experimental filmmaker Jonas Mekas. Music by the Velvet Underground.
VHS: S25793. $75.00.
Jonas Mekas, USA, 1991, 38 mins.

Walden (aka Diaries, Notes & Sketches)

Jonas Mekas kept a film diary since 1950, "reacting to the immediate reality: situations, friends, New York, seasons of the year." This film contains materials from 1965-1969, unedited, in chronological order. The soundtrack includes sounds collected from the same period: voices, subways, street noise, bits of Chopin, and "other significant and insignificant sounds… They tell me I should always be searching but I'm only celebrating what I see. I make home movies—therefore I live—therefore I make home movies" (*Walden* filmmaker Jonas Mekas).
VHS: S30214. $100.00.
Jonas Mekas, USA, 1964-8/1968-9, 175 mins.

Zefiro Torna or Scenes from the Life of George Maciunas

Footage of the Fluxus heavy, Maciunas, depicts his family, various Fluxus events, and scenes from his private life. Shot between 1952-1978, it is set to Monteverdi music and Jonas Mekas reading from *The Diaries* kept during the last years of Maciunas' life.
VHS: S25794. $75.00.
Jonas Mekas, USA, 1992, 35 mins.

STEVEN SODERBERGH

Gray's Anatomy

A truly inspired cinematic collaboration between director Steven Soderbergh (*sex, lies and videotape*) and America's master of monologue, Spaulding Gray (*Swimming to Cambodia*). This somewhat autobiographical tale is a comical look at Gray's middle-age angst, with its impending mortality, and, in his case, a sight distortion in his left eye. After being diagnosed with a rare and mysterious eye condition, Gray recalls his hilarious and obsessive pursuits into alternative healing.
VHS: S32206. $89.95.
Steven Soderbergh, USA, 1997, 80 mins.

Kafka

Steven Soderbergh's follow-up to *sex, lies and videotape* is set in a baroque, sinister Prague. Jeremy Irons plays an insurance underwriter who, following a friend's disappearance, gets entangled with a shadowy anarchist group and an unbalanced doctor performing perverse scientific experiments. The cast includes Theresa Russell, Joel Grey, Ian Holm, Jeroen Krabbe, Armin Mueller-Stahl and Alec Guinness.
VHS: S17789. $92.95.
Steven Soderbergh, USA/France/Great Britain, 1991, 100 mins.

King of the Hill

Steven Soderbergh's splendid, realistic tale of growing up during the Depression in St. Louis, based on the memoirs of A.E. Hotchner. The young Jesse Bradford stars as 12-year-old Aaron, whose perseverance and intelligence help him overcome the incredible odds growing up with a family that's falling apart. With Jeroen Krabbe, Lisa Eichhorn, Karen Allen, Spalding Gray and Elizabeth McGovern. "Simply one of the year's best films" (Siskel & Ebert).
Laser: Letterboxed. **LD72364. $34.98.**
Steven Soderbergh, USA, 1993, 102 mins.

sex, lies and videotape

When an old college buddy drops into the lives of a Louisiana yuppie couple, the bonds of matrimony begin to fray. Soderbergh's accomplished feature film debut scored a big win at Cannes and really annoyed Spike Lee. James Spader also won a Best Actor Award at Cannes for his role as the soft-spoken, sensitive visitor. With Peter Gallagher and Andie MacDowell as the former perfect couple and Laura San Giacomo as the lusty sister-in-law.
VHS: S11693. $19.95.
Laser: CAV. **LD70456. $124.95.**
Laser: CLV. **LD70457. $134.98.**
Steven Soderbergh, USA, 1989, 100 mins.

Steven Soderbergh's Schizopolis

This berserk film, written and directed by and starring Steven Soderbergh (*sex, lies and videotape*), leaps into the uncharted territories of the absurd—a satire of our anxieties as we approach the end of the millenium. Soderbergh is a downtrodden everyman in this timely and uproarious shock comedy that pokes fun at cults, gurus, marriage and dentistry. "A truly wild ride at the movies…a lot more thrilling than the souless blockbusters that aim to flatten you into submission" (*Movieline*).
VHS: S32363. $89.98.
Steven Soderbergh, USA, 1997, 96 mins.

The Underneath

In this thriller, a handsome drifter (Peter Gallagher) named Michael Chambers goes home. There he finds that the good looks and the good luck he relied on while traveling may not be worth much. His mother wants to start a new life while his brother is consumed by jealous rage. Chambers hopes to reignite an old flame, but there is a complication there as well. Soon he is transfixed in a treacherous game of emotional turmoil, joining sex, desire and violence.
VHS: S26991. $19.98.
Laser: LD75430. $34.98.
Steven Soderbergh, USA, 1994, 100 mins.

MONTE HELLMAN

Beast from Haunted Cave

Gangsters hiding out in a mountain cabin find themselves being killed off one by one at the hands of a horrible monster who's the resident of a local cave. A Roger Corman film (although his name doesn't appear in the credits). Great fun. With Michael Forest, Sheila Carol and Frank Wolff.
VHS: S32550. $24.95.
Monte Hellman, USA, 1959, 75 mins.

China 9, Liberty 37

An interesting adult Western from cult director Hellman. Fabio Testi (*The Garden of the Finzi-Continis*) is Clayton Drumm, a gunfighter saved from the gallows by railroad men who want him to kill Matthew Sebanek (Warren Oates) because Sebanek's farm is in the way of their line. Drumm fails to kill Sebanek, but succeeds in sleeping with his wife (Jenny Agutter, *Walkabout*), who believes her husband is dead. Sam Peckinpah is featured in a cameo as a dime store Western novel writer.
VHS: S32953. $19.95.
Monte Hellman, Italy, 1978, 94 mins.

Creature from the Haunted Sea

Roger Corman created this and even appears in a cameo in the story of a gangster who tries to cover his tracks by inventing the story of a sea monster.
VHS: S08431. $29.95.
Roger Corman/Monte Hellman, USA, 1960, 76 mins.

Ride in the Whirlwind

Jack Nicholson wrote the screenplay for this unusual western. When three down-and-out cowpokes run into a gang of thieves, they find themselves wanted for a crime they didn't commit. Jack Nicholson, Cameron Mitchell and Millie Perkins star.
VHS: S25626. $29.98.
Monte Hellman, USA, 1965, 83 mins.

Shatter

In the bustling international port of Hong Kong, Shatter (Stuart Whitman), a tough American assassin, gets tricked into accepting an assignment that turns out to be a deadly trap set by an international drug cartel. Shatter is wanted by British Agent Rattwood (Peter Cushing) and the drug syndicate boss (Anton Diffring) for the drug smuggling info he possesses. Teamed with a martial arts instructor (Kung Fu star Ti-Lung), Shatter battles the drug syndicate goons. Letterboxed.
VHS: S34423. $14.98.
Monte Hellman/Michael Carreras, Great Britain, 1974, 90 mins.

Shooting

An unconventional Western starring Warren Oates and Will Hutchins as two former bounty hunters out for revenge, with a powerful, hair-raising finale. With Jack Nicholson and Millie Perkins.
VHS: S06340. $29.98.
Monte Hellman, USA, 1967, 82 mins.

AFRICAN-AMERICAN INDEPENDENTS

Alma's Rainbow

In this female rite-of-passage romantic comedy drama, the ordered life of a repressed woman devoted to being the "good mother" is threatened by her teenage daughter's sexual awakening and the arrival of her free-spirited sister. An impressive debut film by this African-American woman director. "A lush, vibrant film…You won't see a movie as witty and compelling as this one any time soon—and you won't see one as beautiful" (*Philadelphia City Paper*). "A hip urban sitcom" (*New York Times*).
VHS: S30132. $49.95.
Ayoka Chenzira, USA, 1994, 88 mins.

America's Dream

Danny Glover, Wesley Snipes, Lorraine Toussaint and Jasmine Guy star in this HBO trilogy focused on the enduring African-American spirit. Glover is a farmer desperately trying to do right by his wife, but in his abscence she meets a traveling salesman. As a principal at a small town school, Snipes must defend one of his students even though it could destroy his career. And in the final episode, Toussaint confronts the prejudices that have dogged her career as a jazz musician. 86 mins.
VHS: S29409. $19.98.

Ashes and Embers

This award-winning film is the story of a Vietnam veteran who, nearly a decade later, begins to come to terms with his role in the war and his role as a Black person in America. His transformation from an embittered ex-soldier to a strong and confident man is provoked and encouraged by the love and chastisement of his grandmother and friends.
VHS: S13411. $59.95.
Haile Gerima, USA, 1983, 120 mins.

Big City Blues

Filmed in Chicago, featuring Jim Brewer talking about the links between traditional blues and the new urban sound, as well as performances by Son Seals and harpist Billy Branch.
VHS: S03194. $24.95.
St. Clair Bourne, USA, 28 mins.

Boomerang

Eddie Murphy's first romantic comedy shows him portraying a womanizing advertising executive. The first object of his affections (Robin Givens) is too much for him because of her aggressive approach so he turns to a "nicer" woman (Halle Berry). The cast includes David Allen Grier, Martin Lawrence, Grace Jones, Eartha Kitt, Chris Rock, Tisha Campbell, John Witherspoon and Melvin Van Peebles.
VHS: S21448. $19.95.
Laser: Widescreen. **LD75122. $24.98.**
Reginald Hudlin, USA, 1992, 118 mins.

Bopha!

Morgan Freeman's directorial debut casts Danny Glover as a South African police officer torn between his duty, his conscience, and his family. This tense drama offers a view inside that troubled country.
VHS: S20614. $19.95.
Laser: LD75162. $34.98.
Morgan Freeman, USA, 1993, 120 mins.

Boyz N The Hood

John Singleton made Oscar history as the first African-American to be nominated as best director. He also became, at age 23, the youngest filmmaker to be so honored for this powerful drama about responsibility and survival. Cuba Gooding Jr. delivers a fine performance as Tre Styles, a young man trying to make the right decisions while dealing with the dangers of living in South Central L.A. With excellent work by rapper Ice Cube, Morris Chestnut and Larry Fishburne as Tre's discerning father.
VHS: S15671. $19.95.
Laser: LD71181. $49.95.
John Singleton, USA, 1991, 107 mins.

Buck and the Preacher

Sidney Poitier's first feature as director. Poitier also plays a wagonmaster on the long trek out West as the wagon train is attacked by white nightriders and encounters a group of slaves freed at the end of the Civil War. With Harry Belafonte as a hustler preacher and Ruby Dee.
VHS: S21479. $19.95.
Sidney Poitier, USA, 1971, 103 mins.

Bush Mama

This landmark of African-American cinema reveals the powerful drama of a black woman living on welfare in the Los Angeles ghetto, trying to care for her daughter after being stranded alone by her man's imprisonment for a crime he didn't commit. Though scripted and professionally acted, the film succeeds in capturing the rich style of ghetto language and humor. Its street scenes, where outbursts of violence assume a fantasy-like power, alternate with fantasy scenes, which gain in reality from the juxtaposition. The narrative is loosely structured, flowing readily from real time to flashback, real life to nightmare. A daring film in concept and execution.

VHS: S15644. $59.95.
Haile Gerima, USA, 1976, 100 mins.

Chameleon Street

This debut work by director/writer Wendell B. Harris Jr. is a brilliant portrait of William Douglas Street, a self-educated, high school drop out from Detroit who pulled a series of complicated hoaxes, at various times impersonating a journalist, surgeon, student and lawyer before he was imprisoned. Winner at the 1990 Sundance Film Festival. "Harris is an original and eccentric talent" (*New York Times*). With Paula McGee, Anthony Ennis and Daven Kiley.

VHS: S17244. $19.98.
Wendell B. Harris Jr., USA, 1989, 95 mins.

Child of Resistance and Hour Glass

Two experimental shorts by Haile Gerima are on this video. *Child of Resistance* follows a personal transformation inspired by a dream brought on by Angela Davis' incarceration. In *Hour Glass*, a pro basketball player imagines himself a gladiator before he decides to go home.

VHS: S25566. $39.95.
Haile Gerima, USA, 1972, 57 mins.

Clarence and Angel

When 12-year-old Clarence moves with his family from South Carolina to New York City he finds school can be a major hassle when he can't read. The black kid is befriended by a kung fu crazy Hispanic kid named Angel, who assists him on his road to literacy. Warm and funny. With Darren Brown, Mark Cardova, Cynthia McPherson and Leroy Smith.

VHS: S07131. $59.95.
Robert Gardner, USA, 1980, 75 mins.

The Color of Love

A revolutionary and sexually provocative work that attempts to confront the issues, mixed identity and confusion of interracial relationships while exploring the nature of attraction and taboo sexual themes. 90 mins.

VHS: S18816. $19.95.

Cooley High

This film focuses on several members of the 1964 graduating class of Edwin G. Cooley Vocational High School in Chicago. Director Schultz was intent on presenting black teenagers—their aspirations, exuberance, silliness, awkwardness, and despair—in a more understanding way than any other Hollywood filmmaker had before him. "*Cooley High* is a landmark movie, one of the year's most important and heartening pictures" (Kevin Thomas, *Los Angeles Times*).

VHS: S13765. $79.98.
Michael Schultz, USA, 1975, 107 mins.

Cotton Comes to Harlem

Based on the Chester Himes novel. Two Harlem cops suspect a Marcus Garvey-like preacher is advocating a back-to-Africa movement to cover for a much more elaborate scam. With Godfrey Cambridge, Raymond St. Jacques, Calvin Lockhart and Redd Foxx.

VHS: S17976. $14.95.
Ossie Davis, USA, 1970, 97 mins.

Da Projects

An all-star cast is featured in this realistic film capturing typical everyday life situations that minorities have to deal with living in the urban areas known as the projects. With Monae Shepard (*The Follower*), Stanley McKnight, Debra Ann Byrd (*Dead Presidents*) and Flora F. Gillard (*Malcolm X*). "A great film" (Black Filmmakers Foundation).

VHS: S33196. $19.95.
Doris Renee Wade, USA, 1997, 88 mins.

Daughters of the Dust

This remarkable first feature by Julie Dash follows three generations of African-American women at the turn of the century, structured around the family's migration from Sea Island to the mainland. Beautifully shot by Arthur Jaffa, the film is a poetic series of pastoral images, landscapes, sound, ritual, music, colors and voice. The film is steeped in the highly distinctive, traditional oral black storytelling, told through a highly unusual narrative device, related by an unborn child. The images sing. With Cora Lee Day, Alva Rogers, Barbara-O, Turla Hoosier and Kaycee Moore.

VHS: S16913. $24.95.
Julie Dash, USA, 1991, 113 mins.

Deep Cover

Larry Fishburne's first major role is as an undercover cop from the Midwest imported to infiltrate a West Coast drug ring. Jeff Goldblum plays a lawyer who becomes Fishburne's "partner" in drug dealing.

VHS: S21481. $19.95.
Bill Duke, USA, 1992, 106 mins.

Devil in a Blue Dress

Denzel Washington is terrific in this stylish thriller set in 1940s Los Angeles. Private Eye Easy Rawlins (Washington) thought he was being asked to take a relatively simple case that would make him some easy money. He didn't expect it would lead to his being blackmailed by a crooked politician. Rawlins quickly finds himself in a netherworld of suspense and deceit where the devil must be paid. Jennifer Beals is featured.

VHS: S27347. $19.95.
Laser: LD75497. $34.95.
Carl Franklin, USA, 1995, 101 mins.

Disorderlies

The Fat Boys are the stars of this Three Stooges-like comedy about an incompetent hospital staff. As you might expect they also perform a number of songs. The film is an enjoyable combination of rap music and sheer idiocy.

VHS: S21400. $19.98.
Michael Schultz, USA, 1987, 86 mins.

Don't Play Us Cheap

Restored, re-mastered, and available for the first time in any form, this delightful comedy is based on Melvin Van Peebles' hit Broadway musical about two kids who are sent by the devil to break up a party in Harlem.

VHS: S30061. $79.95.
Melvin Van Peebles, USA, 1973, 104 mins.

Ebony Pearls

A cultural adventure in and around Charleston, South Carolina, exploring sites related to the Denmark Vesey slave insurrection plot of 1822, an ancient art form of sweetgrass basketry, and the origins of the African Church.

VHS: S31703. $19.95.
Erwin Bahan Peters, USA, 1996, 50 mins.

Firehouse

A made-for-television movie about a black fire fighter (Richard Roundtree) who is assigned to an all-white New York City fire station just as an arsonist tries to destroy the black community.

VHS: S18820. $19.95.
Alex March, USA, 1972, 73 mins.

The Five Heartbeats

Robert Townsend's follow-up to *Hollywood Shuffle* is a moreserious film which follows the career of an African-American musical group, The Five Heartbeats. The group's highs and lows as well as their music are chronicled. Features Townsend, Tressa Thomas, Michael Wright, Harry J. Lennix and Diahann Carroll.

VHS: S21433. $19.98.
Robert Townsend, USA, 1991, 120 mins.

Ganja and Hess

A landmark African-American feature which stars Marlene Clark and Duane Jones, who had previously starred in *Night of the Living Dead*. Bill Gunn's *Ganja and Hess*, "once seen as a standard vampire movie, has been reinterpreted as a multi-layered study of conflicts within African-American culture" (Ephraim Katz). Jones plays an anthropologist who contracts a mysterious disease after he is stabbed with an ancient object. The attack makes him immortal but also makes him a vampire.

VHS: S21928. $39.95.
Bill Gunn, USA, 1970, 110 mins.

Ghost Dad

Bill Cosby dies in a cab accident and has only a couple of days to get his finances in order to provide for his children in this family comedy. With Kimberly Russell, Denise Nicholas.

VHS: S21482. $19.98.
Sidney Poitier, USA, 1990, 84 mins.

The Glass Shield

Michael Boatman and Ice Cube star in this intense thriller about a man wrongfully accused of a crime. Ice Cube could be put away for a long time if a rookie cop (Boatman) does not solve a shocking murder case. In the end, Boatman must decide whether to uphold the law or remain loyal to the unspoken code of silence that shields him from the violent streets. With Lori Petty, Elliott Gould.

VHS: S26953. $99.99.
Laser: LD75426. $39.99.
Charles Burnett, USA, 1995, 110 mins.

Go Tell It on the Mountain

James Baldwin's searing autobiographical novel about the African-American experience follows a family's migration from the rural South to Harlem. At the center of the film is a young man who struggles to understand and earn the approval of his stern, moody stepfather. "A remarkable film, *Go Tell It on the Mountain* is powerful enough to lift us off the ground. [The film] soars." (*The Wall Street Journal*). With Paul Winfield, James Bond III, Olivia Cole, Rosalind Cash, Ruby Dee, Linda Hopkins and Alfre Woodard.

VHS: S20385. $69.95.
Stan Lathan, USA, 1984, 97 mins.

Greased Lightning

Richard Pryor plays Wendell Scott, the first U.S. African-American stock car driver in this biographic film most of which was apparently directed by Melvin Van Peebles, but completed and credited to Michael Schultz. With Pam Grier, Cleavon Little, Richie Havens, Beau Bridges.

VHS: S21483. $19.98.
Melvin Van Peebles/Michael Schultz, USA, 1977, 96 mins.

Harlem Nights

Black nightclub owners Richard Pryor and Eddie Murphy team up against the mob and the law in this action comedy. Curiously, Pryor is cast as the more cautious and learned of the two men. Murphy also directed an all-star cast that includes Redd Foxx (with his usual acidic wit), Danny Aiello (*Do the Right Thing*), Della Reese, Jasmine Guy and Arsenio Hall.

VHS: S21446. $19.95.
Eddie Murphy, USA, 1989, 118 mins.

Higher Learning

Laurence Fishburne, Ice Cube, Jennifer Connelly and Tyra Banks star in this thought-provoking film about diversity on a formerly quiet college campus. Race and sexuality are just some of the issues explored in this troubling drama. Sometimes love and understanding are not enough.

VHS: S25847. $19.95.
Laser: LD75004. $39.95.
John Singleton, USA, 1994, 127 mins.

House Party

One night in East St. Louis, Illinois—the "Blackest city in America"—two teens named Kid and Play decide to take advantage of vacationing parents by throwing a bash, a blow out, a house party. Peppered with hip rap music by these real-life musicians, this is the story of that fateful night and the misadventures of the teens and their friends. A def, Black version of *Risky Business*.

VHS: S12749. $19.98.
Reginald Hudlin, USA, 1990, 100 mins.

House Party 2: The Pajama Jam

The stars of *House Party* are back and in college. In order to raise tuition "Kid 'N Play" (Christopher Reid and Christopher Martin) put together a fundraiser. Needless to say, it does not turn out exactly as planned. Features Tisha Campbell, Iman, Queen Latifah and Martin Lawrence.

VHS: S21395. $19.95.
Doug McHenry/George Jackson, USA, 1991, 94 mins.

House Party 3

"Kid N' Play" return for a third *House Party*. This time Kid is on his way to the altar and Play takes it upon himself to plan the bachelor party of all time. The fiance, Veda, becomes suspicious of Kid's party plans resulting in more madcap madness like that featured in the first two installments. The film also introduces female rappers TLC. Features Christopher Reid and Christopher Martin (aka Kid N' Play), Tisha Campbell, Bernie Mac and Michael Colyar.

VHS: S21386. $19.95.
Eric Meza, USA, 1994, 93 mins.

How U Like Me Now

A young man on the south side of Chicago deals with his social climbing girlfriend. She is overly ambitious while he lacks drive. A sort of romantic comedy with a great script. Features Darnell Williams, Salli Richardson, Daniel Gardner and Raymond Whitefield.

VHS: S21445. $92.95.
Daryll Roberts, USA, 1992, 109 mins.

I Know Why the Caged Bird Sings

An eloquent film based on poet Maya Angelou's memories of the hardships, private joys and public pleasures of growing up in the Depression-era South. Ostracized by the social and racial caste systems of the period, Angelou finds self-expression and fulfillment through writing. Written by Leonora Thuna, Ralph B. Woolsey and Angelou. With Diahann Carroll, Esther Rolle, Ruby Dee, Paul Benjamin, Roger E. Mosley and Constance Good (who plays Maya as a young girl).
VHS: S19890. $19.98.
Fielder Cook, USA, 1979, 100 mins.

In Motion: Amiri Baraka

Called "a brilliantly executed documentary" by *The New York Times*, a fascinating exploration of the writer and political activist formerly known as Leroi Jones. Following Baraka from his early days as a poet in New York City's Greenwich Village to his present literary and political activities, *In Motion: Amiri Baraka* is a portrait of a man of singular commitment to social change. Interspersed throughout the film are excerpts from Baraka's powerful play *The Dutchman*, one of the archetypal literary works of the 1960s, as well as scenes from other Baraka plays.
VHS: S10909. $59.95.
St. Clair Bourne, USA, 1985, 60 mins.

Jason's Lyric

This powerful drama follows the efforts of a young man who seeks to change his life against the overwhelming odds that face him on the street. Love can be a redemptive force. Forest Whitaker, Allen Paine and Jada Pinkett star. Music by the Cranberries, Salt 'n' Pepa and others is featured on the soundtrack.
VHS: S23961. $19.99.
Laser: LD74929. $34.95.
Doug McHenry, USA, 1994, 119 mins.

Jo Jo Dancer, Your Life Is Calling

Richard Pryor directs this autobiographical (and self-indulgent) film about a comic reviewing his career from a hospital bed. The film is far heavier than any of Pryor's previous films but still retains a sense of humor.
VHS: S21472. $14.95.
Richard Pryor, USA, 1986, 97 mins.

Juice

Cinematographer Ernest Dickerson's (*Do the Right Thing, Jungle Fever*) directorial debut deals with inner city crime and the search for respect by urban youth. A young D.J. called "Q", is talked into committing a robbery and winds up involved in a murder. The cast includes Omar Epps, Jermaine Hopkins, Tupac Shakur and Samuel L. Jackson.
VHS: S21444. $19.95.
Laser: Widescreen. **LD75212. $34.98.**
Ernest R. Dickerson, USA, 1992, 95 mins.

Just Another Girl on the I.R.T.

Leslie Harris' debut film is a vivid portrait of the panache of a 17-year-old Brooklyn African-American woman. Ambitious and colorful, she is played by astonishing newcomer named Ariyan Johnson, who portrays a street-tough woman with plans to attend college and study medicine. Harris documents life in the projects, from the unique perspective of a young black woman. With Kevin Thigpen, Jerard Washington and Ebony Jerido.
VHS: S19024. $14.98.
Laser: LD75214. $34.98.
Leslie Harris, USA, 1992, 90 mins.

Just Dam' Lucky

From the director of the cult hit *Mala Voodoo* comes this comedy about a young black man who becomes the most popular guy on the block when an elderly woman gives him a large sum of money.
VHS: S30058. $19.95.
Lowry Brooks Jr., USA, 1995, 90 mins.

The Keeper

Paul Lamont (Giancarlo Esposito) is a disillusioned corrections officer at the King's County House of Detention in Brooklyn, whose life changes when he meets Jean-Baptiste (Isaach De Bankole), a Haitian immigrant imprisoned for a rape he swears he did not commit. Moved by the young man's plight, Paul helps Jean-Baptiste with his bail and opens his home to him. Paul and his wife (Regina Taylor) soon find themselves under the spell of this charming stranger.
VHS: S33011. $79.95.
Joe Brewster, USA, 1997, 89 mins.

Krush Groove

Blair Underwood (*LA Law, Posse*) stars in the first all-rap musical. Musicians featured include Kurtis Blow, The Fat Boys and Sheila E.
VHS: S21404. $14.95.
Laser: LD74707. $34.98.
Michael Schultz, USA, 1985, 95 mins.

La Permission

Melvin Van Peebles explores the contrasting European and American attitudes toward race in this story of an African-American soldier who has an affair with a white French woman while stationed in Europe. French with English subtitles.
VHS: S28474. $19.98.
Melvin Van Peebles, France, 1968, 86 mins.

Laurel Avenue

From Carl Franklin, the director of the acclaimed *One False Move*, this HBO miniseries details the intimate joys, sorrows, hardships and family dynamics of the Arnett family in St. Paul, Minnesota over a long weekend. This bold work, gloriously alive and telling in details, is an intimate look at the conflicts and dreams of an African-American family. "The most emotionally layered look at black life ever presented" (James Wolcott, *The New Yorker*).
VHS: S20377. $49.99.
Carl Franklin, USA, 1993, 156 mins.

The Learning Tree

A well-intentioned and beautifully photographed film version of Gordon Parks' autobiographical novel set in Kansas in the mid-1920s. Writer-director-producer Parks recreates his teen years in a small town where a young black learns about life. With Kyle Johnson as Newt and Dana Elcar as the Sheriff.
VHS: S03572. $19.98.
Gordon Parks, USA, 1969, 107 mins.

Let's Do It Again

Sidney Poitier and Bill Cosby reprise their roles in this sequel to *Uptown Saturday Night*. The two men fleece a couple of gamblers in order to build a lodge hall. Features Ossie Davis, Jimmy Walker, John Amos, Denise Nicholas and Calvin Lockhart.
VHS: S21459. $19.98.
Sidney Poitier, USA, 1975, 113 mins.

Let's Get Bizzee

Platinum-selling recording artist Doug E Fresh stars in this comedy as a young rapper who runs for political office to unseat a corrupt politician bent on destroying the local housing project. Also stars Lisa Carson (*Devil in a Blue Dress*).
VHS: S30060. $79.95.
Carl Clay, USA, 1991, 87 mins.

Mahogany

Diana Ross plays a poor secretary from Chicago who rises to the height of the international fashion scene. All she needs is the help of Tony Perkins and the love of Billy Dee Williams. Also making the scene are Beah Richards, Jean-Pierre Aumont and Nina Foch. Sing, Diana, sing. With direction supplied by Motown Records exec Berry Gordy.
VHS: S10831. $14.95.
Berry Gordy, USA, 1976, 109 mins.

Melvin Van Peebles' Classified X

With candor and wit, Melvin Van Peebles (*Sweet Sweetback's Baadassss Song*) examines how Hollywood has aided and abetted the public's perception of African Americans throughout the years. Featuring archival footage from Thomas Edison through present-day Hollywood pictures, Van Peebles explores the institutionalization of racism before *Sweetback* and after.
VHS: S34674. $24.98.
DVD: DV60444. $24.98.
Melvin Van Peebles, USA/France, 1998, 50 mins.

Menace II Society

This stylized inner-city gangster drama is the debut film of Allan and Albert Hughes, 21-year-old fraternal twins. Set in a claustrophobic Watts, the film is constructed as a harrowing collection of brutal vignettes of car hijackings, street assassinations and random violence. The film plays like a black *Mean Streets*. Its theme is the cruel fate of its two lead characters, a relatively good though unfocused kid (Tyrin Turner) who is undone by his allegiance to his pathologically unbalanced best friend O-Dog (Larenz Tate). From the opening scene, a brutal Korean grocery store murder, *Menace II Society* is a pessimistic and wholly unsentimental portrait of late 20th-century American life. With Jada Pinkett, Vonte Sweet, MC Eiht, Ryan Williams, Too $hort, Samuel L. Jackson, Charles Dutton and Bill Duke.
VHS: S19937. $19.95.
Laser: LD76802. $99.95.
The Hughes Brothers, USA, 1993, 97 mins.

Messenger

Vittorio De Sica's groundbreaking film *The Bicycle Thief* inspired this contemporary tale about poverty in urban America. Richard Barboza is determined to stay on the straight and narrow until he is faced with a threat to his livelihood and all he has struggled to achieve. This film shows a side of African-American life missing from the more prevalent "gangsta" films made in Hollywood.
VHS: S27009. $79.99.
Norman Loftis, USA, 1995, 80 mins.

Meteor Man

A meteor crashes to earth endowing a man with super powers which he uses for the good of mankind. An upbeat, largely non-violent superhero film starring director Robert Townsend.
VHS: S21409. $19.95.
Robert Townsend, USA, 1993, 99 mins.

Native Son (1986)

Co-production of the PBS American Playhouse features Victor Love as Bigger Thomas in this adaptation of the Richard Wright landmark novel. With Matt Dillon, Elizabeth McGovern and Oprah Winfrey.
VHS: S05330. $29.95.
Jerold Freeman, USA, 1986, 112 mins.

New Jack City

A drug lord is pursued by an interracial police duo in this violent drama. Wesley Snipes portrays the drug dealer and the "Salt and Pepper" team on his trail are Ice-T and Judd Nelson. The plot is simple but the acting top notch. In addition, the supporting cast includes director Mario Van Peebles and *Saturday Night Live* alumnus Chris Rock (*CB4*).
VHS: S21405. $19.98.
Laser: LD74739. $29.98.
Mario Van Peebles, USA, 1991, 101 mins.

Nightjohn

Carl Lumbly (*Pacific Heights*) is Nightjohn, a plantation slave whose will has not been broken and who has many talents, including one skill forbidden above all others: he can read. When he teaches Sarny, a young slave girl, how to read, she learns an unforgettable lesson about the power of words and discovers the true meaning of freedom in this powerfully "inspiring story of courage and determination" (*The Hollywood Reporter*). With Beau Bridges.
VHS: S30424. $19.95.
Laser: LD76062. $39.98.
Charles Burnett, USA, 1996, 96 mins.

Nothing But a Man

An impressive collaboration between director Michael Roemer (*The Plot against Harry* and cinematographer and writer Robert Young (*The Ballad of Gregorio Cortez*) about racial attitudes in the 1960s South. Ivan Dixon plays a dignified railroad worker whose desire to lead a normal life with a beautiful schoolteacher (jazz virtuoso Abbey Lincoln) is unhinged by racial politics and discrimination. The Motown soundtrack features Stevie Wonder, Mary Wells and Martha and the Vandellas. With Julius Harris, Gloria Foster, Martin Priest, Leonard Parker, Yaphet Kotto and Stanley Greene.
VHS: S20283. $19.95.
Laser: LD74888. $39.95.
Michael Roemer, USA, 1964, 92 mins.

Once Upon a Time When We Were Colored

Al Freeman Jr., Phylicia Rashad and Leon star in this screen adaptation of Clifton L. Taubert's memoir. It depicts the land of cotton after slavery, but before the civil rights movement. Told through the eyes of a young boy, this story tells how people nurtured themselves through tough times with a spirit that cannot be forgotten.
VHS: S29791. $14.98.
Tim Reid, USA, 1996, 113 mins.

One False Move

A small masterpiece, this B-movie thriller features wonderful performances by Bill Paxton and Cynda Williams. A trio of criminals stage a grotesque gangland murder and travel to Arkansas, unaware the local sheriff and two L.A. cops await them. The two principal characters confront their pasts. With Michael Beach, Earl Beach, Jim Metzler and Billy Bob Thornton, who co-wrote the screenplay.
VHS: S17057. $19.95.
Laser: LD71541. $34.95.
Carl Franklin, USA, 1991, 103 mins.

Penitentiary II

Drama about a falsely accused man, "Too Sweat" (Leon Isaac Kennedy), who returns to prison, where he survives the harsh conditions through his prowess as a boxer. With Mr. T., Glynn Turman, Ernie Hudson and Malik Carter.
VHS: S18828. $19.95.
Jamaa Fanaka, USA, 1982, 103 mins.

Penitentiary III

While still exciting, this third part of the series begins to make the audience yearn for an early release for "Too Sweet". Less a social commentary than a "Rocky in Prison", this film still offers a good deal of action. Leon Isaac Kennedy returns.
VHS: S21466. $14.98.
Jamaa Fanaka, USA, 1987, 91 mins.

A Piece of the Action

Sidney Poitier and Bill Cosby are paired in this film about two con men put to work at a community center. A police officer (James Earl Jones) blackmails the two into becoming more productive citizens. Features Denise Nicholas, Hope Clarke, and Tracy Reed.
VHS: S21434. $19.98.
Sidney Poitier, USA, 1977, 135 mins.

Poetic Justice

John Singleton's follow-up to *Boyz n the Hood* features Janet Jackson as a poet and hairdresser who is trying to cope with the senseless murder of her boyfriend. Jackson reluctantly joins a friend on a trip from South-Central Los Angeles to Oakland in a mail truck. She develops a complicated relationship with an ambitious music producer and postal delivery man (Tupac Shakur). The soundtrack includes numbers by Babyface, Tony! Toni! Tone!, Naughty by Nature and The Dogg Pound. The poetry spoken by Jackson was written by Maya Angelou. With Tyra Ferrell, Regina King and Joe Torry.

VHS: S20221. $19.95.
Laser: LD72331. $34.95.
John Singleton, USA, 1993, 109 mins.

Porgy: A Gullah Version

The classic Dubose Heyward play gains authenticity in this version with African-American characters speaking Gullah, an English-based creole language spoken along the South Atlantic coast. This tape captures the world premiere of *Porgy: A Gullah Version*, performed in Charleston, South Carolina. 120 mins.

VHS: S31704. $19.95.

Rage in Harlem

Robin Givens heats up the screen in this action-packed criminal escapade based on a novel by Chester Himes, the author of *Cotton Comes to Harlem*. Givens plays a slick country woman hiding out in the big city with a sizable amount of gold. Actor Bill Duke directs a fine ensemble cast that includes Forest Whitaker, Gregory Hines, Zakes Mokae and Danny Glover as a Harlem gangster known as Easy Money. Bullets fly. Men die. And Givens looks good as the lady in red.

VHS: S15133. $19.98.
Laser: LD71673. $29.98.
Bill Duke, USA, 1991, 90 mins.

River Niger

An adaptation of the Broadway play about the dynamics of an African-American family coping with ghetto life. With James Earl Jones, Louis Gossett Jr. and Cicely Tyson.

VHS: S18830. $29.95.
Krishna Shah, USA, 1976, 105 mins.

Rosewood

Based on actual events of the 1920s, John Singleton's *Rosewood* "has all the power of *Boyz 'N the Hood* in a different time and place" (Jean Wolf, *Jeanne Wolf's Hollywood*). When a white woman from Sumner, Florida, falsely claims that she was assaulted by a black stranger, a town mob declares war on the peaceful residents of Rosewood. In the midst of the savagery and panic, an unexpected alliance forms between a white shopkeeper (Jon Voight) and a heroic, black World War I veteran (Ving Rhames), who cast aside their differences to rescue the town's terrified, fleeing inhabitants.

VHS: S31748. $19.98.
Laser: LD76302. $39.98.
DVD: DV60097. $24.98.
John Singleton, USA, 1997, 142 mins.

Sankofa

This remarkable, independently-made film by African-American filmmaker Haile Gerima (*Bush Mama, Harvest: 3000 Years*) has become a quiet boxoffice sensation entirely by word-of-mouth. *Sankofa* is a Ghanaian word that means returning to the past in order to go forward. Gerima uses this concept to transport a fashion model who is possessed by lingering spirits in the Cape Coast Castle to a sugar plantation where she suffers constant abuse as a slave. *Sankofa* is an attempt to heal the psychic legacy of slavery and to address those in the African Diaspora who neglect their own history. "Engrossing and provocative." (*New York Times*).

VHS: S25625. $64.95.
Haile Gerima, USA/Ghana, 1993, 125 mins.

Sky Is Gray

Based on the short story by Ernest Gaines, and starring Olivia Cole, James Bond III and Cleavon Little. From The American Short Story series.

VHS: S01962. $24.95.
Charles Fuller, USA, 52 mins.

Small Time

This prison drama portrays the gritty reality of doing time. If you do "small time" it can make all the difference. Your life could depend on it. Crude and harsh, this film catches the traumatizing environment which over one million Americans call home.

VHS: S20713. $69.95.
Norman Loftis, USA, 1991, 88 mins.

Soul Food

Sunday dinner at Mother Joe's is a mouth-watering, 40-year tradition, but the good times suddenly stop when bickering tears the family apart. Now it's up to Mother's young grandson to bring everyone back together and teach everyone the true meaning of soul food. With Vanessa Williams, Vivica Fox, Nia Long, Brandon Hammond and Michael Beach.

VHS: S33031. $19.98.
Laser: LD76430. $39.98.
George Tillman Jr., USA, 1997, 114 mins.

South Central

Oliver Stone executive produced this debut work by Steve Anderson about the Los Angeles neighborhood, overrun by Los Angeles gangs. This film tracks one young man's odyssey from gang member to adopting a life of hope and fulfillment. With Glenn Plummer, Carl Lumbly and Byron Keith Minns. "Uncompromising and authentic" (Roger Ebert).

VHS: S17890. $19.98.
Laser: LD71837. $29.98.
Steve Anderson, USA, 1992, 99 mins.

Stir Crazy

Richard Pryor and Gene Wilder team up again in this comedy about two men convicted of a robbery they didn't commit. They wind up involved with psychotic prisoners, tough guards and an irritable warden. One of the top grossing films of 1980.

VHS: S21440. $14.95.
Sidney Poitier, USA, 1980, 111 mins.

Story of a Three-Day Pass

A very unique independent American film directed by Melvin Van Peebles, and shot in France. Despite its very low budget, the film is impressive for its dynamic depiction of an affair between a black American soldier and a white French girl. In English.

VHS: S04620. $29.95.
Melvin Van Peebles, USA/France, 1967, 87 mins.

Straight Out of Brooklyn

Dennis Brown has been raised in the projects of Brooklyn—entrapped in a world of desperation, drugs and danger. His parents tell him to study hard, go to college and be patient, but Dennis can't wait any longer. He plans a robbery that'll take them out of Brooklyn forever, only now the neighborhood threatens to close in on him before he can escape. An astonishing tale of struggle and achievement from 19-year-old director Matty Rich. "A strong film…honest and effective…the truth is there and it echoes long after the film is over" (Roger Ebert).

VHS: S15274. $19.98.
Laser: LD75134. $24.98.
Matty Rich, USA, 1991, 83 mins.

Strapped

A gritty urban thriller centering on the character of Diquan. Desperate to free his pregnant girlfriend, who's in jail for dealing drugs, Diquan decides to play the dangerous double game of becoming a police informant and dealing guns at the same time. When the gun dealer finds out Diquan's an informant, he's "strapped". A hard-hitting, compelling film from Forest Whitaker which won the Best First Feature award at the Toronto Film Festival. With Bokeem Woodbine, Kia Joy Goodwin and Michael Biehn.

VHS: S20485. $19.98.
Laser: LD75266. $34.98.
Forest Whitaker, USA, 1993, 102 mins.

Street Wars

Jamaa Fanaka (*Penitentiary*) directs this tale about a violent struggle for power in the inner city. A high school student at an elite military school decides to avenge the murder of his drug lord brother and take over the business. He also vows to make the business legitimate—eventually.

VHS: S21392. $14.98.
Jamaa Fanaka, USA, 1994, 90 mins.

Sweet Perfection

The low-budget, debut film of Chicago director Darryl Roberts (*How U Like Me Now?*) was released theatrically as *The Perfect Model*, a shrewd, well-meaning romantic comedy about a black film star who returns to his former neighborhood and falls for the beautiful and fiercely independent sister of a young boy requiring a father figure. With Stoney Jackson, Liza Cruzat and basketball star Reggie Theus.

VHS: S18835. $19.95.
Daryll Roberts, USA, 1989, 90 mins.

Sweet Sweetback's Baadassss Song

Melvin Van Peebles wrote, directed, produced, scored and starred in this critically acclaimed, reverse racist blaxploitation movie that has Van Peebles on the run from the police after he kills two cops who were beating up on a black man. With John Amos, Simon Chuckster and Rhetta Hughes. X-rated when first released.

VHS: S06195. $59.95.
Laser: LD76004. $49.95.
Melvin Van Peebles, USA, 1971, 90 mins.

Talkin' Dirty After Dark

Martin Lawrence is cast as a struggling stand-up comedian looking for a shot at headlining at Dukies, an inner-city comedy venue. With Darryl Sivad, Renee Jones, Marvin Wright-Bey and Tiny Lister Jr. As the title implies, the on and off-stage material is definitely blue.

VHS: S16414. $14.95.
Laser: LD72347. $39.99.
Topper Carew, USA, 1991, 89 mins.

To Sleep with Anger

Danny Glover stars as Harry Mention, a mysterious and magnetic visitor from the Deep South who comes to stay with an old friend, named Gideon (Paul Butler), in South-Central Los Angeles. Harry's effect on Gideon and his assimilated black middle-class family is both immediate and profound. He spins tales full of folklore, lucky charms and bad magic that seem exotic and ominous to these urban up-and-comers who have lost touch with the rural tradition.

VHS: S13817. $19.95.
Charles Burnett, USA, 1990, 105 mins.

True Identity

Talented black British comedian Lenny Henry is cast as a struggling American actor who must resort to passing as a white hitman when he learns the secret mob past of a prominent citizen. Frank Langella orders a hit on the New York actor not knowing he has been thoroughly disguised by *Sidewalk Stories* director Charles Lane, his best buddy and a whiz at theatrical make-up. Will Henry stay white and alive long enough for him to audition for *Othello*? With J.T. Walsh, Anne-Marie Johnson, Michael McKean, Peggy Lipton and James Earl Jones as himself.

VHS: S16807. $19.99.
Charles Lane, USA, 1991, 93 mins.

Uptown Saturday Night

Sidney Poitier and Bill Cosby are cheated out of a $50,000 lottery ticket. To get the ticket back they turn to a Black gangster (Harry Belafonte) who bears a striking resemblance to Don Corleone. This comedy's supporting cast includes Lincoln Kirkpatrick, Roscoe Lee Browne, Richard Pryor, Flip Wilson and Calvin Lockhart.

VHS: S21435. $19.98.
Sidney Poitier, USA, 1974, 104 mins.

Waiting to Exhale

Whitney Houston, Angela Bassett, Lela Rochon and Loretta Devine are four African-American women who share their lives and endure a world of romantic ups and downs. Although these are intelligent, educated women, somehow they've all managed to give the best years of their lives to their husbands and boyfriends—to helping the men's careers and fulfilling the men's dreams, while putting their own careers and dreams on hold. Now, as another new year approaches, these women are determined to begin this year with a passion for life that no man can take away. Based on Terry McMillan's best-selling novel, *Waiting to Exhale* is a wise, warm and hopeful film about waiting your whole life for that moment when you exhale—when you stop waiting and start actually living your life. With Gregory Hines, Dennis Haysbert, Mykelti Williamson and an uncredited Wesley Snipes.

VHS: S27534. $19.95.
Laser: LD75546. $39.99.
Forest Whitaker, USA, 1995, 124 mins.

Watermelon Man

A great early American independent film, about a bigoted white man who suddenly turns black and sees his life turned upside down. With Godfrey Cambridge, Estelle Parsons.

VHS: S04321. $14.95.
Melvin Van Peebles, USA, 1970, 97 mins.

SPIKE LEE

Clockers

Newcomer Mekhi Phifer stars as Strike, a "clocker" (24-hour drug dealer) who hopes for advancement but finds himself caught between the police and a killer. Harvey Keitel is Rocco, an honest cop searching for the truth, while his partner (John Turturro) is just out for an easy bust. When Strike's law-abiding brother takes the rap for the murder, it's up to Strike to find the real killer and save his selfless brother. Based on Richard Price's book, this violent and suspenseful tale tells another side of the war on drugs. Produced by Martin Scorsese.

VHS: S27305. $19.95.
Laser: LD75478. $39.98.
Spike Lee, USA, 1995, 129 mins.

Crooklyn

Spike Lee's funny, uplifting look at a family in a crowded but cozy Brooklyn neighborhood in the 1970's. It's a slice of life that gets African-American life just right, catching all the humor and joy of that time and place. The great nostalgic soundtrack includes Stevie Wonder, Curtis Mayfield, and Sly and the Family Stone, as well as many others.
VHS: S22377. $19.98.
Laser: LD74603. $34.98.
Spike Lee, USA, 1994, 114 mins.

Do The Right Thing

Spike Lee's powerful, gritty film set in Brooklyn's Bedford Stuyvesant community, called "a great film" by Roger Ebert. Danny Aiello stars as the pizza parlor owner, Spike Lee himself as the delivery boy. Notable for its uncanny depiction of the community, its focus on the moral issues of racism and non-violence—a gripping experience. With Ossie Davis, Ruby Dee, Richard Edson.
VHS: S11445. $19.95.
Laser: LD70023. $39.98.
Spike Lee, USA, 1989, 120 mins.

Get on the Bus

Spike Lee made cinematic history when he combined the comedy of the classic road movie with the controversy of the Million Man March. Twenty very different men travel from L.A. to Washington, DC, as strangers, but return as blood brothers, destined to ride into history together. With Ossie Davis, Charles S. Dutton, Andre Braugher and Richard Belzer.
VHS: S31206. $19.95.
Laser: LD76180. $39.95.
Spike Lee, USA, 1996, 121 mins.

Girl 6

Spike Lee, Theresa Randle and Isaiah Washington star in this fresh comedy about a fantasy telephone operator. Randle portrays an underemployed actress who happens on a job where she plays to the desires of men over the phone. Making the most of the situation, she soon emerges as the most popular girl on call. Halle Berry, Naomi Campbell, Quentin Tarantino, John Turturro, Debi Mazar and Madonna make appearances.
VHS: S29403. $99.99.
Laser: LD75814. $39.98.
Spike Lee, USA, 1996, 108 mins.

Jungle Fever

An insightful and provocative drama from Spike Lee that examines urban angst, inter-racial romance and the drug problem in New York City. Wesley Snipes stars as a buppie architect whose physical attraction to Annabella Sciorra, his white temp-secretary, colors all areas of his life. With Ossie Davis, Ruby Dee, John Turturro, Lonette McKee, Anthony Quinn, Spike Lee and Samuel L. Jackson, who won a special award at Cannes for his performance as Snipes' drug addicted brother. Songs by Stevie Wonder.
VHS: S15412. $19.98.
Laser: LD71405. $39.98.
Spike Lee, USA, 1991, 132 mins.

Malcolm X

Spike Lee's controversial biography features an astonishing lead performance from Denzel Washington which captures Malcolm's transformation from Boston street hustler and pimp to his prison conversion and reinvention as devoted Muslim. The narrative covers Malcolm's embrace of Islam and his ascension to brilliant orator and black leader who broke with Elijah Muhammad and underwent a final moral and spiritual recovery on his pilgrimage to the Mecca. Arnold Perl, Lee and an uncredited James Baldwin adapted the screenplay. The cast includes Angela Bassett, Albert Hall, Al Freeman, Jr., Delroy Lindo and Lee. Cinematography by Ernest Dickerson. Music by Terence Blanchard.
VHS: S18855. $24.98.
Laser: Letterboxed. **LD71884. $39.98.**
Spike Lee, USA, 1992, 201 mins.

Mo' Better Blues

Denzel Washington stars as Bleek Gilliam, a musician who prefers to put his music before his friends and the women in his life. Spike Lee directs and co-stars as an incompetent jazz group manager with a serious gambling problem. A movie with heart and soul that has a real feel for the jazz scene in New York. With Cynda Williams, Joie Lee, Ruben Blades, John Turturro, Wesley Snipes and Robin Harris.
VHS: S13291. $19.95.
Laser: LD74604. $39.98.
Spike Lee, USA, 1990, 129 mins.

School Daze

Spike Lee produced, wrote, directed and stars in this all-black musical comedy about tensions and social divisions at a southern black university, Mission College. The issues raised are as powerful as the dance numbers. With Larry Fishburne, Joe Seneca, Ellen Holly, Ossie Davis and Tisha Campbell. From the maker of *She's Gotta Have It*.
VHS: S07676. $14.95.
Spike Lee, USA, 1988, 114 mins.

She's Gotta Have It

A brazenly comic foray into sexual politics. Tracy Camila Johns stars as Nola Darling—a beautiful, free-spirited artist who simultaneously shares three men for her pleasure, dominance and one-upmanship. Lee's acute comic perception, innovative cutting and hilarious use of montage aesthetics-where Nola's suitors slay her with opening lines and come-ons-are evidence of a stream-of-consciousness talent and film school sensibility. His father, Bill Lee, composed the music.
VHS: S02777. $14.98.
Laser: LD74463. $49.95.
Spike Lee, USA, 1986, 84 mins.

EARLY BLACK CINEMA

African-American Film Heritage Series I

Facets Video has released six historic, artistically important works that trace the origins of an indigenous black American filmmaking network, highlighted by two important films from the pioneering black filmmaker Oscar Micheaux and the brilliant Austrian-born director Edgar G. Ulmer.

Lying Lips. A late film from the gifted Oscar Micheaux examines racial and sexual repression in the story of a charismatic nightclub singer (Edna Mae Harris) unjustly incarcerated for trumped-up murder charges. With Robert Earl Jones, Carmen Newsome, Armanda Randolph and Frances Williams. Directed by Oscar Micheaux, USA, 1939, 60 mins.
VHS: S00786. $24.95.

Moon over Harlem. Edgar G. Ulmer directs this unusual musical about a Harlem widow who falls for a charismatic gangster trapped by his dangerous attraction to the rackets. The cast is augmented by 20 chorus girls, a choir and a 60-piece orchestra conducted by Donald Heywood. With the superb jazz clarinetist Sidney Bechet, his wife, Marieluise, Bud Harris, Cora Green and Izinetta Wilcois. Screenplay by Sherle Castle. Directed by Edgar G. Ulmer, USA, 1939, 67 mins.
VHS: S02163. $24.95.

Black King. Made by an independent white company, *Black King* concerns an amoral con man who fashions a "Back to Africa" movement as a pretext for an elaborate pyramid scheme. Also known as *Harlem Hot Shot*, the film is read by most as a vigorous satire of Marcus Garvey, the Jamaican-born scholar and charismatic leader who organized a pro-African movement in the 20s and 30s. With A.B. Comathiere, Vivian Baker and Knolly Mitchell. Screenplay by Donald Heywood. Directed by "Bud" Pollard, USA, 1932, 70 mins.
VHS: S07041. $24.95.

Girl from Chicago. Oscar Micheaux's sinister crime melodrama concerns Alonzo Smith (Carl Mahon), a young secret service agent romantically involved with Norma (Starr Calloway), a young Mississippi schoolteacher. The action shifts to New York, where Alonzo, agreeing to intervene for Norma's friend, is accused of murder. With Eunice Brooks, Frank Wilson and Minta Cato. Directed by Oscar Micheaux, USA, 1932, 69 mins.
VHS: S07054. $24.95.

Blood of Jesus. Spencer Williams directed this absorbing work about the scandal that envelops a small rural community when a weak husband accidentally shoots his religious wife, unleashing his own tormented faith and quest for redemption. With Williams, Cathryn Caviness, Heavenly Choir and Juanita Riley. Directed by Spencer Williams, Jr., USA, 1941, 50 mins.
VHS: S07042. $24.95.

Scar of Shame. A powerful silent film about race and class issues. The movie shows the social fissures created by the ill-matched marriage of a black concert pianist who's ashamed of his poor, lower-class wife, whom he conceals from his socially conscious mother. With Harry Henderson, Lucia Lynn Moses, Norman John Stone and Ann Kennedy. The first film produced by the Philadelphia-based Colored Players Film Corp. Directed by Frank Peregini, USA, 1927, 70 mins.
VHS: S15388. $24.95.

African-American Film Heritage Series I. Complete set.
VHS: S18845. $129.95.

African-American Film Heritage Series I and II

All 12 titles.
VHS: S23222. $249.95.

African-American Film Heritage Series II

Six films which continue to represent the largely unknown, early African-American film tradition.

Song of Freedom. One of Paul Robeson's great roles, as an English dockhand who returns to Africa to discover his roots. Features Robeson singing many great songs. England, 1936, 70 mins.
VHS: S01231. $24.95.

Native Son. Richard Wright's landmark novel stars the author himself as Bigger Thomas, the black chauffeur who unintentionally kills a white woman. With Jean Wallace and Gloria Madison. Directed by Pierre Chenal, USA, 1950, 91 mins.
VHS: S03682. $24.95.

Go Down Death. A morality melodrama which puts a minister's reputation in question, bringing him to the brink of Heaven and Hell. With Myra D. Hemmings and Samuel L. Jones. Directed by Spencer Williams, USA, 1944, 50 mins.
VHS: S07043. $24.95.

Duke Is Tops. Lena Horne made one of her earliest film appearances in this all-black musical about a girl who attempts to make it to the big time while her boyfriend joins a travelling medicine show. With Ralph Cooper, Basin St. Boys and Neck Holmes. Directed by William Nolte, USA, 1938, 80 mins.
VHS: S07047. $24.95.

Harlem Rides the Range. A black-cast western musical with Herb Jeffries struggling to keep the villain (Lucius Brooks) from getting control of a radium mine that belongs to his girlfriend's father. USA, 1939.
VHS: S07053. $24.95.

Body and Soul. "An extremely rare film—featuring the first screen appearance by Paul Robeson. Robeson plays the dual role of a preacher who preys on the people and the heroine, and of his brother, a good man. The film, one of the productions of Oscar Micheaux, ran into trouble with the New York censors, and had to change the preacher's role so that he is first a preacher, then detective, and finally an upstanding bourgeois future husband for the heroine, who awakens from her nightmare experience to a happy ending" (*Frame By Frame: A Black Filmography*). Directed by Oscar Micheaux, USA, 1924.
VHS: S10260. $24.95.

African-American Film Heritage Series II. Complete set.
VHS: S20768. $129.95.

The Beulah Show, Vol. 1

This tape contains two episodes of the 50's television series about the lovable maid "Beulah". Hattie McDaniel, the originator of the role on radio, makes an appearance in the first episode. Ernest Whitman (*Green Pastures, Cabin in the Sky*) also appears. The second episode features Ethel Waters (*Cabin in the Sky, Member of the Wedding*) as Beulah. Special guest appearances by Butterfly McQueen and Dooley Wilson. USA, 1951, 60 mins.
VHS: S21389. $24.95.

The Beulah Show, Vol. 2

Louise Beavers appears as the last of the "Beulah"s. She portrays a maid who seems to run the household. The role is an early appearance of African-American film stereotypes on television. Beavers, as well as her predecessors Ethel Waters and Hattie McDaniel, were such solid character actors that the show remains enjoyable today. Ernest Whitman also appears. USA, 1951, 115 mins.
VHS: S21390. $24.95.

Beware

A young man returns to his alma mater, Ware College, to save it from its unscrupulous namesake Benjamin Ware III. In the process he sweeps his old college sweetheart off her feet. The film is a well-made, well-acted musical drama. Features Louis Jordan, Frank Wilson, Emory Richardson and Valerie Black.
VHS: S21419. $24.95.
Bud Pollard, USA, 1946, 60 mins.

The Big Timers

An all-Black cast film featuring "Moms" Mabley and Stepin Fetchit. Bud Pollard, USA.
VHS: S21411. $24.95.

Black Artists Short Subjects, Volume One

These shorts subjects are from the 1940's and are dedicated to important African-Americans in sports, entertainment and industry.
VHS: S21425. $29.95.

Black Artists Short Subjects, Volume Two

Stepin Fetchit, Duke Ellington, Billie Holiday, Cab Calloway, Fester Young and Barney Kessel are all featured in this collection of musical and comedy short films.
VHS: S21426. $29.95.

Black Artists Short Subjects, Volume Three

Spencer Williams, Lena Horne, Teddy Wilson, Fats Waller and Ethel Waters are just some of the important African-American figures who are seen in this collection of comic and musical short subjects.
VHS: S21427. $29.95.

Boardinghouse Blues

Tenant troubles in a show-business boarding house are an excuse for this musical review film notable for its guest appearances by Lucky Millinder's band, Bull Moose Jackson, Una Mae Carlisle and Stump and Stumpy. With Dusty Fletcher, Jackie Moms Mabley.
VHS: S07044. $34.95.
Josh Binney, USA, 1948, 90 mins.

Boy! What a Girl!

All-black cast musical the plot of which revolves around two would-be-producers who are offered half the financing for a show provided they get the other half. With Tim Moore, Elwood Smith, Duke Williams, Al Jackson, Sheila Guyse.
VHS: S07045. $34.95.
Arthur Leonard, USA, 1945, 60 mins.

Broken Strings

A Black cast musical drama concerning a classical violinist who injures his fingers and encourages his son to carry on; however, the son likes swing a lot more than classical music. With Clarence Muse, Cyril Lewis, William Washington, Tommie More.

VHS: S07051. $34.95.

Bernard B. Ray, USA, 1940, 50 mins.

Bronze Buckaroo

Filmed at a Black dude ranch in California, this film is a musical western. "Bob Blake", the hero, and his sidekick, "Dusty", set out to apprehend the men responsible for the death of Blake's father. Features Herbert Jeffries, Lucius Brooks, Artie Young and Flournoy E. Miller.

VHS: S21415. $24.95.

Richard C. Kahn, USA, 1939, 57 mins.

Burlesque in Harlem

The great African-American comedian Pigmeat Markham stars in this dance/musical burlesque. An all-Black cast of dancers, strippers and musicians back him up. 60 mins.

VHS: S21391. $24.95.

Carmen Jones

Dorothy Dandridge plays Carmen, a woman caught between two men and her own unorthodox nature. The men, one a pretty boy and the other a tough sergeant, are portrayed by Harry Belafonte and Brock Peters. Dandridge lures Joe (Belafonte) into deserting from the army and then leaves him for the two-fisted Sgt. Brown (Peters). The supporting cast is every bit as impressive as the main actors and includes Pearl Bailey, Joe Adams and Diahann Carroll in her first film role. Dandridge became the first African-American nominated for a Best Actress Academy Award. The film won a Golden Globe for Best Musical/Comedy in 1955.

VHS: S21385. $19.98.

Laser: LD76970. $24.98.

Otto Preminger, USA, 1954, 105 mins.

Devil's Daughter

A girl returns to take over her late father's Jamaican plantation, where she confronts her jealous half-sister, a crooked overseer and voodoo rituals. Comedy relief from an American servant who believes his soul is embodied in a pig. With Nina Mae McKinney, Jack Carter, Ida James.

VHS: S07046. $34.95.

Arthur Leonard, USA, 1939, 60 mins.

Dirty Gertie from Harlem

A two-timing showgirl, on the run, takes work at an island hotel, where she wins the heart of the hotel owner, until her vengeful ex-boyfriend catches up with her. With Francine Everett, Don Wilson, Katherine Moore.

VHS: S07048. $34.95.

Spencer Williams, USA, 1946, 60 mins.

Double Deal

An all-Black cast drama with a moralistic message. Two men are rivals for the same girl, and one, a gangster, robs a jewelry store, double-crosses his boss, and implicates the honest rival. With Monte Hawley, Jeni Le Gon, Edward Thompson, Florence O'Brien.

VHS: S07049. $34.95.

Arthur Dreifuss, USA, 1939, 60 mins.

Emperor Jones

Dudley Murphy's adaptation of Eugene O'Neill's play about the personal transformation of Brutus Jones (Paul Robeson), an anonymous man catapulted from a socially insignificant train porter and escaped prisoner to the emperor of a Caribbean island. With Dudley Digges, Frank Wilson and Fredi Washington. On the same program is the documentary short, *Paul Robeson: Tribute to an Artist*, directed by Scott Turrell.

VHS: S02627. $19.95.

Laser: LD76785. $49.95.

Dudley Murphy, USA, 1933, 72 mins.

Gang War

Two gangs go head to head over a criminal enterprise: the control of a city's juke box business. Ralph Cooper and Lawrence Criner are the competing hoods but the town isn't big enough for both of them. Features Gladys Snyder and Mantan Moreland.

VHS: S21430. $24.95.

Leo Popkin, USA, 1940, 60 mins.

Girl in Room 20

Geraldine Brock and Judy Jones star in this black-cast feature about a talented, small-town singer who discovers that the show business of New York can be no pot of gold.

VHS: S20544. $19.95.

Spencer Williams, USA, 64 mins.

God's Step Children

Oscar Micheaux's film deals with a light-skinned African-American orphan who refuses to acknowledge her race. She winds up in a convent after being disruptive in her all-Black school. Eventually she marries a dark-skinned man. A serious and moving film featuring Alice B. Russell, Carmen Newsome, Jacqueline Lewis and Ethel Moses.

VHS: S21471. $24.95.

Oscar Micheaux, USA, 1937, 65 mins.

Hi-De-Ho

Cab Calloway does his song "Hi-De-Ho," with specialty numbers by the dancers and other musical routines. With Ida James and Jeni Le Gon.

VHS: S07058. $34.95.

Josh Binney, USA, 1947, 60 mins.

Jericho

An important film because of the seminal presence of Paul Robeson, who plays a convicted soldier who flees from pre-WWII France to Africa, where he lives as a desert sheik, saving his white comrades, and romancing with Princess Kouka. "How American audiences in the South must have reacted to a Negro hero who was twice as intelligent, attractive and heroic as the white characters in the film, one can only hazard a guess," wrote Peter Noble in *The Negro in Films*.

VHS: S02162. $24.95.

Thornton Freeland, Great Britain, 1937, 75 mins.

Juke Joint

Bad News Johnson and July Jones arrive in the West, meet Mama Lou Holiday who takes them in as boarders after they convince her they are actors. With Spencer Williams, July Jones, Inez Newman, Melody Duncan, Katherine Moore.

VHS: S07050. $29.95.

Spencer Williams, USA, 1947, 70 mins.

Junction 88

An early all-Black musical featuring Bob Howard and Pigmeat Markham. USA, 1940, 60 mins.

VHS: S21429. $24.95.

Killer Diller

The story of a magician who does disappearing acts ties together with a variety program of musical numbers including an act by Jackie "Moms" Mabley. With Dusty Fletcher, King Cole Trio, Andy Kirk and Orchestra, and others.

VHS: S07056. $34.95.

Josh Binney, USA, 1948, 80 mins.

Look Out Sister

This film is a musical satire of westerns featuring Louis Jordan and an all-Black cast. Also features Monte Hawley (*Tall, Tan and Terrific*) and Suzette Harbin.

VHS: S21428. $24.95.

Bud Pollard, USA, 1948, 64 mins.

Marching On

Spencer Williams, Jr., directs this docudrama about the all-Black 25th Infantry. He shows the harsh reality of segregation but also makes it clear that the African-American soldier during World War II was a patriotic and dedicated as his white counterparts. USA.

VHS: S21410. $24.95.

Mark of the Hawk

Sidney Poitier stars as a man put on trial for murder in colonial Africa. In the beginning he sides with the liberation movement but in the end makes a speech that is positive about colonialism as a whole. The cast includes Eartha Kitt who performs "This Man Is Mine". Also featured is Juano Hernandez (*Intruder in the Dust*).

VHS: S21412. $24.95.

Michael Audley, Great Britain, 1958, 83 mins.

Midnight Ramble

James Avery narrates this exploration of the early black film industry. Over 500 movies were produced between 1910 and World War II that were commonly known as "race movies." Early on they tried to counteract Hollywood stereotypes. Oscar Micheaux is perhaps the best known director who tackled difficult social issues in Black America. His story and the story of late night segregated screenings, the "Midnight Rambles," are the subject of this documentary. 60 mins.

VHS: S24696. $19.95.

Midnight Shadow

John Criner and Frances Redd star in this black-cast feature about a con man who attempts to marry the daughter of a wealthy landowner to secure her dowry.

VHS: S20543. $19.95.

George Randol, USA, 1939, 54 mins.

Miracle in Harlem

A gang tries to take a piece of the action at a Harlem candy shop. The gang leader winds up dead and it appears the shop owner's daughter had a hand in the killing. A landmark all-Black gangster film featuring one of the day's biggest African-American stars, Stepin Fetchit.

VHS: S21417. $19.95.

Jack Kemp, USA, 1948, 69 mins.

Mistaken Identity

A rare look at independent African-American cinema from the 1940's. This mystery musical with an all-black cast is set against the background of a big city nightclub. With Nellie Hill and George Oliver. Includes the production number "I'm a Bangi from Ubangi." Not to be mistaken for *True Identity*, the recent Charles Lane comedy starring Lenny Henry. USA, 1941, 60 mins.

VHS: S16182. $29.95.

Murder in Harlem

Clarence Brooks (*Harlem Rides the Range, Bronze Buckaroo*) stars in this story of a night watchman accused of murder. When he finds the body of a white woman in the chemical factory he guards, he must prove his innocence in court. Also stars Laura Bowman, Dorothy Van Engle, Andrew Bishop and Alec Lovejoy. A provocative murder mystery from the director of *Girl from Chicago* and *Lying Lips*.

VHS: S21388. $24.95.

Oscar Micheaux, USA, 1935, 102 mins.

Murder on Lennox Ave

An all-Black cast is featured in this gangster film. Mamie Smith appears in one of the musical numbers and is supported by a cast that includes Alec Lovejoy and Edna Mae Harris.

VHS: S21413. $24.95.

Arthur Dreifuss, USA, 1941, 65 mins.

Murder with Music

A musical drama with an all-black cast. Bob Howard stars as a reporter who goes underground to crack the story of a notorious gangster. Also with Nellie Hill and the music of Noble Sissle.

VHS: S12318. $24.95.

George P. Quigley, USA, 1945, 57 mins.

Paradise in Harlem

Frank Wilson, Mamie Smith, Juanita (Bloody Mary) Hall and Edna Mae Harris star in this all-black musical.

VHS: S08458. $29.95.

Joseph Seiden, USA, 1939, 83 mins.

The Proud Valley and Jericho (Dark Sands)

Paul Robeson lends his sweet bass voice to these two films. In *The Proud Valley* (1940), a story about coal miners in Wales, Robeson set out to, in his words, "depict the Negro as he really is—not the caricature he is always represented to be on the screen." 77 mins. *Jericho* (1937) is a high-tension adventure featuring a submarine and camels. According to Robeson biographer Martin Bauml Duberman, "the *Jericho* experience…confirmed Robeson in his fondness for cinema as a vehicle for his voice." 74 mins.

VHS: S28430. $34.95.

Rare Black Short Subjects

A collection of rare short-films featuring African-Americans. It includes *The Negro in Sports, Entertainment and Industry; The All American Newsreel* and *Kilroy Was Here*.

VHS: S15479. $29.95.

Reet, Petite and Gone

Louis Jourdan and His Tympany Five are featured in this drama about the search for a girl whose measurements fit those prescribed in the will of the hero's uncle. With June Richmond, Lorenzo Tucker, Milton Woods.

VHS: S10059. $29.95.

William Forest Crouch, USA, 1947, 65 mins.

Sanders of the River

Alexander Korda produced this, one of the best films starring the great Paul Robeson, in the story of a British colonialist commissioner who maintains peace with the West African chieftain (Robeson) until a group of white slave traders start trouble.

VHS: S02765. $19.98.

Zoltan Korda, Great Britain, 1935, 85 mins.

Scar of Shame

This early "race movie" depicts turmoil within the black community, around the issues of middle-class aspirations and lower- class stigma. A composer marries a woman to save her from the dance halls and gunfights of the ghetto. This silent film was filmed in Philadelphia by a mixed race production, a black producer and a white director. The short experimental musical film *Sissle and Blake*, with Noble Sissle and Eubie Blake, is also included. From the *Origins of American Films* series, a joint project of the Library of Congress and Smithsonian Video.

VHS: S21266. $34.95.

Frank Peregini, USA, 1927, 90 mins.

Sepia Cinderella

One of the best all-Black cast musicals. The musical romance of a songwriter and singer who, after trials and tribulations, get back together to the tune of his "Cinderella Song." Freddie Bartholomew makes a cameo appearance as himself. Original tinted ending.

VHS: S06913. $29.95.

Arthur Leonard, USA, 1947, 67 mins.

Son of Ingagi

An all-Black cast in one of the rarest of horror films; Zack Williams plays a detective in this "African" style melodrama about hidden gold, murder and theft, with a happy ending. With Laura Bowman, Spencer Williams.

VHS: S06912. $34.95.

Richard C. Kahn, USA, 1940, 70 mins.

Spirit of Youth
Joe Louis plays Joe Thomas, a poor black fighter who climbs to the top of the boxing world. With Mantan Moreland, Clarence Muse, Edna Mae Harris.
VHS: S07059. $34.95.
Harry Fraser, USA, 1937, 70 mins.

Sunday Sinners
A musical feature with lyrics and music by Donald Heywood, writer and composer, who was prominently associated with independent black films from 1932 onwards. With Mamie Smith, Alec Lovejoy, Edna Mae Harris.
VHS: S07055. $34.95.
Arthur Dreifuss, USA, 1941, 65 mins.

Swing
Much of this all-black cast musical directed by Oscar Micheaux is built around the music which is performed from Alabama to Harlem, with the Tyler Twins performing the dance numbers, and also featuring Cora Green, Hazel Diaz, Carmen Newsome, Alec Lovejoy.
VHS: S07057. $34.95.
Oscar Micheaux, USA, 1938, 80 mins.

Tall, Tan and Terrific
Mantan Moreland (*Lucky Ghost*) portrays a detective out to clear the name of a Harlem club owner, "Handsome Harry", (Monte Hawley) who is accused of murder. Francine Everett stars as "Miss Tall", a waitress at the club and the object of Harry's affections.
VHS: S21416. $24.95.
Bud Pollard, USA, 1946, 60 mins.

Ten Minutes to Live
A film by Oscar Micheaux, a mystery-musical built around a threatening note which gives the heroine only "ten minutes to live." Song and dance numbers, a comedy routine, with Bill Heywood as the nightclub M.C.
VHS: S05293. $39.95.
Oscar Micheaux, USA, 1932, 65 mins.

Two-Gun Man from Harlem
A bogus preacher from Harlem travels to the old west. As you might suspect from the title, he brings along a couple of guns just in case. Features Herbert Jeffries, Marguerite Whitten and Mantan Moreland.
VHS: S21414. $24.95.
Richard C. Kahn, USA, 1938, 60 mins.

Veiled Aristocrats
Lorenzo Tucker (the "Black Valentino") stars in this story of a lawyer who returns home to find that his light-skinned sister is about to marry a dark-skinned man. His mother has picked a more suitable candidate. Director Oscar Micheaux once again tackles the issue of dark-skinned versus light-skinned African-Americans. Features Laura Bowman.
VHS: S21468. $24.95.
Oscar Micheaux, USA, 1932, 50 mins.

Way Down South
Bobby Breen portrays a young white man who inherits his father's plantation. He battles with a vicious overseer who is appointed caretaker of the land. Clarence Muse stars as "Uncle Caton" in this melodrama which also features musical numbers. The script was co-written by Clarence Muse and Langston Hughes.
VHS: S21431. $24.95.
Bernard Vorhaus, USA, 1939, 62 mins.

Within Our Gates
This is the earliest American feature by an African-American. It tells the story of an African-American woman who seeks a white patron for a school. This film confronts racism directly with depictions of lynching and white-on-black rape in a plot that may be seen as a response to D.W. Griffith's *Birth of a Nation*. From the *Origins of American Films* series, a joint project of the Library of Congress and Smithsonian Video.
VHS: S21262. $34.95.
Oscar Micheaux, USA, 1919

AFRICAN-AMERICAN ISSUES

African Americans in WWII: A Legacy of Patriotism and Valor
Black World War II veterans from all military branches describe their personal experiences, in this film dedicated to seven African Americans who received the Medal of Honor in 1997 for actions performed in WWII. Includes archival footage and a message from former General Colin Powell and President Clinton. 58 mins.
VHS: S33748. $19.95.

African Story Magic
Brock Peters narrates the tale about a young child's odyssey from urban life to discover the power and wonder of ancient African folklore and ritual. 27 mins.
VHS: S17765. $12.98.

African-American Heroes of World War II, Tuskegee Fighter Pilots and Black War Time Radio
Over 400 enemy aircraft were destroyed or damaged by African-American fighters in World War II. This video traces the story of these men from their training on into battle. It also includes popular broadcasts aimed at these keen warriors. 46 mins.
VHS: S27854. $19.95.

Afro-Classic Folk Tales, Vol. I
This collection of Afro-centered folk tales will promote positive self-affirming values among all children. Storyteller Sybil Destu tells two traditional folk tales, about the spider Anansi and about a tiger. The tales are animated. 30 mins.
VHS: S20620. $29.95.

Afro-Classic Folk Tales, Vol. II
This second installment of *Afro-Classic Folk Tales* includes a Brer Rabbit and Woodpecker cartoon, as well as an old African tale told by puppets. 30 mins.
VHS: S20621. $29.95.

Afro-Classic Mother Goose
In this collection the favorite tales of Mother Goose find new expressiveness with an Afro-centric twist. Playtime rhymes are updated in this fresh look at childhood stories. 30 mins.
VHS: S20622. $29.95.

Alex Haley's Queen
This is the powerful story *Roots* creator Alex Haley was preparing at the time of his death in 1992. *Roots* told the story of his mother's side of Haley's family; now comes the story of his father's side: a sweeping, generations-spanning saga with an all-star cast which includes Halle Berry, Danny Glover, Tim Daly, Ann-Margret, Ossie Davis, Jasmine Guy, Martin Sheen and Paul Winfield. "*Queen* is television of uncommon passion and substance" (John J. O'Connor, *The New York Times*).
VHS: S30742. $39.98.

Alice Walker
Pulitzer Prize winner Alice Walker is most famous for novels like *The Color Purple*. In this video she reads passages from that novel, along with works from *Revolutionary Petunias and Other Poems, Horses Make a Landscape Look More Beautiful* and *The Temple of My Familiar*. It was recorded on January 9, 1989, in Los Angeles, but the interview was conducted by Evelyn White at Walker's northern California home. From the *Lannan Literary Videos* series. 60 mins.
VHS: S27121. $19.95.

All God's Children
This documentary shows how the Black Church has embraced African-American lesbians and gay men as dedicated members of its spiritual family. Prominent religious, intellectual and political leaders, family members, and activists speak out about the role of the church and the importance of commitment to equal rights and social justice for all people.
VHS: S34404. $69.95.
Dr. Dee Mosbacher/Frances Reid/Dr. Sylvia Rhue, USA, 1996, 26 mins.

Amiri Baraka
A poet, playwright, novelist, essayist and activist, Amiri Baraka (born Leroi Jones) has long championed black rights. He was instrumental in founding the Congress of African People. On this video he reads works from *Boptrees* and unpublished works, in Los Angeles on February 11, 1991. Baraka then speaks with Lewis MacAdams. From the *Lannan Literary Videos* series. 60 mins.
VHS: S27133. $19.95.

Amistad
Spielberg's Oscar-nominated epic starring Morgan Freeman, Nigel Hawthorne, Anthony Hopkins, Djimon Hounsou, Matthew McConaughey, David Paymer, Pete Postlethwaite, and Stellan Skarsgard. In the summer of 1839, 53 Africans held captive in the cramped cargo holds of the Spanish slave ship *La Amistad* break free of their shackles, arm themselves, take control of the ship and reclaim their freedom as they try to return to Africa. The two surviving members of the crew trick them and they are captured by an American naval ship and put on trial for the murder of the crew. Letterboxed.
VHS: S34573. $106.99.
Steven Spielberg, USA, 1997, 155 mins.

Amos 'n' Andy: Anatomy of a Controversy
This is the first authorized, in-depth look at the landmark, controversial, black comedy team. On top of hilarious clips from the Amos n' Andy TV series and interviews with Redd Foxx, Marla Gibbs and others, find additional footage never before seen on television.
VHS: S15679. $39.95.

Arthur Ashe: Citizen of the World
A moving portrait of a champion in tennis and in life, the late Arthur Ashe. 59 mins.
VHS: S23444. $19.98.

The Assassination of Dr. Martin Luther King, Jr.
This expose considers the clandestine activities of the government, the counterintelligence campaigns of the FBI to discredit King and the civil rights movement, private communications with Lyndon Johnson's top aides, and the final days of King's life. The film uses key FBI files and other government records that have only recently been made public, including the FBI's unsettling request that King take his own life. 90 mins.
VHS: S18512. $19.98.

Autobiography of Miss Jane Pittman
Made for TV tour-de-force for Cicely Tyson, who plays a 110-year-old former slave recalling her life from the Civil War through the civil rights movement. Winner of nine Emmy Awards.
VHS: S00076. $19.95.
John Korty, USA, 1974, 106 mins.

bell hooks on Video: Cultural Criticism & Transformation
bell hooks, distinguished professor of English, City College of New York, and author of 14 books of commentary, criticism and autobiography, makes a compelling argument for the transformative power of cultural criticism, in this extensively illustrated two-part tape. 70 mins.
VHS: S31887. $195.00.

Benjamin E. Mays: Mentor of Martin Luther King, Jr.
This famous author, scholar and philosopher was president of Morehouse College for 27 years. His important influence as an educator and community member was felt by many, including Martin Luther King, Jr. and former President Jimmy Carter. In this documentary the lasting legacy of this great role model is finally revealed.
VHS: S20746. $49.99.
Rex Barnett, USA, 20 mins.

Benjamin O. Davis, Jr.: American
A biography of General Davis, the first 20th century African-American graduate from West Point, who founded the legendary Tuskegee Airmen, the elite World War II unit of black aviators who distinguished themselves during combat. 60 mins.
VHS: S18445. $19.95.

Benny Andrew's The Invisible Line
African-American artist Andrew is a self-styled innovator. He creates collages and paintings that capture the lives of sharecroppers. It is a world he knows firsthand as he grew up amidst these previously invisible people in the 1930s. Narrated by Jeoffrey Holder. 28 mins.
VHS: S28408. $49.95.

Best of Nightline
Louis Farrakhan. 30 mins.
VHS: S14029. $14.98.

Betye and Alison Saar
African-American, mother and daughter artists Betye and Alison Saar are the focus of this tape. Betye is a mixed media artist frequently using "found" objects in her art. Alison is a sculptor whose work is done largely in wood. USA, 30 mins.
VHS: S21456. $49.95.

Black Achievers Video Series
Five volumes.
Everyday Battle: Fannie Lou Hamer. Reports on the life of civil rights leader Fannie Lou Hamer, from her birth in the Mississippi Delta to her unplanned thrust into national prominence in the 1960s as a result of her life-risking convictions against an oppressive system that denied blacks basic human rights. Congressman John Lewis and others comment on the mark left by this woman of limited education, who was alone and largely ignored by the media in the last years of her life. 30 mins.
VHS: S32740. $49.95.

From a Sidewalk Stand: Nathaniel H. Bronner, Sr. An account of how this black businessman, the founder of Bronner Brothers Cosmetics Co. in Atlanta, began selling products on the sidewalk in front of his sister's beauty shop and built one of the most successful enterprises in American business. 30 mins.
VHS: S32743. $745.00.
In Medical Science. Bill Jenkins, Ph.D., M.P.H. and Walter Williams, M.D., M.P.H., two black epidemiologists at the Centers for Disease Control and Prevention in Atlanta, discuss their duties at the CDC and the academic and professional training that led to their current positions.
VHS: S32741. $49.95.
The Leader: Shirley Chisholm. Covers the life and hard climb up the political ladder of Brooklyn-born Shirley Chisholm, who in 1969 became the first African-American woman elected to Congress, and later was the first black woman to to run for president. Congressman John Lewis and others talk about her contribution to the nation and women. 30 mins.
VHS: S32742. $49.99.
One Doctor: Daniel Hale Williams. The first video biography of the black surgeon who, in 1893, was the first person to successfully perform an operation on the human heart. Founder of the first interracial hospital, Dr. Williams toiled relentlessly to aid blacks in reaching legitimate positions in the medical field. Study guide included. 45 mins.
VHS: S32739. $49.99.

The Black Americans of Achievement

This collection studies the sacrifices and achievements of 20th century American heroes, including Booker T. Washington, Colin Powell, Martin Luther King Jr., Jackie Robinson, and Malcolm X. "Excellent archival footage and photographs, interviews with historians and family members... paint a lively portrait of the subject and their achievements" (*Video Librarian*).
Booker T. Washington. 30 mins.
VHS: S17383. $39.95.
Colin Powell. 30 mins.
VHS: S17384. $39.95.
Dr. Martin Luther King, Jr. 30 mins.
VHS: S17385. $39.95.
Frederick Douglass. 30 mins.
VHS: S17386. $39.95.
George Washington Carver. 30 mins.
VHS: S17387. $39.95.
Harriet Tubman. 30 mins.
VHS: S17388. $39.95.
Jackie Robinson. 30 mins.
VHS: S17389. $39.95.
Jesse Jackson. 30 mins.
VHS: S17390. $39.95.
Madam C.J. Walker. 30 mins.
VHS: S17391. $39.95.
Malcolm X. 30 mins.
VHS: S17392. $39.95.
Sojourner Truth. 30 mins.
VHS: S17393. $39.95.
Thurgood Marshall. 30 mins.
VHS: S17394. $39.95.
The Black Americans of Achievement: Boxed Set. 360 mins.
VHS: S17395. $479.40.

Black Americans of Achievement Collection #2

Artists, athletes, scholars and explorers are all people who take risks in order to stretch the limits accepted by ordinary folks. Each of these 30-minute tapes features an African-American whose accomplishments are extraordinary.
Muhammad Ali. He boxed his way to an Olympic gold medal and was the first man to win three world championships.
VHS: S24098. $39.95.
Marcus Garvey. This charismatic leader was tremendously influential with his nationalist doctrine supporting racial purity and separatism.
VHS: S24099. $39.95.
James Baldwin. American novelist, essayist and early civil rights leader, Baldwin is acclaimed for his works *Go Tell It on the Mountain, Nobody Knows My Name and Another Country*.
VHS: S24100. $39.95.
Matthew Henson. Besides the Eskimos, this man was the only other person of color to accompany Robert E. Peary to the North Pole.
VHS: S24101. $39.95.
Jesse Owens. As a four-time Olympic gold medal winner, Owens' triumph discredited Hitler's fantasy of Aryan superiority during the 1936 Berlin Olympics.
VHS: S24102. $39.95.
Alice Walker. A Pulitzer Prize winner for her novel *The Color Purple*, this prolific author was also a feminist and civil rights activist.
VHS: S24103. $39.95.
W.E.B. Du Bois. Beginning with his role as a founder of the National Association for the Advancement of Colored People, Du Bois remained a key figure in the civil rights movement for over 50 years.
VHS: S24104. $39.95.
Mary McLeod Bethune. A pioneer in education, she helped create the Bethune-Cookman College in 1931.
VHS: S24105. $39.95.
Langston Hughes. This "Poet Laureate of Harlem" was also a noted journalist, dramatist and winner of the Harmon Gold Medal.
VHS: S24106. $39.95.
Elijah Muhammad. During his leadership, the African-American Muslim religious movement thrived and gained national recognition.
VHS: S24107. $39.95.
Black Americans of Achievement Collection #2, Set of Ten Videos.
VHS: S24108. $399.50.

Black Artists of the Silver Screen—Harlem Variety Review (Showtime at the Apollo)

With Duke Ellington, Nipsey Russell, Herb Jeffries, Nat "King" Cole, Mantan Moreland, Lionel Hampton and more. 80 mins.
VHS: S32152. $24.95.

Black Artists of the Silver Screen—Proud Valley

Paul Robeson and Edward Chapman star in this story of a Welsh coal-mining village beset by a mine shutdown.
VHS: S32151. $24.95.
Penrose Tennyson, Great Britain, 1940, 75 mins.

Black Brigade

Billy Dee Williams and Richard Pryor star in this World War II film. They are part of an all-Black unit, dropped behind Nazi lines on a sabotage mission, and who are not expected to return. Features Stephen Boyd. USA, 1969, 90 mins.
VHS: S21438. $14.95.

The Black Military Experience

This interesting collection of shorts about black military life includes *The Negro Soldier, The Navy Steward,* and *The Negro Sailor*.
VHS: S15480. $29.95.

Black Panthers: Huey Newton

A film documentary of the "Free Huey Newton" rally in California, with the speakers including Eldridge Cleaver, James Foreman, Bobby Seale, H. Rap Brown, Stokely Carmichael, and Bob Avakian. Includes the short *Black Panther Newsreel*, featuring interviews with Huey Newton in the Alameda County Jail. 1968, 53 mins.
VHS: S03358. $39.95.

Black Power in America: Myth or Reality?

A survey of some of the changes in American society since the civil rights movement of the 60's, *Black Power in America* opens with a focus on Black Americans like Mayor Tom Bradley of Los Angeles and Franklin Thomas of the Ford Foundation by looking at men who have achieved power and influence difficult to attain in the past, looks at contemporary education, and at a wide range of events with provocative insights into Black America.
VHS: S10089. $129.95.
William Greaves, USA, 1988

Black Profiles

The lives of famous African-Americans serve as the inspiration for this documentary. Paul Lawrence Dunbar, Booker T. Washington, Dr. George Carver, and Dr. Martin Luther King are all covered in this inspirational and educational work.
VHS: S20625. $29.95.

Black Studies: Then and Now

This examination of African-American culture traces struggles and accomplishments through a vast historical prism, from the end of slavery to the political and social movements led by Dr. Martin Luther King Jr. to the celebrations of Kwanzaa, June tenth and other holidays. Designed for children in grades 4-6.
Black Heritage Holidays. An African-American family honors its cultural heritage by observing Kwanzaa, a holiday involving elaborate table decorations and the dispensing of gifts to award the children's accomplishments. 20 mins.
VHS: S19988. $65.95.
Dr. Martin Luther King, Jr. The life and legacy of Dr. King are examined. The topics explored include the Supreme Court decision outlawing school desegregation, the Montgomery Bus Boycott and the march to Selma. 15 mins.
VHS: S19987. $65.95.
Rebels and Abolitionists. A historical examination of the cruel legacy of slavery and its impact on African-American freedom, this program studies its pre-Civil War roots to the Emancipation Proclamation to the surrender of Confederate troops at Appomattox. 14 mins.
VHS: S19986. $65.95.
Slavery and Plantation Life. This video presents a subjective view of the experiences of being a slave, what it means and feels to be captured, traded and treated as property. The program also studies the origins of slavery. 14 mins.
VHS: S19985. $65.95.
Black Studies: Then and Now, Set.
VHS: S19989. $229.00.

The Black Unicorn: Dudley Randall and the Broadside Press

Documentary chronicles the life and literary career of a major black American poet, Dudley Randall, the poet laureate of Detroit and publisher/editor of Broadside Press. Interviews with other black poets reveal the extent of Randall's influence on the development of African-American literature. Public performance rights included.
VHS: S33384. $99.95.
Melba Joyce Boyd, USA, 1996, 54 mins.

Black Warriors of the Seminole

This Emmy-Award winning PBS documentary reveals the amazing and historic story of an unusual and lasting alliance between the Seminole Indians of Florida and Southern blacks. A compelling chapter in American history bringing to life the remarkable story of an honorable and courageous people. 1990. 28 mins.
VHS: S34396. $29.95.

Booker

Levar Burton plays the young Booker T. Washington. He saw the demise of slavery and the degradations of the Civil War. Despite all these hardships, he founded the respected Tuskegee Institute, an institution of higher learning for African-Americans. It's a perfect film for kids as it shows this struggle from the viewpoint of the young Booker. Shelley Duvall and Judge Reinhold are also featured. 58 mins.
VHS: S27620. $14.95.

Booker T. Washington's Tuskegee America

Hugh Downs hosts this look at the fascinating life of a man born a slave. Washington realized the power of education and founded the institute that still bears his name. 24 mins.
VHS: S23558. $49.95.
Laser: LD74786. $99.95.

Booker T. Washington: The Life and the Legacy

A candid, investigative docu-drama on the highly controversial leader of Black America at the turn of the century. His policies of Black economic self-reliance and political accommodation were debated nationwide. With Maurice Woods as Booker T. Washington.
VHS: S03419. $79.95.
William Greaves, USA, 1986, 30 mins.

Brother Minister

Investigates the conspiracy surrounding the death of Malcolm X, probes the innocence of two of the convicted assassins, reveals the true identities of the killers, examines the FBI and NYPD clandestine roles in the assassination, and discovers the secret origin of the Nation of Islam and its political and religious legacy in America. Narrated by actor Roscoe Lee Brown, the film uses archival footage and interviews to make the case that Nation of Islam leader Louis Farrakhan was involved in Malcolm X's assassination.
VHS: S33019. $29.95.
Jack Baxter/Jefri Aalmuhammed, USA, 1994, 115 mins.

Buffalo Soldiers

Danny Glover, Mykelty Williamson and Michael Warren star in this spirited salute to the famed African-American U.S. Cavalry corps whose fighting bravery in the West helped carve out a nation and the cavalrymen's rightful place in it.
VHS: S33684. $71.99.
Charles Haid, USA, 1997, 95 mins.

The Buffalo Soldiers

Chronicles the history and accomplishments of the all-black cavalries and infantries during the last half of the 19th century. Utilizes a rare collection of Buffalo Soldier photographs and features the dedication speech by General Colin Powell at the Buffalo Soldier Memorial at Fort Leavenworth, Kansas. 50 mins.
VHS: S34077. $19.95.

By Any Means Necessary

This provocative documentary examines two leading currents in contemporary African-American thinking—Afrocentism and the reparations movement—both of which represent the black community's response to centuries of political, economic and social oppression. Features interviews with leading African-American educators, activists, and intellectuals, as well as scenes from the October 1995 Million Man March in Washington, D.C.

VHS: S34406. $295.00.

Isaac Isitan, USA, 1997, 52 mins.

A Century of Black Cinema

A celebration of the finest African-American entertainers to grace the silver screen. With rare film footage ranging from pioneer director Oscar Micheaux to Spike Lee. With behind-the-scenes takes with Richard Pryor, Sidney Poitier and James Earl Jones, and interviews with Eddie Murphy, Whoopi Goldberg, Denzel Washington, Laurence Fishburne, Danny Glover and Fayard Nicholas. 90 mins.

VHS: S32422. $19.99.

Charles Drew: Determined to Succeed

This documentary reveals the pioneering work undertaken by African-American research scientist Charles Drew. He formulated the technique of using blood plasma for blood transfusions, saving countless lives in World War II. It's a legacy that changed medicine forever. 30 mins.

VHS: S22416. $49.95.

Charlotte Forten's Mission

As part of President Lincoln's "great experiment," a young black woman journeyed south seeking to give newly freed black children a decent education and the chance for a better life. This is the true story of Charlotte Forten. Starring Melba Moore, Ned Beatty and Mary Alice. 113 mins.

VHS: S30618. $24.95.

Charlotte Forten's Mission Half Slave, Half Free Part 2

A compelling story of one woman's determination during the struggle for racial liberation to prove to President Lincoln that the black man is equal to the white man. Starring Melba Moore, Ned Beatty, Moses Gunn and Glynn Turman. 1985, 120 mins.

VHS: S14609. $59.95.

Chester Himes: The Long Climb

Though Himes was in prison at the age of 19, he took hold of his life and became a respected author. Photographs of his life and archival film show how he overcame the disappointments of his earlier experiences and then wrote successful novels which won international acclaim. Narrated by Morehouse College historian Dr. Lester Rodney. 30 mins.

VHS: S29471. $49.95.

Civil War Journal: The 54th Massachusetts

This is the true story behind the movie *Glory*. Over 180,000 black men were in the Union Army at the end of the Civil War. This acclaimed A & E program examines the most famous such company, the 54th Massachusetts, whose heroics at the battle of Fort Wagner are the stuff of legend. But were they chosen for their valor, or because they were deemed expendable? 50 mins.

VHS: S30843. $19.95.

Colin Powell: A Soldier's Campaign

This biographical documentary from A&E tells the story of the highly popular and charismatic general. Born to immigrant parents, he grew up in the Bronx and rose through the ranks in the military to lead the Allied forces in the Gulf War. Includes interviews with his family and friends as well as rare archival footage.

VHS: S27212. $19.95.

Bill Harris, USA, 1995, 50 mins.

Conversation with Richard Wilbur

Richard Wilbur, Pulitzer Prize-winning poet, reads some of his favorite poems and reminiscences about his life and work with Grace Cavalieri, poet and host of the national radio series, *The Poet and the Poem*. Produced by the Library of Congress. 28 mins.

VHS: S08131. $49.95.

The Court-Martial of Jackie Robinson

After experiencing racism on his army base, Jackie Robinson wages his own battle against bigotry. He refuses to move to a seat at the back of an Army bus, and because of this he is court-martialed for insubordination. The nightmarish ordeal that followed that action helped to shape the strong and defiant character of a true American hero.

VHS: S13556. $79.98.

Larry Peerce, USA, 1990, 93 mins.

The Cultural Philosophy of Paul Robeson

The open cultural philosophy of Paul Robeson is revealed through writer Sterling Stuckey. Robeson's research into African and world cultures led to his belief that Black Americans suffer from an inferiority complex, nurtured by white oppression. Includes film footage from Robeson's acting and singing career.

VHS: S21905. $49.95.

Rex Barnett, USA, 1994, 30 mins.

Death of a Prophet

Fanatics tried to firebomb Malcolm X's home; they tried to murder him while he slept. *Death of a Prophet* is a suspense thriller which follows the events in the final 24 hours of the life of religious and political leader Malcolm X. Woodie King, Jr., brilliantly combines documentary footage with reenactments to weave a fascinating work. Starring Morgan Freeman (*Glory*) and Yolanda King (daughter of Martin Luther King, Jr.). The music is composed and performed by jazz legend Max Roach; Ossie Davis narrates.

VHS: S14536. $39.95.

Woodie King Jr., USA, 1981, 60 mins.

Don't Leave Out the Cowboys

An historical overview of the Black Cowboys who seized, settled and developed the Old West from 1865 through the 1880's, through old photographs, prints, slides and a descriptive narrative with much little-known information about the Black Cowboys. 22 mins.

VHS: S10107. $39.99.

Don't Look Back: The Story of Leroy "Satchel" Paige

Satchel Paige was one of the greatest pitchers in the Negro League and possibly the best there ever was. He fought for the day when the Major Leagues would be desegregated. Eventually he would see that day. Stars Louis Gossett, Jr., Beverley Todd, Ossie Davis and Cleavon Little.

VHS: S21387. $19.95.

Richard A. Colla, USA, 1981, 98 mins.

Dr. Martin Luther King, Jr.: A Historical Perspective

A new examination of King's extraordinary life using rare and largely unseen footage and photographs, the program looks at the ideas, thoughts and causes of Dr. King's life. Includes non-profit public performance rights. 90 mins.

VHS: S20542. $59.95.

The Dream Awake

This seven-part video series, told in verse, is a kaleidoscopic portrait of the social, cultural and historical forces that shaped the African-American experience and character. The series looks at Africa, pre-revolutionary and pre-Civil War American life, the rise of the black cowboy and the emergence of the black intellectual. The program studies individualists (Malcolm X, Dr. Martin Luther King) who demanded honor and respect. "Dodson tells the history with pathos and humor, lifting his historic journey to a literary experience" (*Children's House*).

Africa.
VHS: S20004. $39.95.
Resurrection City and the Children.
VHS: S20009. $39.95.
The Amistad, Crispus Attucks, Harriet Tubman, the Emancipation Proclamation.
VHS: S20005. $39.95.
The Black Arts.
VHS: S20010. $39.95.
The Black Cowboy.
VHS: S20006. $39.95.
The Black Quartet.
VHS: S20007. $39.95.
The Martyrs.
VHS: S20008. $39.95.
The Dream Awake, Set.
VHS: S20011. $179.95.

Ebony/Jet Guide to Black Excellence Program 2: The Leaders

Trailblazers L. Douglas Wilder, Governor of Virginia; Marian Wright Edelman, Founder and President of the Children's Defense Fund; and Dr. James P. Corner, Director of Yale University's Child Study Center, explain how they persevered and assumed positions of leadership to open doors for others. 35 mins.

VHS: S16595. $14.95.

Ebony/Jet Guide to Black Excellence Program 3: The Entertainers

TV's No. 1 dad, Bill Cosby; Maya Angelou, author, actress, singer, talk-show host and professor; and Charles Dutton, Broadway, film and TV star, entertain and inspire with their tales of persistence and endurance. 35 mins.

VHS: S16596. $14.95.

Emma Amos: Action Line

Amos is an African-American artist who combines a colorful palette with non-traditional materials like photographs, her own weaving and African cloth in her work. Together these materials express something of her feelings and fears regarding the times we live in. Narrated by Anna Deavere Smith. 28 mins.

VHS: S28409. $49.95.

Entering Oakland

A documentary about the problems of African Americans in Oakland and a look at the city itself. Narration by Erskine Peters of Notre Dame and James Baldwin.

VHS: S33833. $24.95.

Claire Burch, USA, 1990, 50 mins.

Eyes on the Prize

Award-winning PBS series on the Civil Rights movement, covering the years1954–the mid1980s, which brilliantly weaves archival news footage, news materials, and interviews. 2 segments per volume, 7 tapes, 14 hours. **Volume I: Awakenings (1954-1956)** contains early formation of the protest movement orchestrated by civil rights organizations, the church, and local protest leaders to protest Jim Crow laws, "separate but equal" doctrines, the lynching of Emmett Till, the Alabama boycott and rampant segregation. **Fighting Back (1957-1962)** focuses on the struggle for equal education, studying the historic 1954 Supreme Court ruling Brown vs. The Board of Education and James Meredith's life-threatening decision to enter the University of Mississippi in 1962. **Volume II: Ain't Scared of Your Jails (1960-1961)** follows the Freedom Summer and the massive number of activists who poured into the South to test the legal challenges of racial inequality. **No Easy Walk (1961-1963)** studies Martin Luther King's non-violent tactics to attack institutional racism in Georgia and Alabama, where police chief Bull Connor turned attack dogs on the demonstrators. **Volume III: Mississippi: Is This America? (1962-1964)** details the first constitutional struggle, galvanizing the energy and force to empower blacks with the right to vote. **Bridge to Freedom (1965)** the 50 mile walk to Selma is highlighted. **Volume IV: The Time Has Come (1964-1966)** Malcolm X, the early stirring of the Black Panther Party, and the advent of "Black Power" are profiled. **Two Societies (1965-1968)** reveals the divisions between black and white societies, particularly in Chicago where a Martin Luther King march is met with unfriendly spectators. **Volume V: Power! (1966-1968)** The election of the first black mayor of a major city, Black Panther Party advocates community empowerment and social programs, African-American parent activists organize for control over their children's education. **Ain't Gonna Shuffle No More (1964-1972)** Cassius Clay becomes Mohammed Ali and fights for his pacifist principles to the Supreme Court, African-American studies programs appear. **Volume VI: A Nation of Law? (1968-1971)** covers the infamous raid on Black Panther Party headquarters and the murder of Fred Hampton, the storming of Attica State Correctional Facility. **The Keys to the Kingdom (1974-1980)** looks at the issues of busing and affirmative action. **Volume VII: Back to the Movement (1979-mid 1980s)** a look at the acquittal by an all-white jury of police officers accused of beating to death a black salesman stopped for a traffic violation and a renewed fervor for political activism set back in motion by the grassroots organization to elect Harold Washington mayor of Chicago.

VHS:S34690.$149.98

Famous Black Americans

This important series on African-Americans examines their contributions to the country's social, artistic, cultural and political framework. The series covers role models of militant freedom fighters to Civil War heroes, contemporary artists and politicians. Designed for students in grades 4-6.

Black Americans: Artists, Entertainers and More. In recounting the significant artistic accomplishments of painter Henry Tanner, poet Gwendolyn Brooks, opera diva Leontyne Price and actor Sidney Poitier, this program showcases the vast cultural diversity of African-Americans. 20 mins.

VHS: S19996. $65.95.

Black Americans: Political Leaders, Educators, Scientists. The historical legacy of the social, political and civil rights protests is examined through the lives of four figures: Blanche K. Bruce, Thurgood Marshall, Ralph J. Bunche and Shirley Chisholm. 20 mins.

VHS: S19997. $65.95.

Black Heroes: Freedom Fighters, Cowboys & More. This program offers a panoramic study of African-American heroes, from Crispus Attucks, the first patriot to die in the Boston Massacre of 1770, to the seminal contributions of Dr. Martin Luther King Jr., winner of the Nobel Peace Prize. 22 mins.
VHS: S19994. $79.95.
Black Heroes: Builders, Dreamers and More. The historical accomplishments of Dr. Carter Goodwin Wodson, Phyllis Wheatley, Mary McLeod Bethune and Dr. George Washington Carver are highlighted in this special tribute to teachers, preachers and researchers. 23 mins.
VHS: S19995. $65.95.
Famous Black Americans, Set.
VHS: S19998. $229.00.

The Father Clements Story

A touching account of the Chicago priest who works on the city's West Side, and his quest to adopt a troubled young man despite the objections of the Catholic hierarchy. With Louis Gossett Jr., Malcolm-Jamal Warner and Carroll O'Connor.
VHS: S17910. $19.98.
Edwin Sherin, USA, 1987, 100 mins.

FBI War on Black America

Operating under the acronym COINTELPRO (for Counter Intelligence Program), J. Edgar Hoover and the FBI were heavily involved in discrediting and, ultimately, defusing what they saw as a militant threat from Black Americans. This video program rigorously investigates this frightening, government-sanctioned conspiracy. 50 mins.
VHS: S13167. $29.98.

For Us, The Living: The Story of Medgar Evers

In 1958, a civil rights leader emerged in Mississippi who changed the course of black history. Medgar Evers' amazing courage, his lifelong struggle for equal rights and his painfully tragic downfall are recounted here with an extraordinary cast including Howard Rollins Jr., Irene Carra, Margaret Avery and Roscoe Lee Browne. 84 mins.
VHS: S06960. $19.95.

Fort Mose

With the recent discovery of Fort Mose (near St. Augustine, Florida), a new chapter opened in American history. This is the story of the first legally sanctioned settlement for free Africans in America. The men and women of Fort Mose won their liberty through an audacious endeavor and made a valuable contribution to America's multi-ethnic heritage. 1990. 16 mins.
VHS: S34397. $29.95.

Frederick Douglass: An American Life

A fast-paced, yet intimate portrait of the famous 19th century abolitionist and human rights advocate, Frederick Douglass. The film graphically portrays the people and events which influenced his long and remarkable life, including meetings with such notable figures as Harriet Tubman, John Brown and Abraham Lincoln.
VHS: S03420. $79.95.
William Greaves, USA, 1986, 30 mins.

Frederick Douglass: When the Lion Wrote History

The remarkable history of a truly remarkable man: Frederick Douglass, escaped slave, and brilliant orator who gave a powerful and poignant voice to freedom and the struggle for Civil Rights. 90 mins.
VHS: S23524. $19.98.

Freedom Road

A made-for-tv movie starring Muhammad Ali as an ex-slave on his way to becoming a U.S. Senator during the Reconstruction Years after the Civil War. Narration by Ossie Davis. Adapted from the Howard Fast novel. With Kris Kristofferson, Ron O'Neal, Barbara O. Jones and Edward Herrmann. Director Jan Kadar's last film.
VHS: S00465. $69.95.
Jan Kadar, USA, 1979, 186 mins.

From These Roots

Using authentic autographs, the film, narrated by Brock Peters and featuring music by Eubie Blake, recreates a vivid portrait of the Harlem Renaissance during the Roaring Twenties. It documents the artistic, social and political re-birth of Afro-America, and includes such well-known individuals as Cab Calloway, Marcus Garvey, Langston Hughes, James Weldon Johnson, Alain Locke, Claude MacKay, Paul Robeson and Ethel Waters.
VHS: S03421. $79.95.
William Greaves, USA, 1986, 28 mins.

Glory

Matthew Broderick stars as Colonel Robert Gould Shaw, the commanding officer of the 54th Massachusetts, one of the first black regiments to form and see combat in the Civil War. Denzel Washington won a Best supporting Oscar for his role as a rebellious soldier who learns what his true duty is. With Morgan Freeman and Cary Elwes. High marks for historical accuracy, Oscars for sound and cinematography. Letterboxed.
VHS: S12846. $14.95.
Edward Zwick, USA, 1990, 122 mins.

Glory & Honor

Based on the stunning, true story of African-American explorer Matthew Henson (Delroy Lindo, *Get Shorty*), who, along with Commander Robert E. Peary (Henry Czerny, *The Boys of St. Vincent, Clear and Present Danger*), conquered the North Pole but did not receive the recognition he deserved because of his race.
VHS: S35125. $71.99.
Kevin Hooks, USA, 1998, 94 mins.

God's Trombones—A Trilogy

Poems by African-American author/educator James Weldon Johnson are voiced here by James Earl Jones and Dorian Harewood. *The Creation* and *Go Down Death* are visualized by Will Vinton using clay painting, while the *Prodigal Son* is animated in clay by Lindsay Van Blerk. These three, 9-minute short subjects will be an inspiration to everyone.
VHS: S23303. $24.95.

Gordon Parks: "Visions"

Within the fleeting images which his cameras and notebooks have recorded are pictures of a nation and the words of a man whose fascinating life journey achieved a unique personal vision. With Avery Brooks, Roscoe Lee Browne and Joe Seneca. 60 mins.
VHS: S30620. $24.95.

Great Crimes and Trials of the 20th Century: The Assassination of Martin Luther King, The Ku Klux Klan Killings

Martin Luther King's untimely death is the focus of the first half of this video. Then the battle between the U.S. government and The Ku Klux Klan is detailed in the second half. Narrated by Robert Powell. 52 mins.
VHS: S29974. $19.95.

Gullah Gullah Island—Feelings

Nick Jr.'s award-winning children's series. Contains two song-filled episodes—*Special Places* and *Binyah Binyah Parade*—plus the Nick Jr. music video *Feelings*. 46 mins.
VHS: S33762. $9.95.

Hale House: Alive with Love

Dr. Lorraine Hale begins by telling the story of one child, born addicted to heroin. From there the story blossoms into the founding of Hale House, a home for children who are born addicted to drugs. 28 mins.
VHS: S21457. $49.95.

Harlem Diary

Author Terry Williams provided nine Harlem youngsters with notebooks and video cameras to let them document their world. The result is a fresh and honest look at the lives of people in Harlem. Often this place is obscured by stereotypes and fantasies. This documentary shows the hardworking people and the troubles they face everyday in the legendary neighborhood of Harlem. From the Discovery Channel. 100 mins.
VHS: S27821. $19.95.

Hezekiah Walker and the Love Fellowship Crusade Choir

Recorded during a live performance at Morehouse College, this video combines interviews, worship and music to reveal the beliefs and ideas that motivate this captivating figure. The songs "Christ Did It All", "Make It to That City", "Let the Glory", "I Will Go in Jesus' Name", "Calling My Name" and many more are included. 58 mins.
VHS: S21326. $14.95.

A History of the Civil Rights Movement in America

Lynchings, "Separate but Equal" facilities and Jim Crow laws set the stage for a powerful political transformation. This is an insightful and moving visual history of the Civil Rights movement, featuring interviews with Andrew Young, James Farmer and other leading authorities. 30 mins.
VHS: S24458. $39.95.

A History of the Slavery in America

Slavery in the US was an institution from the 1600's to the early days of Reconstruction. This legacy is reviewed through interviews with leading African-American Studies scholars. 30 mins.
VHS: S24459. $39.95.

Horace Pippin

An appreciation of the striking color, originality and directness of self-taught African-American artist Horace Pippin. 28 mins.
VHS: S31744. $39.95.

Ida B. Wells

This famous African-American woman fought for human rights at a time in American history when these concerns were largely ignored. Her work as a journalist shed important light on the injustices faced by African-Americans in the South after the Civil War. This documentary tells the story of her heroic life.
VHS: S20745. $49.95.
Rex Barnett, USA, 1993, 27 mins.

Ida B. Wells: A Passion for Justice

Toni Morrison reads Ida B. Wells in her own words, while Al Freeman narrates the life story of this famed African-American woman. Archival photographs and lithographs, together with expert scholarly opinion, illustrate Wells' activism as a journalist, a suffragist and an anti-lynching crusader. 53 mins.
VHS: S12313. $125.00.

The Incredible Voyage of Bill Pinkney

Bill Cosby narrates this extraordinary chronicle about the first African-American to navigate his ship alone around the globe. Bill Pinkney turned this opportunity into an inspirational event for his students in the US, who learned important lessons in math, science and geography. This documentary, a winner of the Peabody Award, gives everyone the opportunity to share in his inspirational achievement.
VHS: S23672. $39.98.

The Jackie Robinson Story

Jackie appears as himself in this chronicle of his ascent from an all-black league to become the first Black American to play major league baseball. Ruby Dee appears as his wife.
VHS: S06334. $19.95.
Alfred E. Green, USA, 1950, 76 mins.

Jackie Robinson: Breaking Barriers

In 1997 Major League Baseball honored the 50th Anniversary of Jackie Robinson's breaking of the color barrier. This tribute tape features game action, newsreel and collegiate footage, and exclusive interviews with Jackie's wife and children, friends and contemporaries as they relive and celebrate his amazing story. 75 mins.
VHS: S31716. $19.98.

Jacob Lawrence

Lawrence is one of the country's most respected artists. This African-American painter grew up in depression-era Harlem and got his schooling in federal workshops. Today his works on African-American themes, particularly history, are widely prized. Interviews and the works of the artist tell this story of artistic excellence. 25 mins.
VHS: S27622. $29.95.

Jacob Lawrence: The Glory of Expression

This documentary is about the life of African-American painter Jacob Lawrence. His work has consisted primarily of epic depictions of the struggles of African-Americans. Considered one of America's greatest modern painters he was the first African-American to have his work exhibited in a major New York gallery. 28 mins.
VHS: S21454. $49.95.

Jesse Owens Story

One of the best TV sports biographies. Dorian Harewood plays the famous black track star who won four Gold medals at the 1936 Olympics in Berlin—which gave Hitler a lot of grief. From his college days to his later exploitation, the life of Owens is profiled. Cast includes George Stanford Brown, LeVar Burton, Debbi Morgan, Tom Bosley, Ronny Cox, George Kennedy and Ben Vereen.
VHS: S10826. $29.95.
Richard Irving, USA, 1984, 174 mins.

John Edgar Wideman

The evolving role of the black man in today's society is one of the themes John Edgar Wideman incorporates in his writing. Wideman read from *The Stories of John Edgar Wideman* and work in progress in Los Angeles on April 6, 1993. In addition, he discussed his work with Michael Silverblatt. From the *Lannan Literary Videos* series. 60 mins.
VHS: S27141. $19.95.

The Josephine Baker Story

Outrageous, shocking, sensational Josephine Baker (*Lynn Whitfield*) was born poor, but achieved fame and fortune through her sizzlingly exotic and erotic dance performances. Her beauty and ambition ensured that she will always be remembered as the first, and possibly most loved, truly international star.

VHS: S14630. $19.98.

Brian Gibson, USA, 1990, 129 mins.

The Journey of the African-American Athlete

Recounts the history of the African-American athletes who took on the struggle to meet their fellow competitors on a level playing field. Witness some of the world's greatest athletes as they make sports history: boxing's Jack Johnson, Joe Louis and Muhammad Ali; basketball's Dr. J and Michael Jordan; tennis stars Althea Gibson and Arthur Ashe; baseball's Negro Leagues and the breakthrough of Jackie Robinson; and more. Narrated by Samuel L. Jackson. 119 mins.

VHS: S33144. $19.98.
Laser: LD76441. $34.98.

Just Doin' It

A fascinating look at the Black barbershop—which is a lot more than a place to get groomed. It also functions as a community center, a place where gossip and camaraderie mix with philosophy, religion and politics. An engaging view of life in urban black America.

VHS: S03424. $79.95.

William Greaves, USA, 1984, 36 mins.

Kenny & Georgia: The Story of a Homeless African-American Couple

Contains voiceover and images of Kenny and Georgia, a homeless couple, and their homeless friends and acquaintances. With images of homeless break-ins, squats and gatherings in People's Park in Berkeley and original music.

VHS: S33796. $24.95.

Claire Burch, USA, 1994, 58 mins.

King

Paul Winfield stars along with Cicely Tyson and Ossie Davis in this five-hour mini-series which recreates the life and struggle of Dr. King in a sensitive and powerful program. With Howard Rollins, William Jordan and Cliff De Young. 3-tape set.

VHS: S20472. $59.98.

Abby Mann, USA, 270 mins.

Kwanzaa: An African-American Cultural Holiday

This informative video explains the origins, purpose and principles of Kwanzaa, the African-American cultural holiday celebrated from December 26 to January 1 and founded by Dr. Maulana Karenga in 1966. The symbols, terminology and practices associated with the holiday are clearly detailed, with a focus on children and the family.

VHS: S31882. $19.95.

Charles Butler Nuckolls III, USA, 1993, 30 mins.

Legends of the Ring

Muhammad Ali, Jack Johnson and Sugar Ray Robinson are all captured on video in this three-part series. These biographies use abundant footage of fights and interviews to catalogue the careers of the greatest boxing champions. 215 mins.

VHS: S29545. $79.98.

The Life and Times of Deacon A.L. Wiley

Based on the oratory of a minister born into slavery, this story recounts the drama of a charismatic African-American father. Gregory Alan-Williams created this work based on slave narratives collected under the auspices of the Works Progress Administration of the 1930's. It offers an inspired and key addition to African-American history.

VHS: S21856. $29.95.

Jerry Grady, USA, 1992, 58 mins.

The Long Walk Home

Sissy Spacek and Whoopi Goldberg provide unforgettable performances in this retelling of the historic bus boycott in Montgomery, Alabama in 1955. After Rosa Parks refuses to give up her seat on the bus to a white passenger, the Rev. Martin Luther King calls for a boycott. Goldberg plays the maid who must walk to work until Spacek has her consciousness raised. *Driving Miss Whoopi* it's not.

VHS: S14504. $14.98.

Richard Pearce, USA, 1989, 95 mins.

Looking for Langston

Isaac Julien's biography of black American author Langston Hughes interweaves the poetry of Essex Hemphill and Bruce Nugent with archival footage and period music from the Harlem Renaissance. A film about identity, sexuality, racism, repression, role playing and art.

VHS: S16641. $29.95.

Isaac Julien, Great Britain, 1989, 65 mins.

Malcolm X

He was the angry voice of a people kept silent for centuries. But at the height of his power, Malcolm X's outspoken independence led to his assassination. An *A & E Biography*. 50 mins.

VHS: S30119. $19.95.

Malcolm X: El Hajj Malik El Shabazz

This intense documentary examines the life and mysterious death of Malcolm X, considered one of the 20th Century's most charismatic yet controversial civil rights leaders. 60 mins.

VHS: S14605. $19.95.

Malcolm X: His Own Story As It Really Happened

An Oscar-nominated documentary about the turbulent life and times of the legendary black leader, based on his own best-selling autobiography. 92 mins.

VHS: S23442. $19.98.

Malcolm X: Make It Plain

Alfre Woodard narrates this in-depth film portrait of the great leader and religious figure. The story is revealed through the memories of those who knew Malcolm best, including Nation of Islam members and Malcolm's own family. Extensive archival footage of rallies and media interviews is also included. Co-produced by the *American Experience*. 136 mins.

VHS: S24871. $29.95.

Malcolm X: Nationalist or Humanist?

Newsreel footage of this influential thinker, leader and religious figure is compiled on this intriguing video. In addition, there is footage of events leading up to his assassination, and an interview with his wife, Betty Shabazz, filmed just after his death. 14 mins.

VHS: S24589. $95.00.

Martin Luther King Commemorative Collection

Two documentaries on one tape commemorating the late Dr. Martin Luther King: *In Remembrance of Martin* interweaves past and present to take the viewer from the days of the Civil Rights movement to America's first recognition of Martin Luther King National Day; *The Speeches of Martin Luther King* includes some of Dr. King's most famous speeches, including "I Have a Dream" and "I Have Been to the Mountaintop." 115 mins.

VHS: S06540. $29.95.

Martin Luther King, Jr.: I Have a Dream

King's eloquent, passionate speech given August 28, 1963, on the steps of the Lincoln Memorial, before over 200,000 civil rights marchers—a speech that still echoes in our memories. 1986, 25 mins.

VHS: S02361. $14.95.

Martin Luther King, Jr.: Legacy of a Dream

From the successful 1955 boycott of city buses in Montgomery, Alabama, to the signing into law of the Voting Rights Act of 1965, this program examines the life and times of Dr. King, the pioneer of non-violent protest, as well as the meaning of his enduring legacy. Narrated by James Earl Jones. 30 mins.

VHS: S34388. $14.98.

Mary McLeod Bethune: The Spirit of a Champion

Historian Dr. Francine King hosts this documentary about the life of the famous African-American educator. Bethune struggled against terrible odds in the Jim Crow South to win an education. Eventually she went on to build the educational institution which became Bethune-Cookman College. 31 mins.

VHS: S29470. $49.95.

Mean to Be Free: John Brown's Black Nation Campaign

A historical documentary about John Brown, who fought to end slavery and gain the rights of citizenship for all black people. Using historical photos and the words of Frederick Douglass and Harriet Tubman, this video is performed and produced by the students and faculty of the Department of Afro-American Studies, University of California, Berkeley. 53 mins.

VHS: S10106. $39.99.

Melvin Van Peebles' Classified X

With candor and wit, Melvin Van Peebles (Sweet Sweetback's Baadassss Song) examines how Hollywood has aided and abetted the public's perception of African Americans throughout the years. Featuring archival footage from Thomas Edison through present-day Hollywood pictures, Van Peebles explores the institutionalization of racism before Sweetback and after.

VHS: S34674. $24.98.
DVD: DV60444. $24.98.

Melvin Van Peebles, USA/France, 1998, 50 mins.

Miss Evers' Boys

Alfre Woodward stars as Eunice Evers, a nurse who was witness to and participant in the deaths of patients and friends in this powerful and provocative, true story of the Tuskegee Experiment, a government cause which sacrificed the lives of African American men. With Laurence Fishburne, Craig Sheffer and Joe Morton.

VHS: S31770. $19.98.

Joseph Sargent, USA, 1997, 118 mins.

Mrs. Fanny Lou Hamer

This woman was born to sharecroppers, the youngest of 20 children. From these humble beginnings she grew to be one of the most influential voices of the civil rights era. She talks with Gil Noble about her growing political commitment to justice. There is also footage of Civil Rights protests and the 1968 Democratic Convention. 50 mins.

VHS: S24588. $145.00.

Nationtime, Gary

Sidney Poitier and Harry Belafonte narrate the official documentary film record of the First National Black Political Convention held in Gary, Indiana in 1972, which brought together virtually the entire hierarchy of black political power in America. Featured are Reverend Jesse Jackson, Mayor Richard Hatcher, Coretta Scott King, Dick Gregory, Amiri Baraka, Isaac Hayes, Bobby Seale and others. Newly re-edited version. USA, 1974, 58 mins.

VHS: S03423. $149.95.

Negro Soldier

Frank Capra supervised this documentary focusing on black participation in World War II. Langston Hughes hailed it as the most remarkable Negro film ever flashed on the American screen.

VHS: S03347. $19.98.

Frank Capra, USA, 1944, 40 mins.

Nightfighters: The Tuskegee Airmen

In World War II, Lt. Col. Benjamin Davis led an elite black group of bombers, support crew and surgical teams over Italy and North Africa. Though these African-American servicemen valiantly shielded white flyers, the army largely ignored their contribution. This video tells their story. 52 mins.

VHS: S27661. $59.95.

Only the Ball Was White

A superior television documentary on the formation and rise of the baseball Negro Leagues and the great ballplayers who were denied a chance to play in the racially segregated Major Leagues. The program features interviews with Satchel Paige, Roy Campanella, Buck Leonard, Jimmy Crutchfield, David Malarcher, Effa Manley and Quincy Troupe. Narrated by Paul Winfield. 30 mins.

VHS: S20421. $19.98.

Passin' It On

Dhoruba was one of the best-known leaders from the New York chapter of the Black Panther Party until he was convicted of shooting two NYC police officers. He always denied the charges and fought for 19 years to clear his name. Finally, in 1990, it was proved in court that he was framed. This documentary tells his story. 57 mins.

VHS: S21246. $29.95.

Paul Robeson

This famed performer was known throughout the world not just for his singing and acting ability, but also for his commitment to justice as a socialist and tireless civil rights activist. These beliefs caused him to champion causes unpopular with some Americans, resulting in his eventual blacklisting. A Morehouse College historian helps place Robeson in perspective while footage from throughout his career reveals the extraordinary talents of this extraordinary man. 45 mins.

VHS: S20946. $49.95.

Paul Robeson: On His Shoulders Many Stand

A legendary figure, Robeson was sought after as a Hollywood star and stage actor at a time when African-Americans were often used only for the most stereotypical roles. His groundbreaking performances and commitment to the cause of international human rights led him along a unique path. Ultimately he quit the film industry because he was so ahead of his times. 30 mins.

VHS: S22417. $49.95.

Portraits in Black

Program includes three award-winning films highlighting the Black American experience: *Paul Lawrence Dunbar*, an early Black poet; *Two Centuries of Black American Art*; and *Gift of the Black Folk*, which depicts the lives of Frederick Douglass, Harriet Tubman and Denmark Vesey.

VHS: S01050. $39.95.

Carlton Moss, USA, 60 mins.

Prelude to Revolution

Filmmaker John Evans' never-before-seen interview with jailed revolutionary and Black Panther Party Leader Huey P. Newton. 76 mins.

VHS: S33254. $19.95.

The Promised Land

This three-volume documentary, narrated by Morgan Freeman, follows the greatest U.S. migration ever experienced in peacetime. *Take Me to Chicago* records the large-scale movement of African-Americans from the South to the city of big shoulders. In *A Dream Deferred*, growing frustration takes its toll on African-American communities in the North. And finally, *Strong Men Keep a-Comin' On* records the growing success of these communities.
VHS: S24582. $49.95.

Purdy's Station

Based on an historic incident, this drama tells the story of the Underground Railway and the Abolitionist movement as they affect the inhabitants of a small town. Jerusha Moore, a school teacher, discovers that a local black farmer called Purdy is hiding escaped slaves in an abandoned mine. Jerusha must choose between her career and her conscience.
VHS: S21323. $49.95.
Don Coonley, USA, 1990

Race to Freedom: The Story of the Underground Railroad

Tim Reid, Alfre Woodard, Glynn Turman and Courtney B. Vance star in the story of courageous men and women who created America's channel to freedom: the Underground Railroad. 90 mins.
VHS: S23570. $79.95.

Raisin in the Sun (Poitier)

Lorraine Hansberry's famous play is masterfully transformed in a film featuring Sidney Poitier and Ruby Dee. Based on Hansberry's personal life, the film follows the attempts of the impoverished family, blessed with an insurance settlement, to escape their apartment and life.
VHS: S01088. $14.95.
Daniel Petrie, USA, 1971, 128 mins.

Raisin in the Sun (Glover)

This 1989 production, which celebrates the 25th year of the play, stars Danny Glover as Walter Lee, Starletta DuPois as his wife and Esther Rolle as the widowed mother. Timeless in its message, this is the story of being poor, black and proud in 1950s Chicago.
VHS: S12662. $39.95.

The Real Malcolm X

Subtitled *An Intimate Portrait of the Man*, Dan Rather hosts this documentary. The program details Malcolm's odyssey from street hustler and drug peddler to charismatic leader, orator and spokesman of the Nation of Islam, before his break with Elijah Muhammad. The material features archival footage, excerpts from some of his most interesting speeches and interviews with his contemporaries. 60 mins.
VHS: S17683. $19.98.

Repercussions: A Celebration of African-American Music

A seven-part celebration of the roots of African-American music, shot over a three-year period, documenting the journey that traditional music made across the Atlantic.

Part 1. *Born Musicians* and *On the Battlefield*. The first film focuses on the professional musicians of West Africa, and particularly the Mandinka Music of the Gambia; the second, on how African musical sensibility came to be integrated into American gospel music, particularly in Alabama, in the form of traditional unaccompanied male gospel quartets. 120 mins.
VHS: S03173. $29.95.

Part 2. *Legends of Rhythm and Blues* and *Sit Down and Listen: The Story of Max Roach*. *Legends* tells the story and records the music of some of the greatest living Blues performers who migrated from Mississippi to the West, generating the way for rock 'n' roll. Legendary performers like Big Mama Thornton, Hound Dog creator Lowell Fulson and Lloyd Glen are featured. *Sit Down and Listen* concentrates on the Afro-American tradition at its most sophisticated and daring—the art jazz of the post-war East Coast, and on its great leader, drummer Max Roach. 120 mins.
VHS: S03174. $29.95.

Part 3. *The Drums of Dagbon* and *Caribbean Crucible*. The first part focuses on the Dagbamba drummers in northern Ghana, and their complex social role; *Caribbean Crucible* traces the complex and fascinating ties that bind the music of coastal west Africa to the music of Europe, particularly that of England and Spain, in the remote countryside of two Carribean islands. The film explores the sounds of reggae and deejay. 120 mins.
VHS: S03175. $29.95.

Part 4. *Africa Comeback: The Popular Music of West Africa*. Africa's own popular music industry has grown rapidly over the past two decades, and this final program explores the Highlife of Ghana, the Afro-Beat and Juju of Nigeria. The popular music scene in Ghana is explored through its most famous musicians, including Nana Ampadu and the African Brothers, Koo Nimo, Smart Nkansah and the Sunsum Band and Segun Adewale. 60 mins.
VHS: S03176. $29.95.

The Road to Freedom: The Vernon Johns Story

Vernon Johns was a famous preacher who, after moving to Alabama in 1953, urged his new congregation to stand up for their rights. His story of courage and empowerment is a little-known episode that some credit with kicking off the modern civil rights movement.
VHS: S21297. $19.95.
Laser: LD75248. $34.98.

Robert Colescott: The One-Two Punch

This tape is a motivational video dealing with stereotypes from artist Robert Colescott. His work and philosophy are also explored. 28 mins.
VHS: S21455. $49.95.

Rodney King Case: What the Jury Saw in California

This two-hour video is taken from the 150-hour gavel-to-gavel coverage recorded by Court TV in the controversial "police brutality" trial of several Los Angeles police officers earlier this year. Court TV chief anchor and managing editor Fred Graham hosts and interprets the proceedings in an effort to make the legal process understandable to the viewer. USA, 1992, 120 mins.
VHS: S16708. $24.98.

Romare Bearden: Visual Jazz

Narrated by Wynton Marsalis, this video shows how Bearden hopes "to redefine the image of man" in terms of the African-American experience in his paintings and collages. 28 mins.
VHS: S28410. $49.95.

Roots

This monumental six-volume series is presented in a digitally remastered, elaborately designed set. Based on the Pulitzer-prize winning work by author Alex Haley, *Roots* is a rich, multi-layered portrait that traces the origins of Haley's African-American family, from their pre-Revolutionary war capture and forced resettlement in Africa to the Civil War, Reconstructionism and their demands for equality and justice in the post-war South. Winner of nine Emmy Awards, the program stars LeVar Burton, Louis Gossett Jr., Ed Asner, Olivia Cole, Henry Fonda, Georg Sanford Brown, and Sandy Dennis.
VHS: S17435. $149.92.

Roots: The Gift

A made-for-television work picks up the fortunes of captured African warrior Kunta Kinte (LeVar Burton) and American-born slave Fiddler (Louis Gossett Jr.), their violent rebellion and heroic efforts to organize a slave rebellion and move for freedom through the Underground Railroad. With Alex Haley, Michael Learned, Avery Brooks, Kate Mulgrew and Shaun Cassidy.
VHS: S17434. $19.98.
Kevin Hooks, USA, 1988, 94 mins.

Roots: The Next Generation

The epic continuation of Alex Haley's autobiographical investigation of his family's origins, related through a rich collection of anecdotes, remembrances and personal history, covering the Reconstruction through the 1970's. A 7-volume set digitally remastered and encased in a elaborately designed slipcase. With James Earl Jones (as Haley), Al Freeman Jr., Henry Fonda, Olivia De Havilland, Irene Cara, Dorian Harewood, Ossie Davis, Ruby Dee and Debbie Allen.
VHS: S17436. $149.92.

Royal Federal Blues—The Black Civil War Soldiers

This award-winning documentary shows the history of African-American soldiers in the Civil War, from their induction into the Union Army all the way to ferocious battlegrounds that marked the divide between freedom and slavery. 45 mins.
VHS: S22048. $19.98.

Run for the Dream: The Gail Devers Story

Academy Award-winner Louis Gossett Jr. stars in this remarkable true story of three-time Olympic gold-winning track star Gail Devers (Charlayne Woodard) and the extraordinary journey of faith and courage that took her from a wheelchair to become the "fastest woman on earth." With Robert Guillaume. Also includes an interview with Gail Devers and her coach Bob Kersee. "Classy performances make this a standout" (*People*). "Inspiring" (Renee Graham, *Boston Globe*).
VHS: S30595. $19.95.
Laser: LD76106. $39.99.
Neema Barnette, USA, 1996, 99 mins.

Separate But Equal

Sidney Poitier, Burt Lancaster and Richard Kiley star in this dramatic re-enactment of an early skirmish in the battle for civil rights. Set in South Carolina in 1950, an NAACP lawyer fights for the use of a single school bus to transport black youngsters to school. He takes his case to the highest court in the land where Chief Justice Earl Warren is faced with a landmark decision.
VHS: S14476. $19.98.
Laser: CLV. LD72029. $39.98.
George Stevens Jr., USA, 1990, 194 mins.

Seven Candles for Kwanzaa

Alfre Woodward narrates this animated celebration of the unique African-American holiday which commemorates the strength of family ties, respect for ancestors, commitment to the growth of community and gratitude for life's bounties. By Andrea Davis Pinkney. 9 mins.
VHS: S33786. $60.00.

Slave Ship

From The Learning Channel. Dramatic recreations and enlightening interviews bring to life the real story of Sengbeh Pieh, a fearless young African slave whose courageous act of mutiny made him a world-renowned hero. The story that inspired *Amistad*.
VHS: S34907. $19.98.

Small Steps, Big Strides: The Black Experience in Hollywood

A brilliant, fun and fast-paced tribute to the groundbreaking achievements of Hollywood's most renowned African-American actors from 1903-1970. 56 mins.
VHS: S33038. $19.98.

Solomon Northrup's Odyssey

This is the powerful, harrowing and true story of Solomon Northrup, a free black man with a trade in 19th-century America who was kidnapped and carried off into slavery for 12 years. Starring Avery Brooks. "An outstanding movie" (*Miami News*). 113 mins.
VHS: S30619. $24.95.

The Speeches of Martin Luther King

The words of the great leader in a collection of his famous speeches.
VHS: S07027. $19.95.

Story of a People

This series, narrated by Danny Glover and Louis Gossett, Jr., features balanced overviews of some of the most important and divisive issues facing black Americans today. Each tape is 60 mins.

Story of a People: Affirmative Action on Trial.
VHS: S33251. $19.95.
Story of a People: Black Youth.
VHS: S33248. $19.95.
Story of a People: Interracial Relationships.
VHS: S33250. $19.95.
Story of a People: The Black Family.
VHS: S33247. $19.95.
Story of a People: The Roots of Racism.
VHS: S33249. $19.95.

Stride to Glory

This documentary chronicles the Olympic performances of a vast array of exceptional black athletes since the beginning of the century, from household names like Jesse Owens and Jackie Joyner-Kersee to unsung heroes such as John Baxter Taylor and DeHart Hubbard. 73 mins.
VHS: S33252. $19.95.

The Tallest Tree in the Forest

This tape is a look at Paul Robeson, his performances and his political views. From his early days as a performer Robeson refused to be quiet on the issue of race and earned the enmity of many. This along with his views on the Soviet Union (which he regarded in a positive light) led to his blacklisting. USA, 1977, 85 mins.
VHS: S21469. $24.95.

That's Black Entertainment: African-American Contributions in Film and Music 1903-1944

Two-tape set. On tape one, *Race Movies: The Early History of Black Cinema*, discover the beginning of black filmmaking from its earliest days through the '20s. This historic film focuses on the movies that were made and the production companies that produced them. Also included are three original short films that were shown in movie houses prior to feature presentations: *St. Louis Blues*, starring Bessie Smith, *Hi-De-Ho*, starring Cab Calloway and *Boogie-Woogie Dreams*, starring Lena Horne. The elegant sights and sounds from some of the biggest names in American music are compiled on tape two, *Black Music Videos from the 1940s*. These 16 three-minute music videos, called "Soundies," were originally screened on a visual jukebox called Panorams during the 1940s. Artists include Nat "King" Cole, Ida James, Lionel Hampton, Cab Calloway, June Richmond and Count Basie. 106 mins.
VHS: S30948. $29.95.

This House of Power

A documentary about the history of the African-American church, from its origins as a separate "invisible institution" among slaves to its present-day role as a major force for social change. Hosted by CBS anchor Hosea Sanders. 60 mins.
VHS: S20545. $29.95.

To Be Young, Gifted & Black

When *A Raisin in the Sun* opened on Broadway, the world of literature had found an exciting new voice in the work of Lorraine Hansberry. Her uniquely gifted vision is presented in her letters, poems, diaries and plays. Starring Blythe Danner and Ruby Dee. 90 mins.
VHS: S30608. $24.95.

The Tuskegee Airmen

Laurence Fishburne stars along with John Lithgow and Cuba Gooding, Jr., in this tale of heroic African-American World War II fighter pilots. Four new recruits are given the mission to help defend American troops from the air, but their mission also has another important goal. Their success could prove that the courage and skills of African-Americans are equal to those of their countrymen.
VHS: S27725. $19.98.
Robert Markowitz, USA, 1994, 52 mins.

Tuskegee Airmen: American Heroes

Never-before-seen interviews and archival footage combine to tell the gripping true story of the 332nd Fighter Group and the 99th Fighter Squadron of the U.S. Army Air Corps, the Tuskegee Airmen—America's first black combat pilots. Hosted by Ossie Davis. 50 mins.
VHS: S34818. $29.95.

The Voyage of LaAmistad: A Quest for Freedom

Alfre Woodard narrates this story of 53 Africans abducted and sold into slavery in 1839, who took their fight for freedom all the way to the Supreme Court. Court documents and transcripts, letters written by the Africans and their lawyers, newspaper articles and testimony from present-day scholars recount the history of this event. With Charles Durning and Brock Peters.
VHS: S33906. $19.95.
H.D. Motyl, USA, 1998, 65 mins.

Whitewash

When Helene Angel walks home from her school with her older brother she is attacked by a street gang and painted white. The effect on Helene and her family is devastating, and the media descend on their neighborhood, completely disrupting the small family. Inspired by actual events and featuring the voices of Ruby Dee, Serene Henry, Ndehru Roberts and Linda Lavin, the story conveys a powerful message that transcends age and race.
VHS: S33432. $19.95.
Michael Sporn, USA, 1994, 25 mins

Wilma

Cicely Tyson and Denzel Washington star in the true story of Wilma Rudolph, who overcame childhood polio to become an Olympic champion—and one of America's greatest athletes.
VHS: S15491. $14.95.
Bud Greenspan, USA, 1977, 100 mins.

A Woman Called Moses

This is the story of Harriet Ross Tubman, founder of the Underground Railroad, who led hundreds of slaves to freedom in the North before the Civil War. To those she helped get to the Promised Land, she became known as Moses. *Newsweek* called this powerful made-for-TV movie "One of the most moving evocations of the black experience ever." Cicely Tyson is brilliant in the role of Tubman as she matures over a period of eighty years. 200 mins.
VHS: S16561. $89.95.

Women of Brewster Place

Donna Deitch (*Desert Hearts*) directed this potent drama about a group of women (Oprah Winfrey, Cicely Tyson, Robin Givens, Jackee Kelly, Paula Kelly) who work together to get out of the ghetto in which they live. 2 cassettes.
VHS: S11588. $29.95.
Donna Deitch, USA, 1989, 180 mins.

ASIAN-AMERICAN INDEPENDENTS

Chan Is Missing

A mystery set against the backdrop of San Francisco's Chinatown. The story involves two Chinese taxi drivers who are looking for their business partner, Chan Hung, a middle-aged Taiwan immigrant who has vanished with their money. Their search for clues to Chan's whereabouts leads them to his family, friends and acquaintances, who reveal a great diversity of people and cultural backgrounds that make up life in Chinatown. A great hit on its release.
VHS: S10918. $79.95.
Wayne Wang, USA, 1981, 80 mins.

Combination Platter

This winner of the Best Screenplay at Sundance in 1993 tells the story of an undocumented Chinese waiter in a gritty, remarkably powerful, independent feature by Tony Chan. In the pressure laden world he inhabits, a green card holds the greatest promise for a better life. He finds himself contemplating an American wife, only to reject the chosen woman. But he hadn't counted on a visit from immigration.
VHS: S21747. $89.95.
Tony Chan, USA, 1991, 85 mins.

Coming Out Under Fire

This winner of the Special Jury Award at the 1994 Sundance Film Festival tells the story of nine lesbians and gay male veterans of the U.S. military. Based on Alan Berube's book of the same name, this film fleshes out this often misunderstood case of grave social injustice, using declassified documents, rare archival footage, interviews, photographs and more, and touches on the World War II origins of the current "don't ask, don't tell" policy. B&W.
VHS: S26966. $29.98.
Arthur Dong, USA, 1994, 71 mins.

Eat a Bowl of Tea

Chinese-American filmmaker Wayne Wang spins a tale of returning soldiers in search of brides and old men in need of grandchildren. Set in post-WWII New York, he exposes the shoddy treatment of Chinese immigrants and the notorious exclusion laws that kept families apart for much of this century. An entertaining and invigorating film based on the 1961 novel by Louis Chu. Cast includes Russell Wong, Victor Wong, Eric Tsang Chi Wai and Cora Miao, the director's wife, as the bashful bride from the old country who grows up fast.
VHS: S11484. $19.95.
Wayne Wang, USA, 1988, 102 mins.

The Great Wall

Peter Wang's great independent American film is touching and moving, as Leo Fang and his family return to his native China, where they are unprepared for the cultural clashes which occur with their Chinese relatives. English and Mandarin with English subtitles.
VHS: S03567. $19.98.
Peter Wang, USA, 1986, 103 mins.

Iron & Silk

A martial arts movie with a difference. Mark Salzman stars in an engaging film based on his two years of teaching English in the People's Republic of China in the early 1980's. In his spare time, he takes martial arts classes from a strict but genuine master. This warm and always human drama perfectly captures the people and the political climate. Salzman, in his film debut, makes a favorable impression playing a slightly fictionalized version of himself.
VHS: S15071. $19.98.
Laser: LD75127. $24.98.
Shirley Sun, USA/China, 1990, 94 mins.

The Joy Luck Club

The stories of four women and their mothers are interwoven in this moving tale of exile, loss, and new beginnings. Amy Tan's novel *The Joy Luck Club* is well realized in this careful adaptation certain to touch everyone.
VHS: S20609. $19.95.
Laser: LD71969. $39.99.
Wayne Wang, USA, 1993, 139 mins.

The Laser Man

From the director of *A Great Wall* and the producers of *The Killer* comes this funny merging of science fiction and comedy about an average young man's metamorphosis into a daring and capable super hero. With Tony Leung, Marc Hayashi and Sally Yeh.
VHS: S18161. $39.95.
Peter Wang, USA, 1990, 90 mins.

Looking Like the Enemy

This video essay on the paradoxes of race and the ironies of war is a bold exploration into the often horrifying predicaments faced by the Asian-American soldiers who fought in World War II and the Korean and Vietnam Wars. Breaking a legacy of silence, 18 veterans share their experiences, filling in the gaps that official history has often left out. 52 mins.
VHS: S31383. $24.95.

Moving Memories

Hosted by George Takei (*Star Trek*'s Mr. Sulu), this journey into the 1920s and '30s features restored and edited home movies taken by Japanese-American immigrant pioneers. 31 mins.
VHS: S31385. $14.95.

Pushing Hands

A loving comedy from the director of *Eat Drink Man Woman*, *The Wedding Banquet* and *Sense and Sensibility*. Mr. Chu is a widowed tai-chi master who leaves Beijing to live with his only son in a New York suburb. The result of this incongruous meeting of differing cultures is a warm comedy. Though his daughter-in-law has no use for him and everything seems to change too quickly, Mr. Chu responds the way he knows best, with the traditional tai-chi exercise of Pushing Hands. English and Mandarin with English subtitles.
VHS: S27008. $92.99.
Laser: LD75459. $39.95.
Ang Lee, USA, 1995, 100 mins.

Slam Dance

Director Wayne Wang (*Dim Sum, Chan Is Missing*) tries something different in this atmospheric contemporary film noir about an amiable professional cartoonist involved in murder. Tom Hulce (*Amadeus*) is the suspect. With Virginia Madsen, Mary Elizabeth Mastrantonio, Adam Ant and Harry Dean Stanton as a cop.
VHS: S06077. $14.98.
Wayne Wang, USA, 1987, 100 mins.

Smoke

Harvey Keitel, William Hurt, Forest Whitaker, Stockard Channing and Ashley Judd star in this offbeat comedy set in a New York cigar shop. Sparks fly when the manager, played by Keitel, gets involved in the intertwining lives of his colorful customers. A gentle love letter to Brooklyn.
VHS: S26708. $19.95.
Laser: LD75322. $39.98.
Wayne Wang, USA, 1995, 112 mins.

Something Strong Within

This critically acclaimed, award-winning video production was created for the Japanese-American National Museum's exhibition, "America's Concentration Camps: Remembering the Japanese-American Experience." A haunting compilation of never-before-seen home movies of the forced removal and incarceration of Japanese Americans during WWII. Includes portions of the movie *Topaz*, which has been listed in the National Film Registry.
VHS: S31384. $19.95.

The Wedding Banquet

Ang Lee's surprise hit is a poignant and funny story of the gay Taiwanese yuppie (Winston Chao) who lives with his American lover (Mitchell Lichtenstein) and tries to end his family's endless matchmaking attempts by announcing that he's engaged. His parents unexpectedly fly in to see the bride and turn their son's deception into a complicated affair.
VHS: S21895. $94.98.
Ang Lee, USA/Taiwan, 1994, 105 mins.

gay & lesbian cinema

27 Pieces of Me

In this bold, independent feature, Tanya (Tina M. Henning), a lesbian sculptor, is forced to confront her sister Ramona (Angelique von Halle) when she arrives on her doorstep unannounced. Both women have been having relationship troubles. Fortunately, Tanya's roommate Bold (Jonathan Harris) helps the two women begin a rapprochement that they desperately need and want.

VHS: S27479. $39.95.

Gerald Donohoe, USA, 1995, 90 mins.

The 28th Instance of June 1914, 10:50 AM

David McDermott and Peter McGough live in another era though contemporary Manhattan surrounds them. The early 20th and late 19th centuries inspire both their art and the way they live. Without electricity or the basics of modern plumbing, they contend with chamber pots and oil lamps. This documentary shows the homoerotic past they create in their work, and the singular lifestyle they pursue together. Quentin Crisp makes an appearance.

VHS: S27082. $29.95.

Barbara Politsch, USA, 1994, 56 mins.

A.I.D.S.C.R.E.A.M., Ecce Homo and Final Solutions

Three short experimental films by gay filmmaker Jerry Tartaglia are joined on this video. Along with *A.I.D.S.C.R.E.A.M.*, *Ecce Homo* and *Final Solutions* explore fear, rage, the anti-sex and anti-gay movements and the rise of AIDS consumerism. It's an angry, arrogant and unapologetic collection.

VHS: S27222. $59.95.

Abuse

A young boy, abused by his parents, finally discovers some much needed emotional gratification when he becomes the focus of a documentary about abuse. He becomes close to the gay man directing this film. Shot in a documentary style, this film raises tough questions about the nature of intimacy between an adult man and a 14-year-old boy.

VHS: S28068. $79.95.

Arthur J. Bressan, USA, 1995, 93 mins.

Acla's Descent into Floristella

Sold into servitude by his parents, 12-year-old Acla must work underground in sulfur mines. Repeatedly beaten by his owner, the threat of sexual abuse is also ever-present. When he runs away, there are dire consequences for both him and his family. The story is based on the social mores and disturbing sexual practices found in 1930's Sicily. Italian with English subtitles.

VHS: S21544. $69.95.

Aurelio Grimaldi, Italy, 1987, 86 mins.

The Adventures of Priscilla, Queen of the Desert

Terence Stamp returns to the screen in this unlikely farce about three drag queens racing across the Australian outback in order to put on a show. Of course there is more to this film than unbelievably elaborate costumes, campily choreographed lip sync numbers and gay humor. It also tries to say something about love. Great disco numbers from ABBA, Gloria Gaynor, The Village People and Peaches and Herb.

VHS: S24030. $19.95.
DVD: DV60010. $29.95.

Stephen Elliott, Australia, 1994, 102 mins.

All God's Children

This documentary shows how the Black Church has embraced African-American lesbians and gay men as dedicated members of its spiritual family. Prominent religious, intellectual and political leaders, family members, and activists speak out about the role of the church and the importance of commitment to equal rights and social justice for all people.

VHS: S34404. $69.95.

Dr. Dee Mosbacher/Frances Reid/Dr. Sylvia Rhue, USA, 1996, 26 mins.

All of Me

Georgette Dee, the famed transvestite cabaret star from Germany, stars as Orlanda. On a concert tour, Orlanda and his/her wife Elisabeth both fall for the same Polish man. This scenario makes for a witty film, and the musical numbers, particularly the title tune, are terrific. German with English subtitles.

VHS: S26867. $39.95.

Bettina Wilhelm, Germany, 1990, 76 mins.

All Women Are Equal & Pentagon Peace March

A pre-operational transsexual explains her values and beliefs in this insightful study of sexual identity by Marguerite Paris. Then Paris offers an impressionistic view of a 1967 anti-war demonstration. The 8mm originals of these works were transformed by optical printing.

VHS: S27223. $59.95.

Marguerite Paris, USA

The Alley Cats

When Leslie, a member of Europe's wealthy, young swinging set, feels ignored by her fiancee, Logan (who is in the midst of a tempestuous affair with Leslie's best friend, Agnes), she decides to do some swinging herself. Her first lover, the suave, debonair Christian, pleases her, but is called away on business. Frustrated, Leslie responds to the advances of Irena, a beautiful lesbian socialite. Soon she must choose between fiancee Logan and her awakening lesbian feelings.

VHS: S32677. $29.95.

Radley Metzger, USA, 1966, 83 mins.

Amazing Grace

A dramatic story is told in this film about the friendship between 18-year-old Jonathon and 30-year-old Thomas. Jonathon places all his hope for happiness in Thomas, who is HIV positive. Winner of the Wolgin Prize at the 1992 Jerusalem Film Festival and Best Film at Turin's Eighth International Gay-Themed Film Festival. Hebrew with English subtitles.

VHS: S22671. $79.95.

Amos Guttman, Israel, 1992, 95 mins.

Amazing World

Two girls, one car, one killer. Vampire babies attack Vegas. Image of Jesus burnt into toaster. You've got to see it to believe it, as queer tabloid reporters Bing and Nico encounter pyromaniacs, brides of Satan, UFO abductees and mutual lust. When Baskir, a mysterious psychic back from the grave, leads them to the bodies of several murdered women, our intrepid girls step into the ring with a killer. Sarcastic, sexy, smart and suspenseful, this is not your mother's lesbian movie. Exploding with music by Seattle bands. "Fun! Frolicking! Delicious dialogue! A romp!" (Nicole Conn).

VHS: S32676. $29.95.

Denise Ohio, USA, 1997, 96 mins.

And the Band Played On

Based on the influential book of the same name, this star-studded adaptation brings author Randy Shilts's story on the first decade of the AIDS crisis to the screen. Alan Alda, Richard Gere, Anjelica Huston, Steve Martin, Sir Ian McKellen and Lily Tomlin all appear in prominent roles with Matthew Modine starring as the doctor who would stop an epidemic.

VHS: S20872. $19.98.

Roger Spottiswoode, USA, 1993, 140 mins.

Apart from Hugh

Collin and Hugh have been together for one year. A party commemorating this anniversary forces Collin to reconsider his feelings about their relationship. Commitment, growth and above all, love, are the buzzwords in the air as these two men struggle with their feelings for each other.

VHS: S27613. $39.95.

Jon FitzGerald, USA, 1994, 87 mins.

Armistead Maupin's Tales of the City

The BBC funded this film realization of Maupin's acclaimed series of books. Set in 1970's San Francisco, it captures the heady mix of sexual politics and sheer fun that characterized that time and place. Olympia Dukakis is at the center of an ever more complicated plot that comes to involve a whole group of characters searching for their own Atlantis. Complete Set. Great Britain/USA, 1993, 360 mins.

VHS: S20873. $59.95.

Around the World the Lesbian Way

Features five excellent lesbian subject films: Kelli Simpson's *This Marching Girl Thing* (19 mins.), from Australia, starring Toni Collette and Matt Day (*Muriel's Wedding*); Katrin Barben's *Casting* (20 mins.), from Germany, an edgy erotic film, as well as Barben's *Go Girl* (7 mins.), from Switzerland, a light-hearted look at the potential girl of your dreams; Shawna Dempsey's and Lorri Millan's *A Day in the Life of a Bull Dyke* (20 mins.), from Canada, a delightful comedy-drama; and from Scotland, Steven Rimkus' poignant and romantic *Dancing* (22 mins.), with film star Sylvia Sims, recalling a passionate love affair in her youth.

VHS: S32041. $29.95.

Kelli Simpson/Katrin Barben/Shawna Dempsey/Lorri Millan/Steven Rimkus, Australia/Germany/Switzerland/Canada/Scotland, 1995, 88 mins.

The Art of Cruising Men

From the creators of *Max Headroom* comes England's best-selling gay video of all time. This streetwise "video sex guide for the 21st century" traces how men cruise men from prehistoric times to the hedonistic clubs of the '90s. "One of the best gay videos on sale" (*The Pink Paper*). "Great...one brilliant, funny and well-produced video" (*QX Magazine*).

VHS: S30149. $39.95.

Peter Litten, Great Britain, 1995, 70 mins.

As Is

When a talented writer discovers he has AIDS he turns his anger into a zest for life because of the love and loyalty of his ex-lover and friends. With Robert Carradine, Jonathan Hadary and Colleen Dewhurst.

VHS: S03289. $19.98.

Michael Lindsay-Hogg, USA, 1986, 85 mins.

The Athena Award 1996

A collection of films awarded the Athena, sponsored by Northern Arts/NAIAD Press, for independent filmmakers working in lesbian film and videomaking. Includes *but would you take her back?*, the question asked of seven very diverse lesbians in this winner of the Outstanding Achievement in Experimental Film by Judith Redding and Victoria Barnsworth; the poignant *Uncommon Ground*, one day in the life of two sisters, one a lesbian and the other her very disapproving, very straight sister, by Pamela Whyte; and *The Cowgirl Sweetbearts: A Dyke-U-Mentary*, hilarious onstage and offstage fun with a lovable lesbian band, by Beverly Buhr and Melissa Dopp. 53 mins.

VHS: S31360. $19.95.

Ballot Measure 9

This winner of the Special Jury Award at Sundance in 1995 follows the fight around Oregon's Ballot Measure 9. Essentially, the initiative would have denied lesbians and gay men civil rights protection. Though defeated, it was the center of acrimonious debate and tense standoffs. This documentary captures the heroic spirits of the people who stood up against bigotry, even under threat of physical harm.

VHS: S27476. $29.98.

Heather MacDonald, USA, 1995, 72 mins.

Bar Girls

Three women are at the center of a plot about love, desire and the travails of dating in lesbian Los Angeles. The circle grows to include other women, who in turn help and hinder the mating game with advice and miscommunication. It's a fun, honest film about love and romance, for people who understand the importance of relationships. Look for Chastity Bono's cameo on "Scorpio Night."

VHS: S26445. $19.95.
Laser: LD75084. $39.99.

Marita Giovanni, USA, 1995, 95 mins.

Beautiful Mystery

Shinohara is a young bodybuilder who joins a para-military sect in Northern Japan. Amidst the discipline and rigor of the group, his instructor, Takizawa, develops a special interest in this new recruit. Before long, they develop a special and loving relationship. Japanese with English subtitles.

VHS: S29952. $39.95.

Nakamura Genji, Japan, 1983, 60 mins.

The Best Defense, Vol. 1

Every lesbian and gay man could benefit from this demonstration video. It features self-defense that really works. Designed for the average person, it requires no formal training. Nine of the world's best lesbian and gay self-defense instructors show how to protect yourself from hate and ignorance in everyday situations. 50 mins.

VHS: S26817. $29.95.

The Best Way

Marc, the aggressive athletic director at a boys' summer camp, discovers the drama teacher dressed in women's clothes, and is shocked by his attraction to him. Their tense confrontation results in Marc forcing him to confront his suppressed sexuality. French with English subtitles.

VHS: S00120. $49.95.

Claude Miller, France, 1982, 85 mins.

The Black Glove

This visionary noir exercise examines and crosses the boundaries of dominance and submission in its artful escalation of pleasure and pain, bondage and menace, fetishism and foot worship, culminating in the hot wax torture of the slave's most private parts as she writhes in ecstacy.

VHS: S33324. $34.95.

Maria Beatty, USA, 1997, 30 mins.

Black Lizard

A hilarious caper movie written originally for the stage by Yukio Mishima; the plot concerns a female jewel thief who kidnaps nubile youths and ferries them to a glitzoid secret island. There she turns them into naked love statues—one of them bizarrely played by Mishima himself. Miss Lizard is portrayed by the transvestite actor Akihiro Miwa, who flounces around in an impossible collection of boas and chokers and turns every flourish of her cigarette holder into an over-the-top arabesque. Called "a tale of love, passion, greed and necrophilia" by the *New York Times*, and "Naughty Japanese noir. Like something by Almodovar or John Waters" (*Village Voice*). Japanese with English subtitles.

VHS: S16261. $79.95.
Kinji Fukasaku, Japan, 1968, 90 mins.

Black Sheep Boy and Decodings

This tape includes two shorts directed by Michael Wallin. The lyrical and voyeuristic *Black Sheep Boy* explores the sexual thrill and emotional obstacles inherent in fantasies of fetishized youth. Written by Stephen Beachy with music by Erik Walker. 37 mins. "*Black Sheep Boy* is one of the best shorts making the '95 gay film-fest circuit, having artistic links to experimental classics such as Jean Genet's *Un Chant d'Amour* and Kenneth Anger's *Fireworks*" (*San Francisco Weekly*). *Decodings* is "a profoundly moving, allegorical search for identity from the documents of collective memory, in this case, found footage from the '40s and '50s" (*The Village Voice*). "A magical, seamless work that manages to beguile even as it probes areas tender to the touch. Its tale is beautifully told" (*San Francisco Weekly*). "Explodes with Bunuel's sensuousness and a Hitchcockian narrative irony" (*LA Weekly*). 15 mins.

VHS: S30932. $39.95.
Michael Wallin, USA, 1995/1988, 55 mins.

Blue Jeans

A young boy is sent to England to improve his English, where he has his first experience with the opposite sex. When his girl friend takes up with a more experienced young man, the young boy confides in one of his supervisors and is taken advantage of. French with English subtitles.

VHS: S00158. $59.95.
Hugues des Roziers, France, 1978, 80 mins.

Body Without Soul

According to the filmmaker, Prague has become a feasting ground for sexual tourists looking for young men. These boys move from their small towns throughout Eastern Europe to the city in hope of making a better life for themselves working as hustlers and porno models. The film introduces us to a group of these young men, whose personal stories are told with unflinching honesty, providing a disturbing and graphic inside view of their exploitation, pain and pitiful existence. We also meet Pavel, a porn producer who exploits these young men.

VHS: S32628. $39.95.
Wiktor Grodecki, Czech Republic, 1996, 103 mins.

Bound

Pulp prince James M. Cain meets lesbian sexpert Susie Bright in this "sultry slice of noir gamesmanship that boasts clever twists, crackling flirtations, smart, assertive camerawork, and a believable, sensual, sexual relationship between two women" (*Chicago Reader*) by the Wachowski Brothers. A mobster (Joe Pantoliano), his mistress (Jennifer Tilly) and a tough, female ex-con (Gina Gershon) are caught in a dangerous plot starting with $2 million of the Mob's money and ending in seduction and betrayal. "Sleek!" (Janet Maslin, *New York Times*).

VHS: S30825. $14.95.
Laser: LD76078. $34.98.
Andy Wachowski/Larry Wachowski, USA, 1996, 108 mins.

Box of Laughter: The Dueling Pages

Part one of a three-part series highlighting the fetish of tickling. In this episode, two best friends share their love of pinup idol Betty Page, lingerie, bondage and tickling.

VHS: S33325. $39.95.
Maria Beatty, USA, 1998, 40 mins.

Boy's Life

A compilation of three short films, *Pool Days, A Friend of Dorothy* and *The Disco Years*, offers differing bittersweet and humorous accounts of growing up gay. In each the pain of coming out is tempered by the joys of gay life. 90 mins.

VHS: S26670. $59.95.

Boyfriends

Three gay male couples, each at varying stages of couplehood, converge on a beautiful English country house for a supposedly relaxing Easter weekend. What ensues is a witty exploration of gay relationships in the '90s. "A perceptive comedy of modern gay manners, with freewheeling sexual behavior" (*New York Times*).

VHS: S33224. $79.95.
Neil Hunter/Tom Hunsinger, USA, 1996, 82 mins.

Boys in Love

This collection of award-winning gay short films includes four worldwide festival favorites. *Death in Venice, CA* is the story of a repressed academic who is seduced by his landlady's stepson. The animated *Achilles*, by Academy Award-nominated animator Bary Purves, features Greek heroes and lovers Achilles and Petroclus as they battle the Trojans. *My Polish Waiter* focuses on a young man's infatuation with a silent, handsome waiter. In *Miguel, Ma Belle*, a recently spurned Latin man finds love again with the help of a dog. Together the films form a bold look at love and sex in the '90s. 83 mins.

VHS: S28484. $29.95.

Boys in the Band

The first really successful American film to openly deal with homosexuality, Boys in the Band is based on the enormously successful Broadway play by Matt Crowley. An adult, witty and, at times, touching depiction of gay life in the early days of gay liberation. The original nine actors who appeared in the Broadway production take their roles here on film, with exceptional acting by all, but particularly Cliff Gorman being ultra-queeny and Leonard Frey as the birthday boy.

VHS: S00176. $59.98.
William Friedkin, USA, 1975, 119 mins.

Boys' Shorts

This collection of six shorts tackles a variety of issues facing gay communities. AIDS, coming out, relationships, family and, of course, sex, are all explored. *The Dead Boy's Club, Relax, RSVP, Billy Turner's Secret, Resonance* and Marlon Riggs' *Anthem* are included in this video.

VHS: S22950. $39.95.
Christopher et al., USA, 1990-1992, 119 mins.

Breaking the Code

Mathematical genius Alan Turing (Derek Jacobi) designed the computer that cracked the German Enigma code and, quite possibly, won World War II. His admittance to homosexuality, however, at a time when it was illegal, created problems for him, his colleagues and national security. "A riveting, intelligent, provocative play" (Susan Granger, WMVA Radio). 90 mins.

VHS: S31008. $19.98.

Breaking the Surface: The Greg Louganis Story

Based on the best-selling book by four-time American gold medalist diver Greg Louganis. An intimate and unique father-and-son story, starring Mario Lopez (*Saved by the Bell*) as the diver, captured the hearts of Americans at the 1988 Summer Olympics, all the while harboring the secret that he was HIV-positive.

VHS: S31725. $59.95.
Steve Stern, USA, 1996, 95 mins.

Brother Sun, Sister Moon

Lavish costume epic depicts the story of St. Francis of Assisi, a man so gentle wild animals would eat from his hand, as he rejects the pomp of the Catholic Church. With some interesting characters working on this production, including Alec Guinness as the Pope, Lina Wertmuller in screenwriting capacity and 60's pop star Donovan supplying the music. English dialog.

VHS: S02623. $14.95.
Franco Zeffirelli, Italy/USA, 1973, 121 mins.

Bugis Street

The "alternately funny and gritty, wise and touching" (Kevin Thomas, *Los Angeles Times*) coming-of-age story of Lien, a wide-eyed 16-year-old girl (Hiep Thi Le, *Heaven and Earth*) who comes from a rural village to work in the Sing Sing Hotel, not knowing that the hotel is based in the heart of Singapore's red-light district and all the "female" residents are transvestites and transsexuals. Amid the colorful lives of the "girls," Lien discovers the secrets and pains of love, sexuality and womanhood from her new "sisters." "It's Snow White and the Seven Drag Queens" (Dennis Dermody, *Paper*). English and Cantonese with English subtitles.

VHS: S34318. $79.95.
Yonean, Singapore, 1994, 110 mins.

Butterflies on the Scaffold (Mariposas en el Andamio)

A rare documentary of a Havana suburb transformed by a group of beautiful and charismatic drag queens. The first and only "dragumentary" ever produced in Castro's Cuba, the journey moves from on-stage action and backstage preparation to insightful interviews with community leaders, the performers and their families. Spanish with English subtitles.

VHS: S33429. $39.95.
Margret Gilpin/Luis Felipe Bernaza, Cuba, 1995, 74 mins.

Can't Stop the Music

A lavish, gay-themed musical that looks at corruption inside the music-publishing industry. The topliners are the 70s act the Village People, each of whom falls madly in love with Valerie Perrine. "It follows that most of the dialogue is gay in-jokes, with the odd music business joke for variety" (*Time Out*). "YMCA" and "Macho Man" are highlights. With Steve Guttenberg, Tammy Grimes, June Havoc and Barbara Rush.

VHS: S20417. $14.98.
Nancy Walker, USA, 1980, 119 mins.

The Castro

Known internationally as the world's first "gay hometown," San Francisco's Castro district was a quiet, working-class neighborhood of European immigrants only a few decades ago. In this moving documentary, filled with rare archival film and fresh contemporary footage, the story of the Castro's transformation is told by those who lived it, young and old, straight and gay. "Traces 30 years of alternating progress, backlash, flamboyance, joy and heartbreak... with reportorial honesty, a sense of balance, a capacity for compressed storytelling and an appreciation for nuance" (*San Francisco Chronicle*).

VHS: S32065. $29.95.
Peter L. Stein, USA, 1997, 86 mins.

Caught Looking & North of Vortex

These two short films cannily explore issues of homoerotic desire. *Caught Looking* features an interactive computer sex fantasy that samples different styles of erotic experiences. n *North of Vortex* two men and a woman drive across the U.S. in search of adventure.

VHS: S20581. $29.95.
Constantine Giannaris, Great Britain, 93 mins.

The Celluloid Closet

Lily Tomlin, Shirley MacLaine, Tony Curtis, Susan Sarandon, Tom Hanks, Whoopi Goldberg and others provide the commentary to entertaining clips from over 120 films as we learn all the secrets and hear all the stories in this compilation of the history of homosexuality in Hollywood movies. A fun romp with some amazing pre-Breen-code early footage. "An indispensable addition to the history of Hollywood, with the popular appeal of *That's Entertainment*" (Janet Maslin, *New York Times*).

VHS: S30403. $19.95.
Laser: LD76027. $39.95.
Rob Epstein/Jeffrey Friedman, USA, 1996, 102 mins.

Chained Girls

Who and what is a lesbian? Where can they be found? Are they happy with their lives? These are a few of the probing questions asked in this "expose" of New York City lesbians. You'll be fascinated to know that lesbians get married, have cat fights over their femmes, and even initiate young debs into the Daughters of Lesbos. Very rare sleaze from the 60's.

VHS: S23055. $19.98.
Joseph P. Mawra, USA, 1965, 80 mins.

Change the Frame

Angela is a college graduate who has put her life on hold waiting for her girlfriend, Rachel, to finish grad school. Meanwhile, Rachel is too absorbed in school to realize Angela has become frustrated with her life and their relationship. Before long a hot dyke singer from San Francisco becomes the catalyst for a classic love triangle with a lesbian twist.

VHS: S34975. $27.95.
Christina Rey, USA, 1995, 92 mins.

Claire of the Moon

Nicole Conn's pioneering lesbian drama. Claire Jobrowski is a carefree, sexually adventurous novelist who shares a cabin with the stern, rigid Doctor Noel Benedict, who specializes in sexual behavior. They're brought together for a writer's workshop in the Pacific Northwest. "An encouraging debut film about love between adults" (*L.A. Weekly*). With Trisha Todd, Karen Trumbo and Caren Graham.

VHS: S19102. $29.98.
Nicole Conn, USA, 1992, 102 mins.

Classic Foreign Shorts—Volume 3: Un Chant d'Amour, Romance Sentimentale

Un Chant d'Amour is Jean Genet's only film, a legendary and long suppressed film masterpiece. "A song of man's love soaring above the sexual ghetto of prison and non-existence" (*Cahiers du Cinema*). 20 mins. *Romance Sentimentale* is usually attributed to Sergei Eisenstein, and although Eisenstein worked on it, it was probably directed by Grigori Alexandrov. Photographed by Tisse and financed by its only player—a wealthy woman who wanted to appear in an Eisenstein film-*Romance Sentimentale* was filmed in Paris during the winter of 1929-30. The film is a somber experimental poem portraying the emotions aroused in a woman (Mara Gitry) by the realization that love is dead. 20 mins.

VHS: S26947. $29.95.

Clay Farmers

A farmhand named Dan forms a close friendship with a handsome young drifter hired by an absentee landowner. Their friendship is tested when they are seen together bathing in the nude at a swimming hole. What exactly do they feel for one another? Also includes *My First Suit*, a hilarious short from New Zealand about a wistful teenager.
VHS: S21321. $69.95.
A.P. Gonzalez, USA, 1989, 90 mins.

Colegas

From the director of *El Diputado*, the story of three friends and their transition into adulthood. A crisis comes about when one of the friends becomes pregnant, and the youths resort to street hustling to raise the funds to solve the problem. Spanish with English subtitles.
VHS: S01562. $89.95.
Eloy de la Iglesia, Spain, 117 mins.

Coming Out Is a Many Splendored Thing

Debbi Daliege's comedy video premieres with clever segmented stories that cover all those "coming out" issues. These bits and pieces are a hilarious exploration of whimsical "coming-out" adventures. Remember and laugh. 35 mins.
VHS: S21123. $24.98.

Coming Out Under Fire

This winner of the Special Jury Award at the 1994 Sundance Film Festival tells the story of nine lesbians and gay male veterans of the U.S. military. Based on Alan Berube's book of the same name, this film fleshes out this often misunderstood case of grave social injustice, using declassified documents, rare archival footage, interviews, photographs and more, and touches on the World War II origins of the current "don't ask, don't tell" policy. B&W.
VHS: S26966. $29.98.
Arthur Dong, USA, 1994, 71 mins.

Creation of Adam

Andrey is a young man who fears his marriage may fall apart because his wife thinks he is gay. A series of events confirm these suspicions as Andrey meets Philip, an enterprising business man who turns his life around. Philip shows Andrey how to love. Russian with English subtitles.
VHS: S26405. $39.95.
Yuri Pavlov, Russia, 1993, 93 mins.

Crocodiles in Amsterdam

Described as a "slapstick female buddy movie," this Dutch feature stars two friends, Gino and Nina. Though thoroughly different, they manage to wrest friendship from the most inauspicious situations. Nina's rebelliousness and Gino's frivolity place them at each other's mercy, and often in hilarious situations. Dutch with English subtitles.
VHS: S26937. $39.95.
Annette Apon, Netherlands, 1990, 88 mins.

Curse of the Queerwolf

Lawrence Smalbut and Richard Cheese are just average macho guys who court disaster when they pick up two mysterious women. Just as Smalbut realizes that his date is no lady, she/he bites him on the derriere and forever transforms his life. Now when the moon is full, Smalbut finds himself magically transformed into "Queerwolf," a drag queen werewolf. It's a campy horror romp in questionable taste.
VHS: S27659. $14.95.
Mark Pirro, USA, 1994, 90 mins.

Cynara

Described by its maker as "a lesbian *Wuthering Heights*," this video brings the homoerotic tensions inherent in many gothic works out into view. Johanna Nemeth and Melissa Nazila star as the sexy and attractive lovers. From the director of *Claire of the Moon*.
VHS: S29784. $29.95.
Nicole Conn, USA, 1996, 35 mins.

Daddy and the Muscle Academy: A Documentary on the Art, Life and Times of Tom of Finland

Tom of Finland was a pioneering gay pornographer whose classic *Ultimate Leather Men* veers between the erotic and the absurd. "A second film will probably be necessary to complete what are here the beginnings of connected discussions concerning the implications of fascistic attractions, fetish-racism, and other generated identity" (David Overbey). English and Finnish with English subtitles.
VHS: S19525. $49.95.
Ilppo Pohjola, Finland, 1991, 55 mins.

Days of Pentecost

"Totally blowing away the Richter scale of camp" (*Lesbian & Gay New York*), this black-and-Latino cross-dressing musical comedy remake of cult classic *Faster Pussycat! Kill! Kill!* is a drag paean to Russ Meyer's vision of rampaging go-go dancers looking for kicks in the California desert. Non-stop fun with fakey fight sequences, cheezy sound effects and a funky soundtrack by Mario Gardner, the L.A. performance artist who also makes his cinematic debut as the film's lead diva, Melena D'L' Moja. With Marcus Kuiland-Nazario, Andre Pearson and Alexis Arquette. "A low-budget film that just might give *To Wong Foo* a run for its cleavage" (*Bay Area Reporter*).
VHS: S31017. $49.99.
Lawrence Elbert, USA, 1995, 85 mins.

The Dear Boys

A harsh, stylized and feverish piece about dark sexual fantasies and deep romantic longing, the film concerns the romantic and sexual entanglements of a morose, self-absorbed writer and an uninhibited, carefree young man who recklessly pursues thrills and excitement. This groundbreaking, unapologetically gay work is adapted from Gerard Reve's novel. With Hugo Netsers, Hans Dagelet, Bill Van Dijk, and Albert Mol.
VHS: S17444. $69.95.
Paul de Lussanet, Netherlands, 1980, 90 mins.

The Delta

A poignantly twisted take on Huckleberry Finn in which a 17-year-old "straight" boy meets the poor Vietnamese son of an American GI, and the two take a lover's ride down the Mississippi. Voted one of the year's ten best by *Bay Area Reporter, LA Weekly, Sight and Sound* and *NY Press*.
VHS: S34859. $59.95.
Ira Sachs, USA, 1996, 85 mins.

Desert Hearts

Wonderful love story between a repressed English professor who is waiting for a divorce at a dude ranch for women, and a beautiful casino worker in Reno who lives at the ranch with her mother. Adapted from the novel *Desert of the Heart*, by Jane Rule, with a fabulous soundtrack!
VHS: S01919. $19.98.
Laser: LD75919. $39.99.
Donna Deitch, USA, 1985, 96 mins.

Desire

Director Stuart Marshall chronicles the events leading to a crucial chapter in the gay and lesbian movement's history: the imprisonment of homosexuals in Nazi concentration camps during World War II. His film examines the "discovery" of homosexuality by the medical and psychoanalytic professions in the 1890s, and the subsequent movements in Germany during the early years of this century demanding recognition of gay and lesbian rights.
VHS: S16632. $29.95.
Stuart Marshall, Great Britain, 1989, 88 mins.

Desire: An Erotic Fantasy Play

Three good-looking, sexy and interesting women form a romantic triangle in this unique lesbian work. It's a skillfully accomplished video where open expressions of sexuality are handled with as much frankness as passion. "A hot lesbian video!" (*Deneuve Magazine*).
VHS: S27234. $49.95.
Janice Kroesen, USA, 1995, 79 mins.

Devotion

This touching and emotional lesbian love story is based on the book of the same name. A comic and her long-term, live-in lover share everything. It's a passionate film filled with humor and warmth.
VHS: S26945. $69.95.
Mindy Kaplan, USA, 1995, 124 mins.

Different Strokes

Dana Plato (TV's *Diff'rent Strokes*) bares all in this controversial lesbian drama. Jack (Bentley Mitchum) is a successful fashion photographer living in the Hollywood Hills and dating Jill (Landon Hall), a woman whose beauty rivals any of his models. Jack seems to have it all until Jill (Plato), an attractive New York art dealer, enters their lives and opens up new sexual possibilities for the other Jill that will turn Jack's idyllic life upside down.
VHS: S33009. $59.95.
Michael Paul Girard, USA, 1996, 87 mins.

Dominique in "Daughters of Lesbos"

Oversexed women bare it all as they pursue sapphic pleasures in a hothouse of emotion. Their club, known as the New York City Man Haters Society, is not a group to be trifled with. One outrageous peeping tom learns this lesson when he seduces a lesbian by slipping her a mickey. He quickly finds out that a lesbian's vengeance can be swift like a knife. With Claudia Cheer, Jo Sweet, Sue Akers and Carla Costa.
VHS: S27675. $19.98.
Peter Woodcock, USA, 1967, 65 mins.

The Doom Generation

From the maker of *The Living End* comes another installment of violence and sex cooled by stereotypical generation X elan. Two kids meet up with a bleeding dude and set off to terrorize the motorized world. A stop at a convenience store leaves a talking head without its body and a bizarre family murder/suicide, so the three main characters go on the run and all have sex with each other. Can they evade the gang of skinheads?
VHS: S27521. $14.95.
Gregg Araki, USA, 1995, 83 mins.

Dos Fallopia: Pretty Girls, Not Too Bright

Seattle zanies Dos Fallopia (Lisa Koch and Peggy Platt) serve up a stew of hysterical and dysfunctional characters in this debut video. Shot from live performances, the duo brings their hilarious sketch comedy and music through their twisted alter egos. "Seattle's reigning queens of sketch comedy" (*Seattle Gay News*).
VHS: S30423. $19.95.

Dream Boys Revue

Ruth Buzzi and Lyle Waggoner host a talent and beauty contest where all the good looking women are men. Lip-synched versions of Ann-Margret, Liza, Bette Davis, Marilyn Monroe and Barbra Streisand all compete for a crown at this alternative competition held in Texas.
VHS: S03950. $19.95.
Howard Schwartz/John Moriarty, USA, 1985, 74 mins.

Dreamers of the Day

Andra, a writer and filmmaker seemingly in charge of her passion for women, is thrown off course by the appearance of Claire. In this romantic comedy, all the careful plans defining Andra's current project vanish amidst a whirlwind of humor and desire.
VHS: S26971. $39.98.
Patricia Spencer, Canada, 1992, 94 mins.

Drifting

Controversial Israeli film called "The best gay film ever made," winner of Israeli Oscars for Best Director, Best Actor and Best Cinematography. Hebrew with English subtitles.
VHS: S00376. $69.95.
Amos Guttman, Israel, 1982, 80 mins.

Dyke Drama

A compilation of four short lesbian stories. *IFE* (H. Len Keller, 5 mins.) is about a lesbian who vows never to fall in love. In *Maya* (Catherine Benedeck, 10 mins.) therapy money is spent for dance lessons and Maya learns more than the cha-cha. *Things We Said Today* (John Miller-Monzon, 34 mins.) is a vaudevillian romantic comedy about surviving relationships and New York's seamy underside. *A Certain Grace* (Sandra Nettlebeck, 40 mins.) causes Zelda to choose between the safety and comfort of her relationship with Tom and the passion she finds with Alice during a photo shoot. 89 mins.
VHS: S29987. $29.95.

An Early Frost

The landmark 1985 Emmy and Peabody Award-winning drama about one family's struggle with the news their son (Aidan Quinn) is gay and has AIDS. With Gena Rowlands, Ben Gazzara, Sylvia Sidney and John Glover.
VHS: S30446. $19.95.
John Erman, USA, 1985, 120 mins.

El Diputado

A political thriller about a gay man high in the ranks of the Spanish Socialist Party whose love affair with a 16-year-old boy jeopardizes the fate of the nation. The Advocate said the gay love scenes are among the best ever presented in a commercial film. Spanish with English subtitles.
VHS: S00397. $79.95.
Eloy de la Iglesia, Spain, 1983, 111 mins.

El Sacerdote (The Priest)

An early work by Eloy de la Iglesia, this is the shocking story of a troubled priest fighting for his own soul. Father Miguel fights physical and psychic fantasies of sex and suffers from painful memories of a bizarre childhood. Banned at the time of its original release. Spanish with English subtitles.
VHS: S23576. $79.95.
Eloy de la Iglesia, Spain, 1979, 62 mins.

Empty Bed

John Wylie plays Bill Frayne, a gay man in his sixties who reflects on his younger days, the choices he has made, and the prospect of an empty bed. He lives alone, having been unable to commit himself to a relationship because of a variety of social and personal pressures. Told mostly through flashbacks, this film is a time tapestry where past and present weave together to form a poignant picture of his life.

VHS: S14155. $29.95.
Mark Gasper, USA, 1990, 60 mins.

Ernesto

A lushly mounted, sensitively directed, complex depiction of homosexuality with Martin Halm as the boy who cooly tries anything and Michele Placido as the older, seducing man. "Genuinely erotic...*Ernesto* reconciles the legacies of Pasolini and Fassbinder." Italian with English subtitles.

VHS: S00416. $49.95.
Salvatore Samperi, Italy, 1983, 98 mins.

Erotikus: History of the Gay Movies

Specifically, the history of the male gay film, from early films of posed muscle-boys, through the early films featuring male nudity to the hard-core films of the recent period. Narrated by Fred Halsted. 54 mins.

VHS: S02168. $29.95.

Et L'Amour

This poetic vignette features two women engaged in a sensuous and tasteful erotic interlude. There is no dialog. 24 mins.

VHS: S27449. $24.95.

Even Cowgirls Get the Blues

Uma Thurman, Rain Phoenix, Lorraine Bracco and William Hurt star in this adaptation of Tom Robbins' best-selling novel. Gus Van Sant, director of *Drugstore Cowboy* and *My Own Private Idaho*, brings his remarkable visual style to this high camp road movie set in the early 1970's, about a hitchhiker, free love and lesbian passion. Also features Angie Dickinson, Keanu Reeves, Roseanne Arnold, Crispin Glover, Sean Young and Buck Henry. Music by k.d. lang.

VHS: S22383. $19.95.
Gus Van Sant, USA, 1994, 96 mins.

Everything Relative

An eye-opening romantic comedy about a reunited group of women who went to college together. The smart, sassy ensemble cast exchange quick-witted repartee which reveals, with irony, humor and a touch of nostalgia for the '70s, how their lives, their politics and their loves have changed. Think of it as a gay *The Big Chill* or a lesbian *Love! Valour! Compassion!* With Harvey Fierstein.

VHS: S32611. $94.98.
Sharon Pollack, USA, 1997, 105 mins.

Extramuros

Carmen Maura, famed for her riveting portrayals in *Women on the Verge of a Nervous Breakdown* and *Law of Desire*, plays a nun who is challenged by her irrepressible lesbian desires. Set in a convent during the Spanish Inquisition, the film is not only a depiction of repressed passion, but a sharply critical look at the relationship between the Church and political power as the convent vies for fame and money through the faked visions and stigmata of the lesbian sisters. Spanish with English subtitles.

VHS: S24033. $39.95.
Miguel Picazo, Spain, 1985, 120 mins.

The Families We Choose

Four lesbian families are shown in this sensitive and informative tape about the families that we choose. These portraits answer key questions about modern life and point to a whole range of inclusive and accommodating family values. 45 mins.

VHS: S25537. $24.95.

Fanci's Persuasion

The night before Fanci's wedding to her girlfriend Loretta, a spell settles upon San Francisco, catapulting them into a tantalizing dream world where magic takes precedent over reality. "Polysexual screwball farce...a self-contained gay punk boho universe...over the top" (*Variety*).

VHS: S31615. $39.95.
Charles Herman-Wurmfeld, USA, 1995, 112 mins.

Female Misbehavior

Monika Treut's kinky exploration of nonconformist women combines two older short films, *Bondage* (1983), about a sadomasochistic lesbian, and *Annie* (1989), a portrait of former porno star Annie Sprinkle, with two recent documentaries, *Dr. Paglia* and *Max*. The former is a witty send-up of controversial academic Camille Paglia; the latter, a look at a lesbianNative American that shows her transsexual change from woman to man. "Treut is a sexual-political provocateur who in her explorations of the sexual fringe takes us where few filmmakers visit" (*New York Post*).

VHS: S19558. $29.95.
Monika Treut, Germany/USA, 1992, 80 mins.

Female Perversions

Eve Stephens (Tilda Swinton), a beautiful and sexy, high-powered attorney, is up for an appointment as a judge. But below her veneer of self-confidence lies a darker side, one in which she is driven by bizarre visions and sexual fantasies. After a series of events, including rescuing her sister Madelyn (Amy Madigan) after her arrest for shoplifting, being rejected by her lover, John (Clancy Brown), during a surprise visit, and finally meeting with the Governor regarding her judicial appointment, Eve comes unraveled.

VHS: S33316. $99.99.
Susan Streitfeld, Germany/USA, 1996, 114 mins.

Fertile La Toyah Jackson Video Magazine: The Kinky Issue!

Fertile La Toyah Jackson is the perfect transy host for this look at a darker, and infinitely more interesting, side of L.A. glamour. It's violent and obscene, and also features appearances by Karen Black, Raquel Welch, Faye Dunaway, Billy Idol, Vaginal Davis, Jean-Paul Gaultier, Peter Berlin, Joe Delassandro and other personalities. Jackson is the only video idol with a black dildo atop her head! 50 mins.

VHS: S29001. $39.95.

Fiction and Other Truths: A Film About Jane Rule

Jane Rule has written lesbian fiction that has touched countless women, including the classic *Desert of the Heart*, the inspiration for the film *Desert Hearts*. This film explores the author behind the books and features interviews with Helen, her lover of over 40 years. In addition, their political work and their dreams—in short, the essence of their lives—stand revealed in this insightful documentary. Produced by the National Film Board of Canada.

VHS: S27227. $59.95.
Lynne Fernie/Aerlyn Weissman, Canada, 1995, 57 mins.

Finished

Director William Jones' obsession with porn star Alan Lambert and his inexplicable suicide at 25 sparked this "audacious and compelling" investigation into his death and the gay porn industry. Official Selection, Sundance 1997, Best Experimental/Independent Film, Los Angeles Film Critics Association.

VHS: S34628. $39.95.
William Jones, USA, 1997, 75 mins.

Flaming Creatures

Jack Smith's groundbreaking, lyrical queer film is being released in a special limited-edition series to raise funds that will help restore and preserve his other works. This classic may seem tame by current standards, but its great camp style stands the test of time.

VHS: S27242. $195.00.
Jack Smith, USA

Flaming Ears

This edgy, sci-fi lesbian fantasy follows the lives of three women: a comic book artist, a performance artist/pyromaniac and and amoral alien who likes lizards. In this cyberdyke movie, love and revenge vie for supremacy amidst violence and ennui in an anti-romantic plea for love of all kinds. German with English subtitles.

VHS: S26936. $39.95.
Angela Hans Sheirl/Ursula Purrer/Dietmar Schipek, Austria, 1991, 84 mins.

The Flavor of Corn

Lorenzo is a handsome, first-year professor with a quiet demeanor. He brings a passion for teaching to his young charges in a small village. As his relationship with his girlfriend deteriorates, he finds himself spending more time with 12-year-old Duilio. Soon Duilio's stepmother is questioning the nature of this amorous friendship. Italian with English subtitles.

VHS: S21545. $69.95.
Gianni Da Campo, Italy, 1994, 89 mins.

Flickers

Theatrical trailers from some of the most intriguing gay-themed films are collected into this feature presentation. *Caligula, Sebastiane, Prick Up Your Ears, My Beautiful Launderette, Cabaret, Nijinsky, The Ritz, The Gay Deceivers* and other classic film previews offer surprising entertainment. 91 mins.

VHS: S27611. $24.95.

Flow

This mind-blowing exploration of culture, race and sexuality in the '90s is a stylish and energetic compilation of short stories, including a postmodern slasher flick with a knife-wielding drag queen, an impressionistic film noir about a young man who kills his mother on Christmas day, a surrealistic tale of a vampire couple and the story of the trials and errors in romance and relationships of two freshmen—one gay and one straight. Binding these shorts together is a witty mockumentary about the fictional filmmaker of these films, his struggles as an independent filmmaker and his love for rice and boys.

VHS: S31791. $39.95.
Quentin Lee, USA, 1995, 80 mins.

For a Lost Soldier

This haunting, true story follows a boy's wartime sexual awakening. It's controversial because this 12-year-old falls in love with a Canadian soldier who is in Holland just at the end of World War II. Ballet star Rudi van Danzig recreates this memory from his childhood to show how a boy falls in love with his handsome liberator. Dutch with English subtitles.

VHS: S21831. $19.98.
Roeland Kerbosch, Netherlands, 1993, 95 mins.

Forbidden Love: The Unashamed Stories of Lesbian Lives

Tales of lesbian love were luridly exposed in pulp novels of the 1950's. This film mixes documentary footage that shows how important these stories were to lesbians with its own scripted torrid romance. It's a campy homage to the works of fiction that delved into the underworld of 1950's lesbian passion.

VHS: S22054. $69.95.
Aerlyn Weissman, Canada, 1992, 84 mins.

Four Directions: Selections from MIX 94—The NY Lesbian & Gay Film Festival

Four lesbian and gay experimental shorts from the innovative New York-based film festival are joined together on this single video. From desire to politics, these shorts express a wide stylistic and thematic range. Included are *Me and Joe* by Stuart Sherman, *Smoke* by Liz Camps, *Virus* by Stuart Gaffney and *Feeling Anything Being Existing* by Liz Tevaarwerk.

VHS: S27228. $59.95.

Fun Down There

Buddy is a young man living with his very ordinary family in upstate New York. Up till now his only source of sexual gratification has been between the covers of *Playgirl* Magazine. Buddy soon leaves the small town and heads off to New York City; during his first week in the East Village Buddy finds a new job, new friends, (safe) sexual adventure and, perhaps, the beginnings of romance.

VHS: S13508. $29.95.
Roger Stigliano, USA, 1988, 89 mins.

Gay Deceivers

Spoof in which two hunks try to avoid the draft by claiming to be homosexuals. They move into a gay apartment complex and the fun begins.

VHS: S02221. $59.95.
Bruce Kessler, USA, 1968, 97 mins.

Gay for a Day

Three documentaries from Tom Palazzolo dealing with gay issues: *Gay for a Day* is the story of the 1976 Gay Pride Parade; *Costumes on Review* is a hilarious documentary of a gay Halloween party.

VHS: S06112. $39.95.
Tom Palazzolo, USA, 45 mins.

Gay Games IV from A to Q

Highlights include *In the Life* coverage from the Opening Ceremonies as well as *Dyke TV & Network Q* footage showing hunks competing for gold. *Gay Entertainment Television* provides a view of the history and the organization behind the games while *Gay Cable Network* shows the closing ceremonies of this historic event. 60 mins.

VHS: S21702. $24.95.

Gay Gay Hollywood

Stars in drag, gay films, gay murders and eight decades of decadence. In the tradition of *The Celluloid Closet*, the closet door swings wide open to explore the sexual orientation of Hollywood's biggest stars, including Cary Grant, Rock Hudson, Montgomery Clift and more.

VHS: S34875. $39.95.

Gay Youth

Esteemed director Pam Walton shows how information, acceptance and support can make an enormous difference in the lives of young people. 40 mins.

VHS: S31215. $39.95.

Georgia Ragsdale: Honey, Pass That Around

Stand-up comedian Georgia Ragsdale riffs on her resemblance to Jackie O, gay bar behavior, fashion faux pas and movie takeoffs. "Puts a bright, intelligent, witty face on gay comedy" (*Backstage*). 40 mins.

VHS: S31732. $19.95.

Girl Friends

This first-ever theatrical anthology of lesbian short films is an "explosively funny, unstoppably entertaining" (*NY Native*) collection of four films by energetic, inventive American filmmmakers reflecting lesbian life close to home or in the realm of fantasy. Shorts include: *Watching Her Sleep* (Barbara Rose Michaels, 1995, 7 mins.); *Little Women in Transit* (Barbara Heller, 1995, 7 mins.); *Playing the Part* (Mitch McCabe, 1994, 38 mins.) and *Carmelita Tropicana: Your Kunst Is Waffen* (Ela Troyano, 1994, 28 mins.). "Girlfriends is a gas—an entertaining anthology brimming over with quirky observational humor, intriguing stylistic tricks and warm, engaging, three-dimensional characters you haven't seen before onscreen" (Matt Zoller Seitz, *NY Press*).

VHS: S30246. $29.95.

USA, 1994-95, 80 mins.

Go Fish

A beguiling and charming look at the lives and loves of a small group of lesbian women in Chicago. Friends play matchmaker to bring together two very different women: Max, a beautiful, gregarious writer, and Ely, a quiet, thoughtful and almost terminally shy woman. They are, of course, perfect for each other in this gentle and offbeat film.

VHS: S26147. $19.98.

Laser: LD75315. $39.98.

Rose Troche, USA, 1994, 83 mins.

Goodbye Emma Jo

Alex is mourning the loss of her beautiful Emma Jo on what would have been their anniversary. When her car breaks down and she is stranded, she is rescued by Haley, a gorgeous local, who offers her a place to spend the night. These two stunning women turn a disastrous chain of events into a series of heightened sexual interludes.

VHS: S33008. $29.95.

Cheryl Newbrough, USA, 1997, 40 mins.

Grief

Alexis Arquette and Craig Chester are featured in this quirky comedy about behind the scenes intrigues set in the offices of an over-the-top soap opera. Camp humor, unfulfilled longing, male homoeroticism and even that standby of television daytime drama, overnight success, are thrown into this crazy mixed-up world of Hollywood's second string producers.

VHS: S22062. $39.99.

Richard Glatzer, USA, 1994, 87 mins.

Growing Up Gay and Lesbian

Brian McNaught, acclaimed author and lecturer, presents "everything you always wanted to know about homosexuality but were afraid to ask" in a sensitive but straightforward question-and-answer session.

VHS: S23430. $39.95.

Happy Together

With gorgeous, saturated images set to an eclectic soundtrack of classic tangos, torch songs and Frank Zappa instrumentals, Wong Kar-Wai chronicles the stormy affair of a gay couple (Hong Kong superstars Tony Leung and Leslie Cheung) living as expatriates in Buenos Aires. "Stylistically brash. Pulsing with life. Captures the restless, open-to-everything spirit of youth" (Stephen Holden, *New York Times*). Letterboxed. Cantonese with English subtitles.

VHS: S34311. $79.95.

Wong Kar-Wai, Hong Kong, 1997, 98 mins.

Hard

From the folks who brought you *Man for Man*, four steamy, gay, erotic tales: *Grease My Axle*, in which a beefy garage mechanic is oiled up and hosed down by an unexpected customer; *Machine Room*, where two workers stay late in the boiler room for some hot and sweaty overtime; *Wild Side*, where dark figures—not ghosts, but firm flesh and blood in leather—move around the deserted docks by night; and *Built*, in which a hulking demolition man feels the earth move when he finds a condemned building is not as deserted as it looks.

VHS: S32627. $24.95.

Gordon Urquhart, Great Britain, 1993, 50 mins.

Harry Weinberg's Notebook

Yariv Kohn's short essay about sexual politics, ethnicity, intolerance and freedom deals with the emotional aftermath when widower Harry enrolls in a creative writing course taught by a lesbian. The writing assignments force Harry to reconsider his bittersweet feelings about his late wife, and to compose a letter to his late friend, gay activist Harvey Milk. With Nate Garnick, Karen Waddell and Irv Hoffman.

VHS: S19532. $54.00.

Yariv Kohn, USA, 1992, 25 mins.

Heart's Desire

Set on the shores of Provincetown, in Boston's north end, and in the scenic countryside of New England, *Heart's Desire* follows the complications surrounding a single lesbian's search for love. With Betsy Mathieu, Dorian Beach and Kim Weaver, and music by June LaPointe.

VHS: S33220. $19.95.

Betsy Mathieu, USA, 1997, 40 mins.

Heaven's a Drag

Mark and Simon, two men in love, are suddenly separated by AIDS and death. Undone by grief, Simon tries to blot out his intense emotions by diving into the swinging life of a gay bachelor. His deceased ex, a former drag artist, is horrified by Simon's actions and refuses to enter Heaven until he is sure that his memory will live on. That means any prospective new paramour of Simon's will have to deal with a queer, territorial ghost.

VHS: S27429. $29.95.

Peter Mackenzie Litten, Great Britain, 1995, 96 mins.

Holy Mary, Remembrance & Vocation

In these three short, experimental films, filmmaker Jerry Tartaglia looks at the Pope in drag, describes memories of Bette Davis from his queer youth, and catches the lyrical existence of The Radical Faeries at their retreat at the Short Mountain Collective in Tennessee.

VHS: S27229. $59.95.

Jerry Tartaglia, USA

Homo Promo

Trailers from dozens of mainstream and major gay or lesbian films have been collected on this video. These coming attractions comprise a serious but ironic look at a difficult past with some great laughs.

VHS: S24835. $39.95.

Jenni Olson, USA, 1991, 62 mins.

Homophobia in the Media and Society 1993 MIT Panel

This panel discussion brings the views of editors, filmmakers and politicians to the sensitive subject of homophobic media institutions. Warren Blumenfeld, Art Cohen, Michael Duffy and A. Victoria Mederos comprise the panel of experts.

VHS: S24717. $29.95.

Homophobia in the Workplace

Brian McNaught, author and lecturer, discusses the issues of homophobia and discrimination in a revealing look at gender roles and the workplace.

VHS: S23431. $24.95.

Homosexual Desire in Minnesota

Originally shot in super 8, this film details gay life in America's heartland during the 1970s. Its 12 parts chart a course from personal development to political action.

VHS: S27230. $59.95.

Jim Hubbard, USA

The Hours and Times

Christopher Munch's feature debut focuses on the circumstances and possible sexual relationship that existed between John Lennon and the Beatles' manager Brian Epstein during a four-day holiday in Barcelona in Spring 1963. A work of delicacy and heartbreak, the film delves into the inner world of each man, depicting Epstein's erotic obsession and Lennon's confusion and pain as an emerging rock-and-roll icon. With David Angus, Ian Hart and Stephanie Pack.

VHS: S18741. $19.98.

Christopher Munch, USA, 1991, 60 mins.

The Hunger

David Bowie, Catherine Deneuve and Susan Sarandon star in this stylish and moving tale of sophisticated vampires. Deneuve needs new blood in order to keep her 300-year-old lover alive. This film has an erotically charged atmosphere which includes a host of memorable scenes like the lesbian encounters between Deneuve and Sarandon. Ann Magnuson and Willem Dafoe also appear. Letterboxed.

VHS: S26970. $19.95.

Tony Scott, USA, 1983, 100 mins.

Hustler White

This gay romantic comedy starring fashion model Tony Ward as Monti, a streetwise hustler working the streets of Santa Monica Boulevard, follows him through his daily routine of sordid and bizarre encounters with hustlers, johns and pornographers. "A delirious, satirical fantasy" (Kevin Thomas, *Los Angeles Times*).

VHS: S31734. $59.99.

Rich Castro/Bruce La Bruce, USA, 1996, 81 mins.

I Am My Own Woman

The exceptional life of Eastern-bloc transvestite Charlotte von Mahlsdorf is the subject of this film. Her story symbolizes both political resistance and sexual difference under a repressive regime. It's a documentary with a touch of Brecht that features a true queer free spirit. German with English subtitles.

VHS: S22670. $19.95.

Rosa von Praunheim, Germany, 1993, 91 mins.

I Became a Lesbian and Others Too

Four shorts bring humor and insight to the lesbian experience. Included are: *Just a Little Crush*, *I Became a Lesbian*, *Cat Nip* and *Le Poisson d'Amour*. From the girl next door to grandma's secret past, even amongst a bunch of cuddly kitties, who knows where lesbian desire can be found lurking? 52 mins.

VHS: S27757. $29.95.

I Like You, I Like You Very Much

This is one of the few sexually explicit films available from Japan. Yu has a nice college student boyfriend, but that does not stop him from approaching a sexy stranger waiting for a train one evening. There is only one thing he can say: "I like you, I like you very much." Japanese with English subtitles.

VHS: S29951. $39.95.

Oki Hiroyuki, Japan, 1994, 58 mins.

I'll Always Be Anthony

This wacky, dark comedy-drama follows a gay man from childhood through adolescence, presenting these periods abstractly, with stylistic film elegance. Filled with interesting avant-garde camera work, colorful characters, memorable names and lines, and powerful knockout performances, this grassroots independent gay boy/straight boy friendship film uses its creative insanity to transform the topic with which it deals into a matter of universal appeal.

VHS: S32157. $59.95.

Vincent Prezioso, USA, 1997, 80 mins.

I'll Love You Forever...Tonight

The first American gay feature film to be written and directed by a Latino, *I'll Love You Forever...Tonight* is the story of a group of aimless, young gay men who gather for a weekend by the pool in Palm Springs. It's a simple enough premise but it is brought alive by the emotional conflicts unleashed in their near-accidental couplings. Love and sex don't seem to mesh for these troubled figures. With Paul Marius, Jason Adams, Roger Shank and David Poynter.

VHS: S25563. $49.95.

Edgar Michael Bravo, USA, 1993, 80 mins.

Images: A Lesbian Love Story

Claire and Dori have lived together for six years—theirs is a deep bond with an open relationship. Enter Alyx, a dynamic, compelling, sexual, energetic Lesbian who loves life, love, women...and Claire. "At last, a woman-identified and realistic portrayal of women loving women" (Lavender Press).

VHS: S06032. $59.95.

Ruth Barrett/Cynthia Smith, USA, 1987, 54 mins.

Improper Conduct

Controversial, powerful documentary, a series of interviews with fascinating Cuban intellectuals and homosexuals who have been persecuted under the Castro regime. An indictment of Castro, implicating also those who would turn a blind eye toward repression from the left. Spanish with English subtitles.

VHS: S00614. $19.95.

Nestor Almendros, USA, 1984, 112 mins.

In a Glass Cage

A thriller that redefines the horror film. Written and directed by Agustin Villaronga, the story concerns a Nazi concentration camp doctor and his family living in exile in Spain a few years after the war. After a nasty fall leaves him in need of an iron lung, the Nazi finds his new male nurse an indispensable member of the family. With Gunter Meisner, David Sust and Marisa Paredes as Griselda. Spanish with English subtitles.

VHS: S10734. $79.95.

Agustin Villaronga, Spain, 1986, 110 mins.

In the Life

This award-winning TV series reflects the rich diversity and accomplishments of the gay community nationwide. Covers politics, health, global issues, art, culture, current events, and comics. 85 mins.

VHS: S34560. $29.95.

In the Life: The Funny Tape

Kate Clinton, America's first lesbian stand-up comic, hosts this collection of songs and skits featuring some of the best lesbian and gay talent around. Even the commercials are twisted. Lily Tomlin and the late Vito Russo are also featured. 60 mins.
VHS: S21125. $19.98.

The Incredibly True Adventure of Two Girls in Love

Randy is a frolicsome tomboy mechanic who lives with her lesbian aunt and accidentally meets a fellow teen with both a Range Rover and an attitude. Despite their differences, they become the best of friends and eventually realize that there can only be one explanation for their feelings toward one another: They're in love.
VHS: S26816. $19.98.
Laser: LD75406. $39.99.
Maria Maggenti, USA, 1995, 94 mins.

Indigo Girls Watershed

Everything, from the Indigo Girls' biggest hits to their most intimate moments, can be found on this video. Candid and memorable footage from the early years is juxtaposed against clips of them them performing songs like "All Along the Watchtower," "Galileo," "Touch Me Fall," "Least Complicated," "Get Together" and more. 68 mins.
VHS: S26669. $22.98.

An Individual Desires Solution & War Songs

The first of these two experimental films by Lawrence F. Brose confronts AIDS as faced by the artist's HIV-positive lover. In the second work, a poem performance by Paul Schmidt forms the basis for an ode to peace. Together these films manage to create a highly personal view of these important issues.
VHS: S27220. $59.95.
Lawrence F. Brose, USA

Inn Trouble

A hilarious and realistic coming-of-age story about an eclectic group of friends who inherit a bed and breakfast and transform it into a haven for girl bands, girl clubs, girl friends, and overall girl trouble.
VHS: S34974. $27.95.
Christina Rey, USA, 1996, 93 mins.

Inside AMG (The Athletic Model Guild Story)

Since 1945, the Athletic Model Guild has been the seminal purveyor of gay boy beefcake and softcore homoeroticism. Hosted by spunky young Rick Cassidy, this charming feature takes us deep within the bowels of AMG to meet an endless myriad of naked young men, a few shady characters, and AMG founder Bob Mizer.
VHS: S33423. $19.98.
1970

International Sweethearts of Rhythm/Tiny & Ruby: Hell-Divin' Women

These two films from award-winning filmmakers Greta Schiller (*Before Stonewall, Paris with a Woman*) and Andrea Weiss tell the swinging story of America's hottest, multi-racial, all-woman jazz band of the 1940s, The International Sweethearts of Rhythm, featuring Tiny Davis and her partner of over 40 years, drummer-pianist Ruby Lucas. Using rare jazz recordings, live performances and vintage photographs, the film follows the amazing journey of these groundbreaking women from the 1940s to the present.
VHS: S32240. $29.95.
Greta Schiller/Andrea Weiss, USA, 1986, 70 mins.

Jeffrey

Paul Rudnick's off-Broadway smash comic hit is finally a feature-length film. It stars Steven Weber, Patrick Stewart and Michael T. Weiss, and even includes Sigourney Weaver in a bizarre cameo. It all begins as a young gay man discovers that AIDS makes looking for Mr. Right even more complex and bedeviling. Now, as he finds the ravages of the epidemic coming ever closer, he must decide if he can rise to the challenge and meet what life has to offer with openness and love. Olympia Dukakis, Kathy Najimy, Robert Klein and Nathan Lane are also featured in this delightful comedy.
VHS: S27050. $19.98.
Laser: LD75456. $39.95.
Christopher Ashley, USA, 1995, 92 mins.

Jerker

Hugh Harrison adapts Robert Chesley's play about the relationship between two men, which is revealed entirely through anonymous telephone conversations. "Raw, honest and unapologetic in its portrayal of gay sexuality," the *Philadelphia Gay News* wrote. With Tom Wagner and Joseph Stachura.
VHS: S17118. $19.95.
Hugh Harrison, USA, 1991, 120 mins.

The Jim Bailey Experience

Combining elements of the outrageous and avant-garde, Jim Bailey has been on the cutting edge of drag performers. In this compilation tape, Bailey pulls out all the stops with his dead-on impersonations and photo layouts of Judy Garland, Barbra Streisand, Marilyn Monroe and Madonna.
VHS: S16916. $39.95.

Johns

This "*Midnight Cowboy* for the '90s" (Kevin Thomas, *Los Angeles Times*) is a gritty and poignant day in the life of two Los Angeles street hustlers: Santa Monica Boulevard veteran John (David Arquette, *Dream with the Fishes*) and rookie Donner (Lukas Haas, *Witness*). When Donner naively tries to help John he inadvertently sets the stage for an unforgettable climax. With a haunting and evocative score by blues legend Charles Brown.
VHS: S34980. $89.98.
Scott Silver, USA, 1996, 96 mins.

Kamikaze Hearts

Juliet Bashore's dark drama boldly merges documentary and narrative storytelling in a fascinating portrait of the lesbian underground. Sharon ("Mitch") Mitchell, an actress, and Tina ("Tigr") Mennett, a producer, are lovers and junkies. They accentuate the perverse sexual nature of their relationship by making explicit pornographic films. "Only the camera, with verite charm, trembles during kisses here. This dramatic documentary…posits lesbian love as women's place of empowerment within an exaggerated patriarchal world—the real life porn industry" (Alisa Solomon, *The Village Voice*).
VHS: S19104. $59.95.
Juliet Bashore, USA, 1991, 80 mins.

Kate Clinton: The Queen of Comedy

Kate Clinton and special guests serve up lesbian-themed comedy in this "Club Skirts & Girlbar Queens of Comedy Show." 52 mins.
VHS: S28567. $29.95.

Kiss Me, Guido

In this lighthearted *Odd Couple* for the '90s, straight-arrow apartment hunter Frankie Zito (Nick Scotti), a pizza maker from the Bronx, answers a classified ad for a GWM, thinking it stands for "Guy With Money." Frankie comes to terms with Greenwich Village gay culture after he moves in with his new roomie, actor/choreographer Warren (Anthony Barrile), with some humorous and charming results.
VHS: S33338. $99.99.
Tony Vitale, USA, 1997, 90 mins.

Kizuna

In this first Japanese, animated, gay love story, Sam is a handsome, legendary high school fencing champion whose career ends after he is mistakenly run over by a car intending to kill his boyfriend, Enjolji, the son of an Osaka Mafia don. During Sam's recovery, their relationship intensifies but is later threatened by Enjolji's rival half-brother, Sagano, and his junior Mafia boss and substitute father. Based on the Japanese comic book sensation, this groundbreaking love story will thrill Japanese animation enthusiasts, foreign film buffs and romantics of all persuasions. 30 minutes each. Dubbed in English.
Part I.
VHS: S28504. $29.95.
Part II.
VHS: S28505. $29.95.

L'Amour Fou

M.M. Serra's film is both a document of a difficult time and a personal exploration of Serra's gay male friends' sexuality. The serenity of the four seasons becomes a metaphor in this beautifully hand-processed work. It shows the fragility and vibrancy of life in a time dominated by AIDS.
VHS: S27231. $59.95.
M.M. Serra, USA

L'Escorte

"Call it Pasolini lite or the gay version of Renoir's *Boudu Sauve des Eaux*, *L'Escorte* is a wry little comedy of manners about how a hustler upsets the lives of a middle-class same-sex couple" (Dimitri Katadotis). French with English subtitles.
VHS: S31736. $79.95.
Denis Langlois, France, 1996, 91 mins.

L'Homme Blesse (The Wounded Man)

The sensitive story of a French teenager and his discovery of his own homosexuality, this film directed by Patrice Chereau received the French Cesar. Henri, the teenager, tries to stop an attack on a man in a public toilet, is given a sexy kiss by the attacker, and discovers that he is strongly attracted to men. French with English subtitles.
VHS: S06588. $79.95.
Patrice Chereau, France, 1984, 90 mins.

La Cage aux Zombies

Writer, producer and director Kelly Hughes, author of *Blood, Sweat & Sequins* and creator of the popular public-access *Heart Attack Theatre*, achieved celluloid notoriety with this masterpiece of camp, which has been called "the *Naked Gun* of drag queen movies." When Norma (Cathy Roubal) and her lover, Brent (Eric Gladsjo), discover her gangster husband Lenny's (J.R. Clarke) drug money, the two run off with the loot to start a new life together. When Lenny shows up, the lovers, along with Tony the manicurist (William Love), make Lenny's life a real "drag" in this "towering inferno of blood, guts and glamour." Stars Kitten Natividad of Russ Meyer fame and a soundtrack featuring the L'Orielles, Pansy Division, Scissor Girls, Kraaken, Homewreckers and Pussy Tourette.
VHS: S28515. $49.95.
Kelly Hughes, USA, 1995, 84 mins.

Ladyboys

An intimate portrait of Dod and Odd, two young men who leave their impoverished homes in the countryside of Thailand to find fame and fortune as transvestite performers in the glamorous cabarets of downtown Pattaya.
VHS: S31614. $39.95.
Jeremy Marre, USA, 1995, 52 mins.

Last Call at Maud's

A documentary about the closing of San Francisco's oldest-running lesbian bar. The film follows the 23-year history of the bar, related by owner Rikki Streicher, and a larger consideration of empowerment within the gay rights movement. "The documentary makes salient points about lesbians' generally second-league standing to gay men, legalistic problems such as women not being allowed to be bartender, a 70s souring of homosexual pride due to male gay's 'lack of political consciousness,' and the shooting of Harvey Milk" (Derek Elley, *Variety*).
VHS: S19745. $29.95.
Paris Poirier, USA, 1993, 75 mins.

Late Bloomers

Julia Dyer's warm and funny view of gay relationships is set in a suburban Texas town where a married mother of two and a high school math teacher fall in love.
VHS: S33329. $59.95.
Julia Dyer, USA, 1997, 104 mins.

Lavender Limelight

This acclaimed film goes behind the scenes to reveal American's most successful lesbian directors, who enlighten and entertain as they explore their sexual identity, growing up gay, inspirations and techniques, Hollywood vs. Indie, and love and sex—on-screen and off. Featuring, and with scenes from Cheryl Dunye (*The Watermelon Woman*), Rose Troche (*Go Fish*), Jennie Livingston (*Paris is Burning*), Monika Treut (*Virgin Machine*), Maria Maggenti (*The Incredibly True Adventures of Two Girls in Love*), Su Friedrick (*Hide and Seek*), and Heather MacDonald (*Ballot Measure 9*). 57 mins.
VHS: S34319. $29.95.

Le Jupon Rouge

In this lesbian menage-a-trois drama, shifting attractions are played out between three women of different ages. The eldest, Bacha (legendary Italian actress Alida Valli), is a human rights activist and concentration camp survivor. Her younger fashion-designer friend Manuela (Marie Christine Barrault) is her primary emotional support. When Manuela meets the beautiful Claude (Guillemette Groban), the two begin a relationship that incites Bacha's intense jealousy. French with English subtitles.
VHS: S32214. $39.99.
Genevieve Lefebvre, France, 1987, 90 mins.

Lea Delaria: The Queen of Comedy

The Queen of Comedy Show featuring Lea Delaria, with Amy Boyd and Maggie Cassella. In this ritual of comedy excellence, the Club Skirts and Girl Bar Dinah Shore Weekend in Palm Springs, you'll join the laughter, where the girls are. 75 mins.
VHS: S32042. $29.95.

Lesbian Humor

A collection of six films spanning the career of this exciting filmmaker: *Menses* is a wry comedy on the disagreeable aspects of menstruation; *Superdyke*, a comedy about a troop of shield-bearing Amazons; *Our Trip*, an animated film based on a hiking trip in the Andes; *Sync Touch*, a series of film experiments which propose an aesthetic connection between touch and sight; *Doll House*, a rapid montage of objects arranged in reference to the central prop of a doll house; and *No No Nooky T.V.* confronts the feminist controversy around sexuality with electronic language. "Hammer's satiric use of technology corresponds well with the Eighties repression of sexual expression. If you've ever looked up 'lesbian' in a computer thesaurus, you'll know that it's not listed" (*Independent Media*).
VHS: S08608. $59.95.
Barbara Hammer, 1975-87, USA, 59 mins.

Lesbian Sexuality

A collection of four films by Barbara Hammer, including the landmark *Dyketactics*, the first lesbian lovemaking film to be made by a lesbian. A sensual, evocative montage of 110 images edited to images of touch, an "erotic lesbian commercial." Also includes: *Multiple Orgasm*, a sensual, explicit film; *Double Strength*, a poetic study of a lesbian relationship between two trapeze artists; and *Women I Love*, using the camera as a personal extension of the body.

VHS: S08609. $59.95.
Barbara Hammer, USA, 1974-76, 57 mins.

Lesbovision

Ingrid Wilhite's funny and irreverent works have been collected on this video. *L'Ingenue* is about a baby dyke's first cruise bar. In *Lezzie Life* wildly different dykes try to co-exist. Finally, in *Pet Names* lesbian endearments will leave you laughing.

VHS: S25535. $29.95.
Ingrid Wilhite, USA, 1985-1991, 61 mins.

Lessons at the End of Spring

A young boy's loss of innocence within a pre-perestroika Russian prison is the Kafkaesque premise of this harrowing film. The impressive feature debut of writer-director Oleg Kavun, *Lessons at the End of Spring* immediately places him at the forefront of Russia's groundbreaking new wave of angry young filmmakers. A landmark in the evolution of Soviet cinema. Mature themes and extensive male nudity. Russian with English subtitles.

VHS: S15495. $69.95.
Olag Kavun, USSR, 1989, 75 mins.

Lie Down with Dogs

A young gay man, off to enjoy life in Provincetown one summer, lives out the second half of this adage rather too completely. He gets up with fleas but manages to laugh at all the strange romantic and sexual complications which make Provincetown unique. At times clever and sharp, it combines a light comedy with social critique.

VHS: S27075. $19.95.
Laser: LD75444. $39.99.
Wally White, USA, 1995, 84 mins.

Life and Death on the A-List

Actor Tom McBride, as the subject of this gripping documentary, grapples with the very real-life complications of living with AIDS while coming to terms with his inevitable fall from (gay) grace. Facing the tragic disjuncture between his dreams and the fearful realities of his physical decline, he emerges as a metaphor for the obsessive relationship many of us have with sex, physical beauty and success. "Wrenching..., wryly humorous and unflinching" (Kevin Thomas, *Los Angeles Times*).

VHS: S32160. $29.95.
Jay Corcoran, USA, 1996, 45 mins.

Lifetime Commitment: A Portrait of Karen Thompson

After living together as a couple for over four years, Karen Thompson and Sharon Kowalski were hit by a drunk driver. Sharon was disabled, and Karen lost her lover to a legal system that refused to recognize their bond. Sharon's parents did all they could to keep the couple apart, a problem that deepened when Sharon's father, Donald Kowalski, gained full guardianship over his daughter. This video documents the struggle of two women in love, in a system that can't see the value of this bond.

VHS: S19454. $39.95.

Lily Tomlin 3-Pack

The Search for Signs of Intelligent Life in the Universe, *Ernestine: Peak Experiences* and *Appearing Nitely* are the comic standouts joined in this three-tape set. It brings Lily Tomlin's Tony Award-winning performances to video. 120 mins.

VHS: S27478. $59.95.

Lip Gloss

This film exposes the lives of ordinary and extraordinary gender benders. Go shopping with transvestites, drag queens and female impersonators and watch backstage as they transform themselves into an image of glamour and sex.

VHS: S24244. $39.95.
Lois Siegel, Canada, 1992, 75 mins.

Live to Tell

The very first gay and lesbian prom in America is captured on this exciting documentary. It offers a fresh and unique look at growing up lesbian or gay in America. USA, 30 mins.

VHS: S26819. $24.95.

Longtime Companion

The impact of AIDS on the gay community is the subject of this well-received and honestly acted drama. Bruce Davison stands out in a distinguished ensemble cast as a man facing the loss of his life partner. With Stephen Caffrey, Patrick Cassidy, Brian Cousins, John Dosett, Mark Lamos, Dermot Mulroney, Mary-Louise Parker.

VHS: S13301. $19.95.
Norman Rene, USA, 1990, 100 mins.

Los Placeres Ocultos

A closeted banker, middle-aged and successful, falls madly in love with a poor but handsome 18-year-old student—with devastating consequences for the young man. Carefully crafted and insightfully scripted, *Los Placeres Ocultos* was the first openly gay film to emerge from Spain following the death of Franco. Virtually unknown to American audiences, this complex updating of *Death in Venice* is among the most powerful affirmations of gay life ever depicted on film. Spanish with English subtitles.

VHS: S11636. $79.95.
Eloy de la Iglesia, Spain, 1977, 97 mins.

The Lost Language of the Cranes

A moody BBC adaptation of David Leavitt's novel about family secrets and sexual identity. The film centers on a young man's sexual declaration and its volatile and revealing consequences on the rest of the family. "Graced with subtle, intense performances" (*Time Magazine*). With Corey Parker, Brian Cox, Eileen Atkins and Angus MacFadyen.

VHS: S18604. $19.98.
Nigel Finch, Great Britain, 1992, 84 mins.

Love! Valour! Compassion!

Based on Terrence McNally's award-winning play, this "*The Big Chill* meets *The Bird Cage*" is the story of eight friends who leave the city behind for three simple weekends of rest and relaxation in the country. What they find is an outrageous mix of laughter, love and surprises. Featuring an extraordinary cast led by Jason Alexander (TV's *Seinfeld*) and John Glover, reprising his Tony Award-winning role as twin brothers.

VHS: S32504. $19.98.
Laser: LD76385. $29.99.
Joe Mantello, USA, 1997, 90 mins.

Macho Dancer

From world-renowned director Lino Brocka comes a story of sex, violence, and political corruption. Abandoned by his American lover, a handsome teenager from the mountains journeys to Manila in an effort to support his family. With a popular call boy as his mentor, Paul enters the glittering world of the "machodancer"—a world of male strippers, prostitution, drugs, sexual slavery, police corruption and murder. Teeming with sex and erotic Oriental beefcake, *Macho Dancers* is a searing indictment of the hypocrisy and corruption rampant under both the Marcos and Aquino regimes. Uncensored and uncut. Tagalog with English subtitles.

VHS: S14597. $79.95.
Lino Brocka, Philippines, 1988, 136 mins.

Maedchen in Uniform

Legendary film from the German post-Expressionism period, extremely daring for its time in suggesting lesbianism in the story of a young girl whose identity is choked by the authoritarian boarding school she attends. German with English subtitles.

VHS: S02140. $24.95.
Leontine Sagan, Germany, 1931, 87 mins.

Making Love

Michael Ontkean, Kate Jackson and Harry Hamlin star in this film about a love triangle in which two men fall in love. Ontkean is a successful, married doctor who realizes that his perfect marriage has only one problem—he doesn't sexually desire women. Fortunately a young Hamlin is there to show him the way.

VHS: S19448. $69.98.
Arthur Hiller, USA, 1982, 113 mins.

The Making of "Bar Girls"

Meet the producer, director and real personalities behind this lesbian romantic comedy. As *Bar Girls* makes its way across the independent circuit, it leaves in its wake curiosity about its origins. Now this documentary will answer all questions.

VHS: S25751. $29.95.
Jennifer Rodes, USA, 1995, 40 mins.

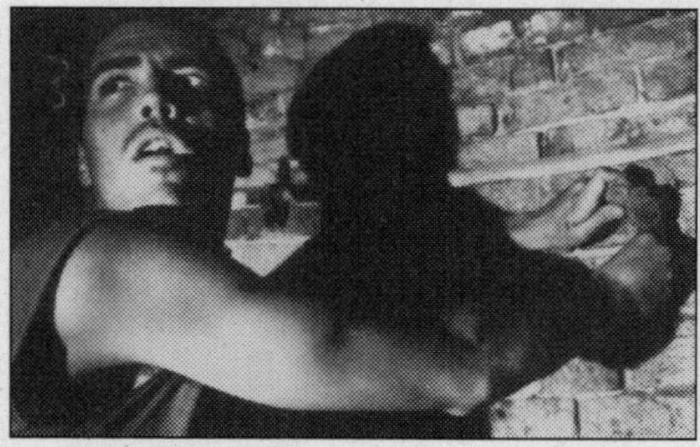

Male Escorts of San Francisco

This documentary tells the story of five male hustlers who advertise in a San Francisco weekly. They have greatly varying interests and experiences. These portraits reveal that commonly held beliefs about the world's oldest profession are often just wrong.

VHS: S22050. $29.95.
Matthew Link, USA, 1992, 42 mins.

Man for Man, Volume I

Four erotic stories feature eight amazing men. They bare all for the camera, in this the first installment of a gay quarterly. There is a costume drama featuring Hercules, a Victorian melodrama, a sculptor and his ideal model, and a luxury evening in a penthouse overlooking London. There are even sections on Ibizia, safer sex, clubs and fashion.

VHS: S22458. $39.95.
Gordon Urquhart, USA, 1993, 59 mins.

Man for Man, Volume II

This sensual all male video is sizzling with a number of exciting scenarios. There is a college boy visiting the steamy South, a Spanish Inquisition dungeon sequence and a gay detective looking for a teenage runaway. Also includes part two of the gay soap opera *Buckingham Place*.

VHS: S24670. $39.95.
Gordon Urquhart, USA, 1993, 55 mins.

Man for Man, Volume III

Stories and travel segments make this third installment of the *Man for Man* series both engaging and erotic. It features stories highlighting Spanish poetry, the epic of Gilgamesh, and Angelo, the sexiest private dick. Visits to Buckingham Palace and Sitges are also included.

VHS: S27174. $39.95.
Gordon Urquhart, USA, 1993, 60 mins.

Man for Man, Volume IV

Fun-filled all-male adventures in this feature-length video quarterly for gay men. Includes *Closed Set*, *Berlin Boy*, and a dramatization of Oscar Wilde's *Teleny*, plus installments of *Buckingham Palace*, England's most popular gay soap opera, and *Angelo*, Britain's dishiest private dick.

VHS: S32966. $39.95.
Gordon Urquhart, Great Britain, 1995, 84 mins.

Man of the Year

Dirk Shafer won the *Playgirl* Man of the Year Award because of his popularity as a nude male centerfold. Unfortunately it meant he had to stay in the closet in order to reap the rewards of his position. This mockumentary follows the hilarious travails of the ultimate poseur.

VHS: S29857. $19.98.
Dirk Shafer, USA, 1995, 85 mins.

Mandragora

Mirek Caslavka stars as a young kid who spurns the workaday robotic lifestyle, continuing from the communist era, which has hung his father out to waste. From his drab origins he is drawn by economic liberties and flashy matrialism to the toxic city of Prague, where everything can be had for a price. He is soon led into the world of male prostitution, teaming up with another boy (David Svec, the film's co-writer) as they try to survive in a world dominated by sex, drugs and teen porn. Czech with English subtitles.

VHS: S33331. $59.95.
Wiktor Grodecki, Czech Republic, 1997, 130 mins.

March in April

Set during the historic march on Washington of 1993, this feature film tells the story of Mark, a man who has never "come out" to his ailing mother. As an assortment of people come to visit him for the big event, he must juggle friends, lovers and family. Keith Meinhold, Barney Frank, Pat Schroeder and Herb Ritts are just some of those who make appearances in this new film.

VHS: S22948. $29.95.
Stephen Kinsella, USA, 1994, 60 mins.

Marching for Freedom: The 1993 March on Washington Video

This video document benefits the National Gay and Lesbian Task Force Policy Institute. Over 700,000 people demonstrated for their rights in Washington D.C. See and hear the joyous sights and sounds of freedom. This country will never be the same again. 78 mins.

VHS: S19453. $29.95.

Massillon

A challenging three-part documentary about a man's sexual dawning and his examination of society's laws restricting sexuality. Filled with colorful minimalist cinematography and a comforting voice-over from the filmmaker as he moves from the personal to the historical issues involved, this "homo road movie" (Lawrence Chua, *Artforum*) is "fiercely demanding yet ever-provocative and decidedly original" (Kevin Thomas, *The Los Angeles Times*).

VHS: S32368. $39.95.
William Jones, USA, 1991, 70 mins.

Meeting Magdalene

Marilyn Freeman's sexy short shows three women trapped in a love triangle overwrought with passion. Sarah is visiting her friend Jean in Olympia, but when Sarah meets Jean's lover, Magdalene, her friendly interests take a dramatic shift. 34 mins.

VHS: S27758. $24.95.

Men in Love

The story of Steven, a young man who has just lost his lover, Victor, to AIDS. Following a moving memorial service in San Francisco, an emotionally drained Steven flies to Hawaii with Victor's ashes—honoring one of his departed lover's last wishes. Struggling with his loneliness and confusion, Steven encounters Peter, a native Hawaiian gardener, and has an affair with him which leads him to a cathartic reawakening of his own sexuality. Starring Doug Self, Joe Tolbe, and Emerald Starr.

VHS: S14086. $29.95.
Marc Huestis, USA, 1990, 87 mins.

Men in Shorts

This collection has something for everyone. Three music videos from John Greyson's feature *Patient Zero* are joined by two juicy Pussy Tourette songs, "Bridgette" and "French Bitch." In addition, *Autobiography* tells of growing up gay in a small Canadian town, while *In View of Her Fatal Inclination, Lilo Wanders Gives Up the Ghost* details a shocking inclination. There is even a bit of history in Pat Rocco's *Kiss*, from 1969.

VHS: S23941. $19.95.

Men in Shorts, Volume 2

Shameless and fun shorts and dance videos featuring comedy, music and men: *Go!* a music video from Pussy Tourette from the feature film *Butch Camp*, starring Judy Tenuta; *Spill Your Seed*, a provocative music video from Chicago-based artist Scott Montgomery; Jorg Fockela's *Spokes*, featuring hot love between two young men from New York City; Eugene Salandra's *Faerie Film*, the beautiful, colorful and truly magical animated tale for the Radical Faeries; and Keith Christensen's music video about cruising in public parks, *No Sign of Life*. Also features film trailers from '70s queer film classics. 90 mins.

VHS: S32210. $19.95.

Midnight Dancers

Banned in the Philippines, this is the story of three young brothers who are trapped in the world of exotic dancing and prostitution which characterizes much of Manila's gay nighttime scene. Though they struggle along different paths, in the end, the violence of the streets brings them all to the brink of desperation. It is reminiscent of the work of Lino Brocka, though more glossy. Filipino with English subtitles.

VHS: S28048. $29.95.
Mel Chionglo, Philippines, 1995, 118 mins.

The Midwife's Tale

Called "*The Princess Bride* for alternative families," this wildly romantic lesbian love story is framed as a bedtime story about Lady Eleanor, a headstrong noblewoman, who finds herself pregnant and falls in love with the beautiful village midwife, Gwenyth. Accusations of witchcraft lead to imprisonment of Gwenyth and the damsels in distress plot an escape. "A tender fable told with affection…the story intelligently avoids male bashing while exploring age-old fear of female sexuality and power" (*Bay Area Reporter*).

VHS: S30135. $49.95.
Megan Siler, USA, 1995, 75 mins.

Mitch Gaylord: The Men's Total Body Workout

Mitch Gaylord is fit, and in this video he explains how to work the upper and lower body and the abdominals, with an emphasis on the importance of nutrition.

VHS: S24735. $24.95.

Mom, Dad...I'm Gay

This guide to coming out offers help to both gay youth and their parents. Interviews reveal personal stories of understanding and acceptance. It's a video that helps demsytify this often troubling and difficult process. 30 mins.

VHS: S25112. $19.95.

Monaco Forever

Set around the 1956 marriage of Grace Kelly and Prince Rainer, the narrative concerns the confusion set off by an enigmatic American who meets a mysterious French woman as they set off on a string of unusual and madcap romantic adventures. The debut film of Jean Claude Van Damme, who plays the "homosexual."

VHS: S18917. $39.95.
William Levey, USA, 1983, 43 mins.

Mondo Rocco (aka It's a Gay World)

This collection of short films by Pat Rocco combines softcore erotica, politics and drag. Rocco was among the first to capture the heady days of Gay Liberation in the late 1960's and 1970's on film. Together these works go some way to preserving that colorful era.

VHS: S25114. $39.95.
Pat Rocco, USA, 1970, 227 mins.

My Father Is Coming

An adventurous German woman receives word from her Bavarian father of his intentions to visit her in New York, where she must pull off an elaborate facade of being married and successful. Her gay roommate poses as her husband but complications ensue when a string of bizarre circumstances result in her father's transformation into an underground sexual icon. With Shelly Kastner, Alfred Edel and Annie Sprinkle.

VHS: S18412. $29.95.
Monika Treut, USA/Germany, 1991, 83 mins.

My Own Private Idaho

In this modern restructuring of the '60s road movie, River Phoenix and Keanu Reeves hustle their way through Seattle, Portland, Idaho and Rome on a quest for River's missing mother. With a meticulous, lyric style, the film combines sprawling landscapes, scenes of passionless sexuality and allusions to Orson Welles' *Chimes at Midnight* as it addresses issues of love, family, politics and homosexuality. A work of great complexity and beauty from the director of *Mala Noche* and *Drugstore Cowboy*.

VHS: S15927. $19.95.
Gus Van Sant, USA, 1991, 102 mins.

Naked Civil Servant

John Hurt delivers a compelling performance in the role of Quentin Crisp, based on Crisp's autobiography as a witty homosexual growing up in England of the 30's and 40's through years of intolerance, ostracism and violence. Hurt's tour-de-force performance brings to life Crisp's unique and often sharp wit at once critical of the society as well as of himself.

VHS: S00914. $19.99.
Jack Gold, Great Britain, 1980, 80 mins.

Neurosia

A sort of *Citizen Queer* in which Orson Welles meets John Waters; this irreverent docu-autobiography shamelessly celebrates gay filmmaker Rosa von Praunheim's life, recapping five decades of activism, guerilla filmmaking and camp by recalling his oeuvre of over 50 films and his role in the birth of the gay rights movement in the 1970s. After Rosa is shot onstage while hosting a tribute to himself, a tabloid reporter travels from Germany to New York to find the motive—and the body. English/German with English subtitles.

VHS: S31351. $29.95.
Rosa von Praunheim, Germany, 1995, 87 mins.

Night Porter

Controversial film about the perverse relationship between a former SS officer from a Nazi concentration camp and a woman, a former inmate at the camp. From one of Italy's few women directors, with Dirk Bogarde and Charlotte Rampling. English dialog. VHS letterboxed.

VHS: S00934. $19.98.
Liliana Cavani, Italy, 1973, 117 mins.

Nighthawks

The first gay feature ever to be theatrically released in England, "*Nighthawks* was the most daring theatrically released gay themed feature of its day" (*Images in the Dark: An Encyclopedia of Gay and Lesbian Film and Video*). A well-liked geography teacher (Ken Robertson), quiet and closeted during the day, goes on the prowl in the gay clubs and discos of '70s London by night. His two worlds collide when he is publicly confronted by his students. "A work of great candor and courage" (*Time Magazine*).

VHS: S34656. $39.95.
Ron Peck, Great Britain, 1978, 113 mins.

Normal Love

Jack Smith's legendary second feature-length film derives from his adoration of B-movie star Maria Montez, best-known for her performance in *Cobra Woman*. It features a variety of '30s horror film monsters, a mermaid, a lecher and other colorful characters performed by a cast which includes Mario Montez, John Vaccaro, Diane DePrima, Francis Francine, Tiny Tim and others. This restored version includes the lost "cobra scene" with Beverly Grant and a musical track from Smith's recovered music collection. Remastered from Smith's camera original; one of the icons of American independent cinema.

VHS: S30532. $325.00.
Jack Smith, USA, 1963, 90 mins.

Not Angels, But Angels

Young boys in the fast changing world of the Czech Republic find the consumer life is available to them through the sale of their own bodies as prostitutes. This documentary lets them describe their experiences plying the world's oldest trade in a new center for sex tourism. Czech with English subtitles.

VHS: S26404. $39.95.
Wiktor Grodecki, Czech Republic, 1994, 80 mins.

Nowhere

This darkly funny film by the acclaimed writer/director of *The Living End* and *The Doom Generation* takes on teen angst with a vengeance in this overtly sexual and achingly real look at an 18-year-old searching for love in a fractured world. A kind of *Beverly Hills 90210* on acid. With Tracy Lords, John Ritter, Shannen Doherty, Christina Applegate, Debi Mazar and Kathleen Robertson.

VHS: S32220. $19.98.
Laser: LD76409. $34.99.
Gregg Araki, USA, 1997, 85 mins.

Odd Gals Out

Canadian lesbian comedy by Sandra E. Fellner and Sharon Jacobs finds its way to the US in this collection of hilarious skits. Everything from hockey to square dancing is lampooned.

VHS: S25536. $24.95.
Lisa King, USA, 45 mins.

Odd Girl Out

Six vignettes detail the coming out process in Tammy Rae Carland's innovative film. From explaining her sexual orientation to her mother to the vagaries of erotic life, coming out remains a complex but exciting experience.

VHS: S27232. $59.95.
Tammy Rae Carland, USA

On Being Gay

A conversation with Brian McNaught, lecturer, counselor, author of *A Disturbed Peace*, Mayor of Boston's Liaison to the Gay and Lesbian Community, and activist, as he talks about the fallacies, the facts, and the feelings of being gay in a straight world. 86 mins.

VHS: S05994. $39.95.

On Common Ground

An idiosyncratic portrait of the tragedy and triumph of the gay liberation movement, from the political urgency tragedy of the 60s to the extreme alienation and social contradictions of the 90s. Using a neighborhood bar as the communal setting, director and writer Hugh Harrison explores the feelings, passions, energy and excitement of a time and place. Cinematography by Ron Hamill.

VHS: S18245. $14.95.
Hugh Harrison, USA, 1992, 90 mins.

One Adventure

An amusing erotic documentary from the early 1970's, this Pat Rocco film follows eight gay Americans across Europe. Bell bottoms are in full bloom, but there was a serious issue in play. Though it is peppered with short erotic vignettes, this film examines the state of gay rights around the world.

VHS: S22956. $39.95.
Pat Rocco, USA, 1994, 90 mins.

Only the Brave

Two wild teenage girls named Vicki and Alex experiment with everything from drugs and sex to violence and just hanging out. Alex wants to write and finds encouragement, along with a little erotic attention, from her English teacher Kate. Vicki wants to sing like Alex's mother did before she disappeared. Together, these girls explore new boundaries in their friendship until events spiral out of their control. Winner of the Best Feature Film award at the 1994 San Francisco Lesbian and Gay Film Festival.

VHS: S26918. $29.95.
Ana Kokkinos, Australia, 1994, 62 mins.

Optical Nerves

Parisian Blinds and *Tourist*, both films by Barbara Hammer, "investigate the nature of spectator perception in an unfamiliar environment." *The Optic Nerve* is a powerful personal exploration of family and aging; *Place Mattes* explores the space between reaching and touching with animation and optical printing used to create travelling mattes for places. *Endangered*, Hammer's most recent work, has light, life and film as endangered in this exquisite film etched with acid.

VHS: S08611. $59.95.
Barbara Hammer, USA, 1984-88, 44 mins.

Oranges Are Not the Only Fruit

This critically acclaimed film, set in '60s northern England, is the tale of Jess, a 16-year-old girl (Geraldine McEwan of BBC-TV's *Mapp and Lucia*) raised to be a missionary, who falls in love for the first time—with another girl. When Jess' strict Evangelist mother (Charlotte Coleman, *Four Weddings and a Funeral*) finds out, she determines to make her daughter renounce her sin, resulting in disaster. Based on Jeanette Winterson's autobiographical prize-winning novel.

VHS: S31261. $29.98.
Beeban Kidron, Great Britain, 1990, 165 mins.

Orlando

Virginia Woolf's ground-breaking novel about a transsexual from the time of Renaissance England has been transformed into a beautiful film. Tilda Swinton stars with Billy Zane as her romantic American lover while Quentin Crisp reigns as Queen Elizabeth the First.

VHS: S20829. $19.95.
Laser: LD74471. $34.95.
Sally Potter, Great Britain, 1993, 93 mins.

Out for Laughs

An irreverent collection of vignettes on lesbian humor, sensibility and outlaw style in this hilarious send-up of images, stereotypes and media representation. USA, 1992, 30 mins.

VHS: S18916. $29.98.

Out in Suburbia

Eleven lesbians between the ages of 23 and 67 speak frankly about their families, their friends and most importantly, their loves. USA, 28 mins.

VHS: S26820. $39.95.

Out in the Garden & You

Two films from Vincent Grenier are included in this video. The first, *Out in the Garden*, is about the dynamic of being HIV-positive. The second film, *You*, offers a more formal examination of perspective, self reflection and narrative.
VHS: S27233. $59.95.
Vincent Grenier, USA

Out Takes

Gay sensibility, homophobia and gender roles on broadcast television are outlined by juxtaposing scenes from two children's shows, and a prime-time sitcom from Japan. Rex Reed's outrageous critique of Pee Wee highlights the self-perpetuating closet of Hollywood and the perceived subversive threat of the show's gay subtext. Reed's opposition to Pee Wee, and Reuben's (Pee Wee) technique of innuendo, double entendre and gender switching, both appear equally repressed compared to the explicit frankness of the Japanese TV series.
VHS: S11638. $39.95.
John Goss, USA, 1989, 13 mins.

Out There

Three 50-minute tapes of loud, proud and outrageous standup comedy by some of today's funniest gay and lesbian comedians, as seen on the Comedy Channel. A portion of the proceeds from the sale of these videos is donated to GLAAD (Gay & Lesbian Alliance Against Defamation). Each tape is 50 mins.
Out There. Hosted by comedienne Lea DeLaria. Performers include Suzanne Westenhoefer, Marga Gomez, PoMo AfroHomos, Steve Moore, Bob Smith, Mark Davis and folksinger Phranc. 50 mins.
VHS: S30435. $12.95.
Out There 2. Hosted by Amanda Bearse (*Married with Children*). Performers include Kate Clinton, Mark Davis, Elvira Kurt, Frank Maya, Scott Silverman and John McGivern. 50 mins.
VHS: S30502. $12.95.
Out There in Hollywood. Hosted by Scott Thompson (*The Larry Sanders Show, The Kids in the Hall*). Performers include Robin Greenspan, Jason Stewart, Sabrina Matthews, Shelly Mars, Rob Nash, Jackie Beat and Lea DeLaria. 50 mins.
VHS: S30503. $12.95.

Outcasts

The most controversial film ever released in Taiwan, *Outcasts* is the story of teenage boys abandoned by their families because they are gay, and the efforts of an aging photographer to provide a home and family for these young people. Chinese with English subtitles.
VHS: S05987. $49.95.
Yu Kan-Ping, Taiwan, 1986, 102 mins.

Paris Is Burning

The title of this lively New York-based documentary is taken from the name of a drag ball. Filmmaker Jenny Livingston spent several years interviewing members of the black and Hispanic gay community and attending their lavish social functions. These costume balls, in a search for expanding the concept of "realness," have gone beyond simple female impersonation to include such categories as butch queens, military attire, executive looks and fierce vogueing competitions. With the participation of such legends as Dorian Corey, Pepper Lebeija, Venus Xtravaganza, Octavia St. Laurent and Willi Ninja.
VHS: S16701. $19.98.
Jennie Livingston, USA, 1990, 71 mins.

Paris Was a Woman

An "intelligent and revealing" (*New York Times*) portrait of the creative community of women writers, artists, photographers and editors who flocked to the Left Bank of Paris between the World Wars. Greta Schiller and writer Andrea Weiss highlight Colette, Djuna Barnes, Gertrude Stein, Romaine Brooks, Marie Laurencin, Berenice Abbott, Gisele Freund, booksellers Sylvia Beach and Adrienne Monnier and *New Yorker* correspondent Janet Flanner.
VHS: S32910. $59.95.
Gretta Schiller, USA, 1996, 75 mins.

Parting Glances

Authentic gay film centering on the final stages of a love affair, featuring fine performances by Richard Ganoung and John Bolger as the couple, and Steve Buscemi as the artist friend doomed by AIDS. Superb photography by Jacek Laskus.
VHS: S02016. $29.95.
Bill Sherwood, USA, 1986, 90 mins.

Perceptual Landscapes

Four works that explore personal landscapes: *Pools*, made with Barbara Klutinis, is an exploration above and under water of two of the first swimming pools designed by the first woman architect in the U.S.; *Pond and Waterfall* is an exploration of verdant pond growth as well as dynamic light and water reflections; *Stone Circles* is a celebration of ancient pre-patriarchal standing mounds and circles including Stonehenge and Asbury; *Bent Time* is one of Hammer's most ambitious films, in "which she attempts to render visually the scientific theory that time, like rays, curves at the outer edges of the universe" (*L.A. Times*).
VHS: S08610. $59.95.
Barbara Hammer, USA, 1981-83, 54 mins.

Personal Best

Two champion female athletes meet at the 1976 Olympic trials. They start out as friends, wind up as lovers and one day meet again as competitors. Mariel Hemingway stars with Patrice Donnelly.
VHS: S01013. $19.98.
Robert Towne, USA, 1982, 129 mins.

Pink Narcissus

It is a gay classic about obsession, beauty and desire. Bobby Kendall stars as a young man who travels from one erotic fantasy to the next, only reality intrudes in the persons of his Johns and the never-ending fear of aging. In this world of want the young man almost doesn't notice that he may become his own most feared apparition, the faded queen.
VHS: S25888. $39.95.
Anonymous, USA, 1971, 70 mins.

Pink Ulysses

Inspired by the earlier, anonymous *Pink Narcissus*, this film pays homage to all those images of vaguely historical but definitely hunky young men captured in 1950's muscle magazines. Longing for a returning hero is the stuff of which legends are made.
VHS: S26698. $39.95.
Eric DeKuyper, USA, 1993, 98 mins.

Plates

Taylor Mead and Bill Rice, two underground, queer art stars, are featured in this funny and remarkable film from playwright and director Gary Goldberg. Shown at the 1991 Berlin International Film festival, *Plates* harkens to the world of silent film even though it employs non-verbal sound to tell its story.
VHS: S27240. $49.95.
Gary Goldberg, USA, 1991, 11 mins.

Poison

An interwoven trilogy, the film uses three distinct stylistic conventions to explore the writings of Jean Genet, arriving at a profound realization of poison in the human mind, body and soul: A gritty prison drama reveals a homosexual's despair at being constantly confronted by forbidden passions; a campy '50s horror film send-up portrays a scientist's search for the essence of sexuality, and draws a compelling parallel to the HIV crisis when things go awry; and a tabloid mystery criticizes religious sentimentality as it reveals the circumstances surrounding the murder of a wife-beater by his own child, who then flew out the window toward heaven. Winner of the Grand Jury Prize at the Sundance Film Festival.
VHS: S15839. $19.98.
Laser: LD72226. $34.95.
Todd Haynes, USA, 1991, 85 mins.

Politically Incorrect: A Special Visit with Camille Paglia

Politically Incorrect host Bill Maher spends two evenings with controversial new-age feminist and author of *Vamps & Tramps* Camille Paglia. In the first episode Maher asks Paglia: Is rape about sex or violence? Are there more lesbian relationships nowadays? And-would the bisexual Paglia prefer Kidman or Cruise, Baldwin or Basinger, Crawford or Gere? In the second episode, Maher and Paglia tackle questions concerning homosexuality, including: Does Camille believe that under the right cirucumstances anyone will have a homosexual encounter? Is homosexual exclusivity natural? Are homosexuals people who couldn't make it in the heterosexual world?—as well as other topics.
VHS: S30626. $12.95.

Postcards from America

Based on the writings of the highly regarded artist David Wojnarowicz, this film follows the troubled life of a young gay man. It includes harrowing depictions from America's underside beginning in the 1960's and leading up to the present. This intense film attempts to fathom the terror and anger of a troubled place.
VHS: S26520. $59.95.
Steve McLean, USA, 1994, 95 mins.

Pretty Boy

In this unflinching and harshly poetic film, the chronicle of a young runaway boy unfolds on the streets of Copenhagen. There he becomes a street hustler. Before the camera, innocence is plundered and finally lost in this compelling exploration of desire. Danish with English subtitles.
VHS: S23290. $69.95.
Carsten Sonder, Denmark, 1993, 87 mins.

The Queen

Almost forgotten, this documentary charts the pressure-laden world of competition surrounding the drag queen event known as the Miss All-America Camp Beauty Queen Pageant from 1967. At times funny and deadly serious, it offers a truly fascinating glimpse of a queer world that existed prior to Stonewall. Crystal, who also appeared in *Paris Is Burning*, is featured.
VHS: S26294. $29.95.
Frank Simon, USA, 1968, 68 mins.

The Question of Equality

Four documentaries, each one hour long, are collected in this video set about the growth of the lesbian and gay rights movement in the last 25 years. They include *Out Rage 69*, the story of what led to Stonewall and the decade following it; *Culture Wars*, the backlash against gay visibility; *Hollow Liberty*, notable court cases surrounding military discharges and state sodomy statutes and *Generation Q*, which features more than 30 gay and lesbian youths talking about growing up gay.
VHS: S27705. $59.95.

Raising Heroes

In this first openly gay action-adventure story, Josh (Troy Sistillio) and Paul (Henry White) are a successful gay couple in the midst of adopting a child when Josh witnesses a mob hit and becomes the next target on their list. Watch as normally mild-mannered Josh maims and kills to protect his loved ones. Will he be able to save his marriage, the adoption, and himself all in one weekend?
VHS: S32493. $39.95.
Douglas Langway, USA, 1996, 85 mins.

Red Ribbons

Quentin Crisp and Georgina Spelvin star in this story about a group of friends paying tribute to a special person. When Frank succumbs to AIDS, his colleagues and former lovers gather in an impromptu memorial service. Part drama and part video diary, this work reveals the feelings of the loved ones left behind.
VHS: S25722. $39.95.
Neil Ira Needleman, USA, 1994, 90 mins.

Reflections: A Moment in Time

"Bright strong Scorpio looking for friendship." So begins Xaviera's ad in a lesbian correspondence club magazine. She finds a friend, and more, in Megan. together they overcome the pain of racism and the fear of trusting and loving. A lesbian-produced and directed original video. 30 mins.
VHS: S06366. $39.95.

Resident Alien

Quentin Crisp, author and professional pansy, has always led a charming, if not charmed, life. While *The Naked Civil Servant* tells of his early and troubled life in Great Britain, this film shows how celebrity in America suited the grand old dame. Fran Lebowitz, Holly Woodlawn, Michael Musto, and other New York scenesters are featured.
VHS: S25103. $19.95.
Jonathan Nossiter, USA, 1990, 85 mins.

Rhinoskin: The Making of a Movie Star

This is the underground film favorite that Hollywood doesn't want you to see! "Rhinoskin" is a slang show business term relating to the thick skin needed by an actor to endure the stress, rejection and failure associated with being a Hollywood hopeful. Armed with a beat-up camera and the guts it takes to get kicked off the studio backlots of Tinseltown, a film crew follows struggling actor Tod DePree in his year-long quest to get "just one line of dialogue on a network sitcom." "A must see for any aspiring actor" (ABC National).
VHS: S30485. $59.95.
Dina Marie, USA, 1993, 82 mins.

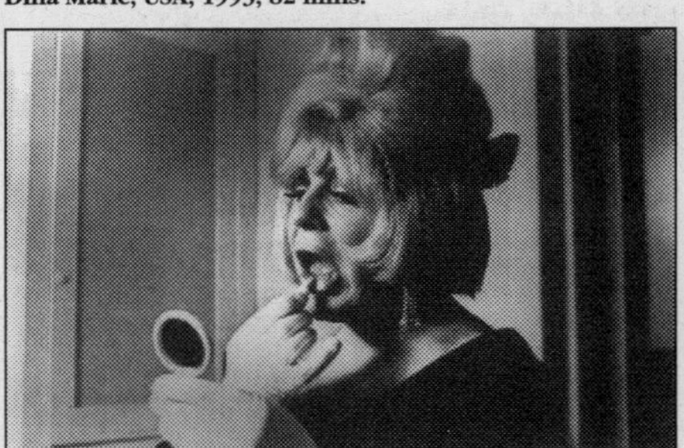

Rich Boy, Poor Boy

A colleague of the late Filipino director Lino Brocka, Piedro de San Paulo's controversial and banned work rips open the Third World taboo. The story concerns an outlawed relationship between a wealthy, Americanized young man and his strong-willed, quiet farmhand. "Brave and brazen, a bittersweet portrait of friendship and desire" (*Bay Area Reporter*). With Victor Viller, Edwyn Casas, Cristina Ocampo. Tagalog with English subtitles. On the same program is *A Boy Named Cocoy*, about a mountain boy's quest to find a better life in Manila.
VHS: S17777. $59.95.
Piedro de San Paulo, Philippines, 1991, 94 mins.

Ritz

Director Richard Lester (*A Hard Day's Night, Three Musketeers*) keeps the pace fast and furious in this crisp farce about Gaetano Proclo hiding out in a men's bathhouse in New York. With Jack Weston, Rita Moreno, Jerry Stiller and F. Murray Abraham.
VHS: S01118. $19.98.
Laser: LD71475. $34.98.
Richard Lester, USA, 1976, 91 mins.

Rock Hudson's Home Movies
With excerpts from some of Rock's most memorable films, this documentary digs into the persona of Hollywood's greatest male sex symbol of the '50s and '60s, whose death from AIDS forever transformed the way America looks at its stars. Mark Rappaport's film was named to multiple Ten Best lists as an original look at an American icon.
VHS: S21090. $29.95.
Mark Rappaport, USA, 1992, 63 mins.

Salmonberries
German director Percy Adlon's political thriller features k.d. lang in her film debut. The story concerns a repressed East German librarian who escapes her oppressive surroundings after her lover is killed trying to scale the Berlin Wall. Devastated and grief stricken, Roswitha (Rosel Zech) travels to Alaska. Trapped in a grim, remote Eskimo outpost, she finds comfort and emotional fulfillment with the sexually ambiguous lang.
VHS: S18844. $29.95.
Percy Adlon, Canada/Germany, 1991, 94 mins.

Savage Nights
Cloaked in controversy because its maker and star, Cyril Collard, died of AIDS just days after the film won the coveted Cesar (French Oscar) award, *Savage Nights* is a story of passion and love in the age of HIV. A bisexual photographer finds his life is shared by those he loves in a way that many would find unforgivable. The film provokes and astonishes with its singular perspective; it is all the more incendiary by being rooted in real life. French with English subtitles.
VHS: S22530. $14.95.
Cyril Collard, France, 1993, 126 mins.

Score
A liberated '70s couple seduces another couple into experimentation with bisexuality and group sex. "Somewhere between *Who's Afraid of Virginia Woolf* and *Love, American Style*" (*Time Out*).
VHS: S33225. $29.95.
Radley Metzger, USA/Yugoslavia, 1972, 90 mins.

Sebastian
From the creators of *Lakki—The Boy Who Grew Wings* comes this sweet story of sexual confusion set in the ultra-liberal social atmosphere of modern Norway. Seventeen-year-old Sebastian and his buddy Ulf are the perfect pals, until one of them decides he wants more. Joy and gentle comedy follow as the boys struggle to understand this new element in their relationship. Norwegian with English subtitles.
VHS: S31414. $59.95.
Svend Wam, Norway, 1995, 88 mins.

The Second Coming
A triumphant mixture of science fiction, political agitpop and experimental montage. Set in the near future, Christian fundamentalists attempt a coup d'etat in the U.S. Meanwhile, Carlos and Ben, two high school classmates in New York, are falling in love despite the homophobic, racist and anti-Semitic attacks of their peers. Together they join forces with an underground resistance led by teenagers who produce and broadcast videos challenging the fundamentalists.
VHS: S32161. $29.95.
Jack Walsh, USA, 1995, 53 mins.

Seduction: The Cruel Woman
Pina Bausch dancer Mechtild Grossman plays Wanda, a dominatrix whose troupe services customers and elaborately stages S&M performances in this "stunning" film from German filmmakers Elfi Mikesch and Monika Treut (*Virgin Machine*). Much more important to Mikesch's insinuating camera than the petty tortures are the settings, costumes, and look of each encounter. This is S&M by Avedon, outfits by Dior...By the way, on her off hours, of which there are few, Wanda prefers women. German with English subtitles.
VHS: S12460. $29.95.
Elfi Mikesch/Monika Treut, Germany, 1985, 84 mins.

Sex Is...
This bold documentary charts the growing sexual awareness among a group of men whose personal histories extend from before Stonewall, through the growing AIDS crises and into today's climate of "in-your-face" sexual politics. It's an in-depth look at how these men coped with change and loss inside the sexual revolution.
VHS: S21134. $29.95.
Marc Huestis, USA, 1993, 80 mins.

Shades of Black
Set in a small town, Kate, a 23-year-old photographer and athlete, finds herself pursued by a seductive older woman, Lilly, an artist from New York. Suspecting that Lilly is cheating on her, Kate confronts her, only to discover that Lilly's manipulative powers hide a dark and dangerous mental instability.
VHS: S33430. $39.95.
Mary Haverstick, USA, 1993, 115 mins.

She Must Be Seeing Things
"A wryly sophisticated comedy...plays like a lesbian homage to *Unfaithfully Yours*," wrote Jay Carr in *The Boston Globe*. Agatha is an international lawyer, Jo a filmmaker. While Jo is on the road with her film, Agatha reads her diary and becomes insanely jealous to the point of dressing up as a man and "shadowing" her. "Groundbreaking in its understated portrayal of sophisticated urban lesbians exploring such dynamics as sex and sexuality, career and commitment, fidelity and companionship. The film gives us characters who are richly realistic and demonstrates that McLaughlin is a complex and refreshingly thoughtful talent..." (*New York Native*).
VHS: S10941. $29.95.
Sheila McLaughlin, USA, 1988, 85 mins.

She's Safe
These hot lesbian short films are also safer sex education. *La Ravissement, Safer Sister, Safe Sex Is Hot Sex, Down on the River, Jill Jacks Off, Current Flow, Cunt Dykula, Girls Will Be Boys, Safe Soap* and excerpts from *Well Sexy Woman* and *Truth or Dare* are joined on this video. 55 mins.
VHS: S24032. $39.95.

Silence=Death
This film serves as an important historical document, exploring the reactions of New York's artistic community to the ravages of AIDS. Responses range from David Wojnorowicz' venomous proclamations and paintings, and painter Rafael Gambas' seething indictment of homophobic bigotry, to Keith Haring's nostalgic longing for the days of care-free sex, and Allen Ginsberg's musing upon his shyer attitude about experimenting sexually. Even with the gentler voices, the film's undercurrent is an angry demand for action and recognition. "Best AIDS film to date..." (*The Guardian*).
VHS: S14148. $29.95.
Rosa von Praunheim/Phil Zwickler, USA, 1990, 60 mins.

Silent Pioneers
Senior members of lesbian and gay communities share their memories about gay life in this documentary. Sometimes tragic, and sometimes funny, their recollections are always personal and poignant. This film offers a unique view of an era less tolerant of sexual minorities.
VHS: S27614. $39.95.
Lucy Winer, USA, 1985, 54 mins.

Silverlake Life: The View from Here
This highly acclaimed documentary was shown on PBS's *Point of View* series. It follows the slow demise of a longtime film and video maker, Tom Joslin, who is dying of AIDS. This unvarnished self-portrait of a man, his lover (Mark Massi), his family and his friends offers an unparalleled look into the heart of the AIDS crises. It won the Sundance Grand Jury Prize.
VHS: S21880. $19.95.
Laser: CLV. LD74626. $39.95.
Tom Joslin/Peter Friedman, USA, 1993, 89 mins.

Sins of Rachel
Someone's bashed in the head of "no-good broad" Rachel Waring, a bloated ex-nightclub entertainer. But the murder investigation turns into an unexpected gay "whodunnit" when the chief suspect becomes her sexually mixed-up, adolescent son, Jimmy. "A seedy little bargain-basement soap opera that's so tacky, badly acted, and wretchedly written...that it's hilariously tragic" (*Video Jones*).
VHS: S30983. $19.98.
Richard Fontaine, USA, 1972, 90 mins.

Siren
Shot on location in London, this erotic lesbian film has all the makings of a delightful fantasy. Ella is captivated by Jodie, a writer of erotic fiction. At Jodie's lavish estate, titillation and more await this young and sexy couple.
VHS: S27448. $29.95.
Sarah Swords, USA/Great Britain, 1996, 45 mins.

Something to Sing About
The 100-member Sydney Gay and Lesbian Choir is the pride of Australia's vibrant gay and lesbian community. Decked in purple waistcoats with the odd touch of chain and leather, the Choir sings everything from Gershwin to Madrigals, spirituals to ABBA, as it takes its audiences on a rich, emotional journey across the continent of Australia to defend its title in the National Choral Competition. "A standing ovation" (*The Australian*).
VHS: S30245. $29.95.
Martin Daley, Australia, 1995, 55 mins.

Split: Portrait of a Drag Queen
International Chrysis was one of Salvador Dali's inner circle. This documentary portrait reveals the person behind the celebrity who appeared as a woman from the waist up, but as a man from the waist down.
VHS: S24245. $39.95.
Ellen Fisher Turk/Andrew Weeks, USA, 1992, 60 mins.

Stiff Sheets
A document of an agitprop/drag fashion show presented by an anonymous collective of gay artists, during a week-long round-the-clock vigil at County/USC Medical Center in Los Angeles. The vigil drew media attention to the lethal lack of public AIDS care and facilities available in L.A.
VHS: S11637. $39.95.
John Goss, USA, 1989, 19 mins.

Stonewall
In this charming and inspirational story of the birth of the gay rights movement, a hustler falls for a transvestite in 1969 New York City and must find the courage to challenge the hatred and discrimination that he and his friends face.
VHS: S31361. $94.99.
Laser: LD76276. $39.99.
Nigel Finch, Great Britain, 1996, 99 mins.

Stonewall 25: Global Voices of Pride and Protest!
Past and present join in this celebration that includes political, sporting and entertainment events. Joan Rivers, Pete Seeger, Lee Grant, Charles Busch, Kate Bornstein, Petulia Clark, Chita Rivera, Nathan Lane, Quentin Crisp, David Marshall Grant and Sir Ian McKellen are just some of the celebrities seen. USA, 1994, 90 mins.
VHS: S21703. $24.95.

Stop the Church
Robert Hilferty's controversial documentary takes an irreverent look at the infamous AIDS activist demonstration that invaded Cardinal O'Connor's own parish church, New York City's St. Patrick's Cathedral. ACT-UP NY meetings and preparations help show what the goal was that these activists hoped to accomplish, which was primarily to stop the Church from interfering in the political crisis occasioned by AIDS.
VHS: S27235. $59.95.
Robert Hilferty, USA

Straight from the Heart
This Academy Award-winning documentary explores the experiences of parents learning to love their lesbian and gay children in a world dominated by homophobia. There is a range of stories touching on a variety of experiences, including a religious Mormon family and an African-American family. 30 mins.
VHS: S26030. $24.95.
Dee Mosbacher/Frances Reid, USA, 1994, 30 mins.

Strip Jack Naked
The unsparing, autobiographical documentary by pioneering British filmmaker Ron Peck about the making of *Nighthawks* and Britain's gay culture over the last 30 years. Archival footage, old photos and magazines recount Peck's life and work. "Groundbreaking" (*Images in the Dark: An Encyclopedia of Gay and Lesbian Film and Video*).
VHS: S34657. $39.95.
Ron Peck, Great Britain, 1991, 91 mins.

The Sum of Us
In this gay romantic comedy a young man finds the search for Mr. Right troubled by his busy-body father. Dad is just concerned for a son who seems unable to find that special someone. Altogether it's a light, amiable tale that is darkened by unexpected misfortune. In sunny Australia, however, things always get bright again. Based on David Stevens' play.
Laser: LD75085. $39.99.
Kevin Dowling/Geoff Burton, Australia, 1995, 99 mins.

Sunday Bloody Sunday
Nominated for four Academy Awards, *Sunday Bloody Sunday* stars Glenda Jackson, Peter Finch and Murray Head in an unusual love triangle on the rocks. Head plays the enigmatic bisexual involved with both a man and a woman.
VHS: S01283. $19.95.
Laser: LD71182. $49.95.
John Schlesinger, Great Britain, 1971, 110 mins.

Super 8½
Bruce La Bruce is back as a tired porn director with a decided lack of lust. With his career in shambles, a documentary about his former glory days offers him the only respite from his currently bleak and empty life. In this campy send-up of art, porn and rip-offs of classic films, queer icons Vaginal Creme Davis and comic Scott Thompson evoke a world grown weary of intimacy. It's rude and funny.
VHS: S26697. $39.95.
Bruce La Bruce, Canada, 1994, 106 mins.

Suzanne Westenhoefer: HBO Comedy Special
Suzanne Westenhoefer is the first openly gay or lesbian comic to have her own *HBO Comedy Special*. This hysterical lesbian comic skewers everything from the military to performing for less than friendly audiences in this, her first cable TV special. USA, 1994, 28 mins.
VHS: S26940. $19.95.

Swoon

A highly stylized black-and-white reconsideration of the Leopold and Loeb case, in which two University of Chicago students attempt the perfect crime: the kidnapping of a 12-year-old boy, that resulted in his death. This film provides a historical and sexual context for the crime, finding its roots in homoerotic fixation. With Daniel Schlachet, Craig Chester and Ron Vawter.
VHS: S18518. $19.95.
Tom Kalin, USA, 1991, 92 mins.

Taxi Zum Klo

A smash hit at the Berlin and New York Film Festivals in 1981, *Taxi Zum Klo* is an autobiographical examination of the director's own sexual escapades and fantasies. Frank Ripploh explores every aspect of gay life in Berlin, with hilarious results. German with English subtitles.
VHS: S01304. $39.95.
Frank Ripploh, Germany, 1981

Teasers

A collection of four short films of lesbian erotica—*Top of the World, Why I'll Never Trust You in 200 Words or Less, Regarde-Moi* and *Double Entente*—and music videos *Love Strikes Hard* and *That's Forever*. 60 mins.
VHS: S32503. $29.95.

Thank You and Goodnight

A highly original film by Jan Oxenberg that uses memory, anecdote and avant-garde representations (such as cardboard cut-outs) to explore the tender, beautiful and emotionally devastating relationship between the filmmaker and her grandmother. "Wildly inventive and unique, it's a cosmic, cerebral comedy of a Woody Allenish sort" (*Toronto Globe*).
VHS: S18269. $19.98.
Jan Oxenberg, USA, 1991, 82 mins.

Therese and Isabelle

Based on the novel by Violette Leduc, *Therese and Isabelle* is a story of love between two students at an exclusive girls' school. Filmed in black and white. English dubbed.
VHS: S01320. $29.95.
Radley Metzger, France, 1968, 102 mins.

The Third Sex

Paula Wesley and Paul Dahlke star in this exploitative look at homosexuality. Parents try to straighten out their son, who is hanging out with a known gay man. It's a shocker. 1959.
VHS: S23187. $24.95.

Third Sex Sinema Volume 1—Vapors

The first volume of the *Third Sex Sinema* series. The notorious short film *Vapors* was banned across America in the 60's and deals with a man's first visit to a New York City gay bathhouse. It was directed by Andy Milligan. Also included is a fun and quirky loop circa early 60's titled *Shoot It Baby*, and the 1960 black and white German import *The Third Sex*, which deals with the sensitive subject of male teacher/male student relations.
VHS: S24737. $19.98.

Third Sex Sinema Volume 2—The Song of the Loon

Richard Armory's novel was realized on film during the height of the sexual revolution. Set in the American West of the 1870's, it follows the growing homoerotic self-awareness and subsequent experiences of a young man. This early gay erotic work is joined by two shorts. *The Coronation* is from the 1960's while *Lot in Sodom* is a silent film from the 1920's.
VHS: S24738. $19.98.
Andrew Herbert, USA, 1970, mins.

Third Sex Sinema Volume 3—The Meatrack

This soft-core relic features a wild plot about a young hustler seemingly lost in a daze of endless cheap sex with men and women until he rescues a young woman. They fall in love and make plans but old habits and traumatic events stand in their way.
VHS: S23060. $19.98.
Michael Thomas, USA, 1970, 71 mins.

Third Sex Sinem Volume 5: Consenting Adults

This obscure study of homosexuality reports on the lifestyles of gay men and women in Great Britain in the mid-'60s. *The Male Nudists* features two burly young men entertaining one another, lounging around, exercising, flexing their huge muscles, oiling themselves up, showering together and wrestling. There's footage from the Gay-In III, sponsored by the Gay Liberation Front, a surrealistic gay encounter on a park bench, wrapped up by *Caught in the Can*, an early '70s short about two guys who dress in drag to take some suckers for a roll.
VHS: S30988. $19.98.

This Special Friendship

A 16-year-old boy becomes infatuated with a young classmate at a strict Jesuit boarding school. "A masterpiece…shocking in the best sense of the word" (L.A. *Times*). A sensitively directed film with a bravura performance by Didier Haudepin. French with English subtitles.
VHS: S01333. $49.95.
Jean Delannoy, France, 1964, 99 mins.

Three

Based on Howard Ruffman's best-selling photography book *Three*, this no-holds-barred documentary chronicles the highs and lows of a three-way love affair between three beautiful and uninhibited boys. 55 mins.
VHS: S34558. $39.95.

Three of Hearts

Yurek Bogayevicz's unconventional romantic triangle concerns a beautiful nurse (Kelly Lynch) who hires a handsome male escort (William Baldwin) to seduce the sexually confused English professor (Sherilyn Fenn) who ended their relationship. An interesting investigation into the nature of attraction, gender and sexual role playing. With Joe Pantoliano and Gail Strickland.
VHS: S19476. $19.95.
Yurek Bogayevicz, USA, 1993, 101 mins.

TimePiece

A surprise birthday party is the catalyst for this story about seven gay men in the 1990's. Though fictional, it feels like a documentary as they discuss highly intimate aspects of their lives. From group sex to monogamy and coming out, this film explores experiences shared by many gay men.
VHS: S25721. $39.95.
Kenn Sprenkel/Brian Petraska, USA, 1994, 58 mins.

To Wong Foo, Thanks for Everything! Julie Newmar

Patrick Swayze, Wesley Snipes and John Leguizamo star as beautiful young drag queens out for a jaunt across America. Along the way, they break some hearts, deepen their sense of fashion and even throw a party. This warm comedy is a perfect gender-bending confection. Stockard Channing and Blythe Danner are both featured.
VHS: S27180. $19.95.
Laser: LD75465. $39.98.
Beeban Kidron, USA, 1995, 109 mins.

Together and Apart

An award-winning musical drama about two former gay lovers who meet again years later, after one has apparently gone straight and married. They reflect, through song and memory flashbacks, the feelings they experience during this painful yet liberating reunion. Public performance.
VHS: S32142. $59.95.
Laurie Lynd, USA, 1986, 26 mins.

The Toilers and the Wayfarers

Gay teens Dieter (Matt Klemp) and his friend Philip (Andrew Woodhouse) are trapped in a puritanical, small-town existence that is slowly suffocating them. Bidding goodbye to this existence sets them adrift to encounter yet another nonexistence. English and German with English subtitles.
VHS: S33330. $59.95.
Keith Froelich, USA, 1996, 75 mins.

Tom Chomont: A Two-Volume Collection

The works of this experimental gay filmmaker are collected on these two videos. *Volume I* contains the short films *Jabbock, The Heavens, Razor Head* and *The Bath*. *Volume II* features *Spider Jan. 16.91, Inner Sanctum, Garden* and *The Mirror*.
Volume I.
VHS: S27237. $69.95.
Volume II.
VHS: S27238. $69.95.
Tom Chomont, USA

Tongues Untied

The late Marlon Riggs was internationally acclaimed for such groundbreaking videos as *Color Adjustment*. Poetry, personal testimony, rap, performance and dance are combined in this singular exploration of the racism and homophobia that black men face daily. Broadcast on the PBS series *P.O.V.*, its beauty and power generated outrage from right-wing politicians. Even so, it remains unmatched for its eloquence.
VHS: S22951. $39.95.
Marlon Riggs, USA, 1989, 55 mins.

The Trials of Oscar Wilde

Peter Finch and John Fraser star in this story based on the loving relationship between Oscar Wilde and Lord Alfred Douglas. John Furnell's *The Stringed Lute* and Montgomery Hyde's *Trials of Oscar Wilde* provide the literary sources for this intriguing film. Also known as *The Man with the Green Carnation*. With Yvonne Mitchell, Lionel Jeffries and Ian Fleming.
VHS: S26878. $24.95.
Ken Hughes, Great Britain, 1960, 123 mins.

Tu Solo

Traditions like bull fighting inevitably depend on venerable institutions. This graceful art is revealed through a true story set in Spain's most prestigious bull fighting school. Students tell their own side of the story, and in a unique tradition, bare all for a nude bullfighting scene.
VHS: S23743. $79.95.
Teo Escamilla, Spain, 1995, 96 mins.

Turnabout: The Story of the Yale Puppeteers

Dan Bessie crafted this documentary about the three gay puppeteers who enchanted Hollywood for 25 years. Their musical extravaganzas, with puppet replicas of celebrities, drew legends like Hitchcock to see their performances. The sophisticated humor of their shows came from a unique camp sensibility, one fostered by these three gay men in a time when being gay was extremely difficult.
VHS: S27492. $39.95.
Dan Bessie, USA, 1992, 55 mins.

Twin Cheeks: Who Killed the Homecoming King?

In this experimental drama by underground filmmaker Osker Wild, a college freshman submits to a sordid underworld of sex and drugs to find out who killed his brother. "It's quite a ride and one that is both funny and delightfully queer" (*Seattle Gay News*). Starring Troy Sinatra and with the bonus music video "Please Don't Hate Me (Because I'm Beautiful)" by Hellen Bedd.
VHS: S31349. $39.95.
Osker Wild, USA, 1996, 60 mins.

Two in Twenty

This lesbian soap opera follows the lives of two households. With humor and suspense, the characters in this soap confront complicated issues such as child custody, lesbian parenting, AIDS, substance abuse, racism, coming out, monogamy, crushes, bisexuality, sex, and of course, therapy. Commercials for fictitious products and services satirize the consumerism at the core of a daytime television experience.
Two in Twenty: Complete Set.
VHS: S16914. $99.95.

Urinal

An innovative first feature, *Urinal* summons seven gay artists from 1937 and gives them an "Impossible Mission": they must research the policing of washroom sex in Ontario, and propose solutions. Each night they convene to present a lecture, with every lecture adopting a different documentary convention. Using interviews with politicians, gay activists and men who have been charged with "gross indecency," hundreds of victims of police entrapment and video surveillance are revealed. A funny and disturbing film that probes into the roots of homosexual discrimination. From Canada's most controversial independent filmmaker.
VHS: S15808. $29.95.
John Greyson, Canada, 1988, 100 mins.

A Valentine for Nelson & Two Marches

New York-based filmmaker Jim Hubbard hand processes his own 16mm film, resulting in intensely personal and moving works. The first is simply a Valentine for his longtime lover. In the second, he contrasts the March on Washington held before AIDS dominated gay life with the later larger gay rights march held in 1993.
VHS: S27221. $59.95.
Jim Hubbard, USA, 1993

Vegas in Space

Drag Queens bring Vegas glamour to an intergalactic battle of outsized proportions. Well, the proportions of the miniature sets are all too obvious, but then so is the drag in this campy, overacted farce. An all-women planet is thrown out of whack by a dastardly crime. Two earth astronauts are sent to help, but there is one condition. They must become women to enter this feminine planet. The rest is showbiz herstory. Features the late Doris Fish.
VHS: S27624. $69.98.
Phillip R. Ford, USA, 1991, 85 mins.

A Very Natural Thing

A young priest drops out of the Church to openly pursue a gay life in New York. He falls in love with a seemingly ideal man, but together they learn that passion and romance take time. Only by learning to respect each other can their love grow. This is the first U.S. film from an openly gay director to be commercially distributed. It captures the feeling of an era when gay men were just beginning to experience greater acceptance.
VHS: S28054. $39.95.
Christopher Larkin, USA, 1973, 85 mins.

Via Appia
A complex film about gay desire and paranoia. A former German steward travels to Rio to find a mysterious man who left a cryptic message, "Welcome to the AIDS Club," following a sexual encounter. "Via Appia, the nickname of a Rio district where male prostitutes hang out, becomes a grim guided tour of the city's gay subculture, its bars, discos, streets and a beach known as the AIDS farm. The documentary-within-the film-format justifies this material" (Vincent Canby). With Peter Senner, Guilherme de Padua and Yves Jansen. German and Spanish with English subtitles.
VHS: S18693. $39.95.
Jochen Hick, Germany/Brazil, 1992, 90 mins.

A Village Affair
Alice Jordan (Sophie Ward) appears to have the perfect life: a handsome, loyal husband, three healthy children, and a beautiful home. But when she meets Clodagh, the aristocratic daughter of the lord of the local manor, a scandalous relationship blossoms between the women which threatens to destroy her perfect life. Originally shown on *Masterpiece Theater*. Based on the best-selling novel by English author Joanna Trollope. 108 mins.
VHS: S30004. $14.98.

Virgin Machine
Called "steamy" by *The San Francisco Chronicle* and "a lesbian *Candide*...deliriously obscene" by *The San Francisco Examiner*, *Virgin Machine* is an offbeat black and white comedy about a journalist researching romantic love. The study takes her from German endocrinologists to San Francisco's porn district where she meets Susie Sexpert, a woman who lectures on the relative merits of various strippers and demonstrates dildos the way some women handle tupperware. German with English subtitles.
VHS: S10940. $29.95.
Monika Treut, Germany, 1988, 90 mins.

A Virus Knows No Morals
A black comedy filled with the worst fears, a savagely funny burlesque on the AIDS crisis, irreverent yet deadly serious. Nurses on the night shift roll dice to see which AIDS patient will die next. An epidemic victim is harassed by a reporter on his death bed—he sticks her with a contaminated syringe. The government opens a quarantine called Hell Gay Land. Gay terrorists capture the Minister of Health. An outrageous and yet extremely honest film by von Praunheim, this controversial film shook West Germany. German with English subtitles.
VHS: S09350. $39.95.
Rosa von Praunheim, Germany, 1985, 82 mins.

Viva Eu! & Ex Voto
Tania Cypriano, an experimental Brazilian filmmaker, explores her most poignant life experiences in these two films. In *Viva Eu!*, Cypriano explores her experiences as a woman living with AIDS. In *Ex Voto*, Cypriano takes a look at her ordeal of surviving terrible burns from a horrible fire she was trapped in. Both films show struggle and a commitment to survival.
VHS: S27241. $59.95.
Tania Cypriano, Brazil

Waking Up: A Lesson in Love
The feature debut of documentary filmmaker Greta Schiller (*Before Stonewall*) is a piercing, emotionally honest dissection of a young woman's journey of self-exploration. The film—shot on location in Austin, Texas—is a collection of painful, funny vignettes unfolding in the casual, loose rhythms of the aggressively hip lesbian bar Petticoat Junction.
VHS: S07854. $39.95.
Greta Schiller, USA, 1988, 60 mins.

We Were One Man
A simple French farmer and a wounded, abandoned German soldier are ultimately united in an openly sexual relationship in this award-winning French film. French with English subtitles.
VHS: S01437. $49.95.
Philippe Vallois, France, 1980, 90 mins.

We Were There
In the year of the American Bicentennial, Pat Rocco created this documentary focusing on the Gay Pride Celebrations in San Francisco and L.A. Rocco was instrumental in making and distributing films about visible, open, gay communities. From 1967-78 he produced, wrote, edited, directed and appeared in over 100 shorts and features. This is one of his best documents, a bit of gay history.
VHS: S22955. $19.95.
Pat Rocco, USA, 1976, 30 mins.

The Wedding Banquet
Ang Lee's surprise hit is a poignant and funny story of the gay Taiwanese yuppie (Winston Chao) who lives with his American lover (Mitchell Lichtenstein) and tries to end his family's endless matchmaking attempts by announcing that he's engaged. His parents unexpectedly fly in to see the bride and turn their son's deception into a complicated affair.
VHS: S21895. $94.98.
Ang Lee, USA/Taiwan, 1994, 105 mins.

West Coast Crones: A Glimpse into the Lives of Nine Old Lesbians
A touching and revealing documentary which focuses on nine women at crossroads in their lives, as they reflect and candidly discuss how they confront aging. A remarkably honest, heartfelt film which plays against stereotype as it humanly and movingly deals with the issues which pit individuals against society and its mores.
VHS: S16832. $39.95.
Madeline Muir, USA, 1991, 28 mins.

Westler: East of the Wall
Before the wall separating East and West Germany came down it divided not just a nation but thousands of families. This film tells a story about the nearly impossible romance between two gay men on opposite sides of the wall. German with English subtitles.
VHS: S24836. $39.95.
Wieland Speck, Germany, 1986, 94 mins.

When a Kid Is Gay
Meet the members of a private peer-support group for gay and lesbian teens in Worcester, Massachusetts, and hear some stories that range from shocking to poignant. A PBS WGBH Boston Special. 60 mins.
VHS: S33093. $19.95.

When Night Is Falling
Two women find one another in this sensitive love story. Camille is a repressed Catholic professor currently involved with a man. Her whole life changes, however, when she meets Petra, an enigmatic performer from a visiting circus. Before long, the two women embark on a romance that startles everyone, including themselves, with an unforseen passion.
VHS: S27541. $89.95.
Laser: LD75925. $39.99.
Patricia Rozema, Canada, 1995, 90 mins.

Wigstock: The Movie
It all began with a bunch of New York drag queens who didn't want to stop partying so they put on a show in Tomkins Square Park—in the daytime. Now it has grown into an annual celebration of queer crossdressers from all over. Underground stars The "Lady" Bunny, Jackie Beat, the Mistress Formica, Lypsinka and Joey Arias are joined by RuPaul, Crystal Waters, Alexis Arquette and Deee-Lite on a trip across a landscape of cosmetic wonders.
Laser: LD75417. $39.99.
Barry Shils, USA, 1995, 82 mins.

Wild Blade
A narcissistic gathering of five people with convulsive sexual desires and unconventional orientation are attracted to a young male prostitute (Stephen Geoffreys) whose married trick dies under mysterious circumstances. The dead man's wife, a deranged pimp and a jealous lover all conspire and negotiate for possession of the hustler. With Sheila Kelley, Carole Scott, Thom Crouch and Geoffrey Paltrowitz.
VHS: S18588. $29.95.
David Geffner, USA, 1992

Wild Life
A video portrait of two 15-year-old gay Latinos, this work by John Goss combines documentary-style interviews with fictional segments in which the young men act out their fantasized day in Los Angeles. As they talk about their lives, we see scenes of them changing into wild style clothes on the street, cruising around "Gay City," meeting their friends at the park, and "throwing attitude." They are questioned about the nature of being gay, relationships with friends and lovers, style and image, and their use of gay language.
VHS: S06509. $49.95.
John Goss, USA, 1985, 40 mins.

Women from Down Under
Australian and New Zealand directors made these lesbian shorts. Italian food, Bulgarian folksinging, truckers and the morning after are just some of the surprising elements that come up in these entertaining works. Included are *Peach, Just Desserts, Excursion to the Bridge of Friendship* and *Jumpin' the Gun*. 52 mins.
VHS: S27609. $19.95.

Word Is Out: Stories of Some of Our Lives
This is the first major film to explore America's gay culture. Involving a diverse range of people in locales from San Francisco to Boston, the study interviews 26 men and women ranging in age from 18 to 77. Speaking tellingly, funnily and movingly of their experiences, these women and men overturn decades worth of accumulated stereotypes. From the director of *Absolutely Positive*.
VHS: S16077. $29.95.
Mariposa Film Group, USA, 1977, 130 mins.

Work
Set against the gritty backdrop of a small Missouri milltown, this major lesbian work tells the tale of Jenny (Cynthia Kaplan), an unemployed housewife in her mid-20s, as she looks for a job and yearns for passion. Jenny divides her days between the search for work and her deepening love affair with June (Sonja Sohn), a young black athlete who lives next door.
VHS: S33867. $29.95.
Rachel Reichman, USA, 1996, 95 mins.

World & Time Enough
Winner of the Audience Award, San Francisco Lesbian & Gay Festival, this is a "...gentle, enchanting comic drama" (*OUT Magazine*) about gay love in which a mellow garbageman and found-object collector, Joey (Gregory G. Giles), and HIV-positive artist/provacateur, Mark (Matt Guidry), work at maintaining a monogamous relationship. Debut film by Minneapolis director Eric Mueller. "...a '90s *Parting Glances*...leaves its pushy, big-budget mainstream kin like *Jeffrey* in their own archaic haze, still mincing and miserable" (*The Village Voice*).
VHS: S30137. $39.99.
Eric Mueller, USA, 1996, 92 mins.

Wrecked for Life: The Trip and Magic of Trocadero Transfer
Before the arrival of AIDS, the underground gay dance scene in San Francisco generated one of the most exciting nightlife sensations ever known. At the center of this scene was the Trocadero Transfer. In this documentary everything about the all-night parties held there is revealed through interviews with the people who made it happen and those who experienced it.
VHS: S21026. $39.95.
John Goss, USA, 1993, 60 mins.

You Are Not Alone
This Danish film honestly explores the boundaries between friendship and love in a boys' school in a film which is full of nuance, gentleness and humor, reminiscent of the early films of Truffaut. Danish with English subtitles.
VHS: S01491. $79.95.
Lasse Nielsen/Ernst Johansen, Denmark, 1982, 90 mins.

Young Hearts, Broken Dreams, Episode 1: The Delivery Boy
Eddie Starr and Mark Cannon star in one of the first gay soap operas, the ongoing saga of a troubled gay movie star, his lover, his friends, sex, drugs, Hollywood and life in the fast lane. Adam Harrington, a delivery boy at Paramount Pictures, finds all his romantic longings fulfilled when he meets and moves in with his idol, gay movie star Scottie Edwards. Unfortunately, Scottie is beholden to a ruthless drug lord, and he and Adam decide to skip town together. In the end, however, they must face reality and return to the oversexed world of gay Hollywood.
VHS: S27722. $49.95.
Gerald Gordon, USA, 1990, 45 mins.

Young Hearts, Broken Dreams, Episode 2: The Search
After the disastrous outcome of the first episode, an entirely new cast of characters comes to the foreground in this steamy sequel. Scottie Edwards' brother Matthew and his best friend, Noah, leave Nebraska to come to Hollywood and avenge Scottie's death. Before long, Matt realizes that he's falling for Zech, the handsome detective assigned to Scottie's murder. *The Search* continues the exciting mix of sex, sensuality and emotional ups and downs found in the first episode of this soap opera. Michael Habusch and Robert Spiewak star.
VHS: S27723. $59.95.
Gerald Gordon, USA, 1995, 83 mins.

Young Hearts, Broken Dreams—Episode 3: He Loves Me He Loves Me Not
The final episode in this truly different '90s soap opera. Find out if Matthew selects Zech over Noah and if the notorious drug lord is capured and put into jail. Matthew has discovered Noah's love for him; but Zech's interested in him too.
VHS: S32913. $49.95.
Gerald Gordon, USA, 1997, 84 mins.

Zero Patience
An outrageous movie musical, this films depicts an imaginary love story between 19th-century Victorian writer and explorer Sir Richard Francis Burton and "Patient Zero", the Canadian flight attendant accused by the media of being the man who brought AIDS to North America.
VHS: S22669. $39.95.
John Greyson, Canada, 1993, 100 mins.

documentary cinema

$8.50/A Barrel! Huit Piastres et Demie and Cajun Visits

Two men, one 82, the other 93, recount what happened in the fishing village of Golden Meadow, Louisiana, during two weeks in the summer of '38. As leaders of opposing sides of the Shrimp War of 1938, each tells the truth, his truth, and each inevitably contradicts the other. Neighbors and relatives don period costumes, drive vintage cars and ride '30s era boats to recreate the shrimp war. Cajun French with English subtitles.
VHS: S06505. $89.95.
Glen Petrie, USA, 58 mins.

28 Up

Beginning in 1964, director Michael Apted turned his camera on a group of 7-year-old boys and girls from both wealthy and poor families in England, recording their thoughts, hopes and dreams with revealing interviews. He then returned to film these same children every seven years, until the age of 28; all of their most personal moments, from the rapture of discovered love to the despair of dreams long forgotten, are brought vividly to life, played out before the viewer with striking emotional power. A moving and utterly memorable work.
VHS: S14291. $19.98.
Michael Apted, Great Britain, 1984, 136 mins.

35 Up

Michael Apted's astonishing documentary, made for Grenada Television, charts the dreams, lives, ambitions and fates of its disparate English characters. The subjects are part of a landmark series, originally titled *Seven Up*. They were chosen as seven-year-olds for a series that would assess the English social, political and ruling systems; the underlying themes are the intermingling of race, class and sex. The documentary picks up their lives in seven-year intervals. (The films in between were *Seven Plus Seven, 21* and *28 Up*.) Apted is brilliant at evoking deep and private feelings about their lives and expectations—Tony had aspirations to be a jockey, while Nick and Peter were fascinated by space. Cinematography by George Jesse Turner. Edited by Claire Lewis and Kim Horton.
VHS: S19020. $19.98.
Michael Apted, Great Britain, 1991, 128 mins.

Abuse

A young boy, abused by his parents, finally discovers some much needed emotional gratification when he becomes the focus of a documentary about abuse. He becomes close to the gay man directing this film. Shot in a documentary style, this film raises tough questions about the nature of intimacy between an adult man and a 14-year-old boy.
VHS: S28068. $79.95.
Arthur J. Bressan, USA, 1995, 93 mins.

An Afternoon with Father Flye

Father James Harold Flye is best known as the life-long friend and mentor of writer James Agee. In this touching portrait of James Flye, the man to whom the *Letters of James Agee to Father Flye* were written, Academy Award-nominated documentary filmmaker Ross Spears gives us a record of several visits with Father Flye spanning a ten-year period and culminating with the occasion of Father Flye's 100th birthday. "Ross Spears is a major talent. His work deserves to be seen by all Americans who want to understand their country better" (Jim Welsh, *Film and History*).
VHS: S30425. $24.95.
Ross Spears, USA, 1995, 30 mins.

Agee

In this Oscar-nominated film, the fascinating story of poet, journalist, film critic, screenwriter and Pulitzer Prize-winning novelist James Agee is told by those who knew him best, including John Huston, Walker Evans, Robert Fitzgerald, Dwight MacDonald, Father James Flye, and Agee's three wives. "Proof of the axiom that a significant subject will inspire an impressive film" (*Booklist*).
VHS: S30145. $24.95.
Ross Spears, USA, 1980, 90 mins.

Aileen Wuornos: The Selling of a Serial Killer

Wuornos is a 35-year-old lesbian prostitute who murdered seven of her male clients along a Florida interstate. She is "adopted" by Arlene Pralle, a "born-again" woman who sells the story to the highest bidders. This crazy set-up also includes a lawyer with a crazy defense and Wuornos' lover, who dupes the killer into confessing over the phone. It's a documentary about the media frenzy that surrounds sensational criminals and obscures justice.
VHS: S23288. $19.98.
Nick Broomfield, USA, 1992, 87 mins.

Albert Schweitzer

Frederic March narrates this fascinating documentary which features Dr. Schweitzer telling his own story about his medical work in Africa. Filmed in France and on location in Equatorial Africa. Winner of the Academy Award for Best Documentary Feature.
VHS: S34193. $19.95.
Jerome Hill, USA, 1957, 80 mins.

All Dressed Up and No Place to Go

Originally shown on Cinemax, this even-handed and often humorous documentary profiles four heterosexual men—an executive, a lawyer, a computer consultant and an engineer—who unabashedly discuss their "unbelievable compulsion" to dress as women. Complete with whimsical fashion and beauty tips, this study of the lifestyles of "drag kings"—and the women who love them—is "an affirmative tribute to the wide spectrum of gender identity, and to human resilience" (John Carman, *San Francisco Chronicle*).
VHS: S31085. $39.95.
Peter Schwartz, USA, 1996, 72 mins.

Alternate Route

This documentary profiles young business owners, from fish to fashion, as they deal with the ups and downs of running their own companies and their lives. These young men and women explain why they are not afraid to take risks and are forging ahead to carve out a place for themselves in society.
VHS: S34405. $165.00.
Denise Withers, USA, 1997, 45 mins.

America & Lewis Hine

The winner of several major awards, including a special Jury Prize at the Sundance Film Festival, *America & Lewis Hine* chronicles the life and art of one of the most influential and recognizable photographers in the world, whose 40-year career recorded the changing face of America in more than 10,000 images. Features hundreds of Hine's photographs, many never seen before. Narrated by Jason Robards, Maureen Stapleton and John Crowley. "Virtuous...superior" (*The New York Times*). "Clearly one of the major American documentaries of recent years" (*Variety*).
VHS: S30583. $24.95.
Nina Rosenblum, USA, 1984, 60 mins.

America in Black & White

A set of three video cassettes featuring five true life video stories by director Scott Jacobs. USA, 89 mins.
Pugs 'N Pols. Featuring three short films by Scott Jacobs: *The Golden Gloves*—a young fighter battles to make his way out of the ghetto through victory in the ring, produced by Scott Jacobs and Tom Weinberg (10 mins.); *Election Night with Jane Byrne*—the historic 1979 triumph of Chicago's first woman mayor over the Democratic machine as seen from inside her private suite, produced by Scott Jacobs, Cynthia Neal and Lilly Ollinger (22 mins.); and *Election Day (Chicago Style)*—vignettes from the key Chicago precincts in Jimmy Carter's 1976 presidential triumph, produced by Scott Jacobs and Valjean McLenighan (7 mins.). USA, 40 mins.
VHS: S13593. $19.95.
The Las Vegas Tapes. Four days and nights on the streets of downtown Las Vegas with Jack the Jam Artist, Toye the Stripper, Angel and The Radio Announcer and Chief Little Fox, the unofficial mayor of Fremont Street. To the tourists, it's glitter gulch; to them, it's home. Directed by Scott Jacobs and Valjean McLenighan. USA, 27 mins.
VHS: S13594. $29.95.
The Real Realness of the Higher Highness. A Bio-Centennial Unity Fair in Golden Gate Park becomes the focal point for this look back at the future past. Greenpeace, Wavy Gravy, Eckankar, Psycho-Acoustics, and Interspecies Communications are featured as old hippies meet the new age in a celebration of the decade to come. Directed by Scott Jacobs. USA, 22 mins.
VHS: S13595. $19.95.
Set of three cassettes.
VHS: S13596. $49.95.

American Dream

The winner of the 1990 Academy award for best documentary, forceful account of the labor strike and political discord in a small, closely knit Minnesota town, at the Hormel Meat Packing plant. Kopple brilliantly covers the issues, background, social and economic context and the key players. The fight literally pitted brother against brother, after some workers crossed the picket line. Kopple strips away the layers of deception and anger to present a startling portrait of Reagan/Bush era greed and the frightening repercussions and break up of a community. Kopple worked on the film for more than seven years.
VHS: S17633. $19.98.
Barbara Kopple, USA, 1990, 90 mins.

Amish: Not to Be Modern

Made in cooperation with the Amish community, this is an exclusive portrait of the intensely private Amish. Filmed over a period of one year, we observe the cycles of life in an Amish community, and the important role that every member plays. 57 mins.
VHS: S13169. $29.98.

And Now Miguel

Produced for the U.S. government by Joseph Krumgold, this motion picture depicts a typical Southwestern American family operating as an economic unit. Its members choose to carry on the traditional occupations from father to son.
VHS: S10555. $24.95.
Manuel Cheves, USA, 1953, 62 mins.

And This Is Free

Chicago's Maxwell Street Market is captured in its entirety through cinema verite techniques in this unique film. The filmmaker originally set out to capture blues singers, but he realized that the whole area contained a much fuller picture that could explain the blues. Since Maxwell Street has been transformed by urban renewal, this may be the only way to see the singular mix of people and music that this area once offered. B&W.
VHS: S27154. $19.95.
Mike Shea, USA, 1964, 50 mins.

Angelyne

Angelyne is an enigmatic but ubiquitous pin-up model in L.A., her hometown. This documentary finally shows the woman with the amazing figure behind all the hype. She reveals everything from her opinions on men to her thoughts on Barbie. The president of her fan club, her psychotherapist and her lingerie consultant offer their opinions of the fascinating Angelyne. 25 mins.
VHS: S26663. $14.98.

Anima Mundi

This collaboration between director Godfrey Reggio (*Koyaanisqatsi*) and composer Philip Glass (*Einstein on the Beach*) is a naturalistic documentary on the relationship between humans and animals. The film uses a series of close encounters between humans and animals of varying sizes to showcase the diversity of the animal kingdom. "The proud procession of life forms has an incandescence and mystery that neither still photographs nor museum exhibitions can begin to capture" (*New York Times*).
VHS: S19593. $19.98.
Laser: CAV. LD72437. $29.99.
Godfrey Reggio, USA, 1993, 50 mins.

Animals Film

A very powerful, unflinching documentary about the shocking treatment of animals in research and in the food process, this feature-length film is narrated by Julie Christie, and has been banned from television for its graphic footage.
VHS: S05363. $79.95.
Victor Schonfeld, Great Britain, 1985, 120 mins.

Anne Frank Remembered

Family members, childhood friends and the people who hid the Franks bring to life the girl behind the diary. Academy Award winner for Best Documentary of 1995, narrated by Kenneth Branagh with selections from Anne's diary read by Glenn Close. German, Dutch and English with English subtitles.
VHS: S28620. $14.95.
Laser: LD75956. $39.95.
Jon Blair, Great Britain/USA, 1995, 117 mins.

Anything I Catch
The rare art and the natural drama of a way of life are shown in this documentary about handfishing. They represent elements of the disappearing Cajun lifestyle and the traditions of this community. 27 mins.
VHS: S22386. $39.95.

Apogee: Life in Motion
Cinematographer Craig McCourry's stunning film, six years in the making, continues the tradition of *Koyaanisqatsi* as he travels the world to capture the visual synergy of man, nature and the built environment. A dazzling collage of music, movement and rhythm from Japan, India, the Seychelles Islands, Hong Kong, Canada and the U.S. 45 mins.
VHS: S21898. $19.98.

Appalachia: No Man's Land
A highly personalized account of the effects of coal mining on several communities on the West Virginia/ Kentucky border. Based on interviews with long-time Appalachians, many of whom have worked for the coal companies, the film is a chronicle of the resilience of a people and their culture in the face of economic and environmental hardships. Produced by Maryknoll Media. 28 mins.
VHS: S04921. $24.95.

The Atomic Cafe
A unique documentary about Cold War paranoia over the Bomb. This chilling documentary by Kevin Rafferty, Jayne Loader and Pierce Rafferty culls newsreel footage and government archives to recreate the hysteria of the Cold War. "A comic horror film, it does more to evoke the what-me-worry social madness of the Cold War than any documentary I've ever seen" (J. Hoberman).
VHS: S00074. $29.95.
Laser: LD75375. $49.98.
Kevin Rafferty, USA, 1982, 88 mins.

The Atomic Filmmakers
This extraordinary documentary chronicles the top secret film studio that for more than 20 years photographed over 300 nuclear weapons tests, from the Nevada desert to remote Pacific atolls to outer space. Among the most spectacular images ever captured on film, the work of these filmmakers created a visual legacy that will serve as an important reference for one of the most dangerous times in world history. 50 mins.
VHS: S33039. $19.95.

Baboona
Fabled explorers and documentary filmmakers Osa and Martin Johnson share their encounters on an African safari, where they discovered the largest baboon community any explorer had ever encountered. The camera captures the lifestyle of this highly intelligent member of the monkey family with an intimacy and agility never before accomplished.
VHS: S31879. $19.95.
Martin Johnson/Osa Johnson, USA, 1935, 73 mins.

Ballot Measure 9
This winner of the Special Jury Award at Sundance in 1995 follows the fight around Oregon's Ballot Measure 9. Essentially, the initiative would have denied lesbians and gay men civil rights protection. Though defeated, it was the center of acrimonious debate and tense standoffs. This documentary captures the heroic spirits of the people who stood up against bigotry, even under threat of physical harm.
VHS: S27476. $29.98.
Heather MacDonald, USA, 1995, 72 mins.

Baraka
Amazing 70mm cinematography tells this global story of human and environmental interdependence. No dialogue is needed in this film that brings the beauty of the earth together with the universal truth of human striving. Music by a number of religious groups and contemporaries like Michael Stearns and Dead Can Dance make this an aural as well as a visual feast. Best Picture, Montreal Film Festival.
VHS: S25539. $29.95.
Laser: LD74951. $39.98.
Ron Fricke, USA, 1992, 96 mins.

Behind the Veil: Nuns
A profoundly stirring record of the turbulent history and remarkable achievements of women in religion from pre-Christian Celtic communities to the radical sisters of the 1980's. Shot on location in Ireland, Italy, Canada and the United States.
VHS: S05800. $29.95.
Margaret Wescott, Canada, 1984, 130 mins.

Benjamin Britten
This collecttion of four shorts from the golden age of British documentaries features three that incorporate the music of Benjamin Britten, including the landmarks *Coal Face* (Alberto Cavalcanti, 1935) and *Night Mail* (Basil Wright and Harry Watt, 1936) produced by John Grierson, as well as *Instruments of the Orchestra* (Muir Mathieson, 1947). The composer featured on the final documentary, *Steps of the Ballet*, is Arthur Benjamin.
VHS: S17420. $29.95
Great Britain, 1935-1948

Berkeley in the Sixties
A moving documentary about the 1960s social, political and sexual revolution at the University of California at Berkeley. The documentary traces the anti-war protest movement, the free speech movement, civil rights protests and the formation of the women's movement. Director Mark Kitchell interweaves archival footage with interviews with key leaders of the movement. The soundtrack includes Joan Baez, Mario Savio, Country Joe and the Fish, The Band, Jimi Hendrix and The Grateful Dead. "Probably the best documentary on the sixties to date" (*Village Voice*).
VHS: S18146. $29.95.
Mark Kitchell, USA, 1990, 117 mins.

Best Boy
An intimate and touching documentary, winner of an Academy Award, Ira Wohl's first feature is the story of his cousin Philly, a 52-year old man with the emotional and intellectual age of an eight-year-old, and of his decision to leave home and work on his own. New York Times wrote, "*Best Boy* records Philly's first four days away from home, though it is always in the company of his cousin-the-filmmaker, who carries the camera ...*Best Boy* is though more than the story of Philly. It's about a family. Even more affecting than Philly's first days in school are the scenes we see played—sometimes at the side of the screen—between Philly's mother and father...The film is about life, and 'a confusion of love and anguish.'"
Laser: CLV. **LD70261. $39.95.**
Ira Wohl, USA, 1979, 110 mins.

The Best of Real Sex
A fun-filled journey through other people's sex lives, from a little S & M to Miss Nude World; from the private life of a peep-show girl to a sex workshop in Hawaii. The best sex is *Real Sex*. From HBO. 60 mins.
VHS: S31619. $14.95.

The Best of Taxicab Confessions
In this Emmy Award-winning HBO program, cameras hidden in New York taxicabs capture exchanges between the drivers and their passengers, from five girls out for a night on the town, to the guy who admits he's a sex addict; from the girl out to catch her boyfriend in the act, to the rescue worker with tales of true-life horror. 60 mins.
VHS: S31618. $14.95.

Beyond the Killing Fields
Millions were killed in the Cambodian civil war. This documentary looks at the efforts made by the people and the organizations that have attempted to help survivors rebuild their lives and their country. Shot on location in Cambodia. 28 mins.
VHS: S23132. $19.95.

The Big Bang
How did the universe begin? What is the human spirit? Filmmaker James Toback (*The Pick-Up Artist*) takes his camera into the lives of the acclaimed and the ordinary—from basketball star Darryl Dawkins, gangster-turned-filmmaker Tony Sirico, violinist Eugene Fodor and former boxing-champ Jose Torres to a model, a mother and a restaurateur—and records their answers to the questions we continue to ask ourselves. "Irresistible" (*N.Y. Times*).
VHS: S15000. $19.98.
James Toback, USA, 1990, 81 mins.

Blacks Britannica
One of the most charged and controversial films of recent years, "a relentless, hard-hitting exposure of the racial and economic oppression of Britain's black population, together with their militant resistance" (Clyde Taylor). The scheduled broadcast on PBS was cancelled, and for the next four years, under a federal court injunction, it could not legally be seen by more than 19 persons at one time. It was condemned as a "danger" by officials of the British government, and its premiere run in a London cinema was stopped by court order. An international campaign to defend the film ultimately succeeded in freeing it from all restrictions. *Blacks Britannica* presents an analysis of racism within the context of British history and the post-war crises of British economy. It reflects the resistance of the Black community to escalating attacks on it, both by organized fascist elements on the streets and by successive British governments. "A startling look at the growing politicization of blacks in Britain and an unsettling portrait of an England in transition" (Variety).
Home Video.
VHS: S10841. $39.95.
Institutional with public performance rights.
VHS: S10846. $89.95.
David Koff, Great Britain, 1978, 58 mins.

Blood in the Face
A darkly humorous and frightening closeup view of today's far right movement, *Blood in the Face* uses archival footage and interviews to reveal the workings of the Ku Klux Klan, the American Nazi Party, the Aryan Nations, and David Duke. One of the most controversial and compelling films of 1991. "Riveting... insidiously spooky...full of outrageous details... first rate journalism" (*New York Times*).
VHS: S15462. $29.95.
Anne Bohlen/Kevin Rafferty/James Ridgeway, USA, 1991

Borneo
A great adventure documentary narrated by Lowell Thomas detailing flying snakes, tree climbing fish and headhunters. USA, 1937, 76 mins.
VHS: S02812. $39.95.

Breasts: A Documentary
Twenty-two women and girls from ages 6 to 84 speak candidly-and naked from the waist up—about their attitudes toward breasts-their own and others'—in this revealing and humorous documentary. They'll introduce you to the secrets, the sensations, the surprises and the stories that lie hidden in their anatomy. It just may change the way you look at the world—and yourself. "Men and women alike can gain much from watching this" (*The Chicago Tribune*).
VHS: S32360. $36.99.
Meema Spadola, USA, 1996, 50 mins.

Briefcases and Bomb Shelters
A survival manual published by the West German government for its citizens states that, in the event of nuclear war, you can protect yourself from fallout by covering your head with a briefcase as you beat a hasty retreat to the nearest bomb shelter. This contribution to atomic absurdity provides the inspiration for this satirical documentary on life in the nuclear age. Written, produced and directed by Bob Hercules.
VHS: S15193. $24.95.
Bob Hercules, USA, 1986, 13 mins.

Broken Noses
Photographer Bruce Weber's first directorial effort is the story of professional lightweight boxer Andy Minsker and his small boxing club for boys in Portland, Oregon. This portrait goes far beyond the realm of boxing as we learn that Minsker was raised in a broken home with a stepfather who beat him. Remarkably unaffected, Minsker reveals both a boxer's machismo and a lifetime of unrealized pain. Set to a smoky jazz score by such greats as Chet Baker, Gerry Mulligan and Julie London.
VHS: S16462. $29.95.
Bruce Weber, USA, 1987, 75 mins.

Brother Can You Spare a Dime?
The chronicle of an unforgettable piece of American history: 12 crazy, painful see-saw years, from the Wall Street Crash to Pearl Harbor. Featuring Eddie Cantor, Cab Calloway, and Ginger Rogers. Golden Globe Nominee for Best Documentary.
VHS: S34195. $19.95.
Phillipe Mora, USA, 1975, 104 mins.

Brother's Keeper
This riveting documentary by Joe Berlinger and Bruce Sinofsky is a reconstruction of the arrest and trial of Delbert Ward in the alleged suffocation and murder of his brother Bill. Set in a small town in upstate New York, Bill, Delbert and their two other brothers lived in a squalid farmhouse with no electricity or running water. *Brother's Keeper* is a powerful work about the nature of justice and community, and the grass-roots campaign to secure Delbert's freedom and exonerate him of the charges.
VHS: S18959. $19.98.
Laser: CLV. **LD74472. $39.95.**
Joe Berlinger/Bruce Sinofsky, USA, 1992, 105 mins.

Buckminster Fuller: Thinking Out Loud
Rising from the depths of despair on Chicago's lakefront, Fuller transformed himself, his life, and ultimately the world with his radical take on the contemporary world. Though he is perhaps best known for his geodesic dome design, this architect and thinker encouraged a new global outlook combining ecology and technology. Morley Safer narrates while Spalding Gray reads Fuller's writings. Includes interviews with Paul Goldberger, Philip Johnson, John Cage, Merce Cunningham, Arthur Penn and others.
VHS: S27909. $39.95.
Karen Goodman/Kirk Simon, USA, 1995, 94 mins.

Cadillac Desert: Water and the Transformation of Nature
Based on Marc Reisner's book, this boxed set chronicles the growth of civilization in the desert, the resistance to this achievement, and the dangers it has created at home and abroad, and examines the real-life drama behind the struggle for water in the modern American West. Narrated by Alfre Woodard. Four programs include *Mulholland's Dream*, *An American Nile*, *The Mercy of Nature*, *Last Oasis*, and, as an added bonus, Roman Polanski's Academy Award-winning classic, *Chinatown*, with Jack Nicholson and Faye Dunaway—the fiction behind the facts of *Mulholland's Dream*.
VHS: S31560. $99.95.

Cannabis Rising
An insider's look at the rapidly growing, quasi-legal cannabis industry in the Netherlands and the issues surrounding it. Sociologists, marijuana tycoons, drug refugees from the U.S. and others explore the debate raging over medical marijuana, the effects of prohibition and America's failed war on drugs, and the results of decriminalization on Dutch society.
VHS: S31104. $19.95.
Daniel Keller/Charles Light, USA, 1996, 35 mins.

Carmen Miranda: Bananas Is My Business

Archival footage, film clips, dramatic re-enactments and interviews document the life story and the lasting influence of the Brazilian Bombshell. This fun and interesting film won Best Documentary at the Chicago International Film Festival and the Film Critic's Award at the Brazilian Film Festival. English and Portuguese with English subtitles.

VHS: S27627. $19.98.

Helena Solberg, USA/Great Britain, 1995, 90 mins.

Catwalk

Supermodel Christy Turlington stands revealed in this behind-the-scenes look at fashion. Whether in Milan, Paris or New York, with Kate Moss, Naomi Campbell, Cindy Crawford or Claudia Schiffer, the backstage world of glamour under pressure that she inhabits is eminently watchable. Designers Giorgio Armani, Jean-Paul Gaultier, Karl Lagerfeld and Valentino are also glimpsed in this singular documentary.

VHS: S27650. $89.99.

Robert Leacock, USA, 1995, 95 mins.

The Champagne Safari

This fascinating film tells the fantastic but true story of wealthy businessman, glamorous playboy and daring adventurer Charles Bedeaux, who rose to wealth and fame in the 1920s after making his fortune by inventing a new method for modernizing industry. Bedeaux, who was lampooned in Chaplin's *Modern Times*, hobnobbed with the rich, powerful and famous all over the globe, even in Nazi Germany. For leisure he planned an elaborate trek through the Canadian Rockies, to be documented for posterity by legendary cinematographer Floyd Crosby (*High Noon*). But soon Bedeaux's opulent world was in danger, as charges of collaboration and treason enveloped him.

VHS: S32650. $59.95.

George Ungar, Canada, 1995, 100 mins.

Chess Kids

With humor and sensitivity, this award-winning documentary goes behind the scenes of the largest World Youth Chess Tournament ever held in the United States, capturing the intensity and excitement of competitive chess. Meet Josh Waitzkin, the real-life subject of *Searching for Bobby Fischer*, and 12-year-old Judit Polgar, the best female player of all time. Featured at the 1996 Chicago International Children's Film Festival. "Chess aficionados and people who simply enjoy a well-made documentary with fascinating interviewees will appreciate this fun film" (R. Pitman, *Video Librarian*).

VHS: S30660. $29.95.

Lynn Hamrick, USA, 1996, 51 mins.

Chicago 1968

Chaos reigned during the 1968 Democratic National Convention in Chicago. As Yippies orchestrated effective protests against the Vietnam war in the streets, Mayor Richard Daley marshalled 25,000 riot police to establish order at all costs. Many thought the ensuing riots spelled the end of the stalemated, two-party political system. This documentary from the American Experience series is narrated by W.S. Merwin. 60 mins.

VHS: S29508. $19.95.

Chicago Maternity Center Story

For more than 75 years, the Chicago Maternity Center provided safe home deliveries for Chicago mothers. But a change in attitude of modern medicine toward home birth and a decline in funding forced its closure. This "powerful and persuasive film" (Roger Ebert) interweaves the story of a young woman about to have her first baby with the history of the center and the fight to keep it open. "A combative, devastatingly researched account of how American medicine has deteriorated since it became a multi-million dollar business" (*Sunday London Times*).

VHS: S27851. $29.95.

Kartemquin Films, USA, 1976, 60 mins.

Chicago Nazis

From the violent confrontations of the American Nazis led by Frank Collins, these two documentaries on one tape, *Marquette Park I* and *Marquette Park II*, offer probing insights into extremism in America. *Marquette Park I* documents a Nazi rally, *Marquette Park II* allows rare insights into the preparation for a planned demonstration. What is remarkable about these films is not only the fact that the filmmaker was allowed to film inside the headquarters, but how he has managed to depict the minds of extremists.

VHS: S06473. $39.95.

Tom Palazzolo, USA, 1976-78, 60 mins.

Chicago Politics: A Theatre of Power

Filmmaker Bill Stamets takes us on a startling and often funny tour of the political arena—Chicago style—into the world of politicians and deal makers, including Mayor Harold Washington and Alderman-turned-Republican Eddie Vrdolyak, in the course of the rituals of office, election and the administration of power. A priceless look at the "inside" of the running of a city.

VHS: S05364. $29.95.

Bill Stamets, USA, 1985-87, 87 mins.

Christo in Paris

Since the days of King Henry IV, Paris' Pont Neuf has inspired artists. Here it is the focus of environmental sculptor Christo Javacheff and his wife Jeanne-Claude, and the millions of Parisians who watch them create an astounding architectural poem. Rich in political intrigue and artistic debate, this "love story" from the Maysles brothers tracks Christo's escape from Bulgaria, his early years as a struggling artist, his romance with Jeanne-Claude and the fulfillment of a ten-year obsession begun in 1975: the wrapping of the Pont Neuf. "*Christo* is another gem from the Maysles, the super stars of cinema verite" (Desson Howe, *Washington Post*). English and French with English subtitles.

VHS: S33770. $39.95.

Albert Maysles/David Maysles, USA, 1991, 58 mins.

Christo's Valley Curtain

Nominated for an Academy Award, a documentary about the construction of Christo's Valley curtain in Rifle Gap, Colorado, in 1972. "It is the finest film I have ever seen about an artist and his work," said *The New York Times*. "The surprise of the film is the enthusiasm with which this project was greeted by the residents of Rifle and by the construction workers who risked limbs and lives on the stunt."

VHS: S07492. $39.95.

Albert Maysles/David Maysles, USA, 1974, 28 mins.

Citizen Diplomat

A compelling portrait of Rama Vernon, a tireless traveler for world peace since 1984 (35 trips to the USSR to date). Share in her unique experiences opening up meaningful communication between private citizens and government officials of the US and USSR. Taped at a special lecture near San Francisco, the viewer learns how Vernon became a citizen diplomat, what it means to her, and how citizen diplomacy has affected us all. A woman's inspiring, insightful story of how "one person *can* make a difference."

VHS: S13719. $29.95.

Paul (Ramana Das) Silbey, USA, 1990, 58 mins.

The City/The Power and the Land

The City is a landmark documentary, co-directed by Willard Van Dyke and Ralph Steiner, with commentary written by Lewis Mumford read by Morris Carnovsky, and with music by Aaron Copland. Notable for its montages, its narrative vignettes and its humor, it is at the same time a powerful social portrait of New York City (1937, 44 mins.). *The Power and the Land* (Joris Ivens, USA, 1940, 39 mins.) is an emotionally powerful documentary about rural electrification, presented by looking at the life of a single farming family.

VHS: S14930. $29.95.

Cityscape Compilations

Includes *San Francisco by the Golden Gate* (10 mins.), *Progress: Los Angeles* (15 mins.), *Long Beach Earthquake* (10 mins.), *In the Street* (13 mins.), *Manhattan* (11 mins.), *Ellis Island* (10 mins.) and *Century of Progress—Chicago* (10 mins.)

VHS: S14931. $29.95.

Classic Documentaries: People and Places

Four important classics of the Grierson documentary movement. *Housing Problems* (Edgar Antsey and Arthur Elton, 1935), a film about the demolition of slums and their replacement with government-financed housing, was revolutionary for its use of slum dwellers as spokesmen, talking directly to the camera. *New Earth* (Joris Ivens, Netherlands, 1934), possibly the most famous of Ivens' films, is a moving record of the draining of the Zuider Zee. Hanns Eisler contributed the dynamic musical score. *Song of Ceylon* (Basil Wright, 1935) is a brilliant, lyrical depiction of the Ceylonese people and culture. And *Night Mail* (Harry Watt and Basil Wright) features narration written by W.H. Auden and music by Benjamin Britten, in a brilliantly edited film about the British mail service.

VHS: S03473. $59.95.

Edgar Antsey/Arthur Elton/Joris Ivens/Basil Wright/Harry Watt, Great Britain/Netherlands, 1930's

Classic Documentaries: The Power and the Land

Three classic documentaries: *The Power and the Land* was commissioned as a companion film to Pare Lorentz' *The River* and it was to do for rural electrification what *The River* did for the TVA. A simple and convincing story of a rural family before and after receiving the benefits of electricity (in 1935 only one farm in ten used electricity), the documentary's extraordinary emphasis on poetry comes from its simple and meticulous closeness to the rhythms of daily life. This tape also contains Lorentz' *The River* and *The Plow That Broke the Plains*. (See description elsewhere).

VHS: S04608. $69.95.

Joris Ivens, USA, 1935, 110 mins.

Colorado Cowboy: The Bruce Ford Story

Bruce Ford is a legend in rodeo. No man has won more championships in the same event. This film explores the roots and horizons of a man pursuing his own dream, a tradition of pride inherited from his father, a legacy of grace. It's a documentary that traces the line between championship and despair in the Western sport of bareback riding.

VHS: S23286. $24.95.

Arthur Elgort, USA, 1993, 78 mins.

Columbus Didn't Discover Us

A politically charged reaction to the events heralding the Columbus quincentennial, this documentary explores the issues discussed in the July 1990 symposium on the cultural, historical and political damage suffered by indigenous cultures and languages through the hemisphere. The historic gathering featured Indian nations from North, South and Central America. "This is an important and valuable testimonial from voices too long suppressed" (Lisa Mitten, American Indian Library Association).

Home Video.

VHS: S17500. $39.95.

Institutional with Public Performance Rights.

VHS: S17686. $89.95.

A Common Destiny:

Walking in Both Worlds—Jewell Praying Wolf James, known as Se-sealth, is an engaging young Lummi tribesman, a hunter and gatherer of the lost and subjugated wisdom of his ancestors. Speaking from a cedar tree-stump in an ancient Northwest forest, he brings to the present the message of his ancestor, chief Seattle, whose name he carries. Directed by Gayil Nalls. *The Hopi Prophecy*—Thomas Banyacya, now in his 80s, is a spokesman for the Hopi high religious leaders. His words come from the heart as he interprets the potentially apocalyptic message of the petroglyph on Second Mesa. Two parts on one tape.

Total length: 60 mins.

VHS: S15436. $24.95.

Consuming Hunger: Getting the Story

News events from the Third World face a tough fight for Western television air time. Yet images determine the Western World's view of the Third World: the dramatic pictures from Ethiopia launched a major relief effort, yet those pictures almost didn't get aired. *Getting the Story* shows how the tragedy in Ethiopia went from just another famine to become the most moving news story of the decade, exploring the "rules" of television news and our own attitudes toward the Third World. 28 mins.

VHS: S05844. $24.95.

Consuming Hunger: Selling the Feeling

Selling the Feeling explores the Madison Avenue treatment of problems such as domestic hunger and homelessness, and the conscious decision by the organizers to avoid the political aspects of the problems. The death of thousands in Ethiopia made us aware of the plight of our own poor, hungry and homeless. Yet when the events are over, are we any different as a nation in our treatment of the poor? Produced by Maryknoll Media. 28 mins.

VHS: S05845. $24.95.

Consuming Hunger: Shaping the Image

Shaping the Images raises questions about the impression of Africa created by television coverage of the Ethiopian famine, and, by extension, the images projected of other suffering peoples. What was our response? Was Live Aid an outpouring of generosity or a celebration of Rock and Roll? Are we ready to listen to Africans and our own poor tell their own story? 28 mins.

VHS: S05846. $24.95.

Coverup: Behind the Iran-Contra Affair

A documentary that investigates the Iran-Contra scandal and alleges a web of lies and deceit that "TV could not tell." USA, 1988, 72 mins.

VHS: S07346. $29.95.

Crumb

Robert Crumb, the multi-talented underground comic book artist, is profiled in this unique, in-depth documentary portrait. Emerging from a dysfunctional family, it's a wonder that Crumb managed to channel his peculiar take on the world into a relatively socially acceptable form. Part of the great fascination of this film is the revelation that his brothers, both also quite gifted, were not as lucky.

VHS: S27253. $19.95.

Laser: LD75491. $39.95.

Terry Zwigoff, USA, 1995, 119 mins.

Cyberpunk

Cyberpunks are young people who fight technology with technology, idealistic and sometimes romantic figures on the margins of society. They use their wits to outsmart the powers that control information and technology. To some their work has terrifying implications; to others, they are the future hope for individual liberty. With William Gibson, Jaron Lanier, Timothy Leary and Michael Synergy.
VHS: S14714. $29.95.
Marianne Trench, USA, 1991, 60 mins.

Daley: The Last Boss

Mayor of Chicago for five consecutive terms, Richard J. Daley was one of the country's most important politicians and, arguably, the last big city boss. His Democratic machine maintained control and order through a system of rewards and intimidation. This unvarnished look details his rise from inner city life to national prominence, a position seriously harmed by changing social pressures and the debacle of the 1968 Democratic Convention.
VHS: S27832. $19.95.
Barak Goodman, USA, 1995, 112 mins.

Damned in the USA

Though the Reverend Wildmon tried to have it stopped by the courts, this documentary was not only screened nationwide, it won an International Emmy Award for Best Arts Documentary. This tape looks at the debates fomented by issues like obscenity and free speech, debates that often embroiled artists and politicians in the late 1980s and early 1990s. Jesse Helms, Christie Hefner, 2 Live Crew, Senator Al D'Amato, Andres Serrano, Jesse Helms and Madonna are just some of the public figures voicing their opinions in this riveting film.
VHS: S27259. $49.95.
Paul Yule, Great Britain, 1991, 126 mins.

The Dancer

Called "the ballet world's equivalent of *Hoop Dreams*" (*Miami Herald*), this documentary follows young ballerina Katja Bjourner on her journey as a student at The Royal Swedish Ballet School as she develops toward a promising professional career. Swedish with English subtitles.
VHS: S31189. $29.95.
Donya Feuer, Sweden, 1994, 96 mins.

Dancing Outlaw

Jesco White is the Dancing Outlaw. His wife says he is three persons: a beautiful man, the Devil himself, and Elvis. He is also "the best mountain dancer in these here parts." Jesco idolized his dad, and keeps his memory alive through Appalachian tap dancing, amid the feuds, poverty, ignorance, violence and natural wildness of Boone County.
VHS: S21882. $49.95.
Jacob Young, USA, 1991, 60 mins.

Dark Circle

Multiple award-winning feature documentary portrait of the nuclear age, told through the lives of those who are directly affected by it. Mixing personal stories with recently declassified footage of the secret world where the hydrogen bomb is tested, built and sold. "Four stars—completely riveting," said Roger Ebert in *The Chicago Sun-Times*.
VHS: S03731. $49.95.
Judy Irving/Chris Beaver/Ruth Landy, USA, 1982, 82 mins.

David Holzman's Diary

Jim McBride's seminal underground film is an autocritique about a young filmmaker (screenwriter L.M. Kit Carson) who makes an autobiographical, cinema verite film. It is a film about identity and self-obsession. With Penny Wohl, Louise Levine and Fern McBride. Selected by the National Film Registry as an American Film Classic.
VHS: S18862. $19.98.
Laser: LD76783. $49.95.
Jim McBride, USA, 1967, 74 mins.

Day After Trinity

This haunting examination of the dawn of the nuclear age focuses on the dramatic events surrounding the development of the first atomic bomb. Featuring interviews with scientists and soldiers, and rare, archival footage, it provides a gripping profile of J. Robert Oppenheimer, the bomb's principal architect, and offers a penetrating commentary on the nature of scientific inquiry, the McCarthy era, and nuclear proliferation.
VHS: S00307. $39.95.
Laser: LD75026. $49.95.
Jon Else, USA, 1981, 88 mins.

Deadly Art of Survival

A Bruce Lee-style docu-epic shot in the housing projects of the Lower East Side, the story revolves around the real and imaginary rivals of an idealistic martial arts school led in actual life by the star of the film, Nathan Ingram. This early super-8 feature fuses ghetto kung-fu culture and what was to become hip hop.
VHS: S22605. $39.95.
Charlie Ahearn, USA, 1979, 58 mins.

Deadly Deception

G.E. does more than "bring good things to life." It also is the industry leader in producing nuclear arms components. This challenging video questions the role of corporate responsibility given the deadly influence exerted by this firm's many nuclear installations. Winner of the Academy Award for Best Documentary.
VHS: S21586. $50.00.
Debra Chasnoff, USA, 1991, 29 mins.

Death in the West

One of the most powerful anti-smoking films ever made. Originally produced for British television and vigorously suppressed by tobacco interests, it juxtaposes the healthy, independent image of the *Marlboro* man, defended in interviews with cigarette company executives, with the stark reality of six smoking cowboys—all dying of smoking-induced illnesses. "A classic film"—C. Everett Koop, former U.S. Surgeon General. 1983, 32 mins.
VHS: S13698. $29.95.

Devil at Your Heels

The late Ken Carter's long-time obsession to be the world's greatest daredevil is the subject of this feature-length documentary. Seen are the five years that are spent in raising $1 million, building a rocket-powered car, and constructing a ten-story take-off ramp for his attempt to jump across a mile-wide stretch of the St. Lawrence River. A portrait of a stunt driver who made his living by risking his life. Produced by the National Film Board of Canada.
VHS: S07672. $79.95.
Robert Fortier, Canada, 103 mins.

Documentary Masterpieces by John Grierson

John Grierson revolutionized the ideas, grammar and shape of the documentary, and this program collects five works he either directed, produced or supervised, from the years 1931 to 1960, beginning with *Industrial Britain*, which was shot by Robert Flaherty; Len Lye's *Color Box*; Edgar Anstey's *Granton Trawler*; Julien Huxley's *The Private Life of the Gannetts*; and Hilary Harris's *Seawards the Great Ships*.
VHS: S17453. $29.95.
John Grierson, Great Britain, 75 mins.

Don't Look Back

One of the best portraits of an artist ever put on film, *Don't Look Back* is about Bob Dylan and the Sixties. Director Pennebaker, known for *Monterey Pop*, filmed Dylan during his 1965 English concert tour, capturing both private moments and public performances. With Joan Baez, Alan Price, Donovan.
VHS: S00357. $19.98.
D.A. Pennebaker, USA, 1967, 95 mins.

Down and Out in America

Academy-Award-winning documentary, narrated by Lee Grant, which takes the viewer into the streets and brings the nightmare home. "It's a war. there's no blood, but there will be!" is a quote from this prophetic documentary which examines the plight of America's homeless.
VHS: S04898. $29.95.
Lee Grant, USA, 60 mins.

Dying for a Smoke

This documentary explores the arguments put forward by the two sides engaged in the furious battle over cigarettes. On one side is the multi-billion dollar industry which manufactures cigarettes. On the other is a powerful anti-smoking lobby determined to prevent the deaths of 49,000 Americans each year from cigarette smoke. Chuck Norris, Gregory Hines, Johnny Mathis and Charleston Heston are just some of the stars involved in this struggle.
VHS: S22419. $59.95.

E.M.B. Classics

British documentarian John Grierson (1898-1972) is one of the most important figures in the history of the medium. With Robert Flaherty and the Soviet directors Eisenstein, Kuleshov and Vertov, they essentially founded the ideas, language and texture of the documentary. Grierson specialized making evocative, gripping, and wholly unsentimental documentaries that expressed a real affinity and feeling for the worker. This program, part of the British Documentary Movement, contains three of his best works: *Drifters* (1929), about turn-of-the-century English workers; *Industrial Britain* (1933), about the labor process; and *Song of Ceylon* (1934), produced by Grierson and directed by Basil Wright, about the British colony Sri Lanka from an Orientalist vantage point.
VHS: S17421. $29.95.

The Electric Valley

This is the first independent film to tell the story of the Tennessee Valley Authority (TVA), one of the most controversial federal agencies ever created and one which, after a half century, continues to shape life in the South. In 1933 the TVA was given the mission to tame the forces of nature, create cheap energy, and produce lasting prosperity in the Depression-wracked Tennessee Valley. *The Electric Valley* is both political parable and human drama, a narrative journey through 50 years of American history with this institution as its focus. "Quite accurately called 'a journal of the American political soul'" (William Sloan, Museum of Modern Art).
VHS: S30426. $24.95.
Ross Spears, USA, 1984, 90 mins.

Elegy for a Street Survivor (Yume)

This piece follows the strange memorial that takes place after Yume, a homeless man who had been a "Buddhist hippie," dies of respiratory distress. A Felliniesque procession follows as his friends perform odd rituals in his honor.
VHS: S33791. $24.95.
Claire Burch, USA, 1995, 45 mins.

England in the Thirties

Three documentary shorts that make up the British Documentary Movement, the brainchild of the brilliant John Grierson, who made films depicting social, political and working conditions in Britain. This volume contains such disparate works as the Edgar Anstey-directed *Granton Trawler* (1934), Alberto Cavalcanti's *Pett and Pott* (1934), and Harry Watt's *North Sea* (1938).
VHS: S17417. $29.95.

Epicenter U.

This first-hand account details the story of a multi-cultural group of students at California State University, Northridge, coping with the aftereffects of the Northridge earthquake. Vice President Al Gore and the Honorable Andrew Young appear in this moving document. 28 mins.
VHS: S26178. $24.95.

The Exiles

A documentary portrait of German intellectuals, artists and writers who fled Hitler and resettled in America, where they made seminal contributions to American culture, science, art, nature, film and music.
VHS: S18695. $39.95.
Richard Kaplan, USA, 1990, 116 mins.

Feed

An entertaining documentary about the relationship of politics and image as captured in the New Hampshire primary in January, 1992. With on-camera reports on Bill Clinton, George Bush, Ross Perot, Pat Buchanan and Jerry Brown, the film is a demystification of the election process. Some of its best moments are the illegally captured "backchannel" footage from satellite coverage.
VHS: S18420. $19.95.
Kevin Rafferty/James Ridgeway, USA, 1992, 80 mins.

Festival of Britain

Three documentaries from the British Documentary Movement: Humphrey Jennings's *Family Portrait* (1951) assesses the fallout of the war, John Eldridge's *Waverley Steps* (1948) is an essay about city life, and Paul Dickson's *David* deals with coal mining in a discussion of Welsh identity.
VHS: S17419. $29.95.

Fifth, Park & Madison

A document of the New York City 1987 bike messenger strike against Mayor Ed Koch's proposed midtown bike ban—bikes in the air!
VHS: S10200. $39.95.
Dragan Ilic, USA, 1987, 45 mins.

The Films of Arne Sucksdorff: The Great Adventure Plus Short Subjects

Distinguished Swedish nature cinematographer Arne Sucksdorff brought the vision of a poet to the wildlife around him and the animals and birds became the principal actors in his films, as these four shorts as well as his acclaimed feature film demonstrate. In *The Great Adventure* (1953, 75 mins.), the rhythms of nature are explored through the eyes of children. Two brothers on a Swedish farm rescue and tame an otter which they keep hidden from their parents. We follow the progress of the forest and its denizens as the seasons change. "A sensuous mixture of beauty and cruelty" (Pauline Kael). *Hunter and the Forest—A Story Without Words* (1956, 6 mins.) is the story of an unusual encounter between a hunter and a family of deer in the forest. On the narrative level it is an idyll, providing an exciting stimulus for creative writing. It also raises more profound questions about man's fundamental attitudes toward hunting as a sport, as well as his sentiments about nature and conservation. The beauty and majesty of the forest and its wildlife is intruded upon by man in the dramatic, touching, magnificently photographed short subject *The Shadow of the Hunter* (1957, 10 mins.). The beautifully photographed short *Struggle for Survival* (1950, 10 mins.) depicts the life cycle of the seagull. The snow-covered woods and its animals are captured in *Shadows on the Snow* (circa mid-1950s, 10 mins.), a dramatic, yet beautiful look at nature and the survival of its creatures.

VHS: S30551. $29.95.

Arne Sucksdorff, Sweden, 1950-57, 115 mins.

Fingers That Tickle and Delight

Named "Deaf Senior of the Year," teacher, storyteller and comedienne Evelyn Zola is a role model for hearing and deaf people alike. Sent away to boarding school at the age of three to study oral and lip-reading tradition, she eventually found "her people" (the signing community) in Chicago. She now does two stand-up comedy shows a night on an all-deaf cruise of 1100 deaf seniors. Interpreted by Sharon Newmann Solow.

VHS: S21982. $35.00.

Elizabeth Sher, USA, 1993, 32 mins.

Fire on the Mountain

"Among the best documentaries about skiing ever filmed" (*Snow Country Magazine*), this is the extraordinary portrait of the men of the U.S. Army's 10th Mountain Division—world-class skiers, mountaineers and climbers who share their exploits in the only mountain and winter warfare division of World War II. Grand Prize winner at the 1995 Telluride Mountainfilm Festival. "Bracing exploits, hearty outdoorsmen, powerfully captured on film" (*New York Times*).

VHS: S31119. $29.95.

Beth Gage/George Gage, USA, 1996, 72 mins.

Forbidden Photographs

Charles Gatewood's *The Video* is the primary work of this documentary, with excursions into Manhattan's sexual underground, the Hellfire Club, Forbidden Tattoos, pierced genitals, Naked City and Mardi Gras Madness, with special appearances by Annie Sprinkle, Spider Webb, and Fakir Musafar. B&W and color. 100 mins.

VHS: S17075. $59.95.

Free at Last

A video celebrating the 25th anniversary of Amnesty International, and its worldwide struggle to protect human rights. A unique look at and inside this Nobel prize-winning organization. 1986, 30 mins.

VHS: S06887. $20.00.

Gay for a Day

Three documentaries from Tom Palazzolo dealing with gay issues: *Gay for a Day* is the story of the 1976 Gay Pride Parade; *Costumes on Review* is a hilarious documentary of a gay Halloween party.

VHS: S06112. $39.95.

Tom Palazzolo, USA, 45 mins.

Getting Around

Students with disabilities at the University of Oregon explain details of their daily lives at school. Despite a number of differing abilities related to missing limbs, blindness or muscular dystrophy, these individual contribute to the community as they further their education. 28 mins.

VHS: S26005. $40.00.

The Ghost of Solid Gold Illusion Meets Danny Boy

A homeless man with a biting sense of humor gives his views, along with psychedelic cut-ins of a series of images that seem to invade his consciousness.

VHS: S33793. $24.95.

Claire Burch, USA, 1995, 30 mins.

Girl Talk

This remarkable documentary tells the no-frills story of three runaway teenagers living by their wits on the mean streets of Boston. You will meet Pinkie, a 14-year-old dreamer, Mars, an underage stripper in the infamous Combat Zone and Martha, a product of 20 foster homes and institutions who is now facing pregnancy. All these young women have seen too much, too soon, but there is always hope. It may not be pretty, but it's real.

VHS: S15942. $19.98.

Kate Davis, USA, 1987, 85 mins.

Golub

Art, politics and the media intersect in artist Leon Golub's nightmarish images of war, torture, death squads and mercenaries. The documentary follows the creation of one of his monumental canvases, *White Squad X*, detailing his complex and unorthodox techniques. Interweaving scenes of Golub at work, archival footage, interviews with museum-goers and TV news, the film challenges us to question our connection to violence in the modern world and to reassess the relationship between art and society. "*Golub* conveys the exhilarating sense that art is inseparable from both the world that engenders it and the world that receives it" (Jonathan Rosenbaum, *Chicago Reader*).

VHS: S27803. $29.95.

Kartemquin Films, USA, 1988, 56 mins.

The Good Fight

It was one of history's most dramatic expressions of international solidarity when 40,000 volunteers from around the world went to fight the armies of Franco, Hitler and Mussolini in the Spanish Civil War of 1936-39. *The Good Fight* tells the story of 3,200 Americans who volunteered to fight on the side of the Spanish Republic. This vivid series of portraits with 12 of the survivors (half the Americans lost their lives in Spain) brings to life the reasons for joining the foreign conflict, and what it was to be a part of a people's army against fascism in the war that was the rehearsal for World War II. An absorbing and passionate account full of humor, pride and deep sorrow, their interviews are illustrated with rare archival footage of the Lincoln Brigade in Spain as well as Hollywood films, songs and newsreels with such notables as Hemingway himself and Henry Fonda. Narrated by Studs Terkel.

VHS: S12206. $69.95.

Noel Buckner/Mary Dore/Sam Sills, USA, 1984, 98 mins.

The Great British Documentary Movement

This comprehensive boxed set features 20 films (1929-1948) presented with the aid of the British Documentary Film Movement, including *Drifters, Family Portrait, Coalface* and *North Sea*. 619 mins.

Laser: LD76752. $199.99.

A Great Day in Harlem

Nominated for an Academy Award, this documentary offers a cross-section of jazz greats. In 1958, Art Kane orchestrated a group portrait of jazz musicians. Archival footage of interviews, performances and home movie footage rounds out the feeling of this day when the best jazz performers were gathered together. Art Blakey, Dizzy Gillespie, Charles Mingus, Thelonious Monk, Count Basie and Coleman Hawkins are just some of the musicians who appeared. 60 mins.

Laser: LD75324. $39.98.

Jean Bach, USA, 1995, 60 mins.

Great Sadness of Zohara

Nina Menkes combines sound, image and fragments of poetry in this moving film about the journey of a young Jewish woman who is drawn to explore the world of the spirit. Her journey takes her to remote and increasingly desolate regions of the Arab lands—alienating her from the orthodox Jewish community in Israel. This mystical quest culminates in her return to Israel where, indelibly marked, she confronts her loneliness and a devastating sense of exile.

VHS: S07374. $39.95.

Nina Menkes, USA, 1983, 40 mins.

Grow Dutch

The first video of its kind to investigate the secrets of Dutch marijuana growing, *Grow Dutch* takes viewers on a tour with Wernard, world-renowned master of marijuana cultivation, through his Positronics Sinsemilla Salon in Amsterdam, to see firsthand how the Dutch grow high-quality Sinsemilla indoors. You'll visit Dutch coffee shops in Amsterdam, one of the only places in the world where customers can purchase and smoke marijuana publicly. Also includes information about the history, ecology, botany, geography and many uses of the fascinating and controversial marijuana plant. With music by Chrissie Hynde of The Pretenders.

VHS: S30917. $19.95.

Ed Rosenthal/Alayn Lowell, 1996, USA, 40 mins.

Growing Up in America

This "intriguing and entertaining" (*New York Post*) time capsule captures '60s luminaries Allen Ginsberg, Timothy Leary, Abbie Hoffman and others then and now who helped shape this tumultuous decade.

VHS: S32027. $29.95.

Morley Markson, USA, 1988, 90 mins.

Guilty Until Proven Not Guilty—Napoleon's Revenge

The incredible story of a hippie dropout from Brooklyn, New York, who, after years in the Far East and Southeast Asia, lands in the oldest prison in France, serving five years for a drug-related "murder without intent." On appeal years later he is finally found not guilty, but through a fluke of French "justice" under Napoleonic laws, his sentence still stands.

VHS: S33825. $24.95.

Claire Burch, USA, 1995, 58 mins.

Hands Across America

The moving story of the Hands Across America project, which involved 6½ million Americans forming a 4,124-mile human chain in support of America's hungry and homeless. With musical highlights by Joe Cocker, James Brown, Harry Chapin, John Lennon, The Pointer Sisters, Prince, Lionel Richie and Kenny Rogers.

VHS: S02267. $14.95.

Harlan County U.S.A.

The Academy Award-winning documentary about the efforts of 180 coal-mining families to win a United Mine Workers contract at the Brookside mine in Harlan County, Kentucky, is a fascinating and moving portrait of the valor and courage of the coal-mining families.

VHS: S00542. $29.95.

Barbara Kopple, USA, 1976, 103 mins.

Harlem Diary

Author Terry Williams provided nine Harlem youngsters with notebooks and video cameras to let them document their world. The result is a fresh and honest look at the lives of people in Harlem. Often this place is obscured by stereotypes and fantasies. This documentary shows the hardworking people and the troubles they face everyday in the legendary neighborhood of Harlem. From the Discovery Channel. 100 mins.

VHS: S27821. $19.95.

Haunted Hills: Ghost Stories

It's been said that a story can be found beyond every hill in the Ozarks. Storytelling, an important segment of Ozark culture, began as a form of entertainment throughout the rural Ozarks. The most popular stories were those of ghosts and haunted places. This award-winning documentary is not only entertaining but serves to preserve the Ozarks' many tales of wonder. With Terry Shirley.

VHS: S30495. $14.95.

Phillip W. Steele, USA, 1994, 55 mins.

Heaven

Documentary from Woody Allen's former girlfriend and co-star, Diane Keaton. She asks a lot of questions about the Celestial Showplace and gets a lot of odd answers from some strange people filmed at uncomfortable camera angles. Film footage from Hollywood films on the subject are the highlights.

VHS: S05523. $14.95.

Diane Keaton, USA, 1987, 80 mins.

Heavy Petting

From the son of the man who invented white bread, a look back at the sexual attitudes and customs of the 1950's. Director Obie Benz, heir to a Delaware baking fortune, has dug into the film vaults for a compilation documentary that includes sex education films, commercials, popular and not-so-popular vintage movies and other archival footage of the news of the day. He also interviews celebrities like Allen Ginsberg, David Byrne, Sandra Bernhard, William Burroughs, Josh Mostel, Spalding Gray, John Oates and Abbie Hoffman and other people not-as-well-known, on what they remember about puberty.

VHS: S11257. $19.98.

Obie Benz, USA, 1988, 88 mins.

Heidi Fleiss: Hollywood Madam

In this bizarre and bawdy documentary the facts behind the controversial madam of tinsel town stand revealed. Though it is odd enough that a woman should find herself under criminal investigation for procuring young women in Hollywood, this film is surprising not just for its candor, but for its revelations.

VHS: S27883. $19.98.

Laser: LD75980. $39.99.

Nick Broomfield, USA, 1995, 106 mins.

Helen Keller in Her Story

Though blind, deaf and mute from the age of 19 months, Helen Keller went on to become one of the most celebrated women of two centuries. Made 13 years before her death in 1968, this feature employs newsreels, interviews and rare footage of Ms. Keller at home in Vermont. An Academy Award-winning documentary narrated by Katharine Cornell.

VHS: S16405. $29.95.

Nancy Hamilton, USA, 1955, 50 mins.

Hello Goodbye Bob Sparks
A piece in four parts, archiving a march to People's Park in memory of longtime park and housing activist Bob Sparks. With music by local musicians.
VHS: S33794. $24.95.
Claire Burch, USA, 1996, 90 mins.

The Hemp Revolution
Hemp, or marijuana, is not just a mild recreational drug. Long before it became notorious for its mind-altering qualities, it was widely grown for its resilient fibers and was used for everything from industrial strength rope to fine cloth.This documentary makes the case that growing hemp is a sound ecological enterprise with very pleasant side effects.
VHS: S29800. $29.95.
Anthony Clark, USA, 1995, 72 mins.

The Hemp Video
Did you know: ...the Declaration of Independence and the Constitution were originally written on paper made of hemp? ...Betsy Ross made the first American flag out of hemp? ...before 1937, Levi jeans were made of hemp? It's all here on *The Hemp Video*! With Johnny Marijuanaseed;The Honorable Robert Sweet, U.S. District Court Judge; Don Fiedler, Executive Director of NORML; and many more."Hemp is the most beautiful and beneficial plant that mankind has ever domesticated on this globe"—Gatewood Galbraith (Candidate for Governor, State of Kentucky).
VHS: S13774. $19.98.

The History of the Condom
A young couple discussing contraception provide the framework for this exploration of the condom. Documentary, dramatization and archival footage, along with the inevitable experts, shed light on these invaluable marital aids. Filmed in six countries, this video provides both a historical understanding and contemporary rationale that explains the usefulness of condoms.The ongoing AIDS crisis is given special emphasis in this respect. 54 mins.
VHS: S26994. $29.95.

Homage to May 19th/Framed
Weather Underground member Kathy Boudin is the subject of a recreated interview in the first film. Photographs, television news footage and written text are used to explore Boudin's transformation. She grew up in middle-class Manhattan but participated in the 1981 Brinks armored vehicle robbery. In *Framed*, dancer/performer Dianne Torr uses material from the French interrogation of Mata Hari.
VHS: S22617. $39.95.
Mary McFerran, USA, 1984-1987, 48 mins.

Homeless in the Nineties (The Video)
A portrait of the friction between society and a potentially explosive, marginalized group: the homeless. Includes interviews with homeless at the Center for Independent Living at Berkeley and original songs and images about homelessness.
VHS: S33795. $24.95.
Claire Burch, USA, 1995, 40 mins.

Hoop Dreams
The groundbreaking documentary about the dream that inspires young men throughout the country: the dream of playing professional basketball for the NBA. Seven years in the making, *Hoop Dreams* is an innovative work that closely focuses on the maze of high school sports, agents and the system as well as on the dreams of escaping the inner city.A remarkable, heartrending piece of history that says a lot about basketball, and about the life we all choose to live. Produced by Kartemquin Films.
VHS: S24386. $19.98.
Laser: Widescreen. **LD74943. $49.99.**
Steve James/Frederick Marx/Peter Gilbert, USA, 1994, 176 mins.

Hotel Terminus: The Life and Times of Klaus Barbie
Marcel Ophuls' award-winning documentary spans 70 years and three continents. Culled from 120 hours of interviews, it traces the 40-year-manhunt for Nazi war criminal Klaus Barbie, the ruthless SS interrogator known as "The Butcher of Lyon.""A shocking, unforgettable film" (Ebert and Siskel).Winner of the Academy Award for Best Documentary and the International Critics Prize at the Cannes Film Festival. Original English-language version (includes French, German and Spanish footage subtitled in English). 2 cassettes.
VHS: S10756. $29.98.
Marcel Ophuls, France/USA, 1988, 267 mins.

House of Un-American Activities
From a maker of "Hoop Dreams"—the riveting story of a filmmaker who looks for the father he never really knew as he draws on a wealth of family archives to uncover his father's persecution by the House Un-American Activities Committee. Also includes *Dream Documentary*, which uses footage from other films to create a surreal and foreboding societal landscape; and *Dreams from China*, a diary-like film essay shot in the wake of Tiananmen Square, presenting a paradox of Chinese politics and society.
VHS: S23209. $29.95.
Frederick Marx, USA, 1989-92, 52 mins.

Houses Are Full of Smoke
Documentary filmmaker Allan Francovich, the award-winning director of *On Company Business*, which investigated the workings of the C.I.A., now turns his cameras on the problems of Central America. Here, from ex-presidents, peasants, and members of the secret police, is what is really going on south of the border. Each of the three volumes focuses on a specific country;Volume I is Guatemala. In Volume 2, Francovich investigates C.I.A. involvement in El Salvador by exposing a cover-up of the death of American citizens as well as of thousands of the local population. Included in this tape is one of the last interviews with Archbishop Oscar Romero before his assassination.Volume 3 centers on Nicaragua.
VHS: S13292. $79.95.
Allan Francovich, USA, 1987, 174 mins.

How to Squash a Squat
This unique documentary chronicles the systematic destruction of a Squatters' building in New York City's East Village by the combined city authorities—Housing and Police—after an arson fire.The squatters fight to save their building, followed by the night and day demolition of their Squat surrounded by the police occupation of three city blocks.A powerful, activist vision of one of the urban nightmares of our time.
VHS: S13349. $39.95.
Franck Goldberg, USA, 1990, 46 mins.

Howard Stern: Shut Up and Listen
A compelling look at the relentless controversy and circus-like atmosphere surrounding the self-proclaimed "king of all media," Howard Stern, and the First Amendment Wars, featuring interviews with Steve Allen, Dr. Joyce Brothers, Pat Cooper,Alan Dershowitz, Morton Downey Jr., Larry Flynt,Anthony Michael Hall, Ed Koch, Dee Snyder, Randi Storm,"Grandpa"Al Lewis, Judith Regan, Rev.Al Sharpton, Bob Peters (President of Morality of Media), Citizens for Better Broadcasting and Citizens for the Return of Stern.
VHS: S31203. $79.95.
Jim Riffel, USA, 1997, 100 mins.

Hoxsey: How Healing Becomes a Crime
In 1924, Harry Hoxsey claimed a cure for cancer—herbal formulas inherited from his great-grandfather.Thousands of patients swore the treatment cured them, and by the 1950's Hoxsey's Texas clinic was the world's largest cancer treatment center, with branches in 17 states. Now Hoxsey's work continues in exile in Mexico and claims a success rate of 80%.Was Hoxsey really a hoax or were "medical experts" trying to suppress alternative therapies? You decide.
VHS: S14578. $29.95.
Ken Ausubel, USA, 1987, 100 mins.

Huit Piastres et Demie!
The shrimp war of 1938 is remembered by two men.The union was pitted against individuals and the drama unfolded in Golden Meadow. 60 mins. In Cajun with English subtitles.
VHS: S22403. $45.95.

The Hutterites
This ethnographic documentary examines the Hutterites, who have survived despite social and religious persecution, forced migration and isolation.The spiritual heirs of Mennonites and Amish, the Hutterites live highly unorthodox lives, outfitted in 16th century dress, cultivate a medieval village pattern and live in collective agrarian societies. Says one minister,"We're in this world, but not of the world." 60 mins.
VHS: S19245. $19.95.

In Motion: Amiri Baraka
Called "a brilliantly executed documentary" by *The New York Times*, a fascinating exploration of the writer and political activist formerly known as Leroi Jones. Following Baraka from his early days as a poet in New York City's Greenwich Village to his present literary and political activities, *In Motion:Amiri Baraka* is a portrait of a man of singular commitment to social change. Interspersed throughout the film are excerpts from Baraka's powerful play *The Dutchman*, one of the archetypal literary works of the 1960s, as well as scenes from other Baraka plays.
VHS: S10909. $59.95.
St. Clair Bourne, USA, 1985, 60 mins.

In Plain English
Julia Lesage's provocative documentary gathers a group of minority and ethnic activists (African-Americans,Asian-Americans, Hispanics, Pacific Islanders and Native Americans) from the University of Oregon to discuss assimilation, racism, the ways to attack discrimination, ethnic identity and their experiences within a wider college curriculum.
VHS: S17437. $50.00.
Julia Lesage, USA, 1995, 42 mins.

In the Blood
A tale of hunter and hunted in the story of two African safaris separated by nearly 80 years.The first, led in 1909 by President Roosevelt, is represented by rare historical footage from the Smithsonian.The President's great-grandson then retraces his ancestor's trail in 1986 and explores the role of the hunter in today's world while pursuing African big game. Brilliant cinematography and a stirring soundtrack depicting the natural magnificence of Africa.
VHS: S12952. $79.95.
George Butler, USA, 1989, 90 mins.

In the Land of the Deaf
A unique and privileged look inside the world of deaf people. A teacher, a woman treated for mental illness because of her deafness, and a newly wed deaf couple offer compelling portraits from a community estimated to comprise 130 million people worldwide in a film which is revealing, moving and often funny. French and French Sign Language with English subtitles.
VHS: S25993. $79.95.
Nicolas Philibert, France, 1994, 99 mins.

In the Shadow of the Stars
Behind the scenes of the San Francisco Opera Company, with chorus singers who aspire to be soloists and who dream of being stars.The film lovingly explores the blurred boundary between private lives and stage spectacles, and creates a rare and privileged look into the grand world of opera. Music by Mozart, Puccini, Rossini, Stravinsky, Verdi, Wagner and others.Winner of the 1992 Academy Award for Best Feature Length Documentary.
VHS: S16640. $24.95.
Irving Saraf, USA, 1992, 93 mins.

Inside the CIA: History
Part One of a three part series, featuring extensive interviews with David A. Phillips, former head of clandestine operations, and John Stockwell, a 14-year CIA veteran who headed up operations in Angola.The History starts at the end of World War II and examines the CIA's role in the Bay of Pigs invasion and the overthrow of Chile's President Allende.
VHS: S02357. $19.95.
Allan Francovich, USA, 1987, 58 mins.

Inside the CIA: Assassination
Part Two of a three part series looks at the use of assassination as a tool of U.S. foreign policy.
VHS: S02359. $19.95.
Allan Francovich, USA, 1987, 49 mins.

Inside the CIA: Subversion
Part Three of this series explores the manner in which the CIA has used subversion to destabilize or topple governments whose policies did not match those of the United States.Areas of emphasis are Latin America, Iran and the overthrow of Allende's government in Chile.
VHS: S02358. $19.95.
Allan Francovich, USA, 1987, 67 mins.

Islands
For two brief weeks in 1983, Christo's *Surrounded Islands* blossomed on the waters of Biscayne Bay, Florida: 11 scrub-pine islands surrounded by 6.5 million square feet of bright pink fabric.A three-year struggle, a political drama interwoven with two other Christo projects—the wrapping of the Pont Neuf in Paris, and the Reichstag in Berlin.
VHS: S07494. $59.95.
Maysles Brothers, USA, 1983, 58 mins.

Italy Wins World War III: 1990 Summit
Visionary TV producer and artist Peter Fend leads a strange live cable colloquium on the shape of the world and nation-states as they might look from space after a series of ecological wars.
VHS: S10172. $14.95.
Peter Fend, USA, 1983, 28 mins.

Jacare
Jack Buck stars in the first feature film documentary shot in the wilds of the Amazon jungle. It is an exciting, suspense-filled adventure story. Music by Miklos Rozsa.
VHS: S23775. $24.95.
Charles E. Ford, USA, 1941, 57 mins.

Julian Samuel Trilogy

This is an intelligent, three-part documentary about frontiers in intellectual history, including the Orient and the Middle East. The first volume, *The Raft of the Medusa: Five Voices on Colonies, Nations and Histories* (99 mins.), focuses on issues of emergent nationalism in Asia, with particular attention to the unique cases of Hong Kong and mainland China, Eastern Modernism and Islamic Fundamentalism. In the second installment, *Into the European Mirror* (56 mins.), Julian Samuel explores the concept of frontiers, both real and imaginary. Highlights include Columbus' voyage of 1492 and the Palestinian/ Israeli question of today. Issues of "euronationalism" are examined by experts in this thought-provoking video. In the final segment, *City of the Dead and The World Exhibitions* (76 mins.), Samuel takes an in-depth look at modern Islamic culture, including the rise of fundamentalism and the role architecture plays in keeping the sexes separate. Also explored in this video are the way turn-of-the-century World Exhibitions created an international perception of Asia and Asian culture, and the effects of terrorism in modern Egypt. English and French with English subtitles.

VHS: $27357. $99.95.

Julian Samuel, Canada, 1993-1995, 231 mins.

Julie: Old Time Tales of the Blue Ridge

Julie Lyon, the sister of Old Time fiddler Tommy Jarrell, lights this gem of a movie like a flower blooming in the wildwood. Nearing 80, she tells tales of childhood and her first romance. A sweet and enduring film. 11 mins.

VHS: $15302. $19.95.

Jupiter's Wife

Maggie is a beguiling homeless woman who lives in Central Park and claims to be the daughter of Robert Ryan and the wife of the god Jupiter. This documentary gets around her enchanting view of the world to discover the real-life mystery behind this cryptic personality.

VHS: $29867. $24.95.

Michel Negroponte, USA, 1994, 78 mins.

Just Between Me & God

An environmental love story about a fisherman and his wife; the Mississippi wildlife that they love is threatened by the construction of a drag race track and a raging chemical fire. This moving documentary was filmed on the edge of Memphis' industrial ruins. USA, 8 mins.

VHS: $15006. $29.95.

Kartemquin Films, Vol. 1: Inquiring Nuns

Set in Chicago in 1967, at the height of the Vietnam War, this disarming, intimate work finds two nuns moving through the city's densely populated streets, asking the question: "Are you happy?" The film pushes beyond the issues of the times and allows its subjects to open their hearts and reveal themselves plainly and simply. "A profound and moving experience for the viewer" (*Chicago Tribune*). USA, 1968, 66 mins.

VHS: $18198. $29.95.

Kartemquin Films, Vol. 2: Winnie Wright, Age 11

Three films by the Kartemquin Films Collective poignantly and honestly deal with personal and social change. In *Winnie Wright, Age 11*, Winnie is the daughter of a steelworker and school teacher watching the dramatic racial and class changes in her neighborhood. She learns valuable and frightening lessons about growing up female, working class and white (1974, 26 mins.). *Now We Live on Clifton*, on the same program, focuses on Pam and Scott Taylor, children who watch their multiracial, working-class neighborhood through an awkward though inevitable gentrification (1974, 26 mins.). *Parents* is an open-ended discussion about a youth group and their feelings about their parents and the "generation gap" (1968, 22 mins.). USA, 1974, 74 mins.

VHS: $18199. $29.95.

Kartemquin Films, Vol. 3: Trick Bag

Three films capture the history and apocalyptic social and personal changes of the Vietnam era. *Trick Bag* (1975, 21 mins.) allows gang members, Vietnam vets and young factory workers to relate their personal experiences of racism. *What the Fuck Are These Red Squares* (1970, 15 mins.) looks at striking students at the School of the Art Institute in the wake of the killing of student protestors at Kent State and Jackson State. *Hum 255* (1969, 28 mins.) traces the activities of two students and their return to the University of Chicago following their expulsion for illegally occupying the Administration building. They confront current students about their attitudes, moral and social values and the meaning of education. USA, 1975, 64 mins.

VHS: $18200. $29.95.

Kartemquin Films: The Complete Set

Volumes 1-3.

VHS: $18201. $74.95.

Kid Nerd

An offbeat reminiscence about nerdhood by adults who have come to terms with their nerdiness. Blending interviews with excerpts from a '40s educational film about teenage social etiquette, *Kid Nerd* finally lets nerds have their say. Includes former nerds Penn Jillette, of Penn & Teller, Josh Weinstein, executive producer of *The Simpsons*, Steven deSouza, screenwriter of *48 Hours* and *Die Hard*, plus an assortment of teachers, architects, cartoonists, editors, and a striptease artist.

VHS: $34409. $275.00.

Shereen Jerrett, USA, 1997, 45 mins.

Koyaanisqatsi

With no dialog, only the music of Phillip Glass, and no characters other than the entire human race and the five elements, this years-in-the making film is a symphony of sound and image, fast-paced, dazzling, hypnotic.

VHS: S00692. $14.95.

Godfrey Reggio, USA, 1983, 87 mins.

The Lash of the Penitents

A reporter investigates a strange cult in the American Southwest. This film represents his findings. 30 mins.

VHS: $23794. $24.95.

Last Call at Maud's

A documentary about the closing of San Francisco's oldest-running lesbian bar. The film follows the 23-year history of the bar, related by owner Rikki Streicher, and a larger consideration of empowerment within the gay rights movement. "The documentary makes salient points about lesbians' generally second-league standing to gay men, legalistic problems such as women not being allowed to be bartender, a 70s souring of homosexual pride due to male gay's 'lack of political consciousness,' and the shooting of Harvey Milk" (Derek Elley, *Variety*).

VHS: $19745. $29.95.

Paris Poirier, USA, 1993, 75 mins.

Last Pullman Car

More than 100 years ago, George Pullman, one of the giants of American industry, built a vast industrial empire. It was supposed to last forever. Yet in 1981, Pullman workers found themselves in the midst of a fight not only for their jobs but the future of the American rail car industry. In this engaging story, 100 years of government, union and corporate policy are traced.

VHS: $27804. $29.95.

Kartemquin Films, USA, 1983, 56 mins.

Legong

A documentary photographed on the island of Bali under the direction of Marquis de la Falaise. "Legong-Dance of the virgins" features an all native cast with authentic native dancing and religious rites. 50 mins.

VHS: $15178. $29.95.

Let Me Be Brave

Narrated by CBS sportscaster James Brown, this tape chronicles the efforts of 12 mentally handicapped athletes in their courageous attempt to scale Mt. Kilimanjaro in February of 1990. USA, 1991, 45 mins.

VHS: $15472. $14.98.

Life and Times Box

Five-volume box set produced by the non-profit James Agee Film Project includes *Agee*, *To Render a Life*, *An Afternoon with Father Flye*, *The Electric Valley* and *Long Shadows*.

VHS: $30427. $99.95.

Life of Adolf Hitler

Paul Rotha's famous documentary uses archival footage to depict the rise of the Nazi party in a powerful study of one of the horrors of history. Much of the footage used by Rotha is rare, including the last films of Hitler before his retreat into the Bunker.

VHS: S00751. $29.95.

Paul Rotha, Great Britain, 1961, 101 mins.

Lifetime Commitment: A Portrait of Karen Thompson

After living together as a couple for over four years, Karen Thompson and Sharon Kowalski were hit by a drunk driver. Sharon was disabled, and Karen lost her lover to a legal system that refused to recognize their bond. Sharon's parents did all they could to keep the couple apart, a problem that deepened when Sharon's father, Donald Kowalski, gained full guardianship over his daughter. This video documents the struggle of two women in love, in a system that can't see the value of this bond.

VHS: $19454. $39.95.

Listen to Britain

Four great poetic documentaries by Humphrey Jennings, all set during World War II by this great English filmmaker: *Listen to Britain*, *The True Story of Lili Marlene*, *A Diary for Timothy* and *The Cumberland Story*.

VHS: S02953. $79.95.

Humphrey Jennings, Great Britain, 1942-47, 120 mins.

Listening to America: 20 Years with Bill Moyers

This program joins some of Bill Moyers' most engaging conversations with notable Americans, including Joseph Campbell, Maya Angelou, Ronald Reagan and Joe Namath. Moyers' series *The Power of Myth* and *A World of Ideas* gave him the opportunity to speak with great thinkers, leaders and heroes, resulting in this insightful work.

VHS: $21378. $19.95.

Little Richard: Keep on Rockin'

Catch the original wildman of rock 'n' roll at his onstage finest! Seen through the camera of D.A. Pennebaker, Little Richard tears through "Tutti Frutti", "Lucille" and six more favorites.

VHS: $16092. $14.98.

D.A. Pennebaker, USA, 30 mins.

Lodz Ghetto

This film covers the years 1940-1944 as it chronicles the 200,000 Jews trapped in the Polish ghettos during the German occupation. The film moves from the past and present; the script was developed from the diaries of the survivors and people left behind. Music by Wendy Blackstone. "Your blood turns to ice. To be unmoved by this film is to be made of stone" (*New York Daily News*).

VHS: $17891. $29.95.

Kathryn Taverna/Alan Adelson, USA, 1991

The Long Way Home

Michael Apted took his camera into recording studios and concert venues to follow Russian rock and roll star Boris Grebenshikov, whose recordings were, until recently, only available on the black market in the Soviet Union. With the coming of glasnost, Grebenshikov finds himself free to travel to New York, where he is invited to record his first album with CBS Records. "A superb documentary…rewarding, both musically and dramatically" (*The Dallas Morning News*).

VHS: $14292. $19.98.

Michael Apted, Great Britain, 1989, 82 mins.

The Long Way Home

This Academy Award-winning documentary details Holocaust survivors' lives from the end of WWII in 1945 to Israel's founding three years later. Narrated by Morgan Freeman, Martin Landau, and Ed Asner. Includes a post-Oscar introduction by producers Richard Trank and Rabbi Marvin Hier of the Museum of Tolerance in Los Angeles.

VHS: $34462. $24.95.

Mark Jonathan Harris, USA, 1997, 120 mins.

Looking for Richard

Al Pacino's critically acclaimed tribute to Shakespeare features Winona Ryder, Kevin Spacey, Alec Baldwin, Estelle Parsons and Aidan Quinn in rehearsals and meetings, allowing the audience to eavesdrop on the behind-the-scenes process that goes into creating characters and mounting a production. In this case, the production is Shakespeare's gripping drama of power and betrayal, *Richard III*. With Sir John Gielgud, Kenneth Branagh, Vanessa Redgrave, James Earl Jones and Kevin Kline.

VHS: $31028. $103.99.

Laser: LD76142. $49.95.

Al Pacino, 1996, USA, 112 mins.

Looking Like the Enemy

This video essay on the paradoxes of race and the ironies of war is a bold exploration into the often horrifying predicaments faced by the Asian-American soldiers who fought in World War II and the Korean and Vietnam Wars. Breaking a legacy of silence, 18 veterans share their experiences, filling in the gaps that official history has often left out. 52 mins.

VHS: $31383. $24.95.

Louisiana Story

The last film of the famous father of the documentary, the story of a new oil derrick and its effect upon the Louisiana Bayou country, the boy and his raccoon. With music by Virgil Thompson.

VHS: S00771. $29.95.

Robert Flaherty, USA, 1948, 79 mins.

Lovejoy's Nuclear War

Awarded the John Grierson award, this 1975 documentary classic follows Sam Lovejoy as he topples a nuclear power plant project tower in Montague, Massachusetts, and turns himself in to the police. "A very thoughtful and provocative account of an original and stubborn one-man war against nuclear power. Muted and underplayed, it is one of the few genuinely consciousness-changing and organically political films of the last few years" (Amos Vogel, *Film Comment*). 60 mins.

VHS: S31095. $29.95.

Daniel Keller, 1977

Madonna: Truth or Dare

The popular musical superstar is the focus, and the executive producer, of this revealing documentary/concert movie that captures the excitement of her 1990 Blonde Ambition world tour. Visit backstage as Madonna chats with Kevin Costner, Sandra Bernhard and Warren Beatty. Come along when she visits her mother's grave. Be there when she leads her dancers and back-up singers in a group prayer. Then sit back and enjoy the sound and fury of blonde ambition in concert.

VHS: S14762. $19.98.

Alek Keshishian, USA, 1991, 118 mins.

The Making of the Holland Tunnel Drive-In Billboard

Artist Leni Schwendinger has created a documentary about the process of designing in light for the large billboard next to the Holland Tunnel. The goal was to transform the viewer's perception of the site, creating conditions for new, previously unquestioned meanings to emerge while engaging the viewer's imagination. Approximately 13 mins.

VHS: S14580. $49.95.

Mama Florence and Papa Cock

Alan Leder's lyrical, heartwarming documentary is a personal account of an elderly Jamaican couple living amidst the growing tourist trade in Negril, Jamaica. Set to the rhythms of reggae music, the film is a warm and often humorous glimpse of the changing tenor of rural Jamaica reflected in the lives of an old village family. Produced by Alan and Jane Leder.

VHS: S01955. $45.00.

Alan Leder, USA, 1983, 17 mins.

The Man Behind the Muppets: The World of Jim Henson

The late Henson began by fashioning his mother's old coat into the most beloved frog in the world, Kermit. The magical world conjured by this visionary is revealed in this video. It began with *Sesame Street* and led to many feature length films. 85 mins.

VHS: S24928. $19.95.

Man of Aran

One of the masterworks of Robert Flaherty, in which Flaherty's "passionate devotion to the portrayal of human gesture and of a man's fight for his family makes the film an incomparable account of human dignity" (Georges Sadoul). Filmed on the island of Inishmore, it depicts the daily life of people on this isolated island off the coast of Ireland, fishing in their tiny curraghs, the difficulty of their existence, the hunting of a basking shark. A masterpiece.

VHS: S09417. $29.95.

Robert Flaherty, Great Britain, 1934, 76 mins.

Manufacturing Consent: Noam Chomsky and the Media

This remarkable Canadian documentary is a riveting look at the political life and times of the controversial author, linguist and radical philosopher, Noam Chomsky. Chomsky provides shocking examples of media deception as he analyzes the media and democratic societies. A film which has achieved cult status in its remarkable call to Chomsky's charge for viewers to "extricate themselves from this web of deceit by undertaking a course of intellectual self-defense."

VHS: S21851. $39.95.

Mark Achbar/Peter Wintonick, Canada, 1993, 180 mins.

Martha & Ethel

Two invincible, 80-year-old nannies offer a portrait of American life in this documentary. Spanning four decades and crossing the barriers of race, class and sex, this film reveals the heart of the American family. *Martha & Ethel* celebrates the extraordinary legacies of love and discipline these women have created, as seen through the eyes of the filmmaker, who herself was brought up by one of the two nannies profiled.

VHS: S26919. $96.99.
Laser: LD75402. $39.98.

Jyll Johnstone, USA, 1994, 80 mins.

Masters of the Congo Jungle

Produced in 1960 by the Belgian International Scientific Foundation, this is a chronicle of Henri Storck's two-year exploration of the Belgian Congo. Untouched for centuries by outside civilization, the jungle is now disrupted by the invasion of modern man. Storck captures remnants of the ancient African continent, plant and animal life and regional natives co-existing in the simple grandeur and rhythm of the earth.

VHS: S17448. $19.95.

Maxwell Street Blues

A unique historical celebration of the street that was "Chicago's unlikely (and extraordinary) commingling of ancient Jewish merchants, young black musicians, and unspecified patrons, set against a landscape that suggests a war has been recently lost there" (Neil Tesser). In an arresting look at the past and present of Maxwell Street, filmmakers Raul Zaritsky and Linda Williams show the history of the blues on the sidewalks, from the "gospel-styled abstractions of Carrie Robertson, to the quieter religiosity of Jim Brewer, to the voice of experience that is Floyd Jones's and Coot 'Playboy' Venson's, to the hard urban blues of the young players working up their chops." But Zaritsky and Williams are not content with a simple portrait of the blues thriving on this urban strip—they portray Maxwell Street Blues against the background of perpetual social change that makes Maxwell Street both "a hustle and an art." With Arvella Gray.

VHS: S03587. $39.95.

Raul Zaritsky/Linda Williams, USA, 1981, 60 mins.

Maya Lin: A Strong Clear Vision

The story of the artist/sculptor/architect who, while an undergraduate at Yale, designed one of the most bitterly debated public monuments, the Vietnam Veterans Memorial. The film follows her throughout the creative process as she produces a succession of eloquent, highly original sculptures and monuments that capture and memorialize significant American social events. Compelling viewing. "The film is absolutely riveting" (Peter Stack, *San Francisco Chronicle*).

VHS: S30482. $59.95.

Freida Lee Mock, USA, 1995, 96 mins.

The Maysles Brothers: Direct Cinema

In this 1969 documentary writer-editor Jack Kroll interviews filmmakers Albert and David Maysles about what they called a "new technique of natural movie making, Direct Cinema." Program includes excerpts from their feature-length film *The Salesman*, about door-to-door sales of *The Bible* to working people in Boston. The Maysles formed a two-man crew and followed the salesmen around in an early example of "cinema verite." They discuss their film techniques, the purpose of working in their verite style, getting the subjects to agree to being documented, and their rejection of the idea that they are reformers. 60 mins.

VHS: S31565. $59.95.

Miracle of Intervale Avenue

This sensitive exploration searches for the secrets of a once thriving Jewish community in the South Bronx that somehow continues despite the decay that surrounds it. The film shows a remarkable reality of Jews, Blacks and Puerto Ricans interacting and helping each other. What makes this film so moving is the cast of vital, complex and moving characters. 65 mins.

VHS: S06576. $59.95.

Miss Sarajevo

First aired on MTV, this award-winning short documentary looks at a city, a people and a time when the very act of living takes on a very surreal quality: an orchestra rehearses in the basement of a TV building because of shelling outside; a rock and roll band spends two days on the front line and two days playing rock and roll at one of the city's remaining clubs; the Miss Sarajevo beauty contest is being held, epitomizing the struggle to survive no matter what the cost. Bono from U2 serves as executive director and performs the title song with Luciano Pavarotti.

VHS: S34718. $99.95.

Bill Carter, USA, 1997

Moana, A Romance of the Golden Age

A great film by Robert Flaherty which followed the success of *Nanook of the North*. Flaherty chose the Samoan cultural tradition; he lived for two years on the islands, with the story gradually evolving out of the lives of the native population. Includes the famous sequences of the tattooing of Moana, a part of the initiation into manhood, and dancing the Shiva before a village virgin. An "intensely lyrical poem on the theme of the last paradise" (Herman Weinberg). Silent with music score.

VHS: S07486. $29.95.

Robert Flaherty, USA, 1926, 76 mins.

Monterey Pop

Directed by one of the foremost factual filmmakers in the cinema-verite style, *Monterey Pop* records the events at the immense Monterey International Pop Festival. Featuring Otis Redding, Jimi Hendrix, Janis Joplin, Jefferson Airplane, Ravi Shankar.

VHS: S00876. $19.98.
Laser: LD70422. $49.95.

D.A. Pennebaker, USA, 1968, 98 mins.

Moving Memories

Hosted by George Takei (*Star Trek*'s Mr. Sulu), this journey into the 1920s and '30s features restored and edited home movies taken by Japanese-American immigrant pioneers. 31 mins.

VHS: S31385. $14.95.

Moving the Mountain

The momentous events surrounding the Tiananmen Square uprisings of May 1989 are at the center of this moving film by Michael (*28 Up, 35 Up*) Apted. Part documentary and part dramatization, it captures the feeling of hope and change that inspired the young demonstrators as they sought democracy and confronted a brutal regime. Newsreel footage and powerful personal testimonies of participants in the Tiananmen Square uprisings make this a powerful and compelling film.

VHS: S26863. $99.98.
Laser: LD75418. $39.99.

Michael Apted, USA, 1995, 83 mins.

Mumia: A Case for Reasonable Doubt?

For the first time, Mumia speaks on camera from behind prison walls in a television interview. Convicted and sentenced to death for the 1981 murder of a 25-year-old white Philadelphia policeman, former NPR radio journalist and activist Mumia Abu-Jamal has voiced his innocence for 14 years. This high-profile case has garnered the interest of such celebrities as Jesse Jackson, Alice Walker, Paul Newman, Whoopi Goldberg, Ed Asner, Mike Farrell and Danny Glover, who believe Abu-Jamal is a political prisoner. Narrated by Marlene Sanders. 74 mins.

VHS: S31672. $19.98.

Ray Frawley, USA, 1997, 74 mins.

Nanook of the North

The original director's cut of the classic documentary of the daily life and hardships of an Eskimo family—a landmark in the history of documentary cinema. Digitally remastered from beautiful source materials and dramatically enhanced with a score conducted by Timothy Brock. Includes an eight-minute interview with the director's wife, Frances Flaherty.

VHS: S34690. $14.98

Robert Flaherty, USA, 1922, 79 mins.

Native Land

Narrated by Paul Robeson, this documentary explores the threats to American values contained in the forces unleashed by economic depression. Many of the artists who worked on this project through the collective called Frontier Films were themselves the victims of the HUAC trials in the 1950's. In the debate on American values this film stands as a powerful testament to the enduring traditions of democratic ideals. This collector's version is mastered from the finest print available.

VHS: S20743. $59.95.

Paul Strand, USA, 1942, 88 mins.

Next Step

A new video produced by Amnesty International and narrated by Glenda Jackson examines both the moral and legal implications of state-sanctioned killing on modern society. The video places the death penalty in the international human rights context and presents compelling arguments for its abolition. *Includes graphic footage*. England, 1989, 22 mins.

VHS: S09779. $19.95.

Nowhere to Hide

In dramatic and often graphic scenes, *Nowhere to Hide* shows a far different reality about the Gulf War than what most Americans saw on the nightly news. Although several networks initially expressed strong interest in the footage, all declined to air it, and NBC ended its long affiliation with director Jon Alpert, a seven-time Emmy-winner.

VHS: S15211. $59.95.

Jon Alpert, USA, 1991, 28 mins.

Occupied Palestine

"A complex, sensitive and brutally authentic movie, *Occupied Palestine* delivers its message with unnerving sharpness and accuracy. The simple realities of what it means to live under and to resist occupation have never been so clearly presented to a Western audience," wrote Professor Joel Beinin of Stanford University. *Occupied Palestine* is a film reflecting the Palestinian experience of Zionism and resistance to it. Dramatic, contemporary footage is combined with the testimony of Palestinians as well as Zionist settlers and officials, to develop a fresh perspective on a critical international issue. "Quite simply the best film ever made about the Palestine question" (*Middle East Report*).

Home Video.
VHS: S10842. $49.95.
Institutional with public performance rights.
VHS: S10847. $99.95.

David Koff, USA/Israel, 1987, 88 mins.

Olympia: Festival of Beauty

Part Two of Riefenstahl's extraordinary film about the 1936 Olympics. Engrossingly beautiful, the film provides a glimpse of the Nazi mystique and idealization of the youthful male body. English dialog.

VHS: S00955. $29.95.
Leni Riefenstahl, Germany, 1936, 97 mins.

Olympia: Festival of the People

Leni Riefenstahl was given unlimited resources and full artistic freedom to produce this film of the 1936 Olympic Games in Berlin. *Festival of the People* is Part One. Famous sequences include the men's diving competition, Jesse Owen's sprint races and Riefenstahl's use of telephoto lenses and slow motion. English dialog.

VHS: S00956. $29.95.
Leni Riefenstahl, Germany, 1936, 115 mins.

Olympia: Parts One and Two

Leni Riefenstahl's films of the 1936 Olympic Games in Berlin: *Festival of the People* and *Festival of Beauty*. English dialog.

Laser: LD76220. $99.95.
Leni Riefenstahl, Germany, 1936, 212 mins.

One Nation Under God

This documentary exposes the chilling world of right-wing Christian conversion techniques employed against lesbians and gay men. Included in this homophobic arsenal is beauty make-overs for lesbians and tough physical contact sports for gay men, especially football. At the center of this documentary is a couple who embody the failure of this quackery.

VHS: S21027. $29.95.
Teodoro Maniaci/Francine Rzeznik, USA, 1993, 83 mins.

Other Prisoners

A unique documentary looking at prison life from a completely original perspective—that of the guard. Winner of awards as both documentary and as art, *Other Prisoners* observes human character and circumstance with irony and darkly funny humor. "We meet car thieves who learned to hot-wire by watching *Adam Twelve* on TV and yard lords who serve the same function in the big house as bankers who charge exorbitant interest to do it in the big world. We watch Cocoa, a gay prisoner who trades sex for cigs (the equivalent of cash inside) and flirts outrageously with a guard, and we hear one of the incarcerated speculate about what would happen to the judges and social workers and police if criminals went on strike…a vivid, haunting work."

VHS: S10931. $59.95.
Stephen Roszell, USA, 1987, 58 mins.

Palazzolo's Chicago

For twenty years Tom Palazzolo has been the purveyor of funny, darkly satirical musings on Chicago, creating low-budget Fellini-esque experimental films on the strange, hypnotic and diverse ethnography of Chicago. This collection of four films is a survey of his best work: *Your Astronauts*, which follows the Apollo 11 parade; *Jerry's*, a classic documentary on a deli owner who prods his customers through blatant terror tactics; *Tattoed Lady of Riverview*, a Diane Arbus-like foray into the freak show carnival as spectacle; and *Enjoy Yourself: It's Later Than You Think*, a panoramic view of a senior citizens' picnic.

VHS: S02655. $39.95.
Tom Palazzolo, USA, 60 mins.

Palazzolo's Chicago Vol. 2

Two priceless gems from filmmaker Tom Palazzolo: *At Maxwell Street* (40 minutes) explores the sounds and textures of the legendary Chicago street on which street peddlers mix with blues musicians; *Labor Day—East Chicago* (25 mins) is a hilarious document of a beauty contest in the neighborhood referred to as East Chicago, Illinois, a steel-town event sponsored by the Lions. A wonderful depiction of hometown rituals.

VHS: S06471. $39.95.
Tom Palazzolo, USA, 65 mins.

The Panama Deception

Barbara Trent's Academy Award-winning documentary explores the ethical and political consequences of George Bush's December 1989 invasion of Panama. Code-named "Operation Just Cause," its strategic intentions were the capture of Panama strongman Manuel Noriega. Trent argues the military offensive masked wide-scale civilian casualties, suppression of the media reports and a pretext for a contemporary Pax Americana. Trent also charges the American media with complicity in refusing to challenge official government reports. Shot on video. Narrated by Elizabeth Montgomery. Music by Sting, Jackson Browne, Jorge Strunz and Ismael Rivera. Banned by the Panamanian government and denied an airing by PBS.

VHS: S18754. $79.95.
Barbara Trent, USA, 1992, 91 mins.

Paradise Lost

Called "true crime reporting at its most bitterly revealing" by *The New York Times*, this gripping documentary from the makers of *Brother's Keeper* is the true story of the brutal slaying of three eight-year-old boys and the investigation that leads to the arrest and trial of three teenagers whose only crime seems to be that they dress in black and listen to heavy metal music. The families, the townspeople and the accused all clash in their efforts to see that justice is served.

VHS: S31169. $59.98.
Joe Berlinger/Bruce Sinofsky, USA, 1996, 150 mins.

Paris Is Burning

The title of this lively New York-based documentary is taken from the name of a drag ball. Filmmaker Jenny Livingston spent several years interviewing members of the black and Hispanic gay community and attending their lavish social functions. These costume balls, in a search for expanding the concept of "realness," have gone beyond simple female impersonation to include such categories as butch queens, military attire, executive looks and fierce vogueing competitions. With the participation of such legends as Dorian Corey, Pepper Lebeija, Venus Xtravaganza, Octavia St. Laurent and Willi Ninja.

VHS: S16701. $19.98.
Jennie Livingston, USA, 1990, 71 mins.

Paris Was a Woman

An "intelligent and revealing" (*New York Times*) portrait of the creative community of women writers, artists, photographers and editors who flocked to the Left Bank of Paris between the World Wars. Greta Schiller and writer Andrea Weiss highlight Colette, Djuna Barnes, Gertrude Stein, Romaine Brooks, Marie Laurencin, Berenice Abbott, Gisele Freund, booksellers Sylvia Beach and Adrienne Monnier and *New Yorker* correspondent Janet Flanner.

VHS: S32910. $59.95.
Gretta Schiller, USA, 1996, 75 mins.

The People vs. Paul Crump

A powerful documentary—the debut film by William Friedkin (*French Connection, To Live and Die in L.A.*)—*The People vs Paul Crump* is an impassioned plea for mercy and justice, based on the true story of Paul Crump—a man who is still in Illinois prison. In 1953, five young black men robbed a food plant in the Chicago Stockyards. Their getaway went awry, one security guard was shot to death, and five employees were severely beaten. Within a week, all five were arrested. The fifth man, Paul Crump, then 22, was sentenced to die in the electric chair. He is sentenced to life in prison, and was at the brink of execution some 15 times between 1953 and 1962. William Friedkin met Paul Crump in jail, and so believed in his innocence, his record of rehabilitation as a model prisoner and his worth as a human being, that he made this artistic tour-de-force which is an impassioned plea for Crump's return to society.

VHS: S06320. $39.95.
William Friedkin, USA, 1962, 52 mins.

A Perfect Candidate

Sometimes horrifying, often hilarious, *A Perfect Candidate* is a twisted journey into the underbelly of American politics. When former Marine Oliver North re-emerged from the Iran-Contra scandal to run for the U.S. Senate, the filmmakers were granted astonishing access to the backroom games played by the candidates, their handlers and the press. "The best American documentary since *Hoop Dreams*…. Invigorating, entertaining and essential" (*Washington Post*).

VHS: S32358. $59.95.
R.J. Cutler/David Van Taylor, USA, 1996, 105 mins.

Peyote Road

The United States Supreme Court denied indigenous peoples the right to use peyote in their centuries-old rituals. Religious freedom is at stake. This documentary explores the effects of this decision and its implications for one of the Western Hemisphere's oldest religions. Peter Coyote narrates. USA, 1993, 59 mins.

VHS: S26895. $29.99.

The Plow That Broke the Plains/ Night Mail

Pare Lorentz's classic documentary *The Plow That Broke the Plains*, with music by Virgil Thomson, is paired with the great classic of the British Documentary Movement, Basil Wright and Harry Watt's *Night Mail*. Total running time 49 mins.

VHS: S03364. $29.95.

The Power and the Land: Four Documentary Portraits of the Great Depression

The program begins with two legendary films by Pare Lorentz. *The River* dramatizes the history of the Mississippi River, while *The Plow That Broke the Plains*, with photography by Paul Strand, focuses on the soil of the Great Plains. H.P. McClure's *The New Frontier* offers an enlightening glimpse into an experimental "Rural Community" while Joris Ivens' *The Power and the Land* observes the daily activities of a farming family in Ohio. This collector's version has been mastered from the finest source materials available.

VHS: S20744. $59.95.
Joris Ivens, USA, 1938, 38 mins.

Pull My Daisy (The Beat Generation)

Inducted in 1996 into the National Film Archives, this 1959 historic beat happening based on the third act of Jack Kerouac's *The Beat Generation* is the documentary comedy of an evening with a young man who is visited by some poet friends at his Greenwich Village pad. Co-directed by Robert Frank, written and narrated by Kerouac, and featuring Allen Ginsberg, Gregory Corso, Larry Rivers, Peter Orlovsky, Delphine Seyrig and David Amram, with original music by Amram. With *The Last Clean Shirt* (1964, 45 mins.), which, "in premise and design, and its concentration on issues of language and speech, repetition and duration beyond the threshold of boredom, anticipates later influential films in the international avant-garde" (Blaine Allen, *The New American Cinema*); and *Birth of a Nation, 1965* (1965, 29 mins.), "a tantalizing, juicy, provocative fragment not only of a legendary lost work but of the '60s themselves: goofy, funny, challenging and unruly in the best sense" (Jonathan Rosenbaum, *Chicago Reader*).

VHS: S34620. $79.95.
Alfred Leslie, USA, 1959/1964/1965, 104 mins.

Pumping Iron

An expose of the motivations of men who undergo grueling training in order to transform their bodies into sculpted works of art. Focusing on the competition for the World Bodybuilding Championship, the film stars Arnold Schwarzenegger and Lou Ferrigno.

Laser: LD74983. $29.99.
George Butler/Robert Fiore, USA, 1976

Pumping Iron II: The Women

Women bodybuilders have changed the definition of the female form, and *Pumping Iron II* documents four of the world's best women's body builders as they prepare for the 1983 Caesars Palace World Cup Championship.

VHS: S01073. $19.95.
George Butler, USA, 1985, 107 mins.

Quiet One

A classic documentary-drama, winner of awards at Venice and Edinburgh, and one of the most penetrating studies of juvenile delinquency ever filmed. The film is the story of a black youth who grows up in Harlem without the love of his parents, and, rejected, falls into delinquency. Sidney Meyers, the director, was apparently influenced by Italian neo-realism and the commentary, written by James Agee, is spoken by Gary Merrill. "A most moving, important and memorable film" (Paul Rotha).

VHS: S06879. $39.95.
Sidney Meyers/Janet Loeb, USA, 1948, 67 mins.

The Race for Mayor

Chicago's 1983 mayoral campaign sparked nationwide interest in the growth of black political awareness. The stunning victory of Harold Washington, a black U.S. congressman, over Chicago's Democratic "machine" heightened the expectations of blacks all over the country. This independent documentary-with Mayor Washington, Jesse Jackson, former mayor Jane Byrne, Richard Daley, and Democratic political boss Edward Vrdolyak—shot in churches, city streets, empty lots, Polish restaurants, political offices and Operation PUSH offices paints a complex picture of the fusing of a new political coalition, and places it in the context of the historic evolution of successive waves of ethnic groups who seek to wrest control from earlier entrenched minorities.

VHS: S02312. $79.95.
Howard Gladstone/James Ylisela, USA, 1983, 29 mins.

Rat

From the award-winning director of *Cane Toads*, this funny and unusual documentary takes a look at the eternal battle of Man vs. Rat in their struggle to control New York City.

VHS: S34627. $19.98.
Mark Lewis, USA, 1997, 60 mins.

The Reluctant Muse

John and Ruth Waddell met at the Art Institute of Chicago over 45 years ago. Their love for the arts and each other brought them together, but at a cost. Ruth channeled her creative energy into their partnership. The concerns of family and finances, and the troubles of infidelity, kept her from fuller artistic expression. This documentary examines what happens when two artists bond. 58 mins.

VHS: S26422. $59.95.
Amy Waddell, USA, 1995, 58 mins.

Rescuers: Stories of Courage—Two Women

Based on the book *Rescuers: Portraits of Moral Courage in the Holocaust*, directed by Peter Bogdanovich and executive produced by Barbra Streisand and Cis Corman, these two true-life dramas feature the courageous stories of two women who risked their lives for the love of humanity in order to defend the Jewish people during the Nazi regime. In *Mamushka*, Gertruda Babilinska (Elizabeth Perkins) is a Polish nanny employed by the wealthy Jewish Stolowitsky family, who devotes her life to the Stolowitskys and travels with them as they flee from the Nazis, agreeing to protect and care for the Stolowitsky's young son, Mickey, and raise him in his Jewish faith after his parents die. *Woman on a Bicycle* is the story of Marie-Rose Gineste (Sela Ward), a single woman employed by the Church who helps counterfeit special identity documents for Jewish refugees. With the aid of her bicycle, Marie-Rose travels to various villages disseminating secret communications to assist the underground resistance movement.
VHS: S34403. $79.99.
Peter Bogdanovich, USA, 1997, 107 mins.

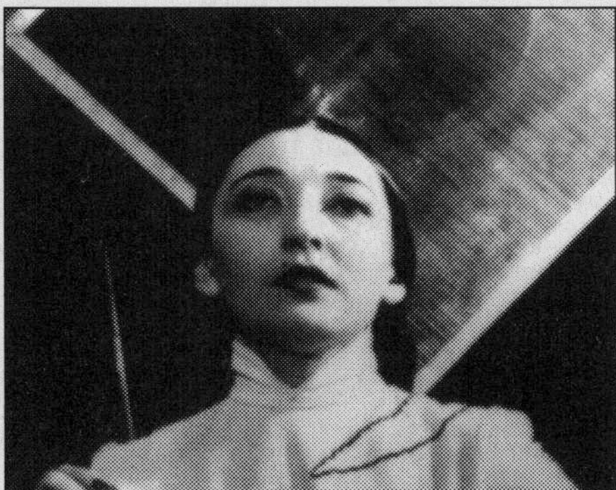

Ring of Fire

The true story of two brothers, Lawrence and Lorne Blair, who voyaged to the East in search of adventure and found themselves into ten years of danger and discovery, in the last of the lands of real kings and queens, dragons and pirates, cannibals and headhunters, mystics and magicians. Indonesia, the world's largest and most mysterious archipelago was where the Blairs sailed with pirates aboard their black-sailed schooners, struggled through rapids and deep jungles searching for elusive nomadic tribes, witnessed veiled forms of human sacrifice, and gained unique access to the ancient palaces of Java. This remarkable BBC-PBS-Australian television co-production is now available on home video.
Part 1: Spice Island Saga. Filmmaker brothers Lorne and Lawrence Blair encounter gypsy pirates, tropical storms, python hunters and the Greater Bird of Paradise as they sail among the islands of the world's largest and least-explored archipelago. Part one of an extraordinary four-part look at the oceans, islands, peoples of Indonesia. 55 mins.
VHS: S08613. $29.95.
Part 2: Dance of the Warriors. The brothers Blair journey to Indonesia's Komodo Island to film the man-eating Komodo dragon. They also witness ritual warfare on the island of Sumba and journey deep into the swamps of New Guinea to find a tribe of headhunters living 50,000 years in the past. 55 mins.
VHS: S08614. $29.95.
Part 3: East of Krakatoa. In this volume, the brothers travel through Java, Bali and the Celebes Islands to discover an erupting volcano, mystical powers and conscious death. 55 mins.
VHS: S08615. $29.95.
Part 4: Dream Wanderers of Borneo. Explorer brothers Lorne and Lawrence Blair encounter blood-sucking leeches, snakes, quicksand and a week-long tropical storm as they trek 800 miles into the heart of Borneo. They meet with a lost nomadic tribe known as the "dream wanderers". 55 mins.
VHS: S08616. $29.95.
Complete 4-volume set.
VHS: S08617. $89.95.
Laser: IMAX. LD74935. $39.95.

The River and The Plow That Broke the Plains

Two important works in the development of the documentary: *The River*, done in 1937, produced by the Farm Security Administration about the Mississippi, and *The Plow that Broke the Plains*, from 1936, about the New Deal's efforts to assist farmers hit by the Dust Bowl in Oklahoma.
VHS: S01121. $39.95.
Pare Lorentz, USA, 1937

Robert Coles: Teacher

This documentary addresses the working methods, structure and achievement of renowned child psychiatrist Robert Coles, the Pulitzer Prize winner who interviews children and records their responses to various racial, social, political and economic issues. 57 mins.
VHS: S17103. $39.95.

Rock Hudson's Home Movies

With excerpts from some of Rock's most memorable films, this documentary digs into the persona of Hollywood's greatest male sex symbol of the '50s and '60s, whose death from AIDS forever transformed the way America looks at its stars. Mark Rappaport's film was named to multiple Ten Best lists as an original look at an American icon.
VHS: S21090. $29.95.
Mark Rappaport, USA, 1992, 63 mins.

Rodrigue: A Man & His Dog

This documentary short subject tells the story of world renowned artist George Rodrigue and his beloved late pet, Tiffany, the blue dog. The film uses the artist's paintings to illustrate the story and features the voices of Academy Award winner Whoopi Goldberg as the voice of Tiffany, Yeardley Smith (Lisa Simpson of *The Simpsons*) and Paige O'Hara ("Belle" of Disney's *Beauty and the Beast*).
VHS: S28566. $19.95.
David Dubos, USA, 1993, 29 mins.

Roger & Me

The funniest movie you will ever see about thousands of people losing their jobs. Journalist Michael Moore turns a jaundiced eye on the closing of several General Motors plants in his hometown of Flint, Michigan. He also attempts to have a face-to-face confrontation with GM president Roger Smith. This non-fiction film uses humor and creative license to bring attention to a serious display of corporate indifference. With Anita Bryant, Pat Boone, Ronald Reagan and Flint native Bob Eubanks.
VHS: S12231. $19.98.
Laser: LD70667. $24.98.
Michael Moore, USA, 1989, 91 mins.

Roses in December

On December 2, 1980, lay missioner Jean Donovan and three American nuns were brutally murdered by members of El Salvador's security forces. With compassion and sensitivity, this film chronicles Jean's brief life—from her affluent childhood in Connecticut, to her decision to volunteer with the Maryknolls in El Salvador, to her tragic death. This award-winning film is an eloquent memorial to a courageous young woman.
VHS: S09442. $39.95.
Ana Carrigan/Bernard Stone, USA, 1982, 56 mins.

Ross McElwee Films

Two pieces by idiosyncratic American regionalist Ross McElwee (*Sherman's March*), whose "nonfiction is equal parts Samuel Beckett, Jean-Luc Godard and Werner Herzog" (*New York Times*). *Charleen* is a poem to Charleen Watson, a South Carolina writer, mother, teacher, eccentric romantic and the subject of *Sherman's March*. It's "an irresistible force, caught beautifully on the run." On the same program is *Backyard*, a collection of small-town Southern charm, community and off-center humor when McElwee turns the camera on his family and friends.
VHS: S17775. $29.95.
Ross McElwee, USA, 1991, 99 mins.

Running Fence

The film depicts the long struggle by Christo to build a 24-mile fence of white fabric over the hills of California disappearing into the Pacific, at a cost of $3 million. After what seemed to be an insurmountable struggle between the artist and the state bureaucracy, the fence, finally unfurled, brings the community together in celebration of its beauty.
VHS: S07493. $49.95.
Albert Maysles/David Maysles, USA, 1978, 58 mins.

Salesman

Albert and David Maysles' landmark documentary focuses on a quartet of Bible salesmen and the hopes and frustrations of one man in particular: Paul Brennan. Labeled as "brutally honest," "funny and touching," and "a great insight into America," *Salesman* is a key work of the American documentary cinema.
VHS: S07491. $79.95.
Albert Maysles/David Maysles, USA, 1968, 85 mins.

The Santa Tapes

His name is Art Baldwin and, according to the *Chicago Tribune*, he was "the only authentic State Street Santa Claus." Warm and compassionate, blunt and irascible, this documentary leads us through his preparations for a day in "The Chair." A fascinating portrait of Santa you've never seen before and will likely never forget.
VHS: S15009. $14.95.
Scott Jacobs, USA, 14 mins.

Seeds of Destiny

Winner of the Academy Award for best documentary subject of 1946, the film portrays the plight of millions of children who were left at the end of WWII without food, clothing or shelter. Under the sponsorship of the UN Relief fund, a team of Signal Corps cameramen were sent to 14 countries to film children in bombed-out cities and refugee camps. The film raised over $200 million for war relief, ironically earning it the status of one of the top moneymaking films of all time. 21 mins.
VHS: S03349. $39.95.

Seeing Red

A powerful documentary by Julia Reichert and Jim Klein that assesses the cultural, political, social and personal evolution of members of the American Communist Party. The film moves from the idealistic fervor and radical intensity of 30s Depression-era humanism to the harsh persecution of ideas during McCarthy-ism and the onset of the Cold War. The documentary is a deft merging of faces and personalities, from the known to the unknown. It captures their pain, triumph, hurt and redemption. The film also considers the disillusionment following the revelations of Stalin's tyranny and looks at the political exploitation of anti-communist hysteria from J. Edgar Hoover, Richard Nixon and Ronald Reagan. "The film is less about dogma than about American idealism" (Vincent Canby).
VHS: S19234. $29.95.
Julia Reichert/Jim Klein, USA, 1983, 100 mins.

Sex Is Sex

This remarkable film containing frank and compelling conversations with male prostitutes breaks through common cliches about prostitution to reveal a world more complex and compelling than popular perception permits. Neither desperately tragic nor overly romanticized, this film presents young New York hustlers telling what they know, whether it be the secret to faking sex, the dangers of crazy tricks, or just the pleasure of easy money. "A remarkable look at a world unseen by the average person…not to be missed" (*The New York Times*).
VHS: S30933. $39.95.
Jennifer Milici/Brian Bergen, USA, 1994, 50 mins.

Sex Is...

This bold documentary charts the growing sexual awareness among a group of men whose personal histories extend from before Stonewall, through the growing AIDS crises and into today's climate of "in-your-face" sexual politics. It's an in-depth look at how these men coped with change and loss inside the sexual revolution.
VHS: S21134. $29.95.
Marc Huestis, USA, 1993, 80 mins.

Shattered Dreams

A massive, chilling, thoughtful and provocative examination of Israel. Born out of the despair of millions as a utopian haven in the desert, *Shattered Dreams* confronts the realities of Israel today against the background of these utopian beginnings. The film passionately documents what more than 20 years of occupation and expansion have done to the soul of Israel. Provocative and unflinching.
VHS: S12305. $19.98.
Victor Schonfeld, Great Britain, 1988, 173 mins.

Sherman's March

Consistently named on ten best lists all over the country,- "uproarious…it'll put you in a pleased delirium and leave you with a happy daze" (*San Francisco Examiner*). The subtitle of the film promises "A Documentary Meditation upon the Possibilities of Romantic Love in the South during an Era of Nuclear Weapons Proliferation," and director Ross McElwee delivers an engaging nonfiction journey through the South in a picaresque tour of contemporary relationships. "If Woody Allen made *Gone with the Wind*, it might resemble *Sherman's March!*" (*People Magazine*).
VHS: S10929. $29.95.
Ross McElwee, USA, 1985, 155 mins.

Shoah

Claude Lanzmann's landmark, monumental epic of the Holocaust, a 9½ hour assemblage of witnesses—death camp survivors and Nazi functionaries—whose combined testimony amounts to one of the most shattering human documents ever recorded. French with English subtitles.
VHS: S01190. $299.95.
Claude Lanzmann, France, 1985, 570 mins.

Short Subject Potpouri

Three intriguing shorts, including Italian director Roberto Rossellini directing his wife Ingrid Bergman in *The Chicken*. The program also includes two ethnographic documentaries, *A Visit to the Smithsonian* and *A Day with the FBI*.
VHS: S18772. $19.95.

Silent Pioneers

Senior members of lesbian and gay communities share their memories about gay life in this documentary. Sometimes tragic, and sometimes funny, their recollections are always personal and poignant. This film offers a unique view of an era less tolerant of sexual minorities.
VHS: S27614. $39.95.
Lucy Winer, USA, 1985, 54 mins.

Simba

Journeying to remote and exotic regions, Martin and Osa Johnson produced, wrote and photographed films celebrating the natural wonders and native tribes of Africa, Asia and the South Seas. For *Simba*, they forded crocodile infested rivers, braved stampeding elephants and stared down angry rhinos in order to film lions in their natural habitat, the veldt. Killing only for food or self protection, the Johnsons became two of Africa's first conservationists. Today, *Simba* is considered the highlight of the Johnson's career.
VHS: S16430. $39.95.
Laser: CLV/CAV. LD72073. $39.95.
Martin Johnson/Osa Johnson, USA, 1928, 83 mins.

Six O'Clock News
Ross McElwee (*Sherman's March*), now a new father concerned about raising a child in a troubled world, becomes obsessed with the dinner-time newscasts and chases after murder, mayhem and catastrophe as he hits the road with his camera, hoping to meet victims of the catastrophes he sees on TV.
VHS: S34130. $59.95.
Ross McElwee, USA, 1997, 102 mins.

Small Wonders
This "real *Mr. Holland's Opus*" (*The Boston Globe*) is the incredible, true story of Roberta Guaspari-Tzavaras, a dedicated teacher who, refusing to let funding cuts stop her, drove from one school to the next in a car packed with violins to bring music to inner city kids. Follow seemingly talentless beginners from first lessons to inspiring performances before a raging crowd at Madison Square Garden and alongside world-renowned musicians at Carnegie Hall in this "magical, moving and inspirational" (*New York Post*) film.
VHS: S31092. $19.95.
Laser: LD76151. $39.99.
Allan Miller, USA, 1996, 80 mins.

Sneakin' and Peekin'
Sneakin' and Peekin' is a funny, revealing trip to a famous nudist camp and its annual Mr. and Mrs. Nude America contest; *I Was a Contestant at Mother's Wet T-Shirt Contest* is a documentary at the Chicago landmark Wet T-Shirt contest at Mother's Bar; *Hot and Nasty* is a very funny look inside the comings and goings of a massage parlor. Americana at its very best (and most hilarious).
VHS: S06111. $39.95.
Tom Palazzolo, USA, 55 mins.

Something Strong Within
This critically acclaimed, award-winning video production was created for the Japanese-American National Museum's exhibition, "America's Concentration Camps: Remembering the Japanese-American Experience." A haunting compilation of never-before-seen home movies of the forced removal and incarceration of Japanese Americans during WWII. Includes portions of the movie *Topaz*, which has been listed in the National Film Registry.
VHS: S31384. $19.95.

Song of Ceylon
One of the masterworks of the documentary, Basil Wright's lyrical impression of Ceylon in four sections: "The Buddha" deals with the coming of the Buddha to liberate the people from devil-worship, "The Virgin Island" depicts the native Ceylonese culture and economy, "The Voices of Commerce" contrasts traditional methods with new technology, and "The Apparel of a God" reflects the continuity of life and tradition. "Its evocative sensual imagery, its construction, and its skillful, often contrapuntal, use of natural life still have a powerful impact" (Georges Sadoul). With sound by Alberto Cavalcanti, produced by John Grierson.
VHS: S09528. $29.95.
Basil Wright, Great Britain, 1934, 40 mins.

Sonic Outlaws
Craig Baldwin presents an energized discourse on copyright infringement, fair use and culture jamming, via a montage of interviews, music and stock footage stemming from the infamous Negativland-U2 case. Phone pranking, billboard alteration, media hoaxing and the digitalization of intellectual property are examined in the light of the law during a period of rapid artistic and technological change.
VHS: S28584. $59.95.
Craig Baldwin, USA, 1995, 87 mins.

South Sea Adventures
Zane Grey's famous sea yarn: a rare 1932 documentary starring Zane Grey himself, deep-sea fishing and encountering the natives of a south sea island. USA, 60 mins.
VHS: S15176. $29.95.

Spanish Earth
Focusing specifically on the small village of Fuenteduena near Madrid, *Spanish Earth* is a stunning documentary on the Spanish Civil War and the drastic land reform that followed. The beautiful commentary was written and delivered by Ernest Hemingway. Directed and photographed by Joris Ivens. Edited by Helen van Dongen.
VHS: S14648. $29.95.
Joris Ivens, USA, 1937, 54 mins.

Starting Place
Robert Kramer achieved notoriety with his 1969 documentary, *People's War*. After 24 years he returns with a documentary that continues to explore the same subjects and once again reveals the other side of Vietnamese society, rarely seen in this country. It is provocative and elegiac at the same time, reflecting a perspective altered in part by the passing of time and the reasoned expectations of an older, more sober outlook.
VHS: S27649. $39.95.
Robert Kramer, France/Great Britain/Vietnam, 1993, 80 mins.

Stoney Knows How
An extended interview with the late Leonard St. Clair, a crippled dwarf, a carnival sword swallower as a child and a tattoo artist since 1928. St. Clair is an ebullient little man with the gift of gab and a fund of bizarre stories about tattooing and other unrelated matters. "Not often does one have the opportunity to meet a man like Stoney," said Vincent Canby in *The New York Times*.
VHS: S09302. $24.95.
Alan Govenar/Bruce Pacho Lane, USA, 1982, 29 mins.

Straight from the Heart
This Academy Award-winning documentary explores the experiences of parents learning to love their lesbian and gay children in a world dominated by homophobia. There is a range of stories touching on a variety of experiences, including a religious Mormon family and an African-American family. 30 mins.
VHS: S26030. $24.95.
Dee Mosbacher/Frances Reid, USA, 1994, 30 mins.

Streetwise
A powerful, emotionally compelling, sensational documentary about the life of teenagers in Seattle, surviving as pimps, prostitutes, muggers, panhandlers and small-time drug dealers. Critically acclaimed throughout the country, *Streetwise* is a powerful, wrenching film.
VHS: S01270. $19.98.
Martin Bell, USA, 1985, 92 mins.

Synthetic Pleasures
This trippy, critically acclaimed documentary takes you on an around-the-world exploration of such cutting-edge technologies as virtual reality, cyber sex, nootropics and plastic beauty. Features commentaries from late cyberguru Timothy Leary and Jaron Lanier, the "father" of virtual reality. "Fascinating, disturbing and quasi-hallucinogenic, a vitally important film, no matter who you are" (John Anderson, *Newsday*).
VHS: S31547. $19.98.
Iara Lee, USA, 1996, 83 mins.

Taylor Chain I and II
These two companion films chart a decade of union democracy and collective bargaining. *Taylor Chain I* tells the gritty realities of a seven-week strike at a small Indiana chain factory. Volatile union meetings and tension-filled interactions on the picket line provide an inside view of the tensions and conflicts inherent in typical negotiations, while *Taylor Chain II* returns to the plant nine years later to show how labor and management are working together to save the plant in a faltering economy. "A tiny stick of dynamite!" (*Chicago Tribune*).
VHS: S27802. $29.95.
Kartemquin Films, USA, 1980-84, 63 mins.

Theremin: An Electronic Odyssey
A cross between Albert Einstein and Ed Wood, Leon Theremin pioneered the electronic music revolution four decades before the rise of Electronic Rock. His invention, the Theremin, produced an eerie, warbling sound, and was used on many Hollywood sound tracks, including *Spellbound*, *The Day the Earth Stood Still* and *The Lost Weekend*, and by rock legends Brian Wilson and Todd Rundgren. At the height of his popularity, Theremin was kidnapped by Soviet agents and forced to develop spy technology for Stalin's KGB. Janet Maslin (*The New York Times*) calls it "fascinating," and it is. Winner at the Sundance and San Francisco Film Festivals.
VHS: S27436. $19.98.
Steven M. Martin, USA/Great Britain, 1995, 84 mins.

Through the Wire
Narrated by Susan Sarandon, this documentary is an award-winning and frank portrait of three uncompromising women convicted of politically motivated crimes and an expose of the secretive prison policy that sent them underground. This controversial film was winner of the 1990 Munich Documentary Film Festival.
VHS: S15266. $19.98.
Nina Rosenblum, USA, 1990

The Thunderbirds
Candice Bergen hosts this high-energy profile of the world-famous elite flyers and their F-16 Fighting Falcons. Cockpit cameras capture the action as the pilots see it. With exclusive interviews with flyers. 100 mins.
VHS: S32989. $19.95.

Tigrero: A Film That Was Never Made
In 1954, armed with a 16mm camera, film, two cases of vodka and 75 boxes of cigars, director Sam Fuller went to Brazil scouting locations for the action-adventure film *Tigrero*. Although this Darryl F. Zanuck production was cast with John Wayne, Ava Gardner and Tyrone Power, the film was never shot because of insurance problems. All that remains of *Tigrero* is Fuller's intriguing footage of the Karaja tribe and their Amazon Rain Forest home. Forty years later, director Mika Kaurismaki ventures back to this location with Fuller and director Jim Jarmusch to talk with the Karaja about the changing world, talk amongst themselves about Fuller's films and the principles of filmmaking, and tell the story of the film that was never made. This film won the International Critics Award at the 1994 Berlin Film Festival.
VHS: S27618. $89.95.
Mika Kaurismaki, Finland/United Germany/Brazil, 1994, 75 mins.

Time Indefinite
This sequel to the highly acclaimed *Sherman's March* continues the stories of the memorable characters the filmmaker (Ross McElwee) encountered on his leisurely jaunt through his native South.
VHS: S20590. $79.95.
Ross McElwee, USA, 117 mins.

Times of Harvey Milk
Academy Award-winning, powerful documentary about the powerful, charismatic, compassionate, gay San Francisco city official Harvey Milk, who was suddenly assassinated. Winner of numerous awards; a powerful document.
VHS: S01348. $39.95.
Rob Epstein/Richard Schmeichen, USA, 1984, 90 mins.

Timothy Leary's Dead
Combines old interviews with the prankster drug guru with recent conversations with Ram Dass, who as Dr. Richard Alpert was Leary's LSD-friendly Harvard colleague; Dr. Ralph Metzner; Summer of Love historian Allen Cohen and writer Claire Burch. "A head trip in every sense of the word" (*Playboy*).
VHS: S34248. $59.95.
Paul Davids, USA, 1996, 80 mins.

Timothy Leary's Last Trip
In the '60s, psychology and consciousness-raising pioneer and self-proclaimed LSD guru Timothy Leary told the nation's youth to "Tune In, Turn On, Drop Out." Diagnosed in 1995 with terminal cancer, Leary chose to "check out" via a media circus, using a new mind-expanding tool: the Internet. Ken Kesey and the Merry Pranksters reunite with the High Priest of LSD for one last psychedelic blowout at Wavy Gravy's annual "Hog Farm Pignic." Includes archival footage of Ken Kesey's Acid Tests and the Merry Prankster's 1964 bus tour across America and features three previously unreleased tracks by The Grateful Dead.
VHS: S30040. $19.98.
DVD: DV60161. $24.98.
A.J. Catoline/O.B. Babbs, USA, 1996, 56 mins.

To Render a Life: "Let Us Now Praise Famous Men" & the Documentary Vision
To Render a Life is the first feature film to be made about *Let Us Now Praise Famous Men*, the brilliant book by writer James Agee and photographer Walker Evans documenting the lives of three poor cotton tenant families in Hale County, Alabama, in 1936. Central to the film is a portrait of a contemporary, poor rural family living under conditions strikingly similar to those facing Depression-era sharecroppers. The film also explores the making of documentary art, featuring outstanding writers and documentary artists Robert Coles, Frederick Wiseman and Ted Rosengarten discussing the ethical and artistic tensions of the documentary process. "Extraordinarily effective, both as an inquiry into the ethics of rendering lives and as a closer look at American poverty" (Georgia Brown, *The Village Voice*).
VHS: S30146. $24.95.
Ross Spears, USA, 1992, 90 mins.

Tom Palazzolo: Films from the Sixties
Filmmaker Tom Palazzolo uses humor as a weapon in an ironic exploration of the puzzle of the turbulent 1960's. The cultural and political change of this crucial decade is revealed in a collection of short films, ranging from a disturbing account of the 1968 Democratic National Convention to a bitter satire on patriotism during the Vietnam era. The result is a completely original unwrapping of history. The collection includes: *The Bride Stripped Bare*—an ironic film about the ritual which surrounds the unveiling of the large Picasso outdoor sculpture in Chicago called "The Woman;" Palazzolo contrasts real and posed shots of all types of women, in an attempt to make us question whether the sculpture is pornography or a matriarchal symbol (1967, 14 mins.). *Campaign*—a disturbing political account of the events surrounding the 1968 Democratic Convention; the threat of violence is underscored by a relentless backdrop of news flashes and Emergency Broadcast Systems tests (1968, 14 mins.). *Love It, Leave It*—themes of freedom and openness in shots of a southern nudist camp evolve into a visual comparison of militarism and abject poverty; scenes of military formations are tied to male sexuality; the frantic montage closing the film provides real insight into the slogan that defined a generation (1970, 14 mins.). *Venus Adonis*—a sarcastic view of modernism in a black-and-white satire of the bridges, beaches and skyline of Chicago; from this context emerges a narrative starring the *perfect* man and the *perfect* woman; on a city beach they act out a romantic but ultimately tragic story of nuptials and the untimely death of Adonis (1966, 15 mins.). Total program length: 57 mins.
VHS: S13701. $39.95.
Tom Palazzolo, USA, 1991

Tompkins Square Park Police Riot
This controversial video has been the focus of a court battle between city authorities and its maker. Patterson said, "I want to show the tape to the public so that the People would be the Grand Jury." Ultimately this work functions as a basic document of recent urban civil strife in the US.
VHS: S22650. $39.95.
Clayton Patterson, USA, 1988, 90 mins.

Tompkins Square Park, 1989/Dinkinsville

In the first film a mini-tour of the park reveals squatters being evicted and an impromtu demonstration. Former NYC Mayor Dinkins called the homeless of Tompkins Square Park "worse than hardened criminals." The second work documents the homeless who named their shantytown Dinkinsville, in tribute to the mayor. They had nowhere to go when the police marched on their homes. The result was explosive.

VHS: S22653. $39.95.

Clayton Patterson, USA, 1989, 58 mins.

Trinity and Beyond: The Atomic Bomb Movie

Narrated by William Shatner, this award-winning, "factually solid, visually stunning, informative documentary" (*Daily Variety*) uses rare archival footage, interviews with scientists and still photos to trace the history of nuclear weapons, from The Manhattan Project of the 1940s to the signing of the Nuclear Test Ban Treaty in 1963.

VHS: S31771. $24.95.

Peter Kuran, USA, 1995, 95 mins.

Triumph of the Will

Enormously controversial film record of a Nazi party solidarity rally at Nuremberg in 1934, crafted by Riefenstahl in her second directorial assignment. A fascinating lesson in the methods used by the Nazis to inspire national support. German with English subtitles.

VHS: S18194. $29.95.

Leni Riefenstahl, Germany, 1936, 80 mins.

Troublesome Creek: A Midwestern

The absorbing, award-winning documentary of an Iowa family's struggle against debt, flawed government policies and a dispassionate local banker to save their family farm, which has been turning out crops by the Jordan family since the 1860s, as told by the youngest daughter of the Jordan family and her filmmaker husband. "A story about loss, about how a time and a place that meant so much to us is being bulldozed under" (John Petrakis, *Chicago Tribune*).

VHS: S31727. $59.99.

Jeanne Jordan/Steven Ascher, USA, 1997, 88 mins.

The True Story of Lili Marlene

One of the famous documentaries produced by Humphrey Jennings for the British Crown Film Unit is this documentary about the famous World War II song, featuring original historical footage.

VHS: S04478. $29.95.

Humphrey Jennings, Great Britain, 1944, 22 mins.

Turnabout: The Story of the Yale Puppeteers

Dan Bessie crafted this documentary about the three gay puppeteers who enchanted Hollywood for 25 years. Their musical extravaganzas, with puppet replicas of celebrities, drew legends like Hitchcock to see their performances. The sophisticated humor of their shows came from a unique camp sensibility, one fostered by these three gay men in a time when being gay was extremely difficult.

VHS: S27492. $39.95.

Dan Bessie, USA, 1992, 55 mins.

Umbrellas

"Veteran verite helmer Albert Maysles adds his name to this highly original and structurally flawless collaboration between Henry Corra and Grahame Weinbren. An ambitious documentary about an ambitious environmentalist arts project by renowned New York-based 'wrap' artist Christo, *Umbrellas* unfolds as an increasingly suspenseful drama" (Howard Feinstein, *Variety*) as Christo and his wife, Jeanne-Claude, erect more than 3,100 20-foot-high umbrellas along stretches of valleys in Japan and California to stunning effect for a two-week period in 1991, with some resistance from nature.

VHS: S33769. $39.95.

Henry Corra/Graham Weinbren/Albert Maysles, Japan/USA, 1994, 90 mins.

The Unquiet Death of Julius and Ethel Rosenberg

On June 19, 1953, Julius and Ethel Rosenberg, the so-called "atomic spies" of the 1950s, were executed at Sing Sing Prison. Their death only fostered the belief of many Americans that the Rosenbergs were innocent, victims of the anti-Communist paranoia of the 50s, rather than spies who had stolen atomic secrets for the Russians. In his landmark documentary *The Unquiet Death of Julius and Ethel Rosenberg*, Alvin Goldstein looks at the facts and procedures of the Rosenberg case, as well as the climate of the times, interviewing jurors, FBI agents, lawyers for both sides, and the two sons of the Rosenbergs. Using documentary and newsreel footage, Goldstein creates a moving human drama, a "thoroughly researched, solidly developed…superb recreation of history, painting with bold strokes the temper of the times" (*Boston Globe*).

VHS: S04736. $59.95.

Alvin Goldstein, USA, 1974, 83 mins.

Unzipped

Isaac Mizrahi, the New York-based fashion designer, is the central subject of this frothy and humorous documentary. This surprisingly intimate film was directed by Mizrahi's former boyfriend. (They broke up during the editing.) It begins with a depressed Mizrahi contemplating his poorly received Spring 1994 collection and ends with the creation of his Fall collection. Along with supermodels Kate Moss, Cindy Crawford, Linda Evangelista and Naomi Campbell, Mizrahi provides witty insights into the world of fashion and artifice.

VHS: S26999. $99.99.

Laser: LD75453. $39.95.

Douglas Keeve, USA, 1995, 73 mins.

Vali: Witch of Positano

A study in beautiful color of a woman along the Amalfi coast of Italy, living in a hermit's house, dressed like a gypsy, weaving dreams and casting spells. A unique film document.

VHS: S01573. $29.95.

Sheldon Rochlin, USA, 1965, 65 mins.

Vezelay

Acclaimed documentary filmmaker Ken Burns and philosopher and painter William Segal pay homage to the magnificent basilica at Vezelay, France, whose magnetism and serene beauty has lured pilgrims from around the world for centuries.

VHS: S31552. $19.95.

Ken Burns, USA, 1996, 31 mins.

Vivre pour Manger

The title means "live to eat", but the film is more than about the food of Louisiana; it is a questioning of the language, culture and ecology of Cajun. Cajun French with English subtitles.

VHS: S08154. $79.95.

Stephen Duplantier, USA, 30 mins.

Waco: The Rules of Engagement

A powerful examination of the tragic series of events outside of Waco, Texas, that led up to the fire at the Branch Davidian compound that took the lives of 70 men, women and children in 1993. Through meticulous research and interviews with both survivors and government authorities, the Academy Award-nominated film attempts to reveal how the Bureau of Alcohol, Tobacco and Firearms, the FBI and the Department of Justice waged an unjustified war against Koresh and his sect and intentionally misled the public about what happened. "It presents testimony from both sides, and shies away from cheap shots. We feel we are seeing a fair attempt to deal with facts" (Roger Ebert, *Chicago Sun-Times*).

VHS: S33273. $24.95.

William Gazecki, USA, 1996, 136 mins.

The War Room

Inside the campaign of President Bill Clinton a new telegenic, electoral style was developed that would appeal to a TV-saturated public. D.A. Pennebaker, the acclaimed documentary maker who covered the 1962 campaigns of Kennedy and McGovern, brings his insight to this presidential hopeful, uncovering that most enduring of American traditions, a sophisticated political machine.

VHS: S20840. $14.95.

Chris Hegedus/D.A. Pennebaker, USA, 1993, 96 mins.

War Stories Our Mothers Never Told Us

In this unique and utterly moving documentary from New Zealand, seven women candidly talk of their loves and their lives during World War II. The poignant interviews are overlaid with restored archival footage and popular songs from World War II years; beautifully shot by Alun Bollinger (*The Piano*).

VHS: S31120. $29.95.

Gaylene Preston, New Zealand, 1995, 95 mins.

Wartime Combat

Two classic documentary works from the British Documentary Movement. The 1943 Oscar-winning *Desert Victory* combines Allied footage and captured Nazi materials to present the full dimension of the punishing Allied victory against Erwin Rommel's forces in the North African campaign. The second program, *Cameraman at War* (1943), is a compilation work of the enormous courage and determination of these professionals to capture the sounds, images and ugliness of the war.

VHS: S17415. $29.95.

Wartime Homefront

The major British documentarian was Humphrey Jennings. This program of the British Documentary Movement contains Jennings's finest works, the brilliant *London Can Take It*, about the individual heroism, valor and sacrifice during the Blitz. The other program is *Fires Were Started*, Jennings's documentary about the Auxiliary Fire Service during 1940/41 German onslaught.

VHS: S17416. $29.95.

Wartime Moments

Three remarkable documentaries from the British Documentary Movement are presented in this volume, highlighting the work of Humphrey Jennings. *Listen to Britain* (1942) chronicles daily life during the war. Harry Watt's *Target for Tonight* (1941) details the precision of a RAF bombing raid on a German depot. Jennings's masterpiece *A Diary for Timothy* (1945), written by E.M. Forster, follows a child's first three months juxtaposed against the massive reconstruction and rebuilding of a physically devastated landscape.

VHS: S17418. $29.95.

Weed

Shot entirely on location in Amersterdam during the 8th Annual Cannabis Cup and Hemp Expo, *Weed* focuses on the Expo's participating Americans and looks at the hash coffeeshops, delves into hemp use and its industrial benefits, ponders legalization of marijuana and touches on spiritual freedom and pot as a religious sacrament. With "great buzzy interviews" (*Village Voice*), *Weed* is a "vicarious stoner's vacation" (*Variety*).

VHS: S33976. $49.95.

Doug Wolens, USA, 1997, 64 mins.

What Sex Am I?

Narrated and directed by Lee Grant, this is a journey into the unseen world of transsexuals, transvestites and "she-males". The filmmakers have drawn out revelations from these outcasts, about their tortured childhoods and the surgery that has given them peace of mind. 58 mins.

VHS: S13174. $59.98.

When Abortion Was Illegal: Untold Stories

If anyone wonders why the battle to keep abortion legal goes on, this documentary makes clear exactly what is at stake. Women were often degraded, physically harmed and scarred. Some even became infertile while others died in search of this medical procedure.

VHS: S22053. $29.95.

Dorothy Fadiman, USA, 1992, 28 mins.

When We Were Kings

Leon Cast's Academy Award-winning documentary is a knockout 20-year labor of love chronicling the famous 1974 "Rumble in the Jungle" heavyweight championship fight between 32-year-old Muhammad Ali and George Foreman in Zaire. Capturing the wit, charisma, intelligence and determination of "the Greatest," Cast's film is a lasting legacy of Ali the boxer, provocateur and political instigator. With interviews with Norman Mailer, George Plimpton and Spike Lee.

VHS: S31675. $19.95.

Laser: Letterboxed. **LD76286. $39.99.**

DVD: DV60129. $29.95.

Leon Cast, USA, 1997, 90 mins.

When Women Kill

Narrated and directed by Lee Grant. A psychological profile of seven trampled women who have been forced to kill. The stories are remarkably similar, their victims most often domineering men. Includes an in-prison confession by Leslie Van Houten, who killed for Charles Manson. 55 mins.

VHS: S13164. $29.98.

Lee Grant, USA, 1989, 55 mins.

Wild Wheels

Harrod Blank directed this excursion into the world of car art. This funky, low-budget film takes the form of a road movie as it examines the car ethos within the textures of Americana. Blank travels the highways to look at the relationship between automobile and its owner, the way a car's styling, design and make-up is connected to freedom and individuality.

VHS: S19742. $29.95.

Harrod Blank, USA, 1992, 64 mins.

Women—For America, for the World

This Academy Award-nominated film celebrates women who have the vision, courage and determination to re-define the meaning of security for the world, as they speak out for our health, educational and economic needs and for the fundamental value in protecting and nurturing our most precious resource-our children. Among the many women appearing in the film are Ellen Goodman, Geraldine Ferraro, Sandra Porter and Joanne Woodward.

VHS: S03792. $29.95.

Vivien Verdon-Roe, USA, 1985, 28 mins.

The Wonderful, Horrible Life of Leni Riefenstahl

An exhaustive, infuriating and unforgettable documentary about Leni Riefenstahl at age 90: actress, filmmaker (*Olympia, Triumph of the Will*), propagandist, personal friend of Goebbels and Hitler, photographer, explorer. Filmmaker Ray Mueller confronts Leni as she seeks to remold her image from that of a master propagandist and Nazi to that of a noble and heroic victim of history. Essential viewing. German with English subtitles.

VHS: S23996. $39.95.
Laser: LD75388. $69.99.
Ray Mueller, Germany, 1993, 180 mins.

Writing in Water and Admiral Bataille & the S.S. Esoterica

Two unique documentaries which challenge the documentary form in their somewhat whimsical approach. Stephen Rozell's *Writing in Water* is a wonderful work about the recollections of a rural Kentucky family, steeped in the southern tradition of storytelling. *Admiral Bataille*, by Jim Newberry, is an experimental documentary about an enigmatic human being, Kris Bataille.

VHS: S05367. $49.95.
Stephen Roszell/Jim Newberry, USA, 43 mins.

LES BLANK

Always for Pleasure

An enjoyable exploration of the mythic quality of New Orleans takes us to a jazz funeral, to a pre-Mardi Gras practice parade, Mardi Gras celebrations, and a St. Patrick's day parade, as well as Mardi Gras celebrations in the black community, including a revival of the black Indian traditions.

VHS: S00040. $49.95.
Les Blank, USA, 1978, 58 mins.

The Best of Blank

Les Blank is one of the true American originals. This program features music arrangements from 15 of his best films, including works from Dizzy Gillespie, Tex Mex, Polish polka, Cajun and zydeco to the American blues (Lightnin' Hopkins).

VHS: S16986. $49.95.
Les Blank, USA

A Blank Buffet

A compilation of the finest scenes of music, people and food selected from thirteen of Les Blank's best films including The Blues Accordin' to Lightnin' Hopkins, Gap-Toothed Women, In Heaven There Is No Beer? and Burden of Dreams.

VHS: S16987. $39.95.
Les Blank, USA, 60 mins.

Blues Accordin' to Lightnin' Hopkins

In his own words, and his "own own" music, Lightnin' Hopkins reveals the inspiration for his blues. He sings, he jives, he ponders. He boogies at an outdoor barbecue and a black rodeo. Les Blank has captured Lightnin's blues in their fullest, darkest power.

VHS: S00160. $49.95.
Les Blank, USA, 1975, 31 mins.

Burden of Dreams

Fascinating, chilling account of the making of Werner Herzog's Fitzcarraldo, a project beset by a series of disasters while shooting in the jungle. Filmmaker Les Blank has made a compelling film about obsessed genius and the creative process.

VHS: S00190. $59.95.
Les Blank, USA, 1982, 94 mins.

Chicken Real

Les Blank brought all his skill to bear on this documentary for an automated chicken-growing operation that produces 156 million chickens each year. It may be his funniest film—surreal images abound.

VHS: S09303. $44.95.
Les Blank, USA, 23 mins.

Christopher Tree

An early film by Les Blank, on the well-known Tibetan temple gong player. Just rediscovered, the film, with its mystical, mesmerizing music and Asian origins, is an interesting look at Tibetan tradition.

VHS: S12929. $19.95.
Les Blank, USA, 1967, 10 mins.

Chulas Fronteras

Chulas Fronteras provides a magnificent introduction to the most exciting nortena, Southern-Texas musicians, working today: Los Alegres de Teran, Lydia Mendoza, Flaco Jimenez and others. The music and spirit of the people is embodied in their strong family life, and their music.

VHS: S00241. $29.95.
Les Blank, USA, 1975, 58 mins.

Cigarette Blues

A microcosmic Les Blank film in which Oakland bluesman Sonny Rhodes simultaneously addresses three of the filmmaker's long-standing obsessions: death, cigarette smoking and the nature of the blues.

VHS: S09299. $29.95.
Les Blank/Alan Govenar, USA, 6 mins.

Dizzy

Les Blank's earliest music film focuses on the trumpet player himself, who, along with Charlie Parker, Tholonious Monk and others, sparked the change from Jazz into Bop in the 40's. Dizzy talks about his beginnings and music theories, and blows hot music on that famous horn.

VHS: S09298. $44.95.
Les Blank, USA, 20 mins.

Dry Wood

The featured music is that of Bois Sec Ardoin and his sons and Canray Fontenot. Theirs is an older, rural style of Cajun music, which, in the film, weaves together incidents in the lives of Fontenot and Ardoin families. The film's highlights include a rollicking country mardi gras, work in the rice fields, a "Mens Only" supper, and a hog-butchering party. Like other Blank films, it expresses respect for living the life.

VHS: S09293. $49.95.
Les Blank/Maureen Gosling, USA, 37 mins.

Gap-Toothed Women

"A love poem to women" (Roger Ebert). An exploration of the self-image of women and pressures to conform to ideals of mass media, concentrating on many unique women who happen to be gap-toothed.

VHS: S02901. $49.95.
Les Blank, USA, 1987, 30 mins.

Garlic Is As Good As Ten Mothers

Blank's gastronomically obsessional film portrait, an exhaustive foray into the history, consumption, cultivation, and culinary and curative powers of garlic, from the kitchens of Chez Panisse and Flint's Bar-B-Que to the international garlic festival.

VHS: S00481. $49.95.
Les Blank, USA, 1977, 51 mins.

God Respects Us When We Work, But Loves Us When We Dance

An original rock music score accentuates this film panorama of the action and more meditative moments occurring at Los Angeles' memorable 1967 Love-In. Earmarks of the alternative abound in this colorful and candid record of a social phenomenon.

VHS: S09297. $44.95.
Les Blank/Skip Gerson, USA, 20 mins.

Hot Pepper

Hot Pepper plunges the viewer deep into the music of Clifton Chenier, and its sources in the surroundings of rural and urban Louisiana. The great French accordionist mixes rock and blues, with his unique version of Zydeco music, a combination of Cajun French and African undertones.

VHS: S00583. $49.95.
Les Blank, USA, 1978, 54 mins.

In Heaven There Is No Beer

A joyous romp through the dance, food, music, friendship, even religion of the polka. Blank takes us through the polka subculture from New London, Connecticut's Polkabration to the International Polka convention—often funny and wry comments on the polka subculture.

VHS: S00616. $49.95.
Les Blank, USA, 1984, 51 mins.

Innocents Abroad

A portrait of the ways American and European cultural, political and social ideas and stereotypes collide. Structured around a group of American tourists, the film observes them moving through London, Amsterdam, Heidelberg, Germany, Venice, Rome, Nice, Avignon and Paris. With music by Bob Dylan and Chuck Berry.

VHS: S16990. $59.95.
Les Blank, USA, 1992, 86 mins.

J'Ai Ete au Bal: I Went to the Dance

The Cajun and Zydeco music of Louisiana is explored by Les Blank, Chris Strachwitz and Maureen Gosling. With rare recordings, stills and footage, interviews and live performances by the greatest names in Cajun and Zydeco music, including Michael Doucet and Beausoleil, Queen Ida and her Bon Temps Zydeco Band, Clifton Chenier, Wayne Toups and many more.

VHS: S12921. $59.95.
Les Blank/Maureen Gosling/Chis Strachwitz, USA, 1989

Marc and Ann

A portrait of Ann and Marc Savoy, the Cajun musical couple: Marc, accordion builder and player, Cajun cook and outspoken defender of his culture, and Ann, an adopted "Cajun" who authored Cajun Music: A Reflection of a People. A more personal look at one Cajun family and their appreciation for their culture in the face of encroaching American mall culture.

VHS: S12923. $49.95.
Les Blank, USA, 1990, 30 mins.

Puamana

Les Blank's joyous examination of Irmgard Farden Aluli and her remarkable family of performers and musicians, part of the vibrant musical scene around the Hawaiian island of Lahaina. The film interweaves of concert footage, archival stills and on-screen text to produce "a cinematic translation of the pulse of island life."

VHS: S16991. $49.95.
Les Blank, USA, 1991, 37 mins.

Six Short Films of Les Blank, 1960-1985

From Running around Like a Chicken with Its Head Cut Off, Blank's first film, done as an homage to Bergman's Seventh Seal, to the 1985 six-minute plea to end smoking entitled Cigarette Blues.

VHS: S02904. $59.95.
Les Blank, USA, 83 mins.

Spend It All

The Cajuns of Southwest Louisiana in scenes such as quarter horse racing, accordion building, cooking and the intoxicating music of the Balfa Brothers, Marc Savoy, Nathan Abshire and others. In English.

VHS: S06504. $59.95.
Les Blank, USA, 41 mins.

Sprout Wings and Fly

A compassionate, life-affirming document on the old-time Appalachian fiddler Tommy Jarrell. A fascinating film on the theme that art, music, dance, food and earthly pleasures help human beings live joyously in the face of certain death. "Jarrell is a fabulous fiddler and ballad singer…a fascinating cast of backwoods characters plus a compelling look at one of the central issues facing a civilization" (Berkeley Monthly).

VHS: S09301. $44.95.
Les Blank, USA, 30 mins.

Sworn to the Drum: A Tribute to Francisco Aguabella

Afro-Cuban drummer Aguabella has brought the rich, complex, religious musical traditions of bata and the the secular conguero traditions to the U.S. and the world of jazz. Now a long time U.S. resident, this video tells both his personal story and of his contribution to Latin Jazz. Dizzy Gillespie, Carlos Santana and Katherine Dunham, among other musicians, appear.

Home Video.
VHS: S29439. $49.95.
Public Performance.
VHS: S29440. $99.00.
Les Blank, USA, 1995, 35 mins.

A Well Spent Life

With Mance Lipscomb's passing, what was always a strong, beautifully filmed portrait of the man and his music has become a precious document—a love song to beat back the silence of death. This film is a deeply moving tribute to the Texas songster, considered by many to be one of the greatest guitarists of all time. Not discovered until 1960, before then Mance lived by sharecropping, surviving the brutality of a system not much better than slavery. The film captures Mance's music, sets it off with scenes of his hometown of Navasota and combines it all with the miracle of his love.

VHS: S09296. $49.95.
Les Blank/Skip Gerson, USA, 44 mins.

Werner Herzog Eats His Shoe

Blank documents German filmmaker Werner Herzog honoring a vow he made to independent filmmaker Errol Morris that Herzog would eat his shoe if Morris ever finished a film. Morris did (Gates of Heaven), and Herzog complies by boiling and consuming his desert boots at the UC Theatre in Berkeley.

VHS: S01443. $39.95.
Les Blank, USA, 1979, 20 mins.

Yum, Yum, Yum!

Les Blank marries his obsession with spicy, down-home food and his fascination for the Cajuns and Creoles of Southern Louisiana, to create this mouth-watering, visceral exploration into the cooking and culture of this region. From the bayous and prairies where this unique cuisine originated to the New Orleans kitchen of celebrity chef Paul Prudhomme, Blank discovers the heart and soul of a people and their cuisine.
VHS: S12922. $49.95.
Les Blank, USA, 1990, 31 mins.

EMILE DE ANTONIO

1968: America Is Hard to See

Veteran documentary filmmaker Emile de Antonio presents a probing analysis of the crucial, kaleidoscopic year 1968, revealing a nation divided: between war and peace, young and old, B&W.
VHS: S07345. $59.95.
Emile de Antonio, USA, 1986, 88 mins.

In the King of Prussia

Emile de Antonio's thought-provoking docu-drama about the Plowshares 8, headed by the Berrigan brothers, who occupied a nuclear weapons plant in Pennsylvania. Martin Sheen stars as the judge presiding over the Berrigans' trial, while Daniel plays himself.
VHS: S00618. $59.98.
Emile de Antonio, USA, 1982, 92 mins.

McCarthy: Death of a Witchhunter

Emile De Antonio's now-classic, rousing film record of the televised 1954 Army-McCarthy hearings dissects the media-clouded history of Cold-War America.
VHS: S01044. $29.95.
Emile de Antonio, USA, 1964, 45 mins.

Millhouse: A White Comedy

Comic and terrifying portrait of Richard Millhouse Nixon. It's all here—Nixon advocating the death penalty for drug dealers, suggesting the use of nuclear weapons in Indochina, photos of Nixon watching go-go dancers in the White House.
VHS: S00857. $39.95.
Emile de Antonio, USA, 1971, 93 mins.

Mr. Hoover & I

The last film from a pioneer of the political documentary, Emile de Antonio, a surprisingly personal reflective work which details de Antonio's decades-long battle with Edgar J. Hoover, who had the FBI spy on him. Over 10,000 documents were compiled on de Antonio's activities, and his battle for justice, independence and his own sanity forms a remarkable tale about a unique and very talented and courageous spirit.
VHS: S31778. $19.98.
Emile de Antonio, USA, 1989, 87 mins.

Painters Painting

Warhol, Rauschenberg, Johns and other American key painters are the subject of De Antonio's documentary which captures the visceral personalities at work.
VHS: S00988. $29.98.
Emile de Antonio, USA, 1972, 116 mins.

Plot to Kill JFK: Rush to Judgment

The film explores the theories of Mark Lane, and provides better than any other document a basis for further exploration of the conspiracy-oriented theories surrounding the assassination of John F. Kennedy.
VHS: S01807. $29.95.
Emile de Antonio, USA, 1983, 50 mins.

Vietnam: In the Year of the Pig

One of the most powerful films ever produced about Vietnam, and an Academy Award nominee. "Passionate and committed, yet it impresses by its sobriety… and will be worth seeing after Vietnam for it raises questions" (*Washington Post*).
VHS: S01416. $39.95.
Emile de Antonio, USA, 1968, 103 mins.

DANNY LYON

Born to Film

A complex and moving picture of a child, played by the filmmaker's son, and within it a film of Danny Lyon's childhood, made 35 years earlier by the filmmaker's father. At last, mythology for the middle class. "Lyon's passionate vision has deepened and grown in resonance, and the film is not just family or even social history, but about human continuity, the power of the instinct to survive, the grace that love and play bring to it, the wonder of being alive."
VHS: S05394. $99.00.
Danny Lyon, USA, 1983, 33 mins.

Dear Mark

Made for Mark di Suvero and his sculpture. "The erection of an heroic, skeletal abstract sculpture by Mark di Suvero in France is Dadaistic light comedy, with its Gene Autry soundtrack. The 'heroic' image of the artist at work is ironically undercut by the soundtrack of a Gene Autry radio episode in which that cowboy 'hero' smokes out illegal Mexican aliens" (*Films from Pictures*).
VHS: S05393. $99.00.
Danny Lyon, USA/France, 1965/1975-80, 15 mins.

El Mojado

Ironically titled *The Wetback*, *El Mojado* pictures a hero of our times, a Mexican who walks a hundred miles to work in America, tracked by the border patrol. "It's just like hunting animals only it's a lot more fun because you're hunting a live human being. *El Mojado* is about my best friend in New Mexico, an undocumented worker from rural Chihuahua….His name is Eddie and I soon came to regard him as a genius. Eddie could do anything, make anything, fix any car or truck, and usually do it with scraps. We built an adobe house together and every spring I would meet him near the border and smuggle him past the border patrol into the United States. He introduced me to the whole unbelievable world of 'illegal aliens'" (Danny Lyon). English and Spanish with English subtitles.
VHS: S05389. $99.00.
Danny Lyon, USA, 1972, 20 mins.

El Otro Lado (The Other Side)

Made with the rare cooperation of large groups of Mexican campesinos as they walk into this country and live as undocumented workers in citrus groves near Phoenix. Filmed in Queretero and Maripoca County, the campesinos work, sing corredos, and laugh at adversity. "Lyon's images are simple and direct. These men do what they have to do in order to survive. And they do it with remarkable spirit and optimism. Nowhere is this more evident than when the men are making music. They look strong, proud and momentarily free" (Nancy Legge, *The Villager*). Spanish with English subtitles.
VHS: S05392. $99.00.
Danny Lyon, USA/Mexico, 1978, 60 mins.

Little Boy

A radical portrait of New Mexico, with Steve Baer's brilliant diatribe on plutonium ("I think a friend has some in his house"), the Navajo Council for Liberation sit-in at tribal headquarters, Ike de Vargas and Bleak Beauty's own hero, Willie Jaramillo, at war with the police. "Named after the atom bomb that destroyed Hiroshima, *Little Boy* is a king of grand *summa*, Lyon's epic view of America focused through the lens of contemporary New Mexico. The bleak, man-made environment is superimposed uneasily on a harsh, unforgiving landscape, and explosively charged with clashing subcultures…robust, pulsating with energy, but also clouded by a kind of doomed fatality" (*San Francisco Chronicle*).
VHS: S05391. $99.00.
Danny Lyon, USA, 1976, 52 mins.

Llanito

The anglos are a group of retarded boys, Alamo is a pueblo Indian who drinks too much, and Willie Jaramillo makes his film debut as a troubled Chicano child. "*Llanito* deals with people who operate on the fringe of society: Indians, Chicanos, and a group of retarded Anglos. Their collective martyrdom to American society is symbolized by the summary of Christ's passion as recounted by one of the retarded boys, unquestionably one of the most bizarre religious testaments ever recorded" (Pamela Allara, *Pictures from Films/Films from Pictures*).
VHS: S05388. $99.00.
Danny Lyon, USA, 1971, 50 mins.

Los Ninos Abandonados (The Abandoned Children)

A classically realistic film made in the streets of a small Colombian city with a cast of abandoned children, that exhibits the emotions of Chaplin, with music composed and sung by the children. "Unobtrusively, Lyon records the boys' aimless daily lives….*Los Ninos Abandonados* is an angry film with the quietest tones imaginable—and is all the more persuasive for being so" (Kevin Thomas, *Los Angeles Times*). Spanish with English subtitles.
VHS: S05390. $99.00.
Danny Lyon, Colombia, 1974, 63 mins.

Media Man

Danny and Nancy Lyon offer a whimsical, quirky and hilarious look at America. Shot in New York, Mississippi and New Mexico, obsessions like blemish-free tomatoes, tattoo contests, rotten pumpkins and fishing reveal some startling truths about this country—like it's a little strange.
VHS: S21873. $99.00.
Danny Lyon/Nancy Weiss Lyon, USA, 1994, 60 mins.

Social Sciences 127

A comedy in a Houston tattoo parlour during the Vietnam War. Featuring the hilarious late, great Bill Sanders in his "painless" tattoo shop. Winner, USA Film Festival. "Mr. Lyon's fondness for bizarre images is balanced by a kind of solemn respect for his subjects. This is particularly true in *Social Sciences 127*, about an eccentric, hard-drinking tattoo artist named Bill Sanders who, while he works, rambles on about Vietnam, lesbians, and the art of what he advertises as 'velvety tattoos'" (Vincent Canby, *The New York Times*).
VHS: S05387. $99.00.
Danny Lyon, USA, 1969, 21 mins.

Willie

A realistic film made in Bernalillo, home of Willie Jaramillo and filmmakers Danny and Nancy Weiss Lyon. Defiantly individual and implacable in the face of authority, Willie is repeatedly thrown into jail for relatively minor offenses. The filmmakers gain access to jail cells, day rooms, lunatic wards and the worst cellblock in the penitentiary where Willie is locked up next to his childhood friend and convicted murderer, Michael Guzman. "Lyon deftly blends footage of Jaramillo as an adult with scenes of his more carefree youth. The effect is powerful. One gets the sense of the ravages of time, coupled with a feel for the devastation wrought by a life wasted" (*New Mexican*).
VHS: S05395. $99.00.
Danny Lyon/Nancy Weiss Lyon, USA, 1985, 82 mins.

ERROL MORRIS

A Brief History of Time

Errol Morris' documentary about the English physicist Stephen Hawking takes its title from Hawking's best seller. The film explores Hawking's groundbreaking work in quantum physics and the study of the origins of the universe, despite his debilitating physical state, brought about by amyotrophic lateral sclerosis. Morris interweaves anecdotes, family dynamics and Hawking's background into a kaleidoscope of images, movements and sound. Music by Philip Glass.
VHS: S18370. $19.95.
Errol Morris, USA/Great Britain, 1991, 84 mins.

Fast, Cheap & Out of Control

Documentary master Errol Morris' magical portrait of the weird and wonderful worlds of an elderly topiary gardner, a retired lion tamer, an expert on mole rats, and a cutting-edge robotics designer. Morris interplays, overlaps and interrelates the lives of these four men who tread the thin line between genius and madness, in order to study humanity, as he raises questions about the future of mankind.
VHS: S34294. $98.99.
Errol Morris, USA, 1997, 82 mins.

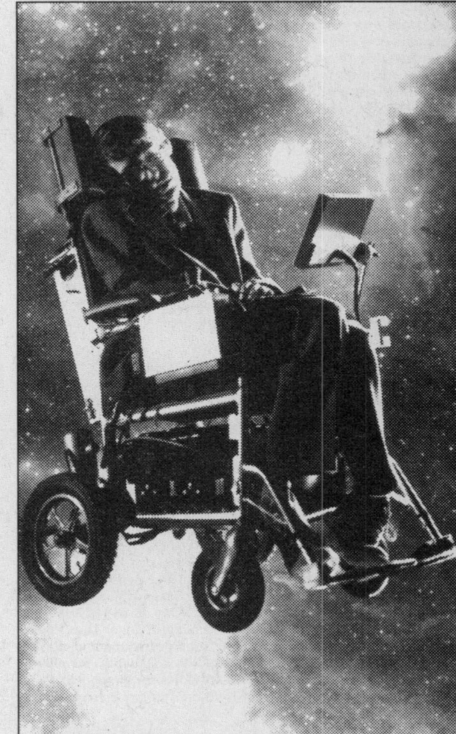

experimental cinema & video

6 Films by Mark Street

This compilation by one of the best of a new generation of filmmakers includes the acclaimed *Winterwheat*, *Excursions*, *Blue Movie*, *Lilting Towards Chaos*, *Echo Anthem* and *Missing Something Somewhere*, and utilizes techniques ranging from hand-manipulated material to recontextualized found footage.
VHS: S28585. $59.95.

8x8 (A Chess Sonata in 8 Movements)

A masterpiece of experimental film and a projection of the surrealist vision into cinema by its outstanding artists. Described by Richter as "part Freud, part Lewis Carroll," it is a fairy tale for the subconscious based on the game of chess. This chess-sonata is played by a host of artists including Paul Bowles, Jean Cocteau, Julian Levy, Jacqueline Matisse, Jose Sert, Yves Tanguy, Marcel Duchamp, Max Ernst and Alexander Calder. "What interested me is…the poetry of images, the melody and rhythm of forms and colors" (Hans Richter).
VHS: S04359. $59.95.
Hans Richter, USA, 1957, 81 mins.

A.I.D.S.C.R.E.A.M., Ecce Homo and Final Solutions

Three short experimental films by gay filmmaker Jerry Tartaglia are joined on this video. Along with *A.I.D.S.C.R.E.A.M.*, *Ecce Homo* and *Final Solutions* explore fear, rage, the anti-sex and anti-gay movements and the rise of AIDS consumerism. It's an angry, arrogant and unapologetic collection.
VHS: S27222. $59.95.

Alexander Alexeieff

The creator of the "pin board" discusses his invention and its application for book illustrations as well as art film. With wife and colleague Claire Parker. Clips from their work, including their film of Gogol's short story *The Nose*. 1966, 28 mins.
VHS: S31600. $59.95.

Alexeieff & Parker

In their Paris studio, Russian-born artist/filmmaker Alexander Alexeieff and his American wife, Claire Parker, show and explain how they create pictures on the instrument they invented, the pinscreen (l'ecran de'epingles), in *Alexeieff at the Pinboard (A Propos de Jivago)* (1960, 8 mins.). *The Nose (Le Nez)* (1963, 11 mins.) is Gogol's celebrated short story in pinscreen animation, without words, in fantastic moving pictures that capture the scene and spirit of 19th century Russia. *Night on Bald Mountain (Une Nuit sur le Mont Chauve)* (1933, 8 mins.) is the first film made on pinboard. In this reknowned illustration of Modest Moussorgsky's tone poem, goblins, skeletons and other fantastic creatures perform outlandish three-dimensional effects. Animator Norman McLaren listed the film "first and foremost" among the animated films he most admired and liked. "Above all it is the quality of Alexeieff's imagination that stirs me profoundly," McLaren said. 27 mins.
VHS: S30223. $75.00.

All Women Are Equal & Pentagon Peace March

A pre-operational transsexual explains her values and beliefs in this insightful study of sexual identity by Marguerite Paris. Then Paris offers an impressionistic view of a 1967 anti-war demonstration. The 8mm originals of these works were transformed by optical printing.
VHS: S27223. $59.95.
Marguerite Paris, USA

American Avant-Garde

Includes three short films from the American avant-garde: *Fall of the House of Usher* (20 mins.), *Lot in Sodom* and *Life and Death of a Hollywood Extra*.
VHS: S14923. $29.95.

American Avant-Garde Films

A collection of five experimental American films spanning 1906-1933; Edwin S. Porter's landmark *Dream of a Rarebit Fiend* (1906, 6 mins., color tints); *Salome*, a bold and stylized version of the Oscar Wilde play starring the dancer Nazimova and based on drawings by Aubrey Beardsley; *The Fall of the House of Usher*, James Watson and Melville Webber's version of Edgar Allan Poe's tale; Watson and Webber's *Lot in Sodom*, an experimental telling of the Old Testament story in terms of homosexuality and the subconscious; and finally Charles Vidor's *The Bridge*, an experimental telling of the Ambrose Bierce story, *Occurrence at Owl Creek Bridge*.
VHS: S09927. $49.95.

Amida/A Mosaic for the Kali Yuga/Arches/Body Count/Hey Joe

"Throughout all of Reeves' videotapes there is a pervasive sense of feeling of the artist's presence, psyche and spirit, of the artist using the medium as a means of understanding himself…the evolution of his work demonstrates…a refined and spare understanding of the relationship of poetry and image," wrote *Afterimage*. A collection of video work concerned with spiritual ideas, *Amida* explores reincarnation by depicting cycles of existence through images of natural beauty juxtaposed with symbols of death. *A Mosaic for the Kali Yuga* is a meditation on the acceleration, fragmentation and devaluation of truth. *Arches* constructs a poem using text, sound and image in an exploration of language and landscapes in the desert; *Body Count* is an emotionally searing work that ironically presents the fascination of youth with military glory. *Hey Joe* is a psychedelic video set to a Jimi Hendrix song.
VHS: S10417. $59.95.
Daniel Reeves, USA, 32 mins.

Antigone: Rites of Passion

Amy Greenfield's daring first feature retells Sophocles' classical tragedy through action, dance and cutting-edge rock music. It transforms the drama of the heroine who defied the State to bury her brother into ceaseless movement and music, haunting sound and words, a mounting outcry against the world's injustices climaxing in an end-of-the-world requiem. A hymn to the extremes of courage, devotion, outrage, eros and death. "Impressive, innovative rock opera film" (*Variety*). With music by Elliott Sharp, Glenn Branca and Diamanda Galas.
VHS: S15437. $29.95.
Amy Greenfield, USA, 1990, 85 mins.

The Aroma of Enchantment

From Chip Lord, one of America's premier videomakers, a video essay that investigates the idea of America in Japan by weaving historical material about General Douglas MacArthur with stories told by collectors or practitioners of Americanization in Japan. Lord relates his own feelings of "otherness" and cultural displacement in 1990s Tokyo, connecting these ideas when General MacArthur arrived on Japanese soil in 1946.
VHS: S31254. $59.95.
Chip Lord, USA/Japan, 1992, 55 mins.

Art Com Video 1: Scandinavia

An indication of the diversity of expression given form through the video medium in Nordic countries—from lyrical abstraction to critique of everyday life to scratch video. Features *Char, en Oversattning* (Karl Druner), *Cricket* (Marikki Hakola), *Elastic Party* (Vibeke Vogel), *The Human Race* (Nicolai Osergard), *Johnny—A Modern Interpretation of Slavology* (Ulrik al Brask), *Menschen* (Ulrik al Bask), *R.E.M.* (Ane Mette Ruge), and other work. 92 mins.
VHS: S13284. $59.95.

Art Com Video 2: Waveforms: Video Japan

A collection of video by artists in Japan that at once represents a diversity of expression, and indicates three themes which underscore Japanese sensibility: Nature, the persistence of cultural traditions, and the embracing of new technology. Features *Mt. Fuji*, Ko Nakajima's electronic interpretation of Hokusai's 19th century woodblock prints; *Flow (3) Part 2*, by Shinsuke Ina, a cascading waterfall rendered and manipulated in video; *Koto Buki*, which documents a ritualistic performance of incantatory music, voice and movement at the tide pools of an inland sea; *Listen the Body*, by Yoshiko Yamaguchi, a body art sound work; *My Gaijin Tengoky*, a humorous view of the idiosyncracies of Japanese culture; and *Alley o Alley*, an unobtrusive journey through a poor community in Osaka. 57 mins.
VHS: S13285. $59.95.

Art Com Video 4: Peter Callas

Selected works from Australian video artist Peter Callas, from 1986-1988. His works explore the relationships between commerce, electro-culture, post-industrial environment and time-based art. 28 mins.
VHS: S14905. $59.95.

Art Com Video 14: Rebel Girls

Leslie Singer's *Flipper* is a strangely funny work about football hero worship, while *Handmirror/Brush Set*, by Liz Canning, brings childhood grooming practice alive through a vinyl practice dummy head. *Untitled II* is Monet Clark's seductive/repulsive ritual that attracts voyeurs. *I Love You Mom*, by Madelaine Altman, shows a secretly recorded mother/daughter argument, and *Goldfinger*, by Meg Mack and Steven Cabella, documents a performance of a blonde who laughs at herself and culture. 55 mins.
VHS: S21274. $59.95.

Art of Memory

Experiment with political and religious forms by acclaimed video artist Woody Vasulka. Documentary images of WW II, the Spanish Civil War and the Russian Revolution appear against vistas of Southwestern landscapes.
VHS: S05398. $59.95.
Woody Vasulka, USA, 36 mins.

The Ascent of Man/ In the Absence of Heroes

In *The Ascent of Man*, broadcast video footage and super-8 film are combined in an experimental investigation of patriotism and virtue, while the video *In the Abscence of Heroes* explores the relationship of warfare to personal trauma and international conflict.
VHS: S21038. $59.95.
Jayce Salloum, USA, 1986/1984, 15 & 40 mins.

Atalanta Strategy

Based on music from the opera *Atalanta* (Acts of God), and using a multi-projector, free-sampling technique to provide video imagery, this is daring video art from Robert Ashley. It is based on the anecdote material of the second episode of *Willard*. There are three kinds of scenes surrounding the main anecdote, which is sung by Robert Ashley.
VHS: S11644. $49.95.
Robert Ashley, USA, 1984, 27 mins.

Avant Garde & Experimental Film

Five early experimental films: Bunuel and Dali's *Un Chien Andalou*, Joris Ivens and Mannus Franken's *Rain*, Erno Metzner's *Uberfall*, Orson Welles' 1934 *Hearts of Age* and Fernand Leger's *Ballet Mecanique*. Silent, with English subtitles. 74 mins.
VHS: S00079. $29.95.

Avant Garde Program #2

Three early silent German and French experimental works: Eggeling's *Symphonie Diagonale*, Man Ray's *L'Etoile de Mer*, and Rene Clair's *Entr'Acte*, starring Man Ray and Marcel Duchamp. 42 mins.
VHS: S00080. $24.95.

Avant Garde Program #11

Features David Lynch's cult-early-classic *Alphabet* (1970, 4 mins), in which the director of *Eraserhead* uses a stunning combination of media to move at breakneck speed through Lynch's vision of the ABC's; Jean Mitry's *Pacific 231*, a film poem which Mitry photographed and cut to fit a twelve-tone musical divertisement which was written by Arthur Honegger some 14 years earlier when Honegger had been aboard the famous train; Marcel Duchamp's *Anemic Cinema* (1926, 5 mins), a series of verbal and visual puns with nonsense phrases.
VHS: S07696. $39.95.

Avant Garde Program #12

Features Germaine Dulac's *Seashell and the Clergyman*, Chris Marker's famous *La Jetee*—both of these are individually available and separately described in the catalog—and Robert Florey/Slavko Vorkapich's *Life and Death of 9413, A Hollywood Extra* , made in 1928, the first important American experimental film, influenced by German Expressionist cinema, a fantasy about an aspiring movie star.
VHS: S07170. $39.95.

Avant Garde Program #14

Three films by the great photographer/artist/filmmaker Man Ray: *Retour a la Raison* (1923, 3 mins) was produced to aggravate audiences at the last great Dada soiree, without the use of a camera, by sprinkling the raw film stock and exposing it light; *Emak Bakia* (1927, 19 mins) is a famous surrealist short in which Man Ray throws the camera into the air; *Les Mysteres du Chateau du De* (1929, 21 mins) features a modern villa designed by Mallet-Stevens as the setting for an unsolved mystery.
VHS: S07169. $39.95.
Man Ray, France, 1921-27, 43 mins.

Avant Garde Shorts/France

Collection of early surreal and avant garde films made between 1914 and 1928: *La Folie du Dr. Tube* (Abel Gance), *Emak Bakia* (Man Ray), *The Smiling Madame Beudet* (Germaine Dulac), *Anemic Cinema* (Marcel Duchamp) and *Charleston* (Jean Renoir). Silent. France, 1914-28.
VHS: S00081. $34.95.

Bachdisc

Music and visuals are beautifully intertwined in this program that combines an accessible and thrilling exploration of J.S. Bach's *Fugue in #4 B minor* and a documentary on the composer's methods and art that captures the full range and excitement of his music.
Laser: LD70102. $49.95.
Juan Downey, USA

Beehive

Film on dance that relates the story of a bumbling drone bee who unwittingly causes the transformation of a worker into a queen. A striking soap opera with dance, animation and high production values.
VHS: S07127. $29.95.
Frank Moore/Jim Self, USA, 1985, 16 mins.

Berks Filmmakers: A Compilation Tape

Works by Gary Adelstein, Jerry Orr, Buddy Kilchesty and Jamie Harrar are combined in this video. Together they offer a view of grassroots filmmaking in Eastern Pennsylvania that is by turns lyrical, psychosexual in focus and critical.
VHS: S27225. $59.95.

Berlin, Symphony of a Great City

Walter Ruttmann's great documentary is a dynamic vision of Berlin, unfolding from dawn until midnight. Ruttmann captured the city's expressive poetry by concealing his camera in vans and suitcases to capture a portrait of the city and its people. Music composed and conducted by Timothy Brock, performed by the Olympia Chamber Orchestra. On the same program is *Opus 1*, a ten-minute essay Ruttman shot in 1922.
VHS: S01931. $24.95.
Walter Ruttmann, Germany, 1927, 62 mins.

The Best of the New York Underground, Year 2

Suicide, intense brutality and steamy sexual situations are found on this extreme video. It includes a number of short independent works, all of which are excessive. *The Operation* is perverse, *Deinstag* is violent, and *Brouhaba* actually features Satan partying. 90 mins.
VHS: S27440. $29.95.

Best of William Wegman

William Wegman is one of the world's most affable subversives. This tape, assembled by Electronic Arts Intermix, is a twenty minute survey of Wegman's vignettes from the years 1970-1978. His dog Man Ray, various props, and the talking stomach are featured in this compilation of Wegman classics which include *Duet, Milk Floor Piece, Stomach Song, Two Lamps, Pocket Bookman, Massage Chair, Deodorant* and *The Spelling Lesson*.
VHS: S06308. $65.00.
William Wegman, USA, 1970-78, 20 mins.

Brains by Revlon

A pattern-obsessive, symmetrical work about three extravagantly costumed women discussing three fates, three graces and three fairy tales from *Sleeping Beauty* in this strange, hypnotic exercise in style.
VHS: S17195. $29.95.
Jack Waters, USA, 18 mins.

Cadillac Ranch/Media Burn

A recent re-edit of two Ant Farm projects, *Cadillac Ranch* documents the burying of 10 Cadillacs in Amarillo, Texas as a monument to the Cadillac fin, plus *Media Burn* , a spectacular performance piece.
VHS: S00200. $59.95.
Ant Farm, USA, 1974-75

Cave Girls

A tape by collaborating women artists who develop a pre-thought fantasy of a prehistoric culture of women. Rife with homemade exoticism, this well-received piece verges on the grand themes of female identity. Conceived by Kiki Smith and Ellen Cooper, with music by Bush Tetras and Y Pants.
VHS: S07112. $29.95.
Cara Brownell, USA, 1982, 28 mins.

Chronos

Chronos, meaning the passage of time, is a visual music journey transcending history from the cradle of civilization to modern day Paris. Startling time-lapse images of the Vatican, the Sphinx, the Great Pyramid and nearly 50 other wonders of our world captivate the senses. Photographed in the world's largest film format for IMAX theatres.
VHS: S16731. $19.95.
Ron Fricke, USA, 1991, 40 mins.

CineBLAST! Vol. 1

Eight short, innovative features from independent directors are collected on this video. Included are: *Tough*(Aiyana Elliot), *Fishmind*(Matthias Freier), *Sheep's Meadow*(Brooke Smith), *Hungreed*(Ira Israel), *Watch with Mother*(Sam Serafy), *The Side of the Road*(David Burris), *The Girl from Mousb*(Garine Torossian) and *Zinky Boys Go Underground*(Paul Tickell). 111 mins.
VHS: S27619. $89.95.

CineBLAST! Vol. 2

Eight independent short films include: *Frog Crossing*, by Jamie Babbit and Ari Gold, the story of an environmental wacko who falls for a junkfood diva while defending mating frogs on a California highway; *Generic Metal Titan*, a powerful, award-winning story of teen angst by Timothy Naylor; *Tick*, by John Hamburg, the Sundance hit comedy about inept bomb disposal experts finding love in the ashes of their careers, starring Michael Showalter of MTV's *The State*; *An Autumn Wind*, by Iara Lee, the director of *Synthetic Pleasures*, a beautiful reflection of Japanese culture with haikus written and read by Allen Ginsberg; *Boom*, by Morgan J. Freeman, starring Brendan Sexton, Jr. (*Welcome to the Doll House*), shot in Virginia, the beautiful drama of the tattered lives of three orphans; *Bad Liver, Broken Heart*, by British director Terry Stacey, an ironic take on Americana in which two fictional types meet and celebrate the Greyhound bus and the passing of their era; *Call Waiting*, by Mimi Steinberg, filmed in Grand Central Station at telephone booths, in which a parade of bizarre New Yorkers passes before the eyes of a young country boy; and *A Counter Fancy*, by Brian D. Cange, the story of a diner waitress whose dishwater life is spiced up by the attentions of a mysterious stranger (Bill Sage). "A welcome antidote to the anti-short mentality that marginalizes some of the best filmmaking in the country" (*Filmmaker Magazine*). 100 mins.
VHS: S30001. $79.95.

Cinema of Transgression

Nick Zedd's *Bogus Man & Go to Hell*, John Spencer's *Shithaus*, Lung Leg's *Worm Movie*, Richard Klemann's *A Suicide*, Erotic Psyche's *Mutable Fire*, Tommy Turner's *Simonland*, Richard Kern's *You Killed Me First & King of Sex*, Michael Wolfe's *Niggernight*, and Manuel de Landa's *Judgment Day* and *Ism, Ism*. Extremely graphic scenes of bodily functions, hokey scenes of trumped up ketchup violence, stabbing and severed limbs, some strangely moving and brilliant filmmaking by a wide collection of drug addicts, outlaws, and perennial outsiders.
VHS: S10161. $49.95.

Clea Waite: Stella Maris

A stylized examination of the female nude, and the impact of movement and light under water. The filmmaker devises "living sculptures" through a bold black and white interpretation of the triple goddess myths. 15 mins.
VHS: S17206. $19.95.

Clothed in Muscle: A Dance of the Body

Gutman described this film as "the most complete evocation of my raison d'etre…as a filmmaker." Gutman uses the film's star—sculptor, writer, and women's body building champion Claudia Wilbourn—posing in the nude, to capture the effect of antique Greek sculpture. "Nature loves variety more than we do and that vaguely is what this film is about" (Walter Gutman).
VHS: S30232. $40.00.
Walter Gutman, USA, 1981, 37 mins.

Colin Campbell

Nine works made between 1972 and 1990 were chosen by Peggy Gale for this video. These pieces have been internationally seen in museums such as the Modern in New York and the Pompidou in Paris. Once, they represented Canada's contribution to the Venice Biennale. 63 mins.
VHS: S29954. $95.00.

Commission

Video artist Woody Vasulka's experiment with narrativity through electronic tools is presented in this operatic work that evokes the friendship between composer Berlioz and the violinist Paganini, whose ill health, loss of voice and habit of gambling led to his death at an early age.
VHS: S05645. $59.95.
Woody Vasulka, USA, 1987, 45 mins.

Communications Update

An intriguing collection of excerpts from the artists' cable TV series that makes room for broad slapstick, pulp drama, horror stories of the streets, and a wry airy speculation on science and loneliness. Includes work by: Milli Iatrou and Ron Morgan, Eric Mitchell and Squat Theatre, Robert Burden and Dictellio Cepeda, Mark Magill, and Stephen Torton. USA, 1982, 58 mins.
VHS: S07113. $59.95.

Critical Art Ensemble

The Tallahassee-Florida based video performance group of seven lays on the post-modern dog, with a collection of short pieces: *Mirror of Reduction, Misappropriation (after Andy Warhol), Baudrillard's Lasso, Collective Oedipal Revolution, Indefinite Concrete Material, Gift-Wrapped Aporia, Art Film, Mondo Familiae, Limnologic Jargon*. 35 mins.
VHS: S10206. $29.95.

Cupid's Infirmary

Mike Kuchar's new, campy soap opera updates Kuchar's 1960s melodramatic drag extravaganzas. This tape features tattooed torsos of sex-starved "she-men" who are in turn laid bare for analysis and cheap thrills.
VHS: S27226. $59.95.
Mike Kuchar, USA

Cyberscape

Computer visionary Beny Tchaicovsky's surreal history of human life and thought is a fast-forward trip from the Garden of Eden to quantum mechanics, with dizzying, often hilarious detours into society's obsessions with time, money and the opposite sex. Soundtrack by Peter Bernstein and DeepRave. 45 mins.
VHS: S31639. $14.95.

The Dead Man and The Color of Love

In *The Color of Love*, Ahwesh takes possession of a decaying strip of counterculture porn (two women carve up a man and have each other over the corpse) and turns it into a *Rose Hobart* for the '90s. *The Dead Man*, based on George Bataille, is elegantly shot in black and white and is stylistically reminiscent of early D.W. Griffith, complete with intertitles between the scenes. The film centers on the story of Marie, who wakes up to a dead lover and travels through various sexual rituals and gender stereotypes between two essentially male positions or fantasies.
VHS: S30852. $89.95.
Peggy Ahwesh, USA, 1990/1994, 48 mins.

The Deliberate Evolution of a War Zone/ A Calculated Forecast of Ultimate Doom

San Francisco's Survival Research Laboratories' largest performance in Europe was held in Graz, 1992, when they presented *The Deliberate Evolution of a War Zone*, subtitled *A Parable of Spontaneous Structural Degeneration*. Their unique art/theater and kinetic sculpture often tackle new ground. One of the Austrian participants even tried to blow himself up. *A Calculated Forecast of Ultimate Doom*, subtitled *Sickening Episodes of Widespread Devastation Accompanied by Sensations of Pleasurable Excitement*, was performed in San Francisco on May 28, 1994. The unique and intricate mechanical props created by the SRL for their unusual performances mesmerize and even terrorize audiences.
VHS: S29945. $25.00.
Leslie Asako Gladsjo, USA, 1992-94, 38 mins.

Delphi 1830 & Next Time Everything Will Be Better

In *Delphi 1830*, filmmaker Rick Minnich uses pixilation to document the experience of a filmmaker at the 1993 Berlin Film Festival. In the second work, *Next Time Everything Will Be Better*, he shows a bunch of carefree types banding together to take back post-Wall Berlin.
VHS: S27239. $49.95.
Rick Minnich, Germany

Dennis Day: Oh Nothing

Oh Nothing is a mediated romance, an urban love story created from 1-second "spots", of desire, design, consumerism and distraction. In the city of Toronto, Rebecca (graphics consultant) and Kevin (systems analyst) battle each other, the corporate sponsors, and their own minds in a continual game of distraction. For them, life is a living commercial in which everything is product and nothing is remembered.

VHS: S12753. $65.00.

Dennis Day, Canada, 12 mins.

Dialectics of Romance

This well received piece by video artist and writer Ann Sargent Wooster takes a structuralist though juicy look at formula romance writing, using miniature sets, faceless close-ups and lush dissolves.

VHS: S22645. $29.95.

Ann Sargent Wooster, USA, 1985, 30 mins.

Diane Teramana: The Knitting Factory Show

This is a collection of video works selected personally by this artist from Cincinnati, Ohio. 77 mins.

VHS: S22578. $50.00.

Diderot

Diderot is a serial anthology of artists' works in video. Published by United Media Arts Studies, each issue contains new work specially produced by invited artists to address specific themes or conditions.

Diderot No. 1—The Emperor's New Clothes. Programs commissioned between 1983 and 1986 and produced by artists normally working in other media, including Mark DeGuerre, Lily Eng, Fast Wurms, Brian Scott, Doug Sigurdson and Suzanne Gillies.

VHS: S11646. $69.95.

Diderot No. 2—Television and the Channels of Culture. A special issue addressing the depth and breadth of television, including work by the artists Michael Balser, Sean Cubbitt, Christine Martin, Andrew J. Paterson and Jeanne Randolph.

VHS: S11647. $69.95.

Diderot No. 3—TV Blong Vanuatu John Watt. This title could be translated as, "a day of television from Vanuatu." Watt went to this island to develop an idea. He hoped to simulate a day of community television programming for a television-less society. The resulting tape comes with a booklet which contains an introduction by Rodney Werden.

VHS: S22563. $58.00.

Die Fettecke

Die Fettecke from 235 Media Cologne includes pieces by the masters Joseph Beuys and Nam June Paik, as well as the works of Konig, Naegeli, Staeck, Cladders and others.

VHS: S22556. $70.00.

M. Bielicky/R. Peredo, USA, 40 mins.

Die Todliche Doris

This video documents the performances and concerts put on by this German video art group. Some of their video work is also included. These pieces cover the years 1981-87. 49 mins.

VHS: S22562. $45.00.

Digital Speech and Pressures of the Text

"Rose's terrific sense of humor and genius at timing make him a cross between an intellectual Eddie Murphy and an old-time vaudeville comedian with a Ph.D.," wrote *Afterimage*. *Digital Speech* uses a traveler's anecdote, a perverse variant of a classic Zen parable, as a vehicle for an exploration of language, thought and gesture. *Pressures of the Text* integrates direct address, invented languages, ideographic subtitles, sign language and simultaneous translation to investigate the feel and form of sense, the shifting boundaries between meaning and meaninglessness.

VHS: S09206. $59.95.

Peter Rose, USA, 1984, 30 mins.

Divine Horsemen: The Living Gods of Haiti

Posthumously edited by Teiji and Cherel Ito, a remarkable document of the Rada, Petro and Congo cults of Haiti whose devotees commune with cosmic powers through invocations, voodoo dances and ritual ceremonies. The sound track conveys the power of ritual drumming and singing.

VHS: S00349. $29.95.

Maya Deren, USA, 52 mins.

Doug Hall: Storm and Stress

Internationally known and acclaimed video artist Doug Hall creates a visual and aural record of turbulent weather systems and industrial and natural energy. The violence of severe storms is juxtaposed with images of hydroelectric plants, wind tunnels, satellite dishes and other technologies that harness or mimic nature. The general theme: merchandising power. 50 mins.

VHS: S12755. $65.00.

Eldon Garnet: Today, Tonight, Tomorrow

The television imagery of this tape is collected from ten broadcast stations during one typical day in the life of a businessman, as recorded during a typical broadcast day. Produced by the Impulse Society for Cultural Productions, Toronto, Canada. 1989. 120 mins.

VHS: S32768. $150.00.

Elisabeth Jappe: Documenta 8—Performance—Action—Ritual

The international art exhibition at Kassel provides the setting for this tape, which includes Allan Kaparow, Charlemagne Palestine, Minus Delta T., Ulrike Rosenbach, Jurgen Klauke and others. 180 mins.

VHS: S22570. $96.00.

Enchanted Landscapes, Volume 2

Visionary nature images set to music by C.H. Deuter, Ray Lynch and Iasos. 40 mins.

VHS: S10227. $29.95.

The End

American avant-garde filmmaker Christopher Maclaine, an eccentric figure of the San Francisco North Beach beat scene, made this film which intercuts color and black-and-white sequences, as well as sound-with-no picture, showing five different people seen on the last days of their lives. Made from a new, restored print with enhanced sound. "No one has ever managed to make a film with the same manic inventiveness as Christopher Maclaine. Neither a late start—he began making films at the age of 30—nor a lack of formal training in the medium proved to be impediments. Coming to the cinema from poetry, Maclaine proceeded to develop his own unique syntax of filmic expression" (J.J. Murphy).

VHS: S30226. $40.00.

Christopher Maclaine, USA, 1953, 35 mins.

Ephemeral Films 1931-1960

Join media archaeologist Richard Prelinger as he explores our recent past. What he has discovered will amaze as much as entertain you. Prelinger has perhaps happened upon one of America's greatest surviving time capsules—educational and industrial movies.

To New Horizons: Ephemeral Films 1931-1945. Lets you share the futuristic dreams of pre-World War II America.

Laser: LD70321. $39.95.

You Can't Get There from Here: Ephemeral Films 1946-1960. Reviews the golden age of American consumerism.

Laser: LD70323. $79.95.

Experience: Perception, Interpretation, Illusion

This tape features the work of diverse Southern California artists. Each artist creates a 30 to 60 second spot that reflects his or her work and personality. Featuring: Carole Caroompas, Karen Carson, Michael Davis, James Doolin, Ann Page, Scott Grieger, Raul Guerrero, William Leavitt, Jerry McMillan, Michael C. McMillen, Margit Omar, John Outterbridge and John Valadez. 14 mins.

VHS: S14585. $19.95.

Experimental Avant Garde Series Volume 19 (Very Serious Fun)

Five short films featuring Hitler, Godzilla, Bambi, JFK and the Grim Reaper: *Bambi Meets Godzilla*—Marv Neuland's wry look at what might happen if these two entertainment legends ever got together. *Lambeth Walk Nazi Style*—Len Lye takes newsreel footage of Hitler and his troops and using freeze frames, jump cuts, repeat action and other techniques, pieces it all together and sets it to a popular British jig. *Loves of Franistan*—a funny take-off of big budget film spectaculars. *The Dove*—a wicked takeoff of Ingmar Bergman films; in one scene Death plays badminton instead of chess. *The JFK Workout*—an offbeat training film made in the 60's to promote JFK's physical fitness; includes a discourse on the inferiority of females. This is not necessarily an avant garde work, but it is so weird and silly we just couldn't leave it out. 60 mins.

VHS: S13504. $39.95.

Experimental Avant Garde Series Volume 20 (The Secret Lives of Inanimate Objects)

Four short films: *Ghosts before Breakfast*—Hans Richter's lively absurdist piece featuring juxtapositions of everyday objects taking on new roles in most unusual settings. *Rhythmus 21*—Richter returns to explore the extremely complex form of the simple square. *H2O*—Ralph Steiner's visually delightful study on water. *The Vanished World of Gloves*—Unusual film by Czechoslovakian Jiri Barta that uses live action and animation to tell this story of some gloves that have come to life. 55 mins.

VHS: S13505. $39.95.

Experimental Avant Garde Series Volume 21 (An Attack on Social, Sexual, and Political Order)

Two short films: *Lot in Sodom*—Watson and Webber's famed filming of the Old Testament story complete with homosexual orgies, sensuous sexual dances and a pillar of salt. *L'Historie du Soldat Inconnu*—Henri Storck uses the signing of the Kellogg-Briand pact to launch his hyperbolic attack on everything including, but not limited to, the bourgeoisie, democracy, religion and capitalism. 45 mins.

VHS: S13506. $29.95.

Experimental Avant Garde Series Volume 22

Knights on Bikes, featuring jousting motorcycle drivers, and *Peepshow* are two of famed director Ken Russell's earliest works. *Happy Anniversary*, by Pierre Etaix and Jean-Claude Carriere, stages a number of gags around the celebration of marital bliss. Finally, director Bert Haanstra exposes the nasty truth about the *The Zoo* in this collection of absurd and serious films. 50 mins.

VHS: S22468. $29.95.

Experimental Avant Garde Series Volume 23

CBS' Harry Reasoner travels to San Francisco to report on *The Hippie Temptation*. It's hilarious and features footage of the Grateful Dead. *Dream Flower*, a short film from 1932, shows how poppies grow into the source of mind-altering substances. 60 mins.

VHS: S22469. $29.95.

Eye Candy

This cutting-edge, three-video package combines computer graphics and music for a new dimension in sight and sound. Journey with Dr. Devious on an incredible cyberspace music video trip in *Dance in Cyberspace*. Experience the music of Grieg, Dvorak, Rimsky-Korsakov, Tchaikovsky and more as Fractal images create extraordinary visual beauty in *Fractasia*. 3-D computer graphics and a modern music compilation provide a powerful combination on *Future Shock*. Features music by Brian Eno, Future Sound of London, Attic Attack, Banco De Gaia and more. 120 mins.

VHS: S30023. $44.98.

Figures

Made by rephotographing original footage, frame by frame, to create a painterly image, James Herbert's work features "nudes photographed with such a disquieting ambivalence—a kind of transcendental nostalgia—otherwise unknown in American cinema" (Laurence Kardish). Also included on this tape are *Automan, Soundings, Two Figures, Carnival* and *Limbo District*.

VHS: S14821. $39.95.

James Herbert, USA, 1990, 85 mins.

Film Portrait

This classic autobiographical film spans the first seven decades of cinema and the 20th century and includes fragments of the painted, surrealistic, and documentary films of Academy Award winner and Anthology Film Archives founder Jerome Hill, from the 1920s to shortly before his death. The film deals with the family of James J. Hill, the family that built the railroads of America, and the development of Jerome Hill himself as a young man and artist. "A beautiful, haunting, aesthetically complete documentary of one man's view of art in society, caught through a very telling mix of emotional filters. An exquisite film!" (Andrew Salkey, BBC London).

VHS: S30225. $40.00.

Jerome Hill, USA, 1972, 81 mins.

Films by Ed Emshwiller

A collection of films by abstract painter-turned science-fiction cover artist-turned filmmaker Ed Emshwiller. *Lifelines* (1960, 7 mins.), which the filmmaker calls "an interplay of line, form and symbol," features abstract, moving line drawings and a motionless nude model clashing in dynamic counterpoint, with both aesthetic and symbolic interest. Includes music by Teiji Ito. *Thanatopsis* (1962, 5 mins.) powerfully organizes images of a contemplative, immobile man against a woman in rapid movement, with sounds of power saws and heartbeats to express the feeling of internal anguish. In *Film with Three Dancers* (1970, 20 mins.), a trio of dancers passes through rituals of movement, first in leotards, then in blue jeans, then nude.

VHS: S30229. $40.00.

Ed Emshwiller, USA, 32 mins.

Films of Charles and Ray Eames

Charles and Ray Eames are among the most influential American designers of this century. Best known for their ground-breaking contributions to architecture, furniture design, industrial design and photography, their legacy also includes over 75 innovative short films. The finest of these programs is in a new series, introduced in a narration by Gregory Peck.

Films of Charles and Ray Eames, Volume 1. *Powers of Ten*, the film that revolutionized the way we view our world, takes us on a breathtaking voyage from the interior of an atom to the furthest reaches of the universe. Starting with the closeup of a man's hand, and increasing the distance from the starting point ten times every ten seconds, this startling adventure in magnitudes illustrates as few films ever have the concepts of space and time. 21 mins.
VHS: S13218. $39.95.
Laser: LD70774. $49.95.

Films of Charles and Ray Eames, Volume 2. The second volume in the series consists of seven short films of dazzling impact and variety. From *Toccata for Toy Trains*, a magical look at antique toy trains, to *The Black Ships*, a subtle view of Admiral Perry's opening of Asia as seen through the Japanese art of the time, this collection illustrates the Eames' remarkable warmth, diversity and intelligence. 62 mins.
VHS: S13219. $39.95.
Laser: LD70775. $49.95.

Films of Charles and Ray Eames, Volume 3. The lives of Benjamin Franklin and Thomas Jefferson spanned 120 years and shaped the course of American history. This film, produced and directed by the famous design team of Charles and Ray Eames, is a masterful tribute to the two founding fathers of American independence. Franklin and Jefferson's philosophies and contributions are viewed against the background of the literary, scientific and artistic developments of their time. Using a visual timeline constructed of portraits, documents and other historical artifacts, the interlocking chapters of each man's story are brought to life. Narrated by Orson Welles and Nina Foch, with original music by Elmer Bernstein. USA, 35 mins.
VHS: S15395. $39.95.

Films of Charles and Ray Eames, Volume 4. This design workshop by Charles Eames features *Design Q & A*, one of the most concise and witty statements about design on film. *Goods*, a discussion of the "new convertables" and one of Eames legendary 3-screen slide shows are also included, as well as *IBM Math Peep Shows, SX-70, Polychris Hapus, The Fiberglass Chairs* and *Copernicus*. 59 mins.
VHS: S21522. $39.95.
Charles Eames/Ray Eames

The Films of Meredith Monk

Two works by dance and performance artist Meredith Monk. *Book of Days* (1986) is a haunting meditation on time and nature, about a perfectly preserved medieval town in Southern France. *Ellis Island* (1981) examines the decaying walls and supernatural presence of the American landmark. 105 mins.
Laser: LD71956. $39.95.

The Films of Scott Bartlett

Visionary—one of America's most celebrated experimental filmmakers. Pioneer—Bartlett's landmark films *Offon* and *Moon 1969* are acknowledged as the earliest expressions of electronic cinema.

Volume 1: The Birth of the Counter Culture. Three landmark films: *Offon*, a classic of experimental film, "a perfect, magical fusion of non-verbal communication and advanced technological filmmaking" (Amos Vogel); *Moon 1969*, "a beautiful, eerie, haunting film, all the more wonderful for the fact that we do not once see the moon—only the manifestations of its powers here on earth" (*L.A. Times*); *1970*, a dramatic autobiographical film that is a multiplexed portrait of the San Francisco sub-culture of the 1960's, "a lasting testament to a time we will never forget" (L.A. Film Festival). 55 mins.
VHS: S05621. $59.95.

Volume 2: The Future of Human Mythology. The serpent embodies the primal chaotic life force in mythic symbology. *Serpent* uses natural and electronic imagery to convey this elusive force in what is "an outstanding piece of art. Striking, kinetic. A beautiful combination of pure visual poetry and ideas about man and the world" (American Film Festival). Also contains *Medina*, an extraordinary, lucid and lyrical documentary of Morocco, "the richest, boldest, most subtly disciplined evocation of a place that I have ever seen on film" (*New York Times*). Also included are *Sound of One*, the unique melding of T'ai Chi Ch'uan and filmmaking, and *Heavy Metal*, which employs elaborate optical techniques to create an instant audio-visual trip back to 1929. 52 mins.
VHS: S05644. $59.95.

Volume 3: The Process of Creation. In the summer of 1967, Scott Bartlett's film loops and Glen McKay's light show liquids were mixed through a video effects bank and the results were filmed by Mike MacNamee. The finished film was called *Offon*. In 1980, Bartlett recreated the event in a video production class at UCLA. The result is *Making Offon*, a video primer. Wipes, keying and feedback are first illustrated and named, then woven into a sound and picture puzzle of the 60's. In *Making Serpent*, Bartlett narrates and describes the creative process behind *Serpent*, his award-winning film. *Making Serpent* is a step-by-step teaching device that explores film techniques such as how to structure a non-verbal narrative, how to shoot film for special editing techniques, how to isolate universal images in nature, and how to make exciting visuals inexpensively. "Eisenstein's *Film Form* continued on film" (Bruce Baillie). 50 mins.
VHS: S05643. $59.95.
Scott Bartlett, USA, 1968-1980

Fireworks

A collection which includes *Fireworks* (a dissatisfied dreamer awakes, goes out in the night seeking a light...), *Rabbit's Moon* (a fable of the unattainable, combining elements of Commedia dell'Arte with Japanese myth), and *Eaux d'Artifice* (a costumed figure moves through Tivoli gardens...), by perhaps the most important American experimental filmmaker of the post-war years. *Eaux d'Artifice* is included in the National Film Registry.
VHS: S00800. $29.95.
Kenneth Anger, USA, 1947-55, 34 mins.

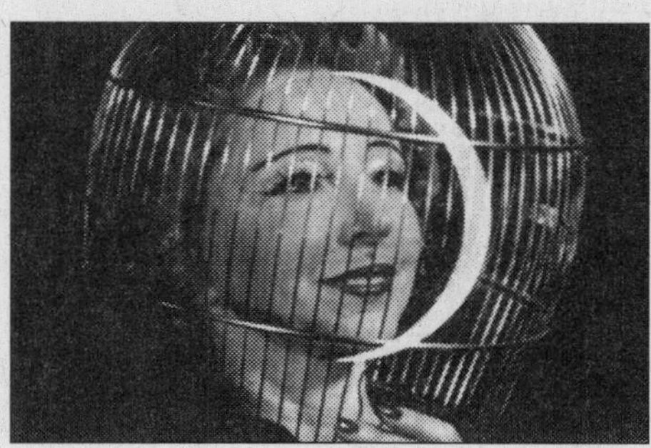

Flaming Creatures

Jack Smith's groundbreaking, lyrical queer film is being released in a special limited-edition series to raise funds that will help restore and preserve his other works. This classic may seem tame by current standards, but its great camp style stands the test of time.
VHS: S27242. $195.00.
Jack Smith, USA

Fluxfilm Anthology

A collection of over 30 short films, ranging from 10 seconds to 10 minutes, all celebrating the ephemeral humor of the Fluxus movement. George Maciunas edited together films by himself, Albert Fine, Dick Higgins, George Brecht, Robert Watts, Joe Jones, James Riddle, Wolf Vostell, George Landow, Peter Kennedy and Mike Parr, Peter Vanderbeek, John Cavanaugh, Jeff Perkins, Yoko Ono, Chieko Shioni, Paul Sharits, John Cale, Nam June Paik and Eric Anderson.
VHS: S30217. $100.00.
1966/1970, 150 mins.

Frank and Koen Theys, Lied Meines Landes II: Die Walkure

This video includes music from *Ring der Nibelungen* by Richard Wagner. Belgium, 1989, 90 mins.
VHS: S22579. $90.00.

Ganapati/A Spirit in the Bush

The artist Daniel Reeves creates a haunting and impressionistic song about the relationship of men and animals, using the poetry of Lorca, Rilke, Kipling and Reeves and location footage of India, Kenya and Thailand matched with archival footage. Reeves's "procession of charged mages involves and implicates the viewer through its silently scrolling text." 45 mins.
VHS: S16736. $59.95.

Gary Hill: Watch Words, Vols. 1-3

The subject of several recent museum exhibitions in Europe and America, Gary Hill's video art is brilliant, witty, and formally spectacular. On these three discs, the work of this acclaimed visionary undergoes a fascinating transformation from the conjunction of audiovisual elements in a new aesthetic vocabulary, to the integration of images and language in a unique and challenging investigation of linguistics and human consciousness. Each volume is 58 mins.
Gary Hill: Watch Words, Vol. 1.
Laser: LD76794. $49.95.
Gary Hill: Watch Words, Vol. 2.
Laser: LD76795. $49.95.
Gary Hill: Watch Words, Vol. 3.
Laser: LD76796. $49.95.

Germaine Dulac: The Smiling Madame Beudet and Seashell and the Clergyman

Two seminal films. *The Smiling Madame Beudet* employs some of the techniques of the "theater of silence" and impressionistic camera. The romantic Madame Beudet is married to a dull and insensitive tradesman who irritates her so much that she dreams of other lovers and of killing him. Silent with sparse inter-titles in French. *Seashell and the Clergyman*, scripted by Antonin Artaud, is composed of a series of episodes using Freudian imagery to express the mental anguish of a clergyman who is committed to his calling to celibacy, but is afflicted by sexual torments he cannot resolve. Musical track.
VHS: S05295. $39.95.
Germaine Dulac, France, 1928, 62 mins.

Gerz Jochen Ti Amo

VHS: S22565. $90.00.
Jochen Gerz, France, 1985, 19 mins.

Gorilla Tapes: Death Valley Days/ Lo Pay No Way!

28 mins.
VHS: S22566. $65.00.

Hans Richter: Early Avant-Garde Films

Richter on Film (1972, 14 mins.) is an interview with Hans Richter at age 83 in his Connecticut home, talking about his early experimental films and their relationship to his paintings, scrolls and collages. The pioneer work *Rhythm 21* (*Rhythmus 21*, 1921-4) orchestrates the squares and rectangles of the film screen, while *Rhythm 23* (*Rhythmus 23*, 1923, 3 mins., silent) features criss-cross patterns, negative reversals, intercut stringed forms and further variations of the rectangle and square. *Film Study (Filmstudie*, 1926, 4 mins.) integrates abstract images with their recognizable counterparts. *Ghosts Before Breakfast* (*Vormittagespuk*, 1927-8, 7 mins.) is Richter's witty, cinegenic mini-classic on the universal theme of the object's revolt and an excellent introduction to avant-garde film for all audiences. *Inflation* (*Inflation*, 1926-9) and *Everything Turns, Everything Revolves* (*Alles Dreht Sich, Alles Bewegt Sich*, 1926-9, 9 mins.) are two cinema essays reflecting life in pre-Nazi Germany, using inventive documentary and avant-garde techniques. *Race Symphony* (*Rennsymphonie*, 1928-9) is an excerpt from Richter's studyof a day at the races in pre-Nazi Germany. *Two-Penny Magic* (1928-9, 10 mins.) is an essay in rhyming images, made to advertise a picture magazine.
VHS: S30215. $100.00.
Hans Richter, Germany, 1921-29, 42 mins.

Hans Richter: Give Chance a Chance

Richter talks of how World War I led to the Surrealist movement, the artists of the period, his early training, Dada, Bauhaus, the antagonism of the Third Reich toward experimentation, crossover from painting to film and experiments with music. With clips from films *Ghosts Before Breakfast*, *Rhythm 21*, *8 X 8* and others. 28 mins, 1973.
VHS: S31591. $59.95.

Heaven and Earth Magic

"Produced in beatnik obscurity during the late 1950s, this hour-long marvel—a bit like dismembered Victorian valentines enacting a vaudeville version of the Egyptian Book of the Dead—is the real Fantasia—a higher form of hieroglyphics," wrote J. Hoberman in *The Village Voice* of Harry Smith's graphic description of initiation, redemption and spiritual transformation, couched in the language of Qabalah, alchemy and experimental psychology. Applying an extension of surrealist and cut up techniques to animate collages of familiar images, Smith transmutes these elements as an alchemist would, extracting the Philosopher's Stone through patience, cinematic pressure and an intense spirituality.
VHS: S09558. $29.95.
Harry Smith, USA, 1957-62, 66 mins.

Hilary Harris

Film critic Amos Vogel talks with Harris about why he makes films, the responsibility of the artist to elevate the audience, and his particular interest in layered sound effects. With clips from *Seaward the Great Ships*, *Generation*, *Highways* and *The Squeeze*. 1964, 28 mins.
VHS: S31593. $59.95.

Holy Mary, Remembrance & Vocation

In these three short, experimental films, filmmaker Jerry Tartaglia looks at the Pope in drag, describes memories of Bette Davis from his queer youth, and catches the lyrical existence of The Radical Faeries at their retreat at the Short Mountain Collective in Tennessee.
VHS: S27229. $59.95.
Jerry Tartaglia, USA

Home of the Brave

More than a concert film, *Home of the Brave* was originally shown in theatres and presents Laurie Anderson's multi-layered version of life in America with an engaging mix of high-tech wizardry, droll satire and 21st century synthesizer music. Includes *Sharkey's Day, Gravity's Angel, Language Is a Virus, Excellent Birds* and other numbers. 90 mins.
VHS: Out of print. For rental only.
Laser: CLV. **LD75394. $39.95.**

Hypnotic Places, Exotic Spaces

A 30-minute scenic music visual fantasy which takes the viewer scuba diving into liquid aqua inner space, strolling 35 acres of misty Canadian gardens, to the tropics, and to the English countryside with castle ruins and fallen abbeys. A mixture of art forms ranging from hand-painted cell animation to computer graphics, produced by photographer and visual designer Carol Davis. The music is an eclectic mix of works in this new-age video, designed for relaxation. 30 mins.
VHS: S08788. $19.95.

Illumination

Ken Jenkins' video of beautiful, flowing images, which unfold one out of another in a seemingly endless progression of radiance. Original music by Iasos and Constance Demby. From the creator of special effects for Shirley MacLaine's *Inner Workout*. 30 mins.
VHS: S10239. $29.95.
Laser: LD70239. $29.95.

In the Street

This short, acclaimed documentary was filmed on the streets of East Harlem in New York during the 1940s by the renowned still photographer Helen Levitt with her friends, Janice Loeb and author James Agee. Stan Brakhage ranks it among the greatest films ever made, with Griffith's *Intolerance* and Eisenstein's *Potemkin*. "...a definite must in both photography and film classes, because it is one of the very few films ever made that possibly bridges both arts" (Gisela Hoelcl, *UFSC Newsletter*).
VHS: S30234. $50.00.
Helen Levitt/Janice Loeb/James Agee, USA, 1941/1952, 15 mins.

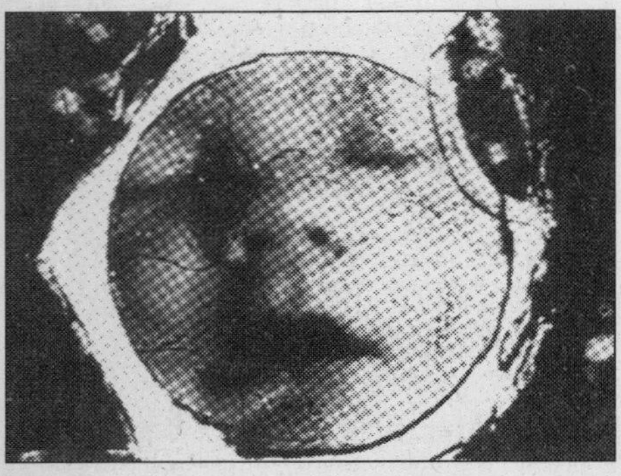

Inauguration of the Pleasure Dome

"A convocation of magicians assume the identity of gods and goddesses in a Dionysian revel....Dedicated to the few and to Aleister Crowley, and the crowned and conquering child" (Anger). One of the key works of American experimental cinema.
VHS: S00801. $29.95.
Kenneth Anger, USA, 1954, 38 mins.

An Individual Desires Solution & War Songs

The first of these two experimental films by Lawrence F. Brose confronts AIDS as faced by the artist's HIV-positive lover. In the second work, a poem performance by Paul Schmidt forms the basis for an ode to peace. Together these films manage to create a highly personal view of these important issues.
VHS: S27220. $59.95.
Lawrence F. Brose, USA

Introduction to the End of an Argument

Combining Hollywood, European and Israeli film with documentary footage and news coverage, this work critiques representations of Arab culture, the Middle East and the Palestinian people. Mimicry serves as a sly entry point for this audio-visual deconstruction of stereotypes.
VHS: S21037. $59.95.
Jayce Salloum/Elia Suleiman, USA, 1990, 45 mins.

It's Clean—It Just Looks Dirty

A collection of short videos assembled by John Giorno: Cabaret Voltaire in *Truth in the Lord*, Husker Du in *The Girl Who Lives on Heaven Hill, Powerline*, Diamanda Galas in two excerpts from *Eyes without Blood*, Einsturzende Neubauten in *Sand*, Robert Frank/Rudy Wurlitzer/Gary Hill in *Energy and How to Get It* featuring William Burroughs and Doctor John, The John Giorno Band in *Scum and Slime*, David Johansen in *Heard the News*, Robert Wilson and the Civil Wars, excerpts from Howard Brookner's film of Wilson's work with music by Shubert, David Byrne and Philip Glass, Swans' *A Screw*, Psychic TV in *Unclean*, and John Waters' *No Smoking in This Theater*. 60 mins.
VHS: S03945. $29.95.

J.S. Bach

Juan Downey's beautiful documentary on J.S. Bach places the famous composer's career and his powerful music in counterpoint with the gritty reality of his life. Downey's tape reflects on the shifting, symbiotic relations of art and the nature and biography of the individual. An insightful reconstruction of another artist's creative path, as well as of his own.
VHS: S08996. $39.95.
Juan Downey, USA, 1986, 28 mins.

Jim Davis: Volume #1

This collection of films by painter and filmmaker Jim Davis includes *Frank Lloyd Wright: Taliesin-West* (1950, 10 mins.), an authorized documentary look at Frank Lloyd Wright's Arizona headquarters and teaching studio; *Frank Lloyd Wright: Taliesin-East* (1950, 10 mins.), a documentary about Wright's Wisconsin home; and *Pertaining to Chicago* (1957, 17 mins.), a city symphony with special attention to the architecture of Wright and Sullivan, and to the processes of urban decay and renewal.
VHS: S30227. $40.00.
Jim Davis, USA, 37 mins.

Jim Davis: Volume #2

This second volume of Davis' films includes *Impulses* (1959, 10 mins.), his most accomplished film and personal favorite; *Pertaining to John Marin* (1950, 10 mins.), a portrait of the modernist painter John Marin, seen in his studio and at his homes in Maine and New Jersey; *Like a Breeze* (1954, 9 mins.), which features close-ups of fabric and water evolving into abstract forms in motion; and *Energies* (1957, 10 mins.), abstract light play, presented at the 1958 Brussels World's Fair Film Festival.
VHS: S30228. $40.00.
Jim Davis, USA, 40 mins.

The Jim Rose Circus Sideshow

A look at the freakish sideshow of impresario Jim Rose, who subjects himself and the members of his troupe to astounding feats of bednailing, regurgitation, body piercing, electrocution and worm eating. The program features Bebe the Circus Queen, the Amazing Mr. Lifto, The Torture King, The Enigma and Matt "The Tube" Crowley. "Lollapolooza's human demolition derby" (*USA Today*).
VHS: S19507. $16.98.

Joan Jonas: Vertical Roll

This classic video by an early pioneer of video art uses one of the primary features of video. The vertical roll that results when two out of sync frequencies meet is interpreted to create perceptual illusions from the rolling image.
VHS: S22587. $65.00.

John Whitney, Sr.

The pioneer computer graphics/film artist explains his early experiments, his camera designs and how he strives to create emotional response to shapes in motion like response to music. With clips from *Matrix 3*, *Catalog*, *Permutations* and *Lapis*. 1975, 28 mins.
VHS: S31594. $59.95.

Juan Downey

Two works by the Chile-born video artist Juan Downey, whose works have been exhibited and collected by countless museums around the world. The first, *Information Withheld*, dramatizes the nature of signs and symbols. From Egypt to Manhattan to Chile, the signs are presented in ascending order of complexity; hieroglyphs to a Michelangelo painting. Also included is *Shifters*, a videotape that aims to "dismantle the narrative mode". Downey distinguishes six recurring themes of imperialism/oppression and uses a subtext concerning class struggle and architecture.
VHS: S12754. $65.00.
Juan Downey, USA, 56 mins.

Just Hold Still

A collection of short films by Jem Cohen, including *Never Change*, a film set to a poem by Blake Nelson, set against the backdrop of rural roads soaked in fog. *Love Teller* is about a carnival side show machine that predicts how passionate a person is. The films are not narrative, but the combination of music, text and imagery create the mood.
VHS: S14820. $34.95.

Klaus Von Bruch: Black Box I

This two-tape package includes Bruch's works *Der Western Lebt* (1984, 4 mins.), *Allierten Band* (1982, 10:30 mins.) and *Verdunstucke* (1990, 60 mins.). Limited edition of 100.
VHS: S22582. $225.00.
Klaus von Bruch, Germany, 1982-90, 14 mins.

La Chute de la Maison Usher

Though directed by Jean Epstein, this French silent version of the Poe classic is also notable for having given apprenticeship to Luis Bunuel. Henri Langlois of the Cinematheque Francaise wrote, "An absolute mastery of editing and rhythm in which slow motion, super-impressions, moving camera shots, and the mobile camera combine to play a totally ungratuitous role. The lighting of the sets transforms them and imparts a sense of mystery. The actors were merely objects."
VHS: S06223. $59.95.
Jean Epstein, France, 1928

Len Lye

Active 1940-1960, New Zealand filmmaker Len Lye developed several of the montage and fast-cutting techniques later used sucessfully in advertising. His interest in light and rhythm also led to experiments in moving sculptures he called Tangibles. Includes interview, demonstrations of a few Tangibles, and clips from films. 1957, 28 mins.
VHS: S31601. $59.95.

Lucifer Rising

Invocation of My Demon Brother (a conjuration of pagan forces), and Anger's most recent, *Lucifer Rising*, "a film about the love generation, the birthday party of the Aquarian Age, showing actual ceremonies to make Lucifer rise."
VHS: S00802. $29.95.
Kenneth Anger, USA, 1969, 39 mins.

MA: Space/Time—In the Garden of Ryoan-ji and AIUEONN Six Features

Pioneer of Japanese experimental film and video Takahito Iimura explores the concept of MA: space and time as a perceptual unity, through a contemplative, tracking camera in the classic Japanese Garden of Ryoan-ji. *AIUEONN Six Features* is a tape version of an installation which was first created at Kirin Plaza in Osaka, featuring six funny faces and Sony system G Real Time Texture Mapping to animate the difference between "image," "letter" and "voice" in Japanese vowels.
VHS: S28578. $89.95.

Macbeth: The Witches Scenes

Adapting scenes from Shakespeare's *Macbeth*, video artist Miroslaw Rogala projects the action from a mythic, barbaric past to a violent, post-apocalyptic future where order and technology have broken down. Rather than "eyes of newt," the magic possessed by the witches is the computer.
VHS: S16042. $19.95.
Miroslaw Rogala, USA, 1988, 18 mins.

Maek/Muscha/Shafer/Trimpop

Decoder, 87 mins.
VHS: S22571. $51.00.

Magic Eye—The Video, Volume 1

3-D moving images are now possible without special glasses. This video is inspired by the exciting *Magic Eye* book series. Includes original music and sound effects in Dolby Surround. 32 mins.
VHS: S22745. $14.95.

Magic Eye II—The Video, Volume 2

At the next plateau of 3-D viewing pleasure lie these abstract images that seem to move in space and time. Original music and sound effects in Dolby Surround. 30 mins.
VHS: S22746. $14.95.

Man Ray Video

Films by the important experimental filmmaker, photographer and surrealist, Man Ray. *Emak Bakia* was described by Man Ray as a "cine poem," (1927, 18 mins.); *L'Etoile de Mer* (1928, 15 mins.) is based on a poem by Robert Desnos and juxtaposes still lives, masked faces, a woman, a starfish and Paris; *Le Retour a la Raison* (1923) weaves abstract and concrete images; *Les Mysteres du Chateau du De* (1929), filmed at the chateau of the Comte de Noailles, explores the structure and dramatic light effects of the forms of the villa.
VHS: S09050. $24.95.
Man Ray, France, 1927-29

The Man Who Could Not See Far Enough

One of the most exciting, powerful works of independent American experimental cinema, *The Man Who Could Not See Far Enough* uses literary, structural, autobiographical and performance metaphors to construct a series of tableaux that evoke the act of vision, the limits of perception, and the rapture of space. Spectacular, moving multiple images, a physical almost choreographic sense of camera movement, and massive, resonant sound have inspired critics to call it "stunning" and "hallucinatory."
VHS: S09207. $59.95.
Peter Rose, USA, 1981, 33 mins.

Maneaters: A Trilogy

Three mondo trasho vignettes, *Girls Can't Help It!* 1986), *World Peace* (1987), and *Squalid Salad* (1988), centered around female empowerment and sexual liberation. Featuring such underground sensations as Counsuelita, Jeep Reis, Randy Rom, Claude Balls, Joey Leatherton and Lucy Poussi.
VHS: S17194. $29.95.

Marcel Odenbach: In the Peripheral Vision of the Witness

Shot on location at Versailles, this videotape examines the conflict between the burden of a heritage of traditions and the desperate attempt to escape from it. West German video artist Marcel Odenbach combines classical and nationalistic images with commercial and media images to illustrate this conflict. A work of tension, comparing individual freedom with the omnipresent mass media.
VHS: S12756. $65.00.
Marcel Odenbach, Germany, 13 mins.

The March on Paris 1914 of General Von Kluck & His Memory of Jessie Holladay

Born in part out of Gutman's memory of World War I and inspired by General Von Kluck, the swing commander of the German attack, who wrote a book on his experience, *The March on Paris*, this is Gutman's witty fantasy story of Von Kluck's two loves: the love of his vast accomplishment, and the love of a woman. "I made up a story in which Von Kluck, before becoming a general, had fallen in love one summer with a young American girl, Jessie Holladay, and he remembered her during the campaign because their affair and the war started from the same place on the Belgian border" (Walter Gutman).
VHS: S30233. $40.00.
Walter Gutman, USA, 1976, 70 mins.

Martina's Playhouse and The Scary Movie

These two complex films, informed by a wide range of issues-including feminism, Lacanian theory, home movie aesthetics and filmic self-reflexivity—play with the Freudian (filtered through Lacan) concept of the female's "lack" of a penis, turning this core issue of psychoanalytic thinking on its head.
VHS: S30856. $89.95.
Peggy Ahwesh, USA, 1989/1993, 29 mins.

Mary Ellen Bute

Clips from *Passages from James Joyce's Finnegan's Wake* with commentary by Bute and Columbia University English professor William York Tindall. 28 mins, 1965.
VHS: S31592. $59.95.

Matta Wagnest and Nicolas Eder: Analog 10001

This combination book and three-tape package is available only within this signed and limited edition of 50 copies.
VHS: S22584. $300.00.

Maurizio Nannucci: Not All at Once

This work comes from the Kasseler Kunstverein in Fridericianum, Kassel, 1993. 15 mins.
VHS: S22572. $35.00.

Maya Deren Experimental Films

A newly re-mastered, top quality reproduction of the leading female experimental filmmaker in cinematic history. Maya Deren's six chamber films included here are: *Meshes of the Afternoon, At Land, A Study in Choreography for Camera, Ritual in Transfigured Time, Meditation on Violence* and *The Very Eye of Night*. Silent.
VHS: S00836. $29.95.
Maya Deren, USA, 1943-49, 76 mins.

Mediamystics

This video collection includes *Blue Moon, Soma Sema, Open Sesame, Fungus Eroticus* and *Dervish Machine*. Honed by frequent live gigs, these works fuse tribal and sacred elements, to explore the mystical knowledge of the body in cybertech.
VHS: S22637. $39.95.
Bradley Eros/Jean Liotta, USA, 1988-92, 60 mins.

Memento Mori

This hand-processed, 16mm Cinemascope meditation on death by Jim Hubbard contrasts the four seasons with the scattering of a person's ashes in the Seine.
VHS: S28579. $59.95.

Menilmontant

An important film made by Dimitri Kirsanov in France, a silent film done without titles which "is not a melodrama but an antecedent to neo-realism, portraying life itself with a sensitive use of natural sets and a feeling for poetry and truth" (Georges Sadoul). In the film, a young girl is seduced by a young man who deserts her when she is pregnant. She contemplates suicide, meets her sister who's since become a prostitute, and is reconciled with her again.
VHS: S07466. $39.95.
Dimitri Kirsanov, France, 1926, 27 mins

Mitch Corber Works

Work by the multi-media performance artist and cable TV pioneer. Includes *Juan in New York*, bike-shot footage mixed with TV soap cuts overlaid with a dense soundtrack of rhetoric and effects; *KGB*, mixed down from a live show on the death of Brezhnev; *Apartheid Aside*, a colorized music video with songs by San Francisco's Toiling Midgets and Morton Subotnick; and *Quiver City*, computer animation and color processing of old people in Brighton Beach.
VHS: S10167. $39.95.
Mitch Corber, USA, 1982-84, 36 mins.

Moving a River

Peter Fend's experimental documentary examines satellite data detailing the ways Iraq's military engineering altered the course of rivers in the Middle East that impacted its physical relationship to Iran.
VHS: S17198. $29.95.
Peter Fend, USA

Music Word Fire and I Would Do It Again: The Lessons

Perfect Lives is an opera commissioned and produced for television by The Kitchen. The Lessons, variations on the theme song from Episode Three of the television opera, introduced the four principal characters in cameo performances. The video and music techniques unique to the seven-episode series are presented in four seven-minute portraits of these four characters.
VHS: S11645. $49.95.
Robert Ashley, USA, 1984, 27 mins.

N. Humbert/W. Penzel: Step Across the Border

90 minutes, 1990.
VHS: S22567. $45.00.

Nam Jun Paik

Profile of avant-garde composer/performance artist Nam Jun Paik. Includes excerpts from video experiments. 1975, 28 mins.
VHS: S31599. $59.95.

Natural Light: Windance

David Fortney's camera dances of light, motion and substance, that are as sensual and alive as the natural world he photographs, scored to the music of W. Aura, R. Burmer, S. Halpern and Synchestra.
Laser: LD70240. $24.95.
David Fortney, USA, 30 mins.

Nature Is Leaving Us

A video opera for prerecorded multi-channel video and sound, live performance and live music, a complex work by video artist Miroslaw Rogala, which addresses the profound subject of man's rupture from nature. This videotape contains both the original program and documentation of the performances and contrasts the immutable rhythms of natural processes with the arhythmia of human urban behavior as reflected in the media.
VHS: S08469. $39.95.
Miroslaw Rogala, USA, 1987, 40 mins.

New Directors: New Short Films

This collection of new works (1993) by young artists includes *Lady Lazarus* by Sandra Lahire, *Weak and Wide Astray* by Tom Paine, *Relax* by Chris Newby and *Floating* by Richard Helsop. In English. Total running time 108 mins.
VHS: S22573. $45.00.

New York Videos

Jens Jurgenson and Jim Spring create art videos for music television. This selection of their work features some of the most innovative groups from the East Village, such as Bongwater, Pussy Galore, Foetus, John Spencer Blues Exploration, Railroad Jerk and Marin Bisi.
VHS: S22638. $29.95.
Jens Jurgenson/Jim Spring, USA, 1988-93

Normal Love

Jack Smith's legendary second feature-length film derives from his adoration of B-movie star Maria Montez, best-known for her performance in *Cobra Woman*. It features a variety of '30s horror film monsters, a mermaid, a lecher and other colorful characters performed by a cast which includes Mario Montez, John Vaccaro, Diane DePrima, Francis Francine, Tiny Tim and others. This restored version includes the lost "cobra scene" with Beverly Grant and a musical track from Smith's recovered music collection. Remastered from Smith's camera original; one of the icons of American independent cinema.
VHS: S30532. $325.00.
Jack Smith, USA, 1963, 90 mins.

O No Coronado

In this black comedy, Craig Baldwin combines found imagery, video-to-filmFX, animated graphics, multiple voices and a time-warped musical mix to restage the 1540 European invasion of the lands known as the American Southwest.
VHS: S28580. $59.95.

Oskar Fischinger

Profile of the early animation artist with clips from *Liebespiel, Komposition in Blau, Spiritual Constructions*, a marching cigarette commercial and others. With his widow Elfriede, writer William Moritz and animator John Canemaker. 1977, 28 mins.
VHS: S31597. $59.95.

Out in the Garden & You

Two films from Vincent Grenier are included in this video. The first, *Out in the Garden*, is about the dynamic of being HIV-positive. The second film, *You*, offers a more formal examination of perspective, self reflection and narrative.
VHS: S27233. $59.95.
Vincent Grenier, USA

Pascal Aubier Films

Six short films by Pascal Aubier: *Flashback* (1985, 4 mins.), in which a fatally wounded soldier remembers the highlights of his young life in the brief moment before his death; *Les Petits Cons* (1986), in which a young factory worker escapes the boredom of his job by locking himself in the bathroom, where he encounters a strange vision; *Le Cendre* (1985, 4 mins.), an amusing tale of the consequences of intolerance, with an anti-smoking slant; *L'Apparition* (1986, 8 mins.), a darkly humorous exploration of faith and ignorance; *Death of a Rat* (1975, 6 mins.), a serio-comic meditation on the pain and inhumanity of modern technological life; and *Santeuse de L'Ange* (without subtitles), a playful study of eating strawberries and high diving.
VHS: S02905. $49.95.
Pascal Aubier, France, 38 mins.

Paulette Phillips and Geoffrey Shea: Work

Two Canadian filmmakers/video artists have combined their talents to create a multi-layered piece that examines the concept of work by using various techniques and intertwining several plots. Documentary-style interviews are interspersed with the narrative structure. Employment is presented as a series of pre-packaged lifestyles that suppress the identity of the individual. 35 mins.
VHS: S12757. $65.00.

A Performance by Jack Smith

This is the only known recorded performance piece by the late artist/actor Jack Smith, made from an optically printed 8mm film original. Included are two works shot in Toronto in 1984: *Dance of the Sacred Application* and *Brassieres of Uranus*.
VHS: S27224. $59.95.
Midi Onodera, Canada, 1984

Peter Callas: Night's High Noon: An Anti-Terrain

This Australian artist's work is from 1988 and is 7.5 minutes long.
VHS: S22561. $90.00.
Peter Callas, Australia, 1988, 7 mins.

Peter Russell: The Global Brain

1991, 35 mins.
VHS: S22576. $70.00.

Peter Thompson Films

Three extremely moving documentaries: *Two Portraits*, a diptych film about the filmmaker's father and mother; *Universal Hotel* records the filmmaker's search for historical graphic evidence on medical experiments in deep cold by Nazi doctors; and *Universal Citizen* records an encounter with a former inmate at Dachau, now a smuggler in the Guatemalan jungle.
VHS: S05650. $59.95.
Peter Thompson, USA, 63 mins.

Pictures Don't Tell You Anything: Selected Films of Ann Marie Fleming

A compilation of 12 award-winning short films spanning 1987-1995 by Canadian filmmaker Ann Marie Fleming, including documentaries, narratives, experimental, music videos and animation: *Waving, You Take Care Now, Drumstix, New Shoes: An Interview in Exactly 5 Minutes, Pioneers of X-Ray Technology: A Film About Grandpa, Buckingham Palace, So Far So…, My Boyfriend Gave Me Peaches, I Love My Work, Jale's Not Happy, Pleasure Film (Ambed's Story)* and *It's Me Again*. "Her powerful, immediate short films display an extremely rare and sometimes acutely troubling honesty and focus. She is without doubt one of the most talented and under-appreciated Canadian filmmakers working today" (Mary Brennan, 5th International Festival of Films by Women Directors). "Fresh, funny, and completely unique" (Atom Egoyan).
VHS: S30439. $39.95.
Anne Marie Fleming, Canada, 106 mins.

Pier Marton (are we and/or do we) Like Men

An intense expose about male vulnerability from Pier Marton. Filled with subverted and challenging images, as well as a deepness of expression.
VHS: S13302. $69.95.
Pier Marton, USA, 1986, 18 mins.

Pier Marton: Collected Works: 1979-84

Features *Heaven is what I've done (for my fellow beings)* (1984), a PSA to measure our (distr)actions against things that must be done; *Tapes* (1979), the unraveling of personal/collective fears; *Telepathos* (1982), a demystification of the "high-tech" satellite broadcast; *Unity Through Strength* (1980-82), revealing fabricated television reality. The subversive art of Pier Marton.
VHS: S13303. $69.95.
Pier Marton, USA, 1979-84, 27 mins.

Pier Marton: Say I'm a Jew

A collage of interviews with Jews who grew up in post war Europe as they describe their experiences. The film progresses from a "memory" of the Holocaust and early self-denial experiences, to a manifesto-like affirmation of Jewish identity. Directed by Pier Marton. 28 mins.

VHS: S13304. $69.95.

Pier Marton, USA

Plates

Taylor Mead and Bill Rice, two underground, queer art stars, are featured in this funny and remarkable film from playwright and director Gary Goldberg. Shown at the 1991 Berlin International Film festival, *Plates* harkens to the world of silent film even though it employs non-verbal sound to tell its story.

VHS: S27240. $49.95.

Gary Goldberg, USA, 1991, 11 mins.

Playboy & Rhonda Goes to Hollywood

Two shorts by the British-born filmmaker Tessa Hughes-Freeland examine sexuality, representation and identity. 35 mins.

VHS: S17197. $39.95.

The Queen of Sheba Meets the Atom Man

Filmmaker Ron Rice—not yet 30—died before he finished shooting this film, which Alberto Moravia called a "violent, childish and sincere" protest against the industrial world. Between 1979 and 1982 Taylor Mead, who also acts in the film, prepared this final version of what was to be a three-hour epic, which not only defied the professional conventions of slick narrative, but seemed to capture the spirit of a rebellious generation.

VHS: S30230. $40.00.

Ron Rice, USA, 1963/1982, 109 mins.

Rain and Uberfall

Two historically significant films: Joris Ivens' *Rain* is an impressionistic study of a rain shower; Erno Metzner's *Uberfall* brilliantly uses in-camera techniques to depict the hallucinations of a man who is the victim of a street robbery.

VHS: S04361. $44.95.

Raindance: The Experience of Light and Celebration

A sumptuous field of visuals and music reveals the multi-facets of light, and a special luminous quality in all living things, in a celebration of inner wholeness. Composed and narrated by Dorothy Fadiman, with music by Klaus Schulze, Will Ackerman, Alex de Grassi; produced by Michael Wiese. 30 mins.

VHS: S10226. $29.95.

Rare Dutch and Belgian Experimental Program

Includes five short films: *Mystic Lamb* (11 mins.), *Rain* (10 mins.), *New Earth* (23 mins.), *Bridge* (15 mins.) and *Umbrella* (30 mins.)

VHS: S14922. $29.95.

Red Grooms and "Fat Feet"

The multi-media pop artist and filmmaker talks about his films and artwork at the start of his brilliant career. Much of his new art is shown as well as two of his films, *Washington's Wig Whammed!* and *Fat Feet*, a humorous pop art view of life in the big city combining animation with live film. 1967, 28 mins.

VHS: S31608. $59.95.

Richard Lester

The film director discusses his career, from early work in commercials to the experimental *Running, Jumping, Standing Still Film* with Peter Sellers and *The Goon Show* cast, through features, including the Beatles' film *A Hard Day's Night, The Knack and How to Get It, How I Won the War, The Bed Sitting Room, The Three Musketeers* and *The Four Musketeers*. Clips from all these works. Lester talks of "the benevolent dictatorship of being a director," his commitment to the subject of his films, his anti-war message and his desire to widen the understanding of the audience. 1973, 60 mins.

VHS: S31603. $59.95.

Robert Cahen: L'Invitation au Voyage/Juste le Temps

These two short videos bracket a span of 10 years during which this artist has continued to create work. *L'Invitation au Voyage* is from 1973, 9 mins. And *Juste le Temp*, 1983, is 13 minutes long.

VHS: S22560. $90.00.

Robert Cahen, USA, 1973-83, 22 mins.

Rome '78

Felliniesque spectacle and Warhol-like degeneration in an underground take-off on *Caligula*, shot in color Super-8 and borrowing fromthe explosive tenets of experimental cinema. With David McDermott, Eric Mitchell and Anya Phillips.

VHS: S17193. $59.95.

James Nares, USA, 1978, 60 mins.

Rudy Burckhardt

Artist/filmmaker Burckhardt, innovator and experimenter in time-lapse photography, describes his work and techniques over numerous clips. 1974, 28 mins.

VHS: S31598. $59.95.

Sabda and Sombra a Sombra

The title *Sabda* refers to the *word*, the original sound of life. Using digital imaging techniques to produce ghostlike, transient figures passing through landscapes, "ancient words and drawn-out beautiful images construct a profound contemplation of human existence." "Reeves' lyrical video poem, a collaboration with some of the great Indian medieval poets. In it Reeves succeeds as few Westerners have in revealing the complex reality that is India" (Deirdre Boyle). *Sombra a Sombra* is an elegy of remembrance and meditation on the architecture of the abandoned as evoked in the writing of the Peruvian poet Cesar Vallejo. Recorded over a period of years in the Alpujanas and Pyrenian mountains of Spain, the tape explores the areas of the heart shaped by the departure of the people and things of this world.

VHS: S06303. $59.95.

Daniel Reeves, USA, 32 mins.

Samadhi and Other Films

Four films by Jordan Belson—"our greatest abstract film poet, he has found how to combine the vision of the outer and the inner eye" (Gene Youngblood). The four films in this volume include *Re-Entry*, an animated metaphor of reincarnation and rebirth; *World*, a dazzling, abstract version of the creation of the world; *Samadhi*, taken from the Sanskrit term meaning "that state of consciousness in which the individual merges with the universal soul"; and *Chakra*, a compelling film re-creating the experience of raising the kundalini through the seven psychic centers in the human being.

VHS: S09557. $19.95.

Jordan Belson, USA, 1964-72, 27 mins.

Sara Hornbacher Early Works

Richly processed and synthesized rapid-cut video by the pioneer video artist. Includes *An American Sequence, Equinox Dance/Polyglot Robot, Raster Relief/ Video Canvas, Writing Degree Z, Diignus Vindice Nodus.*

VHS: S10166. $29.95.

Sara Hornbacher, USA, 30 mins.

See for Yourself

Jerry Tartaglia employs a formalist syntax to create an intimate and moving document of a friend dying from AIDS in this silent film.

VHS: S28582. $59.95.

Simultaneous

A collection of 10 works by Scott Rankin, video artist on the cutting edge of exploring language, perception, association and metaphor: *Simultaneous* is a self-referential work about consciousness and learning using as a metaphor the controversial theory of hemisphere specialization in the brain. Other works included are: *This and That, Fugue, LA 84* (commissioned for the L.A. Contemporary Exhibitions as a portrait of Los Angeles as a city and as a media center), *Synchronicity, French performance, Swedish Two, Swedish One, Magic*, and *Carousel*. Winner of many awards, the work of Scott Rankin offers daring explorations of the video medium.

VHS: S08612. $59.95.

Scott Rankin, USA, 1980-88, 77 mins.

Small Gauge Shotgun

Eight Super 8 films by Danny Plotnick and Jim Sikora, including *Flip About Flip* and *Bring Me the Head of Geraldo Rivera*, are included in this joint compilation which serves to make a strong case for Super 8 filmmaking.

VHS: S28583. $59.95.

Smothering Dreams and Thousands Watch

It does in 23 minutes what *Apocalypse Now* and *Deer Hunter* tried to do in 3 hours…One of the most compelling, eloquently visual denunciations of war in any medium," wrote one critic of *Smothering Dreams*. Based on Reeves' own experiences, the tape is an autobiographical reflection on the Vietnam War, "a cathartic recollection, burning anti-war statement and searing analysis of the mass media's role in inculcating violence and aggression from childhood onward" (Deirdre Boyle). With dramatic re-enactments of the ambush of Reeves' platoon in 1969 and of childhood memories, *Smothering Dreams* is a collage of childhood dreams of battle and adult nightmares of the atrocities of war. *Thousands Watch* is an image-processed work that demystifies the suicidal nature of the use of nuclear weapons. Using 1936 newsreel footage cutting between images of war and domestic tranquility, *Thousands Watch* is a uniquely powerful poetic statement.

VHS: S01221. $59.95.

Daniel Reeves, USA, 40 mins.

Stan Brakhage Selected Films: Vol. 1

Includes six Brakhage short films from 1954-57: *Desistfilm* (1954, 7 mins.), *Reflections on Black* (1955, 12 mins.), *The Wonder Ring* (1955, 4 mins.), *Flesh of Morning* (1956, 25 mins.), *Loving* (1956, 6 mins.) and *Daybreak & Whiteye* (1957, 8 mins.).

VHS: S30216. $100.00.

Stan Brakhage, USA, 1954-1957, 62 mins.

Stan Brakhage Selected Films: Vol. 2

Includes six Brakhage short films from 1959-62: *Cat's Cradle* (1959, 5 mins.), *Window Water Baby Moving* (1959, 12 mins.), *Sirius Remembered* (1959, 12 mins.), *The Dead* (1960, 11 mins.), *Thigh Line Lyre Triangular* (1961, 5 mins.), *Blue Moses* (1962, 11 mins.) and *Mothlight* (1963, 4 mins.).

VHS: S30218. $100.00.

Stan Brakhage, USA, 1959-1962, 60 mins.

Stan Brakhage—Hand-Painted Films

Considered a master in avant-garde circles, Stan Brakhage's theory of representing "closed-eye vision in film has led him to these hand-painted works, a visual tour-de-force." Includes *Night Music* (1986, 30 seconds); *Autumnal* (1993, 5 mins.); *Study in Color and Black and White* (1993, 2 mins., 30 seconds); *Three Homerics* (1993, 6 mins.); *Ephemeral Solidity* (1993, 5 mins.); *The Harrowing & Tryst Haunt* (1993, 5 mins.); *Stellar* (1993, 2 mins., 30 secs.); *Black Ice* (1994, 2 mins., 30 secs.); *Chartres Series* (1994, 9 mins.); and *Naughts* (1994, 5 mins., 30 secs.).

VHS: S35151. $29.95.

Stan Brakhage, USA, 1986/1993/1994, 44 mins.

Stan VanDerBeek: The Computer Generation

The then-pioneering computer expert at MIT talks about computers' interaction with creativity, the potential for artists to create using the new technology, and his hope that all children will learn computing, as he demonstrates new experimental techniques. With clips from *Symmetricks* and other films. 1972, 28 mins.

VHS: S31589. $59.95.

Stephen Forsyth: Passages

"Passages…urban romanticism reflects an openness to nature and the outside world, while surrendering to the siren song within. A tapestry of lyricism of every kind, from the most secretive to the most expressive…now projecting dreams, now capturing the forces of the elements, now voicing the cries of the heart and its echoes."

VHS: S22564. $65.00.

Strange Weather

As the most devastating hurricane in 100 years descends on Miami, what else would a crack addict do but try to score? Reality television is reinvented through the never-ending search for drugs and money. Fearing the police more than the elements, three women and a man cajole money and affection from anyone who will listen, as director Ahwesh yields the Pixelvision camera, the "philosophical" Fisher-Price toy that turns any image into that of a surgeon's internal scope, turning the world inside out for its lesions and scars in the closest of close-ups. With Margie Strosser.

VHS: S30853. $89.95.

Peggy Ahwesh, USA, 1993, 50 mins.

Susan Rynard

Three works by the Toronto-based video artist Susan Rynard, whose videos have been shown in festivals from Hong Kong to Rio. *Absence* is a fragmented narrative about desire and expectation, leaving the viewer to search for explanations and closure. *Untitled—A Tape about Memory* is a recreation of the sensations of memory through texture, color, mood and movement. And *Within Dialogue (Silence)* portrays a young professional city dweller whose idea of ecology is hewn in concrete, broadloom and nouvelle cuisine. Each shot reverberates in a barren web of table settings and freeways. 15 mins.

VHS: S12758. $65.00.

Takahiko Imura: A Journey to Ayersrock

Contains two works: *Moments at the Rock*, which won the Grand Prize at the T. Edison Black Maria International Film Festival and the Golden Gate prize at the San Francisco Film Festival; and excerpts from *Ayersrock*, with music by Richie Beirach, Terumasa Hino and Masahiko Togashi.

VHS: S32769. $78.00.

Takahiko Imura, Japan, 1985, 33 mins.

Takahiko Imura: Concept Tapes (1975-87)

This collection joins excerpts from nine tapes of this artist's works. "Iimura is a significant and singular filmmaker, but also one of the most important conceptual artists working in any medium" (Malcolm LeGrice).

VHS: S22568. $118.95.
Takahiko Imura, USA, 1975-87

Takahiko Imura: John Cage Performs James Joyce

A private performance by composer John Cage is captured on this tape. *Writing for the Fifth Time through Finnegan's Wake* is realized by Cage in three ways—by reading, singing and whispering. 15 mins.

VHS: S22569. $115.00.
Takahiko Imura, USA, 15 mins.

Tear Jerker

This compilation of works by Joel Baird and Rick Philips reveals the hypocritical attitudes common in the United States. It contains the short films *Tear Jerker, With the Good Witch* and *The Evil Cleric.*

VHS: S27236. $59.95.
Joel Baird/Rick Philips, USA

This Is Not Beirut/ There Was and There Was Not

This personal project finds that the conflicts and complexities that affect a Lebanese person in the West are intimately bound together with the experiences of diverse communities and the jarring perceptions that separate them.

VHS: S21036. $59.95.
Jayce Salloum, USA, 1994, 48 mins.

Tina L'hotsky: Barbie and Snakewoman

Two works by the talented New York writer and Hollywood emigre. *Barbie* is a surreal self-portrait of a young woman cooking and eating a doll. *Snakewoman* chronicles the epic exploits in 1930's Africa of adventurer Patti Astor. Both films were shot by Michael Oblowitz.

VHS: S17204. $39.95.
Tina L'hotsky, USA, 45 mins.

Todd Rutt/Arn McConnell: Shock! Shock! Shock!

A black and white work combining film and video to trace the life of Jim Norman, "a loser so lost only trouble could find him." His story unfolds with a pulp terseness, about a young man trying to escape his past and confront the alien beings intent on colonizing earth. 60 mins.

VHS: S17205. $39.95.

Tom Chomont: A Two-Volume Collection

The works of this experimental gay filmmaker are collected on these two videos. *Volume I* contains the short films *Jabbock, The Heavens, Razor Head* and *The Bath. Volume II* features *Spider Jan.16.91, Inner Sanctum, Garden* and *The Mirror*.

Volume I.
VHS: S27237. $69.95.
Volume II.
VHS: S27238. $69.95.
Tom Chomont, USA

Towers Open Fire

William S. Burroughs and Brion Gysin met Ian Sommerville and Antony Balch during their Beat Hotel days in Paris in 1958-59, an amazingly fertile period that saw the publication and attempted suppression of Burroughs' *Naked Lunch*. These films (Towers Open Fire, The Cut Ups, Bill & Tony and *William Buys a Parrot*) convey the consciousness of the period in the visual language of the artists who defined it.

VHS: S09556. $19.95.
Antony Balch, USA, 1962-72, 35 mins.

Trio

Created by the internationally successful Zone Productions, *Trio* consists of three short musical works. *Suspect No. 1* is a murder mystery where investigation and filmmaking become intermixed. *Zzang Toumb Toumb* is a dance piece with music and movement alluding to the Italian Futurists of the early twentieth century. And *Life and Death of an Architect* portrays the life of one person, with the five stages of their life shot in different styles, each reminiscent of a different popular director. 25 mins.

VHS: S12761. $65.00.

A Trip to the Land of Knowledge

Zoe Beloff juxtaposes footage from home movies with melodramatic staged scenes to tell the story of a young girl who escapes from her drab, black-and-white adolescent reality into a Kodachrome fantasy, and comes face-to-face with her worst anxieties, as well as her awakening sexuality.

VHS: S28576. $59.95.

Tripe

Adapted from the play *Ein Mann, Ein Worterbuch* by Franz X. Kroetz (*Hamlet Machine*), this stars Australian director Lindzee Smith as the restless, jobless lover of a lady butcher (Caz Porter), who, much to his discomfiture, keeps a journal.

VHS: S10182. $49.95.
Betsy Sussler, USA, 1980, 58 mins.

Tung, To Parsifal & Castro Street

Tung (1966, silent, 5 mins.), Bruce Baillie's most intensely lyrical film, is a portrait of a friend named Tung, deriving directly from a momentary image on walking, which features shots of a girl dancing in black and white negatives, intercut and superimposed over shots moving along of plants. The ocean and mountains, a boat and railroad train are the central subjects in *To Parsifal* (1963, 16 mins.). Using the European legend as basic structure and hero, and Richard Wagner's music for the soundtrack, the film is a depiction of "he who becomes slowly wise." "A tribute to summer" (Bruce Baillie). "Creating, in a moment of viewing, a great sense of perspective" (Stan Brakhage). *Castro Street* (1966, 10 mins.), perhaps Baillie's best-known work, is a tour-de-force in its use of color and camera movement in expressing a set of complicated, often paradoxical feelings for a locale. Selected into the National Film Registry of the Library of Congress, the film "is inspired by a lesson from Eric Satie; a film in the form of a street—Castro Street, running by the Standard Oil Refinery in Richmond, California...switch engines on one side and refinery tanks, stacks and buildings on the other-the street and film, ending at a red lumber company" (Bruce Baillie).

VHS: S30222. $75.00.
Bruce Baillie, USA, 1966/1963/1966, 31 mins.

TV Party

Writer Glenn O'Brien, a columnist for *Interview* and Artforum, culls vignettes and episodes from his late-night cable talk show in the early 80s, featuring sketches with David Byrne, Debbie Harry, Jean-Michel Basquiat during the outbreak of the Mudd Club's meteoric rise in the downtown art and performance scene. 30 mins.

VHS: S17192. $29.95.

Ulrike Rosenbach: Osho—Samadhi

Germany, 1990, 12 mins.

VHS: S22575. $95.00.

Up to the South

The south of Lebanon is a disputed area where issues like colonialism, terrorism, occupation, resistance, collaboration, experts, spokespeople, leadership, and even the definition of the land itself are hotly disputed. These concerns lead to a critique of documentary traditions and their relationship to a history of representation.

VHS: S21035. $59.95.
Jayce Salloum, USA, 1993, 60 mins.

A Valentine for Nelson & Two Marches

New York-based filmmaker Jim Hubbard hand processes his own 16mm film, resulting in intensely personal and moving works. The first is simply a Valentine for his longtime lover. In the second, he contrasts the March on Washington held before AIDS dominated gay life with the later larger gay rights march held in 1993.

VHS: S27221. $59.95.
Jim Hubbard, USA, 1993

Vanderbeekiana!: Stan VanDerBeek's Vision

VanDerBeek discusses work, found images and inventions, demonstrates his "moviedrome" for seeing films against a hemisphere, and reflects on film as "an experience, not an artifact." Clips from *Will, See Saw Seams*, Image After Image After Image and Poemfield #1. 1968, 28 mins.

VHS: S31590. $59.95.

Variety Is the Spice of Life

Program 5 of the *What Does She Want* series, this program imagines a more generous world in which a variety of love and lovers is not just permitted, but welcomed. Jill Kroesen's *Lowell Moves to New York* stars actor Eric Bogosian who made his mark by creating characters like Lowell, a nerd dwelling beneath the facade of one cool guy. Valie Export's *A Perfect Pair* could refer to the handsome couple on display, or to a part of the heroine's anatomy. Max Almy's *Modern Love* is a series of lovers' discourses. Lynn Blumenthal's *Doublecross* traces the journey of a woman through the tricky terrain of sexual exploration. In Linda Look's *Luchare* the Flamenco, usually performed by a man and a woman, takes on new meaning when danced erotically by two women. Finally *Two in Twenty*, a lesbian soap opera, parodies daytime television with a simulation that just might be real. Produced by the Video Data Bank. 75 mins.

VHS: S06514. $59.95.

Video Art, Tape One

Includes three works. *All Orientals Look the Same* is a brief exploration of the title phrase, which takes a common misperception and turns it on its head. It provokes the viewer to confront his or her own prejudices and misconceptions about Asian-Pacific Americans and the contradictions inherent in those beliefs. *Scratch Video* is a short piece which looks at some of the true sources of allergies, itching and repressed reactions. *New Year, Parts 1 & 2* combines hand-drawn illustrations and found footage to show the conflict of a child caught between her Chinese-American heritage and the expectations created by stereotypical Hollywood images of Asians. Clips of Charlie Chan, Fu Manchu and Suzie Wong illustrate the point.

VHS: S30854. $49.95.
Valerie Soe, USA, 1986/1987, 29 mins.

Video Art, Tape Two

Includes three works. In *Picturing Oriental Girls: A (Re)Educational Videotape*, geisha girls, china dolls and dragon ladies populate a visual compendium of representation of Asian women in American film and television. Juxtaposed with texts from mail order bride catalogs, men's magazines and popular literature, the images of *Picturing* explicate the orientalism and exoticism prevalent in mass media images of "oriental girls." *Walking the Mountain* is an elegy to the artist's Aunt Lula. It recounts the fate of her grandparents' cherished second daughter, born into a climate too arid and dry for her genotype. *Mixed Blood* is an experimental documentary which examines some of the motivations, attitudes and reactions surrounding cross-cultural intimacy.

VHS: S30855. $49.95.
Valerie Soe, USA, 1992/1994, 25 mins.

Video Art: Antonio Muntadas

Three works by Antonio Muntadas, who locates his work in what he calls "the media landscape"—the intersection of art, social sciences and media. *Between the Lines* (1979), focuses on the role of the reporter to deal with the way in which information is selected, scheduled and edited to fit television news programming; *This Is Not an Advertisement* (1985), is a documentation of a 50-second computer-generated message produced by the Public Art Fund's Message to the Public Project, broadcast from the Spectacolor light board in Times Square, and alludes to the fine line between art and advertisement; *Credit* (1984), juxtaposes and edits several TV and film credit sequences together—a rumination on the nature of money and labor.

VHS: S06260. $65.00.
Antonio Muntadas, USA, 1979-85, 55 mins.

Video Art: Ardele Lister

Ardele Lister has produced several award winning tapes, with *Hell*, the work on this tape, winning awards at the Tokyo and other festivals. *Hell* is the modern hell of information storage and retrieval, with "the souls in hell stored on disc and tortured with the latest in digital video effects." Inspired by Dante's Inferno, Lister's *Hell* updates the metaphors and locations. Lister employs a full arsenal of gadgetry to make her art stimulating and accessible, using computers that bend, freeze, tilt and spin images.

VHS: S05353. $65.00.
Ardele Lister, Canada, 1985, 17 mins.

Video Art: Blue Moon

Rodney Werden has worked in video art since 1974. His most recent works develop innovative, narrative structures as vehicles for a more complex view of human sexuality, as overt content, issues of gender roles and sexual identity provide the ground for an exploration of the fiction of artistic subjectivity. In Blue Moon the audience observes the parallel events of a prostitute searching for a client intercut with a film producer visiting an old friend and guiltily offering him money for sex. French with English subtitles.

VHS: S05350. $65.00.
Rodney Werden, Canada, 1983, 14 mins.

Video Art: Come on Touch It (Study No. 4 for a Personality Inventory Channel)

A real-time performance by Ian Murray, overlayed on a dense complex of sound and image. Created as a study of a fictional "interactive" 24-hour television station, it displays the artist as being manipulated by a computer. "A balance between seemingly objective and distanced electronic world and the subjective, emotional and philosophical reality of the artist" (*Signal Approach*). Ian Murray's installation, video and audio work is based in the alteration or manipulation of popular forms and mass media products.

VHS: S05351. $65.00.

Ian Murray, Canada, 1983, 34 mins.

Video Art: Damnation of Faust Trilogy

Dara Birnbaum's trilogy renders the Faustian legend contemporary through examining and reflecting upon scenes of the ritualized behavior of Italian youths in New York City playground. Birnbaum's *Faust* urges an examination of the quest for experience and knowledge…her characters describe and define their own stories, and react and respond to their own placement within the narrative. Concluding with a timeline composed of street demonstrations, mass and student activism, *Damnation of Faust* establishes a social framework which can be enlarged from the personal.

VHS: S06301. $65.00.

Dara Birnbaum, USA, 1983-87, 22 mins.

Video Art: Dana Atchley & Eric Metcalfe

Crime Time Comix Presents Steel & Flesh is the work (1980, 12 mins.) in this tape, which is a fast-moving pastiche of poker faces, guns, knives, and suspense, based on the murder mystery comics which Metcalfe drew in his 1950's childhood. Dana Atchley has worked as a designer, publisher, teacher and television producer and artist; Eric Metcalfe is a noted Canadian videotape artist, whose work is noted for fantasy narratives that manipulate the features of comic strips and detective thrillers. Canada, 1980, 12 mins.

VHS: S05348. $65.00.

Video Art: David Askevold

Two works by David Askevold, a prominent Canadian video artist whose work depends on the imposition of arbitrary systems on obscure, psychological and often mystical "information" to arrive at a structural ambiguity: *Rhea* (1982, 6.5 mins), opens and closes with a wandering spotlight on a dark interior. Faces appear against vague landscapes or without setting to speak the names of others. *Jumped Out* (1984, 12 mins.), is comprised of a sensual drift of images which allude to or trace evidence of psychic energy, a form of energy that surfaces within the image.

VHS: S05352. $65.00.

David Askevold

Video Art: Gary Hill

Four tapes by Gary Hill: *Full Circle*, originally titled "Ring Modulation" sets up a paradoxical circumstance in which a performer attempts to overcome the matter of difference between metal and electronic signals; *Mediations*, an excerpt from a remake of Hill's "Soundings," (1979/1986)—as sand is placed on a loud speaker, it forms patterns which correspond to the frequency of a voice as it is amplified through the speaker; *Around & About* attempts to engage the "positions" of a viewer via a monologue—images are cut to the syllabic rhythm of the spoken word making their content and context susceptible to the utterances of speech.

VHS: S06075. $65.00.

Gary Hill, USA, 1978-86, 12 mins.

Video Art: Helen Doyle

Scars of Memory (*Tatouages de la Memoire*) is a lyrical, spiritual piece by Helen Doyle dealing with the layers of memory; stripping them away to reveal the core of Sarah, the main character in the tape. Helen Doyle describes the tape as an intimate voyage of discovery verging on the indecent…an invitation to the fantasies of a world outlined in myth and colored in dreams. A co-founder of Video Femmes in Quebec, Helen Doyle is a foremost Canadian video artist concerned with social and political issues. 1984, 33 mins.

VHS: S05340. $65.00.

Video Art: Here in the Southwest

Joyan Saunders' recent work is concerned with alternatives to content and structure of traditional narrative. In *Here in the Southwest*, Saunders deals in a sporting manner with the ideas of biological determinism and sexual difference. Elements of pop wisdom or quasi-scientific pronouncements are subjected to an informal process of deductive reasoning and the ostensibly logical conclusions are diametrically opposed to what is generally held to be true.

VHS: S05349. $65.00.

Joyan Saunders, Canada, 1984, 23 mins.

Video Art: Hygiene

A tape by writer, lyricist, performer and musician by Andy Paterson, whose obsession with history leads him to mythologize about contemporary popular information and video. In *Hygiene*, Paterson weaves stories based on a simple premise and embellishes them with his own unique perspective. *Hygiene* is the story of a woman whose men have done her wrong and who finds a greater sense of self-reliance and self-confidence in her relationship with another woman.

VHS: S05339. $65.00.

Andrew Paterson, Canada, 1985, 41 mins.

Video Art: It Starts at Home

Michael Smith has been hearing about cable TV everywhere. What could be better? Hundreds of channels and guaranteed crystal-clear reception definitely added up to a full day of television. So he thought it over and decided to join the ranks with millions of other cable subscribers. Mike was confident making this "state of the art" improvement to his home entertainment program, but what he ordered and what he got was another story. Through some quirk of technology, Mike's private life and all activity in his home would soon be broadcast to the entire world.

VHS: S06307. $65.00.

Michael Smith, USA, 1982, 25 mins.

Video Art: Jan Peacock

Jan Peacock re-shapes the literary and metaphorical content of situations, building narratives, often from autobiographical sources, which expose and question the values and methods by which we construct and share reality. In *Wallace + Theresa*, the work on this tape, the propensity to read and interpret it as a given condition is construed as a layering of images, sounds, printed and written words and voice—all and each of which reciprocally narrate each other.

VHS: S05343. $75.00.

Jan Peacock, Canada, 1985, 14 mins.

Video Art: Leaving the 20th Century and Perfect Leader

Leaving the 20th Century is a trilogy of experimental videotapes by Max Almy which call attention to the fact that we are approaching a point of departure in history. The tape takes a pointedly satirical look at the realities of this century and raises serious questions about the possibilities of the future. *Perfect Leader* is a short experimental tape which utilizes a combination of live action, audio and video special effects, an original score, and computer animation to probe the questions of political image-making and the marketing of a candidate. "Max Almy's work exploits a narrow gap between quotation and parody….
Her high-tech razzle-dazzle videotapes are laden with futuristic special effects and have the breathtaking rhythmic speed of commercials" (*Afterimage*).

VHS: S06300. $65.00.

Max Almy, USA, 1982/83, 15 mins.

Video Art: Les Levine

Levine uses the techniques, tactics and even the sites of popular media—advertising, fashion design and television—and the information they purvey as the target of his work. *Diamond Mind* is a performance tape in which the artist is seen talking about previous experiences in life and showing some of the objects he designed at the time. The performance is concerned with the idea that people are programmed by the images they make for themselves. *Diamond Mind* is in the collection of the Museum of Modern Art and the Centre Georges Pompidou.

VHS: S05341. $65.00.

Les Levine, Canada, 1977, 30 mins.

Video Art: Noel Harding

A retrospective tape of the work of Noel Harding, whose video, film and sculptural installations center around the interaction of props and settings. Through this interaction, he explores very personal notions of illusion and reality, subjective understanding and public perceptions. The works included on the tape are: *Birth's Child*, a mother and child portrait which takes on sculptural qualities; *Simplified Confusions*, a conversational counterpoint and quick cuts which examine the interchange between a woman and a man; *A Serene Composition Suggestive of Pastoral Repose*, a study of combinations of the sensual; *Yellow,M* a fantasy play which reflects the interior landscape; *Out of Control*, a fast-paced, hard-boiled tale of sex, power and intrigue in high places inspired by the story of G. Gordon Liddy; *Houses Belong to Those Who Live in Them*, an examination of the complexities of modern life; and *Elephants*, inspired by the shooting down of the Korean jetliner, composed of image after image to construct an enigmatic work. Total length: 53 mins.

VHS: S05342. $65.00.

Noel Harding

Video Art: Not Dead Yet

Edward Mowbray directed this fast-paced documentary about a second generation of punk rockers living in Toronto, offering insight into this segment of culture by videotaping in the streets, bars and homes of punks. Conversations are intercut with the music of the punk bands at the Core of the scene. "The best in-depth look at Canadian punk scene" (*Vancouver Sun*). Mowbray's work in video employs filmic techniques to create a hybrid style of video art and television.

VHS: S05344. $65.00.

Edward Mowbray, Canada, 1984, 56 mins.

Video Art: Prime Cuts

Paul Wong's work in photography, performance and video can be characterized as a visceral personal response to events and conditions of his and his friends' lives. *Prime Cuts* sets to motion the fantasy world of eternal beauty and glamor as portrayed in the fashion tear-sheet. Wong's puppet-like fashion model characters never stop having fun in their endless pursuit of happiness. Non-narrative in structure, the tape considers notions of style.

VHS: S05345. $65.00.

Paul Wong, Canada, 1981, 20 mins.

Video Art: Red Tapes

A classic work from the poet of the 60's New York school, Vito Acconci, an epic of storytelling. Most of the tape takes place while viewing a blank screen; other segments involve props, voice-overs, appropriated images, sound collages, and most importantly, Vito Acconci himself.

VHS: S06299. $65.00.

Vito Acconci, USA, 1976, 142 mins.

Video Art: Rober Racine

Rober Racine's *J'Aurais Dit Glenn Gould* is half document, half fiction, based on the style of Glenn Gould's little-known CBC radio documentaries. The tape is a sound collage utilizing both English and French and is interspersed with radio interviews with John Jessop, Glenn Gould's radio documentary assistant editor. The video concerns itself with the issues of radio, music and video as it creates "a song to listening." "Racine's work is a vast undertaking aimed at decoding cultural forms" (Aurora Borealis).

VHS: S06302. $65.00.

Rober Racine, Canada, 1984, 28 mins.

Video Art: Shut the Fuck Up

Produced by General Idea, *Shut the Fuck Up* was selected at Documenta 8, and exhibited internationally. The tape examines the relationship between mass media and the artist. They incorporate segments from television and film, along with their own commentary, to humorously point out the media's insistence that gossip and spectacle make art and artists interesting to the public. Canada, 1985, 14 mins.

VHS: S05346. $65.00.

Video Art: Telling Motions

"*Telling Motions* is presented in the musical form of variations on a theme. The work utilizes a musical score and poetic texts to explore meanings which are outside the realm of conventional language. The tape explores repetition and change based on the context and treatment of imagery…Memory and learning are explored as the viewer becomes actively engaged in the process of decoding pluralistic "readings."

VHS: S06306. $65.00.

Bill Seaman, USA, 1985/86, 20 mins.

Video Art: Test Tube

General Idea produced this tape at De Appel, Holland, and the tape incorporates television formats and video special effects in a witty and visually sophisticated production. General Idea uses the media to create a complex visual portrait of the artist in the 80's. The tape represented Canada at the Venice Biennale, 1980. Canada, 1979, 28 mins.

VHS: S05347. $65.00.

Video Art: Tomiyo Sasaki

Two works by Tomiyo Sasaki, a Canadian-born artist who lives and works in New York: *Creatures of the Enchanted Isles* is a study for a five-channel, 20-monitor installation work which utilizes images taped on the Galapagos Islands. "The combination of the bizarre and barren volcanic landscape with the strange and unique creatures which inhabit the land makes one ponder basic aspects of nature as Darwin obviously did." *The Dreams of Christopher Columbus* is a mosaic of images, videotaped in India, a study for a much longer and larger work by the same title consisting of 11 channels and 50-300 monitors arranged in the shape of a mandala.

VHS: S06305. $65.00.

Tomiyo Sasaki, USA, 1984-87, 53 mins.

Video Art: Vital Statistics of a Citizen, Simply Obtained

Martha Rosler's *Vital Statistics* acts out the duality of women's consciousness. In the primary scene, a woman's body is measured in a clinical setting and compared with standard measurement. Voice-overs, symbolic scenes, and photographs suggest the implications of enforcing social standards of measurement-whether by the state through its police functions or, more informally, by "common sense."
VHS: S06304. $65.00.
Martha Rosler, USA, 1977, 40 mins.

Video Congress No. 8

Works by the artists Claude Torey, Der Plan, KAOS, John Cage, Jonathon X Jackson, Tony Allard, Etant Donnes, and others who participated in this congress are included in this two-tape package. 120 mins.
VHS: S22580. $136.95.

Video Congress No. 9

Artists who participated in this second congress have works included on this tape. Didier Bay, Kain Karawahn, Mike Hentz, Viebeke Vogel, Pyrolator, Tony Allard, Yvonne Oerlemans and others are represented. 82 mins.
VHS: S22581. $70.00.

Video Works: Miroslaw Rogala (1980-86)

Four video works by the important video artist Miroslaw Rogala: *Love among Machines* departs from the writings of Carlos Drummond de Andrade to explore the relations of modern technology to manners, movements and motivations of earlier eras; *Polish Dance '80* is a short video dance dedicated to the Workers' movement in Poland; *Questions to Another Nation* is a complex work that reflects on the effort to understand and be understood in a foreign culture; *Remote Faces: Outerpretation* is a 7-channel video installation with 8 channel sound by Lucien Czyzewski and live performance, with both video and audio digitally processed, playfully challenging our concepts of language, communication and meaning.
VHS: S08470. $39.95.
Miroslaw Rogala, USA, 1980-86, 39 mins.

Videotape for a Woman and a Man

Amy Greenfield uses human motion, camera lens, editing and optical techniques to "see into, with and through the body." Shot over a period of six months and edited over four years, *Videotape for a Woman and a Man* is "an absorbing and disturbing inquiry into male-female relationships. Photographed in black and white and color, and performed in the nude by Greenfield and dancer Ben Dolphin, it relentlessly examines the possible physical and emotional encounters between a man and a woman....We marvel at and are moved by the poignant spectacle of the human body as an instrument capable of transcending its own reality" (John Guen, *Dance Magazine*).
VHS: S01415. $19.98.
Amy Greenfield, USA, 1979, 34 mins.

The Videotapes of Elizabeth Sher, Volumes 1-11

I.V. Magazine #1. *I.V. Magazine*—a very creative alternative to the bland network TV magazine shows—combines a pastiche of interviews, humor, satire and music. This edition includes an interview with a policewoman at target practice, a peep behind the scenes at a fantasy phone call service, fashion mutilation set to an industrial score, and more. 60 mins.
VHS: S05674. $45.00.

I.V. Magazine #2. An upbeat amalgam of weird, whimsical and ironic visions, this edition of *I.V. Magazine* includes *Showtime* (with a soundtrack by Minimal Man), an original look at Hong Kong, a chat with a reformed bank robber who lunched with Reagan, ads for products you won't believe exist, and a musical tribute to the roaring 20's featuring a Samurai Tap Dancer. 60 mins.
VHS: S05675. $45.00.

I.V. Magazine #3. A special edition—*Information for People Who Can Take It Straight*—is a full-scale invasion into the computer age conducted by mega-hostess MacDonna. View tips for handypersons and upscale house hunters, the whimsy of computerized martial arts, and an English "industrial music video" set to the tune of tearing velcro, along with computer-animated frenzy in a dumpster with mime Arina Isaacson. 60 mins.
VHS: S05676. $45.00.

What's Inside These Shorts? A witty, humorous series of video-shorts that includes *Juggling*, about the pressures of motherhood and work; *Beat It*, an exercise in frustration; *The Training*, as serious as any potty-training film can be; plus a tongue-in-cheek look at pre-pubescent lust, and a nightmare of a gynecological checkup. 60 mins.
VHS: S05677. $45.00.

Brainwash and Beyond. Explores the parameters of the art-video interface in a charged look at Empty-Vee (MTV), and offers a montage of impressions of contemporary culture, including unusual looks at amusement parks, car washes, and more—with industrial soundtrack works by Phil Hopper. 60 mins.
VHS: S05678. $45.00.

How to Make a Body of Art. Four members of the Arts Community—museum curator, gallery director, art consultant and performance space coordinator—discuss a range of topics from ethics of the art world to some of the tawdry aspects of the art-finance interface. They cover tips on launching art into the marketplace, tax advantages, presentation, and more—in a way that is upbeat with a touch of irreverence. 15 mins.
VHS: S05679. $30.00.

Interviews with Artists: Program 1. A combination of interviews with artists in various media: painter John King; video artist Vee Hotchkin, who talks about her secret of eternal youth; narrative painter M. Louise Stanley; sculptor Tyler Hoare, who replaces the Red Baron with the Sopwith Camel in San Francisco Bay; and members of Survival Research, leading masters of avant-garde irreverence. 45 mins.
VHS: S05680. $39.95.

Interviews with Artists: Program 2. Three minority artists reveal the genesis and motivations behind their art: John Abduljaami, a sculptor, carves poignant stories in wood; painter and printmaker Carmen Lomas Garza shows how her work has evolved; and altar and installation artist Amalia Mesa Bains constructs her personal tribute to Santa Teresa as she begins her own "Renunciation"—a five-month fast—and loses 100 pounds. 30 mins.
VHS: S05681. $35.00.

Women by Women. At an historic exhibition of leading Hispanic artists that portrays woman as healer, mother, sister, abuelita, indegena and worker—held at Galeria de la Raza in San Francisco—women artists explain how they have evolved their own individual voices while paying homage to a common cultural and female heritage. 60 mins.
VHS: S05682. $39.95.

Dancing on the Edge of Success: An Interview with Choreographer Margaret Jenkins. Dancer/ choreographer Margaret Jenkins discusses her sources and influences—Merce Cunningham, Martha Graham and Jose Limon among them-and describes her experiences in the early days of modern dance in New York, the building of her own San Francisco company, and the joys and difficulties of keeping it alive. Discussion is interspersed with a view of her dancers rehearsing and developing a new piece in collaboration with Yoko Ono. 30 mins.
VHS: S05683. $35.00.

Interviews with Artists: Program 3. Realist painter Anton Gintner describes the relation of his inner-city Oakland (California) surroundings and love of the blues to his work; puppeteer and mime Arina Isaacson talks about her "family" of archetypal dolls and her spell-binding method of working with them; and "Arts Plural" artists Chaarles Amirkhanian and Carol Law explain the interaction between his sound/text and her surrealistic pop slide images in their joint performance. 30 mins.
VHS: S05684. $35.00.

Viva Eu! & Ex Voto

Tania Cypriano, an experimental Brazilian filmmaker, explores her most poignant life experiences in these two films. In *Viva Eu!*, Cypriano explores her experiences as a woman living with AIDS. In *Ex Voto*, Cypriano takes a look at her ordeal of surviving terrible burns from a horrible fire she was trapped in. Both films show struggle and a commitment to survival.
VHS: S27241. $59.95.
Tania Cypriano, Brazil

Wheeler Dixon: Selected Films

This compilation of 18 short films by Wheeler Dixon, including *Serial Metaphysics*, *Numen Lumen* and The Children of Light, uses archival footage, sound/image restructuring and diaristic techniques to successfully blend personal cinema with formal aesthetic issues.
VHS: S28577. $59.95.

Whoregasm

The title says it all, a blending of film and video art that stars Susan Manson, Rick Strange and director Nick Zedd. On the same program is *I Shit on God*, a five-minute short. 11 mins.
VHS: S17196. $24.95.

William Wegman Reel 1

This compilation of early video works by Wegman includes *Microphone, Pocketbook Man, Abet and Abtu, The Ring, Randy's Sick, Milk/Floor, Stomach Song, Happy Song, The Door, William Wegman in Chinese, Elbows, Dress Curtain, Hot Sake, Casper, Handy, Cut and In, Plunger Series, Nosy, Firechief, Come In, Hidden Utensil, Contract, Puppet, Shadows, Ventriloquism, Light Trails* and *Cape On*.
VHS: S22589. $65.00.
William Wegman, USA, 1969-70, 30 mins.

William Wegman Reel 2

Wegman videos compiled on this tape include *The Kiss, Sanforized, Coin Toss, Monkey Business, Same Shirt, Diving Board, Straw and String, Product, In the Cup* and *Treat Bottle*.
VHS: S22590. $65.00.
William Wegman, USA, 1972, 19 mins.

William Wegman Reel 3

This is a collection of Wegman tapes from 1973. It includes *Stich and Tooth, Emporer and Dish, Lucky T-shirt, Rage and Depression, Speed Reading, Born with No Mouth, Dual Function, Massage Chair, Raise Treat, Many Ray, Do You Want To?, Crooked Finger, Crooked Stick, Deodorant, Bubblebath* and *47 Seconds*.
VHS: S22591. $65.00.
William Wegman, USA, 1973, 18 mins.

William Wegman Reel 4

From 1973-74 comes this compilation of Wegman videos: *Wake Up, Trip Across Country, Down Time, Laundromat, Saw Movies, Cocktail Waiter, Nail Business, Calling Man Ray, New and Used Car Salesman, On the Ball, Tails, Radar Screen, Air Travel, Criticize, Pyramids, Symbolize, The Letter, Snowflakes, Growl* and The Spelling Lesson.
VHS: S22592. $65.00.
William Wegman, USA, 1973-74, 21 mins.

William Wegman Reel 5

Wegman's works from 1977 have been compiled on this tape: *Stalking, Nocturne, Audio Tape and Video Tape, Dancing Tape, Hobo on Train, Drinking Milk, Copyright, Buying a House, Lerch Hairpiece, Tammy and Can of Plums, Loves Water, Average Guy, Over the Drink, Marbles, Ball Drop* and *Treat Table*.
VHS: S22593. $65.00.
William Wegman, USA, 1977, 27 mins.

William Wegman Reel 6

This is a compilation of William Wegman videos from 1977. *Ball and Can, The Reel, Eyes of Ray, Dog Duet, tube talk, Stereo Systems, Video, Joke* and *Furniture* are all included. 19 mins.
VHS: S22594. $65.00.
William Wegman, USA, 1977, 19 mins.

William Wegman Reel 7

Due to popular demand, Wegman has created another video about his dogs. These are the last works made with the now famous, the late Man Ray. Shot in color, this tape features several comic vignettes by the artist and his talented pet Weimeraner, including *Doctor Joke, Alarm Clock A and B, Smoking, Drop It* and *Piano Hands*. 18 mins.
VHS: S12760. $65.00.
William Wegman, USA

William Wegman Reel 7

Art Metropole's Artist VHS series produced this last tape featuring Wegman's much loved pet Weimaraner, Man Ray. The talented dog is seen in a number of humorous segments, including *Doctor Joke, Alarm Clock A and B, Smoking, Drop It* and *Piano Hands*. 18 mins.
VHS: S29955. $65.00.

Willoughby Sharp's Downtown New York

Distilled from 13 hours of cable TV, this show is hosted by the noted video pioneer and publisher. Artists profiled in on-location clips include: Kathy Acker, Laurie Anderson, Kipper Kids, Gracie Mansion, Michael Smith, Cookie Mueller, Spada and more. Called "a guide for the curious through the dense sub-culture of Downtown New York," Sharp appears with his hilarious sidekick Boris Policeband.
VHS: S07124. $49.95.
Willoughby Sharp, USA, 1986, 58 mins.

The Wind Is Driving Him Towards the Open Sea

Filmmaker David Brooks summarized his film thusly: "a boy travels, while we search for a man, Chandler Moore. He is never found but we see the world he has made for himself." Brooks was one of the first film diarists, but also "one of the most prominent lyricists of the experimental cinema. His work was eclipsed by his early death at age 24...most of his films are preoccupied with the relationship between music and image" (J.J. Murphy). "...a fascinating melancholy...surrounds it. It's a narrative of moods, of reflection, of things lost, gone, like autumn leaves—no tragedy, really, only a mood of melancholy, of sadness—of friends, of ways of life, of cultures gone, of ages coming and going" (Jonas Mekas).
VHS: S30231. $40.00.
David Brooks, USA, 1968, 52 mins.

The Works of Ken Feingold—Distance of the Outsider

India Time (1987, 46 mins.) was recorded between 1985 and 1988, during which time video artist Ken Feingold lived mostly in India and traveled extensively throughout other parts of Asia. The document shows the people of India in their daily work, and often in response to the fact that they are being recorded by the camera. It is as much about the meeting of cultures, and the imposition of Feingold's own perspective on Indian culture, as it is about Indian culture itself. One might consider it a fascinating ethnography of an American in India.
VHS: S15648. $59.95.
Ken Feingold, USA, 1987, 46 mins.

The Works of Ken Feingold—Fictions

A collection of four wide-ranging video shorts from director Ken Feingold, whose intelligent, disjointed and confrontational style has invited favorable comparisons to radical mainstream directors like Nagisa Oshima and Sergei Eisenstein. Includes *The Smallest Particle* (1987, 8 mins.), *In Shadow City* (a collaboration with Constance De Jong, 1988, 13 mins.), *Irony (The Abyss of Speech)* (1985, 29 mins.), and *Un Chien Delicieux* (1991, 19 mins.). Total length: 69 mins.
VHS: S15650. $59.95.
Ken Feingold, USA, 1985-91, 69 mins.

The Works of Ken Feingold—Life in Exile

Life in Exile is Ken Feingold's ambitious two-part video examining the philosophy and political predicament of the Tibetan refugee community in India. This thoughtful, moving document reveals the turmoil of a disenfranchised and much-abused people, while at the same time presenting a clear view of the spiritual and cultural beliefs which have managed to nurture and sustain them through these painful times. It was created in consultation with the Tibetan Government-In-Exile and the Private Office of the Dalai Lama.
VHS: S15649. $59.95.
Ken Feingold, USA, 1988, 90 mins.

The Works of Ken Feingold—Names in Search of a Body

A kaleidoscopic pair of videos from director Ken Feingold: *5 dim/MIND* (1983, 29 mins.) and *The Double* (1984, 29 mins.). These collected images are from around the world, culled from various films and broadcasts, as well as original footage by the artist. The surreal suppression of conventional continuity, achieved through Feingold's freewheeling, associative editing style, creates a series of signs and symbols which appeal directly to the intellect—personally involving viewers in its philosophical meditations on the world as we know it or, rather, should know it. Produced, directed and edited by Ken Feingold. Total length: 58 mins.
VHS: S15647. $59.95.
Ken Feingold, USA, 1983-1984, 58 mins.

The Works of Ken Feingold—Water Falling from One World to Another

A moody and suggestive pair of short works from highly acclaimed video artist Ken Feingold. This collection, which includes *Water Falling from One World to Another* (1980, 34 mins.) and *Purely Human Sleep* (1980, 28 mins.), contemplates the endless, human pursuit of the invisible, especially as it confronts the limits of the body; limitations which often manage to imprison us, reining in our perceptions of the world around us.
VHS: S15646. $59.95.
Ken Feingold, USA, 1980, 62 mins.

The Works of Ken Feingold: The Complete Set

Includes ten films made between 1980 and 1991, ranging from 8 to 90 minutes.
VHS: S18808. $249.95.

JAMES BROUGHTON

The Films of James Broughton

Spanning an artistic career of forty years, the collected films of James Broughton represent a remarkable body of work by a leading avant-garde American filmmaker—an undisputed master of the fusion of spoken poetry with moving images. A poet and dramatist as well as a filmmaker, Broughton has transformed all three of these forms into what Stan Brakhage calls "an art of lifelong montage."

Volume 1: Erotic Celebrations. Contains Broughton's 1968 masterpiece, *The Bed*, a lyrically erotic celebration of just about everything that could happen on a bed, with an all-nude cast, among them some of San Francisco's best-known artists, and *Erogeny* (1976), an intimate exploration of the landscape of the human body. *Hermes Bird* (1979) and *Song of the Godbody* (1977) continue Broughton's sly attacks on sexual taboos and celebrate the ecstasy of physical awareness with close-up camerawork that caresses the body parts it explores. 47 mins.
VHS: S07284. $29.95.

Volume 2: Rituals of Play. Three important black and white films by Broughton, including the classic *Mother's Day* (1948)—an ironic recollection of childhood games in the nostalgic style of a cluttered family album, enacted by adults, and *Four in the Afternoon* (1951) with four poetic variations on the search for love from a girl of 10 to a man of 40. It ends with the comedy *Loony Tom* (1951), picturing the amorous progress of an amiable tramp who makes love to every woman he meets. 48 mins.
VHS: S07285. $29.95.

Volume 3: The Pleasure Garden. A comic fantasy with songs that celebrate the triumph of love and liberty over the forces of restriction. Filmed in the ruined gardens of the Crystal Palace in London with a professional cast, this satiric fairy tale won a prize for poetic fantasy at the Cannes Film Festival of 1954. 38 mins.
VHS: S07286. $29.95.

Volume 4: Autobiographical Mysteries. Includes *Testament* (1974), an exquisite self-portrait in which the poet-filmmaker views his life and work with wit and charm in a rich pageantry of personal imagery, songs, anecdotes and dreams, and *Devotions* (1983), a work made with collaborator Joel Singer which envisions a world where men have abandoned rivalries in favor of comradely devotion, featuring 45 different couples who reveal the many pleasures that men can enjoy together. *Scattered Remains* (1988) is a cinematic performance piece in which Joel Singer creates a multi-faceted portrait of Broughton acting out his verses in unlikely situations and with surprising camera inventions. 57 mins.
VHS: S07287. $29.95.

Volume 5: Parables of Wonder. Five important works by Broughton from the decade of the '70s. *High Kukus* (1973) is a visualization of a Zen teaching accompanied by 14 of Broughton's cuckoo haikus, while *Golden Positions* (1978) is a series of tableaux vivants that follow the form of a liturgical service and glorify the naked human body. *This Is It* (1971) is a playful pseudo-Zen creation myth shot in a home-movie style with a two-year-old Adam in a backyard Eden. *The Gardener of Eden* (1981) is an intense poetic work that celebrates the sexual dance of all creation, set in Sri Lanka. The tape concludes with *Water Circle* (1975), an homage to Lao-Tzu in a joyful poem read by the filmmaker and set to music by Corelli. 56 mins.
VHS: S07288. $29.95.

Volume 6: Dreamwood. A spiritual odyssey into the landscape of the dream in which its poet hero sets forth to rescue the bride of his soul and bring about his own rebirth. 1972, 45 mins.
VHS: S01575. $29.95.

Complete Set.
VHS: S07289. $149.75.

BARBARA HAMMER

Lesbian Humor

A collection of six films spanning the career of this exciting filmmaker: *Menses* is a wry comedy on the disagreeable aspects of menstruation; *Superdyke*, a comedy about a troop of shield-bearing Amazons; *Our Trip*, an animated film based on a hiking trip in the Andes; *Sync Touch*, a series of film experiments which propose an aesthetic connection between touch and sight; *Doll House*, a rapid montage of objects arranged in reference to the central prop of a doll house; and *No No Nooky T.V.* confronts the feminist controversy around sexuality with electronic language. "Hammer's satiric use of technology corresponds well with the Eighties repression of sexual expression. If you've ever looked up 'lesbian' in a computer thesaurus, you'll know that it's not listed" (*Independent Media*).
VHS: S08608. $59.95.
Barbara Hammer, 1975-87, USA, 59 mins.

Lesbian Sexuality

A collection of four films by Barbara Hammer, including the landmark *Dyketactics*, the first lesbian lovemaking film to be made by a lesbian. A sensual, evocative montage of 110 images edited to images of touch, an "erotic lesbian commercial." Also includes: *Multiple Orgasm*, a sensual, explicit film; *Double Strength*, a poetic study of a lesbian relationship between two trapeze artists; and *Women I Love*, using the camera as a personal extension of the body.
VHS: S08609. $59.95.
Barbara Hammer, USA, 1974-76, 57 mins.

Nitrate Kisses

Unlike any other documentary, this work combines Barbara Hammer's unique experimental film style with archival footage to yield a unique view of overlooked lesbian and gay history. From the era of Nazism to today's AIDS epidemic, this work forces everyone to remember the importance of queer lives without evading any aspect of love, from the physical to the sublime.
VHS: S24031. $39.95.
Barbara Hammer, USA, 1992, 67 mins.

Optical Nerves

Parisian Blinds and *Tourist*, both films by Barbara Hammer, "investigate the nature of spectator perception in an unfamiliar environment." *The Optic Nerve* is a powerful personal exploration of family and aging; *Place Mattes* explores the space between reaching and touching with animation and optical printing used to create travelling mattes for places. *Endangered*, Hammer's most recent work, has light, life and film as endangered in this exquisite film etched with acid.
VHS: S08611. $59.95.
Barbara Hammer, USA, 1984-88, 44 mins.

Perceptual Landscapes

Four works that explore personal landscapes: *Pools*, made with Barbara Klutinis, is an exploration above and under water of two of the first swimming pools designed by the first woman architect in the U.S.; *Pond and Waterfall* is an exploration of verdant pond growth as well as dynamic light and water reflections; *Stone Circles* is a celebration of ancient pre-patriarchal standing mounds and circles including Stonehenge and Asbury; *Bent Time* is one of Hammer's most ambitious films, in "which she attempts to render visually the scientific theory that time, like rays, curves at the outer edges of the universe" (*L.A. Times*).
VHS: S08610. $59.95.
Barbara Hammer, USA, 1981-83, 54 mins.

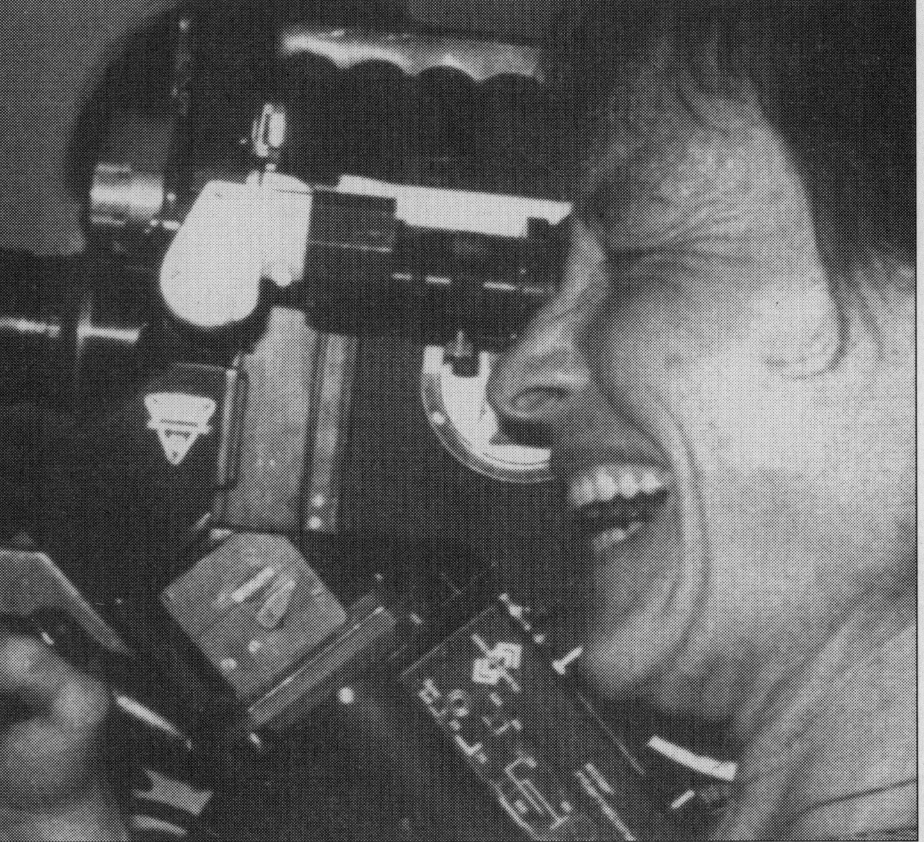

GUILTY pleasures

sci-fi on video

20 Million Miles to Earth
Ray Harryhausen is the original master of monster movie special effects. In this sci-fi thriller he manages to animate a gelatinous mass which escaped from a returning American rocketship.
VHS: S24134. $19.95.
Nathan Juran, USA, 1957, 82 mins.

Alien
Space explorers on a routine mission bring an extremely adaptable life form on board that attaches itself on crew members and reproduces itself. Most of the crew pay for the mistake with their lives. Notable special effects and relentless suspense from the director of *Blade Runner*. Screenplay by Dan O'Bannon.
VHS letterboxed.
VHS: S02337. $19.98.
Laser: LD72430. $49.98.
Ridley Scott, USA, 1979, 116 mins.

Alien Terror
Boris Karloff plays a deranged scientist who discovers a destructive form of energy that threatens the planet Earth and other solar systems. A galactic visitor seeks to destroy this energy and a violent battle is waged to possess the Alien Terror. 90 mins.
VHS: S09256. $9.98.

Alien Trilogy
All three of the *Alien* films are collected in this gift pack, including Ridley Scott's *Alien* (1979), about an alien presence on an expeditionary force; James Cameron's *Aliens* (1986); and David Fincher's *Alien3*, which finds Ripley (Sigourney Weaver) trapped on a penal colony with an interplanetary monster.
VHS: S19094. $49.98.
Ridley Scott/James Cameron/David Fincher, USA, 1979-92, 389 mins.

Alien3
The third entry of the baroque horror/science fiction series finds Lt. Ripley (Sigourney Weaver) the sole survivor of the previous mission, marooned on a lice-ridden, deep-space penal colony inhabited entirely by men, and acutely aware of a regenerated alien's presence. Letterboxed.
VHS: S17770. $19.98.
David Fincher, USA, 1992, 115 mins.

Aliens
An above-average sequel to the Ridley Scott film, this time featuring more thrills than chills. As if one alien weren't bad enough, a return to the infested planet provides the background for a violent confrontation between settlers and the large, futuristic cockroaches.
VHS: S12586. $19.98.
Laser: LD72431. $59.98.
James Cameron, USA, 1986, 138 mins.

Aliens, Dragons, Monsters & Me
Gary Owens and Eric Boardman host this program that features scenes from 13 of the screen's best loved fantasy films, including *King Kong, The 7th Voyage of Sinbad, Mysterious Island* and *Clash of the Titans*. Ray Harryhausen discusses his career and reveals trade secrets.
Laser: CLV. **LD71491. $34.95.**
Richard Jones, USA, 1991, 48 mins.

Andromeda Strain
A mysterious virus has wiped out a small town with the exception of one infant and an old drunk. Scientists want to know why as they race against time in a underground high security lab for the answers. With Arthur Hill, David Wayne, Kate Reid and James Olson. From the novel by Michael Crichton.
VHS: S07798. $19.98.
Robert Wise, USA, 1971, 130 mins.

The Arrival
Sci-fi/action veteran David Twohy *(The Fugitive)* wrote and directed this "science fiction thriller that will keep you on the edge of your seat" *(Los Angeles Times)*. Radio astronomer (Charlie Sheen) has been listening for years for cosmic noise in the middle of the night—an obsession that is the bane of his tough, successful girlfriend (Teri Polo, *Golden Gate*)—until his search for the explanation behind a shockwave from deep space takes him on a journey that makes him realize that an alien invasion might be closer than we think. "The extraterrestrial space ride of the year. Sci-fi at its chilling best" (Bonnie Churchill, *National News Syndicate*). Letterboxed.
VHS: S30509. $19.98.
David Twohy, USA, 1996, 109 mins.

Assignment Outer Space
Rick Von Nutter and Archie Savage star in this beautifully filmed sci-fi feature. The earth is threatened by an addled space ship's massive but haywire force field. Scientists try to save the earth, but Gabriella Farinon manages to distract them from their task just enough to generate suspense.
VHS: S23491. $29.95.
Antonio Margheriti, Italy, 1961, 79 mins.

The Astounding She-Monster
Classic B-movie thriller, with Robert Clarke tempted by a sexy alien she-creature with a deadly touch. Producer-director Ronnie Ashcroft's first feature guided by his mentor, Ed Wood, Jr., whose uncredited help gives this film that unmistakable "scent" of Wood. With Keene Duncan, Marilyn Harvey and Ewing Brown.
VHS: S32114. $19.95.
Ronnie Ashcroft, USA, 1958, 60 mins.

Atlantis, The Lost Continent
A camp science fiction classic from George Pal *(The Time Machine)* set on the mythical island that sank during a volcanic eruption. The story follows the heroic efforts of a fisherman to aid a beautiful young maiden. Adapted from Sir Gerald Hargreaves' play. Cinematography by Harold E. Wellman. With Anthony Hall, Joyce Taylor, John Dall and Edward Platt.
VHS: S19036. $19.98.
George Pal, USA, 1961, 91 mins.

The Atomic Man
Gene Nelson and Faith Domergue are featured in this sci-fi thriller about a living atomic bomb. A man is hauled to safety from the Thames and recognized by a reporter as a well-regarded nuclear physicist. There is only one problem however: the scientist appears to have a double in good health who is hard at work. Even stranger revelations ensue, and the fate of the planet is at risk.
VHS: S24019. $24.95.
Ken Hughes, Great Britain, 1955, 79 mins.

Atomic Submarine
A U.S. atomic sub heads for the north pole to investigate a series of oceanic disasters. There it discovers an underwater flying saucer piloted by an alien monster intent on conquering the world. A drive-in schlocker. With Dick Foran, Brett Halsey and Arthur Franz.
VHS: S32553. $24.95.
DVD: DV60328. $24.99.
Spencer Gordon Bennett, USA, 1960, 72 mins.

Attack from Mars
A blood-thirsty creature from Mars invades a Burbank theater in 1956. Starring legendary Robert Clarke and gorgeous Ann Robinson *(War of the Worlds)*. Mild nudity!
VHS: S32113. $19.95.

Battle for the Planet of the Apes
The fourth and final sequel, so far, to the famous talking ape series. Roddy McDowall returns as Caesar, the leader of the Simian revolution. He is all in favor of living in peace with the remaining humans, but apes like Claude Akins, John Huston, Paul Williams and Lew Ayres don't quite trust human mutants like Severn Darden.
VHS: S12175. $19.98.
J. Lee Thompson, USA, 1973, 86 mins.

The Beast from 20,000 Fathoms
Disturbed by A-bomb testing, a rhedosaurus from the North Pole wakes up from its sleep of ages and lets loose its full fury on New York. Based on a story by Ray Bradbury, this sci-fi film features masterful special effects by the legendary Ray Harryhausen *(Jason and the Argonauts)*.
VHS: S14286. $19.98.
Eugene Lourie, USA, 1953, 80 mins.

The Beast of Yucca Flats
Plan 9 alumni Tor Johnson and Conrad Brooks star in this uncut collector's edition. Johnson plays double roles as a noted Russian scientist carrying secret data of the Russian moon shot who escapes to the U.S. after his family has been killed by Communists, and the Beast he becomes after explosion of the H-Bomb, which burns the scientist and destroys his brain waves. Includes bonus *Misfit Control* trailer.
VHS: S31015. $29.95.
Coleman Francis, USA, 1966, 75 mins.

Beneath the Planet of the Apes
James Franciscus heads up a rescue ship to find out what happened to Charlton Heston and friends. He gets a similar shock and shoddy treatment by talking gorillas and orangutans and a little help from chimpanzees like Kim Hunter. The journey leads to the ruins of the New York subway system, where mutant humans worship the last nuclear weapon. With Linda Harrison, Victor Buono and Maurice Evans.
VHS: S12172. $19.98.
Ted Post, USA, 1970, 100 mins.

Beyond the Time Barrier
A jet pilot from the 20th century breaks through a time barrier in the sky and suddenly finds himself lost in an apocalyptic future. After a disastrous third world war, the Earth is menaced by mutants and a deadly virus. Robert Clarke and Darlene Thompkins star.
VHS: S23157. $29.95.
Edgar G. Ulmer, USA, 1959, 75 mins.

Bimbos B.C.
While hunting, a barbarian woman accidentally stumbles on the fortress of prehistoric bimbos. They are engaged in a desperate race against time. Their queen was bitten by a radioactive beast and now they must venture into the world in search of an antidote.
VHS: S24759. $9.95.
Todd Sheets, USA, 1992, 85 mins.

Blade Runner
A visually expressive adaptation of Philip K. Dick's futurist novel about Deckard (Harrison Ford), a cynical detective assigned to terminate a group of genetically devolved replicants set loose in Los Angeles, circa 2019. In this special director's cut, Deckard's voice-over narration is eliminated and the original ending is restored. With Rutger Hauer, Sean Young, Edward James Olmos and Daryl Hannah. VHS letterboxed.
VHS: S18596. $19.98.
Laser: LD71873. $39.99.
DVD: DV60107. $24.98.
Ridley Scott, USA, 1982, 117 mins.

Body Snatcher from Hell (Goke)
A Japanese airliner crashes in a remote area. Its survivors are menaced by horrible, blob-like monsters from outer space that slither into their victims' skulls, changing them into bloodthirsty vampires who prey on the other survivors. With Hideo Ko and Teruo Yoshida. Dubbed in English.
VHS: S32580. $24.95.
Hajime Sato, Japan, 1968, 83 mins.

Borrower
A twisted tale of an outer space alien who enjoys collecting the heads of foolish earthlings and wearing them in public. His first victim is Tom Towles, Henry's accomplice in murder. With Antonio Fargas, Don Gordon and Rae Dawn Chong as the disbelieving police detective on the track of this most unusual mass murderer. The very juicy special effects are not for the squeamish.
VHS: S14991. $14.95.
John McNaughton, USA, 1991, 97 mins.

A Boy and His Dog
This is a kinky sci-fi tale about a young man, Don Johnson, and his telepathic dog. While searching for food and sex in a destroyed world they happen upon an impotent group of survivors. This group drafts Johnson to father a new generation, but there is little pleasure to be found in their method. Also features Jason Robards and Tiger, the former *Brady Bunch* dog.
VHS: S25715. $29.95.
Laser: Widescreen. **LD75446. $49.95.**
DVD: DV60292. $29.95.
L.Q. Jones, USA, 1975, 87 mins.

The Brain Eaters
Ed Nelson produced and stars in this AIP science fiction thriller based on Robert A. Heinlein's *The Puppet Masters*. Citizens of a small mid-west town are being taken over by hairy parasites that come from beneath the Earth. Ed is out to stop them. Watch for Leonard Nimoy as a bearded old man. B&W.
VHS: S04094. $9.95.
Bruno VeSota, USA, 1958, 60 mins.

Brain from Planet Arous
John Agar stars in this freaky flick about a floating brain named Gor that invades his body and sets out to conquer Earth. Vol, a rival alien brain, borrows the body of Agar's dog to battle Gor and save the planet. Hosted by Elvira, Mistress of the Dark.
VHS: S13514. $19.95.
Nathan Juran, USA, 1958, 70 mins.

Cat Women of the Moon
3D thrills and chills as Moon Rocket 4 and its crew dodge menacing meteors before touching down on the moon's barren surface. In an underground cavern filled with giant, carnivorous spiders the crew discovers some subterranean sweeties dressed in black tights.
VHS: S14683. $12.95.
Arthur Hilton, USA, 1953, 64 mins.

A Century of Science-Fiction
Christopher Lee hosts this two-hour, star-studded program tracing the roots of science-fiction movies from marvelous trick films like *A Trip to the Moon* to mega-hits such as *The Day the Earth Stood Still, The Terminator, The Island of Dr. Moreau* and *Independence Day*. 120 mins.
VHS: S32418. $19.99.

Classic Sci-Fi Trailers Vol. 1
Movie trailers from some of the infamous sci-fi films from the 50's, including *Tarantula, Attack of the 50 Foot Women, Man from Planet X*, and *Enemy from Space*. Great camp fun!
VHS: S04097. $29.95.

A Clockwork Orange
An exploration of Stanley Kubrick's award-winning film with film historian William Everson, Anthony Burgess, the novel's author, and Malcolm McDowell, star of the film, examining the future-oriented story's mix of brutality and humor, its made-up language of Russian and English, its synthesized classical score, and its sex scenes, which almost threatened it with an "X" rating. 1972, 28 mins.
VHS: S31606. $59.95.

Colossus: The Forbin Project
Humanity faces extinction when the central U.S. defense computer finds common cause with its Soviet counterpart. As these machines grow together the world finds itself at their mercy. This sci-fi thriller is a tight adaptation of a novel by D.F. Jones.
VHS: S29949. $14.98.
Joseph Sargent, USA, 1970, 100 mins.

Conquest of the Planet of the Apes
The year is 1990. The intelligent chimp baby of Kim Hunter and Roddy McDowall grows up to look and sound just like his dad. When he feels his fellow primates are being mistreated, he leads an armed revolt against the human masters. With Don Murray, Ricardo Montalban, Nathalie Trundy and Severn Darden.
VHS: S12174. $19.98.
J. Lee Thompson, USA, 1972, 88 mins.

Contact
Jodie Foster and Matthew McConaughey star in this sci-fi journey to the heart of the universe from the Academy Award-winning director of *Forrest Gump* and Pulitzer Prize-winning author Carl Sagan. A scientist receives a dramatic message from deep space and instructions for building a machine that will either usher in a new age or Armageddon. VHS letterboxed.
VHS: S32661. $19.95.
Laser: LD76417. $39.95.
DVD: DV60038. $24.95.
Robert Zemeckis, USA, 1997, 150 mins.

Crash of the Moons
Two civilizations are threatened when their twin worlds head for a collision. Another Rocky Jones adventure featuring special effects, including a dynamite collision of planets. With Richard Crane, Sally Mansfield and Scotty Beckett.
VHS: S32543. $24.95.
Hollingsworth Morse, USA, 1953, 75 mins.

Crawling Eye
A hideous alien creature descends on the Earth in a cloud of radioactive fog, emerging to wreak havoc and terror as it mutilates and then possesses its helpless victims. Forrest Tucker and Janet Munro star.
VHS: S05672. $19.95.
Quentin Lawrence, Great Britain, 1958, 85 mins.

Dagora, the Space Monster
Dagora, an immense, pulsating cell from outer space, visits Japan in search of carbon, which it uses for energy. Rocket attacks cause multiplication. Real estate and diamond thieves are upset. Trucks, bridges and actors' careers are also damaged. Dubbed in English.
VHS: S05485. $29.95.
Inoshiro Honda, Japan, 1965, 80 mins.

Daredevils of the Red Circle
One of the finest serials of all time, the story of three circus stunt men pursuing a ruthless madman known as 39-0-13. Bent on destroying the wealth of millionaire Horace Granville, 39-0-13 imprisons him and assumes his identity in order to accomplish his evil deeds of destruction. 12-episode serial on two cassettes.
VHS: S11570. $29.95.
John English/William Witney, USA, 1938, 195 mins.

Dark City
In this futuristic sci-fi thriller from the director of *The Crow*, John Murdoch (Rufus Sewell) awakens in a strange hotel room to find that he is wanted for a series of brutal murders—only he can't remember a thing. Pursued by the police and haunted by The Strangers, mysterious beings with the ability to stop time and alter reality, he seeks to unravel the riddle of his identity. With Kiefer Sutherland, William Hurt and Jennifer Connelly.
VHS: S34703. $103.99.
Alex Proyas, USA, 1998, 100 mins.

Dark Star
A cult classic that began as a $6,000 project of a group of California students, *Dark Star* is an earth spaceship on a mission to find and destroy any planets likely to cause a supernova. Among the hilarious scenes is the ship's captain, dead, but preserved in cold storage, who talks baseball through electrodes in his head, while bombs which have intelligence threaten to end it all by exploding prematurely..
VHS: S00303. $19.95.
John Carpenter, USA, 1974, 91 mins.

Day of the Triffids
While much of the earth's population is blinded by a brilliant meteor shower, small plants called triffids undergo horrifying mutations causing them to grow, acquire mobility, and feed on humans. From John Wyndham's famed sci-fi/horror novel.
VHS: S00310. $19.95.
Steve Sekely, Great Britain, 1963, 94 mins.

The Day the Earth Caught Fire
Nuclear bombs are set off simultaneously at both ends of the globe. The result of these polar mishaps is that the Earth is knocked off course and begins a dangerous course, pulled by gravity towards the sun.
VHS: S29950. $9.98.
Val Guest, USA, 1962, 95 mins.

Day the Earth Froze
Nina Anderson, Jon Powers and Peter Sorenson are superb in this Finnish/Soviet fantasy epic. An evil witch steals the sun and causes nearly everything on the Earth to freeze. There are magic harps, fields of snakes, a wizard and even a magic mill in this singular film.
VHS: S23195. $29.95.
Gregg Sebelious, Finland/Russia, 1959, 67 mins.

The Day the Earth Stood Still
One of the first films to portray aliens from space as advanced saviors rather than menacing monsters. Michael Rennie stars as Klaatu. Intense, high production values and excellent casting with Patricia Neal and Sam Jaffe.
VHS: S02521. $14.98.
Robert Wise, USA, 1951, 92 mins.

The Deadly Mantis
A huge, freakish killer mantis with stunning capabilities to walk, run and fly is unleashed from a million-year deep freeze and terrorizes New York City.
VHS: S18703. $14.98.
Nathan Juran, USA, 1957, 78 mins.

Demolition Man
This sci-fi thriller and action adventure features Sylvester Stallone and Wesley Snipes. When a dangerous 20th century man is reanimated in the not-too distant future, the stage is set for a classic struggle between two men. They square off amidst a treasure trove of special effects and over-the-top, futuristic scenery.
VHS: S20682. $19.98.
Laser: LD72378. $34.98.
Marco Brambilla, USA, 1993, 115 mins.

Destination Moon
The first major sci-fi film in the U.S., the sets are ingenious and the film won an Academy Award for Special Effects. Co-scripted by Robert A. Heinlein from his novel *Rocketship Galileo*.
VHS: S00326. $19.95.
Irving Pichel, USA, 1950, 91 mins.

Devil Girl from Mars
A female Martian lands in England to recruit Earth males for the purposes of intergalactic breeding. She is accompanied by a robot companion that resembles a thin white toaster with a police-car light on top, only taller. With Hazel Court, Andrienne Corri and Hugh McDermott. B&W.
VHS: S18643. $19.95.
David MacDonald, Great Britain, 1954

The Doomsday Machine
The year is 1975. A spaceship is launched from the Earth on a mission to Venus. As it streaks through space, its passengers are horrified to see on their telescreen that Earth has been destroyed by a nuclear holocaust by the Red Chinese with a nuclear doomsday device. They then devise a plan to save what's left of the human race. An interesting and obscure American sci-fi thriller. With Grant Williams, Henry Wilcoxon, Denny Miller, Casey Kasem and Mala Powers.
VHS: S32563. $24.95.
Lee Sholem, USA, 1967, 80 mins.

Dr. Cyclops
Set in the Peruvian jungle, this 1940 landmark science-fiction adventure follows four explorers as they search for legendary physicist Dr. Cyclops. When they discover their missing colleague, they find his brilliant mind warped by radiation. But the half-blind, half-mad scientist uses an experimental body-altering device to reduce his former friends to one-fifth their normal size. Just terrific.
VHS: S10110. $14.98.
Ernest B. Schoedsack, USA, 1940, 76 mins.

Earth vs. the Flying Saucers
Aliens land at a U.S. Army base seeking help for their dying planet, but are greeted with gunfire by the paranoid armed forces. The aliens are forced to retaliate, which pits earthlings vs. humanoids in a fight for earth's survival. With great early special effects by Ray Harryhausen.
VHS: S03560. $19.98.
Laser: Includes interview with Ray Harryhausen. **LD75042. $34.95.**
Fred F. Sears, USA, 1956, 83 mins.

Earth vs. the Spider
A monster spider attacks and traps two teenagers in a large cave web. With June Kenney, Edward Kramer, Gene Roth and Mickey Finn.
VHS: S16411. $29.95.
Bert I. Gordon, USA, 1958, 75 mins.

The Electronic Monster (Escapement)
A mad scientist conducts sinister experiments on people with a mind-altering, electronic brain machine. Terrific dream sequences are the highlight of this unusual British sci-fi movie. With Rod Cameron, Mary Murphy, Meredith Edwards and Peter Illing.
VHS: S32546. $24.95.
Montgomery Tully, Great Britain, 1957, 77 mins.

Escape from New York

This science fiction film casts a new spin on getting out of the Big Apple. New York is a giant prison where ruthless gangs rule. It's an apocalyptic vision that at times comes close to the violent reality that exists in big cities today. Starring Kurt Russel and Adrienne Barbieau, with Ernest Borgnine, Isaac Hayes and Donald Pleasance.

VHS: S20926. $19.95.

Laser: Letterboxed, special edition includes interview with John Carpenter, trailer and never-before-seen footage. **LD74465. $49.99.**

John Carpenter, USA, 1981, 99 mins.

Escape from the Planet of the Apes

Chimpanzee scientists Kim Hunter, Roddy McDowall and Sal Mineo use Charlton Heston's spaceship to return to the year 1973. When the human military brass considers them a threat to national security, they find refuge in Ricardo Montalban's circus. With Bradford Dillman, Jason Evers, Eric Braeden and William Windom. Mineo's last movie before he was murdered.

VHS: S12173. $19.98.

J. Lee Thompson, USA, 1972, 88 mins.

F.P. 1 Doesn't Answer

One of the earliest science fiction films. F.P. 1 is a gigantic, floating platform used as a mid-Atlantic airfield to allow planes to refuel on their long, Euro-American flights. When the platform cannot be reached by either telephone or cable, sabotage is suspected. Help arrives to find the crew gassed and the platform in immediate danger of being destroyed. English version. With Conrad Veidt, Jill Esmond.

VHS: S10000. $29.95.

Karl Hartl, Germany, 1932, 74 mins.

Fantastic Puppet People

A mad dollmaker invents a shrinking machine that reduces people to a few inches in size. He's a lonely wacko who keeps his victims in small glass tubes, taking them out occasionally to ward off the emotional strains of his solitude. John Agar, himself miniaturized, rallies the other victims against their giant captor. A drive-in classic. With June Kenney and John Hoyt.

VHS: S32549. $24.95.

Bert I. Gordon, USA, 1958, 79 mins.

The Fantastic Voyage

The cult science fiction thriller in which a team of doctors are miniaturized and set inside the body to operate on the blood clot of a scientist. With Stephen Boyd, Raquel Welch, Donald Pleasance and Arthur Kennedy.

VHS: S30661. $14.98.

Richard Fleischer, USA, 1966, 100 mins.

The Fifth Element

In this haute couture-designed, futuristic tour-de-force from Luc Besson, Bruce Willis stars as a cab driver who becomes an unsuspecting hero when he picks up the kind of fare that only comes along every 5000 years: a perfect being, a perfect beauty, a perfect weapon (Milla Jovovich). Together they must save the world. The most expensive French film in history. With Gary Oldman, Chris Tucker and fashions by Gautier. In English.

VHS: S32390. $19.95.

Laser: LD76371. $39.95.

DVD: DV60158. $24.98.

Luc Besson, France/USA, 1997, 126 mins.

First Men in the Moon

A flamboyant adaptation of H.G. Wells's novel about the first settlers in space and their battles with giant warrior ants for control of the moon. Ray Harryhausen did the special visual effects. With Edward Judd, Martha Hyer, Lionel Jeffries, and Erik Chitty.

VHS: S16681. $14.95.

Laser: Widescreen. **LD74632. $34.95.**

Nathan Juran, Great Britain, 1964, 103 mins.

Flash Gordon—Rocketship

The first screen version about Flash Gordon and his adventures on the planet Mongo. Features condensations from the classic serial. With Buster Crabbe, Jean Rogers and Charles Middleton.

VHS: S34479. $29.95.

Frederick Stephani, USA, 1936, 97 mins.

Flight to Mars

Academy Award-winning producer Walter Mirisch presents the first color cinematic journey to Mars in the weird hues of Cinecolor. Starring Arthur Franz, Cameron Mitchell and Marguerite Chapman.

VHS: S32110. $19.95.

Leslie Selander, USA, 1951, 71 mins.

Flying Saucer

The first movie about UFOs, this classic sci-fi thriller allegedly had to be viewed by the FBI prior to its release. Mikel Conrad stars in his own story as a special agent sent to Alaska, where he finds a flying saucer and diabolical Communist scientists. Denver Pyle gets mixed up in the extraterrestrial adventure on the frozen frontier.

VHS: S12385. $19.95.

Mikel Conrad, USA, 1950, 70 mins.

Forbidden Moon

More outer space thrills as a mysterious planetoid is the setting for this science fiction adventure featuring Rocky Jones. With Richard Crane and Sally Mansfield.

VHS: S32544. $24.95.

USA, 1953, 75 mins.

Forbidden Planet

Nervy, funny and very clever science fiction adaptation of Shakespeare's final play, *The Tempest*, set in the year 2200, about a group of space explorers investigating a previous space flight who encounter an embittered expatriate creating his own society on the abandoned planet with his beautiful daughter and trustworthy robot. Beautiful widescreen photography by George Folsey. With Walter Pidgeon, Anne Francis, Leslie Nielsen and Warren Stevens. Available in two versions, a widescreen from Criterion and letterbox from MGM.

VHS: S00458. $14.98.

Laser: CAV, widescreen, Criterion. **LD70989. $99.95.**

Laser: CLV, deluxe widescreen, MGM. **LD70186. $34.95.**

DVD: DV60109. $24.98.

Fred M. Wilcox, USA, 1956, 98 mins.

Gamera

The creature is a jet-powered superturtle reawakened by a nuclear explosion; the turtle wreaks havoc and forces the Army to unleash 'Plan Z.' 79 mins.

VHS: S17540. $9.99.

Gamera vs. Barugon

The jet-powered superturtle Gamera must confront Barugon, a gigantic horned dinosaur hatched from a huge opal, whose horns spew a devastating "rainbow ray."

VHS: S17541. $9.99.

Shigeo Tanaka/Noriaki Yuasa, Japan, 1966, 101 mins.

Gamera vs. Gaos

Gaos, a huge, prehistoric vampire bat, is conjured from an explosion and battles the jet-powered, superturtle Gamera.

VHS: S17542. $9.99.

Noriaki Yuasa, Japan, 1967, 87 mins.

Gamera vs. Guiron

The jet-powered, superturtle Gamera is summoned to outer space when a team of aliens, led by the gigantic, knife-nosed Guiron, abducts a pair of Earth children.

VHS: S17544. $9.99.

Noriaki Yuasa, Japan, 1969, 82 mins.

Gamera vs. Zigra

A giant, alien shark monster descends on the Earth with the intention of conquering the world, though he didn't count on the appearance of the jet-powered, superturtle Gamera.

VHS: S17543. $9.99.

Noriaki Yuasa, Japan, 1971, 90 mins.

Gattaca

In the genetically engineered world of Gattaca, children are born with perfect health, a high IQ and a long lifespan. The bioformed have inherited the earth, and babies who are born naturally become menial laborers, like space center cleaner Vincent (Ethan Hawke). Determined to become a crew member on a Saturn moon expedition, Vincent fights back by borrowing DNA from the paralyzed, but gene-perfect Jerome (Jude Law). With Uma Thurman, Alan Arkin, Tony Shalboub, Gore Vidal, Loren Dean and Ernest Borgnine. "One of the smartest and most provocative of science fiction films, a thriller with ideas" (Roger Ebert, *Chicago Sun-Times*).

VHS: S33955. $104.99.

Andrew Niccol, USA, 1997, 106 mins.

Geisha Girl

William Andrews, Martha Hyer and Archer MacDonald are featured in this nearly forgotten sci-fi gem. A mad scientist invents small explosive pills. When he and his Japanese cohorts utterly destroy a small Pacific isle, their dreams of world domination seem assured. That is, until two wacky American G.I.'s find themselves burdened with the pills. Soon mentalists and spies are trying to help them, but they are happily hiding out in a geisha house.

VHS: S23154. $29.95.

George Breakston, USA, 1952, 67 mins.

Ghidrah the 3-Headed Monster

The all-time great Japanese monster rally: bad monster Ghidrah is pitted against three popular creatures: Godzilla, the fire-breathing reptile; Mothra, the B-52 scaled moth; and Rodan, the mega-pterodactyl. English dialog.

VHS: S00496. $19.95.

Inoshiro Honda, Japan, 1965, 85 mins.

The Giant Behemoth

A rampaging, radioactive brontosaurus menaces England and invades London. With Gene Evans, Andre Morell, John Turner, Leigh Madison, Jack MacGowran and great stop-motion effects by Willis *(King Kong)* O'Brien.

VHS: S31279. $14.95.

Eugene Lourie, Great Britain, 1959, 80 mins.

Giant of Metropolis

A weird, very atmospheric sci-fi adventure. An ancient, scientific super-city is the setting where a mad ruler becomes involved with strange experiments, torture and court intrigue. An "Atlantis"-styled cataclysmic climax. With Gordon Mitchell and Bella Cortez. Dubbed in English.

VHS: S32557. $24.95.

Umberto Scarpelli, Italy, 1961, 82 mins.

The Gifted

This sci-fi thriller follows a black southern family with a special gift. Their supernatural abilities were transported from Africa but possess otherworldly sources. Now they have been discovered by an enemy alien force. A West African king is determined to join his family in America so that The Gifted will not be destroyed.

VHS: S24530. $69.95.

Audrey King Lewis, USA, 1993, 101 mins.

Girl in His Pocket

Jean Marais, Genevieve Page and Jean Claude Brialy star in this unique, French sci-fi adventure. An eccentric scientist discovers a method for shrinking people. He uses his girlfriend as a guinea pig with somewhat comical results.

VHS: S23156. $29.95.

Pierre Kast, France, 1957, 82 mins.

Glen or Randa

A desperate odyssey by the last survivors of an atomic holocaust through the wreckage of a vanished civilization, called "one of the best and most original American films of the year" *(Time)*.

VHS: S00504. $19.95.

Jim McBride, USA, 1971, 94 mins.

Godzilla 1985

Japan's most famous export returns to face his old nemesis. Starring Raymond Burr. Also includes the animated film short *Bambi vs. Godzilla*.

VHS: S32280. $9.99.

Kohji Hashimoto, Japan, 1985, 91 mins.

Godzilla 5-Pack

Oh no, there goes Tokyo. Experience the legend of Godzilla with five classics from the first *Godzilla* director. Spanning 20 years of monstrous destruction, this gargantuan five-pack includes *Godzilla: King of the Monsters, Godzilla Versus Mothra, Godzilla's Revenge, The Terror of Mechagodzilla* and *Godzilla Versus Monster Zero*. All cheesily dubbed in English. With bonus video art gallery, *Godzilla* trailer collection and sci-fi monsters documentary.

VHS: S34638. $59.95.

Inoshiro Honda, Japan, 1954/1964/1965/1969/1975, 538 mins.

Godzilla vs. Biollante

A return of the monster who's been reawakened and threatens world peace and stability. The larger community responds with Biollante, a genetically engineered plant form who feeds off Godzilla. English dubbed.

VHS: S17709. $19.95.

Laser: LD75199. $34.98.

Kazuki Omori, Japan, 1989, 104 mins.

Godzilla vs. Gigan
Alien monsters from outer space threaten to destroy mankind. The evil Gigan and King Ghidrah have been summoned from outer space and mankind is powerless against their vicious wave of destruction. Soon an earth-shattering death struggle rocks Tokyo as Godzilla and Anguiras go head-to-head with the monsters in a ferocious battle.
VHS: S32520. $9.99.
Jun Fukuda, Japan, 1972, 89 mins.

Godzilla vs. Mechagodzilla
Godzilla battles his mechanical double. Controlled by evil space invaders, Mechagodzilla rises from the sea and begins a ferocious rampage of death and destruction. Has Godzilla met his match?
VHS: S32521. $9.99.
Jun Fukuda, Japan, 1974, 84 mins.

Godzilla vs. Megalon
Once the city's nemesis, the fearsome giant reptile becomes Tokyo's defender when, aided by robot buddy Jet Jaguar, he exterminates Megalon, a giant cockroach, and Gigan, a flying mechanical monster, to save Tokyo and the world.
VHS: S32279. $29.95.
Jun Fukuda, Japan, 1976, 80 mins.

Godzilla vs. Monster Zero
A ferocious monster called Ghidra is menacing Planet X. Godzilla and Rodan are recruited to combat this terror. In return they expect help back home on Earth, but suspicious acting aliens may well have other unforseen plans. Letterboxed. Dubbed in English.
VHS: S25028. $14.95.
Laser: LD76956. $39.99.
Inoshiro Honda, Japan, 1970, 93 mins.

Godzilla vs. Mothra
Radiation is once again wreaking havoc in the natural environment. A radioactive egg leads to a mammoth caterpillar and only Godzilla is big enough to do battle with the segmented worm. It's a race against time because as everyone knows caterpillars turn into big mean moths. VHS letterboxed. Dubbed in English.
VHS: S25027. $14.95.
Laser: LD75200. $39.95.
Inoshiro Honda, Japan, 1964, 88 mins.

Godzilla vs. the Sea Monster
Godzilla teams up with former nemesis Mothra, the giant moth, and together they take on Ebirah, a giant lobster unleashed by a totalitarian regime.
VHS: S32277. $29.95.
Jun Fukuda, Japan, 1966, 80 mins.

Godzilla's Revenge
Director Inoshiro Honda's continuation of the *Godzilla* saga takes on an aggressive psychological subtext, tapping into a lonely child's dream patterns and associations built around Godzilla's own child and other monsters. "Good juvenile science fiction" (Leonard Maltin). VHS letterboxed.
VHS: S16894. $9.95.
Laser: LD75201. $39.95.
Inoshiro Honda, Japan, 1971, 70 mins.

Godzilla, King of the Monsters
Raymond Burr stars in this remake of the original Japanese classic. Godzilla is awakened by an atomic blast and all of Tokyo watches his antics in terror. Burr acts as narrator, intercut with the hysterically primitive special effects.
VHS: S25030. $14.95.
Laser: Widescreen. **LD76955. $39.99.**
Inoshiro Honda, Japan/USA, 1956, 79 mins.

Gorgo
A volcanic eruption in the North Atlantic brings to the surface a 65-foot prehistoric monster. Two treasure divers capture the creature and take him to London where he is put on display in a circus. But the creature is only an infant, and soon his mother comes thundering ashore to reclaim her offspring, trashing a generous portion of London in the process. A fun sci-fi story with exciting special effects.
VHS: S09519. $19.95.
Eugene Lourie, Great Britain, 1961, 76 mins.

H.G. Wells' First Men in the Moon
Academy-Award winner Ray Harryhausen created the special effects for this sci-fi adventure starring Edward Judd and Martha Hyer. The terrible creatures of Wells' imagination come to life in this widescreen, deluxe presentation. Peter Finch makes a cameo appearance.
Laser: LD74546. $34.95.
Nathan Juran, USA, 1964, 103 mins.

Hardware Wars
The Farce is back with this cult spoof on *Star Wars*, featuring the adventures of cosmic hero Fluke Starbucker, galactic boy wonder; Princess Anne-Droid; Ham Salad, intergalactic wise guy; robots 4-Q-2 and Artie Deco; Chewchilla, the Wookie Monster; and Augie "Ben" Doggie. A space saga of romance, rebellion and household appliances. Special Edition includes 20 new computer-generated "special defects." 20 mins.
VHS: S33745. $9.99.
Ernie Fosselius, USA, 1977, 20 mins.

The Hidden
Michael Nouri and Kyle MacLachlin star in this suspenseful crime film featuring an extraterrestrial plot. Bizarre and inexplicable robberies and murders leave the L.A. police totally baffled until an FBI agent imparts a startling fact. A demonic creature from outer space is invading ordinary citizens and turning them into extraordinary killers. This sci-fi classic is joined with a second tape containing original trailers, unused footage, and new special effects footage.
VHS: S27856. $14.95.
Laser: Widescreen. **LD75948. $69.95.**
Jack Sholder, USA, 1990, 117 mins.

The High Crusade
In this high-tech science fiction fantasy set on the eve of the crusades, all good English knights are preparing to march on Jerusalem when an alien spaceship lands before them. Unimpressed by the aliens' high-tech weapons, the knights storm the spaceship and order a hostage to fly the craft to the Holy Land in order to put the fear of God into the heathens. The knights are in for a surprise when the hostage switches the automatic pilot to return home. With John Rice Davies.
VHS: S32607. $89.98.
Klaus Knoesel, Great Britain, 1996, 90 mins.

Humanoids from the Deep (Monster)
Vic Morrow and Doug McClure star in this gory sci-fi thriller about humanoid salmon-like ecological mutants that terrorize a sleepy fishing village and bother bikinied women.
VHS: S28613. $14.98.
Laser: LD76177. $39.99.
Barbara Peeters, USA, 1980, 81 mins.

I Married a Monster from Outer Space
Monster-like aliens from another planet inhabit the bodies of people in a small town in hopes of having children with Earth women. Tom Tyron stars as one of these very monsters married to Gloria Talbott.
VHS: S00598. $49.95.
Gene Fowler Jr., USA, 1958, 78 mins.

I Worship His Shadow
This interplanetary action film tells the story of the conflict between the dark forces of "His Shadow" and a daredevil band of intergalactic rebels. What begins as a simple act of defiance soon ignites into the ultimate sci-fi battle with the fate of the galaxy hanging in the balance. With Barry Bostwick and Michael McManus.
VHS: S32630. $92.99.
Paul Donovan, Canada, 1995, 94 mins.

Idaho Transfer
Peter Fonda *(The Hired Hand)* directed this little seen environmental futuristic drama set in the year 2044. A team of young scientists from the present day arrive and discover an ecological nightmare. A chilling study of survival and responsibility. With Keith Carradine, Kelley Bohanan, Kevin Hearst and Caroline Hildebrand.
VHS: S09849. $29.98.
Peter Fonda, USA, 1973, 90 mins.

The Illustrated Man
Based on the Ray Bradbury story, Rod Steiger stars as a man whose body paints pictures of horrors to come. With Claire Bloom.
VHS: S00609. $19.98.
Jack Smight, USA, 1969, 103 mins.

In the Mouth of Madness
A masterful tale of terror starring Sam Neill, this film is an homage to the great sci-fi/horror writer H.P. Lovecraft. It begins in an asylum where a madman awaits the end of mankind at the hands of monstrous demons. He thought it was just a story, but that was only what it appeared to be. Charlton Heston has a cameo.
VHS: S25659. $19.95.
Laser: LD75017. $39.99.
John Carpenter, USA, 1995, 95 mins.

The Incredible Melting Man
The sole surviving member of a doomed space mission returns to Earth, only to find that he has been transformed into "The Incredible Melting Man". This horror classic is unforgettable, with gory make-up supplied by Rick Baker.
VHS: S20928. $14.98.
William Sachs, USA, 1978, 86 mind.

The Incredible Petrified World
John Carradine, Robert Clarke and Phyllis Coates star in this underwater sci-fi adventure. Placed in a special diving bell, a crew is off to explore the ocean floor. Unexpectedly, the cable snaps and they are left to fend for themselves amid a strange series of caves that no one ever imagined possible.
VHS: S24068. $19.95.
Jerry Warren, USA, 1957, 67 mins.

Incredible Shrinking Man
One of the best American science fiction films of the 1950's. Grant Williams and Randy Stuart star in the story of an ordinary businessman who encounters a radioactive mist during a boating trip, and finds his growth process suddenly reversed; in two weeks, he's two inches tall. Terrifying.
VHS: S06556. $14.98.
Jack Arnold, USA, 1957, 81 mins.

Independence Day
One of the biggest box office hits of all time, this all-star, special effects extravaganza delivers the ultimate encounter when mysterious and powerful aliens launch an all-out invasion against the human race. When massive spaceships begin fire-blasting cities all over the planet, the world's fate lies in the hands of a determined band of survivors who unite to strike against the invaders. Stars Will Smith, Bill Pullman, Jeff Goldblum, Mary McDonnell, Judd Hirsch, Margaret Colin, Randy Quaid, Robert Loggia, Harvey Fierstein, Harry Connick, Jr., Viveca Fox and Brent Spiner. Letterboxed.
VHS: S30056. $22.98.
Roland Emmerich, USA, 1996, 145 mins.

Invaders from Mars (1953)
One of the definitive "Cold War" sci-fi films, laced with paranoia, in which no one believes a little boy that aliens have landed until the invaders begin to control the town's inhabitants. A surrealistic nightmare.
VHS: S00632. $19.95.
Laser: LD72257. $54.95.
William Cameron, USA, 1953, 78 mins.

Invaders from Mars (1986)
Remake of the classic 1953 McCarthy era sci-fi film, this from the director of *Poltergeist* and *Texas Chainsaw Massacre*. With Timothy Bottoms, Laraine Newman, Louise Fletcher and Karen Black. Special effects by John Dykstra *(Star Wars)*.
VHS: S02000. $19.95.
Tobe Hooper, USA, 1986, 102 mins.

Invasion of the Body Snatchers (1956)
The great Cold War classic. A small American town is taken over by an alien force which turns everyone into a zombie. Kevin McCarthy and Dana Wynter star.
VHS: S00633. $19.95.
Laser: CAV, widescreen. **LD70384. $79.95.**
Laser: CLV, widescreen. **LD70385. $49.95.**
DVD: DV60275. $24.95.
Don Siegel, USA, 1956, 80 mins.

Invasion of the Body Snatchers (1978)
Intriguing remake of the Don Siegel classic stars Donald Sutherland and Brooke Adams, with cameos by Siegal and original star Kevin McCarthy.
VHS: S02355. $14.95.
DVD: DV60213. $24.98.
Philip Kaufman, USA, 1978, 115 mins.

The Invisible Boy
The robot from *Forbidden Planet*, Robby falls under the control of an alien superhuman computer intent on world domination. A scientist enlists his ten-year-old son with a mysterious potion that renders him invisible to regain the robot's independence. With Richard Eyer and Philip Abbott.
VHS: S19134. $19.98.
Laser: LD76318. $39.99.
Hermann Hoffman, USA, 1957, 89 mins.

Invisible Dr. Mabuse (The Invisible Horror)
Lex Barker, Karin Dor and Wolfgang Preiss star in this stellar example from the sci-fi series featuring the maniacal German Doctor. Barker is an American detective who has a serious problem. He must find the fiend even though he has concocted a formula for invisibility.
VHS: S23159. $29.95.
Harald Reinl, Germany, 1962, 89 mins.

Invisible Invaders

John Carradine and John Agar are featured in this horror film about space creatures. Aliens find human corpses the perfect vessels for their invasion of earth. Before long a beleaguered group of scientists are the world's only hope against their onslaught.
VHS: S27752. $14.95.
Edward L. Cahn, USA, 1959, 67 mins.

It Came from Beneath the Sea

The action is wet and wild in this riveting sci-fi thriller, featuring extraordinary special effects by Ray Harryhausen. Submarine commander Kenneth Tobey and scientists Faith Domergue and Donald Curtis battle an angry sea monster driven from the depths by an H-bomb.
VHS: S13001. $9.95.
Robert Gordon, USA, 1955, 80 mins.

It Came from Beneath the Sea/ 20 Million Miles to Earth

A giant octopus vents its wrath on the city of San Francisco. Kenneth Tobey and Faith Domergue star in the first horror film of this double feature. Ray Harryhausen, the famed special effects animator, joined Charles H. Schneer for their first of many joint efforts. The second feature depicts the rampages of a Venusian monster in the streets of Rome. William Hopper and Joan Taylor star and Ray Harryhausen did the special effects.
Laser: LD74588. $59.95.
Jack Arnold/Nathan Juran, USA, 1953-1957, 79-82 mins.

It Came from Outer Space

Originally shown in 3-D, this classic science fiction adventure was based on a short story by Ray Bradbury. Richard Carlson stars as an astronomer who thinks there is more to the meteor that fell in the desert than meets the eye. With Barbara Rush, Morey Amsterdam and Russell Johnson. B&W.
VHS: S05525. $14.98.
Jack Arnold, USA, 1953, 81 mins.

It! The Terror from Beyond Space

The tension steadily mounts as a space crew tries everything in their power to destroy an alien monster. The climactic scene was described by the *Citizen News* as "fraught with suspense and excitement."
VHS: S14959. $14.95.
Edward L. Cahn, USA, 1958, 70 mins.

Journey Beneath the Desert (L'Atlantide)

George Riviere and Jean-Louis Trintignant are featured in this sci-fi fantasy. Three lost aviators discover the entrance to Atlantis at a nuclear blast site in the desert. They face countless perils and are forced to confront an evil Queen.
VHS: S23158. $29.95.
Edgar G. Ulmer, France, 1961, 105 mins.

Journey to the Center of Time

This science fiction adventure weaves back and forth in time, forcing the protagonists to confront age-old enemies and unheard of and unimagined atrocities from the future. It's a roller coaster of terror through time.
VHS: S21559. $24.95.
David L. Hewitt, USA, 1967, 80 mins.

Journey to the Far Side of the Sun

When scientists a hundred years into the future discover a duplicate Earth on the far side of the sun, the stage is set for science fiction and suspense in an entertaining science fiction film which stars Roy Thinnes and Ian Hendry.
VHS: S06923. $19.98.
DVD: DV60346. $24.99.
Robert Parrish, Great Britain, 1969, 99 mins.

King Kong vs. Godzilla

Before Tyson met Spinks, before Rocky met Apollo, these two heavyweights were using Japan as their own private arena. Watch for the battle royale atop Mt. Fuji. See Kong warm up on a giant octopus. Witness Godzilla, in color for the first time, break out of a frozen iceberg and tackle a nuclear sub. With Mie Hama, James Jagi and Michael Keith as the UN reporter.
VHS: S10378. $19.95.
Inoshiro Honda, Japan/USA, 1962, 90 mins.

Kronos

A titanic robot is sent from another world to steal energy from Earth and destroy it. Even when attacked with H-bombs, the cyborg simply absorbs the blasts, growing more powerful. Can Earth survive? With Jeff Morrow, Barbara Lawrence, John Emery and Morris Ankrum. Presented for the first time in letterbox format.
VHS: S32112. $19.95.
Kurt Neumann, USA, 1957, 78 mins.

Krull

This widescreen, deluxe Dolby presentation reveals the epic fantasy of the original film. A young prince tries to rescue his bride from the evil Beast in this sci-fi action adventure. With Ken Marshall and Lysette Anthony.
Laser: LD74544. $39.95.
Peter Yates, USA, 1983, 122 mins.

The Land Unknown

Underneath the tundra of Antarctica there lies a surprise landscape untouched since prehistoric times. Jock Mahoney and Shawn Smith are part of a naval expedition that is marooned in this place where dinosaurs still prevail.
VHS: S20891. $14.98.
Virgil W. Vogel, USA, 1957, 79 mins.

Last Days of Planet Earth

Doomsday is at hand. There are radioactive clouds and mutant bats overhead while on the ground giant slugs leave trails of slime behind them. Dubbed in English. 88 mins.
VHS: S25031. $19.95.
Laser: LD75218. $34.98.

The Lawnmower Man

A controversial and highly debated science fiction work taken from a short story by Stephen King about a brilliant scientist (Pierce Brosnan) who wants to experiment his revolutionary Virtual Reality system on a gardener, the Lawnmower Man (Jeff Fahey). He is thwarted by sinister underworld forces who want to get their hands on the system. With Jenny Wright and Geoffrey Lewis. This is the unrated director's cut with additional footage. VHS: Out of print. For rental only.
Laser: THX. **LD76006. $59.95.**
Brett Leonard, USA, 1992, 108 mins.

Lost Continent

While searching for a lost atomic-powered rocket, Cesar Romero encounters a land of prehistoric nightmares. This world of weird greenish hue is inhabited by dinosaurs and prehistoric beasts in this sci-fi classic.
VHS: S13061. $19.95.
Sam Newfield, USA, 1951, 86 mins.

The Lost World

Irwin Allen's early special effects trailblazer stars Claude Rains as Professor Challenger, who leads a team of scientists to a remote Amazonian jungle to investigate reports that dinosaurs still live there. With Michael Rennie and Jill St. John.
VHS: S34566. $14.95.
Irwin Allen, USA, 1960, 97 mins.

Marooned

Three astronauts are stranded in space and a rescue mission goes under way in this 60's sci-fi thriller. "It has all the zip, zest and zing of a moon walk, and I suspect a computer-fed dictionary could come up with better dialogue," said Judith Crist.
VHS: S00828. $19.95.
Laser: widescreen. **LD75045. $39.95.**
John Sturges, USA, 1969, 130 mins.

Mars Needs Women

It's a blunt and horrifying idea: Mars needs women. Five Martians invade the Earth to find mates for their dying planet. They are not planning long and thoughtful courtships for their prospective brides. A science fiction classic.
VHS: S20930. $14.98.
Laser: LD76085. $39.99.
Larry Buchanan, USA, 1968, 80 mins.

Martian Chronicles, Volumes 1-3

Based on Ray Bradbury's famous novel. Rock Hudson, Bernie Casey and Gayle Hunnicutt star. In *Martian Chronicles, Volume 1*, a clash develops between the Earth colonists and the highly evolved, telepathic Martian natives. Then, in *Martian Chronicles, Volume 2*, the peaceful but powerful race of Martians try to protect their planet from the invading Earth colonists. Finally, in *Martian Chronicles, Volume 3*, the powerful conclusion of Bradbury's epic, the Earth colonists discover the essence of the Martians' power. USA, 1979, 360 mins.
VHS: S04411. $14.95.

Martian Chronicles Series

Contains the complete three-volume set of *Martian Chronicles*.
Laser: LD71130. $99.95.

Master of the World

Richard Matheson wrote the screenplay by adapting two Jules Verne stories, giving Vincent Price, Charles Bronson and Henry Hull a science fiction film worthy of their talents. Bronson must stop the ingenious scientist, played by Price, from becoming master of the world.
VHS: S20933. $14.98.
William Witney, USA, 1961, 104 mins.

Mesa of Lost Women

Allan Nixon and Jackie Coogan find themselves cast in this strange feature about the terrors of a new race of vicious women. A group of people crash land on a desert mesa where a mad scientist is crossing women with giant spiders.
VHS: S23155. $29.95.
Ron Ormond, USA, 1952, 70 mins.

Missile to the Moon

Elvira hosts this hair-raising adventure into the unknown in a camp remake of the classic *Cat Women on the Moon*.
VHS: S12858. $19.95.
Richard Cunha, USA, 1959, 78 mins.

Mission Stardust

A rare '60s sci-fi odyssey. A space hero, backed by a team of astronauts, heads to the moon to rescue a blonde alien babe who is desperately seeking the aid of a blood scientist to help save her dying race. Space thrills abound as our heroes fight off a marauding force of renegade robots. With Lang Jeffries, John Karlsen and Essy Persson. Dubbed in English.
VHS: S32565. $24.95.
Primo Zegio, Italy/Spain/Germany, 1967, 95 mins.

The Mole People

During an expedition in Asia, three archaeologists discover a subterranean group of albino Sumerians who avoid light and enslave mutant mole men. With John Agar, Cynthia Patric and Hugh Beaumont.
VHS: S18701. $14.98.
Virgil W. Vogel, USA, 1956, 78 mins.

The Monolith Monsters

In this science fiction classic, meteor fragments strewn across the desert grow when they come into contact with water. Geologist Grant Williams and professor Trevor Bardette must stop this stone-cold terror before it envelops the planet.
VHS: S20895. $14.98.
John Sherwood, USA, 1957, 78 mins.

Monster from a Prehistoric Planet

Do you have a yen for large destructive monsters that invade Japan? This time prepare yourself for Gappa the Tripibian, a big reptile bird on display in Tokyo. The trouble really starts when the big bird is found out to be the baby in the family and boy, are his parents steamed!
VHS: S10995. $19.98.
Haruyasu Noguchi, Japan, 1967

The Monster That Challenged the World

In the aftermath of an earthquake, a giant caterpillar awakens and spawns one murderous offspring. The massive creature terrorizes coastal California communities and the Navy must find the means to prevent their spread. With Tim Holt, Audrey Dalton, Hans Conried and Milton Parsons.
VHS: S19135. $14.95.
Laser: Three-disk boxed set. **LD74589. $99.98.**
Arnold Laven, USA, 1957, 83 mins.

Morons from Outer Space

An engaging satire that explodes the myth of higher life forms. A group of stupid aliens with British accents crash land on Earth; the physical comedy is well played by Mel Smith, Griff Rhys Jones and Dinsdale Landen.
VHS: S00883. $14.95.
Mike Hodges, Great Britain, 1985, 87 mins.

Mothra

First class trick photography in this monster film about the giant beast that threatens the Earth. English dubbed.
VHS: S01587. $19.95.
Inoshiro Honda, Japan, 1961, 99 mins.

Multiple Futures

Taylor Mead and Holly Adams are featured in this trio of sci-fi spoofs. Whether poking fun at consumer fashion madness, overpopulation, or even AIDS hysteria, these three worst-case-future scenarios finally put sci-fi seriousness to the ultimate test of satire. 108 mins.
VHS: S26089. $59.95.

Night of the Blood Beast

A spaceship returns to Earth carrying an astronaut who's been impregnated with alien embryos. Also on board is a horrible alien monster that terrorizes a group of research scientists in their mountain laboratory. This movie is great fun in the purest late-'50s schlock tradition.

VHS: S32548. $24.95.

Bernard L. Kowalski, USA, 1958, 65 mins.

Nightfall

Based on the Isaac Asimov story about a civilization dealing with the loss of light and heat from all its suns. David Birney stars as a leader trying to hold his people together using science and logic. Blind shaman Alexis Kanner encourages religious solutions. Minimalist science fiction filmed in a futuristic community in the American southwest.

VHS: S08317. $79.95.

Paul Mayersberg, USA, 1988

The Orbitrons

A cult classic about the political and sexual dynamics on a planet where women control and dominate society, placing men in a subservient position. Music by I Love You, The Drills, Azalea Snail and Alexander Ross. With Diva Haase, Dave Lancet and Lawrence Talbot. Directed by Christopher Frieri.

VHS: S17539. $19.95.

Outland

Sean Connery discovers corruption in mining operations on the moons of Jupiter in this futuristic retelling of *High Noon*.

VHS: S03536. $14.95.
Laser: LD70736. $34.98.
DVD: DV60183. $24.98.

Peter Hyams, USA, 1981, 109 mins.

Panic in Year Zero

Year Zero refers to a post apocalyptic Los Angeles that has been devastated by a nuclear attack. Ray Milland and Frankie Avalon star in this science fiction thriller, where the placid everyday world of the early 60s has been replaced by a brutal environment devastated by unimaginable cataclysm.

VHS: S20927. $14.98.

Ray Milland, USA, 1962, 92 mins.

Perils of the Planet Mongo

Buster Crabbe stars as Flash Gordon. A feature derived from the serial *Flash Gordon Conquers the Universe*. USA, 75 mins.

VHS: S15180. $29.95.

Phantasm III: Lord of the Dead

This sequel to the cult classic *Phantasm* is as murderous and horrifying as the original. Once again, the tall cadaverous mortician is armed with his mysterious and inexplicable shiny spheres. The difference is that this film finally explains the powers contained by these balls.

VHS: S00007. $94.98.
Laser: LD74631. $34.98.

Don A. Coscarelli, USA, 1994, 91 mins.

Phantom from Space

Billy Wilder's brother directed this little sci-fi adventure about an invisible alien (Dick Sands) who crash lands on Earth and then begins killing picnickers.

VHS: S08435. $19.95.

W. Lee Wilder, USA, 1953, 72 mins.

The Phantom Planet

An enjoyable and underrated little sci-fi "B" opus about an astronaut who's stranded on an invisible planetoid. There, he finds a race of miniature people menaced by a fleet of marauding alien monsters. A wonderful stock sci-fi music score. With Dean Fredericks, Coleen Gray, Dolores Faith, Anthony Dexter and Francis X. Bushman.

VHS: S32556. $24.95.

William Marshall, USA, 1961, 82 mins.

Pilot X (Death in the Air)

The country is shocked by a series of horrible plane crashes. Authorities are even more horrified to learn that all the planes were shot down by mysterious killer in a black plane with a large "X" emblazoned across the wing. The suspects are a group of WWI aces who are all invited to a creepy mansion for the weekend by an eccentric doctor. With John Carroll, Lona Andre and Leon Ames.

VHS: S32602. $24.95.

Elmer Clifton, USA, 1937, 64 mins.

Planet of Blood (Queen of Blood)

Roger Corman bought a bad Russian movie with very good special effects and had an entirely new movie made using the space footage of the original. Basil Rathbone heads a crew that includes John Saxon, Dennis Hopper and Forrest J. Ackerman (Famous Monsters Magazine) which finds a female space vampire willing to be rescued.

VHS: S04096. $29.95.

Curtis Harrington, USA, 1966, 81 mins.

Planet of the Apes

Astronaut Charlton Heston crash lands on a distant world where he finds that human beings are not the dominant species. The novel by Pierre Boulle was adapted for the screen by Rod Serling and Michael Wilson and won a Special Oscar for its outstanding achievement in make-up. Kim Hunter, Roddy McDowall, Maurice Evans, and James Whitmore are some of the stars in simian suits. Followed by four sequels and a couple of TV shows.

VHS: S12171. $19.98.

Franklin J. Schaffner, USA, 1968, 112 mins.

Planet of the Vampires

Barry Sullivan and Norma Bengell star in this sci-fi horror flick of intergalactic dimensions. A spaceship is stranded on a mysterious planet where the inhabitants appear to be interested only in sucking the blood of strangers. Dubbed in English.

VHS: S25692. $19.95.

Mario Bava, Italy, 1965, 86 mins.

Planeta Burg

A foreign sci-fi masterpiece! Cosmonauts land on Venus to find themselves in peril by various alien monstrosities. This appears to be the actual print that Roger Corman used to make parts of the negative to *Voyage to the Prehistoric Planet* (the film cans are addressed to Roger). Visually stunning. Based on a story by Stanislav Lem. Russian with English subtitles.

VHS: S15370. $29.95.

Pavel Klushantsev, USSR, 1962, 73 mins.

Project Moonbase

Legendary science fiction novelist Robert Heinlein's 1953 vision of 1970 space travel, complete with orbital rockets, space stations, Commie spies and Donna Martell's gravity-defying bra. Starring Ross Ford and Hayden Rorke (Dr. Bellows on TV's *I Dream of Jeannie*).

VHS: S32111. $19.95.

Richard Talmadge, USA, 1953, 63 mins.

Purple Death from Outer Space

Buster Crabbe stars as Flash Gordon. A feature derived from the serial *Flash Gordon Conquers the Universe*. USA, 75 mins.

VHS: S15179. $29.95.

Purple Monster Strikes

The Purple Monster, sinister vanguard for a Martian invasion of our planet, possesses the body of noted scientist Dr. Cyrus Layton in order to build futuristic weapons of war to assist in the invasion. Only two people, Layton's niece Sheila, and noted criminologist Craig Foster, can stop the Purple Monster and his diabolical plan. 15 episode serial on 2 cassettes.

VHS: S11569. $29.95.

Quatermass 1: The Quatermass Experiment

A single man is found alone on a returning spaceship. Tension grows as he mysteriously changes into an alien creature. The result is a hideous monster with unimagined powers and the will to see his horrible desires through at any cost.

VHS: S27751. $14.95.

Val Guest, Great Britain, 1956, 79 mins.

Quatermass 2: Enemy from Space

The second and best of the three notable *Quatermass* films written by Nigel Kneale. This frightening tale of alien invasion and political paranoia is comparable to *1984* and *Invasion of the Body Snatchers*. With Brian Donlevy as Quatermass.

VHS: S01077. $49.95.
Laser: LD76822. $49.95.

Val Guest, Great Britain, 1957, 85 mins.

Quatermass and the Pit

In this Hammer classic, a London subway excavation abruptly halts when construction workers unearth a cluster of prehistoric skulls and skeletons. Anthropologist Dr. Roney (James Donald), his assistant Barbara Judd (Barbara Shelley) and space expert Professor Quatermass (Andrew Keir) are driven by curiosity and dig deeper to discover a strange "missile" that is not of this earth. Letterboxed.

VHS: S32499. $14.98.
Laser: LD76436. $49.98.

Roy Ward Baker, Great Britain, 1967, 98 mins.

Radar Men from the Moon

Republic serial that introduced Commando Cody, with George Wallace and Clayton Moore. All 12 episodes included on this double tape.

VHS: S07018. $29.95.

Fred Brannon, USA, 1952, 152 mins.

Red Planet Mars

A notorious Cold War parable about American and Russian scientists establishing radio contact with Mars. The radio emissions first elicit panic, leading to a religious revivalism and finally to a personal declaration between the countries to peacefully coexist. With Herbert Berghof, Peter Graves and Andrea King.

VHS: S19136. $14.95.

Harry Horner, USA, 1952, 87 mins.

Reptilicus

When scientists unexpectedly uncover the frozen tail of a dinosaur, they prematurely congratulate themselves on their good fortune. Soon the tail begins to grow and before long the entire horrific creature is complete and ready to roam the world once again.

VHS: S20929. $14.98.

Sidney Pink, Denmark, 1962, 90 mins.

Return of the Fly

Sadly, the son of the original fly-man meets the same fate as his tragic scientist father, with Vincent Price reprising his role from *The Fly* as the understanding family friend. The sins of the fathers are the sins of the sons.

VHS: S14790. $14.98.

Edward Bernds, USA, 1959, 80 mins.

Robocop

The action/science fiction movie of 1987 stars Peter Weller as a Detroit cop gunned down and used as a guinea pig to create a cyborg police officer. All goes well until Robocop starts remembering his past life and enemies. With Nancy Allen, Ronny Cox, Kurtwood Smith and Miguel Ferrer.

VHS: S05637. $19.98.
Laser: CAV/CLV. LD72101. $99.95.

Paul Verhoeven, USA, 1987, 103 mins.

Robot Monster

Ro-man, an ape-like intergalactic exterminator wearing a plastic diving helmet, attempts to vaporize the entire "hu-man" population with his calcinator death ray. When this movie made its debut in 1953 the reviews were so bad its director committed suicide.

VHS: S14682. $12.95.

Phil Tucker, USA, 1953, 62 mins.

Rocketship X-M

Historically, the first serious science fiction film of the Atomic Age. Deftly brought to thrilling life by science fiction producer-director Kurt Neumann, starring Lloyd Bridges and Osa Massen, and introducing Hugh O'Brien. Panchromatic and Sepia Color Color Sequences.

VHS: S32109. $19.95.

Kurt Neumann, USA, 1950, 77 mins.

Rodan

Rodan! Disturbed from his prehistoric slumber by H-Bomb testing in the Pacific. Foolish humans! Rodan comes to wreak havoc on civilization! A classic thriller. English dialog.

VHS: S01127. $9.95.

Inoshiro Honda, Japan, 1956, 72 mins.

The Sci-Fi Files

From fiction to fact, this four-volume program explores the history of this artform using clips from some of Hollywood's blockbuster films, incredible archival footage and interviews with some of the leading experts in the field. Volumes include *Spaceships and Aliens, March of the Machines, Children of Frankenstein* and *Living in the Future*. Each tape is 50 mins.

VHS: S35007. $59.98.

Secret of the Telegian

A very entertaining Japanese sci-fi film in which men are being mysteriously murdered by a vengeful madman known as "the Telegian," who uses a matter-transmitting device to find his intended victims no matter where they hide. With Koji Tsurata and Tadao Nakamura. Dubbed in English.

VHS: S32558. $24.95.

Jun Fukuda, Japan, 1962, 86 mins.

Silent Running

Bruce Dern stars in this sci-fi classic as a botanist preserving the only botanical specimens left on Earth, under huge geodesic domes, whose rebellion takes him on the loneliest adventure of all. Co-scripted by Michael Cimino, with original songs sung by Joan Baez.

VHS: S01200. $19.95.
Laser: LD70079. $34.95.

Douglas Trumbull, USA, 1977, 90 mins.

Son of Godzilla

Godzilla and son are threatened by giant mantises and a huge spider in this good-natured monster rally.

VHS: S32278. $9.99.

Jun Fakuda, Japan, 1966, 86 mins.

Soylent Green

Veteran action director Fleischer invents a science fiction fantasy of the distant future, where an absurdly overpopulated New York City forces its citizens to survive on a wafer-like food plant known as Soylent. Charlton Heston is a laconic detective assigned to uncover the details of a murdered industrialist. The film features a final performance from Edward G. Robinson.

VHS: S02362. $19.98.

Laser: Letterboxed. Includes original theatrical trailer. **LD71509. $34.98.**

Richard Fleischer, USA, 1973, 97 mins.

Space Patrol

Stand by for exciting out-of-this-world action as you blast into the future with Commander Buzz Corry, Cadet Happy and the intrepid crew of the space cruiser Terra. Travel to the farthest reaches of the galaxy on daring missions as the Space Patrol battles mad scientists, zombie-like robots, evil androids and other diabolical 30th century villains in the name of interplanetary justice. Contains not only full episodes but also original commercials in each volume.

Space Patrol Volume 2. 3 episodes. 90 mins.

VHS: S12182. $19.95.

Space Patrol Volume 3. 2 episodes. 60 mins.

VHS: S12183. $19.95.

Spawn—The Director's Cut

Five years after being murdered by corrupt colleagues in a covert government agency, Al Simmons (Michael Jai White) makes a Faustian pact with the devil so that he can be resurrected to see his beloved life Wanda (Theresa Randle) one last time. In exchange for his return to Earth, Simmons agrees to lead Hell's Army in the destruction of mankind. Based on the comic book by Todd McFarlane. With John Leguizamo, Martin Sheen and D.B. Sweeney. Special director's cut includes interview with McFarlane, additional footage and *The Making of Spawn* featurette.

VHS: S32712. $104.99.

DVD: DV60294. $24.98.

Mark A.Z. Dippe, USA, 1997, 94 mins.

Sssssss

From the same special effects creator who brought you *Planet of the Apes* comes this spine-tingling sci-fi classic about a mad scientist who transforms a young man into a king cobra with venomous results. With Strother Martin and Dirk Benedict. "Finally! A horror film we chiller freaks can recommend to our friends" *(Cosmopolitan)*.

VHS: S31081. $14.98.

Bernard L. Kowalski, USA, 1973, 99 mins.

Star Trek Generations

Finally the two captains of the Starship Enterprise, John Luc Picard (Patrick Stewart) and James T. Kirk (William Shatner) are joined in an intergalactic quest. They must join forces to save millions. This film includes the cast of the *Next Generation* crew and both Whoopi Goldberg and Malcolm McDowell.

VHS: S25541. $19.95.

David Carson, USA, 1994, 117 mins.

Star Trek I: The Motion Picture

Most of the television cast was back, with the addition of Persis Khambatta, but director Wise *(Sound of Music)* just does not have the right feel for the material. Widescreen.

VHS: S01582. $19.95.

Robert Wise, USA, 1979, 132 mins.

Star Trek II: Wrath of Khan

Ricardo Montalban plays Khan, who had been banished to a barren planet in a television episode in 1967 and seeks revenge against Captain Kirk. Fast-paced and highly entertaining, starring the entire crew of the Enterprise. Widescreen.

VHS: S01583. $19.95.

Nicholas Meyer, USA, 1982, 113 mins.

Star Trek III: Search for Spock

Leonard Nimoy is given an opportunity to direct and turns out a very credible film in which Kirk and the crew disobey Starfleet Command in order to save the soul of Mr. Spock. Widescreen.

VHS: S01584. $19.95.

Leonard Nimoy, USA, 1984, 105 mins.

Star Trek IV: The Voyage Home

The Enterprise travels back to the 20th century in this entertaining feature and tries to save the Earth with the help of humpback whales. Widescreen.

VHS: S09568. $14.95.

Leonard Nimoy, USA, 1986, 119 mins.

Star Trek IV: The Voyage Home (Director's Cut)

Director Leonard Nimoy leads you through the special-effects magic of the fourth film in the *Star Trek* filmography. In a letter-boxed format, this uninterrupted science-fiction epic takes on glorious new meaning. With an environmentally sound message, the Enterprise travels back to the 20th Century and enlists the help of the humpback whales in an effort to save the Earth. With all the familiar faces from the original series.

VHS: S15710. $29.95.

Leonard Nimoy, USA, 1986, 119 mins.

Star Trek V: The Final Frontier

The crew of the *Enterprise* is hijacked to the center of the universe. A mad Vulcan sets this kidnapping plan in motion and it holds surprisingly deep emotional—even spiritual—effects in store for the intrepid crew. William Shatner and Leonard Nimoy are both along for the mystic ride. Widescreen.

VHS: S26352. $19.95.

William Shatner, USA, 1989, 107 mins.

Star Trek VI: The Undiscovered Country

The Federation and the Klingon Empire are set on a wide-ranging peace summit. Captain Kirk the old warrior has his doubts about the impending peace. These fears are realized when an act of sabotage implicates the crew of the Enterprise as renegade terrorists set on destroying the peace summit. The finale is an effective culmination to a long-building, suspense-laden plot. Widescreen.

VHS: S26353. $19.95.

Nicholas Meyer, USA, 1991, 110 mins.

Star Trek: First Contact

Jean-Luc Picard (Patrick Stewart) and his *Next Generation* crew face their most fearsome enemy—the half-human, half-machine race known as the Borg—in this critically acclaimed film by Treker Jonathan Frakes.

VHS: S31363. $19.95.

Jonathan Frakes, USA, 1996, 111 mins.

Star Trek: The Cage

The part color, part black and white, never-televised original Star Trek debut television series, one of the most sought-after titles. This special edition includes the long-lost color footage, believed to have been destroyed, from Gene Roddenberry's pilot episode of the Star Trek television series. On the first voyage of the Starship Enterprise, Captain Kirk tries to rescue an earth crew that disappeared 18 years ago but that's now imprisoned in a zoo-like cage, studied by a mysterious life form. 64 mins.

VHS: S09327. $24.95.

Star Wars

Already a classic, a blend of pulp magazine sci-fi, comic book action, and old fashioned cliff-hanger story starring Mark Hamill, Harrison Ford and Carrie Fisher.

VHS: S02866. $19.98.

George Lucas, USA, 1977, 121 mins.

The Return of the Jedi

The last chapter in this popular trilogy delivers more thrills and adventure as the forces of good and not-so-good battle on the forest planet of Endor, inhabited by feisty teddy bears called Ewoks. Also, Jabba the Hut in action. Be there when the victory dance begins. With Mark Hamill, Carrie Fisher, Harrison Ford and the voice of James Earl Jones.

VHS: S03478. $19.98.

Laser: LD71300. $69.98.

Richard Marquand, USA, 1983, 133 mins.

Star Wars Trilogy

A special collector's edition of the phenomenal science-fiction trilogy, George Lucas' *Star Wars*, Irvin Kershner's *The Empire Strikes Back* and Richard Marquand's *Return of the Jedi*, available for the first time in a letterboxed, THX format that preserves the original aspect ratio of their theatrical releases.

VHS: S17771. $59.95.

Stargate

Kurt Russell and James Spader star in this sci-fi epic about a gateway to another world. Spader is a professor asked to decode an ancient Egyptian artifact. Before long he and Russell, an Air Force colonel, are on the other side of the universe battling the evil and oppressive Sun god Ra (Jaye Davidson). Great sets and effects. VHS letterboxed.

VHS: S24085. $19.98.

Laser: LD76805. $39.99.

Roland Emmerich, USA, 1994, 119 mins.

Starman

Jeff Bridges and Karen Allen star in this love story about an alien and a human woman. When the alien appears, he takes the form of the woman's recently deceased husband, forcing her to confront a remarkable resurrection. A widescreen, deluxe Dolby presentation.

Laser: LD74545. $34.95.

John Carpenter, USA, 1984, 115 mins.

Starship Troopers

Cult favorite Paul Verhoeven *(Robocop)* directs this highly entertaining futuristic satire of war epics. Giant extraterrestrial insects launch an invasion of the Earth, and it is up to new army recruit Johnny Rico to squash the alien attack. Amazing special effects and over-the-top camp separate this from your run-of-the-mill insect invasion flick. With Casper Van Dien and *Doogie Hauser*'s Neil Patrick Harris.

VHS: S33956. $106.99.

Paul Verhoeven, USA, 1997, 130 mins.

Strange Days

Ralph Fiennes, Angela Bassett and Juliette Lewis form the tense romantic triangle that drives this futuristic thriller. It's the dawn of a new millennium and a strange technology is unveiled which is capable of transmitting the sensations of people's experiences directly to the human brain, offering the world some startling new possibilities. A series of killings makes the most of this new technology, but the deaths serve only to shield a more diabolical plot. VHS letterboxed.

VHS: S27369. $19.99.

Laser: LD75512. $49.95.

Kathryn Bigelow, USA, 1995, 145 mins.

The Stranger from Venus

Helmut Dantine is the stranger from Venus who is concerned about the future of Earth. He encounters Patricia Neal and befriends her but soon finds out that not all Earthlings are as friendly as Neal. An uncredited remake of *The Day the Earth Stood Still* made in England on a very low budget. B&W.

VHS: S03282. $19.95.

Burt Balaban, Great Britain, 1954, 75 mins.

Supersonic Man

Obscure Italian sci-fi complete with a superhero from a distant galaxy who has the power of flight and superhuman strength. Cameron Mitchell is great as the evil mad scientist. Watch for the rocket-shooting robot. With Michael Coby and Diana Polakov. Dubbed in English.

VHS: S32566. $24.95.

Juan Piquer Simon, Spain, 1979, 88 mins.

Suroh: The Alien Hitchhiker

Paul is a reporter for a small newspaper who, while attending a UFO conference, comes across an actual alien. The being has crash landed and needs Paul's help. This premise takes on an entirely new dimension when Paul and the alien initiate an interspecies sexual liason. Despite the emotional depth of this experience Paul must help his new friend to return or face destruction from evil, earth-bound forces.

VHS: S29443. $29.95.

Patrick McGuinn, USA, 1996, 74 mins.

Tarantula

Scientist Leo G. Carrol's experiment to create the world's largest food supply mutates into a gigantic spider that wreaks havoc on the pastoral countryside. "One of the best giant-insect films, with fast pacing and convincing special effects" (Leonard Maltin). With John Agar, Mara Corday and in a small role, Clint Eastwood.

VHS: S18700. $14.98.

Jack Arnold, USA, 1955, 80 mins.

Target Earth

Robots from Venus invade the Earth seizing an American city and leaving scientists helplessly searching for a method to save mankind. With Richard Denning and Virginia Grey.

VHS: S34213. $19.95.

Sherman A. Rose, USA, 1954, 75 mins.

Teenagers from Outer Space

A teenager from outer space tries to alert the planet Earth about his alien race and their diabolical scheme of destruction. He is pursued by a killer because of this plan, but that does not prevent him from becoming infatuated with a teenage girl. This is a camp classic made on a tiny budget that could only have been produced in the 1950's.

VHS: S24069. $14.95.

Tom Graeff, USA, 1959, 86 mins.

The Terminator

Schwarzenegger *is* the villainous Terminator, a cyborg (part man, part machine) sent to present day Earth from the future on a deadly mission. His task: to kill a young woman whose life will have great significance in the revolutionary decades to come. An above-average sci-fi thriller, now considered a classic. Letterboxed.

VHS: S05716. $19.99.

James Cameron, USA, 1984, 89 mins.

Terminator 2: Judgment Day

At over $100 million, James Cameron's sequel to his popular 1984 science-fiction thriller is easily one of the most expensive feature films ever made. Arnold Schwarzenegger is back as the eponymous, time-traveling death machine, only this time he gets to play the "good" guy—meaning that instead of killing everyone in his path he now only injures them seriously. If you can stand the film's pumped-up violence, most of the special effects and stunt sequences are pretty spectacular, and, despite a few attempts at sentimentality which just flat-out fail, the movie functions fairly well as an entertaining roller coaster ride paced with action, fireworks and mild suspense. Written, produced and directed by James Cameron. Also starring Linda Hamilton. Letterboxed.

VHS: S15229. $19.98.
DVD: DV60134. $34.98.
James Cameron, USA, 1991, 139 mins.

Terror Is a Man

A mad scientist transforms a panther into a man-like creature that escapes and goes on a rampage. Plenty of chills and an outstanding music score. An excellent sci-fi/horror opus shot by an all English-speaking cast in the Philippines. With Francis Lederer, Richard Derr and Greta Thyssen.

VHS: S32551. $24.95.
Gerardo de Leon/Eddie Romero, USA, 1959, 89 mins.

Terror of Mechagodzilla

Outer space fiends use a prehistoric sea creature, the Titanosaurus, and Mechagodzilla in their intergalactic plans to destroy Tokyo. Only Godzilla can battle the two titans and save the Japanese capital. Dubbed in English.

VHS: S25029. $14.95.
Laser: LD75271. $39.95.
Inoshiro Honda, Japan, 1978, 89 mins.

Them!

A 50's masterpiece of the cinema of the fantastic. With atmospheric shadow and light photography, memorable performances by James Whitmore and James Arness (pre-Gunsmoke), and assists from 12 foot long ants.

VHS: S01319. $19.98.
Laser: LD74719. $34.98.
Gordon Douglas, USA, 1954, 93 mins.

They Live

John Carpenter's sci-fi thriller about one man's battle against aliens who are systematically gaining control of the earth. Pro-wrestler Roddy Piper stars as the loner who stumbles upon ghoulish creatures masquerading as humans while they lull the public into submission through subliminal advertising messages! Only specially made sunglasses make the deadly truth visible.

VHS: S10111. $19.95.
John Carpenter, USA, 1988, 95 mins.

The Thing

A chilling morality tale about the responsibility of scientists toward humanity, *The Thing* was produced by Howard Hawks and stars James Arness as the extraterrestrial. It concludes with the hysterical admonition: "Keep on looking! Watch the skies!"

Laser: LD70087. $34.98.
Christian Nyby, USA, 1951, 80 mins.

Things to Come

A sci-fi classic, based on the novel by H.G. Wells. World civilization is on the brink of collapse, in the grasp of evil dictatorship. Raymond Massey plays John Cabal, who hopes to restore peace and save civilization through technology. A humanistic film, and one of the all-time science fiction greats.

VHS: S01326. $19.95.
William C. Menzies, Great Britain, 1936, 87 mins.

This Is Not a Test

Social science fiction at its best. A state trooper stops people along a highway after hearing news of an impending nuclear attack. Good drama as citizens quarrel over what to do before the bombs hit. (And they hit big-time.) With Seamon Glass and Mary Morlas.

VHS: S32560. $24.95.
Fredric Gadette, USA, 1962, 80 mins.

This Island Earth

Joseph Newman's science fiction film contains all the classic archetypes: death rays, mutant bugs and, according the the press release, "college sweethearts turned nuclear fission experts." Faith Domergue and Rex Reason star as the lovers/scientists spirited to the planet Metaluna to save it from destruction. A 1955 special effects classic.

VHS: S02613. $19.95.
Laser: LD70088. $34.98.
Joseph M. Newman, USA, 1955, 86 mins.

Threads

The story of the aftermath of a global thermonuclear war, shockingly realistic with graphic effectiveness. Set in Sheffield, England, and told from the vantage points of a working class family and a middle class family.

English Version.
VHS: Out of print. For rental only.
Spanish Version.
VHS: S07291. $64.95.
Mick Jackson, Australia/Great Britain, 1985, 110 mins.

The Three Avengers

Alan Steele stars as Ursus. He must defeat not only a tyrant but an imposter Ursus as well. In the end this hero of mythic proportions manages to defeat all his enemies and save the rightful heir to a powerful kingdom. Dubbed in English.

VHS: S25691. $19.95.
Gianfranco Parolini, Italy, 1964, 97 mins.

THX 1138

Robert Duvall is the androgynous worker who, with his partner, passes up their daily drug requirement in the futuristic society, and begins to feel sexual awakening. George Lucas' first film is a classic science fiction vision of a nightmare future.

VHS: S01340. $19.98.
Laser: Letterboxed. **LD74720. $34.98.**
George Lucas, USA, 1971, 90 mins.

Time Machine

H.G. Wells' classic novel is adapted in a now-classic film directed by George Pal. Rod Taylor is the time traveler who guns his machine into the distant future only to find a civilization devitalized by endless wars.

VHS: S01346. $19.95.
Laser: Widescreen. **LD71156. $34.98.**
George Pal, USA, 1960, 103 mins.

Tobor the Great

Tobor is robot spelled backwards. It is also gifted with telepathic powers which help out a lot when enemy agents threaten the lives of its inventor and his grandson. The science fiction thriller is aimed at kids. With Billy Chapin, Lyle Talbot and William Schallert. B&W.

VHS: S04263. $19.95.
Laser: CLV. **LD72038. $34.98.**
Lee Sholem, USA, 1954, 77 mins.

Twilight Zone—The Movie

Four segments, directed by four different directors in the spirit of the original Rod Serling TV series, including "Kick the Can," "It's a Good Life," "Nighmare at 20,000 Feet," remakes of original episodes and one new episode. Starring Dan Aykroyd, Albert Brooks, John Lithgow, Burgess Meredith, John Larroquette, Scatman Crothers, Selma Diamond, Kathleen Quinlan, Nancy Cartwright, Bill Mumy, Cherie Currie, and Vic Morrow (who died in a helicopter accident while filming).

VHS: S34608. $14.95.
Joe Dante/John Landis/George Miller/Steven Spielberg, USA, 1983, 101 mins.

Unknown World

Using a gigantic drilling machine, a group of scientists are off on an adventure to the interior of the earth in order to escape the perils of the atomic era. An intelligent script and colorful cast make this a worthwhile sci-fi yarn.

VHS: S23152. $29.95.
Terry Morse, USA, 1951, 73 mins.

Valley of the Gwangi

Adventurers in Mexico stumble upon a hidden valley and decide to bring back one of the prehistoric creatures they find, hoping to profit off the venture by displaying him in captivity in a sort of travelling circus. Excellent special effects by Ray Harryhausen (*The Seventh Voyage of Sinbad*).

VHS: S14287. $19.98.
Laser: LD74724. $34.98.
James O'Connolly, USA, 1969, 95 mins.

Village of the Damned/ Children of the Damned (1960)

Two chilling psychological shockers. Wolf Rilla's 1960 British thriller *Village of the Damned* is a perverse adaptation of John Wyndham's novel about a group of strange, detached children created by alien visitors plotting to destroy an English village. Anton Leader's 1964 follow-up, *Children of the Damned* concerns six immensely gifted young children and their ruthless attempt to take over the world. Includes the theatrical trailer for both works.

Laser: LD71653. $39.98.

Village of the Damned

Classic sci-fi thriller about twelve children all born on the same day in a peaceful English village, who terrorize their community with telepathic powers. With George Sanders.

VHS: S02364. $19.98.
Wolf Rilla, Great Britain, 1960, 78 mins.

Village of the Damned (1994)

This remake of the earlier 1960's sci-fi classic captures all the brooding menace of that previous film. Terror is brought to a small town by an unlikely generation of perfect children. They are blond, efficient and alien. As their powers grow, the townspeople realize that no one, not their parents or their teachers, will be able to control them.

VHS: S26369. $19.95.
Laser: Widescreen. **LD75293. $34.98.**
John Carpenter, USA, 1994, 99 mins.

Virtuosity

Denzel Washington is a cop forced to play a deadly game. Somehow, a composite of 200 serial killers has escaped the cyberworld game he inhabits. Now this killer stalks real victims relying on the intelligence and viciousness of the minds used to create him. Washington's character is made all the more disturbed by an intriguing personal connection to this virtual madman.

VHS: S27004. $19.95.
Brett Leonard, USA, 1995, 107 mins.

Voyage to a Prehistoric Planet

Basil Rathbone stars in this sci-fi film about a voyage to Venus in the year 2020. A number of interesting and surprising adventures await the crew of this ship, including dinosaurs, monsters, and most intriguingly of all, invisible Venusians.

VHS: S21557. $24.95.
Jonathan Sebastian, USA, 1965, 80 mins.

Voyage to the Bottom of the Sea

A top cast, thrilling underwater photography, and superb special effects fuel this science fiction classic about an enormous sub trying to save the earth from destruction. Written and directed by the master of the natural disaster genre, Irwin Allen (*The Towering Inferno*). Starring Walter Pidgeon, Joan Fontaine and Peter Lorre.

VHS: S07815. $14.98.
Irwin Allen, USA, 1961, 105 mins.

War of the Gargantuas

A Japanese monster film about the outbreak of war between nasty, green giants called gargantuas and their brown-colored adversaries trying to restore peace. "You're in for a monster extravaganza," says one prominent science fiction magazine.

VHS: S16899. $9.95.
Laser: LD75280. $34.98.
Inoshiro Honda, Japan, 1970, 92 mins.

The War of the Robots

In this Italian *Star Wars*, members of a dying race from planet Anthor cannot reproduce, so they kidnap a famous geneticist from Earth to save them from extinction. Space soldiers venture to Anthor and combat humanoid robots to save Earth. With Antonio Sabato and Yanti Somer. In English.

VHS: S34214. $19.95.
Alfonso Brescia, Italy, 1978, 99 mins.

War of the Worlds

Based on the H.G. Wells novel, this film is everybody's SF classic. Winner of an Oscar for special effects, starring Gene Barry.

VHS: S01430. $14.95.
Byron Haskin, USA, 1952, 88 mins.

Warning from Space

A spaceship full of starfish-shaped aliens visits Earth to warn the human race of impending global destruction. Good special effects highlight this intelligent Japanese sci-fi thriller. Beautiful color. With Toyomi Karita and Keizo Kawasaki. Dubbed in English.

VHS: S32545. $24.95.
Koji Shima, Japan, 1956, 87 mins.

Waterworld

Kevin Costner and Dennis Hopper star in this $90-million extravaganza about the doomed planet Earth. The polar ice caps have melted, turning the entire planet into a vast oceanic expanse. One little girl could hold the key to saving mankind from a precarious existence on artificial atolls where the threat of pirates is ever present. With Tina Majorino and Jeanne Tripplehorn.

VHS: S26950. $19.95.
Laser: LD75423. $44.99.
DVD: DV60143. $26.98.

Westworld

Author and anthropologist Michael Crichton *(The Andromeda Strain)* wrote and directed this study of a regressive futureworld gone awry by the horrors of misdirected technology. A futuristic theme park called Westworld becomes a killing ground when robots begin killing the participants. James Brolin and Richard Benjamin star.

VHS: S02363. $19.98.
Michael Crichton, USA, 1973, 90 mins.

When Dinosaurs Ruled the Earth

A pair of Stone-Age lovers defy rampaging dinosaurs, murderous tribesmen and a tidal wave to be together. A fast-paced, enjoyable prehistoric adventure film with fine special effects. Featuring former Playmate of the Year Victoria Vetri.

VHS: S14288. $19.98.
Laser: LD74725. $34.98.
Val Guest, Great Britain, 1970, 96 mins.

When Worlds Collide

A pioneering classic of science-fiction films, *When Worlds Collide* won the Oscar for its special effects. The potential pulverizing impact of the collision makes a chilling panorama of disaster. The balance between human and planetary drama is excellently maintained as the film builds to its fascinating, unforgettable climax.

VHS: S01446. $14.95.
Laser: LD75366. $44.98.
Rudolph Mate, USA, 1951, 81 mins.

X from Outer Space

Another Japanese giant monster movie. The land of the rising sun is under attack from an outer space organism that mutates into a lizard-like chicken. Expect Tokyo to be severely damaged. Watch for hundreds of extras to flee screaming. This is the movie that set back the Japanese space program for decades.

VHS: S10996. $19.98.
Dazui Nihomatsu, Japan, 1967

The Yesterday Machine

This is a Texas-produced original starring Tim Holt, James Britton and Jack Herman. A fugitive Nazi scientist is plotting from his hideout in the Texas prairie. He invents a time machine so they can go back and save Hitler from suicide. A truly bizzare oddity.

VHS: S23160. $29.95.
Russ Marker, USA, 1963, 85 mins.

Zardoz

Sean Connery delivers a powerful performance in the fantastic vision of a future world divided into two societies, the Eternals and the Brutals. Connery is a superior Brutal who finds his way into the world of the Eternals, setting that society on an entirely new course. The special effects and imaginative vision make for high adventure.

VHS: S01498. $19.98.
Laser: LD71227. $59.98.
John Boorman, Great Britain, 1974, 105 mins.

Zeram

An extravagant science fiction work about a female bounty hunter tracking Zeram, a massive renegade space alien who's drawn to Earth to kidnap humans for the planet Mays. In order to defeat the alien, she must use her smarts, cunning and a warp machine, space bazooka, electric shield and a computer called Bob in this off-center, clever futuristic thriller. English dubbed. Japan, 1992, 92 mins.

VHS: S19326. $19.98.
Laser: Widescreen. **LD74963. $39.99.**

cult films

200 Motels
Frank Zappa and the Mothers of Invention get inventive in this free-for-all film that features Ringo Starr as Frank's twin. Theodore Bikel wears an impressive uniform, and an animated featurette on proper dental hygiene is presented along with lots of music and bizarre humor. Made for those who haven't got the money for drugs but can afford to rent a tape.
VHS: S06227. $19.95.
Laser: LD76153. $39.98.
Frank Zappa/Tony Palmer, USA, 1971, 98 mins.

2000 Maniacs
A classic shocker about six tourists who stumble upon a small town called Pleasant Valley that is in the midst of a Centennial celebration—honoring a Civil War massacre! The innocent tourists become unwilling "guests of horror" at the bloody bash. Directed by Herschell Gordon Lewis in gushing blood color.
VHS: S15142. $19.98.
Herschell Gordon Lewis, USA, 1964, 87 mins.

3-D Video Visions: Vol. 1, Deep Space Videoscapes
This cosmic journey goes beyond our solar system to an unseen universe that lies somewhere between the viewer and the screen. From the creators of *Stereograms* and *Superstereograms*. 25 mins.
VHS: S22900. $9.95.

3-D Video Visions: Vol. 2, Stereogram Videoscapes
Amazing 3-D videoscapes challenge the mind, startle the senses and dazzle the eye in this second volume of animated fantasy. 25 mins.
VHS: S22901. $9.95.

5 Dark Souls
The uncensored director's cut of Jason Paul Collum's *5 Dark Souls*. The kids are bored. They're getting restless. They want to play. Whatever you do, don't go in the woods—your best friends have just become your worst enemies. Starring cult favorites Richard S. Blades *(Kill Zone)*, Karen Dilloo *(Mark of the Devil 666)*, Tina Ona Paukstelis *(The Unearthling)* and Mick Wynhoff *(America's Deadliest Home Videos)*.
VHS: S31539. $29.99.
Jason Paul Collum, USA, 1997, 122 mins.

Affliction
This provocative and controversial work features GG Allin, Annie Sprinkle and convicted artist Mike Diana, along with bands God Loves Over Dose, The Voluptuous Horror of Karen Black (featuring Kembra Phaler), Tit Torture Technical Journal and many more. It's 45 minutes of the most outrageous, terrifying and genuinely abrasive performances you'll ever see. 45 mins.
VHS: S32640. $19.95.

Alice in Acidland
This Z-grade, '60s cult work has virtually no relationship to Lewis Carroll, instead using the psychedelic, surreal episodes of a young woman under the influence of LSD as a cautionary moral tale of abuse and degradation.
VHS: S16961. $24.95.

Aliens Cut My Hair
An extravagantly campy video by Michael McIntosh based on the surreal comic strip *Fabulous Space Stories*, by Gentry Johnson. The story unfolds in an outerspace populated by hairdressers, alien transvestites, a vibrator-shaped space ship, and glitter to convey the transporter sequences. When a young ensign shows insufficient compliments for a haircut, the hairdresser announces eternal revenge. "Every bit as campy as it sounds" (Steven Miller, *Seattle Gay News*).
VHS: S18918. $39.95.

The Alley Cats
When Leslie, a member of Europe's wealthy, young swinging set, feels ignored by her fiancee, Logan (who is in the midst of a tempestuous affair with Leslie's best friend, Agnes), she decides to do some swinging herself. Her first lover, the suave, debonair Christian, pleases her, but is called away on business. Frustrated, Leslie responds to the advances of Irena, a beautiful lesbian socialite. Soon she must choose between fiancee Logan and her awakening lesbian feelings.
VHS: S32677. $29.95.
Radley Metzger, USA, 1966, 83 mins.

Alley Tramp
"She went for anything in pants!" screamed the ads of this notorious, long-thought-lost cult film produced by Herschell Gordon Lewis. The subject is the sexual freedom of 16-year-old Marie. She voyeuristically watches her parents in erotic thrall, an act which unleashes her emerging sexual impulses and she is transformed into a "sex machine." With Annette Courset and Jean Lamee.
VHS: S20096. $24.95.
Armand Pays, USA, 1966

Amazing World
Two girls, one car, one killer. Vampire babies attack Vegas. Image of Jesus burnt into toaster. You've got to see it to believe it, as queer tabloid reporters Bing and Nico encounter pyromaniacs, brides of Satan, UFO abductees and mutual lust. When Baskir, a mysterious psychic back from the grave, leads them to the bodies of several murdered women, our intrepid girls step into the ring with a killer. Sarcastic, sexy, smart and suspenseful, this is not your mother's lesbian movie. Exploding with music by Seattle bands. "Fun! Frolicking! Delicious dialogue! A romp!" (Nicole Conn).
VHS: S32676. $29.95.
Denise Ohio, USA, 1997, 96 mins.

American Messiah
In this quirky low-budget flick, a film crew arrives in Seattle to shoot a feature movie about a former porno film star who thinks she's the Messiah, and the actress who plays the role actually starts to believe she's Jesus Christ. Starring John Keister (Comedy Central's *Almost Live*), Alyce LaTourelle, Ken Boynton and Jon Ward.
VHS: S33377. $19.95.
Adam Gold/Taso Lagos, USA, 1995, 75 mins.

Anatomy of a Psycho
A quintessential B-movie experience about the outlaw relationship of a young psychopath (Darrell Howe) and his strung-out girlfriend (Judy Howard) who go on a rampage to avenge his brother's state-ordered death. With Pamela Lincoln, Russ Bender and Ronnie Burns.
VHS: S18919. $14.95.
Brooke L. Peters, USA, 1961

Around the World with Fanny Hill
Diana Kjaer stars as Fanny Hill in this loose sequel which chronicles a scandal in Stockholm, casting couches in Hollywood, erotic films in Hong Kong, romance in Venice and a strange resolution in Munich.
VHS: S16976. $29.95.
Mac Ahlberg, Sweden, 1974, 102 mins.

As Nature Intended
Considered by many to be the British Russ Meyer, Harrison Marks caused a storm in England when he released this film in 1961. Three young women on holiday innocently meet up with two other women on the road, and soon their exhibitionist nature is revealed. Skinny dipping leads to nudist camping, where even more women are found without their clothes. Pinup stars Pamela Green, Jackie Salt and Bridget Leonard are featured, with narration by cartoon voice-man Dawes Butler.
VHS: S15914. $29.95.
Harrison Marks, Great Britain, 1961, 65 mins.

Assassin of Youth
Luanna Gardner stars in this exploitation film where one puff of a controlled substance turns kids into fiends. Wild parties and the terrors of marijuana use follow a girl's introduction to this drug. Terrifyingly funny.
VHS: S23180. $24.95.
Elmer Clifton, USA, 1937, 70 mins.

The Atom and Eve
Produced in 1965 by a consortium of utility companies to promote electricity use and nuclear power, this blend of male chauvinism and conspicuous consumption now provokes both outrage and uproarious laughter as the film follows a scantily-clad housewife through her all-electric day. Proven popular with womens' and anti-nuclear groups, as well as in classes where the nuclear propaganda battle is a subject. 15 mins.
VHS: S31102. $19.95.

The Atomic Brain (Monstrosity)
One of the greatest turkeys ever made. A mad doctor is hired by a millionaire spinster to transplant her brain into the body of a young girl. He gets ticked off at her and puts it into the skull of a cat instead. A fun party film.
VHS: S34485. $29.95.
Joseph V. Mascelli, USA, 1963, 72 mins.

Babette in "The Return of the Secret Society"
Babette is a hip, young sex kitten who has travelled the world and is now settling down in New York City. In need of employment, she returns to her former career in "the secret society," a world of mail-order porn and prostitution. She quickly befriends Ramon, a kinky photographer, and finds herself drawn to Carla, one of his favorite models. Together, Carla and Babette pose for Ramon and his camera, initiate a new member into the secret society via a far out candlelight orgy, and join a group of horny young housewives called the Daughters of Lesbos. Very rare sleaze from the 60's. With Claudia Cheer, Jo Sweet, Carla Costa and Sue Akers.
VHS: S27628. $19.98.
Peter Woodcock, USA, 1968, 80 mins.

Back Street Jane
When a pair of beautiful young thieves try to extort drugs from an evil femme fatale, their plan backfires and ends in multiple murder. This modern film noir is stylishly shot and superbly acted, with "non-stop double-crosses and plot surprises in the tradition of (Stanley Kubrick's) *The Killing* and (John Huston's) *The Asphalt Jungle*" (Michael Weldon, *Psychotronic Video*). For mature audiences.
VHS: S16677. $14.95.
Ronnie Cramer, USA, 1989, 95 mins.

Back to the Beach
Frankie Avalon and Annette Funicello revisit the beaches of their youth, this time as the parents of two teenagers. A nostalgic romp with lots of guest stars like Bob Denver, Don Adams, Connie Stevens, The Cleaver Family minus Ward, and Pee Wee Herman, who sings "Surfin' Bird." Fun for the sand set.
VHS: S05528. $19.95.
Laser: LD75152. $34.98.
Lyndall Hobbs, USA, 1987, 92 mins.

Bad Girls Go to Hell
Innocent, naive airheads in high heels are forced into a life of sin by sleazeballs and lesbians—this, believe it or not, was the formula for a whole series of movies called "roughies", made between 1964 and 1967. This 1965 morality tale about a penniless, talentless, brainless woman, lost in New York City, is one of the best of the group. Written, directed and produced by Doris Wishman, the only woman making exploitation movies in the 60s.
VHS: S15143. $19.98.
Doris Wishman, USA, 1965, 98 mins.

Batman
The caped crusader and his sidekick Robin in this first, full-length feature film starring Adam West and Burt Ward, as they battle the Fearsome Foursome: the Riddler (Frank Gorshin), the Penguin (Burgess Meredith), the Catwoman (Lee Meriwether), and the Joker (Cesar Romero). Exciting bat-chases and clever traps as the United Nations delegates face the prospect of being turned into small piles of dust.
VHS: S10794. $19.98.
Leslie Martinson, USA, 1966, 105 mins.

The Battle of Love's Return
A Troma comedy full of action, slapstick and unforgettable characters; a combination of satire and wild comedy. Follow Abercrombie, a lovable everyman, through the streets of New York into offices of large corporations and finally into the frenzied battlefields of the Vietnam War. Watch for a surprise appearance from Oliver Stone. "Saucy, satirical comedy…real wit" *(New York Times)*.
VHS: S32643. $14.98.
Lloyd Kaufman, USA, 1971, 80 mins.

Battle of the Bombs
The best scenes from the worst movies ever made, including *Orgy of the Dead, Terror of Tiny Town, I Changed My Sex,* and *Hell Is a Place Called Hollywood.* Total length, 60 mins.
VHS: S05200. $39.95.

Beyond Life with Timothy Leary
The controversial life and death of '60s guru Timothy Leary is explored through flashbacks and interviews with Yoko Ono, Bob Guccione, Jr., Allen Ginsberg, Paul Krasner, Zach Leary, Ramdass, Danny Goldberg, Winona Ryder, Gordon Liddy and Rosemary Leary, from his days at West Point and Harvard to his legendary '60s status and designer Internet-hyped death. 90 mins.
VHS: S31700. $19.95.

Big Bad Mama II
Angie Dickinson reprises her role as the cult heroine Wilma "Big Bad Mama" McClatchie, out to steal a better life for her two teenaged girls. The terrible trio set their gun sites on revenge against a crooked politician by shooting holes in his banks and kidnapping his son. Includes Leonard Maltin's exclusive interview with Roger Corman.
VHS: S32031. $14.98.
Jim Wynorski, USA, 1987, 83 mins.

Big Breakdowns
Hollywood bloopers of the 1930's featuring many of the greatest stars: Humphrey Bogart, Bette Davis, Errol Flynn and the legendary scene of Porky Pig hitting his thumb with a hammer. USA, 27 mins.
VHS: S02233. $19.95.

The Big Doll House
Sexy young women struggle against their sadistic warden. Shocking and violent, this film is perhaps one of the most influential of all women-in-prison films. With Pam Grier.
VHS: S32036. $14.98.
Jack Hill, USA, 1971, 93 mins.

Bizarre Sports and Incredible Feats
A collection of bizarre sports in the far corners of the world: soccer-playing elephants, knuckle-racing Eskimos, and cockroach racing! 36 mins.
VHS: S05380. $9.95.

Blast-Off Girls
Herschell Gordon Lewis' cult item about a corrupt talent agent who discovers a grungy bar band known as the Big Blast and ruthlessly exploits them by signing a one-sided contract. He invents their success with the aid of attractive young women who disrupt their stage shows.
VHS: S20101. $24.95.
Herschell Gordon Lewis, USA, 1967, 83 mins.

Blood Feast
The story of Fuad Ramses, maniac Egyptian caterer, was the most tasteless film ever made when it was released in 1963, and was the first movie to use explicit gore. The only thing more appalling than the bloody special effects is the acting. Directed by the "Godfather of Gore", Herschell Gordon Lewis.
VHS: S15137. $19.98.
Herschell Gordon Lewis, USA, 1963, 78 mins.

Blood Orgy of the Leather Girls
A violent feminist revenge movie far more serious than its mock title implies, this feature by the late Meredith Lucas focuses on the efforts of four radically different women to avenge the terrorist tactics waged on them by the school's fascist bullies. With Robin Gingold, Jo Ann Wyman, Melissa Lawrence and David Nudleman. Special appearance by the Wild Breed.
VHS: S18600. $19.95.
Meredith Lucas, USA, 1988

Blood Shack (Director's Cut)
Ray Dennis Steckler's ghoulish work is about an actress (Carolyn Brandt) who inherits a ranch that many believe is demonized by an ancient Indian devil god called "The Chopper," who is responsible for a string of grisly crimes. With Ron Haydock, Jason Wayne, Laurel Spring and John Bates.
VHS: S20144. $24.95.
Ray Dennis Steckler, USA, 1971, 60 mins.

Bloodsucking Pharaohs in Pittsburgh
A group of cannibalistic crazies looking for eternal life try to turn Pittsburgh into blood soup, in this "hilarious" and "campy" feature-length horror film in the tradition of *The Rocky Horror Picture Show* and *Pink Flamingos.*
VHS: S13714. $79.95.
Alan Smithee, USA, 1990, 89 mins.

The Bloody Brood
Intense and sometimes brutal film about a drug-dealing gang of beatniks who get their kicks by perverse and violent means (including feeding a messenger boy a hamburger laced with ground glass). Low budget brilliance with Peter Falk, Jack Betts and Barbara Lord.
VHS: S32595. $24.95.
Julian Roffman, USA, 1959, 80 mins.

Body Fever
A grim detective saga set in a bleak, corrosive world of drug trafficking and prostitution. The story follows a criminal genius who declares war on a woman he believes ripped her off. Charlie Smith (Ray Dennis Steckler), who worships Humphrey Bogart, is trying to track the woman down before the gangster finds her. Alternate titles: *The Last Original "B" Movie* and *Super Cool.* With Carolyn Brandt, Bernard Fein and Gary Kent.
VHS: S20145. $24.95.
Ray Dennis Steckler, USA, 1971, 80 mins.

Boinng
Herschell Gordon Lewis' hilarious send-up of the film industry about two amateur pornography fanatics who try their hand at making adult movies and discover the business is fraught with terrifying figures and unforseen complications.
VHS: S20107. $24.95.
Herschell Gordon Lewis, USA, 1963, 70 mins.

Boys from Brooklyn
Bela Lugosi stars with Ramona the Chimp in this jungle comedy about a mad scientist. USA, 1952, 65 mins.
VHS: S05462. $29.95.

Bring Me the Head of Geraldo Rivera
A cult classic, heralded as "One of the best underground films of the decade" *(Film Threat Video Guide).*
VHS: S25714. $19.98.
Jim Sikora, USA, 1989, 30 mins.

Bugged
Ghostbusters meets *Aliens* in this bugged-out horror extravaganza from Troma in which sexy homemaker Devine (Priscilla K. Basque) hires a whacked-out group of exterminators to rid her house of disgusting bugs. But it's not long before these bugbusters are combating really big, disgusting bugs. With Ronald K. Armstrong and Jeff Lee.
VHS: S32649. $14.98.
Ron Armstrong, USA, 1996, 90 mins.

Bushwacked
Hosted by comedian and impressionist Jim Morris, this is 30 minutes of jokes, bloopers and twisted syntax taken from ten years of George Bush's speeches, press conferences and public appearances. Witness some of George's best speaking performances—as he forgets the words to the Pledge of Allegiance, or describes the Communist system as an "Economic Rubic's Cone." This tape "kicks ass." 30 mins.
VHS: S15739. $14.95.

Caged Women
When a young female journalist (Laura Gemser, *Emanuelle the Queen*) poses as a female prostitute inmate in order to explore the issues of sex, violence and mistreatment that go on behind bars in a women's prison, her journalistic endeavor becomes a fight for her life. A sort of female *Shock Corridor.*
VHS: S31623. $19.95.
Vincent Dawn, USA, 1984, 90 mins.

Candide Royalle's The Gift
When Liz returns to sell her grandmother's home, little does she know that she will leave with the gift of sensual love and unleashed passion from the other side of life, one that will heal Liz's troubled relationship with Todd and that of every other couple that encounters it. 80 mins.
VHS: S32212. $49.95.

Candy Stripe Nurses
Marisa, Diane and Sandy, three curvaceous teenagers who work as candystripers at a local hospital, are about to embark on some wild adventures. Marisa finds herself trying to save an innocent man from a band of villains. Diane falls in love with a basketball player whose life only she can save, and Sandy gets involved in some sexual games that leave her running forever. With Candice Rialson and Robin Mattson.
VHS: S32035. $14.98.
Alan Holleb, USA, 1974, 77 mins.

Chained for Life
The Hilton sisters, Daisy and Violet, are literally joined in this exploitation film about a marriage involving a pair of Siamese twins. One finally murders the hapless husband, thereby setting in motion a dilemma. Who should be prosecuted?
VHS: S23183. $24.95.
Harry Fraser, USA, 1951, 81 mins.

Child Bride
Shirley Miles and Bob Bolinger star in this film about a severe social problem. A school teacher tries to create a public movement against the practice of older, horny country men taking teenage and even preteen brides. A camp classic, its skinny-dipping scenes are not to be missed. This longer version was transferred from a 35mm nitrate print, and offers the only uncut version available.
VHS: S23181. $24.95.
Harry Revier, USA, 1941

Chillers
From out of the crypt and beyond the darkside, a one-way ticket to terror awaits five lonely travelers stranded in a rural bus depot. The group must fight for their lives as their nightmares come alive to haunt, hunt and horrify. From Troma.
VHS: S32646. $14.98.
Daniel Boyd, USA, 1997, 90 mins.

Chloe
A truly remarkable low-budget gem, broadly described as a romantic voodoo jungle thriller. A gnarled, old black voodoo mistress from the Everglades comes out of the swamp to seek revenge on the white plantation lord responsible for the death of her husband 15 years earlier. Her daughter Chloe (who could pass for white), finds herself torn between the love of a black man and a handsome white foreman. Evidence surfaces that Chloe may actually be the plantation lord's long lost child. With Olive Borden, Reed Howes and Molly O'Day.
VHS: S34486. $29.95.
Marshall Neilan, USA, 1934, 62 mins.

Christine's Secret
A mysterious girl makes repeated visits to a charming country inn in this erotic tale. Winner of the New York Adult Critic Association's Ladies' Choice Award, Best Cinematography, Best Editing, and Best Shot-on-Video Feature. 60 mins.
VHS: S28574. $39.95.

Class of Nuke 'em High
Genetic insanity overtakes the local high school when radioactive sludge from the nearby nuclear power plant seeps into the water supply. Wonderful madness!
VHS: S02912. $9.95.
Richard Haines/Sam Weill, USA, 1986, 84 mins.

Clear Day
Picture Ed Wood shooting a music video while on LSD and you may get something like *Clear Day.* Includes video excerpts of live 1995 Destroy All Monsters concerts from Detroit, Los Angeles and San Diego, with band interview, unreleased tracks, Mexican monster montages, Mike Kelley rants, conspiracy sub-themes and psych-horror teen fun. 60 mins.
VHS: S31889. $34.95.

Cocaine Fiends
An innocent young girl is lured to the glamour of the big city, where she falls into the grasp of a dastardly dope peddler. On the pretense of curing her headache he gives her some soothing powder. Before long she is hopelessly trapped in the throes of addiction. Camp has long since overtaken this once serious melodrama.
VHS: S23177. $24.95.
W.A. O'Connor, USA, 1936, 68 mins.

Cold Turkey
The lure of 25 million dollars for any community that can quit smoking causes havoc in this small-town satiric comedy directed by Norman Lear. Dick Van Dyke is the local minister at the forefront of a campaign created by adman Bob Newhart, who never dreamed that anyone could actually win the money.
VHS: S12234. $19.95.
Laser: LD72171. $34.98.
Norman Lear, USA, 1971, 99 mins.

Commies Are Coming, Commies Are Coming!

From the 1950's, this is the definitive anti-Communist documentary, hosted by Jack Webb. Total paranoia reigns. 60 mins.
VHS: S09969. $39.95.

Common Law Wife

Anne MacAddams, Max Anderson, George Edgely and Lucy Kelly are featured in this film about an uncontrollably lustful woman. She preys on everyone from old men to young studs. It has moments of unintentional hilarity followed quickly with intensely dramatic moments. The climax is gritty and shocking.
VHS: S23190. $24.95.
Eric Sayers, USA, 1963, 81 mins.

Confessions of a Psycho Cat

At a hippie sex party, everyone's waiting for Buddy to show up with some drugs. Instead he shows up with a leg wound and an incredible story: "Psycho Cat" Virginia can't join her brother on safari since she's having a nervous breakdown. She invites three people: junkie Buddy, actor Charles Freeman, and "The Champ" (Jake "Raging Bull" LaMotta) to her trophy room and makes them an offer: $100,000 to the person who can stay alive in Manhattan for 24 hours. A lunatic cult classic.
VHS: S37085. $24.95.
Herb Stanley, USA, 1968

Confessions of a Vice Baron

Willy Castello stars in this story of a thug gone bad, played to the hilt by a real-life gangster. Through drugs and pimping our hero makes it big, only to lose it all for love. Awful acting and a ludicrous script add up to a rip-roaring good laugh.
VHS: S23178. $24.95.
Harvey Thew, USA, 1942, 70 mins.

Corpse Fucking Art

Nekromantik's director, Jorg Buttgereit, reveals his gore-effect secrets in this revealing behind-the-scenes look at his work. Includes stills, unreleased scenes and the early shocker *Hot Love*. 90 mins.
VHS: S26008. $29.95.

Curse of the Wraydons

Tod Slaughter is at it again as a mad spy in the early 1800s who goes around the countryside strangling everyone he can get his hands on. His evil scheme is to destroy the family who once wronged him. His secret lab is complete with a torture chamber that's highlighted in the film's climax. "Without a doubt the most over-the-top, leering, sneering, insidious laughing, totally loony-tunes performance Tod ever gave. A pure horror melodrama from start to finish" (Sinister Cinema).
VHS: S34487. $29.95.
Victor M. Gover, USA, 1946, 94 mins.

Daddy-O

Also known as *Out on Probation*, this low-rent, grade Z work about teenage rebellion and alienation concerns the pressures placed on a young man to drive the getaway car during a heist. With Dick Contino, Sandra Giles, Bruno VeSota, and Gloria Victor.
VHS: S16972. $9.95.
Lou Place, USA, 1959, 74 mins.

Damaged Lives

A guy breaks a date with his fiancee and finds himself having a fling with another girl. The next day he confesses everything to his beloved. There's just one problem: the woman he slept with has VD. When the woman confronts him with this fact, he refuses to believe her. So she does what any self-respecting '30s gal would do: she shoots herself. A camp classic documentary. With Diane Sinclair, Lyman Williams, George Irving and Jason Robards.
VHS: S32598. $24.95.
Edgar G. Ulmer, USA, 1933, 61 mins.

Dark Odyssey

Metzger's first film, shot in 1950s New York City. Athan Karras portrays a young Greek sailor who jumps ship in NYC to avenge the seduction, rape and suicide of his sister, which was caused by a fellow Greek who has fled to the U.S. Unseen director's cut. Contains original theatrical trailer. "Messrs. Kyriakis and Metzger rate a warm welcome to the movie fold. Excellently photographed with a fine, brooding score by Laurence Rosenthal" *(New York Times)*.
VHS: S33226. $29.95.
Radley Metzger/William Kyriakis, USA, 1961, 85 mins.

Deadly Weapons

This historic film stars the amazing 73" bust line of Chesty Morgan. Chesty uses "the only two weapons I've got" to fight the Mob and, of course, she wins. Featuring the famous "droopy-pantyhose" gross-out scene and Chesty's famous ten-inch platform heels. Directed by Doris Wishman; many critics consider the two films she made with Chesty Morgan to be the apex of her career. Well, maybe one critic.
VHS: S15141. $19.98.
Doris Wishman, USA, 1970, 90 mins.

Death Ray of Dr. Mabuse

The magical Dr. Mabuse threatens the world with a death ray. This was the last of the six German Mabuses from the '60s. With Wolfgang Preiss, Peter Van Eyck, Yvonne Furneaux and Toko Yani. Dubbed in English.
VHS: S32562. $24.95.
Hugo Fregonese, Germany, 1964

Death: The Ultimate Mystery

From painstaking hospital surgery to the ghoulish mummies of ancient Mexico, this program scans the common denominator facing all mankind: death. Narrated by Cameron Mitchell. 97 mins.
VHS: S16573. $29.95.

DeathSport

One thousand years into the future, after the Great Neutron Wars, the world is divided into desert wastes and isolated city-states. Lord Zirpola captures Kaz Oshay (David Carradine) to fight to the death in his game, DeathSport. Now Kaz must face his past and fight to save himself and his city from the war that Lord Zirpola is about to wage.
VHS: S32034. $14.98.
Henry Suso/Allan Arkush, USA, 1978, 83 mins.

Deep Throat

Not a documentary about Watergate. Linda Lovelace has disavowed this movie, but it remains the most recognized porno title of all time.
VHS: S00319. $29.95.
Jerry Gerard, USA, 1972, 73 mins.

Delta of Venus

From the guru of erotic films comes this sensuous portrait of a beautiful young writer (Audie England, *Red Shoe Diaries*) on a path of sexual awakening, inspired by the eroticism of renowned author Anais Nin. With Costas Mandylor *(Picket Fences)*. "Tender, passionate and erotic" (Kevin Thomas, *Los Angeles Times*).
VHS: S30894. $19.98.
Zalman King, USA, 101 mins.

Deranged

A chilling work inspired by the depraved psycho Ed Gein, a loathsome serial killer whose acts inspired *Psycho* and *The Texas Chainsaw Massacre*. This film features an anonymous, cruel killer (Roberts Blossom) who preserves his mother's corpse and then randomly pursues other women. The film has been remastered and digitally restored. On the same program is the notorious, underground documentary *Ed Gein: American Maniac*. With Alan Ormsby, Cosette Lee and Leslie Carlson.
VHS: S18839. $39.95.
Jeff Gillen, USA, 1974, 110 mins.

Desperate Teenage Love Dolls

This underground thriller is about the rise and fall of a female road crew cum rock group, who record a smash single ("Come On Up to Me"). The band must also content with a sleazy manager and a rival group, the She Devils.
VHS: S16933. $39.95.

Destroy All Monsters

The ultimate monster movie reunites Godzilla, Rodan, Gidrah, Mothra, Bagara, Spidrah, Minilla, and Manda in a non-stop showdown in which the 40-story lizard decimates New York City, and the capitals of the world are trampled to rubble as a sinister race of alien invaders attempt to use the Earth's own monsters to destroy mankind. Humanity's only hope lies in the courage of the valiant crew of the United Nations Star Ship Moonlight SYS to locate the Klilak's hidden base on the moon, and sever the alien's contol over their titanic beasts of destruction. Deluxe collector's edition letterbox format. Letterboxed. Dubbed in English.
VHS: S34424. $14.98.
Ishiro Honda, Japan, 1968, 90 mins.

Different Strokes

Dana Plato (TV's *Diff'rent Strokes*) bares all in this controversial lesbian drama. Jack (Bentley Mitchum) is a successful fashion photographer living in the Hollywood Hills and dating Jill (Landon Hall), a woman whose beauty rivals any of his models. Jack seems to have it all until Jill (Plato), an attractive New York art dealer, enters their lives and opens up new sexual possibilities for the other Jill that will turn Jack's idyllic life upside down.
VHS: S33009. $59.95.
Michael Paul Girard, USA, 1996, 87 mins.

Dinosaur Valley Girls

When actor Tony Markham finds a magic stone icon that can grant its possessor three wishes, he is instantly transported to a place straight out of his dreams, populated by mammoth prehistoric beasts, grunting cavemen and scantilly clad Jurassic bimbos who can't keep their hands off him. With the legendary Karen Black, William Marshall, Jeff Rector, Denise Ames and Griffin Drew. This director's cut was written and directed by the author of *Star Wars: The Empire Strikes Back*." A masterpiece of arrested development" (Mick Garris, director, Stephen King's *The Stand*).
VHS: S32365. $59.95.
Donald F. Glut, USA, 1997, 94 mins.

Dog Eat Dog

Three hoodlums steal one million dollars from a bank and hide out on an island in the Adriatic in this camp classic. Stars Jayne Mansfield and Cameron Mitchell.
VHS: S16104. $29.95.
Ray Nazarro, USA/Germany/Italy, 1963, 84 min.

Double Agent 73

This film stars the 73" bust line of Chesty Morgan. Chesty is special agent 73; her mission is to expose a gang of drug smugglers by photographing them with the camera implanted in her left bazoom. Of course, to use the camera she must constantly "drop her cover." Chesty has to work fast—the camera is programmed to explode. Directed by Doris Wishman.
VHS: S15147. $19.98.
Doris Wishman, USA, 1971, 72 mins.

Dr. Alien!

The sexy new biology instructor Ms. Xenobia is actually a blue-skinned bug-eyed alien scientist. She may look like blonde and bouncy Judy Landers but she is after sexual data on reproduction on the planet Earth. College freshman Billy Jacoby is her nerd guinea pig. With Troy Donahue, Arlene Golonka and Edy Williams as the comic relief.
VHS: S08274. $79.95.
Laser: LD75183. $34.98.
Dave DeCoteau, USA, 1988, 90 mins.

Dr. Goldfoot and the Bikini Machine

Vincent Price has a diabolical plot to control the world through an army of beautiful, bikini-clad spy machines. These robots will seduce and then embarrass the world into doing his bidding. Frankie Avalon is also featured looking for the beach.
VHS: S25893. $14.98.
Norman Taurog, USA, 1965, 84 mins.

Dr. Goldfoot's the Girl Bombs

Vincent Price is back with yet another diabolical plot to control the world. This time his weapon of choice is a group of even more deadly bikini-clad lovelies. They explode on impact.
VHS: S25894. $14.98.
Mario Bava, USA/Italy, 1966, 79 mins.

Dr. Mabuse vs. Scotland Yard

The spirit of Dr. Mabuse takes over the body of a notable professor. He then begins a new citywide crime wave. With Klaus Kinski, Peter Van Eyck and Wolfgang Preiss. Dubbed in English.
VHS: S32561. $24.95.
Paul May, Germany, 1963, 90 mins.

Drug Propaganda and Satire Compilation

This hilarious collection includes *Mystery of the Leaping Fish* (1916) with Douglas Fairbanks, *Sinister Harvest* (circa 1930s), *Death Weed* (circa 1920s), and *The Pusher* (circa 1955).
VHS: S15486. $29.95.

Eat My Dust

Ron Howard goes berserk in this fast, action-packed car chase/car race thrill ride. Includes Leonard Maltin's exclusive interview with Roger Corman.
VHS: S32032. $14.98.
Charles B. Griffith, USA, 1976, 89 mins.

Edge of Sanity

So you say you've seen every version of Robert Louis Stevenson's classic tale of dual personalities, *Dr. Jekyll and Mr. Hyde*. Well think again. Anthony Perkins as the good doctor hasn't been himself lately since his experiments with cocaine. This suspense thriller was called "ghoulish fun and games" by Vincent Canby. Cast includes Glynis Barber, David Lodge, Ben Cole and Lisa Davis.
VHS: S10352. $89.95.
Gerard Kikione, Great Britain, 1989, 86 mins.

El Frenetico & Go-Girl

El Frenetico (Charlie Pellegrino), a washed-up alcoholic superhero, is lured back to crimefighting by his loyal and spunky sidekick, Go-Girl (Frances Lee). Together they face off against the trilogy of villainy in three episodes: *The Wax Terror, Crimes of Fashion* and *Shades of Crime*. "Take one part Batman and Robin, add Mexican wrestling hero Santo and thrown in the female answer to The Green Hornet's Kato, and you've got the superhero team of El Frenetico and Go-Girl" *(Screem Magazine)*.
VHS: S33222. $19.98.
Pat Bishow, USA, 1997, 92 mins.

Erotic Touch of Hot Skin

A psychotic fantasy—"hot skin" arouses the animal passion in man. In southern France, Irene and Mark, husband and wife with hot skin, have a shared secret. Florence, the cousin not seen in 10 years, a cool blond, and Julian, the outsider, pair up with everyone else, while the body of a man lies rotting under ground. Terrific exploitation. With Fabienne Dali, Sophie Hardy, Jean Valmont.
VHS: S04845. $34.95.
Max Pecas, USA/France, 1964, 77 mins.

Even Hitler Had a Girlfriend
Meet Marcus Templeton, a thirty-year-old bachelor who works the graveyard shift as a security guard. He has no friends and no interests—until one day he discovers that beautiful women are willing to come to his house and have sex with him. Joe Bob Briggs called *Even Hitler Had a Girlfriend* the "best drive-in movie of 1992." For mature audiences.
VHS: S16676. $14.95.
Ronnie Cramer, USA, 1992, 98 mins.

Fanny Hill
An English-language update of John Cleland's 18th century novel about a young woman's sexual awakening. Fanny (Diana Kjaer) leaves the countryside for the big city and discovers sex through closed circuit television.
VHS: S16975. $29.95.
Mac Ahlberg, Sweden, 1968, 92 mins.

Feeding Frenzy
With intimations of Orwell's *1984* and Terry Gilliam's *Brazil*, this is a ferocious, dark work about the cold, impersonal reality of day-to-day life and its negative imprint on the individual, "and how it feeds into the industrial machine." Some surreal, stunning video effects.
VHS: S17157. $29.95.

The Female Bunch
Director Al Adamson decided to shoot this at the Charles Manson ranch so he could get just the right atmosphere. Exploitation sleaze about a gang of man-hating women. Lon Chaney plays a drug pusher in his last released film.
VHS: S15371. $29.95.
Al Adamson, USA, 1972, 86 mins.

Femme
In this debut Candida Royalle production, the steamiest female fantasies are explored: a woman's soap opera star comes to life, a woman meets two men at an art gallery and an erotic encounter ensues, and a rock fan meets her idol for passionate results. Voted top video by adult fans at First Annual POP Awards. 75 mins.
VHS: S28568. $39.95.

First Nudie Musical
One of the zaniest movies, which one-ups Mel Brooks and goes beyond. This double spoof of Hollywood musicals and porno pictures was directed by Bruce Kimmel, and involves an aging Hollywood studio on its last legs of decline. Now known for producing only cheap porno flicks like "Stewardesses in Chains," it is in danger of being turned into a supermarket when it's saved by Kimmel, who convinces the studio to make *The First Nudie Musical*. With Cindy Williams.
VHS: S07780. $29.95.
Bruce Kimmel, USA, 1975, 95 mins.

Fist of Fear Touch of Death
Bruce Lee describes his martial arts techniques in this film from footage shot during the height of his career. In addition to these candid question/answer sessions there is footage of martial arts demonstrations from an exhibition in Madison Square Garden. Fred Williamson is also featured.
VHS: S29473. $19.95.
Matthew Mallinson, USA, 1980, 90 mins.

Flesh Gordon
An outrageous parody! The ads read, "Not to be confused with the original *Flash Gordon*." Flesh Gordon and his companion Dale Ardor save the Earth from the clutches of Emperor Wang, who has created chaos with a mysterious sex ray.
VHS: S00450. $29.95.
Howard Ziehm, USA, 1981, 70 mins.

The Flesh Merchant
Joy Reynolds, Guy Manford and Geri Moffat are featured in this exploitation movie about young girls living in shame. They find themselves organized into prostitution by vice lords. From Dan Sonney. 1955.
VHS: S23185. $24.95.

French Peek-a-Boo
A detective sniffs around a girlie theater and sees more than he ever hoped for in a three-ring circus of can-can girls, show girls, gangster scenarios and some of the most bizarre ballet dances ever filmed. France, 1959. French with English subtitles.
VHS: S23061. $19.98.

Frostbiter
According to Native American lore, the Wendigo, a deadly creature of the North who takes many forms, will rise to strike terror into the hearts of those who desecrate its resting place. When a group of hunters with a lust for blood disturbs the peace on a remote island, they awaken the invincible wrath of the demon frostbiter. Featuring Ron Ashton from Iggy and the Stooges. From the Troma Team.
VHS: S32648. $14.98.
Tom Chaney, USA, 1996, 90 mins.

Gargoyles
An anthropologist and his daughter battle to save Earth from being taken over by a clan of grotesque demons they've discovered in Mexico. With award-winning special effects by Stan Winston *(Terminator 2, Jurassic Park)*.
VHS: S34389. $14.99.
Bill L. Norton, USA, 1972, 74 mins.

Gentlemen Prefer Nature Girls
Gentlemen love the outdoors, and here we get to see them enjoying themselves in their natural habitat. Join them as they forage for wild berries in some of the most exotic bushes the world has to offer.
VHS: S15155. $19.98.

Ghosts on the Loose (East End Kids Meet Bela Lugosi)
Bela Lugosi plays the leader of a Nazi spy ring in this second meeting with the East End Kids. Huntz Hall and Leo Gorcey and their pals find plenty of sliding panels, hidden passageways in a NYC mystery mansion filled with Nazi agents. Ava Gardner plays a newlywed. B&W.
VHS: S04009. $29.95.
William Beaudine, USA, 1943, 64 mins.

Giant from the Unknown
A definitely unusual sci-fi thriller about a group of research scientists who are threatened by a murderous, giant conquistador whose body has been preserved over the centuries and brought back to life by radioactive elements in the soil. With Edward Kemmer, Morris Ankrum, Bob Steele, Sally Fraser and Buddy Bear.
VHS: S34480. $29.95.
Richard E. Cunha, USA, 1958, 77 mins.

Girl Hunters
Mickey Spillane as Mike Hammer! Spillane, in his own creation, gleefully nails that hand of a killer to the floor in this story about a plot involving communist assassins. There's also a bit of booze and lots of beautiful dames. With Lloyd Nolan, Shirley Eaton, Scott Peters.
VHS: S09999. $29.95.
Roy Rowland, USA, 1963, 103 mins.

The Girl, the Body and the Pill
A beautiful, free-spirited health education instructor wants to enlighten her students on the joy of sexual responsibility. The loud objections of the parents and the community forces her instructions underground. The students naturally gravitate to her class in droves.
VHS: S20105. $24.95.
Herschell Gordon Lewis, USA, 1967, 80 mins.

Glitter Goddess of the Sunset Strip
Llana Lloyd's autobiographical, camp melodrama is an impressionistic assembly of Super 8mm home movie footage and period recreations. Lloyd tries to assess the emotional repercussions of her domineering mother's militant lesbian stance. "Mentally intense and satirical, this psycho shocker is shaped to emphasize the fascinating and fragile imperfections of human kind" *(Film Threat Magazine)*. With Lloyd and Diane Nelson.
VHS: S18744. $69.99.
Dick Campbell, USA, 1992, 120 mins.

Go, Go, Go, Go World!
A sensational tour of the odd sights and wicked practices around the world in the tradition of *Mondo Cane*, including an Italian chastity belt store, baby exchanges, strippers, mud wrestlers, snake charmers and much more. For mature audiences only. English narration.
VHS: S13499. $24.95.
Marco Vicario/Anthony Dawson, Italy, 1964, 89 mins.

The Gruesome Twosome
Charming Mrs. Pringle and her sick son Rodney have a blossoming business—selling human hair wigs. In order to replenish their hair supply, they put up a "Room for Rent" sign. Just like at the Bates Motel, young women check in, but they never check out.
VHS: S15145. $19.98.
Herschell Gordon Lewis, USA, 1967, 72 mins.

Gun Is Loaded
Lydia Lunch delivers her brutally frank address of the true state of the union. This video super-realization trails her through New York City as she fires her spoken word manifesto. Identifying herself as "the all-American girl-next-door gone bad", Lydia excavates her own sustained damage as a product of this emotionally ravaging environment.
VHS: S12673. $29.95.

Head
One of the cult films of the 60's, with the Monkees in a kaleidoscope of surreal vignettes, full of 60's psychedelia. Written and produced by Rafaelson *(Five Easy Pieces)* and Jack Nicholson.
VHS: S02531. $19.95.
Bob Rafelson, USA, 1968, 86 mins.

Hell's Angels on Wheels
Great trash features Jack Nicholson as a gas station attendant named Poet, real Hell's Angel Sonny Barger as technical advisor, and splendid photography by Laszlo Kovacs.
VHS: S06899. $9.99.
Richard Rush, USA, 1967, 95 mins.

High School Caesar
John Ashley has the title role in this absurd slice of Americana, as a wealthy teenager with a burning passion to be the vicious overlord of an on-campus protection plan. Al preys on the lunch money and weekly allowances of the unwitting students.
VHS: S05187. $24.95.
O'Dale Ireland, USA, 1956, 75 mins.

High School Confidential
The incomparable Mamie van Doren stars in one of the truly great camp American films of the 1950's in which a tough-talking gang leader comes in contact with a drug ring and its leader-all in the surroundings of the all-American high school. A great rock musical score.
VHS: S00568. $14.98.
Laser: CLV. LD71989. $29.98.
Jack Arnold, USA, 1958, 85 mins.

History of Pornography
The title says it all. Beginning with the erotic literature and drawings of China, Japan and India, the film moves through the first nude photos, comic books and stag films, to the hard-core films of the modern market. The photos, drawings and films are explicit.
VHS: S00574. $29.95.
Hons Wegmunsen, 64 mins.

The Hitler Tapes
This continuation of the compelling, voyeuristic fantasy *Even Hitler Had a Girlfriend* brings more beautiful women to the screen in a variety of kinky, exciting scenarios. From voyeurism to domination to a slow striptease, it's all here and it's all new. 60 mins.
VHS: S26206. $14.95.

Hollywood Dinosaur Chronicles
Doug McClure hosts this historical look back on Hollywood's fascination with the prehistoric. Clips include scenes from *King Kong, Godzilla, The Lost World, Baby* and *Gertie the Dinosaur*. Hear fascinating insights from paleontologists, special effects artists and folks like Charlie Chaplin and Arthur Conan Doyle. 42 mins.
VHS: S13287. $19.95.

Hollywood Outtakes
Cinematic bloopers! A visit with Joan *(Mommie Dearest)* Includes Crawford at home with the kids, Bela Lugosi meeting Betty Boop, and W.C. Fields shooting a film during an earthquake.
VHS: S02100. $59.95.
Bruce Goldstein, USA, 1983, 84 mins.

The Hollywood Strangler Meets the Skid Row Slasher
Two perverse killers strike fear and malaise in the sleazy underside of Hollywood. A deranged loner tracks down models, under the pretense of photographing them, and summarily executes them. Ray Dennis Steckler's feature uses voice-over narration and eerie music. Also known as the *The Model Killer*. With Pierre Agostino and Carolyn Brandt.
VHS: S20146. $24.95.
Ray Dennis Steckler, USA, 1979, 72 mins.

Honky Tonk Girl (Highway Hell)

Mary Chauning is featured in this hilarious exploitation film, in the tradition of *Reefer Madness*. The story is about a hitch-hiking prostitution ring. Catching a lift has never been so much fun. 1937.

VHS: S23179. $24.95.

How to Make a Doll

Herschell Gordon Lewis' science-fiction sex comedy about a computer that creates beautiful women. A professor (Robert Wood) grows impatient after a series of orgies with computer-generated women and longs for the real thing. With his sight impaired, he falls for an unattractive woman whom the computer turns into a rabbit when he tells the computer she is his "dreamy bunny."

VHS: S20102. $24.95.

Herschell Gordon Lewis, USA, 1968

I Was a Teenage Serial Killer

Mary is a serial killer who will gladly kill off any annoying man. The result—she may be America's most popular serial killer. 30 mins.

VHS: S26013. $14.95.

The Immoral Three

A tempting trio of illegitimate sisters must avenge their mother's murder within one year to collect a million bucks each. But, as usual, where there's big money, there's big trouble. Double-crossing, triple-crossing and plenty of undressing ensues in Doris Wishman's action-packed "guns 'n' hooters" classic. I won't give away the ending, but…everybody gets killed. Sorry.

VHS: S15148. $19.98.

Doris Wishman, USA, 1965, 82 mins.

The Incredibly Strange Creatures Who Stopped Living and Became Mixed Up Zombies

A funky horror movie set in a sleazy roadside carnival about a deranged fortune teller who creates a series of grotesque monsters and imprisons them in the back of her tent. Problems ensue when a string of unsolved murders plague the carny. "Truly bizarre film features gorgeously saturated color, awful acting, hideous dialogue, haunting atmosphere and little plot" (Leonard Maltin). With Cash Flagg, Brett O'Hara, Atlas King, Sharon Walsh and Madison Clarke.

VHS: S20140. $24.95.

Ray Dennis Steckler, USA, 1963, 82 mins.

The Intruder

A grisly murder is committed onboard a cruise ship. Before an investigation can begin, the ship is wrecked in a storm and the survivors find themselves shipwrecked on a mysterious jungle island. The survivors are terrorized by weird sounds from the jungle and are horrified when they discover a cave full of skeletons. After a murder occurs, several of the survivors flee into the jungle and encounter a wild man and a killer gorilla.

VHS: S34494. $29.95.

Albert Ray, USA, 1933, 59 mins.

Invasion of the Blood Farmers

A cheesy, sleazy '70s low-budget gem that features lashings of hyperbolic gore and lots of sadistic humor. Young women are being brutally murdered in and around an out-of-the-way New York valley. Behind the heinous crimes is a modern band of bloodthirsty druids who are seeking a rare blood type that will resurrect their queen in time for a ritualistic blood feast.

VHS: S34492. $29.95.

Ed Adlum, USA, 1972, 84 mins.

Invasion USA

A '50s Red Scare movie that portrays a full-fledged invasion of America by "the Enemy." With Gerard Mohr, Peggie Castle, and Dan O'Herlihy.

VHS: S34201. $19.95.

Alfred E. Green, USA, 1952, 74 mins.

Iron Thunder

World championship fighter Anthony "Amp" Elmore stars in this thriller about an ambitious young street fighter trying to ascend to the top of the nefarious, corrupt, kickboxing world. 1989, 90 mins.

VHS: S18825. $19.95.

Jayne Mansfield: Single Room Furnished/The Female Jungle

Jayne Mansfield's bodaciousness is captured in two titillating tapes. In *Single Room Furnished* (93 mins.), Jayne is a buxom blonde who falls from uncorrupted innocence through pregnancies to desperate prostitution. Starring Dorothy Keller. Jayne makes her debut in *The Female Jungle* (69 mins.), a dramatic murder case in which police sergeant Tierney is caught between a rock and a hard place. The prime suspect in a murder case, Tierney discovers a series of clues that implicates his friend (John Carradine). Simply *divoon!*

VHS: S32226. $14.99.

Matt Cimber/Bruno Ve Sota, USA, 1968/1956, 162 mins.

Jimmy, The Boy Wonder

A wickedly subversive "children's film" by cult specialist Herschell Gordon Lewis about a young boy whose soul becomes a battle ground for two magicians. One wants to control him by halting time, and the other tries to reverse the evil deed. The irreverent Lewis enlivens the material with some musical numbers and a half-hour of Italian cartoons blended into the narrative.

VHS: S20100. $24.95.

Herschell Gordon Lewis, USA, 1966

Jive Junction

Unpretentious, occasionally bizarre, World War II era "B" movie about a group of teens who play jitterbug music for the troops. Directed by the master of the "B" movies, screenplay by novelist Irving Wallace.

VHS: S02242. $24.95.

Edgar G. Ulmer, USA, 1943, 62 mins.

Just for the Hell of It

This is the ultimate teenage rebellion film. These kids are really mad—although it's hard to tell exactly why. Maybe it's because they're stoked up on grass, free sex and all that rock music. Roving gangs of teenagers head out onto the streets terrorizing everyone in their way: the old, the crippled, the blind, even infants can't escape their brutality. One question though: Didn't this town have any cops?

VHS: S15152. $19.98.

Herschell Gordon Lewis, USA, 1968, 88 mins.

Kentucky Fried Movie

The '70s comic cult classic from Jerry Zucker, James Abrahams, David Zucker and John Landis. A hilarious, no holds-barred collection of take-offs and put-ons and commericals, news shows, and coming attractions, plus the immortal *Fistful of Yen*. With Donald Sutherland, Henry Gibson, Bill Bixby and Tony Dow. "Inspired…flawless…raunchy. Those easily offended by strong language and steamy sex take notice" *(L.A. Times)*.

VHS: S34461. $19.95.

John Landis, USA, 1977, 84 mins.

Killer Bait (Too Late for Tears)

Lizabeth Scott turns in a great femme fatale performance as a scheming psycho-bitch who eliminates everyone who stands in her way as she tries to make off with 60 grand in blackmail money. An excellent script, top-notch production values, outstanding performances, and a terrific music score make this terrific a film noir. With Don Defoe, Dan Durea and Arthur Kennedy.

VHS: S34493. $29.95.

Byron Haskin, USA, 1949, 99 mins.

Knives of the Avenger

This sequel to Mario Bava's earlier film, *Erik the Conqueror*, follows more Vikings as they pursue their favorite pastimes, namely war and pillage. The story is actually built around the rivalry of two groups, but his plot line really gives Bava free reign to depict the savagery of Norse invaders. Stars Cameron Mitchell. Dubbed in English. 1967.

VHS: S29454. $29.95.

Las Vegas Serial Killer

A dark, ferocious urban thriller about a masochistic killer who is released from prison early and is set loose in Las Vegas, where he preys on showgirls and prostitutes. With Pierre Agostino, Ron Jason, Tara MacGowan and Kathryn Downey.

VHS: S20147. $24.95.

Ray Dennis Steckler, USA, 1985, 90 mins.

The Lemon Grove Kids

A surreal satire of the protective innocence of the Bowery Boys, by cult director Ray Dennis Steckler (aka Cash Flagg). Some demented, gross-out humor is the order of the day in this compilation work of three shorts: *The Lemon Grove Kids, Lemon Grove Kids Meet the Green Grasshopper and the Vampire Lady from Outer Space* and *Lemon Grove Kids Go Hollywood*. Ray's dead-on impression of Huntz Hall is reportedly eerie. With Mike Cannon, Carolyn Brandt and Coleman Francis.

VHS: S20142. $24.95.

Ray Dennis Steckler, USA, 1966, 80 mins.

The Libertine (La Matriarca)

Initially banned in America and challenged all the way to the Supreme Court, *The Libertine* is the story of Mimi, a young woman who discovers that her recently deceased husband had kept a secret apartment equipped to satisfy his unusual sexual desires. With Catherine Spaak and Jean-Louis Trintignant. Italian with English subtitles.

VHS: S33337. $29.95.

Pasquale Festa Companile, Italy, 1969, 90 mins.

The Lickerish Quartet

Filmed in the breathtaking Castle of Balsorano in Italy's Abruzzi Mountains, *The Lickerish Quartet* finds three people obsessed with an erotic film that features a striking, young, blonde woman. When the three—a man, his elegant wife, and her hungry-for-experience son—surreptitiously happen upon the young performer at a local carnival and invite her back to their castle, they soon fall into a maze of truth and illusion, as each fulfills their fantasy in the seduction of the mysterious woman. Presented in its original widescreen format with original theatrical trailer. "An outrageously kinky masterpiece" (Andy Warhol).

VHS: S33433. $29.95.

Radley Metzger, Italy/Germany/USA, 1970, 90 mins.

Little Mother

Before *Evita*, there was Radley Metzger's *Little Mother*. Made when Madonna was still in her training bustier, this retelling of the Eva Peron story presents Evita as a young seductress who sleeps her way to the top of a nation, bedding important ministers and generals. When her new husband becomes President, she finally has all the power she craves, until her shocking downfall.

VHS: S33434. $29.95.

Radley Metzger, USA, 1971, 95 mins.

Living Venus

This is one nudie film that no one should miss, simply because it's Harvey Korman's first feature film role. The tale of *Pagan Magazine*'s rise and fall, *Living Venus* stars Korman as the staff photographer. He and the magazine's obnoxious publisher are both after the cute cover girl. Who will she go for? Good, kind-hearted Harvey or the sleazebucket? Watch and see

VHS: S15150. $19.98.

Herschell Gordon Lewis, USA, 1960, 87 mins.

Love Dolls Superstars

This bizarre sequel to *Desperate Teenage Love Dolls* considers the group's transformation and re-emergence in the alternative music scene. The plot includes elements of the supernatural, prostitution, assassination, religious overkill, genocide and space travel.

VHS: S16935. $39.95.

Love Letter to Edy

A charming, fictionalized biography of Edith Massey, known to fans of John Waters' cult classic, *Pink Flamingos*, as Edy the Egg Lady. Featuring Waters and Mink Stole.

VHS: S31356. $14.95.

Robert Maier, USA, 1973, 15 mins.

Lucky Pierre

This true cult-film classic stars Chicago vaudeville comedian Billy Falbo and hosts of naked women in five vignettes probably written before electricity. With such clever titles as "Drive-in Me Crazy" and "The Plumber's Friend," you can't help but love it. Plus you get the bonus short film "A Hot Night at the Go-Go Lounge." What a deal.

VHS: S15151. $19.98.

Herschell Gordon Lewis, USA, 1963, 73 mins.

Malamondo

This is another of the films made in the 60's that show the seamier sides of our planet. The Malamondo revealed—literally the bad world—is a strange place never before seen on video.

VHS: S23320. $24.95.

Paolo Cavara, Italy, 1963, 100 mins.

Man and Child

A war veteran's adopted daughter is kidnapped by a man looking for his missing granddaughter. The missing girl was an employee for a perfume factory that smuggles drugs. Eddie is the director of the factory and must find the girl to retrieve his own daughter. With Eddie Constantine and Juliette Greco. Dubbed in English.

VHS: S32599. $24.95.

Raoul Andr, France/Italy, 1964

Maniac and Protect Your Daughter

Two cult films from the 1930's. *Maniac* begins like a horror film and then takes off in several directions around a plot in which a lunatic murders a scientist and takes his place experimenting on other psychotics. *Protect Your Daughter* presents a look at the flapper era under the guise of social consciousness.

VHS: S02319. $29.95.
Dwain Esper, USA, 1934, 115 mins.

Microwave Massacre

Jackie Vernon, a frugal GORE-met who likes his flesh done in a flash, loves women, especially between two slices of rye with lettuce and tomatoes. You'll develop a taste for this cannibalistic comedy as Jackie slices sensual sweeties into microwaveable morsels and seasons them with his own brand of horrific humor.

VHS: S14255. $59.95.
Wayne Berwick, USA, 1983, 76 mins.

Miss Melody Jones

A beautiful and talented young woman is exploited and thrown into the seedier underside of Hollywood in this chilling melodrama.

VHS: S18826. $19.95.
Bill Brame, USA, 1973, 86 mins.

Mondo Africana (Original: Africana)

No, this is not just any mondo-sleazo film; this is historically important cinematic sleaze. Although supposedly a "serious" documentary, the filmmakers did go out of their way to film the weird and disgusting—safari hunts, initiation ceremonies, hot-coal walkers, people passing spears through their cheeks and the narrator hams it up as much as possible. Narrated by Quentin Reynolds. For mature audiences only. USA, 80 mins.

VHS: S13501. $24.95.

Mondo Balardo

Boris Karloff narrates this superbly anachronistic addition to the Mondo movie genre. There is a midget rock and roll star, Japanese bondage, an Asian opium den, children coke addicts in Ecuador, a transvestite bar, and other customs that some consider bizarre. It's the film that is truly weird.

VHS: S23191. $24.95.
Robert Montero, USA, 1964, 86 mins.

Mondo Cane

Fascinating and repulsive! *Mondo Cane* was called the "most argued about film" when released in 1963, featured scenes of the bizarre, such as flagellation, nude painting, primitive rituals. French with English subtitles.

VHS: S00871. $29.98.
Gualtiero Jacopetti, Italy, 1963, 107 mins.

Mondo Cane 2

The controversial sequel to *Mondo Cane*, investigating the horrifying, weird, hideous and bizarre.

VHS: S08523. $59.95.
Gualtiero Jacopetti, Italy, 1964, 94 mins.

Mondo Sleazo (The World of Sleaze)

It's unbelievable, but true. Here are 50 trailers to some of the sleaziest movies ever made. Everything is here—drugs, racism, the supernatural, monsters, bikers...you name it. From the 30's to the 80's, this tape will take you on a guided tour of exploitation. Included are: *Love Life of a Gorilla, Maniac, Cocaine Fiends, The Smut Peddler, The Nine Ages of Nakedness, Violated Love, Werewolves on Wheels, Superchick* and literally dozens more. These movies are so slimy, you'll have to wash your hands after viewing this tape. 100 mins.

VHS: S13668. $29.95.

Moonshine Mountain

Herschell Gordon Lewis' baroque hillbilly cult film concerns a once-prominent country singer who returns home and gets caught up in the surreal intrigue of the community's two outlaw families and a corrupt sheriff, who own and operate the world's largest still. With Chuck Scott, Adam Sorg, Jeffrey Allen and Bonnie Hinson.

VHS: S20097. $24.95.
Herschell Gordon Lewis, USA, 1964, 90 mins.

More Moron Movies

An amusing, low-brow, satirical compilation of grade Z works dusted off for home video browsing. Produced by Len Cella, the titles include *Superman at the Psychiatrist, How to Get Fatter, The Bra Unhooking Champion* and *Broccoli Abuse*.

VHS: S02346. $19.95.
Len Cella, USA, 1986, 60 mins.

Moron Movies

Len Cella has brought over 100 comic short films together for this side-splitting compilation tape. *Animals Should Wear Underwear, Dreaded Wheat, Another Use for Tough Meat, How to Aggravate, The Advantage of Having Warts, Schitt for President, How to Exercise if You're Ugly, Exercise for Fat Ears, How to Clean the Toilet Without Gagging, The Truck Wrestler, A Turd Is a Man's Best Friend, King Dong* and *Another Use for Bad Presidents* are all included. 60 mins.

VHS: S23357. $19.95.
Len Cella, USA, 60 mins.

Movie in Your Face!

Described by its makers as "tasteless, sophomoric and hilarious," it's a frantic comedy in the mode of Woody Allen's *What's Up, Tiger Lily?* that combines and recombines several genres, blissfully sending up the movies with a series of cameos and star turns. 1990, 85 mins.

VHS: S18160. $39.95.

Mr. Flathead

Rock and roll discord, mayhem and transformation are the quirky ideas and themes of this cult work about Howard, an unemployed, desperate and lonely man whose life is fundamentally altered when "rock and roll lightning strikes." 1992, 85 mins.

VHS: S18058. $19.95.

Murder by Television

Bela Lugosi plays two parts in this murder mystery, one of them being the investigator of the crime. A greedy businessman's attempt to corner the market on the secrets of a television machine are thwarted by a gadget that turns harmless electronic waves into death rays.

VHS: S03999. $29.95.
Clifford Sanforth, USA, 1935, 60 mins.

The Muthers

Set in a desolate South American jungle, Jayne Kennedy is the mistress of a corrupt warden, who orchestrates a daring liberation of women prisoners to escape the harsh living conditions.

VHS: S18827. $29.95.
Cirio H. Santiago, USA, 1976, 101 mins.

My Surrender

From Femme filmmaker Candida Royalle comes this erotic story of April Hunter (Jeanna Fine), surrounded by the passions of couples who come to her to be filmed as they act out their private fantasies. But her own life is devoid of any real intimacy, until Robert Landon (Alex Sanders) enters her world. Will April surrender to her fears of the past or to the thrill of new love? 83 mins.

VHS: S30828. $39.95.

My Sweet Satan

Cult director Jim Van Bebber concocts a tale of violence, drugs and heavy metal in this story of Satan worship run amok. A remastered version of *Roadkill: The Last Days of John Martin* and the druggie documentary *Doper* are also included on this video. 60 mins.

VHS: S26012. $24.95.

Naked Venus

A boy and a girl torn apart just because she's a nudist? Can they sweep aside the barriers of prejudice and find true happiness in the buff? With Patricia Conelle.

VHS: S12315. $24.95.
Edgar G. Ulmer, USA, 1958, 80 mins.

Naked Youth

A great exploitation film in which Mamie Van Doren hosts this classic featuring psycho-teens who escape from juvenile prison, flee to Mexico for a head-on collision with deadly drugs and dangerous dolls.

VHS: S05198. $24.95.
John F. Schreyer, USA, 1959, 80 mins.

The Narcotic Story

Art Gilmore narrates this lurid expose about the evils of heroin addiction. Originally intended for police seminars only, it was then released to the general public with a sensational ad campaign. The images of burned-out heroin addicts are campily overdone.

VHS: S23186. $24.95.
Robert W. Larsen, USA, 1958, 75 mins.

Nation Aflame and Probation

Two rare films from the 1930's. *Nation Aflame* (Victor Halperin, USA, 1937, 78 mins.) is an indictment against the Ku Klux Klan and Nazism, and remains relevant today. *Probation* (Richard Thorpe, USA, 1932, 70 mins.) features the first screen appearance of Betty Grable, and is a blend of 30's exploitation and social commentary.

VHS: S02320. $29.95.

Naughty Nostalgia #1

Presented as a historical curiosity are two stag films from the 1920's. More amusing than arousing. Nobody takes off their shoes. Ask your grandfather if he remembers the titles *Mixed Relations* or *Bob's Hot Story*. These silent films are for adults only. USA, 1923, 38 mins.

VHS: S05512. $24.95.

Naughty Nostalgia #2

More stag films from the past. These three titles are from the late 1930's. *The Babysitter, The Opium Den* and *A Day in the Country* all provide nostalgia and nudity. Includes "Nightmare," the ugliest woman ever to appear in a porno movie. These are silent films with a musical score. Adults only. ID's will be required. USA, late 1930's, 42 mins.

VHS: S05513. $24.95.

Neutron and the Black Mask (Neutron el Enmascarado Negro)

The black-masked Mexican wrestler/atomic superman fights against a gang of crooks who plot to steal a dangerous neutron formula. Starring Wolf Rubinski, Armando Silvestre and Rosita Arenas.

VHS: S34483. $29.95.
Federico Curiel, Mexico, 1961, 86 mins.

Neutron vs. the Amazing Dr. Caronte

Neutron is up against a mad scientist and his monster-men in what is one of the more popular films of the Neutron series. With Wolf Rubinski, Julio Aleman and Rosita Arenas. Dubbed in English?

VHS: S34484. $29.95.
Federico Curiel, Mexico, 1962, 80 mins.

Neutron vs. the Death Robots (Los Automatas de la Muerte)

One of the best in the Neutron series. Neutron finds himself pitted against a monstrous, blood-consuming brain created with the brains of three dead scientists. Campy fun. Starring Wolf Rubinski and Armando Silvestre.

VHS: S34482. $29.95.
Federico Curiel, Mexico, 1961, 80 mins.

Neutron vs. the Maniac

The black-masked, Mexican wrestler/superhero solves a series of murders in a mysterious sanitarium. With an interesting twist ending. Starring Wolf Rubinski, Gina Romand and Rudolfo Landa.

VHS: S34481. $29.95.
Alfredo B. Crevenna, Mexico, 1961

Night of the Day of the...

Influenced by Woody Allen's *What's Up Tiger Lilly?*, director Lowell Mason has reimagined George Romero's horror masterpiece *Night of the Living Dead* as a burlesque comedy, reshaping the original soundtrack and mixing in new voices and dialogue to alter everyone's perception of the original. "Hilarious, the new cult hit of the 90s is recast with a new soundtrack" *(Mortal Remains)*.

VHS: S18241. $34.95.
Lowell Mason, USA, 1992, 90 mins.

Nude on the Moon

Two rocket scientists use Uncle Ted's inheritance to fly to the moon, where they discover a population of nudist "moon dolls" with pipe-cleaner antennae growing out of their bouffant hairdos. Features the classic romantic ballad, "I'm Mooning over You, My Little Moon Doll," and some of the strangest see-through, dirt-brown panties ever witnessed on any creature in the known universe. Written, directed and produced by Doris Wishman. This is one of Ms. Wishman's least favorite films, "because the people are so ugly."

VHS: S15138. $19.98.
Doris Wishman, USA, 1961, 78 mins.

Olga's House of Shame

Olga, the ultimate sadist, moves her headquarters from Chinatown to upstate New York, where she controls a crime syndicate involving narcotics, prostitution and jewel smuggling. An infamous work of sleaze. USA, 1964.

VHS: S23062. $19.98.

Omoo Omoo, The Shark God

A pretty good "B" jungle/voodoo thriller based on the novel by Herman Melville about the curse of a shark god that follows the despoilers of a jungle idol. With Ron Randall, Devera Burton, Trevor Bardette and Pedro DeCordoba.

VHS: S34488. $29.95.
Leon Leonard, USA, 1949, 58 mins.

One Body Too Many

Bela Lugosi plays a sinister servant in this murder mystery with comedic trimmings. Plot concerns an insurance salesman (Jack Haley) hired to guard the body of an eccentric millionaire overnight. With Lyle Talbot, Jean Parker and Blanche Yurka. B&W.

VHS: S04010. $29.95.
Frank McDonald, USA, 1944, 76 mins.

One Plus One
Leo G. Carroll and Hilda Brauner are featured in this dramatization of the *Kinsey Report*. After participating interviewees talk about it, they go on to do it. Five tales are shown tackling such issues as premarital sex, divorce, affairs and child-bearing.
VHS: S23188. $24.95.
Arch Oboler, USA, 1961, 114 mins.

Palm Springs Weekend
Guys with crew cuts, girls with flips, cars with fins, and fun, fun, fun, as eager young holidaymakers mix and mingle. Starring Troy Donahue, Stefanie Powers, Robert Conrad and Connie Stevens in tight gold lame.
VHS: S12581. $19.98.
Norman Taurog, USA, 1959, 101 mins.

Phantom of Paradise
Outrageous horror-rock comedy featuring pop musician Paul Williams as a notorious record tycoon who sells his soul to the devil for success. William Finley stars as a rock composer victim of an accident that leaves him disfigured and blaming Williams. Macabre and a bit bizarre.
VHS: S01018. $14.98.
Brian DePalma, USA, 1974, 92 mins.

Philosophy in the Bedroom
This contemporary adaptation of a work by the Marquis de Sade is a witty and outrageous comedy chronicling the experiences of Juliette, a young woman who undergoes a deep exploration of her sexuality as she is given a series of special lessons in sex and philosophy by the extremely decadent Dolman, assisted by his equally perverse friend, Angela. During the course of an evening, Dolman and Angela help demolish Juliette's conservative ideology and replace it with their own libertine perspectives.
VHS: S33878. $39.95.
Tony Guzman, USA, 1995, 88 mins.

Pope Must Diet
The original release title did not include the letter "t" in the last word. Robbie Coltrane, a former "Nun on the Run," now upsets the religious community by becoming pope by mistake. With Beverly D'Angelo, Herbert Lom, Paul Bartel, and Alex Rocco as Cardinal Rocco. A good hearted satire with a very controversial title. Watch for *Cinema Paradiso* star Salvatore Cascio as an adorable orphan.
VHS: S15508. $19.98.
Peter Richardson, Great Britain, 1991, 87 mins.

Prehistoric Bimbos in Armageddon City
Old Chicago City is the last outpost of civilization but it is ruled by the evil Nemesis. The prehistoric bimbos, led by Trianna, are the only threat to his evil rule. This wacky film is filled with great action and beautiful but tough women.
VHS: S24593. $19.95.
Todd Sheets, USA, 1993, 70 mins.

Prehistoric Women
The original stone age sex kittens epic that started it all. Filmed in "sin-scope" and "gorgeous cine-color."
VHS: S10057. $9.95.
Greg Tallas, USA, 1950, 74 mins.

The Prime Time
A beautiful, street-smart woman finds herself caught in a sleazy adult world she can't fully handle and seeks out the help of a grim detective she meets at the house of a beatnik artist to save her soul.
VHS: S20104. $24.95.
Herschell Gordon Lewis, USA, 1960, 76 mins.

Primitive Love
The "lost" 1964 Jayne Mansfield movie from Italy, featuring Franchi and Ciccio (Italy's answer to Martin and Lewis?) as two horny bellhops who spy on the bodacious Jayne as she finds every excuse to romp around almost naked. Then, it's *mondo* time as Jayne narrates her shockumentary, featuring topless Asian babes, *real* animal sacrifices and oriental cockfighting.
VHS: S32037. $29.95.
Luigi Scattini, Italy, 1964, 77 mins.

The Psychic
James F. Hurley's critique of celebrity. After an accident, Dan Thomas learns he has psychic capabilities. The power turns him into a sexual predator, as he uses his skills to coerce and manipulate people. He has a series of affairs, leaves his wife and daughter and becomes famous performing a psychic nightclub act. He goes on television and defames a well-known movie star who doubts his powers by declaring she is a lesbian. With Dick Genoa, Robin Guest and Carol Saenz.
VHS: S20103. $24.95.
James F. Hurley, USA, 1968

Pterodactyl Woman from Beverly Hills
Pixie Chandler (Beverly D'Angelo, *Vegas Vacation*), is not your average housewife. When Pixie's archeologist husband, Dick, digs up an ancient burial site, disturbing an eccentric witch doctor (Brion James, *The Fifth Element*), the shaman puts a curse on the meddling scientist's wife. Without warning, Pixie turns into the *Pterodactyl Woman from Beverly Hills*. From the Troma Team. With Moon Zappa.
VHS: S32156. $59.95.
Philippe Mora, USA, 1997, 97 mins.

Puss Bucket
A controversial reconsideration of a biblical tale, framed as a musical comedy, about two dimwitted brothers who are enlisted to "kill for Jesus," and the mayhem that ensues. Billed as "from the Broadway musical." With Terrence Fleming, Eric Hammer, Brian Sullivan and Gina Cammarotta. Directed and photographed by Lisa Houle.
VHS: S18108. $29.95.

Puzzle Channel, Vol. 1
A series of brain teasers that include picture puzzles, wordies, logic problems, number problems and other useless and unconventional tests. 60 mins.
VHS: S13094. $19.98.

Puzzle Channel, Vol. 2
A series of brain teasers that include murder mysteries, picture puzzles, wordies, logic problems, number problems and more. 60 mins.
VHS: S13095. $19.98.

Q the Winged Serpent
In this "genuinely entertaining" (Gene Siskel, *Chicago Tribune*) sci-fi cult tribute to moviedom's mightiest monsters, Quetzalcoatl, a dragon-like Aztec god is summoned to modern-day Manhattan by gory human sacrifices. But just call it "Q," because that's all you'll have time to say before it tears you apart. With winning performances by Michael Moriarty and David Carradine.
VHS: S34426. $14.98.
Larry Cohen, USA, 1982, 92 mins.

Rat Fink a Boo-Boo
A stylized parody of the kitsch 60s television series *Batman* features an inept superhero and his sidekick thrust into a series of perilous situations and life-saving adventures. With Vin Saxon, Carolyn Brandt, Titus Moede and Mike Kannon.
VHS: S20143. $24.95.
Ray Dennis Steckler, USA, 1966, 72 mins.

Really Strange Stories of the Totally Unknown
"Unauthorized parodies" include *The X Wives* (30 mins.) in which "FIB" agents Sox Molder and Zana Sully waste hard-earned taxpayer money investigating a really big chicken who murders ex-wives; *Unresolved Mysteries* (20 mins.) in which host Rubber Sack explores the mystery of an amnesiac Siamese Twin, the really truly final secret of Atlantis, and oh-so-much more; and *Invasion of the Ballroom People* (10 mins.) in which Jason from accounting stumbles onto a heinous conspiracy to replace office personnel with balloons.
VHS: S33197. $19.95.
Stephan Petrucha, USA, 1997, 60 mins.

Red
The visual equivalent of the red tape, this perverse work stars the legendary B-actor Lawrence Tierney in a piece about the damaging repercussion of phone hoaxes. 30 mins.
VHS: S17164. $19.95.

Red Nightmare
The now-famous anti-communist propaganda film, produced for the Defense Department by Warner Brothers, as a small-town American finds his community taken over by communists. Narrated by Jack Webb.
VHS: S04717. $29.95.
George Waggner, USA, 1962, 25 mins.

Reefer Madness
This anti-marijuana propaganda film has become a cult classic. Dave O'Brien plays a twitchy, eye-rolling lunatic who sits around talking to himself as he chain smokes the dreaded weed.
VHS: S01102. $19.95.
Louis Gasnier, USA, 1939, 65 mins.

Return of the Giant Majin
A well-done sequel to *Majin, Monster of Terror*. It's rumble time again for an ancient Japanese god whose spirit inhabits a giant stone statue. He romps around the countryside stomping the bad guys in a medieval feud. With Kojiro Hongo and Shiho Fujimura. Dubbed.
VHS: S34491. $29.95.
Yoshiyuki Kuroda/Kenji Misumi, Japan, 1966, 79 mins.

Revelations
In a not-so-distant future where sex is forbidden unless for procreation, lovemaking goes undercover for the release of repressed passions. Featured as *Penthouse*'s Couple Tape of the Month. Shot on 35mm film. 76 mins.
VHS: S28575. $49.95.

Revenge of the Bee Girls
From the producer of *Enter the Dragon* comes this "wonderfully campy and sexy sci-fi" (Leonard Maltin) about a strange force that turns a group of ordinary small-town California housewives into dangerous and ravishing predators who "love" men to death. Written by a pre-*Seven Percent Solution* Nicholas Meyer.
VHS: S31280. $14.95.
Denis Sanders, USA, 1973, 85 mins.

Ride the Wild Surf
One of the quintessential early 60s beach movies about young men in Hawaii in search of women and fun. Jan and Dean sing the title cut. With Fabian, Tab Hunter, Barbara Eden and James Mitchum.
VHS: S18361. $14.95.
Don Taylor, USA, 1964, 101 mins.

Rites of Passion
In *Shady Madonna*, the dirty mind of a TV evangelist is exposed. *In Search of the Ultimate Sexual Experience* is the story of a young woman who discovers ancient lovemaking secrets from her mysterious Adonis-like "master." 70 mins.
VHS: S28571. $39.95.

Robert Ripley: Believe It or Not
Ripley was a cartoonist, a collector, an explorer, an adventurer, a millionaire and a decided eccentric. This is the first in-depth look at the man who brought oddities to a world-wide audience. In this portrait amazing facts like his morbid fear of the telephone (he thought he would be electrocuted) come to light.
VHS: S21746. $14.98.

Rock 'n' Roll Mobster Girls
A fledgling all-girl band (performed and played by the notorious Doll Squad) is led into a Faustian pact with Bruno Multrock, a psychotic promoter who will stop at nothing to be the group's sole promoter. 110 mins.
VHS: S16934. $79.95.

Rock, Baby, Rock It
A rare 50's rock 'n' roll teenage film, hosted by Mamie Van Doren, and featuring 17 songs by obscure early rock legends like Kay Wheeler and rockabilly wildman Johnny Carroll.
VHS: S05199. $9.95.
Murray Douglas Sporup, USA, 1957, 84 mins.

Rocky Horror Picture Show
Now you can do the Time Warp in the privacy of your own home. The cult movie of cult movies is finally available in the U.S. on video. When Brad and Janet are forced to spend the night at the foreboding castle of the sexually ambitious Dr. Frank-Furter, they had no idea so many people would stay up late to watch them squirm. With Tim Curry, Barry Bostwick, Susan Sarandon, Richard O'Brien, Meatloaf and Little Nell.
Laser: THX. LD76381. $29.99.
Jim Sharman, USA, 1975, 105 mins.

Samurai
A hilarious spy-exploitation film about a Japanese orphan, raised in America, who turns traitor and helps plot the invasion of California. With Paul Fung and Luke Chan.
VHS: S15361. $29.95.
Raymond Cannon, USA, 1946, 62 mins.

Satan in High Heels
Meg Myles and Sabrina Grayson Hall star in this melodrama that exploits the femme fatale image. Meg is a full-figured stripper who ditches her drug-dependent husband and steals $900 from him on the way out. With her booty, she is off to New York, where an older man, and then his son, fall victim to her charms. Eventually she tries to get her forsaken husband to knock off the old codger.
VHS: S23189. $24.95.
Jerald Intrator, USA, 1962, 90 mins.

Schramm

Nekromantik's director Jorg Buttgereit depicts the world of a serial killer in this hypnotizing orgy of sex and violence. It's all seen through the eyes of the killer, Lothar Schramm (Florian Koemer von Gustorf). He is fascinated by a prostitute (Monika M.) and obsessed with death. The result is a well-crafted, surreal vision of love and desire.

VHS: S27510. $29.95.

Jorg Buttgereit, Germany, 90 mins.

Score

A liberated '70s couple seduces another couple into experimentation with bisexuality and group sex. "Somewhere between *Who's Afraid of Virginia Woolf* and *Love, American Style*" *(Time Out)*.

VHS: S33225. $29.95.

Radley Metzger, USA/Yugoslavia, 1972, 90 mins.

Scum of the Earth

An innocent woman is tricked into posing nude for a brutal gang of rednecks. After she is ruthlessly exploited to increase sales of the magazine, she is sexually harassed by one of its members and saved by another of the group.

VHS: S20106. $24.95.

Herschell Gordon Lewis, USA, 1963, 71 mins.

Secrets of Love, Classics of Erotic Literature: Vol. 1

This series of erotic stories is based on works by some of the greatest authors of all time: *The Greenhouse*, by Guy de Maupassant, is a tale of voyeurism. An older couple find their lost passion by watching a younger pair. In *A Country Villa*, adapted from Anton Chekhov's story, a man and wife are captivated by the women of a Turkish-style brothel. 58 mins.

VHS: S23292. $19.95.

Secrets of Love, Classics of Erotic Literature: Vol. 2

The Marquis de Sade's *Augustine* begins this volume of arousing stories. The title character is reputed to be a lesbian until one night when she seduces a man at a ball. In *At the Rose Leaf*, by Guy de Maupassant, a man and his wife find themselves charmed by the same delights. 57 mins.

VHS: S23293. $19.95.

Secrets of Love, Classics of Erotic Literature: Vol. 3

Mandragora, by Niccolo Machiavelli, and *The Contest*, by Geoffrey Chaucer, are adapted in this volume of sexy tales. In the first story a young medical student gets his way with a chaste and virtuous wife through a powerful drug. Then students try to take advantage of an old man with a beautiful wife, leading to surprising consequences. 57 mins.

VHS: S23294. $19.95.

Secrets of Love, Classics of Erotic Literature: Vol. 4

This erotic series brings a unique level of sophistication to romance and sex through well-produced stories written by famous authors. This volume features *The Spanking* by Marguerite de la Navarre and *The Pupil* by Nicolas de la Bretonne. In *The Spanking*, a pretty weaver girl plots revenge against someone who humiliated her. In *The Pupil*, a rich uncle finds that his chambermaids can give his nephew a much needed education.

VHS: S27085. $19.95.

Pierre Grimblat, France, 56 mins.

Secrets of Love, Classics of Erotic Literature: Vol. 5

In Guiseppe Celentano's *The Test of Love*, an heir to the Duke of Mantua must prove his manhood before he can wed a Medici woman. This man must demonstrate his virility with a virgin before several witnesses. In *A Well Deserved Punishment* by Giovanni Boccaccio, a rich merchant tries to control his overly amorous wife.

VHS: S27086. $19.95.

Pierre Grimblat, France, 56 mins.

Secrets of Love, Classics of Erotic Literature: Vol. 6

Jean de la Fontaine's *The Wager of Three Wives* follows three women who engage in adulterous love. *Lady Roxanne*, from Daniel Defoe, concerns a beautiful but poor Lady who must consider the use of her most cherished asset quite carefully. Ingenuity and compromise ensure that contentment is achieved by all concerned, even the Lady's landlord.

VHS: S27087. $19.95.

Pierre Grimblat, France, 56 mins.

Sensual Escape

Fortune Smiles is the funny tale of a couple who have been dating and are about to make the leap into bed. In *The Tunnel*, a young artist's recurring erotic dream leads her to an encounter with a mysterious and passionate stranger. *Adult Video News* choice for Best Actress, Best Performance in a Sex Scene, and Best Director. 67 mins.

VHS: S28569. $39.95.

Sex and the College Girl

Charles Grodin stars in this campy tale of free love and manipulation set on the sands of Puerto Rico. Two college girls head off on a vacation with definite plans—one wants to get married, and one wants to get lucky. Both are in for a big surprise in this tale of sex, sleaziness, lost virginity and lacking morals.

VHS: S15146. $19.98.

Joseph Adler, USA, 1964, 90 mins.

Sex Education Films of the 40's

Five short films include *Dating Do's and Don'ts, USS-VD: The Ship of Shame,* and *Know for Sure*.

VHS: S02586. $34.95.

Sex Madness

Duncey Taylor. Wild dancing and heavy duty makeout sessions lead young ones to pregnancy, social diseases, drugs and even death. Syphilitic madness is the ultimate evil depicted here. This film has all the hallmarks of an enduring exploitation classic. 1937, 50 mins.

VHS: S23176. $24.95.

Sgt. Kabukiman, N.Y.P.D.

Another critically acclaimed hit from the wacky Troma Team. Harry Griswold is a tough New York City police officer. While investigating the murder of a legendary Japanese actor, Griswold is given magic powers through a strange twist of fate. At the same time, an ancient prophecy unleashes an omnipotent evil spirit that Griswold must destroy to save the world. Sgt. Kabukiman, N.Y.P.D., has a variety of high-tech weapons in his arsenal, which include lethal, heat-seeking chopsticks, pyroprojectile parasols and fatal flying sushi. "Colombo with a dash of Jim Carrey" *(New York Times)*. With Rick Gianasi, Brick Bronksi and Susan Byun. Uncut version.

VHS: S32155. $59.98.

Lloyd Kaufman/Michael Herz, USA, 1996, 105 mins.

The Shadow Strikes

Rod La Rocque stars as the famous radio crime fighter who knows what evil lurks in the hearts of men. As a sleuthing lawyer with a secret identity, he stalks a mysterious killer and a gangster chief. All the while the police are trying to pin the crimes on his alter-ego. With Lynn Anders and Walter McGrail. B&W.

VHS: S03338. $39.95.

Lynn Shores, USA, 1937, 61 mins.

Shag

When Southern Belle high school grad Phoebe Cates gets engaged, her three girlfriends embark on a last fling weekend of sun, fun, dancing and romancing in Myrtle Beach in 1963. With Bridget Fonda, Annabeth Gish and Tyrone Power Jr.

VHS: S32703. $14.95.

Zelda Barron, USA, 1988, 98 mins.

Shake a Lizard Tail, Or Rust Belt Rump

Video of techno dancers mixed with old horror footage, Detroit late-nite TV commercials and Japanese monsters, with original, unreleased soundtrack from Detroit cult band Destroy All Monsters, recorded in 1995. 30 mins.

VHS: S31888. $14.95.

Shanty Tramp

A sleazy evangelist puts the move on a small-town shanty tramp. She then makes a move on a local black kid, which eventually gets him killed after her drunken father walks in on them and she yells rape. "Kind of an R-rated sleazy cross between *Elmer Gantry* and *To Kill a Mockingbird*" (Sinister Cinema). With Lee Holland, Kenneth Douglas, Lewis Galen, Bill Rogers and Lawrence Tobin.

VHS: S34495. $29.95.

Joseph G. Prieto, USA, 1966, 72 mins.

She Shoulda Said No

Lila Leeds, Lyle Talbot, Alan Baxter and Jack Elam are the best cast ever assembled in exploitation film history. There are still more horrors caused by marijuana that have not been fully explored elsewhere. Leeds made this film to atone for a real-life marijuana arrest. 1949.

VHS: S23182. $24.95.

She-Devils on Wheels

This cult classic was the first feminist biker movie; the story of the "Man Eaters" gang proves that women can slap men around and use them for sexual meat too. Portrayed by real lady bikers from an organization out of Miami called the "Cut-Throats." Watch for the famous "stud line" scene, and always remember the Man-Eaters' motto: "Sex, Guts, Blood, and all men are Mothers!" Directed by Herschell Gordon Lewis, who fashioned a career out of exploiting the forbidden, the tasteless, and the bizarre.

VHS: S15140. $19.98.

Herschell Gordon Lewis, USA, 1968, 90 mins.

Slave Trade in the World Today

Allen Swift narrates this mondo movie, which documents slavery in the contemporary world. Whole tribes sold into bondage, an auction for a rich shiek's harem, and a variety of brutal practices are revealed in this shocking film.

VHS: S23318. $24.95.

Roberto Malenotti, USA, 1964, 87 mins.

Slaves in Bondage

Lona Andre, Donald Reed, Wheeler Oakman and Florence Dudley are featured in this exploitation classic about the perils of prostitution. Young, innocent, country girls are lured into the big city and recruited into a life of ill repute. Spankings, catfights, alcohol abuse and other unsavory goings-on make this a must-see. 1937.

VHS: S23175. $24.95.

Sleazemania

This compilation tape features highlights and previews from some of the sleaziest and sickest movies of all time. It includes only the very best from classics like *Jailbait Babysitters, The Flesh Merchants, The Young Seducers* and more. 60 mins.

VHS: S26328. $19.95.

Sleazemania Strikes Back

More outrageous highlights and previews have been combined on this over-the-top compilation videotape. Includes footage from *College Girls Confidential, Suburban Roulette, Beach Blanket Bloodbath* and more. 60 mins.

VHS: S26330. $19.95.

Sleazemania: The Good, the Bad and the Sleazy

There are more clips and previews from schlocky classics on this third *Sleazemania* video. Lenny Bruce in *Dance Hall Racket, Striporama, Teenage Zombies* and exploitative delights are represented. 60 mins.

VHS: S26329. $19.95.

Something Weird

A disfigured man with psychic abilities meets a witch who will give him back his beautiful face in exchange for a little action. The next thing you know, we're in Wisconsin trying to solve a serial murder case and tripping on LSD. A must-see if only for the possessed, killer bed sheets scene.

VHS: S15149. $19.98.

Herschell Gordon Lewis, USA, 1967, 87 mins.

Sorority Babes in the Dance-a-thon of Death

Sorority women conjure a demon from an ancient crystal ball. Now two nerdy but randy boys are their only hope in fighting this evil. A great shlocky film with a finale set in a disco.

VHS: S24592. $19.95.

Todd Sheets, USA, 1994, 75 mins.

Stewardess School

The *Police Academy* of the skies, with the wild parties, coed showers and the usual mishaps.

VHS: S04692. $14.95.

Ken Blancato, USA, 1986, 84 mins.

Stick It in Your Ear

David awakens in a gothic building and can't remember how he got there. He wanders through the delirious freedom of the counterculture, consuming drugs and free love in vast quantities. David's absence of an identity leads to his transformation to a cold-hearted assassin. A shadow group hires him to kill a woman, but he would rather have sex with her. With Guido Conte, Lance Revson and Michelle Most.

VHS: S20098. $24.95.

Charles Morgan, USA, 1970

Story of O
The adaptation of the famous novel describing the process of love through discipline and obedience, from the director of *Emmanuelle*. English dubbed.
VHS: S01515. $49.95.
Just Jaeckin, France, 1975, 96 mins.

The Strange Hostel of Naked Pleasures
In a haunted hostel the perverse and unnatural desires of its guests leap out of the dream world to haunt their waking hours. Bizarre scenarios characterize this horror film of surrealistic terror. Portuguese with English subtitles.
VHS: S20750. $24.95.
Marcello Motta, Brazil, 1975

Strictly Speaking
Mistress Karen leads curious couples through this light documentary on S&M. 55 mins.
VHS: S27646. $24.95.

Striporama
The greats of Burlesque, including Sally Rand doing her classic *Bubble Dance*, Betty Rowland *The Ball of Fire*, Virginia Bell, Tempest Storm, Scarlett Knight, Helene Renee, in a classic review of the great days of Burlesque. USA, 50 mins.
VHS: S04846. $29.95.
Jerald Intrator, USA, 1953, 65 mins.

Stuff Stephanie in the Incinerator
Don't throw your love away—burn it. When your wife and best friend are after your hard-earned money, there is only one thing left to do: *Stuff Stephanie in the Incinerator*. A grand cinematic achievement in the tradition of Truffaut, Hitchcock and DePalma.
VHS: S32645. $14.98.
Don Nardo/Peter Jones, USA, 1990, 90 mins.

Suburban Roulette
In 1967 wife-swapping was a taboo subject, even in the movies. So this morality tale about the steamy underside of suburban living was considered lurid and shocking—especially in its depiction of two housewives who are addicted to sex. Made on an extremely low budget, it's so rough around the edges that, in a fight scene, one of the punches misses entirely, but the intended target falls down anyway. Produced and directed by Herschell Gordon Lewis, a Chicago advertising man turned exploitation filmmaker.
VHS: S15139. $19.98.
Herschell Gordon Lewis, USA, 1967, 91 mins.

Superman & the Mole Men
In his first Superman full-length feature, the Man of Steel investigates when curious creatures from the bowels of the Earth surface through an oil-well shaft. Starring George Reeves.
VHS: S06245. $14.95.
Lee Sholem, USA, 1951, 58 mins.

Surf Nazis Must Die
A camp film with a great title in which, in the wake of a killer earthquake, the beaches of California have been taken over by neo-Nazi punks. Their reign of terror comes to a halt when a retired, fat black woman with a .38 stops them dead!
VHS: S05894. $79.95.
Peter George, USA, 1987, 83 mins.

Switchblade Sisters
The "Switchblade Sisters" is a tough, all-women gang fighting for turf. These outrageous teenage hoodlums create mayhem everywhere they go, from the classroom to the steets, and eventually confront one another in a final switchblade fight. With Joanne Nail and Monica Gayle. "A shotgun wedding of mini-skirts and M-16s. Timeless and quite entertaining" *(Newsday)*.
VHS: S30638. $103.99.
Laser: Widescreen. **LD76165. $49.98.**
Jack Hill, USA, 1996, 90 mins.

A Taste of Blood
American cult filmmaker Herschell Gordon Lewis directed this off-center *Dracula* variation about an American who is transformed into a night prowler after swallowing a strange potion. The action shifts from the American Southwest to London, where the stalker goes on a diabolical killing spree.
He is pursued by the avenging Dr. Helsing. Screenplay by Donald Stanford. With Bill Rogers, Elizabeth Wilkinson, Thomas Wood and Otto Schlesinger.
VHS: S20095. $24.95.
Herschell Gordon Lewis, USA, 1967, 120 mins.

Teaserama: David Friedman's Roadshow Rarities, Vol. 1
A fascinating underground history on the origins of the exploitation film, showcasing the extraordinary Betty Page in a collection of erotic vignettes and burlesque madness, opposite the self-named Tempest Storm, Cherry Knight, Honey Baer, Trudy Wayne and Chris La Chris.
VHS: S18439. $24.95.

Teenage Confidential
Wild youth set free with violent passions. They were too young to know any better. Highlights from the greatest and greasiest teen flicks ever made are merged with previews and an in-depth interview on teenage delinquency taken from newsreels and government scare films of the 40s and 50s. 60 mins.
VHS: S05185. $24.95.

Teenage Devil Dolls
Mamie Van Doren hosts this "tough" teen film, with the Devil Dolls. Young Cassandra joins a crazy gang where she starts on reefer, graduates to goofballs, and is soon found groveling in garbage, looking for a fix. Naturally, this lands her in the psycho ward, and eventually back on the streets.
VHS: S05204. $24.95.
B. Lawrence Price, USA, 1953, 70 mins.

Teenage Strangler
Bill Posner's funky variation of the juvenile delinquent angst drama follows the deranged activities of a lipstick killer who is suffocating schoolgirls with stockings in Huntington, West Virginia. A member of a local gang called the Fastdogs, Jimmy is a prime suspect. The film weaves in the social protest and outlaw behavior of the 60s B-movie (including drag races, rumbles and rock and roll) within the trappings of the serial killer movie. With Bill A. Bloom, Jo Canterbury and John Ensign.
VHS: S20108. $24.95.
Bill Posner, USA, 1964, 64 mins.

Terror of Tiny Town
One of the classic camp films: a musical Western enacted entirely by midgets. One of the wonders of Hollywood. With Billy Curtis, Yvonne Moray, Little Billy, John Bambury.
VHS: S03056. $19.95.
Sam Newfield, USA, 1963, 63 mins.

Terror-Creatures From the Grave
Summoned to draw up a will, lawyer Alfred Kovac (Walter *Playgirls and the Vampire* Brandi) arrives at the villa Hauff only to find that Dr. Jeronimus Hauff, an accomplished spiritualist and the man who requested his visit, has been dead almost a year. With the sultry Barbara Steele as the less-than-faithful widow of the dearly departed Dr. Hauff.
VHS: S37086. $24.95.
Masimo Pupillo, Italy, 1966, 90 mins.

Texas Chainsaw Massacre: The Next Generation
Two young couples take a wrong turn down a deserted road and meet up with maniacal cross-dressing chainsaw murderer Leatherface in this bone-chilling sequel to the the horror classic. "Leatherface crosses Divine with Hannibal Lecter" (Thelma Adams, *New York Post*). "A giddy mix of gruesome horror and campy humor" (John Anderson, *Los Angeles Times*). With Renee Zellweger *(Jerry Maguire)* and Matthew McConaughey *(A Time to Kill)*, and Robert Jacks as Leatherface.
VHS: S33229. $104.99.
Kim Henkel, USA, 1994, 94 mins.

Thank God It's Friday
A glittering slice-of-life in a West Coast disco called the Zoo, where an aspiring singer (Donna Summer) keeps trying to convince the club's emcee and deejay to let her sing. Co-starring Jeff Goldblum, Debra Winger and Berlin singer Terri Nunn. Features a live performance by The Commodores with Lionel Richie and the film's Academy Award-winning song, "Last Dance," performed by Donna Summer.
VHS: S32683. $19.95.
Robert Klane, USA, 1978, 89 mins.

That's Offensive
A hilarious, often shocking look at American culture in the days before political correctness. This long-lost footage has been rescued from history's dustbin so you can witness "fat girl diving exhibitions," a Jim Crow watermelon-eating contest, and living, breathing freaks of nature that have made women scream and strong men faint.
VHS: S32158. $14.95.

They Saved Hitler's Brain
One of the great cult classics: a scientist is kidnapped; his daughter traces him to the mysterious island of Mandoras where a cult of Nazi worshippers is manipulated by the severed head of Adolf. 74 mins.
VHS: S05381. $29.95.

They Wear No Clothes
Where this film is lacking under its pretense as a sociological study, *They Wear No Clothes* makes up in bravado. Not too long on commentary, the film examines those who—by choice or profession—choose to undress. Includes the bonus short, *How to Hold a Husband*. 1941, 55 mins.
VHS: S15913. $19.95.

The Third Sex
Paula Wesley and Paul Dahlke star in this exploitative look at homosexuality. Parents try to straighten out their son, who is hanging out with a known gay man. It's a shocker. 1959.
VHS: S23187. $24.95.

Third Sex Sinema Volume 5: Consenting Adults
This obscure study of homosexuality reports on the lifestyles of gay men and women in Great Britain in the mid-'60s. *The Male Nudists* features two burly young men entertaining one another, lounging around, exercising, flexing their huge muscles, oiling themselves up, showering together and wrestling. There's footage from the Gay-In III, sponsored by the Gay Liberation Front, a surrealistic gay encounter on a park bench, wrapped up by *Caught in the Can*, an early '70s short about two guys who dress in drag to take some suckers for a roll.
VHS: S30988. $19.98.

This Nude World
The film that puts the "camp" into Nudist Camp. Travel on a world tour from Camp Olympia in New York (home of the weekend volleyball enthusiasts) to France, Germany and other fun spots on the naked globe. 55 mins.
VHS: S12316. $24.95.

This Stuff'll Kill You
A Herschell Gordon Lewis epic with religious overtones follows the anarchic adventures of some mountain rednecks who set in motion a violent chain of events under the influence of some white lightning.
VHS: S20099. $24.95.
Herschell Gordon Lewis, USA, 1971, 100 mins.

Three Daughters
As Heather Clayton blossoms into a young woman, her parents rediscover the passion between them as they watch their daughters grow up and leave home. Winner of New York Adult Critic Association Best Music Award. 80 mins.
VHS: S28572. $39.95.

The Thrill Killers
Director Ray Dennis Steckler (aka Cash Flagg) made this grubby shocker about a band of marauders who randomly terrorize wealthy Los Angeles suburbs and kill indiscriminately. With Cash Flagg, Liz Renay, Brick Bardo, Carolyn Brandt and Atlas King.
VHS: S20141. $24.95.
Ray Dennis Steckler, USA, 1965, 82 mins.

Ticket of Leave Man
Tod Slaughter, the horror man of Europe, enacts the role of Tiger Dalton. By day, a respected benefactor for an organization dedicated to help ex-convicts. By night, the head of a criminal syndicate. When the police find out, he is chased through a cemetery. Watch out for open graves. With Marjorie Edwards, John Warwick and Jenny Lynn.
VHS: S04044. $29.95.
George King, Great Britain, 1937, 71 mins.

The Tiger and the Pussycat
Vittorio Gassman plays an aging Italian businessman who tries to spice up his life with a fling with an American art student in Rome. Ann-Margret co-stars in this comedy-drama as the subject of the attentions of both the father and the son. With Eleanor Parker as Gassman's somewhat understanding wife, Caterina Borrato and Fiorenzo Fiorentini.
VHS: S12601. $29.95.
Dino Risi, USA/Italy, 1967, 105 mins.

Tokyo Decadence
Japanese novelist and filmmaker Ryu Murakami adapts his novel *Topaz*, about a prostitute's (Miho Nikaido) search for redemption. Ai falls under the spell of a charismatic dominatrix and tries desperately to reverse her slide into cocaine dependency and sexual slavery. "Murakami adeptly throws us off balance, with deadpan black humor and a complex politic involving the notion of 'wealth without pride'" (Toronto Film Festival). With Sayoko Amano, Tenmei Kanou and Masahiko Shimada. Japanese with English subtitles.
VHS: S19176. $29.95.
Ryu Murakami, Japan, 1991, 112 mins.

Too Much, Too Often
A gritty sexual parable from master director Doris Wishman. Women driven to the depths of degradation by the insistent burning of their outsized sexual pangs. The flavor of this film is every bit as enjoyable as its considerable stench.
VHS: S15157. $19.98.
Doris Wishman, USA, 1965

Trader Hornee

A bawdy sex and jungle romp written by David F. Friedman that turns into a hilarious parody of the genre, about a sexy young detective hired to track down the missing heir of the late African explorer and help settle the family estate. What she discovers is everyone is consumed by sex and greed.
VHS: S17038. $29.95.
Tsanusdi, USA, 1970, 72 mins.

Trail of Blood

A dramatization based on the notorious Green River serial murder case, which, despite over 40 female victims, remains unsolved. *Trail of Blood* features some of the most colorful and offbeat characters imaginable, with such personalities as Warhol superstar Taylor Mead, art terrorist and serial killer aficionado Joe Coleman, author William Kotzwinkle *(E.T.)* and philosophical performance guru Copernicus. The film also introduces the master of pop Yiddish humor, Arthur of New York, and actress/model Madonna Chavez (the niece of the late labor leader Cesar Chavez) Directed by Russian filmmaker/painter Ari Roussimof.
VHS: S31135. $49.95.
Ari Roussimof, USA/Mexico, 1996, 105 mins.

Trip to Where?

This outrageous discourse on the evils of LSD was produced by the United States Navy. A group of innocent, upstanding sailors are led astray and experience acid trips that inevitably turn bad (but not quite as bad as the film itself). Highlights include some nice photographic special effects and sexy, young Vic Tayback in a gripping cameo performance as a drug kingpin (before he went legit, opened Mel's Diner and hired Linda Lavin). USA, 56 mins.
VHS: S15386. $24.95.

Trog

A strange creature suspected of murdering students in England is captured and brought to anthropologist Dr. Brockton (Joan Crawford), who believes this "trog" is the missing link between man and ape. She begins to study and educate the Trog when it escapes and abducts a little girl. Dr. Brockton and her colleagues must find Trog before the cops get him.
VHS: S34601. $14.95.
Freddie Francis, Great Britain, 1970, 91 mins.

Troma's War (Director's Cut)

If you liked *The Toxic Avenger*, you'll love *War*. Packed with gargantuan battle scenes, heart-stopping stunts and never-before-seen special effects, this unparalleled action film from Troma features a set of Siamese twins joined at the head, exploding breasts, and the fearless citizens of Tromaville. "Makes *Rambo III* look like *Lassie Come Home" (Variety)*.
VHS: S32644. $14.98.
Lloyd Kaufman/Michael Herz, USA, 1986, 106 mins.

Tromeo & Juliet

The Troma Team does *Romeo & Juliet* in this "sexy, silly, sweet & surreal" *(USA Today)* film that's not just for Troma junkies. Featuring the music of Sublime, Superchunk, Motorhead, Ass Ponys, Unsane, Wesley Willis and Fiasco.
VHS: S31272. $59.99.
Lloyd Kaufman, USA, 1997, 95 mins.

Truly Tasteless Jokes: The Video

Based on the best-selling books compiled by Blanche Knott.
VHS: S04503. $9.98.

Uptown Angel

A stern moral fable with a taut, realistic texture about a promising young actress unable to realize her dreams, who falls into a deadly cycle of prostitution, drugs and violence.
VHS: S18838. $19.95.
Jay Shannon, USA, 1990, 90 mins.

Urban Heat

The camera watches lovers heat up as the summer temperatures soar in the city, where an older woman and a younger man experience lust in an elevator, two dancers take their passion beyond the dance, and rooftop sunbathing turns into an a erotic encounter. Voted best video of the year by the New York Adult Critic Association. 60 mins.
VHS: S28573. $39.95.

Valley of the Dolls

An examination of the dark side of Hollywood and the industry's objectification of a group of actresses, where the vicissitudes and dangers of drugs, sexual exploitation, infidelity, insecurity, jealousy, betrayal and fear intermingle in the lives of the various "dolls," ambitious young women desperate for stardom and recognition. Adapted from Jacqueline Susann's novel. With Patty Duke, Barbara Parkins, Sharon Tate and Paul Burke.
VHS: S18598. $14.98.
Laser: LD76739. $39.98.
Mark Robson, USA, 1967, 123 mins.

Vampire Vixens from Venus

Hideous in their original form, three alien drug smugglers transform into beautiful women on Earth. Their drug is derived from the life essence of men and they're on a mission to drain every last drop. A funny sexy sci-fi thriller.
VHS: S23048. $69.95.
Ted A. Bohus, USA, 1994, 90 mins.

Varietease: David Friedman's Roadshow Rarities, Vol. 2

A color exercise in the art and beauty of the striptease act, with world champion Betty Page taking on all rivals, including Lili St. Cyr, Chris La Chris and Vicki Lynn in the title for Anatomy Award of 1955.
VHS: S18440. $24.95.

Vegas in Space

Drag Queens bring Vegas glamour to an intergalactic battle of outsized proportions. Well, the proportions of the miniature sets are all too obvious, but then so is the drag in this campy, overacted farce. An all-women planet is thrown out of whack by a dastardly crime. Two earth astronauts are sent to help, but there is one condition. They must become women to enter this feminine planet. The rest is showbiz herstory. Features the late Doris Fish.
VHS: S27624. $69.98.
Phillip R. Ford, USA, 1991, 85 mins.

Video from Hell

A compilation of Frank Zappa video releases. Including "Uncle Meat", a project started in 1967 with Haskell Wexler as the cinematographer. Clay animation by Bruce Bickford. The videos "G-Spot Tornado", "You Are What You Is", "St. Etienne". Also the true story of *200 Motels* and *Baby Snakes*.
VHS: S04970. $29.95.
Frank Zappa, USA, 1987, 60 mins.

Violated

A baffling set of murders is at the center of this strange exploitation extravaganza. The killer slays his victims and then gives them a haircut. A psychopathologist is brought in to give the police advice on hair fetishes, in an erie echo of *Glen and Glenda*. Among the suspects are a paunchy old man who lusts after young girls and a sleazy photographer. With Mitchell Kowal, Wim Hollard, Lili Dawn and Vicki Carlson.
VHS: S23184. $24.95.
Walter Strate, USA, 1953, 78 mins.

The Wacky World of Doctor Morgus

Filmed in the back alleys and tacky cafes of New Orleans, Dr. Morgus (a TV horror show host), his comatose girlfriend Zelda and his sidekick Chopsely join in a fiendish plot to take over the country. The evil ruler of Microvania is preparing to smuggle 300 spies into the United States; his secret weapon is the Doctor's "instant people machine" that turns humans into sand—then reanimates them. Enter ace reporter Pencils McCane to foil the dastardly plot. The climax is the icing on the cake in a city famous for its eccentric inhabitants.
VHS: S30733. $29.95.
Roul Haig, USA, 1962, 87 mins.

Weird America

Charles Gatewood's work documents the "Beyond-the-Fringe never-never land of sexual fetishists," according to *Penthouse* magazine. The work explores such unconventional sexual playgrounds as San Francisco's sadomasochistic underground, New York's nude centers, erotic tattooing and body piercing, with forays into mud wrestling bikers, wet T-shirt contests, and coverage of Mardi Gras breakouts. 85 mins.
VHS: S17089. $59.95.

Weird World of LSD

Terry Tessem, Ann Lindsay and Yolanda Morino star in this expose of countercultural drug use. The effects of LSD have never been so bizarrely portrayed as in this schlocky camp classic. 1967.
VHS: S23192. $24.95.

What's the Matter with Helen?

A lurid thriller about two aging film stars (Shelley Winters and Debbie Reynolds) attempting to conceal their pasts, who open a dance school for child stars. With Dennis Weaver, Agnes Moorehead and Michael MacLiammoir.
VHS: S17535. $14.95.
Curtis Harrington, USA, 1971, 101 mins.

White Slaves of Chinatown

Sex and drugs rule in this first of Frank Henenlotter's depraved "Olga" films, in which the sadistic Olga keeps Lola and half a dozen other girls in bondage and throws drug parties in her Chinatown torture headquarters.
VHS: S27547. $29.95.
Joseph P. Mawra, USA, 1964

The White Warrior

Steve Reeves stars as the famous Cossack Agi Murad, the courageous leader of a 19-century rebellion against the Russian Czar. It's a classic Reeves vehicle, featuring a historic backdrop and costumes in a tale loaded with dramatic battles and more individual conflicts. Dubbed in English.
VHS: S29449. $29.95.
Riccardo Freda, Italy/Yugoslavia, 1959, 91 mins.

Whore 2

This sequel builds on the controversial themes originally explored in the original Ken Russell production of *Whore*. It too offers a powerful, stark and compelling look at the world's oldest profession. Nightlife will never have quite the same meaning ever again.
VHS: S22531. $94.99.
Laser: LD75284. $34.98.
Amos Kollek, USA, 1994, 85 mins.

Wild Guitar

The curiosity film from the early 60s, capturing the pre-Beatles scene in America. Arch Hall Jr. stars as a young, naive, pompadoured pixie who motorcycles into Hollywood with nothing more than a "git-tar" and the clothes on his back, and within minutes of his arrival, appears on TV, becomes a superstar, and falls into the clutches of an unscrupulous, cigar-chomping manager.
VHS: S05188. $9.95.
Ray Dennis Steckler, USA, 1962, 92 mins.

Wild Ones on Wheels

A sportscar gang murders an ex-con and forces his wife to locate $240,000 he had buried in the desert. Ray Dennis Steckler is priceless in a supporting role. With Francine York and Robert Blair.
VHS: S32597. $24.95.
Rudolph Cusumano, USA, 1962, 92 mins.

The Wild Women of Wongo

The world of Wongo is filled with hungry alligators, wild women, and sexually unsatisfied tribesmen. It seems the boys are not pleased with their shapeless prehistoric wives, and turn to the gyrating Wongo-ettes for down and dirty tribal dancing. This film must be seen to be believed. Stars Jean Hawkshaw, Johnny Walsh, Mary Ann Webb, Cande Gerrard and Ed Fury.
VHS: S16111. $29.95.
James L. Wolcott, USA, 1959, 80 mins.

The Wild World of Batwoman

The super-heroine battles diabolical evil to save the world in this rare 60's camp feature which pits Bat Woman Katherine Victor and her bevy of beautiful Bat Girls against the evil Ratfink and the scheming Dr. Neon. Racing against their nasty nemesis to find the prototype of a new hearing aid (actually an atomic listening device/nuclear bomb), these sexy super-heroines still have time for their rock'n'rolling bikini beach parties. USA, 1966, 80 mins.
VHS: S10840. $29.95.
Jerry Warren, USA, 1966, 70 mins.

Wild, Wild World of Jayne Mansfield

Jayne Mansfield hosts a tacky tour of Europe's sleaze spots, including topless clubs and nudist camps, providing a droll commentary the whole time. The low point of bad taste is the finale in which gruesome shots of her fatal car accident are followed by a tearful tour of her Purple Palace, hosted by her hubby, Mickey Hargitay.
VHS: S07479. $29.95.
Arthur Knight, USA, 1968, 90 mins.

Witch Doctor in Tails

This one is in the true tradition of Mondo sleazo with visits to a slaughterhouse, firewalkers and a very disgusting look at the sundry rites and mutilations witch doctors perform. For mature audiences only. Narrated, in English, by George Sanders. Italy, 1966, 96 mins.
VHS: S13500. $24.95.

The Wizard of Gore

This mind twister pits unsuspecting women against the gruesome illusions of an evil magician. The beautiful volunteers are magically sawed in half, impaled through the head and gored through the stomach—and then walk away seemingly unharmed. Hours later they are found dead of the same wounds.
VHS: S15144. $19.98.
Herschell Gordon Lewis, USA, 1970, 96 mins

Wizards of the Demon Sword

A Troma adventure in the tradition of *Kull the Conqueror*. In a world of sword and sorcery, the heroic Thane must have a beautiful princess from the evil wizard, Lord Khoura. Along his journey he must face sadistic slave traders, deadly dinosaurs and hellish highwaymen as he struggles to possess the all-powerful Blade of Aktar, the Demon Sword. With Michael Berryman, Lawrence Tierney, Russ Tamblyn and Lyle Waggoner.
VHS: S32647. $14.98.
Fred Olen Ray, USA, 1991, 81 mins.

World's Greatest Movie Challenge

A lot of fun—a VCR game which features film clips from some of the greatest motion pictures, offering a dazzling array of stars including John Wayne, Gary Cooper, Bing Crosby, Bette Davis, Helen Hayes, Abbott and Costello—and a challenge in trivia knowledge to the serious as well as casual devotees of Hollywood, the movies, and the stars of yesterday. Comes complete with a formatted answer pad, an instruction book, and a full-size movie poster from "It's A Wonderful Life." Four gamesin one, graduated by degree of difficulty. 88 mins.
VHS: S06322. $39.95.

RUSS MEYER

Beneath the Valley of the Ultravixens

Russ Meyer's self-described "all-out assault on today's sexual mores" with Lavonia, Eufaula Roop, Junk Yard Sal, and others.
VHS: S03539. $79.95.
Russ Meyer, USA, 1979, 90 mins.

Beyond the Valley of the Dolls

Russ Meyer's excursion into studio filmmaking resulted in this melodrama written by film critic Roger Ebert about an all-girl rock group, their relationship with a transsexual manager and their rise and introduction to the Hollywood netherworld of exploitation and flagrant hedonism. "A delirious comedy soused in self-parody but spiked with dope, sex and thrills" *(Time Out)*. With Dolly Read, Cynthia Myers, Marcia McBroom and John La Zar.
VHS: S18599. $19.98.
Russ Meyer, USA, 1970, 109 mins.

Blacksnake!

On the Caribbean Isle of San Cristobal, the legendary and sadistic Lady Susan presides over a plantation worked by slaves. When her most recent husband, Jonathan, disappears, his brother Charles arrives to infiltrate the island and search for the missing man. In this strange and violent place he uncovers "ton-ton macoute", brutal white overseers, horribly overused slaves, and a host of unusually obsessed sexual beings. It's a campy and sleazy vision of a historical time, deformed through the singular eye of Russ Meyer.
VHS: S27370. $79.95.
Russ Meyer, USA, 1973, 83 mins.

Cherry, Harry and Raquel

A menage a trois, loosely translated by Russ Meyer: "a trio is not necessarily a crowd."
VHS: S03649. $79.95.
Russ Meyer, USA

Common-Law Cabin

A busted-out tourist trap under Arizona's hot desert sun, a way out, raunchy dude ranch..."a slow, simmering look at three fast-boiling women at the mercy of themselves." Directed by Russ Meyer.
VHS: S03620. $79.95.
Russ Meyer, USA

Eve and the Handyman

The King of the Nudies brings his wife to the screen in this, his second film. Like the *Immoral Mr. Teas* before it, Meyer uses narration and music to connect wild imagery as a whirlwind of sex, pinball and modern art sends a handyman mired by conformity into the arms of the voluptuous Eve.
VHS: S16024. $79.95.
Russ Meyer, USA, 1961, 65 mins.

Faster Pussycat! Kill! Kill!

"The story of a new breed of superwomen emerging out of the ruthlessness of our times...." Directed by Russ Meyer.
VHS: S03665. $79.95.
Russ Meyer, USA, 1966, 83 mins.

Finders, Keepers, Lovers, Weepers

"Get a good grip on your popcorn," says Russ Meyer, as this film "socks it to you...the flesh, fantasy and action...unencumbered by parlour analysis or suburban sociology."
VHS: S01527. $79.95.
Russ Meyer, USA, 72 mins.

Good Morning...And Goodbye

"Without compromise, without apology, and without question, Russ Meyer has made an honest motion picture which explores the deepest complexities of contemporary life, as applied to love and marriage in these United States."
VHS: S03648. $79.95.
Russ Meyer, USA

Immoral Mr. Teas

An early Russ Meyer film, "America's first classic skin-flick....Here was a film which dared to laugh at all the pretentiousness of its predecessors, and for the first time depicted the living pin-up."
VHS: S03644. $79.95.
Russ Meyer, USA, 63 mins.

Lorna

"Without artistic surrender, without compromise, without question or apology, an incredibly sensual picture was made. *Lorna*. The story of a woman." Starring Lorna Maitland, "the new standard of beauty by which all women shall be judged."
VHS: S03650. $79.95.
Russ Meyer, USA, 78 mins.

Mondo Topless

Mondo Topless, says Russ Meyer, "captures the basic essence of the (topless) movement...with MOVEMENT! Way out, wild undulatory movement!" Subtitled *Thanks for the Mammaries*.
VHS: S03072. $79.95.
Russ Meyer, USA, 60 mins.

Motor Psycho

Three motorcycle riding hoodlums ravage a small town with their brutal taste for violence. Only they step over the line when they beat and rape Cory's wive, Gail. Teaming up with the licentious Ruby, Cory stalks the killers in this classic blend of gore and sensuality from the Master of Camp.
VHS: S16022. $79.95.
Russ Meyer, USA, 1965, 74 mins.

Mudhoney

A Russ Meyer classic. With Lorna Maitland, Rena Horten, and Lee Ballard as country harlots who have too much fun for one town.
VHS: S03666. $79.95.
Russ Meyer, USA, 92 mins.

Russ Meyer's Up!

"Two-timers, cops, robbers, joints, and mind-boggling, bra-busting women."
VHS: S03315. $79.95.
Russ Meyer, USA, 80 mins.

Russ Meyer: The Vixen Collection

Let your boob tube live up to its potential with this laser version of the titillating Meyer classics: *Vixen* (1968), *Supervixen* (1975) and *Beneath the Valley of the Ultravixens* (1979), with Erica Gavin, Shari Eubank and Kitten Natividad. Accompanying the three movies on this laser version is running commentary from the charming, dirty old man himself.
Laser: LD76315. $119.99.

Supervixens

Meyer calls this film his "epitome of twenty years of gut-tearing film making, a rural Fellini geared for the young and old alike, the sophisticate and the blue-collar. ...A cinematic smorgasbord of erotic fantasy...SIX of the world's most bountiful women...served up from the lusty table of Russ Meyer."
VHS: S03540. $79.95.
Russ Meyer, USA, 1975, 105 mins.

Vixen

Meyer's critical and popular success, as Roger Ebert described it, "a merciless put-on...Erica Gavin is electrifying!"
VHS: S03585. $79.95.
Russ Meyer, USA

Wild Gals of the Naked West

Into this riotous parody of the Hollywood Old West rides our hero, a five-foot shrimp of a man riding a burro! With his powder-blue ten-gallon hat, rhinestone-studded purple cowboy boots and a pistol of obscene dimensions, he cleans up the town, vanquishing the villainous Snake Wolf and stealing away the vivacious Goldie Nuggets.
VHS: S16023. $79.95.
Russ Meyer, USA, 1962, 65 mins.

ROGER CORMAN

Atlas

In this mini-epic, Olympic champion Atlas battles Praximedes over the earthly favors of Candia. The most remarkable thing about this film is its shoestring budget. Actually traveling to Greece for the project, Corman clad a handful of extras (himself included) in cardboard costumes to represent massive armies. Stars Michael Forrest, Frank Wolff, Barboura Morris and Walter Maslow.
VHS: S16105. $29.95.
Roger Corman, USA, 1960, 84 mins.

Attack of the Crab Monsters

This fun baby-boomer classic is one of the greatest schlock "B" sci-fi drive-in movies ever made. A scientific research team finds itself stranded on a small island recently exposed to fall-out from a nearby H-bomb test. All animal life has been destroyed except for seagulls and crabs. Unfortunately, the crabs are mutating into giant, intelligent monsters. The thundering beasts literally dissect the island in search of their human prey. With Richard Farland, Pamela Duncan, Russell Johnson, Leslie Bradley, Mel Welles and Ed Nelson.
VHS: S32547. $24.95.
Roger Corman, USA, 1957, 70 mins.

Big Bad Mama

Angie Dickinson, William Shatner and Tom Skerritt star in this ribald Roger Corman production about a woman and her two daughters who travel through rural Depression-era America robbing banks, selling liquor, picking up men and kidnapping rich daughters. Also stars Susan Sennett, Robbie Lee, Noble Willingham and Dick Miller.
VHS: S28612. $14.98.
Steve Carver, USA, 1974, 85 mins.

Bucket of Blood

Roger Corman's first vision of *Little Shop of Horrors*, with Dick Miller getting that life-like quality to his clay sculptures by building them around life-like dead people.
VHS: S08428. $19.95.
Roger Corman, USA, 1959, 66 mins.

Carnival Rock

A rare rock film of the 50s, which features thrill-crazed kids, grimy gangsters and psycho-teens who all clash together in a seedy carnival nightclub, set to the blistering beat of rockabilly, r&b, and classic rock 'n' roll. Featuring music by The Platters, The Blockbusters, David Houston and Bob Luman and His Shadows.
VHS: S05184. $9.95.
Roger Corman, USA, 1957, 80 mins.

Creature from the Haunted Sea

Roger Corman created this and even appears in a cameo in the story of a gangster who tries to cover his tracks by inventing the story of a sea monster.
VHS: S08431. $29.95.
Roger Corman/Monte Hellman, USA, 1960, 76 mins.

Death Race 2000

David Carradine and a pre-*Rocky* Sylvester Stallone star in this cult favorite in which drivers score points by mowing down pedestrians. Produced by Roger Corman, this quirky audience-pleasing film also features Simone Griffeth, Roberta Collins, Joyce Jameson and Mary Woronov (Andy Warhol's Chelsea girl) as driver Calamity Jane.
VHS: S28609. $14.98.
Paul Bartel, USA, 1975, 79 mins.

It Conquered the World

A horrifying invader from the planet Venus (suspiciously carrot-shaped) terrorizes the planet Earth in this low-budget sci-fi quickie from director Roger Corman. Atmospheric and well acted by Peter Graves and Lee Van Cleef, among others.
VHS: S14276. $29.95.
Roger Corman, USA, 1956, 68 mins.

Last Woman on Earth

Roger Corman's variation on *The World, The Flesh and the Devil*. Two men and a woman appear to be the only survivors of a world-wide nuclear holocaust. Can they survive together? Well-acted with a very literate script. With Anthony Carbone and Betsy Moreland.
VHS: S32552. $24.95.
Roger Corman, USA, 1960, 71 mins.

Little Shop of Horrors

Jack Nicholson is the masochist who thrives on dental pain in this very funny cult classic from Roger Corman. The preposterous plot revolves around a young do-nothing who murders people to feed his carnivorous plant.
VHS: S00762. $19.95.
Roger Corman, USA, 1960, 70 mins.

The Masque of the Red Death

Vincent Price stars in this classic screen adaptation of the Edgar Allan Poe tale. It's a lavishly produced effort featuring amazing sets of the horrific castle of Prince Prospero. There, an indifferent nobility pursues their debauched past-times while the countryside endures the scourge of the red death.

VHS: S01719. $14.98.

Roger Corman, USA, 1964, 86 mins.

Shame (The Intruder)

A rare departure from Roger Corman's usual work, *The Intruder* is a personal statement on race relations in the South, starring William Shatner as a social reformer in a small town.

VHS: S01187. $34.95.

Roger Corman, USA, 1962, 84 mins.

St. Valentine's Day Massacre

A vividly bloody recounting of the infamous Chicago gangland slaying in the mob war between Al Capone and Bugs Moran. This was Roger Corman's first big studio film. Starring Jason Robards, George Segal, Ralph Meeker and, if you look closely, a young Jack Nicholson.

VHS: S13617. $19.98.

Roger Corman, USA, 1967, 100 mins.

Swamp Women

Marie Windsor, Beverly Garland and Michael Connors star in this complicated but campy thriller about a group of women criminals in search of riches and freedom in the Louisiana Bayou. These bad women are guided by two things only: greed and lust.

VHS: S23778. $24.95.

Roger Corman, USA, 1955, 73 mins.

Tales of Terror

Peter Lorre and Basil Rathbone join Vincent Price in these four tales of terror adapted from Edgar Allan Poe stories. It's a classic horror film in which Price has the chance to camp it up.

VHS: S04192. $14.98.

Roger Corman, USA, 1962, 90 mins.

Teenage Caveman

An early Roger Corman AIP knock-off set in a barren, post-apocalyptic landscape stars Robert Vaughn as a young prehistoric caveman in search of salvation and understanding. With Darrah Marshall, Leslie Bradley, and Frank De Corva.

VHS: S16969. $29.95.

Roger Corman, USA, 1958, 66 mins.

The Terror

Boris Karloff and Jack Nicholson square off in this gothic tale set in the Napoleonic Wars. The young officer is determined to save a beautiful, tormented young woman from the spooky old Baron. Karloff's scenes took two days to shoot. Made on the sets of *The Raven*.

VHS: S04026. $19.95.
DVD: DV60271. $19.95.

Roger Corman, USA, 1963, 81 mins.

Tomb of Ligeia

A Roger Corman production based on Edgar Allan Poe's work of the same name, starring Vincent Price. Strange events occur when Price marries after burying his first wife.

VHS: S01357. $14.98.
Laser: LD76054. $39.99.

Roger Corman, USA, 1964, 82 mins.

Tower of London

Roger Corman's gothic translation of Shakespeare's *Richard III* stars Vincent Price as the disfigured warrior Richard Crookback, who's aided by the brutally efficient executioner Mord (Michael Pate). With Joan Freeman, Robert Brown, Justice Eatson and Sara Salby.

VHS: S11286. $14.95.

Roger Corman, USA, 1962, 79 mins.

The Undead

In this camp classic a scientist fixes his gaze on the past and finds a way to magically transport himself into the Dark Ages. Once there he encounters many surprises, including the wholly unexpected Undead.

VHS: S23817. $24.95.

Roger Corman, USA, 1957, 75 mins.

Von Richtofen and Brown

A high-flying tale of famous battles and infamous daredevils. Two of history's most fabled flyboys, Red Baron and Roy Brown, square off in a daring, acrobatic duel of death.

VHS: S31843. $19.98.

Roger Corman, USA, 1971, 96 mins.

Wasp Woman

A Roger Corman sociological study of White Anglo-Saxon Protestant women who turn into demented killers by using an untested beauty cream. Susan Cabot stars as a cosmetics executive who learns, too late, about the side effects of the latest beauty aid. With Anthony Eiseley, Michael Mark, Bruno VeSota and Barboura Morris. Written by Leo Gordon *(Giant Leeches)*. B&W.

VHS: S09133. $29.95.
Laser: LD76055. $39.99.

Roger Corman, USA, 1959, 73 mins.

The Wild Ride

Wild parties, motorcycles and drag races abound in this fun flick from Roger Corman's film company. Jack Nicholson runs down two cops and then kidnaps the girlfriend of a friend who has gone straight. A fun high-speed chase is climaxed with a wild victory celebration. With Georgianna Carter and Robert Bean.

VHS: S32596. $24.95.

Roger Corman, USA, 1960, 80 mins.

X—The Man with the X-Ray Eyes

Ray Milland stars in this classic science fiction film as a scientist who invents a serum that enhances his vision, giving him X-ray eyes. Ultimately it turns out to be a curse. Don Rickles is also featured.

VHS: S06110. $14.98.

Roger Corman, USA, 1963, 79 mins.

JOHN WATERS

Cry Baby

With a decree to "bring back the juvenile delinquent", director John Waters creates a takeoff on 1950's bad kid, teenage hoodlum movies. Johnny Depp is the cry baby: doll, dream boat and delinquent. The seasoned Traci Lords and *Hairspray* star Ricki Lake star as his admirers. Cast includes Susan Tyrrell, Iggy Pop, Amy Locane and a cameo by Patty Hearst. Great soundtrack, as usual.

VHS: S12775. $19.95.
Laser: LD70020. $34.98.

John Waters, USA, 1990, 85 mins.

Desperate Living

A perverse and demented film from the outcast priest of sleaze, John Waters, dealing with his usually upsetting themes of self-expression, violence, alienation, mental anguish, sexual hijinks and political corruption, done in a fragmented, hyper absurd comic style. With Liz Renay, Mink Stole, Susan Lowe and Edith Massey.

VHS: S00324. $19.98.
Laser: LD76262. $39.99.

John Waters, USA, 1977, 90 mins.

Divine

A special tribute to the most beautiful babe in the world. First up, a short, *The Diane Linkletter Story*, starring a very young Divine as a naughty girl who wants to: "get high," "get laid," "...and do my thing, momma...." Thankfully there's a moral lesson here, as Diane kills herself. Following that, the only existing performance of the infamous *The Neon Woman* show. Divine plays the owner of a sleazy strip joint with a lot of problems, including the District Attorney (who doesn't know he's her son) trying to shut the place down, the horny bible-thumping Senator who's just fallen in love with her, and her virginal daughter who has just returned from boarding school and after spending a few minutes in the club has become an alcoholic, heroin-addicted wanton who has just married the black janitor. Now that's high comedy.

VHS: S13498. $39.95.

John Waters, USA, 1990, 110 mins.

Hairspray

John Waters' breakthrough commercial work is a funny, witty and extremely well-made piece of mock nostalgia, about the efforts of a politically conscious white girl to integrate a local television bandstand in 1962 Baltimore. Memorable as Divine's final collaboration with Waters, the casting is superb and Waters has grown tremendously as a stylist, with a particularly shrewd use of color and a shock cutting style reminiscent of early Russ Meyer. With Ricki Lake, Sonny Bono, Debbie Harry, Pia Zadora and Ric Ocasek.

VHS: S07303. $14.98.
Laser: LD76261. $39.99.

John Waters, USA, 1988, 96 mins.

The John Waters Collection, No. 1

American satirist John Waters, whose films deal with politics, sex, style, fashion and class, offers four of his works in a specially bound edition: *Pink Flamingos* (1972), *Desperate Living* (1977), *Polyester* (1981) and *Hairspray* (1988). 373 mins.

VHS: S18167. $59.95.

Love Letter to Edy

A charming, fictionalized biography of Edith Massey, known to fans of John Waters' cult classic, *Pink Flamingos*, as Edy the Egg Lady. Featuring Waters and Mink Stole.

VHS: S31356. $14.95.

Robert Maier, USA, 1973, 15 mins.

Pink Flamingos

The 25th anniversary edition of John Waters' underground trash classic starring Divine in his/her quest to become "the filthiest person alive", has been digitally remastered and features never-before-seen footage, the original theatrical trailer and commentary by Waters. Widescreen.

VHS: S31386. $19.98.
Laser: LD76281. $49.95.

John Waters, USA, 1972, 108 mins.

Polyester

John Waters' lurid satire of middle-class America cast his collaborator Divine as an abused housewife and mother liberated by handsome, campy, drive-in entrepreneur Tab Hunter. The movie is notable for Waters' witty sympathy for outsiders and the exploited. With Edith Massey, Mary Garlington, Ken King, David Samson and Mink Stole.

VHS: S01046. $19.98.
Laser: CLV. LD72109. $59.95.

John Waters, USA, 1981, 86 mins.

Serial Mom

Kathleen Turner is the overly perfect wife and mother of a normal family. When things get just a little too out of hand Mom makes everything all right again with the help of a little murder. Then it becomes a habit, just another of her many ways that make the world a better place for everyone. Sam Waterston and Ricki Lake also star.

VHS: S21505. $19.95.

John Waters, USA, 1994, 93 mins.

PAUL MORRISSEY

Beethoven's Nephew

Paul Morrissey directs this made-in-Europe investigation of Ludwig van Beethoven's obsession with his nephew Karl. The nephew, the sole heir to the Beethoven estate, is not eager for the composer's personal advances. A study in madness that is both touching and humorous.

VHS: S08089. $19.95.

Paul Morrissey, France/Germany, 1985, 103 mins.

Dracula

Warhol's version of the Dracula story finds the Count touring Italy for a marriageable virgin, and there are few to be found. With Joe Dallesandro as a class-conscious estate hand.

VHS: S02301. $14.98.

Paul Morrissey, USA, 1974, 106 mins.

Frankenstein

"Severed limbs, gobs of livid human entrails, a hideously efficient decapitating gadget...are among the treats that slither off the screen...The most outrageously gruesome epic ever unleashed" *(Playboy)*. With Joe Dallesandro, Monique Van Vooren and Udo Kier.

VHS: S02302. $14.98.

Paul Morrissey, Italy/France, 1974, 95 mins.

ED WOOD JR.

Bride of the Monster

Winner of the Golden Turkey Award, this is another classic from the director of *Glen or Glenda* and *Plan 9 from Outer Space*. Starring Bela Lugosi as a mad scientist trying to create a race of giants. Great mad fun!

VHS: S00180. $29.95.

Ed Wood Jr., USA, 1956, 70 mins.

Crossroad Avenger/ Trick Shooting with Kenne Duncan

Tom Keene, Lyle Talbot and Tom Tyler are featured in this half-hour, Western, TV pilot and short feature combination. The first is solid shoot 'em up fare. Then Kenne Duncan displays his amazing sharp-shooting and trick shooter abilities.

VHS: S23171. $29.95.

Ed Wood Jr., USA, 1954

Ed Wood

Johnny Depp portrays the nearly inconceivable cult film director/cross-dresser Ed Wood in this imaginative biographical film that won an Academy Award for Martin Landau in the role of actor Bela Lugosi, who (in real life) died during the making of one of Wood's notorious films. A truly singular Hollywood achievement about a stranger-than-fiction filmmaker whose atrocious films, like *Plan 9 from Outer Space* and *Glen or Glenda*, have become cult classics. With Patricia Arquette and Bill Murray.

VHS: S24321. $19.98.
Laser: Letterboxed. **LD74914. $39.99.**

Tim Burton, USA, 1994, 127 mins.

The Ed Wood Collection

Now the films of this Hollywood original—*Jail Bait: The Director's Cut, Plan Nine from Outer Space* and *The Night of the Ghouls*—are available together. Steve Reeves made his debut for Ed Wood. Despite this flirtation with success, Wood's final film was held by the lab that developed it because he could not pay for its processing. Trailers and commentary about Wood are also included. 224 mins.

Laser: LD74620. $79.95.

The Ed Wood Collection, Vol. 2

Two of Wood's outrageous films starring the immortal Bela Lugosi are joined on this laser disc. *Glen or Glenda* (1953), Wood's first film, is an homage to transvestite men everywhere, and Wood plays himself, the man who bravely must face his wife with his closely held secret. In *Bride of the Monster* (1956), Lugosi is a mad scientist bent on the creation of a race of giants. This film contains the sequence of Lugosi desperately battling an inert rubber octopus that was recreated in Tim Burton's *Ed Wood*. Includes original theatrical trailers.

Laser: LD74937. $69.98.

The Ed Wood Story: The Plan 9 Companion

The career of this strange director is revealed through interviews with cast members Vampira, Gregory Wolcott, Paul Kelton "the cop" Marco and Conrad Brooks. Footage and photos show another side of Wood and there is even a tour of the studio where *Plan 9* was shot. 111 mins.

VHS: S24872. $19.98.

Ed Wood: Look Back in Angora

Conrad Brooks hosts this biographical look at Hollywood's perhaps most inept filmmaker, Ed Wood. Infamous for his camp classics *Plan 9 from Outer Space* and *Jail Bait*, Wood's passion for film was clearly his undoing. Yet his films are unlike anything ever produced before; he was a true original. 50 mins.

VHS: S22334. $19.95.

Elvira's Midnight Madness: Night of the Ghouls

Triple threat (writer/producer/director) Ed Wood Jr.'s amazing follow-up to *Bride of the Monster*, featuring the immortal Criswell—possibly the finest actor the cinema has ever known. The living dead walk again when a phony spiritualist accidentally succeeds in reviving a pack of corpses that bury him alive in a blood curdling climax.

VHS: S14471. $9.95.
Ed Wood Jr., USA, 1959, 69 mins.

Glen or Glenda

One of the funniest exploitation films ever made—starring Bela Lugosi as he tells the story of Glen—or Glenda—who is undergoing a sex change operation, and tells the horror story about fetishism. Not to be missed!

VHS: S00505. $19.95.
Ed Wood Jr., USA, 1953, 64 mins.

The Haunted World of Edward D. Wood, Jr.

The first feature-length documentary of the Orson Welles of low-budget pictures, Ed Wood, produced by Wood's first partner, Crawford John Thompson. See clips from Wood's first, inept attempt at filmmaking, *Crossroads of Laredo*, and hear him comment about his "craft." Bela Lugosi, Jr. discusses his father's unusual relationship with Wood. Also featuring Bela Lugosi, Maila Nurmi, Delores Fuller, Paul Marco, Conrad Brooks, Gregory Walcott and rare appearances by Loretta King, Lyle Talbot, Mona McKinnon and Norma McCarty-Wood.

VHS: S32302. $19.95.
Brett Thompson, USA, 1997, 110 mins.

Jail Bait

Lyle Talbot (first screen Lex Luthor) stars in this first effort of Ed Wood, Jr. While many filmmakers improve during the course of their careers, Wood got worse and created the infamous *Plan 9 from Outer Space*. In this genuine Wood effort, Timothy Farrell leads young Clancey Malone into a life of crime so that when the law closes in, he forces Malone's father to change his face with plastic surgery.

VHS: S06332. $14.95.
Ed Wood Jr., USA, 1954, 70 mins.

Married Too Young

Ed Wood was brought in to finish the last quarter of the script for this explosive melodrama, though he was never credited. A pair of high school sweethearts get married on the sly but find the burdens of life too tough. Trouble comes when they get mixed up with a hot car racket. The film climaxes with a crash. Harold Lloyd, Jr., Anthony Dexter and Jana Lund star.

VHS: S23172. $29.95.
Ed Wood Jr., USA, 1962

Necromania

This low-budget, soft-core horror flick, from master of cult films Ed Wood Jr., was lost until recently. Now this tale about a young couple who happen upon a supernatural sex clinic is available once again. It's a camp classic featuring outrageous dialog, a strange collection of music tracks and offbeat humor.

VHS: S21348. $24.95.
Ed Wood Jr., USA, 1971, 43 mins.

On the Trail of Ed Wood

A personal documentary about the legendary Plan 9 Hollywood director Edward D. Wood Jr., whose grade Z horror movies earned him the unfortunate nickname of the "world's worst filmmaker." Hosted by Conrad Brooks, a friend of the director, the program studies Wood's perennially campy works, including *Plan 9 from Outer Space, Glen or Glenda, Bride of the Monster* and *Orgy of the Dead*.

VHS: S18242. $19.95.

Orgy of the Dead

Ed Wood Jr.'s masterpiece of erotic horror, winner of the Golden Turkey award.

VHS: S05193. $14.95.
Ed Wood Jr., USA, 1965, 90 mins.

Plan 9 from Outer Space

Aliens invade earth and revive corpses from a San Fernando Valley cemetery to aide them in their dreams of conquest. Bela Lugosi is featured in this camp classic, but he died shortly after production began. Fortunately he was replaced by a taller man with a cape over his face. Possibly the worst film ever made.

VHS: S01036. $14.95.
Ed Wood Jr., USA, 1959, 79 mins.

Sinister Urge

One of Ed Wood's least-known films, dedicated to the idea that overweight women in their underwear are the principal cause of juvenile delinquency. Two zealous cops are out to smash the "smut picture racket" and stop a "sex maniac killer" who is motivated by the dirty pictures as the "psycho killer strikes terror in every woman's heart." Originally titled *Sinister Sex*, the title was too risque for the 1960's and had to be changed.

VHS: S22912. $19.95.
Ed Wood Jr., USA, 1960, 75 mins.

Take It Out in Trade—The Outtakes

Slates, flubs, unused sex scenes and Ed Wood himself in a screwball sexploitation comedy that marked his return to the director's chair for the first time since *Sinister Urge*. Three cans of silent *Take It Out in Trade* outtakes, found in a Santa Monica cutting room, feature an androgynous couple making out in a kitchen, posters of foreign countries, and Ed Wood in a lovely lime green dress, blonde wig, and white go-go boots playing a drag queen named "Alecia."

VHS: S23037. $19.98.
Ed Wood Jr., USA, 1970

The Violent Years

This recently re-discovered classic by Ed Wood, Jr. *(Plan 9)* features filthy rich teenage sex kittens who form gangs, rob gas stations, rape rich guys, and strip gown "goody" girls. A cheap thrills masterpiece.

VHS: S05186. $14.95.
Ed Wood Jr., USA, 1956, 60 mins.

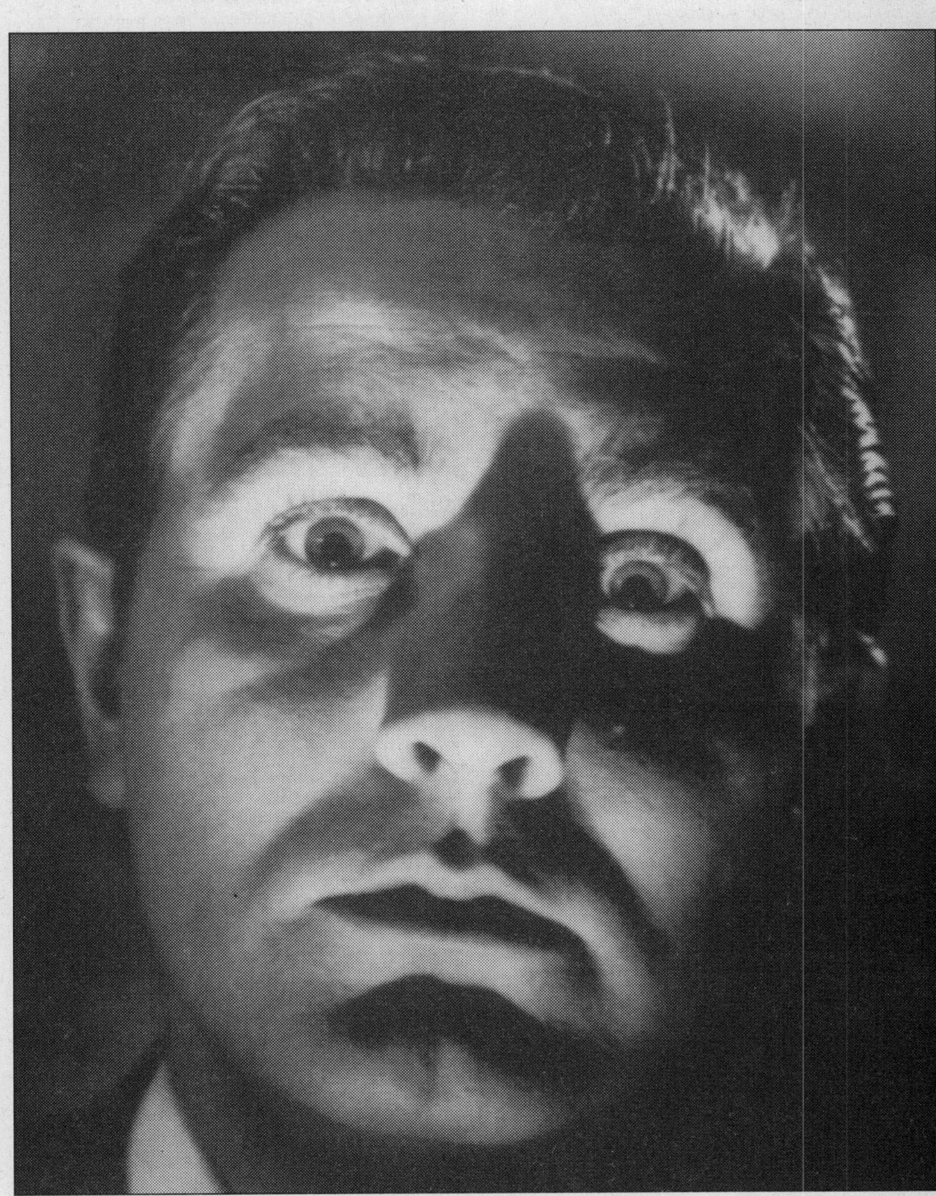

horror flicks

100 Years of Horror

Christopher Lee hosts this two-hour program chronicling the history of movie horror from the earliest experimental chillers through the unforgettable "golden age of movie monsters" and on to today's horrifying fright films. 120 mins.

VHS: S32419. $19.99.

The Abominable Dr. Phibes

The disfigured physician, played by Vincent Price, wreaks havoc on a world that he feels wronged him. His revenge is both terrible and imaginative. You can never guess exactly how Dr. Phibes' enemies will meet their deaths, but rest assured, each one is grisly. Also features Joseph Cotten.

VHS: S20931. $14.98.

Robert Fuest, Great Britain, 1971, 94 mins.

The Alligator People

A horror classic about a doctor who discovers a serum enabling humans to grow back amputated parts of their bodies—with horrible side effects. With Lon Chaney, Jr., Beverly Garland, and Bruce Bennett.

VHS: S34565. $14.95.

Roy Del Ruth, USA, 1959, 74 mins.

The Amazing Colossal Man

In this '50s horror cult classic, an Army officer who's exposed to an atomic blast grows to gigantic proportions. Fueled by alienation and discomfort at his condition, he attacks Las Vegas. With Glen Langan, Cathy Downs and James Seay.

VHS: S17903. $29.95.

Bert I. Gordon, USA, 1957, 80 mins.

Amazing Transparent Man

A great B movie by the incomparable Edgar G. Ulmer. Shot at a Texas state fair because some of the exhibits had a futuristic look, the plot concerns a mad scientist who invents a formula for invisibility in order to make an invisible man his accomplice in bank robberies.

VHS: S06903. $29.95.

Edgar G. Ulmer, USA, 1960, 58 mins.

An Angel for Satan

Barbara Steele has a dual role in this excellent horror film about a woman possessed by the spirit of a statue. This was Barbara's last major Italian horror film. The best video copy available. Italian with NO subtitles.

VHS: S15367. $29.95.

Camillo Mastrocinque, Italy, 1966, 93 mins.

The Ape

Boris Karloff plays an evil doctor obsessed with producing a cure for a dreaded disease by injecting the afflicted with human spinal fluid.

VHS: S13854. $19.95.

William Nigh, USA, 1940, 62 mins.

Apeman

Bela Lugosi literally makes a monkey of himself as a scientist who experiments with a new serum. Also known as *Lock Your Doors*.

VHS: S00065. $19.95.

William Beaudine, USA, 1943, 64 mins.

Army of Darkness

Sam Raimi's film is the third installment of his *Evil Dead III* trilogy. The handsome, appliance store salesman Nash (Bruce Campbell) is sucked through a vortex into the 13th century. While trying to retrieve a text that will return him to the present, Nash inadvertently unleashes a squadron of the walking dead, skeleton figures who lay siege to the village. With Embeth Davidtz.

VHS: S19329. $19.98.

Laser: Letterboxed. **LD71886. $34.98.**

Sam Raimi, USA, 1992, 81 mins.

Asylum

British chiller contains four tales of madness and murder that are told to the new doctor assigned to a mental institution. Cast includes Peter Cushing, Britt Ekland, Robert Powell, Herbert Lom, Barbara Parkins and Patrick Magee. Script by Robert "Psycho" Bloch. Bloody good fun.

VHS: S03766. $29.95.

Roy Ward Baker, Great Britain, 1972, 92 mins.

At Midnight I'll Take Your Soul

A psycho-sexual gothic thriller from Brazil's horror auteur Jose Mojica Marins represents the debut appearance of the evil protagonist Coffin Joe (played by the director). He's a gravedigger whose specter haunts a small town. Coffin Joe is looking for a woman who will bear his child and preserve his demonic reign. Spanish with English subtitles.

VHS: S18982. $24.95.

Jose Mojica Marins, Brazil, 1963

Atom Age Vampire

A mad scientist uses weird, glandular transplants to restore beauty to the horribly scarred face of Jeanette, a stripper he's fallen in love with. When the treatment begins to fail, he undergoes radioactive treatment which turns him into a hideous monster who commits a number of murders in order to help Jeanette. A '60s drive-in staple. With Susanne Loret and Alberto Lupo. Dubbed in English.

VHS: S32559. $24.95.

Anton Giulio Majano, Italy, 1962, 75 mins.

Attack of the Giant Leeches

White trash finds itself on the menu of some oversized swamp pests in this AIP Cheapie executive produced by Roger Corman. When a backwoods bartender finds his trampy wife violating her marital vows, he institutes a shotgun divorce and forces the lovers into the deadly wetlands to meet man-sized monsters in very cheap costumes. With Bruno Ve Sota, Yvette Vickers, Ken Clark and Gene Roth. B&W.

VHS: S09125. $19.95.

Bernard L. Kowalski, USA, 1959, 62 mins.

Audrey Rose

Anthony Hopkins, Marsha Mason and John Beck star in this terrifying tale of soul possession and reincarnation, directed by Robert Wise *(The Day the Earth Stood Still)*. A chilling thriller.

VHS: S14961. $14.95.

Robert Wise, USA, 1977, 113 mins.

Awakenings of the Beast

Banned for 18 years by the Brazilian military dictatorship, this grotesque film is a stylish essay about the dangers of drug experimentation. The title refers to LSD, as a drug addict relies on the psychedelic rush to compensate for his tormented visions of loss and terror. Spanish with English subtitles.

VHS: S18984. $24.95.

Jose Mojica Marins, Brazil, 1968

Awful Dr. Orlof

A mad doctor stalks foggy backstreets in search of young girls whom he kidnaps and murders. He drains their blood and attempts to graft their skin to the horribly disfigured face of his daughter. Sick fun. Considered by many to be Jess Franco's best film. With Howard Vernon, Conrado San Martin, Perla Cristal and Diana Lorys. Dubbed in English.

VHS: S32576. $24.95.

Jess Franco, Spain/France, 1962, 86 mins.

Baron Blood

While restoring an ancient castle for tourists, two college students unknowingly resurrect the ghost of a notorious sadist. Once awakened, the restless spirit goes on a bloody rampage, torturing unsuspecting guests. Includes the original musical score and scenes that were cut from the original U.S. theatrical release. Digitally remastered. Stars Elke Sommer and Joseph Cotten.

VHS: S30438. $14.95.

Mario Bava, Italy, 1972, 90 mins.

The Bat (1926)

One of the great silent horror films. A maniacal killer dressed in a weird bat-like costume terrorizes a group of people in a shuddery, spooky old house riddled with secret passageways. The use of miniatures and the overall cinematography is stunning for its day.

VHS: S15365. $19.95.

Roland West, USA, 1926, 81 mins.

The Bat (1959)

This classic chiller, faithfully adapted from the famous Mary Roberts Rinehart novel, stars Vincent Price and Agnes Moorehead. The Bat, a maniacal killer after a bank book, wreaks havoc on a group of people staying at an old gothic mansion where $1 million is hidden. With Gavin Gordon, John Sutton, Elaine Edwards, Darla Hood, and Lenita Lane.

VHS: S34583. $14.99.

Crane Wilbur, USA, 1959, 80 mins.

The Bat People

When a biologist is bitten by a winged mammal, he turns from a modern, rational man into a blood-craving, shape-altered beast. He finds this puts a severe damper on his honeymoon. The makeup is said to be convincing in this low-budget shocker. With Michael Pataki as the sheriff.

VHS: S05103. $19.99.

Jerry Jameson, USA, 1974, 95 mins.

The Bat Whispers

One of the early great sound films, this remake of the silent 1926 classic *The Bat* is also a great horror film. A group of people gather in an old dark house where they are menaced by a maniacal, yet brilliant, hooded criminal. Hidden in a secret room in the mansion is a fortune in stolen money. Chester Morris and Una Merkel star.

VHS: S23161. $29.95.

Roland West, USA, 1930, 84 mins.

The Beast with Five Fingers

A cult horror movie about a once brilliant pianist now consumed by doubt and self-loathing. Features his classic encounter with the disembodied hand. With Robert Alda, Peter Lorre and Andrea King.

VHS: S17532. $19.98.

Robert Florey, USA, 1946, 88 mins.

The Bela Lugosi Collection: Devil Bat/Scared to Death

Two Bela Lugosi pictures told with unnerving skill. In Jean Yarbrough's *The Devil Bat* (1941), Lugosi experiments with bats and trains them to destroy his enemies. The second feature, Christy Cabanne's *Scared to Death* (1947), was Lugosi's only color film, which chronicles a young woman's death, eerily told from her point of view.

Laser: LD71952. $49.95.

DVD: DV60132. $29.95.

Jean Yarborough/Walt Mattox, USA, 1941-47, 137 mins.

Bela Lugosi Meets a Brooklyn Gorilla

In this spoof of jungle horror movies Bela, as Dr. Zabor, turns one half of a stranded comedy team into a gorilla. The comedy team of Duke Mitchell and Sammy Petrillo are said to be look-alikes of Dean Martin and Jerry Lewis. Screenplay by Irene Ryan's husband Tim.

VHS: S04013. $29.95.

William Beaudine, USA, 1952, 74 mins.

The Bells

When a carnival hypnotist (Boris Karloff, bearing a striking resemblance to Dr. Caligari) arrives in a small town, the local lodge-keeper (Lionel Barrymore) is haunted by the spirit of the man he brutally murdered. Adapted from the story by Edgar Allen Poe. Silent.

VHS: S04084. $24.95.

James Young, USA, 1926, 70 mins.

Big Calibre

Bob Steele must battle a mad scientist on the lone prairie who uses corrosive gas against his foes. Lots of action out west in an unusual match-up. With Peggy Campbell and Forest Taylor. B&W.

VHS: S04080. $29.95.

Robert North Bradbury, USA, 1935, 59 mins.

Billy the Kid Versus Dracula

Mixed genres meet a low budget with a sixty-year-old John Carradine as the Transylvanian bloodsucker and Chuck Courtney as the infamous western backshooter. This horror western was filmed in Shockorama. With Roy Barcroft, Harry Carey Jr. and Melinda Plowman as Betty.

VHS: S05483. $29.95.
William Beaudine, USA, 1966, 73 mins.

The Black Castle

Boris Karloff and Lon Chaney Jr. both appear in this atmospheric horror film set in an Austrian castle. An unscrupulous Count plans the deaths of his enemies with apparent impugnity until a young adventurer becomes concerned about a pair of his friends.

VHS: S29522. $14.98.
Nathan Juran, USA, 1952, 82 mins.

The Black Cat

Edgar G. Ulmer *(Detour)* directs Boris Karloff and Bela Lugosi in this stylish horror work. Ulmer pulled out all the stops in this movie about a young American couple trapped in the house of a demented scientist. With David Manners, Jacqueline Wells, Lucille Lund, and Egon Brecher. From a story by Edgar Allan Poe.

VHS: S17270. $14.98.
Edgar G. Ulmer, USA, 1934, 65 mins.

Black Cat

The short story by Edgar Allan Poe is the inspiration for this Italian-made horror film in which the residents of a small English town find themselves at the mercy of a fiendish feline. Nine lives are more than enough for the revengeful purposes of the cat's owner, an out-of-control clairvoyant. With Patrick Magee, Mimsy Farmer, David Warbec and Al Cliver. Not to be confused with the 1934 and 1941 Bela Lugosi horror films of the same title.

VHS: S15826. $14.98.
Lucio Fulci, Italy/Great Britain, 1986, 93 mins.

Black Friday

Boris Karloff and Bela Lugosi star in this horror film which mixes questionable science with the gangster underworld. In fact, the brain of a professor is placed into the head of a gangster. The result is a man with far too many thoughts for a profession where action is paramount.

VHS: S29523. $14.95.
Arthur Lubin, USA, 1940, 70 mins.

The Black Raven

They lived by blood, this motley crew! And squared their debts with murder! So say the ads for this George Zucco thriller. He runs an inn crowded with strangers on a dark and stormy night. With Wanda McKay and Glenn Strange as the comic relief. B&W.

VHS: S04038. $29.95.
Sam Newfield, USA, 1943, 64 mins.

Black Sabbath

Boris Karloff in this tale of "wurdalaks," a variety of vampires that drink only the blood of loved ones. Filmed in Italy, this is an English language version.

VHS: S00139. $24.95.
Mario Bava, Italy, 1963, 99 mins.

Black Sunday

This Barbara Steele Italian horror movie has nothing to do with Middle Eastern Terrorists or hijacked blimps. In her first horror film she plays a dual role: Asa, a reincarnated vampire-witch, and Katia, her innocent great-granddaughter. Heavy on the atmosphere. With John Richardson and Ivo Garrani. B&W.

VHS: S09126. $24.95.
Mario Bava, Italy, 1961, 83 mins.

The Blob

The 1950's gooiest monster is back in a special 30th anniversary remake of *The Blob*, starring Kevin Dillon as a young outcast who must save the town of Arborville from the gelatin.

Laser: LD70350. $49.95.
Chuck Russell, USA, 1988, 92 mins.

Blood and Black Lace

The beautiful models of a luxurious fashion salon are being fiendishly slain one by one. The killer is a masked maniac wearing a glove with metal claws. The director creates a superb, atmospheric setting filled with horror and dread. Cameron Mitchell and Eva Bartok are featured.

VHS: S23170. $19.95.
Mario Bava, Germany/France/Italy, 1964, 88 mins.

Blood Beast Terror

Peter Cushing stars in this well-crafted British horror film in which Wanda Ventham is the beautiful vampire who tears her lovers to death.

VHS: S04786. $39.95.
Vernon Sewell, Great Britain, 1967, 81 mins.

Blood Fiend (aka Theatre of Death)

Are there vampires on the loose in Paris? The local police are stymied by a series of "blood" related murders. The mystery seems to center around a Grand Guignol stage sensation, a beautiful young actress who seems to be in a hypnotic trance. Unquestionably one of Christopher Lee's better low budget shockers. With Julian Glover and Jenny Till.

VHS: S15368. $29.95.
Samuel Gallu, Great Britain, 1966, 91 mins.

Blood Hook

Local jail bait becomes live bait in this horror movie where water sports take on a new and frightening aspect. Teens are hooked and hacked to bits in the backwoods of Wisconsin. Even though it's clear something fishy is going on, the sheriff won't make any waves. Is it any wonder kids keep disappearing as fish food?

VHS: S22675. $14.95.
James Nallon, USA, 1983, 98 mins.

Blood of Dracula

This AIP production stars Sandra Harrison as a student at a private girl's school who is hypnotized into becoming a vampire by the evil headmistress. The ads proclaimed "In her eyes…DESIRE. In her veins…the Blood of a MONSTER!" With Louise Lewis, Gail Ganley, Thomas B. Henry and Jerry Blaine.

VHS: S16409. $24.95.
Herbert L. Strock, USA, 1957, 68 mins.

Blood of Ghastly Terror

John Carradine stars as a doctor with dubious credentials who needs a human subject to test his artificial brain implant. But the doctor's orders don't work when his victim turns into a psychopathic killer. The film has gone under various other titles, including *The Fiend with the Atomic Brain, Psycho a Go Go!, The Love Maniac*, and *The Man with the Synthetic Brain*.

VHS: S08041. $19.98.
Al Adamson, USA, 1972, 87 mins.

The Blood on Satan's Claw

A highly original thriller. The story unfolds in a 17th century English village, where a group of children are stalked by a devil's claw. Also known as *Satin's Skin*. With Patrick Wymark, Linda Hayden, Barry Andrews and Avice Landon.

VHS: S19131. $14.95.
Piers Haggard, Great Britain, 1970, 93 mins.

The Bloody Exorcism of Coffin Joe

Jose Mojica Marins is on a Christmas break with a seemingly normal family when strange occurrences disturb the festive mood, in this Brazilian-made camp horror classic. It seems there was a pact made with the devil for the hand of the family's eldest daughter. Threatening to renege on this deal leads to mounting terrors, culminating in a perverse, ritualistic ceremony that includes naked devil worshippers and cannibalism. Portuguese with English subtitles.

VHS: S21346. $24.95.
Jose Mojica Marins, Brazil, 1972

The Bloody Pit of Horror

Mickey Hargitay, the husband of sexpot Jayne Mansfield, stars in this Italian horror film based on the writings of the Marquis de Sade. He becomes possessed by the spirit of a sadistic castle owner who enjoys making his guests feel uncomfortable. Five sexy models, among others, are shown that torture chambers can be functional as well as decorative.

VHS: S09138. $29.95.
Max Hunter (Massimo Pupillo), Italy, 1965, 87 mins.

Body Bags

An anthology series of three works by John Carpenter and Tobe Hooper. The action is set in a creepy morgue, where people drop in and never leave. The all-star cast includes Robert Carradine, Stacy Keach, Mark Hamill, Deborah Harry, Sheena Easton, David Naughton, Twiggy and David Warner. Cameos by horror auteurs Wes Craven, Sam Raimi, Roger Corman, Hooper and Carpenter.

VHS: S20190. $19.95.
Laser: LD72439. $34.98.
John Carpenter/Tobe Hooper, USA, 1993, 95 mins.

Bowery at Midnight

Bela Lugosi plays Professor Brenner, a Manhattan psychology prof who secretly runs a Bowery mission to front his criminal activities. His victims, through the aid of a drug crazed medico, are revived and are eager to seek revenge for their shoddy treatment. B&W.

VHS: S04008. $29.95.
Wallace Fox, USA, 1942, 61 mins.

Brainscan

Frank Langella and Edward Furlong star in this horrific tale about high school kids who encounter the deadliest interactive video game ever. A lonely kid thought his obsession was just a game, but soon deception, desire and death are more than state of the art software.

VHS: S22913. $19.95.
John Flynn, USA, 1994, 96 mins.

Bride of Frankenstein

A superior sequel, mixes wit with chills. Boris Karloff is the Monster, Elsa Lanchester plays the created mate as well as Mary Shelley in the prologue. Marvelous score by Franz Waxman. A classic!

VHS: S06386. $14.98.
Laser: LD70019. $34.98.
James Whale, USA, 1935, 75 mins.

Bride of the Gorilla

Raymond Burr lusts after the mistress of a jungle plantation and is willing to murder all those that stand in his way. Intimidation will only go so far when it is matched with a voodoo curse that causes a drastic change in Burr's appearance. With Lon Chaney Jr., Barbara Payton and Tom Conway. B&W.

VHS: S04033. $29.95.
Curt Siodmak, USA, 1951, 76 mins.

The Brides of Dracula

A Hammer Studio film about a beautiful, naive, young French woman who liberates an imprisoned baron. The baron wakes the undead to carry out his perverse agenda, and now the young woman and the indefatigable Dr. Helsing (Peter Cushing) must restore order.

VHS: S17018. $14.98.
Terence Fisher, Great Britain, 1960, 86 mins.

Buried Alive

Once, Ravenscroft Hall was an asylum for the incurably insane. Now, the isolated mansion is a school for troubled teenaged girls run by charismatic psychiatrist Robert Vaughn. Captivated by his charm, a young woman (Karen Witter) joins his staff. She is soon tormented by nightmare visions of the long-dead victims of a nameless killer. When the students begin to disappear, she realizes he still lives…John Carradine and Donald Pleasance star in this classic tale of terror based on an Edgar Allan Poe story.

VHS: S13005. $39.95.
Gerard Kikione, USA, 1989, 97 mins.

Candyman

British director Bernard Rose's American debut transposes Clive Barker's short story *The Forbidden* from Liverpool to Chicago, with Virginia Madsen as a doctoral candidate who inadvertently unleashes the spirit of "Candyman," a mythological 19th-century black serial killer with a hook for his left hand who was brutally murdered by white racists. With Tony Todd, Xander Berkeley and Kasi Lemmons.

VHS: S18323. $19.95.
Bernard Rose, USA, 1992, 108 mins.

Captive Wild Woman

A doctor, played by John Carradine, steals a killer orangutan and then, through the wizardry of chemical injections and plastic surgery, transforms the beast into a beautiful woman, played by Paula Dupree. Despite her make-over she remains a beast at heart, and when jilted goes on a maddened rampage.

VHS: S21729. $14.98.
Edward Dmytryk, USA, 1943, 61 mins.

Carnival of Souls

The best horror movie ever made in Lawrence, Kansas. Candace Hilligoss plays the only survivor of a traffic accident where a carload of young women goes off a bridge. Shaken by the experience, she leaves town to play the pipe organ in Lawrence where she is haunted by very disturbing spectres. Truly eerie despite its low budget. B&W.

VHS: S04077. $19.95.
Herk Harvey, USA, 1962, 80 mins.

Carrie

Director Brian de Palma breathes life into the Steven King novel about a repressed teenager who uses her telekinetic powers to take revenge on her tormenting school peers. Sissy Spacek stars as the sympathetic Carrie; Piper Laurie plays her pious, crazy mother. VHS letterboxed.

VHS: S12742. $14.95.
Laser: LD70743. $89.95.
Brian DePalma, USA, 1977, 101 mins.

Cast a Deadly Spell
The setting is Los Angeles in 1948, home to a bevy of witches and voodoo. This sci-fi horror whodunit centers on Harry P. Lovecraft (Fred Ward), a gumshoe who must rely on street smarts to find the fabled Necronomicon. Fantastic elements coupled with good effects and a driving plot make for a highly watchable yarn. With David Warner, Julianne Moore, Clancy Brown and Alexandra Powers.
VHS: S25872. $89.99.
Laser: LD75123. $24.98.
Martin Campbell, USA, 1991, 93 mins.

Castle of Blood
Barbara Steele is the bait for a daring reporter who bets he can stay the night in a haunted castle. It seems on "The Night of the Dead" everyone who has died violently in the place returns seeking human blood. The moral of this story is, never trust a woman without a heartbeat. With George Riviere and Margaret Robsham. B&W. Based on E.A. Poe's *Dance Macabre*.
VHS: S09131. $29.95.
Anthony Dawson (Antonio Margheriti), Italy, 1964, 85 mins.

Castle of Evil
The faithful robot of a deceased mad scientist has orders to kill all those that show up on this Caribbean island for the reading of the will. Starring Scott Brady, Virginia Mayo and David Brian. A free funeral was promised if you dropped dead watching this film. Be careful—the offer may no longer be valid.
VHS: S04262. $14.98.
Francis D. Lyon, USA, 1966, 81 mins.

Castle of Fu Manchu
Christopher Lee stars as the evil Oriental magnate who experiments with more deadly potions in his castle near Istanbul, pitted against his nemesis, Nayland Smith of Britain's Home Office.
VHS: S03066. $19.95.
Jess (Jesus) Franco, Germany/Italy/Spain/Great Britain, 1968, 92 mins.

Castle of the Living Dead
Christopher Lee is Count Drago, the sinister host who often changes his unfortunate guests into living statues. This allows him to have lots of company and still save on expenses. Donald Sutherland plays a witch and a sergeant of the guard in his film debut.
VHS: S04053. $29.95.
Herbert Wise (Luciano Ricci), Italy/France, 1964, 90 mins.

The Cat and the Canary
A shadowy mansion provides the setting for chills, laughter and amazing Expressionist filmmaking when a family gathers for the reading of an eccentric relative's will. Combining masterful art direction, photography and pacing, Leni's film is the most famous of the classic *Old Dark House* story. Silent.
VHS: S00219. $29.95.
Laser: LD76290. $39.99.
Paul Leni, USA, 1927, 71 mins.

Cat People (1942)
A revolutionary horror picture, in which the horror grows by suggestion rather than being depicted. Val Lewton made his name as producer of *Cat People*. The scare at the swimming pool is a true classic.
Laser: LD75377. $49.98.
Jacques Tourneur, USA, 1942, 73 mins.

Cat People (1982)
Paul Schrader's remake of Jacques Tourneur's 1942 classic about an innocent young woman (Nastassia Kinski) whose incestuous relationship with her brother (Malcolm McDowell) results in a terrifying transformation. With John Heard, Annette O'Toole, Ed Begley, Jr., and John Larroquette.
VHS: S06126. $14.98.
Laser: LD72191. $34.98.
Paul Schrader, USA, 1982, 118 mins.

Cat's Eye
A trilogy of horror tales based on some of Stephen King's most successful short stories. An all-star cast is featured in these three thrilling narratives about a radical way to stop smoking, a man forced to walk along a skyscraper ledge, and a stray cat that comes to a little girl's rescue against an evil troll. Starring James Woods, Robert Hays, Drew Barrymore and Alan King.
VHS: S13972. $19.99.
Lewis Teague, USA, 1985, 93 mins.

Cauldron of Blood
Boris Karloff, at the end of his career, plays a blind sculptor in a Spanish art colony. His wife, Viveca Lindfors, is trying to kill him. She rehearses by murdering other people while Karloff unknowingly uses their skeletons in his work. Made in 1967 but not released until 1971.
VHS: S04257. $14.98.
Edward Mann (Santo Alcocer), Spain/USA, 1967, 95 mins.

Chamber of Horrors (The Door with Seven Locks)
Leslie Banks plays a villainous host who keeps his dungeon adequately supplied with victims. Based on an Edgar Wallace story, a madman terrorizes the lovely Lilli Palmer to learn her secret. With Cathleen Nesbitt and Richard Bird. Low-budget terror. B&W.
VHS: S04060. $19.95.
Norman Lee, Great Britain, 1940, 80 mins.

The Changeling
George C. Scott is a recently widowed musician who moves into an old house inhabited by the spirit of a child who lived there 70 years ago. With Trish Van Devere, Melvyn Douglas and John Corlicos.
VHS: S31897. $9.95.
Peter Medak, Canada, 1979, 109 mins.

Christine
When a teenager (Keith Gordon) buys an old car that needs fixing, it becomes something of an obsession. This harmless tendency turns dangerous when the car responds in kind and becomes a jealous friend. Soon this possessed car is murdering all those who come between it and its owner. Also stars Harry Dean Stanton.
VHS: S22110. $14.95.
Laser: Letterboxed. **LD74551. $34.95.**
John Carpenter, USA, 1983, 110 mins.

Circle of Deceit
Dennis Waterman stars as an agent called back into service as a recently killed IRA soldier. He must convince his assumed family in order to complete his mission, but he has inadvertently fallen in love with the widowed daughter of his primary target. 103 mins.
VHS: S24781. $19.98.

Circus of Horrors
Anton Diffring and Erika Remberg star in this frightening horror film, in which an unethical plastic surgeon and a nurse join a bizarre circus in order to escape a deformed patient threatening their lives.
VHS: S04562. $19.98.
Sidney Hayers, Great Britain, 1960, 89 mins.

The Climax
Boris Karloff is house physician at the Vienna Opera House. Though he loves music, he slowly goes mad and brings disaster to this illustrious institution by attacking first his own mistress, a beloved diva, and then her replacement. Unfortunately for this young singer, her voice is practically identical to that of her illustrious predecessor.
VHS: S29521. $14.98.
George Waggner, USA, 1944, 86 mins.

Coffin Joe's Visions of Terror
This collection of 14 trailers from the films of Brazil's prolific purveyor of gore will show you the very worst that he has to offer. *Macabre Nightmare*, a short excerpt from *Trilogy of Terror*, about a man who dreams of being buried alive, is also included. Portuguese with English subtitles.
VHS: S20747. $24.95.
Jose Mojica Marins, Brazil, 1963-1986

Cold Eyes of Fear (Gli occhi freddi della paura)
A bad boy with a seriously awful English accent threatens a lawyer and his main squeeze in this stylish and ultra-rare '70s thriller, set in a swinging London seemingly populated entirely by bent policeman. A good example of the *giallo* (thriller) genre. Dubbed in English. VHS letterboxed.
VHS: S35002. $19.98.
Laser: LD77001. $29.99.
DVD: DV60376. $24.99.
Enzo G. Castellari, Italy, 1971, 91 mins.

The Comedy of Terrors
Vincent Price stars as an enterprising undertaker who decides to supply his own customers when business gets bad. Peter Lorre, Boris Karloff and Basil Rathbone join in this terrifying farce. A full-service undertaker is a great idea and this cast manages to get every laugh and groan imaginable from the campy plot.
VHS: S25892. $14.98.
Jacques Tourneur, USA, 1963, 84 mins.

Condemned to Live
A married couple escape from Savage Africa and head for New England in the days of the Puritans. The catch is that the wife was pregnant and had been bitten by a vampire bat. Son grows up with a taste for blood and murder. With Ralph Morgan, Maxine Doyle and Mischa Auer. B&W.
VHS: S04057. $29.95.
Frank Strayer, USA, 1935, 67 mins.

The Conqueror Worm
Vincent Price is Matthew Hopkins, a dedicated witch hunter in the days of Cromwell. He uses his power of life and death for his own profit and pleasure and eventually ticks off the local populace. This AIP release had Price read E.A. Poe's poem over credits to justify the name change.
VHS: S05104. $14.98.
Laser: LD76200. $39.98.
Michael Reeves, Great Britain, 1968, 95 mins.

The Corpse Vanishes
Bela Lugosi stars as an orchid loving doctor who kidnaps brides at their weddings and drains their blood in order to preserve his aging wife's beauty. A plucky female reporter tracks him to his secret laboratory which comes complete with a dwarf, an oaf and a sinister old woman. B&W.
VHS: S03067. $19.95.
Wallace Fox, USA, 1942, 64 mins.

Corridors of Blood
Boris Karloff stars as a doctor working on an anesthesia, who becomes obsessed and falls outside the law, with Christopher Lee. Originally titled *Doctor from Seven Dials*.
VHS: S03546. $39.95.
DVD: DV60327. $24.99.
Robert Day, Great Britain, 1958, 90 mins.

Count Dracula
After five Hammer films playing Transylvanian royalty, Christopher Lee left England to try a new approach to the character. This version stars Herbert Lom as Van Helsing and Klaus Kinski as the insect-eating Renfield. Closely based on the Bram Stoker novel.
VHS: S04265. $14.98.
Jess (Jesus) Franco, Spain/Germany/Italy, 1971, 90 mins.

The Craft
Heathers meets *The Witches of Eastwick* in this witty, witchy, "coven-of-age" mall-schlock film. Stars Fairuza Balk, Robin Tunney, Neve Campbell and Rachel True as the teen witches with bad attitudes who rule the school.
VHS: S30022. $19.95.
Laser: LD75962. $34.95.
DVD: DV60014. $29.95.
Andrew Fleming, USA, 1996, 101 mins.

Crawling Hand
When a handsome pre-med student is given the hand of a dead astronaut, Peter Breck rockets off into a frenzy of murder. The teen remake of *The Beast with Five Fingers* features the music of the Livingstons, including the classic "Papa Oom Mow Mow." With Alan Hale Jr., Richard Arlen, Allison Hayes and Sissy Steffen.
VHS: S10967. $19.95.
Herbert L. Strock, USA, 1962, 89 mins.

The Crazies (Code Name Trixie)
A government plane carrying a biological warfare virus suddenly crashes near a small Pennsylvania town resulting in a poisoned water supply. When the residents embark on a chaotic, murderous rampage, the government sends in the army, unannounced, to quarantine the town and resolve the anarchy.
A small war breaks out when the citizens find themselves caught between a lethal disease, their crazed neighbors and an unexplained occupying army.
VHS: S34331. $14.98.
George A. Romero, USA, 1973, 103 mins.

Creature from Black Lake
This fun, light-hearted, low-budget Bigfoot movie features entertaining performances by Jack Elam *(Once Upon a Time in the West)* and Dub Taylor *(Bonnie and Clyde)* as two college students who travel to Louisiana to track Bigfoot. With Dennis Fimple and John David Carson.
VHS: S32954. $19.95.
Joy N. Houck Jr., USA, 1977, 95 mins.

Creature from the Black Lagoon
The classic love story of a girl and a gill-man who meet on a moonlit night in the backwaters of the Amazon. Originally in 3-D. Truly one of the better monster movies. With Richard Carlson, Julie Adams and Ricou Browning as the gill-man when he is swimming. B&W.
VHS: S05524. $14.95.
Jack Arnold, USA, 1954, 79 mins.

Creature of Destruction
Les Tremayne is a mysterious hypnotist who predicts a series of murders by a sea creature at a country club, and uses a girl, a reincarnation of the monster. With Pat Delaney, Aron Kincaid and Scotty McKay.
VHS: S32150. $24.95.
Larry Buchanan, USA, 1968, 80 mins.

The Creature Walks Among Us
The second follow-up to *The Creature from the Black Lagoon*, about the mysterious gill-man who violently reacts against the scientists trying to control him and soften his appearance through plastic surgery. He longs to return to the freedom of the ocean in this strange parable about the dangers of conformity. With Jeff Morrow, Rex Reason and Leigh Snowden.
VHS: S19015. $14.98.
John Sherwood, USA, 1956, 78 mins.

Creepshow
George A. Romero directed a screenplay by Stephen King that is a ghoulish comic tribute to EC Comics. Five tales of the macabre are offered. E.G. Marshall's battle with cockroaches is a standout. King himself acts as a hick farmer who finds something he shouldn't.
VHS: S04184. $19.98.
George A. Romero, USA, 1982, 120 mins.

Crime of Dr. Crespi
Low-budget but fascinating version of Poe's "Premature Burial" with Erich von Stroheim in great form—the entire film was shot in the old Biograph Studios in less than two weeks.
VHS: S06008. $29.95.
John H. Auer, USA, 1935, 60 mins.

Crimes at the Dark House
Tod Slaughter adapts Wilkie Collins' classic *The Woman in White* for one of the best of his staged melodramas to be filmed. As Sir Percival Glyde, he kills his rich wife and replaces her with an escaped lunatic lookalike. With Hilary Eaves, Sylvia Marriott and Hay Petrie as Dr. Fosco. B&W.
VHS: S04046. $29.95.
George King, Great Britain, 1940, 69 mins.

Crucible of Horror
A gothic thriller with a social edge about an abused wife who poisons her destructive husband and goes slowly mad when his corpse mysteriously appears. With Michael Gough, Sharon Gurney and Yvonne Mitchell.
VHS: S19132. $14.95.
Viktors Ritelis, Great Britain, 1971, 91 mins.

Cry of the Banshee
Witches summon Satan to avenge the many deaths caused by the witch-hunting campaign of Vincent Price.
VHS: S06472. $14.98.
Gordon Hessler, Great Britain, 1970, 87 mins.

Crypt of Horror
A witch curses the family of Count Karnstein. The witch herself will someday be reincarnated as one of the Count's offspring. Years later, the Count fears his daughter is the one. With Christopher Lee, Ursula Davis, Jose Campos, and Vera Valmont.
VHS: S34489. $29.95.
Camillo Mastrocinque, Spain/Italy/USA, 1963, 92 mins.

Cult of the Cobra
When six servicemen unwittingly disturb a secret and ancient ceremony, powerful and evil forces are unleashed that threaten to destroy them. The cobra goddess can deceive and kill. This camp horror classic stars Richard Long, Marshall Thompson and Faith Domergue.
VHS: S20892. $14.98.
Francis D. Lyon, USA, 1955, 82 mins.

Cult of the Dead
Dr. van Molder (Boris Karloff) studies the unique behavior of an island population practicing sexual ceremonies and offering human sacrifices to a demonic spirit. Investigations lead to a horrifying confrontation with the cult's diabolical high priestess. 90 mins.
VHS: S09257. $19.98.

Curse of King Tut's Tomb
Based on the book *Behind the Mask of Tutankhamen*, by Barry Wynne. As you might expect with a title like that the word Egypt will be mentioned more than once in the course of this film, which will include both a curse and the burial place of an internationally known member of royalty. Cast includes Robin Ellis, Wendy Hiller, Raymond Burr and Eva Marie Saint. See it if you dare.
VHS: S10386. $19.95.
Philip Leacock, Great Britain, 1980, 96 mins.

Curse of the Demon
One of the very great horror films; when psychologist John Holden's colleague, Professor Harrington, is mysteriously and brutally murdered, Holden denies it's the work of the devil-until he becomes the next target. Great suspense from Jacques Tourneur.
VHS: S02072. $19.95.
Jacques Tourneur, Great Britain, 1958, 95 mins.

Curse of the Undead
Michael Pate's character might seem forbidding enough as a gunslinger, but he is only posing. In actuality this gunman is a vampire. Scores of townspeople in a remote Western spot have been found dead. Eric Fleming, a preacher with gumption who joins both religious conviction with hard-hearted lust for justice, may be the only one who can defeat this creature and save a young rancher woman (Kathleen Crowley).
VHS: S29518. $14.98.
Edward Dein, USA, 1959, 79 mins.

Curse of the Werewolf
A Hammer Film Production, starring Oliver Reed as the blood-thirsty man-beast who is gentle and loving by day and kills by night.
VHS: S02722. $14.98.
Laser: LD71440. $34.98.
Terence Fisher, Great Britain, 1961, 91 mins.

Curse of the Yellow Snake
Atmospheric German adaptation of an Edgar Wallace mystery. An ancient Chinese artifact carries a vicious curse: whoever possesses it will win any war they initiate. The film's hero follows the snake's path from Hong Kong to London, up against Chinese imperialist Fighting Hand and a host of other creepy types. Complete with odd camera angles and eerie lighting effects. Dubbed in English.
VHS: S00289. $29.95.
Franz Gottlieb, Germany, 1963, 98 mins.

Dance of Death
Mathias Morteval (Boris Karloff) calls a reunion of his relatives to determine who inherited the family curse of insanity. One by one the heirs are murdered, suddenly and violently. Who would be next to dance with death?
VHS: S09260. $59.95.
Juan Ibanez, Mexico, 1968, 89 mins.

Danger: Diabolik
In reaction to the suave, sophisticated superspy thrillers that ruled their day, this action piece centers on something far darker and unsettling, the presence of "a psychedelic-era outlaw" named Diabolik, a brilliant, cold and impulsive thief. In English.
VHS: S16890. $19.95.
Mario Bava, Italy, 1968, 99 mins.

The Dark Angel
A psychological horror movie about treachery and deception set against the last vestiges of a decaying Victorian sensibility, Peter O'Toole plays a repressed, depraved old man in line to receive the inheritance of his beautiful, virginal niece, who's come to live with him. With Jane Lapotaire, Beatie Edney and Tim Woodward.
VHS: S17769. $19.98.
Peter Hammond, Great Britain, 1991, 148 mins.

Daughter of Horror
Adrienne Barrett, Bruno VeSota and Angelo Rossitto star in this horrific feature narrated by Ed McMahon. A girl wanders through a series of strange events that culminates in her sawing off the hand of the man she murders. There is hardly any dialog in this odd, dream-like film. Originally banned by the New York Board of Censors.
VHS: S23162. $29.95.
John Parker, USA, 1955, 60 mins.

Daughters of Darkness (Director's Cut)
This classic, cult vampire favorite, originally cut by more than 12 minutes, is restored to the full film that director Harry Kumel intended. A pair of newlyweds stop at a posh French hotel and encounter the Scarlet Countess (Delphine Seyrig), a stunning and seductive woman who, according to the hotel owner, hasn't aged a day in 40 years. Before long, the couple's innocent intrigue leads them into a sexually charged game of cat and mouse as the mysterious countess turns deadly. "Subtle, stately, stunningly colored and exquisitely directed.... The most artistic vampire shocker since *Blood and Roses*" *(The New York Times)*. With Andrea Rau, Danielle Ouimet and John Karlen. In English.
VHS: S31446. $14.98.
Laser: Letterboxed. **LD76337. $49.95.**
DVD: DV60277. $24.95.
Harry Kumel, Belgium/France/West Germany, 1971, 100 mins.

Dawn of the Dead (Director's Cut)
George A. Romero's sequel to *Night of the Living Dead* is a bleak satire of American consumerism. Three men and a woman escape the ravenous walking dead and gain refuge in a sterile, abandoned shopping mall. Romero charts a series of complicated sexual, racial and political relationships as the flesh-devouring zombies lay siege to their "fortress." With David Emge, Ken Foree, Scott H. Reininger and Gaylen Ross.
VHS: S04563. $14.98.
Laser: LD70939. $99.95.
George A. Romero, USA, 1978, 131 mins.

Day of the Dead
The walking dead have taken over the world. Only a small band of scientists and soldiers remain and have taken refuge in an underworld missile silo. Borderline mad scientist Dr. Logan attempts to control the hordes of walking dead by using a zombie as a guinea pig. When a military leader discovers that some of his soldiers have been used as guinea pigs, he retaliates by locking up the remaining scientists with the zombies. Now the remaining human survivors must engage in a horrific last ditch battle for life with thousand of the walking dead.
VHS: S34335. $14.98.
George A. Romero, USA, 1985, 102 mins.

Dead Eyes of London
A German re-make of the Bela Lugosi chiller *Dark Eyes of London*, which was based on an Edgar Wallace short story. Once again the director of a home for the blind will use the place as a front for his criminal activities. With Klaus Kinski and Karin Baal. B&W.
VHS: S04076. $29.95.
Alfred Vohrer, Germany, 1961, 104 mins.

Dead Is Dead
A man is dismembered by a mutant creature and left for dead. Fortunately a woman administers a miraculous drug that saves him. When he pays off a debt with this drug he doesn't realize that it was a bad batch. Now he must get it back somehow.
VHS: S24744. $19.95.
Mike Stanley, USA, 1993, 75 mins.

Dead Men Walk
The reason they walk is that they can't afford to take a bus. But seriously, horror fans, George Zucco plays a double role of brothers with decidedly opposing viewpoints on life and death. There are vampires and mad scientists and Dwight Frye as a maniacal assistant. All in glorious black and white. What more do you want?
VHS: S04037. $29.95.
Sam Newfield, USA, 1943, 67 mins.

The Dead Next Door
A scientist has invented a virus that takes over a corpse's cells. Then the reanimated flesh is trapped in a cycle of feeding. The virus needs more dead human flesh. In response, the government fights back with the Zombie Squad. They must kill the undead to save humankind.
VHS: S24763. $59.95.
J.R. Bookwalter, USA, 1989, 84 mins.

Def by Temptation
In this Troma Team horror film starring Samuel L. Jackson, Kadeem Hardison and Bill Nunn, a young divinity student, in search of an old friend, travels to New York, where he meets a sexy vampire who is hell-bent on destroying Joel through her powers of satantic seduction. One by one, Joel's friends fall victim to the vampire's charms and die hideous deaths, leaving Joel to face up to the temptress and his destiny alone. Great soundtrack by Freedy Jackson and Najee. "Genuine tension and eroticism...excellent special effects" *(Variety)*.
VHS: S32610. $24.95.
James Bond III, USA, 1990, 95 mins.

Dementia 13
Coppola's second film, produced by Roger Corman,is the eerie story of a greedy woman who sets out to gain control of a fortune. Her actions trigger a series of brutal and gory axe murders.The psychological makeup of each suspect is explored in this chilling cult classic filmed in the Republic of Ireland.With William Campell, Luana Anders and Patrick Magee.
VHS: S18175. $19.95.
Laser: LD75940. $49.95.
Francis F. Coppola, USA, 1963, 75 mins.

The Demon Barber of Fleet Street
Tod Slaughter,"the horror man of Europe", stars as Sweeney Todd, the industrious barber who turns potential customers into meat pies that are sold at the bake shop next door.All you need is a sharp razor and a trap door under the barber chair.With Eve Lister. B&W.
VHS: S04041. $29.95.
George King, Great Britain, 1936, 68 mins.

Demons 2
Sally Day's 16th birthday starts with promise but ends with demonic possession and gore.An uninvited guest is lurking in her room with an insatiable appetite. It takes over the innocent girl and transforms her party into a macabre dance with death. Music by the Smiths and Dead Can Dance.
VHS: S24954. $14.99.
Lamberto Bava, Italy, 1986, 88 mins.

Devil Bat
Bela Lugosi as a mad scientist who trains bats to suck the blood of selected victims.With Dave *(Captain Midnight)* O'Brien.
VHS: S03777. $19.95.
Jean Yarbrough, USA, 1941, 69 mins.

The Devil Doll
Lionel Barrymore, disguised as a sweet old granny, shrinks people down to 12 inches using a serum he found while a prisoner on Devil's Island. He uses the little people to gain revenge on his crooked ex- business partners. Great special effects.With Maureen O'Sullivan. B&W.
VHS: S04705. $59.95.
Tod Browning, USA, 1936, 79 mins.

The Devil Rides Out (a.k.a. The Devil's Bride)
Based on the classic novel by Dennis Wheatley.The Duc de Richleau (Christopher Lee) discovers a devil cult that is taking control of innocent people through hynotic spells and demonic ceremonies. Presented in original aspect ratios. Includes original theatrical trailers and TV spots.With Charles Gray. Letterboxed.
VHS: S34976. $14.98.
Terence Fisher, Great Britain, 1968, 95 mins.

The Devil's Commandment
A classic Italian horror film about a mad scientist who captures young women and drains their blood, thereby helping to rejuvenate an aging, evil duchess. Considered the grand-daddy of Italian horror films that followed in the 1960s. Partially lettterboxed in the scope format.With Gianna Canale. Dubbed in English.
VHS: S32572. $24.95.
Ricardo Freda/Mario Bava, Italy, 1956, 90 mins.

The Devil's Daughter
Herbert Lom *(The Dead Zone)* and Kelly Curtis *(Trading Places)* plunge headfirst into a malevolent whirlpool of murder, madness and unholy mayhem in this terrifying supernatural tale of a legion of evil and the woman who uncovers their deadly secret.A supernatural suspense-thriller produced by world-renowned master of shock cinema, Dario Argento.
VHS: S15391. $89.98.
Michele Soavi, USA, 1991, 112 mins.

Devil's Hand (Carnival of Sinners)
A great fantasy/horror film about an artist who buys a hand that seems to bring him luck. It turns out to be the hand of Satan.The devil tells the artist to sell the hand for less than he paid for it within 24 hours or be sent straight to Hell.With Pierre Fresnay, Josseline Gael and Marcelle Monthyl. Dubbed in English.
VHS: S32570. $24.95.
Maurice Tourneur/Jack Raymond, France, 1942, 82 mins.

The Devil's Messenger
Lon Chaney, Jr. is Satan in this bizarre trio of horror stories from the TV series *13 Demon Street* starring John Crawford and Karen Kadler. Satan's messenger goes back to Earth with a formula for a 500-megaton bomb so that everyone can join him in hell.
VHS: S32575. $24.95.
Curt Siodmak, USA, 1961, 84 mins.

Devil's Nightmare
This slice of demented Belgian/Italian sleaze is presented in its full widescreen glory. Featuring a collection of shifty aristos, grumpy servants and a saucy homicidal incubus played by the lickable Erica Blanc. Seventies goth at its campy best. Dubbed in English.VHS letterboxed.
VHS: S35004. $19.98.
Laser: LD77003. $29.99.
DVD: DV60378. $24.99.
Jean Brismee, Belgium/Italy, 1971, 93 mins.

The Devil's Partner
A stranger shows up in a small desert town to claim an inheritance. He brings his satanic beliefs and soon the townsfolk begin to notice changes in their dusty little burg.With Edgar Buchanan, Jean Allison, Ed Nelson and Richard Crane.
VHS: S04070. $29.95.
Charles R. Rondeau, USA, 1961, 75 mins.

The Devil's Rain
A cult leader searches for a satanic book that was stolen from him.The book is needed in order for devil worshippers to deliver souls to Satan.With Ernest Borgnine, Eddie Albert, Ida Lupino, William Shatner, and John Travolta.
VHS: S34208. $19.95.
Robert Fuest, USA, 1975, 83 mins.

The Diary of a Madman
In this eerie adaptation of Maupassant's short story,Vincent Price is Simon Cordier, an apparently simple man who tells a 19th century magistrate that a sinister evil spirit called Horla induces him to murder.With Nancy Kovack, Chris Warfield and Stephen Roberts.
VHS: S11285. $14.95.
Laser: LD76224. $39.98.
Reginald LeBorg, USA, 1963, 96 mins.

Diary of a Nudist
This brilliant expose gets inside the head, and various other body parts, of a proud and practicing American nudist.Witness the purpled mountains' majesty as they hover effortlessly above the fruited plain. God, I love this country.
VHS: S15154. $19.98.

Doctor X
Lionel Atwill is suspected of performing cannibalistic murders by the police.This brings unwanted suspicion on his Long Island research lab. Beware of the one-armed man.Also keep an ear out for Fay Wray, who screams alot in this movie, originally made in Technicolor.
VHS: S04707. $59.95.
Laser: LD70132. $39.98.
Michael Curtiz, USA, 1932, 80 mins.

Dominion
The Dominion is a group of children vampires who give new meaning to the concept of juvenile delinquent.Aside from the usual feasting on human blood, these pint-sized creatures stage a rock concert that actually will conjure their demonic leader.
VHS: S24747. $19.95.
Todd Sheets, USA, 1994, 70 mins.

Don't Look in the Basement
The insane take over the asylum in this super-gory film not for the weak of heart or stomach.With William Bill McGhee and Anne MacAdams.
VHS: S34209. $19.95.
S.F. Brownrigg, USA, 1973, 95 mins.

Donovan's Brain
Curt Siodmak's story of a scientist turned into a controlled killer under the power of the brain of a dead but very determined industrialist had been made before in 1944, but that cast didn't include a future First Lady. Nancy Davis (Reagan) tries to assist a man whose mind is not his own. Practice makes perfect. B&W.
VHS: S04710. $14.95.
Felix E. Feist, USA, 1953, 83 mins.

Dorian Gray
Helmut Berger, fresh from *The Damned*, stars as the title character in this trash update of the Oscar Wilde story of a hedonist who stays young while his portrait ages. Lots of sex in trendy places like horse stables and steam baths.With Herbert Lom, Marie Liljedahl and Beryl Cunningham.
VHS: S04258. $14.98.
Massimo Dallamano, Italy/Lichtenstein, 1970, 92 mins.

Dr. Jekyll and Mr. Hyde (Barrymore)
Recognized as the first great American horror film, this classic tale provided matinee idol John Barrymore with a wonderfully grotesque role as an aristocratic physician who is transformed into a brutal murderer. His zestful rendition of the title character has a grand guignol quality that the later versions of this classic cannot match.
VHS: S05382. $29.95.
John S. Robertson, USA, 1920, 96 mins.

Dr. Jekyll and Mr. Hyde (March)
The uncensored version of the 1932 interpretation of the Robert Louis Stevenson classic that won Fredric March an Oscar.The ten minutes that were cut for its re-release have been restored in its home video debut.Wally Westmore created the transformation make-up for this taut and exciting story of the battle of good and evil in the single body of a man of science.With Miriam Hopkins as Ivy, the prostitute, and Holmes Herbert and Rose Hobart.
VHS: S11217. $19.95.
Rouben Mamoulian, USA, 1932, 98 mins.

Dr. Jekyll and Mr. Hyde (Tracy)
The third screen version of Robert Louis Stevenson's novel is the most popular due to Spencer Tracy's performance as Dr. Harry Jekyll, whose experiments bring out the sexually frustrated Mr. Hyde.With Lana Turner, Ingrid Bergman.
VHS: Out of print. For rental only.
Laser: LD70559. $34.98.
Victor Fleming, USA, 1941, 113 mins.

Dr. Orlof's Monster
The second in the "Orlof" series about the good doctor and his latest monstrosity: a human robot that goes on a destructive rampage.With Jose Rubio and Perla Cristal. Dubbed in English.
VHS: S32577. $24.95.
Jess (Jesus) Franco, Spain, 1964, 88 mins.

Dr. Phibes Rises Again
Vincent Price reprises his role as Dr. Phibes in this sequel. He travels to Egypt hoping to find an elixir that will revive his lovely wife. She remains perfectly preserved for just this purpose. Once again those who threaten this near-sacred quest suffer unimaginable torments.With Peter Cushing and Robert Quarry.
VHS: S20932. $14.98.
Robert Fuest, Great Britain, 1972, 89 mins.

Dracula (Lugosi)
Bela Lugosi stars in his most famous role as the debonair Count in this classic version of Bram Stoker's tale of the bloodsucking fiend. Lots to recommend it, including atmosphere galore and the wonderful Lugosi.
VHS: S00371. $19.95.
Tod Browning, USA, 1931, 75 mins.

Dracula (Palance)
This version recasts the count as a misunderstood genius. Richard Matheson's screenplay is faithful to the original novel.With Simon Ward, Nigel Davenport, Fiona Lewis and Jack Palance as Dracula.
VHS: S17913. $59.98.
Laser: LD71838. $29.98.
Dan Curtis, USA, 1973, 100 mins.

Dracula (Spanish Version)
Filmed simultaneously with Tod Browning's celebrated 1931 English language version, this evocative, atmospheric Spanish translation of Bram Stoker's novel is based on the play by Hamilton Deane and John Balderston, adapted in Spanish by B. Fernandez Cue, shot on the same expressionistic sets.With Carlos Villarias, Lupita Tovar and Pablo Alvarez Rubio.
VHS: S17271. $14.98.
George Melford, Spain, 1931, 104 mins.

Dracula A.D. 1972
Johnny Alucard, a young man performing black magic in the churchyard where Count Dracula (Christopher Lee) was buried 100 years ago, revives the vampire in 1972 London, where the Count goes after the descendents of Professor van Helsing (Peter Cushing).
VHS: S34602. $14.95.
Alan Gibson, Great Britain, 1972, 96 mins.

Dracula Has Risen from the Grave
When Monsignor Muller (Rupert Davies) exorcises Dracula's castle, the Count (Christopher Lee) takes vengeance on him by claiming his beautiful niece Maria (Veronica Carlson) as his bride.
VHS: S34604. $14.95.
Laser: LD76977. $34.98.
Freddie Francis, Great Britain, 1968, 92 mins.

Dracula's Daughter
This sequel stars Gloria Holden as Countess Marya Zaleska, who turns up in London to investigate a series of disappearances where the bodies of beautiful women are found with their blood drained.With Otto Kruger, Marguerite Churchill, and Nan Grey.
VHS: S17272. $14.98.
Lambert Hillyer, USA, 1936, 70 mins.

Dracula's Last Rites
A mortician creates vampires from the recently dead and terrorizes a family that hampers his scheme when they demand a relative's body for a private wake.With Patricia Lee Hammond, Gerald Fielding,Victor Jorge and Michael Lally.
VHS: S19133. $14.95.
Domonic Paris, USA, 1979, 88 mins.

Dracula—A Cinematic Scrapbook

A fabulously fiendish collection of film trailers and trivia about Dracula. Includes clips from classics like *Nosferatu, Son of Dracula* and *Plan 9 from Outer Space*. With Bela Lugosi and Christopher Lee. 60 mins.
VHS: S14461. $9.95.

Dracula: A True Story

This captivating documentary travels to the heart of Transylvania, in today's Romania, where vampire tourism is booming, to uncover the historical truths behind the legend of Dracula. Meet a self-described vampire hunter, who believes that vampires lurk in various forms in Bucharest; a Viennese dermatologist who discusses his theory that porphyria was behind the superstition of vampire's fear of sunlight; and Princess Brianna Caradja as she talks about her famous ancestor, Vlad the Impaler. 45 mins.
VHS: S35123. $24.95.

Dracula: Prince of Darkness

Christopher Lee returns to the role that made him an international star. A chilling wind blows through the sumptuous dining hall as four unwary travelers toast the hospitality of their long-dead host, Count Dracula. Includes original theatrical trailer and a behind-the-scenes home movie with commentary by Christopher Lee, Barbara Shelley, Francis Matthews and Suzan Farmer. Widescreen.
VHS: S31792. $14.98.
Terence Fisher, Great Britain, 1965, 90 mins.

Drums of Jeopardy

Warner Oland, in a pre-Charlie Chan phase, as a mad doctor out for revenge. He holds a certain family responsible for the death of his daughter. Torture and poison gas are but two of his methods to eliminate his victims. With June Collyer and Mischa Auer. B&W.
VHS: S04055. $29.95.
George B. Seitz, USA, 1931

Elvira's Midnight Madness: EEGAH!

Featuring two of the biggest attractions in horror and sci-fi: Richard "Jaws" Kiel and Arch Hall Jr. Dick plays a caveman who schlepps around the desert looking for grub and girls, while Arch and the Archers spend their time rocking out.
VHS: S14466. $9.95.
Nicholas Merriwether, USA, 1957

Elvira's Midnight Madness: Frankenstein's Daughter

This frightening feature stars Dr. Frankenstein's female creation. It's classic teenage monster movie mayhem, as the Frankenstein femme fatale follows family tradition and delivers plenty of horror.
VHS: S14468. $9.95.
Richard Cunha, USA, 1958, 85 mins.

Elvira's Midnight Madness: Giant Gila Monster

An over-sized lizard satisfies its appetite for town folk until our crooning hero, Don Sullivan, turns it into a crispy critter. Scary!
VHS: S14465. $9.95.
Ray Kellogg, USA, 1959, 84 mins.

Elvira's Midnight Madness: I Eat Your Skin

Voodoo Island becomes even creepier than its name when a mad scientist starts messing with the gene pool. What happen's next is not a pretty sight.
VHS: S14463. $9.95.
Del Tenney, USA, 1964, 82 mins.

Elvira's Midnight Madness: She Demons

A thriller about a crazed Nazi scientist who holds an uncharted island in the grip of terror as he performs unnatural human experiments that turn vivacious beauties into voluptuous monstrosities.
VHS: S14470. $9.95.
Richard Cunha, USA, 1958, 80 mins.

Elvira's Midnight Madness: The Brain That Wouldn't Die

A surgeon saves his girlfriend's head after she is decapitated in a gruesome car accident. He then preserves her head in his lab while he looks for a fresh body to hook her up with.
VHS: S14473. $9.95.
Joseph Green, USA, 1960, 92 mins.

Elvira's Midnight Madness: The Hideous Sun Demon

A toxic tale about a scientist who is accidentally exposed to radiation and turns into a lizard-like lunatic every time he's in the sunshine.
VHS: S14472. $9.95.
Robert Clarke, USA, 1959, 75 mins.

The Embalmer

A horrible fiend is on the loose under the streets of Venice. He pulls beautiful girls down into murky canals that catacomb the sewers of the ancient Italian city. He kills and stuffs them, then adds them to his grisly collection of statues that adorn the walls of his underground lair. This rare video is one of the most sought-after Italian horror films. With Maureen Brown, Gin Mart, Luciano Gasper and Anita Tedesco. Dubbed in English.
VHS: S32578. $24.95.
Dino Tavella, Italy, 1966, 85 mins.

Encounter with the Unknown

Rod Serling narrates these three eerie stories based on data from world-famous ghost hunters. The first tale concerns a shockingly accurate death prophesy placed on three young men. Next, a bizarre story of a mysterious "deep hole" located on a farm in which a chilling mist surrounds the area and eerie noises are heard from within the hold. The final tale is of a beautiful ghost who haunts the highway where she and her boyfriend were killed in an accident.
VHS: S34210. $19.95.
Harry Thomason, USA, 1975, 90 mins.

The End of Man

In this more serious horror film, a preacher named Finis Hominis has supernatural powers that aid him as he explores the psychedelic world of hippies and the mysteries of death. By day he cures paraplegics but by night he raises the dead. Portuguese with English subtitles.
VHS: S20749. $24.95.
Jose Mojica Marins, Brazil, 1971

Evil Dead 2: Dead by Dawn

Ash (Bruce Campbell), the sole survivor of *The Evil Dead* returns to the same isolated cabin deep in the woods with his girlfriend, Annie (Sarah Berry). The two discover a mysterious tape recorder and hear the voice of Professor Knoby reciting passages from the *Necromekon*, or *Book of the Dead*. Little do they know that the professor's words are powerful enough to invoke a spell that unleashes the spirit of evil alive in the remote forest surrounding them. "*Rambo, Mad Max* and *Dirty Harry* all rolled into one. A sizzler of a sequel. An absolute scream" *(Daily Mirror)*. Letterboxed.
VHS: S33221. $14.98.
Sam Raimi, USA, 1987, 85 mins.

Evil of Frankenstein

Peter Cushing stars as Baron Frankenstein in this Hammer Films presentation. The Baron teams up with Zoltan the Hypnotist to explore new methods of making the monster a more productive citizen. Once again the townfolk fail to see the scientific value of the project and break out the torches and farm implements. With Peter Woodthorpe, Katy Wild, Duncan Lamont and Kiwi Kingston as the Creature.
VHS: S12254. $19.95.
Freddie Francis, Great Britain, 1964, 84 mins.

The Exorcist—25th Anniversary Edition

View pea soup like never before in this new widescreen version sure to make your head spin. Starring Ellen Burstyn and Linda Blair. With 11 minutes of never-before-seen out-takes and interviews with director William Friedkin and screenwriter William Peter Blatty.
VHS: S01818. $19.98.
DVD: DV60108. $24.98.
William Friedkin, USA, 1973, 121 mins.

The Exorcist—25th Anniversary Edition Set

This widescreen version includes the video, a commemorative book, a CD soundtrack, limited edition lobby card reprints and senitype film frame blowup. With 11 minutes of never-before-seen out-takes and interviews with director William Friedkin and screenwriter William Peter Blatty.
VHS: S34623. $49.98.
William Friedkin, USA, 1973, 175 mins.

Eyes Without a Face

A classic horror film from French filmmaker Georges Franju. A guilt-ridden plastic surgeon attempts to rebuild his daughter's face using the skin from unwilling volunteers. A poetic, artistically made study of madness and guilt. With Pierre Brasseur, Alida Valli, and Edith Scob as the faceless daughter. French with English subtitles. B&W.
VHS: S04481. $29.95.
Georges Franju, France, 1959, 84 mins.

The Face at the Window

A horror movie about the efforts to capture "The Wolf," the killer stalking 1880s Paris. With Tod Slaughter, Marjorie Taylor and John Warwick. On the same program is a stylish Ub Iwerks' cartoon, *Spooks*.
VHS: S04045. $24.95.
George King, USA, 1939, 64 mins.

Face of the Screaming Werewolf

Via hypnosis Dr. Edmund Redding helps a woman recover memories of her past life as an Aztec woman. She leads Redding and associates to the Great Pyramid of Yucatan, where they find two mummified bodies: one a living Aztec; the other a dead modern man who turns out to be a werewolf. Lon Chaney, Jr. stars as The Mummy and The Werewolf.
VHS: S34497. $24.95.
Rafael Lopez Portillo/Gilberto Martinez Solares/Jerry Warren, USA, 1964, 60 mins.

Fall of the House of Usher

Kay Tendeter is Lord Roderick Usher. His sister is dead but he really isn't so sure. This causes great anxiety and a steep decline in property values. With Gwendoline Watford, Irving Steen, Gavin Lee and Lucy Pavey as the Hag. Source material is Edgar Allan Poe.
VHS: S04067. $29.95.
Ivan Barnett, Great Britain, 1952, 70 mins.

Fiend Without a Face

A rocket base in Canada is under attack by a horde of free-moving killer brains with spinal cords that choke their screaming victims. These mutant brains are very fond of human grey matter. For a while they are also invisible. With Marshall Thompson. B&W.
VHS: S04255. $39.96.
Laser: CAV. **LD71983. $29.98.**
Arthur Crabtree, Great Britain, 1958, 78 mins.

The Fiendish Plot of Dr. Fu Manchu

Peter Sellers' final film is full of villainous fun. He plays two roles: a diabolical criminal mastermind *and* his own Scotland Yard nemesis.
VHS: S14568. $19.98.
Laser: LD71473. $34.98.
Piers Haggard, Great Britain, 1980, 100 mins.

Flesh and the Fiends (Mania)

Peter Cushing stars in this gory tale of body-snatching as the dedicated Dr. Knox. He needs fresh corpses for his medical experiments and studies. Donald Pleasance and George Rose are in the cast and seem likely to be able to provide the Dr. with what he needs.
VHS: S04073. $29.95.
John Gilling, Great Britain, 1960, 87 mins.

The Flesh Eaters

One of the greatest low-budget black and white shockers of all time. A mad, ex-Nazi scientist breeds a strain of flesh-devouring bacteria on a desert island, using victims of a shipwreck as his guinea pigs. Some of the gruesome special effects are amazing. This is not one to show to your young children, yet not really a gore film. And the astonishing climax still packs a jolt.
VHS: S00449. $29.95.
Jack Curtis, USA, 1964, 87 mins.

The Fly

Vincent Price is the mad scientist who experiments with his disintegration machine and has his atomic pattern traded with that of a fly in the original version of this now classic sci-fi theme.
VHS: S03366. $14.98.
Kurt Neumann, USA, 1958, 94 mins.

The Fly II

A new generation of terror in this follow-up to *The Fly*, starring Eric Stoltz and Daphne Zuniga.
VHS: S09791. $19.98.
Chris Valas, USA, 1988, 105 mins.

The Fog

A contemporary tale of supernatural horror from the director of *Halloween*, featuring a cast that includes Jamie Lee Curtis, Janet Leigh, Adrienne Barbeau, Hal Holbrook and John Houseman.
Laser: LD72301. $29.99.
John Carpenter, USA, 1979, 94 mins.

Frankenstein (Bergin/Quaid)

David Wickes' stylish adaptation of Mary Shelley's baroque classic about a brilliant doctor (Patrick Bergin) who experiments to build the perfect human. His plans go hideously awry and in the process the doctor creates a beast (Randy Quaid)—which responds by trying to avenge his disfigured state. Cinematography by Jack Conroy *(My Left Foot)*. With John Mills, Lambert Wilson and Fiona Gillies.
VHS: S19535. $92.98.
David Wickes, USA, 1993, 117 mins.

Frankenstein (Gielgud)

Carrie Fisher, Sir John Gielgud, Robert Powell and David Warner star in this modern version of Mary Shelley's classic. Robert Powell is Dr. Frankenstein, Carrie Fisher his fiancee.
VHS: S02658. $19.95.
James Ormerod, Great Britain, 1984, 81 mins.

Frankenstein 1970

Never before on video, decades after his landmark role as Frankenstein, Boris Karloff is at the controls this time as a very mad and very entertaining Dr. Frankenstein.
VHS: S31837. $14.95.
Howard W. Koch, USA, 1958, 83 mins.

Frankenstein Created Woman

In a 19th-century Balkan Village, Baron Frankenstein embarks upon an experiment that is driven by the spirit of evil and its passion for revenge. Starring Peter Cushing and Susan Denberg. Presented in original aspect ratios. Includes original theatrical trailers and TV spots. Letterboxed.
VHS: S34977. $14.98.
Terence Fisher, Great Britain, 1967, 92 mins.

Frankenstein Meets the Wolfman

This Universal horror film provides a sequel that combines two of their most popular monsters. Lawrence Talbot seeks out the help of a certain notorious mad scientist only to find the doctor dead and his creations quite alive. The townspeople are not pleased to find monsters in their neighborhood. With Lon Chaney Jr., Ilona Massey, Patric Knowles, Dwight Frye and Bela Lugosi as Frankenstein's monster.
VHS: S12253. $14.98.
Roy William Neill, USA, 1943, 72 mins.

Frankenstein Must Be Destroyed!

Baron Frankenstein (Peter Cushing) is at it again, working on illegal medical experiments. This time he teams up with Karl Holst (Simon Ward), a young doctor, and his fiancee, Anna (Veronica Carlson), as they kidnap the mentally ill Dr. Brandt (George Pravda) to perform the first brain transplant.
VHS: S34609. $14.95.
Terence Fisher, Great Britain, 1969, 101 mins.

Frankenstein—A Cinematic Scrapbook

A diabolically delicious collection of movie trailers and terrifying trivia about the immortal Frankenstein. Includes clips from the original horror classic and such hilarious spoofs as *Abbot and Costello Meet Frankenstein* and Mel Brooks' modern day masterpiece, *Young Frankenstein*. 60 mins.
VHS: S14460. $9.95.
Ted Newsom, USA, 1991, 60 mins.

Frankenstein—The Restored Version

A restored version (containing footage not seen since censors cut the film at the time of its original release) of one of the great Hollywood horror films, with Boris Karloff in this famous adaptation of Mary Shelley's masterpiece.
VHS: S00462. $14.98.
James Whale, USA, 1931, 71 mins.

Freaks

Tod Browning's classic horror film, with a cast of real side-show "freaks"—dwarfs, midgets, Siamese twins— dominated and exploited by the circus strong man and a beautiful aerialist, who eventually band together in a horrifying revenge.
VHS: S01560. $19.98.
Laser: LD70578. $34.98.
Tod Browning, USA, 1932, 66 mins.

The Fury of the Wolfman

A chiller about a gifted scientist who is transformed into a diabolical wolfman and wreaks havoc on the unsuspecting. With Paul Naschy and Mark Stevens. English dubbed.
VHS: S19352. $19.95.
Jose Maria Zabalza, Spain, 1970, 80 mins.

Galaxy of the Dinosaurs

The rather dimwitted Zyrox, a human-like people with simple desires, stop for lunch on a pleasant looking planet. They never expected a whirlwind of chaotic prehistoric terror, just a nice picnic spot. This is a good, terror-filled film with some great laughs.
VHS: S24754. $9.95.
Lance Randas, USA, 1992, 85 mins.

The Ghost

Barbara Steele stars in this Italian semi-sequel to *The Horrible Dr. Hichcock* as a greedy, scheming, unfaithful wife to the crippled Dr. Hitchcock, a physician with a strong interest in the occult. There was no "t" in the man's name in the first film, but both films have Steele doing what she does best. With Harriet White, Elio Jotta and Peter Baldwin as Dr. Livingstone.
VHS: S09139. $29.95.
Riccardo Freda, Italy, 1963, 96 mins.

The Ghost of Frankenstein

An eerie sequel to *Son of Frankenstein*. Ygor (Bela Lugosi) tries desperately to foil a fiendish plot to switch the monster's brain with the brain tissue of an educated human. With Cedrick Hardwicke, Lon Chaney Jr., Lionel Atwill and Ralph Bellamy.
VHS: S19009. $14.98.
Erle C. Kenton, USA, 1942, 68 mins.

The Ghoul

For years a lost cult classic of British horror films, this stars Boris Karloff, with Cedric Hardwicke and Ralph Richardson. Very effective Gothic mood sustained by atmospheric camera work.
VHS: S02931. $14.98.
Laser: LD75975. $39.99.
T. Hayes Hunter, Great Britain, 1933, 68 mins.

Girls School Screamer

There are seven beautiful coeds at this exclusive finishing school, where they ultimately find themselves finished off. It all begins when they are locked in a dark mansion for a night of unspeakable horrors. Suddenly graduation does not seem so terribly important. Getting out alive does.
VHS: S22676. $14.95.
John P. Finegan, USA, 1985, 85 mins.

Goblin

A newlywed couple move into their own home, but there is an unknown previous inhabitant still in residence. He was accidentally conjured from the depths of hell and is in no mood to move back, because he enjoys spreading terror.
VHS: S24745. $19.95.
Todd Sheets, USA, 1993, 75 mins.

God Told Me To

In this cult epic suspense thriller by Larry Cohen *(It's Alive)*, a series of bizarre, motiveless murders send a religious New York cop on a manhunt for a mysterious cult leader. With Tony Lo Bianco, Sandy Dennis and Deborah Raffin.
VHS: S31680. $14.98.
Laser: Letterboxed. **LD76389. $39.95.**
Larry Cohen, USA, 1976, 89 mins.

Graveyard Shift

Another terror-filled tale from Stephen King. This one is based on one of his short stories about a monstrous, primordial rat living in the tunnels underneath a previously abandoned textile mill. When the mill is re-opened one night, the horror begins.
VHS: S13715. $14.95.
Laser: LD75203. $34.98.
Ralph S. Singleton, USA, 1990, 89 mins.

The Greed of William Hart

Tod Slaughter lends himself to recreating the story of Burke and Hare, the Scottish graverobbers. When the supply of cadavers runs low for the medical schools in Edinburgh, Slaughter and Henry Oscar create access to a fresher product, much to the annoyance of the local populace. With Arnold Bell as Doctor Cox.
VHS: S04047. $29.95.
Oswald Mitchell, Great Britain, 1948, 78 mins.

The Green Slime

This campy, stylish tribute to the sci-fi classics of the 50s stars Robert Horton as a hot-headed commander enlisted to save Earth. Filmed entirely in Japan at Toei Studios in Tokyo with a Japanese director and crew—despite its all-Caucasian cast.
VHS: S14958. $19.98.
Kinji Kukasaku, USA/Japan, 1968, 90 mins.

Grizzly

A grizzly of unbearable ferocity preys on the flesh of unsuspecting humans to satisfy his enormous hunger.
VHS: S03263. $14.95.
William Girdler, USA, 1976, 92 mins.

Half Human

Half man, half beast, but all monster! Low budget Japanese chiller from the director of *Godzilla*. With Inoshiro Honda, John Carradine and Kenneth Crane.
VHS: S12779. $14.95.
Inoshiro Honda, Japan, 1958, 78 mins.

Halloween

Considered one of the scariest films ever made, as well as one of the most successful independent films. The godfather of the subgenre of the high school horror film, with the boogie man who just won't die. With Jamie Lee Curtis and P.J. Soles.
VHS: S00536. $14.98.
Laser: Letterboxed, special edition. **LD74592. $99.98.**
John Carpenter, USA, 1978, 90 mins.

Hallucinations of a Deranged Mind

An anti-government assembly of outlawed footage that's a radical critique of censorship and authoritarianism. Brazil horror auteur Jose Mojica Marins assembled sequences from 10 different films that were altered by the military junta. The scenes include a young man ravaged by images of a Coffin Joe. Portuguese with English subtitles.
VHS: S18985. $24.95.
Jose Mojica Marins, Brazil, 1970

Hands of a Stranger

A variation of *Hands of Orlac*, about a gifted pianist who receives a hand transplant from a demented killer and begins acting out violent rages. With Paul Lukather, Joan Harvey and Irish McCalla.
VHS: S18936. $19.95.
Newton Arnold, USA, 1962, 86 mins.

Hands of Orlac

With Christopher Lee, Mel Ferrer, Donald Wolff. A well-done remake of *Mad Love* has Ferrer as the pianist with the transplanted criminal hands and Lee as the man who torments him. Ferrer does a fine performance as the tormented Orlac, who is obsessed by the hands grafted to his wrists after an accident, that he believes belonged to a psychotic stranger.
VHS: S12328. $19.95.
Edmond T. Greville, Great Britain/France, 1960, 95 mins.

The Harvest

Miguel Ferrer stars in this tense psycho-thriller as a screenwriter who uncovers a black market in human parts, or to be more precise, these crooks discover him and steal one of his kidneys. Not satisfied with that, they want to take its mate.
VHS: S21004. $14.95.
David Marconi, USA, 1992, 97 mins.

Hatchet for a Honeymoon

Mario Bava's baroque chiller about a despondent man, haunted by recurring memories of his dead wife, who abducts and kills young brides. English dubbed.
VHS: S19347. $24.95.
Mario Bava, Italy/Spain, 1971, 93 mins.

Haunted Palace

A man arrives in a New England town to claim his family castle and discovers that the town is populated by mutants. He soon falls under the evil spell of the castle's ancestor. With Vincent Price and Lon Chaney Jr. Based on H.P. Lovecraft's *The Strange Case of Charles Dexter Ward*.
VHS: S31898. $9.95.
Roger Corman, USA, 1963, 85 mins.

The Haunting

Robert Wise's nerve-jangling adaptation of Shirley Jackson's *The Haunting of Hill House* centers on a gathering at a Boston mansion. An anthropologist, a disbeliever and two mediums confront the supernatural terror. With Richard Johnson, Claire Bloom, Julie Harris and Lois Maxwell.
VHS: S01561. $19.98.
Laser: LD72121. $34.98.
Robert Wise, USA, 1963, 112 mins.

Haunting Fear

Based on the E.A. Poe short story *The Premature Burial*. Jan-Michael Vincent stars as an unfaithful husband with a surefire plan to scare his wife to death. He and girlfriend Brinke Stevens hadn't counted on Karen Black's troubled spirit being interested in seeking revenge. With Robert Quarry, Delia Sheppard and Michael Berryman, the spookiest looking actor since Rondo Hatton. Scary stuff.
VHS: S15494. $79.95.
Fred Olen Ray, USA, 1991, 88 mins.

The Head
This German horror film is not to be confused with the Monkees psychedelic comic of 1968. French actor Michel Simon invents serum Z, which keeps a dog's detached noggin alive. Horst Frank as Dr. Ood experiments using human subjects like his boss's head. He also transplants the head of a crippled nurse onto the body of a stripper just for fun. B&W.
VHS: S09135. $29.95.
Victor Trivas, Germany, 1959, 92 mins.

The Headless Ghost
Three young exchange students on holiday in Britain take a tour of the famous Ambrose Castle, reputedly haunted by a headless ghost named Malcom who lost his head leading a rebellion against King Edward. When a portrait of the 4th Earl of Ambrose leaps from the wall asking for their help, the three students try to end Malcom's reign of terror. Letterboxed.
VHS: S34291. $19.99.
Peter Graham Scott, Great Britain, 1959, 63 mins.

Hellish Flesh
George Medeiros, played by Jose Mojica Marins, is a scientist obsessed with devising an acid that can dissolve an entire human body. Tragically disfigured by his scheming wife and her gigolo boyfriend, his plans are sidetracked. Ultimately, however, he manages to make his mark in the world of science and on his conniving spouse as well. Made in Brazil. Portuguese with English subtitles.
VHS: S21347. $24.95.

Hellraiser/Special Edition
Clive Barker wrote and directed this classic horror film featuring outlandish effects. A house is haunted by a mad adventurer. When he was alive, the adventurer found a mysterious box that ultimately killed him. Now as a ghost he seeks human flesh to restore his life. Digitally remastered, this edition also contains theatrical trailers, interviews with the actors, and a letter from Barker.
VHS: S29796. $14.98.
Clive Barker, USA, 1987, 118 mins.

Horror Chamber of Dr. Faustus
The American version of Georges Franju's classic *Eyes without a Face*—a spine-tingling chiller in which the demented physician seeks facial transplants for his disfigured daughter.
VHS: S04074. $29.95.
Georges Franju, France, 1960, 84 mins.

Horror Express
There is a monster defrosting in the baggage car that wants to eat its way through the entire train. Christopher Lee, Peter Cushing and Telly Savalas are determined not to be on the menu when the formerly frozen diner finds it likes to travel by train. Good for its genre.
VHS: S04054. $19.99.
Eugenio Martin, Spain, 1972, 88 mins.

Horror Hotel
A very scary film which concerns witchcraft in New England as a 17th century witch, who is now an innkeeper, lures her victims for their blood and sacrifice to the devil.
VHS: S08432. $29.95.
John Llewellyn Moxey, Great Britain, 1960, 76 mins.

Horror of Dracula
This Hammer film is said to be one of the best vampire movies ever made. Based on the Bram Stoker classic novel, it stars Christopher Lee as the Count and Peter Cushing as his arch foe, Von Helsing. It spawned seven sequels. Sink your teeth in something good.
VHS: S04187. $14.95.
Laser: LD74703. $34.98.
Terence Fisher, Great Britain, 1958, 82 mins.

Horror of It All
Narrated by Jose Ferrer, a look at the dark side of the imagination and movies and some of horror's most popular stars—Boris Karloff, Lon Chaney, Bela Lugosi, John Barrymore, Lionel Atwill, John Carradine and Vincent Price—and a behind-the-scenes examination of how some of horror's most memorable moments were created. 58 mins.
VHS: S05323. $19.98.

Horror of the Blood Monsters
More camp: a scientist traces the wave of vampire killings that's sweeping the earth; John Carradine is the vampire-like inhabitant of a planet whose natives invade earth to feed on human flesh. Also known as *Vampire Men of the Lost Planet, Horror of the Blood Monster, Creatures of the Prehistoric Planet, Horror Creatures of the Prehistoric Planet, Space Mission of the Lost Planet*.
VHS: S08042. $19.98.
Al Adamson, USA, 1970, 85 mins.

Horror Rises from the Tomb
In the 15th century, a knight and his sidekick are beheaded on charges of practicing witchcraft. Revived more than 500 years later, they disrupt a group of vacationers. With Paul Naschy, Vic Winner, Emma Cohen and Helga Line. English dubbed.
VHS: S19351. $19.95.
Carlos Aured, Spain, 1972, 89 mins.

Horrors of the Black Museum
A mystery writer uses his hypnotized assistant to commit a series of killings that baffle Scotland Yard. Features a classic eyeball-gouging binoculars scene. With Michael Gough, June Cunningham, Graham Curnow, Geoffrey Keen.
VHS: S34211. $19.95.
Arthur Crabtree, Great Britain, 1959, 94 mins.

The House of 1000 Dolls
A couple vacationing in Tangiers is befriended by a young man who believes that his fiancee has been abducted into a white slavery ring. With Vincent Price.
VHS: S31895. $9.95.
Jeremy Summers, Great Britain/Spain, 1967, 83 mins.

House of Darkness
In this atmospheric and chilling story, a ghostly narrator presents flashbacks of a man who brutally murders his step-brother in a creepy old haunted house. The stepbrother's ghost returns to haunt his murderer. An ultra-rare, creepy British thriller. With Leslie Brooks, John Stuart and Laurence Harvey in one of his first films.
VHS: S32571. $24.95.
Oswald Mitchell, Great Britain, 1948, 77 mins.

House of Dracula
A gothic sequel to *House of Frankenstein*. The story concerns a doctor who is shocked to watch his personality being turned into that of a destructive monster. With Onslow Stevens, Lon Chaney Jr., John Carradine and Lionel Atwill.
VHS: S19010. $14.98.
Erle C. Kenton, USA, 1945, 67 mins.

House of Frankenstein
Boris Karloff and J. Carrol Naish star in this peculiar horror movie about a twisted scientist and his hunchback assistant who escape from prison, impersonate traveling show performers, and conjure up Dracula, Frankenstein, and Wolfman to carry out their evil intentions. With Lon Chaney, John Carradine, Anne Gwynne, Peter Coe, and Glenn Strange's first appearance as Frankenstein.
VHS: S17275. $14.98.
Erle C. Kenton, USA, 1944, 71 mins.

House of Horrors
Marcel De Lang plays an insane sculptor who befriends an escaped psychopath. It's a rewarding friendship that gives De Lang the opportunity to wreak revenge on all those art critics who have belittled his art works.
VHS: S21728. $14.98.
Jean Yarbrough, USA, 1946, 65 mins.

House of Wax
Vincent Price stars as a demented sculptor who must use human bodies in his wax museum after a fire destroys his hands and his optimistic outlook on life. With Carolyn Jones, Phyllis Kirk and Charles Bronson as the mute assistant. Originally shown in 3-D. Watch for the paddleball man.
VHS: S04188. $19.98.
Laser: LD71809. $34.98.
Andre de Toth, USA, 1953, 88 mins.

The House on Haunted Hill
Vincent Price stars in this classic William Castle film about a group of people who, in order to win a bet with the wealthy Price, try to spend one night in a spooky old mansion with lots of skeletons in its closets.
VHS: S14791. $14.98.
William Castle, USA, 1958, 75 mins.

Human Monster (Dark Eyes of London)
Bela Lugosi in one of the most macabre horror films, as the brilliant but unbalanced Dr. Orloff, who owns an insurance company, works with indigent blind men in his spare time, but is no philanthropist: he is a fiendish killer. Crack Scotland Yard inspector Holt is brought on Orloff's case with hair-raising results.
VHS: S02991. $29.95.
Walter Summers, Great Britain, 1939, 73 mins.

The Hunger
David Bowie, Catherine Deneuve and Susan Sarandon star in this stylish and moving tale of sophisticated vampires. Deneuve needs new blood in order to keep her 300-year-old lover alive. This film has an erotically charged atmosphere which includes a host of memorable scenes like the lesbian encounters between Deneuve and Sarandon. Ann Magnuson and Willem Dafoe also appear. Letterboxed.
VHS: S26970. $19.95.
Tony Scott, USA, 1983, 100 mins.

Hush, Hush, Sweet Charlotte
There are strange goings on at Hollis House, where feeble-minded Bette Davis lives protected by her peculiar housekeeper, Agnes Moorehead. Then cousin Olivia de Havilland comes for a visit, and now Bette will have more than headless ex-boyfriends to worry about. With Bruce Dern and Joseph Cotten. B&W.
VHS: S03912. $19.98.
Robert Aldrich, USA, 1965, 133 mins.

Hyena of London
One of the better German horror films of the 1960s. A mad professor studying the "symptoms of evil" has his assistant inject the brain fluid from a dead killer into his own brain. The results are disastrous as the professor is transformed into a stark, raving maniac himself. With Bernard Price, Diana Martin and Tony Kendall.
VHS: S34490. $29.95.
Germany, 1964

I Bury the Living
At a cemetery, the caretaker has a map of plots and uses white pins for vacant plots and black pins for plots with occupants. When the honorary chairman of the cemetery switches the pins around, live plot owners die and buried tenants revive. Tension builds while waiting to see the consequences of the pin switcharoonie. Does the Chairman of the Morgue have supernatural powers? Very spooky and creepy cult favorite. With Richard Boone, Theodore Bikel.
VHS: S12326. $29.95.
Albert Band, USA, 1957, 77 mins.

I Was a Teenage Mummy (1962)
This classic horror flick is introduced by monster movie maven Forrest J. Ackerman. A professor unearths a mummy that becomes obsessed with revenge. Back in Bridgeport, Connecticut, the entire entourage find themselves plagued by the murderous, overwrapped fiend. Includes an interview with the director.
VHS: S25657. $39.95.
Ralph C. Bluemke, USA, 1962, 73 mins.

I Was a Teenage Mummy (1992)
A low-budget thriller, shot in New Jersey, about a beautiful young girl's transformation into a crazed and unearthly monster. The film stars Chris Tsakis, Ahmed Ben "Leo" Kalib and Mark Fucile, and features the original music of A-Bones.
VHS: S17538. $19.95.
Christopher C. Frieri, USA, 1992

I Was a Teenage Werewolf
One of the best-known cult classics of the Fifties, it launched a wave of "transformed teen" films. Starring Michael Landon as the hirsute and troubled young boy.
VHS: S14275. $29.95.
Gene Fowler, USA, 1957, 70 mins.

Impulse
When some unknown malevolent force reaches the good people of the tranquil farming town of Sutcliffe and unleashes their most primitive urges in full fury, Jennifer and her boyfriend, Stuart, who were somehow spared this transformation, must risk everything to save the doomed town from destruction. With Tim Matheson, Meg Tilly, Hume Cronyn and Bill Paxton. Digitally remastered in full-frame format.
VHS: S34427. $14.98.
Graham Baker, USA, 1984, 93 mins.

The Incredible Doktor Markesan
Boris Karloff is Doktor Markesan, the inventor of a serum that wakes the dead. Actually they are living zombies. The Doktor's nephew and his wife, Dick York and Carolyn Kearney, come to live with him, and their insatiable curiosity sets the stage for terror.
VHS: S21496. $12.98.
Robert Florey, USA, 1962, 50 mins.

The Indestructible Man
No, it's not Arnold Schwarzenegger. But if you guessed Lon Chaney Jr. you may want to see this science fiction tale of a man who returns from the dead to get even with the gang of criminals that did him wrong. With Ross Elliott, Marian Carr and Casey Adams. B&W.
VHS: S04034. $19.95.
Jack Pollexfen, USA, 1956, 70 mins.

The Inner Sanctum: Calling Dr. Death/Strange Confession
Horror legend Lon Chaney, Jr. stars in these two horror classics. In *Calling Dr. Death* (63 mins.), Chaney stars as an accomplished doctor susceptible to the wiles of his inner demon. In *Strange Confession* (62 mins.), Chaney's greedy boss releases a flawed cure for influenza with disastrous consequences. With Lloyd Bridges and Brenda Joyce.
VHS: S31833. $14.98.
Reginald Le Borg/John Hoffman, USA, 1943/1945, 125 mins.

The Inner Sanctum: Dead Man's Eyes/Pillow of Death

In *Dead Man's Eyes* (62 mins.), all eyes turn to an "accidentally" blinded artist (Lon Chaney, Jr.) after his fiancee's father dies mysteriously. *Pillow of Death* (67 mins.), starring Chaney and sultry Brenda Joyce, is a story of humor and horror involving the eccentric Kincaid family.
VHS: S31835. $14.98.
Reginald Le Borg/Wallace Fox, USA, 1944/1943, 129 mins.

The Inner Sanctum: Weird Woman/Frozen Ghost

Weird Woman (64 mins.) is a story filled with sorcery and superstition in which a conniving ex-lover (Evelyn Ankers) seeks revenge on her old beau (Lon Chaney, Jr.). *Strange Confessions* (62 mins.) is a tale of murder and madness in which wax figure creations become all too real.
VHS: S31834. $14.98.
Reginald Le Borg/Harold Young, USA, 1944/1945, 166 mins.

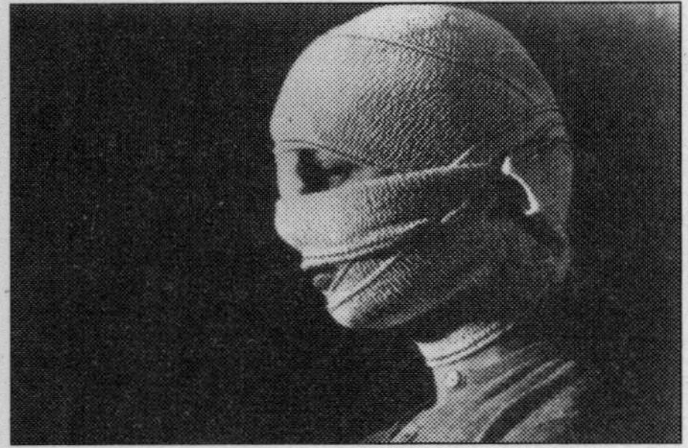

Invasion of the Vampires

Carlos Agosti and Bertha Moss star in this extremely atmospheric "vampire in a castle tale." There is a misty cave chock full of coffins where the troops will be marshalled for the invasion. Could this be an arty Mexican horror film?
VHS: S23164. $29.95.
Miguel Morayta, Mexico, 1961, 78 mins.

Invisible Agent

An irresistible boy's fantasy film about a brave and resourceful young kid who fights the Nazis through his skills to render himself invisible. With Ilona Massey, Jon Hall and Peter Lorre.
VHS: S19016. $14.98.
Edwin L. Martin, USA, 1942, 81 mins.

The Invisible Ghost

One of Bela Lugosi's best films. The story concerns a husband who, when hypnotized by his insane wife, commits many blood-thirsty murders.
VHS: S03333. $29.95.
Joseph H. Lewis, USA, 1941, 64 mins.

The Invisible Man

A super version of H.G. Wells' fantasy, with Claude Rains playing the scientist who experiments with a drug which, while it makes him invisible, also turns him into a megalomaniac murderer. Terrific special effects, with Gloria Stuart playing the sexy heroine.
VHS: S02943. $14.98.
Laser: LD70041. $34.98.
James Whale, USA, 1933, 72

The Invisible Man Returns

Vincent Price stars in this sequel as a brilliant scientist who renders himself invisible. Price is falsely accused of killing his brother and turns invisible to pursue his own investigation. With Sir Cedric Hardwicke, Nan Grey, John Sutton and Cecil Kellaway.
VHS: S17273. $14.98.
Joe May, USA, 1940, 81 mins.

The Invisible Man's Revenge

John Hall is an unstable man who wants to claim an estate. A crazed scientist gives him a serum that makes him invisible, thereby allowing him to realize his plans. Things go awry when they disagree and the invisible man cannot regain his appearance.
VHS: S21731. $14.98.
Ford Beebe, USA, 1944, 77 mins.

Invisible Ray

Bela Lugosi and Boris Karloff are teamed in this classic thriller about a scientist who receives the power to kill with a touch of the hand, from a meteorite found during an expedition in Africa.
VHS: S02721. $14.98.
Lambert Hillyer, USA, 1936, 90 mins.

The Invisible Woman

A genius professor renders a beautiful model invisible. In the confusion, a corrupt industrialist who funded the experiment and a savvy gangster fight for control of the formula. With John Barrymore, Virginia Bruce, John Howard and Charlie Ruggles.
VHS: S19011. $14.98.
A. Edward Sutherland, USA, 1941, 72 mins.

Island of Lost Souls

A terrifying adaptation of H.G. Wells' story about a vivisectionist trapped on a desolate island who alters the biological genetics of jungle animals and changes them into pathological man/animal hybrids. With Charles Laughton, Bela Lugosi, Richard Arlen and Stanley Fields.
VHS: S19013. $14.98.
Erle C. Kenton, USA, 1933, 70 mins.

Island Terror

Mutant monsters resulting from bizarre radiation research terrorize a peaceful island. Now two doctors, Peter Cushing and Edward Judd, must combat the creatures who are rapidly reproducing themselves and could conceivably threaten the whole world.
VHS: S20890. $14.98.
Terence Fisher, Great Britain, 1966, 87 mins.

It Lives Again

The sequel to *It's Alive* features more than one killer baby with an organized government program to isolate and eliminate these freaks of nature. Frederic Forrest and Kathleen Lloyd are the new parents warned by John Ryan that their precious little gift needs special care.
VHS: S04186. $14.95.
Larry Cohen, USA, 1978, 91 mins.

It's Alive

Cult director Larry Cohen delivers the ultimate parental nightmare. John Ryan and Sharon Farrell find that not only is their newborn a physical monstrosity, it is also capable of catching and killing its own lunch. With Michael Ansara, Andrew Duggan, and Guy Stockwell. This one is creepy.
VHS: S04185. $14.95.
Larry Cohen, USA, 1974, 91 mins.

Jack the Ripper (Karloff)

This trilogy of terror blends the familiar with the supernatural, depicting the master of menace, Boris Karloff, as the highlight of each story. Includes *The Murder that Never Happened, Where There's a Will* and a shocking interpretation of the grisly *Jack the Ripper* murders, told from the killer's point of view. 70 mins.
VHS: S15915. $29.95.

Jack the Ripper (Paterson)

The definitive film about the famed English madman. "Jack" commits a series of gruesome slayings in an effort to wipe out prostitution from the streets of London. Brutal and sadistic for its time. With the famed "color" sequence at the end of the film. A well-acted, solid British thriller. With Lee Paterson, Eddie Byrne and Ewen Solon.
VHS: S32573. $24.95.
Robert S. Baker/Monty Berman, Great Britain, 1959, 84 mins.

Jack the Ripper: The Final Solution

A killer stalked late 19th century London. His frenzy of murder remains an unsolved mystery to this day. Using new evidence, this video reveals Jack the Ripper's identity and the conspiracy that kept it a secret for so long. 90 mins.
VHS: S25638. $19.95.

Jack's Back

One hundred years later Jack the Ripper returns to plague Southern California with a duplication of his famous crimes. Is the copy-cat killer the mild mannered medical doctor or his criminal twin brother (both played by James Spader)? Co-worker Cynthia Gibb isn't sure. A creepy and calculating murder mystery and thriller with more red herrings than a fish market in Moscow.
VHS: S07582. $89.95.
Laser: LD75290. $34.98.
Rowdy Herrington, USA, 1988, 97 mins.

Kill, Baby, Kill

Erica Blanc, Max Lawrence and Fabienne Dall star in this atmospheric horror movie driven by vengeance. A young girl's ghost haunts those who caused her death. The only one who understands this deftly woven scenario is ignored until it is too late. All the required horror movie elements are here, including swirling mists, cobwebbed rooms and even a black cat.
VHS: S23169. $29.95.
Mario Bava, Italy, 1966, 83 mins.

Killer Shrews

They may look like dogs dressed up for Halloween but they still can bite, in this low budget horror movie made in Texas. Produced by and starring Ken Curtis (Festus on *Gunsmoke*) as a mad scientist. With James Best and Miss Universe 1957, Ingrid Goude, as people who know that even giant shrews can't bite through a barrel. B&W.
VHS: S09127. $29.95.
Ray Kellogg, USA, 1959, 70 mins.

Killers from Space

Peter Graves plays a scientist raised from the dead by some monsters with bulging eyes who plan to use him as a spy. Will Peter save the earth from these alien creatures?
VHS: S14464. $19.95.
W. Lee Wilder, USA, 1954, 80 mins.

King Kong (60th Anniversary Edition)

The classic 1933 shocker by Ernest B. Schoedsack in a 60th anniversary edition. The film's daring special effects still astonish and are preserved in this archival print and digitally remastered soundtrack struck from the original optical master track. With Fay Wray, Robert Armstrong, Bruce Cabot, Frank Reicher, Sam Hardy and Noble Johnson. B&W.
VHS: S17035. $16.98.
Laser: CAV. LD70389. $74.95.
Ernest B. Schoedsack, USA, 1933, 103 mins.

King Kong Lives

Linda Hamilton *(The Terminator)* and Brian Kerwin *(Murphy's Romance)* star in this exciting sequel to the 1976 Academy Award-winning film *King Kong*. Through the miracle of modern medicine, King Kong is revived after his fall from a skyscraper ten years ago and is brought together with Lady Kong, his lifelong mate. When the two escape, the U.S. military is sent out to track them down.
VHS: S30007. $14.98.
John Guillermin, USA, 1986, 105 mins.

King of the Zombies

Another ambitious scientist has come up with the perfect soldier for WWII, the zombie corps. Developed in the laboratory of a castle on a jungle island, the undead train to hit the beach. The cast includes Dick Purcell, Joan Woodbury, Henry Victor and Mantan Moreland as the comic relief. B&W.
VHS: S04061. $29.95.
Jean Yarbrough, USA, 1941, 67 mins.

Kingdom of the Vampires

Jeff is a liquor store clerk who hides his secret rather well. In actuality he is a vampire with a ghoulish mother at home who snacks on the neighborhood kids. Jeff's troubles are compounded when he falls in love, because mother is just a trifle jealous.
VHS: S24760. $9.95.
J.R. Bookwalter, USA, 1991, 90 mins.

Kiss of the Tarantula

Great camp. In the tradition of *Ben*, Susan, the unusual daughter of a mortuary owner, collects tarantula spiders. Shunned by her schoolmates and friends, she uses her deadly pets in acts of hideous revenge. With Eric Mason, Susan Ling. Color, 85 mins.
VHS: S13232. $19.95.
Chris Munger, USA, 1975, 85 mins.

Kiss of the Vampire

In search of a honeymoon destination, a young couple loses their way in the Bavarian forest. Luckily, a distinguished lord invites them to his castle. A nightmare unfolds there featuring a family of vampires. Only Professor Zimmer and his ancient ritual offer them any hope of leaving this Hammer Horror Collection nightmare behind. With Clifford Evans, Noel Willman, Edward De Souza, Jennifer Daniel and Barry Warren.
VHS: S25569. $14.98.
DVD: DV60332. $29.99.
Don Sharp, Great Britain, 1962, 88 mins.

The Last Man on Earth

Vincent Price stars as a scientist who is the last survivor on Earth after a plague turns the rest of the population into vampires. He escapes contagion because of a jungle virus he once had. While battling the vampires he falls in love with a vampire (Franca Bettoja) who claims to have found a temporary antidote. He tries to free her from the virus before her vampire friends kill him. With Emma Danieli and Giacomo Rossi-Stuart.
VHS: S30407. $19.95.
Sidney Salkow, USA, 1964, 86 mins.

The Leech Woman

A doctor and his wife, played by Phillip Terry and Colleen Gray, venture to Africa together even though age has dampened the doctor's interest in his wife. There they uncover a secret to eternal youth that extracts a terrible price, the blood of young men.
VHS: S20894. $14.98.
Edward Dein, USA, 1960, 77 mins.

The Legend of the Seven Golden Vampires

Professor Van Helsing (Peter Cushing) and Count Dracula (John Forbes-Robinson) meet again in this kung-fu horror spectacular set in the village of Ping Kuei. After learning about the Seven Golden Vampires of the village, Van Hesling, his son, and three guides set out to free the village from the curse of Count Dracula.
VHS: S34421. $14.98.
Roy Ward Baker, Great Britain, 1974, 164 mins.

Lisa and the Devil

An innocent woman (Elke Sommer) is drawn to a mysterious mansion where the evil inhabitants practice sadism and the butler may be the devil himself. Digitally remastered and presented in its uncut, original form. With Telly Savalas.
VHS: S30437. $14.95.
Mario Bava, Italy/Spain, 1973, 116 mins.

The Long Hair of Death

Barbara Steele is back as another vengeful ghost in this Italian horror film. In another life she was the sister of an accused witch who was burned at the stake, while she was hurled to her death by an overreacting Count. Those who deserve punishment are dealt with severely. With Jean Rafferty, Giorgio Ardisson and Halina Zalewska.
VHS: S09132. $29.95.
Anthony Dawson (Antonio Margheriti), Italy, 1964

Lord of Illusions

Scott Bakula stars in this horrifying tale spawned by the dark imagination of Clive Barker. Bakula plays Harry D'Amour, a detective who stumbles upon a mystery. Phillip Swan, a world famous magician, and his wife involve Harry in a murder. If only that were the extent of the troubles. Before long, Harry learns the terrifying truth that illusion is trickery, but magic is real.
VHS: S26859. $19.95.
Laser: Letterboxed. **LD75515. $49.95.**
Clive Barker, USA, 1995, 109 mins.

The Lugosi Files

A salute to the master of menace, who was buried in his Dracula cloak in 1956 but lives on in the hearts of horror film fans forever. Scenes cover his career from 1931-1955 and include the rare trailer narrated by Bela, *Mark of the Vampire*, and his tv appearance on "You Asked for It."
VHS: S04014. $29.95.

The Mad Death

Horror reaches an epidemic scale when family pets become rabid killers. With wild beasts attacking and people going mad, one man is given the powers of a dictator. He unleashes the army on a countryside where the most dangerous animals are humans. Great Britain, 120 mins.
VHS: S14330. $49.95.

The Mad Executioners

A mad scientist decapitates his victims and tries to keep their heads alive. Meanwhile, a group of strange vigilantes are capturing and murdering criminals without benefit of a public trial. Scotland Yard investigates to see if there is any connection. Wolfgang Preiss and Chris Howland star.
VHS: S23197. $29.95.
Edwin Zbonek, Germany, 1963, 94 mins.

The Mad Ghoul

A chemistry professor's research into Ancient Egyptian gases pays off when he uncovers one that induces a strange mental state. The victims of this gas experience a paralysis that robs them of their wills and turns them into zombies.
VHS: S21727. $14.98.
James P. Hogan, USA, 1943, 65 mins.

The Mad Monster

George Zucco steals the show as a crazed doctor who changes a man into a werewolf for the purposes of revenge. No wonder the monster is cranky. With Johnny Downs, Anne Nagel and the ever popular Glenn Strange. Low budget and lots of unintended laughs.
VHS: S04036. $29.95.
Sam Newfield, USA, 1942, 72 mins.

Madame Satan

Please don't confuse this selection with the 1930 Cecil B. De Mille film of the same name. While that film had a wild party on a zeppelin, this video features a seance of sexuality, as a slave of the devil conjures up the Prince of Darkness and it's time for an unholy orgy with whips and chains and naked people. FOR ADULTS ONLY. 60 mins.
VHS: S03660. $29.95.

Madhouse

In this adaptation of Angus Hall's novel *Devilday*, a horror film actor (Vincent Price), after a mental breakdown, makes a TV comeback, then is implicated in a series of homicides. With Peter Cushing.
VHS: S31896. $9.95.
Jim Clark, Great Britain, 1974, 89 mins.

Majin, The Monster of Terror

A top-of-the-line horror-fantasy about a giant stone idol that comes to life and helps a prince and princess regain their thrones from an evil warlord. Fine destruction effects feature villains crushed underfoot and being swallowed up by gaping holes in the earth. An excellent Samurai warrior saga with plenty of action. With Miwa Takada, Yoshiko Aoyama and Jun Fujimaki. Dubbed in English.
VHS: S32579. $24.95.
Kimoyoshi Yasuda/Yoshiyuki Kuroda, Japan, 1966, 84 mins.

The Majorettes

Someone is killing all the beautiful majorettes at a seemingly normal high school. While suspicions abound, no one is able to stop the murderous rampage. Beauty and gore have never been mixed into a more terrifying plot.
VHS: S24752. $9.95.
Bill Hinzman, USA, 1986, 92 mins.

The Man and the Monster

A pianist can't help himself from becoming a hideous monster whenever a certain tune is played. An affliction of this sort is without doubt going to cut down on one's social life and employment possibilities. With Abel Salazar, Marta Roth, and Enrique Rambol.
VHS: S04072. $29.95.
Rafael Baladon, Mexico, 1958, 78 mins.

Man Beast

The abominable snowman has human desires in this fun and bone-chilling '50s monster B-movie. With Rock Madison, Virginia Maynor, George Skaff, Lloyd Nelson and Tom Maruzzi.
VHS: S32103. $9.95.
Jerry Warren, USA, 1955, 65 mins.

The Man They Could Not Hang

Master of horror Boris Karloff stars in this thriller about a brilliant scientist who becomes an insane killer. When Doctor Savaard innocently kills a student to test his life-restoring heart device, he is hanged. When Savaard is restored to life by his assistant, he becomes a maddened killer seeking revenge.
VHS: S13002. $9.95.
Nick Grinde, USA, 1939, 65 mins.

The Man Who Lived Again

Boris Karloff plays a mad scientist with the ability to transfer minds from one living person to another. He sees his work as a short cut to immortality but unfortunately for him, not everyone wants to swap. With Anna Lee and John Loder. B&W.
VHS: S04016. $29.95.
Robert Stevenson, Great Britain, 1936, 66 mins.

Man-Made Monster

Lon Chaney, Jr., stars as a circus man who has built up an immunity to electricity through his circus performances. This unusual ability gives him the power to harm simply with his touch. It's a useful skill, particularly when he is framed by the unscrupulous scientist who originally helped him.
VHS: S21726. $14.98.
George Waggner, USA, 1941, 59 mins.

Maniac Cop

Described as *Frankenstein* meets *The French Connection*, this low-budget thriller has been a surprise worldwide theatrical hit, spawned two sequels and taken its place as one of the most copied films of the last decade. Someone is patrolling the streets of New York City, stalking and murdering. When the citizens discover the murderer is a cop, they panic and start attacking innocent policemen. Featuring an extraordinary cast of veterans, including Tom Atkins, Richard Roundtree and Bruce Campbell, with cameos by Jake "Raging Bull" LaMotta and director Sam Raimi *(Darkman)*. Presented letterboxed, this special edition includes original French key art, theatrical trailers, TV spots, written commentary from the film's director, and scenes created specifically for Japanese television.
VHS: S30938. $14.98.
William Lustig, USA/France, 1988, 85 mins.

Maniac/Special Edition

Joe Spinell stars as one of the cinema's most memorable serial killers. This character was based on several actual murderers and it shows in the intensity of the performance. The maniac stalks women in New York City, but kills others who get in his way. A woman photographer has the misfortune to capture the killer in action. This edition features a digitally mastered widescreen director's cut, along with theatrical trailers and the infamous deleted date scene.
VHS: S29795. $14.98.
William Lustig, USA, 1980, 95 mins.

The Manster

Not a typo but a Japanese/U.S. co-production about a mad scientist named Dr. Suzuki who injects an American reporter with a diabolical serum that causes him to grow another head. That's just for starters, for the evil head grows another body. Unholy population explosion. This is what happens when you keep your mutant wife in a cage. B&W.
VHS: S09136. $29.95.
Kenneth D. Crane/George Breakston, USA/Japan, 1959

Mark of the Devil (Collectors Edition)

Presented for the first time in its original, uncut form, this Spanish shock-horror classic was infamous upon its release for its exploitative advertising campaign and intense violence. Herbert Lom is a long way from *The Pink Panther* in this story of sadism in 18th-century Austria, where Count Cumberland and his evil henchmen torture and kill innocent citizens of the region, accusing them of witchcraft. Starring Herbert Lom, Reggie Nalder and Udo Kier of *Andy Warhol's Frankenstein*. Spanish with English subtitles.
VHS: S05856. $14.98.
Michael Armstrong, Great Britain/Spain, 1969, 90 mins.

Mark of the Devil, Part II

The sequel to the most revolting movie of the decade finds the evil Count Balthasar (slayer of hundreds of innocent women) on a witch hunt and after the lovely Countess Von Solmaneau. With Anton Diffring, Erica Blanc and the incredible Reggie Nalder.
VHS: S04848. $29.95.
Adrian Hoven, USA, 1972, 87 mins.

Mark of the Vampire

Most folks would agree that the mark of the vampire is two small holes over the jugular vein. This Tod Browning sound re-make of *London after Midnight* stars Bela Lugosi as Count Mora and Carroll Borland as his eerie daughter, Luna. With Lionel Atwill, Lionel Barrymore and a special surprise ending. B&W.
VHS: S04706. $59.95.
Tod Browning, USA, 1935, 60 mins.

Martin

Martin is a misunderstood young man who happens to be a vampire...maybe. The sun really just bothers his eyes a little, garlic and crosses have no effect, and he has no fangs. He also doesn't have any vampiric powers, which makes acquiring blood an extremely harrowing experience for all involved. An excellent combination of satire and gore, this cult classic is both frightening and funny, with ironic twists. "*Martin* is a vampire for our age of unbelief" *(Newsweek)*.
VHS: S03445. $14.98.
George A. Romero, USA, 1977, 96 mins.

Mary Shelley's Frankenstein

An all star cast, including Robert De Niro, Kenneth Branagh, Tom Hulce, Helena Bonham Carter, Aidan Quinn and John Cleese, is featured in this lavish but monstrous film. This adaptation follows Shelley's seminal gothic text more closely than past screen incarnations have. VHS letterboxed.
VHS: S24385. $19.95.
Laser: LD74901. $39.95.
Kenneth Branagh, USA, 1994, 123 mins.

The Mask

Elvira, Mistress of the Dark, hosts this camp horror classic also known as *Eyes of Hell*. The discovery of an ancient mask poses unforseen threats to those around it. This 3-D presentation will make the terrors posed by *The Mask* seem uncomfortably close and real.
VHS: S00030. $12.95.
Julian Roffman, USA, 1961, 85 mins.

The Mask of Fu Manchu

An adaptation of the Sax Rohmer novel about a deranged Chinese killer (Boris Karloff) squaring off with an expedition studying the relics of Ghengis Khan's tomb. With Lewis Stone, Karen Morley and a campy, exaggerated Myrna Loy as Fu's mischievous and darkly vicious daughter.
VHS: S17533. $19.98.
Charles J. Brabin, USA, 1932, 72 mins.

Midnight at Madame Tussaud's

A financier finds his life is in danger when he bets he can spend the night in the Chamber of Horrors in a popular London tourist attraction. Filmed on location at Madame Tussaud's. With James Carew as Sir Clive, the intended victim, Lucille Lisle and Kim Peacock.

VHS: S04058. $29.95.

George Pearson, Great Britain, 1936, 63 mins.

Mondo Lugosi—A Vampire's Scrapbook

Bela Lugosi, the world's most beloved blood sucker, is profiled in this collection of rare interviews and highlights from his greatest (and sometimes ghastliest) screen appearances. 60 mins.

VHS: S05189. $19.95.

The Monster and the Girl

Ellen Drew plays a character dragged into a life of prostitution by the mob. The plot gets especially strange when her brother is wrongly executed and his brain is transplanted into the body of a gorilla. Now he seeks revenge for the wrongs done to both him and his sister.

VHS: S21730. $14.98.

Stuart Heisler, USA, 1941, 65 mins.

Monster from Green Hell

Man tampers with the unknown when a rocket carrying test animals crashes in Africa's Green Hell. As the local animal population begins to flee, scientists put the blame on ancient legend, but the real problem may be....giant wasps! With Dallas' Jim Davis, Barbara Turner.

VHS: S04849. $29.95.

Kenneth Crane, USA, 1957, 70 mins.

Monster Maker

Half-crazed scientist puts a fantastic discovery to use: an injection of serum turns men into monsters. With J. Carrol Naish and Ralph Morgan.

VHS: S03336. $19.95.

Sam Newfield, USA, 1944, 66 mins.

Monster of Piedras Blancas

When a seven foot tall sea creature removes the heads of two local fisherman, some of the surviving members of a small community decide there may be some truth to the local legends after all. This low-budget monster movie was chosen as the winner of "The Shock Award" by *Monster Magazine*. Producer Jack Keven designed and wore the killer crustacean suit. Cast includes Lee Tremayne, Forrest Lewis, Don Sullivan, Jeanne Carmen and John Harmon as the superstitious lighthouse keeper. The title translates as the monster from the white rocks.

VHS: S12547. $19.95.

Irvin Berwick, USA, 1959, 72 mins.

Monster of the Island (Island Monster)

Boris Karloff plays Don Gaetano, an elderly philanthropist, who heads a smuggling ring on the island of Ischia. The monster of the title is a human drug importer and a kidnapper of children. Made in Italy, it is said to be Karloff's worst film. For the curious.

VHS: S04024. $29.95.

Robert Montero, Italy, 1953, 87 mins.

Monster on the Campus

When a prehistoric fish is discovered, a rather ordinary academic is accidentally contaminated with its blood, turning him into a rampaging beast. Tranquil Dunsfield University will never be the same. Starring Arthur Franz and Joanna Moore.

VHS: S20893. $14.98.

Jack Arnold, USA, 1958, 76 mins.

The Monster Walks

An eerie movie with some black humor set in a decaying Earlton Manor, a holding pen for the grotesque, a lumbering manservant, a vicious ape, a German maid, a recent corpse and a wheelchair bound relative. The plot concerns the attempted murder of a shrieking heiress. With Rex Lease, Sheldon Lewis and Vera Lewis. On the same program is the Ub Iwerks 1932 horror cartoon, *The Cuckoo Murder Case*.

VHS: S18682. $24.95.

Frank Strayer, USA, 1932, 59 mins.

Monsters Crash the Pajama Party

In this rare film a combination live act was presented at screenings. Teenage girls invade a haunted house only to find a mad scientist at work conducting odd experiments. When the scientist sends for new victims, his henchmen run toward the camera. The screen goes dark. Real people would run through the theater and grab a woman. Magically she would appear on screen. This video also includes a number of trailers for similar live spook shows that once toured movie theaters.

VHS: S23168. $29.95.

David L. Hewitt, USA, 1965

Monsters on the March

Trailers from 14 of your favorite movie monster attractions. Program includes *Isle of the Dead* (Karloff), *The Return of the Fly* (Price), *The Thing (From Another World)*, *The Mummy* (Karloff), *I Walked with a Zombie*, *The Return of Captain Marvel*, and *The Wolfman* (Chaney Jr.). USA, 1932-60, 25 mins.

VHS: S05486. $19.95.

The Mummy

Boris Karloff in a landmark role as the mummy, accidentally revived by British archeologists after being entombed for 3,700 years. A brooding, dream-like masterpiece of the horror genre.

VHS: S00895. $14.98.

Laser: LD70060. $34.95.

Karl Freund, USA, 1932, 72 mins.

The Mummy's Curse

The final effort of a series which chronicles the adventures of the archeologist Kharis and his assistant Ananka. They're in the Louisiana bayou searching for artifacts though they're inadvertently caught up in the death and mayhem of local characters. With Lon Chaney Jr., Peter Coe and Virginia Christine.

VHS: S19014. $14.98.

Leslie Goodwins, USA, 1944, 62 mins.

The Mummy's Ghost

This sequel to *The Mummy's Tomb* is a quickly paced affair about a professor and his protege tracking a woman who's the reincarnation of Princess Ananka. With Lon Chaney Jr., John Carradine, Ramsay Ames and Robert Lowery.

VHS: S19012. $14.98.

Reginald LeBorg, USA, 1944, 60 mins.

The Mummy's Hand

The first in the celebrated *Kharis* series is not a sequel to Karl Freund's *The Mummy*, but an eerie and effective shocker about a group of archaeologists who search for Egyptian Princess Ananka. The cast includes Dick Foran, Wallace Ford, Peggy Moran, Cecil Kellaway and Charles Trowbridge.

VHS: S17276. $14.98.

Christy Cabanne, USA, 1940, 67 mins.

The Mummy's Shroud

A small archeological party discovers the hidden tomb of Kah-to-Bey. When the mystical shroud that covers his body is read aloud, an unstoppable progression of madness results, with deadly consequences. With Andre Morell and John Phillips. Presented in original aspect ratios. Includes original theatrical trailers and TV spots. Letterboxed.

VHS: S34979. $14.98.

John Gilling, Great Britain, 1967, 90 mins.

The Mummy's Tomb

The sequel to *The Mummy's Hand* balances humor and chills. Famed archeologist Kharis (Lon Chaney Jr.) returns stateside to exterminate the surviving members of an expedition force. With Elyse Knox, John Hubbard and Turhan Bey.

VHS: S19018. $14.98.

Harold Young, USA, 1942, 61 mins.

Murder in the Mirror

In this lost episode of the TV series *13 Demon Street*, Lon Chaney, Jr. (in spooky make-up) plays the ghostly host for this suspenseful ghost story about a man who sees a vision of an ages-old murder within a mysterious mirror. Also includes a full reel of vignettes from the rare *Ripley's Believe It or Not*.

VHS: S32574. $24.95.

Curt Siodmak, USA, 1960, 45 mins.

Murder Mansion

A young couple traveling through an eerie landscape are stranded in a castle full of mysterious noises and unexplained phenomena. With Analia Gade, Evelyn Steward and Andres Resino. English dubbed.

VHS: S19350. $19.95.

Francisco Lara Polop, Spain, 1970, 90 mins.

The Murders in the Rue Morgue (1932)

An expressive horror translation of Edgar Allan Poe's short story. Set in Paris, the film stars Bela Lugosi as the brilliant Dr. Mirakle, who prowls the streets to find an experimental companion for his pet gorilla. Famed director John Huston worked on the screenplay. With Sidney Fox, Leon Waycoff, Brandon Hurst and Noble Johnson.

VHS: S17274. $14.98.

Robert Florey, USA, 1932, 75 mins.

The Murders in the Rue Morgue (1971)

Jason Robards and Lilli Palmer star in this film based upon the Edgar Allan Poe masterpiece of terror about a horror theater whose staged murders become all too real.

VHS: S00899. $59.95.

Laser: LD75231. $34.98.

Gordon Hessler, Great Britain, 1971, 87 mins.

The Murders in the Rue Morgue (1986)

George C. Scott, Rebecca De Mornay and Val Kilmer star in this adaptation of Edgar Allan Poe's mystery thriller set in 19th-century Paris. Police are baffled by the murder of a woman and her child, especially since the room where it happened is locked from inside. Dupin (Scott) must solve this riddle before anyone will feel safe again.

VHS: S21706. $14.99.

Laser: LD76393. $39.99.

Jeannot Szwarc, USA, 1986, 92 mins.

Mystery of the Wax Museum

Before there was Vincent Price and *House of Wax*, there was Lionel Atwill, as a semi-crazed sculptor who uses human victims to populate his historical recreations. Fay Wray is a potential and unwilling Marie Antoinette. Filmed in early Technicolor. With Glenda Farrell.

VHS: S04708. $59.95.

Michael Curtiz, USA, 1933, 77 mins.

The Naked Witch

An ancient witch returns to life when a student pulls the stake from her evil heart. She seeks bloody revenge against the local village. Some hilarious shots of her running around naked while someone holds their finger over the camera lens to shield her privates offer priceless cinematic moments.

VHS: S23166. $29.95.

Andy Milligan, USA, 1963, 60 mins.

Needful Things

Based on the novel of the same name by the most famous horror writer of our time, Stephen King, this film is set in a small town that makes a terrible promise. Starring Ed Harris, Max Von Sydow and Bonnie Bedelia.

Laser: LD72426. $39.99.

Fraser C. Heston, USA, 1993, 120 mins.

Night Monster

Bela Lugosi is featured, along with Lionel Atwill and Irene Hervey, in this suspense-laden mystery. Five deaths occur in the large but foreboding home of a man who has lost both legs. Suspicions abound, but the list of possible suspects is especially frustrating as it includes the very man confined to his wheelchair.

VHS: S29524. $14.98.

Ford Beebe, USA, 1942, 73 mins.

Night of Terror

Bela Lugosi stars as a Hindu servant working at the estate of a wealthy family. Soon the grounds are plagued by a strange, murderous lunatic, who sends chills through the inhabitants of this house. Sally Bane and Wallace Ford also star in this macabre thriller with a twisted ending.

VHS: S22884. $19.95.

Ben Stoloff, USA, 1933, 64 mins.

Night of the Living Dead

George A. Romero's brilliant debut film boldly re-imagines horror conventions in this nihilistic thriller about a group of survivors seeking sanctuary in a farmhouse under siege from the walking dead, flesh-eating zombies that patrol the ravaged landscape. With Judith O'Dea, Duane Jones and Karl Hardman.

VHS: S18644. $14.98.

Laser: CLV. LD72009. $34.95.

DVD: DV60269. $19.95.

George A. Romero, USA, 1968, 96 mins.

Night of the Living Dead 25th Anniversary Documentary

George A. Romero, director of *Night of the Living Dead*, is joined by John Landis, Wes Craven, Sam Raimi and other creative filmmakers to discuss the impact of this seminal horror flick.

VHS: S24743. $19.95.

Thomas Brown, USA, 1993, 83 mins.

The Night They Killed Rasputin

An atmospheric retelling of the rise and fall of Rasputin, whose seemingly supernatural powers made the czarina into a hypnotic slave. John Drew Barrymore reprises the role his father played in *Rasputin and the Empress*. A bizarre film. With Edmund Purdon and Gianna Canale. USA, 1962.

VHS: S15369. $29.95.

The Night Visitor

An ingenious tale of Gothic horror and murderous revenge in which a man escapes from an asylum, night after night, to wreak vengeance on his accusers. With Max Von Sydow, Trevor Howard and Liv Ulmann. In English.

VHS: S34215. $19.95.

Laszlo Benedek, USA, 1971, 106 mins.

The Night Walker

William Castle's film about a woman besieged by recurring images and dreams of her dead husband and a handsome, charismatic stranger. With Barbara Stanwyck, Robert Taylor, Lloyd Bochner and Judi Meredith. Screenplay by Robert Bloch.

VHS: S18702. $14.98.

William Castle, USA, 1964, 86 mins.

Nightmare Castle

Barbara Steele plays two sisters tormented by the same husband, the horrible Dr. Arrowsmith. When he finds Barbara #1 fooling around with the gardener he kills them and later marries Barbara #2 to cash in on an inheritance. Grizzly goings on in Italy.

VHS: S04049. $29.95.

Allan Grunewald/Mario Caiano, Italy, 1966, 90 mins.

A Nightmare on Elm Street

Wes Craven's tour-de-fright that spawned a "Freddy" phenomenon. Fierce, fedored, finger-razored Freddy (Robert Englund), the scarred maniac, is out to kill neighborhood teens in their dreams—or is it reality? The kids can fight back—as long as they don't fall asleep. Only a Craven coward would miss this frightfest. With John Saxon, Heather Langenkamp, Ronee Blakely, Amanda Wyss and Johnny Depp.

VHS: S32102. $14.99.

Wes Craven, USA, 1984, 92 mins.

Oasis of the Zombies (La Tumba de los Muertos Vivientos)

A group of European students looking for buried treasure in the Sahara find blood-sucking Nazi zombies instead. With Manuel Gelin and France Jordan. Dubbed in English.

VHS: S34498. $24.95.

Jesus Franco, Spain, 1982, 84 mins.

The Oblong Box

Edgar Allan Poe's classic tale about two brothers and the evil dead; Vincent Price is the British aristocrat tormented by his disfigured brother who's kept in a tower room. With Christopher Lee.

VHS: S04564. $59.99.

Gordon Hessler, Great Britain, 1969, 91 mins.

The Old Dark House

A melodrama with a tongue-in-cheek sense of humor gathers stranded travelers in a mysterious household, where a brutish butler is one of many strange characters. The film stars Boris Karloff, Melvyn Douglas, Charles Laughton, Gloria Stuart, Raymond Massey, and Eva Moore.

VHS: S16180. $24.95.

James Whale, USA, 1932, 71 mins.

The Omen

Gregory Peck and Lee Remick star as a U.S. diplomat and his wife who adopt a child. Soon tragedy strikes near their family, and before long, Peck's character becomes convinced that his son is somehow to blame. This sets off a search for the boy's original family, resulting in more terror and a final, unbelievable secret.

VHS: S29792. $19.98.

Laser: LD76744. $24.98.

Richard Donner, USA, 1976, 111 mins.

Outlaw Drive-In Vol. 1: Horror Comedy Double Feature

Humanoids from Atlantis and *Reanimator* are two over-the-top, grisly films that combine camp humor with terror. In the first, mutated underwater creatures rise to terrorize a small east coast town. It's a graphic opportunity to see seafood gone really bad. Then in *Reanimator* a serum which revives the dead only manages to bring back the worst of human behavior from the great beyond.

VHS: S26467. $14.98.

Ozone

Great effects lift this horror film above the rest. A new drug is accidentally injected into a cop. Suddenly his search for an evil drug lord is transformed into a sinister underworld journey where mutants abound. This drug transforms simple drug users into pawns of a plot for world domination.

VHS: S24590. $29.95.

J.R. Bookwalter, USA, 1994, 83 mins.

Pale Blood

A series of vampire-like murders in Los Angeles attracts the attention of a veteran bloodsucker played by Oscar winner George Chakiris. B-movie action icon Wings Hauser is the cop assigned to investigate in this erotic thriller. With Pamela Ludwig, Diane Frank and Darcy DeMoss as potential blood banks. Highly praised by the Academy of Science Fiction, Fantasy and Horror.

VHS: S15619. $79.95.

Dachin Hsu, USA, 1991, 94 mins.

Pattern for Plunder (Curse of San Michel)

Keenan Wynn, Mai Zetterling and Ronald Howard star in this intriguing British thriller. Some WWII vets decide to find lost Nazi loot. Their search brings them to an ancient castle. Below lies a beach riddled with quicksand where the curse of the tidal wave of San Michel has taken many lives. Mystery and horror are combined in this great B-movie.

VHS: S23193. $24.95.

John Ainsworth, Great Britain, 1962, 73 mins.

The Penalty

A young boy whose legs where amputated by an inept doctor grows up to carry out an elaborate and gruesome vengeance. One of Lon Chaney's most terrifying roles, it was rumored that he suffered permanent spinal damage from the contortions necessary to portray the legless "Blizzard." Silent.

VHS: S25698. $24.95.

Wallace Worsley, USA, 1920, 82 mins.

The People Under the Stairs

A young African-American becomes entangled in an attempt to rob a bizarre couple. His accomplices are murdered and he is left in the house alone. Eventually he finds the house is peopled by the crazed, almost zombified offspring of the couple. As the plot moves along we find that the evil couple are also the ones responsible for the deplorable conditions of his neighborhood.

VHS: S21393. $19.98.

Wes Craven, USA, 1991, 102 mins.

Perversion

A sick millionaire with unusually unhealthy sexual tastes is at the center of this bizarre film. In one instance he bites off a piece of one of his numerous sexual conquests in order to show it to his friends as a trophy. Portuguese with English subtitles.

VHS: S20748. $24.95.

Jose Mojica Marins, Brazil, 1978

Phantasm II: The Ball Is Back

A horror classic like *Phantasm* screams out for a murderous sequel. Once again the psychic teen calls forth the tall mysterious mortician armed with orbs of death. If there was any confusion about the reality of the terrifying world watched over by this tall man it is dissipated in this film forever.

VHS: S21791. $14.98.

Don A. Coscarelli, USA, 1988, 97 mins.

The Phantom Creeps

Evil reigns as the fiendish Dr. Zorka extracts a mysterious substance from a fallen meteor and uses it to create a robot and a mechanical spider. Starring Bela Lugosi.

VHS: S13856. $19.95.

Ford Beebe, USA, 1939, 75 mins.

The Phantom of the Opera (1943)

The burnished color photography of decorated cinematographer Hal Mohr gives a surrealistic glitter to this remake of the classic Gaston Leroux horror tale. Claude Rains is a crazed, masked phantom terrorizing a Paris Opera House, whom he believes has stolen his music. Rains focuses his obsession on a beautiful soprano (Suzanna Foster), which forces a confrontation with Nelson Eddy. With Hume Cronyn.

VHS: S02720. $14.98.

Laser: LD70221. $39.95.

Arthur Lubin, USA, 1943, 93 mins.

The Phantom of the Opera (1962)

A series of mysterious mishaps, culminating in a terrible opening night incident at a London opera house, are not the work of providence. They are deliberate acts of sabotage perpetrated by a madman. A young, new singing star attracts this dangerous, disfigured man, a once brilliant composer betrayed into oblivion. A Hammer Films classic, featuring Herbert Lom, Heather Sears, Thorley Walters and Michael Gough.

VHS: S25568. $14.98.

Terence Fisher, Great Britain, 1962, 85 mins.

The Phantom of the Opera (1989)

Robert Englund, the actor underneath the macabre makeup of Freddy Krueger, is well cast as Erik Destler, a 19th century composer who makes a bad bargain with the Devil. This insures that he spend most of his spare time in a grotto apartment located beneath a big city opera house. For this remake of the Gaston Leroux novel, the locale has been switched from Paris to London. With Jill Schoelen, Alex Hyde-White, and Stephanie Lawrence as the ill-fated diva.

VHS: S11689. $19.98.

Dwight H. Little, USA, 1989, 93 mins.

Phantom of the Rue Morgue

Karl Malden stars as mad Dr. Marais, who trains a gorilla to kill a series of girls and is tracked by police in the classic Poe tale of horror. Look for Merv Griffin as a college student.

VHS: S34610. $14.95.

Roy Del Ruth, USA, 1954, 84 mins.

Pharaoh's Curse

A fanatical Egyptian is out to stop the unearthing of ancient tombs by killing each member of an archeological expedition. As he completes his task he ages until he himself becomes a mummy.

VHS: S08436. $29.95.

Lee Sholem, USA, 1956, 63 mins.

The Plague of the Zombies

Amidst walking corpses, voodoo dolls and empty graves, two inquisitive doctors embark upon an investigation that uncovers a ghastly secret and leads them to the shocking truth. With Andre Morell, Diane Clare and John Carson. Includes original theatrical trailer. Widescreen.

VHS: S31793. $14.98.

Laser: Letterboxed. **LD76342. $39.98.**

John Gilling, Great Britain, 1966, 90 mins.

The Playgirls and the Vampire

One of the last great ones from the Golden Age of Italian Horror, this long-lost, erotic horror classic, completely uncut, is the story of five sexy dancers who take refuge in the Castle of Count Kernassy. "A beautiful blend of old-fashioned booga-booga, complete with a steamin' striptease scene and a bare-breasted vampire babe" (Frank Henenlotter).

VHS: S31216. $24.95.

Piero Regnoli, Italy, 1960, 85 mins.

Poltergeist

When you build a community over a graveyard and don't move the bodies, expect the kind of problems that plague this typically American suburban family. Moving furniture and floating toys lead to alternative dimensions and the lowering of real estate values. With Craig T. Nelson, JoBeth Williams and Heather O'Rourke. Great special effects. Co-written and produced by Steven Spielberg. VHS letterboxed.

VHS: S04502. $19.95.

Laser: CAV, special collector's edition. **LD74490. $39.98.**

DVD: DV60111. $24.98.

Tobe Hooper, USA, 1982, 114 mins.

Poltergeist II

A satire about middle class normalcy and desire as the white bred Freeling family is subjected to strange attacks, mysterious beings, and supernatural forces. The cast includes JoBeth Williams, Craig T. Nelson, the late Heather O'Rourke, Geraldine Fitzgerald and theater director Julian Beck.

Laser: LD70171. $34.98.

Brian Gibson, USA, 1986, 91 mins.

Prince of Darkness

There is something evil in the basement of an abandoned church that fascinates a small group of scientists and grad students and terrifies members of the clergy. With Donald Pleasence, Victor Wong, Lisa Blount, Jameson Parker and Alice Cooper as the leader of a group of street zombies. Chilling and thoughtful.

VHS: S06921. $14.98.

John Carpenter, USA, 1987, 102 mins.

Prom Night

Jamie Lee Curtis and Leslie Nielsen star in one of their earliest roles in this cult horror classic. Curtis is Kim Hammond, the perfect vision of high school popularity, but she has a dark secret in her past. As she is about to be crowned prom queen by her school principal and father (Nielsen), a masked killer stalks the high school halls taking revenge for the dark secret.

VHS: S31641. $14.98.

Paul Lynch, USA, 1980, 91 mins.

Race with the Devil

Thinking they're going to enjoy a fun and peaceful vacation, two couples witness a bloody sacrifice and are then pursued by the coven of witches responsible for it. With Peter Fonda and Loretta Swit.

VHS: S14793. $14.98.

Jack Starrett, USA, 1975, 88 mins.

Rasputin: The Mad Monk

Screen shock and flamboyant costume adventure meld in this tale of the real-life "holy man" whose evil charm held the fate of an entire nation in its grip. With an acclaimed, multi-layered performance by Christopher Lee. Also with Barbara Shelley and Francis Matthews. Includes original theatrical trailer and combo TV spots with *The Reptile*. Widescreen.

VHS: S31794. $14.98.
Laser: Letterboxed. **LD76355. $49.95.**
Don Sharp, Great Britain, 1965, 92 mins.

The Raven

Boris Karloff and Bela Lugosi appear in this horror film based on the works of Edgar Allan Poe, including the title story and *The Pit and the Pendulum*. Lugosi is the doctor with the Poe-obsession, Karloff his innocent victim, about a doctor who blackmails a killer into killing the woman who rejected him.

VHS: S17269. $14.98.
Louis Friedlander, USA, 1935, 62 mins.

Red House

Suspense melodrama about a moody farmer's guilty obsession with an old house in the woods where he murdered his parents. With Edward G. Robinson, Rory Calhoun.

VHS: S04065. $19.95.
Delmer Daves, USA, 1947, 100 mins.

The Reincarnation of Isabel

An ultra-rare example of deluxe sleaze by one of Italy's grand masters of the satanic knee-trembler. Packed full of whippings, impalings, torture, sadistic couplings and a series of mind-blowing, devil-worshipping bunk ups. Italian with English subtitles. VHS letterboxed.

VHS: S35005. $19.98.
Laser: LD77004. $29.99.
DVD: DV60379. $24.99.
Renato Polselli, Italy, 1972, 93 mins.

The Relic

After an anthropologist gets eaten by a mutant monster in Brazil, he winds up wreaking havoc in Chicago's natural history museum. With "evolutionary biologist" Penelope Ann Miller, superstitious homicide cop Tom Sizemore, and Linda Hunt as a publicist for anexhibit on superstitions, trying to hasten the cop's investigation. Special effects by Stan Winston *(Jurassic Park)*.

VHS: S31616. $103.99.
Peter Hyams, USA, 1996, 110 mins.

The Reptile

The terrifying account of a small village's encounter with a horrifying creature, The Reptile. Warned only of its approach by the eerie sound of music, a young couple desperately tries to solve a deadly mystery as the villagers bar their doors in terror. With Noel Willman, Jennifer Daniel and Jacqueline Pearce. Includes original theatrical trailer and combo TV spots with *Rasputin: The Mad Monk*. Widescreen.

VHS: S31795. $14.98.
Laser: Letterboxed. **LD76356. $39.95.**
John Gilling, Great Britain, 1966, 91 mins.

The Return of Chandu

Bela Lugosi stars in this feature version of the serial of the same name which incorporates the first six chapters of this occult thriller about a secret death cult and a mysterious princess they wish to sacrifice. With Maria Alba, Lucien Prival and Dean Benton. B&W.

VHS: S08437. $24.95.
Ray Taylor, USA, 1934, 61 mins.

Return of Dr. Mabuse (The Phantom Meets the Return of Dr. Mabuse)

In this sequel to *The 1000 Eyes of Dr. Mabuse*, Gert Frobe and Lex Barker play detectives on the trail of the maniacal Mabuse, who plots to overrun a giant metropolis with an army of zombies. With Wolfgang Preiss. Dubbed in English.

VHS: S32554. $24.95.
Harald Reinl, Germany/France/Italy, 1961, 89 mins.

The Return of Dracula

In this horror movie the Count (Francis Lederer) assumes the identity of a murdered Czech painter and infiltrates an idyllic small American town, wreaking havoc and discord among the unsuspecting. With Norman Eberhardt, Ray Stricklyn and Jimmie Baird.

VHS: S19137. $14.95.
Paul Landres, USA, 1958, 77 mins.

Return of the Blind Dead

The second of four movies by Ossori featuring the dreaded Templar knights—mummified zombie/vampires who have vowed to return and destroy the ancestors of those who killed them during the Middle Ages. Considered by many to be the most terrifying of the Templar films. Presented in its original uncut form. Dubbed in English.

VHS: S31679. $14.98.
Amando de Ossorio, Portugal, 1975, 90 mins.

Return of the Vampire

Bela Lugosi rises from the crypt in this blood-curdling horror classic. Lugosi is one of a kind as a 200-year-old Hungarian vampire that prowls the English countryside feeding on the jugular of innocent villagers. Roland Varno, Frieda Inescort and Matt Willis also star. 1943.

VHS: S13003. $9.95.
Lew Landers, USA, 1943, 69 mins.

Return to Salem's Lot

Larry Cohen invades Stephen King territory with a terrifying tale of a whole town of vampires in New England. Michael Moriarty is an inquisitive anthropologist aided by director Sam Fuller as a fearless vampire hunter. With Andrew Duggan, June Havoc and Evelyn Keyes.

VHS: S07342. $14.95.
Larry Cohen, USA, 1987, 101 mins.

Revenge of the Creature

This sequel to the horror classic *The Creature from the Black Lagoon* shifts the action from the Amazon to a Florida aquarium theme park as the scientists and citizenry try to fathom the motives and nature of the mysterious gill-man. With John Agar, Lori Nelson, John Bromfield and in a minor role, Clint Eastwood. The movie was originally shown in 3D.

VHS: S19017. $14.98.
Jack Arnold, USA, 1955, 82 mins.

Revenge of the Creature/ The Creature Walks Among Us

Two sequels to the *The Creature from the Black Lagoon* tap into the fears of the outsider. Jack Arnold's 1955 *Revenge of the Creature* finds the mysterious gill-man transferred from the Amazon to a Florida aquarium. In John Sherwood's 1958 sequel, *The Creature Walks among Us*, a group of scientists turn to radical forms of plastic surgery to alter his deformity.

Laser: LD72182. $59.98.

Revolt of the Zombies

Dean Jagger returns dead Cambodian soldiers to a semblance of life and then exploits them for his evil purposes. No wonder they revolt. Stock footage from *White Zombie* featuring Bela Lugosi's eyes is re-used to spice up this tale of voodoo in the Far East. B&W.

VHS: S04059. $29.95.
Victor Halperin, USA, 1936, 65 mins.

Sabaka (The Hindu)

Boris Karloff stars in a tale of an evil cult of fire-worshippers in India. Made on location. His part is small and made to capitalize on a US tv series about an elephant boy. June Foray (the voice of Rocky the Flying Squirrel) is featured as the high priestess of the cult.

VHS: S04025. $29.95.
Frank Ferrin, USA, 1953, 81 mins.

The Sadist

In this phenomenal, low-budget, psycho horror movie, three people encounter disaster on the way to a Dodgers game. They become trapped in an old wrecking yard when their car stalls. A psycho and his girlfriend put these three captives through pure hell.

VHS: S23165. $29.95.
James Landis, USA, 1963, 95 mins.

Salem's Lot: The Movie

TV mini-series based on Stephen King's best-selling novel. Ben Mears, a young novelist (David Soul), returns to Salem's Lot and becomes fascinated with the inheritently evil old Marsden house, located at the top of a hill. The house also attracts suave antiques dealer Straker (James Mason) and his mysterious partner Mr. Barlow (Reggie Nalder), a vampire. With the help of young horror fan Mark (Lance Kerwin), Ben tries to stop Straker and Barlow before they takeover Salem's Lot.

VHS: S34606. $14.95.
Tobe Hooper, USA, 1979, 111 mins.

Samson vs. the Vampire Women

Santo and Lorena Valesquez star in this blood-sucking gore fest. Santo, the masked hero, battles voluptuous vampire women led by Lorena, who employs a number of muscle-bound, caped henchmen. This shlocky classic ends with an hysterical wrestling scene.

VHS: S23163. $29.95.
Alfonso Corona Blake, Mexico, 1961, 89 mins.

The Satanic Rites of Dracula

Christopher Lee made his last appearance as the Count, which Lee described as "a cross between Fu Manchu and Howard Hughes" in this original uncut Hammer film. Dracula returns as the mysterious D.D. Denham, a reclusive billionaire who is never seen in daylight. Professor Van Helsing is called upon to challenge Dracula and save his granddaughter Jessica (a young and *Absolutely Fabulous* Joanna Lumley!). Includes theatrical trailers. Widescreen.

VHS: S34422. $14.98.
Alan Gibson, Great Britain, 1973, 87 mins.

The Scare Game

This double feature begins with a love story gone wrong. A young woman thinks she has found her match but the man she loves may not be all he appears to be. Then a game becomes subject to a demon's caprice for sadistic ritualistic scenes.

VHS: S24762. $29.95.
Eric Stanze, USA, 1994, 120 mins.

Scared Stiff

Not to be confused with Jerry Lewis/Dean Martin comedy remake of *Ghostbreakers*. This is a serious tale of a psychiatrist and a female rock star staying in a haunted Charleston mansion where they are not the only ones to go bump in the night. With Andrew Stevens, Mary Page Keller, Josh Segal and David Ramsey. Called "too explicit for the squeamish" by *Variety*.

VHS: S12546. $19.95.
Laser: CLV. **LD72027. $29.98.**
Richard Friedman, USA, 1986, 85 mins.

Scared to Death

Bela Lugosi plays a mysterious stage magician who wears a Dracula cape and tries to appear ominous most of the time. Filmed in Cinecolor, the plot concerns the plight of Laura, a mental patient in a disturbing sanitarium run by George Zucco. Watch for the green floating masks.

VHS: S04011. $19.98.
Christy Cabanne, USA, 1947, 65 mins.

Schreck

A young horror fan discovers that a murderous Nazi once lived in his home. On the anniversary of the fiend's death they raise his spirit and unleash the ghoul. Now the ghoul is once again free to engage in his deadly rites. 75 mins.

VHS: S24746. $19.95.

Scream

Wes Craven's horror deconstruction, starring Drew Barrymore, Courteney Cox, Neve Campbell, David Arquette, Rose McGowan, Skeet Ulrich and Henry Winkler as a high school principal, toys with both the intellectual and the visceral. A scary movie fan has gone too far, and now a group of friends must follow the universal "rules" of fright movies: don't answer the phone, don't go off alone—and don't scream.

VHS: S31526. $19.95.
Laser: LD76257. $39.99.
Wes Craven, USA, 1997, 111 mins.

Scream 2

One of those rare sequels that is as good as the original. It's been two years since the tragic events at Woodsboro and newswoman Gale Weathers (Courteney Cox), who covered the story of the murders, has written a bestseller about the event which has been turned into the film, *Stab* starring Tori Spelling. As the film's premiere date approaches, the cycle of death begins anew, with a mad slasher in a Halloween ghost mask who stalks the college freshmen who survived the original slashings. With Neve Campbell, David Arquette, Liev Schrieber, and Laurie Metcalf.

VHS: S34355. $106.99.
Laser: DTS. **LD76959. $49.99.**
Wes Craven, USA, 1997, 122 mins.

Scream and Scream Again

Vincent Price stars as a mad scientist driven to create his own race of beings. Only he needs to do a number of experiments on human samples first. This is one of his later horror films and also features Christopher Lee and Peter Cushing.

VHS: S20934. $14.98.
Laser: LD76086. $39.99.
Gordon Hessler, Great Britain, 1970, 95 mins.

Scream of Fear

Penny Appleby (Susan Strasberg) pays a visit to her father's Riviera resort, although she is told that her father is away on business. Continually terrified by sudden appearances of his ghost, the suspense builds until she finds herself at the edge of a cliff. A terrific chiller.

VHS: S09395. $69.95.
Seth Holt, USA, 1961, 81 mins.

Scream of the Demon Lover
A hideously disfigured killer, who seems to get uglier every time the full moon rises, terrorizes a small, remote village. Meanwhile, a beautiful woman and a 19th-century baron work on an experiment to show that matter can never be destroyed. A fine, uncut European horror opus. With Jeffrey Chase, Jennifer Harvey and Agostino Belli. Dubbed in English.
VHS: S32581. $24.95.
J.L. Merino, Spain/Italy, 1971, 98 mins.

Scream of the Wolf
In this made-for-TV movie starring Clint Walker and Peter Graves, a big-game hunter comes out of retirement to track down a killer wolf which he fears can take human form. With JoAnn Pflug.
VHS: S32951. $19.95.
Dan Curtis, USA, 1974

The Screaming Skull
Alex Nicol stars in and directed this shocking supernatural thriller about a man trying to make his wife crazy. The ad for this film promised movie patrons a free burial if they died of fright while watching this picture. I don't know if the offer is still valid, so be careful. With Peggy Webber and John Hudson.
VHS: S04071. $29.95.
Alex Nichol, USA, 1958, 68 mins.

Season of the Witch
When ordinary wife and mother Joan Mitchell (Jan White) and her friends hear of a woman in their community, Marion Hamilton (Virginia Greenwald), who is practicing witchcraft, they are fascinated. Intrigued by this experience and frustrated with her current situation, Joan seeks solace in witchcraft and begins to feel the power of black magic. Before long, Joan begins to have increasingly ominous nightmares that begin to change her life.
VHS: S34332. $14.98.
George A. Romero, USA, 1972, 89 mins.

Serpent and the Rainbow
Who do that voodoo that you do so well? Horror filmmaker Wes Craven gets serious with a dramatic tale of an anthropologist's visit to Haiti. Based on the true-life adventures of Wade Davis. With Bill Pullman, Cathy Tyson, Zakes Mokae and Paul Winfield. Expect the unexpected.
VHS: S12252. $19.95.
Laser: LD70076. $34.95.
DVD: DV60350. $24.99.
Wes Craven, USA, 1988, 98 mins.

Shake Hands with the Devil
Set against the brutal Irish 1921 rebellion, James Cagney stars as a Dublin surgeon who commands an IRA faction and believes violence is the only means to achieve political and social liberation from English tyranny. With Glynis Johns, Don Murray, Dana Wyner and Michael Redgrave.
VHS: S19042. $19.98.
Michael Anderson, USA, 1959, 110 mins.

Shatter Dead
In this violent film, religious fervor is seen in all its unmitigated horror. A young woman simply tries to go home but undead creatures confront her at every turn. These zombies are transfixed by a higher power with blood and gore on its mind. This is one low budget film sure to shock the religious but please all gore fans.
VHS: S24761. $29.95.
Scooter McCrae, USA, 1994, 84 mins.

She Beast (Revenge of the Blood Beast)
Barbara Steele plays a modern English tourist possessed by the spirit of a vengeful witch burned to death in Transylvania two hundred years earlier. Against her will she terrorizes a Carpathian mountain village and decreases its population. Talk about a bad vacation. May be first horror movie with Iron Curtain in-jokes.
VHS: S04051. $29.95.
Michael Reeves, Italy/Yugoslavia, 1966, 74 mins.

Shock Cinema Volumes 1-4
Brinke Stevens hosts this introduction to the masters of schlock horror. He interviews directors, writers, FX artists, actors and actresses. It's a behind-the-scenes look at how to make it in the gory world of Hollywood. 60 mins. each.
Shock Cinema Volume 1. Interviews with Charles Band, Fred Olen, Jeff Burr, Scott Spiegel and more.
VHS: S24755. $9.95.
Shock Cinema Volume 2. Forrest J. Ackerman, Robert Quarry, Steve Neill, Deanna Lund, Melissa Moore and others are interviewed in this volume.
VHS: S24756. $9.95.
Shock Cinema Volume 3. This is the volume filled with bloopers, babes and blood.
VHS: S24757. $9.95.

Sin You Sinners
June Colbourne, Dian Lloyd and Derek Murcott star in this supernatural tale. A has-been exotic dancer gets her hands on an ancient amulet that enables her to project youthfulness. Through its magic she's able to control those around her as though they were zombies. Watch for the abrupt and twisted ending. 1964.
VHS: S23167. $29.95.

The Sinful Nuns of Saint Valentine
An Italian nunsploitation epic in which a demented Mother Superior and rabid collection of mentally disturbed and sex-crazed sisters lose their habits and morals with equal gusto. Inspired in part by *The Devils of Loudun*, this is a classic of the genre. Italian with English subtitles. 93 mins.
VHS: S35003. $19.98.
Laser: LD77002. $29.99.
DVD: DV60377. $24.99.

The Skull
Taken from a story by Robert Bloch: Peter Cushing comes into possession of the Marquis de Sade's coveted skull, and its mysterious powers.
VHS: S16898. $19.95.
Freddie Francis, Great Britain, 1965, 83 mins.

Slime People
From the sewers of Los Angeles come subterranean, lizard-like humanoids who take over the town by releasing a deadly wall of fog. Not a documentary but a low-budget and very small-cast monster movie. Can a brave scientist and his two shapely daughters save the human race before it is too late? With Les Tremayne, Susan Hart, Tom Laughlin, and Robert Hutton, who also directed.
VHS: S10968. $19.95.
Robert Hutton, USA, 1962, 76 mins.

The Snake People (Isle of the Snake People)
Boris Karloff made four Mexican horror movies back to back before he died in 1969. This is one of the two to have been released. It concerns a snake cult which turns its victims into zombies. Karloff is the secret leader of the cult. His scenes were all shot in L.A.
VHS: S04027. $29.95.
Jack Hill/Juan Ibanez, USA/Mexico, 1971, 90 mins.

The Snow Creature
Paula Langston and Leslie Denison are cast in this outrageous horror film about an escaped Yeti. Brought back by a botanist, the creature is held by customs officers. Of course this makes the monster furious and he rampages through Los Angeles. A camp classic.
VHS: S24018. $19.95.
W. Lee Wilder, USA, 1954, 71 mins.

Son of Dracula
Lon Chaney Jr. stars as Count Alucard, a mysterious visitor to the swamp lands of Louisiana. The Count is not the son of Dracula but the authentic bloodsucker himself. Lots of atmosphere in this mis-titled and neglected horror film. With Eveleyn Ankers, Louise Allbritton and Robert Paige.
VHS: S06868. $14.98.
Robert Siodmak, USA, 1943, 80 mins.

Son of Frankenstein
The great cast of Basil Rathbone, Boris Karloff and Bela Lugosi star as the son of Dr. Frankenstein returns to the castle some 25 years after the infamous monster's "death." There he meets Ygor (Bela Lugosi), a mad shepherd hiding the lifeless body of the creature, and the son of Frankenstein can't resist re-awakening the creature.
VHS: S10113. $14.98.
Laser: LD70081. $34.95.
Rowland V. Lee, USA, 1939, 99 mins.

Son of Kong
Sequel to the classic. Adventurer Carl Denham returns to Skull Island and finds Kong's offspring: a 30-foot albino gorilla. Once again, full of first-rate special effects.
VHS: S10665. $19.98.
Ernest B. Schoedsack, USA, 1933, 69 mins.

Son of Monsters on the March
More monster movie trailers from ten cult favorites. Titles include *The Vampire Killers* (Sharon Tate), *Dark Star* (John Carpenter), *One Million Years B.C.* (Raquel Welch), *This Island Earth*, *The Damned*, *I Was a Teenage Frankenstein* and *The Rocky Horror Picture Show*. USA/Great Britain/Italy/West Germany, 1955-77, 27 mins.
VHS: S05487. $19.95.

Spider Baby
Lon Chaney Jr. heads a household of inbred cannibals in this bizarre and many-titled horror cheapie. As if that weren't enough, he also sings the theme song. Included in the cast of wackos are Sid Haig, Carol Ohmart and the ever-popular Mantan Moreland. B&W. It's weird.
VHS: S04035. $14.98.
Laser: LD76967. $24.99.
Jack Hill, USA, 1964, 86 mins.

The Stepford Wives
For two decades this film's title and what it implies have been ingrained into our vocabulary and consciousness. Something strange is happening in the town of Stepford, where the men spend their nights doing something secret and every woman acts like every man's dream of the "perfect" wife—a dream that is really a nightmare. With Katherine Ross, Paula Prentiss, Tina Louise, Dee Wallace, Patrick O'Neal and seven-year-old Mary Stuart Masterson, making her film debut. "I can promise you an eerie, spine-tingling, good shiver down the spine with the *Stepford Wives*" (Rex Reed, *The New York Daily News*).
VHS: S31190. $14.98.
Laser: LD76197. $39.98.
Bryan Forbes, USA, 1974, 115 mins.

Stephen King's It
Made-for-TV movie based on Stephen King's best-selling novel about a supernatural fatal disease known as "It" that plagues the town of Derry, Maine every 30 years, killing children as they fall victim to its manipulative clown form, Pennywise. A series of murders prompts Mike Hanlon (Tim Reid), who met It as a child, to suspect that It's back. Stars Harry Anderson, Dennis Christopher, Richard Masur, Annette O'Toole, Richard Thomas, and Tim Curry.
VHS: S34605. $14.95.
Tommy Lee Wallace, USA, 1990, 193 mins.

Strait-Jacket
This later, terror-filled Joan Crawford film was written by Robert Bloch, who also penned *Psycho*. Crawford is not to be missed as the insane woman with an axe. After doing time for attacking her husband and his lover, she is finally set free to terrorize once again. Also features George Kennedy and Lee Majors in his screen debut. Includes original trailer.
Laser: LD74975. $34.95.
William Castle, USA, 1964, 93 mins.

Strange World of Coffin Joe
Three atmospheric episodes of horror shape this chilling triptych: a perverse dollmaker whose creators take on human form, the allure and dread of necrophilia, and Coffin Joe (Mojica) disguised as a doctor who tortures two unsuspecting travelers who doubt his power. Portuguese with English subtitles.
VHS: S18983. $24.95.
Jose Mojica Marins, Brazil, 1968

A Study in Terror
Jack the Ripper is terrorizing London and there is only one man who can stop him from carving up more English prostitutes. Elementary, dear viewer, it's Sherlock Holmes. John Neville is Holmes and Donald Houston is Watson and the game is soon afoot. A tidy thriller.
VHS: S04384. $69.95.
James Hill, Great Britain, 1965, 94 mins.

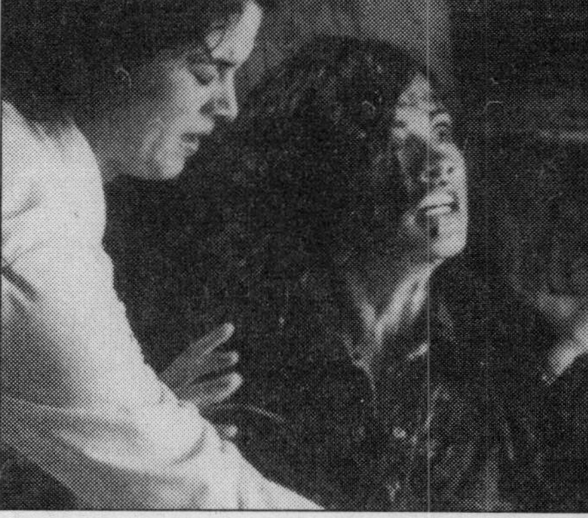

Suspiria
Considered by many to be one of the most terrifying and stylized horror films of recent years, *Suspiria* stars Jessica Harper as Susy Banyon, an American student who has enrolled in a German dance academy. On the very night she arrives, two of the students are brutally murdered. It soon becomes apparent that this is only the beginning of a terrifying nightmare. With Joan Bennett. "The most eagerly awaited horror film of the decade…the most stylish and simply one of the best horror films ever made" (*Fangoria*).
VHS: S10717. $19.98.
Dario Argento, Italy, 1984, 97 mins.

Tales from the Darkside: The Movie

Four ghoulish tales of horror. Watch it if you dare and witness the cat from Hell, the return of the mummy, an artist with a secret terror and a housewife who supplements her food dollar by planning dinner parties around missing children. With Deborah Harry, Christian Slater, David Johansen, William Hickey and Rae Dawn Chong. Based on the works of Stephen King and Arthur Conan Doyle among others.

VHS: S12855. $19.95.
Laser: LD75269. $34.98.
John Harrison, USA, 1990, 93 mins.

Tales of Frankenstein

The classic story, featuring a sharp performance from Anton Diffring. On the same program is Alfred Hitchcock's diabolically witty and entertaining *The Sorcerer's Apprentice*, featuring Diana Dors and Brandon de Wilde.

VHS: S18957. $19.95.

Taste the Blood of Dracula

Christopher Lee is back as Dracula when the Count is reactivated through his last remains.

VHS: S34603. $14.95.
Peter Sasdy, Great Britain, 1969, 91 mins.

Teenage Zombies

Cult favorite Katherine Victor plays a mysterious woman doctor working on a nerve gas that turns anyone into a mindless slave. When she is interrupted by a group of waterskiing teenagers, they prove to be almost as good a subject as her pet gorilla. With Don Sullivan, Bri Murphy and Mitzi Albertson. B&W.

VHS: S05484. $29.95.
Jerry Warren, USA, 1957, 71 mins.

The Tell-Tale Heart (1963)

Edgar Allan Poe's classic story elaborated into a story of a jealous love murder. With Laurence Payne, Adrienne Cori, Dermot Walsh.

VHS: S05053. $24.95.
Ernest Morris, Great Britain, 1963, 81 mins.

The Tell-Tale Heart (1973)

This classic, based on the famous short story by Edgar Allan Poe, is hauntingly filmed in stark black and white to accentuate the good versus evil theme. The viewer cannot help but be captured this carefully woven web of murder, investigation, and the dreadful reality of betrayal from within. Starring Sam Jaffe.

VHS: S14260. $24.95.
Steve Carver, USA, 1973, 26 mins.

Terror Creatures from the Grave (Cemetery of the Living Dead)

Barbara Steele plays a treacherous wife who will feel the wrath of her murdered husband from beyond the grave. In a small village in Central Europe circa 1900, plague ridden corpses from the twelfth century return to do the bidding of a ghost. English dubbed.

VHS: S04050. $29.95.
Ralph Zucker/Massimo Pupillo, Italy, 1965, 85 mins.

Terror in the Haunted House

Classic horror noir about a man returning with his young bride to the house of her nightmare. Filmed in psychorama—a visual process so devastating that it was banned by the Federal Government 25 years ago.

VHS: S05195. $19.95.
Harold Daniels, USA, 1958, 90 mins.

The Texas Chainsaw Massacre

Tobe Hooper's restored cult film is a frightening piece of Americana. This strange subversion of the slasher movie concerns five friends traveling through a flat, nondescript Texas wasteland who encounter a bizarre family and are forced to struggle for their lives. With Marilyn Burns, Allen Danzinger, Paul A. Partain and William Vail.

VHS: S19463. $19.98.
Laser: LD71919. $29.98.
Tobe Hooper, USA, 1974, 81 mins.

The Texas Chainsaw Massacre: A Family Portrait

A curious documentary on the making of Tobe Hooper's 1974 cult classic about five hippies caught in a brutal chase and stalking game with a deranged killer loosely inspired by Ed Gein. The documentary combines interviews with the film's stars and provides previously unseen production photos. 70 mins.

VHS: S19743. $29.95.

Theater of Blood

Vincent Price plays Edward Lionheart, a demented Shakespearean actor who adds murder to his repertoire when he takes gruesome revenge on the eight critics who slighted him. With Diana Rigg, Ian Hendry, Jack Hawkins, Robert Morley and Milo O'Shea.

VHS: S01559. $14.95.
Laser: Letterboxed. **LD76365. $39.99.**
Douglas Bell, Great Britain, 1973, 105 mins.

This Night I Will Possess Your Corpse

Coffin Joe seeks the perfect woman so that she might bear him a perfect child. Along the way he tortures innumerable innocent women by crushing heads and even employing 50 real tarantulas to terrorize his victims. Finally he is dragged off to hell for a taste of his own medicine. Portuguese with English subtitles.

VHS: S20751. $24.95.

Thriller

Boris Karloff hosts this collection of the best episodes from the classic 1960's television series, *Thriller*. Some of these creepy stories even include Karloff as an actor. Grim tales like these have an unnatural life all their own, which keeps this series entertaining and frightening.

Masquerade. Tom Poston and Elizabeth Montgomery are a newly wed couple who accept the hospitality of a fiendish family. But the honeymooners prove more than a match for their hapless hosts. Co-stars John Carradine. 50 mins.

VHS: S21491. $12.98.

The Grim Reaper. William Shatner is a greedy young man who discovers the truth behind the legend of the Grim Reaper. This fiend exacts a terrible revenge on the murderous young man. 50 mins.

VHS: S21493. $12.98.

The Prediction. Boris Karloff hosts and stars in this episode of *Thriller*. Karloff is a mentalist who can predict the deaths of people around him. Those who ignore his predictions must face the dire consequences. 50 mins.

VHS: S21494. $12.98.

The Premature Burial. In this episode a wealthy old man is accidentally buried alive. Karloff is the friend that saves him from this grisly fate. When the old man marries again, his new young wife plans to put him back just where Karloff found him. 51 mins.

VHS: S21495. $12.98.

The Terror in Teakwood. In this episode a wife faces a mortal terror when her musician husband desecrates the grave of his arch rival. Revenge and rivalry know no bounds between life and death. 49 mins.

VHS: S21492. $12.98.

The Tingler

Finally available on laser disc, the cult classic thriller stars Vincent Price as a mad and maddening scientist. Gimmicky director William Castle had theater seats wired with low-voltage electric charges to shock audiences as the "tingler" appeared on screen. Originally presented in PERCEPTO and highly recommended by John Waters, the king of bad taste. Wire your couch!

VHS: S27552. $14.95.
Laser: LD74846. $34.95.
William Castle, USA, 1959, 82 mins.

Tombs of the Blind Dead

Spanish auteur Ossorio made his name in the '70s Spanish horror genre with this tale of horrific and malefic reanimated mummified corpses of 13th-century Templar knights who seek victims through sound alone and drink human blood in order to sustain their own damned existence. The superb, highly influential score by Anton Garcia Abril helps underline the stunning visuals. Despite the trite storylines and hammy acting, "the Templars make Ossorio's grisly, heart-string quartet more than worth the effort, galloping to the rescue of the viewer's sanity like a spectral cavalry charge" (Nigel J. Burrell, March 1995). Digitally remastered collector's edition presented in its original uncut form. Spanish with English subtitles.

VHS: S31002. $14.98.
Amando de Ossorio, Spain, 1972, 102 mins.

Torture Zone

Boris Karloff plays Dr. Mantell, a madman who discovers a lifeform that must be fed human blood to stay alive. Dr. Mantell traps beautiful women, and their blood becomes the life form's nourishment. Who will put an end to The Torture Zone? Also known as *The Fear Chamber (La Camara del Terror)*.

VHS: S09261. $19.98.
Juan Ibanez, USA/Mexico, 1968, 90 mins.

Tower of Evil

What is the ancient secret of the deserted lighthouse on Snape Island? Who is the crazed woman the authorities discover living there? And who is behind the series of brutal psychosexual murders that suddenly start to plague the town?

VHS: S09259. $59.95.
James O'Connolly, USA, 1972, 90 mins.

Tower of Terror

A half-mad lighthouse keeper (Wilfrid Lawson) keeps an eye on the water off the coast of Germany during World War II. Complications arise when a British spy (Michael Rennie) and a female escapee from a concentration camp (Movita) drop by. Much of this movie is said to take place in the dark.

VHS: S04062. $29.95.
Lawrence Huntington, Great Britain, 1941, 80 mins.

Tower of the Screaming Virgins

The notorious Countess Marguerite stages orgies in her castle and then brutally murders her lovers in this lavish European horror tale based on Alexandre Dumas' novel. Featuring equal doses of blood and nudity. Dubbed in English.

VHS: S01652. $24.95.
Frantz Antel, Germany/France/Italy, 1968, 89 mins.

Trail of Blood

A dramatization based on the notorious Green River serial murder case, which, despite over 40 female victims, remains unsolved. *Trail of Blood* features some of the most colorful and offbeat characters imaginable, with such personalities as Warhol superstar Taylor Mead, art terrorist and serial killer aficionado Joe Coleman, author William Kotzwinkle *(E.T.)* and philosophical performance guru Copernicus. The film also introduces the master of pop Yiddish humor, Arthur of New York, and actress/model Madonna Chavez (the niece of the late labor leader Cesar Chavez) Directed by Russian filmmaker/painter Ari Roussimof.

VHS: S31135. $49.95.
Ari Roussimof, USA/Mexico, 1996, 105 mins.

Treasure of Fear (aka Scared Stiff)

In this madcap murder mystery, Jack Haley plays a newspaper reporter who can never get a story straight. Good fare for fans of *The Tin Man*.

VHS: S13861. $19.95.
Frank McDonald, USA, 1945, 66 mins.

The True Story of Frankenstein

Kenneth Branagh, Mel Brooks, Robert De Niro, Gene Wilder, Peter Bogdanovich, Helena Bonham Carter, John Cleese, Roger Corman, Aidan Quinn, Margaret Atwood and more share insights about their work on various versions of Mary Shelley's gothic classic. Roger Moore hosts this documentary and Eli Wallach narrates. Includes clips of all the best Frankenstein films. 100 mins.

VHS: S25098. $19.95.

Twice Told Tales

Vincent Price heads a fine cast in this trilogy of horrific tales from the pen of Nathaniel Hawthorne. Segments include "Rappacini's Daughter", "Dr. Heidegger's Experiment" and the ever-popular "The House of the Seven Gables", none of which were named Clark.

VHS: S04709. $14.95.
Sidney Salkow, USA, 1963, 119 mins.

The Unearthly

The *Citizen Kane* of mad scientist epics, featuring John Carradine, Alison *(Attack of the 50 Foot Woman)* Hayes and Tor Johnson. A mad scientist tries to do right but ends up with a lab full of mutant beings. When his two pending experiments fall in love, Dr. Carradine has trouble.

VHS: S05182. $19.95.
Brooke L. Peters, USA, 1957, 76 mins.

The Uninvited

Lewis Allen's elegant ghost tale about a music critic and his sister attempting to solve the questions of unnatural occurrences and supernatural disturbances at a beautiful old house they've just purchased. Gail Russell stars as a beautiful young woman haunted by the past. With Ray Milland, Ruth Hussey, Donald Crisp and Cornelia Otis Skinner.

VHS: S17017. $14.98.
Lewis Allen, USA, 1944, 99 mins.

Unnatural

Erich Von Stroheim, Hildegard Knef and Karl Boehm star in this beautifully shot, Gothic fantasy. Mixing the genes of a murderer and a prostitute, a scientist creates a femme fatale monster. Neff is beautiful, seductive and souless because she has no real parents, only genetic material donors.

VHS: S23153. $29.95.
Arthur Maria Rabenalt, USA, 1952, 90 mins.

The Val Lewton Collection

Lewton produced nine classic horror films in the 40's. All of them are collected on this compilation disc, including *The Ghost Ship, Cat People, I Walked with a Zombie, The Leopard Man, The Seventh Victim, The Curse of the Cat People, Isle of the Dead, Bedlam* and *The Body Snatcher*. 1942-1946, 639 mins.

Laser: LD75000. $179.99.

The Vampire

The granddaddy of Mexican vampire films. German Robles is Count Lavud and producer Abel Salazar is the hero, who gets top billing. With Ariadne Welter and Carmen Montejo as possible blood donors. Salazar and Robles were featured in a sequel, *The Vampire's Coffin*. B&W.

VHS: S04069. $29.95.
Fernando Mendez, Mexico, 1957, 95 mins.

The Vampire Bat
Lionel Atwill stars as a doctor with a need to murder in order to find a blood substitute. Needless to say he doesn't find many volunteers for his radical approach to health care. With Fay Wray, Dwight Frye and Melvyn Douglas. B&W.
VHS: S04031. $19.95.
Frank Strayer, USA, 1933, 63 mins.

Vampire over London
Bela Lugosi plays a mad scientist working on a robot that will aid him in his conquering the world. He also sleeps in a coffin and has a desire for human blood. Mother Riley (Arthur Lucan in drag) is hired to tidy up the scientist's living quarters and soon finds the secret lab, with comic results. Lots of slapstick.
VHS: S04012. $29.95.
John Gilling, Great Britain, 1952, 72 mins.

Vampire People
Also known as *The Blood Drinkers*, this gothic horror work with a B-movie delirium concerns a mad nobleman and his vampire disciples, who terrorize a small town, setting up a mythic showdown with the town's frightened citizens. With Ronald Remy and Ed Fernandez.
VHS: S18326. $29.95.
Gerardo De Leon, Philippines, 1966, 79 mins.

Voodoo Woman
A horror thriller about a deranged scientist who transforms a beautiful, unsuspecting woman into a monster. With Maria English, Tom Conway, Michael Connors and Lance Fuller.
VHS: S17521. $9.95.
Edward L. Cahn, USA, 1957, 77 mins.

The War of the Colossal Beast
The sequel to *The Amazing Colossal Man* finds the anti-hero attempting to deal with his deteriorating face, and his siege of Los Angeles. With Sally Fraser, Roger Pace and Dean Parkin.
VHS: S17904. $9.95.
Bert I. Gordon, USA, 1958, 68 mins.

Werewolf of London
The first recorded film about werewolves concerns a young botanist's efforts to locate a Tibetan flower who's inadvertently transformed into a diabolical killer who's terrorizing London. With Henry Hull, Warner Oland, Valerie Hobson, and Lester Matthews.
VHS: S17277. $14.98.
Stuart Walker, USA, 1935, 75 mins.

Werewolf vs. the Vampire Woman
When the moon is full different monsters compete for victims in the dead of night. It's all out competition and every monster for him/herself in this deadly race for fresh blood and gore between the blood-sucking women of the night and the demonically inspired werewolf.
VHS: S21558. $24.95.
Leon Klimovsky, Spain, 1970, 82 mins.

Wes Craven's New Nightmare
Robert Englund and Heather Langenkamp reprise their role from the original *Nightmare on Elm Street*. This time, however, they're featured in a plot as the Hollywood insiders who cannot get away from the fame their gory blockbuster spun around them. Something was set in motion by the *Nightmare* movies and it is larger and more deadly than any one movie.
VHS: S24061. $19.98.
Laser: Widescreen. **LD74941. $39.99.**
Wes Craven, USA, 1994, 111 mins.

What Ever Happened to Baby Jane?
An unforgettable performance by Bette Davis as the former child star who torments her bed-ridden sister (Joan Crawford) in one of the great Hollywood horror films.
VHS: S04410. $19.98.
Laser: LD70703. $39.98.
DVD: DV60064. $24.98.
Robert Aldrich, USA, 1962, 132 mins.

What Ever Happened to...
Vanessa and Lynn Redgrave reprise the roles of Blanche and Jane Hudson, characters immortalized by Bette Davis and Joan Crawford in *Whatever Happened to Baby Jane?*. It's the story of two former child stars whose careers were ended by the combination of age and a terrible accident. Now, facing the double hardships of old age and mental illness, sibling rivalry unleashes dark, unforseen terrors.
VHS: S26231. $59.95.
Hank Hines, USA, 1993, 94 mins.

What!
Mario Bava directed this haunting tale. Christopher Lee stars as a sadistic nobleman who whips his brother's wife. Lee turns up dead, but his ghost returns to haunt the castle in this top-notch Italian thriller. This is the uncut, R-rated, theatrically released version.
VHS: S23321. $24.95.
Mario Bava, Italy/France, 1963, 90 mins.

White Zombie
Bela Lugosi followed up his great success in *Dracula* with this disquieting, poetic horror film about Haiti's cult of the "walking dead." Lugosi plays a magician and zombie-master who raises the dead in this film of haunting psycho-sexual imagery.
VHS: S01454. $19.98.
Laser: Collector's Edition. **LD75942. $39.95.**
Victor Halperin, USA, 1932, 73 mins.

The Wicker Man
A British police officer goes to a small island off Scotland to find a missing girl, only to discover that the islanders practice a Celtic religion which worships the phallic symbol, and practices human sacrifice. This film quickly became a cult film, and is considered one of the most intelligent horror films ever made.
VHS: S01457. $19.98.
Robin Hardy, Great Britain, 1973, 102 mins.

Winterbeast
A Native American burial ground lies perilously near a winter resort. Before long there is a strange creature terrorizing this settlement. A park ranger and his bumbling sidekick must discover the secret of the Winterbeast.
VHS: S24751. $9.95.
Christopher Thies, USA, 1992, 80 mins.

The Witch's Mirror
A man disfigures his wife's face and then has the bright idea to use the skin from (hopefully) recently dead people to make amends. This Mexican film sounds suspiciously like Franju's *Eyes without a Face* which opened a year earlier. With Rosita Arenas and Armando Calvo.
VHS: S04075. $29.95.
Chano Urueto, Mexico, 1960, 75 mins.

The Witches (a.k.a. The Devil's Own)
Joan Fontaine stars as school teacher Gwen Mayfield in this suspenseful tale of witchcraft set in a quiet English countryside. Although things appear peaceful, she soon uncovers a series ofdisasters that lead her to the horrible truth. Presented in original aspect ratios. Includes original theatrical trailers and TV spots. Letterboxed.
VHS: S34978. $14.98.
Cyril Frankel, Great Britain, 1966, 91 mins.

The Witching
Two 17-year-old guys think they are forced into another boring Friday night watching grandma. But the house and the family harbor a secret past that places these teenagers in a battle with evil witches from another dimension.
VHS: S24748. $19.95.
Eric Black, USA, 1994, 70 mins.

Wolf
Jack Nicholson and Michelle Pfeiffer are featured in this classy werewolf thriller. While driving, an editor accidentally hits a wolf. As he tries to help the dying animal it bites him, triggering a transformation that ups his aggressiveness, particularly when the moon is full. Before long his assertiveness turns deadly.
VHS: S23221. $19.95.
Laser: LD74664. $39.95.
DVD: DV60136. $24.95.
Mike Nichols, USA, 1994, 125 mins.

Wolf Man
One of the great horror films, with a terrific cast: Bela Lugosi, Claude Rains, Ralph Bellamy, and Lon Chaney as the man cursed by lycanthropy and Rains his unknowing father.
VHS: S04519. $14.98.
Laser: LD70095. $34.98.
George Waggner, USA, 1941, 71 mins.

Wolfen
Albert Finney, Gregory Hines, Tommy Noonan and Diane Venora are featured in this chilling adaptation of Whitley Striber's terror-filled novel. Good effects and superior suspense make this tale of intelligent werewolves a compelling film. It even has an interesting take on environmental and Native American issues.
VHS: S26335. $19.98.
Michael Wadleigh, USA, 1981, 115 mins.

Wolfman: A Cinematic Scrapbook
A compilation documentary featuring Lon Chaney Jr. and his weird assortment of friends with their garish appetites in *Frankenstein Meets the Wolfman, Werewolf in London*, and *I Was a Teenage Werewolf*. A behind-closed-doors look at the personalities who worked on the films. With a look at Chaney's final screen performance in a 1962 Halloween special.
VHS: S17536. $9.95.

Zoltan: Hound of Dracula
An inventive *Dracula* tale about a Transylvanian servant and his voracious dog who travel to contemporary Los Angeles to locate the count's last living descendent. "The style varies between spoof and rather nasty horror" (Leslie Halliwell). With Jose Ferrer, Reggie Nalder, Michael Pataki and Jan Shutan. The film's alternate title is *Dracula's Dog*.
VHS: S19242. $9.98.
Albert Band, USA, 1977, 88 mins.

Zombie
Tisa Farrow, Ian McCulloch and Tom Conway star in this monstrous adventure film. When a man is missing, and only his boat, laden down with zombies, surfaces, his daughter decides to investigate. Soon she finds herself surrounded by zombies on an otherwise idyllic island. Letterboxed. Dubbed in English.
VHS: S25693. $14.98.
Lucio Fulci, Italy, 1980, 91 mins.

Zombie '90: Extreme Pestilence
A military machine crashes into a forest, unleashing chemicals that propagate a population of undead. Only two doctors know this secret. They are forced into a desperate, gory struggle with these zombies. Directed by Andreas Schnass, dubbed, 80 mins.
VHS: S24750. $29.95.

The Zombie Army
Set in an insane asylum, this horror film brings the terrors of war and the undead together. Two deranged inmates create an army of zombies. Only the elite Lethal Ladies combat troop can stop them from escaping into the outside world.
VHS: S24749. $19.95.
Betty Stapleford, USA, 1991, 82 mins.

Zombie Cop
A routine drug bust takes on a horrific, ghoulish cast when the suspect turns out to be a voodoo priest. Both the cop and the suspect die but return to continue their struggle as members of the undead.
VHS: S24753. $9.95.
J.R. Bookwalter, USA, 1991, 90 mins.

Zombie Island Massacre
The bus breaks down. The driver disappears. Surely everyone should realize something terrible is going to happen. Soon frightened tourists are succumbing to Native charm. In this Caribbean vacation, death makes an unwelcome appearance. Playboy covergirl Rita Jenrette is featured.
VHS: S22677. $14.95.
John Carter, USA, 1984, 85 mins.

Zombie Rampage
A young man sets off to meet his friends at the train station and instead finds himself lost in a world of underworld terror. These inner-city gangs are not just sadistic; they are bloodthirsty zombies.
VHS: S24591. $9.95.
Todd Sheets, USA, 1992, 85 mins.

BLAXPLOITATION FILMS

Adios Amigos
Fred Williamson directs and Richard Pryor stars in this mid-70s family western. Pryor is a con man travelling the west and is joined by a cast that includes James Brown, Thalmus Rasulala and Fred Williamson.
VHS: S21418. $19.95.
Fred Williamson, USA, 1975, 87 mins.

Afros Macks 'n Zodiacs
Rudy Ray Moore *(Dolemite)* hosts this funky compilation of trailers from the best black action films of the '70s, including *Blacula, Monkey Hustle, The Mack, Dr Black and Mr. Hyde, Cleopatra Jones, Foxy Brown, Black Caesar* and many more. Plus a surprise music video with a cast of legends. 120 mins.
VHS: S33259. $24.95.

The Arena
Kidnapped and forced to kill, female gladiators beat the Romans at their own game. Starring Pam Grier. Digitally remastered.
VHS: S34863. $14.98.
Steve Carver, USA, 1973, 83 mins.

The Big Bird Cage (Women's Penitentiary II)
Women so hot with desire they melt the chains that enslave them! Pam Grier and Sid Haig star in this sequel to *The Big Doll House* as thieving mercenaries who engineer a prison break from the outside. Digitally remastered.
VHS: S34864. $14.98.
Jack Hill, USA, 1972, 88 mins.

Black Belt Jones
From the makers of Bruce Lee's breakthrough *Enter the Dragon*, this film combines the energy of blaxploitation films, the anger of social protest movies and baroque flourishes of a gangster melodrama. Karate virtuoso Jim Kelly must prevail against the strong-arm tactics of the Mafia, which is trying to destroy his Watts-based self-defense school. With Gloria Hendry, Scatman Crothers, Alan Weeks and Nate Esformes.
VHS: S18928. $19.98.
Robert Clouse, USA, 1974, 87 mins.

Black Caesar
The talented B-moviemaker Larry Cohen wrote and directed this aggressive inner-city gangster drama that chronicles the spectacular rise of its ambitious hero (former pro football star Fred Williamson). With Art Lund, Julius W. Harris, Gloria Hendry and D'Urville Martin.
VHS: S18929. $19.98.
Larry Cohen, USA, 1973, 96 mins.

Black Cobra
A lone cop struggles to protect a female photographer from a gang of psychopathic bikers. With Fred Williamson, Jack Palance, Eva Grimaldi and Karl Langdon.
VHS: S35130. $19.95.
Stelvio Massi, Italy/USA, 1987, 85 mins.

Black Enforcers
Ex-Vietnam General Ahmed is engaged by the U.S. government to operate a Black army. The objective is to stop the traffic in drugs, but drug lords have different plans. Ahmed's chief of staff also has plans which call for an all-out drug war. Initially Ahmed resists this plan, but a personal tragedy pushes him much further than he ever expected to go. This nearly forgotten blaxploitation film combines some radical ideas with over-the-top violence.
VHS: S27865. $19.98.
Lee Frost, USA, 1975, 88 mins.

Black Gestapo
A Black army takes over the ghetto. In the beginning their aim is to help the citizens but they wind up as the oppressors. The film is a violent, crazed morality tale in which power corrupts absolutely. Features Rod Perry, Charles P. Robinson *(Night Court)*, Phil Hoover and Ed Gross.
VHS: S21462. $19.95.
Lee Frost, USA, 1975, 88 mins.

The Black Godfather
In this blaxploitation work of the early 70s, two brothers join a black revolutionary vanguard to prevent the white mob from infiltrating their community and destroying their inner sanctum through a deadly flow of narcotics.
VHS: S18813. $29.95.
John Evans, USA, 1974, 96 mins.

Black Mama, White Mama
Two female prisoners chained together—a black prostitute (Pam Grier) and a white guerilla (Margaret Markov)—escape from a Latin American prison and are on the run from police, gangsters and guerillas. Based on a story by Joseph Viola and Jonathan Demme.
VHS: S30009. $14.98.
Eddie Romero, USA, 1973, 85 mins.

Black Sister's Revenge
A melodramatic revenge from the 70s blaxploitation cycle concerns a naive Mississippi farm girl making the trek to Los Angeles and falling for a street hustler, whose arrest prompts her to make a series of hard decisions.
VHS: S18814. $19.95.
Jamaa Fanaka, USA, 1976, 100 mins.

Black Vengeance
Leslie Uggams is a charismatic singer caught in a strange love triangle with the owners of an isolated motel. With Ted Cassidy, Slim Pickens and Dub Taylor.
VHS: S18815. $29.95.
Richard Robinson, USA, 1989, 90 mins.

Blackenstein
After the use of his arms and legs is restored by a renowned DNA expert, a black Vietnam veteran is turned into a monster when an evil assistant switches his medicine. A Blaxploitation classic.
VHS: S32513. $19.95.
William Levey, USA, 1973, 87 mins.

Blacula
This groove from beyond the grave was named best horror film of 1972 by the Academy of Horror Films and Science Fiction Films. Interior decorators buy the coffin of an African prince (William Marshall), bitten by Dracula centuries before, and bring it back to Los Angeles. The African prince starts feeding his hunger while following a woman who looks like his departed wife. With Vonetta McGee and Denise Nicholas.
VHS: S34619. $14.95.
William Crain, USA, 1972, 92 mins.

Bucktown
Fred Williamson and Pam Grier star in this story of a man returning to his hometown to find that all is not well. He arrives to bury his brother and winds up burying a number of others as well. Grier plays "Aretha", the woman who helps him put the screws to the gang that has terrorized the town.
VHS: S21397. $14.95.
Arthur Marks, USA, 1975, 95 mins.

Cleopatra Jones
A curious blaxploitation work with Tamara Dobson as the title character, a statuesque, beautiful CIA agent who uses her training and martial arts skills to wipe out a nefarious gang of drug dealers. With Shelley Winters, Bernie Casey, Brenda Sykes and Antonio Fargas.
VHS: S18927. $19.98.
Jack Starrett, USA, 1973, 89 mins.

Cleopatra Jones and the Casino of Gold
This film combines the revenge hysteria of a blaxploitation drama (antiauthoritarian political messages) with a high-camp revelry (personified by the outlandish antics of Stella Stevens, a character known as "Dragon Lady"). Coming at the end of the blaxploitation cycle, when the films turned to self-parody, this is a wild, stylized melodrama with cool, suave blacks pitted against hysterical, rampaging whites (including Norman Fell). Ostensibly a sequel to Jack Starrett's 1973 original, the film stars Tamara Dobson as a beautiful CIA agent locked in a mortal duel with drug-empress Stevens. With Tanny, Albert Popwell, Caro Kenyatta and Christopher Hunt.
VHS: S18926. $19.98.
Chuck Bail, USA, 1975, 96 mins.

Coffy
Pam Grier's biggest hit finds her battling the drug dealers who made a junkie out of her young sister. Lots of violent retribution as Nurse Grier becomes a one-woman army against criminal scum. With Allan Arbus, Sid Haig, Bob Minor, Booker Bradshaw and Robert Do Qui as King George.
VHS: S07451. $19.98.
Jack Hill, USA, 1973, 91 mins.

Deadly Drifter
Danny Glover plays a disaffected urban revolutionary whose specialized talents for destruction and death lead to his exploitation and corruption. Also known as *Out*.
With Peter Coyote.
VHS: S18817. $19.95.
Eli Hollander, USA, 1982, 85 mins.

Detroit 9000
Set against the urban squalor of Detroit, rogue cops and petty criminals seek a valuable collection of jewels. With Alex Rocco, Hari Rhodes and Vonetta McGee.
VHS: S18818. $19.95.
Arthur Marks, USA, 1973, 106 mins.

Diamond Shaft (aka Diamonds)
Richard Roundtree is back as Shaft in this heist action film about a suave London merchant who coerces an ex-con and his lover into breaking into an international diamond exchange. Robert Shaw stars in a dual role as a diamond merchant who masterminds a Tel-Aviv break-in and his twin brother.
Also stars Shelley Winters and Barbara (Hershey) Seagull.
VHS: S30059. $24.98.
Menahem Golan, Israel, 1975, 101 mins.

Disco Godfather
Rudy Ray Moore mixes martial arts, rap and of course, disco in this action film. Moore portrays the owner of a disco out to topple the nation's largest producer of angel dust. USA, 93 mins.
VHS: S21461. $29.95.

Dolemite
A pastiche of gangster and karate movies set in a stand-up nightclub and centered around Rudy Ray Moore's loose and comic turn as the dark avenger. With Jerry Jones and Lady Reed.
VHS: S18810. $19.95.
D'Urville Martin, USA, 1987, 91 mins.

Dolemite 2: Human Tornado
Brash sequel to Rudy Ray Moore's earlier *Dolemite*, about the criminal activity in the seedy nightclub circuit. With Lady Reed.
VHS: S18823. $19.95.
Cliff Raquemore, USA, 1976, 98 mins.

Fass Black
Black gangsters face down the mob over the control of Hollywood's hottest disco. Music by soul artist Johnnie Taylor.
VHS: S18819. $14.95.
D'Urville Martin, USA, 1977, 105 mins.

Foxtrap
Fred Williamson stars as a tough, unstoppable private eye hired by a wealthy family. They want him to track down a beautiful woman, and after treks through the south of France and Rome, he succeeds. Back in L.A. he finds that he was mislead. Murder and betrayal force him to seek revenge.
VHS: S26344. $14.98.
Fred Williamson, USA, 1985, 88 mins.

Foxy Brown
Pam Grier goes into action when her undercover cop boyfriend is murdered by drug dealers on her own front porch. She isn't happy at all to find that her drug-dealing brother, Antonio Fargas, dropped the dime on her lover. A violent blaxploitation film with Terry Carter, Juanita Brown, Sid Haig, Bob Minor and Peter Brown, who loses more than his heart to foxy Pam Grier.
VHS: S07449. $19.98.
Laser: LD76971. $39.99.
Jack Hill, USA, 1974, 91 mins.

Friday Foster
Pam Grier stars in the title role as a newspaper photographer who uncovers a plot to assassinate black politicians. Based on the syndicated comic strip, the cast includes Yaphet Kotto, Thalmus Rasulala, Eartha Kitt, Godfrey Cambridge, Scatman Crothers, Ted Lange and Jim Backus as Enos Griffith, the evil mobster pulling the strings of death.
VHS: S07447. $19.95.
Arthur Marks, USA, 1975, 89 mins.

Get Christie Love
The protagonist of novelist Dorothy Uhnak's colorful and vibrant street detective, Christie Love (Teresa Graves), goes undercover to destroy powerful drug barons. With Harry Guardino, Louise Sorel and Paul Stevens.
VHS: S18811. $19.95.
William A. Graham, USA, 1974, 100 mins.

The Guy from Harlem
Harlem's seamy underside and the atmospheric streets and dangerous environment form the setting of this vigorous and chilling work about a black private investigator.
VHS: S18821. $14.95.
Rene Martinez Jr., USA, 1977, 86 mins.

Hell Up in Harlem
In this sequel to *Black Caesar* a young hood (Fred Williamson) rises from the gutter to take on the corrupt NYPD and the mob in a full-fledged war that sets the streets of Harlem on fire.
VHS: S33722. $14.95.
Larry Cohen, USA, 1973, 98 mins.

Hit!
A revenge action movie which stars Richard Pryor, Billy Dee Williams and Paul Hampton. Williams is the federal agent who springs into action after his daughter overdoses. He puts together his own revenge squad in order to get nine heroin dealers in Marseilles.
VHS: S21484. $19.95.
Sidney J. Furie, USA, 1973, 134 mins.

I'm Gonna Git You Sucka
A smart and very funny parody of the blaxpoitation films of the 1970's. Keenan Ivory Wayans stars with Bernie Casey, Jim Brown, Isaac Hayes and Antonio Fargas. When the brother of the hero O.D.'s from wearing too many gold chains, he assembles an over-the-hill group of public avengers to get the dreaded Mr. Big. With John Vernon, Damon Wayans and Steve James.
VHS: S09397. $19.95.
Laser: LD72137. $34.98.
Keenen Ivory Wayans, USA, 1988, 85 mins.

In Your Face
Little-known blaxploitation feature about a black family who are being harassed by their white suburban neighbors. They are helped by a black motorcycle gang. Also known as *Abar, the First Black Superman*.
VHS: S18824. $19.95.
Frank Packard, USA, 1977, 90 mins.

J.D.'s Revenge
Glyn Turman, Joan Pringle and Lou Gossett star in this well-made black horror film about the evil J.D. Walker, whose vengeful spirit returns from beyond the grave to possess an innocent young man.
VHS: S13768. $14.98.
Arthur Marks, USA, 1976, 95 mins.

Joshua
Originally known as *The Black Rider*, this last wave of the blaxploitation works and nominal western stars former football star Fred Williamson as a peaceful man who tracks down the band of killers who viciously murdered his mother. With Isela Vega, Benda Venus and Stacy Newton.
VHS: S18139. $19.95.
Larry Spangler, USA, 1976, 75 mins.

The Legend of Dolemite: Rudy Ray Moore
A living legend from the world of Black comedy, Moore has been hailed as the Godfather of Rap. For over 30 years he has blended a number of styles without shying away from X-rated material. He has influenced all the biggest stars, from Richard Pryor to Whoopi Goldberg. This video is pure Rudy Ray Moore. Features Snoop Doggy Dogg.
VHS: S22460. $24.95.
Rudy Ray Moore, USA, 1994, 75 mins.

The Mack
One of the most popular (and one of the most violent) blaxploitation films made, *Mack* is the story of a Black pimp in Oakland. With Max Julien, Don Gordon, Richard Pryor, Carol Speed, Roger E. Mosley.
VHS: S21485. $9.98.
Laser: LD76316. $39.99.
Michael Campus, USA, 1973, 110 mins.

The Messenger
After doing time in an Italian prison, Jake Turner (Fred Williamson) is free. That night he sees his beloved wife once again but the next day she is brutally murdered. In an orgy of violent revenge he begins killing off the drug suppliers who first hooked his wife on drugs and then killed her. He then meets a strange rich man who encourages him to seek revenge but ultimately betrays him.
VHS: S26343. $14.98.
Fred Williamson, USA, 1986, 95 mins.

Monkey Hustle
An appealing cast, including Yaphet Kotto and Rudy Ray Moore, bolsters this action comedy shot in Chicago. It is the story of a ghetto neighborhood earmarked for leveling in order to make way for a new expressway coming through.
VHS: S13766. $59.98.
Arthur Marks, USA, 1977, 90 mins.

Mr. Mean
Fred Williamson stars as an amoral, ruthless killer and mercenary who reluctantly enters into a contract with the Mafia, setting off a chain of violent and explosive events. Williamson also wrote the screenplay. With Crippy Yocard.
VHS: S18140. $19.95.
Fred Williamson, USA, 1992, 81 mins.

Petey Wheatstraw
An African-American folktale is retold by "Dolemite" himself, Rudy Ray Moore. The story is that of a man so useless that he cuts a deal with Satan himself—he has to marry the devil's ugly daughter.
VHS: S21460. $29.95.
Cliff Roquemore, USA, 1978, 93 mins.

Real Soulja
Woody Strode *(Spartacus)* stars as Mike Martin, a retiring CIA agent who has been persuaded to accept one final mission. His orders are to assassinate a KGB gunrunner in Thailand and replace him with a CIA man. Mike soon finds himself in the thick of the action, and before long he knows the names of all the players—and they know his.
VHS: S35129. $19.95.
USA, 1983, 87 mins.

The Return of Superfly
Curtis Mayfield and Ice-T provide the music for this third sequel to *Superfly*. The plot revolves around "Superfly" and his Harlem exploits—hassling drug dealers and avoiding the cops. Features Margaret Avery, Nathan Purdee and Sam Jackson.
VHS: S21464. $14.95.
Sig Shore, USA, 1990, 94 mins.

Scream, Blacula, Scream
Pam Grier is Lisa, the voodoo princess who must persuade the ferocious black vampire Manuwalde (William Marshall) from draining the life's blood from any more of the black community in Los Angeles. This sequel to *Blacula* features Richard Lawson, Don Mitchell, Lynn Moody and Michael Conrad as the Sheriff. Set in L.A. and Africa.
VHS: S07450. $14.95.
Bob Kelljan, USA, 1973, 95 mins.

Shaft
Richard Roundtree is the title character, a black private detective in New York City who dresses sharp, pleases the ladies and knows just when to crash through a window. Isaac Hayes's theme song won an Oscar. With Moses Gunn, Charles Cioffi, Gwenn Mitchell and Drew Bundini Brown. The action packed script by Ernest Tidyman is based on his own novel.
VHS: S09159. $19.95.
Laser: LD76972. $39.99.
Gordon Parks, USA, 1971, 100 mins.

Shaft in Africa
Richard Roundtree goes to Africa in this action-filled 1970's thriller. Naturally, this lawman brings style and justice to the struggle of black people wherever he goes. In this film he must confront one of mankind's most horrific legacies: that of slavery.
VHS: S26872. $14.95.
John Guillermin, USA, 1973, 112 mins.

Shaft's Big Score
A continuation of the predicaments of the hip and stylish black private eye trying to break up a deadly numbers and racketeering syndicate responsible for the killing of a friend. Features Isaac Hayes' title song, director Gordon Parks' music and a startling climax with Shaft chased by a helicopter. With Richard Roundtree, Moses Gunn and Drew Bundini Brown.
VHS: S18480. $19.98.
Gordon Parks, USA, 1972, 104 mins.

Sheba, Baby
Pam Grier is Sheba Shayne, Private Eye. Her father was murdered by a wealthy white businessman who framed him for some racial riots, and she wants to clear his name. With D'Urville Martin, Austin Stoker, Rudy Challenger, Dick Merrifield as Shark and Charles Broaddus as Hammerhead.
VHS: S07448. $59.98.
William Girdler, USA, 1975, 90 mins.

Slaughter's Big Ripoff
Jim Brown is back as street-smart Slaughter, who returns to help unravel a crime ring. But he'll need to pull off the crime of the century for evidence to bust the Mob. Also stars Gordon Douglas, Brock Peters and Ed McMahon as the syndicate head.
VHS: S30011. $14.98.
Gordon Douglas, USA, 1973, 93 mins.

Soul Brothers of Kung Fu
Illegal immigrants Bruce Li and Lo Meng *(Five Venoms)* find work on a construction site, where they meet kung fu fanatic Carl Scott. The three become fast friends and spend many hours practicing techniques and beating up local thugs. But Lo Meng is lured into the gang of Triad big boss Ku Feng, and he turns on his former brothers. Now Bruce and Carl face the ultimate challenge: can they stand up to the power of the Triads, or will they be crushed by the might of Lo Meng and Ku Feng's Iron Palm Strike? Special collector's edition with extra alternate ending.
VHS: S35131. $19.95.
USA, 1980, 90 mins.

Soul Vengeance
Savagely beaten and convicted on false charges, Charlie is released from prison and pursues the men responsible, wielding an alarming weapon. 91 mins.
VHS: S18833. $14.95.
Jamaa Fanaka, USA, 1975, 91 mins.

Super Soul Brother
An exuberant social and political comedy about a classic underachiever who ingests a strange potion that endows one with supernatural gifts. With Wildman Steve. 80 mins.
VHS: S18834. $14.95.

Superfly
Ron O'Neal plays a rather curious hero in Gordon Parks, Jr.'s *Superfly*. He is a pimp and a drug dealer who defies the system and manages to leave his life of vice with a hefty retirement fund. Features Carl Lee, Julius Harris, Sheila Frazier and Charles McGregor. Curtis Mayfield provides the music.
VHS: S21465. $19.98.
Gordon Parks Jr., USA, 1972, 98 mins.

Superfly TNT
This sequel finds "Superfly" in Europe fighting for the independence of Africa. An arms dealer, the suave Roscoe Lee Browne, enlists the ex-hustler to overthrow a brutal dictatorship. This film is the very definition of blaxploitation. Features Sheila Frazier from *Superfly* and Robert Guillaume.
VHS: S21475. $14.95.
Ron O'Neal, USA, 1973, 87 mins.

Truck Turner
The incomparable Isaac Hayes stars in this incredibly violent "blaxploitation" film about a bounty hunter out to capture bail jumpers. With Yaphet Kotto and a musical score from Hayes himself.
VHS: S13767. $14.98.
Jonathan Kaplan, USA, 1974, 91 mins.

Urban Jungle
Part of the new wave of films resembling 70s blaxploitation pictures, it tells the story of a ruthless Housing Commisssioner who forces the poor out into the streets in order to make a quick buck. Somehow this all relates to S & M and drug dealing priests. The heroes of this picture are a couple of two-bit drug merchants who decide to help the community instead of poison it. Their help however, is brutal violence.
VHS: S21467. $79.95.
Daniel Matmor, USA, 1994, 90 mins.

Way of the Black Dragon
This third film in the Black Dragon series stars world karate champion Ron Van Clief as the Black Dragon, dispatched by Interpol to investigate drug trafficking and white slavery in Indochina. During a stopover in China, he rescues a Thai girl named Ellisin from the clutches of the Triads. The two then head for Bangkok. Upon their arrival, they are joined by Ellisin's brother Ichai (Carter Wong), whose distrust of the Black Dragon leads to a serious confrontation. But soon Ichai realizes that they are both fighting for the same cause, and they join forces to bring down Smith, kingpin of the drug and prostitution ring.
VHS: S35132. $19.95.
Chan Wui Ngai, USA, 1981, 88 mins.

The Wilby Conspiracy
Sidney Poitier is Shack Twala, a Bantu revolutionary in South Africa who has to get out of the country with a cache of diamonds to be used to further the cause. He relies on the reluctant Michael Caine to assist him. An anti-apartheid action thriller with Persis Khambatta, Rutger Hauer, Prunella Gee and Nicol Williamson as the determined pursuer, Major Horn.
VHS: S06064. $14.95.
Ralph Nelson, USA, 1975, 105 mins.

Women in Cages

Boiling passions confined behind concrete walls! Naked lust that builds to a deadly climax! Sex and action with American female prisoners behind bars in a foreign country. Starring Pam Grier. Digitally remastered.
VHS: S34862. $14.98.
Gerardo de Leon, USA, 1971, 78 mins.

COMEDY ACTS

All-Star Toast to the Improv

Hosted by Robert Klein, with Billy Crystal, Richard Lewis, Martin Mull, Paul Rodriguez and Robin Williams, a celebration of 15 years of outrageous comedy at Los Angeles' Improv Club in an evening of stand-up comedy. 60 mins.
VHS: S08144. $39.99.

America's Favorite Jokes

A collection of jokes ranging from the inane to the ridiculous, usually based on such questions as "How do you circumcise a whale?", "What do wide mouth frogs eat?" and "What's the difference between a Porsche and a porcupine?" 30 mins.
VHS: S07443. $16.95.

Anna Russell: The Clown Princess of Comedy

Anna Russell, the failed diva, dubbed "the world's funniest woman" by the *London Times*, delivers three of her timeless routines and tells all in a side-splitting interview. A must for any fan of the "lady who has been reducing audiences to helpless laughter for nearly half a century" *(Washington Post)*. 60 mins.
VHS: S30129. $29.95.

Best of Eddie Murphy—Saturday Night Live

A compilation of the television roles that launched a movie career. More than 30 of Eddie Murphy's most popular sketches are included. See Eddie as Buckwheat, James Brown, Stevie Wonder and Little Richard Simmons as well as the host of "Mr. Robinson's Neighborhood". Relive those great Saturday Nights with Eddie when the show was actually funny. 78 mins.
Laser: LD75119. $24.98.

The Best of Minnie Pearl: Let Minnie Steal Your Joke

The first lady of country comedy brings you classic American humor packed with unforgettable laughs and precious moments from her popular segment with Ralph Emery on the *Nashville Now* TV show. 60 mins.
VHS: S23146. $19.95.

The Best of The Kids in the Hall

A collection of sketches that mix the political, social and scatological—in other words, a non-stop revelry for camp, the Queen and her country. In this hip work by the Canadian ensemble, their exuberant humor takes no prisoners. "It's *Monty Python* with a migraine, anxiety made antic, frantic and hilarious" *(USA Today)*. With David Foley, Mark McKinney, Scott Thompson, Bruce McCulloch and Kevin McDonald.
VHS: S19880. $19.95.

Best of the Not Necessarily the News

A hysterical tape in the Comedy Club's new series. 60 mins.
VHS: S09807. $39.99.

Bette Midler's Mondo Beyond

Bette Midler stars in a nutty performance at The Comedy Club. 60 mins.
VHS: S09808. $19.98.

Blackstone on Tour

The world's foremost illusionist presents a fast-paced demonstration of his remarkable talents—including the mysterious appearance on stage of a live elephant. A masterful demonstration of the art of illusion. USA, 1981, 60 mins.
VHS: S03239. $39.95.

Bob Goldthwait: Is He Like That All the Time?

Hilarious stand-up comedy live from the star of Police Academy. 60 mins.
VHS: S11003. $19.95.

Brett Butler: The Child Ain't Right

This hysterical comic finally is available on video. Her stand-up routine will amply demonstrate that this "child ain't right." Contains adult material. 26 mins.
VHS: S24797. $12.95.

But...Seriously

Comic greats Whoopi Goldberg, Richard Pryor, Lenny Bruce, Lily Tomlin, Eric Bogosian, Jack Paar, Billy Crystal and others are joined in this collection of political comedy. These comedians satirize everything, from the civil rights movement to the L.A. riots. 82 mins.
VHS: S26461. $19.95.

The Classic Schiller's Reel Collection

Finally, 15 of the classic comic shorts by Tom Schiller, that were featured on *Saturday Night Live*, are now available. Comic greats like Bill Murray, Gilda Radner and John Belushi are featured in some of their best performances, in films like *La Dolce Gilda* and *The Acid Generation—Where Are They Now?*. 44 mins.
VHS: S21206. $9.99.

Comedy's Dirtiest Dozen

Top stand-up comics Tim Allen, Chris Rock and Jackie "the Jokeman" Martling *(The Howard Stern Show)* will have you rolling on the floor as they perform their bluest comedy routines, live and uncensored. Also features comedians Bill Hicks, Thea Vidale, Stephanie Hodge and John Fox. 95 mins.
VHS: S33364. $19.99.

Denis Leary: No Cure for Cancer

He was great on *Saturday Night Live*, but here he can really let loose and reveal the true extent of his wit. Contains adult material. 63 mins.
VHS: S24801. $12.95.

Dos Fallopia: Pretty Girls, Not Too Bright

Seattle zanies Dos Fallopia (Lisa Koch and Peggy Platt) serve up a stew of hysterical and dysfunctional characters in this debut video. Shot from live performances, the duo brings their hilarious sketch comedy and music through their twisted alter egos. "Seattle's reigning queens of sketch comedy" *(Seattle Gay News)*.
VHS: S30423. $19.95.

Dr. Katz

Two volumes of *Dr. Katz*, the Emmy and Cable Ace award-winning animated comedy from Comedy Central. Listen to guest comedians (in their animated form) as they share their neuroses with shrink Dr. Katz. Each tape is 50 mins.
Dr. Katz, Vol. 1. Guests include Garry Shandling *(The Larry Sanders Show)*, Larry Miller, Judy Tenuta and Ray Romano.
VHS: S31826. $12.95.
Dr. Katz, Vol. 2. Guests include Jon Stewart, Marc Maron, Bob Odenkirk, Emo Phillips and Ritch Shydner.
VHS: S31827. $12.95.

Eddie Izzard: Glorious

Self-styled Eddie Izzard, a sometimes cross-dressing, always original British comic, brings a psychedelic, glam-rock sensibility to the comic stage. Izzard's *Glorious* is a one-man tour-de-farce, deconstructing everything from dog poo to shampoo. 100 mins.
VHS: S33677. $19.95.

Eddie Murphy Delirious

Eddie Murphy raps about life, sex, childhood and more in this scathing, scatological, stand-up performance.
Laser: LD75186. $34.98.
Bruce Gowers, USA, 1983, 69 mins.

Eddie Murphy: Raw

Eddie Murphy's second stand-up performance film, featuring many of his woman-bashing observations on life.
Laser: LD75185. $34.98.
Robert Townsend, USA, 1987, 90 mins.

Elayne Boosler

Live from the Bottom Line in New York City, the comedy of Elayne Boosler. She's been called the funniest woman in America and this is a golden opportunity to find out why. With special appearances by David Letterman, Bill Cosby, Dr. Ruth, Brother Theodore and Larry "Bud" Melman. 60 mins.
VHS: S08706. $59.98.

Elayne Boosler: Broadway Baby

An all-new stand-up special from one of the funniest comedians in the business, in an hour of comedy about mothers, sports, shopping, sports, contacts, condoms, pets, and, of course, sex. 60 mins.
VHS: S11692. $59.95.

Elayne Boosler: Live Nude Girls

Though this tape contains adult material, there really aren't any nude girls. But it got your attention and that is exactly the kind of all out humor Boosler does best. 59 mins.
VHS: S24798. $12.95.

Fun House

Early Eric Bogosian at the Los Angeles Matrix Theater in all his sweaty, maddened glory. Before *Talk Radio*, pre-*Sex, Drugs, Rock & Roll, Funhouse* features the desperate, hungry actor/writer in the performance of a lifetime.
VHS: S30436. $24.95.
Jo Bonney/Lewis MacAdams, USA, 1986, 80 mins.

Gallagher—Melon Crazy

Happiness to some people is a 30-foot melon and the willingness to destroy a wonderful example of the bounty of the land that could probably feed several needy and deserving individuals. But not if Gallagher is around. Rumor has it he started as a contestant on "The Gong Show." Kids, don't try this kind of stuff at home. 58 mins.
VHS: S10816. $19.95.

Gallagher—Over Your Head

The subtitle is probably referring to some sticky and gooey concoction and not the level of the jokes. In this video concert Gallagher speaks his mind on politicians, ancient history and methods of child-rearing. Be prepared to take notes. Familiar items will be destroyed in the Sledge-O-Matic demonstration. 1984. 58 mins.
VHS: S10817. $19.95.

Gallagher—Stuck in the Sixties

Said to be his most inventive collection of props on display to date in this continuing series of childish mayhem. Gallagher pulls out all the stops in still another high energy comic concert that will feature the infamous Sledge-O-Matic in action. 1984. 58 mins.
VHS: S10818. $19.95.

Gallagher—The Bookkeeper

The messiest comic in the business takes on the IRS in this live video concert. The self-proclaimed king of prop comedy-What, did Rip Taylor die?—assaults his audience with a barrage of one-liners and unusual objects. As usual, the Sledge-O-Matic will conclude the act. 58 mins.
VHS: S10814. $19.95.

Gallagher—The Maddest

In the mood for a concert of comedy featuring mutant sofas and assaults on 7-11's? How about freaky guys who wear striped shirts and suspenders? Gallagher is the one name comedian who goes through props the way Warren Beatty goes through girlfriends. Be prepared for a particularly goopy Sledge-O-Matic finale. 60 mins.
VHS: S10815. $19.95.

Gilda Radner

Saturday Night Live's Gilda Radner created memorable characters that live on. Roseanne Roseanadanna, Baba Wawa and Lisa Loopner are just some of them. This special memoir uses Radner's own recording of her autobiography, *It's Always Something*, to showcase some of her delightful humor. 50 mins.
VHS: S25870. $19.95.

The Groove Tube

Now seventies nostalgia, a wild lampoon series of skits that spoof television which gave Chevy Chase his first big break. 75 mins.
VHS: S04622. $39.95.

The Hungry I Reunion

The world-famous nightclub in San Francisco is host to a comedy salute by some of the stars who performed there. Performers include Mort Sahl, Bill Cosby, Jonathan Winters, The Limelighters, Phyllis Diller and Lenny Bruce. Lenny's contribution is presumably pre-recorded. USA, 1980, 90 mins.
VHS: S06165. $29.98.

In the Life: The Funny Tape

Kate Clinton, America's first lesbian stand-up comic, hosts this collection of songs and skits featuring some of the best lesbian and gay talent around. Even the commercials are twisted. Lily Tomlin and the late Vito Russo are also featured. 60 mins.
VHS: S21125. $19.98.

Jackie Mason

A definitive biography of the equal opportunity offender, this tape is also a hilarious compilation of Mason's best schtick. It includes early appearances on *The Steve Allen Show* and routines from Mason's many Broadway shows. 52 mins.
VHS: S26216. $19.95.

Jay Leno: The American Dream

Jay Leno delves as only he can into the comedic implications of what keeps America a vibrant and hopeful place to be. From Paramount Home video come words and ideas of the man Johnny Carson trusts to host the Tonight Show in his absence. Among the subjects for jest are big cars, flashy clothes and Italian beef sandwiches. In color. USA, 1986, 49 mins.
VHS: S06170. $19.95.

Joan Rivers: Abroad in London

Does "ugly American abroad" mean anything to you? Rivers holds nothing back in this terrific stand-up routine. Contains adult material. 57 mins.
VHS: S24802. $12.95.

Joe Piscopo Live!

One of the sharpest comic impersonators to break out of the comedy circuit in 60 minutes of raucous, rockin' comedy. A panorama of impressions from Phil Donahue and Robert De Niro to Frank Sinatra and David Lee Roth. 60 mins.
VHS: S07572. $39.99.

Kovacs & Keaton

Two rare television appearances by master comedians—Kovacs is silent in *Eugene* (1960) as he mimes his way through life, while Keaton is *Wrestling with Trouble* as he and his buddy get tangled with two real-life wrestlers (1953). USA, 60 mins.
VHS: S01651. $24.95.

Lee Evans Live: The Ultimate Experience

A cross between Jim Carrey and Charlie Chaplin, hyperkinetic British comic Lee Evans *(Mousehunt)* turns the stage into a slightly berserk pinball machine in this program featuring classic Evans routines plus previously unseen footage. 90 mins.
VHS: S33678. $19.95.

Lenny Bruce

Filmed exactly one year before his death in August of 1965, this is the only full-length, unedited recording of America's most brilliant comic. This is not a documentary, but a raw account of Lenny Bruce in performance at a steamy San Francisco nightclub. Includes the animated short *Thank You Mask Man*. 68 mins.
VHS: S16334. $19.95.

Lenny Bruce Without Tears

Fred Baker's personal, off-beat documentary about his friend Lenny Bruce. The film interweaves memoirs and anecdotes from friends and colleagues, including Steve Allen, Paul Krassner, Mort Sahl, Kenneth Tynan, Nat Hentoff and Malcolm Muggeridge. "With anger, biting humor and sorrow the film shows the demise of the iconoclastic comic…so plagued by personal demons" (Linda Gross, *L.A. Times*).
VHS: S18517. $19.98.
Fred Baker, USA, 1992, 75 mins.

Lily Tomlin 3-Pack

The Search for Signs of Intelligent Life in the Universe, Ernestine: Peak Experiences and *Appearing Nitely* are the comic standouts joined in this three-tape set. It brings Lily Tomlin's Tony Award-winning performances to video. 120 mins.
VHS: S27478. $59.95.

Martin Mull Live from North Ridgeville, Ohio

A classic comedy performance—"an impressive catch of comedy talent."
VHS: S07162. $39.95.

Milton Berle Invites You to a Night at La Cage

Uncle Miltie has been known to put on a dress for laughs now and again, so he is a perfect host for an evening of female impersonation and comedy. With Gypsy, the master/mistress of ceremonies at the La Cage Revue. Filmed in Las Vegas. Watch for Berle as Dolly Parton.
VHS: S04215. $29.95.
Milton Berle/Jim Gates, USA, 1986, 75 mins.

The Mr. Bill Collection

This program highlights the postmodern humor of Mr. Bill, *Saturday Night Live's* disembodied man of clay. 50 mins.
VHS: S19407. $14.95.

Niall Tobin Live

Master Irish comedian and cabaret performer—Irish, earthy, open and uproarious, in his first video program after his leading role in the award-winning Broadway plays "Borstal Boy" and "Fearless Frank." 82 mins.
VHS: S09164. $29.95.

Paramount Comedy Theater: Volumes 1-3

Howie Mandel hosts a show featuring four young comics: Bruce Mahler, Judy Carter, Philip Wellford and Bob Saget.
VHS: S01913. $29.95.
Joe Hostettler, USA, 1986, 71 mins.

Paramount Comedy Theater: Volume 4

Howie Mandel hosts *Delivery Men*, featuring five of America's hot new comics: Jimmy Aleck, Maurice LaMarche, Rick Overton, Lou Dinos, Pat Hazell. Jimmy Aleck tells you how *not* to talk to an auto mechanic. Maurice does uncanny impressions of everyone from Wilma Flintstone to Alan Alda. 71 mins.
VHS: S10053. $29.95.

Paramount Comedy Theater: Volume 5

Cutting Up, again hosted by Mandel, features Dale Gonyea, Lois Bromfield, Teddy Bergereon and Louise Duart. Gonyea presents a musical salute to single sex and famous parents, Bergeron tells how he hooked his VCR to his microwave. 60 mins.
VHS: S10054. $29.95.

Pat Paulsen for President

Henry Fonda narrated this one-hour presidential special which aired on CBS in October 1968. A take-off on presidential campaigns, it details Pat Paulsen's early denials of political ambition to his barnstorming antics across the country.
VHS: S33071. $24.95.
Bob Collins, USA, 1968, 60 mins.

Pat Paulsen's Greatest Bits

The late, great, deadpan comic Pat Paulsen won an Emmy in 1968 for his outstanding work on the Smothers Brothers Comedy Hour. This collection contains some of Paulsen's most brilliantly executed mental lapses, painful pratfalls and embarrasing gaffs. Bits include "The Carpenter," "The Humor Lecture," "The Menu," "Farewell to the Smothers," "Six Years Later," "Want Ads," "The Folk Singer," "The Spy Kit," "The Speed Reader," "Self Defense," "Sex Education," "My Fascinating Life," "Walking on Water" and "The Novelty Guy." 60 mins.
VHS: S33072. $24.95.

Paul Reiser: 31/2 Blocks from Home

Paul Reiser, of the hit TV comedy show *Mad About You*, is at his stand-up best in this great video. Contains adult material. 58 mins.
VHS: S24799. $12.95.

Politically Incorrect: A Special Visit with Camille Paglia

Politically Incorrect host Bill Maher spends two evenings with controversial new-age feminist and author of *Vamps & Tramps* Camille Paglia. In the first episode Maher asks Paglia: Is rape about sex or violence? Are there more lesbian relationships nowadays? And-would the bisexual Paglia prefer Kidman or Cruise, Baldwin or Basinger, Crawford or Gere? In the second episode, Maher and Paglia tackle questions concerning homosexuality, including: Does Camille believe that under the right circumstances anyone will have a homosexual encounter? Is homosexual exclusivity natural? Are homosexuals people who couldn't make it in the heterosexual world?—as well as other topics.
VHS: S30626. $12.95.

Politically Incorrect: Political Improvement

Politically Incorrect host Bill Maher is joined by *Home Improvement*'s Tim Allen, *Wings'* Tim Daly, rap singer and actress Queen Latifah *(Set it Off, Living Single)* and seven-time Emmy award-winning actor Ed Asner. Maher poses the following questions: What type of message is the O.J. Simpson trial media blitz sending? Would an occasional use of police force drop the crime rate? And other thought-provoking topics. Two episodes on one tape. 50 mins.
VHS: S30433. $12.95.

Politically Incorrect: Politics Tonight

Politically Incorrect's Bill Maher hosts two episodes with Jay Leno. Guests include George Clooney, Gabrielle Cartaris, Randy Newman, Daryl Gates and Doris Allen.
VHS: S30832. $12.95.

Politically Incorrect: Pulp Politics

Bill Maher is joined by Quentin Tarantino *(Pulp Fiction)*, Corbin Benson *(L.A. Law)*, Dick Clark and Janeane Garofalo *(The Truth About Cats and Dogs)*. Maher poses the following questions: Do rap music's violent lyrics incite violent behavior? Will Americans get nostalgic about almost anything? Why do people join cults? Two episodes on one tape. 50 mins.
VHS: S30434. $12.95.

Politically Incorrect: Really Roseanne

Bill Maher hosts two episodes with Roseanne. Guests include Lorraine Bracca, Matt Lauer and John O'Sullivan.
VHS: S30833. $12.95.

Raised Catholic (Can You Tell?)

Ed Stivender has often been called the Catholic Garrison Keillor. This funny and nostalgic look at growing up Catholic shows why this comparison holds. It contains the best of Stivender's witty humor, which also inspired his best-selling book. 60 mins.
VHS: S29995. $19.95.

Rap Master Ronnie: A Report Card

Jim Morris stars as the President in this comedy created by Garry Trudeau and Elizabeth Swados and performed at The Comedy Club. 60 mins.
VHS: S09809. $39.99.

Rich Little's Christmas Carol

Snow is falling, shoppers are scurrying about, bells are ringing…Christmas time is here…this time with a twist from the comic genius of master impressionist Rich Little. Here, Little plays the whole gang! W.C. Fields is the sourest scrooge you'll ever see. Paul Lynde is poor Bob Cratchit; Richard Nixon is Marley's Ghost.
VHS: S12476. $14.95.

Rich Little—One's a Crowd

One can certainly be a crowd when that one person is Rich Little, the leading impersonator of the famous people. Now available on home video, Mr. Little performs a cavalcade of movie stars, celebrities and political figures. Included in this parade of impressions are John Wayne, Groucho Marx, Jack Nicholson, Jimmy Stewart, Jack Benny and Ronald Reagan.
VHS: S07787. $19.98.

Richard Lewis—I'm Exhausted

The star of TV's "Anything But Love" as he "whines about life with the rhythm, body language and material of a Woody Allen, the posture of a Groucho Marx and the speed of a Mario Andretti." *(People Magazine)*. 60 mins.
VHS: S11253. $19.98.

Richard Pryor Live! In Concert

The incomparable Richard Pryor brings "truth to humor and humor to truth" in this 1979 concert video which showcases Pryor's greatest moments. "The comedian, uncensored, is at his raunchy best" (Leonard Maltin, *Movie and Video Guide*). Richard Pryor raps on subjects ranging from race to death to sex to machismo, and tells such famous stories as the time he shot his car and the time his children thought he was joking when he nearly drowned.
VHS: S27199. $19.98.
Jeff Margolis, USA, 1979, 78 mins.

Richard Pryor: Live & Smokin'

In this live performance filmed at the New York Improvisation on April 29, 1971, you'll see the ingenious comic during his earliest stand-up days. The routine is uniquely Prior: interpretative voices and characterizations, material drawn from his outrageous life, and plenty of comments on racial differences, chemical substances and sex. Includes the now famous "Wino Preacher & Willie the Junkie" sequence.
VHS: S32496. $14.98.

Robert Klein

Multi-talented comic Robert Klein gives a hilarious stand-up and musical performance in this live recording from the campus of New York University. 60 mins.
VHS: S07698. $29.95.

Ron Reagan Is the President's Son/The New Homeowner's Guide to Happiness

The shockingly true and hilariously not-so-true story of Ron Reagan, dancer, journalist, writer, interviewer, TV host and all around President's son, and, in a hilarious second piece, when the peace and prosperity promised by the purchase of an American Dream House is disturbed by the incessant din of barking dogs, our unhappy-go-lucky married couple will try anything for a wholly silent night; but can valium laced raw steaks be anything but a recipe for disaster? 60 mins.
VHS: S08146. $39.99.

Rude: Rudy Ray Moore

A live concert performance of comic and actor Rudy Ray Moore in his best known impersonation, *Dolemite*, taken from the film character. 86 mins.
VHS: S18831. $19.95.

Sam Kinison: Family Entertainment Hour

An irreverent performance by the late shock comedian Sam Kinison, who luxuriates in his scatological mixture of sex, death, religion and intolerance. With the Randy Hansen Band. 50 mins.
VHS: S18719. $19.95.

Sam Kinison: Why Did We Laugh?

A portrait of the late, great preacher-turned-screaming-comedian Sam Kinison. Contains rare, early footage of Sam preaching and performing stand-up at the Comedy Store. Featuring Jay Leno, Richard Pryor, Rodney Dangerfield, Dennis Miller, Larry King and more.
VHS: S33390. $19.98.
DVD: DV60284. $24.95.
Larry Carroll, USA, 1997, 90 mins.

Saturday Night Entertainment

4 volumes of the best (and funniest selections) from comedians who have made Saturday night famous.
The Best of Gilda Radner.
VHS: S09413. $9.99.
The Best of Dan Aykroyd.
VHS: S09414. $14.95.
The Best of John Belushi.
VHS: Out of print. For rental only.
Laser: LD72211. $34.98.
The Best of Chevy Chase.
VHS: S09416. $19.98.

Scrambled Feet

Jeffrey Hadow, John Driver and Roger Neil, the three original award-winning New York cast members, are joined by Madeline Kahn in blackout sketches, comedy routines and jokes. USA, 1982, 100 mins.
VHS: S03238. $39.98.

Steve Allen's 75th Birthday Celebration

Bill Maher (TV's *Politically Incorrect*) serves as master of ceremonies in this all-star comedy and musical event celebrating Steve Allen's 75th birthday and his half-century career in TV and entertainment. Steve performs several of his greatest musical hits with The Steve Allen Big Band and introduces clips of some of his best-loved comedy sketches and ad-libbed routines. 90 mins.
VHS: S33241. $19.98.

Steve Allen's Golden Age of Comedy

The best from Steve Allen's early TV shows, featuring a bevy of stars associated with his funny show. The outrageous comedy skits and music includes appearances by Bob Hope, Johnny Carson, Abbott and Costello, Mel Brooks and Jimmy Durante. 49 mins.
VHS: S03309. $59.95.

Tim Allen: Men Are Pigs

Home Improvement is not the only skill that Tim Allen possesses. Here he shows the comic side of himself that is perfect for a stand-up format. Contains adult material. 30 mins.
VHS: S24800. $12.95.

Toast to Lenny

Bill Cosby, Steve Allen, George Carlin and Mort Sahl (to name a few) gather at Hollywood's Troubadour to pay tribute to the trailblazing comedy of Lenny Bruce. Includes anecdotes, rare film clips and reflections by those who knew him best. 60 mins. 1984.
VHS: S04500. $59.95.

Tunnel Vision

A committee investigating TV's first uncensored network examines a typical day's programming in 1976. This outrageous and irreverent send-up of television launched the careers of comics Chevy Chase, John Candy, Howard Hesseman, Joe Flaherty, Larraine Newman, Betty Thomas, Phil Proctor, Rick Hurst, Reger Bowen, Bill Saluga, Ron Silver, Al Franken and Tom Davis.
VHS: S33334. $19.95.
Neal Israel/Brad Swirnoff, USA, 1976, 70 mins.

Victor Borge: On Stage with Audience Favorites

Two video cassettes with some of his funniest—and classic-performances, released on two separate tapes. At 75 Borge is "still one of the funniest people in the world" *(L.A. Times)*. Volume 1 includes: Introducing Mozart, My Favorite Barber, Early American Folksong, Introducing Marylyn Mulvey, Croatian Folksong, Aria from "Rigor Mortis" by Joe Green, Viennese Dance No. 1 by Friedman-Gaertner, The Timid Page Turner, and Complete Piano Selections. Volume 2 includes: Birthday Improvisations, Sahan Arzruni with the 2nd Rhapsody by Liszt, Salieri Opera, Inflationary Language, Phonetic Punctuation, Viennese Dance No. 2 by Friedman-Gaertner, Danish Lullaby, Improvisation, Complete Piano Selections.
Volume 1.
VHS: S05847. $29.95.
Volume 2.
VHS: S05848. $29.95.

Whoopi Goldberg: Fontaine...Why Am I Straight?

The comic operation on the moral backbone of America from Jim and Tammy Faye Bakker and Jerry Falwell to Jesse Jackson and the Reverend Al Sharpton, with Whoopi Goldberg in a live performance. In the character of Fontaine, she's out of the Betty Ford clinic, and taking on the real world. 51 mins.
VHS: S11004. $59.99.

The Young at Heart Comedians

Comic talk-show host David Brenner introduces seven senior members of a profession that tells jokes for a living. Filmed in front of a live audience and backstage, veteran stand-up comics Henny Youngman, Norm Crosby, Jackie Gayle, George Gobel, Jackie Vernon, Shelly Berman and Carl Ballantine do their stuff. They have over 300 years of experience in the business. USA, 1984, 77 mins.
VHS: S07442. $29.95.

ELVIS PRESLEY

Blue Hawaii

Elvis Presley plays a soldier stationed in Hawaii, singing and surrounded by girls. Angela Lansbury is Presley's mother, who comes to the island to work with a tourist agency.
VHS: S04286. $19.98.
Norman Taurog, USA, 1961, 101 mins.

Clambake

Elvis Presley plays a millionaire's son who trades places with a poor water ski instructor (Will Hutchins) to see if he's got the right stuff to make it on his own on the beach in Florida. He sings seven songs, romances Shelley Fabares and tangles with playboy Bill Bixby.
VHS: S03929. $19.95.
Arthur Nadel, USA, 1967, 99 mins.

Double Trouble

Elvis Presley gets involved with jewel smuggling, teenaged heiresses, and rock and roll in swinging London and Brussels, Belgium. He sings nine songs including "Long-Legged Girls with Short Dresses On" and "Old McDonald". With Annette Day, John Williams and the Wiiere Brothers.
VHS: S03930. $19.95.
Norman Taurog, USA, 1967, 90 mins.

Elvis and Me

Unflinching TV mini-series based on Priscilla Beaulieu Presley's memoirs about her life with the king. Features Presley hits sung by country singer Ronnie McDowell. With Dale Midkiff, Susan Walters, Billy Green Bush, Linda Miller and Jon Cypher.
VHS: S30656. $19.95.
Larry Peerce, USA, 1988, 187 mins.

Elvis on Tour

The King of Rock and Roll is the focus of this concert-documentary that features numerous songs sung in a number of cities. It also examines Elvis the man and takes a private peek at his personal life. Colonel Tom Parker serves as technical advisor.
VHS: S03931. $19.95.
Robert Abel/Pierre Adige, USA, 1972, 93 mins.

Elvis Stories

Titled "hysterical video tabloid and cure for Bambi fever," this fun video features John Cusack as the amazing burger king whose patties transmit messages from Elvis in "Corkey's Elvis Patties." Then "Elvis Lennon" proposes that Elvis and John Lennon were the same person, as Rick Saucedo, Ben Stiller, Joel Murray and others act in this hilarious collection of strange Elvis stories. 30 mins.
VHS: S11258. $14.95.

Elvis—That's the Way It Is

An entertaining and engaging documentary of Elvis, live on stage at the International Hotel in Las Vegas. Photographed by Lucien Ballard. Twenty-seven songs are presented, including "Blue Suede Shoes," "Heartbreak Hotel," "Crying Time" and "That's All Right Mama."
VHS: S03932. $24.95.
Laser: LD71151. $34.98.
DVD: DV60114. $24.98.
Denis Sanders, USA, 1970, 107 mins.

Elvis: The Echo Will Never Die

Tom Jones, B.B. King, Sammy Davis Jr., Ursula Andress and David Marsh join Casey Kasem in this personal tribute to Elvis Presley, recounting his musical roots and rise to fame to his final days. USA, 1983, 50 mins.
VHS: S01806. $29.95.

Follow That Dream

Elvis Presley and his family move to Florida where they try to homestead a prime piece of real estate. Naturally there is serious opposition. With Arthur O'Donnell, Joanna Moore, Simon Oakland, and Jack Kruschen. Elvis sings the title tune and three others.
VHS: S03927. $19.95.
Laser: Letterboxed. **LD72334. $34.98.**
Gordon Douglas, USA, 1962, 111 mins.

Frankie and Johnny

Elvis Presley and Donna Douglas *(The Beverly Hillbillies)* play riverboat entertainers and lovers who like to fight because they make up so well. A popular folk ballad becomes an excuse for Elvis to sing twelve more lesser-known songs. With Nancy Kovack.
VHS: S03928. $19.95.
Laser: LD76068. $39.98.
Fred De Cordova, USA, 1966, 88 mins.

Fun in Acapulco

The King woos Ursula Andress and wows the crowd with a 136-foot cliff dive. Featured songs are "Bossa Nova Baby," "No Room to Rhumba in a Sports Car" and "You Can't Say No in Acapulco." With Alejandro Rey.
VHS: S33274. $14.95.
Richard Thorpe, USA, 1963, 97 mins.

G.I. Blues

G.I. Elvis melts the frosty heart of dancer Juliet Prowse. Featured songs: "G.I. Blues," "Blue Suede Shoes," "Tonight Is So Right for Love" and "Wooden Heart."
VHS: S33275. $14.95.
Norman Taurog, USA, 1960, 104 mins.

Girl Happy

Elvis Presley is hired by a Chicago night club owner to make sure his daughter, Shelley Fabares, stays unmolested on her trip to Fort Lauderdale. It's a tough job but someone has got to do it. With Mary Ann Mobley, Harold J. Stone, Gary Crosby and Fabrizio Mioni as the Florida gigolo. Elvis sings 11 songs including "Wolf Call" and "Do the Clam."
VHS: S08065. $19.95.
Boris Sagal, USA, 1965, 96 mins.

Harum Scarum

Elvis Presley plays a motion picture-recording star kidnapped on a tour of the Middle East. He must escape, stop a royal assassination, romance a princess and still find the energy to sing nine songs, including "Harem Holiday" and "Hey Little Girl". With Mary Ann Mobley.
VHS: S03936. $19.95.
Gene Nelson, USA, 1965, 95 mins.

Heartbreak Hotel

A fictional fable about the King of Rock and Roll. Elvis Presley (David Keith) finds himself kidnapped by an ambitious teenager who wants to cheer up his mother. Tuesday Weld is the big Elvis fan who snaps out of her depression when he decides to stay awhile in her run-down hotel and help with the chores. With Charlie Schlatter and a whole lot of shaking going on.
VHS: S09574. $89.95.
Chris Columbus, USA, 1988, 101 mins.

Jailhouse Rock

Elvis Presley goes to prison for accidentally killing a man in a bar fight, and is signed to a musical contract following his performance on a tv show in prison. He follows a strange road to success and learns what's really important. Seven songs. With Mickey Shaughnessy, Judy Tyler and Dean Jones as the disc jockey who gives him a "break."
VHS: S00648. $19.95.
Laser: LD71157. $34.98.
DVD: DV60113. $24.98.
Richard Thorpe, USA, 1957, 96 mins.

Life with Elvis

Members of Elvis Presley's elite inner circle share their remembrances of the King. With never-before-seen photos of Elvis with friends and family. 31 mins.
VHS: S31741. $9.98.

Live a Little, Love a Little

Elvis Presley is an ambitious photographer working for two different bosses, one of whom wouldn't approve of the job at the girlie magazine. Somehow he finds the time to sing four songs, romance Michele Carey, and see what develops with bosses Don Porter and Rudy Vallee. With Sterling Holloway as the milkman. Based on the novel *Kiss My Firm and Pliant Lips* by Dan Greenburg.
VHS: S08085. $19.95.

Love Me Tender
Elvis makes his film debut in this tale set during the Civil War about two brothers in love with the same girl. Presley sings the title tune as he vies for the lady's heart. With Richard Egan, Debra Paget, Neville Brand, Mildred Dunnock, James Drury and Barry Coe.
VHS: S31163. $14.98.
Robert D. Webb, USA, 1956, 89 mins.

Paradise, Hawaiian Style
Romance is in the air when Elvis takes to the skies as a helicopter charter pilot. With a bevy of Hawaiian beauties. Featured songs: "Paradise, Hawaiian Style," "Drums of the Island," "Queenie Wahine's Papaya" and "This Is My Heaven."
VHS: S33276. $14.95.
Michael Moore, USA, 1966, 91 mins.

Roustabout
Karate-chopping biker Elvis saves Barbara Stanwyck's carny from bankruptcy. Watch for Raquel Welch (in her film debut) asking Elvis for a towel, and a cameo by Teri Garr. Featured songs: "Little Egypt" and "One Track Heart."
VHS: S33277. $14.95.
John Rich, USA, 1964, 101 mins.

Speedway
Elvis Presley plays a winning stock car driver who gets in trouble with the IRS when his manager, Bill Bixby, puts too much of his client's money on slow horses, who race at a different sort of track. The government sends Nancy Sinatra to investigate. With Gale Gordon.
VHS: S03934. $19.95.
Norman Taurog, USA, 1968, 90 mins.

Spinout
Elvis Presley races fast cars and leads a rock and roll band with a girl drummer, as he is pursued by four women. Shelley Fabares, Diane McBain, Dodie Marshall and Deborah Walley as the drummer limit the King to only five songs. What lucky girl will Elvis meet at the altar? Place your bets. The technical advisor for this film was Colonel Tom Parker.
VHS: S08086. $19.95.
Norman Taurog, USA, 196, 95 mins.

Stay Away Joe
Elvis Presley is a Navajo Indian rodeo star with a plan to better the life of his family on the reservation by raising cattle. When he barbecues the bill the government gets upset. With Burgess Meredith and Katy Jurado as his parents and L.Q. Jones as Navajo pal. Elvis sings only two songs and romances Susan Trustman and Quentin Dean.
VHS: S08087. $19.95.
Peter Tewkesbury, USA, 1968, 102 mins.

This Is Elvis
Unusual and quite good documentary combines historical footage with actors playing Elvis at various parts of his life. 144 mins.
VHS: S01329. $19.98.
Laser: LD76982. $39.99.
Malcolm Leo/Andrew Solt, USA, 1981, 144 mins.

Trouble with Girls (a.k.a. How to Get into It)
Elvis Presley manages a traveling Chautauqua show, sings two songs and tries to prevent trouble between the locals and the members of the troupe. With Marlyn Mason, Sheree North, Edward Andrews, John Carradine, Anissa Jones and Dabney Coleman. From the novel by Day Keene and Dwight Babcock.
VHS: S08088. $19.95.
Peter Tewkesbury, USA, 1969, 105 mins.

Viva Las Vegas
One of the King's best films. He co-stars with Ann-Margret as a Grand Prix driver who wants to sing, dance and operate expensive motor vehicles at high speed while in the company of a vivacious redheaded swimming instructor. With Cesare Danova and William Demarest.
VHS: S03935. $19.95.
Laser: LD70701. $34.98.
DVD: DV60112. $24.98.
George Sidney, USA, 1964, 86 mins.

Walkin' in the Shoes of the King
This performance documentary takes you inside the minds and lives of Elvis impersonators as they recreate some of the magic of the King. Join in the preparations that took place to produce and direct a large Elvis fan festival and concert in the San Francisco Bay Area in 1996. 45 mins.
VHS: S32641. $19.98.

SERIALS

Ace Drummond
The Universal serial in 13 chapters, of Captain Eddie Rickenbacker's exploits in the sky, directed by Ford Beebe and Cliff Smith. Featuring aerial stunts and action with John Kind, Jean Rogers, Noah Beery Jr., Lon Chaney Jr. and Ed Cobb. From a very good quality print.
VHS: S13212. $29.95.
Ford Beebe, USA, 1936, 260 mins.

The Adventures of Captain Marvel
A very popular serial from Republic wherein young Billy Batson has only to say the magic word *Shazam* and he turns into Captain Marvel, an adult and very tough crime fighter. The villain of record is the evil Scorpian, who needs five ancient lenses to rule the world. Tom Tyler is the Captain. Frank Coghlan, Jr. is Billy. B&W.
VHS: S06051. $29.95.
Laser: CLV. LD71967. $39.98.
William Witney/John English, USA, 1941, 12 chapters

The Adventures of Frank and Jesse James
The archetypal bad boys of the West undertake a program for restitution to the community they plundered by their search for gold and profit in a silver mine in thrilling serial. 180 mins.
VHS: S18375. $29.98.

The Adventures of Rex & Rinty
A stolen prize horse teams up with a wandering dog to help oust various villains. 12 chapters. USA, 1935, 234 mins.
VHS: S15604. $29.95.

Adventures of Smilin' Jack
Zack Moseley's famous comic-strip character comes roaring to life in this action-packed serial. Daredevil stunt pilot Smilin' Jack Martin takes on the air war in China during the darkest days of WWII. 13 thrilling episodes on two cassettes.
VHS: S13014. $24.95.
Ray Taylor, USA, 1943, 90 mins.

Black Widow (Cliffhanger Serials #5)
An Asian king sends his daughter to America to steal an atomic rocket engine in this lively serial from Republic studios. With Bruce Edwards, Virginia Lindley, Carol Forman. 13 deadly episodes on two videocassettes.
VHS: S15087. $29.98.
Spencer Bennet/Fred Brannon, USA, 1947

Burn 'em Up Barnes
Our hero, "Burn 'em Up", battles gangsters and must endure fiery crashes, explosions and other perils, but still finds time to race everything from cars to speedboats like a bat out of ....!
12 episodes. USA, 1934, 240 mins.
VHS: S15600. $29.95.

Cliffhangers: Adventures from the Thrill Factory
Film historian Leonard Maltin considers the world of the Republic Cliffhanger serials, reflecting on the heroes, stunts, gimmicks and actors. 46 mins.
VHS: S18376. $14.98.

The Clutching Hand
Our hero, Craig Kennedy, faces a myriad of fiendish pitfalls, ruthless gunmen and diabolical devices before he unmasks the sinister master criminal—Clutching Hand. 15 chapters. USA, 1936, 308 mins.
VHS: S15599. $29.95.

The Crimson Ghost
A Republic serial about the efforts of the title character to capture and control a machine that can short circuit electricity. Behind the grinning skull mask and the black shroud lurks Bud Geary using the voice of I. Stanford Jolley. Also in the cast is Clayton Moore *(The Lone Ranger)* as a villainous thug. With serial queen Linda Stirling and Charles Quigley. B&W.
VHS: S06048. $29.95.
William Witney/Fred Brannon, USA, 1946, 12 chapters

Cyclone of the Saddle
A western serial about the loneliness and solitude of the American frontier and a violent range war. With Rex Lease, Bobby Nelson, William Desmond and Yakima Canutt.
VHS: S18902. $19.95.
Elmer Clifton, USA, 1935, 53 mins.

Darkest Africa
Fifteen episodes of a cliffhanger series following the adventures of animal trainer Clyde Beatty in the wild landscapes of Africa. Laser disk contains original theatrical trailer. 270 mins.
VHS: S17410. $29.98.
Laser: LD71703. $49.98.

Dick Tracy
Ralph Byrd stars in this complete 15-episode compilation as Dick Tracy battles the sinister Spide Gang. 255 mins.
VHS: S12857. $24.95.

Don Daredevil Rides Again
In this serial, 12 adventures center around Don Daredevil, a mysterious presence in a border town hired to protect ranchers and their legally gained land from a ruthless baron. 167 mins.
VHS: S18372. $29.98.

Federal Agents vs. Underworld Inc. (Cliffhanger Serials #5)
An archeologist disappears after discovering the legendary Golden Hands of Kurigal, in this adventure serial from the Republic studios. With Kirk Alyn, Rosemary La Planche and Roy Barcroft. 12 episodes on two videocassettes.
VHS: S15085. $29.98.
Fred Brannon, USA, 1949

Fighting Devil Dogs (The Tornado of Doom)
A Republic serial that featured "the Lightning," a popular master of menace who could destroy ships, dirigibles and cities and town with his awesome electronic thunderbolt. Out to stop him are those brave and daring "fighting devil dogs" led by U.S. Marine hero Lee Powell. With Bruce Bennett, Eleanor Steward and Montagu Love. B&W.
VHS: S06050. $29.95.
William Witney/John English, USA, 1938, 12 chapters

The Fighting Marines
The U.S. Marines must battle the "Tiger Shark", a modern day pirate who has thwarted their every effort to build an airstrip on a Pacific island. 12 episodes. USA, 1935, 214 mins.
VHS: S15597. $29.95.

Flash Gordon Conquers the Universe
The third serial adventure starring Buster Crabbe as Alex Raymond's creation Flash Gordon. Carol Hughes is the new Dale. They must battle Ming on the planet of Frigia, meet rock men and borrow costumes from Robin Hood. Charles Middleton plays Ming, as usual, for every drop of villainy he can muster. B&W.
VHS: S05543. $29.95.
Laser: LD75984. $79.95.
Ford Beebe/Ray Taylor, USA, 1940, 235 mins.

Flying Disc Men from Mars (Cliffhanger Serials #5)
A young aviator uncovers a plot by evil Martians to conquer Earth in this science fiction serial from the Republic studios. Starring Walter Reed, Lois Collier, Gregory Gay and James Craven.
12 episodes on two videocassettes.
VHS: S15083. $29.98.
Fred Brannon, USA, 1951, 167 mins.

G-Men vs. the Black Dragon
This thrill-packed 1942 serial exposes the infamous Black Dragon Society, pitting special agent Rex Bennett against the Axis spy ring intent on crippling the U.S. war effort. Expect crackling non-stop action loaded with futuristic robot planes, Oriental torture chambers, and even a deadly raven with a poison-tipped beak. 15 episode serial on 2 cassettes.
VHS: S11566. $29.95.

Great Moments from Serials

Clips from rare silent serials, including *Plunder* (1920), with Pearl White; *The Fatal Ring* (1917); *The Lightning Raider* (1919); *Hazards of Helen* with Helen Holmes; *Leap from the Water Tower—The Iron Claw* (1916), with Sheldon Lewis; *Shielding Shadow* (1917); *Steel Trail* (1923) with William Duncan and Edith Johnson; *Captain Kidd* (1922, with Eddie Polo); *The Third Eye* with Eileen Percy; *White Eagle, The Tiger's Trail and The Timber Queen* with Ruth Roland; and *A Woman in Grey* with Arline Pretty. 64 mins.
VHS: S08864. $24.95.

The Invisible Monster (Cliffhanger Serials #5)

A scientist and criminal mastermind called The Phantom Ruler implements a new plan for smuggling in dastardly aliens in this thrilling serial from Republic. With Richard Webb, Aline Towne, Lane Bradford and John Crawford. 12 episodes on two videocassettes.
VHS: S15086. $29.98.
Fred Brannon, USA, 1950

Jesse James Rides Again

In this rousing, pistol-packing cliffhanger, Jesse flees the law after being wrongly accused of leading the historic 1876 Northfield, Minnesota bank robbery—only to clash with hooded raiders pillaging farmers in his name. A frontier adventure at its gun-slinging best. 13 episode serial on 2 cassettes.
VHS: S11565. $29.95.
Laser: CLV. LD71998. $39.98.

Jungle Drums of Africa (Cliffhanger Serials #5)

A mining engineer puts an end to a villainous hunter on the trail of uranium deposits in this adventure serial loaded with stock wildlife shots. Produced by the Republic studios. With Clayton Moore, Phyllis Coates, Johnny Spencer and Roy Glenn.
VHS: S15088. $29.98.
Fred Brannon, USA, 1953

Jungle Girl

Based on the Edgar Rice Burrough's novel and starring Frances Gifford, this program features 15 action-packed chapters on two cassettes. "The best of all the jungle serials" (Alan G. Barbour, *A Pictorial History of the Motion Picture Serial*).
VHS: S34468. $29.95.
John English/William Witney, USA, 1941

Junior G-Men

The Dead End Kids and The Little Tough Guys join forces with the FBI to foil international terrorists and save the free world in this timeless, action-packed serial. 2-tape set, 250 mins.
VHS: S09211. $24.95.

King of the Rocketmen (Lost Planet Airmen)

Tristram Coffin is Jeff King, alias Rocket Man, who must do his darndest to stop the diabolical Dr. Vulcan from destroying any more of New York City with his decimator. The suit was re-used for the Commando Cody serials and the scenes of destruction are from *Deluge*. With Mae Clarke. B&W. A Republic serial.
VHS: S06053. $29.95.
Laser: CLV. LD72000. $39.98.
Fred Brannon, USA, 1949, 12 dha chapters

King of the Texas Rangers

This Republic serial boasts to be "the all time ace of action". It stars "Slingin' Sammy" Baugh—a popular football hero—as a modern Texas Ranger aided by the pre-Cisco Kid Duncan Reynolds. They must deal with such villainous types as Ray Barcroft, Neil Hamilton, Bud Geary, Jack Ingram and Kenne Duncan, a very tough group of hombres. 12 episodes.
VHS: S08328. $29.95.
Laser: CLV. LD72001. $39.98.
William Witney, USA, 1941, 195 mins.

The Last of the Mohicans

All the excitement and memorable characters of James Fenimore Cooper's classic novel come to life in this gripping adventure starring Harry Carey. 12 chapters. USA, 1932, 214 mins.
VHS: S15601. $29.95.

The Little Rascals Collection

This group of children is responsible for some of the funniest films from the 1930's and 1940's. These beautifully restored and mastered prints are introduced by Leonard Maltin, expert and co-author of the definitive book, *The Little Rascals—The Life and Times of Our Gang*. Each volume is 70 mins.
The Little Rascals, Volume 1. *Fly My Kite, Honkey Donkey, Beginner's Luck* and *Reunion in Rhythm*.
VHS: S21777. $14.95.
The Little Rascals, Volume 2. *Hook and Ladder, The First Round-up, Teacher's Beau* and *Hearts and Thumps*.
VHS: S21778. $14.95.
Laser: LD74823. $124.99.
The Little Rascals, Volume 3. *Teacher's Pet, School's Out, Love Business* and *Spooky Hooky*.
VHS: S21779. $14.95.
The Little Rascals Volume 4. *Readin and Writin, The Kid from Borneo, Sprucin Up* and *Pay as You Exit*.
VHS: S21780. $14.95.
The Little Rascals, Volume 5. *Bouncing Babies, Pups Is Pups, Dogs Is Dogs* and *Glove Taps*.
VHS: S21781. $14.95.
The Little Rascals, Volume 6. *Free Wheeling, Mike Fright, Washee Ironee* and *Fishy Tales*.
VHS: S21782. $14.95.
The Little Rascals, Volume 7. *Helping Grandma, Spanky, Little Papa* and *Two Too Young*.
VHS: S21783. $14.95.
The Little Rascals, Volume 8. *Shiver My Timbers, Choo-Choo!, Divot Diggers* and *Bored of Education*.
VHS: S21784. $14.95.
The Little Rascals, Volume 9. *When the Wind Blows, The Pooch, Mush and Milk* and *Framing Youth*.
VHS: S21785. $14.95.
The Little Rascals, Volume 10. *Birthday Blues, For Pete's Sake!, The Lucky Corner* and *Arbor Day*.
VHS: S21786. $14.95.
The Little Rascals, Volume 11. *The First Seven Years, Hi-Neighbor!, The Pinch Singer* and *Rushin' Ballet*.
VHS: S21787. $14.95.
The Little Rascals, Volume 12. *Boxing Gloves, Mama's Little Pirate, Our Gang Follies of 1938* and *Hide and Shriek*.
VHS: S21788. $14.95.
Gift Set. All twelve volumes.
VHS: S21789. $149.95.

Little Rascals: Divot's Diggers and Mama's Little Pirate

Tee up for outrageous antics as the Rascals take to the fairway; Spanky and his daring gang go hunting for a treasure in a deep, mysterious cave.
VHS: S09242. $9.95.

Little Rascals: Our Gang: Don't Lie

Spanky, Alfalfa, Buckwheat, Froggy and Darla will keep you laughing in five of their most hilarious adventures from the original "Our Gang" series. Includes: *Don't Lie, Bubbling Troubles* and *The Big Premiere*. 54 mins.
VHS: S16853. $12.95.

Little Rascals: Pinch Singer and Framing Youth

When a radio station runs an amateur contest with a $50 prize, the enterprising gang holds a goon-show audition. In *Framing Youth*, comical crooner Alfalfa rehearses for a radio talent contest with the all-too-expert guidance of Spanky.
VHS: S09239. $9.95.

Lost City

The complete 12-chapter series, starring Kane Richmond and George "Gabby" Hayes.
VHS: S10607. $69.95.

Manhunt in the African Jungle

This Republic Serial, the forerunner to the hit film *Raiders of the Lost Ark*, chronicles the action-packed adventures of Secret Service agent Rex Bennett and his quest to obtain a sacred Arab religious artifact. His mission: to thwart the Nazis from obtaining the artifact, who want to use it to turn the Arabs against the Allied forces. 15 episode serial on 2 cassettes.
VHS: S11568. $29.95.
Laser: LD71706. $39.98.

Manhunt of Mystery Island

A brilliant scientist who's discovered a possible solution to the energy crisis has been kidnapped, occasioning a frenzied race to solve the crime or face eternal dependence on oil, in these 15 episodes of the Republic Pictures cliffhanger series. Laser disc contains the original theatrical trailer. 219 mins.
VHS: S17411. $29.98.
Laser: LD71704. $39.98.

Masked Marvel

Twelve exciting episodes in this Republic serial about a heroic masked insurance investigator who must defend this nation of ours against foreign peril. The time is World War II and spies from the land of the rising sun find that some Americans are ready for them. With Tom Steele, William Forrest, Louise Currie and Rod Bacon. USA, 1943.
VHS: S08329. $29.95.

Master Key

Directors Ray Taylor and Lewis D. Collins fashioned this 13-chapter mystery serial about a secret Nazi plan dubbed "The Master Key" to create panic and hysteria in war-time America. With Milburn Stone, Jan Wiley, Dennis Moore and Alfred LaRue. 240 mins.
VHS: S17493. $24.95.

Miracle Rider

The legendary Tom Mix plays a Texas Ranger who vows to save the "Ravenhead" Indian tribe from the ruthless villain "Zaroff." 15 chapters. USA, 1935, 309 mins.
VHS: S15598. $29.95.

The Mysterious Dr. Satan

The title character in this Republic serial wants to, surprise, take over the world. He has a robot to back him up. Only the heroic Copperhead can possibly stop him and protect society. With Eduardo Ciannelli as the Doctor and Robert Wilcox as the hero with the copper mask. B&W.
VHS: S06049. $29.95.
William Witney/John English, USA, 1940, 15 chapters

Mystery Trooper (Trail of the Royal Mounted)

Robert Frazer stars in this 10-chapter classic cliffhanger series.
VHS: S34470. $19.95.
Stuart Paton/Harry S. Webb, USA, 1931, 195 mins.

The New Adventures of Tarzan—Collector's Edition

This 12-chapter adventure serial was made by Edgar Rice Burroughs' own production company, and represents the Tarzan true to Burroughs' original vision from his famous novel. The story follows a brilliant archeologist who discovers an earth shattering secret, and enlists Tarzan to help him on his desperate quest. 244 mins.
VHS: S16631. $24.95.

Nyoka and the Tigermen

An action-packed cliffhanger classic that chronicles the efforts of an African expedition to locate the fabled Lost Tablets of Hippocrates, golden artifacts that contain a cure for cancer. But beautiful Arab ruler Vultura and her band of cutthroats seek the tablets for their own use. 15 episode serial on 2 cassettes.
VHS: S11567. $29.95.
Laser: LD71707. $59.98.

The Original Flash Gordon

A box set of the original Flash Gordon movie serials by King Features—starring the young Buster Crabbe. Action-packed adventure! Includes *The Deadly Ray from Mars, The Peril from Planet Mongo, Spaceship to the Unknown* and *The Purple Death from Outer Space*. Four videocassettes. Total time: 6 hrs.
VHS: S13887. $79.95.

Painted Stallion

An original Republic Cliffhanger serial in twelve chapters. Indians are on the warpath but are subdued by a mysterious masked rider who helps the U.S. government lead the first wagon train safely through the Santa Fe Trail. With Ray "Crash" Corrigan. 212 mins.
VHS: S13229. $29.98.
Laser: CLV. LD72014. $39.98.

Panther Girl of the Kongo

In this Republic Pictures cliffhanger series, 12 episodes of terror and shocks are presented when a demented scientist constructs giant, deadly animals out of ordinary species, unleashing a wave of death and destruction. 167 mins.
VHS: S17412. $29.98.
Laser: LD71705. $39.98.

The Perils of Pauline

Starring Pearl White, this is a ten-chapter serial made in 1914.
VHS: S07490. $39.95.

Perils of the Darkest Jungle

Linda Stirling, the queen of the serials, stars as the appropriately-clad Tiger Woman in the first of her six starring serials for Republic. Rumor has it the jungle is missing in this jungle serial as the villainous LeRoy Mason tries to steal Linda's oil lands. With Allan Lane as the good guy. 12 episodes.
VHS: S08327. $29.95.
Laser: LD71708. $39.98.
Spencer Gordon Bennett, USA, 1944, 196 mins.

Phantom Empire

The most unusual serial of the 1930's and perhaps the entire sound era features the original singing cowboy (Gene Autry) in his premier starring role. From Radio Ranch to the subterranean empire of Murania, Autry battles evil robots, mad scientists and unearthly terrors. 2-tape set, 250 mins.
VHS: S09210. $24.95.

Phantom of the West

An interesting serial containing ten episodes about a Phantom hovering over a western community, where one of its inhabitants is a killer. Ross Lederman directed Tom Tyler, Dorothy Gulliver, Tom Santschi, Kermit Maynard, Joe Bonomo and Tom Dugan.
VHS: S17492. $24.95.
David Ross Lederman, USA, 1931, 185 mins.

The Phantom Rider

A mysterious avenging spirit, known as the Phantom Rider, patrols the countryside, challenging the marauders and bandits and providing peace to the indigenous tribes in this serial. 167 mins.
VHS: S18374. $29.98.

Radar Patrol vs. Spy King (Cliffhanger Serials #5)

International saboteurs threaten America's defense system. Who will come to the rescue? A lively and suspenseful serial from Republic Studios. Starring Kirk Alyn, Jean Dean, Anthony Warde and George J. Lewis. 12 episodes on two videocassettes.
VHS: S15084. $29.98.
Fred Brannon, USA, 1950

The Return of Chandu (The Magician)

As the immortal villain Count Dracula, Bela Lugosi sucked the neck of many a fair maiden. In a rare performance as the romantic Chandu the Magician, he's out to save the neck of an exotic Egyptian Princess who's to be sacrificed on a South Sea island. The hand is quicker than the eye in this suspenseful tropical adventure with plenty of tricks and plot twists. Complete serial. 206 mins.
VHS: S11262. $24.95.

Riders of Death Valley

During the California gold rush, vigilantes protect the mines of decent folk against the evil advances of enemy raiders. 15 chapters. USA, 1941, 285 mins.
VHS: S15603. $29.95.

Robinson Crusoe of Clipper Island

An original Republic Cliffhanger serial in fourteen chapters. An airlines tropical island base is mysteriously destroyed and investigator Ray Mala journeys to Clipper Island to uncover the identity of the saboteurs. Is it a newly arrived passenger or the is it the natives' High Priest? Fourteen segments set in the South Seas. 256 mins.
VHS: S13230. $29.98.
Laser: CLV. **LD72024. $39.98.**

S.O.S. Coastguard

An original Republic Cliffhanger serial presented in twelve chapters. Bela Lugosi is Boroff, a diabolical scientist who has created a deadly disintegrating gas. It's up to Ralph Byrd and the U.S. Coastguard to prevent Boroff from delivering his lethal invention to menacing foreign powers. Good special effects. 224 mins.
VHS: S13231. $29.98.
Laser: CLV. **LD72032. $39.98.**

The Serial Collection

Includes the original crime-fighting superheroes cliffhangers shown as weekly installments in theaters in the '40s and '50s. Each series contains 15 episodes on two tapes.

Batman & Robin. Join the Dynamic Duo as they combat the Wizard, a villain who has all of Gotham City at his mercy, in this action adventure originally shown in theaters in 1949. With Lyle Talbot *(Plan 9 from Outer Space)* as Police Commissioner Gordon. Directed by Spencer Gordon Bennet, USA, 1949, 252 mins.
VHS: S31450. $29.95.

Blackhawk. The Blackhawks, a heroic squadron of international freedom fighters, take to the skies to battle devilish saboteurs in this action serial which was originally shown in theaters in 1952. With Kirk Alyn. Directed by Spencer Benet and Fred F. Sears, USA, 1952, 242 mins.
VHS: S31448. $29.95.

The Shadow. Victor Jory stars as The Shadow, legendary crime-fighting supersleuth of pulp fiction magazines and radio fame, in this action adventure originally shown in theaters in 1940. USA, 1949, 285 mins.
VHS: S31449. $29.95.

Shadow of Chinatown (The Yellow Phantom)

Bela Lugosi stars in this fifteen-chapter serial as Victor Poten, a mad scientist hired to drive Chinese merchants out of business on the West Coast. More money was said to be spent on the salaries of Lugosi and co-star Bruce Bennett than on the production values. B&W.
VHS: S04001. $24.95.
Bob Hill, USA, 1936, 70 mins.

Sky Raiders

Donald Woods stars in one of the most sensational sky-serials ever made. Amazing air adventure as heroes battle spies in the sky. 12 chapters.
VHS: S34469. $19.95.
Ford Beebe/Ray Taylor, USA, 1941

Son of Zorro

Son of Zorro chronicles the efforts of a returning Cavalry officer to battle the forces of outlawry that have left his home in a state of disorder. To combat his foes he dons the garb of his famous ancestor, Zorro, and becomes an avenging masked rider. Told in 13 episodes. 1947, 164 mins.
VHS: S08326. $29.95.
Laser: CLV. **LD72031. $39.98.**

Spy Smasher

Republic's second favorite serial hero after Captain Marvel was also a comic book hero. For the movies Kane Richmond was aided by a newly added twin brother in his fight against the Nazi menace. With Sam Flint, Marguerite Chapman, Hans Schumm and Tristram Coffin. 12 action-packed episodes. USA, 1942.
VHS: S08330. $29.95.

Tarzan and His Mate

Johnny Weissmuller and Maureen O'Sullivan star in this epic story of jungle romance. In this one Tarzan pounces on lions, wrestles crocodiles and defeats a charging rhino to protect his precious mate.
VHS: S14309. $19.98.
Jack Conway, USA, 1934, 93 mins.

Tarzan Escapes

One of the all-time best of the classic MGM *Tarzan* series, *Tarzan Escapes* begins when a safari leader snares Tarzan in a steel cage, planning to exhibit him in a freak show. But as long as they're in the jungle, they're on Tarzan's turf. Johnny Weissmuller and Maureen O'Sullivan star.
VHS: S14310. $19.98.
Richard Thorpe, USA, 1936, 95 mins.

Tarzan Finds a Son

Tarzan (Johnny Weissmuller) and Jane (Maureen O'Sullivan) adopt "Boy," the lone survivor of a plane crash, and fight off the young man's various relatives. With Johnny Sheffield and Ian Hunter.
VHS: S17905. $19.98.
Richard Thorpe, USA, 1939, 90 mins.

Tarzan the Tiger

A complete, early version of Tarzan, directed by Henry MacRae, with Frank Merrill, Natalie Kingston and Al Ferguson. Produced as a serial, this is the complete, 15-chapter version.
VHS: S08863. $49.95.
Henry MacRae, USA, 1929

Tarzan's New York Adventure

Tarzan (Johnny Weissmuller) and Jane (Maureen O'Sullivan) go on a cross-Atlantic journey to rescue "Boy," who's been kidnapped by evil circus promoters. With Johnny Sheffield, Virginia Grey and Charles Bickford.
VHS: S17906. $19.98.
Richard Thorpe, USA, 1942, 72 mins.

Tarzan's Secret Treasure

Tarzan (Johnny Weissmuller) enlists the aid of a skillful photographer when Jane (Maureen O'Sullivan) and "Boy" (Johnny Sheffield) are kidnapped by three greedy gold seekers. With Reginald Owen, Barry Fitzgerald and Tom Conway.
VHS: S17907. $19.98.
Richard Thorpe, USA, 1941, 81 mins.

Tim Tyler's Luck

This rare Universal 12-chapter serial is now available from an excellent original print. Directed by Ford Beebe and starring Frankie Thomas, Frances Robinson, Al Shean, Norman Willis. 235 mins.
VHS: S13276. $29.95.

Trader Tom and the China Seas

Set against a backdrop of romance, danger and espionage, this serial focuses on two undercover agents, an island trader and a shipwrecked woman, who join forces to help the UN safeguard the strategically important Asian corridor. 167 mins.
VHS: S18373. $29.98.

Undersea Kingdom

An original Republic Cliffhanger serial in twelve chapters. When mysterious man-made earthquakes threaten the world, navy lieutenant Ray "Crash" Corrigan leads a submarine expedition to the undersea kingdom of Atlantis. There, naturally, he finds the Atlantians at war with the fiendish Unga Khan, and must use his super-human strength to save the world. 226 mins.
VHS: S13228. $29.98.
Laser: CLV. **LD72041. $39.98.**

The Whispering Shadow

Bela Lugosi plays Professor Adam Strang, the proprietor of the House of Mystery Waxworks. Is he the mysterious madman seeking world domination in this 12-part serial, who kills with a radio death ray and speaks to his followers over a television monitor? Rent this tape and find out. B&W.
VHS: S10103. $29.95.
Al Herman/Colbert Clark, USA, 1933, 228 mins.

Zombies of the Stratosphere (Satan's Satellites)

Judd Holdren *(Commander Cody)* is Larry Martin, a caped rocketeer who goes to Mars to alter an evil plot that could destroy the Earth with Atomic weapons. Leonard Nimoy is featured as an evil Martian henchman named Narab. Much of the footage is borrowed from earlier Republic serials. B&W.
VHS: S06052. $29.95.
Laser: CLV. **LD72042. $39.98.**
Fred Brannon, USA, 1952, 12 chapters

Zorro Rides Again

The super-heroic Zorro keeps justice on track when ruthless raiders attempt a takeover of the California-Yucatan Railroad, in this collection of Cliffhanger Serials.
VHS: S33927. $14.98.
John English/William Witney, USA, 1937, 213 mins.

Zorro's Black Whip

An original Republic Cliffhanger serial in twelve chapters. This Zorro's a woman! Glamorous Linda Sterling dons leather, lace and a black mask to avenge the murder of her brother by a gang of outlaws. She vows to protect the innocent, but first must survive avalanches, explosions and a gun fight a minute. 182 mins.
VHS: S13226. $29.98.
Laser: CLV. **LD72043. $39.98.**

Zorro's Fighting Legion

An original Republic Cliffhanger serial in twelve chapters. When the evil Don Del Oro stirs up the Indians and steals government gold shipments, Diego Vega (Reed Hadley) assumes a black cape and sword to become the legendary swashbuckler. Zorro upholds justice, here accompanied by his gang of "Avengers".
VHS: S13227. $29.98.
Laser: CLV. **LD72044. $39.98.**

TRAILERS & COMMERCIALS

America's Favorite Commercials

Explore how commercials have captured the fashions, sexual climates, personalities and fads of our rapidly changing world, in a fun-filled, nostalgic exploration of modern culture. 60 mins.
VHS: S33369. $19.98.

Baby Boomer Television

Relive television's Golden Years by a look at the promos for dozens of shows, including the NBC Peacock, Mickey Mouse Club, Howdy Doody Show, Flintstones, Honeymooners, Amos 'n Andy, Bewitched, The Lone Ranger and dozens more. 60 mins.
VHS: S26081. $29.95.

Beer Commercials

A collection of dozens of beer commercials from around the country, including Ballantine Ale, Budweiser, Gunther, Miller Party Time, Schlitz, Falstaff, Duquesne, Hamms (featuring Stan and Ollie) and National Bohemian. 60 mins.
VHS: S26077. $29.95.

Best Classic Commercials from the 50's and 60's, Vol. 1

From the Golden Age of Television come messages that urge you to grease your hair with Brylcreme or to drink Bosco Chocolate Drink. There are hilarious promos for Bonomo's Turkish Taffy, Old Gold Dancing Cigarettes and Double Mint with the Double Mint Twins as well. 30 mins.

VHS: S21339. $14.95.

Best Classic Commercials from the 50's and 60's, Vol. 2

Some of TV's early celebrities can be seen making pitches for the products of yesteryear in this great collection of early commercials. George Reeves, the TV Superman, spots Sugar Smacks using his X-ray vision, while Lucy and Desi do their bit for Phillip Morris. Nancy Reagan and Sandra Dee are just some of the other stars that can be seen selling something in this collection. 60 mins.

VHS: S21340. $14.95.

Car Commercials

A 60-minute compilation of 1940's, 50's and 60's commercials for cars, including the Lark, DeSoto, King Kong for Volkswagen and the 1964 Stingray.

VHS: S26071. $29.95.

Cast Commercials

Hollywood stars and characters push their favorite (and most lucrative) stuff. Includes the Beverly Hillbillies for Kellogg's Corn Flakes and Winston, Mr. Ed for Studebaker, Leave It to Beaver for Purina Dog Chow and the Monkees for Kellogg's Rice Krispies. 60 mins.

VHS: S26073. $29.95.

Celebrity Commercials

Louis Armstrong (Suzy Cute), Harpo Marx (Pepsi), Cybil Shepherd (Cover Girl), Willie Mays (Gillette), John Wayne (Camel), Ronald Reagan (Boraxo), Marilyn Monroe (Union Oil Company) and Groucho Marx (De Soto) are among the dozens of stars in this compilation of Americana. 60 mins.

VHS: S26076. $29.95.

Cereal Commercial Tapes

A collection of zany commercials that constitute pure Americana. Cereal Commercial Tapes Volume 1: Soggy Celebrities. Over 70 commercials that pour milk over Superman, Space Patrol, Tom Corbett-Space Cadet, The Lone Ranger, Lost in Space (intro), Captain Midnight, The Monkees, Jimmy Durante, Danny Thomas and a full bowl of others. Color and B&W. 60 mins.

VHS: S09704. $24.95.

Cereal Commercial Tapes Volume 2: Famous Animated Flakies. Bullwinkle in over his head in milk, Bugs Bunny, Elmer Fudd, Yogi Bear and Boo-Boo, Daffy Duck, Snaggle-Puss, Top Cat, Cheerios Kid, Rocky and more of these fine cartoon actors in over 60 commercials. 60 mins.

VHS: S09705. $24.95.

Cereal Commercial Tapes Volume 3: Snap, Crackle, Poppourri. The rarest, obscurest, weirdest, oddest, looniest, and most eccentric cereal commercials to be made. This is the widest variety pack containing 60 different commercials all celebrating what America eats for breakfast. 60 mins.

VHS: S09706. $24.95.

Cereal Commercials

Over four dozen commercials for breakfast cereals, including Kellogg's Raisin Bran, Corn Flakes, Super Sugar Crisp, Coco Krispies, Corn Kix, OK's, Cheerios, Cocoa Puffs and more. 60 mins.

VHS: S26078. $29.95.

Cigarette Commercials

Muriel Cigars, the Flintstones for Winston, Lark, Bel Air, Pall Mall 100's, Kool, Camel, L&M (with Nick Adams), Parliament, Philip Morris, Chesterfield (Men of America) and more than three dozen other commercials are featured in this compilation of tobacco's most memorable ads. 60 mins.

VHS: S26079. $29.95.

Classic Animation Commercials from the 50's and 60's, Vol. 1

Many animators found their way into television when producers realized that animation provided a quicker and easier medium than live talent. Fred Flintstone and Barney Rubble as well as Bugs and Daffy are some of the animated celebrities that are joined by the Gillette Razor Blade Parrot, the Hamms Beer Bear and the Cheerios Kid in this nostalgic collection. 60 mins.

VHS: S21335. $19.95.

Classic Car Commercials from the 50's and 60's, Vol. 1

Campy road trips are the order of the day in this collection of chrome- and finned-filled commercials from the golden era of American cars. Fords, Edsels, Buicks, Chevys and a Volkswagen make the most of their small screen appearances. 60 mins.

VHS: S21338. $19.95.

Classic Cigarette Commercials from the 50's and 60's, Vol. 1

Before the Surgeon General put an end to it, television and its greatest stars were in the business of selling cigarettes. To name just a few, Dick Van Dyke, Joey Bishop and Steve McQueen all make appearances in favor of puffing away. All the well-known brands are here, including some that no longer exist. 60 mins.

VHS: S21336. $19.95.

Classic Commercials

Take a nostalgic trip with this collection of the most memorable TV commercials from the 1950s to the 1970s, featuring famous Hollywood stars, fictional characters old and new, catchy tunes and phrases, and recurring popular themes. Four-volume set. 120 mins.

VHS: S35122. $24.99.

Classic Commercials Volume 1

Classic commercials of the 50's, including Old Gold's dancing cigarettes, Muriel cigars, Garry Moore selling S.O.S., Arthur Godfrey selling Lipton Soup and Dinah Shore selling Chevy, to mention a few.

VHS: S07060. $34.95.

Classic Commercials Volume 2

See King Kong selling Volkswagens, The Lone Ranger selling Pizza rolls, Lucy and Desi selling Philip Morris, Jack Benny for Texaco, Boris Karloff for A-1 steak sauce, Dustin Hoffman selling Toyotas, and more.

VHS: S07061. $34.95.

Classic Commercials Volume 3

Commercials for Hula-Hoop and Frisbee, Billy de Wolfe for Ban, Bob Hope and Dinah Shore for Chevrolet, Edsel, Barbie Doll, Ozzie Nelson for Kodak, Bing Crosby for Ducks Unlimited, 5th Dimension for Jello, and much more.

VHS: S07062. $34.95.

Classic Doll Commercials of the 50's and 60's

Baby boomers will suddenly remember all those dolls they once longed to possess, including Betsy Wetsy, Chatty Cathy, Tuesday Taylor, Tiny Tears, Revlon Dolls, the Playtex Baby and of course Barbie. These are just some of the doll commercials included from the Golden Age of Television.

VHS: S21333. $19.95.

Classic TV Train Commercials

Embark on a nostalgic ride down memory lane with those great toy train commercials of the '50s and '60s. These uncut commercials have been restored to the pristine quality of their original broadcasts over 30 years ago. 30 mins.

VHS: S30486. $9.95.

Commercial Best

Some of the best commercials of the 50's and the 60's, including Coppertone, K-Tel Stars, Alka Seltzer (Cave Man), Charlie the Tuna for Star-Kist, Pan Am and the Houston Astros for Desenex. 60 mins.

VHS: S26074. $29.95.

Commercial Best—2

A second volume of some of the most memorable commercials of the past 30 years, including Morris for 9-Lives, O Cedar, Goober for Country Pop, John Lennon for *TV Guide* and Louise Lasser for Toyota. 60 mins.

VHS: S26075. $29.95.

Commercial Jingles

Some of the unforgettable commercial jingles from America's past, including Coca-Cola's "Zing! What a Feeling," "Make Friends with Kool Aid," Pepsi's "Taste That Beats the Others Cold" and "From the Valley" of—naturally, the Green Giant. 60 mins.

VHS: S26072. $29.95.

Commercial Mania

An hour of the most incredible, insidious, and entertaining commercials from the 50s and 60s. 60 mins.

VHS: S05202. $29.95.

Commercials from Around the World

An international mixture of amusing and creative commercials. 60 mins.

VHS: S13098. $9.98.

The Fine Art of Separating People from Their Money

A visually dazzling, wickedly witty journey through the world of commercial creativity examining advertising's influence on feature films and the techniques that have made commercials an art form on par with motion pictures. Hosted by Dennis Hopper and featuring 60 clips from award-winning all-time favorite commercials with Leslie Nielsen, Dudley Moore, John Cleese and Rowan Atkinson, and offbeat interviews with Spike Lee, Tony Scott, Alan Parker, Harvey Keitel, Anthony Hopkins, David Bowie and Dave Stewart. 115 mins.

VHS: S31695. $19.98.

Good Old Days

Arthur Godfrey, Jimmy Durante, Championship Wrestling, Brenda Lee, Connie Francis, Fats Domino, Barbara Stanwyck, Ford Theater, Loretta Young, Lloyd Bridges, Jane Wyman, Pat Boone and Our Miss Brooks are among the dozens of commercials featured from the golden days of television. 105 mins.

VHS: S26082. $29.95.

Kid-A-Vision

Children are the object of the messages for Wheaties, Funny Face, Time Bomb, Twinkies, Fruit Loops and dozens of other sugar-laden cereals and candies as well as toys, chewing gum, stencils and, naturally, Welch's Grape Juice. 60 mins.

VHS: S26080. $29.95.

Next Week Promos

Dozens of advance promotional TV announcements for television shows, including *77 Sunset Strip, Route 66, Green Hornet, Untouchables, Racket Squad, Gunsmoke, Wild, Wild West, Cheyenne* and *Walt Disney Presents*. 60 mins.

VHS: S26088. $29.95.

Pop Culture Classics from the 50's and 60's

Rootie Kazootie, Howdy Doody, Andy's Gang and Bobby Darin are among the TV stars who appear in this collection of rare and early footage. In addition, there are bloopers from *Gunsmoke, The Red Skeleton Show* and *Twilight Zone*. 60 mins.

VHS: S21337. $19.95.

The President Fights the Japs...And Dirt

Ronald Reagan's career as an actor led to some ironic film roles, considering that he later became President of the U.S. *Recognition of the Japanese Zero Fighter* shows him as a young pilot who is learning to recognize the enemy. In *Borax Spots*, Reagan's turn as pitchman for Borax laundry detergent shows exactly how talented he is at selling soap. 23 mins.

VHS: S24073. $9.95.

The Return of Video Yesterbloop

Warner Brother Studio performers blow lines, get mad and say words that cannot be repeated in church. Among the hotheads are Edward G. Robinson, John Garfield, Bette Davis, James Cagney, Claude Rains and Ronald Reagan. Also Bogart and Bacall, Errol Flynn and Eve Arden. USA, 1941-47, 27 mins.

VHS: S05446. $19.95.

Show Promos

Television commercials for dozens of television's best-remembered shows, including *Love American Style, Bewitched, The Flintstones, FBI, Rifleman, Lawrence Welk Show, Avengers, Outer Limits* and *Lost in Space*. 60 mins.

VHS: S26086. $29.95.

Show Promos 2

Dozens more promotional TV announcements of shows, including *The Brady Bunch, Rifleman, ABC Wide World of Sports, Bullwinkle, Disneyland, My Friend Flicka* and *The Lone Ranger*. 60 mins.

VHS: S26087. $29.95.

Silent Era Trailers

This set includes footage of some of the rarest films of the silent era. Trailers with Greta Garbo, John Gilbert, Victor McLaglen. Included are *Barclays the Magnificent, The Rookies* and many others. 43 mins.

VHS: S13211. $19.95.

Son of Video Yesterbloop

A three-part collection of some of your favorite stars missing lines, messing up, getting mad or making off-color remarks. See Jackie Cooper, William Powell, Lou Costello and Carole Lombard cuss. Witness a cow taking a dump in front of Red Skelton. Also outtakes from *Gunsmoke, The Twilight Zone* and the world of sports. For mature viewers. USA, 1930-70, 54 mins.

VHS: S05458. $24.95.

Teenage-A-Go-Go

Teenagers are at the center of dozens of television commercials for Cheer, Twister, Clark's Teaberry Gum, Clearasil, *Shindig, The Patty Duke Show, Soul Train* and *The Ed Sullivan Show*. 100 mins.
VHS: S26085. $29.95.

Television Toys Vol. 1

A special collection of television commercials honoring marketing gimmicks from the '50s, '60s and '70s. With a focus on favorite shows and serials, toys featured include the Dick Tracy 2-way radio, the Man from U.N.C.L.E. secret bracelet, the Captain Midnight decoder, and Mr. Potato Head. 60 mins.
VHS: S16546. $24.95.

Television Toys Vol. 2

More familiar toy commercials from the '50s, '60s and '70s. Includes Colorforms, Fanner Fifty guns, Twister, Etch a Sketch, the Steve Canyon helmet, Duncan Yo Yo's, G.I. Joe and more! 60 mins.
VHS: S16547. $24.95.

Theatrical Trailers

Twenty-five horror and exploitation trailers from the 1930's through the 1960's, including such great coming attractions as *Killing from Space, Things to Come, Head for the Hills, Weird Woman, Cuban Rebel Girls*, and 20 others.
VHS: S05058. $34.95.

Toon-A-Vision

Animation in the service of commerce in over 50 commercials, including Woody Woodpecker for Kellogg's, *The Road Runner Show, Speed Racer, Rocky and His Friends, Felix the Cat, Beanies, Green Lantern* and *Mighty Mouse Playhouse*. 90 mins.
VHS: S26084. $29.95.

COMICS & THEIR CREATORS

Batmania: From Comics to Screen

The story of Batman from an obscure bat image in the Mary Roberts Rinehart novel, *The Bat*, to the comic book creation of writer/illustrator Bob Kane, to the 15-chapter serial. This is the first story of the career of Batman, from comics to screen. 45 mins.
VHS: S10947. $14.99.

Comic Book Confidential

From Spiderman to Zippy the Pinhead, from the scariness of *Tales from the Crypt* to the sophisticated commentary of *Maus, Comic Book Confidential* brings you into the world of comics. Includes interviews with Stan Lee, William M. Gaines, Lynda Barry and more.
VHS: S14598. $19.95.
Laser: CLV/CAV. **LD70103. $49.95.**
Ron Mann, Canada, 1990, 85 mins.

The Comic Book Greats: Overkill

This volume looks at the personalities and work of illustrators Rob Liefeld and Todd McFarlane in their comic book creation, *Overkill*.
VHS: S16960. $15.95.

The Comic Book Greats: Rob Liefeld

This volume considers the career of the gifted 23-year-old illustrator and his new work, *Die Hard*. Liefeld discusses his working methods and provides insights and lessons on illustration, layout and design.
VHS: S16959. $19.95.

The Comic Book Greats: Sergio Aragones

This work traces the fantastical career of Sergio Aragones, the illustrator whose gift for mining humor in the commonplace begins with his revolutionary work in *Mad Magazine*, animation work in television's *New Laugh In, Speak Up America* and *Dick Clark's Bloopers & Practical Jokes*.
VHS: S16958. $19.95.

The Comic Book Greats: Todd McFarlane

A behind-the-scenes look at Todd McFarlane, whose early assignments with *Batman* and *Coyote* led to comic history with his *Spiderman #1*. Talking candidly about his work with host Stan Lee, Todd reveals his plans for the future and some of his new characters.
VHS: S16419. $19.95.

Crumb

Robert Crumb, the multi-talented underground comic book artist, is profiled in this unique, in-depth documentary portrait. Emerging from a dysfunctional family, it's a wonder that Crumb managed to channel his peculiar take on the world into a relatively socially acceptable form. Part of the great fascination of this film is the revelation that his brothers, both also quite gifted, were not as lucky.
VHS: S27253. $19.95.
Laser: LD75491. $39.95.
Terry Zwigoff, USA, 1995, 119 mins.

The History of the Comics

This complete chronicle of comic book and comic serial history begins in 1900. Complete with colorful examples of familiar and rare characters, and interviews with the artists who created them. The History of the Comics Volume 1. The growth of the press into a mass medium at the turn of the century provided a framework within which cartoons and illustrations became known as "the comics." Among the characters popularized during this period are Little Nemo, Krazy Kat, Betty Boop, Dick Tracy, The Phantom, Little Orphan Annie, Popeye, Flash Gordon and Tarzan. 90 mins.
VHS: S16800. $19.95.

The History of the Comics Volume 2. Superheroes were born shortly before WWII, and saw active duty on the Allied side. This period featured many incredible characters with a variety of superhuman powers. In the '50s and '60s, events created a whole new cast of comic characters for the "baby boom" generation: *Superman, Batman, Captain Marvel, Steve Canyon, Peanuts, Beetle Bailey, Barbarella*. 90 mins.
VHS: S16801. $19.95.

The History of the Comics Volume 3. The underground movement of the sixties produced an alternative tradition using line-art. Many of these comics appeared in the form of "prozines" and "fanzines." Included in this era: *Vampirella, Conan, Furry Freak, Spiderman, Little Annie Fanny, "Creepy"* and *"Eeerie"* magazines, and more. 90 mins.
VHS: S16802. $19.95.

The History of the Comics Volume 4. Comic superheroes have now become more human, and face contemporary concerns like ecological disaster and drugs. Meanwhile, the independent comics carry on, faithful to the spirit of the underground in publications like *"Heavy Metal"* and *"Epic."* The weekly Japanese comic phenomenon *"Manga, Manga"* is often over 300 pages long, and provides a glimpse of what's ahead for comics in the 21st century. 90 mins.
VHS: S16803. $19.95.

The History of the Comics. All four volumes in one pre-pack.
VHS: S16804. $79.80.

Hooked on Comix

Finally a documentary explores the often misunderstood phenomenon of underground comic books. Nineteen of the most famous comics are covered, including *Hate, Yummy Fur, Naughty Bits, Yahoo, Bad Boys, Slutburger, Love and Rockets* and *Cereal Killings*. Music by bands like Beat Happening and Bikini Kill are featured on the soundtrack. 60 mins.
VHS: S23857. $29.95.

Masters of Comic Book Art

Award-winning author Harlan Elison hosts this fascinating look at the new generation of innovative comic book artists, including "maus" creator Art Spiegelman. Each artist is interviewed and their work examined in the context of the comic book art genre. 61 mins.
VHS: S08462. $19.95.

Sex in the Comics

Live characters re-create all the flamboyant, erotic comics from the 1930's and 1940's.
VHS: S01186. $24.95.
Eric von Letch, USA, 1982, 70 mins.

Will Eisner

A video portrait of the cartoonist famed for his strip, "The Spirit."
VHS: S10204. $19.95.
Jordi Torrent, USA, 1986, 15 mins.

fine arts on VIDEO

art on video

15th Century: Renaissance in Full Bloom
The flowering of the Renaissance in 15th Century Italy. Included are Botticelli's *Birth of Venus*, Fra Angelico's beautiful paintings, Venetian architects Codussi and Lombardo, the Bellini's Carpaccio, Andrea del Castagno and many others, as the camera moves from Florence to Rome, Ferrara, Urbino, Mantua and Venice. Produced by Rizzoli. 59 mins.
VHS: S13254. $39.95.

20th Century American Art: Whitney Museum of American Art
Three Whitney Museum of American Art releases.
American Art '85: A View from the Whitney. Documents the 1985 Whitney exhibit with lively commentary from the artists, critics and the curators; featured artists are Dara Birnbaum, Robert Breer, Eric Fischl, Donald Judd, Elizabeth Murray, Susan Rothenberg, David Salle, Kenny Scharf, and Ned Smith. Critics interviewed are Arthur Danto and Carter Ratcliff. 28 mins.
VHS: S07080. $29.95.
American Art Today: A View from the Whitney. An informative and entertaining overview of the Whitney Museum's 1987 biennial exhibition of new American art. Artists Ross Bleckner, Peter Halley, Annette Lemieux, Robert Lobe, Nam June Paik, Tzhar Patkin, Judy Pfaff, Richard Prince talk about their work, and art historian Robert Pincus-Whitten discusses the artists' concepts within the framework of post-modernism. 28 mins.
VHS: S07081. $29.95.
20th Century American Art: Highlights of the Permanent Collection. Presents the dramatic story of American art in the 20th century, offering an enticing look at the Museum's collection of art including such noted artists as O'Keefe, Stella, Warhol, Pollock, Rothko, Hopper, Lichtenstein and de Kooning, exploring Abstract Expressionism, Pop and Minimalism. 28 mins.
VHS: S07079. $29.95.
Gift Pack.
VHS: S07078. $79.95.

20th Century Art at the Metropolitan Museum
Philippe de Montebello, director of New York's Metropolitan Museum of Art, is the host of this tour of the inaugural installation in the museum's new Lila Acheson Wallace wing, which displays selections from more than 8,000 paintings, sculptures, works on paper, and objects of design and architecture created by American and European artists in this century. Featured in this video are works by Klee, O'Keefe, Bonnard, Kandinsky, Picasso, Matisse, Pollack, de Kooning, Rauschenberg and many others. The Metropolitan Museum of Art. 60 mins.
VHS: S05234. $39.95.

Abe Ajay
An intimate visit with the "master engineer, architect, carpenter and poet, all rolled into one" (*ArtsMagazine*), Abe Agay, in his Connecticut studio, as he explores the importance of his family and youth, recounts his student days in New York and examines the role of the Federal Arts project in American art. Manipulating arrangements, testing relationships, he discusses the importance of his craft as well as philosophy.
VHS: S31097. $29.95.
Daniel Keller, USA, 1990, 29 mins.

Academia Museum of Venice
The Academia, Venice's most important museum, holds more than six centuries of art. This program ventures into original locations to highlight the works of Titian, Veronese, Giorgione, the Bellinis, Veneziano, Tiepolo and Canaletto. 60 mins.
VHS: S20185. $39.95.

Africa Between Myth and Reality
Join artist and art educator Betty LaDuke as she travels to the African country of Eritrea to witness the daily rituals and color of village life that form the basis of her artistic vision. Back in her studio, she reveals how her vision is transformed, stage-by-stage, into figurative and symbolic compositions of myth, magic and reality.
VHS: S31080. $39.99.
1996, 28 mins.

African Art
African art, the booty of colonial wars, emerged in the West as a strange and exotic art form that would influence such modernists as Picasso, Matisse and Modigliani. But, as Kirk Varnedoe, Curator of New York's Museum of Modern Art, and Harvard Professors Henry Louis Gates and Cornel West explain, it is important to view African art within its own cultural context, as we travel to Mali to examine the art of the Bamana, Dogon and Djenne people. From the home of the famous Tyi Warra antelope carvings to the ancient walled city of Djenne, local inhabitants explain the function of art and the role of the artist in their society. "A successful and concise analysis. Fascinating viewing" (*Time Out London*). 47 mins.
VHS: S30786. $29.95.

African Art, Women, History
This documentary is about Luba Art and the relationship between women, art and history. Welcome to the world of Lukasa, a memory board, where kings are born only after their spirits have takenpossession of the body of women. Then watch history come alive. 28 mins.
VHS: S35164. $39.95.

African-American Art: Past and Present
A comprehensive survey of African-American art. With more than 65 artists represented, the program is divided into three programs: African Art, 18th and 19th Century Fine Art Survey, and 20th Century Fine Art Survey: In the Artist's Words. 90 mins.
VHS: S20319. $199.00.

African-American Artists: Affirmation Today
Sculptor Frederick Brown and painters Sam Gilliam, Lois Jones and Keith Morrison discuss their work, their influences and the importance of their heritage. These masters detail not only their technique but also how they overcame prejudice to succeed. 29 mins.
VHS: S24867. $85.00.

Alejandro Obregon Paints a Fresco
Demonstrating the techniques and formulas of fresco painting, Colombian artist Obregon works on a moving or portable wall in front of the camera. Many of the artist's most important stylistic traits are shown in this demonstration: exuberant color, emphasis on the horizontal, and masterly handling of glazes. Directed by Jose Gomez Sicre, 21 mins.
English Narration. William D. Clark.
VHS: S06748. $60.00.
Spanish Narration. Luis Vivas.
VHS: S06749. $60.00.

Alexis Smith: Life in America
Alexis Smith works within received forms of found objects. Her art combines storytelling, conceptual art and collage. This documentary explores the facets of Smith's art, related in her voice, words and actions, as she moves through streets and alleys in search of materials and objects. 27 mins.
VHS: S20312. $49.95.

Altering Discourse: The Works of Helen and Newton Harrison
This program interweaves narrative, text, music and visuals to provide insight into the notions of "conceptual environmental artists" Helen and Newton Harrison. 13 mins.
VHS: S20352. $39.95.

American Art at the Huntington
A walking portait of the Huntington galleries, in which a time machine allows us to move from the early colonial period to contemporary times, studying the works of Copley, Stuart, Sargent, Cassatt, Church and Harnett. 15 mins.
VHS: S19638. $19.95.

American Craft: Clay, Functional Pottery
Finished pottery from 48 American artists is shown in this video, including works by Warren MacKenzie, Cynthia Bringle, John Glick, Don Pilcher and Paula Winokur. A variety of forms, functions and techniques are also shown. 20 mins.
VHS: S22189. $39.95.

American Craft: Clayworks
The late 1960's were a time of great change for ceramic art. A wide range of bodies and styles came into view. Raku, bisque-firing, china paints, lustres, underglazes, decals and acrylic paints were just some of them. Artists David Gilooly, Patti Warashina, Jack Earl and Richard Shaw show some of their work. 20 mins.
VHS: S22190. $39.95.

American Craft: Contemporary Ceramics
This is one of the most comprehensive selections of recent functional and non-functional ceramics available. Eighty-five artists are shown on the occasion of the 250th anniversary of Joseph Wedgewood's birth. 20 mins.
VHS: S22192. $39.95.

American Craft: Contemporary Clay—Diverse Soup Tureen Forms
Seventy-five ceramicists, including David Gilooly, Warren MacKenzie, Patti Warashina and Paula Winokur, are featured in this examination of functional works. A variety of traditional forms and recent pop, sculptural and conceptual trends are showcased. 20 mins.
VHS: S22191. $39.95.

American Impressionist: Richard Earl Thompson
Born in 1914, Richard Earl Thompson has often been compared to Monet. Influenced deeply by the masters of Impressionism, his work is the study of brilliant colors and fleeting seasons, and the emotions they evoke. Find dozens of remarkable paintings in this essay on an often overlooked American treasure. 30 mins.
VHS: S16076. $24.95.

Andrew J. Paterson: Controlled Environments
Split-screen dialogue allows the artist to talk as two personas around the issues of art regulation, methodology and bureaucracy.
VHS: S32774. $50.00.
Andrew J. Paterson, Canada, 1994, 33 mins.

Andrew Wyeth: The Helga Pictures
Charlton Heston narrates this portrait filmed at Chadds Ford where many of Wyeth's famous Helga pictures were painted, and examines 44 of the Helga pictures, including 22 nudes that have created a storm of controversy in the art world, examining the meaning and mystery of Wyeth's work.
VHS: S05639. $39.95.
Gene Fairly, USA, 1987, 36 mins.

Andy Warhol
This is the first major profile made since the death of the American Pop Cult leader and self-styled superstar. Featured are conversations with a dozen of his closest associates—discussing his family, the art world, and those he worked with.
VHS: S07604. $39.95.
Kim Evans, Great Britain, 1987, 79 mins.

Andy Warhol: The Scope of His Art
Few individual artists have had the impact of Andy Warhol on contemporary society and its art. This insightful program explores the method and message of Warhol's paintings and graphics from the beginning of his career to his last works. 25 mins.
VHS: S09460. $174.00.

Anti-Credo
Rapid montage in Super 8mm film of the Rivington Street Sculpture Garden in New York City, now destroyed, by Swiss performance artist and founder of the Neoist movement.
VHS: S10194. $39.95.
Monty Cantsin, USA, 1988, 30 mins.

Apprentice to the Gods: Ruben Nakian
Produced by the Smithsonian Institution; an intimate portrait of the late sculptor's pioneering spirit through different phases of his career, from his youth at the Art Students League and Beaux Art to his series of monumental works. Includes rare footage of an artist whose career has spanned the most important periods of art in American history and places him with such Abstract Expressionists as Jackson Pollock and David Smith. 28 mins.
VHS: S06558. $39.95.

Arata Isozaki: Architecture from 1960-1990

An interview with the architect of the Museum of Contemporary Art, and a look at some examples of his symbolically imaginative buildings. Museum of Contemporary Art, Los Angeles. 1992. 7 mins.
VHS: S34316. $13.95.

The Art and Life of Georgia O'Keefe

She is one of the most beloved of American artists. From abstractions to realism, this acclaimed program explores in images and her own words the entire sweep of Georgia O'Keefe's vision. 29 mins.
VHS: S09464. $174.00.

Art and Recreation in Latin America

Games people play and the art and architecture they enjoy are presented. Focus is on the Spanish and Indian influences to be found today. Bilingual English-Spanish narration.
VHS: S07426. $59.95.

Art and Splendor: Michelangelo and the Sistine Chapel

It took Michelangelo four years to complete his masterpiece. The central element tells the story of Genesis, while side panels show famous prophets. This exploration of one of the Vatican's greatest treasures will reveal in detail the majesty of this awe-inspiring work. 35 mins.
VHS: S29923. $19.98.

Art City: Making It in Manhattan

Informed entertainment about the artists, collectors and dealers who bring to life the art capital of the world as it plunges into the 21st century. Presenting a cross-section of artists, the film discusses inspiration, aesthetic issues and the meaning of success. With Louise Bourgeois, Brice Marden, Chuck Close, Neil Jenney, Elizabeth Murray, Pat Steir, Ashley Bickerton, Gary Simmons, Ursula von Rydingsvard, Caio Fonseca, Rirkrit Tiravanija and more. "Anyone who knows anything about the perils of talking heads and flapping tongues on film must marvel at this insightful job" (Andrew Sarris, *N.Y. Observer*).
VHS: S31387. $24.95.
Chris Maybach, USA, 1996, 58 mins.

The Art of Andrew Wyeth

This video journal of discovery into the art of Andrew Wyeth visits Chadds Ford, Pennsylvania and transports you through the years between Brandywine winters and Maine summers, the beloved places which inspired Wyeth's masterpieces. 29 mins.
VHS: S09463. $89.95.
Laser: LD70779. $59.95.

The Art of Central America and Panama

The most well known artists of the region are shown painting in their native environments, demonstrating techniques and styles that distinguish the artists of this area from other artists around the world. Made several years ago, many of the artists shown have had a profound impact on the development of art in their countries. Directed by Jose Gomez Sicre, 29 mins.
English Narration. William D. Clark.
VHS: S06755. $80.00.
Spanish Narration. Luis Vivas.
VHS: S06756. $80.00.

Art of Folk Art

A general survey of the collection from the museum of American Folk Art discussing the definitions of major styles of folk art in America with museum administrators and curators, plus interviews with Pichio Odio and Malcah Zeldis, two prominent American folk artists currently living in New York City. 11 mins.
VHS: S07456. $59.95.

Art of Haiti

A powerful documentary from Chicago filmmaker Mark Mamalakis on the absorbing art movement that has emerged from the rage, poverty and passion of Third World cultures, specifically Haiti. The film includes interviews with artists Philome Obin and Rigaud Benoit and detailed retrospectives of painters Hector Hyppolite and Andre Pierre. The "program is…exquisitely shot and edited, giving the feeling that some of the paintings could have been made from your film." The works of twelve prominent artists are juxtaposed with voice-over narration, interviews and traditional Haitian folk music.
VHS: S03471. $39.95.
Mark Mamalakis, USA, 1982, 26 mins.

Art of Indonesia: Tales from the Shadow World

Girding the Equator like a string of emeralds, the 13,000 islands of Indonesia are dotted with steaming volcanoes, cascading waterfalls and magnificent temple ruins. This documentary explores Indonesia's ancient treasures and its shadow world—the rituals, myths, and performances by which the harmony of the universe is maintained. Shot on location in Java and Bali, produced by the National Gallery of Art and the Metropolitan Museum. 28 mins.
VHS: S13234. $29.95.

Art of the American West

Three sections: Before the White Man (Albert Bierstadt, Thomas Moran, Charles Wimar, Henry Farny, Thomas Hill, Worthington Whittredge, Frederic Remington), Westward Expansion (Charles Christian Nahl, C.M. Russell, Remington, Frank Schoonover and others), and The Old West Is Dead (the influence of modern art in the works of Thomas Hart Benton, Georgia O'Keefe, Ernest Blumenshein, Victor Higgins). 50 mins.
VHS: S07657. $89.50.

Art of the Dogon

Travel to the steep cliffs and arid plains of Mali in West Africa and discover the art of the Dogon people. Possessing one of the richest art traditions in Africa, the Dogon have for centuries created powerful sculpture to use in various rituals and in their daily life. Through rare film footage from the Metropolitan Museum of Art, witness the beauty of Dogon ritual dances and ceremonial worship. 28 mins.
VHS: S08476. $29.97.

Art of the Fantastic

A review of an exhibition of fantastic and magic realist art at the Indianapolis Museum of Art, including an interview with the curators of the exhibition. Narrated in English by Roger Wilkinson. 30 mins.
VHS: S08310. $30.00.

Art of the Western World

Michael Wood hosts this comprehensive survey of the Western World's seminal paintings, sculptures and architecture. This video series offers unusual historical and visual perspectives in four volumes.
Volume 1: The Classical Ideal. A white garment of churches in the Romanesque and Gothic styles are featured in this video. 100 mins.
VHS: S26880. $29.95.
Volume 2: The Early Renaissance. This volume looks at the high Renaissance realms of light and features of the Baroque. 150 mins.
VHS: S26881. $29.95.
Volume 3: An Age of Reason, An Age of Passion. The Age of Reason flowed into an Age of Passion. This video ends with the fresh view pioneered by Impressionism and Post-Impressionism. 100 mins.
VHS: S26882. $29.95.
Volume 4: Into the Twentieth Century—In Our Own Time. The final volume explores the art of our own time. 100 mins.
VHS: S26883. $29.95.

Art of the Western World

A ten-volume PBS series shot on location in Europe and America. Hosted by historian and journalist Michael Wood, the program studies the evolution of Western art, from its origins through the Reformation and Renaissance, Impressionism, Baroque, Modernism, Realism, and other significant movements. With each segment, Wood is joined by leading art historians who offer historical, social and artistic overviews of each period and its leading figures. The laserdisc version offers exciting opportunities to view hundreds of still pictures contained in each volume.
Vol. 1: Greece and Rome. Moving from the Acropolis to the Colosseum, from Athens' Parthenon to Rome's Pantheon, Wood examines the beauty and form of Greek sculpture and architecture.
Laser: LD72183. $99.95.
Vol. 2: Romanesque and Gothic. Michael Wood discusses art produced during the Middle Ages, placing special emphasis on Gothic cathedrals in Chartres, Notre Dame and St. Denis as well as important Romanesque churches.
Laser: LD72231. $99.95.
Vol. 3: The Early Renaissance. The birth of the Renaissance is the focus of this program, highlighted by Michael Wood's journeys through Florence and Venice, where he examines the works of Giotto, Masaccio, Donatello, Botticelli and Bellini, as well as the major Flemish and German artists, van Eyck and Durer.
Laser: LD72232. $99.95.
Vol. 4: The High Renaissance. The Renaissance reaches its zenith with the work of Leonardo da Vinci, Michelangelo and Raphael. Wood travels to Italy, where he studies Leonardo's *The Last Supper*, Michelangelo's *David*, the Sistine Chapel and St. Peter's and Raphael's *School of Athens*. The program also looks at Venetian artists Titian and Veronese and the architect Palladio.
Laser: LD72233. $99.95.
Vol. 5: The Baroque. Michael Wood studies the aesthetic influences of Baroque art and design, from the fountains of Rome to Madrid's Prado Museum to Rubens' baronial mansion in Flanders. Leading historians provide a social context for the work.
Laser: LD72234. $99.95.
Vol. 6: An Age of Passion. Political upheavals and social turbulence are mirrored in the wit and playfulness of Fragonard, the Romantic Delacroix and the neoclassical Ingres. The program also studies the valuable input of Goya and English artists Constable and Turner.
Laser: LD72235. $99.95.
Vol. 7: Realism and Impressionism. This program moves from the birth of modernism, with the flowering of Realism, signified by Courbet, to the birth of impressionism, including the works of Monet, Degas and Manet and the post-impressionists van Gogh, Cezanne, Seurat and Gauguin. The program also studies Pre-Raphaelites, such as England's Millais and Rosetti and America's Homer, Eakins and Whistler.
Laser: LD72236. $99.95.
Vol. 8: Into the Twentieth Century. In the 20th century, art enters a new phase. Picasso and Braque are the leading practitioners of Cubism in Paris. Klimp, Schiele and Kokoschka are behind Vienna's radical avant-garde. The program also considers modernism between the two World Wars, studying the works of Matisse, Leger, Miro, Calder, Mondrian and Frank Lloyd Wright.
Laser: LD72237. $99.95.
Vol. 9: World War II and Beyond. New York emerges as the center of Western art in the aftermath of World War II. This program examines the outbreak of Minimalism, the Pop Art movement, Abstract Expressionism and the Action Paintings of Jackson Pollock, Jasper Johns and Robert Rauschenberg. The volume studies the principal international movements of the 1970s and 80s.
Laser: LD72238. $99.95.

Art on Film/Film on Art

This five-part series of films on art conceived by various teams of filmmakers and art experts is an anthology of 14 films and videos intended to open up discussion of the way people interpret works of art on film and videotape. The films examine the tensions between art expert and filmmaker, the confusion between the art object and the art being depicted and how to reimagine content and form.
Program 1: Balance: Film/Art. The works include *The Payum Portraits* (1988, 15 mins.), directed by Bob Rosen and Andrea Simon; *Funerary Painting of Roman Egypt* (1990, 14 mins); and *MA: Space and Time in the Garden of Ryoan-JI* (1989, 16 mins), by Taka Limura.
VHS: S20330. $79.95.
Program 2: Film Sense/Art Sense. The works contained are *Giorgione's Tempest* (1988, 11 mins), by Stephanie Tepper; *The First Romantic Picture* (1988, 17 mins), by Trevl and Richard P. Rogers; and *A Window to Heaven* (1990, 20 mins).
VHS: S20331. $79.95.
Program 3: Film Form/Art Form. The works are Mark Whitney's *Leonardo's Deluge* (1989, 14 mins), Edin Velez's *A Mosque in Time* (1990, 8 mins), and Nadine Descendre's *Sainte-Genevieve, the Pantheon of Domes* (1989, 16 mins.).
VHS: S20332. $79.95.
Program 4: Film Voice/Art Voice. The works are Keith Griffiths' *De Artificial* and *Perspective or Anamorphosis* (1991, 15 mins.), Richard Greenberg's *Architecture of Transcendence* (1988, 9 mins.), and Anita Thatcher's *Painted Earth: The Art of the Mimbres Indians* (1989, 15 mins.).
VHS: S20333. $79.95.
Program 5: Film/Art: Subject and Expert. The works are Philip Haas' *A Day on the Grand Canal with the Emperor of China or Surface Is Illusion But So Is Depth* (1988, 46 mins.) and Judy Marie's *Gombrich Themes* (1989, 46 mins.).
VHS: S20334. $79.95.
Art on Film/Film on Art, Set. A five-tape boxed set.
VHS: S20335. $399.00.

Art Out Doors: Andre Emmerich's Sculpture Farm

An exclusive tour of this fantastic 150-acre sculpture Top Gallant Farm in upstate New York, and Emmerich's midtown Manhattan galleries. 1990. 15 mins.
VHS: S34011. $19.95.

Art Treasures of Spain

This collection of three videos documents the works of three artists dear to Spain. Goya, El Greco and Hieronymous Bosch were all masters of their time. Today their paintings are part of the rich artistic patrimony of the Iberian Penisula.
El Greco. A warm and brilliant examination of the range and glory of the work of El Greco is presented in this video. This artist used his Byzantine Greek heritage to become the symbol of Spanish thought and art. 60 mins.
VHS: S22922. $19.95.
Goya: His Life and Art. This is an introduction to Goya's work and the critical period in Spanish history which he recorded. Goya's paintings show Spain in the period spanning the decline of neo-classicism, the devastation of the Napoleonic Wars, and the rise of Romanticism and Impressionism. 44 mins.
VHS: S22921. $19.95.
Hieronymous Bosch. Though alive at the time of the Renaissance, this painter epitomizes the Middle Ages, particularly its bitter vision of sin. This video displays the works collected by Phillip II, now housed in the Prado. Bosch's visualization of man on Earth relied on extraordinary detail and imagination. 30 mins.
VHS: S22923. $19.95.
Complete Set.
VHS: S22924. $69.95.

The Artists Talk (Los Artistas Hablan)

Five prominent Latin American artists are interviewed, including Raquel Forner, Enrique Grau, Alejandro Obregon, Ramirez-Villamizar and Fernando de Szyszlo. In Spanish only.
VHS: S21811. $40.00.

Arts of Islam

From Spain to India, from Turkey to Morocco, the art of Islam has molded the cultural eye of millions of people over more than a millennium. This program explores Islamic art as one of the great cultural forces in world history and shows how it captivates the eye and engages the imagination. 26 mins.
VHS: S09462. $174.00.

As Beautiful as I Can Make Them: The Art of Ken Done

A profile of Ken Done, one of Australia's most successful artists. Filmed in Australia, Fiji and Japan, where Done enjoys superstar status, the program focuses on the the artist's paintings as well as his consumer goods and fashion wear designs for his mulitmillion-dollar business. 53 mins.
VHS: S33898. $39.95.

Aurobora Press: The Monoprint Studio

Located in one of the oldest buildings downtown, this firehouse has been revived as a place where artists can work through their ideas in a nurturing, comfortable setting. Includes an interview with the Aurobora Press Gallery director in San Francisco. 1995. 15 mins.
VHS: S34023. $19.95.

Balthus

Explores the career of the acclaimed, reclusive, Polish-Swiss painter, known for his haunting portraits of adolescent girls. Shot on location in Switzerland, Italy, France and England, the program includes interviews with Balthus, his family, and close friends, including actor Phillipe Noiret, and the artist's reflections upon his relationships with Picasso, Giacometti and Rainer Maria Rilke. 51 mins.
VHS: S33897. $39.95.

Beatrice Wood: Mama of Dada

Even at the age of 102, Beatrice Wood continues to influence younger artists with her definitive, free-wheeling ways. She was central to the American Dada movement and is the last surviving member of this group. In this video she recalls her friends Man Ray, Picabia and others, and her ex-husband Marcel Duchamp. USA, 1993, 57 mins.
VHS: S27102. $29.95.

Behind the Scenes

Magicians Penn and Teller host this look at the creative process. The program examines the craft and precision of artist David Hockney, photographer Carrie Mae Weems, jazz percussionist Max Roach and composer Allen Toussaint. The program is designed to encourage children to get involved in the arts and expand their intellectual and creative capacities. 180 mins.
Tape 4: With Max Roach/Allen Toussaint.
VHS: S19361. $14.95.
Tape 5: With JoAnn Falleta/David Parsons.
VHS: S19362. $14.95.
Tape 6: With Julie Taymor.
VHS: S19363. $14.95.
The Complete Set.
VHS: S19364. $99.95.

Ben Nicholson: Razor Edge

Looks back on the life work of the man who jolted 1930's British art out of its doldrums with his uncompromising abstract style. 60 minutes.
VHS: S01780. $39.95.

Benny Andrew's The Invisible Line

African-American artist Andrew is a self-styled innovator. He creates collages and paintings that capture the lives of sharecroppers. It is a world he knows firsthand as he grew up amidst these previously invisible people in the 1930s. Narrated by Jeoffrey Holder. 28 mins.
VHS: S28408. $49.95.

Berthe Morisot: The Forgotten Impressionist

This painter was the only woman among the famed Impressionist practitioners, and she was influential with the better-known men of this movement. Obscured by their fame, she has recently become recognized again for her work. This video is based on the 1987 exhibit that rescued her masterworks from undeserved obscurity. With Teri J. Edelstein.
VHS: S22944. $49.95.

Beyond Tradition: Contemporary Indian Art and Its Evolution

Based on the award-winning book of the same title, this video gives a sensitive overview of American Indian Art and its development through the centuries. Emphasizing southwest cultures and tribes, over 300 examples of prehistoric, historic and contemporary artworks are shown to promote a comprehensive understanding and appreciation of the subject. 45 mins.
VHS: S15763. $29.95.

A Bigger Splash

An innovative blend of fact and fiction reflecting the world of David Hockney, arguably the most important and celebrated artist of our time. This feature incorporates Hockney's art and unabashed lifestyle in bold and daring ways and parallels his brilliant work in painting, design and photography. "Moving, gossipy and just a little bit shocking. Constructed in the studios, the swimming pools, the beds and baths of Hockney and friends who orbit around him" (*Newsday*).
VHS: S08116. $69.95.
Jack Hazan, Great Britain, 1985, 102 mins.

Birth of the Renaissance: Giotto to Masaccio

In this program, the camera travels to Florence, Siena, Pisa, Mantua and Padua to discover early Renaissance masterworks in these cities. Included are the art and architecture of Alberti, Brunelleschi, Luca della Robbia, Donatello, Michelozza, Giotto, Martini, Lorenzetti and Masaccio. Produced by Rizzoli. 58 mins.
VHS: S13255. $39.95.

Bob Branaman: Everybody's a Buddha

Filmmaker/printmaker/painter Bob Branaman's work encompasses a broad range of subject matter, from the treatment of the American Indians to his love of the female form. This interview with producer Juri Koll includes books and artwork not seen since the early '60s. 1994. 15 mins.
VHS: S34026. $19.95.

Breakthrough: A Portrait of Aristides Demetrios

This Cine-Golden Eagle winner profiles San Francisco sculptor Aristides Demetrios, who creates abstract metal monuments of monolithic process, and is an intriguing portrait of an artist's dream as it gets transformed into a massive sculpture—on camera. 45 mins.
VHS: S04646. $39.95.

Brice Marden

In this film, shot over a period of nine years in the artist's studio, Marden paints large monochromatic panel works, diptychs and triptychs, and emerges as an articulate and provocative spokesman for his own work. 22 mins.
VHS: S08275. $39.95.

Bruce Edelstein: The Vessel

A sculptor and painter, Edelstein creates organically shaped vessels of the mind. Includes a conversation with the artist as he works in his studio in New York City. 1990. 7 mins.
VHS: S34037. $13.95.

Burchfield at the Met

John I.H. Baur guides the viewer through a visual presentation of the works of Charles E. Burchfield which are on display at New York's Metropolitan Museum of Art. Viewers learn visual style, techniques and the various stages of his three major works. 23 mins.
VHS: S20307. $39.95.

Burchfield's Vision

Burchfield's Vision examines the peculiar range and power of artist Charles E. Burchfield, who died in 1967 after producing more than 4,000 pieces of work. The program allows glimpses of Burchfield's journals, which offer an inside view of his feelings, philosophy and spiritual growth. 60 mins.
VHS: S20308. $49.95.

Caravaggio and the Baroque

Caravaggio, Correggio, Lotto, Parmigianino, Tintoretto. New masters find deeply emotional directions in art as the High Renaissance gives way to the Baroque. In Venice, we see Sansovino's plans for St. Marks Square, while Palladio invents the country villa. In Rome, architects Bernini and Borromini define the city with graceful fountains and St. Peter's Cathedral. Produced by Rizzoli. 53 mins.
VHS: S13252. $39.95.
Laser: CAV. LD70791. $99.95.

Caravaggio Conspiracy

Reconstructs the true story of an artful sleuthing operation: journalist Peter Watson disguises himself as a shady art dealer, and with the cooperation of Sotheby's, Christie's, and the law, recovers some of the world's most lamented stolen masterpieces. 60 minutes.
VHS: S05126. $39.95.

Carolyn Oberst: Small and Large Works

An interview with the artist in her New York City studio by Willoughby Sharp. 1991. 10 mins.
VHS: S34035. $13.95.

Case Study House Program 1945-1966: An Anecdotal History & Commentary

The Case Study House program, initiated by John Entenza of *Arts & Architecture* magazine in 1945, is one of Southern California's most important contributions to architecture. The program featured designs for 36 experimental modern housing prototypes by some of the most important architects of the region at that time. Of these, 25 were built. Produced in conjunction with an exhibition of the work at the Museum of Contemporary Art, Los Angeles. 58 mins.
VHS: S14588. $39.95.

Caspar David Friederich: The Borders of Time

Peter Schamoni's award-winning film on Caspar David Friederich, one of the greatest of the Romantic artists, uses his paintings, alongside dramatic film of the landscapes which inspired him, to bring the viewer close to his work. Dramatized scenes construct a picture of his life, and put his work in an historical and intellectual context. Heading the cast of fine actors, Helmut Griem takes the role of Friederich's friend and pupil, Carl Gustav Carus, who after his death published *In Memory of the Landscape Painter Friederich*, together with fragments from the artist's own writings. Carus defends his mentor and acts as narrator of his story. Caspar David Friederich himself only appears, like one of the figures in his paintings, with his back to the camera—a small, silent observer of the natural world, in which he saw reflected his inner vision. 39 mins.
VHS: S13750. $39.95.

Centre Georges Pompidou

The Centre Georges Pompidou, which opened in January 1977, is now the world's most-visited center for the arts. This documentary reviews the daily activities of this highly successful cultural center matching the revolutionary concepts of the institution with an imaginative use of video effects. 60 mins.
VHS: S07608. $39.95.

Cezanne: The Riddle of the Bathers

Paul Cezanne is one of Modernity's undisputed founders. Among his paintings, a special preoccupation with a specific theme stands out: that of "the bathers." This film traces the riddle of the bathers, a curious fixation that resonates across Cezanne's entire career as a painter. 57 mins.
VHS: S27566. $19.95.

Chagall

Explores Marc Chagall's life and work and documents the history of the artist who began his life as a poor Russian Jew, yet, before his death, became the grand old man of French Art. 55 minutes.
VHS: S02391. $39.95.
Laser: LD70782. $75.00.

Chancay, The Forgotten Art

The Chancay culture predates the Inca, and is documented in this fascinating film made on location in Chancay, on the Pacific coast line of central Peru. The textiles and pottery shown demonstrate the influences of other cultures on the Chancay as well as giving us a feel for the expressive, imaginative works of art created by this very early civilization. Directed by Jose Gomez Sicre, 17 mins.
English Narration. Paul A. Ritacco.
VHS: S06753. $50.00.
Spanish Narration. Luis Vivas.
VHS: S06754. $50.00.

Charles Santore Illustrates The Wizard of Oz

A major reinterpretation of the myth of Oz is presented by Philadelphia artist Charles Santore in the 1991 edition of *The Wizard of Oz*. This documentary explains Santore's artistic philosophy, reveals his creative techniques and displays pencil drawings and watercolor paintings in the evolution of his vision of Oz. 30 mins.
VHS: S31831. $19.95.

Chilean Indian Legends

"Susana Guevara Mueller, sister of Chilean artist Alvaro Guevara, friend of Picasso, and an artist whose works have been exhibited in the U.S. and overseas, has captured the charm and drama of ancient Indian legends in a series of excitingly colorful, imaginative paintings depicting the creation of the world, mythical monsters, sea sagas and the tale of a sacred tree high in the icy Andes." 12 mins.
VHS: S07537. $39.95.

Chinese Brush Painting

This ancient technique continues to hold great expressive promise for artists of all types. Part one introduces the basic equipment and techniques needed to practice this art, while part two progresses to more complex and challenging projects. 90 mins.
VHS: S24366. $19.95.

Chris Burden: A Video Portrait

During the early 70's, Chris Burden's shockingly simple, unforgettable performances took the jaded art world by surprise. In this documentary, Chris Burden talks about his works of the past 20 years: from the performances of the 70's to the sculpture and installations of the 80's. 28 mins.
VHS: S14582. $39.95.

Christian Boltanski

An interview with the provocative French artist whose works created from found photos and other human relics from rummage sales and junk shops often invoke the memory of the Holocaust and deal explicitly with death. 53 mins.
VHS: S31926. $39.95.

Christo in Paris

Since the days of King Henry IV, Paris' Pont Neuf has inspired artists. Here it is the focus of environmental sculptor Christo Javacheff and his wife Jeanne-Claude, and the millions of Parisians who watch them create an astounding architectural poem. Rich in political intrigue and artistic debate, this "love story" from the Maysles brothers tracks Christo's escape from Bulgaria, his early years as a struggling artist, his romance with Jeanne-Claude and the fulfillment of a ten-year obsession begun in 1975: the wrapping of the Pont Neuf. "*Christo* is another gem from the Maysles, the super stars of cinema verite" (Desson Howe, *Washington Post*). English and French with English subtitles.
VHS: S33770. $39.95.
Albert Maysles/David Maysles, USA, 1991, 58 mins.

Christo's Valley Curtain

Nominated for an Academy Award, a documentary about the construction of Christo's Valley curtain in Rifle Gap, Colorado, in 1972. "It is the finest film I have ever seen about an artist and his work," said *The New York Times*. "The surprise of the film is the enthusiasm with which this project was greeted by the residents of Rifle and by the construction workers who risked limbs and lives on the stunt."
VHS: S07492. $39.95.
Albert Maysles/David Maysles, USA, 1974, 28 mins.

Chromosome XL

Six painters work on a single canvas, sharing and changing each other's images, in this fascinating time lapse view of the artistic process. 1986, 14 mins.
VHS: S10191. $19.95.

Chrysanne Stathacos: India 2063

A work produced in collaboration with composer Andrew Zealley, Stathacos has created a vision of India 2063, her predicted location for the future center of the art world.
VHS: S32773. $65.00.
Chrysanne Stathacos, USA, 1997, 7 mins.

Chuck Close

The world of contemporary artist Chuck Close is explored in this behind-the-scenes look at his life and work. Featuring Philip Glass, Alex Katz, Kiki Smith, Jasper Johns and Robert Rauschenberg. 57 mins.
VHS: S34632. $29.95.

Citizen Barnes: An American Dream

A portrait of the eccentric life and behavior of Dr. Albert C. Barnes (1872-1951), who amassed a huge collection of art. The Barnes Foundation, which opened in 1925 outside Philadelphia, features an amazing number of French works, including 180 Renoirs, 69 Cezannes, 60 Matisses and works by Manet, Monet, Degas, Van Gogh, Rousseau, Picasso and Modigliani.
VHS: S19357. $29.95.
Jaubert/Pilard, France/USA, 1992, 52 mins.

City Louvre (La Ville Louvre)

This documentary goes behind the scenes for the first time at the Louvre. It was shot during the ongoing renovations that culminated with the opening of the pyramid. Now the public will see hidden aspects of this incomparable museum that have never been seen before. French with English subtitles.
VHS: S25106. $59.95.
Nicolas Philibert, France, 1990, 80 mins.

City Wildlife: Mice, Rats & Roaches

Sculptor Christy Rupp produced this TV show of science-oriented information about vermin, then the subject of her art.
An interview with a cockroach expert (who dissects one), curious set-ups, includes the classic shot of a rat eating a Big Mac Hamburger.
VHS: S10202. $29.95.
Christy Rupp, USA, 1980, 28 mins.

Claes Oldenburg

A look at the works and life of the artist whose giant soft sculptures based on food and domestic items helped define Pop Art. Features the artist and his wife, and contemporaries Roy Lichtenstein, Jim Dine and other art experts. 52 mins.
VHS: S31925. $39.95.

Clemintine Hunter

Mrs. Clemintine Hunter is one of the most widely acclaimed African-American folk painters. When she died at the age of 101, she left over 4,000 images behind. Her legacy recreates a past that stretches back to her life on Melrose plantation in Louisiana during the era of Reconstruction. Despite the hardships of that time, Mrs. Hunter's work captures a joy in living that few artists can match.
VHS: S27100. $24.95.
Katina Simmons, USA, 1994, 22 mins.

Cloisters: The Grandeur of Medieval Art

The Cloisters are a branch of the Metropolitan Museum in New York that is dedicated to medieval art. Phillipe de Montebello, the museum director, escorts viewers through these galleries featuring manuscripts, stained glass, precious objects and the well-known Unicorn Tapestries. 27 mins.
VHS: S24273. $29.95.

Collecting America: Folk Art and the Shelburne Museum

A stunning exploration of the thousands of American folk objects housed in Vermont's Shelburne museum. Narrated by Ann Sothern and hosted by John Wilmerding, the film plays homage to the craftsmanship of folk art. More than 100,000 art objects are housed in this unique museum dedicated to preserving American folk art history. 28 mins.
VHS: S06606. $29.95.

Conversation with Roy Lichtenstein and The New German Art

First there is a look at the Whitney exhibition of Lichtenstein works with an interview of the artist in his Southampton studio. In the second short feature, Donald Kuspit and Benjamin Buchloh discuss the neo-expressionist work of Keifer, Penck, *et al.*
VHS: S22655. $39.95.
Ross Skoggard, USA, 1980-1982, 40 mins.

Cowboy Art

Explores this uniquely American genre which helped transform the cowboys and Indians legends into a mythology. Explores the revival of interest in this genre, and shows "cowboy artists" at work at a Pueblo village in New Mexico and at a round-up ranch in Texas. 55 minutes.
VHS: S03584. $39.95.

The Creative Act: Paths to Realization

A nine-part series summarizing the reasons, goals and philosophy regarding the creative work of contemporary artists, including how each of the artists feels as an artist in today's society. Each artist recounts important early experiences which helped shape his or her motivations and ideas regarding creative activity. Illustrations from childhood and adolescence, student days and early works are included. The emphasis is on conscious aspects of the development of concepts and style. The series is based on *The Creative Act: Paths to Realization*, by Franz Geierhaas, associate professor of psychology at Trenton State College and a writer on art. Geierhaas introduces the series, interviews the artists, and summarizes the visits to the artists' studios. Each part is 30 mins.
Clarence Carter: Paintings and Printmaking.
VHS: S07542. $29.95.
Werner Drewes: Paintings and Printmaking.
VHS: S07543. $29.95.
John Goodyear: Kinetic Paintings and Sculptures.
VHS: S07544. $29.95.
Richard Kemble: Woodcuts and Sculptures.
VHS: S07545. $29.95.
Jacob Landau: Paintings and Printmaking.
VHS: S07546. $29.95.
Naoko Matsubara: Woodcuts.
VHS: S07547. $29.95.
Clare Romano: Paintings and Collagraphs.
VHS: S07548. $29.95.
John Ross: Paintings and Collagraphs.
VHS: S07549. $29.95.
Burton Wasserman: Serigraphs and Constructions.
VHS: S07550. $29.95.

Cubism and Non-Objective Art

The work of Braque and Picasso, Gris, Duchamp and Leger are explored, as well as the work of Kandinsky, Mondrian, Brancusi and others. A second segment covers the surrealists through the work of artists such as Dali, Magritte, Arp, Ernst, Miro and Tanguy.
VHS: S09074. $59.95.

Cuenca, Ecuador

A film about the II International Bienal of Painting held in Cuenca, Ecuador in June of 1989. Spanish, 30 mins.
VHS: S15289. $70.00.

Dancing Hands: Visual Arts of Rita Blitt

Unfolds the development of Blitt's art including painting, minimal pastels, acrylic and monumental sculpture inspired by drawings drawn with both hands simultaneously. 25 mins.
VHS: S07636. $59.95.

David Hockney at the Tate

Since he burst onto the art scene in the mid 1960s, David Hockney has become one of the most successful British painters. To mark the artist's 50th birthday, London's Tate Gallery staged a major retrospective of his work. Melvyn Bragg joins Hockney at the Tate for an exclusive, private view of the exhibition in which they discuss works from all stages of Hockney's remarkable career. 55 mins.
VHS: S10266. $39.95.
Laser: LD70115. $39.95.

David Hockney: Portrait of an Artist

In recent years, Hockney's painting has taken a back seat to his work in photography. During the filming of this production, Hockney invited the crew to his London studio, where he applies his photography innovations to motion pictures, and creates an experiment.
VHS: S01624. $29.95.
Don Featherstone, Great Britain, 1983, 55 mins.

David Manzur Paints a Picture

A short documentary showing this well known Colombian painter demonstrating the techniques of fresco painting as it is applied to a modern painting. Made during the artist's figurative period. He is a master of chiaroscuro, flashing beams of light with dramatic intensity across spaces murky with a velvety darkness. Directed by Jose Gomez Sicre. Narrated in English by William D. Clark. 21 mins.
VHS: S06747. $40.00.

David Raymond: Art Out West

A lively interview with David Raymond, an art collector, artist, and editor-in-chief of *Art-West Magazine*, San Francisco. 1995. 10 mins.
VHS: S34032. $13.95.

David Skinner: Paintings on Metal

This artist paints on found metal objects. Watch as he prepares for his opening on a warm Saturday evening in Soho. Willoughby Sharp Gallery, New York City. 1991. 10 mins.
VHS: S34021. $19.95.

David: The Passing Show

Celebrates the story of David (1748-1825), artist of the French Revolution and leader of the Neo-classical movement. Twice taken political prisoner and finally exiled, David continued to work, producing two remarkable landscapes from the view outside his jail cell window. Produced by the BBC. 50 minutes.
VHS: S02382. $39.95.

A Day in the Country: Impressionism and the French Landscape (Kirk Douglas)

Camille Pissarro, Claude Monet, Vincent Van Gogh, Paul Cezanne, Alfred Sisley, Edouard Manet and Pierre-August Renoir are all featured in this video hosted by Kirk Douglas. He takes viewers through the homes and landscapes which inspired the Impressionist movement. 55 mins.
VHS: S23504. $149.95.
Laser: LD74763. $159.95.

A Day in the Country: Impressionism and the French Landscape

Forty of the most important landscape works from the Impressionist movement, featuring the works of Monet, Cezanne, Van Gogh, Matisse, Manet, and others, are shown here. The narration presents an overview of the movement and specific commentary on the paintings, set to music by Debussy. 27 mins.
VHS: S05744. $29.95.

A Day on the Grand Canal with the Emperor of China (or surface is illusion but so is depth)

World-famous artist David Hockney invites the viewer to join him on a magical journey down a 72-foot-long, legendary, 17th-century Chinese scroll. As he unrolls the richly detailed painting, Hockney traces the Emperor Kangxi's grand tour of his southern domains. The bustling streets and waterfronts of 300 years ago come alive as Hockney spins a dazzling discourse on eastern and western perspective and their relationship to his own artistic vision. "Splendid!" (Janet Maslin, *The New York Times*); "A fascinating and quietly moving film" (David Bordwell, *University of Wisconsin at Madison*).
VHS: S14902. $39.95.
Laser: CLV. LD74627. $39.95.
Philip Haas, USA, 1990

Definitive Dali: A Lifetime Retrospective

Archival footage, feature film excerpts and interviews with Salvador Dali's friends and colleagues highlight this extraordinary dramatic portrait of Dali's unique life and career in painting, sculpture, writing, fashion and film. 75 mins.
VHS: S08388. $29.95.

Degas

Enjoy Degas' most important works and a taste of the artist's life in his own words. From the Metropolitan Museum of Art. 58 mins.
VHS: S34100. $39.95.

Degas, Erte & Chagall

Three of this century's most influential artists are studied in this film. *Degas in New Orleans* portrays the artist's little-known visit here. *Diana Vreeland* tells the story of Erte, his life and works, from Paris to Hollywood. In the third segment, *Marc Chagall* gives us a personal view of some of his greatest works.
VHS: S03968. $29.95.

Degas: The Unquiet Spirit

Explores the life and work of a complex man and an unorthodox artist, controversial especially for his treatment of women as subjects whom he often showed in "earthy" and unglamorous activities. Includes many original paintings, drawings and prints to show Degas' favorite settings—the ballet class, racecourse and railway. 65 minutes.
VHS: S02385. $39.95.

Delacroix: The Restless Eye

The film uses the artist's own journal to tell the story of one of France's greatest painters, who was also a passionate lover of music and an accomplished writer. The journal illustrates the places and people Delacroix knew, and treats us to rare glimpses of his childhood drawings as well as a new look at his famous masterpieces. Produced by the BBC. 65 minutes.
VHS: S02384. $39.95.

Delta Solar and the Four Seasons

The kinetic sculpture by the Venezuelan artist Alejandro Otero, set in the garden of the Air and Space Museum in Washington, D.C., is the subject of this short film. The sculpture owes its name to the Delta structure and contains dozens of rust-proof, light weight, steel reels that move with the slightest breeze. Highly polished, each reel reflects the ambience that surrounds it. Set to the music of Vivaldi's *Four Seasons*, the camera has recorded an inspiring visit to this monumental structure during each change of the seasons. Directed by Angel Hurtado, 13 mins.
English Narration. Renee Channey.
VHS: S06798. $40.00.
Spanish Narration. Herbert Morales.
VHS: S06799. $40.00.

Diego Rivera/ Los Murales del Palacio Nacional

Created 1929-1947 in Mexico City, Rivera's murals portray artistic themes and his controversial political views. Includes student and teacher scripts. 30 mins.
English Version.
VHS: S34474. $59.95.
Spanish Version.
VHS: S34473. $59.95.

Drawing on Life

A documentary about David Fincham, a gifted artist who ruminates on his work and life since he was diagnosed with AIDS. His exuberant humor counterbalances the conversations about the nature of art, politics, culture and tensions of being Catholic and gay.
VHS: S19641. $39.95.
Richard L. Harrison, USA, 1992, 30 mins.

Drawing the Line: A Portrait of Keith Haring

Keith Haring, successor to Andy Warhol's pop zeitgeist, was an artist whose playful, simplistic drawings made a serious commentary on the 1980's. His work—kinetic iconography whose roots are to be found in primitivism—speaks to our collective subconscious. As evidence of this, his paintings, drawings and sculptures are to be found throughout the spectrum of mass culture, from skateboards to subway walls. This revealing portrait of Haring's work and world views contains interviews with Leo Castelli, Dennis Hopper and many other leaders of the international art scene.
VHS: S12594. $19.95.
Elisabeth Aubert, USA, 1989, 30 mins.

Dream Window: Reflections on the Japanese Garden

The Japanese garden is for many a reflection of the inner state. In their intricate design and structure, they were conceived as retreats for people to tap into their natural world. The program contrasts the vibrant, dense milieu of contemporary Japanese life with the contemplative and interior landscape of the traditional garden. 85 mins.
VHS: S20320. $29.95.
Laser: LD72242. $34.95.

East Side Story

The artist's sculptural and philosophical essay on breaking glass and light bulbs.
VHS: S10181. $29.95.
Jim Sutcliffe, USA, 1982, 28 mins.

Edouard Manet

Award-winning director Didier Baussy has created an engrossing, comprehensive portrait of the great Impressionist. Close-up views of the artist's works, filmed at splendid Manet exhibitions in Paris and New York, are highlights of this sweeping biography. 60 mins.
VHS: S10268. $39.95.

Edouard Manet: Painter of Modern Life

Presents the work of the great painter in the context of his 19th century world. Manet believed that a serious painter should explore modern life, and his paintings feature Paris, its fashionable society, and friends, such as Baudelaire and Zola, whose writings provide the narrative background for this program. Cine Golden Eagle winner. Produced by the Metropolitan Museum of Art. 27 minutes.
VHS: S02386. $29.95.
Laser: LD70783. $75.00.

Edouardo Chillida

Spain's finest living sculptor draws inspiration from the culture and landscape of his native Basque country. The program profiles both the man and his work, capturing the power of his abstract sculptures. 60 minutes.
VHS: S02392. $39.95.

Edvard Munch

Considered by some the greatest film about an artist ever made, Peter Watkins' feature focuses on Munch's formative years, a life marked by the absence of intimacy. "A long, abortive affair with an older woman joins the ubiquitous ghosts of a childhood scarred by sickness and death. In the end, it's the paintings which do Munch's talking for him....A remarkable film" (Giovanni Dadomo). With Geir Westby, Gro Fraas and Iselin von Hanno Bart. Norwegian with English subtitles.
VHS: S20594. $29.95.
Peter Watkins, Norway/Sweden, 1976, 167 mins.

Edward Hopper: The Silent Witness

The great American realist painter Edward Hopper emerges in this thoughtful docudrama. It traces his steps along the Eastern Seaboard using his works, from museums like the Whitney, the Art Institute of Chicago and MOMA, as clues to his itinerary. 43 mins.
VHS: S25854. $19.95.

Edward Ruscha: Don't Want No Retro...

An exclusive look at some of the finest examples of this modern artist's body of work, from the early 1960s to the present day. He is considered one of the first modern conceptual artists. Museum of Contemporary Art, Los Angeles. 1992. 20 mins.
VHS: S34007. $29.95.

The Eight: The American Independence Movement

A survey of paintings by The Eight, a group of artists attempting to break out of the art establishment that dominated the early part of the 20th Century. The Phillips Collection, Washington, DC. 1991. 15 mins.
VHS: S34016. $19.95.

El Greco

Recreates the career of this great painter against the scheme of the Counter-Reformation which inspired his work. Filmed on location in Toledo and Venice, the film traces El Greco's beginnings as a Byzantine icon painter in Crete, and explores both the religion of El Greco's times and his personal spiritual quest, explored in his masterpieces from the great churches and museums of Madrid to New York. 60 minutes.
VHS: S02379. $39.95.

El Teatro Museo Dali

Visit the museum Salvador Dali designed himself, building up from the ruins left behind after severe shelling during the Civil War. His theater-museum allows the viewer a very personal look inside the mind of Dali—painter, author, designer, filmmaker, and this century's most recognized artist—whose mere presence could cause controversy: paintings hung haphazardly and without titles, divers placed outside the building complete with loaves of bread on their heads, a room that copies the face of Mae West; a virtual Dali universe. With *Un Chien Andalou*. Spanish with English subtitles.
VHS: S30480. $24.95.
Spain, 1993, 60 mins.

Embryo

Embryo is a visual and narrative journey through lost wax bronze casting. Katherine Michaels explores the intricate steps of the process and meditates on the symbolism surrounding the origins of metallurgy. With Native American flute music by R. Carlos Nakai. 28 mins.
VHS: S15744. $49.95.

Emma Amos: Action Line

Amos is an African-American artist who combines a colorful palette with non-traditional materials like photographs, her own weaving and African cloth in her work. Together these materials express something of her feelings and fears regarding the times we live in. Narrated by Anna Deavere Smith. 28 mins.
VHS: S28409. $49.95.

End of the Art World

Andy Warhol, Robert Rauschenberg, Jasper Johns, Michael Snow, Roy Lichtenstein and other prominent artists are the subject of this free-wheeling film by Alexis Krasilovsky. "With a quality of humor possible only with depth of understanding, Alexis Krasilovsky presents a catalogue of interviews with modern artists in which the shooting style as well as the aural material's format rehearses the personal style, the aesthetics, and the assumption of each artist about the nature of his art" (Artforum).
VHS: S07773. $29.95.
Alexis Krasilovsky, USA, 1971, 35 mins.

Esso Salon of Young Artists

A selection of works of prize-winning artists at the Esso Salon of Young Artists. Narrated in Spanish by Luis Vivas. 16 mins.,
VHS: S06752. $40.00.

The Etruscans

Recent art finds are used to depict the daily life of these ancient people, who survived for eight centuries on the Italian peninsula until they were defeated by Rome. 17 mins.
VHS: S15531. $45.00.

Eui Kyu Kim: The Elusive Figure

This well-known Korean artist creates spiritual, beautiful canvases that emphasize the curves of the human body. Includes an interview with the artist in his native tongue. Academy of Art College, San Francisco. 1995. 15 mins.
VHS: S34022. $19.95.

European Video Library

A 12-episode series focusing on European artists and art movements.
Caravaggio. Caravaggio was a revolutionary painter whose subject matter and dramatically lit scenes transformed painting throughout Italy and Europe. Despite the success of his work, he had a difficult career and a short life marked by turbulent interludes. 30 mins.
VHS: S26014. $29.95.
The Early Italian Renaissance: Brunelleschi—Donatello-Masaccio. Brunelleschi transformed architecture, Donatello brought new plasticity to sculpture and Masaccio achieved great breakthroughs in the realm of painting. Together these three men forged new ways, without which the Renaissance would be unimaginable. 27 mins.
VHS: S26017. $29.95.
French Gothic Architecture. French Gothic masterpieces from Chartes, Notre Dame, Amiens, Reims and the Saint Chappelle in Paris are the subject of this video. These works tell a history of technical breakthroughs and plastic innovation expressive of a monumental world view. 25 mins.
VHS: S26018. $29.95.
Giorgione. Even though only a small body of this master's work exists, Giorgione's intriguing style, expressive of a mysterious view of nature, haunts viewers to this day. This video helps explains such enigmatic works as the "Dresden Venus" and the "Tempest." 24 mins.
VHS: S26015. $29.95.
The Italian Romanesque. From Sant'Ambrogio in Milan to the Monreale Cathedral in Sicily, this video depicts the greatest achievements of the Italian Romanesque. It is a tradition of varied richness based on a pious world view. 26 mins.
VHS: S26016. $29.95.
Klee. All aspects of Paul Klee's life and career, 1879-1940, are explored in this video documentary. He left a great legacy of work. Special attention is given to the Bauhaus years and his relation to Kandinsky. 25 mins.
VHS: S26019. $29.95.
Leonardo da Vinci. This documentary offers an overview of da Vinci's life, 1452-1519. From his early works in Florence to the later accomplishments of the "Mona Lisa" and the fresco of the "Last Supper," this genius demonstrated amazing versatility. He also left a great many intriguing drawings illustrating amazing and imaginative machines. 30 mins.
VHS: S26020. $29.95.
Munch and Ensor. Edvard Munch and James Ensor pioneered new expressive methods in paint that helped inspire German Expressionism. This video examines the works and the lives of these two innovative and influential artists. 21 mins.
VHS: S26022. $29.95.
Palladio. This master of classical architecture fused Greek and Roman elements and thereby achieved a new Renaissance architecture. The video begins with a tour of the early Town Hall in Vincenza and continues with a detailed look at the many villas Palladio built in the nearby countryside of the Veneto. 28 mins.
VHS: S26021. $29.95.
Rome: Art and Architecture, Part One. This video offers a unique approach to the great monuments of the eternal city. The narrator follows an itinerary made up of the many fountains which water the city. Some were erected in classical times while others date from the late Renaissance. All the most important sites are visited, including the Forum, Castel Sant'Angelo, the basilicas, Saint Peter and the Pantheon. 39 mins.
VHS: S26024. $34.95.
Rome: Art and Architecture, Part Two. Once again the glorious, eternal monuments of Rome are on view, in this second episode of the series. 39 mins.
VHS: S26025. $34.95.
Titian. Titian's great achievements with color are thoroughly explored in this video. All aspects of this painter's work, including his innovations in composition and light, are illustrated. 27 mins.
VHS: S26023. $29.95.

Everlasting France
This outstanding art film shows the building and major works from the Legion of Honor affiliated with the Fine Arts Museums of San Francisco. Hosted by noted art historian Rosamond Bernier. 30 mins.
VHS: S15049. $29.95.

Exit in 3
A short story saga of a metaphorical investigation into the lives of three artists—Jerry Kearns, Elaine Lustig Cohen, and Hunt Slonem. Using interviews and video portraits interwoven with elements of fiction, this tape made by the New York alternative arts space juxtaposes the works of three different artists as a new approach to documentary that deals with the problem of translating the medium of painting into that of TV.
VHS: S07114. $49.95.
Papo Colo, USA, 1985, 23 mins.

Eye of Painter: Judy Rifka and Frank Mann
Bold statements from two modern painters in their studio are recorded on this video. It is shot with an eye for detail. Rifka and Mann are seen at work, which gives a sense of their aesthetic struggles.
VHS: S22662. $19.95.

Faith Ringgold Paints Crown Heights
African-American artist Faith Ringgold illustrates the folk tales of 12 distinct cultures who call Crown Heights home. This inspirational documentary shows how diverse cultures have contributed to the American spirit, using Ringgold's beautiful paintings. 28 mins.
VHS: S26040. $49.95.

Faith Ringgold: The Last Story Quilt
From the day she learned to draw, Faith Ringgold has worked steadily to master her craft and communicate her vision: to present a realistic view of the black female in society. This film is an insider's look at how one woman has fulfilled her dream of becoming an artist. Cine Gold Eagle Award. 28 min.
VHS: S18392. $49.95.

The Fantastic World of M.C. Escher
In this engaging documentary, the person behind the famous, heavily patterned artworks is revealed at last. From the landscapes in Spain and Italy that inspired him, to accounts from his friends, this film will explore many aspects of Escher and his art. 50 mins.
VHS: S21341. $19.95.

Fauvism and Expressionism
The Fauves emerged as a reaction against Impressionism and Post-Impressionism. Early modern art is explored through the work of Matisse, Rouault, Derain and Vlaminck; in *Expressionism* the work of Nolde, Munch, Kokoschka, Beckmann and others are explored.
VHS: S09072. $59.95.

The Fauvres: Plein Aire Painters
Once called "The Wild Beasts," these artists painted vibrant, colorful landscapes outside in the open air. They were considered radical in their day because of their use of bold colors without regard to naturalistic concerns. Artists such as Henri Matisse, Georges Braque, Claude Derain and their circle are represented from 1904-1908. Los Angeles County Museum of Art, Los Angeles. 1991. 15 mins.
VHS: S34015. $19.95.

The Feast of the Gods
Using computer graphics and animation, *The Feast of the Gods* shows how the 16th century masterpiece of the same name looked at various stages of its history. A collaborative effort of Giovanni Bellini and Titian, the painting was altered several times during its history. Filmed on location in Ferrara, Venice, Mantua and the National Gallery. 27 mins.
VHS: S11755. $29.95.
Laser: LD70114. $39.95.

Fernando de Szyszlo of Peru Paints a Picture
Fernando de Szyszlo was a pioneer in the field of abstract art in his native Peru. Absorbed with pre-Columbian cultures, the camera finds him in his small, secret studio that faces the sky and the sea. He paints undisturbed to the music of Vivaldi and Bach, taking up to three weeks to complete a painting as he works with transparent colors over opaque colors and must wait for each stage to dry. Directed by Jose Gomez Sicre. Narration in Spanish only, by Luis Vivas. 22 mins.
VHS: S06750. $60.00.

First Modern Sculptor: Donatello, 1386-1466
Donatello was the greatest sculptor of the early Italian Renaissance. A pioneer in the use of linear perspective, he also promoted the revival of Greco-Roman culture and realism in art. Filmed in Florence, Siena, Venice, Padua, and London, this program reveals the astonishing variety of his work. Sequences shot in modern day workshops illustrate the sculptor's amazing range of skills. Three eminent contemporary sculptors—Elisabeth Frink, Peter Rockwell, and the late Henry Moore—describe the inspiration they gained from his work. England, 60 mins.
VHS: S13745. $39.95.

Frame and Context: Richard Ross
Photographer Richard Ross discusses his art, life and satirical, deadpan style of photography. 16 mins.
VHS: S20353. $39.95.

Francis Bacon
Widely regarded as the greatest British painter of this century, Bacon's work further fetches more on the open market than almost any other living painter. This program follows Bacon from his studio where he starts work every day at dawn, to his favorite club and gambling joint in Soho, and explores how his way of life affects his vision of the world. 55 mins.
VHS: S07607. $39.95.

Francisco Oller
A film on the life and works of this 19th century Puerto Rican master, made in conjunction with the retrospective of this great artist's work in 1986. Oller, though born in Puerto Rico, studied in Spain and lived part of his life in France, working with such well known artists as Monet, Pissarro and Cezanne. Directed by Angel Hurtado, 25 mins.
English Narration. Renee Channey.
VHS: S06808. $70.00.
Spanish Narration. Ivan Silva.
VHS: S06809. $70.00.

Frans Hals of Antwerp
This program presents an extensive montage of Hals' canvasses and examines the various stages in his work. 54 mins.
VHS: S16599. $39.95.

Frederic Remington: The Truth of Other Days
Near the turn of the century, Frederic Remington popularized the myths, legends and images of the Old West, and this program traces the career of the brilliant painter, sculptor and author. Hundreds of original artworks are showcased while narration by Gregory Peck, interviews, location footage, archival footage and period photographs create an illuminating frame around the works of one of America's finest artists. The program also explores Remington's direct influence on filmmakers such as John Ford and his continuing influence on today's popular culture. 58 mins.
VHS: S12367. $39.95.

Frescoes of Diego Rivera
Explores the great beauty and political expression in Rivera's most extensive body of work, examining the artist and his techniques, using archival footage filmed during his work on murals created for the Ford Motor Company, and location footage of his most recognized efforts. In addition, the film explores the man and his politics, creating a complex and fascinating portrait of one of the geniuses of the twentieth century. 35 mins.
VHS: S10306. $29.95.

Frida Kahlo
Sada Thompson narrates this fascinating look at Frida Kahlo, the center of the Mexican renaissance of the 20's and 30's, both as an artist, a woman and a tragic figure. A catastrophic accident at the age of 16 left Kahlo with severe injuries. During her recuperation, she began to paint, first portraits and later more complex works with the themes of death and her loss of motherhood. *Frida Kahlo* profiles Frida's work, her increasing interest in politics, and her tempestuous relationship with her husband, Diego Rivera. 62 mins.
VHS: S08477. $39.95.

Fusion Arts
Solstice events at the Rivington St. Sculpture Garden in NYC (now destroyed) unfold toward a climax consisting of a noise rock concert on the huge junk sculpture by Demo Moe. 1987, 40 mins.
VHS: S22664. $29.95.

Gaudi
This program details the methods and contributions of the visionary architect who reshaped our ideas and theories about form through his unique applications of function, reality and art. 25 mins.
VHS: S17223. $29.95.

George Bellows: Portrait of an American Artist
This documentary, produced by the Smithsonian, explores the life and works of artist George Bellows, one of the major figures of 20th century American art, with commentary by Margaret Christman, research historian at the National Portrait Gallery. 28 mins.
VHS: S02510. $49.95.

Georgia O'Keefe
For the first time in this film, O'Keefe appeared on camera to talk candidly about her work and life, showing how nature and the mountains and desert of New Mexico figure prominently in her work. Produced by WNET. 60 minutes.
VHS: S02349. $39.95.
Laser: LD70118. $39.95.

Gericault: Men and Wild Horses
The program sets the work of this enigmatic French painter against the background of his time. Events of the early 19th century are presented "newsreel" style, including archival footage from silent movies of the period. Called "The Madman" by his contemporaries, Gericault was a man in conflict with his own age. Produced by the BBC. 60 minutes.
VHS: S03583. $39.95.

The Gods of Beauty: A Portrait of the Visionary Artist: Mona Boulware Webb
A delightful portrait of surrealist artist and outsider Mona Boulware Webb. Now in her 70s, Mona Webb was a protege of Aldous Huxley and Krishnamurti during the 1950s. She creates expressionist art on a grand assemblage scale, and her greatest work is the quirky and mystical house she has spent the past four decades transforming. The entire three-story house is painted and sculpted in wild, psychedelic forms.
VHS: S27165. $35.00.
Niels Nielsen, USA, 1990-1995, 29 mins.

Gothic Art
Enter a shimmering Gothic universe and discover the elements that allowed these master artisans to pile stone upon stone-the development of the rib vault and the flying buttress and how stained glass is made. 27 mins.
VHS: S09491. $174.00.

Graffiti Verite
This fresh video details the history of graffiti art. From the 1930's and 40's when cholos and pachucos first started claiming territory with their names, this public art has developed into a worldwide phenomenon. It combines words and graphics that recall hieroglyphic writing. Over 20 of L.A.'s best artists are included, showing them at work or just relating their experience of tagging. 45 mins.
VHS: S28036. $19.95.

Graffiti/Post-Graffiti
Exhibitions at Sidney Janis, Fashion Moda and Fun Galleries were instrumental in popularizing and promoting the acceptance of graffiti art. This documentary explains the 80's phenomenon and includes interviews with artists Lady Pink, Crash, Keith Haring, John Michel Basquiat, Futura and others. 30 mins.
VHS: S22620. $34.95.
Art New York, USA, 1984, 30 mins.

Great Tales in Asian Art
Four mythic tales are revealed through masterpieces of Asian art in this video. Indian painting, Indonesian sculpture, Javanese shadow play, Korean masked drama and Japanese paintings on screens and scrolls are all explored here. This beautiful joining of literature and the visual arts was filmed on location in four countries. 82 mins.
VHS: S26927. $19.95.

Gustave Caillebotte or the Adventures of the Gaze
Called the Urban Impressionist, Gustave Caillebotte created dynamic cityscapes reminiscent of a series of snapshots. In his masterpiece, *Paris Street; Rainy Day*, a fashionable couple gaze at something outside the picture as people from all walks of life hurry along the boulevards. All of his works—street scenes, interiors, country views—celebrated these ordinary moments with extraordinary skill.
VHS: S31149. $39.95.
Alain Jaubert, France, 1994, 59 mins.

The Hague School
Documents the 19th century group of Dutch artists who took painting out of the studio and into nature, captured the vanishing rural beauty of the Hague, and had a profound influence on Van Gogh and Mondrian. 45 minutes.
VHS: S01800. $39.95.

Hans Hartung: A German Destiny

Born in Germany 1904, Hans Hartung was one of the most influential figures in the development of 20th-century art. A fascinating program that takes a close look at this experimental modernist and his "spontaneous" style. 55 mins.

VHS: S15294. $29.95.

Henry Moore

A moving portrait of the great sculptor of the century, revealing Moore to be a man of humor, compassion and sincerity, with many revealing close-ups of his masterpieces. Moore is interviewed on camera by Sir Hugh Weldon. 52 mins.

VHS: S04350. $49.95.

Hermitage Masterpieces

An 18-program, nine-tape series highlighting masterpieces from every school of Western art residing in one of the world's greatest museums, the Hermitage, in St. Petersburg, Russia. Programs include: *The Museum's Majestic Architecture*; *Highlights of the Masterpieces*; *Russia in the Age of Peter the Great*; *Decorative Arts of Italy, France & England*; *Art from Mesopotamia to Ancient China*; *The Art of Ancient Egypt*; *The Vast Sculpture Collection*; *The Classical World of Greece and Romance*; Art of the Middle Ages; *Art of the Early Italian Renaissance*; *Raphael, DaVinci and The High Italian Renaissance*; *Art of the Netherlands: 15th and 16th Century*; Rubens, Van Dyck and the 17th-Century Flemish Painters; *Rembrandt and the 17th-Century Dutch Masters*; *Velazquez, El Greco, Goya and the Spanish Masters*; *French Classical Style of the 17th and 18th Centuries*; *The Road to Impressionism: 19th-Century France*; and *Modernism: Matisse, Picasso and More 20th Century Painters*. 540 mins.

VHS: S31933. $119.95.

The Hermitage Museum of St. Petersburg—Series 1

This four-disc, boxed set highlights the masterpieces created between the 16th and 20th centuries, including those of El Greco, Goya, Rubens, Van Dyke, 17th century Flemish painters, Rembrandt, the 17th century Dutch Masters, and the French classical style that shaped the 17th and 18th centuries. The program details the emergence of modernism, impressionism and post-impressionism, the works of Matisse and Picasso, and 20th century art. 240 mins.

Laser: LD71765. $189.95.

The Hermitage Museum of St. Petersburg—Series 2

Researched by the Hermitage Museum of St. Petersburg, Russia, this program traces post-Renaissance art and sculpture from Russia in the early 18th century, its Oriental art collection, and the decorative art of Italy, France and England. The program also looks at ancient Egypt and Greek and Roman classicism, the Middle Ages and early Italian Renaissance, and concludes with the High Italian Renaissance and art of the Netherlands, from the 15th and 16th centuries. 300 mins.

Laser: LD71766. $169.95.

The Hermitage: A Russian Odyssey

St. Petersburg's premier museum houses one of the world's greatest art collections, assembled by the Czars of Russia over centuries of conquest and patronage. Noted commentator, journalist and critic Rod Macleish leads the viewer through 300 years of history and art in an exploration of this storied collection.

Part I, Catherine the Great: A Lust for Art. Peter the Great built St. Petersburg for the glory of his dynasty. In this episode the role of this monarch and the pivotal influence of his successor, Catherine, are examined. The Queen is credited with bringing Western culture into Russia. She amassed a great quantity of artworks by such masters as Rembrandt, Rubens, Breughel and Watteau in less than 40 years, resulting in a collection greater than the Louvre had assembled in over 400 years.

VHS: S21366. $29.95.

Part II, Tyrants and Heroes: The Nineteenth Century Czars. The Napoleonic invasion and a succession of weak Czars left their imprint on the Hermitage. It was during this era, however, that the great collection of Scythian gold from prehistoric Russia was discovered and added to the collection.

VHS: S21367. $29.95.

Part III, From Czars to Commissars: A Museum Survives. Preserving this collection during the Russian Revolution and the horrendous 900-day Nazi siege of the city was a momentous task. Despite these depredations, the collection survived and grew to include 20th-century masters like Picasso, Matisse and Renoir.

VHS: S21368. $29.95.

Complete Set. Three tapes.

VHS: S21369. $79.95.

History of Poland in Painting

A survey of the major historical events of the country through the artistic visions of Poland's top painters: Jan Matejko, Wojciech Kossak, Jacek Malczewski, Piotr Michalowski, Artur Grottger. All the best in the tradition of Polish historical painting.

VHS: S15579. $39.95.

Bozena Walter, Poland, 1988, 109 mins.

Hogarth's Progress

Commemorating the 300th anniversary of William Hogarth's birth, this program presents interviews with experts to guide viewers through Hogarth's works, which influenced both the history of art and the English sense of humor. 50 mins.

VHS: S33405. $39.95.

Homage to Chagall

A study of the life and works of the great Russian artist, superbly filmed in color, and with narration by James Mason. Included is rare footage of Chagall and Madame Chagall—"an affectionate and visually beautiful celebration of both the man and his art" (*New York Times*). In English.

VHS: S04722. $79.95.
Laser: LD71044. $19.98.

Harry Rasky, Canada, 1977, 90 mins.

Horace Pippin

An appreciation of the striking color, originality and directness of self-taught African-American artist Horace Pippin. 28 mins.

VHS: S31744. $39.95.

Howard Hodgkin

Profiles Howard Hodgkin, one of the 20th century's foremost British artists. Filmed in Venice and featuring interviews with Hodgkin, artist David Hockney and art critics Andrew Graham-Dixon, Sarah Kent and David Sylvester. 52 mins.

VHS: S33403. $39.95.

Howard Terpning: The Storyteller

Howard Terpning's paintings function as visual stories depicting Native Americans. Along with the works, this video shows the artist at work. His compositions offer a glimpse of a lifestyle rarely seen elsewhere. 30 mins.

VHS: S26806. $49.95.

Howardena Pindell: Atomizing Art

Howardena Pindell is an uncompromising artist with an insight into life spanning from the tiniest particle known to man, the atom, to the largest social issues of our time, including class, racism and sexism. Howardena is a passionate artist and social critic whose art demands an unusually aggressive and challenging process of self-examination. 28 mins.

VHS: S35163. $39.95.

The Hudson River and Its Painters

The mid-nineteenth century saw the growth of America's first native school of landscape painters, artists inspired by the compelling beauty of the Hudson River Valley, who portrayed this and other romantic wilderness areas with an almost mystical reverence. This video explores the life and work of the major artists of what came to be known as the Hudson River School—Thomas Cole, Asher Durand, Frederic Church, Albert Bierstadt, John Kensett, Jasper Cropsey, Worthington Whittredge, Sanford Gifford, and George Inness. It presents more than 200 paintings, prints and photographs of the period and juxtaposes them with dramatic location photography of the Hudson River area. The Hudson Company in association with The Metropolitan Museum of Art. 57 mins.

VHS: S05233. $39.95.

Hungers of the Soul: Be Gardiner, Stone Carver

Shot on location in Honduras and North Carolina, this documentary shows the creative life of the famed Southern sculptor Be Gardiner. Her work is prized throughout the Southeastern United States.

VHS: S27101. $39.95.

Gorham Kindhem, USA, 1994, 54 mins.

II International Biennial of Painting: Cuenca-Ecuador

A special exhibition of contemporary Latin American art was held in the Museum of Modern Art at Cuenca, Ecuador. Mario Martinez narrates this aesthetic journey, which also includes general information about the historic city of Cuenca. Spanish language with no subtitles. 30 mins.

VHS: S21813. $59.95.

Impressionism and Post Impressionism

Developed by Gale Murray, Ph.D. Shows the brilliance of Monet, Renoir, Degas, Manet and others, and then the harmony of work and color in the work of Cezanne, order and permanence of Seurat, dynamism of Van Gogh, Toulouse-Lautrec. 44 mins.

VHS: S07656. $59.95.

Impressionism Boxed Set

Three artists, Monet, Degas and Van Gogh, are revealed in separate tapes devoted to each artist. Their legacy to painting is revealed through careful analysis of their works. 153 mins.

VHS: S24795. $79.95.

Impressionism: A Visual Revolution

Winner of the Gold Medal at the National Educational Film Festival, this colorful history is of the revolutionary Impressionist movement. Viewers observe how principles of color, light, shade, line and form were used by artists that radically introduced a new way of seeing. 40 mins.

VHS: S09468. $174.00.

Impressionists on the Seine

Captures the mystery, beauty and moods of the River Seine and the life of Parisians who worked and played along its banks in the 1870s. Archival photos and over 45 masterpieces by celebrated French impressionists Renoir, Monet, Manet, Sisley, Pissarro, Morisot and Caillebotte give viewers the experience of living in that period of intense creativity (1869-1881) when these Impressionists used the river as their inspiration to establish a new course for Western art. 30 mins.

VHS: S33899. $29.95.

In a Brilliant Light: Van Gogh in Arles

A portrait of van Gogh's climactic 444 days in the south of France, the film focuses on the artist's work rather than on his life, and dispels many of the myths surrounding this legendary painter. Produced by the Metropolitan Museum of Art. 57 minutes.

VHS: S02718. $39.95.

In and Out: The Petrie Court at the Metropolitan

A guided tour of the Museum's breathtaking new outdoor sculpture court, led by one of the world's leading authorities on French and Italian sculpture from the 17th and 18th centuries, Olga Raggio. Sculptures by August Rodin, Maillol, Bernini, Lemoyne, and many others fill this huge, glass-covered wing of the museum. 1990. 15 mins.

VHS: S34012. $19.95.

In the Shadow of Angkor Wat

This release follows the first major exhibition of Cambodian sculpture to be shown in the U.S. and traces the religious, social and political life which still animates Angkor, Cambodia's capital and site of magnificent temples, including the most majestic, Angkor Wat, completed in the 12th century. 55 mins.

VHS: S32205. $29.95.

In the Steel: A Portrait of Mark di Suvero

Documents the installation of a huge sculpture on the grassy knoll near the sands of Venice Beach, California. Includes interviews with the world-renowned sculptor and L.A. Louver Gallery owner Peter Goulds. Hosted by Digby Diehl at the L.A. Louver Gallery, Venice, California. 1990. 24 mins.

VHS: S34002. $29.95.

Ingres: Slaves of Fashion

Investigates the life and work of Ingres (1780-1867), who was in his own day admired by many, but loved by few. The program studies another paradox: how Ingres, known as a revolutionary artist, could have inspired the new Romantic movement. Produced by the BBC. 50 minutes.

VHS: S02383. $39.95.

Interviews with Artists, Program 4: Three Installation Artists

Three installation artists are interviewed. Susan Leibovitz Steinman, an environmental activist/sculptor, discusses the motivation behind her work in site-specific public installation using recycled materials. Jeanne O'Connor combines photography, painting, drawing and sculptural elements to create a sense of memory of places. And M. Luise Stanley talks about her narrative work, her sketchbooks and her building of her own private Pompeii Villa for an exhibition in San Francisco.

VHS: S21981. $35.00.

Elizabeth Sher, USA, 1993, 35 mins.

Isabel Bishop: Portrait of an Artist

The master of romantic realism who captured on canvas the world of New York—the hobos, shop girls, the weary day-to-day existence of life in the city, all painted from the perspective of her studio in Union Square. This program brings to light one of America's true masters in a unique pairing of the artist at work and scenes recreating her most important paintings. 26 mins.

VHS: S10310. $29.95.

Isamu Noguchi

Born of an American mother and a Japanese father, sculptor Isamu Noguchi transcended two worlds to become an artist of international renown, "at once the purest of sculptors and one of the most socially oriented, exulting in large public projects" (Hilton Kramer, *New York Times*). This unique video probes the psyche of a creative genius, exploring the effects of an unusual childhood and the artist's reconciliation with his heritage. Apprenticed to Brancusi, Noguchi embraced the arts of furniture design, calligraphic brush drawings, set design, and took the humble Japanese lantern and developed it into his trademark Akari lamp. 52 mins.
VHS: S10305. $39.95.

Islands

For two brief weeks in 1983, Christo's *Surrounded Islands* blossomed on the waters of Biscayne Bay, Florida: 11 scrub-pine islands surrounded by 6.5 million square feet of bright pink fabric. A three-year struggle, a political drama interwoven with two other Christo projects—the wrapping of the Pont Neuf in Paris, and the Reichstag in Berlin.
VHS: S07494. $59.95.
Maysles Brothers, USA, 1983, 58 mins.

Jack Levine: Feast of Pure Reason

Shows America's foremost Social Realist painter, as he stands before an empty canvas, and with breathtaking virtuosity, creates a painting on-camera. Directed by David Sutherland. 58 minutes.
VHS: S02747. $39.95.

Jack Levine: Out of the Studio

Jack Levine was first exhibited in the Metropolitan Museum of Art in New York during the Depression, painting in a tough style known as Social Realism. Gangsters and their crowd, as well as the art world, remain Levine's favorite subjects. Includes an interview with the artist. Midtown-Payson Galleries, New York City. 1991. 25 mins.
VHS: S34006. $29.95.

Jackson Pollock

This biography of Jackson Pollock looks at his work, his concept of "action painting" and his part in the abstract expressionist movement. 52 mins.
VHS: S17725. $39.95.

Jacob Lawrence

Lawrence is one of the country's most respected artists. This African-American painter grew up in depression-era Harlem and got his schooling in federal workshops. Today his works on African-American themes, particularly history, are widely prized. Interviews and the works of the artist tell this story of artistic excellence. 25 mins.
VHS: S27622. $29.95.

Jacob Lawrence: The Glory of Expression

This documentary is about the life of African-American painter Jacob Lawrence. His work has consisted primarily of epic depictions of the struggles of African-Americans. Considered one of America's greatest modern painters he was the first African-American to have his work exhibited in a major New York gallery. 28 mins.
VHS: S21454. $49.95.

Jacques Lipchitz

A fascinating glimpse of a serious artist and the artistic process, this program allows Lipchitz to tell his own story, recalling his early life in Lithuania, the height of the Cubist movement, and his post WW2 years in New York and Italy. With a handful of artists, he helped forge a new direction in art with his friends and co-workers Picasso, Diego Rivera, Juan Gris, Gertrude Stein, Soutine and Modigliani. Filmed working at the height of his creative powers, the program also demonstrates his warm talent as a storyteller. 58 mins.
VHS: S10304. $39.95.

James C. Christensen: The Art of Imagination

James C. Christensen is a unique artist who changes the rules of reality in his highly imaginative and complex art. Rich symbolism hidden in his work is explained in this video. The result is an invitation to participate in a world of fantasy. 31 mins.
VHS: S26807. $49.95.

Jan van Eyck: The Mystery of Painting

Jan van Eyck and his brother Hubert are traditionally credited with founding the Flemish school and inventing oil painting. Part I gives an in-depth appraisal of Hubert van Eyck's only known work, *Adoration of the Lamb*, which was completed by Jan. Part II spotlights Jan van Eyck's *Madonna with Chancellor Rolin*, the *Madonna with Canon Van der Paele* and *The Marriage of Arnolfini*. Harold van de Perre discusses the symbolic meaning of these breathtaking masterpieces and sheds light on van Eyck's technical skill. Each part is 55 mins.
VHS: S33244. $39.95.

Jasper Johns: Ideas in Paint

A revealing portrait of Jasper Johns which covers his remarkable work that helped usher in Pop Art and Minimalism. The documentary includes intimate conversations and footage of Johns working, with commentary by his colleagues Leo Castelli, the late composer John Cage, choreographer Merce Cunningham and other noted artists and art critics. 56 mins.
VHS: S17728. $39.95.

Jeff Carpenter: The Real Thing

This documents an art opening on the lower east side of Manhattan at Charles Finch's gallery. Includes an interview with the artist. 1990. 7 mins.
VHS: S34038. $13.95.

Jeff Way: Faces and Masks

This artist makes masks and paints startling portraits that are both realistic and abstracted. Includes a conversation with Willoughby Sharp in his studio in New York City. 1991. 11 mins.
VHS: S34019. $19.95.

Jewish Museum

The story behind the thousands of paintings, sculptures, and photographs in the collection of the Jewish Museum in New York City. 18 mins.
VHS: S03888. $29.95.

Joan Miro: Constellations— The Color of Poetry

A retrospective filmed at the Miro Museum in Barcelona, this video offers a unique insight into the visual world of Miro, which fuses passion, sexuality, philosophy and flights of fancy into an ecstatic carnival of symbols. With historic newsreel footage, a tour of Miro's studio and a performance by the La Claca Theater in Miro-designed costumes. 52 mins.
VHS: S21904. $29.98.

Joe Coleman

On a rainy night a visit to Joe's 20th-century bizarre memorabilia museum on New York's Lower East Side offers the perfect art experience. Coleman is a painter and performance artist who was banned in Boston and censored by Bob Barker from *The Price Is Right*. His exploding performances may have something to do with his outre reputation.
VHS: S22651. $29.95.
Clayton Patterson, USA, 1989, 28 mins.

John Baldessari: Some Stories

Presented without commentary, this film reveals the thinking behind his work and provides clues to the understanding of the artist's paintings, photographic work and books. What emerges is a portrait of a thoughtful, quietly rebellious artist who has influenced a large number of younger artists over the last 20 years. 28 mins.
VHS: S14581. $39.95.

John Marin's New York

A video representation of artist John Marin's complex *New York City Series*. Marin's modernist style melded tenets of Impressionism, Cubism and Futurism to create a signature aesthetic. This series examines New York's artistic, social and cultural evolution, from the years 1910-53. With an original jazz score by Derek Smith and Jay Leonhart.
VHS: S19901. $29.98.

John Piper: Piper's Way

Takes a close look at the career of England's foremost neo-Romantic artist. Documents much of Piper's recent work, including his stained glass design for Coventry Cathedral. 55 minutes.
VHS: S01799. $39.95.

Joseph Beuys, Public Dialogues

Famous performance artist Beuys is seen in his first public appearance in the U.S. in this video. He outlines his political and artistic philosophies.
VHS: S22654. $49.95.
Willoughby Sharp, USA, 1974, 120 mins.

Joyce Khozloff: The Erotic Paintings

This painter adapts various style of ancient art into modern artwork. Their erotic content is startling at first glance because of the assumptions the viewer makes about Egyptian art. Robert Berman Gallery, Santa Monica. 1993. 10 mins.
VHS: S34029. $15.95.

Jules Feiffer: Feiffer's Follies

A relaxed visit with one of America's most celebrated political satirists. Filmed at Feiffer's summer home at Martha's Vineyard. Shows Feiffer as he creates a typical Feiffer character on-camera. 55 minutes.
VHS: S03586. $19.95.

Julio Rosado del Valle

A visit to the studio of the prominent Puerto Rican artist, Julio Rosado, in San Juan. Narrated in Spanish by Luis Vivas. 13 mins.
VHS: S06759. $40.00.

Juri Koll: The Artifact in Art

Colorist Juri Koll takes us on a journey up the coast through his paintings of Chumash Indian ceremonial artifacts. 1997. 20 mins.
VHS: S34027. $19.95.

Kazimir Malevich: Breaking Free of the Earth

The most inscrutable of the Russian revolutionary artists, Kazimir Malevich had the misfortune to die in official Soviet disfavor, and to remain under that disapproval for decades afterwards. Now political changes have opened the doors to these hidden storerooms, and Malevich's pictures can be publicly viewed once again. This program documents the first major retrospective of his work since his death more than 50 years ago, providing viewers with analyses and commentary on his work that is vivid, precise and personal. 52 mins.
VHS: S13742. $39.95.

Kenneth Noland: A Look at a Minimalist

A very quick look at this minimalist painter's large painted panels of endless shapes and colors. Salander O'Reilly Gallery, Beverly Hills, California. 1990. 5 mins.
VHS: S34030. $13.95.

Kinetic Sculpture Windcarver

Former architect Merrill Prentice measures the slightest currents of air and designs common materials into delightful, ever-changing sculptures. The wonder of the creative process is revealed along with humorous anecdotes and even a discussion about the philosophy of public and private art. A valuable video for all art students, or even those who simply love great art.
VHS: S14593. $49.95.

Klee

This video biography covers the life and work of Paul Klee (1879-1940), whose vast output coincided with some of the most important developments in modernism. The video highlights Klee's work during the Bauhaus period and focuses on his relationship with Kandinsky. 25 mins.
VHS: S17226. $29.95.

L.A. Art Fair 1990: Another Quick Take

Scenes from an important international art fair in Los Angeles, including interviews and guest speakers. 1990. 5 mins.
VHS: S34031. $13.95.

L.A.—Suggested by Art of Ruscha

Los Angeles is stylishly rendered in Conklin's sunset-hued homage to painter Edward Ruscha. L.A., the city of heretics, malcontents, messiahs, and "the city of pools, palm trees, and real estate," is both inspiration and obsession for Ruscha.
VHS: S00698. $29.95.
Gary Conklin, USA, 1981, 28 mins.

Land & Landscape: Views of America's History & Culture

This program from the Smithsonian Institution's National Museum of American Art examines the history of American landscape painting and photography from the early 19th century to the present. Its goal is to develop a heightened awareness of the significance of America's wilderness, geologic wonders, agricultural abundance and ecological diversity in shaping the nation's social, cultural and political history. Includes a 28-minute video, 56-page study guide and a 32-page workbook.
VHS: S31825. $85.00.

The Landscapes of Frederic Edwin Church

This program studies the work of Frederic Edwin Church, whose style is described as "magnificent, dramatic, sweeping, fantastic and poetic," tracing his career as a important figure in the Hudson River School, the country's leading 19th-century landscape painters. 29 mins.
VHS: S15300. $29.95.

Lascaux Revisited

Prehistoric paintings in a cave were accidentally discovered by French schoolchildren. The drama of this true story is recreated in this video through animation. Even more exciting is the footage of these remarkable ancient works of art which have been closed to the public since 1963.
VHS: S27099. $29.95.
Jacques Willemartt/Norbert Aujolat, USA, 1995, 35 mins.

Lasting Impressions

This documentary profiles lithograph artist and founder/director of the Printmaking Workshop, Robert Blackburn, one of the few black printmakers to emerge from WPA-sponsored arts projects, including the Harlem Art Center, during the '30s. Features interviews with Blackburn, fellow artists, art critics and curators, and many of his current and former students.
VHS: S34429. $250.00.
Gail Jansen, USA, 1997, 30 mins.

Left Right

Sculptor and architect Robert Parker, at home in Guelph, Canada, moves among stones and bones dressed in a loincloth. 1984, 20 mins.
VHS: S22659. $29.95.
Robert Parker, USA, 1984, 20 mins.

Legacy of the Mamluks

Based on the first major international exhibition of the art of the Mamluks at the Smithsonian—the art of the Mamluk Dynasty, one of the most formidable regimes of the Middle Ages, ruling most of the parts of Egypt, Palestine and Syria. An amazing retrospective of work in metalwork, glasswork, illustrated manuscripts, ceramics and woodwork. 30 mins.
VHS: S06561. $39.95.

Lempad of Bali

From the co-director of the acclaimed series *Ring of Fire* comes this remarkable portrait. Lempad was a great Balinese artist who died a fully conscious death (he invited his whole family to attend) at the age of 116. He had become an oracular source for every variation of Balinese mythology, and was known throughout Europe in the 1920s for his extraordinary religious and erotic art.
VHS: S16622. $19.95.
Lorne Blair, USA, 1979, 60 mins.

Leonardo, Michelangelo, Raphael and Titian

Pinnacle of Renaissance artistic achievement. Journey from Florence to the Vatican, Rome and Venice to view masterworks, including Leonardo's *Mona Lisa, The Last Supper* and *Adoration of the Magi*; Michelangelo's *David* and newly restored Sistine Chapel; Raphael's Madonnas and Vatican paintings; Giorgione's *Tempest*; Titian's dramatic portraits and more. Produced by Rizzoli. 56 mins.
VHS: S13253. $39.95.
Laser: LD70790. $99.95.

Leonor Fini

Noted for her surreal fantasy paintings, the Italian-Argentine painter Leonor Fini has a life deeply rooted in her immediate surroundings and in the people and places she treasures. In this program the Belgian film director Chris Vermorcken has created a loving portrait that places what Fini loves side by side with what she paints. The film takes us into Fini's home, where we meet the 19 cats who share her life and who constantly turn up in her paintings. We also view a number of her canvases, which together offer a tribute to the exotic and the erotic. 86 mins.
VHS: S13744. $39.95.

Life of Leonardo da Vinci

A brilliant, massive portrait of Leonardo da Vinci in five parts, produced by Italian State Television and directed by acclaimed Italian filmmaker Renato Castellani. The man who painted the Mona Lisa and the Last Supper, one of the great geniuses of history, comes alive in an exhaustive study of da Vinci and his period. *Part I: 1452-1482*, covers the first 30 years of da Vinci's life, the circumstances of his birth and childhood, as well as his influences. *Part II: 1482-1500*, covers da Vinci leaving Florence for Milan to work for Duke Ludovico Sforza, his scientific studies as well as The Last Supper. At age 50, Leonardo returns to his home in Florence. *Parts IV & V: 1500-1519*. While in Florence, Raphael is introduced to da Vinci, and Leonardo meets and forms a bitter rivalry with Michelangelo. In 1506, he leaves again for Milan. 4½ hours total. 3 cassettes in slipcase.
VHS: S12189. $99.95.

Light of the Gods

This video brings brilliantly to life the world of Homer, Sappho, Herodotus and Sophocles in the engaging story of the evolution of Greek art, narrated by Colleen Dewhurst. The film abounds with examples of Greek representational art, from the stylized stick figures of the Geometric period to the exquisitely carved and painted images of the early classic era, accompanied by quotations from the works of noted thinkers and poets.
VHS: S06712. $29.95.
Suzanne Bauman, USA, 1987, 28 mins.

The Line King

For over 70 years, Al Hirschfeld's drawings have graced the pages of *The New York Times*, bringing to life the stars of Broadway and the silver screen. This thoroughly engaging portrait of one of America's most beloved illustrators features rare home movies, special appearances by his celebrity subjects and interviews with his late wife Dolly Haas and daughter Nina. The artist emerges as a brilliant, delightful, quirky and compassionate observer of humanity.
VHS: S32495. $24.98.
Susan W. Dryfoos, USA, 1996, 126 mins.

Living Monuments in Jewish Spain

The Medieval life of Jewish Spain is recreated through illuminated manuscripts from the period. They are a source of amazing information about everyday family life, including the celebration of festivals and clothing styles. 21 mins.
VHS: S23246. $39.95.

Lori Taschler: Little Objects

This interview by Willoughby Sharp captures the artist's sensibility for the nature of small objects, making art using everyday materials seemingly found around the house. Filmed at the artist's studio in New York City. 1991. 5 mins.
VHS: S34036. $13.95.

Los Angeles Murals

More than 500 murals adorn the walls of Los Angeles, suggesting the vital energy, cultural richness and diversity of the city. This program showcases the city's most talented mural artists and conservators. 11 mins.
VHS: S20356. $39.95.

Louise Nevelson in Process

Nevelson was in her seventies before critics recognized her contribution to sculpture in America. In this documentary, Nevelson creates two new sculptures on camera, providing a rare opportunity to share in the unfolding of her unique process. Produced by WNET. 30 minutes.
VHS: S02719. $29.95.

Louvre (Boyer)

NBC-produced documentary about the most famous art museum in the world, France's Louvre. Narrated by Charles Boyer.
VHS: S01712. $24.95.
John Sughrue, USA, 1978, 53 mins.

The Louvre

The most famous treasure-house of art in the world. Pause and admire such masterpieces as the "Winged Victory", "Venus de Milo" and of course, the "Mona Lisa". Exquisite works beautifully presented. 55 mins. English narration.
VHS: S05280. $69.95.

Louvre 200

A three-part series exploring the evolution of the museum in European culture.
Part 1, A Museum in Time: Louvre 1793-1993. Founded in 1793, the Louvre is the largest museum in the world, holding more than 360,000 works. The program studies the commemoration of the Bicentennial and the openings of the Richelieu wing and the Great Louvre. 60 mins.
VHS: S18847. $29.95.
Part 2, At the Louvre with the Masters. Drawing on the memoirs and published works of Courbet, Degas and Cezanne, this program reveals the extraordinary influence on these 19th century artists in their art and work. The program suggests the multifaceted functions the Louvre served to the leading artists—part school, studio, salon, laboratory and collection of technique and accomplishment. The program also considers the inspiration of Delacroix, Zola, Durantt, Monet, Renoir, Manet and Picasso. 60 mins.
VHS: S18849. $29.95.
Part 3, Selected Places. This program considers the splendor and wonder of the Louvre, highlighted by the old Louvre, the Winged Victory of Samothrace, the Venus de Milo, the Mona Lisa, the great sculpture courts, the installation of Taureax of Khorsabad and the apartments of the Duke de Mornay, among others. 60 mins.
VHS: S18848. $29.95.
Complete Set. Parts 1, 2 and 3.
VHS: S18850. $79.95.

The Louvre: Thousands of Masterpieces

Produced under the aegis of the museum's curators, each videodisc volume is stored with multiple images recreated in color and beautiful detail, with an indexed guide book, on screen catalog information, and motion sequences with a French and English soundtrack that walks you through the museum's greatest works.
Louvre Vol. 1: Paintings and Drawings. More than 2,400 works showcasing 18,000 still frames and 29 motion sequences (with narration) covers the Louvre's groundbreaking Western art section, covering the 13th to mid-19th centuries.
Laser: LD70299. $99.95.
Louvre Vol. 2: Sculptures and Objets d'Art. Some 5,000 still frames and 21 narrated motion sequences capture the extraordinary range and beauty of multiple examples of sculpture, furniture, jewelry and other three dimensional works.
Laser: LD70300. $99.95.
Louvre Vol. 3: Antiquities. With 23 narrated motion sequences and 6,000 still frames, this fascinating program considers the 1,200 ornaments, monuments, textiles, vessels and status borne from the civilizations of Greece, Rome and Egypt.
Laser: LD70301. $99.95.

Magic Work-Shop of Reveron

The fantastic life of the Venezuelan painter as revealed in the objects and dolls at his studios. Co-produced with the National Gallery of Venezuela. 23 mins.
English Narration. Roger Wilkison.
VHS: S06796. $60.00.
Spanish Narration. Hector Myerston.
VHS: S06797. $60.00.

Magicians of the Earth

Philip Haas is the acclaimed director of many films, including the recent *Angels and Insects*. This video collection of four of his documentaries (*The Giant Woman & The Lightning War, Young Man's Dream & A Woman's Secret, Seni's Children* and *Kings of the Water*) shows native artists working in traditional forms. The highly original films are scored by David Byrne.
Laser: LD75012. $89.95.
Philip Haas, USA, 1989-1990, 224 mins.

Making Masterpieces

A behind-the-scenes look at the National Gallery in London presenting six beautifully illustrated programs encompassing centuries of great art and tracing the evolution of the painter's craft. Includes works by Rembrandt, Renoir, Holbein and other masters. Three tapes, six programs, 30 mins. each.
VHS: S33402. $79.95.

Manabu Mabe Paints a Picture

This documentary shows the renowned Japanese-Brazilian artist creating an abstract painting in his studio. His phantasmal images of reality are akin to those executed by his ancestors in old Japan with foliage and clouds and glimmerings of water, more suggestive of environment in Brazil. On large canvases he abstracts and combines the legacy of his ancestors with the vibrancy and music of the world he lives in today. Directed by Jose Gomez Sicre. Narrated in English by William D. Clark. 13 mins.
VHS: S06746. $40.00.

Marcel Duchamp: A Game of Chess

A driving force behind many modern movements—Dada, surrealism, futurism and kinetic/conceptual art—Marcel Duchamp did more than any artist in his century to change the concept of art. 56 mins.
VHS: S15295. $29.95.

Marisol

Discussions with Sydney Janis, art dealer, and Dale McConathy, New York University, on Venezuelan artist Marisol's sculptures and the acquisition of "Madonna, Nino, Santa Ana and San Juan." A detailed visual examination of the wood sculpture is enhanced by the process of packing the sculpture for shipment. 13 mins.
VHS: S07455. $39.95.

Mary Cassatt: Impressionist from Philadelphia

The first film to celebrate Mary Cassatt's remarkable career-her years in Paris, her relationship with Degas, the influence of her socially prominent Philadelphia family, told with on-location footage and stills. The best examples of her work reveal the quality, variety and originality of her work. Produced by WNET/Channel Thirteen. 30 minutes.
VHS: S02389. $29.95.

Masaccio: A View of Mankind

Lawrence Gowing's documentary chronicles the life and times of Masaccio and highlights his frescoes at the Santa Maria Novella and the Church of the Camines' Brancacci Chapel in Florence. 40 mins.
VHS: S18761. $29.95.

Masterpieces of British Art

The Yale Center for British art is home to the most comprehensive collection of British art outside Great Britain. Among its outstanding paintings, the collection includes 15 Turners, 21 Gainsboroughs, 7 Reynolds and 44 Constables. This program highlights major works from this collection. Also included is an interview with Paul Mellon, revealing how his marvelous collection was created. 30 mins.
VHS: S13251. $29.95.

Masterpieces of Italian Art: Greek to Gothic

Beginning with the glorious Greek temples in Sicily's Valley of Temples, the camera lovingly reveals Italy's early artistic masterpieces. Includes Greek sculpture, Etruscan tombs, Roman architecture, the Catacombs, early Christian mosaics in Ravenna, Romanesque churches and the great Gothic cathedrals. Produced by Rizzoli. 58 mins.
VHS: S13256. $39.95.
Laser: LD70787. $99.95.

Masterpieces of the Met

A superb introduction to one of the world's finest art institutions, hosted by museum director Philippe de Montebello, as he leads the viewer on this tour of 5,000 years of world civilization. Included are such noted works as Van Gogh's *Cypresses*, Degas' *The Dance Class*, Vermeer's *Young Woman With a Water Jug*, artifacts from the Egyptian tombs, African sculpture, Oriental painted screens, and art objects from around the world. 55 mins.

VHS: S06349. $29.95.
Laser: LD71133. $29.95.

Masters of Illusion

This program studies the artistic and scientific discoveries of the Renaissance period, studying the theories of light, texture and form through the works of Brunelleschi, Michelangelo, Leonardo da Vinci, Botticelli and Raphael, and their relation to evolving technology and visual innovation. 30 mins.

VHS: S15297. $29.95.

Masterworks of Painting

There is a difference between looking at a painting and seeing a painting. What makes a great painting great? This video museum of the world's great paintings is a private course in art appreciation, illuminating the principles of art: color, line, shape, light, composition and design. 51 mins.

VHS: S09471. $198.00.

Matisse Voyages

Traces the development of the artist's brilliantly colored work, from his early canvasses, images of dance and music, and odalisques, to his cut-out pieces and his decorations for the Chapel of the Rosary at Venice. Filmmaker Didier Baussy draws on a wealth of paintings, archival footage, photographs, and extracts from his *Notes of a Painter* to capture the richness of the artist's legacy and the splendors of his achievements. 58 mins.

VHS: S10267. $39.95.

Max Ernst

This retrospective celebrates the 100th anniversary of the birth of Max Ernst, one of the most influential artists of this century. Revealing what Ernst called "the private brittle places of refuge," this program considers Ernst's involvement with the Surrealist movement, his retreat to Provence, his flight to New York and life in America, and his eventual return to Europe. 90 mins.

VHS: S15994. $39.95.

Max Ernst/Marcel Duchamp

Two documentaries on one tape about two pivotal artists; the first is a 40-minute documentary on the life and work of Max Ernst, the second a 10-minute interview conducted with Marcel Duchamp in the late 1960's.

VHS: S04360. $29.95.

Meishu—Travels in Chinese Art

Combines art history and travelogue for a remarkable journey through China. Guided by art historian Edmund Capon.

Meishu—Travels in Chinese Art: Canal Boat to History. Delves into the problems of communication caused by China's vast size and diversity of landscape, and how these elements have impacted Chinese art throughout the ages. From Shanghai, journey north, exploring the peaks of Chinese culture—the Bronze Age, the Han Dynasty and the Tang Dynasty. 57 mins.

VHS: S33900. $29.95.

Meishu—Travels in Chinese Art: China and the World. Explores China's erratic and difficult contacts with other cultures and ideologies, and how this isolation has allowed China to develop its own great and distinctive artistic traditions. Traces China's evolution through 2,000 years of trading and commercial contacts. 54 mins.

VHS: S33901. $29.95.

Meishu—Travels in Chinese Art: The Chinese Identity. Takes viewers to locations that embody the real and distinctive character of China and the symbols that represent the spirit reflected in China's art: the Forbidden City in Beijing, a classic Chinese garden, and the greatest of the sacred mountains, Huangshan. 55 mins.

VHS: S33902. $29.95.

Memories of Monet

This American Film Festival Blue Ribbon Winner blends superb views of Monet's gardens at Giverny with his paintings. Narration from Claire Bloom is drawn from the memoirs of American Impressionist Lilla Cabot Perry who was a student and friend of the French Impressionist master. 29 mins.

VHS: S16202. $39.95.

Metropolitan Museum Boxed Set

This three-part video collection includes *Masterpieces of the Met*, showcasing some of the Met's many masterpieces; *Merchants and Masterpieces*, a discussion of the people and the art that shaped the history of the Met; and *Cloisters: The Glories of Medieval Art*, about The Cloisters, the branch of the Met devoted to religious and Medieval art. Philippe deMontebello, the director of the Met, narrates. USA, 175 mins.

VHS: S24794. $79.95.

Mexican Arts

This program turns to the crafts of Mexico, revealing the unique style of the natives as a reflection of their Indian and Spanish heritage. Spanish narration with no subtitles. 10 mins.

VHS: S16368. $29.95.

Michael Todd: Jazz

Artist Michael Todd's work has a connection to the rhythms and texture of jazz improvisation. This work studies his art, and the technique and motivation his working methods comprise. 6 mins.

VHS: S20357. $39.95.

Michelangelo

A & E Biography looks at the great artist whose name has become synonymous with the word "masterpiece." 50 mins.

VHS: S30110. $19.95.

Michelangelo: Self Portrait

A two-disc set that contains two feature length works about the art and life of Michelangelo, including *The Titan*, Richard Lyford's 1950 documentary narrated by Fredric March, that won an Academy Award. On the second soundtrack are two hours of readings from Michelangelo's memoirs and diaries that establishes a social, personal and artistic context within the larger Renaissance period.

Laser: LD70305. $99.95.

Miro: Theatre of Dreams

Profiles one of the major figures of 20th century art, the only surrealist whose work survived in the face of new trends. Miro is shown here at the age of 85, working in his studio and embarking on an entirely new venture: an original theatrical production. Produced by the BBC. 60 minutes.

VHS: S02395. $39.95.
Laser: LD70784. $75.00.

Mirtala

This three-part series offers an unparalleled look into the creative process and artistic accomplishments of the sculptor Mirtala. Mandalas: Visions of Heaven and Earth. Mirtala's work blends images of circular sculptures with cosmic sounds of Michael Stern's "Planetary Unfolding," conjuring up origins and roots. "Mirtala's bronzes have the magical quality of uniting reality and illusion; she adds poetry to the human condition and forges it into sculpture" (*Boston Herald*). 22 mins.

VHS: S20313. $39.95.

Poetry in Bronze. This video offers an interview with Mirtala. Her amazing sculptures offer an appreciative audience a path to the self through contemplation of beauty. Introduction by Paul Nagano. 30 mins.

VHS: S24855. $39.95.

The Human Journey. In a series of sculptures by Mirtala, the artist examines freedom and individuality. Beautifully photographed in their natural settings, the sculptures highlight the poetic intensity of Mirtala's work. 25 mins.

VHS: S20314. $39.95.

Mirtala, Complete Set.

VHS: S24856. $110.00.

Mobile: By Alexander Calder

The first work placed in the National Gallery's East Building was the last major work by Alexander Calder, the man who forged an art through mobiles. This is a behind-the-scenes introduction to the architect, engineer and museum officials who met the challenge of building this complex piece. 25 mins.

VHS: S16203. $29.95.

The Modern Masters: Louise Bourgeois

Rosamond Bernier's acclaimed lecture series at the Metropolitan Museum of Art has expanded with this examination of artist Louise Bourgeois. Both the life and work of this French-born American sculptor is detailed, an effort which helps explain the international appeal of this challenging artist. 60 mins.

VHS: S29494. $19.95.

Moire

A look at the kinetic art works of Venezuelan artist Jose Maria Cruxent, who has played a decisive part in the trend in South America. Directed by Angel Hurtado, 8 mins.

English Narration. William D. Clark.

VHS: S06765. $25.00.

Spanish Narration. Amelia Bruce.

VHS: S06766. $25.00.

Mondrian

This program considers the work of Piet Mondrian (1872-1944), whose work was characterized by his search for spiritual enlightenment, order and structure. His paintings of straight perpendicular lines and basic colors represent some of the highest and most mature peaks of abstract art. 30 mins.

VHS: S17225. $29.95.

Mondrian: From Naturalism to Abstraction

Made in collaboration with leading galleries, this impressionistic documentary on the life and formal influences of Dutch painter Mondrian examines his evolution from naturalism to abstraction. 52 mins.

VHS: S19585. $29.95.

Monet Legacy of Light

Monet devoted his life to capturing nature's kaleidoscope of color and light on canvas. Letters, journals, interviews and the painter's own timeless images are used to tell his story. 27 mins.

VHS: S24274. $19.95.

Monroe Wheeler and MOMA

For 35 years, Monroe Wheeler was a close advisor to the directors of the Museum of Modern Art; this unique documentary captures Wheeler at the age of 86, talking about the formative years and his close associations with some of the world's most famous artists and writers, including Matisse, Calder, Pavel Tchelitchew, Somerset Maugham and Katherine Anne Porter. Personal photos and art illuminate his stories. 30 mins.

VHS: S07541. $29.95.

Monsieur Rene Magritte

Magritte said it was the subject, rather than artistic technique, which creates a beautiful painting. This presentation takes us to the places that fired Magritte's imagination. Winner of the Paris International Art Film Festival. 60 minutes.

VHS: S02394. $39.95.

Moscow Treasures and Traditions

More than 200 national treasures were part of a unique exhibit that traveled to the U.S. Icons, paintings, engravings, precious metal work, porcelains, costumes and armor were included to show the range and depth of Russian/Soviet traditions. This video also shows how the exhibit was formed by curators in both the US and Russia. 48 mins.

VHS: S24863. $24.95.

Mountain in the Mind

Hong Kong artist Wucius Wong explains the traditional Chinese approach to landscape painting: the need to create both the essence of nature and the emotion of the artist contemplating it. Follow Wong closely as he visits Minnesota landmark Minnehaha Falls, and then paints it from memory in his studio. 28 mins.

VHS: S15762. $29.95.

Mr. Five Percent: Calouste Gulbenkian

Shrewd Armenian businessman Calouste Gulbenkian collected art from all over world. He amassed the largest private collection attributable to one person in this century. Rare antiquities, jewelry, sculpture and paintings by such masters as Rembrandt, Rubens, Degas and Monet are seen in this documentary, against the backdrop of his favorite cities, including Istanbul, Paris and Venice. 59 mins.

VHS: S20855. $39.95.

Musee d'Orsay

The world's most extensive collection of impressionist and post-impressionist art is on display in this program, featuring the masterpieces of Monet, Degas, Gauguin, Renoir and Whistler. The second side has 11,000 images culled for 2,100 of the museum's finest works. With French and English dialog.

Laser: LD70304. $199.95.

The Museum of Modern Art of Latin America

A guided tour of this unique museum specializing in the collection of contemporary Latin American art with the founder and first director of the Museum, Sr. Jose Gomez Sicre. Gomez Sicre points out the important works by Latin American artists and explains the part each of those artists played in the development of art in their own countries. Directed by Julio Delgado, with narration in English by Renee Channey. 14 mins.

VHS: S06800. $40.00.

Museum Without Walls Series

This series of eight tapes has been called "a splendid art course for art majors or just those who would like an introduction to the great world of art." Color.

Crete and Mycenae. Over a hundred years ago, archeologist Heinrich Schliemann unearthed the massive and fabled Lion Gate, leading him to pronounce that he had found the graves of Agammemnon and his companion. His discovery helped add another piece to the most fascinating and mysterious archeological puzzle, Crete. This documentary, filmed on Crete and at Mycenae, unveils the findings of Schliemann and those who went before and after him. Hans Horsfeld, 1970, 54 mins.

VHS: S02281. $24.95.

Cubist Epoch. Based on an exhibition originally shown at the L.A. County Museum of Art and the Metropolitan Museum, this video studies the works of Picasso, Braque, Gris, Leger, Gleized, Villon, Delaunay and their followers. Bruce Seth Green, 1971, 53 mins.

VHS: S02276. $24.95.

Germany-Dada. Filmed with the cooperation of original Dadaists Hans Richter and Richard Hauelsenbeck, this unique video collage of art, music and poetry is an alphabet of German Dadaism, and also a true Dadaist experience in itself. Helmut Herbst, 1968, 55 mins.

VHS: S02634. $24.95.

Giotto and the Pre-Renaissance. Described as a truly artistic experience, this documentary records each of the major cycles of Giotto's frescoes. Included are his masterpieces at the Upper and Lower Church of San Francesco, Assissi, the Arena Chapel in Padua, and St. Croce in Florence. Lionella Torossi, 1969, 47 mins.

VHS: S02277. $24.95.

Goya. Perhaps no other artist in Spanish history so brilliantly documented the time in which he lived, and this documentary captures Goya's most prominent works: the etchings, war scenes, bullfight sequences, tapestries, and portraits of royalty and friends. Jesus Santos, 1971, 54 mins.
VHS: S02278. $24.95.

Le Corbusier. Explores the revolutionary ideas of author, abstract artist, prophet and teacher Le Corbusier, as it travels through architecture and urban renewal, and conducts an in-depth tour of his most important buildings, from the hills of France to the Himalayas. Filmed by one of Corbusier's own collaborators, Carlos Vilardebo. Carlos Vilardebo, 1970, 46 mins.
VHS: S02282. $24.95.

Picasso: War, Peace and Love. A sensitive and moving tribute to the single most influential figure in the history of 20th century art, Pablo Picasso. The cassette documents Picasso's major works, as well as many previously unknown and unfamiliar pieces, as it travels through museums, galleries and private collections, including a tour of his studio near Cannes. Lucien Clergue, 1970, 51 mins.
VHS: S02275. $24.95.

The Greek Temple. A fascinating journey through the remains of a sacred city that has stood for over 2,000 years in the forbidding regions of southern Italy. The video also travels through the remains of Acropolis, Delphi, Agrigento and Sounion, as it traces the evolution of temples in Magna Grecia through the Doric, Ionic and Corinthian styles and includes models and animated reconstructions of some of the most magnificent of the ancient shrines. Hans Horsfeld, 1969, 54 mins.
VHS: S02280. $24.95.

National Gallery of Art

One of the best art videos, this extensive tour through Washington's National Gallery features a history told by its director, J. Carter Brown, with an examination of the 1,645 important art works held by the gallery, annotated by both Brown and the curators.
VHS: S05638. $39.95.
Laser: LD70778. $98.00.

Native American Indian Artist Series

A profile of seven contemporary artists representing diverse backgrounds and styles. Available individually, or order the complete set of six tapes at a savings.

Charles Loloma. The world famous Hopi jeweler displays some of his most stunning work, and discusses his heritage. His interests, inside and outside the reservation, are revealed in his art, which uses only materials indigenous to his homeland: iron, wood, ivory, coal, turquoise, lapis lazuli and shell. 29 mins.
VHS: S15755. $39.95.

Fritz Scholder. Fritz Scholder, a California Mission Indian, creates prints and paintings that depict today's Indian caught between ancient tradition and modern society. 29 mins.
VHS: S15756. $39.95.

Helen Hardin. Helen Hardin attempts to integrate two parts of herself, the Indian and the artist, painting sophisticated and colorful geometric patterns and traditional motifs of dancers, deer, the sun and seasons. 29 mins.
VHS: S15757. $39.95.

Medicine Flower and Lonewolf. Two potters from Santa Clara Pueblo in New Mexico have revived and extended the traditional forms and techniques of their pre-Columbian ancestors. 29 mins.
VHS: S15758. $49.95.

R.C. Gorman. R.C. Gorman, a Navajo painter and printmaker, is shown in his Taos, New Mexico studio working on one of a suite of paintings dedicated to the Navajo woman. 29 mins.
VHS: S15759. $49.95.

Allan Houser. A Chiricahua-Apache, Allan Hauser creates stone, wood and bronze homages to the American Indian. As he works, Hauser talks of his personal life and beliefs, and explains how his heritage has contributed to his art. 29 mins.
VHS: S15760. $39.95.

Complete set. 6 tapes.
VHS: S15754. $250.00.

Native Grace: Prints of the New World 1590-1876

After Europeans discovered the New World, a long period of exploration followed. Accompanying these explorers were gifted artists—men like DeBry, Catesby, Audubon, Catlin, Bodmer and Moran, who recorded the grandeur they saw in drawings and paintings. Featured in this unique video is the artistic genius of Audubon's birds and mammals, DeBry's depictions of the Indians of the Southeast, Catesby's 18th century color prints of American plants and wildlife. 31 mins.
VHS: S08136. $29.95.

The Nature of the Artist: Homer Winslow

Hosted by art critic and historian John Wilmerding, this program considers the evolution of Winslow's art, from his Civil War illustrations to the primal, beautiful images of nature appearing throughout his work. 29 mins.
VHS: S15299. $29.95.

Nelson: Palette Knife Portraits

Nelson paints on raw wood panels, using oil paint, with only a palette knife. He paints portraits and figures that are at once haunting and sublime, at his studio in San Francisco. 1996. 15 mins.
VHS: S34024. $19.95.

Neoclassicism, Romanticism, Realism

Developed by Dr. Gale Murray. Covers first the period of 1750-1850. revealing the Romantics' interest in nature, picturesque, violent, sublime, through the works of David, Delacroix and others. *Realism* shows the dominance of the movement in 1850 through the works of Courbet, Daumier, Corot and others. 44 mins.
VHS: S07655. $59.95.

New Ways of Seeing: Picasso, Braque and the Cubist Revolution

This program chronicles the landmark exhibition at New York's Museum of Modern Art, hailed by *The New York Times* as "the greatest exhibition ever devoted to a single phase of 20th century art." Filmed on location at the museum, the program presents a provocative view of Cubism and the extraordinary artistic collaboration of Picasso and Braque. 66 mins.
Laser: LD70119. $49.95.

New World Visions: American Art and the Metropolitan Museum

A two-part series that interweaves painting, sculpture, decorative arts and architecture in an exploration of uniquely American art forms. Using the collections of the Museum as a starting point, the programs were shot on location in New York, Pennsylvania, Washington D.C. and New England. A co-production of WNET and the BBC. 58 minutes each.
Part 1: Covers the years 1650-1820.
VHS: S01797. $39.95.
Part 2: Covers the years 1820-1914.
VHS: S01803. $39.95.

Nigerian Art—Kindred Spirits

Actress Ruby Dee narrates this journey into Nigerian art and culture. Talented artists from Africa's most populous country share their history and cultural legacy with viewers. 58 mins.
VHS: S29539. $19.98.

Nine Artists of Puerto Rico

A visit to the studios of Puerto Rico's most prominent artists, with actor Jose Ferrer as narrator. This film discusses the artists of his native land who developed in the 1970's: Lorenzo Homar, Julio Rosado del Valle, Olga Albizu, Rafael Villamil, Rafael Ferrer, Julio Micheli, Luis Hernandez Cruz, Edgardo Franceschi and Jose Alicea. Directed by Jose Gomez Sicre, 16 mins.
English Narration.
VHS: S06762. $40.00.
Spanish Narration.
VHS: S06763. $40.00.

Norman Rockwell's World... An American Dream

This Academy Award-winning video details the artistic life of one of America's best loved illustrators. Using the artwork and the commentary of Rockwell himself in combination with old film footage and staged reenactments, the *Saturday Evening Post* covers once again come alive.
VHS: S03396. $19.95.
Laser: LD70120. $24.95.
Robert Deubel, USA, 1972, 30 mins.

Oil and Water: A Portrait of Gloriane Harris

Gloriane Harris is an artist whose chosen subject is the ocean and its environs. We visit her studio in Mar Vista, California, as she explains her classical glazing technique, and the source of her work, the Channel Islands off the coast of Southern California. 1990. 30 mins.
VHS: S34009. $29.95.

On the Rocks

The famed cave paintings of Lascaux and Altamira, in Southwestern Europe, are the focus of this documentary. Douglas Mazonowicz examines the artistic ability of prehistoric man using his expert knowledge on the subject. 25 mins.
VHS: S22109. $119.00.

Other World of Winston Churchill

As a result of early defeats on the political scene, Winston Churchill undertook a voyage of exploration into painting, stating, "And then it was that the muse of painting came to my rescue." This video portrait of Churchill's "second career" as a painter is told in his own words, and through anecdotes by Paul Maze (his painting instructor), Field Marshall Lord Montgomery, Merle Oberon and others. 54 mins.
VHS: S12763. $29.95.

Otto Dix: The Painter Is the Eyes of the World

The first comprehensive study of German artist Otto Dix looks at the life and works of the much maligned artist who was blacklisted by the Nazis for his paintings depicting the horrors of war. 58 mins.
VHS: S15293. $29.95.

Pablita Velarde: An Artist and Her People

Pablita Velarde is a Native American artist who paints the history of her ancient people. Found materials and other materials supply her pigments. Her work ensures future generations will know the vital traditions and legends of her tribe. 20 mins.
VHS: S26805. $49.95.

Painters Painting

Warhol, Rauschenberg, Johns and other American key painters are the subject of De Antonio's documentary which captures the visceral personalities at work.
VHS: S00988. $29.98.
Emile de Antonio, USA, 1972, 116 mins.

Painting That Fools the Eye: Trompe L'Oeil

Trompe l'oeil means—literally—*fools the eye*. This award-winning program examines how artists create this extraordinary artistic illustration, the set of rules which allow the artists to open up the creative imagination and provide leaps of fantasy within a limited format. 32 mins.
VHS: S09474. $174.00.

Paolo Veronese: Between Art and Inquisition

This film finds the right historical context for Paolo Veronese, his "irreverent" paintings during the Inquisition, and largely religious pieces intended to celebrate Venetian culture and society, the centerpiece of European life. The film examines Veronese's influence on such diverse artists as Eugene Delacroix and Hermann Hesse.
VHS: S18760. $39.95.
Renate Liebenwein, Great Britain, 60 mins.

Paul Cadmus: Enfant Terrible at 80

Cadmus created scandal and controversy in the 30s and 40s with his brash, satirical paintings. In this award-winning production, he recalls those days as he performs on camera the two tasks for which he is best known: drawing the male nude, and painting in the ancient medium of egg yolk tempera. Directed by David Sutherland. 64 minutes.
VHS: S02396. $39.95.

Paul Cezanne: The Man and His Mountain

Focuses on Cezanne's use of a single image—the Mont St. Victoire in Cezanne's native Provence—to define form, color and light. Richly illustrated with his paintings and views of the countryside, the film opens with the artist at the age of 67, at odds with both his peers and critics, and traces Cezanne's career to his final recognition as the father of modern painting. 60 minutes.
VHS: S02388. $39.95.

Paul Gauguin: The Savage Dream

This National Gallery of Art co-production explores the artist's obsessive search for a "savage" alternative to his own culture, which drove him to that far point of the earth and became a critical aspect of Gauguin's art and life. Shot on location in Tahiti and the Marquesas, the film focuses on Gauguin's final years and his monumental artistic achievement during this period. The story is told, to a great extent, in Gauguin's own words. 45 mins.
VHS: S07605. $39.95.

Persistent Women Artists

In inspired conversations, artist Betty LaDuke captures the spirit of three American women artists of diverse heritages: Pablita Verlade, Mine Okubo and Louis Mailou Jones. Their paintings, drawings, lithographs and murals reflect their experiences as Native-, Asian- and African-American women.
VHS: S31076. $39.99.
USA, 1996, 28 mins.

Peru Virreinal

Colonial art from the private collection of Barboza Stern. Exhibited at the Art Museum of the Americas in 1989. Spanish, 20 mins.
VHS: S15288. $50.00.

Peter Paul Rubens: Classical Synthesis-Prophet of Modern Painting

Part I, *Classical Synthesis—Prophet of Modern Painting* (50 mins.), examines Rubens' role as the dominant figure of baroque art in northern Europe, as the great synthesizer of the Antique and Renaissance traditions, and as the prophet of modern art. Part II, *Celebrating the Art of Painting* (51 mins.), contrasts Rubens' work with paintings by Cezanne, Fragonard, Gericault, Turner and Picasso. Commentary by Harold van de Perre.
VHS: S33246. $39.95.

Picasso

For many, the paintings and sculptures of Pablo Picasso represent the crowning achievements of 20th century art. Over 1,500 works are presented here, creating an unmatched resource that documents the range and creativity of this monumental figure. The work is divided into 57 chapters, each beginning with a biographical sequence on Picasso. Featuring essays by Helene Seckel, Brigitte Leal and Marie-Laure Bernadae, curators at Paris's Musee Picasso. 1992, 30 mins.
Laser: CAV. **LD75514. $124.95.**

Picasso (Musee Picasso)

Centered around the recent opening of Musee Picasso in Paris, *Picasso* takes the opportunity to examine the collection created by Picasso, the work he felt would be his personal legacy to the world. The spirit of the artist is echoed in the dramatic theater of corrida, the ring of the bullfight, and the images of regional Spain.
VHS: S08478. $39.95.

Picasso: The Man and His Work

A major, two-part survey of the work of the legendary 20th century artist, which explores more than 600 of his works, many of which have never been seen in public. Director Edward Quinn captures Picasso at work and at play, during the last 22 years of his life. On two cassettes (90 minutes total).
VHS: S02757. $69.95.
Laser: LD72213. $145.00.

Pierre Bonnard

This program explores Bonnard's style through a look at his paintings gathered for a major retrospective at the Paris Centre Pompidou. 55 minutes.
VHS: S02390. $39.95.

Pierre Bonnard and the Impressionist Vision

Using such world-class paintings in the collection of the Minneapolis Museum of Art as Bonnard's *Dining Room in the Country*, Vuillard's *Place St. Augustin* and Pissarro's *Place du Theatre Francais*, this program explores Bonnard's relationship with his contemporaries and his desire to depict the poetry of life in his art. 12 mins.
VHS: S04377. $29.95.

Piet Mondrian: Mr. Boogie Woogie Man

A stirring portrait of this seminal and enigmatic modern artist. The program explores how Mondrian's art influenced painting, architecture, interior decor, furniture, design and typography, and how his passion for jazz music and dance infected his art. Features *Time* art critic Robert Hughes, designer Terence Conran and composer Louis Andriessen. 49 mins.
VHS: S31562. $39.95.

Pieter Brueghel the Elder: A Painter for All Time

Harold van de Perre looks at two aspects of Brueghel's genius: his gift for storytelling and his brilliant technique. Part I, *Prophet for All Seasons* (50 mins.), reveals how Brueghel's paintings form a detailed panorama of village and city life, war, and the gospels. Part II, *Painter for All Seasons* (46 mins.), investigates Brueghel's intricate brushwork and color compositions, and illuminates his realistic style.
VHS: S33245. $39.95.

Poleo and Poetic Figuration

A documentary about the life and work of the world-renowned Venezuelan painter Hector Poleo, who lives in Paris and New York today, but has never escaped the strong attachment for the old Caracas of his childhood. Poleo is considered one of the precursors of the Neo-Realist school of New York. This prolific artist's style is, as he describes it, "a mixture of fusion of abstraction and elements of the dream world..." The artistic development of Hector Poleo reflects the four attitudes which, in turn, he has assumed toward life: the people-oriented man, the skeptic, the pessimist, and the poet which is so beautifully brought out in this short film. Directed by Angel Hurtado, 28 mins.
English Narration. Roger Wilkison.
VHS: S06781. $80.00.
Spanish Narration. Andres Morales and Hector Myerston.
VHS: S06782. $80.00.

The Popes and Their Art: The Vatican Collection

A work that shows the breadth and historical value of the art hanging within the splendor and spectacle of the Vatican. This program looks at the important works of Michelangelo, da Vinci and Raphael. Narrated by James Mason. 60 mins.
VHS: S19236. $24.95.

Portrait of Gustave Caillebotte in the Country

Gustave Caillebotte spent 20 summers on his family's estate at Yerre, the most productive period of his artistic career. *Portaits in the Country*, done in 1876, incorporates the informal poses favored by the Impressionists with Caillebotte's deep linear perspective and attention to detail. Paintings of the estate gardens and river scenes add their luster to this stunning program.
VHS: S31150. $29.95.
Emmanuel Laurent, France, 1994, 25 mins.

Pre-Real Estate

A document of New York artists setting up the insurgent art exhibition that engendered New York's ABC No Rio.
VHS: S10197. $39.90.
Mitch Corber, USA, 1979/80, 28 mins.

Profile of an Artist: Moriziu Gottlieb

Dead at 23, this artist managed to attain a career summed up in the phrase, "the Jewish Rembrandt". Through a vivid and detailed examination of his work, the life of this artist and his world of 19th-century Eastern Europe is brought to life. 40 mins.
VHS: S23254. $29.95.

Public Sculpture: America's Legacy

Sculptures are presented and then the audience is taken on a tour to see and understand how each work functions in a public place. In this way both the nature of the work and its role in history is carefully elucidated. 29 mins.
VHS: S24868. $85.00.

Puerto Rican Painting: Between Past and Present

A review of an exhibition of Puerto Rican art, sponsored by the Squibb Corporation. Interviews with the curators and the artists. In English.
VHS: S08311. $40.00.

Raoul Dufy: Painter and Decorator

Perhaps best-known for his colorful paintings of people at play, Dufy was also one of the most adventurous artists of the 20th century, as evidenced by his variety of ceramics, wall hangings, furniture, and fabric designs. Interviews with friends and colleagues, along with close-up views of his work, reveal why many consider Dufy to be one of this century's most influential designers and an innovative painter who ranks alongside Matisse and Leger. 58 mins.
VHS: S10265. $39.95.

Raphael

This biography of Renaissance artist Raphael examines his breakthrough works in Urbino, Perugia and Florence within the context of his late period at the Vatican. 60 mins.
VHS: S20186. $39.95.

Raphael Series

For four centuries "The Divine Raphael" (1483-1520) was unquestioned as the greatest of all painters, and he is undeniably still the artist of the most far-reaching influence. This three-part series presents a challenge to re-appraise his work. David Thomson, former art critic of the *London Times*, wrote and narrates these three films, which were shot on location in Urbino, Perugia, Florence and Rome—places where Raphael lived and worked. 58 minutes each.
Raphael: Legend and Legacy.
VHS: S02377. $39.95.
Raphael: The Apprentice Years.
VHS: S02375. $39.95.
Raphael: The Prince of Painters.
VHS: S02376. $39.95.

Rauschenberg: Man at Work

Filmed at his studio on Captive Island, Florida, this film presents Robert Rauschenberg's autobiography, a 790-foot multimedia extravaganza begun in 1981. The artist is also shown installing his works for a 1998 Guggenheim retrospective. Friendships and collaborations with Merce Cunningham, John Cage and Jasper Johns are also explored. 50 mins.
VHS: S33233. $39.95.

The Real Estate Show

In this archival video footage artists set up the insurgent art exhibition that spawned ABC No Rio.
VHS: S22661. $29.95.
Mitch Corber, USA, 1979-1980, 28 mins.

Reality and Hallucinations

A look at the life and work of the master draftsman and printmaker, Mexican artist Jose Luis Cuevas. Cuevas begins and completes a drawing in the film and needs no model, as he dispenses with reality and relies on imagination, on remembrances of people and things past. Little by little a form takes shape, comes to life before our eyes. Filmed on location in the artist's studio in Mexico and Paris, during the early career of the artist, this film was awarded the prestigious National Prize of Fine Arts of Mexico in 1981. Directed by Angel Hurtado. Narration by Jose Ferrer. 23 mins.
English Narration.
VHS: S06786. $60.00.
Spanish Narration.
VHS: S06787. $60.00.

Rebellion of the Santos

The carved wooden images of saints made in Puerto Rico during the 18th and 19th centuries. The texts are extracted from the book of the same title by Marta Traba. Filmed on location in the museum of Santos, San Juan. 15 mins.
English Narration. Renee Channey.
VHS: S06810. $45.00.
Spanish Narration.
VHS: S06811. $45.00.

Red Grooms and "Fat Feet"

The multi-media pop artist and filmmaker talks about his films and artwork at the start of his brilliant career. Much of his new art is shown as well as two of his films, *Washington's Wig Whammed!* and *Fat Feet*, a humorous pop art view of life in the big city combining animation with live film. 1967, 28 mins.
VHS: S31608. $59.95.

Red Grooms Talks about Dali Salad

In his work *Dali Salad*, Red Grooms used paper, vinyl, aluminum, wood, steel, plastic and even ping pong balls to create a lively and humorous portrait of Salvador Dali. This behind-the-scenes look at the production process shows Grooms' three-dimensional print as it was made. 4 mins.
VHS: S03311. $29.95.

Red Is Green: Jud Fine

The work of Southern California artist Jud Fine documents social drift and the inability of people to communicate. This video looks at the style, textures and thematic preoccupations of his art. 11 mins.
VHS: S20355. $39.95.

Rediscovering a Forgotten Legacy

Traces the fascinating history of a rare collection of plaster casts that originally graced the halls of Metropolitan Museum of Art until 1938. Rediscovered in 1975 by the Queens Museum, the plaster casts were stored in a warehouse under a viaduct in New York; their discovery and restoration is shown in detail. 9 mins.
VHS: S07510. $39.95.

Rembrandt

A two-part documentary on Rembrandt van Rijn covers the 40-year period between his first and last self-portraits. The second part considers the elaborate, painstaking restoration of Rembrandt's masterpiece, "The Night Watch," which was nearly destroyed by vandals in 1975. 56 mins.
VHS: S17310. $29.95.

Rembrandt and Velazquez: Two Faces of the Seventeenth Century

The film takes an in-depth look at two masterpieces from the Metropolitan Museum of Art: Rembrandt's 1660 Self Portrait, and the 1650 Portrait of Juan de Pareja by Velazquez. The Rembrandt work is viewed in context of many other Rembrandt self-portraits, while the Velazquez painting is viewed by itself. Produced by the Metropolitan Museum of Art. 28 minutes.
VHS: S02380. $29.95.

Rembrandt—1669

The final years of the artist's life and varied career, detailing the tension between his egotistical, self-centered celebrity and the contemplation, insight and emotional refinement of his art. An investigation of a man's art and life, the movie reveals the fascinating process and discoveries Rembrandt's art was heir to. "A fascinating life, a near perfect union of form and content" (*Variety*). With Frans Stelling, Tom de Koff and Aye Fil. Dutch with English subtitles.
VHS: S17766. $79.95.
Jos Stelling, Netherlands, 1977, 114 mins.

Remington & AVA: American Art

Frederic Remington immortalized the wild west in his paintings and sculptures, capturing for all time the intimate drama of the unbridled American spirit. The spirit of Remington lives on in the contemporary frontiers of American art, here paired on video with AVA, the prestigious Awards in the Visual Arts, narrated by Arthur Godfrey.
VHS: S03969. $29.95.
Laser: LD70116. $39.95.

Richard Pousette-Dart: Thinking with the Brush

Richard Pousette-Dart is one of the original Abstract Expressionists, and has recently begun receiving the notoriety other New York School painters have long enjoyed. Includes a conversation between Pousette-Dart and his dealer, Martin Bush. ACA Galleries, New York City. 1991. 25 mins.
VHS: S34004. $29.95.

Rick Prol: Facing the Critics

An artist who received much notoriety in the late 1980s, Prol returned fron self-imposed exile to answer both his fans and his critics. Includes an interview by Willoughby Sharp in the artist's New York City studio. 1990. 10 mins.
VHS: S34020. $19.95.

Riding the Waves: Andre Emmerich on Art

An engaging conversation with Andre Emmerich, on subjects ranging from Titian, to Sam Francis, his relationships with his artists, to the mythology of the "discovered" artist. Andre Emmerich Gallery, New York City. 1990. 40 mins.
VHS: S34003. $29.95.

Rita McKeough: An Excavation

A survey of the artist's work plus documentation of a new site-specific, multi-disciplinary, multi-media performance/installation entitled "Take It to the Teeth" and other works. Two tapes.
VHS: S32770. $37.00.
Rita McKeough, Canada, 1994, 135 mins.

The Roar of the Gods

A fascinating panoramic view of the pre-Hispanic culture found in San Augustin, Colombia. Stray finds of pottery from this area date back in time to the early centuries of the first millennium B.C. Monoliths found here are as tall as four meters—with carvings unique to the area. Directed by Angel Hurtado. 20 mins.
English Narration. Douglas Fairbanks, Jr.
VHS: S06779. $60.00.
Spanish Narration. Gloria Valencia.
VHS: S06780. $60.00.

Robert Colescott: The One-Two Punch

This tape is a motivational video dealing with stereotypes from artist Robert Colescott. His work and philosophy are also explored. 28 mins.
VHS: S21455. $49.95.

Robert Motherwell and the New York School: Storming the Citadel

An investigation of Abstract Expressionism, centered on one of its most important figures, Robert Motherwell (1915-1991). The program considers artists who comprised the movement (Pollock, de Kooning, Mark Rothko, Franz Kline), and the social and political context that deeply influenced their work. 56 mins.
VHS: S17729. $39.95.

Robert Parker

The sculptor, one of the pre-eminent members of the Rivington School, at his forge and on the street scavenging metal. Produced for Japanese Television. 1987, 20 mins.
VHS: S10201. $24.95.

Robert Vickrey: Lyrical Realist

Described as "the world's most proficient artist in egg tempera," Robert Vickrey is observed during the creation of his magic realist paintings. Filmed on location at his studio on Cape Cod and favorite spots in Manhattan, the viewer discovers an enchanted realm of children, nuns and office workers wandering through the labyrinths of contemporary civilization. Cine Golden Eagle. 30 mins.
VHS: S06557. $39.95.

Rodrigue: Acadian Artist

This documentary profiles a well-known Cajun artist. 25 mins.
VHS: S22392. $59.95.

Roland Reiss

Artist Roland Reiss works within extreme forms, from miniatures to large-scale pieces, that are attuned to different emotional and analytical ideas. This program examines his art and ideas, studies his feelings, motivations and thematic concerns. 8 mins.
VHS: S20358. $39.95.

Romanesque Art

This program follows the development of a unique iconography synthesizing the elements found in Roman, Byzantine, Spanish and Islamic as well as Nordic design. 28 mins.
VHS: S09476. $174.00.

Romare Bearden: Visual Jazz

Narrated by Wynton Marsalis, this video shows how Bearden hopes "to redefine the image of man" in terms of the African-American experience in his paintings and collages. 28 mins.
VHS: S28410. $49.95.

Ron English

A self-portrait emerges from interviews and paintings by the outlaw neo-pop artist Ron English. His work and promotional gimmicks exude a homespun populist conviction and shameless hucksterism. His upbeat theme song says it all: "I'm going to make it in the 90's."
VHS: S22626. $14.95.
Ron English, USA, 1992, 30 mins.

Rosamond Bernier: The Metropolitan Museum of Art Lecture Series

This collection of lectures brings Bernier's astounding learning and her unique insights to video. Whether discussing modern masters or royal patrons, her lectures offer a fascinating glimpse into the wonder of art.
Taste at the Top: Francois I/Charles I.
VHS: S25642. $19.95.
Taste at the Top: Christina of Sweden/Catherine the Great.
VHS: S25643. $19.95.
The French Impressionists: The Cast of Characters.
VHS: S25644. $19.95.
The French Impressionists: Modern Art and Modern Manners.
VHS: S25645. $19.95.
The French Impressionists: Paris by Day and by Night.
VHS: S25646. $19.95.
The French Impressionists: An Accessible Paradise.
VHS: S25647. $19.95.
The Modern Masters: The Matisse I Knew/The Matisse Nobody Knew.
VHS: S25639. $19.95.
The Modern Masters: The Picasso I Knew/The Picasso Nobody Knew.
VHS: S25640. $19.95.
The Modern Masters: The Miro I Knew.
VHS: S25641. $19.95.

The Rotund World of Botero

This video is both a tribute and an expose of the famed artist. He tells of his early life in Colombia and his growing international fame. There are also segments that show him at work on a fresco and a sculpture, and most importantly, we see him at work in his home just outside Bogota. 56 mins.
VHS: S24364. $29.95.

Roy Lichtenstein

A rare interview with the influential American artist Roy Lichtenstein, one of Pop Art's pioneers. Lichtenstein talks in an interview about his current work, the Pop explosion and the history of Western Art. 55 min.
VHS: S18391. $39.95.

Roy Lichtenstein: Reflections

As one of the great Pop artists, Lichtenstein offers exciting insights into the artistic process and the source of inspiration. 30 mins.
VHS: S28411. $49.95.

Rudolf Arnheim: A Life in Art

Rudolf Arnheim, Professor Emeritus of the psychology of art, Harvard University, and author of *Art and Visual Perception*, *Film as Art*, *Towards a Psychology of Art*, *Visual Thinking* and *The Power of the Center*, reflects on his life and work and explains some of his most important theories on this educational video. Also includes a biographical section. 58 mins.
VHS: S32425. $49.95.

Running Fence

The film depicts the long struggle by Christo to build a 24-mile fence of white fabric over the hills of California disappearing into the Pacific, at a cost of $3 million. After what seemed to be an insurmountable struggle between the artist and the state bureaucracy, the fence, finally unfurled, brings the community together in celebration of its beauty.
VHS: S07493. $49.95.
Albert Maysles/David Maysles, USA, 1978, 58 mins.

Saint Gaudens: Masque of the Golden Bowl

A lush dramatization of the life and work of Augustus Saint Gaudens, pre-eminent sculptor of the American Renaissance, as seen and recorded in his own words and those of his contemporaries. Shot on Location in Boston, New York and New Hampshire. Produced in association with the Metropolitan Museum of Art. 60 mins.
VHS: S03398. $39.95.

Sam Francis: Another Quick Look

A montage of Sam Francis watercolors from the late 1950s to the early 1960s, at the rise of his popularity. Includes an interview with longtime friend and dealer, Andre Emmerich. Andre Emmerich Gallery, New York City. 1991. 10 mins.
VHS: S34014. $19.95.

Santa Fe: Artists of New Mexico

Native American artists along with other artists are featured on this video. R.C. Gorman, Allan Houser, Jacqueline Shutiva, Marie Romero, Jemez Pueblo, Bunny Tobias, Charles Greeley, Fred Prescott, Paul Lutonsky and David Dear Silversmith are included. 46 mins.
VHS: S26803. $49.95.

The Sculpture of Spaces

Traces Isamu Noguchi's lifelong exploration of his revolutionary vision through works as diverse as his stage designs for Martha Graham, public parks and plazas, innovative playgrounds and the intimate garden designed for his home in rural Japan.
VHS: S32079. $29.95.
Charlotte Zwerin, USA, 1997, 54 mins.

Secret World of Erotic Art

Enter the world of erotic images created by world-renowned artists but rarely seen in museums or art history classes; erotica by Manet, Calder, Toulouse-Lautrec and many others are included in this video. 51 mins.
VHS: S09973. $59.95.

Sergio Moyano: Living the Dance

This documentary follows the Argentinian-born Moyano through his art studies in Argentina as a young boy, to his travels throughout Europe, and finally to his home in Santa Fe.
VHS: S32413. $29.95.
Mark Oliver, USA, 1997, 34 mins.

Seurat: Point Counterpoint

Defines the life and work of Georges Seurat, one of the most influential artists of the Post-Impressionist generation. Highlighted by conversations with artists Henry Moore and Bridget Riley, the program provides a close look at the creator of the pointillist technique. Produced by the BBC. 75 minutes.
VHS: S02387. $49.95.

Shalom of Safed

Shalom lived in Galilee as a watchmaker until his 58th year, when he began to paint. This video explores the vision of Shalom's acclaimed folk art and the spiritual and physical sources that inspired his work. 30 mins.
VHS: S23255. $29.95.

The Shock of Futurism

Italian Futurism was at the forefront of 20th century avant-garde impulses and helped form the basis of modern art. This program concerns the works of Boccioni, Balla, Carra and Severini, and relates how their visions and ideas shaped cubism, Dada and Pop art. 23 mins.
VHS: S17224. $29.95.

Similar Differences: Betye and Alison Saar

Mother and daughter artists, Betye and Alison Saar's work encompasses multi-cultural, racial, generational and religious symbols, elements and concerns. This video offers a glimpse into the similarities and differences of these two unique individuals. 10 mins.
VHS: S14584. $39.95.

The Singing Sculpture

Philip Haas' film was made in honor of the 20-year history of British cabaret performers Gilbert and George's astonishing show, *The Singing Sculpture*. The comics' crazed, inspired performance carries a manic intensity. 20 mins.
VHS: S19640. $39.95.
Philip Haas, USA, 1991, 20 mins.

Sister Wendy in Conversation with Bill Moyers

A free-ranging, in-depth conversation between America's best-known commentator and Britain's best-loved nun and art connoisseur. Topics range from art to spirituality, from sex to solitude, from television to contemplation. Erudite, witty and enlightening, this program is a delightful and inspiring stroll through the world of art and ideas. A PBS WGBH Boston Special. 60 mins.
VHS: S33092. $19.95.

Sister Wendy's Story of Painting

This acclaimed BBC production takes viewers on a unique journey through art and history with best-selling author Sister Wendy. Filmed on location, the five-volume collection covers the history of art down through the ages, sweeping from cave paintings through the Renaissance, and on to the modern art scene in New York's SoHo scene. Volumes include *Early Art*, *The Renaissance*, *Baroque to Modernism*, *The Age of Revolution* and *Modernism*. 60 mins each.
VHS: S32093. $99.98.

The Smart One

A portrait of master Tahltan-Tlingit carver Dempsey Bob, whose work preserves a vision of a once-lost art and a nearly extinct tradition. His work interprets the art and stories of the past and brings them into dynamic and forceful connection with the present.

VHS: S32227. $14.95.

Smithsonian World: The Vever Affair

The intriguing story that details the rediscovery, and eventual acquisition, of The Vever Collection by The Arthur M. Sackler Gallery (The Smithsonian Institution's Museum of Asian Art) is told by leading scholars of Islamic art and international art dealers.

VHS: S29537. $19.98.

Smithsonian World: The Wyeths: A Father and His Family

Both a portrait of the Wyeth family and a tribute to the family's patriarch, N.C. Wyeth, this video shows the unique and troubled relations that bind this creative clan. Home movies and interviews with the various family members, including Andrew, a respected painter in his own right, make this an exhaustive and intimate look at a talented family. 58 mins.

VHS: S27376. $19.98.

Soldner: Thrown and Altered Clay

A new work by the talented avant-garde ceramist Paul Soldner, who revolutionized American-style raku and changed the shape of contemporary ceramics. More than 50 examples of his work are on view in the video. 37 mins.

VHS: S18006. $39.95.

Soto, A New Vision of the Art

A retrospective view of the Venezuelan kinetic artist, Jesus Soto, who is considered one of the major forerunners of the universal kinetic movement. Since his days as a student in Paris, Soto has continued to experiment with the temporal and movement relationships which involve the viewer as an active agent and participant in his work. This film was awarded *Cine*'s Golden Eagle Award. Directed by Angel Hurtado. Narration by Herbert Morales. 45 mins.

English Narration.
VHS: S06772. $120.00.
Spanish Narration.
VHS: S06773. $120.00.

The Spirit of Haida Guaii

This program celebrates the craft, dedication and hard work of artist Bill Reid to produce a 20-foot, seven-tone bronze piece, *The Spirit of Haida Guaii*. The program includes a rare look at the first sequence of animated Haida art. The video also explores the mythology of the creatures rowing the canoe. "Bill Reid has brought back northwest native art to the 20th century" (Levi Strauss). 48 mins.

VHS: S20318. $54.95.

Steve Reinke: The Hundred Videos

For this complete set of his infamous *Hundred Videos*, Reinke designed a box with text and image which becomes part of the piece. The custom-made boxes come in eight different designs; only a few of each have been made. Five one-hour tapes.

VHS: S32771. $150.00.
Steve Reinke, Canada, 1997, 300 mins.

Su Rynard: What Wants to Be Spoken, What Remains to Be Said

In representing what has been lost, this video seeks to affirm a place in history for women, while at the same time, it acknowledges the importance of the act of imagination in the meditation of the past.

VHS: S32772. $50.00.
Su Rynard, Canada, 1992, 25 mins.

Superstar: The Life and Times of Andy Warhol

This is no ordinary documentary. Its subject is one of the most controversial artists of our time, a man who made celebrity an art form. *Superstar* traces Warhol's career from his beginnings as a commercial artist to his jaw-dropping appearance on *The Love Boat* (a brief clip that is alone worth the price of the video). Was Warhol a great artist or a master hypester? In all the postures and roles he assumed, which was the real Warhol? An ambitious film that endeavors to answer the myriad of questions surrounding the man and the myth. USA, 1991.

VHS: S15135. $14.98.

Theatre of Indifference

A document of David Finn's installation projects in New York's East village, on the Bowery and elsewhere. Video artist Mitsuru Hayashi uses an inset frame of local action, setting up a diptych with images of the sculptor at work.

VHS: S10199. $24.95.
Mitsuru Hayashi, USA, 1987, 24 mins.

Thomas Eakins: A Motion Portrait

Shot on location in Philadelphia, the film combines dramatic sequences in which all dialog has been verified as authentic with archival footage, still photographs, and interviews to create a moving portrait of a man who was not recognized as one of America's greatest painters until many years after his death in 1916. Narrated by Sam Waterston. Produced in association with the Metropolitan Museum of Art. 60 mins.

VHS: S03397. $39.95.

Tibor Jankay—The Art of Survival

Jankay is 94 years old, but this highly personal artist had to escape the horrors of the Holocaust in order to pursue such a long life dedicated to his art. His many stories of survival have helped young artists in his adoptive home, Santa Monica, California. This film explores both his life from his time in Hungary to his inspirational impact in California. Many of his paintings, sculptures and sketches have not been exhibited and this film offers a unique opportunity to view Jankay's work.

VHS: S29535. $19.95.
Harlan Steinberger, USA, 1994, 40 mins.

Tintoretto

The words of Jean-Paul Sartre guide this look at Tintoretto. Sartre was fascinated by the Venetian master's rebellion against 16th century convention and by his visionary style. Filmed in Venice. Winner of the 1984 Montreal Festival of Films on Art. 52 minutes.

VHS: S02378. $39.95.
Laser: LD70780. $75.00.

Titan—Story of Michelangelo

An extraordinary documentary presented by Robert Flaherty which re-creates the work, life and times of Michelangelo without showing a glimpse of a human actor. The film is at once an exciting tribute to the work of the master, and an impressive cinematic tour-de-force. With narration by Frederic March.

VHS: S07297. $79.95.
Robert Flaherty, USA, 1950, 67 mins.

Titian

The greatest painter of the Venetian school is one of the most celebrated names in the history of art. This study by award-winning film director Didier Baussy offers an in-depth appraisal of the master's work. 60 mins.

VHS: S12408. $39.95.

Titian: The Prince of Painters

An exclusive look at one of the most important art exhibits of the 20th Century. Includes over 70 of the master's works. This enormously popular exhibition was over 50 years in the making, due to the tremendous expense and difficulty of transporting these revered icons. Includes an interview with National Gallery director J. Carter Brown. National Gallery of Art, Washington, DC. 1991. 25 mins.

VHS: S34005. $29.95.

Torres-Garcia and the Universal Constructivism

A documentary about the life and work of the renowned Uruguayan artist Torres-Garcia, who spent many years in Paris and was among the pioneers of the movement known as Universal Constructivism. Working with Mondrian and Van Doesburg, he founded the "Circle in the Square" group and held to his ideas, reacting to the flamboyant Western culture around him by advocating a return to order and stability, which is clearly seen in his art. Directed by Angel Hurtado, 30 mins.

English Narration. Paul Anthony.
VHS: S06777. $90.00.
Spanish Narration. China Zorrilla.
VHS: S06778. $90.00.

Toulouse-Lautrec

Henri de Toulouse-Lautrec (1864-1901), a great artist and devotee of Parisian night life, painted his haunts with a sharp eye that saw beneath the gay surface to the corruption underneath. In the superb lithographic posters he produced for these clubs, Lautrec pioneered a style that shaped the future of graphic art. He created striking images by focusing on simple but dramatic shapes and using flat, pure colors. This program, produced in conjunction with an exhibit of Lautrec's work at London's Royal Academy, follows his colorful life and groundbreaking work through the presentation of historic photographs, location shots of Montmartre, and present-day lithography print works. Prominent artists, critics and scholars add richness to the program with comments on their favorite works from the exhibition. England, 60 mins.

VHS: S13741. $39.95.

Treasures of the Vatican Museum and Sistine Chapel

This compelling series of 16 videos offers unprecedented access to the 13 Vatican Museums and the Sistine Chapel. Founded in 1503, the Vatican Museums represent 500 years of papal art collections and span all the important historical periods from antiquity (Egyptian, Greek, Etruscan and Roman art) to the present, including a vital ethnological collection. The museums contain secular and non-secular sculptures, paintings and architecture by history's most revered artists, including Michelangelo, Raphael and Botticelli. The video collection also includes *The Restoration of the Sistine Chapel, which features exclusive accounts of this challenging project as well as close-up views of Michelangelo's painting. 30 mins. each. 1995.*

The Ethnological Museum: In Search of the Divine.
VHS: S30687. $29.99.
Greek Art in the Vatican Museums.
VHS: S30688. $29.99.
Modern Art in the Vatican Museums.
VHS: S30689. $29.99.
Pius Clemente Museum.
VHS: S30690. $29.99.
The Raphael Rooms and Logge.
VHS: S30691. $29.99.
The Restoration of the Sistine Chapel.
VHS: S30692. $29.99.
Roman Art in the Vatican Museums.
VHS: S30693. $29.99.
Stories of Etruscan Civilization.
VHS: S30695. $29.99.
The Sistine Chapel.
VHS: S30694. $29.99.
The Vatican, Volume 1.
VHS: S30696. $29.99.
The Vatican, Volume 2.
VHS: S30697. $29.99.
The Vatican Egyptian Museum.
VHS: S30698. $29.99.
The Vatican Historical Museum.
VHS: S30699. $29.99.
The Vatican Picture Gallery.
VHS: S30702. $29.99.
Vatican Museums, Volume 1.
VHS: S30700. $29.99.
Vatican Museums, Volume 2.
VHS: S30701. $29.99.

The Trecento: Italian Art and Architecture in the Fourteenth Century

Dividing the Middle Ages and the Renaissance, the *Trecento* (the Fourteenth Century) represents a complex and vital age of artistic activity which shared characteristics of both periods it separated. Travel through Florence, Assisi, Padua, Venice and other cities while exploring the works of artists like Giotto and the Pisanos. 26 mins.

VHS: S15809. $29.95.

Turner at the Tate

Joseph Mallord William Turner (1775-1851), considered by many to be England's finest painter, was a man of extraordinary energy and initiative. He was enormously successful in his own time and is recognized today as one of the world's great and truly original artists. In 1987 London's Tate Gallery opened a special gallery, The Clore Wing, to house its massive collection of Turner's works. Produced to coincide with the opening, this program explores Turner's genius from a variety of perspectives: artists, designers, and scholars of note comment on their favorite works from the collection. 55 mins.

VHS: S13743. $39.95.

Two from Beirut: Seta Manoukian and Missak Terzian

These two painters are originally from Beirut, Lebanon. Both combine the human figure with various methods of abstraction. Includes interviews with the artists in French and English. Sherry Frumkin Gallery, Santa Monica. 1992. 15 mins.

VHS: S34018. $19.95.

Uffizi, Florence's Treasure House of Art

The fascinating story of one of the world's oldest and most important museums, the Uffizi in Florence, from the beginning to modern times. The splendor of Renaissance life comes to life through the most well-known masterpieces by such artists as Botticelli, da Vinci, Michelangelo, Piero della Francesca, Paolo Uccello and Rafael. 60 mins.

VHS: S07467. $29.95.

Umbrellas

"Veteran verite helmer Albert Maysles adds his name to this highly original and structurally flawless collaboration between Henry Corra and Grahame Weinbren. An ambitious documentary about an ambitious environmentalist arts project by renowned New York-based 'wrap' artist Christo, *Umbrellas* unfolds as an increasingly suspenseful drama" (Howard Feinstein, *Variety*) as Christo and his wife, Jeanne-Claude, erect more than 3,100 20-foot-high umbrellas along stretches of valleys in Japan and California to stunning effect for a two-week period in 1991, with some resistance from nature.

VHS: S33769. $39.95.

Henry Corra/Graham Weinbren/Albert Maysles, Japan/USA, 1994, 90 mins.

Understanding Surrealism: Painters of the Dream

From Dali's highly-charged dream scapes and Magritte's subtle icons to Miro's joyous fantasies of color and playful biomorphic forms, this award-winning study of Surrealism shows how these artists used accident as a technique and how free-wheeling experimentation lead can lead to a surprising and unique metamorphosis of one form into another. 36 mins.

VHS: S09479. $174.00.

Understanding the Art of the Renaissance: Ideas and Ideals

The art of the Renaissance comes alive in this illuminating study of the wide range of styles and schools as seen in painting, sculpture and architecture. 27 mins.

VHS: S09477. $164.95.

Unknown Secrets: Art and the Rosenberg Era

This touring exhibition depicted a variety of artists who have responded to the fate of Julius and Ethel, the only Americans sentenced to death for espionage by a public jury. Using interviews and documentation of the exhibition, this essay focuses on the peculiarities of the case which give rise to question the fatal verdict. Featuring visual works by Picasso and Sue Coe, and readings of Arthur Miller and Adrienne Rich. 1990, 30 mins.

VHS: S16324. $50.00.

Van Gogh Revisited

A documentary made on the van Gogh centenary; Leonard Nimoy narrates this program about the post-impressionist painter's life and work, with period photographs, a catalog of his finest works and excerpts from his letters.

Laser: LD70311. $69.95.

Van Gogh: A Museum for Vincent

This visually stunning documentary about history's most popular painter features the world-famous collection of the Rijksmuseum Vincent van Gogh in Amsterdam—which is dedicated exclusively to van Gogh's work. 32 mins.

VHS: S15095. $29.95.

Vassily Kandinsky

A native of Russia, he taught at the Bauhaus, and became a leader of the abstract impressionist movement in Paris. Kandinsky's emotional use of color and forms pulsates through the film, shot during a major retrospective at the Paris Centre de Pompidou. 60 minutes.

VHS: S02393. $39.95.

Velazquez: The Nobleman of Painting

Didier Baussy's film on Velazquez deals with the special relationship between an artist and his king. Passionate about painting, Philip IV was the largest art collector of his time, and Velazquez was the servant of this passion. Baussy was able to take full advantage of the Velazquez exhibition at the Prado in Madrid. 60 mins.

VHS: S16600. $39.95.

Vermeer: Love, Light and Silence

This is the first film to profile Dutch artist Jan Vermeer, the master of camera obscura, and his art, which was neglected during his lifetime. Offers close-up views of some of Vermeer's most famous paintings and explores the social, economic, scientific and political context of his work. 50 mins.

VHS: S31563. $39.95.

Vibrant Mirror

A kinetic visual work by Venezuelan artist Alejandro Otero. Narrated by William D. Clark.

Vibrant Mirror. English version.

VHS: S06775. $30.00.

Vibrant Mirror. Spanish version.

VHS: S06776. $30.00.

Videotape with Joseph Beuys

An interview conducted by former *Avalanche* magazine publisher Willoughby Sharp with the important underground German artist Beuys, taken at the height of his career. 30 mins.

VHS: S17202. $29.95.

Joseph Beuys

Vincent van Gogh: His Art and Life

In life, he sold but one minor piece. In death, his works command millions of dollars. This award-winning program chronicles the fascinating career of Vincent van Gogh, who painted the majority of his surviving 800 paintings in the brief span of a decade, with his major masterpieces painted in the last four years of his career. 25 mins.

VHS: S09480. $174.00.

Visions of the Arawaks

Over a decade, surreal artist Penny Slinger has realized a body of work inspired by this group, utilizing their images, their authentic instruments and the close symbiotic relationship they share with their environment. Rare, live footage of these people and over 100 paintings by Slinger form the bulk of this rich tapestry. 70 mins.

VHS: S21187. $39.95.

Vizcaya Museum and Gardens

Come discover the magical grandeur and beauty of Vizcaya—a magnificent Italian Renaissance-style villa built by industrialist James Deering and now a renowned museum of European decorative arts. 30 mins.

VHS: S06688. $29.95.

Voices in Celebration

Filmmaker Aviva Slesin explores the multiple functions and possibilities of art, through a penetrating documentary on history, ritual and creative process of the National Gallery. 45 mins.

VHS: S15298. $29.95.

Willem de Kooning: Artist

Paintings by Willem de Kooning are prized the world over as superb examples of the New York school. He worked both abstractly and with the figure. This film shows him at work and in conversation with friends. There are also 31 paintings captured here for home viewing.

VHS: S26718. $29.95.

Robert Snyder, USA, 32 mins.

Willem de Kooning: The Last Picture Show

This is the last known exhibit that Willem de Kooning could ever attend, due to his advanced age. An intimate look at the last picture show. Salander O'Reilly Gallery, New York City. 1993. 10 mins.

VHS: S34028. $15.95.

William Merritt Chase at Shinnecock

Chase changed American art with the nation's first outdoor summer school of painting. From the National Gallery of Art. 25 mins.

VHS: S34101. $29.95.

Willoughby Sharp: The Bronze Commission

Watch as several artists work in the Long Island foundry, making sand casting molds, supervising the pouring of molten bronze, all the way through to the final grinding and patina process. 1992. 20 mins.

VHS: S34010. $29.95.

Willoughby Sharp: The Cutting Edge

This infamous artist-publisher-turned gallery owner has a keen eye for the cutting edge in the art world. A day-in-the-life seen from an intimate perspective. Includes a lively discussion between Mr. Sharp and Charles Finch of the Real Art Gallery. Willoughby Sharp Gallery, New York City. 1992. 25 mins.

VHS: S34008. $29.95.

World Folk Art: A Multicultural Approach

Six new programs which explore the meaning of folk art and how it has been passed down through history within different cultures tied by the thread of common themes. The vast collection of the Museum of International Folk Art has been richly photographed to provide a resource for this excellent series. Includes *An Introductory Overview, The Influence of Tradition, The Influence of Religion and Spirituality, The Influence of Architecture and Natural Designs, A Product of the Community* and *Expression of Cultures*.

VHS: S15492. $185.00.

The World of a Primitive Painter

Film on renowned painter Jose Antonio Velasquez, on location in his village of San Antonio and in Tegucigalpa, Honduras. A barber by trade, Velasquez had a passion to paint, and with no training he created canvas after canvas with intricate detail, painting the cobblestones of the village streets and the tiles of the rooftops. Awarded *Cine*'s Golden Eagle in the U.S. Directed by Angel Hurtado, 20 mins.

English Narration. Shirley Temple Black.

VHS: S06767. $60.00.

Spanish Narration. Maria Elena Walsh.

VHS: S06768. $60.00.

PHOTOGRAPHY

America & Lewis Hine

The winner of several major awards, including a special Jury Prize at the Sundance Film Festival, *America & Lewis Hine* chronicles the life and art of one of the most influential and recognizable photographers in the world, whose 40-year career recorded the changing face of America in more than 10,000 images. Features hundreds of Hine's photographs, many never seen before. Narrated by Jason Robards, Maureen Stapleton and John Crowley. "Virtuous…superior" (*The New York Times*). "Clearly one of the major American documentaries of recent years" (*Variety*).

VHS: S30583. $24.95.

Nina Rosenblum, USA, 1984, 60 mins.

Annie Leibovitz: Celebrity Photographer

A portrait of a celebrated portrait photographer known for her famous subjects. Annie Leibovitz began her professional career at *Rolling Stone* and became *Vanity Fair*'s first contributing photographer, and one of the highest paid photographers of our day. 51 mins.

VHS: S31561. $29.95.

The Art of Erotic Photography

World-famous lensman John Kelly shares his professional secrets. He travels to a lush tropical island to capture four gorgeous amateur models for a calendar promotion. 60 mins.

VHS: S22215. $24.95.

The Art of Nature: Reflections on the Grand Design

Tom Skerritt narrates this meditation on beauty, the language nature uses to communicate with us. Spectacular scenery from all over the world is seen. Time-lapse photography exposes natural processes not otherwise visible to the naked eye. Based on the best-selling photography book of the same title. Featuring the music of Michael Gettel.

VHS: S27313. $19.95.

DVD: DV60032. $29.95.

Gray Warriner, USA, 1995, 50 mins.

Blast 'Em

A guerrilla-style documentary that explores the highly competitive gonzo world of celebrity photographers, or "paparazzi," as they rush to shoot exclusive photographs for tabloids and other publications. The film's focus is on Victor Malafronte, and records his inventive and aggressive pursuits of Michael J. Fox, Willem Dafoe, Robert De Niro, Jack Nicholson and John F. Kennedy Jr. "More star cameos than *The Player*" (Michael Musto, *The Village Voice*). With music by The Cowboy Junkies, Them and Toni Childs.

VHS: S19440. $19.98.

Joseph Blasioli, USA, 1992, 103 mins.

The Classroom Collection

This six-part series discusses techniques, mechanics, aesthetics and style in a comprehensive guide to photography.

Vol. 1: Basic Camera Techniques.

VHS: S20339. $24.95.

Vol. 2: Basic Daylight Exposure and Equivalent Exposures.

VHS: S20340. $24.95.

Vol. 3: Metering and Exposure Controls.

VHS: S20341. $24.95.

Vol. 4: Advanced Camera Techniques.

VHS: S20342. $24.95.

Vol. 5: Black and White Techniques.

VHS: S20343. $24.95.

Vol. 6: Careers in Photography.

VHS: S20344. $24.95.

The Classroom Collection, Set. A set of six tapes.

VHS: S20345. $129.00.

Documentary Urge: Tom Arndt

Narrated by Garrison Keillor, this documentary shows photographer Tom Arndt in action: stalking his prey at the Minnesota State Fair, and preparing for a retrospective of his work. Arndt follows in the tradition of Walker Evans and Robert Frank, his acknowledged heroes, as a photographer of the American scene. 22 mins.

VHS: S02644. $39.95.

Dorothea Lange: A Visual Life

The great photographer is revealed through examples of her work and interviews with both the artist and her family. Lange was pivotal to the development of documentary photography traditions and her work remains an aesthetic achievement that continues to inspire photographers today.
Home Video.
VHS: S24404. $39.95.
Public Performance Rights/Institutional.
VHS: S24405. $199.00.

The Frontier Photographers

Join frontier photographers William Henry Jackson, Jack Hillers and Timothy O'Sullivan as they explore Yellowstone, climb the Teton and Rocky Mountains, navigate the Colorado River and witness the legacy of the Native Americans before they disappeared. Their photographs captured the images of the raw and wild American West and chronicled its transformation through the westward expansion. 90 mins.
VHS: S34821. $14.95.

Harry Callahan, Eleanor and Barbara

Callahan's photographs of his wife and daughter, taken over a period of 25 years, provide an important insight into his creativity. 18 mins.
VHS: S04104. $39.95.

Helmut Newton: Frames from the Edge

One of the world's leading photographers, whose style has been stamped on the image of many of the world's most beautiful people and has enjoyed amazing success as a Svengali of the glitterati. Newton talks of his life and work, his approach to photography, how he selects the right girl. Charlotte Rampling, Catherine Deneuve, Sigourney Weaver and Karl Lagerfeld comment on the man. 60 mins.
VHS: S12409. $39.95.

Henri Cartier-Bresson

This video portrait of one of the century's greatest photographers, produced by Cartier-Bresson's friends and fellow photographers Sarah Moon and Robert Delpire, includes portraits of Ezra Pound, William Faulkner, Alberto Giacometti, and Henri Matisse plus never-before-seen photos of the notoriously private artist himself. 37 mins.
VHS: S34093. $29.95.

Horst P. Horst

A portrait of the first photographer to have an exhibition at the Louvre. Spans the six decades in which Horst set standards in fashion and portrait photography. Includes interviews with Paloma Picasso, Karl Lagerfeld and Jean Marais. 50 mins.
VHS: S32395. $29.95.

Images 150 Years of Photography

This six-part documentary series traces the technical and aesthetic development of early photographers, the birth of the amateur documentary, the objectifying of images, photographs as a use for exploration and science, for documenting social realism, and explores photography as an artistic expression. The works are culled from 20 collections in museums, archives and private collections in the United States, Canada, Britain and France.
Images 150 Years of Photography: Domestic Memories.
VHS: S17299. $29.95.
Images 150 Years of Photography: The Pencil of Nature.
VHS: S17298. $29.95.
Images 150 Years of Photography: The Best or Nothing.
VHS: S17300. $29.95.
Images 150 Years of Photography: The Eyes of the Empire.
VHS: S17301. $29.95.
Images 150 Years of Photography: The Real Thing.
VHS: S17302. $29.95.
Images 150 Years of Photography: The Magic Mirror.
VHS: S17303. $29.95.

Imogen Cunningham: Never Give Up

In 1901, Imogen Cunningham saved up $15 and sent away for a camera and a correspondence course. Over a span of 70 years, she photographed the famous and the unknown (or infamous as she prefers to call them). *Never Give Up* is a philosophy she lived. Though she was 90 years old at the time this fascinating documentary was produced, she never quit working and she never quit dreaming. Produced by Ann Hershey, 28 mins.
Home Video.
VHS: S16833. $29.95.

Lee Miller: Through the Mirror

Follows Lee Miller's work as a New York model, news photographer for *Vogue*, and as a war correspondent from Normandy landings through the end of WWII, and explores her relationships with Picasso and Cocteau. Includes excerpts from Cocteau's *Blood of a Poet*, in which Miller had a minor role, and interviews with Miller's son Antony Penrose and photographer David Scherman. 54 mins.
VHS: S34092. $29.95.

Limites

Peruvian photographer Carlos Quiroz unveils the artistic process behind capturing the male nude as these private photo sessions allow the viewer to witness the intimate relationship between camera and subject.
VHS: S31735. $19.95.
Jose Torrealba, Canada, 1996, 60 mins.

Man Ray: The Bazaar Years

Man Ray was an artist of many talents, not the least of which was his photography, which broke new ground in both the fine art and graphic arts worlds when he was first published in *Harper's Bazaar* magazine in the 1920-40s. Women and fashion figured predominantly in his work during this time, ranging from the sublime to the bizarre. International Center of Photography, New York City. 90 mins. 15 mins.
VHS: S34013. $19.95.

Masters of Photography: Andre Kertesz

Andre Kertesz claimed he was born for the camera; he reflects on his boyhood in Hungary and his life in Paris. Leading a walking tour of New York City, he photographs a young girl, The Cloisters, and his beloved Washington Square. A heartwarming profile of the man his colleagues call "the father of 35 millimeter photography." 30 mins.
VHS: S16206. $29.95.

Masters of Photography: Diane Arbus

The only film profile of this genius who photographed those living on the fringes of society. This video explores her work through her own words and the images that stunned visitors at her show in the Museum of Modern Art. 30 mins.
VHS: S16205. $29.95.

Masters of Photography: Edward Steichen

Steichen died in 1973 at the age of 95. Drawing images from his whole career which range in subject from celebrities to architecture to advertising to nature, he made this profile when he was 86. "You must establish an intimate relationship between yourself and what you're photographing," he says, "whether it's a can of beans or Greta Garbo." 30 mins.
VHS: S16207. $29.95.

NY/New Wave at P.S. 1

This episode from the long running video magazine views the art show that broke Robert Mapplethorpe. *New Wave* is a look at the seminal art show which marked the convergence of art and music in the late 1970's. Curator Diego Cortez is also featured in a rare interview.
VHS: S22619. $34.95.
Art New York, USA, 1984, 30 mins.

On Assignment

A six-tape series of tapes for learning photography and videography, this series is authored by Brian D. Ratty, nationally known photographer and graduate of the Brooks Institute of Photography.
Photographic Design. Fast-paced and packed with information, this tape is designed for any photographer serious about understanding and using the principles of good photographic design. Includes information on camera and lens choices, framing, selective focus, design elements, design principles, light direction, light quality, control of light and color, psychology of color.
VHS: S06939. $29.95.
Photographic Light. Each half-hour chapter explores and illustrates how light works in photography. This video is designed to help better control and manipulate light in photography. Includes information on direction, form, contrast, color, measuring light, tonal control, film latitude, natural light, available light, electronic flash, artificial light.
VHS: S06938. $29.95.
The Business of Photography. How to make a living as a photographer: interviews art directors and editors who buy freelance photography and give profitable assignments. Three half-hour chapters including choosing your direction, portfolios, how the business works, editing, the interview, staff photographer opportunities, breaking in and staying in, reps and stock agencies, major markets and freelancing.
VHS: S06941. $29.95.
The Darkroom. Brian D. Ratty, the nationally known photographer, hosts this educational review of darkroom materials and techniques. Included are an overview of darkroom layouts, equipment, developing methods for both black and white and color films, proofing and even special printing methods, as well as many other important techniques. 90 mins.
VHS: S21083. $29.95.
The Studio. Detailed and practical ideas about how to lay out and equip a photographic studio to gain optimum results for product and people photography. Includes three half-hour chapters covering studio layout and design, lighting for the studio, still life photography, classic view camera, loading sheet film, view camera techniques, shifts, swings and tilts, formal portraits and candids.
VHS: S06940. $29.95.
Video Guide to Basic Photography. *The Video Guide to Basic Photography* is the starting point for any person wishing to learn photography. This is a practical, easy-to-follow guide, containing three half-hour chapters. Includes how the camera works, F Stops, shutter speeds, camera lenses, film, available light, flash photography, steady shooting, finding pictures, portraits.
VHS: S06937. $29.95.
Video Guide to Basic Videography. Lights, camera, action... This basic guide to videography takes the mystery out of shooting effective, entertaining videos. This basic tape is the starting point for any person wishing to learn the exciting world of video, presented in three half-hour chapters. Includes video theory, formats, cameras/recorders, using your camera, pre-production, production, post-production, basic maintenance, lighting for video and video markets.
VHS: S06942. $29.95.

The Photographer's Secrets

Lennart Nilsson reveals the secret state-of-the-art techniques used in the Emmy Award-winning *The Miracle of Life* and much more. From NOVA. 60 mins.
VHS: S31437. $19.95.

Photography

Camera techniques and developing and printing black and white are illustrated by Doug Rinehart, including operation of single lens reflex camera, shutter speeds, lenses, filters, film, enlarging techniques. 44 mins.
VHS: S07652. $59.95.

Photography Video Series—The Classroom Collection

This six-part video series is a perfect education aid for teaching technique, content and style, with the use of computer generated graphics, charts and examples. Each volume is approximately 15 minutes, and covers daylight exposure, meter, advanced camera techniques, black and white technique and possible careers in photography. 90 mins.
VHS: S17681. $129.00.

Pirelli Calendar

One of the world's most famous annual calendars, the Pirelli Tire Company's calendar features the work of top photographers and designers as they combine the female form and the lure of the road (symbolized by the famous Pirelli Tire Tread mark). Follow the evolution of the calendar from its early days to the growing sophistication of today's calendar, including the most recent issue, as Gillian Lynne, award-winning choreographer of *Cats*, works her magic on the dance elements of the '88 calendar. 39 mins.
VHS: S08488. $19.95.

The Real Weegee

A biography of the talented street photographer Weegee (nee Arthur Fellig), whose photographs captured post-war, urban American life. Weegee's dual themes were alienation and loneliness found in the marginal and powerful-hustlers, gangsters, prostitutes, thieves and presidents. The program features more than 100 of Weegee's photographs. 60 mins.
VHS: S18699. $19.95.

Remembering Edward Weston

Weston's photographic work has defined both the field of photography and the course of art history. His clear images of common objects, vegetables, shells and other natural forms has changed our understanding of the medium. This video offers a view of the artist and the man through interviews with close family members and friends. 30 mins.
VHS: S22802. $29.95.

Richard Avedon: Darkness and Light

An illuminating look at one of the most celebrated and controversial fashion and portrait photographers of our time. Highlights Avedon's 50-year career, recalling his work for *Harper's Bazaar*, *Vogue* and *The New Yorker* magazines and featuring his signature portraits of Charlie Chaplin, Dorothy Parker, the Windsors and Natassia Kinski (and snake). 59 mins.
VHS: S32396. $29.95.

Rudy Burckhardt

Artist/filmmaker Burckhardt, innovator and experimenter in time-lapse photography, describes his work and techniques over numerous clips. 1974, 28 mins.
VHS: S31598. $59.95.

Sebastiao Salgado

A portrait of one of the world's leading photojournalists, who has shaped our perception of political and social reality. Presents his monumental photoessay *Workers*, focusing on laborers in Eastern Europe, Cuba, Gdansk, Brazil, India, Sicily, and Bangladesh. Features archival footage and commentary from artists, photographers, critics, and writers such as Arthur Miller and Jorge Amando. 59 mins.
VHS: S34091. $29.95.

Strand: Under the Dark Cloth

Using samples of his exquisite work and interviews with those who knew him, director John Walker has created a unique portrait of one of the most fascinating figures of contemporary art: photographer Paul Strand.
VHS: S14748. $29.95.
John Walker, Canada, 1990, 81 mins.

Telefoto

This documentary profiles several different photojournalists, whose work offers a remarkable witness to current events, and who explain what personally motivates their often dangerous efforts. Focuses on three photographers from the New York-based Contact Press Images agency; legendary French photographer Gilles Carron; and Russian photographer Igor Kostine.
VHS: S34432. $275.00.
Raymond Saint-Jean/Jacques Malaterre, V. Kriptchenko/V. Tarantchenko, USA, 1995, 47 mins.

W. Eugene Smith

The life and work of this brilliant photographer, whose passion for social justice matched his desire to create photographs that were works of art, are explored in this film. In addition to showcasing over 600 of Smith's stunning photos, the program includes a dramatic recreation in which actor Peter Riegert portrays Smith, with dialog taken from Smith's diaries and letters. 87 min.
VHS: S18390. $39.95.

Wegman's World

Observe William Wegman at work with his Weimaraners and visit with the renowned artist at photo sessions with his famous dogs. 58 mins.
VHS: S34083. $19.95.

APPLIED ART

Antiques Roadshow Collectors Edition

Hear the tales of family heirlooms, yard sale bargains and long-neglected items salvaged from attics and basements on this three-volume set which includes *The Best of Antiques Roadshow, Antiques Roadshow: Home Furnishings* and *Antiques Roadshow: Collectibles*. Each tape is 60 mins.
VHS: S31418. $49.95.

Arno Werner, Master Bookbinder

Arno Werner, born in West Germany, studied with the famous Ignatz Wiemeler, a disciple of the Arts and Crafts movement in England. The video examines the history of bookbinding, Werner's step-by-step techniques, and personal and professional opinions about life and the pursuit of distinguished craftsmanship. 28 mins.
VHS: S06563. $39.95.

Art Ache—Art Is Long, Life Is Short?

This program assesses the role of art in contemporary culture, and the way money and the media have changed people's attitudes and ideas about art. 45 mins.
VHS: S18784. $39.95.

Art Ache—The Game of Art and How to Play It

Drawing on the models of Christie's and Sotheby's in New York and the Cologne Art Fair, this documentary examines the issues facing galleries, dealers, collectors and shifting tastes in the art market, assessing issues of money versus conservation, investment versus art. 45 mins.
VHS: S18782. $39.95.

Art Ache—The Image of an Artist

Drawing from Andy Warhol's exhibition at the Museum Ludwig in West Germany, this program explores the complicated issues of an artist's relationship to his career, celebrity, identity and the media. 45 mins.
VHS: S18783. $39.95.

Art Ache—The Complete Set

Includes *Art Is Long, Life Is Short?, The Game of Art and How to Play It* and *The Image of an Artist*.
VHS: S18785. $99.95.

Art in Its Soul: Provincetown Art Colony

Combines oral histories, archival footage, still photos and works of art to trace Provincetown's evolution into a major art colony. Artists recall the early 1900s, when art students came from around the world to study with Charles Hawthorne and the years of Hans Hoffman, who left his indelible mark on abstract impressionism. Includes Halper, Harmon, Soyer, Gross, Stout, Hensch, Moffet, Hopper, Kanths, Dickenson, Frankenthaler, Pollock, Grooms, Kline, Avery, de Kooning and Motherwell. 34 mins.
VHS: S07511. $39.95.

Art of Navajo Weaving

Explores the traditional art of Navajo weaving and its origins, with visits to a contemporary Navajo weaving family, showing how artists create magnificent pieces of art. 56 mins.
VHS: S08304. $29.95.

Banks' Florilegium: The Flowering of the Pacific

A rich mixture of art, history, science and travel, written and narrated by *Time Magazine* art critic Robert Hughes. Joseph Banks was a botanist who accompanied Captain Cook on his first circumnavigation of the globe. The film visits such places as Madeira, Tierra del Fuego, Tahiti and New Zealand, where Banks recorded over 700 new species of plants. Produced by the BBC. 60 minutes.
VHS: S01848. $39.95.

Before You Visit a Museum

This orientation program gives students insightful background so they will get the most out of their museum visit and take advantage of every opportunity to learn. "...this is a useful introduction for intermediate classes who will visit a museum." 16 mins.
VHS: S09465. $115.00.

Commercial Art: General, Vol. 1

An overview of career possibilities in commercial art fields, including graphic design, computer art and neon design. 30 mins.
VHS: S19926. $39.95.

Commercial Art: Media, Vol. 2

This video offers career insights from three artists who have staked out careers in the following disciplines: cartoonist, scenic designer and photographer. 30 mins.
VHS: S19927. $39.95.

Commercial Art: Design, Vol. 3

This volume shows the careers of a fashion designer, industrial designer and architect. 30 mins.
VHS: S19928. $39.95.

Costakis the Collector

George Costakis' private collection of Russian avant-garde art is the most comprehensive record of an art movement ever amassed. This film tells the story of this movement before and after the Revolution and of the man who saved its greatest works from obliteration. 54 mins.
VHS: S13221. $39.95.

Curator's Choice

A 1982 exhibition at the Metropolitan Museum of Art in which no item's price exceeded $5,000 provides a framework for this exploration of the work of a museum's curator. The five department curators who are interviewed discuss their day-to-day work and the long-range value in serving historic preservation. 25 mins.
VHS: S04647. $29.95.

The Decoy

This film traces the history of the seemingly pedestrian duck decoy. First used by the Native Americans, it later became an intricate test of the woodcarver's skill. Dan Brown, a champion carver, shows how these figures evolved and how they continue to be deployed. 30 mins.
VHS: S24365. $19.95.

Dewess Cochran, Doll Artist

A biography of the premiere American artist in the evolution of the doll art movement, who sculpted one-of-a-kind portrait dolls of specific children. Based on her personal papers, diaries, and memorabilia. 82 mins.
VHS: S33946. $39.95.

Dream Weaver

Helena Hernmarch creates tapestries that hang in major buildings all over the world. As she and her assistants work on two new pieces, Hernmarch comments on her development of photo-realism on the loom, the discovery of techniques to stimulate three dimensions on a flat surface, and the concepts of applied creativity and design. 28 mins.
VHS: S15747. $49.95.

The Eighteenth Century Woman

Using the Metropolitan Museum's costume collection as a point of departure, this documentary provides an in-depth look at the role of women in the 18th century when "to be direct was to be dull, and dullness was the greatest of sins." Includes interviews with Philippe de Montebello, director of the museum, as well as costume curator Stella Blum and Vogue Magazine editor Diana Vreeland. 60 mins.
VHS: S04648. $39.95.

Etched in Stone: The Golden Age of Cuban Tobacco Art

The famous "Havana" is treasured by cigar connoisseurs all over the world. In the mid-19th century, the labels, wrappers and bands used to market Cuban tobacco to an international clientele evolved into high art and are now popular collectibles. It was an art of extraordinary detail and beauty, which resulted in what is known as "The Golden Age" of lithography. This entertaining documentary looks at the skill and imagination that created these exquisite gold-embossed and gilded cigar box labels.
VHS: S31854. $19.95.

Ethel Kvalheim, Rosemaler

One of America's foremost folk artists, Ethel Kvalheim, talks about her life and work. This beautifully presented video portrait makes a valuable library resource. 18 mins. Resource guide available.
Resource Guide.
VHS: S25772. $45.00.
Video.
VHS: S25759. $95.00.

Fine Art: General, Vol. 1

This program offers an overview of career opportunities that exist in the visual art field. The video illustrates the various fields of study of fine arts—a painter, a pastel artist, an art appraiser and a gallery owner. 30 mins.
VHS: S19923. $39.95.

Fine Art: Production, Vol. 2

This program presents alternate careers in fine art production, including the professions of a sculptor, a printmaker, and a potter, who offer insights and advice on the correct steps toward becoming a financially independent artist. 30 mins.
VHS: S19924. $39.95.

Fine Art: Education, Vol. 3

This program looks at careers in art restoration, art history and high school level art instruction. 30 mins.
VHS: S19925. $39.95.

Flowers and Gardens

The most familiar use of flowers in art is in painted still life, but flowers at the Metropolitan Museum are also used in huge floral displays arranged weekly, and in the gardens and courtyards of the Museum itself. 25 mins.
VHS: S04649. $29.95.

Forms of Artistic Expression: Glass and Sculpture

"Stained Glass: Painting With Light" explores the beauty and art form of stained glass; "Sculpture—Process of Discovery", the molding of sculpture from rock, and the process of discovery. 31 mins.
VHS: S05842. $19.95.

Four Fashion Horses

Colorful, imaginative studio set ups present clothes by artists and innovative designers. Designed as a sales scheme, the tape vividly presents a little-known convergence of art and fashion.
VHS: S10183. $19.95.
Sophie Vielle, USA, 1983, 28 mins.

Furniture to Go

The Learning Channel's popular Furniture Guys show how to strip, sand and paint an antique Hoosier, refinish a marble top table and reupholster a Victorian sofa. Their easy instructions are made even more palatable by humor and the possibility of turning old relics into useful items. 60 mins.
VHS: S29429. $39.95.

Gathered in Time

The strands of quilters lives, like their patchwork, chronicle the experience of women and their fascinating past. Learn their stories in this film based on the book *Gathered in Time: Utah Quilts and Their Makers, Settlement to 1950*. 90 mins.
VHS: S34822. $14.95.

Gifts from the Fire: The Ceramic Art of Brother Thomas

Brother Thomas Bezanson, a Benedictine monk, is a ceramic artist working with porcelain in the Chinese and Japanese traditions. This film weaves the story of the artist, his work and his philosophy with the technical aspects of the making of a single piece of art. 29 min.
VHS: S18393. $14.95.

Glenville School Computer Graphics

Shows animated designs created by fifth and sixth grade students in Greenwich, CT, on an Apple II computer. Includes a 36-page booklet, *An Easy Guide for Creating Computer Graphics in Elementary Schools*. 8½ mins.
VHS: S06560. $39.95.

Hidden Treasures

Jewelry collector and instructor Christie Romero hosts this informative program on antique and vintage jewelry of the last two centuries, defining major characteristics, style and periods and what to look for in assessing value and worth.
VHS: S18262. $24.95.

I Can't Give You Anything But Love/ Solid Gold Illusion

Includes a selection of Claire Burch's "unusual people drawings" used in the film *Timothy Leary's Dead*, as well as images of paintings from the book *Solid Gold Illusion* by Burch, set to original music.
VHS: S33822. $24.95.
Claire Burch, USA, 1990, 90 mins.

Illustrated Guide to Caricature

The art of making people look ridiculous has influenced politics, society, and the arts for centuries. Luck and Flaw, two contemporary caricaturists, take viewers on an unusual, eye-opening journey through the history of this appealing art form. A survey of works by such early caricaturists as Low, Daumier, Dantan and Cruikshank is enriched by views of contemporary caricature by Gerard Scarfe, Ralph Steadman, Steve Bell and Ralph Sallon. 60 mins.
VHS: S10269. $29.95.

Inside Tips on Discovering Antiques

This instructive guide provides lessons and insights into finding the best buys on antiques. Frank Farmer Loomis IV is an acknowledged expert and appraiser who wanders from outdoor markets to country stores in search of valuable works. He offers a practical guide in the buying and selling of antiques and collectibles. 40 mins.
VHS: S20350. $19.95.

Knights and Armor

The reality of knighthood is captured in this document based on the actual experiences of Sir William Marshall. This video brings the viewer to battlegrounds and ancient courts where knights fought and lived. Includes a visit to Graz, Austria, the site of a great collection of armor. 100 min.
VHS: S24492. $29.95.

L'Art Vetraria (The Art of Glass)

This program goes inside the craft and discipline of art glass, through the objects of Josh Simpson, who discusses the technical and creative mechanics involved, as well as the personal consequences of sustaining a 3000-year old tradition. 30 mins.
VHS: S20309. $39.95.

Lethal Weapons: The Visual Art of Barton Benes

An illustrated, post-museum retrospective interview with artist Barton Benes, who uses his HIV-positive blood as "art supplies." Benes is known for his visual puns and politically rebellious treatment of money.
VHS: S33821. $24.95.
Claire Burch, USA, 1993, 20 mins.

Malagan Art of New Ireland

In the South Pacific of Papua, New Guinea, the New Irelanders honor their ancestors by staging elaborate ceremonies known as malagans. Days of dancing, feasting, singing and speechmaking culminate in the dramatic unveiling of large wooden sculptures, which are hidden in the secret enclosures near the clan's burial grounds. This film documents a contemporary malagan in vivid detail, from the roasting of the pigs to the carving of intricate masks and poles used during this complex cycle of festivities. 28 mins.
VHS: S02631. $29.95.

Maria! Indian Pottery of San Ildefonso

Indian pottery maker Maria Martinez demonstrates the traditional Indian ways of making pottery. Beginning with the spreading of sacred corn, you will see gathering and mixing of clay, construction and decorating of pottery and building of the firing mound. 27 mins.
VHS: S06698. $29.95.

Mark Munski: Funcrime and Art

Mark Munski is an artist who often uses graffiti as a jumping-off point, both for his method and his chosen ground, which usually is an unused wall. Watch while he creates a piece as the sun goes down. Empty Lot, Venice, California. 1993. 15 mins.
VHS: S34025. $19.95.

The Marvelous Toys of Dr. Athelstan Spilhaus

World-famous oceanographer, inventor and toy collector Athelstan Spilhaus shows off more than a hundred of his personal favorite toys. Dating from the 18th and 19th centuries, these one-of-a-kind "automata" spin, waddle, nod and gyrate in hypnotizing detail. 1989, 72 mins.
VHS: S15802. $29.95.

Masks from Many Cultures

This video unveils more than 100 masks, representing the various images with sequences of dances and festivals. The program includes masks from Mardi Gras in New Orleans, Dominican Republic, New Guinea, Bali, China, Tibet, Japan, Korea, Mexico, Guatemala, Bolivia, Native Americans and several African nations. 21 mins.
VHS: S18514. $39.95.

The Medal Maker

This rare 1929 film presents multi-award-winning coin and medal designer/sculptor Laura Gardin Fraser in her New York studio creating the models for the Special Medal of Honor for the National Sculpture Society, America's highest sculptural award. 30 mins.
VHS: S32202. $29.95.

Meet the Caldecott Illustrator: Jerry Pinkney

The award-winning illustrator of *The Talking Eggs* invites viewers into his studio to watch him work on his delightful watercolor and pencil drawings. "My satisfaction," he says, "comes from the actual marks on the paper, and when it sings it's magic." 1991, 21 mins. Public Performance Rights.
VHS: S13892. $164.95.

Merchants and Masterpieces

Meet the collectors whose vision and generosity built the Metropolitan Museum of Art. J. Pierpont Morgan, Robert Lehman, Benjamin Altman, the Rockefellers, and the Webbs were passionate collectors pursuing magnificent art. Based on Calvin Tomkins' history of the museum, this program provides a rare opportunity to discover the people who originally collected the Met's masterpieces. 87 mins.
VHS: S12368. $39.95.

Metropolitan Cats

The cat—as expressed in the art of different cultures through history. In an examination of more than 4,000 years of art housed at New York's Metropolitan Museum, this program explores the charm and mystery of the cat as a vehicle for reflecting both the artist and society. 30 mins.
VHS: S04651. $39.95.

Norman Rockwell and the Saturday Evening Post

A charming video biography of America's popular and beloved artist, Norman Rockwell, through rare footage, photographs and intimate interviews with his friends and colleagues. 60 mins.
VHS: S09872. $39.95.

Norman Rockwell: An American Portrait

Mason Adams hosts this look at Rockwell, the man and his works. A host of commentators including humorist Erma Bombeck and child psychiatrist Robert Coles reflect on Rockwell, his works and impact. 60 mins.
VHS: S12149. $24.95.

Paper and Silk: The Conservation of Asian Works of Art

This program begins with a brittle 18th century Chinese scroll painting in hundreds of fragments. We are led through the restoration process; from the initial piecing together of the work to its re-backing and in-painting and eventual remounting. 26 mins.
VHS: S02697. $39.95.

Quilt on the Wall: Portrait of Jan Myers

Contemporary textile artist Jan Myers weds her utilitarian respect for quiltmaking with her own desire for self-expression. Antique quilts and historical photographs provide the backdrop as we watch Myers make a patchwork quilt from beginning to end. 28 mins.
VHS: S00203. $29.95.

Raggedy Ann and Andy

Collectors will enjoy this documentary that both explores and explains the history of these classic cloth dolls. Dating and distinguishing their origins is a valuable and enjoyable pursuit. In addition, the life of the originator, Johnny Gruelle, is portrayed through interviews and photographs. 90 mins.
VHS: S25744. $49.95.

Shodo, The Path of Writing

Introducing the manifestations of calligraphy in Japan, this program visits advertisers, monks, students and the kabuki theater. Masters demonstrate various techniques, their reverence for special inks and brushes, and the origins of texts and ideograms. 1980, 30 mins.
VHS: S16209. $29.95.

Solid Gold Illusion, Variations I, II and III

Images from the Claire Burch's book *Solid Gold Illusion*, plus new ones, set to original music.
VHS: S33823. $24.95.
Claire Burch, USA, 1991, 90 mins.

The Story of Fashion Box Set

First seen on public television, this three-program box set features commentary by artistic adviser Karl Lagerfeld and goes behind the scenes with world-famous designers, including Donna Karan, to explore the history of fashion. Programs include: *Remembrance of Things Past* (60 mins.), *The Art and Sport of Fashion* (63 mins.) and *The Age of Dissent* (61 mins.).
VHS: S28590. $79.95.

Story of Fashion Volume 1: Remembrance of Things Past

The fashion of the early 20th century had its roots in the 19th, influenced particularly by the work of Charles Worth. This program traces the fashion of haute couture, from Worth through Coco Chanel, as revealed in the rise and fall of the corset and reflected in the wardrobes of the era's most famous women. 60 minutes.
VHS: S07625. $29.95.

Story of Fashion Volume 2: The Art and Sport of Fashion

Innovations in art, such as cubism and surrealism, greatly influenced the fashions of the '20s, '30s, and '40s, as did the glamorous stars of Hollywood. This film explores fashion's evolution from Coco Chanel to Christian Dior. 64 minutes.
VHS: S07626. $29.95.

Story of Fashion Volume 3: The Age of Dissent

From the '50s to today, from Dior to Dynasty, fashion has evolved into a huge international business with a new breed of superstar designers. *The Age of Dissent* shows how fashion is not just a business, but is show business—with theatrical fashion shows, extravagant product launches, and lavish photographic sessions that rival the film industry in opulence and cost. 61 minutes.
VHS: S07627. $29.95.

Studio Melee Sampler

Schematic computer-animated presentation and documentary of an interactive video installation constructed from old machine parts and painted backdrops.
VHS: S10208. $29.95.
Terry Mohre, USA, 1984, 20 mins.

Textile Magicians

A magical journey with five contemporary Japanese fiber artists who left urban centers for cedar forests outside Kyoto in order to live in harmony with nature. With Chiyoko Tanaka, Masakazu Kobayashi, Naomi Kobayashi, Jun Tomita and Hiroyuki Shindo. 58 mins.
VHS: S31849. $29.95.

Threads of Survival

Master weaver Nhu Fang Yang and her daughter-in-law apprentice Ia Moua Yang sit at their traditional bamboo loom and describe the life of the Hmong. Brightly colored and intricately textured story cloths portray such events as the Hmong fleeing Laos after the Vietnam War. 25 mins.
VHS: S26808. $49.95.

The Tournament

Chivalry may be dead, but many of its beautiful artifacts survive in the armour collection of the Metropolitan Museum, one of the world's greatest armories. Collection curator Dr. Helmut Nickel narrates this fascinating glimpse of medieval society. 30 mins.
VHS: S04656. $29.95.

Tradesmen and Treasures: Gothic and Renaissance Nuremburg

Documents the remarkable flowering of art and culture in Nuremberg during the 14th to 16th centuries, as the city evolved from a trade center of the Holy Roman Empire to a Renaissance city. Works of art by Durer, Veit and Kraft are featured. Produced by the Metropolitan Museum and Bayerische Rundfunk. 55 mins.
VHS: S03402. $39.95.

Treasures of the National Postal Museum/Rarities and Oddities of the National Postal Museum
This package of two documentaries provides highlights into the methodology and working conditions of the world's largest stamp museum, produced in association with the museum and the U.S. Postal Service. Each tape is 40 mins.
VHS: S17183. $19.95.

Varga Girls: The Esquire Magazine Images of Alberto Vargas
Vargas's drawings defined an entire era's concept of the beautiful pin-up girl. His images were featured in over 60 published *Esquire* issues. This video examines these works and also offers a personal look at Vargas himself. 55 mins.
VHS: S26292. $19.95.

Vermillion Editions
As one of the country's most distinguished print studios, Vermillion Editions attracts artists from all over the U.S. to Minnesota to work with master printer Steven Andersen. This program opens with a brief overview of modern American printmaking and then goes behind the scenes into the studios to show artists making highly complex prints on paper. 55 mins.
VHS: S04193. $49.95.

A Visit with Tomie dePaola
Acclaimed children's author/illustrator Tomie dePaola opens his home and 200-year-old barn/studio for a tour and some conversation about how he creates his books and artwork. 25 mins.
VHS: S31612. $39.95.

Voyages: The Journey of the Magi
The Biblical journey of the Magi has inspired artists for nearly 2,000 years. This program recreates their actual route, setting the event in both its cultural and archeological contexts. As sites in the journey of the Wise Men are seen, artifacts and coins dating from the period offer additional insight into an event which generated a wealth of art. Narrated by art historian and archeologist Karl Katz; filmed in Jerusalem and Bethlehem. 30 mins.
VHS: S04653. $29.95.

Walls of Light: The History of Stained Glass
Covers the 5,000-year history of leaded and stained glass, from Yemen in the Arabian Peninsula, to Istanbul, Augsburg, Chartres and New York. Includes the stained glass artwork of artists such as Louis Comfort Tiffany, John LaFarge, Frank Lloyd Wright, Marc Chagall, Henry Holiday and William Morris. 85 mins.
VHS: S33257. $29.95.

The Way Things Go
This 1987 cult masterpiece captures the precisely crafted chaos created by visual artists Peter Fischli and David Weiss in their kinetic installations using everyday objects. "This rudimentary yet showy masterpiece would have made Picasso envious" (*Flash Art*).
VHS: S32030. $29.95.
Peter Fischli/David Weiss, Switzerland, 1987, 30 mins.

Wildlife Decoy Carvers
Carving duck decoys has transcended its early uses in hunting and has become a folk art form of considerable accomplishments. This documentary looks at wildlife decoy carvers and their unique art.
VHS: S03417. $19.95.

Windcarver
Former architect T. Merrill Prentice studies the slightest air currents before handcrafting common materials into delicate, moving sculptures. Captured in the heat of his creative process, Tim discusses his philosophies of public and private art with several humorous anecdotes. Many of his works are featured, photographed in mesmerizing detail. 28 mins.
VHS: S15748. $49.95.

With Hand in Heart
A portrait of southwestern Native American artists and their work, ranging from vases and bowls to hand-woven Navajo blankets and storyteller figures. With Lucy Lewis, Jody Falwel, Margaret Tefoya, Tony Roller, Fanny Nampeyo, Thomas Polacca, Mary Reed and Helen Cordero. 30 mins.
VHS: S31850. $24.95.

Work in Process: The Furniture of Larry Hendricks
Laurence Hendricks explores his theory of style and function as an outgrowth of Shaker and Bauhaus traditions. With examples of his work, he discusses the value of apprenticeship and the high level of experience, education and information required to become a master craftsperson in the modern world. Close-up photography of his hands in action follow the creation of a new piece from conception to completion. 28 mins.
VHS: S15745. $49.95.

Wrapped in Glory: Quilts and Bedcovers from 1700-1900
American history is recorded from a unique perspective, in these beautiful and rare examples of figurative quiltmaking. Los Angeles County Museum of Art, Los Angeles. 1991. 15 mins.
VHS: S34017. $19.95.

ART TECHNIQUES

Acrylic
The brushes, palettes, paints, painting surfaces of acrylic, use of various mediums, scumbling, drybrush, spattering, impasto and painting with instruments other than brushes. Gail Price. 37 mins.
VHS: S07644. $59.95.

American Craft Council: Fiber-Coiled Basketry
Illustrates the process of making continuous coil baskets with yarn, raffia, beads, feathers and techniques to alter their form and composition. Shows completed pieces incorporating the described stitches as well as historical basketry. 20 mins.
VHS: S07660. $39.95.

American Craft Council: Masks and Face Coverings
Portrays the many ways man has sought to alter, disguise, protect and immortalize his face. Symbolic, ritualistic, historic and contemporary masks are shown created from a wide range of materials. 21 mins.
VHS: S07661. $39.95.

American Craft Council: Papermaking USA and The Handmade Paper Book
Presents the work of 34 artists who approach papermaking from varied perspectives. The Handmade Paper Book highlights examples by 16 artists who go beyond the traditional book to create unique, three-dimensional art objects. 20 mins.
VHS: S07662. $39.95.

Art Smart Videotape Series
This series of 12 videos on pottery, drawing, printing and jewelry provides hands-on instruction laid out in a clear, step-by-step process. Basic skills are presented for different grade levels, and each video concludes with a summary of major steps covered.

Basic Screen Printing.
VHS: S22104. $49.95.
Basic Jewelry.
VHS: S22105. $49.95.
Cast Jewelry.
VHS: S22106. $49.95.
Figure Drawing.
VHS: S22100. $49.95.
Fundamentals of Drawing.
VHS: S22099. $49.95.
Glazing and Firing.
VHS: S22098. $49.95.
Handbuilt Pottery.
VHS: S22095. $49.95.
Handbuilt Clay Sculptures.
VHS: S22096. $49.95.
Photo Screen Printing.
VHS: S22103. $49.95.
Portrait Drawing.
VHS: S22101. $49.95.
Relief Printing.
VHS: S22102. $49.95.
Wheel Thrown Potters.
VHS: S22097. $49.95.

Artists Are Special People... Just Like You!
Anyone can learn to draw! This stimulating four-part program helps students develop their powers of observation, introduces viewers to the five basic elements of drawing and encourages them to loosen up their creative muscles as they use these basic elements to construct simple and complex pictures and images. 32 mins.
VHS: S09461. $141.00.

Basic Art by Video I: Painting
I in a series of III tapes introduces drawing, design, and color, the building blocks of painting, right in the instructor's studio. Step-by-step, fine artist Charles Haddock teaches classic technique in the tradition of the masters.
VHS: S03994. $19.95.

Basic Art by Video II: Drawing & Design
II in a series of III tapes demonstrates that drawing and design skills, though intuitive, must consciously be nurtured and developed under professional guidance.
VHS: S03995. $19.95.

Basic Art by Video III: Color
III in a series of III tapes demonstrates the poetic nature-colors from Renaissance through Impressionism to Modern, bypassing the raw beginners' colors.
VHS: S03996. $19.95.

Batik as Fine Art
Cloth dyeing and alternate waxing is a staple of folk art. Professor Helen Carkin examines its transformation from textile art to a more accessible fine art. She shows the use of color and its relation to the color wheel, and takes the viewer on a step-by-step process from making a pinning frame to framing the finished work. 30 mins.
VHS: S17209. $39.95.

Beadmaking
Glass, fire and the imagination are the chief building blocks that go into the manufacture of beads. Michael Max, a glass artist and educator, demonstrates his original techniques in a step-by-step process. Anyone can learn to make and decorate these tiny jewel-like wonders. 60 mins.
VHS: S25737. $39.95.

Blizzard's Wonderful Wooden Toys
Richard Blizzard has assembled this special video of seven of his most popular wooden toys and models to make. Here are projects carefully designed to suit all abilities, ranging from an easy-to-make sand pit to his tour-de-force, a 1907 Rolls Royce Silver Ghost, nearly three feet long, which will challenge the most skilled woodworker. 108 mins.
VHS: S07610. $19.95.

Ceramics
Ceramics handbuilding, ceramics mixing, wedging, throwing and ceramics decorating, glazing and firing are demonstrated at the Anderson Ranch Arts Center. 35 mins.
VHS: S07649. $89.50.

Ceramics: Handbuilding
Popular ceramist Ro Mead presents this two-part video.
Ceramics: Handbuilding Part 1. The artist, working in her own studio, demonstrates creative ways to make coil and pinch pots and slab forms. She also creates a drape-mold platter decorated with inlaid colored clays. 45 mins.
VHS: S11657. $29.95.
Ceramics: Handbuilding Part 2. In Part 2, Ro Mead expands on her first video and creates slab forms decorated with inlaid colored clay including a cylindrical vase, a drape-mold bowl and tiles decorated with airbrush. 45 mins.
VHS: S11658. $29.95.
Ceramics: Handbuilding (Complete). Both parts of this 2-part series at a special price.
VHS: S11659. $54.95.

Ceramics: Introduction to Throwing on the Potter's Wheel
Virtuoso potter Stephen Jepson offers a comprehensive, easy-to-follow program on the basics of understanding the Potter's wheel. Jepson runs the viewer through the intricate process step-by-step, with special emphasis on mechanics and methodology. 53 mins.
VHS: S19643. $39.95.

Charles Reid: Flowers in Watercolor
From contour drawing to last brush stroke, you watch a beautiful still life with flowers emerge—seeing it from the artist's point of view. A fascinating study of how Reid achieves the freshness for which his paintings are acclaimed.
VHS: S09712. $69.95.

Clay in a Special Way
Shows the process of teaching clay to students of diverse abilities, including handicapped children, resulting in a successful creative experience as well as developing positive human interaction and communication. 15 mins.
VHS: S07640. $49.95.

Collage Methods
Different kinds of paper are put together demonstrating the basic techniques of two-dimensional collage. Colored and stained paper, tissue, letters and pictures are all arranged using collage methods. 20 mins.
VHS: S22077. $24.95.

Color Perceptions
Illustrates basic color theory and practice including the use of primary, secondary and complementary colors. Artist Arthur Turner emphasizes learning by direct perception of color phenomena. 44 mins.
VHS: S07654. $39.95.

Color: The Artist's Inspiration
Lively illustrations and practical demonstrations bring alive the study of color. This comprehensive, two-volume program displays lively modern and classic paintings to show how color theory is applied by real artists in the studio and how color has been used during various eras in the history of art. 42 mins.
VHS: S09466. $359.00.

Connecting—Grades K-8
An interdisciplinary approach to visual learning for young students. Connecting draws its content from all subjects, stimulating visual, experimental learning. Themes are "webbed" to extend meaning and find relationships, expand understanding and make connections. Covers rhythms and patterns, change and transformation, grids. A 200-page manual accompanies.
VHS: S09087. $269.00.

Contour Drawing
Contour lines free the imagination as it sharpens the viewer's observation. This program helps students understand the power of contour lines and shows them the variation and interest that can be achieved with various materials, including pastel, marker, pencil, crayon and paint. 13 mins.
VHS: S09467. $105.00.

Controlling Watercolor
Tony Couch explains in simple terms the behavior of water, paint and paper in painting and demonstrates control of these elements using brush, water and sponge to create three critical textures. 55 mins.
VHS: S07628. $39.95.

Creating Abstract Art
Abstraction and abstract art are explained using easily understood examples. The simplification of shapes, distortion, emphasis on overlapping shapes and fracturing, contour continuation are explained. Ultimately these examples and techniques reveal how design becomes more important than subject matter in art-making. 20 mins.
VHS: S22076. $24.95.

Creating Nonobjective Paintings
Artist and teacher Gerald F. Brommer shows how to create nonobjective works through a variety of techniques. Texture, color fields, gesture and collage are some of the main issues covered. In addition, noteworthy examples of nonobjective art show students the emotional and creative range of this type of artwork. 26 mins.
VHS: S27639. $24.95.

Creating the Decorative Cloth
A video for highlighting the techniques deployed in creating four different kinds of decorative cloth—tapestry, brocade, embroidery and pile. The expert commentary demonstrates the distinct features that separate the four structures. 45 mins.
VHS: S20351. $39.95.

Creating with Ceramics
Shows a montage of historical ceramic pieces and then illustrates techniques of clay gathering, mixing, wedging, throwing, handbuilding, glazing and firing. Ceramicists demonstrate different techniques and types of pottery. 26 mins.
VHS: S07634. $59.95.

Creating with Watercolor
Cecile Johnson captures the beauty of basic watercolor techniques as she applies them in several demonstration paintings including a barn, a street scene, and a mountain landscape. 20 mins.
VHS: S07633. $39.95.

Crizmac Master Pack
A specially developed art video for students in grades 4-8, this tape explores the life and work of six modern artists, including Monet, van Gogh, Gauguin, Picasso, Kandinsky and Chagall. After introducing the artists, studio activities that relate to the artist's work are demonstrated combining art history and studio skills.
VHS: S09077. $209.00.

Dance of the Wheel
An apprentice and disciple of the legendary potter Michael Cardew, Todd Piker has built one of the few wood-fired tube kilns in the United States. He takes the viewer through the creative and emotional process of the elemental art of pottery: Earth - Water - Fire. For potters at all levels of experience. 28 mins.
VHS: S14595. $49.95.

Drawing and Sketching with Markers
Using step-by-step demonstrations, artist Tony Couch shows the techniques he uses to create fine art with markers—showing that skillful handling of this drawing media can give you exceptional works of art. 60 mins.
VHS: S14133. $39.95.

Drawing I
Drawing with the pencil (basic drawing techniques to render texture, value, shading, negative and positive space), and drawing techniques (use of charcoal, pen and ink, crayon, felt tips and washes on varied textures). Gail Price. 33 mins.
VHS: S07641. $59.95.

Drawing II
Drawing landscapes, seascapes, cityscapes, and drawing people and animals are taught by Gail Price. 39 mins.
VHS: S07642. $59.95.

Drawing III
Includes drawing with charcoal and pastels, drawing with mixed media and drawing with markers. 64 mins.
VHS: S07643. $89.50.

Drawing in the Source: Lita Albuquerque
Extracting the mystical relationship of humankind to earth and earth to the cosmos, Lita Albuquerque has explored a variety of mediums ranging from ephemeral earthworks, stream of consciousness writings and drawings to large scale paintings, sculptures and installations. This profile reveals her thoughts, motivations, inspirations and concerns. 9 mins.
VHS: S15767. $39.95.

Drawing Landscapes with Pencil and Ink
Tony Couch shows you just how easy it is to create professional-looking drawings using basic methods with pencil and ink-and you'll be able to incorporate these techniques into your drawings after viewing this video program. 60 mins.
VHS: S14134. $39.95.

Drawing Methods with Gail Price
A series of nine drawings lead aspiring artists through many methods for enhancing and finishing drawings, including crayon resist. Gail Price employs felt tip markers, ink pens, colored pencils, crayons, and even twigs and a palette knife in this exploration of drawing techniques.
VHS: S20989. $24.95.

Drawing: Learning Professional Techniques
Artist and educator Tony Couch shows the professional drawing techniques he feels are necessary to create a work of art. These include contour drawing, gesture drawing, perspective, cross-hatching and modeling. Then he completes several drawings in pencil, ink, and colored markers using the techniques demonstrated. 55 mins.
VHS: S14132. $39.95.

Elementary Art Appreciation Videos—Understanding Painting Series
Children in grades 3-8 will learn how to view artistic masterpieces by focusing on line, shape and the language of art. Developing a mood in portraiture and the use of color and line to express ideas is thoroughly explained for young audiences.
Abstraction, Light, and Color.
VHS: S26605. $34.95.
Approaching a Painting.
VHS: S26601. $34.95.
Composition and Realism.
VHS: S26602. $34.95.
Landscape, Seascape.
VHS: S26603. $34.95.
Portraits, People.
VHS: S26604. $34.95.
Elementary Art Appreciation: Understanding Painting Video Set.
VHS: S26606. $165.00.

Elements and Principles of Design with Artist Tony Couch
Tony Couch graphically explains how the elements of design, including line, shape, value, color, texture and direction, are used to build a design. He shows how each of the principles of design, balance, harmony, gradation, repetition, contrast, dominance and unity apply to each of the elements. 47 mins.
VHS: S11261. $39.95.

Exploring Color Workshop: Vol. 1: Basic Color Mixing
Nita Leland, author of *Exploring Color*, teaches artists of every level color vocabulary and basic color mixing, exploration of paint characteristics and compatible pigments, and expanded palettes and color schemes. 54 mins.
VHS: S31542. $29.95.

Figure Drawing and Painting with James Kirk
Kirk uses many existing drawings to show the use of dry media (pens, crayons, pencil) in drawing and sketching figures, both human and animals. He defines such concepts as contour line vs. gesture line, value and composition, and then demonstrates the application of the same skills to a watercolor painting of a seated nude. 60 mins.
VHS: S12861. $39.95.

Forrest Bales Presents Basic Latex Mold Making
Forrest Bales has been at the forefront of latex molds for more than 15 years. This instructional video considers the craft, technique, materials and tools needed from conception through completion. The video also provides step-by-step instructions on how to arrange and apply the materials. 32 mins.
VHS: S20338. $39.95.

Graphic Arts Training Library
Clip Art: Use and Fundamentals: Using Pre-Prepared Art Creatively. Teaches the fundamentals of designing and producing effective finished art work using limited-budget, camera-ready graphics in a variety of applications, including newsletters, ads, brochures, and T-shirts. 45 mins.
VHS: S10861. $69.95.

How to Draw Comics the Marvel Way
Stan Lee, the father of Marvel Comics and the creator of Spiderman and the Incredible Hulk shows you how to put your visions of super heroes on paper. 59 mins.
VHS: S08897. $19.95.

How to Visit an Art Museum
Stunningly photographed within the galleries of one of the world's great museums, The Art Institute of Chicago, this video contains practical tips that show parents and teachers how to help children get the most from every museum visit. 30 mins.
VHS: S31451. $19.95.

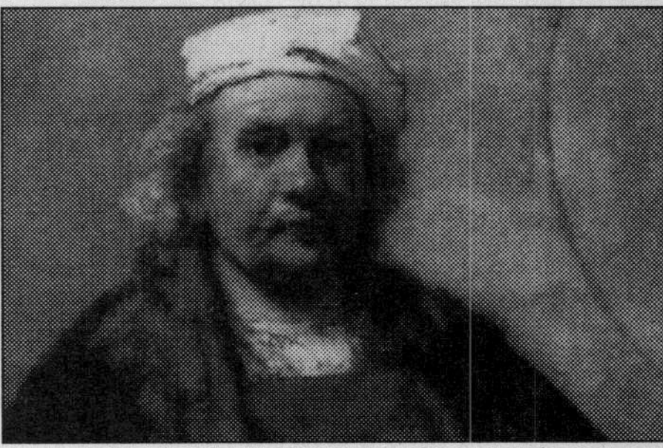

Learning to Paint with Carolyn Berry
This series, featuring professional art instructor Carolyn Berry, is designed for students, hobbyists, amateur painters and professionals. Each video offers an easy-to-follow, step-by-step method for creating a finished painting or drawing. Episodes include *Portrait Painting* (60 mins.), *Portrait Drawing* (60 mins.), *Still Life* (60 mins.), *Field Flowers* (42 mins.), *Water Color Techniques* (30 mins.), *Perspective* (30 mins.), *Basic Color: Vol. 1* (70 mins.) and *Basic Color: Vol. 2* (55 mins.). Public performance.
VHS: S32143. $279.95.
Christian Surette, USA, 1991-94, 407 mins.

Let's Create Art Activities (For Ages 5-10)
An instructional video supervised by teacher Ann Felice, featuring her students as they engage in various exercises, problem solving and creative endeavors, including creative clay, fold-dyed paper, pasta mosaics and snazzy sunglasses. 45 mins.
VHS: S18645. $29.95.

Life Drawing Video Workshops by Ruth Block
An exhaustive series of eight lessons, each beginning with a brief lecture defining the principles of the exercise and following with the necessary demonstrations of technique. Instruction is succeeded by the model(s)' pose, where "real time" is given to allow for participation in the exercise. Each tape comes with an information booklet. The complete set includes eight tapes, 729 minutes all told.
VHS: S15750. $449.00.

Lifting a Curtain: Conservation of Rubens' Crowning of St. Catherine
Documents the cleaning and restoration of Peter Paul Rubens' magnificent painting The Crowning of St. Catherine, in the collection of the Toledo Museum of Art. The viewer has a rare opportunity to see the care given to the masterpieces as paintings conservator Gabrielle Kopelman engagingly explains and demonstrates the techniques required to clean and restore the painting. 30 mins.
VHS: S03562. $39.95.

Making Stained Glass Windows
Learn the delicate art of making stained glass windows from Tim Yockey, master craftsman working in the Pacific Northwest, including the design, glass cutting, leading, soldering, puttying and finishing. 100 mins.
VHS: S09942. $54.95.

Maskmaker
Jackie Miller's video workshop is a guide to the fabrication and painting of *papier mache* masks. The program demonstrates the basic skills required for the process, distilled from a 10-hour course.
VHS: S19644. $39.95.
Jack Johnson, USA, 1992, 130 mins.

Maskmaking Introduction
Carole Sivin demonstrates techniques for using basic materials to make a variety. An instructional program is enriched by historical examples from different cultures. 35 mins.
VHS: S15549. $39.95.

Maskmaking with Clay
Teacher Peggy Flores demonstrates in an articulate and understanding manner the art of creating colorful and decorative masks from clay. 20 mins.
VHS: S31742. $24.95.

Maskmaking with Paper
Peggy Flores demonstrates in an articulate and clear way the art of constructing paper masks. Complete techniques and easily accessible materials are shown. 18 mins.
VHS: S20629. $24.95.

Maskmaking Workshop
Carole Sivin expands on the basic maskmaking techniques to produce interesting examples for performance, decoration, and fantasy. 50 mins.
VHS: S15550. $39.95.

Mobiles: Making Art That Moves
Go mobile! From the first mobiles created by Alexander Calder and exhibited in 1932, this program follows the evolution of style and technique and the endless search for creative expression. 22 mins.
VHS: S09472. $168.99.

Nudes in Limbo
A documentary that closely observes the employment of the unclothed human form in abstract and artistic dimensions and settings. Both the male and the female body will be presented in this color compilation distributed by the MCA corporation. 1983, 53 mins.
VHS: S06160. $29.95.

Oil Painting: Simplifying Outdoor Painting
A video showcasing the simple methods that painter John Stobart has developed during his 35-year career. The video provides an overview of the basic requirements an artist needs in order to paint nature. It includes a lesson on drawing and the nature of perspective, with special emphasis on preparation of canvas and the materials required for a field trip. 60 mins.
VHS: S19645. $24.95.

Oriental Art—Grades 5-12
Students gain new insights into the Chinese and Japanese cultures through calligraphy, paintings and woodblock prints. The philosophy and the art's connection with history is explored.
VHS: S09088. $112.50.

Paint with Strings 'n Things
Julie Abowitt shows how to paint using a ball of string, tempera paint, an old sponge and paper. 30 mins.
VHS: S09888. $9.95.

Paint Without a Brush
Give paintbrushes the brush with this new and create way to paint using just cotton swabs, tempera and construction paper. 30 mins.
VHS: S09887. $29.95.

Painting Barns in Watercolor
Tony Couch prepares a detailed drawing of barn buildings on location. The drawing is a lesson in itself as the artist uses line and value to make his reference drawing. In the studio, he draws a value sketch and prepares the watercolor paper for painting. He illustrates how color, shape, texture and value are used in painting barns, trees, grass and sky. 50 mins.
VHS: S11183. $29.95.

Painting Streams, Rocks and Trees in Watercolor
Well-known artist Tony Couch shows how to paint a mountain stream as he shares his painting skills in lessons on painting trees, mountains, rocks and water. The camera shows step-by-step painting skills with close-up views of his brush and palette. 55 mins.
VHS: S11182. $29.95.

Painting with Stephen Quiller
Crystal Productions presents five new art instruction videos with artist and teacher Stephen Quiller. Each tape focuses on a single topic or medium including watercolor, composition, color, visualization and experimental water media.
Color. Color concepts and different color combinations are presented in an exploration of this vital aesthetic component. Among those issues explored are primary, secondary and intermediate colors, after-image, intensity, contrast, value and monochromatic and analogous color. 18 mins.
VHS: S20898. $24.95.
Composition. Students will learn how to develop compositions from different subjects, and the importance of various shapes and values which can trigger ideas for larger scale paintings. Sketches also figure prominently in this instruction toward landscape painting. 18 mins.
VHS: S20897. $24.95.
Experimental Water Media. Combining different media like graphite, charcoal, colored pencils, pastels and even oil pastels can enliven traditional watercolor. Collage also offers greater creative flexibility. All these techniques are ably demonstrated in this final tape. 19 mins.
VHS: S20900. $24.95.
Visualizing What You Paint. More spontaneous and creative work will result when students are motivated to see and visualize their subjects with the techniques employed in this segment. Negative shapes, painting around the subject, even painting from light to dark and vice versa can all lead to more inspired paintings.
19 mins.
VHS: S20899. $24.95.
Watercolor Methods. Different types of papers, brushes and pigments are explored in this demonstration of watercolor techniques. A variety of key approaches, including wet-on-wet, drybrush and other innovative methods, are included in this easy-to-follow tape. 18 mins.
VHS: S20896. $24.95.
Painting with Stephen Quiller, Set.
VHS: S20901. $99.75.

Paper Play
Julie Abowitt demonstrates how tissue paper can be used to make collages and decorate other items such as bottles, jars and cans. 30 mins.
VHS: S09886. $9.95.

Papermaking and Bookbinding
Sandy Kinnee and Mollie Favour show handmade paper, papermaking techniques, and bookbinding using simple equipment. 59 mins.
VHS: S07650. $89.50.

Pencil Drawing with Gail Price
Using graphite and colored pencils, as well as a variety of papers and techniques, artist Gail Price leads the viewer through a series of ten drawings that illustrate the basics of drawing. Includes examples of scumble, smudge, stipple, hatching and cross-hatching. 20 mins.
VHS: S20988. $24.95.

Philip Pearlstein Draws the Artist's Model
A video workshop focusing on the painting and teaching ideas of one of the most important artists of the century; Pearlstein relates important ideas about art history and drawing the human nude figure to demonstrate techniques available to artists. Adapting sophisticated computer systems to this style of art, Pearlstein demonstrates step-by-step process of how to draw the human figure. 90 mins.
Laser: LD70306. $99.95.

Portraits in Watercolor with James Kirk: Elements of Design
Noted teacher and artist James Kirk covers the elements of design in drawing and painting and demonstrates a series of work-along exercises that lead directly to painting a portrait.
60 mins.
VHS: S09949. $39.95.

Portraits in Watercolor with James Kirk: Magic of Light and Dark
James Kirk guides you through a progression of different approaches to portrait painting. Follow along as Kirk implements and weighs each of the design elements in actual paintings.
60 mins.
VHS: S09950. $39.95.

Potter's Song: The Art and Philosophy of Paul Soldner
Soldner discusses his work and demonstrates the techniques to create his non-functional raku pottery. He also his lifestyle and theories of education for the potter.
VHS: S07635. $39.95.

Printmaking
Sandy Kinnee demonstrates introduction to printmaking and printmaking with basic equipment including relief, intaglio, lithography and serigraphy, and making prints with linoleum blocks, found objects, metal relief plates, plaster relief blocks, stencils, cutout cardboard plates. 38 mins.
VHS: S07651. $59.95.

Raku Ceramics with James Romberg
Raku artist and teacher James Romberg brings a subtle and fascinating form within reach of amateur potters, explaining this serendipitous art rooted in centuries-old Japanese ceremonies which is enjoying a powerful renaissance in the U.S. 75 mins.
VHS: S12865. $39.95.

Sculpture and the Creative Process
Dale Lamphere explores the creative process of the sculptor in his studio starting with initial thumbnail sketches in clay. He then makes the maquette and the armature and sculpts the finished work. 29 mins.
VHS: S16565. $39.95.

Slip Casting
Slip cast moldmaking and slip casting techniques; demonstrates making an original piece of pottery and then preparing it for multiple reproduction, including the complete process of making pottery from slip cast molds. Wendy Lopez, ceramicist. 37 mins.
VHS: S07648. $59.95.

Stretching the Canvas with Guest Host Peter Sellars
Producer/director Peter Sellars visits a number of California artists in their respective environments. A revealing trip inside the studio that depicts the artists at ease with their work.
59 mins.
VHS: S15768. $39.95.

Tempera
Tempera painting and tempera methods are demonstrated by Gail Price including tempera mixing, color mixing, dry brush techniques. 44 mins.
VHS: S07653. $59.95.

Time Exposure
Portrays the history of photography through the work of William Henry Jackson, who made 40,000 glass negatives. Reenactments demonstrate wet-plate photography, developing, solar printing. Includes dramatic on-location filming of the scenes of many of his photographs. 28 mins.
VHS: S09071. $29.95.

Traditional Basketmaking with John McGuire
This high-level professional instructional tape, suitable for both beginning and advanced basketmakers, presents traditional New England basketmaking with nationally acclaimed historian, author and basketmaker, John McGuire. 90 mins.
VHS: S08242. $69.95.

A Very Easy Christmas Ornament
Even beginning crafters can enjoy immediate success with this tape hosted by renowned crafter Julie Adolph, which provides easy-to-follow, step-by-step instructions for making a festive Christmas ornament. 38 mins.
VHS: S30037. $14.95.

A Very Easy Santa Design
Renowned crafter Julie Adolph provides step-by-step instructions for making a festive Santa design. 73 mins.
VHS: S30038. $14.95.

A Very Easy Santa Pillow
Julie Adolph provides easy-to-follow instructions for making a festive Santa pillow. 48 mins.
VHS: S30039. $14.95.

Water Media Techniques: Acrylic and Casein
Stephen Quiller demonstrates the special properties and handling characteristics of acrylic and casein and then shows how they can be used to create both transparent and opaque washes, impasto textures, and special effects. 60 mins.
VHS: S13297. $39.95.

Water Media Techniques: Watercolor and Gouache
Stephen Quiller works with various media and often combines them to create mixed media paintings. In this program, he shows the use of watercolor and gouache through small demonstration studies and then demonstrates landscape painting. 60 mins.
VHS: S13296. $39.95.

Watercolor I

Basic equipment and principles of watercolor, watercolor composition, techniques and watercolor demonstrations. Cecile Johnson. 40 mins.
VHS: S07645. $89.50.

Watercolor II

Mastering watercolor techniques through demonstration and learning watercolor skills through bold, positive, colorful brushwork as well as the construction of objects. Irving Shapiro. 45 mins.
VHS: S07646. $59.95.

Watercolor III

Design and composition in watercolor painting, and watercolor techniques in landscapes and seascapes. Tony Couch. 47 mins.
VHS: S07647. $59.95.

Watercolor Painting Pt. 1: Wet and Spontaneous

Watercolor artist Judy Howard demonstrates the art and techniques of watercolor, introducing color theory and exercises to help understand the behavior of water color paint. 60 mins.
VHS: S09947. $39.95.

Watercolor Painting Pt. 2: Taming the Wet Medium

In this program Judy Howard helps the student gain more control to achieve more harmonious colors and looseness, and to understand the step-by-step development of a painting. 60 mins.
VHS: S09948. $39.95.

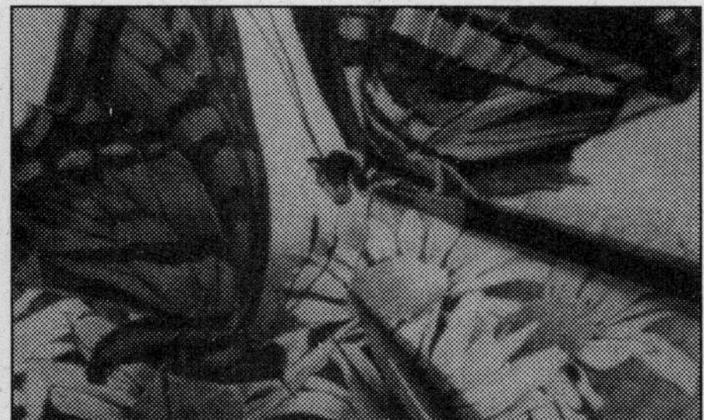

Watercolor Symbols: Rocks, Puddles and Weeds

Demonstrates painting symbols for rocks, puddles, weeds and grasses, as well as the "spatter" technique. 55 mins.
VHS: S07630. $54.95.

Watercolor Symbols: Trees and Water

Demonstrates painting symbols for trees and water. 55 mins.
VHS: S07629. $54.95.

The Way Pots Pour

Potter and teacher Marvin Bartel shows the common problems which afflict many teapots. This video includes basic physics demonstrations about the way liquids pour, as well as advice on how potters can design effective spouts.
VHS: S21990. $35.00.

Winter's Soft Mantle

Tony Couch demonstrates step-by-step how to complete a painting of farm buildings in the snow with special instruction on how to paint rough wood, soft snow and cast shadows. 115 mins.
VHS: S07631. $49.95.

Workshop in Oils with William Palluth

60 minutes each.
Autumn Landscape. William Palluth illustrates step-by-step through the painting of this colorful and detailed autumn landscape. Sketch and color print included.
VHS: S08928. $29.95.
Oil Painting Technique. A must for the serious artist or art teacher, revealing secrets including wood textures, shadows and reflections, soft edges, wet-on-wet, and glazes.
VHS: S08933. $29.95.
Starting to Paint. *For the beginning artist, William Palluth shows the basic brushes, brush strokes and paints to show how to apply oil paints to canvas while keeping colors clean and rich.*
VHS: S08935. $29.95.
Winter Landscape. A nostalgic snow scene featuring a magnificent bare tree in a step-by-step oil painting instruction. Includes a sketch and print.
VHS: S08936. $29.95.
Workshop in Oils: Mountain Landscape. William Palluth instructs how to paint this dramatic scene depicting the Mount of the Holy Cross in Colorado. Follow Bill as he mixes and supplies each color with depth, one of the most sought after effects in landscape painting. Sketch included. 60 mins.
VHS: S15751. $29.95.
Workshop in Oils: Sunset. You'll enjoy painting this nostalgic summer scene with warm light from an evening sky reflecting off a quiet stream. In this workshop, artist William Palluth shows how mixing large pools of color can make painting so much easier, as well as promote harmony in blending. Perfect for beginners. Sketch included. 60 mins.
VHS: S15752. $29.95.

WorldScape

The distinguished American naturalist and maritime artist John Stobart hosts this massive 13-part series. 390 mins.
WorldScape: Beer.
VHS: S19658. $19.95.
WorldScape: Greenwich.
VHS: S19653. $19.95.
WorldScape: Hilton Head.
VHS: S19656. $19.95.
WorldScape: Honfleur.
VHS: S19652. $19.95.
WorldScape: Jersey.
VHS: S19655. $19.95.
WorldScape: Laguna Beach.
VHS: S19650. $19.95.
WorldScape: Lyme Regis.
VHS: S19648. $19.95.
WorldScape: Martha's Vineyard.
VHS: S19654. $19.95.
WorldScape: Maui.
VHS: S19647. $19.95.
WorldScape: Montserrat.
VHS: S19649. $19.95.
WorldScape: Savannah.
VHS: S19651. $19.95.
WorldScape: St. Barthelemy.
VHS: S19646. $19.95.
WorldScape: Westport Point.
VHS: S19657. $19.95.
WorldScape: The Complete Series.
VHS: S19659. $129.95.

Yvonne Jacquette: Autumn Expansion

Yvonne Jacquette discusses the process of painting her 27 foot, three-panel work "Autumn Expansion" during its 1981 exhibition at the Brooke Alexander Gallery. 13 mins.
VHS: S08254. $39.95.

ARCHITECTURE

1071 5th Avenue: Frank Lloyd Wright and the Guggenheim Museum

Although this museum opened in 1959, it did not fulfill all of Wright's original intentions. Sir Richard Rogers explores the disputes, money problems and personality clashes that plagued this building. F. Murray Abraham and Claire Bloom are featured reading Wright's letters, offering still more insights into the drama surrounding the erection of this masterwork.
VHS: S22150. $29.95.

Antonio Gaudi

Compelling portrait of Antonio Gaudi (1852-1926), leading proponent of the Art Nouveau movement in architecture in Spain, whose distinctive style is marked by a fluidity of movement, rich color and sensuality of form and texture. Teshigahara's camera examines buildings designed by Gaudi, including Casa Vicens, Crypt of the Colonia Guell and Park Guell, Casa Batlo, Casa Mila and Barcelona's unfinished landmark, Templo de la Sagrada Familia.
VHS: S34740. $89.98.
Hiroshi Teshigahara, Japan, 1984, 72 mins.

Architect's Journal

A world-class DVD magazine exploring films on architecture and design, interactively involving the viewer in the discipline, process and personalities. Contains nine films, including *Spaces: The Architecture of Paul Rudolph*, *First-Person Singular: I.M. Pei*, *The Loop: Where the Skyscraper Began* and an original film of Frank Gehry's Schnabel House.
DVD: DV60263. $19.95.

The Architecture of Doom

A brilliant documentary which explores the inner workings of the Third Reich and illuminates the Nazi aesthetic in art, architecture and popular culture. Director Peter Cohen uses this analysis of Nazi art and architecture to shed new light on German popular culture, which made Hitler possible. Music by Richard Wagner, footage of Hitler and his Nazi party and rare films and memorabilia are combined to show how a civilized country supported a frustrated artist who became a maniacal despot.
VHS: S26346. $29.95.
Peter Cohen, USA, 1995, 119 mins.

Bob Vila's Guide to Historic Homes

Bob Vila of *This Old House* leads this three-tape video tour of 20 historic private homes, including Jefferson's Monticello and Frank Lloyd Wright's Fallingwater. A plantation in Mississippi, a Shaker home in Massachusetts, a Spanish colonial in Monterey and the peculiar Ace of Clubs House in Texas are also among the highlights. Each tape is 100 mins.
VHS: S29908. $59.95.

Buckminster Fuller: Thinking Out Loud

Rising from the depths of despair on Chicago's lakefront, Fuller transformed himself, his life, and ultimately the world with his radical take on the contemporary world. Though he is perhaps best known for his geodesic dome design, this architect and thinker encouraged a new global outlook combining ecology and technology. Morley Safer narrates while Spalding Gray reads Fuller's writings. Includes interviews with Paul Goldberger, Philip Johnson, John Cage, Merce Cunningham, Arthur Penn and others.
VHS: S27909. $39.95.
Karen Goodman/Kirk Simon, USA, 1995, 94 mins.

Built on the Rock: The Southern Appalachians

Features over 60 old-time mountain churches in four magnificent seasons in the Blue Ridge and Great Smoky Mountains. Includes Baptist, Methodist, Presbyterian and Episcopalian, all against the scenic background of the Appalachian Mountains. 60 mins.
VHS: S32674. $19.95.

Charles Rennie Mackintosh: A Modern Man

Traces the story of Scottish artist, architect and designer Charles Rennie Mackintosh, a precursor of the modernist style and Art Deco movement, and designer of the Glasgow School of Art library and the Glasgow Museum's McLellan Galleries. 45 mins.
VHS: S34888. $29.95.

Chicago's Riverfront: Where the Present Meets the Past

The Chicago River was the link between the Mississippi River and the Great Lakes, fostering the growth of the city of Chicago during the 19th Century. Today it is a showcase of striking modern architecture and historical buildings adapted to new uses. 30 mins.
VHS: S14590. $29.95.

The David Macaulay Series

Awe-inspiring architectural history comes alive in this award-winning PBS series from author/illustrator David Macaulay. Four-video set includes *Castle*, *Cathedral*, *Pyramid* and *Roman City*. Each tape is 60 mins.
VHS: S28448. $79.98.

Frank Lloyd Wright: The Office for Edgar J. Kaufmann

A documentary about the artistry and architectural innovation of Frank Lloyd Wright in designing the office for Edgar J. Kaufmann in 1935-37. The period coincides with Wright's historic Fallingwater House. 28 mins.
VHS: S19637. $29.95.

Frederick Law Olmsted and the Public Park in America

Olmsted's first major work was the composition of New York's Central Park in 1858. The project was fraught with obstacles-political, financial and topographical—yet the completed park serves as a testament to Olmsted's unique and pioneering vision. With a dramatic rhetoric depicting this exceptional undertaking, the film blends documentary elements and dramatizations of actual events. 58 mins.
VHS: S16000. $39.95.

Great Palaces of the World

Across the continents of the world, this Learning Channel production explores the often elusive interiors of key royal buildings. The Summer Palace of Beijing, the Royal Palace of Bangkok and India's Red Fort are highlighted. Both these buildings and the people who ruled from them are detailed in this three part series. 300 minutes.
VHS: S29431. $49.95.

The Homes of Frank Lloyd Wright

Go inside the homes Frank Lloyd Wright designed for himself: Oak Park Home and Studio (1891), Taliesin West (1937) and Taliesin (1911) in Spring Green, Wisconsin. Includes extensive footage of areas off-limits to the public. Features interviews with colleagues and students, including members of Wright's Taliesin Fellowship. 50 mins.
VHS: S33194. $19.95.

In the Footsteps of Peter: The Museums & The Buildings of Vatican City

A visually spectacular, state-of-the-art series of 16 half-hour segments in eight volumes produced by the Edizioni Musei Vaticani for the Jubilee in the Year 2000. Through the wonders of modern technology, this documentary series makes available to everyone the world's most spectacular and sacred repository of art, history and faith. Volumes include *The Vatican Museums: History, Art Works & Personalities*, *Roman & Etruscan Art in the Vatican Museums*, *Greek and Egyptian Art in the Vatican Museums*, *The Origins of Christian Art & The Sistine Chapel*, *The Raphael Rooms*, *The Loggia & The Historical Museum at St. John Lateran*, *The Ethnological Museum & Picture Gallery*, *The Collection of Modern Religious Art & The Apostolic Palace* and *Vatican City & The Great Basilica*. Each volume is 60 mins.
VHS: S32375. $149.95.

The Lakefront: Parks and Plans

"City in a Garden" is the slogan that inspired the Burnham 1909 plan for Chicago. In this video, the development of the Lakefront and Grant Park are detailed as they affected the face of the contemporary Midwestern metropolis. Includes a companion guidebook.
VHS: S27496. $34.95.

The Loop: Where the Skyscraper Began

A unique confluence of forces and events led to the development of this key modern architectural form. Technology and circumstances surrounding the genesis of the skyscraper are at the center of this video. Includes a companion guidebook.
VHS: S27494. $34.95.

Michigan Avenue: From Museums to the Magnificent Mile

At one end it is heavy with retail giants. At the other, this world renowned boulevard is home to key cultural institutions. The growth of Chicago's most fashionable and prestigious Avenue is revealed in this video. Includes a companion guidebook.
VHS: S27495. $34.95.

Modern Marvels Series

A series of tapes which explore major accomplishments of modern engineering and building.
Empire State Building. This is the miraculous story behind the building of the world's most famous skyscraper. It was the world's tallest for over a generation and it remains a monument for the ages. 50 mins.
VHS: S22091. $19.95.
Grand Coulee Dam. This mammoth dam is the result of both engineering bravado and a colossal vision. Many said it couldn't be done because of the obstacles that stood in the way. And yet here it is, a man-made wonder.
VHS: S22090. $19.95.
Las Vegas. Only in the contemporary era of jet travel and publicity could a city emerge that seems to be based on the ephemeral image of a mirage. This unique tourist site's origin is on view in this video. 50 mins.
VHS: S26235. $19.95.
Mount Rushmore. It took over 15 years to create the largest sculpture the world has ever seen. Carved from the raw stone of a living cliff, this memorial to four of America's greatest presidents is a testament to the bold character of the nation. 50 mins.
VHS: S22092. $19.95.
Panama Canal. A story of drama, history and action emerges in this documentary about the building of this ever-vital canal. Its union of the two oceans through the heart of the Western Hemisphere changed the modern face of the Americas. 50 mins.
VHS: S22093. $19.95.
The Eiffel Tower. Originally ridiculed as ugly, Gustave Eiffel's tower came to be regarded as a masterpiece of engineering. Today it is recognized the world over as an icon for Paris, the City of Light. This is the story of an inspired vision. USA/France, 1994, 50 mins.
VHS: S26232. $19.95.
The Golden Gate Bridge. It was originally believed that no bridge could span the San Francisco Bay. Then the longest suspension bridge on Earth opened to the public. A story of an engineering wonder is revealed in this video. 50 mins.
VHS: S26233. $19.95.
The Statue of Liberty. A design emerged in France for a colossal statue. The site in New York harbor required that an entire country, the United States, be convinced that it was possible. 50 mins.
VHS: S26234. $19.95.

Napa Valley Farmhouse Restoration

Join Steve Thomas and master carpenter Norm Abram as they expand and update a kitchen in a 1906 Victorian hip-roofed farmhouse to take advantage of a spectacular view, then tour the region's premier architectural attractions. 240 mins.
VHS: S28658. $29.95.

Notre Dame, Cathedral of Amiens

Two high-tech architectural videos describe 13th-century construction of Amiens Cathedral, one of the world's largest gothic structures. Volumes include *Notre Dame, Cathedral of Amiens: Computer and Architectural Animation* and *Notre Dame: Cathedral of Amiens: Live Walk-Through Video*. 22 mins.
VHS: S32309. $54.00.

Nova—Super Bridge

Play sidewalk supervisor at one of the world's most remarkable and risky bridge projects, the building of the elegant, cable-stayed Clark Bridge spanning the Mississippi at Alton, Illinois. 60 mins.
VHS: S33083. $19.95.

Once There Was a Ballpark

Martin Sheen hosts this informative and entertaining look at the history of baseball stadiums. From the humble beginnings in the streets through the original wooden bleachers, and on to more modern concrete structures, it's all here, including a look at some of the most beloved structures still standing, like Wrigley Field. 108 mins.
VHS: S21707. $19.98.

Philip Johnson: Self Portrait

America's pre-eminent senior architect wittily discusses his life, his work, his critics and his aesthetic in this documentary filmed over a period of ten years in many of the locations that evoke Johnson's long, brilliant and controversial career. Interviewing him is celebrated arts lecturer and writer Rosamund Bernier.
VHS: S30989. $150.00.
1985, 55 mins.

Places We Live: Complete Set

All three volumes of this "Weird and Wonderful Houses" series at a special price.
VHS: S20541. $75.00.

Places We Live: Dream Houses

A person's house is his self image, his autobiography as ghost-written by the architect. Mark Twain's house suited him so well that he became convinced he himself designed it. Other houses visited are Fenway Court in Boston, recreating a Venetian palazzo; the house at Vizcaya; Frank Lloyd Wright's Hollyhock House; Saarinen's Cranbook House and Henry Davis Sleeper's Beauport. 58 mins.
VHS: S20539. $29.95.

Places We Live: Houses for Individualists

A look at some fantastic houses built by individualists—houses built by people with creative dreams, original needs or compulsions and the ability to design and erect the unconventional. The program shows a guest house in the shape of a yellow dragon with slides for stairs, a spherical house, a house shaped like a snail, and many more. 28 mins.
VHS: S20540. $29.95.

Places We Live: Way Out Architecture

Some of the more unusual places Americans have designed as habitats and the kinds of people who design them and live in them are examined in this freewheeling look at modern architecture. Among them are an underwater house, a $3-million concrete tent, space ships and Noah's ark. The program also looks at the unorthodox architects who create the structures. 44 mins.
VHS: S20538. $29.95.

Pyramid

Based on his popular book, David Macaulay brings the mysteries of ancient Egypt to vivid life in this unique documentary. Combining location photography and animation, *Pyramid* describes the planning, construction and cultural significance of the Great Pyramid of Giza, the world's largest pyramid. 57 mins.
VHS: S15761. $69.95.

Salem, Massachusetts Antique Federal/Victorian Renovation

Watch the exciting renovation of this neglected 1768 gem as its Victorian addition undergoes exterior restoration, new kitchen and bath installation, heating system upgrades, and floor refinishing. 9 hrs.
VHS: S28659. $39.95.

Savannah, Georgia Victorian Row House

Watch as some of Savannah's finest restoration craftspeople restore and expand the kitchen, baths and master bedroom of this historically significant 1884 row house to accommodate a young family. 480 mins.
VHS: S28660. $29.95.

Soleri's Cities: Architecture for Planet Earth and Beyond

A portrait of architect Paolo Soleri, a student of Frank Lloyd Wright, who believes the massive population centers have created vast social and environmental threats to daily life. Soleri has proposed rebuilding the American city, which he calls the Arcology, integrating ecological principles within innovative architectural designs, to alleviate stress, overcrowding, urban despair and tumult. 30 mins.
VHS: S20023. $19.95.

Super Structures of the World

Take a tour through the inner workings of our modern structural giants with this visually astonishing, three-part series which examines the innovative thinking and technological advances that have made possible the world's most spectacular construction projects. Volumes include *Eurotunnel*, *Skyscrapers* and *Seawolf*. 156 mins.
VHS: S34904. $39.98.

Taliesin: The Tradition of Frank Lloyd Wright

Frank Lloyd Wright designed over 1,000 structures in a career that spanned more than half a century. Many of his most enduring architectural triumphs came during the time he immersed himself in the vitality and energy of the Taliesin Fellowship.
VHS: S15301. $29.95.

This Old House—Milton, MA—Project One 1701-1718

America's favorite home team renovates a 1724 Colonial and its classic post-and-beam barn in Milton, Massachusetts. The team is working with a respected Boston architect and a team of interior designers to preserve the home's architectural integrity, while at the same time updating it for 21st-century living. 18 half-hour episodes. Nine hours.
VHS: S33103. $39.95.

This Old Pyramid

An Egyptologist advises a stonemason from *This Old House* on how to build a new pyramid, as he reveals the secrets of the ancient pyramids in this NOVA video. 90 mins.
VHS: S28645. $19.95.

The World of Buckminster Fuller

Buckminster Fuller, the visionary creator of the geodesic dome, was influential across a range of fields. He coined the concept of the "Spaceship Earth," and gave voice to ecological concern in a time of unshakable faith in progress. This film from Robert Snyder offers a thorough biography of this unique genius.
VHS: S12220. $29.98.
Robert Snyder, USA, 85 mins.

PERFORMANCE ART

Antigone: Rites of Passion

Amy Greenfield's daring first feature retells Sophocles' classical tragedy through action, dance and cutting-edge rock music. It transforms the drama of the heroine who defied the State to bury her brother into ceaseless movement and music, haunting sound and words, a mounting outcry against the world's injustices climaxing in an end-of-the-world requiem. A hymn to the extremes of courage, devotion, outrage, eros and death. "Impressive, innovative rock opera film" (*Variety*). With music by Elliott Sharp, Glenn Branca and Diamanda Galas.
VHS: S15437. $29.95.
Amy Greenfield, USA, 1990, 85 mins.

Best of Radio Thin Air

Highlights from the best of the long running cable TV poetry/music show are joined in this video. Taylor Mead, John Zorn, Elliot Sharp, Lydia Lunch, Pete Seeger, numerous "New Beat" poets, East Village performance art, poetry and music videos are all included.
VHS: S22663. $29.95.
Mitch Corber, USA, 1990-93, 105 mins.

Burning Man Festival

Since 1986, the wild Burning Man Festival has attracted strange sights to a remote desert location. There, in a mix of pagan exuberance and post-apocalyptic whimsy, individuals stage fearsome performance/rituals. Happenings like the *Drive By Shooting Gallery* or the *Pyrotechnic Couple* are just the warm-up for the spectacular burning of a 40-foot figure to the sounds of beating drums and screaming crowds. 60 mins.
VHS: S27912. $19.95.

Cabaret Voltaire Presents...

A comprehensive video guide to Cabaret Voltaire and their radical incorporation of musique concrete, tribal, tape collage, industrial noise and techno. The 14 tracks include "Diskono," "Trash (Part 1)," "Badge of Evil," "Landslide," and "Seconds Too Late." 90 mins.
VHS: S19614. $19.95.

Carmen

Bizet's tale of temptation, desire, obsessive love and death is placed in the nightclubs and graffiti-laced streets of contemporary New York. Dance images, the sex life of a penguin, and scientific writings on volcanoes and glaciers also play a part in this updated opera.
VHS: S22644. $29.95.
Ann Sargent Wooster, USA, 1990, 20 mins.

Chappaqua

A controversial, startling and hypnotic mix of music and visuals in Conrad Rooks' (*Siddhartha*) semi-autobiographical drama following his journey from addiction to health. Rooks, a young, well-to-do alcoholic and junkie, heads for Switzerland for the "Swiss Sleeping Cure," where he enters a psychedelic, explosive and delusional world of the mind. With William S. Burroughs, Allen Ginsberg, Jean-Louis Barrault and Ornette Coleman; music by Ravi Shankar, Philip Glass and The Fugs. "Exceptionally interesting…a superb feat of imagination" (*The New Yorker*).
VHS: S31116. $19.95.
Conrad Rooks, USA, 1966, 82 mins.

Cirque du Soleil: We Reinvent the Circus

This video captures the original tour of the highly innovative and rightfully famous circus troupe from Canada. Experience the daring feats, the fantastic costumes, and the wonderful music which has captivated audiences the world over. An Emmy Award winning program. 55 mins.
VHS: S15623. $19.95.

Dream Man

An adaptation of James Carroll Pickett's one-man performance stars Michael Kearns as a harsh, Lenny Bruce-like commentator who conjures up elaborate, witty and profane sexual fantasies over the phone lines. "Straight forward, poetically insightful," wrote *Daily Variety*. Includes an interview with the playwright.
VHS: S17117. $19.95.
Hugh Harrison, USA, 1991, 90 mins.

Eric Bogosian: Confessions of a Porn Star

Eric Bogosian performs a variety of routines that cross the line between stand up comedy and performance art. This tape brings together some of his best bits, including selections from *Our Gang, The Pacer, Porno, Beat Poet* and more.
VHS: S26706. $24.95.
Rob Klug, USA, 1995, 60 mins.

The Films of Meredith Monk

Two works by dance and performance artist Meredith Monk. *Book of Days* (1986) is a haunting meditation on time and nature, about a perfectly preserved medieval town in Southern France. *Ellis Island* (1981) examines the decaying walls and supernatural presence of the American landmark. 105 mins.
Laser: LD71956. $39.95.

Gary Goldberg—Four Films: Plates, Mesmer, Usher and TV Head

These shorts feature two icons of the downtown New York underground film/performance scene, Taylor Mead and Bill Rice. Their stage-show-based vignettes reveal quietly seething emotions that boil over into explosive climaxes.
VHS: S22506. $39.95.
Gary Goldberg, USA, 1992, 40 mins.

Ginsberg Sings Blake

Time-travel to the late 18th century and witness visionary William Blake crafting away at this labor of love, *The Songs of Innocence* and *The Songs of Experience*. Then spin back to the present and tune in with bard Allen Ginsberg in concert with Steven Taylor (vocals, guitar) in a hearty neo-Renaissance revival of Blake's classics. 80 mins.
VHS: S30801. $24.95.

Halber Mensch

Electric performances, industrial set design, performance art and superb production values highlight this long-form video, directed by Sohgo Ishii, of Einsturzende Neubauten's classics *Drawings of Patient O.T.* and *Halber Mensch*. The numbers include "Armenia," "Sehnsucht," "Abfackeln," "Z.N.S." and "Schaben." 60 mins.
VHS: S19609. $19.95.

Homage to Hermann Nitsch (Apologies to Don Garlits)

A wild night at No Se No featuring performance artist, poet, critic and curator Michael Carter is captured in this video. Carter indicts modern car culture.
VHS: S22623. $19.95.
Michael Carter, USA, 1987, 20 mins.

Impact Addict Videos

Described as "the Evel Knievel of performance art" (*The Village Voice*), performance artist/stunt man David Leslie performs four harrowing assignments, including being wired with firecrackers, boding the heavyweight amateur champion, and simultaneously dueling with six New York City dojo masters. 30 mins.
VHS: S17199. $49.95.

In a Storm Even Dinosaurs Trip & Invasion of the Amazons

Swiss performance artist Penelope Wehrli creates dreamy films with strong images of female courage. Between heroes and heroines there is often a desert that could be characterized as a place of entrapment. 29 mins.
VHS: S22646. $29.95.
Penelope Wehrli, USA, 29 mins.

Judgment Day

A long-form video of Diamanda Galas' incendiary concert performances, shot by H-Gun Corp in Chicago, during her 1992 *Plague Mass* tour. *Judgement Day* distills her best works from the *Saint of the Pit, Divine Punishment, Red Death* and *Plague Mass* albums. The tracks include "There Are No More Tickets to the Funeral," "Let My People Go," "Blind Man's Day" and "Gloomy Sunday." 60 mins.
VHS: S19610. $19.95.

Love Lion

San Francisco poet and playwright Michael McClure joins Ray Manzarek, keyboardist for legendary group The Doors, in a performance of words and music. 70 mins.
VHS: S14715. $29.95.

Nouvelle Experience: Cirque du Soleil

The French Canadian troupe Cirque du Soleil has transformed the circus into an exciting, novel performance experience. This video reveals the magic of their innovative techniques, where lions and tigers have been replaced with wit and fantasy. 82 mins.
VHS: S25921. $19.95.

A Performance by Jack Smith

This is the only known recorded performance piece by the late artist/actor Jack Smith, made from an optically printed 8mm film original. Included are two works shot in Toronto in 1984: *Dance of the Sacred Application* and *Brassieres of Uranus*.
VHS: S27224. $59.95.
Midi Onodera, Canada, 1984

Performing at the San Francisco Museum of Modern Art Groundbreaking Ceremony

On April 8, 1992, this short and to the point show by Survival Research Labs stopped traffic in downtown San Francisco for 15 minutes. The staging of this event represents a sincere effort by a major art institution to align itself with more edgy, defiant work. 10 mins.
VHS: S26468. $15.00.

The Pleasures of the Uninhibited Excess

Three fast-moving Survival Research Labs performances from 1989-1990 are well documented in this video. It includes *Illusions of Shameless Abundance, ArtSpace Computer-Controlled Installation* and *A Carnival of Misplaced Devotion*.
VHS: S26469. $25.00.
Leslie Asako Gladsjo, USA, 1991, 45 mins.

Return of the Goddess for the New Millennium

This unique video performance blends environmental, sociological, and metaphysical/archetypal imagery with compelling interpretive dance movement and music. Experience archetypal Goddess energy in a vibrant dancer's expression of sensuality, openness and empowerment. Dance concept, choreography and performance by Jamie Miller; music composed and performed by Paul (Ramana Das) Silbey. "Ms. Miller dances with such passion that I kept waiting for smoke to pour out of the VCR…the wildest, most intense, incredibly powerful Goddess invocations that I have ever experienced" (*Harvest Magazine*). "Powerful, controversial, deeply moving" (Lawrence Ferlinghetti). Note: This video contains scenes of partial nudity and erotic dance movement. 1989, 32 mins.
VHS: S13720. $29.95.

The Rocket Movie

A re-enactment of performance artist/stuntman David Leslie's gonzo attempt to scale a mountain of watermelons before a large, adoring crowd. 32 mins.
VHS: S17200. $39.95.

Stars & Scars

Video backdrops from stunts performed by the man *The New York Times* called "the Evel Knievel of Performance Art," David Leslie, as seen in Larry Fessenden's films *Impact Addict Videos, The Rocket Movie* and *Stunt*.
VHS: S32347. $39.95.
Larry Fessenden/David Leslie, USA, 1994, 20 mins.

Stunt: A Musical Motion Picture

In this collage of images, representation and meta-reality, the performance artist and stunt man David Leslie orchestrates a spectacular pageant that pays homage to the respective spirits of James Brown, Evel Knievel, Bruce Lee and Julie Andrews. 35 mins.
VHS: S17201. $39.95.

Survival Research Laboratories

Founded in 1979 by Mark Pauline, this organization of artists and technicians is dedicated to exploring the potential for redirecting the techniques, tools and tenets of industry and science by staging mechanized presentations in the U.S. and Europe. Each performance consists of a unique set of ritualized interactions between machines, robots and special effects devices with humans present only as operators or audience.

Bitter Message of Hopeless Grief. Living in a fictional world all their own, SRL's machines act out scenarios of perpetual torment, exasperating consumption and tragic recognition. 1988, 13 mins.
VHS: S10952. $18.00.

Scenic Harvest from the Kingdom of Pain. Three machine performances from 1983-1984. "Disturbing, fascinating, recommended" (Richard Gere, *L.A. Reader*). 1984, 45 mins.
VHS: S10951. $20.00.

Will to Provoke: An Account of Fantastic Schemes for Initiating Social Improvement. A documentation of SRL's 1988 European tour with shows in Amsterdam and Copenhagen. SRL ferrets out and satirizes assorted icons of cultural pride in two of Europe's more libertarian social democracies. 1988, 48 mins.
VHS: S10950. $24.95.

Videotape for a Woman and a Man

Amy Greenfield uses human motion, camera lens, editing and optical techniques to "see into, with and through the body." Shot over a period of six months and edited over four years, *Videotape for a Woman and a Man* is "an absorbing and disturbing inquiry into male-female relationships. Photographed in black and white and color, and performed in the nude by Greenfield and dancer Ben Dolphin, it relentlessly examines the possible physical and emotional encounters between a man and a woman….We marvel at and are moved by the poignant spectacle of the human body as an instrument capable of transcending its own reality" (John Guen, *Dance Magazine*).
VHS: S01415. $19.98.
Amy Greenfield, USA, 1979, 34 mins.

Virtues of Negative Fascination

This videotape documents the five most recent performance spectacles by the Survival Research Laboratories. Power and intricate, radio-controlled machines clash in parking lots and nightclubs of San Francisco, horrific photo images rotate on stands, bombs explode, fires start. SRL spectacles, frequently covered by national print and TV media, are a cross between mechanized warfare and demolition derbies.
VHS: S10203. $29.95.
Survival Research Labs, USA, 1986, 80 mins.

What's Underground About Marshmallows: Ron Vawter Performs Jack Smith

The complete, extraordinary "reperformance" by Ron Vawter of Jack Smith's 1981 performance piece, "What's Underground About Marshmallows?," in which Jack, strongly against the commodification of art and fearful that people were making illegal copies of his films, accuses Jonas Mekas, the champion of avant-garde film in the early '60s, of this diabolical infringement. In "Marshmallows," Jack tells a funny, pathetic tale "on" himself—a nightmare of failing to catch Mekas—called variously "Uncle Artcrust," "Uncle Fishhook" and sometimes "Old Uncle Oldie"—in the act of duplication.
VHS: S35376. $39.95.
Jill Godmilow, USA, 1996, 60 mins.

dance on video

3 by Martha Graham

Features three original dances choreographed by and starring Martha Graham. One of the giants of American dance, Graham is the subject of a new biography and the inspiration to her company's triumphant return to Broadway. Originally aired on television, this program has been remastered for home video. "Extraordinary" (*New York Times*). USA, 87 mins.
VHS: S15397. $59.95.

Alice in Wonderland: A Dance Fantasy

The Prague Chamber Ballet and The Czech Philharmonic Orchestra bring to life the magical adventures of Alice, the Cheshire Cat, the Mad Hatter and the Queen in this dance fantasy as original as the Lewis Carroll story it tells. A magnificent array of costumes, colors and sets, and an interweaving of ballet, mime, acrobatics and theatre gracefully dramatize the story. 27 mins.
VHS: S34382. $19.98.

Alicia

Cuban by birth, Alicia Alonso is perhaps the most venerated "American" dancer in the history of ballet. This is a portrait of the still active ballerina, including excerpts of the "Black Swan Pas de Deux" from *Swan Lake* and the complete *Carmen Ballet*. 70 mins.
VHS: S07095. $19.95.

All the Best from Russia

The best in ballet, the best in folk-dancing, the best in all-round entertainment from inside Russia. Here are the Bolshoi Ballet and the Don Cossack dancers, the Armenian Folk Ensemble and the incomparable treasures in the fabulous Hermitage Museum, a variety of colorful, exciting entertainment. 52 mins.
VHS: S03965. $29.95.

American Ballet Theater Now

Leading American Ballet Theater dancers perform highlights from ABT's repertoire at New York's City Center. With Alessandra Ferri, Paloma Herrera, Vladimir Malakhov, Jose Manuel Carreno, Susan Jaffe, Amanda McKerrow and Julio Bocca. Features romantic, classical and contemporary pieces, including *Swan Lake, Sleeping Beauty, Don Quixote, Romeo and Juliet* and others. Natalia Makarova introduces the virtuoso performances. 83 mins.
VHS: S34721. $29.95.

Anna Karenina

Maya Plisetskaya and Alexander Godunov star in this ballet choreographed by Plisetskaya to music by Rodion Schedrin and based on Tolstoy's famous novel. A very cinematic rendering of the famous Bolshoi company production never before seen in the U.S. 81 mins.
VHS: S08531. $29.95.

Anna Sokolow

This notable modern dance choreographer speaks about her career with the aid of film clips and demonstrations of her choreographic process. Rehearsals of *Rooms* are particularly illuminating. 20 mins.
VHS: S25972. $39.95.

Anyuta

Brimming with sly humor and graceful balalaika melodies, *Anyuta* captures deftly the delicate color and flavor of Chekhov's Russia. Ekaterina Maximova of the Bolshoi dances in the title role, with the production choreographed by Vladimir Vasiliev and featuring the cream of the Bolshoi, Kirov and Maly ballet companies. 68 mins.
VHS: S03155. $39.95.

The Art of the 20th Century Ballet

This program presents three ballets, introduced by their choreographer, Maurice Bejart. Includes *Bolero, Adagietto* and *Ce qui l'amour me dit*. A pioneering new style of dance combining the traditional with modern techniques. 75 mins.
Laser: LD70276. $34.95.

The Arthur Murray Dance Lesson Series

Hosted by Terry Leone, this series of easy-to-follow dance lessons runs the gamut of dancing styles. Complete with a brief history of each dance and informative notes on timing and measures, this series features top dance couples from around the globe.
Dancin' Dirty.
VHS: S16781. $19.95.
Nightclub.
VHS: S16785. $19.95.
Swing.
VHS: S16789. $19.95.
Waltz.
VHS: S16791. $19.95.

Backstage at the Kirov

A remarkable portrait of the great company which has given the world Balanchine, Nureyev, Baryshnikov and Makarova. 1983, color, 83 mins.
VHS: S02430. $14.95.

The Balanchine Celebration: Part One

Darci Kistler, Nilas Martins and Kyra Nichols are featured in this video, along with Paris Opera Ballet prima ballerina Isabelle Guerin and Kirov ballet star Zhanna Ayupova. Selections from *Apollo, Vienna Waltzes, Union Jack, Theme and Variations*, and other Balanchine works, along with the complete *Scherzo a la Russe*, reveal Balanchine's Russian and European roots.
VHS: S27060. $29.98.
Matthew Diamond, USA, 1993, 86 mins.

The Balanchine Celebration: Part Two

Darcey Bussell and Lindsay Fischer dance a *pas de deux* from *Agon*. Then, American Ballet Theater prima ballerina Susan Jaffe stars with Nikolaj Hubbe in *Western Symphony*, while Damian Woetzel and Margaret Tracey lead in the patriotic *Stars and Stripes*. Finally, *Who Cares?*, featuring Jeremy Collins and Viviana Durante, brings the era of Gershwin alive.
VHS: S27059. $29.98.
Matthew Diamond, USA, 1993, 86 mins.

The Balanchine Essays: Arabesque

Now the inimitable Balanchine style and technique are available on video. Merrill Ashley, of the New York City Ballet, and Suki Schorer, of the School of American Ballet, demonstrate the principles and steps employed by the great choreographer. 45 mins.
VHS: S24683. $29.97.

The Balanchine Essays: Passe and Attitude

The incomparable technique of choreographer George Balanchine is clearly presented in this video. New York Ballet principals Suki Schorer and Merrill Ashley demonstrate Balanchine's interpretation and teaching of passe and attitude. Excerpts from *Agon, Diamonds, La Source, Swan Lake, The Nutcracker* and more are included.
VHS: S27058. $29.98.
Merrill Brockway, USA, 1994, 45 mins.

The Balanchine Essays: Port de Bras and Epaulement

George Balanchine's technique is presented by New York Ballet principals Suki Schorer and Merrill Ashley in this video. It demonstrates Balanchine's interpretation and teaching of port de bras and epaulement and features excerpts from *Divertimento No. 15* and *Symphony in C*.
VHS: S27061. $29.98.
Merrill Brockway, USA, 1994, 43 mins.

The Balanchine Library

The work of George Balanchine is danced by members of the New York City Ballet, featuring Mikhail Baryshnikov, Patricia McBride, Karn Von Aroldngen and Merrill Ashley in *Ballo Della Regina, The Steadfast Tin Soldier, Elegie* and *Tchaikovsky Pas de Deux*. 51 mins.
VHS: S35018. $29.99.

Balanchine: Dancing for Mr. B: Six Balanchine Ballerinas

Anne Belle made this documentary featuring interviews with six Balanchine prodigies who danced for the New York City Ballet. Maria Tallchief, Melissa Hayden, Allegra Kent, Merrill Ashley and Darci Kistler are featured and excerpts from some of Balanchine's most acclaimed ballets are included. 86 mins.
VHS: S24681. $29.97.

Balanchine: Prodigal Son/Chaconne

Mikhail Baryshnikov, the greatest male dancer of modern times, stars with Karin von Aroldingen in the Balanchine/Prokofiev classic from the 1920's, *Prodigal Son*. Suzanne Farrell and Peter Martins, principal dancers from the New York City Ballet, then perform *Chaconne*. 57 mins.
VHS: S24679. $29.97.

Balanchine: Robert Schumann's Davidsbundlertanze

Ib Anderson, Karin von Aroldingen, Jaques D'Amboise, Suzanne Farrell and Peter Martins are just part of an all-star cast called upon to perform Balanchine's final masterpiece. 43 mins.
VHS: S24682. $29.97.

Balanchine: The Four Temperaments, Andante from Divertimento No. 15, Tzigane

The first of these ballets, *The Four Temperaments*, is perhaps Balanchine's greatest achievement. *Tzigane* features the incomparable Suzanne Farrell, and Mozart's *Andante from Divertimento No. 15* features the New York City Ballet and their incomparable, flawless technique. 54 mins.
VHS: S24680. $29.97.

Ballerina: Karen Kain

Rudolph Nureyev has said of this dancer that "in her, the star quality is unmistakable." The first ballerina from North America to perform with Bolshoi Ballet, Miss Kain performs with Roland Petit's corps de ballet in *Carmen*, *Coppelia* and *Romeo and Juliet*. Included also are her insights on dance. 54 mins.
VHS: S03963. $29.95.

Ballerina: Lynn Seymour

Rudolph Nureyey is one of the many male stars performing here with Miss Seymour in performances of Kenneth MacMillan's *Romeo & Juliet*, Sir Fredrick Ashton's *Two Pigeons*, and *Intimate Letters with Galina Samsova*. Here also is recorded the world premiere performance of *Mac and Polly*. 56 mins.
VHS: S03964. $29.95.

Ballerinas

Carla Fracci is featured in a lavish recreation of the golden days of ballet in Paris, portraying dance stars of the 19th century, 10 ballerinas whose art and fame are legendary. Ms. Fracci dances excerpts from such classics as *Giselle, Coppelia, La Sylphide, Sleeping Beauty* and others, and is partnered by such great male dancers as Vladimir Vasiliev, Michael Denard, Richard Cragun and Peter Schaufuss. USA, 1985, 108 mins.
VHS: S04688. $39.95.

Ballet Class for Beginners

David Howard's ballet class for beginners is an excellent learning and teaching tool designed by America's foremost ballet master, introducing the beginning ballet student to the technique and vocabulary of classical ballet. Featuring Allison Potter with music by Whit Kellog.
VHS: S04689. $39.95.

Ballet Class—Intermediate-Advanced

Specially designed by David Howard to expand the classical vocabulary, movement potential, and kinetic awareness of the student. Dancers and teachers alike are given the possibility to participate in this unique class which features Cynthia Harvey and Peter Fonseca of the American Ballet Theatre.
VHS: S05851. $39.95.

Ballet Folklorico Nacional de Mexico

The richness of Mexican culture, its myths and traditions, comes alive through the artistry of the Ballet Folklorico in a production unequaled in pageantry and color. 110 mins.
Spanish Narration.
VHS: S05273. $59.95.
English Narration.
VHS: S05732. $59.95.

Ballet for Children and Adults

Kathryn Anderson, former soloist with the Boston Ballet, hosts this valuable instructional tape. Ballet attire, training methods, equipment and etiquette are all covered by this great ballerina. French terms are explained and there is even a Q & A section for some of the most commonly asked questions about this dance form. 48 mins.
VHS: S22441. $29.95.
Karl Brown, USA, 1932, 63 mins.

Ballet Legends: The Kirov's Ninel Alexandrovna Kurgapkina

This gala performance honors incomparable ballerina Ninel Alexandrovna Kurgapkina, dancing with the Kirov in scenes from some of the most important leading roles of her career. 40 mins.
VHS: S34058. $29.98.

Ballet Ruse

Choreographer Peter Anastos, renowned founder of Les Ballets Trockadero de Monte Carlo, brings his talents to focus on two hilarious ballets for mixed company, in this case his own Garden State Ballet. Winner of three Emmy Awards, *Ballet Ruse* features *Yes, Virginia, Another Piano Ballet*, a parody of the genre to music by Chopin, and *Forgotten Memories*, with music by Tchaikovsky—a wicked takeoff on prime-time soaps. 28 mins.
VHS: S34509. $19.95.

Ballet Russe
From choreographer Peter Anastos comes this hilarious Emmy Award-winning production of a dance parody. New Jersey's Garden State Ballet performs Yes Virginia, Another Piano Ballet and *Forgotten Memories*, which takes dead aim at prime time soap operas.
VHS: S12660. $19.95.

Ballet Workout
An elegant way to achieve a lithe, supple body, improve your carriage and attain the look and grace of a professional dancer. Melissa Lowe, a former soloist and principal dancer with several ballet companies, guides this body re-shaping series of exercises. 83 mins.
VHS: S11446. $19.95.

The Ballet Workout II
Melissa Lowe's instructional program looks at ways to hone and shape up your body, using the rigorous techniques and stretching exercises of the ballet dancer. 70 mins.
VHS: S19688. $19.95.

Ballroom Dancing for Beginners
The basic techniques of ballroom dancing, including elements, dance position, understanding music and patterns for the fox trot, waltz, tango, rumba, cha cha and swing, taught by Teresa Mason and Susan Major. 57 mins.
VHS: S09935. $29.95.

Ballroom Dancing: Advanced
Instructor Theresa Mason showcases six popular social dances, including the Fox Trot, Waltz, Tango, Rumba, Cha-Cha and Swing. She also reviews beginner and intermediate steps. 60 mins.
VHS: S19005. $29.95.

Ballroom Dancing: Intermediate
This tape is designed for those who want to increase their ballroom dancing skills beyond the beginner's level. Master techniques for the most popular dances like the fox trot, the tango, the waltz and more. 48 mins.
VHS: S15094. $29.95.

Baryshnikov at Wolf Trap
This performance from 1975 shows the incredible Mikhail Baryshnikov at the peak of his artistic talents. Recorded at the Wolf Trap Farm Park for the Performing Arts in Virginia, the video features Baryshnikov in a series of solos and *pas de deux* with a variety of partners, including Gelsey Kirkland. Hosted by Beverly Sills. 50 mins.
VHS: S14751. $29.95.

Baryshnikov Dances Carmen
Ballet superstar Mikhail Baryshnikov stars in this sexy dance version of the Bizet classic, co-starring the legendary Zizi Jeanmaire as Carmen, and choreographed by Roland Petit.
VHS: S13059. $29.95.

Baryshnikov Dances Sinatra
Mikhail Baryshnikov dances three classy ballets featuring the choreography of Twyla Tharp: *Sinatra Suite*, a duet for Baryshnikov and Elaine Kudo set to a medley of songs by Sinatra, including "Strangers in the Night"; *Push to Shove*, set to rags by Joseph Lamb and Haydn symphonies; and *The Little Ballet*, featuring Baryshnikov, Deirdre Carberry and three other ABT dancers performing one of Tharp's most balletic works. 60 mins.
VHS: S10876. $19.95.

Bill T. Jones: Dancing to the Promised Land
This video is built around the rehearsal and performance of Jones' epic, *Last Supper at Uncle Tom's Cabin/The Promised Land*. In the process, the work and creative processes of one of the most respected powers in American modern dance is revealed. 60 mins.
VHS: S21868. $29.98.

The Birmingham Royal Ballet in Tchaikovsky's The Nutcracker
A favorite at Christmas, this ballet follows the dreams of a young girl as she awaits Christmas morning. In her amazing journey she meets a handsome prince, a sugar plum fairy and the dreaded Rat King. This traditional work continues to enchant both children and adults. 98 mins.
VHS: S26298. $29.95.

Black Tights
Four sparkling ballets by Roland Petit featuring Petit and three great partners: Zizi Jeanmaire as Carmen and The Diamond Cruncher, Moira Shearer as Roxanne in Cyrano de Bergerac, and Cyd Charisse in A Merry Mourning. Maurice Chevalier is the host.
VHS: S03215. $29.95.
Terence Young, France, 1960, 120 mins.

Blue Angel
Renowned French choreographer Roland Petit's highly acclaimed ballet makes its North American debut in video in a superb stage production featuring the Ballet National de Marseilles. This is the ballet rendition of Heinrich Mann's dramatic story of the alluring Rosa Frohlich, the dancer at the famous Blue Angel Cabaret.
VHS: S10713. $29.95.

Bolshoi at the Bolshoi
Full-length ballet performances featuring the Bolshoi Ballet at the historic Bolshoi Theatre, under the direction of Yuri Grigorovich, newly recorded and mastered in digital stereo sound and digital D-2 video.
Sleeping Beauty. Original choreography by Marius Petipa, featuring Nina Semizorova and Alexi Fadeyechev.
VHS: S10419. $39.95.
The Nutcracker. Original choreography by Lev Ivanov, featuring Irek Mukhamedov and Natalya Archipova.
VHS: S10418. $39.95.

The Bolshoi Ballet
Paul Czinner's highly acclaimed film of the Bolshoi Ballet in performance stars Galina Ulanova in a complete *Giselle* (with Nikolai Fadeyechev) and *The Dying Swan*; plus five shorter ballets including such Bolshoi signature works as the "Walpurgisnacht" from *Faust* (with Struchkova) and *Spring Water* (set to a score by Rachmaninoff). Color, 95 mins.
VHS: S13683. $49.95.

Bolshoi Prokofiev Gala
To celebrate the 100th birthday of Russian composer Sergei Prokofiev in November, 1991, a gala ballet concert was staged at the Bolshoi Theater in Moscow. Yuri Grigorovich directs the dance greats Ludmila Semenyaka, Alexander Vetrov, Yuri Vasyuchenko, Nina Semizorova, Natalya Archipova and many other top performers. Includes excerpts from *Romeo & Juliet*, *Ivan the Terrible* and *Stone Flower*, as well as profiles of the Bolshoi Ballet and the life of Prokofiev. 170 mins.
VHS: S16507. $29.95.

Bolshoi Soloists
A loving tribute to the Bolshoi Ballet, featuring the Bolshoi with music of Tchaikovsky, Albinoni, Adam and Gershwin, in many treasured favorites, and featuring soloists Nina Timofeyeva and Michail Lavroski. 40 mins.
VHS: S06847. $39.95.

Bolshoi: Les Sylphides
With music by Frederic Chopin and the Bolshoi Ballet, choreographed by Mikhail Fokine, featuring Natalia Bessmertnova, Alexandre Beofatyriov and Galina Koslova. 34 minutes.
VHS: S02687. $49.95.

Book of Shadows
This ground-breaking video ballet employs experimental techniques in sound, performance, video and choreography to create a new and moving work. This winner of numerous awards explores the many incarnations of the goddess in a mythic landscape.
VHS: S21065. $29.95.
Janis Mattox, USA, 1993, 25 mins.

Bryony Brind's Ballet—The First Steps
Bryony Brind, Senior Principal Dancer with the Royal Ballet Convent Garden, has created this unique new ballet video which for the first time teaches the viewer the basic principles and movements of ballet. The program has been specifically designed so that it can be used by individuals, groups of friends, or by teachers in a class.
VHS: S10716. $29.95.

Bujones in Class
Fernando Bujones demonstrates his personal ballet technique that has made him one of the most sought-after guest artists in the world. A unique learning and teaching tool, the video was specifically designed by Bujones to teach the techniques of classical ballet. 31 mins.
VHS: S10021. $39.95.

Bujones: In His Image
Considered one of the leading male ballet dancers in the world, this program is a compilation of his greatest performances, with excerpts from "Le Corsair," "Raymonda," "Don Quixote," "7-Greek Dances," "Swan Lake," "Giselle" and "La Bayadere." There are also revealing discussions with Bujones about his life. 62 mins.
VHS: S03613. $39.95.

Cambodian Royal Ballet
The Royal Dancers of Cambodia, once one of the finest Asian troupes in the world, perform two works from their classical repertoire. Asian arts authority Faubion Bowers provides commentary and interviews the young lead dancer, Voan Savay, as she demonstates styles and training methods. These dancers, all women, had just made a successful tour of the United States when this program was made. Soon thereafter the political upheavals in Cambodia virtually destroyed that country. These "apsaras" or "goddess dancers" were all either driven into exile or killed. 1971, 27 mins.
VHS: S32330. $89.95.

Carmen
The Carmen Suite presents ballerina Maya Plisetskaya in one of her critically most acclaimed and popular roles. The music, by Rodion Schedrin, is based on Bizet's score, and the ballet is choreographed by Alberto Alonso. Other works on the tape include *Prelude*, pairing Plisetskaya with Vladimir Vasiliev; *Raymonda*, originally choreographed by Marius Petipa and performed to a score by Glazunov; and *The Dying Swan*, to music by Saint-Saens. 1973, color, 73 mins.
VHS: S02432. $29.95.

The Catherine Wheel
A collaboration between choreographer Twyla Tharp and Talking Heads lead singer David Byrne merges classical dance with non-traditional movement in the story of the 4th century martyr, St. Catherine. "A major event in our theater, (with) dancing of astonishing beauty and power" (*The New Yorker*). 88 mins.
VHS: S02962. $29.97.
Laser: LD71632. $39.97.

Celebration—Royal Ballet
This exuberant program commemorates the 50th anniversary of Britain's Royal Ballet. The company's luminaries, including Sir Frederick Ashton, Dame Alicia Markova, Kenneth Macmillan and Sir Robert Helpman, are featured in a program that combines performances, rehearsals, interviews and archival film to provide a fitting celebration. Glimpses of rare performances including the very young Margot Fonteyn in *Polonia, Giselle, La Fille Mal Gardee*. 50 mins.
VHS: S10307. $39.95.

Celtic Feet
Colin Dunne, star of the hit show *Riverdance* and nine-time world dance champion, teaches you step-by-step how to learn the basics of Irish dance, in this spectacular music and dance-filled video. 55 mins.
VHS: S31543. $19.95.

Charles Weidman: On His Own
The career of modern dance pioneer Charles Weidman (1901-1975) is traced from his roots in Lincoln, Nebraska, to the last work he choreographed in 1974. Includes rare footage. USA, 1990, 59 mins.
VHS: S15334. $49.95.

Checkmate
From the series *Masterpieces of British Ballet* comes this ballet in one act with prologue choreographed by Ninette de Valois and with music composed by Sir Arthur Bliss. Performed by dancers from Sadler's Wells Royal Ballet and Royal Ballet Orchestra. A game of love and death, played according to the rules of chess. 45 mins.
VHS: S13243. $29.95.

Children of Theatre Street
Provides an unprecedented glimpse inside the Kirov Ballet School where Nijinsky, Baryshnikov, Makarova and Nureyev were taught the tricks of their elegant trade. Presented by the late Princess Grace of Monaco and shot on location in Leningrad.
VHS: S02422. $19.95.
Robert Dornhelm/Earle Mack, USA, 1977, 92 mins.

Choreography by Balanchine: Selections from Jewels/Stravinsky Violin Concerto
Great dancers are featured in these excerpts from Balanchine works. Suzanne Farrell and Peter Martins dance in *Diamonds*. Merrill Ashley, Bonita Borne, Gerard Ebitz, Karin von Aroldingen, Heather Watts, Daniel Duell and Sean Lavery perform the ensemble piece *Emeralds*. Then, Peter Martins, Bart Cook, Karin von Aroldingen and Kay Mazzo perform *Stravinsky Violin Concerto*, along with members of the New York City Ballet.
VHS: S27062. $29.98.
Merrill Brockway, USA, 1977, 56 mins.

Cinderella (Bolshoi)

The great 1961 color motion picture featuring the Bolshoi Ballet performing the timeless fairy tale. This unique mixture of film, dance and music stars Raisa Struchkova in the title role and a score by Sergei Prokofiev.
VHS: S01927. $55.00.

Cinderella (Lyon Opera Ballet)

Choreographer Maguy Marin's highly sophisticated, highly imaginative version of the Cinderella story, conceived of and performed by the Lyon Opera Ballet. Marin evokes childlike wonder by envisioning her characters as live dolls, with human feelings projected upon them in the way children identify with their playthings. Prokofiev's wistful score, edited and restructured for this presentation, captures the familiar feelings of childhood and the happy endings all fairy tales promise. 87 mins.
VHS: S12217. $39.95.
Laser: LD71424. $34.95.

Cinderella: A Dance Fantasy

This classic fairy tale is depicted in all of its romantic splendor in this ballet production set to Prokofiev's timeless score. Performed by The Berlin Comic Opera Ballet. 31 mins.
VHS: S34380. $19.98.

Classic Kirov Performances

A rare compendium recreates some of the legendary Kirov Theatre performances, including Anna Pavlova's work as *The Dying Swan*. The program features Natalia Dudinskaya, Galina Ulanova, Vakhtang Chabukiani, Konstantin Sergeyev, Altynai Asylmuratova and Tatyana Terekhova, in performances from *Romeo and Juliet, The Nutcracker, Sleeping Beauty* and *Don Quixote*. 110 mins.
VHS: S18568. $29.95.

Coppelia (Ballets de San Juan)

Features Fernando Bujones, one of the most acclaimed dancers of the American Ballet Theatre, in a 1980 performance with the Ballets de San Juan, Puerto Rico. 110 mins.
VHS: S02417. $39.95.

Coppelia (Lyon National Opera Ballet)

Choreographer Maguy Marin's *Coppelia* is a tremendously entertaining piece of dance theatre. Marin transposes the work from its original rustic setting to a modern, run-down, urban environment and also adds a whole new twist to the story. Features the dancers of the Lyon National Opera Ballet. 62 mins.
VHS: S30877. $29.95.

Creole Giselle (Dance Theatre of Harlem)

Using the story and original classical choreography of this repertory staple, Dance Theatre of Harlem founder Arthur Mitchell has set the ballet in 1841 Louisiana. Giselle is danced by Virginia Johnson, and Eddie J. Shellman co-stars as Albert. This remains one of the Dance Theatre of Harlem's most popular works. 88 mins.
VHS: S13931. $29.95.

Daisy and Her Garden: A Dance Fantasy

This Czech production tells the tale of young Daisy living happily with her enchanted garden with animals and flowers as her companions, until the Winter Witch comes along and tries to banish spring. This original fairy tale combines dance, mime, music and poetic narration with glorious sets and colorful costumes, for a magical introduction to the performing arts. Created by the Czech Television Arts Workshop. 38 mins.
VHS: S34379. $19.98.

Dance and Myth, The World of Jean Erdman Part 1: The Early Dances

Jean Erdman worked with Martha Graham but broke away to pursue her own vision. This video includes her works *The Transformations of Medusa* (1942), *Creature on a Journey* (1943), *Passage* (1946), *Ophelia* (1946), *Hamadrayad* (1948) and *Daughters of the Lonesome Isle* (1945). 60 mins.
VHS: S26742. $29.95.

Dance and Myth, The World of Jean Erdman Part 2: The Group Dances

The Perilous Chapel (1949) and *Solstice* (1950) show the evolving work of Jean Erdman. 60 mins.
VHS: S26743. $29.95.

Dance and Myth, The World of Jean Erdman Part 3: The Later Solos

These works represent the culmination of a life dedicated to dance. Included are *Pierrot, The Moon* (1954), *Changing Woman* (1951) and *Fearful Symmetry* (1957). 60 mins.
VHS: S26744. $29.95.

Dance Basics Plus Curriculum

Designed for public and academic libraries, this six-tape set with support materials, featuring instructor Tony Louis Ridgel, comprises the most comprehensive course available for teaching students to dance. Tapes include Ballroom, featuring Foxtrot, Waltz and Single & East Coast Swings; Country, featuring Two-Step, Texas/Triple-2, Waltz and Single & East Coast Swings; Latin, featuring Rumba, Cha-Cha and Mambo; Line Dance, featuring Bayou Boogie, Cotton Eyed Joe, Electric Slide, 4-Corners, Cowboy Cha-Cha and Tush-Push; Contemporary/Social, featuring Freestyle, Single & East Coast Swing and Slow Dancing; and Hip Hop, featuring more than 30 of the most popular moves.
VHS: S30873. $209.95.

Dance Black America

Narrated by Jeffrey Holder, this four-day festival held at the Brooklyn Academy of Music is a celebration of African-American dance. Includes performances by the Alvin Ailey American Dance Theater and the Charles Moore Dance Theater. 1983, 87 mins.
VHS: S15335. $49.95.

Dance Theater of Harlem

The New York Times has hailed this program as "a sheer utter triumph." Now the energy, creativity and classical perfection of the Dance Theater of Harlem has been captured in dazzling performances of four signature pieces. The American classic *Fall River Legend*, choreographed by Agnes de Mille, tells the notorious story of Lizzie Borden. *Troy Game*, by Robert North, is a dynamic satire of the machismo attitudes inherent in sports. *The Beloved*, a ballet for two dancers by Lester Horton, confronts the themes of violence and fanaticism. *John Henry*, choreographed by Arthur Mitchell, is a celebration of the strength of the human will. 117 mins.
VHS: S12215. $29.95.

Dancers

Mikhail Baryshnikov stars in this drama about the backstage romantic intrigues, travails and triumphs of a world-class ballet company as they prepare to perform the ballet "Giselle."
VHS: S06368. $19.98.
Herbert Ross, USA, 1987, 99 mins.

Dancetime! 500 Years of Social Dance

This program takes you through history from the 1400s to the 1990s. The popular social dances of each era evoke the thrill of Renaissance revelry, Baroque beauty, 19th-Century romance and 20th century energy. Featuring over 100 costumes and 60 musical favorites to accompany historical dances, this video set combines an educational journey, high artistic standards and entertainment. Each tape is 45 mins.
Dancetime! 500 Years of Social Dance—Volume 1: 15th-19th Centuries. Includes Bàlli, So Ben Mi Chi Ha Bon Tempo, La Votta, Galliard, Minuet, Contradances, Folies d'Espagne, Country Dances, Quadrilles, Durang's Hornpipe, Polka, Mazurka, Gallop and Waltz Cotillion.
VHS: S34505. $39.95.
Dancetime! 500 Years of Social Dance—Volume 2: 20th Century. Includes Animal Dances, Castle Walk, Apache, Tango, Black Bottom, Charleston, Marathon, Movie Musical, Big Apple, Jitterbug, Rhumba, Swing, Rock 'n' Roll, Mambo, Twist, Mod, Psychedelic, Disco, Break Dancing, Punk, Moonwalk, Vogueing, Hip Hop and Country Western.
VHS: S34506. $39.95.

Dancing

This 8-part series probes the traditions of dance in communities around the world—from the often misunderstood waltz to the eloquent gestures of an Asante court dance in Ghana, and from the latest hip-hop in Morocco to a ballet class in Russia and a modern dance rehearsal in New York. Filmed on location on five continents, it explores the oldest and most compelling of languages: the art of communication called dance.
Vol. 1: The Power of Dance. In its great diversity, dance is the thread which connects all people—from the great classics of England's Royal Ballet and Japanese Kabuki to Broadway's rich jazz and tap heritage; from the hundreds of children in Jacques d'Amboise's National Dance Institute learning dances from around the world to the latest video art choreography and the Hip Hop dances of New York City streets. 58 min.
VHS: S18394. $29.95.
Vol. 2: The Lord of the Dance. Dancers and dances have been worshipped as divine and feared as manifestations of the devil. Here we trace the cultural belief that shaped the great traditions of sacred and secular dance. Christianity has had an ambivalent view of dance in worship; Hinduism throughout India and the Yoruban religion of Nigeria combined worship and dance to create great dance/theater traditions. 58 min.
VHS: S18395. $29.95.
Vol. 3: Sex and Social Dance. Social dance can be as refined as the waltz or as sexy as the tango. Dance of one community may shock another whose social values and gender roles differ. We all dance, but what social values and ideals are told through the dances we do? 58 min.
VHS: S18397. $29.95.
Vol. 4: Dance at Court. In royal courts of the world, dance not only reached a pinnacle of elegance but played a role in the preservation of power and the maintenance of order and control. This function lives on in European ballet, the imposing dance of Asante kings in Africa, the refinement of Japan's Bugaku and the otherworldliness of the Javanese Bedoyo. 58 min.
VHS: S18396. $29.95.
Vol. 5: New Worlds, New Forms. In the Americas, dance became a medium for cultural fusion among African and European peoples. Here their steps and styles combined, creating dances that can be read as cultural maps. From the Samba in Bahia and Candomble in Salvador, Brazil, to the Lindy Hop in the Catskills, New York State, and Rock and Roll in Baltimore, Maryland, cultural fusion has shaped the great popular dances of the 20th century. 58 min.
VHS: S18399. $29.95.
Vol. 6: Dance Center Stage. The demands of a growing middle class created a new relationship between dancer and audience. Illustrated are the dazzling theatrical traditions of Japan's Kabuki and Russia's Kirov Ballet, both adapted over generations to entertain wider, changing audiences. 58 min.
VHS: S18398. $29.95.
Vol. 7: The Individual and Tradition. This segment features extraordinary individuals who revolutionized dance: Isadora Duncan, Martha Graham, Katherine Dunham, George Balanchine, Twyla Tharp, Eiko and Koma, Sardono Kusumo and Garth Fagin. 58 min.
VHS: S18400. $29.95.
Vol. 8: Dancing in One World. Less than 100 years ago, people from one part of the globe might have had no idea what people from other places looked and sounded like or how they moved. Today, television and satellite bring Rock and Roll to Bali, for example, and Yoruba ritual dances appear in rock videos. Are the traditional dances dying out? The new pan-culturalism is exciting, but will it change the face of dance forever? Are we racing toward a single global culture or will ancient traditions continue into the 21st century? 58 min.
VHS: S18401. $29.95.
Dancing, Complete Set.
VHS: S18402. $199.95.

Daphnis and Chloe

This Sydney Dance Company production features choreography by Graeme Murphy and music by Maurice Ravel. Starring Carl Morrow as Daphnis and Victoria Taylor as Chloe, this sensual ballet tells the story of two young lovers brought together by Cupid who learn the meaning of love and desire. 60 mins.
VHS: S07601. $39.95.

Don Quixote (Ananiashvili)

Prima ballerina Nina Ananiashvili exhibits her technical command in this Russian State Perm Ballet production of composer Leon Minkus' work. Ananiashvili and Aleksei Fadeyetchev dance the lovers Kitri and Basilio. Aleksandr Astafiev is the knight; Evgeny Katusov is his comic squire Sancho Panza. 120 mins.
VHS: S19898. $24.95.

Don Quixote (Kirov Ballet)

The tremendous resources of the Kirov Ballet flash and dash through the four acts of joyous Petipa and Gorsky choreography, making *Don Quixote* a visual treat. The action centers around Don Quixote's quest to perform chivalrous deeds. Tatyana Terekhova and Farukh Ruzimatov are featured as the lovers Kitri and Basilio. Hailed as one of the greatest large cast ballet productions ever recorded on film. 120 mins.
VHS: S08795. $39.95.

Don Quixote (Nureyev)

Rudolf Nureyev stars and co-directs this film version of the famous ballet, with Lucette Aldous and Sir Robert Helpmann in the title roles, with the dancers of the Australian Ballet and choreography by Marius Petipa. 110 mins.
VHS: S06896. $39.95.

Early Dance Part 1: From the Greeks to the Renaissance

A concise history of dance unfolds in this first section of a two-part series. Demonstrations detail the works of early Greek theater and English masques. Music, narration, costumes and performances tell the story of dance. 24 mins.
VHS: S25973. $39.95.

Early Dance Part 2: The Baroque Era

Beginning with the burlesque entertainments of the Louis XIII era, this video traces the evolution of dance through a theatrical tradition that culminates in ballet. Even Louis XIV performed in these ballet spectacles. 30 mins.
VHS: S25974. $39.95.

Erich Hawkins' America

Hawkins' choreography on American themes is evident in the works *Plains Daybreak, Hurrah, Ahab* and *God's Angry Man*. This video also includes portions of his other works *Classic Kite Tails* and *Black Lake*. 57 mins.
VHS: S25874. $49.95.

Erik Bruhn Gala: World Ballet Competition

This gala, presented in honor of the first Erik Bruhn prize, features dancers from four of the companies with which he is most closely associated. Breathtaking performances of pas de deux and variations include choreography by Bruhn, Glen Tetley, Kenneth Macmillan and Antony Tudor. Natalia Makarova makes a special appearance. 90 mins.
VHS: S10270. $39.95.

Essential Ballet

A unique collection featuring the greatest stars of the Russian ballet, in performances in Moscow and London. Part I includes the Kirov Ballet in highlights from *Swan Lake* (with Mikhalina and Liepa), *The Nutcracker* (with the Vaganova Ballet Academy) and Drigo's *Diana and Actaeon*. Part II is a special outdoor performance in Red Square with Maya Plisetskaya in her final performance as the Dying Swan, Nina Ananiashvili in *Sleeping Beauty* and *Don Quixote*, and *Le Corsaire*, *Giselle* and *The Firebird*.
Laser: LD72366. $34.95.

European Dance Theater

European dance theater comes alive through the works and voices of its creators and fascinating narrative about its originators. Archival footage and beautifully filmed and edited excerpts of current repertory demonstrate the forms and power of this genre. 62 mins.
VHS: S32187. $49.95.

An Evening with Ballet Rambert

Three short ballets from one of dance's most innovative companies. Included are "Sergeant Early's Dream," choreographed by Christopher Bruce to British, Irish and American folk tunes; "Intimate Pages," using Janacek's Second String Quartet; and Robert North's "Lonely Town, Lonely Street," a jazz ballet.
VHS: S03738. $39.95.

An Evening with Royal Ballet

Rudolf Nureyev and Dame Margot Fonteyn head a cast of legendary artists performing excerpts from "The Sleeping Beauty," "Les Sylphides" and "Le Corsaire." 87 mins.
VHS: S04424. $29.95.

An Evening with the Bolshoi Ballet

Excerpts from eight ballets made famous by the Bolshoi, permitting viewers to see the Corps de Ballet and soloists, including "Paganini" and music by Rachmaninoff, Ravel's "Bolero" and "Waltz," and Prokofiev's "Stone Flower." 90 mins.
VHS: S03147. $39.95.

Faces of Dance

This documentary offers an overview of the major dance trends of the 20th century by showcasing the work of contemporary dancers and interviewing them about their individual artistic approaches to dance. Featured performers include Evelyn Hart of the Royal Winnipeg Ballet, Rex Harrington of the National Ballet of Canada, flamenco dancer Antonio Canales, Maya Plisetskaya, former Bolshoi Ballet star, and American dancers Andrea Boardman, and Derek Reid.
VHS: S34408. $295.00.
Bernar Hebert, USA, 1996, 65 mins.

A Fantasy Garden Ballet Class

This video is the perfect tool for teaching kids basic ballet dance techniques. It features all the music and lyrics found in the *Fantasy Garden*. Kids will be able to practice at home as they dance along with their favorite garden characters.
VHS: S29497. $19.95.

A Feast of Irish Set Dances

Set dancing has been very much a part of the living tradition in Ireland, especially in rural areas, for at least four centuries. In this vibrant video, you will see young and old keeping the set dancing tradition alive. 56 mins.
VHS: S11999. $29.95.

Fiesta Gitana!

Pilar Perez de Guzman continues his series of Flamenco videos with the help of the incomparable Angelita Vargas, a dancer renowned for her passionate and elegant abilities. They are joined by some of the greatest practicing flamenco dancers, singers and guitar players in this bravado display of Spanish soul. 32 mins.
VHS: S21059. $34.00.

Filming Ballet

Techniques of filming classic dance. Interview of director Herbert Ross and his wife, the former ballerina Nora Kaye, who together made the film *The Turning Point*, starring Baryshnikov and Leslie Browne. With journalist Cliff Jahr. Many clips illustrate the discussion points about angles, pacing, lighting and costume. 1978, 28 mins.
VHS: S31602. $59.95.

Firebird

American choreographer Glen Tetley gives a new look to Stravinsky's *The Firebird*, stylishly performed in this new release by the Royal Danish Ballet. 55 mins.
VHS: S08481. $39.95.

Firestone Dances

These rare performances from *The Voice of Firestone* television series show superstars at the top of their careers. Rudolf Nureyev, Jacques D'Amboise, Melissa Hayden, Maria Tallchief, Carla Fracci, Henning Kronstam, Kirsten Simone and Oleg Tupine dance on this video. 50 mins.
VHS: S26703. $24.95.

Five Dances by Martha Graham

Rarely taped on video, these five dances were recorded at the Palais Garnier in Paris on the occasion of the Martha Graham Dance Company's triumphant 1991 appearance. This tape not only offers the opportunity for dance enthusiasts to enjoy these works, but also reveals the evolution of movements and innovations which Graham developed. 127 mins.
VHS: S28999. $29.95.

Flamenco

A rare treat for Flamenco lovers, this video provides a magnificent portrayal of Flamenco and its performers. The rhythms and lyrics are inherited folklore and part of daily life, but the techniques are arduously studied, and each of the four distinct schools of flamenco in Spain is represented.
VHS: S05588. $39.95.

Folkloric Ballet of Mexico

Created by choreographer Amalia Hernandez in 1952, the Folkloric Ballet combines modern creativity with a thorough research of history. These dances reveal the cultural values of pre-Hispanic Mexico, and its evolution through the centuries. 113 mins.
VHS: S16371. $49.95.

Fonteyn & Nureyev: The Perfect Partnership

A collector's item that traces the famous pair of ballet dancers from their first ballet in 1962, to their grand finale 17 years later. 90 mins.
VHS: S04686. $39.95.

Footnotes: The Classics of Ballet

This acclaimed series explains the world of ballet, utilizing historic clips and interviews with the legends of dance. These exciting programs feature the Bolshoi, Kirov and Royal Ballets as well as superstars Rudolf Nureyev, Margo Fonteyn, Natalia Makarova, Fernando Bujones, Anthony Dowell, Edward Villella, Cynthia Gregory, Darcey Russell and many others. Hosted by Frank Augustyn. 60 minutes each.
Volume 1: Swan Lake and La Sylphide. 60 mins.
VHS: S27814. $19.95.
Volume 2: Romeo and Juliet and Giselle. 60 mins.
VHS: S27815. $19.95.
Volume 3: The Nutcracker and The Sleeping Beauty. 60 mins.
VHS: S27816. $19.95.
Volume 4: Don Quixote & La Bayadere.
VHS: S31373. $19.95.
Volume 5: Cinderella & Coppelia.
VHS: S31374. $19.95.
Volume 6: The Male Dancer & Gala Excerpts.
VHS: S31375. $19.95.

Fred Astaire Dance Series

The Fred Astaire Dance Studios developed this series of six programs, presenting the newest steps and old favorites.
Fred Astaire Ballroom Dancing.
VHS: S09102. $19.99.
Fred Astaire Latin Dancing.
VHS: S09103. $19.99.
Fred Astaire Western Dance.
VHS: S09104. $19.99.

French Folk Dances

Learn three exciting French dances performed by students: Le Branle a Six from Brittany, La Boulangere from Alsace-Lorraine, and La Contra-Danse from Haiti. Also includes audio-cassette, directions and guide with cultural and costume information. 45 mins. English narration.
VHS: S05285. $59.95.

French Folk Dancing Video, Volume 2

More folk dancing in the French language high school classroom, with authentic folk dances performed by high school students. This volume contains Le Branle du Quercy, Saint Ferreol from Catalogne and La Bastringue from Quebec. 35 mins.
VHS: S09058. $49.95.

Gael Force: An Irish Music Event

From the producers of *Riverdance: The Show* comes this true Irish event filmed over six days at the Point Depot in Dublin, featuring the Riverdance Irish Dance Troupe in an all-new performance, Sinead O'Connor, The Chieftains and Clannad. 80 mins.
VHS: S33045. $19.98.

Gaite Parisienne

Victor Jessen followed the Ballet Russe de Monte Carlo around America for several years filming bits and pieces of *Gaite Parisienne*, hoping to put together a complete performance. The finished film is a triumphant and loving tribute to the company and its principles, including Alexandra Danilova, Frederic Franklin and Leon Danielian. 38 mins.
VHS: S07094. $39.95.

Garth Fagin's Griot New York

Choreographer Garth Fagin, jazz master Wynton Marsalis and sculptor Matind Puryear collaborated on this acclaimed dance piece. Griot, the West African term for storyteller, inspired this testament to the diverse stories of New York City. Features the Wynton Marsalis Septet. 87 mins.
VHS: S24726. $24.98.
Laser: LD74903. $29.98.

George Balanchine's The Nutcracker

Macaulay Culkin stars in this ballet masterpiece, composed by Tchaikovsky. The cast includes former NYC Ballet dancers with narration by Kevin Kline. This unforgettable story of a dreamy young girl and her nutcracker soldier unfolds at night when a battle breaks out between a dashing prince and the evil king of the rats. 93 mins.
VHS: S22420. $19.99.
DVD: DV60192. $24.98.

German Folk Dances

Authentic folk dances performed by students include: Siebenschritt from Bavaria, S'Trommt Em Babeli from Switzerland and Das Fenster, danced throughout Germany. Also includes audio-cassette, directions and guide with cultural and costume information. 42 mins. English narration.
VHS: S06838. $59.95.

German Folk Dancing Video, Volume 2

Volume 2 of folk dancing in the German language classroom, with folk dances performed by high school students, contains D'Hammerschmedsgselln from Bavaria, Brandiswalzer from Switzerland and Zillertaler Laendler from Austria. 35 mins.
VHS: S09054. $59.95.

Ghost Dances

Choreographer Christopher Bruce created this contemporary ballet in response to a letter from the widow of Chilean folk singer/writer Victor Jara, murdered during the military junta that brought Pinochet to power, which described the plight of the South American people. Performed to a selection of Jara's work and traditional folk music, *Ghost Dances* evoke the natural gaiety and courage of the South American people. 40 mins.
VHS: S08482. $39.95.

Giselle (Alonso)

Thousands watched transfixed during the MET Opera Centennial Gala as Alicia Alonso danced an excerpt from *Giselle*, the role of her first major triumph. This film, made almost twenty years earlier, offers her complete portrayal of the part, capturing Alonso as one of the most virtuosic and touching Giselles of all time. 99 mins.
VHS: S07096. $19.95.

Giselle (Bolshoi)

A classic production of the Bolshoi's staging of *Giselle*. "I've never seen so sharp and clear a live performance ballet tape. And the stereo sound track is a knock out" (Roy Hemming, *Video Review*).
VHS: S19521. $39.95.

Giselle (Bujones)

Ballet virtuoso Fernando Bujones stars in this brilliant production of *Giselle* with the Ballet Teatro Municipal of Rio de Janeiro. Supreme among the romantic ballets, *Giselle* has never before been delivered with such intensity as in this performance by Bujones, "the finest male classical dancer this country has ever produced" (*NY Post*). 104 mins.
VHS: S13665. $29.95.

Giselle (Malahov)

Vladimir Malahov, the acclaimed Russian ballet star, performs in this classic romantic ballet. Giselle is danced by Ludmilla Vasileva. Shot live at the State Theater Academy in the Kremlin. 100 mins.
VHS: S29854. $19.95.

Giselle (Nureyev)

Rudolf Nureyev and Lynn Seymour are the principal dancers in this recording choreographed by Jules Perrot and Jean Coralli. With Monica Mason and Gerd Larsen. 78 mins.

VHS: S18191. $29.95.

Giselle...The Making of

Marcia Haydee recreates both the choreography of her adaptation of *Giselle* and the creative process of rehearsal and directing that makes this performance possible. The Corps de Ballet of the Stuttgart Ballet Company is featured in this video. 29 mins.

VHS: S27005. $19.98.

Godunov: The World to Dance In

A provocative portrait of a man whose personal odyssey has led from a fatherless childhood and his 1979 defection from the Kirov Ballet to superstardom in the United States. Included are dazzling performances with Cynthia Gregory and Maya Plisetskaya. 60 mins.

VHS: S02421. $39.95.

Green Fire and Ice

The Trinity Irish Dancers are among America's foremost ethnic dance troupes. They have won numerous Gold Medals at the annual World Championships of Irish Dancing in Ireland. This documentary shows the ins and outs of this troupe from rehearsal to performance and international competition. 30 mins.

VHS: S22056. $19.95.

Hamlet Ballet

Vladimir Malahov, Nadia Saidkova and Ludmilla Vasileva perform in this version of Shostakovich's rarely performed ballet. This video offers a chance to see this often overlooked work in a world-class production. 65 mins.

VHS: S29855. $19.95.

Hanya: Portrait of a Pioneer

This video traces the career of dancer/choreographer Hanya Holm—from her early days in Germany in the 1920s, through her work on the Broadway stage, to being regarded as one of the famous "four pioneers" of modern dance. USA, 1985, 60 mins.

VHS: S15338. $49.95.

Holiday of Ballet

In 1981, Amanda McKerrow of Washington D.C. became the first American ever to win the gold medal in the International Competition of Ballet Artists in Moscow. This behind-the-scenes look at the competition captures both the heartbreak and the joy of this annual event.

VHS: S13057. $29.95.

Honi Coles & Cholly Atkins: Over the Top to Bebop

Two masters of tap dance demonstrate its development. Coles and Atkins were a headlining team in the days when dance was on every vaudeville bill. On this program they show what two lives in tap dance have taught them. In conversation with them is Marshall Stearns, world authority on jazz dance in all its forms. 1964, 27 mins.

VHS: S32336. $89.95.

Horton Dance Method

This instructional video demonstrates the modern dance training method created by Lester Horton and used by Alvin Ailey and other noted companies. From warm-up exercises through fortifications, this comprehensive program is both a great workout and a solid foundation for the serious dancer.

VHS: S13054. $29.95.

I Am a Dancer

A portrait of the great Rudolf Nureyev, from his homely beginnings in 1938 to one of the century's great dancers and superstars. Includes excerpts from many of Nureyev's greatest moments, including *Sleeping Beauty, Marguerite and Armond, La Sylphide*. 1970, color, 90 mins.

VHS: S01928. $19.98.

Il Ballarino: The Art of Renaissance Dance

Learn authentic Renaissance court dances—and the gestures and step vocabulary associated with them—from *Il Ballarino*, the first instructional video of its kind. USA, 1990, 33 mins.

VHS: S15339. $44.95.

Ilona Vera's Ballet Class: Developing a Personal Style

Provides instruction in how to get the most out of taking class. Primarily developed for dancers who have reached an intermediate level and aspire for professionalism in their work. Based on the famed Vaganova (Kirov) method, considered one of the most definitive methods of exercising the body. 73 mins.

VHS: S08693. $29.95.

Introduction to Ballroom Dancing

Learn to swing, rumba, cha cha, waltz and fox trot on video in this unique tape featuring instructor Margot Scholz, a member of the Imperial Society of the Teachers of Dance. For those with little or no previous dance experience or a refresher for those with prior experience. 68 mins.

VHS: S10877. $19.95.

Invitation to the Dance

Gene Kelly wrote, directed, choreographed and performed in this three-part tribute to his fascination with movies and movement. "Circus", "Ring around the Rosy" and "Sinbad the Sailor" each incorporate Kelly's love of dance. "Sinbad" is partially animated by the Hanna-Barbera studios. With Claire Sombert, Carol Haney, Tamara Toumanova and Igor Youskevitch.

VHS: S06169. $19.98.

Gene Kelly, USA, 1956, 93 mins.

Irish Dance

Meet the people who keep the Irish dance, culture and tradition alive in this exciting two-tape set, as future Irish dance stars practice for competition and experience the rich history and beauty that has propelled Irish dance into the international spotlight with such hit shows as *Riverdance* and *Lord of the Dance*. Shot on location in Cork, Limerick and Dublin, Ireland; London, England; Queensland, Australia; and North America. 60 mins.

VHS: S31152. $12.99.

Isadora Duncan Dance

The technique and repertory perfected by Duncan are demonstrated by the Isadora Duncan Ensemble in this video. It contains the complete works: *Under the Scarf, Slow Mazurka, Dance of the Blessed Spirit* and *Dubinushka*, as well as a number of excerpts from other works. 60 mins.

VHS: S25873. $49.95.

Israel in Dance: Shalom in Action

The Shalom Dance Company tries to bring all the traditions of the inhabitants of modern Israel together in their unique works. During rehearsal, backstage and in performance this troupe never forgets the importance of its mission. 53 mins.

VHS: S23256. $29.95.

Israel's Folk Dance Festival

A rare and exciting collection of the best Hebrew folk dance groups performing in Israel, filmed at the picturesque Zemach, on the beautiful shores of the Sea of Galilee. 60 mins.

VHS: S05757. $59.95.

Ivan the Terrible Ballet

The original cast stars in one of the most dazzling of all Bolshoi Ballet productions, based on Sergei Eisenstein's classic film of murder and intrigue. With Yuri Vladimirov, Natalia Bessmertnova. USSR, 1977, 91 mins.

VHS: S09226. $29.95.

Jazz Dance Class with Gus Giordano

Covers the warmup, basic jazz techniques, jazz walks, centre barre, and the professional dancer in a teaching tape of elements of jazz dancing. 63 mins.

VHS: S09936. $39.95.

Jazz Workout

An exercise tape which is also designed as an introduction to jazz dancing. It includes a warm-up, floor progressions and dance combinations. Ann Coombes, a dance instructor for over 10 years, leads a class that helps beginners develop a routine and paces accomplished dancers through their workouts. The warm-up sessions include stretches, flexes, stomach and thigh strengthening exercises. 55 mins.

VHS: S10878. $19.95.

Jesus, The Son of Man

An interesting ballet featuring Ivan Marko and other distinguished Hungarian dancers in a modern recreation of the teachings of Jesus that are relevant today—with music by Liszt, Shostakovich, and Xenakis. 72 mins.

VHS: S09629. $29.95.

Jose Greco in Performance

A 1959 performance of Jose Greco that captures the famous dancer at the peak of his career, accompanied by a hand-picked troupe of singers and musicians. Selections include "Pastoral Romance", "Castellana", "Cordoba", "Granada" and "Wedding Dance". 26 mins.

VHS: S13246. $24.95.

JVC/Smithsonian Folkways Video Anthology of Music and Dance of Africa

Features 72 traditional music and dance performances of Africa packaged in a three-volume/three-booklet collection. Featured countries include Uganda, Senegal, Ghana, Nigeria, Egypt, Kenya, Botswana, The Gambia, Liberia, Malawi and South Africa.

VHS: S30173. $149.00.

JVC/Smithsonian Folkways Video Anthology of Music and Dance of Europe

Features 58 music and dance performances of Europe packaged in a two-volume/two-booklet collection. Featured countries include Iceland, The Faroe Islands, Denmark, Ireland, Scotland, Wales, England, Belgium, France, Spain, Italy, The Czech Republic, Hungary, Romania and Serbia.

VHS: S30174. $99.00.

JVC/Smithsonian Folkways Video Anthology of Music and Dance of the Americas

This six-volume anthology is a scholarly survey of American folk traditions featuring 159 music and dance examples from 23 countries, and accompanying booklets. Volume 1: Canada and the United States, Canada: Francophone Traditions, Canada: Native and Anglophone Traditions, and USA: African American Secular Traditions; Volume 2: European Traditions in the New World; Volume 3: The United States: Sacred Traditions; Volume 4: The Caribbean; Volume 5: Central and South America: Belize, Brazil, Chile, Colombia, Guatemala, Guyana; Volume 6: Central and South America: Mexico, Nicaragua, Peru, Venezuela. "...a must-purchase item for ethnomusicologists and multicultural music educators" (*Multicultural Education*). "An exceptional and essential series" (*School Library Journal*).

VHS: S30172. $299.00.

Khmer Court Dance: Cambodian Royal Court Dances

Five authentic dances in the Khmer court repertoire are performed in traditional costume by masters of these dances, with accompanying traditional music performed by the Pinn Peat Ensemble. Solo and group dancers have been filmed so that the hand, feet and body movements can be seen clearly. Dances include Buong Suong, Apsara, Chhouy Chhay, Muni Mekhala and Tep Monorum. 74 mins.

VHS: S30163. $24.99.

Khovanschina

This Bolshoi opera tells the story of the violent and turbulent era of Peter the Great's regency. Shostakovich orchestrated this work by Mussorgsky, who died before he could finish it. The incomparable ballerina Maya Plisetskaya is featured. Russian with English subtitles. USSR, 1959, color, 131 mins.

VHS: S02253. $69.95.

The Kiev Ballet Collection

Long ranked as one of the Soviet Union's outstanding theater groups, the Kiev Schevchenko Ballet is featured in this deluxe boxed set, which includes five outstanding performances: *Swan Lake, Cinderella, La Sylphide, Don Quixote* and *Song of the Woods*. 519 mins.

Laser: LD76755. $149.99.

Kirov Ballet in London

A thrilling program that captures the excitement and visual grandeur of a Kirov Ballet performance on stage in London during 1988, with a special guest appearance by Natalia Makarova, who is reunited with her former company after an absence of 17 years. Includes many favorites, including *Kingdom of the Shades* from *La Bayadere*, selections from *Swan Lake, Don Quixote, Le Corsaire, Le Papillon*. 128 mins.

VHS: S12591. $39.95.

The Kirov Ballet in Tchaikovsky's Sleeping Beauty

Natalia Dudinskaya, Natalia Makarova, Valeri Panov, Alla Sizova and Yuri Soloviev are featured in this classic film version of the ballet as choreographed by Marius Petipa. This Cinemascope masterpiece is presented in letterbox format to preserve the unmatched beauty and integrity of the performance.

VHS: S24889. $29.95.

A. Dudko/K. Sergeyev, Russia, 1964, 84 mins.

Kirov Ballet: Classical Ballet Night

Live performances by the world-renowned Kirov Ballet, featuring some of the famous Pas De Deux of the Classic repertory, including Diana and Actheon, Esmeralda, Flower Festival in Genzano, the Canteen Keeper, Venice Carnival and Pas de Quatre. Dancers include Irina Kolpakova, Gabriela Konleva, Elena Evteeva. 95 minutes.

VHS: S02688. $39.95.

The Kirov Ballet: Coppelia

The Kirov Ballet, with the Maryinsky Theater Orchestra, performs the ballet in two acts based on the story by E.T.A. Hoffmann. Recorded at the Maryinsky Theater in St. Petersburg in 1993. Choreography by Oleg Vinogradov. 92 mins.

VHS: S37094. $29.97.

The Kirov Ballet: Le Corsaire

Recorded at the Kirov Theater in St. Petersburg in 1989, the Kirov Ballet and Kirov Theater Orchestra perform *Le Corsaire*, a ballet in three acts, based on the work by Lord Byron. Original choreography by Marius Petipa. 86 mins.

VHS: S37096. $29.97.

Laser: LD76835. $34.97.

The Kirov Ballet: The Stone Flower
The Kirov Ballet, with the Maryinsky Theater Orchestra, performs the ballet with prologue in three acts based on the fairy tale from the Urals by Pavel Bazhov. Recorded at the Maryinsky Theater in St. Petersburg, 1991, Choreography by Yuri Grigorovich. 112 mins.
VHS: S37093. $29.97.
Laser: LD76836. $34.97.

Kirov Soloists
Irina Kolpakova, the prima ballerina of the Kirov, dances and presents this film dedicated to the work of the principal dancers of the Kirov, including behind-the-scenes looks at rehearsals, and full-fledged performances, giving a glimpse into how the Kirov Ballet tradition is carried from one generation to another. With Sergei Berezhnoi, Olga Tcheytchikova, Tatiana Terekhova, and music by Pugni, Villa-Lobos and Offenbach. 55 mins.
VHS: S06848. $39.95.

L'Enfant et les Sortileges
Ravel's enchanting fantasy ballet, choreographed by Jiri Kylian, tells the story of a naughty child whose temper tantrum brings the objects in his room to life. 52 mins.
VHS: S32416. $29.95.

La Bayadere (Kirov)
Choreographed by Petipa to music by Minkus, and first performed by the Kirov Ballet in 1877, this production was filmed at the Kirov Ballet in Leningrad. 126 mins.
VHS: S02416. $39.95.

La Bayadere (Royal Ballet)
Natalia Makarova choreographed and designed the Royal Ballet's production of *La Bayadere*, using elaborate stage effects, spectacular sets and a brilliant cast headed by Irek Noukhamedov and Darcey Bussell. This Covent Garden production is considered the definitive production. 124 mins.
VHS: S17308. $29.95.

La Sylphide
Winner of the VIRA Award, a reconstitution of the Taglioni ballet, achieved by Pierre Lacotte. The recreation includes original costume and set designs, and features Michel Denard, Ghislaine Thesmar and the Paris Opera Ballet Company. 81 mins.
VHS: S03162. $39.95.

Lady of the Camellias
John Neumeier directs this Hamburg Ballet production. 125 mins.
VHS: S09359. $39.95.

The Land of Sweet Taps
This is a fun-filled adventure for children ages 4-8 who want to learn tap dancing. In addition to the fundamental sounds, rhythms and steps there are shuffles and digs. The lyrics are fun and memorable, helping children remember the timing of the music. 57 mins.
VHS: S21701. $19.95.

Learn the Art of Flamenco (Videos Flamencos de la Luz)
The esteemed instructional series produced by Pilar Perez de Guzman of Madrid, Spain. An invaluable teaching tool that helps you perfect your technique.
Course in Castanets. Develop speed, precision and ease. 54 mins.
VHS: S15323. $40.00.
Course in Rumba. Enjoy the sensuality of Flamenco-Rumba. 45 mins.
VHS: S15324. $40.00.

Legend of Love
Part of the *Bolshoi at the Bolshoi* series, *Legend of Love* ballet is a colorful story set in an opulent, oriental palace in ancient Turkey. Featuring Maria Bilova. 1990, 111 mins.
VHS: S14551. $39.95.

The Leningrad Legend
Natalia Makarova is the narrator for this behind-the-scenes look at today's Kirov Ballet. The company's great past is recalled in film clips, but the focus of the program is on future developments. 71 mins.
VHS: S14749. $29.95.

The Little Humpbacked Horse
Vladimir Vasiliev and Maya Plisetskaya bring to life this 19th century Russian fairytale in one of the Bolshoi's most popular ballets. USSR, 1961, color, 85 mins.
VHS: S02441. $29.95.

Lord of the Dance (Irish)
King of step dancing Michael Flatley, choreographer and star of the worldwide hit *Riverdance*, dazzles audiences again as the principal performer in his own dance spectacle, *Lord of the Dance*, which played to sold-out arenas in the United Kingdom and Australia.
VHS: S30941. $24.95.
Laser: LD76366. $39.99.
DVD: DV60005. $29.95.

Ludmila Semenyaka Bolshoi Ballerina
A selection of jewel-like performances by the legendary prima ballerina, performing excerpts from many of her famous roles, including the Rose Adagio from *Sleeping Beauty*, and selections from *Swan Lake, Spartacus, The Talisman, The Nutcracker*. 60 mins.
VHS: S12592. $29.95.

Macbeth
The Shakespeare masterpiece in a stunning production by the Bolshoi Ballet taped live at Moscow's historic Bolshoi theatre. Choreographed by Vladimir Vasiliev and featuring Alexei Fadeyechev and Nina Timofeyeva. 105 mins.
VHS: S03154. $39.95.

Mademoiselle Fifi
This Canadian Broadcasting Corporation production is the only existing document of ballet's beloved star Alexandra Danilova in a complete performance. Along with her partners from the Ballet Russe de Monte Carlo, Michael Maule and Roman Jasinski, this ballet legend helped popularize the art in North America. 20 mins.
VHS: S19401. $29.95.

Magic of the Bolshoi Ballet
This video is a rare collection of the most historic performances by the leading dancers of the famed Bolshoi Ballet Company. Archival films from the past 50 years feature Soviet dance legends such as Ulanova, Plisetskaya, Vasiliev, Fadeyechev and many others in scenes from *The Sleeping Beauty, Romeo and Juliet, Don Quixote*, and other ballets rarely seen in the West.
VHS: S10714. $29.95.

Magic of the Kirov Ballet
This extraordinary program contains an outstanding selection of highlights from the Kirov's extensive classical repertoire, including dazzling sequences from choreographer Marius Petipa's interpretations of *La Bayadere, Le Corsaire, The Sleeping Beauty, Raymonda, Swan Lake, Paquita* and *Don Quixote*. Current members Farukh Ruzimatov, Tatyana Terekhova and Olga Chenchikova are featured. 60 mins.
VHS: S08794. $29.95.

Makarova Returns
In this emotionally charged program, ballerina Natalia Makarova returns to the Kirov Ballet nearly 20 years after her defection from the USSR. 60 mins.
VHS: S14750. $29.95.

Making Ballet: The Actress
This feature-length documentary goes behind the scenes at The National Ballet of Canada to deconstruct the seemingly magical process of creating a major ballet production. The ballet is The Actress, with Karen Kain, choreographed by James Kudelka. 86 mins.
VHS: S34383. $19.98.

Margot Fonteyn Story
In a career spanning more than four decades, Margot Fonteyn achieved perfection in the most demanding of the arts and thrilled audiences worldwide. On the eve of her 70th birthday, Dame Fonteyn finally agreed to tell her life story in this landmark video. Her candid revelations are augmented by archival film and interviews with mentors, partners and proteges such as Ninette de Valois, Frederick Ashton, Robert Helpmann and Rudolf Nureyev. 90 mins.
VHS: S10271. $29.95.

Mark Morris Dance Group—The Hard Nut
The Mark Morris Dance Group, with the Symphony Orchestra and Chorus of the Theater Royal de la Monnaie, performs this ballet in two acts based on *Nutcracker and the Mouse King* by E.T.A. Hoffmann. Recorded in 1992 at the Theater Royal de la Monnaie, Brussels. 87 mins.
VHS: S37095. $29.97.
Laser: LD76837. $34.97.

Martha Graham Dance Company
This 1976 program is highlighted by a cornerstone work of the 20thcentury repertory, *Appalachian Spring*, with music by Aaron Copland. Also features *Diversion of Angels, Lamentation, Frontier, Adorations*, and *Medea's Dance of Vengeance*.
VHS: S34568. $29.99.
Merrill Brockway, USA, 1976, 90 mins.

Martha Graham: An American Original in Performance
A true pioneer in the American dance, Martha Graham has become a legend, and this film contains three of her historic performances: *A Dancer's World, Night Journey, Appalachian Spring*. 93 mins.
VHS: S07694. $39.95.
Laser: LD72346. $99.95.

Martha Graham: The Dancer Revealed
This famed choreographer has shaped modern dance. She died in 1991 at the age of 97 leaving behind a legacy of achievement that will certainly endure. In this documentary, seven decades of her life and work are chronicled, revealing the person behind the legend. Interviews with Agnes de Mille, Erick Hawkins, Ron Profas and many others are included. 60 mins.
VHS: S21814. $24.95.

Mary Wigman 1886-1973
Here is a vivid film portrait that captures Mary Wigman's enduring historical significance as one of the founders of German expressionist dance. Narrated by Wigman herself, with an accompanying voice-over in English. USA, 1991, 47 mins.
VHS: S15340. $44.95.

The Maryinsky Ballet
The former Kirov Ballet has been transformed into the Maryinsky, and this compilation studies the company's works, including *Chopiniana, Petrushka, Barber's Adagio, Le Corsaire, The Fairy Doll* and *Paquita*. The program highlights its three greatest performers, Altynai Asylmuratova, Larissa Lezhinina and Farukh Ruzimatov. 147 mins.
VHS: S18890. $39.95.

Masters of Tap
This exuberant documentary introduces viewers to the lively history of tap dance with three acknowledged masters, Charles "Honi" Coles, Chuck Green and Will Gaines, serving as a guide and teacher. Coles, often called the greatest living exponent of tap dancing, entertains the audience with his experiences in show business during the 20's and 30's, and demonstrates his mastery with the audience. 61 mins.
VHS: S08483. $39.95.

Mayerling
Kenneth MacMillan's ballet, danced to Franz Liszt's music, is a powerful dramatic work concerning the tragic love affair of Crown Prince Rudolph and 17-year-old Mary Vestera. It captures the elegance of the Austro-Hungarian Empire in its twilight. Performed by the Royal Ballet and the Orchestra of the Royal Opera House. 135 mins.
VHS: S21052. $29.95.

Mazowsze: The Polish Song and Dance Ensemble
Made for Polish television, this is a rare 1971 performance of the Polish ensemble Mazowsze, one of the world's most interesting and popular folk collectives. 40 mins.
VHS: S18551. $29.95.

Medea
Filmed in the Soviet Union and never seen by Western audiences, this extraordinary one-act ballet freely interprets the classic drama by Euripides. With Marina Goderdzishvilli and Vladimir Julukhadze. 70 mins.
VHS: S03153. $39.95.

The Men Who Danced: The Story of Ted Shawn's Male Dancers 1933-1940
The Men Who Danced presents the story of the first all-male dance company in the U.S. It includes historic footage of the company performing in the 1930's, capturing the beauty and rigor of Ted Shawn's brilliant choreography. USA, 1986, 30 mins.
VHS: S15342. $44.95.

Merry Widow Ballet
Choreographed by Ruth Page, this beguiling, romantic ballet features Patricia McBride and Peter Martins in a memorable performance based on the Franz Lehar opera. 60 mins.
VHS: S11767. $39.95.

Mid-Eastern Dance: An Introduction

An award-winning two-hour course, beginning and intermediate levels, in the art of the belly dance, taught by Kathryn Ferguson, internationally recognized performer and teacher of Oriental dance. Includes preparation, understanding of Oriental rhythms, music, finger cymbals, and much more. 122 mins.
VHS: S09799. $39.95.

Moiseyev Ballet

Igor Moiseyev is world-renowned both for his choreography and for the dance company that he founded. This video shows a number of his key works, including *Partisans, Polyanka, Two Boys in a Fight, The Cunning Makanu* and other dances that make clear the source of this troupe's fame. 120 mins.
VHS: S24363. $29.95.

Moiseyev Dance Company: Gala Evening

The non-stop excitement and acrobatic dancing of this world-famous dance ensemble introduces the viewer to the many faces of folk dancing in the Soviet Union. Performed as a part of the cultural spectacle of the 1980 Moscow Olympics, choreographed by Moiseyev, and featuring working the bar and the floor, the Moldavian folk dance, the soccer match, Tajik's Dance of Happiness, Azerbaijan Shepard dance, and Ukrainian Gepak dance. 70 minutes.
VHS: S02615. $39.95.

Murray Louis in Concert Volume 1: Dance Solos

This videotape documents Murray Louis' extraordinary career as a dance soloist, drawing on choreography from his first concert in 1953 to today. None of this live performance footage has been previously released on film or video. USA, 1989, 52 mins.
VHS: S15341. $49.95.

New England Dances: Squares, Quadrilles, Step Dances

This film is a spirited visit to the old dances of New England, featuring Phil Johnson calling squares with the Maple Sugar Band, John Campbell and Norman MacEachern, William Chaisson and Joe Cormier, Arcade Richard and Victor Albert doing quadrilles, and Charlie Mitchell contradances. Also included are bravura dance sequences by Irish step dancers Liam Harney and Deirdre Goulding and by Cape Breton step dancer Harvey Beaton.
VHS: S30165. $24.99.
John M. Bishop, USA, 1995, 29 mins.

Nijinsky

Herbert Ross directs this portrayal of the most celebrated dancer of the early 20th century caught in a love triangle between the ballerina he married and the domineering mentor he loved, Diaghilev. With brilliant dance sequences.
VHS: S09897. $14.95.
Herbert Ross, USA, 1986, 125 mins.

Nina Ananiashvili and International Stars, Vol. 1

This magnificent Russian ballerina, currently with the American Ballet Theater, dances *Le Spectre de la Rose* with Farukh Ruzimatov and *The Sleeping Beauty* with Aleksei Fadeechev. Artists from the Bolshoi, The Royal Danish Ballet and the Kirov are also included. Aleksandr Sotnikov directs the 21st Century Orchestra.
VHS: S21760. $24.95.

Nina Ananiashvili and International Stars, Vol. 2

Ananiashvili dances with Aleksei Fadeechev in *The Dying Swan* and *Moods*. In *Don Quixote* she appears with Farukh Ruzimatov, Irma Nioradze and Rose Gad. Other selections feature artists from the Bolshoi, the Royal Danish Ballet and the Kirov. Aleksandr Sotnikov directs the 21st Century Orchestra.
VHS: S21761. $24.95.

Nina Ananiashvili and International Stars, Vol. 3

Ananiashvili dances with Aleksei Fadeechev in *Ramonda* and with Rose Gad and Tatyana Terekhova in *Pas de Quatre*. This 1993 gala, taped in Japan, also features artists from the New York City Ballet, the Dusseldorf Ballet, the Paris Opera Ballet, the Bolshoi, the Royal Danish Ballet and the Kirov in scenes from still more works. Aleksandr Sotnikov directs the Shinsei Nihon Symphony Orchestra.
VHS: S21762. $24.95.

Nina Ananiashvili and International Stars, Vol. 4

Ananiashvili dances "Grand Pas" from *Don Quixote* with Aleksei Fadeechev. This 1993 gala features premier artists from the New York City Ballet, the Bolshoi, the Royal Danish Ballet and the Kirov in scenes from *Bayaderka, The Talisman* and *Giselle*. Aleksandr Sotnikov directs the Shinsei Nihon Symphony Orchestra.
VHS: S21763. $24.95.

Notes Alive! Nutcracker: The Untold Story

This award-winning production, featuring the music of Tchaikovsky performed by the Minnesota Orchestra, the 3-D animation of Maurice Sendak, and a lively ballet performance, is a new version of the beloved Christmas tale that will enchant children of all ages. Go behind the scenes with Sendak, scriptwriter Pamela Hill Nettleton, and music director and conductor Eiji Oue to learn how this unique production of the original E.T.A. Hoffmann story was conceived and created. 50 mins.
VHS: S33160. $19.95.

Nureyev and the Joffrey Ballet in Tribute to Nijinsky

Rudolf Nureyev joins the Joffrey Ballet in this tribute to Nijinsky, performing three of his famous roles in *Petrouchka, Le Spectre de la Rose* and *L'Apres-Midi d'un Faune*. 79 mins.
VHS: S35019. $29.99.

The Nutcracker (Baryshnikov)

Baryshnikov and Kirkland star in the ballet extravaganza with the ever-popular music of Tchaikovsky. USA, 1984.
VHS: S01813. $19.98.

The Nutcracker (Bolshoi)

The entire corps of the Bolshoi join in this live recording with Vladimir Vasiliev and Ekaterina Maximova in the lead as well as Vjacheslav Gordeyev and Nadia Pavlova. Recorded in 1978, color, 87 mins.
VHS: S08219. $16.95.

The Nutcracker (Kirov)

The Kirov Ballet perform this holiday classic at St. Petersburg's renowned Mariinsky Theater. It's a tale of romance, bravery and honor told through a little girl's fantastic dream. Her Christmas gift, the nutcracker comes alive in a burst of music and dance that every child and adult will enjoy. 95 mins.
VHS: S22885. $29.95.
Laser: LD74621. $34.95.

The Nutcracker (Nureyev)

This historic performance from 1968 captures Rudolph Nureyev at the peak of his career. Nureyev's legendary performance with Merle Park in the Royal Ballet makes this production the definitive *Nutcracker* on video. 100 mins.
VHS: S32105. $29.95.

The Nutcracker (Royal Ballet)

Leslie Collier and Anthony Dowell appear as the leads in this Royal Ballet production. 1983, color, 120 mins.
VHS: S02448. $19.95.

The Nutcracker (Russian State Theatre Academy of Classical Ballet)

The world's favorite Christmas ballet comes to life in this production by the Russian State Theatre Academy of Classical Ballet. Featuring Russia's top dance stars, Ludmilla Vasileva and Alexander Gorbatsevich, this enchanting *Nutcracker* will be a Christmas treasure for dance lovers of all ages. 100 mins.
VHS: S30064. $19.95.

Nutcracker: Fantasy on Ice

Dorothy Hammill and Robin Cousins star in this version of Tchaikovsky's ballet—on ice. 85 mins.
VHS: S03862. $19.95.

On Your Toes...The Making of

George Balanchine made history in 1936 with his brilliant choreographic fusion of ballet and Broadway traditions known as *On Your Toes*. Prima ballerina Marcia Haydee is at the forefront of this 1990 recreation featuring the work of choreographer Larry Fuller. The creative process of rehearsal and directing are included in this video. The Corps de Ballet of the Stuttgart Ballet Company performs. 30 mins.
VHS: S27007. $19.98.

Onegin

The National Ballet of Canada in a delightful production of Tchaikovsky's story ballet, based on a tragic poem by Pushkin. Sabina Alleman dances the young girl who becomes involved with a handsome stranger (Frank Augustyn). Choreographed by John Cranko.
VHS: S03691. $39.95.

Paris Dances Diaghilev

The Ballets Russes perform four works which highlight the revolutionary technique and form of impresario Serge Diaghliev. The works are reproduced in their original sets, costumes and choreography, and filmed at the Paris Opera House in 1990. The four dances are Fokine's *Petrouchka* and *Le Spectre de la Rose*, and Nijinsky's *L'Apres-midi d'un Faune* and *Noces*. 84 mins.
VHS: S17278. $29.97.
Laser: LD71634. $39.97.

The Paris Opera Ballet: Cinderella

The Paris Opera Ballet, with the Orchestre National de l'Opera de Paris, performs this ballet in three acts based on Perrault's fairy tale with music by Sergei Prokofiev. Adapted and choreographed by Rudolf Nureyev. Recorded in 1987. 125 mins.
VHS: S37097. $29.97.

Paris Opera Ballet: Seven Ballets

Seven ballets by the Paris Opera, including their famous performance of *The White Swan*, featuring soloists Patrick Dupond, Sylvie Guillem, Noella Pontois and Manuel Le Gris. 66 mins.
VHS: S06849. $39.95.

Paris Opera Ballet: Six Ballets

Norbert Schmucki choreographed a collection of Pas De Deux ensembles to the music of Shostakovich, Meyerbeer and Tchaikovsky, including The Black Swan from *Swan Lake*. Featuring the Corps de Ballet of the Paris Opera, and Patrick Dupond, Noella Pontois and Sylvie Guillem. 58 minutes.
VHS: S02686. $39.95.

Pas de Deux

A collection of sixteen stars taped at the 1984 Los Angeles International Ballet Festival, including Patricia McBride of New York City Ballet, Michel Denard of Paris Opera Ballet and Yoko Morishita of Matsuyama Ballet. Program narrated by John Clifford.
VHS: S02949. $29.95.

Paul Taylor Dance Company

This 1970s piece, supervised by choreographer, Paul Taylor, includes two of his company's signature works, *Esplanade*, with music by J.S. Bach, and *Runes*, commissioned from composer Gerald Busby. 58 mins.
VHS: S34567. $29.99.

Peter Martins: A Dancer

A behind-the-scenes look at one of the world's foremost male dancers, featuring three full pas-de-deux with Suzanne Farrell, Heather Watts and Daniel Duell. 54 mins.
VHS: S03157. $39.95.

Pilobolus

One of the dance world's most iconoclastic companies is featured in a Merrill Brockway-directed *Dance in America* program from 1977, including *Monkshood's Farewell*, with sets by illustrator Edward Gorey. 59 mins.
VHS: S34569. $29.99.

Plisetskaya Dances

A rare documentary about the legendary Soviet ballerina, capturing her in some of her most famous roles, including scenes in *Romeo and Juliet, Swan Lake, Sleeping Beauty, Spartacus*, and *Don Quixote*. USSR, 1964, B&W, 70 mins.
VHS: S02450. $29.95.

Pointe by Point

The definitive ballet teaching aid based on Barbara Fewster's years of experience in overseeing the training of many of Britain's most talented dancers. An invaluable companion to teachers throughout the world, guiding the dancer's first tentative steps on pointe. The program embraces two levels of training: the course for beginners, and the course at a Pre-Elementary to Elementary level, a logical progression from Part I, designed to increase technique and encourage confidence. 45 mins.
VHS: S11542. $39.95.

Points in Space

The critically acclaimed collaboration for the screen by choreographer Merce Cunningham, composer John Cage and filmmaker Elliott Caplan. The first half features BBC's documentary interviews with Cunningham, Cage and members of the company as well as scenes from rehearsals in New York and London. The second half features *Points in Space*, performed by Cunningham and the Dance Company. 55 mins.
VHS: S11769. $39.95.

Puss in Boots

Featuring the National Ballet of Marseilles, a fanciful ballet adaptation of the famous fairytale to the music of Tchaikovsky, with dancer Patrick Dupond in the role of Puss, and recorded before a live audience. A wonderful introduction for children to the world of ballet, and a delight for audiences of all ages. 90 mins.
VHS: S06350. $29.95.

Rambert Dance Company—Soldat & Pulcinella

The Rambert Dance Company performs two Igor Stravinsky one-act ballets. *Soldat* features the Mercury Ensemble with choreography by Ashley Page. *Pulcinella* features the BBC Symphony Orchestra with choreography by Richard Alston. Recorded in 1989. 66 mins.
VHS: S37098. $29.97.
Laser: LD76838. $39.97.

Raymonda (Bolshoi/Bessmertnova)

A sumptuously staged production of the Bolshoi's *Raymonda*, with music by Aleksandr Glazunov and choreography by Yuri Grigorovich. The performance features Natalia Bessmertnova and Yuri Vasyuchenko.
VHS: S19520. $39.95.

Raymonda (Bolshoi/Semenyaka)

A glorious ballet that boasts a magical score by Alexander Glazunov, filled with melody, color, dazzling costumes, grand scenery and effects. This 1986 production was filmed at the Bolshoi, features choreography by Yuri Grigorovich, and superstars Ludmila Semenyaka and Irek Mukhamedov. 146 mins.
VHS: S05993. $39.95.

Red Shoes

Presentation by the Children's Theatre of Minneapolis of the ballet based upon Hans Christian Andersen's story.
VHS: S02209. $39.95.

Riverdance—The Show

American dancers Michael Flatley and Jean Butler are at the center of this thrilling dance experience. It joins traditional Irish dance and music with the passion of more recent American styles. It is as if a mixture of *Dirty Dancing* with the chemistry of Torvill and Dean were added to Irish folk ways.
VHS: S27643. $24.95.

Riverdance: A Journey

The story behind the creation of *Riverdance*, from its beginnings in Dublin to hit shows in London and New York. 76 mins.
VHS: S31199. $24.95.

Riverdance: Live from New York City

This all-new production from the composer, director and producer of the hit dance show *Riverdance* features brand new pieces never before seen on video. Filmed live at Radio City Music Hall and starring principal dancers Jean Butler, Colin Dunne and Maria Pages, it is supported by an international cast of over 70. 102 mins.
VHS: S31200. $24.95.

Road to the Stamping Ground

Stamping is an important element in aboriginal dance. In 1980, on a remote island off the Australian coast, there occurred the largest gathering of tribal dancers ever held. One of the few outsiders allowed to witness the event was choreographer Jiri Kylian, who subsequently inspired a ballet by what he had seen. 60 mins.
VHS: S02423. $29.95.

The Romance of Dance

A lively, clear and concise approach to ballroom dancing geared toward a younger generation of ballroom dancers. With live music performances with the Bobby Benson Orchestra and singer Nancy Hays.
The Romance of Dance—Instruction Series Overview. Includes the fox trot, swing, tango, waltz, rumba and cha cha. 60 mins.
VHS: S32633. $19.95.
The Romance of Dance—Instruction Tape. 42 mins.
VHS: S32635. $19.95.
The Romance of Dance—Instruction Tape 2. 40 mins.
VHS: S32634. $19.95.

Romeo and Juliet (Bolshoi Ballet 1975)

The Bolshoi's two most dynamic soloists, Natalia Bessmertnova and Mikhail Lavrovsky, give a stunning performance as the ill-fated lovers. This vivid performance was filmed at the Bolshoi Theatre's Bicentennial Anniversary gala. 1975, 108 mins.
VHS: S06895. $29.95.
Laser: LD71310. $49.95.

Romeo and Juliet (Bolshoi Ballet)

A dazzling production of the Bolshoi Ballet's *Romeo and Juliet*, with music by Sergei Prokofiev, choreography by Yuri Grigorovich. The performance is danced by Irek Mukhamedov and Natalia Bessmertnova.
VHS: S19519. $39.95.

Romeo and Juliet (Nureyev)

Margot Fonteyn and Rudolf Nureyev team with the Royal Ballet in the classic of tragic love.
VHS: S01889. $29.95.
Paul Czinner, Great Britain, 1966, 124 mins.

Romeo and Juliet (Preljocaj)

Angelin Preljocaj's new choreography of Sergi Prokofiev's ballet is performed by the Lyon Opera Ballet. With Pascale Doye and Nicolas Dufloux. 90 min.
VHS: S18404. $39.95.

Romeo and Juliet (Ulanova)

Ballerina Galina Ulanova created the role of Juliet when Prokofiev originally wrote his most famous ballet, and here is her historic interpretation preserved for posterity.
VHS: S02746. $29.95.

The Royal Ballet in Tchaikovsky's The Sleeping Beauty

This performance from the Royal Opera House of Covent Garden is a superb realization of the acclaimed ballet. It is based on the age-old tale of a princess forced to slumber for 100 years until a prince comes to her aid. The timeless quality and deepfelt romance of this story appeals to audiences of all ages. 132 mins.
VHS: S26299. $29.95.

Rudolf Nureyev

This startling biography tells Rudolf Nureyev's story in his own words. Drawing from a variety of sources, the program includes news clips, revealing footage of the infamous ballet dancer reflecting on his past, and of course, breathtaking segments of Nureyev in performance. Includes interviews with Ninette de Valois, Margot Fonteyn, Roland Petit and Nureyev's sister, Rosa. 90 mins.
VHS: S15993. $29.95.

Russian Ballet: The Glorious Tradition, Vol. 1

An historical preservation of ground-breaking Russian ballet, including *Don Quixote*, featuring Mikhail Baryshnikov and Lyudmila Semenyaka; *Corsaire*, with Nina Ananiashvili and Andris Liepa; La Bayadere; *The Nutcracker* and *Swan Lake*.
VHS: S18721. $39.95.

Russian Ballet: The Glorious Tradition, Vol. 2

A valuable inner view of the historical and aesthetic shifts in Russian ballet, captured through rare archival materials and films never shown in the West. This two-volume retrospective showcases the form's dominant figures, from Vera Karalli's sublime interpretation of *The Dying Swan* in 1914, through 40s footage of Marina Semenova and Natalia Dudinskaya, to more recent footage of Galina Ulanova, Maya Plisetskaya and Michail Gabovich. The concluding footage is the amazing *Quixote Act Three grand pas de deux*, with Ekaterina Maximova and Vladimir Vasiliev. 71 mins.
VHS: S18994. $39.95.

Russian Ballet: The Glorious Tradition, Vol. 3

As the third installment of this all-encompassing history of Russian Ballet, *The Glorious Tradition* brings more footage of the brilliant stars of the dance world. Galina Ulanova, Maya Plisetskaya, Mikhail Baryshnikov, and Yuri Soloviev are included. 67 mins.
VHS: S20693. $39.95.

Russian Folk and Dance

Tony Randall narrates the performances of these four great Russian troupes. Dance from the Ukraine, song, dance and instrumentalists from Siberia, dance from Samarkand, melodies and dance from northwestern Russia. 70 mins.
VHS: S03149. $59.95.

Sacred Trances in Bali and Java

Invisible spirits are brought down to enter the bodies of trance dancers who perform super feats in Bali and Java. 30 mins.
VHS: S06487. $49.95.

Shakespeare Dance Trilogy

Shakespeare's immortal dramas are powerfully interpreted in a trilogy of ballets, danced by stars of the Kirov and filmed on location at a spectacular medieval castle. With Svetlana Semenova, Nikita Dolgushin, Gabriella Komleva and Andres Williams. 70 mins.
VHS: S34057. $29.98.

Shape Up

A complete exercise program including warm-up, beginner, intermediate, advanced and aerobic routines, specially designed for dancers and non-dancers alike by America's ballet master, David Howard.
VHS: S10064. $39.95.

Sleeping Beauty (Bujones)

Fernando Bujones performs "Sleeping Beauty" as a guest artist of the Ballet del Teatro Municipal in Santiago, Chile, in this 1982 performance. 120 mins.
VHS: S03159. $39.95.

Sleeping Beauty (Kirov/Fedotov)

Featuring Victor Fedotov, this rendition of Tchaikovsky's Sleeping Beauty is presented by the Kirov Ballet with choreography by Marius Petipa and Oleg Vinogradov.
VHS: S15734. $34.95.
Laser: LD71872. $59.95.

Sleeping Beauty (Kirov/HBO)

The Kirov Ballet, joined by the Orchestra of the Leningrad Theatre, with Irina Kolpakova as Princess Aurora, and with Sergei Berezhnoi, Lubov Kunakova and Vladimir Lopukhov. England, 1983.
VHS: Out of print. For rental only.
Laser: LD70288. $59.95.

Sleeping Beauty (Kirov/Zaklinsky)

Tchaikovsky's beloved fairy tale ballet is given a grand performance by the Kirov Ballet at the Maryinsky Theater in Russia. This dazzling production starring famed Kirov dancers Altynai Asylmuratova and Konstantin Zaklinsky features colorful costumes and brilliant orchestration. 160 mins.
VHS: S30063. $19.95.

Sleeping Beauty (National Ballet of Canada)

Rudolf Nureyev and Veronica Tennant star in this Emmy Award-winning production of the ballet classic. This spectacular and historic performance captures Nureyev at the height of his powers with the National Ballet of Canada. 90 mins.
VHS: S27817. $24.95.

Sleeping Beauty on Ice

Adapted from Charles Perrault's original French fairy tale of the sleeping princess, with choreography by Lar Lubovitch and featuring ice skating of Olympic skaters Robin Cousins and Rosalynn Somners.
VHS: S05929. $29.95.
Tom Gutteridge, USA, 1987, 62 mins.

Soviet Army Chorus, Band and Dance Ensemble

A special opportunity to see and hear this internationally popular group, filmed in various locations all over Russia, as they sing, dance and play. 70 mins.
VHS: S03148. $59.95.

Spanish Folk Dances

Learn three authentic dances including the Huaino from Peru, Jesucita en Chichuahua from Mexico and Rado Blanquita from Spain. Also includes audio-cassette, directions and guide with cultural and costume notes. 40 mins. English narration.
VHS: S05254. $59.95.

Spartacus (Bolshoi/Mukhamedov)

A muscular and sumptuous staging of the lyrical ballet that combines exuberant athleticism and compact grace. Irek Mukhamedov dances the title role with a score by Aram Khachaturian. "First class" (*Chicago Sun-Times*). 132 mins.
VHS: S19524. $39.95.
Laser: LD72258. $59.95.

Spartacus (Bolshoi/Vasiliev)

A very important film, performed by the Bolshoi Ballet, interpreting a contemporary work about the Roman slave who sparks a rebellion. Stars Vladimir Vasiliev and Natalia Bessmertnova. Color.
VHS: S02068. $29.95.
Laser: LD71334. $49.95.
Preben Montell, USSR, 1977, 95 mins.

Speaking in Tongues

A breathtaking and imaginative collaboration with the Paul Taylor Dance Company, designer Santo Loquasto (who works with Woody Allen), and musical theorist Matthew Diamond, interlocking dance and music, told in the expressive vernacular of the Company. "A masterwork" (*New York Times*). 54 mins.
VHS: S17279. $24.97.
Laser: LD71635. $34.97.

Stars of the Russian Ballet

Short works exemplify some of the Russian ballet's great works—scenes from *Swan Lake* feature Galina Ulanova, and a rare record of Ulanova and Plisetskaya dancing together in Boris Asafiev's *The Fountain of the Bakhchisarai*. The performers are from both the Bolshoi and the Kirov ballets. 1953, color, 80 mins.
VHS: S02456. $59.95.

Step into Ballet
Former Royal Ballet star Wayne Sleep presents this easy-to-follow and entertaining guide to the art of ballet. Even choosing the correct shoes and costume—those first important steps—are thoughtfully explained. All the early stages of ballet training are shown, including basic positions like the arabesque, pirouettes and many other important techniques. 50 mins.
VHS: S21700. $19.95.

Stomp Out Loud
Members of the hit show perform their unique blend of music, comedy and dance, filmed live in New York City. Features never-before-seen excitement as performers risk their lives dangling from a billboard opposite the Manhattan skyline, dive into Brooklyn Navy Yard, and dance and drum in the streets and alleyways of New York, on land, in water and more. "A sure-fire crowd pleaser which is banged, tapped, swished, clicked and clomped with a rock-and-roll heart" (Stephen Holden, *New York Times*). 55 mins.
VHS: S33133. $19.98.

The Stone Flower
Part of the *Bolshoi at the Bolshoi* series, *The Stone Flower* ballet was inspired by the rich heritage of Russian culture and folk dance. With music by Sergei Prokofiev. 1990, 107 mins.
VHS: S14550. $39.95.

Swan Lake (Ananiashvili)
Tchaikovsky's ballet is performed by the Russian State Perm Ballet, with Nina Ananiashvili dancing the part of Odette. With Aleksei Fadeyetchev. 132 mins.
VHS: S19739. $24.95.

Swan Lake (Bolshoi/Mikhalchenko)
A century after its creation, Tchaikovsky's lyrical ballet remains the most popular piece in the Bolshoi's repertory. Yuri Grigorovich, the company's current artistic director, has adapted the traditional choreography in order to showcase the special talents of today's Bolshoi dancers. Featuring Alla Mikhalchenko, Yuri Vasyuchenko. USSR, 1989, 128 mins.
VHS: S12823. $39.95.

Swan Lake (Bolshoi/Plisetskaya)
Maya Plisetskaya, the legendary ballerina, stars in this famous version of the ballet. USSR, 1957, color, 81 mins.
VHS: S02458. $29.95.

Swan Lake (Kirov/Ivanov)
Filmed in St. Petersburg's Kirov Theater, this production of the Kirov dancing the quintessential Romantic ballet links Tchaikovsky's music with the legendary Ivanov/Petipa staging. Igor Zelensky dances the role of the Prince. "Show-stopping athletic exuberance and proper bravura form" (*The New York Times*). 116 mins.
VHS: S03146. $39.95.
Laser: LD71633. $39.97.

Swan Lake (London Fest/Makarova)
A landmark interpretation of the classical masterpiece in the London Festival Ballet production, with Natalia Makarova realizing her vision born of 20 years experience of dancing the classical ballet. With innovative sets evoking the perfect atmosphere of magic and mystery. 116 mins.
VHS: S12216. $39.95.

Swan Lake (Nureyev)
Rudolf Nureyev choreographed and dances in this historic production of Tchaikovsky's timeless ballet. John Lanchbery leads the Vienna Symphony.
VHS: S12654. $24.95.
Laser: LD71358. $34.95.
DVD: DV60011. $29.95.

Sylvie Guillem
At only 24 years of age, Sylvie Guillem has already enjoyed a most brilliant career dancing all over the world and as a choreographer in her own right. During this one-hour portrait, we discover a young woman whose personality has remained unaffected by this meteoric rise to fame. 54 mins.
VHS: S11753. $39.95.

Tales of Beatrix Potter
The Royal Ballet, in association with the Royal Opera House in Covent Garden, presents a program based on the children's stories of Beatrix Potter. Many of her favorite characters are here, including the two Town Mice, Mrs. Tiggy-Winkle, Squirrel Nutkin and Jeremiah Puddleduck. Music by John Lanchbery.
VHS: S01992. $19.98.
Reginald Mills, Great Britain, 1971, 86 mins.

Tango
The Ballet Ensemble of the Grand Theatre Company of Geneva performs a series of pieces to the vibrant and throbbing rhythms of the tango. Choreographed with great originality by the talented and famous Oscar Araiz and performed by some of the finest dancers in Europe. 57 minutes.
VHS: S03380. $39.95.

Tango: Our Dance
The sensuality and stylized rituals popular with the residents of Buenos Aires are part of the complex art form called the tango. Director Jorge Zanada examines the unique role of this dance within Argentina's social and personal landscape, exploring issues of machismo and passion contained within the dance. With a special appearance by Robert Duvall. Spanish with English subtitles.
VHS: S20380. $29.95.
Jorge Zanada, Argentina, 1988, 71 mins.

Tap Dancing for Beginners
One of the best ways to start dancing life, introduced by Henry le Tang. Coordination, agility, timing and rhythm are stressed.
VHS: S04746. $39.95.

Tap Dogs
Winner of 11 international awards, this smash hit Australian dance show, originated and choreographed by dancer Dein Perry, stars six young Australian men who steal tap from the world of black ties and tails and carry it body and soul into the '90s. "Spectacular! Trimphant!" (*Los Angeles Times*).
VHS: S32651. $19.98.
Aubrey Powell, Australia, 1996, 73 mins.

Tchaikovsky's Swan Lake (Male Cast)
Bourne's Olivier Award-winning production brings a bold, new twist to an old classic. Set in the modern era with an all-male cast, Bourne's creation brings great ballet to an audience it has never before reached, and for cognoscenti it offers a new view of the breadth of possibility in Tchaikovsky's well-loved score. "One of the most gripping, funny and profoundly moving dance works I've seen" (*The Guardian*).
VHS: S32967. $29.97.
Matthew Bourne, Great Britain, 1996, 117 mins.

A Tribute to Alvin Ailey
This two-part program celebrates this dance world legend with performances of four of his works: *For Bird with Love, Witness, Memoria* and *Episodes*. Each dance is introduced by Judith Jamison, the dancer and choreographer whose career was nurtured to stardom by Ailey and who has succeeded him as director of their company. 120 mins.
VHS: S15992. $39.95.

Troy Game
Created for the London Contemporary Dance Theatre by Robert North in 1974, *Troy Game* is a steady fixture in repertoires of both the LCD and the Dance Theater of Harlem. Choreographed to Brazilian folk music, Bob Downes, and drum instrumental pieces, the ballet begins with the London company in warm-up class, led by Artistic Director Robert Cohan, intercut with his commentary on the ballet, and a complete performance. 39 mins.
VHS: S08485. $39.95.

The Tsar's Bride
The Bolshoi performs a quintessential example of the work of Nikolai Rimsky-Korsakov, celebrating the extravagance and pageantry of Tsarist Russia. Russian with English subtitles. USSR, 1966, B&W.
VHS: S02461. $59.95.

Twist
Canadian independent filmmaker Ron Mann, who specializes in cultural documentaries (*Comic Book Confidential*), made this entertaining work about the history of the 50s dance craze. Mann interweaves archival footage and interviews with Chubby Checker, Hank Ballard, Joey Dee and various dancers to comment on the racial, social and artistic implications of the Twist. Mann argues the movement was the catalyst for American rock and roll. Cinematography by Bob Fresco.
VHS: S19732. $9.98.
Laser: LD72280. $49.95.
Ron Mann, Canada, 1992, 78 mins.

The Ultimate Swan Lake
Opulent interpretation is exquisitely danced by the Bolshoi, featuring Natalia Bessmertnova, Boris Akimov and Alexander Bogatyrev. Choreographed by Yuri Grigorovich with the Moscow Symphony Orchestra, narrated by Gene Kelly. 126 mins.
VHS: S03781. $39.95.

Video Dictionary of Classical Ballet
An innovative tool for learning and studying the movements of ballet over and over again, this four-cassette, 270-minute program provides the viewer with an index to over 800 steps, all of them numbered and correspondingly indicated in the accompanying booklet. Produced in association with the Metropolitan Opera Guild and Capezio, the dictionary features Merrill Ashley, Denise Jackson, Kevin McKenzie and Georgina Parkinson. 4 cassettes. 270 mins.
VHS: S03143. $99.95.

White Night of Dance in Leningrad
Two great dance troupes, the Soviet Kirov Ballet and the French Ballet of the 20th century, join together in this rare and extraordinary dance program. Filmed in Leningrad. 83 mins.
VHS: S15092. $29.95.

With My Red Fires/New Dance: Dance Works by Doris Humphrey
Includes two masterpieces of modern choreography by world-renowned choreographer Doris Humphrey. "With My Red Fires" (1936) and "New Dance" (1935) are parts of a dance trilogy, the general theme of which is human relationships. Exciting and evocative work. USA, 1978, 65 mins.
VHS: S15336. $49.95.

World's Young Ballet
This fascinating look at the world of international ballet competitions features a young, pre-defection Mikhail Baryshnikov competing in Moscow in 1969. Ballet legends Maya Plisetskaya and Alicia Alonso are among the judges in this tense and thrilling documentary.
VHS: S13053. $29.95.

Yuri Grigorovich: Master of the Bolshoi
A revealing profile of one of the greatest choreographers of our time, featuring excerpts from great Bolshoi Ballet productions, including *Spartacus, Swan Lake, Ivan the Terrible, The Golden Age, Romeo and Juliet, The Legend of Love*. 67 mins.
VHS: S12593. $29.95.

music on video

OPERA

Abduction from the Seraglio (Dresden)
Mozart's merry song-play is performed by the Dresden State Opera conducted by Harry Kupfer and starring Carolyn Smith-Meyer and Barbara Sternberger. Love and faith overcome power and egotism in this timeless masterpiece. 130 mins.
VHS: S03372. $79.95.

Abduction from the Seraglio (Glyndebourne)
This early Mozart opera is both exotic (set in a harem) and humorous, and stars Ryland Davies and Valerie Masterson. This new Glyndebourne Festival release marks the completion of the VAI series from the Festival.
VHS: S02424. $49.95.

Adriadne auf Naxos (Strauss)
This Metropolitan Opera production features the dramatic soprano Jessye Norman in the title role and Kathleen Battle as Zerbinetta. James Levine conducts the Metropolitan Opera Orchestra with soloists Tatiana Troyanos and James King. In Hi-Fi stereo, 148 mins.
VHS: S16401. $34.95.

Adriana Lecouvreur
This La Scala production of the Francesco Cilea opera dramatizes the story of the celebrated 18th century rivalry of the actress with the Princess of Bouillon for the Count of Saxony's love. The difficult role requires a great soprano, and Mirella Freni sings at the height of her vocal maturity. With Peter Dvorsky, Fiorenza Cossotto and Ivo Vinco. Directed by Lamberto Puggelli. Italian with English subtitles. 157 mins.
VHS: S13188. $39.95.
DVD: DV60334. $49.99.

Agrippina
The rare opera by Handel, telling of the insidious tricks of power-hungry Empress Agrippina, in a remarkable new production by Michael Hampe at the Schwetzingen Palace, featuring Barbara Daniels, David Kuebler, and Gunter von Kannen. Arnold Ostman conducts the Cologne Opera and the London Baroque Players. Performed in Italian with English subtitles. 160 mins.
VHS: S04640. $29.95.

Aida (Downes)
Doomed but fated to be beautifully sung, the romance between Radames the Egyptian prince and Aida, an Ethiopian princess, is a standard of opera repertory the world over. Edward Downes conducts a strong cast which includes Cheryl Studer, Luciana d'Intino and Dennis O'Neill. Sung in Italian with English subtitles. 150 mins.
VHS: S26296. $39.95.

Aida (Gencer, Cossotto, Bergonzi)
The singing is superb. This is the only video that captures these three legendary greats together in Verdi's opera. In Italian, 150 mins.
VHS: S24560. $34.95.

Aida (La Scala)
Luca Ronconi's production of Verdi's much-loved masterpiece conducted by Loren Maazel; Luciano Pavarotti heads an exceptional cast including Ghena Dimitrova, Maria Chiara, Nicolai Ghiaurov. Italian with English subtitles.
VHS: S03685. $29.95.

Aida (Metropolitan Opera)
This very special performance of Verdi's *Aida* won an Emmy. James Levine conducts the Metropolitan Opera Chorus and Orchestra. Performers include Aprile Millo, Placido Domingo, Dolora Zajick, Sherrill Milnes and Dimitri Kavrakos. A treat.
VHS: S15448. $34.95.
Laser: LD70177. $59.95.

Aida (Royal Opera)
The classic Verdi opera in four acts features Cheryl Studer and the Royal Opera with Luciana D'Intino and Dennis O'Neill. This spectacular production has been acclaimed by critics as being "of the highest orchestral, choral and vocal standards." "Spectacular. Studer's pure-toned, dramatic singing says everything that *Aida* has to say" (*Evening Standard*). 150 mins.
VHS: S31132. $29.95.

Aida File
Luciano Pavarotti, Carlo Bergonzi, Grace Bumbry, Dame Eva Turner and Renata Tebaldi delve into the making of one of the most popular operatic works in a rare backstage glimpse featuring excerpts from the famous La Scala production starring Pavarotti and many other well-known performances. 77 mins.
VHS: S11752. $29.95.

Albert Herring
Benjamin Britten's comic opera, adapted from a short story by Guy de Maupassant, tells the story of how the title character becomes the May Queen. Bernard Haitink conducts the London Philharmonic at Glyndebourne Festival. 150 mins.
VHS: S03410. $29.95.

All the Great Operas in Ten Minutes
Behind the long and expansive librettos of most operas lies a kernel of overpowering excitement. In this hysterical ten-minute animation the nutty centers of these works are revealed in brief, pithy manifestations. Among the operas lampooned are; *La Traviata, Aida, Tosca, Tristan and Isolde, Madame Butterfly* and *The Ring of the Nibelungen*.
VHS: S29295. $12.95.

Amahl and the Night Visitors
The most-often performed opera in America, and a Christmas tradition, Giancarlo Menotti's wonderful work stars Teresa Stratas, and other Metropolitan Opera stars Giorgio Tozzi, Willard White and Nico Castel. USA, 1985.
VHS: S01957. $19.95.

Andrea Chenier (Royal Opera)
Placido Domingo stars in the title role of this production from Royal Opera House Covent Garden, with Anna Tomowa-Sintow, Giorgio Zancanaro, and Julius Rudel conducting the Royal Opera House. 118 mins.
VHS: S02411. $29.95.

Anna Russell: The Clown Princess of Comedy
Anna Russell, the failed diva, dubbed "the world's funniest woman" by the *London Times*, delivers three of her timeless routines and tells all in a side-splitting interview. A must for any fan of the "lady who has been reducing audiences to helpless laughter for nearly half a century" (*Washington Post*). 60 mins.
VHS: S30129. $29.95.

Arabella
Sir Georg Solti directs the Vienna Philharmonic Orchestra in Richard Strauss' opera. Gundula Janowitz stars in the title role, and is joined by Rene Kollo, Bernd Weikl, Margarita Lilowa and Martha Modl. In Hi-Fi stereo, 150 mins.
VHS: S17680. $34.95.
Laser: LD71422. $59.95.

Aria
Ten different directors select a different aria and have free rein to do anything that they want. The world of opera meets the medium of film with an eclectic mix of music and imagery. Robert Altman, Ken Russell, Derek Jarman, Jean-Luc Godard, Nicolas Roeg, Julien Temple, Bill Bryden, Franc Roddam, Charles Sturridge and Bruce Beresford go off in different directions. Cast includes Buck Henry, Theresa Russell, John Hurt, Anita Morris and Peter Fonda's daughter Bridget.
VHS: S07452. $14.98.
Ken Russell, et al., Great Britain, 1988, 90 mins.

The Art of Singing
This video tracks the evolution of recorded song from the silent films of Caruso to the early Vitaphone footage with Martinelli and De Luca, culminating with Maria Callas' triumphant performance as Tosca at Covent Garden in 1964. With rare footage, including a never-before-seen film of Kirsten Flagstad singing "Hojotoho" from *Die Walkure* and Rosa Ponselle's screen tests for *Carmen*. Narrated by Penny Gore with insightful commentary by such opera notables as Schuyler Chapin, Magda Olivero, Kirk Browning and Nicola Rescigno. "One of the most involving, enlightening and entertaining productions to hit the market since classical labels began producing videos" (*New York Times*). 117 mins.
VHS: S31282. $29.95.
Laser: LD76204. $34.95.

As Frozen Music
The story of the remarkable Sydney Opera House, now the famous landmark on Sydney's skyline, home to Luciano Pavarotti, Joan Sutherland, Janet Baker and other stars. 55 mins.
VHS: S06562. $49.95.

Attila (La Scala)
La Scala presents a rare revival of this early Verdi masterpiece. The superstar cast includes Samuel Ramey, Cheryl Studer, Giorgio Zancanaro, Kaludi Kaludov. Conducted by Riccardo Muti and directed by Jerome Savary, this production was received with great acclaim by the Italian public. 118 mins.
VHS: S16003. $39.95.
DVD: DV60335. $39.99.

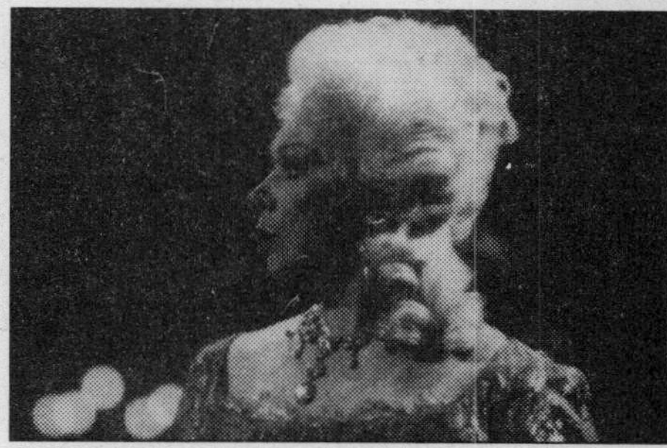

The Australian Opera Series
SONY presents four classic operas, performed by Dame Joan Sutherland with Richard Bonynge conducting the Elizabethan Sydney Opera. Each volume is in stereo and contains a libretto and a playbill.
Die Fledermaus. 142 minutes.
VHS: S02428. $39.95.
Il Trovatore. 138 minutes.
VHS: S02429. $39.95.

Ave Maria
In this 1936 film, Beniamino Gigli is a tenor blackmailed by a woman, who expresses his rage through a performance of *La Traviata*. "Di quella pira," songs and excerpts from *La Boheme* are also performed. "Gigli...is a perfect lover and a fine actor. Beauty of his voice and captivating story keep up the dramatic tension. Photography is outstanding" (*Variety*, 1936). Italian with English subtitles. 76 mins.
VHS: S28425. $34.95.

The Bartered Bride and The Last Waltz
The Bartered Bride features Jarmila Novotna and Willi Domgraf-Fassbaender. This 1932 production was directed by Max Ophuls with music by Smetana. "Fans of Novotna will certainly want to watch these over and over again while fans of the filmmaker's art will probably derive even more pleasure than will purely opera connoisseurs" (*H & B Directory*). Sung in German with German dialog (no subtitles). 76 mins. Novotna also stars in *The Last Waltz* (1935), featuring Harry Welchman, with music by Oscar Straus. English. 73 mins.
VHS: S28429. $34.95.

The Beggar's Opera
Roger Daltrey, lead singer of The Who, and 1986 Academy Award-winning actor Bob Hoskins (of *Mona Lisa*) head a distinguished cast in this British television production of John Gay's ballad opera. Adapted by Jonathan Miller, the exuberant production brings to life the corruption, lust and greed of low-life London.
VHS: S03741. $29.95.
Laser: LD71431. $59.95.

Bellini: La Sonnambula
A stunning historic 1948 feature film version of the delightful Bellini opera about a beautiful young country girl who sleepwalks her way into a love affair. With Gino Sinimberghi, Fiorella Ortis and Franco Tamantini. Sung in Italian with English narration between arias. 90 mins.
VHS: S34054. $29.98.

Beniamino Gigli in Mamma
Beniamino Gigli stars in his most famous film, recorded in 1941, performing the title song and selections from *Otello*. With Emma Gramatica and Luigi Ricci conducting the Rome Opera Chorus and Orchestra. 84 mins.
VHS: S31713. $39.95.

Bergonzi in Luisa Miller
Carlo Bergonzi performs with Cristina Rubin, Sofia Salazar, Giancarlo Pasquetto, Michel Pertusi and Gilberto Zanellato, with Angelo Campori conducting in this 1986 recording. 150 mins.
VHS: S31711. $39.95.

Billy Budd

Adapted from Melville's great novel, Benjamin Britten's gripping opera of sadism and injustice on board a British man-of-war. Britain's leading baritone, Thomas Allen, displays his superb abilities as a singer and his phenomenal acting skills in this splendid English National Opera production. 151 mins.
VHS: S10262. $29.95.

Bizet's Carmen

The definitive version of this classic opera, shot entirely on location in Andalusian Spain, featuring Placido Domingo and Julia Migenes-Johnson. Soundtrack by the Orchestre National de France, conducted by Lorin Maazel. French with English subtitles.
VHS: S01790. $19.95.
Francesco Rosi, France/Italy, 1984, 151 mins.

Bluebeard's Castle

Sir Georg Solti conducts the London Philharmonic Orchestra, under the direction of Miklos Szinetar, in this recording of Bartok's opera. With Sylvia Sass and Kolos Kovats. 58 mins.
VHS: S17679. $24.95.

Caballe Subjugates La Scala

This 1983 performance marks Caballe's return to La Scala's *Anna Bolena* after withdrawing from the production the previous season. With Miguel Zinetti on piano. 118 mins.
VHS: S31712. $39.95.

Carmen (DeMille)

Cecil B. DeMille's much talked-about but seldom-seen version of *Carmen* has been superbly restored with a new soundtrack featuring the London Philharmonic Orchestra. Geraldine Farrar, the Metropolitan Opera's biggest box-office draw from 1906-1922, was engaged by DeMille to recreate one of her greatest roles for the silent screen. The film was rapturously received at its 1915 world premiere performance, with Farrar elevated to Hollywood stardom. Also includes passages of the opera sung by Farrar herself, taken from a recording of the period.
VHS: S30710. $29.95.
Cecil B. DeMille, USA, 1915, 75 mins.

Carmen (Bolshoi)

Bizet's famous work was realized in 1959 through the brilliant pairing of Italian tenor Mario del Monaco with the incomparable company of the Bolshoi Opera. Mezzo-soprano Irina Arkipova stars in the title role while the Armenian baritone Pavel Lisitsyan briefly appears as Escamillo. Sung in Italian and Russian. 68 mins.
VHS: S20694. $39.95.

Carmen (Covent Garden)

Carmen, one of the world's favorite operas, celebrates its first new production at Covent Garden in nearly 20 years. The fateful story of jealousy and passion between the gypsy Carmen and her rival lovers is superbly realized in this all-star cast, including Maria Ewing as Carmen and Luis Lima as Don Jose. Zubin Mehta conducts. Two cassettes, 180 mins.
VHS: S16001. $29.95.

Carmen (Met)

The Metropolitan Opera and Chorus, conducted by James Levine, are featured in this complete performance of Bizet's opera with soloists Agnes Baltsa, Jose Carreras, Leona Mitchell and Samuel Ramey. 2 laser disks.
VHS: S18537. $44.95.
Laser: LD70884. $69.95.

Carole Farley in "The Telephone" and "La Voix Humaine"

The talented American soprano Carole Farley stars in this two 20th-century operas about the relationship between love and the telephone. *La Voix Humaine* is adapted from Jean Cocteau's play. Conducted by Jose Serebrier and the Scottish Chamber Orchestra. 66 mins.
VHS: S17132. $24.95.

Carteri in "La Traviata"

Carteri was 24 when this film of the great opera was made for television in 1954. Her vocal quality is perfect for the role of a woman who was mature in terms of experience but not age. In Italian, 51 mins.
VHS: S24559. $34.95.

Cavalleria Rusticana (Verrett/1990)

American diva Shirley Verret gives a mesmerizing portrayal of Santuzza in Mascagni's masterpiece. Rising tenor star Kristjan Johannsson sings the role of Turiddu with fiery passion and vocal opulence in this live 1990 performance from Siena, staged in honor of the 100th anniversary of the opera's world premiere. 85 mins.
VHS: S13999. $39.95.
Laser: LD70906. $39.95.

Cavalleria Rusticana and I Pagliaci

Herbert von Karajan leads the Orchestra and Chorus of the esteemed La Scala Opera House in moving renditions of these Italian opera favorites.
VHS: S27437. $34.95.
Laser: LD75506. $59.95.

Charles Gounod's Romeo et Juliette

Gounod realized an opera of enduring magic by adapting Shakespeare's tragic romance. Robert Alagna and Leontine Vaduva bring terrific vocal talent to the title roles under the direction of Charles Mackerras. This video does justice to the ideal of unending love. Sung in French with English subtitles. 170 mins.
VHS: S26297. $29.95.

The Charm of La Boheme

Real-life husband and wife tenor and soprano team Jan Kiepura and Marta Eggerth sing and act together in this wonderfully nonsensical 1936 tearjerker. "*The Charm of La Boheme* is notable for the charm of Jan Kiepura…The quality of the film transfer is superb" (Steve Cohen, *The Delaware Jewish Voice* and *The Philadelphia Jewish Times*). Also features Paul Kemp, Oskar Sima and Theo Lingen. German with English subtitles. 97 mins.
VHS: S28427. $34.95.

Cinderella (Berlin)

Grimm's wonderful fairy tale becomes even more magical with Prokofiev's music, here performed by the Berlin Comic Opera with Hannelore Bey as Cinderella and Roland Gawlick as the Prince. 75 minutes.
VHS: S03379. $24.95.

Cinderella (Glyndebourne)

Famous Glyndebourne production of Rossini's witty and vivacious adaptation of the Cinderella story, featuring American mezzo-soprano Kathleen Kuhlman. 155 mins.
VHS: S02413. $39.95.

Classic Views Video Magazine, Volume 2

This is the first magazine on video for opera and classical music lovers. Includes performances, interviews and critics' samples of the best of today's classical music scene. Features of the second volume include: "In Homage: Dmitry Sitkovetsky's Goldberg Variations," "On Reflection: Bryn Terfel," "New Directions: Bobby McFerrin," "Opera on Video: Martin Bernheimer," "On Reflection: John Adams," "Critic's Choice: William Livingstone," "Past Masters: Alexander Nevsky," and "Divertimento: Opera Imaginaire's La Traviata." 95 mins.
VHS: S30131. $9.95.

Claudio Monteverdi: L'Orfeo

Nikolaus Harnoncourt conducts the Monteverdi Ensemble of the Zurich Opera House in this adaptation of *L'Orfeo*. Directed and designed by Jean-Pierre Ponnelle.
VHS: S19108. $24.95.

Corelli in Tosca

Renata Heredia Capnist, Carlo Tagliabue and Antonine Votto join the incomparable Franco Corelli in the Puccini opera. The story revolves around jealousy, love and tragic death.
VHS: S24850. $34.95.
Carmine Gallone, Italy, 1956, 113 mins.

Cosi Fan Tutte (Chatelet Theater)

John Eliot Gardiner's cycle of Mozart operas were the cause of much excitement in Europe. Now Americans can see Gardiner's work in this video recording originally shot on HDTV at the Chatelet Theater in Paris.
VHS: S20644. $44.95.

Cosi Fan Tutte (Glyndebourne)

Mozart's witty look at Romantic foibles is a Glyndebourne Festival production, starring Thomas Allen and Sylvia Linderstrand and conducted by John Pritchard. Italian with English subtitles.
VHS: S02447. $49.95.

Cosi Fan Tutte (La Scala)

Mozart's classic opera and comedy of manners receives lavish treatment in this La Scala production. With Daniela Dessi, Delores Ziegler, Jozef Kundlak, Alessandro Corbelli and Adeline Scarabelli. Directed by Riccardo Muti. Italian with English subtitles. 186 mins.
VHS: S13187. $49.95.
DVD: DV60336. $49.99.

Cosi Fan Tutte (Vienna)

Mozart's great opera about the vagaries of romantic love is captured as it was presented by the Vienna State Opera. Teresa Stratas, Edita Gruberova, Delores Ziegler, Luis Lima, Ferruccio Furlanetto, Paolo Montarsolo and Nikolaus Harnoncourt join the Vienna Philharmonic for this engaging production. 175 mins.
VHS: S21988. $44.95.

The Daughter of the Regiment (Sills)

A spirited production of Donizetti's opera, highlighted by Sills' lead performance. "Her supremely confident form, her zest and vivacity prove infectious with the other performers and the entire audience." With William McDonald, Spiro Malas and Muriel Costa-Greenspon. Conducted by Charles Wendelken-Wilson. 118 mins.
VHS: S17695. $39.95.

The Daughter of the Regiment (Sutherland)

Joan Sutherland is featured in this wonderful Australian Opera production of Donizetti's opera. Italian with English subtitles.
VHS: S09358. $29.95.

Death in Venice

Death in Venice was the last opera by Benjamin Britten, presented here in a highly acclaimed performance from the Glyndebourne Touring Opera. Robert Tear stars as Aschenbach, with Alan Opie and Michael Chance. Graeme Jenkins conducts the London Sinfonietta. Sung in English. 138 min.
VHS: S18382. $29.95.

Del Monaco: The Singing Volcano

Mario Del Monaco is heard here in what is considered his prime, in this 1952-60 recording and 1978 interview. 37 mins.
VHS: S31714. $39.95.

Der Ring

James Levine conducts the Metropolitan Opera Orchestra and Chorus with a host of world renowned soloists, in Wagner's complete "Ring" cycle.
Das Rheingold. The first chapter of Wagner's monumental *Ring*. James Levine conducts the Metropolitan Opera Orchestra with soloists Morris, Ludwig, Jerusalem, Wlaschiha, Zednick, Rootering, Salminen. German lyrics with English subtitles. 162 mins.
VHS: S16048. $34.95.
Laser: LD71194. $59.95.
Die Walkure. Behrens, Norman, Ludwig, Lakes, Morris, Moll are in principal roles. German lyrics with English subtitles. 243 mins.
VHS: S16049. $44.95.
Laser: LD71195. $82.50.
Gotterdammerung. Soloists include Behrens, Saliminen, Ludwig, Raffell, Lisowska and Wlaschiha. German lyrics with English subtitles. 280 mins.
VHS: S16051. $44.95.
Laser: LD71197. $82.50.
Siegfried. Featuring Morris, Zednik, Behrens, Wlaschiha, Svenden, Upshaw and Salminen. German lyrics with English subtitles. 252 mins.
VHS: S16050. $44.95.
Laser: LD71196. $82.50.
Complete Set. Four cassettes, 937 mins.
Laser: LD71198. $307.45.

Der Rosenkavalier (Bavarian State)

Carlos Kleiber conducts the Bavarian State Opera and Chorus, with soloists Gwyneth Jones, Brigitte Fassbaender, Lucia Popp, Manfred Jungwirth, Benno Kusche and Francisco Araiza. In Hi-Fi Stereo. German with English subtitles. 182 mins.
VHS: S16520. $44.95.

Der Rosenkavalier (Schwarzkopf)

Herbert von Karajan conducts and Elisabeth Schwarzkopf stars in this memorable film of Richard Strauss' charming comedic opera. Now available in a double-cassette set with English subtitles and a newly remastered soundtrack. 190 mins.
VHS: S02270. $59.95.

Der Rosenkavalier (Vienna)

Carlos Kleiber conducts Felicity Lott, Barbara Bonney, Anne Sofie Otter and Kurt Moll with the backing of the Vienna State Opera Chorus and Orchestra, in this telling rendition of the Strauss opera. Based on a stage production by Otto Schenk. 193 mins.
VHS: S23909. $44.95.
Laser: LD74797. $69.95.

Destination: Mozart—A Night at the Opera with Peter Sellars

Peter Sellars' recent productions of Mozart, set in contemporary America, are probably the most radical and iconoclastic opera stagings of our time. Mr. Sellars is widely regarded as the most exciting director at work on the international theater and opera scene today. This special program gives viewers a revealing look at Sellars' controversial productions of Mozart's *Don Giovanni, Marriage of Figaro* and *Cosi Fan Tutte*. His unconventional approach to these musical masterpieces led him to set them in the South Bronx, Trump Tower and a Long Island diner, respectively. All the opera excerpts are subtitled, and interviews with Sellars and his collaborators are included. 60 mins.
VHS: S13664. $29.95.

Die Entfuhrung aus dem Serail (Bohm)

This 1980 performance features Karl Boehm conducting the Bavarian State Opera Orchestra and Chorus. Soloists include Edita Gruberova, Reri Grist, Francisco Araiza, Norbert Orth and Martti Talvela. In Hi-Fi Stereo. German with English subtitles. 146 mins.
VHS: S16521. $34.95.

Die Entfuhrung aus dem Serail (Drottningholm)

Mozart's famous opera, set in a Turkish Sultan's harem, is beautifully realized in this staging at the Royal Palace in Stockholm. The famous 18th century Drottningholm theater is used to great effect, including the original costumes, scenery, and machinery from that time, and featuring the Drottningholm Orchestra and Chorus. 133 mins.
Laser: LD72372. $59.95.

Die Fledermaus (Schenk)

Discover the pure pleasure of opera with Otto Schenk's delightful production of Johann Strauss' classic comedy of ruses, revenge and mistaken identity.
VHS: S12653. $34.95.

Die Fledermaus (Sutherland/Pavarotti)

This most effervescent of all Johann Strauss operettas is a perennial favorite, with its tide of bright Viennese dance music and charmingly nonsensical plot. Bidding farewell to the Royal Opera House, Dame Joan Sutherland appears in this Covent Garden production that also hosts Luciano Pavarotti and Marilyn Horne. The cast assembles, paying tribute to Sutherland, in the famous party scene. 180 mins.
VHS: S16005. $29.95.

Die Frau ohne Schatten

Sir Georg Solti conducts the Vienna Philharmonic Orchestra. With Cheryl Studer, Thomas Moser, Eva Marton, Robert Hale and Marjana Lipovsek. 203 mins.
VHS: S19753. $44.95.
Laser: LD71962. $69.95.

Die Meistersinger von Nurnberg (Jerusalem/Bayreuth)

Staged and directed by Wolfgang Wagner, this production includes an all-star cast: Siegfried Jerusalem, Bernd Weikl, Hermann Prey, Graham Clark and Marga Schiml.
VHS: S15446. $44.95.

Die Meistersinger von Nurnberg (The Australian Opera)

Wagner's masterpiece is brought to glorious life by the renowned Australian Opera. An enchanting love story, as well as an intriguing exploration of the conflict between tradition and innovation in art, *Die Meistersinger* is masterfully conducted by Charles Mackerras, who brings absolute sureness of touch to the demanding score. 277 mins., two videocassettes.
VHS: S15168. $29.95.

Die Soldaten

Zimmermann's opera receives a rare staging by the Staatsoper Stuttgart. Bernhard Kontarsky conducts a cast led by Nancy Shade, William Cochran and Mark Munkittrick. German with English subtitles. 111 min.
VHS: S18383. $29.95.

Die Zauberflote (Araiza)

Francisco Araiza, Lucia Popp and Kurt Moll are the featured singers in this magical production of Mozart's charming opera *The Magic Flute*.
VHS: S12652. $34.95.

Die Zauberflote (Battle)

James Levine conducts the Metropolitan Opera Chorus and Orchestra in this production of Mozart's opera. With Kathleen Battle, Luciana Serra and Barbara Kilduff. Production design by David Hockney. 169 mins.
VHS: S17674. $34.95.
Laser: LD71790. $59.95.

Don Carlo (Met)

Placido Domingo, Grace Bumbry, Mirella Freni, Louis Quilico, Nicolai Ghiaurov in Verdi's opera, conducted at the Met by James Levine. Italian with English subtitles. Stereo, 1983, 214 mins. 2 cassettes.
VHS: S02433. $29.95.

Don Giovanni (Glyndebourne)

Benjamin Luxon stars in Mozart's operatic masterpiece, as the wily and roguish Don. Leo Goeke, Elizabeth Gale, and Rachael Yakar also star in this Glyndebourne Festival production. Bernard Haitink conducts the London Philharmonic in this 1977 performance. Italian with English subtitles. 173 mins.
VHS: S03217. $59.95.

Don Giovanni

Finally on video, this sumptuous production of Mozart's great opera was shot on location in Venice, and is one of the great films of Joseph Losey. Ruggero Raimondi, Kiri Te Kanawa and Teresa Berganza are principal singers, with Lorin Maazel conducting the Paris Opera Orchestra. Sung in Italian with English subtitles.
VHS: S07688. $39.95.
Joseph Losey, Italy/France, 1972, 185 mins.

Don Giovanni (Muti)

Mozart's opera is directed by theatrical great Giorgio Strehler, with Thomas Allen in the role of Don Giovanni, in a La Scala production under the direction of Riccardo Muti. 177 min.
VHS: S18385. $49.95.

Don Giovanni (Ruggero Raimondi)

Raimondi discusses the music and performs the title role in selections from Mozart's masterwork. 60 mins.
VHS: S20569. $24.95.

Don Giovanni (Salzburg)

Herbert Von Karajan conducts the Vienna Philharmonic and Samuel Ramey, Kathleen Battle, Ferruccio Furlanetto and Anna Tomowa-Sintow in this performance from the Salzburg Festival. 193 mins.
VHS: S27572. $34.95.
Laser: LD74558. $79.98.

Don Giovanni (Sellars)

In Peter Sellars' interpretation, Mozart's *Don Giovanni* meets modern-day Harlem. Craig Smith conducts the Vienna Symphonic Orchestra and the Arnold Schoenberg Choir. With soloists Eugene Perry, Herbert Perry, Dominique Labelle, Lorraine Hunt, Carroll Freeman, James Patterson, Ai Lan Zhu and Elmore James. In Hi-Fi Stereo, 190 mins.
VHS: S16515. $44.95.

Don Giovanni (Siepi)

The incomparable Cesare Siepi stars in this legendary Salzburg production of Mozart's masterpiece. Wilhelm Furtwangler conducts a cast which also includes Elisabeth Grummer, Lisa Della Casa, Erna Berger, Anton Dermota and Otto Edelmann. Color, 129 mins. (two cassettes)
VHS: S13682. $59.95.

Don Pasquale

Barbara Hendricks performs in this production of Donizetti's opera at the Aix-en-Provence Festival. As Norina she brings her youthful vitality and incisive intelligence to one of the trickiest tragic-comic roles in the repertoire. This artist is captured at work by Hungarian director Marta Meszaros in one of Europe's most beautiful cities. Another in the series *My Favorite Opera*. 60 mins.
VHS: S21294. $24.95.

Elektra (Marton)

Elektra, Richard Strauss' gripping musical interpretation of Sophocles' tale of horror and revenge, is given a compelling production by the innovative East German director Harry Kupfer. Brigitte Fassbaender triumphs with her overpowering portrayal of the mad, guilt-ridden Klytemnestra. Cheryl Studer is radiant as the vulnerable Chrysothemis, and Eva Marton gives an exultant performance as the vengeful Elektra. Under Claudio Abbado's baton, the Vienna Philharmonic gives a superlative account of Strauss' eerie and compelling score. 108 mins.
VHS: S13747. $29.95.

Elektra (Nilsson)

Richard Strauss' 20th century operatic masterpiece features the great Birgit Nilsson as Elektra, with a cast including Leonie Rysanek, Mignon Dunn, Robert Nagy, Donald McIntyre. James Levine conducts the Metropolitan Opera Orchestra. 1980. 112 mins. German, English subtitles.
VHS: S05642. $22.95.

Elixir of Love

Donizetti's opera is performed by the Bratislava Radio Symphony Orchestra with a cast including Melanie Holliday, Miroslav Dvorsky, Alfredo Mariotti. Italian with *no* subtitles.
VHS: S08108. $39.95.
Frank De Quell, Hungary, 1980, 90 mins.

Ernani

Verdi's hot-blooded, romantic opera comes to life with the exemplary performances of Luciano Pavarotti, Leona Mitchell, Sherrill Milnes and Ruggero Raimondi. James Levine conducts the Metropolitan Opera. Sung in Italian with English subtitles. 142 mins.
VHS: S04420. $22.95.

Essential Opera

Twelve selections from Bizet's *Carmen* and Puccini's *Madame Butterfly*, performed by such important figures as Luciano Pavarotti, Placido Domingo, Joan Sutherland, Mirella Freni and James Levine. 56 mins.
VHS: S17431. $24.95.
Laser: LD71756. $29.95.

Essential Opera II

This sequel to *Essential Opera* features Opera's biggest stars singing some of the most popular music in opera, including Pavarotti singing excerpts from *Rigoletto* and Cecilia Bartoli singing her signature aria from the *Barber of Seville*. Joan Sutherland, Placido Domingo, Kiri Te Kanawa, Jose Carreras and conductor Sir Georg Solti are also featured.
VHS: S20645. $29.95.
Laser: LD72376. $34.95.

The Essential Sutherland

Thirteen of Joan Sutherland's great roles at the Australian Opera, prefaced by remarks from Sutherland and her husband, conductor Richard Bonynge. Highlights include several duets, from *La Traviata* with Luciano Pavarotti, and from *Semiramide* with Marilyn Horne. 116 mins.
VHS: S18310. $29.95.
Laser: LD71846. $34.95.

Eugene Onegin (Bolshoi)

Called "one of the great romantic masterpieces yet achieved within the operatic form," Tchaikovsky's opera is performed by the Bolshoi opera singers with some of Russia's best actors doing the acting. Russian with English subtitles. USSR, 1958, color, 106 mins.
VHS: S02067. $39.95.

Eugene Onegin (Covent Garden)

This film of Tchaikovsky's most "Russian" work combines the resources of Covent Garden, a brilliant international cast conducted by Sir Georg Solti, Decca and a great filmmaker, Peter Weigl. The tragic story, based on Pushkin's "verse novel", is cloaked in some of Tchaikovsky's most beautiful and melodic music. Stars Anna Reynolds, Teresa Kubiak, Julia Hamari, Enid Hartle, Bernd Weikl and Stuart Burrows. In Hi-Fi stereo. 116 mins.
Laser: LD71420. $29.95.

Eugene Onegin (Kirov)

The Kirov Opera and Ballet theatre in a dazzling operatic production of the Tchaikovsky opera with text by Pushkin. Stars Evgenia Gorokhovskaya, Tatiana Novikova and Larissa Dyadkova. Russian language, English subtitles. 155 mins., 2 cassettes,
VHS: S04685. $69.95.

Eva Marton in Tosca

Eva Marton stars in the title role in Puccini's great opera, with tenor Lamberto Furlan as Cavaradossi. Conducter Alberto Erede leads the Australian Opera Chorus and the Elizabethan Sydney Orchestra in this stunning production. Sung in Italian with English subtitles. 123 mins.
VHS: S31376. $29.95.

Falstaff (Glyndebourne)

Verdi's final work is a tribute to Falstaff, Shakespeare's roguish hero. Donald Gramm stars and is given strong support by Benjamin Luxon. John Pritchard conducts the London Philharmonic on this Glyndebourne Festival production. English subtitles.
VHS: S02465. $49.95.

Falstaff (Zeffirelli)

James Levine assembled a stellar cast, including Paul Plishka in the title role, Mirella Freni, Marilyn Horne, Barbara Bonney and Frank Lopardo, for this production of Verdi's last opera. Franco Zeffirelli's staging evokes the original Shakespeare play through scenery reminiscent of the theater at Stratford-on-Avon. 126 mins.
VHS: S24874. $34.95.
Laser: LD74908. $59.95.

Fidelio (Covent Garden)

Conducted by Christoph Dohnanyi, Alfred Dresden's production of *Fidelio* moves at a compelling pace and conveys Beethoven's theme: the triumph of love and freedom over forces of evil and oppression. The impressive cast includes Gabriela Benackova, Josef Protschka, Robert Lloyd and Marie McLaughlin. 150 mins.
VHS: S16006. $29.95.

Fidelio (Glyndebourne)

Elisabeth Soderstrom portrays the courageous Leonore in Peter Hall's stirring production of *Fidelio*. Bernard Haitink conducts this Glyndebourne Festival opera presentation. This is a top-quality presentation that all Beethoven fans will cherish.
VHS: S02431. $39.95.

The Fiery Angel

Set in medieval Germany, this five-part opera by Sergei Prokofiev follows the tempestuous tale of a young woman named Renata who has a vision of a fiery angel. The explosive content of this striking work resulted in a ban that was not lifted until 1991. Galina Gorchakova, Sergei Leiferkus and The Kirov Opera and Orchestra join the Royal Opera House, Covent Garden, for this singular operatic experience. 123 mins.
VHS: S26482. $34.95.
Laser: LD75094. $39.95.

Francesca da Rimini

The rare Metropolitan Opera production of Riccardo Zandonai's *Francesca da Rimini* is a legendary production. 1984.
VHS: S10031. $22.95.

Frederick Delius: A Village Romeo and Juliet

Delius' best-known opera, directed by Peter Weigl, with baritone Thomas Hampson, and with Sir Charles Mackerras conducting the ORF Symphony Orchestra and Arnold Schoenberg Choir. Hi-Fi stereo, 113 mins.

VHS: S16776. $24.95.
Laser: LD71516. $39.95.

Fritz Wunderlich—Live

This tape compiles rare kinescope footage of this remarkable tenor singing a number of famous works. Excerpts from *The Magic Flute, Die Entfuhrung aus dem Serail, Onegin* and other operas reveal the musical virtuosity of this singer. 47 mins.

VHS: S24037. $34.95.

The Ghost of Versailles

John Corigliano's opera is the comic completion of the Beaumarchais trilogy, preceded by *The Marriage of Figaro* and *The Barber of Seville*. Conducted by James Levine and performed by the Metropolitan Opera Orchestra and Chorus. With Teresa Stratas, Marilyn Horne, Hakan Hagegard and Gino Quilico. 180 mins.

VHS: S18313. $44.95.
Laser: LD71848. $59.95.

Gigli in Solo per te

Gigli stars in this 1938 recording featuring excerpts from *Andrea Chenier, Un ballo in Maschera* and Bizet's *Agnus Dei*, as well as the picture's title work. With Maria Cebotri and Michael Bohnen. 87 mins.

VHS: S31709. $39.95.

Gilbert & Sullivan: 12 Best-Known Operas

The London Symphony Orchestra and the world-acclaimed Ambrosian Opera Chorus perform the timeless and tuneful lyrics of 12 of Gilbert & Sullivan's best-known operas, specially filmed for television and video.

The Gondoliers. With Keith Mitchell and Eric Shilling. 117 mins.
VHS: S31662. $29.95.
H.M.S. Pinafore. With Peter Marshall and Frankie Howerd. 117 mins.
VHS: S31659. $29.95.
Iolanthe. With Beverly Mills, Derek Hammond-Stroud and Richard Van Allen. 117 mins.
VHS: S31668. $29.95.
The Mikado. With William Conrad and Clive Revill. 117 mins.
VHS: S31663. $29.95.
Patience. With Derek Hammond-Stroud and Donald Adams. 117 mins.
VHS: S31661. $29.95.
The Pirates of Penzance. With Peter Allen and Keith Mitchell. 117 mins.
VHS: S31660. $29.95.
Princess Ida. With Frank Gorshin and Neil Howlett. 112 mins.
VHS: S31669. $29.95.
Ruddigore. With Vincent Price and Keith Mitchell. 115 mins.
VHS: S31664. $29.95.
The Sorcerer. With Clive Revill and Donald Adams. 116 mins.
VHS: S31666. $29.95.
Trial by Jury & Cox and Box. With Frankie Howerd, Kate Flowers, John Fryatt and Russell Smythe. 115 mins.
VHS: S31667. $29.95.
The Yeomen of the Guard. With Joel Grey and Alfred Marks. 116 mins.
VHS: S31665. $29.95.

Giovanna d'Arco

Iconoclastic German film director Werner Herzog joins forces with conductor Riccardo Chailly in this stunning new production of Verdi's seventh opera, the story of Joan of Arc, the maid of Orleans. A fascinating production.

VHS: S15452. $39.98.

Giulio Cesare

This production of Handel's opera was designed by Peter Sellars and transposes the action from Egypt under the Roman Empire to contemporary Middle East. With Jeffrey Gall, Susan Larson, Mary Westbrook-Geha, Lorraine Hunt and James Maddalena. 237 mins.

VHS: S17675. $44.95.

Giuseppe Verdi: Simon Boccanegra

Placido Domingo, Kiri Te Kanawa and, in the title role, Vladimir Chernov are all featured in this superb Metropolitan Opera production. Civil strife between two Italian cities has serious implications for three generations of opposed families. The discovery of a long lost child has the potential to heal this old and bitter enmity. 141 mins.

VHS: S29925. $34.95.
Laser: LD75910. $59.95.

Glyndebourne Festival Opera: A Gala Evening

Before closing for reconstruction, Glyndebourne hosted this extraordinary gala evening. Montserrat Caballe, Felicity Lott, Ruggero Raimondi, Benjamin Luxon, Kim Begley, Frederica von Stade and Cynthia Haymon are just some of the performers featured in this singular video event. 120 mins.

VHS: S24308. $29.95.

The Gold and Silver Gala

Placido Domingo, Roberto Alagna, Angela Gheorghiu and other opera stars celebrate the 50th anniversary of the first performance by the Covent Garden Opera Company. The Gala is also a Silver Jubilee celebration of Placido Domingo's first appearance at Covent Garden; it features favorite opera selections performed by Domingo and company. 90 mins.

VHS: S31370. $29.95.

The Golden Ring

Humphrey Burton's documentary follows Sir Georg Solti's recording of *Gotterdammerung* with the Vienna Philharmonic, featuring Birgit Nilsson, Wolfgang Windgassen and Dietrich Fischer-Dieskau. 89 mins.

VHS: S17678. $24.95.
Laser: LD71794. $34.95.

Gotterdammerung

Daniel Barenboim conducts Siegfried Jerusalem, Phillip Kang, Bodo Brinkman, Gunter von Kannen, Annie Evans and the Bayreuth Festival Choir and Orchestra in the concluding opera of Wagner's *Ring Cycle*. 270 mins.

VHS: S22910. $44.97.
Laser: LD74625. $99.97.

Great Opera Gala for Armenia

At the Bolshoi theater in Moscow, a benefit for war-torn Armenia brought the talents of Alfredo Kraus, Yevgeni Nesterenko, Hermann Prey, Carlo Berganzi and Irina Archipova together for a night of great singing, featuring arias from operas by Verdi, Puccini, Mozart, Wagner, Mussogorsky, Leoncavallo and many more. 120 mins.

VHS: S21062. $24.95.

Great Scenes from Der Ring des Nibelungen

The Ring Cycle at Bayreuth, directed by Patrice Chereau, under the musical direction of Pierre Boulez, used a stellar cast of internationally renowned Wagnerians. This condensed version brings the best moments of this production together on one video. 115 mins.

VHS: S25026. $29.95.

Great Singers from the CBC

Rare television performances of songs and operatic selections, 1957-1965. With Marian Anderson, Marilyn Horne, Richard Tucker and Lisa Della Casa, Peter Pears and Julian Bream, George London, Maureen Forrester and Irmgard Seefried. 52 mins.

VHS: S34392. $29.95.

The Great Waltz

A 1955 television production of the life and art of "The Waltz King," Johann Strauss Jr., featuring opera performers Patrice Munsel and Jarmila Novotna and an appearance by Bert Lahr. 78 mins.

VHS: S18723. $39.95.

Hansel and Gretel (Met)

Though universally acclaimed for its magical evocation of childhood nostalgia, this production of the Metropolitan Opera was greeted by *New York Times* critic John Rockwell as "...artwork very much for adults." Suffused with power by the haunting voices of leads Frederica von Stade and Judith Blegen and the perverse hypnotic spell of Rosalind Elias' witch. Filmed on Christmas Day, 1982.

VHS: S02629. $22.95.
Nathaniel Merrill, USA, 1982, 104 mins.

Hansel and Gretel (Vienna)

There's no sweeter introduction to opera than Humperdinck's charming adaptation of the beloved fairy tale. Sir George Solti conducts the Vienna Philharmonic.

VHS: S12648. $24.95.

The House of Magical Sounds

Based on the book by renowned conductor Claudio Abbado, this is the story of a boy mesmerized by the power of opera, who is determined to conduct great music. This charming and compelling story joins animation, live action and performances by great musicians, including Abbado himself. Narration by Raul Julia.

VHS: S23277. $19.95.

I Pagliacci (Gobbi/Allegro)

The Rome Opera Chorus and Orchestra accompany Tito Gobbi in this film version of the opera *Pagliacci*. Then they join forces again in selected highlights from a 1947 version of *William Tell*. 92 mins.

VHS: S24038. $34.95.

I Pagliacci (Gobbi/Video Yesteryear)

A filmed version which stars Tito Gobbi, Gina Lollobrigida (though not her voice), Onelia Fineschi, Afro Poli, as filmed in 1948, in a classic Gobbi performance. B&W, 89 minutes.

VHS: S03375. $29.95.

I Pagliacci (Zeffirelli)

Franco Zeffirelli directs this lavish film of Leoncavallo's tragic opera. The incomparable Placido Domingo performs one of his most famous operatic arias, "Vesti la Giubba". Georges Pretre leads the chorus and orchestra of La Scala.

VHS: S12657. $24.95.

I Sing for You Alone

Tito Schipa plays a tenor whose stage fright causes his voice to break on a high note. The audience boos him and runs him out of town, but he comes back in the end when he sings a concert in this Marx Brothers-like slapstick farce. "[Schipa] is at his most caressing and works magic on eight songs [in this] lovely print" (Stefan Zucker, *Opera Fanatic's Catalog*). In English, with songs in English, Italian, French and Spanish. 57 mins.

VHS: S28426. $34.95.

I Vespri Siciliani

Giuseppe Verdi's *I Vespri Siciliani* epitomizes the elegant style of the Paris Opera. Under the direction of Riccardo Muti, the La Scala orchestra delivers a blazing tour de force in the large ensemble scenes and a sensitive intimacy to the quieter moments. The excellent cast includes soprano Cheryl Studer and tenor Chris Merritt. 214 mins., two videocassettes.

VHS: S15163. $49.95.
DVD: DV60338. $34.99.

Idomeneo (Drottningholm)

Idomeneo was Mozart's first serious opera. This critically acclaimed production is doubly enhanced by the charming Drottningholm Court Theater in Stockholm, featuring both the Drottningholm Orchestra and Chorus under the direction of Michael Hampe. 143 mins.

Laser: LD72373. $59.95.

Idomeneo (Met)

Metropolitan Opera production features Luciano Pavarotti in Mozart's early masterpiece. With Ileana Cotrubas, Hildegard Behrens, John Alexander; James Levine conducts. 185 mins.

VHS: S04422. $29.95.

Il Barbiere di Siviglia (La Scala)

Directed by Jean-Pierre Ponnelle, conductor Claudio Abbado and members of the Coro e Orhcestra del Teatro alla Scala perform Gioacchino Rossini's comic opera. With Luigi Alva, Enzo Dara and Teresa Berganza. Italian lyrics with English subtitles. 142 mins.

VHS: S17750. $34.95.

Il Barbiere di Siviglia (Met)

Recently recorded live from the stage of the Metropolitan Opera, conducted by Ralf Weikert and sung by some of the greatest voices of our time, including Kathleen Battle and Leo Nucci. 161 mins.

VHS: S14123. $34.95.
Laser: LD71430. $59.95.

Il Matrimonio Segreto

This Cimarosa masterpiece is a gem of the operatic repertoire; the tale of the amorous bumblings of Bolognese gentry masterfully performed by Barbara Daniels, Carlos Feller, Claudio Nicolai and David Kuebler. Cologne Opera production recorded at Schwetzingen Palace's rococco theatre. Performed in Italian with English subtitles. 140 mins.

VHS: S04642. $29.95.

Il Re Pastore

This festive and passionate "serenade", in which action and characters are delineated by the scoring of the arias, is an important step in Mozart's exploration of the operatic medium. Blasi / McNair / Vermillion / Hadley / Ahnsjo. With Sir Neville Marriner and the Academy of St. Martin In the Fields. 116 mins.

VHS: S15733. $29.95.

Il Ritorno d'Ulisse in Patria

Michael Hampe's lavish production of Monteverdi's epic tale of love and steadfastness in a brilliant new realization by Hans Werner Henze has been the triumph of recent Salzburg Festivals. Thomas Allen reveals a gorgeous range of tone as Ulysses, alongside the intensity of Kathleen Kuhlman's performance as the hero's long-abandoned wife, Penelope. 187 mins. 2 cassettes.
VHS: S12407. $29.95.

Il Tabarro/Pagliacci

Filmed at the Metropolitan Opera's 1994 opening night gala, this video showcases Placido Domingo and Luciano Pavarotti with Teresa Stratas, Juan Pons, Dwayne Croft and James Levine performing Puccini's *Il Tabarro* and Leoncavallo's *Pagliacci*. English subtitles. 141 mins.
VHS: S33365. $34.95.

Il Trovatore (Del Monaco)

Musical greats Mario Del Monaco, Gencer, Barbieri and Bastiani star in this 1957 production of the opera directed by Previtali. Together they comprise a production team that knows no equal. 124 mins.
VHS: S24328. $34.95.

Il Trovatore (Levine)

Verdi's heroic composition of 1853 is filled with unforgettable melodies, was an immediate success and always has been one of the most popular of his operas. This Metropolitan Opera performance features superstars Eva Marton and Luciano Pavarotti, conducted by maestro James Levine. 133 mins.
VHS: S15719. $34.95.
Laser: LD70284. $59.95.

Il Trovatore (Pederzini)

Gianna Pederzini, the amazing mezzo soprano, is cast as Azuncena in this classic bel canto work. Verdi's music is sung in the original Italian without subtitles. The burning of Azuncena's mother is realized filmically rather than through the traditional narration.
VHS: S25532. $39.95.
Carmine Gallone, Italy, 1949, 102 mins.

In the Shadow of the Stars

Behind the scenes of the San Francisco Opera Company, with chorus singers who aspire to be soloists and who dream of being stars. The film lovingly explores the blurred boundary between private lives and stage spectacles, and creates a rare and privileged look into the grand world of opera. Music by Mozart, Puccini, Rossini, Stravinsky, Verdi, Wagner and others. Winner of the 1992 Academy Award for Best Feature Length Documentary.
VHS: S16640. $24.95.
Irving Saraf, USA, 1992, 93 mins.

Jenufa

Under the direction of Nikolaus Lehnhoff, the renowned Glyndebourne Festival Opera brings to life Leos Janacek's masterpiece *Jenufa*. This highly acclaimed 1989 production resurrects the Brno version of the opera, unseen and unheard since its 1904 debut. Featuring the London Philharmonic Orchestra conducted by Andrew Davis, and the brilliant soprano Anja Silja. 119 mins.
VHS: S15164. $29.95.

Joan Sutherland: The Age of Bel Canto

This 1963 CBC telecast showcases Sutherland in some of the soprano's greatest operatic roles, including *Semiramide*, *La Sonnambula*, *I Puritani* and *La Traviata*. Tenor Richard Conrad also joins Miss Sutherland in scenes from *La Sonnambula*, *Don Pasquale* and *La Traviata*. 60 mins.
VHS: S30130. $29.95.

Jon Vickers: Four Operatic Portraits

Gala performance from the National Arts Centre, Ottawa, from the video archives of the CBC, Toronto. Four fully staged operatic scenes showcase the tenor's towering interpretations of Handel's *Samson*, Beethoven's Florestan (*Fidelio*), Britten's *Peter Grimes* and Verdi's Otello. A magnificent testament to one of the opera world's most extraordinary singing actors. National Arts Centre Orchestra conducted by Franz-Paul Decker. 52 mins.
VHS: S31872. $29.95.

Julius Caesar

Handel's opera performed in Berlin by the English National Opera Company featuring Janet Baker and Valerie Masterson. 179 minutes.
VHS: S03370. $59.95.

June Anderson: The Passion of Bel Canto

An enticing glimpse into the life and music of a modern-day Diva. See June Anderson rehearse and perform classic bel canto roles from the operas of Donizetti, Rossini and Bellini and follow her through Europe as she performs at some of the world's greatest opera houses. 57 mins.
VHS: S34049. $29.98.

Katya Kabanova

Janacek's incandescent score, played by the London Philharmonic Orchestra, under the baton of Andrew Davis, has seldom achieved such perfect unity with the dramatic action in this landmark production. Tobias Hoheisel's designs—a combination of stark outlines and the flaring colors of Edvard Munch's expressionistic world—provide the setting. Niklaus Lenhoff's intense production achieves a harrowing realism in its depiction of the suffocating and frustrated emotions destroying a straight-laced, middle-class household. 99 mins.
VHS: S13748. $29.95.

Khovanschina (Kirov)

Mussorgsky's unfinished score, completed by Shostakovich, creates a powerful opera drama about 17th-century Russian intrigue. Featuring the Kirov, this production dates from 1953, when the death of Stalin led to a great burst of liberalization. As a result the clash of conservative and progressive forces in this work take on a greater resonance. 205 mins.
VHS: S22220. $49.95.
Laser: LD74596. $61.95.

Khovanschina (St. Petersburg)

St. Petersburg's acclaimed orchestra and opera company present the 1953 production of Mussorgsky's opera about change and progress, set in 17th-century Russia. The struggle between conservative, inward-looking elements and progressives who look to the outside world is especially relevant in today's world.
VHS: S20975. $44.95.
Laser: LD72404. $69.95.

Khovanschina (Vienna State Opera)

A live recording made in February 1989 of Mussorgsky's *Khovanschina* in the performing edition by Dmitri Shostakovich. Conducted by Claudio Abbado and featuring the great Bulgarian bass Nicolai Ghiaurov, with Paata Burchuladze as Dossifei, and Ludmila Semtschuk. 182 mins. 2 cassettes.
VHS: S12410. $29.95.

King Priam

Michael Tippet's operatic retelling of the legend of Troy follows the Homeric characters through their loves, loyalties and vengeance. This Kent Opera production is recorded in English and features Rodney McCann in a compelling portrayal.
VHS: S03742. $29.95.

Kiri Te Kanawa at Christmas

International diva Kiri Te Kanawa performs her most popular seasonal music at Barbican Hall in London accompanied by over 100 singers and musicians from the Philharmonic Orchestra and The Tallis Chamber Choir. 50 mins.
VHS: S34059. $19.98.

Kiri Te Kanawa: My World of Opera

A compilation video selected by Dame Kiri Te Kanawa that reproduces her favorite scenes and features her opposite Jose Carreras, Placido Domingo, Janet Baker, Barbara Bonney, Thomas Allen, Robert Lloyd, Vladimir Altantov, Ileana Cotrubas, Mirella Freni and Neil Shicoff. Highlights include Strauss' *Der Rosenkavalier*, Offenbach's *The Tales of Hoffmann*, Verdi's *Otello* and *Don Carlo*, Puccini's *La Boheme* and Strauss' *Die Fledermaus*. 59 mins.
VHS: S19933. $24.97.
Laser: CLV. LD72180. $29.97.

L'Africaine

Placido Domingo and Shirley Verret star in this acclaimed San Francisco Opera production of Meyerbeer's masterwork, the story of explorer Vasco da Gama, who falls in love with the beautiful and exotic Selika on the African continent. Two cassettes, 190 mins.
VHS: S10261. $29.95.

L'Elisir d'Amore

Luciano Pavarotti stars as the lovesick Nemorino in Donizetti's beloved opera. With Judith Blegen, Sesto Bruscantini and Nicola Rescigno conducting the Metropolitan Opera Orchestra and chorus. Recorded in 1981. Italian, English subtitles, 132 mins.
VHS: S05641. $22.95.

L'Incoronazione di Poppea (Glyndebourne)

Maria Ewing stars in this Glyndebourne Festival production of Monteverdi's opera based on the story of the Roman Emperor Nero. Nero falls for the scheming but seductive Poppea as the allegorical figures of Fortune, Virtue and Love look on. A new production from Peter Hall. 120 mins.
VHS: S24362. $29.95.

L'Incoronazione di Poppea (Zurich)

Monteverdi's masterpiece is performed by the Monteverdi Ensemble and Choir of the Zurich Opera House, conducted by Nikolaus Harnoncourt. Solos by Yakar, Tappy, Schmidt, Esswood. In Hi-fi stereo, 162 mins.
VHS: S16044. $34.95.
Laser: LD71193. $69.95.

L'Innocenza ed il Piacer

Recorded live at the beautiful rococo theatre of Schwetzingen Palace, a double bill of operas by Christoph Gluck commemorating the anniversary of his death in 1787. *Echo et Narcisse* and *Le Cinesi* are performed in original 18th-century costumes, with the acclaimed Concerto Cologne playing authentic Baroque instruments. With Kurt Streit, Sophie Boulin, Christine Hoegnman. French with English subtitles. 130 mins.
VHS: S07084. $29.95.

La Boheme (Levine)

Lavish Metropolitan Opera production filmed live, with costumes and sets designed by Franco Zeffirelli, and with some of Met's greats: Teresa Stratas, Richard Stilwell, Renata Scotto, Jose Carreras, Allan Monk, James Morris. James Levine conducts. Italian with English subtitles. Stereo, 1982, 141 mins.
VHS: S02180. $22.95.

La Boheme (Omnibus)

Alistair Cook hosts this 1953 presentation of an opera by Pucini. Sponsored by AMF Bowling Pinspotters, the opera is sung in English by members of the Metropolitan Opera Company. Featuring Brian Sullivan, Nadine O'Connor, and Brenda Lewis. USA, 1953, 81 mins.
VHS: S05864. $29.95.

La Boheme (Pavarotti)

Luciano Pavarotti stars in this magnificent stage production of Puccini's most beloved opera, performed by the Genoa Opera Company. Filmed live in Peking while the Company toured the People's Republic of China. Italian with English subtitles.
VHS: S10710. $29.95.

La Boheme (San Francisco Opera)

Luciano Pavarotti and Mirella Freni star in this San Francisco Opera production of Puccini's great love story. 120 mins.
VHS: S11749. $29.95.

La Boheme (The Australian Opera)

Baz Luhrmann, the director of *Strictly Ballroom*, updated Puccini's classic opera to Paris in 1950. It gives him the chance to capture something of the glamour of the era and bring out the dramatic romance of this compelling operatic work. Features Julian Smith conducting the Australian Opera.
VHS: S26221. $29.95.
Laser: LD75046. $59.95.

La Boheme (Zeffirelli)

Franco Zeffirelli's historic production of Puccini's grand opera features Mirella Freni. Herbert von Karajan conducts the orchestra of La Scala.
VHS: S12649. $24.95.

La Cambiale di Matrimonio

Gelmetti leads this performance of Rossini's rarely performed *La Cambiale di Matrimonia* at the Schwetzingen Festival.
Laser: LD70210. $39.98.

La Cenerentola (Bartoli)

Cecilia Bartoli recreates the young woman who inhabits a fairytale world of utter despair broken by the promise of love. The Houston Symphony and the Houston Grand Opera Chorus, under the direction of Bruno Campanella, render this unforgettable opera into a vital production. Originally part of PBS's *Great Performance* series.
VHS: S27634. $34.95.

La Cenerentola (Salzburg Festival)

Renowned bel canto specialists Ann Murray and Francisco Araiza, under the masterful baton of Riccardo Chailly, infuse Rossini's Cinderella story with new fire and brilliance. This delightful Salzburg Festival production captures the fairy-tale quality of the opera but also emphasizes Rossini's gentle satire on personal relationships. 160 mins.
VHS: S12369. $29.95.

La Cenerentola (von Stade)

A Dutch adaptation of Cinderella transforms the classic fairy tale into a charming opera, featuring Frederica von Stade in the title role.
VHS: S12650. $34.95.

La Clemenza di Tito (Drottningholm)

A lavish production of Mozart's late opera performed at the Drottningholm Court Theatre, with the Drottningholm Court Theatre Orchestra, featuring Dahlberg, Pulson and Soldh as soloists.
Laser: LD72055. $59.95.

La Clemenza di Tito (Glyndebourne)

A stellar cast, conductor and director combine forces in this Glyndebourne production of Mozart's final opera. Nicholas Hytner (*Miss Saigon*) directs this production conducted by Andrew Davis. The international cast includes Ashley Putnam, Diane Montague and Philip Langridge in a brilliant interpretation of the title role. 150 mins.
VHS: S16007. $29.95.

La Clemenza di Tito (Vienna Philharmonic)

Mozart's last opera, as performed by the Vienna Philharmonic Orchestra and Vienna State Opera Chorus under the baton of James Levine. Soloists include Tatiana Troyanos, Carol Neblett, Catherine Malfitano and Eric Tappy. Recorded in 1980.
VHS: S15634. $34.95.

La Donna del Lago

Rossini's romantic opera, based on Sir Walter Scott's poem *The Lady of the Lake*, is staged in a spectacular production at La Scala. June Anderson leads an all-star cast of top bel canto singers under the direction of Riccardo Muti with staging designed by famed German filmmaker Werner Herzog. 167 mins.
VHS: S21364. $49.95.

La Fanciulla del West

Puccini's neglected masterpiece receives new attention in this glittering production from La Scala. Renowned stage director Jonathan Miller assembles a talented cast: Placido Domingo, Juan Pons and Mara Zampieri. Loren Maazel conducts this "original spaghetti western", set during the 1849 California Gold Rush. 145 min.
VHS: S16004. $39.95.
DVD: DV60337. $49.99.

La Favorita

Donizetti's opera sung by Sofia Lazzaro, Franca Tamantini and Paolo Silveri. Opera sung in Italian, narration in English. Sophia Loren appears in an uncredited, small supporting role.
VHS: S02240. $29.95.
Italy, 1952, 89 mins.

La Forza del Destino

A dramatic production of Verdi's great opera featuring Leontyne Price in a performance at the Metropolitan Opera, taped live in 1984. Italian with English subtitles.
VHS: S07010. $29.95.

La Gazza Ladra

This production boasts a star-studded cast in one of Rossini's most brilliant works for the stage. Ileana Cotrubas stars in this story of a servant girl accused of stealing a silver spoon; Bruno Bartoletti conducts the production. 172 mins.
VHS: S11750. $29.95.

La Gioconda

Placido Domingo and Eva Marton star in this sumptuous Vienna State Opera production of Ponchielli's famous melodrama. Set against an historical background of tyranny and intrigue in Venice. 169 mins.
VHS: S10263. $29.95.

La Scala di Seta

Gianluigi Gelmetti conducts the Stuttgart Radio Symphony Orchestra at the Schwetzingen Festival. Set in Paris, this one-act opera is a comic farce in which two newlyweds plot to hide their wedded bliss from the bride's father. With Alberto Rinaldi, Luciana Serra and Alessandro Corbelli. In Hi-Fi Stereo, 100 mins.
VHS: S16551. $34.97.

La Scala: A Documentary of Performances

A "brilliantly conceived and executed video of La Scala and its history" (Opera Canada) featuring performances by Mario Del Monaco, Tito Gobbi, Tio Schipa, Ferruccio Tagliavini, Arturo Toscanini and others, performing selections from Verdi, Bizet, Rossini, Puccini, and Bellini. A must for opera lovers. 63 mins.
VHS: S34056. $29.98.

La Traviata (Covent Garden)

Covent Garden, under the guidance of Sir Georg Solti, staged this new production of the Verdi favorite. Angela Gheorghiu, Frank Lopardo and Leo Nucci are featured.
VHS: S26450. $34.95.
Laser: LD75087. $59.95.

La Traviata (Glyndebourne)

This 1987 production by Glyndebourne was directed by Sir Peter Hall. It stars Marie McLaughlin as Violetta, Walter MacNeil as Alfredo, and Brent Ellis as Germont. The acclaimed production has been set in its own period by designer John Gunter; one of the main features of the set design is a profusion of mirrors in virtually every scene. A moving and emotional experience. 133 mins. Italian with English subtitles.
VHS: S07602. $39.95.

La Traviata (Moffo)

One of the greatest operatic films ever made, featuring a tour-de-force of Verdi's work by the incomparable soprano Anna Moffo, whose interpretations of Violetta were hailed throughout the world. Supporting cast includes Franco Bonisolli, Gino Vechi and the Orchestra of the Rome Opera House. Color, 113 mins. Italian with English subtitles.
VHS: S14817. $39.95.

La Traviata (Sills)

Giuseppe Verdi's *La Traviata* is conducted by Julius Rudel and performed by the New York City Opera company. Beverly Sills delivers a virtuoso performance as Violetta. With Henry Price and Richard Fredricks. 144 mins.
VHS: S17694. $39.95.

La Traviata (Zeffirelli/Domingo)

Zeffirelli's film of Verdi's *La Traviata* is an exquisitely designed, opulently mounted production made expressly for the movie medium. Placido Domingo, one of the greatest tenors, and Teresa Stratas, a renowned soprano, star, featuring music performed by the New York Metropolitan Opera Orchestra and Chorus, directed by James Levine. Italian with English subtitles.
VHS: S00713. $29.98.
Laser: LD70043. $34.98.
Franco Zeffirelli, Italy, 1982, 105 mins.

La Vie Parisienne

Offenbach's opera, produced by the Opera de Lyon in a production by Alain Francon, starring Helene Delavault, Claire Wauthion, Jean-Yves Chatelais, Jean-Francois Sivadier. Conducted by Jean-Yves Ossonce. 1991, 158 mins. French with English subtitles.
VHS: S20508. $29.95.

Lakme

Norman Ayrton's 1976 production of Delibes' *Lakme* is a tour-de-force for soprano Joan Sutherland. With Huguette Tourangeau, Clifford Grant and Henri Wilden. Sung in French with translated libretto. 154 mins.
VHS: S18386. $29.95.

Le Barbier de Seville

Josette Day, Andre Bauge, the great Charpin and Jean Galland appear in Rossini's opera adaptation. Acted and sung in French, without English subtitles. France, 1934, 52 mins.
VHS: S06986. $24.95.

Le Grandi Primadonne

World renowned sopranos Marilyn Horne and Montserrat Caballe perform arias and duets by Handel, Rossini, Offenbach and Puccini in these excerpts from their concert in Philharmonie Hall in Munich, Germany.
VHS: S15581. $19.95.

Le Nozze di Figaro (Gardiner)

John Eliot Gardiner's restaging of Mozart's operas using period instruments reveals a wholly new perspective on this classic work. Taped on HDTV in Paris, this production employs the Welsh baritone Bryn Terfel, the Monteverdi Choir, and the English Baroque Soloists. 170 mins.
VHS: S22457. $44.95.

Le Nozze di Figaro (Lyon National Opera)

This Lyon National Opera production of Mozart's immensely popular opera is faithful to the composer's 18th-century tale of amorous intrigue. With Giovanna Furlanetto as Figaro, this exceptional performance is a spectacular theatrical and musical experience. 193 mins.
VHS: S30876. $29.95.

Legend of Tsar Saltan

The Dresden State Opera presentation of Rimsky-Korsakov's sparkling fantasy written to celebrate the centennial of Pushkin's birth. Contains the famous "Flight of the Bumblebee." 98 mins.
VHS: S02827. $39.95.

Leonard Bernstein Conducts West Side Story

You are invited into the recording studio to watch an historic performance: Leonard Bernstein conducting his own *West Side Story*, performed by Kiri Te Kanawa and Jose Carreras. A beautiful recording of an historic moment: this was a first for Bernstein.
VHS: S12651. $24.95.

Les Brigands

The Lyon Opera production of Offenbach's operetta transposes the hijinks of the Italian mountain bandits to gangland Chicago. With Michel Tremont, Valerie Chevalier, Colette Alliot-Lugaz. Conducted by Claire Gibault. 1989, 122 mins. French with English subtitles.
VHS: S20507. $39.95.

Les Contes d'Hoffmann

Director Louis Erlo's production of Offenbach's fantasy opera transposes it into a realistic 20th-century setting, in this Lyon Opera production conducted by Kent Nagano and featuring Daniel Galvez-Vallejo, Nathalie Dessay, Barbara Hendricks, Isabelle Vernet and Jose Van Dam. 1993, 110 mins. French with English subtitles.
VHS: S20509. $29.95.

Les Huguenots (The Australian Opera)

Dame Joan Sutherland's farewell performance is a gala triumph of spectacle, pageantry, and drama. This grand production captures the horror and tragedy of the St. Bartholomew's Day Massacre, as well as the splendor and romance of 16th-century France. Richard Bonynge conducts this splendid revival of director Lotfi Mansouri's highly praised 1981 production. 200 mins., two videocassettes.
VHS: S15165. $29.95.

Les Troyens

Hector Berlioz' masterpiece, uncut, with Tatiana Troyanos, Jessye Norman, Placido Domingo, Alan Monk and Paul Plishka, with James Levine conducting at the Metropolitan Opera. French with English subtitles. 253 mins.
VHS: S04419. $29.95.

The Life of Donizetti

This dramatic feature film tells the story of a great artist whose passionate love for his country comes into conflict with his love for a woman. With several arias by Tito Schipa, this tale of love, passion, rebellion and political intrigue is set against the music of one of the 19th Century's most celebrated artists and patriots. Dubbed in English with arias in Italian. 90 mins.
VHS: S34052. $29.98.

Live from the Met Highlights Volume 1

Selected performances from the Metropolitan Opera include excerpts from the Centennial Gala, including *Un Ballo in Maschera, La Boheme, Don Carlo, Tannhauser,* and *Lucia di Lammermoor*. 70 mins.
VHS: S04423. $29.95.

Lo Frate 'nnamorato

Enter the sparkling world of 18th-century *commedia musicale*! Pergolesi's *Lo Frate 'nnamorato* is a jewel of an opera, rediscovered and mounted by Riccardo Muti and the forces of La Scala to universal acclaim. This sumptious production reflects the superb alliance of musical and artistic talent brought together to make this little-known baroque masterpiece a triumph of the stage. 171 mins., two videocassettes.
VHS: S15162. $49.95.

Lohengrin (Bayreuth)

This splendid opera was recorded at the great Wagner Festival held in Bayreuth, Germany—home of the Bayreuth Festival Theatre, designed and built by the composer specifically for the performance of his own operas. 200 mins.
VHS: S14800. $44.95.

Lohengrin (Met)

A *Live from the MET* performance featuring soprano Eva Marton and Leonie Rysanek, along with Peter Hofman in the title role, in Wagner's masterwork. German with English subtitles.
VHS: S07183. $29.95.

Lohengrin (Vienna State Opera)

The power and radiance of Wagner's score expresses his deeply felt belief that love is essentially mystical. The forces of the Vienna State Opera conducted by Claudio Abbado bring this operatic milestone to magnificent realization. The title role is brilliantly performed by tenor Placido Domingo, ably partnered by soprano Cheryl Studer as Elsa. 180 mins., two videocassettes.
VHS: S15167. $29.95.

Love of Destiny

The creative vision of Czech filmwriter/director Peter Weigl, who creates a powerful dramatic story through the combination of dramatic imagery and operatic aria. Opera star Peter Dvorsky evokes in every chosen aria his emotions toward an unknown woman—a fatal guide—which creates a connection between reality and this woman. Arias from *Cavalleria Rusticana, Tosca, Un Ballo in Maschera* and others are featured. 60 mins.
VHS: S11768. $19.95.

Lucia di Lammermoor (Sutherland)

One of Joan Sutherland's most famous roles, here in a MET production with Alfredo Kraus, Pablo Elvira, and Paul Plishka, with Richard Bonynge conducting.
VHS: S07567. $22.95.

Lucia di Lammermoor (Moffo)
Anna Moffo stars as Lucia in this entrancing opera. Filmed on location in Scotland by Mario Lanfranchi, this beautiful video highlights Moffo's expressive coloratura soprano. Also starring Giulio Fioravanti and Paolo Washington. 108 minutes.
VHS: S02273. $49.95.

Lucrezia Borgia
Donizetti's dramatic opera is produced by the Australian Opera, conducted by Richard Bonynge. With Joan Sutherland, Ron Stevens, Richard Allman and Margreta Elkins. Italian libretto with English subtitles. 138 mins.
VHS: S18728. $29.95.

Luisa Miller
Bel Canto specialist June Anderson gives a command performance of this tuneful Verdi masterwork. With Taro Ichihara and Eduard Tarmagian. English subtitles. 150 mins.
VHS: S31836. $29.95.

Macbeth (Deutsche Opera)
Recorded at the Deutsche Opera Berlin, this new production of Verdi's *Macbeth* won immediate critical acclaim. Giuseppe Sinopoli conducts with Renato Bruson and Mara Zampieri in leading roles. Italian with English subtitles, 150 mins.
VHS: S07086. $29.95.

Macbeth (Glyndebourne)
Verdi's operatic version of *Macbeth* is dramatically staged in this Glyndebourne Festival production. Kostas Paskalis and Josephine Barstow star as the doomed Macbeths; John Pritchard conducts the London Philharmonic. English subtitles.
VHS: S02466. $79.95.

Macbeth (Verdi)
Claude d'Anna's acclaimed adaptation of the prestigious Riccardo Chailly recording is shot in a castle in the Ardennes. Featured are Leo Nucci and Shirley Verret. Orchestra is the Teatro Communale di Bologna. 138 mins.
Laser: LD71702. $59.95.

Madama Butterfly (La Scala)
An exquisitely Oriental production of Puccini's great lyrical-tragic opera stars Yasuko Hayashi in the title role, with Hak-Nam Kim, Peter Dvorsky and Giorgio Zancanaro supporting. The production was mounted by Keiuta Asari, with costumes by Hanae Mori and sets by Ichiro Takeda. Italian with English subtitles.
VHS: S03687. $29.95.

Madame Butterfly
This award-winning film from the popular Puccini opera is the heart-wrenching story of a beautiful young geisha who forsakes her family, and ultimately her life, for her American husband. With an international cast of opera stars, including Ying Huang, Richard Troxell of the New York City Opera, Ning Liang and Richard Cowan. Italian with English subtitles.
VHS: S31204. $24.95.
Frederic Mitterand, France, 1995, 129 mins.

Mado Robin Live!
Mado Robin (1918-1960) was the preeminent 20th-century French coloratura. This live performance includes selections from *Lakme*, *Mireille*, *Rigoletto*, *Hamlet*, *Barbiere* and *Lucia*. Be sure to check out the "mad scene" in the latter, in which Robin demonstrates her B-flat above high C which landed her in the *Guinness Book of World Records*. 24 mins.
VHS: S28423. $34.95.

Maestro's Company—Volume 1
An inventive introduction to opera for children. Little Johnny and Tina lose a soccer ball but find a subterranean opera community living under an old theatre. The operatic talents are all played by puppets with the voices of Joan Sutherland, Renata Tebaldi, and Placido Domingo. Volume 1 contains *The Barber of Seville* and *La Traviata*. 60 mins.
VHS: S09116. $29.95.

Maestro's Company—Volume 2
Johnny and Tina continue to learn about the wonderful world of opera from the dedicated Maestro who lives underneath a disused opera theatre. The Maestro may look like a puppet but he know his stuff. Famous opera talents like Joan Sutherland and Placido Domingo lend their voices to the bodies of puppets. With selections from *Rigoletto* and *Hansel and Gretel*. In color. 60 mins.
VHS: S09117. $29.95.

Magda Olivero: The Last Verismo Soprano
Magda Olivero displays her artistry as the last of the verismo sopranos in *Traviata*, *Iris*, *Risurrezione*, *Tosca*, the final 6-1/2 minutes of *Act III* (from a 1960 made-for-TV film, the rest of which is presumed lost), Tost's "Sogno" (late 1970s), "Ave Maria" (Solda, 1991), *Manon Lescaut* (1993), *Adriana* (excerpt with Gigli, 1938), and Adriana (two excerpts, 1993). Still performing in her 80s, Olivero was hailed by one critic as "more expressive and musical than Callas." "No other opera video ever produced is more important than *Magda Olivero: The Last Verismo Soprano*" (Stefan Zucker, *Opera Fanatic's Catalog*). 59 mins.
VHS: S28419. $34.95.

The Magic Flute (Australian Opera)
The Australian opera, renowned for its interpretations of Mozart, reveals its definitive talents in "the most believable and simply beautiful production you are likely to see anywhere." Soprano Yvonne Kenny with Richard Bonynge conducting. Sung in English. 160 mins.
VHS: S08694. $29.95.

The Magic Flute (Gewandhaus Orchestra, Leipzig)
Mozart's opera is performed by the Gewandhaus Orchestra of Leipzig, conducted by Gert Bahner. This lavish production stars Hermann Polster and Magdalena Falewicz. 157 mins.
VHS: S03371. $79.95.

The Magic Flute (Glyndebourne)
Sung in German (with English subtitles), this Glyndebourne Festival production features striking sets by David Hockney. Leo Goeke, Felicity Lott, and Thomas Thomaschke star with Bernard Haitink and the London Philharmonic. 164 mins.
VHS: S02164. $59.95.

Making Opera: The Creation of Verdi's "La Forza del Destino"
Witness two stories: the making of an opera and the opera itself in this exciting and revealing look at the creative process of staging a grand opera during a 21-day rehearsal period. Featuring Stefka Evstatieva, Allan Monk, Judith Forst, Ernesto Veronelli with the Canadian Opera Company. 88 mins.
VHS: S34050. $29.98.

Makropulos Case
A powerful production of Janacek's 20th-century operatic masterpiece, performed by the Canadian Opera Company and Stephanie Sundine. Sung in the original Czech, with English subtitles. 123 mins.
VHS: S13244. $49.95.

The Man Who Mistook His Wife for a Hat
Michael Nyman's chamber opera, adapted from the case studies of Dr. Oliver Sacks (*Awakenings*), examines the difficulties of perception and identity of those suffering from the disease. 75 mins.
VHS: S17287. $39.95.

Manon Lescaut
Puccini's ultimate love story is sung in English in a brilliant performance at the Metropolitan Opera. In the Bel Canto videotape series.
VHS: S02630. $22.95.

The Marriage of Figaro
Kiri Te Kanawa leads a fine cast in this performance of Mozart's story of domestic class struggle. John Pritchard conducts the London Philharmonic. English subtitles. 168 mins.
VHS: S02446. $59.95.

The Medium
Menotti shows a deft hand as a filmmaker in his own film of his own opera, "The Medium," starring Marie Powers and Anna Maria Albergetti. One of the most important contemporary operas, with the symphony orchestra conducted by Thomas Schippers.
VHS: S00842. $39.95.
Giancarlo Menotti, USA, 1950, 80 mins.

Meet the Met
Favorite opera scenes from *Aida, Otello, Turandot, Die Fledermaus* and other works are staged with the Metropolitan Opera Orchestra and Choir under the direction of James Levine and Ralf Weikert. Kathleen Battle, Jessye Norman and Eva Marton are just some of the great singers included in this unique video. 101 mins.
VHS: S23911. $29.95.
Laser: LD74798. $34.95.

Mefistofele
The San Francisco State Opera brings Boito's opera to magnificent realization under the baton of Maurizio Arena, with bass Samuel Ramey. 159 mins.
VHS: S13223. $29.95.

The Merry Widow (The Australian Opera)
The delightful melodies of Franz Lehar's *The Merry Widow*, sung by the incomparable soprano Joan Sutherland. This glittering production is directed with elegance and a glorious sense of fun by Lotfi Mansouri. Conductor Richard Bonynge draws out the charm and beauty of the score and leads the Elizabethan Philharmonic Orchestra with great aplomb. 151 mins.
VHS: S15166. $29.95.

The Metropolitan Opera Gala 1991: 25th Anniversary at Lincoln Center
"A grand scaled tribute to a great opera company" is what the *New York Times* called this "Who's Who" evening of world renowned singers: Pavarotti, Studer, Domingo, Freni, von Otter, Prey, Daniels, Nucci, Ghiaurov, Svenden, Diaz, Hampson, Anderson, Battle, von Stade, Milnes, Ramey, Furlanett, Millo. James Levine conducts the Metropolitan Opera Orchestra and Chorus in Verdi's *Rigoletto [Act III]* and *Otello [Act III]*, as well as J. Strauss' *Die Fledermaus [Act II]*. Also includes the first-ever duet by Pavarotti and Domingo. In Hi-Fi stereo, 167 mins.
VHS: S16053. $34.95.
Laser: LD71199. $69.95.

Midsummer Night's Dream
Peter Hall's magical production of Benjamin Britten's opera, in an unforgettable performance at the Glyndebourne Festival. With Ileana Cotrubas, James Bowman and Curt Appelgren. Bernard Haitink conducts the London Philharmonic. 194 mins.
VHS: S03411. $29.95.

The Mikado (D'Oyly Carte)
In Japan, a timid official is appointed Lord High Executioner and finds that his first intended victim is the Emperor's son, travelling incognito. This first film version of Gilbert and Sullivan's comic opera features the D'Oyly Carte Company, the same company that premiered *The Mikado* in 1885.
VHS: S05357. $39.95.
Stuart Burge, Great Britain, 1939, 93 mins.

The Mikado (Miller)
Jonathan Miller's version of the classic operetta by Gilbert and Sullivan is a wonderfully warm, comic interpretation featuring an art deco set design and top singers and performers. Produced for Thames Television.
VHS: S12550. $39.99.

Mitridate, Re di Ponto (Ponnelle)
Mozart was just 14 when he composed this *opera seria*, a tragedy set in early Roman times. Director Jean-Pierre Ponnelle uses an 18th-century theater in which to stage this production, with Nikolaus Harnoncourt conducting the Concertus Musicus Wien. With Gosta Winbergh, Yvonne Kenny, Ann Murray, Anne Gjevag and Joan Rodgers. Hi-Fi stereo, 124 mins.
VHS: S16777. $34.95.

Mitridate, Re di Ponto (Vick)
This production of Mozart's early masterpiece, written when he was only 14, was staged by Graham Vick for the Mozart Bicentennial celebrations in 1991. It received the 1992 Olivier Award for The Most Outstanding Achievement of the Year in Opera. This brilliant succession of arias and duets illustrates young Mozart's debt to the great Baroque masters. 170 mins.
VHS: S21365. $29.95.

Mlada
Rimsky-Korsakov's rarely performed four-act opera ballet is finally available on home video. Recorded at the Bolshoi in Moscow, this recording features famed members of the Ballet and Opera troupes which carry the Bolshoi name. Alexander Lazarev conducts. 198 mins.
VHS: S22074. $49.97.
Laser: LD74496. $69.97.

Mozart: Die Zauberflote
Filmed at the Concertgebouw in Amsterdam during the 1995 Holland Festival, this third release in John Eliot Gardiner's survey on authentic instruments of the great Mozart operas features the English Baroque Soloists, the Monteverdi Choir and the Pilobolus Choir. German with English subtitles. 160 mins.
VHS: S28642. $34.95.
Laser: LD75961. $59.95.

Music from Wagner's Ring
This program features selected orchestral music from Wagner's *The Ring of the Nibelungen*. Erich Leinsdorf conducts this program, which also includes the Preludes and Interludes from Wagner's final opera, *Parsifal*. 78 mins.
VHS: S22008. $19.95.

My Favorite Opera: Alfredo Kraus, Werther

Alfredo Kraus returns to the site of his debut, the Teatro Sao Carlo in Lisbon, to reprise his favorite role. Jules Massenet's *Werther* gives this tenor the opportunity to portray the ultimate character of the Romantic era, first seen in Goethe's landmark novel. 60 mins.
VHS: S21815. $24.95.

Nicolai Gedda in Concert, Volume 2

Among the top Italian tenors of the day, Gedda performs excerpts from *Elisir*, *Land des Lachelns*, *Onegin*, *Paganini*, *Giuditta* and *Lustige Witwe* in this 1985 recording. 33 mins.
VHS: S31710. $39.95.

Nobel Jubilee Concert: Kiri Te Kanawa

Mezzo-soprano Dame Kiri Te Kanawa and conductor Sir Georg Solti lend their skills in this concert to celebrate the Nobel Foundation's 90th Jubilee and occasion the 200th anniversary of Mozart's death. Kiri Te Kanawa performs five arias. 86 mins.
VHS: S18468. $24.95.

Non Ti Scordar di Me

In this 1935 hit film, Beniamino Gigli portrays a cuckolded Italian singer, performing "Di quella pira," songs and excerpts from *Rigoletto*, *Africana*, *Mignon*, *Favorita*, *Marta* and *Elisir* (a total of four high Cs). "This is Gigli's most popular film, lovingly restored" (Steve Cohen, *The Delaware Jewish Voice* and *The Philadelphia Jewish Times*). English. 73 mins.
VHS: S28424. $34.95.

Norma (Australian Opera)

Joan Sutherland in her signature bel canto opera role filmed in the 1970s and performed by the Australian Opera, conducted by Richard Bonynge. With Margreta Elkins, Ron Stevens and Clifford Grant. Italian libretto with English subtitles. 153 mins.
VHS: S18727. $29.95.

Norma (Canadian Opera)

Joan Sutherland and Tatiana Troyanos star in a complete live 1971 performance of Bellini's bel canto masterpiece. Also starring Francisco Ortiz, Justino Diaz, and the Canadian Opera Company Orchestra and Chorus, with Richard Bonynge conducting. 150 mins.
VHS: S34391. $39.95.

Oedipus Rex (Felicity Palmer)

One of the musical masterpieces of the 20th century, sung in Latin, and recorded at the Carre Theatre, Amsterdam, this production features Felicity Palmer, Neil Rosenhein and Anton Scharinger, with Bernard Haitink conducting. Jean Cocteau's libretto is adapted from Sophocles. Cassette also includes "The Flood," created by Stravinsky for George Balanchine.
VHS: S03744. $29.95.

Oedipus Rex (Jessye Norman)

Peter Gelb directed this film of the 1992 Saito Kinen Festival production with Jessye Norman as Jocasta and the orchestra conducted by Seiji Ozawa. Stage direction by Julie Taymor.
VHS: S20552. $29.95.
Laser: LD72365. $29.95.

Operafest

A gala concert reopening the Zurich Opera House in December 1984, featuring selections from Donizetti's "Don Pasquale", Wagner's "Tannhauser" and Mozart's "Die Zauberflote" along with many others.
VHS: S03941. $49.95.
Gianni Paggi, Switzerland, 1984, 92 mins.

Orfeo ed Euridice (Kowalski)

An award-winning production of Gluck's masterpiece. Male alto Jochen Kowalski gives a riveting performance as Orfeo. French with English subtitles. 84 mins.
VHS: S32106. $29.95.

Orfeo ed Euridice (Kupfer)

Originally conceived for the Berlin Komische Oper and directed by Harry Kupfer, this startling, surreal version of Gluck's masterpiece won the Olivier Award for Most Outstanding Achievement in Opera. Kupfer's Orfeo is a young everyman in jeans and leather jacket whose beloved Euridice dies in a car accident. He sets off, guitar in hand, to charm the beasts of an inner-city concrete jungle who may be able to restore Euridice to life. 89 mins.
VHS: S16598. $29.95.

Orlando Furioso

The San Francisco Opera presents Vivaldi's magnificent opera based on a section of one of the greatest poems of the Italian renaissance by Ariosto. Marilyn Horne sings the virtuoso role with Susan Patterson as Angelica and Kathleen Kuhlman as Alcina.
VHS: S12411. $29.95.

Otello (Berlin)

Verdi's magnificent opera is performed by the Berlin "Komische Opera" and stars Hanns Nocker and Christa Noack Van Kamptz. The tragic story of the Moor, Desdemona, and the treacherous Iago is performed with an operatic cast of hundreds. A unique production. 123 mins.
VHS: S04743. $39.95.

Otello (Del Monaco)

The great tenor Del Monaco stars in this version of Verdi's opera based on the Shakespeare play. Filmed in 1958, Del Monaco's performance is considered a classic of the genre. 134 mins.
VHS: S23960. $34.95.

Otello (Domingo/Solti)

This production of Verdi's opera is conducted by Sir Georg Solti. With Placido Domingo, Kiri Te Kanawa and Russian baritone Sergei Leiferkus. Italian with English subtitles. 146 mins.
VHS: S20418. $29.95.

Otello (Vickers)

Jon Vickers' towering performance highlights Herbert von Karajan's masterful production of Verdi's immortal opera. Also featuring Mirella Freni.
VHS: S12656. $34.95.

Parsifal (Bayreuth)

A splendid interpretation of Wagner's last opera, performed at the Bayreuth Festival Theatre.
VHS: S15735. $44.95.

Parsifal (Berlin)

Richard Wagner's opera is conducted by Daniel Barenboim with the Staatskapelle Berlin, John Tomlinson, Falk Struckman and Waltraud Meier. 244 mins.
VHS: S21736. $44.97.
Laser: LD74495. $89.97.

Parsifal (Met)

James Levine conducts this version of Wagner's opera at the Metropolitan in New York. The story of the Knights of the Holy Grail provided this composer with the tragic and mythical basis for one of his most moving works. Waltraud Meier and Siegfried Jerusalem are featured.
VHS: S20913. $44.95.
Laser: LD72400. $82.50.

Parsifal (Syberberg)

Syberberg's (*Our Hitler*) remarkable homage to Richard Wagner, with Edith Clever. Syberberg explores Wagner's last, mystic opera, with a challenging style, using Wagner's face as a set. The actors perform to a recording expressly made for the film. German lyrics with English subtitles.
VHS: S00995. $79.95.
Hans Jurgen Syberberg, Germany, 1982, 255 mins.

Pavarotti in Central Park

This renowned tenor is joined by members of the New York Philharmonic, the Boys Choir of Harlem and Leone Magiera for an open air concert performance. He sings many great songs, including works by Verdi, Donizetti, Ellington and other great composers.
VHS: S23882. $29.95.
Laser: LD74795. $34.95.

Pelleas et Melisande

Pierre Boulez conducts this staging of Debussy's famed opera with the Welsh National Orchestra, Choir and Opera. This 20th century masterpiece brought the concerns of the symbolists to the operatic stage, shifting the emphasis of this form to recitative and atmosphere.
VHS: S20909. $34.95.
Laser: LD72399. $59.95.

The Perfumed Handkerchief

The classic comedy of manners presents Western opera lovers with their first opportunity to experience Chinese opera in all of its musical and visual splendor. Steve Allen and Jayne Meadows provide commentary on the performance, with English subtitles for the performance. 70 mins.
VHS: S02826. $39.95.

Pergolesi: La Serva Padrona

Metropolitan Opera star Anna Moffo and Paolo Montarsolo are musically perfect in this 1956 film of Pergolesi's masterpiece in the opera buffa tradition, combining pantomime, music and broad comedy. Song in the original Italian and performed by The Rome Philharmonic Orchestra. 63 mins.
VHS: S34053. $29.98.

Peter Grimes

Phillip Landgridge stars as Peter Grimes, a proud fisherman who descends into madness. Benjamin Britten's opera is a bleak tragedy that foregrounds the hypocrisy of a small town. The English National Opera and Chorus perform under the direction of David Atherton.
Laser: LD75095. $69.95.

Pique Dame—The Queen of Spades

The Kirov Opera and Orchestra of St. Petersburg are featured in this two-volume collection of recordings of Tchaikovsky's opera.
VHS: S19918. $44.95.
Laser: LD72045. $69.95.

Placido Domingo: Gala De Reyes

Performed with the Symphonic Orchestra of Madrid, at the National Auditorium, Placido Domingo gives a bravura performance. Domingo is joined by Teresa Verdera, Guadalupe Sanchez and Paloma Perez Inigo. 60 mins.
Laser: LD71934. $29.95.

Prince Igor (Haitink)

Alexander Borodin's full-length masterpiece is directed by Andrei Serban, with members of the Royal Ballet performing the *Polovtsian Dances*, and with the Royal Opera Chorus. Performed by Sergei Leiferkus, Anna Tomowa-Sintow and Paata Burchuladze. Conducted by Bernard Haitink. 186 mins.
VHS: S18311. $44.95.
Laser: LD71847. $69.95.

Prince Igor (Kirov)

A rare treat to see this powerful, lush spectacle by Borodin, with the Polovtsian Dance sequences choreographed by Mikhail Fokine. The full opera score is sung by the Kirov Opera. Russian with English subtitles. USSR, 1972, 110 mins.
VHS: S02451. $69.95.

Queen of Spades (Bolshoi)

Directed by Roman Tikhomirov with the Bolshoi Opera bringing a stunning cinematic adaptation of one of Tchaikovsky's most popular operas. Russian with English subtitles. USSR, 1960, color.
VHS: S02999. $69.95.

Queen of Spades (Glyndebourne)

Tchaikovsky's operatic interpretation of Pushkin's ghost story. This Glyndebourne Festival production features Yuri Marusin, Nancy Gustafson and Sergei Leiferkus. Russian with English subtitles. 168 mins.
VHS: S18729. $29.95.

The Rake's Progress

Stravinsky's operatic masterpiece became a glorious success for the Glyndebourne Festival's 1977 season! Starring Felicity Lott, Leo Goeke, Samuel Ramey and Rosalind Elias, and designed by David Hockney, this is a masterful production. 144 mins.
VHS: S02457. $49.95.

Renata Tebaldi/Louis Quilico: Concerto Italiano

Renata Tebaldi and Louis Quilico are at their vocal and dramatic peaks in this 1965 telecast, highlighted by the finale of Act II of *Tosca*. Miss Tebaldi performs the novelty Rossini song cycle *La Regata Veneziana* as well as "O mio babbino caro," from Puccini's *Gianni Schicchi*. Quilico is heard in the chilling finale of Puccini's *Il Tabarro* and Tosti's *L'ultima canzone*. The CBC Festival Orchestra is conducted by Ernesto Barbini. 60 mins.
VHS: S30128. $29.95.

The Return of Ulysses

Dame Janet Baker gives a virtuoso performance as Penelope in Monteverdi's majestic opera based on Homer's *Odyssey*. This Glyndebourne Festival performance from 1973 also features Benjamin Luxon and Richard Lewis. Raymond Leppard conducts. Italian with English subtitles. 152 mins.
VHS: S02445. $59.95.

Richard Strauss: Arabella

Christian Thielemann has quickly gained attention as one of the world's leading Strauss conductors. In this 1994 performance of Richard Strauss' lyric romantic comedy written in the 1920s, Thielemann demonstrates his gifts as he conducts The Metropolitan Opera. With Kiri Te Kanawa as Arabella and Wolfgang Brendel as Mandryka. "As conducted by Christian Thielemann, the orchestra was also the dominant force of the opera, not supporting the singers as much as daring them to hang on for the lush exotic ride" (*New York Times*).
VHS: S31071. $34.95.
Laser: LD76146. $59.95.
1994, 30 mins.

Richard Wagner Edition—Bayreuth Fest

The unprecedented offering of the ten operas produced every year at the theater Wagner had specially built. Each program is a state-of-the-art recording, with such conductors as Pierre Boulez, Woldemar Nelsson and Horst Stein, expert casting and first-rate stagings. The ten operas are *Das Rheingold, Siegfried, Die Walkure, Gotterdammerung, Der Fliegende Hollander, Lohengrin, Tristan und Isolde, Tannhauser, Parsifal* and *Die Meistersinger von Nurnberg. 35 hours, 30 mins.*
VHS: S17404. $489.95.

Rigoletto (Gobbi)

Gobbi performs the title role in this 1947 production of *Rigoletto* which also features Filippeschi as the Duke, Neri as Sparafucile, and the voice of Pagliughi as Gilda. "This is the quintessential *Rigoletto* for its era. Gobbi, the greatest postwar Rigoletto, gives a riveting dramatic performance, extraordinarily well sung" (Stefan Zucker, *Opera Fanatic's Catalog*). Italian. 101 mins.
VHS: S28422. $34.95.

Rigoletto (Gobbi)

A hunchbacked court jester causes tumult and misfortune in the Court of the Duke of Mantua. Verdi's opera is performed by the Orchestra del Teatro dell'Opera di Roma. With the voices of Tito Gobbi, Mario Del Monaco and Giuseppina Arnaldi. Sung in Italian. Dubbed in English.
VHS: S03374. $49.95.
Giulio Fiaschi, Italy, 1954, 90 mins.

Rigoletto (Miller)

Jonathan Miller's brilliant new interpretation of Verdi's tragic opera shifts the story to mob-controlled Manhattan in the 1950s. This lavish production features inventive staging and memorable performances. Recorded life and sung in English. 140 mins.
VHS: S10911. $39.99.

Rigoletto (Pavarotti)

The legendary Luciano Pavarotti stars in Jean-Pierre Ponnelle's acclaimed production of Verdi's opera of court corruption. Ponnelle's work in stage and television brings a grandly colored vitality to opera interpretations.
VHS: S12658. $24.95.
Laser: LD71302. $59.95.

Rigoletto at Verona

Enjoy Verdi's *Rigoletto*, presented at the ancient Roman amphitheater in Verona, Italy. This beautiful production features top-quality digital hi-fi. 60 mins.
VHS: S02467. $29.95.

Ring Cycle

Wagner's extraordinary *Ring*, from the celebrated staging at the Bayreuth Festspielhaus directed by Patrice Chereau, with the participation of the Bayreuth Festival Orchestra conducted by Pierre Boulez.
Das Rheingold. 144 mins.
VHS: S16772. $34.95.
Laser: LD72289. $59.97.
Die Walkure. 269 mins.
VHS: S16773. $44.95.
Laser: LD72290. $99.97.
Siegfried. 228 mins.
VHS: S16774. $44.95.

Robert Ashley: Perfect Lives

Robert Ashley performs solo voice, and Jill Kroesen and David Van Tieghem sing as the chorus, with "Blue" Gene Tyranny on keyboards and David Van Tieghem providing non-keyboard percussion in this video of Robert Ashley's seven-part opera, originally produced in 1984. The video was produced for television by John Sanborn at New York's The Kitchen. 181 minutes on two cassettes.
VHS: S20866. $95.00.

Roberto Devereux

Donizetti's rarely performed opera features Beverly Sills in her acclaimed portrait of Elizabeth I, supported by John Alexander, Susanne Marsee and Richard Fredericks. Conducted by Julius Rudel. Italian with English subtitles. 145 mins.
VHS: S18344. $39.95.

Rossini: La Cenerentola (Cinderella)

An elaborate 1948 version of Rossini's version of Cinderella, filmed in some of the most beautiful palaces of Italy. Performed by Fedora Barbieri, Afro Poli and members of the Rome Opera under the direction of Oliviero de Fabritiis. Sung in Italian with English narration between the arias. 94 mins.
VHS: S34055. $29.98.

Royal Opera House

This three-volume documentary series examines the glamorous image of one of Britain's most prominent institutions, the Royal Opera House, Covent Garden, the prestigious home of opera and ballet. Contains excerpts from the operas *Carmen, The Marriage of Figaro, Katya Kabanova* and others, as well the ballets *The Sleeping Beauty* and *The Nutcracker*. Volumes include *Star Struck & Horse Trading, Footfault & High Hopes* and *Settling Scores & A Winning Ticket*. Each volume is 100 mins. 3-volume set.
VHS: S31155. $79.95.

Rusalka

David Poutney's acclaimed production of Dvorak's fairy tale fantasy opera, performed by the English National Opera, and re-set in an Edwardian nursery. This English-language production features Eilene Hannan, Rodney McCann and Ann Howard, with Mark Elder conducting.
VHS: S03745. $29.95.

Sadko

The Kirov Opera and Orchestra bring Rimsky-Korsakov's story of love and sacrifice to a unique video offering. Sadko is a minstrel who falls in love with a sea goddess. Though he leaves everything to join her, tragically he must lose her in the end. 174 mins.
VHS: S23908. $44.95.
Laser: LD74796. $59.95.

Salome (Ewing/Hall)

Peter Hall's production of Strauss' *Salome* features American soprano Maria Ewing, tenor Kenneth Riegel and bass-baritone Michael Devlin. Conducted by Edward Downes. German with English subtitles. 103 mins.
VHS: S20419. $29.95.

Salome (Malfitano/Weigl)

From the Deutsche Oper Berlin comes director Peter Weigl's new production of Richard Strauss' one-act opera *Salome*. Catherine Malfitano stars in the title role, Simon Estes is the unfortunate John the Baptist, and Horst Hiestermann is King Herod. Conducted by Giuseppe Sinopoli. In Hi-Fi Stereo, 109 mins.
VHS: S16552. $34.97.
Laser: CLV. LD71485. $39.97.

Salome (Stratas/Boehm)

Richard Strauss' third opera, performed by Karl Boehm and the Vienna Philharmonic Orchestra, with Teresa Stratas and Bernd Weikl. 102 mins.
VHS: S15633. $24.95.

Samson et Dalila

Placido Domingo, Shirley Verret and Wolfgang Brendel star in a magnificent performance of Saint-Saens' moving work. This San Francisco Opera production was unanimously hailed by the critics as a triumphant, extravagant spectacle. 118 mins.
VHS: S10264. $29.95.

Semiramide

Marilyn Horne, Samuel Ramey and June Anderson are cast in this Metropolitan Opera production of Rossini's elaborate opera. John Copely places this superb cast in a strong and effective production that gives firm ground to their accomplished bel canto singing. 220 mins.
VHS: S25853. $39.95.
Laser: LD76439. $34.98.

The Seven Deadly Sins

Peter Sellars' latest bold opera production brings stars Teresa Stratas and Kent Nagano to the Kurt Weill fable *The Seven Deadly Sins*. This London production features the Lyon Opera of France.
VHS: S24687. $29.95.

Siegfried

Daniel Barenboim conducts Siegfried Jerusalem, Graham Clark, John Tomlinson, Gunter von Kannen and the Bayreuth Festival Orchestra in this exciting performance of Wagner's opera. 244 mins.
VHS: S22909. $44.97.
Laser: LD74624. $99.97.

Simon Boccanegra (Milnes)

Sherrill Milnes is Simon Boccanegra in Verdi's opera about a passionate Renaissance ruler willing to die in order to unite his warring countrymen. Taped live at the Met in 1984. Italian with English subtitles.
VHS: S07037. $29.95.

Simon Boccanegra (Te Kanawa)

Conducted by Sir Georg Solti and performed by the Royal Opera House, Giuseppi Verdi's opera was hailed for its performances by Kiri Te Kanawa, Alexandru Agache and Roberto Scandiuzzi. 137 mins.
VHS: S17701. $34.95.
Laser: LD71799. $59.95.

Stiffelio (Carreras)

Conductor Edward Downes leads the Orchestra and the Chorus of the Royal Opera House in this staging of Verdi's middle-period work that was banned by the Italian government censors. Jose Carreras is a Protestant minister whose faith is shattered when he discovers his wife is involved with a family friend. With Catherine Malfitano, Gregory Yurisich, Gwynne Howell and Robin Leggate. Italian with English subtitles.
VHS: S20420. $29.95.

Stiffelio (Domingo)

Placido Domingo stars as Stiffelio, a minister trapped in the throes of a troubling divorce. James Levine conducts the Met's thrilling performance of this long-lost opera by Verdi. It was censored in its day for openly confronting the possibility of divorce, and only uncovered in 1968.
VHS: S27431. $29.95.
Laser: LD75504. $39.95.
Brian Large, USA, 1993, 115 mins.

Sutherland, Horne, Bonynge Gala Concert

This is the Australian Opera's "Night of a Lifetime." On June 12, 1985, the Sydney Opera House hosted the two greatest proponents of the art of "Bel Canto"—Joan Sutherland and Marilyn Horne-with Richard Bonynge conducting. Featured are arias and duets from many classic operas. 142 mins.
VHS: S31377. $29.95.

Tannhauser (Davis)

Wagner believed that *Tannhauser* was the most meaningful of all his operas. It certainly contains some of his most unforgettable music. A bravura international cast, led by Dame Gwyneth Jones, tells the dramatic true story in this famous Gotz Friedrich production, conducted by Colin Davis at Bayreuth. 151 mins.
VHS: S14115. $39.95.

Tannhauser (Marton)

Eva Marton is Elisabeth, Tatiana Troyanos is Venus and Richard Cassily is Tannhauser in Richard Wagner's great opera. German with English subtitles. 1982, 176 mins. 2 cassettes.
VHS: S02007. $29.95.

Tannhauser (Mehta)

Wagner's grand romantic opera is given a modern interpretation by director David Alden, who stirs up the visionary, erotic and archetypal elements of Wagner's masterpiece. This acclaimed Bayerische Staatsoper performance stars Rene Kollo, Waltraud Meier and Bernd Weikl, and is conducted by Zubin Mehta. 195 mins.
VHS: S30878. $29.95.

Three Waltzes

Yvonne Printemps achieved her greatest theatrical success with this 1938 film, a French adaptation of a Viennese operetta which she performed for nearly two years. The film, spanning three generations from 1867 to 1937, recounts the love story of a ballerina, her daughter and her granddaughter. Music by Oscar Straus, with adaptations of music by Johann Strauss I and Strauss II. French with English subtitles. 101 mins.
VHS: S28434. $34.95.

Tosca (Domingo/Behrens)

This 1985 version recorded live at the Metropolitan Opera features Placido Domingo, Hildegard Behrens, Cornell MacNeil, Italo Tajo. The stage director is Franco Zeffirelli. Italian with English subtitles. Stereo, 127 mins.
VHS: S02460. $22.95.

Tosca (Domingo/Malfitano)

Placido Domingo, Catherine Malfitano and Ruggero Raimondi perform in this film set in the time of Tosca. With The Orchestra Sinfonica e Coro di Roma della Rai, conducted by Zubin Mehta. Sung in Italian with English subtitles. "The staggered timing, the complex technology and the settings themselves made the production the first of its kind" (*The New York Times*).
VHS: S37099. $34.97.

Tosca (Domingo/Milnes)

Puccini's tragic drama about the dedicated painter, the passionately jealous singer and the demonic chief of police is performed by Placido Domingo and Sherrill Milnes.
VHS: S12655. $29.95.
Laser: LD71373. $59.95.

Tosca (Marton)

This Arena di Verona production features Eva Marton, Giacomo Aragall and Ingvar Wixell. In Italian. 1984, 124 mins.
VHS: S10097. $24.97.

Tosca (Tebaldi)

A newly discovered film recording of the incomparable Renata Tebaldi at the peak of her vocal and dramatic powers in a 1961 performance of Puccini's masterpiece, filmed live at the Stuttgart Staatsoper. George London portrays Scarpia and the cast also includes Eugene Tobin. Franco Patane conducts. B&W, 130 mins.
VHS: S19398. $39.95.

Tristan and Isolde
Wagner's great romantic opera, with Daniel Barenboim conducting the Choir and Orchestra of the Bayreuther Festspiele with solos from Schunk, Meier, Schwarz, Becht and Kollo. In Hi-Fi stereo, 245 mins.
Laser: LD71189. $89.95.

Trouble in Tahiti
A rare video performance of Leonard Bernstein's 1951 opera. Bernstein conducts the London Symphony Wind Band in a production which incorporates performers singing before an animated set. With Nancy Williams, Julian Patrick, Antonio Burler, Michael Clark and Mark Brown. 46 mins.
VHS: S17312. $29.95.

Turandot (Corelli)
Franco Corelli, "the favorite tenor of the century," performs his signature role as Calaf in this 1958 telecast of *Turandot*. Also features American soprano Lucille Udovick in the title role, Renata Mattioli as Liu, and Plinio Clabassi as Timur. Directed by Mario Lanfanchi. "Franco's only video of his signature role; he looks and sounds stupendous" (Stefan Zucker). Italian. 114 mins.
VHS: S28420. $34.95.

Turandot (New York)
Eva Marton performs Puccini's famous opera. Conducted by James Levine in New York.
Laser: LD71281. $59.95.

Turandot (San Francisco)
Eva Marton stars in the San Francisco Opera production of Puccini's popular work. Famed artist David Hockney designed the sets, and Michael Sylvester, Kevin Langan and Lucia Mazzaria are featured. Together they enliven this story of love triumphant over barbaric cruelty. 123 mins.
VHS: S25917. $29.95.

The Turn of the Screw
Benjamin Britten's 1954 chamber opera based on the Henry James novel is realized in this film by Petr Weigl. In Hi-Fi stereo, 115 mins.
VHS: S16771. $24.95.

Un Ballo in Maschera (Pavarotti/Millo)
Verdi's opera, with Luciano Pavarotti as Gustavo III, Leo Nucci and Aprile Millo. Conducted by James Levine and performed by the Metropolitan Opera Orchestra and Chorus. 137 mins.
VHS: S17673. $34.95.

Un Ballo in Maschera (Pavarotti/Ricciarelli)
Luciano Pavarotti, Katia Ricciarelli and Louis Quilico at the Met in Verdi's opera of political intrigue. Italian with English subtitles. Stereo, 1980, 150 mins.
VHS: S02464. $22.95.

Under the Arbor
Robert Greenleaf's new opera follows the budding romance of two distant cousins in the South. Religion, guilt, magic and voodoo inflect this seemingly simple tale set on Chattahoochee River in 1943. The music is as beguiling as the singers. 112 mins.
VHS: S26376. $29.95.

Verdi (The Opera)
Pierre Cressoy and Anna Marie Ferreo star in this story of the life and work of Italian composer Giuseppe Verdi. With Gaby Andr, Irene Genna, Tito Gobbi, Mario del Monaco, Sandro Ruffini and Laura Gobe.
VHS: S30524. $29.95.
Raffaello Matarazzo, Italy, 1953, 120 mins.

Verdi/Donizetti: An Evening with Joan Sutherland & Luciano Pavarotti
A gala filmed at the MET in 1987, this tape features two of the world's biggest opera superstars in scenes from three of the most famous Italian operas. 115 mins.
VHS: S15635. $24.95.
Laser: LD70281. $34.95.

Verdi: The King of Melody
Starring Metropolitan Opera and La Scala stars Tito Gobbi and Mario del Monaco, this colorfully filmed drama of the life and loves of the great composer, Giuseppe Verdi, is played against a background of the great operas of the 19th Century. Dubbed in English and sung in Italian. 118 mins.
VHS: S34051. $29.98.

Victory over the Sun: A Reconstruction of the 1913 Futurist Performance
One of the first gasps of Russian futurism, this work reconstructs the 1913 opera that featured costumes and sets by Kasimir Malevich, music by Mikhail Matiushin and text by Aleksei Kruchenykh. "As though the Wizard of Oz had met Alice in Wonderland with some help from Doctor Who" (*The London Times*). 39 mins.
VHS: S20316. $250.00.

Wagner: Scenes from "The Ring" at the Met
James Levine conducted Jessye Norman, Siegfried Jerusalem, James Morris and other noted singers in his masterful rendition of the entire Ring cycle. Key scenes from this complex work have been collected on this singular video, offering a wonderful introduction to Wagner's masterpiece. Directed by Brian Large. 86 mins.
VHS: S27633. $29.95.

War and Peace
Valery Gergiev leads the Kirov Opera in this astounding performance of Prokofiev's opera. Based on Leo Tolstoy's famed work, Prokofiev captures the epic sweep of his acclaimed novel. Olga Borodina, Aleksandr Gergalov, Yelena Prokina, Gegam Grigorian and more are featured. 248 mins.
VHS: S27072. $44.95.
Laser: LD75443. $82.50.

Werther
The famous stage director Peter Weigl directs this charming version of Jules Massenet's opera based on Goethe's famous novella: the story of young Werther who falls in love with Charlotte who, however, following the wishes of her mother, marries another man. With Peter Dvorsky, Brigitte Fassbaender, Magdalena Vasary. Sung in French with no subtitles.
VHS: S08111. $39.95.
Peter Weigl, Germany, 1986, 107 mins.

Who's Afraid of Opera
World-famous soprano Joan Sutherland and her magical puppet friends present a series of opera highlight programs designed for the whole family. Each program highlights two operas. Joining Sutherland in these unique programs are her funny puppet friends Sir William, an elderly, erudite goat; his nephew, Little Billy; and Rudy, the boisterous lion. The puppets punctuate storylines with bits of humor which balance the tragic overtones of some of the operas and add great humor and suspense to the lighter, comical ones. Together they relate the stories in English, and the arias are sung in their original language with costumes and sets directly from the opera house. Each of the films is designed to make adults and children who are unfamiliar with opera comfortable with this area of western culture and to appreciate the stories and music of opera. Produced and conceived by Nathan Kroll; the London Symphony Orchestra is directed by Richard Bonynge, with the puppets created by Larry Berthelson.
Who's Afraid of Opera Vol. 1. Features *Faust* and *Rigoletto*. 60 mins.
VHS: S05249. $29.95.
Who's Afraid of Opera Vol. 2. Features *La Traviata* and *Daughter of the Regiment*. 60 mins.
VHS: S05250. $29.95.
Who's Afraid of Opera Vol. 3. Features *The Barber of Seville* and *Lucia di Lammermoor*. 60 mins.
VHS: S05251. $29.95.
Who's Afraid of Opera Vol. 4. Features *Mignon* and *La Perichole*. 60 mins.
VHS: S05274. $29.95.
Who's Afraid of Opera Complete. The complete, four-volume set at a special discount price.
VHS: S05329. $113.81.

William Tell
Rossini's final opera features Chris Merritt in the role of Arnold, produced at La Scala under the direction of Riccardo Muti. Two videocassettes. 239 min.
VHS: S18384. $49.95.

Wolfgang Amadeus Mozart
Three productions of Mozart's da Ponte operas, recorded at Stockholm's Royal Palace, are conducted by Arnold Ostman and performed by Drottningholm Court Theatre Orchestra.
Cosi Fan Tutte.
Laser: LD71851. $59.95.
Don Giovanni.
Laser: LD71849. $59.95.
Le Nozze di Figaro.
Laser: LD71850. $69.95.

Wozzeck
Claudio Abbado conducts the Vienna State Opera in this powerful recording of Alban Berg's gripping drama *Wozzeck*. Franz Grundheber plays the soldier Wozzeck who, driven mad with jealousy, stabs his mistress Marie (sung by Hildegard Behrens) to death before drowning himself. Philip Langridge stars as Andres in this moving performance of one of the great classics of modern music. 98 mins.
VHS: S11758. $29.95.

Xerxes
London's *Financial Times* called this production "one of the glories of the English National Opera's recent history." Handel's comic opera—revolving around the love intrigues of the great Persian King Xerxes—in a performance conducted by Sir Charles Mackerras. 2 cassettes. 180 mins.
VHS: S11751. $29.95.
Laser: LD71700. $69.95.

CLASSICAL MUSIC

Abbado in Berlin: The First Year
This documentary considers the first year in Berlin of conductor Claudio Abbado, the late Herbert von Karajan's successor. The program includes a concert performance of Mahler's *Symphony No. 1*. 114 mins.
VHS: S17671. $29.95.
Laser: LD71787. $34.95.

After the Storm: The American Exile of Bela Bartok
The great Hungarian composer Bela Bartok spent the last five years of his life as a man without a country, a refugee from war-torn Europe. He spent these years, 1940-45, in the United States, where few people understood the greatness of his genius. He struggled with sickness and poverty, yet he composed some of the greatest music of his career, including the *Concerto for Orchestra*, the *Sonata for Solo Violin* and the *Third Piano Concerto*. England/Hungary, 75 mins.
VHS: S13749. $29.95.

Aldo Ciccolini
Pianist Ciccolini performs around the world. In this video he interprets Chopin's *Sonata 3 in B Minor, Op. 58*, Ravel's *Pavane for a Deceased Child* and Schubert's *Sonata 3 in B Flat, Op. 960*. 79 mins.
VHS: S27696. $14.95.

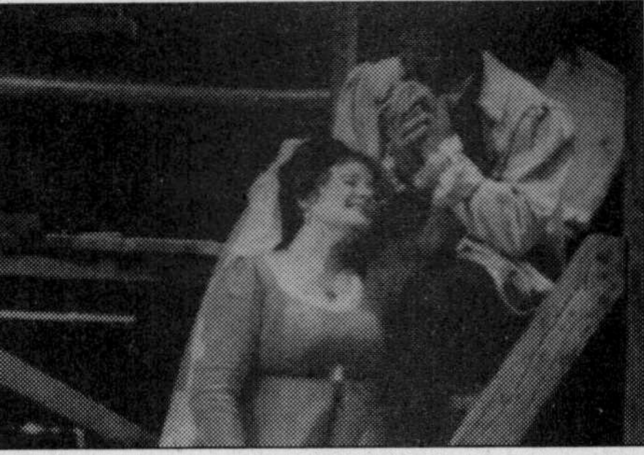

All That Bach
A diverse and brilliant group of musical talents, including jazz pianist Keith Jarrett, the Canadian brass, contralto Maureen Forrester, early-music specialist Christopher Hogwood and the Academy of Ancient Music, join in a celebration of the genius of J.S. Bach. Highlights include excerpts from the Italian Concerto and the French Suite, the Well-Tempered Clavier, and The Art of the Fugue. Canada, 1985, 50 mins.
VHS: S03090. $39.95.
Laser: CLV. LD70771. $34.95.

Andre Rieu, From Holland with Love
Rieu and the Johann Strauss Orchestra bring the ever popular waltz to life in this video performance. A pop chart topper in Europe, Andre Rieu and his music are now available in this country, where he is sure to inspire similar devotion.
VHS: S27780. $29.95.

Andre Rieu: The Vienna I Love, Waltzes from My Heart
"Waltz King" Andre Rieu and the Johann Strauss Orchestra perform some of the most beautiful and romantic music ever written in 3/4 time, including Johann Strauss' *The Voices of Spring*, *Radetzky March*, *Emperor Waltz* and *Fledermaus*, as well as Rossini's *William Tell*, Offenbach's *Barcarole*, *The Skater's Waltz* and more.
VHS: S30770. $19.95.

The Art of Conducting
A miraculous look at great conductors of the past: Toscanini, Furtwangler, Walter, Klemperer, Stokowski, Koussevitzky and Reiner. Adapted from the award-winning BBC television program, this program uses rare archival material, and image and audio restoration to present dramatic—and unprecedented-moments like Wilhelm Furtwangler's hair-raising rehearsal of Brahms' *Fourth Symphony* with the Berlin Philharmonic during the first post-war tour of England. "The most fascinating program ever made about classical music." 120 mins.
VHS: S22461. $29.97.
Laser: LD74756. $34.97.

The Art of Conducting: Legendary Conductors of a Golden Era
Over 100 minutes of rare and never-before-seen footage of such great conducting legends as Wilhelm Furtwangler, Erich Kleiber, Charles Munch, Sergiu Celibidache, Evgeny Mravinsky and others. The historical clips are interspersed with candid, insightful commentary by several of the subjects and their peers.
VHS: S33258. $29.97.
Laser: LD76756. $34.97.

Artur Rubinstein
Two short films of the great pianist: the first part shows Rubinstein at a recording session, playing for his children, and exhibiting his technique with the music of Liszt, Chopin and Mendelssohn; in the second part, Rubinstein performs an all-Chopin program, and together with Heifetz and Piatagorsky interprets the music of Schubert and Mendelssohn. 78 mins.
VHS: S03144. $19.95.

Artur Rubinstein: Piano Concerto #3 and Piano Concerto #1
On the tenth anniversary of his death, this video captures the genius of the virtuoso pianist as he performs these two concerts at Amsterdam's Concertgebouw Hall in August 1973, at the age of 86.
VHS: S16907. $24.95.

Ashkenazy Observed
Barenboim, Harrell and Perlman headline this moving tribute with support from the Swedish Radio Symphony Orchestra.
A Christopher Nupen documentary.
VHS: S15459. $29.98.

At the Haunted End of the Day... A Profile of Sir William Walton
Over 20 pieces of music of Sir William Walton are featured, including a special piece written for the Coronation of King George VI titled "Crown Imperial," and the music for his good friend, Sir Olivier's Shakespeare roles of "Richard III," "Hamlet," and "Henry V." Contributing artists to this Prix Italia winning film are Julian Bream, Ralph Kirschbaum, Yvonne Kenny, Yehudi Menuhin, Sacheverell Sitwell, Lord Olivier. 120 mins.
VHS: S03698. $59.95.

Bach: Goldberg Variations
A complete performance of Bach's *Goldberg Variations* by the pianist Andras Schiff. 81 mins.
VHS: S19631. $29.97.
Laser: LD71927. $34.97.

Bach: Mass in B Minor
Bach scholar Helmuth Rilling leads a performance of one of the most revered works in the history of Western music. This concert was videotaped at the International Bach Festival, Stuttgart, and features soprano Arleen Auger, alto Anne Sophie von Otter, tenor Aldo Baldin, and bass Wolfgang Schone. With Gachinger Kantorei and the Bach-Collegium Stuttgart, conducted by Helmuth Rilling. 28 mins.
VHS: S34507. $29.95.

Bach: Violin Concerto No. 2
Herbert Von Karajan conducts the Berlin Philharmonic in Bach's *Violin Concerto No. 2* and *The Magnificat*.
Laser: LD74575. $29.98.

Battle for Music
A semi-documentary account of the London Philharmonic Orchestra's struggle during World War II. With Joss Ambler, Charles Carson, Mavis Clarke, Anthony Holles, Jack Hylton, Hay Petrie, Ben Williams, and Dennis Wyndham.
VHS: S34502. $24.95.
Donald Taylor, Great Britain, 1943, 79 mins.

Beethoven Concerti
The complete set of all five Beethoven concerti performed by renowned pianist Murray Perahia at the Royal Festival Hall London. Available as a set, or individual volumes.
Beethoven Concerti Vol. 1: Piano Concertos 1 & 3. Murray Perahia joins the Academy of St. Martin in the Fields conducted by Neville Marriner; an additional segment interviews Perahia about Beethoven the man and the musician. 86 mins.
VHS: S09864. $29.95.
Beethoven Concerti Vol. 2: Piano Concertos 2 & 4. Piano concerto Number 4 in G Major, written in 1808, and Piano Concerto No. 2. Performed by Murray Perahia at Royal Festival Hall London. 75 mins.
VHS: S09865. $29.95.
Beethoven Concerti Vol. 3: Piano Concerto 5. The last of the composer's concertos, Number Five in E Flat Major, written in 1811, and known as "The Emperor Concerto." Also contains interviews of the pianist, Murray Perahia, on Beethoven, the composer. 49 mins.
VHS: S09866. $29.95.

Beethoven, Schumann, Brahms
Featuring a selection performed by Alexis Weissenberg on piano, Pierre Amoyal on violin, with Brahms' "Lieders" sung by Teresa Berganza. 55 mins.
VHS: S03829. $19.95.

Beethoven—Klassix 13
Anthony Quayle and Balint Vaszonyi lead this expedition into the extraordinary life of Beethoven, including his home in Bonn, his life in Vienna, his turbulent mind, and the agony over his crushing deafness. 60 mins.
VHS: S10895. $24.95.

Beethoven: Piano Concerto No. 1 and No. 2 (Zimmermann)
Leonard Bernstein had worked with Krystian Zimmermann and the Vienna Philharmonic on the last three Beethoven Piano Concertos. After Bernstein's death the Philharmonic voted to complete the recording cycle with Zimmermann as both soloist and conductor. This recording is the result. 70 mins.
VHS: S20643. $29.95.
Laser: LD72374. $34.95.

Beethoven: Piano Concerto No. 3 and Brahms: Piano Concerto No. 1 (Rubinstein)
The legendary Artur Rubinstein is the pianist in two works by Beethoven and Brahms with the Concertgebouw Orchestra conducted by Bernard Haitink.
VHS: S18535. $24.95.

Beethoven: Piano Concerto No. 3 and No. 4 (Zimmermann)
Leonard Bernstein conducts the Vienna Philharmonic with soloist Krystian Zimmermann.
Laser: LD71797. $34.95.

Beethoven: Piano Concerto No. 4 and No. 5 (Arrau)
The great pianist Claudio Arrau performs with Philadelphia Orchestra and the London Symphony Orchestra under the batons of Riccardo Muti and Sir Colin Davis, respectively.
VHS: S15445. $24.95.
Laser: LD70231. $34.95.

Beethoven: Piano Concerto No. 5, "The Emperor" (Zimmermann)
Pianist Krystian Zimmermann performs Beethoven's fifth piano concerto, *The Emperor*, with conductor Leonard Bernstein leading the Vienna Philharmonic Orchestra.
VHS: S17700. $24.95.
Laser: LD71798. $29.95.

Beethoven: Piano Sonatas No. 21 and No. 23 (Barenboim)
Daniel Barenboim performs two Beethoven Piano Sonatas: "Waldstein" and "Apassionate." 54 mins.
Laser: LD76839. $29.97.

Beethoven: Piano Sonatas 30, No. 31 and No. 32 (Serkin)
Rudolf Serkin performs Beethoven's Piano Sonatas No. 30 op. 109, No. 31 op. 110 and No. 32 op. 111.
VHS: S18542. $24.95.
Laser: LD70871. $34.95.

Beethoven: Symphony No. 1 and No. 2 (Bernstein)
Leonard Bernstein conducts the Vienna Philharmonic in this historic recording. 85 mins.
Laser: LD71792. $34.95.

Beethoven: Symphony No. 1, No. 2, No. 6 "Pastoral" and No. 8 (Karajan)
Herbert von Karajan made these filmed performances of the complete Beethoven symphonies in the '60s and '70s, when he was at the vigorous height of his brilliance. Featuring the Berlin Philharmonic Orchestra. 117 mins.
VHS: S15714. $24.95.

Beethoven: Symphony No. 2 and No. 3 (Karajan)
Herbert von Karajan conducts the Berlin Philharmonic.
Laser: LD74580. $34.48.

Beethoven: Symphony No. 3 ("Eroica") and No. 7 (Bernstein)
Conducted by the legendary Leonard Bernstein, this inspired reading of two of Beethoven's finest symphonies is sure to electrify audiences. The years from 1803 to 1822 were among the most productive of Beethoven's entire life; he composed no fewer than six symphonies—including the two performed here. Witness the epitome of Beethoven's heroic music. 97 mins.
VHS: S13890. $24.95.
Laser: LD70872. $34.95.

Beethoven: Symphony No. 3 ("Eroica") and No. 7 (Karajan)
The Berlin Philharmonic led by Herbert von Karajan is captured in these historic recordings from the '60s and '70s. 84 mins.
VHS: S15716. $24.95.

Beethoven: Symphony No. 4 and No. 7 (Kleiber)
Carlos Kleiber conducts the Concertgebouw Orchestra, Amsterdam, in this recording.
VHS: S18541. $24.95.
Laser: LD70876. $34.95.

Beethoven: Symphony No. 4 and No. 8 (Bernstein)
Leonard Bernstein conducts the Vienna Philharmonic in two Beethoven symphonies and the incidental music to the ballet *The Creatures of Prometheus*. 99 mins.
VHS: S17677. $24.95.
Laser: LD71793. $34.95.

Beethoven: Symphony No. 4, Symphony No. 5, "Coriolan" Overture, "Egmont" Overture
Herbert von Karajan conducts the Berlin Philharmonic in these definitive recordings from the '60s and '70s. 82 mins.
VHS: S15715. $24.95.
Laser: LD74581. $34.48.

Beethoven: Symphony No. 5/Solti
Sir Georg Solti conducts the Chicago Symphony Orchestra in Beethoven's *Symphony No. 5* and the *Egmont Overture*.
Laser: LD74574. $24.98.

Beethoven: Symphony No. 5 and No. 6 (Bernstein)
Leonard Bernstein conducts the Vienna Philharmonic in two symphonies by Beethoven and the Leonore Overture No. 3, Opus 72a.
VHS: S18536. $24.95.
Laser: LD70877. $34.95.

Beethoven: Symphony No. 6 and No. 7 (Karajan)
Herbert von Karajan conducts the Berlin Philharmonic.
Laser: LD74582. $34.48.

Beethoven: Symphony No. 6 and No. 8 (Harnoncourt)
Nikolaus Harnoncourt is shown conducting Beethoven's *Symphonies No. 8* and *No. 6, the Pastoral*. Then a behind-the-scenes look is offered by footage of this great conductor rehearsing the Chamber Orchestra of Europe through *Symphonies Nos. 1-8*. 118 mins.
VHS: S22462. $29.97.

Beethoven: Symphony No. 9 (Bernstein)
Leonard Bernstein conducts the Vienna Philharmonic in Beethoven's *Ninth Symphony*, performed on the 200th anniversary of the composer's birth. Performers include Placido Domingo, Gwyneth Jones, Shirley Verret and Martti Talvela, as well as the Vienna State Opera Chorus. 78 mins.
VHS: S19003. $29.95.
Laser: LD70869. $34.95.

Beethoven: Symphony No. 9 (Karajan)
Herbert von Karajan conducts the Berlin Philharmonic with the Choir of the Deutsche Opera Berlin and soloists Anna Tomowa-Sintow, Agnes Baltsa and Jose van Dam.
VHS: S15717. $24.95.
Laser: LD70873. $34.95.

Beethoven: Violin Concerto (Karajan)
Herbert von Karajan conducts the Berlin Philharmonic.
Laser: LD74587. $29.98.

Beethoven: Waldstein and Appassionata (Barenboim)
The Sonata No. 21, Opus 53 and Sonata No. 23, Opus 57 are performed here by Daniel Barenboim. In Hi-Fi Stereo.
Laser: CLV. LD70209. $29.98.

Berlioz: Symphonie Fantastique, Op. 14
Symphonie Fantastique, recorded at the Conservatoire National Superieur d'Art Dramatique, performed by the Orchestre Revolutionnaire et Romantique, and conducted by John Eliot Gardiner. 55 mins.
VHS: S18317. $29.95.
Laser: LD71855. $29.95.

Bolero/Pictures at an Exhibition
Dutoit and the Montreal Symphony Orchestra perform these works by Ravel and Mussorgsky with dances choreographed by Lar Lubovitch and interpreted by MOMIX. This work received Grand Prize at the 28th Chicago International Film Festival.
VHS: S20908. $29.95.

Boulez in Salzburg
This concert video captures Pierre Boulez's premier performance leading the Vienna Philharmonic at the 1992 Salzburg Festival. Works by Stravinsky, Debussy, Bartok and a piece by Boulez make up this exciting program. 94 mins.
VHS: S24261. $29.95.
Laser: LD74843. $34.95.

Brahms Quartets
Demonstrates how a record is made and features the Brahms *Piano Quartets op. 25* and *op. 26*.
Laser: LD74567. $29.98.

Brahms Sextets
Features the Brahms *Sextets op. 18* and *op. 36* as it shows how a record is made.
Laser: LD74566. $29.98.

Brahms—Klassix 13
Anthony Quayle and Balint Vaszonyi host this drama about the life of Brahms, from his tavern brawls to the writing of his first symphony, to his hopeless love for Clara Schumann. 60 mins.
VHS: S10896. $24.95.

Brahms: German Requiem (Ein Deutches Requiem)
Herbert von Karajan conducts the Berlin Philharmonic in this performance of Brahms' German Requiem.
Laser: LD70178. $34.95.

Brahms: Piano Concerto No. 1 and No. 2 (Bernstein)
Leonard Bernstein conducts the Vienna Philharmonic with pianist Krystian Zimmerman.
VHS: S18538. $24.95.
Laser: LD70891. $39.95.

Brahms: Symphony No. 1 (Ozawa)
Seiji Ozawa conducts the Saito Kinen orchestra's recording of Brahms' first symphony. "The performance maintains a sense of lyrical continuity even when most impassioned" (*The New York Times*). 60 mins.
Laser: LD71545. $29.95.

Brahms: Symphony No. 1 and No. 2 (Karajan)
Herbert Von Karajan conducts the Berlin Philharmonic in Brahms' first two symphonies. 86 mins.
VHS: S17430. $24.95.
Laser: LD71754. $34.95.

Brahms: Symphony No. 3 and No. 4 (Karajan)
The two Brahms symphonies are conducted by Herbert von Karajan and performed by the Berlin Philharmonic Orchestra. 74 mins.
Laser: LD71796. $34.95.

Brendel on Beethoven
In his London home, Alfred Brendel shares his thoughts on Beethoven's sonatas. Then Brendel performs the *Tempest* sonata. Filmed for the BBC. 59 mins.
VHS: S24688. $29.95.

Bridging the Silence
The 1996 strike by members of the Philadelphia Orchestra stilled one of the world's greatest orchestral ensembles. This strike benefit concert brought the musicians back together. This videocassette is the first and only video featuring what many music lovers believe to be America's greatest orchestra. The program of orchestral showpieces, under the expert guidance of conductor Luis Blava, demonstrates the legendary "Philadelphia Sound." 118 mins.
VHS: S31874. $19.95.

Bruckner: Symphony No. 8
Herbert von Karajan conducts the Vienna Philharmonic in a performance of the Bruckner *Symphony No. 8*. In Hi-fi Stereo, 85 mins.
Laser: LD74564. $34.98.

Bruckner: Symphony No. 9
Herbert von Karajan conducts this work with the Berlin Philharmonic.
Laser: LD74584. $34.98.

Bruckner: Symphony No. 9 in D Minor, Te Deum (Vienna)
Herbert von Karajan directed the filming of this 1978 performance in addition to conducting the Vienna Philharmonic Orchestra and Chorus with soloists Anna Tomowa-Sintow, Agnes Baltsa, David Kendall and Jose van Dam. In Hi-Fi stereo, 89 mins.
Laser: LD71465. $34.95.

Bruno Walter: The Maestro, The Man
A rare treasure from the archives of the CBC, Toronto. One of the major musical influences of the 20th century, the legendary maestro Bruno Walter rehearses Brahms' *Symphony No. 2* with the Vancouver International Festival Orchestra and discusses his art with respected music critic Albert Goldberg. This video presents the most extended footage of the esteemed conductor ever available. A must for all fans of the art of conducting.
VHS: S31165. $29.95.
1958, 60 mins.

Burning Poles: Cecil Taylor in Performance
"The American aesthetic landscape is full of idiosyncratic marvels: poet Walt Whitman, the composer Charles Ives, filmmaker D.W. Griffith, the painter Jackson Pollock, and the searing, visionary pianist Cecil Taylor. His playing has been said to resemble Niagara Falls, a volcano, a great river, thunderheads, a high wind, a cannonade, a stampede" (*The New Yorker*). 60 mins.
VHS: S14718. $19.95.

Canadian Brass: Home Movies
The popular Canadian Brass in an entertaining retrospective of their home movies, archival footage, live arrangements and musical performances. The show includes "Thus Spake Zarathustra", "Amazing Grace" and "Pachelbel's Canon". 53 mins.
VHS: S19105. $24.95.
Laser: LD71894. $29.95.

Carlos Kleiber: Mozart Symphony No. 36 and Brahms Symphony No. 2
On the occasion of the 150th anniversary of the Vienna Philharmonic Kleiber conducted this world-renowned orchestra in these two works.
VHS: S18453. $29.95.
Laser: LD71867. $34.95.

A Celebration in Vienna
Leonard Bernstein wrote, narrated, performed and conducted this special program on Beethoven's 200th birthday, with excerpts from *Piano Concerto 1 in C Major*, the "Ode to Joy", and rehearsal and scenes from *Fidelio*. Soloists include Placido Domingo, Gwyneth Jones and Shirley Verret, with the Vienna Philharmonic and the Vienna State Opera Chorus. 90 mins.
VHS: S17313. $29.95.

A Century of Russian Music
A glorious concert video starring Maxim Shostakovich and Viktoria Mullova, recorded live with the London Symphony Orchestra. Glinka, Tchaikovsky and Shostakovich, whose music is synonymous with the heritage of Russian composition, are presented, including performances of Glinka's overture to "Russlan and Ludmila," Tchaikovsky's "Violin Concerto", and Shostakovich conducting the orchestra in a brilliant rendition of his father's response to political repression, the "Symphony No. 5". 95 mins.
VHS: S11543. $19.95.

Charles Ives: Good Dissonance Like a Man
Dramatized biography of the great American composer Charles Ives, which blends words with music and photography to create a moving portrait of the artist. Peabody Award winner. 60 mins.
VHS: S04151. $39.95.

Christmas at Ripon Cathedral
Ripon Cathedral, founded in 664 A.D., is the second oldest Christian place of worship in Great Britain. It is the perfect setting for this inspirational program which features some of Britain's finest musical talents, including Dame Janet Baker, the Huddersfield Choral Society and the Black Dyke Mills Band, performing traditional Christmas music. The cathedral's own choir also sings five beautiful Christmas carols. 60 mins.
Laser: LD70328. $34.95.

Christmas Goes Baroque
Subtitled *Performed in the Style of Bach, Handel and Vivaldi*, this heartwarming Christmas show alternates scenes from Zurich, Switzerland, with musical selections including "Silent Night," "Alle Jahre Wieder," "God Rest Ye Merry Gentlemen," and "O Tannenbaum." With the CSSR State Philharmonic Orchestra, conducted by Peter Breiner.
Laser: LD72245. $29.95.

Classic Views Video Magazine, Volume 2
This is the first magazine on video for opera and classical music lovers. Includes performances, interviews and critics' samples of the best of today's classical music scene. Features of the second volume include: "In Homage: Dmitry Sitkovetsky's Goldberg Variations," "On Reflection: Bryn Terfel," "New Directions: Bobby McFerrin," "Opera on Video: Martin Bernheimer," "On Reflection: John Adams," "Critic's Choice: William Livingstone," "Past Masters: Alexander Nevsky," and "Divertimento: Opera Imaginaire's La Traviata." 95 mins.
VHS: S30131. $9.95.

Classical Christmas
An opulent video presentation with music interpreted through scenes of nature's winter, and classical images from Christmas season, as well as the historic artwork of Currier and Ives. Highlights include "Deck the Halls," "Joy to the World," "Nutcracker Suite," "Silent Night," and "Messiah" selections. 30 mins.
VHS: S05618. $19.95.

Classical Images—A Concert in Nature
Visual interpretations of all-time favorites, including Mozart, Tchaikovsky and Debussy, performed to spectacular visual looks a nature. The New Philharmonic Orchestra performs. 45 mins.
VHS: S04679. $29.95.

Classical Music from Moscow
These programs cater to classical music enthusiasts, celebrating Shostakovich's and Tchaikovsky's artistic achievement and savoring the performances of their compositions. 110 mins.
VHS: S12724. $19.98.

Claudio Arrau—Volumes 1, 2, 3, 4
Widely regarded as one of the great pianists of the century, these historic performances capture Arrau in interpretations of Beethoven's *Emperor Concerto*, and compositions by Liszt, Chopin, Debussy.
Volume 1.
VHS: Out of print. For rental only.
Volume 2.
VHS: S07690. $29.95.
Volume 3.
VHS: S07691. $29.95.
Volume 4.
VHS: S07692. $29.95.

The Cleveland Orchestra: A Portrait of George Szell
This *Bell Telephone Hour* television episode presents a portrait of conductor George Szell. He brought the Cleveland Orchestra to a high standard recognized the world over. Szell's rehearsal of Beethoven's *Symphony No. 5* is especially indicative of his artistic ability. 60 mins.
VHS: S22439. $24.95.

The Cleveland Quartet
The Cleveland Quartet performs Beethoven's *String Quartet in D dur (Op. 18, no. 3)* and Brahms' *Quintet with Piano (Op. 34)*. As a special feature, the celebrated Cleveland Quartet performs Brahms' *Quintet with Piano (Op. 34)* on Paganini's own treasured and virtually priceless Stradivariuses.
VHS: S27197. $14.95.

Concert Aid
Originally produced by Oxfam, this is a spectacular recording of Beethoven's Symphony No. 5 performed by the BBC Symphony Orchestra with Sir Georg Solti conducting. Since 1942, Oxfam has worked with the poor around the world, and all of the profits from the performances for the cassette were donated. 40 mins.
VHS: S04681. $19.95.

Das Konzert
This powerful musical event captures the triumphant concert of Daniel Barenboim and the Berlin Philharmonic that greeted the fall of the Berlin Wall. *Beethoven's Symphony No. 7* and *Piano Concerto No. 1* are on this program. 112 mins.
Laser: LD74557. $29.98.

David Oistrakh in Performance

Virtuoso violinist David Oistrakh masterfully interprets works by Leclair, Prokofiev, Shostakovich, Kreisler, Debussy and Ravel in this rare filmed performance in 1962. 52 mins.
VHS: S09225. $19.95.

David Oistrakh: Remembering a Musician

In rare footage from the musical archives of the Soviet Union, Oistrakh plays scintillating and emotional performances of such works as the intermezzo movement from Lalo's "Symphonie Espagole," excerpts from Shostakovich's F minor Sonata and other works. 60 mins.
VHS: S03166. $39.95.

The Debussy Etudes Performed and Discussed by Mitsuko Uchida

Piano virtuoso Mitsuko Uchida performs the etudes and provides commentary. In Hi-Fi stereo, 70 mins.
VHS: S16047. $29.95.
Laser: LD71190. $34.95.

Diane Bish—Classic Organ Favorites

An hour of continuous classical favorites performed on organs around the world. 60 mins.
VHS: S34266. $19.95.

Diane Bish—Favorite Hymns of Faith

Diane Bish presents an hour of favorite hymns played on the great organs of the world. 60 mins.
VHS: S34267. $19.95.

Diane Bish—J.S. Bach Favorites for Organ

An hour of continuous Bach music for organ.
VHS: S34268. $19.95.

Diane Bish—Mozart: The Man & His Music

The life of Mozart is highlighted as Diane Bish plays his music in locations around the world.
VHS: S34269. $19.95.

Discovering the Music of the Middle Ages

All walks of life, from the nobles and the clergy to the peasants, found music an indispensable part of life during the Middle Ages. It was played in church, in the castle and in the village. 20 mins.
VHS: S23517. $49.95.

Dvorak in Prague: A Celebration

Yo-Yo Ma, Itzhak Perlman, Frederica von Stade, Seiji Ozawa and the Boston Symphony Orchestra join forces on the occasion of the 100-year anniversary of Dvorak's *New World Symphony*. A variety of his music is performed in this Sony production set in Prague.
VHS: S21073. $24.98.

Early Musical Instruments

The authentic, complete and fascinating guide to the instruments of Henry the Eighth, Gabrieli, Byrd, Purcell, Bach and Mozart—shawm, bibiou, dulzaina, zampogna, crumhorn, gemhorn, tromba—the whole range of instruments which are ancestors to the modern instruments. The six-part series is narrated by David Munrow, one of the pioneering authorities on early music, and performed by the Early Music Consort of London, with Christopher Hogwood.

Bowed Instruments. In the 11th century, European musicians tried to make their instruments sound like the human voice; instead of plucking the strings, they began drawing a piece of wood or bone across them to sustain the tone. By Elizabethan times, the viol was the aristocrat of bowed instruments.
VHS: S05594. $29.95.

Flutes and Whistles. The first musical instruments developed when primitive man used tubes of bamboo, bone or wood to produce whistling sounds, later applied to create a wide range of folk and concert instruments.
VHS: S05591. $29.95.

Keyboard and Percussion. A close look at such rarities as the dulcimer and the hurdy-gurdy, as well as better-known instruments like the organ, harpsichord and kettledrums.
VHS: S05593. $29.95.

Plucked Instruments. The roots and foreign branches of the guitar family tree, and a good look at the more important of the many relatives of this instrument.
VHS: S05592. $29.95.

Reed Instruments. The development of reeds from those played loudly by the Saracens to frighten the horses of the Crusaders, to the 17th century forerunners of today's orchestra.
VHS: S05590. $29.95.

Complete six-volume set.
VHS: S05589. $149.00.

Erick Friedman Plays Fritz Kreisler

Friedman plays the works of the beloved Kreisler, the recital consisting of ten selections, including the ever-popular "The Old Refrain." 90 mins.
VHS: S03150. $39.95.

Four American Composers

Unique musical profiles, directed by Peter Greenaway (*Drowning by Numbers, The Cook, the Thief, His Wife and Her Lover*), that offer startling and intimate insights into the music and ideas of four very original American composers. Greenaway takes as his starting point performances given by the artists in London and creates an exciting musical experience. Four volumes.

(1) John Cage. 60 mins.
VHS: S14720. $19.95.
(2) Philip Glass. 60 mins.
VHS: S14721. $19.95.
(3) Meredith Monk. 60 mins.
VHS: S14722. $29.95.
(4) Robert Ashley. 60 mins.
VHS: S14723. $19.95.
Complete four-volume set. 60 mins.
VHS: S14719. $69.95.

The Four Seasons

Antonio Vivaldi's *Four Seasons* is combined with the beautiful countryside of Switzerland in this award-winning presentation. Excellent for music appreciation classes. 14 mins.
VHS: S23503. $49.95.

Four Ways to Say Farewell

In an essay illustrated with rehearsal scenes, Leonard Bernstein offers a moving, lucid analysis of Gustav Mahler's *Ninth Symphony*. The Vienna Philharmonic Orchestra is featured. 57 mins.
VHS: S26794. $19.95.

Frederich Gulda/Mozart No End and the Paradise Band

Gulda is a famed classical musician and jazz performer whose unique interpretations are well-regarded. In this video he presents his own treatments of Mozart works, including *The Marriage of Figaro, Coronation Concerto* and *Piano Sonata in C*, together with his own original works. 96 mins.
Laser: LD74556. $29.98.

From Mao to Mozart

This is the document of the visit of Isaac Stern to the People's Republic of China in 1979. Mr. Stern happily exercised his musical passport to share the best of western classical music with the people of China. Featuring the music of Mozart.
Laser: LD70996. $39.95.
Murray Lerner, USA, 1980, 84 mins.

Gala Tribute to Tchaikovsky

Famed opera singers Kiri Te Kanawa and Placido Domingo join a host of ballet stars like Vivian Durante and conductors Sir Edward Downes, Stephen Barlow and Barry Wordsworth to perform selected highlights of music by Tchaikovsky, Rachmaninoff and Rimsky-Korsakov. 135 mins.
VHS: S21053. $29.95.

George Frederick Handel: Honour, Profit and Pleasure

A remarkable portrait of Handel in the cultural and social context of the England in which he created—and which his creations mirror. Portrayed by Simon Callow, Handel emerges as an extraordinary musician with ordinary motivations.
VHS: S05587. $29.95.

George Gershwin Remembered

A documentary about George Gershwin. The film examines Gershwin's origins in ragtime and Tin Pan Alley through his work on Broadway and in American films, including *Porgy and Bess, An American in Paris, Rhapsody in Blue, Concerto in F* and *Strike Up the Band*. 90 mins.
VHS: S19109. $19.95.

Glenn Branca: Symphony No. 4

Documentary of the musician's European tour with performance footage and music.
VHS: S10193. $19.95.
Arleen Schloss, USA, 1984, 10 mins.

The Glenn Gould Collection

A remarkable series of videos charting the unique career of music's idiosyncratic genius.

Program I: Prologue. Features Beethoven's *Piano Sonata No. 31* (Third Movement), an excerpt from Bach's *Partita No. 2*, the announcement of Glenn Gould's death, Gould discussing Russian music and performing Beethoven's *Eroica Variations*, Bach's *Well-Tempered Clavier II: Prelude and Fugue* and Sir William Walton's *Facade: Scotch Rhapsody*.
VHS: S21936. $29.98.

Program II: Sonatas and Dialogues. Gould in conversation with Yehudi Menuhin and then performing Bach's *Violin Sonata No. 4*, Beethoven's *Sonata for Piano and Violin No. 10*, and Schoenberg's *Phantasy for Violin and Piano Accompaniment*.
VHS: S21937. $29.98.

Program III: End of Concerts. Gould talks about concerts and Paul Hindemith, appears as Karl-Heinz Klopweiser, and performs Bach's *Partita No. 5*, Sweelinck's *Fantasia in D*, Beethoven's *Bagatelle op. 126, no. 3*, Krenek's *Wanderlied im Herbst*, Bach's *Well-Tempered Clavier II: Fugue BWV 891*, Beethoven's *Piano Sonata No. 17* and the fourth movement of Hindemith's *Sonata No. 3*.
VHS: S21938. $29.98.

Program IV: So You Want to Write a Fugue? Gould talks about Beethoven and appears in his "So You Want to Write a Fugue?". He is also shown performing Bach's *Well-Tempered Clavier II: Fugue BWV 876*, Berg's *Piano Sonata op. 1*, Beethoven's *Piano Sonata No. 30*, Bach's *Piano Concerto No. 7* and Bach's *Well-Tempered Clavier II: Prelude and Fugue BWV 878*.
VHS: S21939. $29.98.

Program V: The Conductor. Glenn Gould appears as Sir Nigel Thwitt-Thornwaite, talks about Wava and conducts the Russell Oberlin Orchestra in Bach's *Cantata "Widerstehe doch der Stunde" BWV 43, excerpts from Beethoven's Symphony No. 6, Pastorale* and Bach's *Brandenburg Concerto No. 5*.
VHS: S21940. $29.98.

Program VI: The Earliest Decade. Gould is the soloist in Bach's *Piano Concerto No. 1 BWV 1052*, the first movement of Beethoven's *Piano Concerto No. 1* and Beethoven's *32 Variations*.
VHS: S21941. $29.98.

Program VII: A Russian Interlude. Gould performs Prokofiev's *Visions fugitives No. 2* and *Piano Concerto No. 2*, Scriabin's *Preludes op. 33* and *op. 45*, and Shostakovich's *Piano Quintet op. 57*.
VHS: S21942. $29.98.

Program VIII: Interweaving Voices. Gould performs Bach's *Art of the Fugue BWV 1080 Contrapunctus IV*, Beethoven's *Variations op. 34*, Hindemith's *Das Marienleben: Argwohn Josephs*, Webern's *Piano Variations op. 27* and Beethoven's *Sonata for Piano and Cello No. 3* (with cellist Leonard Rose).
VHS: S21943. $29.98.

Program IX: Mostly Strauss. Gould talks about Strauss and Mozart, and is seen performing Strauss's *Cacilie*, Mozart's *Piano Sonata No. 13* and Strauss's *Burleske for Piano and Orchestra*.
VHS: S21944. $29.98.

Program X: Rhapsodic Interludes. Glenn Gould talks about *Elektra*, discusses *La Valse*, and performs the transcription of an excerpt from Schubert's *Symphony No. 5*, the piano transcription of an excerpt from Strauss's *Elektra*, Schoenberg's *Pierrot Lunaire*, Ravel's *La Valse*, Debussy's *Premiere Rhapsodie pour Clarinette* and Strauss's *Violin Sonata op. 18, 1st Movement*.
VHS: S21945. $29.98.

Program XI: Ecstasy and Wit. Glenn Gould appears as Myron Chianti, talks about Richard Strauss and performs Beethoven's *Piano Sonata No. 17, op. 31, no. 2, Der Sturm*, Scriabin's *Prelude op. 49, no. 2*, Strauss's *3 Ophelia-Lieder op. 67*, Bach's *Goldberg Variations BWV 988* and Casella's *Ricercare No. 1 on B-A-C-H*.
VHS: S21946. $29.98.

Program XII: Epilogue. Glenn Gould discusses *The Emperor Concerto* and performs Bach's *The Well-Tempered Clavier II: Prelude and Fugue BWV 872* and *Prelude and Fugue BWV 891*, and Beethoven's *Piano Concerto No. 5, The Emperor*.
VHS: S21947. $29.98.

Program XIII: The Goldberg Variations: Glenn Gould in Conversation with Bruno Monsaingeon. Gould's first recording of the Goldberg Variations in 1951 was a revelation. It displayed something essential about the creative process and made him a legend besides. Now a film shot in 1981 brings this musician's career full circle. 59 mins.
VHS: S23928. $29.98.

Program XIV: The Question of Instrument: Glenn Gould in Conversation with Bruno Monsaingeon. Gould takes up a key question regarding the original instruments movement: should Bach's work be played on a harpsichord or on a piano, an instrument developed only after Bach's time? This great pianist and thinker offers some provocative insights. 57 mins.
VHS: S23929. $29.98.

Program XV: An Art of the Fugue: Glenn Gould in Conversation with Bruno Monsaingeon. Bach perfected the fugue, a compositional technique of interweaving of voices. Master pianist Glenn Gould explores the philosophical underpinnings of the fugue and its importance beyond music.
VHS: S23930. $29.98.

Program XVI: On the Twentieth Century: Glenn Gould Talks About and Plays Music by Sriabin, Schoenberg, Webern, Strauss, and Hindemith. From the romanticism of Strauss to the scientifically inspired tonal system of Schoenberg, Gould performed the music of this century with passion and conviction. This is a fascinating program of contemporary works. 58 mins.
VHS: S23931. $29.98.

Glenn Gould Collection: Laser

Two programs are featured on each laser disc.

Program I and Program II.
Laser: LD74532. $29.98.
Program III and Program IV.
Laser: LD74533. $29.98.
Program V and Program VI.
Laser: LD74534. $29.98.
Program VII and Program VIII.
Laser: LD74535. $29.98.
Program IX and Program X.
Laser: LD74536. $29.98.
Program XI and Program XII.
Laser: LD74537. $29.98.

Glenn Gould Plays Beethoven

After decades of silence, Glenn Gould is suddenly being rediscovered, perhaps because of the wonderful Canadian biopic *32 Short Films About Glenn Gould*. The newest release is *Glenn Gould Plays Beethoven*, a wonderful concert for Beethoven fans and Gould fans alike. Gould plays *The Emperor Concerto*, *Bagatelle (Op. 26 No. 3)* and the *F-Minor Variations (Op. 34)*. 60 mins.
VHS: S27195. $19.95.

Glenn Gould's Greatest Hits

Highlights from the Glenn Gould Collection include Gould playing Bach's *Goldberg Variations BWV 98*; the *Violin Sonata No. 4, 2nd movement* (with Yehudi Menuhin), Beethoven's *Bagatelle op. 126* and *2nd movement of Sonata for Piano and Cello No. 3* (with Lenn Rose). Then Gould does "So You Want to Write a Fugue." He appears as Sir Nigel Thwitt-Thornwaite, conducts Mahler's *Ulricht*, and plays Walton's *Facade: Scotch Rhapsody* and Scriabin's *Prelude op. 49*.
VHS: S21948. $29.98.
Laser: LD74538. $29.98.

Glenn Gould: Two Portraits

This historic profile of the celebrated pianist comprises two 30-minute programs filmed at the time of Gould's sensational debut upon the music scene. This fascinating glimpse of his early years features a rare studio performance of Gould recording Bach's *Italian Concerto*. 60 mins.
VHS: S30881. $29.95.

Glory of Spain

Tribute to the art and music of Spain, shot at the Prado Museum, and featuring performances by soprano Victoria de los Angeles, pianist Alicia de la Rocha, and guitarist Andres Segovia. Composers Falla, Granados, and Albeniz are featured, along with masterpieces by El Greco, Velazquez and Goya.
VHS: S03216. $49.95.

Going on Fifty

A look at the private and professional life of conductor Zubin Mehta and his work as the musical director of the Israeli Philharmonic Orchestra. 60 mins.
VHS: S07768. $39.95.

Grand Duo: Itzhak Perlman and Pinchas Zukerman

Filmmaker Christopher Nupen captures the 1976 European tour of violinists Itzhak Perlman and Pinchas Zukerman. Filmed at the Royal College of Music in London, selections include Wieniawski's *Etudes Caprices, Opus 18*, Spohr's *Duo Concertante, Opus 67*, Leclair's *Sonata, Opus 3*, Handel/Halvorsen's *Passacaglia in G minor*, Mozart's *Duo No. 1 in G major* and Wieniawski's *Caprice in A minor*. In Hi-Fi Stereo, 90 mins.
VHS: S16512. $29.97.
Laser: LD71460. $34.97.

Great Music from Chicago

Andre Kostelanetz conducts the Chicago Symphony Orchestra. Selections include "Polovetzian Dances" by Borodin, "The Mother Goose Suite" by Ravel, "Rhapsody Espana" by Emanuel Chabrier, and "Intermezzo" by Samuel Barber. Ken Nordine is the program's host. USA, 1957, 55 mins.
VHS: S05519. $24.95.

Great Solos with James Galway and Friends

Presented by the United Nations High Commission for Refugees, this inspiring 1989 Classic Aid Gala Concert from UNESCO in Paris features the brilliant James Galway and the incomparable Lorin Maazel conducting the National Orchestra of France, joined by an international roster of some of the world's most revered musicians and their proteges, including Larry Adler, Yefim Bronfman, Julian Lloyd Weber, Alexis Weissenberg, and others, dedicating their masterful performances to the millions of refugees the world over. 51 mins.
VHS: S30253. $19.98.

The Guarneri Quartet

This world-famous quartet plays two works to the accompaniment of piano soloist Mikhail Rudy, Mozart's *String Quartet in D Dur, K.575* and Brahms's *Quartet No. 1 for Piano and Strings, Op. 25*. The performances captured on this tape testify to the enduring reputation of The Guarneri Quartet. 68 mins.
VHS: S27567. $14.95.

Guitarra

A two-tape series featuring world-renowned classical guitarist Julian Bream, who traces the evolution of the Spanish guitar from 1500 to the present day. Bream plays against a backdrop of the magnificent old buildings and panoramic landscapes of Spain, creating a visual evocation of the culture that spawned this special music. 205 mins.
VHS: S01838. $39.95.

Haydn at Esterhaza Hogwood

Includes a brief documentary that outlines Haydn's remarkable career, followed by a collection of superb performances featuring three complete Haydn symphonies brought to life by conductor Christopher Hogwood and The Academy of Ancient Music. 106 mins.
VHS: S15631. $24.95.
Laser: LD70277. $34.95.

Haydn: Cello Concerto No. 1 and No. 2

Mstislav Rostropovich is the soloist and conductor of the Academy of St. Martin in the Fields in this performance.
Laser: LD71030. $34.95.

Heifetz Master Classes

Maestro Jascha Heifetz, this century's greatest violinist, becomes Professor Heifetz in these rare, filmed seminars from the early 1960's taken from his legendary workshops at USC. The brilliant musician can be seen coaxing, cajoling, inspiring and occasionally terrifying his pupils as he imparts his unquestioned genius and lifetime of musical experience. Learn the secrets of intonation, phrasing and vibrato from the man whose name has become synonymous with the violin. Part 2 contains never-before-released footage showing Heifetz in a rare, humorous parody of a violin student giving an audition.

Heifetz Master Classes Part I. 120 mins.
VHS: S12772. $49.95.
Heifetz Master Classes Part II. 120 mins.
VHS: S12773. $49.95.
Heifetz Master Classes Pre-Pack. Both volumes (240 mins.) of the Heifetz Master Classes at a special combined price.
VHS: S12774. $79.95.

Hermann Scherchen: In Rehearsal—Bach's Art of the Fugue

The great conductor Hermann Scherchen (1891-1966) was throughout his life absorbed with Bach's Art of the Fugue. After years of conducting Graeser's and Vuataz's versions, he composed his own orchestration, which he then performed during the last 12 months of his life. In 1965, the CBC filmed Scherchen's rehearsal of the work with the CBC Toronto Chamber Orchestra and Kenneth Gilbert, harpsichord. 58 mins.
VHS: S31873. $29.95.

High Fidelity

From the director of *From Mao to Mozart* comes this fascinating journey with the Guarneri String Quartet on their recent world tour. *High Fidelity* celebrates the 25 years the quite diverse Guarneri members have managed to stay together to become among the most long-lived, most successful and most popular string quartets in the world. "Pure pleasure" (Vincent Canby).
VHS: S12825. $39.95.
Allan Miller, USA, 1989, 85 mins.

Hoffnung Festival Concert

Music lovers everywhere have delighted in the special madcap parody contrived by Gerald Hoffnung in this gala evening of symphonic caricature featuring the Hoffnung Festival Orchestra. 59 mins.
VHS: S09828. $29.95.

Horszowski: Live at Carnegie Hall

A rare concert performance by the late pianist Mieczyslaw Horszowski as he plays Bach, Beethoven, Schumann, Chopin and Mendelssohn. 94 mins.
Laser: LD71926. $34.97.

Huberman Festival

This series of stereo programs won the Best Program of the Year Award, and features Isaac Stern, Itzhak Perlman, Pinchas Zuckerman, Shlomo Mintz, Henryk Szeryng, Ivy Giltis and Ira Haendel, and Zubin Mehta conducting the Israel Philharmonic Orchestra. Each is 45 minutes.

Volume 2: Mozart: Sinfonia Concertante and Handel: Passcaglia.
VHS: S06399. $19.95.
Volume 3: Tchaikovsky: Concerto in D Minor and Vivaldi: Concerto in A Minor.
VHS: S06400. $19.95.
Volume 4: Mendelssohn: Concerto in E Minor and Bach: Concerto in D Minor.
VHS: S06401. $19.95.
Volume 5: Bach: Brandenburg Concerto No. 6 and Vivaldi: Concerto in B Minor.
VHS: S06402. $19.95.

Igor Stravinsky

A fascinating and intimate 1965 portrait, chronicling a week in the life of one of the most important composers of the century. Stravinsky is seen reminiscing about his life and travelling with his wife aboard ship en route to Hamburg. The highlight of the program is a recording session of Stravinsky conducting his *Symphony of Psalms*, "a vivid demonstration of the process" (*The New York Times*). A rare glimpse of the master and his extraordinary life. 50 mins.
VHS: S32424. $29.95.

Igor Stravinsky's Symphony of Psalms

Stravinsky found inspiration in sources ranging from Greek Orthodox Liturgy to the 19th century composer Verdi. Now this singular work has been preserved on video, capturing its innovative and abstract sounds. 30 mins.
VHS: S22930. $19.95.

In Celebration of the Piano

An all-star tribute to the Steinway piano taped live at Carnegie Hall, and hosted by Van Cliburn. Performances by Murray Perahia, Alfred Brendel, Rudolf Serkin, Alexis Weissenberg, Lazar Berman and 20 others! 100 mins.
VHS: S13241. $39.95.

In Concert: Karl Bohm & Jon Vickers

Complete 1965 live concert from the archives of the CBC, Toronto, features the interpretive brilliance of maestro Karl Bohm and the profound artistry of tenor Jon Vickers. Bohm conducts Mozart's *"Haffner" Symphony*, Beethoven's *Leonore Overture*, and Wagner's *Die Meistersinger* Prelude; Vickers sings Florestan's aria from *Fidelio*, and two arias of Siegmund from *Die Walkure*. With the Toronto Symphony Orchestra.
VHS: S31166. $29.95.
1965, 60 mins.

In the Steps of Chopin: Portrait by Byron Janis

Janis takes us through the stations in Chopin's life, demonstrating the pianistic techniques Chopin taught his pupils, examining differences between manuscript and published versions of some of the pieces, and showing both his technical virtuosity and exceptional affinity with Chopin in performances of a broad range of Chopin pieces.
VHS: S05586. $29.95.

Inspired by Bach: Yo-Yo Ma

Six-part PBS broadcast teams the celebrated cellist with celebrated filmmakers and artists from a variety of disciplines. Each film embarks on an exploration on of Bach's solo cello suites. Each tape is 55 mins.

Inspired by Bach: Yo-Yo Ma—Suite No. 1: The Music Garden. Yo-Yo Ma and garden designer Julie Moir Messervy journey from Boston to Toronto.
VHS: S33919. $24.98.
Inspired by Bach: Yo-Yo Ma—Suite No. 2: The Sound of the Carcieri. 18th-century master architect Giovanni Battista Piransi's dazzling prison etchings are brought to life in a computer-rendered, 3-D, virtual collaboration. Directed by Francois Girard (*32 Short Films About Glenn Gould*).
VHS: S33920. $24.98.
Inspired by Bach: Yo-Yo Ma—Suite No. 3: Falling Down Stairs. This collaboration between choreographer Mark Morris and Yo-Yo Ma yields an astonishing dance.
VHS: S33921. $24.98.
Inspired by Bach: Yo-Yo Ma—Suite No. 4: Sarabande. Director Atom Egoyan (*The Sweet Hereafter*) creates a dramatic film built on a series of encounters and coincidences.
VHS: S33922. $24.98.
Inspired by Bach: Yo-Yo Ma—Suite No. 5: Struggle for Hope. Master Kabuki actor Tamasaburo Bando sets out on a revelatory cross-cultural journey to discover, through traditional Japanese dance, the universality and emotion of Bach's suite.
VHS: S33923. $24.98.
Inspired by Bach: Yo-Yo Ma—Suite No. 6: Six Gestures. Olympic ice skating champions Torville and Dean join Yo-Yo Ma in this film that takes its inspiration from Bach's life as filtered through Ma's masterful performance.
VHS: S33924. $24.98.

The Instrumental Artistry of Vishwa Mohan Bhatt

A combined concert video and self-portrait of an artist who alerted the West to the guitar's radical and new possibilities within India's classical music tradition. Bhatt, accompanied by tabla master Sukhvinder Singh Namadhari, performs four ragas and a folk tune. 90 mins.
VHS: S31758. $29.95.

Isaac Stern: A Life

This video documents the 70th year of the great violinist Isaac Stern. He was honored in his hometown of San Francisco with an endowed chair and a concert for 30,000 people. But this video also shows the busy season performed by Stern, as it follows him across the world performing his favorite works by Beethoven. Gregory Peck narrates. 122 mins.
VHS: S26003. $29.98.

Israel in Egypt

The Jerusalem Symphony Orchestra, under the direction of John Currie, performs "The Exodus" and "Songs of the Sea" on the shore of the Red Sea directly across from Pharaoh's Island. The Scottish National Choir and the Edinburgh Festival Choir sing. Includes English subtitles of the oratorio text. 90 mins.
VHS: S26107. $29.95.

Israel Philharmonic Welcomes Berlin Philharmonic
Zubin Mehta, music director for life of the Israel Philharmonic, brought these two great musical forces together in Tel Aviv. It was an historic moment, cementing a new era in unity and peace. A Sony Music production. 98 mins.
Laser: LD74553. $29.98.

Itzhak Perlman: Virtuoso Violinist
A Christopher Nupen film about virtuoso violinist Itzhak Perlman, who first resolved to play the violin at age 3½ and who went on, despite setbacks, to become an international star of the highest rank. The film was shot during 1975-1977, crucial years in the development of his career.
VHS: S37092. $29.97.
Laser: LD76834. $34.97.
Christopher Nupen, Great Britain, 1978, 80 mins.

IvoPogorelich in Castello Reale di Racconigi
Ivo Pogorelich performs works by Chopin, Mozart and Haydn.
VHS: S18539. $24.95.
Laser: LD71029. $34.99.

Ivo Pogorelich: In Villa Contarini
Pianist Ivo Pogorelich performs music of the 19th century. Includes works by: Scriabin, Chopin (Sonata #2, Polonaise Op. 44) and others. 52 mins.
VHS: S14963. $30.95.

Jacqueline du Pre and the Elgar Cello Concerto
Du Pre performs this lyrical concerto with Daniel Barenboim and the New Philharmonia Orchestra. An intimate portrait of a legendary musician.
VHS: S15460. $29.98.
Laser: LD70218. $34.98.

John Cage: Man and Myth
An intimate visit with the sage of conceptual music and collage poetry. At ease and affable, Cage discusses his new pursuits, theories, memories and friends. Includes several compositions. Directed by Mitch Corber. 60 mins.
VHS: S14104. $49.95.

John Kim Bell: A Profile of the First North American Indian Conductor
John Kim Bell tells the story of a talented and passionate young man who broke through social barriers. From his 1981 conducting debut with the Toronto Symphony to associate to Zubin Mehta of the New York Philharmonic, *John Kim Bell* is a cinematic portrait of a vibrant and charismatic conductor. 41 mins.
VHS: S04682. $29.95.

Karajan Conducts
Herbert von Karajan conducts the Berlin Philharmonic in a series of lighter works, including pieces by Verdi, Bizet, Liszt, Weber and Wagner. 78 mins.
VHS: S17127. $24.95.
Laser: LD71543. $34.95.

Karajan in Salzburg
Susan Froemke and Peter Gelb follow the famous conductor in Salzburg; cinematography by Edward Lachmann.
Laser: LD71074. $34.95.

Karajan: Early Images, Vol. 2 (1965-66)
An anthology of Herbert von Karajan's work with the Vienna Symphony Orchestra. The highlights are Karajan's rehearsal for Schumann's *Symphony No. 4*, and a performance of Mozart's *Concerto for Violin and Orchestra, No. 5*, with Yehudi Menuhin. The film is directed by the important French filmmaker Henri-Georges Clouzot (*The Wages of Fear*).
Laser: LD72002. $34.95.
Henri-Georges Clouzot, France, 89 mins.

Karel Ancerl: In Rehearsal and Performance
The legendary Czech conductor rehearses and performs Smetana's *The Moldau* with the Toronto Symphony Orchestra. This 1969 CBC television production was made just before Ancerl assumed his post as director of the Toronto Symphony. 57 mins.
VHS: S33043. $29.95.

Karl Bohm: The Birth of a Symphony
The legendary conductor directs the CBC Festival Orchestra in a rehearsal segment and complete performance of Beethoven's *7th Symphony*. Historic 1963 CBC telecast. 57 mins.
VHS: S33042. $29.95.

Kyoto Vivaldi: The Four Seasons
Antonio Vivaldi's baroque masterpiece is one of the most popular classical pieces of all time and receives a stunning performance by the Japanese Kyoto Ensemble, with the ancient capital city of Kyoto serving as background for this visual discovery. This unique video interpretation of Vivaldi's timeless classic adds a new dimension to the classic. 45 mins.
VHS: S03821. $19.95.

Landowska: Uncommon Visionary
A fascinating documentary about the life and art of the woman who single-handedly revived interest in the harpsichord. As a bonus, following the documentary Landowska is seen in brief solo performances of Bach: *Concerto in D major*, 3rd movement (excerpt); *Italian Concerto*, 1st movement (abridged); *Concerto in D major* (Bach, after Vivaldi), 2nd movement; and *Branle Simple* by the early 17th-century composer Antoine Francisque. 65 mins.
VHS: S33041. $29.95.

Lazar Berman in Recital
Pianist Lazar Berman performs a number of Chopin's works, including *The Polonaise, Op. 26, No. 1, Op. 40, No. 3, Op. 40, No. 2, Op. 26, No. 2*, Op. 44 and *Op. 53*. In addition he plays Liszt's *Funerailles*. 62 mins.
VHS: S27697. $14.95.

Leonard Bernstein (Candide)
Filmed live at the Barbican Centre in London in 1989, this was the first and only time Bernstein ever conducted *Candide*, and it was Bernstein's last major recording of his own music.
VHS: S15219. $34.95.
Laser: LD71444. $59.95.

Leonard Berstein Conducts Bernstein
Leonard Bernstein conducts the Israel Philharmonic Orchestra in *Chichester Psalms*, with the Wiener Jeunesse-Chor; his Symphony No. 1, *Jeremiah*, with featured soloist Christa Ludwig; and his Symphony No. 2, *The Age of Anxiety*, with pianist Lukas Foss. 80 mins.
VHS: S18467. $29.95.

Leonard Bernstein in Paris: The Ravel Concerts
Bernstein conducts the National Orchestra of France in a program of music by Maurice Ravel, including *La Valse, Tzigane* and *Bolero*. Bernstein also performs Piano Concerto No. 1 and mezzo-soprano Marilyn Horne performs *Sheherazade. 87 mins.*
VHS: S18567. $29.95.

Leonard Bernstein in Vienna: Beethoven Piano Concerto No. 1 in C Major
Leonard Bernstein conducts the Vienna Philharmonic in Beethoven's *Piano Concerto No. 1 in C Major* in honor of the composer's 200th birthday. 45 mins.
VHS: S18704. $29.95.

Leonard Bernstein on Broadway
Though hailed as a masterful conductor, Leonard Bernstein also composed some of Broadway's most innovative theatrical music. Included in this video are songs from his musicals *On the Town, West Side Story and Candide*. Among the unforgettable tunes collected here are "New York, New York," "Maria," "America," "I Feel Pretty" and more, sung by stars like Tyne Daly, Kiri Te Kanawa and Cleo Laine. USA, 74 mins.
VHS: S27208. $29.95.

Leonard Bernstein Place, A Musical in Celebration of Leonard Bernstein's 75th Birthday
Live from Alice Tulley Hall in Lincoln Center, the Bernstein family hosts this concert of songs, chamber music and jazz. Friends like Lauren Bacall, Isaac Stern, Wynton Marsalis, Phyllis Newman and Jerry Hadley contribute to the festivities. 87 mins.
VHS: S22934. $19.95.

Leonard Bernstein's Young People's Concerts: The Collector's Edition
Winner of multiple Emmy, Peabody and Edison Awards, *Leonard Bernstein's Young People's Concerts* with the New York Philharmonic, filmed from 1958 through 1973, shaped an entire generation of music lovers. Twenty-five of the Young People's Concerts are collected on ten VHS videocassettes in a deluxe slipcase.
VHS: S31146. $349.95.

Leonard Bernstein: Schumann/Shostakovich
On a Japanese tour, Leonard Bernstein conducts the New York Philharmonic in Robert Schumann's *Symphony No. 1 (Spring)* and Dmitri Shostakovich's *Symphony No. 5*. 93 mins.
VHS: S19583. $29.95.

Leonard Bernstein: Serenade for Violin and Orchestra
Bernstein wrote this work based on Plato's *Symposium*. Russian virtuoso Dmitry Sitkovetsky, plays the violin accompaniment in this recording of the late composer's vibrant work. 43 mins.
VHS: S29493. $19.95.

Leonard Bernstein: The Gift of Music
This documentary honors the vision and talents of Leonard Bernstein. It reveals Bernstein as a brash showman who intuitively understood the emotional resonance of music on the public. Highlights include excerpts from his "Young People's Concerts," Bernstein conducting the New York Philharmonic in Moscow in 1959, and his interpretations of Beethoven and Mahler. 90 mins.
VHS: S19754. $29.95.

Leonard Bernstein: The Rite of Spring in Rehearsal
Bernstein inspires a youth orchestra to perform with primal force in this production of Igor Stravinsky's groundbreaking masterpiece. As a result, Bernstein's unique genius as both a musician and a teacher comes through. 60 mins.
VHS: S27695. $19.95.

Leonid Kogan
With piano accompaniment by his daughter Nina, dynamic performances of Tchaikovsky's *Melodie* and *Valse Scherzo*, Glazunov's *Entracte*, Brahms' *Scherzo*, Kreisler's *Liebesfreud*, Bizet's *Carmen*, and a set of Paganini variations. 60 mins.
VHS: S03882. $19.95.

Little Drummer Boy
Leonard Bernstein reveals the inner character of a composer close to his heart—Gustav Mahler. This documentary essay explores the influence of Jewish origins on Mahler's life and compositions. 85 mins.
VHS: S26793. $19.95.

Looking at Music with Adrian Marthaler, Vol. 1
Swiss TV and film director Adrian Marthaler is a creative magician who takes pop music video techniques to create imaginative, exhilarating and often hilarious images of classical music. In Volume 1 are Bach's Brandenburg Concerto No. 2, Gershwin's Rhapsody in Blue, Honegger's Concertino, and Saint-Saens' Danse Macabre. Pianist Ilana Vered and Matthias Bamert conducting the Basel Radio Symphony are featured.
VHS: S05615. $29.95.

The Love of Three Orchestras
Leonard Bernstein's generous and loving spirit inspired this autobiographical essay about his relationship to three orchestras. Performances spanning four decades with the New York, Vienna and Israel Philharmonics serve as demonstrations of this love. 88 mins.
VHS: S26475. $19.95.

The Loves of Emma Bardac
Acclaimed classical piano duo Katia and Marielle Labeque portray the daughters of Emma Bardac, the product of her liaisons with composers Debussy and Faure. This award-winning program features the music of Bizet, Debussy and Faure performed by the Labeques. 1991, 60 mins.
VHS: S15801. $24.98.
Laser: LD71477. $34.98.

Mahler: Symphony No. 1 and No. 4
Leonard Bernstein conducts the Vienna Philharmonic.
Laser: LD71123. $34.95.

Mahler: Symphony No. 3
This program features the composer's Third Symphony, conducted by Leonard Bernstein and performed by Vienna Philharmonic Orchestra. The program also features Mahler's unfinished Tenth Symphony.
VHS: S16905. $34.95.
Laser: LD71527. $59.95.

Mahler: Symphony No. 3 in D Minor

Bernard Haitink leads the Berlin Philharmonic with Florence Quivar, the women of the Ernst-Senff Choir and the Tolzer Boys Choir in this rendition of Mahler's *Symphony No. 3*. Filmed at the Schauspielhaus in Berlin, it won an Edison award for fine audio recording. 106 mins.
VHS: S20976. $29.95.

Mahler: Symphony No. 4 in G

Bernard Haitink conducts this work, considered by some to be among Mahler's most accessible. This was filmed at the Schauspielhaus in Berlin with the Berlin Philharmonic. 60 mins.
VHS: S20642. $29.95.

Mahler: Symphony No. 5

Leonard Bernstein's definitive and historic interpretation of Mahler's fifth symphony. Performed by the Vienna Philharmonic Orchestra. 72 mins.
VHS: S15636. $24.95.
Laser: LD70282. $34.95.

Mahler: Symphony No. 6

This performance was filmed in 1976 in Vienna at the Musikverein, and features Leonard Bernstein conducting the Vienna Philharmonic Orchestra. In Hi-Fi stereo, 84 mins.
VHS: S16423. $24.95.
Laser: LD71446. $34.95.

Mahler: Symphony No. 7

Leonard Bernstein conducts the Vienna Philharmonic. 83 mins.
VHS: S17126. $24.95.
Laser: LD71542. $34.95.

Mahler: Symphony No. 8

Edda Moser, Judith Blegen, Hermann Prey and Jose Van Dam are among the soloists in this performance, with Leonard Bernstein conducting the Vienna State Opera Chorus and the Vienna Philharmonic.
Laser: LD71125. $34.95.

Mahler: Symphony No. 9

Leonard Bernstein conducts Berlin Philharmonic in this great 1971 performance. Hi-Fi stereo, 83 mins.
Laser: LD71518. $34.95.

Majestic Marches

A visual tour of the Soldier Museum and the Plassenburg Castle in Germany is offset by musical selections from Wagner, Meyerbeer, Saint-Saens, Van Suppe, Rimsky-Korsakov, Tchaikovsky and Mendelssohn, including "Wedding March," "Marche Militaire," "Coronation March," "Festive March" and the march from *Sleeping Beauty*. With the Slovak Philharmonic Orchestra, conducted by Richard Hayman.
Laser: LD72247. $29.95.

Making Music: The Emerson String Quartet

A close look, through conversation and performance, at the personal and musical qualities that must combine to make an ensemble of excellence. It gives a sense of involvement with the four articulate young men who are the Quartet, while helping to illuminate chamber music. "This is what making music is all about—a warm, personal, and often humorous interaction between the members of a truly first-rate string quartet" (*Choice*). 28 mins.
Public Performance.
VHS: S09271. $89.95.
Home Video.
VHS: S09272. $49.95.

Mendelssohn Symphonies No. 3 & 4

Mendelssohn's "Italian" and "Scottish" symphonies are performed in concert by the Chicago Symphony Orchestra under the direction of Sir Georg Solti. Korean violinist Kyung-Wha Chung joins the orchestra to perform Mendelssohn's *Violin Concerto*. In Hi-Fi Stereo, 97 mins.
VHS: S17409. $24.95.
Laser: LD71425. $34.95.

Midori Live at Carnegie Hall

Works by Mozart, Strauss, Beethoven, Ernst, Chopin and Ravel are performed by this acclaimed violinist, accompanied by Robert MacDonald on piano.
Laser: LD74573. $24.98.

Moussorgsky/Holst/Debussy: Ormandy and the Philadelphia Orchestra

Eugene Ormandy and the Philadelphia Orchestra, American musical legends, perform "La Mer", "The Planets" and "Pictures at an Exhibition." 108 mins.
VHS: S14966. $29.95.
Laser: LD71423. $34.95.

Mussorgsky: Pictures at an Exhibition

A three-part collaboration between filmmaker Christopher Nupen and pianist/conductor Vladimir Ashkenazy. Ashkenazy conducts the Swedish Radio Symphony Orchestra in a 1922 Leo Funtek orchestration, and gives a solo performance filmed in concert at London's Barbican Centre. In Hi-fi Stereo, 96 mins.
VHS: S16510. $29.97.

Mozart (Biography)

History's greatest musical genius is explored in A&E's masterful look at the famous composer, from his beginnings as a child prodigy, which made him the darling of the European courts. Later leading a life of excess, Mozart died alone and poverty-stricken at 35, leaving behind work that would revolutionize nearly every area of music. Featuring musical performances by conductor Zubin Mehta, violinist Isaac Stern and flutist James Galway. 50 minutes.
VHS: S27653. $19.95.

Mozart (Performances)

Three pieces: two for flute, performed by soloist Alain Marion, and one for piano, performed by Jeremy Menuhin. 55 mins.
VHS: S03822. $19.95.

Mozart Ensemble Salzburg

The acclaimed Mozart Ensemble Salzburg performs two of Mozart's Divertimenti as the camera takes us to scenic and historical sites of the great city. Intercut with dancers from La Scala, completing their visual expression of Mozart with traditional costuming. Georg Homosky, violinist and founder of the ensemble, leads the group. 65 mins.
VHS: S16229. $19.95.

Mozart on Tour: Volume 1 (London—The First Journey)

The first part of this documentary/performance series hosted by Andre Previn starts with this childhood visit to the British capital, where Mozart and his family were idolized by the royal court. The London influence was later felt in works like Piano Concerto No. 23, performed here by Vladimir Ashkenazy and the Royal Philharmonic Orchestra. A trip to Paris in 1778 resulted in the Symphony No. 31, performed by Jeffrey Tate and the Salzburg Mozarteum Orchestra. In Hi-Fi stereo, 75 mins.
Laser: LD71448. $34.95.

Mozart on Tour: Volume 2

With an introduction by Andre Previn, this documentary/performance investigation into the history of this great artist continues over the Alps in Italy, where Mozart was introduced to the "Manzuoli style" of virtuoso singing, and to the newly developed pianoforte instrument. In Mantua, Heidrun Holtmann performs *Piano Concerto No. 1 in F* and *Piano Concert No. 4 in G*. Marc Andrae conducts the Orchestra Della in Milan through *Piano Concerto No. 5 in D*, with American pianist Malcolm Frager. In Hi-Fi Stereo, 113 mins.
Laser: LD71466. $34.95.

Mozart on Tour: Volume 3

The third installment depicts Mozart at his musical and emotional turning point, in Mannheim where he meets soprano Aloysia Weber (and her sister Constanze). Gianluigi Gelmetti conducts the Radio Symphony Orchestra of Stuttgart, with pianist Christian Zacharias performing Piano Concertos No. 6 and No. 8. With an introduction by Andre Previn. Hi-Fi stereo, 109 mins.
Laser: LD71515. $34.95.

Mozart on Tour: Volume 4

Set in 1778, this program details Wolfgang Amadeus Mozart's arrival in Paris, the tragic death of his mother, and his return to Salzburg. Over the next two years he works on his important opera, *Idomeneo*, until he's summoned by the Archbishop of Vienna, and commissioned for a new work.
Laser: LD71528. $34.95.

Mozart on Tour: Volume 5

This volume of the video biography of Mozart centers on one of his most creative periods, the writing of his two greatest works, *The Marriage of Figaro* and *Don Giovanni*. Hosted by Andre Previn, the conductor and soloist with the European Chamber Orchestra. 100 mins.
Laser: LD71549. $34.95.

Mozart Piano Concerto No. 23 K. 488 (Horowitz)

Vladimir Horowitz performs Mozart's Piano Concerto No. 23 K. 488 with the Orchestra del Teatro ala Scala Milano conducted by Carlo Maria Giulini.
Laser: LD71047. $29.95.

Mozart Piano Concertos No. 9, K. 271 and Jeunehomme

This program combines images with music, alternating portraits of such important landmarks as Bishops Place, Brixen, Southern Tyrol, the Church of St. Peter and Gratsch in Southern Tyrol with Mozart's piano concertos *No. 9, K. 271* and *Jeunehomme* and *No. 27, K. 595*, performed by pianist Wolf Harden.
Laser: LD72243. $29.95.

Mozart Quintets by the Emerson String Quintet

The highly acclaimed chamber music ensemble performs some of Mozart's clarinet and string quintets.
Laser: LD70214. $34.98.

Mozart Story

Biography of Mozart and his contemporaries Haydn and Beethoven featuring the Vienna Philharmonic. Austria, 1937, 95 mins.
VHS: S02248. $29.95.

Mozart, Smetana, Dvorak, Janacek

Performed by the Czech Philharmonic Orchestra conducted by Vaclav Neuman. 48 mins.
VHS: S03823. $19.95.

Mozart—Klassix 13

Anthony Quayle and Balint Vaszonyi explore Mozart's creative process, his house in Salzburg, the life in Vienna, and the haunting spectre of death which invaded his dreams. 60 mins.
VHS: S10897. $24.95.

Mozart/Barenboim Volume 1

Daniel Barenboim performs Concertos for 2 & 3 Pianos under the direction of Sir Georg Solti and the Berlin Philharmonic Orchestra.
VHS: S15455. $29.98.
Laser: LD70211. $29.98.

Mozart/Barenboim Volume 3

Daniel Barenboim as pianist performs Mozart's Piano Concerto No. 20 and his Sonata No. 8.
Laser: LD70213. $29.98.

Mozart: "Haffner" (Solti)

Sir Georg Solti conducts the Chicago Symphony Orchestra in Mozart's *Symphony No. 35* and Gustav Mahler's *Symphony No. 5*.
Laser: LD74571. $29.98.

Mozart: Concert in Tarascon Castle

The Polish Chamber Orchestra conducted by Jerry Maksymiuk performs a glorious all-Mozart concert within the opulent confines of Tarascon Castle in France. The concert includes flutist Alain Marion's interpretation of Mozart's Flute Concerto No. 2, the Piano Concerto No.9 in E Flat Major. 60 mins.
VHS: S12152. $19.95.

Mozart: Divertimento. K. 334/Strauss: Also Sprach Zarathustra

Herbert Von Karajan conducts the Berlin Philharmonic in this thrilling performance. 81 mins.
Laser: LD74559. $34.98.

Mozart: His Life and Loves

A critical, uncompromising portrait of the great composer Wolfgang Amadeus Mozart, during the breakdown and disintegration of his final, poverty-stricken years. Oskar Werner plays Mozart. 87 mins. English dubbed.
VHS: S17454. $29.95.

Mozart: Serenade K. 361 Gran Partita

Frans Bruggen conducts the Orchestra of the 18th Century in this performance of Mozart's famous serenade.
Laser: LD70287. $29.95.

Mozart: Serenade Posthorn/ Serenade Notturno

A tour of Italy, highlighted by a visit to the Velthurns Castle, built in the 12th century at the foot of the Dolomites, is accompanied by two major works by Wolfgang Amadeus Mozart. The musicians are post hornist Hans Gansch, flutist Vojtech Samec, oboeist Jozef Cejka and bassoonist Peter Gazenl.
Laser: LD72244. $29.95.

Mozart: Symphonies 39-41

Observing the 200th anniversary of Mozart's death, Nikolaus Harnoncourt conducts the Chamber Orchestra of Europe in a selection of the composer's final symphonies. 116 mins.
VHS: S19632. $29.97.
Laser: LD71928. $34.97.

Mozart: The Dissonant Quartet

In a concert filmed exclusively for Voyager, the Angels Quartet gives a stunning performance of the Quartet in C minor, with music scholar Robert Winter's commentary on the second soundtrack.
Laser: LD70303. $49.95.

Murray Perahia in Performance: The Aldeburgh Recital

This recital, recorded in hi-fi at Aldeburgh, offers riveting performances of repertoire all new to the Perahia discography. Featuring works by Beethoven, Schumann, Liszt and Rachmaninoff.
VHS: S15803. $24.98.
Laser: LD74565. $29.98.

Murray Perahia's Mozart

In this high definition video production, Perahia, the acclaimed pianist, performs Mozart's *Piano Concertos K.467* and *K.595*. 119 mins.
Laser: LD74555. $29.98.

Mussogorsky: Pictures at an Exhibition/ Solti

Sir Georg Solti conducts the Chicago Symphony Orchestra.
Laser: LD74568. $24.98.

Nello Santi, Guglielmo Tell

Performance footage and documentary scenes are joined to give an intimate look at this conductor as he contemplates, rehearses and interprets his favorite opera. From the Swiss countryside, where it all happened, to the innermost thoughts of the maestro, this video gives new depth to this operatic work. 60 mins.
VHS: S22931. $24.95.

Neville Marriner Conducts the Academy of St. Martin in the Fields

The historic, stately home of Longleat House provides the ideal setting for the classic music of Bach, Handel, Mozart, Grieg, Pachelbel, Borodin, Gluck and Rossini, performed by the Academy of St. Martin in the Fields. 55 mins.
VHS: S03164. $29.95.

New Sousa Band

Keith Brion conducts this concert of rousing John Philip Sousa music at The Barns of Wolf Trap. Also stars New York City opera star Erie Mills.
VHS: S12424. $29.95.

A New World of Music

Take an 18-day trip of a lifetime to South America with the New England Conservatory Youth Philharmonic Orchestra. Led by vibrant conductor Benjamin Zander, this group of 85 12- to 18- year-olds shares a voyage of discovery, of new lands and new friendships. A PBS WGBH Boston Special. 120 mins.
VHS: S33091. $19.95.

New Year's Eve Concert 1985

Herbert von Karajan conducts the Berlin Philharmonic in this celebratory concert that features music by Weber, Leoncavallo, Puccini, Liszt and Ravel. 55 mins.
VHS: S26705. $29.95.
Laser: LD74563. $29.98.

New Year's Eve Concert 1987

Herbert von Karajan conducts the Berlin Philharmonic in this celebratory concert that features the music of Josef and Johann Strauss.
Laser: LD74577. $34.98.

New Year's Eve Concert 1991—Beethoven in Berlin

This all-Beethoven concert features the *Egmont Overture; Ah! Perfido; Choral Fantasy* and *Leonore III Overture*. With soprano Cheryl Studer and pianist Yevgeny Kissin. Claudio Abbado conducts the Berlin Philharmonic Orchestra. Includes narration by Bruno Ganz. In Hi-Fi stereo, 90 mins.
Laser: LD71191. $34.95.

New Year's Eve Concert 1992

Carlos Kleiber leads the Vienna Philharmonic Orchestra through a recreation of the finest works of Nicolai, J. Strauss I, J. Strauss II, and Josef Strauss. 90 mins.
Laser: LD71701. $34.96.

New Year's Eve Concert 1993

Riccardo Muti and the Vienna Philharmonic Orchestra provide a joyous New Year's performance, with selections from Josef Strauss, Johann Strauss and Joseph Lanner. "Boundless enthusiasm. It was, without a doubt, one of the most joyful New Year's concerts in the history of the event." 100 mins.
Laser: LD71853. $34.95.

New Year's Eve Concert 1994—Wagner Gala

Claudio Abbado leads the Berlin Philharmonic Orchestra in this collection of excerpts from four Wagner operas: *Tannhauser, Lohengrin, Die Meistersinger von Nurnberg* and *Die Walkure*. Cheryl Studer, Waltraud Meier, Siegfried Jerusalem and Bryn Terfel are featured singers.
VHS: S20978. $29.95.
Laser: LD72406. $34.95.

Of Men and Music

A wide-ranging and innovative program on the relationship of art and performance, with five astonishing talents—pianist Artur Rubinstein, violinist Jascha Heifetz, sopranos Nadine Conner and Jane Pierce, and conductor Dimitri Mitropoulos and the Philharmonic Symphony Orchestra—discussing the nature of their work and art. 85 mins.
VHS: S18028. $29.95.

Once at a Border... Aspects of Stravinsky

A unique historical document, a celebration of the life, passions and music of Igor Stravinsky. Features are documents, photographs, and film never before available, including appearances by Marie Rambert, George Balanchine, Nadia Boulanger, as well as "Les Noches," never before seen. 166 mins.
VHS: S03696. $69.95.

Orchestre l'Opera de Paris

Georges Pretre conducts three Mozart works, *Concerto for Bassoon (K. 191), Concerto for Oboe (K. 314)* and *Concerto for Clarinet (K. 622)*. These dramatic interpretations showcase the talents of this singular musical institution under the direction of an accomplished master. 63 mins.
VHS: S29492. $14.95.

Orient Express Panorama Music

This film follows that fabled train from London to Budapest, capturing the beautiful scenery of Europe with music reflecting each place, performed by the quintet *I Salonisti*. 49 mins.
Laser: LD70279. $34.95.

Otto Klemperer's Long Journey Through His Times

A remarkable film about a legendary musician and human being; Otto Klemperer lived and made music through two world wars to become a great interpreter of Brahms, Beethoven, Bach and Wagner. Through rare archival footage and interviews, filmmaker Philo Bregstein takes the viewer on a revealing journey through eight decades and across four continents, as this extraordinary artist battled Hitler, McCarthy and personal tragedy to become one of the supreme artists of our century. German with English subtitles.
VHS: S08220. $59.95.
Philo Bregstein, Germany/Holland, 1984, 96 mins.

Papal Concert to Commemorate the Holocaust

In St. Peter's Basilica this special concert was held to underscore the Catholic Church's recent recognition of the State of Israel. Richard Dreyfuss hosts this event, with Gilbert Levine conducting the London Royal Philharmonic. Music by Beethoven, Bernstein, Schubert and other famed composers is included. 90 mins.
VHS: S22448. $19.98.

Papal Concert: A Musical Offering from the Vatican

From the Pope Paul IV Hall in the Vatican comes this special concert in honor of Pope John Paul II, featuring a select program of deeply inspirational classical music, including *Ave Maria—Opus 12 for Chorus and Orchestra* by Johannes Brahms; *Stabat Mater*, by Krzysztof Penderecki; and *Mass in D Major-Opus 86*, by Antonin Dvorak. World-renowned conductor Gilbert Levine, the Pope's Maestro and conductor of the Krakow Philharmonic in the city of the Pope's birth, leads the Television Italian (RAI) Symphony Orchestra and the Chorus of the Krakow Philharmonic in this concert classic. Illustrated with priceless artwork from the collection of the Vatican museum. 60 mins.
VHS: S30252. $19.98.

Papazian Live

Armenian pianist Artur Papazian's herculean 1995 recital at New York's sold-out Carnegie Hall features the Twenty-Four Preludes, Op. 28 and the Twenty-Four Etudes, Ops. 10 and 25. "The man is a monster pianist" (*The Washington Post*).
VHS: S34513. $29.95.

Pinchas Zukerman: Here to Make Music/The Ghost

Through performance and personal recollection, *Here to Make Music* documents the musical developments of the acclaimed violinist over seven years in six different countries. The performances include Mozart's *Symphony No. 29* with the English Chamber Orchestra. In *The Ghost*, Zukerman is joined by Jacqueline du Pre and Daniel Barenboim for a complete performance of Beethoven's *Piano Trio, Opus 70. In Hi-Fi Stereo, 91 mins.*
VHS: S16511. $29.97.
Laser: LD71459. $34.97.

"Play Bach"—The 1989 Munich Concert

Jacques Loussier, the celebrated french jazz pianist, applies his own distinctive style of jazz to the classics of Bach. This video documents the concert his jazz trio played in Munich in 1989. 84 mins.
VHS: S15046. $34.95.
Laser: LD71442. $34.95.

Polish Chamber Orchestra

A brilliant performance of Mozart's "Eine Kleine Nachtmusik," and Haydn's "Symphony No. 45," conducted by Jerzy Maksymiuk. 60 mins.
VHS: S03165. $29.95.

Prokofiev: Classical Symphony (Karajan)

Herbert von Karajan conducts the Berlin Philharmonic in this thrilling performance. Also includes Tchaikovsky's *Piano Concerto No. 1*.
Laser: LD74578. $29.98.

Prokofiev: Romeo and Juliet

Charles Dutoit conducts the Montreal Symphony Orchestra in a performance of Prokofiev's *Romeo and Juliet*, the orchestra is outfitted in 18th-century costumes and interacts with the audience. "Extraordinary" (*Gramophone*). 58 mins.
Laser: LD71547. $39.95.

Prokofiev: Symphonie Classique (Celibidache)

"I do not make the music. I create the circumstances where the music comes to life" (Sergiu Celibidache). The maestro leads the Munich Philharmonic in a rehearsal and complete performance of Prokofiev's *"Classical" Symphony*. In Hi-Fi Stereo, 57 mins.
VHS: S27000. $29.95.
Laser: CLV. LD71483. $29.97.

Puccini—Two Loves Had I

A biopic of the great composer starring Gabriele Farzetti as Puccini. With Marta Toren and Nadia Gray. Dubbed in English.
VHS: S34501. $24.95.
Carmine Gallone, France/Italy, 1953, 105 mins.

Quartet

An illustrated performance film of Schubert's "Rosamunde" quartet which, among other things, focuses on the craft of instrument-making as compared to the crafts of the composer and musician. Dutch filmmaker Anton van Munster's film won the top prize at the Chicago International Film Festival. 35 mins.
VHS: S15626. $19.95.

Ralph Kirkpatrick Plays Bach

A rare memento of one of the greatest harpsichordists in a recital of J.S. Bach. The performance features the Toccata in D, Chromatic Fantasy and Fugue and Partita No. 5 in G.
VHS: S05585. $29.95.

Remembering Jacqueline du Pre

Christopher Nupen made this inspiring and revealing film portrait of the musician Jacqueline du Pre. Her miraculous musical talent is an inspiration to her fans. 56 mins.
VHS: S26926. $19.95.

Rhapsody Pathetique

The Moscow Philharmonic gives a memorable performance of Robert Nanes' powerful *Rhapsody Pathetique*, "A Hebraic Lament" for Violin and Orchestra, at Tchaikovsky Hall in Moscow. The program includes Nanes' *Symphony for Strings* and his *Grande Etude*, featuring the composer at the keyboard. 60 mins.
VHS: S30062. $19.95.

Richard Nanes in Recital in Moscow and Kiev

A brilliant composer and performer, Nanes performs some of his greatest piano works in this video. *Rhapsody and Fugato No. 2, The Grand Etude No. 2* and the *Piano Concerto No. 2 A/Solo* are included. 60 mins.
VHS: S24830. $19.95.

Richard Nanes—The Holocaust Symphony No. 3

Taped live at the Kiev Opera House during the Kiev International Music Festival, this video preserves the premier of this important and powerful new work. It is a meditation on the Holocaust. The Kharkiv Festival Orchestra performs. 60 mins.
VHS: S22437. $19.95.

Robert Schumann: Piano Concerto in A Minor, Op. 54; Pyotr Ilyich Tchaikovsky: Piano Concerto No. 1 in B Flat Minor, Op. 23

Sergiu Celibidache conducts and Daniel Barenboim is featured on the piano in this recording with the Munich Philharmonic. 77 mins.
VHS: S26907. $29.97.

Rodrigo: Concierto de Aranjuez Pepe Romero

This film tribute to the composer Pepe Romero contains a documentary about this artist as well as the music he composed. This latter segment combines the actual Palace of Aranjuez, where the composer and his wife are seen touring the grounds with his acclaimed musical composition. Joaquin Rodrigo and the Academy of St. Martin in the Fields, with Sir Neville Marriner, are featured. In Spanish and English with English subtitles. 97 mins.
VHS: S22219. $29.95.

Rosalyn Tureck at the Teatro Colon

Pianist Rosalyn Tureck made her stunning video debut in this recital in Buenos Aires, highlighting works by J.S. Bach, Mendelssohn, Schubert and Brahms, with particular emphasis on Bach's *Chaconne in D Minor*. 90 mins.
VHS: S18345. $29.95.

Rosalyn Tureck Plays Bach: Goldberg Variations

The legendary Bach interpreter Rosalyn Tureck in her most technically dazzling and emotionally powerful interpretations of Bach's monumental work. This performance, on piano, was taped live at the Great Hall of the Philharmonic in St. Petersburg during Tureck's historic 1995 tour of Russia. A stunning achievement by one of the keyboard giants of the century. 98 mins.
VHS: S31871. $29.95.

Rubinstein Remembered

1987 marks the 100th anniversary of the birth of the legendary pianist, and this remarkable documentary, hosted by his son, actor-composer-conductor John Rubinstein, traces Artur Rubinstein's career from its beginnings in Lodz, Poland, to its enduring international fame. He performs excerpts from Chopin, his favorite composer, chats and tells his inimitable stories, and is fondly remembered by his family and others. 58 mins.
VHS: S04701. $19.98.

Rudolf Serkin Performs Beethoven

This recital filmed in 1987 at the Konzerthaus, Vienna, features the late American piano virtuoso performing the last three Beethoven sonatas. Digitally recorded in Hi-Fi stereo, 70 mins.
VHS: S16425. $24.95.

Satie and Suzanne: The Passion of a Lifetime

Composer Erik Satie had a passionate affair with alluring painter Suzanne Valadon. The liaison between these two Parisian art world figures is recreated in this film when they meet unexpectedly in a cafe and recall their passionate affair. Satie's piano music and dance from members of the Cirque du Soleil evoke the spirit of their love. 53 mins.
VHS: S28998. $29.95.

Schubert—Klassix 13

Anthony Quayle and Balint Vaszonyi lead us through the Schubert "garage" where his greatest works were written, to the Viennese night life and a gathering of 19th century students in an intriguing portrait of an intriguing composer. 60 mins.
VHS: S10898. $24.95.

Schubert: The Greatest Love and the Greatest Sorrow

Christopher Nupen continues his series of musical portraits with this look at the life of Franz Schubert. Pianist/conductor Vladimir Ashkenazy is featured performing some of Schubert's greatest works and some of those performed much less frequently, such as *Die Stadt*. 84 mins.
Laser: LD74623. $34.97.

Schubert: The Trout

The historic 1969 performance. Pianist Daniel Barenboim, Itzhak Perlman, Jacqueline du Pre, and conductor Zubin Mehta are featured in Schubert's classic.
VHS: S15461. $29.98.
Laser: LD70219. $29.98.

Segovia at Los Olivos

Guitarist Andres Segovia looks back on his stunning career and performs some of the music with which he is most closely associated. This film by Christopher Nupen examines one of the longest performing careers of the 20th century and highlights some of the wonderful music by Andres Segovia. 57 mins.
VHS: S27196. $19.95.

The Segovia Legacy

This video tribute to Andres Segovia presents revealing interviews and historic performance footage of the legendary Spanish guitarist whose career spanned nearly a century. Includes performances on television, in concert halls, and at the White House. A treasure for the many devoted lovers of this man, known as the "father" of the classical guitar. 60 mins.
VHS: S13666. $29.95.

Segovia: The Song of the Guitar

More beautiful and passionate music from the "father" of modern classical guitar. This Christopher Nupen documentary will be a treasure for fans of the master.
VHS: S15458. $29.98.
Laser: LD70235. $34.98.

Seiji Ozawa: Boston Symphony Orchestra

Winner of Tanglewood's highest honor, the Koussevitzky Prize, Seiji Ozawa has led the BSO for 17 years. Recorded live in hi-fi at Osaka Festival Hall in Japan, featuring Richard Strauss' *Also sprach Zarathustra*.
VHS: S15805. $24.98.
Laser: LD71481. $29.98.

Seiji Ozawa: Russian Night

Enjoy an electrifying evening under the stars at the Waldbuhne Berlin with the Berlin Philharmonker as they perform classic Russian masterpieces under the baton of the great conductor Seiji Ozawa. Selections include Rimsky-Korsakov's "Russian Easter Overture"; Tchaikovsky's "Nutcracker Ballet Suite," "1812 Overture" and "Waltz from Serenade for Strings"; Borodin's "Polovtsian Dances"; Stravinsky's "The Firebird"; Khatchaturian's "Sabre Dance"; Johann Strauss' "Radetsky-March" and Lincke's "Berliner Luft." 98 mins.
VHS: S30126. $24.95.

Serebrier Conducts Prokofiev

Jose Serebrier conducts the Sydney Symphony Orchestra and the Melbourne Symphony Orchestra in these live performances of the works of Prokofiev, Tchaikovsky and Beethoven. 134 mins.
VHS: S03151. $39.95.

Soldiers of Music

Mstislav Rostropovich returned to the Soviet Union after more than a dozen years. Though he lost his citizenship he was welcomed as a hero. This documentary includes interviews and tearful private reunions with close friends. The music is unforgettable. 90 mins.
Laser: LD74554. $29.98.

Solti: The Chicago Symphony Orchestra

Sir Georg Solti and the Chicago Symphony perform two staples of the classical repertory: Mozart's *Haffner* and Mahler's *Symphony No. 5*. Hi-fi stereo sound.
VHS: S15807. $24.98.
Laser: LD71480. $54.98.

Song of the Birds: A Biography of Pablo Casals

The program explores Pablo Casals' virtuoso technique and subtle craft. Various musicians and artists such as Yehudi Menuhin, Mstislav Rostropovich, Alexander Schneider and King Juan Carlos comment on Casals' life and work. 66 mins.
VHS: S18566. $24.95.

The Spanish Guitar

Six solo performances by Pedro Sierra, J.L. Morgan and Jose Cortes demonstrate the three basic styles found in this musical tradition—modern, classical and gypsy. A brief explanation follows each solo to explain the technique of flamenco guitar. 45 mins.
VHS: S21058. $40.00.

Stanislav Bunin in Tokyo

Bunin's career was launched after winning first prize in Warsaw's prestigious Chopin competition. Seven of Chopin's most popular compositions form the central part of the recital program which Bunin recorded live in Tokyo. Hi-fi stereo sound.
VHS: S15806. $24.98.
Laser: LD74570. $24.98.

The Story of the Symphony

A remarkable series of programs produced by the BBC, in which Andre Previn conducts the Royal Philharmonic Orchestra in some of the most popular and important works in the concert repertoire. All of the programs are recorded in stereo hi-fi, and the series won the 1984 British Academy Award for Best Television Sound.

Beethoven: Symphony No. 7 and Excerpts from Symphony No. 5.
VHS: S03111. $39.95.
Berlioz: Symphonie Fantastique.
VHS: S03112. $39.95.
Brahms: Symphony No. 4.
VHS: S03114. $39.95.
Haydn and Mozart: Symphony No. 87 and Symphony No. 39. 90 minutes.
VHS: S02713. $39.95.
Shostakovich: Symphony No. 5.
VHS: S01830. $39.95.
Tchaikovsky: Symphony No. 6 (Pathetique).
VHS: S03113. $39.95.

Strauss: Death and Transfiguration

Herbert von Karajan conducts the Berlin Philharmonic in *Death and Transfiguration* and *Metamorphosis*.
Laser: LD74576. $29.98.

Strauss: Don Quixote

Herbert von Karajan conducts the Berlin Philharmonic. 46 mins.
Laser: LD74560. $29.98.

Strauss: Ein Heldenleben

Herbert von Karajan conducts the Berlin Philharmonic. 50 mins.
Laser: LD74561. $29.98.

Strauss: Eine Alpensinfonie

Herbert von Karajan conducts the Berlin Philharmonic. 56 mins.
Laser: LD74562. $29.98.

Strauss: The King of 3/4 Time

This third film from the PBS series *The Composers Specials* continues with a tale featuring the premier master of the waltz, Johann Strauss Jr., and a young boy named Nicholas. Strauss is struggling with demands for ever more virtuosic composing feats while Nicholas lives in fear of his brutal father. These unlikely friends find solace in each other. Features numerable famous waltzes, including *The Blue Danube* and *Tales of the Vienna Woods*. 50 mins.
VHS: S29405. $19.98.

Tchaikovsky Competition: Violin & Piano

"All the musicality of the event laced with all the tension of a thriller..." *London Times*. "Absolutely spellbinding...technique, virtuosity and style...it is Mullova's presence and performance that are the core of the tape...some of the finest sound engineering for home video..." Rob Baker, *N.Y. Daily News*. Pavel Kogan conducts the Moscow Symphony. (HiFi-Stereo).
VHS: S03966. $29.95.

Tchaikovsky: Symphony No. 4 and No. 5

Tchaikovsky's Fourth Symphony in F minor (1876) and Fifth Symphony in E minor (1888) are presented here, conducted by Herbert von Karajan and the Berlin Philharmonic Orchestra.
VHS: S16903. $24.95.
Laser: LD71525. $34.95.

Tchaikovsky: Symphony No. 6 ("Pathetique") & Piano Concerto No. 1

In this richly musical performance film, Alexis Weissenberg and the Berlin Philharmonic, under the baton of Herbert von Karajan, give dazzling exhibitions of virtuosity in these much loved, Romantic works. Impassioned, dramatic, sad, and triumphant. 85 mins.
VHS: S14118. $24.95.

Tchaikovsky: Violin Concerto Op. 35

Itzhak Perlman is the soloist and Eugene Ormandy leads the Philadelphia Orchestra in this performance of Tchaikovsky's Violin Concerto, Op. 35.
Laser: LD71359. $34.95.

Telemann: Recorded Suite Concerto Violins and Concerto for Horns

This travelogue looks at a glass factory and museum at Frauenau, Germany, and the Palace of Thurin and Taxis at Regensburg. The tour also includes views of St. George and St. Martin Monastery Church of Weltenburg-Kelheim.
Laser: LD72246. $29.95.

A Time There Was... A Profile of Benjamin Britten

Prix Italia winning film biography of one of the foremost composers of the 20th century, including excerpts from several major operas, including *Peter Grimes* and *Death in Venice*, as well as priceless footage of Britten rehearsing and conducting, as well as playing Mozart with Sviatoslav Richter, and his home movies. 120 mins.

VHS: S03697. $69.95.

The Unanswered Question: Six Talks at Harvard by Leonard Bernstein

In this critically acclaimed series, Leonard Bernstein examines all types of music, including folk songs, pop hits and symphonies. Drawing on his insights as a master composer and conductor, he explores works ranging from Mozart and Beethoven, through Wagner and Mahler, to Ravel and Copland in search of a musical grammar. Bernstein also analyzes the crisis of twentieth century music, as expressed in Charles Ives' "The Unanswered Question," with a close analysis of works by Schoenberg and Stravinsky. Containing over 13 hours of material, this deluxe boxed set includes six individual programs: (1) *Musical Phonology*; (2) *Musical Syntax*; (3) *Musical Semantics*; (4) *The Delights and Dangers of Ambiguity*; (5) *The Twentieth Century Crisis*; (6) *The Poetry of the Earth*.

VHS: S16799. $149.95.

Victor Borge: Live from London

The incredible Victor Borge in a London performance of his best-loved classic(al) routines. Beginning with some hilarious variations on Chopin's *Waltz in C-Sharp Minor*, Borge moves on to a series of send-ups of other classical greats. A madcap medley as only Victor Borge could interpret it. USA, 50 mins.

VHS: S14932. $29.95.

Vienna in Music

An impressionistic blending of music and images, Peter Lodyinski's film contrasts the sights and traditions of Viennese locations with various Strauss polkas and waltzes, performed by the Vienna Philharmonica conducted by Willi Boskovsky, backed by the Vienna Boys' Choir. Includes "The Blue Danube," "The Emperor" waltzes, "Pizzicato" Polka and "Radetsky" March. 92 mins.

VHS: S19893. $29.95.

Vienna New Year's Concert 1991

Claudio Abbado conducts the Vienna Philharmonic in the 1991 New Year's Concert of works by Johann and Josef Strauss.

VHS: S16402. $24.95.
Laser: LD71445. $34.95.

Vivaldi: Le Quattri Stagioni (The Four Seasons) (Nupen)

Christopher Nupen's 1981 filmed account of Vivaldi's chamber piece, recorded in the Abbey Library in Polling, Germany. Performed by violinist Gidon Kremer, harpsichordist Philip Ledger and the English Chamber Orchestra. 43 mins.

VHS: S17672. $24.95.
Laser: LD71788. $34.95.

Vivaldi: The Four Seasons (Karajan)

Herbert von Karajan conducts the Berlin Philharmonic, featuring Anne-Sophie Muller.

Laser: LD74583. $29.98.

Vivaldi: Violin Concerti

All the most memorable sights of Venice are showcased in this tour. The church of Santa Maria della Salute, the Piazetta San Marco, Doges' Palace, the island of San Giorgio Maggiore and the heart of it all, the Piazzo San Marco, are on view, accompanied by the violin compositions of Antonio Vivaldi. 60 mins.

Laser: LD74752. $29.95.

Vladimir Ashk3enazy

Follows the pianist and conductor on tour in Russia, Sweden and Germany as he discusses his life and career and rehearses and performs Stravinsky, Shostakovich and Tippett's *A Child of Our Time* in Berlin in celebration of the composer's 90th birthday. 45 mins.

VHS: S32228. $19.95.

Vladimir Horowitz in Moscow

The drama and excitement of Vladimir Horowitz's extraordinary 1986 concert in Moscow, his first visit back to Russia since he left in 1925. The program includes Scarlatti sonatas, Mozart's "Sonata in C Major" and a selection of Schubert, Liszt, Chopin, Rachmaninoff and Scriabin, in one of the legendary performances of the 20th century. Color. USSR, 1986, 120 mins.

VHS: S01862. $29.95.

Vladimir Horowitz in Vienna

Witness the musical wizardry of the legendary Vladimir Horowitz in this special 90-minute video capturing one of the last performances he ever gave. Horowitz—the dramatic storyteller, a musical conversationalist who needed no words. 90 mins.

VHS: S13889. $24.95.

Vladimir Horowitz: A Reminiscence

Vladimir Horowitz was perhaps the century's most acclaimed and beloved pianist. Wanda Toscanini Horowitz, his widow and the daughter of the great Toscanini, hosts this collection of home movie footage and his concert hall performances, offering the quintessential profile of a great musician.

VHS: S21075. $24.98.

Vladimir Horowitz: Sergei Rachmaninoff Piano Concerto No. 3

Zubin Mehta and the New York Philharmonic played together with Horowitz at New York's Lincoln Center to produce this singular musical achievement. No other concerto was more closely associated with Horowitz and this is the only video featuring him performing this signature work. 44 mins.

VHS: S26222. $29.95.

Wagner Concert in Leipzig

This exciting video presents an all-Wagner concert performed in the new Leipzig Gewandhaus. Internationally acclaimed conductor Kurt Masur leads the Gewandhausorchester in a thrilling and varied program including the overture to *Tannhauser*, Overture and Liebestod from *Tristan and Isolde*, overture and vocal excerpts from *Die Meistersinger von Nurnberg* and *The Wessendock Lieder*. Bass Theo Adam and soprano Karan Armstrong are featured. 90 mins.

VHS: S11770. $19.95.

Wagner: The Complete Epic

This is the complete, 9-hour epic never before available on videocassette. Richard Burton performs as Wagner— scoundrel, joker, philosopher, con-man, poet, refugee, virulent political orator, a legend in his own time and one of the greatest composers who ever lived. Lensed on location and in more than 200 separate locations in six different countries, and co-starring Sir Laurence Olivier, Sir John Gielgud, Sir Ralph Richardson and Vanessa Redgrave as Cosima Wagner. The music is conducted by Sir Georg Solti. 4 cassettes, 540 mins.

VHS: S11721. $124.95.

The Winner's Gala Concert

This video features performances from the Gala Concert for the International Tchaikovsky Competition of 1990. Performers include Berezovsky, Suwanai, Rivinius, Voigt, and Choi. A brilliant collection of talented, young musicians. 114 mins.

VHS: S15451. $29.98.

Yehudi Menuhin

Tony Palmer's intimate profile of the virtuoso violinist Yehudi Menuhin assembles interviews with his contemporaries Stefan Grappelli and Ravi Shankar, intimate discussions with his mother and footage recording with his son Jeremy. 120 mins.

VHS: S18758. $29.95.

Yehudi Menuhin: Concert for the Pope

Master violinist Yehudi Menuhin gives a magnificent private concert for Pope John Paul II at the Pope's summer residence in Castelgandolfo. The Pope exchanges candid views with Menuhin, the musicians and the audience after this 1983 concert. Includes selections from Vivaldi, Bach and Mozart with The Polish Chamber Orchestra conducted by Jerzy Maksymiuk. 53 mins.

VHS: S34060. $19.98.

Yehudi Menuhin: Tribute to J.S. Bach (1685-1750)

A tricentennial tribute to Johann Sebastian Bach by beloved violinist Yehudi Menhuhin at the Barbican in London. With French baritone Nicolas Rivecq in his debut performance and the English Chamber Orchestra. 90 mins.

VHS: S34061. $19.98.

Yevgeny Kissin in Tokyo

Recorded live in Japan, *Kissin in Tokyo* captures this brilliant artist performing works by Rachmaninoff, Prokoviev, Liszt, Chopin and Scriabin. A young artist who "measures up to his already formidable reputation." Hi-fi stereo sound.

VHS: S15804. $24.98.
Laser: LD74569. $24.98.

Yevgeny Kissin Plays

Yevgeny Kissin 1990 recital at Munich's Bavaria Musikstudios, as he performs pieces by Schubert, Brahms, Bach, Liszt and the melody from "Orphee." 92 mins.

Laser: LD71963. $34.95.

Young People's Concerts

These landmark programs, originally telecast between 1958 and 1964, are vivid proof of Leonard Bernstein's genius for communicating the joys of music to audiences of all ages. Filmed at Carnegie Hall and featuring the New York Philharmonic Orchestra, this sampler set of six concerts is an excellent introduction to music. Using works by Ravel, Strauss, Tchaikovsky and Beethoven, Bernstein shows how music conveys emotions and feelings. From there he explores musical forms such as sonatas and symphonies, explains "classical" music in terms anyone can easily grasp and demonstrates the secrets of a great orchestra. Always engaging, these programs remain fresh and exciting more than 30 years after they were filmed. Five hours, 38 mins. on three videocassettes.

VHS: S30939. $89.95.

CLASSICAL VOICE

Adventures of Don Quixote

Feodor Chaliapin, the famed bass, left this unforgettable record of his talent on film. Though primarily an actor, in this film he sings four songs by Jaques Ibert. Two versions were cast, one in English and the other in French, both of which are included on this videocassette. 118 mins.

VHS: S20695. $39.95.

Anna Russell Farewell Concert

The hilarious comedienne in her farewell concert in her famous routines: "The Ring Cycle," "How to Become a Singer," "Wind Instruments I Have Known," "A Gilbert and Sullivan Operetta," "On Pink Chiffon," "Jolly Old Sigmund Freud" and other folk tunes.

VHS: S00058. $59.95.
Phillip Byrd, Great Britain/USA, 1984, 85 mins.

Ariel Ramirez: Misa Criolla

Jose Carreras is featured in this classic by Argentine composer Ariel Ramirez. It combines traditional Argentine folk music with the striking melodies of this contemporary artist. Damien Sanchez conducts.

VHS: S21989. $29.95.
Laser: LD74540. $29.95.

Bach's Christmas Oratorio

A stunning performance of Bach's oratorio with Katharina Beidler, Heidi Riess, Arnim Ude, and the Dresden Philharmonic and Chorus.

VHS: S05581. $39.95.

Barbara Hendricks

Whether performing at the Met, LaScala or the Berlin Opera, Hendrick's captivating voice make her a true diva. This video includes excerpts from *Der Rosenkavalier, The Marriage of Figaro* and *Rigoletto*, along with songs by Schubert and Rachmaninoff. 47 mins.

VHS: S26215. $19.95.

Beethoven: Missa Solemnis (Karajan)

Herbert von Karajan conducts the Berlin Philharmonic in Beethoven's intensely moving, sacred work—*Missa Solemnis*. The vocalists include Ruza Baldani and Eric Tappy. 83 mins.

Laser: LD70179. $34.95.

Berlioz: Requiem (Bernstein)

Leonard Bernstein conducts the Orchestre National de France, the Orchestre Philharmonique de France and Les Choeurs de Radio France, with lead tenor Stuart Burrows, in a performance of Hector Berlioz's *Requiem*. 98 mins.

VHS: S19410. $29.95.

Birgit Nilsson: The Bell Telephone Hour

Perhaps the leading interpreter of Richard Wagner's opera heroines in this century, the great Swedish soprano Birgit Nilsson is here seen and heard performing a variety of arias written by Puccini, Verdi, and Wagner. Magnificent. 45 mins.

VHS: S14447. $29.95.

Bizet Concert

This program features Montserrat Caballe in a rare performance of *Clovis and Clotilda*. She is joined in the cantata by tenor Gerard Garino and bass Boris Martinovic. Jean-Claude Casadesus conducts the Orchestra National de Lille. Also includes *L'Arlesienne Suite No. 1 and the Symphony in C*. 95 mins.

VHS: S16509. $19.95.

Boast of Kings

The renowned boys' choir of Chapel of King's College, Cambridge University, in a unique blend of travelogue and music performance, featuring "Ave Maria," "Nunc Dimittis", Allegri's "Miserere" as well as popular favorites by Cole Porter and Randy Newman. 60 mins.
VHS: S05905. $39.95.

Carmina Burana (Cardiff)

This performance of Carl Orff's choral masterpiece was filmed during the Cardiff Festival of Choirs in Wales. Soloists Thomas Allen, Norma Burrowes and Kenneth Bowen are joined by the Royal Philharmonic Orchestra, along with the Cardiff Polyphonic Choir, the Dyfed Choir and the Llandaff Cathedral Choiristers. Latin with English subtitles. 60 mins.
VHS: S16230. $19.95.

Carmina Burana (Polygram)

This popular and captivating choral work by Carl Orff is instantly recognizable with its insistent rhythms, its tender settings of love poems and its massive orchestral and choral arrangements. 64 mins.
VHS: S14802. $24.95.
Laser: LD71426. $34.95.

Carols for Christmas

Twenty-four popular carols are lavishly illustrated with works of art and images of Christmas from the Metropolitan Museum of Art in New York. Boy soprano Aled Jones sings. 60 mins.
VHS: S26476. $19.95.

Carols from Christchurch, Oxford

Oxford Cathedral is the setting for this rare musical performance. Christchurch choristers sing such carols as "O Little Town of Bethlehem" and "Silent Night". Alec McCowen and Ian Charleson also provide readings. 30 mins.
VHS: S21821. $19.95.

Cecilia Bartoli—A Portrait

An in-depth look at the career of mezzo-soprano Cecilia Bartoli is followed by a recital at the London Savoy Hotel that features Bartoli singing seven Rossini arias, plus works by Mozart, Vivaldi and Pergolesi. In Hi-Fi Stereo, 90 mins.
VHS: S16426. $24.95.
Laser: LD71447. $34.95.

Christmas Carols from England

A joyous, heartwarming program of words and music of the Christmas season at the majestic York Minister Cathedral, featuring King's Singers, Benjamin Luxon and the Northern Sinfonia, conducted by Robin Stapleton. Carols include "Silent Night" and "O Holy Night." 50 mins.
VHS: S19595. $19.95.

Christmas Time in Vienna

Placido Domingo and Dionne Warwick join the Vienna Boys Choir and the Vienna Symphonic Orchestra to perform this concert of Christmas songs. Filmed at the imposing Hofberg Palace, it includes such favorites as "O Holy Night", "Smile", "As Time Goes By", "Ave Maria" and many more. 75 mins.
VHS: S22875. $19.95.
Laser: LD74758. $34.95.

Christmas with Eleanor Steber

Highlights from Steber's Memorable Firestone Christmas telecasts, including "Silent Night," "White Christmas," "The First Noel," Mozart's "Alleluia," and many more Christmas favorites. 1950-57, 30 mins.
VHS: S13626. $24.95.

Christmas with Jose Carreras

Set in the magnificent Jesuit Church of Luzern, this concert has a gleaming altar for a backdrop. Standards like "White Christmas," "Silent Night" and "Adeste Fidelis" are included in this joyful recording. 60 mins.
VHS: S29490. $19.95.

Christmas with Luciano Pavarotti

A very special program with the great baritone performing Christmas favorites.
VHS: S10722. $19.95.

Dame Kiri Te Kanawa

This biography of Dame Kiri includes footage from some of her best works, including her performance as the Countess in Strauss' *Capriccio*. 106 mins.
VHS: S18757. $29.95.

Del Monaco at His Most Thrilling

In 1969 at age 54, this great tenor performed a concert for television that revealed his talents were wondrously intact. Excerpts from *Norma, Macbeth, Il Trovatore, Otello* and other works are performed by this peerless singer. 37 mins.
VHS: S24329. $34.95.

Ev Viva Belcanto

World renowned sopranos Marilyn Horne and Montserrat Caballe perform works by Vivaldi, Meyerbeer, Mercadante and Rossini in excerpts from their concert in Munich Germany.
VHS: S15580. $19.95.

Eva Marton in Concert

Eva Marton, one of the world's foremost dramatic sopranos, returns to her native Hungary to give a concert of Italian operatic arias. Julius Rudel conducts the Hungarian State Orchestra in this very special concert, which includes selections from some of Marton's most famous roles, including *La Gioconda, Tosca* and *Manon Lescaut* as well as the haunting "Ebben, ne andro lontana" from Catalani's *La Wally*, made famous in the Jean Jacques Beineix film, *Diva*. 90 mins.
VHS: S13746. $29.95.

Evelyn Laye and Conchita Supervia in Evensong

Beverly Nichols wrote the book and play on which this rarely seen film adaptation is based. Beverly's one-time employer, the great Australian soprano Nellie Melba, is at the center of this traumatic story. She was simultaneously adored and exploited. Excerpts from *La Boheme, Cerentola* and *La Traviata* punctuate this amazing tale. 83 mins.
VHS: S24034. $34.95.

Evening with Placido Domingo

This gala benefit was performed on the evening of June 21, 1987 at the Wembly arena in London. It was a memorable event to aid the Save the Children fund. This film of that performance captures Domingo, the artist and humanitarian, in arias of Verdi, Puccini, Lehar and selections from Spanish operas. 55 mins.
VHS: S07684. $19.95.
Laser: LD74969. $29.99.

Faure/Poulenc Concert

Soprano Barbara Hendricks performs Faure's *Requiem* and Poulenc's *Gloria* from the Saint Denis Basilica. 70 mins.
VHS: S17316. $19.95.

Final Romance Starring Jose Carreras

The story of the life and music of the 19th century tenor Julian Gayarre, who was considered the greatest tenor of his age. The production stars Jose Carreras as Gayarre in the story of his singing career and love for his childhood sweetheart, Alicia. It is a passionate and tragically tender tale with musical excerpts from the operas of Donizetti, Verdi, Bizet, Wagner and others. 120 mins. Subtitled in English.
VHS: S11639. $39.95.

Gala Concert with Luciano Pavarotti

This is the video of the famous concert Luciano Pavarotti gave at the magnificent Olympic Hall in Munich, Germany. Pavarotti performs before a wildly enthusiastic crowd of thousands, singing many of his greatest arias and songs.
VHS: S10711. $19.98.

Golden Age of Opera

Programs from the *Voice of Firestone* telecasts, which brought the world's greatest opera singers into the homes of music lovers.

Anna Moffo in Opera and Song. American soprano Anna Moffo achieved instant stardom with a performance of Puccini's *Madama Butterfly* for Italian television. Her captivating performance includes arias from *La Boheme, Madama Butterfly, Faust* and *Pagliacci*; plus songs by Richard Rodgers and others. 1958-63, 30 mins.
VHS: S13627. $24.95.

Bidu Sayao in Opera and Song. From telecasts in 1951-52, selections from *Manon, Madama Butterfly, Gianni Schicchi*, as well as many popular songs. 45 mins.
VHS: S12912. $34.95.

Blanche Thebom in Opera and Song. The great Blanche Thebom is featured in this classic performance. Includes arias from *Il Trovatore, Don Carlo, Samson et Dalila*; plus songs. 1950-59, 30 mins.
VHS: S13690. $24.95.

Easter with Fred Waring. This telecast of March 23, 1959, features Fred Waring and the Pennsylvanians in an inspiring program of Easter music, including "He Is Risen," "Were You There," "Hallelujah" and others. B&W, 25 mins.
VHS: S13684. $24.95.

Eleanor Steber in Opera and Song, Vol. 1. From telecasts in 1949-51, selections from Rodgers and Hammerstein, Charpentier, Victor Herbert, Mozart (*Marriage of Figaro*), and Verdi's *La Forza del Destino*. 50 mins.
VHS: S12911. $34.95.

Eleanor Steber in Opera and Song, Vol. 2. "One of the most ravishing voices and accomplished singers ever produced in the United States" (J. Ardoin on soprano Eleanor Steber). This telecast includes arias from *Ernani, Madama Butterfly* and *Die Fledermaus*; ensembles from *Rigoletto, Faust* and *Lucia*; plus songs. 1951-54, 45 mins.
VHS: S13625. $29.95.

Eleanor Steber in Opera and Oratorio. This telecast, featuring soprano Eleanor Steber, includes arias from *Le Nozze di Figaro, La Boheme, Otello, Lohengrin, Messiah* and others. 1950-56, 45 mins.
VHS: S13685. $34.95.

Eleanor Steber Sings Love Songs. Eleanor Steber performs songs by Jerome Kern, Rodgers & Hammerstein, Cole Porter, Victor Herbert and others. 55 mins.
VHS: S16083. $34.95.

Ferruccio Tagliavini in Opera and Song. This telecast features Ferruccio Tagliavini performing arias from *Tosca, La Boheme, L'Elisir d'Amore, Martha* and songs. 1950-54, 45 mins.
VHS: S13689. $34.95.

George London in Opera and Song. This telecast features bass-baritone George London and special guest sopranos Dorothy Warenskjold and Nadine Conner. Includes arias from *Boris Godunov* and *Le Nozze di Figaro*; songs by Rodgers & Hammerstein, Kern, Romberg and others; plus duets with Warenskjold and Conner. 1953-55, 45 mins.
VHS: S13631. $34.95.

The Great Sopranos: Voices of Firestone Classic Performances. Leontyne Price, Renata Tebaldi, Joan Sutherland, Bidu Sayao, Birgit Nilsson, Eleanor Steber, Licia Albanese, Patrice Munsel, Jeanette MacDonald, Anna Moffo, Roberta Peters and Helen Traubel can all be seen on this compilation video. 58 mins.
VHS: S26701. $34.95.

The Great Tenors: Voices of Firestone Classic Performances. This stellar collection of performers includes some selections which have never been released before. Jussi Bjoerling, Franco Corelli, Nicolai Gedda, James McCracken, Lauritz Melchior, Jan Peerce, Ferruccio Tagliavini, Jess Thomas and Richard Tucker all appear on this video. 58 mins.
VHS: S26702. $34.95.

Helen Traubel in Opera and Song. This telecast includes two arias from *Die Walkure* plus six songs. 1950, 30 mins.
VHS: S13688. $34.95.

Igor Gorin in Opera and Song. Culled from his performances on *The Voice of Firestone* telecasts, this program features Igor Gorin as he performs arias from *La Traviata, I Pagliacci, Herodiade* and *The Barber of Seville*, as well as some popular songs. 55 mins.
VHS: S17427. $34.95.

Jan Peerce in Opera and Song. The glory of Peerce's singing was in the solidity and power of the tone, the consistency of the timbre throughout the range, and the sheer exuberance of his presentation. This telecast includes "Vesti la giubba" from *Pagliacci*, plus songs by Rossini, Rodgers & Hammerstein and Herbert. 1950, 25 mins.
VHS: S13630. $24.95.

Jussi Bjoerling in Opera and Song. Bjoerling sings selections from Victor Herbert, Puccini, Gounod, Strauss, Leoncavallo and *Prayer of Thanksgiving*. 40 mins.
VHS: S12910. $34.95.

Jussi Bjoerling in Opera and Song, Vol. 2. This telecast features Jussi Bjoerling, a first-class tenor of exquisite refinement and effortless grace. Includes the "Flower Song" from *Carmen*, plus songs by Schubert, Leoncavallo and Herbert. 1950, 26 mins.
VHS: S13624. $24.95.

Lauritz Melchior in Opera and Song. From 1951 telecasts, works by Wagner (*Meistersinger, Die Walkure, Flying Dutchman*) and popular songs by Rodgers and Hammerstein and others. 45 mins.
VHS: S12916. $34.95.

Lauritz Melchior in Opera and Song, Vol. 2. This telecast includes arias from *Lohengrin, I Pagliacci* and *The Student Prince*, plus songs. 1950-52, 40 mins.
VHS: S13687. $34.95.

Leonard Warren in Opera and Song. The legendary baritone sings "A Little Bit of Heaven" and "None But the Lonely Heart" as well as selections from *Carmen, Faust, Un Ballo in Maschera*. 45 mins.
VHS: S12914. $34.95.

Leonard Warren in Opera and Song, Vol. 2. This telecast features the dramatic baritone Leonard Warren, and a special guest appearance by soprano Eleanor Steber. Includes arias from *Barber of Seville* (Warren) and *Tosca* (Steber), a duet from *Maytime* (Romberg) plus songs by Speaks, Huhn and Herbert. 1949, 27 mins.
VHS: S13623. $24.95.

Licia Albanese in Opera and Song. From a 1951 telecast, popular songs and selections from *I Pagliacci*. 26 mins.
VHS: S12913. $29.95.

Lisa Della Casa in Opera. The incomparable soprano in a program of arias and duets from *La Boheme* and *Tosca*. With Nicolai Gedda, Richard Tucker and Giuseppe Campora. 30 mins.
VHS: S16081. $24.95.

Patrice Munsel in Opera and Song. Lyric soprano Patrice Munsel became the youngest singer to debut with the Metropolitan Opera in 1943. Her performances on the *Voice of Firestone* programs are recollected, as she performs arias from *The Daughter of the Regiment, Die Fledermaus, La Boheme, Louise and Madama Butterfly*. 55 mins.
VHS: S17428. $34.95.

Presenting Joan Sutherland. Joan Sutherland sings selections from *La Boheme, Semiramide, Les Huguenots*, with Richard Bonynge conducting. 26 mins.
VHS: S12917. $29.95.

Renata Tebaldi and Franco Corelli. Selections from Mascagni's *Cavalleria Rusticana*, Puccini's *Turandot, Tosca, Madama Butterfly*. 35 mins.
VHS: S12909. $34.95.

Richard Tucker in Opera and Song. From 1957, Tucker sings Neapolitan love songs, selections from *Aida, Carmen, The Student Prince, I Pagliacci, Rigoletto*. 45 mins.
VHS: S12918. $34.95.

Riise Stevens in Opera and Song. From 1951 and 1954 telecasts, selections from *Carmen* and popular songs by Rodgers, Berlin, Jerome Kern. 45 mins.
VHS: S12915. $34.95.

Riise Stevens in Opera and Song, Vol. 2. This telecast includes arias from *Samson et Dalila, Carmen* and *Orfeo ed Euridice*, plus songs. 1951-59, 45 mins.
VHS: S13686. $34.95.

Robert Merrill in Opera and Song. This telecast features the pure, mellow baritone of Robert Merrill. It includes arias from *Carmen, The Barber of Seville, Pagliacci, Hamlet* and *Il Trovatore*, plus songs by Weill, Leoncavallo and others. 1955-59, 50 mins.
VHS: S13629. $34.95.

Robert Merrill in Opera and Song, Vol. 2. More songs and arias from America's most beloved baritone. Music by Massenet, Verdi, Gounod, Romberg, Jerome Kern, Rodgers and Hammerstein and others. 55 mins.
VHS: S16084. $34.95.

Roberta Peters in Opera and Song. Her appearances on the "Voice of Firestone" telecasts amply display the brilliant vocalism and delightful personality which made Roberta Peters one of the most famous and beloved sopranos of our time. Includes arias from *The Magic Flute, Lucia, La Traviata* and *Lakme*, plus songs by Arditi, Friml and others. 1952-57, 50 mins.
VHS: S13628. $34.95.

Roberta Peters in Opera and Song, Vol. 2. In this second volume of her work, Peters performs arias from *Don Giovanni, The Tales of Hofmann, Rigoletto* and a string of popular songs and music. 55 mins.
VHS: S17429. $34.95.

Thomas L. Thomas in Opera and Song. The vocal talent of the great Welsh baritone is the focus of this *Voice of Firestone* presentation featuring arias from *Hamlet* and *Un Ballo in Maschera*, as well as songs by Rudolf Friml, Jerome Kern, Rodgers & Hammerstein and others. Also highlighted are traditional folksongs. 55 mins.
VHS: S16082. $34.95.

The Great Caruso

Mario Lanza is cast as Enrico Caruso, the fabled Italian singer who had a voice that could shatter glass as well as hearts. This musical biography follows Caruso from his formative years in Naples to his triumphs in the great opera houses of the world. With Ann Blyth, Dorothy Kirsten and Jarmila Novotna. Story by Dorothy Caruso.
VHS: S06145. $19.98.
Laser: LD72176. $34.98.
Richard Thorpe, USA, 1951, 108 mins.

Haydn: The Creation (Bernstein)

Soloists Lucia Popp, Judith Blegen, Thomas Moser and Kurt Moll are featured in this performance of Haydn's oratorio with the Choir and Orchestra of the Bayerische Rundfunk conducted by Leonard Bernstein.
VHS: S18530. $24.95.
Laser: LD71031. $59.95.

Haydn: The Creation (Muti)

Riccardo Muti conducts the great oratorio by Haydn.
Laser: LD74572. $29.98.

Heart's Desire and Forbidden Music

Richard Tauber was the major tenor star of central Europe in his day and the most popular operetta tenor of all time. *Heart's Desire* includes performances from *Carmen*, "Aus den ostlichen Rosen," "Widmung" by Schumann, and many other songs, including some by Tauber. Also features Tauber's wife, Diana Napier, Leonora Corbett, Paul Graetz and Frank Voster. 79 mins. *Forbidden Music* features Tauper, Napier, June Clyde, Derrick de Marney and Jimmy Durante. 64 mins.
VHS: S28428. $34.95.

I Capuleti e I Montecchi

The great soprano, Katia Ricciarelli, sings her favorite operatic role from Vincenzo Bellini's version of *Romeo and Juliet*. It's set in the illustrious Teatro la Fenice in Venice, where we see her sing both in rehearsal and in performance. 60 mins.
VHS: S20941. $24.95.

I Live for Art—The Great Toscas

A film featuring fifteen world-renowned sopranos, whom we see both in performances, as Tosca, and in candid interviews. The result is a composite portrait of the prima donna, going beyond the conventional image. With Maria Callas, Montserrat Caballe, Renata Tebaldi, Dame Kiri Te Kanawa, Galina Vishnevskaya and others. 91 mins.
VHS: S04683. $39.95.

Jan Peerce, Marian Anderson & Andres Segovia

This historic film captures performances by three legends in the world of music. Jan Peerce and Nadine Conner perform three arias for which they are famous. Included are vignettes of the life of Marian Anderson, including a program of traditional spiritual favorites, and Andres Segovia permits the audience into the seclusion of his Paris studio as he performs traditional and contemporary numbers. 60 mins.
VHS: S11720. $19.95.

Janet Baker Full Circle

Janet Baker began her career singing in the Glyndebourne Chorus, and now, at the peak of her career, makes her farewell to opera from the same Glyndebourne stage. This profile is an intimate look at one year in the life of an international star-the final year in Dame Janet's operatic career. Included are several performance extracts of this great mezzo soprano from her final performances at the Royal Opera House, Covent Garden, the English National Opera and Glyndebourne. 75 mins.
VHS: S03168. $39.95.

Jessye Norman: A Christmas Concert

A revealing collection of Christmas songs by the remarkable Jessye Norman, featuring spirituals ("Go Tell It on the Mountain"); "He Shall Feed His Flock," from Handel's *Messiah*; and the inspired works of Gounod, Bach, Brahms and Schubert. Conducted by Lawrence Foster and the Orchestre de L'Opera de Lyon. 68 mins.
VHS: S17667. $24.95.
Laser: LD71783. $34.95.

Joan Sutherland: Making "Lakme"

Joan Sutherland and Richard Bonynge take you inside their production of Delibes' *Lakme*. Beginning with costume and scenic design, to dance, orchestral, and voice rehearsals, to grand opening night, you'll see the opera bloom under your eyes! 60 mins.
VHS: S02438. $29.95.

Jon Vickers Sings Verdi and Puccini

Rare Canadian Broadcasting Corporation performances by Jon Vickers are collected on this videotape. Act I of *Tosca*, Act II of *Manon Lescaut* and Act IV of *Il Trovatore* are included. Mary Simmons and Louis Quilico are also featured. 80 mins.
VHS: S19400. $39.95.

Jose Carreras

This world-renowned tenor, accompanied by the Vienna State Opera, sings a varied program of works by Puccini, Massenet, Faure and many others. This event has been hailed as the miracle concert, because it was presented just after his recovery from bone marrow treatments for leukemia. 140 mins.
VHS: S20984. $24.95.

Jose Carreras and Friends

The "Royal Gala Evening" held for Their Royal Highnesses Prince and Princess Michael of Kent starred Jose Carreras, Agnes Baltsa, Katia Ricciarelli and Ruggero Raimondi. Accompanied by the London Arts Orchestra conducted by Jacques Delacote, the program includes favorite operatic arias and duets, as well as popular songs. 90 mins.
VHS: S22006. $24.95.

Jose Carreras in Concert

Jose Carreras in a live performance at the Komische Opera in East Berlin, performing arias by Puccini, Leoncavallo, Respighi and others, and in a rousing encore with Bernstein's *Tonight*. 90 mins.
VHS: S07685. $19.95.

Jose Carreras in Salzburg

Tenor Jose Carreras performs *Seven Spanish Songs* by Manuel de Falla at the Great Festival House in Salzburg. Of course the enthusiastic audience is rewarded with a number of encores, including Leoncavallo's *Mattinata* and *Granda*. 111 mins.
VHS: S21061. $24.95.

Jose Carreras' Comeback Recital in Spain

The long-awaited video of Jose Carreras' comeback recital at Peralada Castle in Spain. The tenor, who has undergone two bone marrow transplants in his fight against leukemia, performs a wonderfully varied program of songs by Tosti, Puccini, Massenet, Faure and others. This video record of Carreras' emotional comeback is a treasure. 82 mins.
VHS: S10413. $19.95.

Jose Carreras: A Life Story

This biography of the elusive Spanish tenor Jose Carreras traces his work as a prodigy, performing at age seven; his subsequent opera performances; his collaboration on Bernstein's *West Side Story*; and the private anguish of his battle with cancer. With Montserrat Caballe, Placido Domingo and Luciano Pavarotti. 77 mins.
VHS: S18625. $29.95.
Laser: LD71874. $34.95.

Jose Carreras: A Tribute to Mario Lanza

Acclaimed tenor Carreras performs the songs of matinee idol and pop star Mario Lanza. Filmed in London's Albert Hall with a full orchestra, the songs featured in this tribute have never had more rich or heartfelt interpretations.
VHS: S21734. $29.97.
Laser: LD74494. $34.97.

Jose Carreras: Four Days with the Famous Tenor on the Road

A contemplative documentary about the life, art and off-stage personality of tenor Jose Carreras. The film captures four days in his life, during production on the film *Misa Criolla*. The film shows Carreras during rehearsals, interacting with his admirers and conferring with his son. 31 mins.
VHS: S19897. $19.95.

Jose Carreras: Music Festival in Granada

This live concert was filmed in Granada during one of Spain's largest annual music festivals. Carreras gives an electrifying performance of songs by Tosti, Puccini, de Falla and others. In Hi-Fi stereo, 93 mins.
VHS: S16797. $24.95.

Kathleen Battle at the Metropolitan Museum

Kathleen Battle performs a solo recital with works from Gershwin, Handel, Mozart, Strauss, Liszt and Puccini.
VHS: S17240. $24.95.
Laser: LD71631. $29.95.

The King's Christmas

The King's Singers perform a collection of seasonal tunes, sprinkled with some of their hits, including Randy Newman's "Short People." Recorded at England's Harewood House. 28 mins.
VHS: S34512. $19.95.

King's College Choir: The Festival of Nine Lessons and Carols

Stephen Cleobury conducts the King's College Choir in Cambridge, in the seasonal concert of carols, including "Silent Night," "Hark! The Herald Angels Sing," "Oh Come, All Ye Faithful" and "O Little Town of Bethlehem." On the same program is a 50-minute BBC documentary that presents an inside view of the King's College Choir. 110 mins.
VHS: S19751. $34.95.
Laser: LD71960. $34.95.

The King's Singers in Concert

Taped in England's Harewood House, and introduced by James Galway, The King's Singers present regal performances of music, including folk songs from the British Isles, Rimsky-Korsakov's *The Flight of the Bumblebee*, and *Creole Love Call* by Duke Ellington. 28 mins.
VHS: S34510. $19.95.

Kiri Te Kanawa: Royal Gala Concert

Kiri Te Kanawa in her first solo recital at Royal Opera House, presenting songs by Schubert, Schumann, Strauss, Wolf and others. 60 mins.
VHS: S07686. $19.95.

Kiri! Her Greatest Hits Live

On her 50th birthday Kiri Te Kanawa sang arias by her favorite composers, including works by Mozart, Puccini and Richard Strauss. In London's Royal Albert Hall, she was accompanied by the London Symphony Orchestra and Chorus directed by Stephen Barlow. Show tunes by Gershwin, Rogers and Hammerstein, Bernstein and Andrew Lloyd Webber, as well as music from her Native New Zealand, round out this one-of-a-kind program.
VHS: S21776. $29.95.
Laser: LD74497. $34.95.

La Gran Scena Opera Company

"Impressive...virtuosic...outrageous...very funny" (*New York Times*). A videotaped performance in Munich by New York's very original company.
VHS: S02947. $49.95.

La Grande Notte a Verona
In celebration of the 75th anniversary of the Festival of the Arena di Verona, this concert brought together singers Jose Carreras, Ruggero Raimondi, Montserrat Caballe, Eva Marton, Samuel Ramey, Ileana Cotrubas and many others to benefit the Jose Carreras International Leukemia Foundation. A contribution by Placido Domingo is also included. 122 mins.
VHS: S20985. $24.95.

La Stupenda: A Profile of Dame Joan Sutherland
At the Sydney Opera House on October 2, 1990, Dame Joan Sutherland bade farewell to opera. This tape looks back on her marvelous singing career, which spanned 42 years and brought joy to millions. Includes her final performances as well as interviews with her and some of her closest friends. 90 mins.
VHS: S15629. $24.95.
Laser: LD70280. $34.95.

Last Night of the Proms: The 100th Season
Welsh baritone Bryn Terfel and percussionist Evelyn Glennie are at the center of this riotous night of glorious music. *Last Night of the Proms* is traditionally an unbridled celebration. The BBC Orchestra, under the direction of Andrew Davis, performs music by Bach, Walton, Wood, Elgar, Massenet and others. 112 mins.
VHS: S24971. $29.97.

The Life of Verdi
This is a collector's edition of an epic drama based on the life of Giuseppe Verdi. Filmed in Italy, Leningrad, Paris, and London, it features a stereo score of Verdi's great works sung by Renata Tebaldi, Maria Callas, Luciano Pavarotti, Birgit Nilsson, and others. 600 minutes.
VHS: S03161. $124.95.

Luciano Pavarotti—The Event
The world's favorite tenor gives a gala concert in Milan to celebrate the World Cup heroes. A must for every music buff's collection, as Pavarotti performs the best-loved operatic arias and songs from the works of composers such as Donizetti, Mozart, Verdi, and Puccini. This engaging performance features no less than six encores! Don't miss it. 88 mins.
VHS: S13654. $29.98.
DVD: DV60355. $29.99.

The Maestro and the Diva
Dame Kiri Te Kanawa and Sir Georg Solti join forces in this collection of Richard Strauss songs, including the famed "Four Last Songs." Recorded by Sony Music in Manchester with the BBC Orchestra. 118 mins.
Laser: LD74552. $29.98.

Magnificat for Solo, Chorus and Orchestra
Bach composed this Magnificat for the Christmas Vesper Service in 1723. In keeping with the tradition, Christmas carols, sung by an additional choir in the choir loft, are added to the Magnificat in this performance filmed in the 800-year-old Church of St. Nicholas in Leipzig. With Peter Schreier, Heidi Riess, Gothart Stier, and the New Bach Collegium Maximum.
VHS: S05584. $29.95.

The Magnificent Victoria de los Angeles
From the BBC archives comes de los Angeles in this live 1968 recital, accompanied by the great pianist Gerald Moore. The performance includes songs by Granados, Faure, Ravel and others. 50 mins.
VHS: S16469. $29.95.

Margaret Price: Ruckert Lieder
Margaret Price's clear voice perfectly accentuates the drama of Friedrich Rukert's poems, which have been orchestrated by Gustav Mahler for this production. 30 mins.
VHS: S26925. $19.95.

Maria Callas Concert: 1962 Hamburg
The second, triumphant return of Maria Callas to Hamburg, in a memorable performance which includes Berlioz' *Carnival Romain, Le Cid,* selections from *Carmen, Ernani, La Cenerentola* and *Don Carlo*. 65 mins.
VHS: S03521. $39.95.

Maria Callas: Life and Art
A celebration of the singing and dramatic skills of the great diva, with an exploration of the woman behind the public persona. The film features excerpts from Callas' performances in *Tosca, La Traviata, Norma,* and others, as well as interviews with some of the people who knew her best, including Franco Zeffirelli, Giuseppe Di Stefano, S.A. Gorlinsky and Carlo Maria Giulini. 78 mins.
VHS: S04911. $19.95.

Mario Lanza: The American Caruso
Mario Lanza did more to bring classical music and opera to the masses through the popular art of movies than anyone before or since. Through clips from his most popular films and recordings and through interviews with co-workers like Zsa Zsa Gabor and Anna Moffo, Lanza's turbulent life is frankly presented. The program is guest-hosted by Placido Domingo. 68 mins.
VHS: S14446. $29.95.

Messe Solennelle
Berlioz' composition was lost in the 19th century, only to be rediscovered in an Antwerp organ loft in 1991. This world premiere is performed by the Monteverdi Choir and the Orchestre Revolutionnaire et Romantique and conducted by John Eliot Gardiner. Shot on location in Westminster Cathedral in October 1993. 59 mins.
VHS: S20977. $29.95.
Laser: LD72405. $29.95.

The Messiah (Cardiff)
"This is the way a performance of *The Messiah* is intended to be performed." In this production, the London Baroque Players, the Cardiff Polyphonic Choir and soloists Norma Burrowes, Helen Watts, Robert Tear and Willard White perform *The Messiah* to the original scoring.
VHS: S13362. $19.95.

The Messiah (Marriner)
An all-star performance at the Point Theatre in Dublin, conducted by Sir Neville Marriner and performed by the Orchestra and Chorus of Academy of St. Martin in the Fields. With Sylvia McNair, Anne Sofie von Otter, Michael Chance and Jerry Hadley. 157 mins.
VHS: S18314. $34.95.
Laser: LD71852. $59.95.

Met Centennial Gala
Grace Bumbry, Montserrat Caballe, Eva Marton, Placido Domingo, Jose Carreras and nearly 100 other singers celebrate the centennial of the Metropolitan Opera with Leonard Bernstein and James Levine conducting. Stereo, 1983, color, 231 mins. 2 cassettes.
VHS: S02444. $29.95.

Montserrat Caballe and Jose Carreras in Moscow
Live from the Bolshoi Theatre, a performance of favorite arias and duets by Puccini, Verdi, Rossini, Bellini and others, and a selection of popular Catalan songs. 120 mins.
VHS: S20567. $24.95.

Montserrat Caballe: The Woman, the Diva
A portrait one of this century's great operatic sopranos, one who feels a deep sense of identification with the roles she portrays. Caballe performs arias from ten selections around the world, and offers a deep insight into her life as an opera star. 62 mins.
VHS: S03167. $39.95.

More Songs of Placido Domingo in Mexico, Vol. 2
The beautiful songs of this Latin American country are featured, as sung by this great tenor accompanied by his musical friends. 70 mins.
VHS: S22041. $19.98.

The Moscow Virtuosi
One of the world's greatest chamber ensembles, formed by Vladimir Spivakov, *The Moscow Virtuosi* interprets works by Bach and Mozart, in a concert taped at the Municipal Theater in Torrejon de Ardoz, Spain. 68 mins.
Laser: LD71935. $34.95.

Mozart Mass in C Minor, K.427
Helmuth Rilling is seen both in rehearsal and in a full production of this grand piece in the Knight's Hall, Wolfegg. 60 mins.
VHS: S22007. $24.95.

Mozart: Coronation Mass (Karajan)
Herbert von Karajan conducts the Berlin Philharmonic.
Laser: LD74585. $29.98.

Mozart: Great Mass in C Minor
Leonard Bernstein conducts the Bavarian Radio Symphony Orchestra with soloists Arlene Auger, Frederica von Stade and Frank Lopardo in this April 1990 concert which was organized to celebrate the opening of borders between East and West Germany. In Hi-Fi stereo, 81 mins.
Laser: LD71464. $34.95.

Mozart: Requiem (Bernstein)
A joyous performance film of Mozart's final gift to the world. The Bavarian Radio Chorus and Symphony Orchestra is conducted by Leonard Bernstein, with an all-star cast including Maria Ewing and Jerry Hadley. Filmed in the beautiful Abbey Church, Diessen (Ammersee), Upper Bavaria, July 1988. 65 mins.
VHS: S14116. $24.95.

Mozart: Requiem (Davis)
Mozart's last work is shrouded in mystery and legend. It was commissioned by an enigmatic stranger and never finished. Mozart wrote presciently that he believed that the requiem was for himself. In this unforgettable performance, Colin Davis conducts the Bavarian Radio Symphony Orchestra and Chorus, with internationally renowned soloists Edith Mathis, Trudeliese Schmidt, Peter Schreier and Gwynne Howell. 57 mins.
VHS: S10274. $29.95.

Mozart: Requiem (Karajan)
Herbert von Karajan conducts the Berlin Philharmonic in this Sony Music performance.
Laser: LD74586. $29.98.

Mozart: Requiem K and Mass in C Minor
Virtuoso conductor John Eliot Gardiner leads the Monteverdi Choir and English Baroque Soloists in a performance of Mozart's final two unfinished masses, filmed in Barcelona on the 200th anniversary of the composer's death. With Barbara Bonney, Anne-Sofie von Otter, Anthony Rolfe Johnson and Alastair Miles. 100 mins.
VHS: S19106. $24.95.
Laser: LD71895. $34.95.

Mozart: The Requiem from Sarajevo
Jose Carreras, Zubin Mehta and Ruggero Raimondi join forces to perform this musical masterpiece in war-torn Sarejevo. The Choir of the Cathedral of Sarajevo and the Orchestra of Sarjevo also took part in this remembrance for all those who have died in this city under seige. 50 mins.
VHS: S25635. $19.95.

Music of the Night
Jose Carreras, under the musical direction of George Martin, sings the music of Andrew Lloyd Webber. With Marti Webb, Jane Harrison, and the Choir of St. Paul's Cathedral.
VHS: S15456. $24.98.
Laser: LD70215. $29.98.

Musical Masterpiece at Masada
Stars Zubin Mehta and the Israel Philharmonic. Mehta and company perform Mahler's Second Symphony at the historic mountain of Masada as the grand finale of Israel's 40th Anniversary Celebrations last year.
VHS: S10712. $29.95.

My Heart's Delight
Luciano Pavarotti sang this concert of songs by Puccini and his contemporaries, including Franz Lehar's "You Are My Heart's Delight", in his hometown, Modena, Italy. On this occasion, born of his gratitude to his compatriots, Pavarotti was accompanied by soprano Nuccia Focile. 86 mins.
VHS: S20974. $29.95.
Laser: LD72403. $34.95.

Nicolai Ghiaurov
A tribute to the world-renowned basso Ghiaurov, he is shown performing in his greatest operatic roles. They include Don Giovanni, Don Quixote, Boris Godunov, and Mephistopheles. 120 mins.
VHS: S03373. $59.95.

Ode to Freedom
This program documents the historic live recording of Beethoven's Ninth Symphony in East Berlin's Schauspielhaus on Christmas Day 1989, just after the collapse of the Berlin Wall. The concert features members of three choruses and six orchestras. Hi-Fi stereo, 92 mins.
VHS: S16815. $24.95.
Laser: LD71519. $34.95.

Opera Favorites Sung by Placido Domingo and Kiri Te Kanawa
Two of opera's best known and most exciting performers in magnificent moments from some of the world's greatest operas, recorded live, with English subtitles. Includes highlights from *Die Fledermaus* performed at the Royal Opera House at Covent Garden, *Otello* from Arena di Verona, *Ernani* from La Scala, and selections from *Les Contes d'Hoffman, La Fanciulla del West*. 59 mins.
VHS: S10910. $39.99.

Opera Stars in Concert, Volume 1

Filmed live in Spain, international opera greats Alfredo Kraus, Katia Ricciarelli, Paolo Coni, Lucia Valentini-Terrani and Ruggero Raimondi perform favorite arias and duets. The Symphonic Orchestra of Madrid is conducted by Gian Paolo Sanzogno, opening with Verdi's *I Vespri Sicciliani*, and then quoting the beloved works of *La Traviata, Tosca, I Puritani, Semiramide, Lucrezia Borgia, Don Carlos, Faust* and *Tales of Hoffman*. 60 mins.
VHS: S16506. $24.95.

Opera Stars in Concert, Volume 2

In this compendium of the world's finest performers, filmed live in Madrid, Alfredo Kraus, Katia Ricciarelli and Ruggero Raimondi perform a series of thrilling arias, from Verdi, Puccini, Rossini, Donizetti, including *Rigoletto, Elisir d'Amore*, and *The Barber of Seville*. The program also features Paolo Coni and Lucia Valentini-Terrani. 60 mins.
VHS: S17309. $24.95.

Opera Stars in Concert, Volume 3

Performed live in Barcelona, this program of features Alfredo Kraus, Paolo Coni, Renata Scotto, Mellanie Holiday, Ramon Vargas and Gail Gilmore performing sections from *Macbeth, Don Carlos, Elisir D'Amore* and *Rigoletto*. 80 mins.
VHS: S17315. $24.95.

P.D.Q. Bach's "The Abduction of Figaro"

The infamous P.D.Q. Bach's only full-length opera is presented here by Professor Peter Schickele. It features the "corpse de ballet," the "Dance of the Seven Pails," and more!
VHS: S02191. $49.95.

Pavarotti & Friends

On September 27, 1992, Italian tenor Luciano Pavarotti returned to his hometown and gathered an international cast of pop and opera stars for a gala charity concert to help fund local disease research, performing popular and classical music. With Sting, Suzanne Vega, The Neville Brothers, Bob Geldof, Brian May, Zucchero, Lucia Dalla and Patricia Kaas. 70 mins.
VHS: S18312. $29.95.

Pavarotti & Friends 2

Bryan Adams, Michael Kamen and Andreas Vollenweider join Pavarotti for this collection of songs performed in concert. Featuring a variety of operatic and popular music, including "All for Love," "Please Forgive Me," "Night Fire Dance," "Ave Maria" and "O Sole Mio."
VHS: S25922. $29.95.
Laser: LD75033. $34.95.

Pavarotti & Friends Together for the Children of Bosnia

Luciano Pavarotti joined Bono, the Edge, Brian Eno, Michael Bolton, Meat Loaf, Simon le Bon, Zucchero, Dolores O'Riordan, The Chieftains, Italian rap sensation Jovanotti and conductor Michael Kamen for a special benefit concert on behalf of the children of Bosnia. This video captures the event, staged in Modena, Italy, in September of 1995. Ultimately, Pavarotti's efforts will help build a music center in the Bosnian town of Mostar.
VHS: S27625. $29.95.
Laser: LD75535. $34.95.

Pavarotti and Levine in Recital

Join Luciano Pavarotti and James Levine on the stage of the Metropolitan Opera in New York, in a recital of operatic arias and popular art songs, including works by Rossini, Bellini and Puccini's "Nessun Dorma" from *Turandot*. In Hi-Fi stereo, 72 mins.
VHS: S14113. $24.95.
Laser: LD71419. $24.95.

Pavarotti and the Italian Tenor

Over the course of this hour-long documentary Pavarotti makes clear in both interview segments and musical performances the importance of the Italian tenor tradition to his own career. He comments frankly on his influences, including Caruso and Gaggle. This video also features songs and arias never released on video before.
VHS: S26484. $29.95.
Laser: LD75096. $34.95.

Pavarotti in Concert in China

The great tenor in recital in Beijing, China, from his historic 1986 tour. From Verdi and Puccini arias to Italian classics like *O Sole Mio*, Pavarotti proves once again why he is the world's most beloved opera singer.
VHS: S13058. $29.95.

Pavarotti in Confidence with Peter Ustinov

Pavarotti is the tenor acclaimed for his great voice and ability to bring opera to new audiences throughout the world, from Central Park to the World Cup. Peter Ustinov goes behind the public persona of this singer to uncover the man and the ideas and passions that drive him. Excerpts from folk songs and arias are included. 50 mins.
VHS: S22933. $19.95.

Pavarotti in Hyde Park

An all-new video production that was taken from this summer's concert in London's Hyde Park by the world's favorite tenor Luciano Pavarotti.
VHS: S15218. $24.95.
Laser: LD71443. $34.95.

A Pavarotti Valentine

Pavarotti sings 19 of his greatest hits, including "Nessun Dorma" from *Turandot*, selections from *L'Elisir d'Amore*,, "O Sole Mio," and others, as recorded at a recital from the Teatro Petruzzelli in 1984. 77 mins.
VHS: S14816. $29.95.

Pavarotti—Master Class at Juilliard

Incomparable tenor Luciano Pavarotti sings and coaches top young singers at the Juilliard School of Music. Using arias by Puccini, Mozart and Verdi, Pavarotti guides students through the elements of breath control, phrasing and interpretation. The subtle discipline of opera singing is revealed. 60 mins.
VHS: S12762. $29.95.

Placido Domingo & Rostropovich

Placido Domingo is at his versatile best in a concert from the Roman Theater in Merida, Spain. He not only sings some of his favorite arias, but also conducts the orchestra for Mstislav Rostropovich's performance of a Haydn Cello concerto. Domingo also sings and plays piano to Rostropovich's cello in Massenet's *Elegy*, plus Tchaikovsky's *1812 Overture* and a *Carmen* duet with soprano Olga Borodina. 60 mins.
VHS: S15939. $24.95.
Laser: CLV. LD74628. $34.95.

Placido Domingo: A Musical Life

At last there is a documentary that explores the man behind the opera superstar. This video shows Domingo in private moments with his wife Marta and his three sons at their spectacular Acapulco home. It also shows him at work as he flies to Madrid to record a zarzuela song and conduct an opera by Bellini. 90 mins.
VHS: S24307. $29.95.

Placido Domingo: His 25th Anniversary Concert at the Roman Amphitheater of Verona

Placido Domingo returns to Verona to commemorate his earlier smashing success in the city's ancient outdoor amphitheater. Cecilia Gasdia joins Placido, who sings his favorites from Verdi and Puccini, including Act 1 of *Othello*, Act 3 of *Aida* and Act 3 of *La Boheme*.
VHS: S27173. $19.95.
Drazen Siriscevic/Armando Tasso, Italy, 1995, 100 mins.

Placido Domingo: Hommage a Sevilla

Placido Domingo honors the cultural diversity and historical importance of Seville, the setting for many great operas and the site of Expo '92. With scenes from *Don Giovanni, The Barber of Seville, Carmen* and *Fidelio*, conducted by James Levine of the Vienna Symphony Orchestra.
VHS: S17128. $24.95.
Laser: LD71544. $29.95.

Placido Domingo: Live from Miami

Superstar tenor Placido Domingo performs at the Miami Arena to a standing-room-only crowd. Joined by the talented American soprano Ana Panagulias, Domingo presents a bounty of favorite arias, duets and songs by Puccini, Donizetti, Meyerbeer and others. 60 mins.
VHS: S15938. $24.95.
Laser: CLV. LD71488. $29.95.

Placido Domingo—Zarzuela

Live from the National Auditorium of Madrid, tenor Placido Domingo performs an "all-zarzuela" concert to an enthusiastic crowd which includes Spain's King Juan Carlos and the royal family. Domingo is joined by some of Spain's leading zarzuela performers, including Guadalupe Sanchez, Teresa Verdera and Paloma Perez Inigo. Also featured is the colorful dancing of the Ballet Espanol. 69 mins.
VHS: S16227. $24.95.

Placido Grandisimo

Officially opening the Seville World Expo, Placido Domingo gives a thrilling live concert performance to a capacity crown at the Seville Stadium. He performs favorite arias by Puccini and Bizet, as well as a selection of popular Spanish songs and zarzuelas. Soprano Julia Migenes joins Domingo in a duet from *Carmen*, and also performs solos from Puccini and Gershwin. As the exciting concert reaches its climax, the crowd demands an encore from Domingo, the moving "El Grito de America." 60 mins.
VHS: S16228. $24.95.

Placido in Prague

Placido Domingo performed a concert in the Prague Concert Hall, where he was joined by Angela Gheorghiu. Works by Puccini, Donizetti, Mozart, Verdi and other great composers make this memorable musical evening an incomparable event. 94 mins.
VHS: S24361. $19.95.

Placido: A Year in the Life of Placido Domingo

Travel around the world with Placido Domingo and enjoy his matchless performances in *Tosca, Tales of Hoffmann, Otello, Ernani*, and other great operas. Offstage, you'll get an intimate portrait of the man *Opera News* called "the King of the opera," seeing his methods of training, rehearsal, and everyday life. 105 mins.
VHS: S02453. $19.95.

Puccini

The composer of some of the world's most popular operas, *Madama Butterfly, La Boheme* and *Tosca*, Puccini became involved in an appalling scandal which nearly ruined his career. His tragic story unfolds in this dramatic program which features Robert Stephens, Judith Horwath and Virginia McKenna. The inclusion of a present-day production of his unfinished *Turandot* shows parallels between the composer's life and work. Stereo hi-fi. 135 mins.
VHS: S02749. $29.95.

Renata Scotto in Concert

This live 1991 concert from Budapest offers the complete *Les Nuits d'Ete* of Berlioz, plus arias by Handel, Mozart and Puccini. In Stereo. 68 mins.
VHS: S16080. $29.95.

Renata Scotto: Prima Donna in Recital

Diva Renata Scotto performs in Tokyo, accompanied by pianist Thomas Fulton on this 1984 video. She performs the music of Puccini, Verdi, Liszt, Rossini, and more.
VHS: S02452. $39.95.

Renata Tebaldi Live!

Tebaldi may well have been the leading non-coloratura Italian soprano of the century. Despite a vocal crisis in the 1960's, she recovered to become a viable verismo soprano. This video shows her in all her early greatness and also captures the more glamorized era of her later career. 25 mins.
VHS: S24558. $34.95.

Requiem (Webber)

Andrew Lloyd Webber's *Requiem* was first performed in February, 1985, at St. Thomas' in New York. Captured live, this production stars Placido Domingo and Sarah Brightman, the choirs of Winchester Cathedral and St. Thomas', and the orchestra of St. Luke's conducted by Lorin Maazel. 60 mins.
VHS: S02454. $19.95.

A Requiem for Mozart

The bicentennial performance of Mozart's *Requiem*, presented in the same church where the requiem mass for his memorial service was held. Sir Georg Solti conducts the Vienna Philharmonic Orchestra and the Vienna State Opera Choir. With Cecilia Bartoli, Arlene Auger, Vinson Cole and Rene Pape. In Hi-Fi Stereo, 100 mins.
VHS: S16043. $24.95.
Laser: LD71192. $34.95.

Ruggero Raimondi

In this revealing documentary, Raimondi's life amidst the international world of opera is highlighted by his performances of great male roles. Rossini's *Moses in Egypt*, Massenet's *Don Quichotte* and Mussorgsky's *Boris Godunov* are stellar showcases for Raimondi, but he is especially renowned for *Don Giovanni*, which he conducts himself in this video. 50 mins.
VHS: S26214. $19.95.

Schmidt: My Song Goes Round the World (Ein Lied Geht Um die Welt)

Schmidt plays a man consumed by love, in this film filled with beautiful music. His rendition of "Mal d'amore" is reason enough to see and hear the film. German with English subtitles. 79 mins.
VHS: S24036. $34.95.

Sherrill Milnes' Homage to Verdi

Renowned operatic baritone Sherrill Milnes presents this look at the work of Verdi, including a description of his life and the operas he composed. Milnes performs arias from *La Traviata, Rigoletto, Macbeth, Nabucco*, and others, proving once again that he is America's premiere baritone. 56 mins.
VHS: S03156. $39.95.

Sherrill Milnes: An All-Star Gala

This exciting musical portrait of the great American baritone also features performances by Placido Domingo, Mirella Freni, Julia Migenes and Peter Schreier. Produced by the Italian television network RAI. 60 mins.
VHS: S26430. $24.95.

Shirley Verret

A film biography of the great black diva, following her professional and private life during the course of a year. Performance extracts show her in many of the dramatic opera roles which she made her own: Iphigenie at the Paris Opera, Tosca at the Arena di Verona, Dalila at the Royal Opera House Covent Garden, and Carmen at La Scala. 60 mins.
VHS: S04684. $19.95.

Silent Night with Jose Carreras
A special Christmas journey to Austria, where he sings such favorites as "White Christmas," "O Come All Ye Faithful," and, of course, "Silent Night." 40 mins.
VHS: S07687. $19.95.

The Soldier's Tale (L'Histoire du Soldat)/Symphony of Psalms
The Nederlands Dans Theater appears in *The Soldier's Tale*, conducted by David Porceljin; *Symphony of Psalms* is conducted Leonard Bernstein and performed by the London Symphony Orchestra and English Bach Festival Chorus.
Laser: LD70408. $34.95.

Songs of a Wayfarer/Songs on the Death of Children—Mahler
Leonard Bernstein's final Mahler recording (recorded in Vienna) in collaboration with American baritone Thomas Hampson, who performs three song cycles. "Hampson darkens or lightens his tone in accordance with the sense of the text and responds alertly to Bernstein's subtleties of phrasing" (*Gramophone*). With the Vienna Philharmonic Orchestra. 76 mins.
VHS: S17432. $24.95.
Laser: LD71757. $34.95.

Songs of Mexico: Placido Domingo: Volume 1
The opera superstar sings an exceptional collection of traditional Mexican songs. 75 mins.
VHS: S22040. $19.98.

The Sorceress
This film of seduction, starring Opera's most alluring soprano, Kiri Te Kanawa, features the greatest love songs by Handel. She is accompanied by the Academy of Ancient Music under the direction of Christopher Hogwood. Dressed in elaborate and sumptuous costumes, this enchantress will delight viewers with her famed voice. 50 mins.
VHS: S21328. $29.95.

South Pacific (London Sessions)
A diverse group of international performers, including Kiri Te Kanawa, Jose Carreras, Sarah Vaughan, Mandy Patinkin, and the London Symphony Orchestra gather in London to record the music from *South Pacific*, the great musical, in a new way. A remarkable performance is the result. England, 1986, 60 mins.
VHS: S01773. $19.98.

Spirituals in Concert
Two of the great divas of the opera stage, Kathleen Battle and Jessye Norman, join forces in this unique performance video to sing a collection of well-known and lesser-known Spirituals. James Levine conducts. Including: "Swing Low, Sweet Chariot" and "He's Got the Whole World in His Hands." 91 mins.
VHS: S14120. $24.95.

St. John Passion
Filmed at St. Thomas Church, Leipzig, where Bach conducted the first performance. Performed by Peter Schreier, Venceslava Hruba-Freiberger, Alain Zaepffel, Hermann-Christian Polster, and the Choir of the St. Thomas Church, Leipzig.
VHS: S05583. $39.95.

St. Matthew Passion
Filmed at the St. Thomas Church in Leipzig where Bach himself was the organist for 25 years. With Peter Schreier, Regina Werner, Rosemarie Lang, Siegfried Lorenz, Theo Adam, and the Choir of the St. Thomas Church, Leipzig.
VHS: S05582. $39.95.

The Story of Carol
Christmas carols originated in dances dating back to the seventh century. This documentary traces the pagan roots of these songs. The first printed carol appeared in 1521. Later they were condemned by the Puritans, only to be revived in the Victorian era. 52 mins.
VHS: S21822. $19.95.

Stratasphere
An emotion-packed, intimate film portrait of Teresa Stratas, one of the greatest voices of the present day. In a mixture of revealing interviews and stirring performance footage, Ms. Stratas tells the story of her childhood as the daughter of poor Greek immigrants in Toronto, and her rise to fame on stage of the Metropolitan Opera in New York, as well as her relationships with the famous, including Lotte Lenya and Mother Teresa, to whom Ms. Stratas dedicates a portion of her income. The opera star is seen in rehearsal for Puccini's *La Boheme* with Franco Zeffirelli. 87 mins.
VHS: S12278. $29.95.

The Swingle Singers
James Galway presents this extraordinary octet, whose jazz-inflected arrangements introduced an entire generation to the glories of Bach. This concert offers vintage Swingle, including Bach, Henry VIII, Debussy, The Beatles and Tchaikovsky's *1812 Overture*, complete with cannons. 28 mins.
VHS: S34511. $19.95.

Symphony for the Spire
A spectacle of music and theater in a concert to support the Prince of Wales' Salisbury Cathedral Spire Appeal. The program features Placido Domingo, Jessye Norman, Ofra Harnoy, Kenneth Branagh, Charlton Heston and the English Chamber Orchestra. The highlights include Harnoy's rendition of *The Flight of the Bumble Bee*, Norman's *Morgen Op. 27 No. 4* and Domingo's *Be My Love*. Conducted by Richard Armstrong. 65 mins.
VHS: S19420. $19.95.

Ten Tenors
Bergonzi, Corelli, Gigli, Keipura, Lauri, Volpi, Martini, McCormack, Piccaver, Schipa and Tagliavini are the great tenors seen in this compilation video. These excerpts are taken from various Bel Canto videos.
VHS: S24852. $34.95.

Thomas Hampson: I Hear America Singing
As seen on PBS, baritone Thomas Hampson celebrates America's rich tradition of concert song in this entertaining program. Features enduring American classics by Foster, Copland, Bernstein, Barber and others. Hampson is joined by an all-star cast including Marilyn Horne, Frederica von Stade, Dawn Upshaw, Jerry Hadley and Harolyn Blackwell. 90 mins.
VHS: S30879. $29.95.

The Three Sopranos
This memorable recital presents three of the world's greatest sopranos together on the same stage. Ileana Cortrubas, Elena Obraztsova and Renata Scotto created magic in front of a sold-out crowd at the Roman Ampitheater of Siracuse, Italy, performing selections from favorite operas such as *Carmen, Tales of Hoffmann, Aida, Pagliacci* and more. 67 mins.
VHS: S15940. $24.95.
Laser: CLV. LD71489. $29.95.

The Three Tenors
Jose Carreras, Placido Domingo and Luciano Pavarotti join conductor Zubin Mehta for this singular musical event. On the occasion of soccer's World Cup in 1994, they performed together in Los Angeles. Operatic arias, popular music and even a salute to the music of Hollywood make this an unforgettable collaborative effort.
VHS: S21991. $29.98.
Laser: LD74542. $39.98.

The Three Tenors in Concert: Carreras, Domingo, Pavarotti
The three greatest tenors in the world side by side on the same stage in Rome during the World Cup soccer finals in 1990. Conducted by Zubin Mehta. Don't miss this once-in-a-lifetime musical treasure! 89 mins.
VHS: S14107. $24.95.
Laser: LD70905. $34.95.
DVD: DV60006. $29.95.

Three Tenors: Encore
Tenors Jose Carreras, Placido Domingo and Luciano Pavarotti, under the direction of conductor Zubin Mehta, are captured in this fascinating, backstage documentary culled from hours of video and performance footage of their *In Concert* video that sold a phenomenal 10 million recordings. Narrated by Derek Jacobi. Features *Nessun dorma, A mare chiaro, Rondine al nido*, and *Mattinata*. 1992, 57 mins.
VHS: S17365. $19.95.
Laser: LD72299. $29.95.

Verdi: Requiem (La Scala/von Karajan)
Of the hundreds of recordings of the great Verdi *Requiem* there is one which could be described as definitive. Leontyne Price, Fiorenza Cossotto, Luciano Pavarotti—together with the chorus and orchestra of La Scala, Milan—are conducted by Herbert von Karajan in a performance for the ages. 85 mins.
VHS: S14117. $24.95.

Verdi: Requiem (London/Abbado)
Recorded live from Edinburgh's Usher Hall, Verdi's brilliant choral piece is conducted by Claudio Abbado and performed by the London Symphony Orchestra, the Edinburgh Festival Chorus and four distinguished soloists, Margaret Price, Jessye Norman, Jose Carreras and Ruggero Raimondi. 97 mins.
VHS: S18759. $29.95.

Vespers of the Blessed Virgin
Filmed in the extraordinary setting of St. Mark's Basilica in Venice, where Monteverdi himself served as maestro di capella from 1613 to 1643, this is a 1989 performance of Monteverdi's masterpiece. 111 mins.
VHS: S14803. $29.95.

Victoria de los Angeles in Recital
The first complete recital by the beloved soprano to be released on video, taped at the 1989 Palacio de la Musica in Barcelona, on the 45th anniversary of her recital career. Among the selections are songs by Granados, de Falla, Mompou and Albeniz, and a seductive rendition from *Carmen*.
VHS: S12919. $39.95.

Vienna Boys' Choir Sings Mozart at the Chapel of the Hofburg, Vienna
A thrilling program of Mozart's choral masterpieces, from the early "Waisenhaus-Messe" to the late period "Ave verum corpus", performed by the world-renowned Vienna Boys' Choir, conducted by Uwe Christian Harrer. 72 mins.
VHS: S18316. $29.95.
Laser: LD71854. $34.95.

Visions of Gregorian Chants
The Benedictine Monks of St. Wandrille perform their timeless and traditional meditations to soothe the soul. This music has brought millions solace. Now combined with visuals that awaken the senses and release anxiety, this spiritual experience is available on video. 45 mins.
VHS: S21293. $9.99.

Wagner in Bayreuth
This two-part program interweaves a 25-minute documentary narrated by Wagner's grandson Wolfgang that describes the birth of the Salzburg festival, a behind-the-scenes look at the Festspielhaus, and the second part that features excerpts of *Tannhauser, Lohengrin, Der Fliegende Hollander, Rheingold*, and *Die Walkure*. 70 mins.
VHS: S17405. $9.95.
Laser: LD71699. $34.95.

War Requiem
Benjamin Britten's requiem features Anthony Rolfe Johnson, Luba Orgonasova and Boje Skovhus as soloists with the Monteverdi Choir, the NDR Choir, and the Tolzer Boys Choir, and the NDR Symphony Orchestra conducted by John Eliot Gardiner in this live performance at the Church of St. Mary in Lubeck, Germany, as part of the Schleswig-Holstein Festival. 87 mins. Hi-Fi Stereo.
VHS: S20555. $29.95.
Laser: LD72367. $34.95.

Young Caruso
Musical biography of Enrico Caruso starring Ermanno Randi but featuring the singing of Mario del Monaco of the New York Met. With an early performance by Gina Lollobrigida.
VHS: S02238. $29.95.
Italy, 1951, 77 mins.

Zubin Mehta and Leontyne Price
The magnificent lyric-dramatic soprano Leontyne Price joins the New York Philharmonic's Zubin Mehta for a glorious concert of Mozart, Verdi, and Strauss. Opening with the Philharmonic's stirring performance of Mozart's Jupiter Symphony, this is a magical concert. 94 mins.
VHS: S08712. $22.95.

WORLD MUSIC

African Dance and Drumming
Culturally and artistically rich African music directly inspires dance, song, language and even clothing. Renowned choreographer Margo Blake and master drummer Dr. David Closson present this interactive program suitable for children from elementary school to the high school level.
VHS: S22479. $99.95.

African Drumming
Baba Olatunji is a master of African drumming. He presents essential techniques, rhythmic patterns and concepts for drummers at all levels. The spiritual power of drumming and drums are the focus of this informative video. 60 mins.
VHS: S22707. $39.95.

African Guitar
Anthropologist Gerhard Kubrik's personal field recordings from 1966-1993 are collected on this video. Kubrik is a widely recognized expert who has written several books and countless articles on the music of sub-Saharan Africa. Now the rich textures of African fingerstyle guitar music can be seen and heard in an accessable format.
VHS: S25057. $24.95.

Afrika Bambaata and Family: Electric Dance Hop
This collection features the very first rap music videos. Bambaata is often called the godfather of hip hop music because of his innovative and enduring style. 60 mins.
VHS: S24022. $9.98.

Ahi-Nama in Cuba
Features six music videos all shot entirely in Cuba. A rare glimpse into the diverse musical styles and beautiful scenery that make up the island. 30 mins.
VHS: S34882. $19.95.

Alan Stivell
With his Celtic harp and other exotic instruments, Alan Stivell weaves a mystical spell that transforms his traditional music into modern form. Considered one of Europe's major musical exports, Stivell captivates his audience and carries them through a concert of Celtic magic. 60 mins.
VHS: S15728. $24.95.

Alle Brider: The Flying Bulgar Klezmer Band
Dance and sing along to this music video featuring klezmer music, including a Yiddish folk tune that has a "hidden merengue". 5 mins.
VHS: S23250. $16.95.

Antonio Carlos Jobim: An All Star Tribute
Jobim is world famous as the co-founder and leading composer behind the distinctive Brazilian music known as Bossa Nova. His runaway hit "The Girl from Inpanema" is just a fraction of his output. This video features jazz giants, Herbie Hancock, Shirley Horn, Joe Henderson and Jobim himself performing some of Jobim's greatest works. 60 mins.
VHS: S24666. $19.98.

Ashkenaz: Eastern European Jewry
This video offers a nostalgic look at the music of Eastern European Jewry. Yiddish folk songs, liturgical music, Klezmer melodies and even Yiddish theater tunes are all here. The origins of Ashkenazic music are traced with the help of vintage archival footage taken before World War II. 28 mins.
VHS: S21710. $39.95.

Aswad "Live"
After a long and fruitful career, Britain's premiere rock/reggae band topped the charts with the infectious "Don't Turn Around" followed by "Give a Little Love". These titles plus twelve more songs from a sell-out concert filmed at Hammersmith Odeon in December 1988 are included. Recorded in Hi-Fi stereo, 70 mins.
VHS: S16159. $19.95.

Batouka: The First International Festival of Percussion
Sacred drums from Haiti, Kora from West Africa, Brazilian Birimbau, Ingouma from Burundi—pulsating rhythms from the skin and wood of drums keeping alive the unwritten history of life. The percussion instruments speak the language of rhythm in this unique record of the festival in Guadeloupe which brings together the musical traditions of the great cultures of West Africa, Peruhl, Bambara, Senonfo, Malimko.
VHS: S07745. $24.95.
M. Huraux/F. Migeat, France, 1986, 52 mins.

The Best of Shabba Ranks
One of Jamaica's most famous and successful artists, Shabba is the first dance hall singer to win a Grammy. This compilation of his songs was created from a number of concerts staged in Jamaica. Songs like "Wicked in My Bed", "Them Bow", "Gal You Good" and "Golden Touch" are featured.
VHS: S22201. $29.95.

Bob Brozman
Brozman's talent as a musician and singer lies not only in his feel and understanding for music, but also in his amazing range. He plays a whole variety of acoustic guitar styles and sings everything from the blues and jazz to French chanson. He is a true world music maker. Taped in Berkeley, California. 90 mins.
VHS: S27914. $24.95.

Bob Marley Legend
A personal, musical compilation of Marley's most popular concert appearances and video clips, combined with rare interview footage and video clips. 55 mins.
VHS: S03901. $29.95.

The Bob Marley Story: Caribbean Nights
This award-winning documentary traces the life of Bob Marley, from interviews with his friends and family to rare archive footage of interviews with Marley himself. We remember the brilliant and evocative music he gave the world, music that stretched back over nearly two decades. This program captures the feel and timelessness of that music and the man himself. 100 mins.
VHS: S14108. $19.95.

Border Clash Volume 1
This reggae dance extravaganza features Skull Man, Tonto Metro, Bean Man & Ghost, Bounty Killer & Anthony Red Nose, Lady Saw and Terry Ganzie.
VHS: S21888. $24.95.

Border Clash Volume 2
Ninja Kid, General B, Round Head, Louie Culture, Captain Barkly, Wicker Man, Little Chris, Professor Nut and Daddy Screw are featured in this reggae video.
VHS: S21889. $24.95.

Brian Eno: Imaginary Landscapes
A visual profile of a modern artist at the cutting edge of technological change and popular taste. This video brings together Brian Eno's work in sound, vision and light. It explains the development of his music in visual terms, based on landscapes and images that have shaped his life as an artist. Directed by Duncan Ward and Gabriella Cardazzo. 40 mins.
VHS: S14713. $19.95.

Brother with Perfect Timing
When he left South Africa in the 60's, Abdullah Ibrahim took the unique mixture of Arabic, African, Oriental and European cultures with him. In this film, Ibrahim reveals himself as a casually charismatic storyteller, in an articulate, self-told portrait echoed in music from Ekaya, his band of saxophones, brass and rhythm section.
VHS: S07741. $29.95.
Chris Austin, USA, 1987, 90 mins.

Buju on Top
Little Major, Little Flipper, Lady P., Junior Cat, Little Ray, Super Sass, Itchy Ranks, Rony Rebel, Alton Black, Wayne Wonder and Buju Banton are featured in this reggae video.
VHS: S21890. $24.95.

Cajun Country
Queen Ida, Dewey Balfa, Boozoo Chavis, Wayne Toups, the Savoy-Doucet Band and other Cajun musicians perform the unique music of the Cajun people. Cajuns arrived in Louisiana after being expelled by the British from Nova Scotia. For 200 years, they have preserved their own customs, including a distinctive musical tradition. 60 mins.
VHS: S29482. $19.95.

Cajun Visits
A portrait of the diverse language and ethnicity of traditional Cajun music. Features six of the finest players—Dennis McGee, Wallace "Cheese" Read, Canray Fontenot, Leopold Francois, Robert Jardell and Dewey Balfa—discussing their art. Includes nine songs on the fiddle, Acadian accordion and guitar. In Cajun French with English subtitles.
VHS: S06507. $44.95.
Yasha Aginsky, USA, 29 mins.

Canadian Brass Live
The famous Canadian brass Ensemble featured in what the Washington Post called "an atmosphere of total enjoyment in which laughter freely mingles with gasps of amazement." The program includes "Carnival of Venice," Fats Waller's "Handful of Keys," "Canonza No. 4" by Gabrieli and Bach's "Little Fugue in G Minor." 50 mins.
VHS: S08929. $24.95.

Canadian Reggae Music Awards
The 6th annual Canadian Reggae Music Awards show. Includes appearances by Foxy Brown, John Holt, Leroy Gibbon, Frankie Paul and many, many more.
VHS: S15329. $29.95.

Caribbean Carnival
This exciting program featuring Virgin Island-born steel drum maker Tom Reynolds and his ensemble introduces students to the rhythms and musical styles of the Caribbean area, including soca, calypso, reggae and more. Includes two 30-minute videos and a study guide.
VHS: S34902. $99.95.

Caribbean Music and Dance
The folk music and dance of Honduras, Grenada, Jamaica and Haiti, filmed on location. Narrated in English by Von Martin. 25 mins.
VHS: S06804. $70.00.

Chase the Devil
Nationally-aired PBS documentary gives a street-level perspective of the religious music of the Appalachians, with a behind-the-scenes tour of the provocative culture. From *Beats of the Heart* series.
VHS: S12608. $19.95.

The Chieftains in China
This video presents the Irish group on their tour of China in performance with accomplished Chinese musicians.
VHS: S15706. $24.95.

Chopi Music of Mozambique and Banguza Timbila
A unique look at the Chopi People and their expressive xylophone music and rituals. This most complex of African music has endured despite oppression and war.
VHS: S12927. $49.95.
Ron Hallis/Ophera Hallis, Canada, 1989, 60 mins.

Clifton Chenier: The King of Zydeco
Clifton Chenier and his Red Hot Louisiana Band perform "Black Gal", "Clifton's Zydeco", "Cher Catin", "J'aime pain de mais", "Every Now and Then", "Let the Good Times Roll" and "I'm a Hog for You".
VHS: S10357. $49.95.

Cobra Live
Cobra is wild, mad as shad, dynamic and comical as he performs live in concert at Roy Wilkins Park, Queens, New York City. This young man from St. Mary, Jamaica, is another reggae great who is bringing the world hits like "Flex, Time to Have Sex".
VHS: S22198. $29.95.

Cool Runnings: The Reggae Movie
All the sounds and sights of the 1983 Sun Splash Festival held in Jamaica are available on home video. Directed by Robert Mugge. Artists include Ziggy Marley and the Melody Makers, Gil Scott-Heron, Musical Youth and more.
VHS: S13248. $19.95.
Robert Mugge, Jamaica, 1983, 105 mins.

Country Stars: A New Tradition
Live from the chapel of Fisk University, a county music jamboree. Includes "Ain't Livin' Long Like This," "Don't Be Cruel," "Blues Stay Away from Me," "Blue Moon of Kentucky," "Chill Factor," "You Ain't Woman Enough". 60 mins.
VHS: S11700. $19.95.

Crowning of the Browning
This reggae splash at Roy Wilkins Park features J.D. Smooth, Blacka Ranks, Penny Irie and Little Vicious. Songs like "Man Fi Dead", "Love Black Woman", "Love Mi Browning" and "Stamina Daddy" are included.
VHS: S22207. $29.95.

Dancehall Vibes
A raunchy reggae dance video which features Glammor Wayne, Sugar Minott, Alton Black and Mr. Big Wood.
VHS: S21892. $24.95.

Dennis Brown: The Living Legend
This collection features over 18 reggae songs by this great singer, including "How Could I Live", "Should I", "So Long" and "Sorry".
VHS: S22202. $29.95.

Dewey Balfa—The Tribute Concert
On May 17, 1992, musicians gathered to honor the great Cajun fiddler. 60 minutes of incredible music by this master are featured.
VHS: S22384. $44.95.

Discovering the Music of Africa
African music is demonstrated by a Ghanaian drummer with several of his associates. This demonstration clarifies how drums are used both for music and communication in Africa today. 22 mins.
VHS: S23511. $49.95.

Discovering the Music of India
This sophisticated musical tradition can trace back its origins without interruption nearly 4000 years. The instruments of both northern and southern India are demonstrated in this video, along with the hand gestures and facial expressions of Indian dance. 22 mins.
VHS: S23513. $49.95.

Djabote: Sengalese Drumming & Song from Master Drummer Doudou N'Diaye Rose
This spellbinding film features an Eric Serra audio recording session of Senegalese master drummer Doudou N'Diaye Rose and dozens of other drummers and singers performing as an ensemble.
VHS: S30162. $39.99.
Beatrice Soule/Eric Millot, USA, 1993, 43 mins.

Djembefola
This master of percussion is steeped in the traditions of his native Guinea, West Africa. From his early career with the National Djoliba Ballet to the development of his current unique style, this musician has combined the best of his musical heritage with his own definitive sensibility. French, English and African dialects with English subtitles.
VHS: S20914. $39.95.

Downbeat vs. Addies
This KG Reggae Video production features artists Ackie and Saltfish from Japan, Duggie Fresh, Half Pint and Mac Daddy.
VHS: S22214. $29.95.

El Charanguero: Jaime Torres, the Charango Player
Argentina's Jaime Torres, the world's foremost charango performer, is presented in a never-before-recorded ritual to Pachamama (Mother Earth) by the indigenous people of the Quebrada, Argentina. Features dances and music performed on traditional instruments and the history of the charango, as well as dramatic concert footage. "An appealing portrait of a man, his music and his culture" (Nancy McCray, *Booklist*).
English Version.
VHS: S30167. $24.99.
Spanish Version.
VHS: S30168. $24.99.
Jeffrey Briggs/Simona Munoz-Briggs, USA, 1995, 58 mins.

Esoteric Nature of Music
Explores views in ancient cultures regarding music and its effect on consciousness. 47 mins.
VHS: S06486. $49.95.

Evelyn Glennie in Rio/Fiesta
A unique portrait of Evelyn Glennie, one of the most remarkable young musicians of our time. Though profoundly deaf from an early age, this young Scottish musician triumphed over seemingly impossible odds to become one of the world's finest percussion players. It introduces her early life and career, then follows her visit to the famous Carnival in Rio de Janeiro—a musical voyage of discovery at the world's most colorful and vibrant festival. Includes performances of Bizet's *Carmen Suite* and Rosauro's *Concerto for Marimba and Strings*. With the London Symphony Orchestra. 93 mins.
VHS: S15737. $24.95.
Laser: LD71433. $34.95.

Everyone Sings/Cantemos Todos!
Records Carlos Meija Godo's Misa Campesina at St. John the Divine Church in New York City. A spectacle of poetry and dance recounting the Central American experience.
VHS: S10198. $29.95.
Doug Eisenstark, USA, 1986, 30 mins.

Fela in Concert
Fela Anikulapo Kuti is perhaps the most celebrated Black African musician today, a revolutionary cultural symbol to the people of Nigeria and the world over. A taped concert in Paris in June 1981 captures the charisma Fela exerts on stage. 1981, 57 mins.
VHS: S02111. $29.95.

Fela Live
This tape captures all the excitement of Fela Anikulapo Kuti and his Egypt 80 Band at their peak. Perhaps Africa's most celebrated performing artist, Fela's spectacular stage show extends his musical epics unlike any other performance.
VHS: S15516. $29.95.

Frank Yankovic: America's Polka King
Yankovic extended the polka into popular culture during the 1940's and 1950's. This documentary explores the success of this unique performer and explains how he sold millions of records with tunes like "The Blue Skirt Waltz" and "Just Because". 58 mins.
VHS: S24306. $29.95.

Fresh, Vol. III
Another KG Reggae Video production, this one features reggae artists Freddie McGregor, Tinga Stewart, Ken Booth, China Man, Quata, Lady P., Johnny Nice and Richie Stevens.
VHS: S22206. $29.95.

Hassidut: Hassidic Music
Music is central for the Hassidic community. Famed Rabbi Nahman of Bratslav taught his students that one can pray not only through word but also through song. Filmed in the Hassidic community, beautiful melodies from prayers, celebrations and other significant events are included. 28 mins.
VHS: S21709. $39.95.

Hawaiian Rainbow: The Magic and the Music of the Islands
A unique examination of the music and culture of the island paradise by award-winning filmmaker Robert Mugge. "Mugge clearly felt some of the magic and the mystery—the mana—that gives Hawaiian music its spine, and this rubs off on the viewers in little jolts" (*Honolulu Star-Bulletin*). Mugge's musical portrait combines the sounds of the Hawaiian slack-guitar, the strumming of the ukelele and the a capella and falsetto singing of native Hawaiian musicians to illustrate the intriguing history of traditional Hawaiian music.
VHS: S08699. $29.95.
Robert Mugge, USA, 1989, 90 mins.

Hot Shot
This reggae music video features performances by Papa Beto, Wild Apache, Clement Irie, Chinna Man, Leroy Smart, Papa Skull, Frankie Paul and more.
VHS: S15330. $29.95.

In South Louisiana/ Dedans le Sud de la Louisiane
By featuring an extraordinarily wide variety of Cajun and Creole musicians, this video uses the music to explore the culture it represents. Included are funny interviews with legendary accordionists Nathan Abshire and Bec Fontenot. In Cajun French with English subtitles.
VHS: S06508. $49.95.
Jean Pierre Bruneau, USA, 43 mins.

John Renbourn & Stefan Grossman
Two of the world's premier acoustic guitarists join forces to define and explore the parameters of European and American styles. From traditional folk standards to modern jazz, this program highlights the differences and similarities of these two fine musicians. 60 mins.
VHS: S15725. $24.95.

John Renbourn Group
The John Renbourn Group embraces musical elements as diverse as Renaissance, British folk, modern jazz, classical and blues. Renbourn, one of Britain's preeminent guitarists, leads the group which features the pristine voice of Jacqui McShee. Her vocal rendering of English and Irish ballads woven with flute, bagpipe, dulcimer and guitar can only be described as hypnotic. 60 mins.
VHS: S15730. $24.95.

Johnny McEvoy in Concert
Without a doubt one of the most successful recording stars in the history of Irish music, John McEvoy sings such favorites as *Grandma's Feather Bed, Botany Bay, Town I Loved So Well, Eileen Is Waiting, The West Awake*. 53 mins.
VHS: S06651. $29.95.

Juju Music: King Sunny Ade
King Sunny Ade and Ebenezer Obey perform the urban tribal music of Nigeria, known as juju. which blends lively traditional songs and instruments with Western musical influences. 1988, 51 mins.
VHS: S14741. $19.95.

JVC/Smithsonian Folkways Video Anthology of Music and Dance of Africa
Features 72 traditional music and dance performances of Africa packaged in a three-volume/three-booklet collection. Featured countries include Uganda, Senegal, Ghana, Nigeria, Egypt, Kenya, Botswana, The Gambia, Liberia, Malawi and South Africa.
VHS: S30173. $149.00.

JVC/Smithsonian Folkways Video Anthology of Music and Dance of Europe
Features 58 music and dance performances of Europe packaged in a two-volume/two-booklet collection. Featured countries include Iceland, The Faroe Islands, Denmark, Ireland, Scotland, Wales, England, Belgium, France, Spain, Italy, The Czech Republic, Hungary, Romania and Serbia.
VHS: S30174. $99.00.

JVC/Smithsonian Folkways Video Anthology of Music and Dance of the Americas
This six-volume anthology is a scholarly survey of American folk traditions featuring 159 music and dance examples from 23 countries, and accompanying booklets. Volume 1: Canada and the United States, Canada: Francophone Traditions, Canada: Native and Anglophone Traditions, and USA: African American Secular Traditions; Volume 2: European Traditions in the New World; Volume 3: The United States: Sacred Traditions; Volume 4: The Caribbean; Volume 5: Central and South America: Belize, Brazil, Chile, Colombia, Guatemala, Guyana; Volume 6: Central and South America: Mexico, Nicaragua, Peru, Venezuela. "...a must-purchase item for ethnomusicologists and multicultural music educators" (*Multicultural Education*). "An exceptional and essential series" (*School Library Journal*).
VHS: S30172. $299.00.

Kevin Burke and Michael O'Domhnaill
Two former members of the Irish group Bothy Band, Kevin Burke and Michael O'Domhnaill, present a concert of traditional Irish folk music. 60 mins.
VHS: S19214. $24.95.

Konkome—Nigerian Music
West Africa's thriving pop music scene comes alive in this vibrant program featuring Sunny Ade, Sonny Okosun, Fela and the Ljadu Sisters. Captures the stunning cultures that shape African pop, Highlife, Juju to Afro-rock and reggae.
VHS: S08892. $19.95.

Kumu Hula: Keepers of a Culture
A colorful, expertly lensed and edited documentary by a master documentarian that is a serious look at the history and ancient traditions represented in the dances of the Hawaiian people. The hulas feature various troupes of dancers attired in vibrantly colored costumes performing against the backdrop of some of Hawaii's most scenic panoramas.
VHS: S12331. $29.95.
Robert Mugge, USA, 1989, 85 mins.

Laibach: A Film from Slovenia
Laibach's Eastern block renditions of The Beatles and Rolling Stones classics give their work a distinctive sound and poetic edge. The 17 tracks include "Kinderreich," "Fiat," "Cariamici," "The Great Seal," "Sympathy for the Devil," and "Across the Universe."
VHS: S19612. $19.95.

Land of the Look Behind
Land of the Look Behind started as a documentary on the funeral of Bob Marley. Somewhere along the line it became a spiritual poem/drama about the strange and beautiful lives of the Jamaican people. It is a life of poverty and oppression in the land of paradise, capturing the cries of a people struggling painfully to survive. The film becomes an exploration of man's search for dignity and joy.
VHS: S08937. $19.95.
Alan Greenberg, USA, 1982, 88 mins.

The Last Klezmer
Klezmer music, sometimes called Jewish "soul" music, is a festive Jewish band music which originated in pre-World War II Poland and is enjoying a revival in America, thanks to 69-year-old Klezmer pioneer Leopold Kozlowski. The career of this last of the active Klezmer musicians culminated in roles as actor and musical consultant in *Schindler's List*. 85 mins.
VHS: S27734. $79.95.

Le Mystere des Voix Bulgares: A Bird Is Singing
This amazing Bulgarian women's ensemble was recorded live during their 1993 tour of Bulgaria, Poland and Norway. Their traditional Bulgarian choral music was nominated for two Grammy awards in 1994. 80 mins.
VHS: S22228. $19.98.

Les Blues de Balfa
The Balfa Brothers are the most renowned Cajun musicians of southwest Louisiana, the first Cajun group to take their music outside of Louisiana. Tragically, Rodney and Will Balfa were killed in an auto accident in 1979. In this film, surviving member Dewey Balfa traces the development of his musical family and its contribution to Cajun music. Music includes the Balfa Brothers, Allie Young, Rockin' Dopsie, and the Cajun Playboys.
VHS: S09292. $44.95.
Yasha Aginsky, USA, 28 mins.

Les Creoles
With interviews of Inez Catalon and Revon Reed among others, and music by Bebe Carriere, Delton Broussard and more great musicians, this tape offers a hearty look at Creole culture and music. The continuing rivalry between devotees of musical traditions La la and Zydeco even get a chance to state their competing claims to greater fame. 28 mins.
VHS: S22395. $49.95.

Manu Dibango: King Makossa

Filmed concert in Belgium, December 1981, featuring saxophonist Manu Dibango from Cameroon. Known as Africa's Hippest Hopper, Dibango is influenced by the legacy of Charlie Parker.
VHS: S02112. $29.98.
Philippe Antoine, Belgium, 1981, 55 mins.

Martin Simpson in Concert

Martin Simpson has come a long way from his roots in Lincolnshire, Northern England. Because of his virtuosity as an acoustic guitarist, he has performed all over the world with luminaries like Richard Thompson and Steeleye Span. This concert performance shows Simpson at his best. Taped in Berkeley, California. 70 mins.
VHS: S27913. $24.95.

Master Blaster, Vol. I

Admiral Bailey, Junior Reid, Leroy Smart, Jack Raddics, Little Kirk, Professor Nuts and Wayne Wonder are presented, singing their acclaimed songs "Fight over My Body", "Bad Boys", "Bonafide", "All My Love" and many others. From KG Reggae Video Productions.
VHS: S22196. $29.95.

Master Blaster, Vol. II

In this video, Ken Booth, Tony Rebel, Buju Banton, Simpleton and Capleton are presented singing their acclaimed songs. "Freedom Street", "Wagonist", "Woman No Fret" and "Coco Cola Shape", as well as many other songs, are included.
VHS: S22199. $29.95.

Missa Luba

Featuring music of the African Mass, *Missa Luba* achieved instant fame when it appeared in the acclaimed 1968 film *If*. These haunting folk songs from Kenya pulsate with the colorful and seductive musical experiences of a powerful land and its people, brimming with all the necessary ingredients to become the cult music of the nineties. 51 mins.
VHS: S13888. $24.95.
Laser: LD71232. $29.95.

Mizike Mama

Zap Mama is the acclaimed Zairian-Belgian five-woman a cappella group which has made world music into a truly international phenomenon. They sing in many languages, including Spanish, Creole, Swahili, French, Arabic, Pygmy and even English. This documentary explores the roots of their music and its novel, sophisticated blend of various cultural influences. French, English and African dialects.
VHS: S20915. $39.95.

Moon Drum (Twelve dream song evocations by John Whitney)

An impressionistic evocation of the mood, color, and feel of Native American art, created with computer graphics. Art of the Pueblo, Hopi, Ogala Sioux; iconography, images of animal deities and pictographs, plus much more. Includes 12 short films. 60 mins.
VHS: S14717. $19.95.

Music of the Spirits

A unique look at Zimbabwe's famed mbira master, Stella Madamombe, by Canadian filmmaking team Ron and Ophera Hallis, providing insight into the roots of African music.
VHS: S12930. $49.95.
Ron Hallis/Ophera Hallis, Canada, 1988, 30 mins.

Musica Para Hot Sundays

Documentary of the summer musical series in New York city parks, this colorful tape shows the sweet side of the city as both kids and grown-ups swirl to a salsa-like beat. Produced by Yomoma Arts. 1985, 27 mins.
VHS: S10160. $19.95.

Musicians in Exile

Some of the innovators of world music must now live outside their home countries for political reasons. This film presents their stories and music, uniquely shaped by their living circumstances. Featuring Paquito Riviera and Daniel Ponce. 1990, 75 mins.
VHS: S14739. $19.95.

Mutaburuka: Live! at Reggae Summerfest '93

Mutaburuka is one of Jamaica's most respected and popular dub poets. This video concert features his live performance at Montego Bay, where he sang some of his most powerful songs. 90 mins.
VHS: S29915. $19.95.

The Ninja Man Rides Again

Junie Ranks, Richie Stevens, Ghost and Culture and I Papa Beto are showcased in this KG Reggae Video production.
VHS: S22200. $29.95.

The One and Only Lola Beltran

Often called "Lola la Grande" (Lola the Great), this singer is considered by many fans to be the First Lady of Mexican Music. This two-volume video set captures the excitement of her music. Both music videos were filmed in Paris and are in Spanish.
VHS: S29397. $39.90.

One Hand Don't Clap

This film takes you deep into the Caribbean for an exploration of the vibrant rhythms of Calypso/Soca Music, as performed by two dynamic artists, Lord Kitchener and Calypso Rose. 1988, 92 mins.
VHS: S14742. $19.95.

Our Musical Heritage Series

Ten volumes of music from around the world. 214 mins.
American Folk Music. The indebtedness of American folk music to British and Irish ballads, the development of American folk music through European and African influences. 21 mins.
VHS: S05831. $19.95.
Country and Western Music. The growth of country music from dance parties, casual events, to the formalization of country and western through the advent of western musical instruments. 23 mins.
VHS: S05832. $19.95.
Electronic Music. An exploration of the technology that makes music and sound synthesizing possible, and the complexities achievable through the use of a digital synthesizer. 21 mins.
VHS: S05833. $19.95.
Music of Africa. Focuses on the music of western Africa, with special attention to the music of Ghana, and the rattles, bells and drums of Ghanaian music blended with voice to create a distinctive musical style. 22 mins.
VHS: S05835. $19.95.
Music of India. The coordination of string, wind and percussion instruments which creates a provocative and sensuous style, which, when integrated with movement and voice, provides a primal level of communication. 22 mins.
VHS: S05836. $19.95.
Music of Japan. The five-tone system of Japanese music, reflecting the beauty of nature, and integration with movement and dance. 22 mins.
VHS: S05837. $19.95.
Music of Latin America. Starting with the roots of Indian music, the foundations of Latin music in the co-mingling of wind and percussion and string instruments, the Spanish and Portuguese influences. 20 mins.
VHS: S05838. $19.95.
Music of the Middle Ages. The roots of medieval music in religious or secular pursuits, the solemn rituals, romantic ballads and social tunes of the age of chivalry. 20 mins.
VHS: S05839. $19.95.
Music of the Middle East. An exploration of the diverse instruments and styles of middle-eastern music, its relationship to dance, and its emotional base. 21 mins.
VHS: S05840. $19.95.
Russian Folk Music. The religious and folk foundations of Russian music, its humorous songs and dances, and the robust rhythms characteristic of Russian dances. 22 mins.
VHS: S05841. $19.95.

Rags & Tangos (Rifkin)

Pianist Joshua Rifkin plays a sensational collection of tangos by the Brazilian 'King of Pop Music', Ernesto Nazareth, and ragtime from composer Scott Joplin.
Laser: LD70233. $34.95.

Rainbow: Live Between the Eyes

Ritchie Blackmore and his group Rainbow live in concert. 77 mins.
VHS: S07020. $29.95.

Reggae Beach Rock, Vol. II

Thriller U, Jack Raddics, Shacka Shamba, Ghost and Culture, Pinchers and Ninja Manew are all included in this KG Reggae Video production.
VHS: S22204. $29.95.

Reggae Go-Go Style Dirty Dancing, Vol. III

This video features erotic, X-rated and kinky dancing, all to the music and beat of sensational hard or soft reggae.
VHS: S21891. $24.95.

Rhythm of Resistance

Nationally-aired PBS documentary gives a street-level perspective of Black South African music, with a behind-the-scenes tour of the provocative culture. From *Beats of the Heart* series.
VHS: S12605. $24.95.

Rhythms of the World Anthology

Both Peter Gabriel and Bobby McFerrin, longtime ardent supporters of World Beat music, offer insight into the musical styles of this collection of world bands. Includes performances by Buckwheat Zydeco, Fela Kuti, King Sunny Ade, and many more. 57 mins.
VHS: S15624. $19.95.

Rockers—It's Dangerous

Set within a world of poor Jamaican Rastafarians, this reggae film offers a variation of the legend of Robin Hood. Leroy "Horsemouth" Wallace and Richard "Dirty Harry" Hall star, with a soundtrack that includes reggae greats Burning Spear, Bunny Wailer, Third World, Peter Tosh and many more.
VHS: S23027. $24.95.

The Romany Trail, Part I

Subtitled *Gypsy Music into Africa*, the first part investigates the lost gypsy tribe inside Egypt, as a group travels up the Nile, through the ancient town of Luxor, around the location of pharaoh's tombs. The journey moves from Cairo to Karnak, introducing us to gypsy dancing performers, magicians, acrobats, musicians, fortune tellers and mystics. 60 mins.
VHS: S16967. $24.95.

The Romany Trail, Part II

The second part opens in India, tracing the origins of the initial gypsy families, providing an insider's portrait of this enclosed world, one of bear trainers, puppeteers, actors and musicians. The action shifts to Eastern Europe, with communism on its last legs, and goes inside the workers' hotels, homes and street theater where the gypsies develop their craft and methods. 60 mins.
VHS: S16968. $24.95.

Roots of Rhythm

Harry Belafonte hosts this globe-trotting, star-studded celebration tracing the history of Latin music. With 40 songs performed by Gloria Estefan, Dizzy Gillespie, Desi Arnaz, Celia Cruz, King Sunny Ade, Celia Cruz, Isaac Oviedo, Ruben Blades and more. Three videos. 57 mins. each.
VHS: S32193. $39.95.

Roots, Rock, Reggae

A street-level tour of the vital music scene in Kingston, with rehearsal and concert footage that captures vintage performances by Toots and the Maytals, Jimmy Cliff, the Heptones and Ras Michael.
VHS: S08893. $19.95.

RSW In Video

RSW's 1989 *Soundclash* album reverberated through the United Kingdom and America with its distinctive merging of house, reggae, funk and postpunk sound. The six tracks of this video include "Kray Twins," "Cocaine Sex," "Biting My Nails" and "Probably a Robbery." 30 mins.
VHS: S19613. $19.95.

Sepharad: Judeo-Spanish Music

Five hundred years after the expulsion of Spanish Jewry, the musical heritage of the Sephardim is alive and well. The film focuses on music first sung by Spanish singers in the Middle Ages, lullabies, wedding tunes, synagogue melodies and songs of mourning, performed in the rich traditional style of the Sephardim. 27 mins.
VHS: S21711. $39.95.

Shock Out with Metro Media

100% dance hall, this video features reggae artists Sky Juice, Peter Metro, Danny Dread, Dicky Ranking, Nicodemus and Blacka Ranking.
VHS: S22195. $29.95.

Structures from Silence

A dream flight through soft liquid universes on waves of Steve Roach's almost transparent music. Marianne Dolan's motion paintings offer celestial navigation for the imagination. 30 mins.
VHS: S10228. $24.95.

Super Clash Round I

Featuring Shabba Ranks vs. Ninja Man live in Saint Mary. A devastating reggae performance highlighted by rapid fire gun salute.
VHS: S15328. $29.95.

Talk of the Town: Shabba Ranks

Shabba's reggae hits "Wicked in Bed", "Twice My Age", "Idle Jubbie", "Pay Down Pon It", "Hard and Stiff", "Best Baby Father" and many more are included in this video recorded live at Dinasty.
VHS: S22197. $29.95.

Teiman: Music of Yemenite Jewry

Yemenite Jews have perfected singing and rhythm, drumming and dancing over centuries. World-renowned vocalists Ofra Haza and Noa (Aicinoam Nini) are just some of the talented performers who illustrate the Yemeni rhythms that have conquered the world stage. 27 mins.
VHS: S21712. $39.95.

Tex-Mex

Nationally-aired PBS documentary gives a street-level perspective of the music of the Texas-Mexican borderlands, with a behind-the-scenes tour of the provocative culture. From *Beats of the Heart* series.
VHS: S12609. $19.95.

There'll Always Be Stars in the Sky

An entry from the 14-part series *Beats of the Heart*, this volume explores the Indian film industry. The staple of the country's astonishing output is its lavish, melodramatic, highly stylized musicals. This is an insider's viewpoint, interweaving interviews and behind-the-scenes footage with actors, directors and location shooting. 60 mins.
VHS: S16966. $24.95.

A Tickle in the Heart

A charming portrait of the three Epstein brothers, once the kings of klezmer music. Now retired in Florida and in their 80s, the brothers embark on an international tour. An infectious cinematic snapshot of joie de vivre with "a hearty helping of some of the world's liveliest and most poignant folk music" (*New York Times*).
VHS: S33315. $59.95.
Stefan Schweitert, USA/Germany, 1997, 83 mins.

Time Will Tell: Bob Marley

An engaging documentary about Bob Marley and his band The Whalers, his collaboration with Peter Tosh, and the roots of his music, steeped in Third World ethnography, poverty and social protest. Produced by Rocky Oldham and directed by Declan Lowney, with Marley performing his classics, "One Love," "Stir It Up," "No Woman No Cry," "Get Up Stand Up," "I Shot the Sheriff," and "Redemption Song."
VHS: S17433. $19.95.
Declan Lowney, Great Britain, 1991, 85 mins.

Various Artists Featuring Raymond Kane Ki Ho'alu: That's Slack Key Guitar

Slack Key Guitar is a unique Hawaiian tradition. This unique finger-picking style developed after Spanish cowboys introduced the guitar to Hawaii in the early 1800's. Raymond Kane's story reveals the unique trajectory of this music.
VHS: S25912. $29.95.

Ziveli! Medicine for the Heart

The culture and music of the Serbian-American communities of Chicago and California. Made in association with Serbian-American anthropologist Andrei Simic and the University of Southern California's Visual Anthropology program, the film focuses on the vital culture strengths of these immigrants from Yugoslavia, who helped form the backbone of industrial America. Music, dancing, the Orthodox church, and featuring the Popovich Brothers, the Kapugi Brothers, and Dunav. 1987, 50 mins.
VHS: S02902. $49.95.

Zydeco

Exploration of Louisiana creole culture and the fast-paced music that mixes Cajun, Rhythm and Blues and Afro-Caribbean music into that unique sound called Zydeco.
VHS: S02907. $49.95.
Nicholas Spitzer, USA, 1984, 57 mins.

Zydeco Gumbo

Clifton Chenier and John Delafose, Boo Zoo Chavis, Terence Semian and Willis Prudhomme star in this spicy gumbo of zydeco. From the old dance halls—like Richard's in Lawtell and Slim's-Y-Ki-Ki in Opelousas—to the Zydeco Festival in Plaisance, this tape features the hottest Zydeco performers in Southwestern Louisiana.
VHS: S12344. $19.95.
Dan Hildenbrandt, USA, 1988, 28 mins.

Zydeco: Nite 'n' Day

This colorful documentary takes the viewer to the bayous of the deep south and into the musical world of Zydeco. It focuses on the heritage of Zydeco music while explaining the distinctions between Zydeco, Cajun and Creole music. Featuring Buckwheat Zydeco and Rockin' Dopsie & the Zydeco Twisters. 56 mins.
VHS: S14521. $19.95.

FOLK & COUNTRY MUSIC

America's Music: Country & Western 1

Gene Weed hosts a Country Jamboree with everything from Cajun to Country Rock, and featuring performers including Sylvia, Razzy Bailey, Eddie Dean, Doug Kershaw, and Patti Page. 60 mins.
VHS: S05030. $19.95.

America's Music: Country & Western 2

Gene Weed continues with presentations by Moe Bandy, Jerry Lee Lewis, Terry Gregory, Ricky Skaggs and Terry Gregory. 60 mins.
VHS: S05031. $19.95.

America's Music: Folk 1

Theodore Bikel hosts this review of American folk music, including many of its best-known performers: Glenn Yarbrough, Buffy Ste. Marie, The New Christy Minstrels, Odetta, Hoyt Axton, Theodore Bikel, the Blue Flame String Band, and film clips of The Limeliters, Leadbelly and Burl Ives. 60 mins.
VHS: S05036. $19.95.

America's Music: Folk 2

The Limeliters, Josh White, Jr., Jean Richie, Doc Watson, Dave Van Ronk, Mary McCaslin and Jim Ringer, and John McEuen are featured in the second part of this folk series. 60 mins.
VHS: S05037. $19.95.

An American Songster

A musical portrait of John Jackson, singer/guitarist and banjo player from Virginia. Jackson's career is traced from discovery in a gas station by folklorist Chuck Perdue to international recognition.
VHS: S04167. $19.95.
Renato Tonelli, USA, 1985, 30 mins.

The Art of Fingerstyle Guitar

Folk, blues and ragtime have expanded the range of fingerstyle guitar. This video joins different artists like John Renbourn, Stefan Grossman, Martin Carthy, Bob Brozman and more to show the range of possibilities with this instrument, from the Celtic to the Hawaiian to jazz.
VHS: S25058. $24.95.

Bert Jansch Conundrum

A dominant force in British folk music, Bert Jansch's work as a singer and guitarist has influenced the musical scene on both sides of the Atlantic. Along with violinist/mando-cellist Martin Jenkins and bassist Nigel Smith they formed the Bert Jansch Conundrum. Jansch's intricate guitar style is the focal point of the trio, while Jenkins and Smith add a mixture of traditional acoustic and electric settings that contribute to the group's unusual and arousing sound. 60 mins.
VHS: S15731. $24.95.

Bill Monroe: Father of Bluegrass Music

In this documentary the fiery radical and originator of this true American musical form emerges to contradict the stereotypes of gentle country grandfather who peaceably strums his guitar on the front porch. Ultimately he will be remembered as a true innovator and consummate performer.
VHS: S20755. $19.95.
Steve Gebhardt, USA, 1993, 91 mins.

The Blarney Pilgrim— Celtic Fingerstyle Guitar, Vol. 2

A collection of traditional music from Ireland and Scotland arranged for solo fingerstyle guitar, featuring Pat Kirtley, Martin Simpson, Steve Baughman, Perre Bensusan, Tom Long and El McMeen. With bonus 72-page booklet featuring all the tunes in tablature and standard notation. 59 mins.
VHS: S34459. $29.95.

Carole King in Concert

Filmed live at Hartford's Bushnell Hall during Carole's 1993 *Color of Your Dreams* tour, this program shows the range of this famed vocalist/song writer. 82 mins.
VHS: S22005. $19.95.

Celebrate for the Rain: Featuring the Music of Elizabeth Burch

A young girl plays and sings her original songs at age 14. These haunting melodies help her to come to terms with her father's death when she was six, and the assorted mysteries of growing up in a non-mainstream New York City.
VHS: S33812. $24.95.
Claire Burch, USA, 1994, 40 mins.

The Changer: A Record of Times

Cris Williamson's landmark album, *The Changer and the Changed*, marked the start of women's music. Interviews with the most important singers of this vital musical tradition are featured. Along with Williamson, Meg Christian, Bonnie Raitt, June Millington, Vicki Randall, Holly Near, Margie Adams and many others recall this album on the occasion of Williamson's 1990 concert in Berkeley. Musical clips from 1975 are also featured.
VHS: S19450. $39.95.
Frances Reid/Judy Dlugacz, USA, 78 mins.

Chet Atkins & Friends

The Everly Brothers, Emmylou Harris, Waylon Jennings, Mark Knopfler, Michael McDonald, Willie Nelson in a super session filmed in Nashville brings together the best artists in a tribute to the man and the music. From his moving solo performance of *I Just Can't Say Goodbye* to the rousing, all-on-stage *Corinna, Corinna*, it was music from the heart. 60 mins.
VHS: S05125. $19.99.

Chet Atkins 1955-1975

"Mr. Guitar", Chet Atkins, is featured playing all over the world on this video. From Nashville to Norway, his singular style and virtuosity set a standard which other guitarists can only hope to emulate.
VHS: S27314. $29.95.

Cooler Than Country— The Bluegrass Mountaineers

Formed in the early 60s, the Bluegrass Mountaineers represent the honest, hardworking, traditional music loved across America. Outstanding vocals and inspiring banjo, fiddle, bass, mandolin and guitar accompaniment make this video a musical delight. 43 mins.
VHS: S26505. $19.95.

Cooler Than Country—The Lewis Family

The first family of bluegrass Gospel music, the Lewis Family, are a wellspring of family entertainment. Though they are professional entertainers of the highest order, they remain friendly and sincere upholders of the values of Gospel music. 38 mins.
VHS: S26504. $19.95.

Country Joe McDonald at Provo Park: Earth Day Concert with Wild Mango and Others

Country Joe and his Band perform folk and folk rock favorites on Earth Day, celebrating the installation of the new "Peace Wall," made by individuals in the Berkeley community.
VHS: S33813. $24.95.
Claire Burch, USA, 1995, 58 mins.

Country Joe McDonald: Concerts at People's Park

A stirring video featuring Woodstock musician and activist Country Joe McDonald. Encompasses two concerts, intercutting images from the '60s with current street problems.
VHS: S33814. $24.95.
Claire Burch, USA, 1996, 58 mins.

Dave Van Ronk

A legend in his own time, Dave Van Ronk was one of the central figures in the folk movement that flourished in the late fifties and early sixties, nurturing such performers as Bob Dylan and Phil Ochs. His tough, gravelly voice and intricate guitar style complement his colorful, bawdy personality. 60 mins.
VHS: S15726. $24.95.

Discovering American Folk Music

Both the British Isles and the traditions of Africa have shaped the sounds of American folk music. The transformations of British ballads and lyric songs are traced as they evolved in the US, while the impact of African music is followed through the growth of spirituals and the blues. 21 mins.
VHS: S23519. $49.95.

Discovering Country and Western Music

Country and Western has enjoyed explosive popularity the world over. This program traces the development of this popular style, measuring the impact of mass media and growing urbanization on this enduring music. 23 mins.
VHS: S23510. $49.95.

Doc and Merle Watson

Doc Watson, probably America's greatest flat-picking guitarist, joins his son Merle and Michael Coleman on bass for a concert recorded in 1980. This performance is a showcase of native folk traditions. A visit at home with the Watsons in North Carolina is also included.
VHS: S25911. $29.95.

Doc Watson: Doc's Guitar Jam Featuring Doc Watson, Tony Rice, Dan Crary, Steve Kaufman & Jack Lawrence

Recorded at the 1992 Merle Watson Festival in Wilkesboro, North Carolina, this jam session showcases the talents of five master flatpicking guitarists. They harmonize, improvise and play up a storm. Two bonus tracks feature Doc Watson and his friends David Grisman, Bela Fleck, Mark O'Conner and Jerry Douglas.
VHS: S27317. $29.95.

Doc Watson: Rare Performances 1963-1981

This North Carolina native enriched the 1960's folk music boom with his distinctive music. In fact, he was a major inspiration for the whole movement. This collection of his appearances shows why he has been such an inspiration to countless other folk musicians.
VHS: S24220. $19.95.

Doc Watson: Rare Performances 1982-1993

By the 1980's Doc Watson had redefined the acoustic guitar's role in American folk music. In these later performances he is joined by duet partners Jack Williams, Merle Watson (Doc's son) and Rickey Skaggs, as well as string band performers Mark O'Conner, Tony Rice, Bela Fleck, David Grisman and Jerry Douglas.
VHS: S24221. $19.95.

Elizabeth Cotten

Born in 1893, Cotten inspired every fledgling fingerpicker of the folk boom era with her classic *Freight Train*. A North Carolina native, she is revealed in this video as more than a one song legend. This performance/interview was taped when she was 85. In it, she displays her ease with a variety of musical styles. 59 mins.
VHS: S22492. $19.95.

A Festival of Bay Area Music (Relix Concert)

A documentary commemorating an event sponsored by *Relix* Magazine. Includes the legendary Rambin' Jack Elliot, introductions by J.C. Flyer, and assorted Bay Area bands.
VHS: S34322. $24.95.
Claire Burch, USA, 1995, 58 mins.

Fingerstyle Guitar

The performances in this video series present two generations of artists who advanced the acoustic guitars cause. Folk, blues and country roots offer a springboard into personal harmonic and melodic pathways. Artists who bridged the gap between folk styles and the innovations of folk, baroque, American primitive guitar, New Age, and even new acoustic are all included in this thorough collection.
Volume 1: New Dimensions and Explorations. Peter Finger, Loe Kottke, Brad Jones, Adrian Legg, John Fahey, Bert Jansch, Jorma Kaukonen, Preston Reed and Woody Mann perform on this volume.
VHS: S22494. $19.95.
Volume 2: New Dimensions and Explorations. Dave Evans, John Renbourn, Stefan Grossman, John Knowles, Pat Donahue, Marcel Dadi, Duck Baker, Chris Procter, El McMeen and Joe Miller play on this video collection of acoustic guitar greats.
VHS: S22495. $19.95.
Volume 3: New Dimensions and Exporations. Steve Howe, Larry Coryell, Pepino D'Agostino, Martin Carthy, Martin Taylor, Bob Brozman, Martin Simpson and Tim Sparks are all featured in this last volume.
VHS: S22496. $19.95.

Folk City 25th Anniversary Concert

Recorded live at the legendary Greenwich Village club. The silver anniversary show includes the artistry of Richie Havens ("Freedom"), Arlo Guthrie ("Inch by Inch"), Joan Baez ("Improv Blues"), Tom Paxton ("Yuppies in the Sky"), The Roches ("Face Down at Folk City"), Suzanne Vega ("Crackin'"), Peter Yarrow ("Puff the Magic Dragon") and many more songs and performers. 83 mins.
VHS: S13288. $19.95.

Gentleman Jim Reeves: The Story of a Legend

This famed country singer was tragically killed at the height of his powers in a airplane crash on July 31, 1964. In this absorbing tribute his story is finally told. A number of his hit songs, including "Bimbo", "Four Walls", "He'll Have to Go" and "Adios Amigo", reveal the extent of Jim Reeves' monumental talent.
VHS: S18705. $19.95.

George Jones: Golden Hits

Along with rare interview footage, this video features film clips of Jones performing his hit songs from the times when they were at the top of the charts, from 1959 up until today. "The Door", "Golden Ring", "Near You" and "The Race Is On" are just some of the songs included. 50 mins.
VHS: S21698. $19.95.

Heartworn Highways

James Szalpski's documentary about the rebirth of country music around Austin and Nashville in the mid-70s. The film looks at the artists, music, and maverick performers who rebelled against the Nashville establishment to form a new American idiom. "Superbly conceived and executed, it's by far the best musical documentary I've seen since *Woodstock*" (Austin American-Statesman). With Guy Clark, Townes Van Zandt, David Allan Coe, Barefoot Jerry, Steve Young, Steve Earl and the Charlie Daniels Band.
VHS: S19122. $29.95.
James Szalspski, USA, 1981, 92 mins.

High Lonesome

Mac Wiseman narrates the story of Bluegrass music. It's all here, from the origins of Bluegrass in the Kentucky foothills to the innovations of modern times. Bill Monroe and other seminal figures are featured. Only the music itself could tell a tale that begins with the upheavals of the Great Depression and follows through into our own era. 95 mins.
VHS: S23041. $19.95.

The Highwaymen: On the Road Again

Johnny Cash, Willie Nelson, Kris Kristofferson and Waylon Jennings combine their talents in this concert filmed during a European tour. The highlights are Cash's "Folsom Prison Blues," Nelson's "Always on My Mind" and "Crazy," Kristofferson's "Help Me Make It through the Night" and Jennings' "Luckenbach, Texas." 60 mins.
VHS: S19582. $14.95.

James Galway in Concert

Taped in the Gallery at Harewood House in England's Yorkshire Dales, James Galway performs the music which has made him a concert and recital favorite throughout the world. Accompanied by pianist Phillip Moll, the concert includes works by Saint-Saens, Ravel, Debussy, Faure, Poulenc, Kreisler, Gaubert, and Bizet. 55 mins.
VHS: S34508. $29.95.

Jim McCann & The Morrisseys

Two concerts, filmed in Ireland, featuring Jim McCann, formerly of the Dubliners, and the Morrisseys, one of Ireland's most popular folk groups. 55 mins.
VHS: S06653. $29.95.

Jim Reeves/Ray Price (with Ernest Tubb)

The spirited and classic country entertainers Jim Reeves and Ray Price are highlighted in this video collection, with some additional performances from Ernest Tubb. Jim Reeves' output includes "I've Lived a Lot in My Time", "Then I'll Stop Loving You" and "Down in the Caribbean". Ray Price sings "Crazy Arms", "One Broken Heart Don't Mean a Thing" and "You Done Me Wrong". Ernest Tubb concludes the video with seven songs, including "If I Never Have Anything Else", "Dear Judge" and "I'm with a Crowd". 60 mins.
VHS: S19212. $24.95.

John Fahey/Elizabeth Cotten: Rare Interviews and Performances from 1969

These seminal role models were presented on Laura Weber's 1960's TV series, *Guitar, Guitar*. As exponents of American primitive guitar, they make a perfect combination. Fahey is like the father of the style, while Cotten is like its Grandma Moses. Their comments and their performances are captured in this rediscovered episode.
VHS: S22489. $19.95.

Kingston Trio & Friends Reunion

The original members of the Trio (Nick Reynolds, Bob Shane and Dave Guard) perform their greatest hits as they are joined by Tommy Smothers and Mary Travers, and by Lindsey Buckingham, John Stewart and George Grove and Roger Gambill. Includes "Tom Dooley", "Scotch and Soda", "A Worried Man" and "M.T.A.". 50 mins.
VHS: S20565. $19.95.

Legends of Country Guitar, Featuring Chet Atkins, Merle Travis, Mose Rager & Doc Watson

Captures four of the most influential country pickers, in performances from 1962 to 1987. 58 mins.
VHS: S31760. $29.95.

Legends of Traditional Fingerstyle Guitar

Artists of the fingerstyle guitar, whether using two- or three-finger picking, with or without picks, have fashioned a truly influential body of music. Their innovations inspire musicians to this day. Merle Travis, Elizabeth Cotten, Mance Lipscomb, Brownie McGhee and Josh White demonstrate their virtuosity on this video. 58 mins.
VHS: S22483. $19.95.

Loretta Lynn

This *A & E Biography* tells the rags-to-riches story of the coal miner's daughter who captured the hearts of millions and became country music's greatest star. 50 mins.
VHS: S30109. $19.95.

Marty Robbins/Ernest Tubb

Marty Robbins and Ernest Tubb perform 26 songs. Robbins' include "Singin' the Blues", "Times Goes By", "I Can't Quit" and "Pretty Words". Ernest Tubb performs "Walkin' the Floor over You", "So Many Times", "Tomorrow Never Comes" and "They'll Do It Every Time". 60 mins.
VHS: S19211. $24.95.

Merle Travis: Rare Performances 1946-1981

The great American musician Merle Travis is captured in all his versatility in this collection of film footage spanning over 35 years. His fingerstyle technique is widely influential—after all, he wrote over 900 songs. 60 mins.
VHS: S22484. $19.95.

Mike Seeger: Fret and Fiddle

Seeger is a master of Oldtime music, the basis of hillbilly, bluegrass and country and western music. Before radio and recorded music it was played everywhere on special occasions. Like its musical descendants, Oldtime spoke about a variety of topics, from hunting to love. 55 mins.
VHS: S22487. $19.95.

New England Fiddles: Playing Down the Devil

Traditional New England fiddlers Joe Cormier, Paddy Cronin, Ben Guilemette, Wilfred Guillette, Harold Luce, Jerry Robichaud and Ron Westas are shown playing in their homes and at dances and contests as they pass on their styles to younger fiddlers and comment on their music. "A fascinating film about how people's lives relate to the music they make" (Pete Seeger).
VHS: S30166. $24.99.
John M. Bishop, USA, 1995, 28 mins.

Norman Blake & The Rising Fawn Ensemble

Norman Blake is one of the leading exponents of flatpicking guitar. He performed with such diverse artists as Bob Dylan, Johnny Cash and Kris Kristofferson before forming the Rising Fawn Ensemble. Blending guitar, cello and mandolin, they create dense, evocative music. 60 mins.
VHS: S15727. $24.95.

Peter, Paul and Mary: 25th Anniversary Concert

A moving concert by the timeless troubadours of folk music, with classic hits from their eight gold and five platinum albums, including "Blowin' in the Wind", "Puff, The Magic Dragon", "Leaving on a Jet Plane", "If I Had a Hammer", "This Land Is Your Land". 88 mins.
VHS: S12477. $19.95.

Pure Pete Seeger

Bill Moyers visits the singer, storyteller and activist on his 75th birthday at home in the New York Hudson Valley. This warm, funny video reveals the humane and witty man who fused folk music and political change into a way of life. 60 mins.
VHS: S24926. $29.95.

Ramble to Cashel: Celtic Fingerstyle Guitar

Pierre Bensusan, Martin Simpson, Duck Baker, Pat Kirtley, El McMeen, Tom Long and Steve Baughman bring their own approach, style, technique and feel to Celtic fingerstyle guitar solos. Includes 72-page booklet. 62 mins.
VHS: S33374. $29.95.

The Real Patsy Cline

Patsy Cline's amazing story, from her humble beginnings through her meteoric rise to her tragic end, add up to a gripping documentary. Rare and classic performances of her hits make this an unforgettable tribute to the legendary country music singer. 48 mins.
VHS: S27568. $14.95.

Red Hot + Country

The Red Hot organization organized this concert featuring great country singers and musicians. Clint Black, Billy Ray Cyrus, Sammy Kershaw, Kathy Mattea, Levon Helm (The Band), Carl Perkins, Earl Skruggs and other greats participated in this AIDS awareness musical special. 70 mins.
VHS: S24725. $19.95.

Steeleye Span: A 20th Anniversary Celebration

Formed in 1969, Steeleye Span became the preeminent folk/rock band of the 70s. By the end of the 80s they had recorded over a dozen albums and sold millions. This exciting concert was recorded on their 20th Anniversary tour and features all their greatest hits. Celtic Rock at its best. 60 mins.
VHS: S15705. $24.95.

Talking Feet

A video by Mike Seeger, the renowned Old Time folk musician and instructor. *Feet*, the first documentary in this genre, showcases Southern-style solo mountain dancing, including flatfoot, buck, hoedown, and rural tap dancing.
VHS: S12925. $49.95.
Mike Seeger, USA, 1989, 90 mins.

Telegraph Avenue Street Musicians: The Concert at Ashkenaz

A group of Telegraph Avenue street musicians get together to celebrate a CD completed via a grant to empower the homeless. Their concert at Ashkenaz contains surreal documentary cut-ins that introduce rebellious social issues to the outward reality of their concert.
VHS: S33816. $24.95.
Claire Burch, USA, 1994, 58 mins.

Texas Fiddle Legends

Two contemporary legends of Texas-style fiddling, Benny Thomasson and Dick Barett, are featured here in a rare concert of Texas fiddling filmed in the early 1970s. 50 mins.
VHS: S34394. $19.95.

That High Lonesome Sound

Three films from John Cohen are collected on this video. These works profile musicians from America's rural musical traditions, particularly those of Appalachia. *That High Lonesome Sound* (featuring Roscoe Holcomb), *The End of an Old Story* (ballad singer Dillard Chandler) and *Sara and Maybelle* (with two members of the Carter family) are included. 70 mins.
VHS: S29483. $19.95.
John Cohen, USA, 70 mins.

This Land Is Your Land: The Animated Kids' Songs of Woody Guthrie

American folk legend Woody Guthrie embarks on a magical, animated journey as he introduces his classic children's folk songs, including "This Land Is Your Land," "Take You Ridin' in My Car," "Bling Blang," "Grassey Grass Grass," "Howjido?," "Jig Along Home," "Mail Myself to You," "All Work Together" and "So Long, It's Been Good to Know You." Featuring the voices of Woody Guthrie and Arlo Guthrie.
VHS: S30976. $12.98.
Tom Burton/Claudia Z. Burton, USA, 1996, 23 mins.

Thumbed a Ride to Heaven: The Music of Alfonia Tims and Others

Features music composed and improvised by Alfonia Tims, a young African-American musician, along with others.
VHS: S33818. $24.95.
Claire Burch, USA, 1990, 40 mins.

Times Ain't Like They Used to Be

Subtitled *Early Rural and Popular American Music 1928-1935*, this documentary provides insight into American popular music. The program features the only known footage of pioneer Jimmy Rodgers, who originated country music. The video features archival footage of Whistler's Jug Band, Bob Wills, Jack Johnson's Jazz Band, Otto Gray's Cowboys and Bascom Lamar Lunceford. 70 mins.
VHS: S19209. $24.95.

Tony Rice: The Video Collection

Tony Rice practices flatpicking guitar styles that are praised in both bluegrass and innovative acoustic guitar circles. This tape features three different settings: an all-star jam session with Sam Bush and Bela Fleck, a set with Ricky Skaggs and David Grisman and a performance by the Tony Rice Unit at the 1992 Merle Watson Festival.
VHS: S27318. $29.95.

Traditional Music Classics

Presents rare archival performances from the 1960s by four legends of traditonal music from the Appalachian Mountains: Doc Watson, Roscoe Holcomb, Buell Kazee and Kilby Snow. 70 mins.
VHS: S34393. $19.95.

Troubadours of Folk Music

Great folk artists participated in a two-day concert series at the UCLA campus in Westwood in 1993. This video brings the best of their work to new audiences. Jefferson Starship, Arlo Guthrie, Janis Ian and John Prine are just a few of the artists featured. 54 mins.
VHS: S22463. $19.98.

The Unbroken Circle—Vermont Music: Tradition Change

This crisp, perceptive film traces the path of traditional music in Vermont from unaccompanied ballads to lively fiddle tunes, from radio cowboy bands to square dancing at the Moose Hall. Historic photos accompany the words and music of over a dozen Vermont performers, including Al Cadorette, Cordelia Cerasoli, Wilfred Guillette, The Hurstins, Lee Jollota, Norman Kennedy, Margaret MacArthur, The Pony Boys and Ron West. "A must see for all who care about traditional music" (Joshua Mamis, *Vermont Vanguard Press*).
VHS: S30164. $24.99.
Mark Greenberg, USA, 1995, 59 mins.

A Vision Shared: A Tribute to Woody Guthrie & Leadbelly

Special performances of Guthrie and Leadbelly songs performed by John Mellencamp, Pete Seeger, Arlo Guthrie, Bruce Springsteen, Taj Mahal, Little Richard, U2 and more. USA, 72 mins.
VHS: S15312. $14.98.

The Weavers: Wasn't That a Time

Joyful, Academy Award-winning documentary about the legendary folksingers, The Weavers, who won the hearts of America in the 1950's with such songs as "Goodnight Irene" and "This Land Is Mine." With Pete Seeger, Lee Hays, Ronnie Gilbert, Fred Hellerman, Arlo Guthrie, Holly Near, Don McLean, Peter, Paul and Mary.
VHS: S01439. $19.98.
Jim Brown, USA, 1982, 78 mins.

Webb Pierce/Chet Atkins

Two country masters are captured in this video assembly of their greatest works. Webb Pierce performs "I'm Walkin' the Dog", "More and More", "Slowly", "I'm Gonna See My Baby Tonight" and "He's in the Jailhouse Now". Chet Atkins does spirited renditions of "Pickin' the Blues", "Georgia Camp Meeting" and "Arkansas Traveller". 60 mins.
VHS: S19210. $24.95.

Webb Pierce: Greatest Hits

A compilation distilled from filmed performances of the unique voice of Webb Pierce, the country star who enjoyed popularity. He once had 69 hit songs in a row. This program contains 17 of his best known works, including "Wondering," "There Stands the Glass," "In the Jailhouse Now" and "More and More." 52 mins.
VHS: S19896. $14.95.

World of Fingerstyle Jazz Guitar

Martin Taylor, Jim Nichols, Tommy Crook, Duck Baker and Woody Mann demonstrate their ability to play or imply all aspects of the music—rhythm, chords, bass and melody—without accompaniment. 76 mins.
VHS: S33375. $29.95.

GOSPEL MUSIC

Al Green...Everything's Gonna Be Alright

Al Green Live at the Celebrity Theater in Anaheim, California. 60 mins.
VHS: S21611. $29.95.

Al Green: On Fire in Tokyo

Legendary soul singer Al Green has become one of gospel music's shining lights. This stirring concert performance features Green at his best, singing such inspiring songs as "Everything's Gonna Be Alright," "You Brought the Sunshine into My Life" and "None But the Righteous." 1988, 60 mins.
VHS: S14547. $29.95.

The All-Star Gospel Show

Paul Simon, Andrae Crouch, the Edwin Hawkins Singers, Jennifer Holliday, The Mighty Clouds of Joy, The Oak Ridge Boys and Luther Vandross are featured in this soul-stirring hour of gospel filmed at the First Presbyterian Church in Hollywood. Includes "His Eye Is on the Sparrow," "Oh Happy Day" and the stunning medley "Still Waters Run Deep, Bridge over Troubled Water." 60 mins.
VHS: S00032. $19.99.

Allen & Allen: Live in Florida

This piano sax duo won national acclaim for their hit song "A-Blaizing Grace." Now their versions of standard religious songs like "Silent Night" and "Jesus Is Love" are joined together with original hits on this video. In all their music they bring a fresh feel to Gospel music.
VHS: S26909. $14.95.

Allen T.D. Wiggin

The Gospel performer and Epic recording artist performs live in New York City. 60 mins.
VHS: S21612. $29.95.

Amazing Grace with Bill Moyers

With help from Judy Collins, Johnny Cash, Jessye Norman, Marion Williams and the Boys Choir of Harlem, host Bill Moyers presents a study of the most popular and enduring hymn of the English language. 87 mins.
VHS: S12936. $24.95.

America's Music: Gospel 1

Gospel music, hosted by Levar Burton, with Andrae Crouch, The Winans, The Archers, Marion Williams, Doug Miller, Walter Hawkins Family, and a rare film clip of Mahalia Jackson singing "When the Saints Go Marching In." 60 mins.
VHS: S05042. $19.95.

America's Music: Gospel 2

Sandra Crouch and Friends, Wently Phipps, The Chambers Family, Linda Hopkins, Reba Rambo and Donny McGuire, Mel Carter are featured, together with a film clip of Mahalia Jackson singing "Bless This House." Hosted by Levar Burton. 60 mins.
VHS: S05043. $19.95.

Angelic Gospel Singers

"Sweet Home", "Touch Me Jesus" and "Somebody's Praying for Me" are the featured songs.
VHS: S21613. $29.95.

Arvis Strickling Jones: From the Inside Out

A live performance featuring Dorothy Norwood and the First Union Choir. 60 mins.
VHS: S21614. $29.95.

Bishop Jeff Banks/Revival Mass Choir

Recorded live at A.M.E. Church in Newark, New Jersey. "Didn't I Tell You", "Let Me Talk in the Spirit" and "You Can Make It If You Try" are featured. 60 mins.
VHS: S21615. $29.95.

Bobby Jones Gospel

Ten volumes.

Volume 1. Bobby Jones, New Life Singers, Rejoice, Lloyd Lindroth, Second Coming and Rythem, David Len Jones and a special salute to Coretta Scott King.
VHS: S05529. $29.95.

Volume 2. Bobby Jones, New Life Singers, Williams Brothers and the Savannah Community Choir.
VHS: S05530. $29.95.

Volume 3. Bobby Jones, New Life Singers, The Impressions, Mary Harris and the Jud Edmonds Gospel Troup.
VHS: S05531. $29.95.

Volume 4. Bobby Jones, New Life Singers, The Ray Manning Singers and Rev. Al Green.
VHS: S05532. $29.95.

Volume 5. Bobby Jones, New Life Singers, Betty Griffin and the Spear Family Singers.
VHS: S05533. $29.95.

Volume 6. Bobby Jones, New Life Singers, Margaret Spence, The Futch Brothers and Susie Nelson (Willie's daughter).
VHS: S05534. $29.95.

Volume 7. Bobby Jones, New Life Singers, Myrna Summers, Darnell Hickman, Robin Junson and Jeff Lavalle.
VHS: S05536. $29.95.

Volume 8. Bobby Jones, New Life Singers, Rev. James Moore, Michael Charles and Evelyn Cosby.
VHS: S05537. $29.95.

Volume 9. Bobby Jones, New Life Singers, Stephene Stone Frierson, Milton Biggham and a special salute to Oprah Winfrey.
VHS: S05538. $29.95.

Volume 10: Special Christmas Show. Bobby Jones, New Life Singers, Jimmy Hill, Shirley Ceasar, Rejoice and Dorothy Norwood.
VHS: S05539. $29.95.

Breathe on Me: Rev. James Cleveland

A live performance with the Northern and Southern Community choirs of the G.M.W.A. 60 mins.
VHS: S21616. $29.95.

Chicago Sings—Gospel's Greatest Hymns, Vol. 1

Chicago is the setting for performances of over 15 great gospel hymns, featuring The Trinity United Church of Christ Mass Choir, Evangelist Joyce Haddon, Corener Hines, Bishop Clarence Haddon, Rev. Dan Willis, Dr. L.S. Scott, Damita Haddon, Pat Sanford, Deitrick Haddon, Rodnie Bryant, and Robert Turner.
VHS: S33953. $19.95.

Clark Sisters

A live concert by the Clark sisters recorded at the World of Faith Christian Center in Detroit. 85 mins.
VHS: S21617. $29.95.

Clouds of Joy
A live concert by the Mighty Clouds of Joy. 60 mins.
VHS: S21618. $24.95.

Commissioned in Concert
A concert at the State Theatre in Detroit. With a special appearance by Derrick Brinkley. 90 mins.
VHS: S21619. $29.95.

Dan Willis and the Pentecostals of Chicago
Experience the Gospel Jamaican style in this full-length concert video recorded live in Kingston, Jamaica, and featuring Darius Brooks of the Thompson Community Mass Choir on the soul stirring "One Lord, One Faith."
VHS: S33768. $14.95.

Douglas Miller Live in Houston
Shirley Caesar, Dr. Bobby Jones and Sarah Jordan Powell, as well as many other gospel singers, join Miller for this inspiring concert. Miller is backed by a choir featuring Houston's best singers in songs like "We Are the Ones," "Hold On," "Power," "My Strength" and many more.
VHS: S26223. $14.95.

Down Memory Lane: Rev. James Cleveland
Recorded live at the Mount Pigsah Baptist Church in Chicago. Also features Inez Andrews, Albertina Walker and the Barnet Sisters. 60 mins.
VHS: S21621. $29.95.

Dr. Charles G. Hayes and the Cosmopolitan Church of Prayer
Includes "I'll Never Forget", "My Soul Cries Out" and "Step Back Let God Do It".
VHS: S21622. $29.95.

Glory of Gospel, Vol. 1
Talented young Gospel performers from choirs and colleges across the U.S. perform. 60 mins.
VHS: S21626. $29.95.

Glory of Gospel, Vol. 2
Revival themes and the rhythm of African song are explored. 60 mins.
VHS: S21627. $29.95.

Glory of Gospel, Vol. 3
Part 3 continues with performances by a new generation of Gospel singers. 60 mins.
VHS: S21628. $29.95.

Glory of Gospel, Vol. 4
The U.S. Airforce Choir, Rutgers University Choir and others perform. 60 mins.
VHS: S21629. $29.95.

Gospel
"There is great energy, joy, and faith in this movie... The performers' singing gives glory to the Lord and what we get is very unselfconscious, unrestrained, joyous music" (Roger Ebert). With Edwin Hawkins, The Mighty Clouds of Joy, and Rev. James Cleveland.
VHS: S00519. $39.95.
David Leivick/Frederick A. Ritzenberg, USA, 1982, 92 mins.

Gospel According to Al Green
Though acclaimed for such 1970's standards as "Can't Get Next to You" and "Let's Stay Together," today Al Green is committed toGospel music. This film shows how one of the best loved pop stars of an earlier era found a new home in the traditions of gospel music.
VHS: S26786. $24.95.
Robert Mugge, USA, 1984, 94 mins.

Gospel Keynotes Live
Filmed at Jackson State University.
VHS: S21630. $29.95.

The Gospel Music Workshop of America—Men of Promise
Recorded live at the GMWA convention in Cincinnati, this exciting program features the men of The Gospel Music Workshop of America. Vocalists include Ronnie Daimond (of The Ohio Players), Dr. Leonard Scott, Issace Witmon and others.
VHS: S34725. $15.95.

Gospel's Best from Saturday Night Sing
Culled from the syndicated TV show, these clips offer some of gospel's greatest performers singing their best-known works. The Williams Brothers' "Lord How I Depend on You", Ricky Dillard's "Lift Up Jesus", Daniebelle Hall's "O Se Baba", Daryl Coley's "I'll Be with You", The Fairfield Four's "Swing Down, Chariot", Albertina Walker's "I Can Go to God in Prayer" and other famous Gospel songs are joined on this tape. 45 mins.
VHS: S21327. $14.95.

Greatest Week in Gospel
Marvin and Rickie Johns, Soul Stirrers, Nicholas, The Five Blind Boys, Commissioned, Pop Staples, Higher Dimensions and Deleon all appear.
Part 1. 80 mins.
VHS: S21631. $29.95.
Part 2. 80 mins.
VHS: S21632. $29.95.
Part 3. 80 mins.
VHS: S21633. $29.95.
Part 4. 80 mins.
VHS: S21634. $29.95.

Hallelujah: A Celebration of Psalms
The Book of Psalms is considered to be the most celebrated prayers of all time. Join the Harvey L. Miller Cantorial School Choir in a glorious program of song and celebration, featuring Leonard Bernstein's famous Chichester Psalms in addition to a mix of traditional, modern and original settings of the psalms sung by renowned cantors from across the country. 60 mins.
VHS: S33741. $34.95.

Hallelujah: A Gospel Celebration
The original Five Blind Boys, Inez Andrews and Bishop Kelsey star in this piece of gospel music history. Filmed in 1965 in a cathedral in Germany, this was the first black gospel performance in Europe. 60 mins.
VHS: S14610. $19.95.

Heavenly Host and The Sons of Calvary
Celebration, spectacle and spiritual enlightenment are the themes of this program, with live concert footage of the two Georgia-based gospel acts moving through the South, spreading their words and music.
VHS: S17498. $39.95.

Homecoming
Willie Neal Johnson, the Gospel Keynotes, Robert Blair and the Fantastic Violinaires, the Jackson Southernaires and the Williams Brothers all appear. 55 mins.
VHS: S21635. $29.95.

How Great Thou Art
This program celebrates the wonder of God's country through a unique combination of visual grandeur and favorite hymns. The highlights are a magnificent Haleakala Volcano represented by "How Great Thou Art"; white water rapids and waterfalls viewed to the strains of "Deep River"; a beautiful shot of a full moon overlooking Zion National Park contrasted with "Nearer, My God, to Thee"; the snow-capped landscapes of Yosemite National Park giving way to a haunting rendition of "Ave Maria"; and the surf cascading against the rocks of California's Big Sur to "Ode to Joy." 57 mins.
Laser: LD72249. $34.95.

In a Land Called Israel
The Mormon Tabernacle Choir sings a number of hymns as images of the Holy Land are revealed. The Mount of Olives, The Garden Tomb and Shepherd's Field are among the sights seen while the songs "Jerusalem of Gold," "How Great Thou Art," "The Lord Is My Shepherd" and "When I Survey the Wondrous Cross" are sung. 45 mins.
VHS: S29984. $19.95.

James Hall & Worship and Praise: ...According to James Hall—Chap. III
The video companion to the hot gospel hit by James Hall & Worship and Praise. Selections include "He Reigns," "Great Is Our God," "Been Mighty Good," "Perfect Security," "I'm Not the Same," "Tell the World," "Hold Me," "He Took My Place," "All I Need," "Overcome," "It Pays," "He First Loved Me" and "When He Comes Back in the Clouds."
VHS: S32085. $19.95.

Jesus Paid It All
Recorded live in Atlanta, GA, this tape features Rev. Donald Vails and Rev. R.L. White. USA, 120 mins.
VHS: S21638. $29.95.

L. Barnes & Red Budd Choir: So Satisfied
Recorded at the Center Stage Theater in Atlanta. 55 mins.
VHS: S21639. $24.95.

L.A. Mass Choir
The L.A. Mass Choir is captured live in Anaheim with a guest appearance by Higher Dimension. USA, 60 mins.
VHS: S21640. $29.95.

Legends of Gospel
Five-tape box set features celebrated live in-concert performances by Rev. James Cleveland, The Clark Sisters, Walter Hawkins and the Hawkins family, Shirley Caeser, and The Mighty Clouds of Joy. "Unrestrained, joyous music. It's a great experience and a whole lot of fun" (Roger Ebert). 100 mins.
VHS: S34273. $49.95.

Mahalia Jackson
Mahalia Jackson and *Elizabeth Cotten* are paired here in a duo of filmed biographies of these remarkable ladies. Returning to her origins in New Orleans, Mahalia sings such favorites as "Down by the Riverside" and "A Close Walk with Thee," while the over-80, incomparable Miss Cotten presents her original version of "Freight Train."
VHS: S03967. $29.95.

The Mahalia Jackson Collection
Four hours containing over 75 songs performed by gospel's greatest singer, including many performances never before seen by the public. Plus, the definitive biography, *Mahalia Jackson: The Power and the Glory*. Digitally remastered. Five-volume set. 240 mins.
VHS: S32901. $89.95.

Mahalia Jackson: "Give God the Glory"
Mahalia Jackson's final tour of Europe is the setting for this documentary which studies the singer's life and music. 88 mins.
VHS: S21636. $29.95.

Mahalia Jackson: The Power and the Glory
The life of the world's greatest gospel singer is examined, from her roots as an obscure child singer in a New Orleans ghetto through her rise to Carnegie Hall and the stages of Europe. Features interviews with Rev. Jesse Jackson, Studs Terkel and others.
VHS: S32900. $19.95.

Mahalia Sings the Songs of Christmas
The gospel legend performs "O Come All Ye Faithful," "Silent Night," "A Child of the King," "Sweet Little Jesus Boy," "A Star Stood Still" and other Christmas songs. 40 mins.
VHS: S32927. $14.95.

Matters of the Heart
Commissioned is a fresh gospel group that brings new vigor to their message with help from pop greats like Run D.M.C. In this video they perform their acclaimed songs "Work on Me", "Stand", "Love Is the Way" and "Dare to Believe", as well as many others.
VHS: S22094. $14.95.

McDonald's Gospelfest
Marilyn McCoo and Glynn Turman host this gospel celebration. Featuring Edwin Hawkins, Daryl Coley, and The Conquerors.
Part 1. 60 mins.
VHS: S21641. $24.95.
Part 2. 60 mins.
VHS: S21642. $24.95.

National Baptist Convention Mass Choir: Let's Go to Church
Under the leadership of Dr. Henry Lyons, the National Baptist Convention USA, Inc., boasts a membership of 8.5 million people and 33,000 churches across the country. The organization celebrated its 116 years in existence with this first recording ever of its Choir. Performances include "Devotion/Near the Cross," "Let's Go to Church," "I'll Go," "Not for Himself," "Christ You Made the Difference," "Hallelujah," "I'm Blessed," "Never Alone," "Who Is This Jesus" and "Work That Thing Out." With Albertina Walker, Evelyn Turrentine-Agee, Paul Porter, Kim McFarland and Rev. Clay Evans.
VHS: S30771. $19.95.

New Jersey Mass Choir
The New Jersey Mass Choir is filmed live at the Aaron Davis Hall in New York City. With Donnie Harper and the New Jersey Mass Choir. USA, 1992, 60 mins.
VHS: S21645. $29.95.

New York Restoration Choir: Thank You Jesus

Includes "We Worship You", "Lamb of God" and "Ain't That Love".
VHS: S21646. $29.95.

Oh Happy Day

A foot stampin', hand clappin' reach for the heavens in these live performances of gospel music superstars, including Shirley Caesar, The Mighty Clouds of Joy, Walter Hawkins and the Hawkins Family, Rev. James Cleveland and The Clark Sisters. 60 mins.
VHS: S07175. $29.95.

Pilgrim Jubilees

Recorded live in Jackson, Mississippi. Includes "We're the People" and "Feel the World".
VHS: S21653. $29.95.

Rev. Clay Evans: I'm Going Through

Recorded live at the Fellowship Baptist Church in Chicago.
VHS: S21658. $29.95.

Rev. Ernest Davis, Jr., and the Wilmington Chester Mass Choir: "He's Preparing Me"

Recorded live at the Church of Atlanta Lighthouse. 80 mins.
VHS: S21656. $29.95.

Rev. F.C. Barnes and Co.

A live performance from Atlanta.
VHS: S21654. $24.95.

Rev. James Cleveland and the L.A. Gospel Messengers

Includes "We're on Business for The King", "Great Things" and others.
VHS: S21655. $29.95.

Rick Grundy Chorale

Video performances by Gospels recent stars include "I'm Standin' Here" and "Just Say the Word". 60 mins.
VHS: S21659. $24.95.

Roots of Gospel

The New World Gospel Choir performs in Biblical locations.
Part 1. 60 mins.
VHS: S21660. $24.95.
Part 2. 45 mins.
VHS: S21661. $24.95.

Saturday Night, Sunday Morning: The Travels of Gatemouth Moore

This award-winning documentary reveals the common roots of blues and gospel through the remarkable story of A.D. Gatemouth Moore. Once called "one of the greatest blues singers ever" by blues legend B.B. King, Moore later became an evangelical preacher and gospel disc jockey in the South. Also features B.B. King, Al Green, Rufus Thomas and Benjamin Hooks. "A wonderful documentary…Gatemouth Moore is a warm and thundering presence" (*Los Angeles Times*).
VHS: S30169. $24.99.
Louis Guida, USA, 1996, 58 mins.

Say Amen, Somebody

A joy-filled celebration of Gospel music! "It's one of the happiest movies in a long, long time. There is no way that I can recommend it any more highly," said Roger Ebert.
VHS: S01162. $29.95.
George Nierenberg, USA, 1983, 100 mins.

The Sensational Nightingales: Ministry in Song

Includes "Nichodemus", "It's Gonna Rain" and "Ain't That Love".
VHS: S21662. $29.95.

T'ain't Nothin' Changed

A musical look back at the history of Gospel. Features Dr. Mattie Moss Clark. 60 mins.
VHS: S21663. $29.95.

Tramaine Hawkins

Feature "I'll Give It to You", "Praise the Name of Jesus" and other songs. 90 mins.
VHS: S21664. $24.95.

Walter Hawkins and Love Alive IV

Includes "Solid Rock", "I Can't Bear It", "He Knows" and other songs. 1990, 60 mins.
VHS: S21665. $29.95.

Wanda Nero Butler: New Born Soul

The award-winning gospel singer is captured live in San Francisco. Special guest appearence by Arvis Strickling Jones. 60 mins.
VHS: S21666. $29.95.

We Sing, Gospel's Greatest Hymns

This service has terrific and inspiring gospel music throughout each section of its duration. "He Is Lord," "At the Cross," "Blessed Assurance," "Just As I Am," "Love Lifted Me" and "So Glad" are just some of the hymns heard on this uplifting video.
VHS: S29941. $14.95.

The Winans: Live in Concert

A live performance featuring Vanessa Bell Armstrong. 120 mins.
VHS: S21670. $29.95.

The Winans: Return

Grammy winners The Winans sing selections from their Gospel hit album *Return*. Includes "It's Time" and "Friend of Mine". 81 mins.
VHS: S21671. $24.95.

The Winans: The Lost Concert

Powerful live concert performance by The Winans, The Commissioned (with their original lineup) and Vanessa Bell Armstrong. 80 mins.
VHS: S32928. $14.95.

JAZZ, BLUES & R&B

40 Years of MJQ

The Modern Jazz Quartet got their start in a seemingly unlikely place. They met while working for the bebop big band of Dizzy Gillespie. Since their formation, this quartet has continued to pursue a unique and dignified style influenced by both classical and jazz greats. "Sketch," "Alexander's Fugue," "Adagio from Concierto de Aranjues" and "A Day in Dubrovnik" are among the selections included on this video. 58 mins.
VHS: S24066. $19.98.

Abbey Lincoln: You Gotta Pay the Band

In its 5-star review of Abbey Lincoln's album of the same name, *Down Beat* stated, "Lady Day and Pres must have revisited Earth the day this record was made." The video edition features live and studio versions of the songs on the album, as well as clips of the 1950s and 1960s movies in which Abbey starred. Also includes interviews with Stan Getz, Tony Bennett, Ruth Brown and Spike Lee. 58 mins.
VHS: S15713. $24.95.
Laser: LD70283. $34.95.

Accent on the Offbeat

Jazz original Wynton Marsalis and choreographer Peter Martins joined forces to produce this unusual dance performance. Both the intimate collaborative process and the final performance employing the New York City Ballet on the stage of Lincoln Center are included in this amazing chronicle.
VHS: S21074. $24.98.

After Hours

Coleman Hawkins, Roy Eldridge, Cozy Cole. 27 mins.
VHS: S03192. $24.95.

Airto & Flora Purim: The Latin Jazz All Stars

The infectious sounds and rhythms of Brazilian jazz are showcased in this 1985 Queen Mary Jazz Festival. The highlight is the virtuoso percussionist Airto Moreira and the six-octave vocalist Flora Purim backed by an 11-piece group, including saxophonist Joe Farrel and the Batucaje Dance Troupe. 60 mins.
VHS: S04341. $29.95.

Albert King

Albert King's musical influences are seen and heard in the classic numbers "Blues Riff," "The Grass Ain't No Greener," "Born under a Bad Sign," "They Call It Stormy Monday" and "Let the Good Times Roll."
VHS: S19681. $19.95.

Alberta Hunter: My Castle's Rocking

An impressionistic portrait of the legendary singer and songwriter, including "Downhearted Blues," "Handy Man," the music of Armstrong and her final interview. "Exhilarating and moving" (*L.A. Times*). 59 mins.
VHS: S17611. $19.98.

Alfonia

A memorial tribute to Alfonia Tims, Jr., an innovative African American jazz musician who died at age 26, three weeks before the release of his highly praised album. Includes early conversations, original music and other documentary material.
VHS: S33824. $24.95.
Claire Burch, USA, 1990, 58 mins.

America's Music: Blues 1

Utilizes interviews with the artists, stills, film clips of Bessie Smith and others, and rousing performances from Linda Hopkins (St. Louis Blues), B.B. King, Leata Galloway, Eddie Cleanhead Vinson, Erne Andrews, Vi Redd, "Pee Wee" Crayton. 60 mins.,
VHS: S05032. $19.95.

America's Music: Blues 2

Brock Peters narrates the second volume of the birth of the blues, featuring such blues greats as Joe Williams, Paula Kelly, Esther Phillips, Bobby McGee, Buddy Guy and Junior Wells, Dorothy Donigan, Joe Williams and Addie, with film clips of Mamie Smith, Count Basie and Big Joe Turner. 60 mins.
VHS: S05033. $19.95.

America's Music: Jazz Then Dixieland 1

Al Hirt hosts this look at Dixieland, with film clips and stills, and performances by Woody Herman, Clora Bryant, Scotty Plummer, Della Reese, Al Hirt, Johnny Guarnieri. 60 mins.
VHS: S05038. $19.95.

America's Music: Jazz Then Dixieland 2

Al Hirt continues with music by Bob Crosby, The Hessions, Scatman Crothers, Al Hirt, Teddy Buckner, Judy Carmichael, Irma Thomas. 60 mins.
VHS: S05039. $19.95.

America's Music: Rhythm and Blues 1

Billy Eckstine hosts this look at rhythm and blues, with featured artists including Eckstine, Ruth Brown, Billy Preston, Gloria Lynne, Sheer Delight, and film clips of Amos Milburn, Louis Mordan and Scatman Crothers. 60 mins.
VHS: S05034. $19.95.

America's Music: Rhythm and Blues 2

Brock Peters hosts the second volume of the rhythm and blues series which features Brook Benton, Scatman Crothers, Mary Wells, O.C. Smith, Sam Moore, and film clips of Slim Gaillard. 60 mins.
VHS: S05035. $19.95.

America's Music: Soul 1

Host Leon Kennedy documents the evolution of soul from rhythm and blues through the music of James Brown. With Brown's "Rap Payback," "Jam," Ben E. King's "Spanish Harlem," "I Who Have Nothing," May Bond Davis' "This Is It," Tyrone Davis' "Turn Back the Hands of Time" and "Turning Point," Maxine Nightingale's "Lead Me On," "I Don't Miss You At All" and "Right Back Where We Started From," Tyrone Davis' "In the Mood," and James Brown's "The Man Understand." 60 mins.
VHS: S05040. $19.95.

America's Music: Soul 2

Leon Kennedy continues his documentation of soul music with Gladys Knight and the Pips' "I Will Fight," "Best Thing That Ever Happened," "Midnight Train to Georgia," Rufus Thomas' "Do the Push and Pull," "Walking the Dog," Carla Thomas' "I Like What You Do To Me," Jerry Butler's "Hey Western Union Man," Freda Payne's "Band of Gold," "Bring the Boys Home," Percy Sledge's "You Had to Be There," Gladys Knight and the Pips' "Save the Overtime," "Neither One of Us." 60 mins.,
VHS: S05041. $19.95.

And This Is Free

Chicago's Maxwell Street Market is captured in its entirety through cinema verite techniques in this unique film. The filmmaker originally set out to capture blues singers, but he realized that the whole area contained a much fuller picture that could explain the blues. Since Maxwell Street has been transformed by urban renewal, this may be the only way to see the singular mix of people and music that this area once offered. B&W.
VHS: S27154. $19.95.
Mike Shea, USA, 1964, 50 mins.

Anything for Jazz

A portrait of Jaki Bayrd, pianist, composer and band leader. 25 mins.
VHS: S03184. $19.95.

Archie Shepp: I Am Jazz…It's My Life

One of the most controversial figures on the jazz scene is captured pontificating on his favorite subjects—the African origins and revolutionary purpose of jazz, the social invisibility and isolation of blacks—but in the film's club sequences Shepp, whether on tenor or soprano sax or shouting his poems of protest, swings like bad and expertly builds his solos to an exciting climax. With Siegfried Kessler piano, Wilbur Little bass, Don Mumford and Clifford Jarvis drums and Cheikh Tidiane Fall percussion.
VHS: S12332. $19.95.
Frank Cassenti, France/USA, 1984, 52 mins.

Aretha Franklin: Live at Park West

From the PBS Series *Soundstage*, Aretha Franklin performs many of her soul gold hits, including "Think", "Respect" and "Rock Steady". 60 mins.
VHS: S20491. $19.98.
Laser: LD74840. $29.99.

Arhoolie Records' 25th Anniversary Party

27 songs in thrilling live performance fill this anniversary concert celebrating Arhoolie Records' first quarter century of recording great down-home American music. Features J.C. Burris, Los Campesinos de Michoacan, Dick Oxtot's Golden Age Jazz Band, Charlie Misselwhite Blues Band, Rose Maddox, Michael Doucet, Ann Savoy, Danny Poullard and Cajun All Stars, Katie Webster with Juke Joint Johnny and the Hot Links. 120 mins.
VHS: S10358. $39.98.

Art Blakey and the Jazz Messengers: The Jazz Life

Fuller Love, Little Man, My Ship, New York, Gypsy Folktales, The Theme. Recorded live at Seventh Avenue South, and featuring Wynton Marsalis. 55 mins.
VHS: S07742. $29.95.

Art Ensemble of Chicago: Live from the Jazz Showcase

Members of the quintet perform in quasi-African costumes, masks and face paint, surrounded by two tons of instruments, all the while sharing musical and visual jokes as they go caroming through the history of jazz. The show touches on be-bop, New Orleans jazz, 1960's funk and a ballad, amid percussion interludes. 50 mins.
VHS: S12333. $19.95.

At the Jazz Band Ball

Some of the greatest music, song and dance from the jazz age is captured on sound film between 1925-1933. Duke Ellington's Cotton Club Orchestra, Louis Armstrong, Bill "Bojangles" Robinson, Bessie Smith and the Dorsey Brothers are included in this collection of music legends. Bix Beiderbecke's only appearance on sound film has been found and added to this tape. 60 mins.
VHS: S23059. $19.95.

B.B. King Live at Nick's

From the beginning there has always been just one king of the Blues, B.B. King. This legendary singer is taped live at Nick's in Dallas, proving, as if it needed proving, that the thrill is not gone. 50 mins.
VHS: S21063. $14.95.

B.B. King Live in Africa

B.B. King performs a classic hour of Blues in a legendary performance in Africa, including "Ain't Nobody Home," "The Thrill Is Gone," and "Sweet Sixteen." 52 mins.
VHS: S11701. $19.95.

Barney Kessel 1962-1991

Kessel's legendary guitar music is one of the most original voices produced by jazz. This video captures 30 years of his performances with a number of jazz greats. In the span of his career he played with Lester Young, Charlie Parker, Billie Holiday, Art Tatum and other famed jazz musicians.
VHS: S24219. $19.95.

Barry Harris: Passing It On

A musical portrait of Barry Harris, pianist and teacher. 23 mins.
VHS: S03190. $29.95.

Beale Street

Beale Street is where W.C. Handy wrote the blues, where Boss Crump abused his power, and where Martin Luther King marched days before his death in 1968. Beale Street has been the victim of urban renewal, and this film is a unique oral history of the street. Among the Beale Streeters featured are B.B. King, the Hooks Brothers, Bobby Blue Bland, Prince Gabe, Maurice "Fess" Hulbert, and Rufus Thomas.
VHS: S07770. $39.95.
Alexis Krasilovsky/Rickey/Baldwin, USA, 1981, 28 mins.

Ben Webster: The Brute and the Beautiful

A fascinating look at the legendary jazz saxophonist Ben Webster. The film traces his origins in Kansas City in the 1920s, his collaborations with Duke Ellington, Benny Carter, Teddy Wilson, Gerry Mulligan and Jimmy Witherspoon, and his European exile and final performance in Holland, in September, 1973. 60 mins.
VHS: S17964. $24.95.

Benny Carter: Symphony in Riffs

Winner of the Grammy Lifetime Achievement Award, Benny Carter is known as a principal architect of the Big Band sound. Lena Horne, Dizzy Gillespie, Andre Previn, Ella Fitzgerald, David Sanborn and Quincy Jones are just some of the personalities who contribute to this loving portrait of Carter.
VHS: S26787. $24.95.
Harrison Engle, USA, 1989, 58 mins.

Benny Goodman: At the Tivoli

A filmed concert from the Tivoli Gardens in Copenhagen, where Benny Goodman performs "Lady Be Good", "I Should Care", "Send in the Clowns", "Airmail Special Delivery", "The World Is Waiting" and "For the Sunrise". Goodman is accompanied by violinist Sven Osmussen, drummer Charly Antolini, pianist Don Haas, trumpet player Jimmy Maxwell, guitarist Harry Pepe and bassist Peter Witte. 50 mins.
VHS: S19004. $29.95.

Big Ben: Ben Webster in Europe

A world of heart, tenderness and terror is the world of Big Ben Webster in this picture of the extraordinary musician who played tenor sax in nearly every great band of the thirties and forties, including the Kansas City bands of Andy Kirk and Benny Moten and his long association with Duke Ellington. Music includes "My Romance", "Perdido", "You'd Be So Nice to Come Home To".
VHS: S12334. $19.95.
Johan van der Keuken, Netherlands, 1967, 31 mins.

The Bill Evans Trio

Bill Evans is joined by Marc Johnson and Joe La Barbera in this video of outstanding jazz performances.
VHS: S26788. $19.95.
John Beyer, USA, 1979, 58 mins.

Bix

This famed trumpeter revolutionized jazz. In this first-rate musical biography his life and times are recreated based on the known facts. He is seen playing in some of the original locations including spots throughout the Midwest where *Bix* began. Hoagey Carmichael and Pee Wee Russel are just some of the figures seen accompanying him, performing songs like "Dardenella" and "Stardust." In English.
VHS: S20939. $29.95.
Pupi Avati, Italy/USA, 1990, 100 mins.

Black Jazz and Blues

Three short films: *The St. Louis Blues* featuring Bessie Smith (1929), Duke Ellington and Billie Holiday in *Symphony in Black*, and Louis Jordan with the Fletcher Henderson Orchestra in *Caldonia*. USA, 44 mins.
VHS: S02237. $24.95.

Black Moses of Soul

Isaac Hayes and The Movement serve up a heaping order of Hot Buttered Soul in this live performance which includes such classic songs as "I Stand Accused," The Jackson 5's "Never Can Say Goodbye" and a soulful rendition of The Doors' "Light My Fire." 80 mins.
VHS: S14941. $19.95.

Blues Legends: Son House & Bukka White

Filmed in the 60s, these performances communicate the power and eloquence of legendary blues masters. Introduced by Taj Mahal.
VHS: S15515. $29.95.

Blues Like Shower of Rain

Country blues through historic photographs and field recordings, featuring Paul Oliver. 30 mins.
VHS: S03185. $24.95.

Blues Masters, Vol. 1

An encyclopedic account of the history, personalities and evolution of the American blues masters, including Son House, Leadbelly, Bessie Smith, Mamie Smith, Roy Milton and His Orchestra, Jimmy Rushing, Ethel Waters and Big Bill Broonzy. The documentary merges archival recording footage and photographs. The highlight is a raucous version of "St. Louis Blues" by Leadbelly and Bessie Smith. 51 mins.
VHS: S19163. $19.98.

Blues Masters, Vol. 2

A compendium of vintage performers is a highlight reel of the greatest blues musicians of their era. This program explores the gifts and personal drive that contributed to their distinctive sounds and charismatic voices. Blending archival performance footage and rare photographs, the show spotlights Ida Cox, Billie Holiday, Big Mama Thornton, Muddy Waters, Joe Turner, Joe Williams, Buddy Guy, Jimmy Witherspoon and B.B. King. 51 mins.
VHS: S19164. $19.98.

Blues Up the Country

Diverse country traditions from the Mississippi Delta to the Piedmont region are captured on this collection of country blues. Taped between 1962 and 1970, it reveals a musical landscape which nurtured artists like John Jackson, Pink Anderson, Jesse Fuller and Ethel & George McCoy.
VHS: S26428. $24.95.

Bluesland: A Portrait in American Music

This complete visual history of the blues is hosted by Keith David and includes appearances by Robert Palmer and Albert Murray. Musical footage of legendary greats Bessie Smith, B.B. King, Muddy Waters, Dinah Washington and many more is included. 90 mins.
VHS: S23324. $29.98.

Bob James Live

The gifted pianist and composer Bob James fronts an eclectic septet showcasing Kirk Whalum, performing "Taxi", "Zebra Man", "Unicorn" and "Ruby" at the 1985 Queen Mary Jazz Festival. 56 mins.
VHS: S19227. $19.98.

The Bob Wilber Big Band: Bufadora Blow-up

Wilber's first big band recording of his own music, recorded live in concert at the 1996 March of Jazz by an all-star group of musicians hand-picked by Wilber. 64 mins.
VHS: S31715. $39.95.

Bobby Short at the Cafe Carlyle

The darling of cafe society singer/pianist with his lively interpretations of Tin Pan Alley songs. 65 mins.
VHS: S03384. $29.95.

Boogie in Blue

An ebullient, lively and colorful documentary biography of Harry "the Hipster" Gibson, called "the mad boogie woogie genius" of his era. The film interweaves performance material, archival photography and interviews with Gibson and his family to present a textured portrait of the man and his music. Directed by Gibson's daughter Arlena Gibson and granddaughter Flavyn Feller. 40 mins.
VHS: S17914. $24.95.

Born to Swing

Count Basie alumni Buddy Tate, Jo Jones and Gene Krupa. 50 mins.
VHS: S03193. $19.95.

Branford Marsalis: Steep

Powerful live performances and insightful interviews with soprano/tenor player Branford Marsalis, a rising star in the jazz world. Performances include "Swingin' at the Haven", "Crescent City", "Lament", "Giant Steps" and many more. USA, 89 mins.
VHS: S15309. $14.98.

Brownie McGhee: Born with the Blues 1966-1992

Tennessee-born, Carolina-influenced, New York-based blues legend Brownie McGhee was an articulate spokesman for the blues who was largely associated with the "folk boom" and showed a stylistic range from turn-of-the-century ragtime ("Come On, Keep It Coming") to the lyrical sophistication of such original songs as "Conversation with a River." Other songs include "Kansas City Blues," "Pawn Shop Blues" and "Death of Blind Boy Fuller." 60 mins.
VHS: S31648. $22.95.

Buddy Barnes

I've Been to Town, Don't Fight It, It's Chemistry, Color of My Life, My Ship, Pick Yourself Up, Long Before I Knew You, Guess I'll Hang My Tears Out to Dry, and Penny by Penny. 30 mins.
VHS: S05424. $19.95.

Built by Hand String Trio

Three musicians from New York want to "take the audience on a trip." Charles Burnham on violin, James Emery on guitar and John Lindberg on bass make up the String Trio of New York, and with this tape you can experience their unique, frantic, acoustic psychedelia. Songs include "Wise Old Owl Blues", "Texas Koto Blues", "Multiple Reasons" and "Seven Vice". 30 mins.
VHS: S12335. $24.95.

Carla Bley and Steve Swallow: Very, Very Simple

This duo play the bass and piano in their own inimical way. Their long working relationship and friendship ensure the audience a captivating experience. They play as one without the help of a conductor, which means that together they achieve a special, intimate stage of rapport with their listeners. "Soon I Will Be Done with the Troubles of the World," "Lawns," and "Very, Very Simple" are included in this video. 32 mins.
VHS: S24065. $19.98.

Carmen McRae Live

Jazz's legendary lady gives a supreme vocal performance of 21 standards, including "That Old Black Magic", "I Get Along without You Very Well", "Thou Swell", "But Not for Me" and "What a Little Moonlight Can Do". 82 mins.
Laser: LD70332. $39.95.

Carnegie Hall Salutes the Jazz Masters

Betty Carter, Al Foster, Pat Metheny, Herbie Hancock, Roy Hargrove, Bruce Hornsby and Yosuke Yamashita are just some of the artists who performed during this historic concert. 120 mins.
VHS: S21298. $24.95.
Laser: LD72423. $34.94.

Celebrating Bird: The Triumph of Charlie Parker

The only authorized documentary on the late, great Charlie Parker, tracing his beginnings in Kansas City to his final years in New York, featuring interviews with friends, family, colleagues, as well as archival clips and historic performances of "Confirmation," "Ballade," "A Night in Tunisia," "Just Friends," and more. 58 mins.
VHS: S05401. $29.95.

Charles Mingus: Triumph of the Underdog

A comprehensively researched and involving portrait of the great jazz bassist, composer, and conductor featuring newly unearthed performance footage, previously unpublished photographs, radio broadcasts and private interviews. "One of the finest documentaries about a jazz musician ever made" (*London Observer*).
VHS: S34255. $19.95.
Don McGlynn, USA, 1997, 78 mins.

Chester Zardis: The Spirit of New Orleans

A colorful documentary on the life and art of the revolutionary African-American bassist Chester Zardis, who is seen playing in concert with Danny Barker, Louis Nelsom, Jeanette Kimball, Wendell Brunious and Dr. Michael White. Leading jazz authorities Alan Lomax and William Russell contribute their insights and assessments of Zardis's work.
VHS: S19124. $29.95.
Preston McClanahan, USA, 1989, 88 mins.

Chet Baker: Let's Get Lost

Bruce Weber examines the life and times of a jazz legend who knew the high notes and the low notes. Weber combines fascinating performance footage with candid and rambling interviews with the jazz trumpeter and vocalist just prior to his death. He also locates old friends, fans and the family of the James Dean of jazz for a complex portrait with plenty of music.
VHS: S12249. $29.98.
Bruce Weber, USA, 1989, 119 mins.

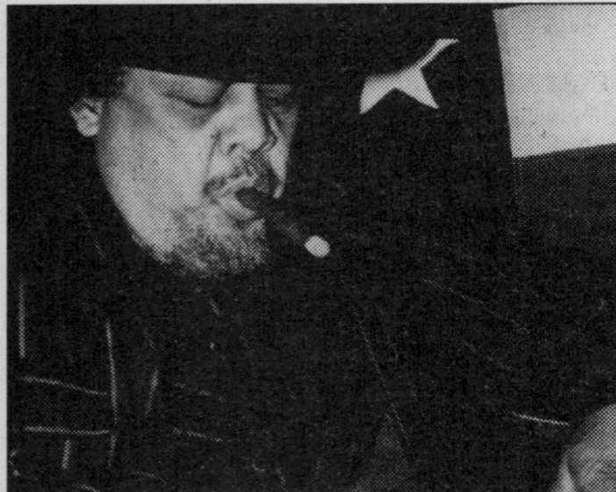

Chicago Blues

A fascinating study of Chicago Blues, including Johnnie Lewis, Muddy Waters, Buddy Guy, Junior Wells and H.B. Hutto, with narration and comments by Dick Gregory.
VHS: S00232. $19.95.
Harley Cokliss, Great Britain, 1972, 50 mins.

Chick Corea Keyboard Workshop

A private lesson with Chick Corea. From Bach's "Goldberg Variations" to his own "Yellow Nimbus", musicians learn methods of composition, improvisation and practice. 60 mins.
VHS: S11523. $39.95.

Chick Corea: Electric Workshop

Chick Corea, Grammy Award-winning keyboardist, guides viewers through the entire composition process, from conception to the finished composition. 60 mins.
VHS: S11522. $39.95.

Chico Hamilton: The Jazz Life

The Theme, Encore, Sweet Dreams Too Soon, The Baron, Space for Stacy, First Light, Clinton Avenue, Erika. 53 mins.
VHS: S05417. $29.95.

Cobham Meets Bellson

All-star drummers Billy Cobham and Louie Bellson face off and alternate in virtuosity. 36 mins.
VHS: S03382. $19.98.

Coltrane Legacy

An hour-long compilation of precious jazz clips that show the reasons for the enormous impact John Coltrane continues to have on the world of jazz.
VHS: S04619. $39.95.

Curtis Mayfield: Live at Ronnie Scott's

One of Curtis Mayfield's last performances before a paralyzing accident, the founding member of the legendary Impressions performs "Little Child Running Wild", "It's Alright", "People Get Ready" and "We Gotta Have Peace". 58 mins.
VHS: S20492. $19.98.

Dave Holland Quartet: Vortex

Dave Holland and his crew—Steve Coleman, Smitty Smith, Kenny Wheeler and Robin Eubanks—join forces for this unique jazz experience. "Vortex," "Homecoming" and "Wiguts Waits for Watts" are three tunes that give these musicians a chance to demonstrate their amazing virtuosity. 62 mins.
VHS: S26039. $19.98.

David, Moffet, Ornette

In the spring of 1966 Ornette Coleman wrote and recorded the soundtrack for a Living Theatre project called *Who's Crazy?*. This film is a record of the three days Ornette spent in the studio making music with virtuoso bass-player David Izenzon and drummer Charles Moffet. The film explores the strength and clarity which three individuals working together can bring to the search for freedom in jazz.
VHS: S07749. $29.95.
Dick Fontaine, USA, 1966, 26 mins.

Devil Got My Woman: Blues at Newport 1966

Alan Lomax recreated the bluesy atmosphere of a juke joint when he captured the performances of Skip James, Howlin' Wolf, Son House, Rev. Pearly Brown and Bukka White at the 1966 Newport Folk Festival. 60 mins.
VHS: S33104. $22.50.

The Dexter Gordon Quartet

Dexter Gordon, the star of '*Round Midnight*, plays alongside his companions George Cables, Rufus Reid and Eddie Gladden. Together they create an unforgettable jazz performance on this videotape.
VHS: S26790. $19.95.
John Beyer, USA, 1979, 58 mins.

Diana Ross Live

Diana Ross reinterprets the works of Billie Holiday, Rodgers and Hart, George Gershwin and Count Basie. Includes "God Bless the Child", "My Man", "Good Morning Heartache" and "The Man I Love" in a 1992 New York concert.
VHS: S18319. $24.95.
Laser: LD71856. $34.95.
Steve Binder, USA, 1992, 90 mins.

Different Drummer: Elvin Jones

A portrait of Elvin Jones with rare footage of John Coltrane. 30 mins.
VHS: S03189. $24.95.

Discovering Jazz

Black American 19th-century traditions are the source of jazz. Rhythmic and melodic innovations transformed European music into an exciting new form. From Dixieland and the blues to swing and bop, jazz is the music of the 20th century. 21 mins.
VHS: S23509. $49.95.

Dizzy Gillespie: A Night in Chicago

In this Chicago concert, Dizzy plays "Swing Low, Sweet Cadillac", "Embraceable You", "'Round Midnight" and "A Night in Tunisia". 53 mins.
VHS: S19173. $19.98.

Dizzy Gillespie: A Night in Tunisia

This dazzling concert performance is followed by Dizzy discussing how Afro-Cuban rhythms altered the form of mainstream American jazz. 28 mins.
VHS: S19224. $19.98.

Dizzy Gillespie: Live in London

A concert recorded at London's Royal Festival Hall features "Manteca", "A Night in Tunisia" and "Moody's Mood for Love". 91 mins.
VHS: S19002. $29.95.

Django, A Jazz Tribute

Bireli Langrene, the groundbreaking young guitarist, performs this musical tribute in honor of Django, accompanied by Django's son Babik Reinhardt. Together they negotiate the complex melodies of the jazz innovator. Django, the leader of the Hot Club of France, composed memorable songs that live on 50 years after they were first recorded. 26 mins.
VHS: S24064. $19.98.

Don Cherry's Multikulti

Together with Ornette Coleman, Cherry assumed a leading position in the jazz vanguard of the 1960's. His interpretations of centuries-old vocal traditions continue to glow. This video documents Cherry's work at the prestigious Days of Jazz in Stuttgart, Germany, and includes "Walk to the Mountain," "Bemsha Swing" and "Trans Love Airways," among others. 57 mins.
VHS: S24067. $19.98.

Dr. John Teaches New Orleans Piano

A complete two-tape series taught by Mac (Dr. John) Rebennack.
Dr. John Teaches New Orleans Piano—Part One. This great video lesson is jammed full of powerful playing, slowed-down instruction, and the wonderful personality of one of the premier artists of our time. Covered are the styles of Professor Longhair, Pine Top Smith, Fats Domino, James Booker and others. 60 mins.
VHS: S09691. $49.95.
Dr. John Teaches New Orleans Piano—Part Two. Continuing his fascinating tour through the dynamic world of New Orleans piano, Dr. John teaches the styles of Huey Piano Smith, Tuts Washington, Allen Toussaint and Mac (Dr. John) Rebennack himself. 60 mins.
VHS: S09692. $49.95.

Dr. John: New Orleans Swamp

New Orleans renegade Dr. John incorporates rhythm and blues, zydeco, Cajun, soul and voodoo refrains as he performs "Walk Right In/Shake, Rattle and Roll", "Whole Lotta Loving", "Every Day I Have the Blues", "Call a Doctor" and "Such a Night". 60 mins.
VHS: S18717. $19.98.

Duke Ellington

With his Orchestra, Duke Ellington plays "Take the A Train," "Satin Doll," "Things Aren't What They Used to Be" and other numbers. 24 mins.
VHS: S19888. $29.95.

Dukes of Dixieland and Friends

In this 75-minute video, The Dukes of Dixieland join the New Orleans Pops Orchestra in an exciting dose of New Orleans Symphonic jazz. The Dukes' program draws on a variety of New Orleans music in the intense, brassy Dixieland style.
VHS: S10150. $29.95.

Eartha Kitt: The Most Exciting Woman in the World

In a live concert performance Eartha Kitt lives up to the sobriquet coined by Orson Welles to describe her musical and performative abilities: the most exciting woman in the world. She sings "C'est Si Bon," "Here's to Life" and many other favorites, proving that she is indeed an undisputed jazz and blues legend. 60 mins.
VHS: S20940. $24.95.

Eddie Jefferson Live from Jazz Showcase

Filmed in Chicago two nights before Jefferson was shot and killed, he is accompanied here by Richie Cole's Quartet. Songs include "Moody's Mood for Love", "I Cover the Waterfront", "Night in Tunisia", "How High the Moon" and a lot more. 50 mins.
VHS: S12336. $19.39.

Electric Hot Tuna: Live at the Fillmore

Hot Tuna, a three-decade wonder band with a prodigious recording longevity and one of the most faithful audiences in popular music, performs live at San Francisco's legendary Fillmore Auditorium at a concert filmed in December 1995. 90 mins.
VHS: S33106. $22.50.

Elvin Jones Jazz Machine

Elvin Jones is recognized as a master drummer of jazz. Since the mid-1960's, when he played with Coltrane's groundbreaking quartet, this drummer has been looked to as a leader within this musical tradition. Sonny Fortune, Chip Jackson, Willie Pickens and Ravi Coltrane accompany Jones in this collection of unmatched musical performances. 58 mins.
VHS: S24063. $19.98.

Ernie Andrews: Blues for Central Avenue

Ernie Andrews, the blues singer, tells his own story from L.A. of the 30's and 40's, as he reminiscences about big bands, after-hours clubs, gambling, bathtub gin and the segregation that was a fact of life. As he talks about his life, he sings the blues in recent performances. With Buddy Collette and Harry (Sweets) Edison.
VHS: S07744. $39.95.
Lois Shelton, USA, 1986, 50 mins.

An Evening with Lena Horne

The legendary Lena Horne was recorded live in a spectacular birthday celebration, backed by the Count Basie orchestra, featuring her signature show stoppers "Come Runnin'", "Squeeze Me", "I've Got the World on a String" and "The Lady Is a Tramp." 72 mins.

VHS: S23569. $19.95.
Laser: LD75923. $39.99.

Fiddlin' Man: The Life and Times of Bob Wills

Fiddler Bob Wills and his Texas Playboys rose out of the dustbowl Depression days to create music that lifted the nation's spirit: Western swing. This documentary takes a nostalgic look back at the heydey of Bob Wills and the Texas Playboys from their early days at KVOO radio, "The Voice of Oklahoma," to the legendary Cain's Ballroom in Tulsa, to national fame in Las Vegas and Hollywood. Features Eldon Shamblin, Clarence Cagle, Bobby Koeffer, Luke and Johnny Lee Wills, Joe Andrews, Johnny Gimble, Mel Tillis, and more. 61 mins.

VHS: S30124. $19.98.

The Fingerpicking Blues of John Jackson

John Jackson details the finer points of the Piedmont style of blues. Turnarounds, slide technique, runs and other elements of his own unique two-finger style are captured on this video. He also teaches several songs and provides some fascinating historical reminiscences. 60 mins.

VHS: S24870. $39.95.

Freddie King in Concert

King's expressive vocals, guitar playing, and bluesy melodic hooks give his work a powerful and individual sound. Footage from concerts given between 1970-75 is collected here to show him at his peak. This tape starts with an interview of the man who performed such hits as "Sweet Home Chicago", "Whole Lotta Love", "Ghetto Woman", "Woke Up This Morning" and many more. 58 mins.

VHS: S22485. $19.95.

Freddie King: Free Stage

On January 20, 1973, Freddie King and a quartet funked up the studio of KERA-TV in Dallas while performing for the *Free Stage* series. This performance is featured along with King describing his career. A singular portrait of King and his music is achieved through this union.

VHS: S23306. $24.98.

Freddie King: The!!!!Beat—1966

Dead at the age 42 in 1976, King still managed to create a body of unforgettable music. This collection of concert performances shows his unique blend of Southern R&B and mid-60's mod. The video concludes with three tunes performed in Sweden in 1973. 60 mins.

VHS: S22491. $19.95.

The Gadd Gang Live

Afficonados will revel in this dynamic performance of R&B-based jazz from the Gadd Gang: Steve Gadd, Eddie Gomez, Ronnie Cuber, Cornell Dupree and Richard Tee. 60 mins.

Laser: LD70329. $29.95.

George Shearing: Lullaby of Birdland

The only known live concert of the virtuoso jazz pianist, filmed in 1991 at the Paul Masson Winery. 56 mins.

VHS: S17610. $19.98.

Gil Evans and His Orchestra

Featuring the Brecker Brothers, Lew Soloff, Mike Mainieri and Billy Cobham, with Gil Evans and his 20-piece orchestra interpreting tunes from Gershwin, Mingus, Monk and Hendrix. 57 mins.

VHS: S03369. $29.95.

Good Mornin' Blues

A documentary about the evolution of country blues. Featuring the work of Bukka White, Big Joe Williams, Furry Lewis, Johnny Shines, Sam Chatmon and Gus Cannon. Recordings by Son House, Charlie Patton and Willie Brown.

VHS: S17998. $24.95.

A Great Day in Harlem

Nominated for an Academy Award, this documentary offers a cross-section of jazz greats. In 1958, Art Kane orchestrated a group portrait of jazz musicians. Archival footage of interviews, performances and home movie footage rounds out the feeling of this day when the best jazz performers were gathered together. Art Blakey, Dizzy Gillespie, Charles Mingus, Thelonious Monk, Count Basie and Coleman Hawkins are just some of the musicians who appeared. 60 mins.

Laser: LD75324. $39.98.
Jean Bach, USA, 1995, 60 mins.

Great Guitarists

Charlie Byrd, Barney Kessel and Herb Ellis are the featured performers in this video on history's greatest jazz guitarists. Also featuring Joe Byrd and Wayne Phillips.

VHS: S26789. $19.95.
John Beyer, USA, 1979, 58 mins.

Great Guitars

The jazz guitar supergroup featuring Herb Ellis, Barney Kessel and Charlie Byrd displays each of these masters in a concert of inspired jazz guitar. "Outer Drive", "Favela", "Alfie", "Agua de Beber" and "Flying Home" are just some of the songs performed by these legendary musicians. 59 mins.

VHS: S22415. $19.95.

Grover Washington, Jr. in Concert

Leading jazz/pop enthusiast Grover Washington, Jr. performs "Just the Two of Us", "Winelight" and other numbers with his band membersRichard Tee, Steve Gadd and Eric Gale. "Perhaps the finest audio of any home video to date" (*Billboard*). 60 mins.

VHS: S19228. $19.98.

The Guitar of Rory Block

A master interpreter of the Mississippi blues, Rory Block shows how to play some of her most requested numbers. This two-tape set is a treasure trove of guitar techniques enlivened by a great performer and her best works.

VHS: S24869. $79.95.

Gypsy Guitar: The Legacy of Django Reinhardt

This program about the gifted jazz guitarist looks at his influences in a Parisian guitar shop, a Liverpool pub, gypsy sites in Holland, and Samois-Sur-Seine, the remote French village where Reinhardt spent the final years of his life. Featured musicians include his son Babik Reinhardt, Bireli Lagrene, Gary Potter and the Gypsy Kids.

VHS: S17963. $24.95.

Hampton Hawes All Stars

Hampton Hawes, piano, Leroy Vinnegar, bass, Bobby Thompson, bass, Joe Turner, vocals, Bobby Thompson, drums, Sweets Edison, trumpet, Sonny Criss, saxophone, and Teddy Edwards, saxophone, drive through "Memory Lane Blues," "Feeling Happy", "Shake, Rattle and Roll," and "Teddy's Blues." 28 mins.

VHS: S07469. $29.95.

Harlem Hotshots

A compilation of the best rhythm and blues and jazz stars of music's golden age. Featured are Lionel Hampton in *Airmail Special, Love You Like Mad,* Dizzy Gillespie in *Dizzy Atmosphere, Boogie in C,* Ruth Brown (*Have a Good Time*), Big Joe Turner, Bill Bailey and others. 50 mins.

VHS: S04852. $29.95.

Harlem Swings Volume 1

This collection of swing greats contains performances by Eubie Blake, Don Redman, Cab Calloway, Louis Armstrong, Duke Ellington, Les Hite and the great jazz bands of the 1930s.

VHS: S21420. $29.95.

Harlem Swings Volume 2

Swing greats Nat King Cole, Lionel Hampton, Sarah Vaughan, Nipsy Russel, Count Basie, Dinah Washington and more perform their classic hits. Also included are *The Nat King Cole Story,* which charts the rise of this singular entertainer, and *Basin Street Review.*

VHS: S21421. $29.95.

Harlem Swings Volume 3

In this collection, swing greats Dusty Fletcher, Ethel Waters, Louis Jordan and comedian Stepin Fetchit perform in all-black cast musical comedy short subjects.

VHS: S21422. $29.95.

Harlem Swings Volume 4

This collection of Harlem legends features the Harlem Hotshots, Louis Armstrong, The Ebony Trio, Lena Horne, Lionel Hampton, Ruth Brown and others.

VHS: S21423. $29.95.

Harlem Swings Volume 5

The "Rock and Roll Review" in this volume features Duke Ellington, Larry Darnell, Coles and Atkins, The Clovers, Nat "King" Cole, Lionel Hampton, Martha Davis and others.

VHS: S21424. $29.95.

Herbie Hancock Trio: Hurricane!

One of modern jazz's brightest stars appears in this electric performance.

VHS: S16727. $19.98.

Hot Tuna: 25 Years and Runnin'—Live at Sweetwater

Jefferson Airplane guitarist Jeff Kaukonen and bassist Jack Casady decided to play some old blues tunes. The result is *Hot Tuna*. Now, 25 years later, they still play the blues. This concert performance was taped at the Sweetwater, a Bay Area landmark. Interview footage and appearances by guests like Bob Weir of the Grateful Dead make this video a terrific musical experience. 60 mins.

VHS: S22493. $19.95.

Hugh Shannon: Saloon Singer

Billie Holiday was one of his biggest fans, and here Shannon performs during a live set at David K's in New York. 55 mins.

VHS: S03386. $29.95.

Imagine the Sound

Enjoy the sounds and performances of Cecil Taylor, Archie Shepp, Paul Bley and Bill Dixon, in this exuberant profile of four legendary figures from the Free-Form Jazz world.

VHS: S13597. $59.95.
Laser: LD70315. $39.95.

Implosions

Cutting-edge work by Stanley Clarke, Randy Brecker, McCoy Tyner, Peter Erskine and more. 50 mins.

VHS: S14967. $19.95.

International Sweethearts of Rhythm/Tiny & Ruby: Hell-Divin' Women

These two films from award-winning filmmakers Greta Schiller (*Before Stonewall, Paris with a Woman*) and Andrea Weiss tell the swinging story of America's hottest, multi-racial, all-woman jazz band of the 1940s, The International Sweethearts of Rhythm, featuring Tiny Davis and her partner of over 40 years, drummer-pianist Ruby Lucas. Using rare jazz recordings, live performances and vintage photographs, the film follows the amazing journey of these groundbreaking women from the 1940s to the present.

VHS: S32240. $29.95.
Greta Schiller/Andrea Weiss, USA, 1986, 70 mins.

It's a Mean Old World & Born in the Blues

Rev. Pearly Brown and Arthur "Big Boy" Crudup are revealed in this pair of insightful portraits. Brown is a bottleneck guitarist and gospel singer, while Crudup is a blues artist. Both musicians share a musical eloquence that succeeds in touching others. 65 mins.

VHS: S26357. $19.95.

Jack Sheldon and New Orleans

Jack Sheldon and New Orleans—a portrait of one of the most original and distinctive trumpet voices in jazz. A rollicking performance shot on Bourbon Street at Lulu White's Mahogany Hall joins Jack with West Coast compatriots Dave Stone, John Pisano, Frank Capp. 60 mins.

VHS: S10153. $29.95.

Jackie McLean on Mars

Conversation and music with J. McLean. 31 mins.

VHS: S03186. $24.95.

Jammin' with the Blues Greats

English Blues met Chicago Blues and Memphis Blues at New Jersey's Capitol Theater in June of 1982. The result was a magical concert where famed blues legends from these three traditions jammed together. John Mayall's Bluesbreakers, Mick Taylor (Rolling Stones), John McVie (Fleetwood Mac), Colin Allen (Rod Stewart's Band), Albert King, Etta James, Buddy Guy, Junior Wells, and the 83 year old Sippie Wallace are all on this video. 90 mins.

VHS: S21985. $19.98.

Jazz

Earl Hines, piano and vocal, with Coleman Hawkins. 28 mins.

VHS: S05834. $19.95.

Jazz Africa: Herbie Hancock/ Foday Musa Suso

Part of the *Jazzvissions* series, this program features Jazz superstar Herbie Hancock leading an ensemble of top African musicians and a few special guests. 54 mins.

VHS: S14968. $24.95.

The Jazz Age

Fred Allen narrates this look at American life between the end of the First World War and the beginning of the Depression. Morals, manners, and even the way Americans thought of themselves were profoundly altered during the Jazz Age. 60 mins.

VHS: S23056. $19.95.

Jazz Hoofer: Baby Laurence

Laurence's only filmed dancing performance. 30 mins.

VHS: S03179. $19.95.

Jazz in America: Gerry Mulligan
Gerry Mulligan is the featured artist in this great series of jazz performance tapes. 60 mins.
VHS: S03140. $19.95.

Jazz in Exile
Some of the finest American jazz musicians have been drawn to Europe, and this classic jazz documentary captures many of them: Richard Davis, Phil Woods, Dexter Gordon, Randy Weston, Johnny Griffin, and many others.
VHS: S00653. $29.95.
Chuck France, USA, 1978, 58 mins.

Jazz Is My Native Language
Vibrant, fast paced documentary gives an in-depth look at the music and life of Toshiko Akiyoshi. "No artist has yet emerged to surpass Toshiko Akiyoshi as a creative composer; her position is comparable to that of Duke Ellington or Stan Kenton in earlier years" (Leonard Feather, *Jazz Critic*).
VHS: S02647. $29.95.
Renee Cho, USA, 60 mins.

Jazz Is Our Religion
Looks at the lifestyles and attitudes of jazz musicians through the photographs and works of the British jazz journalist Valerie Wilmer. The technique is quick-cut stills, with a welter of voices—musicians Jo Jones, Dizzy Gillespie, Sunny Murray, the poet Ted Joans and others—providing a personal and often wryly knowing commentary, with music by drummer Art Blakey, saxophonist Johnny Griffin, and a group of celebrated jazz drummers.
VHS: S04168. $19.95.
Val Wilmer, Great Britain, 1985, 50 mins.

Jazz Masters: Vintage Getz
The work of Stan Getz is showcased in this program, in collaboration with the virtuoso bassist Marc Johnson and drummer Victor Lewis. Volume 1 features "Over the Edge", "From the Heart", "Answer without Question", "Sippin' at Bell's" and "Tempus Fugit". Volume 2 was recorded in Paul Masson's California vineyard and contains the works "Lush Life", "Desafinado", "Alone Together" and "It's You or No One".
Vol. 1.
VHS: S18515. $19.98.
Vol. 2.
VHS: S18516. $19.98.

Jazz Odyssey: Beyond El Rocco
This film noir style docudrama unveils the legendary players and historic venues that defined Australia's Modern Jazz scene for over five decades. The history of bebop, fusion and its crossover inrock and funk make for an engaging story. Shot on location in Australia. A two-volume set, 102 mins.
VHS: S25630. $29.98.

Jazz on a Summer's Day
The concert movie that came first—before *Woodstock, Monterey Pop, The Last Waltz* and Gimme Shelter—is still among the best. On a hot summer's day in Newport, Rhode Island in 1958, jazz greats Louis Armstrong, Thelonious Monk, and Anita O'Day get together with Chuck Berry, Mahalia Jackson, and Dinah Washington among others to make this glorious gem of a movie.
VHS: S12198. $29.95.
Bert Stern, USA, 1958, 85 mins.

Jazz Shorts
Four shorts include: *Honky Tonk Bud*, featuring the music of Edward Wilderson Jr. and the rap poetry of John Toles-Bey; *Bird Lives*, an animation piece directed by Peter Bodge; *Daybreak Express*, which features a ride on a New York subway set to the music of Duke Ellington and directed by D.A. Pennebaker (*Don't Look Back, Monterey Pop*); and *Is That Jazz?*, a performance piece by Gil Scott-Heron directed by Robert Mugge. 30 mins.
VHS: S02995. $19.95.

Jazz: Earle Hines and Coleman Hawkins
Hines sings and plays piano while Hawkins adds saxaphone. Includes "Crazy Rhythm" and "But Not for Me". 28 mins.
VHS: S21676. $24.95.

Jazzball
A musical compilation features the talents of such artists as Duke Ellington, Cab Calloway, Louis Armstrong, Gene Krupa and the song stylings of Miss Peggy Lee. A full hour of jazz so hot it's cool. USA, 1958, 60 mins.
VHS: S07436. $19.95.

Joe Cool Live
New York City's first call players display their incredible abilities with special guest Sadao Watanabe. Jams include "Trans Himalayan", "Dr. Potato Head", "Borderland" and "Sometimes Bubba Gets Down". 90 mins.
VHS: S12007. $34.95.
Laser: LD70330. $34.95.

Joe Pass in Concert
This consumate jazz improvisor was likened to Art Tatum for his ability to combine virtuosity, taste and harmonic invention. Though he accompanied great singers like Ella Fitzgerald and Frank Sinatra, his genius shone brightest as a soloist. Shot at Christ College, Brecon, Wales in 1991, it captures his transformation of a range of styles and standards.
VHS: S23305. $24.98.

Joe Williams: A Song Is Born
In collaboration with pianist George Shearing, this live concert of the redoubtable Joe Williams, voted best male vocalist in the 1992 Down Beat Critics' poll, provides an intimate and up-close portrait of his singing prowess. Filmed in 1991 at the Paul Masson Winery. 58 mins.
VHS: S17609. $19.98.

John Hartford
John Hartford plays music loaded with references to blue grass and old-time traditionalism in this eclectic video collection of his best work. 60 mins.
VHS: S19213. $24.95.

John Lee Hooker & Friends
John Lee Hooker performs with Albert Collins, Ry Cooder, Robert Cray, John Hammond, Charlie Musselwhite, Bonnie Raitt and other musicians on this video. Performances collected here range from 1984 to 1992 and show why Hooker is a serious musician who can still manage to perform on MTV.
VHS: S27491. $22.50.

John Lee Hooker: Rare Performances, 1960-1984
John Lee Hooker is one of the foremost blues performers of the postwar period. Over five decades his music has entertained the world with a sound firmly grounded in the traditions of his home state, Mississippi. This compilation of his performances shows how his music stretched a rich tradition into contemporary times.
VHS: S27490. $19.95.

Journey Through Jazz
The Dan Jordan Trio guides students through the many facets of jazz. Students will enjoy improvisation as they move through the blues to ragtime, swing, be-bop, cool jazz, fusion and the avant garde.
VHS: S22478. $99.95.

Kenny Drew Live
Kenny Drew, one of the most interesting jazz pianists, performs "Hushabye" and "Saint Thomas" with his frequent collaborators Niels-Henningh Orsted Pedersen and Alvin Queen. 55 mins.
VHS: S18380. $19.95.

Koko Taylor: Queen of the Blues
This profile of Koko Taylor recalls the highlights of her career to date, and captures live performances. An inside look at one of the most visible female blues artists. 60 mins.
VHS: S15877. $19.98.

Konitz: Portrait of Artist
Through conversations with the musician and a fair sampling of his work, this film gives a portrait of Lee Konitz, jazz saxophone great from the 1940s. Songs include "Stella by Starlight", "Subconscious Lee", "She's Wild as Springtime" and more. 83 mins.
VHS: S12339. $19.95.

L.A. All Stars: Hampton Hawes
With Big Joe Turner, Sweets Edison and Hampton Hawes doing "Memory Lane Blues", "Feeling Happy", "Shake, Rattle and Roll" and "Teddy's Blues". 28 mins.
VHS: S05634. $24.95.

Ladies Sing the Blues
This program combines concert and archival footage in a bold essay on the evolution of blues and jazz and looks at the personalities who made the music. With Bessie Smith, Lena Horne, Billie Holiday, Dinah Washington and Sarah Vaughn. 60 mins.
VHS: S19223. $29.95.

Lady Day: The Many Faces of Billie Holiday
Considered by many to be the greatest jazz singer of all time, Billie was also the victim of vicious racism, personal tragedy and drug addiction. Yet she remained a fighter, as this video portrait proves in remembrances by fellow jazz stars Carmen McRae, Harry "Sweets" Edison, Milt Gabler and Mal Waldron. And there's plenty of Lady Day herself, from her own words (as read by actress Ruby Dee) to generous film clips featuring her singing her best-loved songs. 60 mins.
VHS: S13929. $29.95.

Last Date: Eric Dolphy
A film about saxophonist Eric Dolphy shot during his final recording session in Hilversum in June, 1964. Dolphy's contemporaries Buddy Collette, trumpeter Ted Curson, pianist Jaki Byard and Richard Davis comment on his art and life.
VHS: S19123. $29.95.
Hans Hylkema, USA, 1991, 92 mins.

Last of the Blue Devils
This great jazz documentary feature documents the world of Kansas City Jazz, with Count Basie and His Orchestra, Big Joe Turner and Jay McShann. "This beautiful film is about life and jazz and how they interact" (*Newsweek*). USA, 1979, 90 mins.
VHS: S00726. $19.95.

The Leaders: Jazz in Paris 1988
The group of Arthur Blythe, Lester Bowie, Cecil McBee, Kirk Lightsey, Chico Freeman and Don Moye make up The Leaders, a jazz band which defines itself as "schizo music". Seven songs are performed here by these singularly great, collectively unique artists. 54 mins.
VHS: S12340. $19.95.

Lee Ritenour and Friends, Vol. 1
In a concert performance at the Coconut Grove, Lee Ritenour is joined by Joao Bosco, Steve Lukather, Ernie Watts, Phil Perry, Bob James, Harvey Mason and Brian Bromberg, in "Night Rhythms," "Harlequin," "Malibu," "Up-Town," "Odile, Odila," "Etude" and "Asa." 58 mins.
VHS: S19660. $19.95.

Lee Ritenour and Friends, Vol. 2
From the Coconut Grove, Lee Ritenour collaborates with Bob James, Tuck and Patti, Ernie Watts, Paulinho da Costa, Brian Bromberg and Alan Broadbent in some virtuoso recordings of "24th Street Blues," "Stolen Moments," "Love Is the Key," "Better Than Anything," "Everything's Gonna Be All Right," "Westchester Lady" and "Bahia Frank." 58 mins.
VHS: S19661. $19.95.

Legends of Bottleneck Blues Guitar
Rare recordings from 1965-70 are joined in this work, resulting in a collection of the best examples of bottleneck guitar styles. Popular in the Deep South, this sound reflects the Hawaiian lap slide technique. Among the great practitioners of the bottleneck blues included here are Son House, Fred McDowell, Mance Lipscomb, Johnny Shine, Furry Lewis and Jesse Fuller. 58 mins.
VHS: S22481. $19.95.

Legends of Country Blues Guitar
Blues was born at the beginning of the 20th century among black rural musicians. Fortunately, the blues was kept alive by a number of fluid and improvisational performers who inspired the blues revival of the 1960's. From the legendary artists Mississippi John Hurt, Son House, Gary Davis, Big Bill Broonzy, Robert Pete Williams and others, this video offers a collection of the best blues. 58 mins.
VHS: S22482. $19.95.

Legends of Country Blues Guitar: Volume 2
The Blues rediscovery of the sixties brought new acclaim to many veteran artists from the "Golden Age" of country blues. Bukka White, Big Joe Williams, Son House, Houston Stackhouse, Rev. Gary Davis, Lead Belly and Sam Chatmon are just some of the legendary performers from that earlier time gathered in this video. 58 mins.
VHS: S22490. $19.95.

Legends of Jazz Guitar, Volume III
Jim Hall, Barney Kessel, Herb Ellis, Charlie Byrd and Tal Farlow are just some of the musicians featured on this third installment of the series. Their performances cover a range of styles, from Cole Porter to the Bossa Nova.
VHS: S25913. $29.95.

Legends of the 1Delta Blues
The Mississippi Delta is the home of the blues. Musical legends Sun House, John Lee Hooker, Johnny Shines and Bukka White are shown on this tape as they performed in the 1960's and 1970's. Earthy and vital, their music has inspired many musicians, including the famed Muddy Waters.
VHS: S26429. $24.95.

Les McCann Trio

Les McCann, piano and vocals, Jimmy Rowser, bass, and Donald Dean, drums, perform "Right On," "Sunny," "With These Hands," and "Compared to What" at Shelly's Manne Hole Club in Los Angeles. 28 mins.
VHS: S04170. $19.95.

Lightnin' Hopkins: Rare Performances 1960-79

Hopkins is the embodiment of Texas country blues. He inspired a host of artists, especially fellow musicians. This video traces his development subsequent to his rediscovery in 1959. It offers a fresh reflection of one of the most creative blues musicians ever heard.
VHS: S23304. $24.98.

Lionel Hampton

Air Mail Special, Smooth Sailing, Hamp's Boogie Woogie. 24 mins.
VHS: S05418. $19.95.

Listen Up: The Lives of Quincy Jones

A feature-film portrait of legendary composer and arranger Quincy Jones. Tracing his illustrious career from a chart-busting pioneer of pop music's early years to composing scores for over 40 movies and producing/ arranging the top selling album of all time—Michael Jackson's *Thriller*. Featuring appearances by Ray Charles, Frank Sinatra, >Rev. Jesse Jackson, Ice-T, Barbra Streisand and dozens more.
VHS: S14105. $19.98.
Laser: LD70614. $29.98.
Ellen Weissbrod, USA, 1990

Live at the Village Vanguard Vol. 1

The hottest sounds from the coolest cats. Freddie Hubbard on trumpet. Ron Carter on bass. Cedar Walton tickles the ivories and Lenny White is on drums. Tunes include "Happy Times", "Guernica", "Little Waltz" and "Fantasy in D". Recorded live at the Village Vanguard.
VHS: S09118. $29.95.
Bruce Buschel, USA, 1982, 59 mins.

Live at the Village Vanguard Vol. 2

The Michael Petrucciani Trio performs jazz just the way you like it in this second volume in the Village Vanguard series. With Palle Danielsson on bass; Eliot Zigmund on drums and guest star Jin Hall on guitar. For your viewing and listening pleasure they play "Gitgo", "All Alone", "Firewaltz" and "Left Alone". In color and stereo. HiFi.
VHS: S09119. $29.95.
Bruce Buschel, USA, 1982, 57 mins.

Live at the Village Vanguard Vol. 3

More hot jazz sounds recorded live at the Village Vanguard. Guitarist John Abercrombie is backed up by Michael Brecker on tenor sax, Peter Erskine on drums and Marc Johnson on bass. They perform "Dreamstepper", "Blues for Sarha", "Tavia's Tune", "Max", "Juicey Brucey" and "Subconscious Lee".
VHS: S09120. $29.95.
Bruce Buschel, USA, 1986, 58 mins.

Live at the Village Vanguard Vol. 4

The Mal Waldron Quartet, featuring Mal Waldron, Woody Shaw, Charles Rouse, Reggie Workman and Ed Blackwell, performs "Git-Go," "All Alone," and other numbers. 56 mins.
VHS: S12192. $29.95.

Live at the Village Vanguard Vol. 5

Lee Konitz and Friends perform "Max", "Dreamstepper", "A Story Often Told," and other numbers. 62 mins.
VHS: S12193. $29.95.

Live at the Village Vanguard Vol. 6

The Dave Murray Quartet performs "Off Season," "Lovers," "Morning Song," and other numbers. 56 mins.
VHS: S12194. $29.65.

Lou Rawls Show with Duke Ellington

Rawls sings "Oh Happy Day" and other gospel and blues standards while Ellington adds his classics including "Satin Doll" and "Sophisticated Ladies". 48 mins.
VHS: S21677. $19.95.

Louie Bellson and His Big Band

Featuring the Brecker Brothers, Lew Soloff, Tom Malone, Herb Geller and Howard Johnson, in an all-star live concert. 55 mins.
VHS: S03383. $29.95.

Louis Armstrong

Backed by his band members Tommy Young, Billy Kyle and vocalist Jewel Brown, Armstrong performs numbers such as "When It's Sleepy Time Down South," "C'est Si Bon" and "When the Saints Go Marching In." 24 mins.
VHS: S19887. $29.95.

Louis Armstrong: The Gentle Giant of Jazz

Satchmo worked his way up from the Dixieland music of New Orleans to Chicago and the world of Jazz, ultimately conquering the whole world with his music. Hugh Downs hosts. 24 mins.
VHS: S23557. $49.95.

Lowell Fulson and Percy Mayfield

Lowell Fulson was one of the greatest blues guitarists to emerge from the California Blues scene. Here is a collection of his greatest songs, including "Every Day I Have the Blues", "Reconsider Baby", "Tramp" and more. 30 mins.
VHS: S12338. $19.95.

Mabel Mercer: A Singer's Singer

A 17-song set that captures the artistry of the grand dame of popular song. 42 mins.
VHS: S03385. $29.95.

Mabel Mercer: Cabaret Artist "Forever and Always"

The last performance of the incomparable *grand dame* of popular song. Live from Cleo's in New York, Mabel performs her unique and timeless renditions of 20 songs from The Great American Songbook. A touching evening of entertainment from the lady who inspired Frank Sinatra. 58 mins.
VHS: S10792. $29.95.

Mance Lipscomb in Concert

This tenant farmer began life as a slave. Despite these hardships, he sang and played the blues all his life. Discovered in 1960, he was soon in demand at festivals, concerts and clubs around the country. This tape presents a rare TV concert recorded in Texas that captures the genius of Mance's music. 58 mins.
VHS: S22488. $19.95.

Mark Naftalin's Blue Monday

Starring John Lee Hooker and Charlie Musselwhite. Hooker's Mississippi origins are combined here in spontaneous performances with the California harmonica sound of Charlie Musselwhite. 30 mins.
VHS: S12337. $24.95.

Martin Taylor in Concert

Guitarist Martin Taylor demonstrates his dynamic solo playing in this concert recorded at the Manchester Craftsmen's Guild in Pittsburgh. 75 mins.
VHS: S31757. $29.95.

Masters of Comic Blues: Mance Lipscomb and Lightnin' Hopkins

Rare archival footage of these Blues greats, shot in the '60s, which vividly captures the eloquence of their visionary music. Hosted by Taj Mahal. 60 mins.
VHS: S15702. $24.95.

Masters of Comic Blues: Rev. Gary Davis and Sonny Terry

Shot in the 60s, this intimate video captures these great Blues artists at their best—communicating the power and brilliance of the American Blues as played by its masters. Hosted by Taj Mahal. 60 mins.
VHS: S15704. $24.95.

Masters of the Blues

Recorded in 1966 at a Toronto studio as part of the CBC *Festival*, this program has finally resurfaced. Includes rare performances by Muddy Waters, James Cotton, Sonny Terry, Willie Dixon, Brownie McGhee, Otis Spann, and Mable Hillary in her only television appearance. Hosted by Canadian blues guitarist Colin James. 60 mins.
VHS: S31613. $19.98.

Max Roach: Jazz in America

An hour of jazz with Max Roach on drums, Calvin Hill on bass, Cecil Bridgewater on trumpet and Odean Pope on tenor sax, recorded live at the Blues Alley in Washington, DC, on March 2, 1981.
VHS: S00834. $19.95.
Stanley Dorfman, USA, 1981, 60 mins.

Mel Lewis and His Big Band

Swinging big-band jazz with Mel Lewis and his 19-piece jazz band. 38 mins.
VHS: S03381. $19.98.

The Memories: Music from The Yank Years, Volume 1

Johnny Desmond, Maxine Sullivan, the Debonaires and friends and the Parke Frankenfield Orchestra join forces to bring back the music of the Swing era. "Sentimental Journey" and "Stardust" are just some of the sentimental oldies performed in this video. 45 mins.
VHS: S23669. $14.95.

The Memories: Music from The Yank Years, Volume 2

Fran Warren, Bobby Burnett, the Debonaires and friends sing along with the Frankenfield Orchestra in this second volume to bring back still more music from the Swing era. "You've Changed", "I'll Get By" and "C'est Si Bon" are only a few of the great tunes that will charm listeners. 45 mins.
VHS: S23670. $14.95.

Messin' with the Blues

Chicago blues legends Muddy Waters, Buddy Guy and Junior Wells perform the music born of bad luck, cheap booze, torrid love and centuries of oppression. Their musical style strongly influenced a generation of rock 'n' roll artists. Recorded June 28, 1974, at the Montreux Jazz Festival, Switzerland, this gritty performance includes such classics as "Messin' with the Kid," and "Got My Mojo Workin." 1974, 54 mins.
VHS: S13676. $19.95.

Michael Feinstein & Friends

Michael Feinstein performs favorites by George and Ira Gershwin, Irving Berlin, Harold Arlen and Duke Ellington. Rosemary Clooney joins Feinstein for several solo numbers and duets. In Hi-Fi stereo, 60 mins.
VHS: S16798. $24.95.

Mike Mainieri: The Jazz Life

Crossed Wires, Flying Colors, Sara's Touch, Bamboo, Song for Seth, Bullet Train, T-Bag. 60 mins.
VHS: S05410. $29.95.

Mingus

A cinema-verite portrait of this great bassist/composer and some of the hard times that came his way. There is superb Mingus in action at a nightclub near Boston, scenes of him conducting his big band, composing, singing and reciting his own poetry. Most of the film, though, takes place in his cluttered New York loft as he awaits eviction in the wake of a legal tangle with New York City.
VHS: S07743. $19.95.
Thomas Reichmann, USA, 1968, 58 mins.

Minnie the Moocher

A rollicking, nostalgic tour of the Harlem clubs of the 30's and 40's. Rare footage shines the spotlight on the great entertainers like Cab Calloway, performing the title song. 55 mins.
VHS: S09245. $19.98.

Mississippi Blues

Tavernier and Parrish approach the Mississippi Delta through its townspeople and its music—Delta Blues and gospel. They explore their own knowledge of this world—Tavernier's from reading Faulkner and Mark Twain, Parrish's from his intimate knowledge of the South. And they skillfully link the drama with such questions as the relationship of the church to politics, and the relationship of music to the life in the Mississippi Delta.
VHS: S09244. $29.95.
Robert Parrish/Bertrand Tavernier, USA/France, 1983, 101 mins.

Modern Jazz Quartet

The grand old gentlemen of jazz (John Lewis on piano, Milt Jackson on vibraphone, Percy Heath on bass and Connie Kay on drums) celebrate their 35th anniversary in a performance at the Arts Festival in Freiburg, Germany. 60 mins.
VHS: S20568. $19.95.

Monk in Oslo

A documentary about the art and music of jazz virtuoso Thelonious Monk. The film has a vivid sense for Monk's gestures and rhythms, as it quietly celebrates the art and dynamic interplay within the quartet as they perform "Lulu's Back in Town", "Blue Monk" and " 'Round Midnight". Produced for the Norwegian Broadcasting Corporation.
VHS: S19120. $19.95.
Harald Heide Steen Jr., Norway, 1966, 33 mins.

Moscow Sax Quintet: The Jazznost Tour

Russia's singular jazz group finds a distinctive sound for American classics as the five virtuoso saxophone players and a rhythm section play riffs on the Beatles, Gershwin, Fats Waller and Charlie Parker. "You hear the breathtaking virtuosity of ensemble work when they take Bird's improvised solos and play them in five-part harmony at breakneck speed, as if there were one single player" (*Jazziz*). 62 mins.
VHS: S19225. $19.98.

Mr. Boogie Woogie

A documentary profile of Moses Vinton, Beale Street's outstanding blues pianist, who was at the center of the Memphis rhythm and blues explosion. The documentary takes up Vinson's life at the present moment, exploring through the recollections of employers, his sister, friends who "made it", and with Vinson himself, the complex causes of his current obscurity. In the process, we discover Vinson as a personality and as a symbol of the minority artist, or, indeed, any artist who finds himself in an inhospitable environment.
VHS: S07769. $39.95.
Alexis Krasilovsky, USA, 1978, 30 mins.

Muddy Waters
A program about the extraordinary Chicago blues artist Muddy Waters. Born on a plantation near Clarksdale, Mississippi, Waters moved to Chicago and developed music which combined the idiom of the Mississippi Delta with the harsh poetry of the Chicago streets. The numbers include "Hoochie Coochie Man," "My Home Is in the Delta," "Baby You Don't Have to Go" and "I'm a King Bee."
VHS: S19679. $19.95.

Music and Comedy Masters (Volume 1)
Includes "Blues and Boogie" with Maxine Sullivan & Nat King Cole, "Murder in Swingtime" with Les Hite & Orchestra, "Ain't Misbehavin'" with Fats Waller & Louis Armstrong, "Bubbling Over" with Ethel Waters, "Boogie Woogie Dream" with Lena Horne, and "Caledonia" with Louis Jordan.
VHS: S15473. $29.95.

Music and Comedy Masters (Volume 2)
Includes: "Minnie the Moocher" (Cab Calloway), "Jittering Jitterbugs" (Hamtree Harrington), "Heavenly Choir" and "St. Louis Blues" (Bessie Smith), "Showtime at the Apollo" (Mantan Moreland, Lionel Hampton & Nat King Cole), and "Hi De Ho" with Cab Calloway.
VHS: S15474. $29.95.

Music and Comedy Masters (Volume 3)
Includes performances by Marian Anderson, Sarah Vaughn, Duke Ellington ("Symphony in Black"), and the Basin Street Review with Lionel Hampton, Nat King Cole, Nipsey Russell and Dinah Washington.
VHS: S15475. $29.95.

Music and Comedy Masters (Volume 4)
Includes: "Come to Baby Do" by the Nat King Cole Trio, "Bundle of Blues" by Duke Ellington, Cab Calloway's "Jitterbug Party," Count Basie & Orchestra, Louis Armstrong, Harlem Hotshots, Sugar Chili, and "Black and Tan" by Duke Ellington.
VHS: S15476. $29.95.

Music and Comedy Masters (Volume 5)
Includes "Sepian Swing" with Cab Calloway and The Nat King Cole Trio, "Sepia Stars on Parade" with Herb Jeffries, Fats Waller, Bill Robinson, Dorothy Dandridge, The Mills Brothers, Louis Armstrong, Nat King Cole and Louis Jordan, and "Rhapsody in Black and Blue" by Louis Armstrong & Orchestra.
VHS: S15477. $29.95.

Music and Comedy Masters (Volume 6)
Includes "Dry Bones" by the Delta Rhythm Boys, "Open the Door Richard" by Dusty Fletcher, "Slow Poke" by Stepin Fetchit, and "Spying the Spy"—a rare 1915 Black short subject on private eye stories.
VHS: S15478. $29.95.

Music Classics, Vol. 2
Includes hit songs by Tex Beneke, Victor Young, Duke Ellington, Artie Shaw, Eubie Blake, Stan Kenton and Gene Krupa. All accompanied by orchestra. 60 mins.
VHS: S15872. $19.98.

Mystery, Mr. Ra
Despite the epic scope of Sun Ra's 35-year career, *Mystery, Mr. Ra* is only the second document of the career of this remarkable musician, band leader, philosopher, shaman, commune leader and cosmic messenger. Acclaimed French filmmaker Frank Cassenti comes up with an entertaining, informative, deeplyfelt report that contains rare footage of the orchestra tuning up and rehearsing, plus a rewarding spectrum of excerpts from Ra's Afro-psychedelic circus of a show. 51 mins.
VHS: S12341. $19.95.

Nancy Wilson at Carnegie Hall
The Grammy Award winning song stylist gives her all in a memorable concert with full-string orchestra…a highlight of the JVC Jazz Festival in New York's Carnegie Hall. 52 mins.
VHS: S10793. $19.98.

The Nat King Cole Story
An exquisite video portrait of singer and jazz pianist Nat King Cole. A moving tribute to this peerless music legend. 30 mins.
VHS: S13882. $29.95.

Nat King Cole: The Unforgettable
A documentary that examines the life and career of Cole, from his beginnings as a jazz pianist to his success as a vocalist and songwriter. 90 mins.
VHS: S09209. $24.95.

The New Music
John Carter and Bobby Bradford. 29 mins.
VHS: S03180. $19.95.

New Orleans: Til the Butcher Cuts Him Down
A superb study of the history and men who played New Orleans jazz, through the eyes of one of its greatest trumpet players, Punch Miller. Kid Punch played with all the greats including King Oliver, Kid Ory, Jelly Roll, Morton, Louis Armstrong. This film is about his life and the changes New Orleans music went through in his lifetime.
VHS: S03191. $29.95.
Philip Spalding, USA, 1971, 53 mins.

Newport Jazz Festival
The 1962 Newport Jazz Festival is preserved on this video, including performances by acclaimed musicians The Oscar Peterson Trio, Lambert Hendricks and Bavan, Roland Kirk, The Clara Ward Singers, Ruby Braff, Pee Wee Russel, Duke Ellington and his Orchestra and many others.
VHS: S21565. $29.95.

A Night in Havana
A celebration of the Afro-Cuban rhythms introduced into American jazz by Dizzy Gillespie as we journey to Cuba with the trumpeter to headline the Fifth International Jazz Festival. With Arturo Sandoval and Gonzalo Rubalcaba.
VHS: S33674. $24.95.
John Holland, USA, 1988, 84 mins.

One Night Stand: Lionel Hampton and an All-Star Jazz Ensemble
Hampton plays vibes, piano and drums in this program hosted by Mel Torme. Buddy Rich, Gene Krupa, Teddy Wilson, Zoot Sims and B.B. King are some of the artists who also appear in this tape. Johnny Mercer even sings a medley of his unforgettable hits.
VHS: S21759. $29.95.

One Night with Blue Note, Part 1
Bouquet, Canteloupe Island, When You Wish upon a Star, Jumpin' Jack, Moanin, Broadside, Little B's Poem. 55 mins.
VHS: S05411. $29.95.

Oregon
One of the most original improvisational jazz bands around, with Ralph Tower, Trilok Gurtu, Glenn Moore and Paul McCandles in their unique combinations of sounds rooted in traditional American jazz. 60 mins.
VHS: S09825. $29.95.

Oscar Peterson: Music in the Key of Oscar
A 40-year musical history of jazz pianist Oscar Peterson is detailed in this documentary. It begins with his early days as a Montreal boogie-woogie sensation and continues into the present. Peterson himself narrates. Quincy Jones, Ella Fitzgerald, Dizzy Gillespie and more jazz greats are also featured. A two-volume set, 106 mins.
VHS: S25631. $29.98.

Out of the Blacks Into the Blues
An interesting two-part work about the political, social and artistic impulses of the American blues.
Part One: Along the Old Man River. Features Bukka White, Furry Lewis, Roosevelt Sykes, Robert Pete Williams, Brownie McGhee and Sonny Terry.
VHS: S17999. $24.95.
Part Two: A Way to Escape the Ghetto. This program looks at self-expression and the pure joy of playing, considering the works of B.B. King, Willie Dixon, Mance Lipscomb, Brownie McGhee, Junior Wells, Buddy Guy, Sonny Terry and Arthur "Big Boy" Crudup.
VHS: S18000. $24.95.

Outside in Sight: Music of the United Front
Portrait of the San Francisco jazz group United Front featuring percussionist Anthony Brown, bassist Mark Izu, Lewis Jordan on sax and George Sims on trumpet.
VHS: S03920. $40.00.
G. Chapnick/Sam Wood, USA, 1986, 60 mins.

Papa John Creach: Setting the Record Straight
Legendary 71-year-old Papa John jams with Eddie "Cleanhead" Vinson, Jorma Kaukonen, Red Callender and George Winston in this unique documentary. Through interviews, rehearsals and major concert appearances over a five-year period, Papa John is revealed as a violinist capable of an unprecedented variety of musical styles. 60 mins.
VHS: S23302. $29.95.

Paris Reunion Band
From the mid 50's to the late 60's Paris was the jazz capital of the world. Its guru was Kenny Clarke and to his memory the Paris Reunion Band was constituted for this live taping at Stuttgart of some of the greats of this era: Woody Shaw and Nat Aderley, Joe Henderson and Nathan Davis, Curtis Fuller, Idris Muhammad, Walter Bishop Jr. and Jimmy Woode. 57 mins.
VHS: S09824. $24.95.

Pat Donohue in Concert at the Freight & Salvage
The wit, songwriting artistry and superb guitar skills of Pat Donohoe are in evidence in this concert performance. Songs include "Midnight Man," "Maple Leaf Rag," "West Coast Blues," "High Society," "St. Louis Blues" and others. 65 mins.
VHS: S31756. $29.95.

Percy Mayfield: Poet Laureate of the Blues
When Percy Mayfield died in 1984, the day before his 64th birthday, the blues lost one of its truly unique personages. In this mixture of performance and reminiscence with pianist Mark Naftalin, the film captures Mayfield at the height.
VHS: S07748. $29.95.
S. Sutherland/M. Prussian/F. Miguet, USA, 1986, 30 mins.

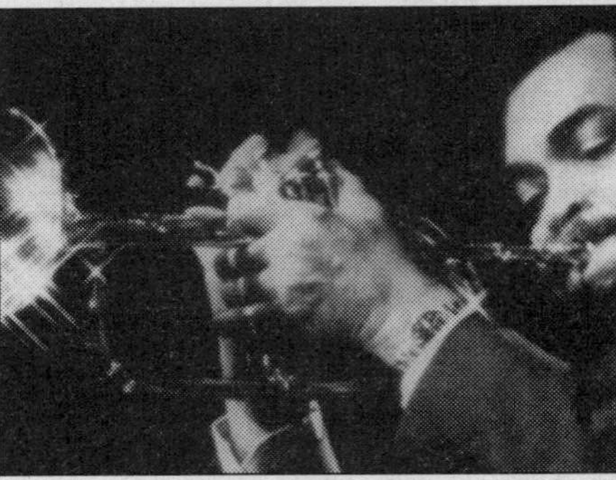

Phil Woods in Concert: With Joe Sudler's Swing Machine
A collaboration between bop altoist Phil Woods and Joe Sudler's Swing Machine, a sinuous collective of great soloists, performing the emotionally charged, exuberant numbers "Groovin' High", "Body and Soul" and "Blues in Ecstasy". 67 mins.
VHS: S19229. $29.98.

The Phil Woods Quartet
Mike Melillo, Steve Gilmore and Bill Goodwin round out the Phil Woods Quartet. They make some of the best jazz to be heard anywhere.
VHS: S26791. $19.95.
John Beyer, USA, 1979, 58 mins.

Piano Legends
Chick Corea narrates a look at the great piano jazz performers, from Fats Waller and Jelly Roll Morton to Oscar Peterson and Thelonious Monk. 60 mins.
VHS: S03213. $39.95.

Quincy Jones: A Celebration
Ray Charles and James Ingram are among the stars performing in this musical tribute to the great Quincy Jones. 60 mins.
VHS: S21672. $14.95.

Reed Royalty
This documentary traces the uses and development of jazz reed playing. Narrated by Branford Marsalis, who also performs two soprano saxophone numbers, the work includes archival footage of Omer Simeon, Artie Shaw, Woody Herman, Benny Goodman, John Coltrane, Ornette Coleman and others. 60 mins.
VHS: S17425. $29.95.

Renee Rosnes: Jazz Pianist
Pianist Renee Rosnes, one of the brightest lights in the 1990s jazz scene, is featured here in an intimate trio performance and candid interview.
VHS: S33765. $19.95.
Daniel Berman/David W. Brady, USA, 1997, 45 mins.

Robert Altman's Jazz '34: Remembering Kansas City Swing
In the midst of making his film, *Kansas City*, Robert Altman decided to recreate an all-night jam session as it might have taken place in a Kansas City club during the Depression era. This modern reinterpretation of classic jazz features talented musicians of today, including Craig Handy and Joshua Redman, performing the music of Coleman Hawkins, Lester Young, and many others. Narrated by Harry Belafonte.
VHS: S34251. $19.95.
Robert Altman, USA, 1997, 75 mins.

Ron Carter & Art Farmer: Live at Sweet Basil
The musicianship of Ron Carter and Art Farmer has brought them each renown in their separate ventures.
VHS: S16728. $19.98.

Ron Carter Live: Double Bass

The jazz great is captured live at NHK 101 Studio in New York, recorded in digital sound and thoughtfully shot on high definition video. Among his many mind-blowing selections are "Double Bass", "Waltz", "Blues for D.P.", "The Third Plane" and "Eight—Sometimes I Feel Like a Motherless Child". 55 mins.
VHS: S16002. $19.95.

Roy Ayers Live

Roy Ayers' melding of disparate jazz styles has made him one of most intriguing figures since the 60s. In this performance, Ayers is accompanied by Rex Rideout, Dennis Davis, Donald Nicks and Zachary Breaux and performs such classics as "Hot", "Mystic Voyage" and "Night in Tunisia". 52 mins.
VHS: S18381. $19.95.

Sarah Vaughan: The Divine One

Friends, family and fellow musicians including Billy Eckstine, Roy Haynes, Joe Williams and others talk about this unmatched songstress. Her performances of "Misty," "Someone to Watch over Me," "I've Got a Crush on You" and "Send in the Clowns" are among her legendary standards included here.
VHS: S26857. $19.95.
Matthew Seig, USA, 1991, 60 mins.

Saturday Night, Sunday Morning: The Travels of Gatemouth Moore

This award-winning documentary reveals the common roots of blues and gospel through the remarkable story of A.D. Gatemouth Moore. Once called "one of the greatest blues singers ever" by blues legend B.B. King, Moore later became an evangelical preacher and gospel disc jockey in the South. Also features B.B. King, Al Green, Rufus Thomas and Benjamin Hooks. "A wonderful documentary...Gatemouth Moore is a warm and thundering presence" (*Los Angeles Times*).
VHS: S30169. $24.99.
Louis Guida, USA, 1996, 58 mins.

Saxophone Colossus

Robert Mugge's stirring tribute to American musical genius Sonny Rollins, an electrifying record of a supreme jazz artist at work, featuring his *G-Man, The Bridge, Concerto for Tenor Saxophone and Orchestra*, and *Don't Stop the Carnival*.
VHS: S05651. $29.95.
Laser: LD71333. $39.95.
Robert Mugge, USA, 1986, 101 mins.

The Search for Robert Johnson

A documentary about the visionary rhythm and blues performer Robert Johnson. His life and art are reproduced through documentary footage and interviews with his contemporaries (John Hammond, David "Honeyboy" Edwards, Johnny Shines) and the musicians whose work he influenced (Keith Richards, Eric Clapton).
VHS: S16882. $19.98.

Shady Grove: Old Time Music from North Carolina, Kentucky & Virginia—featuring Kilby Snow, Dock Boggs, Tommy Jarrell & Roscoe Holcomb

Poignant and exciting blues-flavored musical performances are presented by four highly expressive and individualistic makers of traditional, old-time country music. 60 mins.
VHS: S31761. $29.95.

Shelly Manne Quartet

Shelley Manne, drums, Ray Brown, bass, Hampton Hawes, piano, and Bob Cooper, saxophone, perform "Blues in the Basement," "Stella by Starlight," and milestones at Shelly's Manne Hole Club in Los Angeles. 28 mins.
VHS: S04169. $19.95.

Sippie

A portrait of blues singer, songwriter Sippie Wallace. 23 mins.
VHS: S03195. $24.95.

The Smithsonian Jazz Series

Six concerts taped at the Smithsonian Institute.
Alberta Hunter. The Grand Lady of the Blues, the late Alberta Hunter, is featured in this toe-tapping concert taped at the Smithsonian Institute. Alberta's down-and-dirty blues and tender ballads are performed with her trademark sass and sensitivity.
VHS: S05421. $29.95.
Art Blakey. Superstar siblings Wynton and Branford Marsalis join the amazing drummer Art Blakey in this hard bop concert at the Smithsonian. Grammy-winner Wynton solos in Kurt Weill's "My Ship," demonstrating the trumpet virtuosity that has made him one of the best-selling jazz artists of all time.
VHS: S05425. $29.95.
Art Farmer. Few trumpeters have ever made their instrument sound as tender as Art Farmer, as this concert video clearly proves. Pianist Fred Hersch, bassist Dennis Irwin and drummer Billy Hart accompany Farmer as he spins his wistful magic around a group of classic ballads.
VHS: S05429. $29.95.
Benny Carter. The legendary composer/arranger/trumpeter/saxophonist performs jazz standards like "Misty" and "Take the A Train." Carter, 74 years young at the time, performs with a quintet that also features Kenny Barron on piano and George Duvivier on bass.
VHS: S05426. $29.95.
Joe Williams. He's become famous twice in a lifetime, as Count Basie's star vocalist and as Bill Cosby's father-in-law on *The Cosby Show*. He's Joe Williams, the King of the Blues, performing in concert with Kirk Stuart on piano, Keeter Betts on bass and Steve Williams on drums.
VHS: S03828. $29.95.
Mel Lewis. The late drummer fronts the big band that has performed every Monday night for more than a decade at New York's legendary Village Vanguard. This young, 17-piece ensemble rips through three pieces by Herbie Hancock and one by Bob Brookmeyer, proving that the jazz orchestra is alive and well.
VHS: S03831. $29.95.

Solo Flight: The Genius of Charlie Christian, 1919-1942

Solo Flight traces the life of jazz guitar legend Charlie Christian, who revolutionized jazz with his amplified single-string solos, elevating guitar from background instrument to focal point of the music. This documentary traces Christian's beginnings, from his birthplace in Oklahoma City through his legendary tenure with the Benny Goodman Sextet, and on to the late-night sessions at Minton's in Harlem with Dizzy Gillespie, Kenny Clarke, Thelonious Monk and Charlie "Bird" Parker, where Christian contributed to the birth of BeBop. 31 mins.
VHS: S30125. $19.98.

Solo Tribute: Keith Jarrett

The magician of the keyboard casts his spell with "The Night We Called It a Day", "Sweet and Lovely", "I Got It Bad", "That Ain't Good", "Summertime" and 10 more classics. 102 mins.
Laser: LD70777. $39.95.

Sonny Rollins Live at Loren

37 mins.
VHS: S03182. $24.95.

Sonny Terry & Brownie McGhee: Red River Blues 1948-1974

A video retrospective featuring 16 country blues performances by this superb duo. Songs include "John Henry," "Easy Rider," "Red River Blues," "Crow Jane," "Whoopin' the Blues," "Born with the Blues" and others. 60 mins.
VHS: S31759. $29.95.

Sonny Terry: Whoopin' the Blues 1958-1974

A retrospective of the influential blues harp player who began as a blind street musician in North Carolina and teamed up with some of blues' best, including Blind Boy Fuller and Brownie McGhee. Songs include "Crazy About You Baby," "Hand Jive," "Shoutin' the Blues," "Sweet Woman Blues," "John Henry," "My Baby's So Fine," "Midnight Special" and "Whoopin' the Blues." 55 mins.
VHS: S31647. $22.95.

Sound??

John Cage's enigmatic questions about sound are intercut with some of the most ambitious experiments of Rahsaan Roland Kirk. While Kirk plays three saxes at once, switches to flute, incorporates tapes of birds played backwards, and finally hands out whistles to the audience and encourages them to accompany him, Cage is preparing a piece for musical bicycle with David Tudor and Merce Cunningham.
VHS: S07747. $24.95.
Dick Fontaine, USA, 1967, 27 mins.

Space Is the Place

This unclassifiable work combines the crude energy and militant outrage of the blaxploitation film with footage of Ra's Intergalactic Arkestra performing their classics "Watusi", "Outer Spaceways Inc." and "The Satellites Are Spinning". "Sun Ra's *Close Encounter* with *Sweet Sweetback* is somewhere between *The Seventh Seal* and *El Topo*" (Michael Shore, *MTV News*).
VHS: S19121. $24.95.
John Coney, USA, 1974, 63 mins.

Stan Getz: A Musical Odyssey

In 1977, Getz went "home" to Israel and jammed with Israeli musicians for three weeks. It was a moving experience which also allowed Getz to showcase his improvisational talents as he worked with an Arab quartet, a Yemenite dance troupe, the Piamenti Brothers Band, and renowned Klezmer clarinetist Giora Feldman.
VHS: S24304. $72.00.
Herbert Dorfman, USA, 1978, 60 mins.

Standards II: With Keith Jarrett

"With a Song in My Heart", "When You Wish upon a Star", "On Green Dolphin Street", "Blame It on My Youth" and "Georgia on My Mind" lead a dazzling jazz showcase performed by three of the greats: Keith Jarrett, Gary Peacock and Jack DeJohnette. 91 mins.
Laser: LD70334. $39.95.

Stanley Jordan: Magic Touch

When You Wish upon a Star, Touch of Blue, Jumpin' Jack, Lady in My Life. 19 mins.
VHS: S05409. $16.95.

Stanley Turrentine: In Concert

This video concert stars one of the best-selling jazz musicians of all time, Stanley Turrentine. Turrentine's warm, masculine tenor sax sound has made him a favorite with both jazz fans and the general public for decades. Now, in this concert recorded at New York's Village Gate, Stanley talks about his career and plays the songs he's known for all around the world. 60 mins.
VHS: S13930. $29.95.

Stefan Grossman

Stefan Grossman's solo concert performances reflect a panorama of fingerstyle techniques and styles ranging from country blues to ragtime to Celtic melodies to jazz-based compositions. Beginning his studies with guitar legend Rev. Gary Davis at age 15, he became an integral part of the infamous "blues mafia." 60 mins.
VHS: S15729. $24.95.

Stephane Grappelli in New Orleans

A front row seat in a terrific French Quarter Club performance of the great jazz violinist at work. 60 mins.
VHS: S10151. $29.95.

Stephane Grappelli—Live in San Francisco—1985

Excellent coverage of the 78-year-old jazz violinist in two early 1980's Bay Area performances—at the Paul Masson Vineyards in Saratoga and at the Great American Music Hall in San Francisco. Grappelli and his trio of accompanists romp through an eclectic set of tunes. 60 mins.
VHS: S12343. $19.95.
C. Broullon/R. Poirer, USA, 1985, 60 mins.

Steve Allen's Jazz Scene USA

The brainchild of life-long jazz devotee Steve Allen, this four-tape set showcases the very best California-based jazz performers and TV appearances by outstanding national acts from the series critics have called the best jazz show ever done for television. Hosted by Oscar Brown, Jr., the series features jazz musicians at their peak, including the Cannonball Adderley Sextet, Teddy Edwards Sextet, Frank Rosolino Quartet, Stan Kenton & His Orchestra, Shelly Manne and his Men, Shorty Rogers & His Orchestra, Phineas Newborn, Jr. Trio and Jimmy Smith Trio. Each tape contains two episodes.
VHS: S34395. $69.95.

Steve Lacy: Lift the Bandstand

A portrait of Steve Lacy, with his music. 50 mins.
VHS: S03181. $29.95.

The Story of Jazz

In this impressive array of jazz performance clips over 30 artists can be seen, including Louis Armstrong, Count Basie, John Coltrane, Miles Davis, Ella Fitzgerald, Dizzy Gillespie, Benny Goodman, Billie Holiday, Thelonious Monk, Charlie Parker, Sarah Vaughn, Lester Young and more. 90 mins.
Laser: LD74754. $39.98.

Straight No Chaser: Thelonious Monk

A revealing portrait of the great Monk, featuring more than 25 Monk songs, including "Round Midnight", "Ask Me Now" and "Ruby, My Dear", and featuring an amazing insight into the personal life of the troubled but extraordinary musician.
VHS: S13023. $19.98.
Charlotte Zwerin, USA, 1989, 89 mins.

Sun Ra: A Joyful Noise

Sun Ra and his Arkestra into the space age by way of Ancient Egyptian mythology. 60 mins.
VHS: S03177. $19.95.

Super Drumming
A who's who of the world of drums and drummers: Louie Bellson, Ian Paice, Gerry Brown, Simon Phillips, Nippy Noya, Cozy Powell and Pete York. Highlights include Bellson's "Deep Skin" and "The Laid Back Heart Attack Tango". 53 mins.
VHS: S09823. $19.95.

Swing: Best of the Big Bands Vol. 1
Contains 18 complete performances including Tommy Dorsey (Opus One); Rosemary Clooney and Tony Pastor (Movie Tonight), Billie Holiday (God Bless the Child); Duke Ellington (Frankie & Johnny) and also featuring Hi-Los, Ray Anthony, Benny Carter, Harry James, Charlie Barnet and Gene Krupa. 50 mins.
VHS: S07529. $24.95.

Swing: Best of the Big Bands Vol. 2
20 complete performances including The Dorsey Brothers (Yes, Indeed), Nat King Cole (Route 66); Woody Herman (Caldonia); Sarah Vaughn (Don't Blame Me); and also Charlie Barnet, Lionel Hampton, Ralph Marterie, Gene Krupa, Stan Kenton, Tex Benecke and Glenn Miller Orchestra. 50 mins.
VHS: S07530. $24.95.

Swing: Best of the Big Bands Vol. 3
19 performances including Count Basie (Red Bank Boogie); Gene Krupa (Stompin' at the Savoy); The Ink Spots (If I Didn't Care); Harry James (Brave Bulls) and also featuring Jimmy Dorsey, Les Brown, Duke Ellington, Teresa Brewer and Charlie Barnet. 50 mins.
VHS: S07531. $24.95.

Swing: Best of the Big Bands Vol. 4
18 complete performances including Tex Beneke and the Glenn Miller Orchestra (Little Brown Jug); The Mills Brothers (Paper Doll); Louis Prima (That Old Black Magic); Buddy Rich (Burn) and also featuring Count Basie, Ray Anthony, Jimmy Dorsey, The Skylarks and Ray Kenton. 50 mins.
VHS: S07532. $24.95.

Taj Mahal
The self-taught Taj Mahal plays more than 12 instruments, including guitar, piano, harmonica, banjo and mandolin. His music alternates between funk and sophisticated charm, in "Cakewalk into Town," "Fishin' Blues," "Sweet Home Chicago," "Going up the Country Paint My Mailbox Blue" "My Little Sugar Mama."
VHS: S19682. $19.95.

Talmage Farlow
A portrait of Tal Farlow with Tommy Flanagan. 58 mins.
VHS: S03178. $29.95.

Tenor Legends: Coleman Hawkins in Brussels, 1962
Hawkins' performances in the 1920's with Fletcher Henderson's Band established the tenor sax as a major instrument for jazz solos. At the Adolphe Sax festival this innovator was recognized for his accomplishments. Over two days backed by George Arvanitas, Mickey Baker, Jimmy Woode and Kansas Fields, Hawkins' magic was captured on film. 57 mins.
VHS: S22414. $19.95.

Tenor Titans
This documentary explores the early pioneers, in particular the radical contributions and innovations of Coleman Hawkins, with commentary from Branford Marsalis. This invaluable program showcases Hawkins, Bud Freeman, Lester Young, Stan Getz, and performances by Sal Nistico, Eric Dion, Frank Foster and Eddie "Lockjaw" Davis, Dexter Gordon, Charlie Rouse, to the rhythm and blues influence of Sam Taylor and Illinois Jacquet, to the modern era of John Coltrane, Sonny Rollins and David Murray. 60 mins.
VHS: S17426. $29.95.

Texas Tenor: The Illinois Jacquet Story
The life, art and music of Illinois Jacquet, who developed a revolutionary, highly improvised sound that established the tenets of rhythm and blues while performing with Lionel Hampton's band. The documentary reproduces the shiny, ecstatic moments of orchestral jazz as well as any film made, its beauty and rounded shapes and sharp punctuations, the delirium and sensuality of performance, the congregational ecstacy" (Peter Watrous, *New York Times*).
VHS: S19119. $29.95.
Arthur Elgort, USA, 1991, 81 mins.

Three Piano Portraits
Three jazz documentaries on videocassette: *Anything for Jazz: Kalo Byard* (25 mins.), an intimate view of pianist Jaki Byard; *Nutman's Got the Blues: Cyrus Chestnut Solo Piano* (15 mins.), pianist Cyrus Chestnut captured in a solo sold-out performance; and *Barry Harris: Passing It On* (23 mins), a portrait of self-proclaimed be-bop pianist Barry Harris.
VHS: S33764. $19.95.
Dan Algrant/Daniel Berman/David Chan/Ken Freundlich, USA, 1980/1997/1985, 63 mins.

Time Groove
Original compositions by Harold Farberman performed by an all-star percussion ensemble made up of renowned jazz artists Alex Acuna, Louie Bellson, Vic Firth, Steve Gadd, Harvey Mason, and Dave Samuels. 70 mins.
VHS: S13632. $29.95.

Toots Thielmans in New Orleans
The great jazz harmonica player surrounds himself with a young surging rhythm section featuring Fred Hersch and Harvie Swartz, in a stirring live performance. 60 mins.
VHS: S10152. $29.95.

The Toshiko Akiyoshi Jazz Orchestra: Strive for Jive
Composer and pianist Toshiko Akiyoshi's band grafts the bebop of the Western big band with the music of the East. The program is a live performance of the 16-piece band, performing "Yellow Is Mellow", "Strive for Jive", "Autumn Sea" and "Warning, Success May Be Hazardous to Your Health". 48 mins.
VHS: S19172. $19.98.

Tribute to John Coltrane
Wayne Shorter, Eddie Gomez, Jack DeJohnette, Dave Liebman and Richie Beirach pay tribute to the master jazzman in this once-in-a-lifetime session. 57 mins.
Laser: LD71379. $29.95.

Tribute to Sidney Bechet
Saxophonist Bob Wilbur and the Smithsonian Jazz Repertory Ensemble salute the master of the soprano sax, Sidney Bechet. The great New Orleans traditional jazz musician is remembered in songs he helped popularize, such as "Summertime" and "Daydreams."
VHS: S13055. $29.95.

Trumpet Kings
Wynton Marsalis hosts this look at the great trumpet players of jazz, from Louis Armstrong to Miles Davis and Lester Bowie. 72 mins.
VHS: S03212. $39.95.

The Universal Mind of Bill Evans
Legendary composer and pianist Evans teaches the viewer the meaning of jazz, through live performance and engaging discussion. Hosted by Steve Allen. 1966, 45 mins.
VHS: S14740. $19.95.

Vassar Clements
This concert highlights the virtuoso fiddler Vassar Clements, whose music is steeped in country, modern jazz, swing and blue grass. 60 mins.
VHS: S19215. $24.95.

We Like the Blues: Vol. 1
Featuring blues-influenced contemporary performers such as Dr. John, The Fabulous Thunderbirds, Steve Marriott, Ten Years After, and more. 51 mins.
VHS: S03825. $19.95.

We Like the Blues: Vol. 2
Featuring John Martyn, Dr. John with Chris Barber's New Orleans Jazz Band, Climax Blues Band and more. 51 mins.
VHS: S03826. $19.95.

Willie Dixon
Chicago blues artist Willie Dixon interweaves traditional elements of black folklore and storytelling with the pessimism and soulful intensity of country blues. The numbers include "29 Ways," "I Think I Got the Blues," "It Don't Make Sense," "Gonna Rock This House Tonight" and "T'ain't Nobody's Business."
VHS: S19680. $19.95.

Wynton Marsalis: Blues and Swing
Live performances, interviews and master classes with jazz trumpeter Wynton Marsalis. Selections include "Knozz Moe King", "Caravan", "Big Butter and Egg Man", "Cherokee" and many more. USA, 79 mins.
VHS: S15310. $14.98.

Zoot Sims Quartet
Zoot Sims, saxophone, Roger Kellaway, piano, Larry Bunker, drums, Chuck Berghofer, bass, sparkle in "Zoots Piece," "My Old Flame," "On the Trail," and "Motoring Along" at Dontes Jazz Club in Los Angeles. 28 mins.
VHS: S04171. $24.95.

OTHER MUSIC

America's Music: Bulk Pack
The complete set: *Blues, Volumes 1 & 2; Country & Western, Volumes 1 & 2; Folk, Volumes 1 & 2; Gospel, Volumes 1 & 2; Jazz Then Dixieland, Volumes 1 & 2; Rhythm and Blues, Volumes 1 & 2*; and *Soul, Volumes 1 & 2*.
VHS: S05044. $279.30.

The Andy Williams Christmas Show
The Osmond Brothers and Lorrie Morgan join Williams at the Moon River Theater in Branson, Missouri, for a holiday celebration. Among the songs they perform are "It's the Most Wonderful Time of the Year," "Sleigh Ride" and "Joy to the World." 78 mins.
VHS: S29491. $14.95.

Andy Williams in Concert at Branson
This phenomenal pop star sings some of his most memorable hits at the theater named for him in Branson, Missouri. "Born Free", "Days of Wine and Roses" and even the theme from *The Godfather* are included in this exciting program, along with many other great songs. 85 mins.
VHS: S22004. $14.95.

Angel Chants
Beautiful chant music is paired in this video with some of history's most celebrated artists. Van Gogh, Botticelli, Raphael and Rubens are just some of the painters represented in this singular video experience.
VHS: S22744. $9.95.

Barbra Streisand: A Happening in Central Park
Includes the songs "People", "Second Hand Rose", "Cry Me a River" and "Silent Night". 60 mins.
VHS: S22023. $19.98.

Barbra Streisand: Putting It Together— The Making of the Broadway Album
This is a behind-the-scenes look at recording sessions from Barbra's popular *Broadway Album*. Includes several tracks recorded for this album as well as music videos.
VHS: S22025. $19.98.

Cage/Cunningham
For 45 years, composer John Cage and choreographer Merce Cunningham have collaborated. On this video, the importance of their association and their interaction with other leading figures in art, literature, dance and music are explored. 95 mins.
VHS: S26792. $19.95.

Chantmania
It all began when Father Connif was excommunicated for teaching his choral ensemble "99 Bottles of Grog on the Wall". This classic is joined by a number of other soulful but mindless ditties, like "Losing My Religion", "We Will Rock You", "Smells Like Teen Spirit" and "Do Ya Think I'm Sexy", for a hilarious but religious experience.
VHS: S22536. $12.98.

COMM3TV Vol. 1
An overview of the hard rock and distinctive sounds putout by the Brooklyn-based label, including Brenda Kahn, Poopshovel, Arson Garden, Zuzu's Petals, Big Trouble House and Cattle Prod. 50 mins.
VHS: S19618. $19.95.

Disarmament: Savage Republic
A performance video of the group's 1986 concert for the participants of the Great Peace March for Nuclear Disarmament. "Muted color ghosts images of the republic float over and under all around one another, breaking down, dissolving, changing, reassembling, repeating. [It is] somewhat psychedelic" (Jon Killough). 55 mins.
VHS: S19629. $19.95.

Discovering Electronic Music
Electronics are now used to alter music through scientific understanding of the physical basis of music. The sound synthesizer can create, envelop and even filter sound, resulting in new and more precise aural compositions. 23 mins.
VHS: S23516. $49.95.

Eddie Fisher: A Singing Legend

The 50s' most popular singer had a string of hits that made him a household name. In this collection of his best performances are renditions of "Wish You Were Here," "You Oughta Be in Pictures," "Thinking of You," "In Old New York," "May I Sing to You" and many more. 40 mins.
VHS: S21219. $19.98.

Endless Summer: Donna Summer's Greatest Hits

In celebration of the Disco Diva's 20th anniversary, this collection of her hits is available on video. Her classic tunes "I Feel Love", "Last Dance", "MacArthur Park", "She Works Hard for the Money", "Unconditional Love" and many more are included. 60 mins.
VHS: S23433. $19.95.

Experimental Audio Research—Millennium Music: A Meta-Musical Portrait

This brain-baking collage of rich analogue sounds features live recordings by Sonic (Spacemen 3, Spectrum), Eddie Prevost (A.M.M.), Pete Bassman (Spacemen 3) and Tome Prentice (God). Intended as a soundscape reflecting time from pre-history and the dinosaur age through modern digital communication and 20th-century travel. Pieces includes *Delysid* and *Digitania*. 45 mins.
VHS: S34085. $19.98.

Flashbacks: Easy Lovin'

Tom Jones, Linda Ronstadt, The Carpenters, Kenny Rogers and Bobby Darin are all included, singing some of the most beautiful ballads of yesteryear. 30 mins.
VHS: S24669. $14.98.

Flashbacks: Pop Parade

Dionne Warwick, Jim Croce, Raquel Welch, The 5th Dimension, Sonny & Cher and many other superstar pop singers are included in this blast from the past. 30 mins.
VHS: S24668. $14.98.

Flashbacks: Soul Sensations

Ike & Tina Turner, Gladys Knight and the Pips, Lou Rawls and more soul icons from the 1960's are included on this amazing look back at a great time in music. 30 mins.
VHS: S24667. $14.98.

Frank Sinatra: His Life & Times

Includes interviews, with film of Sinatra, film excerpts, photographs, singing performances and TV appearances. Includes singing performances with Elvis Presley and comedy roles opposite Bob Hope, Dean Martin, Jack Benny and Johnny Carson. 100 mins.
VHS: S32668. $29.99.

George Crumb: The Voice of the Whale

A unique portrait of Pulitzer Prize-winning American composer George Crumb; his life, his art, and the connections between the two. Included in this film are performances from Crumb's "Vox Balaenae for Three Masked Players," samples of the rural gospel music which has influenced him, demonstrations by Crumb of the exotic instruments and unusual effects which figure in his compositions.
VHS: S07746. $24.95.
Robert Mugge, USA, 1976, 54 mins.

House of Usher—Malice in Wonderland

This music video provides insight into the musical development and parallel evolution of 3-D computer animation that defines Formaldehyde, the record label from Berlin, Germany. It offers a collaborative format, where composers and computer animators were free to fuse these different art forms. 30 mins.
VHS: S22227. $14.98.

Jeanette MacDonald in Performance

A 1950 performance that stands as a testament to the artistry of Jeanette MacDonald, with selections including "If I Could Tell You", "California Here I Come", "Will You Remember", "Italian Street Song", "In My Garden" and more. 23 mins.
VHS: S13245. $24.95.

John Cage

Conversation between avant-garde composer John Cage and Jack Kroll, senior arts editor at *Newsweek*. Cage was a composer and a philosopher of aesthetics, whose revolutionary definitions of music influenced a whole generation of artists. Here he discusses his life and work, the purpose of music and his experiments. 1969, 27 mins.
VHS: S32335. $89.95.

John Cage: I Have Nothing to Say and I Am Saying It

The visionary avant-garde composer John Cage reflects on his art and music as he discusses his philosophy, creative habits and the chance element of composing. In addition artist Robert Rauschenberg and choreographer Merce Cunningham discuss *Minutiae*, their collaboration with Cage. The late composer's *4'33"* is also performed. With Laurie Anderson, Yoko Ono, Paul Jacobs and David Tudor. 56 mins.
VHS: S18731. $29.95.

Karen Akers: On Stage at Wolf Trap

Cabaret singer Karen Akers interprets the work of Steven Sondheim, Jacques Brel, Peter Allen and Andrew Lloyd Webber in this live performance. "The quintessential cabaret singer" (*The New York Times*). 59 mins.
VHS: S19230. $29.98.

Keiko Matsui: Light Above the Trees

Created as a celebration and reflection of Keiko Matsui, America's #1 female instrumentalist, this sumptuous program captures Keiko's stunning concert at the Palace of Fine Arts in San Francisco and her solo piano improvisations at the enchanting 1200-year-old Itsukushima Shrine in Miyajima Island in Japan. Kyogen dancer Mannojo Nomura complements Keiko's compositions. 90 mins.
VHS: S34218. $19.98.

Kurt Bestor Christmas

In this live concert of Christmas music, award-winning composer Kurt Bestor weaves heartfelt and joyous melodies of age-old carols with the earthiness of acoustic folk instruments, the ancient pulse of world percussion, and the richness and warmth of a classical orchestra. Performances include "Deck the Halls," "Bring a Torch Jeanette Isabella," "Angels We Have Heard on High," "It Came Upon a Midnight Clear," "Joy to the World," "Sundance," "Silent Night," "Sage of Lamberene" and "Prayer of the Children." 56 mins.
VHS: S30441. $14.95.

Legendary Theatre Organists

Rare footage from American films of the 1930's is combined with solo presentations, pictorials and sing-alongs celebrating the legendary organ accompanists to silent film. Featuring Jesse Crawford, Ann Leaf, Reginald Foort, Lew White, Dick Liebert and Don Baker. The program is hosted by organist Gaylord Carter.
VHS: S01659. $39.95.

Legends of Old Time Music

Though widely acknowledged as the source of bluegrass and country, Old Time music is an exciting genre in its own right. This video explores Old Time music's many varieties and demonstrates its blend of Celtic, African and American influences.
VHS: S24372. $29.95.

Liberace

From A & E comes this first authorized biography of the flamboyant Las Vegas showman who became the highest-paid and best-loved entertainer in the world. 50 mins.
VHS: S30108. $19.95.

Liberace Collection

A comprehensive collection of this audacious performer's vast output. All the diamonds, dazzle and dashing that make his music so popular are showcased in this three-volume set.
Volume 1. 75 mins.
VHS: S15874. $19.98.
Volume 2. 75 mins.
VHS: S15875. $19.98.
Volume 3. 75 mins.
VHS: S15876. $19.98.

Light Dance

Santana's music will lead you through this visual exploration of the natural world. The patterns of light and color found in a variety of mystical landscapes are revealed in this inspired video. From the outermost vistas of the universe to fields of wildflowers, this tape offers a visual feast. 40 mins.
VHS: S26092. $19.98.

Live at the Bradford

Powerful performances from the Mission of Burma's *Vs.* and *Calls and Marches* albums, including some breathtaking versions of "That's How I Escaped My Certain Fate," "Mica," "Outlaw," "Peking Spring," "He Is, She Is," "Fun World," "Max Ernst" and "Academy Fight Song." 35 mins.
VHS: S19624. $19.95.

Lyrics by Tim Rice

Britain's most famous lyricist is the object of this special musical tribute. Marti Webb, Elaine Paige and David Essex join to perform a selection of Tim Rice's most popular songs, including hits co-written with Andrew Lloyd Webber, such as "Jesus Christ Superstar" and "Don't Cry for Me, Argentina". 52 mins.
VHS: S21699. $14.95.

!Male! (In Excelsis Corruptus Deluxe)

The Foetus Inc. line-up, comprised of Clint Ruin, Norman Westberg (Swans), Al Kizys (Of Cabbage and Kings) and David Ouimet (Cop Shoot Cop), gathered for this live performance of their recent American tour. The numbers include "Free James Brown," "Fin," "Honey I'm Home," "Butterfly Potion" and "Death Rape 2000." 75 mins.
VHS: S19616. $19.95.

Material Witness

Michael Eric Dyson, one of the foremost commentators and theorists on popular culture and race, focuses on the controversial race, identity and political issues associated with "gangsta rap." 42 mins.
VHS: S28444. $195.00.

Michael Crawford: A Touch of Music in the Night

Talented vocalist Michael Crawford is seen performing in the studio, singing classics like "When You Wish upon a Star" and "If You Could See Me Now". His newer hits "The Power of Love" and "She Used to Be Mine" are also included, along with many more favorites. 40 mins.
VHS: S20689. $19.98.
Laser: LD72379. $29.98.

The Mills Brothers Story

This nostalgic documentary about one of the most beloved vocal groups spans more than 50 years of their show business history. Through film clips dating back to 1932, you'll hear many timeless Mills Brothers songs, including "Paper Doll", "You Always Hurt (The One You Love)", "Till Then" and "Yellow Bird". 56 mins.
VHS: S15856. $29.95.

Music for the Movies: Bernard Herrmann

This documentary was nominated for an Academy Award because it so successfully illustrates the importance of music to the movies. Herrmann worked on over 50 films during his career, including the legendary *Citizen Kane*. Though most widely known for his work with Hitchcock on films like *The Man Who Knew Too Much* and *Psycho*, he also collaborated with other great directors, such as Martin Scorsese on *Taxi Driver*. Includes clips from these and other films.
VHS: S26668. $24.98.
Laser: LD75108. $24.98.
Josh Waletzky, USA, 1992, 58 mins.

Music for the Movies: The Hollywood Sound

During the golden age of Hollywood, from the 1930's to the 1950's, musical accompaniment in American film reached a high point. Based on the achievements of 19th century masters, these scores transformed films into overwhelming sensory experiences. This BBC documentary explains their evolution. Under the direction of John Mauceri, the BBC National Orchestra of Wales performs this tribute to Hollywood films like *Laura* and *Casablanca*.
VHS: S26917. $24.98.
Laser: LD75401. $29.98.
Josh Waletzky/Margaret Smilow, Great Britain, 86 mins.

Music Moves the Spirit

This music video is an all-night concert dedicated to the talented post-World War II musicians and writers who came together to forge a resonating era which encapsulates the searching spirit of the Beats. Features poet Michael McClure, the Doors' Ray Manzarek, David Amram and his Quartet, Allen Ginsberg, late screenwriter Terry Southern and poet Ted Joans with Village Gate impresario Art D'Lugoff. 80 mins.
VHS: S30800. $24.95.

Music with Roots in the Aether

Performances by and interviews with David Behrman, Philip Glass, Alvin Lucier, Gordon Mumma, Pauline Oliveros, Terry Riley and Robert Ashley, in this 14-hour (seven 2-hour cassettes) overview of the contemporary American composing scene. Produced in 1976.
VHS: S20867. $450.00.

The Nativity Story

More than a concert, this is a look at how cultures all over the world celebrate the birth of Jesus Christ and interpret the story of Christmas. This command performance of the world-famous Mormon-Tabernacle Choir will thrill and inspire you with their performances of such Christmas favorites as "Angels We Have Heard on High," "O Come All Ye Faithful," "Deck the Halls," "Away in a Manger," "I Saw Three Ships," "O Come O Come Emmanuel" and others. 48 mins.
VHS: S30442. $14.95.

Natural Selections

A merging of visuals and progressive instrumental music offers selections from Tangerine Dream, Jan Hammer, David Lanz & Paul Speer, Michael Stearns and James Reynolds. "A feast of sight of sound" (*Los Angeles Times*. 50 mins.
VHS: S19594. $14.95.

Nature of Music
What is music? Why has every society throughout the world-and throughout history—regarded it as so important? To answer these questions, award-winning producer/director Jeremy Marre travels the globe examining everything from the throat songs of Inuit Eskimos to Wagner's *Ring* at Bayreuth. 135 mins.
VHS: S11756. $29.95.

Nova Scotia International Tattoo 1997
The Nova Scotia International Tattoo is the world's largest indoor show, featuring more than 2,000 international military and civilian performers and the great military bands of the world. Includes the world's best fife and drum corps, as well as singers, dancers, comedians and gymnasts. 90 mins.
VHS: S32398. $29.95.

Ozric Tentacles—Live at the Fridge
This stereo video by the Ozric Tentacles was recorded live in Brixton, U.K. The tracks "Space Jam", "OG-HA-BE", "Erpland", "Sunscape", "The Throb", "Sniffing Dog" and many other songs are included.
VHS: S22229. $19.95.

Paris Waltz (La Valse de Paris)
Considered one of the last *monstres-sacres* of the French musical stage, Yvonne Printemps portrays Jacques Offenbach's beautiful and tempestuous prima donna, Hortense Schneider (1833-1920) in this beautifully photographed film with music by Offenbach and gowns by Dior. Also stars Printemps' real-life husband, Pierre Fresnay, as Offenbach. "Delightful, witty, with 20 songs. In a selection from *Fortunio*, Printemps' is singing that is sensed in the soul" (Stefan Zucker, *Opera Fanatic*). French with English subtitles.
VHS: S28433. $34.95.
Marcel Archard, France, 1948, 92 mins.

Perfect Harmony
A celebration of Tanglewood's 50 years of music is featured in this concert hosted by Marvin Hamlisch. Seiji Ozawa, John Williams and a host of Tanglewood fellows from around the world are also featured. Includes musical selections from Beethoven's *Leonora Overture #3*, John William's *E.T.* and Tchaikovsky's *1812*. 48 mins.
VHS: S26219. $19.95.

Rosemary Clooney's Demi-Centennial
An all-star tribute to the woman Frank Sinatra called the "symbol of good, modern American music." Rosemary sings classic tunes from her legendary career and is joined by Tony Bennett, Bette Midler and others.
VHS: S31297. $19.95.

Scoring Films: Bernard Herrmann
A profile of composer Bernard Herrmann (1911-1975), whose scores set a new standard in American cinema. Includes selections from *Citizen Kane, Jane Eyre, The Ghost and Mrs Muir, Psycho, North by Northwest, Taxi Driver* and other films. Herrmann's early classical training, his techniques for matching music to mood, and his unconventional ideas are discussed. With commentary by friend and music professor David Raksin. 1976, 28 mins.
VHS: S31584. $59.95.

Scoring Films: Marvin Hamlisch
Marvin Hamlisch comments on difficulties in capturing the personality of a film, how music enhances film, writing to click-track and working with an orchestra to fit his music to scenes from *Starting Over*. Includes clips from several films that feature his music, and interviews with theater friend Joel Grey and others. 1979, 28 mins.
VHS: S31583. $59.95.

Sinatra
This five-hour authorized biography of Frank Sinatra, produced by his daughter Tina, traces his extravagant life, his rise as the premier singer to Hollywood matinee idol, turbulent personal life, highly publicized marriages, alleged mob connections and complicated relationships with the Kennedys. With Olympia Dukakis, Rod Steiger, Philip Kasnov as Sinatra, Nina Siezmaszko, Marcia Gay Harden and Gina Gershon.
VHS: S17708. $29.98.
Laser: LD71801. $69.98.
James Sadwith, USA, 1992, 245 mins.

So Wrong They're Right
Over 20 interview segments from 8-track tape and player fanatics—or "trackers," as dubbed by the magazine *8-Track Mind*—ranging from rants and reminiscences to diatribes, fantasies, fix-it tips and sales pitches. "Perfectly expresses future shock and warmly embraces a naivete that is regrettably lacking in this country" (*Ink*).
VHS: S31399. $24.95.

Russ Forster, USA, 1995, 92 mins.
Sound: Rahsaan Roland Kirk and John Cage
Two experimental musicians of the first rank here team up in a mesmerizing work. Recorded in 1967, 27 mins.
VHS: S21678. $24.95.

The Spike Jones Story
The first documentary made about this innovative musical humorist. Discover Spike Jones' personal and professional history, including some of his most popular recordings: "Cocktails for Two", "Der Fuehrer's Face", "All I Want for Christmas Is My Two Front Teeth", as well as rarely seen 1950's rock & roll parodies. Meet personal friends, family members, and the zaniest of his collaborators, The City Slickers. 60 mins.
VHS: S15857. $29.95.

Stompin' at the Savoy: World of Slide Guitar, Volume 2
Modern slide guitar masters Bob Brozman, Vishwa Mohan Bhatt, Martin Simpson, Mike Auldridge and Freddie Roulette perform Delta blues, Indian ragas, bluegrass and pop tunes. 80 mins.
VHS: S33376. $29.95.

Symphony of Wonders
Locations such as the Taj Mahal, the Colosseum, St. Peter's Basilica, the Eiffel Tower, the Great Pyramids, the Amazon, Ayers Rock, Machu Picchu, Mt. Rushmore, the Statue of Liberty and the Grand Canyon are set to musical scores composed specifically for the program. 52 mins.
Laser: LD72248. $34.95.

The Tahitian Choir Volume II
On Rapati Iti, an isolated South Sea island, the chants and dances remains pure, recalling an earlier time. This second volume contains music from this place that once again beguiles listeners with its haunting simplicity and undeniable strength.
VHS: S22413. $19.95.

Tony Bennett: The Art of the Singer
Joseph Mantegna narrates this retrospective look at Tony Bennett's life and music. Despite his incredible run of hits in the 1950's, Bennett ran into trouble with changes in musical taste in the late 1960's. Now he may be enjoying his greatest popularity ever. 60 mins.
VHS: S26916. $19.98.

Ute Lemper Sings Kurt Weill
Twenty-one Weill songs are included in this performance based on Lemper's show at the Paris cabaret Les Bouffes du Nord. This songstress brings her own compelling interpretation to standards like "The Ballad of Mack the Knife," "September Song," "Trouble Man," "Die Rote Rosa" and more.
VHS: S23910. $29.95.

A Visit with Alan Jay Lerner
This lyricist wrote words to songs in many hit musicals. "My Fair Lady," "Camelot," "Brigadoon," "Paint Your Wagon" and the smash "Gigi" are his creations. Of course, there are even more, and they are also included in this video collection.
VHS: S25787. $24.95.

A Visit with Arthur Schwartz
Schwartz is the famed songwriter who collaborated with many lyricists, but he is especially well-known for his work with Howard Dietz. "Dancing in the Dark," "Alone Together," "Make the Man Love Me" and "That's Entertainment" are just some of the songs included on this video, that give an idea of his range.
VHS: S25789. $24.95.

A Visit with Burton Lane
This great songwriter not only discovered Judy Garland and worked with the biggest stars, including Astaire, Crawford and Gable, he also composed the tunes "Old Devil Moon," "Everything I Have Is Yours," "Too Late Now," "How About You," "On a Clear Day" and more.
VHS: S25788. $24.95.

A Visit with Charles Strouse
Master songwriter Strouse penned a number of great songs. Hits like "Tommorrow," "One Boy," "Bye Bye Birdie," "Applause," "Easy Street," "One Last Kiss" and other unforgettable tunes are featured on this video.
VHS: S25786. $24.95.

A Visit with E.Y. "Yip" Harburg
The great songwriter is featured on this musical video. Songs like "Over the Rainbow," "It's Only a Paper Moon," "April in Paris," "Brother, Can You Spare a Dime?," "Old Devil Moon" and more are included.
VHS: S25785. $24.95.

A Visit with Kander and Ebb
Liza Minnelli worked with this songwriting duo so much that it is only fitting she introduce this video. "Maybe This Time," "All That Jazz," "New York, New York" and "Cabaret" offer just some indication of the intense but humorous demeanor behind this great team.
VHS: S25790. $24.95.

A Visit with Mitchell Parish
An amazing Tin Pan Alley songwriter, Parish wrote songs that are still popular. On this video, "Stairway to the Stars," "Volare," "Sweet Lorraine" and "Stardust" reveal the magic of his lyrics.
VHS: S25791. $24.95.

A Visit with Sheldon Harnick
Harnick's songs are distinctively witty, complex and often dark. This video includes his signature works "Sunrise, Sunset," "If I Were a Rich Man," "Matchmaker, Matchmaker" and many more.
VHS: S25792. $24.95.

Weathered and Torn
A documentary on the final tour of The Dream Syndicate offers live and unreleased versions from their albums *Medicine Show, Ghost Stories* and *Out of the Grey*, including "Now I Ride Alone," "Weathered and Torn," "Drinking Problem," "Still Holding On to You," "The Side I'll Never Show" and "Boston." 65 mins.
VHS: S19620. $19.95.

Wildlife Fantasia
A video that matches music to images of wildlife in search of freedom, joy and spontaneity. In Borneo's rain forest, orangutans slumber under the green canopy through the haunting strains of Roger's "The Virgin Slumber Song"; dolphins and sea lions frolic to the swirl of Debussy's "Reflections on the Water"; Antarctic penguins are captured to Bizet's "Jeux d'Enfants"; and a bald eagle sweeps across the Yellowstone National Park to the strains of a Brahms symphony. 48 mins.
Laser: LD72250. $34.95.

ROCK PORTRAITS & SUPERSTARS

11th and B: East Village Summer of Love
A French group made this music video featuring the music of Alan Vega, Marty Rev (both of Suicide) and the False Prophets. Each song is bracketed by a verite documentary of Scott Borofsky spray-painting a mural on a tenement wall. Together these elements capture the feeling of this art-filled New York neighborhood.
VHS: S22649. $19.95.
Marie Martine, USA, 1985, 20 mins.

33-1/3 Revolutions per Monkee
Peter! Mike! Mickey! Davy! It's Monkee mania revisited with this rare Monkees television special, available for the first time on video—more than 25 years after the last recording of the group. Newly remastered with superior sound quality. 60 mins.
VHS: S30743. $19.98.

Alf Bicknell's Personal Beatles Diary
The only video NOT produced by the Beatles that is fully licensed, *Alf Bicknell's Personal Beatles Diary* is your ticket to ride on a personal two-year tour with the most influential rock band of our time, as chronicled by the Beatles' driver and road manager from 1964 and 1966. The course of your travels provides you with a never-before-seen look at life on the road, inside the studio and through the pulsing pop clubs of the tumultuous '60s. Party with the Rolling Stones, watch Ringo take driving lessons and go behind the scenes at famous recording sessions at Abbey Road. Also includes original footage by Paul McCartney.
VHS: S30584. $19.95.

American Pop
An amazing soundtrack which includes The Doors, Janis Joplin, Jimi Hendrix, The Mamas and the Papas, Lynyrd Skynyrd, Pat Benatar, Lou Reed and Bob Seger accompanies this incredible animated film from Ralph Bakshi (*Fritz the Cat*), the story of four generations whose lives revolve around the beat of American pop music.
VHS: S33317. $19.98.
Laser: LD76758. $34.95.
DVD: DV60198. $24.95.
Ralph Bakshi, USA, 1980, 96 mins.

Anything Boys Can Do
This film covers 15 underground New York "girl groups" with styles of music and performances ranging from mild to nakedly aggressive. It is charged with questions about sex, sexual orientation, feminism, politics, other musicians and artistic integrity. These questions are dealt with through interviews with the bands, their fans and others, intercut with liberal doses of performance footage. Bands include Tribe 8, The Horror of Karen Black, Sexpod, Thrust and 12 others.
VHS: S31187. $29.95.
Ethan Minsker, USA, 1996, 75 mins.

The Band: The Authorized Video Biography
Some of The Band's best music is featured in this video, along with clips of their appearances from *American Bandstand, The Ed Sullivan Show* and *The Last Waltz*. Musical giants Eric Clapton, Emmylou Harris, Van Morrison, Todd Rundgren, George Harrison and others testify to the lasting influence of The Band's down-to-earth rock style.
VHS: S26518. $19.95.
Laser: LD75325. $39.98.

Barnes and Barnes Zabagabee

A star-studded retrospective of the world's popular music video artists, featuring Rae Dawn Chong, Mark Hamill, Jose Ferrer, Shaun Cassidy, Stephen Stills, Rosemary Clooney, Weird Al Yankovic, Dr. Demento and featuring the "Original Fish Heads." 40 mins.
VHS: S05197. $19.95.

The Beatles

This tribute to the Fab Four covers their career from the early days in Liverpool to the tragic murder of John Lennon in New York City. A concise history complete with highlights of their performances. 60 mins.
VHS: S16556. $19.95.

The Beatles Anthology

After three decades, The Beatles remain the most captivating and popular musical group of all time. The story of the Fab Four's meteoric rise to stardom and their continued popularity is told for the first time by The Beatles themselves in this collection of archival footage, including photos, interviews, backstage and rare studio clips, home movies, live concerts, and of course, music. Twice the length of the November 1995 ABC broadcast, this anthology features five additional hours of exclusive footage. Contains ten volumes of 75-minute tapes.
VHS: S29958. $159.98.

Beatles Collection

A priceless collection of video history with *The Beatles: The First U.S. Visit*, and complete versions of *A Hard Day's Night, Help!* and *Magical Mystery Tour*. Four cassettes in slipcase collector set.
VHS: S20547. $79.98.

The Beatles Story: Days of Beatlemania 1962-1970

Rare footage recreates the mania which surrounded this pop group from their earliest Liverpool days. The phenomenon quickly spread from England to America. This video includes interviews with band members at critical points in their careers, as well as interviews with members of the Beatles' inner circle. 60 mins.
VHS: S27698. $14.95.

The Beatles' First U.S. Visit

A day-to-day audio-visual diary of the Beatles' first American visit in 1964. Includes rare news, concert and television footage as you go behind the scenes with the Beatles at their hotels and on the road. Also featuring numerous live performances of some of their greatest early hits. England, 85 mins.
VHS: S15172. $24.98.

The Best of 120 Minutes

For six years and still counting, MTV's *120 Minutes* program has offered a weekly showcase of music videos from the best and brightest in cutting edge rock. Includes videos by such artists as: Sonic Youth, Love and Rockets, Violent Femmes and more. 40 mins.
VHS: S14943. $14.95.

The Best of New Wave Theatre, Vol. 1

Highlights from this award-winning cable show, featuring 45 Grave, Suburban Lawns, The Unknowns, Fear, The Blasters, Surf Punks, The Plugz and more, hosted by Peter Ivers. 60 mins.
VHS: S05191. $29.95.

The Best of New Wave Theatre, Vol. 2

Featuring Legal Weapon, Killer Pussy, The Circle Jerks, Fear, The Angry Samoans, Top Jimmy and the Rhythm Pigs and more. 60 mins.
VHS: S05192. $29.95.

Beyond the Doors

An investigation of three cult figures of the music scene of the 60's—Jimi Hendrix, Janis Joplin and Jim Morrison—with the theory that all three were assassinated. Gregory Allen Chatman plays Jimi Hendrix, Riba Meryl is Janis Joplin, and Bryan Wolf plays Jim Morrison. 117 mins.
VHS: S11598. $79.95.

Big Black "Live"

Chicago's powerhouse band rips their way through the detritus to perform startling numbers from their albums *Atomizer* and *Bulldozer and Lungs*. The numbers include "Dead Billy," "Jordan MN," "Kerosene" and "Steelworker." 50 mins.
VHS: S20249. $19.95.

Bizarre Music Television

A collection of the most insane, bizarre and outrageous music videos ever made, including Julie Brown's "Home Coming Queen's Got a Gun," Barnes and Barnes' "Fish Heads," and more. 60 mins.
VHS: S05201. $19.95.

Black Easter

A collection from Flaming Lips, including "2001 Intro," "Ode to C.C. (Part Two)," "Dream Sequence for Lou Reed," "Can't Stop the Spring," "Ungplugged," "With You," "Prescription Love," "Maximum Dream for Evil Knievel" and "Staring at the Sound." 55 mins.
VHS: S19627. $19.95.

Brian Wilson: "I just wasn't made for these times"

Brian Wilson, the musical visionary behind the Beach Boys, stands revealed in this feature length documentary. Made by record producer Don Was, it manages to get inside Wilson's life, his eccentricities, his troubled childhood and the strange home life he himself led as a distant father. Though some delicate points are not investigated, including the death of Wilson's brother, Beach Boy drummer Dennis Wilson, this film is good at explaining the source and achievements of Brian Wilson's pop innovations.
VHS: S26949. $19.99.
Don Was, USA, 1995, 69 mins.

Buried Treasures: Volume 2—Reggae Classics

This compilation has a reggae theme and has been carefully compiled from nearly two decades worth of videos. Includes performances by Black Uhuru, Bob Marley and the Wailers, and more. 30 mins.
VHS: S15625. $14.95.

Buried Treasures: Volume 3—Rap Source

Captures the unique genesis of the rap movement in music video. Highlights of the program include the earliest works by Eric B. & Rakim and the rare 1992 live version of "Bring the Noise," a collaboration between Anthrax and Public Enemy. With Def Jeff, Isis and Professor X. 35 mins.
VHS: S16684. $14.95.

California Rock

A greatest hits anthology of early 60s California rock, extolling freedom and youth. The titles include Canned Heat's "Let's Work Together", Santana's "Jingo", The Byrds' "So You Want to Be a Rock and Roll Star" and The Grateful Dead's "One More Saturday Night". 33 mins.
VHS: S19314. $14.98.

Carpenters—Yesterday Once More

This retrospective of the music of Karen and Richard Carpenter offers a rare look at a legendary career. For more than a decade, the camera's eye tracked the entertainment phenomenon of the Carpenters—giving this classic collection a wonderful variety. Including performances of some of their greatest hits, including: "We've Only Just Begun" and "Top of the World." 55 mins.
VHS: S14109. $19.95.

Casey Kasem's Rock and Roll Goldmine: The British Invasion

Casey Kasem hosts a nostalgic musical trip back to the city with flowers in its hair. The Summer of Love and all those cool sounds from groups like The Grateful Dead, Santana, Country Joe and Fish, Big Brother and The Holding Company with Janis Joplin, and Van Morrison. Heavy. 39 mins.
VHS: S08035. $19.98.

Chuck Berry: Hail! Hail! Rock and Roll

A documentary-concert film about one of the founding fathers of rock and roll made on the occasion of his sixtieth birthday bash at the Opera House in St. Louis. Chuck doesn't say anything he doesn't want to, but lets the music do all the talking he needs. With Keith Richards, Julia Lennon, Etta James, Robert Cray and many others.
VHS: S06076. $79.95.
Taylor Hackford, USA, 1987, 120 mins.

Chuck Berry: Live at the Roxy

Chuck Berry performs with his trademark abandon in this exuberant rock and roll concert. Displaying his showmanship, Berry performs "Move Over Beethoven," "Hail, Hail Rock and Roll," "Reelin' and Rockin'" and "Johnny B. Goode," among others. Berry is joined in a special appearance by Tina Turner. 60 mins.
VHS: S19895. $14.95.

Chuck Berry: Rock and Roll Music

The founding father of Rock and Roll is featured live in this 1969 performance. Filmmaker D.A. Pennebaker of *Don't Look Back* fame captures his best-known songs, including *Johnny B. Goode, Maybelline,* and *Sweet Little Sixteen*. 45 mins.
VHS: S16089. $14.98.

The Clash: Rude Boy

This award-winning semi-documentary captures the social hurricane that swept through the decaying failure of England through the eyes of an unemployed anarchist named Ray Gange. At the eye of that storm was the rock band, the Clash. An interesting film about one of the most important bands in the recent history of popular music.
VHS: S15470. $19.98.
Jack Hazan, Great Britain, 1980, 130 mins.

COMM3TV Vol. 1

An overview of the hard rock and distinctive sounds putout by the Brooklyn-based label, including Brenda Kahn, Poopshovel, Arson Garden, Zuzu's Petals, Big Trouble House and Cattle Prod. 50 mins.
VHS: S19618. $19.95.

Compleat Beatles

Everything the Beatles did best, from the early days at the Cavern Club through eight incredible years to the rooftop goodbye concert during the recording of "Let It Be." The Beatles in concert, in films and in rare footage. Narrated by Malcolm McDowell. England, 1982, 119 mins.
Laser: Re-mastered. LD74484. $34.98.

The Concert for Bangladesh

This groundbreaking concert documentary brought together some of the rock and roll world's great figures. The highlights include a collaboration of Ringo Starr and George Harrison, Bob Dylan's return to live performing following a two-year absence, and a virtuoso turn by guitarist Eric Clapton. With Billy Preston, Leon Russell, Ravi Shankar and Klaus Voormann. "One of the proudest and most remarkable moments in the colorful history of rock and roll" (Robert Hilburn, *Los Angeles Times*).
VHS: S00262. $19.95.
Laser: LD75306. $39.98.
Saul Swimmer, USA, 1972, 95 mins.

The Creation of the Woodstock 1969 Music Festival: Birth of a Generation

Archival photographs, rare film footage and interviews with the producers, planners and performers from this event recall some of the magic of the fabled gathering. 500,000 young people claimed a place and a time for their music and inadvertently named a generation, the Woodstock generation. 60 mins.
VHS: S24313. $19.99.

Crosby, Stills and Nash: Acoustic

Crosby, Stills and Nash perform their greatest hits live at San Francisco's Warfield Theater in November, 1991, with these favorites: *Deja Vu, Helplessly Hoping, Guinnevere, Marrakesh Express, Suite: Judy Blue Eyes, Wooden Ships*, and many more! 80 mins.
Laser: LD72295. $29.95.

Cure—Staring at the Sea

A collection of videos featuring the nihilistic British band The Cure. Songs include "Killing an Arab", "Boys Don't Cry", "Play for Today", "Close to Me" and more. 82 mins.
VHS: S04583. $24.98.

The Cutting Edge

A two-volume collection of the best of The Cutting Edge. Features the highlights from the MTV program featuring The Fleshtones. With Dale Alvin, REM, Willie Dixon, Tom Waits, Jonathan Richman and the Modern Lovers, The Blasters, The Alarm, Red Hot Chili Peppers, Benjamin Weisman, Stan Ridgeway, and Husker Du. Each volume 60 mins.
Volume 1.
VHS: S05205. $24.95.

David Bowie—The Glass Spider Tour

A live two hour concert featuring the vocal talents of entertainer and musician David Bowie. An uncut performance to be released after a 44 minute version is shown on tv on ABC. Musical guests include Peter Frampton.
VHS: S06608. $29.95.
David Mallet, 1988, 120 mins.

Dead Can Dance: Toward the Within

This film provides an in-depth look at the music of Dead Can Dance. It features excerpts from a mesmerizing performance at the Mayfair Theater in Santa Monica and revealing interview footage. Together these elements provide a glimpse into the workings of this singular musical partnership. 75 mins.
VHS: S22508. $19.98.
Laser: LD74609. $34.98.

Decline of Western Civilization—Part II—The Metal Years
Penelope Spheeris follows up her high-decibel look at the punk rock scene with another loud and outrageous concert documentary interview show. Groups include Megadeth, Lizzie Borden, Odin, Seduce and Poison in concert. The truth about backstage and on-the-road revelations from Ozzy Osbourne, Kiss, Aerosmith and Motorhead. Sex, groupies, Satan and make-up tips are discussed.
VHS: S08345. $19.95.
Penelope Spheeris, USA, 1988, 90 mins.

Devo: The Complete Truth About De-Evolution
A look at Devo, whose distinctive voice, enigmatic lyrics and heady stage shows secured their reputation. The numbers include "Whip It," "Beautiful World" and "Satisfaction."
Laser: LD71931. $49.95.

Direct Art, Good Lovin' Guitar Man and Other Works
Includes music videos of the Jickets. With Chett Grant, Larry Lame. Includes *Good Lovin' Guitar Man, Heterosexual Love, Bloody Stump*.
VHS: S10207. $29.95.

Dominoes: Portrait of a Decade
Called "one of the few pieces to authoritatively capture the view from inside the counterculture" by *Video Review*, *Dominoes* is a unique audio-visual portrait of the 60s, conveying the director's view that in the turbulent decade "one thing led to another like dominoes." Composed of footage from both TV news and independent filmmakers, juxtaposed with a soundtrack including B.B. King's "The Thrill Is Gone" and the Rolling Stones' "Gimme Shelter".
Laser: CAV. **LD70106. $49.95.**
John Lawrence Re, USA, 1989, 59 mins.

Don't Look Back
One of the best portraits of an artist ever put on film, *Don't Look Back* is about Bob Dylan and the Sixties. Director Pennebaker, known for *Monterey Pop*, filmed Dylan during his 1965 English concert tour, capturing both private moments and public performances. With Joan Baez, Alan Price, Donovan.
VHS: S00357. $19.98.
D.A. Pennebaker, USA, 1967, 95 mins.

The Doors
Oliver Stone investigates the life of poet-musician Jim Morrison and discovers the rock idol couldn't handle drugs, women or success. Val Kilmer does a reasonable job impersonating the lead singer of *The Doors*, but as wild as the film concerts get, the albums are better. With Meg Ryan, Kyle MacLachlan and Crispin Glover as Andy Warhol. This is the end, my friend.
VHS: S14534. $14.98.
Oliver Stone, USA, 1991, 138 mins.

Dope, Guns and Fucking Up Your Videodeck, Vol. I
A raucous collection of cutting edge video clips by Dr. Sphincter ("Your Guest Host with the Most"), Helmet ("Bad Mood"), Helios Creed ("The Rant"), Cows ("Cartoon Corral"), King Snake Roost ("Top End Killer") and Tar ("Les Paul Worries"). 50 mins.
VHS: S19623. $19.95.

Dope, Guns and Fucking Up Your Videodeck, Vol. II
A radical collection of exuberant videos, most of them shot on high quality 16mm, features the distinctive lyrics and hard-edged soul of Helmet, Cows, Helios Creed, Surgery, Vertigo, Boss Hog, Tar, Godbullies, Cosmic Psychos, The Crows and With Your Host. 50 mins.
VHS: S19619. $19.95.

Dr. Demento's 20th Anniversary Collection
For the first time ever, over a dozen classic twisted tunes have been captured on this spectacular video put together by the doctor himself. Featuring madcap artists such as Spike Jones and Weird Al Yankovic, as well as jazz giants Cab Calloway and Fats Waller. Celebrate two decades of musical lunacy. 45 mins.
VHS: S13794. $19.95.

Enrico Macias Live at the Olympia
Experience the many moods of Enrico Macias in this 1985 performance in front of a sellout audience in Paris. 1985, 105 mins.
VHS: S16191. $69.95.

Freedom Beat: The Video
UK artists against apartheid freedom concert, recorded live on January 5, 1988, including performances by Peter Gabriel, Sade, Elvis Costello, The Style Council, Princess, Maxi Priest and others. 70 mins.
VHS: Out of print. For rental only.
Laser: LD70993. $39.95.

Gimme Shelter
In 1969, the Maysles Brothers followed the Rolling Stones on their North American tour, the climax of which was a free concert for 300,000 fans in Altamont, California. Featuring some of the Stones' most beloved songs, as well as appearances by Tina Turner, Jefferson Airplane and The Flying Burrito Bros., *Gimme Shelter* remains much more than a performance film.
Laser: LD71467. $34.95.
Maysles Brothers/Charlotte Zwerin, USA, 1970

Girls Bite Back
A collection of live recordings from leading alternative groups of the 80s, including Siouxsie & the Banshees, The Slits, Nina Hagen and Girlschool a.m., supplemented by interviews and footage of backstage rehearsals.
VHS: S18257. $19.95.
Wolfgang Buld, USA, 1992, 45 mins.

Go Go Big Beat
This rare rock film presents many of the top 60's British Beat groups in a concert setting, including The Hollies, The Animals, Lulu, The Mersey-Beats and many more.
VHS: S05203. $29.95.
Kenneth Hume, Great Britain, 1964, 25 mins.

Grateful Dead Movie
Both concert footage, and behind-the-scenes backstage mechanics, with Jerry Garcia and Leon Gast—and The Grateful Dead in their original, full-length feature.
VHS: S04787. $39.95.
Jerry Garcia, USA, 1976, 131 mins.

The Great Rock and Roll Swindle (The Sex Pistols)
Julien Temple's strange and brilliant essay about the decadence of the extraordinary British punk act, the Sex Pistols. The film intersperses early footage with late period set pieces, including Sid Vicious' elegant and dark cover of *My Way*. "It adds up to the most innovative comic strip fantasy since Tashlin" (*Time Out*). With Malcolm McLaren, Sid Vicious and Johnny Rotten.
VHS: S18405. $24.98.
Julien Temple, Great Britain, 1979, 104 mins.

Grokgazer
Todd Rundgren's music is paired with fantastic computer-generated art reminiscent of pop/psychedelic imagery from the 1960's. This visual concert hall for the mind showcases intricate and evolving forms, colors and shapes. 45 mins.
VHS: S26091. $14.95.

Grow Live Monsters
A compilation of early films (1971-1976) of Detroit cult band Destroy All Monsters by founding member Cary Loren, including live performances of the band. "This insane one-hour comp is pre-'76 underground-style music videos from the original Destroy All Monsters Band...crammed with FX, multi-layered horror and hallucination images, found footage (Godzilla, John Agar, Vampira, The Ghoul! and even some live Iggy) and visual focal point Niagara appears as a vampire, a mermaid, a cannibal (and naked)" (*Psychotronic Video*).
VHS: S30410. $19.95.

Guitar Legends
This program looks at the techniques of acoustic and electric guitar players and considers their musical roots and influences. The works include Jeff Beck's "Definitely Maybe", Johnny Winter's "Johnny B. Goode", B.B. King's "Heartbreaker", Jimi Hendrix's "Hey Joe" and Eric Clapton's (with Delaney and Bonnie) "Tribute to Robert Johnson". 33 mins.
VHS: S19315. $14.98.

Hated: GG Allin and the Murder Junkies
A portait of GG Allin, the punk artist who was found dead from a drug overdose on the Lower East Side in June, 1993. Allin's sado-masochistic act resulted in more than 50 arrests. The songs include "Die When You Die," "Snakeman's Dance," "I Wanna Kill You" and "Bite It You Scum." "*Hated* lies somewhere between the satiric world of *Spinal Tap* and the tragic world of *Dream Deceivers*" (*The Village Voice*).
VHS: S19699. $29.95.
Todd Philipps, USA, 1993, 60 mins.

Heart and Soul
The official Monkee videography, featuring music videos from their album *Pool It*, as well as interviews. 40 mins.
VHS: S05877. $16.95.

Hullabaloo (Chuck Berry et al.)
This four-volume boxed set brings back all the best 60's music from the hit television show *Hullabaloo*. Sonny and Cher, Petula Clark, The Supremes, The Yardbirds, Sammy Davis, Jr., The Everly Brothers, Trini Lopez, The Mamas and the Papas, and Chuck Berry are just a few of the legendary performers featured on this collection. Even the Hullabaloo dancers are back again. Each volume is 60 minutes long.
VHS: S24086. $79.98.

Hullabaloo (Simon & Garfunkel et al.)
The fondly remembered music variety show from the '60s showcases rock artists performing the biggest hits of the decade along with the legendary Hullabaloo dancers and a special celebrity guest host for each program. The Supremes, The Righteous Brothers, and Simon and Garfunkel are among the 50 featured musical acts. Features bonus segments from London hosted by Beatles manager Brian Epstein. Four-volume boxed set includes Vols. 9-12. 260 mins.
VHS: S34089. $79.95.

Hype!
Doug Pray's critically acclaimed rockumentary chronicles the Northwest grunge rock explosion and the birth of the "Seattle sound." Features interviews and rare performances from more than 20 bands, including Nirvana, Mudhoney, Love Battery and 7 Year Bitch, recorded during the golden age of grunge. "The funniest rock film since *Spinal Tap*" (Tim Appelo, *The Oregonian*).
VHS: S31790. $19.95.
Doug Pray, USA, 1995, 84 mins.

Imagine: John Lennon
Subtitled the definitive film portrait. Lennon himself eerily narrates his life story, taken from the tapes he made previous to his murder. Culled from over 200 hours of material supplied by his widow, Yoko Ono. 36 songs are featured.
VHS: S08498. $24.98.
Laser: LD70598. $24.98.
Andrew Solt, USA, 1988, 100 mins.

In Love with These Times
The program features numbers by Verlaines, Gordons, Tall Dwarfs, The Chills, Snapper, Headless Chickens and Straightjacket Fits. 60 mins.
VHS: S19626. $19.95.

It's Hullabaloo!
Shows of the popular music show from 1965-66 are collected in this set of four volumes. Famous guest hosts like Frankie Avalon, Annette, Soupy Sales and Petula Clark will inspire uncontrollable outbreaks of nostalgia. But it's music from The Shangri-Las, Marianne Faithfull, Brenda Lee, The Rolling Stones, The Supremes, Lola Falana, The Everly Brothers and more that make this collection so worthwhile. Each video is approximately 60 mins.
VHS: S27638. $79.98.

James Brown
Get to know "the Godfather of Soul," whose explosive energy and innovative sound revolutionized popular music, in this *A & E Biography*. 50 mins.
VHS: S30099. $19.95.

James Brown & Guest B.B. King
James Brown, the "Godfather of Soul," in a taped concert at the Beverly Theater, where he performs "It's a Man's World," "Papa's Got a Brand New Bag," "Hot Pants" and "Sex Machine." Also featured are B.B. King—who performs his legendary "Thrill Is Gone"—and Michael Jackson, who does a song and dance number. 66 mins.
VHS: S19581. $14.95.

James Brown: The Lost James Brown Tapes
Discovered in the archives of producer Alan Douglas, this is a previously unseen 1979 performance of "Mr. Dynamite" himself. Highlights include a heart-stopping 20-minute rendition of *Sex Machine*. 60 mins.
VHS: S16090. $14.98.

Janis
Rock immortal Janis Joplin in the best cinematic portrait of her stellar but troubled career. Through interviews and concert footage, the documentary traces the gritty-voiced rocker from her childhood to superstardom.
VHS: S03310. $19.95.
Howard Alk/Seaton Findlay, Canada, 1974, 97 mins.

Jerry Lee Lewis: I Am What I Am
The real-life story of "The Killer" as told by Lewis himself and a host of celebrities, including Kris Kristofferson, Roy Orbison, Johnny Cash, Chuck Berry, Dick Clark and Mickey Gilley. Loaded with live performances of Lewis' great hits, including "Great Balls of Fire", "Whole Lotta Shakin' Goin' On", "Breathless" and "Crazy Arms".
VHS: S09608. $19.95.

Jimi Hendrix Live at the Isle of Wight, 1970
Filmed 18 days before Hendrix's death, this series of Isle of Wight concerts held on East Afton Farm in England captures one of the greatest performances of the guitar legend ever recorded. Features Mitch Mitchell on drums and Billy Cox on bass.
VHS: S30248. $19.98.
Laser: LD76072. $29.99.
DVD: DV60354. $24.99.
Murray Lerner, USA, 1970/1991, 59 mins.

The Jimi Hendrix Story

A documentary on Jimi Hendrix, perhaps the most innovative player in history. The filmmakers interweave concert footage and interviews with the enigmatic figure and his confidantes and collaborators. The songs include "Purple Haze," "Wild Thing" and "Johnny B. Goode," directed by Joe Boyd, John Head and Gary Weis.

VHS: S02818. $19.98.

Joe Boyd/John Head/Gary Weis, USA, 1973, 102 mins.

Jimi Hendrix: Experience

Narrated by British blues master Alexis Korner, *Experience* features Hendrix on- and off-stage in 1967. The program also includes a rare acoustic performance.

VHS: S16091. $14.98.

Peter Neal, Great Britain, 33 mins.

Jimi Hendrix: Woodstock

This legendary rock star was perhaps the finest guitarist and vocalist of his generation. Now on the occasion of the 25th anniversary of the amazing event that was Woodstock, his performance from this concert has been transferred to laserdisc. 57 mins.

Laser: LD74498. $24.98.

Jimi Plays Berkeley

Classic Hendrix live at the 1970 Berkeley Memorial Day Concert with Mitch Mitchell on drums and Billy Cox on bass.

VHS: S00655. $19.98.

Peter Pilafian, USA, 1971, 55 mins.

Jimi Plays Monterey

An historic, electrifying Hendrix performance with band members Noel Redding and Mitch Mitchell. Songs: "Can You See Me," "Sgt. Pepper's Lonely Hearts Club Band," "Wild Thing," "Monterey," "Killing Floor," "Foxy Lady," "Like a Rolling Stone," "Rock Me Baby," "Hey Joe," "The Wind Cries Mary" and "Purple Haze." 50 mins.

VHS: S31656. $14.98.

Joe Cocker: Mad Dogs & Englishmen

This neglected work is considered by many to be one of the classic rock films of the 1970s, along with *The Last Waltz* and *Woodstock*. This outrageous rock tour comes complete with traveling groupies, psychedelic drugs, families and their dogs—a fantastic, loving portrait of an excessive musical era which will likely never be repeated again. Presented in letterbox format.

VHS: S15742. $19.95.

Pierre Adige, USA, 1971, 119 mins.

John Lennon: The Bed-In

On May 26, 1969, John Lennon and Yoko Ono moved into Room 1742 of the Queen Elizabeth Hotel in Montreal, and for seven days, from their bed, talked about peace to anyone who would listen. This program features 74 minutes of conversations with Timothy Leary, Tommy Smothers and Al Capp among others. Also includes the classic live bedroom recording of "Give Peace a Chance", "Instant Karma", "Remember Love", John's acoustic version of "Because" and many more.

VHS: S18223. $24.95.

Killdozer "Li'l Baby Huntin'" Live

This hard-edged trio from Madison perform some dazzling works from their *Burl and Snakeboy* album. The highlights are covers of Neil Diamond and Neil Young, as well as "Hamburger Martyr" and "King of Sex." 50 mins.

VHS: S20247. $19.95.

Latino Session

Latin artists combine their distinct sounds for a powerful anthology. The major works include Carlos Santana's versions of "America the Beautiful" and "Mandela", Ruben Blades' "Ojos De Perro Azul" and "Muevete", and collaborations with Celia Cruz, Tito Puente and Poncho Sanchez. 60 mins.

VHS: S19317. $19.98.

Led Zeppelin: Song Remains the Same

The midnight cult favorite on video! Led Zeppelin's legendary 1973 concert appearance at Madison Square Garden, featuring 13 of the band's best songs. USA, 1976, 137 mins.

VHS: S02915. $19.98.

Lifestyles of the Ramones

This program looks at the evolution of the music of the Ramones, with interviews with the members of the band they influenced, Talking Heads, and Debbie Harry. 58 mins.

Laser: LD70263. $29.95.

Little Richard: Keep on Rockin'

Catch the original wildman of rock 'n' roll at his onstage finest! Seen through the camera of D.A. Pennebaker, Little Richard tears through "Tutti Frutti", "Lucille" and six more favorites.

VHS: S16092. $14.98.

D.A. Pennebaker, USA, 30 mins.

Live Skull "Skullf*ck"

This mercurial, brooding act is captured live during a 1987 *Cloud One* tour, with additional works from their albums *Bringing Home the Bait* and *Pusherman*. The numbers include "Fort Belvedere," "Sparky" and "Wallow in It." 45 mins.

VHS: S20248. $19.95.

Lou Reed

Legendary Lou Reed performs all of his best-known hits, including songs from The Velvet Underground. 60 mins.

VHS: S06551. $19.98.

Lou Reed: Rock & Roll Heart

Overflowing with archival performance footage, this documentary spans over three decades, from the formation of the Velvet Underground, to Reed's extensive solo career, to a collaboration on the futuristic rock opera *Time Rocker*. Interviews with Reed, his friends and band members and commentary on Reed's influence by David Bowie, David Byrne, Patti Smith, Suzanne Vega, Dave Stewart, and Philip Glass. 75 mins.

VHS: S34561. $19.98.

Madonna: Truth or Dare

The popular musical superstar is the focus, and the executive producer, of this revealing documentary/concert movie that captures the excitement of her 1990 Blonde Ambition world tour. Visit backstage as Madonna chats with Kevin Costner, Sandra Bernhard and Warren Beatty. Come along when she visits her mother's grave. Be there when she leads her dancers and back-up singers in a group prayer. Then sit back and enjoy the sound and fury of blonde ambition in concert.

VHS: S14762. $19.98.

Alek Keshishian, USA, 1991, 118 mins.

Magical Mystery Tour

One of the Beatles' last appearances together, this musical fantasy features such songs as "I Am the Walrus" and "Fool on the Hill." 60 mins.

VHS: S04691. $19.98.
Laser: CLV. LD72095. $29.98.
DVD: DV60124. $19.98.

Mamas & The Papas: Straight Shooter

The life, loves and music of John Phillips, "Mama" Cass Elliott, Michelle Phillips and Denny Doherty in one of the archetypal 60's recreations. 80 mins.

VHS: S09793. $19.95.

Message to Love: The Isle of Wight Festival: The Movie

Capturing what many have called the last great rock festival, this 1970 film of "Britain's Woodstock" features legendary performances by The Who, Joan Baez, Leonard Cohen, Miles Davis, Donovan, Bob Dylan, Kris Kristofferson, Joni Mitchell, Free, The Moody Blues, John Sebastian, Taste, Ten Years After and Jethro Tull, the debut performance of Emerson, Lake and Palmer, the last stage performance by Jim Morrison with the Doors, and Jimi Hendrix, 18 days before his death. "A vintage concert film...that dwarfs its contemporaries" (*Spin*).

VHS: S31625. $19.95.
DVD: DV60141. $24.98.

Murray Lerner, Great Britain, 1970, 120 mins.

Metal Roots

This heavy metal sampler includes Black Sabbath's "Iron Man" and "Black Sabbath", Alice Cooper's "Eighteen", Steppenwolf's "Rock Me" and Deep Purple's "Highway Star". 38 mins.

VHS: S19316. $14.98.

The Mike Douglas Show— John Lennon & Yoko Ono

The week that John Lennon and Yoko Ono hosted the Mike Douglas Show made for five strange days that changed the course of television. Guests included Chuck Berry, George Carlin, Black Panther leader Bobby Seale, consumer advocate Ralph Nader, Frank Gorshin and others. Includes 48-page hardcover book with new and rare interviews and previously unpublished photos. Five-tape box set. Each tape is 75 mins.

VHS: S34257. $99.95.

Ministry: In Case You Didn't Feel Like Showing Up

A documentary on Ministry's last tour, combining visuals and music and the crazed attention and energy of its audience. "This live concert is an unmitigated classic" (*Video Review*).

Laser: LD70257. $29.95.

Monterey Pop

Directed by one of the foremost factual filmmakers in the cinema-verite style, *Monterey Pop* records the events at the immense Monterey International Pop Festival. Featuring Otis Redding, Jimi Hendrix, Janis Joplin, Jefferson Airplane, Ravi Shankar.

VHS: S00876. $19.98.
Laser: LD70422. $49.95.

D.A. Pennebaker, USA, 1968, 98 mins.

Music for Montserrat

Legendary producer George Martin assembled some of the world's greatest music stars in this benefit concert for the island of Montserrat. Performing their hits in this all-star show are Elton John, Phil Collins, Sting, Eric Clapton, Jimmy Buffet, Paul McCartney, Carl Perkins, Mark Knopfler and Arrow. 112 mins.

VHS: S34917. $19.95.
Laser: LD77000. $29.99.
DVD: DV60374. $24.99.

My First Name Is Maceo

James Brown's longtime alto sax man steps forward to blow his horn in this portrait of the musician better known as a sideman than as a star. When Brown when to prison in the late '80s, Maceo became a bandleader in his own right with funk pioneers trombonist Fred Wesley and tenor saxophonist Pee Wee Ellis. Includes 1994 concert and rehearsal footage in New York, New Orleans and on the road, as well as revealing interviews. With George Clinton and Kim Mazelle.

VHS: S32686. $19.95.

Markus Gruber, USA, 1996, 87 mins.

New Wave Hits of the '80s, Volume 1

This is the most comprehensive series of 80's music ever. "Video Killed the Radio", "Star", "Love Plus One", "Come on Eileen", "Girls on Film", "I Eat Cannibals", "I Want Candy" and "Twilight Zone" are just some of the tunes included in this video. 35 mins.

VHS: S22446. $14.98.

New Wave Hits of the '80s, Volume 2: Just Can't Get Enough

This is the continuation of the most comprehensive series of 80's music ever. Included are "Pop Muzik", "I Ran (So Far Away)", "Mickey", "In a Big Country", "True", "Stand By", "One Thing Leads to Another", "Metro" and many more. 35 mins.

VHS: S22447. $14.98.

Nico Icon

An "entrancingly lurid" (Owen Gleiberman, *Entertainment Weekly*) documentary about the German *uber*model from cover girl to cameo in Fellini's *La Dolce Vita*; from European pop diva to Andy Warhol superstar and Velvet Underground zombie chanteuse in the late '60s; from self-destructive heroin addict to her death in 1988 from a cerebral hemorrhage at age 49. A scrupulous assemblage of home movies, performance clips and interviews with director and fellow Warhol superstar Paul Morrissey, Jackson Browne (Nico's lover when he was 17) and Nico's son by Alain Delon (although he denied paternity), Ari, whom she turned on to heroin.

VHS: S32679. $59.98.
DVD: DV60164. $24.98.

Susanne Ofteringer, Germany, 1995, 75 mins.

No Alternative

Alternative rock bands like Soul Asylum, Smashing Pumpkins and Soundgarden join directors Tamra Davis (*Guncrazy*), Derek Jarman (*War Requiem*), Nick Gomez (*Laws of Gravity*), Jennie Livingston (*Paris Is Burning*) and Hal Hartley (*Simple Man*) in a compilation of short films and music videos that serve as a massive public education campaign for HIV/AIDS prevention among millions of teenage and twenty-something music fans worldwide. 65 mins.

VHS: S21040. $14.95.

Orchestral Tribute to the Beatles

Joan Collins hosts this program which features the Royal Philharmonic Orchestra in classic renditions of famous Beatles songs, performed for the Queen of England. 52 mins.

VHS: S04945. $14.95.

Otis Redding: Shake

One of Redding's few live performances on film. Featuring heart-stopping versions of "Shake," "Respect," "I've Been Loving You Too Long," "(I Can't Get No) Satisfaction" and "Try a Little Tenderness." 19 mins.

VHS: S31657. $12.98.

Paul Anka '62

An insightful documentary filmed in 1962, when Anka was at the crest of his popularity, featuring excerpts of many of his greatest hits, including "Lonely Boy", "Diana", "Put Your Head on My Shoulder" and others. 34 mins.

VHS: S20566. $14.95.

Peter Gabriel: Secret World Live
This pop star's exciting show combines spectacle and music. Filmed live at Modena, Italy, it captures the performance of Gabriel's many hits, including "Steam", "Digging in the Dirt", "Red Rain", "Kiss That Frog", "Don't Give Up" and many more.
VHS: S22534. $24.95.
Laser: LD74815. $39.99.

Pink Floyd: The Wall
Bob Geldof stars as Pink, the burned-out rock star slowly going out of control. Conceived and written by Pink Floyd's Roger Waters, with animation by Gerald Scarfe and songs off the album.
Laser: LD70654. $34.98.
Alan Parker, Great Britain, 1983, 95 mins.

Pointer Sisters Live in Africa
The dazzling Pointers team up with a native African band in a sizzling hour of swing and standards. Includes "Ring Ding Do," "Salt Peanuts" and "Steam Heat." 45 mins.
VHS: S11702. $19.95.

Prince: Sign "O" the Times
Prince's new, critically-acclaimed concert film, which intersperses dramatic vignettes with Prince's top singles.
VHS: S06618. $19.95.

Psychedelic High
It's a collection of psychedelic hits hosted by VH-1's Peter Noone, including The Byrds, The Moody Blues, The Who, Blue Cheer, Small Faces, The Rice, Thunder Clap Rewman, and even The Crazy World of Arthur Brown. 32 mins.
VHS: S20980. $14.98.

Punk and Its After Shocks
In this absorbing documentary, filmmaker Wolfgang Buld shot live recordings by The Clash, The Police, Sex Pistols, Madness, Jam and other seminal acts from December 1979 to January 1980, crosscut with interviews that establish the political, social and artistic flowering of the movement.
VHS: S18256. $19.95.
Wolfgang Buld, USA, 1992, 85 mins.

The Punk Rock Movie
Vulgar, chaotic, noisy and rude, *The Punk Rock Movie* captures the era's great bands and safety-pinned fans in all their raw glory. Candid on- and offstage footage provides a rare look at young rock 'n' rollers who uncompromisingly dared to believe in themselves and their music. With Siouxsie and the Banshees, The Sex Pistols, The Clash, Generation X with Billy Idol and more. 80 mins.
VHS: S12180. $39.95.

Pussy Galore: Maximum Penetration
An ode to the honesty and power of Pussy Galore, the New York band fronted by lead singer Jon Spencer. "They're the blood and guts of New York City. Homeless bums in subway stations, the Tompkins Square Riot, dirt, the Hudson river, smut and drug addicts all somehow get wrapped up, dropped in the meat grinder, and squeezed into the grooves of every…album" (Rich Shupe, *Reflex Magazine*). 50 mins.
VHS: S19628. $19.95.

Quadrophenia
A compelling adaptation of the Who's classic rock opera featuring Sting. Inspired soundtrack by the Who, and startling images of the street fighting between Mods and Rockers in 1964 England.
VHS: S01076. $19.95.
Franc Roddam, Great Britain, 1979

Rainbow Bridge
A psychedelic journey featuring Jimi Hendrix at his concert in Maui, the film follows a woman's search to see what lies beyond our realities. Inner space of the mind is explored through the use of drugs, the outer space of consciousness is explored through music and meditation.
VHS: S01653. $19.95.
Laser: LD76230. $49.98.
Chuck Wein, USA, 1971, 74 mins.

Remembering the Summer of Love and Other Songs
A musical tribute to Bill Graham. Also includes several songs from the musical play by Claire Burch: *It's a Blues to Be Called Crazy When Crazy's All There Is.*
VHS: S33815. $24.95.
Claire Burch, USA, 1992, 30 mins.

The Residents: Twenty Twisted Questions
This "alternative music" group began breaking the boundaries and corrupting notions of pop in 1971. Self-made pioneers of the music video, they became—and remain—the definitive audiovisual concept band. *Twenty Twisted Questions* documents two decades of musical innovation, bold experimentation and independent vision. 60 mins.
Laser: CAV. LD71486. $49.95.

Ringo Starr and His All-Starr Band
The legendary drummer of The Beatles is joined by musicians Joe Walsh, Burton Cummings, Todd Rundgren, Nils Logfren, Dave Edmunds and Zak Starkey as they perform versions of "Yellow Submarine," "I Can't Tell You Why," "Bang on the Drum," "American Woman," "In the City," With a Little Help from My Friends," "You're Sixteen," "Rocky Mountain Way," "No Time," "I Hear You Knocking" and many others. 120 mins.
VHS: S19914. $19.98.

The Road to God Knows Where
Cinema verite that follows the experiences of Nick Cave and the Bad Seeds during a recent road tour. Bracketed by five video clips, the film offers memorable covers of John Lee Hooker's "Mini Skirts," "I'm Gonna Killa That Woman" and Johnny Cash's "The Singer." The 24 tracks include "Sorrow's Child," "Getting to Phoenix," "Saint Huck" and "Wade in the Water." 113 mins.
VHS: S19611. $19.95.

Rock in the UK
The Hollies, The Spencer Davis Group with Stevie Winwood, The Kinks, Jethro Tull and even The Bee Gees are just some of the recording artists singing their most popular hits in this collection hosted by Peter Noone of VH-1. 32 mins.
VHS: S20979. $14.98.

Rock, Rock, Rock
The film debut of Tuesday Weld. She plays a teenager with a problem. She needs to raise money for a strapless formal for the prom after father took away her charge card. Made in the Bronx in nine days. Great bands include Frankie Lymon and the teenagers, LaVern Baker, Chuck Berry, The Moonglows and rock promoter Alan Freed. Connie Francis supplies the singing voice for the 13-year-old Weld. B&W.
VHS: S10389. $24.95.
Will Price, USA, 1956, 85 mins.

Rockroots
This educational musical journey traces the roots and rhythms of American pop music from its rural beginnings to the latest technology. The Rockroots Band takes a live audience through all the trends, including folk, blues, swing, R&B, country, rockabilly, Motown, British invasion, rap and more.
VHS: S22477. $99.95.

The Rolling Stones Rock & Roll Circus
On December 11, 1968, the Rolling Stones, led by head ringmaster Mick Jagger, assembled some of their friends, including John Lennon and Yoko Ono, The Who, Eric Clapton, Marianne Faithfull, Jethro Tull, Taj Mahal, and the Jimi Hendrix Experience's Mitch Mitchell for a swinging two-day musical circus in London. Twenty-eight years later, this quirky, incomplete chapter in rock history is available for the first time on video. "*The Rolling Stones Rock & Roll Circus* is a time capsule.
Two days in December 1968 that in many ways capture the spontaneity, aspirations and communal spirit of an entire era… for a brief moment it seemed that rock 'n' roll would inherit the earth" (David Dalton).
VHS: S30142. $24.95.
Michael Lindsay Hogg, Great Britain, 1968, 65 mins.

Rolling Stones—25 x 5: The Continuing Adventures of the Rolling Stones
The definitive history of the Rolling Stones, told for the first time ever by the band themselves. Rocking with a soundtrack of nearly 40 songs, this video-document takes you inside the Stones' personal archives. 129 mins.
VHS: S15311. $19.98.

Rrrecords "Testament" Vol. II
This work penetrates an obscure though growing phenomenon, the emerging international industrial underground that highlights clips from Japanese act Merzbow and Americans Arcane Device, Chop Shop, Generator, Monty Cantsin and works from Naram Sin, Takell-Kizimecca and Pile of Cows. 55 mins.
VHS: S20246. $19.95.

Running out of Luck
Mick Jagger's feature-length film, the story of a rock and roll superstar (Mick) who's isolated from the real world by the beautiful-people hangers-on, features nine songs from Mick's *She's the Boss* solo album.
VHS: S01522. $79.98.
Julien Temple, USA, 1985, 88 mins.

San Francisco Sound
Casey Kasem showcases the sounds of Haight-Ashbury and the "Summer of Love" in this video flashback to one of rock's most experimental periods. Van Morrison, Carlos Santana, Janis Joplin and The Grateful Dead are featured. 39 mins.
VHS: S08036. $19.98.

Shindig! British Invasion, Vol. 1
A collection works from the best English groups of the 60s, including Gerry and the Pacemakers ("Don't Let the Sun Catch You Crying"), Manfred Mann ("Doo Wah Diddy"), Searchers ("Needles and Pins"), The Honeycombs ("Have I the Right") and Freddy and the Dreamers ("I'm Telling You Now"). 30 mins.
VHS: S19635. $9.98.

Shindig! British Invasion, Vol. 2
One of the most important developments in rock and roll is recounted in this program of musical acts who changed the shape and texture of American music, featuring Freddy & the Dreamers, Manfred Mann, The Zombies, The Animals, Gerry & the Pacemakers, The Yardbirds, and The Searchers. 30 mins.
VHS: S17403. $14.95.

Shindig! Frat Party
Presenting an all-star lineup of talent, this fast-stepping music and dance program is guaranteed to get you onto the dance floor. Featuring The Kingsmen, The Isley Brothers, and the sensational Little Richard. 1965, 30 mins.
VHS: S13927. $14.95.

Shindig! Groovy Gals
Screaming teens dance to songs of first love, heartache and undying devotion performed live by the legendary ladies of pop music. Includes Aretha Franklin, Tina Turner and Petula Clark. 30 mins.
VHS: S14688. $12.95.

Shindig! Jackie Wilson
This volume of the popular series features electrifying performances by Jackie Wilson—lighting up the stage like only he could, with acrobatic moves, an illustrious voice, and a raw sexuality that helped turn him into a legend. 1965, 30 mins.
VHS: S13928. $14.95.

Shindig! Jerry Lee Lewis
It's "The Killer" setting the stage ablaze with his fancy licks and rip-roaring voice. Includes "Great Balls of Fire" and "Whole Lotta Shakin'". 30 mins.
VHS: S15642. $14.95.

Shindig! Legends of Rock 'n' Roll
A compendium of classic rock and roll performances culled from the '60s music series, featuring The Righteous Brothers, Jerry Lee Lewis, Aretha Franklin, Tina Turner, Bo Diddley, Little Anthony and the Imperials, Johnny Cash, the Everly Brothers, Chuck Berry, and the Godfather of Soul, James Brown. 30 mins.
VHS: S17402. $14.95.

Shindig! Motor City Magic
This episode of the classic prime-time pop music show features performances from The Four Tops, The Supremes, Smokey Robinson and the Miracles, The Temptations, and Marvin Gaye. 1964, 30 mins.
VHS: S13926. $14.95.

Shindig! Sixties Superstars
Get an eye- and earful of the hottest rock acts of the '60s. Includes performances by The Byrds and The Mamas & Papas. 30 mins.
VHS: S15643. $14.95.

Shindig! Soul
Your heart will ache and feet will fly as the sensual and soothing sounds of sweet soul music are performed live by some of the all-time greats. Includes Booker T and the MGs, James Brown and Aretha Franklin. 30 mins.
VHS: S14687. $12.95.

Shindig! The Kinks
This great 60s group is captured in the numbers, "You Really Got Me," "Set Me Free," "See My Friends," "All Day and All of the Night" and "I'm a Lover Not a Fighter." 30 mins.
VHS: S19636. $9.98.

Shindig! The Righteous Brothers
The Righteous Brothers perform their hits "Unchained Melodies," "You've Lost that Lovin' Feeling," "Little Latin Lupe Lu," "Justine" and "Night Time Is the Right Time." 30 mins.
VHS: S19634. $9.98.

Simon and Garfunkel: The Concert in Central Park
On September 19, 1981, Paul Simon and Art Garfunkel set foot on a stage in front of half a million adoring fans who were gathered in Central Park in New York City to witness musical history—the reunion, after 11 long years, of two of the most talented performers to make music during the turbulent 60's. USA, 1982, 87 mins.
VHS: S15345. $14.98.

Stone Temple Pilots: Live
The energy of today's hottest band, winner of a Grammy for Best Hard Rock Performance with Vocal, is captured in this video that features footage from their breakthrough tour. "Vasoline", "Silvergun Superman", "Crackerman", "Meatplow", "Still Remains", "Creep", "Andy Warhol" and "Plush" are among the songs included. 80 mins.
Laser: LD74644. $29.98.

Storytelling Giant: The Talking Heads Retrospective

Ten music videos featuring The Talking Heads plus original segments made especially for this collection. Includes *Crosseyed and Painless, Once in a Lifetime, Wild Wild Life, Love for Sale, This Must Be the Place, Burning Down the House, And She Was, Stay Up Late, Road to Nowhere, The Lady Don't Mind*. 60 mins.
VHS: S06638. $19.98.

Thin White Rope: The Axis Calls

A documentary of The Rope's final tour was shot on location in Europe. A fascinating companion piece to their recent *One That Got Away*, the film contrasts the difficulties of the road with their exuberant stage shows at huge festival gigs. The musical highlights are live versions of "Ruby Sea," "Hunter's Moon," "Red Sun" and "The Fish Song." 75 mins.
VHS: S20250. $19.95.

Tie-Died: Rock 'n' Roll' s Most Deadicated Fans

Though the original Grateful Dead no longer exist since the death of Jerry Garcia, the fans of this quintessential rock band will keep the memory of the music alive. These followers are known for the caravan atmosphere they created around the band's tours. In this unabashed documentary, these fans share their dreams and their desires.
VHS: S27882. $19.98.
Laser: LD75977. $39.99.
Andrew Behar, USA, 1995, 88 mins.

Time Warner Presents the History of Rock 'n' Roll

Over 10,000 hours of concert and archival footage have been culled to compile this complete history of Rock 'n' Roll. Ten volumes, each covering a specific aspect of this cultural phenomenon, show everything from Elvis to the MTV revolution.
Volume 1: Rock 'n' Roll Explodes. Blues, gospel and jazz are fused into a new musical sound. This volume features Elvis Presley, Chuck Berry, Fats Domino, The Beatles and more.
VHS: S24087. $19.98.
Volume 2: Good Rockin' Tonight. Buddy Holly, Dick Clark, Bono, The Ronettes, and even The King were all caught up in the 50's teen idol craze. *American Bandstand* made idols overnight and set alight a new dance fad every week.
VHS: S24088. $19.98.
Volume 3: Britain Invades, America Fights Back. The Beatles and The Stones vied for influence against Motown and the California sound.
VHS: S24089. $19.98.
Volume 4: Plugging In. Dylan, The Byrds, Jimi Hendrix, The Who and The Beatles all participated in the musical experimentation of the 1960's.
VHS: S24090. $19.98.
Volume 5: The Sounds of Soul. Motown transformed popular music with stars like Sam Cooke, Sam and Dave, Ray Charles, The Jackson 5, Whitney Houston and so many more.
VHS: S24091. $19.98.
Volume 6: My Generation. A full-fledged counterculture emerged and rock played a major role shaping this new cultural force. The Jefferson Airplane, Janis Joplin, The Doors, Neil Young, The Grateful Dead and a host of other performers made the music that transformed a generation.
VHS: S24092. $19.98.
Volume 7: Guitar Heroes. Hendrix, Van Halen, Duane Allman, Clapton, Townsend, Slash, U2 and other guitar heroes set new standards for rock and roll.
VHS: S24093. $19.98.
Volume 8: The 70's: Have a Nice Decade. Metal, glam, disco, reggae and funk were innovations from new stars like Elton John, Steely Dan, Pink Floyd, Frampton and Springsteen.
VHS: S24094. $19.98.
Volume 9: Punk. Before Nirvana and Green Day there were The Sex Pistols, Iggy Pop, The Ramones, Elvis Costello, The Talking Heads and other musical icons.
VHS: S24095. $19.98.
Volume 10: Up from the Underground. Rap and alternative conquered musical worlds through MTV. R.E.M., U2, Smashing Pumpkins, Salt'n'Pepa, and even Michael Jackson made it big through music videos.
VHS: S24096. $19.98.
Time Warner Presents the History of Rock 'n' Roll, Complete Set.
VHS: S24097. $159.92.
Laser: LD74966. $199.99.

True Story of 200 Motels

A one-hour documentary on the making of Frank Zappa's bizarre 1971 comic musical. Vintage private footage from Frank's personal archives plus behind-the-scenes of the actual shooting and recording. With Ringo Starr, Theodore Bikel, Keith Moon and such songs as "Sleeping in a Jar," and "Strictly Genteel." The inside history of the first feature-length film to be shot on video in 6 days. 60 mins.
Laser: LD70196. $39.98.

Tupac Shakur: Thug Immortal

Details the life of rap artist Tupac Shakur through never-before-seen home video footage and interviews with those who knew him best. 90 mins.
VHS: S33256. $19.98.

Twelve O'Clock High, Vol. 1

A vivid collection of the hippest sound in alternative music, with works by Pussy Galore, Savage Republic, Crime and the City, Thin White Rope, Live Skull, Mudhoney, Tall Dwarfs, American Music Club and Soul Asylum. 58 mins.
VHS: S19625. $19.95.

Twelve O'Clock High, Vol. 2

A collection of leading video clips, including vital works from The Flaming Lips, Bad Brains, Babes in Toyland, Foetus, Inc., David Atherton, Thin White Rope, Afghan Whigs and Buffalo Tom. 50 mins.
VHS: S19622. $19.95.

U2: Rattle and Hum

A concert film from the hot Irish group of musicians as they tour the United States and visit places like Elvis Presley's Graceland and a church in Harlem. Songs include "Where the Streets Have No Name", "With or Without You" and "Pride (In the Name of Love)". With the musical talents of Larry Mullen Jr., Adam Clayton, Bono and The Edge.
VHS: S09924. $19.95.
Laser: LD75279. $34.98.
Phil Joanou, USA, 1988, 90 mins.

Video Band War Dance

A collection of music video art from the San Francisco-based War Dance. Includes *War Dance, Reagan Commercials, California Zones*, and other pieces. 30 mins.
VHS: S10210. $29.95.

Video Network Program One

An eclectic collection of videos from leading Pacific Northwest indy bands, including Nirvana, Mudhoney, Mark Lanegan, The Fluid, Thee Headcoats, Dwarves, Tad, Afghan Whigs, Seaweed, Beat Happening and Walkabouts. 50 mins.
VHS: S19621. $19.95.

Video Network Program Two

A provocative collection of 21 music videos by leading alternative music groups. With cover art by Peter Bagge. The numbers include Sub Pop's "It," Fastbacks' "Gone to the Moon," Big Chief's "Drive It Off," Pond's "Agatha" and Codeine's "Realize." 70 mins.
VHS: S19615. $19.95.

Video Void VIII

A collection of rock, jazz music and poetry recorded at Neither/Nor, the now-closed East village bookstore and performance space. This tape is fresh and lively.
VHS: S10192. $37.95.
Rick van Valkenburg, USA, 1987, 30 mins.

Virge Piersol Short Pieces

A fixed camera black-and-white documentary of musical performances at Jeffrey Lohn's loft. A good portrait of the NYC "art band" aesthetic, featuring solo performances by Laurie Anderson, Rhys Chatham, Glenn Branca.
VHS: S10190. $49.95.
Virge Piersol, USA, 1978, 58 mins.

The Wavy Gravy Birthday Benefit for Seva Foundation

Documents a benefit concert for Seva Foundation and Camp Winnarainbow on activist Wavy Gravy's birthday, featuring Bob Weir of the Grateful Dead, Paul Kantner of Jefferson Airplane, Maria Muldauer, and others.
VHS: S33819. $24.95.
Claire Burch, USA, 1997, 58 mins.

We've Come for Your Daughters

A compilation work of the emerging acts on the vibrant Seattle label, including Treepeople, Icky Joey, Deadspot, Tonedogs, Vexed, Hammerbox and Coffin Break. 40 mins.
VHS: S19617. $19.95.

Welcome to My Nightmare

Alice Cooper's original hell-raising rock 'n' roll spectacular is now available on video. For the uninitiated, Alice is only a stage name for an energetic guy with a fondness for large snakes and the Grand Guignol. Songs include "Eighteen", "School's Out" "Only Women Bleed" and "The Awakening". An elaborate rock theatre production from 1975. USA, 1975, 84 mins.
VHS: S09853. $19.95.

Women in Rock

A collage of rare historical footage, music videos, and interviews featuring Brenda Lee, Carole King, Tina Turner, Janis Joplin, Bangles, Madonna, Grace Slick in Jefferson Airplane, and many more.
VHS: S01993. $29.95.
Stephanie Bennett, USA, 1986, 57 mins.

Woodstock

Never-before-seen performances by rock legends Canned Heat, Janis Joplin, Crosby Stills and Nash, Jefferson Airplane, Jimmy Hendrix and many others bring alive the spirit of the event that defined a generation. This newly available director's cut of the highly acclaimed documentary, winner of the Academy Award in 1970, shows how three days of peace and music changed the world. VHS letterboxed.
VHS: S06044. $24.98.
Laser: LD70712. $49.98.
DVD: DV60119. $24.98.
Michael Wadleigh, USA, 1970, 225 mins.

Woodstock 94

This recreation of the original Woodstock concert brought a whole new generation to the ideals of peace, love and music, through a collection of legendary and new performers. Aerosmith, Melissa Etheridge, Peter Gabriel, Metallica, Red Hot Chili Peppers, Salt N' Pepa and more played in the greatest musical weekend since the original concert took place over 25 years ago. 165 mins.
VHS: S22877. $24.95.
Laser: LD74944. $49.99.

Words for the Dying

An examination of the musical collaboration between John Cale, a member of the 60s band Velvet Underground, and avant-garde theorist and producer Brian Eno. Filmmaker Ron Nilsson shows the process of recording a new album, *Words for the Dying*, based on four Dylan Thomas poems. 80 mins.
VHS: S18642. $19.95.

Yessongs

The musical rock group Yes is featured in this concert film that follows their 1973 World Tour. Songs include "Roundabout" and "All Good People". Musical fans of this major rock group will not be disappointed. With the video you can have all the encores you want. 70 mins.
VHS: S02252. $14.98.
Laser: LD75023. $39.99.

You Can't Do That: The Making of A Hard Day's Night

When the early Beatles film *A Hard Day's Night* started shooting in Chicago in 1964, few expected that either the film or its subjects would be so wildly successful. Now, over 30 years later, the story behind this film is available on video. Phil Collins appeared as an extra in the film and he appropriately hosts this documentary. 65 mins.
VHS: S24382. $19.98.

MUSIC INSTRUCTION

Acoustic Guitar Musicianship

Russ Barenber teaches this intensive course to help the acoustic guitarist add style and musicality to his or her playing. Russ shows how to achieve good tone, keep solid time, understand accenting and articulation, compose solos, and improvise freely using hammers and pulls, melodic ornamentation, slides, variations, vibrato, damping and syncopation; a variety of great tunes are taught, including "For J.L.", "Old Joe Clark", and others.
VHS: S09702. $49.95.

Banjo Picking Styles

Learn a variety of techniques as played by the hottest young player, Bela Fleck. Bela shows the stylistic innovations that will add sparkle, interest and new repertoire to your playing. 60 mins.
VHS: S09688. $49.95.

Basic Guitar Set-Up and Repair

Harvey Citron guides this clear step-by-step instruction on how to take care of the minor repairs and set-up that will have your instruments playing perfectly. 90 mins.
VHS: S09678. $49.95.

Beginning Bluegrass Piano
Perfect for those who want to play banjo in the style of Earl Scruggs and other bluegrass pickers—from scratch. Learn basic rolls, left-hand fingerpicking and nine all-time favorite bluegrass songs. With Pete Wernick. 120 mins.
VHS: S09686. $49.95.

Beginning Blues Piano
The only requirement for taking this video course is to want to play blues, boogie woogie or rock and roll piano. With no written music to learn and David Cohen's easy-to-follow instructions, even a beginner will be improvising blues riffs, and sound great doing it. 60 mins.
VHS: S09689. $49.95.

Beginning Electric Bass
A two-tape series taught by Roly Salley.
Beginning Electric Bass—Part One. Here is the easiest way to learn the electric bass. Within five minutes the student is getting hands-on experience from a professional, learning the fundamentals of bass playing. This video teaches left and right-hand techniques, scales, theory and a number of great bass lines in country, blues, rock and R&B styles. 60 mins.
VHS: S09684. $49.95.
Beginning Electric Bass—Part Two. On his second one-hour video lesson, bassist Roly Salley moves on to more complex bass lines and patterns. He teaches left-hand exercises, 12-bar blues, inversions, turn-arounds and a wide range of helpful tips on performing, playing with a rhythm section, and equipment. 60 mins.
VHS: S09685. $49.95.

Bluegrass Mandolin
Sam Bush details the dominant mandolin styles, from Bill Monroe to Newgrass. You'll see, up close, Sam's amazing right-hand picking techniques and left-hand fingering as he teaches ten great tunes. 90 mins.
VHS: S09694. $49.95.

Choreography of the Hands: The Work of Dorothy Taubman
Taubman is well-known among pianists for her summer institute at Amherst College, where she helps ailing musicians. Through the study of physiological principals she locates the movements which lead to chronic pain and then sets about correcting these dangerous repetitive motions. Now this video brings her theories and techniques to a wider audience.
VHS: S22943. $79.95.

Contest Fiddling Championship Style
Mark O'Conner, a true champion, takes apart three of his award-winning tunes, showing up close the fine points of his playing to help you improve yours. In addition, Mark is shown in performance with a band as he would play in a Texas-style fiddle contest. 60 mins.
VHS: S09682. $49.95.

Drum Course for Beginners with Louie Bellson
Drummer Louie Bellson shows how to play drums at its most basic level. Bellson illustrates hand positions, note and rest values, time signatures, staff and dynamics. 53 mins.
VHS: S12153. $29.95.

Elementary Guitar Practice and Theory with Barney Kessel
The grand master of the guitar introduces students to the guitar parts, strings, tuning, tone production and music theory, and then follows guides for sight reading, chords and songs to play. 77 mins.
VHS: S12154. $29.95.

Frank Gambale: Monster Licks and Speed Picking
Innovative guitarist Frank Gambale demonstrates his speed/sweep picking technique and presents a method for developing Monster Licks. Playing each example slowly twice through, Gambale demonstrates his picking technique in the context of scales, pentatonics, arpeggios and triad examples.
VHS: S11524. $39.95.

The Hammer Dulcimer
This easy to follow, comprehensive beginner's course on video makes it easy to see the way the hammers are held, where the notes are found, and how to make exciting music almost immediately. Taught by John McCutcheon. 90 mins.
VHS: S09696. $49.95.

How to Play Flutes of the Andes
Learn to play the haunting and powerful music of the Andes mountains. The members of Sukay teach two of the most popular wind instruments: the zampona (pan pipes) and the recorder-like kena. Quentin Howard and Carlos Crespo demonstrate the songs and techniques, and the entire quartet plays them as they would in performance. 45 mins.
VHS: S09698. $49.95.

An Intimate Lesson with Tony Rice
Here is the fabulous Tony Rise picking style, slowed down and brought up close so you can clearly see what he is doing and how he's doing it. Tony demonstrates a variety of techniques through six songs and instrumentals taken from his most recent albums. 60 mins.
VHS: S09677. $49.95.

Jazz Class for Kids
Jazz choreographer Bob Rizzo is a jazz dance instructor for kids 9-16. Joined by the Riz-Biz Kidz, the program offers training in beginning, intermediate and advanced levels. The class floor stretches and progressions feature turns, jumps and step-by-step combinations. 55 mins.
VHS: S19411. $29.95.

Jerry Douglas' Dobro Techniques
One of the world's top Dobro players shares years of experience as he teaches the dynamic techniques and musical skills that make his Dobro playing so powerful. Jerry demonstrates the left and right hand positions, bar pull-offs and hammer-ons, forward and reverse bar slants, string pulls and picking sequences, as well as invaluable tips on musicianship and equipment. Note-by-note breakdowns of great tunes like "Fireball Mail" and "Cincinnati Rag" are also included.
VHS: S09700. $49.95.

Learn to Play Autoharp
A wonderful one-hour video lesson in which John Sebastian provides a step-by-step learning guide to the autoharp, one of our most beautiful—and easiest—traditional instruments. Includes the use of fingerpicking techniques and how to pick out melodies and play instrumentals in the styles of the great traditional players. 60 mins.
VHS: S09695. $49.95.

Learning Blues Piano—Intermediate Level
This lesson is for those who have some background in blues piano. Taught in a clear and easy style, David Cohen covers theory, blues scales and improvisation techniques, shuffle and straight rhythms, endings, intros, turnarounds, and more. 60 mins.
VHS: S09690. $49.95.

Learning the Bluegrass Fiddle
Kenny Kosek shows how to hold the instrument, proper use of the bow and other techniques that will make starting or continuing fiddle playing easy and fun. You'll learn riffs, double-stops and exciting solos to numerous hot fiddle tunes. 90 mins.
VHS: S09681. $49.95.

Learning to Fingerpick—Intermediate Level
A perfect follow-up to *Learning to Fingerpick*, this is a challenging and exciting step into blues and country fingerpicking with more complex instrumentals and new left- and right-hand techniques. Taught by Harry Traum. 60 mins.
VHS: S09674. $49.95.

Learning to Fingerpick—Level 1/2
An elementary knowledge of guitar chords is all you'll need to get started picking out syncopated melodies while maintaining a steady bass accompaniment in the styles of Merle Travis, Mississippi John Hurt and others. 60 mins.
VHS: S09670. $49.95.

Learning to Flatpick
Harry Traum guides this beginner's video to the joys of country and bluegrass flatpicking. You'll see how to hold the pick and play scales, bass runs, hammer-ons, and melodies to some of America's favorite songs. 60 mins.
VHS: S09676. $49.95.

Learning to Play Blues Guitar—Part 1
Harry Traum teaches the right- and left-hand techniques of traditional finger-style blues. Chord progressions, turnarounds, walking basses, picking techniques, blues riffs, and several complete songs and instrumentals are taught, along with the elements of blues improvisation. 60 mins.
VHS: S09675. $49.95.

Learning to Play Blues Guitar—Part 2
Delves into the many possibilities and intricacies of blues in the key of A, as played by Brownie McGhee, Big Bill Broonzy and other blues masters. Happy Traum teaches new chord positions, bass runs, turnarounds, licks and solos, and the tape includes several wonderful songs with which to practice.
VHS: S09699. $49.95.

Legends of Flatpicking Guitar
In the 1960's Doc Watson proved that fiddle tunes could flow as well under an acoustic guitar pick as under a fiddle's bow. His work inspired a number of other American folk musicians including Norman Blake, Dan Crary and Tony Rice. 90 mins.
VHS: S24369. $29.95.

Legends of Jazz Guitar, Volume I
Since the 1920's jazz has been enlivened by the sounds of the acoustic guitar. Wes Montgomery, Joe Pass, Barney Kessel and Herb Ellis are just some of the musicians featured on this video.
VHS: S24370. $29.95.

Legends of Jazz Guitar, Volume II
More jazz greats are on offer in this video. For example, Wes Montgomery is featured on a pair of 1965 BBC performances while Barney Kessel can be seen playing the BBC Blues. Joe Pass also contributes two pieces and Charlie Bird shows how a classical guitar can swing.
VHS: S24371. $29.95.

Let's Play the Piano and All Those Keyboards
This revolutionary video teaching technique will have the student reading music and playing a popular tune with chord accompaniment after only two half-hour lessons. It prepares students to play any form of music—classical, jazz, pop, country. The video course contains the equivalent of over one year of private keyboard instruction.
VHS: S10715. $39.95.

Listening for Clues: Wynton on Form
Structure and form, Wynton Marsalis maintains, are the key to following music, like a good story. In this episode from the BBC series, he shows listeners how to discern a number of forms using music from Prokofiev, Gershwin, Ellington and Ives. 54 mins.
VHS: S25685. $19.98.

Mastery of the Flamenco Guitar
Guillermo Rios studied for 17 years in Spain with the masters of flamenco guitar. Now this video and the enclosed 28-page booklet condense the bulk of his experiences. Its 16 exercises are useful for beginners and advanced students alike. 95 mins.
VHS: S21060. $49.95.

Play Bluegrass Banjo by Ear
Bill Keith conveys an understanding of basic music theory for the banjo that opens vast possibilities for all players. Includes details of right-hand rolls, harmonized scales, pentatonic runs and licks, and more. 60 mins.
VHS: S09687. $49.95.

Rick Danko's Electric Bass Techniques
For the first time, the dynamic bassist of The Band details some of the exercises, picking techniques and musical ideas that have formed his style through the years. Rick teaches scales, exercises, and great bass lines to get you really rocking. 60 mins.
VHS: S09683. $49.95.

Rock and Roll Rhythm Guitar
A complete two-tape series taught by Amos Garrett.
Rock and Roll Rhythm Guitar Part One. A master of rhythm guitar styles and techniques teaches the chops of the great rock and soul rhythm players. Covered in this lesson are the styles of Chuck Berry, Bo Diddley, Wilson Pickett and James Nolin. Also taught are damping techniques, alternate chord shapes, two-guitar drills. 90 mins.
VHS: S09679. $49.95.
Rock and Roll Rhythm Guitar Part Two. This video documents and teaches the styles of Steve Cropper and the Memphis Sound, Al Green, Albert King, and others. Included are drills and exercises plus tips on holding the pick, getting the best tone, keeping time and other invaluable information. 73 mins.
VHS: S09680. $49.95.

Singing for Tin Ears
This tape is an encouraging and enjoyable lesson that will turn listeners into singers. It will help break down inhibitions, teach pitch perception and basic music theory, and get anyone started making wonderful vocal music. Taught by Penny Nichols. 60 mins.
VHS: S09697. $49.95.

Snare Drum Rudiments with Pat Petrillo
Renowned New York studio drummer Pat Petrillo explains and demonstrates snare drum rudiments, including the roll, diddle, flam and drag. Each rudiment is demonstrated at slow, medium and fast speeds. 30 mins.
VHS: S11527. $34.95.

Sousa to Satchmo: Wynton on theJazz Band
The transformation of European symphonic music in the American marching band and Ragtime traditions led to jazz. Wynton Marsalis traces this history into New Orleans. Music from Sousa, Joplin and Armstrong are featured in this BBC episode. 55 mins.
VHS: S25686. $19.98.

Stephen Sondheim: Anatomy of a Song

Examination of the song "Someone in a Tree" from *Pacific Overtures*, Sondheim's favorite at the time. Filmed in his home, Sondheim describes how he wrote the song and discusses the creative process with playwright John Weidman and critic Frank Rich. The song is performed by cast members of the show, with Sondheim at the piano. 1976, 27 mins.
VHS: S32325. $89.95.

Steve Smith, Part 1

Named Best Instructional Music Video by the American Video Conference, this definitive drumming clinic with former Journey drummer Steve Smith details jazz and rock styles, concepts and practicing methods. 55 mins.
VHS: S11525. $39.95.

Steve Smith, Part 2

A demonstration of more advanced styles and concepts of drumming. Smith covers fusion drumming, soloing, creativity, double bass drumming and creating a drum part. Concert and performance footage features Smith's groups Steps Ahead and Vital Information. 52 mins.
VHS: S11526. $39.95.

Tackling the Monster: Wynton on Practice

In this video both Yo-Yo Ma and Wynton Marsalis discuss their strong negative reactions to the necessity of practice. Fortunately, Marsalis has a 12-point plan to combat this challenge. Marsalis and Yo-Yo Ma work through Ellington's "Mood Indigo." 54 mins.
VHS: S25687. $19.98.

Trumpet Course Beginner-Intermediate with Clark Terry

The jazz trumpet player and teacher introduces the trumpet, its accessories and the usage of mutes, and provides music theory in relation to actual performance. Then Clark Terry presents warm-up exercises utilizing simple intervals, harmonics and scales. 52 mins.
VHS: S12155. $29.95.

Why Toes Tap: Wynton on Rhythm

Wynton Marsalis focuses on rhythm in this educational video from the BBC. Using two renditions of the Nutcracker, he shows how composers use rhythm to create distinctive sounds and evoke a variety of emotions. 53 mins.
VHS: S25684. $19.98.

You Can Play Guitar

Happy Traum teaches this three-part course.

Chords and Chord Progressions. Shows the beginner, close up, the proper way to play chords on the guitar and how they fit together in creating music. Includes songs, exercises, playing ideas and advice. 60 mins.
VHS: S09671. $49.95.

Right-Hand Techniques. Strumming and picking techniques, and how they can be used to enhance songs and make them more exciting. Includes rhythmic variations, left and right-hand damping, alternating bass notes, hammering-on, classical-style arpeggios and the basics of traditional fingerpicking.
VHS: S09672. $49.95.

Understanding the Guitar. An exploration of the fingerboard to provide a solid understanding of the relationships of notes, frets and strings. Guitarists at all levels will benefit from this lesson, gaining a more complete understanding of the instrument. 60 mins.
VHS: S09673. $49.95.

You Can Play Jazz Piano

You will see as well as hear how to play jazz and pop piano, learning chord progressions, scales and modes, proper fingering and improvising, on both blues and standard tunes. Clear and concise, with no music to read, especially created for beginning/intermediate jazz players. Three-tape set.
VHS: S09693. $119.95.

children's VIDEO

children's video

Abuela's Weave

Esperanza's *abuela*, her grandmother, is unmatched in her weaving skills. She shares the gift of traditional Mayan tapestry with her granddaughter. Together they decide to sell their wares in the market, but Abuela's birthmark may frighten away customers. Esperanza must sell their works alone.
VHS: S21884. $44.95.

Adventures from the Book of Virtues

Based on the best-selling books by William J. Bennett, this PBS for Kids series of programs helps children learn the value of virtues as they join Zach and Annie, two animated, ordinary kids who experience everyday adventures and learn some of life's most important lessons.

Compassion. When Zach watches a fire destroy an immigrant family's home, his indifference about getting involved slowly wanes as Plato recounts inspiring stories of compassion, including "The Good Samaritan" (Bible), "The Legend of the Dipper" (Norse), "Androcles and the Lion" (Greek) and the poem "The New Colossus." 30 mins.
VHS: S30857. $12.95.

Courage. When Annie takes a tumble during a track race, she loses her confidence and lets her fear and embarrassment discourage her from racing again. Her friends help to restore her spunk and bolster her determination by sharing heroic tales of gallantry, valor and dauntless spirit, including "The Minotaur" (Greek), Aesop's "The Brave Mice," "William Tell" (Swiss) and the inspirational poem "If." 30 mins.
VHS: S30858. $12.95.

Honesty. To escape blame for breaking his father's camera, Zach concocts a story, instead of telling the truth, prompting his friends at Plato's Peak to help him focus on the importance of honesty with the stories of "The Frog Prince" (English), "George Washington" and his infamous cherry tree, "The Indian Cinderella" (Native American) and a poem about truth.
VHS: S30859. $12.95.

Responsibility. When Annie's mother presents her with a new bicycle to deliver cakes, she promises to take care of it. Instead she wrecks it—along with the cakes—after impulsively accepting the challenge of a race. Plato points out the consequences of irresponsibility in "Icarus and Daedalus" (Greek), "King Alfred and the Cakes" (English), and "The Chest of Broken Glass" (English). 30 mins.
VHS: S30860. $12.95.

Self-Discipline. When Zach's preoccupation wih earning money spirals out of control, it prompts him to throw a furious tantrum at home. Plato and Aurora help Zach draw parallels between his own behavior and that of King Midas in "The Golden Touch" (Greek) and Ghengis Khan in "The King and His Hawk" (Asian). The penalties of impatience depicted in "The Magic Thread" (French) leave Zach with an appreciation of the Ecclesiastes poem, "For Everything There Is a Season." 30 mins.
VHS: S30861. $12.95.

Work. When a raging storm wrecks Plato's Peak, Sock the bobcat learns "it's all in the attitude," as he grows to understand the value of a hard day's work with the stories "How the Camel Got His Hump" (English), "The Bundle of Sticks" (Greek) and Mark Twain's "Tom Sawyer Gives Up the Brush" (American).
VHS: S30862. $12.95.

Adventures in Dinosaur City

When three totally hip teens get accidentally zapped into the prehistoric stomping grounds of freaked-out dinosaurs, they find themselves in a stone age fantasy. Joining forces with a crime-fighting tyrannosaurus named Rex and his right-claw reptile Tops, they embark on a fossil-fueled mission to retrieve a stolen power cell and save Saur City from melting down into a big Jurassic jacuzzi.
VHS: S16814. $89.98.
Laser: CLV. **LD71966. $29.98.**
Brett Thompson, USA, 1992, 88 mins.

The Adventures of a Two-Minute Werewolf

In this comic adventure, Walt has two major concerns. One is a bully, the other is a werewolf. Walt finds that he can't stop himself from transforming into a werewolf. Before long, however, he discovers that there are some advantages to this problem. 29 mins.
VHS: S23475. $49.95.

Adventures of Babar

Babar, King of the Elephants and hero of the classic children's story, is brought to life in these volumes, each 60 minutes in length.

Volume 1. Eleven episodes, including Babar's arithmetic lesson, Babar's car, a meal at the old lady's house, Babar and the flower vendor and more. USA, 1985.
VHS: S00017. $19.95.

Volume 2. Eleven episodes, in which Babar takes a fishing trip, learns to read music, goes on a picnic, makes pastry and more. USA, 1985.
VHS: S00018. $19.95.

Volume 3.
VHS: S04861. $19.95.

Volume 4.
VHS: S04862. $19.95.

Volume 5.
VHS: S04863. $19.95.

Volume 6.
VHS: S04864. $19.95.

Volume 7.
VHS: S04865. $19.95.

The Adventures of Blinky Bill: Blinky Bill's Zoo/Magician

In *Blinky Bill's Zoo* the animated Koala bear Blinky gets together with his "mates" to build a zoo for a human girl that they have discovered. In *Magician* a magic show leads to disaster for Blinky. 48 mins.
VHS: S24247. $12.99.

The Adventures of Blinky Bill: Blinky's Fire Brigade/Fund Run

Blinky Bill, the animated koala bear from down under, decides to set up the town's first fire brigade. Then in *Blinky Bill's Fund Run*, Blinky turns to fundraising for charity. Greedy dingos threaten his plans however. 48 mins.
VHS: S24248. $12.99.

The Adventures of Chico

Young Chico describes his escapades with wild animals-including a pet bird who saves him from a snake—in this heartwarming, live-action film set in Mexico. B&W, 54 mins.
VHS: S10577. $24.95.

The Adventures of Corduroy

Based on the award-winning classic children's story by Don Freeman, these colorful, animated stories from the makers of *The X-Men* and *The Tick* follow the adventures of the little department store stuffed bear who longs for a home and a friend. With theme music performed by Linda Ronstadt.

The Adventures of Corduroy—Home. He's been on a department store shelf a long time. Maybe his missing button is why no one has taken him home. When the store is closed, Corduroy sets out to find a button. Based on the original Corduroy Christmas story. 22 mins.
VHS: S32293. $9.95.

The Adventures of Corduroy—The Circus. Corduroy looks for his missing friend under the Big Top. 27 mins.
VHS: S32296. $9.95.

The Adventures of Corduroy—The Dinosaur Egg. A museum trip brings excitement when a chicken egg hatches inside the dinosaur exhibit and Corduroy thinks the newborn is a baby dino. 22 mins.
VHS: S32294. $9.95.

The Adventures of Corduroy—The Puppy. The new puppy Lisa brings home leaves Corduroy feeing alone, unloved, and determined to find a new home. 27 mins
VHS: S32295. $9.95.

The Adventures of Tintin: Cigars of the Pharaoh

Since the '30s the adventures of this ordinary man have been recognized throughout the world for both charm and suspense. In this story, Tintin's vacation to Egypt is detoured by a tombful of ancient mummies and a case of international diamond smuggling. 45 mins.
VHS: S23933. $12.98.

The Adventures of Tintin: The Secret of the Unicorn

Once again this seemingly ordinary fellow is caught in a story of mystery and suspense. Tintin and his loyal dog Snowy are involved in a swashbuckling quest for sunken treasure. It all begins innocently enough, with an ancient map. 45 mins.
VHS: S23934. $12.98.

The Adventures of Wayan and the Three R's

Six-year-old Wayan learns the value of the three R's: reduce, reuse and recycle, when he finds plastic litter around his village on the island paradise of Bali. This video is an entertaining way to introduce elementry school students to the three R's and inspire creative class projects. 15 mins.
VHS: S30089. $59.95.

Alabaster's Song

Alabaster is a little angel, high on the top of a Christmas tree, whose remarkable song is heaven-sent. It is the tender music of the heart that unites a little boy, his father and a glorious night long ago in Bethlehem. Based on Max Lucado's best-selling Christmas book. 30 mins.
VHS: S33288. $14.95.

Alejandro's Gift

Alejandro plants a garden in the desert that attracts a number of animals. When he digs a well even more animals show up, rewarding him for his thoughtfulness with their company. It's a delightful read-along video that kids will love. 7:28 mins.
VHS: S22345. $39.95.

Alexander and the Terrible, Horrible, No Good, Very Bad Day

Everything goes wrong for Alexander in this animated version of Judith Viorst's delightful book. From gum in his hair to bullies in the yard, the world seems to conspire against Alexander until he decides to move to Australia. 30 mins.
VHS: S23276. $12.95.

Alexander, Who Used to Be Rich Last Sunday

Based on the book by Judith Viorst. Alexander's grandparents gave him five dollars making him rich on Sunday. After a spending spree his fortune is lost. This video will teach students the value of saving. 14 mins.
VHS: S23445. $69.95.
Laser: LD74760. $99.95.

All I See

Cynthia Rylant's story about friendship between a young boy and a painter is strikingly brought to life by Peter Catalanotto's illustrations in this iconographic video presentation. 8 mins. Public Performance Rights.
VHS: S13891. $104.00.

All the Colors of the Earth

Sheila Hamanaka's multicultural sketch features evocative text and beautiful art along with a captivating musical score and narration to celebrate the glorious diversity of children laughing, loving and glowing with life. 8 mins.
VHS: S33782. $60.00.

All the Money in the World

Quentin saves a leprechaun from a well and is granted three wishes. He wastes two but on his third try he asks for all the money in the world. The world economy is brought to a standstill, turning his money into a worthless commodity. This gives him a new appreciation of that which money cannot buy. Based on the book by Judith Viorst. 23 mins.
VHS: S22372. $49.95.

All the Troubles in the World

Isaac Asimov wrote this story about a civilization run by an all-powerful computer called the Multivac. A boy's father tries to sabotage the machine, and his son is drawn into the plot. Despite this scheme the Multivac has a far more powerful but unforseen enemy. 22 mins.
VHS: S23450. $49.95.

Alvin and the Chipmunks: Love Potion #9

In *Love Potion #9*, Valentine's Day finds the Chipmunks at the mercy of Cupid. But that is only the first of four shorts collected on this video. *Theodore and Juliet, Dear Diary* and *Dr. Simon and Mr. Heartthrob* continue the theme of comic romance featuring the antics of the lovable rodents. 25 mins.
VHS: S27363. $12.99.

The Amazing Bone and Other Stories

The adventures of various humans and animals are shown in this collection of four award-winning animated films taken from favorite children's literature. The title piece, narrated by John Lithgow, is about a young pig who spends her time with a talking bone. 30 mins.
VHS: S11226. $14.95.

The American Dream Contest
Kids between the ages of nine and seventeen were asked to create a concept for a short film on something that's special about our country. Host Michael Landon, in one of his last projects, presents the twelve winners: refreshing and inspiring views of America, filled with humor and heart, imagination and surprises. USA, 47 mins.
VHS: S15003. $29.95.

Amos Fortune, Free Man
Haunting spirituals furnish the background for this sensitive adaptation of the Newbery Award-winning story of Prince Atmun, who was captured, sold at auction, and freed as Amos Fortune. 46 mins.
VHS: S08401. $119.00.

Anansi and the Talking Melon
Eric Kimmel's book is brought to life in this delightful children's video. Anansi is trapped inside a melon. Elephant thinks he has grown a talking fruit and sets off to present this treasure to the king. 11 mins.
VHS: S24720. $37.95.

Animals Are Beautiful People
A program which looks at the creatures living in Africa. This documentary will fascinate and educate children with its magnificent footage. *The Gods Must Be Crazy* filmmaker Jamie Uys spent four years filming African animals.
VHS: S03886. $19.98.

Animals of the Bible
Ostriches, lions, lambs, camels, donkeys and more are all included in this video for children ages 6-10. For each animal listed in the video a story from the *Bible* is related. 30 mins.
VHS: S23123. $14.95.

Anna Marie's Blanket
In this read-along video, Anna must explain to her favorite blanket that she must go alone to nursery school. Of course the blanket is sad to be left behind. This is the story of how Anna helps her blanket overcome its loneliness. 10:15 mins.
VHS: S22358. $39.95.

Archer's Adventure
A wonderful family film from Australia about a daring young boy who takes a prize-winning racehorse across the wild outback in order to compete in the big race in Melbourne.
VHS: S04952. $19.95.
Denny Lawrence, Australia, 1985, 120 mins.

Are You Afraid of the Dark? "Ghostly Tales"
In this pair of spooky episodes, *Tale of the Frozen Ghost* and *Tale of the Shiny Red Bicycle*, there are enough chills for the whole family. Melissa Joan Hart makes a surprise appearance. A new music video compiled from horror story highlights is also included. 50 mins.
VHS: S20661. $14.98.

Are You My Mother?
P.D. Eastman's appealing children's stories *Are You My Mother?*, *Go, Dog Go* and *The Best Nest* are transformed into charming animated shorts that kids will love. 30 mins.
English Narration.
VHS: S22016. $14.95.
Spanish Narration.
VHS: S22015. $14.95.

Arthur's Eyes
The popular animated PBS series based on Marc Brown's award-winning books. Follow the imaginative adventures of eight-year-old Arthur, his little sister, D.W., and their friends and family. Contains two episodes. 30 mins.
VHS: S31440. $12.99.

Arthur's Pet Business
Marc Brown's popular storybook character returns in this iconographic video. Arthur learns about patience and responsibility when he starts his own pet business. 10 mins.
VHS: S12258. $19.95.

Astronomy 101: A Family Adventure
Subtitled *A Beginner's Guide to the Night Sky*. Join Michelle and her mother as they show you how they explore the night sky together. Astronomy proves to be a fascinating family activity. This video really helps kids get started. It is most refreshing to see the mother/daughter team as the focus of the activity. Filmed on location at the Chicago's Adler Planetarium, this video combines science and fun. 25 minutes.
VHS: S24358. $19.95.

At Home in the Coral Reef
A living coral reef is the subject of this read-along video. In this tropical underwater tour children will see all kinds of unique and colorful wildlife. It's informative and beautiful to see. 11:15 mins.
English Version.
VHS: S22362. $39.95.
Spanish Version.
VHS: S22363. $39.95.

Babar's First Step
In this story, Babar the elephant tells his son Alexander about a incident from his childhood. A hunter terrorizes the herd, causing the death of a loved one. Babar's anger gives him the strength to confront the hunter while the rest of the herd escapes. An animated fable of growing up and responsibility. 49 mins.
VHS: S12813. $12.95.

Babar: Babar Returns
This charming episode finds Babar and his daughter Flora in the kitchen whipping up some midnight snacks, when Babar begins to tell Flora and the audience an enchanting tale with an important lesson about concentrating on our strengths rather than our weaknesses. 1989, 49 min.
VHS: S13443. $14.95.

Baby-Sitter's Club Videos
The popular Scholastic Book series is every bit as popular on video. Seven diverse girls start a business, and together they can solve any problem. Live action. USA. Ages 6-12. 30 minutes each.
The Baby-Sitters' Club: Christmas Special (1991). A very moving Christmas story, with the girls at a hospital Christmas party, when diabetic Stacey lands in the hospital herself after too many cookies.
VHS: S24356. $14.95.
The Baby-Sitters' Club: Claudia and the Missing Jewels. The mystery unfolds when Claudia launches a jewelry-making business, and a pair of earrings is stolen.
VHS: S24354. $14.95.
The Baby-Sitters' Club: Claudia and the Mystery of the Secret Passage. Claudia follows a note found in a secret passage, as the Baby-Sitters hope to settle an ancient feud.
VHS: S24344. $14.95.
The Baby-Sitters' Club: Dawn and the Dream Boy. Concerns the rivalry between two sisters thinking of going to a teen dance with the same boy. Note: the subject is dating.
VHS: S24355. $14.95.
The Baby-Sitters' Club: Dawn and the Haunted House. Dawn thinks Claudia is spending too much time with the neighborhood "witch," in this story about appreciating differences.
VHS: S24351. $14.95.
The Baby-Sitters' Club: Dawn Saves the Trees. When the city plans to build a road through the local park, Dawn leads the Baby-Sitters in a fight to save the trees. Deals with recycling and conservation.
VHS: S24346. $14.95.
The Baby-Sitters' Club: Jessi and The Mystery of the Stolen Secrets. The Baby-Sitters go undercover to find out who is stealing club secrets.
VHS: S24347. $14.95.
The Baby-Sitters' Club: Kristy and the Great Campaign. A third-grader's bid for class president yields a look at self-concept and gender stereotypes.
VHS: S24353. $14.95.
The Baby-Sitters' Club: Mary Ann and the Brunettes (1990). Two girls' clubs find a rational way to work out their differences. Note: the subject concerns teenage girls and conflict over two girls who want to date the same boy.
VHS: S24350. $14.95.
The Baby-Sitters' Club: Stacey Takes a Stand. The Baby-Sitters help Stacey figure out what to do when she is torn between her divorced mom and dad.
VHS: S24348. $14.95.
The Baby-Sitters' Club: Stacey's Big Break. Stacey has a chance at fashion modelling. A dialogue ensues concerning priorities and anorexia.
VHS: S24352. $14.95.
The Baby-Sitters' Club: The Baby-Sitters Remember. A very nice review of the best and funniest adventures.
VHS: S24349. $14.95.
The Baby-Sitters' Club: The Baby-Sitters and The Boy Sitters. The boys start their own baby-sitting club!
VHS: S24345. $14.95.

Bach's Fight for Freedom
Produced for HBO, this involving children's story concerns a young boy who reluctantly becomes an assistant to the great German composer Johann Sebastian Bach. At first they don't work well together. In the end, however, they do find an understanding between them. This is a tale about the positive power of ambition. From *The Composers' Specials* series. 53 mins.
VHS: S26745. $19.98.

Ballet Shoes
Refusing to let a money crunch hinder their ballet career, three young girls decide to pursue their dreams. The possibilities and realities of fame and fortune are creatively displayed in this live-action film based on the Noel Streatfield children's novel of the same name. 120 mins.
VHS: S12636. $29.95.

Barry's Scrapbook: A Window into Art
Join Barry Louis, a singer and writer of children's songs, as he visits an art museum and meets a collage artist, an illustrator and a sculptor. He sings about art and recyclables.
VHS: S22130. $26.95.

Bartholomew and the Oobleck
A jazz-loving boy's dreams come true when he plays a real musician's trumpet in this adaptation of Rachel Isadora's book. 11 mins.
VHS: S08403. $62.00.

Basil Hears a Noise
A vigorous and heartwarming Muppets musical tale with Basil and his friends trapped inside an enchanted forest where they must find the inner courage to overcome their fear and conquer their personal demons. Special appearance by Elmo, the furry red monster. 28 mins.
VHS: S19159. $12.98.

BBC Children's Favorites
This BBC video of the animated pieces "Ivor the Engine," "Bagpuss" and "Clangers" promises to be delightful time after time. 55 mins.
VHS: S12638. $19.95.

The Bear
In this story by William Faulkner, a boy discovers the value of wilderness as he confronts a bear. Nicknamed Old Ben, this bear has eluded the boy's father and his friends for years. Tension mounts as the boy grows up until he finally must confront this legendary creature himself. 24 mins.
VHS: S23471. $79.95.

Bear in the Big Blue House
This hit pre-school series from Jim Henson features an insatiably curious bear and his playful friends as they explore themes such as friendship and helping others, in fun, creative ways using music and storytelling.
Bear in the Big Blue House—Volume 1. In *Home Is Where the Bear Is*, Bear and his friends share their secret, special places as they tour the Big Blue House; in *What's in the Mail Today?*, when Tutter gets his first letter ever from his grandmother, Bear teaches him how to double the excitement by writing back.
VHS: S35011. $12.95.
Bear in the Big Blue House—Volume 2. In *Friends forLife*, Ojo learns the importance of keeping your old friends while making new ones; in *The Big Little Visitor*, Bear and his friends explore the fun and love of family as they prepare for the arrival of Tutter's Grandma Flutter.
VHS: S35012. $12.95.

Beebtots
Four animated films which are BBC Children's Favorites. In this collection, the King of the Nogs may have an unwelcome party guest, Clangers are visited by a Gladstone bag, Bagpuss receives a gift and Ivor the Engine is slowed by falling snow. 52 mins.
VHS: S12637. $19.95.

Beezbo
A lesson in manners for the neighborhood kids takes place when a furry alien, Beezbo, crashes his spaceship on earth and he transforms himself to look human. While looking human is easy, behaving so is not. Recommended for ages up to 10 years old.
VHS: S03484. $14.95.
R.C. Bailey, USA, 1985, 48 mins.

Beneath the Ghost Moon
Jane Yolen narrates this video presentation of her Halloween tale of a courageous mouse. She convinces her friends that their home is worth fighting for and reminds them of the importance of forgiveness, especially after the mean-hearted creepy-crawlies destroy the mice's costumes designed for the upcoming Ghost Eve Ball.
VHS: S31441. $44.99.

Bernard and the Genie

Lenny Henry *(True Identity)* showcases his gift for mimicry in this comedy which transfers the Aladdin legend to a contemporary London context, with the genie (Henry) helping a shy young London man overcome his fears about a dazzling young woman. With Rowan Atkinson and musician Bob Geldof.
VHS: S19095. $19.98.

Best Christmas Pageant

Loretta Swit stars in this heartwarming adaptation about what happens when the nastiest bunch of kids in town decide they want to participate in this year's Christmas pageant. 60 mins.
VHS: S08405. $19.95.

Best Friends Part I

A video for children with or without pets, this series of animated stories demonstrates how to act responsibly toward our animal friends and our environment in general. A mouse, dog, turtle, rabbit and frog tell what they want to receive from a human friend in the first part of a two-program series. 25 mins.
VHS: S14990. $14.95.

Best Friends Part II

A fish, cat, guinea pig, pony and bird take their turns in telling entertaining animated stories informing children how to respect and care for our best pet friends. 25 mins.
VHS: S15240. $19.95.

Best of Babar, Vol. 1

Six complete episodes of new adventures with the King of the Elephants, Babar. Included are *Babar Gets Sunstroke, Babar and the Bicycle, Babar and the Cheese Fondue* and more. USA, 1986, 30 mins.
VHS: S02620. $14.95.

Best of Babar, Vol. 2

The King of Elephants and his friends have more fun in this laugh-filled collection of six episodes about a billiard game, a masked ball, a postman, astronomy, sewing and theater. 30 mins.
VHS: S02621. $14.95.

The Best of ZOOM—The Early Years

The best bits from the early years of the Emmy award-winning '70s PBS kids' show, the first inspired, written and performed by kids. Watch the original ZOOMers build things, play games, conduct experiments, enact stories, speak Ubbi-Dubbi, sing, dance, laugh and learn along with kids all over America. 60 mins.
VHS: S34780. $19.95.

Best Offer

Horse-crazy 12-year-old Kyle must sell her horse and does her best to delay the inevitable and stay by his side to the end. At the ranch where he's to be sold, she meets Ray, a saddle-bronc rider. By the time he takes over the sale of her horse, Ray's made a profound impression on Kyle. Public performance.
VHS: S32127. $59.95.
Lisa Krueger, USA, 1992, 28 mins.

The Best Valentine in the World

Getting a head start early in November, Ferdinand Fox gathers sticks, flowers, ribbon and lace to make something different for Florette: a purple valentine. He works long and hard until it's all finished. But when Valentine's Day comes, things don't turn out the way he expects. At least not at first...
VHS: S16338. $44.95.

The Big Fat Fabulous Bear

The Big Fat Fabulous Bear is already a well known character in children's books by Janosch. Now he is featured in this collection of animated films surrounded by a host of lovable animal characters. Together they experience a number of adventures that also impart important lessons to kids.
VHS: S23993. $24.95.

The Biggest Bears

All kinds of bears in their wild habitat are shown in this exciting documentary narrated by a five-year-old Alaskan boy. The makers travelled across Alaska, Canada and Russia in order to create this unparalleled musical adventure.
VHS: S22160. $14.95.

Bizet's Dream

Young Michelle is inspired by the newest operatic work written by her piano teacher, Georges Bizet. The plot of *Carmen* leads her to imagine a scenario involving her parents in a love scandal. This delightful story mixes fact and fiction to offer an intriguing portrait of the great composer Bizet. 53 mins.
VHS: S26213. $19.98.

The Bollo Caper

Art Buchwald's book about a magnificent golden leopard called Bollo is adapted in this animated show. Bollo escapes fur hunters and manages to get to Washington D.C., where he saves his life by being listed on the endangered species list. 23 mins.
VHS: S23451. $49.95.

The Boy Who Cried Wolf

Jack Otis Moore has reinterpreted Aesop's fable in an illustrated children's book. This video is directly photographed from this charming book. 6 mins.
VHS: S24910. $42.95.

Brenda Brave

From Astrid Lindgren, author of the children's classic *Pippi Longstocking*, comes this Christmas story of Brenda, who lives with her grandmother in a village. When Grandma slips and injures her leg, Brenda takes care of her and saves her business, selling peppermint sticks from a stall in the town square. 30 mins.
VHS: S31764. $19.95.

Bugs Don't Bug Us

Insects, spiders and other invertebrates interact with children in this tape. Some of the most common of these creatures are revealed in a friendly and casual way. Detailed views of motion and eating habits as well as the complete transformation of a caterpillar to a butterfly make this an exceptional viewing experience. 35 mins.
VHS: S22381. $19.95.

Buron B. Blackbear and Beyond the Stars

From Mother Earth to the outer reaches of our Universe, this delightful duo of animated stories will fill a child with wonder, awe, laughter and joy. USA, 1985, 30 mins.
VHS: S04767. $14.95.

Buster and Chauncey's Silent Night

A whimsical, animated Christmas tale of how the beloved hymn "Silent Night" was created. When two musical mice, Buster and Chauncey, befriend a poor little orphan girl, they accidentally create a holiday miracle and make Christmas history. Featuring the voices of Phil Hartman, Tom Arnold and Marie Osmond.
VHS: S34922. $12.95.

By the Light of the Halloween Moon

Join the fun as a brave young girl, who would rather play a trick than be gobbled up as a treat, is the star of this spirit romp under an old wooden bridge by the light of the spooky Halloween moon. Story by Caroline Stutson. Narrated by Sherry Stringfield *(ER)*. 6 mins.
VHS: S33783. $60.00.

Caddie Woodlawn

The hardships and pleasures of the pioneer life is the life of Caddie Woodlawn in this compelling adaptation of Carol Ryrie Brink's Newbery Medal-winning book. 38 mins.
VHS: S07689. $119.00.

Call It Courage

This video presentation of Armstrong Sperry's book tells the story of a Polynesian chief's son called "The Boy Who Was Afraid," who has to overcome his fear of the sea. 50 mins.
VHS: S08406. $119.00.

Can I Be Good?

Children see themselves as a golden retriever sees them in this enjoyable read-along video. A puppy tries to be good, but he can't help being just a puppy. Finally he becomes an indispensable member of the family that loves him just as he is. 11 mins.
VHS: S22359. $39.95.

Candles, Snow and Mistletoe

This original music fantasy unfolds as Sharon, Lois and Bram take a trip home for the holidays. On the way, they meet an assortment of eccentric fellow passengers, including an adorable elephant. Together they take the ride of their lives and rediscover the true meaning of the holiday season. 50 mins.
VHS: S22224. $9.98.

The Canterville Ghost

The delightful animated tale, based on the book by Oscar Wilde, of Sir Simon, a 300-year-old ghost who attempts to scare the human inhabitants from his house until he gets a proper burial. 22 mins.
VHS: S30726. $19.95.

Cap'n O.G. Readmore Meets Dr. Jekyll and Mr. Hyde

In this latest animated adventure of the well-read cat, Cap'n O.G. Readmore spins a yarn based on Robert Louis Stevenson's classic *Dr. Jekyll and Mr. Hyde*. The Cap'n is transported to 19th-century London, where he's got an appointment with the notorious Dr. Henry Jekyll. 24 mins.
VHS: S34948. $12.95.

Carnival of Animals

Carnival of Animals is the tale of Camille, a young boy who writes a magical musical story of an imaginary carnival. Before your eyes a tea set floats away, and dancing turtles and chickens turn into clowns. 30 mins.
VHS: S16755. $19.95.

The Carrot Highway

This fun-to-watch video, created by carrot farmer and parent Ron Wyss, includes delightful music, great animation, a host of colorful characters, and a bit of history, geography and science to help children of all ages understand how carrots go from seeds to the marketplace. 40 mins.
VHS: S28637. $14.95.

A Caterpillar's Wish

Written and illustrated by first graders in Washington, D.C., this inventive tale follows Chad Caterpillar, who longs for wings like the kind his friend Janet Ladybug sprouts. Fortunately, Chad is eventually transformed into a yellow butterfly. 6 mins.
VHS: S19603. $39.00.

Chanuka at Bubbe's

Delightful Muppet-like characters create an irresistible cast in this program explaining the traditions and significance of Chanuka. Great family entertainment. USA.
VHS: S14949. $19.95.

Charles the Clown

Watch Charles Kraus become a clown right before your eyes. A fascinating look at the fine art of clowning. Live action. Ages 3-8. 30 minutes.
VHS: S24515. $9.98.

Cherries and Cherry Pits

Bidemmi is a child with a rich imagination who loves to draw with her colored markers, and tell stories. One day Bidemmi draws pictures of herself as she buys a bag of cherries. One by one, she eats the cherries, but she saves the pits for her own special purpose.
VHS: S16339. $44.95.

Chicken Sunday

A story by Patricia Polacco about loss, acceptance and assimilation. A young Russian-American girl is initiated into a neighbor's family following the death of her grandmother. She must stake out a series of new relationships and friendships and learns about trust, love and family bonds.
VHS: S19999. $44.95.

A Child's Garden of Verses

This animated interpretation of Robert Louis Stevenson's collection of poems for children is beautifully interpreted. 26 mins.
VHS: S19545. $12.95.

Chingis Khan

This is the story of a great leader and military strategist who learned to survive the hard lessons of the Mongolian steppe as a young boy. Children will be fascinated by the story of this genius who conquered China and Persia and established the greatest contiguous land empire in the world.
VHS: S16340. $44.95.

Choo Choo Trains: Close Up and Very Personal

In this episode from the *Close Up* series, preschoolers learn about the mystery and importance of these amazing machines. Along with the close-ups, there are plenty of panoramic views of Colorado and New Mexico where trains transport both people and goods. 30 mins.
VHS: S24218. $14.95.

Christmas Carousel

Four heartwarming cartoon tales certain to become a part of everyone's holiday traditions are featured on this video. They include *The Little Brown Burro, The Christmas Racoons, Tukiki and his Search for a Merry Christmas* and *Santa's Pocket Watch*. Two-volume set, 120 mins.
VHS: S23145. $24.95.

The Christmas Collection

This program celebrates the cheer of Christmas. The highlight of the collection is the story of Good King Wenceslas. The program features sacred and secular musical pieces that honor popular Christmas traditions. Designed for children from kindergarten through 3rd grade.

Christmas Celebrated in Song, Vol. 1. This program answers long-standing questions about the history of Christmas hymns, their origins and the people who created them. The program uses pictures and music to illustrate eight different hymns. 17 mins.
VHS: S19982. $37.95.

Christmas Celebrated in Song, Vol. 2. Highlighted by music, this special program explores the traditions of gift giving, caroling, Christmas trees and St. Nicholas. 11 mins.
VHS: S19983. $37.95.

The Story of Good King Wenceslas. A faithfully researched history of the ancient legend charges this tale of the avuncular and lovable king. 15 mins.
VHS: S19981. $37.95.

The Christmas Collection, Set. A set of three tapes.
VHS: S19984. $99.00.

Christmas Reunion

A classic children's story stars James Coburn and Edward Woodward as they travel back in time 50 years to discover a wholesome past.
VHS: S23478. $69.95.

Christmas Star

A recreation of the journey of the Magi and the Nativity while studying ancient Babylonian and Roman astronomical statistics and modern scientific principles to legitimize the authenticity of the Star of Bethlehem. 60 mins.
VHS: S19547. $19.95.

Christmas Stories

Four favorite stories suitable particularly for children ages 3-10, including *The Twelve Days of Christmas; Little Drummer Boy; Morris's Disappearing Bag*, about a magical gift to the youngest child in a family; and *The Clown of God*, about a juggler who performs in a church on Christmas Eve.
VHS: S01685. $14.95.
Freitag/Michael Sporn, USA

Christmas Unwrapped

Take an enchanting tour through the history of this beloved holiday and trace the origins of its enduring traditions. 50 mins.
VHS: S34901. $19.95.

Circus: 200 Years of Circus in America

Jack Perkins hosts this look at the history of the Big Top and its many attractions. Clowns, acrobats, magicians and animal trainers have delighted audiences for generations. This definitive work explores the past, present and future of this enduring entertainment. 60 mins.
VHS: S24209. $19.95.

Clarissa Explains Dating

From Nickelodeon's top-rated show, the precocious star of *Clarissa Explains It All* offers teenagers advice and smart ideas about the etiquette of dating.
VHS: S20287. $14.98.

Clarissa Explains It All: "Take My Brother, Please"

From the popular *Nickelodeon* serial of the same name come these two episodes: *Darling Wars* and *Brain Drain* show Clarissa and her obnoxious brother Ferguson at their combative best. The brother you can do without is always easy to annoy. 55 mins.
VHS: S20662. $14.98.

Clarissa Explains It All: Ferguson Explains It All

Ferguson is Clarissa's obnoxious little brother, the infamous character from the popular *Nickelodeon* series. In the title episode Ferguson is bent on controlling the minds of those around him. In the second episode he reaches new lows while campaigning for school president. 60 mins.
VHS: S24721. $14.98.

Classroom Holidays

A continuation of the stories about Jim and his first-grade classmates. Created by Miriam Cohen and illustrated by Lillian Hoban, the stories highlight issues of trust, warmth, independence, humor and compassion. Intended for children from kindergarten through 3rd grade.

Bee My Valentine: A Valentine's Day Story. Little George is hurt when he receives fewer valentines than his peers. He hides out in a coatroom until Jim devises a music fest that uplifts George's spirits. 8 mins.
VHS: S20060. $44.95.

Don't Eat Too Much Turkey: A Thanksgiving Story. When Anna Maria writes a Thanksgiving play, she believes that entitles her to cast and direct the work, which upsets her classmates. The teacher intervenes and settles the dispute by getting the entire class involved in the production. 8 mins.
VHS: S20058. $44.95.

Liar, Liar, Pants on Fire: A Christmas/Chanukah Story. Alex has difficulties adjusting to his new environment and starts telling a string of lies to cover up his discomfort. At the Christmas party, he summons up enough strength to tell the truth. 7 mins.
VHS: S20059. $44.95.

Starring First Grade: An Anytime Celebration. Jim is upset when he is forced to play a tree rather than a troll in the school play. The kids have to deal with adjustments and problem solving in arguing over roles. 8 mins.
VHS: S20061. $44.95.

Classroom Holidays, Set. A collection of four programs on the joys and confusion of first grade. 31 mins.
VHS: S20062. $159.95.

Clementine's Enchanted Journey

With a lot of hope, endless determination and the help of a very special guardian angel, this 10-year-old adventurer trades in his wheel chair for a magic flying bubble, and embarks on travel through time to meet Leonardo da Vinci and Pinocchio. Animated. 95 mins.
VHS: S09624. $19.95.

Cloudy with a Chance of Meatballs

Adaptation of Judy Barrett's fantasy about the land of Chewandswallow and the day the skies stopped raining their sensible, square meals three times a day. 15 mins.
VHS: S08408. $44.95.

The Clown of God

Giovanni, a once-famous juggler now old and penniless, gives one last, unforgettable performance on Christmas Eve. Story by Tomie de Paola. Animated. 10 mins.
VHS: S33789. $49.95.

Colonial Life for Children

This three-tape set takes students on a journey back in time to investigate the beginnings of our nation. Follow along in this dramatization as modern-day kids blast back in time to the actual sites of these settlements to learn what daily life was like and how colonists and Native Americans came to live there. Volumes include *Jamestown, Plimouth Plantation* and *St. Augustine*. Each volume is 23 mins.
VHS: S34914. $89.95.

A Colt Called Lucky

This is the story of a wild mustang living in the desert mountains of the Southwest. 14 mins.
VHS: S23459. $49.95.

Construction Ahead

This new *How We Work 2 Pack* includes "Road Construction" and "Building Construction." Foreman Scott will show kids how everyone works together with cranes, bulldozers and trucks to build massive buildings. Then he will show how demolition works. In the consecutive piece road building on site is featured. 70 mins.
VHS: S21311. $14.98.

A Conversation with Magic

Nickelodeon produced this show with Linda Ellerbee to explain to kids the exact differences between the HIV virus and AIDS, as well as how this disorder is transmitted, and how to interact with people with AIDS. This is a frank look at an important subject, geared toward children.
VHS: S21257. $29.95.

Corletto and Son

Young Mike Corletto wants to follow in his father's footsteps as an ironworker, but his father has big college plans for him. Against the advice of parents and teachers, Mike sees no reason to prepare for college, and a day in health class provides him with life-saving instruction that helps him save his father's life and re-evaluate his goals. 27 mins.
VHS: S09875. $14.95.

Cougar

In this Mississippi River adventure two children find themselves trapped in a house with a wild cougar. Though they escape from this animal, one of the children is kidnapped. Now, they must rely on the wild animal they once feared. 28 mins.
VHS: S23497. $49.95.

Courage of Sarah Noble

During pioneer times, eight-year-old Sarah Noble and her father journey into the wilderness to build a new home. Adapted from Alice Daigliesh's Newbery Award-winning book. 49 mins.
VHS: S08409. $119.00.

Critter Songs

This upbeat video captures a mixture of live action visuals and children's art work in a celebration of our connection with the animal world. The video shows children how they can be a part of nature. Ages 3 to 12.
VHS: S23358. $39.95.

Curious George

Based on the books by Margaret and H.A. Rey featuring the adventures of the mischievous little monkey George. Ages 2-6. The Adventures of Curious George. A puppet animation version. 1986.
VHS: S24771. $12.95.

d'Aulaire's: Abraham Lincoln

This d'Aulaire book on Abraham Lincoln won a Caldecott Medal for its comprehensive look at an American hero from his humble beginnings to his mighty accomplishments. Part of the children's *Holidays* series.
VHS: S14180. $44.95.

d'Aulaire's: Benjamin Franklin

As a writer, printer, inventor, politician, diplomat and statesman, Benjamin Franklin helped shape the country and change the world. Part of the children's *Holidays* series.
VHS: S14179. $44.95.

d'Aulaire's: Christopher Columbus

Beginning when Columbus was a young boy in Genoa, Italy, this video follows him through shipwreck and war, to the New World and back again. Part of the children's *Holidays* series.
VHS: S14177. $44.95.

d'Aulaire's: George Washington

When George was born the country was little more than wilderness, but he was instrumental in mapping its future. Part of the children's *Holidays* series.
VHS: S14178. $44.95.

d'Aulaire's Holiday Biographies: Complete Set

Includes *Christopher Columbus, Abraham Lincoln, Benjamin Franklin* and *George Washington*. Four titles on one video cassette.
VHS: S14181. $159.95.

Daddy Can't Read

In this ABC Afterschool Special a girl joins an adult literacy program and discovers that her father can't read. This enjoyable show explores the stigma attached to illiteracy and treats it as a social problem that can be solved through patience and effort. This film is part of the Project Literacy U.S. (PLUS) Campaign. 28 mins.
VHS: S23470. $49.95.

Dan Crow's Oops!

Crow, respected as an educator as well as a songwriter/performer, stars in this concert video guaranteed to keep his fans happy. He's also the voice performing the title song for *The Adventures of Milo and Otis*. 30 mins.
VHS: S15307. $14.98.

Dancing with the Indians

Based on the book by Angela Shelf Medearis, this award-winning video tells the story of a young Black girl and her family's annual visit to and participation in the ceremonies of the Seminole tribe that during the Civil War, some 70 years earlier, had given sanctuary to her grandfather, an escaped slave. Ages 6-12. 8 minutes.
VHS: S24521. $37.95.

Daniel and the Towers

Streetwise 10-year-old Daniel Guerra forms an unlikely friendship with eccentric Italian immigrant Sam Rodia, who spent over 30 years building the Watts Towers in Los Angeles. Through Rodia, Daniel gains hope and a new set of values, and he crusades to save Rodia's lifework when the county slates it for demolition. With Alan Arbus, Carmen Zapata, Michael McKean and Miguael Alamo. 58 mins.
VHS: S16013. $29.95.

David the Gnome—Volume 1

Based on the best-selling Dutch children's books, *Gnomes* and *The Secret of the Gnomes*, the story of Gnome-Doctor David, who has magical powers and cures the mentally and physically sick and wounded creatures. Forever on the run all over the world, he is often in danger by the troublesome Trolls, sneaky Snotgurgles, fires and floods. 45 mins.
VHS: S03292. $19.95.

The Day Boy and the Night Girl

A 19th-century fantasy story, based on the book by George MacDonald, about an evil woman and two children who overcome her cruelty. This exquisite adaptation features beautiful cinematography and an engaging Scottish narrator who guides children through an intriguing good vs. evil story. 29 mins.
VHS: S30725. $19.95.

The Day Jimmy's Boa Ate the Wash

This collection of four animated shorts is perfect for kids. In addition to the story of the title, there is a story about *Monty*, an alligator taxi; *The Great White Man-Eating Shark*, a cautionary tale; and *Fourteen Rats and a Rat Catcher*. 35 mins.
VHS: S22168. $14.95.

Dear Mr. Henshaw

Adaptation of Beverly Cleary's book about a young boy who becomes author Boyd Henshaw's number one fan and begins a series of personal letters that help him find his own place in the world.
VHS: S08410. $119.00.

Diamonds on Wheels

Three English teenagers looking forward to entering a 24-hour road ralley find a second-hand driver's seat in an old junkyard. Little do they know that it is filled with stolen gemstones and villainous mobsters are eager for their return. With Peter Firth *(Equus)*. From Disney. Great Britain, 1973, 84 mins.
VHS: S06901. $69.95.

Dig Hole, Build House

Joe is a builder and Susan is an architect. They join forces with a cast of kids to show how concrete is poured into a hole in order to form the foundation of a house. It's perfect for truck crazy kids ages 3-10, 30 mins.
VHS: S25531. $14.95.

The Dingles

From the National Film Board of Canada, *Dingles* is the outlandish adventures of a grandmother and her three energetic cats. Other shows on the tape include *Little Red Riding Hood* (cell animation conjures up a world of children, wolves, grandmothers and wood choppers), *The Boy and the Snow Goose* (special relationship between a shy young boy and the goose he encounters), and *The Lion and the Mouse* (a delightful reworking of the Aesop fable). 30 mins.
VHS: S18562. $14.98.

The Discovery of the Americas

The discovery of the Americas is told with clear language and panoramic illustrations. Long before Columbus, many other movements and migrations took place in the Americas over thousands of years. There were Stone Age explorers, the Mayan civilization, the voyages of the Vikings as well as Columbus, Magellan and Balboa. Told by Betsy and Giulio Maestro.
VHS: S16342. $44.95.

Discovery Stories

Imaginative situations are presented through beautifully illustrated stories to make children aware of the world in which they live, and the need to protect it and find positive ways in which to live. 25 mins.
VHS: S10316. $29.95.

Disney Presents Bill Nye the Science Guy: Dinosaurs, Those Big Boneheads

What large ferocious creatures are loved by every kid on the planet? Dinosaurs of course, and Bill Nye is just the guy to explain to kids the science behind these prehistoric creatures. In-home experiments and special guests help make this another kid-pleasing science adventure. 47 mins.
VHS: S22337. $12.99.

Disney Presents Bill Nye the Science Guy: Outer Space Way Out There

Kids love the puns, jokes and cool science facts that Bill Nye tells. This video is so way out, it's stratospheric. It presents the hard science on outer space in an MTV like format with in-home experiments and special guests. 47 mins.
VHS: S22336. $12.99.

Disney Presents Bill Nye the Science Guy: The Human Body

Bill will take kids on a journey to the inner most parts of the human body. There is no more fun way to explore the cardiovascular system or the nervous system. 47 mins.
VHS: S22338. $12.99.

Divorce Can Happen to the Nicest People

A video specially designed for kids who ask the toughest questions. In a half hour of video animation, the video employs love, honesty and a sense of humor to explain some of life's toughest questions...helping to take the mystery and pain out of this difficult time. USA, 1987, 30 mins.
VHS: S04762. $19.95.

Doctor De Soto and Other Stories

Doctor De Soto is the Academy-Award short film about a dentist who finds a way to treat a crafty fox with a sore tooth. Other films on the tape are *Curious George Rides a Bike*, *The Hat* and *Patrick*.
VHS: S00353. $14.98.

The Dog Days of Arthur Cane

Arthur Cane is a spoiled child who scoffs at the magic powers of an amulet worn by James, an exchange student from Africa. Magically transformed, Arthur becomes a guide dog for a blind man and learns about love, kindness and friendship. Based on T. Ernesto Bethancourt's book. 29 mins.
VHS: S23452. $49.95.

The Dog Who Had Kittens

Based on the book by Polly M. Robertus. Baxter the Basset Hound adopts Eloise the cat's kittens. Ages 5-8. 14 minutes.
VHS: S24522. $37.95.

Dogsong

A 14-year old Eskimo, uncomfortable with the modern ways adopted by his people, embarks on a grueling 1,400 mile journey by dog sled across mountains, tundras and ice fields in this adaptation of Gary Paulsen's Newbery Award-winning book. 40 mins.
VHS: S08155. $119.00.

A Dozen Dizzy Dogs

Count up to twelve and back again with a lively, entertaining crew. Checkered dogs, dogs with stripes, dogs with spots, dogs with funny hats...all these dogs and more populate this funny, zany counting adventure. From the *Bank Street Read-Along Story Video* series. The story is told twice—once to familiarize children with the characters and story; the second time with words printed onscreen so children can easily follow along. For ages 3-8. 30 mins.
VHS: S13528. $14.99.

Dr. Zoology: The Tamarin Mystery

Dr. Zoo leads an undercover operation called the Eco-Adventures Travel Agency. Together with his assistant Nabe and a computer, The Magic Ring, a virtual rain forest, and Kidspower, Dr. Zoo is able to save Tammie, one of the mysterious and endangered Golden Lion Tamarins, from the evil PolyMorfus. In fact, his efforts save the globe from ecological disaster will teach kids that they too have the power to save the planet. Ages 5-10.
VHS: S27694. $19.95.
Ron Hankison, USA, 1995, 25 mins.

Dragonfly's Tale

When the Ashiwi tribe celebrates abundant food with a joyous food fight the Corn maidens are disappointed and show their disdain with a poor harvest and famine. The villagers leave to find a better life and leave two small children behind. They fashion the first firefly from a withered cornstalk, which flies to the Corn maidens. Soon the plentiful harvest returns, as do the villagers, who are wiser and kinder.
VHS: S21883. $44.95.

The Easter Bunny

The secretive Easter Bunny fools foxes, enters houses without a sound, leaves his Easter eggs and silently slips away. A charming story by Winifred Wolf.
VHS: S16344. $44.95.

The Easter Story Keepers

In the dark days of Roman persecution, Christian storykeeper Ben the Baker and his friends spread the inspiring tale of Easter and of Jesus' death and resurrection. This action-packed, animated story will captivate children while it teaches them about faith, family values and the importance of the Easter holiday. Featuring the celebrity vocal talents of Robert Guillaume, Debbie Boone and Jonathan Taylor Thomas. 70 mins.
VHS: S33234. $14.98.

Ed & Chester Bible Stories

Selected Bible stories come to life with these puppet plays by talented African-American puppeteer Ed Winters. 30 mins.
VHS: S20624. $29.95.

Ed & Chester Show

Puppet plays and skits by Ed Winters illustrate delightful tales that instruct and teach African-American values. 55 mins.
VHS: S20623. $29.95.

Eggs Mark the Spot

Pauline is a hen that can lay an egg that bears the image of whatever she is looking at. Find out how she becomes a heroine when she provides the clues to catch a burglar. Written and illustrated by Mary Jane Auch.
VHS: S30470. $37.95.

Elmopalooza!

Some of the biggest names in showbiz have gathered to sing their favorite Sesame Street Songs, and to celebrate 30 years of laughter, learning and fun. There's just one hitch: the host of the show is locked in his dressing room. Since the show must go on, Elmo takes over as host, and Big Bird, Ernie, Bert, and their friends pitch in to make sure that the evening is a hit. With Gloria Estefan, En Vogue, The Mighty Mighty Bosstones, Rosie O'Donnell, Fugees, Shawn Colvin, Steven Tyler, Jimmy Bufett, Celine Dion, Kenny Loggins, David Alan Grier, Chris Rock, Cindy Crawford, Tyra Banks, Richard Belzer, Jon Stewart, and Conan O'Brien. 55 mins.
DVD: DV60246. $24.98.
VHS: S33949. $12.98.

Emerald City of Oz

Margot Kidder narrates this animated adaptation of Frank Baum's continuing adventures of Dorothy. USA, 1988.
VHS: S08412. $19.98.

The Empty Pot

Based on a tale by Demi, *The Empty Pot* focuses on the efforts of Ping, an excellent gardener, to win the Emperor's unusual test in selecting an heir, the one who is able to raise flowers from a seed furnished by the emperor. Ping is frustrated when his seed won't sprout. "Demi's story is gracefully and sparely told, accompanied by delicately detailed artwork filled with plants, animals, and traditions that clearly place the story in ancient China" *(The Horn Book)*.
VHS: S20000. $44.95.

The Enchanting Travels of Benjamin of Tudela

In this animated short Benjamin is seen travelling to the communities he described in his *Book of Travels*. Barcelona, Constantinople, Jerusalem, Baghdad and Cairo are just a few of the places he visited. 9 mins.
VHS: S23260. $24.95.

Encyclopedia Brown: The Boy Detective— The Case of the Missing Time Capsule

Idaville's favorite pint-sized sleuth does some tricky detective work and saves the town's centennial celebration from disaster. Live action. 50 mins.
VHS: S11236. $14.95.

End of the Game

Julio Cortazar wrote a short story about a teenage girl named Jen who goes to visit her cousins Julie and Samantha. Through adventure and fantasy they learn about rivalry and change. 17 mins.
VHS: S23454. $79.95.

Ernst

Elisa Kleven's charming story about a young crocodile who loved to think "what if?" is an entertaining story lyrically narrated and set against sprightly music. 1991, 10 mins. Public Performance Rights.
VHS: S13895. $62.00.

Esteban and the Ghost

A merry tinker decides to investigate the mournful howl that echoes through Grey Castle and finds a strange figure unlike anything he ever imagined. A presentation of Sibly Hancock's story.
VHS: S08411. $62.00.

Eureeka's Castle: Sing Along with Eureeka

Eureeka, a wizard-in-training, and her friends Magellan, Batly and the Fish Tomes, rock the castle with 11 favorite songs from the *Parents' Choice* award-winning puppet character preschool series. Songs include "Pop Goes the Weasel," "I've Been Working on the Railroad," and a special rap version of "Old MacDonald Had a Farm." 30 mins.
VHS: S31443. $9.99.

Ewok Adventure
The impish, furry creatures from *Return of the Jedi* are now in their own film. After a crash landing on the planet of Endor, two Earthling youngsters befriend the magical Ewoks and embark on a thrilling quest to find their captive parents. USA, 1984, 96 mins.
VHS: S14558. $14.95.

The Ezra Jack Keats Library
This animated children's video includes the Ezra Jack Keats stories *The Snowy Day, Whistle for Willie, Peter's Chair, A Letter to Amy, Pet Show* and *The Trip*. 45 mins.
VHS: S22161. $14.95.

The Fall of Freddie the Leaf
Freddie the Leaf began as a small healthy sprout on a tree top. With the first frost he shivers with cold and fear. Fortunately his wise friend Daniel helps him prepare for change and the mystery of death. Based on the book by Leo Buscaglia. 16 mins.
VHS: S22367. $79.95.
Laser: LD74597. $99.95.

A Family Concert Featuring the Roches
Live concert footage, mime segments and animation enliven this video. It features music from the 1994 Parent's Choice Award winning album, *Will You Be My Friend?* Undoubtedly the Roches won this award because their music appeals to children and adults alike. 60 mins.
VHS: S26623. $14.95.

The Family Farm: Thomas Locker
A brother and sister design a plan using pumpkins and flowers to save their family's farm in this animated film showing contemporary rural life. Fun, toe-tapping bluegrass music encourages children to follow the story. 12 mins.
VHS: S14197. $44.95.

The Farmer's Huge Carrot
Written and illustrated by kindergarten children in West Columbia, Texas, this engaging story details the efforts of a farmer and his wife to grow a vegetable garden in the midst of a summer drought. 4 mins.
VHS: S19602. $39.00.

Fat Charlie's Circus
Fat Charlie loves the circus. He tries to duplicate a circus act by jumping from a tree into a glass of water. Fortunately Charlie learns an important lesson from his Grandmother, who saves him. This read-along video is an inspiring moral tale. 10:30 mins.
VHS: S22361. $39.95.

Father Christmas
Father Christmas' preparations for the Big Night are an exhausting, year-round affair, and he decides it's time he took a vacation. He converts his sleigh into a camper trailer, hitches it to the reindeer and flies off into the sky for a globe-hopping vacation to France, Scotland and Las Vegas. Based on the books by Raymond Briggs *(The Snowman)*. 25 mins.
VHS: S32195. $14.95.

Fay's 12 Days of Christmas
Renowned artist William Wegman celebrates the joy of Christmas with his dog Fay and her offspring, Batty, Chundo and Crooky. Kids will love watching these dogs decorate and prepare for the season. There is even a dream sequence of Santa's workshop as the dogs dream of Christmas morning. Ages 3 and up.
VHS: S26142. $12.95.
William Wegman, USA, 1995, 30 mins.

Fiesta
Sesame Street is having a fiesta, complete with floats, costumes and Elmo's favorite new dance, the Conga-Wiggle. Sing and dance along with Maria, Gabi and Rosita. With special performances by Linda Ronstadt and Celia Cruz. All the songs are in English and Spanish. 30 mins.
VHS: S32663. $9.95.

Fine White Dust
Cynthia Rylant's Newbery honor book is adapted in this presentation of her story about a 13-year-old boy who learns that appearances can be deceiving, when he falls under the spell of a charismatic stranger.
VHS: S08413. $69.95.

Fire and Rescue
Fact-filled and exciting, this video takes kids into a fire station, and shares the facts of the job of firefighting. The video shows men and women of diverse backgrounds. Ages 4+. 30 minutes.
VHS: S25040. $29.95.

First and Second Grade Feelings
Adolescence is evoked in these prize-winning tales by Miriam Cohen, illustrated by Lilliam Hoban, that deal with fraternity, independence, self-realization and honesty. "A multi-ethnic classroom, a loving teacher…amusing antics of Jim and the other children, natural sounding dialogue: who could ask for anything more?" *(Bulletin of the Center for Children's Books)*. Intended for children in kindergarten through third grade.
Jim's Dog, Muffins. Following the death of his dog, Jim is withdrawn and pensive and refuses to speak to his first-grade classmates. As his friends try to understand Jim's reaction to death, Paul helps him deal with his sorrow and loss. "Numerous books have dealt with the effect of a pet's death on a child, but few are as true to a child's feelings" *(The Horn Book)*. 7 mins.
VHS: S20041. $44.95.
So What? Jim feels ostracized because he is smaller than everybody else in the first grade. He tries to start a club and people abandon him. But a sympathetic girl from Chicago helps him overcome his insecurity and teaches him valuable lessons in independence. 8 mins.
VHS: S20042. $44.95.
See You in Second Grade! Jim, Paul, Danny, George and Anna Maria celebrate at the end-of-the-year picnic on the beach. The teacher helps them recall the fantastic experiences of First Grade and they eagerly await the forthcoming year in Second Grade. 7 mins.
VHS: S20044. $44.95.
The Real-Skin Rubber Monster Mask. Jim is excited about wearing his real-skin rubber monster mask until he seeks his reflection on Halloween and fears that he's being transformed into a monster. Willy comes to his aid. 11 mins.
VHS: S20043. $44.95.
First and Second Grade Feelings, Set. A collection four titles. 33 mins.
VHS: S18696. $159.95.

Five Lionni Classics
The power of imagination is the theme of these five animated pieces based upon Leo Lionni's popular animal fables. Frederick, Cornelius and Swimmy are featured in animation by Lionni and Giulio Gianini.
VHS: S02846. $19.95.
Giulio Gianini, Italy, 1986, 30 mins.

Fledgling
An adaptation of Jane Langton's Newbery Honor fantasy tells the story of eight-year-old Georgie, who longs to fly. Her dream comes true after she meets a mysterious Canadian goose. 38 mins.
VHS: S09902. $110.00.

A Flight to the Finish
A race is being held in Odyssey, and Dylan and Sherman are in the thick of it. Taunted by their new neighbors, Holly and her mischievous cat Jasper, Dylan and Sherman are determined to beat them to the finish line. But when Holly's car careens out of control, Dylan must choose to either follow his conscience and help her or continue on and win the race. His dilemma provides an exciting lesson in caring for others. USA, animated, 30 mins.
VHS: S15054. $14.98.

The Flyaway Pantaloons
After they're blown off a clothesline, a pair of women's pantaloons undertake a colorful odyssey through the streets, markets, corners and textures of a Renaissance city. 9 mins.
VHS: S20001. $36.95.

Follow My Leader
Jimmy must undergo rehabilitation after an accident involving a firecracker. He was blinded and is naturally angry at the friend responsible for the accident. As Jimmy learns to forget his anger, his guide dog emerges as a vital link in his effort to enjoy life once more. Based on James B. Garfield's book. 29 mins.
VHS: S23472. $79.95.
Laser: LD74762. $99.95.

Follow the Drinking Gourd
Ron Richardson narrates this iconographic video presentation of Jeannette Winters' moving story about Peg Leg Joe and a brave group of runaway slaves who follow the Drinking Gourd north to freedom on the Underground Railroad. 12 mins.
VHS: S12259. $62.00.

The Fool of the World and the Flying Ship
Meet Pyotr, a peasant boy who wins the hand of a beautiful princess, with a little help from some talented friends. Pyotr and his friends journey to the Czar's palace, where they successfully complete three impossible tasks and prove that the most humble of people can defeat power and greed. Claymation. A PBS WGBH Boston Special. 60 mins.
VHS: S33086. $14.95.

Four for Thrills, Edgar Allan Poe, Etc.
Here is a quartet of exciting and colorful animated shorts containing Edgar Allan Poe's classic *Masque of the Red Death*, Harry Belafonte's presentation of *The Hand* and the immortal *Casey at the Bat*, and the story of *The Hangman* as told by Herschel Bernardi.
VHS: S03957. $19.95.

The Fourth King
An original, animated Christmas story featuring sing-along songs, loveable animals and an important lesson about friendship and humility. USA, 30 mins.
VHS: S15221. $14.95.

Frog
Arlo Anderson adds a magic frog who is really a prince to his reptile collection, and the web-footed wizard turns his life upside down with wacky results. Shelley Duvall, Elliott Gould, Paul Williams star.
Laser: LD71063. $29.98.
David Grossman, USA, 1987, 95 mins.

Garden of Abdul Gasazi
A boy lets his dog wander into a magician's forbidden garden in this award-winning tale of Chris Van Allsburg's cautionary tale. 8 mins.
VHS: S08157. $114.00.

Gentle Giant
The feature film that launched the tv series *Gentle Ben*. A gentle, orphaned bear cub grows very large and causes some problems in public relations for Dennis Weaver and Vera Miles.
VHS: S04237. $39.95.
James Neilson, USA, 1967, 93 mins.

Gerbert Is Ben Franklin
This delightful video will entrance kids with an historic look at the life of Ben Franklin as played by Gerbert. One of America's founding fathers, Franklin was not just a gifted leader, but a man of charm and wit.
VHS: S26289. $14.95.
Richard Tiffany, USA, 1992, 30 mins.

Gerbert Is Marco Polo
Gerbert and his pal Roary are off to China as Gerbert imagines himself to be the Italian explorer Marco Polo. This puppet's tale will intrigue children with the historic achievements of this intrepid figure from the past.
VHS: S26291. $14.95.
Richard Tiffany, USA, 1992, 30 mins.

Gerbert Is Mozart
The 18th-century musical genius will come alive for kids in this historic recreation of Mozart's life starring the puppet Gerbert. Gerbert starts by fantasizing about being the composer, but soon realizes that it takes talent, hard work and practice to reach any goal.
VHS: S26290. $14.95.
Richard Tiffany, USA, 1992, 30 mins.

Gerbert Is Tom Sawyer
Kids will love this historically inspired cartoon featuring Gerbert Sawyer. He travels down the Mississippi with America's most original humorist, Mark Twain.
VHS: S26151. $12.99.
Richard Tiffany, USA, 1992, 30 mins.

Ghost Writer: Into the Comics
The Children's Television Workshop has created another hip, fresh, comic mystery adventure. This one features a contest and a surprise appearance by Spike Lee. 99 mins.
VHS: S22194. $14.98.

Ghost Writer: Who Burned Mr. Brinker's Store

From the creators at Children's Television Workshop comes this hip, fresh and funny series. In this video a mystery adventure is set in motion to find the culprit who burned Mr. Brinker's store. The truth will either set Jamal free or get him burned. 95 mins.
VHS: S22193. $14.98.

Giving Thanks: A Native-American Good Morning Message

Known as the Thanksgiving Address, this Native-Amerian good morning message is based on the belief that the natural world is a precious and rare gift, from the moon and the stars to the tiniest blade of grass. Written and narrated by Chief Jake Swamp in English and the Mohawk language. 7 mins.
VHS: S33784. $60.00.

Glass Slipper

This sentimental, musical version of the classic Cinderella story alternates between dramatic setpieces and rich, romantic fantasy sequences filled with song and dance. Stars Leslie Caron and Keenan Wynn.
VHS: S13643. $19.98.
Charles Walters, USA, 1955, 94 mins.

Golden Voyage of Sinbad

A spectacular adventure set in mysterious ancient lands inhabited by incredible creatures. Sinbad (John Philip Law) finds an intriguing map and sets sail for the uncharted island of Lemuria. His companions: a mysterious and intriguing slave girl and Prince Koura.
VHS: S12999. $14.95.
Gordon Hessler, USA, 1973, 105 mins.

Good King Wenceslas

Illustrator Jamichael Henterly's rich medieval details and deep warm colors convey the warmth of this beloved holiday story about a kindly king who is moved by the unfortunate plight of a peasant. 6 mins.
VHS: S12260. $57.00.

Good Morning Miss Toliver

Acclaimed teacher Kay Toliver takes us to her New York City school, where we glimpse her incredible combination of math, art, acting and fun. First seen on PBS. Ages 8+. 26 minutes.
VHS: S24981. $24.95.

Granpa

This beautifully animated video about exploring the imaginary worlds of each other's future and past is based on John Burningham's prize winning book and was created by the same team responsible for the perennial best-seller *The Snowman*. Narrated by Peter Ustinov. 30 mins.
VHS: S15305. $14.98.

Great Bible Stories

Narrated and animated bible stories for children, with two complete stories on each video. Each tape is 30 minutes.
Abraham/Naaman and the Slave Girl.
VHS: S07411. $14.99.
Apostle Paul/Prodigal Son.
VHS: S07419. $14.99.
David and Goliath/Gideon.
VHS: S07409. $14.99.
Moses/Samuel and Saul.
VHS: S07410. $14.99.
Noah's Ark/Joshua.
VHS: S07408. $14.99.
Story of Peter/Phillipian Jailer.
VHS: S07417. $14.99.

The Greedy Man in the Moon

Rick Rossiter retells this ancient Chinese folk tale about a poor village boy who rescues a wounded bird and is rewarded for his kindness. In not quite the same kind-hearted spirit, the boy's neighbor tries to copy him. For grades K-3.
VHS: S31442. $44.99.

Greg & Steve Live! In Concert

Greg & Steve perform "ABC Rock", "The World Is a Rainbow", "Friends" and other popular children's favorites. 60 mins.
VHS: S20468. $19.95.

Greg & Steve Musical Adventures

Greg & Steve sing their way through six different musical adventures, including "The Three Little Pigs", "Heavenly Music", "We've Got the Whole World", "Down by the Bay" and more. 30 mins.
VHS: S20469. $14.95.

Greyling

Jane Yolen based this original story on Scottish fishermen's tales of "selchies," the magical creatures who are human on land and seals in the water. A sad, childless couple live on one of the islands off the coast of Scotland. Their lives change one day when the fishermen bring home an orphaned seal pup (who turns out to be a selchie) and whom the fisherman and his wife view as their own beloved son.
VHS: S16347. $44.95.

Gullah Gullah Island—Feelings

Nick Jr.'s award-winning children's series. Contains two song-filled episodes—*Special Places* and *Binyah Binyah Parade*—plus the Nick Jr. music video *Feelings*. 46 mins.
VHS: S33762. $9.95.

Gullah Gullah Island: Dance Along with the Daise Family

Ron and Natalie Daise, a real-life couple from Sea Island, off South Carolina's coast, invite you to dance along to 14 of the hip-hoppingest tunes ever spun on Gullah Gullah Island. 30 mins.
VHS: S31444. $9.99.

Gulliver's Travels

Gulliver has been trapped by the tiny Lilliputians. After he wins their trust, he learns they are engaged in a war with the nearby island of LaFuscoe. It all began over the preparation of pasta. Only his gigantic size can stave off disaster in this miniature animated kingdom. From the *Enchanted Tales* series.
VHS: S27371. $14.95.
Diane Eskenazi, USA, 1996, 48 mins.

H.R. Pufnstuf Live at the Hollywood Bowl

Before there was Barney, there was a lovable clown-like dragon named Pufnstuf who brightened many a Saturday morning for a generation of larval Gen X-ers. Get nostalgic with Puf, Jimmy, Witchiepoo, Lidsville and the rest of Sid & Marty Krofft's most popular characters in this live performance. Also featuring the Brady Bunch kids in a rare live performance. 50 mins.
VHS: S32063. $12.95.

Halloween

This iconographic presentation of Gail Gibbon's book explores the history, meanings and trappings of one of childhood's most favorite and colorful holidays. 6 mins.
VHS: S24914. $37.95.

Handel's Last Chance

Set in 18th-century Dublin, this enchanting film for kids—the last in the award-winning Composers' Specials series—tells the captivating story of Jamie, a boy with a golden voice who is down on his luck, and Handel, the great composer, whose career is failing. Given one last chance to prove themselves, Jamie and Handel learn to trust each other and believe in their own talents. Joining forces, the two make the first performances of *The Messiah* a resounding success. 50 mins.
VHS: S30652. $19.98.

Harbor Tugs at Work

This video follows in the traditions of the children's video *I Love Toy Trains*. It shows how harbor tugs work for an audience ages two and up. Captain Evans and his crew are helpful and informative guides to the modern world of harbors and their cargo. 30 mins.
VHS: S24357. $14.95.

The Hardly Boys in Hardly Gold

In William Wegman's first feature film, doggy detectives the Hardly Boys, have returned to Rangeley Lake for another relaxing summer at the Hardly Inn with their friend, Chip Mason. But soon the boys find themselves enmeshed in a perplexing mystery that puts their sleuthing kills and secret dog powers to the test.
VHS: S33003. $19.95.
William Wegman, USA, 1997, 30 mins.

Harold and the Purple Crayon and Other Harold Stories

Gene Deitch, the world's foremost animator of classic children's books, explains how he learned from Crockett Johnson. *Harold and the Purple Crayon, Harold's Fairy Tale* and *A Picture for Harold's Room* are animated shorts that make this video a delight for children. 30 mins.
VHS: S22166. $14.95.

Harry and the Lady Next Door

In this award-winning film based on the books by Gene Zion, the lady next door, an opera singer, has a high voice that hurts Harry the dog's ears. Harry tries everything to drown out the lady's singing and his eventual solution provides plenty of laughs. 20 mins.
VHS: S30719. $19.95.

Harry the Dirty Dog

This hilarious, award-winning, live-action adaptation of Gene Zion's popular children's story tells of Harry, a care-free, fun-loving dog—who hates baths. When bathtime comes, Harry hides the scrub brush and runs away, landing him into all kinds of trouble. 18 mins.
VHS: S30718. $19.95.

Henry Hamilton: Graduate Ghost

Former Civil War soldier Hamilton is having a hard time as a ghost because he's too nice. The Specter Inspector is not convinced Henry can haunt a great mansion so he is assigned to the Landry family as a test of his spooking abilities. Henry loses no time and teaches the Landrys a host of self-affirming ideals. 29 mins.
VHS: S23448. $49.95.

Hercules

Journey back in time to an age of ancient mysteries, superhuman deeds and breathtaking, mythical adventures in this exciting, animated story of the most powerful hero to walk the earth. 48 mins.
VHS: S30500. $14.98.

Here Comes a Roller Coaster

Dave and his son Taylor will show kids some of the most daunting roller coasters at Six Flags Theme Park. Also includes a look at the Batman ride and the Log Jammer. Ages 3-8, 35 mins.
VHS: S24488. $12.95.

Here Comes the Cat and Other Cat Stories

Animated features *The Cat and the Collector, Cat and Canary* and *Millions of Cats* are joined with the title story for a collection sure to please cat lovers of all ages. 30 mins.
VHS: S22167. $14.95.

Here We Go—Vol. 1

An informative show that captures children's fascinations with some of the most exciting vehicles ever made, including zeppelins. Narrated by Lynn Redgrave, Parents' Choice award. 33 mins.
VHS: S04996. $12.95.

Here We Go Again

Featuring 14 thrilling sequences from around the world, *Here We Go Again* continues the educational series on transportation. Lynn Redgrave provides valuable information and excitement at each intriguing location. Among other vehicles, kids will get to ride on a San Francisco cable car, farm tractor, police car, and propeller airplane. 60 mins.
VHS: S16759. $12.95.

Herman & Marguerite

A tale of an insecure worm and a frightened caterpillar (later a butterfly) who learn to look at themselves and each other with love and respect as they help bring spring to the earth. A discussion guide which suggests ways of using storytelling accompanies. Told by master storyteller Jay O'Callahan. Public performance rights included.
VHS: S09268. $19.95.

The Holiday Collection

In this series, children discover the foundations and traditions of our national holidays. They learn how April 1st evolved into a day of pranks and the strange tradition behind the groundhog's search for his shadow on February 2nd. The series also looks at the origins of St. Patrick's Day, Thanksgiving and Christmas. Designed for children from kindergarten through 3rd grade.
Special Spring Days. Children learn the background of three spring holidays: the origins of Groundhog Day; the story of St. Patrick; and how the first day of April became a day for trickery. 19 mins.
VHS: S19991. $37.95.
Thanksgiving Tales. Two versions of the Thanksgiving holiday, the familiar telling of the pilgrims and the First Thanksgiving, and the story of an Indian who befriends a group of strangers and helps them adjust to the rugged frontier life. 29 mins.
VHS: S19990. $37.95.
The Twelve Days of Christmas. Children are taught the private joys and special pleasures behind an enduring season classic, the popular carol that discusses the epiphanies of the 12 days. 13 mins.
VHS: S19992. $37.95.
The Holiday Collection, Set.
VHS: S19993. $99.00.

Holidays for Children Video Series

This 12-volume set offers an interactive children's video experience. It explores the customs, rituals and folklore underlying some of the major traditional American holidays. Traditional music, animation and live-action sequences hosted by Michael Keck make this series an entertaining but educational resource for children. Each volume is 30 mins.

Arbor Day.
VHS: S24460. $29.95.
Chinese New Year.
VHS: S24461. $29.95.
Christmas.
VHS: S24462. $29.95.
Cinco de Mayo.
VHS: S24463. $29.95.
Easter.
VHS: S24464. $29.95.
Halloween.
VHS: S24465. $29.95.
Hanukkah/Passover.
VHS: S24466. $29.95.
Independence Day.
VHS: S24467. $29.95.
Kwanzaa.
VHS: S24468. $29.95.
Rosh Hashana/Yom Kippur.
VHS: S24469. $29.95.
Thanksgiving.
VHS: S24470. $29.95.
Valentine's Day.
VHS: S24471. $29.95.
Holidays for Children Video Series. 12-volume set.
VHS: S24472. $359.40.

Homer Price Stories

Two Homer Price stories, based on Robert McCloskey's now classic stories, set in fictional town of Centerburg, with Homer, the 10-year-old boy, growing up in the world of the 50's. 40 mins.
VHS: S03519. $14.95.

How a Car Is Built

Kids will travel down a Ford assembly line nine miles long. They will see how the Ford Mustang is built. Everything from precision robots to powerful metal presses to the arduous painting process is fully detailed. 30 mins.
VHS: S26004. $14.95.

How Beaver Stole Fire

In this sand animation short, a Native American tale about the origin of fire is beautifully realized. 12 mins.
VHS: S23507. $39.95.

How It's Done: From Baseball Bats to Potato Chips

This fascinating behind the scenes look at the production of everyday objects will fascinate kids. Detective Howie Dunn leads kids on a tour that explains how bats, orange juice, cherries, and even potato chips are made. 34 mins.
VHS: S23964. $9.99.

How It's Done: From Roller Coasters to Ice Cream

Howie Dunne does it again. This time his tour shows how roller coasters, ice cream, softballs, TV news broadcasts and more are prepared and made available to consumers. 32 mins.
VHS: S23965. $9.99.

How to Hide Stories

Ruth Heller has composed six beautiful tales involving birds, amphibians and reptiles engaged in clever games of hide-and-seek with Mother Nature. The stories deal with transformation and how animals camouflage in nature, realized through striking illustrations and a rhyming text. Designed for children in kindergarten through 3rd grade.

How to Hide a Butterfly and Other Insects.
VHS: S20020. $44.95.
How to Hide a Crocodile and Other Reptiles.
VHS: S20015. $44.95.
How to Hide a Gray Treefrog and Other Amphibians.
VHS: S20019. $44.95.
How to Hide a Polar Bear and Other Mammals.
VHS: S20016. $44.95.
How to Hide a Whip-Poor-Will and Other Birds.
VHS: S20017. $44.95.
How to Hide an Octopus and Other Sea Creatures.
VHS: S20018. $44.95.
How to Hide Stories, Set.
VHS: S20021. $239.95.

Human Race Club: A Story About Fights Between Brothers and Sisters

Sibling rivalry and handling uncomfortable feelings are the topics dealt with in this volume of the animated children's series created by Joy Berry. The stories include *Casey's Revenge* and *The Lean Mean Machine*. 60 mins.
VHS: S10990. $29.95.

Human Race Club: A Story About Making Friends, a Story About Prejudice and Discrimination

Children learn about discrimination, prejudice and friendship in the animated stories *The Fair Weather Friend* and *Unforgettable Pen Pal*. From Joy Berry, the founder of the Human Race Club. 60 mins.
VHS: S10989. $29.95.

Human Race Club: A Story About Self-Esteem, a Story About Earning Money

A fully animated children's series that emphasizes proper values and valuable tips on growing up. This volume deals with self-esteem and earning money in the stories *The Letter on Light Blue Stationery* and *A High Price to Pay*. Created by Joy Berry, the best-selling author of over 250 self-help books for children. 60 mins.
VHS: S10988. $29.95.

The Hunchback of Notre Dame

Victor Hugo's touching and dramatic love story is transformed in this animated musical. Quasimodo plays the bells for his only friends, the bats at the top of the Notre Dame belfry. Then one day he happens to see the beautiful gypsy girl, Melody, walking by. His desire for her leads him down to the streets of Paris, where he must protect her from the dastardly Captain of the Guard. USA, 1996, 48 mins.
VHS: S27418. $14.98.

Hundred Dresses

Based on Eleanor Estes' Newbery Award-winning book about Wanda Petronski, who wears the same faded blue dress every day. When she tells two classmates that she has a hundred dresses at home, she becomes the target of a daily game of tease. 36 mins.
VHS: S08159. $119.00.

I Can Build

A family works together to build a two-story playhouse. The family cooperation of big sister, younger brother, mom and dad is nice. The step-by-step process is shown, from shopping to sawing to hammering. Combining live action and 3-D animation, this video shows youngsters how a house is constructed from the ground up. Ages 2-8. 25 mins.
VHS: S24547. $14.95.

I Have a Friend

A small boy tells of his very special friend, who keeps his dreams secret and safe. At night his friend disappears, but will be waiting for him with the sun. The friend is the small boy's shadow. 7 mins.
VHS: S12261. $62.00.

I Need a Hug!

In this rhyme, composed and illustrated by first-grade students at Clara Barton Elementary in Bordertown, New Jersey, a sad, lonely bug who longs for love and acceptance wants a hug, except the other bugs are too busy to notice his pain. Finally he finds a soulmate. 6 mins.
VHS: S19600. $39.00.

I Want to Be an Artist When I Grow Up

This video, designed for children in grades K-5, provides an overview of the various careers the art field offers. 15 mins.
VHS: S19929. $28.99.

I'll Fix Anthony

Anthony can read, but he won't read to his younger brother Nicholas. Nicholas dreams of revenge when he turns six years old. This is a charming story of sibling rivalry sure to delight viewers. Based on the book by Bill Britain. 14 mins.
VHS: S22371. $69.95.
Laser: LD74600. $99.95.

I'm Not Oscar's Friend Anymore and Other Stories

Four book-based stories centered on friendship, including: *Creole*, with a bird whose appearance frightens the other animals; *Hug Me*, with a porcupine desperate for a hug; and *Birds of a Feather*, about differences. Ages 4-9. 30 minutes.
VHS: S24533. $9.95.

Imaginit

This computer-animated ride through the imagination contains 14 segments filled with bright, colorful animation and catchy sing-along tunes by acclaimed children's recording artist Craig 'n Co., that will be enjoyed by kids and parents alike. This is the third title in the award-winning Imagination Series. Directed by Grammy-nominated Michael Boydstun, project director for the multi-platinum *Beyond the Mind's Eye*. "...a bonafide children's success. It will interest parents...as much as their kids" *(Billboard)*.
VHS: S30154. $12.98.
Michael Boydstun, USA, 1996, 35 mins.

In Coal Country

This iconographic video presentation evokes the flavor of Judith Hendershot's award-winning story about the life of a miner's family in the 1930's, seen through the eyes of a young girl. 11 mins.
VHS: S12262. $62.00.

In My Own Backyard

In this read-along video children will learn about all the things that used to live in their backyard. From agrarian America all the way back to the time of the dinosaurs, it's a fascinating look at history, geology and more. 11:17 mins.

English Version.
VHS: S22364. $39.95.
Spanish Version.
VHS: S22365. $39.95.

Ira Says Goodbye

Based on Bernard Waber's story, Ira is upset when his best friend Reggie has to move away. Ages 5-9. 1989, 18 mins.
VHS: S24532. $37.95.

Ira Sleeps Over

Michael Sporn's whimsical animation is based on Bruce Weber's children's story about the trepidation and fears experienced by Ira on his first night away from home, when he sleeps over at Reggie's house. Adapted from Weber's musical *Lyle, Lyle Crocodile*. 27 mins.
VHS: S19546. $12.98.

It Could Always Be Worse

A poor man learns to count his blessings when he asks his rabbi for advice on how to cope with his crowded household. A charming adaptation of Margot Zemach's award-winning Yiddish tale. 9 mins.
VHS: S08160. $65.00.

It's in Every One of Us

Enchanting to both adults and children, this video blends Wernher Krutein's heart-warming images of the global family with David Pomeranz's music and lyrics as a celebration of the human spirit. 5 mins.
VHS: S10230. $17.95.

It's Like This, Cat

A delightfully-illustrated adaptation of Emily Neville's Newbery Award-winning book tells the story of 14-year-old David, who is launched into a series of neighborhood adventures after he acquires a cat. 34 mins.
VHS: S08161. $119.00.

It's Me, Claudia! & My Grandson Lew

Two popular children's books on one video. In *It's Me, Claudia!*, based on the book by Alyse Newman, we meet 9-year-old Claudia, who hides herself under a big, floppy hat because she hates her big ears. Life gets pretty lonely until Claudia bumps into Paul, who is hiding under a hat, too. Together the two learn not to be self-conscious. In *My Grandson, Lew*, based on the book by Charlotte Zolotow, a young boy learns that his grandfather has died. The young boy and his mother share their memories of the old man and this helps them overcome the loneliness of life without him. 32 mins.
VHS: S30722. $19.95.

It's Not Always Easy Being a Kid

The puppets at The Judy Theatre help children acquire skills for living. In this video, young Charlie comes to grips with his failure at school by working with a tutor. Then a fable and song examine the temptation to smoke cigarettes and help find an alternative for feeling good about oneself. Ages 7-10.
VHS: S24713. $19.95.

Jacob Have I Loved

Amanda Plummer plays Louise in this adaptation of Katherine Paterson's Newbery Award-winning novel about a young girl growing up on a tiny, isolated Chesapeake island and her relationship with her twin sister. 55 mins.

VHS: S07697. $119.00.

Jaguar Trax

Featuring a talented cast of young TV actors and recording artists, this entertaining tale is designed to teach students about the value of tropical rainforests and how they might be saved. 40 mins.

VHS: S30090. $65.00.

The James Marshall Library

A Tale of Two Chickens, Goldilocks and the Three Bears, The Three Little Pigs and *Red Riding Hood* are all told by the witty James Marshall. These delightful children's animated tales are complemented by a brief documentary about Marshall himself. 43 mins.

VHS: S22684. $14.95.

Janey Junkfood's Fresh Adventure

Emmy award-winning TV special, wildly fun, which aims to excite and educate children (and families) about healthy food. Ages 5-13.

VHS: S24768. $99.00.

Janosch

The unusual storytelling bear presents a collection of stories in which objects have regained their magic, stories of lasting friendship, fables about being strong, being weak, about dreams and daydreams. Based on the acclaimed children's stories by Janosch, whose books have won innumerable international awards. Fully animated. 116 mins.

VHS: S10332. $39.95.

Jay O'Callahan: A Master Class in Storytelling

Storytelling sparks imagination. In *Master Class*, O'Callahan shows what makes a story work and how characters can be brought to life. "Jay O'Callahan is a one-man cultural renaissance. These tapes should be required viewing for all between the ages of five and ninety-five" *(Video Librarian)*. 33 mins. color, with workshop guide. Public performance rights included.

VHS: S09265. $59.95.

Jazz Time Tale

A sensitive work about a young girl's social and personal transformation following her encounter with the legendary piano player Fats Waller. Narrated by Ruby Dee.

VHS: S17764. $9.95.

Michael Sporn, USA, 29 mins.

Jeremy Around the World

The adventures of Jeremy and his pal Raven as they search for Cousin Hector, who has been captured by the greedy Wolf. Jeremy's amazing suitcase turns into an auto, a helicopter, a jeep or any other vehicle. 90 mins.

VHS: S03845. $29.95.

Jessi Sings Songs from Around the World

Jessi Colter performs 25 international children's songs, including such favorites as "La Cucaracha", "This Land Is Your Land", "Funiculi, Funicula", "London Bridge", "Too Ra Loo Ra Loo Ral", and even "Aloha Oe". 57 mins.

VHS: S21875. $14.98.

Jimbo and the Jet-Set

Here's the lovable little junior jet with big ideas. Follow the world-wide adventures of Jimbo to fun and excitement in far-off lands. Two precious volumes.

Jimbo and the Jet-Set, Volume 1. 50 mins.

VHS: S16143. $12.98.

Jimbo and the Jet-Set, Volume 2. 54 mins.

VHS: S16144. $12.98.

Jing, A Chinese Girl

Jing is an 11-year-old girl at the center of this chronicle. Over two days her experiences reveal intriguing aspects of life among those living in the world's most populous country. This video explores a number of issues affecting the quality of life for the Chinese people, including population control and competition. 18 mins.

VHS: S23720. $145.95.

Jingle Bell Rap!

Members of the all-dog band, the K9 Four, are all tuned up for a special hometown Christmas concert and gala tree lighting ceremony. Then their town's search for the proper pooch to play the part of Santa Claws runs into some heavy sledding. 25 mins.

VHS: S13031. $9.98.

Josephine's Imagination

Based on the story by Arnold Dobrin, the video features his illustrations. The story is about a young Black Haitian girl and her mother, who earns a living selling at the colorful market. Josephine makes little dolls from the throw-away bits of things from the market. Soon she has a good little business going. Even the boys like her dolls. Told with a simple, lovely French/Haitian Creole dialect, this is a very warm, gentle film, which shows Haitian culture at its best. 14 minutes.

VHS: S24537. $69.95.

Journey Home: The Animals of Farthing Wood

Heroic Fox, dutiful Badger, shy Mole, playful Weasel and their friends are on the move. The Animals of Farthing Wood are looking for a land far from civilization, a safe place they can call home. Feature-length animated film based on the best-selling children's books. Featuring the voice of Ralph Macchio. 90 mins.

VHS: S33237. $14.98.

The Jousters

This children's film features two young boys, best friends, who regularly play games together, imagining themselves as medieval knights. Inspired by the classroom tales of the legend of Sir Lancelot, and learning of the existence of a real castle near their homes, the two youngsters set out on their own adventure, during which they experience a real scare and learn the value of true friendship. Public performance.

VHS: S32122. $79.95.

John Muccigrosso, USA, 1989, 16 mins.

Jumanji

Fantasy and reality combine in this adaptation of Chris Van Allsburg's Caldecott Medal winning story about two bored children who find a mysterious game which startlingly comes to life. 13 mins.

VHS: S08163. $65.00.

The Jungle Books, Set I

This dramatic presentation of the all-time children's classic features sound effects ingeniously recorded at the London Zoo. Includes *Mowgli's Brothers, Rikki-Tikki-Tavi, Tiger! Tiger!* and *Toomai of the Elephants*. For Grades 2-6.

VHS: S14208. $139.95.

A Jungle for Joey

A baby orangutan gets himself a new home. 14 mins.

VHS: S23461. $49.95.

Laser: LD74761. $99.95.

Jungle King

Being king of the jungle is not just a privilege, it's a responsibility. In this funny, animated feature a lion has his paws full learning how to rule over the wild animals of hisdomain. Overcoming his easy-going nature and discovering the majesty within himself is a recipe for good-natured humor.

VHS: S21363. $14.98.

Junglies: First Day at School

A vivid collection of vignettes which dramatize individual situations of young children caught up in the awe and wonder of adolescence. 30 mins.

VHS: S19433. $14.99.

The Keeping Quilt

This iconographic presentation captures the warmth of Patricia Polacco's AJL Sidney Taylor Book Award story of her ancestors that traces the history of the clothing back home to Russia. Over the course of a century, a coverlet serves as a Sabbath tablecloth, a wedding canopy and a blanket for new-born babies.

VHS: S31445. $44.99.

A Kid's Eye View of Ecology

Kids will want to sing along with children's entertainer Michael Mish's lively introduction to environmental preservation for young people. Mish and three children present a fast-paced overview of a wide range of topical environmental issues. USA, 1991, 28 mins.

VHS: S15200. $59.95.

The Knight Travellers

Dylan Taylor discovers the important parts of life when he and his dog, Sherman, become involved with the rescue of a time transport machine from a diabolical villain. This animated video is based on the radio program *Adventures in Odyssey*. 30 mins.

VHS: S15053. $14.98.

Knots on a Counting Rope

In this poignant story of love, hope and courage, the counting rope is a metaphor for the passage of time and the boy's emerging confidence in facing his greatest challenge—his blindness. Grades P-3.

VHS: S14198. $44.95.

Lassie's Great Adventure

Taken from the long-running television series and not the collection of MGM series, this enchanting children's work charts the episodes of the determined, eager dog and her amazing tales. With June Lockhart and Jon Provost.

VHS: S18897. $24.95.

Lassie: Mother Knows Best

Only Mom can rival Lassie for intelligence, resourcefulness and loyalty. In these two episodes June Lockheart shares center stage with the famed canine. First *The Wrong Gift* surprises Mom, then *The New Refrigerator* leaves Lassie out in the cold. 55 mins.

VHS: S25517. $9.98.

Lassie: To Fetch a Thief

Two episodes show Lassie sleuthing her way through mystery. Only a fearless young boy called Timmy and his trusty collie can save two people wrongly accused of crime. 55 mins.

VHS: S25519. $9.98.

Lassie: To the Rescue

The two episodes on this video show Lassie at her heroic best. Both are literally cliffhangers. In the first, a precarious cliff road gives way, while in the second little Timmy gets too close to the edge of the Grand Canyon. Includes Nickelodean's Lassie Camping Quiz. 55 mins.

VHS: S25518. $9.98.

Leader of the People

John Steinbeck wrote this widely anthologized story about the Tiflins, a ranching family who figure in the *The Red Pony* cycle of stories. Valuable as literature, this work also reveals much about the American frontier. 23 mins.

VHS: S23447. $79.95.

Les Miserables

Victor Hugo's classic novel is translated in an easy-to-follow animated production, spanning 40 years of French history. 60 mins.

VHS: S09189. $24.95.

Let's Make a Map

First a street and its buildings are rendered as cardboard models, then as wooden blocks, and then as pieces of cloth. From these last elements a two-dimensional world emerges that reflects the real world of three dimensions. 11 mins.

VHS: S23726. $49.95.

Lights: The Miracle of Chanukah

Judd Hirsch narrates this animated feature about the origins and meaning of the candles that are lit over the eight days of Chanukah. Kids will be fascinated by the significance of this vital story. The voices of Leonard Nimoy and Paul Michael Glaser are featured.

VHS: S22071. $16.95.

The Lilith Summer

Based on the book by Hadley Irwin. Ellen, 11 years old, and Lilith, 77, are tricked into taking care of each other. They overcome their initial resentment of having to "sit" one another and develop a sincere affection. 28 mins.

VHS: S22369. $99.95.

Laser: LD74599. $119.95.

Liszt's Rhapsody

Franz Liszt craved the creative outlet of musical composition and was acclaimed for his skills as a pianist. In this story, a young Gypsy violinist appears who helps him achieve his greatest success. This film is perfect for children. It is the third episode from the Emmy Award-winning *The Composer's Specials* series.

VHS: S27417. $19.98.

David Devine, USA, 1995, 53 mins.

The Little Horse That Could

Children and adults alike will enjoy listening to and watching Erin Go Braugh, a Connemara Irish stallion, as he and his trainer, Carol Kozlowski, take you behind the scenes to see all that is involved in the caring for and training of a champion. Lilting Irish music accompanies Erin Go Braugh's narrative, delivered in a delightful Irish brogue. 60 mins.

VHS: S30120. $12.95.

Stirlin Harris, USA, 1996, 60 mins.

Little Lou and His Strange Little Zoo

The adventures of a young black boy who lives in the city. Author/illustrator Mark Rubin offers children an interesting way to become involved in learning activities in language arts, social studies and guidance, with a special emphasis on brotherhood, human relations and cooperation.

VHS: S06726. $29.95.

Little Monk and the Tiger

Narration, music and sound effects complement the color illustrations which accompany this tale from Thailand about a small Buddhist monk and a tiger that has been stalking a little village.

VHS: S30560. $49.99.

Thailand, 1996, 10 mins.

Little Nezha Fights Great Dragon Kings

Animation brings traditional Chinese mythology to life in the story of Nezha, the boy who challenges the mighty Dragon King of the Eastern Sea. 59 mins.

VHS: S16149. $14.98.

Little Sister Rabbit

A witty portrait of the activities and movements of Big Brother Rabbit and his fiercely individualistic and stubborn younger sister. 25 mins.

VHS: S18022. $12.95.

The Little Troll Prince

This endearing story tells of the once frozen heart of the Little Troll Prince melting upon receiving the greatest Christmas gift of all. Features the animation artistry of Hanna-Barbera and voice performances by Vincent Price, Jonathan Winters, Cloris Leachman and Don Knotts. 45 mins.

VHS: S33287. $12.95.

Living and Working In Space: The Countdown Has Begun

Interviews with space professionals. Famous calculus teacher Jaime Escalante and a former student look at outer space activities. Ages 8+. 60 minutes.

VHS: S24982. $19.95.

Living in the World Around Us Series

Commercialization. "Drugs: A Primary Film" shows the benefits and dangers inherent in the drugs in a common medicine cabinet; "Seeing through Commercials" is an explorations of how commercials are structured to influence our daily lives. 24 mins.

VHS: S05827. $19.95.

Cooperation. "I Want... You Want" teaches how a boy who only said "I Want" learns cooperation and sharing; "Pulling Together" are the further cartoon adventures which emphasize cooperation; and "A Time And Place" teaches that there is a time and place for everything. 25 mins.

VHS: S05828. $19.95.

May We See Ourselves. "All about Bobby" teaches how to understand others; "Old Eyemo Sees the Truth", how to see oneself through understanding others. 28 mins.

VHS: S05829. $19.95.

Perception. "Use Your Ears" explores the nature of sounds-warnings, sharing, identification, happiness; "Use Your Eyes", how to see the real image; "Light Is Many Things", the life, knowledge, energy that comes from light. 31 mins.

VHS: S05830. $19.95.

A Look Around Endangered Animals

Did you know that rhinos don't see very well? Elephants like to have a lot of company? The cuddly panda isn't a bear at all? *A Look around Endangered Animals* includes segments on the Siberian tiger, the manatee and the gray wolf, among others.

VHS: S16345. $44.95.

Look What Happens at the Car Wash

From soap to wax, this kid's video shows exactly how both an automated and a hand car wash work. Kids will learn important skills and ten new words along the way. This lively and entertaining tape uses great videography, animation and music. 30 mins.

VHS: S26218. $12.95.

M.C. Higgins, The Great

Sarah Mountain is threatened by strip mining and 13-year-old M.C. Higgins dreams of escape for himself and his impoverished family. Based on Virginia Hamilton's Newbery Award-winning book. 42 mins.

VHS: S08164. $119.00.

Ma's Motors

A handicapped Taiwanese boy struggles successfully for a career in auto mechanics. His family, the church and a boy he does not know get involved. They demonstrate how, through love and concern, the handicapped can flourish and fulfill their potential. Produced by Maryknoll Media. 28 mins.

VHS: S04931. $24.95.

Magic Eye—The Video for Kids

This video is aimed at children and seeks to educate them about the possibilities of 3-D images that seem to move in both space and time. Includes original music and sound effects in Dolby Surround. 30 mins.

VHS: S22747. $14.95.

The Magic of Lionel Trains 3-Video Set

Lionel toy trains are world renowned. Tom McComas shows the viewer some of the largest and most elaborate set-ups ever devised for Lionel trains. There are charming anecdotes, great train accessory action, and tips that explain to kids how they can build their own layouts. 30 mins.

VHS: S24215. $49.95.

The Magic Thinking Cap

A family is on their way to the Judy Theater for their usual puppet workshop, but a crisis sours the mood and Dad gets abusive. Fortunately the Magic Thinking Cap, a contraption that examines underlying thoughts and emotions, helps them get a grip on what the family really thinks and feels. 30 mins.

VHS: S21275. $19.95.

A Magical Field Trip to the Denver Mint

Rosie O'Flanigan takes a group of children along for an inside look at the way money is made. The people and machines that make coins are explained in this educational video. 14 mins.

VHS: S23728. $79.95.

A Magical Field Trip to the Post Office

Rosie O'Flanigan shows a young girl the many activities that take place in a post office. In addition to the importance of various jobs and machines, this video clarifies the role of stamps, showing how they are made and used. 15 mins.

VHS: S23729. $79.95.

Maps: Symbols and Terms

Reading maps requires simple skills that this video explains. With these skills youngsters will have the whole world at their fingertips. 13 mins.

VHS: S23725. $49.95.

Maps: Where Am I? (3rd Edition)

A helicopter ride gives children the opportunity to see a neighborhood as it might appear from a map. It's a process that helps them relate the world of solid objects to the abstract markings of two-dimensional maps. 11 mins.

VHS: S23727. $49.95.

Marc Brown's Play Rhymes

From the author and illustrator of *Arthur's Eyes*, this captivating program invites young viewers to explore language and rhymes.

VHS: S08397. $89.00.

The Marvelous Land of Oz

At the center of this cartoon is Tip, a young boy who escapes to Oz in order to evade his evil guardian, the witch Mombi. There Tip encounters all the familiar characters, the Scarecrow, Glinda and Dorothy, as well as other new friends. A plot threatens the Emerald City but a forgotten heir to the throne of this fabled land may just save the day. 90 mins.

VHS: S24229. $19.98.

The Mask of the Dancing Princess

In an imaginary kingdom of the 17th century, 10-year-old Princess Rosamond demands a birthday present she should not have: a child identical to herself. In this tale of mistaken identity, she is carried away by a group of gypsy actors and begins a hard new life in a strange land before she develops into a gracious and worthy ruler.

VHS: S16349. $44.95.

Master of the World

An animated adventure of a mad scientist and his attempt to rule the civilized world from the deck of his deadly flying machine, the Albatross. Robur the Conqueror is the brainchild of Jules Verne and is part of the Classics for Kids Collection. 1976, approx. 50 mins.

Laser: Widescreen. **LD74980. $39.99.**

Mathnet: The Case of The Unnatural

In the *Mathnet* series by Children's Television Workshop, a young detective team investigates answers while learning concepts related to math. Lefty Cobbs is a washed up pitcher, but something strange is happening to him. Suddenly he is hitting one-handed homers, pitching faster than anyone in history and sending crazy code messages to his pal Babs. This is a case for Mathnet. Ages 8-12.

VHS: S24550. $9.95.

Maurice Sendak's Little Bear—Parties & Picnics

From celebrated children's author and illustrator Maurice Sendak, four classic animated tales: *Party at Owl's House, Little Bear's Sweet Tooth, Picnic on Pudding Hill* and *Duck, Babysitter*. 33 mins.

VHS: S33763. $9.95.

Max's Christmas

Irrepressible Max wants to stay up late on Christmas so he can see Santa Claus. Story by Rosemary Wells. Animated. 5 mins.

VHS: S33790. $49.95.

Merlin and the Dragons

Old Merlin the Magician tells young Arthur stories that inspire him to become the magnificent King Arthur. Narrated by Kevin Kline. Children's Video Report Top 15 Kidvids. 27 minutes, ages 5-12.

Home Video.

VHS: S17007. $12.98.

Merry Christmas Space Case

The Goober twins swagger toward Buddy McGee in their red sweat shirts with the big G's on the front. Are they from outer visiting Buddy for Christmas? James Marshall has once again created hilarious characters that will have children roaring with laughter.

VHS: S16354. $44.95.

The Mighty River

This animated film recreates the grace, beauty and tragedy of nature, presenting a passionate lesson about human impact on our fragile natural resources. Academy Award nominee. Ages 11 to adult. 24 mins.

VHS: S23361. $89.00.

Milk Cow. Eat Cheese.

A multicultural group of kids learns the relationship between cows and dairy products in this video. Kids will love seeing how everyday things are made. There's even a visit to an ice cream factory. Ages 3-10.

VHS: S26094. $14.95.

Bonnie Scott, USA, 1995, 30 mins.

Mole's Christmas

On Christmas Eve, Mole and his friend, the Rat, find themselves stranded in the snow. Soon they are thinking of home and in a flash they are there, warming themselves against a fire. The joy of this scene is completed when a group of carolling mice happen by. With the voices of Richard Briers, Peter Davison and Imelda Staunton. From *The Wind in the Willows* Collection.

VHS: S26673. $12.98.

Martin Gates, Great Britain, 1995, 28 mins.

Molly's Pilgrim

This Academy Award-winning live-action short subject examines the plight of a young Russian Jewish emigrant who has come to the United States to escape religious persecution. It carries a message about American values, Thanksgiving, growing up and religious tolerance. 24 mins.

VHS: S33787. $89.00.

Mona's Pets

In this comic portrait of a dysfunctional American family, punky older sister Ramona unexpectedly returns home to where her mother and two young brothers live, with a suitcase full of cockroaches, which soon infest their home. As the roach invasion forces the famiy to interact, Mona and her "pets" become a catalyst for changing the family.

VHS: S34430. $59.95.

John D. Allen, USA, 1992, 32 mins.

Money Rock

This addition to the Emmy Award-winning *Schoolhouse Rock* collection features seven short musical sketches, with song and dance, to teach children everything from how money was invented and how checks get paid, to how to pay taxes, balance your allowance and make investments on Wall Street. 30 mins.

VHS: S34916. $14.95.

Monsters of the Greek Myths

Based on the Wonder-Book and Tanglewood Tales of Nathaniel Hawthorne, these ancient stories tell of the confrontations of great heroes with the horrific monsters that populated the mythical Greek landscape. Includes *The Chimaera, The Gorgon's Head, The Minotaur* and *The Dragon's Teeth*. For Grades 4-9.

VHS: S14203. $159.95.

Mouse Soup

John Matthews' stop animation is used to tell the story of a mouse who manages to save himself from becoming dinner. The weasel who captures him is so taken by the mouse's stories that he forgets his hunger pangs. Buddy Hackett provides the mouse's voice.

VHS: S21260. $12.98.

John Matthews, USA

A Movie Star's Daughter

A young adult drama about fitting in and following your heart. Dena is the new kid in school but it helps that her dad is a Hollywood heartthrob. Still, she wonders how much of the attention is due to her dad and who her real friends will turn out to be. With Frank Converse as the famous father. 1979, 46 mins.
VHS: S10984. $14.95.

Mrs. Piggle-Wiggle

Shelley Duvall presents this new series for kids of all ages. Jean Stapleton stars as the lovable lady with a knack for helping kids—and their parents—out of the stickiest situations. From the top of her piled-up red hair to the tips of her funky platform shoes, she's a genius when it comes to finding uncommon solutions to common, everyday challenges.
Mrs. Piggle-Wiggle: The Answer-Backer Cure and The Chores Cure.
VHS: S22874. $12.98.
Mrs. Piggle-Wiggle: The Not-Truthful Cure and The Radish Cure.
VHS: S22872. $12.98.
Mrs. Piggle-Wiggle: The Pet Forgetters Cure and The Never-Want-To-Go-To-Bedders Cure.
VHS: S22873. $12.98.

The Mud Family

Paul Morin's illustrations evocatively complement Betsy James's story about a young Native-American girl, whose family depends on rainfall. For grades K-3.
VHS: S31447. $44.99.

The Murky Water Caper

Follow the adventures of Billie Beaver, Molly Duck, Devin the Dolphin, Toots the Trout and a host of other characters as they seek the help of Detective Trout to discover who's been polluting the local stream. Written by children's playwright Deborah Rodney Pex. Ages 6-10. 30 mins.
VHS: S23360. $59.95.

Music and Magic

"Positive Music Videos for Today's Kids." These MTV-style videos promote positive values. Ages 5-11.
VHS: S24714. $9.98.

Musical Tales

Introduce children to the beauty and enchantment of the classics with these beautifully animated puppet films of fairy stories set to the music of Tchaikovsky, Stravinsky and Delibes.
Volume 1: *The Nutcracker* and *Petrushka*. 35 mins.
VHS: S16147. $12.98.
Volume 2: *Coppelia* and *The Sleeping Beauty*. 32 mins.
VHS: S16148. $12.98.

Mutzmag

A live action adaptation of the Appalachian folktale, set around 1920, about a young woman named Mutzmag, and her adventures with her half-sisters, gullible young women Mutzmag saves from two backwoods ogres. The tale unfolds in the vernacular and idiom of the Appalachians.
VHS: S17413. $59.00.
Tom Davenport, USA, 1993, 53 mins.

My Brother Sam Is Dead

Winner of the Newbery Honor Book, James Lincoln Collier and Christopher Collier's historical story focuses on the Meekers, a nonpartisan family which is affected by the Revolutionary War. 26 mins.
VHS: S08166. $119.00.

My Family and Other Animals

A charming program about one boy's experience on a strange and beautiful island where he encounters many bugs and other small animals. 23 mins.
VHS: S13207. $14.98.

My Principal Lives Next Door

Ben Johnson thought life was a breeze until Mrs. Strictly, the school's principal, moved in next door, setting off a panic. After experiencing trouble with his math papers, he discovers that the principal is a nice person to turn to. Written and illustrated by third-grade students of Sanibel, Florida Elementary School. 8 mins.
VHS: S19599. $39.00.

My Side of the Mountain

Ted Eccles and Theodore Bikel star in this adaptation of Jean Craighead George's novel. It features a 13-year-old who sets out on an adventure in the wilderness. 38 mins.
VHS: S23457. $49.95.

The Mysterious Island

Jules Verne's science fiction masterpiece is told in this Classics for Kids series as a young boy and his friends face amazing perils when they are shipwrecked on a strange, exotic island.
VHS: S03018. $24.95.
Laser: Includes interview with Ray Harryhausen. **LD75044. $34.95.**
Leif Gram, USA, 1987, 49 mins.

The Mysterious Tadpole and Other Stories

Based on a story by Steven Kellogg, *The Mysterious Tadpole* concerns a birthday gift from Uncle McAllister that appears to be a tadpole—but turns out to be much more! Louis' affection for his pet, and his determination to keep it, make this story heartwarming and lots of fun. Other stories included are: *The Five Chinese Brothers*, by Claire Bishop; *Jonah and the Great Fish*, retold and illustrated by Warwick Hutton; and *The Wizard*, by Jack Kent. Animation. 30 mins.
VHS: S11225. $19.95.

Mystery of Harris Burdick

In the introduction, Chris Van Allsburg relates how a man named Harris Burdick illustrated and wrote 14 stories. Now, years later, all that remain are the illustrations with their titles and brief captions. A wonderful creative experience for children.
VHS: S14190. $44.95.

National Geographic Geo Kids: Bear Cubs, Baby Ducks, and Kooky Kookaburras

Sunny Honeypossum, Bobby Bushbaby and Balzac de Chameleon tell how different wild animals grow from infancy to young adulthood. The footage of a mother monkey caring for her baby is unforgettable.
VHS: S21961. $12.95.

National Geographic Geo Kids: Camouflage, Cuttlefish, and Chameleons Changing Color

Once again the animated characters Bobby Bushbaby, Uncle Balzac and Honeypossum introduce animal wonders to children five and under. The camouflage of these various creatures will fascinate viewers. 35 mins.
VHS: S23947. $12.95.

National Geographic Geo Kids: Chomping on Bugs, Swimming Sea Slugs, and Stuff that Makes Animals Special

In this combination of animation and live footage children will be introduced to the wonders of nature through Bobby Bushbaby and Honeypossum. The sticky tongue chameleon is sure to be a hit, especially with children five and under. 35 mins.
VHS: S23948. $12.95.

National Geographic Geo Kids: Cool Cats, Raindrops, and Things That Live in Holes

While playing hide-and-seek, Sunny Honeypossum and Bobby Bushbaby discover a tree hole. Balzac de Chameleon then explains to them the variety of animals that make their home in these natural crevices.
VHS: S21962. $12.95.

National Geographic Geo Kids: Flying Trying and Honking Around

The delightful characters Sunny Honeypossum, Bobby Bushbaby and Balzac de Chameleon host this fascinating look at birds. These characters are all created by the maker of the Muppet Babies. Together they help kids explore the world of flight.
VHS: S21960. $12.95.

National Geographic Geo Kids: Tadpoles, Dragonflies and the Caterpillar's Big Change

Animated characters Bobby Bushbaby, Uncle Balzac and Honeypossum explore live action footage of amazing wildlife for children five and under. These characters experiment with transformations, but their fooling around cannot compete with the butterfly that emerges from a cocoon. 35 mins.
VHS: S23946. $12.95.

National Geographic Really Wild Animals

This series of documentaries will take kids to exotic locations to see how the animals they love really live. An animated globe called Spin narrates, with the voice by Dudley Moore.
Polar Prowl. This video is set in the Artic and the Antartic. Spin gives kids the kind of narration that brings these exotic locales and their unique creatures alive. 47 mins.
VHS: S29850. $14.95.
Dinosaurs and Other Creature Features. *T. rex* is related to contemporary reptiles like snakes and alligators. This video makes the creatures of the past into features of interest for today's children. 47 mins.
VHS: S29851. $14.95.
Monkey Business and Other Family Fun. Spin shows kids how animal families the world over care for and nurture one another. 47 mins.
VHS: S29852. $14.95.
Awesome Animal Builders. Check out some amazing animal abodes and how they're built as Spin takes you on a tour of some of the wildest construction sites around.
VHS: S32404. $14.95.
Farmyard Friends. Join Spin in two episodes about life on the farm and the real-life story of animal rescuers. 46 mins.
VHS: S32510. $14.95.
Hot Dogs and Cool Cats. In this whirlwind worldwide adventure, Spin sets out to prove that our tame house pets have some really rowdy relatives. The wilds mixes with the mild as we discover what's behind the dog's growl and the cat's meow. 47 mins.
VHS: S32509. $14.95.
Secret Weapons and Great Escapes. Detect and inspect the hidden weapons of the animal world with Spin.
VHS: S32405. $14.95.

Nature Stories

Four stories deal with various subjects, including eggs, mammals, flowers and plants. Designed for children in grades 1-4. 25 mins.
VHS: S20026. $159.95.

New Coat for Anna

Anita Lobel's illustrations bring to life Harriet Ziefert's book, set in post-World War II, as Anna and her mother decide to use their most cherished possessions in order to get the coat Anna has dreamed about.
VHS: S08398. $59.00.

Nick Jr.: Eureeka's Castle: Wide Awake at Eureeka's Castle

Eureeka is a wizard in the making. In this video she and her entire castle full of friends take kids on a special tour of all their favorite sleepless nights. USA, 1995, 35 mins.
VHS: S27312. $12.95.

Nick Jr.: Gullah Gullah Island: Play Along with Binyah and Friends

Kids will enjoy this video that encourages them to play along with their Gullah Gullah Island friends. They will dance and clap as they learn one game after another. This video offers a unique opportunity to experience one of the oldest African-American traditions surviving in the United States. USA, 1995, 30 mins.
VHS: S27310. $12.95.

Nina's Strange Adventure

A young river otter uses special magic to travel to the land of her dreams. 14 mins.
VHS: S23460. $49.95.

No Greater Gift

Based on a real-life account, the poignant drama of Nick Santana and Keith Williams, two 12-year olds from different backgrounds who are drawn together by their illnesses, but torn by the realization that they will soon be separated. When Nick accepts the fact that his disease is fatal, he must make a decision that could save his new friend's life. USA, 1986, 45 mins.
VHS: S04764. $19.95.

Noah's Ark

Embark on one of the greatest adventures of all time as Academy Award-nominee James Earl Jones narrates this beautifully animated adaptation of Peter Spiers' acclaimed children's book, complemented by a dynamic, evocative score from Grammy-winner Stewart Copeland. Winner of the Action for Children's Television Award and CINE Golden Eagle. Recommended by American Library Association and *Video Librarian*. Ages 5-12. 27 minutes.
VHS: S11415. $12.98.

A Norman Rockwell Christmas

Eddie Albert hosts this nostalgic, heartwarming look at Christmas scenes based on the illustrious world created by Norman Rockwell. Music accompaniment by the world famous Pacific Chorale augments the perfect worlds created by this famous American painter and illustrator. 50 mins.
VHS: S21810. $19.98.

Norman the Doorman and Other Stories

Although Norman's job is to stand guard at the mouse entrance to the Museum of Art, his ambition is to become an artist, in the adaptation of the story by Don Freeman. Other stories include *Brave Irene*, by William Steig, and *Lentil*, by Robert McCloskey. Animated. 30 mins.
VHS: S11228. $14.95.

Not Now, Bernard

Five charming *Anytime Tales* stories by David McKee which are inventive tales about personal self-expression. 35 mins.
VHS: S19431. $14.99.

Notes Alive! Nutcracker: The Untold Story

This award-winning production, featuring the music of Tchaikovsky performed by the Minnesota Orchestra, the 3-D animation of Maurice Sendak, and a lively ballet performance, is a new version of the beloved Christmas tale that will enchant children of all ages. Go behind the scenes with Sendak, scriptwriter Pamela Hill Nettleton, and music director and conductor Eiji Oue to learn how this unique production of the original E.T.A. Hoffmann story was conceived and created. 50 mins.
VHS: S33160. $19.95.

The Notorious Jumping Frog of Calaveras County

Based on the classic story by Mark Twain. Jim Smiley would bet on anything, and his frog, Dan'l Webster, was his favorite betting animal. Dan'l Webster could jump farther than any other frog alive. Smiley never lost a bet with Dan'l until the stranger came to town. 24 mins.
VHS: S30727. $19.95.

The Nutcracker

Dudley Moore narrates and the Moscow State Orchestra performs music by Tchaikovsky in this delightful animated version of the classic childhood romance. A host of lovable characters, including a charming prince, a plum fairy and a young girl, Marie, will delight all kinds of audiences. It is especially useful for introducing youngsters to classical music. From the *Storyteller's Classics* series, animated. 27 mins.
VHS: S26342. $9.98.

Nuzzling with Nozzles: A Magical Adventure

Starring in their first animated feature, Blinky, Pinky and Sandy go from one delightful adventure to another in a splendid mix of reality and fantasy. 110 mins.
VHS: S10333. $39.95.

Off on a Comet

Jules Verne's story of Captain Sevadec, who finds that he has been swept off the earth with a small group of others and is hurtling out into space. An animated classic.
VHS: S04425. $19.95.
R. Slapczynski, USA, 1979, 52 mins.

Officer Buckle and Gloria

John Lithgow narrates this animated video based on the Caldecott Medal-winning story by Peggy Rathmann about Officer Buckle of the Napville Police Department and a police dog named Gloria who has her own way of demonstrating safety tips. 11 mins.
VHS: S33781. $60.00.

The Old Curiosity Shop

An animated version of the Charles Dickens story about Little Nell and her grandfather and their many adventures in 18th century England. When they are evicted from the Old Curiosity Shop these two brave and optimistic souls must fend for themselves. 1984, 72 mins.
VHS: S06161. $79.95.

Old Man of Lochnagar

From the BBC, a children's story written and narrated by the Prince of Wales. It's about ticklish eagles, tame grouse, sea haggis and the Gorms—tiny people who live in the Scottish hillsides. 20 mins.
VHS: S12640. $19.95.

On Christmas Eve

Peter Collington's award-winning tale is an imaginative rumination on the mysteries of Christmas, as a young girl becomes concerned about the physical obstacles which surround Father Christmas on his hazardous journey. 25 mins.
VHS: S19434. $14.99.

Once When I Was Scared

The drama and power of Ted Rand's imaginative paintings bring to life Helena Clare Pittman's heartening story of the conquest of a young boy's fear of the cold, dark wood. 11 mins.
VHS: S12263. $57.00.

One Terrific Thanksgiving

Irving Morris Bear asks his friends to hide his Thanksgiving food so he doesn't eat it before the feast. When he tries to locate it anyway, he learns that there's more to Thanksgiving than food. From the storybook by Marjorie Weinman Sharmat.
VHS: S16350. $44.95.

Orange Cheeks

A hilarious tape of a young boy's visit with his wise grandmother, from whom he learns about love, told by master storyteller Jay O'Callahan. Complements *Jay O'Calllahan: A Master Class in Storytelling*. 8 mins. Public performance rights included.
VHS: S09266. $39.95.

Orca Whales and Mermaid Tales

Meet the huge Orca whales and the mysterious manatees, once thought to be mermaids! Watch a baby manatee and find out about the Orca's blowhole. Nature. Ages 4-12.
VHS: S24614. $14.95.

Owl Moon and Other Stories

Five short animated films based upon popular children's literature charmingly tell the stories of people and animals learning about themselves. The title piece shows a child who looks for the great Horned Owl with his father. 35 mins.
VHS: S13969. $14.95.

Ozma of Oz

Dorothy's return to Oz sets off a series of adventures as she tries to save the Royal Family of Ev. Her old friends the Tin Man, the Lion and the Scarecrow brave harrowing travails with her, including the evil but magical Nome King. This joyful, animated film will delight children. 90 mins.
VHS: S24230. $14.95.

Paddle to the Sea

This Academy Award-nominated live-action film is based on the Caldecott Honor children's picture book from Holling C. Holling. A young Native American boy carves a boat with a passenger. He sets it in a small stream with hopes that his toy will reach the sea. Along the way it encounters numerous possible obstructions, from industrious beavers to Niagara Falls.
VHS: S29959. $12.95.
William Mason, Canada, 1966, 30 mins.

Paper Bag Princess

Hits the question of sex-role stereotyping head-on. After rescuing the prince from a dragon, when the prince is not only unappreciative but downright rude, the princess leaves him to fend for himself. Turns traditional princess stories, fairy tales and dragons on their heads. All ages. Animation/Fairy Tales. Canada, 1993. 25 minutes.
VHS: S24616. $12.95.

Paper John

A strange, gentle fellow comes to a town by the sea. Paper John folds paper into all sorts of shapes: flowers, kites, even houses and furniture. By accident he catches a small gray devil on his fishing line. An enchanting fable told with economical language and imaginative illustrations. Written and illustrated by David Small.
VHS: S33725. $37.95.

Paws, Claws, Feathers and Fins

Dogs, cats, gerbils, hamsters…even a pony! An award-winning video to help families consider the ups and down of taking a pet into their home. Ages 4-12. 30 minutes.
VHS: S24617. $14.95.

PBS Kids Pack of Pals

This four-tape gift set includes *Families Are Special*, starring Barney; *Theodore's Big Adventure; Generosity*, featuring *Mr. Rabbit's Thanksgiving*, from the *Adventures from the Book of Virtues* series; and Sesame Street's Elmo in *Basil Hears a Noise: A Musical Adventure*.
VHS: S32402. $53.92.

Peeping Beauty by Mary Jane Auch

Poulette the Hen is starstruck and dreams of becoming a famous ballerina. A slick talent scout, a fox, offers her the lead in his production of "Peeping Beauty." Now she must stay on her toes to avoid debuting as dinner. 10 mins.
VHS: S24911. $37.95.

Pegasus

Mia Farrow tells the enchanting life of Pegasus, the winged horse in Greek myths that was transformed into a dazzling star constellation. *Parents Magazine* selected this animated adventure for its Best of the Year List, Parent's Choice Award. 25 mins.
Home Video.
VHS: S16162. $12.98.
Public Performance Rights.
VHS: S17145. $50.00.

People

Cara and her grandfather embark on an animated journey across a wide cultural array of peoples and traditions. Various styles of animation and 11 original songs make this video highly entertaining as well as educational. Music by Heavy D, Al Jarreau, Chaka Khan, Vanessa Williams and others is featured. 60 mins.
VHS: S26485. $12.95.

Pepito's Dream

An adaptation of the *Pepito* trilogy, three books by John and Margaret Travers-Moore, this heartwarming tale chronicles a young boy's determination to quell the violence and discord in his neighborhood, and his long-held dream to deliver a speech before the United Nations. 27 mins.
VHS: S17280. $14.95.

Peppe the Lamplighter

Turn-of-the-century New York is hard for an Italian immigrant. Peppe lights lamps, a job his father finds disappointing. But when Peppe's sister disappears, Peppe's job proves essential in finding her. This tale of pride is a beautifully illustrated read-along video.
VHS: S22346. $39.95.

Pepper and All the Legs

Pepper is a tiny dachshund whose viewpoint never gets above the legs of his owners. He feels lonely when he sees the legs of his owners go upstairs to places his short legs can't take him. One day, he hides in a laundry basket before it is taken upstairs and gets himself into a series of mishaps. Based on the book by Dick Gackenback. 22 mins.
VHS: S30717. $19.95.

Peter Ustinov: The Orchestra

This award-winning program features 28 excerpts from the classical repertoire, all carefully selected to be appealing to the young listener. Each excerpt is used to illustrate musical concepts of the sound of a particular instrument.
VHS: S13409. $19.98.

Peter-No-Tail

Not to be confused with *Peter Cottontail*. This animated children's story concerns the adventures of a country kitten who travels to the big city. Such familiar voices as Ken Berry, Dom DeLuise, Larry Storch, June Lockhart and Tina Louise are to be heard in the tale of a cat who is missing an important appendage.
VHS: S06164. $79.95.
Stig Lasseby/Jan Gissberg, USA, 1983, 22 mins.

Philip Hall Likes Me, I Reckon

Ruby Dee narrates this adaptation of Bette Greene's Newbery Award-winning book about a bright, 11-year-old black girl who has a crush on the smartest boy in her class. 29 mins.
VHS: S08167. $119.00.

A Picture Book of Martin Luther King, Jr.

Based on the book by David A. Adler. A straightforward, fact-filled text joins with warm, realistic illustrations to capture the life and times of Dr. King, fostering an appreciation and understanding of his efforts to secure equal rights for all people. Deals with historical events in a positive manner. Ages 6-10. 9 minutes.
VHS: S24618. $37.95.

Picturebook Classics: Complete Set

Includes *Adam's Smile, The Porcelain Cat, The Beast in the Bathtub* and *Five Secrets in a Box*. Four video cassettes.
VHS: S14196. $139.95.

Picturebook Classics: Adam's Smile

Adam's grandmother says his smile could light the world. When he is taken to a dark, hidden world, Adam finds that only he can save the world from the creatures of darkness—through the power of his smile. For Grades 1-3.
VHS: S14192. $44.95.

Picturebook Classics: Five Secrets in a Box

Virginia, the younger daughter of Galileo, opens her father's gold box to find five objects that reveal the world to her—and us-in new and wonderful ways. For Grades 1-6.

VHS: S14195. $44.95.

Picturebook Classics: The Porcelain Cat

When the old sorcerer decides to turn a porcelain cat into a real one that will catch the rats that are gnawing on his books, he sends his apprentice, Nickon, on a quest to find the charm needed for the enchantment. For Grades 1-3.

VHS: S14193. $44.95.

Piggy Banks to Money Markets

A group of kids share the facts about money: saving, investing, spending, earning…in an exciting manner. Produced with consultation from the American Banking Association, National Council on Economic Education and *Inc. Magazine*. Includes original songs, computer graphics and a fun group of kids. Ages 5-12. 30 minutes.

VHS: S24619. $14.95.

The Pigs' Wedding and Other Stories

Porker and Curlytail are two pigs in love. When they invite all of their favorite friends to their wedding, everyone comes-including the rain. The lovely music and animation will capture your heart. Also includes *The Selkie Girl, The Happy Owls, A Letter to Amy* and *The Owl and the Pussy Cat*. All ages. 39 mins.

VHS: S14492. $14.95.

Pirate's Dagger

This fantasy-adventure film is the story of 12-year-old Sam, who, after being confined to his room as punishment by his mother, escapes in his imagination to engage in a series of fantastic adventures with his friend, the fierce pirate Captain Jack Rackham. Public performance.

VHS: S32126. $59.95.

Steven Sorensen, USA, 1992, 30 mins.

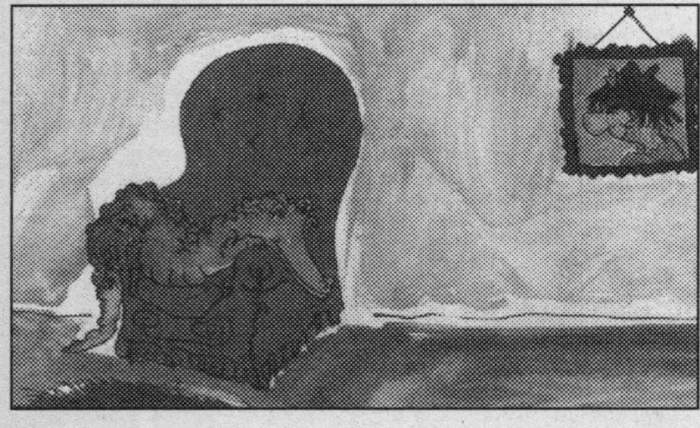

Pocahontas (Animation)

The Indian princess Pocahontas falls in love Captain John Smith from the Old World. She saves his life, but is separated from him and travels to England, accompanied by her animal friends, to find him. This charming animated film follows her adventures as she struggles to find true love. From the *Enchanted Tales* series. 48 mins.

VHS: S25887. $14.98.

Pocahontas (Stop-Motion Animation)

The story of legendary Native American woman Pocahontas is told in this well-crafted, stop-motion animation. As the savior of Jamestown settlers (including John Rolfe, her future husband), her story has fascinated Americans for over 300 years.

VHS: S27433. $9.95.

John Matthews, USA, 31 mins.

Pocahontas: Her True Story

At age 12, this Native American princess saved the life of Captain John Smith and changed forever the course of history of the British American colonies. This documentary charts her achievements as an ambassador, stateswoman, peacemaker and visionary. 50 mins.

VHS: S25837. $19.95.

Pollyanna

Elizabeth Archand stars as the orphaned Pollyanna Whittier, who comes to a small English town to live with her stern Aunt Polly and ends up spreading happiness wherever she goes, in this BBC version of the classic story.

VHS: S19093. $24.98.

Jayne Wyndham-Davis, Great Britain, 1973, 155 mins.

The Portrait

Julie is a promising young art student recovering from a suicide attempt. While recuperating she is inspired by a young girl named Sarah who is terminally ill with cancer. Sarah's enthusiasm helps Julie realize the preciousness of life. 30 mins.

VHS: S22373. $149.95.

Laser: LD74601. $169.95.

Pryor's Place

Sid & Marty Kroft's Emmy Award-winning series for kids starring Richard Pryor features special guests Robin Williams, Henry Winkler, Sammy Davis Jr., Ron Cey, Willie Nelson, John Ritter, Lily Tomlin, Kareem Abdul Jabbar, Pat Morita and others. Each 60-minute tape contains two episodes.

Pryor's Place—Volume 1. In *Readers of the Lost Art*, young Richard Pryor and his friends learn the joy of reading. Henry Winkler guests as himself in *Home Free*, which deals with avoiding strangers. 60 mins.

VHS: S32744. $12.95.

Pryor's Place—Volume 2. In *High Noon at 5:30*, just when young Richard Pryor thinks he has to face a bully alone, his friends show up to help. In *The Kimosabe Blues* Richard learns the meaning of true friendship. 60 mins.

VHS: S32745. $12.95.

Pryor's Place—Volume 3. In Episode 1, *Sax Education*, when Richie loses Chill's saxophone, he quickly learns a lesson about responsibility. With Robin Williams, Marla Gibbs, Rip Taylor and Ron Cey. In Episode 2, *Too Old Too Soon, Too Smart Too Late*, Richie learns to appreciate old people when his Uncle Moes disappears and later shows up playing one-on-one against Kareem Abdul Jabbar. With Scatman Crothers.

VHS: S34360. $12.95.

Pryor's Place—Volume 4. In Episode 1, *To Catch a Little Thief*, Richie steals a basketball to impress some older boys, but his guilty conscience gets the best of him. With Sammy Davis, Jr. In Episode 2, *Cousin Rita*, Richie has to convince his best friend Wally that cousin Rita isn't in love with him. With Lily Tomlin and Kim Fields.

VHS: S34361. $12.95.

The Puzzle Place

From the producers of the Emmy Award-winning *Reading Rainbow* and *Storytime, The Puzzle Place* is a magical realm where kids will discover what makes them different, what makes them the same and what makes each one of them special.

Friends Don't Tease. The Puzzle Place kids discover that the best part of playing sports is being a good sport. 48 mins.

VHS: S31230. $12.95.

Working Together. The Puzzle Place gang learns to get by with a little help from its friends as it discovers that teamwork is the key to getting the job done right. 48 mins.

VHS: S31229. $12.95.

The Puzzle Place: Accentuate the Positive

In *The Puzzle Place* kids can discover how they are the same as other kids and how they are different. Ultimately, they will realize that everyone is special. Two imaginary adventures are featured on this video. 60 mins.

VHS: S29213. $12.95.

The Puzzle Place: Rock Dreams

Kids will learn about themselves in these charming episodes from the popular Puzzle Place kids. They visit a recording studio and laugh about their own experiences with musical fortune and fame. Includes performances by The Boys Choir of Harlem and a Native American rock band called Red Thunder. 55 mins.

VHS: S24685. $14.98.

The Puzzle Place: Sing-Along Songs

All the favorite friends from *The Puzzle Place* are featured on this video leading kids through memorable songs. It's easy to learn the words and sing along because the lyrics are shown at the bottom of the screen. Includes over a dozen songs. 30 mins.

VHS: S29212. $12.95.

The Puzzle Place: Tuned In

Children learn that there is more to life than what they see on television in this video featuring the Puzzle Place kids. Lessons like these are invaluable. 55 mins.

VHS: S24686. $14.98.

Quarterback Princess

Can a girl find happiness and popularity as a star quarterback? Helen Hunt stars as the daring heroine of this movie based on a true story.

VHS: S05898. $59.98.

The Rainbow Fish

Based on the best-selling, award-winning series by Marcus Pfister, this two-story set features colorful animation and original music to delight children and adults. In *The Rainbow Fish*, the most beautiful fish in the entire ocean discovers the real value of personal beauty and friendship. In *Dazzle the Dinosaur*, a story about friendship and bravery, Dazzle discovers how special he is when his dazzling spine saves his best dino-pal. 30 mins.

VHS: S31034. $12.95.

The Rainforest for Children Series

Animals of the Rainforest, People of the Rainforest and *Plants of the Rainforest* are three titles included in this video set. Together these tapes reveal a comprehensive view of some of the world's most intriguing ecosystems, in Brazil, Costa Rica, Indonesia and Papua New Guinea. Each video is 25 mins.

VHS: S29948. $89.85.

Rechenka's Eggs

Old Babushka is preparing her famous eggs for the Ukrainian Easter Festival when she takes in an injured goose whom she names Rechenka. They live happily together until one terrible day when Rechenka accidentally breaks all of Babushka's lovingly crafted eggs. From the award-winning book by Patricia Polacco.

VHS: S16351. $44.95.

Red Balloon

A classic childhood fantasy with appeal for viewers of every age. This is a story of Pascal, a French boy who befriends a red balloon which follows him everywhere. A touching allegory of the magic powers of love and friendship. No dialog.

VHS: S01098. $14.95.

Albert Lamorisse, France, 1956, 34 mins.

Red Balloon/White Mane

Albert Lamorisse's *Red Balloon* is a priceless classic about a young boy's friendship with a red balloon. 1956, 38 mins. His *White Mane* explores man's relationship to nature; it chronicles the efforts of bandits to capture a wild white stallion, and a young boy who rescues him. Winner of the International Grand Prize, Best Short Film, Cannes Film Festival. 1952, 38 mins.

VHS: S18762. $24.95.

Laser: LD70443. $29.95.

Rembrandt's Beret

It is rumored that a secret hall spans the Arno River in Florence linking two great museums, the Uffizi Gallery and the Pitti Palace. Tiberius finds more than a rumor as he discovers the Hall of the Old Masters. When some of the paintings come to life, Tiberius gets to talk with Rembrandt, and receives the master painter's beret and brushes as a first step to becoming a great artist himself.

VHS: S16352. $44.95.

Rescue Party

Arthur C. Clarke's story is adapted in this thought-provoking film. A surveying spaceship is diverted to Earth in order to save its population. Students join this ship as the planet is doomed. The outcome of this story will leave the audience pondering the significance of these aliens' actions. 20 mins.

VHS: S23473. $79.95.

The Return of the Borrowers

Mary Norton's popular children's books have already inspired the original *The Borrowers*. Now another feature-length film continues the enchanting family adventures of the wee people. Their presence is magical and mesmerizing. 165 mins.

VHS: S29822. $14.98.

Rings Around the World

Don Ameche hosts a lively program of circus acts from around the world. For the entertainment of the entire family come spectacular performers from Sweden, Germany, Switzerland and the US, as well as other parts of the globe. The big top is now on video, where every seat is at center ring. 1967, 79 mins.

VHS: S06830. $69.95.

Rip Van Winkle

Washington Irving's classic tale of man who fell asleep in one era and wakes up in another is adapted for this new video. This character tried to escape his wife, but found that he got far more than he bargained for. 18 mins.

VHS: S23495. $79.95.

Roll of the Thunder

Original watercolor and pastel illustrations highlight this award-winning adaptation of Mildred Taylor's Newbery Award-winning book based on her experiences growing up with her close-knit black family during Depression-era Mississippi. 46 mins.

VHS: S07703. $119.00.

The Rory Story

Rory *(Kidrock)* stars in this funny, fictitious story about how she broke into the recording business. Her adorable puppet, and back-up singers, The Incredible Piglets, are also along for the ride in this entertaining children's film. 60 mins.

VHS: S15306. $14.98.

Rossini's Ghost

Produced by Emmy Award-winner David Devine *(Beethoven Lives Upstairs)*, *Rossini's Ghost* is the fifth program in The Composers' Specials series. Set in 1816, it is the story of a composer whose friends never lose faith in him, even when everything is going wrong. With an invisible little girl as his assistant, Rossini overcomes the disastrous opening night of *The Barber of Seville* to give the world one of its most beloved operas.

VHS: S30585. $19.98.

David Devine, USA, 1994, 50 mins.

Roxaboxen
Alice McLerran's treasured *Roxaboxen* is a hill of sand and rocks and old wooden boxes. But Marion and her sisters, neighbors and friends all remember it as a special place: a sparkling world of jeweled homes, streets edged with the whitest stone, and two ice cream shops.
VHS: S16353. $44.95.

Rudolph & Frosty's Christmas in July
Rudolph the Red Nosed Reindeer and Frosty the Snowman team up for a joyous holiday celebration in July. Voices of Red Buttons, Ethel Merman, Jackie Vernon & more.
VHS: S29061. $9.95.
Rankin/Bass, USA, 1979, 96 mins.

Rudolph the Red Nosed Reindeer
The delightful tale of the North Pole's favorite reindeer and how he saved Christmas. Told and sung by Burl Ives.
VHS: S10795. $12.95.
Rankin/Bass, USA, 1964, 53 mins.

Rudolph's Shiny New Year
Aided by a whale and a caveman, Rudolph sets out to find Happy, the missing baby New Year. If Aeon, a monstrous bird, finds Happy first, Dec. 31st will last forever. Voices of Red Skelton and Frank Gorshin.
VHS: S29060. $9.95.
Rankin/Bass, USA, 1979, 50 mins.

A Rugrats Thanksgiving
Includes the double-length Holiday special *The Turkey Who Came to Dinner*, plus two bonus cartoons, *Chuckie Is Rich* and *Home Movies*. 47 mins.
VHS: S32505. $12.95.

Rugrats—Mommy Mania
Nickelodeon's popular, award-winning animated series. Contains double-length video cartoon *Mother's Day*, plus bonus episodes *Game Show Didi, Family Feud* and *Mommy's Little Assets*. 57 mins.
VHS: S33760. $12.95.

Rugrats: A Baby's Gotta Do What a Baby's Gotta Do
Three episodes.
VHS: S19087. $9.95.
Nickelodeon, USA, 1997, 47 mins.

Rugrats: A Rugrats Chanukah
A special double-length episode.
VHS: S32095. $12.95.
Nickelodeon, USA, 1997, 35 mins.

Rugrats: A Rugrats Passover
A special double-length episode.
VHS: S27080. $9.95.
Nickelodeon, USA, 1997, 35 mins.

Rugrats: A Rugrats Vacation
In this special double-length cartoon, the Rugrats gang is heading to Las Vegas. Spotting a billboard for a Siegfried and Roy-type animal act, the babies undertake to free the kitties. Plus two bonus cartoons.
VHS: S32462. $12.95.
Nickelodeon, USA, 1997, 55 mins.

Rugrats: Angelica the Divine
Three episodes.
VHS: S32468. $9.95.
Nickelodeon, USA, 1997, 47 mins.

Rugrats: Bedtime Bash
Includes five not-so-sleepy cartoons from Nickelodeon's *Rugrats* gang. 56 mins.
VHS: S32096. $12.95.

Rugrats: Chuckie the Brave
Three episodes.
VHS: S32467. $9.95.
Nickelodeon, USA, 1997, 48 mins.

Rugrats: Diapered Duo
Five cartoons.
VHS: S32942. $12.95.
Nickelodeon, USA, 1997, 57 mins.

Rugrats: Dr. Tommy Pickles
Five cartoons: *Hiccups, Autumn Leaves, Potty Training Spike, Chicken Pops* and *Grandpa's Bug*.
VHS: S32941. $12.95.
Nickelodeon, USA, 1997, 57 mins.

Rugrats: Grandpa's Favorite Stories
Four episodes.
VHS: S32463. $12.95.
Nickelodeon, USA, 1997, 58 mins.

Rugrats: Phil & Lil—Double Trouble
Four episodes.
VHS: S32466. $12.95.
Nickelodeon, USA, 1997, 63 mins.

Rugrats: Return of Reptar
Four episodes.
VHS: S32464. $12.95.
Nickelodeon, USA, 1997, 57 mins.

Rugrats: Tales from the Crib
Three episodes.
VHS: S19086. $9.95.
Nickelodeon, USA, 1997, 48 mins.

Rugrats: The Santa Experience
A special double-length episode.
VHS: S32098. $9.95.
Nickelodeon, USA, 1997, 35 mins.

Rugrats: Tommy Troubles
Four episodes.
VHS: S32465. $12.95.
Nickelodeon, USA, 1997, 63 mins.

Runaway Ralph
In this sequel to The Mouse and the Motorcycle, Fred Savage plays a kid at summer camp who has no friends till he meets the rambunctious mouse, Ralph. Based on the book by Beverly Cleary. 42 mins.
VHS: S16580. $9.98.

Rupert
The animated adventures of Rupert the Bear and his friends Bill Badger, Tiger-Lilly and Jack Frost in a faraway land of dragons and sea-serpents, reached only by the animal underground railway. Narration by Ray Brooks. 57 mins.
VHS: S13204. $14.98.

Rupert and the Runaway Dragon
More stories about Rupert the Bear, in a world where dragons run away, robbins turn yellow, eggs hatch fire birds and trees house goblins. 37 mins.
VHS: S13205. $14.98.

Rupert—Caring and Sharing with Friends
Launch into a dazzling new world of animated enchantment and wonder as Rupert and his unforgettable friends embark on magical, globe-trotting adventures sure to spark young imaginations while offering gentle and humorous lessons about growing up. Tape includes two Rupert adventures: "Rupert and the Dragon Race" and "Rupert and the Carousel." 48 mins.
VHS: S30499. $14.98.

Ruth Heller's Nature Stories
Questions about plants and animals are asked and answered in meaningful and amusing stories that young children will love. Includes four programs: *Animals Born Alive and Well, Chickens Aren't the Only Ones, Plants That Never Ever Bloom* and *The Reason for a Flower*. For Grades 1-4.
VHS: S14175. $139.95.

Sadako
Eleanor Coerr's story of an ill Japanese adolescent girl is narrated by Liv Ullmann with music by George Winston. Sadako has leukemia because of the residual radiation left by the bombing of Hiroshima. She is beset by the threat of despair when a friend reminds her of the belief that a thousand paper cranes may cause the gods to grant her a wish. Ages 8 and up. 30 mins.
VHS: S24930. $195.00.

Santa Claus and the Magic Drum
Christmas is just days away as Santa explores the busy workshops chock full of terrific toys. Soon Santa realizes he's being followed by a noisy little mischief maker with a magic drum, and through an amazing discovery, we learn that sometimes the best Christmas presents aren't toys at all. 50 mins.
VHS: S32707. $12.95.

Sarah, Plain and Tall
Set on the Midwestern prairie, this video presentation of Patricia MacLachlan's book tells the story of Sarah, who answers a pioneer's ad for a wife, but misses her home in Maine, the ocean and her family. 30 mins.
VHS: S08400. $119.00.

Savannah Smiles
A touching children's film about Savannah, a six-year old runaway, who is thrown together with two escaped convicts in a crazy comedy of errors.
VHS: S04298. $14.95.
Pierre de Moro, USA, 104 mins.

Scholastic Productions
Series of pre-teen videos combining entertainment with insights into the world around them. 60 minutes each.
The Great Love Experiment. This is the Emmy-Award-winning story of a "love experiment"—four seniors try to change a nerd's luck, through friendship.
VHS: S04165. $19.95.

Scuffy the Tugboat and Friends
Remember the Golden Books you read as a kid? *Scuffy the Tugboat* is now in video format. Also included are other Golden Book titles: *What Was That!* and *Theodore Mouse Goes to Sea*. Ages 2-6. 30 minutes.
VHS: S24989. $5.95.

Sea Dream
A lively animated film about a girl who escapes into an underwater fantasy after having a bad day. She "dives" through her quilt into the sea where she joins a friendly octopus for tea. After a wonderful day together, the little girl swims back to her bed, refreshed by a trip into fantasy. With the hallucinatory *Nebule* and *The Sound Collector*. 30 mins.
VHS: S15793. $19.98.

Seabert: Good Guys Wear White
A fun-filled adventure with Seabert, who is out to make a better world for all by fighting poachers, hunters and other evil forces that threaten wildlife. Animated.
VHS: S09188. $49.95.

Seal Morning
Along the desolate Norfolk coast of England, an orphaned girl is sent to live with her reclusive aunt. The girl, Rowena, adjusts to her new surroundings by exploring the wild countryside of the region. Her discovery of a baby seal helps her aunt break out of her seclusion toward a new family life. 103 mins.
VHS: S25060. $19.95.

Season on the Water
Heather and Billy's father is reluctant to take them out on the water because he was lost at sea for two days. Heather's determination changes his mind however, providing valuable insights about family relationships. 26 mins.
VHS: S23453. $79.95.

Seasons and Holidays Around the World
These are colorful, dramatic stories that tell how real people in Mexico, China, Britain and Sweden celebrate the holidays most meaningful to them. Many diverse cultures and societies are explored in holiday gatherings around the world. In England, they celebrate with a party that originated in the Druid religion. The Swedes have a special Christmas tale about Jultomenten arriving in his sleigh. Explore!
Halloween in Britain.
VHS: S16362. $34.95.
Christmas in Mexico.
VHS: S16363. $34.95.
Chinese New Year.
VHS: S16364. $34.95.
Christmas in Sweden.
VHS: S16365. $34.95.

A Second Chance
Starring Richard Mulligan. Friendship, loyalty, guilt and regret come under scrutiny as events lead up to the accidental shooting of a boy's best friend. 27 mins.
VHS: S23446. $79.95.

The Secret World of Alex Mack: In the Nick of Time

Alex was accidentally drenched with strange chemicals from the Paradise Valley Chemical Plant. In these two episodes she manages to outwit the company employees who try to track her down and even cope with the usual teenage troubles. It's all made possible by her special and amazing powers. USA, 1996, 55 mins.

VHS: S26915. $9.98.

Seven Candles for Kwanzaa

Alfre Woodward narrates this animated celebration of the unique African-American holiday which commemorates the strength of family ties, respect for ancestors, commitment to the growth of community and gratitude for life's bounties. By Andrea Davis Pinkney. 9 mins.

VHS: S33786. $60.00.

Shamu & You

Featuring live kids, animation, wild-life footage and songs. Ages 4-10. 30 minutes each video.

Shamu & You: Exploring the World of Birds.
VHS: S24637. $14.98.
Shamu & You: Exploring the World of Fish.
VHS: S24638. $14.98.
Shamu & You: Exploring the World of Mammals.
VHS: S24639. $14.98.
Shamu & You: Exploring the World of Reptiles.
VHS: S24640. $14.98.

Sherlock Holmes Cliffhangers

Students led through these gripping and dramatic puzzles practice observation, organization, sequencing and reasoning as they uncover the evidence from the clues presented. At a key point, the students must match wits with the master sleuth by answering focus question. Includes four tales: *The Musgrave Ritual, The Adventures of the Priory School, The Adventure of the Norwood Builder* and *A Case of Identity*. For Grades 5-12.

VHS: S14204. $159.95.

Sherlock Holmes Spellbinders

These four tales show the master at his best. Holmes inspires viewers to follow his methods of scholarly research, careful observation and acute deduction. Includes *The Adventure of the Three Students, The Adventure of the Reigate Puzzle, The Adventure of the Solitary Cyclist* and *The Adventure of the Lion's Mane*. For Grades 5-12.

VHS: S14176. $159.95.

Sherlock Holmes' Greatest Cases

The sleuth of sleuths is called upon to render assistance where simple mortals are totally perplexed. Each case challenges the viewer to think like the detective and come up with the solution. Includes four classic mysteries: *A Scandal in Bohemia, Silver Blaze, The Adventure of the Dancing Man* and *The Red-Headed League*. For Grades 5-12.

VHS: S14205. $159.95.

Showdown at Lonesome Pellet

Wild and furry days with the coney people on the frontier is the subject of this read-along children's video. The notorious Pointy Brothers are the meanest outlaws in the West. They have come to terrorize the quiet coney town of Lonesome Pellet. But a stranger promises to clean up the town in three days. Is he coney enough to do the job?

VHS: S22352. $39.95.

Silas Marner

Alison de Vere's animated adaptation of George Eliot's masterly Victorian novel about the fall and redemption of the weaver Silas Marner, a man who loses everything, but regains his strength and identity through a beautiful baby girl. 28 mins.

VHS: S16995. $59.95.

Silent Mouse

The story of the famous carol "Silent Night" starts in a little town in Austria where a chain of strange events happened on Christmas Eve 1887. In *Silent Mouse*, Lynn Redgrave reveals a curious and charming story of mice and men. 1990, color, 60 mins.

VHS: S14989. $19.95.

A Singing Stream: A Black Family Chronicle

This film charts the living tradition of black gospel music in the lives of an ordinary family, the Creedmoors from North Carolina. Shape note singing, backyard harmonizing, quartet programs and church services are just part of the way this music inspires and preserves family life. 60 mins.

VHS: S26356. $19.95.

Six Stories About Little Heroes

Jay O'Callahan's original tales on the universal themes of courage, friendship and truth are examples of how all of us can draw upon the power of the imagination to create our own stories. In *Six Stories*, the subjects include O'Callahan's creations of a king, various children and assorted frogs and bees. 38 mins. Public performance rights included.

VHS: S09267. $19.95.

Something Good (plus Mortimer)

This is the tale of Tyya, a little girl whose dad refuses to buy her any "good stuff"—like cookies and candy—at the market. Plus Mortimer, who's unwilling to be quiet and go to bed. Animated stories by Robert Munsch. Ages 2-7. 30 minutes.

VHS: S24987. $12.95.

Sometimes I Wonder

A brother and sister run away from home to Grandma's ranch, where their favorite mare is beginning to foal. The children gain insights about the special gifts family life brings. 45 minutes, ages 5-12.

VHS: S17141. $14.95.

Sound Around

This tape explores the sounds made by toys, household objects and appliances, as well as those sounds made by animals and people. It's a great tool for understanding human similarities and differences as children are seen listening to, generating and imitating these sounds. 27 mins.

VHS: S22382. $19.95.

Soviet Bedtime Stories—Films for Children

Included on this tape are *A Monkey Leads the Band, The Wolf and the Tailor, The Miracle Frost, Little Cucumbers Adventures* and more. Each film is a fable, with a wide range of animation techniques rendered. 60 mins.

VHS: S12725. $19.98.

Space Case

A fun Halloween story in which a thing from outer space comes to earth to visit Buddy McGee. "A terrific comedy, crisply told, and illustrated by James Marshall's inimitable caricatures." From the storybook by Edward Marshall.

VHS: S16361. $44.95.

Spirits of the Rainforest

Children boat down an actual river, sharing myths, magic and legends of the Michiguenga Indians, who still live in the rainforest. Ages 8+.

VHS: S24767. $19.95.

Spooky Stories

A collection of strange and eerie stories about wild animals, old hunters, small women, monsters, tailors and a greedy old fat man, created by Paul Galdone. Intended for children from kindergarten through 4th grade.

The Greedy Old Fat Man. A greedy fat man devours his breakfast and in succession, a boy, a girl, a dog, a cat, a fox and several rabbits. A squirrel challenges him, declaring, "You can't catch me, old man!" 7 mins.
VHS: S20066. $44.95.

The Monster and the Tailor. The Grand Duke hires a tailor to design a pair of trousers, but he insists the craftsman make them in a ghoulish graveyard populated by a wild and spooky monster. 9 mins.
VHS: S20065. $44.95.

The Tailypo. An old hunter detaches the tail of a wild varmint, and the animal responds by stalking him each night, calling for his "Tailypo." 11 mins.
VHS: S20063. $44.95.

The Teeny-Tiny Woman. A small woman discovers a teeny-tiny bone and encounters strange noises emanating from a teeny-tiny cupboard. 7 mins.
VHS: S20064. $44.95.

Spooky Stories, Set. A collection of four programs. 34 mins.
VHS: S20067. $159.95.

Spoonbill Swamp

On a typical day in the swamp, an alligator mother and a spoonbill mother tend to their young. Children will be fascinated by the similarities and differences between these two animals as they read along with this video. 9:30 mins.

VHS: S22354. $39.95.

The Star Child

Oscar Wilde's tale is brought to life in this Claymation adaptation. A woodcutter finds a child at the site of a fallen shooting star. He takes the child home and raises him into a mischievous youngster, until a beggar woman appears and transforms the child.

VHS: S26618. $14.95.
Will Vinton, USA, 27 mins.

A Star for Jeremy

This warm, animated story relates the friendship of young Jeremy, who dreams about God's assigned position for all the stars, and the special task that awaits Sam, the smallest star who's called to carry out a heroic endeavor. 22 minutes.

VHS: S04140. $14.95.

Starstruck

An Emmy award winning short about a talented 16-year-old girl who doesn't know how best to use her musical ability. Young Alice is torn between listening to her mother or pursuing her dreams. With Rini Alvarado and Lee Curreri from *Fame*. 1981, 32 mins.

VHS: S08692. $14.95.

The Stolen Necklace

Anne Rockwell's book about a princess who loses her necklace is adapted by William Clairborne in this video. Apparently, mischievous monkeys are to blame for this theft. 9 mins.

VHS: S23494. $39.95.

Stories from the Black Tradition

A Story—A Story, Mufaro's Beautiful Daughters, Why Mosquitoes Buzz in People's Ears, The Village of Round and Square Houses and *Goggles* are now enjoyable children's animated shorts. These cartoons will instill children with pride. 52 mins.

VHS: S22685. $14.95.

Story of a Silent Night

Featuring the Vienna Boys Choir, this video uncovers the story of this popular Christmas carol as it was written in 1818 by Father Joseph Mohr. Now translated into over 120 languages, this beautiful carol has become a timeless Christmas favorite. 55 mins.

VHS: S23143. $29.95.

The Story of Lassie

Lassie touched Americans in her feature films, over the radio and on television. Interviews with famous stars featured in Lassie stories, like Roddy McDowall and Janet Leigh, are interspersed with clips from some of the most memorable moments of Lassie's long career. Hosted by June Lockhart. 60 mins.

VHS: S25996. $24.95.

Storybook

Eight-year-old Brandon finds himself inside a magical storybook world where he must believe in himself in order to survive. Fortunately his dog Leo and a host of new and outlandish friends are there to help him battle the dark rule of Queen Evilia. Milton Berle is featured in a surprise cameo.

VHS: S26041. $19.95.
Lorenzo Doumani, USA, 1995, 88 mins.

Storytelling with Sandy Jenkins: Learning and Sharing

Jenkins reveals how to tell children wonderful stories that are not only entertaining but also educational and enriching. This advice can help anyone at any level of ability. 45 mins.

VHS: S25968. $24.98.

The Sun the Wind and the Rain

This is the story of two mountains. The earth made one. Elizabeth in her yellow sun hat made the other. Lisa Westberg Peters describes the creation and evolution of mountains by comparing the centuries-long geological process to Elizabeth's sand sculptures. Ted Rand's spectacular paintings illuminate the basic concepts of the story. The result is an unusually evocative first lesson in geology.

VHS: S16355. $44.95.

Swan Lake

Music by the great Russian composer, Tchaikovsky, is featured in this animated film. Narration by Dudley Moore and a musical performance by the Moscow State Orchestra make this new version of the classic story a must for children, which will help them grow to appreciate serious music. From the *Storyteller's Classics* series, animated. 27 mins.

VHS: S26340. $9.98.

Swiss Family Robinson

Based on the story by Johann Wyss, this is an animated adaptation of the classic story. A family shipwrecked on an island faces adventure and mystery as they try to build a new life.

VHS: S03019. $19.95.

Tail of the Tiger

The story of a boy's fascination with airplanes and his friendship with a crusty old war veteran who owns a real Tiger aircraft.

VHS: S02683. $59.95.

Tales of Washington Irving

An animated look at one of the world's least animated men, Rip Van Winkle. The literary creation of 19th Century American author Washington Irving, that old sleepy head has his story told along with that of the Headless Horseman in *The Legend of Sleepy Hollow*. 1970, approx. 48 mins.

VHS: S03632. $24.95.

The Talking Reference Library

This introductory program employs claymation and live-action to teach children how to utilize a library's resources, including the use of encyclopedias, dictionaries, atlas and almanac. Offers valuable, easy lessons in understanding key terms, indexes, maps, graphs and cross-referencing. "[The] claymation techniques bring books to life. This series is an excellent teaching resource for all elementary/middle school learning centers and libraries" *(School Library Journal)*. Designed for children in grades 4-6.

The Animated Dictionary. The dictionaries on the library shelf boldly come alive and help a student, struggling with his creative writing assignment, in the correct spelling of a word. 22 mins.
VHS: S19950. $65.95.

The Animated Atlas. A young student enchanted by the story of Amelia Earhart and her historic flight across the Atlantic Ocean visits the reference shelf, and voices from the books aid her in learning about maps and atlases. 20 mins.
VHS: S19951. $65.95.

The Animated Encyclopedia. Through claymation effects, an entire shelf of reference books assumes three-dimensional shape and life. The video helps students understand the contents of the encyclopedia. 17 mins.
VHS: S19952. $65.95.

The Animated Almanac. Claymation is used to demonstrate how almanacs are indexed and organized. 15 mins.
VHS: S19953. $65.95.

The Talking Reference Library, Set. A set of four programs on how to use reference books. 60 mins.
VHS: S19954. $229.00.

Tara the Stonecutter

When Tara is granted his wish for wealth and power, he learns that he is actually more powerful simply being himself. 8 mins.
VHS: S23505. $39.95.

Telephone Tips for Kids, Volume 1

This video shows what can happen when a telephone message is mishandled. Auntie Bella and her life-sized puppet house guests are at the center of this funny story. The Telephone Doctor then shows kids how to take messages and how to dial an emergency phone number. Produced by Telephone "Doctor," ages 3 and up. 21 mins.
VHS: S25891. $9.95.

Tell Me Why:

This series of encyclopedias is based on the book and newspaper series by Arkady Leokum. Each volume presents and answers over 50 questions with colorful graphics and film footage, guaranteed to capture any child's imagination.

Americana. 30 mins.
VHS: S12800. $19.95.

Anatomy and Genetics. 30 mins.
VHS: S12808. $19.95.

Animals and Arachnids. 30 mins.
VHS: S12804. $19.95.

Beginnings: Civilization and Gov't. 30 mins.
VHS: S12812. $19.95.

Birds and Rodents. 30 mins.
VHS: S12802. $19.95.

Tell Me Why: Customs and Superstitions.
VHS: S26309. $19.95.

Tell Me Why: Electricity and Electric Safety.
VHS: S26310. $19.95.

Fish, Shellfish and Underwater Life. 30 mins.
VHS: S12805. $19.95.

Tell Me Why: Flight.
VHS: S26307. $19.95.

Flowers, Plants and Trees. 30 mins.
VHS: S12797. $14.95.

Gems, Metals and Minerals. 30 mins.
VHS: S12798. $19.95.

Tell Me Why: Geography.
VHS: S26312. $19.95.

Tell Me Why: How Things Work.
VHS: S26308. $19.95.

Insects. 30 mins.
VHS: S12799. $19.95.

Life Forms and Animal Oddities. 30 mins.
VHS: S12801. $19.95.

Mammals. 30 mins.
VHS: S12803. $19.95.

Medicine. 30 mins.
VHS: S12809. $19.95.

Prehistoric Animals and Reptiles. 30 mins.
VHS: S12806. $19.95.

Science, Sound and Energy. 30 mins.
VHS: S12811. $19.95.

Space, Earth and Atmosphere. 30 mins.
VHS: S12795. $19.95.

Sports and Games. 30 mins.
VHS: S12810. $19.95.

Tell Me Why: Time, Money, and Measurement.
VHS: S26311. $19.95.

Water and Weather. 30 mins.
VHS: S12796. $19.95.

Tell Me Why: 24-Volume Set.
VHS: S26407. $478.80.

Ten Tall Soldiers

There is a Royal Reward to any citizen or soldier for the positive identification of the nasty and naughty monster that has been prowling the castle with the express purpose of disrupting the Royal Routine and badly scaring the Royal Personage. A witty text full of alliteration to rhyme with Hilary Knight's childlike humor and imaginative drawings.
VHS: S16356. $44.95.

The Tenth Good Thing About Barney

When Barney the cat died his family gave him a funeral in the backyard. To help her son through his grief, his mother suggests he think of ten good things about Barney. Based on the book by Judith Viorst. 13 mins.
VHS: S22368. $49.95.
Laser: LD74598. $99.95.

Thanksgiving Day by Gail Gibbons

This adaptation of Gibbons' book details the rich history, traditions and customs surrounding the celebration of Thanksgiving. Graphic illustrations and clear text are used throughout. 6 mins.
VHS: S24912. $37.95.

There's a Cricket in the Library

Written by fifth-grade students of McKee School in Oakdale, Pennsylvania, this charming tale follows the adventures of a cricket caught in the library, who displays no manners or good library behavior and has to be reminded by the children of about the need to obey rules. Illustrated by Morgan Windsheimer. 4 mins.
VHS: S19601. $39.00.

There's a Witch Under the Stairs

Anyone who has ever worried about witches (or ghost or monsters or other scary creatures) will know exactly how Frances feels. She knows there's a witch under the stairs to the basement. She has tried lots of tricks to get rid of that witch but so far nothing has worked. She makes her own special witch's brew but that doesn't make the witch disappear.
VHS: S16357. $44.95.

Thirteen Moons on Turtle's Back

Subtitled *A Native American Year of Moons*, Abenaki Indian Joseph Bruchac and poet Jonathan London discuss the history of Native American legend and mythology, focused on the belief of the thirteen moons of the year. The writers contrast legends within different Native American tribes to show how the cultures identified the cycles of the moon with the seasons.
VHS: S20002. $44.95.

The Three Robbers and Other Stories

Three fierce robbers terrify the countryside until they meet a little girl named Tiffany whose charm turns their gold to good. Other films on the program are *Leopold the See-Through Crumbpicker, The Island of the Skog* and *Fourteen Rats and a Rat Catcher*.
VHS: S01336. $14.95.

Thunder Cake

A loud clap of thunder booms and rattles the windows of Grandma's old farmhouse. "This is Thunder Cake baking weather," calls Grandma, as she and her granddaughter scurry around the farm gathering the necessary ingredients. A real Thunder Cake must reach the oven before the storm arrives—but the list is long, not easy to follow and the storm is coming closer every minute. From the award-winning story by Patricia Polacco.
VHS: S16358. $44.95.

Thunderbird 6

The Tracy brothers, leaders of an International Rescue team, are back and this time are faced with a plot to steal their fabulous fleet of rescue planes. 1968, 90 mins.
VHS: S16856. $19.98.

Thunderbirds Are Go

Streak through uncharted worlds of adventure with the incredible Tracy team! Earth's favorite electronic puppets launch a dangerous rescue in space. 1966, 94 mins.
VHS: S16855. $19.98.

Tickle Tune Typhoon: Let's Be Friends

This live concert outing by the Tickle Tune Typhoon entourage features a "typhoon" of award-winning songs with messages ranging from racial tolerance to an understanding of differently abled persons: "Skin" reveals a harmony in our multiracial society; "Everyone Is Differently Abled" focuses on what people *can* do, not what they can't; "Pearly White Waltz" stresses the importance of brushing one's teeth. 60 mins.
VHS: S16758. $14.98.

Timmy's Gift

Little Timmy the angel is given the greatest honor in all of Heaven: to deliver the jeweled crown to the newborn Prince. But he's sure that they have made some sort of mistake. He's much too little for such a long and difficult journey, and who knows what frightful things lie ahead. 23 mins.
VHS: S33286. $12.95.

Tinka's Planet

An entertaining introduction for elementary-school children to the need for recycling. When Tinka discovers that not all trash needs to be thrown away, she begins to collect her family's cans, bottles and newspapers. On her first visit to the local recycling center she learns how recycling can help preserve the environment. Inspired to do something more for the environment, she convinces other kids in the neighborhood to join her in a recycling campaign.
VHS: S12321. $55.00.
Ben Swets/Donna Worden, USA, 1990, 12 mins.

Tom Thumb Meets Thumbelina

Enter a thrillingly animated kingdom of mischievous fairies, wicked princes and a pair of very little people caught up in a very big adventure on this tape brimming with original songs and delightful characters. 48 mins.
VHS: S30501. $14.98.

Too Many Pumpkins

Ever since she was a little girl growing up during the Great Depression, Rebecca Estelle has hated pumpkins because her family had nothing to eat but baked, stewed or mashed pumpkins. Rebecca learns to make amends with her pumpkin phobia when an enormous pumpkin smashes in her yard and begins to sprout and she finds herself in a sea of pumpkins. Story by Linda White, illustrated by Megan Lloyd.
VHS: S30471. $37.95.

The Toothbrush Family

The bathroom becomes a land of discovery for Susie Sponge, Flash Fluoride, Countess de Comb and young toothbrushes Molly and Max in this animated adventure. 90 mins.
VHS: S34915. $19.95.

The Toytown Story Adventures

Five wonderful animated shorts, produced in the Toytown tradition by director Hendrick Baker, are collected on this video. Larry the Lamb and other Toytown Pals, including a pig and a dog among others, will delight children and parents alike.
VHS: S28071. $14.98.
Hendrick Baker, USA

Treasure Island

Robert Louis Stevenson's classic epic of the high seas will delight children in this animated version. Charming animated characters (including a talking parrot and a wisecracking cat and mouse duo) make this cartoon even more appealing to kids. From the *Enchanted Tales* series. USA, 1996, 48 mins.
VHS: S26914. $12.98.

Treasury of Animal Stories, Set I

Delightful video versions of Beatrix Potter's perennial classics. Includes four stories: *The Tale of Peter Rabbit, The Tale of Benjamin Bunny, The Tale of Squirrel Nutkin* and *The Tale of Jeremy Fisher*. For Grades 3-4.
VHS: S14210. $159.95.

Tribal Design Grades 4-12

A multicultural program introduces tribal art from different cultures, including Africa, New Guinea, pre-Columbian Mexico, Alaska and Pacific Northwest Coast Indian. Demonstration of studio activities are also illustrated.
VHS: S09076. $249.00.

Urashima Taro & Cabbages and Kings

Two programs are included on this video. *Urashima Taro* is an animated adaptation of an ancient Japanese folk tale about a fisherman who saves a sea turtle's life and is rewarded by a visit to the kingdom under the sea. *Cabbages and Kings* is the story of a vain princess who spurns and ridicules every suitor until her father decrees that she marry the next beggar who shows his face at the castle. 30 mins.
VHS: S30724. $19.95.

The Veldt

In this Ray Bradbury story the house of a family does all the housework. It cooks, cleans, and even reads to and comforts the children. In the playroom it brings the children's fantasies to life. Soon ominous images of the African Veldt bring this sci-fi story to a traumatic conclusion. 24 mins.
VHS: S22374. $79.95.

Video Storybreak

Bob Keeshan, "Captain Kangaroo," hosts this animated series of four books that children themselves have put on the best-seller lists.

Arnold of the Ducks. A young boy, lost in the wild, is rescued and reared as their own by ducks. When he is found and returned to his human parents, they must learn to adapt to a son who goes "quack." 25 mins.
VHS: S08250. $14.98.

C.L.U.T.Z. This story is set in the very near future, when servants are robots. The Pentax family, which can't afford the latest mechanical butler, settles for an older model, a good-hearted robot whose comical imperfections earn him his name. 25 mins.
VHS: S08252. $14.98.

Chocolate Fever. When chocolate-lover Henry Green breaks out in "measles", made of pure chocolate, he learns too much of anything can make for disastrous results. 25 mins.
VHS: S08253. $14.98.

How to Eat Fried Worms. Having bet he can eat a worm a day for 15 days, Billy is in for some unusual meals. His friends try to sabotage the bet but Billy devises a clever plan that will allow him to keep his honor and still win. 25 mins.
VHS: S08251. $14.98.

The Visitor

State-of-the-art special effects and an original musical score highlight this powerful science fiction story about human greed and treachery. Based on the Ray Bradbury story. 22 mins.
VHS: S22375. $79.95.
Laser: LD74602. $99.95.

Voyage en Ballon

From the director of *The Red Balloon*, a marvelous adventure as Little Pascal and his grandfather take off across France in a 60-foot-tall balloon with many humorous and suspenseful adventures which ensue. Dubbed in English.
VHS: S01421. $19.95.
Albert Lamorisse, France, 1962, 82 mins.

Waiting for Grandma

This claymation film features Allegra, who is so excited about Grandma's visit that she can hardly sit still. Fortunately, Allegra learns to make time fly until Grandma arrives with stories, songs and special surprises. Features the song "Holiday with Grandma." 30 mins.
VHS: S26635. $12.95.

A Walk in the Wild

Youngsters will learn about ecology and the environment through this read-along video. The illustrations are based on an actual visit to the Arkansas National Wildlife Refuge in Texas. 9:30 mins.
VHS: S22357. $39.95.

Wanted: The Perfect Guy

A young boy concerned about his mother devises a wacky scheme to find her Mr. Right. He places a personal ad which leads to a series of Mr. Wrongs, until the right one turns up. An ABC afterschool special. 28 mins.
VHS: S23449. $49.95.

A Week in the Life of a Chinese Student

Young students from Beijing are the subjects of this documentary about life in the People's Republic of China. 20 mins.
VHS: S23722. $99.95.

When the Wind Stops

Charlotte Zolotow's book about an inquisitive child is adapted in this charming short. Questions about wind, ocean waves, ships, airplanes and much more reveal the interconnectedness of life. 11 mins.
VHS: S23456. $49.95.

Where Did I Come From?

Based on the best-selling book, this animated film proves, among other things, that sex education is quite possibly fun. This film tells the story of conception through birth and takes the chance of laughing along with its subject. It answers questions parents may have chosen to avoid. An informative, educational tool to sex education.
VHS: S02459. $19.95.
Steve Walsh, 1985, 27 mins.

Where in the World/Kids Explore

With a pen pal and a secret clubhouse, viewers join the live-action journey to some interesting spots around the world. Using a combination of colorful graphics, animation and dance, we see real kids finding out about the culture, geography, geology, ecology and history of their destination. Ages 5-11. Each video is 30 minutes.

Where in the World Volume 1. Kids Explore Mexico. Investigate the mysteries of the Aztec and Mayan ruins, have dinner with a fun-loving Mexican family, join guitar players and flamenco dancers, see festivals, visit Mexico City, have fun!
VHS: S24945. $9.95.

Where in the World Volume 2. Kids Explore Alaska. Pan for gold, join "Gold Rush Days," race with a sled dog team, share a little Eskimo life, meet the Coastal Indians and visit a wilderness bush family.
VHS: S24946. $9.95.

Where in the World Volume 3. Kids Explore Kenya. Meet nomadic herders; unearth ancient skulls in the Great Rift Valley; find out about tribal family life; enjoy music, dance and a visit to Nairobi.
VHS: S24947. $9.95.

Where in the World Volume 4. Kids Explore America's National Parks. Explore the rain forests and seashore of Olympic; see the granite walls and giant Sequoia trees of Yosemite and look at pioneer life at Fort Vancouver. Yellowstone, Grand Canyon, Everglades and more—walks, wildlife, waterfalls…whew!
VHS: S24948. $9.95.

Where the Lilies Bloom

Based on the Newbery Award-winning book by Vera and Bill Cleaver, *Where the Lilies Bloom* tells the story of four children who are left orphaned by the death of their father. Determined to stay together despite all odds, the children hide their father's death from the state and learn to fend for themselves.
VHS: S16848. $14.95.
William A. Graham, USA, 1973, 97 mins.

Which Way, Weather?

One of the award-winning Bo Peep Productions. This video is made with the developmental needs of the youngest viewers in mind. The tape features the weather, and demonstrates ways for young children to enjoy various weather conditions. See multicultural children swimming, sailing, flying kites, ice skating, sledding, pumpkin picking, puddle stomping and more. Ages 18 months to 6 years. 30 minutes.
VHS: S24658. $19.95.

Whiffle Squeek

Ted Rand's swashbuckling illustrations have been partially animated in this iconographic video presentation of Caron Lee Cohen's story of Whiffle Squeek, the sea-sailing cat. 10 mins.
VHS: S12266. $62.00.

The Whipping Boy

In this Newbery Award-winning tale, Jemmy, an orphaned rat-catcher, and the arrogant Prince Bat exchange identities to confuse kidnappers and learn valuable lessons in compassion, loyalty and friendship. 38 mins.
VHS: S20040. $59.00.

Whistlepunks & Sliverpickers: A Fun Look at Forestry

Children will love this video field trip through the logging industry. Full of fun, games, and plenty of noise, this tape shows everything there is to know about logging and milling jobs. The scenery is breathtaking.
VHS: S25542. $19.98.
Ibex Communications, USA, 1994, 30 mins.

Whitewash

When Helene Angel walks home from her school with her older brother she is attacked by a street gang and painted white. The effect on Helene and her family is devastating, and the media descend on their neighborhood, completely disrupting the small family. Inspired by actual events and featuring the voices of Ruby Dee, Serene Henry, Ndehru Roberts and Linda Lavin, the story conveys a powerful message that transcends age and race.
VHS: S33432. $19.95.
Michael Sporn, USA, 1994, 25 mins

The Wild Christmas Reindeer

A marvelously original Christmas story in which Santa asks Teeka to get his reindeer ready to fly on Christmas Eve. Teeka is both excited and worried because she has never worked with the reindeer before, and they've been running wild and free on the tundra. Can she catch them, and groom them? Once she finds the reindeer, Teeka's strong hand does more harm than good, and soon the reindeer are wilder than ever. How will she get them ready to pull Santa's sleigh on time?
VHS: S16359. $44.95.

Wildlife Symphony

Combines symphony music with animals at play in their native habitats. Ages 2+.
VHS: S24814. $29.95.

Will We Miss Them? Endangered Species

The bald eagle, the mountain lion, the rhinoceros and the giant panda are just some of the creatures examined in this carefully illustrated read-along video. Over a dozen species are discussed. 9:30 mins.
VHS: S22356. $39.95.

William Wegman's Mother Goose

Everyone's favorite childhood rhymes get the wry Wegman touch with his canine companions Batty, Crooky, Chundo and Chip, as Mother Goose attempts to teach her son Simon the art of rhyming with some surprising advice from Grandmother Goose.
VHS: S31642. $9.95.
William Wegman, USA, 1997, 30 mins.

Wind and Water

For all ages. Bustling Hong Kong is background for this story of an aged widow and an aging missioner. He helps her find shelter and she helps him discover a deeper meaning in life. A dramatic story of person-to-person caring. Produced by Maryknoll Media. 28 mins.
VHS: S04938. $24.95.

The Wind in the Willows, Volume #1

A beautiful, full-length animated version of the classic children's book with extraordinary animation and voices supplied by some of England's leading stage and film actors.
VHS: S01465. $14.99.
Mark Hall, Great Britain, 1984, 78 mins.

The Wind in the Willows, Volume #2

Three animated adventures based on the popular children's story *Wind in the Willows*, with the characters of Badger, Mole, Ratty and the flamboyant Toad of Toad Hall.
VHS: S01466. $14.99.
Mark Hall, Great Britain, 1983, 60 mins.

The Wind in the Willows, Volume #3

Three adventures featuring characters from Kenneth Grahame's stories: *Great Steamer, Buried Treasure* and *Mole's Cousin*.
VHS: S00716. $14.99.
Mark Hall, Great Britain, 60 mins.

The Wind in the Willows, Volume #4

Three adventures based on Kenneth Grahame's classic: *Grand Annual Show, Open Road Again* and *Wayfarers All*. Populated by Badger, Mole, Ratty, and the Toad of Toad Hall.
VHS: S01467. $14.99.
Mark Hall, Great Britain, 1983, 60 mins.

The Wind in the Willows: Four Seasons Set

Originally a children's book, this four-volume video set brings 12 episodes, featuring the characters of this book, to the screen. Badger, Mole, Ratty and Toad inhabit a wonderful world of seasonal change and lovely countryside. Their antics will delight children. Each video is 60 mins.
VHS: S29977. $39.99.

Wings: A Tale of Two Chickens and Other Stories by James Marshall

Finally Marshall's stories appear in charming animated versions. *Wings: A Tale of Two Chickens, Goldilocks and the Three Bears, The Three Little Pigs* and *Red Riding Hood* are all included. 43 mins.
VHS: S22165. $14.95.

Winter Wolf

This award-winning video is an exciting way for children to understand the age-old conflict between man and wolf. Kids follow the adventures of a 14-year-old Native American girl who discovers a lone wolf living on her family's ranch and learns the importance of the wolf in her heritage through stories told by her grandmother. Grades 1-8, 1996, 30 mins.
VHS: S31905. $49.95.

The Wish That Changed Christmas

An enchanting animated adaptation of *The Story of Holly and Ivy*. Ivy, a disillusioned orphan, boards a train on Christmas Eve and entertains no thoughts of happiness until she receives a mysterious message that catapults her on a magical odyssey to find the grandmother she's always longed for. Voices by Paul Winfield and Jonathan Winters. 23 mins.

VHS: S19178. $12.98.

Wishbone: Bone of Arc

Mark Twain and Joan of Arc are the inspiration for this Wishbone episode. It follows two young girls who are determined to fetch victory for their teammates and their countrymen. 30 mins.

VHS: S29943. $12.95.

Wishbone: Frankenbone

Mary Shelley's gothic classic serves as the inspiration for this episode about the dog who continually remakes history. Wishbone helps get a science project that went out of control back in the bag, and also manages to inspire kids with the artistry of Shelley's original novel. 30 mins.

VHS: S29942. $12.95.

Wishbone: Homer Sweet Homer

Wishbone imagines himself in another scenario sure to inspire kids to read. In this episode he is transported back to ancient Greece as Odysseus, the hero of Homer's *The Odyssey*. The goddess Calypso would ensnare Wishbone, but he thinks of his sweet Emily and somehow finds his way back home. 30 mins.

VHS: S27068. $12.95.

Wishbone: Salty Dog

Buried treasure lures Wishbone the dog into a south sea adventure. Inspired by Robert Louis Stevensons's *Treasure Island*, this live-action children's video has everything a kid could want, including pirate's gold, mutiny on the high seas, and the legend of Blackbeard. 30 mins.

VHS: S27779. $12.95.

Wishbone: Terrified Terrier

Wishbone the dog stars in this live-action children's video inspired by Stephen Crane's *The Red Badge of Courage*. Left alone when Joe finds new basketball buddies, Wishbone sets out to earn his very own badge of courage. 30 mins.

VHS: S27778. $12.95.

Wishbone: The Prince and the Pooch

Mark Twain's *The Prince and the Pauper* is cleverly reinterpreted for today's kids in this charming episode. While Joe merely wants to be a coach, Wishbone ends up as both the Prince of Wales and a lowly pauper in this tale of role switching and big trouble. 30 mins.

VHS: S27070. $12.95.

Wishbone: The Slobbery Hound

Wishbone is the sleuthing dog who inspires kids to read. In this episode based on Sir Arthur Conan Doyle's *The Hound of the Baskervilles*, Wishbone dons a cape and demeanor reminiscent of Sherlock Holmes. It's up to him to track down the mystery curse of the Baskerville family. 30 mins.

VHS: S27067. $12.95.

Wishbone: Twisted Tail

Kids will want to read Charles Dickens' *Oliver Twist* after watching Wishbone in *Twisted Tail*. Joe's house is burglarized and fingers start pointing to the new kid, Max. Meanwhile, Wishbone is trapped by a gang of colorful criminals on the streets of London. 30 mins.

VHS: S27069. $12.95.

The Wombles

Developed by the creators of Paddington Bear, *The Wombles* are fury creatures obsessed with the care and preservation of the environment. They live in an expansive park in London in the area around Wimbledon. These works use technology and puppet animation and vivid storytelling to convey their message of hope and inspiration.

The Wombles: Orinoco & the Ghost. 50 mins.
VHS: S17176. $14.98.
The Wombles: Sticky End. 50 mins.
VHS: S17175. $14.98.

Working Together

Winnie the Pooh and his friend, Christopher Robin, star in three short, animated films on this video. In *Shovel, Shovel, Toil and Trouble* gophers go crazy over a new power shovel. Next, Rabbit comes up with a plan to ground the bouncy Tigger in *Tigger's Shoes*. In the last short, *Easy Come, Easy Gopher*, the ultimate tunnel becomes even more imposing under Rabbit's supervision. 33 mins.

VHS: S29844. $12.99.

A World Alive

Spectacular wildlife footage encourages children to appreciate the diverse lives and beauties of this planet's creatures. Narrated by James Earl Jones, this video received the National Educational Film Festival Award and includes a dramatic musical score by Kit Walker. 25 mins.

Home Video.
VHS: S13839. $14.95.
Laser: LD76797. $49.95.
Public Performance Rights.
VHS: S17146. $34.95.

The World Through Kids' Eyes

This series of six short programs provides an intimate and unique insight into the reality and dreams of children from six countries: Philippines, Peru, Brazil, India, South Africa and the U.S. Each story reflects one of the articles of the United Nations Convention on the Rights of the Child but from the uncensored and oftentimes unsparing viewpoint of the children themselves. 56 mins.

VHS: S33232. $29.95.

The Worlds Below

Sweeping sea lions...snowstorms of plankton...starfish in motion...forests as majestic as any on land. Swim with a newborn seal and slide into a wondrous journey of wave-swept rocks, vast submerged plains, and the mysterious depths of the ocean. 50 minutes, family.

Home Video.
VHS: S17135. $19.95.
Public Performance Rights.
VHS: S17147. $34.95.

Yonder

Using one and two-part harmony, this icononographic video presentation transforms Tony Johnston and Lloyd Bloom's narrative poem into a beautiful song. One family's history is illuminated through the planting of a plum tree. 11 mins.

VHS: S12267. $57.00.

You Can Choose

A ten-volume series.

Volume 1: Cooperation. Part of a series which imparts positive social values in a fun manner. Moose learns how to cooperate. Ages 6-11.
VHS: S24701. $59.95.
Volume 2: Being Responsible. Rhonda Bird must choose between having a good time and her responsibilities. This video reminds us that positive social values can be imparted through media. This is best when done in a fun, engaging, dramatic manner, as this video does. Ages 5-8.
VHS: S24702. $59.95.
Volume 3: Dealing with Feelings. When Tuggy Turtle tries to hide his fears about going on a weekend camp out, his friendship with Moose is almost ruined. Together they discover the importance of accepting feelings and expressing them honestly and positively.
VHS: S24703. $59.95.
Volume 4: Saying No. Missie Mouse has to choose whether to say no to a friend or do something she knows is wrong. When Missie's best friend Rhonda tries to pressure her into smoking cigarettes, Missie agonizes over her options before discovering that there are many ways to say no.
VHS: S24704. $59.95.
Volume 5: Doing the Right Thing. Two girls struggle over a money-filled wallet, which they find on the playground. A good effort at imparting good values. Ages 6-11.
VHS: S24705. $59.95.
Volume 6: Dealing with Disappointment. Missie Mouse must learn to handle disappointments in a positive way when her baseball team falls into last place.
VHS: S24706. $59.95.
Volume 7: Appreciating Yourself. Tuggy learns that being himself is better than pretending to be something he's not. When Tuggy becomes troubled by feelings of inadequacy, his friends help him to recognize and appreciate his positive inner qualities.
VHS: S24707. $59.95.
Volume 8: Asking for Help. Moose learns not to let pride or embarrassment get in the way of asking for help. After ruining a group science project, Moose finds that the only good way to cope with his secret reading problem is to get the help he needs to overcome it.
VHS: S24708. $59.95.
Volume 9: Being Friends. Rhonda, Missie and Fiona learn about the complex nature of friendship. When Missie is not invited to the "in" party, the three girls are forced to deal with differences in their relationships with each other.
VHS: S24709. $59.95.
Volume 10: Resolving Conflicts. Tuggy and Rhonda learn that there are ways to resolve disagreements without fighting. When a dispute between them puts their class art project in jeopardy, Tuggy and Rhonda learn to work out interpersonal conflicts in a peaceful and positive way.
VHS: S24710. $59.95.
Complete Set. The ten-volume set.
VHS: S24829. $549.50.

Young Cinematographer

A DVD video magazine of great films, animation, kid stars and more made by, for and about kids aged 6 to 18.

DVD: DV60262. $14.95.

Zero Hour

Based on the Ray Bradbury story. Mink plays a strange game with her friends called "Invasion." At first Mink's mother discounts the precision and zeal of the children, but after a barrage of explosions the parents lock themselves in the attic. Now Mink has a surprise end for her special game. 20 mins.

VHS: S22376. $79.95.

Zlateh the Goat

With the holiday season approaching, poor Reuven, the furrier, has no recourse but to sell the family's beloved goat for supplies. But Aaron has other ideas. Story by Isaac B. Singer. Live action. 20 mins.

VHS: S33788. $49.95.

FAIRY TALES

The Adventures of Peer Gynt

Based on the classic story, Peer Gynt travels through an exciting world of witches, trolls and wild animals. Green Hilda, the powerful Mountain King and Peer Gynt vividly come to life in this production designed by master puppeteer Jim Gamble. 30 mins.

VHS: S16754. $19.95.

Aesop & His Friends

A delightful cartoon film festival of family entertainment which includes most of Aesop's best-loved stories, from *The Fox and the Crow* to *The Boy Who Called Wolf*.

VHS: S03956. $19.95.

African Story Magic

Brock Peters narrates the tale about a young child's odyssey from urban life to discover the power and wonder of ancient African folklore and ritual. 27 mins.

VHS: S17765. $12.98.

Afro-Classic Folk Tales, Vol. I

This collection of Afro-centered folk tales will promote positive self-affirming values among all children. Storyteller Sybil Destu tells two traditional folk tales, about the spider Anansi and about a tiger. The tales are animated. 30 mins.

VHS: S20620. $29.95.

Afro-Classic Folk Tales, Vol. II

This second installment of *Afro-Classic Folk Tales* includes a Brer Rabbit and Woodpecker cartoon, as well as an old African tale told by puppets. 30 mins.

VHS: S20621. $29.95.

Afro-Classic Mother Goose

In this collection the favorite tales of Mother Goose find new expressiveness with an Afro-centric twist. Playtime rhymes are updated in this fresh look at childhood stories. 30 mins.

VHS: S20622. $29.95.

Aladdin and His Magic Lamp

An early adaptation of one of the stories from *One Thousand and One Nights*, about an impoverished boy whose possession of a magic lamp endows him with superior powers and imagination. With Patricia Medina, Richard Erdman and John Sands.

VHS: S18024. $9.95.
Lew Landers, USA, 1952, 68 mins.

Ashpet: An American Cinderella

Set in the rural South in the early years of World War II, *Ashpet* is a humorously touching version of Cinderella, the world's most popular fairy tale. From the Brothers Grimm Series. Includes Public Performance Rights.

VHS: S12251. $35.00.
Tom Davenport, USA, 1988, 45 mins.

The Banshee

In this nighttime fantasy, a mysterious Banshee comes to a village in search of someone to share her loneliness. But among the village folk there is a special kind of strength and security that is far more powerful than the compelling song of the lonely Banshee. An enchanting tale by award-winning author Karen Ackerman, with illustrations by David Ray.

VHS: S16337. $44.95.

Bearskin (Or the Man Who Didn't Wash for Seven Years)

A young man triumphs over the Devil through endurance and force of character. Based on the Grimm Brothers' fairy tale, the setting is transposed to the South just after the Civil War. All ages.

VHS: S04370. $30.00.
Tom Davenport, USA

Beauty and the Beast

A beautifully animated version of the famous story, featured on PBS's Long Ago and Far Away. CINE Golden Eagle, Chicago International Children's Film Festival, TV Guide 10 Best Videos. Recommended by American Library Association, Parents' Choice Award. 30 minutes, ages 5-12.
VHS: S11416. $12.98.

Bill Cosby: Aesop's Fables

Bill Cosby stars as Aesop the master storyteller in a program that combines live action and animation. Featured story is *The Tortoise and the Hare*. USA, 1986, 30 mins.
VHS: S02514. $14.95.

Brer Rabbit and the Wonderful Tar Baby

The comic adventures of that original American troublemaker, Brer Rabbit—Bugs Bunny's great grandfather—are among the funniest and most cherished stories of our culture. The classic and hilarious tale of how he outsmarts his wily nemesis, Brer Fox, with a clever contraption he calls a "tar baby", in the story read by Danny Glover.
VHS: S12475. $9.95.

Bristlelip

An American version of Grimm's "King Thrushbeard," in which a haughty young woman learns how to treat other people. Recommended for all ages. 20 minutes,
VHS: S04373. $30.00.

Children's Stories from Africa

Meet Capusee the Clever Monkey, Bushpig and Warthog, Empesa the Hyena, Infene the Baboon, Gafumbi the Brave Boy and other new friends, in this unique blend of live storytelling, valuable lessons and values, whimsical drawings, African rhythms, and song and dance. Four-tape boxed set. 100 mins.
VHS: S32935. $44.95.

Cinder-Elly

Fairy tale magic and fast-paced rhyming make this read-along video a delight for children. A modern day Cinderella tries to win the affections of a Prince Charming, a local basketball player. Only her fairy godmother, a shopping cart lady, can give her the help and confidence she needs.
VHS: S22347. $39.95.

Cinderella

The timeless story of the cinder girl who becomes a princess comes alive in this Rankin/Bass Studio animation. 30 mins.
VHS: S03595. $11.95.

Classic Christmas Stories

A collection of children's Christmas favorites, including *Rudolph the Red-Nosed Reindeer, Silent Night, Jingle Bells* and *The Story of the Nutcracker*. Designed for children from kindergarten through 3rd grade.
Rudolph the Red-Nosed Reindeer Stories. In these holiday programs, the fabled reindeer Rudolph not only saves Christmas but helps some rabbits who are missing. 25 mins.
VHS: S19977. $34.95.
Silent Night/Jingle Bells. Two separate programs about the wonder of Christmas. *Silent Night* tells the history of a carol which was used for a Christmas service in 1854. *Jingle Bells* is an adventure set to the heart-warming music. 20 mins.
VHS: S19978. $34.95.
The Nutcracker. This program introduces children to the classic ballet. 16 mins.
VHS: S19979. $34.95.
Classic Christmas Stories, Set.
VHS: S19980. $89.00.

Davy Crockett and the River Pirates

Davy Crockett, King of the Wild Frontier, meets Mike Fink, King of the River, in this classic Disney adventure. This film launched the Crockett-mania of the mid-1950's. 81 mins.
VHS: S22982. $19.99.

Dreadlocks and the Three Bears

Draws on the works of collage artists Leo Lionni, Romare Bearden and Varnette Honeywood to tell the story of Dreadlocks, who finds herself in the home of the Three Bears, in Teddy Bear Forest, while visiting her aunt. Written and illustrated by Alile Sharon Larkin.
VHS: S18327. $14.95.

Elephant's Child

From Rudyard Kipling's *Just So Stories*, the story of how the elephant got his trunk. Narrated by Jack Nicholson, music by Bobby McFerrin.
VHS: S02843. $14.95.
Mark Sottnick, USA, 1986, 30 mins.

The Emperor's New Clothes and Other Folktales

The emperor leads a parade of his loyal subjects against a background of lively jazz music; wait until you see the emperor's new clothes! Based on the famous story by Hans Christian Andersen. Also includes *Why Mosquitoes Buzz in People's Ears* and *Subo and the White Horse*. For ages 4-9. 30 mins.
VHS: S14489. $19.95.

Enchanted Tales: Beauty and the Beast

An animated adaptation of the timeless classic about seeing beyond appearances, featuring whimsical songs. 48 mins.
VHS: S32670. $9.95.

European Folk Tales

This collection has been assembled from the work of the world's most talented animators. *European Folk Tales* will delight both children and adults. Produced by British animator John Halas.
Volume One. *The Lovelorn Giant, The Trumpeter* and *The Tower of Mice*. 34 mins.
VHS: S23485. $49.95.
Volume Two. *The Vixen and the Hare, The Lady and the Apple* and *The Unlucky Boy*. 38 mins.
VHS: S23486. $49.95.
Volume Three. *The Christmas Feast, The Ass and the Stick* and *The Green Mountain*. 35 mins.
VHS: S23487. $49.95.
Volume Four. *The Cinderella Barber, The Pear Tree* and *The Chameleon Cat*. 34 mins.
VHS: S23488. $49.95.
Volume Five. *The Princess and the Goat Boy, Enormous Lies* and *The Bag of Winds*. 35 mins.
VHS: S23489. $49.95.
Volume Six. *The Laughing Mirror, Katalina and Katalin* and *The Seven Flames*. 34 mins.
VHS: S23490. $49.95.

Fables and Fairy Tales

This collection of fables and fairy tales features stories with a moral which engage the mind with playful wit. "These fables have been teaching stories for centuries. Their simple problems and morals illustrate basic, universal values; their characters and situations have become part of our language" *(Landers Film Reviews)*. Designed for children in kindergarten through 3rd grade.
Aesop's Fables. A delightful collection of animal tales, myths and legends that is humorous and entertaining. 30 mins.
VHS: S19968. $37.95.
Fairy Tale Masterpieces. A collection of stories—including *The Tortoise and the Hare, The Wolf in Sheep's Clothing* and *Rumpelstiltskin*—are dramatized to help children develop language and listening skills. 24 mins.
VHS: S19970. $37.95.
The Art of Storytelling: Tall Tales. The precise craft and daring rhythm of a gifted storyteller are involved through two familiar folk tales about Pecos Bill and Annie Christmas. 20 mins.
VHS: S19969. $37.95.
Fables and Fairy Tales, Set.
VHS: S19971. $99.00.

Faerie Tale Theatre

The fairy tale series produced by Shelley Duvall features well-known actors and top directors in live-action realizations of the tales. All of the tapes run 60 minutes, are closed captioned, with many in hi-fi stereo.
Beauty and the Beast. Klaus Kinski, Susan Sarandon. Directed by Roger Vadim, USA, 1983, 60 mins.
VHS: S02877. $9.98.
Cinderella. With Jennifer Beals, Matthew Broderick and Jean Stapleton. 1984.
VHS: S02879. $9.95.
Dancing Princesses. With Lesley Ann Warren, Peter Weller and Roy Dotrice. Directed by Peter Medak, USA, 1984, 60 mins.
VHS: S02880. $14.98.
Emperor's New Clothes. Alan Arkin, Art Carney, Dick Shawn. 1984.
VHS: S02881. $9.98.
Frog Prince.
VHS: Out of print. For rental only.
Little Mermaid. Pam Dawber, Helen Mirren, Treat Williams. 1984.
VHS: S02885. $9.98.
Little Red Riding Hood.
VHS: Out of print. For rental only.
Pinocchio.
VHS: Out of print. For rental only.
Princess and the Pea. With Tom Conti, Liza Minnelli and Beatrice Straight. 1983.
VHS: S02890. $14.98.
Princess Who Had Never Laughed. Ellen Barkin, Howard Hesseman, Howie Mandel. 1984.
VHS: S02891. $9.98.
Puss in Boots. Gregory Hines, Ben Vereen. 1984.
VHS: S02892. $9.98.
Rapunzel. Jeff Bridges, Shelley Duvall, Gena Rowlands. 1982.
VHS: S02893. $9.98.
Rip Van Winkle. With Harry Dean Stanton and Talia Shire. 1985.
VHS: S04100. $9.98.
Sleeping Beauty. Beverly D'Angelo, Bernadette Peters, Christopher Reeve. 1984.
VHS: S02895. $9.98.
Snow Queen.
VHS: Out of print. For rental only.
Tales of the Frog Prince.
VHS: S04098. $9.98.
Three Little Pigs. Billy Crystal, Jeff Goldblum, Valerie Perrine. 1984.
VHS: S03597. $9.98.
Thumbelina.
VHS: Out of print. For rental only.

Fairy Tale Classics

A fresh version of familiar fairy tales in full color and complete sound production to motivate reading and stimulate interest in reading as a source of pleasure for young learners.
Volume 1: The Ugly Duckling, The Shoemaker and The Elves.
VHS: S06716. $29.95.
Volume 2: Puss in Boots, The Fisherman and His Wife.
VHS: S06717. $29.95.
Volume 3: Tom Thumb, The Three Pigs.
VHS: S06718. $29.95.
Volume 4: King Midas and the Golden Touch, The Three Bears.
VHS: S06719. $29.95.
Volume 5: Snow White and Rose Red, Jack and the Beanstalk.
VHS: S06720. $29.95.
Volume 6: Little Red Riding Hood, The Happy Prince.
VHS: S06721. $29.95.
Volume 7: Paul Bunyan, The Story of Pecos Bill.
VHS: S06722. $29.95.
Volume 8: Cinderella, Peter and the Magic Goose.
VHS: S06723. $29.95.
Volume 9: Johnny Appleseed, The Golden Blackbird.
VHS: S06724. $29.95.
Volume 10: Rip Van Winkle, Old Stormalong.
VHS: S06725. $29.95.

Fairy Tales from Exotic Lands

Treasures from children's literature which reflect the ancient tradition of storytelling that is the heritage of children the world over. The tapes reveal insights into different cultures and traditions. Each tape is 30 mins.
Tales from Europe: The Ugly Duckling, The Good Woman (Norway), The Glass Ax (Hungary), The Hobyahs (England).
VHS: S06731. $29.95.
Tales from Africa (Central): Old Man and Deer, The Origin of the Animals, The Law of Mapaki, Musar and His Parents.
VHS: S06732. $29.95.
Tales from Asia: Hok Lee and the Dwarf (China), The Rajah's Son and the Princess (India), The Jellyfish and the Monkey (Japan).
VHS: S06733. $29.95.
Tales from the North American Indians: Hiawatha and the Magic Arrows, The Monster of Niagara, The Green Mouse and the Buffalo, Nanook—The Eskimo Boy.
VHS: S06734. $29.95.

Flower Storm

Two boys prevent their countries from going to war with one another in this charming Iranian folk tale. This animated short evokes the style of Persian miniatures. 9 mins.
VHS: S23506. $39.95.

Forever Fairytales—Hans Christian Andersen

This two-volume gift set features four lesser-known gems from the beloved storyteller's vast collection. The heroines in both Andersen's *The Wild Swans* and *The Brave Duckling* must overcome great adversity to restore happiness in their lives. *The Woodcutter's Wish* and *The Amazing Gift* are two tales in which heroes are given a gift of magic. 128 mins.
VHS: S32423. $19.98.

The Frog King

A wonderful adaptation of the famous fairy tale about the importance of valuing others as well as the awkwardness of growing up. When a young princess breaks her promise of friendship to a frog, the frog follows her home, and is ultimately transformed into a handsome prince. Notable Children's Film, American Library Association, Blue Ribbon Winner, American Film Festival.
VHS: S04376. $30.00.
Tom Davenport, USA, 1983, 15 mins.

The Gingerbread Man

Eric Kimmel's retelling of the classic tale is brought directly to video. A fast runner is no match for a sly fox and it's a very important lesson if you are a delicious gingerbread man. 6 mins.
VHS: S24913. $37.95.

The Golden Goos e

An act of kindness pays off when a peasant simpleton finds himself in line to marry a princess. But first he must meet three conditions the king has set. They seem impossible from the start but he gets help from an old beggar who isn't what he seems to be. Featuring the voices of Richard Lewis, Sinbad, Loretta Devine, Heavy D., and Robert Guillaume. 30 mins.
VHS: S33128. $9.95.

Golden Tales and Legends, Vol. 1

Delightful, live-action stories for bedtime. Includes *The Fir Tree, The Great Fish of Maui* and *Billy Goat's Gruff*. 60 mins.
VHS: S13067. $39.98.

Golden Tales and Legends, Vol. 2

More bedtime stories for children. Includes *The Juggler, The Golden Apple* and *The Iron Mountain*. 60 mins.
VHS: S13068. $24.98.

The Goose Girl

An ancient folktale about endurance and the ultimate triumph of virtue through honorable means. As the story opens, a widow sends her daughter on a journey to be married. Along the way, the daughter's maid takes advantage of the girl's vulnerability and forces her to exchange places, with the real bride forced to tend geese. Cine Golden Eagle.
VHS: S04372. $30.00.
Tom Davenport, USA, 1983, 18 mins.

Hallo Spencer Presents Robin Hood and Sleeping Beauty

The Spencerville Players, puppeteers, present rich and funny interpretations of two classic tales. 45 mins.
VHS: S19663. $9.99.

Hansel and Gretel, An Appalachian Version

A wonderful adaptation of the famous fairy tale, set in an Appalachian setting, with all the actors cast local townspeople. "With this film, [Davenport] has translated a European folk story into the American idiom, making it part of our common heritage" *(Previews)*. Winner of the Cine Golden Eagle.
VHS: S04375. $30.00.
Tom Davenport, USA, 17 mins.

Happily Ever After Fairy Tales

This series of animated videos gives a new, multicultural look to classic fairy tales. Harry Belafonte, Danny Glover, Cheech Marin, Rosie Perez, Denzel Washington, B.D. Wong, the series narrator, Robert Guillaume, and other stars are featured.
Beauty and the Beast (African American). Gregory Hines, Vanessa Williams (Beauty) and Debbie Allen provide the voices for this animated, multicultural version of the favorite children's story. The African theme is just one element that makes this video so different. It also features terrific Broadway-style music and singing. 30 mins.
VHS: S29845. $9.98.
Cinderella.
VHS: S25875. $9.98.
Hansel and Gretel.
VHS: S25879. $9.98.
Jack and the Beanstalk.
VHS: S25880. $9.98.
Little Red Riding Hood.
VHS: S25881. $9.98.
Rapunzel.
VHS: S25878. $9.98.
Rumpelstiltskin.
VHS: S25882. $9.98.
The Emperor's New Clothes.
VHS: S25876. $9.98.
The Frog Prince.
VHS: S25877. $9.98.

Happy Birthday Moon and Other Stories

Frank Asch's *Happy Birthday Moon*, about the Bear misreading the echoes of his own voice as the moon's response to his invitation, is the centerpiece of the five tales. The others are: Ezra Jack Keats' *Peter's Chair*, Audrey Wood's *The Napping House*, Eric Blegvad's retelling of *The Three Little Pigs*, and Edward Lear's *The Owl and the Pussy Cat*.
VHS: S11224. $14.95.

Jack and the Dentist's Daughter

Based on Grimm's *The Master Thief*, and set in small-town America in the 1930's, this wonderful adaptation of the fairy tale is the comical story about a clever hero who wins his true love by using his head. Jack, a poor farmer's son, wants to marry the daughter of the town dentist, can't come up with the money, and has to resort to being a Robin Hood to win his love. Cine Golden Eagle.
VHS: S04371. $30.00.
Tom Davenport, USA, 1984, 38 mins.

Katharine Hepburn: World of Stories

Katharine Hepburn recalls her grandfather's storytelling prowess in this vivid, finely crafted collection of six short stories for young children. The stories are *Jack and the Beanstalk, The Nightingale, The Musicians of Bremen, Beauty and the Beast, The Emperor's New Clothes* and *Tattercoats*. 78 mins.
VHS: S19737. $19.95.

Light Princess

A classic story of love and hope based on George McDonald's inventive fairy tale about an evil witch who curses a Princess with total levity, as a result of which the girl can never take anything seriously. A deft mix of live action and dazzling animation highlights this wonderful BBC production.
VHS: S07180. $19.98.
Andrew Gosling, Great Britain, 1985, 56 mins.

The Little Match Girl

New Year's Eve 1999 finds homeless little Angela selling matches on the streets of Times Square in this updated adaptation of a Hans Christian Andersen story from animator Michael Sporn. Narrated by F. Murray Abraham. For ages 5 and up. 30 mins.
VHS: S13904. $14.95.

The Magic Voyage of Sinbad (Sadko)

The colorful Russian fantasy is about a bearded hero from Novgorod who is on a quest to find the bird of happiness. He apparently isn't particular about the exact color. He also isn't Sinbad. A neat ploy to recruit an American audience for '61 release with anglicized cast names.
VHS: S04087. $29.95.
Alexander Ptushko, USSR, 1952

The Marzipan Pig

Narrated by Tim Curry, this is the touching tale of a marzipan pig whose sweetness is enchanting. A beautiful film from animator Michael Sporn. For ages 5 and up. 30 mins.
VHS: S13905. $14.95.

Mikhail Baryshnikov's Stories from My Childhood

Based on the works of acclaimed writers, these delightful fairy tales, hand-picked by world-renowned dancer and actor Mikhail Baryshnikov from the completely restored animated archives of Russia's premier production studio, Soyuzmultfilm, will entertain all generations and cultures. The series has earned awards at the Venice, London and Moscow film festivals. A portion of the proceeds from these titles will be donated to The Audrey Hepburn Hollywood for Children Fund.
Beauty and the Beast: A Tale of the Crimson Flower. Amy Irving, Tim Curry and Robert Loggia star in Pushkin's version of this timeless love story.
VHS: S30506. $12.98.
The Twelve Months. Lolita Davidovich and Amanda Plummer are featured in this tale of a young girl who is sent by her mean stepmother into the woods to find snow flowers for the Queen, who has promised gold to anyone who brings her these rare and beautiful flowers.
VHS: S30508. $12.98.
Alice and the Mystery of the Third Planet. Kirsten Dunst, Jim Belushi and Harvey Fierstein provide the voices for this adventure story which chronicles the crew of the space ship *Pegasus* as they search for unusual and exotic animals to bring back to a zoo on earth.
VHS: S30507. $12.98.

Mother Goose

The whole town is turned upside down when Mother Goose has had enough of storytelling: Little Bo Peep hasn't lost her sheep, Mary's little lamb is missing, Little Miss Muffet can't find her spider and Humpty Dumpty won't fall down. Can Old King Cole persuade Mother Goose to stay? Featuring the voices of Whoopi Goldberg, Denzel Washington, Salt-N-Pepa and Jimmy Smits. "An imaginative boost to an old standard" *(Hollywood Reporter)*. 30 mins.
VHS: S33127. $9.95.

The Nutcracker

Based on the classical music tale by Peter Tchaikovsky and performed with a full symphony orchestra, this adaptation features wonderful puppet performances from Jim Gamble, master puppeteer for the Los Angeles Music Center. Watch as the Sugar Plum Fairy guides Clara through a fantasy world of Toy Soldiers, Cossack Acrobats, Arabian Dancers, Chinese Dragons and a Christmas tree that comes to life. 30 mins.
VHS: S16752. $19.95.

Once Upon a Brothers Grimm

An enchanted forest provides the setting when Jacob and Wilhelm Grimm meet the fairy-tale characters from their most famous stories: Hansel and Gretel, Little Red Riding Hood, Sleeping Beauty and others. With Dean Jones, Paul Sand, Teri Garr, Arte Johnson and Ruth Buzzi. 102 mins.
VHS: S16570. $39.95.

Peter and the Wolf (Animation)

Dudley Moore and the Moscow State Orchestra join forces to bring this classic fairy tale into a contemporary animated form. The woods are brimming with humorous characters that all fear the wolf. This cartoon has a surprise ending that emphasizes living together in harmony. It also makes a good introduction to the music of Sergei Prokofiev. From the *Storyteller's Classics* series, animated. 28 mins.
VHS: S26341. $9.98.

Peter and the Wolf (Live Action and Animation)

Chuck Jones provides the animation for this live-action/animated feature. It's inspired by Sergei Prokofiev's musical tale, which in turn drew on older Russian folktales. Kirstie Alley and Lloyd Bridges are among the cast featured in this beguiling family film. 60 mins.
VHS: S27527. $9.98.

Peter and the Wolf (Live Action and Puppetry)

Sting provides all the voices, live actors play Peter, the Grandfather and the Hunters wearing Marx Brothers masks, and puppets from the cutting-edge U.K. puppeteers Spitting Image are featured. This new production of Prokofiev's fantasy is accompanied by the Chamber Orchestra of Europe conducted by Claudio Abbado. 50 mins. Hi-Fi stereo.
VHS: S20556. $29.95.
Laser: LD72368. $29.95.

Peter and the Wolf: Moscow Musical Theatre for Children

Natalia Sats, who collaborated with Sergei Prokofiev to create *Peter and the Wolf*, narrates this musical classic in English for the first time. This video is a souvenir of Sat's 50th anniversary performance with the Moscow Musical Theatre for Children. 1986, 58 mins.
VHS: S13893. $19.95.

The Pied Piper

When the town of Hamlyn finds itself overrun with rats, the mayor and his council turn in desperation to a mysterious piper. But after he rids them of the plague, they deny him his payment. The piper teaches the townsfolk a lesson in this classic fairy tale, which features the voices of Samuel L. Jackson, Grant Shaud, Wesley Snipes, Tico Wells and Robert Guillaume. 30 mins.
VHS: S33129. $9.95.

The Pied Piper/Cinderella

Wonderful British puppet animation of two classic tales. 70 mins.
VHS: S04552. $14.95.

Pinocchio (Animated)

A "delightful, hip and sparkling" *(Hollywood Reporter)*, animated retelling of the classic tale of the toymaker who longs for a son and fashions a boy out of wood who magically comes to life. Featuring the voices of Will Smith, Chris Rock, Della Reese and Robert Guillaume. 30 mins.
VHS: S33130. $9.95.

Pinocchio (Live Action)

Sandy Duncan stars in this musical version of the classic tale about a puppet called Pinocchio who becomes an irrepressible little boy. Danny Kaye plays Gepetto, the wood carver. 76 mins.
VHS: S16571. $39.95.

Prince Cinders

This prince is stuck at home doing housework while his three brothers live it up around town. Suddenly everything changes when a magical fairy godmother appears. She makes Prince Cinders into a he-man, but that is the beginning of his troubles, as he encounters the problems of masculinity. 30 mins.
VHS: S24211. $14.95.

The Princess and the Goblin

This animated feature brings to life the timeless fairy tale by master storyteller George MacDonald about a peaceful kingdom that is menaced by an army of monstrous goblins, and a brave and beautiful princess who joins forces with a resourceful peasant boy to rescue the noble king and his people. 82 mins.
VHS: S34435. $29.95.

Princess and the Swineherd

A charming adaptation of the fairy tale by Hans Christian Andersen, as the Prince sends the Princess he wants to marry precious gifts—a rose and a nightingale. But the Princess only wants things artificial, and so the Prince dons the clothing of a swineherd to be near his beloved, and charms the cool Princess. In English. Germany, 1960, 82 mins.
VHS: S07507. $29.95.

The Rabbit Ears Collection

The universal traditions of storytelling and music are charmingly celebrated in the animated programs of the Rabbit Ears *We All Have Tales* series. Each narrated by famous actors like Kathleen Turner and Denzel Washington, these entertaining programs showcase the folklores of peoples around the world and are set to the sounds of various musicians. Grammy and Parents' Choice awards have been given to Rabbit Ears.

A Gingerbread Christmas. Susan Saint James narrates this effervescent tale about the Prince and Princess of Gingerbread, called into action to save the town of Gloomsbury, where Christmas has been cancelled. Music by Van Dyke Parks. 30 mins.
VHS: S17773. $19.98.

Aladdin and the Magic Lamp. Distinguished British actor John Hurt displays his virtuosity as he tells this engaging story from *The Tales from 1001 Arabian Nights*. Mickey Hart supplies the music for this animated film.
VHS: S24048. $19.98.

Anansi. Reggae hit-makers UB40 and Oscar-winner Denzel Washington unite to recount the Jamaican tale of Anansi the spider, who outwits a prideful snake and wins all stories for himself. In the end, Anansi gets caught in his own web of lies—losing his hair in the process. 30 mins.
VHS: S14454. $19.98.

Annie Oakley. Keith Carradine reprises his prize-winning stage role of American humorist Will Rogers to narrate this spirited, wonderfully textured tale of Annie Oakley, the sharpshooter whose extraordinary skills demythologized the American West and made her the international star of Buffalo Bill's Famous Wild West Show. 30 mins.
VHS: S17025. $19.98.

Brer Rabbit and Boss Lion. Actor Danny Glover narrates this lively installment in the Rabbit Ears "American Heroes & Legends" series. When the peaceful folk of Brer Village are threatened by mean old Boss Lion, it is up to Brer Rabbit to teach the troublemaker a powerful lesson in how to properly behave. Blues legend Dr. John supplies a down-home score full of gritty Bayou blues. For ages 5 and up. USA, 1992, 30 mins.
VHS: S16811. $19.98.

David and Goliath. Branford Marsalis' jazz score finds the proper mood and tempo in Mel Gibson's retelling of the story of the preordained shepherd boy chosen to be the king of the Israelites. Illustrated by Douglas Fraser.
VHS: S18004. $19.98.

Davy Crockett. Nicholas Cage narrates the story of the legendary American woodsman, known to some as "The King of the Wild Frontier." He claimed to be half-alligator, half-snapping turtle with a touch of earthquake thrown in. This bodacious entry in the Rabbit Ears series of "American Heroes & Legends," includes the knee-slapping music of David Bromberg. For ages 5 and up. USA, 1992, 30 mins.
VHS: S16812. $19.98.

East of the Sun, West of the Moon. Internationally renowned actor Max von Sydow and award-winning composer Lyle Mays dramatically retell this Scandinavian tale of a young girl who, in order to reclaim her lost love, enlists the help of the four winds.
VHS: S14103. $19.98.

Emperor and Nightingale. Glenn Close narrates the famous Hans Christian Andersen story about the Emperor who is given a gift of a mechanical singing bird only to learn that the genuine song of the real nightingale is truly the best of all. With music by Mark Isham and illustrations by Robert Van Nutt. 40 mins.
VHS: S04904. $14.95.

Emperor's New Clothes. When two swindlers cleverly announce that the magical garments they are weaving for the Emperor are invisible to anyone lacking intelligence, who has the courage to speak the truth? Sir John Gielgud tells the Hans Christian Andersen fairytale.
VHS: S12474. $14.95.

Finn McCoul. Hero Finn McCoul and his clever wife work together to defeat a brutish giant in this modern re-telling of an Irish folk tale. Narrated by comedienne Catherine O'Hara, this animated video contains music performed by the Irish quintet Boys of the Lough. 30 mins.
VHS: S16996. $19.98.

Follow the Drinking Gourd. Subtitled *A Story of the Underground Railroad*, Morgan Freeman narrates this tale, adapted from the folksong, about one family's bid for freedom, achieved through the Underground Railroad. The gritty blues score is by Taj Mahal. 30 mins.
VHS: S17888. $19.98.

How the Leopard Got His Spots. Narrated by Danny Glover.
VHS: S09506. $14.95.

How the Rhinoceros Got His Skin and How the Camel Got His Hump. Jack Nicholson narrates, Bobby McFerrin performs and Tim Raglin draws in this animated video showing the moral sources of the rhino's skin and the camel's hump according to Rudyard Kipling's *Just So Stories*. 30 mins.
VHS: S04903. $14.95.

Jack and the Beanstalk. Monty Python's own Michael Palin returns this classic tale about Jack and a dimwitted ogre to its decidedly English origins as only he can. Music by Dave Stewart of the Eurythmics.
VHS: S14102. $19.98.

John Henry. Denzel Washington narrates a poetic, dreamy and mythic tale about the physically imposing, tireless nation builder who singlehandedly defeated the steam drill in a steel driving competition. Legendary blues performer B.B. King provides a gritty, textured score. 30 mins.
VHS: S17887. $19.98.

Johnny Appleseed. This cartoon is narrated by Garrison Keillor, author and radio personality. It tells the tall tale that explains how apples came to be so prevalent in the young United States. Music by Mark O'Conner.
VHS: S24040. $19.98.

Jonah and the Whale. Jason Robards recounts the fantastic and amazing tale of the man who must summon up all his creativity, will and imagination to save the people of Nineveh when he's swallowed by a whale. Illustrated by Jeffrey Smith; music by George Mgrdichian.
VHS: S18005. $19.98.

King Midas and the Golden Touch. Narrator Michael Caine adds a regal touch to the classic Greek tale of *King Midas*, in which a misguided monarch learns that there are some things in life more precious than gold. Music by Ellis Marsalis and Yo-Yo Ma. For ages 5 and up. 30 mins.
VHS: S14681. $19.98.

Koi and the Kola Nuts. Oscar-winner Whoopi Goldberg humorously retells this African folktale about the proud son of a chief who sets out to find his rightful place in the world. Grammy and Oscar-winning composer Herbie Hancock provides the inimitable score. 30 mins.
VHS: S16549. $19.98.

Legend of Sleepy Hollow. Glenn Close narrates Washington Irving's classic tale about timid schoolmaster Ichabod Crane and his encounter with the legendary Headless Horseman. Illustrated by Robert Van Nutt. 40 mins.
VHS: S08128. $14.95.

Mose the Fireman. Michael Keaton tells the story of this legendary fireman. His bravery was without equal. An animated short with music by John Beasley and Walter Becker. Perfect for kids.
VHS: S24039. $19.98.

The Night Before Christmas. Meryl Streep narrates this traditional retelling of the holiday classic. The program also includes some of the best loved yuletide carols sung by the Edwin Hawkins Singers, the Christ Church Cathedral Choir and the Oscar-winning Miss Streep. For ages 5 and up. USA, 1992, 30 mins.
VHS: S16813. $19.98.

Noah and the Ark. Kelly McGillis narrates the poetic and heroic tale of Noah. Illustrated by Lori Lohstoeter; music by Paul Winter Consort.
VHS: S18003. $19.98.

Paul Bunyan. Jonathan Winters reads the story that captures the spirit of early America. The hilariously exaggerated exploits of Paul's logging adventures in the northern United States represent the best in the proud tradition of American storytelling.
VHS: S12473. $14.95.
Laser: LD71820. $24.95.

Peachboy. The story of a peasant couple who discover a boy inside a giant peach; they take him in and he grows up to become a great warrior who sets off to vanquish a band of ogres. Sigourney Weaver's tender reading and Ryuichi Sakamoto's (Oscar winner—*The Last Emperor*) rich score combine to tell Japan's most revered children's story. For ages 4 and up. 30 mins.
VHS: S13779. $19.98.

Pecos Bill. One of the most popular tall tales of the old American Wild West—the legend of Pecos Bill, raised by coyotes from an early age until he discovered cowboys and became king of the range. Narrated by Robin Williams, with illustrations by Tim Raglin. 30 mins.
VHS: S07166. $14.95.

Pinocchio. Danny Aiello narrates this animated version of the novel written by Italian author Carlo Collodi about a lonely, frustrated toymaker named Gepeto and his astonishing creation, a wooden marionette who comes to life. Music by the Les Miserables Brass Band. 30 mins.
VHS: S18132. $19.98.

Princess Scargo and the Birthday Pumpkin. Geena Davis recounts this Native American myth about the selfless act of a young girl who refuses her priceless birthday gift in order to help her village. With music by Michael Hedges. 30 mins.
VHS: S18131. $19.98.

Puss in Boots. Tracey Ullman's comedic genius and veteran jazz violinist Jean Luc Ponty's spirited score animate this hilarious version of the beloved French story. 30 mins.
VHS: S15640. $19.98.

Red Riding Hood and Goldilocks. Meg Ryan reads the classic story of Little Red Riding Hood and the much-beloved tale of Goldilocks and the Three Bears.
VHS: S12472. $14.95.

Rip Van Winkle. Academy Award-winning actress Anjelica Huston tells the amusing tale of a man who somehow managed to sleep so long that he woke up in a new era. A great animated film sure to be enjoyed by everyone, kids and grown-ups alike. Jay Unger and Molly Mason provide the music.
VHS: S24042. $19.98.

Rumpelstiltskin. Kathleen Turner retells this popular Grimm's fairytale about a young woman who is forced to promise her firstborn child to a mysterious little man in return for the ability to spin straw into gold. Tangerine Dream provides the haunting musical score. In Hi-Fi Stereo, 30 mins.
VHS: S16548. $19.98.

Squanto. The very first Thanksgiving, when the pilgrims learned to share and celebrate the bounty of the New World, emerges from the past in this animated short. Graham Greene, Native American actor, narrates. Music by Paul McCandles.
VHS: S24041. $19.98.

Stormalong. John Candy relates the fantastic and hilarious adventures of the rude, brutish captain and his magnificent times on the seven seas. 30 mins.
VHS: S17774. $19.98.

Tailor of Gloucester. The poor tailor of Gloucester is worn to a ravelling, for he has no more twisted silk for his buttonholes thanks to his naughty cat Simpkin, but with the help of special friends, finds that a kind favor is returned. Narrated by Meryl Streep; illustrations by David Jorgensen. 30 mins.
VHS: S07167. $14.95.

The Boy Who Drew Cats. A touching story in which a Japanese boy, whose only talent is in drawing cats, sets out alone into a countryside haunted by a mysterious demon. Narrated by William Hurt; music by Mark Isham. For ages 5 and up. 30 mins.
VHS: S14680. $19.98.

The Bremen Town Musicians. Bob Hoskins tells the story of a group of mesmerizing musicians. Eugene Friesen supplies the music.
VHS: S24052. $19.98.

The Firebird. Hollywood great Susan Sarandon narrates this classic Eastern European folk tale about a prince, a beautiful girl and the magical firebird. Music by Mark Isham.
VHS: S24049. $19.98.

The Fisherman and His Wife. Narrated by Jodie Foster.
VHS: S09499. $14.95.

The Gingham Dog and the Calico Cat. The Gingham Dog and the Calico Cat are two Christmas presents who just don't get along—until Christmas Eve when they fall out of Santa's sleigh and get lost in a great forest. Narrated by Amy Grant; music by Chet Atkins. For ages 5 and up. 30 mins.
VHS: S14679. $19.98.

The Monkey People. Raul Julia brilliantly narrates this fantastical fable from the Amazon rainforest about a village of people whose extreme laziness has hilarious and devastating consequences. Music by Lee Ritenour. 30 mins.
VHS: S15641. $19.98.

The Savior Is Born. Actor Morgan Freeman gives a resonant reading of the first Christmas, from the gospels of Matthew and Luke. Beautifully illustrated by Robert Van Nutt. Music by the Christ Church Cathedral Choir of Oxford, England.
VHS: S18002. $19.98.

The Tale of Jeremy Fisher and the Tale of Peter Rabbit. Two famous English stories, animated, about the disobedient bunny Peter Rabbit and the angler frog, Mr. Jeremy Fisher. Based on Beatrix Potter's tales, with a narration by Meryl Streep, music by Lyle Mays, and illustrations by David Jorgensen. 30 mins.
VHS: S04902. $14.95.

The Tiger and the Brahmin. Ben Kingsley and Ravi Shankar, master of the sitar, weave a colorful retelling of this traditional Indian tale about a Brahmin who makes the deadly mistake of freeing a hungry tiger from its cage. 30 mins.
VHS: S14455. $19.98.

The White Cat. Emma Thompson, famed British actress, tells the story of a charming creature. Joe Jackson provides the music.
VHS: S24050. $19.98.

Three Little Billy Goats Gruff/The Three Little Pigs. Narrated by Holly Hunter.
VHS: S09498. $14.95.

Thumbelina. Narrated by Kelly McGillis.
VHS: S09497. $14.95.

Tom Thumb. John Cleese, the comedic actor who achieved fame in the *Monty Python Show*, brings his gift for humor to this tale of the wee man no bigger than his father's thumb. Elvis Costello supplies the music for this animated short.
VHS: S24046. $19.98.

Rapunzel, Rapunzel

Suspense—with a happy ending— with 19th century Shaker songs played by a flute and cello, in the American setting of Grimm's tale about Rapunzel, who lets down her hair, and is finally rescued and her sight restored by the handsome prince.
VHS: S04374. $30.00.
Tom Davenport, USA, 16 mins.

Reader's Digest Children's Classics

Animated series of the best loved children's stories. Each tape is in color, 26 minutes in length.

Remarkable Rocket. David Niven narrates this Oscar Wilde story of a conceited rocket who learns a lesson in humility.
VHS: S02838. $14.95.

Red Riding Hood
Isabella Rossellini and Craig T. Nelson star as the faithful little girl must brave the forest and the big, bad wolf in order to bring her grandmother a basket of goodies.
VHS: S09815. $14.95.
Laser: CAV. **LD70337. $99.95.**
Laser: CLV. **LD70338. $49.97.**
Adam Brooks, USA, 1988, 84 mins.

Red Shoes
The story *The Red Shoes*, by Hans Christian Andersen, is a charming favorite that receives a hip and delightful updating by animator Michael Sporn with music by reggae star Jimmy Cliff. As today's story goes, Lisa and Jennie are best friends. They share everything until Lisa's parents win the lottery and the now jealous and selfish Lisa steals a pair of magical red shoes from Jennie. With the shoes on her feet, she is caught in an energetic dance which she can stop only when she realizes that friendship is the most precious gift of all.
VHS: S12353. $9.95.
Michael Sporn, USA, 1990, 30 mins.

Singing Princess
A snake charmer, his beautiful sweetheart, a wicked prince and a magic genie. Winner of the Grand Prize at the International Children's Film Festial, this enchanting animated musical fantasy features the voice of Julie Andrews as the singing princess. 66 mins.
VHS: S08127. $24.95.

The Snow Queen
Gerda is a little girl who sets out to rescue a friend under the spell of the evil Snow Queen in this Hans Christian Andersen fantasy. The tale is magically told with actors, animated characters and beautiful illustrations. 54 mins.
VHS: S16150. $19.98.

The Snow Queen
Sigourney Weaver narrates this expressive adaptation of Hans Christian Andersen's moving tale about a young girl's fantastic efforts to rescue her playmate from the ice prison of the Snow Queen. Animated by a group of Russian artists whose work is on view for the first time, *The Snow Queen* is taken from the picture book by Susan Jeffers and Amy Ehrlich. Music by Jason Miles. 30 mins.
VHS: S17970. $12.98.

Steadfast Tin Soldier
The Hans Christian Andersen story narrated by Jeremy Irons featuring captivating illustrations by David Jorgensen and an original score by Mark Isham.
VHS: S02845. $14.95.
Mark Sottnick, USA, 1986, 30 mins.

Story of the Dancing Frog
Renowned animator Michael Sporn directed this charming story about George, who is no ordinary frog. He is a multi-talented entertainer whose leaps and bounds bring him to fame and fortune. George and his devoted friend Gertrude set out to dance their way around the world in this adventure based on the story by Quentin Blake, narrated by Amanda Plummer.
VHS: S12003. $14.95.
Michael Sporn, USA, 1986, 30 mins.

Strega Nonna and Other Stories
Big Anthony finds himself ankles deep in trouble (and pasta) when he tries to use Strega Nonna's magic pasta pot without her permission. Blue Ribbon winner at the American Film Festival. Also includes *Tikki Tikki Tembo, The Foolish Frog* and *A Story—A Story*. Ages 4-9. 35 mins.
VHS: S14491. $14.95.

The Swan Princess III and the Mystery of the Enchanted Treasure
In this animated adventure, Zelda, an evil sorceress, kidnaps the Swan Princess to hold her ransom until the Prince turns over a magical treasure that gives its keeper unlimited powers.
VHS: S34688. $14.95.
Richard Rich, USA, 1998, 73 mins.

The Swan Princess: Escape from Castle Mountain
Action and humor and a great tale are combined in this sequel based on Swan Lake, featuring Prince Derek and Princess Odette as they fight to save their kingdom from the evil magician Clavius.
VHS: S31751. $19.96.
Richard Rich, USA, 1997, 75 mins.

Tall Tales: Annie Oakley
Jamie Lee Curtis gives a spirited performance as "Little Sure Shot" Annie Oakley in this colorful biography of the master sharpshooter. Co-starring Brian Dennehy as Buffalo Bill and featuring actual footage of Annie filmed in 1903 by Thomas Edison. 53 mins.
VHS: S10751. $9.98.

Tall Tales: Pecos Bill
Steve Guttenberg gives Texas its unique style as Pecos Bill, the King of the cowboys, in this high-flying tall tale about one of the most colorful legends in American history. With Martin Mull, Rebecca De Mornay and Claude Akins. 50 mins.
VHS: S10750. $9.98.

The Tin Soldier (Plummer)
A heartwarming adaptation of the Hans Christian Andersen tale about the comic adventures of two lonely mice who inadvertently place the Tin Soldier in danger and then set out to rescue him. Narrated by Christopher Plummer. 30 mins.
VHS: S08727. $9.95.

The Tin Soldier (Struthers)
Children will enjoy this engaging ballet story narrated by Sally Struthers. It's about a toy soldier given to a little boy. When the toy soldier falls in love with a beautiful paper doll ballerina, an unexpected confrontation with a jealous and evil Jack-in-the-Box sends him on a dangerous adventure. Only his love for the ballerina can help him overcome insurmountable odds. 63 mins.
VHS: S22107. $19.95.

The Ugly Duckling (Cher)
The unforgettable fairy tale by Hans Christian Andersen narrated by Cher and illustrated by the striking paintings of Patrick Ball.
VHS: S02844. $14.95.
Mark Sottnick, USA, 1986, 30 mins.

The Ugly Duckling (Children's Circle)
Three fairy tales: Hans Christian Andersen's *The Ugly Duckling; The Stonecutter*, a Japanese fable about a stonecutter who seeks great riches; and *The Swineherd*, another Hans Christian Andersen classic about a princess who scorns the love of an honorable prince.
VHS: S01392. $14.98.
Gene Deitch, USA, 1986

The Velveteen Rabbit (Plummer)
Christopher Plummer narrates this charming, animated adaptation of Margery Williams' timeless story. 25 mins.
VHS: S09891. $14.95.

The Velveteen Rabbit (Streep)
Meryl Streep narrates this children's classic, first published in 1922. George Winston provides the music, David Jorgensen the illustrations.
VHS: S05108. $14.95.
Mark Sottnick, USA, 1985

Victor Borge Tells Hans Christian Andersen Stories
Hans Christian Andersen's children's tales, including *The Princess and the Pea, The Emperor's New Clothes* and *The Ugly Duckling*, are brought to life by master storyteller Victor Borge. Illustrations by Rob Gilbert and Cecilia Laureys.
VHS: S19696. $24.95.

Wisdom of the Gnomes: Klaus the Judge & The Stolen Mirror
Dany must help Klaus the Judge solve all kinds of problems for their fellow Gnomes and animal friends in these delightful adventures. 50 mins.
VHS: S16583. $9.98.

Wonderful World of the Brothers Grimm
A top notch adaptation of fairy tales by the Brothers Grimm woven together with a depiction of the lives of the Brothers. Laurence Harvey, Claire Bloom, Oscar Homolka, Barbara Eden, Buddy Hackett and others star, and one of the highlights is the animated sequence created by George Pal in which Hackett battles a fire-breathing dragon.
VHS: S11156. $19.95.
Laser: LD70135. $39.98.
Henry Levin, USA, 1962, 129 mins.

PRE-SCHOOL VIDEO

The Adventures of Jay Jay the Jet Plane
Model airplanes come to life in the storybook land of Tarrytown. This is the setting for stories filled with heart, humor and humanity. Joyful lessons about life, family and friends—those things that really matter—are on this delightful children's tape. Ages 2-8, 25 mins.
VHS: S22941. $12.95.

All About ABC's
Children have fun visiting Alphabet Land with Letter Lizard and Magic Man. Ages 2-6.
VHS: S24359. $6.99.

Allegra's Window— Sing Along with Allegra & Lindi
Features seven favorite songs starring everyone's favorite three-year-old, Allegra, from the award-winning Nick Jr. series. 28 mins.
VHS: S33761. $9.95.

Alphabet Soup
Artist William Wegman's dog Fay and her offspring, Batty, Chundo and Crooky, teach kids the about the alphabet. They do everything to make these lessons memorable, from balancing a boat on Fay's head to making alphabet soup. Don't forget the apples and zucchini! Ages 3 and up.
VHS: S26141. $12.95.
William Wegman, USA, 1995, 30 mins.

Angela's Airplane (plus The Fire Station)
Angela wanders onto a huge, empty plane, pushes some buttons and winds up flying it. Also includes a short story, *The Fire Station*. Animated stories by Robert Munsch. Ages 2-5. 25 minutes.
VHS: S24985. $12.95.

Baby Animal Fun
Live footage of baby animals interacting with kids. All ages. 1989, 30 mins.
VHS: S24596. $29.95.

Baby Animals Just Want to Have Fun
Peter Puppy, Raindance the Pony and other favorite baby animals romp around in five humorous adventure stories. Enchanting songs and live photography in this video will make children adore baby animals even more.
VHS: S02996. $14.95.

Baby Goes...Songs for the Season
Original sing-alongs that bring toddlers and Christmas together are featured on this video. Kids will learn about baking cookies and enjoy sledding, skating and even shopping. Finally it's time to wrap the presents and wait for Santa. For ages 1-6. 30 mins.
VHS: S25967. $9.95.

Baby Goes...Songs to Take Along
Children ages six and under will enjoy these songs that help them learn by doing. This video goes everywhere, from the market to the beach, and shows how a number of different tasks are accomplished, like counting, dressing and getting ready for bed. 30 mins.
VHS: S23943. $12.95.

Baby Songs
Live action music video for young kids from singer/songwriter Hap Palmer. Ten songs include "Piggy Toes" and "Security". USA, 1987, 30 mins.
VHS: S03520. $14.95.

Baby Songs Series
A very good series of live action music videos for pre-schoolers, ages 1-5. 30 minutes each.
Baby Songs 2: More Baby Songs. Hap Palmer is back! Good for babies; relates at their level: tickling, playing, walking—fun! This video combines live action and animation for the very young, ages infant to 8. 30 mins.
VHS: S24337. $12.98.
Baby Songs Christmas. Interesting, singable, multicultural, fun. 1991.
VHS: S24597. $14.95.
Baby Songs Presents: Baby Rock. Ten songs by original artists are presented in this live action/animation video for the very young, ages infant to 8. 30 mins.
VHS: S24339. $12.98.
Baby Songs Presents: Follow Along Songs with Hap Palmer. Songs designed for children to enact the lyrics, including "The Mice Go Marching," "Parade of Sticks," and "Homemade Band."
VHS: S24772. $12.95.
Baby Songs Presents: John Lithgow's Kid-Size Concert. Acoustic guitar, a wonderful actor and a chance to sing along. With "I Can Put My Clothes on By Myself," "Getting Up Time," and "What a Miracle I Am." Songbook included. 1990.
VHS: S24341. $12.98.
Baby Songs: Even More Baby Songs. Ten charming songs by Hap Palmer that reach into a child's everyday life for their subject matter. More catchy tunes are featured in this video which combines live action and animation for the very young, ages infant to 8. 30 mins.
VHS: S24338. $12.98.
Baby Songs: Sing Together. Nine sing-alongs. 1992.
VHS: S24598. $14.95.
Baby Songs: Super Baby Songs. More great sing-along tunes for tykes with Hap Palmer. This video combines live action and animation for the very young, ages infant to 8. 30 mins.
VHS: S24340. $12.98.

Baby Vision
Fascinating films made for children from 9 to 36 months of age! From New Zealand. For infant to age 3. 45 minutes each tape.
Baby Vision Volume 1. *Volume 1* centers on soft images, a bit of narration and music related to toys and animals.
VHS: S24342. $14.95.

Baby's Bedtime

Judy Collins invites young viewers on a gentle journey into dreamland with this new collection of best-loved lullabies. Tuck your child in to the beautiful animation and memorable melodies of "Hush Little Baby", "The Land of Nod", "Lullaby and Good Night" and other classics. Parents' Choice Award. 26 minutes, infant to age 6.
Home Video.
VHS: S11417. $12.98.

Baby's Morningtime

Greet the day with a song and a smile as Judy Collins sings the works of Robert Browning, Emily Dickinson, Gertrude Stein and others. Enhanced by Ernest Troost's winsome score and Sesame Street's Daniel Ivanick's animation. 25 minutes, infant to age 6.
Home Video.
VHS: S17136. $12.98.
Public Performance Rights.
VHS: S17149. $50.00.

Baby's Storytime

Singer-songwriter Arlo Guthrie brings his whimsical wit and music to this warm, lighthearted re-telling of such children's classics as "The Three Little Pigs", "Henny Penny" and "Little Red Riding Hood". A delightful adaptation of Kay Chorao's children's book animated by Oscar nominee Michael Sporn. 26 minutes, infant to age 6.
Home Video.
VHS: S11418. $12.98.

Bananas in Pajamas

Kids love the comic antics of these oversized banana characters. Their other animal friends also appeal to young children. This live-action series is already gaining on other established children's shows like *Sesame Street* because of its humor and good nature.
Bananas in Pajamas: Birthday Special. B1 and B2 go all out to prepare for birthday fun. Preschoolers will love the fun, music and humor of these festive goings-on. USA, 1995, 25 mins.
VHS: S27194. $9.95.
Bananas in Pajamas: It's Music Time. Go a little bananas with this video and special audio cassette package featuring music from *It's Singing Time*, a collection of nursery rhymes. 25 mins.
VHS: S32243. $12.95.

Barney and the Backyard Gang

A series with a strong quality focus, combining favorite, traditional songs and rhymes, live action and animation. Each show features Sandy Duncan as "Mom" to kids Michael and Amy. The children and their neighborhood friends have a special pal, Barney the dinosaur, who magically comes to life to lead the Backyard Gang through the shows.
A Day at the Beach. Contains video, storybook and audio cassette.
VHS: S09787. $24.95.
Barney Goes to School. Barney and pals enjoy finger painting, creative learning and the search for Zippity the hamster. 1990.
VHS: S24599. $14.95.
Barney in Concert. Barney and the two-year-old Baby Bop perform fun songs which encourage interaction. 1991.
VHS: S24600. $14.95.
Barney's Best Manners. A picnic, with songs and games which teach manners, including "Does Your Chewing Gum Lose Its Flavor," "Please and Thank You," and "Snackin' on Healthy Food."
VHS: S24601. $14.95.
Barney's Birthday. Birthday songs and birthday customs from around the world. 1993.
VHS: S24602. $14.95.
Barney's Campfire Sing-Along. Fun with camping, animals, stars and forest safety.
VHS: S24603. $14.95.
Barney's Home Sweet Homes. Discover the variety of homes—homes for animals and homes for people—around the world and under the sea.
VHS: S24604. $14.95.
Barney's Magical Musical Adventure. When the Backyard Gang builds a sand castle, Barney takes them to a real castle. 1992.
VHS: S24605. $14.95.
Rock with Barney. Barney sings some of his favorite songs.
VHS: S24606. $14.95.
Waiting for Santa. Barney and the Gang travel to the North Pole to learn the true meaning of Christmas. 1991.
VHS: S24607. $14.95.

Barney's Adventure Bus

The purple dinosaur is back as bus driver with the whole gang and you're invited to cruise along as they visit their favorite imaginary destinations. 50 mins.
VHS: S31853. $14.95.

Barney's Imagination Island

Fun with songs, rhymes and problem solving. Barney helps his friends go sailing and they discover a toy inventor who learns about sharing from the visitors. 1994. 48 minutes.
VHS: S24940. $19.99.

Barney's Safety Video

Kids join B.J., Barney and firefighter Frank to learn about important safety issues such as crossing the street and safety at home. 48 minutes.
VHS: S24942. $14.95.

Barney's Sense-sational Day

Join Jason, Tosha, Carlos, Kim and that popular purple dinosaur as they use their imaginations, along with Barney's video camera, to capture the fun-filled events of the day—everything they see, hear, smell, taste and touch.
VHS: S30531. $14.95.

Barney—Good Day Good Night

When Barney uses his special "Night Timer" to create night during the day, the kids enjoy a long day's night complement of their big purple pal. 50 mins.
VHS: S32185. $14.95.

Beady Bear

Based on the book by Don Freeman, a stuffed bear realizes he needs more than just a cave—he needs love! 8 minutes.
VHS: S24508. $37.95.

The Bear Who Slept Through Christmas

Little Ted E. Bear wants to discover the meaning of Christmas, while the rest of the town sleeps.
VHS: S24360. $12.95.

Berenstain Bears Videos

Based on the best-selling books by Jan and Stan Berenstain, the videos are of high quality, featuring a charming bear family which works out problems in a thoughtful and entertaining manner. Animated. 20-30 minutes each.
Berenstain Bears and the Messy Room. Brother and Sister's room is a mess. Mama is about to toss everything out when Papa Bear offers a neat solution. 30 mins.
VHS: S07716. $14.95.
Berenstain Bears and the Missing Dinosaur Bone. Also includes "Bears in the Night" and "The Bear Detectives." 30 mins.
VHS: S12771. $9.95.
Berenstain Bears and the Trouble with Friends. The new girl cub in the neighborhood is the same age as Sister Bear—and just as bossy. Mama Bear helps both cubs learn that you can't always have your own way if you want to be friends. 30 mins.
VHS: S09230. $14.95.
Berenstain Bears and the Truth. Brother and Sister bear learn that breaking Mama Bear's trust in them is worse than breaking her lamp. 30 mins.
VHS: S07715. $14.95.
Berenstain Bears and Too Much Birthday. Is there such a thing as too much birthday? Sister doesn't think so, but she learns the hard way when she coaxes Mama and Papa to throw a big bash for her sixth birthday.
VHS: S09229. $14.95.
Berenstain Bears Christmas Tree. Papa Bear realizes that Christmas trees are also animals' homes.
VHS: S24509. $9.98.
Berenstain Bears Forget Their Manners. Mama Bear is determined to teach Papa Bear and her kids the necessity of patience and politeness, with hilarious results. In "Berenstain Bears and the Wicked Weasel Spell," the evil Archweasel McGreed orchestrates a dastardly plan to rule Bear County.
VHS: S18615. $14.95.
Berenstain Bears Get in a Fight. Brother and Sister Bear turn a minor disagreement into a major war, and it is up to Mama Bear to call a truce. 30 mins.
VHS: S07713. $14.95.
Berenstain Bears Get Stage Fright. Sibling rivalry comes in the form of the stage play *Grizzlystiltskin*, in which Brother and Sister Bear have leading roles. In "Berenstain Bears Go Bonkers over Honkers," Bigpaw's four small pet geese wreak havoc on the idyllic Bear County.
VHS: S18616. $14.95.
Berenstain Bears in the Dark. When Brother reads Sister a scary story, she can't fall asleep in the dark. Papa Bear helps sister conquer her fear. 30 mins.
VHS: S09231. $14.95.
Berenstain Bears Learn About Strangers. When Papa Bear tells the cubs they should never talk to strangers, Sister thinks all strangers are ominous. It's up to Mama to bring some common sense to the problem. 30 mins.
VHS: S07714. $14.95.
Berenstain Bears: No Girls Allowed. Brother Bear and his friends create a mysterious clubhouse strictly off limits to Sister Bear and her friends. In "Berenstain Bears and the Missing Dinosaur Bone," the Bear Detectives pursue the trail of a rare dinosaur bone stolen from Actual Factual's Museum.
VHS: S18614. $14.95.

The Best Christmas Surprise Ever

Have a very Scarry Christmas with the title story and two other stories from The Busy World of Richard Scarry. 25 mins.
VHS: S32242. $9.95.

Bethie's Really Silly Clubhouse

Silly songstress Bethie is the perfect host who always enjoys a good knock-knock joke. This video features a good story that will teach kids about animals even as it entertains them. Ages 2-8.
VHS: S24512. $14.98.

Big Bird Gets Lost

When Big Bird and Maria go to the ABCD-Mart to buy some skates for Snuffy's birthday, Big Bird forgets all about sticking together and takes off after a runaway skate. Now that he's lost, will he remember what to do and where to go for help? 30 mins.
VHS: S32704. $9.95.

Big Red

Real firefighters offer kids a unique view of the preparation, tools and large trucks that go into fighting big fires. Kids will even learn valuable safety lessons in this enjoyable and educational tape.
25 mins.
VHS: S23087. $24.95.

Big Rigs: Close Up and Very Personal

This episode from the *Close Up* series shows preschoolers the intricacy and power of these great machines. The big rigs are seen inside and out, in order to explain how they work and how they function as transportation for goods. 30 mins.
VHS: S24216. $14.95.

The Birthday Dragon

The magic continues in this animated film about Emily and the Railway Dragon. They play and fly together as they celebrate a very special day. Ages 3 and up. 30 mins.
VHS: S24513. $9.98.

Bloopy's Buddies: Body Knowledge

Bloopy lives by the motto "Be well. Eat well. Live well. Learn well." In this video, the large puppet character puts this motto into practice. Kids will Bloopycise and learn all about maintaining the body. Special guest conductor Jon (Jonathan Winters) is also ready to entertain kids with a story. 30 mins.
VHS: S29210. $12.95.

Bloopy's Buddies: Yummy in Your Tummy

It's International Food Day at the Snack Attack Cafe, so Bloopy and his pals learn how to cook some delicious treats. Then it's time to Bloopycise at the Gym Shoe before finally hearing a story from Andre the Artist (Jonathan Winters). Kids will even learn safety tips for car travel in this engaging kids' video. 30 mins.
VHS: S29211. $12.95.

Blue Ribbon Stories Vol. 1

Two stories, *The Three Billy Goats Gruff* and *The Little Red Hen*, are featured in this animated video from Scholastic Productions, including activity segments featuring two puppets who encourage young viewers to participate.
VHS: S04136. $14.95.

Blue Ribbon Stories Vol. 2

Two more stories from Scholastic's Blue Ribbon Storybook Video: *Harold and the Purple Crayon* and *The Bremen Town Musicians*. 30 mins.
VHS: S04155. $14.95.

Bluetoes the Christmas Elf

It's Christmas Eve at the North Pole and all of Santa's helpers are busy packing the sleigh for takeoff…all except for one sad, unnamed elf, who is too young and entirely too clumsy to help. Then in a dream come true, the little elf is airborne with Santa, delivering toys to all the girls and the boys of the world. On this wondrous journey through the winter night, the tiny elf makes a heartwarming sacrifice that helps Santa and ultimately earns him the name Bluetoes. 27 mins.
VHS: S12480. $14.95.

Brum: The Big Adventures of a Little Car

Motoring in from England, Brum is a spunky, miniature, 1920's-style car. He is always ready to roll to the rescue. Each volume in this series contains three live-action Brum misadventures. From Random House Home Videos, 30 minutes each.
Volume 1: Brum and the Baby Carriage.
VHS: S22975. $9.95.
Volume 2: Brum and the Bank Robbers.
VHS: S22976. $9.95.
Volume 4: Brum to the Rescue.
VHS: S22978. $9.95.

Bump—My First Video

An evocative adaptation of six stories narrated by Simon Cadell detailing the whimsical adventures of the precocious elephant Bump and his peculiar friend Birdie. 30 mins.
VHS: S19423. $12.98.

The Busy World of Richard Scarry: Mr. Frumble's New Car

Three episodes from the popular cartoon series seen on *Nick Jr.* and *Showtime* are joined on this video. 25 mins.
VHS: S26625. $9.95.

The Busy World of Richard Scarry: Summer Picnic

Adventure awaits Richard Scarry and his animal friends when they set off for a picnic. It's a warm and funny video, perfect for younger children. 25 mins.
VHS: S29529. $9.95.

The Busy World of Richard Scarry: The Best Babysitter Ever

Based on the successful children's books, these animated adventures of Richard Scarry and his other animal friends are perfect entertainment for children. In addition to the episode mentioned in the title, there are two more stories included on this video. 25 mins.
VHS: S29528. $9.95.

The Busy World of Richard Scarry: The Busiest Firefighters Ever

Three episodes from the delightful animated television series are included on this video. Kids love it on *Nick Jr.* and *Showtime*. Now these cartoons, with their animated animal characters, are available at any time to delight children. 25 mins.
VHS: S26624. $9.95.

The Busy World of Richard Scarry: The Snowstorm

Snow storms are the stuff of childhood dreams. The world is covered in white, and if it's an especially snowy day, school might even be cancelled. This story and two others featuring Lowly Worm, Huckle Cat and their friends in Busytown are joined on this videotape based on Richard Scarry's popular books. 25 mins.
VHS: S27422. $9.95.

The Cat and the Fiddler

This story about a traveling fiddler and his cat is adapted from Jackey Jeter's book, illustrated by Lionel Kalish. Produced by Thomas Sand. 11 mins.
VHS: S23493. $39.95.

Catch Me If You Can

An entertaining and educational way for younger children to learn about animal behavior and its importance for animal survival. Includes two complete programs: *The Predators* and *The Grazers*. Each is 26 minutes.
VHS: S23359. $39.95.

Christmas Sing-Along Video Album

A collection of Christmas favorites, including "We Wish You a Merry Christmas", "Silent Night", "Jingle Bells" and others, in a special sing-along program.
VHS: S10726. $19.95.

Classic Stories for Children

Beautifully designed and dressed puppets tell four classic children's stories using voice-over narration, dramatic action (puppets) and musical numbers. Includes *Rapunzel, The Frog Prince, Rumpelstiltskin* and *Jack and the Beanstalk*.
VHS: S15134. $24.95.
Peter Babakitis, USA, 1990, 37 mins.

Clean Your Room, Harvey Moon!

Harvey Moon's room is a mess! Socks, marbles, trains and even a map of the brain are crowding on his rug and hiding under his bed, and his mother won't let him watch cartoons until his room is spotless. This Saturday morning cleaning spree is told in upbeat verse with a true-to-life humor. Pat Cummings won the Coretta Scott King Award for illustration.
VHS: S16341. $44.95.

Clifford's Fun with Numbers

Clifford and his friends lead children through fun and games with numbers in this fully animated learning adventure. 30 mins.
VHS: S13732. $12.95.

Clifford's Fun With...Series

Clifford the Big Red Dog and his owner Emily Elizabeth are the stars of these Scholastic Learning Library videos developed by early childhood specialists, geared toward ages 3-8. (The books have sold millions of copies.) 30 minutes each.

Clifford's Fun with Opposites. Clifford shows kids about things that are different. The big red dog will delight kids as he instructs them about the concept of opposites in this animated short.
VHS: S24517. $12.95.

Clifford's Fun with Rhymes. Clifford and Emily Elizabeth want to join the Rhyme Cats, but must solve these rhyming riddles. Engaging.
VHS: S24516. $12.95.

Clifford's Fun with Shapes and Colors. In this short animation, the big red dog teaches kids about shapes. Join the scavenger hunt searching for shapes and colors. Full of songs and fun.
VHS: S24518. $12.95.

Clifford's Fun with Sounds. In this short animation, the big red dog shows kids how to have fun with sounds.
VHS: S24519. $12.95.

Clifford's Sing-Along Adventure

Clifford and his friends lead children at home in a musical adventure that gets them to sing, dance, clap and compose their own songs. Features old and new music classics, live action and video animation. 30 mins.
VHS: S04154. $14.95.

Cookie Monster's Best Bites

Annette Benning drops by to help Cookie Monster, one of Sesame Street's most beloved muppets, sort out the difference between a "Cookie Here and There." A large assortment of treats awaits kids in this song-filled, cookie-crunching delight. 30 mins.
VHS: S26659. $12.98.

Corduroy Bear

Three bear stories! *Corduroy* is a loveable stuffed bear who goes searching for a missing button; *Blueberries for Sal* is about an adventure of a little girl and a baby bear; *Panama* is about the search for a wonderful smell, with Little Bear and Little Tiger.
VHS: S00270. $14.95.
Gary Templeton, USA, 1986, 38 mins.

Cranberry Birthday

The birthday of that cantankerous yet loveable old salt, Mr. Whiskers, seems to be everyone's favorite holiday except for Mr. Whiskers himself! A potluck supper birthday party and surprise present from Maggie help change his mind.
VHS: S14187. $39.95.

Cranberry Easter

With Easter approaching, the town of Cranberryport anticipates the fun and celebration of the Easter Egg hunt, until Seth spoils everybody's mood with the shocking announcement he's moving.
VHS: S20013. $44.95.

Cranberry Holidays: Christmas

Mr. Whiskers is caught in a double dilemma: his fussy sister is coming to take him out of his messy house, and nasty neighbor Mr. Grape claims his ice skating pond. A last-minute house cleaning saves the day.
VHS: S14184. $44.95.

Cranberry Holidays: Halloween

Mysterious pirates try to capture Maggie and Mr. Whiskers on their way to the Halloween party with money for the new dock.
VHS: S14182. $44.95.

Cranberry Holidays: Thanksgiving

Who is trying to steal Grandma's bread recipe? Is it the slick gentleman who "smells of lavender" or the rough and tumble, "fishy" Mr. Whiskers?
VHS: S14183. $44.95.

Cranberry Holidays: The Complete Set

Includes *Halloween, Thanksgiving, Christmas* and *Valentine*. Four titles on one videocassette.
VHS: S14186. $159.95.

Cranberry Holidays: Valentine

In the continuing adventures of Maggie and charming Captain Whiskers, we visit Cranberryport to discover who is secretly sending the old seafarer sweet valentines.
VHS: S14185. $44.95.

Cranberry Mystery

Mr. Whiskers and Maggie pursue a group of nefarious thieves who are stealing valuable antiques and relics from Cranberryport. 11 mins.
VHS: S20014. $44.95.

Cranberry Summer

In this animated series, Mr. Whiskey and Maggie experience a host of complications from attending to a lost donkey in Cranberryport. The donkey's demands for food and shelter force them to stage an unforgettable Fourth of July fundraiser.
VHS: S20012. $44.95.

Creative Dance for Preschoolers

Imparts the fun of movement together with important basic principles. Ages 3-6. 60 minutes.
VHS: S24608. $42.95.

Cro

The Children's Television Workshop produced this animated series that spins entertaining and informative problem-solving stories from the perspective of a hip woolly mammoth named Phil. Normally these creatures are extinct, but Phil was thawed out by Dr. C and her lab assistant Mike. Phil often fondly recalls the old days when he and Cro, a Cro-Magnon boy, used to solve problems together. 45 mins. each.

Adventures in Woolyville.
VHS: S22979. $9.95.
Have Mammoths Will Travel.
VHS: S22980. $9.95.
It's a Wooly Wooly World.
VHS: S22981. $9.95.

Danny and the Dinosaur and Other Stories

Danny's friend for the day is the very Dinosaur that he had just been admiring in the Museum. What child wouldn't want to ride, go for a swim and play hide-and-seek with a real, live dinosaur? Also includes *The Camel Who Took a Walk, The Happy Lion* and *The Island of Song*. 35 mins.
VHS: S14494. $14.95.

A Day at the Zoo

Desi Arnaz, Jr. hosts this fascinating look at animals from around the world. Action footage and interesting facts about the creatures found at the zoo make for an enjoyable children's video. 30 mins.
VHS: S22760. $14.98.

A Day with Horses

Casey introduces kids to one of their best animal friends, the horse. Kids will see how horses take baths and even get to kiss a wobbly baby horse. Sing-a-alongs included. 30 mins.
VHS: S24494. $10.95.

A Day with Lions and Other Cats

Casey introduces kids to some fascinating facts about felines. For example, tigers love to swim and lions live in families just like people. Sing-a-alongs included. 30 mins.
VHS: S24495. $10.95.

A Day with Monkeys

This volume from the highly entertaining children's series *Real Animals* introduces kids to lovable monkeys using sing-alongs, important facts and just plain fun. 30 mins.
VHS: S24820. $10.95.

A Day with Whales

Another of the children's series *Real Animals*, this video introduces kids to intriguing whales using sing-alongs, important facts and just plain fun. 30 mins.
VHS: S24819. $10.95.

Doing Things: Eating, Washing, In Motion

This Bo Peep video compares children engaged in everyday activities like eating, washing and playing. Some animals like the same foods as kids and everyone likes a mud bath. This non-narrated tape has musical accompaniment that makes it suitable for a variety of situations. 27 mins.
VHS: S22378. $19.95.

Don Cooper: Mother Nature's Songs

Entertainer Don Cooper encourages imaginations to blossom as children see, hear and imitate nature in this delightful sing-along video featuring "The Not Ready for Bedtime Players." USA, 30 mins.
VHS: S15321. $19.95.

The Donkey's Dream

The little donkey is drowsy. He and his master approach Bethlehem...This poetic re-telling of the Christmas story from the point of view of the patient donkey is a perfect first introduction for small children. By Barbara Helen Berger.
VHS: S16343. $44.95.

Dot and Dash, Volume 1

These two puppets inhabit a world where dots, lines, shapes, and colors come together in fun and whimsical ways. From these simple means they bring forth a rich and imaginative understanding of the world.
VHS: S26153. $12.99.
Nikki Tilroe, USA, 1993, 30 mins.

Down Buttermilk Lane

This read-along video is beautifully illustrated by John Sanford's paintings, which depict the Pennsylvania Dutch Country. It tells the story of an Amish family and includes scenes from their everyday life. Images of horse-drawn carriages, traditional cooking and socializing make this vivid video an ideal introduction to another culture. 7:25 mins.
VHS: S22349. $39.95.

Dr. Seuss

These videos, based on the books by Dr. Seuss, receive a special mention. They are loved by adults and kids alike, who often find in them a special life-affirming message important today. The stories are wildly imaginative, often focusing on a positive theme in a positive manner, usually presenting males and females in multi-dimensional ways. The videos are also noted for stimulating an interest in reading the books they are based upon.
Dr. Seuss' ABC. ABC fun plus two other stories: *I Can Read with My Eyes Shut* (featuring the Cat in the Hat) and *Mr. Brown Can Moo—Can You?*, full of interactive fun. Animation/book based. Ages 2-6. 30 minutes.
VHS: S24523. $14.95.
Dr. Seuss' Sleep Book. An epic poem recreates the classic book with narration by Madeline Kahn. Follow these crazy creatures as they prepare to sleep. Ages 2-7. 30 minutes.
VHS: S24813. $9.95.
Dr. Seuss: Hop on Pop. Three Dr. Seuss stories for the youngest readers. *Hop on Pop* is simple rhyming fun. *Oh Say Can You Say?* tells a story in tongue twisters kids love. And *Marvin K. Mooney, Will You Please Go Now!* completes the set of three wonderful word worlds whirling, whew! Ages 3-6. 30 minutes.
VHS: S24525. $14.98.
Dr. Seuss: Horton Hatches the Egg. Horton the Elephant helps out Mayzie the lazy bird by sitting on her egg while she goes on vacation. Ages 3-8.
VHS: S24811. $9.95.
Dr. Seuss: Horton Hears a Who. Dr. Seuss teams up with the wonderful Chuck Jones to bring Horton, the lovable elephant, and his wild and woolly friends to life. Filled with songs and tongue-twisting verse. "A person's a person. No matter how small." Also includes *Thidwick the Big-Hearted Moose*. Ages 3+. Chuck Jones, 1970, 26 mins.
VHS: S24810. $9.95.
Dr. Seuss: I Am NOT Going to Get Up Today! A little boy claims that he will not get out of bed. Other stories: *The Shape of Me and Other Stuff, Great Day for Up* and *In a People House*. Interesting animation. Nice for the under 6 year olds. Animation/book based. Ages 2-6. 25 minutes. 1991.
VHS: S24812. $9.95.
Dr. Seuss: The Cat in The Hat Comes Back. With three Dr. Seuss stories: *The Cat in the Hat Comes Back*, this time with bunches of little cats, *Fox in Socks*, the amazing rhyming tongue twister and *There's a Wocket in My Pocket*. Ages 3+. 30 minutes.
VHS: S24524. $14.98.

Eight Super Stories from Sesame Street

A video twin-pack featuring Oscar the Grouch, Big Bird, Cookie Monster, Grover and the rest of the gang. 30 minutes.
VHS: S24993. $12.95.

Ella Jenkins Live at the Smithsonian

Legendary folksinger Ella Jenkins performs with the children of the Smithsonian Institute's Early Enrichment Center. Lots of fun, playful songs for children. 1991.
VHS: S15497. $14.95.

Ella Jenkins: For the Family

Ella Jenkins, a recognized national treasure, sings eleven favorite children's songs. Ages 3-7. 30 minutes.
VHS: S25036. $14.95.

Elmo Says Boo!

That giggling sensation Elmo and the ever-calculating Count star in Sesame Street's first-ever Halloween special. 30 mins.
VHS: S32061. $9.95.

Farm Animals: Close Up and Very Personal

Close-ups of cows, pigs, sheep, donkeys, goats, ducks, chickens, turkeys and horses make this episode from the *Close Up* series particularly appealing to preschoolers. They can see all these animals without any fear, and it's allergy free. 30 mins.
VHS: S24151. $14.95.

Fingermouse, Yoffy and Friends

Children will be intrigued by the stories of discovery as told by Yoffy, Fingermouse and other finger-puppet friends in this 3-tape series that includes music and sound effects. With educational lessons accompanying each story, the American Library Association calls the series a "combination of imaginative play and substantive story." 180 mins.
VHS: S15539. $100.00.

Five Sesame Street Stories

Included in this collection are five exciting adventures, including *Super-Grover* and *Big Bird Brings Spring to Sesame Street*. Ages 2-6. 30 minutes.
VHS: S24992. $5.95.

Five Stories for the Very Young

The five stories are *Changes*, about the adventures of two wooden dolls; *Harold's Fairy Tale* reveals how the title character employs purple crayons to create stories; *Whistle for Willie* teaches Peter how to whistle. The other tales are *Drummer Hoff* and the famous story, *Caps for Sale*. Animated.
VHS: S00447. $14.95.
Gene Deitch, USA, 1986

Follow That Bunny!

This "hoppin'" claymation musical shows the adventures of some energetic bunnies when Spring almost never came one year. 27 mins.
VHS: S18023. $12.95.

Follow That Fish

Take a ride on a turtle's back and swim past eels, octopi, glowing fish—even a shark! From the *Bank Street Read-Along Story Video* series. The story is told twice-once to familiarize children with the characters and story; the second time with words printed onscreen so children can easily follow along. 30 mins.
VHS: S13529. $14.99.

Frog and Toad Are Friends

Five short stories by Arnold Lobel of the two best friends, including *Spring, The Story, A Lost Button, A Swim,* and *The Letter*. Amazing animation. Ages 4-7. 18 minutes.
VHS: S24765. $12.95.

Frog and Toad Together

Easy-going Frog and excitable Toad share several amusing adventures and make some important discoveries. The *Dragons and Giants* story could be a bit frightening. This multiple award-winner, directed by John Matthews, is presented in stop-action animation. Ages 4-7. 30 minutes.
VHS: S24988. $12.95.

Get Ready for School

Based on Richard Scarry's popular characters. Young Brewster's first day of nursery school finds him overcoming his fears and having a great time learning things and making friends. Ages 3-7. 30 minutes.
VHS: S25034. $9.95.

A Golden Treasury of Nursery Rhymes

A mosaic of children's classic nursery rhymes is visualized in this fully animated video collection. 40 mins.
VHS: S19430. $14.99.

Good Morning Sunshine

"Songs For a Day Full of Wonder," by Patti Dallas and Laura Baron. Fascinating instrumentation with dulcimers and recorders. Real kids dance and play. Ages 2-6. 30 minutes.
VHS: S24895. $14.95.

Good Morning, Good Night: A Day on the Farm

Wake up with a little child and then watch as all the farm animals start a new day. First there's a little breakfast and then a romp, even some chores. Finally the day is done and everyone, a little tired, goes to sleep once again. Folk songs accompany this delightful video, perfect for sing-alongs. 17 mins.
VHS: S22379. $19.95.

Good Morning, Granny Rose!

Children will love this romp in the Ozarks with Granny Rose and her old dog, Henry. "Don't just lay there like a sack of potatoes, Henry!," Granny Rose says as they hurry off after breakfast to watch the sunrise. From the story by Warren Ludwig.
VHS: S16346. $44.95.

A Good Thing About Spots

A shy leopard cub learns to appreciate his spots. 14 mins.
VHS: S23458. $49.95.

A Great Day for Singing

James Durst performs 25 traditional songs and nursery rhymes for young children. Any child will find this treasury of sing-alongs simply irresistible. "Old MacDonald" and "Row, Row, Row Your Boat" are just some of the favorites included. 30 mins.
VHS: S24217. $14.95.

Happy Birdy

In this birthday video, a bird hosts the party. Combining animation and puppetry, the words to songs are spelled out on the screen, encouraging viewers to sing along. 30 minutes.
VHS: S25033. $9.98.

Happy Pooh Day

Three short animated films starring Winnie the Pooh are featured on this video. In *April Pooh*, Pooh and his friends are on the lookout for a silly trickster. Then wily crows trigger a lively mystery in *Tigger Got Your Tongue*. Finally, Pooh is feted with too many candles at his birthday party in *The Wise Have It*, resulting in a surprise declaration. 33 mins.
VHS: S29843. $12.99.

Hello Kitty

Animated adventures of the cute kitty.
Hello Kitty: Kitty and the Beast. Includes *Grinder Genie and the Magic Lamp, Hello Mother Goose*, and *Little Red Bunny Hood*. 45 mins.
VHS: S33371. $9.95.
Hello Kitty: Wizard of Paws. Includes *Snow White Kitty, Sleeping Kitty* and *Peter Penguin*. 45 mins.
VHS: S33370. $9.95.

Henry and Mudge in Puddle Trouble

It's spring and Henry and his 180-pound dog Mudge encounter the first spring flower, a gigantic puddle and a box full of kittens.
VHS: S08464. $71.95.

Henry and Mudge in the Green Time

Summer, the perfect time for a boy and his dog to picnic in the park—presentation of Cynthia Rylant's story of two best friends—Henry and his dog, Mudge.
VHS: S08414. $71.95.

Henry and Mudge Under the Yellow Moon

Henry and his dog Mudge never do things the same way, and falling leaves, scary Halloween tales and a Thanksgiving visitor provide fun for the two friends.
VHS: S08395. $71.95.

Henry's Cat: The Birthday Caper

Henry's Cat is the enormously popular British cartoon, created for children 3 and up. This tape contains two episodes: *The Birthday Caper* and *The Great Adventure*. 32 mins.
VHS: S09001. $9.95.

Hey, What About Me?

A warm, straight-forward attempt to talk to Pre-Schoolers about adjusting to new siblings. Teaches games, lullabies and bouncing rhymes. American Film Institute Video Award, American Academy of Pediatrics suggested media list. 25 minutes, ages 2-6.
Home Video.
VHS: S10149. $14.95.
Public Performance Rights.
VHS: S17154. $14.95.

Horses: Close Up and Very Personal

This episode from the *Close Up* series emphasizes the physical attributes of these magnificent animals so that preschoolers will understand their power. Horses are seen in a variety of environments, from the workaday world of the farm to the world of sports. 30 mins.
VHS: S24214. $19.95.

The Huggabug Club: I'm One of a Kind

This live-action children's show is full of songs and dance numbers that can brighten a kid's day. All the lovable flowers and bugs of the Huggabug Club join in the fun for an uplifting message that will make kids glad to be themselves. 27 mins.
VHS: S27501. $12.98.

The Huggabug Club: School Days

Kids can be worried about the inevitable first day of school. This video shows the Huggabug Club members singing their way through this anxious moment in a young person's life. It has lessons that can turn school into an exciting new part of a child's experience. 27 mins.
VHS: S27502. $12.98.

The Huggabug Club: You Can't Win 'em All

Sometimes children have trouble with losing at games or even just waiting their turn. Songs from the Huggabug Club gang teach vital lessons that can show kids winning isn't everything. Playing by the rules and staying focused on fun is more important. 27 mins.
VHS: S27503. $12.98.

Hullabaloo

Preschoolers will learn about numbers, colors, time and more in a fun and exciting way. Games, animation, and the lovable Ted Bear use repetition and reinforcement to build a secure relationship with kids that makes these lessons highly effective and entertaining. Each episode is 30 mins.

All About Opposites.
VHS: S24976. $12.95.
All About Shapes!
VHS: S24977. $12.95.
Colors!
VHS: S24972. $12.95.
Count with Me!
VHS: S24973. $12.95.
Everything Grows!
VHS: S24974. $12.95.
Making Fun!
VHS: S24978. $12.95.
Nature Friends!
VHS: S24975. $12.95.
Time!
VHS: S24979. $12.95.

Huxley Pig

The creation of children's storyteller and illustrator Rodney Peppe, *Huxley Pig* has a magical personality given to flights of fancy and dreams. He hates Horace the Rodent, heights, water, but he compensates through his favorite activities, eating, performing, dressing up or day dreaming. Each film contains five 10-minute adventures.

Huxley Pig and the Sea Monster.
VHS: S17173. $14.98.
Huxley Pig at the Beach.
VHS: S17172. $14.98.
Huxley Pig Makes a Movie.
VHS: S17174. $14.98.

I Love Big Machines

Big machines of every type are shown and explained to kids in fun but informative ways. Trains, airplanes, excavators, steam tractors, bull dozers and giant cranes are featured in this fascinating children's video. 30 mins.
VHS: S24213. $14.95.

I Love Toy Trains 3-Video Set

Toy trains of all sorts are shown on some of the most intricate set-ups in this fascinating video series. Kids will love this snappy and funny program that informs without ever becoming preachy or boring. It's perfect for toy trains lovers of all ages. Each tape is 30 mins.
VHS: S24212. $39.95.

Imagine That!

Nice video about a young boy adjusting to preschool. Would be helpful to either kids in preschool or children preparing to go to preschool. Ages 3-6. 30 minutes.
VHS: S24534. $9.95.

In the Tall, Tall Grass

If you were a fuzzy caterpillar crawling through the tall, tall grass on a sunny afternoon, what would you see? You'd see ants and bees and birds—hip-hopping bunnies too. This backyard tour, created with bold, colorful paintings and large simple words, is one no child wants to miss.
VHS: S16348. $44.95.

It Zwibble: Earthday Birthday

This animated film features a clan of dinosaur babies that will delight children even as they remind kids about the importance of the environment. Join a dinosaur family that wants to protect the earth. After a journey seeing the beauty as well as the destruction of the Earth, we see that even small gestures can help our Earth.
VHS: S24514. $9.98.
Michael Sporn, USA, 30 mins.

It's Not Easy Being Green

The Muppets sing 13 crowd-pleasers, with Kermit on his ukulele. Includes "Bein' Green," "Somewhere over the Rainbow" and "In a Cabin in the Woods." Ages 2-7. 37 minutes.
VHS: S24941. $12.99.

It's the Muppets!

The acclaimed *Muppet Show*, now in a video series, presents highlights. Hear Kermit's "It's Not Easy Being Green," Pig-Latin musicals, episodes of *Pigs in Space*, and more! 38 minutes each tape.

Meet the Muppets!
VHS: S24711. $12.99.
More Muppets!
VHS: S24712. $12.99.

Ivor the Engine

Ivor the Engine contends with elephants on the line and fire-breathing Welsh dragons in these charming stories. Two volumes set in the gentle landscape of the Valley of Wales.

Ivor the Engine and the Dragons. 59 mins.
VHS: S16146. $14.98.
Ivor the Engine and the Elephants. 60 mins.
VHS: S16145. $14.98.

Jane Hissey's Old Bear Stories: Friends, Friends, Friends

Once again the characters of the "Old Bear" books delight viewers with their toy room antics. Whether escaping from a musty old attic in *Old Bear* or taking a midnight ride with a baby owl in *Hoot*, Old Bear turns imaginative play into beguiling children's entertainment.
VHS: S27415. $9.98.
Kevin Griffiths, Great Britain, 1996, 30 mins.

Jane Hissey's Old Bear Stories: Happy Birthday Old Bear

The characters from the "Old Bear" storybooks come alive in the three stop-motion episodes collected on this video. First, in *Ruff*, Ruff the dog's friends realize that Ruff has never had a birthday. They soon set things right, and the fun grows in the stories *The Birthday Band* and *Fancy Dress Parade*.
VHS: S27416. $9.98.
Kevin Griffiths, Great Britain, 1996, 30 mins.

Joe Scruggs First Video

A blend of animation, live action and enchanting songs for ages 3-8. Recommended by the American Library Association, Video Librarian, Parents' Choice Award. 30 minutes.
VHS: S17139. $14.95.

Joe Scruggs in Concert

Children's music videos for the whole family. Includes Joe, his guitar, puppets and giant props. The audience is fascinating as they sing along, clap along and sign along. 51 minutes.
VHS: S24536. $14.95.

Joey Runs Away and Other Stories

When Joey the kangaroo tires of hearing his mother's complaints about his messy room (her pouch), he tries out other accommodations, like a pelican's bill and finally a mail pouch, before deciding that there really is no place like home. Also includes *The Cow Who Fell in the Canal, The Bear and the Fly* and *The Most Wonderful Egg in the World*. 28 mins.
VHS: S14490. $14.95.

Just Grandma and Me

One of Mercer Mayer's best-loved stories comes to life in this 1995 release. Ages 4-9. 30 minutes.
VHS: S25000. $12.95.

Just Me and My Dad

Mercer Mayer's ever-popular "Little Critter" is off to the woods for his first camp-out with Dad. Based on the book of the same title. 30 minutes.
VHS: S24999. $12.95.

Just So Stories, Set I

Kipling's tales have been entertaining children since the turn of the century. This valuable and imaginative edition is no exception. Includes four tales: *How the Whale Got His Throat, How the Camel Got His Hump, How the Rhinoceros Got His Skin* and *The Sing-Song of Old Man Kangaroo*. Grades P-3.
VHS: S14209. $139.95.

Kids Love the Circus

The second in the *Kids Love...* series, this video takes kids into the world of the circus. Beyond that, it encourages them to explore the power of their own imaginations, a realm where high-wire acts and clowns rule supreme. 30 mins.
VHS: S23120. $14.95.

Kino's Story Time, Vol. 1

Stories read by Tom Selleck, John Ritter, Valerie Bertinelli and Kim Karnsrithong are featured in this first volume hosted by the lovable puppet Kino. These well crafted stories were first available on Public Television. Kids will love hearing them and seeing some of their favorite TV personalities at the same time.
VHS: S21983. $12.98.

Kino's Story Time, Vol. 2

John Goodman, Mark Ritts, Tatyana Ali, Shari Belafonte and Zachary Bryan read stories along with Public Television's puppet star Kino in this collected volume. These favorite children's tales are newly rendered by famous personalities. Kids will certainly enjoy these classics.
VHS: S21984. $12.98.

Kino's Story Time, Vol. 3

Ellen DeGeneres *(Ellen)*, Patricia Richardson *(Home Improvement)*, Elena Epps and Kelly Williams *(Family Matters)* and Meshach Taylor *(Designing Women)* are featured on this video, reading stories to the puppet Kino and his children friends. Kids will learn about the exciting world of books from this video. 60 mins.
VHS: S26392. $12.98.

Kitten Companions

This program examines the friendships between children and kittens, as children see the actions and behavior of kittens and learn how to respond to them. 30 mins.
VHS: S18225. $14.95.

Kukla, Fran and Ollie: Be a Clown, Be a Clown

Enjoy a fun-filled day at the circus with Kukla, Fran and Ollie! Kukla plays ringmaster, Ollie's a roustabout, Fletcher Rabbit's a clown, and Beulah performs as an aerialist—without her broom! Songs include "Big Top," "Be a Clown" and "Here We Are." Includes special short subject, *The Best of Madame Ooglepuss*. 45 mins.
VHS: S28631. $14.95.

Kukla, Fran and Ollie: Get on the Dragon Wagon

Just in time for election year, it's Ollie's "Do-It-Yourself Campaign Kit." Watch Ollie play politician as he demonstrates how to deflect questions from reporters, how to smile all the time, and the importance of a campaign song. Songs include "Get on the Dragon Wagon," "A Fella Needs a Girl" and "Here We Are." Includes special short subject, *The Best of Kukla*. 45 mins.
VHS: S28630. $14.95.

Kukla, Fran and Ollie: Kukla Discovers America

When Ollie, as King Ferdinand, attempts to retell the legend of Columbus Day in his pageant, rather than giving it a twist, he rewrites history. Songs include "Lady of Spain," "Kukla, Fran and Ollie's Birthday Song" and "Here We Are." Includes special short subject, *The Best of Ollie*. 45 mins.
VHS: S28629. $14.95.

Kukla, Fran and Ollie: Madame O's Merry Musicale

Baby boomers can take a trip down memory lane with their children as they enjoy this blast from the past. Diva Madame Ooglepuss stars in a musicale and Beulah takes the phrase "break a leg" too literally, all adding up to to Kukla, Fran and Ollie hilarity. Songs include "Here We Are," "Roses" and "It's a Most Unusual Day." Includes special short subject, *The Best of Fletcher*. 45 mins.
VHS: S28627. $14.95.

Kukla, Fran and Ollie: Tis the Season to be Ollie

Make your Christmas jolly with Kukla, Fran and Ollie! When Ollie brings home a scrawny Christmas tree after squandering his money on a chocolate soda, the Christmas Fairy (or is it Beulah?) makes the skinny tree glow with lights. Includes five Christmas songs: "Deck the Halls," "Bye, Bye, Baby Dear," "Poor Little Christmas Tree," "A Kuklapolitan Christmas" and "Here We Are." Includes special short subject, *The Best of Buelah*. 45 mins.
VHS: S28628. $14.95.

Lamb Chop in the Land of No Numbers

Puppeteer Shari Lewis and her beloved sidekick Lamb Chop are featured in this wonderful children's video that is sure to please all kids. 48 mins.
VHS: S24249. $12.95.

The Land of Pleasant Dreams

This is a series of animated videos in which children fall off to sleep and enter a lovely dreamland where their experience helps them know what to do in real life. 1987. 30 minutes each video.

A Fence Too High. Lacey, the quilted lamb, is convinced she can't win the fence-jumping contest. Peter helps her realize that she'll never succeed if she doesn't try. Includes *A Tailor-Made Friendship*.
VHS: S24543. $14.95.
Bearly There At All. Threads, the bear, wants to be special like his other animal friends. He simply needs a friend to remind him that he too has something special. Also includes *A Girl with the Pop-Up Garden* 30 mins.
VHS: S24545. $14.95.
Is It Soup Yet? RicRac, the rabbit, is brewing a pot of luscious soup, but when his friends ask to add their favorite ingredients, they learn that too many cooks can spoil the soup. 30 mins.
VHS: S24544. $14.95.

Let's Create for Pre-Schoolers

Six exciting projects are featured in this video that will lead children through concepts dealing with color and shape. It's educational, informative, and certain to keep young minds engaged. Kids learn about colors and shapes in these six art projects accompanied by music.
VHS: S24546. $24.95.

The Little Ant

Professional storyteller David Novak offers a unique perspective on the traditional folktale in this read-along video. The Little Ant sets off a chain reaction of accusation when he accuses a snowflake of making him trip. Perfect for children.
VHS: S22351. $39.95.

Little Bear

This Cable Ace-nominated series brings to the screen the stories of the curious cub and his friend who discover the world around them. Based on the *Little Bear* books by Else Holmelund Minarik and illustrated by Maurice Sendak. 37 mins.
Family Tales. Includes the stories "Pudding Hill," "Father's Flying Flapjacks," "Little Bear and the Wind" and "Doctor Little Bear."
VHS: S31877. $9.99.
Meet Little Bear. Includes the stories "What Will Little Bear Wear?," "Hide and Seek," "Little Bear Goes to the Moon" and "Gone Fishing."
VHS: S31878. $9.99.

A Little Duck Tale

This tender, heart-warming story portrays the true life adventures of "Chibi" and his duckling brothers and sisters as they struggle for survival in downtown Tokyo. Children and parents alike will find joy in this tale of determination and triumph. 55 mins.
VHS: S17012. $19.95.

The Little Engine That Could

The classic tale of imagination, perseverance and hope to overcome existing hurdles and obstacles is boldly re-imagined in this warm, animated adaptation. 30 mins.
VHS: S18252. $12.95.

A Little Girl and Gunny Wolf

Wilhemina Harper's story is adapted for this video by an actual inner-city kindergarten class. It tells the story of a little girl who is captured by a Gunny Wolf but escapes by singing the wolf a song. 6 mins.
VHS: S23492. $39.95.

Little People Videos

Based on the Fisher-Price toy characters, these fun videos have high production quality and also promote positive values, such as friendship. 30 minutes each.
Little People: Christmas Fun.
VHS: S24806. $14.95.
Little People: Favorite Songs.
VHS: S24807. $14.95.
Little People: Fun with Words.
VHS: S24808. $14.95.
Little People: Three Favorite Stories.
VHS: S24809. $14.95.

Little Toot

The brave tug boat Little Toot sets off on the adventure of his life carrying three motherless puppy-dog children in search of their father.
VHS: S16750. $12.95.
Don Spencer, USA, 1992, 52 mins.

Look and Learn

Lessons in letters, numbers and words for kids 3-6.
Alphabet Soup. Sing-Along, Flying Pictures, Flipping Words and Jaunty Rhymes, animated.
VHS: S06449. $19.95.
Barefoot Bear. Features read-along word recognition and story words that change color at a read-along pace.
VHS: S06451. $19.95.
Bear Dreams. Teaches word recognition games and road-to-reading with lessons of friendship.
VHS: S06452. $19.95.
Hello Numbers. Features a one-to-one numbers games and songs with count-a-long to ten and by tens to 100.
VHS: S06450. $19.95.

Lyle, Lyle Crocodile: The House on East 88th Street

He cooks! He cleans! But he's a crocodile...and he's living in the bathtub of the Primm's new house. Narrated by Tony Randall. Fully animated. 25 mins.
VHS: S11237. $14.95.

Madeline and the Easter Bonnet

Madeline and the girls become the hit of the fashion show when their horse's tattered hat is transformed into a wonderful Easter bonnet. Narrated by Christopher Plummer. 30 minutes.
VHS: S24997. $12.95.

Madeline and The Toy Factory

The girls go on a tour of a toy factory. Madeline poses as a doll herself and becomes the prized possession of a sad and lonely little girl. Narrated by Christopher Plummer. Ages 3-12. 30 minutes.
VHS: S24998. $12.95.

Madeline Collection

The tales of Madeline's adventures at boarding school.
Madeline and The Dog Show. Madeline and the rest of the boarding school arrive to register Genevieve the dog (who saved Madeline in *Madeline's Rescue*) for a dog show. Unfortunately, Genevieve is rejected for lack of a pedigree. Find out how she wins anyway!
VHS: S24764. $12.95.
Madeline in Cooking School. Madeline makes a very important choice. Recommended.
VHS: S24888. $12.95.
Madeline in London. Madeline and the rest of the boarding school visit a friend in London. Madeline gets caught up in adventures and even receives a medal from the queen. 30 minutes.
VHS: S24548. $12.95.
Madeline's Christmas. Everyone at the boarding school is sick, so Madeline changes her holiday plans to help them. The show ends with a rhyme about love. 24 mins.
VHS: S24549. $12.95.

Madeline's Rescue

The chairman of the trustees decides to enforce a no pets rule. The girls can't bear to part with Genevieve, and her triumphant return provides a surprise and happy ending. 1990, 25 mins.
VHS: S13334. $14.95.

Make Way for Ducklings and Other Classic Stories by Robert McCloskey

These stories are now wonderful animated shorts that children will enjoy. *Lentil, Blueberries for Sal, Time of Wonder* and *Burt Dow: Deep Water Man* are included with the favorite, *Make Way for Ducklings*. 60 mins.
VHS: S22162. $14.95.

The Maurice Sendak Library

Three great stories by Maurice Sendak. First, four little poems set to music from Sendak's *The Nutshell Library: Alligators All Around, Pierre, One Was Johnny* and *Chicken Soup with Rice*. Then, *Where the Wild Things Are*, one of Sendak's classics. Finally, *In the Night Kitchen*, a little boy dreams of a special time in the kitchen when bakers bake cake, dough airplanes fly, and everyone dances to the deliciously syncopated music. Includes *Getting to Know Maurice Sendak*, a personal talk with the author/illustrator! 35 mins.
VHS: S11229. $14.95.

Max's Chocolate Chicken

This collection of popular children's stories makes a wonderful animated video. *Max's Chocolate Chicken*, by Rosemary Wells, is joined by Janet and Allan Ahlberg's *Each Peach Pear Plum*, Emily Arnolds McCully's *Picnic*, and Maud and Miska Petersham's *The Circus Baby*. 36 mins.
VHS: S22163. $14.95.

Meet Your Animal Friends

Lynn Redgrave hosts this visit with baby animals, to the delight of infants and toddlers, who giggle with glee at the funny antics of sheep, deer, horses, dogs and other species. 60 minutes.
VHS: S17013. $12.95.

Mike Mulligan and His Steam Shovel

Three treasured children's books are adapted into three animated video pieces in which a whale rescues Burt Dow, the Moon Man visits Earth and the collection's title duo are helped by a little boy. 30 mins.
VHS: S00854. $14.95.
Morton Schindel, USA, 1986, 30 mins.

Mine and Yours

Live-action and animated stories and songs in this colorful, well-produced video which carries a message about sharing and cooperation. Katie wants to keep Renee's birthday present. 25 minutes.
VHS: S24554. $9.95.

Mister Rogers' Neighborhood: Circus Fun

Joining the circus with the acclaimed PBS children's show virtually guarantees that children will be entranced by this episode. The emphasis is on fun.
VHS: S23024. $9.98.

Mister Rogers' Neighborhood: Going to School

This PBS television series won countless awards for excellence and was popular with an entire generation of kids. In this episode the issue of going to school is calmly dealt with in a way that will reassure nervous youngsters. USA, 28 mins.
VHS: S27155. $9.98.

Mister Rogers' Neighborhood: Kindness

Tommy Tune joins Mr. Rogers in this episode from the long running PBS children's show. This series has been a staple of pre-schooler television viewing for a generation. Parents have long relied on the simple charms and humor of the acclaimed show.
VHS: S23023. $9.98.

Mister Rogers' Neighborhood: Learning Is Everywhere!

Mr. Rogers shows children how they can turn any experience into a learning experience. It's perfect for children who might think that learning can't be fun. USA, 28 mins.
VHS: S27156. $9.98.

Mister Rogers' Neighborhood: Love

Who could explain the complexities of this central emotion better than Mr. Rogers on his long-running PBS children's show? Of course, he gets some help from his teddy bear.
VHS: S23026. $9.98.

Mister Rogers' Neighborhood: Making Music

From the long-running PBS children's show comes this episode, enlivened by a visit from the acclaimed cellist Yo-Yo Ma. Kids will love this easy-going introduction to the world of classical music.
VHS: S23025. $9.98.

Mister Rogers' Neighborhood: Our Earth: Clean and Green

Important lessons about the relationship between humans and the environment are at the center of this episode from the classic PBS series. USA, 28 mins.
VHS: S27157. $9.98.

Mister Rogers' Neighborhood: The Doctor, Your Friend

Visiting a physician, while important, can be a frightening experience for children. In this video, Mister Rogers explains why doctors are to be trusted. After all, they really are trying to help. USA, 28 mins.
VHS: S27158. $9.98.

Mister Rogers: Dinosaurs & Monsters

Mister Rogers helps young people understand what scary monsters are and are not about. Mister Rogers visits a museum to show dinosaurs, and with the help of Lady Aberlin and Handyman Negri, he clears up confusion about what is real and what is fantasy. USA, 1986, 64 mins.
VHS: S00893. $19.98.

Mister Rogers: Music and Feelings

Mister Rogers, aided by Ella Jenkins, explores the many moods of music along with cellist Yo-Yo Ma and the entire gang from the Neighborhood of Make-Believe. 65 mins.
VHS: S05012. $19.98.

Mister Rogers: Musical Stories

Mister Rogers invites children into a land of musical make-believe with two musical stories for children: *Potato Bugs and Cows* and *A Granddad for Daniel*. 59 mins.
VHS: S05897. $19.98.

Mister Rogers: What About Love

A trolley will take you to the enchanting Neighborhood of Make Believe in this reassuring program about the value of love and the confusing feelings that can come along with it. 51 mins.
VHS: S05011. $19.98.

Mister Rogers: When Parents Are Away

Mister Rogers advises parents and their children on how to handle the times of separation. It covers babysitters and day-care and contains songs, outings and a special visit to the "neighborhood of make believe" with King Friday and Queen Sara Saturday. Can you say, "We'll be back soon?" USA, 1987, 66 mins.
VHS: S04380. $19.98.

Moira's Birthday (plus Blackberry Subway Jam)

Moira's birthday is coming and she wants a big party! The video also includes *Blackberry Subway Jam*, about a subway that pulls into Jonathan's house, where all the passengers pile out. Animated stories by Robert Munsch. 25 minutes.
VHS: S24996. $12.95.

Mommy's Office

Watercolor illustrations make this story of a little girl visiting mom at work especially charming. She realizes that mommy's office work is similar to her own school day activities. Just the right message for working mothers to impart to their own children through this read-along children's video. 6:19 mins.

VHS: S22348. $39.95.

Monster in My Pocket with The Schnozzes

This video joins two delightful animated adventures. *Monster in My Pocket* is the story of a whole cast of good and bad monsters struggling against each other after they have been rendered tiny in an escape attempt. *The Schnozzes* are animals with big noses who try to make the most of their prominent schnozzes. Great for kids. 30 mins.

VHS: S26097. $12.99.

Mop Top

Based on the story by Don Freeman. Moppy finally sees himself as others do. (His head is literally mistaken for a mop.) He begins to appreciate a neat-looking appearance. 10 minutes.

VHS: S24555. $37.95.

More Preschool Power

Pre-School age "teachers" show how to tie shoes, brush teeth, make fruit salad and play with shadow puppets. Packed with songs, music, jokes and tongue-twisters. Recommended by Parents Magazine, Parents' Choice Award, California Children's Video Award. 30 minutes, pre-school.

VHS: S17008. $14.95.

More Stories for the Very Young

The Little Red Hen, Petunia, Not So Fast Songololo, The Napping House and *Max's Christmas* are cartoons small children will enjoy. 38 mins.

VHS: S22686. $14.95.

Morris the Moose

Two stories from Bernard Wiseman's beginning reading books are realized through stop motion animation in this video. *Morris the Moose Goes to School* introduces Morris to the alphabet and numbers. Then in *Morris Has a Cold*, Boris the Bear tries to nurse his friend back to health. 28 mins.

VHS: S23278. $12.95.

Move Like the Animals

This exercise-movement tape helps children develop balance, coordination and motor sequencing skills while moving to original songs and music. Moshe Feldenkrais' movement awareness lessons are captured in this lively musical exercise video for children. As kids learn to walk like a bear, roll like a cat and crawl like an alligator they will develop coordination and motor sequencing skills. 24 mins.

VHS: S24551. $19.95.

Moving Machines

In this tape children experience the excitement of big machines. A bulldozer, a cement truck, a crane and many others are included. Children play with toy machines that will help other kids to identify with the use of these powerful machines. Fun percussion musical accompaniment. 25 mins.

VHS: S22380. $19.95.

Mr. Bubble Gum

Having a little brother can be a big pain! Eli's older brother calls him Mr. Bubble Gum, because he sticks to him like gum. Follow along as the kids and their best pal Roberta invent a new soft drink, go trick-or-treating, and find out that having a little brother may not be so bad after all. From the *Bank Street Read-Along Story Video* series. The story is told twice—once to familiarize children with the characters and story; the second time with words printed onscreen so children can easily follow along. 30 mins.

VHS: S13527. $14.99.

Mr. Monster

Five-year-old Eli's monster collection is taking over the whole bedroom! Everybody thinks Eli's monster phase is cute-everybody but his big brother, that is. Find out what happens when Eli's brother and his friend Roberta hatch a plot to get rid of the monsters forever. From the *Bank Street Read-Along Story Video* series. The story is told twice—once to familiarize children with the characters and story; the second time with words printed onscreen so children can easily follow along. 30 mins.

VHS: S13530. $14.99.

Mr. Popper's Penguins

The fun begins when mild-mannered Mr. Popper unexpectedly receives an Antarctic penguin and decides to keep it as a pet. Jim Backus narrates this adaptation of Richard and Florence Atwater's classic story. 42 mins.

VHS: S10050. $119.00.

Mrs. Frisby and the Rats of Nimh

Mrs. Frisby, a widow-mouse, needs to find a new home before her family is uprooted by the farmer's plow. She receives unexpected help from a secret society of super-intelligent rats. An award-winning adaptation of Robert O'Brien's Newbery Award-winning book. 29 mins.

VHS: S08165. $119.00.

Muppet Treasure Island

The Robert Louis Stevenson swashbuckling classic gets the Muppet treatment in this musical comedy high-seas adventure featuring over 400 Muppets, including Kermit as Captain Smollet, Miss Piggy as jungle queen Benjamina Gunn, and Fozzie Bear as Squire Trelawney. Also features more human actors than have ever appeared in a Muppet movie, including Tim Curry as Long John Silver, Jennifer Saunders *(Absolutely Fabulous)*, Billy Connolly, and Kevin Bishop as Jim Hawkins.

VHS: S30055. $22.99.
Laser: LD76056. $39.99.
Brian Henson, USA, 1996, 99 mins.

Muppet Treasure Island Sing-Alongs

Kermit the Frog and his Muppet buccaneers storm the high seas with comic fervor and pirate songs in this charming video. Sing-alongs with new characters, including Pirate Girl and her pirate friends, Monty, Polly and Clueless, make this great entertainment for kids and parents alike. Featuring two songs from the Muppet feature film *Muppet Treasure Island*.

VHS: S27434. $12.99.
Brian Henson, USA, 1996, 30 mins.

Muppets on Wheels

Kermit hosts this show featuring a new Muppet character called Lindy. She is precocious, and together with Kermit she indulges a passion for cars, trains and trucks. Soon they happen upon a group of kids and other Muppets who share their fascination. Perfect for preschoolers. 30 mins.

VHS: S25914. $12.99.

Murmel, Murmel, Murmel (plus The Boy in the Drawer)

The story of a little girl who discovers a real, live baby in her sandbox. The tape includes the story *The Boy in The Drawer*, about a boy the size of a sock who lives in Shelly's dresser drawer. Animated stories by Robert Munsch. 30 minutes.

VHS: S24986. $12.95.

My Sesame Street Home Video

Featuring the Jim Henson cast of *Sesame Street Muppets* and the *Sesame Street Live* cast.

A New Baby in My House. Mrs. Snuffleupagus helps older brother Snuffy understand his feelings about his new baby sister. Snuffy's little sister makes him upset when she breaks his toy. Mrs. Snuffleupagus then tells her two children a story about a prince who feels neglected because of his new baby sister. With a story-within-a-story and six little musical numbers. From the acclaimed Children's Television Workshop. Ages 2-6.
VHS: S24557. $9.98.

Bedtime Stories & Songs. Big Bird, Kermit the Frog and the Cookie Monster tell stories and sing lullabies that children will ask for night after night.
VHS: S02836. $9.98.

Big Bird's Favorite Party Games. Big Bird's having a party and everyone's invited. There's music, participation games, and even a game of "Oscar says."
VHS: S07710. $9.98.

Big Bird's Story Time.
VHS: S24630. $9.98.

Count It Higher: Great Music Videos from Sesame Street. A collection of Sesame Street music videos. Enjoy the Doo Wop Hop and others!
VHS: S07712. $9.98.

Getting Ready to Read. Big Bird and Bert and Ernie present songs, stories and rhymes designed to show children how some words look and sound, and how letters can be blended to become words.
VHS: S02832. $9.98.

Getting Ready for School. The crowd shares basic skills for getting along in school.
VHS: S24631. $9.98.

I'm Glad I'm Me. Bert and Ernie encourage children to identify parts of their own bodies and to develop a sense of pride and self-esteem.
VHS: S02835. $9.98.

Learning About Letters. Big Bird and his friend Alphabet Day introduce the entire alphabet, with help from the rest of the Muppets. Cookie Monster's favorite letter is "C", of course, because it stands for "cookie."
VHS: S02833. $9.98.

Learning About Numbers. Children will learn to count from 1 to 20 with the help of the Count and Big Bird.
VHS: S02834. $9.98.

Learning to Add and Subtract.
VHS: S24632. $9.98.

Play Along Games & Songs. Big Bird and his friends present some of the most popular games from the television show, games that will familiarize children with counting, reading and reasoning skills.
VHS: S02837. $9.98.

The Alphabet Game. Sunny Friendly is the host of a new game show, Alphabet Treasure Hunt. There are prizes and surprises, and children can play along.
VHS: S08172. $9.98.

The Best of Ernie and Bert. When Sesame's Big Bird turns the pages of Ernie's scrapbook, each picture comes to life and everyone relives the adventures of Bert and Ernie.
VHS: S07711. $9.98.

The Best of Elmo. From the acclaimed Children's Television Workshop comes the furry Elmo and some charming songs for preschoolers.
VHS: S24511. $9.98.

The New Adventures of Peter Rabbit

An all new version of Beatrix Potter's delightful character is featured in this animated video. Peter and his friends journey through the countryside and discover new adventures and thrills. Along the way they sing memorable songs and generate big laughs. 48 mins.

VHS: S23932. $14.98.

Nick Jr.: Allegra's Window: Storytime Sing-Along

Allegra and her friends introduce kids to ten irresistible songs. The result is a popular sing-along video that kids will be able to watch and participate with. USA, 1995, 35 mins.

VHS: S27311. $12.95.

The Night Before Christmas (Edwards)

Clement Clarke Moore's beloved Christmas classic is brought to life with exquisite illustrations and festive music. Narrated by Anthony Edwards *(ER)*. 6 mins.

VHS: S33785. $60.00.

The Night Before Christmas (Styner)

Jerry Styner provides the narration and original music for this adaptation of the holiday classic. Children will love this version of Clement C. Moore's enduring poem. 10 mins.

VHS: S23474. $49.95.

Noel

The story of a magical Christmas tree ornament that comes to life as it is passed down from one generation to the next.

VHS: S24612. $12.95.

Nonsense and Lullabyes: Nursery Rhymes

A collection of eighteen nursery rhymes updated with new twists and beautifully animated by renowned filmmaker Michael Sporn. Original music and songs are by Caleb Sampson and the all-star roster of narrators includes Karen Allen, Eli Wallach, Linda Hunt, Courtney Vance, Heidi Stallings and Phillip Schopper.

VHS: S16466. $9.98.
Michael Sporn, USA, 27 mins.

Nonsense and Lullabyes: Poems for Children

Classic poems like Edward Lear's "The Owl and the Pussycat" and Robert Louis Stevenson's "Autumn Fires" are featured with new children's poems like Russel Hoban's "Homework" to make up this collection. With the voices of Karen Allen, Eli Wallach, and Linda Hunt.

VHS: S16467. $9.98.
Michael Sporn, USA, 27 mins.

"Not Now!" Said the Cow

Crow asks for help planting corn. "Not Now!" answers Cow. "I'm asleep," baas Sheep. "Nix, Nix!" peep the Chicks. Find out what Crow really wants—and what he does when turned down by all the other animals. From the *Bank Street Read-Along Story Video* series. The story is told twice—once to familiarize children with the characters and story; the second time with words printed onscreen so children can easily follow along. 30 mins.

VHS: S13531. $14.99.

On Our Way to School

Shari Lewis, Lamb Chop and friends lead kids in a romp through activities which help prepare pre-schoolers.

VHS: S24613. $9.95.

One Fish Two Fish Red Fish Blue Fish

Three classic Dr. Seuss stories—*One Fish Two Fish Red Fish Blue Fish; Oh, The Thanks You Can Think* and *The Foot Book*—are now animated shorts. Kids will enjoy the offbeat humor of these cartoons. 30 mins.

Spanish Narration.
VHS: S22017. $14.95.
English Narration.
VHS: S22018. $14.95.

One, Two, Buckle My Shoe

A heartwarming and engaging collection of more than 35 traditional nursery rhymes. 35 mins.

VHS: S19432. $14.99.

One-Minute Bible Stories (New Testament)

Shari Lewis and Lamb Chop are joined by Florence Henderson to recreate these charming stories from the New Testament. 26 different tales are animated and narrated, bringing these enduring stories to young audiences. 30 mins.
VHS: S21380. $14.99.

One-Minute Bible Stories (Old Testament)

Five-time Emmy Award-winner Shari Lewis brings 26 stories from the Hebrew Bible to life with the help of her hand puppet, Lamb Chop. In under one minute's time, these two use their unique comic style and animation to tell these delightful tales in a new and refreshing way that preserves their essential values. 30 mins.
VHS: S21379. $14.99.

Original Tales and Tunes

Little K.J. is the guide for a song-filled journey combining live action and puppetry.
VHS: S24615. $14.95.

Peep and the Big Wide World

Three simple, amusing and fresh episodes on the adventures of Peep, a newly hatched chick. Quack, a cantankerous duck and Chirp, an excitable robin, accompany Peep on her thrilling travels. Sure to enrich the imaginations of the very young. Smart animation, with the voice of Peter Ustinov. 30 mins.
VHS: S15790. $14.95.

Pete Seeger's Family Concert

Join the live outdoor concert. A mix of folk songs, favorite kids songs and originals from the folk master. Ages 4-6. 45 minutes.
VHS: S24620. $14.95.

Pictures and Letters: A Video Picture Dictionary

The real world of children is presented in alphabetical order to provide an interesting review of the letters of the alphabet, and an interesting vocabulary-building activity for parents and teachers. 30 mins.
VHS: S10318. $29.95.

Pigs and David's Father

Join the chase when Megan lets the pigs out. Then join Julie when she meets her neighbor's unusual dad.
VHS: S24766. $12.95.

Poky Little Puppy's First Christmas

Sweet little Poky is now on video. While the family searches for the perfect Christmas tree, Poky wanders off, falls into a deep hole and meets his rescuer, a little skunk named Herman. Narrated by Donald Sutherland. 30 minutes.
VHS: S25001. $9.95.

Poky's Favorite Stories

These Golden Book favorites are now on video. Parents probably read them as kids. This compilation features the animated stories *The Poky Little Puppy and The Patchwork Blanket, The Sailor Dog* and *Little Toad to the Rescue*. Ages 2-5. 30 minutes.
VHS: S24990. $5.95.

Postman Pat's 123 Story

Postman Pat teaches young children the basics of counting in this humorous, simple tale. 30 mins.
VHS: S19422. $12.98.

Preschool Power #3

Pre-Schoolers learn to do things for themselves—things like putting on gloves, making a paper fan, sweeping up spills, making French bread, making giant bubbles, setting up dominoes. Recommended by the American Library Association. 30 minutes, pre-school.
VHS: S17010. $14.95.

Preschool Power: Jacket Flips & Other Tips

How to button, buckle, zip, wash hands, put on jackets, tidy rooms, make snacks and pour without spilling a drop. Featuring the proven methods of Maria Montessori, Pre-Schoolers will learn the lasting gift of self-reliance. New York Film Festival Award. Recommended by American Library Association. 30 minutes, pre-school.
VHS: S17009. $14.95.

Puff the Magic Dragon

Puff, the magic dragon made famous by Peter, Paul and Mary, comes alive in this animated version with the voice of Burgess Meredith as Puff. USA, 1984, 45 mins.
VHS: S01071. $14.98.

A Rainbow of My Own

Based on the book by Don Freeman. After a rainy afternoon of playing imaginary games with a rainbow, a boy goes home to find a real rainbow waiting in his room. 5 minutes.
VHS: S24621. $37.95.

The Real Story Videos Series

Well known celebrities are the voices for the leading characters in this series of reinvestigations of well-known children's stories, songs and rhymes. While the actual story may be short, the videos imagine an entire life surrounding the material. Contemporary, upbeat, imaginative and surprising. Ages 4-8. Each video is approximately 25 minutes.

The Real Story of Baa Baa Black Sheep.
VHS: S25047. $12.95.

The Real Story of Happy Birthday to You.
VHS: S25045. $12.95.

The Real Story of I'm A Little Teapot.
VHS: S25042. $12.95.

The Real Story of Itsy Bitsy Spider. Recommended. With *Cosby* show star Malcolm Jamal-Warner and singer Patti LaBelle. Very engaging.
VHS: S25041. $12.95.

The Real Story of Rain, Rain Go Away.
VHS: S25044. $12.95.

The Real Story of Three Little Kittens.
VHS: S25043. $12.95.

The Real Story of Twinkle Twinkle Little Star.
VHS: S25046. $12.95.

Richard Scarry Series

The leader in educational preschool programming teaches children the fundamentals of spelling and numbers in a fun, entertaining way. The videos are as enjoyable as the well-liked books. Join the fun in Busytown with Huckle Cat, Lowly Worm and friends. Great for the ages 2-6 set. Each tape is 25 mins.

Richard Scarry's Best Busy People Video. A fun look at jobs and occupations in Busytown.
VHS: S24623. $9.95.

Richard Scarry's Best Counting Video. The friends are back all over town—count down! 20 mins.
VHS: S24625. $9.95.

Richard Scarry's Best Ever ABC Video. This time, the fun is centered at the Busytown School. 20 minutes.
VHS: S24624. $9.95.

Richard Scarry's Best Learning Songs Ever. Join the Busytown crowd singing about letters, numbers, shapes and other fun things.
VHS: S24626. $9.95.

Richard Scarry's New Friend on the Block. Animated animals populate the three stories joined on this video. Cats, dogs, mice and an earthworm are all part of the gang who welcome a new friend in the title story. This video is perfect for kids. 25 mins.
VHS: S29816. $9.95.

Richard Scarry's Now I Know My 1 2 3's.
VHS: S31701. $9.95.

Richard Scarry's Sally's First Day at School. Three stories, collected on this video, follow the adventures of animated animals including cats, dogs, mice and an earthworm. Kids will get a kick out of these creatures and their ability to get through life's little crises. 25 mins.
VHS: S29815. $9.95.

Richard Scarry's Sergeant Murphy's Day Off and Two Other Stories. There are three stories from the popular cable television children's s show on this video. It contains more imaginative and colorful characters. 25 mins.
VHS: S25920. $9.95.

Richard Scarry's The Best Birthday Present Ever and Two Other Stories. In addition to the title story, this video of the popular Nick Jr. cable network cartoon show includes two other stories. Kids love these tales featuring a variety of talking animals. 25 mins.
VHS: S25919. $9.95.

Richard Scarry's The Best Spelling Bee Ever.
VHS: S31702. $9.95.

Richard Scarry's The First Halloween Ever. This very Scarry Halloween video features Richard Scarry's first Halloween title and two other stories. 25 mins.
VHS: S32064. $9.95.

Romper Room: Ask Miss Molly

Where do bananas come from? How do you count money? Where does Shamu the Killer Whale live? A fascinating introduction for children about the wonders of nature. 40 mins.
VHS: S06361. $14.98.

Romper Room: Kimble's Birthday

Miss Molly and friends give Kimble the Bear a birthday celebration complete with magic tricks, a pinata, and of course, a cake. A birthday present any pre-schooler will love. 30 mins.
VHS: S06362. $14.98.

Romper Room: Outta Space

The Romper Room gang investigates the stars, visits a spaceship, and interviews a real-life astronaut. An entertaining introduction to out-of-this-world wonders. 30 mins.
VHS: S06363. $14.98.

Rosenschontz: The Teddy Bears' Jamboree

These children's music pioneers perform 15 of their greatest hits on this video compilation. Kids will love the sing-alongs accompanied by ample teddy bear hugging, dancing and tossing. In fact, it's an interactive experience for the whole family. 62 mins.
VHS: S24207. $12.98.

Rosie's Walk and Other Stories

An over-eager fox stalks an innocent hen to a catchy barnyard tune. Winner of the CINE Golden Eagle award. Also includes *"Charlie Needs a Cloak", The Story about Ping* and *The Beast of Monsieur Racine*. 32 mins.
VHS: S14493. $19.95.

Sammy and Other Songs from Getting to Know Myself

Singer/songwriter Hap Palmer is back, encouraging the audience to join in this exploration of body movement and feelings. This movement participation video gets kids to stretch, jump, and just enjoy the feeling of moving about. It also covers body image, the position of the body in space, identifying body parts, as well as moods and feelings.
VHS: S24627. $19.95.

Sesame Songs

Stories, games, songs and the wonderful Sesame Street crowd. 30 minutes each. Ages 2-6.

Sesame Songs: Dance Along! The Muppets and other Sesame Street characters demonstrate such dances as The Count's "Batty Bat" and Bert's favorite, "Doin' the Pigeon."
VHS: S12769. $9.98.

Sesame Songs: Elmo's Sing-Along Guessing Game. Kids sing along the clues as they try to guess the answers to Elmo's questions in this TV game show take-off. 1991.
VHS: S24628. $9.98.

Sesame Songs: Monster Hits! Ten *Sesame Street* hit songs performed by the loveable and furry monsters. Sing along with "C is for Cookie," "That Furry Blue Mommy of Mine" and "Fuzzy and Blue."
VHS: S12264. $9.98.

Sesame Songs: Rock & Roll! Sesame Street characters call in their requests to DJ Jackman Wolf. Songs include "Count up to Nine," and "The Word Is No."
VHS: S12768. $9.98.

Sesame Songs: Sing Yourself Silly! James Taylor is the musical guest for this potpourri of *Sesame Street*'s silliest songs, including the "Honker Duckie Dinger Jamboree," "The Everything Is in the Wrong Place Ball," "Jellyman Kelly" and the ever popular "Lady Bug Picnic." Also includes visits from Pete Seeger, Paul Simon and Rhea Perlman.
VHS: S12265. $9.98.

Sesame Songs: Sing, Hoot and Howl. Big Bird hosts such sing-along favorites as "Proud to Be a Cow," "The Insects in Your Neighborhood," and "Cluck Around the Clock."
VHS: S24629. $9.98.

Sesame Songs: Sing-Along Earth Songs. Join *Sesame Street*'s Grover to find out about the importance of protecting the earth.
VHS: S24649. $9.98.

Sesame Songs: We All Sing Together. The *Sesame Street* crowd is back! This time, Herry the anchor monster discovers the variety of shapes, colors and sizes of different kids. Full of songs, fun and favorite Sesame Street characters.
VHS: S24656. $9.98.

Sesame Street Home Video Visits

Pre-schoolers love Sesame Street's "get-acquainted" approach to making places like the firehouse and the hospital less frightening. 30 minutes each.

Sesame Street Visits the Firehouse. After Oscar's trash can catches on fire, the crew visits the firehouse.
VHS: S24634. $9.98.

Sesame Street Visits the Hospital. Big Bird is afraid when he has to go to the hospital; but after he finds out more, he feels better.
VHS: S24635. $9.98.

Sesame Street Kids' Guide to Life: Learning to Share

Elmo has trouble with learning to share. Fortunately, Big Bird, the Cookie Monster, Oscar, Elmo's best friend Zoe and special guest Katie Couric can teach him how. This video is a great way for kids to learn key values. It also includes a number of delightful songs.
VHS: S26913. $12.98.
Lisa Simon, USA, 1996, 45 mins.

Sesame Street Kids' Guide to Life: Telling the Truth

Telly learns that a little lie can become a big problem when he tries to impress his friends by telling them his uncle, special guest Dennis Quaid, is a ringmaster at the circus. Will his friends be mad when they learn the truth? Designed to help parents and kids smooth the sometimes bumpy road to growing up.
VHS: S30888. $12.95.
Lisa Simon, USA, 1997, 30 mins.

Sesame Street Presents: Follow That Bird!

Big Bird is lost—trying to get home to Sesame Street. With the help of his Muppet friends, he'll find his way, but not before he runs into meanies like Chevy Chase, John Candy, Joe Flaherty, and other special stars.
VHS: S04388. $19.98.
Laser: LD74702. $34.98.

Sesame Street Specials

Travel with Big Bird and the Sesame Street gang to exciting and often faraway places such as China, Japan and the Metropolitan Museum of Art in these award-winning Sesame Street specials.
Big Bird in China. Big Bird's desire to find the legendary Chinese phoenix bird leads him and Barkley, the dog, to an exciting adventure in China. Along the way, they visit with Chinese schoolchildren and learn some Chinese words and songs. 75 mins.
VHS: S05373. $12.98.
Big Bird in Japan. Join Big Bird and Barkley the Dog on their visit to Japan. Meet with Japanese people as well. 75 minutes.
VHS: S24633. $12.98.
Christmas Eve on Sesame Street. Holiday skits and songs, with Big Bird figuring out "How does Santa Claus, who is 'built like a dump truck', get down all those skinny little chimneys?" The whole gang is involved in this charming story which uncovers the true Christmas spirit. 60 mins.
VHS: S05379. $12.98.
Don't Eat the Pictures: Sesame Street at the Met. This one-hour musical follows the adventures of Big Bird, Snuffy, Cookie Monster, and the rest of the Sesame Street gang as they find themselves accidentally locked in the Metropolitan Museum overnight. 60 mins.
VHS: S05374. $12.98.
Put Down the Duckie. Sesame Street's Ernie learns to play the saxophone. Originally aired as a PBS special in 1988, this all-star musical combines Gladys Knight and the Pips, Danny DeVito, Patti LaBelle, Barbara Walters, James Taylor, Paul Simon and many other celebrities. 45 mins.
VHS: S23130. $12.98.
Sesame Street CelebratesAround the World. Join the party as the Sesame Street crowd celebrates New Year's Eve around the world: Mexico, Japan, Portugal, Israel, Norway and Germany. Shot on location, this video features a global New Year's Eve party filled with culturally diverse music and customs. Originally broadcast on New Year's Eve 1993, it features an appearance by Lily Tomlin. 60 mins.
VHS: S23129. $12.95.
Sesame Street's 25th Birthday:A Musical Celebration. A musical birthday party featuring an hour of musical favorites. Twenty musical numbers, including favorites like Ernie's "Rubber Duckie." Also includes new magic, like a finale with the South African *a capella* singing group Ladysmith Black Mambazo. Ages 4-7. 60 minutes.
VHS: S24636. $12.98.
DVD: DV60002. $24.95.

Sesame Street Start to Read Books

These videos are based on the popular "Start to Read Books" series. Large print permits children to read along with Big Bird, the well known Sesame Street character. Suitable for ages three and up. Each tape features three stories and is 30 minutes long.
Don't Cry Big Bird and Other Stories.
VHS: S21949. $14.95.
Ernie's Big Mess and Other Stories.
VHS: S21950. $14.95.
Ernie's Little Lie and Other Stories.
VHS: S21951. $14.95.
I Want to Go Home and Other Stories.
VHS: S21952. $14.95.

Sesame Street: Big Bird Sings!

Big Bird invites his pal Snuffy to look through his precious scrapbook. Snuffy is amazed at the array of memories recalled by photos, souvenirs and handmade trinkets. Kids will join right in the fun, especially the 11 sing-along songs. 30 minutes.
VHS: S26621. $12.98.

Sesame Street: Do the Alphabet

Baby Bear cannot remember all his letters. Big Bird has an amazing method including games, songs and special surprises that make learning the ABC's easy and fun. Kids learn best with the help of friends like Big Bird.
VHS: S26912. $12.98.
John Ferraro, USA, 1996, 45 mins.

Sesame Street: Elmo Saves Christmas

Wishing for even more Christmas, Elmo magically finds himself in a world where every day is Christmas. Though he makes a new friend, Lightning the reindeer, Elmo's wish may have given him more holiday cheer than he can bear. 55 mins.
VHS: S29849. $12.98.

Sesame Street: Elmocize

Elmo's exercise camp is a fun-filled place where kids play games with *Sesame Street* characters. Bending, stretching and hopping are made especially easy by the many featured catchy songs. 30 mins.
VHS: S27812. $12.95.

Sesame Street: Quiet Time

Big Bird loves to sing and dance and play, but when his Granny Bird tells him it's quiet time, he's not sure what to do. Fortunately Oscar, Telly, Rosita and his other Sesame Street friends have plenty of great ideas, like reading stories, playing quiet games and more. Special guest Daphne Rubin-Vega joins Big Bird to sing a special quiet time song. Come along to Sesame Street, where quiet time is fun time too.
VHS: S30887. $12.95.
Ted May, USA, 1997, 30 mins.

Sesame Street: Sing Yourself Sillier at the Movies

Oscar and Telly are the hosts of Sneak Peek Previews, where they review the silliest movies you've ever seen, featuring the silliest songs you've every heard. Will these daffy ditties rate a "wow" or a "phooey?" Telly and Oscar just can't agree. But one thing's for sure: with songs this silly, you'll have no choice but to sing yourself sillier.
VHS: S30889. $12.95.
Victor DiNapoli, USA, 1997, 30 mins.

Sesame Street: Slimey's World Games

Slimey the worm loses in the winter games but with the help of his coach, Oscar the Grouch, he manages to turn his sports career around. This entertaining children's video features lovable *Sesame Street* characters like Big Bird and memorable songs. 30 mins.
VHS: S27813. $12.95.

Shari Lewis: 101 Things for Kids to Do

A fun activity tape, including arts & crafts, games, magic tricks and more. 60 minutes.
VHS: S24642. $9.95.

Shari Lewis: Don't Wake Your Mom

This innovative program gives kids something to do for 45 minutes while a parent takes that needed break. With characteristic charm, Shari Lewis makes magic out of the classic question, "Is it time *yet*?" 45 mins.
VHS: S16158. $14.95.

Shari Lewis: Kooky Classics

Join Shari and friends as they tour the world of classical music, from Brahms to Mozart. 55 minutes.
VHS: S24641. $19.95.

Shari Lewis: Lamb Chop in the Haunted Studio

Shari Lewis and Lamb Chop are determined to film their show in a studio bedeviled by the hilarious antics of Count Dracula, Frankenstein and the Phantom. These monsters create an atmosphere of levity and make-believe scariness that is just right for children. 60 mins.
VHS: S26454. $12.95.

Sharon, Lois & Bram's Elephant Show

Featuring the veteran children's entertainers and a life-sized puppet elephant, this multiple award-winning series was designed to impart social skills, to strengthen preschool-age developmental abilities and to provide pre-reading and language experiences in a fun manner. Uses music, sing-along, games, live action, visits with real people, and on-location visits to interesting places. Each video is 30 minutes each.
Sleepover. 12 songs, including *Where's My Pajamas, Ham 'n Eggs* and *Ten in the Bed*. 30 mins.
VHS: S16491. $14.95.
Live in Your Living Room. 10 songs, including *Little Rabbit Foo Foo, Pufferbellies* and *Canadian Jig Medley*. 30 mins.
VHS: S16492. $14.95.
Back by Popular Demand...Live. 10 songs, including *Jelly, Jelly in My belly, Keep on the Sunny Side and Chugga-Chugga*. 30 mins.
VHS: S16493. $14.95.
Treasure Island. 9 songs, including *Lot's of Worms, Going over the Sea* and the *The Shanty Medley*. 30 mins.
VHS: S16494. $14.95.
Who Stole the Cookies? 10 songs, including *Cookie Jar, My Little Rooster* and *Apple Pickers Red*. 30 mins.
VHS: S16495. $14.95.
Soap Box Derby. 10 songs, including *Get Out and Get Under, Going to Kentucky* and *I'm a Little Piece of Tin*. 30 mins.
VHS: S16496. $14.95.
Pet Fair.
VHS: S24645. $14.95.
Radio Show.
VHS: S24646. $14.95.

Shelley Duvall's Bedtime Stories (Collection)

Seven of the best of these children's stories are joined in the special collection. Included are *Elbert's Bad Word, Weird Parents, Patrick's Dinosaurs, What Happened to Patrick's Dinosaurs, There's a Nightmare in My Closet, There's an Alligator Under my Bed* and *There's Something in My Attic*. 78 mins.
VHS: S23223. $39.98.

Shelley Duvall's Bedtime Stories: Aunt Ippy's Museum of Junk

Jodi and Jimi love visiting Aunt Ippy's shop, a hotbed of recycling and rebuilding. One day they explore the entire fascinating kingdom in search of a special object. Narrated by Kathy Bates. *Uncle Wizmo's New Car*, the story of Jodi and Jimi in a used car lot, is also included. Ed Begley, Jr., narrates. 26 mins.
VHS: S21806. $12.98.

Shelley Duvall's Bedtime Stories: Bootsie Barker Bites

Lisa has trouble playing with the beastly Bootsie. But one day, she turns the table on her biting friend. Narrated by Rhea Perlman. Then Shelley Long narrates *Ruby the Copycat*. Ruby copies the prettiest girl in class and learns an important lesson; it's better to be yourself. 26 mins.
VHS: S21805. $12.98.

Shelley Duvall's Bedtime Stories: Elbert's Bad Word and Weird Parents

Elbert's Bad Word: At a very proper party, little Elbert overhears a most improper word; then the word pops out of Elbert's mouth at the worst possible moment. Narrated by Ringo Starr. *Weird Parents*: Once there was a boy whose parents were so weird and kooky he was embarrassed to be seen with them, until he realized they were very special. Narrated by Bette Midler.
VHS: S16992. $12.95.

Shelley Duvall's Bedtime Stories: Elizabeth and Larry and Bill and Pete

Elizabeth and Larry: For years, Elizabeth and her pet alligator Larry were the best of friends. But when Larry discovers he doesn't look anything like Elizabeth, it causes an alligator identity crisis. Narrated by Jean Stapleton. *Bill and Pete*: On the banks of the river Nile, Bill the alligator and his pal Pete the Toothbrush Bird work together to keep Bill from being made into a suitcase. Narrated by Dudley Moore.
VHS: S16993. $12.95.

Shelley Duvall's Bedtime Stories: Little Toot and the Loch Ness Monster and Choo Choo

Little Toot and the Loch Ness Monster: Full of curiosity about creatures of the deep, the tugboat little Toot sails to Scotland to search for the Loch Ness Monster. Narrated by Rick Moranis. *Choo Choo*: Deciding to see the wide world for herself, a little steam engine runs away from the train yard. Narrated by Bonnie Raitt.
VHS: S16994. $12.95.

Shelley Duvall's Bedtime Stories: Moe the Dog in Tropical Paradise

Moe, the family dog, works at an ice cream factory in the frozen north. He and a friend dream of an expensive tropical holiday until Moe resourcefully finds a unique solution. Narrated by Richard Dreyfuss. Then Morgan Freeman narrates *Amos, The Story of an Old Dog and His Couch*. 26 mins.
VHS: S21771. $12.95.

Shelley Duvall's Bedtime Stories: My New Neighbors

Billy Crystal narrates this story about a young boy who meets his neighbors and discovers that they are very strange indeed. Also included is *Rotten Island*, a place where monsters and mayhem rule, narrated by Charles Grodin. 26 mins.
VHS: S21770. $12.95.

Shelley Duvall's Bedtime Stories: The Christmas Witch

Angela Lansbury narrates and Shelley Duvall hosts this animated tale about a witch who was no good at being bad. Instead, the witch decides to spread the spirit of Christmas. This delightful children's tale features three original holiday songs. 27 mins.
VHS: S26437. $12.98.

Shelley Duvall's Bedtime Stories: The Little Rabbit Who Wanted Red Wings

Shelley Duvall narrates this story of an imaginative rabbit who gets his wish for wings, only to discover that being yourself is really the best thing. *Katy No-Pocket* has a problem. She's a mother kangaroo with no pouch for her baby, until she finds the perfect all-purpose pocket. Narrated by Mary Steenburgen. 26 mins.
VHS: S21804. $12.98.

Shelley Duvall's Bedtime Stories: Tugford Wanted to be Bad

This animated feature follows Tugford the mouse in his adventures to be like the bad guys in the movies. But his outlaw scheme backfires and he almost foils his own birthday party. Narrated by Steve Martin. *Little Penguin's Tale*, narrated by Candice Bergen, is also included. It's the story of a penguin who almost meets disaster. 26 mins.
VHS: S21769. $12.95.

Shelley Duvall's Tall Tales and Legends

This hour-long program from the creator of the beloved *Faerie Tale Theatre* features celebrities such as Elliot Gould, Beverly D'Angelo, Jamie Lee Curtis, Brian Dennehy, Carol Kane, Steve Guttenberg, Martin Mull, Martin Short, Randy Newman, Ed Asner and Molly Ringwald in stories ranging from *Johnny Appleseed* and *Casey at the Bat* to *Annie Oakley* and *The Legend of Sleepy Hollow*.
VHS: S25784. $54.98.

Sign Songs: Fun Songs to Sign and Sing

Sign language can enhance the learning of all children. This is a great tape for kids, who can learn new songs/new signs and sign-along. Eleven delightful songs by Ken Longquist, who sings and plays guitar, are signed by John Kinstler. 29 minutes.
VHS: S24983. $49.95.

Simon the Lamb

Simon the lamb turns bright blue. The rest of the flock reject him because he's different. Find out how they come to accept him.
VHS: S24936. $12.95.

Simply Magic: Episode 2

Joanie Bartell is an substitute teacher who leads students on journeys to different places, times and planets.
VHS: S24648. $14.98.

Simply Magic: The Rainy Day Adventure

Joanie Bartell leads a sing-along program about a poolside party and a magical car. 1993. Ages 3-10. 45 minutes.
VHS: S24647. $14.98.

Smile for Auntie and Other Stories

Smile for Auntie is the hilarious tale of silly Auntie who sings, dances, does anything to make a baby smile. Other films are *Make Way for Ducklings, The Snowy Day*, and *Wynken, Blynken and Nod*.
VHS: S01218. $19.95.

Spot Goes to School

The pages of Eric Hill's best-selling pop-up books come to life in this charming program. In the first of five stories, new student Spot learns just how much fun going to school can be. 30 minutes, from Walt Disney Home Video.
VHS: S22974. $14.99.

Stories to Remember: Bedtime

Judy Collins sings 17 lullabies to music by Ernest Troost. This fully animated video is just right for those before-bedtime moments, especially for preschoolers.
VHS: S27401. $9.95.

Stories to Remember: Rhymin' Time!

Phylicia Rashad (*The Cosby Show*), accompanied by the music of Jason Miles, sings 36 nursery rhymes on this video. Animated shorts, adapted from the books of Kay Chorao, accompany this episode of the *Stories to Remember* series.
VHS: S27399. $9.95.

Stories to Remember: Singing Time!

Judy Collins sings 18 poems to beautifully animated films. The soothing imagery is perfect for children ages five and under. This series has won seven Parent's Choice Awards and is widely known through the Disney Channel. Music by Ernest Troost.
VHS: S27398. $9.95.

Stories to Remember: Storytime!

Arlo Guthrie sings and tells 11 charming children's stories. This fully animated video is a terrific source of entertainment for preschoolers.
VHS: S27400. $9.95.

The Storytellers Collection

With its entertaining blend of regional and ethnic sources, this unique collection of stories told by four of America's most accomplished storytellers offers an enchanting look at a tradition as old as the spoken word. Four volumes.
Animal Stories. A cast of lovable creatures with lessons. 30 mins.
VHS: S14775. $14.95.
Magic Tales. Enter a world of fantasy and moonlight. 30 mins.
VHS: S14773. $14.95.
Scary Stories. Creepy creatures and slithery slimies. 30 mins.
VHS: S14774. $14.95.
Tall Tales, Yarns and Whoppers. Featuring giant animals and superhuman feats. 30 mins.
VHS: S14772. $14.95.
Complete four-volume set.
VHS: S14776. $59.80.

The Tailor of Gloucester

A mixture of dance and Christmas carols enlivens this story of a tailor who falls ill just as an important garment must be completed. The tailor takes to his bed, and a host of little creatures manage to finish his work and save the day. 45 mins.
VHS: S29978. $19.98.

Tales of Beatrix Potter

These animated cartoons bring the delightful antics of Peter Rabbit directly to kids. They will love his adventures in the beautiful English countryside, modeled on the illustrations of Beatrix Potter. 43 min.
VHS: S24496. $12.98.

Tales of Beatrix Potter: Vol II

This is a delightful, animated collection of stories featuring the tiny creatures of the English countryside as only Beatrix Potter can imagine them. Peter Rabbit is always up to some mischief in the garden. 46 mins.
VHS: S24497. $12.98.

Tawny Scrawny Lion's Jungle Tales

These Golden Book favorites are back, now on video. This tape includes the classics *The Saggy Baggy Elephant, The Tawny Scrawny Lion* and *Rupert the Rhinoceros*. 30 minutes.
VHS: S25002. $5.95.

Teddy Bears' Jamboree

Gary Rosen and Bill Shontz present 15 of their greatest hits live in concert. Great humor and smart songs entertain the live concert audience of kids, parents and bears. Ages 1-10. 60 minutes.
VHS: S24653. $12.98.

The Teddy Bears' Picnic

The teddy bears come alive to a party in the forest for one day each year. This time a real girl, Amanda, gets to attend. Ages 4-8. 30 minutes.
VHS: S24652. $9.95.

Teletubbies

Tinky, Winky, Dipsy, Laa-Laa and Po live over the hills in Teletubbyland, where anything can happen. When the wind blows, a magic windmill brings pictures from far away, joining the Teletubbies to the world of real children celebrating the joy of play. 60 mins.
Teletubbies—Dance with the Teletubbies
VHS: S35236. $14.95.
Teletubbies—Here Come the Teletubbies
VHS: S35237. $14.95.

There Goes a Boat

Come with Captains Becky and Dave into the wonderful world of big ships in this fascinating voyage of discovery for children about tankers, freighters, passenger ships and submarines.
VHS: S23006. $10.95.

There Goes a Bulldozer

A children's video which features a live action introduction to heavy construction. Foreman Dave guides youngsters around the heavy earth-moving machinery that shapes our environment. 30 mins.
VHS: S20605. $10.95.

There Goes a Fire Truck

Fireman Dave indulges children's fascination with all the trappings of fire fighting, including fire department trucks, boats, and even helicopters. 30 mins.
VHS: S20606. $10.95.

There Goes a Helicopter

Becky and Dave take kids on an adventure to the world of whirly gigs. Helicopters can rise straight up in the air and fly at fantastic speeds. This makes choppers ideal for the military, and is vital to saving lives. Ages 3-8, 35 mins.
VHS: S24487. $12.95.

There Goes a Monster Truck

Becky and Dave take kids on the wildest ride imaginable. These monster trucks are powerful; they can even crush cars. And yet this video is completely safe. Ages 3-8, 35 mins.
VHS: S24489. $12.95.

There Goes a Motorcycle

Kids will get a front row seat along with Becky and Dave as they explore these two-wheeled motorized machines. It's all here from stunt bikes to racing. Ages 3-8, 35 mins.
VHS: S24486. $12.95.

There Goes a Police Car

Officers Becky and Dave lead children through the paces that these hard-working cars endure everyday. Kids will be thrilled to see the inside of these vehicles that serve the nation's lawmakers as they do their duty. 35 mins.
VHS: S21253. $10.95.

There Goes a Race Car

The green flag goes down and the action never stops as drivers Becky and Dave learn about race cars and the people who make them go.
VHS: S23007. $10.95.

There Goes a Spaceship

Astronauts Becky and Dave visit the Kennedy Space Center and Space Camp, experience the challenges of living in space and find out what it takes to be a NASA astronaut.
VHS: S23008. $10.95.

There Goes a Train

Engineer Dave stars in this videotape aimed at children. Kids will learn in this fun but educational tape about the ways trains work, how they travel and how they are powered, as well as the ins and outs of the job. 35 mins.
VHS: S21251. $10.95.

There Goes a Truck

Dave is joined by Becky in this jaunt aboard a large truck, capable of traveling many miles with a heavy load. These machines carry nearly everything we use. Kids will be fascinated by their power and the ingenuity of their design as well as the romance of the road. 35 mins.
VHS: S21254. $10.95.

There Goes an Airplane

Flying with Pilot Dave is fun and kids will learn things too, including how these wonders of the modern age achieve the miracle of flight. Jet fighters are among the most exciting aircraft available today. 35 mins.
VHS: S21252. $10.95.

Things That Fly Sing-Alongs

Everything from hot air balloons to helicopters to hang gliders to rockets are explored by Kermit the Frog and his friends in this video. All "song barriers" are broken as Kermit and his friends sing seven delightful and original Muppet sing-alongs.
VHS: S27435. $12.99.
Brian Henson, USA, 1996, 30 mins.

Thomas the Tank Engine & Friends

From *Shining Time Station*, the award-winning PBS children's show that is heralded for presenting a fascinating learning environment, filled with positive values. Very young kids everywhere have fallen in love with Thomas the Tank Engine, whose character was popularized in *The Railway Series* written by Rev. W. Awdry.
Trust Thomas & Other Stories. 40 mins.
VHS: S16485. $12.98.
Thomas Gets Tricked & Other Stories. 40 mins.
VHS: S16486. $12.98.
James Learns a Lesson & Other Stories. 40 mins.
VHS: S16487. $12.98.
Tenders & Turntable & Other Stories.
VHS: Out of print. For rental only.
Thomas Breaks the Rules & Other Stories.
VHS: Out of print. For rental only.
Better Late than Never & Other Stories. 40 mins.
VHS: S16490. $12.98.
Perry's Ghostly Trick & Other Thomas Stories. This wonderful children's video is from the wildly successful series featuring Thomas the Tank Engine.
VHS: S21986. $12.98.

Thomas' Christmas Party & Other Favorite Stories. George Carlin is the storyteller for this special animated video. It joins eight stories featuring the charming train engine Thomas. Two are for Christmas while the other six are sturdy favorites.
VHS: S21987. $12.98.
Rusty to the Rescue. This collection of stories features Thomas the Tank Engine and his assorted friends as they engage in a variety of live-action animation adventures. Perfect for kids. 37 mins.
VHS: S23966. $12.98.
The Special Letter and Other Stories. These new, animated adventures featuring the charming locomotive Thomas the Tank have never been shown on TV. Kids will love visiting the Island of Sodor to see Thomas and the gang, including Rusty, Sir Handel, Daisy and all the rest. Features a host of great songs. 37 mins.
VHS: S26212. $12.98.
Thomas & His Friends Help Out. This special hour-long collection features the best stories in which Thomas and his pals learn to help others. George Carlin tells the stories in which the pack of train friends help a group of villagers stranded in a snowstorm, Percy brings Annie and Clarabel safely through a thunderstorm, and James pulls his own when he helps out a very long train that's in trouble. From Thomas' *Helping Collection*. Directed by David Mitton, USA, 1993, 60 mins.
VHS: S27309. $12.98.
The Gallant Old Engine and Other Thomas Stories. Thomas and his friends, Percy, Stuart, Falcon, Duke and Henry, are all featured in this video. Whether it involves saving a stuck elephant or carrying passengers home during a dangerous storm, this collection of stories will enthrall children. 35 mins.
VHS: S29965. $12.98.
Get Along. Thomas, Sir Topham Hatt, Percy and their friends have learned many lessons about working together. They have selected their favorite stories to create this collection about getting along with each other. Narrated by George Carlin. 56 mins.
VHS: S33227. $12.98.

Three Sesame Street Stories
Included in this collection are three tales, starring Big Bird, Oscar the Grouch and the Cookie Monster. 30 minutes.
VHS: S24991. $5.95.

Thumpkin and the Easter Bunnies
The lovable and charismatic Bumbling Thumpkin is the centerpiece of this warmhearted and endearing family classic about the heroic quest for the original Easter egg hunt. 26 mins.
VHS: S18021. $12.95.

Timmy's Special Delivery
Timmy the Angel is touched when a brother and sister make their Christmas wish—that the other will receive a gift. 30 minutes.
VHS: S25003. $12.95.

To Bathe a Boa
A clever boa tries all kinds of evasive techniques in order to avoid a bath. Children may very well recognize someone very familiar as they read along to this fun, rhyming video. 8 mins.
VHS: S22355. $39.95.

Today Was a Terrible Day
Based on the book by Patricia Reilly Giff. On a day with one mishap after another, young Ronald finally has a reason to smile, when he discovers he can read by himself. 8 minutes.
VHS: S24655. $37.95.

Treasury of Children's Stories: Stories to Help Us Grow
Beginning with an alligator who learns not to be scared of the dark, this collection of three delightfully illustrated stories shows how other friendly animals deal with common problems of insecurity. 25 mins.
VHS: S10315. $29.95.

Trolls and the Christmas Express
Children will be charmed by this wonderful animated video in which mischievous trolls bring some humbug into Santa's workshop. 1981, 25 mins.
VHS: S13043. $12.95.

Truck Song
Diane Siebert celebrates trucks and truckers with rhymed verse that evokes the driving rhythm of a transcontinental truck journey. 13 mins.
VHS: S22370. $49.95.

Tubby the Tuba
Dick Van Dyke and Pearl Bailey provide the voices for this charming animated feature. It's based on the popular children's album about a tuba who performs in the Great Orchestra. He is frustrated with playing only "oompahs," so he sets off into the world and strikes it big in the circus.
VHS: S25889. $12.95.
Alexander Schure, USA, 1977, 81 mins.

Waltzing Matilda
Animated clay animals sing this famous Australian folk song. Kangaroos, koalas, emus and many other bush inhabitants sing along. 8 mins.
VHS: S23455. $49.95.

Water Is Wet
A very special children's film produced by the Erikson Institute for Early Childhood Education which was made to engage the imaginations and learning spirit of urban and rural pre-schoolers who weren't pre-disposed by their home environment to "learn" in the classroom. *Water Is Wet* is a visual and auditory exploration of simple elements, always striving to engage the child's imagination and sense of discovery in learning more about them. The film's unique accomplishment is to do so in a fun, fast-paced way, engaging the child on his/her own level.
VHS: S03490. $39.95.
Gordon Weisenborn, USA, 1968, 65 mins.

We Learn About the World
Available in both an English and a Spanish version, this tape introduces young viewers into the world of shapes, colors, feelings, and concepts of big and little numbers.
English Version.
VHS: S06727. $29.95.
Spanish Version.
VHS: S06728. $29.95.

Welcome Back Wil Cwac Cwac
Everyone's favorite little duckling is back with a waddle and a quack as Wil Cwac Cwac and his barnyard buddies share delightful lessons about love, friendship and growing up. Animated. 40 mins.
VHS: S11601. $14.95.

What Do You Want to Be When You Grow Up? Heavy Equipment Operator
Kids learn all about the big machines that go into heavy construction, including bulldozers, scrapers, excavators, backhoes and more. It's all here, from moving mountains of earth to transporting tons of steel overhead. 30 mins.
VHS: S23980. $15.95.

What Do You Want to Be When You Grow Up? Railroaders
Three kids, Allison, Armondo and Jacob, go for a train ride and learn all about engines, boxcars, flatcars, hoppers, tankers and more. They talk with engineers, brakemen, switchmen and even tie gangs. Perfect for kids fascinated with trains. 30 mins.
VHS: S23981. $15.95.

What's Under My Bed and Other Creepy Stories
Four animated films, all of which are scary adaptations of children's books: *What's under My Bed* by James Stevenson, narrated by Barnard Hughes; *The Three Robbers* by Tomi Ungerer; *Georgie*, by Robert Bright; and *Teeny-Tiny and the Witch-Woman*, by Barbara Walker, illustrated by Michael Foreman. 35 mins.
VHS: S13332. $19.95.

Where the Wild Things Are/ Higglety Pigglety Pop!
Two delightful one-act operas taped live at Glyndebourne Festival Opera are joined in this title. Both feature the stories and designs of Maurice Sendak, acclaimed children's book author. The first introduces Max the lovable monster, while the second features the adventures of Sendak's own pet terrier. 105 mins.
VHS: S22947. $29.97.
Laser: LD74645. $34.97.

Where's Spot
This is a well-regarded set of stories featuring a puppy who has entertaining adventures. Based on the books by Eric Hill, the six stories on the tape include *Spot Goes Splash* and *Spot Finds a Key*. Ages 2-4. 30 minutes.
VHS: S24657. $14.99.

Who Will Be My Friend?
A film which helps kids deal with starting school. Molly brings her toy dinosaur to school. Conflict resolution, full of songs and stories. 25 minutes.
VHS: S24659. $9.95.

Winnie the Pooh
Using the original illustrations of E.H. Shepard, this video includes four stories from the classic A.A. Milne books. 60 mins.
VHS: S13206. $14.98.

Winnie the Pooh: Clever Little Piglet
Pooh misplaces Piglet, and the search is on in *Where, Oh Where Has My Piglet Gone?*. Piglet masters his fears to bravely save his dearest friend in *Gone With the Wind*. Then, learn why being a hero is hard work in *My Hero*. In *Owl Feathers*, Owl takes heart when he takes flight, thanks to Piglet's confidence in his friend's ability to fly. 44 mins.
VHS: S34276. $12.95.

Winnie the Pooh: Imagine That, Christopher Robin!
Pooh invites children to share in the lessons of these heartwarming tales that express the value of friendship. After cloud watching with Christopher Robin, Pooh thinks he's broken the sky in *Pooh Skies*. Then, in *Oh, Bottle*, Pooh and company rescue Captain Robin and it'll be smooth sailing ever after. And in *Up, Up, and Awry* best friends stick together to save Pooh from himself by locking him up for breaking the law of gravity. 44 mins.
VHS: S34274. $12.95.

Winnie the Pooh: Making Friends, Learning
Three stories with Pooh, Piglet and Tigger. About "sharing, caring and growing up." Animated. Ages 1-5.
VHS: S24660. $12.99.
USA, 27 mins.

Winnie the Pooh: Three Cheers for Eeyore & Rabbit!
Thinking Rabbit gave Eeyore a worthless old seed, his friends try to stem his disappointment in *Eeyi, Eeyi, Eyore*. Then, *The New Eeyore* hopes some of Tigger's popularity will rub off on him until he realizes that not being himself rubs his friends the wrong way. After discarding his favorite bunny bookend in *Honey for a Bunny*, Rabbit thinks he's found his mate, or has he? Then chaos reigns at home and garden when *Rabbit Takes a Holiday*. 44 mins.
VHS: S34275. $12.95.

Winnie the Pooh: Un-Valentine's Day
Winnie the Pooh and his pals are set on celebrating Valentine's Day by giving each other cards, but Rabbit insists they cancel the holiday. Last year too much litter was generated by these notes of affection. This video also has a version of *The Three Little Piglets*. 30 mins.
VHS: S27365. $12.95.

The Witch Who Turned Pink
Spooky witches, pet werewolves, singing pumpkins and a clairvoyant owl come together to create this animated tale of Halloween magic. USA, 24 mins.
VHS: S15220. $14.95.

The Witch's Hat
A witch's magical brew turns out to be a mischief maker. What is the witch to do when the pot plays tricks on her? A delightful story by Tony Johnston thoughtfully illustrated by Margot Tomes.
VHS: S16360. $44.95.

The World of Baby Animals
This two-volume set contains videos about a variety of young creatures. Every kind of animal is shown, from bobcats and kangaroos to elephant seals, bison and horned owls. Six award-winning cinematographers made it possible. 100 mins.
VHS: S25062. $29.95.

World of David the Gnome: Rabbits, Rabbits Everywhere
From the pages of Will Huygen's best-selling book, an enchanting, magical adventure with Tom Bosley as the voice of David the Gnome, the world's smallest doctor. 45 mins.
VHS: S09893. $14.95.

Xuxa Celebration with Cheech Marin
The fun starts with a cheery tune-filled tale about a kooky school bus ride courtesy of Cheech Marin. Then Xuxa's own games begin. Watch out for the gooey Gloop. Learn how to build a monster with Xuxa or do the Xuxa Cha-cha. In addition kids will learn about the planets, the moon, hawks and owls and much more.
VHS: S20665. $14.98.

Xuxa: Fantastic Birthday Party
Xuxa is the world's most famous children's entertainer, from Brazilian television. Her kinetic energy inspires peppy song and dance numbers which will entertain everyone, especially kids. This blond dynamo will make any birthday memorable. 40 mins.
VHS: S20664. $14.98.

Yes, I Can Help
Kermit helps his nephew Robin learn all about the world and how to fit in. It all began when Kermit was a Muppet Baby. These reminiscences offer perfect, insightful lessons for preschoolers. 30 mins.
VHS: S25915. $12.99.

Yes, I Can Share
Kermit shares more memories of his Muppet Baby days with his young nephew Robin. 30 mins.
VHS: S25916. $12.99.

You Can Do It
Shari Lewis uses her delightful puppets, Lamb Chop, Hush Puppy and Charley Horse, to help her teach kids how to make their own puppet shows and magic tricks. USA, 1984, 60 mins.
VHS: S04441. $19.95.

The Z Was Zapped
Chris Van Allsburg presents a trip through the alphabet with the help of vivid verbal descriptions and three-dimensional drawings. Whimsical and sophisticated, this is an educational program that will keep children on their toes.
VHS: S14191. $44.95.

Zeezel the Zowie Zoon in the Color Chase
Kids will love following Zeezel on his imaginative, fun-filled chase to recapture his missing colors. This exciting live action short contains live singing and dancing, as well as vivid animation. 30 mins.
VHS: S24859. $12.98.

Ziggy's Gift
Ziggy, one of the most popular children's characters, comes to home video in a stocking-stuffer price.
VHS: S01580. $24.95.

Zoobilee Zoo
This Emmy Award-winning series hosted by Ben Vereen uses stories to encourage and educate children about their own self-worth. Endorsed by the American Federation of Teachers and recommended by the National Education Association each tape contains three full episodes.
Blue Ribbon Zooble and Other Stories. Learning that honesty is its own reward or discovering that even when it's difficult, doing the right thing is worth the effort, are just some of the lessons brought up by the Blue Ribbon Zooble. Children will see that accepting friends means accepting their similarities and differences. 70 mins.
VHS: S20676. $9.95.
Land of Rhymes & Other Stories. Favorite childhood singalongs like "Old MacDonald Had a Farm," and "Three Blind Mice" can teach youngsters about rhymes. Most importantly they will learn the value of listening to friends. 70 mins.
VHS: S20672. $9.95.
A Sticky Situation and Other Stories. Making mistakes is a normal part of learning, a lesson easily garnered from the Zoobles when they accidentally get glued together. Children will also love Backwardville, where everything is done backwards. 70 mins.
VHS: S20675. $9.95.
Zooble Hop and Other Stories. Children will be keen to get up and dance the Zooble dance steps, but they will also understand that even those who can't dance should be treated nicely. Doing something for yourself and not having someone do it for you is another lesson found in this interactive tape.
VHS: S20674. $9.95.

WONDERWORKS

African Journey
In this fast-paced adventure, Luke, a high school student from Canada, and Themba, an African youth, forge a lasting friendship despite their vastly different cultures. With Jason Blicker, Alan Jordon, Pedzisai Sithole and Eldinah Tshatedi. 174 mins.
VHS: S15785. $79.95.

Almost Partners
Teenager Molly McCue finds herself enmeshed in New York City's biggest mystery when she joins forces with a reluctant police detective. Their unlikely partnership develops into a special friendship. With Paul Sorvino and Royana Black. 58 mins.
VHS: S14480. $29.95.

And the Children Shall Lead
In this compelling story taken from our recent history, a young black girl is profoundly moved by the coming of the civil rights movement to her sleepy Mississippi town. Starring Danny Glover, Levar Burton and Denise Nicholas. From the Rainbow Television Workshop. 60 mins.
VHS: S12404. $14.95.

The Boy Who Loved Trolls
More than anything, 12-year-old Paul wishes that all the wonderful stories he reads about trolls and mermaids and far away kingdoms could be real. Imagine his amazement when one day a loveable old troll named Ofoeti appears and transports him to a fabulous fantasy world. Starring Sam Waterston and Susan Anton. 58 mins.
VHS: S14481. $29.95.

Bridge to Terabithia
Katherine Paterson's powerful story about a poor boy and an imaginative girl who share a secret hiding place they call Terabithia. But their friendship is severed when she is accidentally killed. 33 mins.
VHS: S13235. $14.95.

Brother Future
A slick, inner-city kid from Detroit named T.J. is knocked unconscious while fleeing the police. He wakes up in 1822 Charleston, South Carolina, where he is taken captive as a slave. Before he can get home, T.J. must learn some hard lessons about life and what it takes to keep the dream of freedom alive. USA, 1991, 110 mins.
VHS: S15786. $29.95.

Caddie Woodlawn
This fanciful story is based on the Newbery Award-winning book by Carol Ryrie Brink. A high-spirited frontier girl actively opposes warlike frontiersmen who try to ambush a Native American tribe. Ages 8 and up, 120 mins.
VHS: S24275. $19.95.

The Canterville Ghost
Strange, unexplained occurrences in an old English manor are turning the Otis family's dream vacation into a nightmare. One night they meet the long-dead Sir Simon de Canterville—and discover just how cowardly a ghost can be. Starring Richard Kiley. 1991, 58 mins.
VHS: S14483. $14.95.

The Chronicles of Narnia
This video collection features the magical land of Narnia, with its mythical creatures, menacing villains and marvelous heroes. Based on the wonderful series of books by C.S. Lewis.
Prince Caspian and the Voyage of the Dawn Treader. The magical land of Narnia is ruled by the corrupt King Miraz. His nephew Prince Caspian calls on Lucy, Peter, Susan and Edmund to help him defeat Miraz and restore Narnia to its former glory. Their adventure leads them to a golden lake, a giant sea serpent, a fierce dragon, and finally the edge of the world. A WonderWorks/BBC co-production starring Richard Dempsey, Sophie Cook, and Jonathon Scott. Great Britain, 174 mins.
VHS: S14158. $29.95.
The Lion, the Witch, and the Wardrobe. In a strange castle in the English countryside, four children open the door of an old wardrobe—and find themselves transported to the magical kingdom of Narnia. The children discover that the evil White Witch has turned all of her enemies to stone, and they are the only ones capable of defeating her. A WonderWorks/ BBC co-production starring Barbara Kellerman, Richard Dempsey, and Sophie Cook. Great Britain, 174 mins.
VHS: S14157. $29.95.
The Silver Chair. In this best-selling adaptation of the C.S. Lewis classic novel, two school friends enter the land of Narnia, where they meet the lion-king Alsan, who has a special, risky request. *The Chicago Tribune* calls this BBC production "first-rate entertainment." 174 mins.
VHS: S14159. $29.95.
The Chronicles of Narnia, Complete Set. Set of three 2-tape volumes.
VHS: S19403. $79.95.

City Boy
Adapted from Gene Stratton Porter's novel *Freckles*, this children's work is about a young man who leaves Chicago and unexpectedly finds romance in the majestic forests of the Pacific Northwest. Set at the turn of the century, the film explores the relevant issues involved in the heated conflict between loggers and conservationists. With Christian Campbell, James Brolin and Christopher Bolton.
VHS: S19508. $29.95.
John Kent Harrison, Great Britain/Canada, 1993, 120 mins.

Clowning Around
14-year-old Sim has grown up in a series of foster and welfare homes. Although life was tough, his dream of becoming a world-class clown survived. Despite various odds and his new foster parents' objections, he is determined to make his dream a reality. Filmed on location in Australia and Paris, and featuring Clayton Williamson, Jean-Michel Dagory, Ernie Dingo and a special appearance by Van Johnson. 174 mins.
VHS: S16012. $29.95.

Clowning Around 2
This charming children's film continues the story of 16-year-old Sim, who isn't content to be just a traditional clown. The film is an emotional journey from Paris to Montreal and Australia, where Sim finally has the chance to own a circus and control his own destiny. With Clayton Williamson, Frederique Fouche, Jean-Michel Dagory and Ernie Dingo. 180 mins.
VHS: S19510. $29.95.

The Fig Tree
Upset by the mysterious passing of her mother, a nine-year-old girl lives unhappily with the fear of death. This live-action adaption of the Pulitzer Prize-winning short story by Katherine Anne Porter has been praised by *The New York Times* as "a memorable little gem." 58 mins.
VHS: S13524. $14.95.

Frogs!
In this whimsical sequel to the 1987 award-winning *Frog*, Gus, a would-be singer who was turned into a frog then restored to human form, once again disrupts the life of his friend Arlo. Now Arlo must deal with a wicked witch and a polluted city pond in addition to his own teenage trials and tribulations. Starring Shelley Duvall, Elliott Gould, Scott Grimes, Judith Ivey and Paul Williams. 116 mins.
VHS: S16009. $29.95.

A Girl of the Limberlost
A poetic adaptation of Gene Stratton Porter's sensitive study about a young girl's maturity in the rural countryside of the Midwest at the turn of the century. With Joanna Cassidy and Annette O'Toole. 111 mins.
VHS: S13239. $19.95.

Gryphon
With a little bit of magic, a substitute teacher in an inner-city school changes the life of a Hispanic boy. This film is based on a Charles Baxter short story with the message about "not dismissing people who care for you" (*Variety* magazine).
VHS: S13525. $14.95.

The Haunting of Barney Palmer
In this suspenseful tale of the supernatural, young Barney Palmer fears he has inherited the Scholar family curse when he is haunted by the spirit of his dead great uncle. But there is more here than meets the eye. His older sister Tabitha is guarding a shocking secret! Alexis Banas, Ned Beatty, Eleanor Gibson, Meridith Braun and Michelle Leuthart star. 58 mins.
VHS: S16014. $29.95.

Hector's Bunyip
When mistakenly placed in an orphanage, young Hector relies upon a giant imaginary best friend to return him to his family, in this PBS live-action movie. 58 mins.
VHS: S13526. $14.95.

Hiroshima Maiden
Susan Blakely and Richard Masur star in this moving drama inspired by a true story. After World War II, a group of young Japanese women called the Hiroshima Maidens were brought to live with American families while undergoing plastic surgery for scarring caused by the bomb. This is the gripping story of one such woman and the impact she has on her American family, particularly the young son. Winner of many international film and television awards. 60 mins.
VHS: S12398. $29.95.

Hoboken Chicken Controversy
When the Bobowicz family asked their son Arthur to pick up a turkey for Thanksgiving, they weren't expecting him to bring home a 266-pound live chicken named Henrietta. Neither was Hoboken, in this wild comedy from the multiple Emmy-award-winning production team. With Gabe Kaplan, Dick Van Patten and Peter Billingsley. 60 mins.
VHS: S12403. $14.95.

Home at Last
Billy, a streetwise kid from New York City, is sent to a Nebraska farm to live with a Swedish immigrant family. At first fearful and resentful, he rejects the Andersons until a crisis threatens them all, and Billy must find his inner strength to realize that he truly belongs. Based on the Orphan Trains which resettled children in the Midwest at the turn of the century. 58 mins.
VHS: S15789. $29.95.

The House of Dies Drear
The Small family discovers too late that their new home hides some dark and frightening secrets. Wait until Walter Small and his son Thomas uncover the murderous mysteries that still haunt the old house. Starring Howard Rollins, Gloria Foster and Moses Gunn. 116 mins.
VHS: S14484. $29.95.

How to Be a Perfect Person in Just Three Days

Based on Stephen Manes' hilarious book, this shrewd comedy studies the monumental fall and rise of a bright, gifted 12-year-old outsider who seeks help from the notorious Dr. K. Pinkerton. With Wallace Shawn and Ilan Mitchell-Smith.
VHS: S13236. $19.95.

Jacob Have I Loved

Based on the popular novel by Katherine Paterson. Bridget Fonda stars in this thoughtful study in sibling rivalry. Louise (Fonda) has always felt that her sister was the favored child and so sets out to find her own special place in her small world. Produced by KCET-TV. 60 mins.
VHS: S12396. $19.95.

Konrad

In this hilarious, heartwarming story, factory-made "instant child" Konrad is perfect in every way, and mistakenly delivered to the eccentric Mrs. Bartolotti. When the factory realizes its mistake, it demands Konrad's return, but his new mom has other ideas! With Max Wright, Polly Holliday, Huckleberry Fox and Ned Beatty. 116 mins.
VHS: S16010. $29.95.

The Little Princess

Based on the classic by Francis Hodgson Burnett, this is the story of Sara Crewe, the little rich girl forced into a life of poverty when her father dies penniless. Once the prize pupil at her boarding school, Sara becomes a servant for the cold-hearted school mistress and her heretofore jealous classmates. Three parts. Produced by London Weekend Television. 180 minutes total.
VHS: S12401. $29.95.

The Lone Star Kid

11-year-old Brian Zimmerman lives in Crabb, Texas—population 400. To obtain adequate police and emergency services, and to keep Houston from swallowing up the tiny burg, Brian decides to modernize his town. With the help of his parents and friends, young Brian makes history when he is elected mayor. Starring Chad Sheets, James Earl Jones and Charlie Daniels. 58 mins.
VHS: S16008. $29.95.

Maricela

A young girl struggles to find her place in American culture when her mother, who was a schoolteacher in El Salvador, must now work as a live-in housekeeper to an affluent family. Can Maricela fit in at her new home and school and still remain true to her old values? 58 mins.
VHS: S15787. $29.95.

The Mighty Pawns

An impassioned work about the efforts of an idealistic young teacher who offers valuable alternatives to inner city kids, the intricate, fascinating world of chess. Winner of the Silver Plaque at the 1987 Chicago International Film Festival. 60 mins.
VHS: S13238. $14.95.

Miracle at Moreaux

Loretta Swit stars in this compelling drama based on a true story. In World War II occupied France, a nun and her young charges risk their lives to harbor a group of Jewish children escaping from the Nazis. 60 mins.
VHS: S12402. $14.95.

My Friend Walter

While visiting the Tower of London, Bess encounters the ghost of her ancestor—Sir Walter Raleigh. Bess enlists Raleigh's help to save her family's farm. With Ronald Pickup, Prunella Scales and Polly Grant. 93 mins.
VHS: S19509. $29.95.

Necessary Parties

A fundamentally loving family is jeopardized when the parents decide to divorce. Fifteen-year-old Chris Mills is unable to accept his parents' decision and is determined to fight the divorce by legal means. He has learned in school that young people have rights too and he dares to claim those rights for himself with his six-year-old sister. With the help of an eccentric part-time lawyer/mechanic and the support of some good friends, Chris pleads to the court for the right to intervene in the divorce action as a "necessary party," thus forcing a situation that changes the course of all their lives. Alan Arkin, Barbara Dana and Adam Arkin star. 120 mins.
VHS: S12399. $19.95.

Runaway

Based on Felice Holman's novel *Slake's Limbo*, this film concerns the plight of a boy who retreats from society, living underground in the subway ducts underneath New York City's massive subway system for believing he caused the accidental death of a friend. With Charles S. Dutton, Jasmine Guy and Gavin Allen. 59 mins.
VHS: S13237. $14.95.

Spirit Rider

Adapted from Mary-Ellen Lang Collure's novel *Winners*, this quiet children's story focuses on the social dislocation experienced by Native American Jesse Threebears. Growing up in a series of foster homes, Jesse is reluctantly repatriated to the reservation where he was born. Both resisting change and struggling to fit in, Jesse travels the rocky road to forgiveness and acceptance. His journey climaxes in a thrilling horse race that will decide his future. With Herbie Barnes, Gordon Tootossis, Michelle St. John, Graham Greene and Adam Beach. 115 mins.
VHS: S19511. $29.95.

Sweet 15

Marta Delacruz is a typical American teenager who can't wait to wear makeup, date boys and be treated like an adult. In the Mexican tradition, when a girl turns 15, she is symbolically ushered into adulthood by a Mass and a party known as a Quinceanera. Samuel Delacruz (Tony Plana), Marta's hard-working, traditional father, is having a difficult time letting his little girl become a woman. But Marta is forced to grow up quickly when she accidentally discovers that her father has never become an American citizen. It is then that she realizes that becoming an adult means more than a festive Quinceanera. 120 mins.
VHS: S12400. $19.95.

Taking Care of Terrific

An imaginative teenager, her boyfriend, and a sheltered little boy team up with a street musician to plan a joyous evening for several bag ladies living in the local park. However, their well-intentioned efforts get them in trouble. Featuring Melvin Van Peebles as the street musician. 58 mins.
VHS: S15788. $29.95.

Walking on Air

Confined to a wheelchair, young Danny's greatest dream is to be able to fly. During a physical therapy class he discovers the wonderful feeling of weightlessness that swimming can bring. Taking his dream one more step, Danny fights friends, family and NASA so that he and his handicapped friends can become part of the space program. Starring Lynn Redgrave, this futuristic drama is based on a story by Ray Bradbury and won the Red Ribbon at the American Film Festival. 60 mins.
VHS: S12397. $14.95.

Waltzing Through the Hills

Andy and his little sister Sammy live in a small town in western Australia. When their mother dies, Andy fears he and Sammy might be separated. He resolves to take Sammy to their grandparents in England but in order to get to the boatyards in Perth, they must make a dangerous, secret journey through the wilds of the Australian outback. Winner of many international awards. 60 mins.
VHS: S12395. $19.95.

Words by Heart

In the early 1900's, Lena Sills and her parents are the only black people living in Bethel Springs, Missouri. When Lena wins a Bible recitation contest at school, the commandment "love thy neighbor" clashes with the townspeople's prejudice. Charlotte Rae and Robert Hooks star. 116 mins.
VHS: S14482. $29.95.

FEATURE FILMS FOR KIDS

Adventures of Milo and Otis

A live action children's adventure story about the exploits of Milo the dog and Otis the cat, narrated by Dudley Moore. Called "delightfully pure and fresh" by the *L.A. Times*. See for yourself how much mischief one canine and one feline can get into in the Land of the Rising Sun.
VHS: S11483. $19.95.
Masanori Hata, Japan/USA, 1989, 89 mins.

The Adventures of Pinocchio

Academy Award-winner Martin Landau *(Ed Wood)* and *Home Improvement* star Jonathan Taylor Thomas team up with the special effects magic of Jim Henson's Creature Shop to bring to life this popular family classic of the rambunctious puppet who longs to be a boy. Also stars Rob Schneider *(Men Behaving Badly)* and Bebe Neuwirth *(Cheers)*.
VHS: S30051. $19.98.
Steve Barron, USA, 1996, 94 mins.

Alice in Wonderland

An enchanting children's version of Lewis Carroll's story is remade as a vibrant musical by the Children's Theatre Company and School, under the direction of John Clark Donahue. Music by Hiram Titus.
VHS: S18990. $39.98.
John Driver, USA, 1982, 81 mins.

All I Want for Christmas

Leslie Nielsen and Lauren Bacall star in this story of a teenager and his younger sister whose ultimate Christmas gift would be for their divorced parents to reunite. 92 mins.
VHS: S30032. $14.95.

The Amazing Panda Adventure

Ryan Slater, brother of Christian Slater, stars opposite one of the world's most lovable creatures, the endangered Panda. This feature-length adventure film was shot on location in the wilds of mainland China. It tells how one boy struggles to save this miraculous creature from destruction.
VHS: S26931. $19.98.
Laser: LD75405. $34.98.
Christopher Cain, USA, 1995, 85 mins.

An American Tail 2-Pack

Features *An American Tail* and *An American Tail: Fievel Goes West*.
VHS: S34940. $32.95.

An American Tail

Follow the delightful, animated tale of Fievel, the brave little mouse who journeys from Russia to America with his family to seek a new life free from cat persecution. But when Fievel is lost at sea, he washes ashore in New York Harbor, where his amazing adventure is only beginning. With the voices of Dom DeLuise, Madeline Kahn, Christopher Plummer and Phillip Glasser.
VHS: S34939. $19.95.
Don Bluth, USA, 1986, 81 mins.

An American Tail: Fievel Goes West

In this rip-roaring adventure, our brave little hero Fievel is lured out west by the evil double-dealer Cat R. Waul, who plans to turn the settlers into mouse-burglars. But with the help of his friend Tiger, Fievel joins forces with the legendary lawdog Wiley Burp to try and stop the sinister scheme. With the voices of John Cleese, Dom DeLuise, Amy Irving and Phillip Glasser.
VHS: S34938. $19.95.
Phil Nibbelink/Simon Wells, USA, 1991, 75 mins.

Andre

This film is based on the book *A Seal Called Andre*, by Harry Goodridge and Lew Dietz. It tells the true story of a seal who befriends a harbor master and his family. Starring Tina Majorino, Keith Carradine and Chelsea Field.
VHS: S23435. $14.95.
Laser: Widescreen. **LD75148. $34.98.**
George Miller, USA, 1994, 94 mins.

Anne of Avonlea

The critically-acclaimed sequel to the award-winning *Anne of Green Gables*, with Colleen Dewhurst, Wendy Hiller and Megan Follows as Anne Shirley. "Destined to tug at hearts, young and old, for decades to come" *(San Francisco Chronicle)*.
VHS: S11443. $29.95.
Laser: LD70838. $39.99.
Kevin Sullivan, Canada, 1987, 224 mins.

Anne of Green Gables

A tender and humorous coming-of-age tale starring Anne Shirley and Tom Brown.
Laser: LD70839. $39.99.
George Nicholls, USA, 1934, 79 mins.

Any Friend of Nicholas Nickleby Is a Friend of Mine

Humorous tale of friendship based on a story by Ray Bradbury and set in a small Illinois town. Stars Fred Gwynne.
VHS: S02671. $59.95.
Ralph Rosenblum, USA, 1981, 55 mins.

Babe
Wonderful special effects make this film a magical and captivating experience that kids and adults can both enjoy. Babe, a pig, arrives on a farm where all the animals have a purpose. Through his ambitions, he makes friends among all the animals and changes forever the utilitarian view that would have destined him for the dinner table. George Miller *(Mad Max)* co-produced this wonderful barnyard fable.
DVD: DV60155. $24.98.
VHS: S27088. $14.98.
Laser: LD75448. $34.98.
Chris Noonan, USA, 1995, 92 mins.

Bach and Broccoli
A truly wonderful film for children—and family—from Andre Melancon, the director of *The Dog Who Stopped the War*, winner of the Best Film prize at the 1987 Chicago International Festival of Children's Films. In *Bach and Broccoli*, 11-year-old Fanny meets her uncle Jonathan for the first time. They are strong-willed, independent people who are worlds apart. Fanny's best friend, Broccoli, her pet skunk, adds to the hilarity in this humorous tale of the odd couple as they learn to love and need each other. Produced by Rock Demers.
VHS: S06616. $14.95.
Andre Melancon, Canada, 1987, 96 mins.

Baker's Hawk
Clint Walker and Burl Ives star in this family film that captures the essence of father-son relationships. Filmed in the mountains of Utah, the story is told through the eyes of a boy in the year 1876.
VHS: S00087. $39.95.
Lyman Dayton, USA, 98 mins.

Barney's Great Adventure—The Movie
Join Barney and his friends as they rush to find a special rainbow-colored egg before it hatches. Includes special effects and performances of some of Barney's all-time classic songs. You'll also get to meet Barney's newest friend, Twinken.
VHS: S34918. $22.95.
Steve Gomer, USA, 1998, 78 mins.

Beanstalk
This great kid's movie follows young Jack Taylor as he schemes to make it big. His chance comes when a wacky scientist (Margot Kidder) unloads her recently discovered seed pods on him. Soon an enormous beanstalk leads him on the path to riches and adventure. He never expected a family of giants, however.
VHS: S22902. $19.95.
Michael Paul Davis, USA, 1994, 80 mins.

Beethoven Lives Upstairs
It is 1820s Vienna, and Ludwig Van Beethoven is desperately trying to compose his Ninth Symphony. As he struggles to balance his musical obsession with the reality of his increasing deafness, Beethoven rents the upstairs flat in the depressed household of ten-year-old Christoph. He watches and listens as Beethoven swiftly turns his house into chaos.
VHS: S16706. $19.98.
David Devine, USA, 1990, 51 mins.

Beethoven's 2nd
Charles Grodin stars in this story of dog family life. Beethoven the St. Bernard meets Missy, and the result is a houseful of puppies. Sadly Missy is the pawn in a human divorce. Debi Mazar plays the cruel kidnapper who jeopardizes this young canine family. It's a perfect film for kids.
VHS: S21865. $19.95.
Laser: Letterboxed. **LD74933. $24.98.**
Rod Daniel, USA, 1993, 88 mins.

Benji
America's most lovable mutt, in his first feature film. Benji saves two kids from kidnappers and wins a home and a place in everyone's heart.
VHS: S04866. $19.99.
Joe Camp, USA, 1974, 86 mins.

Benji Takes a Dive at Marineland
America's huggable hero takes on Marineland, and comes up swimming.
VHS: S06342. $24.95.
Joe Camp, USA, 60 mins.

Benji the Hunted
The canine superstar is separated from his trainer Frank Inn and must survive by his wits in a wilderness section of the Pacific Northwest. In addition to looking out for his own well-being, he becomes the guardian of an orphaned litter of cougar pups and annoys a local woodsman.
VHS: S06831. $19.95.
Joe Camp, USA, 1987, 89 mins.

Benji's Very Own Christmas Story
Benji and his friends journey to a magical kingdom to meet Kris Kringle and learn how Christmas is celebrated all over the world.
VHS: S04452. $14.99.
Joe Camp, USA, 1983, 60 mins.

Bingo
Chuckie is a little boy separated from the dog he loves when his family moves from Denver to Green Bay. Fear not, Bingo is a most resourceful pooch and should be able to catch up, if he can only escape from the pound. With Robert J. Steinmiller, David Rasche and Cindy Williams.
VHS: S15667. $14.95.
Matthew Robbins, USA, 1991, 87 mins.

Black Beauty (1933)
Esther Ralston, Alex Kirkland and Hale Hamilton star in this film adaptation of Anna Sewell's delightful novel. A young girl comes to the rescue of an injured race horse. This noble beast touches all who come to know and respect his pristine character. A delight for children and adults alike.
VHS: S22601. $19.95.
Phil Rosen, USA, 1933, 70 mins.

Black Beauty (1971)
Based on the classic novel by Anna Sewell, *Black Beauty* is the story of a friendship between Mark Lester and his horse. Outstanding family entertainment.
VHS: S00136. $14.95.
James Hill, Great Britain, 1971, 105 mins.

Black Beauty (1994)
A superb British cast, including Sean Bean, David Thewlis and Andrew Knott, is featured in this most faithful film version of Anna Sewell's delightful novel. Children have always loved this story of an indomitable black horse who personifies freedom. Everyone who came into contact with this magnificent animal was touched by his spirit.
VHS: S22412. $19.98.
Laser: LD74605. $34.98.
Caroline Thompson, USA, 1994, 88 mins.

The Black Stallion
An exciting viewing experience for all ages, *The Black Stallion* follows the adventures of a young boy and his magnificent Arabian horse. With Teri Garr, Hoyt Axton and Mickey Rooney, presented by Francis F. Coppola.
DVD: DV60103. $24.98.
VHS: S00140. $19.95.
Laser: LD70527. $34.98.
Carroll Ballard, USA, 1979, 118 mins.

The Black Stallion Returns
A sequel to the popular *Black Stallion* in which Kelly Reno loses his horse in Morocco and only gets him back after a series of hair-raising adventures.
VHS: S12428. $19.98.
Laser: LD76194. $39.98.
Robert Dalva, USA, 1983, 93 mins.

Born Free
This wonderful story is based on the best-selling novel about a lioness raised in captivity. On the beautiful open savannah, a game warden is forced to kill a dangerous lioness. He and his wife adopt and raise one of her cubs until they realize this young lion must adapt to the wild.
VHS: S26177. $12.95.
James Hill, USA, 1965, 94 mins.

The Borrowers (1993)
Based on the best selling classic by Mary Norton, this wonderful children's film follows the adventures of a wee family who live under the floorboards of an English house until they decide to leave for the great outdoors. Starring Ian Holm and Sian Phillips, and hosted by Richard Lewis.
VHS: S21055. $14.98.
Laser: LD74461. $49.99.
John Henderson, Great Britain, 1993, 199 mins.

The Borrowers (1998)
John Goodman stars as evil realtor Ocious P. Potter, who battles the four-inch high people who live under the floorboards of a house he wants to destroy in order to build luxury apartments.
VHS: S34691. $22.95.
Laser: Dolby Digital. **LD77023. $39.99.**
DVD: DV60362. $24.95.
Peter Hewitt, USA, 1998, 86 mins.

The Brave Frog
A poor treefrog named Jonathon moves to the woodland community of Rainbow Pond and tries to fit in. With his musical reed pipe and his girlfriend Pookie, he battles cats, snakes and sea monsters, and most of all the selfish King Leopold. Dubbed in English.
VHS: S23330. $14.95.
Laser: LD74839. $34.95.
Tatsunoko/Harmony Gold, Japan, 1985, 90 mins.

Call of the Wild
Rick Schroeder and Mia Sara star in Jack London's classic tale of a young man's adventure in Alaska during the Yukon Goldrush in 1897.
VHS: S31845. $14.98.
Alan Smithee, USA, 1993, 97 mins.

Camel Boy
From the creator of *Dot and the Kangaroo*, an animated adventure story about the unique friendship between Ali, an Arabian boy, and his camel during a journey across the Great Victoria Desert in Western Australia.
VHS: S02703. $89.95.
Yoram Gross, Australia, 1984, 78 mins.

Care Bears Adventure in Wonderland
When an evil wizard kidnaps the Princess of Wonderland, the Care Bears join the characters of *Alice in Wonderland* to rescue her. Features the songs of John Sebastian.
Laser: LD75604. $34.95.
Nelvana, Canada, 76 mins.

Care Bears Movie II: A New Generation
A little girl is tricked into trapping the doting bears, but later has a change of heart when she learns the truth. Written by Peter Sander. Directed by Dale Schott.
VHS: S28034. $14.95.
Nelvana, Canada, 1986, 77 mins.

Casper
Amazing special effects render this tale of a friendly ghost more real and exciting than previous tales of good-humored haunting. Bill Pullman is a ghost therapist hired by a pair of greedy crooks, Eric Idle and Cathy Moriarty, to help rid a manor of spooks.
VHS: S26372. $22.98.
Laser: LD75078. $34.98.
Brad Silberling, USA, 1995, 101 mins.

Challenge to Lassie
This pleasant adventure with America's favorite collie involves a dispute over her ownership. Featuring solid performances from Edmund Gwenn, Geraldine Brooks, Reginald Owen, Sara Allgood, and, of course, Lassie.
VHS: S13640. $19.98.
Richard Thorpe, USA, 1949, 76 mins.

The Challengers
After the death of her father, 11-year-old Mackie Daniels moves to a small town. Even if life has not been fair to her, she has a plan for the future, and before long she has made new friends, joined a band and become a Challenger. Everything seems fine, or is it?
VHS: S21156. $89.95.
Eric Till, USA, 1989, 97 mins.

Charlotte's Web
E.B. White's classic novel is translated to the screen in this musical version. Voices by Paul Lynde, Henry Gibson, Debbie Reynolds and Agnes Moorehead.
VHS: S00230. $14.95.
Laser: LD75846. $34.95.
Hanna-Barbera, USA, 1973, 94 mins.

A Child's Christmas in Wales
A wonderful adaptation of Dylan Thomas' memories of Christmas in Wales, reliving the child's youth in one magical evening.
VHS: S07446. $12.98.
Don McBrearty, Canada, 1988, 55 mins.

The Children of Noisy Village
Before World War II, six boisterous children find adventure and old-fashioned fun around their home town of Noisy Village. Simply exploring the lush countryside of fields and woods inspires these kids to invent a slew of imaginative games. The result is a childhood grounded in seemingly endless possibilities. Based on the best-selling novel from author Astrid Lindgren, who also wrote *Pippi Longstocking*.
VHS: S28997. $24.95.
Lasse Hallstrom, Sweden, 1995, 88 mins.

Chitty Chitty Bang Bang
Dick Van Dyke is a slightly offbeat inventor in this modern fairy tale about a magical car. Charming songs, whimsical humor, wonderful special effects and enough suspense to make this a treat for the whole family.
VHS: S00236. $14.95.
Laser: Letterboxed, chapter search. Includes original theatrical trailer. **LD71647. $39.98.**
Ken Hughes, USA, 1968, 143 mins.

Christmas Story
Based on a novel by best-selling author Jean Shepherd, this slightly twisted tribute to the original, one-hundred-percent, red-blooded, two-fister American Christmas is set in Indiana during the 1940s and follows the adventures of Ralphie (Peter Billingsley) as he pursues the gift of his dreams. Roger Ebert called it "Norman Rockwell crossed with Mad Magazine."
VHS: S01832. $14.95.
Bob Clark, USA, 1983, 90 mins.

Clarence the Cross-Eyed Lion
Solid, old-fashioned family entertainment. This alternately comic and dramatic adventure story takes place in the jungles of Africa. Starring Betsy Drake, Richard Haydn, and Marshall Thompson.
VHS: S13642. $19.98.
Andrew Marton, USA, 1965, 98 mins.

Courage of Lassie
The lovable animal hero Lassie stars as a young pup who is rescued by a teenager (Elizabeth Taylor) and nursed back to health after being accidentally shot.
VHS: S16845. $19.98.
Fred M. Wilcox, USA, 1946, 93 mins.

The Crossbow
William Lyman is the reluctant hero William Tell, a man chosen by destiny to become a symbol of resistance against tyranny. Filmed among medieval castles and villages of Europe, *Crossbow* is a heroic adventure for all ages.
VHS: S31846. $14.98.
George Mihalka, USA, 1989, 92 mins.

Curly Top
Shirley Temple is the mop-topped charmer adopted by a millionaire in love with her beautiful sister. Shirley sings "Animal Crackers in My Soup."
VHS: S05899. $19.98.
Irving Cummings, USA, 1935, 74 mins.

The Deerslayer
The James Fennimore Cooper novel from his *Leatherstocking Tales* is presented as a family drama about two men from different cultures who rescue a Mohican princess. With Steve Forrest as Hawkeye and Ned Romero as Chingachgook.
VHS: S06866. $19.95.
Richard Friedenberg, USA, 1978, 98 mins.

A Dog of Flanders
A heartwarming children's story based on the novel by Ouida about a young child's desire to be a painter; the young boy and his grandfather find their lives changed significantly upon the arrival of a stray dog. Upon his grandfather's death, the boy calls upon the dog to help realize his potential.
VHS: S02523. $19.95.
James B. Clark, Great Britain, 1959, 96 mins.

Dot & Santa Claus
Dot travels around the world in search of her missing baby kangaroo. Along the way she finds the true meaning of Christmas.
VHS: S10742. $9.95.
Yoram Gross, Australia, 1979, 73 mins.

Dot & The Bunny
Dot tries to help out her friend Funnybunny, who wants to become a kangaroo.
VHS: S00361. $14.95.
Yoram Gross, Australia, 1982, 79 mins.

Ele, My Friend
A heartwarming children's tale about the unbreakable bond created when a small, shy boy must summon enough strength and courage to rescue his best friend, an endangered baby elephant known as Ele.
VHS: S19917. $89.95.
Dharan Mandrayar, India, 1993, 104 mins.

Far from Home: The Adventures of Yellow Dog
After a storm a teenage boy is washed ashore in the Pacific Northwest with only his dog. Together they make do in the wilderness even as the boy's family desperately tries to locate him. This is an entertaining, heartwarming film perfect for any age group.
VHS: S24853. $19.98.
Laser: Widescreen. **LD74979. $39.99.**
Phillip Borsos, USA, 1994, 81 mins.

Fearless Frida and the Secret Spies
Frida (Annette Brandt) is a curious little girl who always leads her friends into mischief. Armed with a camcorder, Frida and her friends accidentally discover truly illicit activity. Once they have the tape to prove it, these kids are under the gun to outwit the criminals. If they succeed they could become heroes. Dubbed in English.
VHS: S27166. $59.95.
Soren Ole Christensen, Denmark, 1995, 71 mins.

Five Weeks in a Balloon
An unlikely crew sets off on a daring balloon expedition across uncharted Africa, in this lighthearted version of a Jules Verne fantasy. Starring Cedric Hardwicke, Red Buttons, Fabian, and Peter Lorre.
VHS: S04602. $19.98.
Irwin Allen, USA, 1962, 101 mins.

Flipper
Set in the Florida Keys and starring an incredibly talented dolphin, this adventure is the story of a fisherman's son who befriends a dolphin. With Chuck Connors, Luke Halpin.
VHS: S12427. $19.98.
James B. Clark, USA, 1963, 87 mins.

Flipper's New Adventure
The further exploits of the world's brightest and most personable dolphin. Flipper and Luke Halpin thwart an extortion plot by some escaped convicts, all set against the exotic backdrop of the Bahamas and Key Biscayne. Bring the kids.
VHS: S13641. $19.98.
Leon Benson, USA, 1964, 103 mins.

For the Love of Benji
The sequel to the original, with Benji pitted against an international espionage ring.
VHS: S04451. $19.99.
Joe Camp, USA, 1977, 85 mins.

Fowl Play
There's trouble afoot in this live-action feature film when the Drakes, duck rulers from a parallel world, slip through a young girl's magical mirror with a dastardly plan for duck domination.
VHS: S30640. $19.95.
Ted Nicolaou, USA, 1996, 89 mins.

Free Willy
Willy is a three-ton Orca whale who was captured and put on display at a Pacific Northwest aquatic park. He's befriended by a troubled 12-year-old boy (Jason James Richter), who orchestrates a daring and dangerous plan to set him free. "The most rousing family adventure since *E.T.*" (Bob Campbell, *Newhouse News*).
DVD: DV60193. $24.98.
VHS: S19727. $19.98.
Laser: LD71933. $39.98.
Simon Wincer, USA, 1993, 98 mins.

From the Mixed-Up Files of Mrs. Basil E. Frankweiler
This light-hearted adventure starring Lauren Bacall is perfect for the whole family. Claudia is a young girl who decides to run away from home as part of her Claudia Appreciation plan. Together with her brother she takes up residence in New York's Metropolitan Museum. As the children dodge guards they become entranced by a mysterious statue. They resolve to discover something of its origins, and that's when they meet the odd and reclusive Mrs. Frankweiler, played by the legendary Lauren Bacall.
VHS: S26695. $14.98.
Laser: LD75416. $39.99.
Marcus Cole, USA, 1995, 92 mins.

George's Island
When a spineless social worker and a meddling schoolteacher show concern for a "troubled" child, ten-year-old George is forced into an evil foster home away from the eccentric grandfather he loves. The boy, his grandfather and friend Bonnie make a wild escape attempt and end up stranded on George's Island. Top prize at the 1990 Chicago International Children's Film Festival. With Sheila McCarthy, Maury Chaykin and Nathaniel Moreau.
VHS: S16040. $19.95.
Laser: LD72298. $34.95.
Paul Donovan, Canada, 1990, 90 mins.

Gold Diggers: The Secret of Bear Mountain
Two girls, Christina Ricci and Anna Chlumsky, join forces to uncover a legendary treasure in gold. Friendship and loyalty give them the courage to brave the treacherous caverns of Bear Mountain, a locale shrouded in mystery and superstition.
VHS: S27654. $99.99.
Laser: LD75560. $39.99.
Kevin Dobson, USA, 1995, 94 mins.

Goldy, The Last of the Golden Bears
Gold prospector Ned Rivers teaches two young orphans how to survive in the wilds of the California Sierra Mountains. Jesse is an 11-year-old tom girl and her friend Goldy is the last of the Golden Bears. This peaceable trio is interrupted when a circus steals Goldy away. But Jesse won't give up her best friend without a fight.
VHS: S20981. $14.98.
John Quinn/Trevor Black, USA, 1984, 91 mins.

Goldy II: Saga of the Golden Bear
Once again Jesse, a young girl who dreams of becoming a cowboy, and her friend, the last Golden Bear, find their friendship endangered by interfering adults. This time Jesse turns to the whole gamut of circus animals to save Goldy from a lifetime of confinement.
VHS: S20982. $14.98.
Trevor Black, USA, 1986, 92 mins.

Goldy III
This is a tender story about the friendship that develops between a young girl and a bear. A sly magician played by Cheech Marin tries to buy Goldy the bear, but Jesse rescues the animal and runs away with him. While hiding in the forest she meets Freedom (Mr. T), who has mysterious powers. This adventure is a wonderful story for kids and parents alike. 104 mins.
VHS: S22128. $92.98.
Laser: LD75202. $34.98.

The Goodbye Bird
A purloined parrot teaches a boy a lesson in compassion in this heartwarming story of courage and friendship. With Wayne Rogers, Cindy Pickett, Christopher Pettiet and Concetta Tomei. 91 mins.
VHS: S31535. $14.98.

The Great Land of Small
A magical family film, set in a maple forest. Only the wise fool Mimmick can see the entrance of Fritz, the hobbit-like creature from the enchanted Land of Small. So begins the magical tale of two youngsters old enough to explore but still young enough to dream. Smart, capable Jenny, 12, and the mischievous David, 7, are about to be treated to the most harrowing, mystical and wonderful adventures imaginable.
VHS: S05311. $14.95.
Vojtech Jasny, Canada, 1987, 94 mins.

Gypsy Colt
An inspirational story about a spirited horse. After the parents of a girl are forced to sell the horse to a racing stable, the horse escapes and travels 500 miles to be reunited with her. With Donna Corcoran, Ward Bond, Frances Dee and Larry Keating.
VHS: S19035. $19.98.
Andrew Marton, USA, 1954, 72 mins.

Harriet the Spy
Louise Fitzhugh's classic children's story about 11-year-old Harriet (Michele Trachtenberg), who dreams of being a writer. Harriet's nanny and best friend Golly (Rosie O'Donnell) tells Harriet to start by writing down everything she sees. But soon Harriet gets into trouble with her friends when they find her secret spy notebook. Featured at the 1996 Chicago International Children's Film Festival. "One of the top ten family films of all time" (Ted Baehr, *Movie Guide*).
VHS: S30462. $19.95.
Laser: Letterboxed. **LD76171. $39.98.**
Bronwen Hughes, USA, 1996, 102 mins.

Heidi (1937)
A family classic that should be part of every childhood, featuring curly-haired Shirley Temple as the orphaned girl who goes to live with her grandfather on a Swiss mountaintop.
VHS: S00560. $19.98.
Allan Dwan, USA, 1937, 88 mins.

Heidi (1953)
Winner of the Grand Prize at the Venice Film Festival, this adaptation of the Johanna Spyri book was especially made for a children's audience. With Elsbeth Sigmund as Heidi. English version.
VHS: S03790. $29.95.
Luigi Comencini, Switzerland, 1953, 98 mins.

Hideaways
Based on the popular Newbery Award-winning book *From the Mixed-Up Files of Mrs. Basil E. Frankweiler*. The legendary Ingrid Bergman headlines this wondrous tale of two children who run away to a secret hideout brimming with intrigue and excitement: New York's Metropolitan Museum of Art. Also starring Richard Mulligan and Madeline Kahn.
VHS: S02715. $19.98.
Fielder Cook, USA, 1973, 105 mins.

Hills of Home
Lassie and a lonely Scottish highlands country doctor confront the elements, local superstition and abject poverty. The doctor receives Lassie as payment for services and the two develop a deep bond.
VHS: S19138. $19.98.
Fred M. Wilcox, USA, 1948, 97 mins.

The Indian in the Cupboard
A young boy experiences a series of unexpected adventures when one of his toys, an Indian figure, miraculously comes alive. There is also a diminutive cowboy action figure that shares the fun. Together they experience conflicts and humorous situations in a plot that is sure to delight kids.
VHS: S26661. $19.95.
Frank Oz, USA, 1995, 97 mins.

Iron Will
This feature film is based on a true-life story about a young man and his team of sled dogs. Together they race across the snow-covered fields of the frozen North to secure a $10,000 prize that can save the family farm. It's a Disney classic.
VHS: S21105. $19.95.
Charles Haid, USA, 1993, 105 mins.

Island of the Blue Dolphins
Based on Scott O'Dell's award-winning children's classic, the heart-warming adventure of a 19th century Indian girl who becomes stranded on a remote island off the California coast.
VHS: S05331. $59.95.
James B. Clark, USA, 1964, 99 mins.

Jack Frost
Buddy Hackett narrates and Robert Morse, Paul Frees and Dave Garroway supply voices to bring Jack Frost to life through the puppet animation technique of "Animagic."
VHS: S28310. $9.95.
Rankin/Bass, USA, 1979, 50 mins.

Jack the Giant Killer
Dazzling special effects and adventures transform the original *Jack and the Beanstalk* legend into an exciting film with Jack the farmer saving the beautiful Princess from numerous monsters.
VHS: S13644. $14.95.
Laser: LD72138. $34.98.
Nathan Juran, USA, 1961, 94 mins.

James & The Giant Peach
Henry Selick's latest feature combines live action and stop-motion animation to bring to life Roald Dahl's famous children's story. Every bit as state-of-the-art as *Nightmare Before Christmas*, this film also has the same sort of scary-but-safe atmosphere. James boards a magical giant peach filled with anthropomorphized insects and embarks on a fantastic odyssey. Music by Randy Newman.
VHS: S28523. $22.95.
Allied/Disney, USA, 1996, 79 mins.

Josh Kirby...Time Warrior! Journey to the Magic Cavern
In this adventure, Josh Kirby travels underground to the lair of the Mushroom People. There he must confront the powers of the mind-melding metalhead, Dr. Zoetrope. He must succeed and rescue the lovely Princess Azabeth. With Corbin Allred, Jennifer Burns, Derek Webster and Matt Winston.
VHS: S27419. $89.95.
Ernest Farino, USA, 1995, 93 mins.

Jumanji
Robin Williams stars as man who was unwittingly trapped inside a mysterious board game. Two modern-day kids inadvertently activate the game and bring both him and a host of computer generated safari animals out of a world of fantasy and into the everyday world of their small-town home. With Kirsten Dunst, Bonnie Hunt, David Alan Grier and Bebe Neuwirth.
VHS: S27652. $19.98.
Laser: LD75559. $39.99.
Joe Johnston, USA, 1995, 104 mins.

A Kid in King Arthur's Court
Thomas Ian Nicholas plays 14-year-old Calvin Fuller, a bright, typical Little Leaguer. When an earthquake rumbles his California hometown, he is magically transported to 12th-century Camelot and the Court of King Arthur. Before long, he is fighting the good fight against the villainous Lord Belasco.
VHS: S27367. $19.99.
Michael Gottlieb, USA, 1995, 90 mins.

The Kid Who Loved Christmas
Cicely Tyson, Michael Warren, Sammy Davis, Jr., and Vanessa Williams star in this story of a child whose adoption may be revoked. Can Santa help? 94 mins.
VHS: S30033. $14.95.

Kids of the Round Table
Malcolm MacDowell stars as Merlin in this modern-day adventure filled with medieval magic. Eleven-year-old Alex and his fellow home-made heroes are having a knights-in-shining-armor blast. The fantasy soon becomes a marvelous reality with a touch of a sword. With Michael Ironside and Johnny Morina.
VHS: S31848. $14.98.
Robert Tinnell, USA, 1995, 89 mins.

Land of Faraway (Mio in the Land of Faraway)
Based on the story by Swedish author Astrid Lindgren *(Pippi Longstocking)*, this is an adventure tale about young boy with an important mission to perform. He must battle the evil knight Kato for control of the land of Faraway. With Timothy Bottoms, Christopher Lee, Susannah York, Christian Bale and Nicholas Pickard as Mio. Available only in EP mode.
VHS: S07973. $9.99.
Vladimir Grammatikov, Norway/Sweden/USSR, 1987, 95 mins.

Lantern Hill
Colleen Dewhurst won an ACE award in this story of Jane Stewart, a young girl who has been sent to live with her wealthy grandmother after her mother is stricken with polio. Cut off from her former friends and enrolled in a private school, Jane has a great deal of trouble adjusting. But she is soon distracted from these everyday trials when she finds out that her missing father (Sam Waterston) is still alive. Based on the book by Lucy Maude Montgomery.
VHS: S13546. $29.95.
Kevin Sullivan, USA, 1990, 112 mins.

Lassie
The canine hero of all times is back in this full-length adventure film. When the Turner family moves to Virginia, they encounter a number of problems, both financial and domestic. Fortunately the relationship between a boy and his dog can weather even the most insurmountable troubles.
VHS: S22889. $95.95.
Daniel Petrie, USA, 1994, 95 mins.

Lassie Come Home
The first and the best of the Lassie films: the story of a poor family that's forced to sell its dog, but she makes a remarkable journey to return to them. One of the all-time great tearjerkers, with Roddy McDowall, Elizabeth Taylor, Donald Crisp.
VHS: S12429. $19.98.
Fred M. Wilcox, USA, 1943, 88 mins.

Leapin' Leprechauns
An American hopes to build a theme park at a beautiful location in Ireland. Unfortunately, there is a group of leprechauns whom he must displace. The tiny creatures fight back, using all their mischievous powers to thwart his greedy plans. This antic film is a great family comedy, chock full of magical humor.
VHS: S25739. $14.95.
Ted Nicolaou, USA, 1995, 84 mins.

Legend of Black Thunder Mountain
The magic of the wilderness comes to life as two children become separated and then lost from their family while traveling by wagon train to their new home. Jamie and Anna face many dangers while on their exciting adventure. Along the way, a young Indian boy and his animal friends help the kids on their incredible journey through Black Thunder Mountain and back to safety. 90 mins.
VHS: S32183. $9.95.

Legend of Sea Wolf
Adaptation of the Jack London tale starring Chuck Connors as Captain Wol Larson, with Barbara Bach and Joseph Palmer.
VHS: S02701. $24.95.
Joseph Green, USA, 92 mins.

Legend of the White Horse
Jim Martin is a geologist with the unfortunate habit of standing up for his principles. Now it's gotten him fired—again. Eager for work, he accepts a surveying job in a distant country, and sets off with his young son. Arriving in the remote land, they move into the mountain home of a reputed witch and her beautiful, blind ward, Jewel (Allison Balson). But there is another inhabitant in the wild mountain wilderness—a magical white horse.
VHS: S15068. $59.98.
Jerzy Domaradzki/Janusz Morgenstern, USA, 1985, 91 mins.

The Leopard Son
This beautifully photographed, award-winning film is the story of a leopard cub's passage from innocent infant to skilled, proud adult. Narrated by Sir John Gielgud. "Breathtaking...beautiful... a real life *Lion King* (Philip Murphy, *L.A. Parent Magazine*).
VHS: S31144. $14.98.
Hugo van Lawick, USA, 1996, 84 mins.

Linnea in Monet's Garden
From the bestselling book—a charming tale of a little girl's exploration of Claude Monet's paintings and life.
VHS: S22181. $19.95.
Christina Bjork & Lena Anderson

The Lion, The Witch and the Wardrobe
The first tale in C.S. Lewis' *The Chronicles of Narnia*—one of the best loved works of children's literature. A wardrobe closet becomes the passageway to a wonderland of mythical creatures and talking animals. Winner of the Emmy Award for Best Animated Special.
VHS: S19158. $12.95.
Children's TV Workshop, USA, 1993, 95 mins.

Little Lord Fauntleroy
Alec Guiness and Ricky Schroder star in this adventure of a poor boy taken from the squalor of a New York slum to the splendor of aristocratic England.
VHS: S00760. $19.95.
Jack Gold, USA, 1980, 98 mins.

The Little Prince
Antione de Saint-Exupery's book is brought to life through Will Vinton's Claymation technique. A young boy searches for matters of consequence and realizes that trivia often obscure the most important things. Narrated by Cliff Robertson.
VHS: S26616. $14.95.
Will Vinton, USA, 27 mins.

The Little Princess
Young Sara Crewe has the perfect life with her father in fabled India. All that ends with the onset of war. Sara is sent to a New York boarding school, where she clashes with a strict headmistress. Somehow she overcomes the hardships of this fate and manages to change both her own life and the fortunes of those around her.
DVD: DV60194. $24.98.
VHS: S26210. $19.98.
Laser: LD75041. $34.98.
Alfonso Cuaron, USA, 1995, 97 mins.

The Littlest Angel
Sixties baby-boomers may remember this delightful musical rendition of Charles Tazwell's best-selling Christmas story, which first aired on TV in 1969. A little boy, Michael (Johnny Whitaker, of TV's *Family Affair*), has a fatal fall and lands in heaven. Patience (Fred Gwynne) is assigned as his guardian angel. But the little angel cannot adjust to heavenly life and wants to return to earth to retrieve his special hand-made box of found treasures. He learns a valuable lesson about the spirit of giving. Also stars Tony Randall, Connie Stevens, Cab Calloway, and E.G Marshall as God. 77 mins.
VHS: S30187. $12.95.

Long John Silver
Robert Newton (Disney's *Treasure Island*) once again stars as the swashbuckling pirate in this delightful color film based on the Robert Louis Stevenson children's classic. In this film, Long John Silver seeks hidden treasure, rescues the governor's daughter and battles his arch-enemy on Treasure Island. Featuring Rod Taylor as Israel Hand.
VHS: S27335. $19.95.
Byron Haskin, Australia, 1954, 106 mins.

Looking for Miracles
Based on the novel by A.E. Hotchner. A coming-of-age tale, set in Depression-era Canada, about two long-separated brothers with almost nothing in common who renew their relationship over the course of one long summer.
VHS: S13547. $29.95.
Kevin Sullivan, Canada, 1989, 90 mins.

Man and Boy
A family film which stars Bill Cosby as a Civil War veteran who, together with his son, takes off after the thief who stole their horse. With Gloria Foster, Leif Erickson.
VHS: S21486. $59.98.
E.W. Swackhamer, USA, 1972, 98 mins.

Matilda
This story of a super-smart little girl, Mara Wilson *(Mrs. Doubtfire)*, who takes hilarious revenge on the unjust grown-ups in her world, will delight kids and adults alike. Danny DeVito and Rhea Perlman star as the bad parents. From the author of *James and the Giant Peach* and *Willy Wonka and the Chocolate Factory*. "A family classic for all generations. Whimsical and wonderful" (Alan Silverman, *Voice of America*).
DVD: DV60012. $29.95.
VHS: S30254. $22.99.
Laser: LD76002. $34.95.
Danny DeVito, USA, 1996, 98 mins.

Maya

A natural wildlife story built around the relationship between a father and son. A young boy (Jay North) estranged from his father, a wildlife hunter whom he blames for losing his nerve, befriends a young native boy. The two undertake a perilous journey in the bush, putting their lives in danger and forcing the young man to reevaluate his father. With Clint Walker, I.S. Johar, Sajid Kahn and Jairag.

VHS: S19033. $19.98.
John Berry, USA, 1966, 91 mins.

Misty

The creators of *A Dog of Flanders* work their magic again in this warmhearted tale of two lonely children and a beautiful, wild pony. Based on Marguerite Henry's award-winning children's novel *Misty of Chincoteague*. Great family entertainment. With David Ladd and Pam Smith.

VHS: S14282. $19.95.
James B. Clark, USA, 1961, 92 mins.

Moon Stallion

A mystical tale from the BBC, enchanting for both adults and children. A professor researches the legend of King Arthur and a strange apparition of a wild, white horse is seen. These mysteries lead the man's blind daughter into adventures far removed from the 20th century. 90 mins.

VHS: S12635. $29.95.

More About the Children of Noisy Village

From Lasse Hallstrom, the director of *What's Eating Gilbert Grape* and *My Life as a Dog*, and Astrid Lindgren, the creator of *Pippi Longstocking*, comes this story of six children who find adventure in their home town, Noisy Village. Set before World War II, the children explore the idyllic countryside, invent wondrous games, and romp and frolic around their tiny village. A delightful tale that brings back an age of simple fun and good times.

VHS: S34982. $24.95.
Lasse Hallstrom, Sweden, 1994, 85 mins.

Mousehunt

Nathan Lane *(The Birdcage)* and Lee Evans *(Funny Bones)* star as down-on-their luck brothers Lars and Ernie Smuntz who inherit a crumbling mansion and discover it's worth millions. But before they cash in, they've got to rid the house of its current occupant: a tiny and tenacious mouse. With Christopher Walken.

VHS: S33944. $22.99.
Gore Verbinski, USA, 1997, 98 mins.

Mrs. Santa Claus

Angela Lansbury stars in this delightful Christmas classic as Mrs. Santa Claus, who believes her holiday contributions go unappreciated as Santa (Charles Durning) busily prepares for the Big Night. When she takes the sleigh to check out a new route, one of the reindeer is injured and Mrs. Claus must make an emergency landing in New York City, where she warms the hearts of New Yorkers. But back at the North Pole, Santa is lost without her.

VHS: S32189. $14.98.
Laser: LD76396. $39.99.
Terry Hughes, USA, 1997, 91 mins.

My Dog Shep

Silent star William Farnum heads the cast in this family entertainment about an old man who teams up with a young runaway boy and his German shepherd, Shep. Together they foil kidnappers and greedy relatives. With Tom Neal, Grady Sutton, Al St. John and Flame.

VHS: S05706. $29.95.
Ford Beebe, USA, 1946, 70 mins.

My Family Treasure

A magical children's tale about a woman's search for a family treasure bequeathed by the Czar to her family before the Russian Revolution. The complex story unfolds over decades, and charts the heroism of a young woman to restore her eccentric family's wounded pride. With Theodore Bikel, Dee Wallace Stone, Bitty Schram and Alex Vincent.

VHS: S19734. $79.95.
Rolfe Kanefsky/Edward Staroselksy, USA, 1992

My Friend Flicka

Roddy McDowall stars as a young boy determined to tame and befriend a wild horse in this screen version of Mary O'Hara's acclaimed novel. This poignant story of trust, love and hope was one of the most popular family films of the forties. With Preston Foster.

VHS: S14211. $14.98.
Harold Schuster, USA, 1943, 89 mins.

Namu, The Killer Whale

An adventure story about a dedicated marine biologist (Robert Lansing) who captures a massive killer whale, begins to study its nature and manner and eventually develops a relationship with the whale. With Lee Meriwether, John Anderson and Richard Erdman.

VHS: S19032. $14.95.
Laszlo Benedek, USA, 1966, 88 mins.

Napoleon

A charming children's film about an adorable dog who goes on a spirited adventure in the Australian countryside and discovers his own strength of character and heroism in the process.

VHS: S34711. $14.95.
Mario Andreacchio, Australia, 1994, 81 mins.

National Velvet

Classic family film starring Elizabeth Taylor at her loveliest as the spunky young girl who hopes to enter and win Britain's Grand National Steeplechase race. With the help of a rascal stableboy (Mickey Rooney), she may just achieve her dreams. Great family entertainment.

DVD: DV60105. $24.98.
VHS: S01789. $19.98.
Laser: LD70636. $69.98.
Clarence Brown, USA, 1944, 125 mins.

Never Cry Wolf

From the director of *Black Stallion*, a spectacular film about the odyssey of a young biologist sent to study the habits of wolves in the Arctic. With Charles Martin Smith and Brian Dennehy, based on the book by Farley Mowat.

VHS: Out of print. For rental only.
Laser: LD71254. $34.95.
Carroll Ballard, USA, 1983, 105 mins.

The Neverending Story

Wolfgang Petersen immerses the audience in a classical fairytale, the story of a young boy for whom the tale of *The Neverending Story* is so real, he becomes the hero in a mythical empire populated by magical beings. His task is, of course, to save this magical world from destruction.

VHS: S00926. $14.95.
Laser: Letterboxed. **LD70639. $34.98.**
Wolfgang Petersen, Germany/USA, 1984, 94 mins.

The Neverending Story II: The Next Chapter

A continuation of Wolfgang Petersen's 1984 surprise about a young boy struggling to come to terms with his mother's death and his father's detachment, who escapes to a magical world called Fantasia, where he's pressed to save the life of a beautiful young girl.

Laser: LD70640. $29.98.
George Miller, USA/Germany, 1990, 89 mins.

The Neverending Story III: Return to Fantasia

This third in the "Neverending Story" series is the enchanting live-action fantasy of Bastian (Jason James Richter, *Free Willy*), a teenager who, in order to escape the school bullies, flees into another world by using the magical "Neverending Storybook" that he finds in the library. Features breathtaking special effects from the Henson Creature Shop.

VHS: S30599. $14.95.
Peter MacDonald, Germany/USA, 1994, 95 mins.

The New Adventures of Black Beauty

This two-volume set follows the continuing saga of that childhood favorite, the horse Black Beauty. It begins when 12-year-old Vicky is introduced to a horse and then finds herself involved in adventure. Despite her growing attachment to Black Beauty she may have to leave for New Zealand. 120 mins.

VHS: S25061. $29.95.

New Adventures of Pippi Longstocking

A brand new film based on the classic children's books by Astrid Lindgren, with Pippi back for fun, laughter and a lot of mischief in brand new adventures.

VHS: S08062. $14.95.
Ken Annakin, USA, 1988, 100 mins.

Our Little Girl

Shirley Temple runs away from home in this sentimental tale about a little girl who comes to believe her parents don't love her. Joel McCrea co-stars.

VHS: S09994. $19.98.
John S. Robertson, USA, 1935, 65 mins.

The Painted Hills

A Lassie adventure story set against an 1870 California gold backdrop, in the High Sierras. Lassie must avenge the death of a kindly prospector murdered by his greedy partner after the old man struck a rich gold vein. Adapted from Alexander Hull's novel *Shep of the Painted Hills*. With Paul Kelly, Bruce Cowling, Gary Gray and Art Smith.

VHS: S19140. $19.98.
Harold F. Kress, USA, 1951, 70 mins.

The Peanut Butter Solution

Winner at the 1986 Children's International Festival of Children's Films, the story of Michael, an average boy living in Montreal, with a vivid imagination. When he concocts a peanut butter solution which makes his hair grow forever, he becomes the object of a kidnapping.

VHS: S02600. $19.95.
Michael Rubbo, Canada, 1985, 96 mins.

The Phantom Tollbooth

Milo drives through the Phantom Tollbooth and into an animated fantasy land, The Kingdom of Wisdom, to end the terrible feud between numbers and words. Co-directed by Chuck Jones with voices of Mel Blanc, Hans Conreid and others.

VHS: S01020. $19.95.
Laser: LD76386. $29.98.
MGM, USA, 1969, 89 mins.

The Pied Piper of Hamelin

Van Johnson and Claude Rains are featured in this delightful retelling of the famous children's tale. The rats disappear, but in the end they don't go alone, as the children of the village find themselves mesmerized by the Pied Piper.

VHS: S23799. $24.95.
Bretaigne Windust, USA, 1957, 87 mins.

Pippi Longstocking

Astrid Lindgren's classic character turns her straight-laced village upside-down with a series of musical misadventures in this theatrically released feature film. A co-production among Canadian, Swedish and German studios.

VHS: S32461. $19.95.
Nelvana, Canada, 1997, 75 mins.

The Point

Harry Nilsson wrote the songs (including the hit "Me and My Arrow") and script for this thought-provoking TV special. Ringo Starr narrates the tale of a child who must leave his homeland because his round head makes him a freak among his countrymen, the cone-heads.

VHS: S25004. $14.95.
Murakami-Wolf-Swenson, USA, 1971, 74 mins.

Pound Puppies and the Legend of Big Paw

Every dog has his day as Cooler and the gang make their feature film debut with this musical full-length animated adventure. 76 mins. 1988.

VHS: S09892. $24.95.

Prancer

This heart-warming holiday fantasy stars Rebecca Harrell as a nine-year-old girl who discovers a wounded deer and becomes convinced that it is Santa's own Prancer. Her attempts to heal the wounded animal and return it to Santa Claus before Christmas unite her troubled family and touch the residents of the small town. With Sam Elliott, Rebecca Harrell and Cloris Leachman.

VHS: S13351. $14.95.
John Hancock, USA, 1989, 102 mins.

Prince Brat and the Whipping Boy

George C. Scott stars in this enchanting children's fairy tale about a princely brat who gets mixed up with a young orphan. It's a case where mistaken identity creates the chance for both a little comeuppance and a lot of fun. Based on Sid Fleischmann's novel *The Whipping Boy*.

VHS: S26948. $19.95.
Laser: LD75428. $34.95.
Syd Macartney, USA, 1995, 96 mins.

Quark the Dragonslayer

Quark, a baby giant, is capable of conquering dragons, robbers and Vikings. Narrated by John Cleese.

VHS: S29036. $24.95.
Nordisk Film, 1987, 70 mins.

A Rat's Tale

Lauren Hutton, Jerry Stiller and Beverly D'Angelo star in this film that combines the magic of marionettes with state-of-the art special effects. Enter a world beneath the streets of New York City filled with cute and cuddly creatures, including a warm-hearted rodent named Marty, who must save the rodent population from being wiped out by a developer.

VHS: S33685. $19.95.
Michael F. Huse, USA/Germany, 1997, 90 mins.

The Return of the Sand Fairy

Based on the book by Edith *(Railway Children)* Nesbit, this is a British adventure about a fantastic, furry gremlin who can make wishes come true and the four children he befriends. Great Britain, 1993, 139 mins.

VHS: S21973. $89.98.

Ring of Bright Water

Fine acting and beautiful cinematography spark this intelligent, heartwarming tale of a man's love for his pet otter. A Disney-like fable for animal lovers, adapted from the bestselling book by Gavin Maxwell. With Bill Travers and Virginia McKenna.

VHS: S14223. $14.98.
Jack Couffer, Great Britain, 1969, 107 mins.

The Road Home

Kris Kristofferson, Danny Aiello and Charles Martin Smith star in this tale of two orphaned brothers. They face poverty and a dreary orphanage that wants to separate them in the East. Only the promise of Father Flannagan's Boys'Town in Nebraska seems to guarantee them some measure of respite from the Great Depression, so they set off across the country. Ultimately their journey inspires a nation. Mickey Rooney makes a cameo appearance as Father Flannagan. Winner at the Chicago International Children's Film Festival.

VHS: S27410. $14.98.
Dean Hamilton, USA, 1995, 90 mins.

Samson & Sally: The Song of the Whales

This three-time award winner in Europe is adapted from Bent Haller's story. Samson & Sally are two young whales searching for Moby Dick. First-rate animation.

VHS: S10966. $14.95.
Nordisk Film, Denmark, 1984, 70 mins.

The Sand Fairy

A BBC adaptation of Edith Nesbith's novel about a strange and wondrous creature who is a canny combination of E.T. and Yoda. He befriends a group of outcast children and dazzles them with magic and hope, sending them through time and history to help them realize their enchanting dreams. 139 mins.

VHS: S19067. $89.98.

The Sandlot

Baseball, the American sports obsession, is the central part of this charming family entertainment. A shy young boy joins a funny ragtag team and learns that how you play the game is the best route to acceptance and belonging.

VHS: S20668. $19.98.
David Mickey Evans, USA, 1993, 100 mins.

Santa Claus: The Movie

Enchanting, heartwarming tale of a master toy maker who discovers a magical kingdom of elves at the north pole. Featuring Dudley Moore as Patch, an eager-to-please elf who becomes mixed up with a toy tycoon's plan to take over Christmas.

VHS: S04800. $19.95.
Jeannot Szwarc, USA, 1985, 104 mins.

Sarah and the Squirrel

Mia Farrow plays a young girl separated from her family who learns to survive the wilds with the help of animals in this story which mixes live action with animation. USA, 1983, 73 mins.

VHS: S04604. $29.98.

Sarah, Plain and Tall

Glenn Close and Christopher Walken star in this acclaimed Hallmark Hall of Fame production about an opinionated Maine schoolteacher who travels to Kansas in 1910 to look after the children of a widowed farmer. With Lexi Randall, Margaret Sophie Stein, Jon de Vries and Christopher Bell. Based on the Newbery Medal winning children's novel by Patricia MacLachlan. Nominated for nine Emmys.

VHS: S15617. $14.98.
Laser: CLV. LD72026. $29.98.
Glenn Jordan, USA, 1991, 98 mins.

The Secret Garden (1949)

A well-made adaptation of Frances Hodgson Burnett's classic children's novel about the transcendent powers of a young girl to change and influence the dark and foreboding residents of a depressed Victorian estate. With Margaret O'Brien, Herbert Marshall, Dean Stockwell and Gladys Cooper.

VHS: S18564. $19.98.
Fred M. Wilcox, USA, 1949, 92 mins.

The Secret Garden (1987)

This Hallmark adaptation of Frances Hodgson Burnett's story about an isolated, abandoned young orphan who discovers a magical garden and unlocks its hidden power and beauty. Shot in the baroque Highclere Castle in England. With Gennie James, Barret Oliver, Jadrien Steele, Derek Jacobi and Billie Whitelaw. "Very handsome and engrossing" *(Washington Post)*.

VHS: S17033. $14.98.
Laser: LD71540. $29.98.
Alan Grint, USA, 1987, 100 mins.

The Secret Garden (1993)

Agnieszka Holland's haunting adaptation of Frances Hodgson Burnett's 1909 classic about an orphaned young girl (Kate Maberly) dispatched to her uncle's remote English estate. With the help of her painfully withdrawn cousin (Heydon Prowse) and a local boy (Andrew Knott), she discovers an enchanting garden. Holland beautifully captures the painful social isolation of childhood. Maggie Smith plays the tyrannical housekeeper.

DVD: DV60195. $24.98.
VHS: S20217. $19.98.
Laser: LD72328. $34.98.
Agnieszka Holland, USA, 1993, 102 mins.

The Secret Garden (1994)

Based on the book by Frances Hodgson Burnett. Orphaned Mary Lennox is sent to live with her uncle in Yorkshire. She discovers a secret garden on the grounds that no one has entered for ten years. What she and her friends find there will change them forever. The home video contains extra footage not aired on TV.

VHS: S22519. $16.95.
Laser: LD74919. $44.95.
ABC, USA, 1994, 72 mins.

The Secret of the Seal

Based on a best-selling book. Find out how Tottoi, an adventurous young boy, discovers two Mediterranean seals believed to be extinct. Too excited to keep his find a secret, Tottoi soon finds himself battling to save the lives of his new friends.

VHS: S19419. $24.95.
Nippon Animation, Japan, 1992, 90 mins.

Sherlock the Undercover Dog

Two courageous kids team up with a fast-talking police dog to collar a gang of bumbling smugglers in this hilarious comedy.

VHS: S22893. $19.95.
Richard Harding Gardner, USA, 1995, 80 mins.

Shiloh

In this "modern day *Old Yeller*," a boy learns about responsibility, commitment and friendship while trying to rescue a beagle pup from mistreatment by its owner. Adapted from the Newbery Award-winning novel. With Michael Moriarty, Rod Steiger, Scott Wilson and Blake Heron.

VHS: S31298. $19.98.
Laser: LD76727. $34.98.
Dale Rosenbloom, USA, 1996, 94 mins.

Shipwreck Island

Share an exciting live-action adventure with eight boys whose sailing yacht is shipwrecked on a deserted island. A two-week vacation soon becomes a two-year adventure when one boy accidentally sets their boat adrift. Floating aimlessly, the boat eventually runs aground on an island inhabited only by wild animals. Here the boys must learn to hunt and survive the challenges of nature without the help of grown-ups. Don't miss the excitement when a band of renegade sailors arrive and try to take Shipwreck Island for themselves! Color.

VHS: S13884. $19.95.
USA, 1961, 85 mins.

Sinbad and the Eye of the Tiger

A sequel to the rousing children's adventure story *Golden Voyage of Sinbad* has the title hero (Patrick Wayne) dueling monsters to break the spell of an evil sorceress. Special visual effects by Ray Harryhausen. With Jane Seymour, Taryn Power, and Margaret Whiting.

VHS: S16682. $14.95.
Sam Wanamaker, Great Britain, 1977, 113 mins.

Skylark

A lyrical sequel to *Sarah, Plain and Tall*, Patricia MacLachlan's evocative children's book about a Maine school teacher (Glenn Close) drawn to a widowed Midwestern farmer (Christopher Walken) and his family. With Lexi Randall, Christopher Bell and Margaret Sophie.

VHS: S18750. $14.98.
Joseph Sargent, USA, 1992, 98 mins.

Smoke

Before there was "Eat My Dust," there was this Disney drama starring Ron Howard. The title refers to the name of an ailing dog that teenaged Ronny and his stepfather (Earl Holliman) nurse back to health, only to have the dog's true owner show up.

VHS: S10068. $69.95.
Vincent McEveety, USA, 1970, 89 mins.

The Snow Queen

Hans Christian Anderson's classic about two small children, Gerta and Kay, and Gerta's search for her brother after he was kidnapped by the evil Snow Queen and taken to live in her Ice Castle. An interesting and beautifully animated Soviet feature that was masterfully re-scored and dubbed in English. Directed by Lev Atamanov. Live-action prologue with Art Linkletter. EP Speed.

VHS: S29081. $19.95.
Soyuzmultfilm, USSR, 1957, 55 mins.

Snow White

The famous Grimm fairy tale is brought to life in this German version. There is a lovely young woman, seven dwarves and a prince to charm everyone, except, of course, the evil witch.

VHS: S25705. $19.95.
Erich Kobler, Germany, 1955, 76 mins.

Snowy River, The McGregor Saga: The Race

Based on the ballad *The Man from Snow River*. Australia, 1993, 87 mins.

VHS: S22014. $14.98.

Son of Lassie

Now grown to manhood, Joe Carraclough has gone off to the RAF training school, leaving behind his beloved Lassie and her pup Laddie. Ever faithful Laddie follows Joe to the academy and stows away aboard Joe's plane as it embarks on a dangerous mission.

VHS: S16847. $19.98.
S. Sylvan Simon, USA, 1945, 100 mins.

Song Spinner

Patti LuPone and John Neville are opposing characters in this mythical story about a young girl named Aurora who receives a magical gift. In the tiny world where she lives, noise of any kind is illegal, as decreed by King Frilo (Neville). When the mysterious Zantalalia (LuPone) arrives, she brings with her a "song-spinner," a glistening gift for Aurora that makes music. Now Aurora's gift for song promises to change the kingdom of Shandrilan from a silent and gloomy place to a joyful, music-laden paradise.

VHS: S27420. $19.95.
Laser: LD75511. $39.99.
Randy Bradshaw, USA, 1995, 95 mins.

Sounder

Paul Winfield stars as a Black sharecropper in Louisiana who steals food in a desperate attempt to feed his family. Cicely Tyson portrays his wife, providing love and strength to keep the family together.

VHS: S01235. $14.95.
Laser: LD75336. $29.98.
Martin Ritt, USA, 1972, 105 mins.

Stone Boy

A family drama starring Glenn Close and Robert Duvall as parents of a 12 year old who inadvertently kills his older brother while hunting. Wilford Brimley is featured as the understanding grandfather.

VHS: S02026. $59.98.
Christopher Cain, USA, 1984, 93 mins.

The Story of Seabiscuit

Shirley Temple stars as Margaret O'Hara. Haunted by her jockey brother's death, she agrees to marry Ted Knowles only if he gives up riding. But when her meddling uncle convinces Ted that a horse named Seabiscuit will triumph only with Ted in the saddle, the clever Irishman must convince his niece that she'll come out a winner, too!

VHS: S16849. $19.98.
David Butler, USA, 1950, 93 mins.

Summer with Selik

This spectacular film shows the developing bond between a teenage girl and a baby seal that she finds on the Norwegian coast. Sadly, the girl grows to love her new friend Selik but as he grows he must be returned to the sea. It's a touching film about a key right of passage to adulthood for this teenager. 60 mins.

VHS: S25995. $29.95.

The Sun Comes Up

A lonely widow (Jeanette MacDonald) blames her son's dog Lassie for her husband's death but eventually learns about Lassie's friendship and loyalty through a young orphan's (Claude Jarman Jr.) love for the dog. MacDonald's last film; she performs five songs. With Lloyd Nolan, Dwayne Hickman, Percy Kilbride and Margaret Hamilton. Music by Andre Previn.

VHS: S19139. $19.98.
Richard Thorpe, USA, 1948, 93 mins.

Susannah of the Mounties

Shirley Temple helps tame the West as the lone survivor of an Indian raid who's taken in a by a kindly Mountie. When all-out war threatens, it's Shirley who saves the day and shows the adults how to live in peace. Co-stars Randolph Scott.

VHS: S09997. $19.98.
William A. Seiter, USA, 1939, 79 mins.

Swallows and Amazons

Arthur Ransome's wondrous adventures of six children on holiday in England. 89 mins.

VHS: S31541. $14.98.

Swallows and Amazons Forever!: Coot Club

This BBC adaptation of a series of books written by Arthur Ransome set on English waterways and lakes in the 1930's continues with the adventures of children in the Coot Club. They are dedicated to protecting nesting sites and let loose a ship they fear will damage one. Now they may well find trouble from the sabotaged crew.

VHS: S24827. $29.95.
Andrew Morgan, Great Britain, 1995, 90 mins.

Swallows and Amazons Forever!: The Big Six

Originally a series of books written by Arthur Ransome set on English waterways and lakes in the 1930's, two of these stories have now been made into captivating films by the BBC. This first film introduces the six children who make up the central characters. They explore a world of skill, nature and friendship.

VHS: S24828. $29.95.
Andrew Morgan, Great Britain, 1995, 90 mins.

The Swan Princess

From the director of *The Fox & The Hound* comes a new animated musical adventure. It's the story of Princess Odette, who is transformed into a swan by an evil sorcerer's (voice of Jack Palance) spell. Held captive at an enchanted lake, she befriends Jean-Bob the Frog (voice of John Cleese), Speed the Turtle (voice of Steven Wright) and Puffin the Bird. Despite their struggle to guard the princess, only a vow of everlasting love can break the spell.

VHS: S25610. $14.95.
Laser: LD75029. $29.95.
Nest Prods, USA, 1994, 90 mins.

The Swan Princess: Escape from Castle Mountain

Richard Rich directs this direct-to-video sequel to his well-regarded 1994 theatrical feature. Prince Derek, Princess Odette and the rest fight to save their kingdom from the evil magician Clavius.

VHS: S32470. $19.95.
Nest Entertainment, USA, 1997, 75 mins.

Swiss Family Robinson

Jonathon Wyss' book of the same name is adapted for the screen in this early version of the much admired tale. A man decides to move his family to Australia, but the ship is destroyed, forcing them to make do on a deserted island. There the harshness and beauty of the landscape challenge and inspire this family to be better than they thought they could be.

VHS: S21560. $24.95.
Edward Ludwig, USA, 1940, 92 mins.

Tadpole and the Whale

The story of a 12-year-old girl and her relationship with some of the world's most spectacular undersea creatures, including Elvar the dolphin, her best friend in the world. Academy of Canadian Television and Cinema Award, London Film Festival Award, International Ecological Film Festival Award. Family.

VHS: S17134. $29.95.
Dominique Ricard, Canada, 1987, 91 mins.

Tall Tale

Patrick Swayze, Scott Glenn and Oliver Platt star in this imaginative recombination of legendary tall tales. Pecos Bill, Paul Bunyan and John Henry come to the aid of a young boy who must go head-to-head with a greedy land-grabber in this epic from Disney.

VHS: S26150. $99.98.
Jeremiah Chechik, USA, 1994, 97 mins.

The Thief and the Cobbler

Nearly 30 years in the making, *The Thief and the Cobbler* is almost literally Richard William's life work. Some of animation's greatest names have contributed to the production over the years, and the lush animation and breathtaking Escher-like backgrounds are a feast for the eyes. Unfortunately, Williams was not able to complete the film on time, so the money men took it away from him—hastily slapping together something that could pass as a complete movie. The resultant version that appears on this tape is a disappointing patchwork of breathtaking Williams animation interspersed with hack fill-in scenes, lame Disney-esque musical numbers, and a jarringly inappropriate soundtrack. Despite all that, every film animation devotee must have this film just for the Williams segments that remain intact.

VHS: S30598. $14.95.
Laser: LD72461. $29.95.
Richard Williams, UK, 1996, 73 mins.

Third Stone from the Sun

A strange sailing ship that speaks (Linda Hunt is the voice) guides a young boy on a mysterious but important journey. He must retrieve a lost treasure. Along the way he discovers the importance of the natural world and his place in it.

VHS: S24741. $19.98.
Jan C. Nickman, USA, 1994, 85 mins.

The Three Worlds of Gulliver

The special effects wizardry of Ray Harryhausen highlight this tale of Gulliver (Kerwin Matthews) and his voyages to the lands of Liliput and Brobdignag. Filmed in Superdynanation. The classic satire of Jonathan Swift comes in three sizes. With Jo Morrow, June Thorburn and Peter Bull. Also giant alligators and squirrels in this live-action fantasy.

VHS: S06829. $14.95.
Laser: Includes interview with Ray Harryhausen. **LD75043. $34.95.**
Jack Sher, Great Britain, 1960, 98 mins.

Thumbelina

From Don Bluth comes one of his lushest-looking animated features yet. The diminutive heroine must fend off the amorous advances of beetles, moles and frogs while she searches for her lost Fairy Prince. Adaptation by Don Bluth, musical score by Barry Manilow, songs and voices by Gilbert Gottfried and Charo... 'nuff said.

VHS: S21255. $24.95.
Laser: Widescreen. **LD72421. $34.95.**
Don Bluth, USA, 1994, 86 mins.

Tom Thumb

Russ Tamblyn is the miniature forest boy from the famed Grimm Brothers story. He is taken in by a kindly couple, but finds his unusual size an advantage when it becomes necessary to outwit the villainous Terry-Thomas and his evil henchman Peter Sellers.

VHS: S16852. $19.98.
George Pal, Great Britain, 1958, 98 mins.

Trailing the Killer

Very much like a Disney true-life nature series, this is the story of a sheep dog, part wolf, accused of killing sheep. Cast: Ceasar, the wolf dog, Frances MacDonald, Heinie Conklin, Tom London.

VHS: S10372. $19.95.
Herman C. Raymaker, USA, 1932, 63 mins.

Travels of Marco Polo

The brave Marco Polo fights for peace and justice in the exotic Far East in this classic tale of wondrous adventure.

VHS: S03021. $24.95.
William Novik, France, 1953, 48 mins.

Two Bits and Pepper

A pet pony and brave horse foil would-be kidnappers. Starring Joe Piscopo. 90 mins.

VHS: S31534. $14.98.

Where the Red Fern Grows

A young boy yearns for two Red-bone coon hounds amidst the splendor of the Ozarks. But life is hard in Depression-era Oklahoma. Facing adventure and tragedy with his new canine friends, Billy ultimately learns of love and hope. With James Whitmore, Beverly Garland and Stewart Peterson.

DVD: DV60268. $19.95.
VHS: S01447. $19.98.
Norman Tokar, USA, 1974, 108 mins.

Where the Red Fern Grows, Part II

A continuation of Wilson Rawls' classic novel about a young boy's coming of age, helped along by his special relationship with two Redbone hound puppies. With Wilford Brimley, Doug McKeon, Lisa Whelchel and Chad McQueen.

VHS: S17875. $89.95.
Jim McCullough, USA, 1992, 105 mins.

Whiskers

In this "engaging, cornball (or should I say furball) comedy" (*New York Daily News*), a shy boy learns what friendship really is when a desperate wish turns his rambunctious cat into a full-grown, 30-year-old man, in this tale of magic, adventure and hilarious fun.

VHS: S31294. $99.99.
Laser: LD76217. $39.99.
Jimmy Kaufman, USA, 1997, 94 mins.

White Fang and the Hunter

Another screen version of the Jack London novel about a boy and his dog in the great white north. Starring Robert Wood and Pedro Sanchez and featuring lots of snow and scenic vistas.

VHS: S03640. $19.98.
Laser: LD71208. $39.99.
Alfonso Brescia, Italy, 1985, 87 mins.

Wild Hearts Can't Be Broken

Gabrielle Anwar stars in the inspirational true story of Sonora Walker, a young girl who thrilled thousands of visitors to Atlantic City during the 1930's and 1940's. Even after she was blinded in an accident, she continued to dive off a 40-foot tower into a tank of water on horseback. With Matt Schoeffling, Kathleen York and Cliff Robertson as wild west showman W.F. Carver, a former partner of Wild Bill Cody.

VHS: S15530. $19.95.
Steve Miner, USA, 1991, 88 mins.

Willa: An American Snow White

In this award-winning production, the classic tale of envy, death and redemption from the Brothers Grimm is set in the countryside of Virginia's Faulkier county, with a cast selected from Washington, D.C.'s renowned Shakespeare Theatre.

VHS: S31705. $39.95.
Tom Davenport, USA, 1997, 85 mins.

Willie Wonka and the Chocolate Factory

Amusing and unconventional story based on the children's book by Roald Dahl features Gene Wilder as a madcap candy man. With Jack Albertson.

VHS: S01604. $19.98.
Laser: LD70707. $34.98.
Mel Stuart, USA, 1971, 94 mins.

Willow

From master storytellers George Lucas *(Star Wars)* and Ron Howard *(Cocoon)* comes this odyssey of unlikely heroes, villains and innocent souls caught in a mysterious realm of battle, magic and comaraderie. Willow Ufgood (Warwick Davis) leaves his village to carry a special child to safety who is destined to bring everlasting peace and freedom to the land.

VHS: S30255. $14.99.
Ron Howard, USA, 1988, 130 mins.

The Wind in the Willows

Rankin/Bass' version of Kenneth Grahame's classic story featuring the voices of Charles Nelson Reilly, Roddy McDowall and Eddie Bracken.

VHS: S29773. $14.95.
Rankin/Bass, USA, 96 mins.

The Wind in the Willows

Vanessa Redgrave narrates this animated film adaptation of Kenneth Grahame's classic children's story about a wise Badger, a clever Rat, and a sensible Mole, who do their best to control the excesses of Toad when they embark on an unpredictable journey. This satire of Victorian society features the voices of Michael Palin *(Monty Python's Flying Circus)*, Alan Bennett, Rik Mayall *(The Young Ones)* and Michael Gambon *(Two Deaths)*. Top-notch animation from the crew who produced the Beatles' *Yellow Submarine* and *Heavy Metal*. Winner of the Gold Special Jury Award for Best Family Film at Worldfest Houston.

VHS: S30241. $14.95.
Dave Unwin, Great Britain, 1996, 74 mins.

The Winter Stallion

A teenage orphan confronts the loss of her family's farm and her beloved stallion after her grandfather's sudden death. A story of love and hope set in the exquisite Welsh countryside. 96 mins.

VHS: S30908. $19.99.

The Yearling (1946)

Twelve-year-old Jody confronts the joys and pains of growing up when the needs of his beloved pet fawn compete with those of his struggling family. Marjorie Kinnan Rawlings' novel is touchingly brought to the screen by Gregory Peck, Jane Wyman and Claude Jarman, Jr., who received an Academy Award for portraying a child enduring harsh pioneer life.

VHS: S01488. $19.95.
Laser: LD70716. $44.98.
Clarence Brown, USA, 1946, 129 mins.

The Yearling (1994)

In the aftermath of the Civil War, a family experiences the poverty and turmoil that beset the South. In this setting, a boy finds a young orphaned deer that soon becomes the object of his affections. This heartwarming story is perfect family entertainment, based on Marjorie Kinnan Rawlings' classic novel. Peter Strauss and Jean Smart star.

VHS: S22442. $19.95.
Rod Hardy, USA, 1994, 98 mins.

Young Ivanhoe

The story of young Ivanhoe and how, with the help of Robin Hood and the Black Knight, he grew from a playful boy to a serious warrior. Starring Stacy Keach, Margot Kidder and Nick Mancuso.

VHS: S31847. $14.98.
Ralph L. Thomas, USA, 1995, 96 mins.

Young Magician
A wonderful children's film from producer Rock Demers. Peter's got magical power, but no practical control…and this spells trouble for his family, his friends, and the whole city. He ends up on the run until another boy genius teaches him the real, not-so-magical, power of practice and discipline.
VHS: S07034. $14.95.
Waldemar Dziki, Canada/Poland, 1987, 99 mins.

Young People
Shirley Temple gets to reprise some of her best moments in this stirring melodrama. Older footage reveals why this young girl needs a normal home in a normal town. Though her parents take her to an ideal place, the town residents are suspicious and treat them rather coldly, until disaster strikes.
VHS: S25910. $14.98.
Allan Dwan, USA, 1940, 79 mins.

Zebra in the Kitchen
When twelve-year-old animal lover Chris is hired at the city zoo, he is less than happy about the run-down facilities. So naturally, the mischievous assistant unlocks all the cages, creating mass hysteria as the mild mannered creatures wander into toy stores, butcher shops and bedrooms. Stars Jay "Dennis the Menace" North.
VHS: S16844. $19.98.
Ivan Tors, USA, 1965, 92 mins.

Zeus and Roxanne
What could be sweeter than the story of a boy and his dog? A boy, his dog and a dolphin. Single parents Terry (Steve Guttenberg) and Mary Beth (Kathleen Quinlan), a marine biologist, and their kids are brought together when Jordan's rowdy dog, Zeus, and Roxanne, the dolphin Mary Beth's studying, begin communicating in this "irresisible" *(Variety)*—and sweet—tale of friendship, freedom and love from the director of *The Man from Snowy River*.
DVD: DV60106. $24.98.
VHS: S31284. $19.98.
Laser: LD76285. $39.99.
George Miller, USA, 1996, 98 mins.

CHILDREN'S ACTIVITIES

All About Kids' Safety
How safe is your child when he rides his bicycle or walks down the street? If there was a fire in your home, what would your child do? This animated program effortlessly teaches children basic rules about bicycle, pedestrian, and fire safety. Produced by Fred Calvert in cooperation with the National Safety Council. 40 mins.
VHS: S13220. $19.95.

Alphabet Library
A child's home and world become a library where things familiar to children are presented in an alphabetical review. Each volume of this series is 30 mins.
Alphabet City.
VHS: S10319. $29.95.
Alphabet House.
VHS: S10321. $29.95.
Alphabet Zoo.
VHS: S10322. $29.95.

Amazing Things, Vol. 1
Dr. Misterio is a magician and a prankster. He also encourages children to participate in the creative process by turning basic household objects into toys and performing simple feats of magic. 56 mins.
VHS: S13070. $9.98.

Amazing Things, Vol. 2
More interactive, make-it-yourself magic from Dr. Misterio. Perfect for parties and rainy afternoons. 55 mins.
VHS: S13071. $9.98.

Animal Alphabet
This unique program lets kids and their parents travel the globe with live action animal photography and colorful animated letters.
VHS: S04134. $14.95.

Art Lessons for Children
Art teacher Donna Hugh demonstrates how easy it is to produce beautiful art projects using simple, inexpensive materials. Each volume several complete lessons.
Volume 1: Easy Watercolor Techniques. All you need is a box of watercolor paints, a brush, construction paper, a black crayon and a black felt-tipped pen for these four lessons: (1) Watercolor Flowers; (2) Watercolor Discovery; (3) Desert Scene; (4) Opaque Watercolors.
VHS: S16155. $29.95.
Volume 2: Easy Art Projects. These three lessons each use a limited number of readily available materials to open the creative minds of children everywhere: (1) Working with Oil Pastels; (2) Foil Art; (3) Printmaking.
VHS: S16156. $29.95.
Volume 3: More Fun with Watercolors. Watercolors, using simple, commonplace materials. Four lessons. 53 mins.
VHS: S17843. $29.95.
Volume 4: Felt Pen Fun. Four more lessons from art teacher Donna Hugh. 58 mins.
VHS: S17844. $29.95.
Volume 5: Animals of the Rain Forest. Beginning with oil pastels, white tempera paint, a brush and black crayon, this video will take children on an art-making expedition through the rain forest. Three animals—a toucan, a baby iguana and an anteater—are not only used as models, but each is carefully described emphasizing their relationship to the environment in which they live.
VHS: S22089. $29.95.
Volume 6: Plants of the Rain Forest. In this tape children can see how plants grow in the rain forest, one of the earth's most fascinating climates. Then art teacher Donna Hugh demonstrates techniques used to make beautiful artworks depicting these interesting and unusual plants. 48 mins.
VHS: S21250. $29.95.

The Best of Beakman's World
The quirky scientist Beakman takes his viewers on an intellectual odyssey as he provokes children into asking important and fundamental questions about life, art, science, nature and their existence. Beakman finds an accessible means of conveying scientific information, using wit, visual shocks and surprise to issue challenges, offer facts, solve problems and demonstrate experiments that can be accomplished at home. 60 mins.
VHS: S19160. $14.95.

Boy Scout Advancement Program: First Class
An instructional video designed to assist the Scout in obtaining the next level of Scouting achievement. Map-making and tracking techniques are covered as well as cooking, camping and conservation skills. The rules of safe swimming are reviewed in this supplemental tape to the Official Boy Scout handbook. 45 mins.
VHS: S07518. $24.95.

Boy Scout Advancement Program: Second Class
This video using real Scouts continues the Scouting program on the second rank. Demonstrations in first aid, life saving techniques, and tips on hiking, camping and communicating are all covered. Be prepared to learn how the Scout Law applies to everyday life. 51 mins.
VHS: S07517. $24.95.

Boy Scout Advancement Program: Tenderfoot
Based on the number two best seller of all time, *The Official Boy Scout Handbook*. Featuring real Scouts in real situations demonstrating the skills needed to obtain the rank of Tenderfoot. Program includes pitching a tent, basic wilderness training and how to make a safe campfire. 63 mins.
VHS: S07516. $24.95.

Child of Mine: The Lullaby Video
Thirteen different female artists perform an eclectic and touching collection of lullabies that acknowledge the special bonds between mother and child. The artists include Mary-Chapin Carpenter, Rosanne Cash, Gloria Estefan, Dionne Warwick and Carole King.
VHS: S20300. $19.98.

Children's Chants and Games
Playground chants and games are illustrated in this video. Some of these games reflect ancient origins while others mirror contemporary tensions and conflicts. 15 mins.
VHS: S23520. $49.95.

Creative Movement: A Step Towards Intelligence
Melissa Lowe's instruction is designed to help children develop self-awareness and confidence and develop their expressive capabilities. The program shows children having fun singing, clapping and moving to music, learning motor skills and coordination. 80 mins.
VHS: S19687. $19.95.

E-Z Bread Dough Sculpture
Young viewers will be rolling in dough after they learn how to create twists, animals and braids with ordinary bread dough. 30 mins.
VHS: S09885. $29.95.

Ei Ei Yoga
Catchy country tunes, friendly barnyard characters and clear demonstrations from Max Thomas as flexible farmer Yogi Oki Doki make this entertaining video a great yoga primer to get kids *mooving*. 38 mins.
VHS: S32078. $14.95.

The Flying Fruit Fly Circus
A documentary on the Flying Fruit Fly Circus, an Australian-based, youth performing arts company that was founded in 1979. The program offers thrilling spectacle, as the 40-member troupe—entirely made up of children—perform various tumbling acts. 50 mins.
VHS: S19642. $24.95.

Fun in a Box
These award-winning animated and live-action films promote positive values and offer ideas for fun and games.
Fun in a Box -: *Ben's Dream*. From acclaimed author Chris Van Allsburg. Also includes *Fish* and *The Red Ball Express*. 30 mins.
VHS: S16309. $14.95.
Fun in a Box #2: New Friends. Howard, by James Stevenson, is the highlight of this program that also includes Metal Dogs of India and Why Cats Eat First. 30 mins.
VHS: S16308. $14.95.
Fun in a Box 3: *The Birthday Movie*. This interactive video is hosted by the birthday spirit who knows all about fun and games. 30 mins.
VHS: S16307. $14.95.

Fun with Clay
Young viewers learn the basics of clay, including the pinch, coil and slab method of clay, working with household objects. 30 mins.
VHS: S09881. $9.95.

Ghostwriter
A blend of expressive graphics, innovative effects and celebrity guest stars highlight this children's game about a team of youthful sleuths who are befriended by the ghostwriter. He's a secret friend who communicates clues and signals through reading and writing. 105 mins.
VHS: S19157. $14.98.
Laser: LD72189. $34.98.

Globalstage
Globalstage travels the world to select the best live, professional theatre productions for kids ages 7 to 14. Creatively filmed and edited by the BBC, each program is hosted by Professor Elizabeth McNamer, a dynamic guide who explores the cultural, literary, and historical significance of the plays with her 11-year-old sidekick, Preston. Both kids and parents will be delighted with the thought-provoking subjects, creative staging, and entertaining stories that these videos capture.
Globalstage—Cyrano. The exquisite avant-garde adaptation of Rostrand's French classic about the power of the written word, and the speciousness of ephemeral beauty. The internationally acclaimed theater company Blauw Vier of Antwerp, Belgium portrays this poetic comedy of a mismatched love triangle. Filmed on location in Antwerp. Directed by Jo Roets, Great Britain/Belgium, 1998, 100 mins.
VHS: S34554. $24.95.
Globalstage—Frankenstein. Masterful direction combines with vivid costumes and sets in this Stage One production of Mary Shelley's classic tale. Professor Elizabeth McNamer provides background on Mary Shelley and the 19th-century Romantic movement and comments on the story's key themes. Filmed on location in Louisville. Directed by J. Clements, Great Britain/USA, 1997, 90 mins.
VHS: S34555. $24.95.
Globalstage—Pinocchio. A live Stage One performance musical of the classic story about the wooden puppet who struggles to become real, but disobeys his father's wishes to go to school. Examines the themes of unconditional love, the importance of education to our success in life, and how we determine what is right and wrong. Performed in the style of the commedia dell'arte, the colorful set and costumes take the viewer back to Renaissance Florence with original songs, dancing, and creative staging. Includes a behind-the-scenes interview with writer and lyricist Moses Goldberg and composer Scott Kasbaum. Filmed on location in Louisville. Directed by J. Clements, Great Britain, 1997, 90 mins.
VHS: S34553. $24.95.

Great Ape Activity Tape
Three activity experts demonstrate 15 activities to chase away boredom or rainy day blues for children 3-8 as they learn a variety of crafts, tricks and games. 30 mins.
VHS: S04156. $14.95.

How to Fold a Paper Crane
A pair of speaking, that is signing, hands, are accompanied by voice-over to explain *How to Fold a Paper Crane*. The paper crane is a symbol of peace and this video makes this simple but delicate craft available to everyone. Perfect for the classroom. 30 mins.
VHS: S24931. $125.00.

I Can Dance
An insightful introduction to ballet, specially designed for children. Professional dancer Debra Maxwell has developed a program forgirls and boys aged seven years and older. The program familiarizes children with plies, center work and the five basic positions. 30 mins.
VHS: S17314. $19.95.

I'm a Ballerina Now

This video was designed to aid and inspire hopeful children. Dance exercises are shown and illustrated with lyrics that help children remember the proper steps. Then a true adult ballerina is seen performing the same steps. 40 mins.
VHS: S24831. $19.95.

In Search of the Missing Numbers

Presents basic addition and subtraction concepts in a fun format as Brad and Melissa go into Blasteria in the search of missing numbers. For ages 6-9. 60 mins.
VHS: S09964. $19.95.

Joshua's Masai Mask

With a jazzy text and splashy illustrations, this read-along video is a special experience for all children. Joshua loves playing his kalimba, a traditional African musical instrument, even though his friends all like rap. His uncle gives him a magical mask that helps Joshua overcome this problem. 11:30 mins.
VHS: S22353. $39.95.

The Joy of Life

In this charming interactive tape, children can be guided through the mysteries of human sexuality with the help of their parents. Five-minute segments slowly build to cover a wide range of topics. The story concerns two cousins who ask their grandmother about the facts of life. Everything crucial is covered, from sexual attraction to safe sex and AIDS. 72 mins.
VHS: S22867. $39.95.

Juggle Time

Learn confidence while learning to juggle in this fun-filled program designed to teach juggling in slow motion by using scarves. Three colorful scarves included in package. Questar/Mercom Gold Award, National Educational Film and Video Festival Award. 30 minutes, ages 5-12.
VHS: S17138. $14.95.

Kids by the Bay

The first children's film by Emmy Award-winning directors Judy Irving and Christopher Beaver shows how much fun it is to pitch in and restore the environment. Features rare footage of endangered species. Grades K-5. 1997, 20 mins.
VHS: S31903. $49.95.

Kids Get Cooking: The Egg

This celebration of food and cooking will thrill kids as they learn recipes, experiments, crafts and more. Puppets Herb and Bea add to the comedy, cooking and songs. Endorsed by the National Education Association. 30 minutes, ages 4-10.
Home Video.
VHS: S10148. $14.95.
Public Performance Rights.
VHS: S17152. $34.90.

Kids Kitchen: Making Good Eating Great Fun for Kids!

Join the juggling nutrition magician and her diverse group of kids as they learn to create delicious, nutritious snacks without cooking. Ages 5-10.
VHS: S24769. $99.00.

Kids Learning Through Fun

These 13 tapes offer both valuable skills and important values to children through an engaging cast of puppets. Music and guests round out the charming elements that make each episode in the series come alive. These tapes are not just fun, but upbeat and positive. 30 mins. each.
A Good Education.
VHS: S26255. $14.95.
A Good Attitude.
VHS: S26264. $14.95.
A Good Sense of Humor.
VHS: S26265. $14.95.
A Helping Hand.
VHS: S26262. $14.95.
Being Conscientious.
VHS: S26266. $14.95.
Completing a Task.
VHS: S26256. $14.95.
Enthusiasm.
VHS: S26261. $14.95.
Good Manners.
VHS: S26257. $14.95.
Planning Your Time.
VHS: S26258. $14.95.
Positive Thinking.
VHS: S26260. $14.95.
Responsibility.
VHS: S26263. $14.95.
Special Friends.
VHS: S26267. $14.95.
Training and Practice.
VHS: S26259. $14.95.

Kidsongs Music Video Stories

A series of sing-a-long music videos, which are designed for children from pre-school to ten years old, featuring performances by the Kidsongs Kids, multi-racial, multi-ethnic, multi-talented boys and girls. Based on the PBS series, the videos also include themes and concepts which are developmentally important. The content is geared toward 2-6 year olds, but also interests older kids, as the subplot involves the older children who produce the show. We see children doing interviews, kids using cameras, kids in the control rooms. Ages 2-10. 25 minutes each tape.
A Day with the Animals.
VHS: S06640. $14.98.
A Day at the Circus.
VHS: S06647. $14.98.
A Day at Camp.
VHS: S24538. $14.95.
A Day at Old MacDonald's Farm. The Kidsongs Kids take a trip to Old MacDonald's farm in this music-filled story.
VHS: S32532. $9.95.
Kidsongs: Baby Animal Songs. This charming music video takes kids on a song-filled adventure with the Kidsongs Kids, Billy and Ruby Biggle, and dozens of their adorable baby animal friends.
VHS: S32533. $9.95.
Boppin' with Biggles.
VHS: S24722. $14.95.
Cars, Boats, Trains and Planes.
VHS: S06641. $14.98.
Country Sing-Along.
VHS: S24723. $14.95.
Good Night, Sleep Tight.
VHS: S06642. $14.98.
I'd Like to Teach the World to Sing.
VHS: S06643. $14.98.
If We Could Talk to the Animals.
VHS: S24539. $14.95.
Let's Play Ball!
VHS: S24540. $14.95.
Ride the Roller Coaster.
VHS: S24541. $14.95.
Sing Out, America!
VHS: S06644. $14.98.
The Wonderful World of Sports.
VHS: S06645. $14.98.
Very Silly Songs.
VHS: S24542. $14.95.
We Wish You a Merry Christmas.
VHS: S24784. $12.95.
What I Want to Be. The Kidsongs Kids take to the high seas, the fire station, the police academy, Hollywood and more as they explore through song and dance what they'd like to be when they grow up.
VHS: S32534. $9.95.

Kratts' Creatures

The creature-crazy zoologist/biologist team of Martin Kratt and Chris Kratt takes you on a high-energy, jam-packed wildlife adventure. Explore with Martin and Chris as they search for fascinating creatures all over the planet. Each tape is 30 mins.
African Creature Quest. It's a scavenger hunt in Africa as Martin looks for the Big Five and Chris looks after the little five.
VHS: S31867. $12.95.
The Great Bear Show. Haul off into Canada's North Woods in search of the great black bear and sit around the campfire as Martin and Chris figure out how humans and bears can share the planet.
VHS: S31868. $12.95.
Maximum Cheetah Velocity. It's a high-speed chase as Chris and Martin catch up with the cheetah, the fastest animal on the planet.
VHS: S31869. $12.95.

The Land of Sweet Taps

This is a fun-filled adventure for children ages 4-8 who want to learn tap dancing. In addition to the fundamental sounds, rhythms and steps there are shuffles and digs. The lyrics are fun and memorable, helping children remember the timing of the music. 57 mins.
VHS: S21701. $19.95.

Landmark

A three-volume set of imaginative, interactive programs that instruct children on the important lessons of problem solving, analysis, questions, play games, learn valuable skills and how to have fun. With audio, video and visual guidelines and 45 minutes of historic newsreel footage.
Fun and Games.
Laser: LD70297. $39.95.
The First National Kidisc: Vol. 1.
Laser: LD70296. $39.95.
The History DisQuiz.
Laser: LD70298. $39.95.

Language Primer

A blend of animation, music and sound effects is used to relate wordless stories about Max, a mouse. The program is designed to encourage children to take an active role in the learning process. The video instructs children on basic language skills: sequencing, recognizing a main idea, recalling details, storywriting and storytelling. The programming is "very effective, providing appealing contrast while learning writing skills" *(Video Rating Guide for Libraries)*. Designed for children in kindergarten through 3rd grade.
Adventuresome Max: Discovering the World. In eight vignettes, Max establishes friendships with an army of ants, an outcast snail and an alien from another world, in the process learning valuable information about himself and the outside world. 18 mins.
VHS: S19960. $49.95.
Max in Motion: Developing Language Skills. Eight stories are expressed without words, each focusing of Max, an eccentric mouse with an innovative flair for problem solving. 18 mins.
VHS: S19959. $49.95.
Max's Library: Beginning to Write. With the aid of puppets and animation, children learn how to create a short story—from conception through execution. They develop storytelling by learning to define a beginning, a middle and an end. 16 mins.
VHS: S19961. $49.95.
Language Primer, Set. A set of three programs. 48 mins.
VHS: S19962. $129.00.

Let's Create a Better World

This how-to video shows kids environmentally safe projects. In addition, it increases awareness of nature and underscores the importance of environmentalism. Ages 6-12. 70 mins.
VHS: S25612. $29.95.

Let's Create for Halloween

Just right for the holidays, this tape shows how to make six art projects with a Halloween theme. Music and special surprises will not only delight kids, but also help motivate them. This video offers a safe way for children to participate in Halloween. USA, 1995, 60 mins.
VHS: S25613. $29.95.

Let's Create for Thanksgiving

In this video kids will see the family holiday of Thanksgiving through an artistic lens. The art projects included here both inform children about Thanksgiving and celebrate the best of this holiday. There is even a demonstration that can transform turkey. USA, 1995, 60 mins.
VHS: S25614. $29.95.

Let's Create Fun Jewelry for Boys and Girls

The art club creates jewelry from everyday items. Children will be amazed at the rings, medallions, pins and other accessories they can make. Many make great gifts. 60 mins.
VHS: S25611. $29.95.

Let's Sing Along

Interactive music and sounds provide the inspiration for kids to play along with the child hosts on the video. Ages 2-6. 25 minutes.
VHS: S25038. $14.95.

Macmillan Video Almanac for Kids

Indoor Fun. Contains four individual *chapters* on one 30-minute cassette, each of them an informative and interactive segment meant to be viewed while using simple household materials: body talk, making faces, a close look at volcanoes and a short journey into space. "A real milestone in children's video." 30 mins.
VHS: S08105. $26.95.
Rainy Day Games. Includes Soap Bubble Magic, A Secret Language, Kite Flying, String Figures. Each of the segments is viewed while using simple household materials. 30 mins.
VHS: S08106. $26.95.

Make a Puppet, Make a Friend

Learn how an ordinary paper bag can be transformed into a playful puppet. 30 mins.
VHS: S09882. $29.95.

Making Music in the Classroom, Program 3, Ages 3-7

The third in the series contains more of John Langstaff's enjoyable musical educational method. Step-by-step techniques prove especially effective with children ages 3-7. Both classroom tapes include an instructional guide for teachers.
VHS: S23683. $24.95.

Making Music in the Classroom, Program 4, Ages 7-11

Absorbing, fun and instructive, this final installment of John Langstaff's musical video series is as much fun as the first.
VHS: S23684. $24.95.

Making Music with Children, Program 1, Ages 3-7

In this introductory video, John Langstaff demonstrates, easily and effectively, basic musical principals for children ages 3-7. Rhythm games, movement activities, simple percussion accompaniments and singing games help children learn in a fun way. Booklets with words and music are included with all these tapes.
VHS: S23681. $24.95.

Making Music with Children, Program 2, Ages 7-11

Langstaff's inspirational teaching method will captivate children in this second video, aimed at children ages 7-11. It contains still more story songs, street cries, sea chanties, folk songs and rounds. Even musical elements like pitch are covered, and the value of music from different cultures is emphasized.
VHS: S23682. $24.95.

Math Rock Countdown

Concentrates on building basic multiplication and division skills and developing strategies for solving problems in the format of a music show as Treva Sue and the Bleaters use math facts to tell their country rock music story. For ages 6-9. 60 mins.
VHS: S09965. $19.95.

Monkey Moves

Based on the acclaimed movement and learning methods of Dr. Moshe Feldenkrais, this marvelous musical exercise-movement tape helps children develop balance, coordination and motor sequencing skills while moving to original songs and music. Put together by Dr. Stephen Rosenholtz, a well qualified educator, known also for his Feldenkrais movement videos for adults. Ages 3-8, 26 mins.
VHS: S24552. $19.95.

Mr. Men: In the Great Alphabet Hunt

Mr. Men is an inventive brand of cartoon figures which aid children in understanding the alphabet and language. 30 mins.
VHS: S19426. $12.98.

My First Activity Series

A fun, intellectually stimulating series of videos adapted from the *My First Book Series*, providing instructional, easy-to-follow guidelines to a series of activities, including the construction of musical instruments, awareness of ecology and environmental issues, unlocking creativity, understanding nature, conducting science experiments and learning how to make interesting and fun things to eat. Backed by lively musical accompaniment. "The production is excellent, with carefully spoken narration and clear, simple cinematography" *(Video Review)*.
My First Music Video.
VHS: S20293. $14.98.
My First Green Video.
VHS: S20294. $14.98.
My First Activity Video.
VHS: S20295. $14.98.
My First Nature Video.
VHS: S20296. $14.98.
My First Science Video.
VHS: S20297. $14.98.
My First Cooking Video.
VHS: S20298. $14.98.
My First Magic Video. This video explains how to stage a magic show at home using simple but captivating illusions. Step-by-step instructions are provided by a professional magician. 45 mins.
VHS: S25520. $14.95.
My First Party Video. Chock full of creative ideas, this video will help make any party more enjoyable. Crazy hats, crocodile invitations, birthday cake, masks and more are all explained in clear, colorful demonstrations. 45 mins.
VHS: S25521. $14.95.

My New York

Premier folk artists reveal vibrant New York City's through vivid and detailed illustrations in this read-along video. Central Park Zoo, Chinatown, the ferry to Ellis Island and the Empire State Building are depicted. Children will love it.
VHS: S22350. $39.95.

Nickelodeon Presents How to Throw a Double Dare Party

The Double Dare award-winning action game show on video stars Marc Summers as host, with each game demonstrated with a list of required props and ingredients, with some classics such as Whip Cream and Cherry Pie Wheelbarrow included. 60 mins.
VHS: S11196. $14.98.

Printmaking Gadgets

With just some paper, old toys and tempera paint, children can create their own pictures, greeting cards, pen holders and wrapping paper. 30 mins.
VHS: S09883. $9.95.

Problems for Young Consumers

Presenting real consumer problems for children to face and solve—problems they are likely to meet in their everyday lives—such as an advertisement that misleads and leaves a child disappointed and unhappy. Includes *What Do You Pay?* (unit pricing), *The Big Sale* (comparable value), *Buy Now—Pay Later* (Credit), and *The Street Vendor* (guaranteed quality). 25 mins.
VHS: S10313. $29.95.

Professor Iris

The series that makes education fun, as originally aired on The Learning Channel.
Animal Antics. Professor Iris goes on a safari looking for elephants. Kids will love this delightful puppet series episode that is rich in both educational possibilities and simple, plain fun. 40 mins.
VHS: S26057. $12.95.
Art Party. Professor Iris is at it once again with her amusing antics. Now this puppet professor sets to work painting a masterpiece. 40 mins.
VHS: S26058. $12.95.
Birthday Party. In this video kids will learn how to organize and cooperate as they party with Professor Iris and her friends at the Learning Channel.
VHS: S23018. $19.95.
Creepy Critters. Professor Iris is back, this time introducing kids to snakes, bats, bugs and bees, in this entertaining and educational pre-science lesson. First aired on The Learning Channel. Ages 2-6. 40 minutes.
VHS: S24520. $12.95.
Let's Do It. From the Learning Channel comes this creative and fun video featuring Professor Iris. Kids will learn about sports, dancing and games as they discover new ways to play.
VHS: S23017. $19.95.
Music Mania. Kids learn about musical instruments as they sing and play with Professor Iris in this video from the Learning Channel. Professor Iris is the perfect puppet companion to take kids on a musical, educational journey.
VHS: S23016. $19.95.
My Body Me. Professor Iris will make kids laugh even as they learn about their bodies and themselves. 40 mins.
VHS: S26059. $12.95.

Raffi in Concert with the Rise and Shine Band

A young children's concert with the incomparable Raffi and his Rise and Shine Band. Songs feature: "Time to Sing," "Bathtime," "Apples and Bananas" and "Everything Grows." Great Fun! 50 mins.
VHS: S14110. $19.95.
Laser: LD71290. $29.98.

Rainy Day Magic Show

Magician Mark Mazzarella instills a sense of wonder while demonstrating how to turn everyday things into an entire magic show. For ages 6 and up. USA.
VHS: S14952. $19.95.

See How They Grow

This collection of four tapes takes children inside the mysteries of animal behavior—charting from infancy to adulthood the growth of pets, farm animals, wild animals and insects and spiders. Each video contains four different animals, and is set off by musical accompaniment. "This timeless video collection will bring kids and parents back again and again" *(The Playground)*.
See How They Grow: Farm Animals.
VHS: S20290. $14.98.
See How They Grow: Insects and Spiders.
VHS: S20291. $14.98.
See How They Grow: Pets.
VHS: S20289. $14.98.
See How They Grow: Wild Animals.
VHS: S20292. $14.98.

The Sign for Friends

Follow the signs for music, laughter and happy faces. This video teaches kids how to sign as they sing and count along. Host David Parker shows his young friend how it's done. Perfect for kids ages 4-8. 30 min.
VHS: S24490. $14.95.

Silly Tales and Tunes

Disc jockey K.J. is back, hosting comical stories and sing-along songs. Ages 2-8.
VHS: S24644. $12.95.

Sing 'n' Sign for Fun!

Both hearing and hearing-impaired children can sing, dance and sign along with Gaia and her friends from KidSign Club in this musical adventure into the world of signing. Age 3 and up. Closed captioned. 42 mins.
VHS: S28594. $14.95.

Sing-Alongs

Hosted by "The Lionhearts," an adorable feline family which leads kids in singing along, this popular tape series features songs from MGM musicals and animated hits, including *Babes in Toyland, Meet Me in St. Louis, The Pebble and the Penguin, Gulliver's Travels, Chitty Chitty Bang Bang,* the *All Dogs Go to Heaven* films, *Take Me Out to the Ballgame, Tom Sawyer,* Dr. Seuss' *How the Grinch Stole Christmas, The Pink Panther* cartoon series, *Anchors Aweigh* and more.
Being Happy.
VHS: S31066. $12.95.
Friends.
VHS: S31067. $12.95.
Having Fun.
VHS: S31064. $12.95.
Searching for Your Dreams.
VHS: S31065. $12.95.

Skating Safe for Kids

This hip video uses a fun story to instruct kids ages six and up how to skate safely. Gail Shrawder is a recognized instructor who will explain "10 Rules of the Road." She also instructs kids on basics like how to balance themselves, stop, and turn. 30 mins.
VHS: S23858. $24.95.

Something Special

Develops awareness of the importance of the arts for a balanced education. Children are shown in classes in the visual arts, music, dance and theatre, illustrating the value of art for children. 28 mins.
VHS: S07638. $39.95.

Spinning Tops and Tickle Bops

This animated children's collection features three different stories: *The Animal's Picnic Day, Spinning Tops* and *The Planet of the Tickle Bops*. For those viewers who are wondering what a tickle bop is, and why they rate an entire planet, the answer can only be found by watching this tape. USA, 30 mins.
VHS: S03642. $14.95.

Squiggles, Dots and Lines

Ed Emberly presents his drawing alphabet, a tool for kids to unlock their creativity. Fourteen kids share their fun-telling stories and create a giant mural. Parents' Choice Award. 30 minutes, ages 5-12.
Home Video.
VHS: S10147. $14.95.
Public Performance Rights.
VHS: S17153. $34.90.

Stop, Look and Cook!

Set in a dairy farm, an apple orchard and a nice kitchen, this video teaches kids how to make some nutritious recipes along with a side of sign language. Host David Parker is effective and appealing, perfect for kids ages 4-8. 20 min.
VHS: S24491. $19.95.

Table Manners for Kids: Tots to Teens

A series of vignettes designed to instruct children and young adults on proper etiquette and how to apply those rules in an actual restaurant setting.
VHS: S19662. $14.95.

This Pretty Planet

This collection features 13 folk songs by Tom Chapin, who is joined by special guests Jon Cobert and Michael Mark. The songs include "Alphabet Soup" and "Sing a Whale Song." "These songs are wittier and catchier than most in kiddom, and Chapin may be the most charming performer on earth" *(Forbes Newspapers)*.
VHS: S20299. $14.98.

Trailsigns North: Poop, Paw & Hoof Prints

In this informative and educational video, kids of all ages will learn how to identify many trail signs that are left behind by animals that live in the Northern United States, Canada and Alaska. 1996, 26 mins.
VHS: S31904. $29.95.

Twinkle Twinkle Little Star

Seventeen songs and rhymes that have always been popular with children are showcased in this charming video. Children will learn to sing along to all their favorites in this simple and straightforward illustration of childhood songs. 40 mins.
VHS: S21532. $14.95.

Vegetable Print Shop

Children learn to use fruits and vegetables to create pictures, including using sliced artichokes, apples and pears as printmaking tools. 30 mins.
VHS: S09884. $29.95.

Wee Sing Series

This series of videos continues the positive tradition of the popular book/audio cassette series which has brought song to so many. Aimed for ages 2-8.
Wee Sing: Grandpa's Magical Toys. Peter and his friends visit the world's most wonderful Grandpa. In turn, Grandpa shows them the importance of remaining young at heart. Grandpa leads the children into a special world where toys come alive and songs are fun to sing. 1988. 60 minutes. Ages 2-8.
VHS: S24843. $12.95.
Wee Sing: King Cole's Party. Jack and Jill, Little Boy Blue and Mary and her Little Lamb voyage to King Cole's Castle to celebrate 100 years of peace. This charming live-action children's video includes over 20 favorite nursery rhymes engagingly performed. 54 mins.
VHS: S26360. $12.98.
Wee Sing: The Best Christmas Ever. Twenty holiday songs and a variety of fingerplays will enchant kids in this video trip to the North Pole. Four kids set off to help Santa save the holiday. Together these friends learn how to overcome personal challenges with help from each other. 56 mins.
VHS: S26362. $12.98.
Wee Sing: The Big Rock Candy Mountains. Lisa and her friends the Snoodle Doodles travel together to a fantasyland of candy. Along the way they learn about the importance of friendship, kindness, recycling and the joys of healthy food. 61 mins.
VHS: S26359. $12.98.
Wee Sing: The Marvelous Musical Mansion. A great cast of characters performs over 20 songs, in every room of this mansion. Oddly, however, there is a mystery afoot. Who stole the missing musical treasures? Kids will love the music and intrigue, and will enjoy an important lesson about self-esteem and consideration for others. 61 mins.
VHS: S26361. $12.98.
Wee Sing in Sillyville. This video features a girl and a boy who bring harmony to the land of Yellow Spurtlegurgles and Green Jingleheimers. 20 nonsense songs. Parents will remember some of these classics. 1990. 30 minutes.
VHS: S24842. $12.95.
Wee Sing Together. Encourages kids to sing along in this mixture of live action and special effects. 1985. 60 minutes.
VHS: S24841. $12.95.
Wee Sing Train. Kids ride along, making exciting stops along the way, singing, dancing and learning. Ages 2-8.
VHS: S24844. $12.95.
Wee Sing Under the Sea. When Granny painted an underwater seascape, she never expected it to come alive. Now she and her grandson Devin can explore a new world where they meet amazing creatures. This delightful children's video is full of songs and information about environmentalism. 60 mins.
VHS: S23273. $14.95.
Wee Singdom. In this song-filled adventure from the award-winning *Wee Sing* series, *Wee Sing* kids Annie and Tim introduce children to the game of "Wee Singdom," which transports them and favorite characters from past videos into the magical, musical center of *Wee Sing* world, Singalingaland. "These are among my favorite video tapes for kids" (Leonard Maltin, *Entertainment Tonight*). 64 mins.
VHS: S30054. $12.98.

Wizkids: Careers in Science

This award-winning show encourages girls and children of color to pursue careers in science. An African-American agronomist and a Native American geneticist explain the gratifications of science. 25 mins.
VHS: S23275. $165.00.

Workout with Daddy & Me

Combining physical activities with games and songs to enhance learning, coordination and socialization, *Workout with Daddy and Me* provides a fun and easy way to exercise with your child. Complete with an activity book. 30 mins.
VHS: S16483. $12.98.

Workout with Mommy & Me

Millions of parents have attended *Mommy and Me* classes for more than 15 years. Now you and your child can take the class at home. Complete with an activity book, this fun-filled exercise program is led by award-winning gymnastics and dance instructor Barbara Peterson Davis. 30 mins.
VHS: S16482. $12.98.

"You Can" Videos

A series of unique, reality-based family and educational programs targeting kids ages 2-6 which aims at empowerment through positive, nurturing messages. Non-violent and aiming to show girls and boys equally. 30 minutes each video. Ages 2-6.
You Can Be an Artist.
VHS: S24938. $12.95.
You Can Fly a Kite.
VHS: S24939. $12.95.
You Can Ride a Horse. Come along with the You Can Kids as they visit a stable, watch a blacksmith at work, learn about horseback riding and more. Full of fascinating facts about horses, with catchy sing-alongs and nice musical backdrop. Perfect for children ages 2-8, this video demonstrates basic horseback riding skills together with catchy original songs performed by kids and the chorus Peaceful Generation. In addition there are grooming demonstrations and exciting stunts. 30 mins.
VHS: S24770. $12.95.

You on Kazoo!

The video comes with a kazoo. Seven kids have a blast inviting the viewers to join the kazoo fun as they mimic animals and machines. Ages 3-8. 30 minutes.
VHS: S25037. $14.95.

Zillions TV: A Kid's Guide to Toys and Games

Zillions TV warns children about the foolish linkage of money and quality. This program teaches kids how to use science, math and problem-solving capabilities in order to assess the quality of video games, walkie-talkies, food, movie tickets, boom boxes and mountain bikes, among other products. The work features two songs, "Check It Out," a rap music video, and "Shop Around," a cover of the classic song that promotes comparison shopping. 30 mins.
VHS: S20024. $19.95.

FOREIGN LANGUAGES FOR CHILDREN

20,000 Lenguas de Viaje Submarino

The incredible animated adventures of Nautilus and Captain Nemo at the bottom of the sea. In Spanish. 60 mins.
VHS: S34437. $19.95.

Aladdin and the Magical Lamp (Aladino y La Lampara Maravillosa)

This is a charming film adaptation of the delightful tale concerning the discovery of a magical lamp. Clavillazo, Ana Bertha Lepe and Oscar Pulido star. Spanish with NO subtitles. 89 mins.
VHS: S23921. $24.95.

Alicia en el Pais de las Maravillas

In this marvelous animated fantasy, Alicia follows the white rabbit into a magical underground world full of fantastic adventures. In Spanish. 60 mins.
VHS: S34438. $24.95.

Anna, Schmidt & Oskar

Follow the adventures of a teenager, a magician and a puppy through these videos produced in conjunction with the Goethe Institute. Based upon one of Germany's most popular TV programs, its portrayal of everyday culture will help improve comprehension and listening skills. Each of the comical misadventures is a self-contained unit and includes songs, games and language exercises which can be used by beginning and intermediate students.
Anna, Schmidt & Oskar Ubungsbuch. Includes exercises, songs and games. 100 mins.
VHS: S33268. $13.00.
Anna, Schmidt & Oskar, Vol. 1. Six segments. 100 mins.
VHS: S33266. $51.00.
Anna, Schmidt & Oskar, Vol. 2. Six segments. 100 mins.
VHS: S33267. $51.00.
Anna, Schmidt & Oskar: Set of 2.
VHS: S33269. $93.00.

Arc-en-Ciel

The next best thing to being there—total immersion in French, via video. The place is Paris, the characters are four French teenagers and an English friend, who explore realistic situations in Paris. Each of the six episodes is followed by a repetition and display of key expressions. The Video Guide provides a synopsis of each episode. 70 mins.
VHS: S11199. $49.95.

Asterix

This inventive program charts the amazing tales of Asterix. In French. 220 mins.
Asterix et Cleopatre.
VHS: S19807. $39.95.
Asterix le Gaulois.
VHS: S19809. $39.95.
Douze Travaux d'Asterix.
VHS: S19808. $39.95.

Asterix in Britain

With his magical potion and Obelisk at his side, Asterix prevents Caesar's invading legions from conquering ancient Britain. Very high production values and wit from director Pino Van Lamsweerde.
VHS: S12527. $14.95.
Gaumont, France, 1986, 85 mins.

Asterix vs. Caesar

Asterix and Obelisk decide Caesar's troops have wandered too far from Rome. They battle legions of centurions with the mystical help of a strength-giving magic potion.
VHS: S12526. $39.95.
Gaumont, France, 1985, 85 mins.

Avantage

This lively collection of 12 mini-programs will strengthen the French language skills of teen-agers. Part I introduces intermediate students to the daily life of French students. Part II explores everyday activities, including a trip to the Ecole du Cirque in Amiens, where film students are trained. Contextualizing grammar and vocabulary makes these lessons both valuable and entertaining.
Part I: Video and Book.
VHS: S19787. $49.95.
Part II: Video and Book.
VHS: S19788. $49.95.

Babar et le Pere Noel

This French adaptation of de Brunhoff's classic has won the 1987 Gemini Best Animated Program. Babar is on a journey to find Father Christmas. Threatening his search is Babar's arch enemy, Rataxas the Rhinoceros. Throughout, the animation is lively and colorful. French without subtitles. 24 mins.
VHS: S09053. $39.95.

Babar le Film

A wonderfully touching, animated treatment of de Brunhoff's classic stories about the king of elephants. *Babar le Film* relates the story of how he saved Celesteville. French with *no* subtitles. 77 mins.
VHS: S19804. $49.95.

Bonjour les Amis!

Moustache is France's most beloved animated character. Now this charming cat helps introduce the French language to children in a collection of three tapes which combine animation and live action. 50 mins each.
Bonjour les Amis! Volume 1.
VHS: S23608. $19.95.
Bonjour les Amis! Volume 2.
VHS: S23609. $19.95.
Bonjour les Amis! Volume 3.
VHS: S23610. $19.95.
Bonjour les Amis! Set of 3 Volumes.
VHS: S23611. $54.95.

Caribbean Kids

Stories about real kids of Hispanic backgrounds who live and learn in today's world. Original entertaining musical backgrounds. 55 mins.
English Version.
VHS: S06729. $29.95.
Spanish Version.
VHS: S06730. $29.95.

Carlitos, Dani y Luis Alfredo

Three puppets and their human companion use song, movement and dialogue to teach basic language and social skills. Four different segments cover colors, shapes, health, conservation and healthy eating. The program is accompanied by a parent/teacher guide with vocabulary, language exercises and followup tasks. Spanish and English. 30 mins.
VHS: S19775. $39.95.

Chanter pour S'Amuser

This Canadian series involves song, dance and movement to make an impression with young students. Each program introduces vocabulary through movement and songs. *L'Album de Marie-Soleil* concentrates on the parts of the body, animals and prepositions. *Une Journee avec Marie-Soleil* deals with the alphabet, numbers and adjectives. 50 mins.
L'Album de Marie-Soleil.
VHS: S19784. $35.00.
Une Journee avec Marie-Soleil.
VHS: S19785. $35.00.
Chanter pour S'Amuser, Set.
VHS: S19786. $62.00.

Chantons Disney Ensemble

Jiminy Cricket hosts this ensemble, which offers the most memorable songs of Disney's movies, sung in French. On-screen French lyrics allow students to sing along. 30 minutes each.
Beauty & the Beast.
VHS: S30572. $19.95.
Peter Pan.
VHS: S30569. $19.95.
Snow White.
VHS: S30568. $19.95.

The Lion King.
VHS: S30571. $19.95.
The Little Mermaid.
VHS: S30570. $19.95.
Set of 5.
VHS: S30573. $89.95.

Chicken Minute (Not Just for Kids)

This children's comedy charts the relations of Mama Chicken, blues enthusiast and virtuoso cook, and Minute, a charming vegetarian fox. The colorful cast includes Anatole Bonbon the alligator and Mudbelly, the local monster. English and French with English subtitles. 120 mins.
Laser: LD71940. $39.95.

Classic Stories in Spanish

Children will delight in seeing these familiar favorites in Spanish. The colorful animation will hold the attention of young students as they listen to the story unfold. Perfect for those just learning Spanish. *Don Quixote* and *The Three Little Pigs* are the stories included. 23 mins.
VHS: S06833. $39.95.

Conversations Entre les Jeunes au Sujet des Jeunes

This inventive program offers practical insights into the nature and personality of the French teenager, based on questions most prominently asked by their American contemporaries. The video is organized into various units—fashion, movies, fast food, education and cross cultural attitudes. In French. 120 mins.
VHS: S19806. $39.95.

The Curious Adventures of Mr. Wonderbird (La Bergere et Le Ramoneur)

In this visually striking French animated feature, the outrageous Mr. Wonderbird (voiced by Peter Ustinov) narrates the story of a most bizarre enchanted castle. Paintings of a shepard girl and a chimney sweep come to life, and the evil, conceited King decides he must have the girl for himself. When she and the chimney sweep run away, it takes all the help that Mr. Wonderbird and his friends can muster to save them from the pursuing King. The final sequence of a gigantic mechanical monster and destruction of the palace contains stunning imagery that rivals the best examples of Japanimation. French dubbed in English. LP Speed.
VHS: S25703. $24.95.
Paul Grimault, France, 1953, 64 mins.

Discovering France

Discover the splendor and pleasure of la Belle France from Brittany and Mont-Saint-Michel to the chateaux of Chambord and Chenonceau. All levels of French students will enjoy the music and narration of this colorful program, which explains such traditions as the bulls at the Bayonne Festival. An outstanding survey of France's cultural and geographical diversity. "An excellent overview for anyone wishing to become familiar with the country" *(Video Rating Guide)*. 75 mins.
VHS: S30574. $39.95.

Disney Canta con Nosotros

Jiminy Cricket hosts this series of memorable Disney movie songs with on-screen lyric titles in Spanish. Students will be able to confidently sing along and reinforce their listening, reading and speaking skills. *Snow White, Peter Pan, The Little Mermaid* and *Beauty and the Beast* are covered in four volumes. Spanish narration, 30 mins.
VHS: S24785. $148.25.

Don Quijote

The animated adventures of one of the most captivating and everlasting characters in Spanish literature. In Spanish. 60 mins.
VHS: S34439. $19.95.

Dragon Flyz: The Legend Begins

In the 41st century, the Dragon Flyz—three brave brothers, their valiant sister and their dragon counterparts—protect the floating sky city of Airlandis. The mutant lord of the netherworld, Dread Wing, attempts to steal the crystals that keep the city aloft. The first three episodes of this French-produced TV series. Clamshell case sports a nifty 3-D lenticular cover.
VHS: S30052. $19.95.
Gaumont, France, 1996, 70 mins.

El Pequeno Tren (The Little Train)

A trip to fantasyland offers the perfect opportunity to meet Little Red Riding Hood, the Little Soldier and other characters from classic children's stories. Animated. Spanish with NO subtitles. 1985, 89 mins.
VHS: S23914. $24.95.

An Elephant Named Illusion (Un Elefante Color Ilusion)

Pablo Luis Codevilla and Ubaldo Martinez star in this whimsical adventure story. A young boy decides to steal a young and friendly elephant. Spanish with NO subtitles.
VHS: S23920. $24.95.
Derlis Maria Beccaglia, Argentina, 1970, 85 mins.

Erase Una Vez

A prince and a princess are separated by war in this animated adventure/romance. Windaria is the magical world they call home. Spanish with NO subtitles. 1987, 92 mins.
VHS: S23915. $24.95.

Es Increible! (Hanna-Barbera in Spanish)

An exclusive collection of Hanna-Barbera cartoons in Spanish, chosen for their easy-to-follow storylines. Beginning Spanish students will be motivated to learn unfamiliar vocabulary, and intermediate students will be challenged to concentrate on the application of more difficult vocabulary and construction. Includes extensive vocabulary and activity worksheets and a Spanish transcript. 39 mins. each.
Volume 1.
VHS: S31237. $18.95.
Volume 2.
VHS: S31238. $18.95.

Fairyland

A series of 12 Polish cartoons for children from popular animation series such as Leon the Fox, Gus and Caesar, Hip-Hop Kangaroo, and Plasticines, from Polish Animation Studios. 110 mins.
VHS: S11291. $39.95.

Fizz and Martina

This program uses the cartoon characters of two high school classmates to relate task-oriented exercises in the solving of math problems and building Spanish language skills. Contains a teacher's guide, 30 student exercise books and reproducible masters. 60 mins.
VHS: S19774. $179.95.

Fox Leon and Others

A series of short animation pieces for children, a sequel to the compilation *Fairyland*. Polish with NO subtitles.
VHS: S11292. $39.95.

French Fairy Tales—Blanche Neige

Fully animated stories selected from the classics in children's literature. Includes: Blanche Neige and Les Troit Petits Cochons. French with no subtitles.
VHS: S06884. $39.95.

French Fairy Tales—Le Petit Chaperon

Fully animated stories in French with no subtitles. Includes two stories: Le Petit Chaperon Rouge and La Belle et la Bete.
VHS: S06885. $39.95.

Heidi

This is an animated version of the classic tale of a young girl who frolics amidst the alpine landscape and brings happiness to her grandfather and a crippled girl. Spanish with NO subtitles. 1975, 93 mins.
VHS: S23913. $34.95.

Hola Amigos

Paco and his sister Lupe, two loveable chihuahuas, and the Perez family help children ages 4-9 learn Spanish words and phrases while introducing them to counting and numbers, colors and the world of animals. Three-volume set. Each tape is 55 minutes.
VHS: S31753. $54.95.

In My Own Backyard

In this read-along video children will learn about all the things that used to live in their backyard. From agrarian America all the way back to the time of the dinosaurs, it's a fascinating look at history, geology and more. 11:17 mins.
English Version.
VHS: S22364. $39.95.
Spanish Version.
VHS: S22365. $39.95.

Ivanhoe

The animated story of knights and maidens during the time of the Great Crusades. In Spanish. 60 mins.
VHS: S34441. $19.95.

Jay Jay the Jet Plane and His Flying Friends

Model planes come to life in the storybook land where not even the sky is the limit. (Yes, some of the planes are female.) With joyful lessons about life, family, friends and things that really matter. Ages 2-8. 30 minutes.
Volume 1. Tito Turbinitas y Sus Amigos Voladores/El Primer Vuelo de Tito Turbinitas y Otros Tres Cuentos. This collection of four stories features Tito Turbanitas and his other airplane friends in four animated shorts. Children will enjoy these non-violent and educational stories. Spanish language, ages 2-8, 30 mins.
VHS: S24584. $12.95.
Volume 2. Old Oscar Leads the Parade and Three Other Stories. This collection features Old Oscar and his other airplane friends in four animated shorts. Children will enjoy these non-violent and educational stories. Ages 2-8, 30 mins.
VHS: S24575. $12.95.

Kaliman, El Hombre Incredible (Kaliman, the Incredible Man)

Jeff Cooper, Nino del Arco, Susana Dosamantes and Adriana del Arco star in this film based on the adventures of the well-known comic book character. Children treasure his heroic exploits. Spanish with NO subtitles.
VHS: S23923. $24.95.

Katy Meets the Aliens

A Mexican/Spanish theatrical co-production directed by Santiago Moro. Katy the butterfly's caterpillar children are so anxious to grow up, they sneak off one night to find a flying teacher. Along the way they meet all manner of forest animals, as well as some aliens who are eyeing the Earth as a new source of food. The animation is quite competent and the designs are pleasing. A good kids' film. HiFi. Stereo.
VHS: S31504. $14.95.
Televicine/Moro, Mexico, 1987, 85 mins.

La Ibla del Tesoro

Pirates and treasures fill this story of animated adventures. In Spanish. 60 mins.
VHS: S34442. $19.95.

La Musique Folklorique

This video contains 11 of the best known French songs, performed in evocative settings such as a castle and a horse-drawn carriage. Each song contains a short note on its origins. The songs include "Au Clair de la Lune," "Frere Jacques" and "Chevaliers de la Table Ronde." 48 mins.
VHS: S19801. $39.95.

La Publicite en France—Volume 1

A fascinating look into the world of French TV commercials. See how the French advertise a variety of products. Explore the similarities and differences with our own TV ads. Includes script. 35 mins.
VHS: S05743. $49.95.

La Publicite en France—Volume 2

A new volume of commercials from France, with the subjects including clothing, cosmetics, perfumes, automobiles, supermarkets, and more. 26 mins.
VHS: S11200. $49.95.

La Rana Valiente (The Brave Frog)

In this touching animated film two frogs team up against the cruel King of Rainbow Pond. If only they can get him to change his ways so that their home becomes a peaceful place to inhabit, then it might be the best kind of home imaginable. In Spanish with no English subtitles. 91 mins.
VHS: S23917. $24.95.

Las Aventuras de Pinocchio

This animated version of the Pinocchio story will delight children. A lonely old puppet maker carves a puppet who magically becomes the son he always hoped for. Spanish with NO subtitles. 1986, 95 mins.
VHS: S23924. $24.95.

Las Aventuras de Tom Sawyer

This animated tale of adventures with Tom Sawyer and Huckleberry Finn ends with the discovery of a treasure which makes them both very wealthy. In Spanish. 60 mins.
VHS: S34443. $19.95.

Las Minas del Rey Solomon

A dangerous trip in search of the treasure that was said to be hidden in the legendary mines of King Solomon in Africa. Animated. In Spanish. 60 mins.
VHS: S34444. $19.95.

Le Noel de Mickey

This program reimagines Mickey Mouse as a French-speaking Bob Cratchit in the wonderful Disney adaptation of Dickens' immortal *A Christmas Carol*. French with no subtitles. 25 mins.
VHS: S19811. $24.95.

Les Jeunes Entrepreneurs

Designed for advanced beginners and students at the intermediate level, this story relates the tale of French-Canadian teenagers who build a robot. Verification of comprehension is made possible by post-viewing activities that stress creativity, listening, speaking, reading and writing. Each video is 25 mins. C'est un Choix Difficile.
VHS: S19802. $29.95.

Les Pompiers

Two young friends find themselves in a fire truck chase, confront a scary monster, and try to rescue a cat in big trouble. This engaging animated film will thrill the intermediate- and advanced-level French student while providing listening comprehension practice. 48 mins.
VHS: S30566. $19.95.

Lettres de France

An advanced beginning-to-intermediate level French program based upon the idea of writing to a pen pal in another country. There are five 10-minute themes, ranging from the market and out-of-school activities to Christmas and New Year activities, which stimulate discussion. Centering around several events in the life of a young Norman, the five episodes tell his story, which enables students to identify with the main character. Includes a teacher's guide providing numerous suggestions on the use of the video and a 50-minute audio cassette with guide.
VHS: S30567. $69.95.

The Little Engine That Could

The enchanting children's tale about desire, hope, courage and optimism is beautifully animated within a French and Spanish context. 30 mins.
Spanish Narration.
VHS: S19813. $22.00.

Los Tres Mosqueteros

The animated story of D'Artagnan, the Three Musketeers, and how they preserved the honor of the queen of France. In Spanish. 60 mins.
VHS: S34445. $19.95.

Lyric Language French

Students will participate in real life adventures with animated characters from *Family Circus* while building fluency in French in this two-volume set. On-screen lyric titles make singing along easy. Vol. 1 includes the zoo, the supermarket, the seasons and seven other trips. Vol. 2 has ten topics, including the family and the senses. 35 minutes each.
VHS: S24792. $32.90.

Lyric Language French Teacher's Guide

Interactive, entertaining activities reinforce the French vocabulary covered in this video. These activities encourage and motivate students to learn a second language even as they develop multicultural understanding. The Natural Approach and the TPR method engage the viewer in four skill areas.
VHS: S24793. $19.95.

Lyric Language Spanish

Students will participate in real life adventures with animated characters from *Family Circus* while building fluency in Spanish. On-screen lyric titles in Spanish make singing along easy. A two-volume set, Vol. 1 includes the zoo, the supermarket, the seasons and seven other trips. Vol. 2 has nine topics, including the family, the senses and a picnic. 35 minutes each.
VHS: S24788. $45.00.

Lyric Language Spanish Teacher's Guide

Interactive, entertaining activities reinforce the Spanish vocabulary covered in this video. These activities encourage and motivate students to learn a second language even as they develop multicultural understanding. The Natural Approach and the TPR method engage the viewer in four skill areas.
VHS: S24789. $19.95.

Magical Coqui—Puerto Rico—Mi Tierra!

Aimed at younger viewers, this cassette contains a delightful original story about a small boy and his pet Coqui (tree frog) in Puerto Rico. Also, there is a presentation of music and beautiful pictures about life in Puerto Rico designed to present the viewers with an appreciation for the island and a taste of its culture. The program is presented first in English, and then repeated in Spanish. 40 mins.
VHS: S10789. $59.95.

Mon Ane: Au Clair de la Lune

This delightful collection of 15 traditional French songs features colorful animation and French subtitles for sing-alongs. Includes "Au clair de la lune," "Sur le pont d'Avignon" and "Frere Jacques." A fun way to promote oral and listening comprehension for beginning and intermediate students of French. 35 mins.
VHS: S31239. $32.00.

My First Series

These two videos combine easy-to-follow instructions for creative activities with Spanish language instruction. Students will develop new vocabulary and be stimulated into conversation. *My First Activity* demonstrates crafts made from everyday materials, while *My First Cooking* shows some easy fun recipes.
VHS: S24786. $35.95.

Peter Pan

Experience the animated adventures of Peter Pan in Never Never Land, with Captain Hook and the lost children. In Spanish. 60 mins.
VHS: S34440. $19.95.

Posada Navidena

Pepe Serna is Scrooge in this Spanish-language version of the Charles Dickens classic *A Christmas Carol*. As the ghosts of Christmas visit the old, greedy businessman Scrooge, he has a change of heart and learns the true meaning of the holiday season.
VHS: S23345. $19.95.

Ravioli

The daily life, activities, incidents and drama of a German family called the Duewels are explored in this prize-winning series, personalizing their struggles and pain, and the often difficult intergenerational relationships. German *without* subtitles.
Ravioli I. 75 mins.
VHS: S17231. $59.95.
Ravioli II. 75 mins.
VHS: S17232. $59.95.
Ravioli III. 75 mins.
VHS: S17233. $59.95.
Ravioli IV. 97 mins.
VHS: S17234. $59.95.

Reflejos Latinos

Gabriela de la Paz performs traditional, folkloric and children's songs from Mexico, Peru and Puerto Rico. Includes on-screen graphics for sing-alongs and a study guide with transcript, notes and discussion questions. 59 mins.
VHS: S30565. $39.95.

Reir, Jugar, Hablar

A new Spanish video for teaching poems, dialogs, activities, games and songs. Created by a dynamic "master" teacher in the New York City school system, who demonstrates her methods with a beginning level FLES Spanish class. An invaluable media tool for teacher training. 70 mins.
VHS: S05282. $44.95.

Robin Hood

The animated adventures of Robin Hood and the men of Sherwood Forest. In Spanish. 60 mins.
VHS: S34446. $19.95.

Sesame Street: Plaza Sesamo

Sesame Street is finally available in Spanish! For use in teaching Spanish, the videos can work for ages 2-12. Each video is 30 minutes.
De Campamento Con Montoya: Big Bird Goes Camping. Camping with the crew from Sesame Street is an opportunity to experience the wonders of nature. At the same time, this camping trip gives kids a chance to learn about the many things one encounters in the wild. In Spanish.
VHS: S19757. $25.00.
El Alfabeto de Montoya: Learn the Alphabet with Bert and Ernie. Sesame Street characters, including Big Bird, help kids learn the alphabet by talking about animals. Actual footage of these creatures will fascinate kids even as it helps them remember their ABC's. In Spanish.
VHS: S19760. $25.00.
Plaza Sesamo Canta: Favorite Songs from Past Shows. Stories, games, songs and the wonderful Sesame Street crowd make this video a trip to the imagination. In Spanish.
VHS: S19758. $25.00.
Vamos a Imaginar: Learn About Sounds and Shapes. It's great fun to take a trip using only your imagination. Sesame Street characters employ just a few shapes and sounds to bring kids a world of diversion, fun and possibility. In Spanish.
VHS: S19759. $25.00.
Viaja Con Nosotros: Big Bird and Oscar Go to Venezuela and Mexico. This special tour of Latin America voyages to Machu Pichu, Buenos Aires and the Amazon. Kids will be entertained and amazed; and they will learn something about the world. In Spanish.
VHS: S19756. $25.00.
Plaza Sesamo Complete Set. The children's program *Sesame Street* is finally available in Spanish. 150 mins.
VHS: S19761. $110.00.

Shalom Sesame

It's a long way from Sesame Street to Israel. Violinist Itzhak Perlman and Broadway and television star Bonnie Franklin team up with the Muppet and Israeli casts of "Rechov Sumsum", the Israeli version of Sesame street, to introduce American children to the people, places, cultures and languages of Israel. Each program is 30 mins.
Aleph-Bet Telethon. Subtitled *Discovering the Hebrew Letters*, Kippi ben Kippod and Jerry Stiller are called to action when the Hebrew alphabet mysterious vanishes, so the two respond by holding a special telethon to track down the mysterious letters.
VHS: S17122. $22.95.
Chanukah. *Shalom Sesame* celebrates the Festival of Lights as Jeremy Miller goes on an exploration through memory and time in the ancient village of Modi'in in the land of the Maccabees.
VHS: S17119. $22.95.
Jerusalem. Experience the golden beauty of Israel's City of Peace as Itzhak Perlman, Bonnie Franklin and their young Israeli friends take you on a tour of Jerusalem from the Old City to the holy places of the Christian, Moslem, Armenian and Jewish Quarters.
VHS: S08386. $22.95.
Journey to Secret Places. Jeremy Miller and Kippi ben Kippod move through a strange tunnel that transports them into the unsettling, vibrant cultures of Israel's exotic, mysterious regions.
VHS: S17121. $22.95.
Kibbutz. Bonnie Franklin travels to Kibbutz Ein Gedi on the shore of the Dead Sea and shares with the kibbutz kids their unique way of life.
VHS: S08384. $22.95.
Kids Sing Israel. In this glorious finale, Kippi, Sarah Jessica Parker and the children of Israel host a rousing mixture of traditional Israeli and Hebrew songs with the best loved *Sesame Street* tunes.
VHS: S17124. $22.95.
Land of Israel. Meet your new Israeli friends from "Rechov Sumsum," including an oversized porcupine, Kippy ben Kipod; Moishe Oofnick, the neighborhood grouch; Bentz and Arik. Mary Tyler Moore joins Bonnie Franklin and Itzhak Perlman in this tour of Israel.
VHS: S08382. $22.95.
Passover. In this film subtitled *Jerusalem Jones and the Lost Afikomann*, the talented young actor Sarah Jessica Parker *(L.A. Story)* stars as Jerusalem Jones. Parker must find the lost afikomann and determine whether Miriam's bread will rise.
VHS: S17123. $22.95.
People of Israel. They came from Sweden, Russia, Ethiopia, Egypt, India and America. Now they're Israeli kids. Join them and Itzhak Perlman as they explore the colorful mix that makes up Israel's people.
VHS: S08385. $22.95.
Sing Around the Seasons. In this educational program about the landscape, people and culture of Israel, the *Sesame Street* gang orchestrate a sing-along, celebrate the country's changing seasons, and explore holidays and festivals and its flair for celebration and ritual.
VHS: S17120. $22.95.
Tel Aviv. Itzhak Perlman introduces his hometown, including the colorful, bustling Carmel Market, the Tel Aviv boardwalk and beach, and the ancient city of Jaffa.
VHS: S08383. $22.95.

Singing French Songs for Children (Les Petits Chanteurs de Paris)

Enjoy the musical mastery of the world famous National Boys Choir of Paris as they sing numerous traditional French songs. Includes "Au Clair de la lune", "Le pont d'Avignon" and "Il pleut bergere".
VHS: S14206. $49.95.

Spanish Cartoon Classics

Three cartoon heroes, Bugs Bunny, Woody Woodpecker and Porky Pig, are available in Spanish. Each video is 30 mins. Woody El Pajaro Loco.
VHS: S19836. $9.95.

Spanish Club: Fiesta!

A live-action video featuring Senora Reyes and her Spanish language club as they explore the meaning of fiesta. The program uses traditional Hispanic songs and stories to teach culture as well as language. For children ages 2-8.
VHS: S21923. $19.95.

Spanish Club: Los Animales!

Senora Reyes and the Spanish Club Kids explore the world of animals in Volume 2 of this series, which uses traditional Hispanic songs and stories for children ages 2-8.
VHS: S21924. $19.95.

Spot

These animated tales are a valuable educational tool for relating familiar objects and activities viewed by Spot that mirror the experience of his young viewers. 30 mins.
Spot's Adventure—German.
VHS: S19854. $29.95.
Spot's Adventure—Spanish.
VHS: S19825. $29.95.
Spot's First Video—French.
VHS: S19794. $29.95.
Spot's First Video—German.
VHS: S19853. $29.95.
Spot's First Video—Spanish.
VHS: S19824. $29.95.

Tell Me Why (Spanish)

This bilingual immersion class teaches the use of content-based materials to learn the subject matter in Spanish. The programs offer a kaleidoscopic range of learning through live-action video, animated slides and charts. 90 mins.
Prehistoric Animals.
VHS: S19762. $29.95.

Un Premier Prix—Perdu, Un Robot

Three Canadian teenagers, determined to win the school science prize, build a robot. Frustrated because it doesn't work, they leave it behind—then the robot takes off. This delightful, live-action story told in simple French is geared to beginning and intermediate French students. 50 mins.
VHS: S05286. $39.95.

ANIMATION

animation

hollywood studio animation

The 2000-Year-Old Man
Mel Brooks and Carl Reiner's comedy sketch about a 2000-year-old man's views on life and history is animated to a recording of the two performing live.
VHS: S03917. $14.95.
Leo Salkin, USA, 1975, 25 mins.

25 Classic Cartoons
Three full hours of color cartoons in each volume, featuring Bugs Bunny, Mighty Mouse, the Three Stooges, Superman and many more. USA, 180 mins. each.
25 Classic Cartoons: Vol. II.
VHS: S15035. $19.95.
25 Classic Cartoons: Vol. IV.
VHS: S15037. $19.95.

Adventures of an American Rabbit
The bravest, most endearing and longest-eared super hero, in one hair-raising escapade after another as he protects America from evil, in enchanting, non-violent animation. 81 mins.
VHS: S08600. $14.95.
Fred Wolf/Nobutaka Nishizawa, USA, 1986, 81 mins.

Adventures of Batman & Robin: Batman
Two episodes. Batman teams up with Gray Ghost to thwart a mysterious bomber.
VHS: S31405. $9.95.
Warner Bros., USA, 1995, 45 mins.

Adventures of Batman & Robin: Fire and Ice
Two episodes. A close encounter with Maxie Zeus and Mr. Freeze plunges the Dark Knight into a life-or-death battle against Fire and Ice.
VHS: S31406. $9.95.
Warner Bros., USA, 1995, 45 mins.

Adventures of Batman & Robin: Poison Ivy
Two episodes. Armed with fatal toxins, killer plants and her hypnotic poisoned kisses, Poison Ivy continues to make life itchy for the dynamic duo.
VHS: S31408. $9.95.
Warner Bros., USA, 1995, 45 mins.

Adventures of Batman & Robin: Robin
Two episodes: In *Robin's Reckoning Part 1*, we learn who Robin was before he became Batman's ward and crime-fighting sidekick. In *Robin's Reckoning Part 2*, the Boy Wonder has waited a long time for a showdown with the murderer of his parents.
VHS: S29595. $9.95.
Warner Bros., USA, 1994, 45 mins.

Adventures of Batman & Robin: The Joker
Two episodes: In *Christmas with The Joker*, it's no Silent Night—not when he commandeers TV stations for a show of his own. In *The Laughing Fish*, it's happy haddock, smiling smelts, amused mackerel. When all seafood looks like the Joker, something fishy's going on.
VHS: S29594. $9.95.
Warner Bros., USA, 1994, 45 mins.

Adventures of Batman & Robin: The Penguin
Two episodes. Batman and Robin go up against The Penguin, the deadliest bird of prey in Gotham City.
VHS: S31407. $9.95.
Warner Bros., USA, 1995, 45 mins.

Adventures of Batman & Robin: The Riddler
Two episodes from the Batman Animated Series: In *If You're So Smart, Why Aren't You Rich?*, the caped crimefighters match wits with the Riddler inside his life-sized computerized game grid. In *Riddler's Reform*, he's got a crooked way of going straight. But Batman has a way to stop him: a riddle that can drive a devious puzzler mad!
VHS: S29592. $9.95.
Warner Bros., USA, 1994, 45 min. mins.

Adventures of Batman & Robin: Two-Face
Two episodes from the Batman Animated Series: In *Shadow of the Bat Part 1*, when Two-Face's scheme lands Commissioner Gordon in jail, help arrives from an unexpected source—Batgirl! In *Shadow of the Bat Part 2*, the Commissioner's in jail and Batman and Robin are trapped in a flooded subway. Two-Face has everyone where he wants them—or does he?
VHS: S29593. $9.95.
Warner Bros., USA, 1994, 45 mins.

Adventures of Droopy
Seven titles: *Wags to Riches* ('49), *Dumbhounded* ('43), *The Shooting of Dan McGoo* ('45), *Droopy's Good Deed* ('51), *Drag-Along Droopy* ('51), *The Chump Champ* ('50) and *Deputy Droopy* ('55).
VHS: S28185. $12.95.
MGM, USA, 1943-55, 53 mins.

The Adventures of Popeye, Vol. 2
Seven more adventures, including *Fright to the Finish, Bride and Gloom, Gopher Spinach, Out to Punch, Parlez Voo Woo, A Haul in One, I Don't Care*. Color, 50 mins.
VHS: S04855. $29.95.

Aesop's Fables & Associates Vol. 1
Eight titles: *Circus Capers, The Last Dance, College Capers, Jail Breakers, The Office Boy, Minnie's Yoo Hoo* (Disney), *Down in Dixie* and *Dizzy Days*.
VHS: S29596. $24.95.
Terry/Disney, USA, 1920's, 60 mins.

Aesop's Fables Volume 1
Paul Terry cartoons—silent shorts with music added; includes *Up in the Air, Flying Hoofs, Rooster and the Eagle, Wicked City, Red Hot Sands, Hitting the Rails, Runaway Balloon, Fable of the Alley Cat*.
VHS: S08956. $29.95.

Aesop's Fables Volume 2
More Paul Terry animated treasures: *Jungle Sports, Home Sweet Home, Sweet Adeline, Venus of Venice, Puppy Love, Wolf and the Crane, Troubles on the Ark, Cross Country Run*.
VHS: S08957. $29.95.

Aesop's Fables Volume 3
Eight more Paul Terry silent (music added) classics: *In Vaudeville, Picnic, Donkey Tricks, Champion, Sport of Kings, Dissatisfied Cobbler, Rat's Revenge, By Land and Air*.
VHS: S08959. $29.95.

Aesop's Film Fables
This collection features the silent, black-and-white cartoons of Paul Terry from the early '20s. All with original organ score. Seven titles: *The War Bride* ('22), *In Again—Out Again* ('27), *Fable of the Jolly Rounders* ('23), *Wolf and the Kid* ('21), *Captain Kidder* ('22), *Rural Romance* ('24) and *One Good Turn* ('24).
VHS: S27965. $19.95.
Paul Terry, USA, 1921-27, 55 mins.

Aladdin & Jasmine's Moonlight Magic
Disney characters Aladdin, Jasmine and Genie find new adventures in these romantic, magic-laced cartoons. In *Moonlight Madness*, Aladdin entices Jasmine to join him on a date but he gets distracted by the promise of treasure. Then, in *Some Enchanted Genie*, Genie falls in love. 45 mins.
VHS: S27358. $12.99.

All Dogs Go to Heaven
Set in colorful New Orleans circa 1939, this film's tender and syrupy story focuses on a roguish German Shepard (Burt Reynolds) who finds himself guardian of a lonely little orphan girl. Also features voices of Dom DeLuise and Charles Nelson Reilly. HiFi Stereo.
VHS: S12541. $14.95.
Laser: LD75594. $34.95.
Laser: CAV. **LD75595. $39.95.**
Don Bluth, USA, 1989, 85 mins.

All Dogs Go to Heaven 2
The story continues in this made-for-video sequel to the 1989 Don Bluth film. Featuring the voices of Charlie Sheen, Sheena Easton, Ernest Borgnine and Dom DeLuise! Laserdisc is letterboxed. HiFi Stereo.
VHS: S29294. $19.95.
Laser: LD75769. $34.95.
MGM, USA, 1996, 82 mins.

All Singing, All Dancing
Eight titles: *Freddie the Freshman* ('32), *Smile, Darn Ya, Smile* ('31), *Crosby, Columbo & Vallee* ('32), *Bosko at the Beach* ('31), *Yodeling Yokels* ('30), *You Don't Know What You're Doin'* ('31) and *Hittin' the Trail for Hallelujah Land* ('31). B&W.
VHS: S27966. $17.95.
Warner Bros., USA, 1930-32, 60 mins.

All Star Cartoon Parade
Six titles: *Raggedy Ann & Raggedy Andy* ('41), *The Friendly Ghost* ('45 Casper), *Indoor Outing* ('44 Little Lulu), *The Constable* ('40 Gabby), *Happy You and Merry Me* ('36 Betty Boop) and *Winter Draws On* ('48 Screen Song).
VHS: S27915. $29.95.
Fleischer/Famous, USA, 1936-48, 54 mins.

Anastasia
Don Bluth and Gary Goldman created this impressive first effort for Fox's new animation studio. The lost heiress to the Russian throne gets the Bluth musical treatment this time around, and celebrity voices are provided by Meg Ryan, John Cusack, Kelsey Grammar, Christopher Lloyd, Hank Azaria, Bernadette Peters and Angela Lansbury. Also available in a widescreen version that includes "making of" footage. Dolby Digital.
VHS: S33691. $26.98.
VHS: Widescreen. **S34844. $29.95.**
Fox Animation, USA, 1997, 94 mins.

Anastasia Sing-Along
Clips from Fox Animation Studio's first animated feature are presented in a sing-along format.
VHS: S32486. $12.95.
Fox, USA, 1997, 30 mins.

Animalympics
In this animated spoof of the Olympics, animals compete from all over the world. Voices of Gilda Radner, Billy Crystal, Harry Shearer and Michael Fremer.
VHS: S29598. $12.95.
Lisberger, USA, 1979, 79 mins.

Animaniacs Sing-Along: Mostly in Toon
Weirdwide, worldwide fun. The Animaniacs are brainiacs too when they come up with clever tunes about Presidents, planets, the Panama Canal and more. 12 songs, including *Panama Canal, The Ballad of Magellan, A Quake a Quake* and *The Big Wrap Party*.
VHS: S30355. $12.95.
Warner Bros., USA, 1996, 30 mins.

Animaniacs Sing-Along: Yakko's World
Sing along with Yakko, Wakko and Dot to 14 of the most popular Animaniacs tunes, including the wonderful geography lesson *Yakko's World*, Dot's irresistible I'm *Cute*, Wakko's *America* and the zany *I'm Mad*. HiFi Stereo.
VHS: S27931. $12.95.
Warner Bros., USA, 1994, 30 mins.

Animaniacs Stew
It's mass hysterical when many Animaniacs favorites—the Warners, Slappy Squirrel, Pinky & the Brain, toddler Mindy and her devoted dog Buttons—all cut loose with comic results. Highlights: Dot's beatnik recital of *Mary Had a Little Lamb* and the Brain's voiceover recording session. HiFi Stereo.
VHS: S27929. $12.95.
Warner Bros., USA, 1994, 45 mins.

Animaniacs: A Pinky & The Brain Christmas

The Brain and Pinky travel to the North Pole—the true seat of power—in an attempt to use Santa in a scheme for world domination. Bonus adventure: *That Smarts!*

VHS: S30353. $12.95.
Warner Bros., USA, 1996, 30 mins.

Animaniacs: Helloooo, Holidays!

Tis the season for Yuletide hilarity, from *Twas the Day Before Christmas* and *The Little Drummer Warners* to a truly unique rendition of *Jingle Bells* and a typically zany retelling of *A Christmas Carol*. Plus a wonderful story by Steven Spielberg about the life and hard times of a sheet of gold wrapping paper. HiFi Stereo.

VHS: S27930. $12.95.
Warner Bros., USA, 1994, 45 mins.

Animaniacs: Pinky & The Brain: World Domination Tour

The two lab mice have their sights on a bigger cage—the world!—in a globe-trotting collection that leaps from Russia to England to Switzerland to a confrontation with Gollyzilla in Japan.

VHS: S30356. $12.95.
Warner Bros., USA, 1996, 37 mins.

Animaniacs: Spooky Stuff

In *Draculee Dracula*, the Count thirsts for company…until Dot, Yakko and Wakko show up. In *Phranken-Runt*, the brainless canine may be the donor for a monstrous laboratory creation. Bergman's *The Seventh Seal* is lampooned in *Meatballs or Consequences*, Slappy and Skippy go trick-or-treating in *Scare Happy Slappy* and *Witch One* revisits the Salem witch trials. Also *Hot, Bothered and Bedeviled*.

VHS: S30354. $12.95.
Warner Bros., USA, 1996, 60 mins.

Animaniacs: The Warners Escape

Meet Yakko and Wakko, the Warner brothers, and Dot, the Warner sister. Find out how the troublemakers first got sentenced to the Warner Bros. water tower and what happens when they're turned loose in a psychiatrist's office, the studio executive suite, a movie set and inside a video store after hours. HiFi Stereo.

VHS: S27927. $12.95.
Warner Bros., USA, 1994, 45 mins.

Animaniacs: You Will Buy This Video!

This seems to be a harmless assortment of the best adventures of lab mice Pinky & the Brain. In reality it contains subliminal messages that will hypnotically render you the Brain's willing puppet in a plan of global domination—after just a few repeated viewings. HiFi Stereo.

VHS: S27928. $12.95.
Warner Bros., USA, 1994, 45 mins.

Babes in Toyland

In this direct-to-video musical feature, Jack and Jill must stop their evil Uncle Barnaby from shutting down the Toyland Factory and spoiling Christmas. Voices of James Belushi, Bronson Pinchot, Christopher Plummer, Charles Nelson Reilly and others.

VHS: S32186. $19.95.
MGM, USA, 1997, 74 mins.

Balto

Part husky, part wolf, Balto doesn't know where he belongs. He's an outcast in his home in Nome, Alaska, except among his true friends. When a dog sled team carrying vital medicine is lost in a blizzard, Balto risks his life to save the town. Based on a true story. Voices of Kevin Bacon, Bridget Fonda, Phil Collins and Bob Hoskins. THX, CC.

VHS: S27430. $19.95.
Laser: LD75503. $34.95.
Amblin/Universal, USA, 1995, 78 mins.

Bambi Meets Godzilla and Other Weird Cartoons

Includes *Betty Boop in Crazy Town*, Max Fleischer creations and many other animated classics. 30 mins.

VHS: S11259. $9.95.

Batman & Mr. Freeze: Subzero

Batman returns in a feature-length, direct-to-video animated adventure. Cryogenic super criminal Mr. Freeze kidnaps Batgirl in a plot to save the life of his beloved wife. Surround.

VHS: S32444. $19.95.
Laser: LD76442. $34.95.
Warner Bros., USA, 1998, 70 mins.

Batman (DC Superpowers Collection)

Five episodes: *How Many Herrings in a Wheelbarrow, A Bird out of Hand, From Catwoman with Love, The 1001 Faces of The Riddler* and *The Cool Cruel Mr. Freeze*.

VHS: S27947. $9.95.
Filmation, USA, 1967-69, 60 mins.

The Batman/Superman Movie

The New Adventures of Batman/Superman TV series comes to video in this feature-length adventure. When Lex Luthor and The Joker team up in a diabolical scheme, only the combined forces of Batman and Superman can save Metropolis. Free Batman comic book in each video.

VHS: S34576. $14.95.
Warner Bros., USA, 1998, 80 mins.

Batman: Mask of the Phantasm

This animated feature arose out of the phenomenally successful *Batman: The Animated Series* TV show. An engaging storyline, a great design sense, good voice acting and an over-the-top performance by Mark Hamill as The Joker. HiFi Stereo.

VHS: S20959. $19.95.
Laser: Widescreen. **LD72402. $39.95.**
Warner Bros., USA, 1993, 77 mins.

Bell Science Series: About Time

Did you know ships couldn't find their way around without an accurate timepiece and that our clocks are set to the earth's rotation? These and other amazing facts are revealed through wonderful animation (by WB animator Phil Monroe) and live action sequences.

VHS: S14940. $9.95.
Jack Warner, USA, 1959, 53 mins.

Bell Science Series: Gateway to the Mind

A wonderful excursion through the senses: touch, smell, taste, sight and sound. Discover that grasshoppers can hear with their stomachs, fish can taste with their bodies, and sometimes things we see aren't what they appear to be. Animation sequences by Chuck Jones.

VHS: S14226. $9.95.
Jack Warner, USA, 1958, 58 mins.

Bell Science Series: Hemo the Magnificent

Take a tour of the body's amazing plumbing system, featuring the most powerful and mysterious muscle, your heart. Learn that blood is not always red, why we stretch in the morning and why small animals' hearts beat so quickly. Animation by Shamus Culhane.

VHS: S14939. $9.95.
Frank Capra, USA, 1958, 54 mins.

Bell Science Series: Our Mr. Sun

An absolutely wonderful installment of the Bell Telephone Science Hour. Eddie Albert and Dr. Frank Baxter relate everything you wanted to know about the sun, with the aid of animation by UPA. Written and directed by Frank Capra.

VHS: S13925. $9.95.
Frank Capra, USA, 1956, 60 mins.

Bell Science Series: The Alphabet Conspiracy

Aided by the Mad Hatter (Hans Conreid) and Jabberwock, Dr. Frank Baxter takes a young girl on an exploration into the intriguing world of language. Animation segments directed by Friz Freleng.

VHS: S13924. $9.95.
Jack Warner, USA, 1959, 56 mins.

Bell Science Series: The Strange Case of the Cosmic Rays

The mysteries of the universe are revealed in this fun- and fact-filled galactic thriller. Elements of the atom, powerful particles and radiation research are presented in a simple and easily understood format. Puppetry by Bil & Cora's Marionettes. Animation by Shamus Culhane.

VHS: S14227. $9.95.
Frank Capra, USA, 1957, 55 mins.

Bell Science Series: The Thread of Life

People knew a few things about you before you were born by looking at your parents, grandparents and others in your family. Dr. Frank Baxter helps unravel how heredity and environment shape our looks, tastes in food, allergies and other specific traits. Features animation and microscopic time-lapse photography. Animation by Robert McKimson.

VHS: S15090. $9.95.
Jack Warner, USA, 54

Bell Science Series: Unchained Goddess

The Goddess of Weather, along with other characters like Wind, Clouds and Rain, helps explain what weather really is. How the poles and equator make wind and what clouds are made of are explained through animation and amazing live footage of hurricanes, tornadoes and extreme weather. Animation by Shamus Culhane.

VHS: S16333. $9.95.
Frank Capra, USA, 54

Best of Betty Boop

Nine titles: *Stop That Noise* ('35), *No No! A Thousand Times No!!* ('35), *Betty Boop's Ker-Choo* ('33 with Bimbo & Koko), *Betty Boop with Henry, The Funniest Living American* ('35), *Little Nobody* ('35 with Pudgy), *We Did It* ('36 with Pudgy), *Betty Boop & The Little King* ('36 with The Little King), *Betty Boop & Little Jimmy* ('36) and *Be Human* ('36 with Grampy). B&W.

VHS: S02229. $19.95.
Fleischer, USA, 1933-36, 56 mins.

Best of George Pal

Before George Pal went on to win five Oscars for Special Effects in the 1950's for such films as *When Worlds Collide, Destination Moon* and *Tom Thumb*, he produced puppet-cartoons for Paramount Pictures. Included here are *Sky Pirates, Captain Kidding* and *Jasper*.

VHS: S00118. $24.95.
George Pal, USA, 1934-, 70 mins.

Best of the Van Beuren Studio

Seven classic pieces of animation by an almost forgotten studio: included are Fox's comic-strip gang—the folks who run the Toonerville Trolley Ride, with Katrinka, The Terrible-Tempered Mr. Bang and the others in *The Toonerville Trolley, Toonerville Ahoy*, and *Toonerville Picnic*. Also included are Felix the Cat in *Bold King Cole, Neptune's Nonsense* and *The Goose That Laid the Golden Egg*, as well as the rare *Waif's Welcome*. 50 mins.

VHS: S04858. $29.95.

Betty Boop & Friends

Nine titles: *The Hot Air Salesman* ('37), *More Pep* ('36), *Poor Cinderella* ('34), *Baby Be Good* ('35), *My Friend the Monkey* ('39), *Housecleaning Blues* ('37), *The Candid Candidate* ('37) and *Happy You and Merry Me* ('36).

VHS: S27968. $19.95.
Fleischer, USA, 1934-39, 54 mins.

Betty Boop Classics in Color

A collection of NTA re-colored versions, from the original masters. Ten titles: *Betty Boop's Big Boss* ('33), *Betty Boop & Little Jimmy* ('36), *Betty Boop's Bizzy Bee* ('32), *Betty Boop's Kerchoo* ('33), *Stop That Noise* ('35), Judge for a Day ('35), *Language All My Own* ('35), *Keep in Style* ('34) and *Whoops, I'm a Cowboy* ('37).

VHS: S00122. $19.95.
Fleischer, USA, 1933-37, 60 mins.

Betty Boop Collection Vol. 1

Eight titles: *Betty in Blunderland, Stop That Noise, Swat That Fly, So Does an Automobile, Rhythm on the Reservation, Poor Cinderella, House Cleaning Blues* and *Little Jimmy*.

VHS: S29605. $24.95.
Fleischer, USA, 60 mins.

Betty Boop Confidential

The Queen of "Boop-Oop-a-Doop" is featured in two classic cartoons of Fleischer's famous "Bouncing Ball Screen Songs" series, along with three vintage "color classics," including Betty's only color epic. 82 mins.

VHS: S32996. $9.95.

Betty Boop Definitive Collection Vol. 1: The Birth of Betty

The first volume of the collection leads off with an introduction by Max Fleischer's son, Richard, followed by eight of the earliest Betty cartoons. The first few show Betty as an nameless walk-on playing to the top-billed star, Bimbo. This proto-Betty sports long dog-ears (but nothing else especially canine) that gradually become less prominent as both she and Bimbo evolve away from dogginess in later appearances. The final cartoon on the tape shows Betty as we're accustomed to seeing her, and also gives her top billing for the first time. Eight titles: *Dizzy Dishes* ('30), *Barnacle Bill* ('30), *Mysterious Mose* ('30), *The Bum Bandit* ('31), *Silly Scandals* ('31), *Bimbo's Express* ('31), *Minding the Baby* ('31) and *Mask-A-Raid* ('31).

VHS: S30344. $7.95.
Fleischer, USA, 1930-31, 62 mins.

Betty Boop Definitive Collection Vol. 2: Pre-Code & Jazzy Guest Stars

The first half of the tape features Betty's more racy outings from the pre-Hays Code days. Then the second half showcases the great musical cartoons, guest-starring Louis Armstrong, Cab Calloway and others. Fourteen titles. Pre-Code: *Boop-Oop-A-Doop* ('32), *S.O.S.* ('32), *Chess-Nuts* ('32), *A Hunting We Will Go* ('32), *Betty Boop's Bizzy Bee* ('32), *Betty Boop's Bamboo Isle* ('32) and *Betty Boop for President* ('32). Jazzy Guest Stars: *Minnie the Moocher* ('32), *I'll Be Glad When You're Dead You Rascal You* ('32), *Snow-White* ('33), *The Old Man of the Mountain* ('33), *Kitty from Kansas City* ('31), *Rudy Vallee Melodies* ('32) and *You Try Somebody Else* ('32).

VHS: S30345. $9.95.
Fleischer, USA, 1931-33, 108 mins.

Betty Boop Definitive Collection Vol. 3: Surrealism & Prime Betty

The first half of the tape highlights the trademark Fleischer surrealism with some of the wildest shorts Betty made, and the second half is packed with a variety of the choicest Boop cartoons. Sixteen titles. Surrealism: *Bimbo's Initiation* ('31), *The Robot* ('32), Crazy Town ('32), *Betty Boop M.D.* ('32), *Betty Boop's Ups and Downs* ('32), *Betty Boop's May Party* ('33), *Red Hot Mamma* ('34) and *Betty Boop in Ha! Ha! Ha!* ('34). Prime Betty: *Admission Free* ('32), *Just a Gigolo* ('32), *Betty Boop's Museum* ('32), *Is My Palm Read* ('33), Betty Boop's Penthouse ('33), *Betty Boop's Birthday Party* ('33), *Betty Boop's Ker-Choo* ('33) and *Morning Noon and Night* ('33).

VHS: S30346. $9.95.
Fleischer, USA, 1931-33, 110 mins.

Betty Boop Definitive Collection Vol. 4: Musical Madness & Fairy Tales

This tape features eight of Betty's music-driven cartoons and seven Betty Boop-style fairy tales. Musical Madness: *Any Little Girl That's a Nice Little Girl* ('31), *The Dancing Fool* ('32), *I Heard* ('33), *Let Me Call You Sweetheart* ('32), *Oh! How I Hate to Get Up in the Morning* ('32), *Romantic Melodies* ('32), *Popular Melodies* ('33) and *Sally Swing* ('38). Fairy Tales and Fantasy: *Mother Goose Land* ('33), *Parade of the Wooden Soldiers* ('33), *Poor Cinderella* ('34), *Jack and the Beanstalk* ('31), *Dizzy Red Riding Hood* ('31), *Betty Boop's Hallowe'en Party* ('33) and *Betty in Blunderland* ('34).

VHS: S30347. $9.95.
Fleischer, USA, 1931-38, 106 mins.

Betty Boop Definitive Collection Vol. 5: Curtain Call & Betty and Grampy

Eight of Betty's stage show musical cartoons and eight cartoons with the crazy inventor Grampy are featured. Curtain Call: *Betty Boop's Crazy Inventions* ('33), *Stopping the Show* ('32), *The Limited* ('32), *A Language All My Own* ('35), *Keep in Style* ('34), *Making Stars* ('35), *The New Deal Show* ('37) and *A Song a Day* ('36). Betty & Grampy: *Betty Boop and Grampy* ('35), *Grampy's Indoor Outing* ('36), *Be Human* ('36), *House Cleaning Blues* ('37), *The Impractical Joker* ('37), *The Candid Candidate* ('37), *Service with a Smile* ('37) and *Zula Hula* ('37).

VHS: S30348. $9.95.
Fleischer, USA, 1932-37, 110 mins.

Betty Boop Definitive Collection Vol. 6: Betty's Boys & New Friends

This volume features eight cartoons with Betty's various suitors, and eight outings with various featured buddies. Betty's Boys: *Any Rags* ('32), *Betty Boop's Life Guard* ('34), *She Wronged Him Right* ('34), *No! No! A Thousand Times No!* ('35), *Betty Boop's Prize Show* ('34), *Betty Boop and The Little King* ('36), *There's Something About a Soldier* ('34) and *Wiffle Piffle in The Hot Air Salesman* ('37). New Friends: *Betty Boop's Big Boss* ('33), *Betty Boop with Henry the Funniest Living American* ('35), *Betty Boop and Little Henry* ('36), *The Foxy Hunter* ('37), *On with the New* ('38), *Betty Boop's Trial* ('34), *Judge for a Day* ('35) and *Betty Boop's Rise to Fame* ('34).

VHS: S30349. $9.95.
Fleischer, USA, 1932-38, 108 mins.

Betty Boop Definitive Collection Vol. 7: Betty's Travels & Betty and Pudgy 1

Seven cartoons with a travel theme, and nine cartoons featuring Betty's precious litlle puppy Pudgy. Betty's Travels: *When My Ship Comes In* ('34), *So Does an Automobile* ('37), *Stop That Noise* ('35), *Be Up to Date* ('38), *Wiffle Piffle in Whoops! I'm a Cowboy* ('37), *Musical Mountaineers* ('39) and *Rhythm on the Reservation* ('39). Betty & Pudgy 1: *Betty Boop's Little Pal* ('34), *Taking the Blame* ('35), *Swat the Fly* ('35), *A Little Soap and Water* ('35), *Little Nobody* ('35), *The Scared Crows* ('39), *Not Now* ('36), *We Did It* ('36) and *More Pep* ('36).

VHS: S30350. $9.95.
Fleischer, USA, 1934-39, 100 mins.

Betty Boop Definitive Collection Vol. 8: Betty and Pudgy & Pudgy and Pals

Eight more cartoons with Betty and Pudgy, plus six assorted Betty cartoons. Also features closing comments by Richard Fleischer. Betty & Pudgy: *You're Not Built That Way* ('36), *Happy You and Merry Me* ('36), *Training Pigeons* ('36), *Making Friends* ('36), *Pudgy Takes a Bow-Wow* ('37), *Pudgy Picks a Fight* ('37), *Ding Dong Doggie* ('37) and *Riding the Rails* ('38). Pudgy & Pals: *Out of the Inkwell* ('38), *The Swing School* ('38), *The Watchman* ('38), *Thrills and Chills* ('38), *My Friend the Monkey* ('39) and *Baby Be Good* ('35).

VHS: S30351. $9.95.
Fleischer, USA, 1934-39, 94 mins.

Betty Boop Definitive Collection: Boxed Set

All eight tapes in a collector's slipcase. Includes a mini-booklet, *Boopliography*.

VHS: S30002. $69.95.
Fleischer, USA, 1930-39, 798 mins.

Betty Boop's Dizzy Dozen

Twelve shorts with the witty and seductive siren as Betty Boop is joined by Koko, the Mills Bros. and Singing Sam. Includes *Judge for a Day, One More Chance* and *Betty Minds a Baby*. 90 mins.

VHS: S17847. $24.95.

Bobby's World: Me and Roger

VHS: S32450. $5.95.
USA

Boop Oop A Doop

Steve Allen narrates this retrospective of Betty Boop cartoons. There are plenty of complete cartoons along with numerous clips illustrating the evolution of Betty from a dog sidekick of Bimbo to a human girlfriend of Bimbo to Bimbo's owner. Much attention is paid to Betty's sex appeal, and the toning down of the character in the post Hayes era. Entertaining, informative, and a chance to see some film of Betty never before released on home video.

VHS: S18026. $14.95.
USA, 1986, 74 mins.

Bosko Cartoons Vol. 1

Mastered from the best film prints available and presented in their original aspect ratio. Nine titles: *Bosko the Talk-Ink Kid* ('29), *Congo Jazz* ('30), *Big Man from the North* ('31), *Ups 'n Downs* ('31), *Yodeling Yokels* ('31), *The Tree's Knees* ('31), *Bosko the Doughboy* ('31), *Bosko's Fox Hunt* ('31) and *Battling Bosko* ('32). B&W.

VHS: S29606. $29.95.
Warner Bros., USA, 1929-32, 65 mins.

Bosko Cartoons Vol. 2

Nine titles: *Sinking in the Bathtub* ('30), *Hold Anything* ('30), *Box Car Blues* ('30), *Ain't Nature Grand* ('31), *Dumb Patrol* ('31), *Bosko's Holiday* ('31), *Bosko Shipwrecked* ('31), *Bosko's Soda Fountain* ('31) and *Bosko at the Zoo* ('32). B&W.

VHS: S29607. $29.95.
Warner Bros., USA, 1930-32, 67 mins.

Bosko Cartoons Vol. 3

Nine titles: *The Booze Hangs High* ('30), *Big-Hearted Bosko* ('32), *Bosko and Bruno* ('30), *Bosko's Party* ('31), *Bosko's Dog Race* ('31), *Bosko at the Beach* ('31), *Bosko's Store* ('31), *Bosko the Lumberjack* ('31) and *Bosko and Honey* ('32). B&W.

VHS: S29608. $29.95.
Warner Bros., USA, 1930-32, 67 mins.

Bugs & Daffy's Carnival of the Animals

All new animation produced, directed and written by Chuck Jones—combined with live action as Bugs and Daffy accompany Michael Tilson Thomas in a performance based on the music of Camille Saint-Saens and the comic poetry of Ogden Nash.

VHS: S12623. $12.95.
Warner Bros, USA, 1976, 24 mins.

Bugs & Daffy: The Wartime Cartoons

Leonard Maltin introduces this collection of 11 shorts: *Herr Meets Hare* ('45), *Super Rabbit* ('43), *Draftee Daffy* ('45), *Plane Daffy* ('44), *Daffy the Commando* ('43), *Falling Hare* ('43), *Russian Rhapsody* ('44), *Swooner Crooner* ('44), *Little Red Riding Rabbit* ('44), *The Weakly Reporter* ('44) and *Fifth Column Mouse* ('43).

VHS: S09121. $19.95.
Laser: LD70537. $34.95.
Warner Bros, USA, 1943-45, 80 mins.

Bugs Bunny Classics

Seven titles: *Heckling Hare* ('41), *Racketeer Rabbit* ('46), *Acrobatty Bunny* ('46), *Rabbit Punch* ('48), *Hare Trigger* ('45), *Bugs Bunny Rides Again* ('48) and *Haredevil Hare* ('48).

VHS: S09124. $14.95.
Warner Bros, USA, 1941-48, 60 mins.

Bugs Bunny Classics/ Starring Bugs Bunny Laser

A double-feature of *Bugs Bunny Classics* and *Starring Bugs Bunny* combined on one video disc. For individual information, see separate listings.

Laser: LD70535. $34.95.
Warner Bros, USA, 120 mins.

Bugs Bunny in King Arthur's Court

Also known as *A Connecticut Rabbit in King Arthur's Court*, this TV special contains all new animation—produced and directed by Chuck Jones. Bugs ends up in King Arthur's (Daffy) court and is captured by a knight (Elmer) who thinks he's a dragon transformed into a rabbit. Merlin is played by Yosemite Sam.

VHS: S12624. $12.95.
Warner Bros., USA, 1977, 24 mins.

The Bugs Bunny Mystery Special

Porky opens with his impression of Alfred Hitchcock, and Bugs is involved in a mini-crime spree through a case of mistaken identity. Complete showing of *Big House Bunny*, plus clips from many others.

VHS: S18149. $12.95.
Warner Bros., USA, 1980, 24 mins.

Bugs Bunny on Parade

Five titles: *Elmer's Pet Rabbit* ('41), *Buckaroo Bugs* ('44), *Super Rabbit* ('43), *Jack Wabbit & The Beanstalk* ('43) and *Hold the Lion, Please* ('42).

VHS: S28004. $12.95.
Warner Bros., USA, 1941-44, 35 mins.

Bugs Bunny Superstar

Narrated by Orson Welles, this collector's classic features behind-the-scenes interviews with legendary cartoon geniuses Bob Clampett, Tex Avery and Friz Freleng. No cartoon library should be without this documentary, which includes nine complete cartoon shorts: *What's Cookin Doc?* ('44), *A Wild Hare* ('40), *I Taw a Putty Tat* ('48), *Rhapsody Rabbit* ('46), *A Corny Concerto* ('43), *Walky Talky Hawky* ('46), *The Old Grey Hare* ('44), *My Favorite Duck* ('42) and *Hair Raising Hare* ('46).

VHS: S06353. $14.95.
Warner Bros, USA, 1975, 90 mins.

Bugs Bunny's Bustin' Out All Over

Three all new shorts produced and directed by Chuck Jones in this TV special. First a preteen Bugs & Elmer endure a summer vacation in *Portrait of the Artist as a Young Bunny*, then a grownup Bugs is whisked off to Mars by Marvin Martian in *Spaced Out Bunny*, and finally Wile E. Coyote stalks the Roadrunner once again in *Soup or Sonic*.

VHS: S15833. $12.95.
Warner Bros., USA, 1980, 24 mins.

Bugs Bunny's Comedy Classics

Five titles: *Acrobatty Bunny* ('46), *Easter Yeggs* ('47), *Falling Hare* ('43), *Racketeer Rabbit* ('46) and *The Hare-Brained Hypnotist* ('42).

VHS: S13565. $12.95.
Warner Bros., USA, 1942-48, 39 mins.

Bugs Bunny's Creature Features

Three recent cartoons from the team of Greg Ford and Terry Lennon: *Invasion of the Bunny Snatchers* ('89), *The Duxorcist* ('87) and *Night of the Living Duck* ('88).

VHS: S16723. $12.95.
Warner Bros., USA, 1987-90, 25 mins.

Bugs Bunny's Cupid Capers
New animation directed by Hal Geer bridges some classic footage clips as Cupid (Elmer) shows Bugs how the world needs his help.
VHS: S15414. $12.95.
Warner Bros., USA, 1979, 24 mins.

Bugs Bunny's Easter Funnies
New animation by DePatie-Freleng bridges classic Warner shorts in this Easter special. When the Easter Bunny falls ill, it's up to Bugs to take his place, with help from the usual gang. Includes *Knighty-Knight Bugs.*
VHS: S15834. $12.95.
Warner Bros., USA, 1977, 50 mins.

Bugs Bunny's Festival of Fun
Five titles: *Hare Ribbin* ('44), *Rhapsody Rabbit* ('46), *Baseball Bugs* ('46), *The Wacky Wabbit* ('42) and *The Wabbit Who Came to Supper* ('42).
VHS: S28006. $12.95.
Warner Bros., USA, 1942-46, 35 mins.

Bugs Bunny's Greatest Hits
Five titles: *Bugs Bunny & The Three Bears* ('44), *Bugs Bunny Gets the Boid* ('42), *Gorilla My Dreams* ('48), *Slick Hare* ('47) and *The Big Snooze* ('46).
VHS: S28007. $12.95.
Warner Bros., USA, 1942-48, 35 mins.

Bugs Bunny's Hare-Brained Hits
Five titles: *My Bunny Lies over the Sea* ('48), *Big House Bunny* ('50), *Baton Bunny* ('59), *Captain Hareblower* ('54) and *Hillbilly Hare* ('50).
VHS: S28008. $12.95.
Warner Bros., USA, 1948-59, 35 mins.

Bugs Bunny's Hare-Raising Tales
Six titles: *A Lad in His Lamp* ('48), *Knight-Mare Hare* ('55), *The Windblown Hare* ('49), *Rabbitson Crusoe* ('56), *Rabbit Hood* ('49) and *A Witch's Tangled Hare* ('59).
VHS: S12625. $12.95.
Warner Bros., USA, 1948-59, 45 mins.

Bugs Bunny's Howl-Oween Special
With new bridging animation directed by David Detiege, Abe Levitow and Maurice Noble, this special features the complete 1966 Daffy & Speedy cartoon *A-Haunting We Will Go*, plus clips from *Broomstick Bunny, Transylvania 6-5000, Scaredy Cat* and *Claws for Alarm.*
VHS: S28012. $12.95.
Warner Bros., USA, 1978, 24 mins.

Bugs Bunny's Looney Christmas Tales
This 1979 TV special features three all-new cartoons: *Bugs Bunny's Christmas Carol*, a Friz Feleng version of Dickens' *Christmas Carol*, starring Yosemite Sam, Porky and Bugs; *Freeze Frame*, a new Chuck Jones cartoon in which Wile E. Coyote tries to utilize snow to capture Roadrunner; and *Fright Before Christmas*, a Friz Freleng cartoon in which Bugs' nephew Clyde leaves milk & cookies for Santa only to have Taz drop down his chimney.
VHS: S13035. $9.95.
DePatie-Freleng/WB, USA, 1979, 25 mins.

Bugs Bunny's Lunar Tunes
New animation features Bugs standing trial for crimes against the universe in a Martian court, with Marvin Martian as the prosecutor. The testimony in the case is illustrated with vintage film clips of Bugs and Marvin's past encounters.
VHS: S18147. $12.95.
Warner Bros., USA, 24 mins.

Bugs Bunny's Mad World of Television
Station QTTV appoints Bugs as the new director of programming. But Bugs must contend with a plotting Yosemite Sam as he reviews the performing talents of Tweety, Pepe Le Pew and others. Bridging animation by David Detiege with clips from *The Ducksters, Wideo Wabbit, What's Up Doc?, Past Perfumance* and others.
VHS: S18148. $12.95.
Warner Bros., USA, 1982, 24 mins.

Bugs Bunny's Mother's Day Special
New animation by Jim Davis links clips of classic Warner cartoons in this TV special. Bugs & Granny meet the stork in the park on Mother's Day, and are regaled with a series of flashbacks of some of his more oddball adventures. Mostly complete showings of *Stork Naked* and *Apes of Wrath*, plus clips from *Busby Hare, Goo Goo Goliath, Mother Was a Rooster* and *Quackodile Tears.*
VHS: S15835. $12.95.
Warner Bros., USA, 1979, 23 mins.

Bugs Bunny's Overtures to Disaster
A concerted comedy effort, with Maestro Bugs leading the concert that raises the roof and brings the house down. Incorporates classic clips of musical cartoons.
VHS: S18150. $12.95.
Warner Bros., USA, 24 mins.

Bugs Bunny's Thanksgiving Diet
Bugs is head of a diet clinic specializing in Thanksgiving overeating. Full showings of *Bedevilled Rabbit* and *Rabbit Every Monday*, along with new bridging animation by David Detiege and clips from *Beep Beep, Canned Feud, Trip for Tat* and others.
VHS: S28013. $9.95.
Warner Bros., USA, 1979, 24 mins.

Bugs Bunny's Wild World of Sports
New animation by Greg Ford and Terry Lennon and classic clips. At a sports banquet, Bugs, Sam and Daffy recall events that qualify them as "World's Greatest Sportsman."
VHS: S15415. $12.95.
Warner Bros., USA, 1989, 24 mins.

Bugs Bunny's Zaniest Toons
Five titles: *Tortoise Wins by a Hare* ('43), *Tortoise Beats Hare* ('41), *Rabbit Transit* ('47), *Hare Trigger* ('45) and *Buccaneer Bunny* ('48).
VHS: S13566. $12.95.
Warner Bros., USA, 1941-48, 39 mins.

Bugs Bunny/Roadrunner Movie
A compilation of Chuck Jones cartoons bridged together with new animation by most of his old staff. In addition to five complete cartoons—*Hareway to the Stars* ('58), *What's Opera Doc?* ('57), *Duck Amuck* ('53), *Bully for Bugs* ('53) and *Rabbit Fire* ('51)—excerpts from eight others are shown, along with an 11-minute *Roadrunner* compilation consisting of 31 gags from 16 cartoons.
VHS: S01781. $14.95.
Warner Bros, USA, 1979, 98 mins.

Bugs Bunny: 1001 Rabbit Tales
In this Friz Freleng compilation feature, Daffy and Bugs are rival salesmen for Rambling House Publishers. In the Arabian desert, Bug encounters Sultan (Yosemite) Sam and his bratty son, Prince Abadaba. Classic cartoon excerpts include *Ali Baba Bunny, Apes of Wrath, Bewitched Bunny, Cracked Quack, Goldimouse & The Three Cats, Mexican Boarders, One Froggy Evening, Pied Piper of Guadalupe, Red Riding Hoodwinked, Tweety & The Beanstalk* and *Wise Quackers.*
VHS: S14614. $14.95.
Warner Bros., USA, 1982, 74 mins.

Bugs Bunny: All-American Hero
When Bugs' nephew Clyde asks for help with a history test, Bugs recalls his own version of historical events. Classic clips and new animation by Friz Freleng.
VHS: S15413. $12.95.
Warner Bros, USA, 1981, 24 mins.

Bugs Bunny: Hare Beyond Compare
Fourteen titles: *Rabbit Fire* ('51), *Hare Lift* ('52), *Big Top Bunny* ('51), *Robot Rabbit* ('53), *Rabbit Every Monday* ('51), *Bedevilled Rabbit* ('57), *8-Ball Bunny* ('50), *Mutiny on the Bunny* ('50), *To Hare Is Human* ('56), *Beanstalk Bunny* ('55), *Knights Must Fall* ('49), *14 Carrot Rabbit* ('52), *Rebel Rabbit* ('49) and *Bunker Hill Bunny* ('50).
Laser: LD72392. $34.95.
Warner Bros., USA, 1949-57, 100 mins.

Bugs Bunny: Here Comes Bugs
Five titles: *A Wild Hare* ('40), *The Unruly Hare* ('45), *Fresh Hare* ('42), *Hare Remover* ('46) and *Wabbit Twouble* ('41).
VHS: S13572. $12.95.
Warner Bros., USA, 1940-46, 37 mins.

Bugs Bunny: Hollywood Legend
Five titles: *Hair Raising Hare* ('46), *Hare Force* ('44), *Hare Tonic* ('45), *A Hare Grows in Manhattan* ('47) and *Hare Conditioned* ('45).
VHS: S13564. $12.95.
Warner Bros., USA, 1944-47, 37 mins.

Bugs Bunny: Truth or Hare
Five titles: *The Fair Haired Hare* ('51), *Dr. Devil & Mr. Hare* ('64), *Wideo Wabbit* ('56), *Hare-Way to the Stars* ('58) and *Water, Water Every Hare* ('52).
VHS: S16717. $12.95.
Warner Bros., USA, 1951-64, 33 mins.

Bugs Bunny: Winner by a Hare
Fourteen titles: *The Fair Haired Hare* ('51), *Bully for Bugs* ('53), *Hare Do* ('49), *Captain Hareblower* ('54), *My Bunny Lies over the Sea* ('48), *High Diving Hare* ('49), *Rabbit Seasoning* ('52), *Bunny Hugged* ('51), *Ballot Box Bunny* ('51), *Box Office Bunny* ('91), *Big House Bunny* ('50), *Rabbit Hood* ('49), *Hare Trimmed* ('53) and *Mississippi Hare* ('49).
Laser: LD71758. $34.95.
Warner Bros., USA, 1949-91, 101 mins.

Bugs vs. Daffy: Battle of the Music Video Stars
New animation by Greg Ford and Terry Lennon bridges clips of classic Warner shorts. Daffy's music video station, KPUT, is getting clobbered in the ratings by Bugs' WABBIT. Daffy decides that this means war.
VHS: S15416. $12.95.
Warner Bros., USA, 1988, 24 mins.

Bugs vs. Elmer
Seven titles: *Fresh Hare* ('42), *Wabbit Twouble* ('41), *Slick Hare* ('47), *Unruly Hare* ('45), *Stage Door Cartoon* ('44), *Hare Remover* ('46) and *The Big Snooze* ('46).
VHS: S28010. $14.95.
Warner Bros., USA, 1941-47, 48 mins.

Bugs!
Seven titles: *Bugs Bunny & The Three Bears* ('44), *Hare Ribbin* ('44), *Bugs Bunny Gets the Boid* ('42), *Gorilla My Dreams* ('48), *Tortoise Wins by a Hare* ('43), *Baseball Bugs* ('46) and *Rabbit Transit* ('47).
VHS: S06354. $14.95.
Warner Bros, USA, 1942-48, 60 mins.

Bugs: The Very Best of Bugs
Five titles: *What's Cookin, Doc?* ('44), *Rabbit Punch* ('48), *Little Red Riding Rabbit* ('44), *Wackiki Wabbit* ('43) and *The Heckling Hare* ('41).
VHS: S28011. $12.95.
Warner Bros., USA, 1941-48, 35 mins.

Cadillacs and Dinosaurs: Rogue & Dino Drive
Based on Mark Schultz's comic book *Xenozoic Tales*, this sci-fi saga has been adapted as an animated series by Nelvana studios. Two episodes.
VHS: S27553. $9.95.
Nelvana, Canada, 1993, 46 mins.

Cadillacs and Dinosaurs: Wild Child & Pursuit
Two episodes.
VHS: S27554. $9.95.
Nelvana, Canada, 1993, 46 mins.

Carrotblanca
1995's theatrical short *Carrotblanca* is available on home video for the first time, along with 1990's *Box Office Bunny* and four classic shorts. Six titles: *Carrotblanca* ('95), *Dripalong Daffy* ('51), *Hare Do* ('49), *You Ought to Be in Pictures* ('40, colorized version), *The Scarlet Pumpernickel* ('50) and *Box Office Bunny* ('90).
VHS: S30357. $12.95.
Warner Bros., USA, 1940-95, 45 mins.

Cartoon Classics in Color #1: Comicolor/Van Beuren
Eight titles: Comicolor Cartoons directed by Ub Iwerks: *Little Black Sambo* ('35), *Jack Frost* ('34), *Sinbad the Sailor* ('35), *Simple Simon* ('35) and *Ali Baba* ('36). Van Beuren Cartoons: *Molly Moo Cow & The Butterflies* ('35) and *The Toonerville Trolley* ('35). Max Fleischer Color Classic: *Somewhere in Dreamland* ('36). Marginal film/video quality.
VHS: S05456. $19.95.
USA, 1934-36, 60 mins.

Cartoon Classics in Color #2: Fleischer/Warners
Eight titles: Max Fleischer Color Classics: *You Can't Shoe a Horsefly* ('40), *Little Lamby* ('37) and *Ants in the Plants* ('40). MGM: *Jerky Turkey* ('45, directed by Tex Avery). Warner Brothers cartoons: *Falling Hare* ('43, with Bugs), *Ali Baba Bound* ('40, with Porky), *Yankee Doodle Daffy* ('43, with Porky & Daffy) and *Robinhood Makes Good* ('39, directed by Chuck Jones). Marginal film/video quality.
VHS: S02231. $19.95.
USA, 1937-45, 60 mins.

Cartoon Classics in Color #3: Wartime Warner Bros.
Eight titles: *A Corny Concerto* ('43, with Bugs Bunny, Porky, Daffy & Elmer), *Foney Fables* ('42), *The Wacky Wabbit* ('42, with Bugs & Elmer), *Have You Got Any Castles?* ('38), *Fifth Column Mouse* ('43), *To Duck or Not to Duck* ('43, with Daffy & Elmer), *The Early Worm Gets the Bird* ('40) and *Daffy the Commando* ('43, with Daffy). Marginal film/video quality.
VHS: S02226. $19.95.
Warner Bros., USA, 1938-43, 60 mins.

Cartoon Classics in Color #4: Classic Warner Bros.

Seven titles: *The Wabbit Who Came to Supper* ('42, with Bugs & Elmer), *A Tale of Two Kitties* ('48), *Case of the Missing Hare* ('42, with Bugs), *Hamateur Night* ('38), *Wackiki Wabbit* ('53, with Bugs), *Daffy Duck & The Dinosaur* ('39, with Daffy) and *Fresh Hare* ('42, with Bugs & Elmer).
VHS: S05475. $19.95.
Warner Bros., USA, 1938-53, 54 mins.

Cartoon Classics Vol. 1: Looney Tunes & Merrie Melodies

Eight titles: *The Queen Was in the Parlor* ('32), *Freddy the Freshman* ('32), *Red Headed Baby* ('32), *Battling Bosko* ('31 with Bosko), *You're Too Careless with Your Kisses* ('33), *It's Got Me Again* ('32), *Moonlight for Two* ('32) and *You Don't Know What You're Doin'* ('32). B&W.
VHS: S28073. $19.95.
Warner Bros., USA, 1931-33, 56 mins.

Cartoon Classics Vol. 2: Warner Brothers

Seven titles: *Porky Pig's Feat* ('43, with Porky & Daffy), *Smile, Darn Ya, Smile* ('32), *Get Rich Quick, Porky* ('37, with Porky & Gabby), *One More Time* ('32), Yodeling Yokels *('31, with Bosko)*, Scrap Happy Daffy *('43, with Daffy) and* Porky's Preview *('41, with Porky)*.
VHS: S28074. $19.95.
Warner Bros., USA, 1931-43, 51 mins.

Cartoon Classics Vol. 3: The Early Pioneers

This volume contains some extremely rare and ancient silent cartoons by early pioneers in American animation. Six titles: Paul Terry: *Farmer Al Falfa's Wayward Pup* ('17); *Newman Laugh-O-Grams* ('21, very early Disney), *Puss in Boots* ('22, Laugh-o-gram) and *Alice the Toreador* ('25, Alice in Cartoonland by Disney/ Iwerks); J.R. Bray Studios: *Bobby Bumps Puts a Beanery on the Bum* ('18, directed by Earl Hurd); Thomas Edison Studio: *The Dinosaur & The Missing Link—A Prehistoric Tragedy* ('17, directed by Willis O'Brien). B&W. Silent.
VHS: S28075. $19.95.
USA, 1917-25, 54 mins.

Cartoon Classics Vol. 5: The Other Studios

Van Beuren: *Brownie Bucks the Jungle* (Mild Cargo) ('34), *An Ill Wind* (Humpty Dumpty Jr.) ('35), *In Darkest Africa (On The Pan)* ('33 Little King) and *A Little Bird Told Me* ('34); Walter Lantz Tuneful cartoon: *Boy Meets Dog* ('37); Comicolor Cartoon: *Tom Thumb* ('36); *Felix the Cat: April Maze* ('30); Warner Bros: *Ain't Nature Grand?* ('30, Bosko).
VHS: S02232. $19.95.
USA, 1930-37, 60 mins.

Cartoon Classics Vol. 6: Early Animation

Nine titles: *Humorous Phases of Funny Faces* (1906, J. Stuart Blackton), considered by some to be the first animated cartoon, *Action Antics* ('26, Bart Foss), *Modeling* ('23, Out of the Inkwell), *Adam Raises Cain* ('20, Tony Sarg), *Princess Nicotine* ('09, Blackton), *The Evils of Alcohol* ('21, France), *Swat the Fly*, a.k.a. *Miracles in Mud* ('16, USA), *Morpheus Mike* ('16, USA) and *RFD 10,000 BC* ('17, Willis O'Brien). Silent with organ score.
VHS: S28078. $19.95.
1906-26, 56 mins.

Cartoon Classics Vol. 7: Early Animation

Seven titles: *Gertie* ('14, by Winsor McCay), *Invisible Revenge* ('26, Mutt 'N Jeff by Raoul Barre & Charles Bowers), *Cramps* ('16, Mutt & Jeff), *Dog-Gone* ('26, Bonzo by Bud Fisher), *Goodrich Dirt, Cowpuncher* ('18, by J.R. Bray), *Willi's Nightmare* ('20, by Paul Peroff) and *The Animated Grouch Chaser* ('15, by Raoul Barre). Silent with organ.
VHS: S28079. $19.95.
USA, 1914-26, 56 mins.

Cartoon Classics Vol. 8: Early Thirties

Eight titles: *Sultan Pepper* ('34, Little King), *Old Anything* ('33, Bosko), *The Shanty Where Santy Claus Lives* ('33), *The Lion Tamer* ('34, Amos & Andy), *Grandfather's Clock* ('34, Burt Gillett Toddle Tale), *Molly Moo Cow & Rip Van Winkle* ('34), *Three Little Kittens* ('33) and *The Mechanical Man* ('32).
VHS: S28080. $19.95.
USA, 1932-34, 59 mins.

Cartoon Classics Vol. 9: Early Pioneers

Eight titles: *Scrub Me Mammy with a Boogie Beat* ('41, Walter Lantz), *A Day at the Zoo* ('39, Egghead), *Ups 'n Downs* ('31), *Christmas Toyshop* ('34), *Funny Face* ('33, Flip the Frog), *Puzzled Pals* ('33, Tom & Jerry), *The Fresh Vegetable Mystery* ('34, Fleischer) and *Presto Change-o* ('29, Paul Terry).
VHS: S28081. $19.95.
USA, 1929-41, 58 mins.

Cartoon Collection Vol. 1: Porky in Wackyland

Sixteen titles: Warner Bros. cartoons: *Porky in Wackyland, Corny Concerto, All This and Rabbit Stew, Daffy Duckaroo, Scrap Happy Daffy* and *Hollywood Steps Out*. Disney Cartoon: *The Spirit of '43*. Fleischer cartoons: *The Friendly Ghost, I'm in the Army Now, Customers Wanted, Poop Deck Pappy, I Ski Love Ski You Ski, Eugene the Jeep, She Sick Sailor, Minnie the Moocher* and *Betty Boop's Rise to Fame*.
VHS: S29610. $19.95.
USA, 115 mins.

Cartoon Collection Vol. 2: Classic Warner Bros.

Sixteen titles: *Bugs Bunny in Fresh Hare, The Wacky Wabbit, Falling Hare, Case of the Missing Hare, The Wabbit Who Came to Supper* and *Wackiki Wabbit*. Daffy Duck in *To Duck or Not to Duck, Daffy Duck & The Dinosaur, The Daffy Commando, Henpecked Duck* and *Daffy's Southern Exposure*. Porky Pig in *Notes to You, Porky's Midnight Matinee, Porky's Pastry Pirates, Porky's Railroad* and *Porky's Preview*.
VHS: S29611. $19.95.
Warner Bros., USA, 115 mins.

Cartoon Collection Vol. 3: Coal Black & De Sebben Dwarfs

Sixteen titles: Porky Pig in *Calling Dr. Porky, Ali Baba Bound, Porky's Picnic, Little Beau Porky, Porky's Phony Express, Kristopher Kolumbus, Confusions of a Nutsy Spy* and *Scalp Trouble. Daffy Duck in The Daffy Doc* and *Tom Turk & Daffy*. Bosko in *Hold Anything* and *Bosko the Speed King*. Merrie Melodies include *Those Beautiful Dames, Coal Black and De Sebben Dwarfs, Eating on the Cuff* and *Billboard Frolics*.
VHS: S29612. $19.95.
Warner Bros., USA, 115 mins.

Cartoon Collection Vol. 4: Warner Bros. & Fleischer

Sixteen titles: Betty Boop in *Making Stars, Ha-Ha-Ha, Dizzy Red Riding Hood, Mother Goose Land* and *Betty in Blunderland*. Popeye in *You're a Sap, Mr. Jap, Spinach Roadster, Blow Me Down* and *Females Is Fickle*. Porky Pig in *The Case of the Stuttering Pig*. Musical cartoons: *Crosby, Columbo and Valle; I'm Afraid to Come Home in the Dark; Smile, Darn Ya, Smile; I Love a Parade; Sleepy Time Down South* and *One More Time*.
VHS: S29613. $19.95.
WB & Fleischer, USA, 115 mins.

Cartoon Collection Vol. 5: Racial Cartoons

Sixteen titles: *Bugs Bunny Bond Rally, Sing-a-long with Popeye, Plane Dumb, Porky's Hare Hunt, Mickey's Song, Little Black Sambo, Porky's Pooch, Joe Glow the Firefly, Porky's Movie Mystery, The Lone Stranger, Japoteurs, The Ballad of John Henry, Congo Jazz, I'll Be Glad When You're Dead, You Rascal You, Snap Happy, Jungle Jive and preview trailers and intermission trailers. B&W/Color.*
VHS: S29614. $19.95.
USA, 120 mins.

Cartoon Collection Vol. 6: The Ducktators

Sixteen titles: Little Lulu in *Loose in the Caboose, Bored of Education* and *Musical Lulu*. Porky Pig in *Porky's Hired Hand* and *Porky's Garden*. Bosko in *Bosko Shipwrecked* and *Bosko's Soda Fountain. It's a Hap-Hap-Happy Day, The Ducktators, Hollywood Capers, Ding Dog Daddy, Presto-Change-o, Foney Fables, Yankee Doodle Donkey, Felix the Cat and the Goose That Laid the Golden Eggs* and *The Talking Magpies*. B&W/Color.
VHS: S29615. $19.95.
USA, 115 mins.

Cartoon Collection Vol. 7: Tokyo Jokio

Sixteen titles: Bugs Bunny in *The Unruly Hare* and *Hare-Um Scare-Um*. Porky Pig in *Boom Boom*. Daffy Duck in *Yankee Doodle Daffy*. Tweety in *A Tale of Two Kitties*. Betty Boop in *Betty Boop & Grampy. Tokyo Jokio, It's Got Me Again, Sinkin' in the Bathtub, Moonlight for Two, The Early Worm Gets the Bird.* Felix in *Oceantics. From Van Beuren Studios: In a Cartoon Studio, Piano Tooners*. The Little King in *Saddle Daze* and *Redskin Blues*. B&W/Color.
VHS: S29616. $19.95.
USA, 115 mins.

Cartoon Collection Vol. 8: Private Snafu

Nineteen titles: Private Snafu in *Snafuperman, Rumors, Spies, Censored!, Going Home, It's Murder She Says, The Goldbrick* and *Malaria Mike*; Little Lulu in *Bargain Counter Attack, A Bout with a Trout, Chick and Double Chick* and *A Scout with the Gout*; Betty Boop in *Crazy Inventions, Betty and Henry, Judge for a Day, Not Now* and *You're Not Built That Way*; Porky Pig in *Get Rich Quick Porky*; Van Beuren Studio: *Gypped in Egypt*. B&W/Color.
VHS: S29617. $19.95.
USA, 120 mins.

Cartoon Crazys

Fully restored classic cartoons with enhanced Dolby soundtrack, sounds and effects. Features great performances from Bugs Bunny, Daffy Duck, Elmer Fudd, Porky Pig, Felix the Cat and more. Each program is 100 mins.
Cartoon Crazys, Vol. 1.
VHS: S34815. $14.95.
DVD: DV60370. $19.95.
Cartoon Crazys, Vol. 2.
VHS: S34816. $14.95.
DVD: DV60371. $19.95.

Cartoon Holidays

Six titles: *Betty Boop's Halloween Party* ('33), *Snow Foolin* ('49), *Santa's Surprise* ('47), *Hector's Hectic Life* ('48), *Rudolph the Red Nosed Reindeer* and *Christmas Comes But Once a Year* ('36).
VHS: S09237. $9.95.
Fleischer/Famous, USA, 1933-49, 48 mins.

Cartoon Madness: The Fantastic Max Fleischer Cartoons

Leonard Maltin narrates a retrospective of Fleischer animation, covering the spectrum and providing rare, behind-the-scenes footage of the 3-D tabletop system and the new Florida studio. Many clips and much intelligent commentary. Eight complete cartoons: *She Reminds Me of You* (Screen Song), *Koko's Earth Control* ('27), *Bimbo's Initiation* ('31), *Snow White, Poor Cinderella, Dancing on the Moon, Raggedy Ann & Andy* and *Betty Boop's May Party. Unbelievably clean film prints. The show glosses over Popeye and Superman, but is nonetheless well worth watching.*
VHS: S28082. $14.95.
Fleischer, USA, 1993, 94 mins.

Cartoonal Knowledge: Confessions of Farmer Gray

Seven titles: *A Cat's Life, Magic Boots, Chemistry Lesson* ('22), *Day at the Park, Wonders of the Deep, Closer Than a Brother* ('25) and *The Window Washers* ('25). B&W/Sient.
VHS: S28083. $19.95.
Paul Terry, USA, 1920's, 54 mins.

Cartoonal Knowledge: Farmer Gray & The Mice

Seven titles: *Snapping the Whip* ('29), *Through Thick & Thin* ('26), *Where Friendship Ceases* ('26), *The Water Cure* ('29), *In the Bag* ('28), *She's In Again* ('24) and *Watered Stock* ('26). B&W/Silent.
VHS: S28084. $19.95.
Paul Terry, USA, 1924-29, 54 mins.

Cartoonal Knowledge: Farmer Gray Goes to the Dogs

Seven titles: *Small Town Sheriff* ('27), *Cracked Ice* ('27), *The Huntsman* ('26), *The Medicine Man* ('27), *Mouse's Bride* ('27), *Monkey Shines* ('27) and *Coast to Coast* ('26). B&W/Silent.
VHS: S28087. $19.95.
Paul Terry, USA, 1926-27, 54 mins.

Cartoonal Knowledge: Farmer Gray Looks at Life

Seven titles: *In Dutch* ('25), *Two of a Trade* ('22), *Why Argue* ('26), *Static* ('28), *Wooden Money* ('29), *Smart Salesman* ('23) and *The Windjammers* ('26). B&W/Silent.
VHS: S28085. $19.95.
Paul Terry, USA, 1922-29, 54 mins.

Cartoonal Knowledge: The Return of Farmer Gray

Seven titles: *Sunday on the Farm* ('28), *Buck Fever* ('26), *Short Circuit* ('27), *Wedding Bells, The Cat & The Magnet* ('24), *One Hard Pull* ('23) and *On the Air*. B&W/Silent.
VHS: S28086. $19.95.
Paul Terry, USA, 1923-29, 54 mins.

Cartoongate!
An anthology of politically themed cartoons, including Chuck Jones' *Hell-Bent for Election*, in which Roosevelt's "Win the War Special" runs against the "Defeatist Limited." Ten titles: *Cartoongate!* ('96, Greg Ford), *Hell-Bent for Election* ('44, Chuck Jones), *Eisenhower Spots* ('52-'56), *No Substitute* ('96, Russell Calabrese), *A Political Cartoon* ('74, Joe Adamson), *Popeye for President* ('56, Famous Studios), *Jimmy Who?* ('75), *Reaganocchio* ('84, Ken Kimmelman), *Now Is the Time for All Good Men* ('60) and *Political Basketball* ('92, Greg Ford).
VHS: S28506. $14.95.
USA, 1944-96, 55 mins.

Cartoons for Big Kids
Leonard Maltin introduces these classic cartoon shorts with "adult" themes. Four titles: *King Size Canary* (MGM/Tex Avery), *The Great Piggy Bank Robbery* (WB/Clampett), *The Big Snooze* (WB/Clampett) and *Red Hot Riding Hood* (MGM/Tex Avery).
VHS: S29618. $19.95.
Laser: LD75845. $29.95.
WB & MGM, USA, 44 mins.

Cartoons Go to War
This A&E documentary celebrates the wonderful shorts, mixing rare vintage animation with first-time interviews of those directly associated with the war movie projects…an ultimate collection of WWII cartoons. Including creations like the U.S. Navy's *Hook* and Disney's *Der Fuehrer's Face*, these cartoons offer a funny and fascinating look at the politics, goals and culture of the times.
VHS: S27623. $19.95.
Sharon K. Baker, USA, 1995, 50 mins.

Cartoons That Time Forgot Vol. 1: All Singing! All Dancing!
The first volume in a series of classic Ub Iwerks and Van Beuren cartoons, assembled by Greg Ford. Ten titles: *Fiddlesticks!* ('30), *The Soup Song* ('31), *The Little Red Hen* ('34), *The Village Smithy* ('31), *Mary's Little Lamb* ('35), *The Village Barber* ('31), *Old Mother Hubbard* ('35), *Humpty Dumpty* ('35), *The Bremertown Musicians* ('35) and *Summertime* ('35). Color/B&W.
VHS: S18205. $24.95.
Ub Iwerks, USA, 1930-35, 75 mins.

Cartoons That Time Forgot Vol. 2: Down & Out with Flip the Frog
Ten titles: *The Milkman* ('32), *The New Car* ('31), *Ragtime Romeo* ('31), *What a Life!* ('32), *The Bully* ('32), *Funny Face* ('33), *Movie Mad* ('31), *The Nurse Maid* ('32), *Room Runners* ('32) and *The Office Boy* ('32). B&W.
VHS: S18206. $24.95.
Ub Iwerks, USA, 1931-33, 76 mins.

Cartoons That Time Forgot Vol. 3: Things That Go Bump in the Night
Ten titles: *The Cuckoo Murder Case* ('31), *Stratos-Fear* ('33), *Jack Frost* ('34), *A Chinaman's Chance* ('33), *Hell's Fire* ('34, excerpt), *Techno-Cracked* ('33), *Soda Squirt* ('33), *The Headless Horseman* ('34), *Spooks* ('32) and *Balloon Land* ('35). Plus bonus short *Willie Whopper in Hell*. B&W/Color.
VHS: S18207. $24.95.
Ub Iwerks, USA, 1931-35, 75 mins.

Cartoons That Time Forgot Vol. 4: Willie Whopper's Fantastic Adventures
Ten titles: *The Air Race* ('33/36), *Tom Thumb* ('36), *Insultin' the Sultan* ('34), *Sinbad the Sailor* ('35), *Rasslin' Round* ('34), *Ali Baba* ('36), *Viva Willie* ('34), *Don Quixote* ('34), *Good Scout* ('34) and *Happy Days* ('36). B&W/Color.
VHS: S18208. $24.95.
Ub Iwerks, USA, 1933-36, 75 mins.

Cartoons That Time Forgot Vol. 5: Free-Form Fairytales
Ten titles: *Aladdin & His Wonderful Lamp* ('34), *Jack & The Beanstalk* ('33), *The Brave Tin Soldier* ('34), *Puss in Boots* ('34), *Little Boy Blue* ('35), *The Queen of Hearts* ('34), *Simple Simon* ('35), *The Valiant Tailor* ('34), *The Three Bears* ('35) and *Dick Whittington's Cat* ('36).
VHS: S18209. $24.95.
Ub Iwerks, USA, 1933-36, 77 mins.

Cartoons That Time Forgot Vol. 6: The Odd & The Outrageous
Eleven titles: *Opening Night* ('33), *In a Cartoon Studio*, a.k.a. *Making 'em Move* ('31), *Tuba Tooter* ('32), *Silvery Moon*, a.k.a. *Candy Town* ('33), *The Sunshine Makers* ('35), *Piano Tooners* ('33), *Molly Moo Cow & Rip Van Winkle* ('35), *Joint Wipers* ('32), *Neptune Nonsense* ('36), *Christmas Night*, a.k.a. *Pals* ('33) and *Toonerville Picnic* ('36). Color/B&W.
VHS: S18210. $24.95.
Van Beuren, USA, 1931-36, 77 mins.

Cartoons That Time Forgot Vol. 7: Rainbow Parades
From the Van Beuren studio in lush Technicolor, Burt Gillett's Rainbow Parades. Ten titles: *Molly Moo Cow & The Butterflies* ('35), *Felix the Cat in Bold King Cole* ('36), *It's a Greek Life!* ('36), *Molly Moo Cow & The Indians* ('35), *Felix and the Goose That Laid the Golden Eggs* ('36), *Toonerville Trolley* ('36), *Cupid Gets His Man* ('36), *Molly Moo Cow & Robinson Crusoe* ('36), *A Waif's Welcome* ('36) and *Trolley Ahoy!* ('36).
VHS: S18211. $24.95.
Van Beuren, USA, 1935-36, 72 mins.

Casper Cartoons Vol. 1
This disc includes the contents of the videotape collections *Casper's Favorite Days, Casper's Good Deeds* and *Casper's Fairy Tales*.
Laser: LD75613. $34.95.
Famous Studios, USA, 1953-58, 75 mins.

Casper Cartoons Vol. 2
This disc includes the contents of the videotape collections *Casper's Halloween, Casper's Animal Friends* and *Casper's Travels*.
Laser: LD75614. $34.95.
Famous Studios, USA, 1953-58, 75 mins.

Casper Cartoons Vol. 3
This disc includes the contents of the videotape collections *Casper's Magic Touch, Casper's Outdoor Sports* and *Casper's City Trips*.
Laser: LD75615. $34.95.
Famous Studios, USA, 1953-58, 76 mins.

Casper Cartoons Vol. 4
This disc includes the contents of the videotape collections *Casper's Friend Wendy, Casper's Tall Tales* and *Casper's Brave Acts*.
Laser: LD75616. $34.95.
Famous Studios, USA, 69 mins.

Casper Cartoons Vol. 5
This disc includes the contents of the videotape collections*Casper's Outer Space, Secret Powers, Ghost Buddies* and *Furry Friends*.
Laser: LD75617. $34.95.
Famous Studios, USA, 92 mins.

Casper Meets Wendy
Harvey Comics' Wendy the Witch makes her full-length motion picture debut as she and Casper forge a boo-tiful friendship and join forces to foil an evil warlock's dastardly plot. With Cathy Moriarty, Teri Garr, Shelley Duvall, George Hamilton and Hilary Duff.
VHS: S35235. $19.98.
Sean McNamara, USA, 1998, 88 mins.

Casper's Animal Friends
Four titles: *Keep Your Grin Up* ('55), *Boo Kind to Animals* ('55), *By the Old Mill Scream* ('53) and *Good Scream Fun* ('58).
VHS: S17242. $9.95.
Famous Studios, USA, 1953-58, 25 mins.

Casper's Brave Acts
Four titles: *Lonesome Giant, The Absent-Minded Robot, Greedy Giants* and *Red Robbing Hood*.
VHS: S28093. $9.95.
Famous Studios, USA, 23 mins.

Casper's City Trips
Four titles: *Ghost of Honor* ('57), *Boo Bop* ('57), *Not Ghoulty* ('59) and *Boo Hoo Baby* ('51).
VHS: S28094. $9.95.
Famous Studios, USA, 1953-58, 25 mins.

Casper's Fairy Tales
Four titles: *Mother Goose Land, Little Bo Peep* ('53), *Once upon a Rhyme* ('50) and *Dutch Treat* ('56).
VHS: S17254. $9.95.
Famous Studios, USA, 1950-56, 25 mins.

Casper's Favorite Days
Four titles: *Casper's Birthday Party* ('59), *Doing What's Fright* ('59), *Do or Diet* ('53) and *Weather or Not*.
VHS: S17253. $9.95.
Famous Studios, USA, 1953-59, 25 mins.

Casper's Friend Wendy
Four titles: *Growing Up, Wendy's Wish, Twin Trouble* and *The Enchanted Prince*.
VHS: S28096. $9.95.
Famous Studios, USA, 23 mins.

Casper's Furry Friends
Four titles: *Ground Hog Play, Boo Ribbon Winner, Pig-A-Boo* and *Bedtime Troubles*.
VHS: S28097. $9.95.
Famous Studios, USA, 23 mins.

Casper's Ghost Buddies
Four titles: *Little Lost Ghost, Hide and Shriek, City Snicker* and *Hooky Spooky*.
VHS: S29621. $9.95.
Famous Studios, USA, 23 mins.

Casper's Good Deeds
Four titles: *Boos and Saddles* ('53), *Zero the Hero* ('54), *Puss 'n Boos* ('54) and *Spook No Evil* ('53).
VHS: S17255. $9.95.
Famous Studios, USA, 1953-54, 25 mins.

Casper's Halloween
Four titles: *To Boo or Not to Boo* ('51), *Which Is Witch* ('58), *Fright Day the 13th* ('53) and *The Witching Hour*.
VHS: S17241. $9.95.
Famous Studios, USA, 1951-58, 25 mins.

Casper's Magic Touch
Four titles: *Red White & Boo* ('55), *Kings of Toyland, The Magic Touch* and *Spree Under the Sea* ('50).
VHS: S28099. $9.95.
Famous Studios, USA, 1950-55, 25 mins.

Casper's Outdoor Sports
Four titles: *Ice Scream* ('57), *Line of Screammage* ('56), *Boo Scout* ('51) and *Boos and Arrows* ('54).
VHS: S28100. $9.95.
Famous Studios, USA, 1951-57, 25 mins.

Casper's Outer Space
Four titles: *A Visit from Mars, Professor's Problem, Cold Wave* and *Down to Mirth*.
VHS: S28101. $9.95.
Famous Studios, USA, 23 mins.

Casper's Secret Powers
Four titles: *Super Spook, Fright from Wrong, Small Spooks* and *Casper Genie*.
VHS: S28102. $9.95.
Famous Studios, USA, 23 mins.

Casper's Tall Tales
Four titles: *The Enchanted Horse, Heart of Gold, Timid Knight* and *Wandering Ghost*.
VHS: S28103. $9.95.
Famous Studios, USA, 25 mins.

Casper's Travels
Four titles: *Spooking with a Brogue* ('55), *Penguin for Your Thoughts* ('56), *Heir Restorer* ('58) and *Bull Fright* ('55).
VHS: S17243. $9.95.
Famous Studios, USA, 1955-58, 25 mins.

Cat's Meow: Kitty Kartoons by Paul Terry
Seven titles: *Spanish Love* ('26), *The Wicked Cat* ('22), *Soldiers of Fortune* ('24), *The Wicked King* ('25), *Motorcycle Hero* ('22), *Our Hero* ('26) and *Money Mad* ('24). Silent with organ score.
VHS: S28088. $19.95.
Paul Terry, USA, 1922-26, 55 mins.

Cats Don't Dance
Cats Don't Dance was one of the best animated features released last year, but if you blinked you missed its one-week showing in the theatres. Warner Bros. spared every effort to properly release this high-quality cartoon musical they acquired from Turner Feature Animation. The good news is that they've released it on video to be discovered by hungry cartoon fans looking for something different. It's a clever spin on an old Hollywood story, in which young, optimistic Danny comes to L.A. with a dream to be a big star, only to learn that Tinsel Town is a cruel, heartless town. The character design is fun, the animation is full and at times spectacular, and even the songs are good. If you're looking for an alternative to the epic fairytales that today's animated features have become, this film is the answer. CC.
VHS: S31640. $19.98.
Laser: Widescreen. **LD76249. $34.95.**
Turner, USA, 1997, 77 mins.

Chariots of Fur

In 1995, Chuck Jones released the first new Roadrunner theatrical cartoon in over 30 years. *Chariots of Fur* is now on home video for the first time, along with five classic shorts: *Beep Beep* ('52); *Operation: Rabbit* ('52, with Bugs); *Hook, Line and Stinker* ('58); *Ready, Woolen and Able* ('60, Ralph Wolf and Sam Sheepdog) and *Zip 'n Snort* ('61).
VHS: S30358. $12.95.
Warner Bros., USA, 1952-95, 39 mins.

A Christmas Carol

In this direct-to-video feature, Dickens' classic tale is retold once more in a song-filled version featuring the voices of Tim Curry, Whoopi Goldberg, Michael York and Ed Asner. CC.
VHS: S32308. $19.95.
DIC, USA, 1997, 72 mins.

Christmas Cartoon Classic

Rudolph the Red Nosed Reindeer (Fleischer), *Christmas Toy Shop*, *A Christmas Dream*, *Christmas Comes But Once a Year* (Grampy), *Somewhere in Springtime*, *Hector's Hectic Life* and *Merry Christmas* (Castle short subject).
VHS: S29619. $24.95.
USA, 60 mins.

Chuck Amuck: The Movie

The man behind the madness! Warner Bros. animation legend Chuck Jones takes you on a fun-filled and cartoon-packed tour of his fascinating career. Chuck talks about the Warner characters and the studio personnel, and he draws Bugs, Porky and others while he talks about their construction and personalities. In addition to his many other talents, Jones is a thoughtful and articulate speaker.
VHS: S14619. $14.95.
Great Britain, 1991, 51 mins.

Classic Cartoon Christmas Treasures

Eight titles: Halas & Batchelor: *The Candlemaker* ('57) and *The Christmas Visitor* ('59); Famous Studios: *Toys Will Be Toys* ('49), *Santa's Surprise* ('47) and *Hector's Hectic Life* ('48); Van Beuren: *Toyland Caper* ('32); Lotte Reininger: *Star of Bethlehem* ('56); Fleischer: *Christmas Comes But Once a Year* ('36).
VHS: S29620. $29.95.
1932-59, 70 mins.

Classic Shorts Compilation #12: Winsor McCay

A collection of six short animated films by Winsor McCay, a pioneer in the world of animation. McCay's early style involved delicate line drawings against a plain background; seen today, they still have considerable beauty and charm. This compilation includes *Gertie the Dinosaur* (1911), *Dream* (1922), *Bug Vaudeville* (1912), *Little Nemo* (1911), *The Pet* (1913) and *The Sinking of the Lusitania* (1919).
VHS: S15062. $29.95.
Winsor McCay, USA, 1911-1922, 60 mins.

Classic Shorts Compilation #14: Felix the Cat

Ten rare, early shorts featuring one of the most popular cartoon characters of all time, Felix the Cat. Includes *April Maze* (1930), *Felix All Puzzled* (1936), *Felix Dines and Pines* (1926), *Felix Gets Broadcasted* (1923), *Felix Goes West* (1924), *Felix in Fairyland* (1924), *Felix Turns the Tide* (1924), *Futuritzy* (1928), *Non-Stop Freight* (1927) and *Polly-Tics* (1928). B&W. 65 mins.
VHS: S15064. $29.95.

Color Adventures of Superman

All color adventures of Superman beautifully animated by the Fleischer studio with the voice of Bud Collyer as Superman. Includes *Superman, The Mechanical Monsters, The Magnetic Telescope, The Japoteurs, The Bulleteers, Jungle Drums* and *The Mummy Strikes*.
VHS: S05474. $24.95.

Columbia Cartoon Classics Vol. 2: Mr. Magoo

Four Cinemascope titles: *Magoo Beats the Heat* ('56), *Magoo Breaks Par* ('57), *Magoo Goes Overboard* ('57) and *Magoo Goes West* ('56).
VHS: S28113. $12.95.
UPA, USA, 1956-57, 26 mins.

Columbia Cartoon Classics Vol. 3: Gerald McBoing Boing

Four titles: *Gerald McBoing Boing* ('51, Oscar winner), *Gerald McBoing Boing on the Planet Moo* ('56, Oscar nominee), *Gerald McBoing Boing's Symphony* ('53) and *How Now McBoing Boing* ('54).
VHS: S00490. $12.95.
UPA, USA, 1951-56, 29 mins.

Columbia Cartoon Classics Vol. 4: Cartoon Classics

Four titles: *Christopher Crumpet's Playmate* ('55), *The Emperor's New Clothes* ('53), *The Jay Walker* ('56, Oscar nominee) and *The Man on the Flying Trapeze* ('54).
VHS: S28115. $12.95.
UPA, USA, 1953-56, 27 mins.

Columbia Cartoon Classics Vol. 5: Mr. Magoo

Seven titles: *Stage Door Magoo* ('55), *Magoo's Glorious Fourth* ('57), *Sloppy Jalopy* ('52), *Magoo's Homecoming* ('59), *Trouble Indemnity* ('50, Oscar nominee), *Fuddy Duddy Buddy* ('51) and *Magoo's Masquerade* ('57).
VHS: S28106. $12.95.
UPA, USA, 1950-59, 45 mins.

Columbia Cartoon Classics Vol. 6: Cartoon Classics

Eight titles: *Pete Hothead* ('52), *Unicorn in the Garden* ('53), *Family Circus* ('51), *Ballet-Oop* ('54), *Christopher Crumpet* ('53, Oscar nominee), *Popcorn Story* ('50), *The Rise of Duton Lang* ('55) and *Four Wheels and No Brake* ('55).
VHS: S28107. $12.95.
UPA, USA, 1950-55, 55 mins.

Columbia Cartoon Classics Vol. 7: Mr. Magoo

Eight titles: *The Grizzly Golfer* ('51), *Pink & Blue Blues* ('52, Oscar nominee), *Magoo's Masterpiece* ('53), *Madcap Magoo* ('55), *Meet Mother Magoo* ('56), *Magoo's Canine Mutiny* ('56), *Terror Faces Magoo* ('59, last Magoo cartoon) and *Magoo's Young Manhood* ('58).
VHS: S28108. $12.95.
UPA, USA, 1951-59, 54 mins.

Columbia Cartoon Classics Vol. 8: Mr. Magoo

Eight titles: *When Magoo Flew* ('55, Oscar winner), *Captains Outrageous* ('52), *The Dog Snatcher* ('52), *Gumshoe Magoo* ('58), *Magoo's Private War* ('57), *Rockhound Magoo* ('57), *Safety Spin* ('53) and *Scoutmaster Magoo* ('58).
VHS: S28109. $12.95.
UPA, USA, 1952-58, 52 mins.

Columbia Cartoon Classics Vol. 9: UPA Classics

Eight titles: *The Tell-Tale Heart* ('53), *Gerald McBoing Boing* ('51, Oscar winner), *Unicorn in the Garden* ('53), *Ragtime Bear* ('49, first Magoo), *Rooty Toot Toot* ('52, Oscar nominee), *Madeline* ('52, Oscar nominee), *Magoo's Puddle Jumper* ('56, Oscar winner) and *Robin Hoodlum* ('48, Oscar nominee).
VHS: S28110. $12.95.
UPA, USA, 1948-56, 50 mins.

Columbia Cartoon Classics Vol. 10: Mr. Magoo

Eight titles: *Calling Dr. Magoo* ('56), *The Explosive Mr. Magoo* ('58), *Hotsy Footsy* ('52), *Kangaroo Courting* ('54), *Love Comes to Magoo* ('58), *Magoo Goes Skiing* ('54), *Magoo's Check-Up* ('55) and *Magoo's Cruise* ('58).
VHS: S28111. $12.95.
UPA, USA, 1952-58, 55 mins.

Columbia Cartoon Classics Vol. 11: Lil' Abner

These theatrical shorts were produced by Dave Fleischer at Columbia/Screen Gems in Technicolor. Five titles: *Amoozin' But Confoosin', Sadie Hawkens Day, A Pee-Kool-Yar Sit-chee-ay-shun, Porkuliar Piggy* and *Kickapoo Juice*.
VHS: S29623. $12.95.
Screen Gems, USA, 1944-45, 55 mins.

Columbia Cartoon Classics Vol. 12: Mr. Magoo

Eight titles: *Magoo Makes News* ('55), *Magoo's Express* ('55), *Magoo Slept Here* ('53), *Magoo's Lodge Brother* ('59), *Magoo's Moose Hunt* ('57), *Magoo's Problem Child* ('56), *Magoo's Three-Point Landing* ('58) and *Matador Magoo* ('57).
VHS: S28112. $12.95.
UPA, USA, 1953-59, 55 mins.

Daffy Duck & Co.

Seven titles: *To Duck or Not to Duck* ('43), *Birth of a Notion* ('47), *Conrad the Sailor* ('42), *The Hep Cat* ('42), *The Dover Boys* ('42), *House Hunting Mice* ('48) and *Daffy Duck & The Dinosaur* ('39).
VHS: S29625. $12.95.
Warner Bros., USA, 1939-48, 49 mins.

Daffy Duck's Easter Egg-Citement

Three all new short cartoons by Friz Freleng in this TV special. Daffy & Sylvester battle for Prissy's golden egg in *The Yolks On You*, security guard Daffy fends off Speedy Gonzalez's attacks on a chocolate factory in *The Chocolate Chase* and Daffy decides to hitchhike rather than fly in *Daffy Goes North*.
VHS: S15836. $12.95.
Warner Bros., USA, 1980, 25 mins.

Daffy Duck's Madcap Mania

Six titles: *The Super Snooper* ('52), *Daffy Duck Hunt* ('49), *You Were Never Duckier* ('48), *Golden Yeggs* ('50), *Dime to Retire* ('55) and *A Star Is Bored* ('56).
VHS: S12626. $12.95.
Warner Bros., USA, 1948-56, 45 mins.

Daffy Duck's Movie: Fantastic Island

A full-length satire of *Fantasy Island* by Friz Freleng, with Daffy as Mr. Roarke and Speedy Gonzalez as Tattoo. Classic cartoon excerpts include *Buccaneer Bunny, Stupor Duck, Greedy for Tweety, Banty Raids, Louvre Come Back to Me, Tree for Two, Curtain Razor, A Mouse Divided, Of Rice and Hen* and *From Hare to Heir*.
Laser: LD75622. $29.95.
Warner Bros., USA, 1983, 78 mins.

Daffy Duck's Quackbusters

A compilation feature with quite a lot of new animation directed by Greg Ford & Terry Lennon. Daffy inherits a million dollars from J.P. Cubish, and organizes a "Ghostbusters"-type company to destroy Cubish's ghost, who is trying to take away his inheritance. The tape includes recent WB theatrical shorts: *The Duxorcist* and *Night of the Living Duck*, as well as classic cartoon excerpts from *Prize Pest, Water Water Every Hare, Hyde and Go Tweet, Claws for Alarm, The Abominable Snow Rabbit, Transylvania 6-5000, Punch Trunk* and *Jumpin' Jupiter*.
VHS: S14615. $14.95.
Laser: LD75623. $24.95.
Warner Bros., USA, 1988, 76 mins.

Daffy Duck's Thanks-For-Giving Special

Using the framing device from *The Scarlet Pumpernickel*, Daffy tries to sell J.L. on two complete shorts: *Duck Dodgers and the Return of the 24th-1/2 Century* ('80) and *His Bitter Half* ('50). The Duck Dodgers short was produced and directed by Chuck Jones in 1980 after renewed interest in the original short. It was intended for theatrical release, but the studio had second thoughts once it was completed. Also clips from Robin Hood Daffy and Drip Along Daffy.
VHS: S16724. $9.95.
Warner Bros., USA, 1981, 27 mins.

Daffy Duck: Duck Victory

Fourteen titles: *Duck Dodgers in the 24th & 1/2 Century* ('53), *Duck! Rabbit! Duck!* ('53), *Drip-Along Daffy* ('51), *The Super Snooper* ('52), *Daffy Duck Hunt* ('49), *Muscle Tussle* ('53), *Don't Axe Me* ('58), *Stork Naked* ('55), *Robin Hood Daffy* ('58), *Ali Baba Bunny* ('57), *Cracked Quack* ('52), *Daffy Dilly* ('48), *Golden Yeggs* ('50) and *Duck Amuck* ('53).
Laser: LD71759. $34.95.
Warner Bros., USA, 1948-58, 99 mins.

Daffy Duck: Just Plain Daffy

Eight titles: *Hollywood Daffy* ('46), *Nasty Quacks* ('45), *Daffy Duck Slept Here* ('48), *Tick Tock Tuckered* ('44), *Along Came Daffy* ('47), *Ain't That Ducky* ('45), *Duck Soup to Nuts* ('44) and *The Wise-Quacking Duck* ('43).
VHS: S09123. $14.95.
Warner Bros., USA, 1943-48, 60 mins.

Daffy Duck: Tales from the Duckside

Five titles: *Wise Quackers* ('49), *The Impatient Patient* ('42), *Porky & Daffy* ('38), *Porky Pig's Feat* ('43) and *Stork Naked* ('55).
VHS: S16718. $12.95.
Warner Bros., USA, 1938-55, 33 mins.

Daffy!
Eight titles: *Book Revue* ('46), *The Great Piggy Bank Robbery* ('46), *Slightly Daffy* ('44), *Yankee Doodle Daffy* ('43), *Daffy Duck in Hollywood* ('38), *Mexican Joyride* ('47), *Daffy Duck & Eggbead* ('38) and *The Upstanding Sitter* ('47).
VHS: S06355. $14.95.
Warner Bros, USA, 1938-47, 60 mins.

Daffy! & Porky!
A double-feature of both programs combined on one video disc. For individual information, see separate listings in this catalog.
Laser: LD75848. $34.95.
Warner Bros., USA, 120 mins.

Disney Animation
Your child will delight to these videos of their favorite Disney characters.
Canine Commando Starring Pluto.
VHS: S03046. $14.95.
Importance of Being Donald.
VHS: S03045. $14.95.
Tale of Two Chipmunks.
VHS: S03048. $14.95.

Disney Sing-Alongs
Sing along to classic Disney tunes with these captioned clips from famous Disney cartoons.
Disney's Sing-Along Songs: Zip-A-Dee-Doo-Dah.
VHS: S03049. $14.95.

Dr. Seuss Collection
Laser: LD75854. $39.95.
USA

Dr. Seuss Video Festival
Two Dr. Seuss favorites: *Horton Hears a Who* and *How the Grinch Stole Christmas*. 48 mins.
VHS: S01700. $29.95.

Dr. Seuss' Daisy-Head Mayzie
A newly-discovered and previously unpublished Dr. Seuss story. Mayzie unaccountably finds a daisy growing out of her head, and her meteoric rise to stardom offers a cautionary lesson about the drawbacks of fame and fortune.
VHS: S24805. $9.95.
USA, 1994, 40 mins.

Dr. Seuss' The Butter Battle Book
Includes Huckleberry Hound in *Cluck & Dagger*.
VHS: S12843. $9.95.
USA, 30 mins.

Dr. Seuss: Green Eggs & Ham & Other Stories
Three episodes: *The Sneetches*, *The Zax* and *Green Eggs and Ham*. Voices of Allan Sherman and Hans Conreid. New sing-along format.
VHS: S21536. $9.95.
DePatie-Freleng, USA, 1973, 30 mins.

Dr. Seuss: Grinch Night
The Grinch's plan to provoke the people of Whoville into leaving because of a "sour-seet wind" is foiled by young Ukariah. Hans Conreid narrates. New sing-along format. Formerly titled *Halloween Is Grinch Night*.
VHS: S10095. $9.95.
DePatie-Freleng, USA, 1977, 30 mins.

Dr. Seuss: Horton Hears a Who
In this Peabody Award-winning special, Horton the elephant rescues the tiny inhabitants of Whoville. Voice: Hans Conreid.
VHS: S00582. $12.95.
Chuck Jones, USA, 1970, 26 mins.

Dr. Seuss: How the Grinch Stole Christmas
CBS-TV thought so much of this special, they paid $315,000 for it. It has gone on to become an annual classic. The cruel Grinch steals all the Christmas presents in Whoville and must be taught the real meaning of Christmas. Narrated by Boris Karloff.
VHS: S03534. $12.95.
Chuck Jones, USA, 1966, 26 mins.

Dr. Seuss: Pontoffel Rock and His Magic Piano
The kind-hearted bungler Pock is fired from a dill pickle factory. The fairy McGillicuddy provides him with a magic piano that takes him anywhere at the touch of a button. Pock madly pushes buttons and is whisked off to magical worlds, where he eventually regains his confidence. New sing-along format. Formerly titled *Pontoffel Rock, Where Are You?*
VHS: S10094. $9.95.
DePatie-Freleng, USA, 1980, 30 mins.

Dr. Seuss: The Cat in the Hat
Two bored kids turn the house upside down looking for the cat's moss-covered, three-handled Gredunza. New sing-along format.
VHS: S10096. $9.95.
DePatie-Freleng, USA, 1971, 30 mins.

Dr. Seuss: The Grinch Grinches the Cat in The Hat
The Grinch is so annoyed when the Cat in The Hat drives across his path that he plans a variety of self-made contraptions to get revenge. Instead, he is taught a lesson in manners by the amiable Cat. Emmy Winner. New sing-along format.
VHS: S29631. $9.95.
Marvel, USA, 1982, 30 mins.

Dr. Seuss: The Hoober-Bloob Highway
The Hoober-Bloob Highway is actually a ribbon of light that leads to a floating island where young humans are sent by Mr. Hoober. New sing-along format.
VHS: S10093. $9.95.
DePatie-Freleng, USA, 1975, 30 mins.

Dr. Seuss: The Lorax
A sad environmental tale about loggers (Once-lers) who greedily harvest all specimens of the beautiful, brightly colored, imaginary Truffulu trees. Dr. Seuss's book was actually banned from the school libraries in the California logging town of Laytonville. Now in sing-along format.
VHS: S10092. $9.95.
DePatie-Freleng, USA, 1972, 30 mins.

Early Warner Brothers Cartoons
Eight favorites from the early 1930's, including *Lady Play Your Mandolin*, *Freddie the Freshman* and *I Love a Parade*. B&W. USA, 1931-32, 55 mins.
VHS: S00387. $24.95.

The Easter Bunny Is Coming to Town
The traditions of Easter are narrated by Fred Astaire in this puppet stop-motion animated TV special.
VHS: S18153. $12.95.
Rankin/Bass, USA, 1976, 50 mins.

Elmer Fudd's School of Hard Knocks
Five titles: *Each Dawn I Crow* ('49), *Pest for Guests* ('55), *Upswept Hare* ('53), *Don't Axe Me* ('58) and *Robot Rabbit* ('53).
VHS: S12616. $12.95.
Warner Bros., USA, 1949-58, 35 mins.

Elmer!
Seven titles: *Good Night Elmer* ('40), *Elmer's Candid Camera* ('40), *A Pest in the House* ('47), *What Makes Daffy Duck?* ('48), *The Wabbit Who Came to Supper* ('42), *The Wacky Wabbit* ('42) and *Hare-Brained Hypnotist* ('42).
VHS: S06356. $12.95.
Warner Bros, USA, 1940-48, 60 mins.

Fantasy Film Worlds of George Pal
A wonderful tribute to the great genius of animation and special effects, George Pal, tracing the career that won him eight Oscars, with rare film clips and demonstrations of his revolutionary techniques. USA, 1986, 93 mins.
VHS: S04763. $19.95.

Fearless Fortune Hunter
Scrooge McDuck's vast fortune tumbles into the underground home of the Terry Fermies in *Earth Quack!*, touching off an earthshaking caper to recover it. In the second adventure, *Masters of the Djinni*, Scrooge's quest for Aladdin's legendary lamp produces a mystical madcap mess. 44 mins.
VHS: S06594. $19.95.

Felix the Cat Silent Films Vol. 1
Beautiful black-and-white film prints transferred to standard play tape. Seven titles: *Sure Locked Homes, Eats Are West, Felix the Cat Ducks His Duty, Whys and Otherwise, False Vases, The Land of Fancy* and *Switches Witches*. B&W.
VHS: S29634. $24.95.
Pat Sullivan, USA, 1925-29, 60 mins.

Felix the Cat Vol. 1
Seven beautifully restored Felix shorts with original organ scores. Film and video quality are top-notch. *Felix Saves the Day* ('22), *Felix in the Swim* ('22), *Felix Turns the Tide* ('22), *Felix Lends a Hand* ('22), *Felix Minds the Kid* ('22), *Felix in the Bone Age* ('22), and *Paramount Magazine* ('19—contains Felix's debut, *Feline Follies*, plus Earl Hurd's Bobby Bumps in *Their Master's Voice* and Frank Moser's Bud and Susie in *Down the Mississippi*). B&W.
VHS: S29632. $29.95.
Pat Sullivan, USA, 1919-22, 64 mins.

Felix the Cat Vol. 2
Nine beautifully restored Felix shorts with original organ scores. Film and video quality are top-notch. *Felix the Ghost Breaker* ('23), *Felix Wins Out* ('23), *Felix Revolts* ('23), *Felix Gets Broadcasted* ('23), *Felix in Hollywood* ('23), *Felix in Fairyland* ('23), *Felix Out of Luck* ('24), *Felix Goes A-Hunting* ('23) and *Felix Finds 'em Fickle* ('24). B&W.
VHS: S29633. $29.95.
Pat Sullivan, USA, 1923-24, 63 mins.

Felix the Cat—Silent—Volume 1
Contains *Felix Wins Out* (1925), *Felix in Fairyland* (1927), *Felix Whoos Whoppie* (1927), *Felix Pines* (1927), *Felix in Hollywood* (1927). 56 mins.
VHS: S11466. $19.95.

Felix the Cat—Silent—Volume 2
Contains *Felix Turns the Tide* (1924), *Felix Switches Witches* (1927), *Forty Winks* (1930), *One Good Turn* (1929), *Felix Busts a Bustle* (1926) and *Outdoor Indoor* (1929). 62 mins.
VHS: S11467. $19.95.

Felix the Cat: Sound & Silent
Twelve titles. Silent cartoons with original organ score are *Comicalamities* ('28), *With the Cowboys, In Dutch, Felix Minds the Kid, Felix Revolts* and *Polly-Tics* ('28). Sound cartoons are *Tee Time* ('30), *Forty Winks* ('29), *Outdoor Indore* ('28), *The Oily Bird* ('28), *False Vases* ('29) and *Oceantics* ('30).
VHS: S06983. $24.95.
Pat Sullivan, USA, 1928-30, 88 mins.

Felix!
Produced by Lumivision and the Cinematheque Quebecoise, this videotape includes Felix's debut as a free-wheeling cat about town in *Feline Follies* (1919); an amazing baseball comedy, *Felix Saves the Day* (1922); the great cat's meeting with his peers—Chaplin, Fairbanks, Swanson, DeMille etc. —in *Felix in Hollywood* (1923); the fabulous *Felix Dopes It Out* (1924); surrealistic masterworks *Futuritzy* (1928) and *Felix Woos Whoopee* (1930); the hilarious *Comicalamities* (1928); and lastly, rare footage of Felix's creator, Otto Messmer. B&W.
VHS: S19674. $39.95.
Pat Sullivan, USA, 1918-30, 60 mins.

FernGully: The Last Rainforest
The adventures of Zak, a human who is shrunken and goes to live in the rain forest with a wild assortment of elves, fairies, bats, beetles and reptiles. Features the voices of Robin Williams, Christian Slater, Tim Curry and Cheech & Chong among others.
VHS: S16858. $14.95.
Laser: LD75669. $29.95.
Laser: CAV, widescreen. **LD71552. $39.95.**
Bill Kroyer, USA, 1992, 72 mins.

FernGully II: The Magical Rescue
This direct-to-video animated musical reunites Batty Koda, Crysta, Pips and the Beetle Boys in an all-new adventure.
VHS: S32487. $19.95.
Fox, USA, 1997

The First Christmas
Sister Theresa cares for a little blind boy, Lukas. Through her caring and help, the boy regains his sight on Christmas Eve.
VHS: S13038. $9.95.
Rankin/Bass, USA, 1975, 23 mins.

The First Easter Rabbit
Burl Ives narrates the animated, tuneful story of Stuffy, the child's toy who magically becomes the first Easter Rabbit after defeating the cold-hearted ice creature Zero. Voices by Paul Frees, Stan Freberg and Robert Morse.
VHS: S18152. $12.95.
Rankin/Bass, USA, 1976, 25 mins.

Fleischer & Famous Studios
Seven titles: *Lamb in a Jam, Old McDonald Had a Farm, Leprechaun Gold, The Bored Cuckoo, Dancing on the Moon, You Can't Shoe a Horsefly* and *Yankee Doodle Donkey*.
VHS: S29635. $24.95.
Fleischer/Famous, USA, 60 mins.

Fleischer Color Classics
Eight great cartoon classics from the creator of Betty Boop, including *Dancing on the Moon, Fresh Vegetable Mystery*, and *Rudolph, The Red Nosed Reindeer*.
VHS: S01628. $24.95.
Dave Fleischer, USA, 1934-40, 55 mins.

Flip the Frog Vol. 1
Eight titles: *Fiddlesticks, The Cuckoo Murder Case, The Soup Song, The Village Specialist, Puppy Love, Circus, Funny Face* and *A Chinaman's Chance*.
VHS: S29636. $29.95.
Ub Iwerks, USA, 1930-33, 60 mins.

Flip the Frog Vol. 2
From Bosko Video's complete *Flip the Frog* collection come eight more cartoons mastered from pristine originals: *Flying Fists* ('30), *The Village Smitty* ('31), *Spooks* ('31), *Nurse Maid* ('32), *School Days* ('32), *The Goal Rush* ('32), *Coo-Coo the Magician* ('33) and *Pale-Face* ('33).
VHS: S30418. $29.95.
Ub Iwerks, USA, 1930-33, 60 mins.

Flip the Frog Vol. 3
From Bosko Video's complete *Flip the Frog* collection come eight more cartoons mastered from pristine originals: *Puddle Pranks* ('30), *Laughing Gas* ('31), *Movie Mad* ('31), *Fire-Fire* ('32), *The Bully* ('32), *Phoney Express* ('32), *Flip's Lunch Room* ('33) and *Soda Squirt* ('33).
VHS: S30419. $29.95.
Ub Iwerks, USA, 1930-33, 60 mins.

Flip the Frog Vol. 4
From Bosko Video's complete *Flip the Frog* collection come seven more cartoons mastered from pristine originals: *Little Orphan Willie* ('30), *Ragtime Romeo* ('31), *Africa Squeaks* ('31), *The Milkman* ('32), *The Office Boy* ('32), *The Music Lesson* ('32) and *Techno-Cracked* ('33).
VHS: S30420. $29.95.
Ub Iwerks, USA, 1930-33, 60 mins.

Flip the Frog Vol. 5
From Bosko Video's complete *Flip the Frog* collection come seven more cartoons mastered from pristine originals: *The Village Barber* ('30), *The New Car* ('31), *Stormy Seas* ('31), *Jail Birds* ('31), *What a Life!* ('32), *Room Runners* ('32) and *Bulloney* ('33).
VHS: S30421. $29.95.
Ub Iwerks, USA, 1930-33, 60 mins.

For Better or Worse
Lynn Johnston's famous, nationally distributed, comic serial, based on the travails of family life as experienced by the Pattersons, is now an animated feature. Three kids and a dog are sure proof that laughter is simply a necessary part of everyday life. 90 mins.
VHS: S21355. $24.95.

Fox Terrytoons
Early animation from the 1930's by Paul Terry and Frank Moser are collected on this video. *Noah's Outing, Grand Uproar, South Pole or Bust, The First Snow, Fox Hunt, Billy Goat's Whiskers, Bug Carnival, Trailer Life* and *Their Last Bean* are the cartoons included.
VHS: S23315. $19.95.

From Hare to Eternity
Five classic Warner shorts plus the new short *From Hare to Eternity*.
VHS: S32399. $12.95.
Warner Bros., USA, 41 mins.

Gabby (Cartoonies)
Gabby was a supporting character from the Fleischer feature *Gulliver's Travels*, who was spun off into his own series of theatrical shorts. Seven titles: *King for a Day* ('40), *The Funshine State* ('49), *It's a Hap-Hap-Happy Day* ('41), *Gobs of Fun* ('50), *All's Well* ('41), *Win Place & Show Boat* ('50) and *Two for the Zoo* ('41).
VHS: S09234. $14.95.
Laser: LD75857. $29.95.
Fleischer/Famous, USA, 1940-50, 49 mins.

George Dunning
The master animator explains his work and techniques. With clips from the Beatles' film *Yellow Submarine*, *The Flying Man* and *Damon the Mower*. 1973, 28 mins.
VHS: S31596. $59.95.

Golden Age of Looney Tunes Vol. 2
Five-disc boxed laserdisc set. Seventy titles. SIDE ONE: Musical Madness: *You Don't Know What You're Doin', Goopy Geer, Three's a Crowd, We're in the Money, Honeymoon Hotel (first color WB cartoon), The Lady in Red, The Penguin Parade.* SIDE TWO: Early Wabbits: *Prest-o Change-o, Hare-Um Scare-Um, Elmer's Candid Camera, Elmer's Pet Rabbit, Hiawatha's Rabbit Hunt, Hold the Lion Please, Fresh Hare.* SIDE THREE: Frank Tashlin: *The Major Lied Till Dawn, Cracked Ice, Brother Brat, Plane Daffy, A Tale of Two Mice, Behind the Meatball, Hare Remover.* SIDE FOUR: Chuck Jones: *The Little Lion Hunter, The Draft Horse, Flop Goes the Weasel, Lost and Foundling, Fair and Worm-er, What's Brewin' Bruin?, Rabbit Punch.* SIDE FIVE: Bob Clampett: *Goofy Groceries, The Wacky Wabbit, Buckaroo Bugs, An Itch in Time, Gruesome Twosome, Draftee Daffy, Bacall to Arms.* SIDE SIX: McKimson & Davis: *Acrobatty Bunny, Hollywood Canine Canteen, The Mouse-merized Cat, One Meat Brawl, Mexican Joyride, Mouse Menace, Catch As Cats Can.* SIDE SEVEN: Fables & Fairy Tales: *Beauty & The Beast, Little Red Walking Hood, A-Lad-In Bagdad, Robin Hood Makes Good, Tom Thumb in Trouble, A Gander at Mother Goose, Jack Wabbit & The Beanstalk.* SIDE EIGHT: Daffy: *Yankee Doodle Daffy, The Wise Quacking Duck, Daffy the Commando, The Stupid Cupid, Birth of a Notion, To Duck or Not to Duck, What Makes Daffy Duck?* SIDE NINE: Best Supporting Players: *The Hardship of Miles Standish, Hop Look & Listen, Roughly Squeaking, The Goofy Gophers, Scent-imental over You, Crowing Pains, Of Fox & Hounds.* SIDE TEN: Variations on a Theme: *Tick Tock Tuckered, Good Night Elmer, Bedtime for Sniffles, A Pest in the House, Trap Happy Porky, The Unbearable Bear, Daffy Duck Slept Here.*
Laser: LD71160. $99.95.
Warner Bros., USA, 1931-48, 530 mins.

Golden Age of Looney Tunes Vol. 3
Five-disc boxed laserdisc set. Seventy titles. SIDE ONE: Harman-Ising: *One More Time, Red-Headed Baby, Pagan Moon, A Great Big Bunch of You, The Shanty Where Santy Claus Lives, One Step Ahead of My Shadow, The Dish Ran Away with the Spoon.* SIDE TWO: Bugs Bunny: *Wackiki Wabbit, Hare Force, Super Rabbit, Herr Meets Hare, Bugs Bunny and the Three Bears, Stage Door Cartoon, Easter Yeggs.* SIDE THREE: Chuck Jones: *The Squawkin' Hawk, Inki and the Minah Bird, From Hand to Mouse, Fin 'n Catty, Fresh Airedale, The Eager Beaver, House Hunting Mice.* SIDE FOUR: Friz Freleng: *Pigs Is Pigs, The Cat's Tale, Lights Fantastic, Ding Dog Daddy, The Wacky Worm, Peck Up Your Troubles, Racketeer Rabbit.* SIDE FIVE: Early Avery: *I Wanna Be a Sailor, Circus Today, Aviation Vacation, Aloha Hooey, Holiday Highlights, Crazy Cruise, The Cagey Canary.* SIDE SIX: Tashlin/Clampett: *Little Pancho Vanilla, Booby Hatched, I Got Plenty of Mutton, Farm Frolics, Falling Hare, Birdy and the Beast, Russian Rhapsody.* SIDE SEVEN: Sports: *Freddy the Freshman, Boulevardier from the Bronx, Along Flirtation Walk, Sport Chumpions, Greetings Bait, Screwball Football, Baseball Bugs.* SIDE EIGHT: The Evolution of Egghead: *Egghead Rides Again, Count Me Out, Johnny Smith and Poker Huntas, A Day at the Zoo, Believe It or Else, A Feud There Was, Confederate Honey.* SIDE NINE: Porky and Daffy: *Daffy Duck and the Dinosaur, Slightly Daffy, Ain't That Ducky, Wagon Heels, Along Came Daffy, Nothing But the Tooth, The Up-Standing Sitter.* SIDE TEN: Politically Incorrect: *Wake Up the Gypsy in Me, He Was Her Man, Sioux Me, The Mighty Hunters, A Feather in His Hare, The Early Worm Gets the Bird, Inki and the Lion.*
Laser: LD71817. $99.95.
Warner Bros., USA, 1931-48, 530 mins.

Golden Age of Looney Tunes Vol. 4
Five-disc boxed laserdisc set. Seventy-two titles. SIDE ONE: Bugs Bunny: *The Wabbit Who Came to Supper, The Hare-Brained Hypnotist, The Case of the Missing Hare, Hare Conditioned, Buccaneer Bunny, Rhapsody Rabbit, Any Bonds Today, A Wild Hare.* SIDE TWO: Early Chuck Jones: *The Good Egg, Ghost Wanted, Snow Time for Comedy, The Bird Came C.O.D., Dog Tired, Fox Pop, The Weakly Reporter.* SIDE THREE: Friz Freleng: *Trial of Mr. Wolf, Double Chaser, The Sheepish Wolf, Hiss and Make Up, Holiday for Shoestrings, The Gay Anties, Of Thee I Sting.* SIDE FOUR: Cartoon All-Stars: *Tom Turk and Daffy, I Taw a Puddy Tat, Two Gophers from Texas, Conrad the Sailor, Doggone Cats, A Horsefly Fleas, Hobo Bobo.* SIDE FIVE: Radio Daze: *Crosby Columbo and Vallee, The Woods Are Full of Cuckoos, Let It Be Me, Little Blabbermouse, Malibu Beach Party, Quentin Quail, Hush My Mouse.* SIDE SIX: The Frantic Forties: *Hop Skip and a Chump, A Hick a Slick and a Chick, Meatless Flyday, The Foxy Duckling, Bone Sweet Bone, The Rattled Rooster, The Shell-Shocked Egg.* SIDE SEVEN: Wacky Blackouts: *Land of the Midnight Fun, Wacky Wildlife, Ceiling Hero, Fresh Fish, Saddle Silly, Foney Fables, Bug Parade.* SIDE EIGHT: Ben Hardaway & Cal Dalton: *Love & Curses, Gold Rush Daze, Bars & Stripes Forever, Hobo Gadget Band, Fagin's Freshmen, Busy Bakers, Snafuperman, Spies.* SIDE NINE: Sniffles: *Naughty But Mice, Little Brother Rat, Sniffles & The Bookworm, The Egg Collector, Sniffles Bells the Cat, Toy Trouble, Brave Little Bat.* SIDE TEN: Merrie Melodies: *The Queen Was in the Parlor, I Love a Parade, The Organ Grinder, Billboard Frolics, Flowers for Madame, September in the Rain, You're an Education.*
Laser: LD75674. $99.95.
Warner Bros., USA, 1932-48, 520 mins.

Golden Age of Looney Tunes Vol. 5
Four-disc boxed laserdisc set. Forty-nine more cartoons. SIDE ONE: Black & White Classics: *It's Got Me Again, Moonlight for Two, A Great Big Bunch of You, You're Too Careless with Your Kisses, I Wish I Had Wings, Young and Healthy, I Like Mountain Music.* SIDE TWO: Early Avery: *Don't Look Now, I Only Have Eyes for You, Ain't We Got Fun, A Sunbonnet Blue, The Sneezing Weasel, Mice Will Play, Detouring America.* SIDE THREE: Freleng Follies: *She Was an Acrobat's Daughter, Sweet Sioux, The Lyin' Mouse, My Little Buckaroo, The Fighting 69th-1/2, Rookie Revue, Fifth Column Mouse.* SIDE FOUR: Musical Madness: *Merry Old Soul, Mr. and Mrs. Is the Name, Into Your Dance, The Country Mouse, Bingo Crosbyana, The Fella with the Fiddle, Now That Summer Is Gone.* SIDE FIVE: Pesky Pets: *The Cat Came Back, The Country Boy, Dog Daze, Doggone Modern, Curious Puppy, Stage Fright, Snowman's Land.* SIDE SIX: Objects d'Art: *Those Beautiful Dames, Little Dutch Plate, I'd Love to Take Orders from You, Toytown Hall, My Green Fedora, Streamline Greta Green, Shop Look and Listen.* SIDE SEVEN: Animal Antics: *Pop Goes Your Heart, I Wanna Play House, I'm a Big Shot Now, When I Yoo Hoo, At Your Service Madame, A Star Is Hatched, Plenty of Money and You.*
Laser: LD75861. $99.95.
Warner Bros., USA, 1932-43, 420 mins.

Golden Age of Looney Tunes: Vol. 5, Chuck Jones
Devilish wit and amazing colors are the highlights of this collection, led by *The Night Watchman, Old Glory, Sniffles Takes a Trip* and *The Aristo-cat*.
VHS: S17756. $12.95.

Golden Age of Warner Brothers Cartoons
Interviews and reminscences with Friz Freleng, Mel Blanc, Chuck Jones and Bob Clampett, and clips from their works from 1934-1964, featuring Bugs Bunny, Road Runner, Porky Pig and Daffy Duck. With demonstrations on drawing, painting cells and voice recording, and discussions on how Bugs evolved, how voice is matched to picture, characters that didn't catch on, adults as the audience for cartoons and the Warner vs. Disney school of animation. Hosted by animation expert John Canemaker. 1975, 28 mins.
VHS: S31595. $59.95.

Great & Minor Animation Volume 1
Eight titles: Disney: *The Mad Doctor* ('33) and *Alice's Tin Pony* ('25); MGM: *Doggone Tired* ('49); Terrytoons: *Talking Magpies* ('46); Warners: *Hollywood Steps Out* ('41); Van Beuren: *Candy Town* ('33); Modern Sales Corp: *Westward Whoa* (Mutt & Jeff); Van Beuren: *Neptune Nonsense* (Felix, '36).
VHS: S29641. $24.95.
USA, 60 mins.

Great & Minor Animation Volume 2
Seven titles: *Flat Heads* (New Three Stooges), *Boy Meets Dog, Cavalcade of Music* (Pal), *Jasper & The Haunted House* (Pal), *At the Devil's Ball, Jerky Turkey* (Tex Avery) and *Swing Cleaning* (Gabby).
VHS: S29642. $24.95.
USA, 60 mins.

Great & Minor Animation Volume 3
Seven titles: *Spirit of '43* (Donald Duck), *A Coach for Cinderella* (Jam Handy), *Alice in Wonderland* (Lou Bunin), *Vitamin Hay* (Hunky & Spunky), *Beach Comber* (Oswald Rabbit), *Pantry Panic* (Woody Woodpecker) and *Loose in the Caboose* (Little Lulu).
VHS: S29643. $24.95.
USA, 60 mins.

Great & Minor Animation Volume 4
Eight titles: *Cookie Carnival* (Disney), *Dingbat Land* (Gandy Goose), *Flip Flap, We're in the Honey, Scotty Finds a Home, Gabby Goes Fishing, Scrappily Married* and *Always Kickin* (Hunky & Spunky).
VHS: S29644. $24.95.
USA, 60 mins.

Guffaw and Order: Looney Tunes Fight Crime
Fourteen titles: *Bugsy and Mugsy* ('57), *My Little Duckaroo* ('54), *Catty Cornered* ('53), *The Blow Out* ('36, B&W), *Don't Give Up the Sheep* ('53), *Porky's Movie Mystery* ('39, B&W), *Baby Buggy Bunny* ('54), *The Stupor Salesman* ('48), *Bye Bye Bluebeard* ('49), *Boston Quackie* ('57), *Riff Raffy Daffy* ('48), *Dough Ray Me-ow* ('48), *Rocket Squad* ('56) and *Bugs and Thugs* ('54).
Laser: LD72395. $34.95.
Warner Bros., USA, 1936-57, 99 mins.

Gulliver's Travels
This is the film the Fleischers moved to Miami to make. Issued as an answer to Disney's *Snow White*, this Fleischer animated feature recounts Swift's story of Gulliver and the Lilliputians.
VHS: S18185. $19.95.
Fleischer, USA, 1939, 75 mins.

Gumby: The Movie
Gumby is back in an all-new feature film from the master's hand. When Gumby's dog hears the new band perform, he cries tears that turn into pearls. This results in a dognapping and many zany adventures.
VHS: S26692. $19.95.
Art Clokey, USA, 1995, 90 mins.

Happy Birthday Bugs!
The all-star TV special combining classic film clips and testimonials from Milton Berle, Whoopi Goldberg, William Shatner and more.
VHS: S12860. $12.95.
Warner Bros., USA, 1990, 47 mins.

Hercules & Xena: The Animated Movie
This direct-to-video animated feature stars the characters of the live-action TV series *Hercules: The Legendary Journeys* and *Xena: Warrior Princess*. With the voices of the live-action TV series' stars, Kevin Sorbo as Hercules and Lucy Lawless as Xena.
VHS: S32191. $19.95.
Universal, USA, 1997, 90 mins.

Here Comes Droopy!
Six titles: *Dixieland Droopy* ('54), *Droopy's Double Trouble* ('51), *Three Little Pups* ('53), *Senor Droopy* ('49), *Droopy Leprechaun* ('58) and *Daredevil Droopy* ('51).
VHS: S28186. $12.95.
MGM, USA, 1949-58, 45 mins.

How Bugs Bunny Won the West
Hosted by Denver Pyle, this TV special assembles clips of vintage cartoons into a montage of Bugs Bunny western scenarios. Bridging animation by Jim Davis.
VHS: S18151. $12.95.
Warner Bros., USA, 1978, 24 mins.

James & The Giant Peach
Henry Selick's latest feature combines live action and stop-motion animation to bring to life Roald Dahl's famous children's story. Every bit as state-of-the-art as *Nightmare Before Christmas*, this film also has the same sort of scary-but-safe atmosphere. James boards a magical giant peach filled with anthropomorphized insects and embarks on a fantastic odyssey. Music by Randy Newman.
VHS: S28523. $22.95.
Allied/Disney, USA, 1996, 79 mins.

The Ketchup Vampires
Elvira, mistress of the Dark, narrates this animated comic tale of creepy Transylvanians. It mixes Dracula, vegetarianism, a kooky castle and a bunch of bat brats into a laugh-inducing story that is perfect for kids. 90 mins.
VHS: S26365. $24.95.

Koko the Clown, Volume 2
Seven more gems from the Max Fleischer studio, including *Koko in Reverse, Koko's Storm, Koko's Kid, Koko Kills Time, Koko Smokes, Koko's Barnyard* and *Koko's Balloons*. All silent with music track, 50 mins.
VHS: S07481. $24.95.

The Land Before Time
After losing his mother to a vicious Tyrannosaurus Rex, a young brontosaurus named Littlefoot, along with some newfound friends, sets off in search of the legendary Great Valley.
VHS: S09598. $19.95.
Laser: LD75862. $24.95.
Laser: CAV. **LD74945. $49.95.**
Don Bluth, USA, 1988, 70 mins.

The Land Before Time II: The Great Valley Adventure
A direct-to-video sequel starring the same cast of characters as the feature film, with several musical numbers written and performed by The Roches.
VHS: S28665. $19.95.
Laser: LD75863. $24.95.
Universal/Amblin, USA, 1994, 74 mins.

The Land Before Time III: The Time of the Great Giving
Another direct-to-video effort starring the same characters as the original Don Bluth theatrical film.
VHS: S28666. $19.95.
Laser: LD75864. $24.95.
Universal, USA, 1995, 71 mins.

The Land Before Time IV: Journey Through the Mists
Littlefoot and his friends are back in a brand-new, direct-to-video animated feature.
VHS: S30367. $19.95.
Laser: LD76015. $24.95.
Universal, USA, 1996, 74 mins.

The Land Before Time V: The Mysterious Island
Stereo. CC.
VHS: S32705. $19.95.
Laser: LD74444. $24.95.
Universal, USA, 1997, 74 mins.

The Land Before Time, Vols. I-IV
The first four of *The Land Before Time* features in a collector's slipcase sleeve. HiFi Stereo. CC.
VHS: S31505. $79.95.
Amblin/Universal, USA, 1988-96, 288 mins.

The Land Before Time: Sing-Along Songs
Ten original songs from *The Land Before Time* series, with on-screen lyrics. Also includes a limited edition CD-ROM. HiFi Stereo. CC.
VHS: S31506. $12.95.
Universal, USA, 1997, 30 mins.

Life with Louie: For Pete's Sake
VHS: S32458. $5.95.
USA

Life with Louie: The Masked Chess Boy
VHS: S32459. $5.95.
USA

Little Lulu (Cartoonies)
Seven titles: Little Lulu in *I'm Just Curious, Man's Pest Friend, Dog Show-Off* and *Lulu at the Zoo*; Screen Songs: *The Big Drip* and *The Little Brown Jug*; Fleischer Color Classic: *A Car-Tune Portrait*.
VHS: S09236. $14.95.
Fleischer/Famous, USA, 1937-49, 49 mins.

Little Lulu and Friends
A collection of Little Lulu cartoons including *Super Lulu* (47); *A Scout with Gout* (47); *A Lamb in a Jam* (45); *Bored Cuckoo* (48); *Naughty But Mice* (47); *Loose in a Caboose* (47); *Chick and Double Chick* (46).
VHS: S05059. $34.95.

Longitude & Looneytude: Globetrotting Looney Tunes Favorites
Fourteen titles: *Mouse Mazurka* ('49), *Frigid Hare* ('49), *A Pizza Tweety Pie* ('58), *French Rarebit* ('51), *The Timid Toreador* ('40, B&W), *Trip for Tat* ('60), *Little Beau Pepe* ('52), *Sahara Hare* ('55), *Polar Pals* ('39, B&W), *A Scent of the Matterhorn* ('61), *Roman Legion Hare* ('55), *Dough for the Dodo* ('49), *The Cat's Bah* ('54) and *Hare We Go* ('51).
Laser: LD72396. $34.95.
Warner Bros., USA, 1939-61, 98 mins.

The Looney Looney Looney Bugs Bunny Movie
This Friz Freleng compilation is in three acts: first Yosemite Sam raises hell with the devil in a remake of *Devil's Feud Cake* ('63); then Bugs outwits Rocky and Mugsy who are holding Tweety hostage; and finally Bugs acts as host for a parody of Hollywood award ceremonies. Classic cartoons shown include *Knighty Knight Bugs, Sahara Hare, Roman Legion Hare, High Diving Hare, Hare Trimmed, Wild and Wooly Hare, Catty Cornered, Golden Yeggs, The Unmentionables, Three Little Bops* and *Show Biz Bugs*.
VHS: S14618. $14.95.
Warner Bros., USA, 1981, 79 mins.

Looney Tunes After Dark
Fourteen titles: *Jumpin' Jupiter* ('55), *Water Water Every Hare* ('52), *Bewitched Bunny* ('54), *Hyde and Hare* ('55), *Night of the Living Duck* ('88), *Transylvania 6-5000* ('63), *The Wearing of the Grin* ('51), *Scaredy Cat* ('48), *Broomstick Bunny* ('56), *Hyde and Go Tweet* ('60), *Hare-Way to the Stars* ('58), *The Abominable Snow Rabbit* ('61), *The Duxorcist* ('87) and *Hasty Hare* ('52).
Laser: LD71760. $34.95.
Warner Bros., USA, 1948-88, 99 mins.

Looney Tunes Assorted Nuts
Sixteen titles: *A Bear for Punishment* ('51), *Dog Gone South* ('50), *Boyhood Daze* ('57), *Pests for Guests* ('55), *Mouse Wreckers* ('49), *A Sheep in the Deep* ('62), *Rabbit's Kin* ('52), *Feed the Kitty* ('52), *The Hypo-Chondri-Cat* ('50), *From A to Z-Z-Z-Z* ('54), *Chow Hound* ('51), *Strife with Father* ('50), *Bear Feat* ('49), *Feline Frame Up* ('54), *Gone Batty* ('54) and *A Hound for Trouble* ('51).
Laser: LD71762. $34.95.
Warner Bros., USA, 1949-62, 112 mins.

Looney Tunes Curtain Calls
Fourteen titles: *Rabbit of Seville* ('50), *One Froggy Evening* ('55), *Hillbilly Hare* ('50), *Curtain Razor* ('49), *What's Up Doc?* ('50), *Nelly's Folly* ('61), *The Scarlet Pumpernickel* ('50), *Show Biz Bugs* ('57), *Three Little Bops* ('57), *Baton Bunny* ('59), *High Note* ('60), *Long-Haired Hare* ('49), *Tweety's Circus* ('55) and *What's Opera Doc?* ('57).
Laser: LD71763. $34.95.
Warner Bros., USA, 1949-61, 92 mins.

Looney Tunes Sing-Along
Classic WB cartoon clips are presented in a "sing-along" format, with lyrics superimposed on screen. Songs include: "This Is It," "Jeepers Creepers," "The Three Little Bops," "Hooray for Hollywood," "What's Up Doc" and seven others.
VHS: S34272. $12.95.
Warner Bros., USA, 1998, 30 mins.

Looney Tunes Video Show Volume 1
Seven titles: *Devil May Hare* ('54), *Birds of a Father* ('61), *The Ducksters* ('50), *Zipping Along* ('53), *Mexicali Schmoes* ('59), *Ant Pasted* ('53) and *Room & Bird* ('51).
VHS: S12628. $12.95.
Warner Bros, USA, 1950-61, 49 mins.

Looney Tunes Video Show Volume 2
Eight titles: *14 Carrot Rabbit* ('52), *Quackodile Tears* ('62), *All Fowled Up* ('55), *An Egg Scramble* ('50), *Cats & Bruises* ('65), *Two Scents Worth* ('55) and *The Hole Idea* ('55).
VHS: S12629. $12.95.
Warner Bros., USA, 1950-65, 48 mins.

Looney Tunes Video Show Volume 3
Seven titles: *Eight Ball Bunny* ('50), *The Quacker Tracker* ('67), *Scaredy Cat* ('48), *A Fractured Leghorn* ('50), *Louvre Come Back* (Pepe LePew), *Feline Frame Up* ('54) and *Double or Mutton* ('55).
VHS: S12630. $12.95.
Warner Bros., USA, 1948-67, 42 mins.

Man's Best Friend
Eight titles: *Helter Shelter* ('55), *Man's Best Friend* ('41), *Dog Tax Dodgers* ('48), *Private Eye Pooch* ('55), *Crazy Mixed-Up Pup* ('55, Tex Avery), *Swiss Misfit* ('57), *Dig That Dog* ('54) and *Get Lost! Little Doggy* ('64).
VHS: S28347. $14.95.
Walter Lantz, USA, 1941-64, 51 mins.

Marvin the Martian & K9: 50 Years on Earth
Six classic cartoons.
VHS: S34846. $9.95.
Warner Bros., USA, 45 mins.

Marvin the Martian: Space Tunes
Six classic cartoons.
VHS: S34845. $9.95.
Warner Bros., USA, 45 mins.

Max Fleischer Presents Koko the Clown
The fantastic, sublime and common intermingle in nine animated works from Max and Dave Fleischer, covering the years 1915-27, including *Auto Ride, Chinaman, Clown's Little Brother, Koko's Cartoon Factory* and *Perpetual Motion*. 60 mins.
VHS: S17455. $29.95.

Max Fleischer's Superman
Collector's edition features nine original sci-fi animated shorts from the world-famous Fleischer Studio. Fully restored. 100 mins.
VHS: S34814. $19.95.
DVD: DV60369. $19.95.

MGM Cartoon Christmas
Four titles: *Peace on Earth* ('39), *Alias St. Nick* ('35), *The Peachy Cobbler* ('50) and *The Pup's Christmas* ('36).
VHS: S28349. $9.95.
MGM, USA, 1935-50, 35 mins.

MGM Cartoon Classics: Happy Harmonies

In the 1930s and '40s, Hugh Harman and Rudy Ising created a series of cartoons for MGM known as *Happy Harmonies*. Here are many of their best, along with other works done for MGM, in a four-disc laserdisc boxed set. Forty-two titles: 1934: *Tale of the Vienna Woods, Toyland Broadcast*; 1935: *The Chinese Nightingale, Honeyland, The Old Plantation, Hey Hey Fever, The Calico Dragon, Barnyard Babies, Poor Little Me*; 1936: *To Spring, Bottles, Little Cheezer, Two Little Pups*; 1937: *Little Buck Cheezer, Swing Wedding, Bosko's Easter Eggs*; 1938: *Pipe Dreams*; 1939: *Goldilocks and the Three Bears, The Bear That Couldn't Sleep, Peace on Earth, The Bookworm, The Little Goldfish, Art Gallery, The Mad Maestro, The Blue Danube*; 1940: *The Fieldmouse, Mrs. Ladybug, Home on the Range, The Fishing Bear, The Milky Way, Romeo in Rhythm, The Lonesome Stranger, Tom Turkey and His Harmonica Humdingers*; 1941: *The Alley Cat, The Flying Bear, The Little Mole, Dance of the Weed, Abdul the Bulbul Ameer*; 1942: *Barney Bear's Victory Garden, The Bear and the Beavers*; 1943: *The Boy and the Wolf, The Uninvited Pest*.
Laser: LD75691. $99.95.
MGM, USA, 1934-43, 475 mins.

MGM Cartoon Magic

Seven titles: *Unwelcome Guest* ('45, Barney Bear), *The Captain's Christmas* ('38, Capt. & The Kids), *The Lonesome Stranger* ('40), *Screwball Squirrel* ('44, Tex Avery), *Little Rural Riding Hood* ('49, Tex Avery), *King Size Canary* ('47, Tex Avery) and *The Blue Danube* ('39).
VHS: S04979. $14.95.
MGM, USA, 1938-49, 55 mins.

Mowgli's Brothers

Roddy McDowell narrates the story of a small boy raised by wolves and taught about love, justice and the jungle code of loyalty. EP Speed.
VHS: S03015. $9.95.
Chuck Jones, USA, 1976, 30 mins.

The Nightmare Before Christmas

Tim Burton's original story is brilliantly realized through stop-motion puppet animation of a technical level never before seen. Jack Skellington, the Pumpkin King of Halloween Town, discovers the joys of Christmas Town and attempts to fill Santa's shoes. Animation is directed by Henry Selick and musical score is contributed by Danny Elfman.
VHS: S21295. $14.95.
Laser: LD75699. $29.95.
Tim Burton, USA, 1993, 76 mins.

The Nightmare Before Christmas Collector's Edition

The special boxed edition also contains *The Making Of* documentary, several deleted scenes from the film, storyboards and sets, Henry Selick's 1990 short *Slow Bob in The Lower Dimensions*, Tim Burton's 1982 animated short *Vincent* and his 1984 live-action short *Frankenweenie*.
Laser: LD75700. $99.95.
Tim Burton, USA, 1993, 76 mins.

The Nine Lives of Fritz the Cat

In this non-Bakshi sequel to Fritz the Cat, a married and henpecked Fritz gets high on pot and experiences some of the better times from his past and his imagination—seducing his kid sister, acting as Hitler's orderly and blasting off to Mars, among other things. ADULTS ONLY.
VHS: S05912. $29.95.
Steve Krantz, USA, 1974, 76 mins.

Oliver Twist

Originally released as a theatrical feature, the film was also shown as a prime-time TV special in 1981. In mid-19th-century London, an orphan boy finds he is heir to a large fortune, in this musical adaptation of the Dickens novel. Voice talents include Larry Storch and Davy Jones.
VHS: S19429. $14.95.
Filmation, USA, 1974, 75 mins.

Once upon a Forest

One day in Dapplewood Forest, three young friends—Abigail mouse, Edgar Mole and Russell Hedgehog—find their idyllic lives threatened. The humans' toxic chemical spill has nearly destroyed the forest and brought their friend Michelle near death. Aided by the teachings of their wise tutor, Cornelius, the three set off into the unknown to seek help for Michelle and Dapplewood. Some good songs, interesting situations and pretty fair animation.
VHS: S19346. $14.95.
Hanna-Barbera, USA, 1993, 71 mins.

Oskar Fischinger

Profile of the early animation artist with clips from *Liebespiel, Komposition in Blau, Spiritual Constructions*, a marching cigarette commercial and others. With his widow Elfriede, writer William Moritz and animator John Canemaker. 1977, 28 mins.
VHS: S31597. $59.95.

Otto Messmer

The creator of *Felix the Cat* cartoon series discusses training, animation and surrealism in his technique. With clips from *Felix* and other work. 1977, 28 mins.
VHS: S31588. $59.95.

The Pagemaster

Bookish and timid little Richard Tyler takes refuge from a storm in the library. He is sent on a wondrous journey where he meets literary greats such as Captain Ahab, Long John Silver and Dr. Jekyll. Combining live action and animation, with Macauley Culkin, Christopher Lloyd, Ed Begley Jr. and Mel Harris.
VHS: S29665. $14.95.
Laser: Widescreen, side two CAV. **LD75866. $29.95.**
USA, 1994, 75 mins.

Paramount/Famous Studios Volume 1

Seven titles: *The Friendly Ghost* ('45, Casper), *The Enchanted Square* ('47, Raggedy Ann), *Land of the Lost* ('48), *Butterscotch & Soda* ('48, Little Audrey), *Musica-Lulu* ('47, Little Lulu), *Bored of Education* ('46, Little Lulu) and *The Goal Rush* ('46, Noveltoon).
VHS: S29666. $24.95.
Famous Studios, USA, 1945-48, 60 mins.

Paramount/Famous Studios Volume 2

Eight titles: *Boo Moon* ('54, Casper), *Crazy Town* ('54), *Raggedy Ann & Raggedy Andy* ('41), *Suddenly It's Spring* ('44), *The Mite Makes Right* ('48), *Seapreme Court* ('54, Little Audrey), *A Haunting We Will Go* ('49, Casper) and *The Wee Men* ('47).
VHS: S29667. $24.95.
Fleischer/Famous, USA, 1941-54, 60 mins.

Paramount/Fleischer Studios Volume 1

Six titles: *Small Fry* ('39), *Play Safe* ('36), *The Fresh Vegetable Mystery* ('39), *Somewhere in Dreamland* ('36) and *Hunky and Spunky* ('38).
VHS: S29668. $24.95.
Fleischer, USA, 1936-39, 45 mins.

Paramount/Fleischer Studios Volume 2

Seven titles: *Dinah* ('33, with the Mills Bros.), *The Old Shell Game* ('48), *Song of the Birds* ('49), *Hepcat Symphony* ('49), *Musical Memories* ('35), *The Kids in the Shoe* ('35) and *Tubby the Tuba* ('47, George Pal).
VHS: S29669. $24.95.
Fleischer/Famous, USA, 1933-49, 55 mins.

Paramount/Fleischer Studios Volume 3

Eight titles: *Naughty But Mice* ('47), *It's a Hap Hap Happy Day* ('41), *Kick in Time* ('40), *Goofy Goofy Gander* ('50), *Tarts & Flowers* ('50), *Farm Foolery* ('49), *The Lone Star State* ('48) and *The Big Flame Up* ('49).
VHS: S29670. $24.95.
Fleischer/Famous, USA, 1940-50, 60 mins.

The Pebble and the Penguin

Original songs by Barry Manilow. Voices of Martin Short, Jim Belushi and Tim Curry.
VHS: S29682. $14.95.
Laser: Letterboxed. **LD75875. $34.95.**
Don Bluth, USA, 1995

The Phantom of the Opera

In the eaves, the tunnels, the trap doors and back stairs of the Paris Opera, the phantom is watching. An animated version of the classic story.
VHS: S29023. $29.95.
Emerald City, 1987, 60 mins.

The Phantom Tollbooth

Milo drives through the Phantom Tollbooth and into an animated fantasy land, The Kingdom of Wisdom, to end the terrible feud between numbers and words. Co-directed by Chuck Jones with voices of Mel Blanc, Hans Conreid and others.
VHS: S01020. $19.95.
Laser: LD76386. $29.98.
MGM, USA, 1969, 89 mins.

The Pink Panther

Nine titles: *Slink Pink, Come on In! The Water's Pink, Pink Aye, Pink-A-Boo, Bobolink Pink, Bully for Pink, In the Pink of the Night, Extinct Pink* and *Smile Pretty, Say Pink*.
VHS: S29013. $9.95.
DePatie-Freleng, USA, 1968-75, 56 mins.

Pink Panther Animation Archive Vol. 1

Side One: Pink Panther movie opening titles: *The Pink Phink* ('64), *Pink Pajamas* ('64), *We Give Pink Stamps* ('65), *Dial P for Pink* ('65), *Pink Punch* ('66), *Come on In! The Water's Pink* ('68) and *Pinkfinger* ('65). Side Two: Opening titles for four Pink Panther movies: *The Pink Blueprint* ('66), *Psychedelic Pink* ('68), opening titles for *A Shot in the Dark, The Great DeGaullestone Operation* ('65) (The Inspector cartoon) and *Pink Plunk Plink* ('66).
Laser: LD75703. $34.95.
DePatie-Freleng, USA, 1964-68, 100 mins.

Pink Panther's Laugh Festival

Six titles: *Scarlet Pinkernel, It's Pink But Is It Mink?, Sherlock Pink, Pink Campaign, Pink Ice* and *The Pink Sphinx*.
VHS: S29020. $9.95.
DePatie-Freleng, USA, 38 mins.

Pink Panther: A Pink Christmas

This superb TV Special was adapted from O. Henry's "The Cop & The Anthem." The Panther is alone, cold and hungry on a Central Park bench in 1890s New York. His pursuit of a meal leads him to the true meaning of Christmas.
VHS: S13065. $9.95.
DePatie-Freleng, USA, 1978, 23 mins.

The Pink Panther: Jet Pink

Eight titles: *In the Pink of the Night, Jet Pink, Little Beaux Pink, Pet Pink Pebbles, Pink Blueprint, Pink Phink, Think Before You Pink* and *Toro Pink*.
VHS: S32056. $12.95.
DePatie-Freleng, USA, 1964-75, 45 mins.

The Pink Panther: Pink Bananas

Eight titles: *Pink Aye, Pink Bananas, Pink Flea, Pink on the Cob, Pink Pranks, Pink Punch, Supermarket Pink* and *Trail of the Lonesome Pink*.
VHS: S32058. $12.95.
DePatie-Freleng, USA, 1964-75, 45 mins.

The Pink Panther: Pink Elephant

Eight titles: *Pink Blue Plate, Pink Elephant, Pinkfinger, Pink Pill, Pink Pull, Pink Streaker, Pinktails for Two* and *Yankee Doodle Pink*.
VHS: S32059. $12.95.
DePatie-Freleng, USA, 1964-75, 45 mins.

The Pink Panther: Pink-A-Rella

Tickled Pink, Pinkadilly Circus, Pink-A-Rella, Pink Arcade, Pink Daddy, Pink Pest Control, Pink Pistons and *Pink Sphinx*.
VHS: S32057. $12.95.
DePatie-Freleng, USA, 1964-75, 45 mins.

The Pink Panther: Prehistoric Pink

Eight titles: *Pink Breakfast, Pink of the Litter, Pink Plasma, Pink Posies, Pink S.W.A.T., Prehistoric Pink, Twinkle Twinkle Little Pink* and *Pinto Pink*.
VHS: S32060. $12.95.
DePatie-Freleng, USA, 1964-75, 45 mins.

Pinocchio's Christmas

In this Animagic production, Pinocchio wants to earn money for a Christmas gift for Geppetto. As he tells one fib after another, his nose grows, until Cricket and a fairy help him discover the true meaning of the season. Featuring the voices of Alan King and George S. Irving.
VHS: S29024. $9.95.
Rankin/Bass, USA, 1980, 23 mins.

The Point

Harry Nilsson wrote the songs (including the hit "Me and My Arrow") and script for this thought-provoking TV special. Ringo Starr narrates the tale of a child who must leave his homeland because his round head makes him a freak among his countrymen, the cone-heads.
VHS: S25004. $14.95.
Murakami-Wolf-Swenson, USA, 1971, 74 mins.

Popeye Cartoons & The History of Animation

Four classic Popeye cartoons: *Insect to Injury* ('56), *I Don't Scare* ('56), *Me Musical Nephews* ('42) and *Customers Wanted* ('39). Plus a rare, untitled film circa 1960 teaching the history of animation from drawings; Muybridge, Edison, Terry, Disney, McCay; creating an episode of *Magilla Gorilla* and more.
VHS: S29686. $24.95.
Fleischer/Famous, USA, 1939-56, 60 mins.

Popeye for President

Nine titles: *Shuteye Popeye* ('52), *Bride and Gloom* ('54), *Popeye for President* ('56), *Greek Mirthology* ('54), *A Haul in One* ('56), *Cookin' with Gags* ('54), *Taxi-Turvey* ('54), *Ancient Fistory* ('52) and *Popeye's 20th Anniversary* ('54).
VHS: S29027. $19.95.
Famous Studios, USA, 1952-56, 55 mins.

Popeye the Sailor

Three two-reel, full-animation cartoons directed by Fleischer: *Popeye the Sailor Meets Sinbad the Sailor, Popeye the Sailor Meets Ali Baba's Forty Thieves* and *Popeye the Sailor and His Wonderful Lamp.*
VHS: S01048. $24.95.
Dave Fleischer, USA, 1936, 54 mins.

Popeye the Sailor

Here are the three two-reel Technicolor special Popeyes made during the 1930's.The first two feature some of Max's dazzling 3-D backgrounds. *Popeye Meets Sinbad* ('36), *Popeye Meets Ali Baba's Forty Thieves* ('37) and *Popeye in Aladdin and His Wonderful Lamp* ('39).
VHS: S29028. $19.95.
Fleischer, USA, 1936-39, 54 mins.

Popeye Vol. 1

For reasons known only to themselves, King Features has blocked the video release of the classic black-and-white *Popeye* cartoons for years. Fortunately for us, a handful of these cartoons have fallen into the public domain.This compilation offers excellent prints and some breathtaking 3-D backgrounds. Eight titles: *Little Swee'Pea* ('36), *I'm in the Army Now* ('36), *The Paneless Window Washer* ('37), *I Never Changes My Altitude* ('37), *A Date to Skate* ('38), *Customers Wanted* ('39), *With Poopdeck Pappy* ('40), *Me Musical Nephews* ('43) and a 1960s Popeye "Soaky" TV commercial.
VHS: S34849. $14.95.
Fleischer/Famous, USA, 1936-43, 55 mins.

Porky Pig & Co.

Six titles: *Old Glory* ('39), *Wagon Heels* ('45), *Tom Turk & Daffy* ('44), *Mouse Menace* ('46), *The Aristo-Cat* ('43) and *Roughly Squeaking* ('46).
VHS: S29033. $12.95.
Warner Bros, USA, 1939-46, 45 mins.

Porky Pig Tales

Six titles: *The Awful Orphan* ('49), *The Pest That Came to Dinner* ('48), *Jumpin Jupiter* ('55), *My Little Duckaroo* ('54), *Dog Collared* ('51) and *China Jones* ('59).
VHS: S12627. $12.95.
Warner Bros, USA, 1948-59, 44 mins.

Porky Pig: Days of Swine and Roses

Five titles: *Porky's Party* ('38), *Patient Porky* ('40), *Thumb Fun* ('52), *Porky's Hero Agency* ('37) and *Bye Bye Bluebeard* ('49).
VHS: S16719. $12.95.
Warner Bros., USA, 1937-52, 33 mins.

Porky Pig: Ham on Wry

Fourteen titles: *Often an Orphan* ('49), *You Ought to Be in Pictures* ('40, B&W), *The Pest That Came to Dinner* ('48), *The Ducksters* ('50), *Dog Collared* ('51), *Porky in Wackyland* ('38, B&W), *Deduce You Say* ('56), *Porky Pig's Feat* ('43, B&W), *Claws for Alarm* ('54), *The Prize Pest* ('51), *The Case of the Stuttering Pig* ('37, B&W), *Thumb Fun* ('52), *Awful Orphan* ('49) and *Boobs in the Woods* ('50).
Laser: LD71761. $34.95.
Warner Bros., USA, 1937-56, 105 mins.

Porky!

Eight titles: *I Haven't Got a Hat* ('35), *I Love to Singa* ('36), *Brother Brat* ('44), *Little Orphan Airedale* ('47), *Daffy Doodles* ('46), *Baby Bottleneck* ('46), *Kitty Kornered* ('46) and *My Favorite Duck* ('42).
VHS: S06357. $14.95.
Warner Bros, USA, 1935-47, 60 mins.

Private S.N.A.F.U.

Seven hilarious episodes of the rarely seen Warner Bros. cartoon figure Private Snafu, that were written by Dr. Seuss (Ted Geisel) and directed by the legendary animator Chuck Jones. Originally intended as an off-center guide to military regulations for enlisted men. 30 mins.
VHS: S17109. $9.95.

Private S.N.A.F.U. Cartoon Festival

A collection of adult-oriented cartoons produced during WWII, intended to teach G.I.'s the finer points of military life.
VHS: S10584. $19.95.

Private S.N.A.F.U. Vol. 1

Private Snafu was a character created by Warner Bros. during WWII for the *Army-Navy Screen Magazine*.These cartoons were shown only to servicemen, and were intended to convey serious messages behind the typical Warner humor. Bosko Video has done a great job transferring them to video from very nice-looking B&W prints.The shorts are even letterboxed, with director and release credits. Fourteen titles: *Coming! Snafu!, Gripes, Spies, The Goldbrick, The Infantry Blues, Fighting Tools, The Home Front, Rumors, Booby Traps, Snafuperman, Snafu vs. Malaria Mike, A Lecture on Camouflage, Gas* and *Going Home.*
VHS: S29687. $29.95.
Warner Bros., USA, 1943-44, 62 mins.

Private S.N.A.F.U. Vol. 2

The second volume of the set contains the balance of the Warner Bros. S.N.A.F.U. shorts as well as two from UPA and one rarity from Harman-Ising. Fourteen titles: *The Chow Hound, Censored, Outpost, Payday, Target Snafu, A Few Quick Facts: Inflation* (UPA), *Three Brothers, In the Aleutians, A Few Quick Facts: Fear* (UPA), *It's Murder She Says, Hot Spot, Operation Snafu, No Buddy Atoll* and *Private Snafu Presents Seaman Tarfu* (Harman-Ising).
VHS: S29688. $29.95.
WB/Others, USA, 1944-46, 73 mins.

Pupettoon Movie

From special-effects wizard George Pal comes this "Fantasia" of puppet animation. Hosted by Gumby and Pokey, *The Pupettoon Movie* features characters like Tubby the Tuba, Jasper in a Jam, hip jazz from Charlie Barnet and Louis Armstrong, and as many as 5,000 individually-carved puppets per short. 80 mins.
VHS: S06541. $12.98.

Quest for Camelot Sing-Along

Cartoon clips are presented in a "sing-along" format, with lyrics superimposed on screen.Three songs from the latest WB animated feature are: "On My Father's Wings," "If I Didn't Have You" and "I Stand Alone." Also songs from classic WB shorts, and even "We're Off to See the Wizard."
VHS: S34271. $12.95.
Warner Bros., USA, 1998, 30 mins.

Rainbow Parades Vol. 2

Six titles from the Burt Gillet Rainbow Parade series: *It's a Greek Life* ('36), *Molly Moo Cow & Rip Van Winkle* ('35), *The Toonerville Trolley* ('36), *Toonerville Picnic* ('36), *The Hunting Season* ('35) and *Grandfather's Clock* ('34, Toddle Tales). Film prints are fair to poor.
VHS: S29689. $17.95.
Van Beuren, USA, 1934-36, 50 mins.

Return of the King

The conclusion of Tolkein's trilogy: while the evil might of Sauron swarms out to conquer Middle Earth, Frodo and Sam struggle to defeat the dark lord. Voices of John Huston, William Conrad, Orson Bean and Roddy McDowell.
VHS: S15185. $14.95.
Rankin/Bass, USA, 96 mins.

Rikki-Tikki-Tavi

This outstanding TV special from Chuck Jones about a brave mongoose is a wonderful adaptation of Rudyard Kipling's *Jungle Book*. Rikki-Tikki-Tavi, the mongoose adopted by a British family in India, fights to protect the people who've been so kind to him. Narrated by Orson Welles. EP Speed.
VHS: S03017. $9.95.
Chuck Jones, USA, 1975, 30 mins.

Roadrunner & Wile E. Coyote's Crash Course

Five titles: *Going! Going! Gosh!* ('52), *Ready Set Zoom!* ('55), *There They Go Go Go* ('56), *Hip Hip Hurry* ('58) and *Scrambled Aches* ('57).
VHS: S29694. $12.95.
Warner Bros., USA, 1952-58, 33 mins.

Roadrunner & Wile E. Coyote: The Scrapes of Wrath

Five titles: *Whoa-Be Gone* ('58), *Guided Muscle* ('55), *Hopalong Casualty* ('60), *Stop Look and Hasten* ('54) and *Rabbit's Feat* ('60).
VHS: S16720. $12.95.
Warner Bros., USA, 1954-60, 33 mins.

Roadrunner vs. Wile E. Coyote: If at First You Don't Succeed

Fourteen titles: *Fast and Furry-ous* ('49), *Beep Beep* ('52), *Going! Going! Gosh!* ('52), *Operation: Rabbit* ('52), *Zipping Along* ('53), *Stop! Look! and Hasten!* ('54), *Ready Set Zoom!* ('55), *Guided Muscle* ('55), *Gee Whiz-z-z* ('56), *There They Go-Go-Go!* ('56), *Scrambled Aches* ('57), *Zoom and Bored* ('57), *Whoa Be-Gone!* ('58) and *Hopalong Casualty* ('60).
Laser: LD72393. $34.95.
Warner Bros., USA, 1949-60, 94 mins.

Rock-A-Doodle

Don Bluth's tale of Chanticleer the Rooster, who is shamed into exile when the sun comes up without him one morning. Chanticleer moves to Vegas and does a fair impression of Elvis. A live-action boy named Edmond reads of his plight and enters the storybook world as a kitten in order to redeem Chanticleer and bring him back to stop the rain that's destroying Edmond's world. Some very powerful scenes may be frightening for small children. Voices of Glen Campbell, Sandy Duncan, Phil Harris, Charles Nelson Reilly and others.
VHS: S16638. $14.95.
Laser: LD71811. $24.95.
Don Bluth, USA, 1992, 75 mins.

The Secret of NIMH

Considered by many to be the best animated feature since the golden days of Disney, Don Bluth's tale of the adventures of a widow mouse is more than just a children's tale. Voiced by Dom DeLuise, Peter Strauss and John Carradine.
Laser: LD75882. $34.95.
Don Bluth, USA, 1982, 83 mins.

Space Jam

Merchandising juggernauts join forces as Michael Jordan and Bugs Bunny star in this live action/animation feature. The plot involving the Monstar aliens stealing the skills of some NBA stars in order to crush the [Looney] Tune Squad in a high-stakes basketball game is a thin excuse for the animators to try their hand at every Warner Brothers cartoon character—even the most obscure supporting players. Having Jordan come to the rescue is the pretext for abundant, reverent slo-mo sequences of His Airness in action. Stereo. CC.
VHS: S30893. $19.98.
Laser: LD76080. $34.95.
Warner Bros., USA, 1996, 88 mins.

Starring Bugs Bunny!

Seven titles: *Easter Yeggs* ('41), *Hare Conditioned* ('45), *Buccaneer Bunny* ('48), *A Feather in His Hare* ('48), *Hare Force* ('44), *Hare Tonic* ('45) and *A Hare Grows in Manhattan* ('47).
VHS: S08295. $14.95.
Warner Bros., USA, 1941-48, 54 mins.

Stars of Space Jam: Bugs Bunny

All six titles on this compilation are new to video: *Hot Cross Bunny* ('48), *Barbary Coast Bunny* ('56), *Homeless Hare* ('50), *Apes of Wrath* ('59, with Gruesome Gorilla), *Forward March Hare* ('53) and *Hare Splitter* ('48).
VHS: S30012. $9.95.
Warner Bros., USA, 1948-59, 42 mins.

Stars of Space Jam: Daffy Duck

Five of the six titles on this compilation are new to video. *Fool Coverage* ('52, with Porky), *The High and the Flighty* ('56, with Foghorn Leghorn), *Person to Bunny* ('60, with Bugs and Elmer), *Holiday for Drumsticks* ('49), *Stupor Duck* ('56) and *Boston Quackie* ('57, with Porky).
VHS: S30013. $9.95.
Warner Bros., USA, 1949-60, 41 mins.

Stars of Space Jam: Roadrunner & Wile E. Coyote

One of the six titles on this compilation is new to video. *Gee Whiz-z-z-z* ('56), *Zoom and Bored* ('57), *Fast and Furry-ous* ('49), *Zip 'n Snort* ('61), *Hook, Line and Stinker* ('58) and *Hot-Rod and Reel!* ('59).
VHS: S30014. $9.95.
Warner Bros., USA, 1949-61, 39 mins.

Stars of Space Jam: Sylvester & Tweety

All six titles on this compilation are new to video: *Canary Row* ('50), *Puddy Tat Twouble* ('51), *Snow Business* ('53, with Granny), *Sandy Claws* ('55, with Granny), *Tree Cornered Tweety* ('56) and *Tweet Zoo* ('57).
VHS: S30015. $9.95.
Warner Bros., USA, 1950-57, 43 mins.

Stars of Space Jam: The Tazmanian Devil

Two of the six titles on this compilation are new to video. *Devil May Hare* ('54, with Bugs), *Bedevilled Rabbit* ('57, with Bugs), *Ducking the Devil* ('57, with Daffy), *Bill of Hare* ('62, with Bugs), *Dr. Devil and Mr. Hare* ('64, with Bugs) and *The Fright Before Christmas* ('79, with Bugs and Clyde).
VHS: S30016. $9.95.
Warner Bros., USA, 1954-79, 40 mins.

Stars of Space Jam: Five-Tape Boxed Set

All five videotapes in a collector's slipcase, and a free Space Jam embroidered cap (mail-in offer).
VHS: S30017. $49.95.
Warner Bros., USA, 1948-79, 205 mins.

Superior Duck

Five classic Warner shorts plus the new Chuck Jones cartoon *Superior Duck* (aka *Father of the Bird*).
VHS: S32400. $12.95.
Warner Bros., USA, 40 mins.

Superman

The 17 original cartoons created by the brilliant animators Max and Dave Fleischer from 1941 to 1943 that subverts the Marvel Comics iconography for a surreal exploration of heroism and identity. Includes the legendary work *Snafuperman*. Transferred from 35mm prints. 150 mins.
VHS: S18259. $24.95.

Superman (50th Anniversary)

Is it a bird? Is it a plane? No it's Superman in this special 50th birthday collectors set which includes all 17 original animated full-color adventures of the Man of Steel. First released to theaters between 1941 and 1943, these Technicolor classics have been made from mint 35mm prints into high-grade video tape. These episodes represent the pinnacle of animation during its Golden Age. Included are: *Superman, The Mechanical Monsters, Billion Dollar Limited, Arctic Giant, Bulleteers, Magnetic Telescope, Electrical Earthquake, Volcano, Terror on the Midway, Japoteurs, Showdown, Eleventh Hour, Destruction, Inc., Mummy Strikes, Jungle Drums, Underground World* and *Secret Agent*.
VHS: S30185. $12.95.

Superman: The Complete Cartoon Collection

The Man of Steel's best cartoons by the master Max Fleischer are joined on this one video. Seventeen classics tell the story of America's most important superhero. His adventures recall a time when right and wrong were clearly defined and opposing forces. And of course, Superman always did the right thing. 142 mins.
VHS: S21081. $24.95.

Sylvester & Tweety's Bad Ol' Putty Tat Blues

Fourteen titles: *A Bird in a Guilty Cage* ('52), *Canned Feud* ('51), *All a Bir-r-r-d* ('50), *Greedy for Tweety* ('57), *Bad Ol' Putty Tat* ('49), *Pop 'Em Pop* ('50), *Gift Wrapped* ('52), *A Mouse Divided* ('53), *Birds Anonymous* ('57), *Kit for Cat* ('48), *Tweety's SOS* ('51), *Stooge for a Mouse* ('50), *Dog Pounded* ('54) and *Tree for Two* ('52).
Laser: LD72394. $34.95.
Warner Bros., USA, 1949-57, 100 mins.

Sylvester & Tweety's Tale Feathers

Five titles: *Muzzle Tough* ('54), *A Street Cat Named Sylvester* ('53), *Satan's Waitin'* ('54), *Dr. Jerkyll's Hide* ('54) and *Ain't She Tweet* ('52).
VHS: S29735. $12.95.
Warner Bros, USA, 1952-54, 34 mins.

Sylvester & Tweety: The Best Yeows of Our Lives

Five titles: *All a Bir-r-rd* ('50), *Tweet and Sour* ('56), *Tweet Tweet Tweety* ('51), *Home Tweet Home* ('50) and *A Bird in a Guilty Cage* ('52).
VHS: S16721. $12.95.
Warner Bros., USA, 1950-56, 33 mins.

Tex Avery's Screwball Classics 1

Eight titles: *Little Tinker, Swing Shift Cinderella, Magical Maestro, Bad Luck Blackie, Lucky Ducky, The Cat That Hated People, Symphony in Slang* and *Who Killed Who*.
VHS: S07967. $14.95.
MGM, USA, 59 mins.

Tex Avery's Screwball Classics 2

Eight titles: *Red Hot Riding Hood, One Ham's Family, Happy Go Nutty, Slap Happy Lion, Wild & Wolfy, Ventriloquist Cat, Big Heel Watha* and *Northwest Hounded Police*.
VHS: S29739. $14.95.
MGM, USA, 60 mins.

Tex Avery's Screwball Classics 3

Six titles: *The Screwy Truant* ('45), *House of Tomorrow* ('49), *Flea Circus* ('54), *Hound Hunters* ('47), *Batty Baseball* ('44) and *TV of Tomorrow* ('53).
VHS: S13555. $12.95.
MGM, USA, 1945-54, 44 mins.

Tex Avery's Screwball Classics 4

Six titles: *What Price Fleadom* ('48), *TV of Tomorrow* ('53), *The Counterfeit Cat* ('49), *Blitz Wolf* ('42), *The Cuckoo Clock* ('50) and *What's Buzzin' Buzzard?* ('43).
VHS: S15665. $12.95.
MGM, USA, 1942-53, 46 mins.

Tex Avery's Screwball Classics LD

Sixteen titles: *Little Tinker, Swing Shift Cinderella, Magical Maestro, Bad Luck Blackie, Lucky Ducky, The Cat That Hated People, Symphony in Slang, Who Killed Who, Red Hot Riding Hood, One Ham's Family, Happy Go Nutty, Slap Happy Lion, Wild & Wolfy, Ventriloquist Cat, Big Heel Watha* and *Northwest Hounded Police*.
Laser: LD75887. $34.95.
MGM, USA, 118 mins.

Tex Avery: All This and Tex Avery, Too!

Fifteen titles: *Blitz Wolf* ('42), *Dumb Hounded* ('43), *The Screwy Truant* ('45), *King-Size Canary* ('47), *Screwball Squirrel* ('44), *What Price Fleadom* ('48), *Half-Pint Pygmy* ('48), *Little Rural Riding Hood* ('49), *Doggone Tired* ('49), *Wags to Riches* ('49), *Counterfeit Cat* ('49), *The Cuckoo Clock* ('50), *House of Tomorrow* ('49), *Droopy's Double Trouble* ('51) and *Flea Circus* ('54).
Laser: LD70151. $34.95.
MGM, USA, 1942-54, 115 mins.

Tex Avery: The Compleat Tex Avery

Every single cartoon directed by Tex Avery while at MGM—collected here in a five-disc (ten sides) boxed laserdisc set—presented in chronological order. 1942: *The Blitz Wolf, The Early Bird Dood It*. 1943: *Dumb Hounded, Red Hot Riding Hood, Who Killed Who?, One Ham's Family, What's Buzzin' Buzzard?* 1944: *Screwball Squirrel, Batty Baseball, Happy-Go-Nutty, Big Heel-Watha*. 1945: *The Screwy Truant, The Shooting of Dan McGoo, Jerky Turkey, Swing Shift Cinderella, Wild and Woolfy*. 1946: *Lonesome Lenny, The Hick Chick, Northwest Hounded Police, Henpecked Hoboes*. 1947: *Hound Hunters, Red Hot Rangers, Uncle Tom's Cabana, Slap Happy Lion, King-Size Canary*. 1948: *What Price Fleadom, Little Tinker, Half-Pint Pygmy, Lucky Ducky, The Cat That Hated People*. 1949: *Bad Luck Blackie, Senor Droopy, The House of Tomorrow, Doggone Tired, Wags to Riches, Little Rural Riding Hood, Outfoxed, Counterfeit Cat*. 1950: *Ventriloquist Cat, The Cuckoo Clock, Garden Gopher, The Chump Champ, The Peachy Cobbler*. 1951: Cock-A-Doodle Dog, Daredevil Droopy, Droopy's Good Deed, Symphony in Slang, Car of Tomorrow, Droopy's Double Trouble. 1952: *Magical Maestro, One Cab's Family, Rock-A-Bye Bear*. 1953: *Little Johnny Jet, TV of Tomorrow, The Three Little Pups*. 1954: *Drag-Along Droopy, Billy Boy, Homesteader Droopy, Farm of Tomorrow, The Flea Circus, Dixieland Droopy*. 1955: *Field and Scream, The First Bad Man, Deputy Droopy, Cellbound*. 1956: *Millionaire Droopy (Cinemascope)*. 1957: *Cat's Meow* (Cinemascope).
Laser: LD71656. $99.95.
MGM, USA, 1942-55, 540 mins.

Thumbelina

From Don Bluth comes one of his lushest-looking animated features yet. The diminutive heroine must fend off the amorous advances of beetles, moles and frogs while she searches for her lost Fairy Prince. Adaptation by Don Bluth, musical score by Barry Manilow, songs and voices by Gilbert Gottfried and Charo... 'nuff said.
VHS: S21255. $24.95.
Laser: Widescreen. **LD72421. $34.95.**
Don Bluth, USA, 1994, 86 mins.

Tiny Toon Adventures Vol. 1: The Best of Buster & Babs

Two episodes: Buster Bunny takes a chance and asks Babs to a dance in *Prom-Ise Her Anything*. And in *thirteensomething*, Babs hopes to land a part on a show whose zip code may be 9021-uh-oh!
VHS: S18489. $12.95.
Warner Bros., USA, 44 mins.

Tiny Toon Adventures Vol. 2: Tiny Toon Music Television

Two episodes: TT-MTV is on the air! In *The TT Music Television* and *Toon TV*, VJs Babs and Buster give "The Name Game," "Particle Man," "Nothing Compares to You," "Yakkity-Yak" and more tunes the TOON treatment.
VHS: S18490. $12.95.
Warner Bros., USA, 44 mins.

Tiny Toon Adventures Vol. 3: Tiny Toons in Two-Tone Town

Two episodes: Babs and Buster meet the first-ever Warner cartoon stars. The pair of hares help down-and-out '30s toonsters revive their careers in *Two-Tone Town*. And Babs finds her role model in the *Field of Dreams* spoof *Fields of Honey*.
VHS: S18491. $12.95.
Warner Bros., USA, 44 mins.

Tiny Toon Adventures: How I Spent My Vacation

This theatrical feature never made it to the theatres, going straight to video instead. Plucky Duck and Hampton head for (gasp and drool!) Happy World Land, Buster & Babs turn a squirt-gun fight into a globe-hopping adventure, and Elmyra treats the ferocious beasts in a drive-through safari park like cute widdle puddy tats. The animation is very good, and the energy level remains high for all 80 minutes.
VHS: S29741. $19.95.
Laser: LD75888. $29.95.
Amblin/Warner, USA, 1991, 80 mins.

Tiny Toon BIG Adventures

Two episodes: Buster and Babs quake rattle & roll in *Journey to the Center of Acme Acres*; and time-traveling Plucky must rush back to the present to finish his homework in *A Ditch in Time*.
VHS: S20493. $12.95.
Warner Bros., USA, 42 mins.

Tiny Toon Fiendishly Funny Adventures

Two episodes: Plucky's imagination gets the best of him in *Duck in the Dark*; Hampton's diet puts him cheek-to-crumb with the *Little Cake of Horrors*; *The Night of the Living Pets* closes in on Elmyra; and Babs and Buster get really mad at a mad scientist in *Hare-Raising Night*.
VHS: S20494. $9.95.
Warner Bros., USA, 38 mins.

Tiny Toon Island Adventures

Two episodes: The Tooners find out where a treasure map leads in *No Toon Is an Island*; and they have some wicky wacky fun in *Buster and Babs Go Hawaiian*.
VHS: S20495. $12.95.
Warner Bros., USA, 42 mins.

Tiny Toons: It's a Wonderful Christmas Special

What would Acme Acres be like if Buster Bunny never starred on *Tiny Toon Adventures?* Guardian rabbit angel Harvey provides the answer in this spoof of the classic Jimmy Stewart film.
VHS: S30377. $12.95.
Warner Bros., USA, 1996, 23 mins.

Tiny Toons: Night Ghoulery

Babs gives a Rod Serling-esque presentation of a collection of macabre paintings. A tale of horrific household appliances unfolds in *The Telltale Vacuum*. Montana Max is plunged into Heck in *The Devil and Daniel Webfoot*. *Hold That Duck* holds monsters in the closet for Buster and Plucky. And a pesky airline traveler munches engine number four in *Gremlin on a Wing*. Also *Sneezer the Sneezy Ghost, Devil Dog of the Moors, Fuel, Night of the Living Dull* and *Franken Myra*. Nine great segments in all.
VHS: S30376. $12.95.
Warner Bros., USA, 1996, 45 mins.

Tom & Jerry & Friends #1

Eight titles: *Tightrope Tricks* ('33), *Happy Hoboes* ('33), *Candyland* ('33), *House Cleaning Time* ('32), *Feathered Follies* ('32), *Ship Ahoy* ('30), *Custard Pies* ('29) and *Ball Game* ('29).
VHS: S05054. $17.95.
Van Beuren, USA, 1929-33, 60 mins.

Tom & Jerry & Friends #2

Eight titles: *Gypped in Egypt* ('30), *The Jail Breakers* ('29), *A Dizzy Day* ('33), *Tuning In* ('29), *Western Whoopee* ('30), *Snow Time* ('30), *Venice Vamp* ('32) and *The Haunted Ship* ('30).
VHS: S05055. $17.95.
Van Beuren, USA, 1929-33, 60 mins.

Tom & Jerry & Friends #3

Eight titles: *Barnyard Bunk* ('32), *Three Little Kittens* ('33), *The Cat's Dilemma* ('32), *A Fireman's Life* ('33), *Hokum Hotel* ('32), *Noah Knew His Ark* ('30), *In Vaudeville* ('26) and *Radio Racket* ('31).
VHS: S05056. $17.95.
Van Beuren, USA, 1926-33, 60 mins.

Tom & Jerry & Friends #4

Six titles: *Plane Dumb* ('32), *Magic Art* ('32), *Dixie Days* ('30), *Galloping Hooves* ('33), *The Lion Tamer* ('34, Amos 'n Andy) and *The Rasslin Match* ('34, Amos 'n Andy).
VHS: S05057. $17.95.
Van Beuren, USA, 1930-34, 60 mins.

Tom & Jerry & Friends #5

Eight titles: *A Swiss Trick* ('31), *Picnic Problems* ('33), *The Fly's Bride* ('29), *AM to PM* ('33), *Farm Foolery* ('30), *Xmas Night* ('33), *Singing Saps* ('30) and *The Panicky Pup* ('33).
VHS: S29745. $17.95.
Van Beuren, USA, 1929-33, 60 mins.

Tom & Jerry & Friends #6

Eight titles: *Puzzled Pals* ('33), *College Capers* ('31), *Happy Polo* ('32), *The Farmerette* ('32), *Cowboy Blues* ('31), *The Animal Fair* ('31), *Robin Hood Rides Again* ('33) and *Good Old School Days* ('30).
VHS: S29746. $17.95.
Van Beuren, USA, 1930-33, 60 mins.

Tom & Jerry & Friends #7

Eight titles: *The Magic Mummy* ('33), *Runaway Blackie* ('33), *Donkey Tricks* ('20s), *Wild Goose Chase* ('32), *Bring 'em Back Half Shot* ('32), *Fisherman's Luck* ('31), *A Close Call* ('29) and *Old Hokum Bucket* ('31).
VHS: S06971. $17.95.
Van Beuren, USA, 1929-33, 60 mins.

Tom & Jerry & Friends #8

Eight titles: *The Phantom Rocket* ('33), *The Iron Man* ('30), *Golden Goose* ('31), *Chinese Jinks* ('32), *The Bully's End* ('33), *Jest of Honor* ('34), *In Darkest Africa* ('33) and *The Big Cheese* ('30).
VHS: S29747. $17.95.
Van Beuren, USA, 1929-33, 60 mins.

Tom & Jerry & Friends #9

Eight titles: Aesop's Fables: *Cinderella Blues* ('31), *Laundry Blues* ('30), *A Stone Age Romance* ('29), *Circus Capers* ('30) and *Red Riding Hood* ('31). Plus *A Royal Good Time* ('34, Little King), *Love's Labor Won* ('33, Cubby Bear) and *Redskin Blues* ('32, Tom & Jerry). Fairly good film prints.
VHS: S29748. $17.95.
Van Beuren, USA, 1929-34, 60 mins.

Tom & Jerry Classics

Fourteen titles: *Puss Gets the Boot* ('40, first cartoon), *Dog Trouble* ('42), *Cat Fishin'* ('47), *Mouse in the House* ('47), *Yankee Doodle Mouse* ('43, Oscar winner), *Heavenly Puss* ('49), *Part Time Pal* ('47), *The Midnight Snack* ('41), *Salt Water Tabby* ('47), *The Mouse Comes to Dinner* ('45), *Quiet Please* ('45), *Old Rockin' Chair Tom* ('48), *Jerry and Jumbo* ('53) and *Solid Serenade* ('46).
Laser: LD75891. $34.95.
MGM, USA, 1940-53, 120 mins.

Tom & Jerry on Parade

Six titles: *Cruise Cat* ('51), *Designs on Jerry* ('53), *His Mouse Friday* ('51), *Little School Mouse* ('52), *Pet Peeve* ('54) and *Pushbutton Kitty* ('52).
VHS: S15663. $12.95.
MGM, USA, 1951-54, 41 mins.

Tom & Jerry's 50th Birthday Classics 1

Seven titles: *Puss Gets the Boot ('40, first cartoon), Dog Trouble* ('42), *Cat Fishin'* ('47), *Mouse in the House* ('47), *Yankee Doodle Mouse* ('43), *Heavenly Puss* ('49) and *Part Time Pal* ('47).
VHS: S29742. $12.95.
MGM, USA, 1940-49, 57 mins.

Tom & Jerry's 50th Birthday Classics 2

Six titles: *Zoot Cat* ('44), *Cue Ball Cat* ('50), *Cat Concerto* ('47), *Million Dollar Cat* ('44), *Cat Napping* ('51) and *Fraidy Cat* ('42).
VHS: S29743. $12.95.
MGM, USA, 1942-51, 45 mins.

Tom & Jerry's 50th Birthday Classics 3

Six titles: *Johann Mouse* ('53), *Mice Follies* ('54), *Mouse Trouble* ('44), *The Night Before Christmas* ('41), *The Dog House* ('52) and *Mouse Cleaning* ('48).
VHS: S29744. $12.95.
MGM, USA, 1941-54, 45 mins.

Tom & Jerry's Cartoon Cavalcade

Six titles: *Casanova Cat* ('50), *Jerry's Cousin* ('51), *Fine Feathered Friend* ('42), *Jerry & The Lion* ('50), *Mouse for Sale* ('53) and *Southbound Duckling* ('54).
VHS: S15662. $12.95.
MGM, USA, 1942-54, 42 mins.

Tom & Jerry's Comic Capers

Six titles: *Downhearted Duckling* ('53), *Fit to Be Tied* ('52), *The Flying Sorceress* ('55), *Hatch Up Your Troubles* ('48), *Polka Dot Puss* ('48) and *Puppy Tale* ('53).
VHS: S15660. $12.95.
MGM, USA, 1948-55, 42 mins.

Tom & Jerry's Festival of Fun

Six titles: *Blue Cat Blues* ('56), *Little Quacker* ('50), *Sufferin' Cats* ('42), *Tennis Chumps* ('49), *Touche Pussycat* ('54) and *The Truce Hurts* ('47).
VHS: S15661. $12.95.
MGM, USA, 1942-56, 43 mins.

Tom & Jerry's The Night Before Christmas

Four titles: *The Night Before Christmas* ('41, Tom & Jerry), *The Captain's Christmas* ('38, Capt. & The Kids), *One Ham's Family* ('43, Tex Avery) and *Toyland Broadcast* ('35).
VHS: S14561. $9.95.
MGM, USA, 1935-41, 45 mins.

Tom & Jerry: Starring Tom & Jerry!

Seven titles: *The Midnight Snack* ('41), *Salt Water Tabby* ('47), *The Mouse Comes to Dinner* ('45), *Quiet Please* ('45), *Old Rockin' Chair Tom* ('48), *Jerry and Jumbo* ('53) and *Solid Serenade* ('46).
VHS: S08294. $12.95.
MGM, USA, 1941-53, 54 mins.

Tom & Jerry: The Art of Tom & Jerry Vol. 1

Every single Tom & Jerry cartoon from 1940 through 1953 in a five-disc (10 sides) boxed laserdisc set. Seventy-seven titles presented in chronological order: 1940: *Puss Gets the Boot*. 1941: *The Midnight Snack, The Night Before Christmas*. 1942: *Fraidy Cat, Dog Trouble, Puss 'n' Toots, The Bowling Alley Cat, Fine Feathered Friend*. 1943: *Sufferin' Cats, The Lonesome Mouse, Yankee Doodle Mouse, Baby Puss*. 1944: *The Zoot Cat, The Million Dollar Cat, The Bodyguard, Puttin' on the Dog, Mouse Trouble*. 1945: *The Mouse Comes to Dinner, Mouse in Manhattan, Tea for Two, Flirty Birdy, Quiet Please*. 1946: *Springtime for Thomas, The Milky Waif, Trap Happy, Solid Serenade*. 1947: *Cat Fishin', Part Time Pal, The Cat Concerto, Dr. Jekyll & Mr. Mouse, Salt Water Tabby, A Mouse in the House, The Invisible Mouse*. 1948: *Kitty Foiled, The Truce Hurts, Old Rockin' Chair Tom, Professor Tom, Mouse Cleaning*. 1949: *Polka-Dot Puss, The Little Orphan, Hatch Up Your Troubles, Heavenly Puss, The Cat & The Mermouse, Love That Pup, Jerry's Diary, Tennis Chumps*. 1950: *Little Quacker, Saturday Evening Puss, Texas Tom, Jerry & The Lion, Safety Second, Tom & Jerry in the Hollywood Bowl, The Framed Cat, Cueball Cat*. 1951: *Casanova Cat, Jerry & The Goldfish, Jerry's Cousin, Sleepy-Time Tom, His Mouse Friday, Slicked-Up Pup, Nit-Witty Kitty, Cat Napping*. 1952: *The Flying Cat, The Duck Doctor, The Two Mouseketeers, Smitten Kitten, Triplet Trouble, Little Runaway, Fit to Be Tied, Pushbutton Kitty, Cruise Cat, The Dog House*. 1953: *The Missing Mouse, Jerry and Jumbo, Johann Mouse, That's My Pup* and *Just Ducky*.
Laser: LD71655. $99.95.
MGM, USA, 1940-53, 540 mins.

Tom & Jerry: The Art of Tom & Jerry Vol. 2

The balance of the Hanna-Barbera Tom & Jerry cartoons on three discs (six sides) with cinemascope cartoons letterboxed (denoted by an *). Side Six contains miscellaneous Hanna-Barbera shorts, including two Captain & The Kids shorts from 1938—their directorial debut. Forty-nine titles: 1953: *Two Little Indians, Life with Tom*. 1954: *Puppy Tale, Posse Cat, Hic-cup Pup, Little School Mouse, Baby Butch, Mice Follies, Neopolitan Mouse, Downhearted Duckling, Pet Peeve, Touche Pussycat!* 1955: *Southbound Duckling, Pup on a Picnic, Mouse for Sale, Designs on Jerry, Tom and Cherie*, Smarty Cat, Pecos Pest, That's My Mommy**. 1956: *The Flying Sorceress*, The Egg and Jerry*, Busy Buddies*, Muscle Beach Tom*, Down Beat Bear*, Blue Cat Blues*, Barbeque Brawl**. 1957: *Tops with Pops*, Timid Tabby*, Feedin' the Kiddie*, Mucho Mouse*, Tom's Photo Finish*, Give and Tyke*, Scat Cats**. 1958: *Happy Go Ducky*, Royal Cat Nap*, The Vanishing Duck*, Robin Hoodwinked*, Tot Watchers**. Miscellaneous Shorts: *Good Will to Men** ('55), *Blue Monday* ('38), *What a Lion!* ('38), *Swing Social* ('40), *Gallopin' Gals* ('40), *The Goose Goes South* ('41), *Officer Pooch* ('41), *War Dogs* ('43), *Anchors Aweigh* ('44, excerpt) and *Dangerous When Wet* ('53, excerpt).
Laser: LD75889. $69.95.
MGM, USA, 1938-58, 340 mins.

Tom & Jerry: The Art of Tom & Jerry Vol. 3 (The Chuck Jones Era)

A three-disc boxed laserdisc set of all the cartoons made during the Chuck Jones years. Thirty-four titles: 1963: *Penthouse Mouse*. 1964: *The Cat Above and the Mouse Below, Is There a Doctor in the Mouse?, Much Ado About Mousing, Snowbody Loves Me, The Unshrinkable Jerry Mouse*. 1965: *Ah, Sweet Mouse-story of Life, Bad Day at Cat Rock, The Brothers Carry-Mouse Off, The Cat's Me-ouch, Haunted Mouse, I'm Just Wild About Jerry, Jerry-Go-Round, Of Feline Bondage, Tom-ic Energy, Year of the Mouse*. 1966: *The A-Tominable Snowman, Catty Cornered, Duel Personality, Filet Meow, Jerry Jerry Quite Contrary, Love Me, Love My Mouse, Matinee Mouse, Puss 'n' Boats*. 1967: *Advance and Be Mechanized, Cannery Rodent, Cat and Dupli-Cat, Guided Mouse-ille, The Mouse from H.U.N.G.E.R., O Solar Meow, Purr-Chance to Dream, Rock 'n' Rodent, Shutter Bugged Cat, Surf-Bored Cat*.
Laser: LD75890. $69.95.
MGM, USA, 1963-67, 300 mins.

Tom & Jerry: The Movie

Tom and Jerry return to the silver screen in a musical feature. The twosome helps out a runaway little girl who is searching for her father, and trying to avoid her nasty Aunt Figg. The two not only cooperate in this new story, they even talk! Produced and directed by Phil Roman, with six original songs by Henry Mancini and Leslie Bricusse.
Laser: LD75276. $34.95.
Film Roman, USA, 1993, 84 mins.

Tom & Jerry: The Very Best of Tom & Jerry

Six titles: *The Little Orphan* ('49), *The Bowling Alley Cat* ('42), *Tee for Two* ('45), *The Flying Cat* ('52), *Saturday Evening Puss* ('50) and *The Bodyguard* ('44).
VHS: S13571. $12.95.
MGM, USA, 1942-52, 44 mins.

Toon Up the Volume

Stick Stickly and Holly B. Wood host this DJ fest of Nickelodeon cartoon music videos. *Kilted Yaksmen Anthem, Rugrats Rap, Ren's Specs* and *Rugrats Rock* are just some of the toons that get this video grooving. 40 mins.
VHS: S27782. $12.99.

Toonland USA

Over six hours of 50 fun-filled cartoons featuring Popeye, Casper the Friendly Ghost, Donald Duck, Little Lulu, Betty Boop, Little Audrey, Baby Huey, Superman, Hector the Dog and many more. These classic cartoons have been carefully restored, digitalized and transferred from high-quality film prints to provide you and your family with hours of fun. 365 mins.
VHS: S30186. $12.95.

Tweety & Sylvester

Eight titles: *Tweety Pie* ('47, Oscar winner), *A Tale of Two Kitties* ('42), *The Gruesome Twosome* ('45), *Birdie and the Beast* ('44), *Life with Feathers* ('45), *Crowing Pains* ('47), *Back Alley Oproar* ('48) and *I Taw a Putty Tat* ('48).
VHS: S09122. $14.95.
Warner Bros, USA, 1942-48, 60 mins.

Ub Iwerks' Famous Fairytales

The animator who was Disney's right-hand man in a collection of priceless animation of some famous fairy tales: *The Headless Horseman, Aladdin and His Lamp, The King's Tailor, Dick Whittington's Cat, Mary's Little Lamb, Puss in Boots*, and *Jack and the Beanstalk*. Color, 56 mins.
VHS: S04856. $29.95.

Van Beuren & Commonwealth

Very nice prints and video transfer of these Rainbow Parades. Seven titles: *Toonerville Picnic, Cupid Gets His Man, It's a Greek Life, Molly Moo Cow and Robinson Crusoe, Trolley Aboy, A Waif's Welcome* and *Molly Moo Cow and Rip Van Winkle*.
VHS: S29761. $24.95.
Van Beuren, USA, 1935-36, 60 mins.

Van Beuren Cartoons #1: Tom & Jerry

Excellent quality filmprints from Bosko Video. Eight titles: *Wot a Night, Trouble, Jungle Jam, A Swiss Trick, The Rocketeers, Rabid Hunters, In the Bag* and *Pots and Pans*.
VHS: S29762. $29.95.
Van Beuren, USA, 1930's, 70 mins.

Van Beuren Cartoons #2: Cubby Bear

In 1933, Manny Davis created Cubby Bear for Van Beuren. Lost in the mists of time for decades, Cubby has been rescued by Bosko Video. Bosko has gone to great lengths to find the best source material available, and has meticulously transferred the films to video—even slightly letterboxing them. Nine black-and-white titles: *Opening Night, Love's Labor Won, The Last Mail, Bubbles and Troubles, Barking Dogs, Fresh Ham, Indian Whoopee, Nut Factory* and *World Flight*.
VHS: S29763. $29.95.
Van Beuren, USA, 1933, 67 mins.

Van Beuren Cartoons #3: The Little King

In 1933, Van Beuren began a series based on Otto Soglow's *Little King* comic strip. Bosko Video has collected all of these cartoons and two *Sentinel Louie* cartoons and presented them here in chronological order. As usual with Bosko, the films are meticulously transferred and letterboxed. Eleven black-and-white titles: *A Dizzy Day* and *AM to PM* (Sentinel Louie); *The Fatal Note, On the Pan, Pals, Jest of Honor, Jolly Good Felons, Sultan Pepper, A Royal Good Time, Art for Art's Sake* and *Cactus King*.
VHS: S29764. $29.95.
Van Beuren, USA, 1933-34, 84 mins.

Van Beuren Studio, Volume #1

A collection of early animation from the 20s and 30s, including *Custard Pies* (Paul Terry), *Barnyard Melody* (John Foster), *Jungle Fool* (John Foster and Mannie Davies), *Summer Time* (1929, John Foster), *Piano Tuners* (Tom and Jerry, 1932, John Foster & George Rufle) and *Happy Hoboes* (Tom and Jerry, 1933). 55 mins.
VHS: S22009. $14.95.

Van Beuren Studio, Volume #2

A collection of Aesop's fables produced by the Van Beuren animation studio. Includes *A Close Call* (Harry Bailey), *A Romeo Robin* (John Foster & Mannie Davis), *The Ball Game* (1932, John Foster & George Rufle), *Play Ball, Cat's Canary, Noah Knew His Ark* and *Cowboy Cabaret*. 57 mins.
VHS: S22010. $14.95.

Waldo Kitty: Even Cats Can Dream

Two episodes: *The Lone Kitty Rides Again* and *Robin Cat*. EP Speed.
VHS: S29073. $9.95.
Filmation, USA, 1975-76, 51 mins.

Warner Bros. Collection Vol. 1: Tokyo Jokio

Eight titles: *Smile, Darn Ya Smile* ('31), *Freddy the Freshman* ('32), *Crosby, Columbo & Vallee* ('32), *Scrap Happy Daffy* ('43), *We're in the Money* ('33), *I Only Have Eyes for You* ('37), *The Case of the Missing Hare* ('42) and *Tokyo Jokio* ('43).
VHS: S29766. $24.95.
Warner Bros., USA, 1931-43, 60 mins.

Warner Bros. Collection Vol. 2: Wackiki Wabbit

Eight titles: *Hamateur Night* ('39), *Have You Got Any Castles?* ('38), *A Corny Concerto* ('43), *Jungle Jitters* ('38), *Daffy Duck & The Dinosaur* ('39), *Wackiki Wabbit* ('43), *I Wanta Be a Sailor* ('37) and *Farm Frolics* ('41).
VHS: S29767. $24.95.
Warner Bros., USA, 1938-43, 60 mins.

Warner Bros. Collection Vol. 3: Private Snafu

Eight titles: *Home Front, Spies, The Gold Brick, It's Murder She Says, A Lecture on Camouflage, Three Brothers, Snafu-perman* and *Booby Trap*.
VHS: S29768. $24.95.
Warner Bros., USA, 60 mins.

Warner Bros. Collection Vol. 4: The Dover Boys

Seven titles: *Falling Hare* ('43), *A Great Big Bunch of You* ('32), *A Tale of Two Kitties* ('42), *The Dover Boys* ('42), *The Wabbit Who Came to Supper* ('42), *The Haunted Mouse* ('41) and *Inki & The Mynah Bird* ('43).
VHS: S29769. $24.95.
Warner Bros., USA, 1932-43, 60 mins.

Warner Bros. Collection Vol. 5: Porky Pig

Seven titles: *Get Rich Quick Porky* ('37), *Porky Pig's Feat* ('43), *Coy Decoy* ('41), *Henpecked Duck* ('41), *Fox Pop* ('42), *Prest-O Change-O* ('39) and *A Day at the Zoo* ('39).
VHS: S29770. $24.95.
Warner Bros., USA, 1937-43, 60 mins.

We're Back! A Dinosaur's Story

Imagine if some goofy dinosaurs came back from extinction and showed up in modern day New York. Now imagine a Tyrannosaurus Rex with the personality of John Goodman. That's what you get in this latest effort from Steven Spielberg's animation studio, and the result is an impressively animated and amusing tale of kids, dinosaurs and evil circus promoters. Voices also include Jay Leno, Walter Cronkite, Rhea Perlman and Martin Short.
Laser: Widescreen. LD72370. $29.95.
Amblimation, USA, 1993, 71 mins.

The White Seal

A baby seal vows to save his fellow seals from the annual slaughter by hunters. He manages to find a safe island for his tribe but then must persuade them that change can be good. Voice of Roddy McDowell. EP Speed.
VHS: S03016. $9.95.
Chuck Jones, USA, 1975, 30 mins.

Who Framed Roger Rabbit?

1988's smash theatrical hit about a rabbit framed for the murder of R.K. Maroon—owner of Toontown. This live-action and animation movie was so successful and so influential that many credit it for a resurgent interest in animation in general. Down and out Private Eye Eddie Valiant is hired to clear cartoon star Roger Rabbit of murder charges. Stars Bob Hoskins and Christopher Lloyd, with voices of Kathleen Turner and Charles Fleischer.
VHS: S10337. $22.99.
Laser: LD75895. $29.95.
Laser: CAV, widescreen. **LD71209. $39.95.**
Amblin/Disney, USA, 1988, 104 mins.

Wild and Woody

Eight titles: *Puny Express* ('51), *Stage Hoax* ('52), *Hot Noon* ('53), *Pistol Packin' Woodpecker* ('60), *Panhandle Scandal* ('59), *Wild and Woody* ('48), *Woodpecker Wanted* ('65) and *Short in the Saddle* ('63).
VHS: S29771. $14.95.
Walter Lantz, USA, 1948-65, 51 mins.

Wince upon a Time: Foolhardy Fairy Tales & Looney Legends

Fourteen titles: *A-Lad-In His Lamp* ('48), *Little Red Rodent Hood* ('52), *The Windblown Hare* ('49), *Yankee Dood It* ('56), *Pied Piper Porky* ('39, B&W), *Lumberjack Rabbit* ('54), *Goldimouse and the Three Cats* ('60), *Knighty-Knight Bugs* ('58), *Porky's Hero Agency* (37, B&W), *Tweety and the Beanstalk* ('57), *Rabbitson Crusoe* ('56), *Porky the Giant Killer* ('39, B&W), *Red Riding Hoodwinked* ('55) and *Paying the Piper* ('49).
Laser: LD72397. $34.95.
Warner Bros., USA, 1937-60, 101 mins.

The Wind in the Willows

Rankin/Bass' version of Kenneth Grahame's classic story featuring the voices of Charles Nelson Reilly, Roddy McDowall and Eddie Bracken.
VHS: S29773. $14.95.
Rankin/Bass, USA, 96 mins.

Woody Woodpecker 50th Anniversary Vol. 1

Four titles: *The Cracked Nut* ('41), *Banquet Busters* ('48), *Born to Peck* ('52) and *The Redwood Sap* ('51).
VHS: S13918. $12.95.
Lantz, USA, 1941-52, 30 mins.

Woody Woodpecker 50th Anniversary Vol. 2

Four titles: *The Coo Coo Bird* ('47), *Well Oiled* ('47), *Ace in the Hole* ('42) and *Arts and Flowers* ('56).
VHS: S13919. $12.95.
Lantz, USA, 1942-56, 30 mins.

Woody Woodpecker Collector's Edition

Both volumes on one video disc.
Laser: LD75897. $34.98.
Lantz, USA, 1941-56, 60 mins.

Yosemite Sam's Yeller Fever

Five titles: *Hare Trimmed* ('53), *Southern Fried Rabbit* ('53), *This Is a Life?* ('55), *Hare Lift* ('52) and *Bunker Hill Bunny* ('50).
VHS: S29778. $12.95.
Warner Bros., USA, 1950-55, 35 mins.

Yosemite Sam: The Good, The Bad and the Ornery

Five titles: *Mutiny on the Bunny* ('50), *Sahara Hare* ('55), *Honey's Money* ('62), *Wild and Wooly Hare* ('59) and *Rabbit Every Monday* ('51).
VHS: S16722. $12.95.
Warner Bros., USA, 1950-62, 33 mins.

WALT DISNEY FILMS

101 Dalmatians

Glenn Close chews the scenery as the flamboyantly wicked Cruella DeVil, along with 101 black-and-white canines, in this live-action Disney hit based on the Disney animated classic. With Jeff Daniels, Joan Plowright and Joely Richardson. Produced and written by John Hughes.
VHS: S31391. $26.99.
Laser: THX. **LD76378. $29.99.**
Stephen Herek, 1996, USA, 103 mins.

The Adventures of Huck Finn

Stephen Sommers wrote and directed this Disney adaptation of Mark Twain's classic novel about the shifting friendship between Huck Finn (Elijah Wood), an energetic, go-for-broke kid, and Jim (Courtney B. Vance), a runaway slave who is desperately trying to secure his freedom. With Robbie Coltrane, Jason Robards, Ron Perlman and Dana Ivey.
VHS: S19726. $19.95.
Laser: Letterboxed. **LD72340. $39.99.**
Stephen Sommers, USA, 1993, 108 mins.

The Adventures of Ichabod & Mr. Toad

The original theatrical version of Disney's classic animated retellings of *The Wind in the Willows* and *The Legend of Sleepy Hollow*. Narrated by Bing Crosby and Basil Rathbone.
Laser: LD75677. $29.95.
Disney, USA, 1949, 68 mins.

Aladdin & Jasmine's Moonlight Magic

Disney characters Aladdin, Jasmine and Genie find new adventures in these romantic, magic-laced cartoons. In *Moonlight Madness*, Aladdin entices Jasmine to join him on a date but he gets distracted by the promise of treasure. Then, in *Some Enchanted Genie*, Genie falls in love. 45 mins.
VHS: S27358. $12.99.

Aladdin and the King of Thieves

Robin Williams returns as the voice of the genie in this direct-to-video feature. Just before Aladdin and Jasmine are to be wed, the Forty Thieves spoil everything in a desperate search for the Hand of Midas—a treasure that turns all it touches into gold. The genie helps Aladdin track them (and his long-lost father) down.
VHS: S29834. $24.95.
Disney, USA, 1996, 80 mins.

Alice in Wonderland

Walt Disney's adaptation of the Lewis Carroll tale is animated in the traditional lavish Disney style, though lacking the grandiosity of earlier Disney features. Directors: Clyde Geronomi, Hamilton Luske and Wilfred Jackson.
Laser: LD74998. $36.95.
Disney, USA, 1951, 75 mins.

Alice in Wonderland Archive Edition

This deluxe CAV laserdisc also includes *One Hour in Wonderland* (a period TV special), excerpts from other TV specials, design concepts, theatrical trailers, TV spots, character designs and more. HiFi Stereo.
Laser: LD75842. $99.95.
Disney, USA, 1951, 75 mins.

Anne of Green Gables

Canadian actress Megan Follows, Tony Award winner Coleen Dewhurst and Richard Farnsworth are featured in this award-winning epic that follows the provocative life drama of Anne Shirley, an endearing orphan, from her struggles as an adolescent to her triumphs as a young woman.
VHS: S05376. $59.95.
Kevin Sullivan, Canada, 1985, 197 mins.

Ariel's Undersea Adventures: Whale of a Tale

Two short, animated films from Disney, *Whale of a Tale* and *Urchin*, show the enchanted underwater realm first seen in *The Little Mermaid*. Ariel is joined by Sebastian and Flounder as well as other new, lovable characters in these cartoons. 44 mins.
VHS: S27364. $12.99.

The Aristocats

Available on home video for the first time, *The Aristocats* was the last film supervised by Walt himself. When a millionairess names Duchess and her three kittens as her sole heirs, the faithful old butler plots to do away with the adorable felines. Duchess enlists the aid of a band of jazz-playing alley cats and a couple of hillbilly basset hounds to secure her inheritance. HiFi Stereo.
VHS: S27539. $26.95.
Laser: LD74873. $29.95.
Disney, USA, 1970, 78 mins.

Bambi

This 55th Anniversary Edition is restored to its original beauty. The gentlest of Disney animated features, *Bambi* served as a format for many of Disney's later true-life features.
VHS: S08700. $26.95.
Laser: CLV. **LD72454. $29.95.**
Laser: CAV. **LD72453. $49.95.**
Disney, USA, 1942, 69 mins.

Beauty and the Beast: The Enchanted Christmas

Angela Lansbury, Robbie Benson, Tim Curry and Bernadette Peters lend their voices to this direct-to-video sequel to the Disney feature. In this story of a Christmas past, Belle vows to warm the Beast's cold castle with the spirit of the season.
VHS: S32445. $26.95.
Disney, USA, 1997, 89 mins.

Bedknobs & Broomsticks

An amateur witch and her young friends help the British forces during WWII. Combines animation with live action.
VHS: S27951. $24.95.
Laser: LD75592. $36.95.
Disney, USA, 1971, 112 mins.

Ben and Me

This featurette tells the story of Amos mouse, who claims to have helped Ben Franklin with almost all of his inventions and achievements. Directed by Hamilton Luske.
VHS: S27959. $12.95.
Disney, USA, 1953, 25 mins.

Ben and Me/Bongo
Both programs on one video disc. For individual information, see listings.
Laser: LD75593. $29.95.
Disney, USA, 72 mins.

Best of Roger Rabbit
The three stand-alone Roger Rabbit theatrical shorts (*What's Cookin'* is incorporated into the *Who Framed Roger Rabbit?* feature) are collected at last on one tape. In *Tummy Trouble*, Roger takes Baby Herman to the hospital after he swallows his rattle; in *Roller Coaster Rabbit*, Roger takes Baby Herman to a fair; and in *Trail Mix-Up*, the pair go hiking in the woods. All three cartoons are brilliant homages to the Tex Avery and Bob Clampett school of 1940s Hollywood cartoons, but done with lush production values only Disney could bankroll.
VHS: S29697. $12.95.
Disney/Amblin, USA, 21 mins.

The Big Green
Disney is behind this inspiring tale, featuring Olivia d'Abo and Steve Guttenberg. D'Abo is a new teacher at the local school who decides to use soccer in order to energize her students. With the help of a local sheriff (Guttenberg), the kids discover the pride and purpose of preparing for a match against a team from a neighboring town.
VHS: S27366. $19.99.
Holly Goldberg Sloan, USA, 1995, 99 mins.

The Black Cauldron
The Black Cauldron stands out in the Disney canon for many reasons: it's the only Disney cartoon feature to earn a "PG" rating, it's only the second to be shot in 70mm widescreen (*Sleeping Beauty* was the first), and it's one of the few Disney cartoon features to flop badly at the box office. Now that it's finally being issued, *Song of the South* is left as the only Disney "classic" never released on video. Young Taran battles the Horned King for possession of the "Black Cauldron" and control of its supernatural powers, in a swords-and-sorcery adventure.
VHS: S34856. $26.95.
Disney, USA, 1985, 80 mins.

Bongo
From the 1947 featurette *Fun & Fancy Free*, *Bongo* is the story of a small circus bear who escapes and finds happiness in the countryside.
VHS: S27992. $12.95.
Disney, USA, 1947, 36 mins.

The Brave Little Toaster Goes to Mars
Inspired by the original Disney feature, this delightful animated film reunites everyone's favorite appliances as they charge through space on a race to Mars. Along the way, it teaches children about sharing, loyalty and teamwork. Featuring an all-star celebrity voice cast, including Farrah Fawcett, Carol Channing, Wayne Knight, Fyvush Finkel, Stephen Tobolowski, Alan King and DeForest Kelley. 73 mins.
VHS: S34585. $22.95.

The Brave Little Toaster
Five electrical appliances in a country cottage suddenly feel "dumped" when their young owner mysteriously disappears. Together they set off for the big city in search of their master.
VHS: S14257. $22.95.
Kushner-Locke, USA, 90 mins.

Cinderella (1950)
The fully restored classic feature has charming music and endearing supporting characters. Cinderella's homely stepsisters conspire to keep her away from the prince's ball, but with the help of her fairy godmother, she makes it anyway.
VHS: S07785. $26.95.
Laser: LD75847. $29.95.
Disney, USA, 1950, 76 mins.

Cinderella (1997)
Disney's new presentation of sibling rivalry, love at first sight and beauty within. Featuring the voices of Whitney Houston as the fairy godmother, Brandy as Cinderella, Whoopi Goldberg, Jason Alexander and Bernadette Peters and the music of Rogers and Hammerstein.
VHS: S32932. $19.99.

Disney Animation
Your child will delight to these videos of their favorite Disney characters.
Canine Commando Starring Pluto.
VHS: S03046. $14.95.
Importance of Being Donald.
VHS: S03045. $14.95.
Tale of Two Chipmunks.
VHS: S03048. $14.95.

Disney Cartoon Classics Special Edition: Fun on the Job!
Four titles: *Clock Cleaners* ('37), *Baggage Buster* ('41), *Mickey's Fire Brigade* ('35) and *The Big Wash* ('48).
VHS: S28153. $12.95.
Disney, USA, 1935-48, 31 mins.

Disney Cartoon Classics Special Edition: GOOFY
Contains the three tape volumes *Goofy World of Sports, Fun on the Job* and *Happy Summer Days*.
Laser: LD75624. $29.95.
Disney, USA, 90 mins.

Disney Cartoon Classics Special Edition: Happy Summer Days
Four titles: *Father's Lion* ('52), *Tea for Two Hundred* ('48), *The Simple Things* ('53) and *Two Weeks Vacation* ('52).
VHS: S28154. $12.95.
Disney, USA, 1948-53, 27 mins.

Disney Cartoon Classics Special Edition: The Goofy World of Sports
Four titles: *The Olympic Champ* ('42), *Donald's Golf Game* ('38), *The Art of Skiing* ('41) and *Aquamania* ('61, Oscar nominee).
VHS: S28152. $12.95.
Disney, USA, 1938-61, 32 mins.

Disney Cartoon Classics Vol. 1: Here's Mickey!
Three titles: *Mickey's Garden* ('35), *Orphan's Benefit* ('41) and *Mickey's Birthday Party* ('42).
VHS: S03032. $12.95.
Disney, USA, 1935-42, 27 mins.

Disney Cartoon Classics Vol. 2: Here's Donald!
Three titles: *Wide Open Spaces* ('47), *Crazy with the Heat* ('47) and *Donald's Ostrich* ('37).
VHS: S03033. $12.95.
Disney, USA, 1937-47, 22 mins.

Disney Cartoon Classics Vol. 3: Here's Goofy!
Three titles: *For Whom the Bulls Toil* ('53), *Lion Around* ('50) and *A Knight for a Day* ('46).
VHS: S03034. $12.95.
Disney, USA, 1945-53, 22 mins.

Disney Cartoon Classics Vol. 4: Silly Symphonies!
Three titles: *Water Babies* ('35), *Toby Tortoise Returns* ('36) and *Three Little Wolves* ('36).
VHS: S03036. $12.95.
Disney, USA, 1935-36, 25 mins.

Disney Cartoon Classics Vol. 5: Here's Pluto!
Three titles: *Mail Dog* ('47), *Pantry Pirate* ('40) and *Springtime for Pluto* ('44).
VHS: S03035. $12.95.
Disney, USA, 1941-47, 23 mins.

Disney Cartoon Classics Vol. 6: Mickey & Minnie
Three titles: *The Little Whirlwind* ('41), *Hawaiian Holiday* ('37) and *The Brave Little Tailor* ('38).
VHS: S29626. $12.95.
Disney, USA, 1937-41, 27 mins.

Disney Cartoon Classics Vol. 7: Donald & Daisy
Three titles: *Don Donald* ('37), *Donald's Double Trouble* ('46) and *Donald's Diary* ('54).
VHS: S28144. $12.95.
Disney, USA, 1936-53, 23 mins.

Disney Cartoon Classics Vol. 8: Animals by Two
Three titles: *Father Noah's Ark* ('33), *Peculiar Penguins* ('34) and *The Tortoise & The Hare* ('35).
VHS: S28145. $12.95.
Disney, USA, 1933-35, 26 mins.

Disney Cartoon Classics Vol. 9: Chip 'n Dale
Three titles: *Working for Peanuts* ('53), *Donald Applecore* ('52) and *Dragon Around* ('54).
VHS: S28146. $12.95.
Disney, USA, 1951-54, 22 mins.

Disney Cartoon Classics Vol. 10: Pluto & Fifi
Three titles: *Society Dog Show* ('39), *Pluto's Blue Note* ('47) and *Pluto's Quin-Puplets* ('37).
VHS: S28147. $12.95.
Disney, USA, 1937-47, 24 mins.

Disney Cartoon Classics Vol. 11: Mickey & The Gang
Three titles: *Boat Builders* ('38), *Canine Caddy* ('41) and *Moose Hunters* ('37).
VHS: S28148. $12.95.
Disney, USA, 1937-41, 25 mins.

Disney Cartoon Classics Vol. 12: Nuts About Chip 'n Dale
Three titles: *Two Chips and a Miss* ('52), *Food for Feudin'* ('50) and *Trailer Horn* ('50).
VHS: S28149. $12.95.
Disney, USA, 1949-51, 28 mins.

Disney Cartoon Classics Vol. 13: Donald's Scarey Tales
Three titles: *Donald Duck & The Gorilla* ('44), *Duck Pimples* ('45) and *Donald's Lucky Day* ('39).
VHS: S28150. $12.95.
Disney, USA, 1939-45, 22 mins.

Disney Cartoon Classics Vol. 14: Halloween Haunts
Three titles: *Pluto's Judgement Day* ('35), *Lonesome Ghosts* ('37) and *Trick or Treat* ('52).
VHS: S28151. $12.95.
Disney, USA, 1937-52, 22 mins.

Disney Cartoon Classics: Here's Donald/Here's Goofy
Both programs on one video disc.
Laser: LD75626. $24.95.
Disney, USA, 1937-53, 55 mins.

Disney Cartoon Classics: Here's Mickey/Here's Pluto
Both programs on one video disc.
Laser: LD75625. $24.95.
Disney, USA, 1935-47, 55 mins.

A Disney Christmas Gift
Contains a collection of animated sequences from great Disney classics, including *Peter Pan, The Sword in the Stone* and *Cinderella*.
Laser: LD75628. $24.95.
Disney, USA, 47 mins.

Disney Love Tales
Three titles: *Mickey's Delayed Date* ('47), *Pluto's Heart Throb* ('50) and *Mr. Duck Steps Out* ('40).
VHS: S27361. $12.95.
Disney, USA, 1940-50, 25 mins.

The Disney Primitive Collection: Alice
Between 1925 and 1927, Disney released a series of silent shorts with the adorable character, Alice. Includes *Alice in the Jungle, Alice Jailbird, Alice Orphan, Alice Rattled by Rats, Alice the Toreador, Alice's Tin Pony, Alice Solves a Puzzle, Alice Chop Suey* and *Alice's Eggplant*. 70 mins.
VHS: S16263. $29.95.

Disney Sing-Alongs
Sing along to classic Disney tunes with these captioned clips from famous Disney cartoons.
VHS: S03049. $14.95.

Disney's Sing-Along Songs: Zip-A-Dee-Doo-Dah.

VHS: S03049. $14.95.

Disney Sweetheart Stories

Mickey and Minnie Mouse reminisce about the most cherished moments from their animated romance. Donald Duck and Pluto join in the fun. Included are *Mickey's Rival*, *In Dutch* and *Nifty Nineties*. 23 mins.

VHS: S27360. $12.99.

Disney's Beginnings

Eight early Disney efforts, some from his days in Kansas City from his first company, called Laugh-O-Grams, the remainder done in Hollywood from the series known as Alice in Cartoonland. Includes *Mechanical Cow*, *Alice Rattled by Rats* and *Great Guns*.

VHS: S00347. $24.95.

Walt Disney, USA, 1920-27, 55 mins.

Disney's Sing-Along Songs Vol. 1: Heigh Ho

Heigh-Ho; The Dwarfs Yodel Song; Up, Down and Touch the Ground; Hi Diddle Dee Dee; Yo Ho; A Cowboy Needs a Horse; The Three Caballeros; Theme from Zorro; The Siamese Cat Song and *Let's Go Fly a Kite*.

VHS: S03038. $12.95.

Disney, USA, 28 mins.

Disney's Sing-Along Songs Vol. 2: Zip-A-Dee-Doo-Dah

Songs from *Peter Pan, Cinderella, Song of the South* and more.

VHS: S28159. $12.95.

Disney, USA, 26 mins.

Disney's Sing-Along Songs Vol. 3: You Can Fly!

Songs from *Peter Pan, Lady & The Tramp, The Jungle Book, Bedknobs & Broomsticks* and more.

VHS: S28160. $12.95.

Disney, USA, 28 mins.

Disney's Sing-Along Songs Vol. 4: The Bare Necessities

Songs from *The Bare Necessities, The Aristocats, Dumbo, The Jungle Book, Cinderella* and more.

VHS: S28162. $12.95.
Laser: LD75620. $49.95.

Disney, USA, 27 mins.

Disney's Sing-Along Songs Vol. 5: Fun with Music

Songs from *Oliver & Company, Snow White, Alice in Wonderland* and more.

VHS: S28163. $12.95.

Disney, USA, 28 mins.

Disney's Sing-Along Songs Vol. 6: Under the Sea

Ludwig Von Drake introduces a collection of songs and scenes from *Peter Pan, The Rescuers, The Little Mermaid* and many others. Sebastian the Crab teaches the lyrics to *Under The Sea* and *Kiss the Girl*.

VHS: S28164. $12.95.

Disney, USA, 28 mins.

Disney's Sing-Along Songs Vol. 7: Disneyland Fun

A musical day at Disneyland with Mr. Owl. See Mickey & Minnie bustle behind the scenes at the park, ride Star Tours, Splash Mountain and the Matterhorn as you sing along to 12 Disney tunes.

VHS: S28165. $12.95.

Disney, USA, 29 mins.

Disney's Sing-Along Songs Vol. 8: Merry Christmas Songs

From All of Us to All of You, Deck the Halls, Jingle Bells, Joy to the World, Up on the Housetop, Let It Snow, Sleigh Ride, Parade of the Wooden Soldiers, Winter Wonderland, Here Comes Santa Claus, Rudolph the Red-Nosed Reindeer, Silent Night and *We Wish You a Merry Christmas*.

VHS: S28166. $12.95.

Disney, USA, 27 mins.

Disney's Sing-Along Songs Vol. 9: I Love to Laugh

I Love to Laugh, Supercalifragilistic-expialodocius, Oo-De-Lally, Who's Afraid of the Big Bad Wolf, Pink Elephants on Parade and five other songs.

VHS: S28167. $12.95.

Disney, USA, 30 mins.

Disney's Sing-Along Songs Vol. 10: Be Our Guest

Includes *Be Our Guest* and many others.

VHS: S28168. $12.95.

Disney, USA, 29 mins.

Disney's Sing-Along Songs Vol. 11: Friend Like Me

Includes *Friend Like Me* and *A Whole New World*, along with many others.

VHS: S28169. $12.95.

Disney, USA, 1993, 30 mins.

Disney's Sing-Along Songs Vol. 12: 12 Days of Christmas

VHS: S28170. $12.95.

Disney, USA, 30 mins.

Disney's Sing-Along Songs: Be Our Guest/Fun with Music

Tape volumes 5 & 10 on one video disc.

Laser: LD75662. $24.95.

Disney, USA, 56 mins.

Disney's Sing-Along Songs: Circle of Life (Lion King)

Songs include *Circle of Life, Part of Your World, Prince Ali, I Just Can't Wait to Be King, Belle, Everybody Wants to Be a Cat* and *When You Wish upon a Star*.

VHS: S22984. $12.95.
Laser: LD75850. $24.95.

Disney, USA, 1994, 30 mins.

Disney's Sing-Along Songs: Colors of the Wind (Pocahontas)

Featuring musical numbers from Disney features, with lyrics appearing on screen.

VHS: S29628. $12.95.
Laser: LD75852. $29.95.

Disney, USA, 1995, 30 mins.

Disney's Sing-Along Songs: Friend Like Me/Disneyland Fun

Tape volumes 7 & 11 on one video disc.

Laser: LD75663. $24.95.

Disney, USA, 60 mins.

Disney's Sing-Along Songs: Pongo & Perdita

More sing-along songs, featuring the new live-action 101 Dalmatians movie.

VHS: S30359. $12.95.

Disney, USA, 1996, 30 mins.

Disney's Sing-Along Songs: The Bare Neccessities/You Can Fly

Tape volumes 3 & 4 on one video disc.

Laser: LD75629. $24.95.

Disney, USA, 56 mins.

Disney's Sing-Along Songs: Topsy Turvy (Hunchback)

Featuring musical numbers from Disney features, with lyrics appearing on screen.

VHS: S29627. $12.95.
Laser: LD75851. $29.95.

Disney, USA, 1996, 30 mins.

Disney's Sing-Along Songs: Under the Sea/I Love to Laugh

Tape volumes 6 & 9 on one video disc.

Laser: LD75660. $24.95.

Disney, USA, 56 mins.

Disney's Sing-Along Songs: Zip-A-Dee-Doo-Dah/Heigh Ho

Tape volumes 1 & 2 on one video disc.

Laser: LD75661. $24.95.

Disney, USA, 54 mins.

Donald in Mathmagic Land

Donald stars as a kind of modern Alice in Wonderland as he explores the mysterious world of math. A very popular educational short directed by Hamilton Luske.

VHS: S06593. $12.95.

Disney, USA, 1959, 27 mins.

Dumbo

Disney's shortest animated feature is in many ways one of the best. With luck, determination and the help of Timothy Mouse, the clumsy baby elephant becomes the flying star of the circus. Especially loved by animation fans for the sequence where a drunken Dumbo experiences the D.T.'s.

Laser: LD75856. $36.95.
Laser: CAV. LD70959. $49.95.

Disney, USA, 1941, 63 mins.

Fantasia

The magic of Disney animation is gloriously blended with the music of eight classical pieces conducted by Leopold Stokowski. Relive those memorable moments with dancing mushrooms and hippos, dinosaurs, demons, abstract shapes, centaurs, and a certain sorcerer's apprentice who Walt felt needed a career boost.

VHS: S14755. $24.99.

USA, 1940, 116 mins.

Fun and Fancy Free

This is a great film for fans of classic Disney animation. Like Disney's later *Ichabod and Mr. Toad* (1949), this film essentially contains two stories linked together with some delightful Jiminy Cricket animation and Edgar Bergen and Charlie McCarthy technicolor footage. But the main thing here is *Bongo*, the story of a circus bear who finds adventure in the forest, and *Mickey and the Beanstalk*, a classic Mickey, Donald and Goofy adventure. The print quality is superb and a nice "making of" short is attached at the end. These package films are a lot of fun and one hopes Disney will next release *Make Mine Music* and *Melody Time*.

VHS: S31508. $26.95.
Laser: LD72467. $49.95.

Disney, USA, 1947, 73 mins.

Gargoyles: The Movie

Inspired by the success of the *Batman* animated series is this new Disney TV series. *Gargoyles* shows the origins of Gargoyle leader Goliath, along with his loyal followers. Frozen in stone for 1000 years, they awaken in modern Manhattan and confront the criminal mastermind Xanatos and the fallen Gargoyle Demona.

VHS: S29638. $19.95.
Laser: LD75859. $29.95.

Disney, USA, 1994, 80 mins.

A Goofy Movie

Goofy takes his teenage son Max on a cross-country trip to try to regain the closeness they once felt. Despite his dad's relentless klutziness, Max eventually learns to appreciate him, in this heavily sentimental story. Songs by Tevin Campbell.

VHS: S29639. $24.95.
Laser: LD75860. $29.95.

Disney, USA, 1995, 78 mins.

Great Expectations

For the first time, Disney tackles Dickens. Bound to have family appeal, this is an award-winning adaptation of Dickens' masterpiece with a strong cast, including Jean Simmons, Anthony Hopkins and John Rhys-Davies.

VHS: S13016. $49.95.

Heavyweights

Camp Hope is place for overweight kids to get lean and mean. Disney finds in this comic situation a story that gets to the lighter side of feeling left out as a kid. The out-of-shape youngsters manage to change their hard-edged fitness guru (Ben Stiller) and even have fun at summer camp.

VHS: S27537. $14.99.

Steven Brill, USA, 1994, 97 mins.

Heidi

Johanna Spyri's beloved novel about a young girl in the Alps is beautifully realized in this Disney adaptation. Jason Robards, Jane Seymour, Patricia Neal and Noley Thornton as Heidi are all featured in this new version, shot in Austria, of the children's classic.

VHS: S21867. $19.99.

Michael Rhodes, USA, 1993, 167 mins.

Hercules
Disney's animated romp through the magical world of mythology features the vocal talents of Tate Donovan, James Woods, Danny DeVito, Rip Torn, Charlton Heston, Bobcat Goldthwaite and Susan Egan.
VHS: S33347. $26.95.
John Musker/Ron Clements, USA, 1997, 92 mins.

High-Flying Hero
Disney's heroic new adventurer—Launchpad McQuack —finds his courage put to the test in *Hero for Hire* in which the Beagle Boys trick him into performing good deeds that turn out to be crimes, and in *Launchpad's Civil War*, his participation in an annual Civil War pageant explodes into pandemonium. 44 mins.
VHS: S06596. $14.95.

The Hunchback of Notre Dame
Disney's take on the story of Quasimodo is given the usual Broadway musical treatment, but the design, animation and voice acting are all quite excellent. Featuring Kevin Kline, Demi Moore, Jason Alexander, Tom Hulce and David Ogden Stiers.
VHS: S30821. $26.95.
Disney, USA, 1996, 91 mins.

The Incredible Journey
Accidentally left behind when a family moves away, three pets find themselves stranded and alone. This Disney classic charts the perilous journey faced by these animals as they make their way across the Canadian wilderness to their new home.
VHS: S21864. $19.99.
Fletcher Markle, USA, 1963, 80 mins.

Jiminy Cricket's Christmas
Join your host Jiminy Cricket for this all-star musical salute to the Christmas season. Includes scenes from Disney classics featuring such songs as "The Dwarf's Yodel Song," "I've Got No Strings" and "When You Wish upon a Star." Also includes *Mickey's Good Deed* (1932).
VHS: S28315. $12.95.
Laser: LD75683. $24.95.
Disney, USA, 47 mins.

The Jungle Book (1967)
Digitally remastered 30th-anniversary edition. The classic animated musical based on Kipling's story of Mowgli, an Indian boy who is raised as a wolf cub and later returned to his people. Voices of Phil Harris, Sebastian Cabot, Louis Prima, George Sanders and others. Includes a "making of" program.
VHS: S32313. $26.95.
Laser: CAV. **LD76404. $49.99.**
Laser: CLV. **LD76383. $29.99.**
Disney, USA, 1967, 78 mins.

The Jungle Book (1994)
Jason Scott Lee, Sam Neil, Cary Elwes and John Cleese are featured in this Disney live-action remake of Rudyard Kipling's adventure. A youngster lives in the jungle with wild animals as his best friends until the presence of civilization and his own human nature challenge this idyllic life.
VHS: S24773. $22.99.
Laser: Widescreen. **LD74956. $39.99.**
Stephen Sommers, USA, 1994, 111 mins.

The Legend of Sleepy Hollow
Disney's animated version of Washington Irving's classic ghost story. Narrated by Bing Crosby, who also sings the film's three songs.
VHS: S28326. $12.95.
Disney, USA, 1949, 45 mins.

The Lion King
Among the highest grossing films of all time, Disney's smash-hit feature is the story of little Simba, who must learn to grow up and take his place in the Great Circle of Life. The all-original story features great vocal performances by James Earl Jones, Whoopi Goldberg and Jeremy Irons. Directed by Roger Allers and Rob Minkoff.
VHS: S23053. $24.95.
Disney, USA, 1994

Little Mermaid, The
Ron Clements and John Musker directed this smash hit musical feature. The film is the first of the new generation of Disney animated features that have restored the studio's absolute dominance of the art form. Available on video again for a limited time, *Mermaid* has been the most-requested film by video collectors since its first release in 1990. THX.
VHS: S33372. $26.95.
Disney, USA, 1989, 82 mins.

Man of the House
In this Disney comedy, 12-year-old Ben (Jonathan Taylor Thomas) rebels when his mother (Farrah Fawcett) falls for a new man (Chevy Chase). Even though the boy was abandoned by his real father six years before, he is determined to thwart his mother's romance. Comic anarchy reigns as his plan to drive away his mother's suitor misfires.
VHS: S27536. $14.99.
James Orr, USA, 1995, 96 mins.

The Many Adventures of Winnie the Pooh
Disney's 22nd animated feature is a compilation of three featurettes: *Winnie the Pooh and the Honey Tree* (1966), *Winnie the Pooh and the Blustery Day* (1968) and *Winnie the Pooh and Tigger Too* (1974), which were released theatrically as a package in 1977. This is the first time these films have been released on video in their originally packaged theatrical format. Also includes a "Making of" program.
VHS: S27480. $26.95.
Laser: LD75513. $29.99.
Disney, USA, 1977, 74 mins.

Mary Poppins
Disney first conceived it as an animated feature, later turning it into a combination of live action and animation.
VHS: S01589. $24.95.
Laser: LD71132. $44.95.
Disney, USA, 1964, 110 mins.

Melody Time
While several of its segments have been released as featurettes, this marks the first time that this musical compilation has been seen in its original 1948 theatrical version. The best of the three Disney compilation "features," *Melody Time* includes seven animated segments: *Johnny Appleseed*, sung by Dennis Day; *Little Toot*, sung by The Andrews Sisters; *Blame It on the Samba*, with Donald Duck and Joe Carioca; *Pecos Bill*, told and sung by Roy Rogers; *Once upon a Wintertime, Bumble Boogie* and *Trees*.
VHS: S34881. $22.95.
Disney, USA, 1948, 75 mins.

Mickey & The Beanstalk
Part of *Fun & Fancy Free*, this special tells of the adventures of Mickey, Donald & Goofy with Willie the Giant.
VHS: S06592. $12.95.
Disney, USA, 1947, 25 mins.

Mickey & The Beanstalk/ Reluctant Dragon
Both programs on one video disc.
Laser: LD75906. $36.95.
Disney, USA, 57 mins.

Mickey Loves Minnie
Disney's Mickey and Minnie Mouse join Donald and Daisy Duck, Pluto and Fifi for love, laughter and romance. *Society Dog Show, Donald's Double Trouble* and *The Brave Little Tailor* are included. 25 mins.
VHS: S27359. $12.99.

Mickey Mouse: The Black & White Years
Five-disc CAV laserdisc boxed set of the black-and-white Mickey Mouse cartoons. This collection contains 34 newly restored and remastered vintage shorts, many unseen in over 60 years. In addition, bonus supplemental materials include animator's story sketches, rare B&W pencil tests, and Mickey's first appearance in color—a recently rediscovered short specially done for the 1932 Academy Awards, unseen for 60 years. Thirty-three titles: 1928: *Steamboat Willie*. 1929: *Gallopin' Gaucho, Plane Crazy, Mickey's Follies.* 1930: *Fire Fighters, The Chain Gang, Gorilla Mystery, Pioneer Days*. 1931: *Birthday Party, Mickey Steps Out, Blue Rhythm, Mickey Cuts Up, Mickey's Orphans*. 1932: *Duck Hunt, Mickey's Revue, Mickey's Nightmare, The Whoopee Party, Touchdown Mickey, The Klondike Kid*. 1933: *Building a Building, The Mad Doctor, Ye Olden Days, The Mail Pilot, Mickey's Gala Premiere, Puppy Love, The Pet Store, Giant Land*. 1934: Camping Out, Gulliver Mickey, Orphan's Benefit, The Dog Napper, Two Gun Mickey. 1935: *Mickey's Service Station*.
Laser: LD75693. $124.95.
Disney, USA, 1928-35, 256 mins.

Mickey's Christmas Carol
Dickens' tale is retold with Mickey as Bob Cratchit and Scrooge McDuck as Mr. Scrooge. The first new Mickey Mouse short in 30 years.
VHS: S28350. $12.95.
Laser: LD75692. $24.95.
Disney, USA, 1983, 25 mins.

Mickey's Fun Songs: Beach Party
VHS: S28672. $12.95.
Disney, USA, 30 mins.

Mickey's Fun Songs: Campout
VHS: S28673. $12.95.
Disney, USA, 30 mins.

Mickey's Fun Songs: Circus
VHS: S28674. $12.95.
Disney, USA, 30 mins.

Mighty Ducks: The Movie: The First Face-Off
Featuring the voice talents of Ian Ziering, Dennis Franz and Jim Belushi, this is the first animated program from *The Mighty Ducks* TV series, about some serious hockey quacks.
VHS: S30930. $14.95.
Disney, USA, 1996, 66 mins.

Mr. Toad's Wild Ride
Monty Python meets Walt Disney in this wonderful tale that will delight kids and adults alike. Based on the Kenneth Grahame children's novel *The Wind in the Willows*, *Mr. Toad's Wild Ride* sends Mr. Toad, Rat and Mole on an exciting journey filled with fun and misadventure. Starring Pythoners John Cleese, Eric Idle, Terry Jones and Michael Palin. 88 mins.
Laser: LD76353. $39.99.

Old Yeller— 40th Anniversary Limited Edition
Disney's classic boy-and-his-dog film is presented in this special, fully restored, 40th-anniversary edition. With Chuck Connors. "Still one of the best!" (Leonard Maltin).
VHS: S32290. $19.95.
Laser: THX. **LD76379. $29.99.**
Robert Stevenson, USA, 1957, 84 mins.

Oliver & Company
Loosely based on the themes of *Oliver Twist*, this feature marked the beginning of Disney's one-per-year animated feature film output, and just under 11 minutes contain computer-assisted animation. Cute little kitten Oliver makes friends with the street-mutt Dodger and his gang of scavengers. Their heartless human master, Fagin, orchestrates a ransom scheme involving a rich girl, but all turns out for the best eventually. Voices of Billy Joel, Cheech Marin and Bette Midler.
VHS: S29886. $26.95.
Disney, USA, 1988, 72 mins.

Oliver Twist
Richard Dreyfuss stars as Fagin, Elijah Wood (*The Ice Storm*) as The Artful Dodger, and Alex Trench as Oliver in this Disney adaptation of the Dickens classic about a poor orphan boy who befriends a neighborhood thief and is thrown into the tough and colorful world of 19th-century London as he searches for his real family. 92 mins.
VHS: S33278. $19.99.
Tony Bill, USA, 1997, 89 mins.

Paul Bunyan
Vividly animated in a clear, simple style, Disney's take on the legend of Paul Bunyan and Babe the blue ox is a fine example of the stylistic experimentation happening at Disney in the late 1950s. Directed by Les Clark. Also on this tape: *Little Hiawatha* ('37, Silly Symphony).
VHS: S28680. $12.95.
Disney, USA, 1958, 25 mins.

Pete's Dragon
As the one and only friend of a young orphan named Pete, Elliot the dragon can also be a big problem. When the town tries to capture Elliot, the dragon's ability to breath fire could well save the day, in this mix of live action and animation.
VHS: S01590. $24.95.
Laser: LD75701. $39.95.
Disney, USA, 1977, 128 mins.

Peter Pan
Disney's *Peter Pan* is back on video again for a limited time, remastered in THX and including a "making of" featurette.
VHS: S33373. $26.95.
Disney, USA, 1953, 76 mins.

Pocahontas
Disney's beautifully animated feature retells the love story of John Smith and the beautiful Indian princess Pocahontas. Featuring the hit soundtrack of Alan Menken and Stephen Schwartz.
VHS: S26928. $26.95.
Laser: LD75876. $29.95.
Disney, USA, 1995, 82 mins.

Pocahontas Special Edition
The deluxe CAV laserdisc includes a "Making of" documentary, deleted musical numbers, running audio commentary by all the principal creative people, character designs, conceptual art and much more.
Laser: LD75877. $99.95.
Disney, USA, 1995, 82 mins.

Pooh's Grand Adventure
Picking up where Walt Disney's 22nd masterpiece—made 20 years ago—left off, Pooh and friends set off on a grand journey through the great unknown to rescue Christopher Robin.
VHS: S31861. $24.99.
Karl Geurs, USA, 1997, 70 mins.

Prince & The Pauper/ Willie/Peter & The Wolf

Seven titles: *Prince & The Pauper, Willie The Operatic Whale, Peter & The Wolf, Ferdinand the Bull, Lambert the Sheepish Lion, Music Land* and *Symphony Hour*. Side One is CAV.
Laser: LD75705. $29.95.
Disney, USA, 75 mins.

The Reluctant Dragon

A remarkable live-action/animation featurette directed by Alfred Werker. A dragon would much rather sit around sipping tea, reciting pun-ny poetry and singing songs until a young boy and a reknowned dragon-fighter team up to teach him ferociousness. This tape includes just the animated portion. Also includes *Morris the Midget Moose*.
VHS: S03040. $12.95.
Disney, USA, 1941, 28 mins.

The Rescuers

Bob Newhart provides the voice of Bernard and Eva Gabor is Miss Bianca in this charming feature set in the Southern swamps. The two mice set out to recue young Penny from the evil Mme. Medusa.
VHS: S35064. $26.95.
Disney, USA, 1977, 77 mins.

The Return of Jafar

Disney's first major made-for-video movie, featuring five new songs. The story picks up where *Aladdin* left off, with all the major characters returning. Noticeably absent is Robin Williams as the voice of the Genie.
VHS: S29048. $19.95.
Laser: LD75706. $29.95.
Disney, USA, 1994, 66 mins.

Robin Hood

Following on the success of *Jungle Book*, Disney came out with this feature directed by Woolie Reitherman. Robin Hood (a fox) and Little John (a bear) combine cunning and ingenuity to defeat the villainous Prince John (a lion) and the slimy Sir Hiss (a snake).
VHS: S02183. $24.95.
Laser: LD75707. $29.95.
Laser: CAV. **LD75708. $39.95.**
Disney, USA, 1973, 83 mins.

The Shaggy D.A.

In this fun sequel to Disney's *The Shaggy Dog*, Wilby Daniels' career goes to the dogs as he fears the unleashing of his doggy doppelganger during a run for District Attorney. With Dean Jones, Tim Conway, Suzanne Pleshette and Keenan Wynn.
VHS: S32312. $19.95.
Laser: LD76380. $29.99.
Robert Stevenson, USA, 1976, 90 mins.

The Shaggy Dog

Magical words spoken from the inscription of an ancient ring turn young Wilby Daniels into a shaggy pooch leading to canine high jinks in this classic Disney shaggy dog story starring Fred MacMurray.
VHS: S32311. $19.95.
Charles Barton, USA, 1959, 101 mins.

Sleeping Beauty

Aurora, daughter of the good King Stephen, falls victim to an evil spell that puts her to sleep. Only a loving kiss will awaken her.
VHS: S31509. $26.95.
Laser: CAV, THX. **LD72468. $99.99.**
Laser: CLV, THX. **LD72469. $29.99.**
Disney, USA, 1959, 75 mins.

Snow White and the Seven Dwarfs

Walt Disney's masterpiece tells the unforgettable story of a young woman who dreams of meeting Prince Charming but is foiled by a jealous woman. Of course she is helped in her struggle with this evil witch by those charming little people, the seven dwarfs.
VHS: S21316. $26.99.
Walt Disney, USA, 1937, 83 mins.

So Dear to My Heart

This live-action and animation feature stars Burl Ives, telling a story of a determined young country boy and his mischievous black lamb. While daydreaming of winning a blue ribbon at the county fair, Jeremiah's scrapbook comes to life with delightful animated sequences.
VHS: S29704. $24.95.
Laser: LD75883. $36.95.
Disney, USA, 1949, 82 mins.

The Spirit of Mickey

A new collection of classic Mickey Mouse shorts featuring 11 cartoons: *The Band Concert* (1935), *Thru the Mirror* (1936), *Lend a Paw* (1941), *Orphan's Picnic* (1936), *The Worm Turns* (1937), *Mickey's Surprise Party* (1939), *Mickey and the Seal* (1948), *Mickey's Trailer* (1938), *Canine Caddy* (1941), *Mr. Mouse Takes a Trip* (1940) and *Steamboat Willie* (1928).
VHS: S34855. $22.95.
Disney, USA, 1928-48, 90 mins.

Squanto: A Warrior's Tale

Based on the true story of Squanto, the Native American who was kidnapped by 17th-century English settlers. Transported back to Plymouth, he escaped and found refuge in a monastery. Eventually he returned home and fostered peace between the English and his tribe, culminating in the first Thanksgiving.
VHS: S27538. $14.99.
Xavier Koller, USA, 1993, 101 mins.

The Sword in the Stone

A young scullery boy named Wart is taught amazing lessons by Merlin, who turns him into a fish, a bird and a squirrel so that he might understand the mysteries of life. These lessons help him remove the enchanted sword from the stone to be crowned Arthur, King of England.
Laser: LD75884. $36.95.
Laser: CAV. **LD74999. $49.95.**
Disney, USA, 1963, 79 mins.

That Darn Cat

Disney redoes Disney in this remake of the classic about a teenager (Christina Ricci, *The Addams Family*) whose boredom with her sleepy hometown disappears when her tomcat D.C. (Darn Cat) delivers an important clue in a mysterious kidnapping. She teams up with a rookie FBI agent (Doug E. Doug, *Cool Runnings*), leading to goofy entanglements and misunderstandings.
VHS: S31698. $103.99.
Laser: LD76293. $39.99.
Bob Spiers, USA, 1997, 89 mins.

The Three Caballeros

Starring Donald Duck, Jose Carioca and Panchito, this combination of live action and animation was made as a companion piece to *Saludos Amigos*, a goodwill gesture by Disney toward our South American allies. Donald celebrates his birthday down south, opening a wondrous collection of gifts that evolve into musical journeys with a Latin beat. Three titles: *Baja, The Cold-Blooded Penguin* and *The Flying Gauchito*.
VHS: S07527. $24.95.
Laser: LD75885. $36.95.
Disney, USA, 1944, 71 mins.

Three Caballeros/Saludos Amigos LD

This special Archive Edition CAV laserdisc set also includes the *Saludos Amigos* feature that has never before been released on home video.
Laser: LD75886. $99.95.
Disney, USA, 1942/44, 120 mins.

Three Little Pigs

On this latest compilation are found the Oscar-winning *Three Little Pigs* and two "sequels" from the Silly Symphonies series. All three cartoons are mastered from the original United Artists prints. In *Three Little Pigs* ('33, Oscar Winner) the Big Bad Wolf is only thwarted by the hardworking pig's house of bricks. In *The Big Bad Wolf* ('34, Silly Symphony) Little Red Riding Hood is rescued not by the woodsman, but by our well-prepared third pig. In *Three Little Wolves* ('36, Silly Symphony) the two silly pigs stand in for The Boy Who Cried Wolf and must once again be rescued by the earnest third pig.
VHS: S30490. $12.95.
Laser: Also contains the cartoons on 'Disney's Favorite Stories: Paul Bunyan.' **LD76014. $24.95.**
Disney, USA, 1933-36, 28 mins.

Timon and Pumbaa's Wild Adventures: Don't Get Mad, Get Happy

The animated episode *Yosemite Remedy* finds the meerkat/warthog duo frustrated by a cop who cannot capture a thief. In *Kenya Be My Friend*, the pair celebrate their friendship, but almost spoil their bond through a silly misunderstanding. 31 mins.
VHS: S29534. $12.99.

Timon and Pumbaa's Wild Adventures: Live and Learn

Disney's famous meerkat and warthog duo are featured in two delightful animated shorts on this video. *Law of the Jungle* finds Timon avoiding jail for using a forbidden stick to scratch himself. Then Timon's friendship with a pachyderm in *Uganda Be an Elephant* provokes an identity crisis in Pumbaa. 34 mins.
VHS: S29532. $12.99.

Timon and Pumbaa's Wild Adventures: Quit Buggin' Me

Timon and Pubaa are besides themselves in *Frantic Atlantic* because they cannot find ants to eat in Antarctica. Then the two are off on a chocolate-drenched adventure to Switzerland in *Swiss Missed*. 29 mins.
VHS: S29533. $12.99.

Tom and Huck

Disney is behind this updated film version of Mark Twain's classic novel *The Adventures of Tom Sawyer*. After witnessing a murder Tom and Huck must leave town to evade the perpetrator. Fortunately, there is a map for buried treasure in this tale, giving the boys a perfect entree to adventure.
VHS: S27640. $19.99.
Laser: LD75573. $29.99.
Peter Hewitt, USA, 1995, 91 mins.

Toy Story

John Lasseter's talents as an animator make this film work, and Pixar's expertise with computer animation gives it a stunning look—together they have created a real knockout of a movie. When Andy's favorite toy, Woody, is forced to compete for his attention with the glamorous Buzz Lightyear, a comic adventure ensues. Voicework by Tim Allen and Tom Hanks is superb, and the supporting cast of characters and voice actors all contribute great performances.
VHS: S29809. $26.95.
Laser: LD75989. $29.95.
Pixar/Disney, USA, 1995, 81 mins.

Toy Story Deluxe Collector's Edition

The deluxe edition contains the videocassette of the movie, a bonus video, *The Story Behind Disney's Toy Story*, a special collector's edition book, *The Art of Disney's Toy Story* and a one-of-a-kind, 3-D lenticular artwork.
VHS: S30018. $79.95.
Laser: LD75985. $124.95.
Pixar/Disney, USA, 1995, 81 mins.

A Walt Disney Christmas

Six titles: *Once upon a Wintertime* ('48, from Melody Time), *Santa's Workshop* ('32), *The Night Before Christmas* ('33), *Pluto's Christmas Tree* ('52), *Donald's Snow Fight* ('42) and *On Ice* ('35).
Laser: LD75894. $24.95.
Disney, USA, 1932-52, 46 mins.

Willie, The Operatic Whale

Originally titled *The Whale Who Wanted to Sing at the Met*, from Make Mine Music ('46), this wonderful short is sung and narrated by Nelson Eddy. Also on this tape: *Ferdinand the Bull* ('38) and *Lambert, The Sheepish Lion* ('52).
VHS: S14549. $12.95.
Disney, USA, 1946, 25 mins.

The Wind in the Willows

J. Thaddeus Toad's mania for motorcars drives his pals Moley, Rat and Angus MacBadger into a frenzy.
VHS: S01464. $12.95.
Disney, USA, 1949, 34 mins.

Winnie the Pooh & A Day for Eeyore

Pooh tries hard to make Eeyore feel better when everyone forgets his birthday.
VHS: S03039. $12.95.
Disney, USA, 1983, 25 mins.

Winnie the Pooh & Christmas Too

The stubby little bear forgets to deliver the gang's wish list to Santa, so he and Piglet dress up as Santa and a reindeer to deliver everyone's gifts. Despite his efforts, it's Christopher Robin who saves the day.
VHS: S29774. $14.95.
Disney, USA, 1991, 38 mins.

Winnie the Pooh & The Blustery Day

This second Pooh featurette won the Oscar in 1968. A storm descends on Hundred Acre Wood so terrible it washes Pooh away.
VHS: S03042. $12.95.
Disney, USA, 1968, 24 mins.

Winnie the Pooh & The Honey Tree

The first of four Pooh featurettes. Pooh eats so much honey he gets himself wedged in his doorway.
VHS: S03041. $12.95.
Disney, USA, 1966, 25 mins.

Winnie the Pooh & Tigger Too

Pooh's third featurette. Tigger's enthusiastic greetings lead Pooh to try and 'unbounce' him.
VHS: S03043. $12.95.
Disney, USA, 1974, 25 mins.

TV ANIMATION

AaaHH!!! Real Monsters: Meet the Monsters

Four episodes about three young monsters who live beneath the city dump. As students in one of the world's elite monster academies, they learn to scare the daylights out of people.
VHS: S27783. $9.95.
Klasky-Csupo, USA, 1997, 58 mins.

AaaHH!!! Real Monsters: Monsters' Night Out

Four episodes about three young monsters—Ickis, Krumm and Oblina.
VHS: S32443. $9.95.
Klasky-Csupo, USA, 1997, 57 mins.

Aeon Flux

Aeon Flux charges through a futuristic landscape full of hidden motives, ominous machines and deceptive appearances. Constantly chancing death and traveling between two battling nations, she is locked in surreal combat with Trevor Goodchild, her lover and sworn enemy. Four full-length episodes, plus the original shorts from *Liquid Television*. Stereo.
VHS: S27616. $14.95.
Peter Chung, USA, 1990-92, 120 mins.

Aeon Flux: Mission Infinite

Three episodes of Peter Chung's stylish and haunting MTV animated series. In *Reraizure*, a strange, illicit trade in an amnesia drug extracted from alien Nargyles leads Aeon to a confontation with Trevor. In *Chronophasia*, Aeon catches a deadly engineered virus that causes insanity, and comes up against a mutant killer baby. In *End Sinister*, bizarre humanoid aliens land on Earth…or are they highly evolved humans from the future? Stereo.
VHS: S31035. $14.95.
Peter Chung, USA, 1996, 75 mins.

Aeon Flux: Operative Terminus

Whether investigating the mysterious disappearance of former Breen leader Clavious, trying to rid Earth of the influence of a powerful God-like being or attempting to liberate a scientist held against his will, independent operative Aeon Flux uses her skill and hardware to uncover the truth. Always at the heart of her plight is the dashing but disturbed Trevor Goodchild. Will the nimble Aeon resist his charms and expose him or will she fall prey to his secret intentions? Includes *Utopia or Deuteronpia*, *The Demiurge* and *Ether Drift Theory*. 75 mins.
VHS: S33035. $14.95.

Beavis and Butt-Head Do America

The doltish duo star in a feature-length film about their road trip across America. It grossed $62 million at the box office.
VHS: S31388. $19.95.
USA, 1996, 90 mins.

Beavis and Butt-Head Do Christmas

Tis the season to get stupid, as Beavis and Butt-Head star in their own twisted versions of two holiday classics. In *Hub Hub Humbug*, the Ghosts of Christmas Past, Present and Future struggle to reach a Scrooge-like Beavis. In *It's a Miserable Life*, Charlie the Angel comes down from Heaven to show Butt-Head how much better life would be without him.
VHS: S28499. $14.95.
MTV, USA, 1996, 40 mins.

Beavis and Butt-Head: Chicks 'n' Stuff

VHS: S26303. $14.95.
USA

Beavis and Butt-Head: Feel Our Pain

VHS: S27532. $14.95.
MTV, USA, 1994, 50 mins.

Beavis and Butt-Head: Innocence Lost

VHS: S31537. $14.95.
MTV, USA, 50 mins.

Beavis and Butt-Head: Law-Abiding Citizens

Stereo.
VHS: S31481. $14.95.
MTV, USA, 50 mins.

Beavis and Butt-Head: The Final Judgement

VHS: S25886. $14.95.
USA

Beavis and Butt-Head: There Goes the Neighborhood

No music videos. No commercials. Just eight episodes featuring Beavis and Butt-Head's most victimized neighbor, Tom Anderson: *Home Improvement, Lawn and Garden, Good Credit, Washing the Dog, Vs. the Vending Machine, Mr. Anderson's Balls, Pool Toys* and *The Trial*.
VHS: S23747. $14.95.
MTV, USA, 1994, 45 mins.

Beavis and Butt-Head: Work Sucks!

No music videos. No commercials. Just eight episodes featuring Beavis and Butt-Head's days at Burger World and their numerous get-rich-quick schemes: *Burger World, Customers Suck, The Butt-Head Experience, Be All You Can Be, Cleaning House, Sperm Bank, Blackout* and *Closing Time*.
VHS: S23746. $14.95.
MTV, USA, 1994, 45 mins.

The Best of Liquid Television

Forty-five minutes of the bizarre, inventive and award-winning animation featured on MTV's *Liquid Television* showcase. Four installments of Peter Chung's stylish *Aeon Flux* series, two episodes of Jim Matison's *Crazy Daisy Ed*, three episodes of Robin Steele's minimalist *Stick Figure Theatre, Uncle Louie's Travels* (Denis Morela), *Dr. Zum Explains…* (George Evelyn), *The Dangwoods: Nightmare in Trailer City* (Michael Dougan), *The Big City* (Ed Bell), *One Less Ant* (Kevin Lofton) and *Smart Talk with Raisin* (John R Dilworth).
VHS: S23748. $12.95.
USA, 1994, 45 mins.

The Best of the Simpsons, Vol. 1

There's No Disgrace Like Home and *Life on the Fast Lane*. Plus a short from *The Tracey Ullman Show*.
VHS: S32447. $9.95.
Clasky-Csupo, USA, 50 mins.

The Best of the Simpsons, Vol. 2

Bart the General and *Moaning Lisa*. Plus a short from *The Tracey Ullman Show*.
VHS: S32448. $9.95.
Clasky-Csupo, USA, 50 mins.

The Best of the Simpsons, Vol. 3

The Crepes of Wrath and *Krusty Gets Busted*. Plus a short from *The Tracey Ullman Show*.
VHS: S32449. $9.95.
Clasky-Csupo, USA, 50 mins.

The Best of The Simpsons, Vol. 4

Tree House of Horror (Simpsons Halloween Special) and *Bart Gets an "F."* Plus a short from *The Tracey Ullman Show*.
VHS: S34850. $9.95.
Clasky-Csupo, USA, 50 mins.

The Best of The Simpsons, Vol. 5

Two Cars in Every Garage and Three Eyes on Every Fish and *Bart vs. Thanksgiving*. Plus a short from *The Tracey Ullman Show*.
VHS: S34851. $9.95.
Clasky-Csupo, USA, 50 mins.

The Best of The Simpsons, Vol. 6

Bart the Daredevil and *Itchy, Scratchy and Marge*. Plus a short from *The Tracey Ullman Show*.
VHS: S34852. $9.95.
Clasky-Csupo, USA, 50 mins.

The Best of The Simpsons, Vol. 7

Bart Gets Hit by a Car and *One Fish, Two Fish, Blowfish, Blue Fish*. Plus a short from *The Tracey Ullman Show*.
VHS: S34447. $9.95.
Clasky-Csupo, USA, 50 mins.

The Best of The Simpsons, Vol. 8

The Way We Was and *Homer vs. Lisa and the 8th Commandment*. Plus a short from *The Tracey Ullman Show*.
VHS: S34448. $9.95.
Clasky-Csupo, USA, 50 mins.

The Best of The Simpsons, Vol. 9

Three Men and a Comic Book and *Lisa's Substitute*. Plus a short from *The Tracey Ullman Show*.
VHS: S34449. $9.95.
Clasky-Csupo, USA, 50 mins.

The Best of the Simpsons, Vols. 1-3, 3-Pack

Volumes 1-3 in a collector's slipcase.
VHS: S32446. $24.95.
Clasky-Csupo, USA, 150 mins.

The Best of The Simpsons, Vols. 4-6 3-Pack

Volumes 4-6 in a collector's slipcase.
VHS: S34853. $24.95.
Clasky-Csupo, USA, 150 mins.

The Best of The Simpsons, Vols. 7-9 3-Pack

Volumes 7-9 in a collector's slipcase.
VHS: S34450. $24.95.
Clasky-Csupo, USA, 150 mins.

Bozo the Clown Vol. 1: Ding Dong Dandy Adventures

The original Bozo cartoons from the '50s, with new live-action bridges. Sixteen titles: *Square Shootin' Square, Little Naggin' Dragon, Car Thief Chief, Big Cake Bake, Show Biz Whiz, Manhunt Stunts, Broad Sword Discord, Big Boo Boo on a Fast Choo Choo, Lake Resort Sport, Big Dealer on a Stern Wheeler, Charter Service Nervous, Sidewalk Peddler's Meddler, Four Flusher Gusher, High Fly Rug Spy, Freeloader Railroader* and *Happy Gas Gasser*.
VHS: S27993. $29.95.
Larry Harmon, USA, 1958, 90 mins.

Bozo the Clown Vol. 2: Wowie Kazowie Clown Tales

Sixteen titles: *Glutton for Mutton, Papoose on the Loose, Bozo's Icy Escape, Hop Chest Quest, Dance of the Ants, Ballpark Lark, Pie in the Eye Guy, Real Gone Leprechaun, Food Pest Jest, Razzle Dazzle Castle Hassle, Gate Crasher Smasher, Whipper Snapper Snipper, Okey Dokey Hokey Pokey, Flim Flam for Ali Kablam, Kooky's Snack Attack* and *Mill Pond Thrill Chill*.
VHS: S27994. $29.95.
Laser: LD75599. $24.95.
Larry Harmon, USA, 1961, 90 mins.

Bozo the Clown Vol. 3: Just Keep Laughing

Nine titles: *Big Flop Train Hop, Eagle's Nest Pest, Fish Tanks Pranks, Teeny Weeny Meany, Chicken Burglar Bungler, Big Tree Spree, Ski Lodge Hodge Podge, Pie in the Eye Guy* and *Hurricane Belinda*.
VHS: S27995. $12.95.
Larry Harmon, USA, 1961, 60 mins.

Bozo the Clown Vol. 4: Crazy Clown Capers

VHS: S27996. $12.95.
Larry Harmon, USA, 1958, 60 mins.

Bugs Bunny's World of Animals

Laugh and learn about animals with Bugs Bunny and his friends, as great live-action animal footage combines with animated Looney Tunes characters. Each tape is 30 mins.
Bugs Bunny's Elephant Parade. Kids won't forget this African journey to learn about elephants, giraffes, hippos and other majestic giants.
VHS: S33368. $9.95.
Bugs Bunny's Funky Monkeys. Monkey business takes center stage as kids learn about apes, monkeys, gorillas and nature's other swingers.
VHS: S33367. $9.95.
Bugs Bunny's Silly Seals. Kids discover the underwater world of seals, sea otters, whales and more.
VHS: S33366. $9.95.

Clutch Cargo Vol. 2

Four episodes, including *Ripcord Van Winkle*.
VHS: S16662. $14.95.
Cambria, USA, 1957, 30 mins.

Colonel Bleep Vol. 1

Col. Bleep—Space Ranger from the planet Futura. Along with Squeak (a marionette) and Scratch (a super strong caveman), he preserves law and order throughout the Milky Way. The first TV cartoon in color, created by Jack Schleh and Robert D. Buchanan at Miami's Soundac studio.
VHS: S15236. $14.95.
Soundac, USA, 1956, 30 mins.

Colonel Bleep Vol. 2

Colonel Bleep blasts off from Zero Zero Island in his new spaceship, the Trav-a-lab, to update the map of Outer Space. Dr. Destructo tries every trick in the book to thwart Bleep, including joining forces with the most evil villains in the Galaxy.
VHS: S16660. $14.95.
Soundac, USA, 1956, 30 mins.

Daria

As Beavis and Butt-Head's only female friend, 16-year-old Daria Morgendorffer is much brighter than her bonehead buddies, and offers dry witticisms at every turn. From her career-obsessed parents to her snooty sister, Daria delivers some biting social commentary that appeals to more than just the teen crowd. Includes three episodes plus the original black-and-white pilot.
VHS: S32232. $12.95.
MTV, USA, 1997, 70 mins.

Daria—Disenfranchised

Beavis and Butt-head's sarcastic classmate valiantly struggles to cope with the illogical world of American adolescence in *Cafe Disaffecto*, *Malled* and *This Year's Model*. 80 mins.
VHS: S32987. $12.95.

Earthworm Jim: Assault and Battery/Trout!

Two episodes: *Assault and Battery* and *Trout!* Includes interviews with the animators and free trading card.
VHS: S27425. $9.95.
Universal, USA, 1995, 40 mins.

Earthworm Jim: Book of Doom/The Egg Beater

Two episodes: *The Book of Doom* and *The Egg Beater*. Includes interviews with the animators and free trading card.
VHS: S27426. $9.95.
Universal, USA, 1995, 40 mins.

Earthworm Jim: Bring Me the Head of Earthworm Jim/Sword of Righteousness

Based on the popular video game and the characters created by Doug TenNapel. Two episodes: *Bring Me the Head of Earthworm Jim* and *Sword of Righteousness*. Includes interviews with the animators and free trading card.
VHS: S27423. $9.95.
Universal, USA, 1995, 40 mins.

Earthworm Jim: Conqueror Worm/Day of the Fish

Two episodes: *Conqueror Worm* and *Day of the Fish*. Includes interviews with the animators and free trading card.
VHS: S27424. $9.95.
Universal, USA, 1995, 40 mins.

Eek! Stravaganza

America's favorite animated cat, Eek!, is the most helpful, friendly and courteous scout imaginable. Though he claims it never hurts to help, Sharky the psychotic sharkdog, Elmo the elk and his girlfriend constantly prove Eek wrong. Two episodes: *Catsanova* and *Hawaii-Eek-5-0*.
VHS: S25622. $9.98.
Nelvana, USA, 40 mins.

The Family Dog (Amazing Stories: Book 2)

Designed by Tim Burton, this delightfully funny animated tale centers on the life of a middle-class suburban family as seen through the eyes of their dog. Also: *Go to the Head of the Class*.
VHS: S28203. $19.95.
Laser: CAV. LD75667. $34.95.
Brad Bird, USA, 1987, 30 mins.

Family Dog Vol. 1

Two episodes from the TV series: In *Enemy Dog* the Binfords keep up with the neighbors, and in *Show Dog* the Family Dog shows off his talent for cat-astrophe.
VHS: S20549. $12.95.
Nelvana/Amblin, USA, 1992, 47 mins.

Family Dog Vol. 2

Two episodes from the TV series: In *Doggone Girl Is Mine* the Family Dog is in puppy love, and in *Family Dog Goes Homeless* the Family Dog befriends a homeless "woman."
VHS: S20550. $12.95.
Nelvana/Amblin, USA, 1992, 47 mins.

Family Dog Vol. 3

Two episodes from the TV series: In *Hot Dog at the Zoo* F.D. gets a little too close to the action, and in *Eye on the Sparrow* the Family Dog turns bird dog.
VHS: S20551. $12.95.
Nelvana/Amblin, USA, 1992, 47 mins.

Family Dog, Laserdisc Set

Ten episodes from the TV series: *Enemy Dog, Show Dog, Doggone Girl Is Mine, Family Dog Goes Homeless, Hot Dog at the Zoo, Eye on the Sparrow* and four additional episodes.
Laser: LD75668. $89.95.
Nelvana/Amblin, USA, 1992, 235 mins.

Fantastic Four: The Origin of the Fantastic Four

As seen on the UPN network.
VHS: S32451. $9.95.
USA

The Flintstones Deluxe Laserdisc Set

This long-awaited four-disc laser collection is more than merely the first 14 episodes of *The Flintstones*. It also includes a wealth of supplemental materials, such as a 24-page color booklet of summaries and commentary by John Kricfalusi and Earl Kress. The seven CLV sides of cartoons benefit from brighter, enhanced colors than any prints previously on video, and the 8th CAV side contains title sequences, commercials, pencil tests, collectibles and profiles of the animators and voice actors. Includes *The Swimming Pool, The Flintstone Flyer, The Prowler, The Babysitters, The Engagement Ring, No Help Wanted, At the Races, The Drive-In, Hot Lips Hannigan, The Split Personality, The Snorkasaurus Story, Hollyrock Here I Come, The Girls' Night Out* and *The Monster from the Tar Pits*.
Laser: LD72456. $124.95.
Hanna-Barbera, USA, 1960-61, 370 mins.

The Flintstones: A Flintstone Christmas

This hour-long Christmas special is available on video for the first time.
VHS: S30362. $12.95.
Hanna-Barbera, USA, 60 mins.

The Flintstones: A Flintstones Christmas Carol

Fred, Barney and the gang star in this version of the Dickens classic. When Fred is cast as Scrooge in the community theatre play, he begins to take his role too seriously. It's up to Wilma to bring him back to Earth.
VHS: S30360. $14.95.
Hanna-Barbera, USA, 1993, 90 mins.

The Flintstones: A Haunted House Is Not a Home

Two episodes with a ghostly theme.
VHS: S30364. $12.95.
Hanna-Barbera, USA, 60 mins.

The Flintstones: Babe in Bedrock

Two episodes: In *The Blessed Event*, Pebbles is born. In *Daddy's Little Beauty*, Fred enters her in a beauty contest. Digitally remastered. Includes "restored" footage.
VHS: S28225. $12.95.
Hanna-Barbera, USA, 1963, 50 mins.

The Flintstones: Bedrock 'n Roll

Two episodes: Fred has a hit record in *Girl's Night Out* and Fred becomes a rock 'n roll sensation in *The Twitch*.
VHS: S28230. $12.95.
Hanna-Barbera, USA, 1961-62, 50 mins.

The Flintstones: Christmas in Bedrock

Two episodes.
VHS: S30361. $12.95.
Hanna-Barbera, USA, 60 mins.

The Flintstones: Dino's Two Tales

Two episodes: Dino runs away from home in *Dino Disappears*, and he gets an audition for the Sassie TV show in *Dino Goes Hollyrock*.
VHS: S28229. $12.95.
Hanna-Barbera, USA, 1962-63, 50 mins.

The Flintstones: Fearless Fred Strikes Again

Two episodes: Fred attends the Water Buffalo Convention in Frantic City in *The Buffalo Convention*. In *Mother-In-Law's Visit*, Fred is at war with his mother-in-law. Digitally remastered. Includes "restored" footage.
VHS: S28226. $12.95.
Hanna-Barbera, USA, 1962-63, 50 mins.

The Flintstones: Fred Takes the Field

Two episodes: Fred is drafted as a college quarterback in *Flintstone of Prinstone* and he's drafted by a major league baseball team in *Big League Freddie*.
VHS: S28231. $12.95.
Hanna-Barbera, USA, 1961-63, 50 mins.

The Flintstones: Hooray for Hollyrock

Two episodes: In *The Return of Stoney Curtis*, Tony Curtis provides his own voice, and in *Ann Margrock Presents*, Ann-Margret provides her own voice in a visit to Bedrock. Digitally remastered. Includes "restored" footage.
VHS: S28227. $12.95.
Hanna-Barbera, USA, 1963-65, 50 mins.

The Flintstones: How the Flintstones Saved Christmas

Fred's holiday job as a part-time Santa at a Bedrock department store lands him in the real Santa's shoes on Christmas Eve in this half-hour TV special originally titled *A Flintstone Christmas*.
VHS: S28224. $9.95.
Hanna-Barbera, USA, 1977, 26 mins.

The Flintstones: I Yabba-Dabba Do

Three episodes with a romantic theme.
VHS: S31493. $14.95.
Hanna-Barbera, USA, 75 mins.

The Flintstones: Love Letters on the Rocks

Two episodes with a romantic theme.
VHS: S31494. $12.95.
Hanna-Barbera, USA, 50 mins.

The Flintstones: Rocky Bye Babies

Two episodes: The Rubbles adopt a baby in *Little Bamm-Bamm* and Fred and Barney start a feud in *The Most Beautiful Baby in Bedrock*.
VHS: S28232. $12.95.
Hanna-Barbera, USA, 1963-64, 50 mins.

The Flintstones: Wacky Inventions

The hilarious stone-age gadgets that made the Flintstones famous. Digitally remastered. Includes "restored" footage.
VHS: S28228. $12.95.
Hanna-Barbera, USA, 50 mins.

Frightfest, Nickelodeon

Three episodes: Doug in *Halloween Adventure*, Ren & Stimpy in *Haunted House* and Rugrats in *Candy Bar Creep Show*.
VHS: S21733. $12.95.
USA, 55 mins.

Frosty Returns

A new TV special that's a sequel to the 1969 Rankin/Bass film. Narrated by Jonathan Winters, and featuring the voice of John Goodman as Frosty.
VHS: S28233. $12.95.
USA, 1993, 25 mins.

Frosty the Snowman

When Frosty is accidentally brought to life, he must weather a storm of adventures and the dastardly plans of an evil magician before he can find safety and happiness at the North Pole. Told and sung by Jimmy Durante.
VHS: S10797. $12.95.
Rankin/Bass, USA, 1969, 30 mins.

Frosty's Winter Wonderland

Features the well known song. Voices of Andy Griffith, Shelley Winters and Jackie Vernon.
VHS: S28234. $9.95.
Rankin/Bass, USA, 23 mins.

A Garfield Christmas

Jon goes home to the farm for the holidays. While Odie works on a mystery gift, Garfield plans to surprise Grandma. Emmy nominee.
VHS: S14794. $9.95.
Film Roman, USA, 1987, 24 mins.

Garfield Gets a Life

Jon attends the School for the Personality Impaired, but it's Garfield who teaches him the real lessons of life.
VHS: S28252. $5.95.
Film Roman, USA, 1978, 30 mins.

Garfield Goes Hollywood

When "Pet Search" announces a talent contest, Jon devises an act for himself, Garfield & Odie: Jonny Bop & The Two Steps. Progressing to the finals in Hollywood, Garfield and Odie dump Jon from the act to become The Dancing Armandos. Emmy nominee.
VHS: S12785. $9.95.
Film Roman, USA, 1987, 30 mins.

Garfield in the Rough

Garfield's enthusiasm wanes when he learns Jon's vacation plans involve camping out. Life in the wild gets dangerous when an escaped panther shows up. Emmy winner.
VHS: S29645. $9.95.
Film Roman, USA, 1984, 30 mins.

Garfield on the Town

On the way to the vet, Garfield escapes and attempts to survive as a street cat. He discovers his birthplace and family in the inner city. Emmy award winner.
VHS: S12786. $9.95.
Mendelson-Melendez, USA, 1983, 30 mins.

Garfield's Feline Fantasies

Garfield's active imagination whisks him in and out of fantasies as an airline pilot, a superspy and a western hero.
VHS: S28254. $5.95.
Film Roman, USA, 1990, 30 mins.

Garfield's Halloween Adventure

Dressed up as pirates for trick-or-treating, Garfield and Odie wind up at a haunted house where ghostly pirates are expected any minute. Emmy winner.
VHS: S28251. $9.95.
Film Roman, USA, 1985, 30 mins.

Garfield's Thanksgiving

Garfield goes on a pre-Thanksgiving diet and Liz the veternarian agrees to have Thanksgiving dinner with Jon. When Jon destroys the meal, Grandma arrives to save the day and end Garfield's fast. Emmy winner.
VHS: S28255. $9.95.
Film Roman, USA, 1989, 30 mins.

Garfield: Babes & Bullets

VHS: S28253. $9.95.
USA, 30 mins.

Garfield: His Nine Lives

In this TV special, we see all of Garfield's nine incarnations: prehistoric cave cat, Pharoah's kitty, stunt cat, a pianist's prized pet, a terrified lab animal, his present slothful self, and a futuristic feline battling slobbery space aliens.
VHS: S28256. $12.95.
Film Roman, USA, 1988, 30 mins.

George of the Jungle Triple-Pack

This three-pack contains nothing but *George of the Jungle* cartoons, and is sold only as a set. Tape #1, *Monkey Business*, contains *Witch Doctor, Chi Chi Dog, Oo-Oo Bird* and *Monkey Business*. Tape #2, *Jungle Fever*, contains *Gold Mine, Dr. Scrupritzer, Mr. Noodnick* and *Ring-A-Ding Circus*. Tape #3, *Animal Power*, contains *The Pearl, The Agent, Animal Power* and *Little Scissors*.
VHS: S32453. $14.95.
Jay Ward, USA, 1967, 75 mins.

George of the Jungle: Gullible Travels

Four episodes: George opposes rich tycoon Seymour Noodnick for King of the Jungle; Tom Slick is in Transylvania to win the Monte Carloff Monster Rally; in Super Chicken's heaviest case, elephants begin appearing all over the city; and Tom Slick competes in the 9th Annual Balloon Race Across the English Channel. EP Speed.
VHS: S15780. $9.95.
Jay Ward, USA, 1967, 34 mins.

George of the Jungle: In George We Trust

Ring-A-Ding Brothers Circus needs a new trapeze artist and George is just the swinger they're looking for. Plus episodes of Tom Slick and Super Chicken and "Watch Out for That Tree" music video starring Savion Glover. EP Speed.
VHS: S28278. $9.95.
Jay Ward, USA, 1967, 34 mins.

George of the Jungle: It's a Mad, Mad, Mad, Mad Jungle

George is mad about Ursula, and mad at Dr. Chicago the mad scientist for stealing her with his mad, thieving plants. Plus episodes of Tom Slick and Super Chicken and "Watch Out for That Tree" music video starring Savion Glover. EP Speed.
VHS: S28279. $9.95.
Jay Ward, USA, 1967, 34 mins.

George of the Jungle: The Man from J.U.N.G.L.E.

Termites help George and Ape recover the Sultan's 300-pound pearl. Plus episodes of Tom Slick and Super Chicken and "Watch Out for That Tree" music video starring Savion Glover. EP Speed.
VHS: S28276. $9.95.
Jay Ward, USA, 1967, 34 mins.

Gerald McBoing Boing: Dusty of the Circus

Includes *The Five-Cent Nickel, Lion on the Loose, The Elephant Mystery* and *The Bear Scare*.
VHS: S13437. $9.95.
UPA, USA, 1956, 31 mins.

Gerald McBoing Boing: Favorite Animals

Includes *Miserable Pack of Wolves, Pee-Wee the Kiwi Bird, Lion Hunt, Three-Horned Flink, Mr. Buzzard, I Had a Bird, Prehistoric Horse* and *The Sad Lion*.
VHS: S13435. $9.95.
UPA, USA, 1956, 31 mins.

Gerald McBoing Boing: Favorite Painters

Includes *The Invisible Moustache of Raoul Dufy, Meet the Artist Sharaku: Day of the Fox* and *Meet the Artist Henri Rousseau: Merry-Go-Round in the Jungle*.
VHS: S13436. $9.95.
UPA, USA, 1956, 30 mins.

Gerald McBoing Boing: Favorite Sing-Along Songs

Commissioned by CBS, this was the first cartoon show made in part for TV and including educational elements. UPA produced 13 films starring their Oscar-winning theatrical character, directed by George Dunning and Ernest Pintoff. Premiered in 1956. Includes *Old McDonald, The Little White Duck, A Little Journey (Frere Jacques, Sur le pont d'Avignon), Two by Two, Good Ole Country Music* and *Alouette*.
VHS: S13434. $9.95.
UPA, USA, 1956, 28 mins.

Gerald McBoing Boing: Favorite Stories & Tales

Includes *Turned Around Clown, The Unenchanted Princess, The Freezee Yum Story, The Little Boy Who Ran Away* and *Matador and the Troubador*.
VHS: S13439. $9.95.
UPA, USA, 1956, 30 mins.

Gerald McBoing Boing: The Silly Twirliger Twins & Their Funny Friends

Includes *Follow Me, Average Giraffe, The Ballet Lesson, The Two Musicians, The Violin Recital, Punch & Judy* and *Alphabet Song*.
VHS: S13438. $9.95.
UPA, USA, 1956, 28 mins.

The Gift of Winter

The voices of Dan Akroyd and Gilda Radner star in this original animated Christmas special about a land that becomes frozen and bleak every winter. In protest to Winter himself are two unlikely rebels, Goodly and Nicely, who eventually persuade Winter to bestow his gift upon the world. EP Speed.
VHS: S29640. $7.95.
Rankin/Bass, USA, 1974, 30 mins.

Goosebumps: The Haunted Mask

This is the pilot from the current hit on the Fox Kids Network. It all began innocently enough when a girl, tired of being teased by boys, put on a frightening mask. It worked, but she soon discovered she couldn't take off the mask.
VHS: S27192. $14.98.
R.L. Stine, USA, 1995, 44 mins.

Goosebumps: The Werewolf of Fever Swamp

From the #1-ranked television show among kids 2-11, based on R.L. Stein's #1 book series, comes another howlingly frightful *Goosebumps* adventure.
VHS: S31062. $14.98.

Greatest Adventure: Daniel & The Lion's Den

Courage in the face of evil comes to life in this spellbinding story of Daniel's unjust imprisonment in Babylon, and his test in a cell of raging lions.
VHS: S29648. $9.95.
Hanna-Barbera, USA, 1987, 30 mins.

Greatest Adventure: David & Goliath

Every child's best loved Bible story, about the bravery of little David, chosen by the Israelites to battle the Philistine giant with only a sling and his faith.
VHS: S29647. $9.95.
Hanna-Barbera, USA, 1987, 30 mins.

Greatest Adventure: Jonah

Jonah, thrown overboard, is swallowed by a great fish. He remains in its belly for three days until he is released through his faith in God.
VHS: S29650. $9.95.
Hanna-Barbera, USA, 1992, 30 mins.

Greatest Adventure: Joseph & His Brothers

Jealous over his precious "coat of many colors," young Joseph's brothers sell him into slavery in Egypt. Eventually Joseph rises to governor of Canaan and hold the lives of his brothers in his hand.
VHS: S29651. $9.95.
Hanna-Barbera, USA, 1990, 30 mins.

Greatest Adventure: Joshua & The Battle of Jericho

God vindicates Joshua's faith in spectacular fashion as the Hebrews assault Jericho, the walled fortress and stronghold of their enemies, the Canaanites.
VHS: S29652. $9.95.
Hanna-Barbera, USA, 1987, 30 mins.

Greatest Adventure: Moses

An epic saga of the power of God at work in Moses' leadership of the Hebrews in their struggle against Egyptian slavery and their flight across the wilderness.
VHS: S29654. $9.95.
Hanna-Barbera, USA, 1985, 30 mins.

Greatest Adventure: Noah's Ark

An all-time favorite Biblical story: Noah is chosen by God to escape the coming flood in an ark, and to renew life on Earth after the flood waters recede.
VHS: S29656. $9.95.
Hanna-Barbera, USA, 1987, 30 mins.

Greatest Adventure: Queen Esther

How a beautiful orphan girl becomes the queen of Persia and saves her people from destruction.
VHS: S29657. $9.95.
Hanna-Barbera, USA, 30 mins.

Greatest Adventure: Samson & Delilah

An ageless Biblical classic: Delilah's treachery in delivering Samson into Philistine bondage, and God's thunderous wrath upon them in an awesone climax.
VHS: S29658. $9.95.
Hanna-Barbera, USA, 1986, 30 mins.

Greatest Adventure: The Creation

The timeless classic of *Genesis*, of Adam & Eve's banishment from the Garden of Eden and mankind's beginning.
VHS: S29646. $9.95.
Hanna-Barbera, USA, 30 mins.

Greatest Adventure: The Easter Story

Told through the eyes of the apostle Mark, this is the story of the entrance by Jesus into Jerusalem and his triumphant resurrection.
VHS: S29649. $9.95.
Hanna-Barbera, USA, 1989, 30 mins.

Greatest Adventure: The Miracles of Jesus

Join Benjamin, the widow's son brought back to life by Jesus, as he walks the roads Christ himself walked, recalling His wondrous works.
VHS: S29653. $9.95.
Hanna-Barbera, USA, 1989, 30 mins.

Greatest Adventure: The Nativity

The wondrous and moving classic of God's prophesy fulfilled, as the Christ child is born to Joseph and Mary amid the three Magi in a Bethlehem manger.
VHS: S29655. $9.95.
Hanna-Barbera, USA, 1987, 30 mins.

The Halloween Tree

Written and narrated by Ray Bradbury, this is the story of four youths who try to save the spirit of their friend Kip from the ghosts of Halloween past. They meet the mysterious Moonshroud (voiced by Leonard Nimoy), who takes them on a journey back 4000 years and teaches them the traditions of Halloween.
VHS: S21754. $14.95.
Hanna-Barbera, USA, 1993, 70 mins.

The Head

All 13 episodes of the MTV series.
VHS: S26304. $14.95.
MTV, USA, 120 mins.

Here Comes Peter Cottontail

Danny Kaye sings the eponymous song that inspired this TV special about the Easter Bunny oversleeping and failing to distribute the annual eggs. Made in "Animagic" stop-motion puppetry and featuring voices of Kaye, Casey Kasem and Vincent Price. EP Speed.
VHS: S11600. $12.95.
Rankin-Bass, USA, 1971, 53 mins.

Hey Arnold!: Arnold's Christmas
VHS: S32094. $12.95.
Nickelodeon, USA, 1997, 59 mins.

Hey Arnold!: Love Stinks
A double-length Valentine's special plus three romantic cartoons.
VHS: S32943. $12.95.
Nickelodeon, USA, 1997, 57 mins.

Hey Arnold!: The Helga Stories
Four episodes of the football-headed kid, featuring his stalker, Helga.
VHS: S32455. $12.95.
Nickelodeon, USA, 1997, 59 mins.

Hey Arnold!: Urban Adventures
Four episodes of the nine-year-old in his contemporary, urban, multi-ethnic world.
VHS: S32454. $12.95.
Nickelodeon, USA, 1997, 59 mins.

The Hunter: The Fox's Foul Play
Thirteen episodes: The Hunter in *Foul Play* and *Hula Hoop Havoc*; The King & Odie in *Long Laugh Leonardo*; Underdog in *Pain Strikes Underdog Parts 1 through 4*; Go Go Gophers in *The Great White Stallion*; Commander McBragg in *Rainbow Island* and *Mystifying McBragg*; Klondike Kat in *Up a Tree*; Tooter Turtle in *Anchors Awry*; Tennessee Tuxedo in *Phunnie Money*. EP Speed.
VHS: S28301. $9.95.
Leonardo-TTV, USA, 1967, 60 mins.

Iron Man: The Origin of Iron Man
As seen on the UPN network.
VHS: S32457. $9.95.
USA

It's a Mystery, Charlie Brown
Woodstock's nest is missing. Donning a cape, hat and pipe, Snoopy does his best to imitate the scourge of Scotland Yard, Sherlock Holmes. All the Peanuts gang are seen in this delightful story, including Lucy acting as a judge at the closing trial. 25 mins.
VHS: S29963. $9.95.

Jetsons: The Movie
The Jetsons Movie is a passably well-done adaptation of the popular TV series.
VHS: S28314. $14.95.
Laser: LD75682. $34.95.
Hanna-Barbera, USA, 1990, 82 mins.

Jonny Quest vs. The Cyber Insects
Join Jonny, Hadji, Race and the crew in their final classic Quest adventure. Team Quest faces their most challenging adventure ever as they battle the diabolical Dr. Zin.
VHS: S27516. $14.95.
Hanna-Barbera, USA, 1964, 90 mins.

Jonny Quest, The Real Adventures: Escape to Questworld
VHS: S29983. $12.95.
Hanna-Barbera, USA, 1996, 60 mins.

Jonny Quest, The Real Adventures: Rage's Burning Wheel
VHS: S29982. $12.95.
Hanna-Barbera, USA, 1996, 60 mins.

Jonny Quest, The Real Adventures: The Alchemist
This new Cartoon Network series brings back the original characters—updated for a '90s kind of high-tech version. New to the series is Jessie, Race's independent teenage daughter.
VHS: S29980. $12.95.
Hanna-Barbera, USA, 1996, 60 mins.

Jonny Quest, The Real Adventures: The Darkest Fathoms
VHS: S29981. $12.95.
Hanna-Barbera, USA, 1996, 60 mins.

Jonny Quest: Bandit—Adventure's Best Friend
Two original episodes featuring Bandit: *Attack of the Tree People* and *Terror Island*. Plus classic *Space Ghost* and *Two Stupid Dogs*. Includes collector's comic book.
VHS: S27520. $12.95.
Hanna-Barbera, USA, 1964, 60 mins.

Jonny Quest: Dr. Zin—Master of Evil
Two original episodes featuring Dr. Zin: *Riddle of the Gold* and *The Robot Spy*. Plus classic *Space Ghost* and World Premiere Toon *Cow and Chicken*. Includes collector's comic book.
VHS: S27519. $12.95.
Hanna-Barbera, USA, 1964, 60 mins.

Jonny Quest: Hadji—Mysteries of the East
Two original episodes featuring Hadji: *Calcutta Adventure* and *Pirates from Below*. Plus classic *Space Ghost* and World Premiere Toon *Johnny Bravo*. Includes collector's comic book.
VHS: S27518. $12.95.
Hanna-Barbera, USA, 1964, 60 mins.

Jonny Quest: Race Bannon—An Army of One
Two original episodes featuring Race Bannon: *Mystery of the Lizard Men* and *Double Danger*. Plus classic *Space Ghost* and World Premiere Toon *Dexter's Laboratory*.
VHS: S27517. $12.95.
Hanna-Barbera, USA, 1964, 60 mins.

Laurel & Hardy in Camera Bugged
The animated version of the classic comedy team, animated by Hanna-Barbera for Larry Harmon Pictures. Ten episodes: *Camera Bugged, Plumber Pudding, Robust Robot, Copper Bopper, Fued for Thought, Love Me Love My Puppy, Squawking Squatter, Goofy Gopher Goof-Up, Sassy Sea Serpent* and *Handle with Care. LP Speed.*
VHS: S28325. $7.95.
Larry Harmon/H-B, USA, 1966, 45 mins.

Liquid Television 2
The second collection of bizarre animation that premiered on MTV. Let the Liquid Lips lead you through a hypnotic succession of strange shorts, where you'll get a sinister glimpse at the cheery 1950s, watch a bloody encounter with a monster from outer space and catch a roller coaster ride straight to hell. Includes *Winter Steele, Billy & Bobby, Brad Dharma: Psychedelic Detective, Cut-Up Kamera* and *Rocky*. 45 mins.
VHS: S31281. $12.95.

The Little Drummer Boy
A lonely little boy discovers the greatest gift of all on a winter's night in Bethlehem. Voices of Jose Ferrer and Greer Garson.
VHS: S10796. $12.95.
Rankin/Bass, USA, 1968, 30 mins.

The Little Drummer Boy, Book II
In this sequel, Aaron sets out to rescue some silver bells from the tax collector and carry them to the manger in Bethlehem. Filmed in Animagic.
VHS: S13036. $9.95.
Rankin/Bass, USA, 1976, 23 mins.

Little Mermaid Vol. 1: Whale of a Tale
Two episodes from the syndicated TV series: *Whale of a Tale* and *Urchin*.
VHS: S28330. $12.95.
Disney, USA, 1992, 44 mins.

Little Mermaid Vol. 2: Stormy, The Wild Seahorse
Two episodes from the syndicated TV series: *Stormy, The Wild Seahorse* and *The Great Sebastian*.
VHS: S28331. $12.95.
Disney, USA, 1992, 44 mins.

Little Mermaid Vol. 3: Double Bubble
Two episodes from the syndicated TV series: *Double Bubble* and *Message in a Bottle*.
VHS: S28332. $12.95.
Disney, USA, 1992, 44 mins.

Little Mermaid Vol. 4: In Harmony
Two episodes from the syndicated TV series: *In Harmony* and *Charmed*.
VHS: S28333. $12.95.
Disney, USA, 1992, 44 mins.

Little Mermaid Vol. 5: Ariel's Gift
Two episodes from the syndicated TV series: *Ariel's Gift* and *Trident True*.
VHS: S28334. $12.95.
Disney, USA, 1992, 44 mins.

Little Mermaid: Ariel's Undersea Adventures Vol. 1
The contents of tape volumes 1 and 2 on laserdisc.
Laser: LD75687. $29.95.
Disney, USA, 1992, 88 mins.

Little Mermaid: Ariel's Undersea Adventures Vol. 2
The contents of tape volumes 4 and 5 on laserdisc.
Laser: LD75686. $29.95.
Disney, USA, 1992, 88 mins.

The Magic School Bus
Based on the best-selling book series and top-rated PBS show, these Emmy Award-winning animated videos provide unlimited fun as children learn about science. Each tape is 30 mins.

The Magic School Bus Blows Its Top. Ms. Frizzle gives the kids the last piece to their Earth puzzle, an undiscovered island. When they go to claim the isle, they learn it is still within an underwater volcano on the ocean floor. Though initially dismayed, the kids get to learn how islands are made.
VHS: S29961. $12.95.

The Magic School Bus Flexes Its Muscles. Ralphie wants to build a robot to do his chores while he plays ball. As he and his classmates struggle to make the robot, they discover the importance of understanding how joints and muscles work together.
VHS: S31059. $12.95.

The Magic School Bus for Lunch. Lily Tomlin is the voice of Ms. Frizzle in this animated science series. Her adventures on the magic bus bring a host of scientific problems and principles to life. Other stars, such as Malcolm Jamal-Warner, Little Richard and Ed Begley, Jr., are also featured.
VHS: S23296. $12.95.

The Magic School Bus Gets Eaten. Lily Tomlin is host for this undersea adventure featuring The Magic School Bus. It's a tough but enjoyable underwater lesson in the law of the jungle.
VHS: S25109. $12.95.

The Magic School Bus Gets Lost in Space. Lily Tomlin plays Ms. Frizzle, the go-getting heroine of this animated science series. On the magic bus, a host of other stars, such as Robby Benson, Carol Channing, Tyne Daly and Dom Deluise, join Tomlin to explore the wonders of science.
VHS: S23297. $12.95.

The Magic School Bus Hops Home. Lily Tomlin is the voice of Miss Frizzle on these animated educational adventures. Kids will love this trip to inland waterways.
VHS: S25108. $12.95.

The Magic School Bus Inside Ralphie. This time The Magic School Bus takes an interior journey to see what makes Ralphie tick. Kids will love this educational look at the human body.
VHS: S25110. $12.95.

The Magic School Bus Inside the Haunted House. Lily Tomlin is the voice of Ms. Frizzle, the school teacher who leads her students on the magic bus into yet another exciting adventure. This time the class is thrilled about a trip to the sound museum until they realize it is in a spooky mansion.
VHS: S26176. $12.95.

The Magic School Bus: Getting Energized. When their ferris wheel breaks down, the class brainstorms about alternative energy sources. 30 mins.
VHS: S32918. $12.95.

The Magic School Bus: Going Batty. Ms. Frizzle leads a fascinating discussion on nocturnal animals, which sets off a strange rumor. Is she a vampire? This story shows how The Friz overcomes this bad rap and convinces everyone that bats are not a threat.
VHS: S29960. $12.95.

The Magic School Bus: Out of This World. Ms. Frizzle and her class go on an out-of-this world adventure to learn about space rocks. 30 mins.
VHS: S32919. $12.95.

Taking Flight. After Wanda asks how to fly, the class is shrunk inside Tim's model airplane. In a series of high adventures, the students personally discover how wings and moving air cause flights.
VHS: S31057. $12.95.

The Busasaurus. Ms. Frizzle takes the class to a dinosaur dig. She completes this field trip by traveling back 67 million years to see what those ancient reptiles, including *T. rex*, were really like.
VHS: S31058. $12.95.

The Maxx
He's large, he's homeless, he's a homeless superhero…he's The Maxx, a hero hovering between alternate universes: New York City, where he's a dumpster dweller, and The Outback, where he and his sidekick, social worker Julie Winters, fight evil and face adventure. But which universe is real, and which is imaginary? 13 episodes from the original series.
VHS: S28671. $14.95.
MTV, USA, 120 mins.

Mega Man: 20,000 Leaks Under the Sea
In the first episode on this video, Mega Man and his sidekick Roll and Rush, the robo dog, find themselves lured into an underwater trap. The adventure continues in *The Strange Island of Dr. Wily*. This time, Dr. Wily has a plan involving a remote island that spells disaster for Mega Man. Suitable for ages 8 and up. 45 mins.
VHS: S27557. $9.99.

Mega Man: Robosaur Park
Mega Man and his sidekick Roll and Rush, the robo dog, blast into action in this fully animated series. In the title episode, Mega Man leads the Robo Commandos into action against robotic dinosaurs which have been programmed to attack. In *The Ice Age*, the second episode included on this tape, Ice Man and Dr. Wily hope to start a new ice age. Mega Man is set to foil their evil plan. Great for kids ages 8 and up. 45 mins.
VHS: S27556. $9.99.

Mega Man: The Beginning
Mega Man and his robo dog, Roll and Rush, confront the good-bots pressed into service by the diabolical Dr. Wily. This opening episode of the action-packed children's series could be both the beginning and the end if Mega Man fails. Next, in *Electric Nightmares*, Dr. Wily devises an intriguing plot to turn ordinary appliances against his nemesis, Mega Man. For ages 8 and up. 45 mins.
VHS: S27555. $9.99.

Mr. Magoo in Sherwood Forest
Mr. Magoo, as the jolly Friar Tuck, joins up with Robin Hood and his merry men to thwart the evil designs of King John.
VHS: S28357. $12.95.
Laser: LD75696. $29.95.
UPA, USA, 1964, 83 mins.

Mr. Magoo in the King's Service
Three tales featuring Mr. Magoo as D'Artagnan, Cyrano de Bergerac and Merlin.
VHS: S28355. $24.95.
UPA, USA, 1964, 97 mins.

Mr. Magoo Literary Classics: Cyrano de Bergerac/A Midsummer Night's Dream
In *Cyrano de Bergerac*, Magoo plays the title role—helplessly in love with Roxanne, but embarrassed by his huge nose. As Puck in *A Midsummer Night's Dream*, Magoo is the catalyst in Shakespeare's amorous mix-ups.
VHS: S13424. $12.95.
UPA, USA, 1964, 50 mins.

Mr. Magoo Literary Classics: Don Quixote
The cantankerous cartoon star brings Cervantes' classic to life. Would-be knight Don Quixote de la Mancha (Magoo) sets out with squire Sancho Panza to joust windmills, search for fair Dulcinea and generally revive chivalry.
VHS: S13422. $12.95.
UPA, USA, 1965, 50 mins.

Mr. Magoo Literary Classics: King Arthur/The Count of Monte Christo
Eye of newt and dragon's wing: as the wizard Merlin, Magoo prepares young Arthur for the throne in *King Arthur*. Then Magoo plays the Count of Monte Christo, plotting revenge on the villain who falsely imprisoned him.
VHS: S13423. $12.95.
UPA, USA, 1964, 50 mins.

Mr. Magoo Literary Classics: Little Snow White
VHS: S13420. $12.95.
UPA, USA, 1964, 60 mins.

Mr. Magoo Literary Classics: Sherlock Holmes/Dr. Frankenstein
In *Sherlock Holmes*, Magoo plays Dr. Watson—who is more likely to stumble across clues than to collect them. In *Dr. Frankenstein*, Magoo plays the title role with a blind determination to show off the monstrous consequences of his genius.
VHS: S28358. $12.95.
UPA, USA, 1964, 50 mins.

Mr. Magoo Literary Classics: The Three Musketeers
Magoo stars as d'Artagnan in this retelling of the Dumas classic. Cardinal Richelieu is plotting to arrest Queen Anne on a trumped-up charge of treason. Who else but the Three Musketeers can help the lady in distress?
VHS: S13421. $12.95.
UPA, USA, 1964, 60 mins.

Mr. Magoo Show Vol. 1
Five episodes: *Magoo's Last Stand, Short Order Magoo, Lost Vegas, Cupid Magoo* and *Cuckoo Magoo*.
VHS: S13412. $9.95.
UPA, USA, 1960, 25 mins.

Mr. Magoo Show Vol. 2
Five episodes: *Three-Ring Magoo, Marshal Magoo, Magoo's TV Set, Slim Trim Magoo* and *Foot Loose Magoo*.
VHS: S13413. $9.95.
UPS, USA, 1960, 25 mins.

Mr. Magoo Show Vol. 3
Five episodes: *Buffalo Magoo, Gasser Magoo, Hermit's Hideaway, From Here to Fraternity* and *Tycoonland*.
VHS: S13414. $9.95.
UPA, USA, 1960, 25 mins.

Mr. Magoo Show Vol. 4
Five episodes: *Fire Chief Magoo, Angler Magoo, Requiem for a Bull, Gangbuster Magoo* and *Magoo's Gnu*.
VHS: S13415. $9.95.
UPA, USA, 1960, 25 mins.

Mr. Magoo Show Vol. 5
Five episodes: *Magoo & The Beanstalk, Magoo's Gorilla Friend, The Real McCoys, Magoo Meets Frankenstein* and *Cast Iron Magoo*.
VHS: S28359. $9.95.
UPA, USA, 1960, 25 mins.

Mr. Magoo Show Vol. 7
Five episodes: *Bar-B-Q Magoo, Magoo's Western Exposure, Buccaneer Magoo, The Vacuum Caper* and *Magoo & The Medium*.
VHS: S28361. $9.95.
UPA, USA, 1960, 25 mins.

Mr. Magoo Show Vol. 8
Five episodes: *Piggy Bank Magoo, Magoo Meets McBoing Boing, Robin Hood Magoo, Fuel in the Sun* and *First Aid Magoo*.
VHS: S28362. $9.95.
UPA, USA, 1960, 25 mins.

Mr. Magoo Show Vol. 9
Five episodes: *Magoo's Roof Goof, Teenage Magoo, Cyrano Magoo, Magoo's Surprise Party* and *Magoo's Dutch Treat*.
VHS: S28363. $9.95.
UPA, USA, 1960, 25 mins.

Mr. Magoo Show Vol. 10
Five episodes: *Skipper Magoo, Private Eye Magoo, Muscles Magoo, What's Zoo Magoo* and *Digger Magoo*.
VHS: S28364. $9.95.
UPA, USA, 1960, 25 mins.

Mr. Magoo's Christmas Carol
Magoo is Ebenezer Scrooge in this first-rate musical of Charles Dickens' story. Songs are by Jule Styne and Bob Merrill.
VHS: S13042. $9.95.
UPA, USA, 1962, 53 mins.

Mr. Magoo...Man of Mystery
Magoo plays Dr. Watson to Sherlock Holmes, Dr. Frankenstein and the Count of Monte Christo, and detects alongside Dick Tracy.
VHS: S13425. $24.95.
UPA, USA, 1964, 96 mins.

Mr. Magoo: Uncle Sam Magoo
Magoo walks us through the history of America, from the pilgrims to the moon landing.
VHS: S13419. $12.95.
UPA, USA, 1970, 54 mins.

Muppet Babies: Be My Valentine
Jim Henson's award-winning Muppet Babies lead kids through lessons for making Valentines as the Muppet Babies make some Valentines themselves. Meanwhile, Baby Gonzo is playing Cupid to win Baby Piggy's heart. This animated short is both informative and fun to watch. 25 mins.
VHS: S27362. $12.99.

Mushfest: Nickelodeon
A collection of Nickelodeon's most inspired romantic moments are preserved in hilarious vignettes from *Rugrats, Hey Dude* and *Doug*.
VHS: S20288. $14.98.

Peanuts Double Feature: Charlie Brown's All Stars & It's Spring Training, Charlie Brown
In *Charlie Brown's All Stars*, Charlie takes a stand when the league won't let girls or dogs play in its baseball games.
In *It's Spring Training*, the team decides it needs uniforms. A businessman promises to provide them…if they first win a game!
VHS: S28682. $12.95.
Mendelson/Melendez, USA, 48 mins.

Peanuts Double Feature: He's Your Dog, Charlie Brown & A Charlie Brown Thanksgiving & You're Not Elected, Charlie Brown
Laser: LD75870. $24.95.
Mend./Melendez, USA, 1968/84, 48 mins.

Peanuts Double Feature: He's Your Dog, Charlie Brown & It's Flashbeagle, Charlie Brown
In *He's Your Dog, Charlie Brown*, Snoopy is sent to obedience school for a refresher course. In *It's Flashbeagle, Charlie Brown*, Snoopy is dragging because he's been sneaking out at night to go disco dancing.
VHS: S28378. $12.95.
Laser: LD75869. $24.95.
Mend./Melendez, USA, 1968/84, 48 mins.

Peanuts Double Feature: Life's a Circus, Charlie Brown & Snoopy's Getting Married
In *Life's a Circus, Charlie Brown*, Snoopy joins the circus after falling head over paws for one of the trained poodles. Emmy Winner. In *Snoopy's Getting Married*, Charlie helps make plans for Snoopy's wedding and reception, but there are a few kinks.
VHS: S28683. $12.95.
Mendelson/Melendez, USA, 48 mins.

Peanuts Double Feature: Play It Again, Charlie Brown & She's a Good Skate, Charlie Brown
Lucy has it all arranged for Schroeder to debut as a rock musician. Then Snoopy coaches Peppermint Patty toward a career in figure skating.
VHS: S26167. $12.95.
USA

Peanuts Double Feature: There's No Time for Love & Someday You'll Find Her
In *There's No Time For Love, Charlie Brown*, Peppermint Patty has a crush on Charlie, but he can only think about The Little Red-Haired Girl. In *Someday You'll Find Her, Charlie Brown*, Charlie enlists Linus' help in wooing a new girl, but it turns out that Linus himself is the one she's interested in.
VHS: S28684. $12.95.
Mendelson-Melendez, USA, 1973/81, 49 mins.

Peanuts Double Feature: What a Nightmare, Charlie Brown & It's Magic, Charlie Brown
At first Snoopy doesn't realize that he's dreaming. Then he inadvertently succeeds as a magician.
VHS: S26166. $12.95.
USA

Peanuts Double Feature: You're in Love, Charlie Brown & It's Your First Kiss, Charlie Brown
In *You're in Love, Charlie Brown*, Charlie falls for the Little Red-Haired Girl, but he's too shy to approach her. In *It's Your First Kiss, Charlie Brown*, Charlie becomes the escort for the homecoming queen—The Little Red-Haired Girl.
VHS: S28685. $12.95.
Mendelson-Melendez, USA, 1967/77, 49 mins.

Peanuts Double Feature: You're Not Elected, Charlie Brown & It Was a Short Summer, Charlie Brown
In *You're Not Elected*, Charlie runs against Linus for student body president. In *It Was a Short Summer*, Charlie reminisces about his typically trying summer vacation.
VHS: S28379. $12.95.
Mend./Melendez, USA, 1972/69, 48 mins.

Peanuts Double Feature: You're the Greatest, Charlie Brown & Snoopy's Reunion
In *You're the Greatest, Charlie Brown*, Charlie enters the Junior Olympics and faces opposition from Freddie Fabulous and the disguised beagle known as Masked Marvel. In *Snoopy's Reunion*, Snoopy remembers growing up on Daisy Hill Puppy Farm and meeting Charlie Brown, and attends a reunion with his brothers and sisters.
VHS: S28377. $12.95.
Mend./Melendez, USA, 1979/91, 48 mins.

Peanuts Feature Film: A Boy Named Charlie Brown

In this first Charlie Brown theatrical feature, Charlie enters a national spelling bee in New York City and makes it to the finals.
VHS: S07813. $14.98.
Mendelson/Melendez, USA, 1969, 85 mins.

Peanuts Feature Film: Bon Voyage, Charlie Brown

In their fourth theatrical feature, the Peanuts gang are sent to France as exchange students.
VHS: S28381. $14.95.
Mendelson/Melendez, USA, 1980, 76 mins.

Peanuts Feature Film: Race for Your Life, Charlie Brown

Charlie and his friends battle the summer camp bullies and race down a rampaging river in their third theatrical feature.
VHS: S28380. $14.95.
Mendelson/Melendez, USA, 1977, 76 mins.

Peanuts Feature Film: Snoopy, Come Home

In this second theatrical feature (generally considered the best), Snoopy is missing and Charlie, Linus and Lucy spare no effort to find him.
VHS: S07814. $14.95.
Mendelson/Melendez, USA, 1972, 80 mins.

Peanuts Holiday Special: A Charlie Brown Christmas

In this Emmy and Peabody Award-winning special, Charlie is sent to select a tree for the Christmas pageant but adopts an especially forlorn specimen. While Snoopy decorates in a gaudy, commercial way, and Lucy theorizes that Christmas is run by a big eastern syndicate, Charlie wanders through the snow hoping to find a more spiritual understanding of the season. The moody and beautiful soundtrack by jazz pianist Vince Guaraldi, together with a low-key but incisive script, add up to a surprisingly powerful film.
VHS: S09513. $12.95.
Mendelson/Melendez, USA, 1965, 25 mins.

Peanuts Holiday Special: A Charlie Brown Thanksgiving

In this Emmy Award-winning special, Charlie serves up a Thanksgiving dinner with his friends, consisting of potato chips, popcorn, jelly beans, buttered toast and ice cream.
VHS: S26162. $12.95.
Mendelson/Melendez, USA, 1973, 25 mins.

Peanuts Holiday Special: Be My Valentine, Charlie Brown

Poor Charlie Brown waits and waits at his mailbox for his valentines cards to arrive. When none appear, he takes his briefcase to school in anticipation of many cards, only to be the only kid in school to receive not a single card.
VHS: S28681. $12.95.
Mendelson-Melendez, USA, 1975, 25 mins.

Peanuts Holiday Special: Happy New Year, Charlie Brown

Charlie has to read *War & Peace* over the school break, so he lugs it around everywhere, including Peppermint Patty's New Years Eve bash.
VHS: S26163. $12.95.
Mendelson/Melendez, USA, 1986, 25 mins.

Peanuts Holiday Special: It's Arbor Day, Charlie Brown

It's baseball season! But where will Charlie Brown play when the pals commemorate Arbor Day by turning his field of dreams into an arboretum?
VHS: S28686. $9.95.
Mendelson/Melendez, USA, 25 mins.

Peanuts Holiday Special: It's the Easter Beagle, Charlie Brown

In this Emmy-nominated TV special, the Peanuts gang is busy getting ready for Easter, but Linus insists no preparation is necessary—the Easter Beagle will take care of everything.
VHS: S28382. $12.95.
Mendelson/Melendez, USA, 1974, 25 mins.

Peanuts Holiday Special: It's the Great Pumpkin, Charlie Brown

In this classic TV special, Linus convinces everyone that the Great Pumpkin will arrive with his bag of toys for all the good children.
VHS: S26161. $12.95.
Laser: LD75868. $24.95.
Mendelson/Melendez, USA, 1966, 25 mins.

Peanuts Special: A Charlie Brown Celebration

Good time tales and vignettes include Sally's school days, Peppermint Patty's dog daze, Charlie's case of the woozies, and more.
VHS: S28687. $9.95.
Mendelson/Melendez, USA, 48 mins.

Peanuts Special: Is This Goodbye, Charlie Brown?

Growing up sometimes means saying goodbye. That doesn't make it any easier when Charlie Brown learns his best buddy Linus is moving. Emmy nominee.
VHS: S28688. $9.95.
Mendelson/Melendez, USA, 1983, 24 mins.

Peanuts Special: It Was My Best Birthday Ever, Charlie Brown

Linus has invited all of his friends to his birthday party. Most of all, the birthday boy wants Mimi, the girl he just met, to be there. But will she show up?
VHS: S32490. $12.95.
USA, 25 mins.

Peanuts Special: It's a Mystery, Charlie Brown!

Who stole Woodstock's nest? Snoopy turns sleuth and Lucy is judge at the trial of the suspect he turns up.
VHS: S30370. $9.95.
M/Melendez, USA, 25 mins.

Peanuts Special: It's an Adventure, Charlie Brown

A grab-bag of sketches featuring Charlie Brown and more favorite characters, plus a good-time mix of Peanuts-style adventure.
VHS: S28689. $9.95.
Mendelson/Melendez, USA, 1983, 47 mins.

Peanuts Special: It's Christmastime Again, Charlie Brown

Snow on the ground, goodwill in the air and—good grief!—another Christmas play to perform. Have fun, and keep an eye out for a sidewalk Santa that looks suspiciously like a bearded beagle!
VHS: S30369. $9.95.
M/Melendez, USA, 1992, 23 mins.

Peanuts Special: It's the Girl in the Red Truck, Charlie Brown

Spike (Snoopy's Brother) and his pickup-driving buddy Jenny share desert vistas and adventure in this happy blend of live action and animation.
VHS: S28690. $9.95.
Mendelson/Melendez, USA, 48 mins.

Peanuts Special: Snoopy the Musical

It's usually a sit-up, roll-over, play dead world—but Snoopy's not just your usual dog in this musical salute.
VHS: S28691. $9.95.
Mendelson/Melendez, USA, 48 mins.

Peanuts Special: What Have We Learned, Charlie Brown?

When the gang visits the French countryside, it turns into a special trip when they visit the Normandy beaches of the D-Day invasion. Peabody and Emmy winner.
VHS: S28692. $9.95.
Mendelson/Melendez, USA, 1983, 23 mins.

Peanuts Special: Why, Charlie Brown, Why?

When one of Charlie Brown's classmates is ill, he learns that it's in times of trouble that friends need each other most of all.
VHS: S25547. $9.95.
Mendelson/Melendez, USA, 25 mins.

Peanuts Special: You Don't Look 40, Charlie Brown!

No gray around his temples! This 40th anniversary celebration of favorite moments, interviews with Charles Schulz, and much more shows why Peanuts remains a timeless treat for old and young alike.
VHS: S30371. $9.95.
USA, 1990, 47 mins.

Peanuts Special: You're a Good Man, Charlie Brown

Based in part on the stage play, this animated special is a cartoon tribute in which the Peanuts gang celebrates the sometimes wishy-washy but always honest Charlie Brown.
VHS: S25546. $9.95.
Mendelson/Melendez, USA, 49 mins.

Peanuts Special: You're a Good Sport, Charlie Brown

Tennis is just not Snoopy's racket after a surprise opponent out-volleys him fair and square. Then the Peanuts gang enters an exciting moto-cross race. Emmy winner.
VHS: S28693. $9.95.
Mendelson/Melendez, USA, 1975, 25 mins.

Peanuts: Charlie Brown & Snoopy Show Vol. 1

In *You Can't Win, Charlie Brown*, Charlie's team finally wins a baseball game, Lucy locks Linus' blanket in a closet, and Patty's teacher won't let her move out from under a dripping ceiling. In *Linus' Security Blanket*, Snoopy fights with the cat next door, Charlie learns how not to fly a kite, and Linus puts aside his blanket…maybe.
VHS: S29671. $9.95.
Laser: LD75871. $24.95.
Mend./Melendez, USA, 1983/85, 45 mins.

Peanuts: Charlie Brown & Snoopy Show Vol. 2

In *Snoopy's Cat Fight*, Snoopy again battles the cat next door when it refuses to give up Linus' blanket, the red-haired girl comes to Charlie's game, and Lucy tells Schroeder what sort of men make good husbands. In *Linus and Lucy*, Lucy clobbers Linus with a snowball, makes him say "thank you" over and over for bringing him a slice of toast, and fails to make Schroeder notice her.
VHS: S29672. $9.95.
Laser: LD75872. $24.95.
Mend./Melendez, USA, 1983/85, 45 mins.

Peanuts: Charlie Brown & Snoopy Show Vol. 3

Snoopy: Man's Best Friend and *The Lost Ballpark*.
VHS: S29673. $9.95.
Mendelson/Melendez, USA, 45 mins.

Peanuts: Charlie Brown & Snoopy Show Vol. 4

Snoopy: Team Manager and *Lucy Loves Schroeder*.
VHS: S29674. $9.95.
Mendelson/Melendez, USA, 45 mins.

Peanuts: Charlie Brown & Snoopy Show Vol. 5

Snoopy the Psychiatrist and *Lucy vs. the World*.
VHS: S29675. $9.95.
Mendelson/Melendez, USA, 45 mins.

Peanuts: Charlie Brown & Snoopy Show Vol. 6

Snoopy's Football Career shows how lean and mean a Beagle can be. Then in *Chaos in the Classroom*, pandemonium breaks out among the Peanuts gang.
VHS: S25548. $9.95.
Mendelson/Melendez, USA, 45 mins.

Peanuts: Charlie Brown & Snoopy Show Vol. 7

In *It's That Team Spirit, Charlie Brown*, the gang tries to rouse the positive energy that will help the team on the baseball diamond. *Snoopy and the Giant* is a humorous retelling of *Jack and the Beanstalk*, starring Snoopy and Woodstock.
VHS: S25549. $9.95.
Mendelson/Melendez, USA, 45 mins.

Peanuts: Charlie Brown & Snoopy Show Vol. 8

In *Snoopy's Brother Spike*, the well-traveled Beagle comes for a visit. Then, *Snoopy's Robot* is the story of a labor-saving device with a difference—making sure someone does all the work.
VHS: S26164. $9.95.
Mendelson/Melendez, USA, 45 mins.

Peanuts: Charlie Brown & Snoopy Show Vol. 9

In *Peppermint Patty's School Days*, Patty takes on the education system. In *Sally's Sweet Baboo*, the troubled romance of Charlie's little sister and Linus faces Linus' indifference.
VHS: S26165. $9.95.
Mendelson/Melendez, USA, 45 mins.

Peanuts: This Is America LD #1: The Great Inventors/The Wright Brothers at Kitty Hawk

Laser: LD75873. $24.95.
Mendelson/Melendez, USA, 1988, 50 mins.

Peanuts: This Is America LD #2: Building the Transcontinental Railroad/The Mayflower Voyagers

Laser: LD75874. $24.95.
Mendelson/Melendez, USA, 1988, 50 mins.

Peanuts: This Is America Vol. 1: The Great Inventors

Sally gives a school report that covers three great inventors: Alexander Graham Bell, Thomas Edison and Henry Ford.
VHS: S29676. $9.95.
Mendelson/Melendez, USA, 1989, 24 mins.

Peanuts: This Is America Vol. 2: The Wright Brothers at Kitty Hawk

See what happens when the Wright Brothers send their airplane aloft at Kitty Hawk.
VHS: S29677. $9.95.
Mendelson/Melendez, USA, 1988, 24 mins.

Peanuts: This Is America Vol. 3: Building the Transcontinental Railroad

Charlie Brown tells the story of the first coast-to-coast railroad.
VHS: S29678. $9.95.
Mendelson/Melendez, USA, 1988, 24 mins.

Peanuts: This Is America Vol. 4: The Mayflower Voyagers

An informative look at the *Mayflower* as only the Peanuts gang can do it.
VHS: S29679. $9.95.
Mendelson/Melendez, USA, 1988, 24 mins.

Peanuts: This Is America Vol. 5: The NASA Space Station

The Peanuts gang become part of the NASA Space Station crew.
VHS: S29680. $9.95.
Mendelson/Melendez, USA, 1988, 24 mins.

Peanuts: This Is America Vol. 6: The Birth of the Constitution

The Peanuts gang help the founding fathers compose the Constitution.
VHS: S29681. $9.95.
Mendelson/Melendez, USA, 1988, 24 mins.

Peanuts: This Is America Vol. 7: The Music and Heroes of America

Schroeder shows how tunes known by nearly every kid in the country are actually related to an important event in American history.
VHS: S25550. $9.95.
USA

Peanuts: This Is America Vol. 8: The Smithsonian & The Presidency

When the Peanuts gang visits the Smithsonian, it inspires an imaginary visit to the life and times of Abe Lincoln, Teddy Roosevelt and FDR.
VHS: S25551. $9.95.
USA

Pinky and the Brain: Cosmic Attractions

Two world-dominating adventures in space and on the high seas.
VHS: S32298. $12.95.
Warner Bros., USA, 1997, 50 mins.

Pinky and the Brain: Mice of the Jungle

Pinky and the Brain face their greatest challenge as they confront their arch-rival, Snowball, in two episodes from the TV series.
VHS: S32297. $12.95.
Warner Bros., USA, 1997, 50 mins.

Reboot: Talent Night

Dot prepares a surprise birthday event for her younger brother, Enzo.
VHS: S27152. $12.95.
USA, 1995, 25 mins.

Reboot: The Great Brain Robbery

Megabyte takes over Enzo's Brain. Only a miniaturized Bob can save the day. Once he is small enough, he is sent into Enzo's head to battle Megabyte on the terrain that is Enzo's mind.
VHS: S27153. $12.95.
USA, 1995, 25 mins.

Ren & Stimpy in Disguise

Two John K. episodes and one by Bob Camp. *Monkey See...Monkey Don't*: Ren & Stimpy masquerade as monkeys at the zoo in search of free eats; *Firedogs*: Ren & Stimpy masquerade as dalmatians and end up fighting fires; and *The Boy Who Cried Rat*: Stimpy poses as a rat catcher and Ren as a rat in a scam that requires Stimpy to chew up Ren. Also *Ren's Pecs* Music Video.
VHS: S20663. $14.98.
Spumco/Games, USA, 1991-93, 45 mins.

Ren & Stimpy on Duty

Contains *In The Army*: Ren & Stimpy join up and suffer the usual indignities of boot camp, and *Royal Canadian Kilted Yaksmen*: R&S are Mounted Yaksmen in charge of finding deposits of Canada's most precious resource. Also *Firedogs* Music Video.
VHS: S20286. $14.98.
Spumco/Games, USA, 1992, 40 mins.

Ren & Stimpy Vol. 1: The Classics

Three episodes from the first season, all directed by John K. *Space Madness*: Commander Hoek and Cadet Stimpy are on a 36-year voyage together and Ren gets paranoid delusions; *Untamed World*: Stimpy plays Jim Fowler to Ren's Marlon Perkins in a parody of *Wild Kingdom* that only Kricfalusi could concoct; and *Stimpy's Invention*: Stimpy invents the Happy Helmet and introduces the ubiquitous "Happy Happy Joy Joy" song. Also includes Log ads and bumpers.
VHS: S19080. $14.95.
Spumco, USA, 1991-92, 40 mins.

Ren & Stimpy Vol. 2: The Stupidest Stories

Three first season episodes directed by John K. *Stimpy's Big Day*: The first episode aired after the pilot follows Stimpy's rise to stardom after winning a Muddy Mudskipper write-in contest; features the first Log commercial and Mr. Horse. *Robin Hoek*: Stimpy conjures his own mad-libs version of the Robin Hood legend, including the Rapunzel nose-hair gag. And *The Big Shot*: the second half continuation of *Stimpy's Big Day*. Also bumpers and Stimpy's breakfast tips.
VHS: S19081. $14.95.
Spumco, USA, 1991, 40 mins.

Ren & Stimpy Vol. 3: The Stinkiest Stories

Two episodes by John K. and a third completed after his firing: *Nurse Stimpy*: An epic gross-fest as Stimpy nurses Ren back to health with daily spleen-flensings; *The Cat That Ate the Golden Hairball*: Another gross-fest as Stimpy goes into commercial production of hairballs; and *Ren's Toothache*: in which we learn things we never wanted to know about Ren's oral cavity. Includes Powdered Toast Man appearance.
VHS: S19082. $14.95.
Spumco/Games, USA, 1991-92, 40 mins.

Ren & Stimpy: As Stinky As They Wanna Be

VHS: S29693. $14.95.
USA

Ren & Stimpy: Classics II

Contains two double episodes: in *Stimpy's Fan Club* the duo receive a mountain of mail—all for Stimpy. In *Sven Hoek* Stimpy's distant Scandinavian cousin finds a kindred spirit in Stimpy. Also included: *Action Log*.
VHS: S29043. $14.95.
Spumco/Games, USA, 1992, 50 mins.

Ren & Stimpy: Essential Collection

Laser: LD75878. $29.95.
USA

Ren & Stimpy: Incredibly Stupid Stories

Three episodes from the Nickelodeon TV series: *An Abe Divided, Jiminy Lummox* and *Rubber Nipple Salesmen*. Also two commercials: the "fisterrific" Cheese Fist and Flod—that "most perfect cube of fat!"
VHS: S29692. $14.95.
USA, 40 mins.

Ren & Stimpy: More Stinky Stories

The Big Baby Scam: the duo impersonate infants in hopes of being pampered, but eventually get pounded by their "siblings"; *A Yard Too Far*: R&S must get past a guard baboon to a plate of hog jowls in this tribute/spoof of Hanna-Barbera formulae; *Mad Dog Hoek*: a straightforward spoof of pro-wrestling with R&S as a tag-team. Also includes two appearances by Mr. Horse.
VHS: S29044. $14.95.
Spumco/Games, USA, 1992, 45 mins.

Ren & Stimpy: Nothing But Shorts

Ren & Stimpy host an exclusive to video retrospective of favorite shorts and commercial parodies, including 22 classics like *Log, Dr. Stupid*and *Powdered Toast Man*. Brand new animation links the short segements, which include 11 never before released on video.
VHS: S27081. $14.95.
USA

Ren & Stimpy: Stinky Little Christmas

This tape features the complete episode *Son of Stimpy* (also known as *Stimpy's First Fart*), in which a despondent Stimpy embarks on a Christmas Eve search for the fruit of his first flatulent event—one of John K.'s most bizarre installments of the series. Also on the tape are two "music videos" composed of stock R&S footage edited together to two original yuletide tunes: "Cat Hairballs" ("Jingle Bells") and "Fleck the Walls."
VHS: S19083. $9.95.
Spumco, USA, 1993, 30 mins.

Rocko's Modern Life: Machine Madness

Three episodes from the Nickelodeon TV series created by Joe Murray: *Unbalanced Load, Suck-O-Matic* and *Trash-O-Madness*. Also *How to Tell If Your Dog Is Brainless*.
VHS: S29696. $9.95.
Nickelodeon, USA, 1994, 40 mins.

Rocko's Modern Life: Modern Love

Five cartoons.
VHS: S32944. $9.95.
Nickelodeon, USA, 1997, 60 mins.

Rocko's Modern Life: Rocko's Modern Christmas

VHS: S32097. $9.95.
Nickelodeon, USA, 1996, 41 mins.

Rocko's Modern Life: With Friends Like These...

Three episodes from the Nickelodeon TV series created by Joe Murray: *No Pain No Gain, The Good the Bad and the Wallaby and Bedfellows*. Also "The Bellybutton Song" from the Ren & Stimpy Show.
VHS: S29695. $9.95.
Nickelodeon, USA, 1994, 40 mins.

Rudolph & Frosty's Christmas in July

Rudolph the Red Nosed Reindeer and Frosty the Snowman team up for a joyous holiday celebration in July. Voices of Red Buttons, Ethel Merman, Jackie Vernon & more.
VHS: S29061. $9.95.
Rankin/Bass, USA, 1979, 96 mins.

Rudolph the Red Nosed Reindeer

The delightful tale of the North Pole's favorite reindeer and how he saved Christmas. Told and sung by Burl Ives.
VHS: S10795. $12.95.
Rankin/Bass, USA, 1964, 53 mins.

Rudolph's Shiny New Year

Aided by a whale and a caveman, Rudolph sets out to find Happy, the missing baby New Year. If Aeon, a monstrous bird, finds Happy first, Dec. 31st will last forever. Voices of Red Skelton and Frank Gorshin.
VHS: S29060. $9.95.
Rankin/Bass, USA, 1979, 50 mins.

A Rugrats Thanksgiving

Includes the double-length Holiday special *The Turkey Who Came to Dinner*, plus two bonus cartoons, *Chuckie Is Rich* and *Home Movies*. 47 mins.
VHS: S32505. $12.95.

Rugrats—Mommy Mania

Nickelodeon's popular, award-winning animated series. Contains double-length video cartoon *Mother's Day*, plus bonus episodes *Game Show Didi, Family Feud* and *Mommy's Little Assets*. 57 mins.
VHS: S33760. $12.95.

Rugrats: A Baby's Gotta Do What a Baby's Gotta Do

Three episodes.
VHS: S19087. $9.95.
Nickelodeon, USA, 1997, 47 mins.

Rugrats: A Rugrats Chanukah
A special double-length episode.
VHS: S32095. $12.95.
Nickelodeon, USA, 1997, 35 mins.

Rugrats: A Rugrats Passover
A special double-length episode.
VHS: S27080. $9.95.
Nickelodeon, USA, 1997, 35 mins.

Rugrats: A Rugrats Vacation
In this special double-length cartoon, the Rugrats gang is heading to Las Vegas. Spotting a billboard for a Siegfried and Roy-type animal act, the babies undertake to free the kitties. Plus two bonus cartoons.
VHS: S32462. $12.95.
Nickelodeon, USA, 1997, 55 mins.

Rugrats: Angelica the Divine
Three episodes.
VHS: S32468. $9.95.
Nickelodeon, USA, 1997, 47 mins.

Rugrats: Bedtime Bash
Includes five not-so-sleepy cartoons from Nickelodeon's *Rugrats* gang. 56 mins.
VHS: S32096. $12.95.

Rugrats: Chuckie the Brave
Three episodes.
VHS: S32467. $9.95.
Nickelodeon, USA, 1997, 48 mins.

Rugrats: Diapered Duo
Five cartoons.
VHS: S32942. $12.95.
Nickelodeon, USA, 1997, 57 mins.

Rugrats: Dr. Tommy Pickles
Five cartoons: *Hiccups, Autumn Leaves, Potty Training Spike, Chicken Pops* and *Grandpa's Bug*.
VHS: S32941. $12.95.
Nickelodeon, USA, 1997, 57 mins.

Rugrats: Grandpa's Favorite Stories
Four episodes.
VHS: S32463. $12.95.
Nickelodeon, USA, 1997, 58 mins.

Rugrats: Phil & Lil—Double Trouble
Four episodes.
VHS: S32466. $12.95.
Nickelodeon, USA, 1997, 63 mins.

Rugrats: Return of Reptar
Four episodes.
VHS: S32464. $12.95.
Nickelodeon, USA, 1997, 57 mins.

Rugrats: Tales from the Crib
Three episodes.
VHS: S19086. $9.95.
Nickelodeon, USA, 1997, 48 mins.

Rugrats: The Santa Experience
A special double-length episode.
VHS: S32098. $9.95.
Nickelodeon, USA, 1997, 35 mins.

Rugrats: Tommy Troubles
Four episodes.
VHS: S32465. $12.95.
Nickelodeon, USA, 1997, 63 mins.

Schoolhouse Rock: America Rock
Ten episodes: *No More Kings, Fireworks, The Shot Heard 'Round the World, The Preamble, Elbow Room, The Great American Melting Pot, Mother Necessity, Sufferin' Till Sufferage, I'm Just a Bill* and *Three-Ring Government*.
VHS: S26414. $14.95.
USA, 1974, 30 mins.

Schoolhouse Rock: Grammar Rock
Nine episodes: *Unpack Your Adjectives, Lolly Lolly Lolly Get Your Adverbs Here, Conjunction Junction, Interjections!, Rufus Xavier Sasparilla, Verb: That's What's Happening, A Noun Is a Person Place or Thing, Busy Prepositions* and *The Tale of Mr. Morton*.
VHS: S26412. $14.95.
USA, 1973, 30 mins.

Schoolhouse Rock: Multiplication Rock
Eleven episodes: *My Hero Zero, Elementary My Dear, Three Is a Magic Number, The Four-Legged Zoo, Ready or Not Here I Come, I Got Six, Lucky Seven Sampson, Figure Eight, Naughty Number Nine, The Good Eleven* and *Little Twelvetoes*.
VHS: S26415. $14.95.
USA, 1973, 30 mins.

Schoolhouse Rock: Science Rock
Eight episodes: *The Body Machine, Do the Circulation, Electricity Electricity, The Energy Blues, Interplanet Janet, Telegraph Line, Them Not-So-Dry Bones* and *A Victim of Gravity*.
VHS: S26413. $14.95.
USA, 1978, 30 mins.

Scooby's All Star Laff-A-Lympics: Heavens to Hilarity
Each video features around-the-world triple-team competition between the Yogi Yahooeys, the Scooby Doobys and the Really Rottens. Join as each team, along with announcers Snagglepuss and Mildew Wolf, travels to exotic locations such as Africa and Italy, participating in the most hilarious Olympic events. Two episodes per tape.
VHS: S29701. $7.95.
Hanna-Barbera, USA, 1977, 50 mins.

Scooby's All Star Laff-A-Lympics: On Your Marks, Get Set—Go Scoobys!
Each video features around-the-world triple-team competition between the Yogi Yahooeys, the Scooby Doobys and the Really Rottens. Join as each team, along with announcers Snagglepuss and Mildew Wolf, travels to exotic locations such as Africa and Italy, participating in the most hilarious Olympic events. Two episodes per tape.
VHS: S29698. $7.95.
Hanna-Barbera, USA, 1977, 50 mins.

Scooby's All Star Laff-A-Lympics: Something Smells Really Rotten
Each video features around-the-world triple-team competition between the Yogi Yahooeys, the Scooby Doobys and the Really Rottens. Join as each team, along with announcers Snagglepuss and Mildew Wolf, travels to exotic locations such as Africa and Italy, participating in the most hilarious Olympic events. Two episodes per tape.
VHS: S29700. $7.95.
Hanna-Barbera, USA, 1977, 50 mins.

Scooby's All Star Laff-A-Lympics: Yippee for the Yogi Yahooeys!
Each video features around-the-world triple-team competition between the Yogi Yahooeys, the Scooby Doobys and the Really Rottens. Join as each team, along with announcers Snagglepuss and Mildew Wolf, travels to exotic locations such as Africa and Italy, participating in the most hilarious Olympic events. Two episodes per tape.
VHS: S29699. $7.95.
Hanna-Barbera, USA, 1977, 50 mins.

Scooby-Doo and a Mummy Too
In the very first Scooby-Doo episode, *What a Night for a Knight*, the gang solves a mystery of forged paintings, ghost knights and a missing archaeologist. In *Scooby-Doo and a Mummy Too*, the gang solves the mystery of the forbidden pyramid. Plus bonus cartoons: a classic Huckleberry Hound episode and the World Premiere Toon *Dexter's Laboratory*.
VHS: S29412. $12.95.
Hanna-Barbera, USA, 1969-70, 60 mins.

Scooby-Doo Goes Hollywood
In this one-hour TV special, Scooby wants to be a serious actor, and with Shaggy as his manager, anything is possible. While Scooby is off becoming famous, his old pals miss him, and reminisce about the first day they met. Meanwhile, a creepy creature wants to stop Scooby's film.
VHS: S32291. $14.95.
Hanna-Barbera, USA, 1979, 51 mins.

Scooby-Doo in Arabian Nights
Scooby and Shaggy travel to Arabia to become the Caliph's royal food tasters and are forced to run for their lives! With their genie (Yogi Bear) and Sinbad (Magilla Gorilla), it's an adventure of mistaken identities and exotic locations.
VHS: S29416. $14.95.
Hanna-Barbera, USA, 80 mins.

Scooby-Doo on Zombie Island
An all-new, direct-to-video, feature-length Scooby adventure. Scooby, Shaggy and the gang reunite to solve the mystery of a bayou island haunted by zombies. Soundtrack features Third Eye Blind performing the Scooby Theme. Voices of Mark Hammil and Adrienne Barbeau.
VHS: S34840. $19.95.
Hanna-Barbera, USA, 1997, 70 mins.

Scooby-Doo: A Gaggle of Galloping Ghosts
Two of the most requested original Scooby-Doo episodes, plus a bonus classic Hanna-Barbera cartoon and a World Premiere Toon.
VHS: S29415. $12.95.
Hanna-Barbera, USA, 1969-70, 60 mins.

Scooby-Doo: A Halloween Hassle at Dracula's Castle
VHS: S30372. $12.95.
Hanna-Barbera, USA, 60 mins.

Scooby-Doo: Foul Play in Funland
Two of the most requested original Scooby-Doo episodes, plus a bonus classic Hanna-Barbera cartoon and a World Premiere Toon.
VHS: S29413. $12.95.
Hanna-Barbera, USA, 1969-70, 60 mins.

Scooby-Doo: Mystery Mask Mix-Up
Two original episodes from *Scooby-Doo, Where Are You?*: *Mystery Mask Mix-Up* and *What the Hex Is Going On?* Plus a bonus cartoon, *Dexter's Laboratory*. HiFi.
VHS: S34841. $12.95.
Hanna-Barbera, USA, 1969-70, 60 mins.

Scooby-Doo: Nutcracker Scoob
VHS: S30366. $12.95.
Hanna-Barbera, USA, 60 mins.

Scooby-Doo: That's Snow Ghost
Two original episodes from *Scooby-Doo, Where Are You?*: *That's Snow Ghost and Go Away Ghost Ship*. Plus a bonus cartoon, *Power Puff Girls*. HiFi.
VHS: S34842. $12.95.
Hanna-Barbera, USA, 1969-70, 60 mins.

Scooby-Doo: The Haunted House Hang-Up
Two original episodes from *Scooby-Doo, Where Are You?*: *The Haunted House Hang-Up* and *A Night of Fright Is No Delight*. Plus a bonus cartoon, *Cow and Chicken*. HiFi.
VHS: S34843. $12.95.
Hanna-Barbera, USA, 1969-70, 60 mins.

Scooby-Doo: The Headless Horseman of Halloween
VHS: S30373. $12.95.
Hanna-Barbera, USA, 60 mins.

Scooby-Doo: Wedding Bell Boos
VHS: S31495. $12.95.
Hanna-Barbera, USA, 60 mins.

Scooby-Doo: Which Witch Is Which?
Two of the most requested original Scooby-Doo episodes, plus a bonus classic Hanna-Barbera cartoon and a World Premiere Toon.
VHS: S29414. $12.95.
Hanna-Barbera, USA, 1969-70, 60 mins.

Siegfried & Roy: Masters of the Impossible
The Las Vegas animal-training showmen bring their inspiration to a feature-length animated fantasy adventure about the quest to return magic to a once-enchanted land. Originally broadcast on the Fox Children's Network.
VHS: S30374. $14.95.
DIC, USA, 1996, 76 mins.

The Simpsons Christmas Special
The Simpsons are in a Yuletide jam—there's no money for presents and they may have to cancel Christmas. So Homer gets a job as a Santa, Bart gets a tattoo, and the whole family gets into the act.
VHS: S29080. $9.95.
Klasky-Csupo, USA, 1990, 30 mins.

Snick Vol. 1: Nick Snicks Friendship
One episode each from *Clarissa Explains It All, Roundhouse, Are You Afraid of the Dark?* and *Ren & Stimpy*. Ren & Stimpy episode: *The Littlest Giant:* Stimpy the Giant is an outcast until he meets Wee Ren.
VHS: S19085. $14.95.
Nickelodeon, USA, 80 mins.

Snick Vol. 2: Nick Snicks the Family
One episode each from *Clarissa Explains It All, Roundhouse, Are You Afraid of the Dark?* and *Ren & Stimpy*. Ren & Stimpy episode: Ren adopts a 400-pound, seven-year-old jailbird.
VHS: S19084. $14.95.
Nickelodeon, USA, 80 mins.

South Park Vol. 1

Trey Parker and Matt Stone's rude, crude animated series on Comedy Central is now available on home video. In *Cartman Gets an Anal Probe*, alien visitors kidnap Kyle's little brother, mutilate cows and give Eric Cartman an anal probe. The boys must overcome flaming farts and Wendy Testaburger in order to rescue little Ike. In *Volcano*, Stan's Uncle Jimbo and his Vietnam buddy Ned take the boys on a camping trip. An erupting volcano and a mysterious creature named Scuzzlebutt threaten the expedition and the whole town as well.
VHS: S34134. $14.95.
Parker/Stone, USA, 1997, 45 mins.

South Park Vol. 2

In *Weight Gain 4000*, Cartman's environmental essay wins a national contest and Kathie Lee Gifford comes to South Park to present his award. As Cartman is bulking up for his TV appearance, Mr. Hat and Garrison are busy hatching a plot to murder Kathie Lee! In *Big Gay Al's Big Gay Boat Ride*, Uncle Jimbo's nephew Stan becomes confused and depressed when he discovers that his new dog is queer. A mysterious and magical new friend, Big Gay Al, helps Stan understand the wonders of being gay and sends him back to play in the big football game.
VHS: S34135. $14.95.
Parker/Stone, USA, 1997, 45 mins.

South Park Vol. 3

In *An Elephant Makes Love to a Pig*, Kyle decides to cross-breed his mail-order elephant with Cartman's pig to make potbellied elephants. When they try to enlist the help of the mysterious geneticist Mephesto, Mephesto makes an evil clone from Stan's DNA and now the boys must stop the clone from destroying the town. In *Death*, Stan's 102-year-old grandfather asks Stan to assist him in suicide. When the parents in town leave to protest the boys' favorite TV show, the kids are left to face the Grim Reaper on their own.
VHS: S34136. $14.95.
Parker/Stone, USA, 1997, 45 mins.

Space Angel Vol. 1

Commander Scott McCloud leads a thrilling secret life as Space Angel—the masked interstellar agent of Earth Intelligence. From space station Evening Star, Scott, Crystal and Taurus patrol the space lanes in *The Starduster*—the fastest spaceship ever built. Created and designed by Alex Toth, this series features the bizarre "Synchro-Vox" technique of superimposing live-action lips over animated faces. Two episodes, including *The Little People*.
VHS: S15238. $14.95.
Cambria, USA, 1962, 30 mins.

Space Angel Vol. 2

Two more episodes of the ultra-camp space cartoon: *The Gladiators* and *The Light Barrier*.
VHS: S16664. $14.95.
Cambria, USA, 1962, 30 mins.

Space Goofs

From Fox Kids Network, five of the funniest aliens you'll ever meethave crash-landed on Earth. Join Candy, Gorgious, Bud, Stereo and Ethno as they try to adust to their new surroundings on one of the strangest planets in the universe.
Space Goofs—Alien Antics. Includes *Once upon a Time—Part 1, Once upon a Time—Part 2, Venus Junior* and *One Minor Technicality*. 45 mins.
VHS: S34694. $9.95.
Space Goofs—Animal Crack-Ups. Includes *Old MacDonald Had a House, Bats in the Belfry, You Can't Go Home* and *Clowning Around*. 45 mins.
VHS: S34696. $9.95.
Space Goofs—Cartoon Tales. Includes *Toon In, Drop Out—Part 1, Toon In, Drop Out—Part 2*, TV Connection and *Showdown in Tiny Town*. 45 mins.
VHS: S34695. $9.95.

Spawn Edited Edition

A compilation of the cliffhanger episodes shown at midnight on HBO. Our "hero" alights on Earth from Hell supposedly to do the Devil's dirty work. A normal human who has been transformed, he spends many of the initial episodes trying to recall and revisit his former life. He is tailed by a creepy clown from Hell who directs him to do evil as Spawn stumbles into the city's filthy underbelly. This tamer, "PG" version is still pretty strong stuff.
VHS: S32492. $19.95.
HBO, USA, 1997, 90 mins.

Spawn Uncut Collector's Edition

Includes interview footage with *Spawn* creator Todd McFarlane. Uncut episodes include nudity, sex and gore. Main characters include a child-murdering pedophile, a crooked senator, a double-dealing CIA agent, and numerous cruel policemen and mobsters.
VHS: S31863. $22.95.
DVD: DV60387. $24.95.
HBO, USA, 1997, 147 mins.

Speed Racer

The teenage hero-star of the most successful animated TV series, for the first time on video. Courageous, smart, resourceful, Speed Racer has the fastest futuristic car in the world, and has been applauded as a positive role model. "I have simply loved Speed since I first saw him. I was going to marry him. Well, I'm no longer a little girl. I'm 19 and yes, I'm still in love with Speed Racer," wrote one fan to the video manufacturer.
The Great Car Wrestling Match. 30 mins.
VHS: S12740. $14.98.
The Trick Race. 30 mins.
VHS: S11547. $14.98.

Spider-Man: The Hobgoblin

As seen on UPN.
VHS: S32469. $9.95.
USA

Star Trek Volume 1

Two episodes: *More Tribbles, More Troubles* and *The Infinite Vulcan*.
VHS: S29718. $12.95.
Filmation, USA, 1973, 48 mins.

Star Trek Volume 2

Two episodes: *Yesteryear* and *Beyond the Farthest Star*.
VHS: S29719. $12.95.
Filmation, USA, 1973, 48 mins.

Star Trek Volume 3

Two episodes: *The Survivor* and *The Lorelei Signal*.
VHS: S29720. $12.95.
Filmation, USA, 1973, 48 mins.

Star Trek Volume 4

Two episodes: *One of Our Planets Is Missing* and *Mudd's Passion*.
VHS: S29721. $12.95.
Filmation, USA, 1973, 48 mins.

Star Trek Volume 5

Two episodes: *The Magicks of Megus-Tu* and *Time Trap*.
VHS: S29722. $12.95.
Filmation, USA, 1973, 48 mins.

Star Trek Volume 6

Two episodes: *The Slaver Weapon* and *The Ambergris Element*.
VHS: S29723. $12.95.
Filmation, USA, 1973, 48 mins.

Star Trek Volume 7

Two episodes: *Jihad* and *The Terratin Incident*.
VHS: S29724. $12.95.
Filmation, USA, 1973, 48 mins.

Star Trek Volume 8

Two episodes: *The Eye of the Beholder* and *Once upon a Planet*.
VHS: S29725. $12.95.
Filmation, USA, 1973, 48 mins.

Star Trek Volume 9

Two episodes: *Bem* and *Albatross*.
VHS: S29726. $12.95.
Filmation, USA, 1973, 48 mins.

Star Trek Volume 10

Two episodes: *The Pirates of Orion* and *The Practical Joker*.
VHS: S29727. $12.95.
Filmation, USA, 1973, 48 mins.

Star Trek Volume 11

Two episodes: *How Sharper Than a Serpent's Tooth* and *The Counter-Clock Incident*.
VHS: S29728. $12.95.
Filmation, USA, 1973, 48 mins.

Star Wars Droids: The Pirates and The Prince

The animated TV series spun off from the *Star Wars* movies, featuring R2D2 and C3PO.
VHS: S30869. $14.95.
Nelvana, Canada, 1985

Star Wars Ewoks: The Haunted Village

The animated TV series spun off from the *Star Wars* movies, featuring the Ewoks and their forest home on the Moon of Endor.
VHS: S30870. $14.95.
Nelvana, Canada, 1985

The Stingiest Man in Town

This TV special is yet another variation on Dickens' *A Christmas Carol*, featuring the voices of Tom Bosley, Walter Matthau and Paul Frees. The cast breaks into song frequently during the story.
VHS: S13039. $9.95.
Rankin/Bass, USA, 1978, 50 mins.

Superboy (DC Superpowers Collection)

Eight episodes: *The Revolt of Robotville, The Great Kryptonite Caper, Krypto's Calamitous Capers, Double Trouble, Double Doom, Superboy Meets Mighty Lad, The Black Knight, Krypto, Super Seeing-Eye Dog* and *The Jinxed Circus*.
VHS: S29732. $9.95.
Filmation, USA, 1967-69, 60 mins.

Superman (DC Superpowers Collection)

Seven episodes: *Superman Meets Braniac, Luminians on the Loose, The Pernicious Parasite, The Prankster, The Chimp Who Made It Big, The Toy Man's Super Toy* and *Luther's Fatal Fireworks*.
VHS: S05471. $9.95.
Filmation, USA, 1967-69, 60 mins.

Superman Cartoons Vol. 1

The complete collection on two Standard Play VHS tapes. The quality of these tapes is so good, it's superior to the laserdisc version. All episodes are transferred from the finest prints and letterboxed. Eight titles: *Superman, The Mechanical Monsters, Billion Dollar Limited, Arctic Giant, Bulleteers, Magnetic Telescope, Electric Earthquake* and *Volcano*.
VHS: S29733. $19.95.
Fleischer, USA, 1941-43, 76 mins.

Superman Cartoons Vol. 2

The complete collection on two Standard Play VHS tapes. Eight titles: *Terror on the Midway, Japoteurs, Showdown, Eleventh Hour, Destruction Inc., The Mummy Strikes, Jungle Drums, Underground World* and *Secret Agent*.
VHS: S29734. $19.95.
Fleischer, USA, 1941-43, 76 mins.

Superman: The Last Son of Krypton

The new animated Superman series is kicked off with this feature-length special. The background of the series is laid, as we see the progression from the planet Krypton blowing up to when Clark Kent becomes a reporter at the *Daily Planet*. From the producers of the animated Batman series, this show has much the same stylish look.
VHS: S30375. $14.95.
Warner Bros., USA, 1996, 75 mins.

Swat Kats: Deadly Dr. Viper

Two episodes: The Swat Kats battle evil alliances and hideous plant monsters when Dr. Viper makes a house call on Megakat City in *Destructive Nature* and *Katastrophe!* Bonus episode: Space Ghost in *Zorak*.
VHS: S31497. $12.95.
Hanna-Barbera, USA, 52 mins.

Swat Kats: Metallikats Attack

Two episodes: With an arsenal of giant attack robots and amazing gadgets at their disposal, the Metallikats terrorize Megakat City in The Metallikats and *Metal Urgency!* Bonus episode: Space Ghost in *Space Armada*.
VHS: S31498. $12.95.
Hanna-Barbera, USA, 52 mins.

Swat Kats: Strike of Dark Kat

Two episodes: In *The Wrath of Dark Kat* and *Night of Dark Kat*, the Swat Kats lock bytes with Dark Kat and the evil techno-villain Hard Drive. Bonus episode: Space Ghost in *Space Ark*.
VHS: S31499. $12.95.
Hanna-Barbera, USA, 52 mins.

Tazmania: Taz-Maniac

From the popular Fox Network Saturday morning TV series. Four episodes: *Not a Shadow of a Doubt, Food for Thought, Gone to Pieces* and *Deer Taz*.
VHS: S19046. $12.95.
Warner Bros., USA, 1993, 34 mins.

Tazmania: Taz-Manimals

From the popular Fox Network Saturday morning TV series. Three episodes: *The Dog the Turtle Story* and *Here Kitty Kitty Kitty Parts I & II.*
VHS: S19045. $12.95.
Warner Bros., USA, 1993, 34 mins.

Tazmania: Taz-Tronaut

From the popular Fox Network Saturday morning TV series. Four episodes: *Airbourne Airhead, Taz and the Pterodactyl, Astro Taz* and *Bottle Cap Blues.*
VHS: S19044. $12.95.
Warner Bros., USA, 1993, 34 mins.

Tennessee Tuxedo: Brushing Off a Toothache

Ten titles: Tennessee Tuxedo in *Brushing Off a Toothache, Zoo's News* and *Telescope Detectives;* Tooter Turtle in *Sea Haunt;* Klondike Kat in *The Candy Mine;* Go Go Gophers in *Who's a Dummy;* Underdog in *March of the Monsters;* Commander McBragg in *Flying Traps;* The Hunter in *Frankfurter Fix;* The King & Odie in *Call Out the Kids.* EP Speed.
VHS: S29736. $9.95.
Leonardo Prod., USA, 1967, 60 mins.

The Tick

It's night in the city and there's a new superhero in town! He's seven feet tall, he's blue, he's an idiot, and he has powers unknown to mortal men. Join him and his sidekick Arthur as they battle all manner of outrageous villains. Two episodes: *The Tick vs. the Idea Men* and *The Tick vs. Chairface Chippendale.*
VHS: S25617. $9.95.
USA

The Tick vs. Arthur?

Two more episodes from the TV series.
VHS: S32471. $5.95.
USA

The Town That Santa Forgot

VHS: S30365. $9.95.
Hanna-Barbera, USA, 45 mins.

Underdog Vol. 1: The Great Gold Robbery

Thirteen episodes: Underdog in *The Great Gold Robbery Parts 1-4;* Tennessee Tuxedo in Rainmakers; The King & Odie in *How High Is Up* and *Drumming Up the Bongos;* Go Go Gophers in *Gatling Gophers;* Klondike Kat in *Rip a Tree;* Tooter Turtle in *Two-Gun Turtle;* The Hunter in *Fort Knox Fox;* Commander McBragg in *Fish Story* and *Himalya.* EP Speed.
VHS: S29755. $9.95.
Leonardo Prod., USA, 1967, 55 mins.

What's New Mr. Magoo? Volume 1

Four episodes: *What's Zoo Magoo?, Museum Magoo, Magoo's Monster Mansion* and *Mountain Man Magoo.*
VHS: S13416. $12.95.
DePatie-Freleng, USA, 1977-78, 42 mins.

What's New Mr. Magoo? Volume 2

Four episodes: *Baby Sitter Magoo, Mr. Magoo's Concert, For the Birds, Magoo* and *A Magoo Bagatelle.*
VHS: S13417. $12.95.
DePatie-Freleng, USA, 1977-78, 42 mins.

What's New Mr. Magoo? Volume 3

Four episodes: *Caveman Magoo, Motorcycle Magoo, Lion Around Magoo* and *Unglued Magoo.*
VHS: S13418. $12.95.
DePatie-Freleng, USA, 1977-78, 42 mins.

What's New Mr. Magoo? Volume 4

Four episodes: *Magoo's Yacht Party, Boo Magoo, Choo Choo Magoo* and *King Tut Magoo.*
VHS: S28675. $12.95.
DePatie-Freleng, USA, 1977-78, 42 mins.

What's New Mr. Magoo? Volume 5

Four episodes: *Good Neighbor Magoo, Magoo's Pizza, Magoo's Kidnap Caper* and *Gold Rush Magoo.*
VHS: S28676. $12.95.
DePatie-Freleng, USA, 1977-78, 42 mins.

What's New Mr. Magoo? Volume 6

Four episodes: *Come Back Little McBarker, Roamin' Magoo, Magoo's Fountain of Youth* and *Miniature Magoo.*
VHS: S28677. $12.95.
DePatie-Freleng, USA, 1977-78, 42 mins.

What's New Mr. Magoo? Volume 7

Four episodes: *McBarker the Wonder Dog, Jungle Man Magoo, Space Man Magoo* and *Secret Agent Magoo.*
VHS: S28678. $12.95.
DePatie-Freleng, USA, 1977-78, 42 mins.

What's New Mr. Magoo? Volume 8

Four episodes: *Magoo's Driving Test, Shutterbug Magoo, Millionaire Magoo* and *Rip Van Magoo.*
VHS: S28679. $12.95.
DePatie-Freleng, USA, 1977-78, 42 mins.

A Wish for Wings That Work

From Pulitzer Prize-winning comic artist Berkeley Breathed, creator of "Bloom County" and "Outland," it's a holiday special starring Opus the Penguin and Bill the Cat. Determined to realize his life-long dream of flight, Opus turns to St. Nick. When Father Christmas finds himself in hot water on Christmas Eve, the holiday suddenly depends on Opus' heroism.
VHS: S19592. $12.95.
Laser: LD71925. $24.95.
Universal, USA, 1993, 25 mins.

Wishbone: Bone of Arc

Mark Twain and Joan of Arc are the inspiration for this Wishbone episode. It follows two young girls who are determined to fetch victory for their teammates and their countrymen. 30 mins.
VHS: S29943. $12.95.

Wishbone: Frankenbone

Mary Shelley's gothic classic serves as the inspiration for this episode about the dog who continually remakes history. Wishbone helps get a science project that went out of control back in the lab, and also manages to inspire kids with the artistry of Shelley's original novel. 30 mins.
VHS: S29942. $12.95.

Wishbone: Homer Sweet Homer

Wishbone imagines himself in another scenario sure to inspire kids to read. In this episode he is transported back to ancient Greece as Odysseus, the hero of Homer's *The Odyssey.* The goddess Calypso would ensnare Wishbone, but he thinks of his sweet Emily and somehow finds his way back home. 30 mins.
VHS: S27068. $12.95.

Wishbone: Salty Dog

Buried treasure lures Wishbone the dog into a south sea adventure. Inspired by Robert Louis Stevensons's *Treasure Island,* this live-action children's video has everything a kid could want, including pirate's gold, mutiny on the high seas, and the legend of Blackbeard. 30 mins.
VHS: S27779. $12.95.

Wishbone: Terrified Terrier

Wishbone the dog stars in this live-action children's video inspired by Stephen Crane's *The Red Badge of Courage.* Left alone when Joe finds new basketball buddies, Wishbone sets out to earn his very own badge of courage. 30 mins.
VHS: S27778. $12.95.

Wishbone: The Prince and the Pooch

Mark Twain's *The Prince and the Pauper* is cleverly reinterpreted for today's kids in this charming episode. While Joe merely wants to be a coach, Wishbone ends up as both the Prince of Wales and a lowly pauper in this tale of role switching and big trouble. 30 mins.
VHS: S27070. $12.95.

Wishbone: The Slobbery Hound

Wishbone is the sleuthing dog who inspires kids to read. In this episode based on Sir Arthur Conan Doyle's *The Hound of the Baskervilles,* Wishbone dons a cape and demeanor reminiscent of Sherlock Holmes. It's up to him to track down the mystery curse of the Baskerville family. 30 mins.
VHS: S27067. $12.95.

Wishbone: Twisted Tail

Kids will want to read Charles Dickens' *Oliver Twist* after watching Wishbone in *Twisted Tail.* Joe's house is burglarized and fingers start pointing to the new kid, Max. Meanwhile, Wishbone is trapped by a gang of colorful criminals on the streets of London. 30 mins.
VHS: S27069. $12.95.

X-Men: The Phoenix Saga Part 1: The Sacrifice

Professor Xavier dispatches the X-Men to the space station Starcore, where they encounter the villainous Erik the Red—an agent of the Sh'iar Empire who is conspiring to tear a hole in the fabric of space! EP Speed.
VHS: S25690. $9.95.
Saban, USA, 25 mins.

X-Men: The Phoenix Saga Part 2: The Dark Shroud

A powerful psychic probe is attempting to contact Professor Xavier. Is this the mysterious force that has transformed Jean Grey into the enigmatic Phoenix? EP Speed.
VHS: S25689. $9.95.
Saban, USA, 25 mins.

Year Without a Santa Claus

When Santa decides to take a year off, Mrs. Claus and the elves must convince him how important he is to the children of the world. His elves fall into trouble with the miserable Snowmiser and Heatmiser. Stop-motion animation with Mickey Rooney voicing Santa Claus.
VHS: S29776. $12.95.
Rankin/Bass, USA, 1974, 51 mins.

Yes, Virginia, There Is a Santa Claus

Many years ago, a newspaper editorial assured a little girl that her belief in Santa Claus was the soul of the Christmas spirit. Now the story comes to life in this animated holiday special.
VHS: S13040. $9.95.
Wolper/Melendez, USA, 1974, 25 mins.

Yogi Bear's All-Star Comedy Christmas Caper

Yogi and Boo-Boo sneak off to the city and make Christmas merry for a lonely little rich girl, Judy Jones, with some help from their old friends, in this All-Star TV special.
VHS: S29779. $9.95.
Hanna-Barbera, USA, 1982, 30 mins.

Yogi the Easter Bear

A prime-time TV special featuring the voice of Jonathan Winters. Pauly and Ernest have kidnapped the Easter Bunny and are intent on creating an all-plastic world, beginning with Easter eggs. Yogi and Boo-Boo must come to the rescue. Bonus short *Yakky Duck in Easter Duck.*
VHS: S29777. $12.95.
Hanna-Barbera, USA, 55 mins.

Zorro

Contains two episodes from the animated TV series *The Adventures of Zorro.*
Zorro: Beastly Battle.
VHS: S34350. $9.95.
Zorro: Double Trouble.
VHS: S34349. $9.95.
Zorro: High Seas Hero.
VHS: S34353. $9.95.
Zorro: Night of Terror.
VHS: S34352. $9.95.
Zorro: The First Encounter.
VHS: S34351. $9.95.

INTERNATIONAL & INDEPENDENT

Aaron's Magic Village

This European musical co-production is based on stories by Isaac Bashevis Singer. Young Aaron and his wisecracking goat, Zlateh, journey to Chelm—an idyllic village of fools which has come under attack by an evil sorcerer. Aaron embarks on a comical journey to foil the sorcerer and his gargantuan beast, Golem. CC.
VHS: S32196. $19.95.
France, 1995, 80 mins.

Abel's Island

While picnicking with his beloved wife Amanda, Abelard Hassam di Chirico Flint, the elegant mouse, is swept away to a deserted island by a sudden storm and must learn to survive using only his wits and his newly awakened creativity.
VHS: S29591. $14.95.
Michael Sporn, USA, 30 mins.

Adventures of Prince Achmed

The first animated feature film—a landmark of cinema created in Weimar Germany with Lotte Reiniger's unique paper cutout silhouette technique. The stories, based on tales from *The Arabian Nights,* come wonderfully alive in this sensitive and imaginative work. A truly beautiful film that must be seen to be believed. Transferred from an original tinted and toned print. B&W.
VHS: S22881. $19.95.
Lotte Reiniger, Germany, 1927, 65 mins.

Alchemist of the Surreal

Five mixed-media animated stop-motion short films from the director of *Alice: Jabberwocky* (1971), *Dimensions of Dialogue* (1982), *The Last Trick* (1964), *Punch & Judy* (1966) and *Etcetera* (1966).

VHS: S14554. $24.95.

Jan Svankmajer, Czechoslovakia, 1964-82, 60 mins.

Alexander Alexeieff

The creator of the "pin board" discusses his invention and its application for book illustrations as well as art film. With wife and colleague Claire Parker. Clips from their work, including their film of Gogol's short story *The Nose*. 1966, 28 mins.

VHS: S31600. $59.95.

Alexeieff & Parker

In their Paris studio, Russian-born artist/filmmaker Alexander Alexeieff and his American wife, Claire Parker, show and explain how they create pictures on the instrument they invented, the pinscreen (l'ecran de'epingles), in *Alexeieff at the Pinboard (A Propos de Jivago)* (1960, 8 mins.). *The Nose (Le Nez)* (1963, 11 mins.) is Gogol's celebrated short story in pinscreen animation, without words, in fantastic moving pictures that capture the scene and spirit of 19th century Russia. *Night on Bald Mountain (Une Nuit sur le Mont Chauve)* (1933, 8 mins.) is the first film made on pinboard. In this reknowned illustration of Modest Moussorgsky's tone poem, goblins, skeletons and other fantastic creatures perform outlandish three-dimensional effects. Animator Norman McLaren listed the film "first and foremost" among the animated films he most admired and liked. "Above all it is the quality of Alexeieff's imagination that stirs me profoundly," McLaren said. 27 mins.

VHS: S30223. $75.00.

Alice

Jan Svankmajer, the Czech master of animation, has fulfilled a lifetime ambition in this interpretation of *Alice in Wonderland*. Svankmajer's Alice remains true to Carroll's original, but bears the stamp of his own distinctive style and obsessions. Combination of animation and live action.

VHS: S10942. $19.95.

Jan Svankmajer, Czechoslovakia, 1988, 84 mins.

Alice in Wonderland

One of the most faithful adaptations of Lewis Carroll's satirical daydream, this long-lost masterpiece was produced and directed by master puppetoonist Lou Bunin in England. The film starts with a live-action prologue, then enters the abstract Wonderland with incomparable puppets and Carol Marsh as Alice.

VHS: S06599. $24.95.

Lou Bunin, USA, 1951, 80 mins.

Alice in Wonderland in Paris

Gene Dietch directed this compilation film of various shorts. Alice meets Francois Mouse, who promises to take her to Paris to meet her heroine, Madeline. The story serves as a bridge between five stand-alone animated shorts: *Madeline & The Bad Hat, Madeline & The Gypsies, Anatole, The Frowning Prince* and *Many Moons*. LP Speed.

VHS: S17452. $19.95.

Rembrandt Films, USA, 52 mins.

All the Great Operas in Ten Minutes

Behind the long and expansive librettos of most operas lies a kernel of overpowering excitement. In this hysterical ten-minute animation the nutty centers of these works are revealed in brief, pithy manifestations. Among the operas lampooned are; *La Traviata, Aida, Tosca, Tristan and Isolde, Madame Butterfly* and *The Ring of the Nibelungen*.

VHS: S29295. $12.95.

Allegro Non Troppo

Bruno Bozzetto's irreverent tribute to Disney's *Fantasia*. From outrageously funny satire to breathtaking lyricism, this film visualizes six popular works by Debussy, Dvorak, Ravel, Sibelius, Vivaldi and Stravinsky. Maurizio Nichetti stars in the live-action interludes between each piece, which are now subtitled.

VHS: S00035. $29.95.

Bruno Bozetto, Italy, 1976, 85 mins.

American Pop

After years of box-office and critical up-and-downs, in 1981 Ralph Bakshi directed this ambitious allegorical tale about contemporary music. It's a retrospective of American pop music as told through the lives of four generations of musicians. Made during Bakshi's heavy rotoscope period, the film offers a soundtrack loaded with the likes of Gershwin, Porter, Brubeck, Dylan, The Doors, Hendrix, The Mamas and Papas, Pat Benatar, Lou Reed, Bob Seger and many more.

VHS: S33317. $13.95.
Laser: LD76758. $34.95.
DVD: DV60198. $24.95.

Ralph Bakshi, USA, 1981, 96 mins.

An American Retrospective Through Animation

These educational short films illustrate how great the American free-enterprise system is. They are well-animated, well-written and entertaining, and convey a great sense of postwar American values. Six titles: an inventor becomes a soap tycoon in *Going Places*; the American worker leads the world in *Meet King Joe*; inflation is explained in *Why Play Leap Frog*; the socialist system is mercilessly parodied in *Albert in Blunderland*; business competition is illustrated in *Inside Cackle Corner*; and the American consumer is celebrated in *The Littlest Giant*.

VHS: S29597. $19.95.

John Sutherland, USA, 1948-54, 60 mins.

AMIGA Animation: Volume 2

This second volume features a more advanced look at the area of home computer animation.

VHS: S16982. $24.95.

Ancient Alien

Propels you on an astonishing computer animated journey in search of mythic realms, gravity-defying beings, molten chrome oceans and fantastic volcanic archipelagoes. Integrated with exotic electronic music, these digital visuals create a powerfully immersive cyber-odyssey. 45 mins.

DVD: DV60260. $24.95.
VHS: S34577. $14.95.

Animaland

David Hand was one of the key figures in developing the Disney style of full animation. He directed *Snow White* and *Bambi* plus many Oscar-winning *Silly Symphonies*. Following WWII, Hand went to England to produce a series of 19 films for the J. Arthur Rank Organisation. The films range from stylized fantasies of regional Britain to fully realized character animation featuring Ginger Nutt. Film print quality varies. Four titles: *Ginger Nutt's Forest Dragon* ('50), *Ginger Nutt's Bee Bother* ('49), *A Fantasy on London Life* ('50) and *It's a Lovely Day* ('49).

VHS: S16647. $19.95.

GB Animation, UK, 1949-50, 30 mins.

Animaland

David Hand was one of the key figures in developing the Disney style of full animation. He directed *Snow White* and *Bambi* plus many Oscar-winning *Silly Symphonies*. Following WWII, Hand went to England to produce a series of 19 films for the J. Arthur Rank Organisation. The films range from stylized fantasies of regional Britain to fully realized character animation featuring Ginger Nutt. This new compilation has very good prints. Nine titles: *Platypus* ('48), *Ginger Nutt's Christmas Circus* ('49), *Ginger Nutt's Forest Dragon* ('50), *The Cuckoo* ('48), *Ginger Nutt's Bee Bother* ('49), *The Lion* ('48), *The Ostrich* ('49), *The House-Cat* ('48) and *Ginger Nutt in It's a Lovely Day* ('49). HiFi.

VHS: S16649. $14.95.

G.B. Animation, UK, 1948-50, 80 mins.

Animated Commercials #1

Did you know that Winston cigarettes originally sponsored the Flintstones? Gaze in wonderment as Fred and Barney hide out behind the house puffing on cigs. A wonderful compilation of animated characters, including classic Raid commercials, Shamus Culhane's Muriel Cigars commercials, the Hamm's Bear, EZ-Pop popcorn, Maypo and Westinghouse.

VHS: S29599. $24.95.

USA, 60 mins.

Animated Commercials #2

Heinz Beans, Yoo Hoo soft drink, Mr. & Mrs Potato Head with Hasbro Kid, B.C. gang for Marathon, Screaming Yellow Zonkers: Celebrities, Alka Seltzer: When You and Your Stomach Disagree (voice of Gene Wilder), Schweppes Bitter Orange, Schweppes Bitter Lemon, Elsie the Cow, Old Gold Cigarettes, Good 'n Plenty, Cocoa Puffs, Hostess Choco-Diles, Chesterfield Cigarettes, Nabisco, Hydrox Cookies, Winston Cigarettes: Pixilated Matchbooks, Rinso Detergent, Chunky Chocolate, Old Nick Chocolate, Bumble Bee Tuna, Clanky Chocolate Syrup, Muriel Cigars: Fresh Tin, Puma Soft Drink, Ipana Toothpaste, FrostyOs, Trix and many, many more!

VHS: S29600. $24.95.

USA, 60 mins.

Animated Commercials #3

Beech Nut Fruit Stripe Gum, Cheerios Kid, Bromo Seltzer, Lustre Creme, Ideal Toys: Mr. Machine, Esso, Bab-O Cleanser, Wildroot, Band-Aid, P.F. Flyers, Mattell: Thunder Burp Machine Gun, Cheerios Kid, Ipana, Armour Star Franks, Baker's Instant Chocolate: Jiminy Cricket, Trix, Snickers, Hostess: Captain Cupcake, Frosty-O's, Lucky Charms, Twinkles, Hamms Bear: Pie Fight, Ritz Crackers, Oreos, Fig Newtons, Lorna Doones, Sugar Wafers, Chocolate Chip Pecans, Vanilla Wafers, Shredded Wheat, Peter Pan Peanut Butter: Tinkerbell, Jell-O, Log Cabin Syrup, Peter Pan Peanut Butter: P-Nuttiest, Canada Dry: Dumbo, General Mills: Pick A Pack, Matty's Funday Funnies: Casper The Ghost, and many, many more!

VHS: S29601. $24.95.

USA, 60 mins.

Animated Commercials #4

Ajax: Foaming Cleanser Elves, Muriel Cigars: Pick Me Up & Smoke Me Sometime (Culhane), Quaker Puffed Wheat & Rice, Playhouse 90 Opening Title, Peter Pan Peanut Butter: Tinkerbell/Shadow Pictures, Cheerios Kid, Hi Ho Crackers: Sunshine Bakers, Coca Cola, Nabisco Wheat & Rice Honeys: Buffalo Bee, Lorna Doones, Keebler Cinnamon Crisp, Beech Nut Gum: Jazz Combo, Yellow Pages, Gillette Super Speed Razor, Dixie Cup Dispenser, Campbells BBQ Beans, DX Gasoline, Star Kist: Charlie The Tuna/Studious Type, Colgate Toothpaste, Count Chocula & Frankenberry, Funny Face Drink Mix, Cheerios: Bullwinkle/Watch Where You're Going, Vaseline Hair Tonic: Talking Sink and many, many more!

VHS: S29602. $24.95.

USA, 60 mins.

Animated Commercials #5

Fig Newton, Salada, Bond Bread, Coke, D-Frost, Macintosh Apple, Nabisco, Cheerios, Quisp & Quake, Cocoa Puffs, Corn Bursts, Whistle Snack, Sugar Smacks, Milk Bone, Bosco, Good 'n Plenty, Zoom Cereal, Ideal Bread, RCA, Sylvania, Lucky Stripe, Vitalis and many more.

VHS: S29603. $24.95.

USA, 60 mins.

Animated Commercials #6

An internal sales film for Aurora's "New Generation" toy line (ca. 1967) starring Fred & Barney, an interview with Lou Gifford discussing his studio's TV commercial animation (Lestoil) and the technique of storyboarding and cel animation, Rocky & Bullwinkle for General Mills cereals, Charlie the Tuna, Frito Bandito, Cheerios Kid, Trix Rabbit, Tony Tiger, the 1969 Plymouth cars with the Roadrunner and Wile E. Coyote, Quisp & Quake, Donald Duck and Porky Pig Soaky Toys, the 1964 Falcon with Charlie Brown and Linus, Chrysler cars and much, much more!

VHS: S29604. $24.95.

USA, 60 mins.

Animation Celebration Vol. 1

Twenty-three titles: *Animation Has No Borders* (Peter Sweenen/Holland), *Augusta Makes Herself Beautiful* (Csaba Varga/Hungary), *Cat and Mouse* (Kirk Henderson/USA), *Characters* (Evert De Beijer/Holland), *The Chicken* (Sotir Gelev/Bulgaria), *The Chore* (Joe Murray/USA), *Come Back to Sorrento* (Donio Donev/Bulgaria), *Cuckoo* (Velislav Kasakov/Bulgaria), *Dino Alley* (Chiodo Brothers/USA), *Disconnected* (Craig Welch/Canada), *Happy Hour* (Brett Koth/USA), *It's an OK Life* (George Griffin/USA), *Moebius Play* (Tita Cooley/USA), *Mongo Makongo* (Michael Posch/USA), *Oh What a Knight* (Paul Driessen/Holland), *Quasi's Cabaret Trailer* (Sally Cruikshank/USA), *Quest: A Long Ray's Journey into Light* (Michael Scuilli/USA), *Rope Dance* (Raimond Krumme/Germany), *Second Class Mail* (Alison Snowden & David Fine/UK), *Sunbeam* (Paul Vester/UK), *The Strange Case of Mr. Donnybrook's Boredom* (David Silverman/USA), *Traveling Light* (Jane Aaron/USA) and *The Wreck of the Julie Plante* (Weston & Grant/UK).

VHS: S17041. $29.95.
Laser: CAV. **LD71772. $49.95.**

90 mins.

Animation Celebration Vol. 2

Seventeen titles: *ASIFA Children's Film Beat Dedication* (Bob Sabiston/USA), *A Crushed World* (Boyo Kanev/Bulgaria), *Eternity* (Sheryl Sardina/USA), *Finger Wave* (Gyula Nagy/Hungary), *Goodnight Norma... Goodnight Milton* (John Schnall/USA), *Lady and the Lamp* (John Lasseter/USA), *Lazar* (Gavrilo Gnatovich/USA), *Paradisia* (Marcy Page/USA), *Pencil Dance* (Chris Casady/USA), *Propagandance* (Tom Sito/USA), *Quinoscopo #2 (Juan Padron/Cuba), Salome* (Maurizio Forestieri/Italy), *A Salute to Olive Jar* (USA), *Scaredy Cat* (Paul Clarehout/USA), *Suspicious Circumstances* (Jim Blashfield/USA), *25 Ways to Quit Smoking* (Bill Plympton/USA) and *Umbabarauma* (Susan Young & Mike Smith/UK).

VHS: S25826. $29.95.

90 mins.

Animation Celebration Vol. 3

Twenty titles: *The Animated Star Spangled Banner* (Skip Battaglia/USA), *Bonehead* (Michael A. Kory & Peter Conn/USA), *Darkness, Light, Darkness* (Jan Svankmajer/Czechoslovakia), *Fumo* (Giorgio Guglielmetti/Italy), *Lava Jr.* (Randy Bauer/USA), *Mr. Tao* (Bruno Bozetto/Italy), *New Fangled* (George Griffin/USA), *A Nice Day in the Country* (Chris Hinton/Canada), *Personality Software* (Sylvie Fefer/Canada), *Plymptoons* (Bill Plympton/USA), *Poumse* (Mikhail Aldashin/USSR), *Prehistoric Beast* (Phil Tippett/USA), *The Reading Room* (John Schnall/USA), *Snowie and The Seven Dorps* (Candy Kugel & Vincent Cafarelli/USA), *Still Life* (Georges Le Piouffle/France), *This Is Not Frank's Planet* (Mike Wellins & Mark Swain/USA), *War Story* (Peter Lord/UK), *Welcome* (Alexei Karaev/USSR), *Wiseman* (Bill Plympton/USA) and *Zeno Reads a Newspaper* (Ferenc Cako/Hungary).

VHS: S25825. $29.95.

90 mins.

Animation Celebration Vol. 4

Nineteen titles: *The Boss* (Alison Snowden & David Fine/UK), *The Button* (Robert Sakayants/Armenia), *Canfilm* (Zlatin Radev/Bulgaria), *Dancing* (Bruno Bozetto/Italy), *Fantastic Person* (Candy Guard/UK), *The Green Beret* (Stephen Hillenburg/USA), *The Hunter* (Mikhail Aldashin/USSR), *Madcap* (Phil Denslow/USA), *Office Space* (Mike Judge/USA), *Okay Tex* (Rumen Petkov/Bulgaria), *Pre-Hysterical Daze* (Gavrilo Gnatovich/USA), *Quinoscopo #3* (Juan Padron/Cuba), *RRRINGG!* (Paul de Nooijer/Netherlands), *A Smaller World "Big Baby"* (Corky Quakenbush/USA), *The Song of Wolfgang the Intrepid* (Mikhail Tumelya/USSR), *The Tale of Nippoless Nippleby* (DNA Productions/USA), *Tarzan* (Taku Furukawa/Japan), *Unsavory Avery* (John Schnall/USA) and *Weeds* (Thomas Stellmach/Germany).
VHS: S25827. $29.95.
90 mins.

Animation Dreams

This magical tapestry of 12 incredible, computer-animated sequences is among the most amazing collection available on video. Human figure animation is a highlight of this imaginative journey where anything is possible—even dolphins fly. John Flommer created the original soundtrack.
VHS: S22418. $9.99.

Animation for Fallen Catholics

Nuns on wheels, priests in purgatory, heavy guilt and lots of laughs. Ten titles: *Opening Dance* (Michael Wheeler), *Divine Miracle* (Daina Krumins), *Regina Coeli* (Maria Elena Rodriguez), *Heavenly Taste* (Kevin Bourque), *Landscape with the Fall of Icarus* (Christopher Sullivan), *Intermission Song* (Michael Wheeler), *Alterations* (Patti Tauscher), *Simply Divine* (Kevin Bourque), *Divine Departure* (Jeff Bloomer) and *Finale Dance (Michael Wheeler)*.
VHS: S16474. $19.95.
USA, 60 mins.

The Animation Game

Illustration, three-dimensional models and cut-out animation are all explored in this video. Featuring the award-winning animator David Johnson. 15 mins.
VHS: S23498. $49.95.

Animation in the '30s

Nine titles: *Crosby, Columbo and Vallee* ('32/WB), *Three's a Crowd* ('33/WB), *Hollywood Capers* ('35/WB), *Songs You Like to Sing—"Margie"* ('29), *Grampy's Indoor Outing* ('36/Fleischer), *Betty in Blunderland* ('34/Fleischer), *Let's Sing with Popeye* ('34/Fleischer), *Happy You and Merry Me* ('36/Fleischer) and *Sinkin' in the Bathtub* ('30/WB).
VHS: S27964. $19.95.
USA, 1929-36, 57 mins.

Animation in The Netherlands

This documentary of Dutch animation covers such illustrious figures as George Pal, Borge Ring *(Anna and Bella)* and Paul Dreissen. Also shown are the works of Joop Geesink *(Dollywood)*, Martin Toonder, Gerrit van Dijk *(Pas a Deux)*, Ellen Meske *(The Inflatable Alphabet)* and many, many more.
VHS: S17053. $19.95.
Nico Crama, Holland, 30 mins.

Animation Propaganda

Four non-theatrical animated shorts. *Easy Does It* (1946/Hugh Harman) is a moral tale promoting Stokely VanCamp foods which is distinguished by its lavish production values. As good as anything Harman did at MGM, this short contains adult sexual innuendo and lots of campy laughs. *Winky the Watchman* (1951/Hugh Harman) is another lavish production promoting good dental hygiene. *Cleanliness Brings Health* (1946/Disney) teaches our backwards South American neighbors the rudiments of sanitation and disease prevention. *The Winged Scourge* (1954/Disney) shows the Seven Dwarfs eradicating the mosquito to prevent malaria.
VHS: S09709. $17.95.
Disney/Harman, USA, 1946-54, 60 mins.

Animation Vol. 1: The Beginning

A survey of animation from 1906 to 1927, including *Humorous Phases of Funny Faces, La Rateleur, Fantasmagoria, Mobiliu Fedele, Little Nemo, Revenge of the Kinematograph Cameraman, Professor Bonehead Is Shipwrecked, Gertie the Dinosaur, Dinosaur and the Missing Link, The Sinking of The Lusitania, Bobby Bumps Puts a Beanery on the Bum, Modelling/Bubbles, Laugh-O-Grams, Puss 'n Boots, Alice on the Farm, Small Town Sheriff, Felix in Hollywood, Oswald* and *The Mechanical Cow*. B&W.
VHS: S04816. $29.95.
1906-27, 120 mins.

Animation Vol. 2

More early animation, including *Dream of a Rarebit Fiend* (1906), *Gertie* (the true 1914 McCay version), *Krazy Kat* (1916), *The Flying House* (1921), *Surprise* (1923), *Felix in Fairyland* (1925) and *Alice's Egg Plant* (1925). B&W.
VHS: S08869. $24.95.
USA, 1906-25, 66 mins.

Annabelle's Wish

A lovable calf named Annabelle, born on Christmas Eve, wishes she could fly like one of Santa's reindeer. Based on the farm legend that Santa gives voices to the animals for one day each year. Voices of Randy Travis, Cloris Leachman, Jerry Van Dyke, Jim Varney and Alison Krauss. CC. Stereo.
VHS: S32190. $16.95.
Baer Animation, 1997, 54 mins.

Aquaman (DC Superpowers Collection)

Eight episodes: *Where Lurks the Fisherman, The Microscopic Monster, Mephisto's Marine Marauders, The War of the Quantix & The Bimphars, Onslaught of the Octomen, Treacherous Is the Torpedoman, Trio of Terror* and *To Catch a Fisherman*.
VHS: S27932. $9.95.
Filmation, USA, 1967-69, 60 mins.

Asterix in Britain

With his magical potion and Obelisk at his side, Asterix prevents Caesar's invading legions from conquering ancient Britain. Very high production values and wit from director Pino Van Lamsweerde.
VHS: S12527. $14.95.
Gaumont, France, 1986, 85 mins.

Asterix vs. Caesar

Asterix and Obelisk decide Caesar's troops have wandered too far from Rome. They battle legions of centurions with the mystical help of a strength-giving magic potion.
VHS: S12526. $39.95.
Gaumont, France, 1985, 85 mins.

Attack of the Cohl Pumpkins

A collection of early primitives by pioneering animator Emile Cohl: *The Pumpkin Race, The Joyous Microbes, Neo-Impressionist Painter* and *Bewitched Matches*. B&W.
VHS: S05793. $24.95.
Emile Cohl, France, 30 mins.

Attic in the Blue

A stop-motion puppet animation by three Canadian filmmakers. An aging mariner joins a comical octopus-like creature on a search for "where lost things go." Their voyage takes them to the Attic in the Blue.
VHS: S18930. $14.95.
Adam Ciolfi, Canada, 1992, 27 mins.

B'raesheet

John Teton's student film is the lyrical voyage of a human embryo and the fantastic vision it experiences prior to birth. Set to Stravinsky's "Firebird," this multi-award-winning short is a mesmerizing experience.
VHS: S34935. $19.95.
John Teton, USA, 1973, 8 mins.

Babar: The Movie

Babar must save his kingdom from certain destruction by Rataxes and his band of invading rhinos in this full-length theatrical feature. EP Speed.
VHS: S11696. $12.95.
Nelvana, Canada, 1988, 79 mins.

Back to the Forest

When tree-chopping townspeople invade their forest home, the heroic birds and animals outwit them with sheer ingenuity. HiFi Stereo.
VHS: S12583. $14.95.
Nippon, Japan, 1989, 75 mins.

Banjo the Woodpile Cat

Don Bluth literally made this film in his garage while a disaffected Disney employee. It was his attempt to relearn the "lost" techniques of classical animation that he felt Disney had abandoned after Walt's death. Banjo, a mischievous kitten, hops a truck and explores the big city. Chased by dogs, lost and alone, he is befriended by Crazy Legs (Scatman Crothers), who cheers him up with songs while they search for another truck to take Banjo home. The technical virtuosity and storytelling conventionality for which Bluth became known are clearly in evidence in this first solo effort.
VHS: S34175. $9.98.
Don Bluth, USA, 1979, 27 mins.

Bebe's Kids

When Robin meets the beautiful Jamika, he's smitten. But on their first date, she greets him with four small surprises: her son Leon and girlfriend Bebe's three trouble-seeking kids. Based on the popular characters created by late comedian Robin Harris, featuring the voices of Nell Carter and rapper Tone-Loc. Also features Hyperion's seven-minute animated short *Itsy Bitsy Spider*. Stereo.
VHS: S21453. $14.95.
Laser: LD75118. $34.95.
Hudlin Bros, USA, 1992, 74 mins.

The Best of Bruno Bozzetto

In this unique compilation video, Italian animator Bruno Bozzetto presents the shorts he considers most representative of his work. Introducing each of the program's four parts, he shares his inspiration for *Self-Service*, his vision of the insect world; *Mr. Rossi Wins an Award*, featuring his most popular character; the Oscar-nominated *Grasshoppers*; and other colorful fantasies. Fourteen titles: *Self-Service, Baeus, Drop, Life in a Tin, Baby Story, Sigmund, Dancing, Mr. Rossi Wins an Award, Mr. Rossi Buys a Car, Ego, Big Bang, Man and His World, Pickles* and *Grasshoppers*.
VHS: S34341. $29.95.
Italtoons, 81 mins.

Best of the Fests 1990

Eleven shorts: *Dr. Ded Bug* (Ethan Cohen-Sitt), *Geologic Time* (Skip Battaglia), *The Measurements of Oxford* (Barry Kimm), *Rumba* (Charles Weiner), *Middle Grays* (Sherann Johnson), *Song from an Angel* (David Weissman), *Macha's Curse* (Rose Bond), *No Pain No Gain* (Tom Brozovich), *Triangle* (Robert Doucette), *An Urban Tragedy* (Wendell Morris) and *Spartacus Rex* (L. Phillipps).
VHS: S13833. $19.95.
USA, 1990, 90 mins.

Best of the Fests 1991

Eleven shorts—four animated, seven live-action: *Six Point Nine* (Dan Bootzin), *Why We Fight* (Byron Gush), *Balloon Head* (Eric Whitfield), *Walls in the Woods* (Sal Giammona), *Post No Bills* (Clay Walker), *Wanting for Bridge* (Joan Stavely), *In Transit* (Kevin Bourque), *Harvest Town* (Tom Schroeder), *Stealing Altitude* (Roger Teich & John Starr), *Madcap* (Phil Denslow) and *Man Descending* (Neil Grieve).
VHS: S15543. $19.95.
USA, 1991, 90 mins.

Best of the Fests, 5th Annual

Fourteen shorts. Animated shorts are *Tabare Se Mueve* (Imagenes Studio/Uruguay), *Bob the Frog in 'Burp'* (Darren Kiner/USA), *Faith & Patience* (Sheila M. Sofian), *Enough* (Emily Hubley/USA), *Milk of Amnesia* (Jeffrey N. Scher) and *The Listener* (Christopher Landreth). Non-animated shorts are *Don't Touch That Dial* (David Pace/Victor Bellomo), *My Birthday Cake* (Whitney Ransick), *You'll Change* (Kelley Baker), *Omnibus* (San Karmann), *Waiting for Max* (Julian Stone), *Le Beatnik Sophistique* (Tony Vegas), *Through an Open Window* (Eric Mendelsohn) and *A Lobster Tale* (Marc Lazzard).
VHS: S17873. $19.95.
1993, 90 mins.

Best of the Fests: For Kids

Eight shorts: *Pumpkin Madness II* (David Gray), *Metal Dogs of India* (Chel White), *The Rooster* (Jonathon Lyons), *Skip It* (Bill Snider), *Housecats* (Peg McClure Moudy), *Fanaround* (David Gau), *Charlie's Boogie Woogie* (Valerie Swanson) and *Travels of a Dollar Bill* (Phil McKenney).
VHS: S13834. $14.95.
40 mins.

Beyond the Mind's Eye

A new compilation of the latest computer animation clips, set to an original score by Jan Hammer. Includes animation from "Lawnmower Man."
VHS: S17600. $19.95.
Laser: LD75695. $29.95.
Michael Boydstun, 1992, 45 mins.

The Big Friendly Giant

In this animated adaptation of Roald Dahl's story, a young orphan named Sophie and a 25-foot-tall giant embark on a journey to rid the world of gruesome, bone-crunching giants.
VHS: S27481. $14.95.
Cosgrove-Hall, UK, 1990, 95 mins.

Black Anthology Vol. 1: Cannibals, Carusoes & Uncle Toms

Seven titles: *Uncle Tom's Cabana* ('47/MGM/Tex Avery), *Uncle Tom's Bungalow* ('37/WB/Tex Avery), *Eliza on Ice* ('44/Mighty Mouse), *It Happened to Caruso* ('38), *Voodoo in Harlem* ('38/Walter Lantz), *Popeye Ala Mode* ('45/Famous Studios) and *Swing Wedding* ('37/MGM "Happy Harmonies"). Note: Picture quality is fair to poor.
VHS: S27977. $19.95.
USA, 1937-47, 60 mins.

Black Anthology Vol. 2: Little 'Ol Bosko

Seven Bosko cartoons: *The Old House* ('36), *Bosko's Easter Eggs* ('37), *Bosko and the Pirates* ('37), *Bosko and the Cannibals* ('37), *Bosko in Bagdad* ('38), *Bosko the Doughboy* ('31) and *Hold Anything* ('31). Note: Picture quality is fair to poor.
VHS: S27978. $19.95.
Warner/MGM, USA, 1931-38, 60 mins.

Black Anthology Vol. 3: Ones Mammy Toad Me Not To Watch

Seven titles: *Scrub Me Mama with a Boogie Beat* ('41/Lantz Swing Symphony), *John Henry & The Inky Poo* ('45/George Pal Puppetoon), *Jasper in a Jam* ('46/Puppetoon), *Rasslin' Match* ('34/Van Beuren/Amos N'Andy), *The Lion Tamer* ('34/Amos N' Andy), *The Early Worm Gets the Bird* ('40/WB/Tex Avery) and *The Little Broadcast* ('43/Puppetoon). Note: Picture quality is fair to poor.
VHS: S27979. $19.95.
USA, 1934-46, 60 mins.

Blaxploitation Cartoons

A collection of seldom-seen cartoons from the 1930s and '40s, including Amos 'n' Andy, Little Black Sambo, Jungle Jitters and more. 60 mins.
VHS: S35225. $24.95.

The Brave Frog

A poor treefrog named Jonathon moves to the woodland community of Rainbow Pond and tries to fit in. With his musical reed pipe and his girlfriend Pookie, he battles cats, snakes and sea monsters, and most of all the selfish King Leopold. Dubbed in English.
VHS: S23330. $14.95.
Laser: LD74839. $34.95.
Tatsunoko/Harmony Gold, Japan, 1985, 90 mins.

British & Australian Cartoons

Six titles by British Animated Productions (Bubble & Squeak), Eric Porter, David Hand Productions, plus Ub Iwerks' "Gran Pop" cartoons (UK release only): *Rabbit Stew* ('38 Aus), *Bimbo's Auto* ('36 Aus), *Big City* ('47 GB), *Ginger Nutt's Xmas Circus* ('49 GB), *A Busy Day* ('39 Gran' Pop) and *Beauty Shoppe* ('39 Gran' Pop). Color/B&W.
VHS: S28003. $17.95.
1936-49, 60 mins.

The British Animation Invasion

Twenty-two titles: *Bluefields Express* (Charlie Fletcher Watson), *Body Beautiful* (Joanna Quinn), *Childhood of a Prophet* (David Lodge), *Creature Comforts* (Nick Park), *Dolphins* (Ian Andrew), *Door* (David Anderson), *Going Equipped* (Peter Lord), *Ident* (Richard Goleszowski, *Jollity Farm* (David Stone), *Jonathan Hodgson Showreel* (Jonathan Hodgson), *Snapper Showreel* (Matt Forest), *Mike Smith Showreel* (Mike Smith), *Moanalogue* (Candy Guard), *Next* (Barry Purves), *Night Visitors* (Richard Ollive), *Picnic* (Paul Vester), *Prophet and Loss* (Jonathan Bairstow), *Strangers in Paradise* (Andrew Staveley), *Susan Young Showreel* (Susan Young), *Them* (Bill Mather), *What About Me* (Candy Guard) and *Wishful Thinking* (Candy Guard).
VHS: S25824. $29.95.
UK, 90 mins.

British Animation Vol. 2

Six rare British animated shorts, including *The Lion* (Animaland), *Platypus (Animaland), and* Old Manor House (Bubble and Squeek).
VHS: S08958. $29.95.

The Brothers Quay Vol. 1

About as far from Disney as you can get—the work of these expatriate American twins, the Brothers Quay, takes puppet animation to its furthest extremes. Terrence Rafferty calls their work "the loveliest, most hypnotic, most profoundly disturbing films ever made in that particular form." Two titles: *The Street of Crocodiles* ('86) and *The Cabinet of Jan Svankmajer* ('84). EP Speed.
VHS: S14160. $19.95.
Laser: LD72097. $59.95.
Atelier Koninck, UK, 1984-86, 35 mins.

The Brothers Quay Vol. 2

With their exquisitely surreal animated puppets, Stephen and Timothy Quay create innovative short films with unsurpassed skill and dark humor. Three titles: *Epic of Gilgamesh* ('81), *Rehearsals for Extinct Anatomies* ('88) and *Nocturna Artificiala* ('79).
VHS: S14146. $19.95.
Laser: CAV. LD72098. $59.95.
Atelier Koninck, UK, 1979-88, 60 mins.

Bruno Bozzetto: Animator, Vol. 1

This program looks at the eccentric body of animated and live action pieces by the talented creator of *Allegro Non Troppo*. Includes *Grasshopper, Baby Story, A Man and His World* and *The Sandwich*. 30 mins.
Laser: CAV. LD72087. $39.95.

Bruno the Kid

Bruce Willis supplies the voice of Bruno, a juvenile superspy, in this animated TV series from Film Roman.
VHS: S31482. $14.95.
Film Roman, USA, 1996, 72 mins.

Calvin & The Colonel Vol. 1

In an attempt to avoid the sort of criticism directed at the TV adaptation of their long-running *Amos 'n' Andy* radio series, Freeman Gosden and Charles Correll produced and voiced a cartoon version animated by Creston Studios *(Crusader Rabbit)*. The cigar-smoking bear Calvin J. Burnside stood in for Andy Brown, while Colonel Montgomery J. Klaxton was not far removed from George "Kingfish" Stevens. The scripts were usually quite witty—no surprise, since many of them were recycled word-for-word from the original *Amos 'n' Andy* radio scripts. Two episodes. In *Thanksgiving Dinner* the Colonel invites 36 relatives for Thanksgiving, thinking they'll forget. When they show up, he can't afford to feed them. In *Sister Sue's Sweetheart*, the Colonel's sister is getting married. This means he'll lose $300 a month, so he tries to stop the wedding.
VHS: S34847. $14.95.
Creston, USA, 1961, 50 mins.

Calvin & The Colonel Vol. 2

Two episodes. In *Sycamore Lodge*, the Colonel sublets his flooded-out vacation cottage to Calvin, but Maggi Belle and Sister Sue have also rented it out to someone. In *Wheeling and Dealing*, the Colonel is not supposed to drive a friend's car that he's storing. When he wrecks it, his next stop is the insurance company. Both episodes with original commercials.
VHS: S34848. $14.95.
Creston, USA, 1961, 50 mins.

Camel Boy

From the creator of *Dot and the Kangaroo*, an animated adventure story about the unique friendship between Ali, an Arabian boy, and his camel during a journey across the Great Victoria Desert in Western Australia.
VHS: S02703. $89.95.
Yoram Gross, Australia, 1984, 78 mins.

The Cameraman's Revenge: The Amazing Puppet Animation of Ladislaw Starewicz

Ladislaw Starewicz created some of the most imaginative and lovely works of puppet animation ever filmed. While working in Russia, he directed the legendary *The Cameraman's Revenge* (1912), a story of love and infidelity among the insects, and the newly rediscovered *The Insect's Christmas* (1913), a dazzlingly beautiful film of the yuletide celebrations of a Christmas tree ornament and his tiny friends. After relocating to Paris, he made the political allegory *Frogland* (1922), the hand-colored fable *Voice of the Nightingale* (1923), the irresistible *The Mascot* (1933) and the snowland fantasy *Winter Carousel* (1958). B&W and hand-colored.
VHS: S17860. $39.95.
Laser: LD76187. $39.95.
Ladislaw Starewicz, Russia/France, 1912-58, 80 mins.

Camouflage

A rare WWII army training film attributed to Paul Terry with a typical "slap the Japs" look. It presents a fascinating overview of camouflage techniques and concepts.
VHS: S28023. $9.95.
Paul Terry, USA, 1943, 21 mins.

Captain of the Forest

Famed canine detective Captain Schnauzer doggedly pursues his arch enemy, Zero the Cat. He goes undercover to foil Zero's plot to destroy a beautiful forest community, teaming up with his sidekick Eddie, a girl bear named Dorka and a wacky bat named Vinny. Directed by Atilla Dargay. Dubbed in English.
VHS: S29609. $24.95.
Pannonia Film, Hungary, 1989, 80 mins.

Cartoons Cel-ing Commercials Vol. 1

Animated commercials: Fred and Barney sneak cigarettes and Mr. Magoo pours beer. Superman and Tennessee Tuxedo sell soap. The Cheerios Kid saves Donald Duck from sharks. And sure you'd buy a Nash from Brer Rabbit. Mickey Mouse drawn by UPA for the 55 Rambler. Talking engines, giant safety eyes, Funny Face drinks, Mr. Bubble and more.
VHS: S13799. $19.95.
USA, 60 mins.

Cartoons Cel-ing Commercials Vol. 2

Animated commercials: Wash Tinkerbell's Peter Pan peanut butter down with Fred Flintstone's "Yabba Dabba Dew." Bucky Beaver and Annette Funicello, Alice in Wonderland and Alvin the Chipmunk sell Jell-O. Charlie Brown sells bread while Snoopy hawks dog food. Pink Panther Flakes and a UPA-drawn Donald Duck drives a Nash Rambler.
VHS: S13800. $19.95.
USA, 60 mins.

Cartoons That Time Forgot, Laserdisc Set Vol. 2

This two-laserdisc set contains the last two videotape volumes of the VHS tape series. B&W/Color.
Laser: LD72020. $49.95.
Van Beuren, USA, 1931-36, 155 mins.

The Cheese Stands Alone

These animated shorts by Mike Wellens reveal a unique and hilarious comic sense complimented by an innovative style. The nine works include *Au Revoir Mon Frigidaire*, about a man and his lovely refrigerator, and *The Big Fat World of Science*, a spoof of scientific illustration.
VHS: S24395. $24.95.
Mike Wellens, USA, 1994, 87 mins.

Chord Sharp

A 10-minute film which, using innovative animation, tells the story of one street musician's sudden rise to fame.
VHS: S12928. $19.95.
Joachim Kreck, Germany, 1989, 10 mins.

A Christmas Carol

Richard Williams' Oscar-winning short film was co-produced with Chuck Jones. Narrated by Michael Redgrave and voiced by Alistair Sim, this is an eerie, compelling version of the Dickens classic. The striking, hand-colored pencil rendering look contributes to the beautiful but grim atmosphere of Dickens' writing.
VHS: S22515. $9.95.
Richard Williams, Great Britain, 1972, 25 mins.

A Christmas Gift

Eight short films animated by the National Film Board of Canada, all reflecting the spirit of the season, including the hilarious *Great Toy Robbery, The Story of Christmas, The Sweater, December Lights, The Energy Carol, An Old Box, The Magic Flute*, and Oscar nominee *The Christmas Cracker*. 65 mins.
VHS: S13342. $29.95.

Classic Cereal Commercials from the '50s & '60s

Tony the Tiger introduces George Reeves and the Superman gang hawking Sugar Smacks at the Daily Planet. Trix are for kids. Do you remember the flying Twinkles elephant with the storybook package? You'll find it a tasty treat watching rare spots from Lucky Charms, Pebbles, Rice & Wheat Honeys with Buffalo Bee, Quisp & Quake and much more.
VHS: S21334. $24.95.
USA, 60 mins.

Classics in Clay

Four claymation shorts are joined on this video. *Good Advice, Fast Food, Bumble-Boogie* and *Jamaica No Problem* combine the best animated clay techniques with humor and insight. USA, 1993, 25 mins.
VHS: S27167. $14.95.

A Claymation Christmas Celebration

A Will Vinton claymation special. The California Raisins join a host of others in song and dance renditions of Christmas carols. Included are a trio of shuffling camels in *We Three Kings* and Quasimodo conducting the *Carol of the Bells*. EP Speed.
VHS: S28104. $12.95.
Will Vinton, USA, 1987, 27 mins.

A Claymation Comedy of Horrors

A Will Vinton claymation Halloween special. Wilshire Pig and his reluctant sidekick Sheldon Snail go off to find Dr. Frankenswine's monster. At the castle they must overcome a riotous jamboree of ghouls, goblins and spooks. EP Speed.
VHS: S17039. $9.95.
Will Vinton, USA, 1992, 27 mins.

A Claymation Easter

This Emmy Award winning Claymation TV special tells the story of the villainous Wilshire Pig, who has kidnapped the Easter Bunny and wants to be his replacement. EP Speed.

VHS: S18020. $12.95.

Will Vinton, USA, 1990, 27 mins.

Computer Animation Celebration

Twenty-three award-winning computer-animated shorts from international competitions such as Imagina, Londo Effects & Animation Festival, Softimage Student Animation Contest, Siggraph Electronic Theater and ResFest. 50 mins.

VHS: S35219. $14.95.

DVD: DV60495. $24.95.

Computer Animation Classics

A new compilation of milestone computer graphics clips—many from the 1980s.

VHS: S31492. $14.95.

USA, 58 mins.

Computer Animation Festival

From the producers of The Mind's Eye comes a new showcase of 20 cutting-edge computer-animated shorts. Each short from around the globe is shown in its entirety. Also includes Iwerks Entertainment TurboRide footage.

VHS: S29835. $14.95.

Laser: LD76050. $24.95.

Odyssey Prods, 1996, 58 mins.

Computer Animation Festival Vol. 1.0

21 award-winning computer animation shorts, including PDI's *Locomotion*, MIT's *Grinning Evil Death* and Todd Rundgren's music video *Change Myself*.

VHS: S18589. $9.95.

Laser: LD75618. $29.95.

Odyssey, 1993, 55 mins.

Computer Animation Festival Vol. 2.0

22 more award-winning shorts, including *Technological Threat*, Todd Rundgren's *Theology* and Peter Gabriel's *Liquid Selves* and *Steam*.

VHS: S27644. $9.95.

Laser: LD75619. $29.95.

Odyssey, USA, 1994, 58 mins.

Computer Animation Magic

A colorful expose on computer graphics, including logos, chrome dinosaurs and a night club piano player. These are just a few samples. 58 mins.

VHS: S13097. $9.95.

Computer Animation Showcase

A collection of 21 cutting-edge, international cyberart shorts from today's hottest computer graphics visionaries, including apioneering short from PIXAR, creators of *Toy Story*. Shorts include Luxo Jr. in *Light and Heavy, Walking Around, Joe & Basket: Mostly Sports, Dreammaker, Dutch Nelson, Galaxy Guy, Bluebird Penguin, Prelude to Eden, Tosio, Operating Manual for Spaceship Uterus, Fan-tasy, Displaced Dice, Amphibian Blues, Stomach Pump, JuJu Shampoo, Matador, A Time for Love, Tiny, Tinkle Terror, The Green Man, Puff* and *Beyond the Walls*. 46 mins.

VHS: S31752. $12.95.

Computer Dreams (Dream Machine Vol. 2)

A compilation of the latest computer graphics from over 100 artists and animation studios the world over, including Rhythm & Hues, PDI, Pixar, Cubicomp and much more. 174 clips.

VHS: S09848. $9.95.

Laser: LD70108. $49.95.

Geoffrey DeValois, 1989, 58 mins.

Computer Visions

Join Ray Tracy, the world's first computer-generated television host, on an international, behind-the-scenes sojourn through a spectacular universe of images and stories created by artists on the cutting edge of computer animation. 58 mins.

VHS: S30404. $9.95.

Computer Visions (Dream Machine Vol. 3)

The third volume in Voyager's Dream Machine series. Hosts Sharon Sheehan and the computer-generated Ray Tracy show how computers are being used to simulate complex real-world phenomena such as gravity, fire and motion, with behind the scenes peeks at JPL, Ohio State and MIT.

Laser: LD70122. $49.95.

60 mins.

The Coneheads

The animated version of the popular *Saturday Night Live* characters, with voices of the original cast.

VHS: S28116. $12.95.

Rankin/Bass, USA, 1983, 23 mins.

Cool World

Bakshi's most ambitious film is a combination of animation and live action starring Kim Basinger and Brad Pitt. The creator of cartoon bombshell Holli Would is pulled by his creation into Cool World, a land where all the cartoon characters ("doodles") live and occasionally interact with visiting humans. *Cool World* has been compared to *Who Framed Roger Rabbit*, but taken to extremes only Ralph Bakshi would dare attempt.

VHS: S28122. $19.95.

Laser: Letterboxed. **LD75621. $34.95.**

Ralph Bakshi, USA, 1992, 101 mins.

Coonskin

One of the most controversial films ever made, *Coonskin* is an angry, violent portrayal of Harlem street life and the black condition of the 1970s. Live action and animation, starring Barry White, Scatman Crothers and Philip Michael Thomas. Original, uncut version. ADULTS ONLY.

VHS: S29624. $29.95.

Ralph Bakshi, USA, 1975, 89 mins.

Crash Corrigan: One More Chance

Sean, the son of a naval pilot, is drawn to excitement and danger, which he pursues through his racing career. When his confidence is shaken by a serious accident, his friends wonder if he can recover for the year's most treacherous race, the Alpine Rally. USA, 1992, 90 mins.

VHS: S18212. $29.95.

Creating Animation on a Computer

Tanya Weinberger, an award-winning animator, explains how she uses computer and video technology to animate her characters. 27 mins.

VHS: S23502. $49.95.

Creative Process: Norman McLaren

A penetrating examination of the art of Norman McLaren, the pioneering filmmaker who made intricate works without the use of cameras and created music without the benefit of instruments. His avant-garde techniques involved direct painting and drawing onto the film strip and music hand carved from a multitude of squiggles. The film draws on previously unviewed footage from McLaren's vaults, including his experimental use of pixilation. *Norman McLaren* is an impressionistic portrait of the artist, distilled from radio and film interviews, artwork, photographs, home movies and various completed and unfinished films. "At last, something new in the art of drawing" (Pablo Picasso). 116 mins.

Laser: LD72230. $69.95.

Creature Comforts

A collection of clay animated shorts from England's Aardman Animations. Four titles: *Creature Comforts*, Nick Park's Oscar-winning comment on life at the zoo; *Wat's Pig*, the 1996 Oscar-nominated tale of knights and daze involving two brothers; *Not Without My Handbag*, a darkly hilarious story of a deceased auntie who won't stay in Hell without a proper handbag; and *Adam*, Peter Lord's whimsical tale of the Creation.

VHS: S32415. $14.95.

Aardman Animations, UK

The Cricket in Times Square

This Chuck Jones production is the tale of a country cricket named Chester who finds himself in the Big Apple. He befriends Tucker the Mouse and Harry the Cat while teaching jaded humans to care about each other. Parent's Choice Award winner. EP Speed.

VHS: S07763. $12.95.

Chuck Jones, USA, 1973, 30 mins.

The Curious Adventures of Mr. Wonderbird (La Bergere et Le Ramoneur)

In this visually striking French animated feature, the outrageous Mr. Wonderbird (voiced by Peter Ustinov) narrates the story of a most bizarre enchanted castle. Paintings of a shepard girl and a chimney sweep come to life, and the evil, conceited King decides he must have the girl for himself. When she and the chimney sweep run away, it takes all the help that Mr. Wonderbird and his friends can muster to save them from the pursuing King. The final sequence of a gigantic mechanical monster and destruction of the palace contains stunning imagery that rivals the best examples of Japanimation. French dubbed in English. LP Speed.

VHS: S25703. $24.95.

Paul Grimault, France, 1953, 64 mins.

Cut-Out Animation

Cutting out paper figures is only the first step to this type of animation. Award-winning animator David Johnson's group of animated characters show how it is done. 8 mins.

VHS: S23501. $49.95.

Danger Mouse Vol. 1: Trouble with Ghosts

Danger Mouse and his sidekick, Penfold, take on the evil Baron Greenback, a power-mad frog who wants to take over their TV show. Four episodes.

VHS: S00295. $9.95.

Cosgrove/Hall, UK, 1982, 70 mins.

Danger Mouse Vol. 2: Public Enemy No. 1

Four episodes: *Who Stole the Bagpipes?, The Odd-Ball Run-Around, The Return of Count Duckula* and *Public Enemy*.

VHS: S00296. $9.95.

Cosgrove/Hall, UK, 1982, 60 mins.

Danger Mouse Vol. 3: Chicken Run

Five episodes: *The Chicken Run, The Dream Machine, The Strange Case of the Ghost Bus, The Four Tasks of Danger Mouse* and *The Planet of the Cats*.

VHS: S00297. $9.95.

Cosgrove/Hall, UK, 1984, 60 mins.

Danger Mouse Vol. 4: The Day of Suds

Four episodes: *Die Laughing, The Day of the Suds, 150 Million Years Lost* and *Rogue Robots*.

VHS: S00298. $9.95.

Cosgrove/Hall, UK, 1984, 60 mins.

Danger Mouse Vol. 5: Lord of the Bungle

Four episodes: *Lord of The Bungle, The Invasion of Colonel K, Tower of Terror* and *Ice Station Camel*.

VHS: S04345. $9.95.

Cosgrove/Hall, UK, 1984, 60 mins.

Davey & Goliath: Caring for Others

Three episodes: In *Lost in a Cave* Davey learns that God cares when he gets lost; in *Pilgrim Boy* Davey learns how God provided for the Pilgrims through the Indians; in *The Zillion Dollar Combo* Davey's new band learns there are more important things than money.

VHS: S28127. $9.95.

Art Clokey, USA, 1962, 45 mins.

Davey & Goliath: Christmas Lost & Found

Davey decides to give away something of personal importance and discovers the true meaning of Christmas.

VHS: S28128. $14.95.

Art Clokey, USA, 1965, 30 mins.

Davey & Goliath: Forgiveness

Three episodes: In *Not for Sale* when Davey loses a ski he works odd jobs to make it up; in *The New Skates* Davey falls through some ice and loses a skate; in *Officer Bob* Davey fears his friendship with Officer Bob will be broken when Davey breaks a bicycle safety rule. EP Speed.

VHS: S28125. $9.95.

Art Clokey, USA, 1962, 45 mins.

Davey & Goliath: Halloween WHO DID IT?

Davey must make amends for Halloween night mischief.

VHS: S28129. $14.95.

Art Clokey, USA, 1977, 30 mins.

Davey & Goliath: Happy Easter

This half-hour special helps children understand the concept of life after death.

VHS: S28130. $14.95.

Art Clokey, USA, 1967, 30 mins.

Davey & Goliath: Helping Others

Three episodes: In *Good Neighbor* Davey helps a little girl find her way home; in *A Dillar, A Dollar* Davey & Teddy are late for school because Teddy's mom is ill; in *Boy in Trouble* Davey & Jonathan give their pop bottle money to a needy friend. EP Speed.
VHS: S28124. $9.95.
Art Clokey, USA, 1962, 45 mins.

Davey & Goliath: Lost & Found: The Movie

Five episodes: *The Good Bad Luck, The Runaway, Sudden Storm, Good Neighbor* and *Boy Lost*.
VHS: S28131. $24.95.
Art Clokey, USA, 70 mins.

Davey & Goliath: New Year Promise

When Davey makes his New Year's resolution, it leads to hurt feelings, a snowy adventure and a valuable lesson learned just in time for the New Year.
VHS: S28132. $14.95.
Art Clokey, USA, 1967, 30 mins.

Davey & Goliath: School: Who Needs It?

Davey & his friends get back into school activity by involving themselves in a week-long safety project.
VHS: S28133. $14.95.
Art Clokey, USA, 1971, 30 mins.

Davey & Goliath: Summer Camp to the Rescue

At church camp, everyone learns to respect God's creation, and, when they must help two plane crash victims, they learn the importance of being prepared.
VHS: S28134. $14.95.
Art Clokey, USA, 1975, 30 mins.

Davey & Goliath: Thanksgiving Special

Two Thanksgiving episodes on one tape: in *The Pilgrim Boy* Davey learns of God's provision through the Pilgrim's story. In *The Big Apple* Davey & Sally learn about sharing.
VHS: S28135. $14.95.
Art Clokey, USA, 30 mins.

Davey & Goliath: Trusting

Three episodes: In *The Bridge* Davey, Goliath & Sally cross a footbridge that breaks and leaves Sally on a ledge; in *Stranded on an Island* Sally, Davey & Goliath's boat is beached by a low tide; in *All Alone* Davey gets trapped in a railroad car when he tries to filch some bananas. EP Speed.
VHS: S28126. $9.95.
Art Clokey, USA, 1962, 45 mins.

David & The Magic Pearl

Directed by Wieslaw Zieba, this "new wave" mixture of animation styles tells the story of what happens when a kid from Chicago meets the wilds of the jungle, baby animals, space creatures and magic.
VHS: S12381. $39.95.
Miniatur Filowych, 1987, 75 mins.

Daydreamer

In this live-action/animation story, young Chris is on an adventurous journey in search of "The Garden of Paradise." Along the way, he encounters characters from The Ugly Duckling to The Little Mermaid.
VHS: S17369. $19.95.
Rankin/Bass, USA, 98 mins.

Dazzle

Computer wizard James Shiflett brings years of computer programming skill to this brilliant video set to music from leading ambient composer John Serrie. A kaleidoscope of changing imagery is the result, using over two million colors and seemingly endless numbers of patterns and images.
VHS: S27645. $19.95.
John Shiflett, USA, 45 mins.

Decade (Miramar)

A collection of the best clips from Miramar's computer Video Album series, including *The Mind's Eye, Computer Animation Festival* and many others.
Laser: LD75849. $34.95.
USA, 68 mins.

Dick Deadeye

Dick Deadeye, that scurrilous villain of Gilbert & Sullivan's *H.M.S. Pinafore*, has been transformed into the most unlikely cartoon hero thanks to the animated designs of Ronald Searle, music of Jimmy Horowitz and direction of Bill Melendez. Dick has been commissioned by the Queen to retrieve the Ultimate Secret from the Sorcerer and the Pirate King.
VHS: S12750. $29.95.
Bill Melendez, USA, 1975, 80 mins.

A Doonesbury Special

Garry Trudeau and the Hubleys collaborated on this Academy Award-nominated film. All the Doonesbury characters are here as Zonker takes a trip down memory lane after seeing Jimmy Thudpucker on television.
VHS: S22868. $19.95.
John & Faith Hubley, USA, 1977, 26 mins.

Dot & Santa Claus

Dot travels around the world in search of her missing baby kangaroo. Along the way she finds the true meaning of Christmas.
VHS: S10742. $9.95.
Yoram Gross, Australia, 1979, 73 mins.

Dot & The Bunny

Dot tries to help out her friend Funnybunny, who wants to become a kangaroo.
VHS: S00361. $14.95.
Yoram Gross, Australia, 1982, 79 mins.

Doug Vol. 1: How Did I Get into This Mess?

Three episodes from the Nickelodeon series: *Doug's Dental Disaster, Doug's Lost Weekend* and *Doug on His Own*.
VHS: S19088. $9.95.
USA, 1992, 40 mins.

Doug Vol. 2: Patti, You're the Mayonnaise for Me

Three episodes: *Doug's Out in Left Field, Doug's Dinner Date* and *Doug's Fair Lady*.
VHS: S19089. $9.95.
USA, 1992, 40 mins.

Doug: Christmas Story

When his dog porkchop is falsely accused, Doug rallies to defend him.
VHS: S28183. $9.95.
USA, 30 mins.

Dr. Devious: Dance in Cyberspace

The latest trend, previously only available in clubs, is now featured on this video. It's a graphic psychedelic experience for the 1990's. 3-D glasses are included. 45 mins.
VHS: S22045. $24.98.

Dr. Seuss: How the Grinch Stole Christmas/Horton Hears a Who

Digital remaster of both programs.
Laser: LD75855. $29.95.
USA, 60 mins.

Dragon Flyz: The Legend Begins

In the 41st century, the Dragon Flyz—three brave brothers, their valiant sister and their dragon counterparts—protect the floating sky city of Airlandis. The mutant lord of the netherworld, Dread Wing, attempts to steal the crystals that keep the city aloft. The first three episodes of this French-produced TV series. Clamshell case sports a nifty 3-D lenticular cover.
VHS: S30052. $19.95.
Gaumont, France, 1996, 70 mins.

The Dragon That Wasn't (Or Was He?)

The adventures of a baby dragon, Dexter, who thinks that Ollie the Bear is his father. When he grows up to monster proportions, Ollie realizes he must return Dexter to the Realm of Dragons beyond the mountains.
VHS: S06132. $19.95.
United Dutch Film, Holland, 1983, 83 mins.

Dream Tales: The Sacred Ways Collection

In the first of these animated myths, five stories from the Watunna tribe of Venezuela explain the origin of the world and the nature of human sexuality. Then Faith Hubley tells six stories, including one about the Moon Lady, who leads the dead to paradise along the Milky Way.
VHS: S21594. $24.95.
Faith Hubley, USA, 35 mins.

Dreaming of Paradise

Directed by Denmark's J. Hastrup, this story is set in a future when humans have polluted the Earth so much they have to live underground. Spike and her small band gain hope from the myth that one day man will return to Paradise above. Winner of Best Animated Feature at Chicago International Children's Film Festival.
VHS: S15007. $24.99.
Metronome Prod., 1987, 75 mins.

Droits au Coeur (Rights from the Heart)

Seven short films illustrating the ideals proclaimed by the United Nations Convention on the Rights of the Child: *1 2 3 Coco, Papa, TV Tango, The Orange, Door to Door, A Family for Maria* and *To See the World*.
VHS: S18966. $39.95.
NFB of Canada, Canada, 1993, 40 mins.

Droopy & Company

Four of the later Droopy cartoons in Cinema-scope directed by Michael Lah and two non-Droopy cartoons: *Mutts About Racing* ('58 /Lah), *Grin and Share It* ('57/Lah), *The Hungry Wolf* ('42/Harman), *Sheep Wrecked* ('58/Lah), *Officer Pooch* ('41/Hanna-Barbera) and *One Droopy Knight* ('57/Lah).
VHS: S15664. $12.95.
MGM, USA, 1941-58, 44 mins.

Early Animation Vol. 1

Seven titles: Felix the Cat in *Roameo* ('27), *Two-Lip Time* ('26) and *Arabiantics* ('28); Farmer Al Falfa in *Picnic (20's);A Life Cartoons: Red Hot Rails* ('26) and *Local Talent* ('27); Disney's Alice in *Alice's Balloon Race* ('26). Silent with score.
VHS: S28189. $17.95.
USA, 60 mins.

Early Animation Vol. 2

Six titles: Felix the Cat in *Skulls & Sculls, Forty Winks, Oceantics* and *Polly-Tics*; Mutt & Jeff in *Slick Sleuths* (re-colored); Keystone's *Man in the Moon*. Silent with score.
VHS: S28190. $17.95.
USA, 60 mins.

Elroy's Toy

The fun starts when a couple of zany characters, Chip (a computer chip) and his dog Sparky, suddenly pop up on Elroy's computer screen and take him into a magical world of stories. Colorful computer animation and original music.
VHS: S24130. $9.95.
Laser: LD75421. $29.99.
Third Planet, USA, 1994, 31 mins.

Everybody Rides the Carousel

Based on the work by psychoanalyst Erik Erikson, the viewer goes on eight "rides" through the different stages of life. With distinctive and poetic animation, the Hubleys explore the inner feelings and conflicting emotions experienced during each stage of personality development.
VHS: S22869. $39.95.
John & Faith Hubley, USA, 72 mins.

Fabulous Adventures of Baron Munchhausen

A masterpiece of animation by Karel Zeman—a fabulous fantasy that mixes live action, antique engravings and animation in a dazzling tour-de-force of fantasy. One of the great works of the cinema. English language version.
VHS: S11474. $29.95.
Karel Zeman, Czechoslovakia, 1965, 75 mins.

Fabulous World of Jules Verne

Based on Jules Verne's classic novel *A Deadly Invention* and directed by visionary director Karel Zeman, this special visual effects masterpiece features incredible creatures, fabulous flying machines and volcanic cities which explode from the screen in "Mystimation," a combination of live actors, foreground miniatures, glass matte paintings and animation. Verne's hero, Simon Hart, searches for his kidnapped mentor, whose experiments have created the ultimate doomsday machine. Now its a race against time as a madman threatens global destruction with the stolen technology. Also includes behind-the-scenes documentary featurette *The Magic World of Karel Zeman* and the original theatrical film trailer.
VHS: S35466. $19.95.
Karel Zeman, USA, 1961/1963, 83 mins./15 mins.

A Family Circus Christmas

Daddy, Mommy, Billy, PJ, Dolly and Jeffy decorate the tree, wrap their presents and celebrate the yuletide season.
VHS: S28200. $9.95.
Cullen-Kasdan, USA, 1975, 30 mins.

A Family Circus Easter

Billy, Dolly and Jeffy succeed in trapping the Easter Bunny to find out why it hides its eggs.
VHS: S28201. $9.95.
Cullen-Kasdan, USA, 1979, 30 mins.

A Family Circus Special Valentine

The kids compete to see who can make the prettiest valentine.
VHS: S28202. $9.95.
Cullen-Kasdan, USA, 1978, 30 mins.

Fantastic Planet

A French/Czech full-length animated fantasy which won a Gran Prix at the 1973 Cannes Film Festival. Animated and scored in an avant-garde style, the film tells the story of the revolt of the Oms—descendents of survivors of Earth who are kept as pets by the Draags. LP Speed.
VHS: S00432. $9.95.
Rene Laloux, France, 1973, 72 mins.

Faust

Jan Svankmajer's long-awaited follow-up to his acclaimed *Alice* is an equally bizarre version of the myth of Dr. Faustus. Combining live action with stop-motion animation, Svankmajer has created an unsettling universe presided over by diabolic life-size marionettes and haunted by skulking human messengers from hell.
VHS: S29877. $24.95.
Jan Svankmajer, Czechoslovakia, 1994, 97 mins.

Ferdy the Ant

The adventures of Bugville are presented in this cartoon based on the works of Ondrej Sekora.
VHS: S03293. $14.95.
1984, 50 mins.

The Films of Oskar Fischinger—Optical Poetry

A collection of abstract animation by the legendary German-born animator Oskar Fischinger, whose work was considered "degenerate" by the Nazis and too experimental and progressive for Hollywood. This first collection features seven of Fischinger's works from the '20s, '30s and '40s, which combine animated abstract, geometric forms with music in a kind of brilliant visual symphony. Shorts include *Muratti Gets in the Act* (1934), *Spiritual Constructions* (1927), *Study #7* (1931), *Study #8* (1932), *Kreise* (1933), *Allegretto* (1936) and *Motion Painting #1* (1936). 35 mins.
VHS: S35160. $40.00.

Five Lionni Classics

The power of imagination is the theme of these five animated pieces based upon Leo Lionni's popular animal fables. Frederick, Cornelius and Swimmy are featured in animation by Lionni and Giulio Gianini.
VHS: S02846. $19.95.
Giulio Gianini, Italy, 1986, 30 mins.

Flash Gordon: The Movie: Marooned on Mongo

A new, animated version of the classic comic character.
VHS: S32452. $9.95.
Lacewood Prod., USA, 1996, 75 mins.

Flash Gordon: To Save Earth

The action is fast and furious as Flash takes refuge in Arboria, where Prince Barin's Forest Fighters battle the Metalmen and the Molemen. Flash and his friends commandeer the giant Mole Machine for a last-ditch effort to save Earth from Ming. EP Speed.
Laser: LD75672. $24.95.
Filmation, USA, 1979, 60 mins.

Flight of Dragons

Directors Jules Bass and Arthur Rankin use cel animation to bring this fantasy to the screen. The good wizards select a man to stop the red wizards, and send him back in time to capture a magic crown. Voices of James Earl Jones, Harry Morgan, Victor Buono and James Gregory.
VHS: S17371. $14.95.
Rankin/Bass, USA, 1982, 102 mins.

Follow That Goblin

Produced with claymation technology and featuring a series of brisk, funny musical numbers, *Follow That Goblin* is about a young boy and his sister, trapped in a haunted house, where they befriend Gerbert the Goblin, who's lost the capability to frighten. 28 mins.
VHS: S17040. $9.95.

Fractal Experience

This new dimension of entertainment pairs the mathematical permutations offered by fractal geometry, as realized in computer graphics, with accompaniment from ambient music. 30 mins.
VHS: S22042. $24.98.

Fractal Fantasy: The Art of Mathematics

Fractal Fantasy is an artistic study of unusual areas within a mathematically defined region known as the Mandelbrot Set. The Set was discovered by Dr. Mandelbrot while studying a class of shapes which he labeled Fractals. The unique Fractal images seen in this video are actually enlarged areas along the edge of the Set. Large amounts of mainframe computer time were required to generate these magnified images; over 20 different regions are animated in this 30-minute journey with beautiful color palettes and special effects in a unique merging of art, science, music and mathematics. Fractal images, animation and software by Charles Fitch; music by Michael Strasmich.
VHS: S07322. $29.95.

Fractal Universe

A special program of highlights on fractals, including the Mandelbrot Sets and Julia Sets, dynamical systems, and the frontiers of chaos, serving as an introduction to some of the finest fractal animations to date. The images are accompanied by a variety of unusual electronic soundtracks. 25 mins.
VHS: S11000. $29.95.

Fractasia

In this tape fractal computer-animated imagery is choreographed to classical music by Bach, Wagner and other well-known composers. 32. mins.
VHS: S22043. $24.98.

Frank Film

Frank Mouris' autobiographical, animated film won the Academy Award in 1974. The 11,592 collages are sequenced to illustrate the chronology of the filmmaker's life. The visual bombardment, together with the double soundtrack, is an intense and moving experience. Includes public performance rights.
VHS: S32638. $24.95.
Frank Mouris, USA, 1973, 9 mins.

Freddie the Frog

Freddie the Frog is F.R.O.7—the world's top secret agent. Together with a lot of brains, a little magic, and a band of loyal friends, Freddie battles the forces of evil to stop his wicked Aunt Messina from conquering the Earth. Voices of Ben Kingsley and James Earl Jones. Soundtrack by George Benson, Patti Austin, Grace Jones, Asia, and Boy George.
VHS: S25741. $19.95.
UK, 1995, 72 mins.

Free Radicals, Vol. 1

A compilation of eight of Len Lye's films, including *Free Radicals* (1958/1989, 4 mins.); *Color Cry* (1952, 3 mins.); Tal Farlow (1980, 2mins.); *Colour Flight* (1938, 4 mins.); *Rhythm* (1957, 1 min.); *Particles in Space* (1979, 4 mins.); and *Tusalava* (1929, 10 mins.)
VHS: S35490. $75.00.

French Animation Festival

A collection of four short films by the great cinema pioneer Emile Cohl.
VHS: S05180. $29.95.

Fritz the Cat

The infamous Ralph Bakshi feature that made his reputation was the first animated film to receive an X rating (now re-classified as R). Based on R. Crumb's underground comic character, Fritz is a college-age feline wandering the hippie-era streets of New York in search of political, sexual and chemical experiences. This video version does not use the best film print in the world, but it's uncut, and still deserving of the R rating. ADULTS ONLY.
VHS: S29637. $29.95.
Bakshi/Krantz, USA, 1972, 78 mins.

Future Shock

Specially created visionscapes are accompanied by mesmerizing music. A true "Technopagan" experience. 43 mins.
VHS: S22044. $24.98.

Gadget

Based on the popular CD-ROM. Computer animation.
Laser: LD75858. $39.95.

Gallavants

It's no picnic for Shando, a young ant trying to grow into an adult. His quest leads him through various adventures until he realizes what being an adult is.
VHS: S25111. $14.95.
Marvel, USA, 100 mins.

The Gate to the Mind's Eye

The latest edition of the popular computer animation series features the most spectacular clips yet. Original soundtrack by Thomas Dolby.
VHS: S23009. $19.95.
Laser: LD74646. $29.95.
M. Boydstun, 1994, 45 mins.

Gay Purr-ee

Directed by Abe Levitow with contributions from Chuck Jones. A *Lady & The Tramp* for the feline set, this classic film features the voices of Judy Garland, Robert Goulet, Red Buttons, Hermione Gingold and Paul Frees.
VHS: S13441. $14.95.
Laser: LD70580. $34.95.
UPA, USA, 1962, 85 mins.

The Genesis of Animation, Volume One

Early and rare animated shorts are joined on this video. *Humorous Phases of Funny Faces*, by J. Stuart Blackton, starts off this line-up. Then, works like *The Evils of Alcohol, Princess Nicotine, Swat The Fly, Morpheus Mike, Alice the Whaler* and more are included. 55 mins.
VHS: S27485. $19.95.

George Pal Puppetoons

Eight titles: *Phillip's Cavalcade* ('38), *Jasper in a Jam* ('46), *Love on the Range* ('37), *Aladdin & His Lamp* ('47), *A Date with Duke* ('47), *Jasper & The Haunted House* ('42), *Oleo for Jasper* ('46) and *Together in the Weather* ('46). Note: film prints vary in quality. B&W/Color.
VHS: S28257. $17.95.
George Pal, USA, 1937-47, 60 mins.

Greentoons: Environmentally Aware Animation

Fourteen environmentally oriented films from animators across North America: *Whale Songs* (Mary Beams), *Global Warming* (Adrian Raeside), *Do You Care About the Earth?* (Kristine Albrechi), *Bob the Frog in "Burp"* (Damen Kiner), *How the Loon* (Gary W. McQuay), *Ozone* (Adrian Raeside), *Oregon Country* (Ken O'Connell), *Only the Cat Saw It* (Celia Kendrick), *All That Power Goes Up in Smoke* and *A Safer Job Pays a Lot Longer* (Sol Levine), *Lady Tree* (Howard Danelowitz), *Oh Dad II* (Jonathan Amday), *Food Additives* (Adrian Reaside) and *Water* (Kristine Albrecht).
VHS: S16917. $14.95.
USA/Canada, 45 mins.

Griffiti

Selected films by independent animator George Griffin. Thirteen titles: *Academy Leader Variations* ('84), *Trikfilm 3* ('73), *Head* ('75), *The Club* ('75), *Viewmaster* ('76), *It's an OK Life* '80), *Thicket* ('85), *Flying Fur* ('81), *Commissioned Work* ('88-'90), *Lineage* ('79), *Ko-Ko* ('88), *New Fangled* ('92) and *A Little Routine* ('94).
VHS: S35161. $39.95.
George Griffin, USA, 1973-90, 90 mins.

Guido Manuli: Animator

In the outlandish dreamscapes of Manuli, one of Italy's premiere animators, offbeat ideas and audacious themes are translated into hilarious visual excitement. Eleven titles: *SOS, Opera, Plus One Minus One, Fantabiblical, Incubus, Erection, Stripy, Serenissima, I Wanna Be Your Lover, Jay Duck* and *Mr. Hiccup*.
Laser: CAV. LD72091. $49.95.
Italtoons, Italy, 60 mins.

Harry Smith: Early Abstractions

Seven abstract films from the wizard of animation that include the first hand-painted abstract films made in America. Smith's early non-figurative works are among the most respected avant-garde cartoons ever made.
VHS: S01576. $29.95.
Harry Smith, USA, 1941-57, 24 mins.

Heavy Metal

The wildly popular animated feature based on the adult comic anthology *Heavy Metal* is finally legally available after years of video pirating. The soundtrack features Black Sabbath, Blue Oyster Cult and Devo. This remastered version also contains the three-minute sequence "Neverwhere Land," which was cut from the original release. Starring the voices of John Candy and Harold Ramis.
VHS: S27756. $19.95.
Laser: LD75579. $39.95.
Gerald Potterton, USA, 1981, 93 mins.

Heavy Traffic

Ralph Bakshi's follow-up to *Fritz the Cat* is a mixture of live action and animation. A downbeat look at the urban life of a young New Yorker depressed by sights and sounds around him, who finds refuge at a drawing board.
VHS: S28292. $29.95.
Ralph Bakshi, USA, 1973, 90 mins.

Hey Good Lookin'

An outrageous, affectionate look at coming of age in the Eisenhower era in Brooklyn. Vinnie is the leader of the Stompers, his girl Roz adores him, and Crazy Shapiro would die for him. Sort of an animated *Happy Days* done with Bakshi's peculiar style and set against live-action NYC backdrops.
VHS: S28293. $19.95.
Ralph Bakshi, USA, 1982, 77 mins.

Highlander: The Adventure Begins

Seven hundred years after his coming was foretold, young Quentin MacLeod is visited by an immortal warrior and informed that only he can save mankind from the evil Kortan. Wise Don Vincente Ramirez undertakes to protect young Quentin until he is ready to meet Kortan in battle.
VHS: S29659. $14.95.
Gaumont TV, 1994, 77 mins.

Highlander: The Animated Series, The History Lesson

Two more new episodes, *The Cursed* and *The History Lesson*, follow the adventures of Quentin MacLeod in his epic pursuit of lost human knowledge. 44 mins.
VHS: S29480. $9.95.

Highlander: The Animated Series, The Suspended Village

Quentin MacLeod, the last Highlander, battled Lord Kortan for the lost knowledge of mankind in the original feature-length animated film. This video contains two new episodes from this ongoing mythic battle, *The Suspended Village* and *Exodus*. 44 mins.
VHS: S29479. $9.95.

Highlander: The Animated Series, The Valley of Thorn Pods

The Valley of Thorn Pods and *Fall Out* find Quentin MacLeod, the last Highlander, engaged in continuing struggles on behalf of mankind. 44 mins.
VHS: S29481. $9.95.

History of the Amiga

This video is about the conception, design and implementation of the Amiga computer and its multiple uses for art, computer graphics and production design.
VHS: S18220. $29.95.

The Hobbit

All the enchantment, warmth and excitement of J.R.R. Tolkien's classic in this TV special. Bilbo Baggins leads a quest through Middle Earth to recover stolen treasure from the dragon Smaug and finds a magical ring. Voices of John Huston, Orson Bean and Hans Conreid.
VHS: S03846. $14.95.
Rankin/Bass, USA, 1977, 76 mins.

Hubley Collection Vol. 1

Three films by Faith Hubley: *Enter Life* ('81), symbolically tracing the evolution of life; *Who Am I?* ('89), visualizing a child's discovery of his five senses; and *Upside Down* ('91), illustrating the delicate relationship between Man and Earth. Also included is *Blake Ball* ('88) by Emily Hubley, inspired by the poet William Blake.
VHS: S15396. $39.95.
Faith/Emily Hubley, USA, 1981-91, 36 mins.

Hubley Collection Vol. 2

Five titles: *Time of the Angels* ('87) is a mixture of poetry, music and vibrant visuals exploring Central and South America; *People, People, People* ('75) is a brief recap of North American population expansion; *W.O.W. Women of the World* ('75) is a collage of the changing relationships between the sexes; *Amazonia* ('89) is a plea to save the tropical rain forest and its peoples; and *Yes We Can* ('88) tells how we can help Gaia heal herself.
VHS: S19162. $39.95.
John/Faith Hubley, USA, 1975-88, 36 mins.

Hubley Collection Vol. 3

Two films by John & Faith Hubley: *Moonbird* ('59), in which two brothers hunt an imaginary bird in an adventure capturing the wonder of a child's world, and *Windy Day* ('67), a creatively visualized film conveying two sisters' views of love, death and marriage. Two films by Faith Hubley: *Tall Time Tales* ('92), ethereal images, surrealist landscapes, and an evocative soundtrack, and *Cloudland* ('93), which draws upon Australian aboriginal art and mythology.
VHS: S21523. $39.95.
John/Faith Hubley, USA, 1959-93, 36 mins.

Hubley Studio: Of Men and Demons

In *Of Men and Demons* ('70), when the weather gods ruin a simple farmer's life, the war is on between nature and machines. Music by Quincy Jones. Also includes *Of Stars & Men* ('61), the story of evolution from microorganisms to space travel, narrated by Harlow Shipley. (Note to Schools & Libraries: Public performance rights included.)
VHS: S24277. $29.95.
John/Faith Hubley, USA, 1961-70, 63 mins.

Hubley Studio: The Cosmic Eye

The story of three musicians from outer space who land on Earth and spread the message of world peace. In the process, they observe a variety of ideas about the origins and destiny of planet Earth. Music by Benny Carter, Ella Fitzgerald, Oscar Peterson and Quincy Jones. (Note to Schools & Libraries: Public performance rights included.)
VHS: S24276. $29.95.
Faith Hubley, USA, 72 mins.

Hubley Studio: The Hole

Three titles: Two construction workers debate the fate of the world in the Academy Award-winning short *The Hole* ('62). Voices of Dizzy Gillespie and George Mathews; in improvised dialog, Dizzy Gillespie and Dudley Moore portray two opposing soldiers who argue over a dropped helmet in *The Hat* ('64); in the musical fantasy *Dig*, a boy and his dog follow a talking boulder under the Earth's crust. Music by Quincy Jones. (Note to Schools & Libraries: Public performance rights included.)
VHS: S24278. $29.95.
John/Faith Hubley, USA, 1962-64, 58 mins.

Hubley Studio: Voyage to Next

Six titles: Mother Earth (Maureen Stapleton) and Father Time (Dizzy Gillespie) observe the state of life on our planet in *Voyage to Next* ('74), an Academy Award-nominee with music by Dizzy Gillespie. The song "Tenderly" provides a musical backdrop for the love story in *Tender Game*. The Goddess of Fertility and Death fight over mankind's future in *Eggs* ('71). A runaway city on legs matches wits with a wily farmer in *Urbanissimo*. The paintings of Gregorio Prstopino convey the sights of Harlem in *Harlem Wednesday*. Benny Carter and Lionel Hampton provide the musical backdrop for *Adventures of An ** ('55), as a baby grows up and regains his appreciation of life through the birth of his own child. (Note to Schools & Libraries: Public performance rights included.)
VHS: S24279. $29.95.
John/Faith Hubley, USA, 1955-74, 63 mins.

The Idea

Based on a book of woodcuts by the same name by Franz Masereel, this masterwork of early animation is a serious film about ideas, creativity and self-ultimacy. The film's main character is a slender, female nude, representing the artist's ideal in an oppressive, materialistic society. *The Idea* is also an amazing work given the circumstances by which it was made. Bartosch was in poor health most of his life and worked for over two years alone in a tiny 10x12 workstation where he created over 45,000 individual frames—some with over 18 superimpositions perframe—using such oblique objects as glass, soap, tissue paper, cardboard and tracing paper to create his unique animation effects. Arthur Honegger's score is thought to be the first to use an electronic instrument in a motion picture. "The first serious, poetic, tragic work in animation" (Alexander Alexeieff).
VHS: S30224. $65.00.
Berthold Bartosch, USA, 1930-2, 27 mins.

Imaginaria

From the producers of *The Mind's Eye* comes a new computer-animation compilation geared toward children. Original music by Gary Powell serves as background for clips including *Locomotion, Andre & Wally B, Rubber Duckies, Night Magic, Styro the Dog* and many other state-of-the-art computer graphic examples.
VHS: S20649. $9.95.
Laser: LD75678. $24.95.
1993, 40 mins.

In a Cartoon Studio

Some very early Van Beuren cartoons featuring Tom & Jerry and Cubby Bear. Nine titles: *In a Cartoon Studio* ('31), *Cinderella Blues* ('31), *Redskin Blues* ('32), *The Ball Game* ('32), *Galloping Hoofs* ('33), *Gay Gaucho* ('33), *Happy Hoboes* ('33), *Indian Whoopee* ('33) and *Brownie's Victory Garden* ('34).
VHS: S28304. $19.95.
Van Beuren, USA, 1931-34, 60 mins.

In Search of Dr. Seuss

As a newspaper reporter attempts to compile background information for a tribute to Ted Geisel (Dr. Seuss), she is given a guided, musical tour of the great man's life by The Cat in the Hat (Matt Frewer). Despite the stagey presentation of the show, there is quite a lot of good biographical material, and clips are shown of all the animated adaptations of Dr. Seuss stories. Celebrity appearances and skits by Christopher Lloyd, Patrick Stewart, Billy Crystal and Robin Williams. Laserdisc is 120 mins—includes *Daisy Head Mayzie* and *The Butter Battle Book*.
VHS: S24804. $9.95.
Laser: LD75486. $49.95.
Turner, USA, 1995, 90 mins.

Incredible Animation Collection: Vol. 1

A collection of animated shorts from the National Film Board of Canada. Includes *Juke Bar, If Only to Be, The Cat Came Back, Special Delivery* and *Kid Stuff*. 60 mins.
Laser: LD70206. $44.95.

Incredible Animation Collection: Vol. 2

More animation from the National Film Board of Canada: *Every Child* (Eugene Fedorenko), *Real Inside* (John Weldon/David Verrall), *Evolution* (Michael Mills), *Get a Job* (Brad Caslor), and *Cat's Cradle* (Paul Driessen). 60 mins.
Laser: LD70220. $44.95.

Incredible Hulk Laserdisc

Tape volumes 1 and 2 on one laserdisc.
Laser: LD75680. $24.95.
Marvel, USA, 1982, 49 mins.

The Incredible Hulk: Return of the Beast

As seen on the UPN network.
VHS: S32456. $9.95.
USA

Incredible Manitoba Animation

This collection of animation from Manitoba includes two Academy Award nominees: *The Cat Came Back* and *The Big Snit*. In addition there are *Getting Started, The Cat Strikes Back, Carried Away* and many more humorous shorts on this great video.
VHS: S25829. $39.95.

The Incredible Mr. Limpet

This animation/live action combination is in the class of the best of Disney. Don Knotts is transformed into a dolphin and becomes the allies' WWII secret weapon. Six songs by Sammy Fain and Harold Adamson.
VHS: S11662. $19.95.
Laser: LD75681. $24.95.
Warner Bros., USA, 1964, 99 mins.

Inside Termite Terrace Vol. 1: Daffy the Commando

Eleven titles: *Bosko the Talk-Ink Kid* ('29), *Congo Jazz* ('30), *Boxcar Blues* ('30), *Goopy Geer* ('32), *The Queen Was in the Parlor* ('32), *Porky's Pooch* ('41), *Robinson Crusoe Jr.* ('41), *Porky Pig's Feat* ('43), *Prest-O Change-O* ('39), *A Tale of Two Kitties* ('42) and *Daffy the Commando* ('43).
VHS: S29660. $24.95.
Warner Bros., USA, 1929-43, 82 mins.

Inside Termite Terrace Vol. 2: Tokyo Jokio

Twelve titles: *Sinkin' in the Bathtub* ('30), *Bosko Shipwrecked* ('31), *Red-Headed Baby* ('31), *Smile, Darn Ya, Smile* ('31), *Three's a Crowd* ('33), *Pagan Moon* ('32), *Porky's Bear Facts* ('41), *Tokyo Jokio* ('43), *Daffy Duck and the Dinosaur* ('39), *The Wacky Wabbit* ('42), *A Corny Concerto* ('43) and *Bugs Bunny Bond Rally* ('42).
VHS: S29661. $24.95.
Warner Bros., USA, 1930-43, 87 mins.

Inside Termite Terrace Vol. 3: Jungle Jitters

Twelve titles: *Big Man from the North* ('31), *It's Got Me Again* ('32), *Boom Boom* ('36), *Jungle Jitters* ('38), *Hamateur Night* ('39), *Early Worm Gets the Bird* ('40), *Fresh Hare* ('42), *The Sheepish Wolf* ('42), *Flop Goes the Weasel* ('43), *Wackiki Wabbit* ('43), *Operation Snafu* ('45) and *Great Gag Shot of Cartoon Directors* ('39).
VHS: S29662. $24.95.
Warner Bros., USA, 1931-45, 87 mins.

Inside Termite Terrace Vol. 4: Bosko

Twelve titles: *Hold Anything* ('30), *One More Time* ('31), *Freddy the Freshman* ('32), *Crosby, Columbo and Vallee* ('32), *Let It Be Me* ('36), *Robinhood Makes Good* ('39), *Bars and Stripes Forever* ('39), *The Case of the Missing Hare* ('42), *Pigs in a Polka* ('43), *To Duck or Not to Duck* ('43), *Outpost* ('44, Snafu) and *Harry Von Zell & Arlo Wilcox at the NBC Studio* ('45, live action).
VHS: S29663. $24.95.
Warner Bros., USA, 1930-45, 85 mins.

Inside Termite Terrace Vol. 5

Eleven titles: *The Booze Hangs High* ('30), *You Don't Know What You're Doin'* ('31), *Moonlight for Two* ('32), *A Great Big Bunch of You* ('32), *The Henpecked Duck* ('41), *Sport Chumpions* ('41), *Rookie Review* ('41), *The Wabbit Who Came to Supper* ('42), *Foney Fables* ('42), *Booby Traps* ('44) and *Harry Von Zell & Harlow Wilcox at CBS* ('45, includes live clip of Arthur Q. Bryan).
VHS: S29664. $24.95.
Warner Bros., USA, 1930-45, 85 mins.

International Tournee of Animation Volume 1

[19th Tournee] Fourteen titles: *Anijam* (Marv Newland, Canada), *Bottom's Dream* (John Canemaker, USA), *Bitz Butz* (Gil Alkabetz, Israel), *Tony De Peltrie* (NFB, Canada), *Sigmund* (Bruno Bozetto, Italy), *Skywhales* (Austin/Hayes, UK), *Moa Moa* (Bruno Bozetto, Italy), *Romeo & Juliet* (Dujan Petricic, Yugoslavia), *Jumping* (Osamu Tezuka, Japan), *Conversation Pieces: Early Bird* (Lord/Sproxton, UK), *Incubus* (Guido Manuli, Italy), *Luncheon* (Csaba Varga, Hungary), *Anna & Bella* (Borge Rin, Holland, 1985 Oscar Winner) and *Charade* (Jon Minnis, Canada, '84 Oscar Winner).
VHS: S17045. $29.95.
1986, 88 mins.

International Tournee of Animation Volume 2

[20th Tournee] Sixteen titles: *The Frog, The Dog & The Devil* (Bob Stenhouse, New Zealand), *Set in Motion* (Jane Aaron, USA), *Success* (Zoltan Lehotay, Hungary), *Garbage In, Garbage Out* (Terry Wozniak, USA), *Carnival* (Susan Young, UK), *Baeus* (Bruno Bozetto, Italy), *Academy Leader Variations* (various), *Greek Tragedy* (N. Van Goethem, Belgium), *Plus One, Minus One* (G. Manuli, Italy), *Your Face* (Plympton, USA), *Break* (G. Bardin, USSR), *Gravity* (F. Rofusz, Hungary), *Augusta Feeds Her Child* (Csaba Varga, Hungary), *Girl's Night Out* (J. Quinn, UK), *Drawing on My Mind* (Bob Kurtz, USA) and *Snookles* (Juliet Stroud, USA).
VHS: S17046. $29.95.
1987, 86 mins.

International Tournee of Animation Volume 3

[21st Tournee] Ten titles: *Arnold Escapes from the Church* (USA), *Lights Before Dawn* (Sandor Bekesi), *Pas a Deux* (Van Dijk/Renault, Holland), *78 Tours* (George Schwizgebel), *When Bats Are Quiet* (Fabio Lignini, Italy), *Augusta Kneading* (Csaba Varga, Hungary), *Living in a Mobile Home* (Neville Astley, England), *Quinoscopo* (Juan Padron, Cuba), *Technological Threat* (Bill Kroyer, USA, 1988 Oscar Nominee) and *The Writer* (Paul Driessen, Holland).
VHS: S17047. $39.95.
Laser: CAV. **LD75898. $39.95.**
1988, 52 mins.

International Tournee of Animation Volume 4

[22nd Tournee] Eighteen titles: *All My Relations* (Joanna Priestly, USA), *Animated Self Portraits* (various), *The Arnold Waltz* (Craig Bartlett, USA), *Balance* (C. & W. Lauenstein, Germany, '89 Oscar Winner), *The Bedroom* (Maarten Koopman, Holland), *Cat and Rat* (James Richardson, USA), *The Cow* (Alexander Petrov, USSR, '89 Oscar Nominee), *Gisele Kerozene* (E. Cayo & J. Kounen, France), *Kakania* (Karen Aqua, USA), *Pictures from Memory* (Nedjeljko Dragic, Yugoslavia), *Plymptoons* (Bill Plympton, USA), *Sand Dance* (Richard Quade, USA), *Shadrach* (Chris Casady, USA), *A Touch of Deceit* (Michael Gagne, Canada), *Train Gang* (Paul Driessen, Holland), *A Very Very Long Time Ago* (B. Jarcho & M. Manning, USA), *Vykrutasy* (Garri Bardin, USSR) and *A Warm Reception in L.A.* (V. Cafarelli & C. Kugel, USA).
VHS: S17042. $29.95.
1989, 90 mins.

International Tournee of Animation Volume 5

[23rd Tournee] Sixteen titles: *At One View* (Paul De Noojier, Netherlands), *The Big Bang* (Bruno Bozetto, Italy), *Breakdown* (Klaus Geoggi, Germany), *Capital P* (Stephen Barnes, Canada), *Fast Food Matador* (Vincent Cafarelli & Candy Kugel, USA), *Getting There* (Paul Driessen, Canada), *Grey Wolf & Little Riding Hood* (Garri Bardin, USSR), *I Should See* (Paul De Noojier, Netherlands), *Les Daisons Quatre a Quatre* (Daniel Suter, Switzerland), *The Lift* (Alexander Tatarsky, USSR), *Ode to GI Joe* (Gregory Grant, USA), *Oral Hygiene* (David Fain, USA), *Photocopy Cha Cha* (Chel White, USA), *Potato Hunter* (Timothy Hittle, USA), *Push Comes to Shove* (Bill Plympton, USA) and *The Wrong Type* (Candy Guard, UK).
VHS: S25823. $29.95.
Laser: CAV. **LD75679. $49.95.**
1990, 90 mins.

International Tournee of Animation Volume 6

[24th Tournee] Fourteen titles: *Get a Haircut* (Mike Smith), *The Stain* (Marjut Rimminen), *We Love It* (Vince Cafarelli & Candy Kugel), *The Ride to the Abyss* (Georges Schwizgebel), *The Square of Light* (Claude Luyet), *Prehistoric Beast* [excerpt] (Phil Tippett), *The Man Who Yelled* (Mo Willems), *I Think I Was an Alcoholic* (John Callahan), *Gahan Wilson's Diner* (Gahan Wilson), *The Billy Nayer Show* (Cory McAbee & Bobby Lurie), *Little Wolf* (An Vrombaut), *The Sandman* (Paul Berry), *Words Words Words* (Michaela Pavlatova) and *Mr. Resistor* (Will Vinton Studio).
VHS: S25818. $29.95.
1993, 90 mins.

J. Lyle

Animator Bill Plympton combines the best of his well-honed, drawn-animation technique with live action in his second feature-length film. A ruthless young man is set on ripping down his building for a toxic waste site. Everything changes, however, when this landlord finds himself transported to other people's bodies.
VHS: S27853. $59.95.
Bill Plympton, USA, 1995, 75 mins.

Jack Frost

Buddy Hackett narrates and Robert Morse, Paul Frees and Dave Garroway supply voices to bring Jack Frost to life through the puppet animation technique of "Animagic."
VHS: S28310. $9.95.
Rankin/Bass, USA, 1979, 50 mins.

Jay Ward & Bill Scott TV Commercials Vol. 1

Jay Ward and Bill Scott were a brilliant team, Ward with story and animation and Scott with story and voices. Here are 45 of their television commercials starring Rocky & Bullwinkle, Quake and Quisp, Simon, Peabody and Sherman, Aesop & Son, Dudley Do-Right and Boris Badenov. Film and video transfer quality varies.
VHS: S18048. $19.95.
Jay Ward, USA, 45 mins.

Jay Ward & Bill Scott TV Commercials Vol. 2

Forty-nine more TV commercials from 1964 to 1972, starring Captain Crunch, John LaFoote, Caryle, Brunhilde, Smedley, Crunchberry Beast, Seadog, Wilma, Alfie, King Vitain, Waffle Whiffer and Guppy. Film and video transfer varies.
VHS: S18049. $19.95.
Jay Ward, USA, 45 mins.

John the Fearless

He's the "Rocky" of the 15th century, defender of the poor, enemy of evil, champion of justice. Based on a classic novel by Constant De Kinder.
VHS: S28316. $14.95.
Cinar Films, 1987, 80 mins.

Journey Back to Oz

In this animated sequel, Dorothy reunites with her friends, but also meets Mombi—the most wicked of all witches—who takes over the Emerald City. Voices of Liza Minnelli, Paul Lynde, Milton Berle, Ethel Merman, Mickey Rooney, Danny Thomas, Herschel Bernardi and Margaret Hamilton. LP Speed.
VHS: S10720. $9.95.
Filmation, USA, 1971, 90 mins.

Journey Through Fairyland

This critically acclaimed animated feature has orchestral masterpieces like *Flight of the Bumblebee* and *Waltz of the Flowers*, recorded by the Tokyo Philharmonic.
VHS: S09168. $19.95.
Sanrio, Japan, 1985, 95 mins.

Karate Kat: Aristokratic Kapers

The misfit of martial arts and the klutz of karate stars in three episodes: *The Katzenheimer Kaper, The Sardine Turnover Kaper* and *The Mousemobile Kaper*.
VHS: S28318. $9.95.
Rankin/Bass, USA, 1987, 30 mins.

Katy Meets the Aliens

A Mexican/Spanish theatrical co-production directed by Santiago Moro. Katy the butterfly's caterpillar children are so anxious to grow up, they sneak off one night to find a flying teacher. Along the way they meet all manner of forest animals, as well as some aliens who are eyeing the Earth as a new source of food. The animation is quite competent and the designs are pleasing. A good kids' film. HiFi. Stereo.
VHS: S31504. $14.95.
Televicine/Moro, Mexico, 1987, 85 mins.

The Ken Southworth Basic Animation Kit

Ken Southworth, animator for Disney, Lantz, MGM and Hanna-Barbera, hosts this most worthy home video course on animation. Seated at his animation stand, Ken shows you many of the important ideas and principles needed to be a good animator, including inbetweening, the "rule of three," the silhoutte principal, anticipation and many more. He also demonstrates exposure sheets, trucks, pans, dissolves, rolling drawings and other technical considerations. The package includes the videotape, an instruction booklet and a set of animation pegs. Definitely the best home-instruction course we've ever seen, and fun to watch even if you never pick up a pencil.
VHS: S33750. $50.00.
Inkwell Images, USA, 1997, 30 mins.

Koko the Clown, 1915-27

Four Out of the Inkwell cartoons produced for J.R. Bray, circa 1915-20: *The Tantalizing Fly, The Clown's Little Brother, Perpetual Motion* and *Ouija Board. Five Koko cartoons produced by Fleischer: Bubbles* ('22), *Modeling* ('21), *Ko-Ko Song Car-Tune* ('27), *Koko the Cop* ('27) and *Koko's Earth Control* ('27). B&W/Silent.
VHS: S00691. $24.95.
Fleischer, USA, 1915-27, 49 mins.

Koko the Clown, 1927-29

Ten titles from the Inkwell Imps series: *Chemical Koko, Koko the Kid, Koko's Courtship, Koko's Harem Scare-Um, Koko Hops Off, Koko's Big Sale, Koko's Conquest, Koko's Hot Ink, Koko's Hypnotism* and *Koko's Reward. Digital master from film negative. B&W/Silent.*
VHS: S16502. $19.95.
Laser: CAV one side only. **LD75684. $29.95.**
Fleischer, USA, 1927-29, 70 mins.

Ladislas Starevitch

Ladislas Starevitch is one of the most admired pioneers of stop-motion puppet animation. He began his career in Russia in 1909, but soon moved to France, where he worked through the 1950s. This tape contains three of his sound classics. *The Mascot* ('34) is a nightmarish vision in which the dustbins of Paris disgorge skeletal demons who gather for midnight Saturnalia. *Nose to the Wind* ('56) is the story of a bear who escapes school to join a fox and a rabbit as a traveling minstrel. *Winter Carousel* ('58) is a winter adventure with a bear, rabbit, fox and scarecrow-turned snowman.
VHS: S14527. $29.95.
Ladislas Starevitch, France, 1934-58, 60 mins.

The Last Unicorn

The voice talents of Mia Farrow, Jeff Bridges and Angela Lansbury bring to life this animated theatrical feature tale of a lonely unicorn who sets out on an extraordinary quest. Based on the novel by Peter S. Beagle.
VHS: S04605. $14.95.
Rankin/Bass, USA, 1982, 93 mins.

Legend of the North Wind

For centuries, the great Bay of Whales was protected by a solemn Indian pact. But when hunters set their sights on it, it seems no one but young Elliot, his sister Anne and their Indian friend Watuna can save it. Stereo.
VHS: S30405. $14.95.
Nelvana, Canada, 1996, 74 mins.

Len Lye

Active 1940-1960, New Zealand filmmaker Len Lye developed several of the montage and fast-cutting techniques later used sucessfully in advertising. His interest in light and rhythm also led to experiments in moving sculptures he called Tangibles. Includes interview, demonstrations of a few Tangibles, and clips from films. 1957, 28 mins.
VHS: S31601. $59.95.

The Leprechauns' Christmas Gold

A young cabin boy lost on an uncharted island unwittingly frees a caterwauling Banshee who tries to steal the leprechauns' pot of gold. Voices of Art Carney and Peggy Cass.
VHS: S28327. $9.95.
Rankin/Bass, USA, 1981, 23 mins.

The Life and Adventures of Santa Claus

This Animagic production tells the story of Santa Claus, who was raised by Immortals in the valley of Ho Ha Ho and gained immortality himself through his yuletide good deeds.
VHS: S13037. $9.95.
Rankin/Bass, USA, 1985, 49 mins.

Light Years

An animated, full-length, science fiction adventure with an English screenplay by Isaac Asimov. A mysterious evil force threatens the tranquility of an idyllic world. A brave warrior and his courageous female companion must travel one thousand years into the future to confront the enemy. With the voices of Glenn Close, Christopher Plummer, Jennifer Grey and Penn and Teller.
VHS: S07173. $14.95.
Rene Laloux, France, 1988, 83 mins.

Linnea in Monet's Garden

From the bestselling book—a charming tale of a little girl's exploration of Claude Monet's paintings and life.
VHS: S22181. $19.95.
Christina Bjork & Lena Anderson

The Lion, The Witch and the Wardrobe

The first tale in C.S. Lewis' *The Chronicles of Narnia*—one of the best loved works of children's literature. A wardrobe closet becomes the passageway to a wonderland of mythical creatures and talking animals. Winner of the Emmy Award for Best Animated Special.
VHS: S19158. $12.95.
Children's TV Workshop, USA, 1993, 95 mins.

The Little Fox

A fine piece of Disney-like animation about the life of an orphaned baby fox growing up in the wild. Pannonia's attempt at a *Bambi*-like film was so popular in Hungary, a commemorative set of postage stamps was issued. Directed by Atilla Dargay. This version is the director's cut.

VHS: S22440. $14.95.

Pannonia, Hungary, 1981, 80 mins.

Little Nemo: Adventures in Slumberland

Based on Winsor McCay's comic strip, this impressive film was ten years in the making. An American/Japanese production, directed by William Hurtz and Masami Hata, Nemo captures something of McCay's rich period look while utilizing lavish animation techniques. Songs by the Sherman Brothers add a lovely mood to the visual feast. Ray Bradbury's screen treatment calls for Little Nemo to save the life of a noble king, outmatch the power of a mighty monster, and win the heart of a lovely princess.

Laser: Widescreen. **LD75688. $34.95.**

Hemdale/TMS, USA/Japan, 1992, 86 mins.

The Little Prince

Antione de Saint-Exupery's book is brought to life through Will Vinton's Claymation technique. A young boy searches for matters of consequence and realizes that trivia often obscure the most important things. Narrated by Cliff Robertson.

VHS: S26616. $14.95.

Will Vinton, USA, 27 mins.

Lotte Reiniger Compilation

Lotte Reiniger pioneered the cut-out silhouette technique of animation in Potsdam, Germany, during the 1920s, and is credited with making the first feature-length animated film, *The Adventures of Prince Achmed*. In the 1950s, she and her husband established Primrose Productions in England and continued making silhouette films. This tape includes *Cinderella, The Frog Prince* ('55), *Hansel and Gretel* ('55), *The Little Chimney Sweep* ('54) and *The Three Wishes* ('55). Also included is *The Art of Lotte Reiniger*, a documentary of the filmmaker in which she takes us through the creation of a film step by step.

VHS: S15063. $29.95.

Primrose Prod's, UK, 1954-55, 70 mins.

Luminous Visions

From computer animation virtuoso Yoichiro Kawaguchi, this spellbinding journey will propel you through 11 discrete cyberworlds overflowing with 3-D morphogenic wonders, powered by the music of Tangerine Dream.

VHS: S34270. $19.95.

Laser: LD76961. $29.99.

The Magic Flute

A magic flute helps a fearless prince rescue a beautiful princess from peril in this action-packed, animated adventure based on Mozart's *The Magic Flute*. Voices of Mark Hamill and Michael York.

VHS: S24021. $14.95.

Laser: LD74982. $29.99.

Greengrass, 1994, 44 mins.

Magic Horse

The first cartoon feature film from the Soviet Union, based on one of the most popular children's folk tales, about a boy who befriends a magical horse. With sound dubbed into English.

VHS: S00798. $29.95.

Ivanov Vano, USSR, 1941, 56 mins.

The Magic Pony

The youngest of three brothers catches a magical horse. The horse bargains for his freedom by giving the boy a magic pony instead. The boy eventually becomes king and wins the hand of the Moon Maiden. A Soviet film directed by Ivan Ivanov-Vano: this version is dubbed with the voices of Jim Backus, Hans Conreid and Erin Moran.

VHS: S02547. $14.95.

Soyuzmultfilm, USSR, 80 mins.

The Magic Voyage of Sinbad (Sadko)

The colorful Russian fantasy is about a bearded hero from Novgorod who is on a quest to find the bird of happiness. He apparently isn't particular about the exact color. He also isn't Sinbad. A neat ploy to recruit an American audience for '61 release with anglicized cast names.

VHS: S04087. $29.95.

Alexander Ptushko, USSR, 1952

Magic Voyage, The

In 1492, Christopher Columbus (Dom DeLuise) believed the world was square. Together with his woodworm pal Pico (Corey Feldman), he set off to discover America. But once there, Marilyn—a magical firefly—is captured by the evil "swarm-lord." It's up to Pico, Columbus and the gang to save the day. Narrated by Mickey Rooney.

Laser: LD75689. $34.95.

MS/Bavaria Film, Germany, 1991, 82 mins.

The Magical Forest

When Kiki the frog's feet are frozen in ice, Belinda the butterfly can't fly, and Skippy the firefly can't light up without burning his shoes, it's up to Maria and Mirabella to find the Fairy Mother and save them. Live action and animation.

VHS: S28346. $24.95.

A.I.P., Italy, 1990, 70 mins.

Manxmouse

Based on the 1968 novel by Paul Gallico of Manxmouse and Manxcat, children will love this tale about a long-eared mouse who looks like a rabbit.

VHS: S12380. $14.95.

Nippon, 1989, 75 mins.

Martin the Cobbler

This Claymation adaptation of Leo Tolstoy's engaging short story is narrated by his daughter, Alexandra. A cobbler who has lost his family is all alone and angry at God. When a holy man leaves him a Bible, he finds new inspiration by reading the tale of a rich merchant who invited the Lord to be his guest.

VHS: S26615. $14.95.

Will Vinton, USA, 27 mins.

Masters of Animation Vol. 1: USA & Canada

USA: Interviews: Chuck Jones, Bill Littlejohn and others. Film Excerpts: *Steamboat Willie, Rooty Toot Toot, The Great Cognito* and others. NATIONAL FILM BOARD OF CANADA: Interviews: Norman McLaren and others. Film Excerpts: *Hen Hop, Blinkety Blank, The Street, Every Child* and others. CBC-RADIO CANADA/INDEPENDENTS: Interviews: Frederic Back and others. Film Excerpts: *Crac, George & The Star, Hooray for Sandbox Land* and others.

VHS: S07613. $29.95.

Educational Film Centre, 1986, 85 mins.

Masters of Animation Vol. 2: Great Britain, Italy & France

GREAT BRITAIN: Interviews: John Halas, Joy Batchelor and others. Film Excerpts: *Animal Farm, Yellow Submarine* and others. ITALY: Interviews: Emanuele Luzzatti, Guilio Gianini and Bruno Bozzetto. Film Excerpts: *Labyrinth, Allegro Non Troppo* and others. FRANCE: Interviews: Yannick Piel. Film Excerpts: *Drame Chez Les Fantoches, The Nose, Asterix in Britain* and others.

VHS: S07614. $29.95.

Educational Film Centre, 1986, 87 mins.

Masters of Animation Vol. 3: USSR, Poland, Yugoslavia & Hungary

USSR: Film Excerpts: *The Snow Queen, Nutcracker Suite, The Tale of Tales* and others. YUGOSLAVIA: Interviews: Dusan Vukotic, Nedeljko Dragic and others. Film Excerpts: *Mask of the Red Death, Per Aspera ad Astra, Second Class Traveler* and others. POLAND: Film Excerpts: *Little Black Riding Hood, The Red & The Black* and others. HUNGARY: Film Excerpts: *Story of a Beatle, Kidnapping of the Sun & Moon* and others.

VHS: S07615. $29.95.

Educational Film Centre, 1986, 113 mins.

Masters of Animation Vol. 4: Japan & Computer Animation

JAPAN: Interviews: Osamu Tezuka. Film Excerpts: *House of Flame and Dojoji Temple, Broken Down Film, Jumping* and others. COMPUTER ANIMATION PART 1: Interviews: Bob Abel, John Whitney Jr. and Charles Csuri. Artists: Charles Csuri, Carl Rosendahl and others. COMPUTER ANIMATION PART 2: Artists: Bob Abel, Art Durinski, Eihachiro Nakamae and others.

VHS: S07616. $29.95.

Educational Film Centre, 1986, 84 mins.

Masters of Russian Animation

Animated films produced by Moscow's world renowned Soyuzmultfilm Studio, including 12 award-winning films.

Masters of Russian Animation: Volume 1. Includes *Film Film Film* (Fyodor Khitruk, 1969, 20 mins.); *Girlfriend* (Yelena Gavrilko, 1990, 10 mins.); *Hunt* (Eduard Nazarov, 1979, 10 mins.); and *Ballerina on a Boat* (Lev Atamanov, 1970, 17 mins.). Total length: 57 mins.

VHS: S33844. $24.95.

Masters of Russian Animation: Volume 2. Includes *Island* (Fyodor Khitruk, 1974, 10 mins.); *Singing Teacher* (Lev Atamanov, 3 mins.); *Last Hunt* (Valentine Karavayev, 1984, 10 mins.); *Old Stair* (Alexander Gorlenko, 1995, 7 mins.); and *Liberated Don Quixote* (Vadim Kurchevsky, 18 mins.). Total length: 48 mins.

VHS: S33845. $24.95.

Masters of Russian Animation: Volume 3. Includes *Contact* (Vladimir Tarasov, 1979, 10 mins.); *Travels of an Ant* (Eduard Nazarov, 1984, 10 mins.); *Cat & Company* (Alexander Guriev, 1991, 10 mins.); and *Tale of Tales* (Yuri Norstein, 1980, 30 mins.). Total length: 60 mins.

VHS: S33846. $24.95.

Masters of Russian Animation: Volume 4. Special children's collection includes *Travels of an Ant* (Eduard Nazarov, 1984, 10 mins.); *Ballerina on a Boat* (Lev Atamanov, 1970, 17 mins.); *Last Hunt* (Valentine Karavayev, 1984, 10 mins.); *Cat & Company* (Alexander Guriev, 1991, 10 mins.); and *Hunt* (Eduard Nazarov, 1979 10 mins.). Total length: 57 mins.

VHS: S33847. $24.95.

Masters of Russian Animation: Volume 5. Includes *Battle of Kerjenets* (Yuri Norstein, 1972, 10 mins.); *Seasons* (1970, 10 mins.); *Heron and Crane* (1975, 10 mins.); *Hedgehog in the Fog* (1977, 10 mins.); and *Tale of Tales* (30 mins.). Total length: 70 mins.

VHS: S33848. $24.95.

Masters of Russian Animation: Volume 6—The Works of Fyodor Khitruk & The Works of Eduard Nazarov. Includes the Khitruk short films *Film Film Film* (1969, 20 mins.); *Island* (1974, 10 mins.); *Lion and Ox* (1984, 10 mins.); and the Nazarov films *Hunt* (1979, 10 mins.); *There Was a Dog* (1983, 10 mins.); and *Travels of an Ant* (1984, 10 mins.). Total length: 70 mins.

VHS: S33849. $24.95.

Masters of Russian Animation: Volume 7. Includes *Firing Range* (Anatoly Petrov, 1978, 10 mins.); *Ball of Yarn* (Nikolai Serebriakov, 10 mins.); *Wolf and Calf* (Mikhail Kamanetsky, 1986, 10 mins.); *My Green Crocodile* (Vadim Kurchevsky, 10 mins.); and *Alter Ego* (Nina Shorina, 10 mins.). Total length: 50 mins.

VHS: S33850. $24.95.

Matt the Gooseboy

When Matt, a simple peasant boy, is unjustly punished by a cruel and wicked tyrant, he sets out to defend himself and his honor against overwhelming odds, leading Lord Blackheart on a wild goose chase.

VHS: S23874. $24.95.

Pannonia, Hungary, 80 mins.

Meet the Feebles

An adult fantasy film, *Meet the Feebles* relates the events that led up to the infamous "Feebles Variety Massacre," the day that rocked the puppet world. The film, directed by Peter Jackson *(Dead Alive, Heavenly Creatures)*, who describes it as "a kind of *Roger Rabbit* meets *Brazil*," is set in a contemporary world like ours, with one major difference: there are no human beings. The Feebles' world is entirely populated by puppets-living, breathing, eating puppets with larger-than-life human characteristics and weaknesses...*Meet the Feebles* is a darkly comic satire on greed, lust and jealousy...part satire/soap opera/ musical that is a wildly original feature" (Charles Coleman).

VHS: S26868. $89.95.

Peter Jackson, New Zealand, 1988, 97 mins.

The Mighty Kong

A direct-to-video musical version of *King Kong*, with songs by the Sherman Brothers. Voices of Dudley Moore and Jodi Benson.

VHS: S34262. $22.95.

Lana Film Co., USA, 1997, 78 mins.

The Mind's Eye

Clips from over 300 computer-animated pieces are edited together and backed by a new-age music bed composed and performed by James Reynolds. Some of the clips are *Creation, Heart of the Machine, Post Modern, Leaving the Bonds of Earth, Civilization Rising, Technodance, Love Found* and *The Temple*.

VHS: S14596. $19.95.

Laser: LD72214. $34.95.

Nickman, 1991, 40 mins.

The Mouse & The Motorcycle

Some delightful stop-motion puppet animation is used in this film about a motorcycle-riding mouse. Based on Beverly Cleary's book, it's about Ralph Mouse, who helps young Keith find the medicine he needs to fight off a bad fever and get well again. EP Speed.

VHS: S16579. $9.95.

Churchill Films, USA, 1986, 42 mins.

Mouse on the Mayflower

This classic tale provides a delightful message about our country's early history. Voices of Tennessee Ernie Ford, Eddie Albert, June Foray and Paul Frees.

VHS: S18863. $12.95.

Rankin/Bass, USA, 1968, 48 mins.

Mr. Rossi's Dreams

Further adventures of Mr. Rossi and his faithful dog Harold by *Allegro Non Troppo* animator Bruno Bozzetto. Mr. Rossi pretends he is the king of the jungle, a daring astronaut, Zorro, and many other heroic characters.

VHS: S01721. $39.95.

Bruno Bozzetto, Italy, 1983, 80 mins.

The Nanna & Lil' Puss Puss Show

The collected work of Dallas' wackiest animators, *The Nanna & Lil' Puss Puss Show* is like no other comedy duo. They're all here: Soggi, Captain Weird Beard, Nippoless Nippleby and the cast of Hard Edition. Nineteen shorts: *In a Pinch, Weird Beard, Cocks, Fe Fi Fo Fooey, Baby Boom, Weird Beard Act I, Hard Edition, Wipe Out, Weird Beard Act II, Downbeat Dowager, Weird Beard Act III, The Tale of Nippoless Nippleby, Off the Record, Weird Beard Act IV, One Ration Under God, Weird Beard Epilogue, The Honeymoonies, Scaredy Cat* and *Who Calcutta the Cheese?*

VHS: S25819. $29.95.

DNA Prods, USA, 1994, 50 mins.

The National Film Board of Canada's Animation Festival

Sixteen titles: *The Balognie Birdman* (Les Drew,'91), *Ottawa '90 Signal Films* ('90), *Every Dog's Guide to the Playground* (Les Drew,'91), *Para-Sight* (John Weldon,'91), *Two Sisters* (Caroline Leaf,'91), *The Irises* (Gervais & Giraldeau,'91), *Jours de Plaine* (Bedard & Leduc,'91), *Strings* (Wendy Tilby,'91), *The Lump* (John Weldon,'91), *The Apprentice* (Richard Condie,'91), *Blackfly* (Chris Hinton,'91) and two-minute excerpts from *George and Rosemary* (Snowden & Fine,'87), *The Big Snit* (Richard Condie, '85), *Juke Bar* (Martin Barry,'89), *Get a Job* (Brad Caslor,'86) and *The Cat Came Back* (Cordell Barker,'88).
VHS: S25830. $29.95.
Laser: LD71937. $49.95.
NFB of Canada, Canada, 90 mins.

Nestor, The Long-Eared Christmas Donkey

In this Animagic special, Nestor is ridiculed for his long ears until he is befriended by a cherub. Together they journey to Bethlehem and meet Mary & Joseph on the way. Nestor protects Mary in a sandstorm, then carries her to Bethlehem.
VHS: S13034. $9.95.
Rankin/Bass, USA, 1977, 23 mins.

New British Animation: The Best from Channel 4

This tape shows off some of the best work coming out of England today. From David Anderson's spooky "deadtime" story, *Deadsy*, to the joyous spontaneity of Erica Russell's *Feet of Song*, this tape was made for the animation fan looking for a peek at the future. Plus *Babylon, Black Dog, Conversation Pieces, Late Edition, Sales Pitch* and *The Victor*.
VHS: S17050. $29.95.
UK, 60 mins.

NFBC—Cartoon Festival: The Sweater

Seven award-winning animated shorts with a Christmas theme, from the National Film Board of Canada: *The Great Toy Robbery, The Sweater, The Story of Christmas, The Magic Flute, Lucretia, Christmas Cracker* (Oscar nominee) and *The Energy Carol*.
VHS: S29962. $12.95.
NFBC, USA, 60 mins.

NFBC: An Animated Christmas

A Christmas collection of animated shorts from the National Film Board of Canada. Six titles: *Lucretia, An Energy Carol, The Great Toy Robbery, Bear's X-Ones, An Old Box* and *Christmas Cracker*.
Laser: LD71938. $39.95.
NFB of Canada, Canada, 60 mins.

NFBC: Animation for Kids Vol. 1

A children's collection of animated shorts from the National Film Board of Canada. Seven titles: *Dingles, Every Dog's Guide to Home Safety, The Tender Tale of Cinderella Penguin, Every Dog's Guide to the Playground, Blackfly, Mr. Frog Went A-Courting* and *The Sound Collector*.
Laser: LD71939. $39.95.
NFB of Canada, Canada, 60 mins.

NFBC: Cartoon Festival: Cactus Swing

Four short films from The National Film Board of Canada: *Cactus Swing, The Tender Tale of Cinderella Penguin* (Oscar nominee), *Every Dog's Guide to Complete Home Safety* and *The Sand Castle* (Oscar winner).
VHS: S28043. $12.95.
NFB of Canada, Canada, 40 mins.

NFBC: Cartoon Festival: The Cat Came Back

Five short films from The National Film Board of Canada: *The Cat Came Back* (Oscar nominee), *Blackberry Subway Jam, The Log Driver's Waltz, The Dingles* and *Summer Legend*.
VHS: S28042. $12.95.
NFB of Canada, Canada, 40 mins.

NFBC: Christmas Cracker

In *Christmas Cracker*, a man builds a spaceship to gather a star for the top of his Christmas tree. *The Story of Christmas* uses cut-out historical figures to narrate the joy of Christmas. *The Great Toy Robbery* recasts Santa as a western cartoon ambushed by a deranged trio of bandits. *The Energy Carol* reworks Dickens' Scrooge into a miserly energy company autocrat who learns a valuable lesson about excessive consumption.
VHS: S18563. $14.95.
NFB of Canada, Canada, 30 mins.

NFBC: Every Child

1979 Oscar-winner *Every Child* is the story of a baby that appears on the doorstep of a busy executive, and is subsequently passed around from household to household. Also *The Magic Flute, The Log Driver's Waltz* and *The Town Mouse and the Country Mouse*.
VHS: S15794. $14.95.
NFB of Canada, Canada, 30 mins.

NFBC: Leonard Maltin's Animation Favorites from the National Film Board of Canada

Maltin selects some of his favorite cartoons in this A&E documentary special. Nine titles: *Begone Dull Care* (Norman McLaren), *Mindscape* (Jacques Drouin), *Log Driver's Waltz* (John Weldon), *The Cat Came Back* (Cordell Barker), *Getting Started* (Richard Condie), *The Sweater* (Sheldon Cohen), *The Street* (Caroline Leaf), *Pas de Deux* (Norman McLaren) and *Anniversary* (Aubry & Hebert).
VHS: S25821. $29.95.
NFBC, Canada, 95 mins.

NFBC: The Box

The Box explores alternate realities of fantasy, animation and live action about an artist's creation that comes to life. *The Story of Cinderella* reinterprets the classic tale with charming illustrations executed by fifth grade students. *Mary of Mile 18* is a warm and simple work about a young woman whose life is transformed when she finds an abandoned puppy.
VHS: S18560. $14.95.
NFB of Canada, Canada, 30 mins.

NFBC: The Sand Castle

1977 Oscar-winner *The Sand Castle* is a stop-motion story of the Sandman who sculpts magical creatures who build a sand castle and then celebrate their new home. Also includes *The North Wind and the Sun, Alphabet and the Owl* and *The Lemming*.
VHS: S15795. $14.95.
NFB of Canada, Canada, 30 mins.

NFBC: The Sweater

The Sweater is a charming tale of the trauma a young boy suffers when a mail-order mixup delivers him the wrong hockey sweater. Also includes *The Ride* and *Getting Started*.
VHS: S15791. $14.95.
NFB of Canada, Canada, 30 mins.

NFBC: The Tender Tale of Cinderella Penguin

This whimsical twist casts Cinderella as a penguin who loses her magic flipper. A kingdom-wide search sees Prince Charming uncover the right webbed foot. Also includes *Metamorphoses, Mr. Frog Went A-Courting, The Sky Is Blue* and *The Owl and the Raven*.
VHS: S15792. $14.95.
NFB of Canada, Canada, 30 mins.

The Nutcracker Prince

This lushly animated feature highlights the music of Tchaikovsky. Voices of Kiefer Sutherland, Phyllis Diller and Peter O'Toole.
VHS: S15098. $14.95.
Laser: LD75865. $29.95.
Paul Schibli, USA, 1990, 74 mins.

Odyssey into the Mind's Eye

The latest installment in the computer animation anthology series is accompanied by the music of Kerry Livgren (Kansas). Clips of the latest CGI blend into a mesmerizing tapestry of fantastic imagery.
VHS: S29807. $19.95.
Laser: LD76049. $29.95.
Odyssey, 1996, 62 mins.

Off on a Comet

Jules Verne's story of Captain Sevadec, who finds that he has been swept off the earth with a small group of others and is hurtling out into space. An animated classic.
VHS: S04425. $19.95.
R. Slapczynski, USA, 1979, 52 mins.

On the Comet

Jules Verne's science fiction adventure is brought to life by Czech animator Karel Zeman. Since the early 1950's Zeman has been directing highly imaginative films that combine animation and live action and are marked by their fantastic trick effects. A film for the whole family! English dialog.
VHS: S00958. $24.95.
Karel Zeman, Czechoslovakia, 76 mins.

Opera Imaginaire

Twelve popular arias are brought to life through the interpretations of some of Europe's most talented animators. All styles of animation are represented, including computer animation. Films by Ken Lidster, Monique Renault, Pascal Roulin, Jonathan Hills, Jimmy Murakami, Raimund Krumme, Stephen Palmer, Hilary Audus, Guionne Leroy and Jose Abel.
VHS: S23751. $14.95.
1995, 50 mins.

Origins of American Animation

From the Library of Congress video collection. Among 21 complete films and two fragments are samples of early live-action animation and pioneering examples of stop-motion, clay-, puppet-, and cutout-animation. Titles include *Krazy Kat, The Katzenjammer Kids, Bobby Bumps Starts a Lodge, Keeping Up with the Joneses* and *The Phable of a Phat Woman*.
VHS: S21264. $34.95.
USA, 1900-21, 84 mins.

Outrageous Animation Vol. 1

Twelve titles: *An Inside Job* (Aidan Hickey/Ireland), *Haploid Affair* (Kaminski & Lidster/Canada), *One of Those Days* (Bill Plympton/USA), *The Four Wishes* (Michel Ocelot/France), *Instant Sex* (Bob Godfrey/England), *Rondino* (Csaba Szorda/Hungary), *Full of Grace* (Nicole Van Goethem/Belgium), *Lupo the Butcher* (Danny Antonucci/Canada), *Striptease* (Bruno Bozzetto/Italy), *Great British Moments* (Peter Mudie/UK), *Love at First Sight* (Pavel Koutsky/Czechoslovakia) and *Vice Versa* (Aleksander Sroczynski/Poland).
VHS: S17043. $29.95.
60 mins.

Outrageous Animation Vol. 2

Eighteen titles: *Adam* (J. Ananiades/Greece), *Another Great Moment* (P. Mudie/UK), *The Club* (G. Griffin/USA), *Dialog* (D. Vunak/Yugoslavia), *Eldorado* (B. Bozzetto/Italy), *Erection* (G. Manuli/Italy), *Jac Mac & Rad Boy... Go!* (W. Archer/USA), *The Jump* (N. Astley & J. Newitt/UK), *Maxi Cat's Lunch* (Z. Grgic/Yugoslavia), *Mr. Gloom* (B. Kopp/USA), *Observational Hazard* (B. Kopp/USA), *The Prayer* (R. Gvozdanovic/Yugoslavia), *Quod Libet* (G. Van Dijk/Holland), *Royal Flush* (J. McIntyre/USA), *Sweet Dreams Luv* (D. Dames/Holland), *Toilet Bowl* (M. Jone/USA), *You Can't Teach an Old Dog New Tricks* (J. Foray/USA) and *Zwisch* (T. Sivertsen/Norway).
VHS: S17048. $29.95.
Laser: LD72086. $39.95.
60 mins.

Ovide and the Gang

Winner of the Gemini Award for Best Animated Series, this collection of ten misadventures follows Ovide and his animal friends as they turn their island paradise upside down imitating what they see on television. 120 mins.
VHS: S09590. $39.95.

Paul Driessen: Animator

Dutch-born Paul Driessen is considered by many one of the most talented and original creators of modern animation. His often bizarre animation, including work on *Yellow Submarine*, has achieved a cult status among animation fans around the world. This tape contains 11 examples of his finest work.
VHS: S18123. $29.95.
Paul Driessen, Holland, 60 mins.

The Paul Glabicki Animation Tape

Four intricately constructed films from animator Paul Glabicki, whose hand-drawn geometric animation is so precise it looks computer-generated. Four films: *Diagram Film* ('78) overlays photographed highways and found footage with Rube Goldberg diagrams. *Five Improvisations* ('80) is a rapid-fire series of B&W lines and dots. *Film-Wipe-Film* ('84) is a formal stream of consciousness in which 100 film sequences are joined by 100 animated film wipes. *Object Conversation* ('85) is a series of dialogues created between source objects such as scissors, chairs and a barbell.
VHS: S15645. $29.95.
Paul Glabicki, USA, 1978-85, 55 mins.

Pioneers in Animation Vol. 1

Winsor McCay's *Little Nemo* and *The Sinking of The Lusitania*; Edison Studio's *Raoul Barre's Cartoons on Tour* (part of the Grouch Chaser series); Max Fleischer and Koko in *The Cure* and *The Reunion*; Mutt & Jeff in *Slick Sleuth*.
VHS: S29683. $24.95.
USA, 60 mins.

Pioneers in Animation Vol. 2

Crusader Rabbit Series where Dr. Frank En Stein is terrorizing a western village when Crusader and Rags come to the rescue; Woody Woodpecker in *Pantry Panic*; Oswald Rabbit in *Beachcomber*; Porky in *Porky's Preview* and *Pigs in a Polka*.
VHS: S29684. $24.95.
USA, 55 mins.

Pioneers in Animation Vol. 3

Eight titles: *Mighty Mouse in Wolf! Wolf!*; *An Itch in Time* (Warner Bros.), *Chicken a la King* (Fleischer), *The Big Bad Wolf* (Ub Iwerks), *The Timid Toreador* (Warner Bros.), *Ali Baba Bound* (Warner Bros.), *Notes to You* (Warner Bros.), *The Stupidstitious Cat* (Buzzy the Funny Crow). Fair to poor print quality.
VHS: S29685. $24.95.
USA, 60 mins.

Pippi Longstocking

Astrid Lindgren's classic character turns her straight-laced village upside-down with a series of musical misadventures in this theatrically released feature film. A co-production among Canadian, Swedish and German studios.
VHS: S32461. $19.95.
Nelvana, Canada, 1997, 75 mins.

Planetary Traveler

This all-digital production from the producer of *The Mind's Eye* was created on the Internet in a virtual studio and produced entirely on desktop computers. It uses the theme of a visual flight log by alien spacefarers to stitch together multiple imagery of alien landscapes. Paul Haslinger provides an original score.
VHS: S32372. $19.95.
DVD: DV60035. $29.95.
Jan C. Nickman, USA, 1997, 40 mins.

Plymptoons: The Complete Works of Bill Plympton

Twenty-one titles: *Self Portrait* ('88), *The Turn On* ('68), *Lucas—The Ear of Corn* ('77), *Boomtown* ('85), *Drawing Lesson #2* ('87), *Your Face* ('87), *Love in the Fast Lane* ('87), *One of Those Days* ('88), *How to Kiss* ('89), *25 Ways to Quit Smoking* ('89), *245 Days* ('89), *Noodle Ear* ('89), *Human Rights* ('89), *Acid Rain* ('89), *Trivial Pursuit* ('90), *Sugar Delight* ('91), *Previous Lives* ('91) and *Plymptoons* ('90).
VHS: S16931. $29.95.
Laser: LD72092. $34.95.
Bill Plympton, USA, 1968-91, 60 mins.

Princess & The Goblin

When a peaceful kingdom is menaced by an army of goblins, a brave and beautiful princess joins forces with a resourceful peasant boy to rescue the people. A multi-national production directed by Jozsef Gemes.
Laser: LD72464. $34.95.
Siriol/Pannonia, Hungary, 1993, 82 mins.

Professor Bunruckle's Guide to Pixilation

Award-winning animator David Johnson's guide to animating people, animals and even inanimate objects is possible using pixilation techniques. The Professor shows how it's done. 16 mins.
VHS: S23499. $49.95.

Puppet Animation

Animated puppet Dennis the Dragon hosts this presentation that highlights the techniques of puppet animation. By award-winning animator David Johnson. 17 mins.
VHS: S23500. $49.95.

Puppet Masters

Three masters of puppet animation are presented. Ladislas Starevitch's *The Mascot* (1934) is the surreal tale of a lost dog who enters a world of devilish characters; Jiri Trnka's *Song of the Prairie* (1952) is a wonderful spoof of Hollywood Westerns; Ray Harryhausen's *King Midas* (1953) is one of his charming early works. Film and video quality is fair.
VHS: S04857. $29.95.
1934-53, 54 mins.

Quark the Dragonslayer

Quark, a baby giant, is capable of conquering dragons, robbers and Vikings. Narrated by John Cleese.
VHS: S29036. $24.95.
Nordisk Film, 1987, 70 mins.

Ray Harryhausen Compilation

Before perfecting the stop-motion animation technique featured in *Jason and the Argonauts* and *Seventh Voyage of Sinbad*, animator Ray Harryhausen made a series of short films based on fairy tales. This tape includes *Hansel and Gretel, Little Miss Muffet, The Story of King Midas, Rapunzel* and *Little Red Riding Hood*.
VHS: S16264. $29.95.
Ray Harryhausen, USA, 60 mins.

Rime of the Ancient Mariner

This evocative work features a recitation by Sir Michael Redgrave accompanied by images both real and animated. Part One is a carefully researched biography of Samuel Coleridge. Part Two is a unique visualization of the man's famous poem. Gold Medal winner at the Int'l. Film & TV Festival of NY.
VHS: S03758. $39.95.
Raul da Silva, USA, 60 mins.

Rip Van Winkle

Washington Irving's short story is brought to life in this Claymation adaptation. A farmer who dozes for 20 years has great difficulty explaining his absence and adjusting to a new era. Narrated by Will Geer.
VHS: S26619. $14.95.
Will Vinton, USA, 27 mins.

The Rocketship Reel

Direct from Vancouver, B.C.—The Canadian Riviera—comes the incredibly bizarre, twisted, and extremely funny animation of Marv Newland's International Rocketship studio. Eleven titles: *Bambi Meets Godzilla* (Marv Newland), *Sing Beast Sing* (Marv Newland), *Anijam* (Marv Newland), *The Butterfly* (Dieter Mueller), *Hooray for Sandbox Land* (Marv Newland), *Points* (Dan Collins), *Dry Noodles* (Dan Collins), *Lupo the Butcher* (Danny Antonucci), *Dog Brain* (Jay Falconer), *Waddles* (Dan Collins) and *Black Hula* (Marv Newland).
VHS: S25828. $29.95.
Laser: CAV. LD71496. $39.99.
Int'l Rocketship, Canada, 60 mins.

Rover Dangerfield

This Rodney Dangerfield project, directed by Jim George and Bob Seeley, is lavishly animated and the canine caricature of Dangerfield is nicely designed and implemented. Vegas star Rover Dangerfield is hijacked to a country farm, where he falls in love with the local country cutie. There's lots of Rodney's stand-up dialogue.
VHS: S29054. $19.95.
Laser: LD75710. $29.95.
Hyperion, USA, 1991, 90 mins.

Samson & Sally: The Song of the Whales

This three-time award winner in Europe is adapted from Bent Haller's story. Samson & Sally are two young whales searching for Moby Dick. First-rate animation.
VHS: S10966. $14.95.
Nordisk Film, Denmark, 1984, 70 mins.

Scenes from the Surreal

Three short films: In *Darkness Light Darkness*, a fragmented man emerges out of the darkness to construct his physical self. In *Manly Games*, a soccer match is interpreted by Svankmajer with balls banging off coffins. In *Death of Stalinism*, Svankmajer examines the myth and downfall of Czech communist doctrine. Also on this tape is *The Animator of Prague*, a BBC documentary by James Marsh. In addition to a look at Svankmajer's works, we join him at work on his latest creation and witness many of his trademark techniques.
VHS: S17912. $19.95.
Jan Svankmajer, Czechoslovakia, 1992, 58 mins.

Schimmelstein

This is a claymation satire on the music biz, starring the Jickets. World Music Inc. conspires to defraud the down-home band. There are many odd domestic and corporate scenes.
VHS: S22636. $19.95.
Direct Art, USA, 1985, 25 mins.

Scientific Visualization

Produced by the National Center for Supercomputing Applications, this tape presents the aesthetic highlights of scientific visualization projects of the Center. The projects envision large, mostly three-dimensional Supercomputer data sets of scientific research from astrophysics, chemistry, geophysics and biology. Included are segments about storms, a tornado's complexity modeled by mathematical equations, simulated air flow. 15 mins.
VHS: S10999. $29.95.

The Secret Adventures of Tom Thumb

In this highly acclaimed stop-motion animated feature, the classic tale of Tom Thumb takes a dark and sinister turn more evocative of science fiction and horror films. Through pixelation and clay animation, a world of seedy slums and sinister laboratories emerges. When Tom is stolen from his parents for experimentation, he meets other small, oppressed creatures and fights with them against the tyranny of the "giants."
NOT SUITABLE FOR CHILDREN.
VHS: S26444. $14.95.
Laser: LD75881. $29.95.
Dave Borthwick, UK, 1994, 57 mins.

The Secret Garden (1994)

Based on the book by Frances Hodgson Burnett. Orphaned Mary Lennox is sent to live with her uncle in Yorkshire. She discovers a secret garden on the grounds that no one has entered for ten years. What she and her friends find there will change them forever. The home video contains extra footage not aired on TV.
VHS: S22519. $16.95.
Laser: LD74919. $44.95.
ABC, USA, 1994, 72 mins.

The Secret of the Seal

Based on a best-selling book. Find out how Tottoi, an adventurous young boy, discovers two Mediterranean seals believed to be extinct. Too excited to keep his find a secret, Tottoi soon finds himself battling to save the lives of his new friends.
VHS: S19419. $24.95.
Nippon Animation, Japan, 1992, 90 mins.

Serendipity, The Pink Dragon

Stranded on a tropical oasis, a courageous little boy meets a magical dragon. Music by Bullets and Takawo Watanabe.
VHS: S12776. $14.95.
Zuiyo, Japan, 1983, 90 mins.

Sextoons: An Erotic Animation Festival

Sexually explicit animation ranging from tenderly erotic to laughably crude to outright disturbing. Featuring the sought-after Buried Treasure featuring Eveready Harton—reputed to be an after-hours project of a major animation studio of the '20s. Sixteen titles: *Boobs a Lot* (Bernard Ellis, sing along), *Armchair Inventions* (Gary Moore), *Little Genitalia* (Barry Brilliant), *A Child's Alphabet* (Thomas Spence), *The Further Adventures of Super Screw* (B&W), *Jack in the Fox* (Karl Krogstad), *Hearts and Arrows* (Roy Fridge), *Snow White & The Seven Dwarfs* (German, ca. 1930's), *Buried Treasure* (B&W, ca. 1924), *Out of Order (B&W, ca. 1920's, with Krazy Kat look-alike), Crocus* (Suzan Pitt Kraning), *Little Ms. Muffet* (Mark Seiderburg, 1974), *Seed Reel #1* (Mary Beems, 1975), *L'Ombre de la Pomme* (Lapoujade), *Show Biz* (Algas Nakis) and *Boobs a Lot* (photo montage).
ADULTS ONLY.
VHS: S17689. $19.95.
1920-75, 70 mins.

Shakespeare Vol. 1: The Twelfth Night

The arrival of shipwrecked twins in the land of Illyria creates havoc in this comical story of love in disguise.
VHS: S21935. $14.95.
Dave Edwards, UK, 1992, 30 mins.

Shakespeare Vol. 2: A Midsummer Night's Dream

An enchanted wood is the setting for a hilarious night of confusion when four young lovers try to resolve their passions despite some meddling from mischievous forest spirits.
VHS: S21932. $14.95.
Dave Edwards, UK, 1992, 30 mins.

Shakespeare Vol. 3: Romeo and Juliet

A pair of young lovers are destroyed by the hatred of their rival families in what is perhaps the greatest tragic love story of all time.
VHS: S21933. $14.95.
Dave Edwards, UK, 1992, 30 mins.

Shakespeare Vol. 4: Hamlet

Prince Hamlet must face the challenge of avenging his father's murder in this tragic story of revenge.
VHS: S21930. $14.95.
Dave Edwards, UK, 1992, 30 mins.

Shakespeare Vol. 5: The Tempest

An outcast duke has a chance to avenge himself and his daughter in this tale of love and sorcery.
VHS: S21934. $14.95.
Dave Edwards, UK, 1992, 30 mins.

Shakespeare Vol. 6: Macbeth

A great soldier is tempted by the prophecies of three witches into murdering the king and seizing the crown of Scotland.
VHS: S21931. $14.95.
Dave Edwards, UK, 1992, 30 mins.

Shame of the Jungle

A wild, animated spoof of Tarzan features showing how the jungle inhabitants were trying to cope with all the problems we face today. A kind of X-rated *George of the Jungle*. Created by animator Picha, this adult comedy features the writing talents of *Saturday Night Live*'s Anne Beats and Michael O'Donahue as well as the voices of John Belushi, Bill Murray, Brian Doyle-Murray, Christopher Guest and Johnny Weissmuller, Jr.
VHS: S32184. $9.95.
Picha/Boris Szulzinger, France/Belgium, 1975, 70 mins.

The Snow Queen

Hans Christian Anderson's classic about two small children, Gerta and Kay, and Gerta's search for her brother after he was kidnapped by the evil Snow Queen and taken to live in her Ice Castle. An interesting and beautifully animated Soviet feature that was masterfully re-scored and dubbed in English. Directed by Lev Atamanov. Live-action prologue with Art Linkletter. EP Speed.
VHS: S29081. $19.95.
Soyuzmultfilm, USSR, 1957, 55 mins.

The Snowman

Based on the book by Raymond Briggs, this is the story of a young boy who builds a snowman that comes to life on Christmas Eve. Academy Award nominee.
VHS: S01222. $14.95.
John Coates, 1983, 30 mins.

The Soldier's Tale

Conceived and designed by *New Yorker* cartoonist Blechman, *The Soldier's Tale* is a dazzling animation adaptation of a classic Russian folk tale about a soldier tricked by the devil into giving up his violin. The music is by Igor Stravinsky, with voices by Max Von Sydow and Dusan Makavejev. In this version, Blechman makes ingenious use of paints, crayons, color pencil and collages to depict temptation and apocalypse.
VHS: S01228. $49.95.
R.O. Blechman, USA, 1984, 56 mins.

Spike & Mike's Festival of Animation Vol. 1

Twelve titles: *How to Kiss* (Bill Plympton), *Snookles* (Juliet Stroud), *Primiti Too Taa* (Ed Akerman), *Thing What Lurked in the Tub* (David Wasson), *A Story* (Andrew Stanton), *Particle Dreams* (Karl Sims), *Charade* (John Minnus, Oscar Winner), *Western* (Gabor Hamolya), *Feet of Song* (Erica Russell), *Winter* (Pete Doctor), *Lea Press on Limbs* (Chris Miller) and *Bambi Meets Godzilla* (Marv Newland).
VHS: S15237. $29.95.
1991, 45 mins.

Spike & Mike's Festival of Animation Vol. 2

Eighteen titles: *Jean Jean and the Evil Cat* (Walter Santucci/USA), *License to Kill* (Teresa Lang/Canada), *La Pista* (G. Toccafundo/Italy), *Adam* (Peter Lord/UK), *Negative Man* (Cathy Joritz/USA), *Singing Ding a Lings* (Lance Kramer/USA), *The Log* (S. Kushnevrov/Russia), *Next Door* (Pete Docter/USA), *Creature Comforts at Home* (Nick Park/UK), *Street Sweeper* (Serge Elissalde/France), *Visions from the Amazon* (Nancy Kato/Brazil), *Amore Baciami* (Oliver Harrison/UK), *Grasshoppers* (Bruno Bozzetto/Italy), *Manipulation* (Daniel Greaves/UK, Oscar Winner), *Panspermia* (Karl Sims/USA), *Big Fat World of Science* (Mike Wellins/USA), *Dinko's Day* (Mike Cachuela/USA) and *Creature Comforts* (Nick Park/UK, Oscar winner).
VHS: S27549. $39.95.
1993, 65 mins.

Spike & Mike's Festival of Animation Vol. 3

A new collection of eight short animated films from the Spike & Mike touring revue: *Screenplay* (Barry J.C. Purves/UK, 10:50): Oscar-nominated puppet animation of a tragic Japanese love story; *Frannies Christmas* (Mike Mitchell/USA, 2:00): A poetic story of Frannie learning there's no Santa; *Streetsweeper* (Serge Elissalde/France, 6:20): The tragicomic story of a Chaplin-esque streetsweeper, rendered in pencil; *Dirdy Birdy* (John R. Dilworth/USA, 7:00): A longtime festival favorite—a starcrossed attraction taken to a hilarious Avery-esque extreme; *Blindscape* (Stephen Palmer/UK, 8:00): The animator takes us into the world of a blind man via colored pencil renderings; *The Monk and the Fish* (Michael Dudok De Wit/France/Holland, 6:00): Oscar-nominated watercolor animation of an obsessed fisherman monk; *Iddy Biddy Beat Boy* (Mo Willems/USA, 4:30): A comic tale of censure that fans of beat poetry will love; *Britannia* (Joanna Quinn/UK, 7:30): Oscar-nominated satire as a bulldog teaches us the history of Mother England.
VHS: S28625. $29.95.
Various, 1996, 53 mins.

Spike & Mike's Sick & Twisted Festival of Animation Vol. 1

The first two years of Mike & Spike's infamous collection of cult animated shorts: they may be gross, they may be outrageous, they may even be pornographic, but they certainly do get your attention! Fourteen titles: *How Much Is That Window in the Doggie?* (John Callahan), *Pink Komkommer* (Driessen/Newland), *Bladder Trouble* (Webster Colcord), *Discoveries* (Dan Smith), *Thanks for the Mammaries* (Cindy Banks), *Dog Pile* (Miles Thompson), *Beavis and Butthead in Peace Love & Understanding* (Mike Judge), *One Man's Instrument* (Max Bannah), *Nana and Lil' Puss Puss in Downbeat Dowager* (DNA Prod.), *Lullaby* (Ken Bruce), *Bulimiator* (Newton/Kellman), *Deadsy* (David Anderson), *Performance Art Starring Chainsaw Bob* (Brandon McKinney) and *Lupo the Butcher* (Danny Antonucci). ADULTS ONLY.
VHS: S27550. $29.95.
1993, 70 mins.

Spike & Mike's Sick & Twisted Festival of Animation Vol. 2

A second volume of the most sarcastic and disgusting animated short films around. Twenty titles: *Horndog* (Sean Mullen), *Brian's Brain* (Miles Thompson), *Woeful Willie* (Chris Louden), *The Cat, Cow and Beautiful Fish* (Walter Santucci), *Finger Food* (Cindy Banks) *Slaughter Day* (Webster Colcord), *Petey's Wake* (Walt Dohrn), *Mutilator II* (Eric Fogel), *Dog Pile II* (DNA Productions), *Oh Crappy Day* (Sean Mullen), *Big Top* (Zac Mayo/Fernella Boggs), *Triassic Parking Lot* (Mike Wellins), *Spaghetti Snot* (Miles Thompson), *Chainsaw Bob in a Cult Classic* (Brandon McKinney), *Tennis* (Peter Hixson), *Poetic Jaundice* (Tom Lamb/Dan Brisson), *Stubbs* (Miles Thompson), *A Hole in One* (Dave Smith), *Lloyd's Lunchbox* (Greg Ecklund) and *Wrong Hole* (Mark Oftedal). ADULTS ONLY.
VHS: S27551. $29.95.
1994, 56 mins.

Spike & Mike's Sick & Twisted Festival of Animation Vol. 3

Fifteen new, totally disturbed animated shorts: *Puke a Pound* (Cindy Banks/Dave Smith), *No Neck Joe* (Craig McCracken), *Gun, Zipper, Snot* (Miles Thompson), *Empty Roll* (Miles Thompson), *Hut Sluts* (Spike & Mike), *Rick the Dick in Hospital Hell* (Zac Mayo/Fernella Bogs), *Wastes Away* (Anthony Loi), *Phull Phrontal Phingers* (Mike Wellins), *The Birth of Brian* (Miles Thompson), *Dirty Birdy* (John R. Dilworth), *I Never Ho'd for My Father* (Tony Nitolli), *Adam's Other Rib* (Eric Schneider), *Phuk Yew* (Bob McAfee), *Home, Honey, I'm High* (Kevin Kalliher) and *Lloyd Loses His Lunch* (Gregory Eckland). ADULTS ONLY.
VHS: S28626. $29.95.
1996, 50 mins.

The Star Child

Oscar Wilde's tale is brought to life in this Claymation adaptation. A woodcutter finds a child at the site of a fallen shooting star. He takes the child home and raises him into a mischievous youngster, until a beggar woman appears and transforms the child.
VHS: S26618. $14.95.
Will Vinton, USA, 27 mins.

A Star for Jeremy

This warm, animated story relates the friendship of young Jeremy, who dreams about God's assigned position for all the stars, and the special task that awaits Sam, the smallest star who's called to carry out a heroic endeavor. 22 minutes.
VHS: S04140. $14.95.

Star Wrek Zone: The Unauthorized Parody

A clay-animated film by Milco Davis that parodies both the Kirk and Picard versions of *Star Trek*. The U.S.S. *Rent-a-prize*, captained by Jon-Nuke Pickacard, is pulled into a space anomaly and transported back 100 years. There the crew meets the original *Rent-a-prize*, engaged in a full-scale battle. Lots of charicatures and parody dialog, animated in a crude but engaging style.
VHS: S31496. $12.95.
Cinellusion, USA, 1995, 17 mins.

The Story of 15 Boys

Based on the Jules Verne story *Two Years Vacation*, this is the animated tale of 15 boys cast ashore on a desert island who find their lives changed forever.
VHS: S16757. $14.99.
Nippon, Japan, 1987, 80 mins.

Stowaways On The Ark

A beautifully animated children's film in the Disney style from Germany's Wolfgang Urchs. In this version of the Biblical story, there's a surprise visitor—Willie the Woodworm. Translated by Harmony Gold.
VHS: S11695. $19.95.
Wolfgang Urchs, Germany, 1986, 90 mins.

Street Fight

One of the most controversial films ever, *Streetfight* (aka *Coonskin*, aka *Harlem Nights*) is an angry, violent portrayal of street life. Live action and animation, with Philip Michael-Thomas.
VHS: SP recording. **S32488. $19.95.**
VHS: EP recording. **S32489. $9.95.**
Ralph Bakshi, USA, 1975, 89 mins.

Sunshine Porcupine

From the producer of *Yellow Submarine* comes a musical Easter tale. Eggwood, the Easter egg capital of the world, scrambles to get all the eggs ready after the evil Uglyunks waste all their electricity. Sunshine the Porcupine invents a plan that gets production going again. LP Speed.
VHS: S29731. $9.95.
Al Brodax, 25 mins.

The Swan Princess

From the director of *The Fox & The Hound* comes a new animated musical adventure. It's the story of Princess Odette, who is transformed into a swan by an evil sorcerer's (voice of Jack Palance) spell. Held captive at an enchanted lake, she befriends Jean-Bob the Frog (voice of John Cleese), Speed the Turtle (voice of Steven Wright) and Puffin the Bird. Despite their struggle to guard the princess, only a vow of everlasting love can break the spell.
VHS: S25610. $14.95.
Laser: LD75029. $29.95.
Nest Prods, USA, 1994, 90 mins.

The Swan Princess: Escape from Castle Mountain

Richard Rich directs this direct-to-video sequel to his well-regarded 1994 theatrical feature. Prince Derek, Princess Odette and the rest fight to save their kingdom from the evil magician Clavius.
VHS: S32470. $19.95.
Nest Entertainment, USA, 1997, 75 mins.

Sword and the Dragon

Beautiful fairytale from Soviet director Alexander Ptushko in which a magic potion and a legendary sword lead a simple farmer into battle against the invading Tugars and their evil leader. Amid galloping hooves and clashing swords, Ilya and his mighty warriors battle to defend their homeland. English dubbed.
VHS: S09194. $19.95.
Alexander Ptushko, USSR, 1960, 81 mins.

Tanka

This prize-winning work by David Lebrun is an animated translation of the Tibetan book of the dead. Tanka means "a thing rolled up." Photographed by Tibetan scroll paintings moving through the 16th and 19th centuries, the program is a cyclical visualizing of ancient gods and demons. "Dazzling and vibrantly colored" *(The Los Angeles Times)*. 9 mins.
VHS: S17457. $29.95.

Terrytoons: The Cats & Mice of Paul Terry

Seven titles: *The Wild West, Short Vacation, China Doll, Sunny Italy* ('28), *Stars of the Circus, Sharpshooter* ('24) and *Ship Ahoy*.
VHS: S05604. $19.95.
Terrytoons, USA, 1920's, 55 mins.

The Thief and the Cobbler

Nearly 30 years in the making, *The Thief and the Cobbler* is almost literally Richard William's life work. Some of animation's greatest names have contributed to the production over the years, and the lush animation and breathtaking Escher-like backgrounds are a feast for the eyes. Unfortunately, Williams was not able to complete the film on time, so the money men took it away from him—hastily slapping together something that could pass as a complete movie. The resultant version that appears on this tape is a disappointing patchwork of breathtaking Williams animation interspersed with hack fill-in scenes, lame Disney-esque musical numbers, and a jarringly inappropriate soundtrack. Despite all that, every film animation devotee must have this film just for the Williams segments that remain intact.
VHS: S30598. $14.95.
Laser: LD72461. $29.95.
Richard Williams, UK, 1996, 73 mins.

Thirties Magic Vol. 1

Eight titles: Walter Lantz's Oswald the Rabbit in *Mechanical Man* ('32), *Beachcombers* ('36) and *Quail Hunt* ('35); *L'il Eightball in Silly Superstition* ('39) and *A Haunting We Will Go* ('39); Krazy Kat in *Bars & Stripes* ('31); *Marty the Monk* ('30's) and *To Spring* ('36).
VHS: S29737. $17.95.
USA, 1932-39, 60 mins.

Thirties Magic Vol. 2

Seven titles: *Daffy Duck & The Dinosaur* ('39, WB), *Betty in Blunderland* ('34, Betty Boop), *Goofy Goat Antics, Lighthouse Keeping* ('32, Krazy Kat), *Westward Whoa* ('36, Porky Pig), *Ding Dong Doggie* ('37, Betty Boop) and *False Vases* ('30, Felix the Cat). Film prints are fair to poor.
VHS: S29738. $17.95.
USA, 1930-39, 55 mins.

The Three Musketeers

In their quest to save the reputation of the Queen of England, the Musketeers cross swords with an evil Cardinal, battle secret agents, and encounter full scale armies out to stop them.
VHS: S29740. $14.95.
John Halas, Great Britain, 1977, 85 mins.

Tiny Toy Stories

The five groundbreaking, computer-animated shorts directed by John Lasseter for Pixar, that led to the making of the feature-length *Toy Story: The Adventures of Andre and Wally B* (1984), *Luxo, Jr.* (1986), *Red's Dream* (1987), *Tin Toy* (1988 Oscar Winner) and *Knicknack* (1989 Oscar Nominee).
VHS: S30600. $9.95.
John Lasseter/Pixar, USA, 1984-89, 20 mins.

Toccata for Toy Trains

This work by Charles and Roy Eames is an imaginative journey about the function of trains as they travel through a universe of movement, sound, noise and landscapes. Toy trains of various size and shape move from the railyard to the roundhouse to a busy station. On the same program is *Parade* a bright and colorful mosaic of mechanized toys played to a vibrant John Philip Sousa score. 22 mins.
VHS: S19161. $19.95.

Tony Vegas' Animated Acidburn Flashback Tabu

Eleven animated shorts of varying degrees of weirdness, from student films to independent animator's warped visions: *Life Is Flashing (Before Your Eyes)* by Vincent Collins; *Ace of Light* by Dennis Pies; *Delivery Man* by Emily Hubley; *Reasons to Be Glad* by Jeffrey Noyes Scher; *Impetigo* by James Duesing; *Lunch* by Michael Dwass; *Parataxis* by Skip Battaglia; *One Nation Under TV* by Ruth Peyser; *Bus Stop* by Andrea Gomez; *200* by Vincent Collins and *Rapid Eye Movements* by Jeff Carpenter & Mary Lambert.
VHS: S16473. $19.95.
USA, 1991, 60 mins.

Too Outrageous Animation

Twenty-seven films: *This Is Your Brain on Animation* (Karl Staven), *Expiration Date* (Eric Fogel), *Weird Beard* (DNA Prod's), *Let's Chop Soo-E!* (Eric Pigors), *9 Seconds and a Half* (Vincenzo Gioanola), *Liver, Lust or Louie* (Caren Scarpulla), *Mad Doctors of Borneo* (Webster Colcord), *Snake Theatre* (Will Panganiban/ Aaron Smith), *Pirates (The Lift)* (Alexander Tatarsky), *Use Instructions* (Guido Manuli), *Rakthavira* (Voltaire), *Guano!* (Federico Vitali), *The Four Wishes* (Michael Ocelot), *Nanna & Lil' Puss Puss in Off the Record* (DNA Prod's), *Little Red Riding Hood* (Cassandra Einstein), *Little Rude Riding Hood* (Mike Grimshaw), *Hard Edition* (DNA Prod's), *Organ House* (Masayoshi Obata), *Vice Versa* (Aleksander Sroczynski), *Skippy the Dog Food Taster* (Larry Royer), *Gring Gallet's Reward* (Vincent Lavachery), *Tampon* (Justine Whitehead/Scott Ingalls), *Beaker and Homeslice Get Out of Hand* (Justin Conant), *Birdy Birdy* (Aaron Tardos), *Yes Timmy, There Is a Santa Claus* (Steven Fonti), *Molly* (Aaron Smith) and *Nanna & Lil' Puss Puss in Who Calcutta the Cheese* (DNA Prod's).
VHS: S29751. $29.95.
88 mins.

The Toytown Story Adventures

Five wonderful animated shorts, produced in the Toytown tradition by director Hendrick Baker, are collected on this video. Larry the Lamb and other Toytown Pals, including a pig and a dog among others, will delight children and parents alike.
VHS: S28071. $14.98.
Hendrick Baker, USA

Treasure Island

Originally released as a theatrical feature, this film was also shown as a prime-time TV special in 1980. Young Jim Hawkins and his friend Hiccup Mouse take to the high seas in this musical version of the Robert Louis Stevenson novel. Voice talents include Richard Dawson, Larry Storch and Davy Jones.
VHS: S29750. $14.95.
Filmation, USA, 1972, 75 mins.

A Tribute to Winsor McCay

An excellent collection of good quality, complete film prints with well-done original organ scores. *The Sinking of The Lusitania* is a tour-de-force rendering of the doomed ship's last moments; *Dreams of the Rarebit Fiend: The Flying House* shows how far one man will go to avoid paying mortgage interest; *Little Nemo* is the result of McCay's wager to make 4,000 drawings in one month; *Dreams of a Rarebit Fiend: The Pet* shows the folly of taking in stray animals; *Gertie the Dinosaur* is the filmed version of McCay's famous stage act—which reportedly required 10,000 drawings; *Dreams of a Rarebit Fiend: Bug Vaudeville* is the rumination of a hobo about the world of insects.
VHS: S01371. $24.95.
Winsor McCay, USA, 1909-21, 55 mins.

A Troll in Central Park

Stanley is a sweet-natured troll with a green thumb that can turn anything into flowers. When wicked Queen Gnorga discovers his secret, she banishes him to New York City. He leads two city kids into the adventure of their lives, and shows them that if you believe in yourself you can do anything.
VHS: S23113. $19.95.
Laser: Widescreen. **LD74837. $34.98.**
Don Bluth, USA, 1994, 76 mins.

The Tune

Bill Plympton's one-man animated feature film is a tour de force. It's a series of musical shorts linked together by the story of Dell, who has to come up with a hit song within the hour. The songs are provided by Maureen McElheron and cover such subjects as Flooby Nooby, Lovesick Hotel and No Nose Blues. Plympton's distinctively warped style lends itself well to the subject matter. Tape also includes "Draw," and "The Making of the Tune."
VHS: S19061. $29.95.
Laser: LD75488. $39.99.
Bill Plympton, USA, 1992, 80 mins.

'Twas the Night Before Christmas

Santa is boycotting the town of Junctionville because doubting Albert Mouse published a letter denouncing the St. Nick myth. The town must work feverishly to repair the damage before Christmas Eve.
VHS: S13033. $9.95.
Rankin/Bass, USA, 1974, 24 mins.

Twice upon a Time

Heroes Ralph and Mum search for the Magic Mainspring among the strange Rushers of Din. Filmed in Lumage—a new technique enabling depth, translucent colors and textures impossible to achieve in cel animation. Co-directed by Sesame Street animator John Korty.
VHS: S13442. $14.95.
Laser: LD75892. $34.95.
Korty/Lucasfilm, USA, 1983, 75 mins.

Twisted Toons: The Warped Animation of Bill Plympton

This documentary reveals the true story behind the one-of-a-kind animator. Working alone in his New York City loft, Plympton has created scores of animated shorts, MTV IDs and television commercials, and even two full-length features. We talk to and watch the animator at work in his studio, and see clips of many of his films, especially his one-man feature *The Tune*.
VHS: S27852. $59.95.
USA, 1993, 60 mins.

Ub Iwerks Comicolor Classics

Six titles: *Summertime* ('35), *Jack Frost* ('34), *Balloon Land* ('35), *Sinbad the Sailor* ('35), *Simple Simon* ('35) and *Tom Thumb* ('36).
VHS: S29752. $17.95.
Ub Iwerks, USA, 1934-36, 60 mins.

The Velveteen Rabbit

Margery Williams' story is brought to life in this Claymation adaptation. After a toy rabbit receives lavish attention from a little boy, the love makes it actually turn real. Also includes *The Twelve Months*.
VHS: S26617. $14.95.
Will Vinton, USA, 27 mins.

Vip My Brother Superman

From Bruno Bozzetto, the creator and animator of *Allegro Non Troppo*, comes this eccentric piece about the Vips, modern day inheritors of the superhuman performing a series of legendary adventures. 90 mins.
Laser: CAV. **LD72094. $49.95.**

Wallace & Gromit Collection

Three short claymation films featuring Wallace, an eccentric English inventor, and his trusty, bookworm dog, Gromit, are joined in this set. In addition to the Academy Award-winning *The Wrong Trousers* (1994, 30 mins.) and *A Close Shave* (1995, 30 mins.), there is the Academy Award-nominated *A Grand Day Out* (1994, 30 mins.). Once you've experienced the terror of the mastermind penguin, you will understand how the *Wallace & Gromit* phenomenon started.
VHS: S29999. $24.95.
Nick Park, Great Britain, 1994/1995, 90 mins.

Wallace & Gromit Laserdisc

A Grand Day Out and *The Wrong Trousers* together on one CAV laserdisc.
Laser: LD75893. $39.98.
Nick Park, UK, 1990-94, 60 mins.

Wallace & Gromit: A Close Shave

Nick Park's latest Wallace and Gromit featurette won the 1995 Academy Award for animated short film. The inimitable pair return in a new adventure every bit as hilarious as their previous shorts.
VHS: S29926. $9.95.
Nick Park, UK, 1995, 30 mins.

Wallace & Gromit: A Grand Day Out

Nick Park's charming clay animation brings to life the comically pedestrian Englishman Wallace and his dog Gromit. In this Academy Award-nominated featurette, when the pair run out of cheese for their tea-time biscuits, they build a spaceship in the basement in order to fly to the moon. Once there, they meet a truly outlandish moon creature that takes exception to their cheese-harvesting mission.
VHS: S26395. $9.95.
Nick Park, UK, 1990, 30 mins.

Wallace & Gromit: The Wrong Trousers

In this Academy Award-winning featurette, Wallace and Gromit are forced to take in a boarder—a comically sinister penguin. Wallace's latest invention, the techno-trousers (with the hapless Wallace wearing them), is comandeered by the penguin to execute a daring jewel robbery. Fortunately, an alert Gromit intercedes at the last moment, and the film climaxes with a hilarious chase sequence that also represents a new pinnacle in the technique of stop-motion animation.
VHS: S25660. $9.95.
Nick Park, UK, 1994, 30 mins.

Wartime Cartoons

Nine adult-oriented WW2 shorts made exclusively for the armed forces. Four Private Snafu shorts: *Fighting Tools, Rumors, The Aleutians* and *Snafu-perman. Five rare "Commandments for Health" by Hugh Harman: Taking Medicine, First Aid, Personal Cleanliness, Drinking Water* and *Native Food.*
VHS: S06970. $17.95.
USA, 60 mins.

Watership Down

The odyssey that a small group of rabbits undertakes after one of them has a vision of evil things coming to destroy their homes. This project was years in the works, originally begun and then abandoned by John Hubley.
VHS: S01605. $14.95.
Laser: Widescreen. LD72398. $34.95.
Martin Rosen, UK, 1978, 92 mins.

Weird Cartoons Vol. 1

Nine titles: *Alice's Egg Plant* (Disney Alice Comedy), *Frogland* (Russian Art Society of Paris), *Crazy Town* (Betty Boop), *Little Black Sambo* (Ub Iwerks), *In a Cartoon Studio* (Jungle Jinks Cartoons), *Scrub Me Mammy with a Boogie Beat* (Walter Lantz Swing Symphony), *Haser's Delirium* (B&W silent), *The Devil's Ball* (puppet animation) and *The Cobweb Hotel* (Fleischer Color Classic).
VHS: S01442. $29.95.
60 mins.

Weird Cartoons Vol. 2

Eight titles: *Alice the Toreador* (Disney Alice Comedy), *Old Anything* (Bosko), *Betty Boop's Crazy Inventions, Inki and the Mynah Bird* (Chuck Jones), *It's a Bird* (stop-motion animation), *The Non Stop Fright* (Felix the Cat), *Scrap Happy Daffy* (Warner Bros) and *Small Fry*.
VHS: S05183. $29.95.
60 mins.

West & Soda

Bruno Bozzetto's *(Allegro Non Troppo)* work is a madcap animated feature that mixes the operatic Westerns of Sergio Leone with the lunatic, freewheeling sensibilities of the Three Stooges, in this grand, flamboyant shoot-em-up. 90 mins.
Laser: CAV. **LD72093. $49.95.**

Will Vinton's Festival of Claymation

A compilation of Claymation shorts, hosted by Herb and Rex, two Siskel and Ebert-esque dinosaurs who introduce each film. Includes *The Great Cognito* (Oscar nominee), *Dinosaur, Legacy* and *The Creation* (Oscar nominee), plus *Mountain Music, A Christmas Gift* and special scenes from the film *Claymation*.
VHS: S29772. $29.95.
Will Vinton, USA, 1987, 53 mins.

Willis O'Brien Primitives

A collection of stop-motion shorts by the great animation pioneer, including *Prehistoric Poultry Creation, RFD 10,000, Dinosaur and the Missing Link* and excerpts from his feature *The Lost World*.
VHS: S05792. $29.95.
USA, 60 mins.

The Wind in the Willows

Vanessa Redgrave narrates this animated film adaptation of Kenneth Grahame's classic children's story about a wise Badger, a clever Rat, and a sensible Mole, who do their best to control the excesses of Toad when they embark on an unpredictable journey. This satire of Victorian society features the voices of Michael Palin *(Monty Python's Flying Circus)*, Alan Bennett, Rik Mayall *(The Young Ones)* and Michael Gambon *(Two Deaths)*. Top-notch animation from the crew who produced the Beatles' *Yellow Submarine* and *Heavy Metal*. Winner of the Gold Special Jury Award for Best Family Film at Worldfest Houston.

VHS: S30241. $14.95.

Dave Unwin, Great Britain, 1996, 74 mins.

The Wind in the Willows, Volume #1

A beautiful, full-length animated version of the classic children's book with extraordinary animation and voices supplied by some of England's leading stage and film actors.

VHS: S01465. $14.99.

Mark Hall, Great Britain, 1984, 78 mins.

The Wind in the Willows, Volume #2

Three animated adventures based on the popular children's story *Wind in the Willows*, with the characters of Badger, Mole, Ratty and the flamboyant Toad of Toad Hall.

VHS: S01466. $14.99.

Mark Hall, Great Britain, 1983, 60 mins.

The Wind in the Willows, Volume #3

Three adventures featuring characters from Kenneth Grahame's stories: *Great Steamer, Buried Treasure* and *Mole's Cousin*.

VHS: S00716. $14.99.

Mark Hall, Great Britain, 60 mins.

The Wind in the Willows, Volume #4

Three adventures based on Kenneth Grahame's classic: *Grand Annual Show, Open Road Again* and *Wayfarers All*. Populated by Badger, Mole, Ratty, and the Toad of Toad Hall.

VHS: S01467. $14.99.

Mark Hall, Great Britain, 1983, 60 mins.

Winsor McCay: Animation Legend

Winsor McCay was one of the most influential artists in the history of animation. This exclusive collection contains every surviving film made by McCay, transferred from beautiful 35mm Cinematheque Quebecoise archival prints. The highlight of the collection is a stunning, hand-colored copy of *Little Nemo* (1911), taken directly from the only known 35mm print in existence. Also included are *How a Mosquito Operates, Gertie the Dinosaur, The Sinking of The Lusitania, Gertie on Tour, The Centaurs* and *Flip's Circus*. The collection also features extensive liner notes by John Canemaker, an article by the Cinematheque's curator, Louise Beaudet, and comments from producer Albert Miller regarding the film-to-tape transfer. In addition to a newly composed score by R.J. Miller, all films were digitally recorded at the proper speed, and letterboxed in the original 1.33:1 aspect ratio. Color & B&W.

VHS: S19675. $39.95.

Laser: LD72089. $69.95.

Winsor McCay, USA, 100 mins.

Witch's Night Out

Gilda Radner provides the voice of a washed-up witch who turns two small children into the monsters of their choice only to fulfill the fantasies of the town's adults.

VHS: S32491. $9.95.

Leach/Rankin, USA, 1978, 25 mins.

Wizards

An evil twin brother/wizard named Blackwolf seeks to extend the evil sphere of his domain in the land of Scortch. He battles for supremacy against his brother Avatar, wizard of Montagar, who is totally the opposite of Blackwolf in personality and beliefs.

VHS: S02910. $19.95.

Laser: LD75896. $34.95.

Ralph Bakshi, USA, 1977, 80 mins.

Works

Stop-motion puppet animations convey post-feminist concerns through wry humor and visual wit in these films. Included are *Rumzababalaars*, in which a Frankenstein woman creates her own destiny; *Psychophony*, which shows girls dancing down into Wall Street; and *Journey to the Afternoon*.

VHS: S22635. $19.95.

Lisa Barnstone, USA, 1990-92, 20 mins.

Works, 1978-79

Terry Mohre, an acclaimed video artist, is revealed in this collection as master of synthesizer and computer animations. There is even a sexy document of a camping trip, where freeze frames assure that nothing goes unseen.

VHS: S22639. $29.95.

Terry Mohre, USA, 1978-1979, 70 mins.

The World of Andy Panda

Eight titles: *Apple Andy* ('46), *Andy Panda's Pop* ('41), *Under the Spreading Blacksmith Shop* ('42), *Goodbye, Mr. Moth* ('42), *Crow Crazy* ('45), *The Wacky Weed* ('46), *The Nutty Pine Cabin* ('42) and *Meatless Tuesday* ('43). HiFi.

VHS: S27967. $14.95.

Walter Lantz, USA, 1941-46, 62 mins.

The World's Greatest Animation

Sixteen independent animated short films, including 11 Oscar winners and five Oscar nominees: *Creature Comforts* ('90), *Balance* ('89), *Technological Threat* ('88), *The Cat Came Back* ('88), *Your Face* ('87), *A Greek Tragedy* ('86), *Anna and Bella* ('85), *The Big Snit* ('85), *Charade* ('84), *Sundae in New York* ('83), *The Great Cognito* ('82), *Tango* ('82), *Crac* ('81), *The Fly* ('80), *Every Child* ('79) and *Special Delivery* ('78).

VHS: S25652. $29.95.

Laser: Includes 15 minutes of supplemental materials. **LD75462. $99.95.**

1978-90, 90 mins.

LARRY JORDAN

H.D. Trilogy

A loving portrait of "H.D."—imagist poet and novelist Hilda Doolittle—a merging of images, Joanna McClure's reading of H.D.'s long poem "Hermetic Definitions" and the traditional music of the Mediterranean by filmmaker Larry Jordan. The three parts of the film, *The Black Oud, The Grove* and *Star of Day*, look at Hilda Doolittle through the life of Joanna McClure during the years 1990 through 1992.

VHS: S23210. $29.95.

Larry Jordan, USA, 1994, 115 mins.

Live Short Films by Larry Jordan

Three live action films by filmmaker Larry Jordan which explore the dualities of myth and levels of reality, and one of which is a moving tribute to the American film master Joseph Cornell. In *Visions of a City*, poet Michael McClure emerges from all-reflection imagery of glass shop and car windows, bottles and mirrors, in a dual portrait of both McClure and the city of San Francisco. In *Cornell 1965*, Jordan documents the only film footage which exists of pioneer artist Joseph Cornell—"If you are a Cornell fan, there *isn't* any other film on him." *Magenta Geryon* is a film in three parts: *Adagio* is a nude study of a beautiful woman named Psyche and a nude man called Eros. *In a Summer Garden* explores the mystery roots of the filmmaker's own passion for the world of bright blossoms, the mystical rose, and the ancient gardens of Beardsley and King Arthur. And *Winter Light* is filmed in the dawn hours of California winter and explores the endless permutations of light and illumination as representatives of the Demeter-Persephone myth of the withdrawal of life through the winter months.

VHS: S09419. $59.95.

Larry Jordan, USA, 1977-89, 35 mins.

Rime of the Ancient Mariner

A fully animated film narrated by Orson Welles. Using the classic engravings of Gustave Dore and a cut-out style of animation, the film follows Samuel Taylor Coleridge's long dream of an old mariner who kills an albatross and suffers the pains of the damned for it.

VHS: S09418. $59.95.

Larry Jordan, USA, 1977, 42 mins.

The Sacred Art of Tibet/ The Visible Compendium

The Sacred Art of Tibet (1972, 28 mins.) was inspired by a gallery showing of unique Tibetan thankas, religious scroll paintings, rupas and other sacred images and artifacts. Jordan set out to present a visual experience of Tibetan Tantric Buddhism, and the resulting film rises above conventional documentary form to become a beautiful and autonomous work of art in its own right. *The Visible Compendium* (1990, 17 mins.) is an animated film that took two years to make and is one of Jordan's most technically refined works to date. It takes the viewer on a trip through idyllic lands where plants smile, an image of a tiger appears in the sun, and nude women wander about comfortably within an enchanted landscape. A beautiful and densely constructed work, rich in enigmatic and allusive images.

VHS: S14552. $59.95.

Larry Jordan, USA, 1972/90, 45 mins.

Short Animations by Larry Jordan

Eight titles: *Duo Concertantes, Patricia Gives Birth to a Dream by the Doorway, Gymnopedies, Our Lady of the Spheres, Moonlight Sonata, Once upon a Time, Carabosse* and *Masquerade*.

VHS: S09420. $59.95.

Larry Jordan, USA, 1964-85, 56 mins.

Sophie's Place

The masterpiece of Jordan's full, hand-painted cut-out animation and the result of five years of work, this film begins in a garden resembling Paradise and proceeds to the Mosque of St. Sophia, then develops into episodes centering on the forms of Sophia.

VHS: S09421. $59.95.

Larry Jordan, USA, 1986, 90 mins.

japanese animation

3 X 3 Eyes Part 1: Altered States
Based on a popular Japanese comic by Yuzo Takada. Pai, a 3-eyed, 300-year-old "adolescent" and last of a mysterious race of immortals, seeks an ancient artifact that can change her into a human. Yakumo is skeptical of her story until Pai resurrects him from an accidental death. Together they travel to Hong Kong in search of the legendary Ningen. Dubbed.
VHS: S17354. $9.95.
Kodansha/Plex, Japan, 1991, 30 mins.

3 X 3 Eyes Part 2: Yakumo
Yakumo and Pai return to Tokyo after failing to turn Pai into a real human. Yakumo goes back to school, but the monsters follow and attack a schoolmate. Yakumo realizes he and Pai must leave again to complete their quest. Dubbed.
VHS: S17362. $9.95.
Kodansha/Plex, Japan, 1991, 30 mins.

3 X 3 Eyes Part 3: Life and Death
The mysterious statue reappears and is immediately stolen by new demons. Pai and Yakumo join warrior-maid Meishin to break in on a deadly ceremony and discover the secret of the statue. Dubbed.
VHS: S17529. $9.95.
Kodansha/Plex, Japan, 1991, 30 mins.

3 X 3 Eyes Part 4: Blind Flight
The exciting conclusion to the series. Yakumo learns of the destruction of Pai's people as the three-eyed Triclops who killed them returns for the statue that will make him ruler of the world. Dubbed.
VHS: S17530. $9.95.
Kodansha/Plex, Japan, 1991, 30 mins.

3 X 3 Eyes Compilation
The four-part *3 X 3 Eyes* series.
VHS: S25064. $19.95.
Laser: Multi-audio. **LD71944. $39.95.**
Kodansha/Plex, Japan, 1991, 120 mins.

8 Man
This is the original cyborg superhero. A ruthless band of drug dealers gun down a promising young cop. The Chief Inspector cannot bear to see him die so he authorizes an experimental operation. A cyborg with an electronic brain results, who then works with Tokyo police to rid the city of violence and crime. Dubbed in English. 91 mins.
VHS: S23289. $19.95.
Laser: LD74964. $39.99.

8 Man After Vol. 1: City of Fear
Based on the popular '60s manga and anime superhero series, this production introduces a brand-new 8 Man in *City of Fear*. The city is being terrorized by drug-maddened street-gang cyber-junkies whose weapons are grafted into their bodies. This production moves away from its obvious nostalgic roots to achieve an overall effect that is part Philip K. Dick, part Philip Marlowe. Dubbed.
VHS: S21695. $9.95.
ACT, Japan, 1993, 29 mins.

8 Man After Vol. 2: End Run
A ruthless politician seeks support by creating a winning football team. Can 8-Man save innocent spectators when the "amplified" football team goes kill-crazy? Dubbed.
VHS: S24892. $29.95.
ACT, Japan, 1993, 29 mins.

8 Man After Vol. 3: Mr. Hallowe'en
Daigo, the would-be crime lord, is overthrown by his own drug-maddened cyborg henchmen. They don't want to rule the city—they want to destroy it. Can Hazama, the new 8 Man, learn to control his powers in time to stop them? Dubbed.
VHS: S22408. $9.95.
ACT, Japan, 1993, 29 mins.

8 Man After Vol. 4: Sachiko's Decision
When underworld boss Mr. Hallowe'en is murdered, his psychotic underling, Tony Gleck, takes over. He kidnaps Sachiko to lure 8-Man into a trap and wants to transplant his brain into 8-Man's body. Dubbed.
VHS: S23339. $9.95.
ACT, Japan, 1993, 29 mins.

8 Man After: Perfect Collection
Compiling the entire *8 Man After* OAV series into a stand-alone, feature-length presentation, the thrilling exploits of the original robot cop come across like a point-blank blast from a double-barrel shotgun. Dubbed. Violence and nudity.
VHS: S25727. $19.98.
ACT, Japan, 1993, 116 mins.

8th Man Vol. 1
8th Man, a super android, was endowed with the likeness and memory of a slain police detective. Remade into Tobor the 8th Man, he resumed the chase for his killer, Saucer Lip, under his own name, Peter Brady. Created by Jiro Kuwata and Kazumasa Hirai with Japan's TCJ Animation Center, and dubbed in English by Joe Oriolo Studios. Five episodes: *Dr. Spectra, Evil Jaw & The Devil Germs, Baron Stormy, Attack of the Horrible Honeybees* and *Pounce, The Robot Tiger*. Dubbed.
VHS: S17106. $34.95.
TCJ, Japan, 1965-72, 120 mins.

8th Man Vol. 2
Five episodes: *The Battle of the Brothers, The Monstrous Eeler, The Atomic Ghost, The Gold Beetle of the Orient* and *The Return of Napoleon Bonaparte*. Dubbed.
VHS: S17107. $24.95.
TCJ, Japan, 1965-72, 120 mins.

8th Man Vol. 3
Five episodes: *Target 8th Man!, The Passenger Rocket Adventure, The Threat of Disaster, The Belligerent Bodyguard* and *The Freezing Ray*. Dubbed.
VHS: S17108. $34.95.
TCJ, Japan, 1965-72, 120 mins.

8th Man Vol. 4
Five episodes: *The Solar Satellite, Rascal Fish and His Pirate Sub, The Armored Man, The Electronic Tyrant* and *Bat Master and His Robot Bats*. Dubbed.
VHS: S17522. $24.95.
TCJ, Japan, 1965-72, 120 mins.

AD Police Files Hybrid LD #1
Two episodes: *The Phantom Woman* and *The Ripper*. One side of disc is dubbed; second side is subtitled.
Laser: LD75715. $39.95.
Japan, 1990, 80 mins.

AD Police Files Hybrid LD #2
Contains *The Man Who Bites His Tongue* plus dubbed AD Police music videos. One side is dubbed; second side is subtitled.
Laser: LD75716. $39.95.
Japan, 1990, 81 mins.

AD Police Files Laserdisc
Files 1, 2, and 3 compiled on one laserdisc. Subtitled.
Laser: LD72333. $39.95.
Japan, 1990, 120 mins.

AD Police: File #1: Phantom Woman
Set in the mid 2020s, the *AD Police Files* chronicle three investigations involving rookie AD Police officer Leon McNichol as he and his comrades attempt to cope with the criminal consequences of the Genom Corporation's artificially intelligent androids, the "Boomers."
VHS: Dubbed. **S29084. $19.95.**
VHS: Subtitled. **S18622. $24.95.**
Japan, 1990, 40 mins.

AD Police: File #2: The Ripper
Detective Ailis Kara investigates a string of brutal murders of prostitutes. Along the way, she meets a female executive who has had augmentation surgery to get ahead in business. Is there a relationship between the newly available implants and the murders?
VHS: Dubbed. **S29085. $19.95.**
VHS: Subtitled. **S18623. $24.95.**
Japan, 1990, 40 mins.

AD Police: File #3: The Man Who Bites His Tongue
Officer Billy Fanword, critically wounded in battle with a runaway Boomer, is used as an experimental subject for a cyber-operation, and reborn as an invincible cyborg policeman. But Billy, who can only confirm his humanity by biting his tongue, soon learns that invincibility isn't all that it's cracked up to be.
VHS: Dubbed. **S29086. $19.95.**
VHS: Subtitled. **S18624. $24.95.**
Japan, 1990, 40 mins.

Ai City (Love City)
Kei is part of an experiment to increase Psi power in humans, who has escaped from the Fraud corporation with a little girl, Ai. Why is it that both Kei and Fraud are so desperate to control this girl? Subtitled.
VHS: S24908. $24.95.
Japan, 86 mins.

Akai Hayate Vol. 1: Episodes 1 and 2
For 1000 years, Japan was secretly ruled by a society of ninja, until their finest warrior, Hayate Kunama, rebelled and murdered their leader—his own father! Guilty of patricide, Hayate fled. But his enemies landed a fatal blow. With only minutes left to live, Hayate took a desperate gamble and transferred his soul into the body of his sister, Shiori. Now, Shiori is wandering the streets of Tokyo, under the alias "Yukiko." Nudity and violence. Subtitled.
VHS: S25024. $29.95.
NextArt, Japan, 1992, 60 mins.

Akai Hayate Vol. 2: Episodes 3 and 4
Master strategist Shuri consolidates his hold over Nanso, at the eastern edge of Tokyo. It's a battle that will pitch the tools of technology against the ancient mystic arts, as Shuri fights to the death to keep the freedom he's so recently acquired. Whatever the outcome, the real showdown must come at Shinogara's heart—at the palatial headquarters hidden at the base of Mt. Fuji. Here, all questions will be answered. Nudity and violence. Subtitled.
VHS: S26099. $29.95.
NextArt, Japan, 1992, 60 mins.

Akira
In the 21st Century, 30 years after a devastating global nuclear war, mankind is once again on the brink of total annihilation. In a world populated by rival motorcycle gangs and petty politicians, a powerful psychic force, known only as "Akira," suddenly resurfaces in Neo-Tokyo. A milestone in the history of Japanese animation.
VHS: Subtitled, letterboxed, remastered. **S16691. $39.95.**
VHS: Dubbed, full frame. **S15233. $19.95.**
VHS: Dubbed, letterboxed. **S29087. $29.95.**
Akira Comm., Japan, 1989, 124 mins.

Akira Laserdisc
The three-disc CAV laserdisc set from the Voyager Criterion Collection includes the *Akira Production Report* along with rough pencil tests by director Katsuhiro Otomo, storyboard-to-film comparison, and excerpts from Epic's *Akira* comic book series, including the entire first issue. Transferred to video with Voyager's customary care. Widescreen version, with both English and Japanese audio tracks. Letterboxed.
Laser: LD75717. $59.95.
Laser: CAV. **LD71555. $124.95.**
Akira Comm., Japan, 1989, 124 mins.

Akira Production Report
In 1989 Katsuhiro Otomo created a ground-breaking, animated, feature-length film adapted from his provocative graphic novel series *Akira*. In this fascinating documentary, Otomo and his associates discuss the production process and techniques of this state-of-the-art animated feature.
VHS: S15234. $24.95.
Akira Committee, Japan, 1989, 52 mins.

Alakazam the Great!

Magical Majutsoland has a brave new animal king: Alakazam the Great. But he's a rude young monkey who complains about everything, and when he learns the magic of Merlin, his great powers make him even more arrogant. He must join human Prince Amat on a pilgrimage to learn the meaning of virtue. Finally, Alakazam gains the experience to be a true leader. Together, Alakazam and Dee Dee, his loyal admirer, will rule the animal kingdom and live happily ever after. Voices of Frankie Avalon, Dodie Stevens, Jonathan Winters, Sterling Holloway and Arnold Stang. Dubbed.
VHS: S27074. $14.95.
VHS: Widescreen. **S29088. $19.95.**
Laser: LD75487. $39.95.
Toei, Japan, 1961, 84 mins.

Ambassador Magma Vol. 1: Episodes 1-3

Episode 1, *My Name Is Goa*: Fumiaki and Miki Asuka are keepers of Goa and Ambassador Magma's spirits. After Fumiaki is captured by aliens and releases Goa's spirit, Miki discovers the true purpose of her life . Episode 2, *The Gold Giant*: Goa fails to capture Miki and Ambassador Magma returns to Earth. However, Goa sends humanoid creatures to quietly begin his plan. Episode 3, *Silent Invasion*: As Atsushi and Junya seek evidence of Goa's existence, a mysterious stranger appears. Mamoru and Tomoko are attacked by a savage canine and fight to stay alive. Violence. Dubbed.
Laser: LD75718. $34.95.
Tezuka Prods/Plex, Japan, 1993, 90 mins.

Ambassador Magma Vol. 2: Episodes 4-5

Episode 4, *The Two Mamorus*: Determined to find "Earth," Goa captures Mamoru and sends one of his creatures to terrorize Atsushi and Junya. Episode 5, *The Government Strategy*: The Defense Intelligence Agency (DIA) is eager to discover what the aliens plan for planet Earth. Meanwhile, Mamoru is attacked by a creature but receives help from "Earth's" new rocket-humanoid assistant, Gamu. Violence. Dubbed.
Laser: LD75719. $34.95.
Tezuka Prods/Plex, Japan, 1993, 45 mins.

Ambassador Magma Vol. 3: Episodes 6-7

Episode 6, *The Questionable Warrior*: Mamoru follows Kunisaki to DIA headquarters to learn the origin of Earth. The government believes Magma is responsible for a deadly tsunami created by Goa. Mamoru risks his life to help a friend. Episode 7, *Gigantic Task*: While searching for Onitono Shrine, Atsushi and Sekita find a girl who may lead them to Goa. Mamoru and Umemura are abducted by Udo. Violence. Dubbed.
Laser: LD75720. $34.95.
Tezuka Prods/Plex, Japan, 1993, 45 mins.

Ambassador Magma Vol. 4: Episodes 8-9

Episode 8, *Hunted Whistle*: Goa sends assassins to retrieve Mamoru's mystic whistle. Mamoru and his mother vanquish them with the help of Mr. Imai, and meet Midori, the Imai's only daughter. Episode 9, *The Resurrection of Udo*: Mamoru blames Goa for the deaths of those close to him. When it appears that his mother may be the next target, he decides to go after the evil Goa. Finding an ominous cave under a questionable shrine, Mamoru, the intelligence bureau and Gamu face off against the newly resurrected Udo. Violence. Dubbed.
VHS: S29089. $19.95.
Laser: LD75721. $34.95.
Tezuka Prods/Plex, Japan, 1994, 45 mins.

Ambassador Magma Vol. 5: Episodes 10-11

Episode 10, *Mother and Her Love*: Mamoru's life is saved by a guardian angel. He discovers the identity of his rescuer. When Udo uses Atsushi, Sekida, and Umemura as barter to capture Magma, the stranger appears again. Episode 11, *Rage of the Earth*: Along with the battling Ambassador Magma and Udo a group of people are transported back in time. While the two titans clash, Magma is aided by a former opponent. A temporal distortion with a path returning back to their period appears, but will everyone be able to return? Violence. Dubbed.
VHS: S26423. $19.95.
Tezuka Prods/Plex, Japan, 1995, 60 mins.

Ambassador Magma Vol. 6: Episodes 12-13

Episode 12: *Death of Magma*: Udo and Magma clash till death, but when Goa becomes involved who is the real victor? When Udo is about to demolish Ambassador Magma, he suddenly turns on Goa and attacks him instead. Is there some reason to this madness? Episode 13, *The Planet of Love*: Mamoru learns the shocking origin of mankind. With Magma gone who will save the humans from Goa? Watch this final climactic episode and find the answers. Concludes the series. Violence. Dubbed.
VHS: S26424. $19.95.
Tezuka Prods/Plex, Japan, 1995, 60 mins.

Angel Cop Vol. 1: Special Security Force

The Special Security Force was formed to protect Japan from international terrorism. Their newest member—the cold, beautiful and deadly Angel—has to face the greatest threat they've ever known. The Red May have targeted Japan as a wave of bombings and murders sweep through the streets of Tokyo. Part 1 of 6. Dubbed. Violence and nudity.
VHS: S26240. $9.95.
Soeishinsha, Japan, 1994, 30 mins.

Angel Cop Vol. 2: The Disfigured City

The Red May threat is growing, and a shadowy government organization has its eye on the members of the SSF. Angel's partner disappears, and a trio of hunters with amazing psychic powers are killing the terrorists before the Special Security Force can get to them. A strange super-powered cyborg appears just as the situation seems desperate. Dubbed. Violence and nudity.
VHS: S26241. $9.95.
Soeishinsha, Japan, 1994, 30 mins.

Angel Cop Vol. 3: The Death Warrant

With the leader of The Red May in the custody of the SSF, details emerge of a high-level, government conspiracy that threatens the future of Japan. Meanwhile, the three enigmatic "psychic hunters" also target the SSF and Angel has found her missing partner, Raiden, transformed into an incredibly powerful, armored cyborg! Dubbed. Violence and nudity.
VHS: S26379. $9.95.
Soeishinsha, Japan, 1994, 30 mins.

Angel Cop Vol. 4: Pain

The SSF race to conceal their last living witnesses to the secret "H File" project, one of whom is the only survivor of the terrorist group The Red May. If the truth behind the "H Files" is ever released, it could mean the end of corrupt forces within the Japanese government. To add to the SSF's problems, the "psychic hunters" are still on their trail, and their leader—he incredibly powerful Lucifer—has decided that not only do the terrorists deserve to die, but so do the members of the SSF. Dubbed. Violence and nudity.
VHS: S26639. $9.95.
Soeishinsha, Japan, 1994, 30 mins.

Angel Cop Vol. 5: Wrath of the Empire

The army closes in on Angel and the last remaining members of the SSF who are trapped within Doctor Ichihara's research facility. It's up to Raiden's combat-enhanced cyborg body to save them. As the battle rages throughout the research center, Raiden and the SSF hold their own, until the mad "psychic hunter" Lucifer appears to finish the job she started. Dubbed. Violence and nudity.
VHS: S26766. $9.95.
Soeishinsha, Japan, 1994, 30 mins.

Angel Cop Vol. 6: Doomsday

With most of the members of the SSF now either missing or dead, Angel is left alone to face the insane fury of the deranged "psychic hunter" Lucifer. Will Angel have what it takes to destroy this menacing foe once and for all? As the body count grows, the stakes heighten and this desperate struggle concludes. Completes the series. Dubbed. Violence and nudity.
VHS: S27346. $9.95.
Soeishinsha, Japan, 1994, 30 mins.

Angel Cop—The Collection

The Special Security Force was formed at the end of the 20th century to protect Japan's economic security from the deadly threat of international terrorism. This elite, 10-man team, with special authorization to prevent terrorist activities and ensure public safety, has been granted a license to kill. Their newest member, the cold, beautiful and deadly Angel, has to face the greatest threat they've ever known. Features six episodes. 150 mins. Dubbed in English.
VHS: S32529. $24.95.

Animated Classics of Japanese Literature: A Roadside Stone, Pts 1 & 2

Born into a poverty-stricken family, Goichi learns to deal with hardship from a very early age. Through it all, he manages to put forth an earnest effort as he struggles to overcome the most severe of circumstances.
VHS: S24269. $29.95.
Yamamoto Yuzo, Japan, 52 mins.

Animated Classics of Japanese Literature: Ansunaro Story/ Story of Koyasu Dog

13-year-old Ayuta learns a life lesson when a "bad girl" comes to stay with his family. Then Hisao adopts Shiro, the only remaining example of the Koyasu dog breed.
VHS: S20819. $29.95.
Yasushi/Togawa, Japan, 52 mins.

Animated Classics of Japanese Literature: Botchan, Parts 1 & 2

New math teacher Botchan has arrived and school will never be the same as he challenges both his students and superiors alike in one hilarious situation after another.
VHS: S24268. $29.95.
Natsume Soseki, Japan, 52 mins.

Animated Classics of Japanese Literature: A Ghost Story/ The Theater of Life

In *A Ghost Story*, by Koizumi Yakumo, a blind lutist finds himself playing for the long deceased Heiki family. In *The Theater of Life*, by Ozaki Shiro, Hyokichi takes his father's teachings of courage to heart.
VHS: S20814. $29.95.
Japan, 52 mins.

Animated Classics of Japanese Literature: Harp of Burma, Pts 1 & 2

In this story by Takeyama Michio, news of Japan's surrender is greeted with disbelief and soldiers continue to die in vain. Private Mizushima is dispatched to persuade his comrades to stop fighting.
VHS: S20812. $29.95.
Takeyama Michio, Japan, 52 mins.

Animated Classics of Japanese Literature: Incident in the Bedroom Suburb / Voice from Heaven

In *Incident in the Bedroom Suburb*, the Mabuchi family thinks that their neighbors are trying to force them out of their apartment. Is there a dark secret that must be concealed at all costs? In *Voice from Heaven*, a mysterious voice rings out at midnight from a recently empty apartment. The tenants are not anxious to discover where it comes from.
VHS: S24271. $29.95.
Akagawa Jiro, Japan, 52 mins.

Animated Classics of Japanese Literature: The Izu Dancer/ The Dancing Girl

The Izu Dancer, by Nobel Prize winner Kawabata Yasunari, is a tale of summer romance between a student and a strolling dancer. *The Dancing Girl*, by Mori Ohgai, portrays a love affair between a businessman and a ballerina.
VHS: S20811. $29.95.
Kawabata Yasunari/Mori Ohgai, Japan, 52 mins.

Animated Classics of Japanese Literature: The Martyr/ The Priest of Mt. Kouya

The Martyr is set in 16th-century Nagasaki at a time when Christianity was not widely accepted. Lorenzo, a devout Christian, plunges into a flaming house to rescue a baby. The Priest of Mt. Kouya is lost deep in the mountains when he comes upon a lone house. He is intrigued by the voluptuous beauty who owns it, unaware of the danger he faces.
VHS: S24272. $29.95.
Akutagawa Ryunosuke, Japan, 52 mins.

Animated Classics of Japanese Literature: The Season of the Sun/Student Days/The Grave of the Wild Chrysanthemum

In *The Season of the Sun*, by Ishihara Shintaro, Tsugawa has never had a lasting relationship until Eiko. In *Student Days*, by Kume Masao, Kenchiki wonders how his gift of a lucky charm will affect his studying for the school exam. In *The Grave of the Wild Chrysanthemum*, by Ito Sachio, Tamiko is commited to an arranged wedding even though her heart belongs to Masao.
VHS: S20813. $29.95.
Shintaro/Masao/Sachio, Japan, 78 mins.

Animated Classics of Japanese Literature: Shanshiro The Judoist, Parts 1, 2 & 3

Sanshiro is chosen to prove judo is stronger than jujustu, in a much publicized bout.
VHS: S20817. $29.95.
Tomita Tsuneo, Japan, 52 mins.

Animated Classics of Japanese Literature: Tale of Shunkin/Friendship

A beautiful, blind harpist has her face burnt by one of her students in *Tale of Shunkin*. Always devoted to her, Sakichi resorts to drastic measures to preserve the memory of her lovely face forever. In *Friendship*, there is nothing like the healthy rivalry between friends—except when they compete for a woman's affection.
VHS: S24270. $29.95.
Junichiro/Saneatsu, Japan, 52 mins.

Animated Classics of Japanese Literature: The Sound of Waves, Pts 1 & 2

18-year-old Shinji has fallen in love with Hatsue, but battles Yasuo's interference.
VHS: S20816. $29.95.
Mishima Yukio, Japan, 52 mins.

Animated Classics of Japanese Literature: The Wind Rises/ The Fruit of Olympus

Love blossoms between a writer and a young girl in the Alps. Also, the Japanese Olympic Team prepares for the games.
VHS: S20818. $29.95.
Tatsuo/Hidemitsu, Japan, 52 mins.

Animated Classics of Japanese Literature: Walker in the Attic/Psychological Test/Red Room

Goda plots the perfect murder as he spies on his neighbors from the attic. Then, murderer Seichiro is exposed through a psychological test. Finally, a man who murders for amusement requests help to commit suicide.
VHS: S20820. $29.95.
Edogawa Rampo, Japan, 52 mins.

Animated Classics of Japanese Literature: Wandering Days/Growing Up

In *Wandering Days*, by Hayashi Fumiko, young Fumiko wanders the countryside with her parents, wondering if she'll become a great writer. In *Growing Up*, by Higuchi Ichiyo, Shinnyo joins a gang only to find rival gang members beginning to make trouble for good friend Midori.
VHS: S20815. $29.95.
Hayashi Fumiko/Higuchi Ichiyo, Japan, 52 mins.

Appleseed

An explosive OVA cyberpunk tale of urban combat. In the utopian megacity Olympus, humans and bioroids peacefully coexist until an anti-bioroid terrorist group wreaks havoc. Special SWAT officers are assigned to track down the terrorists. Dubbed.
VHS: S16064. $19.95.
Gainax, Japan, 1988, 70 mins.

Arcadia of My Youth

Captain Harlock comes to the big screen. Set against the conquest of Earth by an alien empire, and drawing parallels to the post-WWII occupation of Japan, Captain Harlock and his comrades battle against tyranny no matter what the cost. This is the first time that this classic of Japanese animation has been available to U.S. audiences in its original, uncut form. Subtitled.
VHS: S18617. $39.95.
Laser: LD74794. $59.95.
Japan, 1982, 130 mins.

Area 88 Act I: The Blue Skies of Betrayal

In the Middle East, Asran is rocked by civil war. Shin Kazama is a fighter pilot at the mercenary airbase, Area 88, who was tricked into joining the Air Force by his friend Kanzaki, who wanted Shin's girlfriend. There are only three ways to leave the Mercenary Air Force: to serve for three years, pay a $1.5 million penalty, or...desertion. Nudity.
VHS: Subtitled. **S18921. $29.95.**
VHS: Dubbed. **S28451. $14.95.**
Laser: Subtitled. **LD74500. $34.95.**
Project 88, Japan, 1985, 57 mins.

Area 88 Act II: The Requirements of Wolves

Kazama's comrades rescue him from escaped killers. In Japan, Ryoko refuses Kanzaki's marriage proposal, and Kanzaki buys large quantities of Yamato Airlines' stock. Ryoko learns Shin is still alive, which enrages Kanzaki, who hires a professional killer to eliminate Shin. A twist of fate brings Ryoko, Kanzaki and Area 88 commander Saki Vashutal together on a passenger jet to the Middle East, but bombs have been set on the plane to eliminate Saki. Subtitled.
VHS: S18922. $29.95.
Laser: LD74501. $34.95.
Project 88, Japan, 1985, 57 mins.

Area 88 Act III: Burning Mirage

Kazama must kill a wounded comrade, rather than endanger the squadron. Kanzaki, now president of Yamato Airlines, brings the company to the brink of financial ruin with his purchase of cheap, defective jets. Ryoko decides to sell her airline stock to raise money to buy Shin's freedom from the Asran military. She must seek help from Kanzaki, but his terms are more than she can bear. Concludes the series. Subtitled.
VHS: S18923. $29.95.
Laser: LD74502. $39.95.
Project 88, Japan, 1986, 96 mins.

Ariel

Two episodes. To save Earth from alien invaders, Dr. Kishida builds Ariel—the ultimate feminine fighting robot. But he can't get his granddaughters to agree to pilot it. Things aren't going too well for the invaders, either. Earth should have surrendered long ago, but now the Accounting Office is warning about cost overruns, and the head of the home office has arrived to personally oversee operations. Subtitled.
VHS: S27344. $29.95.
Japan, 60 mins.

Armageddon

Four billion years ago, an ancient race instituted the Omega Program to seed the universe with new sentient races. Now the products of this program, including the human race, are destined to clash in violent opposition. Earth's last hope is the Delta Boy—living avatar of the supercomputer that began life on Earth. KOREAN. Violence and nudity. Dubbed.
VHS: S32263. $19.95.
Daewoo, Korea, 1996, 90 mins.

Armitage III Polymatrix: The Movie

The OAV series is edited together into a feature film, with some new animation, and with voices provided by Kiefer Sutherland and Elizabeth Berkley. Violence. Dubbed.
VHS: S33408. $19.95.
Laser: Multi-audio. **LD76765. $24.95.**
DVD: Multi-Audio. **DV60201. $29.95.**
AIC, Japan, 1997, 90 mins.

Armitage III, Part 1: Electro Blood

The place: Mars, during the terra-forming process. As soon as Detective Ross Sylibus arrived at the spaceport, he got involved in a murder. The victim was Kelly McCanon, the popular singer. Ross discovered something shocking: the corpse was not a human, but a "Third," a much more advanced robot than the "Seconds" which are currently in common use. Ross must team up with Armitage of the MPD (Martian Police Department) to chase the killer, Rene D'anclaude, who is destroying the "Thirds" one by one. Violence.
VHS: Dubbed. **S29629. $24.95.**
VHS: Subtitled. **S24240. $29.95.**
Laser: CAV multi-audio. **LD74819. $39.95.**
AIC, Japan, 1994, 50 mins.

Armitage III, Part 2

A new mystery unfolds when another bullet-ridden "Third," Lavinia Whately, is found dead at an industrial power plant. However, Armitage is still missing. "Yet...isn't D'anclaude supposed to be in the police hospital?!" Another victim brings new confusion to the MPD, still echoed by D'anclaude's mocking laughter. And now, Armitage's mysterious disappearance places her under immediate suspicion.
VHS: Dubbed. **S29093. $19.95.**
VHS: Subtitled. **S25680. $24.95.**
Laser: CAV multi-audio. **LD74993. $34.95.**
AIC, Japan, 1995, 45 mins.

Armitage III, Part 3: Heart Core

The MPD decides to drop the investigation of the Third Type murders. They are now focusing on an investigation of a terrorist case involving the Seconds. Ross instead heads to Shinora General Hospital to find out if the true D'anclaude is really there. Meanwhile, Armitage discovers a video still photograph of D'anclaude and Asakura together in earlier days. What secret do they hold together involving the development of the "Thirds?" The key to this whole mystery lies with D'anclaude in a hospital bed in Shinora.
VHS: Dubbed. **S29094. $19.95.**
VHS: Subtitled. **S27097. $24.95.**
Laser: CAV multi-audio. **LD75450. $34.95.**
AIC, Japan, 1995, 30 mins.

Armitage III, Part 4: Bit of Love

Armitage and Ross finally find Dr. Akasura, the developer of "Third Type" robots. But Akasura's memory has been erased and he can't remember Armitage. Can Armitage and Ross find the purpose of "Thirds?" The concluding episode of the series.
VHS: Dubbed. **S29095. $19.95.**
VHS: Subtitled. **S27096. $24.98.**
Laser: CAV multi-audio. **LD75451. $34.98.**
AIC, Japan, 1995, 30 mins.

Armored Trooper Votoms, Stage 1

A 52-episode TV series featuring specially bred perfect soldiers, lots of battle action and mecha designs by Kunio Okawara *(Gundam, Gatchaman). The video release refers to each TV season as "Stage 1," "Stage 2," etcetera.*

Volume 1: Episodes 1-3. A century of bloodshed between warring star systems has plunged nearly 200 worlds into the flames of war. Chirico Curvie, a special-forces powered-armor pilot, is suddenly transferred into a unit engaged in a secret and highly illegal mission. Now a renegade, hunted by both the conspirators and military intelligence, Chirico is driven by a haunting image of a mysterious and beautiful woman—the objective of the traitorous mission. Episode 1: *War's End*, Episode 2: *Uoodo* and Episode 3, *The Encounter*. Stereo. Subtitled. 72 mins.
VHS: S29879. $24.95.

Volume 2: Episodes 4-6. The Secret Society is watching Chirico's every move, waiting for an opportunity to strike. Meanwhile, Gotho pushes Chirico to compete in the Battling, a futuristic form of gladiatorial combat using modified Armored Troopers. But the contest turns deadly when Chirico discovers that his opponent is one of the commanders from the Lido mission—and he's fallen into their trap! Stereo. Subtitled. 72 mins.
VHS: S29884. $24.95.

Volume 3: Episodes 7-9. Chirico is finally ready to launch a serious strike against the conspiracy that destroyed his career and made him a fugitive. With the assistance of Gotho, Vanilla, Coconna and a fully-armed Scopedog, Chirico plans to hijack an entire shipment of jijirium meant for the pockets of the Secret Society. Stereo. Subtitled. 72 mins.
VHS: S29881. $24.95.

Volume 4: Episodes 10-11. After being chased from their homes, the idea of fighting back is starting to sound really good. But to take the fight to the police, they're going to need some serious firepower—and the Battling arena is fully stocked with Armored Troopers. Meanwhile, the Phantom Lady is having serious reservations about returning to battle. The solution: she must kill Chirico! Stereo. Subtitled. 50 mins.
VHS: S29882. $24.95.

Volume 5: Episodes 12-13. Chirico must fight his way out of Police Headquarters—with Proto-One at his side. But the city has been plunged into chaos. As Chirico's companions fight to rescue him, Melkian forces parachute into the city for a full-scale invasion—courtesy of Captain Rochina. But the conspirators have reinforcements of their own, and as the inhabitants race to evacuate Uoodo, will Chirico be able to escape? Stereo. Subtitled. 50 mins.
VHS: S29883. $24.95.

Boxed Set: Episodes 1-13. Tape volumes 1-5 in a collector's case. Includes color liner notes. Stereo. Subtitled. 316 mins.
VHS: S30258. $99.95.
Kunio Okawara, Japan, 1983

Armored Trooper Votoms, Stage 2

The second season of the TV series by Kunio Okawara.

Volume 1: Episodes 1-3. Separated from his friends—and Fyana—after the fall of Uoodo, Chirico travels to the war-torn jungles of Kummen, where he signs on as a mercenary Armored Trooper pilot in a bloody civil war. Chirico's hopes are raised when he encounters a mysterious, blue AT aiding the rebels. Who else but Fyana could be so fast and deadly? But when he attempts to contact the pilot, the blue AT launches a devastating attack! Includes a recap of *Stage 1: Uoodo City*. Stereo. Subtitled. 72 mins.
VHS: S30183. $24.95.

Volume 2: Episodes 4-6. After his last confrontation with the mysterious, blue Armored Trooper, Chirico comes to a startling conclusion: the pilot MUST be a Perfect Soldier...but it isn't Fyana! With his Scopedog AT damaged in battle, Chirico escapes into the jungle, where he is captured and taken to the rebels' secret base. There, Chirico is not only reunited with Fyana, but he also comes face-to-face with the pilot of the blue AT! Stereo. Subtitled. 72 mins.
VHS: S30184. $24.95.

Volume 3: Episodes 7-9. Chirico is ordered to lead a joint Kummen-Melkian operation against the rebel forces, beginning with an assault against Prince Kanjelman's stronghold. Their objective: the capture of a live Perfect Soldier! But Borough has plans of his own. He believes that if Ypsilon kills Chirico—and Fyana is forced to watch—the Secret Society will finally break Chirico's hold over her. But no one is prepared for how far Fyana will go to protect Chirico. Stereo. Subtitled. 72 mins.
VHS: S30180. $24.95.

Volume 4: Episodes 10-12. Fyana is now on the run from Borough and the Secret Society...but Chirico has no intention of losing Fyana again. As the rebel soldiers and Chirico's squad stand poised for battle, Ypsilon prepares to exact his revenge upon Chirico. And as the mercenaries of Assemble EX-10 are air-lifted to join the fight, Prince Kanjelman is forced to make a decision that will shake the faith of even his most ardent followers. Stereo. Subtitled. 72 mins.
VHS: S30181. $24.95.

Volume 5: Episodes 13-14. Prince Kanjelman's palace is turned into a blazing ruin as all the forces converge in a fiery finale! Chirico's squad mate searches for the treasonous Prince—determined to make him pay for the devastation he brought to Kummen. Meanwhile, Ypsilon bursts forth in a powerful new AT. His sole objective: kill Chirico! And as the forces of Assemble EX-10 prepare to crush the rebels, the Melkian forces move in to eliminate whomever stands between them and their stolen Perfect Soldier—Fyana! Stereo. Subtitled. 50 mins.
VHS: S30182. $24.95.

Boxed Set: Episodes 1-14. Tape volumes 1-5 in a collector's case. Includes color liner notes. Stereo. Subtitled. 338 mins.
VHS: S30259. $99.95.
Kunio Okawara, Japan, 1984

Armored Trooper Votoms, Stage 3

The third season of the TV series by Kunio Okawara.

Volume 1: Episodes 1-3. Chirico and Fyana are stranded on a mysterious spaceship with a mind of its own, taking them straight into enemy territory. Ypsilon pursues them to the battle-scarred desert planet of Sunsa. Includes a recap of the series to this point. Subtitled. 72 mins.
VHS: S30898. $24.95.

Volume 2: Episodes 4-6. Chirico is injured and lies dying in the mysterious starship. Fyana decides the only way to save him is to surrender herself to the Balarant. Subtitled. 72 mins.
VHS: S30899. $24.95.

Volume 3: Episodes 7-9. Stranded on Sunsa, Chirico meets Zophie, leader of a pack of scrap weapons dealers. While Zophie begins a mission of vengeance on Chirico, Fyana realizes her supply of jijirium is almost gone, and without it she'll die. Subtitled. 72 mins.
VHS: S30900. $24.95.

Volume 4: Episodes 10-12. Chirico is captured and given an ultimatum: face Ypsilon in a battle to the death or his friends will die. But the pair are trapped in a cave-in and must cooperate to survive. As the two warriors settle old matters, a devastating revelation awaits Chirico at the end of the battle. Subtitled. 72 mins.
VHS: S30901. $24.95.

Boxed Set: Episodes 1-12. Tape Volumes 1 through 4 in a collector's slipcase with color liner notes. Subtitled. 288 mins.
VHS: S30914. $89.95.

Kunio Okawara, Japan, 1984

Armored Trooper Votoms, Stage 4

The final season of Kunio Okawara'TV series.

Volume 1: Episodes 1-3. Chirico travels to Quent to learn if he's a Perfect Soldier, or perhaps something more. He moves closer to uncovering the mysteries of the planet Quent and his own past. Includes a recap of *Stage 3*. Subtitled. 72 mins.
VHS: S33416. $24.95.

Volume 2: Episodes 4-6. Chirico and Shako journey deep into the ancient machinery hidden beneath Quent's surface. Within the planet, an ancient intelligence waits for Chirico to finally make contact. Subtitled. 72 mins.
VHS: S33417. $24.95.

Volume 3: Episodes 7-9. The Balarant and Gilgamesh fleets in orbit around Quent have awakened an incredible power. As the skies burn, Chirico, Rochina and Killy discover their link to the mysterious intelligence that has guided them for so long. Subtitled. 72 mins.
VHS: S33418. $24.95.

Volume 4: Episodes 10-11. After his meeting with Quent's ancient intelligence, Chirico emerges a changed man. But to claim his inheritance, he must first survive the combined might of the two greatest superpowers known to space. Subtitled. 50 mins.
VHS: S33419. $24.95.

Volume 5: Episodes 12-13. Chirico races for Wiseman's stronghold. Hopelessly outnumbered, he needs a miracle to survive…but what's that to a man promised godhood? All is revealed in this final volume of the Votoms saga. Subtitled. 50 mins.
VHS: S33420. $24.95.

Boxed Set: Episodes 1-13. Tape Volumes 1-5 in a collector's slipcase with liner notes. Subtitled. 316 mins.
VHS: S33438. $99.95.

Kunio Okawara, Japan, 1985

Art of Fighting

Based on the hit video game. When Ryo and Robert witness a mob hit, they're shot at and nearly blown to pieces. But when Mr. Big kidnaps Ryo's sister, the only way to get her back is to find a missing diamond that the dead man had hidden from Mr. Big. Violence. Dubbed.
VHS: S33421. $19.95.

SNK/Fuji TV, Japan, 1993, 46 mins.

Astro Boy 30th Anniversary, Vol. 1

Two episodes: *Vampire Vale* and *Phoenix Bird*.
VHS: S19716. $14.95.

Mushi, Japan, 1963, 50 mins.

Astro Boy 30th Anniversary, Vol. 2

Two episodes: *Cleopatra's Heart* and *Funnel to the Future*.
VHS: S19717. $14.95.

Mushi, Japan, 1963, 50 mins.

Astro Boy 30th Anniversary, Vol. 3

Two episodes: *The Deadly Flies* and *Astro Boy Goes to School*.
VHS: S19718. $14.95.

Mushi, Japan, 1963, 50 mins.

Astro Boy 30th Anniversary, Vol. 4

Two episodes: *General Astro* and *The Vikings*.
VHS: S19719. $14.95.

Mushi, Japan, 1963, 50 mins.

Astro Boy 30th Anniversary, Vol. 5

Two episodes: *Dolphins in Distress* and *The Wonderful Christmas Present*.
VHS: S19720. $14.95.

Mushi, Japan, 1963, 50 mins.

Astro Boy LD #1

Four episodes: *The Birth of Astro Boy, The Monster Machine, The Terrible Time Gun* and *One Million Mammoth Snails*.
Laser: LD75722. $34.95.

Mushi, Japan, 1963, 100 mins.

Astro Boy LD #2

Four episodes: *Vampire Vale, Phoenix Bird, Funnel to the Future* and *Cleopatra's Heart*.
Laser: LD75723. $39.95.

Mushi, Japan, 1963, 100 mins.

Astro Boy Volume 1

Two episodes: *The Birth of Astro Boy* and *One Million Mammoth Snails*.
VHS: S15960. $19.95.

Mushi, Japan, 1963, 50 mins.

Astro Boy Volume 2

Two episodes: *The Terrible Time Gun* and *The Monster Machine*.
VHS: S15961. $19.95.

mushi, Japan, 1963, 50 mins.

Astro Boy Volume 3

Two episodes: *Super Brain* and *Mystery of the Amless Dam*.
VHS: S15962. $19.95.

Mushi, Japan, 1963, 50 mins.

Astro Boy Volume 4

Two episodes: *The Magic Punch Card* and *The Great Rocket Robbery*.
VHS: S15963. $19.95.

Mushi, Japan, 1963, 50 mins.

Astro Boy Volume 5

Two episodes: *Shipwreck in Space* and *Gift of Zeo*.
VHS: S15964. $19.95.

Mushi, Japan, 1963, 50 mins.

Astro Boy Volume 6

Two episodes: *Mystery of the Metal Men* and *Gangor, The Monster*.
VHS: S15965. $19.95.

Mushi, Japan, 1963, 50 mins.

Astro Boy Volume 7

Two episodes: *Brother Jetto* and *Dogma Palace*.
VHS: S15966. $19.95.

Mushi, Japan, 1963, 50 mins.

Astro Boy Volume 8

Two episodes: *The Mad Beltway* and *Mission to the Middle of the World*.
VHS: S15967. $19.95.

Mushi, Japan, 1963, 50 mins.

Astro Boy Volume 9

Two episodes: *The Hooligan Whodunit* and *Return of Cleopatra*.
VHS: S15968. $19.95.

Mushi, Japan, 1963, 50 mins.

Astro Boy Volume 10

Two episodes: *Inca Gold Fever* and *Hullabaloo Land*.
VHS: S15969. $19.95.

Mushi, Japan, 1963, 50 mins.

Astro Boy Volume 11

Two episodes: *Silver Comet* and *Robot Olympics*.
VHS: S16978. $19.95.

Mushi, Japan, 1963, 50 mins.

Astro Boy Volume 12

Two episodes: *Three Robotiers* and *Angels of Alps*.
VHS: S16979. $19.95.

Mushi, Japan, 1963, 50 mins.

Astro Boy: The Lost Episode

Two episodes: *The Beast from 20 Fathoms* was created during the 1963 television run by a handpicked team of animators. The show's creator was unhappy with it and ordered all prints destroyed. One print sent to NBC for dubbing still survives, and here it is. Also *The Snow Lion*, which features an early version of Kimba the White Lion. Dubbed.
VHS: S24909. $14.95.

Mushi, Japan, 1963, 50 mins.

Attack of the Supermonsters

Set in the year 2000, Earth is under siege from the sudden reappearance of deadly, powerful dinosaurs, unleashed from their subterranean caverns by the evil Emperor Tyrannus. Man's only hope for survival is the Gemini Command. 83 mins.
VHS: S17524. $19.99.

Ayane's High Kick

Ayane Mitsui is a high school student with dreams of becoming a pro wrestler. But what will she do when the top contender of the All-Japan Kickboxing League challenges her to a duel? Violence.
VHS: Dubbed. **S33998. $19.95.**
VHS: Subtitled. **S33999. $24.95.**

Takahiro Okao, Japan, 1996, 60 mins.

Babel II Part 1: The Awakening

Hidden psychic powers are unleashed in a reluctant hero who is transformed from a mild-mannered student into Babel II, a supernatural warrior, who must battle an army of zombies led by a ruthless "Magus." Dubbed. Graphic violence.
VHS: S26172. $9.95.

Hikara Prod's, Japan, 1992, 30 mins.

Babel II Part 2: First Blood

Learning the origin of his remarkable powers, Babel proceeds to do battle with a cult of telekinetic assassins. He is joined in his fight by a trio of powerful alien warriors as well as a team of special agents working for the UN. Dubbed. Graphic violence.
VHS: S26173. $9.98.

Hikara Prod's, Japan, 1992, 30 mins.

Babel II Part 3: Crossroads

Seeking revenge against Babel and his alien allies for defeating her master, Juju devises a foolproof plan to destroy her unsuspecting enemy. Her scheme calls for Babel to drain his energy battling an endless stream of psychic zombies. Once Babel has been worn down, Juju will come in for the kill. Dubbed. Graphic violence.
VHS: S26174. $9.98.

Hikara Prod's, Japan, 1992, 30 mins.

Babel II Part 4: Final Conflict

One by one, Babel confronts his powerful foes. Each new battle drains his strength, but with no chance to stop to recharge his psychic reservoir, he quickly realizes that it will take a miracle just to survive the day. The concluding episode in the series. Dubbed. Graphic violence.
VHS: S26175. $9.98.

Hikara Prod's, Japan, 1992, 30 mins.

Babel II Perfect Collection

Hidden psychic powers are unleashed in a reluctant hero who is transformed from a mild-mannered student into Babel II, a supernatural warrior, who must battle an army of zombies led by a ruthless "Magus." All four episodes of the series: *The Awakening, First Blood, Crossroads* and *Final Conflict*. Includes free limited edition collectible phone card. Dubbed.
VHS: S27810. $19.95.

Hikara Prod's, Japan, 1992, 104 mins.

BAOH

A secret organization called "Doress" has developed a new parasite code-named "BAOH." Organisms infested by BAOH become virtually indestructible survival machines able to mutate their body structure. The first of the human guinea pigs, Hashizawa Ikuroo, has escaped with a psychic young girl and Doress operatives must find him before the parasite fully manifests.
VHS: Subtitled. **S24264. $24.95.**
VHS: Dubbed. **S29100. $19.95.**
Laser: Multi-audio. **LD74886. $44.95.**

Toho, Japan, 1989, 50 mins.

Barefoot Gen

Drawn from Keiji Nakazawa's true-life experiences in the aftermath of the atomic bombing of Hiroshima, *Barefoot Gen* tells the story of one family's struggle to survive against overwhelming odds. Six-year-old Gen has lived practically his entire life in the shadow of war. Yet, he is not prepared for the horrors which follow the bombing of Hiroshima. In adapting Nakazawa's critically acclaimed, autobiographical graphic novel into animation, producer Masao Muruyama has created a vivid, poignant, powerful and genuine depiction of this historic event. Dubbed.
VHS: S25890. $29.95.

Keiji Nakazawa, Japan, 1983, 85 mins.

Battle Arena Toshinden

For one year, Master Swordsman Eiji Shinjo has been haunted by his aborted battle with the renegade champion Gaia. Now someone is hunting down the champions of the Battle Arena, and that someone might be Eiji's long-lost brother, Sho. Based on the hit video game. Violence and nudity. Dubbed.
VHS: Uncut. **S30924. $19.95.**
VHS: Edited. **S30925. $29.95.**
DVD: Multi-audio. **DV60202. $29.95.**

Takara, Japan, 1996, 85 mins.

Battle Can-Can

Femme Fatales Sophia, Diane, Jill, Mariana, Lily and their faithful robot companion Harold battle bad guys, rescue stolen treasure and save the galaxy from unsavory space pilots. In order to return a stolen artifact to its rightful owners, the gals must subdue the pirates, have sex with the aliens and confront a traitor from within. Subtitled.
VHS: S32767. $24.95.

Japan

Battle Royal High School

High school student Hyoudo Riki has the misfortune of being the doppelganger of Byoudo, Master of the Dark Realm. When a dimensional gate between our world and Byoudo's opens, the evil Fairy Master tricks Byoudo into attempting to conquer our world. Now poor Riki is semi-possessed by his opposite number, and the Fairy Master is mutating his classmates into hideous, lustful monsters. To make matters worse, the commotion has attracted the attention of Zankan of the Space-Time Police!

VHS: Dubbed. **S29101. $19.95.**
VHS: Subtitled. **S27710. $24.95.**
Laser: Hybrid. **LD75569. $39.95.**
Tokoma, Japan, 1987, 60 mins.

Battle Skipper 1

Sayaka Kitaoji is the richest girl in the world, and the ruthless leader of the Debutante Club. She and her fellow members plan to use their colossal combat suits (Battle Skippers) to take over the St. Ignacio School for Girls—and then the world! The only hope lies with the five valiant members of the Etiquette Club and their secret squad of prototype combat suits. It's the zaniest high school comedy since *Project A-Ko*. Dubbed.

VHS: S29102. $12.95.
Japan, 30 mins.

Battle Skipper 2

The Debutantes are determined to salvage their reputation after the humiliating defeat at the hands of the Etiquette Club. As always, Sayaka has a plan. Meanwhile, Saori finds herself in serious trouble—only to be rescued by the handsome and mysterious Brother Gilbert. Only who is Brother Gilbert? Is he destined to be Saori's first love—or does he plan to exploit her for his own nefarious purposes? It's up the the Etiquette Club to save the day. Nudity. Stereo. Dubbed.

VHS: S30260. $12.95.
Japan, 30 mins.

Battle Skipper 3

Sayaka's master plan is unfolding—and it spells trouble for the Etiquette Club. First, she'll kidnap the president of the Etiquette Club, and lure the rest of the club into a trap. Then she'll be free to invade the clubhouse and steal the secrets of the Battle Skipper combat suits! Can this be the end of the Exstars? Nudity. Stereo. Dubbed.

VHS: S28602. $12.95.
Japan, 30 mins.

Be Forever Yamato

In 2202, the Dark Empire threatens to destroy Earth with a hyperon bomb. Kodai and the old crew escape to the *Yamato* and set course for the Empire's home base to deactivate the weapon's trigger. They are amazed to learn they have warped 200 years into the future and are back on a conquered Earth. The *Yamato* crew decides to return in time through hyperspace and change history. They are intercepted by an enormous floating fortress and make another incredible discovery that changes the fate of the world. Subtitled.

VHS: S29347. $29.95.
Japan, 149 mins.

Big Wars

A mysterious race of aliens has returned to halt mankind's expansion into space—by force. Now, mankind fights a desperate battle with every weapon at its disposal, but will it be enough against the aliens' mind-control plague? Our last hope lies with Captain Akuh and the crew of the Battleship Aoba—but his girlfriend is showing the first signs of alien subversion. Subtitled.

VHS: S29103. $29.95.
Japan, 75 mins.

Bio Hunter

A strange virus attacks the human genetic code and transforms people into demonic monsters. One of these is stalking Tokyo and devouring young women's livers. Two molecular biologists must reach a psychic and his beautiful daughter before the Demon Virus conquers the world. Directed by Yoshiaki Kawajiri. Violence and sexual situations.

VHS: Dubbed. **S32245. $19.95.**
VHS: Subtitled. **S32246. $29.95.**
Hosono/Toho, Japan, 1995, 58 mins.

Black Jack: Clinical Chart 1

In a world where death could come at any time, there is a mercenary doctor for hire: Black Jack. He asks no questions and his legendary medical skills can keep the dying alive—for a price. Violence, nudity, profanity and gore. Dubbed.

VHS: S31077. $19.95.
Tezuka Prod., Japan, 1993, 50 mins.

Black Jack: Clinical Chart 2

Six months after he treated them, four girls fall ill again. Two are dead, one is insane, and the fourth is hanging on by a thread. Black Jack must try to save her and also figure out what happened in his absence. Violence, nudity, profanity and gore. Dubbed.

VHS: S31300. $19.95.
Tezuka Prod., Japan, 1993, 50 mins.

Black Jack: Clinical Chart 3

Black Jack must keep a rebel leader alive long enough to return him to his own country where he may die in peace. Violence, nudity, profanity and gore. Dubbed.

VHS: S31301. $19.95.
Tezuka Prod., Japan, 1993, 50 mins.

Black Jack: Clinical Chart 4

It's a perplexing question of faith when Black Jack is hired to keep a movie starlet from dying of anorexia. Unable to hold her food down, the young star has become desperate. Since she is considering suicide to end her torment, Black Jack must race against time to save her. Violence, nudity, profanity and gore. Dubbed.

VHS: S31302. $19.95.
Tezuka Prod., Japan, 1993, 50 mins.

Black Jack: Clinical Chart 5

Black Jack must help a young man plagued by a supernatural affliction. What could cause the bizarre visions and phantom bullet wounds that appear on his body, and who is the strange woman who beckons him to return to a town he's never visited? Violence, nudity, profanity and gore. Dubbed.

VHS: S33413. $19.95.
Tezuka Prod., Japan, 1993, 50 mins.

Black Jack: Clinical Chart 6

A stand-alone story. In the middle of a strange blizzard, Black Jack finds himself trying to rescue a dying princess. He is forced to question what's real when he opens up the girl and finds a demon inside. Violence, nudity, profanity and gore. Dubbed.

VHS: S33414. $19.95.
Tezuka Prod., Japan, 1993, 50 mins.

Black Jack: Six Pack

All six volumes in a collector's slipcase. Violence, nudity, profanity and gore. Dubbed.

VHS: S33415. $99.95.
Tezuka Prod., Japan, 1993, 300 mins.

Black Lion

The year is 1580 and Nobunaga Oda is working to consolidate his power over all the provinces of Japan. His weapons, are rapid-fire machine guns, lasers, missiles, and Ginnai Doma, the immortal ninja killer. After an entire fort is destroyed, the sole survivor must avenge his friends and the woman he loved by killing Ginnai Doma. 60 mins.

Dubbed Version.
VHS: S34532. $19.95.
Subtitled Version.
VHS: S34533. $29.95.

Black Magic M-66

Based on the story *Boobytrap* from the original manga *Black Magic*, this is the story of Sybel, a futuristic video journalist. She becomes involved in a military fiasco when two top secret android assassins are lost in an accident. The deadly M-66 units have a deadly mission that only Sybel can head off. Dubbed.

VHS: S16063. $14.95.
Masamune Shirow, Japan, 1987-93, 48 mins.

The Blade of Kamui

On a faraway planet, a mysterious priest trains Jiro, an outcast, to be a powerful and feared Ninja warrior. The young boy soon masters the extraordinary arts of stealth, mind control and karate. When he is called to embark on a perilous mission, Jiro learns that the Blade of Kamui he has inherited from his father holds the key to his past…and will control his future. Will he win the battle with the evil warlord or will he face the same fate as others before him? Dubbed.

VHS: S25017. $9.95.
Haruki Kadokawa, Japan, 1985, 133 mins.

Blood Reign: Curse of the Yoma

To avenge the woman and friends he loved, one lone warrior must seek out and destroy his former comarade in arms. But how does one slay the dead? Dubbed. 90 mins.

VHS: S34653. $19.98.

Blue Seed, Collection 1

All four episodes contained in tape volumes 1 and 2. Multi-audio.

Laser: LD75828. $59.95.
Yuzo Takada, Japan, 1995, 120 mins.

Blue Seed, Collection 2

All four episodes contained in tape volumes 3 and 4. Multi-audio.

Laser: LD75829. $59.95.
Yuzo Takada, Japan, 1995, 120 mins.

Blue Seed, Vol. 1

The story of the TAC, a secret government unit founded to combat the Aragami, a race of beings whose millennia-long attempts to conquer humanity have given rise to many of man's ancient legends of shape-shifting monsters and demons. Joining the TAC in their battle is Momiji Fujimiya, a young Japanese girl who carries an unborn Aragami, a "Blue Seed," inside her chest, and Mamoru Kusanagi, a cat-eyed servant of the Aragami with superhuman powers who rebels against the will of his masters to protect Momiji. Nudity and violence.

VHS: Dubbed. **S29104. $24.95.**
VHS: Subtitled. **S27022. $29.95.**
Yuzo Takada, Japan, 1995, 60 mins.

Blue Seed, Vol. 2

After she is accidentally implanted with a "Blue Seed," teenager Momiji Fujiyama becomes the recipient of bizarre psychic powers. Destined to be sacrificed to the Aragami, will Momiji find protection in the mutated human, Mamoru, and the badly outnumbered TAC? Nudity and violence.

VHS: Dubbed. **S29105. $24.95.**
VHS: Subtitled. **S27461. $29.95.**
Yuzo Takada, Japan, 1995, 60 mins.

Blue Seed, Vol. 3

As the strain of the war against the Aragami begins to take its toll, the TAC finds itself under increasing pressure from within as well as without. When Yaegashi's inexperience with weapons almost costs Kome her life, Yaegashi must live with the result. Later, as a giant jellyfish creature attacks Tokyo, Matsudaira must deal with her feelings of inadequacy when she forgets her son's birthday. Nudity and violence.

VHS: Dubbed. **S29106. $24.95.**
VHS: Subtitled. **S27686. $29.95.**
Yuzo Takada, Japan, 1995, 60 mins.

Blue Seed, Vol. 4: The Kushinada Project

Six-year-old Yukiko is kidnapped by the Aragami to force her father to release data from the Kushinada Project. As a result of her popularity after rescuing Yukiko, Momiji is nominated to perform for the Kanto Pop-idol Scout Caravan. However, the contest's climactic singing duel, which pits Momiji against Sakura Yamazaki, a magic-using young lady with her eye on Maoru, is interrupted by the attack of a ginko tree Aragami. Nudity and violence.

VHS: Dubbed. **S29551. $24.95.**
VHS: Subtitled. **S29554. $29.95.**
Yuzo Takada, Japan, 1995, 60 mins.

Blue Seed, Vol. 5: A Date with Danger

A new breed of Aragami has appeared in Tokyo. Taking the form of hunting dogs, these Hell Hounds are stronger, faster and meaner than all the Aragami that have come before. Add their mysterious master and his giant fire-breathing toad and the TAC's resources and Kusanagi's abilities will be stretched to the breaking point. Nudity and violence. HiFi Stereo.

VHS: Dubbed. **S29839. $24.95.**
VHS: Subtitled. **S29837. $29.95.**
Yuzo Takada, Japan, 1995, 60 mins.

Blue Seed, Vol. 6: Impending Disaster

It's an entomologist's dream come true when the world of the TAC is invaded by a host of insectoid Aragami. The fun begins with little black spiders in control of Momji's classmates at school. No sooner is the spider invasion squashed than a giant, skyscraper-scaling centipede appears to terrorize downtown office workers. Nudity and violence. HiFi Stereo.

VHS: Dubbed. **S30378. $24.95.**
VHS: Subtitled. **S30379. $29.95.**
Yuzo Takada, Japan, 1995, 60 mins.

Blue Seed, Vol. 7: Rebirth

The Aragami are turning the battle with a nightmarish wave of mutated monsters. Mankind's last trump card: sacrificing Momji and unleashing the awesome power of the Kushinada Effect. Nudity and violence.

VHS: Dubbed. **S30505. $24.95.**
VHS: Subtitled. **S30504. $29.95.**
Yuzo Takada, Japan, 1995, 60 mins.

Blue Seed, Vol. 8: Sea Devils

Momji's sister Kaede unexpectedly reappears, fighting on the side of the Aragami. While investigating sea monster sightings, Momji questions her own worth after hearing stories told by Kaede's friends. Nudity and violence.

VHS: Dubbed. **S31303. $24.95.**
VHS: Subtitled. **S31305. $29.95.**
Yuzo Takada, Japan, 1995, 60 mins.

Blue Seed, Vol. 9: When Gods Walk the Earth

Momji is plauged by a recurring vision of a hexagram that presages the appearance of the Stone Door of Heaven. Meanwhile, the rapidly growing infant-god, Susano-O, plans a holocaust that will wipe Japan off the face of the Earth. And the Aragami known as Nozuchi swallows Momji and Sakura alive. Nudity and violence.

VHS: Dubbed. **S31304. $24.95.**
VHS: Subtitled. **S31306. $29.95.**
Yuzo Takada, Japan, 1995, 60 mins.

Blue Seed, Vol. 10: Fate & Destiny

The Aragami are awake and the time nears for the final ceremony that will bring their ruler, Susano-O, to full power. Can Momiji and Kusanagi stop them? Nudity and violence.

VHS: Dubbed. **S33441. $24.95.**
VHS: Subtitled. **S33440. $29.95.**
Yuzo Takada, Japan, 1995, 60 mins.

Blue Seed, Vol. 11: Sacrifice

With Kusanagi missing and presumed dead, the government decides to use Momji as a human sacrifice and it's up to Kunikada and the TAC to rescue her. Nudity and violence.

VHS: Dubbed. **S33443. $24.95.**
VHS: Subtitled. **S33442. $29.95.**
Yuzo Takada, Japan, 1995, 60 mins.

Blue Seed, Vol. 12: Betrayal

Matsudaira discovers the factor behind the Kushinada's power. However, despite this exciting discovery, the Japanese government makes a stunning announcement: Momji Fujimiya must be found and used as a human sacrifice. To top things off, Kunikida reveals the government's dreadful "final option" to deal with the Aragami. Nudity and violence.

VHS: Dubbed. **S33445. $24.95.**
VHS: Subtitled. **S33444. $29.95.**
Yuzo Takada, Japan, 1995, 60 mins.

Blue Seed, Vol. 13: Nightfall

The day of the eclipse has dawned and the end of the world is at hand. Will Momji's faith in humanity be enough to save Japan? Or will the specter of eternal darkness be broken by the hellish brilliance of a nuclear fireball? Concludes the series. Nudity and violence.

VHS: Dubbed. **S33447. $24.95.**
VHS: Subtitled. **S33446. $29.95.**
Yuzo Takada, Japan, 1995, 60 mins.

Blue Sonnet Vol. 1

The ultimate weapon is a teenage girl. Code named "Blue Sonnet," she was rescued from the slums and surgically rebuilt as a combat cyborg. She is now totally loyal to her creator, the grotesque Dr. Merikus, who fears espers. Sonnet is dispatched to Japan to investigate a powerful esper known only as the "Red Fang." Subtitled.

VHS: S21833. $29.95.
Laser: LD75048. $34.95.
M. Shibata, Japan, 1989, 90 mins.

Blue Sonnet Vol. 2

With the capture of Lan Komatsuzaki, Talon's plans to conquer the world seem more real. Deep inside the most secure stronghold in Japan, Lan is running out of time. Talon plans to turn Lan's body into a factory for producing an army of super-espers through artificial insemination and cloning. Meanwhile, Sonnet and Red Fang come face-to-face in a battle to the death. Subtitled.

VHS: S23080. $29.95.
Laser: LD75725. $34.95.
M. Shibata, Japan, 1990, 60 mins.

Bomber Biker Mecha Pack

Tires burn and fists fly in *Shonan Bakusozoku—Bomber Bikers of Shonan*. Eguchi Yoosuke is the leader of a high school biker gang and the school's handicrafts club. Between fist fights and fancy needlework, he cuts a strange figure, until you consider the other members of the gang. *Madox-01-Metal Skin Panic* tell the story of Koji, a teenager who gets trapped in a highly automated personal battle tank. Japanese with English subtitles.

VHS: S23436. $65.00.

Bounty Dog

In the future, mankind has colonized the moon, but there are forces that want mankind to fail. Only one man can stop them, a member of the Bounty Dog investigation unit. The Bounty arrive on the moon to investigate strange waves of energy. They find themselves caught up in a desperate attempt to destroy "The Sleeper," a centuries-old alien power, before it awakens and obliterates all traces of mankind. Dubbed.

VHS: S27472. $19.95.
Japan, 60 mins.

Bubblegum Crash 1: Illegal Army

The cyberpunk saga which started in *Bubblegum Crisis* continues. An armored mercenary force commits a series of daring bank robberies, masterminded by a mysterious "Voice." Meanwhile, the Knight Sabers are...breaking up? Priss is getting her big singing break, Linna is making a fortune in the stock market, Nene is still stuck in the AD Police, and Sylia has vanished!

VHS: Dubbed. **S29107. $19.95.**
VHS: Subtitled. **S15954. $24.95.**
Laser: Hybrid. **LD75726. $39.95.**
Artmic, Japan, 1991, 45 mins.

Bubblegum Crash 2: Geo Climbers

Dr. Haynes creates new A.I. software that gives Boomers human reasoning abilities. Using his Boomer assassins, Yuri murders Haynes and his staff, and steals Adama, a prototype Boomer that uses the new A.I. technology. His plans go awry when Adama escapes into the depths of MegaTokyo.

VHS: Dubbed. **S29108. $19.95.**
VHS: Subtitled. **S15958. $24.95.**
Laser: Hybrid. **LD75727. $39.95.**
Artmic, Japan, 1991, 45 mins.

Bubblegum Crash 3: Meltdown

In the final chapter of the trilogy, the mysterious "Voice" is infecting Boomers with his purloined A.I. technology, recruiting an army that shares his desire for a new world order. The resulting commotion will keep the Knight Sabers busy while the real plot unfolds.

VHS: Dubbed. **S29109. $19.95.**
VHS: Subtitled. **S15959. $24.95.**
Laser: Hybrid. **LD75728. $39.95.**
Artmic, Japan, 1991, 45 mins.

Bubblegum Crash LD

In MegaTokyo circa 2034 the Combat Boomers attempt to remake society by stealing top technologies. The Knight Sabers are the only ones who can stop them, but will they forgo this battle to pursue their own careers? Japanese animation, 135 mins.

Laser: LD72387. $49.95.

Bubblegum Crisis Collector's Boxed Set: Vol. 1-8

MegaTokyo 2032 A.D.—As the city struggles to rebuild itself in the aftermath of a devastating earthquake, a small band of high-tech mercenaries fight a lonely war against the evil GENOM corporation and its sinister android Boomers. This collector's set includes the complete eight-episode BGC saga in dubbed format. Dubbed in English. 344 mins.

VHS: S33001. $160.00.

Bubblegum Crisis Collector's Suite

This boxed set of eight Anime episodes tells a story set in MegaTokyo in 2032 AD. The city is struggling to rebuild after a devastating earthquake, but an evil corporation and its androids have other plans. Only a small band of high tech mercenaries can oppose the evil GENOM corporation. Japanese with English subtitles, partial nudity.

VHS: S25717. $190.00.

Bubblegum Crisis Music Video: Hurricane Live 2032

Elements of the *Bubblegum Crisis* series in an MTV-styled rock video. Clips from the series are combined with the music of Kinuko Omori and the Knight Sabers. Subtitled.

VHS: S16672. $19.95.
Artmic, Japan, 30 mins.

Bubblegum Crisis Music Video: Hurricane Live 2033

Elements of the *Bubblegum Crisis* series in an MTV-styled rock video. Clips from the series are combined with the music of Kinuko Omori and the Knight Sabers. Subtitled.

VHS: S16673. $19.95.
Artmic, Japan, 30 mins.

Bubblegum Crisis Vol. 1

In the year 2032, Mega Tokyo is rebuilding after the great Kanto earthquake. The greatest threat to civilization is the release of the bio-engineered creatures called "Boomers." Standing between the Boomers and the complete subjugation of humanity are the "Knight Sabres"—an all-girl band of mercenaries for hire.

VHS: Subtitled. **S16065. $24.95.**
VHS: Dubbed. **S22335. $19.95.**
Artmic/Youmex, Japan, 1987, 53 mins.

Bubblegum Crisis Vol. 2: Born to Kill

Linna Yamazaki, one of the Knight Sabres, grows close to Irene. Irene has captured the attention of the Genom Corp., which created the Boomers, and her life is at risk.

VHS: Subtitled. **S16066. $24.95.**
VHS: Dubbed. **S22451. $19.95.**
Artmic/Youmex, Japan, 1987, 53 mins.

Bubblegum Crisis Vol. 3: Blow-Up

The Genom Corp.'s Brian J. Mason has deduced the identity of the Knight Sabres' leader and arranges for a decisive final conflict.

VHS: Subtitled. **S16067. $24.95.**
VHS: Dubbed. **S22449. $19.95.**
Artmic/Youmex, Japan, 1987, 53 mins.

Bubblegum Crisis Vol. 4: Revenge Road

When marauding motorcycle gangs go too far, J.B. Gibson builds a car for the purpose of killing gang members. Complete with artificial intelligence, "Griffon II" is more than a match for the AD Police.

VHS: Subtitled. **S16068. $24.95.**
VHS: Dubbed. **S22450. $19.95.**
Artmic/Youmex, Japan, 1987, 53 mins.

Bubblegum Crisis Vol. 5: Moonlight Rambler

From an orbiting space station, a new generation of Boomers escapes. These Boomers must have blood to survive, and start a string of vampire killings and introduce a new terror weapon—"D—D."

VHS: Subtitled. **S16069. $24.95.**
VHS: Dubbed. **S29096. $19.95.**
Artmic/Youmex, Japan, 1987, 53 mins.

Bubblegum Crisis Vol. 6: Red Eyes

Priss, a founding member of the Knight Sabres, is hanging up her hardsuit, but there is a band of phony Knight Sabres terrorizing the city and a killer satellite controlled by the Boomers.

VHS: Subtitled. **S16070. $24.95.**
VHS: Dubbed. **S29097. $19.95.**
Artmic/Youmex, Japan, 1987, 53 mins.

Bubblegum Crisis Vol. 7: Double Vision

"Vision" (Leika), a popular singer, is Irene's sister. She's engaged in a personal vendetta against the Genom Corp., and her GD-42 battlesuit is more than a match for those of the Knight Sabres.

VHS: Subtitled. **S16073. $24.95.**
VHS: Dubbed. **S29098. $19.95.**
Artmic/Youmex, Japan, 1987, 53 mins.

Bubblegum Crisis Vol. 8: Scoop Chase

The daughter of the AD Police Chief discovers Nene Romanova's identity, just when Genom is unleashing its newest creation.

VHS: Subtitled. **S16074. $24.95.**
VHS: Dubbed. **S29099. $19.95.**
Artmic/Youmex, Japan, 1987, 53 mins.

Bubblegum Crisis LD #1

Episodes 1-3 on laserdisc. Subtitled.

Laser: LD71832. $39.95.
Artmic, Japan, 1987, 150 mins.

Bubblegum Crisis LD #2

Episode 4 and Hurricane Live music videos on laserdisc. Subtitled.

Laser: LD71833. $39.95.
Artmic, Japan, 1987, 90 mins.

Bubblegum Crisis LD #3

Episodes 5 and 6 on laserdisc. Subtitled.

Laser: LD71834. $59.95.
Artmic, Japan, 1987, 96 mins.

Bubblegum Crisis LD #4

Episodes 7 and 8 on laserdisc. Subtitled.

Laser: LD71835. $39.95.
Artmic, Japan, 1987, 105 mins.

Burn Up W! File 1: Skin Dive

In the near future, high-tech crime is running rampant! But a special SWAT unit, WARRIOR, is ready to hit the streets. Terrorists take over a luxury hotel and WARRIOR must get the hostages out. If that involves granting a few unreasonable demands, that's a small price to pay....That's what Rio keeps telling herself as she prepares to make the world's highest nude bungee jump. Nudity and violence.

VHS: Dubbed. **S29111. $19.95.**
VHS: Subtitled. **S27680. $24.95.**
Laser: Hybrid. **LD75729. $39.95.**
AIC, Japan, 1995, 35 mins.

Burn Up W! File 2

WARRIOR is back in a new episode from the creator of *Tenchi Muyo*! Nudity and violence.

VHS: Dubbed. **S29563. $19.95.**
VHS: Subtitled. **S29552. $24.95.**
Laser: Multi-audio CAV. **LD75830. $39.95.**
AIC, Japan, 1995, 35 mins.

Burn Up W! File 3: Policetown Assault Part 1

When the mind-altering effects of a virtual drug cause a police supervisor to go mad, Team WARRIOR must take back their own building from a force of terrorists. Nudity and violence.

VHS: Dubbed. **S31307. $19.95.**
VHS: Subtitled. **S31309. $24.95.**
AIC, Japan, 1995, 30 mins.

Burn Up W! File 4: Policetown Assault Part 2

As the drug-crazed forces of Cerebus take over Policetown, Team WARRIOR must stop the killing machines that have already massacred much of the Police Corps. Nudity and violence. Dubbed.

VHS: Dubbed. **S31308. $19.95.**
VHS: Subtitled. **S31310. $24.95.**
AIC, Japan, 1995, 30 mins.

Burn Up!

When pretty young Yuka, a female police cadet, is kidnapped while investigating a white slavery ring run by an important businessman, her two partners, Remy and Maki, launch an all-out commando raid on the villain's heavily fortified estate. Graphic violence and nudity. Dubbed.

VHS: Dubbed. **S29110. $19.95.**
VHS: Subtitled. **S19891. $29.95.**
NCS/AIC, Japan, 1991, 50 mins.

Capricorn

From Johji Manabe, the acclaimed creator of *Outlanders* and *Carvan Kid*. In the blink of an eye, high school student Taku Shimamura finds himself transported to the bizarre world of Slaphrase, where strange, intelligent creatures rule and the ruling class, led by the villainous Zolba, is plotting the invasion of the world known as Capricorn: the Earth. Taku must also gain the love and trust of the last of the Yappie, the ancestral guardians of Slaphrase, a cute young female dragon. Japanese with English subtitles.

VHS: S32275. $29.95.
Johji Manabe, Japan, 1991, 45 mins.

Casshan: Robot Hunter: Perfect Collection

Casshan is the legendary Robot Hunter who is mankind's only hope to defeat the heartless mechanical monsters who have beaten and enslaved civilization. All four episodes of the series: *Return from the Myth, Journey to the Past, Blitz on the Bridge* and *The Reviver*. Includes a free, limited-edition, collectible phone card. Dubbed.

VHS: S27809. $19.95.
Tatsunoko, Japan, 1993, 101 mins.

The Castle of Cagliostro

A fast and furious slapstick production, boasting a lead character, Wolf, who is more memorable than many live actors. There are gun fights, air attacks, steel-plated mutant ninjas, incredible visual effects, classic lines and a terrific showdown inside a giant clock. Screenplay and direction by Hayao Miyazaki. Animation from this movie was used in the videogame "Cliffhanger." Dubbed.

Laser: LD74814. $39.99.
Monkey Punch/TMS, Japan, 1980, 100 mins.

Cat Girl Nuku Nuku Vol. 1: Episodes 1 and 2

Akiko Mishima runs a huge industrial conglomerate and employs all her muscle to get her son back from ex-husband Kyusaku Natsuma. Natsuma is an inventor, and to protect his son Ryunosuke, he develops a super-powerful android. Oddly enough, he chooses the brain of his son's dead cat to transfer into the android's body. Thus is born Cat Girl Nuku Nuku. Nudity. Subtitled.

VHS: S23227. $29.95.
Movic, Japan, 1992, 60 mins.

Cat Girl Nuku Nuku Vol. 2: Episodes 3 and 4

Combat android NK-1124, better known as Nuku Nuku, must control the damage when Kyusaku and Akiko attempt to reconcile and move back in together. This is a couple who argue with tanks and anti-aircraft weapons! In addition, Nuku Nuku must face an even cuter android replacement who wants her job. Nudity. Subtitled.

VHS: S23228. $29.95.
Movic, Japan, 1992, 60 mins.

Cat Girl Nuku Nuku Vol. 3: Episodes 5 and 6

Nuku Nuku takes a job waitressing at a restaurant owned by Ryu's mom. Arisa and Kyouko are about to spice up the menu with their own special recipe for trouble. Next, when a new Mishima Weapons satellite malfunctions, Akiko finds herself the target of an automated extermination program, and Nuku Nuku's mission backup is none other than Eimi! Nudity. Subtitled.

VHS: S23229. $29.95.
Movic, Japan, 1992, 60 mins.

Chimera

Rei, code name Chimera, is an expert marksman, a silent assassin and more woman than meets the eye, and leaves nothing but death and grief in her path. How much longer can she continue to kill, searching for the key that will free her from her mysterious past and her unknown future? 57 mins.

VHS: S34104. $29.95.

The Complete Adventure Kid

Nineteen-year-olds Norikazu and Midori must battle the evil and vengeful Masago when they get sucked into a World War II-era computer. In Midori, Masago sees a perfect replacement for his long-dead wife and only Norizaku's love for her can save them both from eternal hell. Dubbed. 115 mins.

VHS: S34793. $29.95.

Crusher Joe: The Movie

When even the United Space Force is at a loss, the Crushers come in—skilled troubleshooters who deal with any problem for a fee. And there's nobody better than Crusher Joe. When Joe's team evacuates an heiress to the planet Miccola, she's stolen during a hyperspace jump—and Joe is blamed. To clear his name, Joe's team must take on the galaxy's most notorious pirate, Big Murphy. This "Star Wars"-type space opera features the very first appearance of Kei and Yuri—the "Dirty Pair."

VHS: Dubbed. **S31334. $29.95.**
VHS: Subtitled. **S31335. $34.95.**
Laser: Hybrid. **LD76212. $59.95.**
Japan, 125 mins.

Crusher Joe: The OVA's

In *The Ice Prison*, the Crushers are hired to keep a cometary core from falling out of orbit. Problem is, the core is in use as a prison and the powers that be hope it burns up and the Crushers die trying to save it. In *Last Weapon ASH*, the Crushers are hired to recover a stray top-secret weapon designed to eradicate all biological life. But the ASH weapon has come down near an abandoned R&D facility populated by biomechanical robots programmed to hunt and destroy anything that looks remotely human.

VHS: Dubbed. **S33449. $29.95.**
VHS: Subtitled. **S33450. $34.95.**
Laser: Hybrid. **LD76766. $59.95.**
Japan, 102 mins.

Crying Freeman Vol. 1: Portrait of a Killer

Crying Freeman is a faithful adaptation of the acclaimed erotic manga *Shades of Death*. Yo Hinomura has been brainwashed by the 108 Dragons, the "Chinese Mafia," to turn his body into a super-assassin. Cruelly, his mind is left free, so he can cry for his victims as he kills them. Emu Hino witnesses Yo kill a Yakuza boss. He is subsequently ordered to eliminate her, but victim and assassin form an immediate attraction and mutual bond.

VHS: S20721. $19.95.
Toei, Japan, 1988, 60 mins.

Crying Freeman Vol. 2

A rival criminal syndicate challenges Freeman's leadership in the 108 Dragons. Its methods include assassination, and humiliation at the hands of Baya San—the powerful granddaughter of the former leaders of the 108 Dragons. Eventually, Freeman must engage in deadly hand-to-hand combat with Kitche, a cunning female assassin.

VHS: S21693. $19.95.
Toei, Japan, 1989, 50 mins.

Crying Freeman Vol. 3

Emu is accepted by the Dragons as Freeman's wife, Fu Ching Ran (Tiger Orchid). But Fu must prove that she is a Tiger in spirit as well as name. African Tusk, a new terrorist gang, tries to muscle in on the 108 Dragons. Freeman personally challenges the leaders of the Tusk, Jigon and Shikebaro. Meanwhile, the 108 Dragons receive the Muramasa, a priceless but accursed ancient samurai sword. To prevent the curse from striking Freeman, Emu travels to the Chinese criminal hellhole of Gauronsai.

VHS: S22907. $19.95.
Toei, Japan, 1990, 50 mins.

Crying Freeman Vol. 4

Naitai, a powerful and driven fanatic, schemes to use the 108 Dragons' influence to spread his Great Bear God religion. He plans to replace Freeman with a perfect double, a brainwashed cultist who is under their control. Their success depends on the support of Oshu Togoku, the almost superhuman world wrestling champion.

VHS: S22407. $19.95.
Toei, Japan, 1991, 50 mins.

Crying Freeman Vol. 5

The daughter and grandchild of an aging Chinatown crime lord are missing. Working with the crime lord's other daughter, a Pentagon computer expert, Freeman constructs an elaborate sting which seems to backfire—placing him in enemy hands. The lone Freeman is now forced to deal with the K.O.—a crime cartel made up of ex-military personnel which specializes in high profile kidnappings. Nina Heaven, the leader of this band of renegades, has an ulterior motive for not immediately murdering Freeman. Fascinated with his legendary skill as both lover and killer, the love-starved sadist gives Freeman a choice: live as her sex slave or face death a thousand times at the hands of her trained army of killers. Freeman comes up with his own solution.

VHS: S23338. $19.95.
Toei, Japan, 1992, 50 mins.

Crystal Triangle

Philanthropic archaeologist Koichiro Kamishiro has acquired the Crystal Triangle, which makes possible access to the Message of God. He has only noble intentions, but others do not—and they lead him on a bizarre adventure featuring everything from the Ten Commandments to the Nemesis re-creation theory, and everyone from Tibetan monks to CIA agents. Subtitled.

VHS: S16639. $14.95.
Laser: LD74503. $34.99.
Movic, Japan, 1987, 86 mins.

Cyber City Oedo 808: Data One

In the year 2808, three criminals are returned to Earth as agents of the Cyber Police, each fitted with a booby-trapped, high-explosive collar. For every criminal caught, the agents receive a bounty that reduces their total sentence. Terrorists have taken over a skyscraper holding the primary nodes for the city's computer grid, and 50,000 people are still trapped inside! There's no time to waste, because the collars have a 24-hour time limit. Violence.

VHS: Dubbed. **S29114. $19.95.**
VHS: Subtitled. **S24569. $29.95.**
Laser: Hybrid. **LD75730. $34.95.**
MadHouse, Japan, 1990, 48 mins.

Cyber City Oedo 808: Data Two

A member of the Cyber Police has turned traitor and sold confidential police data to a mysterious customer who could destroy the Cyber Police forever. But before that can happen, the heroes have 24 hours to uncover the plot. The trail leads to an illegal black market dealing in stolen body parts. Goggles is reunited with his ex-partner-in-crime, and together, they find themselves face-to-face with MOLCOS, the military's ultimate killing machine. Violence.

VHS: Dubbed. **S29115. $19.95.**
VHS: Subtitled. **S24570. $29.95.**
Laser: Hybrid. **LD75731. $39.95.**
MadHouse, Japan, 1990, 52 mins.

Cyber City Oedo 808: Data Three

The Vampire Case. Genetics researchers are turning up dead—all with fang wounds on their necks. The most recent victim used his own blood to scrawl a cryptic message on the wall and left notes for a very unusual retro-virus on his computer. The trail leads Benten to a cryogenic suspension facility tethered at the top of a space elevator. But the frozen death of cryogenic sleep may not have any meaning to one of the undead...and vampires can be very hungry when they wake up. Violence.

VHS: Dubbed. **S29116. $19.95.**
VHS: Subtitled. **S24571. $29.95.**
Laser: Hybrid. **LD75732. $34.95.**
MadHouse, Japan, 1990, 49 mins.

Cyber Ninja

This epic fantasy adventure follows Saki, a princess kidnapped amid the turmoil that results from a brutal civil war. Only Cyber Ninja can save her from the Dark Overlord and his evil plans to make her into a human sacrifice. Should the Dark Overlord succeed, he will unleash a hideous tide of evil upon the land.

Laser: LD74984. $39.99.

Cybernetics Guardian
In the near future, the City of Tomorrow is being devoured by the violence bred in its hellish slums. When the Central Guard Company is hired to clean up the slums, two researchers compete to find a solution. When John Stalker is sent to test a prototype Guard Suit, one of the researchers sees the perfect opportunity to test his Genocyber Killing Machine! But no one could've predicted the dark secret lurking within John Stalker.
VHS: Subtitled. **S27092. $29.95.**
VHS: Dubbed. **S30380. $19.95.**
Japan, 45 mins.

Cyborg 009: Legend of the Super Galaxy
In the far-flung regions of interstellar space, the race is on. Zoa, the evil space alien, plots to capture the Vortex, the most powerful force in the universe. With that power, no one will be able to stop the diabolical maniac. Only the Galaxy Legion, nine invincible cyborgs—each designed with extraordinary powers: superhearing, Herculean strength, telepathic minds—can save the universe. Led by the fearless Cyborg 009, the army of cyborgs challenges the all-powerful Zoa in the most spectacular battle in the cosmos. Dubbed.
VHS: S25020. $19.95.
Toei, Japan, 1980, 130 mins.

The Dagger of Kamui
On the eve of the Meiji Restoration, an innkeeper finds a baby named Jiro adrift in a boat with a glittering blade—the dagger of Kamui. When Jiro is 13, his adoptive family is murdered and Jiro is blamed, only to be rescued by the priest Tenkai. Jiro is tutored as a Ninja, and after many plot twists, Jiro must travel as far away as America to retrieve some treasure and perhaps exact revenge on the murderer who killed his family. Subtitled.
VHS: S18618. $39.95.
Laser: LD74662. $59.95.
Toei, Japan, 1985, 132 mins.

Dallos
The Earthlings have conquered the moon and enslaved the moonmen. Forced to work in labor camps and wear electronic ID bands, the Lunarians helplessly watched their beautiful planet being destroyed as they only dream of freedom and brotherhood. From the depths of despair, a lone rebel emerges to lead his people against the Earthlings and regain control of the moon. But first he must overcome his own fears and twisted loyalties. As the battle begins, the lunar freedom fighters face incredible odds…and an all-out war on the moon's surface looks inevitable. Dubbed.
VHS: S29117. $9.95.
Pierrot, Japan, 1985, 83 mins.

Dancougar Vol. 1: Episodes 1-5
Led by the traitor Shapiro, the Earth faces the threat of invasion by the alien forces of Emporer Muge. Our only hope lies in a secret robot unit called the Cyber-Beast Force and Earth's ultimate secret weapon—Super Beastial Machine God Dancougar! Subtitled.
VHS: S29119. $19.95.
Japan, 120 mins.

Dancougar Vol. 2: Episodes 6-10
Emporer Muge continues his relentless assault on planet Earth, but now there's a human defense system—the Cyber Beast Force! Finally able to transform themselves into colossal robots and match the Emperor weapon for weapon, Earth's only chance for survival lies in the courage and cunning of its heroes and Super Beastial Machine God Dancougar. Subtitled.
VHS: S29564. $19.95.
Japan, 120 mins.

Dancougar Vol. 3: Episodes 11-15
Now capable of "humanoid" transformations, the Cyber Beast Force is called into action as the Empire unleashes its newest weapon—a death-spewing monster of unearthly proportions! The only good news for the CBF is the savage infighting between two of the Empire's most formidable commanders: Death Gaia and the Earthling turncoat Shapiro Keats! HiFi Stereo. Subtitled.
VHS: S28601. $19.95.
Ashi Prod., Japan, 1985, 120 mins.

Dancougar Vol. 4: Episodes 16-20
The Cyber Beast Force is off to the Gobi Desert in a desperate attempt to disable the aliens' deadly laser system, when they discover they lack the energy they need to power their transforming weapon system. HiFi Stereo. Subtitled.
VHS: S30381. $19.95.
Ashi Prod., Japan, 1985, 120 mins.

Dancougar Vol. 5: Episodes 21-25
The struggle to save Earth shifts to Europe, where Emperor Muge and Shapiro launch a wave of terror against the European Union. But with the Cyber Beast Force now able to transform themselves into the mighty Dancougar, civilians of the war-torn continent still have a chance at survival. Subtitled.
VHS: S30931. $19.95.
Ashi Prod., Japan, 1985, 120 mins.

Dancougar Vol. 6: Episodes 26-30
In a pivotal episode, Gil Dorom has discovered the hidden location of the Cyber Beast Force base. Trapped and cornered by the forces of General Helmut, the CBF still has an ace up their sleeve—the Dragon Base Gundor. Subtitled.
VHS: S31311. $19.95.
Ashi Prod., Japan, 1985, 120 mins.

Dancougar Vol. 7: Episodess 31-35
With the General of the Cyber Beast Force now dead, his son Allan bears the responsibility of carrying out his father's wish: a space assault from their flying Dragon Base Gundor. However, Emperor Muge and General Helmut have been constructing a covert military base on the moon from which they plan to launch an all-out attack. Subtitled.
VHS: S31312. $19.95.
Ashi Prod., Japan, 1985, 120 mins.

Dancougar, Vol. 8: Episodes 36-40
As Luna betrays him and General Gil Dorom seizes command of the troops, Shapiro's dream of becoming god of the universe seems improbable. But by secretly constructing bases on Mars and the asteroids, the aliens have gained an advantage over the earthlings. Subtitled.
VHS: S31313. $19.95.
Ashi Prod., Japan, 1985, 120 mins.

Dangaio
Tarsan is the unscrupulous space scientist who develops psyonic mecha warriors to sell to the highest bidder. He claims that Mai, Pai, Lamba and Roll are his new creations. They are actually kidnapped victims, stripped of their own identities. This popular animated serial follows the four young mecha warriors on their search to find out who they really are, in three action-packed volumes. Original character design by Haruhiko Mikimoto. Japanese with English subtitles.
Dangaio Part 1. 45 mins.
VHS: S13330. $34.95.
Dangaio Part 2. 45 mins.
VHS: S15956. $34.95.
Dangaio Part 3. 45 mins.
VHS: S15957. $34.95.

Dangaioh
Brought together by the mysterious Doctor Tarsan, these four psychic warriors are able to unite to form Dangaioh—the most powerful weapon in the universe. Using their full cyonic force, they alone can stop the bloody tyranny of Captain Garimoth. But is their psychogenic wave strong enough to destroy his evil henchmen? Or will the warriors fall to Garimoth's trickery, which finds weakness in their forgotten pasts? Dubbed.
VHS: S29118. $19.95.
Japan, 90 mins.

Dangaioh: Hyper-Combat Unit
Four psychic warriors, brought together by the mysterious Dr. Tarsan, now form Dangaioh, the world's most powerful combat unit. Together they offer hope to a cosmos terrorized by the tyranny of Captain Garimoth and his evil henchmen. Anime, dubbed in English, 90 mins.
VHS: S27471. $19.95.

Dangard Ace
Young pilot Winstar must battle the evil Komisar Krel, aided by the super-robot Dangard Ace. In *Enter Captain Mask*, Winstar and the crew at the World Space Institute meet Capt. Mask, who has escaped from Krel's slave station. In *Down from Mach 2*, Capt. Mask becomes the pilot instructor on Dangard Ace. Dubbed.
VHS: S18591. $17.95.
Toei, Japan, 1982, 46 mins.

The Dark Myth Part 1
Brahman is the force of pure truth and knowledge, while Atman is the energy of the human soul. Only through true enlightenment can they be reconciled. This enlightenment bears a terrible price, as youg Takahashi knows only too well. Violence. Dubbed.
VHS: S30904. $19.95.
Japan, 50 mins.

The Dark Myth Part 2
Takahashi has left the carnage at Osaka behind. In his possession is one half of the Golden Seal of Yamatai—the only artifact that can summon the God of Darkness back to Earth. Violence. Dubbed.
VHS: S31185. $19.95.
Japan, 50 mins.

Dark Warrior: First Strike
When computer genius Joe Takami hacks into a top-secret computer system, he uncovers evidence of a secret government experiment. Now he's running for his life, and everyone, including his best friend and his PC, has turned against him. Nudity and graphic violence. Subtitled.
VHS: S27685. $29.95.
S. Takeshima, Japan, 1991, 60 mins.

Dark Warrior 2: Jihad
As a ruthless team of high-tech ninjas follows his trail, Joe must depend on the unsuspected powers that lie buried in his past in order to survive. Nudity and graphic violence. Subtitled.
VHS: S29555. $29.95.
S. Takeshima, Japan, 1991, 60 mins.

Darkside Blues
In the gothic landscape of the future, the Persona Century Corporation owns 99% of the world. But a lawless free zone, Kabuki Town, is a haven for misfits, criminals and rebels. Now a dark mystic has appeared to challenge the global dictatorship. Violence and nudity. Subtitled.
VHS: S31078. $29.95.
Toho, Japan, 1996, 83 mins.

Debutante Detective Corps
Five wealthy girls at an exclusive private school moonlight as detectives. Two police detectives have their hands full when the girls are marked for death, and the principal spends as much time rebuilding the school as monitoring class schedules. Violence and nudity. Subtitled.
VHS: S33452. $29.95.
Toho/Head Room, Japan, 1996

Deluxe Ariel 1
Those aliens are still plotting to conquer Earth! The only obstacle in their path is the giant, feminine robot Ariel. But the young pilots have lives of their own. When Kazumi receives a mysterious love letter from a secret admirer, should she cancel her first date, just to save Earth? Subtitled.
VHS: S27676. $29.95.
Japan, 45 mins.

Deluxe Ariel 2
Things have not gone well for the invaders. Their budget has been slashed and their technology is falling apart, but now their star drive has failed and their immense starship is about to crash into Tokyo! And unless something is done really soon, the impact will start a chain reaction that will extinguish all life on Earth! Stereo. Subtitled.
VHS: S27684. $29.95.
Japan, 45 mins.

Demon City Shinjuku
Within Tokyo, the tyrannical Levih Rah has created a Demon City - teeming with street punks, fugitives and monsters. The beautiful Sayaka Rama must enlist the help of Kyoya, a streetwise Tokyo teenager, to rescue her father from this terrible place. Together with the mystical ancient Mephisto, they must stop Levih Rah. Violence.
VHS: Subtitled. **S20473. $29.95.**
VHS: Dubbed. **S29120. $19.95.**
Laser: Subtitled. **LD75733. $39.95.**
Hideyuki Kikuchi, Japan, 1993, 82 mins.

Detonator Orgun, Part 1
Tomoru Shindo is almost ready to graduate college when his dreams are invaded by an alien life form, warning him of impending danger to Earth. As Earth researchers try to unlock the secrets of an alien suit of armor, the suit has an agenda of its own—prompting the aliens to dispatch a killing machine to destroy the renegade: Orgun. Subtitled.
VHS: S21101. $29.95.
Laser: LD75734. $34.95.
Darts/Artmic, Japan, 1991, 57 mins.

Detonator Orgun, Part 2
City #5 is again under fire as Orgun is hunted, and Tomoru prefers to keep his connection to Orgun unexplored. Now Michi is having her dreams invaded by the aliens as well, and what she learns may be enough to convince Tomoru to join with Orgun. Subtitled.
VHS: S21102. $29.95.
Laser: LD75735. $34.95.
Darts/Artmic, Japan, 1991, 49 mins.

Detonator Orgun, Part 3
With the Evoluder battle planet only three months away, Tomoru finally deciphers Orgun's advanced weapons systems. Earth's armies scramble to build their new hardware—but will they be ready in time? Subtitled.
VHS: S21103. $29.95.
Laser: LD75399. $34.95.
Darts/Artmic, Japan, 1991, 53 mins.

Devil Hunter Yohko 1
Yohko Mano is a typical high school student until she learns she is the 108th generation of a family of professional devil hunters. Only she can stop an invasion of demons who will do anything to get rid of her. LD is subtitled. Dub VHS has bonus footage. Nudity, violence & adult situations.
VHS: Subtitled. **S18064. $29.95.**
VHS: Dubbed. **S27020. $19.95.**
Laser: Subtitled, CAV. **LD74479. $34.95.**
Toho, Japan, 1990, 45 mins.

Devil Hunter Yohko 2 & 3

Part 2: A local shrine is destroyed and Yohko has the task of shoving the vengeful spirits back into their graves. She also must train Azusa; and Yohko's pal Chigako has her own agenda for exploiting her friend's new talents. *Part 3*: Yohko finds herself kidnapped to a strange alternate dimension where she must battle Harpy, Griffon and Dragonewt in deadly mortal combat. At stake: the life of Biryu, the handsome son of Ryu-O, the Dragon King. Nudity, violence and adult situations. Subtitled.
VHS: S21704. $24.95.
Toho, Japan, 1992, 60 mins.

Devil Hunter Yohko 4 & 5

Devil Hunter Yohko 4-Ever and Devil Hunter Yohko 5 on one tape Nudity, violence and adult situations. Subtitled.
VHS: S29121. $34.95.
Toho, Japan, 1993, 75 mins.

Devil Hunter Yohko 4-Ever!

This is a compilation of original animation, live action and animated clips from *Devil Hunter Yohko Parts 1, 2* and *3*, all combined with a soundtrack designed to drive Yohko-holics into a frenzy. Nudity, violence and adult situations. Subtitled.
VHS: S21705. $19.95.
Toho, Japan, 1993, 30 mins.

Devil Hunter Yohko 5: The Death of Yohko

She's cheated death before, but now bouncy teenage exorcist Yohko Mano steps beyond the veil into the greatest mystery of all. All hell literally breaks loose when the shadow demons possess the body of Yohko's new boyfriend, then use the body of another friend to open the door to the demon plane. Yohko will find some way to stop the forces of evil, even if it literally kills her! Graphic sex and violence. ADULTS ONLY. Subtitled.
VHS: S24227. $29.95.
Toho, Japan, 1994, 50 mins.

Devil Hunter Yohko 6

A new girl who looks just like Yohko shows up at school and begins infringing on a certain teenage exorcist's private hunting grounds. It's bad enough when this impersonator beats Yohko to the punch in putting the moves on a sexy new teacher, but when the Yohko clone starts fighting demons as well, with a young assistant who looks like Yohko's own Azusa, things are really getting out of hand! Nudity, violence and adult situations. Subtitled.
VHS: S26439. $29.95.
Toho, Japan, 1995, 45 mins.

Devil Man Vol. 1: Genesis

A prehistoric carving discovered by Professor Asuka reveals visions of the demon world and knowledge that an invasion draws near. To kill a demon, the killer must become a demon too, and only one who is pure of heart has the will to possess a demon. Nudity, profanity and violence.
VHS: Subtitled. **S18925. $19.95.**
VHS: Dubbed. **S29122. $14.95.**
Dynamic Prod., Japan, 1987, 55 mins.

Devil Man Vol. 2: Siren, The Demon Bird

As Devilman, Akira must face new horror as bizarre creatures challenge him for the fate of the world. His girlfriend is attacked by the evil Geruwel, and Devil Man battles Jinmen, who carries the souls of his victims embedded in his shell—and the seductive, evil Siren may finally be his match. Nudity, profanity and violence.
VHS: Subtitled. **S19710. $19.95.**
VHS: Dubbed. **S29123. $14.95.**
Dynamic Prod., Japan, 1987, 55 mins.

Dirty Pair Flash Act 1

When the galaxy-wide 3WA unleashes the Dirty Pair, it's every sentient being for itself. Meet Kei and Yuri, two junior agents with a proclivity for being in the wrong place at the wrong time with just enough firepower to blow their way out of a bad situation and into something worse.
VHS: Dubbed. **S34047. $19.95.**
VHS: Subtitled. **S34048. $29.95.**
Japan

Dirty Pair Flash Act 3

Massive space fleets, killer kindergartners, gun-wielding stewardesses and baby head-bangers are only a few of the obstaclesKei and Yuri must overcome to stop a madman from taking over the universe through the galactic communications system. 60 mins.
Dubbed Version.
VHS: S34810. $19.95.
Subtitled Version.
VHS: S34811. $29.95.

Dirty Pair: Affair on Nolandia

Adapted from Haruka Takachiho's popular stories, the Dirty Pair films have been decribed as *Barbarella* meets *Beverly Hills 90210*. Kei and Yuri are special agents of WWWA who have gained their unflattering nickname due to their unfortunate habit of inadvertently causing mass destruction and leaving chaos in their wake as they fight crime. Nudity. Dubbed.
VHS: S17167. $19.95.
Laser: LD76019. $39.95.
Sunrise/Studio Nue, Japan, 1985, 55 mins.

Dirty Pair: Flight 005 Conspiracy

A departure from the usual high-spirited antics of the Dirty Pair, *Flight 005 Conspiracy* is a complex thriller. The WWWA is called to investigate a mysterious explosion which destroyed Dubahl Spaceliner Flight 005, as well as to look into the disappearance of a key scientist. Kei and Yuri—the agency's hottest investigators—are assigned to both cases. Shuttling between the planets Dahl, Dubahl and Zahl, the "Dirty Pair" get caught up in a deadly web of intrigue. Nudity. Dubbed.
VHS: S21694. $19.95.
Matsuke/Sunrise, Japan, 1990, 60 mins.

Dirty Pair: Project Eden

Haruku Takachiho's stormy, sexy space sleuths in their only theatrical feature-length adventure. Kei and Yuri are sent to Agerna to secure the only supply of pure Vizorium from two warring nations. Professor Wattsman thickens the plot with his belief that Vizorium actually contains life within its atomic structure. By the time the credits roll, the Dirty Pair have solved the problem and treated Agerna to their own brand of "planetary makeover." Nudity. Dubbed.
VHS: S21755. $19.95.
Matsuke/Sunrise, Japan, 1987, 80 mins.

Dog Soldier: Shadows of the Past

When an American scientist carrying a cure for the AIDS virus is kidnapped by a notorious arms merchant, John Kyosuke Hiba is forced back from retirement. This former Green Beret accepts the assignment to recapture the vaccine, only to get a Japanese intelligence operative off his back. But after learning the true identity of those he must pursue, his mission takes on a personal meaning. Graphic violence.
VHS: Subtitled. **S16059. $19.95.**
VHS: Dubbed. **S29124. $14.95.**
Laser: Subtitled. **LD74504. $29.95.**
Movic, Japan, 1989, 45 mins.

Dominion II, Vol. 1

In this animated feature an elite anti-terrorist unit, the Tank Police, is desperately trying to preserve order in Newport City. Their zeal frightens many residents, forcing the mayor to rein in their power. Now they must respond to a threat far graver than any they had prepared for. Dubbed in English. 60 mins.
VHS: S23878. $14.95.

Dominion Tank Police Act I

In the year 2010, the environment is so polluted, people must wear gas masks. The cat sisters Annapuna and Unipuma are attacking society under the direction of the evil cyborg Buaku. Enter the Tank Police—the only defense against futuristic terrorism. Nudity. Subtitled.
VHS: S16056. $19.95.
Koichi Mashimo, Japan, 1989, 40 mins.

Dominion Tank Police Act II

The Tank Police hound Buaku and the sexy/wicked Cat sisters as they try to rob the "hospital for healthy people" of its valuable collection of human excretions. Nudity. Subtitled.
VHS: S15953. $19.95.
Koichi Mashimo, Japan, 1989, 40 mins.

Dominion Tank Police Act III

The evil Buaku gang have set a trap for Leona, the newest member of the Tank Police, as they plot their heist of the last great work of art done while the world was healthy: an 80-year-old nude painting of Buako himself. Nudity. Subtitled.
VHS: S16055. $19.95.
Koichi Mashimo, Japan, 1989, 40 mins.

Dominion Tank Police Act IV

Finally, we learn the truth about Buaku's origins. Could there be something noble in the half-human, half-cyborg blood of this reknowned gang leader? Nudity. Subtitled.
VHS: S16058. $19.95.
Koichi Mashimo, Japan, 1989, 40 mins.

Dominion Tank Police Pt. 1: Acts I & II

This is the English-dubbed version of the popular Japanese series already available on home video in subtitled form. Dubbed.
VHS: S17870. $29.95.
Koichi Mashimo, Japan, 1989, 80 mins.

Dominion Tank Police Pt. 2: Acts III & IV

This is the English-dubbed version of the popular Japanese series already available on home video in subtitled form. Dubbed.
VHS: S17871. $29.95.
Koichi Mashimo, Japan, 1989, 80 mins.

Doomed Megalopolis Part 1: The Haunting of Tokyo

Tokyo is under siege as occult forces lay claim to the burial site of Taira No Masakado, a founder of the centuries-old city. The necromancer Kato hopes to free the soul of this ancient warrior and gain ultimate control of this budding metropolis. Standing in the way of Kato's quest for power are an aging priest, an innocent virgin and a group of untested heroes. But, they soon learn that the sadistic Kato is not an easy enemy to defeat.
VHS: S17743. $19.95.
OZ/Toei, Japan, 1991, 50 mins.

Doomed Megalopolis Part 2: The Fall of Tokyo

Realizing he cannot resurrect the spirit of Masakado through traditional means, Kato subjects an innocent victim to the ultimate debasement as he forces his seed into her unwilling body. The group of honorable men who stand opposed to him are driven to the brink of madness by Kato's evil. The final conflict causes a massive earthquake that rips Tokyo apart.
VHS: S19487. $19.95.
Toei/Oz, Japan, 1992, 50 mins.

Doomed Megalopolis Part 3: The Gods of Tokyo

Following the devastating earthquake of 1923, rebuilding plans for Tokyo include a subway system. Kato schemes to use the construction process to awaken and control Masakado—the ancient warrior spirit. Keiko, a Shinto priestess, puts up a spiritual barrier, but finds Kato's power is not so easily defeated.
VHS: S20429. $19.95.
Toei/Oz, Japan, 1992, 47 mins.

Doomed Megalopolis Part 4: The Battle for Tokyo

Frustrated in his attempts to control Masakado, the evil necromancer Kato plots revenge. When the Moon starts falling toward the Earth, Keiko knows Kato is responsible. She and Masakado join forces to stop the impending global catastrophe in the conclusion to this spellbinding miniseries by Rin Taro.
VHS: S20722. $19.95.
Toei/Oz, Japan, 1992, 47 mins.

Dragon Ball Z, Vol. 1: Arrival

Episodes 1-4. The popular show fron the Saban Kids Network. The story begins when Goku's big brother, Raditz, lands on Earth and Goku discovers he's a Saiyan warrior from the planet Vegeta. Goku's son Gohan is kidnapped by Raditz, so Goku challenges his more powerful brother. Joined by his archrival Piccolo, Goku heads towards Raditz's hideout to rescue Gohan. The first four episodes of the series. Dubbed.
VHS: S33411. $14.95.
Bird/Toei, Japan, 1997, 80 mins.

Dragon Ball Z, Vol. 2: The Saiyans

Three episodes. Dubbed.
VHS: S33568. $14.95.
Bird/Toei, Japan, 1996, 65 mins.

Dragon Ball Z, Vol. 3: Snake Way

Three episodes. Dubbed.
VHS: S33569. $14.95.
Bird/Toei, Japan, 1996, 65 mins.

Dragon Ball Z, Vol. 4

Three episodes. Dubbed.
VHS: S33570. $14.95.
Bird/Toei, Japan, 1996, 65 mins.

Dragon Ball Z, Vol. 5

Three episodes. Dubbed.
VHS: S33571. $14.95.
Bird/Toei, Japan, 1996, 65 mins.

Dragon Ball Z, Vol. 10: Rebirth

Bulma, Gohan and Krillin face trial after trial on their journey to Namek to find the original Dragon Balls and wish their friends back to life. Includes Episode 29, *Friends or Foes*; Episode 30, *Hunt for a Dragon Ball* and Episode 31, *Who's Who*. Dubbed. 65 mins.
VHS: S34797. $14.95.

Dragon Ball Z, Vol. 11: Namek

Bluma, Gohan and Krillin finally arrive on the planet Namek. Unfortunately, Vegeta and his powerful boss, Frieza, are already there, terrorizing the natives and looking for the Dragon Balls. Includes Episode 32, *Touchdown on Namek*; Episode 33, *Face Off on Namek* and Episode 34, *The Ruthless Frieza*. Dubbed. 65 mins.
VHS: S34798. $14.95.

Dragon Ball Z, Vol. 12: Betrayal

Goku continues his long journey to Namek, while the Namekians continue their struggle against Frieza's aggressive search for the Dragon Balls. Includes Episodes 35, 36 and 37. Dubbed. 65 mins.
VHS: S34933. $14.95.

Dragon Ball Z, Vol. 13: Zarbon!

The long journey continues for Goku, just as the long journey to King Kai's ends for Piccolo and the other warriors defeated by Vegeta. On Namek, Gohan and friends learn about the Eldest Namek and Krillin decides to look for the last Dragon Ball. Includes Episodes 38, 39 and 40. Dubbed. 65 mins.
VHS: S34934. $14.95.

Dragon Ball Z: The Movie: Dead Zone

The complete, uncut Japanese theatrical release.
VHS: Dubbed. **S32755. $19.95.**
VHS: Subtitled. **S32756. $24.95.**
Laser: Multi-audio. **LD76421. $29.95.**
DVD: Multi-audio. **DV60203. $29.95.**
Japan

Dragon Ball Z: The Movie: The Tree of Might

An evil alien plants a tree on Earth that will absorb all the living energy of the planet into its fruit. Goku and the rest of Earth's Special Forces gather together to battle this strong enemy for the fate of our planet. Violence.
VHS: Dubbed/Uncut. **S34044. $19.95.**
VHS: Subtitled/Uncut. **S34045. $24.95.**
VHS: Dubbed/Edited. **S34046. $14.95.**
Laser: Multi-audio. **LD76833. $29.95.**
DVD: Multi-audio. **DV60248. $29.95.**
Toei/Bird, Japan, 1997, 60 mins.

Dragon Ball Z The Movie: The World's Strongest

Mad scientists Dr. Wheelo and Dr. Kochin plot to take over the world with their fearsome biotechnology. Dr. Wheelo dies, and now his brain, living in a glass jar, needs a home in the strongest, healthiest body. Dr. Kochin and his android warriors kidnap Piccolo and Master Roshi in a quest to find the world's strongest fighter. Goku, Gohan and Krilian come to their friends' rescue, but will they save the day or lose their minds? 60 mins.
VHS: Dubbed. **S34298. $19.95.**
VHS: Subtitled. **S34299. $24.95.**
Laser: LD76946. $29.95.

Dragon Ball, Vol. 1: Secret of the Dragon Ball

Two episodes from the TV series: Episode 1: *Secret of the Dragon Ball* and Episode 2: *The Emporer's Quest*. Dubbed.
VHS: S29970. $12.95.
Toei, Japan, 1987, 44 mins.

Dragon Ball, Vol. 2: The Nimbus Cloud of Roshi

Two episodes from the TV series: Episode 3: *The Nimbus Cloud of Roshi* and Episode 4: *Oolong the Terrible*. Dubbed.
VHS: S29971. $12.95.
Toei, Japan, 1987, 44 mins.

Dragon Ball, Vol. 3

Episode 5: Yamcha the Desert Bandit and *Episode 6: Keep an Eye on the Dragon*. Dubbed.
VHS: S31128. $12.95.
Toei, Japan, 1986, 44 mins.

Dragon Ball, Vol. 4

Episode 7: The Ox-King on Fire Mountain and *Episode 8: The Kamehameha Wave*. Dubbed.
VHS: S31129. $12.95.
Toei, Japan, 1986, 46 mins.

Dragon Ball, Vol. 5

Episode 9: Boss Rabbit's Magic Touch and *Episode 10: The Dragon Balls Are Stolen*. Dubbed.
VHS: S31130. $12.95.
Toei, Japan, 1986, 44 mins.

Dragon Ball: Curse of the Blood Rubies

Dragon Ball is the story of Goku, a brave, innocent, young boy with incredible powers who is plunged into a mystical adventure that is played out in exotic lands filled with noble warriors, beautiful princesses, shape-changing monsters, armies of ruthless villains and a kooky old wise man. This is a TV special. Dubbed.
VHS: S29969. $12.95.
Toei, Japan, 1987, 48 mins.

Dragon Half Parts 1 and 2

When a Knight and a Dragon meet and fall in love, the result is Mink, a precocious young female who's half human, half dragon and all trouble! Exactly how much trouble? Well, having vestigial wings and tail isn't a problem most teenage girls have to bear, but when Mink insists on compounding her difficulties by falling in love with a professional dragon slayer, Dick Saucer, she really has put her heart before her head. Violence and nudity. Subtitled.
VHS: S24226. $29.95.
Ryuusuke Mita, Japan, 1993, 55 mins.

Dragon Slayer

Disappear into a bygone time, to a mystical land where demons and sorcery build kingdoms as surely as swords and armies; where shapeshifting warriors clash in bloody battle and a boy reaches manhood tempered by the flame of a dragon's breath. Violence.
VHS: Dubbed. **S32289. $19.95.**
VHS: Subtitled. **S33456. $29.95.**
Japan, 50 mins.

E.Y.E.S. of Mars

Thirty thousand years ago, the people of Mars live dangerously close to extinction after destroying their environment. Deep beneath the surface, Eve, Sarah and other young children are sheltered at the E.Y.E.S. Institute, where they are being taught "mindpower." The government wants to evacuate everyone to Earth, but a rebel group wants Eve to use her power to contact an ancient spirit who can give them the key to saving their own planet. Dubbed.
VHS: S32188. $19.95.
JKB Daira, Japan, 1995, 80 mins.

Earthian

Based on the popular Japanese comic book, *Earthian* is the story of a pair of angelic investigators, Kagetsuya and Chihaya, sent to Earth by the Arc Angel Michael, one to investigate the positive side of the Earthians, the other the negative. The fate of all humanity rests in their hands. Each tape is 45 mins.
Earthian—Angelic Destroyer, Dubbed Version.
VHS: S34803. $24.95.
Earthian—Angelic Destroyer, Subtitled Version.
VHS: S34800. $29.95.
Earthian—Fallen Angel, Dubbed Version.
VHS: S34802. $24.95.
Earthian—Fallen Angel, Subtitled Version.
VHS: S34799. $29.95.
Earthian—Final Battle, Dubbed Version.
VHS: S34804. $24.95.
Earthian—Final Battle, Subtitled Version.
VHS: S34801. $29.95.
Earthian—The Beginning, Dubbed Version.
VHS: S34172. $24.95.
Earthian—The Beginning, Subtitled Version.
VHS: S34103. $29.95.

El Hazard Vol. 1: The First Night

Two episodes: *The War Zone* and *El Hazard*. It all begins with the discovery of mysterious ruins beneath the school. Katsuhiko Jinnai, a high school student, believes that Makato Mizuhara is his destined rival, and lures Makato to the school late one night for his own nefarious reasons. Once there, Makato is summoned by a mysterious woman who shows him the way to El Hazard, The Magnificent World. Pulled this way and that by the threads of destiny, Makato and several others venture into this incredible new land.
VHS: Dubbed. **S29128. $24.95.**
VHS: Subtitled. **S25977. $29.95.**
Laser: CAV multi-audio. **LD75736. $39.95.**
A.I.C., Japan, 1995, 50 mins.

El Hazard Vol. 2: The Second Night and Third Night

In *The Second Night: The World of Beautiful Girls*, Makoto resembles the missing Princess Fatora, and is persuaded to impersonate her. In *The Third Night: The World of Hot Springs*, Makoto & Company visit the site of the annual Purification Ceremony and end up in a vast desert containing the Spring of Arliman.
VHS: Dubbed. **S29129. $24.95.**
VHS: Subtitled. **S26630. $29.95.**
Laser: CAV multi-audio. **LD75102. $39.95.**
A.I.C., Japan, 1995, 60 mins.

El Hazard Vol. 3: Episodes 5 and 6

Makoto can finally meet the three priestesses. But they learn that Bugrom's troop is on the way to the forbidden island to wake the legendary evil called Ifleata. They intend to use Ifleata's power as a weapon against "God's Eye." The three priestesses, Makoto and his company hurry there to stop Bugrom, but what Makoto finds there is the girl who transferred him to El Hazard!
VHS: Dubbed. **S29130. $24.95.**
VHS: Subtitled. **S29132. $29.95.**
Laser: CAV multi-audio. **LD75737. $39.95.**
A.I.C., Japan, 1995, 60 mins.

El Hazard Vol. 4: Episodes 6 and 7

The allied countries are gradually destroyed by Ifleata, but Rune Venus receives even worse news—the Phantom tribe occupies the "stairs to heaven" leading to "The God's Eye." Jinnai succeeds in abducting Princess Fatora from the Phantom tribe and plans to use her as a human shield. Makoto, Mr. Fujisawa and the three priestesses are waylaid by Ifleata and the Bugrom troops on their way to help Fatora. The conclusion of the series.
VHS: Dubbed. **S29131. $24.95.**
VHS: Subtitled. **S27692. $29.95.**
Laser: CAV multi-audio. **LD75586. $44.95.**
A.I.C., Japan, 1995, 75 mins.

El Hazard 2, Vol. 1

Miz finally got Fujisawa to propose to her while he was drunk. On the day of their wedding, Fujisawa goes on a walkabout, leaving Makota to break the news to everyone. Fatora, disguised as Makoto, begins to play the field by making a pass a Nanami and Shayla-Shayla with very explosive results. 60 mins.
VHS: Dubbed. **S34789. $24.95.**
VHS: Subtitled. **S34790. $29.95.**

Ellcia

Long ago, the inhabitants of Megaronia discovered the forgotten technology of a dead civilization. Their king used this knowledge to lead them down a path of unstoppable conquest. Once again, rumors of forgotten knowledge are circulating. This time it could bring about the ultimate weapon. Only a small band of outlaws can prevent total world domination. It's good vs. evil in this Anime video featuring swords, sorcery and powerful machines. 50 mins.
Dubbed Version.
VHS: S29840. $24.95.
Subtitled Version.
VHS: S29838. $29.95.

Ellcia 2: Ghost Ship

The first phase of the ancient Eijan prophesy has come to pass as Eira's comrades discover the legendary Ship of God—Ellcia. Now armed with the mightiest weapon on the sea, the young band of pirates take on King Nabosu's armored fleet. Graphic violence.
VHS: Dubbed. **S31314. $24.95.**
VHS: Subtitled. **S31315. $29.95.**
Jam Creations, Japan, 1993, 50 mins.

Ellcia 3: Ironclads

As Eira and her band of pirates from the Gods' ship, Ellcia, prepare to take on the Megaronian Empire, a new player enters the game. It's plot and counter-plot as Phelkis launches his own campaign to conquer the world. Graphic violence.
VHS: Dubbed. **S33575. $24.95.**
VHS: Subtitled. **S33574. $29.95.**
Jam Creations, Japan, 1993, 50 mins.

Ellcia 4: Ship of God

The final chapter of the series, as Eira and her pirates must face down the combined forces of Nobosu, Phelkis and Crystel. Will the arming of the Ship of God be completed in time to stave off the ultimate genocide? Graphic violence.
VHS: Dubbed. **S33576. $24.95.**
VHS: Subtitled. **S33577. $29.95.**
Jam Creations, Japan, 1993, 50 mins.

Ellcia: The Legend Begins

In a far away place and time, the inhabitants of Megaronia discovered the ruins of a civilization long dead. Many years have passed, and now the Sacred Book of the land of Eija, long thought to have been burned, has been rediscovered and with it the legends of a mysterious and all-powerful ship. Princess Crystal of Megaronia has set forth on a quest to recover the ship. Swords, sorcery and technology blend to form a mesmerizing tale of good versus evil. HiFi Stereo.

VHS: Dubbed. **S30382. $24.95.**
VHS: Subtitled. **S30383. $29.95.**
Jam Creations, Japan, 1993, 50 mins.

Explorer Woman Ray

Archaeologist and black belt extraordinaire Ray Kizuki has come to a remote corner of the world to explore an ancient temple. She carries a mysterious mirror-like object that may hold the key to a lost civilization. But the Tachibana sisters lose it, and they must all struggle to keep the deadly secrets out of the hands of Rig Veda. Subtitled.

VHS: S18427. $19.95.
Laser: LD74505. $34.95.
A.I.C., Japan, 60 mins.

Farewell to Yamato: In the Name of Love

Derek Wildstar and Nova must postpone their wedding when the original crew of the famous space battleship *Yamato* reunites for a last voyage. Prince Zordar's enormous dreadnought, disguised as a comet, is on a diabolical mission to enslave every planet in the galaxy. Although Yamato is outgunned, Commander Wildstar prevails, but at a terrible cost in lives.

VHS: Dubbed. **S29348. $29.95.**
VHS: Subtitled. **S29349. $29.95.**
Japan, 120 mins.

Fatal Fury: Legend of the Hungry Wolf

When world-class martial artist Jeff Bogard is murdered before his sons' eyes, young Terry and Andy Bogard devote their lives to bare-knuckled street-fighting techniques to stand a chance of avenging their father's death. As the King of Fighters tournament approaches, only one will be chosen to learn the Hakkyokuseiken technique. Based on the videogame. Violence. Dubbed.

VHS: S23333. $19.95.
SNK, 1992, 50 mins.

Fatal Fury 2: The New Battle

After defeating Geese Howard, the man responsible for the murder of his father, Terry "Hungry Wolf" Bogard spars one night with deadly German nobleman Wolfgang Krauser. Krauser leaves Terry with his life but not much else, and the embittered street fighter must gather up what's left of his pride and start down the lonely road to recovery. A scrappy young street punk named Tony may be able to give Terry back his will to live, but what good is passion when honor is gone? Violence. Dubbed.

VHS: S24574. $19.95.
SNK, Japan, 1993, 70 mins.

Fatal Fury: The Motion Picture

A full-length theatrical feature. Prideful young Laocorn Gaudeamus has scoured archaeological sites for the legendary "Armor of Mars." To prevent her brother from acquiring it, Laocorn's beautiful, estranged twin sister, Sulia, enlists the aid of the only man in the world powerful enough to challenge him…Terry "Hungry Wolf" Bogard. Unless Terry can stop him, Laocorn will don the final piece of armor and become invincible. Nudity and violence. Dubbed.

VHS: S26247. $19.95.
SNK, Japan, 1994, 100 mins.

Fatal Fury 1-2 Punch

Fatal Fury 1 and *Fatal Fury 2*. Subtitled.

VHS: S32286. $29.95.
SNK, Japan, 1992-93, 120 mins.

Fatal Fury Boxed Set

All three *Fatal Fury* videos in a collector's slipcase. Dubbed.

VHS: S30266. $54.95.
SNK, Japan, 1992-94, 220 mins.

Final Fantasy, Vol. 1: Legend of the Crystals

Planet R's beautiful existence is maintained by four magical crystals: Earth, Water, Fire and Wind. Three have been stolen and young Linaly and Prettz are all that remain to protect the final Crystal of Wind from evil forces. Directed by Rin Taro, based on the popular role-playing game.

VHS: Dubbed. **S32776. $19.95.**
VHS: Subtitled. **S32778. $29.95.**
Square/NTT, Japan, 1994, 60 mins.

Final Fantasy, Vol. 2

Rouge, the leader of a leather-clad army of female pirates, must team up with Prettz to fight the common evil. Together they must travel to the Black Moon, face a swarm of alien soldiers, and retrieve Linaly and the four crystals before the Deathgyunos force is set free.

VHS: Dubbed. **S33458. $19.95.**
VHS: Subtitled. **S33457. $29.95.**
Square/NTT, Japan, 1994, 60 mins.

Final Yamato

The final film appearance of the characters in the *Star Blazers* TV series. Admiral Okita assumes command of Space Battleship *Yamato* in 2203, replacing Kodai. During a climactic battle with the Uruku, Kodai is saved by Lugarl's own son, but the *Yamato* crew seems doomed until Dethlar comes to the rescue. Okita orders the crew to abandon *Yamato*, and pilots it to Aquarius. Okita destroys the water planet by fusing energy from *Yamato*'s wave motion gun, forming a hydrogen bomb. The battleship sinks into the same kind of watery grave from which it was originally rescued. Subtitled.

VHS: S29350. $29.95.
Japan, 163 mins.

Fobia 1

Someone or something is raping and devouring women at Enoshima College and it is up to students Mutsumi and Megumi to stop it. Together they must fight these powerful beasts and save the world from extinction. Subtitled. 46 mins.

VHS: S34791. $29.95.

Gaiking

From the golden age of Japanese giant robot cartoons: Fighting warrior Gaiking and his mystical space dragon protect Earth from the evil King Davius and his minions. In *Aries Joins the Team*, Darius and his Black Horror Corps plan to save Zela from a black hole, and Aries Astonopolons, a baseball player, is recruited to pilot the giant robot Gaiking. In *Right Down the Middle*, Aries learns to pilot Gaiking, but he may be quitting…until he meets the Garwings. Dubbed. EP Speed.

VHS: S18595. $17.95.
Toei, Japan, 1982, 46 mins.

Galaxy Express 999: Adieu Galaxy Express

Two years after the events of the first movie, Earth has become a battlefield and Tetsuro is summoned aboard the 999 once more. He embarks on a journey whose destination is unknown even to Engine C6248 itself. New characters are introduced: Metalmena, a cold-hearted replacement for the warm-hearted Claire; Faust the Black Knight; Meowdar the brave feline partisan from La Met‡l; and more.

VHS: Dubbed. **S31343. $24.95.**
VHS: Subtitled. **S31344. $29.95.**
Toei, Japan, 1981, 135 mins.

Galaxy Express 999: The Signature Edition

On Earth of the near future, humanity has for the most part cast aside their bodies in favor of a variety of machines. Now it's easier than ever for the have's to dismiss the have-not's. Galaxy Express 999 is the name of a train which travels through space, beginning at Megalopolis Station and terminating at the other end of the galaxy at Andromeda. But it's also a metaphor for life itself, with passengers boarding, debarking, and dreaming along the way. Tetsuro Hoshino is a young man who promises to accompany a mysterious woman to Andromeda, where he is told he can get a new machine body for free and avenge the cruel death of his mother. But nothing in this life is truly free, and Tetsuro is about to learn the true price for boarding GE999. Director Taro Rin's classic adaptation of Leiji Matsumoto's manga is uncut and unedited. HiFi Stereo.

VHS: Dubbed. **S28462. $24.95.**
VHS: Subtitled. **S28465. $29.95.**
Toei, Japan, 1979, 120 mins.

Galaxy Fraulein Yuna

Cosmic cooking contests, house-destroying wake-up calls and kidnapped puppies are all in a day's work for Yuna and her sidekick Yuri, the incredible eating machine. But is the new girl at school really what she seems? And what about those two around the corner? Yuna better watch out! The aliens have arrived and they're after her! Contains silly violence. Subtitled.

VHS: S27463. $29.95.
Japan, 35 mins.

Galaxy Fraulein Yuna 2

After watching a person she believes to be Yuna destroy large portions of the city, Galactic Investigator Misaki takes Yuna in to stand trial on charges of treason. Much to the dismay of a bemused Yuna, she is found guilty and sentenced to die by being thrown into a black hole. Is this the end for our heroine? Or will Taro-chan, the kidnapped puppy, prove to be the loose thread that will unravel Fraulein D's nefarious plans? Contains silly violence. HiFi Stereo. Subtitled.

VHS: S29889. $29.95.
Japan, 35 mins.

Gall Force 1: Eternal Story

Famous for its nouveau animation style and ingenious script, Gall Force is set deep in space, where two warring races—the all female Solonoids and the biomechanical Paranoids—have not seen peace for 1000 years. Ordered to their new homeworld, Chaos, in the 9th Star System, the seven surviving crew members of the Solnoid cruiser *Star Leaf* are cut off from the rest of their fleet. As they battle their way to Chaos, the young women find themselves pawns in the plans of the high commands of both sides. Evocative of an all-female *Magnificent Seven*. Nudity.

VHS: Subtitled. **S17364. $19.95.**
VHS: Dubbed. **S28598. $19.95.**
Laser: Subtitled. **LD74507. $29.95.**
Movic, Japan, 1986, 86 mins.

Gall Force 2: Destruction

Now, others take up the fight—Ace pilot Lufy, survivor of the ill-fated *Star Leaf*, rejoins the Solnoid army just as both the Paranoid and Solnoid home planets have been destroyed. Now it seems no planet is safe, and the next world targeted for destruction is the one that has been selected for a bold experiment that could end the fighting forever. Nudity. Subtitled.

VHS: S19693. $19.95.
Laser: LD75738. $34.95.
Movic, Japan, 1987, 50 mins.

Gall Force 3: Stardust War

With the destruction of DAMIA, the new race on the planet Terra is free to develop in peace. Gathering together their remaining ships and Planet Destroyers, the Solnoid have retreated to a forgotten star system to await their enemies. As both races prepare themselves for Armageddon, Lufy and the last survivors of the Lorelei fleet scramble to avert the inevitable. Nudity. Subtitled.

VHS: S21100. $19.95.
Laser: LD74950. $34.95.
Movic, Japan, 1988, 60 mins.

Gall Force Earth Chapter 1

In 2085, Earth is a wasteland ruled by lethal war machines. When humanity fled to Mars, only a handful of warriors were left behind. Now, if Sandy Newman and her comrades could only reach one of the unlaunched nuclear missiles, the main stronghold of the cyberoid war machines could be destroyed. Sandy's team discovers a secret underground retreat where the Geo Chris religious sect has been quietly worshipping their "Tree of Revival." Subtitled.

VHS: S22763. $29.95.
Laser: LD75291. $34.95.
Artmic, Japan, 1989, 48 mins.

Gall Force Earth Chapter 2

Mankind, banished to Mars, races desperately against time to build an immense plasma cannon which could destroy the MME citadel in a single blast. Meanwhile, Sandy Newman and her comrades are staging a desperate fight from their hidden Australian bases. At the same time, Gorn's plans for the destruction of humanity are dangerously near completion. Subtitled.

VHS: S22764. $29.95.
Laser: LD75400. $34.95.
Artmic, Japan, 1990, 50 mins.

Gall Force Earth Chapter 3

The soldiers of the resistance grimly prepare for their final battle. But on Mars, General McKenzie is planning a massive return to Earth. But the crucial contest may come deep inside the half-mile tall MME citadel as Sandy Newman comes face-to-face with the computer leader Gorn. Subtitled.

Laser: LD75739. $34.95.
Artmic, Japan, 1990, 58 mins.

Gall Force: New Era 1

Generations ago, humanity's war against the Cyberoid war machines left our planet a desolate wasteland. Now, dozens of hyper-modern "ecropolis" habitats dot the landscape, containing both humans and the genetically engineered "Yumans." Some Yumans believe they are superior to humans, and wish to seize power for themselves. Only the android Catty has the ability to gather the seeds of mankind's salvation. Subtitled.

VHS: S26251. $29.95.
Laser: LD75740. $34.95.
Artmic, Japan, 1992, 50 mins.

Gall Force: New Era 2

Mankind is dead, destroyed by the evil computer intelligence Gorn. The only survivors are six young women shot deep into space by Catty. But Gorn is close behind, and through brain surgery and implants, now inhabits the body of Nova, its human tool. The six young women wait by their radio, hoping for news that someone else has survived the holocaust, not realizing that Gorn can insert himself into any computer. Subtitled.

VHS: S26252. $29.95.
Laser: LD75544. $34.95.
Artmic, Japan, 1993, 49 mins.

Garaga

An explosion in the engine room sends the starship *XeBeC* hurtling out of control. Making an emergency landing on the planet Garaga, they face attacks from dinosaur-like monsters and powerful ape creatures. Rescued by a telepathic woman, they discover the crash was caused by a saboteur! The mystery unfolds—a powerful general, a ruthless pilot and a race of psychics. It's up to our hero, Jay M. Jay, to save the crew, the girls and the galaxy! Subtitled.
VHS: S26898. $29.95.
Japan, 49 mins.

Gatchaman, Vol. 1: The Dragon King

This recent OAV series is based on the 1972-74 TV series. Revamped for the '90s, the new OAVs modernize the original characters (Ken, Joe, June, Rocky and Jimmy) without sacrificing the design of the original. A huge warship seeks to destroy The Mantel Plan: a worldwide energy network. As it heads for its next target, the Gatchaman team launches a counterattack with their own ship, *The Phoenix*. Violence and nudity.
VHS: Dubbed. **S32247. $19.95.**
VHS: Subtitled. **S32248. $29.95.**
Tatsunoko, Japan, 1994, 45 mins.

Gatchaman, Vol. 2: The Red Specter

Summoned to avenge a surprise attack on a submarine, the Gatchaman team discovers the secret headquarters of the alien Gallacter. The team struggles against Gallacter's mighty Jupiter Death Brigade and the evil Black Bird Battalion in a fierce air and undersea battle. Violence.
VHS: Dubbed. **S32282. $19.95.**
VHS: Subtitled. **S32283. $29.95.**
Tatsunoko, Japan, 1994, 45 mins.

Gatchaman, Vol. 3: The Final Countdown

As the Gallacter initiate their invasion battle plans, hordes of spaceships attack the planet. The conclusion of the miniseries ties together the lives and deeds of the Gatchaman team and their mysterious ally, the Red Specter. Violence.
VHS: Dubbed. **S32288. $19.95.**
VHS: Subtitled. **S32287. $29.95.**
Tatsunoko, Japan, 1994, 45 mins.

Genesis Survivor Gaiarth: Stage 1

Gaiarth—a world devastated by a cataclysmic war, where pockets of humanity struggle to survive amidst the rubble of technologies made magical by ignorance. Gaiarth—a world where artificially intelligent machines doggedly pursue their programmed imperatives, to protect, or to destroy, humanity. Gaiarth—the world of Ital del Labard, a young man raised by an aging Warroid, Sahari, the leader of a band of Junk-hunters, and Zaxon, an amnesiac Warroid who may be a link to the fabled past. Nudity and violence. Dubbed.
VHS: Dubbed. **S29133. $19.95.**
VHS: Subtitled. **S18347. $24.95.**
Laser: Hybrid. **LD75741. $39.95.**
Artmic, Japan, 1990, 40 mins.

Genesis Survivor Gaiarth: Stage 2

After defeating the Beast-Master, Ital, Zaxon and Sahari travel to Metro City, where a gigantic Kampfdraken has reportedly awakened. When the Draken is finally defeated, they discover that it is guarding a treasure, an egg containing a mysterious Elf, a synthetic human named Sakuya—the same Sakuya that the Beast-Master was searching for. But when Sakuya awakens, the mysterious General is able to set his terrible plan into motion. Nudity and violence. Dubbed.
VHS: Dubbed. **S29134. $19.95.**
VHS: Subtitled. **S18620. $24.95.**
Laser: Hybrid. **LD75742. $39.95.**
Artmic, Japan, 1992, 46 mins.

Genesis Survivor Gaiarth: Stage 3

After the defeat of the Kampfdraken, a mysterious Elf named Sakuya awoke from a century-long slumber, only to be captured by the diabolical General, who plans to use her to dominate the world—or destroy it in the attempt. Can Ital, Sahari, Fayk and Zaxon the Warroid rescue Sakuya, defeat the General and save Gaiarth from a fate worse than Armageddon? Nudity and violence. Dubbed.
VHS: Dubbed. **S29135. $19.95.**
VHS: Subtitled. **S27023. $29.95.**
Laser: Hybrid. **LD75743. $39.95.**
Ooba Hideaki, Japan, 1993, 45 mins.

Genocyber Part 1: Birth of Genocyber

The Japanese Kyuryu Group has discovered a weapon which will tip world power in their favor—two sisters: one whose body is mostly machine and the other with unbelievable psychic powers. If these two could be combined into one, a weapon beyond anything ever conceived would be created: Genocyber—a cybernetic monster strengthened with pure psychic energy! Subtitled.
VHS: S21319. $29.95.
Laser: LD74826. $34.95.
Artmic, Japan, 1993, 46 mins.

Genocyber Parts 2 & 3: Vajranoid Showdown

After the destruction of Hong Kong, the Genocyber's rage is unleashed against its creators. Wandering into a small nation's war of aggression, Elaine is embroiled in the Kuryu Group's latest weapons test: The Vajranoid, a biomechanical monstrosity designed to be the ultimate fighter pilot. Capable of merging with almost any piece of machinery, the Vajranoid is the only one who can sense the dangerous power within this innocent-looking girl's cybernetic body. Subtitled.
VHS: S21835. $29.95.
Laser: LD75744. $34.95.
Artmic, Japan, 1993, 50 mins.

Genocyber Parts 4 & 5: The Legend of Ark de Grande

On the eve of its final battle with the last remnants of Kuryu's forces, Genocyber mysteriously vanishes. Some 300 years later, mankind has only barely recovered from the destruction. In the city of Ark de Grande, two young lovers arrive to start a new life, and are swept up in the plots rippling through the city. As one is unwittingly linked with the growing rebel movement, the other is mistaken for a heavenly messenger by a cult devoted to the legend of Genocyber. For 300 years Genocyber has slept, but now the time for its rebirth is almost at hand. Subtitled.
VHS: S23081. $29.95.
Laser: LD75745. $34.95.
Artmic, Japan, 1993, 60 mins.

Ghost in the Shell

Japan, 2029—The digital sea of information has washed over every aspect of society. Amidst this electronic chaos surfaces an internationally notorious computer criminal. Codenamed "The Puppet Master" for its ability to control the minds of innocent victims, this unique and mysterious super-hacker is suspected of a multitude of offenses, including stock market manipulation, illegal data gathering, terrorist acts and infringement of cybernetic ethics. Section 9, Japan's elite secret service unit, is called in to capture this elusive criminal, only to discover that the elaborate web of evidence leads back to Japan's own Ministry of Foreign Affairs and an intelligence without physical form...a ghost in search of its shell. From the producers of *Akira*. Violence, nudity and profanity. HiFi Stereo. Dubbed.
VHS: Dubbed. **S28057. $19.95.**
VHS: Subtitled. **S28056. $29.95.**
Laser: CLV multi-audio. **LD76017. $34.95.**
Laser: CAV multi-audio. **LD76018. $49.95.**
Masamune Shirow, Japan, 1995, 82 mins.

Ghost in the Shell—Special Edition

Digitally remastered version of the award-winning anime feature film that questions our own human existence in the fast-paced world of the information age. Seamlessly merging traditional cel animation with the latest computer graphic imagery, this stunning sci-fi spectacle broke through the boundaries of mainstream animation with its detailed artistic direction and uniquely intelligent story line. Includes the bonus program *The Making of Ghost in the Shell*. "Unusually intelligent and challenging science fiction, aimed at smart audiences" (Roger Ebert).
Dubbed.
VHS: S32251. $24.95.
Subtitled.
VHS: S32252. $34.95.
Mamoru Oshi, Japan, 1997, 120 mins.

Giant Robo, Vol. 1

A nefarious organization known as "Big Fire" attempts to control a powerful energy source to conquer the Earth, waging war through a combined use of physics and giant robots. 55 mins.
VHS: S18341. $24.95.

Giant Robo, Vol. 1: Episodes 1 and 2

In Episode 1, *The Black Attache Case*, Big Fire assigns Lord Alberto to capture Shizuma and a prototype Shizuma Drive. Can Daisaku and Giant Robo stop them? In Episode 2, *The Tragedy of Bashtarlle*, the Experts of Justice and Dr. Shizuma narrowly escape Big Fire, only to be trapped by the terrible Ivan. Giant Robo, unable to penetrate a force field, witnesses the conflict with Ivan, who explains the power of the Shizuma Drive over the city of Bashtarlle. Dubbed.
VHS: S25545. $19.95.
Hikaru, Japan, 1992, 90 mins.

Giant Robo, Vol. 2: Episode 3: Magnetic Web Strategy

When an energy-sucking orb advances toward the last power source on Earth (the Shanghai oil refinery), all the Experts of Justice except Tetsugyu, Daisaku and Robo are ordered there. Disobeying orders, the three arrive in Shanghai. One by one the Magnetic Web Devices fail because of sabotage. All hope seems lost when Robo and Daisuku charge after the Orb and are defeated. Even Robo's tremendous strength is no match for the menacing eyeball.
VHS: Dubbed. **S25726. $14.95.**
VHS: Subtitled. **S33706. $24.95.**
Laser: CAV, multi-audio. **LD75748. $34.95.**
Hikaru, Japan, 1992, 45 mins.

Giant Robo, Vol. 3: Episode 4: Twilight of the Superhero

Even Giant Robo's punch has no effect on the menacing Eye of Folger. When Magnetic Web Devices are sabotaged, Taison and Alberto battle for the ultimate destiny of Earth. Elsewhere, members of Big Fire attack the Greta Garbo and Gynrei must protect Daisaku, even if it means sacrificing her life. She makes a startling discovery when she comes face to face with her father. Dubbed.
VHS: S26239. $14.95.
Laser: CAV, multi-audio. **LD75749. $34.95.**
Hikaru, Japan, 1994, 45 mins.

Giant Robo, Vol. 4: Episode 5: The Truth of Bashtarlle

Inside the fiery Greta Garbo, Daisaku plummets into the icy depths of the Himalayan mountains. Gynrei and Tetsugyu desperately search for their fallen comrade, who has been sucked into the darkness of the snowy mountains. As Daisaku lies unconscious, he dreams of his past and the origins of Giant Robo. Dubbed.
VHS: S26638. $14.95.
Hikaru, Japan, 1992, 45 mins.

Giant Robo, Vol. 5: Episode 6: Conflict in the Snow Mtns.

Big Fire and the Magnificent Ten attempt to follow through with "Operation Earth Stand Still." Using their newest weapon, "The Big Balloon"—a device that absorbs energy—Big Fire hopes to annihilate the Earth. Giant Robo and comrades team up once again to protect the sample and to stop the detonation of "The Big Balloon." Dubbed.
VHS: S26767. $14.95.
Hikari, Japan, 1992, 45 mins.

Giant Robo—The Night the Earth Stood Still, Vol. 1

Includes two exciting episodes. In *The Black Attache Case*, Lord Alberto is assigned to capture Dr. Shizuma and a prototype of his "Shizuma Drive" that will usher in Earth's greatest age of darkness. In *The Tragedy of Bashtarelle*, the Experts of Justice and Dr. Shizuma narrowly escape the clutches of Big Fire, only to be trapped by the terrible Ivan. Japanese with English subtitles. 90 mins.
VHS: S32264. $24.95.

Gigantor Retrospective 30 Vol. 1

Two episodes: *World in Danger* and *Badge of Danger*. Dubbed.
VHS: S21287. $19.95.
TJC, Japan, 1964, 50 mins.

Gigantor Retrospective 30 Vol. 2

Two episodes: *The Smoke Robots* and *The Freezer Ray*. Dubbed.
VHS: S21288. $19.95.
TJC, Japan, 1964, 50 mins.

Gigantor Retrospective 30 Vol. 3

Two episodes: *The Magic Multiplier* and *The Submarine Base*. Dubbed.
VHS: S21289. $19.95.
TJC, Japan, 1964, 50 mins.

Gigantor Retrospective 30 Vol. 4

Two episodes: *Treasure Mountain* and *The Mystery Missile*. Dubbed.
VHS: S21290. $19.95.
TJC, Japan, 1964, 50 mins.

Gigantor Retrospective 30 Vol. 5

Two episodes: *The Giant Cobra* and *The Great Hunt*. Dubbed.
VHS: S21291. $19.95.
TJC, Japan, 1964, 50 mins.

Gigantor Vol. 1

Gigantor is a jet-propelled robot controlled by Dr. Sparks' ("Dr. Kaneda") 12-year-old son, Jimmy ("Shotaro"), to assist the Japanese police in their fight against crime. Fifty-two black-and-white episodes produced by Japan's TCJ Animation Center. Edited for American syndication by Al Singer & Fred Ladd, 1963-67. Three episodes: *Struggle at the South Pole, Battle at the Bottom of the World* and *Sting of the Spider*. Dubbed.
VHS: S15970. $29.95.
TCJ, Japan, 1964, 75 mins.

Gigantor Vol. 2

Three episodes: *Return of the Spider, Spider's Revenge* and *Secret Valley*. Dubbed.
VHS: S15971. $29.95.
TCJ, Japan, 1964, 75 mins.

Gigantor Vol. 3

Three episodes: *The Diamond Smuggler, Dangerous Dr. Diamond* and *Force of Terror*. Dubbed.
VHS: S16700. $29.95.
TJC, Japan, 1964, 75 mins.

Gigantor—30th Anniversary
A lunchbox-shaped device controls the world's most powerful robot, owned by a young boy named Jimmy Sparks. This robot can unleash immense powers and fly effortlessly around the world. Jimmy joins forces with his robot friend to fight crime, leading them on spectacular adventures in exotic locales around the globe. Originally a TV series, these episodes are presented just as they were aired. Dubbed in English, 120 mins.
Laser: LD74608. $39.95.

Gigantor—30th Anniversary Vol. 2
Four episodes: *The Spider's Revenge, The Secret Valley, The Diamond Smugglers* and *Dangerous Dr. Diamond*. Dubbed.
Laser: LD74829. $39.95.
TJC, Japan, 1964, 120 mins.

The Girl from Phantasia
When young Akihiro discovers a magic carpet, the very female sprite Malon pops into his hands! Akihiro is faced with not only the mischievous Malon, but also her combative brownie buddies Short and Monbran, the psychotic Magician-In-Exile, Roll, and, worst of all, an extremely annoyed Michiko! Nudity. Subtitled.
VHS: S20522. $19.95.
Star Child, Japan, 1993, 40 mins.

Go Shogun: The Time Etranger
The Go Shogun Team are reunited at the deathbed of former teammate Remy Shimada, who battles a relentless evil that deftly maneuvers her toward oblivion. Buried alive at the age of 10, caught in a nightmare at age 20, ravaged by disease at age 70, she faces a darkness which promises only death. Subtitled.
VHS: S25682. $29.95.
Ashi, Japan, 1985, 90 mins.

Godmars
Godmars has: Gaia, one of the most famous combining super-robots; climactic robot battles; constantly twisting storyline as more plot is revealed; a desperate brother-against-brother struggle; a central character who is exploring his emotions as his world is coming apart. Super-robot fans: this one's for you! Subtitled.
VHS: S22766. $24.95.
Hikari/TMS, Japan, 1982, 93 mins.

Golden Boy
Aspiring computer programmer Kintaro finds himself employed by T.N. Software, a company staffed entirely by women. When they discover that his programming ideas are a little unusual, he is demoted to office boy. Does this mean the end of his dreams, or will his skills make him the golden boy of the software business? Nudity and adult situations.
VHS: Dubbed. **S29136. $19.95.**
VHS: Subtitled. **S27713. $24.95.**
Laser: CAV multi-audio. **LD75571. $39.95.**
KSS, Japan, 1995, 30 mins.

Golden Boy 2
Kintaro's back! After leaving the lovely ladies at T.N. Software, Kintaro takes a job working for the political campaign of a wealthy businessman. Then it happens. He meets the young lady of his dreams, who just happens to be the boss's daughter. When the young lady in question asks Kintaro to help her with her "homework," things begin to heat up. But is it really his body she's after? Or is she only interested in Kintaro's mind? Nudity and adult situations. HiFi Stereo.
VHS: Dubbed. **S29842. $19.95.**
VHS: Subtitled. **S29841. $24.95.**
Laser: CAV, multi-audio. **LD75902. $39.95.**
KSS, Japan, 1995, 30 mins.

Golden Boy 3: Danger! The Virgin's First Love!
Kintaro bounces from job to job and finally ends up making noodles. When he uncovers a plot to steal a family-owned noodle shop by seducing the daughter, Kintaro steps in to rescue the fair maiden. Nudity and Adult Situations.
VHS: Dubbed. **S31319. $19.95.**
VHS: Subtitled. **S31320. $24.95.**
KSS, Japan, 1995, 30 mins.

Golden Boy 4: Swimming in the Sea of Love
When an infatuation with a lovely swimming instructor turns into a winner-takes-all swim match, Kintaro's in for the challenge of his life. Nudity and Adult Situations.
VHS: Dubbed. **S32625. $19.95.**
VHS: Subtitled. **S32624. $24.95.**
KSS, Japan, 1995, 30 mins.

Golden Boy 5: B@!!s to the Wall
Reiko is a sexy biker babe who knocks Kintaro out with her combination of burning rubber and perfume. It's all he can do to keep pace with her. Nudity and Adult Situations.
VHS: Dubbed. **S33460. $19.95.**
VHS: Subtitled. **S33459. $24.95.**
KSS, Japan, 1995, 30 mins.

Golden Boy 6: Animation Is Fun!
Kintaro's latest job is as a production assistant in an animation studio, where he gets to meet his idol, a popular erotic illustrator. When the studio gets behind schedule, Kintaro calls in reinforcements and brings things abreast of schedule. Nudity and Adult Situations.
VHS: Dubbed. **S33462. $19.95.**
VHS: Subtitled. **S33461. $24.95.**
KSS, Japan, 1995, 30 mins.

Golden Boy Collection 1
Tapes 1-3 in a collector's slipcase.
VHS: Dubbed. **S33858. $49.95.**
VHS: Subtitled. **S33857. $59.95.**
KSS, Japan, 1995, 90 mins.

Golgo 13: Queen Bee
Golgo's next mission is to terminate the infamous Queen Bee—the leader of a dissident South American liberation army—before she kills a high-profile Presidential candidate. However, Queen Bee isn't your average radical, and when Golgo 13 discovers her true identity, he decides to step aside and let Queen Bee's personal feud climax in tragedy. From the director of *Space Adventure Cobra*. 60 mins.
Dubbed Version.
VHS: S35166. $19.95.
Subtitled Version.
VHS: S35165. $29.95.

Grandizer
Orion Quest and his super spaceship, *Grandizer*, must thwart the evil Vagans who threaten Earth. In *Robot Back to Action*, Lance arrives at the institute in a cocky mood, but is soon taken down a peg. In *Beware the Red Moon*, Bellicose orders an attack on Earth, Panhandle takes a plane ride and Lance learns Johnny's true identity. EP Speed. Dubbed.
VHS: S18594. $17.95.
Toei, Japan, 1982, 46 mins.

Grappler Baki
Baki Hanma is a mysterious new fighter who's taking the Karate Championship by storm. But in this underground fighting circuit, if he loses he's dead. Graphic Violence. Dubbed.
VHS: S31321. $19.95.
Keisuke Itagaki, Japan, 1994, 45 mins.

Grave of the Fireflies
When fire bombing destroys their home, 14-year-old Seita and his four-year-old sister wander the ruined countryside. Unable to sustain themselves, the children eventually die. Just before the Americans land, an old janitor finds a small metal candy container and unwittingly frees the children's spirits. Subtitled.
VHS: S18628. $29.95.
Laser: Widescreen. **LD75750. $39.95.**
Akiyuki Nosaka, Japan, 1988, 88 mins.

Great Conquest: The Romance of the Three Kingdoms
The true story of Liu Pei, the father of historical China, *Great Conquest* is a spectacular animated motion picture filled with action and intrigue. Set in Imperial China, circa 169 AD, the story—adapted from the well-known historical epic—follows the key characters who would come together to forge a brave new nation out of the flames of chaos and the unrelenting sufferings of the oppressed. Narrated by Pat Morita. Dubbed.
VHS: S25066. $19.95.
Enoki, Japan, 1992, 118 mins.

Green Legend Ran
Extraterrestial objects landed on the polluted Earth and sucked up the air, water and living creatures into their wombs. In Episode 1, *Departure*, a hot-blooded young boy, Ran, tries to join the anti-Rodo group Hazzard. In Episode 2, *Green 5*, Ran is rescued from near death by Jeke, then Rodoist troops attack the Hazzards, capturing Aira. In Episode 3, *Holy Green*, Ran goes into the holy green to rescue Aira and Jeke learns the secret of Rodo, joining hands with Kiba to help the operation.
VHS: Dubbed. **S29137. $49.95.**
VHS: Subtitled. **S29138. $69.95.**
Laser: CAV, multi-audio. **LD75751. $99.95.**
AIC, Japan, 1992, 151 mins.

Grey: Digital Target
Trapped in a mysterious military society which rewards killing with the promise of a better life, laconic trooper Grey—the legendary "Grey Death"—seeks only to survive.
VHS: Dubbed. **S33563. $19.95.**
VHS: Subtitled. **S33564. $19.95.**
Japan, 80 mins.

Gunbuster Vol. 1
Gunbuster is the saga of an Earth invasion by monstrous space creatures. *Episode 1:* Noriko is struggling at the Space High School for Girls. Surprisingly, she is selected to join Kazumi Amano and advance to the Earth Space Force. *Episode 2:* The pair arrives in space and Kazumi is challenged by the pilot "genius" Jung-Freud. Noriko and Kazumi are sent to investigate an alien object which has entered the solar system. HiFi Stereo. Subtitled.
VHS: S13329. $19.95.
Gainax, Japan, 1988, 60 mins.

Gunbuster Vol. 2
Episode 3: As the *Exelion* and the Earth Fleet prepare to engage the enemy forces, Noriko discovers romance in the form of male pilot Smith Toren. Kazumi and Noriko's relationship becomes strained as Kazumi loses confidence in Noriko's abilities. *Episode 4:* Noriko tries to cope with the loss of a friend as the final phases of her training are completed and she is given command of the Earth Space Force's top-secret ultimate fighting machine, the monolithic Gunbuster. HiFi Stereo. Subtitled.
VHS: S16061. $19.95.
Gainax, Japan, 1989, 60 mins.

Gunbuster Vol. 3
In *Episode 5*, Noriko and Kazumi graduate from the Space Academy. The alien forces are preparing a massive attack on Earth. Ota devises a revolutionary plan as Kazumi and Noriko once again fight for Earth's survival. In the final episode, the year is 2048 AD (15 years after *Episode 5*), and the alien forces are regrouping for a final assault. Earth Space Force has devised the ultimate weapon, The Black Hole Bomb, to destroy the alien menace once and for all. Courage and bravery propel Noriko, Kazumi and their comrade Jung-Freud into a battle of epic proportions. *Episode 6* is black and white, letterboxed. HiFi Stereo. Subtitled.
VHS: S16062. $19.95.
Gainax, Japan, 1989, 60 mins.

Gunsmith Cats 1: Episodes 1 and 2
From Kenichi Sonoda (*Gall Force, Bubblegum Crisis*) comes Rally Vincent, the professional bounty hunter and gun expert extraordinaire. Together with her streetwise partner, the luscious Minnie-May, Rally's going to clean up the streets of Chicago with a few blasts from her pump-action sidearm—for a price. Violence and profanity.
VHS: Dubbed. **S29139. $19.95.**
VHS: Subtitled. **S29140. $24.95.**
Laser: CAV, multi-audio. **LD75439. $39.95.**
Japan, 30 mins.

Gunsmith Cats 1: Special Edition
Includes a bonus 40-minute "Making of Gunsmith Cats" featurette. Subtitled. Violence and profanity.
VHS: S27021. $34.95.
Japan, 70 mins.

Gunsmith Cats 2
When gun runner James Washington asks the girls for help, they're not inclined to believe him. However, when Washington and a host of agents are gunned down in an ATF safehouse mere minutes after the girls depart, Rally is forced to go looking for the killer. Then, when May is kidnapped by a psychotic Russian, the resulting chase through Chicago leaves traffic a shambles.
VHS: Dubbed. **S29141. $19.95.**
VHS: Subtitled. **S27712. $24.95.**
Laser: Multi-audio. **LD75570. $39.95.**
Japan, 30 mins.

Gunsmith Cats 3
The Cats are back and Rally proves that her intuition is something to be respected. The ATF case is far from over and when Radinov, a true femme fatale, reappears, she is out for blood...of the feline sort. Add a handful of surprisingly high-placed gun runners who are after their coats as well, and Rally and Minnie May are going to need every one of their nine lives just to make it through the day! Violence. HiFi Stereo.
VHS: Dubbed. **S30384. $19.95.**
VHS: Subtitled. **S30385. $24.95.**
Japan, 30 mins.

The Guyver Data 1: Genesis of the Guyver
The Guyver is a mysterious bio-booster armor of alien design. When activated, the unit interfaces with human subjects, transforming them into powerful combatants. The three Guyver units are stolen from the enigmatic Chronos Corporation in Japan. A high school student named Sho Fukamachi accidentally discovers Guyver 1 and triggers the control metal. He becomes the Guyver and battles biomorphic Zoanoids controlled by Chronos. Episode 1 of 12. Violence and profanity. Dubbed.
VHS: S27368. $12.95.
K.S.S., Japan, 1989, 30 mins.

The Guyver Data 2: Battle of the Guyvers

Lisker, an agent of Chronos headquarters, unwittingly joins with Guyver 2. He abducts Sho and his friend Tetsuro in an attempt to locate the other missing units. Sho summons the Guyver and the two are thrust into a deadly battle. Collector's card included. Violence and profanity. Dubbed.
VHS: S29144. $12.95.
K.S.S., Japan, 1989, 30 mins.

The Guyver Data 3: Mysterious Shadow

Commander Guou arrives from Chronos headquarters to lead the recovery of the Guyver units. Meanwhile, Chronos Japan creates the Zoanoid "Zerububuse" in a final desperate attempt to eliminate the Guyver. To bait the trap for Sho, Mizuky is kidnapped and Sho must become the Guyver and face the challenge of Zerububuse as well as the mysterious shadow, Guyver III. Free collector's card included. Violence and profanity. Dubbed.
VHS: S29145. $12.95.
K.S.S., Japan, 1989, 30 mins.

The Guyver Data 4: Attack of the Hyper Zoanoid-Team 5

Sho is finally convinced by his friend Tetsuro to publicly expose the existence of the evil Chronos organization. But before they have a chance, Commander Gyou attacks with Chronos' five most powerful hyper Zoanoids. Escaping only to face a further sudden attack from the deadly cyborg warriors, it is clear that Guyver 1 will not survive the battle alone. Includes collector's card. HiFi Stereo. Dubbed.
VHS: S27717. $12.95.
K.S.S., Japan, 1989, 30 mins.

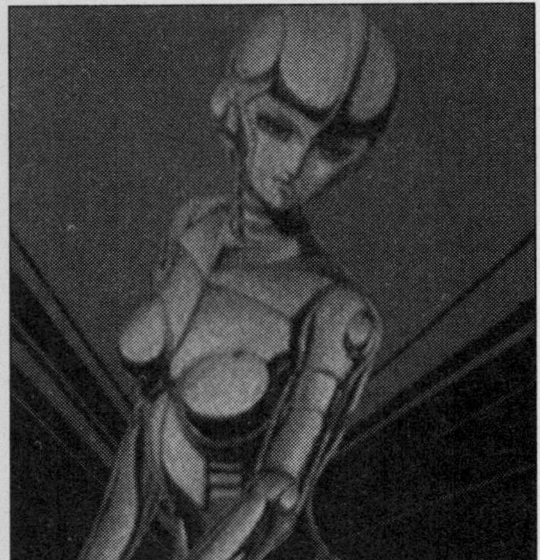

The Guyver Data 5: Death of the Guyver

The desperate Commander Gyou commands his men to transform Makishama into a Zoanoid armed with an enzyme capable of disintegrating the Guyver armor. Gyou kidnaps Sho's girlfriend and her brother and forces them to watch Sho and Makishama in a battle to the death. HiFi Stereo. Dubbed.
VHS: S30262. $12.95.
K.S.S., Japan, 1989, 30 mins.

The Guyver Data 6: Terminal Battle

Mizuki and Tetsuro are imprisoned under heavy guard at Chronos' Headquarters. With Sho believed dead, Tetsuro fears the worst as he begins to comprehend the enormous power of Chronos. Meanwhile, Guyver III's identity is finally revealed as he initiates his plan to destroy Chronos and Commander Gyou. But can Guyver 1 regenerate in time to save his girlfriend and her brother? HiFi Stereo. Dubbed.
VHS: S30263. $12.95.
K.S.S., Japan, 1989, 30 mins.

The Guyver Data 7: The Battle Begins

Having destroyed the evil Commander Gyou and his branch of the Chronos organization, the Guyver's battle to defeat them has only just begun. Chronos' leading scientist, Dr. Balcus, takes command and devises a plan to destroy the Guyver. HiFi Stereo. Dubbed.
VHS: S30264. $12.95.
K.S.S., Japan, 1989, 30 mins.

The Guyver Data 8: The Lost Unit

Sho's horrifying nightmare continues as he heads for Chronos headquarters at Mount Minakami, where death threatens Mizuki and his father. Spying on Sho's every move, Dr. Balcus decides to test out his research and orders the "lost units"—enzymes with unlimited powers—to challenge and destroy the Guyver. Will the Guyver have the strength to defeat him? HiFi Stereo. Dubbed.
VHS: S28479. $12.95.
K.S.S., Japan, 1989, 30 mins.

The Guyver Data 9: Transformation Tragedy

The Guyver's mission to save his father and Mizuki appears accomplished as they all attempt to escape from Mount Minakami. Dr. Balcus is unalarmed by this because he has programmed Sho's father to transform into a terrifying deadly Zoanoid, and using his psychic powers he commands him to kill the Guyver. Faced with this moral dilemma, will the Guyver fight back and kill his father to save his own life? HiFi Stereo. Dubbed.
VHS: S30265. $12.95.
K.S.S., Japan, 1989, 30 mins.

The Guyver Data 10: Haunted Village

Sho and his friends, desperate to escape Mount Minakami, work out an escape route. Guyver III returns to Chronos to intercept Dr. Balcus' evil plans to destroy the Guyver, but is in serious danger when the secret of his identity is revealed. Meanwhile, Sho and the others have fallen into Dr. Balcus' trap, having arrived at a village full of Zoanoids controlled by Dr. Balcus. Traumatized by his father's death, Sho is unable to transform into the Guyver. HiFi Stereo. Dubbed.
VHS: S30261. $12.95.
K.S.S., Japan, 1989, 30 mins.

The Guyver Data 11: Terminal Battle

Hiding from Dr. Balcus, Sho and his friends are in danger of attack from Zoanoids. Agito is desperate to know the secrets of Chronos and persuades Murakami to reveal all he knows. Violence. Dubbed.
VHS: S30905. $12.95.
K.S.S., Japan, 1989, 30 mins.

The Guyver Data 12: Reactivation

Sho and Mizuki are saved from Balcus' Zoanoids by Aptom, the only survivor of the lost units. Seeking vengeance for the death of his friends, he draws on his superhuman powers to torture and destroy the Guyver. Concludes the series. Violence. Dubbed.
VHS: S31186. $12.95.
K.S.S., Japan, 1989, 30 mins.

Hades Project Zeorymer Vol. 1: Episodes 1 and 2

The Hakkeshu—a team of eight giant robots built to bring the forces of Hau Dragon world domination. Zeorymer of the heavens, the most powerful of these robots, is stolen along with the frozen embryo of its genetically engineered pilot. Fifteen years later it is finally time for Zeorymer to awaken. As powerful forces gather to battle for the fate of the world, a teenager is swept into the heart of the action. Subtitled.
VHS: S20865. $29.95.
Laser: LD75752. $34.95.

Artmic, Japan, 1988, 60 mins.

Hades Project Zeorymer Vol. 2: Episodes 3 and 4
Masato's last battle with Aen and Tau unleashed a frightening new personality, and now all wonder if they really understand the true relationship between Masato and the Zeorymer robot. Masato was born to be the Zeorymer's pilot…or was he? No one is sure who is behind the plot which will either lead to world domination or absolute extinction. Subtitled.
VHS: S21292. $29.95.
Laser: LD75753. $34.95.
Artmic, Japan, 1989, 60 mins.

Hakkenden Vol. 1: Episodes 1 and 2

The story of eight young warriors and their struggle to find justice in ancient Japan. Episode 1, *The Kaleidoscope*: The year is 1457 and Princess Fuse is forced into matrimony with her dog, Yatsufusa. Ultimately, the princess and the dog are killed, and at the moment of Fuse's death, eight spirit beads from her necklace disperse and the legend of the dog warriors begins. Episode 2, *Dark Music of the Gods*: Coming of age, Shino Inukuka is entrusted by his father with a legendary sword, the Murasame. Devastated by his father's tragic death, Shino somehow comes into possession of a small bead, on which the Chinese character "KO" appears, symbolizing filial devotion.
VHS: Dubbed. **S29146. $24.95.**
VHS: Subtitled. **S25976. $29.95.**
Laser: CAV, multi-audio. **LD75034. $39.95.**
A.I.C., Japan, 1993, 60 mins.

Hakkenden Vol. 2: Episodes 3 and 4

Episode 3, *The Futility Dance*: Sosuke is ordered by Kamezasa to kill Shino. The two warriors, however, soon realize the extent to which fate has connected them, and make a pledge of brotherhood. Episode 4, *Horyu Tower*: In Otsuka village arrives evil itself, personified by the jindai. Only Sosuke is able to stand up to them. Meanwhile, Shino arrives in Koga and is granted an audience with the Shogun, Nariuji Ashikaga.
VHS: Dubbed. **S29147. $24.95.**
VHS: Subtitled. **S26633. $29.95.**
Laser: CAV, multi-audio. **LD75105. $39.95.**
A.I.C., Japan, 1993, 60 mins.

Hakkenden Vol. 3: Episodes 5 and 6

Episode 5, *Demon's Melody*: Innkeeper Kobungo Inuta rescues Shino and Genpachi, who fell into the river from Hiryu Tower. Kobungo's brother-in-law alerts the authorities, and during an intense battle, he mistakenly kills his wife. Episode 6, *The Cicada Spirit Cry*: The three warriors take Nui's infant son Daihachi and set off for Otsuka village, where Sosuke faces a death sentence after being charged with the murders of his stepmother and father.
VHS: Dubbed. **S29148. $24.95.**
VHS: Subtitled. **S26632. $29.95.**
Laser: CAV, multi-audio. **LD75104. $39.95.**
A.I.C., Japan, 1993, 60 mins.

Hakkenden Vol. 4: Episode 7 and Digest

This volume features a compilation episode, *The Hakkenden Digest*, which summarizes the first six episodes of the series. In addition, a bonus music clip of the ending theme song, "Blue Skies," is included. In Episode 7, *Spirits*, six of the eight Dog Warriors have assembled. Chudai, Shino, Sosuke, Genpachi, Kobungo and Dosetsu learn they must work for the Satome clan. Although the young warriors are confused, their destinies are leading them to the war.
VHS: Dubbed. **S29149. $24.95.**
VHS: Subtitled. **S27095. $29.95.**
Laser: CAV, multi-audio. **LD75452. $39.95.**
A.I.C., Japan, 1993, 60 mins.

Hakkenden Vol. 5: Episodes 8 and 9

In Episode 8, Kobungo kills an intruder in self-defense while traveling through a small village. When he is arrested as a suspect, he meets a dog warrior in disguise. In Episode 9, Genpachi puts his life in jeopardy as he pays a visit to the dojo of a famous swordsman. When the swordsman's son harbors Genpachi at his mountain hideaway, Genpachi saves him from a legendary Ghost Cat.
VHS: Dubbed. **S29150. $24.95.**
VHS: Subtitled. **S29152. $29.95.**
Laser: CAV, multi-audio. **LD75754. $39.95.**
A.I.C., Japan, 1993, 60 mins.

Hakkenden Vol. 6: Episodes 10 and 11

In Episode 10, Hamaji's spirit reappears and talks Sosuke into thinking about killing Shino. In the meantime, Shino is caught in a bear trap while wandering about on a mountain. In Episode 11, on the way to see Yoshizane, the seven dog warriors encounter an old foe—one that may have the secret of the eighth dog warrior.
VHS: Dubbed. **S29151. $24.95.**
VHS: Subtitled. **S29153. $29.95.**
Laser: CAV, multi-audio. **LD75585. $39.95.**
A.I.C., Japan, 1993, 60 mins.

Hakkenden Vol. 7: Episodes 12 and 13

In Episode 12, the eight dog warriors finally gather under the Satomi flag. They plan a strategy to attack Hikita's castle and rescue Princess Hamaji, who is being held captive as a human shield by Aboshi and Hikita. In Episode 13, Hikita's troops manage to escape the downed castle and occupy the Satomi's castle instead. The dog warriors must now devise a plan to rescue their brothers and the Princess from the Satomi castle. The fate that the dog warriors are born to gradually leads them into a living hell. The finale to the series.
VHS: Dubbed. **S29553. $24.95.**
VHS: Subtitled. **S29556. $29.95.**
Laser: CAV, multi-audio. **LD75831. $39.95.**
A.I.C., Japan, 1993, 60 mins.

Harmagedon

This futuristic animation is set in a post-nuclear society, as humans defend Earth from raging psychotic demons and a determined, malevolent space god. Character design by *Akira*'s Katsuhiro Otomo.
VHS: Subtitled. **S18745. $29.95.**
VHS: Dubbed. **S28599. $19.95.**
Laser: Subtitled. **LD74508. $49.95.**
Kadokawa, Japan, 1983, 132 mins.

Here Is Greenwood Vol. 1: Episodes 1 and 2

Kazuya Hasukawa is just a regular teenager who wants to live a normal life. But when his first love marries his older brother and moves into their house, Kazuya has to move out to preserve his sanity! He discovers he's been assigned to the strangest dorm on campus—Greenwood—where weirdos, outcasts and lunatics at Ryokuto Academy reside. Stereo.
VHS: Dubbed. **S28458. $24.95.**
VHS: Subtitled. **S28459. $24.95.**
Laser: Multi-audio. **LD75946. $39.95.**
Pierrot, Japan, 1991, 60 mins.

Here Is Greenwood Vol. 2: Episodes 3 and 4

As Ryokuto Academy prepares for its annual school festival, the residents at Greenwood are planning the unthinkable—they're making a movie. If they are voted as the winning group, they'll win enough cash to throw the biggest party the dorm has ever seen. Once the school festivities are over, terror strikes Greenwood! Mitsuru is being haunted by a teenage ghost named Misako, whom at first, everyone but Mitsuru welcomes. And before she passes on to the next world, her only wish is to possess Shinobu's body and kiss Mitsuru! Stereo.

VHS: Dubbed. **S28604. $24.95.**
VHS: Subtitled. **S28605. $24.95.**
Laser: Multi-audio. **LD75955. $39.95.**
Pierrot, Japan, 1991, 60 mins.

Here Is Greenwood Vol. 3: Episodes 5 and 6

Greenwood is in turmoil when a mysterious girl suddenly appears late one night. Mistaken for a gang leader, she's on the run from a rival gang of girl thugs, and begs Mitsuru to let her stay at the dorm. Acting as the new dorm president, Kazuya decides to help the endangered girl, with whom he soon falls in love. The problem: Miya has been involved with another boy for the last ten years! Will Kazuya once again come between a relationship, or has he found true love?

VHS: Dubbed. **S28606. $24.95.**
VHS: Subtitled. **S28607. $24.95.**
Laser: Multi-audio. **LD75954. $39.95.**
Pierrot, Japan, 1991, 60 mins.

Heroic Legend of Arislan, Part 1

When Daryoon, a young but highly skilled officer, voices his reluctance to send men into battle, he is banished for his "cowardice." Daryoon's new mission is to guard the king's only son, Prince Arislan. Daryoon and Prince Arislan convince both Lord Narsus and the archer Elam to join their quest. Meanwhile, a traveling minstrel, Gieve, encounters Pharangese—the beautiful and skilled servant of the Goddess Misra. Pharangese is charged with protecting the prince as well, and soon the group has grown to six.

VHS: Dubbed. **S29154. $19.95.**
VHS: Subtitled. **S19885. $19.95.**
Laser: Subtitled. **LD75755. $34.95.**
Movic, Japan, 1992, 60 mins.

Heroic Legend of Arislan, Part 2

Prince Arislan and his band of warriors must survive a confrontation with 300,000 trained Lusitanian soldiers, among them Silvermask—who also claims to be heir to the throne. Arislan seeks help from the Palse, but must agree to a personal battle to determine the rightful heir to the throne.

VHS: Dubbed. **S21318. $19.95.**
VHS: Subtitled. **S21317. $19.95.**
Laser: Subtitled. **LD74827. $34.95.**
Movic, Japan, 1992, 60 mins.

Heroic Legend of Arislan, Parts 3 & 4

Betrayed from within and overwhelmed by sorcery, Palse's army was burned alive by the religious fanatics of Lusitania, but Arislan escaped to the farthest corner of his realm. Lord Silvermask is chosen to cement the Lusitanian victory by eliminating the fanatic priest Jon Bodan.

VHS: Subtitled. **S23335. $19.95.**
VHS: Dubbed. **S28453. $19.95.**
Laser: Subtitled. **LD75398. $34.95.**
Movic, Japan, 1993, 60 mins.

The Humanoid

Dr. Watson is a scientific genius whose crowning achievement is Antoinette, a chrome-bodied android. She commands a strikingly beautiful form and vast knowledge. Yet, she is as a child confronted by a world which seems to elude her intuitive grasp. Amidst political intrigue, Antoinette pursues her Pinocchio-like search for the elusive quality known as humanity.

VHS: Dubbed. **S29155. $14.95.**
VHS: Subtitled. **S15955. $19.95.**
Laser: Subtitled. **LD75756. $29.95.**
Hiro Media, Japan, 1986, 45 mins.

Hyper Doll Act 1

Mew and Mica are cute high school students—and also aliens! They're androids from outer space who came to Earth to capture a creature, but then are ordered to stay to preserve peace on the planet. However, when jellyfish and locust monsters invade Tokyo, Mew and Mica join forces to protect Earth.

VHS: Dubbed. **S29156. $24.95.**
VHS: Subtitled. **S29157. $29.95.**
Laser: Multi-audio. **LD75757. $34.95.**
Japan, 40 mins.

Hyper Doll Act 2

Mew and Mica go to see a fireworks show, but the real fireworks begin when the worm monster Mimizu-man goes after Akai and Shoko! It's Hyper Dolls to the rescue in this action-packed sci-fi comedy from the writer of *Moldiver*!

VHS: Dubbed. **S29158. $19.95.**
VHS: Subtitled. **S29159. $24.95.**
Laser: LD75758. $34.95.
Japan, 40 mins.

Iczelion! Acts 1 & 2

From Toshihiro Hirano comes the climax to his famous Icz-series. Nagisa Kai is a normal girl until fate makes her the combat partner of the intelligent alien battlesuit Iczelion. Now, with three other young women, Nagisa must save the Earth from conquest and total subjugation at the hands/tentacles of an insidious army of invading aliens. It's the "Babes in Battle Armor" adventure every anime fan has been waiting for. Nudity and violence. Subtitled.

VHS: S24700. $24.95.
KSS, Japan, 1994, 60 mins.

Iczer 3 Vol. 1

Years ago, Iczer 1 defeated the evil forces of Big Gold, saving Earth from her monstrous army. But Big Gold left many of her progeny still at large in the galaxy. Iczer 1, now protector of the Cthuwulf, has finally tracked down and destroyed all but the mightiest of Big Gold's children—Neos Gold. Earth's fate suddenly falls into the hands of Iczer 1's younger sister, Iczer 3, who is sent by the Cthuwulf to defend the planet until Iczer 1 can regain her strength. Nudity. Subtitled.

VHS: S21284. $29.95.
Laser: LD75759. $34.95.
Artmic, Japan, 1991, 60 mins.

Iczer 3 Vol. 2

Now, without two of her best allies and the trust of her new Earth comrades, Iczer 3 must prepare for battle alone. While Iczer 3 leaves the ship to fight Neos herself, Neos is busily experimenting with her newly captured power source and creates a new opponent made especially to battle the diminutive warrior. In the midst of a battle with the beast woman Bigro and her deadly pet, Iczer 3 encounters Atros, an exact copy of herself! Now Iczer 3 must face an opponent with all her power and knowledge. Nudity. Subtitled.

VHS: S21285. $29.95.
Laser: LD75050. $34.95.
Artmic, Japan, 1991, 60 mins.

Iczer 3 Vol. 3

As the crew of the *Queen Fuji* finally reaches Neos' base and Iczer 1 arrives to help, Iczer 3 has her hands full dealing with Atros, Golem and the newly-revived Iczer 2. While Iczer 2 helps finish Atros' job, Atros is becoming more and more confused as to where her loyalties lie. The saga of the Iczers concludes in an epic struggle of violence and sacrifice, as Neos reveals her new, terrifying form to us while the world edges closer to absolute destruction. Nudity. Subtitled.

VHS: S21286. $29.95.
Laser: LD75397. $34.95.
Artmic, Japan, 1991, 60 mins.

Iczer-One Vol. 1: Acts One & Two

The Earth has been targeted for invasion by the alien Cthuwulf. Nagisa Kano becomes the key to Earth's defense when she is forced to become the partner of Iczer-One: a rebel battling the alien invaders. In *Act One*, Nagisa and Iczer-One meet when the Cthuwulf attack. In *Act Two*, Nagisa befriends a young girl while Iczer-One investigates the Cthuwulf fortress. Screenplay, character design and direction by Toshihiro Hirano. Nudity & violence. Dubbed.

VHS: S18107. $14.95.
Kubo Shoten/A.I.C., Japan, 1985/86, 60 mins.

Iczer-One Vol. 2: Act Three

Nagisa and Iczer-One battle Iczer-Two's mecha, Iczer-Sigma. Later, Big Gold, the leader of the Cthuwulf, orders Nagisa's capture and conversion into Iczer-Two's partner. Nudity & violence. Dubbed.

VHS: S18169. $14.95.
Kubo Shoten/A.I.C., Japan, 1987, 48 mins.

The Complete Iczer-One

Contains *Iczer-One Acts 1* through *3* in a subtitled format. Nudity and violence. Subtitled.

VHS: S30271. $24.95.
Kubo Shoten/A.I.C., Japan, 1985-87, 108 mins.

Iria: Zeiram the Animation Vol. 1: Episodes 1 and 2

Zeiram is a monster feared in every corner of the galaxy. Iria, an apprentice bounty hunter, accompanies her brother and his boss on a mission to rescue a VIP and a mysterious cargo from the hijacked starship *Karma*. A corporation has imported Zeiram for use as a new bio-weapon, but now it's loose. Only Iria and her sidekick, Kei, can halt the monster's rampage.

VHS: Subtitled. **S27343. $29.95.**
VHS: Dubbed. **S28595. $19.95.**
Japan, 60 mins.

Iria: Zeiram the Animation Vol. 2: Episodes 3 and 4

Iria's on the run from a major conspiracy, and someone's out to silence her before she can learn the truth. All she knows is that she holds the key to exposing the Tedan Tippedai Corporation and their link to the monster Zeiram. But Iria is not alone. A mysterious client has hired another bounty hunter to keep her alive.

VHS: Subtitled. **S27405. $29.95.**
VHS: Dubbed. **S28596. $19.95.**
Japan, 60 mins.

Iria: Zeiram the Animation Vol. 3: Episodes 5 and 6

All hell breaks loose in the finale to the series. Iria faces Zeiram for their final battle and discovers the awful truth behind her brother's disappearance and her own connection to the monster. She has a dangerous plan to discover Zeiram's weakness, but will she be able to escape the trap the authorities have set?

VHS: Subtitled. **S27406. $29.95.**
VHS: Dubbed. **S28597. $19.95.**
Japan, 60 mins.

Iron Virgin Jun

When the Asuka family arranges a marriage for their lovely daughter Jun, she rebels and runs off with a trusted servant. Convinced that her aversion to the marriage is due to unfamiliarity with sex, the family hires a gang to hunt her down and introduce her to the carnal pleasures. Little does the gang realize that she's not called the "iron" virgin for nothing. Sex and violence. Subtitled.

VHS: S33567. $29.95.
Go Nagai, Japan, 1992, 45 mins.

The Irresponsible Captain Tylor 1: Most Irresponsible Man in Space

This 26-episode TV series has been at the top of anime fans' "must-see" list for years. In the distant future, the Raalgon Empire has declared war on the over-extended UPSF defense force. Knowing they're desperate for recruits, the complacent, bumbling Justy Tylor manages to charm his way into command of a UPSF starship. Disliked and distrusted even by his own crew, the new Captain Tylor takes his ship out to search of the enemy in defense of the homeland. Serendipity triumphs over incompetence as the bumbling Tylor manages to luck into enough success to acquire an unearned reputation as a brilliant tactician. Episodes 1-4. Subtitled.

VHS: S32355. $19.95.
Japan, 100 mins.

The Irresponsible Captain Tylor 2: Bring Me the Head of Capt. Tylor!

Four episodes. Subtitled.

VHS: S32356. $19.95.
Japan, 100 mins.

The Irresponsible Captain Tylor 3: Boldly Going Nowhere

Three episodes. Unable to deal with Tylor's embarrasing successes, his commanders have banished him to the boondocks. However, if he can get planetside and complete the paperwork, Tylor will be spared the ultimate humiliation. Subtitled.

VHS: S33580. $19.95.
Japan, 75 mins.

The Irresponsible Captain Tylor 4: Escape Times Three

Three episodes. Fed up with Tylor's dumb luck, the Raalgon have targeted his ship specifically. Admiral Donan is authorized to dedicate a sizeable portion of the fleet against the Soyokaze and its crew. Subtitled.

VHS: S33581. $19.95.
Japan, 75 mins.

The Irresponsible Captain Tylor 5: Strange Love

Three episodes. With Admiral Donan gone, the Raalgon go all out to capture Tylor alive. The only way to save his crew is to surrender himself. Subtitled.

VHS: S33860. $19.95.
Japan, 75 mins.

The Irresponsible Captain Tylor 6: Irresponsibly Responsible

Three episodes. As the Soyokaze races back to him (against orders), Tylor finds himself targeted by both the Raalgon fleet and his own UPSF. Subtitled.

VHS: S33861. $19.95.
Japan, 75 mins.

The Irresponsible Captain Tylor: A Farewell to Responsibility

To win the war, Captain Tylor must figure out a way to have both the UPSF and the Raalgon forces emerge victorious. Japanese with English subtitles. 75 mins.

VHS: S34301. $19.95.

The Irresponsible Captain Tylor: Leave It to Tylor

This time Tylor has gotten himself in so much trouble that he's scheduled to be executed for treason. He'll have to single-handedly defeat the entire Raalgon armada to get out of this one. Japanese with English subtitles. 75 mins.

VHS: S34300. $19.95.

The Irresponsible Captain Tylor: Prepack 1
The first 14 episodes. Subtitled.
VHS: $33582. $79.95.
Japan, 350 mins.

Johnny Sokko and His Flying Robot: Episodes 1 and 2
The evil alien Emperor Guillotine is set on world domination. Though Johnny Sokko is a young boy, together with his robot friend he alone can save the world from Emperor Guillotine's terrifying plans. This video includes the first two episodes of the series: *Dracalon, The Great Sea Monster* and *Nucleon, The Magic Globe*.
VHS: $27076. $9.98.

Johnny Sokko and His Flying Robot: Episodes 3 and 4
This tape features the third and fourth episodes of the *Johnny Sokko* series: *Gargoyle Vine, A Space Plant* and *Tyrox, A Strange Monster*.
VHS: $27077. $9.98.

Johnny Sokko and His Flying Robot: Episodes 5 and 6
In *Destroy the Dam* and *The Transformed Humans*, Johnny and his 100-foot tall robot friend once again save the planet from the evil Emperor Guillotine.
VHS: $27078. $9.98.

Johnny Sokko and His Flying Robot: Episodes 7 and 8
The final volume in the *Johnny Sokko* series, this tape features *Dragon, The Ninja Monster* and *The Gigantic Claw*, both of which offer more exciting stories of Johnny and his robot friend.
VHS: $27079. $9.98.

Judge
Ryuichi Murakami is a successful corporate executive involved in embezzlement and murder. But there's more to this world than corporate greed and the laws of man. The dead have their own code, and they've chosen the Judge of Darkness and his Demons of Hell to enforce it. Yet when vengeance seems certain, even the damned have rights and the screen erupts in cataclysmic battles. In the most terrifying courtroom case ever presented, the trial reaches its climax before the Ten Kings of Hell. Nudity and violence. Subtitled.
VHS: Subtitled. **$21836. $29.95.**
VHS: Dubbed. **$28452. $14.95.**
Futabasha, Japan, 1991, 50 mins.

Key: The Metal Idol, Vol. 1
Her nickname is "Key," as in the key to a strange mystery. She is an android who appears just like an ordinary girl, but when her creator dies, she is left with a body that will never age. A mysterious message suggests she can become more human if she wins the love of 30,000 people. Three episodes.
VHS: Dubbed. **$31000. $24.95.**
VHS: Subtitled. **$31001. $29.95.**
Japan, 90 mins.

Key: The Metal Idol, Vol. 2: Awakening
After running into her old school chum, Sakura, in the city, Key now has a place to stay. When she sees a performance by famous pop singer Mihuo Utuse, she begins to get an idea how to find 30,000 friends. Two episodes.
VHS: Dubbed. **$33586. $24.95.**
VHS: Subtitled. **$33583. $29.95.**
Japan, 55 mins.

Key: The Metal Idol, Vol. 3: Believing
Key has been the center of many disasters since coming to the city, from deadly experimental robots to strange "flashes" of humanity. Is it any wonder she believes a strange priest who claims her powers could inspire 30,000 followers? Two episodes.
VHS: Dubbed. **$33587. $24.95.**
VHS: Subtitled. **$33584. $29.95.**
Japan, 55 mins.

Key: The Metal Idol, Vol. 4: Dreaming
Sakura decides to boost Key's career and asks the president of Miho Utsuse's fan club to introduce them to the right people. At an audition, the producer is intrigued even though Key does nothing at all. Two episodes.
VHS: Dubbed. **$33588. $24.95.**
VHS: Subtitled. **$33585. $29.95.**
Japan, 55 mins.

Key: The Metal Idol, Vol. 5: Searching
Key is discovered by a producer who can do anything for a rising star. In this case, he claims he can fulfill her wish to become human. Then Shuichi journeys to Key's hometown to find out more about her past. Two episodes.
VHS: Dubbed. **$32763. $24.95.**
VHS: Subtitled. **$32762. $29.95.**
Japan, 55 mins.

Key the Metal Idol, Vol. 7: Knowing
Key is the "key" to the mystery of the PPOR robots. In this penultimate adventure in the series, Key may become a live human if she can win the love of 30,000 people. 95 mins.
VHS: Dubbed. **$34786. $24.95.**
VHS: Subtitled. **$34787. $29.95.**

Kiki's Delivery Service
This story of a young witch who makes her way in a strange new city was Japan's biggest box-office hit of 1989. Miyazaki brings his beautiful sense of design and atmosphere to this visually sumptuous film that reminds the viewer why he's the Steven Spielberg of Japanese animation. This is the first home video release from the package of eight Miyazaki films picked up by Disney last year. Dubbed.
VHS: $34137. $59.99.
Hayao Miyazaki, Japan, 1989

Kimagure Orange Road Vol. 1
Kyosuke's just your average high-school kid, except that he and his family are cursed with psychic powers they prefer to keep a secret. In a new town, Kyosuke finds two beautiful girls are in love with him, and he can't decide whom he prefers. Two episodes: In *First I'm a Fish, Then I'm a Cat*, Kyosuke has an accident with a family heirloom and swaps souls with the family goldfish and cat. In *Hurricane! Polymorphic-Girl Akane*, Kyouke's cousin Akane visits, complete with her shape-changing powers. Subtitled.
VHS: $16668. $24.95.
Toho/Pierrot, Japan, 1989, 50 mins.

Kimagure Orange Road Vol. 2
Two episodes: In *White Lovers*, an avalanche traps Kyosuke and Madoka in a cave full of the ghosts of young lovers. In *Hawaiian Suspense*, Hikaru is mistaken for a billionaire's daughter and kidnapped. Subtitled.
VHS: $16669. $24.95.
Toho/Pierrot, Japan, 1989, 50 mins.

Kimagure Orange Road Vol. 3
Two episodes: In *Heart of Fire: Spring Is an Idol*, singing idol Hayakawa comes to town and Kyosuke inadvertantly swaps bodies with him. In *Heart of Fire: A Star Is Born*, Kyosuke tries to convince Hayakawa not reveal Kyosuke's powers, while Madoka tries to win the song contest. Subtitled.
VHS: $16670. $24.95.
Toho/Pierrot, Japan, 1989, 50 mins.

Kimagure Orange Road Vol. 4
Two episodes: In *The Unexpected Situation*, Kyosuke has a date with Akane. In *Message in Rouge*, Madoka runs away from home and seeks refuge with Kyosuke. Subtitled.
VHS: $16671. $24.95.
Toho/Pierrot, Japan, 1989, 50 mins.

Kimagure Orange Road Vol. 5: I Want to Return to That Day
A special OAV also known as "The Kimagure Orange Road Movie." Kyosuke and Madoka walk together on the grounds of a University. A chance comment overheard and Kyosuke's thoughts range back…to the previous summer, when he was struggling to prepare for the all-important examinations, amid the myriad distractions of youth…to the previous summer, when Madoka and he finally admitted their feelings for each other…to the previous summer, when he tried not to break Hikaru's heart. Subtitled.
VHS: $17531. $24.95.
Toho/Pierrot, Japan, 1988, 70 mins.

Kimagure Orange Road, Collector's Suite
This Anime boxed set of five videos follows the comic travails of an indecisive teenager who must choose between the love of two girls. The only problem is that he must not reveal his family's secret. They possess psychic gifts. Japanese with English subtitles.
VHS: $25716. $120.00.

Kimagure Orange Road, Laserdisc #1
Contains the first four OVAs in the series (tape volumes 1 & 2). Subtitled.
Laser: LD75760. $39.95.
Toho/Pierrot, Japan, 1989, 100 mins.

Kimagure Orange Road, Laserdisc #2
Contains the second four OVAs in the series (tape volumes 3 & 4). Subtitled.
Laser: LD75761. $39.95.
Toho/Pierrot, Japan, 1989, 100 mins.

Kimagure Orange Road, Laserdisc #3
Contains the "I Want to Return to That Day" movie (tape volume 5). Subtitled.
Laser: LD75762. $39.95.
Toho/Pierrot, Japan, 1989, 73 mins.

Kimba The Lion Prince: Insect Invasion
Two episodes: In *Insect Invasion*, Kimba must stop millions of locusts from eating all the animals' food. In *Troublemaker*, Kimba's evil uncle BooBoo is plotting to turn the animals against each other. With lioness cub Lea, he sets a trap to catch BooBoo and the hyenas. Dubbed.
VHS: $29568. $12.95.
Mushi, Japan, 1966-67, 45 mins.

Kimba The Lion Prince: Jungle Thief
Two episodes: In *Jungle Thief*, the animals look to Kimba to solve a drought and stop a thief who's stealing emergency supplies. In *A Friend Indeed*, Bongo the leopard cub and Kimba start out as enemies, but find friendship. Dubbed.
VHS: $29567. $12.95.
Mushi, Japan, 1966-67, 45 mins.

Kimba The Lion Prince: Legend of the Claw
Two episodes: *Legend of the Claw* is the episode that started it all as Kimba follows in his father's paw prints to become the pride of the jungle. In *The Wind in the Desert*, Kimba is rescued from hunters by his human friend Jonathan. Dubbed.
VHS: $29565. $12.95.
Mushi, Japan, 1966-67, 45 mins.

Kimba The Lion Prince: River Battle
Two episodes: In *River Battle*, Kimba battles a giant python but must still prove he's as wise and strong as his father. In *Human Friend*, Jonathan shows that not all humans are hunters. Dubbed.
VHS: $29566. $12.95.
Mushi, Japan, 1966-67, 45 mins.

Kimera
At war with humanity and each other, and driven by the most terrifying of genetic imperatives, vampires walk the Earth. Like wasps seeking a spider, they have come to this planet to perpetuate their species. Nudity and graphic violence.
VHS: Dubbed. **$33863. $19.95.**
VHS: Subtitled. **$33862. $29.95.**
Toho/Animate, Japan, 1996, 60 mins.

Kishin Corps #1: Episode 1
The Kishin Corps guards Earth with the help of a giant robot developed from captured alien armor. *Episode 1*: In October 1941, a Manchurian train is stopped and boarded by a Kanto Army division looking for Takamura and his "black lunch box." As aliens descend from the sky, Takamura's son Taishi escapes with the box in the confusion, only to quickly be trapped again.
VHS: Dubbed. **$29160. $24.95.**
VHS: Subtitled. **$23065. $29.95.**
Laser: CAV, multi-audio. **LD74653. $39.95.**
AIC, Japan, 1993, 57 mins.

Kishin Corps #2: Episodes 2 and 3
Surprise Attack! and *The Battle*: Will the Kishin Corps and Taishi be able to retrieve the module as they head out to the Kanto Army's Fortress Island? And will they obtain the Kanto Army's module body as they battle head-to-head on the railroad tracks of Manchuria?
VHS: Dubbed. **$29161. $24.95.**
VHS: Subtitled. **$23066. $29.95.**
Laser: CAV, multi-audio. **LD74654. $39.95.**
AIC, Japan, 1993, 60 mins.

Kishin Corps #3: Episodes 4 and 5
Kishin vs. Panzer Knight Parts 1 and *2*: The Nazis' alliance with aliens has created the Panzer Kavalier! This new foe appears as the Kishin Heidan attempts to protect an important scientist. But the module is stolen again!
VHS: Dubbed. **$29162. $24.95.**
VHS: Subtitled. **$24239. $29.95.**
Laser: CAV, multi-audio. **LD74818. $39.95.**
AIC, Japan, 1993, 60 mins.

Kishin Corps #4: Episodes 6 and 7
Storming The Base of the Alien Foe and *Youth to the Rescue*: The Kanto Army pursues Taishi and his module. If taken from Taishi, the module can strengthen the Kanto Army. Meanwhile, the Nazis use the aliens' technology to pursue their conquest of the world.
VHS: Dubbed. **$29163. $24.95.**
VHS: Subtitled. **$25677. $29.95.**
Laser: CAV, multi-audio. **LD74990. $39.95.**
AIC, Japan, 1993, 60 mins.

Kishin—The Symphony
The heart-pounding music of the Kishin Heidan series is performed by the Shinsei Japan Orchestra and the Shinsei Nikkyo Chorus under the direction of Kaoru Wada at the Showa Women's University. Also includes other musical excerpts. Japanese with English subtitles, 60 mins.
Laser: LD74991. $39.98.

KOR Whimsical Highways LD Set

Can an indecisive teenager choose between two girls who love him without exposing his family's psychic gifts? There is never a dull moment on whimsical Kimagure Orange Road in this feature length animated film.
Laser: **LD74606. $110.00.**

Landlock, Part 1

The land of Zer'lue is in turmoil, ravaged by the technological might of Chairman Sana'ku and his evil, militaritic Zul'earth forces. In a rapidly unfolding story of treachery, deceit and betrayal, only one boy holds the power to defeat such overwhelming odds…a boy named Lue'der, who possesses a mysterious red eye and the ability to control the power of the wind. Violence and nudity.
VHS: Dubbed. **S33704. $19.95.**
VHS: Subtitled. **S33705. $24.95.**
Japan, 30 mins.

Leda: The Fantastic Adventures of Yohko

Yohko Asagiri is a typical high school student with a crush on a boy. She composes a song to explain her feelings to him, but there's a problem. The song magically transports her to the dimensional sister-world of Earth, Ashanti. She and her new friends there must stop an army from invading Earth.
VHS: Dubbed. **S31159. $19.95.**
VHS: Subtitled. **S31158. $19.95.**
Japan, 75 mins.

Legend of Lemnear

As the Dark Lord's legions spread across the land, Lemnear, the fabled Champion of Silver, searches for vengeance. She hunts for the wizard Gardein and his evil master to avenge the slaughter of her people. Within Lemnear lies an invincible power that could change the course of history and free mankind—a power the Dark Lord will do anything to possess. Subtitled.
VHS: S26899. $29.95.
Japan, 45 mins.

Legend of the Forest

An experimental mini-epic from Osamu Tezuka, set to Tchaikovsky's 4th Symphony. The story deals with the environmental theme of deforestation, while the animation style evolves from black-and-white Winsor McCay-ish to lush-color Disney-esque. A visually stunning and beautifully conceived film that pays visual homage to every major stylistic influence in animation history.
VHS: S21283. $12.95.
Laser: Includes two *Astro Boy* episodes. **LD75055. $39.95.**
Osamu Tezuka, Japan, 1987, 30 mins.

Leo the Lion Vol. 1: The First Adventure

Young Chris is abandoned in the jungle and befriended by Leo. Chris, Leo and Leah then set out to find Chris's kidnapped grandfather.
VHS: S29388. $6.95.
Japan, 25 mins.

Leo the Lion Vol. 2: The Map of Danger

Leo sends his jungle friends out to survey the danger spots and enemies.
VHS: S29389. $6.95.
Japan, 25 mins.

Leo the Lion Vol. 3: The Blue Lion

While seeking a cure for his wife Leah's illness, Leo encounters Zamba, the ferocious Blue Lion.
VHS: S29390. $6.95.
Japan, 25 mins.

Leo the Lion Vol. 4: Leo Becomes a Father

Leah gives birth to Roonie and Rookie.
VHS: S29391. $6.95.
Japan, 25 mins.

Leo the Lion Vol. 5: The Mighty Gorilla

Rookie makes friends with Dwimog the gorilla, and helps him battle the mandrills.
VHS: S29392. $6.95.
Japan, 25 mins.

Leo the Lion Vol. 6: The Golden Bow

Leo meets the king of another tribe and together they conquer a new enemy.
VHS: S29393. $6.95.
Japan, 25 mins.

Leo the Lion Vol. 7: The Case of the Moonlight Stone

British agent Sterling Bond enlists Leo in a search for the famous Moonlight Stone.
VHS: S29394. $6.95.
Japan, 25 mins.

Leo the Lion Vol. 8: The Saber-Toothed Tiger

Leo and Roonie travel back in time and befriend a mammoth and a sabertooth.
VHS: S29395. $6.95.
Japan, 25 mins.

Locke the Superman

The intergalactic wars have begun. The federal army is no match for Lady Chan's legion of robotic soldiers. Defeat is at hand. Only the super-powered Locke, now a peace-loving civilian, can save the Earth. Will Locke come to the rescue of his doomed planet? Can he resist the beautiful but traitorous Jessica, sent to destroy him? Are his superhuman powers and untra-destructive lightning sword strong enough to defeat the villainous onslaught? The final showdown awaits aboard a monstrous asteroid spaceship. Dubbed.
VHS: S29164. $19.95.
Nippon Anim., Japan, 1984, 120 mins.

Luna Varga Vol. 1

What comes between a girl and her dragon? If she's Princess Luna, absolutely nothing! Mostly because Luna has inadvertantly invoked the ancient spell that summoned Varga, a 200-foot-tall mythical beast. In doing so, Luna finds herself stuck on her dragon's forehead…permanently. The bad news is that it's her rear end attached to the dragon. The good news is that Varga can shrink himself down to a vestigial tail that only ruins the cut of Luna's dress. Nudity, violence and profanity. Subtitled.
VHS: S27016. $29.95.
Japan, 60 mins.

Luna Varga Vol. 2

The insanity continues as Luna and her giant dragon Varga battle an army of invading demons, a giant sea serpent, a mad magician, a gluttonous general, an extremely ill-behaved barbarian berserker and a slew of shape-changing soldiers. Can Luna and Varga stop them? The conclusion of the series. Nudity, violence and profanity. Subtitled.
VHS: S27345. $29.95.
Japan, 60 mins.

Lupin III #1: Albatross: Wings of Death

Taken from Tokyo Movie Shinsha's classic TV series of the world's greatest cat burglar, this exceptional episode written and directed by Hayao Miyazaki is a fine example of the golden age of Japanese TV animation. Wolf tries to catch a flipped out billionaire who's blackmailing the government with a nuclear-armed airship. Dubbed.
VHS: S17742. $9.95.
TMS, Japan, 1980, 25 mins.

Lupin III #2: Aloha, Lupin

Originally broadcast as the final episode of the second *Lupin III* TV series, studio TMS gave director Hayao Miyazaki carte blanche in order to let the series go out with a bang. The result is the essence of the wit and cleverness of *Lupin III* distilled into one superb effort. A powerful flying robot is stolen from a top secret military arsenal, and Lupin is the suspect. Inspector Zenigata vows to finally capture The Wolf and put an end to his nefarious career. Dubbed.
VHS: S21793. $14.95.
TMS, Japan, 1980, 25 mins.

Lupin III's Greatest Capers

Two episodes from Tokyo Movie Shinsha's classic TV series of the world's greatest cat burglar. *Albatross: Wings of Death* is an exceptional episode directed by Hayao Miyazaki, in which Wolf tries to catch a flipped-out billionaire who's blackmailing the government with a nuclear armed ship. *Aloha Lupin* was broadcast as the final episode of the second *Lupin III* TV series, and director Miyazaki was given carte blanche to make the series go out with a bang. A powerful flying robot is stolen from a top secret military arsenal, and Lupin is the suspect. Dubbed.
VHS: S25065. $19.95.
TMS, Japan, 1980, 50 mins.

Lupin III: The Mystery of Mamo

An exciting, satirical and amorous feature-length animated film. Lupin succeeds in pulling off a series of seemingly impossible capers in order to score "big-time" with Fujiko, his beautiful arch-rival. Curiously, all of the capers involve some arcane object associated with eternal life. But there is more to Lupin's schemes than a simple one-night stand. His efforts result in a date with destiny as he faces the mysterious Mamo—his most deadly opponent. Nudity. Dubbed.
VHS: S25069. $29.95.
Monkey Punch, Japan, 1978, 102 mins.

Machine Robo: Revenge of Cronos, Vol. 1

Episodes 1-5. The planet Cronos is populated by humanoids with metal bodies and transforming machines with human-like personalities. But the forces of the evil Gandora are on their way to capture Master Kirai and the mystical knowledge he holds. Only Kirai's son, Rom, can stop them. Subtitled.
VHS: S32273. $24.95.
Japan

Machine Robo: Revenge of Cronos, Vol. 2

Episodes 6-10. From the home of the mysterious Rock People and the animal-like Leo Clan to the lost island of the Mu civilization, Rom and his allies battle Gandora's Devil Commanders and their allies, the tribes of Cronos. Subtitled.
VHS: S32274. $24.95.
Japan

Macross II: The Movie

Hibiki Kanzaki, an investigative reporter for SNN, inadvertantly allies himself with Ishtar, an enigmatic Zentraedi princess. Enlisting the help of Valkyrie pilot Silvie Gena, Hibiki refuses to save Ishtar from imminent "reprogramming" by hostile Zentraedi. Silvie and Hibiki must broadcast the truth about the Zentraedi invasion and convince the powerful U.N. Spacey to reactivate the Macross fortress and defend Earth one more time. Nudity and profanity.
VHS: Dubbed. **S26640. $19.95.**
VHS: Subtitled. **S29165. $29.95.**
Big West, Japan, 1992, 120 mins.

Macross Plus Part 1

In 2040 AD on the colonial planet Eden, the Ministry of Defense is developing transforming aircraft to counter alien attacks. Isamu Dyson is a jet fighter maverick assigned as a new test pilot on Project Super Nova. He discovers that his old rival Guld is test pilot for the competing project. The arrival of Myung, a mutual ex-girlfriend, adds more tension to the conflict. From the director of *Macross* (*Robotech* in the US). Nudity.
VHS: Dubbed. **S25544. $14.95.**
VHS: Subtitled. **S26236. $24.95.**
Laser: CAV, multi-audio. **LD75763. $34.95.**
Big West, Japan, 1994, 40 mins.

Macross Plus Part 2

Computer-generated mega-pop star Sharon Apple packs in the crowds. Amongst the fans are Isamu Dyson and Yang, who is about to pull off the biggest computer-hacking stunt ever. A computer-transmitted message alarms the pilots that Myung is in danger and both rush to her rescue. Guld emerges a hero and Isamu is jealous. Sparks fly and rivalry turns violent as they meet in aerial combat. Nudity.
VHS: Dubbed. **S29166. $14.95.**
VHS: Subtitled. **S26237. $24.95.**
Big West, Japan, 1994, 40 mins.

Macross Plus Part 3

The UN unveils its hidden agenda and cancels Dyson and Bowman's experimental star fighters in favor of a new, artificially intelligent aircraft. Myung heads for Earth while Dyson hijacks the YF-19 fighter and heads after her. Only one other plane can catch him—the rival YF-21. Bowman climbs aboard and the chase is on. Meanwhile on Earth, the computerized Sharon Apple has become self-aware. Nudity.
VHS: Dubbed. **S29167. $14.95.**
VHS: Subtitled. **S26238. $24.95.**
Big West, Japan, 1994, 40 mins.

Macross Plus Part 4

Isamu and Yang head toward Earth to get even with the pilot-less Valkyrie, *Ghost X-9*. Guld goes after them for a final battle. The two fighters clash amidst interceptor missiles being fired from Earth. Meanwhile in Macross City, Sharon Apple absorbs Myung's thoughts and twists them in a terrifying fashion. She now has full control over the city as well as the minds of its citizens. Sharon sends the *Ghost X-9* after Isamu and Guld. Concludes the series. Nudity.
VHS: Dubbed. **S29168. $14.95.**
VHS: Subtitled. **S27716. $24.95.**
Big West, Japan, 1994, 40 mins.

Macross Plus: The Movie

The OAV series combined into a feature-length film, including 15 minutes of new footage. Nudity. Subtitled.
VHS: S31322. $24.95.
Big West, Japan, 1994, 180 mins.

Madox-01

A parody of the "robot suit" genre. Ace female test pilot Kusomoto Elle defeats macho tank driver Lt. Kilgore in the first demonstration of the advanced personal battle tank, the Madox. Kilgore vows revenge, and gets his chance when the army carelessly loses the prototype in Tokyo. Meanwhile, the Madox is found by Sujimoto Koji, who presses buttons before he has completely read the manual and ends up zooming around trapped in a machine he doesn't quite know how to operate.
VHS: Dubbed. **S26637. $19.95.**
VHS: Subtitled. **S16071. $24.95.**
FujiSankei, Japan, 1987, 48 mins.

Madox-01/Riding Bean Laserdisc

Both films on one video disc. Nudity and violence. Subtitled.
Laser: LD75764. $39.95.
Japan, 94 mins.

Magical Princess Gigi

Our loveable princess from out of this world visits Earth to join her friends for light-hearted adventure and laughs in this Japanese theatrical feature directed by Hiroshi Watanabe.
VHS: S29169. $14.95.
Ashi Prod., Japan, 1985, 80 mins.

Magical Twilight: The HeX Files

Contains all three Magical Twilight episodes. When one innocent mortal becomes the object of three sexy, young witches' desires, the roof of the victim's house isn't the only thing that's ever going to get blown when all three seductive sorceresses square off in a bare everything showdown.
Magical Twilight: The HeX Files, General Release. 75 mins.
VHS: S34813. $29.95.
Magical Twilight: The HeX Files, Uncut. 90 mins.
VHS: S34812. $29.95.

Maison Ikkoku, Vol. 1: Welcome to Maison Ikkoku

Maison Ikkoku is a love story which takes place in Japan—but that doesn't mean it couldn't happen anywhere. You'll fall in love with the wacky inhabitants of the boarding house Maison Ikkoku all over again! Based on the best-selling manga about a bumbling college student who falls in love with his lovely, young, widowed apartment manager.
VHS: Dubbed. **S27457. $24.95.**
VHS: Subtitled. **S29630. $29.95.**
Japan, 52 mins.

Maison Ikkoku, Vol. 2: Ronin Blues

Two episodes. Yusaku is a ronin, a student studying to re-attempt the college entrance exams, but the other residents of his home, the run-down boarding house Maison Ikkoku, are hell-bent on preventing him from hitting the books!
VHS: Dubbed. **S27678. $24.95.**
VHS: Subtitled. **S30272. $29.95.**
Japan, 52 mins.

Maison Ikkoku, Vol. 3: Spring Wasabi

Two episodes. Manager Kyoko panics when Godai's grandmother pays an unannounced visit and Godai is AWOL. But manager Kyoko has secret problems of her own. Now, Godai and the other tenants of Maison Ikkoku are about to find out that even springtime can have its sadness.
VHS: Dubbed. **S29569. $24.95.**
VHS: Subtitled. **S30788. $29.95.**
Japan, 52 mins.

Maison Ikkoku, Vol. 4: Soichiro's Shadow

Godai has finally passed the college entrance exam! But now that his ronin days are behind him, he has to think about finding a part-time job. A request from Kyoko's father-in-law to tutor his granddaughter Ikuko provides Godai with the perfect chance to both earn some spending money and endear himself to Kyoko through her extended family. Then again, Kyoko may not be ready to accept his efforts, not with memories of her beloved late husband Soichiro weighing so heavily on her heart these days. HiFi Stereo. Dubbed.
VHS: S28461. $24.95.
Kitty Films, Japan, 1996, 52 mins.

Maison Ikkoku, Vol. 5: Playing Doubles

Convincing Kyoko that he wasn't some modern-day Tokyo slacker was hard enough, but now Yusaku Godai must face a new rival—a handsome, charming, sophisticated rival who plays a mean game of tennis! Godai is going to have to clean up his act if he ever hopes to score with Maison Ikkoku's beautiful manager. HiFi Stereo. Dubbed.
VHS: S30273. $24.95.
Kitty Films, Japan, 1996, 52 mins.

Maison Ikkoku, Vol. 6: Love Love Story

Two episodes. Now that Kyoko is being romanced by handsome tennis coach Mitaka, she can't exactly complain about an innocent date between Yusaku and his cute young coworker Kozue.
VHS: Dubbed. **S31324. $24.95.**
VHS: Subtitled. **S33593. $29.95.**
Kitty Films, Japan, 1996, 52 mins.

Maison Ikkoku, Vol. 7: Call Me Confused

Two episodes. Yusaku's social calendar suddenly fills up after joining a campus club…but all those phone calls!
VHS: Dubbed. **S30912. $24.95.**
VHS: Subtitled. **S33594. $29.95.**
Kitty Films, Japan, 1996, 52 mins.

Maison Ikkoku, Vol. 8: No Strings Attached

Two episodes. Godai realizes that if Kyoko had not met Soichiro, she would probably be in college herself right now. Then when Kyoko is hurt playing tennis, Godai and coach Mitaka fall all over themselves to comfort her.
VHS: Dubbed. **S31160. $24.95.**
VHS: Subtitled. **S33596. $29.95.**
Kitty Films, Japan, 1996, 52 mins.

Maison Ikkoku, Vol. 9: A Winter's Yarn

Two episodes. Godai happens upon the gift he never gave Kyoko that first special year she came to the boarding house. In return, she gives him a lovingly handmade gift he can wrap himself up in to keep warm. But is he the only special one on her Christmas list?
VHS: Dubbed. **S33597. $24.95.**
VHS: Subtitled. **S32765. $29.95.**
Kitty Films, Japan, 1996, 52 mins.

Maison Ikkoku, Vol. 10: Home for the Holiday

Two episodes. While others plan New Year's trips, Godai looks forward to a low-budget evening with Kyoko and Akemi in front of the TV. When Akemi plans to take a ski trip that means he'll be all alone with Kyoko with no one else in the house.
VHS: Dubbed. **S33599. $24.95.**
VHS: Subtitled. **S33598. $29.95.**
Kitty Films, Japan, 1996, 52 mins.

Maison Ikkoku, Vol. 11: Kyoko & Soichiro

Two episodes. When Godai agrees to take on a house guest, his eavesdropping housemates jump to conclusions. Meanwhile, Manager Kyoko's parents try to convince her to leave her job.
VHS: Dubbed. **S33595. $24.95.**
VHS: Subtitled. **S33592. $29.95.**
Kitty Films, Japan, 1996, 52 mins.

Maison Ikkoku: She's Leaving Home

There's a new threat coming on the horizon: Kozue. While Godai's involved in compromising positions up in Kozue's bedroom, Daddy has a shotgun downstairs. Dubbed in English. 52 mins.
VHS: S32759. $24.95.

Make Way for the Ping Pong Club

The Boys' Ping Pong Club is hormonally driven, distracted by pubescent diversions, and constantly humiliated by the Girls' Team. Salvation rests in the hands of their captain and the intelligence of their new manager. Follow the misadventures of these misfits as they journey toward impending ping-pong doom. Subtitled. 120 mins.
VHS: S34794. $29.95.

Maps 1 & 2

Gen Tokishima and his girlfriend Hoshimi are confronted by half-naked Space Hunter Lipumira and her 60-story-tall spaceship. They are told that as a result of thousands of years of genetic programming, Gen is the only being in the universe who can locate the long-lost crystal Maps that show the way to a priceless artifact hidden millenia ago by a mysterious race of aliens! Immediately, a second hunter's ship arrives and begins destroying the city in search of Gen. This convinces the two to join Lipumira on an interstellar quest for the ultimate treasure. Nudity and violence. Subtitled.
VHS: S25674. $29.95.
KSS/TMS, Japan, 1994, 60 mins.

Maps 3 & 4

For hundreds of years Hunters have searched in vain for the Flowing Light, a priceless artifact hidden by an ancient race, but the beautiful Hunter Lipumira had found the key in the form of Gen. Having located the first set of maps, Gen. Lipumira and Hoshimi are the focus of a galaxy-wide manhunt, with the ultimate treasure as the prize. But first Lipumira must confront a dark shadow from her past and Gen will find himself face-to-face with the most unusual alien of all. Concludes the four-part OAV series. Nudity and violence. Subtitled.
VHS: S25675. $29.95.
KSS/TMS, Japan, 1994, 60 mins.

MD Geist

Using advanced bio-technology, one race has created the MD's: the Most Dangerous Soldiers. MD Geist, the second of these created, finds his way back to his homeworld Jerra to find it threatened with Armageddon. Only he can save his world from the "Death Program."
VHS: Subtitled. **S16703. $14.95.**
VHS: Dubbed. **S29570. $19.95.**
Laser: Subtitled. **LD74511. $34.95.**
Hiro Media, Japan, 1986, 50 mins.

MD Geist II: Death Force

The Death Force has been unleashed and the murderous robots are slaughtering every living thing on the planet. As the surviving remnants of humanity hatch a dangerous plan to destroy the Death Force, Geist goes head-to-head with the prototype Most Dangerous Soldier! Dubbed.
VHS: S29571. $19.95.
Japan

Megami Paradise 1

Enter a world where every girl is literally a goddess! Shielded from the corruption of the outside universe by the purifying Astrostar, the Megami Paradise has long been desired by the evil followers of the Dark Goddesses. Can Lilith and her companions Rurubell, Stasia and Julliana defeat the Dark Goddesses' fearsome champion, or will the Megami Paradise be destroyed? Violence and nudity. Subtitled.
VHS: S27462. $29.95.
Movic, Japan, 1995, 30 mins.

Megami Paradise 2

The forces of the Dark Goddess kidnap Lilith and Astrostar as Lilith prepares to ascend to the position of Mother Goddess. Stasia and Juliana race to the fortress of the Dark Goddess to rescue Lilith before she is sacrificed. Will their combined power be enough to stop the Dark Goddess and rescue their friend? Violence and nudity. Subtitled.
VHS: S27629. $29.95.
Movic, Japan, 1995, 30 mins.

Mermaid's Scar

The sequel to *Mermaid Forest* (see ***Rumik World***). Two ageless wonders, the handsome Yuta and the beautiful Mana, are traveling through Japan to find an end to their immortality. During the journey, they encounter some characters who further unravel the mystery and the curse of the mermaid. Violence and nudity. Dubbed.
VHS: S20148. $19.95.
Rumiko Takahashi, Japan, 52 mins.

Metal Fighters Miku Vol. 1

Episode 1, ***Miku Enters the Ring***; Episode 2, ***Miku Starts Training*** and Episode 3, ***Miku Gets Special Training***. Women's Neo-Pro Wrestling is the most popular sport in the year 2061. It's wrestling with the added twist of equipping its contestants with high-tech powered Metal Suits. Entering this highly competitive sport is The Pretty Four. Miku, Ginko, Sayaka and Nana face the likes of the monstrous Crushers and the deadly Lady Ninjas. Subtitled.
VHS: S26270. $24.95.
Enoki Films, Japan, 90 mins.

Metal Fighters Miku Vol. 2

Episode 4, ***Miku Under Suspicion: The Pretty Four vs. The Maskers*** and Episode 5, ***Miku Turns Chicken: The Pretty Four vs. The Beauties of Nature***. With the arrival of a new girl to join the ranks of the TWP, it looks as though Miku's found both a doting fan and a new friend. But when mysterious accidents begin striking everyone on the team except Miku herself, she's soon under suspicion by everyone around her. Subtitled.
VHS: S26271. $24.95.
Enoki Films, Japan, 60 mins.

Metal Fighters Miku Vol. 3

Episode 6, *Miku Falls Head over Heels: The Moonlight Jewels vs. The Amazons* and Episode 7, *Miku Tells All: The Pretty Four vs. The Star Wolves*. Shibano and his son Naoya are still trying to destroy the TWP, and they've come up with their most devious plot yet: set the Pretty Four up to destroy themselves! This cunning plan takes the form of a two-pronged strike on the girls' morale, with Naoya playing the doting new boyfriend for an unsuspecting Miku while offering Ginko a chance at stardom in the American Neo-Pro Wrestling leagues. Subtitled.

VHS: S26272. $24.95.

Enoki Films, Japan, 60 mins.

Metal Fighters Miku Vol. 4

The Pretty Four leave the semifinals behind in a blaze of victory! But now, Miku and the rest of the girls must prepare for their greatest challenge yet—and their training and skills will be completely useless! The Pretty Four must step into the ring and sing! And now, as the girls try to prepare for their final match against the Moonlight Jewels, can they focus on anything but trying to get the edge on Sapphire's killer team? Subtitled.

VHS: S26273. $24.95.

Enoki Films, Japan, 60 mins.

Metal Fighters Miku Vol. 5

Since the last match was declared invalid, Miku prepares for a rematch with Sapphire. Despite Yohko's insistence that Sapphire can beat Miku fair and square, Shibano plays an underhanded trick anyway, and this time it's all-out war. Subtitled.

VHS: S26274. $24.95.

Enoki Films, Japan, 60 mins.

Metal Fighters Miku Vol. 6

Miku is slated to face the great Aquamarine, the JWMF Champion and Queen of the Neo-Pro Wrestling world, in a one-on-one battle royale, but Miku's starting to have second thoughts. Concludes the series. Subtitled.

VHS: S26275. $24.95.

Enoki Films, Japan, 60 mins.

Mighty Space Miners

Only the bravest and most resourceful of individuals can ever become Mighty Space Miners, the hardworking pilots, scientists and technicians who keep Earth supplied with priceless metals and isotopes from deep-space asteroid mines in the year 2060. This is a stunning film that depicts what happens when a military satellite triggers a catastrophic disaster on a remote asteroid colony. Told from the point of view of a young boy, this film documents the surviving colonists' desperate battle to survive in a hostile environment in which every moment carries the possibility of instant death by fire, cold, radiation or explosive decompression. Featuring realistic depictions of man in space, *Mighty Space Miners* is accurate in every detail.

VHS: Dubbed. **S29180. $19.95.**
VHS: Subtitled. **S26438. $19.95.**

KSS, Japan, 1994, 60 mins.

Miyuki-Chan in Wonderland

She's late! She's late! And When Miyuki-chan meets a skateboarding Playboy bunny, she's going to be even later! Wonderland's never been stranger, as everything from the door to the door-mouse takes on a feminine form. Created by the group of talented artists known as CLAMP, this beautifully animated, condensed version of the classic tale is a visual delight. Subtitled.

VHS: S29574. $29.95.

CLAMP, Japan, 35 mins.

Moldiver #1: Metamorforce

Tokyo 2045: the year the Mysterious Superhuman appears. Name: Moldiver. Mira Ozora discovers his true identity: her brother Hiroshi. Hiroshi, discoverer of the Supersuit; when worn, endows the wearer with absolute, infinite power—power to twist the laws of physics and repel all forces of the outer world. Mira is young, gorgeous and helpful. She becomes the Moldiver, too! Nudity.

VHS: Dubbed. **S29174. $19.95.**
VHS: Subtitled. **S23067. $24.95.**
Laser: CAV, multi-audio. **LD74647. $34.95.**

AIC, Japan, 1993, 30 mins.

Moldiver #2: Overzone

Hiroshi is off to Florida for a business trip. Nozumo tags along to attend a concert by Amy Lean. Mirai remains in Japan to pay off her numerous bills, but when she finds that her admired Mr. Misaki is in Florida with her love rival Mao, duty must be set aside. A very piqued Mirai changes into Moldiver and soars off to Florida. Meanwhile, at the concert, the Space Shuttle is hijacked by Machinegal in yet another of his evil plans. Nudity.

VHS: Dubbed. **S29175. $19.95.**
VHS: Subtitled. **S23068. $24.95.**
Laser: CAV, multi-audio. **LD74648. $34.95.**

AIC, Japan, 1993, 30 mins.

Moldiver #3: Longing

An ecstatic Mirai arranges to meet Mr. Misaki, but they miss each other. Frustrated, she searches everywhere with Metamorforce. The Machinegal dolls gather after tracking her Mol reaction and a tremendous battle ensues over Tokyo, causing even greater inconvenience. Nudity.

VHS: Dubbed. **S29176. $19.95.**
VHS: Subtitled. **S23069. $24.95.**
Laser: CAV, multi-audio. **LD74649. $34.95.**

AIC, Japan, 1993, 30 mins.

Moldiver #4: Destruction

Professor Amagi directs the *Yamato* salvage, but his actual motive is to continue his grandfather's unfinished study: The Ultra Dimension System, which sank with the *Yamato* 100 years before. However, Nozomu covertly discovers the secret of The Moltron, and starts the system, causing a mysterious power to overtake the Yamato and Moldiver! Nudity.

VHS: Dubbed. **S29177. $19.95.**
VHS: Subtitled. **S23070. $24.95.**
Laser: CAV, multi-audio. **LD74650. $34.95.**

AIC, Japan, 1993, 30 mins.

Moldiver #5: Intruder

The Mol-unit is successfully divided into #1 and #2. But the rocket that Misaki will board is on the way to a launch site at Mount Fuji. Hurriedly Mirai transforms to Moldiver II and pursues him, coming face-to-face with Machinegal's Superdolls, who plan to stop the project from going forward. Nudity.

VHS: Dubbed. **S29178. $19.95.**
VHS: Subtitled. **S23071. $24.95.**
Laser: CAV, multi-audio. **LD74651. $34.95.**

AIC, Japan, 1993, 30 mins.

Moldiver #6: Verity

Sakigake continues to speed up in preparation for launch; however Moldiver II tries to stop the proceedings. The *Sakigake* is launched into space, where there is yet another obstacle. Then Isabelle challenges Mirai to defend her dignity. Can Mirai keep her word to Misaki and save the *Sakigake*? The final episode of the OAV series. Nudity.

VHS: Dubbed. **S29179. $19.95.**
VHS: Subtitled. **S23072. $24.95.**
Laser: CAV, multi-audio. **LD74652. $34.95.**

AIC, Japan, 1993, 30 mins.

My Dear Marie

When a mad scientist attempts to build a robotic duplicate of his dream girl, Marie is the result. But he built her too well and Marie has a mind of her own and a whole host of questions to go with it. Includes three episodes. Japanese with English subtitles. 90 mins.

VHS: S34534. $29.95.

My My Mai Vol. 1

Mai is a super counselor with blazing sex appeal. She'll be happy to solve anyone's problems or troubles with a lot of devotion and motherly love—but male clients are preferred. In *Part 1*, Mai is consulted by the family of a dying girl, and must locate the mysterious Dr. Shinobi. But time is running out, and Mai has no idea what the good doctor looks like or where to find him! In *Part 2*, Mai must cure a famous rock star of his phobias—using her own, special brand of shock therapy! Nudity and adult situations. Stereo. Dubbed.

VHS: S28454. $19.95.

Y. Masakazu, Japan, 1993, 45 mins.

My My Mai Vol. 2

In *Part 1*, Kazumi's near death, and Mai and Dr. Shinobi haven't shown up yet! A mysterious stranger, Yua, arrives and diagnoses the problem as demonic possession! In *Part 2*, Mai and company take some time off and head for a summer resort—which turns out to be haunted! Will Mai be able to solve the mystery and exorcise the "non-paying residents" once and for all? Nudity and adult situations. Stereo. Dubbed.

VHS: S30175. $19.95.

Y. Masakazu, Japan, 1993, 45 mins.

My Neighbor Totoro

Written, produced and directed by Hayao Miyazaki, *Totoro* is a lovely, delicate story touching on many Shinto traditions. Upon moving to the country, two young girls discover the magical forest creature Totoro, and develop a friendship. The visual design is lushly beautiful and the story is charming. To use an overworked term, this film is delightful. Dubbed.

VHS: S21354. $19.95.
Laser: LD74635. $29.95.

Tokuma, Japan, 1993, 87 mins.

My Youth in Arcadia

When aliens conquer and enslave the human race, all hope for freedom is abandoned. But one man will not give up. Captain Harlock, a brave space pilot, leads the resistance and vows to oust the aliens and restore freedom to his planet. Harlock and his rebel band adopt the fighting strategies of ancient marauders and become known as The Space Pirates…with a skull and crossbones on their atomic-powered spaceship. But the revolution is not without a price and The Space Pirate must make a difficult choice. Dubbed.

VHS: S29181. $19.95.

Toei, Japan, 1982, 130 mins.

Nadia Movie Compilation

The 39-episode TV series *Nadia: Secret of the Blue Water* was animated by Gainax Ltd., the studio which created the theatrical feature *The Wings of Honneamise* and the OAV series *Gunbuster*. The plot construction is crafted so that every four episodes of the 39 total form a sort of "mini-feature." In the first four, presented here, Nadia and Jean are introduced to each other, they begin their adventure, and conclude their first encounter with Captain Nemo. Multi-audio. HiFi Stereo.

Laser: Multi-audio. **LD71943. $39.95.**

Gainax, Japan, 1989, 90 mins.

Neo-Tokyo

Three fantastic adventures by Japan's top animation artists including *Labyrinth*, directed by Rin Taro; *The Running Man*, featured on MTV's *Liquid Television*, a cyberpunk thriller; and *The Order to Stop Construction*, a grim sci-fi comedy in which a bureaucrat manages robots deep in the Amazon. 50 mins. English language version.

Laser: LD75031. $34.99.

Neon Genesis Evangelion, Genesis 0:1

In the year 2015, the awesome alien war machines The Angels return to Tokyo. Only the humanoid fighting machine Evangelion, piloted by teenager Shinji Ikari, stands in their way. Can Shinji find the courage and strength to not only fight, but survive, or risk losing everything? HiFi Stereo.

VHS: Dubbed. **S29578. $24.95.**
VHS: Subtitled. **S29575. $29.95.**

Gainax, Japan, 60 mins.

Neon Genesis Evangelion, Genesis 0:2

With the lives of every soul on Earth at stake, the Evangelion pilots must reach down deep for the courage to meet the Angels head on, and NERV must pierce the veil of mystery surrounding the Angels. Why was Earth attacked? And why were the only Evangelion-qualified pilots all born exactly nine months after the giant meteor impact that annihilated half the human race? HiFi Stereo.

VHS: Dubbed. **S30488. $24.95.**
VHS: Subtitled. **S30489. $29.95.**

Gainax, Japan, 60 mins.

Neon Genesis Evangelion, Genesis 0:3

High-tech action, blistering battles and spectacular visuals merge in the animated series that exceeds space opera to question the very nature of being human. One of the most controversial series ever produced in Japan. HiFi Stereo.

VHS: Dubbed. **S30395. $24.95.**
VHS: Subtitled. **S30396. $29.95.**

Gainax, Japan, 60 mins.

Neon Genesis Evangelion, Genesis 0:4

When a low-cost replacement for the EVAs malfunctions, Shinji and Masato must stop it before it destroys the city and military base at Atsugi. Then, the convoy transporting a new EVA is attacked by an Angel and Unit 02 is activated for an underwater battle.

VHS: Dubbed. **S31325. $24.95.**
VHS: Subtitled. **S31327. $29.95.**

Gainax, Japan, 1995-96, 60 mins.

Neon Genesis Evangelion, Genesis 0:5: Magma Diver

NERV is faced with an Angel that splits into two. Shinji and Asuka must learn to coordinate in order to challenge it. Then, Asuka dives into a volcano to retrieve a dormant Angel.

VHS: Dubbed. **S31326. $24.95.**
VHS: Subtitled. **S31328. $29.95.**

Gainax, Japan, 1995-96, 60 mins.

Neon Genesis Evangelion, Genesis 0:6: Day Tokyo 3 Stood Still

When a power failure cripples Tokyo 3, Gendo and Ritsuko must prepare the EVAs for combat anyway. As the largest Angel yet attacks, Shinji, Asuka and Rei must find their way through NERV's subterranean crawlways to the launch bays.

VHS: Dubbed. **S33605. $24.95.**
VHS: Subtitled. **S33600. $29.95.**

Gainax, Japan, 1995-96, 60 mins.

Neon Genesis Evangelion, Genesis 0:7: Invasion

As the three EVA pilots sit unprotected in their cockpits, a new Angel attacks Tokyo 3's supercomputers. Waves of neural attacks slam NERV while Ritsuko races to decipher the secrets buried inside the MAGI.
VHS: Dubbed. **S33606. $24.95.**
VHS: Subtitled. **S33601. $29.95.**
Gainax, Japan, 1995-96, 60 mins.

Neon Genesis Evangelion, Genesis 0:8: Lies & Silence

Betrayals erupt across NERV as Kaji becomes loyal to a higher authority. The discovery of what's inside a top-secret hanger is enough to shake anyone's faith in mankind. An Angel absorbs Unit 01 and Shinji's mind begins to collapse as hallucinations assault his sanity.
VHS: Dubbed. **S33607. $24.95.**
VHS: Subtitled. **S33602. $29.95.**
Gainax, Japan, 1995-96, 60 mins.

Neon Genesis Evangelion, Genesis 0:9: The Fourth Child

The first test of the new EVA Unit 03 turns into a disaster when the giant bio-humanoid goes insane and runs amok. The monstrous power of Unit 01 is unleashed and it becomes horrifyingly apparent that the EVAs are far more than machines.
VHS: Dubbed. **S33608. $24.95.**
VHS: Subtitled. **S33603. $29.95.**
Gainax, Japan, 1995-96, 60 mins.

Neon Genesis Evangelion, Genesis 0:10: Weaving a Story

In order to save his friends, Shinji must not only conquer his fears, but also fight for his very life and soul in the belly of the beast itself. Discover the terrifying truth behind the sinister mask of the EVA.
VHS: Dubbed. **S33609. $24.95.**
VHS: Subtitled. **S33604. $29.95.**
Gainax, Japan, 1995-96, 60 mins.

Neon Genesis Evangelion, Genesis 0:11

The secret workings of NERV and Gendo Ikari's agenda are becoming clear and mind-reeling possibilities may soon become reality. What was once God's domain has become NERV's playground.
VHS: Dubbed. **S34040. $19.95.**
VHS: Subtitled. **S34041. $29.95.**
Gainax, Japan, 1995-96, 60 mins.

Neon Genesis Evangelion, Genesis 0:12: Rei III

With Asuka traumatized from her last Angelic encounter and unable to fight, Rei must make a terrible sacrifice in order to save NERV. As the survivors sift through the wreckage of their lives in a desperate bid to come to terms with the horrible consequences of the latest battle, a guilt-ridden Ritsuko summons Shinji and Misato to a secret chamber for an even more startling revelation. 60 mins.
VHS: Dubbed. **S34808. $24.95.**
VHS: Subtitled. **S34809. $29.95.**

Neon Genesis Evangelion, Genesis 0:13: A World Ending

The shocking conclusion to the controversial animated series. Third impact has occurred, the world has ended, and now Shinji must go alone where Angels fear to tread. At last the circle of life will be complete.
VHS: Dubbed. **S34530. $24.95.**
VHS: Subtitled. **S34531. $29.95.**

Neon Genesis Evangelion: Deluxe Collection LD

The first four episodes on a multi-audio CAV laserdisc.
Laser: **LD76025. $59.95.**
Gainax, Japan, 1995-96, 120 mins.

New Dominion Tank Police Vol. 1: Episodes 1 and 2

Kobe, Japan—2100 AD. Terrorism runs rampant in the ruins of Newport City. Led by Leona and her tank Bonepart, the Tank Police strike back. Thrown into the mix are the mercenary Puma Sisters, who will side with anyone willing to pay their price. Episode 1, *Launch Tank Police*: Ignoring the mayor's orders to tone down their tactics, the Tank Police blast their way into the middle of a mysterious terrorist attack involving the chief of police. Episode 2, *Charles Brenten, Master Detective*: Leona's friend is murdered. Bent on revenge, Leona quits her job to track down the killer, and finds herself captured by the terrorists. Nudity. Dubbed. HiFi Stereo.
VHS: **S25543. $14.95.**
S. Masamune, Japan, 1993, 60 mins.

New Dominion Tank Police Vol. 2: Episodes 3 and 4

In *Limit the Tube Way*, a Dai Nippon Giken truck is out of control, destroying everything in its path. Its cargo: enough Liberium W23 to obliterate a city. Headquarters attempts to shut down its automatic pilot, but unknown terrorists have taken control of the truck via satellite. In *The Chase*, under cover of the biochemical smog engulfing Newport City, the Cat Sisters manage to steal Bonaparte on behalf of a mysterious gang. The gang plans to eliminate the Cat Sisters after retrieving secrets hidden within Bonaparte. Nudity. Dubbed. HiFi Stereo.
VHS: **S26243. $14.95.**
S. Masamune, Japan, 1993, 60 mins.

New Dominion Tank Police Vol. 3: Episodes 5 and 6

In *Conflict City*, Leona and Brenten report to the mayor's house and see a high-maneuver combat robot. Leona rescues the wounded mayor and finds out the robot is the property of the Dainihon Giken Corporation. In *The End of Dreaming*, the two military research corporations plan an all-out assault on the mayor at Newport City Hospital. The Tank Police surround the building and wait in anticipation for a surprise attack by Coldsman's combat robot. Concludes the series. Nudity. Dubbed. HiFi Stereo.
VHS: **S26378. $14.95.**
S. Masamune, Japan, 1993, 60 mins.

Night on the Galactic Railroad

Based on the 1927 Japanese literary classic, this is a fable of magic and symbolism. Giovanni is a poor boy whose life is filled with hardship. But his life is about to change. While staring into the starry sky, a mysterious galactic train appears. Together with his only friend, Campanella, Giovanni travels the constellations of the Milky Way, where he witnesses inspiring beauty, tragic loss and the splendors of the universe. Together, the boys experience a voyage of inner discovery that will transform them forever. Subtitled. Stereo.
VHS: **S27453. $29.95.**
Japan, 115 mins.

Night Warriors— Darkstalkers' Revenge, Vol. 1

Supernatural sisters Mei-ling and Hsien-Ko are freelance Darkstalker Hunters who find that a mysterious monk has already done their work for them. However, a mad general in a suit of accursed armor is laying waste to the countryside, but he too must face the one powerful man who only wished for The Dark expunged from everywhere in the world. Dubbed in English. 45 mins.
VHS: **S34173. $19.95.**

Night Warriors— Darkstalkers' Revenge, Vol. 2

Hipper, sexier and harder-edged than the *Darkstalkers* TV animation aired in the U.S., *Darkstalkers' Revenge* will thrill animation and video game fans alike with non-stop action, explosive fight scenes and gorgeously animated characters. Based on the best-selling video game series. 45 mins.
Dubbed Version.
VHS: **S34529. $19.95.**
Subtitled Version.
VHS: **S34528. $19.95.**

Nightmare Campus, Vol. 1: The Resurrection of the Demon Lord Esedess

Nineteen-year-old student Masao Sera stumbles upon a bloody sacrificial rite and becomes the final victim of a mysterious priestess. She uses him to release demons from the underworld into our world and into his college. Dubbed. 40 mins.
VHS: **S34303. $29.95.**

Nightmare Campus, Vol. 2: The Resurrection of the Demon Lord Esedess

Nineteen-year-old student Masao Sera stumbles upon a bloody sacrificial rite and becomes the final victim of a mysterious priestess. Dubbed. 40 mins.
VHS: **S34784. $29.95.**

Nightmare Campus, Vol. 3: The Great Ambitions of the Gods

Masao has learned that his best friend, Akira, is the demon lord Aquifiel, and that his own sexual relationship with his companion, Yuuko, is the source of his private anguish. Dubbed. 40 mins.
VHS: **S34785. $29.95.**

Nightmare Campus: Collector's Boxed Set

What began with a deadly ceremony, will become the prelude to world Armageddon. An entire college campus is possessed by a mysterious force from the underworld, turning it into the Nightmare Campus. After 19-year-old Masao Sera is possessed by a demon, he must learn to control it and help save mankind from total obliteration. Contains 1-5 of the series. Dubbed in English. 200 mins.
VHS: **S34302. $129.95.**

Ninja Scroll

Jubei is a masterless ninja who travels feudal Japan, selling his services. When a village succumbs to a terrible plague, an investigating team of ninjas is wiped out by a fearsome man-monster, leaving only one alive—Kagero, a beautiful female ninja, whose touch can bring instant death. Jubei rescues her and unwittingly becomes drawn into the web of treachery. He is soon faced with his greatest challenge—an enemy for whom death holds no fear, with the power to destroy Jubei's world. Nudity and violence. HiFi Stereo.
VHS: Dubbed. **S29186. $19.95.**
VHS: Subtitled. **S25724. $24.95.**
VHS: Espanol. **S29187. $19.95.**
Mad House, Japan, 1993, 94 mins.

Odin: Photon Space Sailor Starlight

In the year 2099, the spacecraft *Starlight* ventures forth. Equipped with an experimental gravity control drive, the vessel is staffed by wizened officers and impetuous youngsters eager for adventure. Pausing to rescue a girl from the wreck of a spaceship, the crew is mystified by her familiarity with alien artifacts. She is able to decipher the location of what she calls Odin…apparently the birthplace of humanity itself! Defying orders to return to Earth, the *Starlight*'s young crew mutinies against its officers and plunges into the depths of the galaxy…where a seemingly infinite army of robotic foes blocks the gates of paradise itself. Stereo.
VHS: Dubbed. **S29188. $19.95.**
VHS: Subtitled. **S18426. $14.95.**
Laser: Subtitled. **LD74513. $49.95.**
WestCape, Japan, 1985, 139 mins.

Ogre Slayer

Two episodes. From the fading warmth of his mother's cooling corpse, an ogre in the form of a young human boy is born. His destiny? To kill his own kind. He bears an ogre-killing sword. Believing that he will become human once all his kind are extinct, he travels the land, sword in hand, daring to dream. He has no human name. Mankind refers only to his sword, "Onikirimaru." Nudity and violence. Dubbed. HiFi Stereo.
VHS: **S26425. $24.95.**
KSS, Japan, 1995, 60 mins.

Ogre Slayer 2: Grim Fairy Tale

Two episodes: A desperate mother prays for a child at a temple with a terrible curse. Alas, any child conceived with the aid of prayers made at this site is destined to die by the age of five, when the ogre that lives at the temple appears to claim it! In the second grisly episode, the clock is turned back to the era of Japan's Meiji Restoration. In that time, there lived an elusive ogre which could hide its presence even from Ogre Slayer. Nudity and violence. Dubbed. HiFi Stereo.
VHS: **S27091. $24.95.**
KSS, Japan, 1995, 60 mins.

Oh My Goddess! Vol. 1: Moonlight & Cherry Blossoms

College freshman Morisato Keiichi runs into Belldandy, an honest-to-goodness goddess, who grants him one wish. When he wishes for a girlfriend just like Belldandy, that's exactly what he gets! Complications ensue as the two must find a new place to live and Morisato must work up the nerve to put the moves on a truly divine babe. HiFi Stereo.
VHS: Dubbed. **S29190. $14.95.**
VHS: Subtitled. **S21181. $19.95.**
Kodansha, Japan, 1994, 29 mins.

Oh My Goddess! Vol. 2: Midsummer Night's Dream

Keiichi has still not managed a kiss with Belldandy after five months. Belldandy's big sister Urd tries to help him with sexy videos and trips to the seashore, but every scheme goes hilariously askew. Will her ultimate weapon, a love potion, turn the trick? HiFi Stereo.
VHS: Dubbed. **S29191. $14.95.**
VHS: Subtitled. **S21182. $19.95.**
Kodansha, Japan, 1994, 29 mins.

Oh My Goddess! Vol. 3: Burning Hearts on the Road

Little sister Skuld pays Belldandy a visit because she's lonely up in heaven without her, and besides, she needs help maintaining the Universal Force System. HiFi Stereo.
VHS: Dubbed. **S29192. $14.95.**
VHS: Subtitled. **S21183. $19.95.**
Kodansha, Japan, 1994, 29 mins.

Oh My Goddess! Vol. 4: Evergreen Holy Night

System Bugs are escaping from the Heavens, upsetting the balance of the earthly plane, and the Lord recalls Belldandy because the bugs appear whenever she and Keiichi get close. HiFi Stereo.
VHS: Dubbed. **S29580. $14.95.**
VHS: Subtitled. **S21184. $19.95.**
Kodansha, Japan, 1994, 29 mins.

Oh My Goddess! Vol. 5: For the Love of Goddess

As the clock ticks down to Belldandy's recall, Urd and Skuld attempt to solve the bug problem. Meanwhile, Keiich is working himself to the bone to buy a ring for Belldandy. HiFi Stereo. Dubbed.
VHS: Dubbed. **S29581. $14.95.**
VHS: Subtitled. **S21185. $19.95.**
Kodansha, Japan, 1994, 29 mins.

Oh My Goddess! Collector's Suite

It all begins with a call for takeout that accidentally conjures up a beautiful goddess. This Anime boxed set of five videos follows the wacky, sexy, romantic adventures that ensue between this divinity and her ordinary mortal friend. Japanese with English subtitles, partial nudity.
VHS: S25718. $95.00.

Oh My Goddess! Hybrid LD #1

Episodes 1 and 2 on one videodisc. HiFi Stereo. Dubbed one side, subtitled on the other.
Laser: LD75576. $39.95.
Kodansha, Japan, 1994, 54 mins.

Oh My Goddess! Hybrid LD #2

Episodes 3 and 4 on one videodisc. HiFi Stereo. Dubbed one side, subtitled on the other.
Laser: LD75833. $39.95.
Kodansha, Japan, 1994, 58 mins.

Oh My Goddess! Hybrid LD #3

Episode 5 on videodisc. HiFi Stereo. Dubbed one side, subtitled on the other.
Laser: LD75832. $39.95.
Kodansha, Japan, 1994, 40 mins.

One-Pound Gospel

Based on Rumiko Takahashi's manga. Kosaku Hatanaka is the first pro boxer produced by Mukaida's gym. Unfortunately, he has a passion for eating, which plays havoc with his weight class. Can Sister Angela, a nun at St. Mary's, help the young boxer control his gluttony? Stereo. Subtitled.
VHS: S29193. $29.95.
Japan, 55 mins.

Orguss 02, Vol. 1

Two episodes: *The Fool's Choice* and *Where Angels Fear to Tread*. For 200 years they lay silent on the ocean floor. Now, two armies race to unearth these massive Decimators, drawing innocent victims into the deadly conflict. Lean is a young mechanic working on a routine excavation of a submerged Decimator, until an ambush by the hostile Zafrins forces him to pilot the armor in order to survive. The ensuing battle changes Lean's life as he sets out on a risky mission to eliminate their Decimators. HiFi Stereo. Dubbed.
VHS: S23483. $14.95.
Big West, Japan, 1993, 55 mins.

Orguss 02, Vol. 2

In Episode 3, *Fugitives*, war is declared between Revillia and Zafrin while Lean is trapped behind enemy lines. With him is a mysterious young girl. In Episode 4, *Searcher*, the Zafrin army unveils the most powerful Decimator ever seen! Lean finally reaches safety, only to be betrayed by a close friend. As the mysterious young girl is delivered into the hands of the Revillian army, Lean must choose between his country or the girl who saved his life. HiFi Stereo. Dubbed.
VHS: S25725. $14.95.
Big West, Japan, 1993, 55 mins.

Orguss 02 Vol. 3

In Episode 5, *Destroyer*, Lean and the mysterious girl meet an enigmatic stranger who needs their help. At last, the secret of the Decimators is revealed, and the ancient stranger reveals his plans to return the world to peace. In Episode 6, *Those Who Wish for Tomorrow*, as the Prince of Revillia leaves a path of destruction, Lean and his friends battle desperately to stop him! They cannot bring peace to the world until the last, greatest Decimator is destroyed forever. The conclusion of the series. HiFi Stereo. Dubbed.
VHS: S26377. $14.95.
Big West, Japan, 1994, 55 mins.

Otaku No Video

Two Original Video Animations: *Otaku No Video 1982* and *More Otaku No Video 1985*. A treat for fans of any genre, *Otaku No Video* ("Fan's Video") is an outrageous mock-umentary combining the superb animation that made Gainax one of Japan's best animation studios with truly strange interviews with "real fans." The result is a thinly fictionalized history of Gainax that segues into a truly strange Sci-Fi adventure. Sit back and enjoy as a small band of otaku (fans) sets out to "otakunize" the human race! HiFi Stereo. Subtitled.
VHS: S18348. $39.95.
Gainax, Japan, 1982, 93 mins.

Outlanders

Aliens from the Santovasku Empire will purify Earth by destroying humanity. But Santovasku's Princess Kahm has fallen in love with a human named Tetsuya. Her marriage to the Earth "primate" would save humanity and this enrages her Emperor father. Kahm is thrust into an intergalactic battle against the fleet commanded by Counselor Progress. Progress' true agenda is to usurp the throne but Geobaldi and the sexy feline Battia aid Kahm in her struggle. Nudity & violence. HiFi Stereo. Dubbed.
VHS: S19340. $19.95.
Tatsunoko, Japan, 1986, 48 mins.

Panda & The Magic Serpent

Narrated in English by Marvin Miller (the man who distributed checks on TV's *The Millionaire*), the animation is lovely and delicate. Panda and Mimi the raccoon travel with Hsu Hsien through the Chinese countryside and meet wizards, magic snakes and fish. A Chinese fairy tale of Pai Niang, a goddess who falls in love with a human and gives up her immortality to save his life. Directed by Kazuhiko Okabe. Dubbed.
VHS: S05473. $24.95.
Japan, 1961, 74 mins.

Patlabor 1 Movie

The year is 1999 and advanced robots called Labors are used to fight criminals. When Patlabor cops Noah Izumi and Azuma Shinohara investigate a wave of rogue Labors rampaging across the city, they uncover a sinister plot to infect Tokyo's eight thousand Labor population with the deadly Babel virus. With the future of the city hanging in the balance and a typhoon poised to trigger the devastation, Noah, Azuma and their teammates must destroy the source of the virus—the giant Babylon Project tower. HiFi Stereo.
VHS: Dubbed. **S29194. $19.95.**
VHS: Subtitled. **S26242. $24.95.**
VHS: Espanol. **S29195. $19.95.**
Headgear, Japan, 1989, 100 mins.

Patlabor 2 Movie

The date is 2002, three years after the events of *Patlabor 1—Mobile Police*. The destruction of a United Nations Labor team in Southeast Asia signals the beginning of a deadly terrorist plan that threatens to send shockwaves throughout Japan's military. With evidence of an impending military takeover, the scattered members of the original SVD must gather to defend the city against danger. To make matters worse, the mastermind behind the operation is Nagumo's former teacher and ex-lover Tsuge. HiFi Stereo.
VHS: Dubbed. **S29196. $19.95.**
VHS: Subtitled. **S26765. $24.95.**
Headgear, Japan, 1989, 108 mins.

Patlabor Mobile Police Original Series Vol. 1

Episodes 1-3. In the near future, the world has come to rely upon Labors—humanoid, multi-purpose construction machines. But these machines also created a new menace: Labor crimes. To combat this threat, the Tokyo Police established the "Special Vehicles Section 2," comprising specially designed Patrol Labors—Patlabors. Violence. Stereo. Subtitled.
VHS: S30288. $24.95.
Headgear, Japan, 1988, 90 mins.

Patlabor Mobile Police Original Series Vol. 2

Episodes 4-5. After a member of the Second Unit loses his cool and resolves a delicate hostage situation with his Patlabor's revolver cannon, Captain Goto sends the whole SV2 back to training camp. But will all their training pay off when a rogue element of Japan's Self-Defense Force lays seige to Tokyo—and the SV2 finds itself without any equipment? Violence. Stereo. Subtitled.
VHS: S30289. $24.95.
Headgear, Japan, 1988, 60 mins.

Patlabor Mobile Police Original Series Vol. 3

Episodes 6-7. On the run from the police, Captain Goto mounts a counter-offensive against the ringleader of the coup—his former teacher, Kai. But can Goto stop Kai before he plays his nuclear trump card? And nothing is what it seems when the SV2 is asked to recover a stolen Labor, due to be unveiled at an upcoming Labor show. Who is the man who stole the prototype from the thieves, and why is the manufacturer so secretive about the new design? Violence. Stereo. Subtitled.
VHS: S30290. $24.95.
Headgear, Japan, 1988, 60 mins.

Patlabor Mobile Police Original Series, Boxed Set

Episodes 1-7, Volumes 1-3 in a collector's slipcase. Violence. Stereo. Subtitled.
VHS: S30291. $69.95.
Headgear, Japan, 1988, 210 mins.

Patlabor Mobile Police New Files Vol. 1

Episodes 1-4. The second OAV series. The SV2's nemesis, the Griffon, is back for a rematch. Discovering that a group of international Labor experts have come to Tokyo, the police race against time to capture Utsumi, the man behind the Griffon Project. Meanwhile, Noa and the SV2 face the seemingly invincible Black Labor. Violence. Subtitled.
VHS: S30398. $29.95.
Emotion/Headgear, Japan, 1992, 120 mins.

Patlabor Mobile Police New Files Vol. 2

Episodes 5, 6 and 7. Violence. Subtitled.
VHS: S31329. $29.95.
Emotion/Headgear, Japan, 1992, 90 mins.

Patlabor Mobile Police New Files Vol. 3

Episodes 8-10. Asuma recalls a time when a civil war erupted within SV2's maintenance squad after the chief banned alcohol and videogames from the barracks. Later, Ohta awakens surrounded by the bloody bodies of his co-workers, and he has no memory of what happened. Violence. Subtitled.
VHS: S31079. $29.95.
Emotion/Headgear, Japan, 1992, 90 mins.

Patlabor Mobile Police New Files Vol. 4

Episodes 11-13. News of a giant, albino alligator laying pearl-like objects in the zoo sends the SV2's maintenance squad into the sewers in search of treasure. Violence. Subtitled.
VHS: S33610. $29.95.
Emotion/Headgear, Japan, 1992, 90 mins.

Patlabor Mobile Police New Files Vol. 5

Episodes 14-16. Noa stumbles on the secret headquarters of an Earth-defense organization. When aliens unleash a giant monster, will Noa be able to summon the power of Ingra-Man? Violence. Subtitled.
VHS: S33611. $29.95.
Emotion/Headgear, Japan, 1992, 90 mins.

Patlabor Mobile Police New Files, Boxed Set

All five tape volumes in a collector's slipcase. Violence. Subtitled.
VHS: S30397. $119.95.
Emotion/Headgear, Japan, 1992, 450 mins.

Patlabor: The Mobile Police—The TV Series: Vol. 1

As the 20th Century was nearing its end, a new Industrial Revolution brought forth unprecedented advances in robotics. The invention of the Labor—a humanoid-type, multipurpose construction machine—emerged as the wave of the future. Making older industrial equipment virtually obsolete, the Labor also became a terrorist weapon. To combat the rise in Labor crimes, the Tokyo Metropolitan Police Department establishes specially designed Patrol Labors: Patlabors. Japanese with English subtitles. 120 mins.
VHS: S34309. $29.95.

Peacock King—Spirit Warrior 1

The Neo-Nazis led by Siegfried von Mittgard plan to pick up where Hitler left off. Utilizing an occult ceremony and a mystical Dragon Orb, and sacrificing young mystic Tomoko, they intend to blanket the world in darkness. However, four heroes oppose them, and the race for the Orb takes them all the way to the Nazi's fortress in Germany. Nudity and graphic violence. Dubbed.
VHS: S32268. $19.95.
Shueisha/Pony Canyon, Japan, 1994, 49 mins.

Peacock King—Spirit Warrior 2

With Tomoko and the mystical Dragon Orb in his possession, von Mittgard now has everything he needs to become the Regent of Darkness. As Siegfried prepares to use the Orb to unlock darkness, Kujaku must come to terms with his fantastic destiny. Nudity and graphic violence. Dubbed.
VHS: S32269. $19.95.
Shueisha/Pony Canyon, Japan, 1994, 49 mins.

Peacock King—Spirit Warrior: Castle of Illusion

Kujaku and his supernatural allies must defeat Nobunaga Oda—the Sixth King of Evil—before he can revive the unholy power hidden within the crumbling walls of Azuchi Castle. If Kajaku should fail, the world will collapse into a fiery pit deeper than Hell. Nudity and graphic violence. Dubbed.
VHS: S33612. $19.95.
Japan

Peacock King—Spirit Warrior: Festival of the Ogres' Revival

A sinister sorcerer has stolen an ancient artifact containing a deadly secret. Now Kujaku and Onimaru must stop him before he unleases the evil and tears apart the heavens. Nudity and graphic violence. Dubbed.
VHS: S33613. $19.95.
Japan

Phantom Quest Corp. Vol. 1

Incident File 01, *Kiss of Fire*: In Shinjuku city is an exorcist detective agency named Phantom Quest Corporation. The Transylvanian ambassador hires this trio of psychics when Dracula's casket is found empty and recent murders are believed to have been committed by the resurrected vampire. Incident File 02, *End of the World*: One night a drunken Ayaka is in a taxi when she senses danger. She escapes disaster, but causes a multi-car pile-up that kills the driver in the process. Ayaka is convinced someone has made a pact with the devil and caused his death. Nudity. HiFi Stereo.
VHS: Dubbed. **S29197. $24.95.**
VHS: Subtitled. **S24573. $29.95.**
Laser: CAV, multi-audio. **LD74828. $39.95.**
MadHouse, Japan, 1994, 60 mins.

Phantom Quest Corp. Vol. 2

Incident File 03, *Love Me Tender*: The "Curse of the Sahara" is spooking workers in the ancient Sahara exhibit. Phantom Quest Corp is assigned to calm the workers. Incident File 04: *Lover Come Back to Me*: President Ayaka Kisaragi has been chasing a werewolf around in the middle of the night. A man named Mukyo, together with a group of monks, quickly terminates the werewolf. Mukyo, leader of a Buddhist Group, Hadja, declares that from now on they will perform all exorcisms in the city. As time goes on, Phantom Quest Corp finds itself being squeezed out of more assignments. HiFi Stereo. Nudity.
VHS: Dubbed. **S29198. $24.95.**
VHS: Subtitled. **S25679. $29.95.**
Laser: CAV, multi-audio. **LD74992. $39.95.**
MadHouse, Japan, 1994, 60 mins.

Phoenix 2772

In the future, the people of Earth are born in laboratories, raised by robots and ruled by a tyrannical government. Into this bleak world, Godah is born, a sensitive boy who will soon hold the future of the world in his hands. While training to become a spaceship pilot, Godah learns of the Legend of the Phoenix, a mystical space Firebird with magical blood. Whoever controls the Firebird will have immortality and everlasting power. When an evil scientist orders Godah to retrieve the Firebird, the young hero is determined to use its powers to rejuvenate a dying Earth. Dubbed.
VHS: S29199. $19.95.
Tezuka Prod's, Japan, 1980, 121 mins.

Planet Busters

On a forgotten planet, a boy, a girl, two bounty hunters and an army of death-dealing robots come together for one wild chase after another. A wild animated feature that leads our heroes on a journey to solve the greatest mystery of the universe. Japan, 80 mins.
VHS: S16643. $29.95.

Please Save My Earth Vol. 1

Ever since she was a little girl, plants and animals have seemed to love Alice—a young high school student. Her classmates tell her about a recurring dream they have of scientists living on the moon who are collecting data about Earth. She discounts their story until she has the same dream, too! Voted best OVA of 1994 by Japanese fans. Stereo. Dubbed.
VHS: S27321. $24.95.
Japan, 1994, 60 mins.

Please Save My Earth Vol. 2

Alice continues to be haunted by the "Lunar" dreams. Rin now joins Alice and her friends as they gather to discuss these strange dreams. That Rin is in love with Alice is no secret, but what hold does he have over Haru Kasama, a gentle-eyed boy with a heart condition and strange powers? Is history doomed to repeat itself, even when that history carries over from a previous life? Stereo. Dubbed.
VHS: S29200. $24.95.
Japan, 1994, 60 mins.

Please Save My Earth Vol. 3

Rin Kobayashi is an eight-year-old child with an oddly adult way about him. With his whole life before him, he's burdened by a terrible sadness, and he must endure pain, loneliness and even madness for the chance to love a wonderful woman named Mokuren. The final volume of the OAV series. Stereo. Dubbed.
VHS: S29201. $24.95.
Japan, 1994, 60 mins.

Poltergeist Report

Armed with awesome supernatural powers, five sentinels from the Spirit World must battle the demonic hordes of Lord Yakumo for possession of five mystical sites…before our world becomes the new Netherworld. Violence.
VHS: Dubbed. **S33615. $19.95.**
VHS: Subtitled. **S33614. $29.95.**
Toho, Japan, 1997, 90 mins.

Power Dolls

In 2535, the planet Omni declared its independence from Earth. The new weapon in the ensuing war is the Power Loder: huge, humanoid tanks, heavily armored and armed. The Omni military drew on all segments of its forces to create a special unit of elite loder pilots known as the "Dolls." Now, in the year 2540, as the Earth forces continue to encroach into Omni territory, the Dolls are facing their toughest assignments yet. Based on the popular Japanese video game. Nudity. HiFi Stereo.
VHS: Dubbed. **S29888. $19.95.**
VHS: Subtitled. **S29887. $24.95.**
Laser: Multi-audio. **LD75952. $39.95.**
Japan, 35 mins.

Princess Minerva

Princess Minerva, who doesn't like being the princess, has been sharpening up her basic sword and sorcery skills and has taken on a secret identity with the aid of her loyal bodyguard Blue Morris. However, Wisler is a pretty dull place to live so her career as a crusading heroine has gone nowhere until the sinister sorceress Dynastar accidentally kidnaps Blue Morris instead of Minerva! So it's up to Minerva and a ferocious flock of Amazon battlemaids to stage a daring rescue. Nudity & violence. HiFi Stereo. Subtitled.
VHS: Subtitled. **S25022. $29.95.**
VHS: Dubbed. **S34535. $19.95.**
Toho, Japan, 1995, 45 mins.

Project A-Ko

In the near future, A-ko and C-ko are lively 17-year-olds attending Graviton High School for Girls. When classmate B-ko decides she wants C-ko, she must go up against the invincible A-ko with her arsenal of power-suits. Meanwhile, what is the connection between these girls and a monstrous alien spaceship plying its way toward Earth? Stereo. Nudity.
VHS: Dubbed. **S17842. $19.95.**
VHS: Subtitled. **S16057. $29.95.**
Laser: Subtitled, widescreen. **LD71831. $39.95.**
Soeishinsha, Japan, 1986, 86 mins.

Project A-Ko 2: Plot of the Daitokuji Financial Group

It's summertime and A-Ko vows to lose weight. B-Ko devises a new plot to get rid of A-Ko so she can have C-Ko all to herself. What will happen when B-Ko's father, Mr. Daitokuji, uses her designs for an anti-A-Ko robot to create a monstrous attack weapon to help his company gain posession of the disabled spaceship's technological secrets? Nudity. Stereo.
VHS: Dubbed. **S21320. $19.95.**
VHS: Subtitled. **S21111. $29.95.**
Laser: Multi-audio. **LD75768. $39.95.**
Soeishinsha, Japan, 1987, 70 mins.

Project A-Ko 3: Cinderella Rhapsody

A-Ko daydreams as she tries on an outrageous dress, while C-Ko is almost run over by handsome motorcyclist K. A-Ko waits on K at a local restaurant and falls in love, but B-Ko also has her eye on K. Laserdisc is multi-audio. Stereo. Nudity.
VHS: Dubbed. **S29202. $19.95.**
VHS: Subtitled. **S21112. $29.95.**
Laser: Multi-audio. **LD74835. $34.95.**
Soeishinsha, Japan, 1988, 50 mins.

Project A-Ko 4: Final

Archaeologists discover an ancient hexagram that matches the insignia of a spacefleet headed for Earth. C-Ko discovers her teacher holding a mysterious pendant. Miss Ayumi announces her intent to marry K. Stereo. Nudity.
VHS: Dubbed. **S22767. $19.95.**
VHS: Subtitled. **S21113. $29.95.**
Laser: Multi-audio. **LD75771. $34.95.**
Soeishinsha, Japan, 1989, 59 mins.

Project A-Ko Vs. Battle 1: Grey Side

C-Ko escapes kidnappers by plummeting down to a planet and landing on A-Ko's equipment pack. Before A-Ko and B-Ko can collect the reward for her return, she is re-kidnapped. While trying to rescue her, B-Ko is killed and A-Ko mourns. Stereo. Nudity.
VHS: Dubbed. **S29303. $19.95.**
VHS: Subtitled. **S21114. $29.95.**
Laser: Multi-audio. **LD75047. $34.95.**
Soeishinsha, Japan, 1990, 54 mins.

Project A-Ko vs. Battle 2: Blue Side

B-Ko and C-Ko find the Kotobuko fleet hot on their trail. C-Ko summons the dragon to destroy the fleet. Meanwhile, A-Ko and Maruten are in pursuit of Gail and sneak aboard her ship as the battle ensues. Nudity. Stereo.
VHS: Dubbed. **S29304. $19.95.**
VHS: Subtitled. **S21115. $29.95.**
Laser: Multi-audio. **LD75292. $34.95.**
Soeishinsha, Japan, 1990, 52 mins.

Psycho Diver

In a dark world of private terrors, haunted by memories of a dark and violent past, Yuki is discovering that she possesses extraordinary psycho-kinetic powers that are out of her control. Only the psycho-diver can free her before she kills again. Violence and nudity.
VHS: Dubbed. **S32284. $19.95.**
VHS: Subtitled. **S32285. $29.95.**
Japan, 45 mins.

Rail of the Star

A child and her family must endure the unendurable in their bid to reach the promised land of South Korea by rail and by foot, guided by the light of a star. An unforgettable true story of courage and the triumph of the human spirit. Dubbed.
VHS: S32757. $24.95.
TV Tokyo/JVC, Japan, 80 mins.

Ranma 1/2 Anything Goes Vol. 1: Darling Charlotte

The first installment of the second *Ranma 1/2* series that picks up where the first series left off. Two episodes: Precious Ice Princess Azusa Shiratori kidnaps Akane's beloved P-Chan. To get P-Chan back, Ranma and Akane must battle Azusa and her partner in a martial arts figure skating fight. HiFi Stereo. Dubbed.
VHS: Dubbed. **S23760. $24.95.**
VHS: Subtitled. **S29203. $29.95.**
Kitty Films, Japan, 1994, 52 mins.

Ranma 1/2 Anything Goes Vol. 2: It's Fast or It's Free

Two episodes: A stranger shows up on the Tendos' doorstep claiming to be Ranma's long-lost dad. It seems a lost and starving Genma once traded baby Ranma to a stranger in exchange for food. The stranger now demands that Ranma marry his daughter and carry on the Daikoku School of Martial Arts Restaurant Takeout. HiFi Stereo.
VHS: Dubbed. **S29204. $24.95.**
VHS: Subtitled. **S27679. $29.95.**
Kitty Films, Japan, 1994, 52 mins.

Ranma 1/2 Anything Goes Vol. 3: Cat-Fu Fighting

Two episodes: Poetry-spouting swordsman Tatewaki Kuno is determined to find Ranma's weak spot. It turns out not to be his achille's heel, but rather a location more unusual. HiFi Stereo.
VHS: Dubbed. **S29296. $24.95.**
VHS: Subtitled. **S29205. $29.95.**
Kitty Films, Japan, 1994, 52 mins.

Ranma 1/2 Anything Goes Vol. 4: Chestnuts Roasting on an Open Fire

Two episodes: Ranma needs the "Phoenix Pill" to reverse the curse of Shampoo's great-grandmother. He must take a part-time job at the infamous Cat cafe to make her hand it over. HiFi Stereo.
VHS: Dubbed. **S26036. $24.95.**
VHS: Subtitled. **S29576. $29.95.**
Kitty Films, Japan, 1994, 52 mins.

Ranma 1/2 Anything Goes Vol. 5: Cold Competition

Two episodes: Ranma, still unable to stand even lukewarm water, tries a new cure in a "Martial Arts Snowman-Carry Race" sponsored by the Cat Cafe. If he wins, he gets a ski-tour with Shampoo and the Phoenix Pill. Then, Ranma is looking forward to the final result of his date with Shampoo: never to be a girl again! Meanwhile, Akane is back home fighting off a challenger to the Tendo dojo singlehandedly. HiFi Stereo.
VHS: Dubbed. **S25978. $24.95.**
VHS: Subtitled. **S29577. $29.95.**
Kitty Films, Japan, 1995, 52 mins.

Ranma 1/2 Anything Goes Vol. 6: The Breaking Point

Two episodes: Ryoga Hibiki discovers that while he was away, Ranma was mixing it up with Cologne. When Ranma and Genma head to the woods for some heavy training, will Akane's offer to cook for them prove their undoing? Then, Ryoga makes great progress with his bakusai tenketsu, a martial arts technique based on the assumption that every living thing has one "breaking point" which, when touched in just the right way, causes the victim to shatter into a thousand pieces! HiFi Stereo. Dubbed.

VHS: Dubbed. **$26248. $24.95.**
VHS: Subtitled. **$30286. $29.95.**
Kitty Films, Japan, 1995, 52 mins.

Ranma 1/2 Anything Goes Vol. 7: Fowl Play

Two episodes: A mysterious masked man takes Akane hostage! Ranma's sent out to follow the trail to the circus, where he becomes the target for a spectacular knife-throwing trick. If Ranma doesn't answer the summons to the circus, Akane's going to get a healthy dose of Yahzu-Nii-Chuan, cursed water from the "Spring of Drowned Duck"! The latest person to take the Jusenkyo plunge is Mousse, Master of Hidden Weapons and All Things Avian, and he's not above a little, uh, fowl play to get his revenge. HiFi Stereo.

VHS: Dubbed. **$26426. $24.95.**
VHS: Subtitled. **$30386. $29.95.**
Kitty Films, Japan, 1995, 52 mins.

Ranma 1/2 Anything Goes Vol. 8: The Evil Wakes

Two episodes: A string of seemingly unconnected bad omens all makes hideous sense when a sleeping demon long thought vanquished by Soun and Genma once again rears its ugly head. Then, after a brief skirmish with Ranma, Ryoga's map to a magical "Japanese Nan-nii-chuan" or "Spring of Drowned Man" just like the one in China leads to where the magical spring is supposed to be: the girls' locker room at Furinkan High School! HiFi Stereo. Dubbed.

VHS: $26629. $24.95.
Kitty Films, Japan, 1995, 52 mins.

Ranma 1/2 Anything Goes Vol. 9: Goodbye "Girl-Type"

Two episodes: When the three Nan-nii-chuan urns are brought together, the waters of Japan's Nan-nii-chuan will rise once more, putting an end to the Jusenkyo curse. The first urn was found beneath the girls' locker room. Then, after much suffering at the hands of the Brother and Sister Kuno, Ranma & Co. have acquired the second urn. All they'll have to do is find the third one. HiFi Stereo. Dubbed.

VHS: $26853. $24.95.
Kitty Films, Japan, 1995, 52 mins.

Ranma 1/2 Anything Goes Vol. 10: Tough Cookies

Two episodes: Akane's whipped up a batch of cookies, and is bound and determined to see Ranma eat them. But given Akane's bad cooking, he'd rather starve! Then, concerned members of the neighborhood watch committee turn to the Tendo dojo for help in finding the notorious panty-stealing prowler currently terrorizing the area. Soun and Genma know all too well who it is...but neither one wants to confront the aged martial arts master with his crimes. HiFi Stereo. Dubbed.

VHS: $26896. $24.95.
Kitty Films, Japan, 1995, 52 mins.

Ranma 1/2 Anything Goes Vol. 11: Ranma and Juliet

Two episodes: Akane is thrilled to be chosen to play Juliet in this year's Furikan High drama production...until she finds out who's playing Romeo! Then, when the water heater breaks down at the Tendo residence, Ranma & Co. set out for the public bathhouse for a long soak in a theraputic bath. Unfortunately, panty-snatching Happosai's idea of "therapy" is nothing like yours or mine! HiFi Stereo. Dubbed.

VHS: $27320. $24.95.
Kitty Films, Japan, 1995, 52 mins.

Ranma 1/2 Anything Goes, Special Collector's Boxed Set

Packed with animation based upon characters created by Rumko Takahashi, the best-selling female comic artist in the world, this ultimate Ranma Collection includes 11 videos of the *Ranma 1/2 Anything Goes Martial Arts* series. Follow the adventures of Ranma Saotome on his/her decade-long martial arts training mission and watch as a splash of cold water magically transforms Ranma into a beautiful, red-haired woman. Contains a bonus CD with the bouncy opening and closing themes in Japanese. Dubbed in English. 572 mins.

VHS: $31161. $199.95.
Kitty Film, Japan, 1995, 572 mins.

Ranma 1/2 Collector's Edition Vol. 1

Episodes 1-3 of the first TV series: *The Strange Stranger from China, School Is No Place for Horsing Around* and *A Sudden Strom of Love...Hey, Wait a Minute!* Nudity. HiFi Stereo. Subtitled.

VHS: $27151. $34.95.
Kitty Film, Japan, 1994, 75 mins.

Ranma 1/2 Collector's Edition Vol. 2

Episodes 4-6 of the first TV series: *Ranma and...Ranma? If It's Not One Thing It's Another, Love Me to the Bone! The Compound Fracture of Akane's Heart* and *Akane's Lost Love...These Things Happen You Know*. Nudity. HiFi Stereo. Subtitled.

VHS: $29206. $34.95.
Kitty Film, Japan, 1994, 75 mins.

Ranma 1/2 Collector's Edition Vol. 3

Episodes 7-9 of the first TV series: *Enter Ryoga, The Eternal Lost Boy, School Is a Battlefield! Ranma vs. Ryoga* and *True Confessions! A Girl's Hair Is Her Life!* Nudity. HiFi Stereo. Subtitled.

VHS: $25681. $34.95.
Kitty Film, Japan, 1994, 75 mins.

Ranma 1/2 Collector's Edition Vol. 4

Episodes 10-12 of the first TV series: *P-P-P-Chan! He's Good for Nothin', Ranma Meets Love Head On! Enter the Delinquent Juvenile Gymnast* and *A Woman's Love Is War! The Martial Arts Rhythmic Gymnastics Challenge*. Nudity. HiFi Stereo. Subtitled.

VHS: $20905. $34.95.
Kitty Film, Japan, 1994, 75 mins.

Ranma 1/2 Collector's Edition Vol. 5

Episodes 13-15 of the first TV series: A Tear in a Girl-Delinquent's Eye? The End of the Martial Arts Rhythmic Gymnastics Challenge, Pelvic Fortune-Telling? Ranma Is the No. 1 Bride in Japan and *Enter Shampoo, The Gung-Ho Girl! I Put My Life in Your Hands*. Nudity. HiFi Stereo. Subtitled.

VHS: $25979. $34.95.
Kitty Film, Japan, 1994, 75 mins.

Ranma 1/2 Collector's Edition Vol. 6

Episodes 16-18 of the first TV series: *Shampoo's Revenge! The Shiatsu Technique That Steals Heart and Soul, I Love You Ranma! Please Don't Say Goodbye* and *I Am a Man! Ranma's Going Back to China!?* Nudity. HiFi Stereo. Subtitled.

VHS: $26641. $34.95.
Kitty Film, Japan, 1994, 75 mins.

Ranma 1/2 Collector's Edition: The OAV's Vol. 1

Three OAVs: *Shampoo's Sudden Switch! The Curse of the Contrary Jewel, Tendo Family Christmas Scramble* and *Akane vs. Ranma! I'll Be the One to Inherit Mother's Recipes*. Nudity. HiFi Stereo. Subtitled.

VHS: $26854. $34.95.
Kitty Films, Japan, 1994, 90 mins.

Ranma 1/2 Collector's Edition: The OAV's Vol. 2

Three OAVs: *Stormy Weather Comes to School! Growing Up with Miss Hinako* and *The One to Carry On, Parts One* and *Two*. Nudity. HiFi Stereo. Subtitled.

VHS: $26897. $34.95.
Kitty Films, Japan, 1994, 90 mins.

Ranma 1/2 Hard Battle Vol. 1: Ukyo Can Cook

Two episodes: Say hello to Furinkan High's newest transfer student, Ukyo—spatula-wielding warrior and okonomiaki chef par excellence. Lots of people around town have their reasons for despising Ranma, but Ukyo's grudge against him goes way way back—all the way to their childhood. HiFi Stereo. Dubbed.

VHS: Dubbed. **$27456. $24.95.**
VHS: Subtitled. **$32760. $29.95.**
Kitty Film, Japan, 1995, 52 mins.

Ranma 1/2 Hard Battle Vol. 2: Dim Sum Darling

Two episodes: Shampoo still hasn't given up on the only man who's ever defeated her in combat. A new recipe which produces a post-hypnotic suggestion-like willingness to please (artfully hidden in some tainted dim sum delicacies) seems the perfect plan...until Shampoo accidentally sneezes during a crucial moment! Now, whenever he hears a sneeze, Ranma is compelled to throw himself into the arms of whoever is close by. The bad news is, Akane's coming down with the sniffles. HiFi Stereo. Dubbed.

VHS: $29301. $24.95.
Kitty Film, Japan, 1995, 52 mins.

Ranma 1/2 Hard Battle Vol. 3: Dharma Chameleon

Two episodes: Ukyo Kuonji's origin story is revealed as Ukyo attempts to evade the coquettish camouflager Tsubasa Kurenai without loosing her own doggedly stubborn "problem" on Akane or girl-type Ranma. Also, Soun Tendo is elected to stop an underwear thief, and gets a surprise when the next victim is a scaly seductress. HiFi Stereo. Dubbed.

VHS: $29302. $24.95.
Kitty Film, Japan, 1995, 52 mins.

Ranma 1/2 Hard Battle Vol. 4: Once Upon a Time in Jusenkyo

Two episodes: Akane eats some magic supper noodles that make her super strong, and she can't wait to enter a local ping-pong tournament so she can beat Shampoo and Ranma both. Then, there is a swordsman on the loose, and he's after Ranma and anyone else who has been transformed by the magic waters of Jusenkyo! HiFi Stereo. Dubbed.

VHS: $29579. $24.95.
Kitty Film, Japan, 1995, 52 mins.

Ranma 1/2 Hard Battle Vol. 5: Pretty Womanhood

Two episodes: In *Am I Pretty? Ranma's Declaration of Womanhood*, an accidental thwack on the noggin has Ranma thinking like a girl. When Ranma declares "she" abhors violence and wants to leave the dojo, Genma arranges a heart-to-heart talk. In *Final Facedown! Happosai vs. The Invisible Man*, Soun and Genma must recall the "Super Secret Special Attack" they once learned from Master Chingensai. They hope to use it against Happosai, the so-called "most evil master in Japan." HiFi Stereo. Dubbed.

VHS: Dubbed. **$30287. $24.95.**
VHS: Adapted in English. **$28603. $24.95.**
Kitty Films, Japan, 1995, 52 mins.

Ranma 1/2 Hard Battle Vol. 6: Suddenly Sasuke

Two episodes: When Kuno's bullying becomes too much for Sasuke, running away seems the only option. Then, Ranma and Akane plan a ghost-bustin' expedition to their alma mater, while Ukyo plans to peddle her Okonomiyaki to the hungry students. Dubbed.

VHS: $30787. $24.95.
Kitty Film, Japan, 1995, 52 mins.

Ranma 1/2 Hard Battle Vol. 7: Melancholy Baby

Two episodes: Panty-snatching Happosai plans to use love potion pills on a trip to the beach. Then, after Ryoga/P-Chan's life-changing dunk in Jusenkyo's cursed springs, is there another with the same reason to hate Ranma? Dubbed.

VHS: $30909. $24.95.
Kitty Film, Japan, 1995, 52 mins.

Ranma 1/2 Hard Battle Vol. 8: Back to Happosai

Two episodes. A priceless Amazon treasure sends old lecher Happosai back to the days of his youth, when he traveled the world and happened upon a village of Amazons in the Chinese mountains...and a beautiful young woman named Cologne. Dubbed.

VHS: $31337. $24.95.
Kitty Film, Japan, 1995, 52 mins.

Ranma 1/2 Hard Battle Vol. 9: Da-Doo Ling-Ling, Lung-Lung

Two episodes. Ranma thinks he's seeing double when Chinese Amazon twins Ling-Ling and Lung-Lung show up on his doorstep to give him the "kiss of death" Shampoo failed to carry out. Plus, Happosai falls prey to a fatalistic fortune-telling that cuses him to lose his will to live. Dubbed.

VHS: $33622. $24.95.
Kitty Film, Japan, 1995, 52 mins.

Ranma 1/2 Hard Battle Vol. 10: Smells Like Evil Spirit

Two episodes. Attempting to set Ranma's female side free, Happosai's incense burning separates his good and bad sides. Girl-type Ranma soon becomes a real bad girl. Then, a copycat martial artist can make himself the exact double of anyone he wants…even Ranma. Dubbed.
VHS: S33624. $24.95.
Kitty Film, Japan, 1995, 52 mins.

Ranma 1/2 Hard Battle Vol. 11: Soap Gets in Your Eyes

Two episodes. Shampoo acquires a special waterproofing soap that allows the Jusenkyo-cursed to get drenched and not turn into their "cursed" form. Then, the Anything-Goes Obstacle Course Race. Dubbed.
VHS: S33623. $24.95.
Kitty Film, Japan, 1995, 52 mins.

Ranma 1/2 Hard Battle Vol. 12: Mirror Mirror

Two episodes. Happosai's magic mirror comes back into play as Ranma and Happosai go back in time to change the past, and end up bouncing around time, even to a future where Ryoga is married to Akane. Plus, the tomboyish Ukyo shows up wearing a skirt, and nobody recognizes her. Dubbed.
VHS: S32764. $24.95.
Kitty Film, Japan, 1995, 52 mins.

Ranma 1/2 Movie #1: Big Trouble in Nekonron China

Lychee comes to settle a score with Happosai—the martial arts teacher of Genma and Soun. He gave her great-grandmother half of a legendary scroll guaranteed to bring happiness, and the women in Lychee's family are growing tired of waiting. But as soon as Akane gets the scroll, she's swept off to her prince's castle in Nekonron with the whole crew in pursuit. HiFi Stereo.
VHS: Dubbed. **S29299. $34.95.**
VHS: Subtitled. **S20904. $34.95.**
Kitty Films, Japan, 1994, 74 mins.

Ranma 1/2 Movie #2: Nihao My Concubine

Ranma & Co. are shipwrecked on a deserted island, and the girls start disappearing. It turns out they've been kidnapped by Prince Toma, youthful ruler of the floating island Togenkyo. Because of a magical spring that turns anything it touches instantly male, would-be bridegrooms have to kidnap girls…and Ranma's fiance Akane is one of them. Nudity. HiFi Stereo.
VHS: Dubbed. **S29300. $34.95.**
VHS: Subtitled. **S27458. $34.95.**
Kitty Film, Japan, 1994, 60 mins.

Ranma 1/2 OAV #1: Desperately Seeking Shampoo

TwoOAVs: In *Shampoo's Sudden Switch! The Curse of the Contrary Jewel*, Shampoo selects a cursed brooch which either enhances one's feelings of love or one's feelings of hatred. In *Tendo Family Christmas Scramble*, the entire cast of the show turns up on the Tendos' doorstep to indulge in holiday-themed mayhem. Nudity. HiFi Stereo. VHS is dubbed. Laserdisc is multi-audio.
VHS: S19892. $34.95.
Laser: LD75770. $39.95.
Kitty Films, Japan, 1994, 52 mins.

Ranma 1/2 OAV #2: Like Water for Ranma

Two OAVs: In *Akane vs. Ranma*, youngest Tendo daughter Akane assumes the cooking duties, and must hide her real identity from Nodoka by becoming "Ran-Ko." In *Stormy Weather Comes to School*, we meet Hinako Ninomiya. She's a new teacher sent to discipline the students, and she gets into a comedic competition to determine who rules the roost at Furinkan High. Nudity. HiFi Stereo. VHS is dubbed. Laserdisc is multi-audio.
VHS: S21838. $34.95.
Laser: LD75519. $39.95.
Kitty Films, Japan, 1994, 52 mins.

Ranma 1/2 OAV #3: Akane and Her Sisters

In the two-part story *The One to Carry On*, two strange girls appear at the Tendos to claim their heritage—The Tendo Martial Arts Hall. Can Akane and Ranma defeat them? HiFi Stereo. Dubbed.
VHS: S29297. $34.95.
Kitty Films, Japan, 60 mins.

Ranma 1/2 OAV #4: An Akane to Remember

In Reawakening Memories, Parts 1 and 2, Akane sees a newscast about "monster sightings" in remote Japan, which triggers a fleeting recollection of being rescued by a boy bearing a horn whistle. Akane sets out and finds this boy, with Ranma coming behind to bring her back to safety. HiFi Stereo. Dubbed.
VHS: S29298. $29.95.
Kitty Film, Japan, 1995, 60 mins.

Ranma 1/2 OAV #5: One Grew over the Kuno's Nest

Two OAVs: In *Team Ranma vs. The Legendary Phoenix*, Kuno schemes to employ the power of a legendary Phoenix egg to defeat Ranma. But before he can carry out his plan, the egg hatches and the Phoenix latches onto him like glue! In *The Tunnel of Lost Love*, Ranma and company spend their vacations near a haunted cave. Legend has it that any couple that enters will exit ready to take out personal ads! HiFi Stereo. Dubbed.
VHS: Dubbed. **S27090. $29.95.**
VHS: Subtitled. **S31162. $29.95.**
Kitty Film, Japan, 1995, 60 mins.

Ranma 1/2 OAV #6: Faster Kasumi, Kill! Kill!

Two OAVs: An ogre possesses gentle Kasumi. How long can the devil in Miss Tendo hold the whole household hostage to terror before somebody takes matters into their own hands? Then, an evil doll switches consciousness with Akane. As eerie Doppleganger menaces Ranma, tiny Akane has to find a way to warn him of the danger he's in…but how can she when she can't even talk? HiFi Stereo. Dubbed.
VHS: Dubbed. **S27677. $29.95.**
VHS: Subtitled. **S32766. $29.95.**
Kitty Film, Japan, 1995, 60 mins.

Ranma 1/2 Outta Control: My Fiance, The Cat

In *Ryoga…Beyond the Pleasure and Pain*, stranded in the lonely mountains, and plagued by memories of his thwarted love Akane, Ryoga pauses to remember not only his grudge against his rival Ranma, but his true and unchanging love for Akane herself. In *My Fiance, the Ghost-Cat*, according to legend, whoever it is that possesses one of two matching bells is destined to be wed. In *Beauty and the Beast* like marries a mysterious hulking monster with a weakness for catnip. Dubbed.
VHS: S34174. $24.95.

Ranma 1/2 TV Series Vol. 1

Episodes 1 and 2: Mr. Tendo and his daughters await the return of Genma Saotome and his son Ranma from China. They're in for a surprise when a giant Panda and a girl enter Mr. Tendo's martial arts studio and introduce themselves as the Saotomes. Both have a Chinese curse which changes them into a girl and a panda when they're doused by cold water, and back again when doused with hot water. Nudity. HiFi Stereo. Dubbed.
VHS: S20149. $29.95.
Kitty Film, Japan, 1994, 50 mins.

Ranma 1/2 TV Series Vol. 2

Episodes 3 and 4. Kuno is smitten by the lovely wench he knows only as the "pig-tailed girl." Naturally, Ranma doesn't react too well to Kuno's come-ons, and a battle is arranged. Meanwhile, Nabiki has discovered a new source of income…selling "French postcards" of female Ranma to a lovesick Kuno! Nudity. HiFi Stereo. Dubbed.
VHS: S20150. $29.95.
Kitty Film, Japan, 1994, 50 mins.

Ranma 1/2 TV Series Vol. 3

Episodes 5 and 6. Kuno continues his assault on male Ranma for alleged lechery against female Ranma, and when Genma counsels Ranma to be nicer to his intended, Ranma grudgingly admits that Akane may not be so bad. Nudity. HiFi Stereo. Dubbed.
VHS: S20151. $29.95.
Kitty Film, Japan, 1994, 50 mins.

Ranma 1/2 TV Series Vol. 4

Episodes 7 and 8. Ryoga Hibiki is a martial artist with a grudge against Ranma. Hampered by a tendency to get lost easily, he may not make it to Furinkan High to settle a score with his rival. Nudity. HiFi Stereo. Dubbed.
VHS: S33941. $29.95.
Kitty Film, Japan, 1994, 50 mins.

Ranma 1/2 TV Series Vol. 5

Episodes 9 and 10. Newly coiffed Akane learns Ranma isn't always a jerk. Newly humbled Ranma learns his problems with Ryoga run deep. Newly aquaphobic Ryoga learns to keep out of the rain…or else. Nudity. HiFi Stereo. Dubbed.
VHS: S20906. $29.95.
Kitty Film, Japan, 1994, 50 mins.

Ranma 1/2 TV Series Vol. 6

Episodes 11 and 12. Akane is elected champion gymnast for an upcoming match against a girl from another school. Why is there such a strong resemblence between this girl and Kuno? Then, an accident forces Akane to withdraw from the upcoming match. Could it be that the champion fighting to decide who'll go steady with Ranma is…Ranma? Nudity. HiFi Stereo. Dubbed.
VHS: S24894. $29.95.
Kitty Film, Japan, 1994, 50 mins.

Ranma 1/2 TV Series Vol. 7

Episodes 13 and 14. Can Ranma beat Kodachi "The Black Rose" at her own game? And does Dr. Tofu's mother really know best about matchmaking? Nudity. HiFi Stereo. Dubbed.
VHS: S24893. $29.95.
Kitty Film, Japan, 1994, 50 mins.

Ranma 1/2 TV Series Vol. 8

Episodes 15 and 16. Ranma discovers there's a price for being a girl, especially when Shampoo is around. By the custom of her tribe, one defeated by a man must wed that man, while those defeated by a woman must kill that woman! Then, Shampoo's going to wash that Ranma right out of Akane's hair with a secret memory-erasing shampoo formula. Nudity. HiFi Stereo. Dubbed.
VHS: S23082. $29.95.
Kitty Film, Japan, 1994, 50 mins.

Ranma 1/2 TV Series Vol. 9

Episodes 17 and 18: The last installment of the first *Ranma 1/2* series. Shampoo will give Ranma the formula to restore Akane's memory if he promises to "almost kill" female Ranma. When Saotome announces he's returning to China, Ranma and Genma reminisce and review their adventures so far in the series. Nudity. HiFi Stereo. Dubbed.
VHS: S23334. $29.95.
Kitty Films, Japan, 1994, 52 mins.

Ranma 1/2: Immortal Kombat

The exciting *Ranma* conclusion. The terrifying secret of the powerful Heavenly Dragon is revealed and perverted martial arts master Happosai is determined to withhold the battle aura that Ranma really needs. A visit from Ranma's mom makes the adventure complete. Dubbed. 52 mins.
VHS: S34788. $24.95.

Raven Tengu Kabuto

Kabuto is a fast-paced and sexy fusion of traditional Japanese mythology and cyberpunk technology that could only come from the mind of Buichi Terasawa *(Space Adventure Cobra, Midnight Eye Goku)*. Contains nudity and sexual situations. Subtitled.
VHS: S18339. $19.95.
Buichi Terasawa, Japan, 1992, 45 mins.

Record of Lodoss War Vol. 1

Episode 1: *Prologue to the Legend*, Episode 2: *Blazing Departure* and Episode 3: *The Black Knight*. Lodoss has seen wars for thousands of years, but now a greater evil than ever before has drawn together six people: Parn the fighter, Deedlit the elf, Ghim the dwarf, Etoh the priest, Slayn the magician and Woodchuck the thief. HiFi Stereo.
VHS: Dubbed. **S29305. $19.95.**
VHS: Subtitled. **S23765. $29.95.**
Group SNE, Japan, 1990, 86 mins.

Record of Lodoss War Vol. 2

Episode 4: *The Grey Witch* and Episode 5: *The Desert King*. In the midst of the invasion of Lodoss, Parn and his cohorts must warn the remaining free kingdoms, but first they must fight off Karla, the mysterious Grey Witch, who attempts to kidnap Princess Fianna. As the heroes are honored at a court party, a powerful new ally is introduced. HiFi Stereo.
VHS: Dubbed. **S29306. $19.95.**
VHS: Subtitled. **S23766. $29.95.**
Group SNE, Japan, 1990, 55 mins.

Record of Lodoss War Vol. 3

Episode 6: *The Sword of the Dark Emperor* and Episode 7: *The War of the Heroes*. Beld's forces sweep across the island. Reaching Valis, our heroes advise the king that Karla is the last descendent of an ancient kingdom of sorcery. King Fahn invites Parn to serve in his army of Holy Knights. Once out on the blazing battlefield, Parn confronts the Black Knight, Ashram—the man upon whom he swore vengeance at the fall of Myce. HiFi Stereo.
VHS: Dubbed. **S29307. $19.95.**
VHS: Subtitled. **S23767. $29.95.**
Group SNE, Japan, 1990, 55 mins.

Record of Lodoss War Vol. 4

Episode 8: *Requiem for Warriors* and Episode 9: *The Scepter of Domination*. Pursuing Ghim to Karla's castle, the heroes encounter Shiris and her partner, Orson. Ghim faces the witch in a duel of wills in an attempt to free Leylia. Meanwhile, the forces of Marmo are in disarray as Ashram prepares to take up the struggle where Beld left off. Urged on by the dark wizard Wagnard, he sets off for Fire Dragon Mountain to obtain the Scepter of Domination. HiFi Stereo.
VHS: Dubbed. **$29308. $19.95.**
VHS: Subtitled. **$23768. $29.95.**
Group SNE, Japan, 1991, 55 mins.

Record of Lodoss War Vol. 5

Episode 10, *The Demon Dragon of Fire Dragon Mountain*, and Episode 11, *The Wizard's Ambition*. Kashue and Ashram race one another for the Scepter of Domination, but it's guarded by a formidable obstacle: the dragon Shooting Star. The evil of Kardis the Destroyer stirs beneath the dark island of Marmo, and Wagnard takes the final steps toward her resurrection. HiFi Stereo.
VHS: Dubbed. **$29309. $19.95.**
VHS: Subtitled. **$23769. $29.95.**
Group SNE, Japan, 1991, 55 mins.

Record of Lodoss War Vol. 6

Episode 12: *Final Battle! Marmo the Dark Island* and Episode 13: *Lodoss—The Burning Continent*. As Kashue and the remaining armies of Lodoss move to stop the resurrection of Kardis, Parn and his friends arrive just ahead of them. But the island of Marmo holds the evil dragon Narse. As Parn and the others rush to stop this dark rite underground, Kashue and his army face the demonic forces of Kardis on the surface. Concludes the series. HiFi Stereo.
VHS: Dubbed. **$29310. $19.95.**
VHS: Subtitled. **$23770. $29.95.**
Group SNE, Japan, 1991, 55 mins.

Record of Lodoss War, Gift Box

This wide-ranging epic fantasy spans a cosmos peopled by fantastic creatures with great powers. They are engaged in a tremendous struggle, the outcome of which will affect the universe. It's an anime feature series with stunning imagery, compelling characters and gruesome monsters. Japanese with English subtitles. Six volumes.
VHS: $24231. $129.95.
Akinori Nagaoka/Shigeto Makino/Katsuhisa Yamada, et al., Japan, 1990, 355 mins.

Red Hawk

In this Korean film, terror reigns in the land of Chungwon. Honglyung sets out with her friends to find the only one who can save the country—Red Hawk. To defeat the Camellia Blossoms war gang, Red Hawk must kill his own brother. Violence and profanity. Dubbed.
VHS: $33864. $19.95.
Dai Won, Korea, 1995, 90 mins.

Renegade Force

A maverick security force enlists a karate champion to operate a powerful, high-tech, armed robot called Magnon. In conjunction with its sister ship, the Magnetta, they battle deadly and sinister aliens for control of the universe. 90 mins.
VHS: $18265. $29.95.

Return of the Dinosaurs

A mysterious comet crash lands on Earth, causing a gravitational pull that plunges the planet back into the prehistoric ages and occasions the return of the dinosaurs. When the climate heals the dinosaurs begin dying out and the international community must act to preserve these majestic, astounding animals from certain death. Japanese animation wizard Akira Tsuburaya created this work. 70 mins.
VHS: $17523. $19.99.

RG Veda, Part 1

At the dawn of time, General Taishakuten brutally slaughters the ruler of the universe. Legend says that six super-powered warriors will rise to restore the world to a golden age. But now there are only five: Yasha, Ashura, Ryuoh, Karura and Sohma. Will they be able to find the sixth? Stereo. Subtitled.
VHS: $19884. $29.95.
Laser: LD75787. $34.95.
Clamp, Japan, 1992, 45 mins.

RG Veda, Part 2

The warriors' quest leads them right into the heart of Taishakuten's castle. As his guards descend on Ashura, the youngest and most powerful warrior, she is mysteriously transported in a blaze of white light to another time and dimension. Will she return safely and in time to rescue Yasha, who now lies beneath Taishakuten's sword? Stereo. Subtitled.
VHS: $20864. $29.95.
Laser: LD74834. $34.95.
Clamp, Japan, 1992, 45 mins.

Rhea Gall Force

The Solnoid race is long since annihilated, but their descendents survive on Earth. In 2085, the East-West war has reduced Earth's cities to rubble. With the killing machines on the loose, the only chance for survival seems to be evacuation to Mars. Stereo. Subtitled.
VHS: $21839. $29.95.
Laser: LD75049. $34.95.
Movic, Japan, 1989, 60 mins.

Riding Bean

Ace courier Bean Bandit operates on both sides of the law. His latest cargo is a 10-year-old girl worth 50 Grand when delivered home. But Bean is about to be framed for a kidnap, and the Chicago Police are hot on his trail. For laserdisc see *Madox 01/Riding Bean*. Nudity and violence. HiFi Stereo.
VHS: Dubbed. **$20752. $19.95.**
VHS: Subtitled. **$16072. $24.95.**
Youmex, Japan, 1989, 46 mins.

Robotech Vol. 1

Episode 1: *Boobytrap*. Episode 2: *Countdown*.
VHS: $18879. $14.95.
Harmony Gold, Japan, 1985, 45 mins.

Robotech Vol. 2

Episode 3 : *Space Fold*. Episode 4: *The Long Wait*.
VHS: $18880. $14.95.
Harmony Gold, Japan, 1985, 45 mins.

Robotech Vol. 3

Episode 5: *Transformation*. Episode 6: *Blitzkrieg*.
VHS: $18881. $14.95.
Harmony Gold, Japan, 1985, 45 mins.

Robotech Vol. 4

Episode 7: *Bye Bye Mars*. Episode 8: *Sweet Sixteen*.
VHS: $18882. $14.95.
Harmony Gold, Japan, 1985, 45 mins.

Robotech Vol. 5

Episode 9: *Miss Macross*. Episode 10: *Blind Game*.
VHS: $18883. $14.95.
Harmony Gold, Japan, 1985, 45 mins.

Robotech Vol. 6

Episode 11: *First Contact*. Episode 12: *The Big Escape*.
VHS: $18884. $14.95.
Harmony Gold, Japan, 1985, 45 mins.

Robotech Vol. 7

Episode 13: *Blue Wind*. Episode 14: *Gloval's Report*.
VHS: $18885. $14.95.
Harmony Gold, Japan, 1985, 45 mins.

Robotech Vol. 8

Episode 15: *Homecoming*. Episode 16: *Battle Cry*.
VHS: $18886. $14.95.
Harmony Gold, Japan, 1985, 45 mins.

Robotech Vol. 9

Episode 17: *Phantasm*. Episode 18: *Farewell Big Brother*.
VHS: $18887. $14.95.
Harmony Gold, Japan, 1985, 45 mins.

Robotech Vol. 10

Episode 19: *Bursting Point*. Episode 20: *Paradise Lost*.
VHS: $18888. $14.95.
Harmony Gold, Japan, 1985, 45 mins.

Robotech Vol. 11

Episode 21: *Blue Wind*. Episode 22: *Battle Hymn*.
VHS: $25574. $14.95.
Harmony Gold, Japan, 1985, 45 mins.

Robotech Vol. 12

Episode 23: *Reckless*. Episode 24: *Showdown*.
VHS: $25575. $14.95.
Harmony Gold, Japan, 1985, 45 mins.

Robotech Vol. 13

Episode 25: *Wedding Bells*. Episode 26: *The Messenger*.
VHS: $25576. $14.95.
Harmony Gold, Japan, 1985, 45 mins.

Robotech Vol. 14

Episode 27: *Force of Arms*. Episode 28: *Reconstruction Blues*.
VHS: $25577. $14.95.
Harmony Gold, Japan, 1985, 45 mins.

Robotech Vol. 15

Episode 29: *The Robotech Masters*. Episode 30: *Viva Miriya*.
VHS: $25578. $14.95.
Harmony Gold, Japan, 1985, 45 mins.

Robotech Vol. 16

Episode 31: *Khyron's Revenge*. Episode 32: *Broken Heart*.
VHS: $25579. $14.95.
Harmony Gold, Japan, 1985, 45 mins.

Robotech Vol. 17

Episode 33: *A Rainy Night*. Episode 34: *Private Time*.
VHS: $25580. $14.95.
Harmony Gold, Japan, 1985, 45 mins.

Robotech Vol. 18

Episode 35: *Season's Greetings*. Episode 36: *To the Stars*.
VHS: $25581. $14.95.
Harmony Gold, Japan, 1985, 45 mins.

Robotech Vol. 19

Episode 37: *Dana's Story*. Episode 38: *False Start*.
VHS: $25582. $14.95.
Harmony Gold, Japan, 1985, 45 mins.

Robotech Vol. 20

Episode 39: *The Southern Cross*. Episode 40: *Volunteers*.
VHS: $25583. $14.95.
Harmony Gold, Japan, 1985, 45 mins.

Robotech Vol. 21

Episode 41: *Half Moon*. Episode 42: *Danger Zone*.
VHS: $25584. $14.95.
Harmony Gold, Japan, 1985, 45 mins.

Robotech Vol. 22

Episode 43: *Prelude to Battle*. Episode 44: *The Trap*.
VHS: $25585. $14.95.
Harmony Gold, Japan, 1985, 45 mins.

Robotech Vol. 23

Episode 45: *Metal Fire*. Episode 46: *Stardust*.
VHS: $25586. $14.95.
Harmony Gold, Japan, 1985, 45 mins.

Robotech Vol. 24

Episode 47: *Outsiders*. Episode 48: *Deja Vu*.
VHS: $25587. $14.95.
Harmony Gold, Japan, 1985, 45 mins.

Robotech Vol. 25

Episode 49: *A New Recruit*. Episode 50: *Triumvirate*.
VHS: $25588. $14.95.
Harmony Gold, Japan, 1985, 45 mins.

Robotech Vol. 26

Episode 51: *Clone Chamber*. Episode 52: *Love Song*.
VHS: $25589. $14.95.
Harmony Gold, Japan, 1985, 45 mins.

Robotech Vol. 27

Episode 53: *The Hunters*. Episode 54: *Mind Game*.
VHS: $25590. $14.95.
Harmony Gold, Japan, 1985, 45 mins.

Robotech Vol. 28

Episode 55: *Dana in Wonderland*. Episode 56: *Crisis Point*.
VHS: $25591. $14.95.
Harmony Gold, Japan, 1985, 45 mins.

Robotech Vol. 29

Episode 57: *Day Dreamer*. Episode 58: *Final Nightmare*.
VHS: $25592. $14.95.
Harmony Gold, Japan, 1985, 45 mins.

Robotech Vol. 30

Episode 59: *The Invid Connection*. Episode 60: *Catastrophe*.
VHS: $25593. $14.95.
Harmony Gold, Japan, 1985, 45 mins.

Robotech Vol. 31

Episode 61: *The Invid Invasion*. Episode 62: *The Lost City*.
VHS: $25594. $14.95.
Harmony Gold, Japan, 1985, 45 mins.

Robotech Vol. 32

Episode 63: *Lonely Soldier Boy*. Episode 64: *Survival*.
VHS: $25595. $14.95.
Harmony Gold, Japan, 1985, 45 mins.

Robotech Vol. 33

Episode 65: *Curtain Call*. Episode 66: *Hard Times*.
VHS: $25596. $14.95.
Harmony Gold, Japan, 1985, 45 mins.

Robotech Vol. 34
Episode 67: *Paper Hero*. Episode 68: *Eulogy*.
VHS: S25597. $14.95.
Harmony Gold, Japan, 1985, 45 mins.

Robotech Vol. 35
Episode 69: *The Genesis Pit*. Episode 70: *Enter Marlene*.
VHS: S25598. $14.95.
Harmony Gold, Japan, 1985, 45 mins.

Robotech Vol. 36
Episode 71: *The Secret Route*. Episode 72: *The Fortress*.
VHS: S25599. $14.95.
Harmony Gold, Japan, 1985, 45 mins.

Robotech Vol. 37
Episode 73: *Sandstorms*. Episode 74: *Annie's Wedding*.
VHS: S25600. $14.95.
Harmony Gold, Japan, 1985, 45 mins.

Robotech Vol. 38
Episode 75: *Separate Ways*. Episode 76: *Metamorphosis*.
VHS: S25601. $14.95.
Harmony Gold, Japan, 1985, 45 mins.

Robotech Vol. 39
Episode 77: *The Midnight Sun*. Episode 78: *Ghost Town*.
VHS: S25602. $14.95.
Harmony Gold, Japan, 1985, 45 mins.

Robotech Vol. 40
Episode 79: *Frostbite*. Episode 80: *Birthday Blues*.
VHS: S25603. $14.95.
Harmony Gold, Japan, 1985, 45 mins.

Robotech Vol. 41
Episode 81: *Hired Gun*. Episode 82: *The Big Apple*.
VHS: S25604. $14.95.
Harmony Gold, Japan, 1985, 45 mins.

Robotech Vol. 42
Episode 83: *Reflex Point*. Episode 84: *Dark Finale*. Episode 85: *Symphony of Light*.
VHS: S25605. $14.95.
Harmony Gold, Japan, 1985, 75 mins.

Robotech Perfect Collection Macross Vol. 1
Robotech Macross episodes 1 & 2, dubbed. Original *Macross* episodes 1 & 2, subtitled.
VHS: S29312. $19.95.
Tatsunoko, Japan, 1982, 100 mins.

Robotech Perfect Collection Macross Vol. 2
Robotech Macross episodes 3 & 4, dubbed. Original *Macross* episodes 3 & 4, subtitled.
VHS: S29313. $19.95.
Tatsunoko, Japan, 1982, 100 mins.

Robotech Perfect Collection Macross Vol. 3
Robotech Macross episodes 5 & 6, dubbed. Original *Macross* episodes 5 & 6, subtitled.
VHS: S29314. $19.95.
Tatsunoko, Japan, 1982, 100 mins.

Robotech Perfect Collection Macross Vol. 4
Robotech Macross episodes 7 & 8, dubbed. Original *Macross* episodes 7 & 8, subtitled.
VHS: S29315. $19.95.
Tatsunoko, Japan, 1982, 100 mins.

Robotech Perfect Collection Macross Vol. 5
Robotech Macross episodes 9 & 10, dubbed. Original *Macross* episodes 9 & 10, subtitled.
VHS: S22409. $19.95.
Tatsunoko, Japan, 1982, 100 mins.

Robotech Perfect Collection Macross Vol. 6
Robotech Macross episodes 11 & 12, dubbed. Original *Macross* episodes 11 & 12, subtitled.
VHS: S23340. $19.95.
Tatsunoko, Japan, 1982, 100 mins.

Robotech Perfect Collection Macross Vol. 7
Robotech Macross episodes 13 & 14, dubbed. Original *Macross* episodes 13 & 14, subtitled.
VHS: S29316. $19.95.
Tatsunoko, Japan, 1982, 100 mins.

Robotech Perfect Collection Mospeada Vol. 1
Robotech New Gen. episodes 1 & 2, dubbed. Original *Mospeada* episodes 1 & 2, subtitled.
VHS: S29322. $19.95.
Tatsunoko, Japan, 1983, 100 mins.

Robotech Perfect Collection Mospeada Vol. 2
Robotech New Gen. episodes 3 & 4, dubbed. Original *Mospeada* episodes 3 & 4, subtitled.
VHS: S29324. $19.95.
Tatsunoko, Japan, 1983, 100 mins.

Robotech Perfect Collection Mospeada Vol. 3
Robotech New Gen. episodes 5 & 6, dubbed. Original *Mospeada* episodes 5 & 6, subtitled.
VHS: S29325. $19.95.
Tatsunoko, Japan, 1983, 100 mins.

Robotech Perfect Collection Mospeada Vol. 4
Robotech New Gen. episodes 7 & 8, dubbed. Original *Mospeada* episodes 7 & 8, subtitled.
VHS: S29326. $19.95.
Tatsunoko, Japan, 1983, 100 mins.

Robotech Perfect Collection Mospeada Vol. 5
Robotech New Gen. episodes 9 & 10, dubbed. Original *Mospeada* episodes 9 & 10, subtitled.
VHS: S22411. $19.95.
Tatsunoko, Japan, 1983, 100 mins.

Robotech Perfect Collection Mospeada Vol. 6
Robotech New Gen. episodes 11 & 12, dubbed. Original *Mospeada* episodes 11 & 12, subtitled.
VHS: S23342. $19.95.
Tatsunoko, Japan, 1983, 100 mins.

Robotech Perfect Collection Mospeada Vol. 7
Robotech New Gen. episodes 13 & 14, dubbed. Original *Mospeada* episodes 13 & 14, subtitled.
VHS: S29327. $19.95.
Tatsunoko, Japan, 1983, 100 mins.

Robotech Perfect Collection Southern Cross Vol. 1
Robotech Southern Cross episodes 1 & 2, dubbed. Original *Southern Cross* episodes 1 & 2, subtitled.
VHS: S29317. $19.95.
Tatsunoko, Japan, 1984, 100 mins.

Robotech Perfect Collection Southern Cross Vol. 2
Robotech Southern Cross episodes 3 & 4, dubbed. Original *Southern* Cross episodes 3 & 4, subtitled.
VHS: S29318. $19.95.
Tatsunoko, Japan, 1984, 100 mins.

Robotech Perfect Collection Southern Cross Vol. 3
Robotech Southern Cross episodes 5 & 6, dubbed. Original *Southern Cross* episodes 5 & 6, subtitled.
VHS: S29319. $19.95.
Tatsunoko, Japan, 1984, 100 mins.

Robotech Perfect Collection Southern Cross Vol. 4
Robotech Southern Cross episodes 7 & 8, dubbed. Original *Southern Cross* episodes 7 & 8, subtitled.
VHS: S29320. $19.95.
Tatsunoko, Japan, 1984, 100 mins.

Robotech Perfect Collection Southern Cross Vol. 5
Robotech Southern Cross episodes 9 & 10, dubbed. Original *Southern Cross* episodes 9 & 10, subtitled.
VHS: S22410. $19.95.
Tatsunoko, Japan, 1984, 100 mins.

Robotech Perfect Collection Southern Cross Vol. 6
Robotech Southern Cross episodes 11 & 12, dubbed. Original *Southern Cross* episodes 11 & 12, subtitled.
VHS: S23341. $19.95.
Tatsunoko, Japan, 1984, 100 mins.

Robotech Perfect Collection Southern Cross Vol. 7
Robotech Southern Cross episodes 13 & 14, dubbed. Original *Southern Cross* episodes 13 & 14, subtitled.
VHS: S29321. $19.95.
Tatsunoko, Japan, 1984, 100 mins.

Robotech II: The Sentinels
Originally conceived as a 65-episode follow-up to the 85-episode *Robotech* saga, *Robotech II* was never completed. What remains are four partially completed episodes. This feature film is compiled from that animation and additional "rediscovered" footage. The crew of the SDF-3 watches a hostile alien race annihilate the home world of the Robotech Masters. Dubbed.
VHS: S16659. $19.95.
Tatsunoko, Japan, 1988, 90 mins.

Robotech Macross LD #2
Episodes 5-8.
Laser: LD75773. $34.95.
Harmony Gold, Japan, 1985, 90 mins.

Robotech Macross LD #3
Episodes 9-12.
Laser: LD75774. $34.95.
Harmony Gold, Japan, 1985, 90 mins.

Robotech Macross LD #4
Episodes 13-16.
Laser: LD75775. $34.95.
Harmony Gold, Japan, 1985, 90 mins.

Robotech Macross LD #5
Episodes 17-20.
Laser: LD75776. $34.95.
Harmony Gold, Japan, 1985, 90 mins.

Robotech Macross LD #6
Episodes 21-24.
Laser: LD75777. $34.95.
Harmony Gold, Japan, 1985, 90 mins.

Robotech Macross LD #7
Episodes 25-28.
Laser: LD75778. $34.95.
Harmony Gold, Japan, 1985, 90 mins.

Robotech Macross LD #8
Episodes 29-32.
Laser: LD75779. $34.95.
Harmony Gold, Japan, 1985, 90 mins.

Robotech Macross LD #9
Episodes 33-36.
Laser: LD75780. $34.95.
Harmony Gold, Japan, 1985, 90 mins.

Roots Search
An alien life form capable of fatal psychic projection has boarded a lone research satellite. This monster is infecting the minds of the crew, killing them one by one. Moira and Buzz are two crewmates who manage to dodge the alien's fierceness long enough to fall in love. Their romance seems eternal yet their death seems imminent. Stereo. Subtitled.
VHS: S17525. $19.95.
Laser: LD74514. $34.95.
Nippon, Japan, 1986, 45 mins.

Roujin Z
In this film written and directed by *Akira's* Katsuhito Otomo, an elderly invalid is volunteered for a bizarre experiment. The Z-001 can monitor, bathe, feed, exercise and entertain by linking with Takazawa's brainwaves. However, when it begins providing for his every need, the Z-001 transforms into an unstoppable robot that smashes out of the hospital and battles through police barricades! Stereo.
VHS: Dubbed. **S29311. $19.95.**
VHS: Subtitled. **S27455. $29.95.**
Japan, 80 mins.

Ruin Explorers
Lovely young adventurers Fam and Ihrie take on a dangerous assignment to recover a fabled weapon of unbelievable power that could shake an entire civilization to its foundations. 60 mins.
Dubbed Version.
VHS: S34805. $19.95.
Subtitled Version.
VHS: S34806. $29.95.

Rumik World: Firetripper

Blown 500 years into the past by a gigantic storage tank explosion, Suzuko lands on top of a medieval battlefield. With her new home also in flames, time begins to loop back on itself. Suzuko and Shukumaru, the warrior who saves her, cope with mystery, tragedy and disaster as time unravels amidst the roaring flames. Nudity. Stereo.

VHS: Subtitled. **S17867. $14.95.**
VHS: Dubbed. **S30280. $14.95.**
Laser: Subtitled. **LD74506. $29.95.**
Japan, 1992, 50 mins.

Rumik World: Maris the Chojo

Maris is a Thanatosian with an alcoholic father and an airhead mother. She's also an accident-prone policewoman with superhuman strength. When she's assigned to rescue the wealthy and handsome Kogane Maru, will she seize the opportunity or once again fumble her assignment? Nudity. Stereo.

VHS: Dubbed. **S30282. $14.95.**
Laser: Subtitled. **LD74510. $39.95.**
Rumiko Takahashi, Japan, 1986, 50 mins.

Rumik World: Mermaid Forest

Legend has it that eating Mermaid flesh will give you immortality. The truth is far worse: the lucky ones die while the unlucky ones turn into hideous, immortal monsters. Yuta, a sailor cursed with immortality, has traveled the world for centuries seeking a mate. Mana may be the one, but first she must be rescued from the evil Dr. Shina. Nudity. Stereo.

VHS: Subtitled. **S17868. $14.95.**
Laser: Subtitled. **LD74512. $39.95.**
Rumiko Takahashi, Japan, 55 mins.

Rumik World: The Laughing Target

Yazuru and his cousin Azusa had an arranged marriage at age six. Ten years later, Yazura is dating Satomi when Azusa returns to fulfill their childhood vows. Terrible things have happened to Azusa that are hidden by her shy demeanor. Nudity. Stereo.

VHS: Dubbed. **S30281. $14.95.**
Laser: Subtitled. **LD74509. $34.95.**
Rumiko Takahashi, Japan, 1992, 50 mins.

Rupan III: Legend of the Gold of Babylon

Also known as *Lupin III*. It's thugs vs. thieves when Rupan & Co. go up against a fearsome, fly-swatting, Polish Mafia boss, a bevy of beauty-contest policewomen, Inspector Zenigata, a mysterious bag lady, and even his own girlfriend, in a transcontinental trek. HiFi Stereo. Subtitled.

VHS: S23761. $24.95.
Laser: LD74793. $39.95.
YTV, Japan, 1987, 100 mins.

Rupan III: The Fuma Conspiracy

Also known as *Lupin III*. The tranquility of a Japanese wedding is shattered when the bride is kidnapped by evil Ninja who demand the key to a hidden treasure as ransom! Rupan and Co. go after the girl and the gold as they try to stay ahead of Inspector Zenigata. HiFi Stereo.

VHS: Dubbed. **S29328. $19.95.**
VHS: Subtitled. **S23759. $24.95.**
Laser: Subtitled. **LD74792. $39.95.**
Toho, Japan, 1987, 73 mins.

Sailor Moon Vol. 1: A Moon Star Is Born

Two episodes. In *A Moon Star Is Born*, the ditzy schoolgirl Serena is introduced, along with Darien (aka Tuxedo Mask) and the talking black cat, Luna. In *Talk Radio*, callers who contact a mysterious talk show are afflicted with a strange sleeping disease—can the floral brooches they receive from the radio station be the cause? Dubbed.

VHS: S33409. $12.95.
Toei, Japan, 1992, 44 mins.

Sailor Moon Vol. 2: Scouts Unite!

Two episodes. In *Computer School Blues*, Serena suspects Amy, a new girl in school, of being an alien from the Negaverse. But after their teacher mutates into the real alien, Amy turns out to be Sailor Mercury. In *An Uncharmed Life*, young girls who buy lucky charms from an alien in disguise suddenly disappear. Sailor Moon helps Raye transform into Sailor Mars. Dubbed.

VHS: S33618. $12.95.
Toei, Japan, 1992, 44 mins.

Sailor Moon Vol. 3: Evil Eyes

Two episodes. In *Cruise Blues*, Serena is jealous when Raye wins cruise tickets and invites Amy instead of her. In *Shutter Bugged*, a photographer who is possessed by the evil Neflite takes Amy and Raye's picture, and with it, their energy. Dubbed.

VHS: S33619. $12.95.
Toei, Japan, 1992, 44 mins.

Samurai Shodown: The Motion Picture

Based upon the SNK video game (originally *Samurai Spirits* in Japan). Fans of the game will thrill to the continued adventures of Charlotte, Wan Fu, Nakoruru, Galford and Tamtam as they search the feudal province of Edo in quest of their lost comrade, Haohmaru, and their sworn nemesis, Shirou Amakusa. Violence. HiFi Stereo. Dubbed.

VHS: S23873. $19.95.
Fuji 8, Japan, 1994, 80 mins.

Satanika

The popular Verotik character Satanika comes to life in full Japanese animation. Produced by Mad House Studios, this beautiful anime pilot features storyboards by the renowned Rintaro and character designs by Yoshiaki Kawajiri. Also included are interviews with series creator Glenn Danzig (The Misfits, Danzig) and Mad House staff Rintaro, Takuji Endoh and Mad House producer Masao Maruyama.

VHS: S34518. $19.95.
Tajuji Endoh, Japan, 1997, 25 mins.

The Secret of Blue Water, Vol. 1: The Adventure Begins

Episodes 1-4. The Paris International Exposition of 1889 provides the backdrop for this Jules Verne-inspired serial. The adventure begins when Jean, a young French inventor, accidentally meets Nadia, an indentured circus acrobat, at the Eiffel Tower. The wheels are set in motion for an adventure which will eventually take the two young orphans on a journey to distant lands in search of answers they know little of. Complicating matter is Lady Grandis, an opportunist who will stop at nothing to get what she wants. And what she wants is a powerful amulet—The Blue Water—which is in Nadia's possession. EP Speed. Dubbed.

Laser: LD72466. $39.95.
Gainax, Japan, 1989, 94 mins.

Shadow Skill

Two men stand atop a towering pinnacle of stone. One is Scarface, a disfigured champion of the Shadow Skill. The other is Gau Ban of the Black Howling. Violence, nudity and profanity.

VHS: Dubbed. **S32249. $19.95.**
VHS: Subtitled. **S32250. $24.95.**
Megumu Okada, Japan, 1996, 90 mins.

Shadow Skill Part 2

While Ella Ragu prepares for a confrontation with the demon beast Barsalf, her adopted brother Gau is given the strength to triumph over the mighty Goa X by a mysterious masked figure. Later, they join spellcaster Fowari and young fighter Quo in an attempt to defeat a carnivorous demon known as "The King of the Moon." Violence, nudity and profanity.

VHS: Dubbed. **S32530. $19.95.**
VHS: Subtitled. **S32531. $24.95.**
Megumu Okada, Japan, 1996, 90 mins.

Sherlock Hound: Dr. Watson, I Presume?

Five episodes: Sherlock & Watson meet on a cruise liner and defeat pirates; Moriarty tries to steal the Crown of Marsalene; Moriarty builds a mechanical sea-monster to devour rich cargo ships; Moriarty steals Big Ben's bell; and Moriarty tries to win a big airplane race by stealing McBane's secret engine. Dubbed.

VHS: S29330. $39.95.
TMS, Japan, 1984, 120 mins.

Sherlock Hound: Moriarty Unleashed

Dubbed.

VHS: S29331. $39.95.
TMS, Japan, 1984, 120 mins.

Sherlock Hound: Tales of Mystery

Dubbed.

VHS: S29332. $39.95.
TMS, Japan, 1984, 120 mins.

Sherlock Hound: The Dogs of Bowserville

Sherlock trails Moriarty by plane, train, ship, submarine, auto and horse carriage. Dubbed.

VHS: S29329. $39.95.
TMS, Japan, 1984, 120 mins.

Sherlock Hound: The White Cliffs of Rover

Five episodes: Sherlock Hound thwarts Professor Moriarty's attempt to steal Sir Focus' gold shipment; Sherlock protects Ellen from the Professor; Moriarty steals the jeweled lobsters; Moriarty robs a bank for gold to cast a statue of himself; and Moriarty tries to steal the secret of the Sacred Sword of The Wizards. Dubbed.

VHS: S29333. $39.95.
RAI/TMS, Japan, 1984, 120 mins.

Shonan Bakusozoku: Bomber Bikers of Shonan

In Japan, the country that inspired the slogan "Born to Be Mild," the blood of young men still runs hot. So some of them do something very un-Japanese. They strap on a big bike, roar around annoying people, and pound anyone they consider dishonorable. Meet Eguchi Yoosuke, leader of a high school biker gang and the school's handicrafts club. Violence. Stereo. Subtitled.

VHS: S18619. $34.95.
Toei, Japan, 1986, 52 mins.

Shuten Doji—The Star Hand Kid 1

Imagine you're a time-travelling, space-jumping, intergalactic troll who was adopted. Now imagine there are other creatures out to get you, and one of them has possessed your teacher and kidnapped your girlfriend to use as a sacrifice to open an interdimensional barrier and destroy all mankind. That's what it's like to be Shuten Doji—from the creator of *Devilman, Cutey Honey* and *Kekko Kamen*. Graphic violence and nudity. HiFi Stereo. Subtitled.

VHS: S27019. $29.95.
Go Nagai, Japan, 55 mins.

Shuten Doji—The Star Hand Kid 2

Go Nagai's masterpiece of erotic horror continues as Jiro tries to solve the mystery of his birth. The newly revealed warrior in the conflict between the forces of light and darkness must cross time and space to find a way to defeat the awesome power of the Oni. Graphic violence and nudity. HiFi Stereo. Subtitled.

VHS: S27460. $29.95.
Go Nagai, Japan, 50 mins.

Shuten Doji—The Star Hand Kid 3

Jiro and Miyuki's space journey is interrupted by a horde of demons intent on killing the Shuten Doji, and they become separated in time. Miyuki is stuck in feudal Japan, while Jiro is flung into the far future, where his arrival aboard an interstellar spaceship spells disaster for the hapless crew. Graphic violence and nudity. HiFi Stereo. Subtitled.

VHS: S27711. $29.95.
Go Nagai, Japan, 50 mins.

Shuten Doji—The Star Hand Kid 4

Left mentally unstable after Jiro's abduction in Part 2, his foster mother continues to cover the walls of her hospital room with paintings of Oni. Meanwhile, after his narrow escape in Part 3, Jiro returns to the land of his birth, where he must defeat the combined might of the Oni. Concludes the series. Graphic violence and nudity. HiFi Stereo. Subtitled.

VHS: S29836. $29.95.
Go Nagai, Japan, 50 mins.

The Silent Service

The Seabat is the most advanced nuclear submarine ever designed. Covertly developed by the U.S. and Japan, the Seabat is Japan's first nuclear submarine. During the shakedown cruise, the crew declare their sovereignty as an independent nation, provoking a major international incident, and straining U.S. Japanese relations to the breaking point. 100 mins.

Dubbed Version.
VHS: S34304. $24.95.
Subtitled Version.
VHS: S34305. $29.95.

Slayers Vol. 1: Episodes 1-4

It's a world of fantasy where magic rules and monsters lurk around every corner. This is where you'll find the wackiest bunch of fantasy characters ever to set out on a quest. There's cute little Lina, a fireball-hurling sorceress named Gourry, the mysterious Zelgadis, the great humanitarian sage Rezo, and a handsome mercenary swordsman. Stereo.

VHS: Dubbed. **S29334. $19.95.**
VHS: Subtitled. **S27683. $19.95.**
Japan, 100 mins.

Slayers Vol. 2: Episodes 5-7

Zelgadis is trying to keep Lina alive at all costs—to the point of fighting his own henchmen. And then, there's Rezo, the Red Priest. Why is this legendary humanitarian now trying to kill Lina and her newfound bodyguard? To add to the trouble, it's that time of the month in which Lina's powers disappear! Now, without the use of her powers, Lina is running for her life, carrying a mysterious statue that everyone wants! Stereo.

VHS: Dubbed. **S29572. $19.95.**
VHS: Subtitled. **S29573. $19.95.**
Japan, 75 mins.

Slayers Vol. 3: Episodes 8-10

Rezo threatens to turn an entire village into stone if Lina does not bring the Philosopher's Stone to his tower. When Rezo tries to use it to cure his blindness, the Dark Lord Shabranigdo takes over his body. Lina and Zelgadis find magic won't work against the monster, and neither will Gourry's Sword of Light—at least not until Lina calls upon the Lord of Nightmare to cast a spell on it. Stereo.

VHS: Dubbed. **S28455. $19.95.**
VHS: Subtitled. **S28456. $19.95.**
SOFTX, Japan, 1995, 75 mins.

Slayers Vol. 4: Episodes 11-13

When Lina learns that Prince Philionel is secretly travelling the countryside, she makes it her number one priority to meet—and possibly marry—the prince. The problem is, he's not exactly Prince Charming and his daughter, Amelia—an obsessive defender of justice—targets our heroes when she discovers that they are wanted by the local authorities! Will Lina and Gourry make it out alive? Stereo.

VHS: Dubbed. **S30178. $19.95.**
VHS: Subtitled. **S30179. $19.95.**
SOFTX, Japan, 1995, 75 mins.

Slayers Vol. 5: Episodes 14-16

You'd think Lina Inverse would get a little credit for killing the Dark Lord. But now there's a bounty on Lina and Gourry's heads. Between fighting sorceresses, appearing in a play, and possible wedding bells, Lina and Co. make their way to the city of Sairaag to find who's responsible for all this.

VHS: Dubbed. **S33632. $19.95.**
VHS: Subtitled. **S33631. $19.95.**
SoftX, Japan, 1995, 75 mins.

Slayers Vol. 6: Episodes 17-19

VHS: Dubbed. **S33633. $19.95.**
VHS: Subtitled. **S33634. $19.95.**
SoftX, Japan, 1995, 75 mins.

Slayers LD 1

Episodes 1 and 2. Multi-audio.

Laser: LD75834. $39.95.
Japan, 50 mins.

Slayers LD 2

Episodes 3 and 4. Multi-audio.

Laser: LD75835. $39.95.
Japan, 50 mins.

Slayers LD 3

Episodes 5 and 6. Multi-audio.

Laser: LD75836. $39.95.
Japan, 50 mins.

Slayers LD 4

Episodes 7 and 8. Multi-audio.

Laser: LD76209. $39.95.
Japan

Slayers LD 5

Episodes 9 and 10. Multi-audio.

Laser: LD76134. $39.95.
Japan

Slayers LD 6

Episodes 11, 12 and 13. Multi-audio.

Laser: LD76210. $39.95.
Japan

Slayers—The Motion Picture

Teaming up to fight the demonic masters of the mystical isle, the curvaceous Nahga and Lina the Inverse stumble upon an ancient evil and lovers cruelly parted. Dragged into the vortex of time, Lina must change the past and alter history itself. 75 mins.

VHS: Dubbed. **S34985. $19.95.**
VHS: Subtitled. **S34984. $29.95.**

Sohryuden Vol. 1: Episodes 1 and 2

Episode 1: *The Four Brothers Under Fire*, and Episode 2: *The Legend of Dragon Springs*. The four Ryudo brothers are endowed with almost superhuman abilities. But the rich and powerful Kamakura no Gozen is envious. He's spent his life trying to unravel a secret to which the brothers hold the key. When their friends become victims, it's time to get tough. Unfortunately, no one knows how powerful the brothers really are. Stereo. Subtitled.

VHS: S25982. $29.95.
Kitty Films, Japan, 1991, 97 mins.

Sohryuden Vol. 2: Episodes 3 and 4

Episode 3: *Black Dragon King Revealed*, and Episode 4: *Tokyo Bay Rhapsody*. Until now, Kamakura no Gozen has trusted his underlings to bring the brothers under his control. But now it's time for more desperate action. First he'll kidnap the brothers' only living relatives: their cousin Matsuri and her family. Then he'll force the brothers to stage a rescue attempt in the middle of an army munitions range. Lastly, he's planned one final bit of treachery: an elite combat team with the latest military hardware. Stereo. Subtitled.

VHS: S25983. $29.95.
Kitty Films, Japan, 1991, 97 mins.

Sohryuden Vol. 3: Episodes 5 and 6

The four Ryudo brothers are descended from dragons—which makes them all the more intriguing to Dr. Tamezawa. The deranged doctor has gained most of his twisted medical knowledge by dissecting living subjects. Now, with his pack of cybernetic Dobermans, the mad doctor is turning a hungry eye toward the unsuspecting brothers. Stereo. Subtitled.

VHS: S27093. $29.95.
Kitty Films, Japan, 1991, 97 mins.

Sohryuden Vol. 4: Episodes 7 and 8

Dr. Tamozawa has discovered the Ryudo brothers' secret—they are descended from dragons. The mad doctor and his army of surgically created cyborgs will never rest until he has realized his dream of dissecting one of the brothers alive. Meanwhile, all of Tokyo is in an uproar, following the appearance of a gigantic, fire-breathing dragon—and the subsequent destruction left in its wake. Stereo. Subtitled.

VHS: S27454. $29.95.
Kitty Films, Japan, 1991, 97 mins.

Sohryuden Vol. 5: Episodes 9 and 10

The Mulligan Foundation's top agent, Lady L, has kidnapped one of the youngest Ryudo brothers. The researchers of the Foundation hope that, with the proper persuasion, the remaining brothers will agree to become agents of the Foundation—as assassins and saboteurs. Stereo. Subtitled.

VHS: S27673. $29.95.
Kitty Films, Japan, 1991, 97 mins.

Sohryuden Vol. 6: Episodes 11 and 12

The battle unfolds as the four brothers must unite to fight the evil mastermind who has manipulated their lives for so long. The ultimate battle will pit all four dragons against an invincible and immortal enemy, while the fate of the planet hangs in the balance! HiFi Stereo. Subtitled.

VHS: S27674. $29.95.
Kitty Films, Japan, 1991, 97 mins.

Sol Bianca

There's only one thing the all-female crew of the spaceship *Sol Bianca* likes more than treasure…more treasure! Naturally, they can't resist stealing the fabled "Gnosis," destroying a few cities and liberating an entire civilization in the process. Voted best OAV at the 1993 Anime Expo. Graphic violence and nudity. HiFi Stereo. Subtitled.

VHS: S18333. $29.95.
Laser: CAV. **LD74480. $39.95.**
NEC, Japan, 1990, 60 mins.

Sol Bianca 2

Unfortunately for the all-female crew of the *Sol Bianca*, an army is exactly what they're up against when they try to corner the interstellar market on pasha, the most valuable substance in the known universe. Actually, make that two armies: a bloodthirsty band of ruthless space hijackers and the galactic police! And then there's also a mysterious stranger who seems much more interested in collecting the *Sol Bianca* and her crew than the pasha. Graphic violence and nudity. HiFi Stereo. Subtitled.

VHS: S24379. $29.95.
NEC, Japan, 1991, 60 mins.

Sonic Soldier Borgman 1: Last Battle

The last three bio-enhanced humans find themselves pitted against the monstrous by-products of their own evolution. Can former lovers put aside differences long enough to solve the mystery of Heaven's Gate? Subtitled.

VHS: S33644. $24.95.
NTV/Toho, Japan, 1989, 80 mins.

Sonic Soldier Borgman 2: Lover's Rain

The last three bioenhanced humans on Earth find themselves pitted against the most monstrous foe they have ever faced. The Borgman team must conquer their worst fears before combating an army of the undead. Subtitled.

VHS: S33645. $24.95.
NTV/Toho, Japan, 1990, 50 mins.

Space Adventure Cobra

In the Seventh Galaxy, the corrupt Mafia Guild is after Cobra nd his female counterpart, Jane Flower. And the evil Crystal Boy is willing to help find them both.

VHS: Dubbed. **S33993. $24.95.**
VHS: Subtitled. **S33994. $29.95.**
Japan

Space Battleship Yamato

This is the first Yamato feature film of the five eventually made. It is the theatrical version of the first *Star Blazers* TV series, *Quest for Iscandar*. The *Yamato* has only 365 days to make a 148,000-light-year voyage from Earth to the planet Iscandar and return with a neutralizer that will cleanse Earth's irradiated atmosphere. On the trip, the Yamato survives oceans of concentrated sulfuric acid, a metal-eating gas attack in space and a battle with Lord Desler's fleet. It is in this seminal film that we first meet Susumu and Mamory Kodai, Yuki Mori, Captain Okita, Dr. Sado, Shiro Sanada, IQ-9 and the mysterious Stasha of Iscandar. Subtitled.

VHS: S29345. $29.95.
Japan, 135 mins.

Space Battleship Yamato: The New Voyage

Terrorist attacks by the Black Star Cluster Empire destroy Gamilus and blast Iscandar out of orbit, hurtling Queen Stasha, her child and Mamoru into the galactic unknown. The refitted *Yamato* is ordered to seek and assist Stasha. Also warping to keep up with the runaway planet are Gamilus leader Desler and General Medlers, commander of the Dark Empire's fleet. All forces meet in an apocalyptic battle at Iscandar. Queen Stasha once again intercedes and saves the *Yamato* in a spectacular act of love and sacrifice. Subtitled.

VHS: S29346. $29.95.
Japan, 1979, 93 mins.

Space Warriors

An infamous space pirate has embarked on a mission of revenge against the chairman of an influential corporation. Now, a psychic warrior must uncover the connection between the pirate and an innocent schoolteacher—a secret that could topple one of the largest corporations in the galaxy! Stereo. Dubbed.

VHS: S30393. $19.95.
Japan, 75 mins.

Space Warriors Baldios

As evil aliens flee their polluted planet in search of another land to destroy, a lone outcast follows them in his robotic spaceship, *Baldios*. When they select the Earth as their next target, the courageous pilot vows to stop them. Armed with fierce missiles, indestructible armor and an invincible halogen sword, the *Baldios* is ready to fight. But first, the people of Earth must be convinced of the impending doom. Dubbed.

VHS: S25018. $19.95.
Toei, Japan, 1981, 99 mins.

Spaceketeers

Two episodes from the *Force Five* series. In *Aurora Accepts the Challenge*, Aurora learns that she is the only one who can save the galaxy from the evil Dekos ebergy. She leaves on her mission and meets Jesse Dart, a cyborg, who becomes her first Spaceketeer. In *The Invincible Warrior*, after Jesse rescues Aurora from the grotesque liquid called "Trakeal," he tells her how he came to be a cyborg. Dubbed.

VHS: S18592. $17.95.
Toei, Japan, 1980, 46 mins.

Speed Racer Vol. 1: The Great Plan

This is the original episode of the teen super-car racer. It introduces the entire family of race-car wizards and the Mach 5's fantastic devices are explained by Speed Racer himself! Speed is determined to win the dangerous Sword Mountain Race. But it's not going to be easy—someone is out to steal the designs and will stop at nothing to get them. Dubbed. EP Speed.
VHS: S29336. $12.95.
Tatsunoko, Japan, 1967, 50 mins.

Speed Racer Vol. 2: The Secret Engine

Speed Racer attempts to stop a mysterious gang led by escaped convict Tongue Blaggard. The gang is after a Model T car owned by kindly Lightfingers Klepto, who inherited the car years before. What no one but Blaggard knows is that the Model T's engine is the key to a fantastic treasure. Dubbed. EP Speed.
VHS: S29337. $12.95.
Tatsunoko, Japan, 1967, 50 mins.

Speed Racer Vol. 3: The Fastest Car on Earth

Years ago, Pops had to bury the fantastic GRX engine that was so fast, it took its drivers into another dimension. Now the devilish Oriena has unearthed the engine and invented a formula that enables the driver's reflexes to survive the GRX's fantastic speeds—at least temporarily. Dubbed. EP Speed.
VHS: S29338. $12.95.
Tatsunoko, Japan, 1967, 50 mins.

Speed Racer Vol. 4: The Race Against Time

Amidst a Sahara Desert race, Speed finds Dr. Digger O. Bone being killed by a death-dealing airplane. The dying doctor asks Speed to find his daughter Calcia, who has disappeared. Speed and Trixie find her in Cleopatra's tomb, being manipulated by the evil Femur, and Speed must face lions, a swordsman and a race against time to save Trixie from a fiery death.. Dubbed. EP Speed.
VHS: S29339. $12.95.
Tatsunoko, Japan, 1967, 50 mins.

Speed Racer Vol. 5: Crash in the Jungle

World reknowned biologist Professor Carnivore is kidnapped. After crashing in the jungle, Speed must fight off beasts of colossal proportions. Trixie, Spridle and Chim Chim search for Speed, but are captured by the evil General Smasher and his crackpot colleague, Dr. Loon, who are also holding Carnivore captive. Unless the professor agrees to cooperate in a mad scientific experiment to develop an army of giants, Trixie and Spridle will be dropped into a pool of flesh-eating piranhas. Dubbed. EP Speed.
VHS: S29340. $12.95.
Tatsunoko, Japan, 1967, 50 mins.

Speed Racer Vol. 6: The Desperate Desert Race

Speed is in Sandoland competing in the grueling Desert Race. He runs into trouble when the notorious Black Tiger, driven by competitor Kim Jugger, is sabotaged, and Spridle and Chim Chim are blamed. Speed is taken hostage by a rebel army led by Kim's father, General Abdul Noble. But there's a traitor in the army—a one-eyed spy named Ali Ben Schemer who wants Speed and Kim out of the way so that he can overthrow the general. Dubbed. EP Speed.
VHS: S29341. $12.95.
Tatsunoko, Japan, 1967, 50 mins.

Speed Racer Vol. 7: The Girl Daredevil

Circus star Twinkle Banks is forced to perform a deadly tightrope trick above Niagara Falls by the evil Cornpone Brotch. While attention is focused on Twinkle, Cornpone and his gangsters search for hidden Indian treasure below. When Speed blows their cover, they steal the mighty Mach-5. Speed and Twinkle locate the hideout where the Mach-5 is stashed and Twinkle's father is held prisoner. Cornpone unleashes his vicious black panthers on the intruders and Spridle and Chim Chim befriend the beasts. Dubbed. EP Speed.
VHS: S29342. $12.95.
Tatsunoko, Japan, 1967, 50 mins.

Speed Racer Vol. 8: The Royal Racer

Pops Racer is building a mini race car for Prince Jam of the kingdom of Sackaren, where the Baby Grand Prix is to be held. Spridle begs to compete, but he's too young. When the prince is kidnapped, however, Spridle is mistaken for the young monarch and gets his chance to race after all. But Spridle discovers that the king's evil minister, Offendum, has sabotaged the mini car so that the half-witted Prince Sugarin can take over the kingdom instead. Dubbed. EP Speed.
VHS: S29343. $12.95.
Tatsunoko, Japan, 1967, 50 mins.

Speed Racer Vol. 9: Challenge of the Masked Racer

Speed enters the perilous Trans-Country Race. His arch-competitor is the Masked Racer—a mysterious driver who allegedly wins every race because he causes others to crash. Preparing for the big event, Speed winds up in a stormy midnight race against the Masked Racer. After Speed loses control of the Mach-5, his strange rival rescues him and warns him not to attempt the dangerous race. Suspense shifts into high gear when Speed is kidnapped by Wiley's depraved gang. Dubbed. EP Speed.
VHS: S11548. $12.95.
Tatsunoko, Japan, 1967, 50 mins.

Speed Racer Vol. 10: The Fire Race

Speed is about to experience the strangest race of his career—an event to decide whether Chief Zuma will have to open the borders of his country of Kapetapeck. Speed will be facing the greatest racer of all time, Kabala, who is rumored to be fierce and unscrupulous. Mysterious Racer X and the ominous Kadar, who is out to steal Kapetapeck's treasure, will also compete. When the volcano erupts and creates an 800-mile tunnel, the hazardous Fire Race begins. Dubbed. EP Speed.
VHS: S26253. $12.95.
Tatsunoko, Japan, 1967, 50 mins.

Speed Racer Vol. 11: The Secret Invaders

Speed Racer tries to stop a gang of ruthless assassins from taking over the country of Avalonia, also the site of the treacherous Twist and Turn Race. The assassins suspect that one of the racers is a secret agent out to thwart their evil plan…and Speed is their prime target. Soon our brave hero finds himself not only fighting for his own life but racing to the rescue of President Mountebank, whose microphone is rigged to blow up as he welcomes the racers. Dubbed. EP Speed.
VHS: S26254. $12.95.
Tatsunoko, Japan, 1967, 50 mins.

Speed Racer Vol. 12: The Car with a Brain

In *The Car with a Brain*, a mad scientist has programmed a monster car to destroy all in its path, and only Speed Racer can save a Scottish county from total obliteration. The evil vehicle's power is so tremendous, even tanks and torpedoes cannot demolish it. In *Junk Car Grand Prix*, the wealthy Baron Von Vondervon is holding a race in honor of his long-lost daughter, and the winner will share his fortune. When the conniving Mr. Freeload discovers the valuable missing heiress, Speed must race to her rescue so she can inherit her rightful fortune. Dubbed. EP Speed.
VHS: S11546. $12.95.
Tatsunoko, Japan, 1967, 50 mins.

Speed Racer: The Movie

This is the theatrical compilation from Streamline Pictures that combines two *Speed Racer* TV episodes with a *Colonel Bleep* TV episode. First, Speed, Trixie and the gang are in a desperate race to save hundreds of lives in *The Car Hater*. Then, Colonel Bleep and his pals are off through outer space in *The Treacherous Pirate*. Next, Speed battles evil in *The Race Against the Mammoth Car*. Interspersed are three '60s vintage TV commercials, and there's even a new Speed Racer "music video." Dubbed.
VHS: S29335. $14.95.
Japan, 1993, 80 mins.

Spirit of Wonder: Miss China's Ring

In the 19th century, a young Asian girl has made a place for herself as owner of a restaurant and boarding house. Yet "Miss China" is depressed because she has a mad scientist living upstairs and she's pining for a young man. But the mad scientist has come up with an incredible invention, and the young man has a plan to use it. Laserdisc is hybrid. HiFi Stereo.
VHS: Dubbed. **S29344. $19.95.**
VHS: Subtitled. **S26798. $24.95.**
Laser: Hybrid. **LD75115. $39.95.**
Tsuruta Kenji, Japan, 1992, 45 mins.

Star Blazers Volume 1

The Quest for Iscandar, Episodes 1 & 2.
VHS: S17800. $19.95.
Sunwagon, Japan, 1974, 44 mins.

Star Blazers Volume 2

The Quest for Iscandar, Episodes 3 & 4.
VHS: S17801. $19.95.
Sunwagon, Japan, 1974, 44 mins.

Star Blazers Volume 3

The Quest for Iscandar, Episodes 5 & 6.
VHS: S17802. $19.95.
Sunwagon, Japan, 1974, 44 mins.

Star Blazers Volume 4

The Quest for Iscandar, Episodes 7 & 8.
VHS: S17803. $19.95.
Sunwagon, Japan, 1974, 44 mins.

Star Blazers Volume 5

The Quest for Iscandar, Episodes 9 & 10.
VHS: S17804. $19.95.
Sunwagon, Japan, 1974, 44 mins.

Star Blazers Volume 6

The Quest for Iscandar, Episodes 11 & 12.
VHS: S17805. $19.95.
Sunwagon, Japan, 1974, 44 mins.

Star Blazers Volume 7

The Quest for Iscandar, Episodes 13 & 14.
VHS: S17806. $19.95.
Sunwagon, Japan, 1974, 44 mins.

Star Blazers Volume 8

The Quest for Iscandar, Episodes 15 & 16.
VHS: S17807. $19.95.
Sunwagon, Japan, 1974, 44 mins.

Star Blazers Volume 9

The Quest for Iscandar, Episodes 17 & 18.
VHS: S17808. $19.95.
Sunwagon, Japan, 1974, 44 mins.

Star Blazers Volume 10

The Quest for Iscandar, Episodes 19 & 20.
VHS: S17809. $19.95.
Sunwagon, Japan, 1974, 44 mins.

Star Blazers Volume 11

The Quest for Iscandar, Episodes 21 & 22.
VHS: S17810. $19.95.
Sunwagon, Japan, 1974, 44 mins.

Star Blazers Volume 12

The Quest for Iscandar, Episodes 23 & 24.
VHS: S17811. $19.95.
Sunwagon, Japan, 1974, 44 mins.

Star Blazers Volume 13

The Quest for Iscandar, Episodes 25 & 26.
VHS: S17812. $19.95.
Sunwagon, Japan, 1974, 44 mins.

Star Blazers Volume 14

The Comet Empire, Episodes 27 & 28.
VHS: S17813. $19.95.
Sunwagon, Japan, 1978, 44 mins.

Star Blazers Volume 15

The Comet Empire, Episodes 29 & 30.
VHS: S17814. $19.95.
Sunwagon, Japan, 1978, 44 mins.

Star Blazers Volume 16

The Comet Empire, Episodes 31 & 32.
VHS: S17815. $19.95.
Sunwagon, Japan, 1978, 44 mins.

Star Blazers Volume 17

The Comet Empire, Episodes 33 & 34.
VHS: S17816. $19.95.
Sunwagon, Japan, 1978, 44 mins.

Star Blazers Volume 18

The Comet Empire, Episodes 35 & 36.
VHS: S17817. $19.95.
Sunwagon, Japan, 1978, 44 mins.

Star Blazers Volume 19

The Comet Empire, Episodes 37 & 38.
VHS: S17818. $19.95.
Sunwagon, Japan, 1978, 44 mins.

Star Blazers Volume 20

The Comet Empire, Episodes 39 & 40.
VHS: S17819. $19.95.
Sunwagon, Japan, 1978, 44 mins.

Star Blazers Volume 21

The Comet Empire, Episodes 41 & 42.
VHS: S17820. $19.95.
Sunwagon, Japan, 1978, 44 mins.

Star Blazers Volume 22

The Comet Empire, Episodes 43 & 44.
VHS: S17821. $19.95.
Sunwagon, Japan, 1978, 44 mins.

Star Blazers Volume 23

The Comet Empire, Episodes 45 & 46.
VHS: S17822. $19.95.
Sunwagon, Japan, 1978, 44 mins.

Star Blazers Volume 24

The Comet Empire, Episodes 47 & 48.
VHS: S17823. $19.95.
Sunwagon, Japan, 1978, 44 mins.

Star Blazers Volume 25

The Comet Empire, Episodes 49 & 50.
VHS: S17824. $19.95.
Sunwagon, Japan, 1978, 44 mins.

Star Blazers Volume 26

The Comet Empire, Episodes 51 & 52.
VHS: S17825. $19.95.
Sunwagon, Japan, 1978, 44 mins.

Star Blazers Volume 27

The Bolar Wars, Episodes 53 & 54.
VHS: S17826. $19.95.
Sunwagon, Japan, 1980, 44 mins.

Star Blazers Volume 28

The Bolar Wars, Episodes 55 & 56.
VHS: S17827. $19.95.
Sunwagon, Japan, 1980, 44 mins.

Star Blazers Volume 29

The Bolar Wars, Episodes 57 & 58.
VHS: S17828. $19.95.
Sunwagon, Japan, 1980, 44 mins.

Star Blazers Volume 30

The Bolar Wars, Episodes 59 & 60.
VHS: S17829. $19.95.
Sunwagon, Japan, 1980, 44 mins.

Star Blazers Volume 31

The Bolar Wars, Episodes 61 & 62.
VHS: S17830. $19.95.
Sunwagon, Japan, 1980, 44 mins.

Star Blazers Volume 32

The Bolar Wars, Episodes 63 & 64.
VHS: S17831. $19.95.
Sunwagon, Japan, 1980, 44 mins.

Star Blazers Volume 33

The Bolar Wars, Episodes 65 & 66.
VHS: S17832. $19.95.
Sunwagon, Japan, 1980, 44 mins.

Star Blazers Volume 34

The Bolar Wars, Episodes 67 & 68.
VHS: S17833. $19.95.
Sunwagon, Japan, 1980, 44 mins.

Star Blazers Volume 35

The Bolar Wars, Episodes 69 & 70.
VHS: S17834. $19.95.
Sunwagon, Japan, 1980, 44 mins.

Star Blazers Volume 36

The Bolar Wars, Episodes 71 & 72.
VHS: S17835. $19.95.
Sunwagon, Japan, 1980, 44 mins.

Star Blazers Volume 37

The Bolar Wars, Episodes 73 & 74.
VHS: S17836. $19.95.
Sunwagon, Japan, 1980, 44 mins.

Star Blazers Volume 38

The Bolar Wars, Episodes 75 & 76.
VHS: S17837. $19.95.
Sunwagon, Japan, 1980, 44 mins.

Star Blazers Volume 39

The Bolar Wars, Episode 77.
VHS: S17838. $19.95.
Sunwagon, Japan, 1980, 44 mins.

Starvengers

Two episodes from the Force Five series. In "Who'll Fly the Poseidon," the new, ten-times more powerful Starvenger is revealed and the search for a pilot for the *Poseidon* is underway. The search is successful and Foul Tip gets the job. In "Dragon Formation…Switch On!," the Starvengers combat the Pandemonium Empire as it makes its first attempt to get the star energizer. Dubbed. EP Speed.
VHS: S18593. $17.95.
Toei, Japan, 1980, 46 mins.

Street Fighter II V, Vol. 1: Beginning of a Journey

Episodes 1-3. Directed by Gisaburo Sugii, this television series adopts the darker tone of the animated movie, and depicts events that predate the storyline of the feature film. *Episode 1: Start of a Journey, Episode 2: The Air Force King* and *Episode 3: The Challenge in the Matou Cave*. Ken and Ryu separate and then reunite years later in America. They tangle with Guile, an Air Force officer who teaches them the shortcomings of their training.
VHS: Dubbed. **S30903. $19.95.**
VHS: Subtitled. **S30902. $24.95.**
Group TAC/Amuse, Japan, 1986, 90 mins.

Street Fighter II V, Vol. 2: Darkness at Kowloon

Episode 4: Darkness at Kowloon Palace, Episode 5: Hot-Blooded Fei Long and Episode 6: Appearance of the Secret Technique.
VHS: Dubbed. **S31183. $19.95.**
VHS: Subtitled. **S31184. $24.95.**
Group TAC/Amuse, Japan, 1986, 90 mins.

Street Fighter II V, Vol. 3: Revenge of Ashura

Episode 7: The Revenge of Ashura; Episode 8: Trap, Prison and The Scream of Truth; and *Episode 9: The Superstar of Muay Thai.*
VHS: Dubbed. **S31332. $19.95.**
VHS: Subtitled. **S31333. $24.95.**
Group TAC/Amuse, Japan, 1986, 90 mins.

Street Fighter II V, Vol. 4: Dark Omen

Episode 10: Dark Omen, Episode 11: Visitation of the Beasts and *Episode 12: The Deadly Phantom Faceoff.*
VHS: Dubbed. **S32209. $19.95.**
VHS: Subtitled. **S32208. $24.95.**
Group TAC/Amuse, Japan, 1986, 90 mins.

Street Fighter II V, Vol. 5: Legend of Hadouken

Episode 13: The Legend of The Hadouken, Episode 14: The Bloodthirsty Prince and *Episode 15: Clash of the Titans.*
VHS: Dubbed. **S32253. $19.95.**
VHS: Subtitled. **S32254. $24.95.**
Group TAC/Amuse, Japan, 1986, 90 mins.

Street Fighter II V, Vol. 6: The Unveiled Ruler

Episode 16: The Unveiled Ruler, Episode 17: The Despot's Commander and *Episode 18: The Beautiful Assassin.*
VHS: Dubbed. **S32255. $19.95.**
VHS: Subtitled. **S32256. $24.95.**
Group TAC/Amuse, Japan, 1986, 90 mins.

Street Fighter II V, Vol. 7: The True Ruler

Episode 19: The True Ruler Appears, Episode 20: The Order of The Tyrant and *Episode 21: The Beautiful Assassin with the Evil Cross.*
VHS: Dubbed. **S32261. $19.95.**
VHS: Subtitled. **S32262. $24.95.**
Group TAC/Amuse, Japan, 1986, 90 mins.

Street Fighter II V, Vol. 8: Rising Dragon

Episode 22: Rising Dragon, Into the Sky; Episode 23: The Icy Light of Their Eyes; and *Episode 24: Nightmare Reunion.*
VHS: Dubbed. **S32527. $19.95.**
VHS: Subtitled. **S32528. $24.95.**
Group TAC/Amuse, Japan, 1986, 90 mins.

Street Fighter II V, Vol. 9: Fight to the Finish

Episode 25: Fight to the Finish [Round One], Episode 26: Fight to the Finish [Round Two] and *Episode 27: Fight to the Finish [Round Three].* Ken realizes that a cyberchip implant has taken control and erased Ryu's memory. Vega has programmed Ryu to kill Ken and Ken must break the chip's control somehow.
VHS: Dubbed. **S33642. $19.95.**
VHS: Subtitled. **S33643. $24.95.**
Group TAC/Amuse, Japan, 1986, 90 mins.

Street Fighter II V, Vol. 10: Episodes 28-29

Episode 28: Fight to the Finish (Round Four) and *Episode 29: Fight to the Finish (Final Round).*
VHS: Dubbed. **S33640. $19.95.**
VHS: Subtitled. **S33641. $24.95.**
Group/TAC/Amuse, Japan, 1986, 60 mins.

Street Fighter II: The Animated Movie

The not-too-distant future is a dark place where the forces of Shadowland attempt to harness psycho power. If they succeed, it could mean the end of civilization. Only the legendary Ryu, the greatest street fighter on the planet, can alter the balance of power. Based on the popular video game. Music by Alice in Chains, Korn, Silverchair, KMFDM and others. Violence. HiFi Stereo. Dubbed.
VHS: Unrated. **S26924. $14.95.**
VHS: Edited. **S29351. $14.95.**
Laser: Unrated. **LD75788. $29.95.**
CapCom, Japan, 1994, 96 mins.

Suikoden—Demon Century

Takateru Suga searches for his missing sister in a lawless 21st-century Tokyo. What he does not realize is that he is the reincarnation of Soko Kohogi, the leader of 108 Chinese heroes who received the protection of the stars but are fated to return time and again to combat the forces of evil in the "Great Battle." The "Stars" have begun to gather and the fight to rescue Takateru's sister from the gang which kidnapped her is just the beginning. HiFi Stereo. Graphic violence and profanity.
VHS: Dubbed. **S29582. $29.95.**
VHS: Subtitled. **S29583. $29.95.**
Laser: Multi-audio. **LD75838. $39.95.**
Japan, 45 mins.

Sukeban Deka 1

When Saki left high school, she changed her uniform for prison grays. Now the Feds need someone to infiltrate a ruthless crime syndicate that masquerades as an exclusive high school and they think Saki's the girl for the job. Armed with a secret weapon that only looks like a yo-yo, Saki is lovely, lethal and back on the streets. Violence and nudity. HiFi Stereo.
VHS: Dubbed. **S29352. $29.95.**
VHS: Subtitled. **S27464. $29.95.**
Laser: Multi-audio. **LD75837. $39.95.**
Shinji Wada, Japan, 1991, 60 mins.

Sukeban Deka 2

The girl with the killer yo-yo is back! When Saki's friend is kidnapped by Remi Mizuchi, who wants her paintings, Saki is arrested for the crime. But before Saki can convince the authorities of her innocence, her friend is murdered by another of the Mizuchi sisters. Saki's on the warpath now, and aided by a lethal case of sibling rivalry, she'll make short work of the Mizuchi sisters! Violence. HiFi Stereo.
VHS: Dubbed. **S29353. $29.95.**
VHS: Subtitled. **S27630. $29.95.**
Shinji Wada, Japan, 1991, 60 mins.

Super Atragon 1

Near the end of World War II, a super-secret Japanese submarine meets its American counterpart, and both are lost to history. Now, some 50 years later, the descendants of the submarine officers are part of a U.N. task force investigating the unusual phenomena which have begun occurring in Antarctica. Faced with a mysterious, deadly, black cylinder, the task force faces certain destruction until the reappearance of the Japanese submarine. HiFi Stereo.
VHS: Dubbed. **S29354. $29.95.**
VHS: Subtitled. **S27714. $29.95.**
Laser: Multi-audio. **LD75853. $39.95.**
Kaitei Gunkan, Japan, 1995, 60 mins.

Super Atragon 2

The U.N. task force watches in horror as the entire naval force is crushed beneath giant gravitronic rings that are the vanguard of an invasion by malevolent beings from beneath the Earth! After 50 years, the Japanese secret weapon that was never used is pressed into service again. HiFi Stereo.
VHS: Dubbed. **S29584. $29.95.**
VHS: Subtitled. **S29585. $29.95.**
Kaitei Gunkan, Japan, 1995, 60 mins.

Super Deformed Double Feature

Contains two programs: *Ten Little Gall Force*: The ten members of Gall Force, who all appeared in the original three-part space opera, are gathered together for this variety video full of short gags that parody the original. Also includes "The Making of the Gallforce Song"—a live segment featuring all ten voice actresses. *Scramble Wars*: A parody of anime, gathering together the popular Artmic characters and mecha. It's a big race set in the lawless land of Gaiarth, sponsored by the no-good Quincy, chairman of Genom Corp. Entrants include the Knight Sabers, Gall Force, and Ital and Sahrai from Gaiarth. Subtitled.
VHS: S18621. $34.95.
Artmic/Movic, Japan, 1988/92, 67 mins.

Super Dimensional Fortress Macross

When two giant Bionoid armies attack, the Earth forces send their indestructible space fortress Macross to battle the invading armies. The Bionoids mercilessly assault the helpless Macross with huge robot-like spaceships. The Earthlings appear doomed until they notice the strange effect music is having on the invaders. Incredibly, the survival of the human race may depend on a female rock star! Dubbed.
VHS: S29368. $9.95.
Big West, Japan, 1984, 115 mins.

Sure Death: Brown, You Bounder

Bicycle-riding English spies led by the evil Mr. Brown are out to seize an ancient secret weapon with the power to destroy the government, and only Mondo's band of assassins can stop them. Japanese with English subtitles. Widescreen. 122 mins.
VHS: S34295. $29.95.

Sword for Truth

In this action-packed anime adventure, Shuranosuke is hired by the Tokugawa Shogunate to rescue Princess Mayu from the clutches of a group of bandit ninjas. They will stop at nothng to prevent him from succeeding and call on the undead spirits of the Seki Ninjas in Hell to assist them. 60 mins.
Dubbed Version.
VHS: S34549. $19.95.
Subtitled Version.
VHS: S34550. $24.95.

Takegami: Guardian of Darkness Vol. 1: Shrine of the Eight-Headed Dragon

From the director of *Battle Arena Toshinden* and *Voltage Fighter Gowcaizer*. According to legend, three dragons shall appear to wreak havoc upon the land. Only the power of an ancient warrior-god can fulfill the prophecy and defeat the growing evil. But can his host—a schoolboy named Koichi—be convinced to fight? Nudity and violence. Dubbed.
VHS: S32270. $19.95.
JVC, Japan, 1990, 43 mins.

Takegami: Guardian of Darkness Vol. 2: Legend of the 800 Priestesses

Following the ancient prophesies of her family, Sayo is aware of the power within Koichi and the imminent emergence of the second dragon—The Dragon of Heaven. But Koichi's will to fight was shattered by the destruction of his alter ego. Nudity and violence. Dubbed.
VHS: S32271. $19.95.
JVC, Japan, 1991, 46 mins.

Takegami: Guardian of Darkness Vol. 3: The Mystery of Hiruko

Koichi has made a horrifying discovery: Susanoo suffered his one and only defeat at the hands of Hiruko, and his host was killed in the battle. Is Koichi destined to share the same fate as his predecessor? Nudity and violence. Dubbed.
VHS: S32272. $19.95.
JVC, Japan, 1992, 41 mins.

Takegami: Guardian of Darkness, 3-Pack

Volumes 1-3. Dubbed.
VHS: S33646. $49.95.
Japan, 130 mins.

The Tale of Genji

This faithful adaptation of Murasaki Shikibu's literary masterpiece evokes the grandeur of the Heian era—a time when Japan passionately pursued the finer arts of music and literature. Hikaru Genji, a nobleman who was born the son of an emporer, was made a commoner. He was the most handsome man in the nation, with abilities in poetry and music that were unparalleled. This is the story of his life and loves. Stereo. Subtitled.
VHS: S26250. $29.95.
Asahi, Japan, 1987, 110 mins.

Techno Police 21C

The year is 2001 and the criminals have taken over Centinel City. Even the Techno Police, a special anti-crime squad, find the situation hopeless until a wise-cracking cop joins the force. When a powerful experimental tank is hijacked, the Techno Police and their newest recruit go to work. Equipped with an ultrasonic car and crime-fighting Technoids, the rookie cop sets out on a death-defying, high-speed chase through the streets...trying to capture the crooks and trying to stay alive. Dubbed.
VHS: S25019. $19.95.
Toho, Japan, 1982, 80 mins.

Tekkaman Vol. 1

In the year 2037, evil alien robots invade the solar system and close in on Earth! Earth's greatest scientist creates an indestructible suit of space armor made from a revolutionary alloy called "Tekka." Young space pilot Barry Gallagher dons this armor to become Tekkaman the Space Knight. Three half-hour episodes. Dubbed.
VHS: S17366. $19.95.
Tatsunoko, Japan, 1975, 86 mins.

Tekkaman Vol. 2

Three half-hour episodes. Killer alien robots threaten the Earth and Barry Gallagher is subjected to a new series of challenges from his foes, who have developed deadlier tools of destruction. Dubbed.
VHS: S17367. $19.95.
Tatsunoko, Japan, 1975, 86 mins.

Tekkaman: Blade II, Stage 1

Ten years have passed since the original series and a new breed of Tekkaman face off against the mysterious and powerful Radham. Yumi, Natasha, Hayato, and David must deal with their own demons from the past as they prepare to battle against extreme odds with the fate of humanity at stake. 60 mins.
VHS: Dubbed. **S34544. $19.95.**
VHS: Subtitled. **S34545. $29.95.**

Tekkaman: Blade II, Stage 2: The Alien Intruder

The raging battle against the evil Radham and the stormy intra-conflict between the Tekkaman teammates continues as a new, powerful enemy appears. Yumi falls in love with the mysterious leader, D. Boy, but later discovers that Aki is involved with him. Hurt and jealous, Yumi unwisely attempts to confront the enemy herself by risking the lives of her teammates.
VHS: Dubbed. **S35167. $19.95.**
VHS: Subtitled. **S35168. $29.95.**

Tenchi Muyo! Vol. 1: The Reincarnation of Ryoko

When high schooler Tenchi Masaki accidentally releases an imprisoned demon from an ancient shrine, he is amazed to find that the demon is a beautiful young girl. Using her supernatural powers, Ryoko the demon begins a terrifying midnight pursuit of Tenchi throughout his school.
VHS: Dubbed. **S29355. $19.95.**
VHS: Subtitled. **S23073. $24.95.**
Laser: CAV, multi-audio. **LD74655. $34.95.**
A.I.C., Japan, 1992, 30 mins.

Tenchi Muyo! Vol. 2: Here Comes Ayeka!

Princess Ayeka has traveled from her home planet in search of her lost fiance, only to run across Ryoko, her mortal enemy from distant stars. As she and Ryoko engage in battle, poor Tenchi is caught in the middle.
VHS: Dubbed. **S29356. $19.95.**
VHS: Subtitled. **S23074. $24.95.**
Laser: CAV, multi-audio. **LD74656. $34.95.**
A.I.C., Japan, 1992, 30 mins.

Tenchi Muyo! Vol. 3: Hello Ryo-Ohki

Ayeka and Sasami are stranded when their spaceship is wrecked in a battle with Ryo-Ohki, and to top it off, an infant Ryo-Ohki hatches from a spaceship egg.
VHS: Dubbed. **S29357. $19.95.**
VHS: Subtitled. **S23075. $24.95.**
Laser: CAV, multi-audio. **LD74657. $34.95.**
A.I.C., Japan, 1992, 30 mins.

Tenchi Muyo! Vol. 4: Mihoshi Falls to the Land of Stars

It's fall and the group visits a hot springs resort. While Ryoko tries to seduce Tenchi in her birthday suit, Ayeka panics when Tenchi sees her naked, and Tenchi's father tries hard to take a peek at the ladies' side of the hot springs. One such day, a new character appears before our group: Mihoshi, a female cop with the Galaxy Police.
VHS: Dubbed. **S29358. $19.95.**
VHS: Subtitled. **S23076. $24.95.**
Laser: CAV, multi-audio. **LD74658. $34.95.**
A.I.C., Japan, 1992, 30 mins.

Tenchi Muyo! Vol. 5: Kagato Attacks

Mihoshi joins the group as a new roomate, making Tenchi's life as lively as ever. One day Kagato, one of the most wanted criminals in the universe, appears before the group. He claims to be Ryoko's creator and he's after Tenchi's sword. Despite Tenchi's and his grandfather's struggle, Kagato kidnaps Ryoko and flees to outer space.
VHS: Dubbed. **S29359. $19.95.**
VHS: Subtitled. **S23077. $24.95.**
Laser: CAV, multi-audio. **LD74659. $34.95.**
A.I.C., Japan, 1992, 30 mins.

Tenchi Muyo! Vol. 6: We Need Tenchi

After losing Tenchi, the girls storm Kagato's spaceship. But Ayeka falls into Kagato's hands! Meanwhile, Ryoko and Mihoshi are confined in a different dimension, where they meet Washu, a scientific genius. To their surprise, she reveals herself as Ryoko's creator. Just as the destruction ray fired at Earth is about to reach its destination, Tenchi is resurrected and reappears!
VHS: Dubbed. **S29360. $19.95.**
VHS: Subtitled. **S23078. $24.95.**
Laser: CAV, multi-audio. **LD74660. $34.95.**
A.I.C., Japan, 1992, 30 mins.

Tenchi Muyo! Vol. 7: Ryo-ohki Special—The Night Before the Carnival

The Kagato incident is over, but Tenchi is at no loss for trouble, with five beautiful girls and Ryo-Ohki around him. Ryoko's and Ayeka's war for Tenchi's love, Washu's organic experiment on Tenchi and the case of disappearing carrots caused by a divided and multiplied Ryo-Ohki... Here's the Special (sequel) to the popular series.
VHS: Dubbed. **S29361. $19.95.**
VHS: Subtitled. **S23079. $24.95.**
Laser: CAV, multi-audio. **LD74661. $39.95.**
A.I.C., Japan, 1992, 30 mins.

Tenchi Muyo! Mihoshi Special

Mihoshi's a bit of a scatterbrain but she's a real Galaxy Policewoman. And, according to her, one of the best! Nobody believes her but maybe they'll acknowledge her abilities after she recounts how she and her partner, Kiyone, solved the galaxy's most notorious case. Tenchi as the Investigator, Ryoko as the space pirate, and Sasami as the Magical Girl Pretty Sammy!? A special episode.
VHS: Dubbed. **S29362. $19.95.**
VHS: Subtitled. **S24238. $24.95.**
Laser: CAV, multi-audio. **LD74817. $34.95.**
A.I.C., Japan, 1992, 30 mins.

Tenchi Muyo! Episodes 8 & 9

In *Hello! Baby*, Tenchi's aunt arrives with her grandson one day, asking Tenchi & Co. to take care of the baby for a while. Ryoko and Ayeka compete to impress Tenchi and Mihoshi remains good-natured. In *Sasami & Tsunami*, Tenchi & Co. return to the hot springs resort, where a ghost is sighted wandering about the inn. Sasami recalls the attack on the royal palace on Planet Jurai by Ryoko, years ago.
VHS: Dubbed. **S29363. $24.95.**
VHS: Subtitled. **S24572. $29.95.**
Laser: CAV, multi-audio. **LD74825. $39.95.**
A.I.C., Japan, 1992, 60 mins.

Tenchi Muyo! Episodes 10 & 11

In *I Love Tenchi*, the Mass, a strange space creature kept in Washu's lab, picks up Ryo-Ohki's desire to help Tenchi, which causes the situation to head in an unexpected direction. In *The Advent of the Goddess*, super-scientist Dr. Clay heads for Earth to capture Washu. Tokimi, a high-level dimensional life-form, wishes to meet Washu in person. Dr. Clay has his assassin Zero, an artificial life-form, impersonate Ryoko.
VHS: Dubbed. **S29364. $24.95.**
VHS: Subtitled. **S25676. $29.95.**
Laser: CAV, multi-audio. **LD74989. $39.95.**
A.I.C., Japan, 1992, 60 mins.

Tenchi Muyo! Episodes 12 & 13

In *Zero Ryoko*, Ryoko's imposter, Zero, is on a deadly mission—to assassinate Tenchi! In addition, Zero has taken Ryoko hostage. In *The Royal Family Has Come*, Tenchi's family is broken up. Now that the royal family of the planet Jurai has arrived on Earth, who do they want to bring back to Jurai? The answer is in this grand finale of the second *Tenchi Muyo!* series.
VHS: Dubbed. **S29365. $24.95.**
VHS: Subtitled. **S29367. $29.95.**
Laser: CAV, multi-audio. **LD75789. $44.95.**
A.I.C., Japan, 1992, 60 mins.

Tenchi Muyo! The Magical Girl Pretty Sammy

Sasami Kawai is a cheerful 4th grader. One day, she meets a strange lady named Tsunami, who claims she comes from a Magical Kingdom called Juraihelm. She asks Sasami to help make the Earth a better place by using the magical powers she can bestow upon Sasami. Sasami's career as a Magical Girl thus begins.
VHS: Dubbed. **S29366. $24.95.**
VHS: Subtitled. **S26631. $29.95.**
Laser: CAV, multi-audio. **LD75103. $39.95.**
A.I.C., Japan, 1992, 60 mins.

Tenchi Muyo! The Magical Girl Pretty Sammy 2

This time the stage is set at Akihabara, the electronics district of Tokyo. Sammy meets a new enemy, Biff Standard, who plots to monopolize the worldwide computer network and then target Akihabara. Stars the voice of Chisa Yokoyama.

VHS: Dubbed. **S31088. $24.95.**
VHS: Subtitled. **S31087. $29.95.**
Laser: Multi-audio. **LD76147. $39.95.**
Japan

Tenchi Muyo—Magical Girl Pretty Sammy 3: Super Kiss

As Pretty Sammy (Sasami) was losing a battle against Pixy Misa in outer space, the sudden arrival of a giant meteorite saved her. The meteorite continued on to crash at a resort beach in Japan—the same beach Sasami and her friends are supposed to go to on vacation. There, Sasami falls in love with a mysterious boy with a secret and meets a man who wants to destroy Sasami and Tsunami. 45 mins.

VHS: Dubbed. **S34296. $24.95.**
VHS: Subtitled. **S34297. $29.95.**

Tenchi Muyo! In Love

Galaxy Police detectives Mihoshi and Kiyone are on routine patrol near Earth when they find out that the Galaxy Police headquarters has been blown up by a notorious terrorist and escaped prisoner named Kain. Kain possesses a power so strong that he can even warp time and space. Tenchi and friends decide to take a trip 26 years into the past, courtesy of Washu's "Time Cause/Effect Controller."

VHS: Dubbed. **S29586. $19.95.**
VHS: Subtitled. **S29588. $24.95.**
Laser: CAV, multi-audio. **LD75841. $49.95.**
A.I.C., Japan, 1992, 90 mins.

Tenchi the Movie 2: The Daughter of Darkness

A stand-alone story. One day a fetching young girl, Mayuka, appears to Tenchi, calling him Daddy. Jealousy follows as Ryoko and Ayeka battle for Tenchi's attention while they try to figure out who the mother is. Meanwhile Yuhuza, the Demoness of Darkness, plots to use Mayuka to steal Tenchi away to the Dimension of Darkness.

VHS: Dubbed. **S34042. $19.95.**
VHS: Subtitled. **S34043. $24.95.**
Laser: Multi-audio. **LD76832. $29.95.**
DVD: Multi-audio. **DV60247. $29.95.**
A.I.C., Japan, 1997, 60 mins.

Tenchi Universe, Vol. 1: Tenchi on Earth I

Episodes 1-4. A new story line plus some new characters are included in this exciting expanded series. Episode 1: *No Need for Discussions!:* The first episode opens with Tenchi's monologue as he reminisces about "those days." Episode 2: *No Need for a Princess!:* The rivalry between Ryoko and Ayeka goes far back to their childhood. What facts could possibly build the kind of childhood stories they tell? See Ryoko as a little girl for the first time. Episode 3: *No Need for Worries!:* Like any other pets, our Ryo-ohki has her favorite food; carrots! As for Sasami, you can enjoy watching her both in her space suits and everyday clothes. Episode 4: *No Need for Monsters!:* With her spaceship crippled, Sasami happily joins Mihoshi, Ayeka and Ryoko to live with Tenchi's family.

VHS: Dubbed. **S30491. $24.95.**
VHS: Subtitled. **S30492. $29.95.**
Laser: Multi-audio. **LD76021. $44.95.**
A.I.C., Japan, 1995, 100 mins.

Tenchi Universe, Vol. 2: Tenchi on Earth II

Episodes 5-7.

VHS: Dubbed. **S31339. $24.95.**
VHS: Subtitled. **S31340. $29.95.**
Laser: Multi-audio. **LD76213. $44.95.**
A.I.C, Japan, 1995, 65 mins.

Tenchi Universe, Vol. 3: Tenchi on Earth III

Episodes 8-10.

VHS: Dubbed. **S33662. $24.95.**
VHS: Subtitled. **S33668. $29.95.**
Laser: Multi-audio. **LD76771. $44.95.**
A.I.C, Japan, 1995, 65 mins.

Tenchi Universe, Vol. 4: Time & Space

Episodes 11-13.

VHS: Dubbed. **S33663. $24.95.**
VHS: Subtitled. **S33669. $29.95.**
Laser: Multi-audio. **LD76772. $44.95.**
A.I.C, Japan, 1995, 65 mins.

Tenchi Universe, Vol. 5: Space I

Episodes 14-16.

VHS: Dubbed. **S33664. $24.95.**
VHS: Subtitled. **S33670. $29.95.**
Laser: Multi-audio. **LD76773. $44.95.**
A.I.C, Japan, 1995, 65 mins.

Tenchi Universe, Vol. 6: Space II

Episodes 17-19. Tenchi and his gang are heading to Planet Jurai to find out what is really going on, while Ayeka and Sasami are being chased by the Galaxy Police and the Jurai Army.

VHS: Dubbed. **S33665. $24.95.**
VHS: Subtitled. **S33671. $29.95.**
Laser: Multi-audio. **LD76774. $44.95.**
A.I.C, Japan, 1995, 65 mins.

Tenchi Universe, Vol. 7: Space III

Episodes 20-22. When part-time jobs repairing the starship *Yagami* don't pay well enough, everyone enters a swimsuit contest. Disguising themselves as a tour group, they try to pass a security checkpoint and reach planet Jurai. Later, Katsuhito asks Tenchi to revive the legendary knights Azaka and Kamidake.

VHS: Dubbed. **S33666. $24.95.**
VHS: Subtitled. **S33672. $29.95.**
Laser: Multi-audio. **LD76775. $44.95.**
A.I.C, Japan, 1995, 65 mins.

Tenchi Universe, Vol. 8

Episodes 23-25.

VHS: Dubbed. **S33673. $24.95.**
VHS: Subtitled. **S33667. $24.95.**
Laser: Multi-audio. **LD76776. $44.95.**
A.I.C, Japan, 1995, 65 mins.

They Were 11

Ten cadets at the Cosmo Academy are set adrift in a derelict spaceship for 53 days. The group of human and alien cadets soon discover that they are actually a group of 11, and the tense situation becomes ripe for explosion. Stereo.

VHS: Subtitled. **S17798. $19.95.**
VHS: Dubbed. **S30176. $19.95.**
Kitty, Japan, 1986, 91 mins.

Those Obnoxious Aliens!

English-language versions of the first two episodes of the *Urusei Yatsura TV Series*. Dubbed.

VHS: S23762. $19.95.
Kitty Films, Japan, 1981, 50 mins.

Tokyo Babylon 1

In this supernatural mystery, Sinji Nagumo seems to lead a charmed life, while his fellow skyscraper builders have been fatally unlucky. It's up to the powerful medium Subaru Sumeragi to determine if there's some sinister force at work. Stereo.

VHS: Dubbed. **S29369. $19.95.**
VHS: Subtitled. **S24241. $29.95.**
Laser: Hybrid. **LD75790. $34.95.**
Clamp, Japan, 1992, 52 mins.

Tokyo Babylon 2

A killer is stalking the subways. With nowhere else to turn, Mirei Hidaka, a psychic "postcognitive," is called in. But just as the threads are starting to come together, Mirei's own life is in jeopardy! It's now up to Subaru Sumeragi, Japan's most powerful medium, to save the day. Stereo.

VHS: Dubbed. **S29370. $19.95.**
VHS: Subtitled. **S24242. $29.95.**
Clamp, Japan, 1992, 52 mins.

Tokyo Private Police Vol. 1

Subtitled.

VHS: S32761. $24.95.
Japan

Tokyo Private Police Vol. 2

Subtitled.

VHS: S33660. $24.95.
Japan

Tokyo Revelation

Akito has plans for the human race that revolve around magnetite, the element that forms the living essence of every human soul. Combined with his demonic software, enough magnetite would release a plague of devils upon the Earth. It is Akito's classmate Kojiro who must find the ultimate power within himself to stop this evil plan. Violence, nudity and profanity.

VHS: Dubbed. **S32257. $19.95.**
VHS: Subtitled. **S32258. $24.95.**
Sony, Japan, 1994, 60 mins.

Tokyo: The Last Megalopolis

The total devastation of Tokyo and creature designs by H.R. Giger *(Alien, Species)* highlight this grim tale of ambition, supernatural horror and undying evil in which a prophet, a physicist and a businessman unite to protect Tokyo from a spiritual invasion. 135 mins.

VHS: S34652. $19.98.

Toward the Terra

Evacuating Earth, mankind has settled on the planet Atarakusha—20,000 light years distant. The new government ruthlessly seeks out and destroys any dissident elements, especially the MU—a new race of man possessing incredible mental powers. HiFi Stereo. Subtitled.

VHS: S21282. $29.95.
Laser: Letterboxed. **LD74887. $39.95.**
Toei, Japan, 1980, 112 mins.

Twilight of the Cockroaches

Written, produced and directed by Hiroaki Yoshida. An innovative combination of live action and animation. The film traces the rise and fall of an (animated) cockroach kingdom in the home of (live action) Mr. Saito. The cockroaches worship Saito and all humans as gods. Filmed with snorkel camera from the insect's viewpoint. HiFi Stereo. Dubbed.

Laser: CLV. **LD71494. $39.99.**
TYO Prod., Japan, 1987, 102 mins.

Twilight of the Dark Master

From the beginning of time, Earth is enslaved by grotesque Ogres, challenged only by the noble Guardians. Eons later…Neo-Shinjuku City, in the year 2089, few Ogres or Guardians remain. Humans are seemingly free of the horrible Ogres, but deep beneath the city the Supreme Ogre is still alive and preparing to once again enslave the human race. Violence and sexual situatons.

VHS: Dubbed. **S33661. $19.95.**
VHS: Subtitled. **S32777. $29.95.**
Japan, 50 mins.

The Ultimate Teacher

It's the worst high school in Tokyo City. The buildings are crumbling, the teachers are nowhere to be found, and the neighborhood looks like a demilitarized zone. But watch out—here comes the newest teacher…half human, half cockroach. HiFi Stereo.

VHS: Dubbed. **S29372. $14.95.**
VHS: Subtitled. **S19437. $29.95.**
Laser: Subtitled. **LD74516. $34.95.**
Movic, Japan, 1988, 57 mins.

Ultraman: The Adventure Begins

The animated adventure begins as three Ultra family members battle a mutated creature attacking Earth. This unique co-production was produced by Tsuburuya Productions and Hanna-Barbera and features unique Ultra battle action. Dubbed.

VHS: S18338. $14.95.
Tsuburuya/Hanna-Barbera, Japan, 1987, 70 mins.

Ultraman II

Sleek Japanese animation from Akira Tsuburaya and Hiroshi Jinzenji that grafts the pulp and violence of the American superhero onto a Japanese aesthetic, as Ultraman must defend his planet from dark powers that threaten its safety. 86 mins.

VHS: S18590. $19.99.

Ultraman: Towards the Future

Ultraman is an intergalactic guard interested in preserving the galaxy. Ultraman has entered the body of astronaut Jack Shindo by fusing with his molecular structure. Jack transforms himself into Ultraman through a special Delta Plasma Pendant. An original English production.

Vol. 2, Episode 2. The mysterious Gudis Bacteria has provoked a global warming, melting the polar ice caps, awakening the dormant Gigasaurus. The monster freezes everything in its wake and Ultraman must summon all his strength and resources to defeat the monster. 23 mins.

VHS: S18335. $14.95.

Vol. 3, Episode 3. The Gudis invade the body of Jimmy Martin, who controls a giant Gerukadon that is wreaking havoc on the city. Ultraman and his young friends confront the savage being. 23 mins.

VHS: S18336. $14.95.

Vol. 4, Episode 4. In *The Storm Hunter*, Jack Shindo and Lloyd Wilder explore a whirlwind that attacked two hunters. They control the force through Aboriginal magic, until a search party attacks the spirit and unleashes its awesome powers and forces Ultraman into an epic struggle. 23 mins.

VHS: S18337. $14.95.

Vol. 5, Episode 5. In *The Blast from the Past*, the UMA regiments stage a ferocious battle with a mysterious enemy, Barraki. Stanley Haggard is recruited by the UMA to circumvent the monstrous beast. Stanley kidnaps Jean Echo, setting in motion a mammoth conflict between Ultraman and Barraki to protect Jean from the sinister Gudis' forces.
VHS: S19712. $14.95.
Vol. 6, Episode 6. In *The Showdown*, Ultraman is engaged in his greatest challenge when the Gudis collect enough cells to be reborn. Strengthed by a violent assault by the armed forces, Gudis descend on the Earth from a volcanic womb. Ultraman prepares for battle.
VHS: S19713. $14.95.
Vol. 7, Episode 7. In *The Forest Guardian*, the UMA forces have only 24 hours to track down a young girl separated from her mother while she was fleeing a Gazebo monster. Ultraman and the monster engage in an epic battle over a mushroom that paralyzes the monster.
VHS: S19714. $14.95.
Vol. 8, Episode 8. When a crop duster plane is attacked by a colossal mutant creature in *The Bitter Harvest*, the UMA forces investigate the incident and discover the monster's origins and location. Succesfully fending off one of the monsters, UMA forces quickly see that only Ultraman can save them from certain destruction.
VHS: S19715. $14.95.
Vol. 10, Episode 10. Japanese television character Ultraman was at the center of a incomparable science fiction serial. Now this 1960's superhero is back. Aliens visiting the Earth are just looking for a good time. Unfortunately Charles doesn't realize this when he falls in love with one of them. Can Ultraman solve this romantic intergalactic mess? 23 mins.
VHS: S20484. $14.95.
Vol. 11, Episode 11. Ultraman is an animated galactic guardian interested in the preservation of the galaxy. In Episode 11, *The Survivalists*, Jean Echo is kidnapped by a criminal scientist who was presumed killed in an auto accident. Echo is forced to help Norberg attack UMA headquarters, and only Ultraman can stop this plot. Dubbed in English, 23 mins.
VHS: S22906. $14.95.
Vol. 13, Episode 13. In this episode, Nemesis, the intergalactic guardian, must find a disk that predicted the chaos currently plaguing the Earth. Like the 1960's live-action television series, this animated feature contains giant monsters and amazing battle scenes. Dubbed in English. 23 mins.
VHS: S23764. $14.95.

Urusei Yatsura Movie 1: Only You

Lum goes ballistic when she learns that Ataru is planning to wed Elle. She abducts Ataru, only to have Elle's fleet capture the wedding party and re-abduct them to her planet. Ataru decides not to wed Elle and the skies light up with the biggest shotgun wedding of all time. Subtitled.
VHS: S17740. $24.95.
Laser: LD75795. $39.95.
Kitty Films, Japan, 1983, 101 mins.

Urusei Yatsura Movie 2: Beautiful Dreamer

Director Oshii Mamoru's magnum opus, combining the comedy that made the TV series such a hit with a deeply philosophical tale of time and space. Life is but a dream, but who is the dreamer? Subtitled.
VHS: Subtitled. **S17739. $14.95.**
VHS: Dubbed. **S30177. $19.95.**
Laser: LD75796. $39.95.
Toho, Japan, 1984, 90 mins.

Urusei Yatsura Movie 3: Remember My Love

When Lum was born, a postal mixup caused a witchy friend to feel slighted. She laid a curse on Lum to never be happy with her true love. At an amusement park opening, Ataru gets turned into a pink hippopotamus—for real! When Lum tracks down the witch that transformed her darling, things get very weird. Subtitled.
VHS: S17741. $24.95.
Laser: LD75797. $39.95.
Kitty Films, Japan, 1985, 93 mins.

Urusei Yatsura Movie 4: Lum the Forever

Strange things are happening in Tomobiki Town. When a great cherry tree is cut down while Lum & Co. are out making a movie, Lum loses her horns—and her powers! Thus begins the strangest and most lyrical of the *Urusei Yatsura* movies. Subtitled.
VHS: S18652. $24.95.
Laser: LD75798. $39.95.
Kitty Films, Japan, 1986, 94 mins.

Urusei Yatsura Movie 5: The Final Chapter

The fifth film is an animated representation of "Boy Meets Girl," the finale of the original manga series. With the appearance of Lum's fiance, a boy named Lupa, Lum and Ataru's game of tag to avert the crisis of Earth's destruction unfolds. Subtitled.
VHS: S20731. $24.95.
Kitty Films, Japan, 1988, 85 mins.

Urusei Yatsura Movie 6: Always My Darling

Lupica, a space princess, abducts Ataru. Lum gives chase, assisted by friends Oyuki and Benten. Lupica not only wants Ataru for his great looks, but for the greatest love potion in the galaxy. Subtitled.
VHS: S20724. $24.95.
Laser: LD75800. $39.95.
Kitty Films, Japan, 1986, 77 mins.

Urusei Yatsura OVA #1: Inaba the Dreammaker

The full title of the Inaba TV Special is *Urusei Yatsura '87: Introduces Inaba the Dream-maker—What Will Become of Lum's Future?* This episode centers around what happens to Lum, Ataru, Shinabu and the gang when they get a glimpse of their possible futures—thanks to a chance meeting with a group of interdimensional doommakers in rabbit suits. Subtitled.
VHS: S18349. $24.95.
Kitty Films, Japan, 1987, 55 mins.

Urusei Yatsura OVA #2: Raging Sherbert & I Howl at the Moon

Two episodes. *Raging Sherbert*: Hiding from the Tokyo heat at the Sherbert Factory on Neptune, Lum, Ran and Benton plot to take a magical Sherbert bird for themselves. *Nagisa's Fiance*: Lum, Ataru and the gang visit Ryuunosuke and her father at their shop. But it's on an uninhabited island where the ghosts start appearing. Subtitled.
VHS: S18350. $24.95.
Kitty Films, Japan, 1988, 55 mins.

Urusei Yatsura OVA #3: Catch the Heart & Goat and Cheese

Two episodes. *Catch the Heart*: A mischievous spirit gives Ran a candy that makes a magical heart appear over the eater's head and whoever catches it captures the heart of that person. *Goat and Cheese*: When Mendou's father takes a picture in front of the statue of Great-Grandfather's goat, only Sakura and Onsenmark can ward off the ancient family curse. Subtitled.
VHS: S18351. $24.95.
Kitty Films, Japan, 1989, 55 mins.

Urusei Yatsura OVA #4: Date with a Spirit & Terror of Girly-Eyes Measles

Two episodes. *Date with a Spirit*: A young girl's ghost falls for Sakura's fiance and Ataru struggles to fondle a babe with no body; *Terror of the Girly-Eyes Measles*: Ten gives Ataru a very contagious disease that turns people's eyes into big, cute, adorable girly-eyes. Subtitled.
VHS: S18367. $24.95.
Kitty Films, Japan, 1989, 55 mins.

Urusei Yatsura OVA #5: Nagisa's Fiance & Electric Household Guard

Two episodes. *Nagisa's Fiance*: Ryuunosuke and her father open an inn that turns out to be on a haunted island; *The Electric Household Guard*: Shingo becomes Mendou's private ninja, but quickly falls for his sister Ryoko. Subtitled.
VHS: S18648. $24.95.
Kitty Films, Japan, 1989, 55 mins.

Urusei Yatsura OVA #6: Ryoko's Tea Party & Memorial Album

Two episodes. At Ryoko's September tea party guests' pasts are revealed and we learn all about the Mendou family. Both feature clips from the original series mixed with new animation. Subtitled.
VHS: S18650. $24.95.
Kitty Films, Japan, 1989, 90 mins.

Urusei Yatsura TV Series Vol. 1

Episodes 1-4: Ataru Moroboshi, the world's unluckiest teenager, is forced to play a game of tag with the beautiful alien princess Lum. If he loses, the aliens will foreclose on Earth. When Ataru wins, Lum takes his victory cry as a marriage proposal. Then Lum's relatives start visiting and things start to get really weird. Subtitled.
VHS: S16980. $24.95.
Kitty Films, Japan, 1981, 100 mins.

Urusei Yatsura TV Series Vol. 2

Episodes 5-8: Ataru runs into the arms of the sorceress Sakura; Ataru tries to two-time Lum but unleashes an annoying devil; Lum starts playing with alien voodoo dolls; Oyuki opens an interdimensional portal and Ataru lands in the dinosaur age. Subtitled.
VHS: S17526. $24.95.
Kitty Films, Japan, 1981, 100 mins.

Urusei Yatsura TV Series Vol. 3

Episodes 9-12: Princess Kurama decides to remake Ataru into a perfect husband; Megane plots to discredit Ataru with Lum; pre-incarnations of everyone battle baby-nappers from the future; Tsubame turns a nightclub into "Disco Inferno"; and Kurama's dad will teach Ataru swordsmanship. Subtitled.
VHS: S17527. $24.95.
Kitty Films, Japan, 1981, 100 mins.

Urusei Yatsura TV Series Vol. 4

Episodes 13-16. The gang goes to Hawaii; Mendou begins causing trouble for the guys; the annual End of Winter fight takes place; it's visiting day at school and Lum, Ataru and Mendou's mothers meet. Subtitled.
VHS: S18352. $24.95.
Kitty Films, Japan, 1981, 100 mins.

Urusei Yatsura TV Series Vol. 5

Episodes 17-20. Mendou's camera means trouble for Ataru; Ran tries to steal Ataru; a diary falls into the wrong hands; an alien baby is in Ataru's locker and the classroom becomes a sorcerer's battlefield. Subtitled.
VHS: S18353. $24.95.
Kitty Films, Japan, 1981, 100 mins.

Urusei Yatsura TV Series Vol. 6

Episodes 21-24. Ataru suffers a split personality; Ataru's mother recaps the series so far; the gang does public service announcements; Ataru is pitted against a gang of female Ninja; Lum's impatient dad decides to match Lum with another man. Subtitled.
VHS: S18354. $24.95.
Kitty Films, Japan, 1981, 100 mins.

Urusei Yatsura TV Series Vol. 7

Episodes 25-28. Ataru gets kidnapped by mythological demons; the gang runs afoul of transmigratory earmuffs; a giant caterpillar runs amok; Little Ten gets the hots for sexy Sakura. Subtitled.
VHS: S18646. $24.95.
Kitty Films, Japan, 1981, 100 mins.

Urusei Yatsura TV Series Vol. 8

Episodes 29-30: An amorous Dracula hits town; Lum travels back in time to re-educate and reform a young lad named Ataru; love blooms when Ten and Ataru fall for a lady florist; and trouble looms for Ataru when an evil rain-spirit dumps all over him. Subtitled.
VHS: S18647. $24.95.
Kitty Films, Japan, 1981, 100 mins.

Urusei Yatsura TV Series Vol. 9

Episodes 31-34. Ten's horn has fallen out; the balance of the book world is being destroyed; a new teacher at school is out of step with Darling; a swimming pool goblin causes trouble. Subtitled.
VHS: S18649. $24.95.
Kitty Films, Japan, 1981, 100 mins.

Urusei Yatsura TV Series Vol. 10

Episodes 35-38. Ran makes another attempt to steal Ataru from Lum; chaos reigns supreme when Rei drops in for a visit; the return of the "Red Cloak" sets up a night of Disco terror; and Lum tries to thwart Ran's latest scheme by duplicating her darling! Subtitled.
VHS: S18651. $24.95.
Kitty Films, Japan, 1981, 100 mins.

Urusei Yatsura TV Series Vol. 11

Episodes 39-42. Lum and Ataru go on a date; a trip to the seaside results in a run-in with a cursed watermelon; a typhoon treads on Tokyo; and Lum and Ten get smashed on high-octane pickled plums! Subtitled.
VHS: S18653. $24.95.
Kitty Films, Japan, 1981, 100 mins.

Urusei Yatsura TV Series Vol. 12

Episodes 43-46. Lum wants to see if Ataru really wants to be rid of her; Lum's friends descend upon the high school and the teachers mobilize for all-out war. Voted "Best Episode" by Japanese viewers! Subtitled.
VHS: S20022. $24.95.
Kitty Films, Japan, 1981, 100 mins.

Urusei Yatsura TV Series Vol. 13

Episodes 47-50: Lum brings a fossil bird to life; goblins try to find a mate for the lovely Princess Kurama; Ten infects the school with a contagious alien toothache; and Mendou is mortified when his younger sister Ryooko puts the moves on Ataru. Subtitled.
VHS: S20725. $24.95.
Kitty Films, Japan, 1981, 100 mins.

Urusei Yatsura TV Series Vol. 14

Episodes 51-54. Jaritan meets Kotatsu (giant white half-ghost kitty) and invites him home. It turns out the ghost cat died of cold and now he he won't leave the heater. Subtitled.
VHS: S20726. $24.95.
Kitty Films, Japan, 1981, 100 mins.

Urusei Yatsura TV Series Vol. 15

Episodes 55-58. Ataru is cast as a food thief and ends up running from Sakura; Lum and Mendou meet a giant monkey; her mother kicks Lum's father out; Lum and Ataru go on a ski trip. Subtitled.
VHS: S20727. $24.95.
Kitty Films, Japan, 1981, 100 mins.

Urusei Yatsura TV Series Vol. 16

Episodes 59-62: Ataru and Lum try to act as Cupid for Mako; a crystal ball will reveal a person's true mate; the Mendo family's masquerade war escalates into a battle; Lum infects everyone with a virus that causes humans to get orange and green stripes! Subtitled.
VHS: S20728. $24.95.
Kitty Films, Japan, 1981, 100 mins.

Urusei Yatsura TV Series Vol. 17

Episodes 63-66: Ataru, Lum and the Gang meet Ryunosuke for the first time; Shinobu mistakenly believes that Ataru is going to give up Lum; Ran meets and falls in love with Ryo. Despite Ataru and Lum's efforts, Ran refuses to believe that Ryo is a girl! On Ataru's birthday he wants to be free of Lum! Subtitled.
VHS: S26636. $24.95.
Kitty Films, Japan, 1981, 100 mins.

Urusei Yatsura TV Series Vol. 18

Episodes 67-70: Lum's bad cooking is the least of the problems facing the gang; those pesky Tengu crows find a near-perfect match for their princess, Kurama, and they set out to fix that one little problem that keeps "him" from being eligible; a letter in a bottle leads to chaos; and Mendou's deadly rival, the scion of the second-richest family in Japan, arrives on the scene. Subtitled.
VHS: S27655. $24.95.
Kitty Films, Japan, 1981, 100 mins.

Urusei Yatsura TV Series Vol. 19

Episodes 71-74: Shinobu meets a mysterious stranger who plunges her into a perilous predicament, movie-making gets mangled by extraterrestrial technology, Lum's inedible cooking turns the Moroboshi household into a battlefield for spacefleets and angry spirits, and a spooky story sets nerves on edge when it becomes more real than anyone bargained for.
VHS: S31341. $24.95.
Japan

Ushio & Tora Vol. 1

Episodes 1 and 2. Young Ushio discovers a 500-year-old demon in his basement who is attracting other nasty creatures to the neighborhood. In a most unlikely buddy story, Ushio forms an uneasy alliance with the demon in order to rid the town of all the unwanted visitors. Violence. Subtitled.
VHS: S29890. $29.95.
Toho, Japan, 1992, 60 mins.

Ushio & Tora Vol. 2

Episodes 3 and 4. When one of Tora's schemes to eat Ushio fails, he gets revenge by telling an itinerant monster-hunter that Tora was the one who ate the man's family 15 years ago. Meanwhile, repair work on an old waterwheel inadvertantly releases a peculiar monster who wants to "reward" Asako by killing all her relatives and carrying her off. Violence. Subtitled.
VHS: S33647. $29.95.
Toho, Japan, 1992, 60 mins.

Ushio & Tora Vol. 3

Episodes 5 and 6. Tora goes to town in search of dinner and eventually finds a morsel to his liking. Unfortunately, it's Ushio's friend Mayuko. Even worse, a quintet of demonic Gamin heads have settled on the same bill of fare. Violence. Subtitled.
VHS: S33648. $29.95.
Toho, Japan, 1992, 60 mins.

Ushio & Tora Vol. 4

Episodes 7 and 8. A trip to the seashore turns into a disaster when Ushio and his classmates go to sea with Tora in tow. First The Old Man of the Sea comes looking for help and then the horrendous Ayakashi starts swallowing everything in sight, including Asako and Tora. Violence. Subtitled.
VHS: S33649. $29.95.
Toho, Japan, 1992, 60 mins.

Ushio & Tora Vol. 5 & Super-Deformed Special

Ushio and Tora bite off more than they can chew when they confront a trio of unhappy wind demons. In a bonus super-deformed special, a creature named Dirt-Licker offers to help Ushio clean the bathroom, Tora encounters a kitten, and the whole thing ends up in a bizarre tribute to silent movies. Violence. Subtitled.
VHS: S33650. $29.95.
Toho, Japan, 1992, 90 mins.

Vampire Hunter D

In 12,090 A.D., vampires act as feudal land barons ruling over hopeless pockets of civilization. These soulless scions are challenged by a mysterious vampire hunter known only as "D". Dubbed.
VHS: S16646. $19.95.
Epic/Sony, Japan, 1985, 80 mins.

Vampire Princess Miyu #1

Episodes 1 & 2: *Unearthly Kyooto* and *Marionette Banquet*. When a medium investigates a string of vampire murders, she meets the enigmatic vampire princess Miyu and her demon slave, Labaa. Miyu and a demonic puppeteer both attempt to seduce a handsome high school student with the promise of eternal life. HiFi Stereo.
VHS: Dubbed. **S29373. $19.95.**
VHS: Subtitled. **S16666. $24.95.**
Laser: Hybrid. **LD75794. $39.95.**
Sooeishinsha, Japan, 1988, 50 mins.

Vampire Princess Miyu #2

Episodes 3 & 4: *Brittle Armor* and *Frozen Time*. Himiku, the medium, is surprised when Miyu asks her help in rescuing Labaa. She agrees in return for information about Miyu and her gods. Himiku then learns the truth about the strange bond between her and the vampire princess. HiFi Stereo.
VHS: Dubbed. **S29587. $19.95.**
VHS: Subtitled. **S16667. $24.95.**
Laser: Hybrid. **LD75840. $39.95.**
Sooeishinsha, JAPAN, 1988, 50 mins.

Vampire Princess Miyu Series

Contains volumes 1 and 2.
Laser: LD71511. $64.95.

The Venus Wars

In the 21st century, mankind has colonized Venus and thrived there for four generations. But old feuds survive and as the war with Earth commences, Hiro Seno (a hotshot motorcycle jockey) and his countrymen are plunged into the tense drama. Stereo.
VHS: Subtitled. **S18325. $14.95.**
VHS: Dubbed. **S29374. $19.95.**
Laser: Dubbed. **LD74520. $34.95.**
Bandai, Japan, 1989, 104 mins.

Violence Jack Part 3: Slum King

A huge comet erupts from the depths of space, hurling into the Earth and blasting away the last remnants of civilization. In the wake of this cataclysm, one man has risen to power in the corpse-strewn wasteland that was once Japan. His name is Slum King, and his rule over Kanto is harsh and absolute. Only Violence Jack has the courage to challenge his rule. Enraged at this defiance, Slum King demands the death of his giant enemy, while the arrival of a huge, fanged warrior in the nearby village of Trench Town signals the beginning of incredible carnage. Explicit violence and adult situations. HiFi Stereo. ADULTS ONLY.
VHS: Dubbed, edited. **S30277. $19.95.**
VHS: Subtitled, uncut. **S30391. $24.95.**
VHS: Dubbed, uncut. **S30392. $24.95.**
Go Nagai, Japan, 55 mins.

Voltage Fighter Gowcaizer Round 1

It is the dawn of the 21st Century and the planet has been rocked by a series of natural disasters—the handiwork of Shizuru Ozaki. Ozaki aspires to something greater than mere mortality—even if that means destroying the Earth. But one young man has the power to stop him: the armored hero Gowcaizer. Based on the hit videogame. Nudity and violence. Dubbed.
VHS: S33410. $19.95.
Japan, 45 mins.

Voltage Fighter Gowcaizer Round 2

To avert the approaching apocalypse, Gowcaizer and Hellstinger must fight a desperate battle against the omnipotent Omni Exist. Their only hope is to prove that mankind is essentially good before the planet is cleansed of human beings. Nudity and violence. Dubbed.
VHS: S33651. $19.95.
Japan, 45 mins.

The Wanderers, El Hazard TV Series Quest #6

Join the heroic band as they aid their friends in desperate need of help, in this bizarre and wonderful TV series. Contains episodes 19, 20, 21 and 22.
Dubbed Version.
VHS: S34796. $24.95.
Subtitled Version.
VHS: S34795. $29.95.
Laser: Multi-lingual. **LD76999. $39.95.**

The Wanderers

This TV series is the follow-up to the OAV series *El Hazard*. While Makoto Mizuhara is working on a chemistry project, Katsuhiko Jinnai causes a ruckus and a strange chemical reaction transports them to El Hazard. Mr. Fujisawa and Jinnai's sister Nanami are also whisked away.
Episodes 1 and 2.
VHS: Dubbed. **S33657. $19.95.**
VHS: Subtitled. **S33654. $24.95.**
Laser: Multi-audio. **LD76767. $39.95.**
Episodes 3 and 4.
VHS: Dubbed. **S33653. $19.95.**
VHS: Subtitled. **S33658. $24.95.**
Laser: Multi-audio. **LD76768. $39.95.**
Episodes 5 and 6. Nanami makes an entrance. Will she ever meet Makoto again?
VHS: Dubbed. **S33655. $19.95.**
VHS: Subtitled. **S33659. $24.95.**
Laser: Multi-audio. **LD76769. $39.95.**
Episodes 7 and 8. Dubbed.
VHS: S33656. $19.95.
Laser: Multi-audio. **LD76770. $39.95.**

Wanna-Be's

In the futuristic world of ladies' wrestling, the Foxy Ladies reign supreme. To defeat these beasts, it requires the superhuman strength that the delicate duo of Eri and Miki acquire. And that's just the beginning of a plot involving biochemistry, corruption and a great deal of body-crushing. Stereo. Subtitled.
VHS: S17072. $14.95.
Laser: LD74521. $29.95.
Movic, Japan, 1986, 45 mins.

A Wind Named Amnesia

In an America reduced to barbarism, a mysterious wind sweeps the land. Everyone it touches forgets...everything: who they were, how to speak, how to use the implements of civilization. Two years later, a young man who has been miraculously re-educated embarks on a coast to coast journey. Stereo. Nudity.
VHS: Subtitled. **S21099. $29.95.**
VHS: Dubbed. **S28600. $19.95.**
Laser: Subtitled. **LD74949. $39.95.**
Japan H.V., Japan, 1993, 80 mins.

Windaria

Two rival kingdoms vie for fresh water and in the process end up destroying their entire society. As seen through the eyes of an innocent go-between, this tragic story details the depths to which loyalty and love must be tested in a futile attempt to save a world. Dubbed.
VHS: S16644. $19.95.
Laser: LD74961. $39.99.
Kaname Prod., Japan, 1986, 95 mins.

Wings of Honneamise

An epic tale of a civilization's first faltering steps into space, set in an alien world that is strangely familiar. When cadet Shiro Lhadatt signs up with the Royal Space Force, he encounters ridicule and apathy from manipulative leaders and a cynical public. A chance encounter with a devout young woman spurs Shiro on towards his destiny—to become the first man in space. While military leaders conspire to use the space program to spark an all-out war, Shiro and a team of aging scientists race against time to complete the first launch. HiFi Stereo. Nudity.
VHS: Dubbed. **S29376. $19.95.**
VHS: Subtitled. **S25723. $24.95.**
Bandai, Japan, 1987, 125 mins.

Wrath of the Ninja: The Yotoden Movie

A theatrical compilation of the Yotoden OVA series, featuring never-before-seen footage, and the design work of Junichi Watanabe (Dangaioh and Ariel). Violence and nudity. Dubbed.
VHS: S34039. $19.95.
JVC, Japan, 1987-89, 87 mins.

Yotoden Chapter 1: Break Out

In 1580, an ominous comet dominates the heavens and Lord Nobunga Oda's bloody military campaign spreads darkly across Japan. Narrowly escaping the slaughter of the Kasumi ninja clan, Ayame and two other renegade ninja—each armed with magical blades—unite to fulfill an ancient prophesy. Violence and nudity. Subtitled.
VHS: S32265. $24.95.
JVC, Japan, 1987, 41 mins.

Yotoden Chapter 2: Demon's Cry

For two months, the three shadow warriors delayed the Warlord's advance, but now the rebellion is all but crushed and there may be a traitor in their midst. Ayanosuke and Ryoma vow to continue the quest, but how can the prophesy of three swords be fulfilled without Sakon's sword? Violence and nudity. Subtitled.
VHS: S32266. $24.95.
JVC, Japan, 1988, 40 mins.

Yotoden Chapter 3: Flames of Anger

The three shadow-ninja must unite one final time before the Demon Prince can open a gate to the Kingdom of Darkness and unleash the minions of Hell. Will they be able to close the gate and fulfill the ancient prophesy of Yotoden? Violence and nudity. Subtitled.
VHS: S32267. $24.95.
JVC, Japan, 1988, 45 mins.

You're Under Arrest! Ep. 1: And So They Met

Tokyo Highway Patrol Officers Natsumi and Miyuki get off to a bad start when Miyuki busts Natsumi for reckless moped driving on her way to work. Things get worse when they find out they're going to be partners. But when they run into "The Fox," a mysterious figure who tools around defying every traffic regulation yet invented in an unbelieveably customized Morris Minor, they'll need all their wits and every RPM in Miyuki's Nito-Boosted Mini Patrol Car to successfully hound their opponent. From the creator of *Oh My Goddess!* HiFi Stereo.
VHS: Dubbed. **S29377. $14.95.**
VHS: Subtitled. **S26006. $19.95.**
F. Kousuke, Japan, 1994, 25 mins.

You're Under Arrest! Ep. 2: Tokyo Typhoon Rally

A fierce typhoon bears down upon the city. Into the darkness and wind steals a mysterious yellow Lancia, taking advantage of the deserted streets to indulge in some high-speed harassment. Meanwhile, back at Bokutoo Police Station, is that love, or just negative ions? Intrepid police officers Natsumi and Miyuki can deal with the chaos of a giant storm. But when they are faced with the challenge of transporting a desperately ill, pregnant patient to a specialist hospital during a city-wide blackout, there's no time to lose. There is, however, a cop-hating yellow Lancia. HiFi Stereo.
VHS: Dubbed. **S29378. $14.95.**
VHS: Subtitled. **S26007. $19.95.**
F. Kousuke, Japan, 1994, 25 mins.

You're Under Arrest! Ep. 3: Love's Highway Stars

Matchmaking goes awry when Natsumi and Yoriko become convinced that Ken is about to lose Miyuki to an old high school boyfriend. HiFi Stereo.
VHS: Dubbed. **S29379. $14.95.**
VHS: Subtitled. **S27323. $19.95.**
F. Kousuke, Japan, 1994, 25 mins.

You're Under Arrest! Ep. 4: On the Road Again

Natsumi is offered the chance to go and be a member of the motorcycle patrol, but to do so means breaking up her partnership with Miyuki. HiFi Stereo.
VHS: Dubbed. **S29380. $14.95.**
VHS: Subtitled. **S27324. $19.95.**
F. Kousuke, Japan, 1994, 25 mins.

You're Under Arrest! Hybrid Laserdisc #1

Episodes 1 and 2. Laserdisc is dubbed one side, subtitled second side.
Laser: LD75036. $39.95.
F. Kousuke, Japan, 1994, 50 mins.

You're Under Arrest! Hybrid Laserdisc #2

Episodes 3 and 4. Laserdisc is dubbed one side, subtitled second side.
Laser: LD75801. $39.95.
F. Kousuke, Japan, 1994, 50 mins.

Yu Yu Hakusho: The Movie

Based on the popular Japanese comic book, TV series and video game. When Yusuke Urameshi dies in an accident trying to save a child, he finds himself in the Spirit World. When he finds that his name is not listed in the Book of Enma, he becomes a half-dead, half-alive agent for Koenma, son of the ruler of the Spirit World. Anime. 30 mins.
Dubbed Version.
VHS: S34171. $24.95.
Subtitled Version.
VHS: S34170. $24.95.

Zeguy, Parts 1 & 2

Miki falls through a "cloud road" and lands in a parallel Cloud World exotic enough to rival Oz. But Miki, noble swordswoman and scholar, stumbles onto a plot to control both worlds and is pitted against werewolf warriors, deadly cyborgs and a mad inventor. Stereo. Nudity. Subtitled.
VHS: S24336. $29.95.
Laser: LD75545. $34.99.
S. Kageyama, Japan, 1993, 79 mins.

Zenki the Demon Prince Vol. 1

Episode 1, *The Demon Lord Stands Before You!*; Episode 2, *Karma the Malevolent*; and Episode 3, *Chiaki in Trouble*. Long ago, there was a demon lord whose life had been bound to a mountain-dwelling monk. He was Zenki, the great and powerful. Under the control of the monk, Enno Ozuno, Zenki battled the forces of darkness before they were sealed for all time. Now, 1200 years and 55 generations later, the most powerful of all demon lords is needed once more! With the coming of the malevolent god Karma, evil forces are at work in the world, and the one person who can stand against them is a high-school girl! Chiaki is the latest descendent of the legendary Enno Ozuno, and heir to the control of the mighty Zenki. Stereo. Subtitled.
VHS: S26642. $24.95.
Kitty Films, Japan, 90 mins.

Zenki the Demon Prince Vol. 2

Episodes 4 & 5: The race to unleash the Seeds of Possession continues as Gohra arrives in Shikigami-cho for this attempt. This time around, a Seed is in the legendary "Jar of Desires," a valuable piece of pottery which Master Jukai would do almost anything to possess. But when a greedy collector buys the jar before he can, the Seed hiding inside finds a willing host for it to do its mischief. Stereo. Subtitled.
VHS: S26643. $24.95.
Kitty Films, Japan, 60 mins.

Zenki the Demon Prince Vol. 3

Episodes 6 & 7: One is a lonely young boy, who only wants to make friends. The other is a high school track star, obsessed with improving his record. Together, they will become the latest pawns in Karma's scheme to subjugate the Earth—and once again, only Chiaki and Zenki can stop her. Stereo. Subtitled.
VHS: S26644. $24.95.
Kitty Films, Japan, 60 mins.

Zenki the Demon Prince Vol. 4

Episodes 8 & 9: Karma's invasion of Earth is stalling, but she sends Guren to attack Chiaki and Zenki. Their vacation at Nami's resort is literally blown to hell when Zenki smells a Seed of Possession inside the hotel. When guests start disappearing, Zenki suspects a mysterious monk is actually Guren. Stereo. Subtitled.
VHS: S26645. $24.95.
Kitty Films, Japan, 60 mins.

Zenki the Demon Prince Vol. 5

Episodes 10 & 11: When Chiaki visits a schoolmate's kennel to see his new puppies, Gohra attacks the Enno shrine himself! But when Chiaki's friend is consumed by a Seed of Possession, the battle moves to two fronts. Chiaki and Zenki will have to combat a double possession, because someone else's personality is still linked to the Possession Beast—and this Beast may be more than any of them can handle. Stereo. Subtitled.
VHS: S26646. $24.95.
Kitty Films, Japan, 60 mins.

Zenki the Demon Prince Vol. 6

Episodes 12 & 13: A severe snowstorm turns deadly when Chiaki and Zenki come face to face with a "Snow Woman" right out of mythology. Also, the village New Year celebration seems to be going well, but when evil Gohra opens his shrine outside town, visitors start vanishing mysteriously! Stereo. Subtitled.
VHS: S26647. $24.95.
Kitty Films, Japan, 60 mins.

Zillion

Champ, Apple and J.J. star in this all-action animated adventure series adapted from the popular Japanese television show. Each volume contains a new installment in the adventures of our high-tech heroes as they try to combat a powerful alien invasion force. Not for children.
Zillion: Volume 1. *They Call Me, J.J.* 25 mins.
VHS: S15239. $14.95.
Zillion: Volume 2. *Hang Fire.* 25 mins.
VHS: S16651. $14.95.
Zillion: Volume 3. *Split Second Chance.* 25 mins.
VHS: S16652. $14.95.
Zillion: Volume 4. *Target: The White Knights.* 25 mins.
VHS: S16653. $14.95.
Zillion: Volume 5. *Judgement Call.* 25 mins.
VHS: S16654. $14.95.

Zillion: The Beginning

In the 24th century, the peaceful colony of Maris is under attack by a warrior race, the Noza. The Marisians' conventional weapons cannot stop the enemy. The newly discovered Zillion Weapon System is their only hope of salvation, Three fearless freedom fighters, the White Knights, have been entrusted with the Zillion guns. Their mission: to save the planet from certain annihilation. Episodes 1-3 of the TV series. Dubbed.
VHS: S19689. $19.99.
Tatsunoko, Japan, 1987, 65 mins.

Zillion: Burning Night

In the peaceful aftermath of the Noza Wars, "The White Knights" have shifted their talents from freedom fighting to music making. JJ, Dave, Champ and Apple have re-emerged as the rock & roll group "The White Nuts." But peace on Maris is short lived, as a new evil threatens the colonial settlers. Apple is kidnapped by the Odama clan—a family of ruthless killers—based in a heavily fortified mountain retreat. JJ and company attempt a daring rescue armed only with makeshift Zillion weapons and a limited supply of ammo. This extra-length Zillion special features edge-of-your-seat action, suspense, songs and surprises. Dubbed.
VHS: S16655. $22.95.
Laser: LD74968. $34.99.
Tatsunoko, Japan, 1988, 45 mins.

Zillion 1-5 Laserdisc

In the 24th century, mankind has entered a new phase of its ongoing development by establishing numerous off-world colonies. One such colony, on the planet Maris, now faces annihilation at the hands of a ruthless alien race. The Earthborn colonists' only hope for salvation rests in a mysterious weapon system known as the Zillion Gun. With only three of these alien super guns, an elite team of freedom fighters, dubbed the White Knights, wage a life-and-death battle for their planet. All five episodes of the OVA series. Stereo. Dubbed.
Laser: LD76022. $49.95.
Tatsunoko, Japan, 1987, 150 mins.

VIDEO non-fiction

historical documentary

The 1964 World's Fair

Part futuristic exhibition, part strip mall, the 1964 New York World's Fair was planned amid the optimism of the late '50s, but the two-year run of the brawling and costly event often mirroredthe chaos of the '60s. With archival footage and narration by Judd Hirsch. 60 mins.
VHS: S34905. $24.95.

60 Minutes: 25 Years

This special celebration of America's longest-lasting and most watched news program provides an in-depth look at this vital newsmagazine. There are reprises and updates of some of the most memorable feature stories by the famed correspondents. Profiles of George Burns, Ray Charles, Barbra Streisand, Jackie Gleason, Oprah Winfrey and Lena Horne are also included. Hosted by Charles Kuralt. 95 min.
VHS: S21715. $19.98.

Aces

This program traces the evolution of fearless aerial warrior pilots from World War I to Vietnam. Includes high-tech dogfight footage. 60 mins.
VHS: S13114. $19.98.

Aces: Story of the First Air War

Rare archival footage and first-hand accounts bring to life the story of history's first combat pilots, in this fascinating program which chronicles the lives and exploits of World War I's "Knights of the Air" and the rapid evolution of aerial strategy, fighter tactics and aircraft technology. 93 mins.
VHS: S31522. $19.95.

Age of Anxiety (1952-1958)

During Eisenhower's presidency, the first Republican president in 20 years, the world took on an ominous cast. Though the Korean War ended, and Stalin's death brought a smiling Khrushchev to power, many troubles remained, particularly the arms race. And the end ofthe decade witnessed the birth of Castro's Cuba. 24 mins.
VHS: S23597. $99.95.

Agriculture Hall of Fame

This official shrine honors and preserves the history of U.S. agricultural achievement which is now presented on this video. There is an 1854 train station, a 1917 schoolhouse, a blacksmith shop and a vast array of agricultural antiques from across the country. 32 mins.
VHS: S23427. $24.95.

Air Force One: Flight II: The Planes and the Presidents

Elliott Sluhan, consultant for the feature film *Air Force One*, wrote, produced and directed this story of the evolution of "the flying White House" from FDR to George Bush. Hosted by Charlton Heston. 90 mins.
VHS: S31525. $14.98.

The Alamo

Using rare archival materials, eyewitness accounts and dramatic reenactments, *American Heritage* magazine and the History Channel take viewers back in time to the 1830s to relive the bloody showdown between Santa Anna's 4,000-man army and the band of 189 Texas volunteers in this two-volume set. Each tape is 50 mins.
VHS: S28496. $29.95.

Alligator Hunting: A Louisiana Legacy

Lifestyle traditions and the way they have changed around this age-old practice are explored in this fascinating documentary. 60 mins.
VHS: S22393. $49.95.

America Fever

The title refers to the wave of emigration that swept 19th-century Norway. This is the story of one woman who, after careful preparations, made the long trek to a new land. Includes public performance rights.
VHS: S22149. $126.50.

America Over There: The United States in World War I: 1917-18

The first officially released motion picture of America's part in World War I, this documentary, shot by U.S. Army Signal Corps, covers the period of 1917-18 when America entered the war, and its involvement with allies during the period. Contains actual footage of the arsenal of weapons developed and used by the United States during this war as well as the retaking of Catigny, Chateu Theirry, Selleua Wood, Soissons, St. Mihiel, Meuse-Argonne, and the Southern rail line through the Sedan. Originally produced in 1927, the film has been re-mastered and enhanced with voice track and music.
VHS: S30496. $29.95.
USA, 1996, 72 mins.

The American Experience: Spy in the Sky

Throughout the Cold War, the U.S. relied on a number of military missions, including the highly successful U-2 spy plane program. Recently declassified information and newly available footage tell the story of this secretive but effective espionage mission. 60 mins.
VHS: S29914. $19.95.

The American Experience: The Wright Stuff

Though they were only the proprietors of a small bicycle shop in Dayton, Ohio, the Wright Brothers surprised the world with their ingenuity. In the process, they also outdid the world's best scientific minds. This video tells of their achievement. 60 mins.
VHS: S29913. $19.95.

American Gunmaker: John Moses Browning

The story of the greatest firearms inventor in history, John M. Browning, from his first crude musket built at age ten to his discovery by Winchester. Features rare archival footage from museums around the world, period photography and recreated vignettes. 58 mins.
VHS: S34824. $14.95.

American History Birth of a Nation Series

Critical moments in the transformation that brought America from colonial status to independence are documented in this insightful series of seven videos.
Colonial America in the 1760's. 17 mins.
VHS: S23526. $49.95.
Taxation Without Representation. 16 mins.
VHS: S23527. $49.95.
Prelude to Revolution. 16 mins.
VHS: S23528. $49.95.
Lexington, Concord, and Independence. 17 mins.
VHS: S23529. $49.95.
Fighting for Freedom. 18 mins.
VHS: S23530. $49.95.
A Nation in Crisis. 16 mins.
VHS: S23531. $49.95.
The Living Constitution. 16 mins.
VHS: S23532. $49.95.

The American Revolution

A&E presents this super-documentary about the birth of the nation, in six volumes. Kelsey Grammar, Bill Daniels and Cliff Robertson narrate events, posing as the founding fathers. Dramatic re-enactments employ on-site locations and period detail to bring this epic struggle to the screen. The battles are incredible. Each episode is 50 mins. Available only as a 6-volume set.
VHS: S23612. $99.95.

The American Woman: Portraits of Courage

This award-winning program uses re-enactments, interviews and historical information to bring to life the courageous acts of the famous and not-so-famous women in our history, from Sybil Ludington's heroic ride to warn the American militia to Susan B. Anthony's quest for voting rights to Rosa Parks' defiance of segregation. Narrated by Patricia Neal. 60 mins.
VHS: S34075. $29.95.

American Women of Achievement Video Collection

This series provides in-depth biographies of notable historic women. As a group they overcame the barriers placed in their way, to transform not only their own time but also our current legacy as Americans. Each 30-minute-long volume relies on archival resources and expert opinion.
Abigail Adams. (1744-1818) Women's rights advocate.
VHS: S24436. $39.95.
Jane Addams. (1860-1935) Social worker.
VHS: S24437. $39.95.
Marian Anderson. (1902-1993) Singer.
VHS: S24438. $39.95.
Susan B. Anthony. (1820-1912) Woman suffragist.
VHS: S24439. $39.95.
Clara Barton. (1821-1912) Founder, American Red Cross.
VHS: S24440. $39.95.
Emily Dickinson. (1830-1890) Poet.
VHS: S24441. $39.95.
Amelia Earhart. (1897-1937?) Aviator.
VHS: S24442. $39.95.
Helen Keller. (1880-1968) Humanitarian.
VHS: S24443. $39.95.
Sandra Day O'Connor. (1930 - Present) Supreme Court Justice.
VHS: S24444. $39.95.
Wilma Rudolph. (1940 - Present) Champion Athlete.
VHS: S24445. $39.95.
American Women of Achievement Video Collection. 10-volume set.
VHS: S24446. $399.50.

Americans on Everest

A spectacular documentary of the first American ascent up the world's tallest mountain. Shot by the mountaineers themselves and including the first motion pictures ever taken from Everest's summit, the film is a stirring record of one of the greatest adventures of our time. Originally presented as a National Geographic special, *Americans on Everest* is narrated by Orson Welles. USA, 50 mins.
VHS: S15001. $39.95.

Anarchy U.S.A.

Made in 1966, this shameful propaganda piece maintains that the Civil Rights movement is part of a worldwide communist plot to destroy America. Its description of an untenable conspiracy for a "Soviet Negro Republic" might be humorous were it not so vile. 78 mins.
VHS: S24080. $24.95.

Anatomy of a Riot

This video looks at the roots of the Los Angeles riots in the aftermath of the first Rodney King trial. The program offers video accounts and eyewitness interviews with people who witnessed the violence. 47 mins.
VHS: S20422. $19.98.

Atomic Stampede

In the 1950s, as the Cold War rapidly escalated, tens of thousands of prospectors flocked to the Colorado Plateau in search of fortune and fame and uranium to create the atom bomb. 60 mins.
VHS: S32406. $14.95.

B-29 Frozen in Time

Expedition team members test their physical endurance as they recover a rare plane from the North Pole after 50 years. 60 mins.
VHS: S28661. $19.95.

Battle for Korea: How the War Was Won

This is a fascinating account of how the United States and her Allies won the battle for Korea. It is a powerful story of how the various elements in our military came together to overcome great odds and emerge victorious over the Chinese and North Koreans. This is not an overview of the whole war, but an examination of the strategic and tactical efforts by the entire military teams to overcome a much larger force. With interviews with combat veterans, 1950s newsreels and archival battle footage.
VHS: S30653. $29.95.

Battle of the Alamo

Hal Holbrook hosts this Discovery Channel documentary about the siege that figures so large in the history of both the U.S. and Mexico. Actual letters and diaries from participants grant this new film greater insight into the actual events of the battle. Davy Crockett, Jim Bowie and General Santa Ana are among the combatants whose roles are explored in this film. 50 mins.
VHS: S29423. $19.95.

Battle of Washington/ Monocacy/Bill Shore

This re-enactment traces the battles of Jubal Early's army up to and including the threat posed to the U.S. Capitol. Civil War buffs will be riveted by this unique view of the war between the states. Narrated by Bill Shore. 59 mins.
VHS: S22046. $14.98.

The Beer Hunter

Renowned British beer expert Michael Jackson leads this behind-the-scenes tour of breweries in England, Holland, Austria and Germany. It's a three-volume set from the Discovery Channel that is perfect for all beer lovers. 180 mins.
VHS: S25084. $49.95.

Belle Case La Follette: 1859-1931

The dramatic life of a charismatic leader and writer in the suffrage movement is revealed from a dramatic first-person perspective in this historical video. It's ideal for women's studies collections. 15 mins. Resource guide available.
Video.
VHS: S25758. $95.00.
Resource Guide.
VHS: S25771. $45.00.

Benjamin Franklin

Let *A & E Biography* introduce you to America's ambassador to the world, Benjamin Franklin, a man who came to symbolize the inventiveness and industriousness of an entire nation. 50 mins.
VHS: S30105. $19.95.

The Best of Times (1920-1924)

E.G. Marshall hosts this look at a nation enamored by motion picture stars. Chaplin, Keaton, Will Rogers and Fatty Arbuckle are just some of the celebrities that emerge on film and radio. Harding maintains his popularity despite a number of scandals. 25 mins.
VHS: S23584. $99.95.

Between the Wars (1918-1939)

Eric Sevareid narrates this look at the tumultuous era between the wars. Prosperity and peace gave way to bust and international tension. In the public eye, sports heroes, film stars and daredevils took people's minds off the troubles of the times. 25 mins.
VHS: S23589. $99.95.

Bloody Korea: The Real Story

The role of the United States Marines in the battle for South Korea is not well known despite the vital participation of this branch of the armed forces in the Korean War. Rare archival footage, interviews with Congressional Medal of Honor recipients and interviews with the Marines who served in Korea are combined in this documentary about the forgotten heroes of "The Forgotten War."
VHS: S27245. $29.95.
Paul Hansen, USA, 1994, 60 mins.

Blue Water: Great Naval Traditions

Naval history overflows with rich legend and lore. These on-going traditions have a direct impact on life aboard warships today. This video offers a tale any old or new "salt" will enjoy. 60 mins.
VHS: S23122. $19.95.

The Brave New Age (1903-1912)

E.G. Marshall narrates this documentary. The introduction of the Model T, a beginning crusade for prohibition, and even the San Francisco earthquake give some indication of the momentous changes ahead. Roosevelt's presidency ushered in this era, but even his energy could not keep him at the nation's helm. 25 mins.
VHS: S23578. $99.95.

Breakout

Over barbwire, through tunnels, by boat, by plane, here is the history of the world's greatest prison escapes. From the Tower of London and "Devil's Island" to Alcatraz and Leavenworth; from the Nazi Stalags to the Soviet Gulags; from Union Army soldiers to WWII Alied Generals to Peruvian revolutionaries; this three-volume set brings to life the schemes, dreams, and courage of these prisoners and the dangers they faced in their quest for freedom. Volumes include: *P.O.W.*, *Fortress*, and *Island*. Narrated by Stacy Keach. 150 mins.
VHS: S34496. $39.98.

Brigham Young

One of the most compelling figures of the West, Brigham Young was the last American to simultaneously wield the authority of spiritual leader, colonizer, political power broker and economic master planner. His vision defined the Mountain West, his conflicts shaped the role of American government and his influence is felt to this day. 60 mins.
VHS: S32411. $24.95.

Cajun Crossroads

This informed cultural portrait reveals the evolution of the historical roots and expressions of the Cajun people. 59 mins.
VHS: S22385. $49.95.

Camelot

Kathleen Turner narrates this documentary about the fabled court of King Arthur. Eminent scholars venture through England and Wales searching for clues to the fate of this kingdom. Tintangel Castle and Arthur's alleged burial mound at Glastonbury are just two sites visited on this video. From the A&E *Ancient Mysteries: New Investigations of the Unsolved* series.
50 mins.
VHS: S27001. $19.95.

Cavaliers & Craftsmen— Colonial Williamsburg and Jamestown

Explores two of America's earliest and most important colonies. Panoramic vistas provide the timeless backdrop for the rich details of colonial life—the clothes, the crafts and the artifacts. 30 mins.
VHS: S11122. $19.95.

The Celts: Rich Traditions and Ancient Myths

This three-tape set explores the bold approach to life, richly evocative music, poetry, art, tradition and ancient mythology of the Celts. Features the music of Enya. Over 300 minutes of programming.
VHS: S33236. $49.98.

A Century of Women

Jane Fonda narrates this series, which documents and celebrates the women of the 20th century. An incredible group of performers have been collected for this task, including Sally Field, Meryl Streep, Glenn Close, Erica Jong, Gloria Steinem, Joan Baez, Twyla Tharp, Chris Evert and Maya Angelou.
A Century of Women: Image and Popular Culture. A fascinating exploration of the changing concepts of "ideal beauty" illuminates the discrepancy between the way women are supposed to appear and their own self image. Clips of fashions reveal how this ideal repeatedly denied the physical reality of a woman's body.
VHS: S21744. $19.98.
A Century of Women: Sexuality and Social Justice. This comprehensive look at women's efforts to shape their own destinies and establish a system of justice shows that they fought not only for themselves, but for all Americans.
VHS: S21743. $19.98.
A Century of Women: Work and Family. The balancing act of labor and family love is not an invention of the 1990's. For many women in the early years of the century, it was a matter of life or death.
VHS: S21742. $19.98.
Complete Set.
VHS: S21745. $49.98.

Charlemagne

The life and times of medieval Europe's most heroic figure are brilliantly portrayed in an epic telling of intense passions, bloody betrayals and the political intrigues that surround this extraordinary leader. It is also the compelling story of one man, Charles, whose great loves and private sorrows must be set aside for the public good. Faced with the overwhelming task of bringing Christianity and political order to a world racked by ignorance and corruption, *Charlemagne* traces the rise of a prince to his place in history as the first Emperor of The Holy Roman Empire. With Christian Brendel. 5-tape set, 300 mins.
VHS: S27396. $89.95.

Cheniere au Tigre: Island of the Marsh

Dances and stories recall significant events from the 1920's to the 1940's and reveal aspects of Cajun life long forgotten by some, but not everyone. 28 mins.
VHS: S22390. $49.95.

Chicago and Its Gangsters

Dubbed a "travelogue with a difference," this program debunks the myths and media-driven association of Chicago gangsters by detailing the characters, figures and deeds of the leading underground figures.
VHS: S16974. $19.95.

The Churchills

Spanning two centuries and three generations, *The Churchills* chronicles the public and private lives of one of Britain's most celebrated political dynasties and the 20th-century statesman whose remarkable achievements brought glory to his nation and family name. Parts include *Aristocratic Adventures*, *Moment of Destiny* and *Born a Churchill*. 150 mins.
VHS: S34330. $49.95.

Cipango

A video concerning the dramatic interplay between Christopher Columbus, Queen Isabella and Martin Pinzon. The author compresses the events of four different voyages and concentrates on the shifting relationship between Columbus and Queen Isabella. 48 mins.
VHS: S20244. $39.95.

Cleopatra

She used her beauty to rule a mighty civilization and to subdue the world's most powerful men. She was the woman no man could resist, but what drove her to commit suicide at such a young age? An *A & E Biography*.
VHS: S30842. $19.95.

Clouds of War (1916-1917)

A number of key political events occurred in this year. America entered World War I, while Pancho Villa provoked the American military along the border. The A.F. of L. was founded as women and African Americans fought for their rights, and President Wilson was re-elected. Narrated by E.G. Marshall. 24 mins.
VHS: S23580. $99.95.

CNN 1994: The Year in Review

O.J. Simpson, the U.S. military in Haiti, the L.A. earthquake, and peacemaking in Israel and Northern Ireland are just some of the groundbreaking events covered in this look back at the top news stories of 1994, by the top news channel—CNN. Hosted by Bernard Shaw.
VHS: S25742. $14.98.

Cold War

From the producer of *The World at War*, this eight-volume, 24-episode CNN program chronicles the people and events that shaped the last 50 years, through moving testimonials, rarely seen footage and engaging storytelling. Narrated by Kenneth Branagh. 20 hours.
VHS: S35133. $119.95.

Colonial Williamsburg

Filmed entirely on location, these programs provide a portrait of what life was like in Colonial America.
Basket Making in Colonial Virginia. The crafting and many uses of the basket are explored in this film. 28 mins.
VHS: S07824. $24.95.
Chelsea Porcelain from the Williamsburg Collection. Narrated by Graham Hood, curator and director of the Colonial Williamsburg Department of Collections, this video explains the history of Chelsea porcelain, and how it came to America. 22 mins.
VHS: S07835. $24.95.
Colonial Clothing. The early Virginia colonists surrounded themselves with elegant, often extravagant fashions and furnishings. This program shows the fashions of 200 years ago. 17 mins.
VHS: S07836. $24.95.
Colonial Naturalist. Based on the life and work of English naturalist Mark Catesby, an exploration of 18th century Virginia. 55 mins.
VHS: S07825. $24.95.
Cooper's Craft. Master Cooper George Petengell demonstrates why the resident Cooper was an indispensable craftsman in colonial Virginia. 28 mins.
VHS: S07826. $24.95.
Doorway to the Past. Like a modern detective manual, this video shows how archaeologists skillfully uncovered and interpreted a host of artifacts to re-create the life and lifestyles of colonial Williamsburg. 28 mins.
VHS: S07840. $24.95.
Flower Arrangements of Williamsburg. Flowers were a year-round pleasure in colonial Williamsburg, and this video demonstrates how the colonists brightened their lives. 30 mins.
VHS: S07839. $24.95.
Forged in Wood, Building Anderson's Blacksmith Shop. James Anderson was a blacksmith and entrepreneur who played an essential role in the American revolution. This film tells the story of the re-creation of Anderson's shop, a project that was undertaken for, and often with the help of, visitors to colonial Williamsburg. 32 mins.
VHS: S07841. $24.95.
Glorious System of Things. A dramatization which shows how the early American colonists learned of important scientific discoveries through "circuit lecturers." 58 mins.
VHS: S07837. $24.95.
Gunsmith of Williamsburg. The gun was a vital part of life and this docu-drama demonstrates the loving care that went into the making of each firearm. 59 mins.
VHS: S07828. $24.95.
Hammerman in Williamsburg. Details the work and involvement in the community of the local blacksmith at a modest Williamsburg forge of the 1770 period. 37 mins.
VHS: S07827. $24.95.
Music of Williamsburg. Virginia's 18th century capital provides the background for this exploration of the music and instruments of colonial America. 40 mins.
VHS: S07834. $24.95.
Musical Instrument Maker of Williamsburg. The results of the instrument maker's craft is a tribute to one of our country's most specialized groups of artisans. 53 mins.
VHS: S07838. $24.95.
Search for a Century. Covers the excavation and interpretation of the early 17th century settlement of Martin's Hundred, lying within Carter's Grove Plantation along the James River in Virginia. 58 mins.
VHS: S07833. $24.95.
Silversmith of Williamsburg. A visual essay on the art of silversmithing as it was practiced in 18th-century Virginia. 4 mins.
VHS: S07829. $24.95.

Williamsburg Sampler. Details the architecture, gardens, textiles, furniture, and other facets of the colonial heritage in a snapshot of 18th-century American life. 28 mins.
VHS: S07830. $24.95.
Williamsburg—Story of a Patriot. A reenactment of the crucial years when every colonist faced the issue of taxation without representation and the forces which led to the commitment for total independence. 36 mins.
VHS: S07831. $24.95.

Columbus: Man and Myth
Part of an extraordinary series produced to commemorate the anniversary of Columbus' arrival in America, this volume covers the origins, the power and the personalities involved with Columbus' travels, with the fact separated from the fiction. Public performance rights included. 35 mins.
VHS: S12641. $149.95.

Coming of Age (1924-1928)
E.G. Marshall narrates this documentary about the flapper era. Despite peace, prosperity and prohibition, the nation was influenced by momentous events and personalities. Footage of Lon Chaney in *The Phantom of the Opera*, Al Capone in Federal Court and Lindbergh's transatlantic flight are included in this video. 25 mins.
VHS: S23585. $99.95.

Communism Boxed Set
People from behind the iron curtain tell how their lives were affected by this new world order, from the storming of the Winter Palace in Tzarist Russia in 1917 to the swift implosion of communist regimes around the world in the 1980s. Includes *Red Flag* (1917-1936), *Brave New World* (1945-1962), *Fallout*, *Great Leap* (1949-1977), *Guerilla Wars* (1954-1981) and *People Power* (1980-1993). Six one-hour cassettes.
VHS: S34747. $79.95.

Conquerors
From Peter the Great to Alexander the Great, from Suleyman the Magnificent to Napoleon, the Learning Channel presents some of the most dramatic moments in world history and shows how masterful strategies and misguided obsessions have shaped the ages.
VHS: S30836. $29.95.
Nigel Maslin/Robert Marshall, USA, 1996, 240 mins.

Construction of Hoover Dam
In this classic documentary (vintage 1936, B&W) you will witness Hoover Dam's construction and re-live the almost insurmountable problems faced by its engineers and builders. 35 mins.
VHS: S06690. $29.95.

Crawfish
This little critter is at the center of an industry key to Cajun traditions. From the economy to gastronomy, crawfish are vital. 27 mins.
VHS: S22388. $59.95.

Crime Inc.
A series of seven documentaries produced by Thames Television on the American gangster underworld.
All in the Family. What the Mafia is really like—as told by the insiders who tell all. 50 mins.
VHS: S09019. $14.99.
Birthright of the Gangsters. The link between organized crime and gambling. 52 mins.
VHS: S09025. $14.99.
Make It Legitimate. How the Mob takes over legitimate businesses for their own use. 51 mins.
VHS: S09024. $14.99.
Making of the Mob. A history of mob activity in Chicago—America's Crime Capital. 50 mins.
VHS: S09020. $14.99.
Mob at Work. A revealing portrait of the Mob's stranglehold on organized labor. 51 mins.
VHS: S09023. $14.99.
Old Mob and the New. A shocking portrait of the drug abuse explosion in America and the criminals who fuel it. 51 mins.
VHS: S09022. $14.99.
Racket Busters. How today's Strike Force is fighting organized crime. 51 mins.
VHS: S09021. $14.99.

Cronkite Remembers
For more than half a century former CBS News anchor Walter Cronkite has celebrated America's greatest achievements and helped the nation and the world through some of the most difficult times in history. This two-hour special is a powerful remembrance of our times as lived, witnessed and reported by America's premier broadcast journalist. 120 minutes.
VHS: S31224. $19.98.

Crusades
Terry Jones from Monty Python is featured in this historical series that presents an overview of the great crusades. They represent one of Europe's largest mass migrations. This series is shot on location in Europe and the Middle East to show the facts behind the mythology of knights and their chivalric codes. Features animated mosaics and statues along with computer graphics. Four videos are included, each 50 mins.
VHS: S24956. $59.95.

David Halberstam's The Fifties
An engaging, inventive, definitive look at the decade that defined post-WWII America, based on the *New York Times* bestseller by Pulitzer Prize-winning author David Halberstam. With classic TV and movie clips and interviews. Six videos. 390 mins.
VHS: S33143. $99.95.

Deadly Duels
This three-box set, narrated by Stacy Keach, chronicles a time when the sword and pistol spoke for tradition, family and honor, and justice was measured in paces and quick reflexes. *Duels of Chivalry* covers dueling in the Age of Knights from the 6th to the 16th century; *Duels of Honor* explores the ancient values and ethics of combat expressed in the new codes of fencing throughout Europe, from the 16th-century renaissance through today; *Dueling in the New World* captures the spirit of the European aristocrat warrior reincarnated in the United States as Southern gentlemen and outlaws of the wild west.
VHS: S31175. $39.98.

Dealers in Death
This is it! All the true stories of America's most notorious mobsters and murderers from the bloody Twenties and Thirties. Authentic footage of Al Capone, John Dillinger, Bruno Hauptmann, Bonnie & Clyde, and more. Narrated by Broderick Crawford. 60 minutes.
VHS: S02473. $19.95.

The Democratic Party, 1960-1992
Highlights from the history of this political party are collected in a new documentary. From the turbulent 1960's, when Kennedy and Johnson led the nation, through the Carter years and the disappointing 1980's, this video tells the story which culminates in a Democratic victory upon the election of Bill Clinton. 58 mins.
VHS: S29495. $19.95.

Disasters/Crime and Terrorism
Disasters looks at some of the natural and manmade disasters that have occurred around the world over the past century. Using archival footage, the program revisits the sites of some of the country's world disasters, including erupting volcanoes, and features interviews with experts in disaster relief and management, emergency service workers, environmental experts and survivors of some of the disasters. 48 mins. *Crime and Terrorism* takes a look at British gangster Frankie Fraser and features psychologist David Canter, a pioneer in criminal profiling, who explains the current phenomenon of the serial killer. Also explores the role of organized crime in this century and examines the history of terrorism in the Middle East and Northern Ireland.
VHS: S30414. $39.95.

The Doomsday Plan
In investigating U.S. preparedness for attack from either a hostile country or a terrorist group, *The Doomsday Plan* first looks back at past plans, ranging from the viable to the ridiculous. Also explored are the several instances of how close the United States came to nuclear engagement with the Soviet Union during the Cold War. 45 mins.
VHS: S34598. $19.98.

The Doughboys: Heroes of WWI
Through rare archival footage this documentary tells the story of America's heroes in WWI from the early great battles to the momentous victory celebration. 40 mins.
VHS: S37078. $19.95.

Downfall of the Monarchies/ The Surviving Monarchies
Downfall of the Monarchies looks at the royal families who fell from grace, from mighty empires like Austria-Hungary to smaller players like Egypt's Farouk and Albania's Zog, and India's maharajahs. Includes appearances by Otto, heir to the Hapsburg throne, and former King Michael of Romania. 48 mins. *The Surviving Monarchies* examines the House of Windsor after the crisis of the abdication of Edward VIII, the Japanese Imperial throne after Japan's defeat in World War II, the Hashimite monarchy of Jordan after the creation of Israel and the rise of Nasser's Egypt, the Belgian monarchy after accusations of capitulation to the Nazis, and the Spanish monarchy after the death of Franco. 48 mins.
VHS: S30412. $39.95.

Edison's Miracle of Light
Though many greeted his prediction that his new invention, the electric light, would make oil lamps and gas light obsolete with profound skepticism, Thomas Alva Edison proved to be more than right. Despite his foresight, Edison lost control of the very industry he founded. Peter Coyote narrates this look at how "the wizard of Menlo Park" lost control of his greatest invention in a maze of patents, corporations and industry. From PBS' *The American Experience* series. USA, 60 mins.
VHS: S27341. $19.95.

The Eighties
Respected anchor persons Jane Pauley and Tom Brokaw host this startling collection of stories and events that rocked the '80s, marking a decade of radical changes. A revealing encapsulation drawing interviews and images from the extensive press coverage of the NBC News Team. 90 mins.
VHS: S15898. $14.95.

Eleanor Roosevelt
One of the century's most respected and admired figures, Eleanor Roosevelt was a humanitarian who transformed the place of women in society and in the White House. An *A & E Biography*. 50 mins.
VHS: S30113. $19.95.

Ellis Island
This "lovingly assembled" (*People Magazine*) three-tape program uses hundreds of interviews, photographs, films and recreations from the Ellis Island Oral History Project to tell the incredible stories of immigration to America through the "golden door," whose entrance, for over half a century, meant an opportunity for a new life. Narrated by Mandy Patinkin. Three 50-min. tapes.
VHS: S31296. $49.95.
Lisa Bourgoujian, USA, 1997, 150 mins.

The Entrepreneurs: An American Adventure
Hosted by Robert Mitchum, this six-part series focuses on a variety of self-made executives.
(1) The Entrepreneurs. A focus on inventors who created and marketed their own products. 50 mins.
VHS: S16194. $19.98.
(2) The Land and Its People. Featuring entrepreneurs who developed the land's resources. 50 mins.
VHS: S16195. $19.98.
(3) Expanding America. Depicting those behind our ever-expanding network of transportation systems. 50 mins.
VHS: S16196. $19.98.
(4) Made in America. People who refined mass production factories are the focus of this episode. 50 mins.
VHS: S16197. $19.98.
(5) Giving 'Em What They Want. Profiles entrepreneurs who identified consumers' appetites. 50 mins.
VHS: S16198. $19.98.
(6) Instant America. Represents professionals who built communications and information systems. 50 mins.
VHS: S16199. $19.98.

Epic Voyages of History
Tim Severin retraces five of the epochal voyages of the past in this series. Using the best available evidence, he tries to capture the feeling of these early travelers, through an examination of their means of travel and a close look at their itinerary. In the process he brings the past alive.
In Search of Genghis Khan. This episode explores both the legend and traces left behind by this military giant, as well as the people descended from the legendary Mongol hordes. Their lives are largely unchanged from the 13th century, when Khan first burst forth onto the world stage. 54 mins.
VHS: S22919. $19.95.
The Brendan Voyage. In the 6th century, the Irish monk Brendan is said to have sailed a leather boat across the Atlantic to Newfoundland. The crew of this episode recreate the "Stepping Stone Route," enduring gales and ice floes as they travel through the Hebrides and the Faroes, then on to Iceland, and finally, along the coast of Greenland. 54 mins.
VHS: S22915. $19.95.
The First Crusade. The 2500-mile route from Northern Europe to Jerusalem comprises the greatest land journey of the Middle Ages. Starting at the castle of Duke Godfrey de Boulion, a hero of the First Crusade, they plodded along with a one-ton medieval battle charger toward the Holy Land. 54 mins.
VHS: S22918. $19.95.
The Jason Voyage: The Quest for the Golden Fleece. The exciting legend of Jason and the Argonauts is relived by the crew of a new ship based on a 20-oar replica of a Bronze Age galley. Along the 1500-mile route of legend they discovered many of the same hardships endured by Jason, as well as plausible explanations for some of the fantastic experiences retold by legend. 54 mins.
VHS: S22917. $19.95.
The Sinbad Voyage. Was Sinbad simply a fictional character, or were his travels based on the real experiences of Arab sailors along the silk and spice route to China? A crew of 20 sailed a ship, held together with 400 miles of coconut rope, over 6000 miles. They traveled from the Arabian Sea to India and China living as a real life Sinbad might have. 54 mins.
VHS: S22916. $19.95.
Epic Voyages of History, Set.
VHS: S22920. $99.95.

Equality: A History of the Women's Movement in America
Comprehensive coverage of the U.S. women's movement from the 18th century onward is found in this important video. It details the compelling story of the challenges and triumphs encountered by women seeking equality. USA, 30 mins.
VHS: S26746. $39.95.

Exploration/Inventions

Exploration takes a look at exploration throughout the 20th century, and the consequences arising from man's exploration of the earth. Includes interviews with Sir Ranulph Fiennes, who crossed the Antarctic continent by foot; Buzz Aldrin, who walked on the moon in 1969; and scientist Richard Taylor, who discusses the next frontiers in space exploration. 48 mins. *Inventions* explores the changes brought by mass production, the invention of new materials, how the needs of war fueled rapid technological progress, and how the invention of products for the home changed everyday life. 48 mins.

VHS: S30413. $39.95.

Famous for 15 Minutes/ Mad, Mad Century

In 1968 Andy Warhol remarked that "everyone will be world-famous for 15 minutes." This prescient observation has come to encapsulate our increasingly short attention span and the power of television to create instant fame around the world. *Famous for 15 Minutes* looks at the "footnotes to history": the basically insignificant people in this century who nonetheless helped shape great events, from the Watergate burglars, to the secret lovers of famous people, to people who achieved instant fame through stunts. 48 mins. *Mad, Mad Century* explores newsreels and the people who made them. Two cameramen who filmed all over the world and an editor recount their tales from the front. Features humorous clips and eccentric oddities in the world of newsreels. 48 mins.

VHS: S30411. $39.95.

FDR

Although physically weak and unable to walk, FDR marched the nation to victory in the greatest conflict in world history. An *A & E Biography*. 50 mins.

VHS: S30114. $19.95.

Fire Fighters

This gripping two-tape collection is an up-close look at the Chicago and New York City Fire Departments, with amazing dramatic footage capturing the awesome force and incredible danger of fire. Volumes include *Brothers in Battle* and *In the Heat of the Blaze*. Each tape is 50 mins.

VHS: S33690. $19.95.

Fires of Kuwait

One of the most harrowing visual memories during the Gulf War was the destruction of Kuwait's oil fields, and the raging fires unleashed as the routed Iraqi troops set fire to more than 600 oil wells. "A mesmerizing spectacle of something unique and unspeakable" (*Los Angeles Times*). 36 mins.

Laser: LD71946. $39.95.

Fleet Firepower

Liberated by the end of the Cold War, the United States Navy has a new mission: protecting American power around the globe. This two-tape series looks at how this new mission and new technology have combined to make the U.S. Navy the most powerful force the U.S. has ever fielded. Each tape is 80 mins. Fleet Firepower: New Doctrine.

VHS: S32343. $19.95.

Fleet Firepower: New Technology.

VHS: S32344. $19.95.

The Foreign Legion

The Foreign Legion is the most secretive and most feared mercenary army in the world. Being granted unprecented access to the Legion, this incredible two-part program accompanies the volunteers and reveals the rigors of their remarkable training and service missions.

VHS: S30880. $29.95.
DVD: DV60345. $24.99.

Forty Days of Musa Dagh

An international production about the genocidal policies of the Turks against the Armenians in the early part of the 20th century, the story follows the life of one man who leads Armenian fighters from the top of Mount Musa Dagh for 40 days.

VHS: S02185. $69.95.
Sarky Mouradian, USA, 105 mins.

Four Hours a Year: The March of Time

The March of Time newsreel series covered the news before the advent of television. Topics include reporting styles, logistical difficulties with 35mm cameras and big lights, the use of reenactments, the difference between the "truth of yesterday and the truth of today and how truth in film is perishable"; reflections on "the natural look," work without zooms or panning; flat lighting, wide angle lens and distortions; and *The March of Time*'s influence on today's television journalism. Many famous excerpts from the series, including Father Coughlin, the Ku Klux Klan, New York's Mayor LaGuardia, Huey Long in Louisiana, 1938 Maginot Line, a 1934 speakeasy raid, New England in 1940 and American youth. 1974, 60 mins.

VHS: S31605. $59.95.

Freedom's Heritage— The Miracle of America

This program examines the political and social framing of America, how the key concepts of liberty, equality and individuality—shaped out of the Spirit of 1776—evolved into a national platform. The program outlines key phrases and important early writings that defined American patriotism. 26 mins.

VHS: S20272. $29.95.

From Stump to Ship: A 1930 Logging Film

More than a documentary about logging, this is an essential American document—a film about the last surviving long log drive on the Machias River in Maine. Not only are the techniques, danger and excitement captured in this unique and only film record, but the 1930 film, which was newly reconstructed by scholars and filmmakers, represents a remarkable look at a vanished way of American life.

VHS: S08259. $39.95.
Alfred Ames, USA, 1930-88, 28 mins.

Frontline: Waco

Behind the scenes of the momentous incident in Waco, Texas, lies a web of conflicting evidence. This *Frontline* episode explores what the government knew, or should have known, before approving a plan that led to the death of David Koresh and 80 of his followers.

VHS: S27379. $19.95.

General Bradley Story

General Omar N. Bradley, according to General Eisenhower, had brains, a capacity for leadership and a thorough understanding of the requirements of modern battle. After his retirement from the Army he served as an elder statesman and advisor in Washington. 1963, 29 mins.

VHS: S32073. $19.95.

George Washington

This *A & E Biography* portrait looks at the father of our country: the gentleman farmer from Virginia and brilliant and bold tactician who proved equally adept at leading men into battle and a young nation into the future. 50 mins.

VHS: S30118. $19.95.

George Washington: The Man Who Wouldn't Be King

This video takes an unconventional look at our first president, deified for over 200 years, yet understood by few Americans. 60 mins.

VHS: S28656. $19.95.

George Washington: The Unknown Years

Explores the early years of Washington, an accomplished surveyor and landowner who, at 21, left behind the life of a country squire in search of glory in the military. 52 mins.

VHS: S31398. $19.95.

Great American Monuments: The Presidential Memorials

A number of intriguing questions are answered in this informative video. For example, it discloses who stole stones from the Washington Monument and reveals the identity of President Nixon's secret four a.m. rendezvous at the Lincoln Memorial. Many of these stories are told for the first time. USA, 50 mins.

VHS: S26932. $19.95.

Great American Monuments: The War Memorials

This touching examination of America's heroic tributes covers a number of unforgettable sights. From Arlington's endless white crosses to the stirring Vietnam Memorial, these monuments inspire both sadness and pride. USA, 50 mins.

VHS: S26933. $19.95.

Great American Monuments: The White House

An historical tour of the "People's House" is featured on this video. Built with slave labor, it saw happier times, such as the occasion of Trisha Nixon's wedding. Modern day operations are also explained. USA, 1994, 50 mins.

VHS: S26934. $19.95.

Great American Speech Series: Lincoln's Gettysburg Address

Charlton Heston reads this important American speech, which is illustrated by original art, archival photographs, graphics and historical re-enactments. The historical events are effectively recalled in this video. 15 mins.

VHS: S23523. $49.95.

Great American Speech Series: Patrick Henry's "Liberty or Death"

Barry Sullivan reads this important American speech. The historic events leading to Henry's call for independence are evoked through original art, archival photographs, graphics and historical re-enactments. 15 mins.

VHS: S23521. $49.95.

Great American Speech Series: Washington's Farewell

This great American speech is read by William Shatner. Original art, archival photographs, graphics and historical re-enactments help illustrate the political and personal context in which this address was originally presented. 15 mins.

VHS: S23522. $49.95.

Great American Speeches

Narrated by former Carter Press Secretary Jody Powell, this educational video traces the history of visually recorded oratory from Theodore Roosevelt's 1912 independent Bull Moose campaign to the mid-1980s. Includes vintage newsreels and films of orations by FDR, LaFollette, Huey Long, Eugene Talmadge, Charles E. Coughlin, George S. Patton, John L. Lewis, Douglas MacArthur, Gerald L.K. Smith, Joseph McCarthy, Richard Nixon, Hubert Humphrey, Joseph Welch, JFK, Martin Luther King, Jr., Malcolm X, Nelson Rockefeller, Barry Goldwater, Ronald Reagan, Barbara Jordan, Jesse Jackson and Mario Cuomo. Two 120-min. tapes.

VHS: S28587. $34.95.

The Great Campaign (1917-1918)

E.G. Marshall narrates this look at the year when America fought to make the world safe for democracy. Chaplin, Fairbanks and Mary Pickford did their bit to keep the nation's morale high. 25 mins.

VHS: S23581. $99.95.

Great Crimes and Trials of the 20th Century: John Wayne Gacy, Richard Speck

Only one receipt linked Gacy to his more than 30 young male victims, many of whom were buried under his home. Speck killed eight women in one night, but one who hid became a witness who helped put him away for life. Both cases are narrated by Bill Kurtis. 52 mins.

VHS: S29973. $19.95.

Great Crimes and Trials of the 20th Century: Murph the Surf, The Boston Brink's Robbery

Bill Kurtis narrates the story of Murph the Surf. This surfing jewel thief was easy to capture, but his booty proved remarkably elusive. The Boston Brink's Robbery took over six years to solve and cost $29 million, all for an original $1.5 million stolen in 1950. Narrated by Robert Powell. 52 mins.

VHS: S29972. $19.95.

Great Crimes and Trials of the 20th Century: The Assassination of Martin Luther King, The Ku Klux Klan Killings

Martin Luther King's untimely death is the focus of the first half of this video. Then the battle between the U.S. government and The Ku Klux Klan is detailed in the second half. Narrated by Robert Powell. 52 mins.

VHS: S29974. $19.95.

Great Crimes and Trials of the 20th Century: The Massacre of the Tsar, Stalin and Katyn

The Tsar and his royal family were not only deposed by Russian Revolutionaries, they were also executed by them. Their story is followed by the intriguing case of 3,000 Polish soldiers whose bodies were found buried in a mass Grave at Katyn. Many could not believe Stalin was responsible, but this video reveals the truth. Narrated by Robert Powell. 52 mins.

VHS: S29975. $19.95.

Great Crimes and Trials of the 20th Century: Trial of Adolf Eichmann, Hitler and the Nuremberg Trials

Bill Kurtis narrates the opening segment of this video which is an account of Adolf Eichmann's trial. Eichmann was a notorious Nazi war criminal responsible for the plans of the "Final Solution." This video ends with the Nuremberg Trials, in which Hitler's Nazis were tried for their crimes against humanity. Narrated by Robert Powell. 52 mins.
VHS: S29976. $19.95.

Great Crimes of the Century

Five of the most devastating and the most talked about crimes of the century are the subject of this tape. Using rare archival footage shot during the original investigations, this is the story of Charles Manson, Clifford Irving, Leopold and Loeb, D.B. Cooper and the Boston Strangler. 60 mins.
VHS: S13166. $39.98.

Great Days of the Century Collector's Boxed Set

Relive the greatest moments of the 20th century with this program highlighting the century's wars, despots, revolutions, heroes and major historical landmarks through archival footage. Includes World Wars I and II, The Russian Revolution, Mussolini and Hitler, The Spanish Civil War, The Founding of Israel, Gandhi, The Communist Invasion of Budapest, De Gaulle, Political Revolution in the Far East, and John F. Kennedy. Nearly 12½ hours of viewing on five tapes.
VHS: S34792. $99.95.

The Great Depression

Mario Cuomo hosts this illuminating four-volume portrait on the Great Depression from the Crash of 1929 to the coming of World War II, filled with photos by Dorothea Lange and newsreel footage of pivotal events. Profiles FDR, Pretty Boy Floyd, Upton Sinclair, Douglas MacArthur and more. Each tape is 50 mins.
VHS: S34342. $59.95.

The Great Egyptians

Three-volume set from The Learning Channel includes *The Mystery of Tutankhamen, The Real Cleopatra* and *The King of the Pyramids*. Each tape is 50 mins.
VHS: S31944. $49.95.

The Great Egyptians II

The pharoah who declared a singular god and radically downsized Egypt's feared army is exposed in *Akhenaten*; a cross-dressing queen gets the royal treatment in *Queen Hatshepsut*; and *Ramses the Great* exposes the leader's giant structures and family of 200 children. Three tape-set from The Learning Channel.
VHS: S34278. $49.98.

The Great Pharaohs of Egypt

From the bloody wars fought by Namer, who united the kingdoms of the Nile to become the first pharaoh, to the final defeat of Cleopatra, this fascinating program explores the 3,000-year history and stunning legacy of the pharaohs. With extensive location footage of the pyramids, the Sphinx, Karnak and Luxor, and more. Features rare archival films of early pyramid exploration and discoveries and visits never-before-seen royal tombs. Four-volume set. 50 mins.
VHS: S32373. $59.95.

The Guillotine

A fascinating look at the history of capital punishment, this video explores the early technology of one of history's most infamous murder machines and its bloodstained career throughout Europe.
VHS: S31177. $19.98.

The Guns of August

An absorbing portrait of warfare during World War I, adapted from Barbara Tuchman's Pulitzer prize-winning book. The film combines archival footage, photographs, narrative and graphics to reveal the horrors of the great war. Narration by Fritz Weaver.
VHS: S18253. $19.98.
Laser: LD71845. $34.98.
Nathan Kroll, USA, 1964, 99 mins.

Harry S. Truman

A & E Biography looks at the man who turned to politics only because he needed a job, and emerged a dominant world power in post-war America. 50 mins.
VHS: S30116. $19.95.

Harry S. Truman: His Life and Library

Follows Truman from his early years on a farm to his service in WWI to his eventual rise to the highest office in the land. Visit the Harry S. Truman Library and Museum in Independence, Missouri.
VHS: S34073. $29.95.

Headline Stories

Four volumes of headlines and newsreel footage from 20th-century American history and culture.
Headline Stories: America in Sports. A collection of newsreel footage on the most important American sporting events from the late 19th century to the modern era, following the exploits and personalities of Bobby Jones, Knute Rockne, Babe Ruth, Babe Didrikson, Jesse Owens, Joe Louis, Joe DiMaggio, Arnold Palmer and the birth of the Super Bowl. 95 mins.
VHS: S18797. $29.95.
Headline Stories: The Complete Set.
VHS: S18800. $79.95.

The Heartbeat of America

A probing investigative look at the mega-giant automobile manufacturer General Motors. A combination of historical footage and personal interviews portray the rise and fall of the corporation and look at one of the most important issues facing the future: the mass production of "clean cars." 87 mins.
VHS: S23386. $79.00.

Her Own Words: Pioneer Women's Diaries

The spontaneous observations of pioneer women from the upper Midwest are at the core of this intriguing video. Their experience is brought to life through first-person narration. 15 mins. Resource guide available.
Video.
VHS: S25761. $95.00.
Resource Guide.
VHS: S25774. $45.00.

The Hidden Army: Women in World War II

American women represented an unexpected source of strength which proved vital to the overall war effort. This video shows how they worked at home and in factories and how they contributed in both the European and Pacific theaters of war. 57 mins.
VHS: S27855. $19.95.

The History of American Funeral Directing

A heavily illustrated view of the world of mortuaries, embalming, caskets and funeral practices all over America, with a fascinating narration by an ex-funeral director.
VHS: S33843. $24.95.
Claire Burch, USA, 1995, 45 mins.

The History of Blue Jeans

The most complete history of blue jeans ever produced. Traces blue jeans from Renaissance Europe to the Gold Rush, from farm and cowboy wear to social statement in the 1960s, to the worldwide trend-setting fashion of today. 50 mins.
VHS: S34719. $19.95.

The History of Talk Radio

Larry King, Dr. Laura Schlessinger, Bob Grant, Morton Downey Jr., Ollie North and other famous and controversial figures from this incendiary radio show format innovation are featured in this informative documentary. Marvin Scott hosts. 60 mins.
VHS: S29853. $19.95.

The History of the Bikini

Named after the Pacific atoll where the H-bomb was tested, the Bikini exploded onto the fashion scene in 1946 and changed women's fashion forever. *Baywatch*'s Gene Lee Nolin hosts this fun and fascinating look at the fashion sensation of the century. 60 mins.
VHS: S31773. $19.95.

History's Turning Points

This series of six videos, first screened by the Learning Channel, presents 13 key historical moments from the last 2000 years, including history of the Black Death, the Great Wall of China, the siege of Constantinople, the conquest of the Incas and the marriage of Pocahontas. Exciting events that span the globe, from Ancient Greece to the detonation of the atom bomb, are included.
VHS: S25835. $149.95.

Hooray for Abbie!

This video tribute to Abbie Hoffman features the Abbie memorials from the Summer of 1989—The Palladium New York—plus the picnic at Washington's Crossing. There are fond remembrances by many friends, including Peter Yarrow, Paul Krassner, Allen Ginsberg, Norman Mailer, Jerry Rubin, The Fugs, Bobby Seale, Dave Dellinger, David Amram, Richie Havens and William Kunstler. Also features brother Jack Hoffman and his wife, Anita. 76 mins.
VHS: S21846. $39.95.

In Service to America

The most comprehensive documentary on women in the military ever produced, *In Service to America* interviews a wide range of knowledgeable sources, from military experts to the women in uniform themselves. It covers the entire history of women in the United States military from the Revolutionary War to Operation Desert Storm. USA, 60 mins.
VHS: S27243. $29.95.

Iowa: An American Portrait

This heartfelt program, written by *Time* magazine's Hugh Sidney and narrated by Tom Brokaw, chronicles the enduring bonds between the past and present and explores the human spirit nourished by a deep and pervasive love of land, community and family in Iowa. Dramatic readings by Simon Estes, Alex Karras, Cloris Leachman and Sada Thompson complement evocative historical photographs.
VHS: S31890. $19.99.
USA, 1996, 65 mins.

The Iron Road

Recounts the six years of harsh labor, searing heat, Indian attacks and frontier lawlessness that railroad men endured in their quest to build America's first transcontinental railroad as the country was torn apart by the Civil War. 60 mins.
VHS: S17177. $19.95.

Journey to Freedom: The Immigrant Experience

Over the last century, mass immigration has shaped this country. Newsreel footage, artwork and vintage photos capture this fascinating story. 13 mins.
VHS: S23742. $89.95.
Laser: LD74787. $109.95.

Ken Burns' America

These seven films earned documentary filmmaker Ken Burns (*The Civil War, Baseball*) universal acclaim and over 100 awards, including Academy Award nominations and Emmy awards.
Brooklyn Bridge. This unparalleled technical achievement is examined in this Academy Award-nominated film. 58 mins.
VHS: S27727. $14.98.
Empire of the Air: The Men Who Made Radio. Jason Robards narrates this film examining the history of radio from 1906 to 1955. Features archival photographs and newsreels of the period, as well as interviews with Garrison Keillor, Red Barber and radio dramatist Norman Corwin. 120 mins.
VHS: S16153. $14.98.
Huey Long. The life of the legendary Louisiana governor and U.S. Senator who controlled a corrupt political machine is examined in this film. 88 mins.
VHS: S27730. $14.98.
The Congress. Rare newsreel footage and historical photographs of this American institution are presented in this film. 90 mins.
VHS: S27728. $14.98.
The Shakers. A look into the lives of these dedicated and disciplined people who put "their hands to work and their hearts to God." 58 mins.
VHS: S27731. $14.98.
The Statue of Liberty. Rare footage of the creation of this national treasure is presented in this Academy Award-nominated and Emmy-winning film. 58 mins.
VHS: S27726. $14.98.
Thomas Hart Benton. This film looks at the life of the man Harry Truman called "the best damned painter in America." 86 mins.
VHS: S27729. $14.98.
The Complete Set
VHS: S27732. $89.95.
Ken Burns, USA, 1996, 558 mins.

Kent State

Fine dramatization of the killings of four students at Kent State by Ohio National Guardsmen in Spring 1970. Originally made for television, co-written by Emmy winner Gerald Green.
VHS: S02156. $39.95.
James Goldstone, USA, 1981, 120 mins.

Korea: MacArthur's War

Described as "the sour little war", over 2,033,000 people lost their lives in a war that ended in a stalemate. Perhaps the most fierce battle of the war was the one fought between General MacArthur and President Truman, this is the story of both battle of wills and battle for blood. 60 mins.
VHS: S13135. $24.98.

The Korean War

An authoritative, ten-hour video series on the Korean War, produced by Korean Television Network. The program welds archival footage with interviews. The five-volume set details the origins of conflict, the strategies and battles, the armistice and uneasy truce that still exists today. Narrated by James Whitmore.
Volume 1: The Division & North and South. 120 mins.
VHS: S17319. $19.95.
Volume 2: The Omens of War & Tempest. 120 mins.
VHS: S17320. $19.95.
Volume 3: To the North & A Different War. 120 mins.
VHS: S17321. $19.95.
Volume 4: Stalemate of Truce & War on the Homefront. 120 mins.
VHS: S17322. $19.95.
Volume 5: Truce & Epilogue-Reflections. 120 mins.
VHS: S17323. $19.95.
Complete Five-Volume Set. 600 mins.
VHS: S17324. $99.75.

Lewis & Clark

This latest installment in Ken Burns' prolific American Lives series is the definitive work on Lewis & Clark, presented from a "you-are-there" perspective as the explorers search for a water route from east to west on their journey with the Corps of Discovery. Two-tape set.

VHS: S32367. $29.98.

Ken Burns, USA, 1997, 240 mins.

Liberty! The American Revolution

Critically acclaimed and lauded, this six-hour PBS documentary series chronicles the events leading up to the declaration of war, and the lasting effects these events had on shaping our country today. Features dramatic readings from letters and diaries of the period and recreations. With Roger Rees, Campbell Scott, Terrence Mann and Donna Murphy.

VHS: S34614. $59.98.

Life in a California Mission in 1790

Within the Spanish-speaking missions of Colonial California, self-sufficient communities took shape. 14 mins.

VHS: S23534. $49.95.
Laser: LD74765. $99.95.

Life in a Gold-Mining Camp 1850

The thrill of the gold rush is relived in this video about life in a mining town. 18 mins.

VHS: S23536. $49.95.
Laser: LD74767. $99.95.

Life in a Midwestern Small Town 1910

Inventions and cultural changes transformed American rural life just after the turn of the century. This program documents these key changes. 18 mins.

VHS: S23538. $49.95.
Laser: LD74769. $99.95.

Life in America 1800

This is an in-depth look at a farming family in central New York State at the dawn of the 19th century. 16 mins.

VHS: S23535. $49.95.
Laser: LD74766. $99.95.

Life in an Eastern Seaport Town 1870

Shipbuilding, sailmaking and ropemaking are unique skills that were at the center of town life in the late 19th century. This video explains the historical importance of these techniques. 17 mins.

VHS: S23537. $49.95.
Laser: LD74768. $99.95.

Life in the 30's

Despite the ravages of the depression, this decade spanned a surprisingly multi-faceted time in American culture. Alexander Scourby narrates this look at an era famous for Benny Goodman and the birth of Swing, even as millions were desperate for a better life. 60 mins.

VHS: S23057. $19.95.

The Lincoln Assassination

Although revered today as one of America's greatest presidents, in his time many hated Lincoln because of his policies and strong convictions. This video explores the various plots hatched by assassin John Wilkes Booth and his cohorts in their efforts to destabilize the union. They even planned to kill all the members of Lincoln's cabinet. 50 mins.

VHS: S26662. $29.95.

Louisiana Boys: Raised on Politics

The history of politics in Louisiana, a state which has been historically ruled by notorious figures who governed by a combination of smarts and terror. With its free-spending and high-rolling elections, Louisiana's political campaigns resemble a charged, carnival atmosphere. The documentary traces the disparate political fortunes of Huey "The Kingfish" Long, his brother Earl, Jimmie Davis, Edwin Edwards and David Duke. 52 mins.

VHS: S19412. $19.95.

Mafia: The History of the Mob in America

This documentary series is a cold-blooded examination of organized crime in the 20th century. Beginning with the imposition of Prohibition, the origins of these gangs are traced up through the Second World War. By this time, they had emerged as permanent features on the American scene in the shape of enduring family enterprises. In the first volume, *The Prohibition Years, Birth of the American Mafia*, Congress' move to outlaw alcohol in 1919 spawned an unforseen side effect—the growth of an underground market that could never be wiped out. Jewish and Irish gangs were among the first to emerge. Then the Mafia is seen coming from Sicily to take over this business, with murderous methods (100 mins.) The second volume is *The Kennedys and the Mob*. Between the imposition of prohibition and the emergence of Camelot, Joe Kennedy, the father of a powerful clan, kept up his dealings with underworld figures. But his sons had a different opinion of these men and persecuted them from Washington (50 mins.) In *Unions and the Mob*, the third volume, we see how traditional union strength was muscled over into a new and potent force, mob-controlled trade unions. They fought ruthlessly with the communists for sympathy and won. Even the Ford Company was not safe from the influence of these teamsters (50 mins.) And in the fourth volume, *Empire of Crime*, World War II and the Allied invasion offer great growth opportunities to the mob. From Sicily they expanded throughout Italy to cover the country with their influence in the blackmarket, while they also used the years of occupation to expand their legitimate business interests in the U.S. (50 mins.) Narrated and hosted by Bill Kurtis.

VHS: S21247. $59.95.

Maggie Kuhn: When Biography and History Intersect

Kuhn is the founder of the Gray Panthers, an advocacy group for the aging. At age 87, her boundless intelligence, fierce determination and tremendous courage are a testament to the ageless quality of the human spirit. 56 mins.

VHS: S23199. $29.95.

Man and the State: Hamilton and Jefferson on Democracy

Conflicting intellectual currents helped shape the growth of American democracy. Hamilton and Jefferson debate their views on significant crises experienced in the development of the nation. 26 mins.

VHS: S23701. $79.95.

Man and the State: Roosevelt and Hoover on the Economy

Hoover and Roosevelt are forced to debate their opposing views on the role of government in the face of the Great Depression. The open-ended nature of this film leaves the viewer free to decide who is right regarding the welfare of the general public. 25 mins.

VHS: S23700. $79.95.

The Man Who Saw Tomorrow

Nostradamus, the 16th century physician and philosopher, predicted many of the events that have transpired in modern times. Orson Welles narrates this tantalizing documentary on the man and his accurate forecasts. 96 minutes.

VHS: S02487. $19.98.

March of Time: American Lifestyles

Originally produced as a newsreel by *Time Magazine, The March of Time* was seen monthly for sixteen years by more than 20 million people in more than 50,000 theatres around the world. This unique documentary provides a fascinating look at the American world in the first half of the 20th century. Narrated by Westbrook Van Voorhis, produced by Louis de Rochemont.

Show Business: The War Years 1939-1945. American lifestyles are documented through a 40-year history of filmmaking, including features on Charlie Chaplin and Al Jolson, Bob Hope on one of his first USO tours, the British challenge to Hollywood with Stewart Granger, Ann Todd, Ronald Colman, Ida Lupino. 73 mins.

VHS: S03025. $19.95.

Show Business: The Post-War Years 1946-1950. The Nightclub Boom shows pleasure-hungry Americans heading for nightclubs with scenes featuring Jimmy Dorsey, Eddie Condon, Ed Wynn, Bert Lahr, the heyday of radio and the ever-popular soap opera, the glamour of New York theatre with Rex Harrison, Charles Boyer, Maxwell Anderson, Robert Sherwood, Maggie Garland, the development of the LP record, and Beauty At Work—the look at the "glamour" life of a top model. 92 mins.

VHS: S03026. $19.95.

American Family: The War Years 1941-1945. The role of ethnic groups in building industrialized America, the contribution of men and women to the war effort, America's food supply and its role in the War, and why the U.S. can't provide enough meat during the war. 89 mins.

VHS: S03027. $19.95.

American Family: The Post-War Years 1946-1948. Child development coupled with the oftentimes hilarious outcome of the "scientific study of babies," the booming black market in babies, and the explosive circumstances of adoption, the effect of the war, radio, comics and the Atomic Age on children, the growing segment of an aging population, and the increasing problems of divorce. 89 mins.

VHS: S03028. $19.95.

America's Youth 1940-1950. Case histories of debutante daughters and the depression-ridden children of the poor, the effect of war on children, the role models for teenage girls, the fight for more modern schools, and educational techniques and facilities in the 40s. 90 mins.

VHS: S03029. $19.95.

American Fashion and Leisure 1945-1950. The role of being beautiful, from Fifth Avenue's most exclusive salons of mysterious beauty concoctions, Americans traveling in Mexico, the story of the fashion industry, the popularity of boxing, a funny look at Americans vacationing, and men fighting baldness, exercising at a health club and trying to stay slim. 105 mins.

VHS: S03030. $19.95.

March of Time: American Lifestyles, Giftpack. The complete set.

VHS: S05336. $99.95.

Marines in Combat

Lt. General Holland M. (Howlin' Mad) Smith, commander of the Marines during WWII at Tinian and Iwo Jima, hosts this look at marines in combat from World War II to the Korean War. Episodes include Battle for Airfields, Pelileu, Iwo Jima, Okinawa, Marines Between Battles, After the A-Bomb, Landing at Pusan, Pusan Perimeter Battles, Inchon Landing, Chinese Counterattack, Helicopter in Korea, and Korean War Summary.

VHS: S34517. $79.95.

Merlin, Arthur & The Holy Grail

This magical collection of three riveting programs explores the connection between these men and the Holy Grail, all the while uncovering the romance, mystery and truth behind the world's most intriguing legends. Includes dramatic recreations, such as the 12th-century Crusades, and features historical locations, such as King Arthur's castle. 78 mins.

VHS: S34893. $19.95.

Merrily We Go Along

Subtitled *The Early Days of the Automobile*, this documentary examines the evolution of the automobile in American society. The role is captured through a succession of transitions, from horse and buggy to horseless carriages. 60 mins.

VHS: S19249. $19.95.

Military Channel

The Military Channel cable network features a variety of military documentaries and boasts one of the most comprehensive, privately held military and aviation footage libraries in North America. The library comprises over 4,000 hours of raw video footage and 550 hours of raw film footage, including Department of Defense footage from World War I to the present.

Frontline Pilots. The pilots who fly the world's deadliest high-performance aircraft describe their missions in detail never before heard. Four-tape boxed set. Each tape is 48 mins.

VHS: S31880. $49.95.

Tools of the Trade. A fast-paced and informative look at the digital battlefield, seen through the eyes of those whose lives depend on it. Four-tape boxed set. Each tape is 57 mins.

VHS: S31881. $49.95.

The Mob

From Lucky Luciano to the Teflon Don, American mob bosses have always written their own rules. Today the Feds are breaking down their walls of silence with new technology and tougher laws. Mob insiders, Federal officers, Mafia experts and other figures from both sides of the war are featured in this expose from A&E. 250 mins.

VHS: S26691. $59.95.

Mob Law

A scintillating portrait of Las Vegas attorney Oscar Goodman, who represents gangsters. Narrated by Anthony LaPaglia, this program features interviews with Oscar's friends and family, the mobsters he's represented, and the FBI agents who have tried to entrap him. 92 mins.

VHS: S35017. $19.98.

A More Perfect Union: The Story of the U.S. Constitution

Combining illustrations and text, this program details the events in Philadelphia during the framing of the United States Constitution. Intended for children in grades 2-5. 15 mins.

VHS: S20056. $44.95.

Motion Picture History of the Korean War

From the hip anarchy of Robert Altman to the personal anti-war heroics of war vets Sam Fuller and Robert Aldrich, the Korean War has been served well in fictional film. Now a short documentary with newsreel footage provides an unsettling period piece of a nearly forgotten, tragic war.

VHS: S02581. $34.95.

Mount Vernon—Home of George Washington

This sensitive and artfully filmed program marks the first time that Mount Vernon has been filmed in its entirety, including its architecture and furnishings, its gardens and the surrounding plantation. Tells about George Washington the man, his personal interests, and life in 18th century Virginia. 30 mins.

VHS: S11476. $29.95.

Mountbatten: The Last Viceroy

In the grand tradition of *Lawrence of Arabia* and *Ghandi*, this grandly staged, $15-million epic tells the story of India's struggle for independence in 1947. With sweeping cinematography and a cast of thousands, including Nicol Williamson, Dame Wendy Hiller and Janet Suzman. "Impressive, richly produced and a major contribution to dramatizing history" (*Variety*).
VHS: S31763. $89.95.
Tom Clegg, Great Britain, 1987, 107 mins.

Mr. Sears' Catalogue: The Sears Roebuck Company and Its Impact on Life in America 1890-1930

In 1893, visionary businessman Richard Warren Sears founded an empire that revolutionized the lives of millions of rural Americans: a 1,500-page mail order catalogue that provided farm families with all their earthly needs, as well as a common language for their ambitions and dreams. More than the story of the company that pioneered home shopping, *Mr. Sears Catalogue* is an affectionate portrait of America during a period of rapid change. 60 mins.
VHS: S30579. $19.95.

Multicultural Peoples of North America Series

These videos celebrate the heritage of 15 diverse cultural groups of North America, blending folklore, customs, traditions and family dynamics to illustrate immigration history. "[A] noteworthy series especially valuable as a North American resource" (*Booklist*). 30 minutes each.
African Americans.
VHS: S20359. $39.95.
The Amish.
VHS: S20360. $39.95.
Arab Americans.
VHS: S20361. $39.95.
Central Americans.
VHS: S20362. $39.95.
Chinese Americans.
VHS: S20363. $39.95.
German Americans.
VHS: S20364. $39.95.
Greek Americans.
VHS: S20365. $39.95.
Irish Americans.
VHS: S20366. $39.95.
Italian Americans.
VHS: S20367. $39.95.
Japanese Americans.
VHS: S20368. $39.95.
Jewish Americans.
VHS: S20369. $39.95.
Korean Americans.
VHS: S20370. $39.95.
Mexican Americans.
VHS: S20371. $39.95.
Polish Americans.
VHS: S20372. $39.95.
Puerto Rican Americans.
VHS: S20373. $39.95.
Multicultural Peoples of North America. The complete 15-volume set.
VHS: S24408. $599.25.

Murder of the Century

Harry K. Thaw shot and killed Stanford White, New York's leading turn-of-the-century architect. Behind this cold-blooded murder was a steamy tale of intrigue, jealousy and passion. Both men were involved in an unlikely love triangle with model and showgirl Evelyn Nesbit and each man wanted her for himself alone. David Ogden Stiers narrates this fascinating documentary about the so-called "Murder of the Century." From PBS' *The American Experience* series. USA, 60 mins.
VHS: S27340. $19.95.

National Geographic Video: Inside the White House

Narrated by Morgan Freeman, this video reveals facts about the mysterious but ever-prominent White House. Along with some surprising secrets, it details intriguing historical tidbits. The human side of the American presidency becomes highly tangible as a result. 87 mins.
VHS: S29917. $19.95.

National Geographic Video: Search for Battleship Bismarck

This video relives the final days of the ill-fated battleship, interviews the survivors of the 1941 battle, and explores the haunting underwater remains discovered in June 1989 by Dr. Robert Ballard, who led the exploration of the R.M.S. *Titanic*. 60 mins.
VHS: S11656. $19.95.

NBC White Papers

This landmark documentary series launched by NBC and narrated by Chet Huntley captured the events, issues and personalities of the day.

NBC White Papers: The Birth of the Cold War. The death of Josef Stalin in 1953 plunged the communist superpower into political chaos. While the world awaited the outcome, Stalin's henchmen waged a five-year battle for control. Ten years later, with the Cold War raging, this award-winning program captured one of the great stories of the century. Two tapes, 50 mins. each.
VHS: S33344. $29.95.
NBC White Papers: The Kennedy Era. Made shortly after JFK's death, this program captures his career and life, as well as the mood of a nation still shaken by the tragedy of his loss. Friends, family and staff reveal intimate details of his life, while reporters and colleagues reflect on his career and consider his legacy. With excerpts from his writings read by Henry Fonda. Hosted by Tom Brokaw. Two tapes, 50 mins. each.
VHS: S33345. $29.95.

New Beginnings (1895-1904)

During these key years President McKinley was assassinated and Theodore Roosevelt became President. Technological wonders also left their mark on the era. Footage of the first flight at Kitty Hawk and the opening of the New York subway show the importance of innovation during this time. E.G. Marshall narrates. 25 mins.
VHS: S23577. $99.95.

The New Europeans

This program demonstrates the repercussions of European unification. The works point out the inevitable tensions between extreme nationalism and the fear of cultural imperialism, the loss of ethnic identity and the difficulties in resolving the issue of a common currency. The series offers a historical view of unification, of past successes and failures. "To understand what's happening in Europe, and the impact of unification on the United States, this series is a must" (*New York Daily News*). 180 mins.
Program 1: Road to Unity.
VHS: S19366. $29.95.
Program 2: Global Agendas.
VHS: S19367. $29.95.
Program 3: Regional Dreams.
VHS: S19368. $29.95.
The New Europeans, Set.
VHS: S19369. $79.95.

New York the Way It Was

58 minutes each.
New York the Way It Was. This is a nostalgic look at Coney Island and other quintessentially New York traditions, from egg creams to the Giants and the Dodgers. Everything that made New York the most exciting place to be in the 30's, 40's and 50's is lovingly recreated for one last look.
VHS: S23118. $19.95.
New York the Way It Was: The Old Neighborhood. A sentimental tour of old time New York neighborhoods is featured on this video. Famous New Yorkers Tito Puente and former mayor Ed Koch are just some of the celebrities who help recall those homey but exciting sections found throughout the five boroughs.
VHS: S26676. $19.95.
New York the Way It Was: Wish You Were Here. Coney Island, the Catskill Mountains, the Rockaway beaches and many other sites were fun places dear to New Yorkers. In this nostalgic video journey memories of these places are brought back for one more special visit. 58 mins.
VHS: S26675. $19.95.
New York the Way It Was: The Series. Includes all three titles.
VHS: S26674. $59.85.

Nova—Disguises of War

The many sides of military deception are examined—from simple camouflage to the ultra-sophisticated Stealth Bomber. 60 mins.
VHS: S14501. $14.98.

Nova—Search for the Lost Cave People

Nova follows an international team of archaeologists and spelunkers into the Rio la Venta Gorge deep in the Chiapas jungle of South America. In a rugged canyon they find caves filled with startling remains of a people called the Zoque who lived hundreds of years before the Maya. Moving downstream from the caves the team finds a legendary city hidden in a tangle of jungle vines. 60 mins.
VHS: S33099. $19.95.

The Oldest Living Confederate Widow Tells All

Diane Lane, Donald Sutherland, Cicely Tyson and Anne Bancroft star in this humorous and irreverent look at the history of the Civil War. Great performances explain why this film was nominated for nine Emmy Awards. Also features Blythe Danner, E.G. Marshall and Gwen Verdon. 180 mins.
VHS: S26449. $14.98.
Laser: LD76403. $49.99.

Our Century

From the dawn of this century through 1990, this five-part series showcases the events that have shaped our world. Using rare footage and newsreels to explore trends, advances and tragedies, the world as we know it is slowly revealed. Each tape covers approx. 20 years, chronologically highlighting the events of those decades. From the *Titanic*, World Wars I and II, royal weddings and the space race to the fall of Communism, this is a fascinating look at ourselves and our world. The first four episodes are 110 minutes, while the final installment is 51 mins.
VHS: S29499. $89.95.

Outlaws and Lawmen

The Discovery Channel's two-volume video set about the Old West is an exciting eye-opener. Jesse James, Bat Masterson, Wyatt Earp, Pretty Boy Floyd and Bonnie and Clyde are some of the trigger-happy varmints described in this set. Their mythic exploits may have defined our heritage but their stories are told in these videos. 200 mins.
VHS: S29902. $29.95.

Over There, 1914-1918

An excellent documentary compiled in France from newsreel footage and government film of the period. The result is an examination of World War I, but with a difference; this time the point of view is that of a lowly foot soldier. 90 mins.
VHS: S16262. $29.95.

The Passing Storm (1931-1933)

In America entertainers like Jack Benny, Mae West, Gable and Garbo provided some relief from the world's troubles. Europe, however, turned to despots like Hitler and Mussolini for help. E.G. Marshall hosts this account of the tense 1930's. 24 mins.
VHS: S23588. $99.95.

Patchwork: A Kaleidescope of Quilts

The narrator of this video calls quilts her diaries and albums. Exploring these meaningful and utilitarian folk art objects reveals critical information about the people who make them. 15 mins. Resource guide available.
Video.
VHS: S25763. $95.00.
Resource Guide.
VHS: S25776. $45.00.

Paul Revere: The Messenger of Liberty

Cliff Robertson narrates this look at Paul Revere, the patriot who was instrumental in alerting the colonists of the advancing British troops and much more. 24 mins.
VHS: S23556. $49.95.
Laser: LD74785. $99.95.

A Place to Stand

This newly-produced video is a fast-paced overview of the history of the United Nations, highlighting its major accomplishments and the unrealized possibilities for its future. The tremendous variety of work performed globally by the UN is revealed through personal stories of people working for the benefit of the world's children, health, human rights, the environment, and peace. 12 mins.
VHS: S30095. $59.95.

Policing the Peace (1948-1951)

After the war, a series of events demanded vigilance and commitment from the great powers. Gandhi was assassinated and North Korean troops crossed into South Korea, while in the Middle East, Egypt took control of the Suez Canal and Israel invaded Sinai. 24 mins.
VHS: S23596. $99.95.

Power and Prejudice (1926-1928)

Hosted by E.G. Marshall, this documentary reveals an era of controversy. Bootlegging, mobsters, Sacco and Vanzetti, the KKK and communism all offered cause for anxiety to the American public. Footage of Babe Ruth's sixtieth home run and Hoover's election are also included in this video. 24 mins.
VHS: S23586. $99.95.

Prairie Cabin: A Norwegian Pioneer Woman's Story

An immigrant pioneer woman learns to love the American prairie, which becomes her new home. 15 mins. Resource guide available.
Video.
VHS: S25764. $95.00.
Resource Guide.
VHS: S25777. $45.00.

Prairie Quilts: A Celebration of the Tall-Grass Prairies
Embroidered and patchwork quilts celebrate Midwestern tallgrass prairie life. It's a dazzling display of a simple native art form. 15 mins. Resource guide available.
Video.
VHS: S25765. $95.00.
Resource Guide.
VHS: S25778. $45.00.

The Presidents Collection
From PBS, a collection of stories for all Americans about the people who shaped the nation.
The Presidents Collection I. Three double-cassette gift set featuring LBJ, the Kennedys and Nixon.
VHS: S32392. $69.98.
The Presidents Collection II. Two double-cassette gift set featuring Teddy Roosevelt and FDR.
VHS: S32393. $59.98.
The Presidents Collection III. Two double-cassette gift set featuring Ike and Truman.
VHS: S32394. $59.98.

The Price of Peace (1917-1918)
Though America has won the war, prisons are full of conscientious objectors. E.G. Marshall narrates this look at a country of startling contrasts. 24 mins.
VHS: S23582. $99.95.

The Prohibition Era
This A & E documentary explores the glamorous era of bootleggers, bathtub gin, illicit speakeasies and Al Capone's whiskey-fueled empire as it journeys from the mining towns of Kansas to the rum-running island of St. Pierre to tell the real, unvarnished story of prohibition. Take a look at the saloon-smashing Carrie Nation, the teetotalling tycoon Henry Ford, and George Remus. Discover how Prohibition's first President, Warren Harding, served cocktails in the White House. Meet Al Capone's oldest brother, a successful enforcement agent in Nebraska. The three-video set includes *The Dry Crusade*, *The Roaring Twenties* and *The Road to Repeal*. Each tape is 50 mins.
VHS: S32626. $39.95.

Ramparts We Watch
The first feature-length film produced by the staff of March of Time, the film was begun in 1939 as an account of the forces which drew the country into World War I, but what emerged was a propagandistic document urging people to prepare for defense as World War II approached. The movie re-creates the 1914-18 era as reflected in the lives of several people in a small New England town; interwoven with dramatic incidents is actual newsreel footage, including clips from the Nazi film *Feuertaufe*, an account of the German invasion of Poland.
VHS: S06878. $39.95.
Louis DeRochemont, USA, 1940, 90 mins.

The Real Las Vegas
From the mobsters who made Vegas their version of the American dream to the tycoons of today's family mega-resorts, here is the ultimate insider's tour of America's neon oasis. Never-before-seen footage and rare interviews recall its wild early days and insiders remember the city's most powerful players, including its would-be king, the high-flying mobster Bugsy Siegel.
VHS: S30945. $59.95.
Jim Milio/Melissa Jo Peltier, USA, 1996, 50 mins.

The Real Richard Nixon
Historian Frank Gannon hosts this exhaustive, three-volume look at the real Richard Nixon. Exclusive, newly released interview footage, photographs and rare home movies reveal an amiable man who destroyed the prestige of the office he served. Everything is covered, from his Quaker upbringing to his work in California and Washington. Gannon also describes his feelings for his wife and the trauma of his resignation. This 3-volume set includes *The Real Richard Nixon: Early Life*; *The Real Richard Nixon: Pat* and *The Real Richard Nixon: Twenty Eight Days*. USA, 1995, 202 mins.
VHS: S26967. $49.99.

Red Bull Division: 34th Infantry Division
The lot of the common infantryman is hardship, suffering, cold, heat, rain and death in many forms. This authentic documentary will chill the viewer with its depiction of stark misery in the mountains of Italy. Colonel Quinn shows army awards and medals (North Africa and Italy, 1943-45). 1953, 29 mins.
VHS: S32071. $19.95.

Rediscovering America
Finally, the secrets and myths of a forgotten culture are revealed. It's our American culture that needs de-mystifying. Roger Kennedy, Director of the Smithsonian Institution's National Museum of American History, offers a fascinating, fresh perspective on the legends and legacies found in our own backyard. 60-100 minutes each.
Vol. 1: The Real American Cowboy.
VHS: S21797. $19.95.
Vol. 2: Indians Among Us.
VHS: S21798. $19.95.
Vol. 3: Railroads, Robbers and Rebels.
VHS: S21799. $19.95.
Rediscovering America, Set.
VHS: S21800. $49.95.

The Republican Party, 1960-1992
A comprehensive look at the "Grand Old Party" shows the recent history of the other dominant American party. Goldwater, Nixon, Ford, Reagan and Bush have all played a major part in the contemporary face of the Republican Party. This documentary shows the evolution which leads to their loss of the White House in 1992. 52 mins.
VHS: S29496. $19.95.

The Revolutionary War
Charles Kuralt narrates this three-part series about the American Revolutionary War. The struggle for independence forever imprinted the American character with a military spirit of which many are proud. From rebels and redcoats to Washington and Jefferson, this series details the birth of a nation. 300 mins.
VHS: S29432. $49.95.

The Rights of Passage (1919-1920)
Even as President Wilson proposes his ill-fated League of Nations, Bolsheviks are coming to power in Russia. At home, Americans are preoccupied with peace-time activities like making money and going to the flicks. Hosted by E.G. Marshall. 24 mins.
VHS: S23583. $99.95.

Rivals: Capone vs. Ness
When prohibition officer Eliot Ness took on the infamous crime king Al "Scarface" Capone, the liquor flowed and the bullets flew in one of America's most colorful eras and intense rivalries. With interviews and rare footage. 46 mins.
VHS: S33162. $9.95.

Rivals: J.F.K. vs. Khruschev
When President John Kennedy refused to let Soviet Premier Khruschev move nuclear missiles to Cuba in 1962, two superpowers wrestled for control while the world teetered on the brink of destruction. With interviews and rare footage. 46 mins.
VHS: S33163. $9.95.

Rivals: King vs. Wallace
Alabama governor George Wallace fueled the fire of racial antagonism while civil rights leader Rev. Martin Luther King preached to end bigotry at all costs. With interviews and rare footage. 46 mins.
VHS: S33164. $9.95.

Rivals: Manson vs. Bugliosi
America's most notorious madman is prosecuted for murder by district attorney Bugliosi in one of the century's most fascinating trials. With interviews and rare footage. 46 mins.
VHS: S33161. $9.95.

Royal Secrets
This three-volume set from the Discovery Channel details some of the most amazing secrets behind Europe's illustrious royal families. Debauchery, inbreeding, devious plots, murders and magic are among the exploits of the historic figures—including the real Count Dracula—described in this collection. 300 mins.
VHS: S29903. $99.95.

Russia's War: Blood upon the Snow
Hosted by former Secretary of State Henry Kissinger, this compelling five-volume documentary contains rare, never-before-seen footage of the Russian Army during World War II. Five-volume set includes *The Darkness Descends*, *Between Life and Death*, *The Fight from Within*, *The Citadel* and *The Fall of the Swastika*. 10 hours.
VHS: S31767. $69.98.

S.A.S.: The Soldier's Story
A remarkable and unique view from inside Britain's elite crack regiment: the S.A.S.—the premiere anti-terrorist organization in the world, featuring live mission footage. Originally broadcast on British television. Two-video set. 80 mins.
VHS: S34415. $29.98.

The Schwartzkopf Four-Pack
Four programs on the nature of war and battle, hosted by Gen. Norman H. Schwartzkopf (Ret.), the former general commander of American ground forces in the Gulf War. The works are *Hitler and Stalin*, about the unholy alliance between two authoritarians; *The Year of the General*, stories about the men who altered the complexity of World War II; *Remember Pearl Harbor* which reconstructs the activities of Dec. 7, 1941 through Japanese footage and previously unveiled readings of letters, diaries and personal documents; and *Schwartzkopf in Vietnam: A Soldier Returns*, a personal essay as the general returns to Vietnam for the first time since 1970, and openly discusses his feelings. 300 mins.
VHS: S19541. $99.98.

The Secret Service
The history and techniques of the most celebrated bodyguards of modern times are revealed in this four-volume boxed set. Assassinations and high tech innovations have shaped the elite force. Interviews, commentary and behind-the-scenes footage reveal the true story behind the Secret Service.
VHS: S26095. $59.95.
Benjamin Magliano, USA, 1995, 200 mins.

Secrets of Alcatraz
This tape tells the story of Alcatraz through exclusive interviews with former guards, inmates and historians and rare film footage and photographs, including the home movies of prison staff and the 1969 occupation by native Americans. Viewers are taken into the cells of Alcatraz's most notorious inmates, such as Al Capone and The Birdman, underneath the cellblock to walk the mysterious corridors of a buried former Union Civil War fort, along the dangerous routes of Alcatraz's most famous escape attempts, and to hidden corners of the island rich with unexpected natural beauty.
VHS: S30654. $19.95.

Secrets of the Rock: Return to Alcatraz
Documentary footage and the actual narratives of former prisoners recreate the horrific legacy of the "the Rock," America's most notorious prison. Legendary escape attempts, infamous prisoners, the "Battle of Alcatraz," and the brutal facts of solitary confinement are all detailed. USA, 60 mins.
VHS: S27391. $19.95.

Sex and Justice
This document explores the complicated issues of class, race, sex and male sexual aggression within the context of the gripping Anita Hill/Clarence Thomas hearings. With commentary by Gloria Steinem.
VHS: S18986. $24.95.
Julian Schlossberg, USA, 1993, 76 mins.

Smithsonian World
A broad intellectual journey into history, science, nature and travel, following the aims and principles of the Smithsonian Institute. The series is a kaleidoscopic and impressionistic account of scientific and technological accomplishment which examines different relations—man to society, the individual to art, and social and cultural movements and their historical context.
Smithsonian World: A Usable Past. An impressionistic and vibrant travelogue that moves through time and across continents to explore different cultures, landscapes and people. 56 mins.
VHS: S19200. $14.98.
Smithsonian World: Heroes and the Test of Time. A vivid look at two radically different men: the military general George A. Custer and the painter Thomas Eakins. 58 mins.
VHS: S19196. $14.98.

The Speeches Collection
This comprehensive collection of important speeches captures the spirit of liberty and equality, spanning three centuries and competently exploring four distinct chapters in U.S. history.
The Speeches of Sitting Bull. Re-enacted by Native American E. Donald Two Rivers, this tape features a representative sample of heartfelt addresses from the legendary Indian leader, conveying his disappointment over the injustice faced by his people, including his meeting with American representatives before and after Little Bighorn. 35 mins.
VHS: S31243. $19.95.
The Speeches of Malcolm X. This volume covers an era in the controversial black nationalist leader's public life during which his attitudes were evolving. Includes excerpts from the 1964 "The Ballot or the Bullet" and famous "By Any Means Necessary" speeches. 41 mins.
VHS: S31244. $19.95.
The Speeches of the Civil War. This brief chronology features different views expressed during the Civil War, from the words of abolitionist John Brown to former slave Frederick Douglass' speech against Independence Day as a "sham", from General Lee's 1865 surrender at Appomattox to Union General Sherman's martial law address to evacuate Atlanta, and President Lincoln's 1863 Gettysburg address. 37 mins.
VHS: S31245. $19.95.
The Speeches of Our Founding Fathers & The American Revolution. This tape features a broad sample of writings and addresses from great thinkers who were inspired by the events that led to America's independence from England, including Patrick Henry's "Give me liberty or give me death" speech, General George Washington's inspiration to this troops before the Battles of Long Island and Trenton, Thomas Jefferson's Declaration of Independence, excerpts from Thomas Paine's infamous "These are the times that try men's souls" tract, and Benjamin Franklin's discussion of the opportunities awaiting emigres to the new country. 40 mins.
VHS: S31246. $19.95.

The Speeches of Franklin D. Roosevelt
The speeches of America's great President.
VHS: S07028. $19.95.

The Speeches of Winston Churchill
Some of the most memorable speeches of the great British leader.
VHS: S07035. $19.95.

Stalking the President
Subtitled *A History of American Assassins*, this revealing documentary examines the various assassination attempts in the history of the American presidency. The film also considers issues of motivation and conspiracy in the attempted assassinations of Presidents Lincoln, Garfield, McKinley, Roosevelt, FDR, Truman, Kennedy, Nixon, Ford and Reagan. 50 mins.
VHS: S18136. $19.95.

The Story of the Statue of Liberty
Examines the assembling of the statue, built and designed by French architect Frederic Bartholdi, that was bequeathed to the United States as an enduring symbol of liberty, equality and freedom. Intended for children in grades 2-5. 7 mins.
VHS: S20057. $44.95.

Studs Terkel's Chicago
Studs Terkel is Chicago's self-appointed chronicler. During the course of a career that began in the Great Depression, Studs has been a radio soap opera gangster, host of his own television show, disc jockey, jazz critic, and Prix Italia-winning broadcaster. He is most famous for his books of oral history, recording America's past and present in the words of the ordinary people he interviews so sympathetically. This program presents a history of Chicago in the words of its people and the music of its incomparable blues players, all filtered through the unique lens of Studs' viewpoint. 60 mins.
VHS: S13751. $19.95.

The Tarnished Dream (1929-1931)
E.G. Marshall tells the story of a country devastated by the crash of 1929. Vivid images of a population out of work bring home the gravity of this time, when one in four Americans could not find a job. 25 mins.
VHS: S23587. $99.95.

Theodore Roosevelt
This sickly child became one of the United States' most vigorous presidents. He made his fame waging war—yet was the first American to win the Nobel Peace Prize. An *A & E Biography*.
VHS: S30840. $19.95.

There's No Such Thing as Woman's Work
An engaging, upbeat video that explores women's changing work roles from 1900 to the present. The modern style and animation combined with period music and historical newsreels will appeal to students and adults alike. 30 mins.
VHS: S33739. $39.95.

Thomas Jefferson
From the acclaimed filmmaker on the American experience, Ken Burns (*The West*), comes this definitive film on the life of Thomas Jefferson, the man who wrote the Declaration of Independence, doubled the size of our country, served as our third president and helped fuel the fires of the American and French revolutions. Includes extra footage not seen in the PBS broadcast. Narrated by Ossie Davis. With Sam Waterston as Thomas Jefferson.
VHS: S30582. $29.98.
Ken Burns, USA, 1996, 180 mins.

Thomas Jefferson: A View from the Mountain
Though renowned as a champion of freedom, former President Thomas Jefferson also owned slaves. Famed documentarian Martin Doblmeier, with the help of narrators Sissy Spacek, Danny Glover and others, examines this seemingly contradictory figure. He even explores the most salacious aspect of Jefferson's life: his purported liaison with his Monticello slave, Sally Hemmings.
VHS: S27509. $29.98.
Martin Doblmeier, USA, 1995, 114 mins.

Those Crazy Americans
George Gobel narrates this kooky nostalgia trip through American fads and follies of the '20s, '30s, '40s and '50s.
VHS: S33904. $14.95.

Titanic (The Learning Channel)
This two-part set from The Learning Channel shares compelling and rarely told personal tales of the *Titanic*. *Great Adventures of the 20th Century: Titanic* recalls how passengers transcended tragedy to alter American culture, the landscape and the future of the country. *Titanic Voyage: Untold Stories* follows historian Charles Hass 12,000 feet down to the ship's watery grave, exposing heartwrenching first-hand stories of tycoon John Jacob Astor, Captain Edward J. Smith, American millionaire Benjamin Guggenheim and many others.
VHS: S34910. $29.98.

Titanic: The Final Chapter
This definitive chronicle of history's worst maritime disaster tells the complete story of the *Titanic*, from design through her fatal voyage. Includes archival footage and never-before-seen photos, chilling exclusive eyewitness interviews with the last living *Titanic* survivor, and historic footage of the sunken ship filmed on the ocean floor. 55 mins.
VHS: S32675. $14.95.

Titanic: Treasure of the Deep
Walter Cronkite hosts this extraordinary journey to the bottom of the North Atlantic Sea, where the doomed luxury liner *Titanic* found its final resting place. 47 mins.
VHS: S35127. $14.95.

Trail of Hope: The Story of the Mormon Trail
This conduit to the West was used by more than 70,000 emigrants on their journey to the Great Basin. The great majority of these pioneers made the trek on foot across windblown plains, sunbaked deserts and frozen mountain valleys, each step a triumph in the face of tragedy. Award of Excellence recipient. Narrated by Hal Holbrook.
VHS: S32234. $24.95.
Lee Groberg, USA, 1997, 120 mins.

Treating the Casualties of the Gulf War
A unique look at the human aftermath of the war. While American casualties were light, some American soldiers suffered disabling injuries or severe stress. The video also examines the fact that our intense bombing virtually wiped out Iraq's ability to treat its victims, a high percentage of whom were children. USA, 1991, 29 mins.
VHS: S15213. $25.00.

Trial of the Avco Ploughshares
A real life political trial is dramatically recorded in this unique video—the only time cameras have been permitted in a courtroom to film a trial of political activists. Seven men and women, including a mother of 13, were charged with trespass and malicious damage for hammering on computer systems and office equipment in AVCO Systems Division, a manufacturer of nuclear weapons components in Massachusetts. This program captures the emotionally charged struggle between prosecution, judge and defendants over "defense of justification."
VHS: S11495. $39.95.
Julie Gustafson/John Reilly, USA, 1987, 60 mins.

United States Naval Academy: 150 Years in Annapolis
Beginning with the legendary John Paul Jones, this unique American institution has forged the men who run the nation's Navy. Everything is here, including painful memories of the time when graduates fought each other during the Civil War.
VHS: S26935. $19.95.
Don Horan, USA, 1995, 50 mins.

The Unquiet Death of Julius and Ethel Rosenberg
On June 19, 1953, Julius and Ethel Rosenberg, the so-called "atomic spies" of the 1950s, were executed at Sing Sing Prison. Their death only fostered the belief of many Americans that the Rosenbergs were innocent, victims of the anti-Communist paranoia of the 50s, rather than spies who had stolen atomic secrets for the Russians. In his landmark documentary *The Unquiet Death of Julius and Ethel Rosenberg*, Alvin Goldstein looks at the facts and procedures of the Rosenberg case, as well as the climate of the times, interviewing jurors, FBI agents, lawyers for both sides, and the two sons of the Rosenbergs. Using documentary and newsreel footage, Goldstein creates a moving human drama, a "thoroughly researched, solidly developed…superb recreation of history, painting with bold strokes the temper of the times" (*Boston Globe*).
VHS: S04736. $59.95.
Alvin Goldstein, USA, 1974, 83 mins.

Valley Forge
The Pennsylvania Association of the Sons of the Revolution filmed this program at the actual historic site of a battle waged in the winter of 1777. There, the Continental Army defended the cause of liberty despite crushing hardship. 24 mins.
VHS: S23731. $49.95.

Vietnam: They Were Young and Brave
Eleven vets return to the site of a decisive battle, the Ia Drang Valley. This story charts the importance of this battle and the impact it had on these men. Their memory of the hellish scene speaks volumes about this horrible conflict, which has been called "a turning point in the Vietnam War." 60 mins.
VHS: S29485. $19.95.

Virtual 60's
Dr. Timothy Leary is the perfect host for this 1990's look at the decade of expanded consciousness, the 1960's. The concept of virtual reality makes this series not only different but completely unique. Some of the biggest rock stars of the era are shown, including Canned Heat, Iron Butterfly, Humble Pie and Blood, Sweat and Tears, as well as many others. It's almost as if a 60's-style rock festival were available on video. Each tape is 50 mins.
The Consciousness Tape.
VHS: S21818. $14.95.
The Love Tape.
VHS: S21817. $14.95.
The Peace Tape.
VHS: S21816. $14.95.
Virtual 60's, Pre-Pack Special.
VHS: S21819. $39.95.

Votes for Women?! 1913 U.S. Senate Testimony
Kate Douglas Wiggin, the author of *Rebecca of Sunnybrook Farm*, argues against the vote for women. Progressive writer Belle Case La Follette offers an opposing view and testifies in favor. 15 mins. Resource guide available.
Video.
VHS: S25767. $95.00.
Resource Guide.
VHS: S25780. $45.00.

War & Civilization
From history's first recorded battle, Meggido, to the end of the knight's reign with the first use of gunpowder, to the dropping of the atomic bomb, this eight-part series from The Learning Channel chronicles the history of war and questions what direction war will take as more states come to own nuclear weapons, threatening worldwide peace.
VHS: S34909. $119.98.

War Machines of Tomorrow
Take a look back at the war technology employed in the Gulf War, "Operation Desert Storm," and preview some military machines of the future. 60 mins.
VHS: S28662. $19.95.

The War That Changed War Deluxe Boxed Set
This four-tape series uses footage and information, kept classified for decades, to show how science and strategy forever altered the way war is fought. Volumes include *Armor*, *Aircraft*, *Carriers* and *Secret Weapons*. Each tape is 60 mins.
VHS: S32345. $49.95.

Wars in Peace
This series looks at battles waged across the frontiers of a number of countries. Many of these wars involved the great powers, as they struggled with issues of politics, religion and economics.
Wars in Peace: 6-Tape Brick. 468 mins.
VHS: S25990. $149.95.
Wars in Peace: Iran/Iraq—Afghanistan. Iran and Iraq consumed vast quantities of resources fighting to control that incredibly valuable resource—oil. The former USSR sought to destroy the growing Islamic fundamentalist fervor emerging in Afghanistan. 80 mins.
VHS: S25987. $29.95.
Wars in Peace: Korea—Vietnam. Though it began as a border dispute, the war in Korea escalated into a red-hot war that engaged the principal protagonists of the Cold War. It was also the United Nations' first war. Vietnam was the first war waged nightly on television, and it marked the growing importance of helicopters in warfare. 80 mins.
VHS: S25984. $29.95.
Wars in Peace: Terrorism—Lebanon. Terrorism relies on random, extreme violence that forces the world to acknowledge intractable conflicts. In *Lebanon*, the Israelis attack the PLO in order to stop its forays into Israel and the occupied territories. 80 mins.
VHS: S25986. $29.95.
Wars in Peace: The Falklands—Special Forces. Argentina's push to gain territory in the South Atlantic underestimated the force of the British response. Special Forces are specially trained troops sent to areas where regular forces dare not venture. 80 mins.
VHS: S25988. $29.95.
Wars in Peace: The Gulf War. Sadam Hussein plunged into Kuwait, but his forces were ultimately repelled and the tiny kingdom was regained. Nevertheless, Iraqi forces left a considerable amount of destruction behind. 68 mins.
VHS: S25989. $29.95.
Wars in Peace: The Six Day War—Yom Kippur. Israel defeated the combined forces of three Arab countries in just six days. Unfortunately, the Israelis did not anticipate the Arab reprisal, launched on the holiest day of the Jewish year. 80 mins.
VHS: S25985. $29.95.

Watergate Scandal and Resignation of President Nixon
The complete story of the Watergate maelstrom, Nixon's near impeachment, and his final dark days prior to his sudden resignation. From ABC News. 60 mins.
VHS: S12681. $24.98.

Watergate—The Deluxe Boxed Set
This series of three videos reveals the truth behind the government scandal that shocked the nation and destroyed the presidency of Richard Nixon. Interviews with actual participants and never-before-seen interviews with Nixon himself make this Discovery Channel presentation a unique historic document.
VHS: S23870. $49.95.

Watergate: The Secret Story
Mike Wallace attempts to shed new light on the political circumstances and events behind Nixon's motives that led to Watergate and his humiliating resignation from the Presidency. 60 mins.
VHS: S17684. $19.98.

The Western Frontier: The First to Let Women Vote

The women of Wyoming, Utah, Colorado and Idaho were the only womenin 19th-century America who had the right to vote. Witness their experiences in this fascinating documentary that includes archival photographs, historical political cartoons, contemporary recreations and cinematography. 90 mins.
VHS: S34823. $14.95.

The Wild West

This ten-hour miniseries is a mosaic of two-bit hustlers and visionary dreamers, of vicious outlaws and true believers. "Scholarly and lively, *The Wild West* tells a big story by telling a lot of little stories" (Bob Wisehart, *The Sacramento Bee*). Narrated by Jack Lemmon. Parts voiced by more than 40 actors, including Joe Don Baker, Lloyd Bridges, Tim Curry, Dana Delaney, Larry Fishburne, Lee Grant, Graham Greene, Christine Lahti, Lyle Lovett and Wes Studi. Directed by Academy Award-winning documentarian Keith W. Merrill (*The Great American Cowboy*).
Volume 1: Cowboys/Settlers. In this two-episode program, *Cowboys* documents the rugged individualism of the mythic American figure. *Settlers* examines the stress and personal toll of wagon trains and the determination of the men and women who survived. 90 mins.
VHS: S19125. $19.98.
Volume 2: Gunfighters/Townspeople. In this two part program, *Gunfighters* extols the legends, actions and circumstances behind the notorious gunslingers, including Bat Masterson, Wyatt Earp and the Daltons. *Townspeople* looks at the determination of the anonymous shopkeepers, professionals and people who forged communities. 90 mins.
VHS: S19126. $19.98.
Volume 3: Indians/Soldiers. In *Indians*, Native American tribes fight for their land, property and right to exist, as Sitting Bull, Geronimo and Red Cloud adopt desperate measures to ensure their survival. In *Soldiers*, Civil War veterans, emancipated slaves and resettled immigrants secure the vastly expanding American outposts. 90 mins.
VHS: S19127. $19.98.
Volume 4: Dreamers and Wayfarers/Chroniclers. *Dreamers and Wayfarers* celebrates the craft, skills and effort of the innovative thinkers and eccentric technicians who developed the transcontinental railroad. *Chroniclers* charts an emerging social and aesthetic evolution, the number of artists, writers, journalists and photographers who left to capture the West's voice, physical representation and mythic nature. 90 mins.
VHS: S19128. $19.98.
Volume 5: Searchers/Mythmakers. *Searchers* examines the efforts of explorers to assess the full dimension of the West and preserve its legacy and vast riches for future generations. *Mythmakers* is a kaleidoscopic investigation of the characters and outsized figures of the New West, as dime novelists transform Annie Oakley, Wild Bill Hickok and Sitting Bull into larger-than-life characters. 90 mins.
VHS: S19129. $19.98.
The Wild West, Complete Set.
VHS: S19130. $75.92.

Winds of Change (1912-1916)

Chaplin, Keaton, Will Rogers, Fatty Arbuckle and Sarah Bernhardt left their indelible impression on this era as the first international stars. Their fame is juxtaposed with the disaster of the age, the sinking of the *Lusitania*. E.G. Marshall narrates. 25 mins.
VHS: S23579. $99.95.

A Woman's Place

Julie Harris narrates this tribute to "Remarkable American Women," highlighting achievements by women in the arts, science, business, athletics, and more. Rare footage and photographs highlight this uplifting celebration of the women who dared to be the best. 25 mins.
VHS: S05745. $39.95.

Women and the American Family

The struggle of women for equal rights has led to some of the most controversial problems of our times. This program examines the issue from a historical perspective, looking at the role of women in the next century, and the related problem of the changes that will occur with respect to the American family and its place in American society. 28 mins.
VHS: S10784. $29.95.

Women First & Foremost: Volume One: "Remember the Ladies"

Rita Moreno and Dee Wallace Stone host this video about inspiring women who pioneered new paths in a variety of professions. Journalism, education, and medicine are all areas that were once off limits to women. Through determination and talent, the women detailed in this volume changed all of that.
VHS: S27046. $24.95.
Scott Mansfield, USA, 1995, 60 mins.

Women First & Foremost: Volume Two: "Touching the Clouds with Pen and Plane"

Few have heard of the bravery which characterized women soldiers like Revolutionary War hero Deborah Gannet. That may be because she was forced to assume a man's identity and fight under the name Robert Shurtleff. Rita Moreno and Dee Wallace Stone host this second volume about women who trailblazed new areas in a number of professions.
VHS: S27047. $24.95.
Scott Mansfield, USA, 1995, 60 mins.

Women First & Foremost: Volume Three: "A Lady in the Spotlight"

Though women movie stars are very well known, the women who work behind the scenes in the entertainment industry are often overshadowed by their male colleagues. Rita Moreno and Dee Wallace Stone host this volume which details the work of many women, including the first woman film director, a leading Broadway lyricist and the first woman network co-anchor.
VHS: S27048. $24.95.
Scott Mansfield, USA, 1995, 60 mins.

Women in American Life

Hundreds of historical photographs combine with a lively-paced narrative and carefully chosen music to create a compelling and lively introduction to women's history for secondary and adult audiences. The five short programs include *1861-1880: Civil War, Recovery, & Westward Expansion*; *1880-1320: Immigration, New Work and New Roles*; *1917-1942: Cultural Image and Economic Reality*; *1942-1955: War Work, Housework, and Growing Discontent*; and *1955-1977: New Attitudes Force Dramatic Changes*. 87 mins.
VHS: S33738. $325.00.

Women on Cane River

Beginning with Coin Coin, a free woman of color and the founder of Melrose, this documentary explores the lives of interesting women from old Acadia. Cammie Henry was an arts patron at Melrose, while Clementine Hunter was a primitive artist and former slave there. Kate Chopin, a writer ahead of her time, captured Creole and Cajun life at Clouterville. 20 mins.
VHS: S22402. $49.95.

Women Speak Up: A Collection of Women's Voices from Around the World

This documentary is a colorful collage of plenaries, workshops, interviews, spontaneous events and music from the Fourth United Nation's International Women's NGO (non-governmental organization) Forum that took place in Huairou and Beijing, China, August 30-September 8, 1995, and was attended by 30,000 women from 189 countries. "The video is absolutely gripping and leads to excellent discussion when shown to a women's studies class or a women's conference" (Ruth Harriet Jacobs, PhD, author of *Women Who Touched My Life*).
VHS: S30171. $19.99.
Linda Leehman/Esther Farnsworth, USA, 1996, 58 mins.

A World on Display

The largest and grandest of all international expositions, the 1904 St. Louis World's Fair, displayed America's economic and artistic resources, the latest inventions, and models for urban life. The Fair's organizers also brought more than 2,000 indigenous peoples from around the world to live in supposedly authentic villages. This video utilizes first-person accounts from elderly Americans who attended the Fair, interviews with historians, rare archival footage and previously unpublished photos to situate the St. Louis Fair in the social and cultural context of American society at the turn of the century. Public performance.
VHS: S32118. $79.95.
Eric Breitbart, USA, 1994, 53 mins.

World War I Complete Set

CBS News produced this historic overview of the issues, events and dominant personalities of the First World War, painstakingly rendered through the use of vivid archival and combat footage. The five-volume program examines the causes of the war, the rise of nationalism, the assassination of Archduke Ferdinand and the German sinking of the Lusitania, the expansion of the war and America's belated involvement. The program studies the major strategic campaigns in Europe and Asia, the barbaric nature of trench warfare at Verdun, the massive destruction and casualties suffered on all sides, the emergence of air power and the long-term consequences of the war. The program concludes with a complex reading of the political issues that led to the peaceful negotiation of the armistice that brokered a precarious peace. 530 mins.
VHS: S19536. $139.98.

The Year of the Generals

From CBS News Videos, General Norman H. Schwarzkopf and Charles Kuralt consider the greatest commanders and strategically important battles of World War II, interweaving combat footage, memoirs and readings by the actors Mel Gibson and Anthony Hopkins. 94 mins.
VHS: S17776. $19.98.

WORLD WAR II

The 10th Mountain Division Ridge Runners

The 10th Mountain Division consisted of an elite group of expert mountain climbers trained by the U.S. Army to combat the Nazis entrenched in the mountains of Italy during WWII. Through rare and unusual film footage, the combined accounts of the Americans, Italians and Germans are woven together to offer a first-hand account of what it was like on the front lines. 45 mins.
VHS: S32388. $19.95.

Admiral Nimitz Story

On the last day of 1941 Admiral Chester Nimitz took command of what was left of the U.S. Pacific Fleet at Pearl Harbor. Fighting defensively, he bought time for the new fleet under construction in American shipyards. By 1943 the Pacific offensive that would reach Japan itself in 1945 was under way. 1963, 29 mins.
VHS: S32072. $19.95.

Adolph Hitler's Home Movies

Eva Braun, mistress of Hitler, filmed these silent home movies which show top Nazi officials relaxing in Hitler's mountaintop estate. It is incredibly eerie to watch men like Albert Speer, Martin Borman, Joseph Goebbels and Heinrich Himmler in this domestic setting. Musical score provided. 53 mins.
VHS: S24070. $14.95.

African Americans in WWII: A Legacy of Patriotism and Valor

Black World War II veterans from all military branches describe their personal experiences, in this film dedicated to seven African Americans who received the Medal of Honor in 1997 for actions performed in WWII. Includes archival footage and a message from former General Colin Powell and President Clinton. 58 mins.
VHS: S33748. $19.95.

After Mein Kampf?

Produced in war-time England, the first actual documentary footage and dramatic reconstruction of the rape of Poland, the seizure of the low countries, and the attacks on Great Britain. Probably the first non-German production about Hitler, obviously meant as war-time propaganda, but remarkable. England, 1940, 43 mins.
VHS: S01620. $24.95.

After the Cloud Lifted: Hiroshima's Stories of Recovery

This documentary shows how Hiroshima's atomic bomb survivors overcame personal tragedies and rebuilt their lives, and how their stories of reconciliation continue to inspire the world today. Find out how one survivor used art to help him overcome the horror of having watched his family burn to death, and how a woman swore revenge against the airmen who dropped the bomb and later came face-to-face with the co-pilot of the *Enola Gay*. And meet two disfigured women who chose different paths toward healing. 35 mins.
VHS: S34717. $150.00.

Air Force Training Films

Two films featuring Lieutenant Ronald Reagan and Lieutenant Burgess Meredith: *The Rear Gunner* and *Snoopers and How to Blast Them*.
VHS: S10586. $29.95.

Allied Fighting Machines of World War II

A look at the evolution of Allied fighting units during World War II captured in historical footage and subgrouped into three one-hour sections: *Allied Fighters*, detailing the Mustangs, Spitfires, the Lightnings and Corsairs; *Allied Bombers*, about American and British bomber offenses, the Flying Fortresses, the Lancasters and Liberators; and *Allied Armor*, about the fierce fighting on the eastern and western fronts, as the Sherman, Churchill and T-34 divisions changed the course of the war. 180 mins.
VHS: S18791. $59.95.

America at War

This wide-ranging program looks at the military and political campaigns of the American military, beginning with Pearl Harbor and moving through the Persian Gulf, with specific attention on Korea, the Bay of Pigs, Vietnam, Grenada, Panama and Operation Desert Storm.
VHS: S17954. $29.95.

America Goes to War
Veteran CBS journalist Eric Sevareid relives the war-torn years on the American home front during World War II with wartime newsreels. Four-volume set. 3½ hours.
VHS: S34713. $69.95.

America: The Way We Were: The Home Front 1940-1945
In this three-volume series, journey back to the home front and relive America's memory years from 1940 to 1945: victory gardens, fireside chats, Your Hit Parade, Rosie the Riveter, Glenn Miller, FDR, Joe DiMaggio and V-J Day. 3 hours.
VHS: S31480. $69.99.

Appointment in Tokyo
A documentary compiled from archive footage taken from the vaults of various government agencies. This World War II video emphasizes the Pacific theatre of operations as told from the perspective of the war fought in the air. Expect dogfights, bombing runs, aircraft carriers and kamikazes. B&W, 56 mins.
VHS: S09521. $19.95.

The Architecture of Doom
A brilliant documentary which explores the inner workings of the Third Reich and illuminates the Nazi aesthetic in art, architecture and popular culture. Director Peter Cohen uses this analysis of Nazi art and architecture to shed new light on German popular culture, which made Hitler possible. Music by Richard Wagner, footage of Hitler and his Nazi party and rare films and memorabilia are combined to show how a civilized country supported a frustrated artist who became a maniacal despot.
VHS: S26346. $29.95.
Peter Cohen, USA, 1995, 119 mins.

Army-Navy Screen Magazine
Army-Navy Screen Magazine was a biweekly news and information short that was shown before the feature film in all military motion picture theaters during World War II. Each show consisted of five segments, with stories ranging from homefront news to news about the war to entertainment shows. By the end of the war, it reached a weekly audience of over four million men and women stationed all over the world. Segments include *Hollywood Canteen, G.I. Journal, By Request, Command Performance, Jubilee*, Mail Call and the popular G.I cartoon *Private Snafu*. Hollywood celebrities include Lucille Ball, Bob Hope, Dinah Shore, Eddie Cantor, Lena Horne, Jimmy Durante and Abbott & Costello performing their classic, "Who's on First?" 58 mins.
VHS: S32636. $19.95.

Atrocities of the Orient
The Japanese invasion and occupation of the Philippines is the subject of this exploitation drama that combines combat bloodthirstiness with a strange love story. A Filipino kills his girlfriend so that the Japanese will not defile her. Looting, torturing, bombing and bayonetting are also featured. USA, 1959, 80 mins.
VHS: S05437. $29.95.

Attack in the Pacific
Armed Forces Information Film #3 details the fight against the Japanese during World War II in the Pacific.
VHS: S02588. $19.95.

Axis Fighting Machines of World War II
A documentary about Axis power military weaponry and forces of World War II, captured in historical footage subdivided into three one-hour sections. *Axis Fighters* shows German and Japanese bombers such as the ME-109, FW-190 and Zero; *Axis Bombers* looks at the German and Japanese blitzkriegs, the Stukas, HG-111s and ground attack aircraft; and *Axis Armor* focuses on the Panzers and Tigers of the Nazi blitzkrieg, as well as sections on Japanese and Italian armor. 180 mins.
VHS: S18792. $59.95.

The Battle of Arnhem
Drawing on British, German and Dutch photo and sound archives, this program looks at Field Marshall Montgomery's ambitious though problematic "Market Garden" strategy, the campaign to capture the river crossings in Holland during the final push on Berlin.
VHS: S17955. $29.95.

Battle of London
Actual war footage of the first serial attacks on London are featured in this documentary. Though bombers devastated the city, Londoners persevered. 1941, 16 mins.
VHS: S26677. $19.95.

The Battle of Midway
Roosevelt insisted that this documentary about the decisive World War II Pacific Battle be made for the mothers of America. John Ford directed this terrific film that was edited in secret and released just days after its completion. Henry Fonda narrates. 20 mins.
VHS: S21993. $19.95.

Battle of San Pietro/ Marines Have Landed
The U.S. War Department presents two documentaries of Marine action during World War II. Music by the Mormon Tabernacle Choir.
VHS: S02587. $19.95.

The Battle of the Bulge
By mid-1944 it seemed that Allied victories were irreversible, until this battle broke any hint of complacency. Eisenhower threw 250,000 men into the struggle, hoping to end the war. The grueling experiences of the fighting men who endured freezing cold and terrible carnage is finally told in this documentary. 90 mins.
VHS: S24697. $19.95.

Battlefield
This four-volume definitive history of the decisive battles of World War II features rare archival footage and state-of-the-art computer graphics. Volumes include *The Battle of Stalingrad, The Battle of Midway, The Battle of Britain* and *The Battle of Normandy*. 110 mins.
VHS: S31646. $69.95.

Best of Nightline
Austrian President Kurt Waldheim. 30 mins.
VHS: S14050. $14.98.
Klaus Barbie and His Connections. 30 mins.
VHS: S14028. $14.98.

Blitzkrieg, The Lightning War
Be there as Nazis storm the democracies of Western Europe with venomous tank warfare. From the series *The Nazis*. 50 mins.
VHS: S12729. $24.98.

Blood & Iron: The Story of the German War Machine
Co-produced by A & E, FR3 and Discovery Europe, this three-volume box set explores the secret underpinnings of German power in this century and examines the men and technology behind the two World Wars. Episodes include: *The Great War Comes, Fatal Alliances* and *From Nuremberg to NATO*. 180 mins.
VHS: S27699. $79.98.

Bob Hope Remembers World War II
Bob Hope offers a nostalgic tribute to the G.I. generation in this look at the European Theatre and D-Day. Contains a full-length video, a souvenir book, and two audio cassettes.
VHS: S23047. $49.95.

Bombardier: The Real Story
Rare footage from the National Archives and interviews with famous bombardiers reveal the importance of bombardiers to the Allies' winning of World War II. 50 mins.
VHS: S27249. $24.95.

Bombers
The plane and bomb have formed a pact that has changed the way wars are fought and won. See how balloons and zeppelins are used to drop bombs, how the first bombers were utilized in 1921, and how they have become increasingly complicated. 60 mins.
VHS: S13123. $19.98.

Breakthrough
D-Day, the infamous day marking the beginning of the end of World War II in Europe, was a success because of the dedication of thousands of young men. This film shows the courageous warriors who made it happen, including actual footage of the battle.
VHS: S21028. $19.98.
Lewis Seiler, USA, 1950, 91 mins.

Cameramen at War
The story of the British Film Unit newsreel cameramen during both world wars, produced by the British Ministry of Information and compiled by Len Lye. Special highlights include sensational footage from campaigns in France, Norway, and North Africa, as well as over the skies of England. 26 mins.
VHS: S03346. $29.95.

Chameleon Cameraman (Changing Roles)
Henry von Javorsky, Jewish cameraman of the Third Reich, learned to survive by changing roles, working first in Nazi Germany, then for the Soviets in Berlin, and then for the Allies. Saved by his camera, Javorsky made films with Leni Riefenstahl and Luis Trenker, aerial shots for war movies like *Pour le merite*, Cologne in flames in 1944, and Soviet newsreel coverage of the trial of the Sachsenhausen concentration camp war criminals. He moved to America in 1952, where he made industrial films for Volkswagen and won an Academy Award for his short film about breaking the on-water speed record. English voice-over.
VHS: S32069. $29.95.
Jurgen Stumphaus, Germany, 1994, 63 mins.

Civilians in War—Then and After: Poland and World War II
Almost 60 million civilians died in World War II; Warsaw alone lost more people to the bombings than did Hiroshima. This dramatic documentary combines haunting classical music, rare archival footage and fascinating current interviews with Polish Resistance fighters and other civilians who survived World War II. "This film stands out for the use it makes of the lives and experiences of ordinary people and for the directness and simplicity with which their stories are told" (Solon Beinfeld, Washington University).
VHS: S30558. $39.95.
Katherine McCarthy, USA, 1996, 55 mins.

Combat America
American propaganda financed by the Army Air Corps concerns the heroism, skill and courage of the 351st Air Bombardment Group, stationed in England. Narrated by Clark Gable, an Air Force captain.
VHS: S18953. $19.95.

Crusade in Europe
A series on the American campaign in Europe, based on General Dwight D. Eisenhower's memoirs. The series employs war footage taken from the U.S. Army, Navy and Coast Guard, the British War Office, the National Film Board of Canada and captured Nazi materials. The program highlights strategic sessions with Allied and Axis power leaders and generals. Narrated by Westbrook Van Voorhis and Hugh James. 520 mins.

Vol. 1: War Declared. Subtitled *America Joins the Fight*, the program considers Hitler's rise, the Japanese attack on Pearl Harbor, the first draft, Churchill's visit to America and Eisenhower's appointment as head of military operations in the European theater. 60 mins.
VHS: S18707. $19.95.

Vol. 2: The First Offensive. The program considers the North African campaigns and the assaults on Algiers, Oran and Casablanca, and portrays Eisenhower's strategies and his showdowns with German Field Marshal Erwin Rommel, the "Desert Fox." 77 mins.
VHS: S18708. $19.95.

Vol. 3: Assault on Italy. As Allied forces gain strategic control of North Africa, Eisenhower settles on Mussolini's fractured Fascist base in Italy. This program looks at the psychological implications of war and reconstructs Mussolini's rise and bloody fall from power.
VHS: S18709. $19.95.

Vol. 4: D-Day. Subtitled *The Turning Point*, this program considers the accumulation of power and material as Allied forces invade Normandy, the Battle of the Beachhead, the Nazi surrender of Paris to de Gaulle and the continued pursuit of Nazi forces through France. 101 mins.
VHS: S18710. $19.95.

Vol. 5: Hitler's Last Stand. This program examines the final German offensive, the Battle of the Bulge, the Battle of Walcheren Island and the Allies' last major offensive against the Nazis. The show also looks at Churchill's crossing of the Rhine, the Battle of Berlin and the Allies' crushing victory. 101 mins.
VHS: S18711. $19.95.

Vol. 6: Victory. In *The Forging of Peace*, the ramifications of the war and the tense and uneasy peace that exists are explored through the Four-Power Pact, the Nuremberg trials, the Yalta Conference and the formation of the United Nations. The program also provides a series overview. 81 mins.
VHS: S18712. $19.95.

Vols. 1-6: Collector's Edition.
VHS: S18713. $99.95.

Crusade in the Pacific
Six volume collection exploring the land and sea battles that ravaged the Pacific during World War II.

Volume 1. The Pacific in Eruption, Awakening in the Pacific, The Rise of the Japanese Empire, America Goes To War in the Pacific. 115 mins.
VHS: S03131. $19.95.

Volume 2. The U.S. and the Philippines, The Navy Holds—1942, Guadalcanal: America's First Offensive, War in the North—The Aleutians, and The Road Back—New Guinea. 130 mins.
VHS: S03132. $19.95.

Volume 3. Up the Solomons Ladder: Bougainville; Attack in the Central Pacific: Makin and Tarawa; The War at Sea; Speeding Up the Attack—the Marshalls. 115 mins.
VHS: S03133. $19.95.

Volume 4. Stepping Stones to the Philippines; Battle for the Marianas; The War in the China-Burma-India Theatre; Palau: The Fight for Bloody Nose Ridge; MacArthur Returns to the Philippines. 115 mins.
VHS: S03134. $19.95.

Volume 5. Bloody Iwo:The Capture of Iwo Jima;At Japan's Doorstep: Okinawa;The Air War on Japan;The Surrender and Occupation of Japan. 115 mins.
VHS: S03135. $19.95.
Volume 6. Shifting Tides in the Orient;War in Korea;The Problem of Asia and the Pacific. 115 mins.
VHS: S03136. $19.95.

D-Day: The Great Crusade

The storming of the Normandy beaches on D-Day, June 6, 1944, began the final chapter of World War II.This historic video is a unique and detailed record of the events of D-Day.The planning and preparation of Operation Overlord, its code name, was one of the greatest military maneuvers of all time. 112 mins.
VHS: S04900. $39.95.

The Darkest Hour (1939-1941)

In this video the effects of war throughout Europe are shown. Though FDR pledges to keep the U.S. out of war, Pearl Harbor changes everything. Before long war has broken out all over the world. Eric Sevareid narrates. 25 mins.
VHS: S23592. $99.95.

Day of Freedom—Our Fighting Forces

Leni Riefenstahl (*Triumph of the Will*) directs this propaganda documentary on the armed forces of Nazi Germany. Military parades, lots of flags and leaders. Planes fly in a swastika formation.This short film was thought to have been lost. No dialog or narration. Original music score.
VHS: S05504. $19.95.
Leni Riefenstahl, Germany, 1935, 17 mins.

December 7th, Midway, Bougainville

This award-winning film focuses on three crucial episodes in the Pacific Theatre, including the infamous sneak attack on Pearl Harbor, and the Battle of the Midway. 60 mins.
VHS: S10026. $19.95.

Desert Victory

The longest chase in military history, the British Eighth Army's pursuit of Rommel's Afrika Korps from El Alamein to Tripoli, is shown via authentic footage. Of the 26 cameramen who filmed *Desert Victory*, four were killed, six wounded and seven captured. Tobruk was actually taken by the film unit, which arrived several hours before the fighting forces. Directed by Colonel David MacDonald of the Army Photographic Unit, *Desert Victory* was important as a propaganda film, bringing home to English audiences the first evidence of a turning point in the North Africa war. 60 mins.
VHS: S04479. $39.95.

Die Deutsche Wochenschau #1 (The German Weekly Newsreel)

Four newsreels from Nazi Germany are presented in this collection now available on video. Combat footage of the Luftwaffe over Greece and Crete. Winter fighting in Finland and Russia. U-Boats in the North Atlantic. Also fabric being made from waste paper. German with no subtitles. WWII as seen from another viewpoint. Germany, 1941, 50 mins.
VHS: S05500. $24.95.

Dr. Todt: Mission and Achievement

This lavishly documented 1943 German propaganda film supplies extensive and rare footage of the life and work of one of the most powerful men of the Third Reich: Dr. Fritz Todt, builder of the West Wall and the Autobahn. German with English subtitles. 1943. 36 mins.
VHS: S33107. $29.95.

The Eagle Has Landed

The fully-restored adaptation of Jack Higgins's World War II adventure novel about a Nazi plot to kidnap Winston Churchill. With Robert Duvall, Michael Caine, Jenny Agutter, Donald Pleasance and Donald Sutherland.
VHS: S17281. $9.98.
John Sturges, Great Britain, 1976, 134 mins.

The Eagle's Nest: Hitler's Secret Center of Power

A fascinating documentary series which chronicles the rise and fall of the Third Reich. You'll see rare color footage of the inner circle of Nazi fanatics, unique contemporary interviews with Albert Speer and other survivors, and much more.
Vol. I: The Early Years. As Germany struggles with the aftermath of WW I, the unstable Weimar Republic finds itself unable to control the splinter parties of both Left and Right. Failed artist Adolf Hitler discovers his true calling, politics, and becomes a member of the rising National Socialist party. Eventually, Hitler takes command of Germany, stirring it to a frenzy of nationalism and racism. German economic strength and military might increases, and Hitler hosts the '36 Olympic games. 60 mins.
VHS: S13660. $29.95.
Vol. II: Europe Falls before the Reich. A now fascist Germany annexes Austria. Hitler meets with Mussolini at the Berghof, while plans are laid to march into Czechoslovakia. Hitler's bold plan begins with the seizure of the Sudetenland, followed by the cynical non-aggression pact with Stalin. 60 mins.
VHS: S13661. $29.95.
Vol. III: A World War. In the summer of 1939 Europe realizes the awesome power of the Reich, but it is already too late. German armor rolls over most of the continent. The mask is removed, and the face of Germany's "New Order" becomes terrifyingly clear to the world. This program ends with the Swastika flying over Red Square in Stalingrad and, for a brief moment, it appears that the "master plan" has succeeded. 60 mins.
VHS: S13662. $29.95.
Vol. IV: The End of the Reich. The tide turns, as Hitler's forces, spread too thin and short of supplies, must assume the defensive. The prolonged war on the Eastern Front has drained Germany, and defeat becomes inevitable, though Germans continue to fight frantically to keep their hold. The U.S. has entered the war and the allies deliver the "coup de grace." A postscript shows a defeated Germany immediately after the war. 60 mins.
VHS: S13663. $29.95.

End of the Ordeal (1943-1945)

After D-Day the Yalta conference sets the stage for a divided Europe. The U.S. ends the war in the Pacific by bombing Hiroshima and Nagasaki. Eric Sevareid hosts this look at the final days of a terrible era. 24 mins.
VHS: S23594. $99.95.

Enola Gay and the Atomic Bombing of Japan

A&E crafted this video which shows every step of the military action that ended the war. From the development of the bomb to the devastation wrought on Japanese cities, dramatic footage shows the methodical process that changed the face of warfare. 75 mins.
VHS: S26690. $19.95.

Entertaining the Troops: American Entertainers in World War II

"As bad a time as that was," says Dorothy Lamour, "there was a happy atmosphere around Hollywood. It was like everybody was trying to hold up everybody else's morale." This unique documentary tells how Hollywood pitched in on the war effort, through film clips, reminiscences and newsreel footage, as American entertainment marshalled its forces to raise not only money but the spirits of the country's fighting men. With Abbott and Costello, Jack Benny, Bob Hope, Andrews Sisters, Lucille Ball, Dorothy Lamour, Mel Blanc, Bill Crosby, Lena Horne and many others.
VHS: S10945. $14.95.
Robert Mugge, USA, 1989, 90 mins.

The Eternal Jew

Dr. Fritz Hippler was responsible for this vicious anti-Semitic propaganda "documentary." Yiddish with English subtitles.
VHS: S34067. $29.95.
George Roland, USA, 1933, 63 mins.

The Eye of the Third Reich

Walter Frentz was Leni Riefenstahl's chief cameraman and a personal cameraman for Adolf Hitler. In this acclaimed film, director Jurgen Stumphaus has woven together interviews with Frentz, excerpts from Frentz's diaries from the '40s and today, and many samples of his work, to depict a man who made countless carefully composed pictures ennobling an inhuman regime. "An excellent documentary with excellent photography" (*Frankfurter Allgemeine Zeitung*).
VHS: S32068. $29.95.
Jurgen Stumphaus, Germany, 1994, 61 mins.

Fahnen Junker

From bayonet fighting to blasting bunkers, glacier climbing to sniper fire, here is the tough training that molded the leaders of Nazi armies. This original 1943 Nazi film depicts the life at German schools for infantry officers. 17 mins. German with English subtitles.
VHS: S08313. $24.95.

Famous Third Army

General George S. Patton commanded the U.S. Third Army during 281 days of incessant combat with the Germans in 1944 and '45. This documentary is a record of the Third Army's drive through France, Belgium, Luxembourg, Germany, Austria and Czechoslovakia. It features a fast-moving narrative of the strategy and tactics employed by the only American general considered by the Germans to be the equal of their best Panzer generals. 1950, 22 mins.
VHS: S32075. $19.95.

Festive Nuremberg (Festlisches Nurnberg)

Picking up where Leni Riefenstahl's *Triumph of the Will* left off, this German propaganda film features highlights from Party rallies at Nuremberg in 1936 and 1937. From Hitler's airfield arrival and motorcade, to mass folk-dance performances, parachute drops, cavalry, infantry and Panzer formations, artillery fire, live explosions and fireworks, torchlit marches and night rallies, the film argues its case for an ever-growing bond between party and nation. German with English subtitles. 1937, 21 mins.
VHS: S33105. $29.95.

Fight for the Sky

This British series utilizes rare footage, much of it obtained from archives in Eastern Europe, to document the air war during WWII. Available as a pre-pack (four tapes) at a discount, or individually.
Battle of Britain. With the surrender of France in 1940, the threat of invasion hung heavily over Britain and the British strategy to meet the German threat was due to one man—Sir Hugh Dowding. This documentary, using much newly discovered footage, gives full justice to the exceptional commander and to all the men and women who, during the dark summer of 1940, inflicted the first defeat on German arms. 60 mins.
VHS: S12455. $29.95.
Elite Forces. The paratroopers played a crucial role in WWII, providing some of the war's greatest heroes. The supposedly impregnable Belgian fortress of Eban-Emael, designed to stop an army, was eliminated by a handful of airborne attackers; the capture of Crete in 1941 by a purely airborne assault remains the great classic of its kind. This is their unique story. 60 mins.
VHS: S12453. $29.95.
Fighter Aces. The story of Air Aces charts the history of aerial combat from the Great War to the dawn of the jet age, using archive footage, much of which has been unavailable in the West since World War II, and documenting such aces as Baron von Richtofen, Oswald Boelcke, Billy Bishop, Herman Goering, Joseph Frantisek, Erich Hartman and others. 60 mins.
VHS: S12457. $29.95.
History of the Luftwaffe. The Luftwaffe became the handmaiden of Hitler's dream of conquest and a vital component of the blitzkrieg. But the fuhrer's continual demands upon his air force as he fanatically pursued his grand design forced the Luftwaffe into the role of a workhorse. 60 mins.
VHS: S12454. $29.95.
Pre-pack.
VHS: S12458. $113.81.

Fight of the Sky

Explores the lifestyle and heroism of the American Fighter Pilots who flew missions over Germany in World War II, illustrating the various types of fighters used to escort the bombers deep into enemy territory. 54 mins.
VHS: S10029. $29.95.

Fire on the Mountain

"Among the best documentaries about skiing ever filmed" (*Snow Country Magazine*), this is the extraordinary portrait of the men of the U.S. Army's 10th Mountain Division—world-class skiers, mountaineers and climbers who share their exploits in the only mountain and winter warfare division of World War II. Grand Prize winner at the 1995 Telluride Mountainfilm Festival. "Bracing exploits, hearty outdoorsmen, powerfully captured on film" (*New York Times*).
VHS: S31119. $29.95.
Beth Gage/George Gage, USA, 1996, 72 mins.

Fire Storm over Dresden

On the night of February 13th, 1945, began one of the most controversial raids of World War II: the bombing of Dresden. This film combines archival images of pre-war Dresden with a night of remembrance 45 years later in the Palace of Culture. Using information from Winston Churchill's diaries, the outspoken historian David Irving paints a comprehensive picture of the time, the background to the bombing, and the strategies employed. English commentary and German with English subtitles. 77 mins.
VHS: S33285. $29.95.

Franklin D. Roosevelt: The New Deal

The early years of this presidential giant are illuminated through photographs and newsreel appearances. 23 mins.
VHS: S23559. $49.95.

Franklin D. Roosevelt: The War Years

From 1941 to 1945, crucial events, anxieties and hard work kept this American President occupied with weighty matters that impacted the whole world. 20 mins.
VHS: S23561. $49.95.

Franklin D. Roosevelt: War Comes to America

The growing threat of European and Asian dictators is explored in this look at America before the Second World War. 20 mins.
VHS: S23560. $49.95.

Fuhrer: Rise of a Madman

Adolph Hitler's rise to power is plotted, from the many unsuccessful attempts to gain German leadership, to the horror of WWII and finally his suicide in the bunker. 108 mins.
VHS: S09253. $39.95.

Gable and Stewart in the Air Force

Winning Your Wings and *Wings Up* with Lieutenant James Stewart and Captain Clark Gable. 40 mins.
VHS: S32148. $24.95.

General Marshall Story

General George C. Marshall became the professional head of the U.S.Army on September 1, 1939. He was in charge of creating an army of more than eight million men, that would eventually defeat the armed forces of Germany, Japan and Italy. After the war he played an important part in managing the Cold War with communism. 1963, 29 mins.

VHS: S32076. $19.95.

George Stevens: A Filmmaker's Journey

An intimate documentary about the Hollywood director, the film weaves interviews, remembrances, on-camera interviews with his collaborators and colleagues, footage from his films and footage he shot during World War II. The interviews include Warren Beatty, Katharine Hepburn, Fred Astaire, Frank Capra and John Huston. "A wonderfully informative tribute, lit together with love, intelligence, wit and, most important of all, a knowledge of film history" (Vincent Canby).

Laser: LD71556. $49.95.
George Stevens Jr., USA, 1984, 111 mins.

George Stevens: D-Day to Berlin

Director George Stevens shot this documentary footage which depicts American efforts in Europe during World War II. It includes some of the most extensive color footage available of both the Normandy invasion and the fall of Berlin. This film won 3 Emmy Awards and was originally commissioned by Dwight D. Eisenhower. George Stevens, Jr. narrates. With William Saroyan, Irwin Shaw and Ivan Moffat.

VHS: S26760. $19.98.
George Stevens, USA, 50 mins.

Good Morning Mr. Hitler

Six weeks before the outbreak of World War II, a three-day festival in Munich celebrated "2,000 Years of German Culture." An amateur cameraman wangled permission to film the event. The result is this unique look at Hitler and the German people celebrating Nazi ideals. The contemporary filmmakers who retrieved this long-lost footage frame the material by showing an audience of elderly Germans watching this extraordinary home movie. Included is the daughter of the man who published *Mein Kampf*. It was she who had always said, "Good morning, Mr. Hitler," at Hitler's request.

VHS: S26995. $29.95.
Luke Holland/Paul Yule, Germany, 1994, 52 mins.

Gorch Fock

This exceptional German propaganda film depicts life and work aboard one of the German navy's training ships, the squarerigger *Gorch Fock*. Alternating shots juxtapose the ocean's rhythms with those of sailors at work, capturing both the exhilaration and rigors of life at sea. German with English subtitles.

VHS: S33109. $24.95.
Dr. Martin Rikli, Germany, 1934, 15 mins.

Great Days of History

A new series which culls rare footage of world archives to provide a comprehensive history of major events of the 20th century.

D-Day: 6 June 1944. This program relives the landings in Normandy in June, 1944. It shows the planning, the assembly of air, sea and land forces by Allied command, the embarkation from England across the Channel, the attack and landings, and the fierce German defense. 52 mins.

VHS: S09432. $29.95.

Mediterranean Front. This unique visual record shows the efforts of the Free French to gather and train in North Africa for the landing and reconquest of France from the south. The campaign that followed the Mediterranean landings is documented to its end in Marshall Keitel's final surrender. 26 mins.

VHS: S09431. $29.95.

World War II: Part 1—Munich to the Battle of Britain. The signposts of the war: Mussolini's adventure in Ethiopia, Franco's brutal insurrection in Spain, Hitler's annexation of the Sudetenland. This program begins with the Anschluss of Austria and the Munich nonaggression pact. Includes rare footage from German War archives, including the destruction of Warsaw, the phony war, Dunkirk, the invasion of France, the Battle of Britain. 51 mins.

VHS: S09428. $29.95.

The Great Escapes of World War II

From the prisoners of Stalag Luft II, the "White Mouse" of the French Resistance and the rescuers of Dunkirk, former POWs, resistance fighters, soldiers and guards tell the incredible stories of their plots, escapes and life-and-death secret missions during World War II. Two 50-minute tapes.

VHS: S31706. $29.95.

The Greatest Battle

Combining action, adventure and romance, this explosive wartime tale is set during the last North African campaigns of World War II, with action centering on the German Panzer Corps in Tunisia. Henry Fonda stars as an American general returning to active duty; German major Stacy Keach is his adversary. Features newsreel footage narrated by Orson Welles.

VHS: S31291. $14.98.
Umberto Lenzi, Italy, 1977, 97 mins.

Guadalcanal & The Shores of Iwo Jima

The Japanese depended heavily on two Pacific islands from which to launch their aggressive air attacks: Guadalcanal and Iwo Jima. The Marines were called on to wrest these islands from the Japanese, and both times were successful. This program examines these battles. 60 mins.

VHS: S13137. $19.98.

Guadalcanal Diary

Based on an eye-witness account of the Marine invasion of the Solomon Islands during World War II, this is war cinema at its most evocative and realistic. First-rate. With Preston Foster, Lloyd Nolan, William Bendix.

VHS: S12164. $19.98.
Lewis Seiler, USA, 1943, 93 mins.

Guilty Men

This short film shows a variety of guilty men. Included are scenes depicting the Nuremberg trials, executions of war criminals, the organization of Hitler Youth Camps, the Versailles Peace Treaty, Trotsky's storming of the Winter Palace in St. Petersburg, Trotsky's speech against Stalin, the progression of anti-Jewish propaganda and Gestapo terrorist acts. 1946, 40 mins.

VHS: S26683. $19.95.

Gulf of Danzig: German Once Again

Prepared by the German navy's own propaganda unit, this film features what were, literally, the opening salvos of World War II, as the battleship *Schleswig-Holstein* opens fire on Polish installations in Danzig harbor at daybreak September 1, 1939, and subsequent other blitzkrieg tactics are used on Poland.

VHS: S33110. $24.95.

Gung Ho!

Randolph Scott leads an assault on Mackin Island against the Japanese defenders. Lots of action in this fact-based chronicle of Carlson's Raiders. Some of the tough gyrenes participating are Robert Mitchum, Rod Cameron, Noah Beery Jr. and J. Carrol Naish. Watch out for snipers.

VHS: S04250. $19.95.
Ray Enright, USA, 1943, 88 mins.

Guns of Navarone

A first-rate World War II action film about a group of Allied commandos who are plotting to destroy German guns. Winner of an Academy Award for Special Effects. With Gregory Peck, David Niven, Anthony Quinn and Stanley Baker. VHS letterboxed.

VHS: S30921. $19.95.
Laser: Includes trailer. **LD72447. $49.95.**
J. Lee Thompson, USA, 1961, 157 mins.

Hans-Joachim Marseille: The Star of Africa

The story of one of the greatest fighter pilots of all time, the legendary "Star of Africa," who made his name flying with the Luftwaffe in the North African campaign before dying over El Alamein. Includes previously unavailable film footage and exclusive interviews from Marseille's commanding officer and survivors from his squadron. English narration. 47 mins.

VHS: S33283. $29.95.

Here Is Germany

Considered one of the most impressive documentaries made by the U.S. government during WWII, this film took over two years to produce. It draws heavily on hundreds of German motion-picture sources, tracing the development of Germany as a military power from the time of Frederick the Great to the end of the Third Reich. 52 mins.

VHS: S03348. $29.95.

The Heroes of Telemark

This explosive, epic war drama from the acclaimed director of *El Cid* stars Kirk Douglas and Richard Harris as resistance fighters who thwart the Nazis' endeavor to create an atomic bomb. Co-starring Sir Michael Redgrave and Ulla Jacobsson, this suspenseful winner is based on a true-life episode of World War II. Filmed on location for authenticity, *Telemark* features amazing action set pieces which Bosley Crowther of *The New York Times* praised as "brilliant and breathtaking."

VHS: S30774. $19.95.
Anthony Mann, USA, 1965, 130 mins.

Hidden Army

The 18,000,000 women who worked in American industry during World War II were the "hidden army" whose efforts helped the US and its allies vanquish their enemies. Produced by the U.S. Army Signal Corps to bolster sagging morale and lagging production, this film features hard-to-find footage of women performing "men's" jobs, from electronics assembly to fork-lift operation, providing valuable insight into this vital but underrated aspect of the war effort. 17 mins.

VHS: S06255. $59.95.

Hiroshima - Nagasaki, August 1945

In August 1945 the Japanese government commissioned filmmaker Akira Iwasaki, jailed during WWII for his antiwar beliefs, to document the effects of the new atomic weapon. The U.S. military classified this raw footage—the first shot following the bombings of Hiroshima and Nagasaki—as "secret" for over 20 years before making it public. In 1970, Prof. Barnouw obtained the historic footage and edited together this unforgettable film, adding a factual, eloquently understood narration. "Objective and poetic…strongly moving" (*The Village Voice*). 17 mins.

VHS: S30093. $79.00.

The History of World War II: Battle of Midway

John Ford's documentary on the Battle of Midway, the large-scale naval engagement that irrevocably changed the course of the war, giving the momentum to the American forces. Ford was hurt during the shooting.

VHS: S19677. $19.95.
John Ford, USA, 1943, 18 mins.

The History of World War II: December 7th

John Ford re-staged the Japanese attack on Pearl Harbor by using Hollywood sound stages to approximate the confusion, panic and disorder. Winner of the Academy Award for Best Documentary Production in 1943.

VHS: S19676. $19.95.
John Ford, USA, 1943, 34 mins.

The History of World War II: Desert Victory

This British-made documentary chronicles the battles of the American Army and German Nazi units under the command of Field Marshall Rommel, the Desert Fox. During the making of the film, four British cameramen were killed, seven wounded and six captured. Winner of the 1943 Academy Award for Best Documentary Feature. 54 mins.

VHS: S19678. $19.95.

Hitler

Learn how a sexually-confused nobody rose to power and turned his sick beliefs into a national ideology. From the series *The Nazis*. 50 mins.

VHS: S12733. $24.98.

Hitler Youth Quex

This Nazi propaganda film tells the story of a boy at odds with his abusive and unemployed communist father. At a communist camp, the boy is disturbed by his comrades and joins the Nazis instead. Ultimately a group of Left-wing radicals hunts him down. Based on K.A. Schenzinger's novel. German with English subtitles.

VHS: S23801. $24.95.
Hans Steinhoff, Germany, 1933, 100 mins.

Hitler's Constructions

This 1938 German propaganda film illustrates Hitler's call for a new German art following the glories of earlier Gothic and Baroque construction and Germany's architectural "decay" represented by the Bauhaus school. Hitler's National Socialist "architectural legacy" of construction would include youth hostels and party schools, bridge projects, the Autobahn, ministries and party buildings, the Zeppelinfield at Nuremberg, and the Olympia Stadium complex in Berlin. German with English subtitles. 1938, 17 mins.

VHS: S33108. $29.95.

Hitler's Henchmen (MPI)

Made by the United States government, this film was pulled from circulation in 1946 because of its attack on the German people. Originally titled *Here Is Germany*, this is a classic propaganda documentary on the "Germanic War Spirit." 58 mins.

VHS: S13112. $39.98.

Hitler: The Final Chapter

This video documentary puts to rest the myths about Adolf Hitler's final days. Many wondered if he lived, but this tape offers the facts about the madman's demise. 51 mins.

VHS: S25991. $29.95.

Hitler: The Whole Story

This is the story behind the madman who oversaw the cataclysmic destruction of World War II, Adolph Hitler.
The ruthless would-be ruler of all Europe is revealed in this documentary, using detailed biographical materials and historic research.

VHS: S20938. $49.95.

Home of the Brave

The story of racial abuse against a black soldier in a combat squad in WW II is a hard-hitting drama. James Edwards is the G.I. under fire from his own buddies. With Lloyd Bridges, Steve Brodie, Frank Lovejoy and Jeff Corey as the shrink.
VHS: S04252. $19.98.
Laser: CLV. **LD71990. $29.98.**
Mark Robson, USA, 1949, 86 mins.

How Hitler Lost the War

A provocative account that challenges a lot of conventional theories about the Germans' defeat in World War II, suggesting Allied victory was due to Hitler's strategic mistakes. The film is told from the perspective of high-ranking Third Reich military officers and uses animated maps, documentary footage and interviews. 67 mins.
VHS: S18135. $29.95.

Hymn for a Nation

Arturo Toscanini conducts the NBC Orchestra in this World War II tribute to the fight against Facism and Nazism. Music by Verdi. USA, 1944.
VHS: S02592. $34.95.

I'm a Civilian Here Myself!

The U.S. Navy hired Robert Benchley to explain how the Navy was making civilians out of sailors. Included are such tidbits on the advantages of civilian life as the right to choose the company of any pretty girl, civil service jobs, insurance. Ava Gardner appears briefly. 25 mins.
VHS: S06931. $19.95.

The Invisible War

The history of technological warfare and its impact on world politics is explored from World War II to the computerized warfare of Desert Storm. Three-tape set. Each tape is 50 mins.
VHS: S31635. $39.98.

Jud Suess

Still banned in Germany (except for educational viewings), this scandalous, classic Nazi anti-Semitic propoganda film caused riots at its screenings and disaster for its cast and crew. The Third Reich's most notorious fictional expression of policy, it is the story of a Jew who rises to power under the duchy of Wuerttemberg by abusing and raping Aryans. German with English subtitles.
VHS: S34066. $29.95.
Veit Harlan, Germany, 1940, 100 mins.

Kamikaze

Extraordinary newsreel footage is deployed in this documentary about the conflict between the U.S. and Japan during World War II. Kamikaze pilots were a tactic used by the Japanese when they sensed that the tide had turned against them. The US response was a controversial measure. Atomic war was seen as a final solution that would lead to the surrender of Japan.
VHS: S24083. $19.95.
Perry Wolf, USA/France, 1961, 85 mins.

Kamikaze: Death from the Sky

The Allied forces were utterly confounded by the emergence of the Kamikaze fighter pilots from Japan during the end of World War II—soldiers on a suicide mission who would crash their bomb-laden aircraft onto the decks of U.S. naval carriers in the Pacific. This is the remarkable story of the doomed Kamikaze. 60 mins.
VHS: S13139. $29.98.

Life of Adolf Hitler

Paul Rotha's famous documentary uses archival footage to depict the rise of the Nazi party in a powerful study of one of the horrors of history. Much of the footage used by Rotha is rare, including the last films of Hitler before his retreat into the Bunker.
VHS: S00751. $29.95.
Paul Rotha, Great Britain, 1961, 101 mins.

Listen to Britain

Four great poetic documentaries by Humphrey Jennings, all set during World War II by this great English filmmaker: *Listen to Britain, The True Story of Lili Marlene, A Diary for Timothy* and *The Cumberland Story*.
VHS: S02953. $79.95.
Humphrey Jennings, Great Britain, 1942-47, 120 mins.

The Lonely Struggle: Marek Edelman, Last Hero of the Warsaw Ghetto Uprising

This cardiologist from Lodz is the last surviving member of the leadership that marshalled the heroic forces of resistance which fought the Nazis under hopeless circumstances. This insider's account vividly recreates a moment of unparalleled courage. 60 mins.
VHS: S23236. $39.95.

March of Time: America at War

A six-volume series.
American Defense, Part 1. America's New Army; Men of the Fleet; Prelude to Victory; We Are the Marines. 112 mins.
VHS: S05090. $19.95.
American Defense, Part 2. The Navy and the Nation; Invasion!; Airways to Peace; Naval Log of Victory; Back Door to Tokyo; Uncle Sam, Mariner? The Unknown Battle. 126 mins.
VHS: S05091. $19.95.
Friend and Foe, Part 1. Battlefields of the Pacific, Far East Command, The Argentine Question, India in Crisis, India at War, the Fighting French, One Day of War—Russia, 1943. 116 mins.
VHS: S05086. $19.95.
Friend and Foe, Part 2. The New Canada; Inside Fascist Spain, Then Japan, Portugal—Europe's Crossroads; Sweden's Middle Road; South American Front— 1944. 87 mins.
VHS: S05087. $19.95.
Friend and Foe, Part 3. The Irish Question, Underground Report; British Imperialism—1944; What To Do with Germany; Inside China Today; Report of Italy; Memo from Britain. 113 mins.
VHS: S05088. $19.95.
On the Homefront. Our America at War; Then Air Raids Strike; Men in Washington—1942; The FBI Front; Bill Jack vs. Adolf Hitler; The West Coast Question; Spotlight on Congress. 114 mins.
VHS: S05089. $19.95.
March of Time: America at War, Gift-Pack. All six volumes of the March of Time America at War series, with a special collector's edition gift-pack.
VHS: S06406. $99.95.

March of Time: Post War Problems and Solutions

A new series of March of Time compilations, winner of the Special Academy Award in 1936, hosted by Westbrook Van Voorhis.
America's Post-War Problems, Part 1. Post-war jobs? Post-war farms. The returning veteran wanted: more homes. Problem drinkers. Is everyone happy? The American cop. 125 mins.
VHS: S06454. $19.95.
America's Post-War Problems, Part 2. The teachers' crisis. Your doctors—1947. New trains for old. T-men in action. The presidential year. Stop—Heavy Traffic. The nation's mental health. 119 mins.
VHS: S06455. $19.95.
Post-War Problems Beyond, Part 1. The new U.S. frontier. Palestine problem. 18 million orphans. Justice comes to Germany. Report on Greece. The new France. 107 mins.
VHS: S06456. $19.95.
Post-War Problems Beyond, Part 2. World Food problem. The Soviet's neighbor, Czechoslovakia. Germany—handle with care. Storm over Britain XIII/13. Turkey's 100 million. End of an Empire? Policeman's holiday. 125 mins.
VHS: S06457. $19.95.
Modern Main Street U.S.A. Public relations.... This means you. White collar girls. Farming pays off. Mid century: half-way to where? Where's the fire? 120 mins.
VHS: S06458. $19.95.
Post-War Problems and Solutions Gift-Pack. All five volumes of this March of Time series, at a special price.
VHS: S06453. $89.95.

March of Time: Trouble Abroad

A continued look at the world during the first half of the 20th century.
Germany and Other Problems. Inside Nazi Germany, Russians in Exile, Old Dixie's New Look, One Million Mission, Arms and the League, Brain Trust Island, Nazi Conquest — No. 1, Crime and Prison. 93 mins.
VHS: S08052. $19.95.
Spotlight on War. Men of Medicine, G-Men of the Sea, Threat to Gibraltar, Man at the Wheel, Prelude to Conquest, Father Divine's Deal, The British Dilemma, U.S. Fire Fighters. 91 mins.
VHS: S08053. $19.95.
Tensions Increase. Junk and War, England's DORA, Fiorello La Guardia, Crisis in Algeria, U.S. Secret Service, Alaska's Salmon War, Britain's Gambling Fever. 76 mins.
VHS: S08051. $19.95.
Uncle Sam: The Observer. Inside the Maginot Line, Uncle Sam: The Good Neighbor, The Refugee — Today and Tomorrow, State of the Nation, Mexico's New Crisis, Young America. 75 mins.
VHS: S08054. $19.95.
War Abroad: Depression at Home. Poland and War, The Dust Bowl, Goods for Sale, The 49th State, Babies Wanted, Rockefeller Millions, Rehearsal for War, The Spoils System, Youth in Camps. 71 mins.
VHS: S08050. $19.95.
War, Peace and America. The Mediterranean — Background for War, Japan — Master of the Orient, Dixie — U.S.A., War, Peace and Propaganda, Metropolis — 1939. 91 mins.
VHS: S08055. $19.95.
Complete Set.
VHS: S08049. $119.70.

March of Time: War Breaks Out

A six-volume series.
Americans Prepare, Part 1. Uncle Sam, the Farmer (with war raging in Europe, the farmer's task of feeding Americans at home and abroad is enormously increased) and The Ramparts We Watch (controversial feature which explores the effect war has on citizens of an average American town). 118 mins.
VHS: S05080. $19.95.
Americans Prepare, Part 2. Labor and Defense; Uncle Sam: The Non-Belligerent; Men of the FBI (The FBI combats espionage); New England's Eight Million Yankees (New England prepares for war); Thumbs Up, Texas! and Main Street, U.S.A. 113 mins.
VHS: S05081. $19.95.
Praying for Peace. The Vatican of Pius XII (Pope Pius XII tries to bring about peace) and The Story of the Vatican. 71 mins.
VHS: S05085. $19.95.
The Military Prepares. Soldiers with Wings; Crisis in the Pacific, the U.S. Navy: 1940; Gateways to Panama; Arms and the Men: U.S.A.; Crisis in the Atlantic; Sailors with Wings. 124 mins.
VHS: S05082. $19.95.
The Battle Beyond, Part 1. Battle Fleets of England; Newsfronts of War: 1940; The Republic of Finland; Canada at War; The Philippines: 1898-1946; Spoils of Conquest. 107 mins.
VHS: S05083. $19.95.
The Battle Beyond, Part 2. On Foreign Newsfronts; Britain's Royal Air Force; Mexico: Good Neighbor's Dilemma; Australia at War; China Fights Back; Peace: By Adolf Hitler; Norway in Revolt. 112 mins.
VHS: S05084. $19.95.
March of Time: War Breaks Out, Gift-Pack. All six volumes of the March of Time War Breaks Out series in a special gift-pack.
VHS: S03031. $99.95.

March to the Fuhrer

A propaganda classic produced during Hitler's reign in Germany—a showcase for Hitler's means of building mass hysteria. German with NO subtitles.
VHS: S10592. $29.95.

Marine Raiders

Pat O'Brien and Robert Ryan co-star as devil-dogs in action both on and off the battlefields in a fast-paced action drama. Another flag-waver to boost U.S. morale.
VHS: S12379. $19.98.
Harold Schuster, USA, 1943, 90 mins.

The Marines Are Coming

Conrad Nagel and William Hayes are featured in this melodramatic short film. A marine lieutenant is confronted with a beautiful Latin dancer who will simply not leave him alone. 1934, 71 mins.
VHS: S26684. $19.95.

The Marines at Tarawa/ To the Shores of Iwo Jima

These two documentaries bring the terrifying reality of Pacific World War II battlefields to the screen. *To the Shores of Iwo Jima* even won an Oscar for Best Documentary. Few works show the details of war with this kind of graphic intensity. 20 mins each.
VHS: S21992. $19.95.

Marines Have Landed

This program tells the story of the U.S. Marines, unmatched in their fight against the Axis during World War II. Their most celebrated battles are recounted here, using dramatic footage. 60 mins.
VHS: S13136. $19.98.

Masters of War

A 13-tape series.
Masters of War—Battle for North Africa. One of the crucial battles of WWII showcases the different styles of two great leaders: the methodical and calculating Field Marshall Bernard "Monty" Montgomery and the brilliantly daring "Desert Fox," General Erwin Rommel. 45 mins.
VHS: S33974. $19.98.
Masters of War—Battle for the Boot. From Salerno to Rome, U.S. General Mark Clark and British General Sir Harold Alexander slug their way up the Italian boot, facing crack German divisions commanded by wily Luftwaffe Field Marshall Albert Kesselring. 47 mins.
VHS: S33964. $19.98.
Masters of War—Blitzkrieg Battle: The Battle for France. Bold and innovative, General Heinz Guderian was the leading exponent of Germany's Blitzkrieg tactics. In 1944, U.S. General Omar Bradly employed huge "land fleets" of mechanized armor to take back France, using the very same Blitzkrieg tactics. 45 mins.
VHS: S33965. $19.98.
Masters of War—Day of Decision. Operation Overlord—the invasion of France. D-Day pitted the best Allied leaders—Eisenhower, Montgomery, Marshall and Bradley—against Axis warriors Rommel and Von Runstedt in a battle of what has been called "The Longest Day." 45 mins.
VHS: S33975. $19.98.

Masters of War—Endgame: The Cold Warriors. Civilization teetered on the edge of extinction as Kennedy and Krushev fought a deadly battle of brinksmanship. Relive the Cuban Missile Crisis, when the U.S. and the U.S.S.R. caused the world to hold its breath. 47 mins.
VHS: S33968. $19.98.
Masters of War—Guerilla Warfare: Vietnam. Peasant General Vo Nguyen Giap vs. U.S. General William Westmoreland—these men commanded armies that pounded and pursued each other throughout Indochina. See the consequences during Ia Drang in 1965, and the Tet Offensive in 1968. 46 mins.
VHS: S33971. $19.98.
Masters of War—In the Lair of the Bear. Zhukov, the brilliant and ruthless Russian General, stops the Nazi Panzers at the gates of Moscow. A year later, he masterminds the offensive that annihilates the methodical General von Paulus' 6th Army at Stalingrad. 46 mins.
VHS: S33963. $19.98.
Masters of War—Operation Pointblank. U.S. General Carl Spaatz and British Air Marshall Sir Arthur "Bomber" Harris direct the largest air campaign ever—the strategic bombing of Germany. Repelling the assault are the Luftwaffe fighters of Goering—"The Fat One." 46 mins.
VHS: S33970. $19.98.
Masters of War—Patton's Charge. Maverick, pistol-packing General George Patton mounts a rapid, full-scale assault behind the German lines, driving his tank corps night and day, racing to save the besieged 101st Airborne. 45 mins.
VHS: S33969. $19.98.
Masters of War—The Battle for Leyte Gulf. When Japanese Admiral Toyoda divides his forces, Admiral Halsey charges after the decoy carriers. But Admiral Sprague's carriers and Admiral Oldendorf's Battlewagons carry the day in the battle that broke the back of the Japanese Navy. 45 mins.
VHS: S33973. $19.98.
Masters of War—The Knights of Desert Storm. Believing no Arab nation would ever unite with "infidels," Saddam Hussein defied the world and invaded Kuwait. Watch General Schwarzkopf's coalition forces, including Arabs, Americans, French and British, shatter Hussein's illusions. 47 mins.
VHS: S33966. $19.98.
Masters of War—The Turning Point at Guadalcanal. Guadalcanal was the bloody seesaw campaign that began America's march across the Pacific to ultimate victory. Watch General Alexander Vandegrift and Admiral William F. "Bull" Halsey square off aginst the legendary Japanese Admiral Yamamoto. 44 mins.
VHS: S33972. $19.98.
Masters of War—Wolfpack: The Hidden Enemy. Watch German Admiral Carl Donetz lead his U-Boat wolfpacks in an effort to sever England's maritime lifeline. The English fight back with convoys, patrol planes and sophisticated code-breaking to ferret out the hidden enemy. 45 mins.
VHS: S33967. $19.98.

Mein Kampf
The most credible and accurate depiction of the actual steps taken by Adolf Hitler to conquer the world. In this specially remastered and re-released original length version, the mind-numbing truth of these events is laid bare. Every shot in this film is authentic, including never-before-seen footage from the secret archives of the Nazi SS Elite Guard.
VHS: S02548. $39.95.
Erwin Leiser, USA, 1960, 120 mins.

Mein Krieg (My Private War)
An eerie compilation of home movies and oral histories of six Wehrmacht soldiers who were involved in the Nazi invasion of the former Soviet Union. The images of the war (soldiers swimming in the Black Sea, bombed out landscapes and literally thousands of dead bodies) are contrasted with the soldiers' memories and reminiscences of their experiences. "*Mein Krieg* is annotated only by the veterans themselves as they explicate the material they produced nearly a half-century before" (J. Hoberman, *The Village Voice*).
VHS: S19859. $79.95.
Harriet Eder/Thomas Kufus, Germany, 1990, 90 mins.

Memoirs of a Barbed Wire Surgeon: An Interview with Elmer Shabart M.D., FACS
One surgeon's incredible legacy as a prisoner of the Japanese during World War II. Elmer Shabart was a survivor of the Bataan Death March who managed to continue practicing his profession throughout the ordeal, without instruments, anesthetics, antibiotics, medicines, or simple supplies.
VHS: S33828. $24.95.
Claire Burch, USA, 1996, 70 mins.

Men Against Tanks/ Engineers to the Front
A Nazi-produced documentary, as German soldiers re-enact combat exploits for this elaborate and frightening film showing how infantrymen battle Soviet armored attacks. In *Engineers to the Front*, German engineer/soldiers—the men who paved the way for the blitzkrieg—lift mines, build bridges and force river crossings under fire. 58 mins. German with English subtitles.
VHS: S08312. $39.95.

Mig Alley
Mig Alley was a combat zone in Northwest Korea where formations of up to 200 jets would dogfight at speeds up to 1200 m.p.h. This program is a recording of this fantastic period. 60 mins.
VHS: S13119. $19.98.

Mine Eyes Have Seen the Glory: The Women's Army Corps
Mariette Hartley, award-winning actress and the author of the best-selling autobiography *Breaking the Silence*, narrates this look at the Women's Army Corps. Known as WAC, the Corps was founded during World War II, paving the way for today's gender-integrated armed forces. Includes interviews with former directors, officers and enlisted women of the WAC.
VHS: S27301. $29.95.
Dane Hansen, USA, 1996

More Than Broken Glass: Memories of Kristallnacht
The night of November 9, 1938 is forever etched in the minds of the Jewish people. Through archival footage, photographs and interviews with witnesses, a sharp portrait is created of the time and place. 57 mins.
VHS: S12904. $39.95.

Mussolini: Rise and Fall of a Dictator
New facts revealed about Italy's controversial figure, from his sexual relationship with his mistress to his love/hate relationship with his father. 105 mins.
VHS: S09252. $39.95.

Nagasaki Journey
This compelling production portrays the aftermath of the atomic bomb dropped on the city of Nagasaki from both an American and Japanese perspective, and presents moving personal stories from two Japanese survivors and eyewitness recollections from U.S. Marines. Includes never-before-seen color footage shot during the occupation by Marine cinematographers, as well as striking black-and-white still photos taken the day after the blast by Japanese Army photographer Yosuke Yamahata. 27 mins.
VHS: S30092. $79.00.

National Geographic Video: Last Voyage of the Lusitania
When the Lusitania was sunk by a German U-boat, few thought that anyone would ever look upon this magnificent ship ever again. Now underwater photography grants us a close look at the remains of a disaster that claimed 1200 innocent lives in 18 minutes.
VHS: S21150. $19.95.

National Geographic Video: The Lost Fleet of Guadalcanal
Dr. Robert Ballard leads a joint expedition with the U.S. Navy in the South Pacific to unearth the ships, planes, materials and wreckage from the fierce World War II battles. The program blends archival footage of the battles with stories and anecdotes related by survivors and participants. 60 mins.
VHS: S18991. $19.95.
Laser: LD71889. $29.95.

Nazi War Crime Trials
This collection contains five newsreels, one theatrical trailer and a short documentary from the Soviet Union on the Nuremberg Trials. Includes footage of executions by firing squad and by hanging of Nazi war criminals. Also the trial of Yamashita, the Tiger of Malaya, is covered, even though he was not a Nazi. USSR film in English. USA/USSR, 1945, 67 mins.
VHS: S05506. $29.95.

Nazi War Crimes
Witness the Nazis' shocking slaughter of over 200,000 innocent civilians at the Ukrainian Babi-Yar ravine. From the series *The Nazis*. 50 mins.
VHS: S12731. $24.98.

Nazi War Crimes: Babi-Yar
Babi-Yar, a pastoral Ukrainian ravine outside Kiev, was occupied by the Nazis in 1941 and used for human extermination experiments. Testimonies of victims who escaped complete a portrait of an incident in history never to be forgotten. 50 mins.
VHS: S12711. $19.95.

Nazis Strike
The Nazis move through Europe, taking over Czechoslovakia and Poland. Using rare documentary footage, this film looks at the Nazi conquest of Europe. 40 mins.
VHS: S03059. $19.95.

Nazis...Lest We Forget!
The first film on this tape, *Nuremberg und Sein Lehre* (*Nuremberg and Its Lesson*), was created to show the German people the full extent of Nazi atrocities. Footage from camps makes it quite unnerving. Narrated in English. Then, to the strains of Luftwaffe songs, *Flieger am Feind* (*A Nazi Newsreel*), shows how the Nazis used air power to terrorize urban populations and fight the allies. 35 mins.
VHS: S24077. $19.95.

Never So Few
John Sturges's World War II epic about jungle fighting, its story centers around American soldiers advising Burmese guerrillas, written by blacklisted writer Dalton Trumbo (under the pen name Millard Kaufman), from the novel by Tom Chamales. With Frank Sinatra, Gina Lollobrigida, Peter Lawford, Steve McQueen and Paul Henreid.
Laser: LD71165. $39.98.
John Sturges, USA, 1959, 124 mins.

The Newsreel Library of World War II
While the war raged in distant European lands, the newsreel brought pictures of battles to the local theater screen. This was the only opportunity the country had to search for familiar faces fighting overseas. Emotional images that united the nation included the rise of Hitler, France's surrender, the battles of Normandy, Patton's amazing offensive, and the dramatic end of the war.
VHS: S15949. $29.95.

Nightfighters: The Tuskegee Airmen
In World War II, Lt. Col. Benjamin Davis led an elite black group of bombers, support crew and surgical teams over Italy and North Africa. Though these African-American servicemen valiantly shielded white flyers, the army largely ignored their contribution. This video tells their story. 52 mins.
VHS: S27661. $59.95.

None But the Brave
U.S. Marine Frank Sinatra crash lands on a Pacific atoll during World War II...and discovers it's held by Japanese troops. After some taut action and suspense the enemies eventually make peace. Believe it or not, this anti-war melodrama was directed by Frankie himself.
VHS: S13620. $19.98.
Laser: LD70645. $34.98.
Frank Sinatra, USA, 1965, 106 mins.

Normandy Invasion
The largest sea invasion ever attempted is chronicled in this detailed account of the June 6, 1944 assault on the beaches of Normandy, using rare documentary footage.
VHS: S02580. $19.95.

Normandy: The Great Crusade
Normandy was the site where the great reclamation of the European continent began ending the iron grip of the Third Reich. This documentary tells the history of that famous battle with expert documentation based on genuine archival and biographical sources.
VHS: S20937. $19.95.

Nostalgia World War II Video Library #1
Produced by the U.S. War Department, these three short films made in 1944- 45 let the folks on the homefront know we were winning but it wasn't over just yet. *Battle Wreckage* shows the need for more steel. *The Wars Speed Up*, narrated by Jose Ferrer, with Robert Mitchum in a brief role, reminds us "that the war begins every day." *It Can't Last* expresses the hope of all involved. USA, 1944-45, 46 mins.
VHS: S05502. $24.95.

Nostalgia World War II Video Library #2
The early days of the war on the American homefront. The building of the Alcan highway. Veronica Lake cuts her hair to benefit work safety in war factories. Unnecessary personal travel tips. The biography of a ball bearing. Plus much more. Camouflage in New Guinea. USA, 1942-43, 51 mins.
VHS: S05505. $24.95.

Nostalgia World War II Video Library #3
U.S. combat footage from the land, the sea and the air courtesy of the Signal Corps and the U.S. Coast Guard. Beach landings in the Mediterranean. Dogfights over England. Bombing missions in the Pacific. The building and launching of a new transport ship, from luxury liner to troop transport. And much more. USA, 1944, 61 mins.
VHS: S05496. $24.95.

Nostalgia World War II Video Library #4
An unusual collection of Hollywood and U.S. Government film shorts which include nine dramatic episodes. Performers include Ronald Reagan, Burgess Meredith, Susan Hayward and Richard Arlen. Songs include "The Marine Hymn," "Keep 'Em Rolling," and "We've Got Another Bond to Buy," sung by Bing Crosby. USA, 1943-45, 61 mins.
VHS: S05494. $24.95.

Nostalgia World War II Video Library #5
The aftermath of the war is dealt with in two short subjects. *Diary of a Sergeant* is a dramatized documentary of the life of Harold Russell, who lost both hands in the war and later won an Oscar for his role in *The Best Years of Our Lives*. The second short, *The Atom Strikes*, traces the development of the A-Bomb and visits Nagasake and Hiroshima for the dramatic results of science at war. USA, 1945, 53 mins.
VHS: S05510. $24.95.

Nostalgia World War II Video Library #6
The fight against Japanese imperialism is documented in this three-part collection. *Inside Fighting China* (1942), *Target Japan* (1944), and *The Fleet That Came to Stay* (1946), which is directed by Budd Boetticher, each reflect the feelings of the time. See America fight back.
VHS: S05497. $24.95.
Budd Boetticher, USA, 1942-46, 52 mins.

Nostalgia World War II Video Library #7
Combat footage from Tarawa beach. Hawaiian Jungle Training. P-47's in action over England. A hill in Italy that took $2 million to take. Also Elisha Cook Jr. as a scared GI in *Baptism of Fire* (1943), a short film so realistic it was nominated for an Oscar for Best Documentary. USA, 1943-44, 57 mins.
VHS: S05498. $24.95.

Nostalgia World War II Video Library #8
Selected footage of the Big One as seen by the Signal Corps. See "dead Japanese, stinking in the sun." Witness "American soldiers with war in their faces." From New Guinea to Anzio beach to Burma and Britain. Also a "Private Snafu" cartoon with the voice of Mel Blanc. American propaganda at its finest. USA, 1944, 59 mins.
VHS: S05495. $24.95.

Nostalgia World War II Video Library #9
Ronald Reagan narrates *The Fight for the Sky*. Vice President Henry A. Wallace explains *The Price of Victory*. And the Signal Corps documents our men in uniform and bombing raids over Germany and in the Pacific. Highlights of the Army and Air Force in action. USA, 1942-44, 61 mins.
VHS: S05499. $24.95.

Nostalgia World War IIVideo Library #10
San Pietro is the unforgettable documentary by John Huston that shows in detail a key World War II battle over an Italian farming valley. *Story of a Transport* is also a documentary about war produced by the American armed forces. It shows how troops were transported by ship overseas. 59 mins.
VHS: S24079. $14.95.

Nostalgia World War IIVideo Library #11
This collection of short documentaries tells the story of the US at war. It includes *What Makes a Battle, The Fifth Army Report from the Beachhead, Freedom Comes High, The 957th Day* and *We Said We'd Come Back*. 60 mins.
VHS: S24072. $19.95.

Nostalgia World War IIVideo Library #12
These seven short films detail a number of specific issues about the US effort in the Second World War. *Objective...Security, The Army Nurse* (includes footage of Gary Cooper), *Photography Fights, Lt. General Holland M. Smith, Sixth War Loan Appeal, RAF and 8th Air Force Report from Britain* and *Target Invisible* are all included in this compilation. 67 mins.
VHS: S24084. $24.95.

Nova—Echoes of War
At the beginning of World War II, radar was a crude warning device. By 1945, it was a sophisticated electronic eye that could pinpoint and track aircraft and guide bombing missions at night. This program explores the unprecedented collaboration between civilian scientists and military that turned the war into a technological chess match. 60 mins.
VHS: S11650. $14.98.

Nuremburg
This captured footage of Nazi concentration camps is quite disturbing and not for those who are easily upset. 1945, 23 mins.
VHS: S26681. $19.95.

Of Pure Blood
The secret details of Hitler's plan to transform Germany into a pure Aryan nation are uncovered. From the series *The Nazis*. 50 mins.
VHS: S12734. $19.98.

Operation Crossbow
Michael Anderson's superb World War II thriller written by Emeric Pressburger about a group of highly skilled commandos assigned an apparent suicide mission to break up Hitler's secret wartime experiments with rocket weapons, the V-1 and V-2. With George Peppard, Sophia Loren, Trevor Howard, Tom Courtenay and Anthony Quayle. Letterboxed.
VHS: S21021. $19.98.
Laser: LD71660. $39.98.
Michael Anderson, USA, 1965, 116 mins.

Our Job in Japan
A U.S. propaganda film like this shows how much attitudes have changed since the war. It describes how the defeated Japanese should be regarded once they were no longer a clear military threat. 1943, 18 mins.
VHS: S26682. $19.95.

Our Soviet Allies, World War II
Four historical programs combine authentic WWII footage with recollections of misty-eyed veterans to document the great Soviet victories of World War II. From the *Inside the Soviet Union* series. 80 mins.
VHS: S12710. $19.95.

Out of the Ashes (1945-1949)
As the trials at Nuremberg and the military tribunal in Tokyo condemn Nazis and war criminals to death, the Cold War begins and communism is established in China. 24 mins.
VHS: S23595. $99.95.

P.O.W.—Americans in Enemy Hands: World War II, Korea and Vietnam
This inspiring documentary tells the stories of nine different men who were captured in three wars. With amazing candor they describe the imprisonment and torture that they survived. Their stories provide a glimpse into the resiliency of the human spirit. Directed by Carol L. Fleischer. 93 mins.
VHS: S21248. $19.95.

Patton: Old Blood and Guts
Ronald Reagan narrates Patton's warrior legacy in this program about the American commander who led his men farther, faster and harder. 25 mins.
VHS: S09251. $19.95.

Payoff in the Pacific
This World War II documentary focuses on the land war in the Pacific. Produced by the U.S. government, archive footage follows the Marines and the Army as they fight island to island against a well entrenched enemy. Authentic combat footage is presented in black and white. 59 mins.
VHS: S09523. $19.95.

Pearl Harbor: Two Hours That Shook the World
ABC News joined forces with Japan's oldest and largest network to produce this retrospective of the attack on Pearl Harbor. 100 mins.
VHS: S15879. $19.98.

Piece of Cake: Complete Set
During World War II, an RAF Hornet Squadron must undergo the rites of passage that will make them seasoned fighter pilots. Their aristocratic CO is arrogant and overconfident. Eventually the concerns of his squadron overtake his attitude as adventure and heartache build toward the climactic battle.
VHS: S21689. $99.98.
Ian Toynton, Great Britain, 1994, 650 mins.

Prelude to War (1935-1939)
Eric Sevareid hosts this documentary about the years just before the outbreak of World War II. As the Axis powers align for war, Japan conquers one third of China. When Stalin suddenly signs a peace pact with Hitler, the U.S. prepares for war. 22 mins.
VHS: S23591. $99.95.

Private Film Collection of Eva Braun
Life at Hitler's mountain refuge—the Berghof—filmed by his mistress, Eva Braun. Spectacular Alpine panoramas highlight scenes of Nazi leaders, foreign diplomats, and local visitors, with candid views of Hitler in war and peacetime chatting with children, conferring with subordinates, relaxing after victories, and recovering after Stalingrad offer a unique picture of the Fuehrer's private life. English commentary. Color. 60 mins. Germany 1936-43.
VHS: S08314. $29.95.

PT 109
Oscar-winner Cliff Robertson is the war hero (and subsequent president) John F. Kennedy in this somewhat routine WW II drama about the U.S. patrol boats that tried to cut off Japanese supply lines in the Solomon Islands. When the craft is nearly sliced in half by a Japanese destroyer, a young Jack Kennedy struggles to save the crew. Also on tap are several shorts and "trailers" to upcoming releases on this two-cassette package. Letterboxed.
VHS: S02562. $19.98.
Laser: LD70737. $39.98.
Robert McKimson, USA, 1963, 159 mins.

Raid on Rommel
In North Africa during World War II, a British officer releases his prisoners of war and leads them on an assault on Tobruk. Stars Richard Burton, John Calicos, Clinton Greyn and Wolfgang Preiss.
VHS: S16301. $14.95.
Henry Hathaway, USA, 1971, 99 mins.

Remember Pearl Harbor
This deeply moving 50th anniversary commemoration of the attack on Pearl Harbor is presented in a style similar to the highly acclaimed *Civil War* series. It features exclusive interviews and commentary, as well as never-before-seen Japanese footage. USA.
VHS: S15352. $14.98.

Report from the Aleutians
American forces live under tough conditions from which they raid Japanese bases. Written and directed for the U.S. Armed Forces by John Huston, and narrated by John Huston with additional narration by Walter Huston. 45 mins.
VHS: S02589. $34.95.

Return to Iwo Jima
Hosted by Ed McMahon, a documentary about four American and two Japanese veterans as they return to Iwo Jima. Produced by PBS for the February 19, 1985 anniversary commemorating the 40 years since the famous island battle.
VHS: S02405. $29.95.

The Rise and Fall of Adolf Hitler (Films for the Humanities)
This exhaustive biography covers the tumultuous career of the failed Austrian artist who nearly conquered the world: a series of events and people, a chemistry of history and current happenings, a confluence of economic, psychological, and political forces that turned a thousand minor, innocuous events into a huge and murderous whole. There had been wars before, and slave labor and genocide, and treaties made to be broken and propagandists who came to believe their own propaganda; what made this experience different is documented in this program: its vast scope, its documentation on film, and its central character, Adolf Hitler. 150 mins.
VHS: S13361. $39.94.

The Rise and Fall of Adolf Hitler (History Channel)
Presented by the History Channel and created by ZDF, this remarkable program is the only German-produced account of Hitler available. Examines Hitler's background, rise to power, rule and downfall, using rare documents, never-before-seen film footage and extensive interviews with people who served under him. Includes six 50-minute videos.
VHS: S32181. $99.95.

Road to Rome/Thunderbolt
The film focuses on World War II and the crucial air war over Italy as the 12th Air Force and the 57th Fighter Group took control of the skies over Italy. 57 mins.
VHS: S10061. $29.95.

Rolling Thunder
Rolling Thunder was a bravado U.S. operation against North Vietnam in the first years of the war. Aerial bombing helped immobilize the enemy, and Vietnam provided the biggest airlift in history. 60 mins.
VHS: S13116. $19.98.

Rommel—The Desert Fox
The complete story of the Nazi Field Marshal who masterminded the Blitzkrieg in Europe and North Africa. From the series *The Nazis*. 50 mins.
VHS: S12730. $24.98.

Run Silent Run Deep
Clark Gable and Burt Lancaster star in one of the better World War II submarine dramas. The crew of the Nerka isn't pleased when their new captain seems obsessed with sinking the Japanese destroyer that lost Gable his last posting in the silent service. With Jack Warden, Brad Dexter, Nick Cravat, Don Rickles as Ruby. Beware of the Bongo straits.
VHS: S13310. $19.98.
Robert Wise, USA, 1958, 93 mins.

The Russian-German War

This three-hour documentary series is a rare look at one of the worst horror stories in the long, infamous history of warfare. The first program in the series, *The Politics of Fear*, looks at the early days of the approaching war. The second program, *The Killing Ground*, begins in Russia in 1941. The last program, *Breakout to Berlin*, tells of the defeat at Stalingrad early in 1943, which was the beginning of the end for Nazi Germany. The series features captured German and Russian footage, much of which has never been seen in the United States. Each tape is 47 mins.

VHS: S30974. $49.95.

The Saga of World War II Boxed Set

This epic documentary set presents the world before, during and after World War II through the stories of ordinary people caught up in those tumultuous times. Includes *Lost Peace* (1919-1936), *Breadline* (1929-1936), *Great Escape* (1925-1946), *Sporting Fever* (1900-1939) and *On the Line* (1908-1939). Eight one-hour cassettes.

VHS: S34746. $99.95.

Sahara

Humphrey Bogart is Sergeant Joe Gunn with his battalion stranded in the great African desert during World War II. Bogie has to lead his desert-weary men in a desperate battle hoping that British reinforcements will arrive in time.

VHS: S07695. $14.95.

Zoltan Korda, USA, 1943, 97 mins.

The Sands of Iwo Jima

One of John Wayne's best films. He plays Sgt. John M. Stryker, who trains his men hard so that they can fight even harder. When these Marines hit the beach, it retreats. With John Agar, Forest Tucker, Richard Jaeckel and Martin Milner. Tarawa and Iwo Jima co-star. Digitally mastered. Contains trailer and *The Making of The Sands of Iwo Jima*. Introduction by Leonard Maltin.

VHS: S04238. $19.95.

Allan Dwan, USA, 1949, 109 mins.

The Scharnhorst, Part 1: The Early Years

The battleship *Scharnhorst* and her sister ship *Gneisenau* heralded the first large German warships since 1918. The construction of so-called "speed battleships" began in the mid-'30s with these two models. This film covers the period from construction, sea trials and early active service through the dash along the English Channel in broad daylight home to Wilhelmshaven, Germany, in February 1942. English commentary and subtitles. 75 mins.

VHS: S33284. $29.95.

Secret Life of Adolf Hitler

The rise and fall of the Third Reich told with actual footage, interviews with Hitler's sister, a fellow prisoner with Hitler before he came to power, and others. Unusual and seldom-seen footage, including Eva Braun's home movies; narrated by Westbrook van Voorhis. USA, 1958, 53 mins.

VHS: S01621. $24.95.

Seeds of Discord (1933-1936)

As Hitler and Mussolini eye world domination, Gandhi dreams of freeing India from the British. Batista seizes power in Cuba, Japan invades Manchuria, and King Alexander of Yugoslavia is assassinated in France. FDR allies the U.S. with the Soviet Union. Eric Sevareid hosts this look at the political turmoil of the 1930's. 24 mins.

VHS: S23590. $99.95.

The Silent Service: The Story of Submarine Warfare in the Pacific

The compelling account of America's successful submarine campaign in World War II. Due to security considerations, America's submarine force was the "silent service" during the war. After victory, this film was made in belated commemoration. Several recreations of underwater combat were staged, combining authentic detail, gritty camerawork and actual combat footage.

VHS: S32070. $19.95.

Jurgen Stumphaus, Germany, 1946, 37 mins.

Silent Victory

Few people realize that U.S. submarines sank over five million tons of Japanese shipping during World War II, accounting for more than half the shipping sunk during World War II. This accomplishment stands as one of the all-time greatest achievements of naval history. USA, 50 mins.

VHS: S27250. $24.95.

The Silver Fleet

Ralph Richardson, Esmond Knight and Googie Withers star in this World War II drama. Though he appears to collaborate with the Nazis, a Dutch shipbuilder is actually leading a double life. In fact, he heads a group of anti-Nazi resistors.

VHS: S23811. $24.95.

Gordon Wellesley, Great Britain, 1943, 87 mins.

Sinai Commandos

This thriller deals with a suicide squad during the Six-Day War, which is responsible for a mission vital to the survival of Israel. 99 mins.

VHS: S03061. $29.95.

The Smashing of the Reich

A documentary on the last days of the German war machine. Archive footage includes the landing at Normandy, Bastogne, the Elbe River crossing, concentration camp survivors and the liberation of Paris. Told without hysterics. See how to win a war in 84 minutes. USA, 1962, 84 mins.

VHS: S10067. $29.95.

Song of Survival

They survived 3½ years of Japanese prison camp in World War II. These courageous Dutch, Australian and British women were helped by the music of Beethoven, Schubert and Chopin, which they created without instruments in a unique choir. Using rare archival footage and recreation of the music, this tape tells the stirring story of brave women in a remote prison camp in Sumatra. 57 mins.

VHS: S05806. $29.95.

Soviet War Stories from World War II

Four short programs that explore mixed memories of World War II, from a variety of Soviet perspectives. Included are *The Great Exploit, Classmates, Heroic Exploit* and *Celebration on Victory Day*. 115 mins.

VHS: S12709. $24.95.

The Speeches of Adolf Hitler

Utilizing English subtitles, this starting video presents Adolf Hitler's most dramatic speeches: revealing the demonic phases the evil Fuhrer used to hypnotize the German people. 50 mins.

VHS: S12308. $19.98.

Stalingrad

From the same production team that brought the world *Das Boot*, this film brings the bloodiest battle in the history of warfare to the screen: the legendary battle of Stalingrad. With German forces following Hitler's orders to neither retreat nor surrender, over two million Russians and Germans lost their lives in what came to be a turning point in the defeat of Germany in the Second World War. One of the most unflinchingly realistic war films ever made, *Stalingrad* stands alone in its searing, unforgettable imagery, "powerfully underscoring the adage that war is hell" (*The New York Times*). German with English subtitles. Letterboxed.

VHS: S30467. $29.95.

Joseph Vilsmaier, Germany, 1996, 150 mins.

Stillwell Road

A study of the building of the Burma road, an important supply route carved out of the mountains. Narrated by Ronald Reagan, produced by the U.S. Army. 1945, 51 mins.

VHS: S03062. $19.95.

Submarine Warfare

Gene Kelly narrates this documentary which was produced by the U.S. Department of Defense. Rare footage includes looks at the USS *Guadalcanal*, the Naval Task Force in pursuit of a 1944 German submarine. 53 mins.

VHS: S03065. $29.95.

Survivors

This film presents a remarkable portrait of Japanese-American survivors caught in the atomic bombings of Hiroshima and Nagasaki, as they describe what they saw and felt when the bombs dropped. Also profiled are Americans who face a range of physical, psychological and social problems, corroborated in the video by doctors at the U.S. Public Health Service and Yale University. "Strong…affecting…unsentimental…It's a film every American should see" (*National Catholic News*). 35 mins.

VHS: S30094. $89.00.

The Tanks Are Coming

Sam Fuller wrote the story for this engrossing World War II movie about an armored division's trek to Berlin. A ruthless sergeant leads the group through a war-ravaged landscape, showing little mercy for the enemy and his own men. Stars Steve Cochran and Phil Carey.

VHS: S24728. $19.98.

Lewis Seiler, USA, 1951, 91 mins.

Target for Tonight

This British documentary on a bombing raid on Germany won an Oscar in 1941. Filmed with the cooperation of the Royal Air Force, it uses everyone from the Commander-in-Chief to the air mechanic doing their jobs for the camera. "A direct hit," says Walter Winchell. England, 1941, 50 mins.

VHS: S05508. $24.95.

Terror of the Third Reich

This video follows the rise of Hitler's Nazi Germany in three parts: *Terror of the Third Reich, Hitler Youth Movement* and *Day of Freedom*. The first segment focuses on Hitler and the second describes the indoctrination of young people. The last segment is directed by the uniquely gifted but controversial director Leni Riefenstahl. It records the training procedures of the German army. 62 mins.

VHS: S26556. $19.95.

Through Hell and High Water

This video details the little-known role of the Merchant Marine during the Second World War. Their valor and dedication is the stuff of legend. 30 mins.

VHS: S27248. $24.95.

Time Capsule: War in Europe

Europe was in flames. Great Britain was on the verge of being conquered. The Russian border had been crossed by Nazi troops. From across the ocean, the fighting forces of the US came to join the French, British and Russian soldiers to forge the winning alliance that changed the course of the war. 30 mins.

VHS: S22716. $19.95.

Time Capsule: War in the Pacific

It began in Hawaii. The blue skies over this tropical paradise turned black with smoke from the surprise Japanese attack. Unprepared but undaunted, America rose up to build a formidable array of forces. The war in the Pacific stands as a testimony to the will of the American people. 30 mins.

VHS: S22717. $19.95.

To Hell and Back

Based on his autobiography, Audie Murphy portrays his own experiences which popularized him as the most decorated infantryman in American war history. Excellent battle sequences depict Murphy's breathtaking heroic exploits. Stars Marshall Thompson, Susan Kohner, Charles Drake, Jack Kelly and Gregg Palmer.

VHS: S16305. $14.95.

Jesse Hibbs, USA, 1955, 106 mins.

To the Shores of Iwo Jima

A rousing film about the assault of the Marines on Iwo Jima and the 25-day siege, as well as a history of the battle of Guadalcanal, one of the bloodiest battles of World War II. 41 mins.

VHS: S03064. $29.95.

Town Meetings: Pearl Harbor

Ted Koppel links viewpoints around the nation as he looks back at the historical issues of the attack on Pearl Harbor 50 years ago. 50 mins.

VHS: S15884. $19.98.

Train

Director John Frankenheimer delivers a World War II drama about an effort to stop retreating Nazis from leaving France with stolen art treasures in 1944. Burt Lancaster stars as a courageous French railroad inspector and member of the French Resistance who is determined to thwart the latest mission of Col. Von Waldheim (Paul Scofield). With Jeanne Moreau, Albert Remy, Wolfgang Preiss and Michel Simon as the stubborn engineer Papa Boule. No models or processed shots were used in the making of this exciting film in which several camera units were destroyed in crashes and explosions. Frankenheimer replaced original director Arthur Penn at Lancaster's request.

VHS: S16442. $19.98.

John Frankenheimer, USA/France/Italy, 1964, 140 mins.

Traitors to Hitler

Documentary on the plot to assassinate Hitler in 1944 by his generals and others. Contains extremely rare, previously unreleased footage of the infamous trial of the anti-Nazi plotters. German dialog with English narrative.

VHS: S30236. $29.95.

Great Britain, 69 mins.

True Glory (Gen. Dwight D. Eisenhower)

Garson Kanin and Carol Reed directed this testimonial to the men who fought in Europe from D-Day to VE Day. Stars Peter Ustinov and Frank Harvey.

VHS: S10578. $19.95.

Tunisian Victory

Produced jointly by the U.S. and British governments, this wartime documentary looks at the struggle for North Africa, from the initial landings to the ultimate victory. 74 mins.

VHS: S03063. $29.95.

The Turning Point (1941-1944)

Hitler faces a crushing loss on the Russian front, while MacArthur leads the U.S. forces in the Pacific. Finally Eisenhower leads the Allies to their first decisive victory in Europe. As Germany prepares for a forceful attack, Italy surrenders and the Japanese are stopped at the Battle of Midway. Eric Sevareid hosts. 23 mins.

VHS: S23593. $99.95.

The Twisted Cross

Using Allied military footage, Nazi propaganda films, newsreels of the period and reconstructed dramatic sequences simulating key events in Hitler's career, *The Twisted Cross* presents a vivid panorama of events leading up to WWII. Among the more disturbing moments captured from pre-Third Reich history is Hitler's "Beer Hall Putsch of 1923", and his dictation of *Mein Kampf to confidant Rudolf Hess. USA, 1956, 53 mins.*

VHS: S04446. $29.95.

Tyranny of Adolf Hitler

From the creators of the acclaimed series *The World at War* comes this special 3-part documentary about life in Hitler's Germany. Using archive footage and interviews, *The Third Reich* follows Hitler's rise to power, his mobilization against Europe, and Germany's crippling defeat in World War II. Told in the compelling words of ordinary people who survived an extraordinary time. Available individually, or as a three-part set.
Third Reich 3-Pack.
VHS: S10254. $39.99.

The Unknown Soldier

Hosted by World War II Navy Veteran Jason Robards, this originally-aired PBS documentary presents the life stories of six American servicemen who died in action during World War II and whose bodies were never recovered or identified. The personal profiles are told through combat footage of the battles they fought, mementoes, letters, and interviews with family members. 60 mins.
VHS: S02406. $29.95.

V for Victory

The Second World War is explored in this documentary series that recounts the battles, campaigns, strategies, political fortunes and global importance from the Japanese bombing of Pearl Harbor to the emergence of atomic warfare. Hosted by veteran journalists Eric Sevareid and Edwin Newman. It "lets you see the face of war in gritty detail" (*Philadelphia Inquirer*).
Vol. I: Pearl Harbor to Midway. Japan's daring predawn raid plunges America into the global war. 45 mins.
VHS: S18287. $14.95.
Vol. II: Guadalcanal and the Pacific Counterattack. This program looks at the American assault on Japan's strategic dominance in the Pacific theater. 45 mins.
VHS: S18288. $14.95.
Vol. III: North Africa and the Global War. This episode considers the deployment of American troops, airmen and sailors to various parts of the world, from North Africa to Burma, the Atlantic Ocean and the European airfields. 45 mins.
VHS: S18289. $14.95.
Vol. IV: Anzio and the Italian Campaign. The difficult and harsh American offensive in Italy. 45 mins.
VHS: S18290. $14.95.
Vol. V: D-Day and the Battle for France. This episode studies the Normandy Invasion and the largest amphibious assault in history, codenamed Operation Overload. 45 mins.
VHS: S18291. $14.95.
Vol. VI: Tarawa and the Island War. This program studies the painful and tragic repercussions of the island war in the Pacific. 45 mins.
VHS: S18292. $14.95.
Vol. VII: Women at War—From the Home Front to the Front Lines. From the factories to the battlefield, this program considers the contributions, pain and sacrifice of the American women. 45 mins.
VHS: S18293. $14.95.
Vol. VIII: The Battle of the Bulge and the Drive to the Rhine. The Third Reich's last major offensive and counterattack of the Allies' penetration into Germany is chronicled in this episode. 45 mins.
VHS: S18294. $14.95.
Vol. IX: Iwo Jima, Okinawa and the Push on Japan. Two of the war's seminal battles are recounted in this portrait of American and Japanese encounters in the Pacific theater. 45 mins.
VHS: S18295. $14.95.
Vol. X: The Eagle Triumphant. The final installment looks at the hard-fought victories in Europe and Asia. 45 mins.
VHS: S18296. $14.95.
V for Victory, Boxed Set.
VHS: S18297. $99.95.

Victory at Sea, Volumes 1 to 6

Now *Victory at Sea* is available in a new format—six volumes in a Collector's Edition Gift Set. Each volume contains compilations of the individual episodes listed above and runs 120 minutes.
Volume 1: Episodes 1-4.
VHS: S02210. $19.98.
Volume 2: Episodes 5-8.
VHS: S02211. $19.98.
Volume 3: Episodes 9-12.
VHS: S02212. $19.98.
Volume 4: Episodes 13-16.
VHS: S02213. $19.98.
Volume 5: Episodes 17-21.
VHS: S08900. $19.98.
Volume 6: Episodes 22-26.
VHS: S08901. $19.98.
Boxed Set (6 Volumes; 26 Episodes).
VHS: S02195. $99.00.

Victory Gardens of WWII

Find out how, at the suggestion of the Agriculture Department in 1943, 20 million backyard and city roof-top victory gardens produced 50% of America's vegetables, playing a major role in winning the war. 50 mins.
VHS: S34692. $19.95.

Visions of War

A multi-volume series covering the history of modern warfare, using archival footage and interviews in color.
Cassino. One of the most harrowing battles of the war, involving soldiers from 16 countries. 50 mins.
VHS: S10087. $19.95.
Memorial Flight. The historical Battle of Britain Memorial Flight showcases British aviation's most revered aircraft, the Lancaster, Spitfire, and Hurricane. 50 mins.
VHS: S10049. $19.95.
The Bulge. The largest single pitched battle of the Western Front, involving over one million troops. 50 mins.
VHS: S10086. $19.95.
Warsaw. The tragic story of the 1944 Warsaw Uprising, one of the most controversial epics of the war. 50 mins.
VHS: S10085. $19.95.

Waldheim: Commission of Inquiry

A video tribunal searches out the "real" story in the conflicting reports about the past of Austria's President Waldheim, who was also the former secretary of the United Nations. USA, 1988.
VHS: S07305. $79.99.

Walk in the Sun

One of the best Hollywood dramas of men at war; follows American infantrymen pursuing objective in Italy during World War II. With Dana Andrews, Richard Conte and Lloyd Bridges.
VHS: S03005. $39.95.
Laser: CLV. **LD70258. $39.95.**
Lewis Milestone, USA, 1945, 118 mins.

War Chronicles Volume 1— The Greatest Conflict

Presents a breathtaking overview of World War II, from 1939 to 1945. 35 mins.
VHS: S02119. $14.95.

War Chronicles Volume 6— Bomber Offensive: Air War in Europe

Graphically depicts the most disastrous air encounters of the War. 35 mins.
VHS: S02124. $14.95.

War Chronicles Volume 8— The Battle of Germany

Shows the American forces breaking through at Saint-Lo and entering Nazi concentration camps. 35 mins.
VHS: S06411. $14.95.

War Chronicles Volume 10— Jungle Warfare: New Guinea to Burma

In addition to the Japanese troops, American soldiers fought disease, heat and millions of things that crawled and slithered. The video series continues in its efforts to provide compelling documentary footage of the hard fought war in the Pacific. In black and white and color, with host Patrick O'Neal. When these GI's say its a jungle out there, they mean it. 35 mins.
VHS: S09857. $14.95.

War Chronicles Volume 12— The Bloody Ridges of Peleliu

Veterans and history buffs will find something of value in this video home library of World War II. This installment, hosted as usual by Patrick O'Neal, shows intense footage of the U.S. Marines under fire, about 600 miles east of the Philippines. For five months they battled the Japanese who retreated to fight from caves on this volcanic island in the West Caroline Islands group. 35 mins.
VHS: S09859. $14.95.

War Chronicles Volume 13— Return to the Philippines

General Douglas MacArthur promised he would return to the Philippines when he was evacuated on March 16, 1942 to the safety of Australia. He kept that promise when he returned on October 20, 1944 and landed on Leyte. This installment of the video history of that great conflict details the bombardments and frontal assaults that freed the Philippines from the Japanese invaders. 35 mins.
VHS: S09860. $14.95.

War Chronicles Volumes 1-8—Pre-Pack

The first eight volumes of The War Chronicles in a bonus edition library collector's case.
VHS: S06412. $119.60.

War on Land and Sea

This British-produced series documents key elements of WWII, using rare, previously unavailable footage. Available in individual volumes, or as a 4-pack.
Churchill's War. This video takes us through Churchill's war, using much newly discovered footage and featuring, where possible, original recordings of the great speeches, in a look at Churchill the statesman and Churchill the Commander. 60 mins.
VHS: S12450. $29.95.
D-Day-Assault on Fortress Europe. Four years in the planning, two in the organizing, and one day in execution, the landing in Normandy was easily the largest and most extraordinary combined military operation ever attempted, and a crucial one. Using rare footage, this documentary examines this historic day which turned the tide in the war. 60 mins.
VHS: S12452. $29.95.
Dunkirk: The Battle for France. Dunkirk, the brilliantly-executed withdrawal of land forces minus all their equipment across the Channel which came to be regarded as almost a major victory, became a bitter symbol of British betrayal for the French. The visions conjured up of a ragged fleet of fishing boats, yachts and dinghies sailing the channel, their pilots risking life and limb to save soldiers from certain defeat or captivity, is vividly realized using very rare footage. 60 mins.
VHS: S12451. $29.95.
Waffen SS. The SS had its beginnings in the turbulent street politics of the Weimar Republic. It became Heinrich Himmler's personal power base, and under him the SS grew into a vast private army and state-within-the-state. After the war, the Waffen SS were burdened with the near-exclusive blame for the most hideous crimes of the Nazi regime. 60 mins.
VHS: S12456. $29.95.
4-pack.
VHS: S12459. $113.81.

War Stories

Combining the recollections of combat veterans, personal photographs and archival footage, *War Stories* captures the history of World War II as never before. A gripping tribute to all the men and women who lived and fought in the second World War. Five volumes.
Airmen of World War II. 50 mins.
VHS: S14778. $19.95.
D-Day. 50 mins.
VHS: S14781. $19.95.
Remembering Pearl Harbor. 50 mins.
VHS: S14777. $19.95.
The Fighting Marine: 1942-45. 50 mins.
VHS: S14779. $19.95.
The Merchant Marines. 50 mins.
VHS: S14780. $19.95.
Complete five-volume set.
VHS: S14782. $99.75.

War Stories Our Mothers Never Told Us

In this unique and utterly moving documentary from New Zealand, seven women candidly talk of their loves and their lives during World War II. The poignant interviews are overlaid with restored archival footage and popular songs from World War II years; beautifully shot by Alun Bollinger (*The Piano*).
VHS: S31120. $29.95.
Gaylene Preston, New Zealand, 1995, 95 mins.

The War Years: Britain in World War II

An anthology of familiar men and famous battles that set the tone of British involvement in the Second World War. The program considers the human scale and dimension—the people who remained behind the lines to endure the Blitz, enlisted in the Home Guard and prepared for a possible invasion.
Vol. 1: The Phoney War. In the aftermath of the Hitler/Chamberlain agreement for "peace in our time," Britain declares war following the Nazi invasion of Poland and Czechoslovakia. The program looks at the early stages of the war, the Navy campaigns, Dunkirk and the political ascension of Winston Churchill.
VHS: S17949. $29.95.
Vol. 2: The Battle of Britain. Britain sustains heavy casualties as western Europe falls under German occupation, and Hitler initiates his massive bombing campaigns on British civilian and military targets. Air raid shelters are part of everyday texture. The Blitz is on.
VHS: S17950. $29.95.
Vol. 3: The Blitz. Despite massive bombing raids, Hitler can't achieve air superiority, though major sections of London are in ruin. German U-boats intercept Atlantic convoys and more than 40,000 are killed.
VHS: S17951. $29.95.
Vol. 4: The Tide Turns. Despite a series of military setbacks that lead to chronic food and supply shortages, women take an active presence in the factories, armed forces and civil defense. Britain's military fortunes change with the American intervention and the German debacle on the Russian front.
VHS: S17952. $29.95.
Vol. 5: The Final Chapter. German forces are crushed in Russia, and following D-day, 300,000 Allied soldiers are waging battle in the French countryside. Despite its last gasp technological offensive, the V-1 and V-2 rocket launchers, Berlin is surrounded by enemy forces and Hitler commits suicide.
VHS: S17953. $29.95.

Warlords

A series of seven videos capturing the heroes and tyrants of Word War II, narrated by Hal Holbrook.

Churchill: The Private War. A monumental leader, Churchill defied Hitler's onslaught to the very end. The story of a man who found himself through war. 30 mins.
VHS: S09031. $14.99.

Hitler's Master Race: The Mad Dream of the S.S. They swore to fulfill Hitler's dream of German Supermen. New archival footage exposes the madness that almost succeeded. 30 mins.
VHS: S09030. $14.99.

Hitler: Portrait of a Tyrant. Even in his early days, the sadistic side of Adolf Hitler reigned unsuppressed. 30 mins.
VHS: S09028. $14.99.

Kamikaze: Mission of Death. Their lives were a rehearsal for death. Rare footage exposes the training and preparation for their deadly missions. 30 mins.
VHS: S09032. $14.99.

MacArthur: The Defiant General. American superhero and military genius. Defiance was his badge of courage and his downfall. 30 mins.
VHS: S09027. $14.99.

Patton: The Man Behind the Myth. Uncovered: Patton's merciless approach to war, his lust for glory. 30 mins.
VHS: S09026. $14.99.

Rommel: The Strange Death of the Desert Fox. He crushed Europe and Africa beneath his iron fist. New evidence uncovers Hitler's fear of the man known as "the desert fox." 309 mins.
VHS: S09029. $14.99.

Warsaw Uprising Chronicle (Kroniki Powstania Warszawskiego)

A unique documentary from 1944 Poland about the Warsaw Uprising against Nazi occupation. The film was confiscated and badly mutilated by communist censors; here it is restored to its best available form. Moving footage from a turbulent time.
VHS: S15562. $39.95.

Why We Fight

A seven-part series produced for the U.S. War Department, designed to convince the American public that WWII deserved their support.

No. 1: Prelude to War. Produced by Frank Capra, this film skillfully combines newsreel footage of the Japanese invasion into Manchuria, the Italian incursion into Ethiopia, and the German blitz of Eastern Europe. Directed by Ernst Lubitsch, USA, 1942, 53 mins.
VHS: S01052. $19.95.

No. 2: The Nazis Strike. Directed by Frank Capra and Anatole Litvak, this documentary uses newsreel footage and scenes from *Triumph of the Will* to prove that Nazis are not nice people. Also a British comic short, *Schichlegruber Doing the Lambeth Walk*. USA, 1942, 44 mins.
VHS: S05503. $24.95.

No. 3: Divide and Conquer. The German war machine continues its march through Europe, Denmark and Norway fall, the Maginot Line in France crumbles and the country surrenders. The British Army is defeated on the continent and crosses the Channel from Dunkirk. 1943, 60 mins.
VHS: S03057. $19.95.

No. 4: Battle of Russia. The battle of Stalingrad climaxes this account of the Nazi invasion of the Soviet Union. 1943, 83 mins.
VHS: S00104. $19.95.

No. 5: Battle of Britain. An account of the unbreakable spirit of London residents during the six week bombing blitz by the German Luftwaffe. Narration by Walter Huston. Directed by Frank Capra, USA, 1943, 52 mins.
VHS: S00102. $19.95.
Laser: LD70862. $59.95.

No. 6: Battle of China. This look at China focuses on the way in which the people harnessed all the country's resources to oppose the Japanese invasion. 1944, 67 mins.
VHS: S00103. $19.95.

No. 7: War Comes to America. Documents the gradual shift of opinion from isolationism to support of the US entry into World War II. Narration by Walter Huston. Directed by Frank Capra, USA, 1945, 66 mins.
VHS: S01428. $19.95.

Wings of the Luftwaffe Fighter Attack

The Discovery Channel produced this video which reveals the superior aircraft of the Luftwaffe. For example, the FW 190 was a deadly success, while the ME 262 was the only true successful jet fighter bomber. These were among the greatest aircraft of the era. 60 mins.
VHS: S25093. $9.95.

Wings over Europe

Stukas, Yaks, Spitfires and the Flying Fortress are just some of the planes that soared into history during the Second World War. This *Discovery Channel* documentary explores the evolution of these aircraft as fighting machines. 60 mins.
VHS: S26049. $19.95.

World at War

This massive, 26-volume series covers virtually all of World War II.

World at War Vol. 1: A New Germany.
VHS: S09363. $19.98.
World at War Vol. 2: Distant War.
VHS: S09364. $19.98.
World at War Vol. 3: France Falls.
VHS: S09365. $19.98.
World at War Vol. 4: Alone—Britain.
VHS: S09366. $19.98.
World at War Vol. 5: Barbarossa.
VHS: S09367. $19.98.
World at War Vol. 6: Banzai—Japan Strikes.
VHS: S09368. $19.98.
World at War Vol. 7: On Our Way—America Enters the War.
VHS: S09369. $19.98.
World at War Vol. 8: Desert—The War in North Africa.
VHS: S09370. $19.98.
World at War Vol. 9: Stalingrad.
VHS: S09371. $19.98.
World at War Vol. 10: Wolfpack.
VHS: S09372. $19.98.
World at War Vol. 11: Red Star.
VHS: S09373. $19.98.
World at War Vol. 12: Whirlwind.
VHS: S09374. $19.98.
World at War Vol. 13: Tough Old Gut.
VHS: S09375. $19.98.
World at War Vol. 14: It's a Lovely Day Tomorrow.
VHS: S09376. $19.98.
World at War Vol. 15: Home Fires.
VHS: S09377. $19.98.
World at War Vol. 16: Inside the Reich.
VHS: S09378. $19.98.
World at War Vol. 17: Morning.
VHS: S09379. $19.98.
World at War Vol. 18: Occupation.
VHS: S09380. $19.98.
World at War Vol. 19: Pincers.
VHS: S09381. $19.98.
World at War Vol. 20: Genocide.
VHS: S09382. $19.98.
World at War Vol. 21: Nemesis.
VHS: S09383. $19.98.
World at War Vol. 22: Japan.
VHS: S09384. $19.98.
World at War Vol. 23: Pacific—The Island to Island War.
VHS: S09385. $19.98.
World at War Vol. 24: The Bomb.
VHS: S09386. $19.98.
World at War Vol. 25: Reckoning.
VHS: S09387. $19.98.
World at War Vol. 26: Remember.
VHS: S09388. $19.98.

The World at War

This documentary recounts the international unrest that led to America's involvement in World War II. Narrated by Paul Stewart, all footage is authentic. B&W, 44 minutes.
VHS: S02926. $19.95.

World War II: A Personal Journey

In this 50-year commemorative collection, join Glen Ford to see the drama of World War II through the eyes of distinguished Americans who fought in the epic battle of the war. Four volumes include *1941-42: The First 1,000 Days*, *1943: At Home & Abroad*, *1944: Victory in Sight* and *1945: "V" for Victory*. Three hours.
VHS: S31478. $79.99.

World War II: From Breadlines to Boomtimes

This three-volume documentary set describes how America responded to the global conflict. Still afflicted by the historic depression, on December 7, 1941, the nation was irrevocably drawn into war. Men and women mobilized to convert the economy into a war machine, a process that transformed the US so that it emerged as the most powerful country in the world. 170 mins.

World War II: From Breadlines to Boomtimes Volume 1.
VHS: S22713. $24.95.
World War II: From Breadlines to Boomtimes Volume 2.
VHS: S22714. $24.95.
World War II: From Breadlines to Boomtimes Volume 3.
VHS: S22715. $24.95.
World War II: From Breadlines to Boomtimes, Complete Set.
VHS: S22712. $69.95.

World War II: Hearst Metronome News

From the archives of the Hearst Metronome News Library, actual newsreel footage that documents World War II. Each volume is 51 mins.

World War II: Volume 1.
VHS: S08139. $19.95.
World War II: Volume 2.
VHS: S08140. $19.95.
World War II: Volume 3.
VHS: S08141. $19.95.
World War II: Volume 4.
VHS: S08142. $19.95.

World War II: The Eastern Front

Goya paintings and Russian poems are combined with historic footage of the Second World War to expose the inhumanity of war. The Soviet Union suffered terrible ravages and tribulations during this tragic conflagration. 30 mins.
VHS: S23739. $99.95.

World War II: The War Chronicles

This seven-volume series documents the whole tragic unfolding of the global conflict whose effects dominated our century. North Africa, Normandy, Anzio, the Battle of the Bulge and the war in the Pacific, including Okinawa, are all places which live on in memory. Now combat footage and expert commentary explain the strategies and forces that behind these battles. Each volume is 70 mins.
VHS: S24388. $59.95.

WWII: Beyond the Battle

In the tradition of *America in the '40s*, this thrilling program not only documents the war, but the war years: from tilling Victory Gardens, to setting up U.S.O. shows, to the front lines. 57 mins.
VHS: S34636. $14.95.

Yankee Samurai: The Little Iron Men

This program highlights the accomplishments of the 100-442nd regiment during World War II, 4,800 Japanese-American soldiers who formed the most decorated American unit in the war. While 120,000 other Asians were being held in "internment camps" in western states, these Americans were intent on proving their loyalty to the States and fought with incredible valor and sacrifice. 50 mins.
VHS: S13138. $29.98.

The Young Lions

One of the best of the World War II studies, based on a novel by Irwin Shaw, features Marlon Brando as a German officer, and Montgomery Clift as an American soldier. With Dean Martin and Hope Lange.
VHS: S03499. $19.98.
Edward Dmytryk, USA, 1958, 167 mins.

THE HOLOCAUST

The 81st Blow

An historical document made up of footage and stills shot by the Nazis. A compilation of testimony from witnesses who appeared at the Eichmann trial provides a telling narrative. The film's title refers to the story of a Jewish boy in one of the ghettos, who was struck with 80 blows. He survived and immigrated to Israel, where he found that no one believed his story—which for him was the 81st blow. Academy Award nominee.
VHS: S06570. $79.95.
Jacquot Ehrlich/David Bergman/Haim Gouri, Israel, 1974, 115 mins.

Act of Faith

This classic Holocaust documentary on the plight of the Jews in Denmark during World War II. Contains historical film material from Denmark during those years, including actual interviews with rescuers and others. English narrative.
VHS: S30239. $29.95.
Denmark, 45 mins.

America and the Holocaust: Deceit & Indifference

Hal Linden narrates this troubling look at the US. Beset by anti-Semitism and a government determined to keep critical information suppressed, the chance to rescue hundreds of thousands from the Nazis was lost. B&W, 60 mins.
VHS: S23051. $19.95.

Anne Frank Remembered

Family members, childhood friends and the people who hid the Franks bring to life the girl behind the diary. Academy Award winner for Best Documentary of 1995, narrated by Kenneth Branagh with selections from Anne's diary read by Glenn Close. German, Dutch and English with English subtitles.
VHS: S28620. $14.95.
Laser: LD75956. $39.95.
Jon Blair, Great Britain/USA, 1995, 117 mins.

Art in the Holocaust

Documentary on Jewish artists and their fate from the 1920s until the end of World War II. Contains rare film footage, including color footage of these artists' works. English narrative.
VHS: S30240. $29.95.
Great Britain, 60 mins.

Because of That War

An extraordinary look at what happens when two of Israel's leading rock musicians, both the children of Holocaust survivors, decide to confront their disturbing past. Exploring the different realities of two generations, haunted by the same horrifying legacy, the film is a stirring tribute to the human spirit, filled with the power and passion of the events that inspired it. Berlin and Leningrad Film Festival winner; voted Israel's best film. "Original, sensitive and beautiful" (Elie Weisel). Hebrew with English subtitles.
VHS: S32020. $89.95.
Orna Ben-Dor Niv, Israel, 1989, 90 mins.

Blood Money: Nazi Gold

As the situation grew dim for Jews in the late 1930s, many families moved their life savings into bank accounts in neutral Switzerland. Fifty years later, most Holocaust survivors are still trying to free their money from Swiss bank accounts. The world has finally taken note and major investigations have been launched. 100 mins.
VHS: S33181. $39.95.

Bound for Nowhere: The St. Louis Episode

Witness the dramatic voyage of over 900 Jews, among them 200 children, who fled Nazi Germany. Turned away from their expected Cuban refuge, they are forced back to European countries. This document stands as testimony to the indifference of other nations to assist the Jews. 1939, 9 mins.
VHS: S16310. $60.00.

Camp of Hope and Despair: Westerbork Concentration Camp, 1939-45

From this camp in Eastern Holland more than 100,000 Dutch Jews were deported at the hands of the Nazis. Despite the terror that awaited them, Jewish classes, celebrations, religious services and weddings continued at Westerbork on a regular basis. Eyewitness accounts from survivors, photographs and films are joined to tell this story of strained normalcy in the face of doom. 70 mins.
VHS: S23237. $39.95.

Chasing Shadows

Filmmaker Naomi Gryn accompanies her father to his Carpathian hometown, Berehovo. Evoking the world of his childhood when half the town was Jewish, Hugo provides his daughter with beautiful memories that all lead to one bitter end: the Jews being shipped to the crematorium at Birkenau. A deeply personal film augmented by rare footage showing Carpathian Jewish farmers and newsreels of the Hungarian troops "liberating" Berehovo.
VHS: S16320. $54.00.
Naomi Gryn, Great Britain, 1990, 52 mins.

Child in Two Worlds

To save their lives, many Jewish parents gave their children over to Christian foster parents. These babies, now in their 50's and 60's, tell their amazing stories of survival and how they returned to their parents' way of life. Consider Halinka, who as a baby was thrown, wrapped in a pillow, over the Warsaw ghetto wall into the hands of a Polish policeman. Winner of the Golden Calf Award for Best Documentary, 1993. Dutch with English subtitles. 60 mins.
VHS: S23235. $39.95.

Choosing One's Way: Resistance in Auschwitz/Birkenau

Crematorium #4 was destroyed by inmates who succeeded in smuggling gun powder past Nazi guards. This act of heroism uses archival footage to tell a story nearly forgotten. Ellyn Burstyn narrates. Winner of the Hugo, 1994 Chicago Film Festival. 30 mins.
VHS: S23244. $39.95.

Christian Boltanski

An interview with the provocative French artist whose works created from found photos and other human relics from rummage sales and junk shops often invoke the memory of the Holocaust and deal explicitly with death. 53 mins.
VHS: S31926. $39.95.

Courage to Care

This documentary shows the courage of the many civilians who saved or hid children from the Nazis during World War II. Contains rare footage and actual interviews with rescuers in Poland, Holland and France. English narrative.
VHS: S30206. $29.95.

The Cross and the Star

Subtitled *Jews, Christians and the Holocaust*, John Michalczyk's documentary interweaves archival footage of Nazi Germany, propaganda films, television shows, and contemporary interviews to make a connection between the death camps, Nazi Nuremberg laws and the possible complicity and collaboration of the institutional churches and orders of the Catholic and Protestant leaders. A former Jesuit priest, Michalczyk considers the Gospel of St. John, the sermons of St. Augustine, and the writings of Martin Luther to trace the evolution of anti-Semitism. 55 mins.
VHS: S17102. $29.95.

Dark Lullabies

A very moving film: they are the children of survivors and of the perpetrators of the Holocaust. Polarized as their heritage is, many of this generation share a legacy of silence. Filmmaker Irene Angelico, herself a child of survivors of concentration camps, takes a deeply personal journey: she asks, what happened, and why? Through interviews with survivors and their children, she searches for comprehension in this powerful and emotional quest. Produced by the National Film Board of Canada.
VHS: S07663. $69.95.
Irene Angelico/Abbey Jack Neidik, Canada, 1982, 82 mins.

The Death March of the Jews from the Camp at Flossenberg

Flossenberg was the third-largest Nazi concentration camp in Germany. From 1938-1945, more than 100,000 inmates from all over Europe were imprisoned in the main camp and its more than 100 subcamps. Utilizing archival footage, the illustrations and diaries of the survivors, and interviews with many who participated in the 50th anniversary of the camp's liberation, we are given a first-hand glimpse at the horror that was Flossenberg. 45 mins.
VHS: S33179. $39.95.

Demjanjuk Trial: The State of Israel vs. John Demjanjuk

This is the trial of the Cleveland auto mechanic accused of being "Ivan the Terrible", the man who supervised the gas chambers at Treblinka. Israel won extradition, but the case became entangled in legal issues larger than the man's guilt or innocence. In this video, the courtroom drama and surrounding issues are unveiled. 50 mins.
VHS: S12905. $49.95.

The Double Crossing: The Voyage of the St. Louis

A film about the May 1939 voyage from Hamburg to Havana of some 900 Jewish refugees, that was aborted when Cuban authorities reneged on their promise and refused them admittance. The documentary includes archival footage and contemporary interviews with survivors of the journey. 29 mins.
VHS: S17942. $39.95.

Escape to the Rising Sun

The story of 20,000 Jews who fled Nazi persecution in Europe and took refuge in Shanghai throughout WWII. Using archival footage of the Japanese occupation, as well as first-hand accounts from fifteen Jewish survivors, the film examines living conditions before the liberation of Shanghai. English narration and subtitles.
VHS: S16323. $90.00.
Diane Perelsztejn, Belgium, 1990, 95 mins.

Exile

A remarkable attempt by a filmmaker to come to terms with her family's past—Alexis Krasilovsky, the filmmaker, travels to Czechoslovakia, Austria and Florida to discover the reason for her family's secrecy through talks with relatives who suffered persecution during Hitler's time. "Remarkable" (*Los Angeles Times*).
VHS: S07771. $39.95.
Alexis Krasilovsky, USA, 1984, 28 mins.

Flames in Ashes

Using testimony of eyewitnesses and recently discovered film footage, this video explores how Jews in innumerable ways resisted the Nazis. The voices of those who survived the horrors of the Holocaust, both murderers and resistance fighters, tell the story that defines the differing dimensions of Jewish resistance in Europe before and during the war. 90 mins.
VHS: S06572. $79.95.

For the Living: The Story of the U.S. Holocaust Memorial Museum

Ed Asner narrates this in-depth view of the nation's premier museum devoted to the Holocaust. The Museum's architect, designers and curators are all seen exploring the complexity of this historical event from Auschwitz and Treblinka to the Warsaw Ghetto and the forests of Poland. 50 mins.
VHS: S20903. $19.95.

Force of Evil

Interviews with a Danish Jew rescued from a concentration camp, a Jehovah's Witness, a German emigre in Shanghai, a Dutch woman who risked her life to rescue Jewish children and a former Hitler youth combine with archival footage to trace the career of Nazi war criminal Adolph Eichmann. Narrated by Lindsay Crouse.
VHS: S16312. $100.00.
Steven Schlow, USA, 1989, 60 mins.

Great Crimes and Trials of the 20th Century: Trial of Adolf Eichmann, Hitler and the Nuremberg Trials

Bill Kurtis narrates the opening segment of this video which is an account of Adolf Eichmann's trial. Eichmann was a notorious Nazi war criminal responsible for the plans of the "Final Solution." This video ends with the Nuremberg Trials, in which Hitler's Nazis were tried for their crimes against humanity. Narrated by Robert Powell. 52 mins.
VHS: S29976. $19.95.

Hanna's War

The heroic resistance of Hanna Senesh, a Hungarian Jew who was trained as a commando and a spy by the British in Palestine and sent back into Nazi-controlled Europe. Maruschka Detmers is cast as Hanna with Ellen Burstyn as her courageous mother. An epic war movie written and directed by Canon Films' Menahem Golan. With Anthony Andrews, David Warner, and Donald Pleasance as the police interrogator. Based on a true story.
VHS: S09842. $19.98.
Menahem Golan, Hungary/Iceland/USA, 1988, 149 mins.

Holocaust (Chomsky)

Meryl Streep stars in this fictional account of two families in Hitler's Germany between 1935-1945. Inge (Streep) watches as her family is torn apart and strewn across a war-torn land, while the Dorf family joins the war effort, with Erik Dorf (Michael Moriarty) penetrating to the heart of the despised SS. This dramatic series won eight Emmy Awards. Also features James Woods.
VHS: S20936. $39.98.
Marvin J. Chomsky, USA, 1978, 390 mins.

Holocaust (Sontag)

In *Dark Places*, writer and social critic Susan Sontag, with a group of present day students, explores the meaning of Hitler's genocide. This powerful documentary is complemented by *How Came Israel?*, *The Good Omen*, and Herschel Bernardi's narrating *The Hangman*, three gripping shorts which probe and elaborate on the same theme.
VHS: S03984. $29.95.

The Holocaust and Yad Vashem: Displaced Persons

These two films are co-produced by Yad Vashem and the Israel Film Service. The first traces the rise of Nazism from its beginning in 1918 through to its terrifying results. Not only are events like Kristallnacht documented, there are important segments devoted to Jewish partisans and the Warsaw Ghetto uprising. *Displaced Persons* tells the story of the SS *Fearless*, an illegal immigrant ship that brought many survivors of Nazism to Palestine.
VHS: S24250. $14.98.

The Holocaust as Seen Through the Eyes of a Survivor

Through documentary footage and artwork, David Bergman, a survivor of the Holocaust, personalizes his experience for viewers. 30 mins.
VHS: S23741. $69.95.

The Holocaust in Memory of Millions

Walter Cronkite leads this tour of the United States Holocaust Memorial Museum. Bone-chilling re-creations, searing photographs and the poignant testimony of survivors are all found in this monument to the human spirit. From the Discovery series.
VHS: S23015. $19.95.

Holocaust, Polish Jews (Holocoust, Zydzi Polscy)

Moving depictions of the miserable life Polish Jews suffered through while living in the Warsaw Ghetto during World War II. These are among the most significant postwar Eastern European documentaries made. Three short films are included: *Requiem for 500 Thousand* (directed by Jerzy Bossak, one of the founders of modern Polish cinema—the teacher of Wajda and Polański), *An Ordinary Day of SS-man Schmidt* and *Silence*. 50 mins.
VHS: S15566. $39.95.

The Illegals

Author Meyer Levin joined the Haganah's European underground after World War II and recorded on film this fantastic story of the "Aliyah Bet"—the clandestine movement of the Holocaust survivors to Palestine. Made available through the Steven Spielberg Jewish Film Archive in Jerusalem.
VHS: S30526. $39.95.

Ivan and Abraham

Winner at the Cannes Film Festival, this powerful film is the story of the friendship of Abraham, a volatile Jewish boy, and Ivan, an older Christian boy, who flee 1930s Poland, where political tensions are mounting, to the vast and perilous countryside. The runaways are followed by Aaron, a young Communist outlaw, and Abraham's teenage sister, Rachel, whose love for Aaron has estranged her from her family. Expertly interweaving personal drama and and historical perspective, the film centers on these four outcasts as they try to detach themselves from a world hurtling into chaos and violence. "Dazzling in its beauty, its audacity, its intelligence, its subtlety, its freedom" (Claude Lanzmann, director of *Shoah*). Yiddish, Polish, Russian and Gypsy dialog with English subtitles. Letterboxed.

VHS: S31191. $89.95.

Yolande Zauberman, France, 1993, 105 mins.

The Janovska Camp at Lvov

Between 1941 and 1944, 200,000 Jews (around one third of the Jews in Galicia) were taken to Janovska, just outside Lvov, Ukraine. Only 300 survived. In 1990, some of the survivors returned to reconstruct a memory of that place. Simon Wiesenthal and Rabbi David Kahane, former Chief Rabbi of the Israeli Air Force, are among those who offer their testimony. English and Hebrew with English subtitles. 52 mins.

VHS: S23241. $39.95.

Joseph Schultz

This documentary/dramatization is the story of a Nazi soldier who refused his high command's order to massacre Jews in his village during World War II. 20 mins. English narrative.

VHS: S30209. $29.95.

The Journey of Butterfly

Charles Davidson's choral work *I Never Saw Another Butterfly* was at the center of commemorative proceedings marking the 50th anniversary of the establishment of the Ghetto Theresienstadt in Czechoslovakia. This ghetto was part of the Nazi final solution. Interviews with survivors and the musical performers round out this documentary about a painful memory. 60 mins.

VHS: S27637. $19.95.

Last Sea

When survivors of the Holocaust realized that they had neither a home to return to nor families to welcome them, thousands set out on the perilous journey to the Land of Israel. They travelled by truck or by train, many went by foot over the Alps; they had to cross the sea aboard dangerously overcrowded ships. The faces of the witnesses are never shown; only their voices are heard, as they retell stories of survival and redemption. "A film should not explain but show…The film recounts an extraordinary epic, astounding in truth, gigantic in scope" (Elie Wiesel). 90 mins.

VHS: S06571. $79.95.

The Last Seven Months of Anne Frank

This international Emmy Award-winning documentary picks up where Anne Frank's diary left off. Eight women who knew the Frank family recount the travails of the Franks in the concentration camps of Westerbork, Auschwitz, Birkenau and Bergen-Belsen. 75 mins.

VHS: S23251. $49.95.

Le Chambon: La Colline aux Mille Enfants

The French village of Le Chambon-sur-Lignon was inhabited by rough farmers of Huguenot descent. During World War II when Hitler imposed his heinous laws and set out to arrest all Jews, this village would not stand for it. Under the courageous leadership of a Christian pastor, this village risked extermination by the Nazis to provide safety and refuge for 5,000 Jewish children. Winner, International Emmy for Best Drama. French with English subtitles. 118 mins.

VHS: S34527. $29.95.

Liberation

Ben Kingsley, Whoopi Goldberg and Patrick Stewart all narrate this documentary about the liberation of Europe from the Nazis. As Allied forces gathered their strength, Jews across the continent faced a continued onslaught of terror. Newsreel footage, radio broadcasts and stories from European Jews make this a compelling look at a disastrous era. 100 mins.

VHS: S26513. $14.98.

The Long Way Home

This Academy Award-winning documentary details Holocaust survivors' lives from the end of WWII in 1945 to Israel's founding three years later. Narrated by Morgan Freeman, Martin Landau, and Ed Asner. Includes a post-Oscar introduction by producers Richard Trank and Rabbi Marvin Hier of the Museum of Tolerance in Los Angeles.

VHS: S34462. $24.95.

Mark Jonathan Harris, USA, 1997, 120 mins.

The Lost Children of Berlin

In April 1942, the Gestapo closed the last Jewish school in Berlin. Half a century later, 50 of its former students travelled from around the world to the re-opened school for an extraordinary reunion. *The Lost Children of Berlin* weaves together a portrait of the social and political landscape of pre-war Berlin, detailing its rich Jewish life that existed there. Hosted by Anthony Hopkins, with testimonies compiled by Steven Spielberg's Shoah Foundation. 50 mins.

VHS: S32370. $19.95.

Married with a Star

Wax Werkendam wed Clara de Vries in the heart of Amsterdam's Old Jewish Quarter during the Nazi occupation. The film of this wedding bears silent witness to a forgotten place. It is now the focus of the story of this couple and their guests, most of whom did not survive. 33 mins.

VHS: S23238. $39.95.

Max and Helen: A True Story

Martin Landau stars as Nazi hunter Simon Wiesenthal in this tense tale of survival and love about Max, his fiancee Helen and her sister Miriam, who are sent from Poland to a Nazi work camp. Max begs Helen to join him in escaping the brutal conditions of the camp, but her sister is too ill. Max flees to Russia but is arrested and exiled to Siberia. It is 20 years before he is free to search for Helen, whose memory has become his only reason for living. With Treat Williams, Alice Krige. Based on the book by Simon Wiesenthal.

VHS: S12312. $14.98.

Great Britain, 1990, 94 mins.

Murderers Among Us: The Simon Wiesenthal Story

Ben Kingsley is cast as the famous Holocaust survivor who became the premiere Nazi hunter. *Variety* praised this made-for-cable epic film for its "enormous power and suspense." With Renee Soutendijk, Craig T. Nelson, Jack Shepherd and Paul Freeman. Script co-written by Abby Mann.

VHS: S14006. $19.98.

Brian Gibson, USA/Great Britain/Hungary, 1989, 157 mins.

Nazi Medicine

Featuring startling footage of Hitler's death camps, *Nazi Medicine* is a shocking yet important study of the role of doctors during the Third Reich. Chronicles the road traveled by the Nazi physicians, from providing medical justification for the 1933 Nuremberg sterilization laws to trying to justify their role in the Holocaust as defendants in the 1946-47 Nuremberg Doctors' Trial. "The horror of Nazi eugenics and experimentation…this is a work of truth and timeliness" (Allan A. Ryan, Director, U.S. Department of Justice, Office of Special Investigations).

VHS: S32672. $29.95.

Night and Fog

A newly mastered version of what Francois Truffaut called "the greatest film of all time": Alain Resnais' incredibly powerful, searing, unforgettable film on Nazi concentration camps, truly a film for all time. Edited by Chris Marker. French with English subtitles.

VHS: S00930. $19.95.

Alain Resnais, France, 1955, 32 mins.

Nightmare

Documentary covering the nightmare years during the Nazi Holocaust. English narrative. 40 mins.

VHS: S30208. $29.95.

Not Like Sheep to the Slaughter: The Story of the Bialystok Ghetto

A historically important work about the heroic Jewish resistance during the Holocaust, set during the summer of 1943, centering on the underground activities of Mordechai Tenenbaum, who led the fight against the Nazi program to liquidate the Bialystok ghetto. The program uncovers new evidence and archival materials. English language version. 150 mins.

VHS: S17940. $79.95.

The Only Way

In the tradition of *The Holocaust, The Hiding Place* and *Playing for Time*, this is the true and magnificent saga of Denmark's valorous actions to save Danish Jews from Nazi extermination at peril of death. With Jane Seymour and Martin Potter.

VHS: S34203. $19.95.

Bent Christensen, Denmark/Great Britain, 1970, 86 mins.

Opening the Gates of Hell: American Liberators of the Nazi Concentration Camps

A harrowing documentary that interviews a number of American servicemen who liberated the Nazi concentration camps, recalling their shock and dread at what they experienced. The innocent Jews re-imagine the bravery, generosity and humanity of the troops. "Most of all, they remember with great clarity the day they opened the gates of hell." 45 mins.

VHS: S17943. $39.95.

Preserving the Past to Ensure the Future

Ray Errol Fox's film deals with the one and a half million children who were murdered under Nazi persecution. He talks with people from all walks of life as they express their profound shock at the incomprehensible realities which are confronted upon visiting the children's memorial in the Yad Vashem museum in Jerusalem. Current news footage of racist violence around the world is juxtaposed with images from the children's museum to make a powerful experience for the viewer. 15 mins.

VHS: S12903. $29.95.

The Rails to Hell...and Back

David Bergman survived the Holocaust. In this film he recounts the suffering experienced by his family and millions of others because of Nazi persecution. 66 mins.

VHS: S23740. $99.95.

Raoul Wallenberg: Between the Lines

Through interviews with colleagues, Holocaust survivors, newsreels and rare footage shot by Nazi camera crews and others, this controversial story of Raoul Wallenberg's heroic campaign to save thousands of Jews from Budapest is relived. With diplomatic maneuvers and ingenious tactics, this Swedish diplomat stood fast against Nazi leader Adolph Eichmann's scheme of mass extermination. When the Russians invaded Budapest, Wallenberg was imprisoned and Soviet officials claim to this day that he died in July of 1947, disputing evidence of sightings, as late as 1979, which appear to prove otherwise. 1984, 90 mins.

VHS: S13677. $29.95.

Rescuers: Stories of Courage— Two Women

Based on the book *Rescuers: Portraits of Moral Courage in the Holocaust*, directed by Peter Bogdanovich and executive produced by Barbra Streisand and Cis Corman, these two true-life dramas feature the courageous stories of two women who risked their lives for the love of humanity in order to defend the Jewish people during the Nazi regime. In *Mamushka*, Gertruda Babilinska (Elizabeth Perkins) is a Polish nanny employed by the wealthy Jewish Stolowitsky family, who devotes her life to the Stolowitskys and travels with them as they flee from the Nazis, agreeing to protect and care for the Stolowitsky's young son, Mickey, and raise him in his Jewish faith after his parents die. *Woman on a Bicycle* is the story of Marie-Rose Gineste (Sela Ward), a single woman employed by the Church who helps counterfeit special identity documents for Jewish refugees. With the aid of her bicycle, Marie-Rose travels to various villages disseminating secret communications to assist the underground resistance movement.

VHS: S34403. $79.99.

Peter Bogdanovich, USA, 1997, 107 mins.

The Righteous Enemy

Beginning with the story of his father who was interned by Italians occupying Yugoslavia's Adriatic coast during WWII, Rochlitz enlarges his account to show how Italian officials prevented the deportation of some 40,000 Jews in Italian-occupiedzones of France, Greece and Yugoslavia. English commentary and subtitles.

VHS: S16318. $90.00.

The Road to Wannsee: Eleven Million Sentenced to Death

On January 20, 1942, 11 million Jews were sentenced to death at Wannsee. The trajectory that led to this death sentence-Hitler's political rise to power, the neutralizing of his opponents, and his obsession with eliminating the Jews—is the subject of this documentary. Archival footage and interviews with respected historians are featured. Dutch with English subtitles. 50 mins.

VHS: S23233. $39.95.

Schindler

The black marketeer, womanizer, gambler and Nazi spy who saved over 1,000 Jews from Hitler's death camps is revealed, in this documentary, through interviews with witnesses of his deeds and the survivors of his efforts. Schindler's widow, his driver Richard Rechen (who drove Schindler to safety at the war's close), and the mistress of Amon Goeth (the "Butcher of Plaszow"), speaking just hours before her suicide, are included in this fascinating, British-produced portrait of Oskar Schindler.

VHS: S21096. $19.98.

Schindler (The True Story)

Amidst the tragedies of the Third Reich, Oskar Schindler emerged as a hero who saved many of his Jewish employees despite the risk it posed to his own safety. This documentary records the enormity of his achievement. 52 mins.

VHS: S26600. $19.95.

Shoah

Claude Lanzmann's landmark, monumental epic of the Holocaust, a 9½ hour assemblage of witnesses—death camp survivors and Nazi functionaries—whose combined testimony amounts to one of the most shattering human documents ever recorded. French with English subtitles.

VHS: S01190. $299.95.

Claude Lanzmann, France, 1985, 570 mins.

Shtetl: A Journal of the Holocaust

The true story of Bransk, a small Polish shtetl that died overnight when all its Jewish residents were transported to Treblinka's gas chambers. A haunting story with tragic consequences emerges through interviews, photographs and personal stories. From FRONTLINE. Two videos. 180 mins.
VHS: S31422. $39.95.

Simon Wiesenthal: Freedom Is Not a Gift from Heaven

This is the life story of the world's greatest Nazi hunter, from his childhood in Ukraine, to his wartime experiences in various concentration camps, through his liberation by Americans in 1945, all told on the occasion of his 85th birthday. 60 mins.
VHS: S23234. $39.95.

So Many Miracles

A haunting memory piece about two Holocaust survivors, Israel and Frania Rubinek, who, joined by their actor son Saul, return to the small Polish village of Pinczow for an emotional reunion with Zofia and Ludwig Banya. Along with their son Maniek, the Banyas sheltered the Rubineks from the Nazis for 28 months.
VHS: S19533. $36.00.
Smalley/Sarin, Canada, 1987/93, 58 mins.

Sorrow: The Nazi Legacy

Six Swedish teenagers, two of whom are Jewish, travel to Auschwitz. Beginning in Wannsee, they embark on an emotional journey that cannot help them comprehend the full weight of that terrible time. They meet a survivor who inspires them with hope, and the son of Hans Frank, the Nazi governor General of Poland, upon their return. 33 mins.
VHS: S23240. $39.95.

Sosua

In 1938, 32 nations met at the Evian Conference to find new homes for endangered European Jews. Only the Dominican Republic offered sanctuary. In 1940, a group of Jews escaping Nazi persecution found a haven on this beautiful Caribbean island of Sosua. This is their courageous story. 30 mins.
VHS: S12891. $34.95.

Station of Sorrow

This Holocaust documentary focuses on a train station in France where Jews were transported, and the story of the fate of the many people who passed through it. English narrative. 45 mins.
VHS: S30207. $29.95.

The Summer of Aviya

The story of one summer in the life of Aviya, a ten-year-old girl, the daughter of a Holocaust survivor, during the first years of Israel's independence. Aviya's mother had been a partisan fighter during the war and walked the thin line between sanity and madness; Aviya lived in orphanages most of her life. This was the summer she would return home. Based on the life of Gila Almagor, writer/producer and star of the film. Winner of the Silver Bear, Berlin Film Festival and three silver Menorah awards, Israel. "The emotionally powerful story…reveals the scars, both mental and physical, that Holocaust survivors brought with them to Israel" (American Historical Review). Hebrew with English subtitles.
VHS: S30527. $79.95.
Eli Cohen, Israel, 1989, 96 mins.

Survivors of the Holocaust

Steven Spielberg, in association with the Survivors of the Shoah Visual History Foundation, brings this intimate collection of survivor testimonials to video. In addition, there is archival footage and extra material hosted by Ben Kingsley. "A superlative chronicle of the Holocaust…heartrending yet uplifting…an outstanding living history lesson" (*TV Guide*).
VHS: S27402. $19.98.
Laser: LD75922. $39.99.

Theresienstadt: Gateway to Auschwitz

More than 140,000 Jews were interned at the Czech fortress town of Terezin. This model ghetto was a transit camp for Auschwitz. Of the 15,000 in Theresienstadt who were under 15, less than 100 survived. Now the story of hope that was nourished by these children through a variety of cultural activities stands revealed in this prize-winning documentary. 57 mins.
VHS: S23242. $39.95.

They Risked Their Lives: Rescuers of the Holocaust

From 1986-1988 Gay Block and Malka Drucker interviewed and photographed more than 100 Gentile Holocaust rescuers who defied the Nazis to shield Jews during the war. Block's video chronicles the passionate and heroic acts of these brave men and women, their selfless courage and manifest honor. 54 mins.
VHS: S17941. $39.95.

Tibor Jankay—The Art of Survival

Jankay is 94 years old, but this highly personal artist had to escape the horrors of the Holocaust in order to pursue such a long life dedicated to his art. His many stories of survival have helped young artists in his adoptive home, Santa Monica, California. This film explores both his life from his time in Hungary to his inspirational impact in California. Many of his paintings, sculptures and sketches have not been exhibited and this film offers a unique opportunity to view Jankay's work.
VHS: S29535. $19.95.
Harlan Steinberger, USA, 1994, 40 mins.

Together at Last

Aaron Zeigelman thought that he, his mother and his sisters were the only Zeigelmans to survive the Holocaust. A genealogist discovered that in fact a large branch of the family had survived. In celebration, Aaron invited the entire family to New York. 58 mins.
VHS: S23248. $39.95.

The Trial of Adolf Eichmann

A compelling documentary about the trial that marked the beginning of Holocaust consciousness, containing actual trial footage of one of the most notorious men in history. Hosted by David Brinkley. 120 mins.
VHS: S31404. $19.95.

Tsvi Nussbaum: Boy from Warsaw

For many the defining icon of the wide-scale Jewish suffering and oppression was the young boy, his arms held up, as the Nazis held their guns at his back. This provocative, revealing documentary considers the intervening life of that young man, Dr. Tvsi C. Nussbaum, as "well as a moving testimony of that era." 50 mins.
VHS: S17944. $39.95.

The Visas That Saved Lives

Chiune Sugihara awoke one summer morning in 1940 to discover that 200 people were awaiting his help. He was the Japanese consul in Lithuania, and he took it upon himself to write 1600 visas that saved an estimated 2000-6000 lives. This is the story of a man who sacrificed his own career to help those no one else would. Japanese with English subtitles. 115 mins.
VHS: S23252. $49.95.

Visualizing Memory...A Last Detail

Peter Kleinman, a native of Czechoslovakia, was deported in 1941 to Auschwitz and selected for forced labor at Gross-Rosen, from where he was sent on a death march to Flossenberg. This unique educational video is composed of five vignettes: The Fallacy of Race, Appropriate Memorials, Liberation, Moral Responsibility, and Thinking Critically. Using Kleinman's experiences, these topics of both contemporary and historic relevance are thoroughly examined. 53 mins.
VHS: S33180. $39.95.

The Warsaw Ghetto

Taken in part from the photo albums and cinefilms of Nazi Heinrich Himmler, this film augments those images with an extremely rare collection of newsreel footage depicting the Warsaw ghetto during the Nazi occupation of Poland. From its inception to its fiery demolition in 1943, this film documents the lives of the over 500,000 Jews who were crowded into the one-square-mile area that was the Warsaw Ghetto, put to work by the Third Reich in Nazi factories, and given only fractions of the rations allotted to "Aryan" Germans and Poles.
VHS: S05179. $29.95.
Poland, 1969, 52 mins.

Warsaw Story

This award-winning short drama movingly recounts the true story of the escape of a Jewish family (the filmmaker's own family) from Poland in 1939, miraculously eluding the occupying Nazi forces and preserving their young son's innocence. Public performance rights included.
VHS: S33385. $59.95.
Amir Mann, USA, 1996, 18 mins.

We Were So Beloved

More than 20,000 German Jewish refugees settled in Washington Heights in Upper Manhattan during the 30's and created a solid, secure middle-class enclave dubbed "Frankfurt-on-the-Hudson." Director Manfred Kirchheimer, one of the refugees, unravels the complexities of the people who were his friends, neighbors and parents, all of them powerfully shaped by the Nazi experience. "Though *We Were So Beloved* is mostly about those who escaped the immediate effects of the Holocaust," wrote Vincent Canby in *The New York Times*, "it is a no less harrowing examination of conscience than *Shoah* and Marcel Ophuls' *Sorrow and the Pity*. In this limited, quite commonplace landscape of Washington Heights, Mr. Kirchheimer finds ghosts not always visible to the naked eye."
VHS: S09443. $65.00.
Manfred Kirchheimer, USA, 1986, 145 mins.

We Were There: Jewish Liberators of the Nazi Concentration Camps

Among the liberators of the Nazi Concentration Camps were numerous Jewish G.I.s. This video chronicles the moving accounts of the Jewish American soldiers who were present at the liberation of the camps, the unforgettable atrocities they witnessed, and the victims of the Holocaust that they liberated. Many of the G.I.s developed lifelong friendships with the Holocaust survivors they rescued. Ultimately, this film tells a story of love and renewal that grew out of horrific circumstances.
VHS: S27251. $24.95.
Paul Hansen, USA, 1994, 40 mins.

Who Shall Live and Who Shall Die?

Laurence Jarvik's searing documentary on the role of American Jewry in World War II as the U.S. government and American Jewish community fail to respond to the atrocities across the Atlantic.
VHS: S04723. $29.95.
Laurence Jarvik, USA, 1978, 90 mins.

Witness to Genocide

A brutal expose about Hitler's twisted plan to eliminate an entire race through torture and execution. From the series *The Nazis*. 50 mins.
VHS: S12732. $24.98.

Witness to the Holocaust: Trial of Adolf Eichmann

This record presents the extensive testimony and evidence which revealed the scope of Eichmann's responsibility, including numerous eye-witness accounts. The first comprehensive examination of Eichmann. 90 mins.
VHS: S06633. $39.95.

The World of Anne Frank

This docudrama highlights selected moments of Anne Frank's important diary. Rare film footage, photographs, and interviews with Anne's father and those who risked their lives hiding her, bring important background information to the story of this young girl. 28 mins.
VHS: S23243. $39.95.

THE VIETNAM WAR

The 317th Platoon

A brilliant evocation of the senselessness of war during the last days of the French occupation of Indochina, based on the director's own experiences of being taken prisoner at Dien Buen Phu. The film tells of the platoon's retreat, focusing on a career soldier and the commanding young lieutenant as they make their way through ambushes, betrayals, rain, jungle, villages, pain, disease and inexorable fatigue to inevitable annihilation. With awesome cinematography by Raoul Coutard. With Jacques Perrin, Bruno Cremer, Pierre Fabre and Manuel Zarzo. French with English subtitles.
VHS: S13224. $59.95.
Pierre Schoendoerffer, France, 1965, 100 mins.

Anderson Platoon

One of the great films about Vietnam, directed by Pierre Schoendoerffer, the documentary focuses on an integrated combat unit led by Black West Pointer Lt. Joseph B. Anderson, and captures the tension, anger, hopelessness and pathos of armed conflict. Winner of the Academy Award for Best Documentary Feature.
VHS: S02404. $19.95.
Pierre Schoendoerffer, France, 1967, 65 mins.

Choosing Sides: I Remember Vietnam

This program introduces you to heroes, draft dodgers, peace activists, nurses and POWs who recount the most difficult decisions they made during the Vietnam War. First-person narratives juxtaposed with stunning archival footage, set against a backdop of '60s music, take you from the killing fields of the Vietnamese highlands to one-on-one combat in Hue.

Choosing Sides: I Remember Vietnam—Fields of Fire. Meet Robert Holcomb, a man who was presented with a choice of informing on the black panthers or going to war; Senator John McCain, who chose to remain in a POW camp, rather than receive preferential treatment; and Jan Barry, a disillusioned West Point graduate who decided to join the peace movement. 48 mins.

VHS: S34219. $19.98.

Choosing Sides: I Remember Vietnam—The War at Home. This program follows Dr. Howard Levy who was court-martialed and jailed for refusing to train Green Berets; Harry Maruer, a university student who got a psychiatric deferral to evade the draft; and Tom Cornell, a civil rights activist who was one of the first to get arrested for burning his draft card. 48 mins.

VHS: S34220. $19.98.

Dear America: Letters Home from Vietnam

More than 30 celebrities read the actual letters of Vietnam veterans accompanied by striking visual footage and nostalgic music of the times. A touching salute to those who fought and to those who died. Readers include Robin Williams, Martin Sheen, Matt Dillon, Willem Dafoe, Tom Berenger, Howard Rollins Jr., Michael J. Fox, Sean Penn and Kathleen Turner. Based on the book by the same name.

VHS: S09921. $19.98.

Bill Couturie, USA, 1988, 87 mins.

The Fall of Saigon

For three days panic reigned in Saigon, the former capital of South Vietnam. As crowds filled the streets, helicopters filled the skies offering hope of a way out. Those who left and those who stayed behind offer chilling testimony to that troubled critical moment in time that marked the end of the war in Vietnam in this *Discovery Channel* production. 90 mins.

VHS: S26043. $19.95.

Great Days of History: Prelude to Vietnam

The rise and fall of French imperial ambitions in Indochina from the 18th century to the battle of Dien Bien Phu are detailed here using rare footage from the French Army Archives. 56 mins.

VHS: S09437. $29.95.

Hitchhiking Vietnam: Letters from the Trail

Karin Muller, a 28-year-old former management consultant, leads a fascinating solo trek through an enchanted Vietnam far off the tourist map, from the hustling backstreets of Saigon and Hanoi to a remote Hmong tribal mountain village few foreigners have ever seen. A PBS WGBH Boston Special. 60 mins.

VHS: S33087. $19.95.

Kindred Men of a Dark War

Beyond the politics and controversy which surrounded the Vietnam War were the men who served on the battle lines. This video is the simple testimony of three decorated Vietnam War heroes. The candid and often emotional video examines the human bond among those who find themselves in great danger. Each of the men has a unique story to tell about fear, uncommon valor and an unbreakable love for their brothers in combat. 28 mins.

VHS: S10136. $24.95.

Maya Lin: A Strong Clear Vision

The story of the artist/sculptor/architect who, while an undergraduate at Yale, designed one of the most bitterly debated public monuments, the Vietnam Veterans Memorial. The film follows her throughout the creative process as she produces a succession of eloquent, highly original sculptures and monuments that capture and memorialize significant American social events. Compelling viewing. "The film is absolutely riveting" (Peter Stack, *San Francisco Chronicle*).

VHS: S30482. $59.95.

Freida Lee Mock, USA, 1995, 96 mins.

No Time for Tears—Vietnam: The Women Who Served

Seven oral histories from former nurses, Red Cross volunteers and intelligence officers are intricately woven into a moving documentary. The entire story is here, from their having to adjust to horrific conditions to their troubling homecomings. Includes period music from The Beach Boys and Credence Clearwater Revival.

VHS: S26453. $75.00.

Elizabeth Bouiss, USA, 1993, 60 mins.

Of Heroes & Helicopters

A fascinating account of the role played by helicopter pilots during the Vietnam War is offered on this video. Powerful stories from these men, including two Congressional Medal of Honor Winners, describe how they helped "save the day" for thousands of soldiers. USA, 60 mins.

VHS: S27246. $29.95.

Program for Vietnam Veterans

Charles Haid ("Hill Street Blues") hosts an evening of speeches and entertainment aimed at Vietnam era vets.

VHS: S02743. $29.95.

Situation Critical: The USS Forrestal

The true story of fire aboard an aircraft during the Vietnam War that claimed over 100 lives. Relive the tragedy and witness the heroism of the sailors who fought to save their ship.

VHS: S32719. $19.98.

Peter Mullett, USA, 1997, 50 mins.

The Story of the Vietnam Veterans Memorial: The Last Landing Zone

Narrated by decorated Vietnam Veteran and former Pittsburgh Steeler running back, Rocky Bleier, this video evokes the emotional turmoil of the Vietnam War and shows how this Memorial has reconciled Vietnam Veterans with their country. 40 mins.

VHS: S37079. $29.95.

Terror in the Minefields

Investigate the terror and tragedy of Cambodia's deadly legacy of mine fields. 60 mins.

VHS: S28663. $19.95.

Turbulent End to a Tragic War: America's Final Hours in Vietnam

The story of the fall of Saigon, America's last desperate bastion in the Vietnam War, of the soldiers and civilians who fled on the final day, as well as those left behind. From ABC News. 60 mins.

VHS: S12690. $24.98.

Vietnam

This seven-volume series, produced by CBS News, studies the roots of the conflict, the American involvement during the French Indochina war, the partitioning of the country, the American military "advisors" dispatched to Saigon, the Gulf of Tonkin episode, the escalation of the war, the Tet Offensive, Richard Nixon's political victory, the invasion of Cambodia and the restricted role of American support troops. With the conclusion of the war, the fall of Saigon, the program studies the personal and social implications, the countercultural protests to end the war and the psychologically scarred veterans who returned, victims of post-traumatic stress disorder (PTSD). With reporting by Dan Rather, Ed Bradley and Charles Kuralt. Hosted by Walter Cronkite. 750 mins.

VHS: S19540. $139.98.

Vietnam Experience

Images of the Vietnam War are combined with the music and lyrics of Country Joe McDonald. 30 mins.

VHS: S04527. $19.95.

Vietnam Home Movies

Powerful personal documentaries of the Vietnam War featuring the amateur footage shot in 8mm by soldiers during their tour of duty. Each veteran narrates his own segment of the tape.

Vietnam Home Movies Vol. 1. 30 mins.

VHS: S11915. $19.99.

Vietnam Home Movies Vol. 2. 30 mins.

VHS: S11916. $19.99.

Vietnam War Story III

Three new, award-winning, true-to-life stories based on the Vietnamese experience. *Malone* is the story of a flippant soldier who is lost in the jungle; *Dusk to Dawn*, the story of a young marine's self-doubts; and *The Promise*, the story of Mary, a young nurse who arrives for her tour of duty, facing the agony of wounded and dying men. 90 mins.

VHS: S11008. $79.99.

Vietnam—The Hot Red War

This is the first film released in the United States that gives enthusiastic, partisan voice to our enemies in Vietnam, the communists of the North, the "patriots of Nam". A powerful film that will fuel explosive emotions. 55 mins.

VHS: S12714. $24.95.

Vietnam: A Television History

The landmark, 13-hour Emmy award-winning television documentary that records the events from the 1945 revolution against the French in Vietnam to the U.S. evacuation following the fall of Saigon in April 1975. Produced by WGBH in Boston, the six-year project carefully analyzes the costs and consequences of the American military involvement in Vietnam, the strife at home and the psychological scars of the national soul.

Volume 1: *The Roots of War, The First Vietnam War (1946-1954).*

VHS: S02729. $29.95.

Volume 2: *America's Mandarin (1954-1963)* and *LBJ Goes to War (1964-1965).*

VHS: S02730. $29.95.

Volume 3: *America Takes Charge (1965-1967)* and *With America's Enemy (1954-1967).* A view of Vietnam from some of the soldiers who were sent there and a view of the war as told by the North and South Vietnamese communist fighters, who fought Americans. 120 mins.

VHS: S02731. $29.95.

Volume 4: *Tet, 1968* and *Vietnamizing the War (1969-1973).* The lunar New Year offensive and its military and political consequences. Nixon's troop withdrawals, increased bombing and arms infusion to Saigon. 120 mins.

VHS: S02732. $29.95.

Volume 5: *No Neutral Ground: Cambodia and Laos* and *Peace Is at Hand.* Despite technical neutrality, Vietnam's neighbors are drawn in. The prolonged Paris peace talks within the context of other political events. 120 mins.

VHS: S02733. $29.95.

Volume 6: *Homefront, U.S.A.* and *The End of the Tunnel (1973-1975).* A focus on the hearts and minds of Americans as they evaluate the undeclared war. The South Vietnamese, denied U.S. support, are defeated. 120 mins.

VHS: S02734. $29.95.

Volume 7: *Legacies.* The lessons, consequences and questions summarized by the metaphor "Vietnam." 60 mins.

VHS: S02735. $19.95.

Complete Set.

VHS: S02736. $99.95.

Vietnam: Chronicle of War

CBS News produced this documentary which traces the steps of U.S. involvement in Vietnam, narrated by Walter Cronkite. 89 mins.

VHS: S02642. $19.98.

Vietnam: In the Year of the Pig

One of the most powerful films ever produced about Vietnam, and an Academy Award nominee. "Passionate and committed, yet it impresses by its sobriety… and will be worth seeing after Vietnam for it raises questions" (*Washington Post*).

VHS: S01416. $39.95.

Emile de Antonio, USA, 1968, 103 mins.

Vietnam: Remember

Documentary footage traces the pivotal battle of Khe Sahn and how the American G.I.'s survived the fierce jungle fighting. Also: on patrol on a deadly search for Vietcong. 60 minutes.

VHS: S02314. $39.95.

Vietnam: The Secret Agent

The first comprehensive look at the history, effects and implications of the deadly contaminant used in the defoliant called Agent Orange. The film exposes the climate of fear and frustration among veterans exposed to Agent Orange while in Vietnam.

VHS: S01998. $29.95.

Jacki Ochs, USA, 1983, 56 mins.

Vietnam: The Ten Thousand Day War

This award-winning series, written by Pulitzer Prize winner and CNN correspondent Peter Arnett and narrated by Richard Basehart, offers objective insight into the real story behind the longest, most controversial war in modern history. With amazing wartime footage shot by both sides. Six-tape set. 6½ hours.

VHS: S34825. $99.95.

Vietnam: Time of the Locust

A collection of short films addressing several sides of the Vietnam War: *Time of the Locust*, funded by the American Friends Service Committee, containing suppressed footage shot by Japanese television; *A Day in Vietnam*, narrated by Jack Webb; and *The Battle*, another government-sponsored film in which Marines are shown driving Vietnamese out from caves. USA, 55 mins.

VHS: S01997. $29.95.

Vietnam: Two Decades and a Wake Up

This documentary follows eight battle-scarred veterans as they return to the land of their nightmares in order to free their wounded psyches and make peace with the past. 60 mins.

VHS: S13886. $19.98.

War at Home

A major film about the anti-war movement in America, concentrating on the growth of the anti-war movement in Madison, Wisconsin. The film emerges as a compelling story of how this movement grew as a genuine revolt against government policy, and documents how both policy and values were challenged and changed.

VHS: S01999. $29.95.

Glenn Silber, USA, 1976, 100 mins.

We Can Keep You Forever

A dramatic documentary that examines the possibility that many of America's M.I.A.'s are still alive and being held captive in Vietnam and Laos. Called "compelling" by *The New York Times*, and endorsed by former POW senator John McClain. Based on a year-long investigation by British TV journalists. 75 mins.

VHS: S07678. $59.95.

The Wild Ones: The Air Cavalry in Vietnam

The Air Cavalry was perhaps the most effective flying force ever conceived. These hunter-killer helicopter teams were relentless in their Vietnam War search-and-destroy missions. Given the difficulty of their task, these forces developed bonds with one another that would last a lifetime. USA, 50 mins.

VHS: S27247. $29.95.

THE CIVIL WAR

America's Civil War

This dramatic 10-volume series features reenactments on actual battle sites of major Civil War conflicts. Volumes include 1861: 1st Manassas: Amateurs Collide at Bull Run, 1862: Shiloh: Surprise & Slaughter in Tennessee, 1862: Antietam: the Rebels Strike North, 1863: Chancellorsville: Rebel Victory, Rebel Loss, 1863: Bloody Standoff in Pennsylvania, 1863: Vicksburg: Key to the Mississippi, 1864: Spotsylvania: The Epic Duel of Grant & Lee, 1864: Atlanta: Yankees Invade the Deep South, 1864: Franklin: The Death of Hood's Army and 1865: Appomattox: Collapse of the Confederate Dream. 7½ hours.
VHS: S31479. $129.99.

American History: The Civil War

Famous events from the Civil War are recounted and analyzed, including Lincoln's campaign for President, John Brown's Abolitionist movement, the battles of the *Merrimac* and the *Monitor*, Bull Run and Gettysburg. 30 minutes.
VHS: S02136. $29.95.

Atlanta Cyclorama—The Battle of Atlanta

Relive the Battle of Atlanta with a visit to the world-famous Atlanta Cyclorama. See the entire Cyclorama show, learn the complete story of this key Civil War battle, the events that led up to it and the story behind the restoration of the Cyclorama. 30 mins.
VHS: S11478. $29.95.

Battle of Antietam

Focusing on the battle of Antietam, the single bloodiest day in American history, and what many consider the turning point in the War between the States, this battlefield tour is led by historian William K. Brown as he points out crucial spots in the fight, and with the aid of photographs, sketches and maps, describes the various strategies of the Confederate and Union armies. 56 mins.
VHS: S08019. $29.95.

Blue and the Gray

The Civil War is refought with an impressive grouping of big stars and a cast of thousands. This TV mini-series includes the talents of Stacy Keach, Lloyd Bridges, Colleen Dewhurst, Warren Oates, Rory Calhoun, John Hammond, Rip Torn, Geraldine Page, Paul Winfield and Gregory Peck as Abraham Lincoln. Great battle scenes. Story by John Leekly and Bruce Catton.
VHS: S12845. $29.95.
Andrew V. McLaglen, USA, 1988

The Civil War (Ken Burns/PBS)

Ken Burns' brilliant nine-part documentary about the American Civil War from PBS chronicles the Civil War from its causes in 1861 through the assassination of Lincoln in 1865. Five years in the making, this staggering achievement should be required viewing for anyone interested in American history. Complete set.
VHS: S14823. $149.98.
Ken Burns, USA, 1990, 680 mins.

The Civil War (Parade Video)

Experience the greatest battles of the Civil War with this series of five collector's editions. (This series is not to be confused with the PBS series directed by Ken Burns.)
Antietam: The Bloodiest Day in American History. Narrated by Dr. Jay Luvass, co-editor of the U.S. Army War College Guide.
VHS: S13543. $14.95.
Chickamauga: River of Death. Narrated by John Cissell, Chief Interpreter, National Park Service.
VHS: S13545. $14.95.
Gettysburg: July 1st-3rd, 1863. The Civil War's greatest battle. Narrated by Bruce Catton and Stacy Keach.
VHS: S13542. $14.95.
New Market: Field of Honor. Narrated by Joseph W.A. Whitehorne, U.S. Army Historian.
VHS: S13544. $14.95.
The Civil War Photographers. Featuring the photographs of Matthew B. Brady, Alexander Gardner, George N. Barnard, George S. Cook, Timothy H. O'Sullivan, James Gibson and many others. Narrated by Gary Merrill.
VHS: S13541. $14.95.

The Civil War

The story of America's Civil War is told through original black-and-white illustrations, created during the war by artists at the scene of the battles. See Manassas, Gettysburg, Shiloh, Vicksburg, and other moments come alive in this vivid program. 30 minutes.
VHS: S02470. $29.95.
Laser: LD72292. $229.95.

Civil War Diary

Based on the award-winning novel *Across Five Aprils*, this is the story of a courageous young man struggling to save his family from the devastation brought on by the Civil War. Winner of the coveted International Heritage Award 1990. USA, 82 mins.
VHS: S15276. $79.95.

Civil War Journal

In 13 episodes this thorough documentary sifts through diaries and historical photographs for a glimpse of our nation's most traumatic historic crises. It combines little known facts with personal observations and factual re-enactments. From the opening canon blast at Fort Sumter Danny Glover will lead you through this highly entertaining look at America's Civil War.
VHS: S20597. $119.95.

Civil War Journal, Set II

This six-volume collection continues the story of the war between the states. It includes *Robert E. Lee, Fredericksburg, The War Reporters, Lincoln and Gettysburg* and many more. Altogether there are 13 50-minute episodes detailing every aspect of this wrenching historic event.
VHS: S25867. $119.95.

Civil War Journal: The 54th Massachusetts

This is the true story behind the movie *Glory*. Over 180,000 black men were in the Union Army at the end of the Civil War. This acclaimed A & E program examines the most famous such company, the 54th Massachusetts, whose heroics at the battle of Fort Wagner are the stuff of legend. But were they chosen for their valor, or because they were deemed expendable? 50 mins.
VHS: S30843. $19.95.

Civil War Journey

This riverboat tour of historic sites along the South's most scenic rivers brings to life both sides of the Civil War with commentary about the rivers, boats and places that played an important role in the outcome of the war, including the Battles of Shiloh, Vicksburg, Fort Donelson, Chickamauga and Chattanooga. 50 mins.
VHS: S31397. $19.95.

Civil War Legends

Four great personalities from the Civil War—*Stonewall Jackson, Ulysses S. Grant, Abraham Lincoln* and *Robert E. Lee*—are featured in this biographical video set. Photos, period art, documents and the commentary of noted historians are brought together in each tape to reveal not only the trajectory of these men's life stories, but also the unique personality behind these monumental figures. Each episode is approximately 30 minutes long.
VHS: S27784. $39.85.

The Civil War: 125th Anniversary Series

A series of exciting and informative videotapes, for sale on an individual basis only, dramatizing the greatest battles of the Civil War.
1st Manassas.
VHS: S14886. $29.95.
Shiloh.
VHS: S14887. $29.95.
Antietam.
VHS: S14888. $39.95.
Chancellorsville.
VHS: S14889. $29.95.
Gettysburg.
VHS: S14890. $39.95.
Vicksburg.
VHS: S14891. $29.95.
Spotsylvania.
VHS: S14892. $39.95.
Atlanta.
VHS: S14893. $39.95.
Franklin.
VHS: S14894. $29.95.
Appomattox.
VHS: S14895. $39.95.

Civil War: The Fiery Trial

Recounts the enduring drama of America's bloodiest conflict. On site photography, archival photographs, period art and music tell the story of the war's major campaigns, battles and leaders. Narrated by Edwin Newman.
VHS: S08461. $19.95.

The Divided Union

An extraordinary series of six one-hour tapes on the Civil War—perhaps the most ambitious project ever undertaken to document the history, feelings, and contradictions of an America divided. The set, featuring hundreds of rare photographs, documents, and interviews with top experts on the Civil War, comes complete with an annotated index which refers to numbered sections within each tape, a facsimile of the Gettysburg Address, and other supplementary informative material. This very limited designer edition is available for a limited time only. Complete six-tape set.
VHS: S06108. $99.95.

Faces of Battle Series

Exciting dramatizations of famous Civil War conflicts. Filmed on the privately-owned battle sites. Three videocassettes for sale on an individual basis only.
Bentonville. The Appomattox of the West.
VHS: S14898. $29.95.
Cedar Mountain. Led by Stonewall Jackson.
VHS: S14896. $29.95.
Petersburg. Excellent re-creation of African-American troops in action.
VHS: S14897. $29.95.

Gettysburg (Documentary)

The Battle of Gettyusburg, fought from July 1-3, 1863, is authentically recreated on location by a cast of thousands in this thrilling video history of one of America's fiercest conflicts. 40 mins.
VHS: S09946. $29.95.

Gettysburg (Martin Sheen)

The Civil War's most famous battle, at Gettysburg, is the center of this epic featuring stars Tom Berenger and Martin Sheen. It combines costume drama detail and riveting war scene footage to bring that troubled event to life.
VHS: S20616. $24.98.
Ronald F. Maxwell, USA, 1993, 254 mins.

Gettysburg Battlefield Tour

This inspiring video tour of the Gettysburg National Military Park takes the viewer chronologically through the decisive battles of the Civil War, and concludes with a stirring rendition of Lincoln's Gettysburg Address. 35 mins.
VHS: S09945. $29.95.

Grant and Lee

Grant and Lee experienced the Civil War from opposite sides. Here they both discuss their decisions and personal views. If Grant experienced his fight as a battle for justice, Lee saw in his utter defeat the end of a way of life. 33 mins.
VHS: S23734. $79.95.

Great Campaigns of the Civil War: Touring Civil War Battlefields, Volumes I and II

Great battles from the West, including Shiloh, Vicksburg, Chickamauga, Ft. Donelson and New Orleans, are portrayed in this documentary. Two-volume set, 120 mins.
VHS: S23133. $49.95.

Great Union Presidents

A documentary that probes the personal and public lives of two complicated, fascinating presidents, Abraham Lincoln and Ulysses S. Grant. 60 mins.
VHS: S19664. $9.99.

Guns of the Civil War

This documentary series of three tapes examines the weapons which fought the war between the States.
Vol. 1: A Greater Moral Force.
VHS: S20601. $24.95.
Vol. 2: Measure for Measure.
VHS: S20602. $24.95.
Vol. 3: Against the Thunderstorm.
VHS: S20603. $24.95.
Complete set.
VHS: S20600. $69.95.

Ironclads: The Monitor and the Merrimac

Tells the story of the two astonishing vessels that fought the most memorable naval battles of the Civil War, and forever revolutionized maritime warfare. Noted experts discuss how the distinctive ships came to be built, how they influenced later fighting craft. Period prints, etchings, photographs and paintings re-create the first battle between iron ships, with dramatic undersea images of the Monitor now resting on the floor of the Atlantic Ocean. Narrated by Edwin Newman. 30 mins.
VHS: S11125. $19.95.

Lincoln

This four-hour program is a biography of the 16th President which interweaves the personal and political with background materials and commentary provided by actors playing Lincoln's important contemporaries. The program utilizes rare archival materials and Lincoln-era memorabilia. With the voices of Arnold Schwarzennegger, Oprah Winfrey, Jason Robards, James Earl Jones, Glenn Close, Eli Wallach, Ossie Davis, Olympia Dukakis, Maureen Stapleton and Richard Thomas.

Vol. 1: The Making of the President. An accumulation of personal details, images of his home, books and personal effects, that reveal roots and origins.
VHS: S18111. $14.98.

Vol. 2: The Pivotal Year: 1863. At the height of the Civil War, Lincoln led the Union in the formation of the Emancipation Proclamation and the freeing of the slaves. The program focuses on the events and stories behind the president's Gettysburg Address.
VHS: S18112. $14.98.

Vol. 3: "I Want to Finish this Job": 1864. The fractured political and social order of the Civil War was the dominant issue of Lincoln's 1864 re-election campaign. He was determined to maintain his promise to preserve the Union.
VHS: S18113. $14.98.

Vol. 4: "Now He Belongs to the Ages": 1865. The filmmakers move beyond the fanaticism of John Wilkes Booth to explore the collective guilt and rage of those who felt the president turned back their heritage and traditions.
VHS: S18114. $14.98.

Lincoln, Complete Set.
VHS: S18110. $49.98.

Long Shadows: The Legacy of the American Civil War

This documentary explores the ways in which the echoes of the Civil War still resonate in American society: from politics to economics, from civil rights to foreign policy, from individual to collective memory, and from South to North to West. Features Robert Penn Warren, Studs Terkel, Jimmy Carter, Robert Coles, Tom Wicker, Albert Murray, John Hope Franklin, James Reston, Jr. and C. Vann Woodward, as well as weekend soldiers, blues singers, battlefield guides, relic collectors, West Pointers, Vietnam veterans, old movie stars and civil rights activists. "A profound vision of the war's meaning for America's regions, races and national identity" (*Cineaste*). "A brilliant film!" (*Chicago Historical Society*).
VHS: S30147. $24.95.
Ross Spears, USA, 1987, 90 mins.

Mr. Lincoln's Springfield

Return to President Lincoln's cherished hometown and the only home he ever owned. Through historic photographs, this program conveys a vivid impression of Mr. Lincoln's relationship with his family and fellow townspeople. 30 minutes.
VHS: S02488. $29.95.

A Nation Asunder

Imagine that the spectacle of the American Civil War was unfolding right before you. *A Nation Asunder* is the first program on the Civil War to interweave photographs, documents and footage of war veterans with early filmed dramatizations. The result is a frighteningly real landscape of battle and emotional testimony taken from actual Civil War transcriptions. A stunning, two-volume (each sold separately) re-creation of the Civil War.

Part I: Brother Against Brother (1861-1863). 55 mins.
VHS: S15686. $19.98.

Part II: The Tide Turns (1863-1865). 55 mins.
VHS: S15688. $19.98.

Robert E. Lee

History comes alive in this video biography of Robert E. Lee, from his birth in the Virginia aristocracy to the fiery battlefields of the Civil War and his presidency of an emerging Southern University. Original music by Grammy-winner Jon Carroll complements footage of the landmarks of his life, historic photographs, paintings and images. 30 mins.
VHS: S09489. $19.95.

Royal Federal Blues—The Black Civil War Soldiers

This award-winning documentary shows the history of African-American soldiers in the Civil War, from their induction into the Union Army all the way to ferocious battlegrounds that marked the divide between freedom and slavery. 45 mins.
VHS: S22048. $19.98.

Smithsonian's Great Battles of the Civil War

In this comprehensive seven-volume history, the battles and strategic importance of the Civil War's seminal conflicts are played out within their vast social, military and political implications. The episodes mix re-enactments of the various campaigns, eyewitness accounts, period reconstruction and photographs, paintings and artifacts, original illustrations, period music and interviews with important scholars and historians. The series was written and directed by filmmaker Jay Wertz. Each episode is 60 mins.

Volume I.
VHS: S17094. $29.95.
Volume II.
VHS: S17095. $29.95.
Volume III.
VHS: S17096. $29.95.
Volume IV.
VHS: S17097. $29.95.
Volume V.
VHS: S17098. $29.95.
Volume VI.
VHS: S17099. $29.95.
Volume VII.
VHS: S23230. $29.95.

Songs of the Civil War

Featuring 25 popular songs from the Civil War era—folk, country, bluegrass, gospel—some standards, others rare. And each is introduced with insightful narrative and performed just as they were 130 years ago. Co-produced by Ken Burns, director of the Award-winning PBS series *The Civil War*. 60 mins.
VHS: S14603. $19.98.

The Speeches of Abraham Lincoln

An historic presentation of Lincoln's immortal words authentically illustrated with visual records of America's past. Includes rare photographs of Lincoln's life and times, original newspaper clippings, and texts of the actual speeches. All of Lincoln's most famous speeches are presented here, including, of course, The Gettysburg Address. 45 mins.
VHS: S15689. $19.98.

Stones River National Battlefield

This National Park Service program explores the history, tactics and strategies of the Battle of Stones River, the Civil War's single bloodiest day of fighting in Tennessee. It also features fascinating living history demonstrations of firing artillery, the key arm in deciding battle's outcome. 35 mins.
VHS: S09182. $29.95.

Stonewall Jackson

Tells the remarkable life story of the legendary Confederate General from his orphaned youth in Appalachia to his daring exploits on Civil War battlefields. Historians discuss Jackson's idiosyncratic personality and his great campaigns, from his boyhood in western Virginia to his early combat success in the Mexican War to his bold feats and tragic death in the War between the States. Contemporary photography, archival photographs and rare manuscripts and art work highlight this biography. 309 mins.
VHS: S11117. $19.95.

Touring Civil War Battlefields

A unique journey to the actual battlefields as they were and as they are today, where the heroic encounters of the Civil War actually happened. Thousands of authentically-trained volunteers re-enact the battles of Appomattox, the first and second Bull Run, Antietam, Fredericksburg, Gettysburg, and the final surrender at Appomattox. USA, 1986, 60 mins.
VHS: S04697. $39.95.

Ulysses S. Grant

Tells the extraordinary story of the one-time shop clerk who became commander of the Civil War's victorious union armies, and the 18th President. Traces Grant's life from his upbringing in rural Ohio to his troubled tenure as president. Historians unlock Grant's distinctive temperament, his military ingenuity, his peacetime woes through archival photographs and rare documents, as well as contemporary photography of the major sites of Grant's life. 30 mins.
VHS: S11118. $19.95.

War Between the States (1800s)

Negro slavery and divided sentiments among the states of the North and South are the subjects vividly portrayed here, conflicts of interest which led inevitably to the bloodiest conflict in American history and which are still of grave concern even today.
VHS: S03973. $64.95.

Women and the Civil War

This program looks at the heroism and struggles of women in the Union and Confederate armies during the Civil War. The program profiles the achievements of two women, Belle Reynolds and Kady Brownell, who marched alongside and fought with their husbands in battle. 30 mins.
VHS: S20271. $29.95.

Yankee Thunder, Rebel Lightning!

Two comprehensive, one-hour videos tell the story of the Civil War from beginning to end, covering the major campaigns of both Eastern and Western theaters, political considerations, African-American troops, the Nurses' Corps and more.
VHS: S14899. $59.95.

cultural documentary

An African in America
Join journalism student Alfred Mutua as he flies thousands of miles from his native home in tropical Kenya to the land of cowboys, Indians, hamburgers, and the cold winters of Spokane, Washington for humorous and insightful observations of American culture. 58 mins.
VHS: S34453. $24.95.

America's Castles
Visit the homes of seven of America's most powerful turn-of-the-century industrialists and entrepreneurs. Their "castles" brought a scale of grandeur and opulence hitherto unknown to this side of the Atlantic. In this documentary it's all visible, from the imposing grounds to the majestic interiors. 100 mins.
VHS: S21066. $29.95.

America's Castles II
During the Age of Invention (1913-1929) the wealthy built sumptuous residences that served as fantasyland homes to America's dreamers. Homes from the Rockefellers, the Fords and others are featured. Perhaps Donald Trump's Palm Beach residence, Mar-a-Lago, outdoes them all. 100 mins.
VHS: S25926. $29.95.

The Amish Folk
An overview of the Amish of southeastern Pennsylvania, including their origins, church meetings, crafts, homes, farms, and schools. With Amish songs and hymns on the soundtrack. 32 mins.
VHS: S15535. $45.00.

Art Meets Science
Five groups of speakers who are experts from different disciplines share their ideas. 58 minutes each.
Crisis of Perception. Four radically different speakers—artist Jacques van der Heyden, scientist Francisco Varela, Carmelite nun Mother Tessa Bielecki and economist J.M. Pinheiro Neto—contrast Buddhist theories of knowledge with modern science. They debate the conflict between the "unknown" nature of reality and what we perceive, examining the relationship between the subject and object of what they're seeing. "The fundamental act of perception is precisely that drawing out into the visible something that wasn't there previously" (Francisco Varela).
VHS: S18631. $29.95.
From Fragmentation to Wholeness. A symposium on creativity, featuring four speakers—artist Robert Rauschenberg, physicist David Bohm, the Dalai Lama and Russian economist Stanislav Menshikov—articulating concepts about science, nature, art and biology. The speakers talk about the ways of implementing these ideas and theories and creating a compassionate and caring society.
VHS: S18629. $29.95.
The Chaotic Universe. Five renowned speakers—composer John Cage, artist John Chamberlain, physicist Ilya Prigogine, philosopher Huston Smith and bank executive F. Wilhelm Christians—examine order and breakdown. They discuss the nature and organization of living systems, the creativity and wonder found in chaos and an unconventional world that makes up multiple perspectives.
VHS: S18630. $29.95.
The Shifting Paradigm. A group of experts, including artist Marina Abramovic, physicist Fritjof Capra, priest and Hindu scholar Raimon Panikkar and former IMF director H.J. Witteveen, discuss the primary ecological threat to the planet, why people dread change and the place of creativity in altering perceptions of reality.
VHS: S18632. $29.95.
The Transforming World. Artist Lawrence Weiner, biologist Rupert Sheldrake, Tibetan Buddhist teacher Sogyal Rinpoche and Credit Lyonnais director J.M. Leveque discuss art and the breakdown of science, reincarnation and the morphogenetic field. They examine shifting trends in biology and physics, a closer study of the living earth and a particular emphasis on the contributions and insights of Third World societies and culture.
VHS: S18633. $29.95.
Art Meets Science, Complete Set.
VHS: S18846. $129.95.

Atrocities of the Drug War: Ram Dass Speaks Out
Ram Dass (Richard Alpert) was one of the noted speakers at a Human Rights Forum conducted at Fort Mason Center in San Francisco in 1995. This piece communicates his moving and sensitive suggestions towards solutions to the injustices described in the Forum's exhibit of photographs and case histories.
VHS: S33830. $24.95.
Claire Burch, USA, 1995, 30 mins.

Black Warriors of the Seminole
This Emmy-Award winning PBS documentary reveals the amazing and historic story of an unusual and lasting alliance between the Seminole Indians of Florida and Southern blacks. A compelling chapter in American history bringing to life the remarkable story of an honorable and courageous people. 1990. 28 mins.
VHS: S34396. $29.95.

Burger Town
A lively tour of the best burger joints on the planet. View L.A's history of great coffee shops, car hops and drive-ins and vintage commercials and enjoy a rare interview with McDonald's founder Richard J. McDonald. 50 mins.
VHS: S34072. $19.95.

Civilization
Historian Kenneth Clark explores the civilization of mankind from the Dark Ages to the 20th century, in 13 programs.
Programs 1 & 2. In *The Skin of Our Teeth*, Clark undergoes a spiritual quest of the Dark Ages, exploring the Byzantine Ravenna, the Celtic Hebrides, Norwegian Vikings and Charlemagne's chapel at Aachen. In *The Great Thaw*, the program studies the rebirth of European civilization in the 12th century.
VHS: S18733. $19.95.
Programs 3 & 4. Clark assesses the accomplishments and evolution of late Middle Ages architecture and culture in France and Italy in *Romance and Beauty*. In *Man—The Measure of All Things*, Clark examines the revitalization of classicism, exploring the Renaissance centers of Urbino and Mantua.
VHS: S18734. $19.95.
Programs 5 & 6. In the first program, *The Hero as Artist*, Clark examines the Papal Room in the 16th century and its influence on the art of Michelangelo, Raphael and da Vinci. In *Protest and Communication*, Clark considers the impact of Reformation and the various artists influenced in Germany, France and England.
VHS: S18735. $19.95.
Programs 7 & 8. In *Grandeur and Obedience*, Clark looks at Rome and the Counter-Reformation, the place of Michelangelo and Bernini, the impact and extensive influence of the Catholic Church, and the dreamy splendor of St. Peter's. In the second program, *The Light of Experience*, technological innovations such as the telescope and microscope allow for greater information and detailed interpretation.
VHS: S18736. $19.95.
Programs 9 & 10. Clark notes how rococco architecture is mirrored in the musical flow and complex symmetry of 18th century composers Bach, Handel, Haydn and Mozart in *The Pursuit of Happiness*. In the follow-up program, *The Smile of Reason*, dissention and uproar in 18th century Paris suggests the pre-revolutionary dissatisfaction with the ancien regime. Clark also studies the expansive European palaces and Jefferson's Monticello.
VHS: S18737. $19.95.
Programs 11 & 12. In *The Worship of Nature*, the belief that divinity guides nature undermined Christianity's authority and unleashed the Romantic Movement. In *The Fallacies of Hope*, Clark explores the dissolution of the French aristocracy and how the Revolution led to Napoleon and a collection of authoritarian bureaucracies. The Romantic artists reveal their disillusionment.
VHS: S18738. $19.95.
Program 13. In *Heroic Materialism*, Clark concludes the series by assessing the materialism and humanitarianism of 20th century ideas and thought, from Britain's industrial landscape to the functional skyscrapers of contemporary New York City.
VHS: S18739. $19.95.
Civilization, Complete Set.
VHS: S18740. $119.95.

Connections
James Burke is back making connections between the discoveries and inventions that criss-cross history, joining disparate places, people and events. The odd and surprising chain of happenstance occurrences that result in objects and processes which are integral to modern life will continue to surprise any viewer. Complete Set.
VHS: S20973. $179.95.

Connections: The Journey Continues
This series, featuring James Burke, presents a history of technology and culture that reveals the present-day world in a wholly new light. The 10 half-hour episodes were created especially for the Learning Channel.
New Harmony. The discovery of cobalt, a blue dye used in Ming vases, has proved crucial to the development of computer chips. In addition, microscopic bugs inspired the novel *Frankenstein*, which in turn inspired the ideology of socialism.
VHS: S25855. $19.95.
Hot Pickle. There is a strong connection between tea, Chinese opium dens, the jungle adventurer who founded the London zoo, and a switch that releases bombs.
VHS: S25856. $19.95.
The Big Spin. A medical accident begins a chain of events that leads through a search for Helen of Troy, police blotters, 17th century flower power, soda pop, the discovery of oil, microfossils and earthquake detection.
VHS: S25857. $19.95.
Bright Ideas. The inventor of the bottle cap could never have forseen the effects of his discovery. It led to razors and clock springs which enable the Hubbell telescope to measure the universe.
VHS: S25858. $19.95.
Making Waves. Hairdressers, Gold Rush miners, English parliamentarians, Scotsmen, Irish potato farmers, Revolutionary War loyalists and innovative printers are all connected in this episode.
VHS: S25859. $19.95.
Routes. A sick lawyer changes farming and thereby triggers the French Revolution. This cataclysmic event is only one effect of the ailing man's actions. His work also led to the invention of radio.
VHS: S25860. $19.95.
One Word. One medieval word triggers a trip to Istanbul. From there it's back to England, where the effects of this word help foment the Industrial Revolution. Then a Swedish connection links these events to the invention of cultural anthropology.
VHS: S25861. $19.95.
Sign Here. Dutch piracy inspires the establishment of international law and French probability math. But this story continues through phonetics, Victorian seances and, ultimately, the invention of mechanical flight.
VHS: S25862. $19.95.
Better Than the Real Thing. Jefferson uncovered some technology in Paris that led to the zipper. But this chain of events had far more momentous implications. It led to the discovery that vitamins are essential to human health.
VHS: S25863. $19.95.
Flexible Response. Robin Hood stands at the beginning of this adventure that threads through medieval showbiz, Dutch swamp draining, decimals, the US currency and ends with the Tornado Fighterbomber.
VHS: S25864. $19.95.
Connections: The Journey Continues Series.
VHS: S25865. $149.95.

The Cousteau Odyssey
Blind Prophets of Easter Island. An exploration of the riddles of the colossal, 1000-year-old stone heads on Easter Island, and the puzzling history of the islands' inhabitants. 58 mins.
VHS: S08359. $24.95.

Disappearing World: Ongka's Big Moka, The Kawelka of Papua, New Guinea
Ongka, an endearing and charismatic tribal leader of the Kawelka tribe of New Guinea, has spent five years as an orator and negotiator to amass the 600 pigs and assorted valuables which he will give away in a festive ceremony, a moka. Unforeseen events threaten his largesse, stirring up rumors of sorcery and a threat of war. 60 mins.
VHS: S23043. $19.95.

Disappearing World: The Herders of Mongun-Taiga, The Tuvans of Mongolia
Along the Siberian-Mongolian border in the Sacred Wilderness, the descendents of the aboriginal Siberian people continue to live in yurts, movable felt tents. These nomads herd yaks, sheep, horses and goats. Farming is impossible. Under these harsh conditions, they must produce all their basic necessities on the spot. 60 mins.
VHS: S23046. $19.95.

Disappearing World: The Island of Malaita, The Lau of the Solomon Islands

The extraordinary Lau people live on man-made coral islands in a South Sea lagoon. Their traditional culture, the "Life of Custom," is threatened by the imminent demise of their two, aged spiritual leaders. Though islands neighboring their home show modern influences, they continue to sing their choral music without any traces of encroaching Christian traditions. 60 mins.
VHS: S23044. $19.95.

Disappearing World: The Kayapo, Indians of the Brazilian Rainforest

Life changed dramatically for the fiercely independent Kayapo when gold was discovered on their land in 1982. The Amazon was opened up for prospecting and thousands of Brazilians invaded their homeland, creating one of the world's largest gold mines. The Kayapo were forced to adapt to a life of business or see their traditions destroyed. 60 mins.
VHS: S23045. $19.95.

Disappearing World: The Masai Women, The Masai of Kenya

The Masai herd animals in the East African Rift Valley of Kenya and Tanzania. They are proud of their cattle, but only the men have rights to the herds. Women are wholly dependent. With a Masai elder as a guide, this video explains what it means to be a woman in this male dominated society. 60 mins.
VHS: S23042. $19.95.

Easter Island

A documentary filmed on location on Easter Island, exploring the mysterious monolithic stone monuments. 25 mins.
English Narration. Joan Crawford.
VHS: S06757. $70.00.
Spanish Narration. Felicia Montealegre.
VHS: S06758. $70.00.

Easter Island: A Vanished Culture

Its inhabitants once called it "Te Pito o te Hanua," or the Navel of the World. The gigantic stone statues, artistic temple platforms and mysterious writings have puzzled explorers and anthropologists. This program examines theories that attempt to uncover exactly who created these artifacts and what then happened to them. Information from the recently deciphered "rongo runes" is highlighted. 44 mins.
VHS: S22926. $19.95.

Essential Alan Watts: Man in Nature and Work as Play

Alan Watts gives two lectures. The first examines the differences between nature and man, the confusion of symbols with reality, and the oversimplification of language. In the second program, Watts talks about the extreme divisions between work and play. 58 mins.
VHS: S20423. $29.95.

Explore!

New Age explorer Douchan Gersi and his camera travel to the world's most remote regions in search of primitive peoples, exotic animals and adventure. Hosted by James Coburn and Douchan Gersi. 60 minutes each.
And the Gods Moved to Aiwan/Between Gods and Men.
VHS: S24288. $19.95.
Blue Men of the Sahara/From Timbuktu to the Stars.
VHS: S24285. $19.95.
Dancers of Evil/The Tooth of Buddha.
VHS: S24291. $19.95.
Headhunters of Borneo/Jungles of Borneo.
VHS: S24281. $19.95.
In the Footsteps of Genghis Khan/ Once Upon a Time, Afghanistan.
VHS: S24292. $19.95.
Journal from India/The Wheel of Karma.
VHS: S24289. $19.95.
Kaaba, Center of the Universe/ Bandits, Pirates and Flying Carpets.
VHS: S24286. $19.95.
Land of Living Gods/Kingdom Beneath the Sky.
VHS: S24293. $19.95.
Land of Sheba/Sanctuaries of Stone.
VHS: S24283. $19.95.
Lost Road to Nubia/Bodies of Art, Bodies of Pain.
VHS: S24282. $19.95.
Orphans of the Sun/Magic Healing, Magic Death.
VHS: S24284. $19.95.
The Last Empire of Sailing Ships/Festival of Tears.
VHS: S24290. $19.95.
Wolves of Freedom/Puppets of God.
VHS: S24287. $19.95.
Complete 13-Volume Gift Set. 780 mins.
VHS: S24294. $239.00.

A Fine and Long Tradition

This lively music video featuring historical images from family albums and archives around the country is a "wonderful introduction to Women's History Month. It provides a framework for readings and discussions on a range of women's history topics for students of all ages" (Susan McGee Bailey, Center for Research on Women, Wellesley College). "The combination of music and photographs provides a moving tribute to all women who have made a difference in the lives of others, whether on a grand scale or with simple deeds" (Roberta Dyrsten, General Federation of Women's Clubs).
VHS: S30655. $39.95.

A Glorious Accident

In this series eminent scientists expound on the place of man in the cosmic puzzle, first in individual interviews, and then as a group at a fascinating round table discussion. It's an exhaustive and comprehensive attempt to address the most puzzling questions of our secular age. Eminent biologist Stephen Jay Gould looks at the puzzle which life presents. In *Disturbing the Universe*, physicist Freeman Dyson discusses his theories on the nature of an all-encompassing concept. In *Wittgenstein's Vienna*, scientific historian Stephen Toulmin charts the key influence of the 20th-century philosopher who first examined the significance of language in the shaping of human perception. In *Consciousness Explained*, philosopher Daniel C. Dennet argues that consciousness not just a matter of awareness. *New Science of Life* features biochemist Rupert Sheldrake. *Awakenings* offers a glimpse of how the human mind actually works, by neuroscientist Oliver Sacks. And *A Clash of Minds, Parts 1 & 2*, is a roundtable discussion at which these six recognized leaders of their respective fields bring their disparate perspectives together. This fascinating meeting of minds reconfigures the perceptions that govern our world. Only available as a set.
VHS: S21377. $179.95.

Highlights of Atrocities of the Drug War

Paul Krassner, Jello Biafra and others continue the symposium begun by Ram Dass (Richard Alpert). Featuring photos from the exhibit Give Peace a Chance, set to readings of a new Human Rights manifesto.
VHS: S33831. $24.95.
Claire Burch, USA, 1995, 45 mins.

The History of Santa Claus

Everyone recognizes Santa yet few actually know who he really is or where he comes from. This fascinating docudrama recreates the history of this figure, tracing his origins back through history and even pre-history across the globe. Ancient Shamanic cave paintings, pagan Germanic gods, St. Nicholas and even the home of reindeer are shown. 54 mins.
VHS: S21823. $19.95.

History of the '80s

ABC News revisits the events, people and places that created headlines and shaped history during one of the most turbulent, provocative decades of the 20th century. 10 one-hour tapes.
History of the '80s—1980.
VHS: S34369. $19.98.
History of the '80s—1981.
VHS: S34370. $19.98.
History of the '80s—1982.
VHS: S34371. $19.98.
History of the '80s—1983.
VHS: S34372. $19.98.
History of the '80s—1984.
VHS: S34373. $19.98.
History of the '80s—1985.
VHS: S34374. $19.98.
History of the '80s—1986.
VHS: S34375. $19.98.
History of the '80s—1987.
VHS: S34376. $19.98.
History of the '80s—1988.
VHS: S34377. $19.98.
History of the '80s—1989.
VHS: S34378. $19.98.
History of the '80s—10-Volume Set.
VHS: S34368. $199.98.

Hunters and Gatherers

This documentary is a lighthearted look at the world of pop-culture paraphernalia—from lunch boxes to Pez dispensers, Elvis memorabilia, Titanic artifacts, comic books and toys, to unusual collectibles like bread tabs, barbed-wire, sugar packets and human hair. With hilarious and intriguing interviews with devoted collectors.
VHS: S31153. $19.95.

Kon-Tiki

On April 28, 1947, to the ridicule of the scientific establishment, Norwegian biologist Thor Heyerdahl and his five crew members embarked on a 4,300 mile expedition across the Pacific Ocean from Peru to Polynesia by raft in an attempt to duplicate the legendary voyage of an ancient race of settlers led by the mythical hero Kon-Tiki. Hailed as one of the most fantastic feats of daring and courage of its time, the expedition attracted worldwide interest. This exciting release celebrates the 50-year anniversary of the legendary voyage which was documented in Heyerdahl's classic book and recorded in this astonishing, Academy Award-winning, black-and-white film.
VHS: S31014. $24.95.
Thor Heyerdahl, Sweden, 1951, 58 mins.

La Belle Epoque

Douglas Fairbanks Jr. narrates how the elite of London, Paris and New York society lived in that carefree age when the pursuit of beauty and romance was a way of life, aided by newsreel clips, paintings, photographs, period costumes and re-enactments. Interviews with La Belle Epoque greats Erte, Jacques-Henri Lartigue and suffragist leader Enid Goulden-Bach provide individual and often idiosyncratic memories of the age. 105 mins.
VHS: S04650. $39.95.

Language and Consciousness

Professor Stephen Pinker guides the viewer through four half-hour segments about language and consciousness. His studies at the Center for Cognitive Neuroscience make him eminently qualified to lead this amazing video series. 120 mins.
VHS: S23632. $44.95.

Legacy

Author Michael Wood (*Search for Trojan War*) traces the rise and fall of the Asian and Western civilizations that flourished and altered our cultural perspective.
China: The Mandate of Heaven. This program considers the valuable resources discovered in China and introduced to the west, particularly iron-casting, gunpowder and printing. 60 mins.
VHS: S18230. $29.95.
Egypt: The Habit of Civilization. As the first great nation, Egypt remains a powerful player in world politics and culture. 60 mins.
VHS: S18231. $29.95.
Iraq: The Cradle of Civilization. The centerpiece of the first cities built 5,000 years ago on the banks of Euphrates in southern Iraq, where it commands a terse hold on the fragile social order. 60 mins.
VHS: S18227. $29.95.
The Barbarian West. As the world enters the 21st century, this program considers the violent histories of western civilization and its exploitation of other cultures. 60 mins.
VHS: S18228. $29.95.
Legacy, Complete Set. The complete set at a special price.
VHS: S19377. $149.95.

Marija Gimbutas: The World of the Goddess

An absorbing view of the culture, religious beliefs, symbolism and mythology of the prehistoric, pre-patriarchal cultures of Old Europe, who revered and celebrated the Great Goddess of Life, Death and Regeneration in all her many forms: of plants, of stone, of animals and humans. By the scholar who has made the exploration of these cultures her life work. Marija Gimbutas, Ph.D., is professor of archaeology at UCLA and the author of *The Language of the Goddess*. Directed by Ralph Metzner. A video presentation of the *Green Earth Foundation*. USA, 1990, 103 mins.
VHS: S14933. $29.95.

The Maya: Temples, Tombs and Time

This program brings to life a culture long shrouded in historical misconceptions. Old myths are shattered as we learn of the majestic yet turbulent history of these spiritual and complex people, from their roots in the great Olmec civilization to their rise to power throughout Mesoamerica. 60 mins.
VHS: S30036. $29.99.

Millennium: Five-Tape Boxed Set

A specially priced, five-tape boxed set of the PBS series that interweaves documentary and dramatization to study divergent cultures and societies. Hosted by Harvard anthropologist David Maybury-Lewis. 600 mins.
VHS: S17063. $99.95.

Muslims in America

In addition to examining the tenets of the Muslim faith, this ABC News Nightline program focuses on the stereotypes and hasty judgements made in connection to Muslims whenever a terrorist act occurs anywhere in the world. Several practicing Muslims candidly discuss what it is like to be Muslim in America. 22 mins.
VHS: S34366. $19.98.

A New Connection: The Video

Interview with Dr. John Frykman, former director of drug services at the Haight Ashbury Free Clinic, presently clinical director at Ross Hospital in Marin County.
VHS: S33835. $24.95.
Claire Burch, USA, 1991, 45 mins.

Nomads of the Wind

This five-part mini-series details the arduous process of colonization and cultural development that is the history of Polynesia. The people who settled these islands developed a sturdy sea-faring way of life. In the process they have had a lasting impact on the land and the sea. Each episode is 60 mins.

Episode 1: The Faraway Heaven. Two thousand years ago the first Polynesian peoples voyaged to the Pacific islands currently known as Tahiti and the Marquesas. They brought plants, animals, fishing skills and horticulture to volcano-dominated landscapes containing blue lagoons and bountiful reefs.
VHS: S23974. $19.95.

Episode 2: Crossroads of the Pacific. The west Pacific islands of Fiji, Tonga and Samoa are the cradle of Polynesia. From these beautiful islands these unique people spread their influence ever further eastward.
VHS: S23975. $19.95.

Episode 3: Burning Their Boats. The story of the mutinous seamen from the HMS *Bounty* echoes the story of the people and wildlife of Polynesia. As these English sailors burned their boat and resolved to live indefinitely on Pitcairn Island, Polynesians living nearby worshiped giants who had made a similar commitment to Easter Island.
VHS: S23976. $19.95.

Episode 4: Distant Horizons. The final great migrations of the Polynesians were their most ambitious. To the North lay Hawaii's tropical splendor while to the Southwest lay New Zealand and its unique but challenging ecosystems.
VHS: S23977. $19.95.

Episode 5: The Pierced Sky. Captain Cook and other European explorers changed Polynesia forever. The characterization of their influence continues to veer between an ideal of discovery and simple exploitation.
VHS: S23978. $19.95.

Nomads of the Wind, Set.
VHS: S23979. $89.95.

Old-Fashioned Christmas

A nostalgic look at the tradition of Christmas as celebrated in America and Europe over the years. Starring Jane Morgan, John Raitt, The Lennon Sisters, Florence Henderson, Earl Wrightson, Mildred Miller, Rosemary Clooney, Thomas Mitchell, Howard Keel, and Phyllis Curtin. 55 mins.
VHS: S08472. $19.95.

Points of Convergence

An extensive panorama of pre-Columbian cultures of Costa Rica: the Choreotega, the Huetar and the Brunca. Also included in this film is the beautiful gold collection of pre-Columbian works from the Central Bank of Costa Rica. Through the pottery, gold work and other artifacts shown in this film, one develops an appreciation for the rich imagination and expressive power of all three cultures. Directed by Angel Hurtado. Narration by John Gavin.

English Narration.
VHS: S06770. $40.00.
Spanish Narration.
VHS: S06771. $40.00.

Portrait of Civilization

Host Edwin M. Adams relates the history of frescoes beginning with ancient Minoan culture, and draws a line to the High Museum of Art in Atlanta and the Church of the Frescoes in North Carolina, where artist Jeff Mims creates a new fresco step-by-step. An informative study of a unique art form which suggests that the frescoes of today will offer future civilizations a continuing portrait "as long as the wall shall stand." 30 mins.
VHS: S15749. $29.95.

The Presence of the Goddess

The development and history of the Goddess in western civilization is finally uncovered and documented in this intriguing video. Her influence has had a humanizing effect throughout successive ages. Her inspiring ways connect all people with the earth we live on. 46 mins.
VHS: S21599. $39.95.

Quest

This adventure series, directed by award-winning documentary filmmaker Jim Burroughs, travels to all ends of the earth in search of the myths, miracles, beliefs and facts that have given meaning to people's lives. In *Part I—Last of the Stone Agers*, famed French explorer Herve de Maigret, co-producer of the Academy Award-winning documentary *The Sky Above, The Mud Below*, returns to New Guinea 30 years after he made contact with the cannibalistic and head-hunting tribes along the Asmat coast. In *Part II—Way of the Warriors*, acclaimed Hollywood stuntman Henry Kingi credits his success to his Cherokee ancestry and a mysterious "warrior" spirit that guides him. At age 50, he decides to impart his spiritual heritage to his 14-year-old son, as he takes the boy to his people's ancient homeland near Sedona, Arizona. In *Part III—Lost World of the Maya*, the Lacandron sect, which has dwindled to barely 300 people, are the sole survivors of the great Mayan culture, with roots traceable to pre-Columbian times. But the recent death, at age 110, of their revered leader has cast an ominous shadow on their ancient calendar, which predicts the end of the world in 2006. Three-tape set.
VHS: S33195. $39.98.
Jim Burroughs, 150 mins.

The Shakers

Ben Kingsley narrates this documentary about the New World Shakers. Originating in the French Huguenot community of Manchester, England, these people earned their name because of their violent religious paroxysms. Today their utilitarian way of life continues to fascinate outsiders. 52 mins.
VHS: S24924. $29.95.

The Shakers in America

This tape examines the history and major contributions of the influential Shaker movement, which began in America in 1774. With interviews, songs, and a look at the art and architecture of the people. 29 mins.
VHS: S15533. $50.00.

Siena: Chronicles of a Medieval Commune

Siena's reputation for a thriving merchant community, as an environment for artists and craftsmen, and for its saints, established the city as one of the major centers of Medieval and Renaissance culture. This film, based on contemporary sources and shot in Tuscany, focuses on the civic and religious institutions of Siena, and captures Sienese life and society during its golden age. 27 mins.
VHS: S08479. $29.95.

Smithsonian World: The Living Smithsonian

The vast range of world-wide activities which this institution supports are explored and explained in this video. It offers a behind-the-scenes look at the people who create the exhibits which document America's ambitions and accomplishments. 58 mins.
VHS: S27377. $19.98.

South Americans in Cordoba

A documentary about the Cordoba Biennial in Argentina, a major exhibition of painting and sculpture from South America. Narrated in Spanish by Luis Vivas. 13 mins.
VHS: S06751. $40.00.

The Spirit of the Mask

Harvard professor and author Wade Davis (*The Serpent and the Rainbow*) hosts this documentary about the cultural and social origins of Canada's Northwest Coast native people. The program describes their secret and elaborate uses of masks, myths, gestures and rituals and explores relations between the natural and the spiritual. 50 mins.
VHS: S19114. $19.95.

The Story of Carol

Christmas carols originated in dances dating back to the seventh century. This documentary traces the pagan roots of these songs. The first printed carol appeared in 1521. Later they were condemned by the Puritans, only to be revived in the Victorian era. 52 mins.
VHS: S21822. $19.95.

The Story of Inanna, Queen of Heaven and Earth

Through voice, gesture and song, acclaimed storyteller Diane Wolkstein recreates the legend of the ancient Sumerian goddess Inanna. This epic tale was lost for 4,000 years and only recently translated from long-buried clay tablets. Includes images of Sumerian art and the landscape of Sumer.
VHS: S25918. $65.00.
Diane Wolkstein, USA, 1988, 50 mins.

Streetwise

A close look at people and events on Telegraph Avenue in Berkeley and Haight Ashbury in San Francisco. Punctuated by original music, and heartfelt encounters with street people young and old.
VHS: S33801. $24.95.
Claire Burch, USA, 1998, 58 mins.

Sukhavati: Place of Bliss

Joseph Campbell's (*The Power of Myth*) first feature film. A journey tracing mythological symbols from Stonehenge and Glastonbury to Tibet and Nepal. By reawakening the myths that have been lost to us, Campbell gives us a message of spiritual significance for our times. 80 mins.
VHS: S34866. $29.95.

Suleyman the Magnificent

Explores the political, social and cultural background of the Ottoman Empire, focusing on the reign of Sultan Suleyman (1520-1566), under whose auspices the Empire spread to encompass parts of Africa, Europe and Asia. Art and architecture flourished under the Sultan. Produced by the National Gallery of Art and the Metropolitan Museum of Art. 57 mins.
VHS: S03399. $39.95.

Technologies of the Gods: The Case for Pre-Historic High Technology

From the creators of *Atlantis Rising* magazine. The first video to document a new scientific scenario for the dawn of civilization with breakthrough evidence from researchers John Anthony West, Robert Bauval, Richard Noone and Colin Wilsom. 60 mins.
VHS: S34867. $19.95.

Thor Heyerdahl: Explorer and Scientist

A portrait of the colorful 82-year-old Norwegian explorer and scientist who became world famous with his Kon-Tiki expedition in 1947 when, with a crew of five, he drifted 8000 kilometers on a balsa raft from Peru to Polynesia. 52 mins.
VHS: S32387. $24.95.

Tibet: On the Edge of Change

An in-depth look at this hidden land and the enduring ancient culture and lifestyle of the Tibetan people as they approach the end of the century. Filmed in locations that few Westerners have ever seen, this documentary takes a close look at the way Tibetans have existed for thousands of years and the many changes being brought about by the occupying Chinese. 58 mins.
VHS: S31368. $29.95.

Tong Tana— A Journey into the Heart of Borneo

Deep within Borneo's lush rainforest, Bruno Manser, a 34-year-old Swiss, has rejected western civilization to live with the nomadic Penan Indians and help them confront the logging companies that threaten their existence. In ten years Borneo's rainforest—the oldest in the world—may be gone forever, and so will be the Penans. Bruno Manser may be one of their last hopes. "A strong environmentalist message...of high artistic order" (Variety). Sweden, 1990, 88 mins.
VHS: S14151. $29.95.

Treehouse People: Cannibal Justice

The Korowai are an elusive people who have maintained their unique way of life for thousands of years in the rain forest. On this Smithsonian Expedition, this isolated group of people is revealed in all their mystery. They may even practice ritual cannibalism. 50 mins.
VHS: S25869. $24.95.

Vicus

A documentary about pre-Columbian ceramics and jewelry of the Vicus culture of Peru—a nation of hunters who may have reached the agricultural stage of development, who settled in the region of Vicus a century before the birth of Christ. Directed by Jose Gomez Sicre. Narration by Dolores del Rio. 18 mins.

English Narration.
VHS: S06760. $50.00.
Spanish Narration.
VHS: S06761. $50.00.

The Wedding of Palo

Dr. Knud Rasmussen, the famed explorer, was filming a documentary about Greenland when he passed away in 1933. This film is what remains. It shows telling details about the native peoples of this frozen region and includes hunting sequences and courting traditions. 72 mins.
VHS: S24081. $24.95.
Friedrich Dalsheim/Knud Rasmussen, Denmark, 1935, 72 mins.

Women Speak Up: A Collection of Women's Voices from Around the World

This documentary is a colorful collage of plenaries, workshops, interviews, spontaneous events and music from the Fourth United Nation's International Women's NGO (non-governmental organization) Forum that took place in Huairou and Beijing, China, August 30-September 8, 1995, and was attended by 30,000 women from 189 countries. "The video is absolutely gripping and leads to excellent discussion when shown to a women's studies class or a women's conference" (Ruth Harriet Jacobs, PhD, author of *Women Who Touched My Life*).
VHS: S30171. $19.99.
Linda Leehman/Esther Farnsworth, USA, 1996, 58 mins.

Xingu: Land of No Shame

This anthropological film documents daily life in Xingu National Park, situated in Brazil's Southern Amazon Basin, a 9,000-square-mile natural preserve which is home to 3,500 Native Brazilians comprising 15 different tribes. Featuring an informative narration and English voice-over translation of Indian conversations, as well as graphic representations of Xingu legends and fables, this video provides a remarkable look at the last stronghold of an endangered civilization.
VHS: S34434. $350.00.
Michael Engel, USA, 1997, 60 mins.

ANCIENT CIVILIZATIONS

Alexander the Great

The exploits of this historic figure transformed the world, leaving a lasting impact on both eastern and western civilization. This documentary traces his accomplishments from the Adriatic to the Himalayas. English dialog.
VHS: S22049. $29.95.

Ancient Egypt

Explores the art and architecture of ancient Egypt through paintings and sculpture of kings, queens and noble persons and temples, tombs and pyramids. Available in three versions.
Ancient Egypt—Elementary School.
VHS: S09078. $125.95.
Ancient Egypt—High School.
VHS: S09080. $199.00.
Ancient Egypt—Middle School.
VHS: S09079. $125.95.

Ancient Greece

Basic concepts of Greek architecture are discussed and related to Stonehenge, Crete and archaic Greek temples. The temples on the Acropolis and sculpture show achievements during the Golden Age of Greece. Available in three versions.
Ancient Greece—Elementary School.
VHS: S09081. $125.95.
Ancient Greece—High School.
VHS: S09083. $189.00.
Ancient Greece—Middle School.
VHS: S09082. $109.00.

Ancient Greece Volume 1

Filmed on location, these two programs, *Art in Ancient Greece* and *Mining in Ancient Greece*, give the modern viewer a fresh perspective on two key cultural and technological achievements. 120 mins.
VHS: S25648. $29.95.

Ancient Greece Volume 2

Bacchus, the God of Wine and *Fire Walking in Greece* present important insights into the religious and philosophical beliefs of Ancient Greece. The attitudes and concepts forged there continue to influence the modern world. 120 mins.
VHS: S25649. $29.95.

Ancient Mysteries

Using modern technology, scientific analysis, high-tech evidence and recent archaeological developments, the films in the *Ancient Mysteries* series are on the cutting edge of discovery.
The Odyssey of Troy. For 3000 years, the legend of Troy has inspired human imagination. Now this video exposes new evidence about the fabled Trojan Horse and the illustrious figures of Helen and Achilles. Narrated by Kathleen Turner. USA, 1995, 50 mins.
VHS: S26101. $19.95.

The Ancient Romans: An Urban Lifestyle

This film traces the influence of Rome's urban society on contemporary Western ways. 12 mins.
VHS: S23705. $99.95.

The Ancient Romans: Builders of an Empire

The structures erected by this civilization reflect the political, commercial and artistic life of its people. 14 mins.
VHS: S23703. $99.95.

The Ancient Romans: People of Leisure

Great theater and sporting events filled the many Roman amphitheaters, to delight the population of this mighty civilization. 13 mins.
VHS: S23704. $99.95.

Ancient Rome

Art and architecture are explored and students see how the arch, vault, and dome relate to the aqueduct, Coliseum, Baths and Pantheon. Sculptures and mosaics trace Roman history. Available in three versions.
Ancient Rome—Elementary School.
VHS: S09084. $124.95.
Ancient Rome—High School.
VHS: S09086. $189.00.
Ancient Rome—Middle School.
VHS: S09085. $125.95.

Ancient Warriors

The Discovery Channel produced this three-volume documentary about warlike societies that shaped the face of history. *Barbarian Forces* shows how warring hordes impacted peaceful peoples. Then the clash between religion and war is explored in *Soldiers of the East. Classical Warriors* reveals that the success of Western civilization was often won by the sword.
VHS: S24583. $49.95.

Athens and the Greek Spirit

Explore this vibrant city with this colorful tour, featuring the history, customs, food, and fun of the Greek culture. 30 mins.
VHS: S05784. $24.95.

Dawn of the Greek Gods

Here are the ultimate symbols of the heroic gods of Greek mythology—a time before light and darkness, when chaos was the only force in the universe. Includes four programs: *From Chaos to Chronos, Titans vs. Olympians, The Powers of the Olympians* and *The Reign of Zeus*. For Grades 5-10.
VHS: S14200. $159.95.

Greek Fire

A provocative, visually startling documentary series that explores the pervasive influence of ancient Greece to our lives today. Features the classicists and writers Oliver Taplin, George Steiner, Kenneth Dover and Bernard Knox. Five volumes.
(1) Source and Myth. 56 mins.
VHS: S14708. $24.95.
(2) Politics and Sex. 56 mins.
VHS: S14709. $24.95.
(3) Tragedy and Architecture. 56 mins.
VHS: S14710. $24.95.
(4) Science and Art. 56 mins.
VHS: S14711. $24.95.
(5) Ideas and War. 56 mins.
VHS: S14712. $24.95.
Complete five-volume set. 280 mins.
VHS: S14707. $99.95.

Hail Caesar

From Julius to Justinian, Constantine to Hadrian, Nero to Augustus, this is a captivating portrait of the most celebrated rulers in human history: the emperors of ancient Rome. Six videos. 50 minutes each.
VHS: S34900. $99.99.

Heroes of the Greek Myths

Four superb dramatizations of classic Greek myths. Includes *Hercules and the Golden Apples, The Golden Fleece, Hector and Achilles* and *The Cyclops Cave*. For Grades 7-9.
VHS: S14201. $159.95.

Heroines and Goddesses of the Greek Myths

The four myths presented in this series are told to Arete, an imaginary young lady of ancient Athens. And each can be appreciated on several levels for its insights into life and its moral teaching. Includes *Atalanta, Athene and Arachne, Demeter and Persephone* and *Pandora*. For Grades 5-10.
VHS: S14202. $159.95.

King Tut: The Face of Tutankhamen

A four-part series about King Tut. The series begins in Egypt, 1922, when archeologist Howard Carter discovers the vast treasure of the boy pharaoh Tutankhamen. Host and author Christopher Frayling reveals the disruptions and misfortune that followed Carter, including the strange "curse," the death of Carter's benefactor, and the cultural influence of Tut on music, film, art, fashion and architecture. 200 mins.
VHS: S19062. $59.95.
Laser: CLV. **LD72218. $69.95.**

King Tut: Tomb of Treasure

This program describes archeologist Howard Carter's obsessive, eight-year search for the sacred burial chamber of King Tutankhamen, who was buried with a king's ransom upon his death when he was 18 years old. The program also looks at the ancient shrine, and goes inside the Cairo Museum and the New Orleans Museum of Art for a view of the amazing artifacts. 25 mins.
VHS: S17693. $29.95.

Macedonia, The Land of a God, Vol. 1: Aina, Aiges, Dion and Pella

This first part of the definitive series begins an in-depth look at the land north of Greece. Its powerful rulers spread Hellenic culture to the frontiers of ancient civilization. Dimitri Pandermalis, the noted Greek scholar of classical archeology, supervised these videos. 90 mins.
VHS: S25650. $29.95.

Macedonia, The Land of a God, Vol. 2: Aina, Aiges, Dion and Pella

The second part of this series continues to examine both the influence and the achievements of Macedonia. Once again Dimitri Pandermalis, the noted Greek scholar of classical archeology, supervised this scholarly video. 90 mins.
VHS: S25651. $29.95.

Mummies and the Wonders of Ancient Egypt

This four-volume video collection recreates the awe-inspiring majesty of Ancient Egypt. It unravels the mysteries behind hieroglyphic writing, as well as the secrets of the pyramids, the Sphinx, and King Tut's tomb. Each tape is 50 mins.
VHS: S29906. $59.95.

The Mysteries and Splendors of Ancient Egypt

Travel 1,000 miles through Egypt, from the Pyramids of Giza to the Sudan border and discover the wonder of the ancient civilization that prospered there. See Giza, Luxor, Karnak, Abu Simbel, and the Egyptian Museum.
VHS: S05773. $24.95.

The Mysterious Origins of Man: Jurassic Art

Pry open the locked storerooms of museums and peer into the dens of Peruvian graverobbers to investigate the controversial Ica Stones and the Acambaro Figurines, which depict the impossible: a people who lived with dinosaurs. Do these collections represent the greatest archeological finds of our time or the greatest hoaxes in history? 46 mins.
VHS: S31033. $19.95.

Myths of the Pharaohs

The myths found in Egyptian tomb paintings are the source for this animated short film. Through these myths the ways of ancient Egyptians are brought alive for contemporary audiences. 12 mins.
VHS: S23715. $49.95.

National Geographic Video: Egypt: Quest for Eternity

This video offers a relatively low cost guided tour of the world of ancient Egypt. It comes complete with pyramids, temples, sand and the River Nile. You bring the snacks. 60 mins.
VHS: S03675. $19.95.

National Geographic Video: In the Shadow of Vesuvius

Discover the secrets of Herculaneum and Pompeii, buried in the violent volcanic eruption of A.D. 79. 60 mins.
VHS: S09931. $19.95.

Nile: River of Gods

The Nile's ancient course has inspired mankind from time immemorial. This documentary from the *Discovery Channel* reveals the unique relationship of this river to God, man and nature through 5000 years of recorded history. 100 mins.
VHS: S26042. $19.95.

Nova—Ancient Treasures from the Deep

Amazing discoveries from a centuries-old underwater wreck and its golden cargo. 60 mins.
VHS: S14502. $14.98.

Nova—Mysterious Mummies of China

Perfectly preserved 3,000-year-old mummies have been unearthed in China's remote Takla Makan desert. They have long, blonde hair and blue eyes, and don't appear to be the ancestors of modern-day Chinese people. *Nova* investigates the identity of these people. 60 mins.
VHS: S33098. $19.95.

Nova—Search for the Lost Cave People

Nova follows an international team of archaeologists and spelunkers into the Rio la Venta Gorge deep in the Chiapas jungle of South America. In a rugged canyon they find caves filled with startling remains of a people called the Zoque who lived hundreds of years before the Maya. Moving downstream from the caves the team finds a legendary city hidden in a tangle of jungle vines. 60 mins.
VHS: S33099. $19.95.

Nova—Treasures of the Sunken City

Search for one of the long-missing Seven Wonders of the World, the lost city of Alexandria, as *Nova* dives below the surface into a watery graveyard of sunken archaeological treasures. 120 mins.
VHS: S33084. $19.95.

The Odyssey

This ambitious adaptation of Homer's epic is a four-hour mini-series produced by Francis Ford Coppola and Robert Halmi Sr. and starring Armand Assante, Greta Scacchi, Isabella Rossellini, Vanessa Williams, Eric Roberts, Christopher Lee, Geraldine Chaplin, Jeroen Krabbe and Bernadette Peters, complete with slick special effects by Jim Henson's Creature Shop and colossal props, including a to-scale Trojan horse. "A major entertainment event" (*The New York Times*).
VHS: S31747. $19.95.
Laser: LD76301. $49.98.
Andrei Konchalovsky, USA, 1997, 165 mins.

The Pyramids and the Cities of the Pharaohs

Egyptologists and video artists recreate the era of Ancient Egypt. This splendid civilization created imposing monuments using simple tools that are still awe-inspiring. Both the pyramids and the Lighthouse at Alexandria are covered. 65 mins.
VHS: S24368. $29.95.

Sacred Sites: Prehistoric Monuments of Europe

Sites included in this documentary are the avenues of Megaliths at Carnac in Brittany; the nearby royal tomb at Gavrinis; the temple under the sea on the isle of Er-Lanic, in Corsica; the oldest sculptures in Europe, the Nuraghens in Sardinia; and more. 43 mins.
VHS: S22929. $19.95.

Secrets of the Lost Empires Gift Set

NOVA five-volume set includes *Pyramid*, *Obelisk*, *Colosseum*, *Stonehenge* and *Inca*. Each tape is 60 mins.
VHS: S31435. $69.95.

Secrets of the Mummy

A long-dead Egyptian grudgingly yields ancient secrets to a multitalented team of scientists through the first filmed autopsy of an actual mummy.
VHS: S22542. $19.95.

Seven Wonders of the Ancient World

Philo of Byzantium, approximately 2,000 years ago, compiled a list consisting of two statues, a temple, a roof-top garden, two tombs, and a lighthouse. Ancient Romans considered these to be the seven wonders of the world. Only the Great Pyramid of Giza still stands in its original form, and is the oldest wonder, built around 2560 B.C. This fascinating video reveals the story behind each wonder, and the people responsible for the construction and function of each. 60 mins.
VHS: S12292. $29.95.

The Story of Rome and Pompeii

This program uses computer technology to conjure up the spectacle and grandeur of Rome and Pompeii. The program covers the social and political atmosphere of Rome, such as the Circus Maximus and Colosseum. 60 mins.
VHS: S20189. $29.95.

Time Life's Lost Civilizations

Sam Waterston hosts this *Time Life Books* ten-volume series about earlier civilizations. Gripping reenactments and stunning photography help reanimate long-dead cultures from four continents. Each volume is 60 mins.

Aegean: Legacy of Atlantis. The fabled lost city of Atlantis has inspired explorers and adventurers for centuries. This volume shows how the search for the city of Troy led to discoveries confirming the existence of an Aegean civilization that dates back 6000 years. USA, 1995.
VHS: S26885. $19.99.

Africa: A History Denied. Europeans maintained that sub-Saharan Africa held no significant advanced civilizations. Now archeologists and scholars have confirmed that African empires organized trade which enriched Europe with gold and ivory. This volume explores the legacy of these forgotten people. USA, 1995.
VHS: S26886. $19.99.

China: Dynasties of Power. Imperial China began with the ancient Shang people over 4000 years ago. Often attributed to legend, contemporary scientists have now uncovered evidence of their shadowy existence. Lucky accidents involving construction crews were instrumental to this scholarly breakthrough. USA, 1995.
VHS: S26887. $19.99.

Egypt: The Quest for Immortality. This volume opens with a recreation of the 70-day embalming ceremony performed for Ramses the Great, Egypt's mightiest pharaoh. It spans 3½ millennia to show both the glory of Ancient Egypt and the blunders performed by primitive archeologists. USA, 1995.
VHS: S26888. $19.99.

Greece: A Moment of Excellence. In a brief historical period, Greece, led by Athens, gave the world trial by jury, the Symposium, the Olympic Games, and most importantly, democracy. Even the Acropolis stands as a testament to this enduringinnovative spirit. USA, 1995.
VHS: S26889. $19.99.

Inca: Secrets of the Ancestors. The Incas ruled the mountainous spine of South America prior to the Spanish conquest. Their culture was only the latest of many South American civilizations dating back thousands of years. USA, 1995.
VHS: S26890. $19.99.

Maya: The Blood of Kings. Scientifically advanced, the Maya have confounded archaeologists for decades because of their mysterious disappearance. After building elaborate cities and road networks they simply abandoned these works for the jungles of Central America.
VHS: S26891. $19.99.

Mesopotamia: Return to Eden. *Time Life* was granted special access to the site on Ancient Sumer in Iraq for this volume. The Sumerians established the world's first civilization 4000 years ago. USA, 1995.
VHS: S26892. $19.99.

Rome: The Ultimate Empire. Almost 2000 years ago Ancient Rome established a transportation system with nearly a quarter of a million miles of road. This network bound an empire that stretched from Scotland to the Holy Land. Within this region, language, technology and culture shaped a world in the image of Rome itself. USA, 1995.
VHS: S26893. $19.99.

Tibet: The End of Time. Tibetan civilization faces dissolution through the ravages of the 20th century. The current Dalai Lama, Tibet's god-King, may well be the last sovereign crowned in his native land. Fortunately, his ascension to the throne in 1940 has been preserved on film. USA, 1995.
VHS: S26894. $19.99.

Tut: The Boy King

An eyewitness account of the traveling exhibit; in Egypt, 1922, archeologist Howard Carter discovered the vast riches and astonishing treasures within the tomb of the boy pharaoh Tutankhamen, known as King Tut. This work reveals the fullness of the splendor and excitement. Narrated by Orson Welles. 55 mins.
VHS: S04447. $24.95.

Tutankhamen: The Immortal Pharaoh

The University of Houston produced this singular view of the wonderfully preserved contents of this young king's tomb. 12 mins.
VHS: S23716. $49.95.

IDEAS & PHILOSOPHY

bell hooks on Video: Cultural Criticism & Transformation

bell hooks, distinguished professor of English, City College of New York, and author of 14 books of commentary, criticism and autobiography, makes a compelling argument for the transformative power of cultural criticism, in this extensively illustrated two-part tape. 70 mins.
VHS: S31887. $195.00.

Carl Gustav Jung: Artist of the Soul

Draws on the first chapters of the unfinished autobiography begun in 1957 by the 82-year-old Jung and delves into workings of the great psychoanalyst's brilliant mind.
VHS: S32080. $29.95.
Werner Weick, USA, 1997, 60 mins.

A Certain Age

Aging in America is both an individual process and a transformation which affects the entire society. *A Certain Age* explores the effects of aging on both these fronts through a variety of different perspectives. 58 mins.
VHS: S29543. $19.98.

The Doors of Perception

Between the external world of "reality" and the internal world of human conciousness is an area bounded by perception. This video shows a number of human efforts which have attempted to transform everday reality. Includes an interesting look at the work of poet and artist William Blake. 58 mins.
VHS: S29544. $19.98.

Dreamworlds: Desire/Sex/Power in Rock Video

Editing together excerpts from 165 different rock videos, Sut Jhally demonstrates the negative and dangerous representations of women contained in popular television images. The program recontextualizes pop culture to reveal the role videos play in how young people think and behave. 55 mins.
VHS: S16420. $195.00.
Sut Jhally, USA, 1990, 55 mins.

Focus for the Future

Willis Harman, president of the Institute of Noetic Sciences and author of the book *Global Mind Change*, presents an overview of today's rapidly changing world as an era of great evolutionary opportunity. He contrasts industrial-age views with entirely new perspectives. 97 mins.
VHS: S10142. $39.95.

Gender: The Enduring Paradox

Gender's role in contemporary society is being challenged by a number of new trends. This video examines the roots of traditional gender in early childhood and the socially constructed roles arising to define masculinity and feminity. The divide between these two opposing forces continues to fascinate many. 58 mins.
VHS: S29541. $19.98.

Greatest Thinkers Series

A series of 30-minute videotapes developed by the International Center for Creative Thinkers. Hosted by Dr. Edward de Bono of Cambridge University, the series explores the philosophy of major thinkers. In-studio demonstrations highlight various principles which are further illustrated in dramatized sequences.

Aristotle.
VHS: S11502. $49.50.
Clausewitz.
VHS: S11503. $49.50.
Columbus.
VHS: S11504. $49.95.
Descartes.
VHS: S11505. $49.50.
Freud.
VHS: S11506. $49.95.
Jesus.
VHS: S11507. $49.50.
Machiavelli.
VHS: S11508. $49.50.
Marx.
VHS: S11509. $49.50.
Moses.
VHS: S11510. $49.50.
Nietzsche.
VHS: S11511. $49.50.
Pavlov.
VHS: S11512. $49.50.
Rousseau.
VHS: S11513. $49.50.
Wiener.
VHS: S11514. $49.50.

Hero's Journey

Explore the worlds of mythology and religion, as they affect modern man, and how they shaped the life of Joseph Campbell. Campbell, famous scholar and teacher, was best known for his compelling interpretations of myth, and how the images and symbols of those myths bring logic and meaning to our lives. *Hero's Journey* portrays the development of Campbell's personal philosophies as they evolve and how they were influenced by the events of his life. Drawing on rare footage of Campbell's lectures and workshops, the film is a remarkable look at an equally remarkable man. 51 mins.
VHS: S08487. $39.95.

Jacques Lacan's Psychoanalysis Part One

A priceless document for anyone interested in contemporary thought and analysis. In interviews with Jacques-Alain Miller, Jacques Lacan, the famous French psychoanalyst called by many the French Freud, exposes with unexpected simplicity his most complex theories of the unconscious; the cure, the difference between psychoanalysis and psychotherapy, love and women. "For anyone hoping to understand the institutionalization of Freudian thought and the challenge Lacan represents, this is an essential work." French with English subtitles.
VHS: S18142. $69.95.
Benoit Jacquot, France, 1974, 60 mins.

Jung on Film

Share a special viewing experience! This compelling film interview with Carl Gustav Jung represents a rare record of an original genius. In *Jung on Film* the pioneering psychologist tells us about his collaboration with Sigmund Freud, the insights he gained from listening to his patients' dreams, and the fascinating turns taken by his own life. Dr. Richard I. Evans, a 1989 Presidential Medal of Freedom nominee, interviews Jung, giving us a rare glimpse into the life and career of this important historical figure. 77 mins.
VHS: S13738. $29.95.

Love, Death and Eros

Controversial psychiatrist and author R.D. Laing, one of the pioneers of radical psychotherapy, explores the topics of sex and love. 58 mins.
VHS: S12207. $29.95.

Man and the State: The Trial of Socrates

Sentenced to death for his ideas, Socrates' trial and sentence represents a momentous event of great significance for Western civilization. Can a society repress ideas it feels are dangerous? Does a man have a moral obligation to ignore unjust laws? 29 mins.
VHS: S23698. $79.95.

Matter of Heart: The Extraordinary Journey of C.G. Jung into the Soul of Man

An affectionate but probing documentary of the enormous contribution of Carl Gustav Jung to modern psychology, this remarkable film has become not only a boxoffice hit, but a must-see film for anyone even remotely interested in the foundations of psychoanalytic thought. USA, 90 mins.
VHS: S04719. $79.95.

Men and Women: Talking Together

A no-holds-barred discussion by two provocative voices on issues relative to the men's and women's movements, author Deborah Tannen (*You Just Don't Understand*) and poet Robert Bly (*Iron John*). "Together they examine how gender dialect works and reveal disturbing truths about the male power elite" (*Publishers Weekly*). 58 mins.
VHS: S20213. $29.95.

Mythos with Joseph Campbell

Just before he died in 1987, Joseph Campbell made a final tour of the United States. Based on this tour, this essential five-part series presents the first volume of Campbell's compelling vision of the "One Great Story" of our human nature. The first in a series entitled *The Shaping of Our Western Tradition, Mythos* showcases what Campbell did best—telling profound and powerful stories from the wealth of the world's great cultures. Commentary by Susan Sarandon. 5 hours on five videocassettes.
VHS: S30981. $99.95.

Power of Myth (Joseph Campbell)

The brilliant historian/mythologist/thinker Joseph Campbell, in a dialogue with Bill Moyers, explores the foundations of culture and our being in this incredible six-part series.
First Storytellers. On myths and the environment—In this program, Campbell discusses the importance of accepting death as rebirth (as in the myth of the buffalo and the story of Christ), the rite of passage (in primitive societies), the role of mystical Shamans, and the decline of ritual in today's society. 60 mins.
VHS: S07387. $24.95.

Hero's Adventure. Long before medieval knights charged off to slay dragons, tales of heroic adventures were an integral part of all world cultures. Heroic stories are still being told. In fact, Joseph Campbell says modern technology is reflected in works such as George Lucas' *Star Wars Trilogy*. Campbell discusses how the hero's journey is possible today in everyday life, and challenges everyone to see the presence of a heroic journey in his or her own life.
VHS: S07385. $24.95.

Love and the Goddess. On women in mythology—In addition to love of God, Campbell talks about romantic love, beginning with the 12th-century troubadours. According to Campbell, the troubadours were "the first ones in the West who really considered love in the same sense we think of it now, as a person-to-person relationship." Then Campbell addresses questions about the image of women—as goddess, virgin, Mother Earth. 60 mins.
VHS: S07389. $24.95.

Message of the Myth. On the relevance of myths—Campbell begins this hour comparing the creation story in Genesis with creation stories from around the world. His discussion with Bill Moyers includes the question, why do we need myths? Myths, Campbell believes, are clues to the spiritual potentialities of human life. Because the world changes, religion has to be transformed and new mythologies created. Unfortunately, Campbell says, people today are stuck with old metaphors and myths that don't fit their needs. 60 mins.
VHS: S07386. $24.95.

Masks of Eternity. On divinity—In the culminating hour of the series, Campbell provides challenging insights into the concepts of God, religion and eternity, as revealed in the Christian teachings and the beliefs of Buddhists, Navajo Indians, psychologist Carl Jung, and others. 60 mins.
VHS: S07390. $24.95.

Sacrifice and Bliss. On the meaning of sacrifice and following your bliss—Campbell begins this program stressing the need for every one of us to find our sacred place—"a place of creative incubation." In the midst of today's fast-paced, technological world, we all need a sacred place, he says, to sense a true feeling for life. Campbell also discusses the role of sacrifice in myth, which he says symbolizes the necessity for rebirth. He also talks about the significance of sacrifice—in particular, a mother's sacrifice for her child, and the sacrifice to the relationship in marriage.
VHS: S07388. $24.95.

Complete Set.
VHS: S07590. $124.95.

The Simple and the Complex

Nobel Laureate Dr. Murnay Gell-Mann addresses the relationship between everyday experience and the sub-atomic realm. Chaos theory reveals that initial conditions are critical to the unfolding of large-scale events. 60 mins.
VHS: S23626. $34.95.

Soul

A complex documentary that investigates the relationship of science and religion and notes how the theoretical breakthroughs in thinking and science have opened up discussion on the origins of the universe and the inner workings of the mind. Originally produced by the BBC, this three-volume series charts the spiritual repercussions of innovative scientific reasoning, with commentary from noted physicist Stephen Hawking (*A Brief History of Time*), theoretical physicist Paul Davies and the science writer and philosopher Danah Zohar. 210 mins.
Soul 1: Soul of the Universe.
VHS: S18306. $19.95.
Soul 2: The Evolving Soul.
VHS: S18307. $19.95.
Soul 3: Silicon Soul.
VHS: S18308. $19.95.
Soul: The Complete Set.
VHS: S18309. $59.85.

Wisdom of the Dream: C.G. Jung and His Work in the World

This three-part series traces Jung's work and message throughout his life—his split with Freud, the major works published on dreams and the psychology of religion, his travels, in particular to New Mexico, and his discovery of the collective conscious. The director uses authentic visual references of Jung's home and consulting room and the film contains previously undiscovered home movies shot during Jung's travels to Africa, plus an interview recorded in 1956.
Wisdom of the Dream Vol. 1.
VHS: S10303. $29.95.
Wisdom of the Dream Vol. 2.
VHS: S10311. $29.95.
Wisdom of the Dream Vol. 3.
VHS: S10312. $29.95.

With a Silent Mind

A richly detailed biographical portrait of Krishnamurti's life and teachings produced by Evelyne Blay. The film blends Krishnamurti's own deep insights with the impressions of scientists, authors, educators, students and friends, and with extraordinary archival footage from India, England and America in the 20's and 30's. 60 mins.
VHS: S12482. $29.95.

The World Within

A new and enlightening film focusing on Jung's Red Book, in which he recorded images from his unconscious. These are creations, Jung comments, "which have carried me out of time into seclusion; out of the present into timelessness." A fascinating glimpse into the philosophy and personal life of C.G. Jung.
VHS: S14747. $59.95.
Suzanne Wagner, USA, 1990, 80 mins.

The World's Philosophies

Dr. Huston Smith, emeritus professor of philosophy at Syracuse, points out the three essential relationships of existence: the relationship to nature, other people and ourselves. This understanding helps him synthesize various world philosophies. 60 mins.
VHS: S23631. $34.95.

NATIVE AMERICAN CULTURE

500 Nations

Kevin Costner hosts and produced this extraordinary eight-volume series about the many peoples who lived in North and Central America long before the arrival of Europeans. This series was filmed on location from Central American jungles to the Canadian Arctic. Computer animation also is deployed to recreate the actual history of this land. Each volume is 47 mins.
VHS: S24383. $139.98.
Laser: LD74900. $139.92.

Ancient America: Indians of the Northwest

Wes Studi, the famed Native American Cherokee who played in *Last of the Mohicans, Geronimo: An American Legend* and *Dances with Wolves*, narrates this in-depth look at the original inhabitants of the Northwest. 60 mins.
VHS: S21601. $59.95.

Ancient America: Indians of the Southwest

In America's beautiful Southwestern lands Native Americans have left traces of their culture dating back thousands of years. Join Wes Studi, the "scene stealer" from a number of recent successful Hollywood Westerns including *Dances with Wolves*, for a fascinating look at the peoples who shaped this unique landscape. 60 mins.
VHS: S21602. $59.95.

Ancient Indian Cultures of Northern Arizona

Explore the ruins of ancient Indian cultures as you wander the mesas and deserts of Arizona. Visit five national monuments: Montezuma Castle, Wupatki, Tuzigoot, Walnut Canyon, and Sunset Crater, and discover the Sinagua and Anasazi civilizations. 30 minutes.
VHS: S02469. $29.95.

Art of Navajo Weaving

Explores the traditional art of Navajo weaving and its origins, with visits to a contemporary Navajo weaving family, showing how artists create magnificent pieces of art. 56 mins.
VHS: S08304. $29.95.

Bear Tribe Storytelling

A fresh collection of Native American folktales and legends, related by Moriah Vecchia, a renowned storyteller and songstress. 60 mins.
VHS: S18094. $34.95.

Brooke Medicine Eagle: Dancing Awake the Drum

Brooke will lead the viewer through the transforming effects of the Sacred Circle. Dancing, singing and drumming are just some of the necessary preparations needed to begin this spiritual journey. Brooke will explain how to prepare for the changing earth. 60 mins.
VHS: S21231. $29.95.

Contemporary and Native American Readings

Richard Chamberlain's gentle creative spirit shines as he recites some consciousness raising excerpts from a work by Joseph Campbell. He also includes an address to the President of the United States by Native Americans reminding us of our obligation as protectors and wardens of the earth. 82 mins.
VHS: S10219. $29.95.

The Dakota Conflict

The personalities, events and conflicts that were a part of the war for America's Great Plains are depicted in this program narrated by Garrison Keillor and Floyd Red Crow Westerman. 60 mins.
VHS: S19630. $19.95.

Discovering American Indian Music

The songs and dances of Native Americans comprise a rich musical tradition. Ceremonial functions and the social significance of these musical works are discussed. The pieces are presented by performers in authentic costumes. 24 mins.
VHS: S23508. $49.95.

Dragonfly's Tale

When the Ashiwi tribe celebrates abundant food with a joyous food fight the Corn maidens are disappointed and show their disdain with a poor harvest and famine. The villagers leave to find a better life and leave two small children behind. They fashion the first firefly from a withered cornstalk, which flies to the Corn maidens. Soon the plentiful harvest returns, as do the villagers, who are wiser and kinder.
VHS: S21883. $44.95.

The Education of Little Tree

James Cromwell (*Babe*) stars in this heartwarming adaptation of the acclaimed bestseller about an orphaned eight-year-old Cherokee boy sent to live with his grandparents in Tennessee's Smoky Mountains during the 1930s.
VHS: S34277. $92.99.
Richard Friedenberg, USA, 1997, 117 mins.

End of the Trail

During the great Westward migration, Native Americans were continuously and rapaciously displaced for a greedy, young nation. This is a sobering if honest account of a tragic time in the history of the US. 60 mins.
VHS: S23058. $19.95.

Feminine— Ancient Vision, Modern Wisdom

Wabun Wind of the Bear Tribe draws on her own life experiences as well as years of research to discuss matriarchy and the beginning of patriarchy to elucidate not only the origin of anger between men and women, but also shed new light upon the subjects of women's power, the moon cycles and menstrual cycles, stereotyping of women, sexuality, relationships and raising children. 77 mins.
VHS: S07725. $34.95.

Four Corners of Earth

The roles and culture of Seminole women are documented in this unique portrait of vanishing Seminole life. Traditional values and changes brought about by the 20th century are seen through the eyes of women living on the Seminole reservations in South Florida.
VHS: S06959. $59.95.

From the Heart of the World: The Elder Brother's Warning

Deep in the mountains of Colombia, the descendants of an ancient Tairona priesthood still rule. In cities more than a thousand years old, the ascetic Kogi tribe has preserved the culture and concepts of an advanced civilization wiped out by the conquistadors. This is the original, uncut, feature-length version of the edited *Nature* program shown on PBS. USA, 88 mins.
VHS: S15435. $29.95.

Fulfilling the Vision

The Lakota generation of the 70's and 80's has its own story, related to the continuity of Lakota spirituality. Beginning in 1990, this video examines the social and political reality of this people today. It goes on to relate the lessons contained in the Vision Quest and the Sun Dance, lessons that could benefit anyone. 30 mins.
VHS: S21595. $29.95.

Geronimo

A true story which tells how a Native American brave becomes the most feared Apache war chief. He was legendary for the ferocious battles he fought on behalf of his people and his amazing ability to dodge capture by the US army. Originally shown on the Turner Home Entertainment channel. 102 mins.
VHS: S20637. $92.98.

Geronimo and the Apache Resistance

In 1886, the United States government mobilized 5,000 men to capture one man: the legendary Apache, Geronimo. In this moving testament to the human spirit, we follow Geronimo through decades of injustices. This is a missing piece of American history that tells the truth about the settling of the frontier. 60 mins.
VHS: S13807. $19.95.

Geronimo: The Last Renegade

In this two-tape set, the story of competing legendary frontiersmen is told in detail. Geronimo avoided capture by the U.S. Cavalry after inspiring his people to fight for their lands. *Custer and the 7th Cavalry* tells the story of this flamboyant and eccentric military man who met his fate at Wounded Knee. Both videos are 50 mins.
VHS: S21548. $19.95.

Giving Thanks: A Native-American Good Morning Message

Known as the Thanksgiving Address, this Native-Amerian good morning message is based on the belief that the natural world is a precious and rare gift, from the moon and the stars to the tiniest blade of grass. Written and narrated by Chief Jake Swamp in English and the Mohawk language. 7 mins.
VHS: S33784. $60.00.

Her Mother Before Her: Winnebago Women's Stories of Their Mothers & Grandmothers

Contemporary Native American women talk about their childhoods and their families. Despite cultural differences, the experiences of these women are profoundly universal. 22 mins. Resource guide available.
Video.
VHS: S25760. $95.00.
Resource Guide.
VHS: S25773. $45.00.

How Beaver Stole Fire

In this sand animation short, a Native American tale about the origin of fire is beautifully realized. 12 mins.
VHS: S23507. $39.95.

Howard Terpning: The Storyteller

Howard Terpning's paintings function as visual stories depicting Native Americans. Along with the works, this video shows the artist at work. His compositions offer a glimpse of a lifestyle rarely seen elsewhere. 30 mins.
VHS: S26806. $49.95.

I Will Fight No More Forever

In the 19th century, the United States government made 1,000 treaties with Indian tribes throughout the country. They honored less than 100. *I Will Fight No More Forever* is the tragic story from this time, about the Nez Perce and their 1,700-mile, 108-day fighting retreat, led by the courageous Chief Joseph. Highly recommended, this docu-drama is a rare and accurate portrayal of the plight of the 19th century American Indian. With James Whitmore, Sam Elliott and Ned Romero.
VHS: S12764. $29.95.
David Wolper, USA, 109 mins.

In the Land of the War Canoes

Edward S. Curtis devoted his life to documenting the world of dwindling Native American cultures. In this film, Curtis told a story of love and revenge among the Kwakiutl Indians of Vancouver Island. Curtis spent three years with the Kwakiutl to meticulously recreate their way of life before the white man came. In addition to the magnificent painted war canoes, the film pictures authentic costumes, ceremonial dances and religious rituals. Silent with soundtrack from 1972 restoration.
VHS: S16431. $39.95.
Laser: LD71816. $34.95.
Edward S. Curtis, USA/Canada, 1914, 47 mins.

Incident at Oglala

Michael Apted's documentary about Leonard Peltier, the Native American activist who's served more than 15 years in federal prison for the murder of two FBI agents, despite evidence suggesting prosecutorial misconduct, perjury and other testimony contradicting the government's case. Narrated and produced by Robert Redford, with much of its research derived from Peter Matthiessen's *In the Spirit of Crazy Horse*.
VHS: S17442. $19.98.
Michael Apted, USA, 1991, 92 mins.

The Indian & His Homeland: American Images, 1590-1876

This video features the art of noted explorer artists such as Catlin, Bodmer, Audubon and Catesby, providing a 300-year survey of the impact of European civilization on the New World—in particular, its devastating effect on the lives and cultures of the American Indians and native wildlife. USA, 30 mins.
VHS: S15080. $29.95.

Indians of North America, Collection I

Based on the book by Chelsea House, this ten-volume series describes the histories and cultures of America's native peoples through examinations of their music, crafts and ceremonies. Archival footage and photographs help uncover the truth behind the myths and stereotypes that obscure the original inhabitants of this land. 30 minutes each.
The Apache.
VHS: S20990. $39.95.
The Aztec.
VHS: S20991. $39.95.
The Cherokee.
VHS: S20992. $39.95.
The Cheyenne.
VHS: S20993. $39.95.
The Comanche.
VHS: S20994. $39.95.
The Iroquois.
VHS: S20995. $39.95.
The Maya.
VHS: S20996. $39.95.
The Navajo.
VHS: S20997. $39.95.
The Seminole.
VHS: S20998. $39.95.
The Yankton Sioux.
VHS: S20999. $39.95.
Indians of North America, Collection I, Set. Includes *The Cherokee, The Cheyenne, The Comanche, The Iroquois, The Maya, The Navajo, The Seminole, The Yankton Sioux, The Apache* and *The Aztec.*
VHS: S23649. $399.50.

Indians of North America, Collection II

The well-regarded book from Chelsea House Publishers inspired this video series about Native Americans. Both historical and contemporary struggles are examined by consulting historians and living tribe members. This series tackles the myths and misconceptions that have long obscured the truth about the first Americans. Each episode is 30 minutes long.
The Chinook.
VHS: S23638. $39.95.
The Creek.
VHS: S23639. $39.95.
The Crow.
VHS: S23640. $39.95.
A History of Native Americans.
VHS: S23641. $39.95.
The Huron.
VHS: S23642. $39.95.
The Lenape.
VHS: S23643. $39.95.
The Menominee.
VHS: S23644. $39.95.
The Narragansett (Enishkeetompauog).
VHS: S23645. $39.95.
The Potawatomi (Bode wad mi).
VHS: S23646. $39.95.
The Pueblo.
VHS: S23647. $39.95.
The Ten-Volume Set.
VHS: S23648. $399.50.

Ishi, The Last Yahi

In this chronicle, narrated by Linda Hunt, the story of Ishi unfolds. He was the sole surviving member of the Yahis of California, a Native American tribe exterminated by the U.S. After 40 years alone and near starvation, he left the land and entered the world of the white man. Photos, archival footage, recordings and commentary are used in this indictment of "manifest destiny." B&W, 60 mins.
VHS: S23052. $19.95.

Joy Harjo

As a member of the Muscogee (Creek) nation, the poet Joy Harjo draws on the experience of her people. This winner of an American Book Award read from *She Had Some Horses* and *In Mad Love and War* in Laguna Beach, California, on February 18, 1989. Lewis MacAdams conducted the interview. From the *Lannan Literary Videos* series. 60 mins.
VHS: S27118. $19.95.

Lakota Woman

Irene Bedard makes her screen debut in this drama about the actual Native American protest at Wounded Knee in 1973. A Native American cast gives this film great passion, enabling it to depict the struggle against silence waged by a united group of 2000 who vowed never to be silenced again.
VHS: S23942. $79.98.
Laser: LD74917. $39.99.
Frank Pierson, USA, 1994, 113 mins.

Legacy of the Generations

In the tradition of *The Daughters of the Anasazi*, an examination of Native American culture and women in the arts. Narrated by Buffie St. Marie. 30 mins.
VHS: S34634. $19.95.

Life in the Woodlands Before the White Man Came

Through re-enactments the day-to-day life of Native Americans is demonstrated in this video. 12 mins.
VHS: S23533. $49.95.
Laser: LD74764. $99.95.

Maria! Indian Pottery of San Ildefonso

Indian pottery maker Maria Martinez demonstrates the traditional Indian ways of making pottery. Beginning with the spreading of sacred corn, you will see gathering and mixing of clay, construction and decorating of pottery and building of the firing mound. 27 mins.
VHS: S06698. $29.95.

Mesa Verde

Visit the world-famous cliff dwellings of Mesa Verde to study the ruins of an ancient Indian civilization that flourished for 1,000 years and then vanished forever. 23 mins.
VHS: S06489. $29.95.

Monument Valley: Navajo Homeland

Discover the majestic beauty of Monument Valley and the mystical bond between the Navajo and their ancient homeland. This is a spectacular land shaped over eons of time, a land of vast open spaces and towering buttes, of natural arches and prehistoric ruins. The culture and craft of the Navajo men and women is also examined. USA, 30 mins.
VHS: S15081. $29.95.

The Moon's Prayer: Wisdom of the Ages

Native Americans preserved the beauty and utility of the American Northwest for centuries. Then settlers invaded these lands and transformed them through deforestation and the proliferation of dams. Today Native Americans are again fighting to preserve and in some cases restore the vitality of this region, using age-old techniques and modern methods. 51 mins.
VHS: S21574. $85.00.

More Than Bows and Arrows

Finally, a documentary that charts how the achievements of Native Americans have contributed to the shape of modern North America. From religion to science, art and even architecture, the ingenuity of ancient ways have informed and built the contemporary world. 60 mins.
VHS: S20732. $29.95.

Mountain Wolf Woman: 1884-1960

A Winnebago woman's own words are used to tell the story of her life. Her granddaughter, Naomi Russell, narrates. This video is based on the book by anthropologist Nancy Oestreich Lurie. 17 mins. Resource guide available.
Resource Guide.
VHS: S25775. $45.00.
Video.
VHS: S25762. $95.00.

Native American Herbology for Beginners

Holistic health educator Kay Moon Dreamer offers some advice for the gathering and use of various native herbs. 55 mins.
VHS: S20155. $24.95.

Native American Indian Artist Series

A profile of seven contemporary artists representing diverse backgrounds and styles. Available individually, or order the complete set of six tapes at a savings.
Charles Loloma. The world famous Hopi jeweler displays some of his most stunning work, and discusses his heritage. His interests, inside and outside the reservation, are revealed in his art, which uses only materials indigenous to his homeland: iron, wood, ivory, coal, turquoise, lapis lazuli and shell. 29 mins.
VHS: S15755. $39.95.
Fritz Scholder. Fritz Scholder, a California Mission Indian, creates prints and paintings that depict today's Indian caught between ancient tradition and modern society. 29 mins.
VHS: S15756. $39.95.
Helen Hardin. Helen Hardin attempts to integrate two parts of herself, the Indian and the artist, painting sophisticated and colorful geometric patterns and traditional motifs of dancers, deer, the sun and seasons. 29 mins.
VHS: S15757. $39.95.
Medicine Flower and Lonewolf. Two potters from Santa Clara Pueblo in New Mexico have revived and extended the traditional forms and techniques of their pre-Columbian ancestors. 29 mins.
VHS: S15758. $49.95.
R.C. Gorman. R.C. Gorman, a Navajo painter and printmaker, is shown in his Taos, New Mexico studio working on one of a suite of paintings dedicated to the Navajo woman. 29 mins.
VHS: S15759. $49.95.
Allan Houser. A Chiricahua-Apache, Allan Hauser creates stone, wood and bronze homages to the American Indian. As he works, Hauser talks of his personal life and beliefs, and explains how his heritage has contributed to his art. 29 mins.
VHS: S15760. $39.95.
Complete set. 6 tapes.
VHS: S15754. $250.00.

Native American Indians

A vivid and enlightening look at the people whose proud heritage and rich culture are a national treasure. *Native Americans* captures the history of three distinct tribes; *Indians of the Plains* discusses the traditions of the tribes who inhabited the midsection of the country and depended upon the buffalo to survive; *Indians of the Southwest* describes the lifestyle of the Navajos and their mythical relationship with nature; and *Indiansof California* looks at the Yokuts, the largest tribe to inhabit California. 57 mins.
VHS: S34838. $19.95.

Native American Prophecy & Ceremony

Gain insight into the Native American sacraments of the peace pipe, sweat lodge, and ritual dancing. Honored medicine men present challenging prophecies regarding how our civilization must return to a way of life in harmony with nature and the Great Spirit or face destruction. 25 mins.
VHS: S10394. $24.95.

Native American Ritual: Healing Way Song

Oh Shinnah Fastwolf, a healer and entertainer of Mohawk and Apache ancestry, shows the methods of sensitizing the hands to the field of psychic energy that flows between them. She teaches an ancient song, which includes a healing rite never before permitted to be recorded. 24 mins.
VHS: S06925. $29.95.

Native American Sweat Lodge Ceremony

Experience the sacred Native American sweat lodge ceremony from beginning to end. Learn about the health and spiritual benefits that Native Americans have known for centuries. 90 mins.
VHS: S10392. $39.95.

The Native Americans

This six-part series of 40-minute long videos tells the story of America's original inhabitants. Native Americans are themselves the writers and the directors, as well as the featured subjects, of this series. Set against a backdrop of majestic lands, five distinct geographic regions (the Northeast, tribal peoples of Northwest, tribes of the Southeast, the Great Plains and natives of the Southwest) emerge, each with its own distinctive beauty and traditions. Robbie Robertson wrote the original score.
VHS: S25752. $59.98.

Native Americans—An Overview

American Indian traditions are explored through the rituals of a contemporary powwow. Through dance and the elaborate design of costumes, Native Americans reenact the daily life of their ancestors. 30 mins.
VHS: S20270. $49.95.

Native Land: Nomads of the Dawn

The highly regarded Native American author Jamake Highwater traces the steps of the nomads who discovered the Americas. These peoples created complex social structures where nature, the animal world and the cosmos were intimately entwined in widely held moral beliefs and ideals. 57 mins.
VHS: S27529. $19.98.

Navajo Code Talkers

Shortly after the onset of World War II, Phillip Johnson, the son of Navajo reservation missionaries, realized that a code in Navajo would be impenetrable to the Japanese. Twenty-nine Navajos were recruited to work as radio operators, thereby providing the US war effort with a top-secret communications link. This film tells their story of service and heroism. 27 mins.
VHS: S22801. $29.95.

Nomadic Indians of the West

Across the majestic wilds of the West, Native Americans have lived, hunted and traveled for centuries. In this documentary Wes Studi hosts the concluding episode. 60 mins.
VHS: S22880. $59.95.

On the Pow Wow Trail

On the Pow Wow Trail is an entertaining and informative focus on the preservation of Native American customs, traditional dress and dance. Follow young Chad Killscrow and friend Mike Roberts as they travel from pow wow to pow wow on the majestic plains of Oklahoma, New Mexico, Colorado and Montana, and recreate ceremonies established centuries before them. 45 mins.
VHS: S15850. $14.95.

Pablita Velarde: An Artist and Her People

Pablita Velarde is a Native American artist who paints the history of her ancient people. Found materials and other materials supply her pigments. Her work ensures future generations will know the vital traditions and legends of her tribe. 20 mins.
VHS: S26805. $49.95.

Paha Sapa: The Struggle for the Black Hills

The story of the Lakota Sioux Indians' past and present struggle for the Black Hills of South Dakota is movingly portrayed in this documentary, which was nominated for an Emmy Award as Best Documentary of the year. 60 mins. 1994.
VHS: S23331. $29.95.

People of the 7th Fire

Native American oral traditions, teachings and prophecies reveal overlooked ways to care for our selves and our environment. This is a collaborative message from many North American native nations that emphasizes co-existence with the earth. A fascinating and comprehensive look at Native Americans in today's society. 55 mins.
VHS: S27657. $24.95.

Peyote Road

The United States Supreme Court denied indigenous peoples the right to use peyote in their centuries-old rituals. Religious freedom is at stake. This documentary explores the effects of this decision and its implications for one of the Western Hemisphere's oldest religions. Peter Coyote narrates. USA, 1993, 59 mins.
VHS: S26895. $29.99.

Picuris Indians

This visually stunning production examines the unrehearsed moments of the Picuris Indians at the location of their ancient pueblo, nestled in a "shangri-la" set in the rock formations of the Picuris mountains of north central New Mexico. 60 mins.
VHS: S20317. $150.00.

The Primal Mind

Jamake Highwater's book of the same name caused a sensation for its insights regarding the different perceptions experienced by Native Americans and Americans of European descent. This documentary shows how Native American techniques and customs influenced and transformed the work of famous artists like Jackson Pollock, Martha Graham, Pablo Picasso and others. 57 mins.
VHS: S27528. $19.98.

Quest for Wisdom

Bear Heart, a traditional elder, medicine man and spiritual and tribal leader, discusses the philosophy of Native people, detailing their relationship and intimate connection to nature and the interconnection between ceremony and daily life. 50 mins.
VHS: S18035. $24.95.

Return to the Sacred Hoop

Native American grandfather Wallace Black Elk, a Lakota healer, teacher and leader of the new generation of Earth Warriors, offers insights and messages about achieving harmony and balance. 45 mins.
VHS: S20160. $29.95.

Rolling Thunder: Healer of Meta Tantay

Rolling Thunder is the controversial medicine man and prophetic Cherokee healer who worked with the Grateful Dead as a spiritual leader. He collaborated on a book with this rock group that brought him widespread notoriety in the 1970's. Now his spiritual ways, including his shocking prophecies for the future, have been updated for the 90's in this fascinating video. 58 mins.
VHS: S21598. $29.95.

Santa Fe: Artists of New Mexico

Native American artists along with other artists are featured on this video. R.C. Gorman, Allan Houser, Jacqueline Shutiva, Marie Romero, Jemez Pueblo, Bunny Tobias, Charles Greeley, Fred Prescott, Paul Lutonsky and David Dear Silversmith are included. 46 mins.
VHS: S26803. $49.95.

The Search for Ancient Americans

A revealing documentary about the long-term archeological finds of five separate discoveries that have helped scientists to unlock the mysteries of ancient civilizations.
VHS: S17730. $14.98.

The Shadow Catcher: Edward S. Curtis and the North American Indian

Photographer, anthropologist and filmmaker Edward S. Curtis forged a tradition among American eccentric genius that worked its way out of the frontier and into the mainstream of the 20th century. Spending over three decades with Native Americans (1896-1930), Curtis completed the most intensive anthropological study ever taken with over 40,000 photographs, 20 volumes of text and some of the earliest motion pictures capturing Native American religious ceremonies.
VHS: S16619. $29.95.
Teri McLuhan, USA, 1976, 88 mins.

Sioux Legends

Native Sioux act out the legends of their philosophy and religion against the backdrop of the Black Hills and the Badlands of South Dakota. The forces of nature are central to their world view. 20 mins.
VHS: S23733. $49.95.

Sisters & Friends: Winnebago Women's Stories

Contemporary Native American women share their stories with each other and, through video, with the viewer. This video is filled with love and laughter. 15 mins. Resource guide available.
Video.
VHS: S25766. $95.00.
Resource Guide.
VHS: S25779. $45.00.

Sun Bear on Power

During this time of earth changes, Sun Bear emerges as a powerful figure who has successfully guided many people who are in search of fuller and happier lives. Sun Bear is a man of Ojibwa descent who has studied with medicine people from many tribes and traditions. In this video, he teaches gentleness as a source of great strength. "In past generations, people knew how to find and follow their path to power. Today we have been taught to give our power away to a society that often misuses it." Produced by the Bear Tribe. 65 mins.
VHS: S06258. $49.95.

Sun Bear: Earth Changes

"The Earth Changes prophesied by many Native traditions have already begun. People need look no further than the daily news to see proof of this. These times of great change are a time of cleansing, and of moving forward. The people who are going to survive the changes are people who can walk in a sacred manner, who live in harmony with each other and the earth. This is what we are being prepared for by the changes." (Sun Bear). Sun Bear is a man of Ojibwa descent who has studied with medicine people, whose life forms a bridge between Native and non-Native cultures. Produced by the Bear Tribe. 65 mins.
VHS: S06259. $49.95.

The Sun Dagger

A fascinating documentary about the discovery of the celestial calendar of New Mexico's ancient Anasazi tribe. With commentary written by Joseph Campbell, the show examines the ethnographic evidence of this vibrant culture that thrived in the desolate desert environment more than 1000 years ago. Narrated by Robert Redford. 60 mins.
VHS: S19113. $19.95.

Tahtonka

Buffalo represented a key element of life for the Native Americans who lived on the Great Plains. In this historical re-enactment, the culture of these original Americans is examined, beginning before the European invasion and continuing up until the Wounded Knee massacre. 30 mins.
VHS: S23732. $49.95.

Thirteen Moons on Turtle's Back

Subtitled *A Native American Year of Moons*, Abenaki Indian Joseph Bruchac and poet Jonathan London discuss the history of Native American legend and mythology, focused on the belief of the thirteen moons of the year. The writers contrast legends within different Native American tribes to show how the cultures identified the cycles of the moon with the seasons.
VHS: S20002. $44.95.

Thunderheart

Michael Apted's documentary-like feature was inspired from actual events in the mid '70s. This work stars Val Kilmer as a half-Sioux FBI agent assigned to investigate the murder of a militant Native American in the South Dakota, Oglala nation. He uncovers a possible government conspiracy, appalling social conditions, and tribal and ethnic warfare between pro-government Indians and the progressive, traditionalists. With Sam Shepard, Fred Ward, and Graham Greene as a reservation police officer.
VHS: S17220. $19.95.
Laser: LD71578. $34.95.
Michael Apted, USA, 1992, 119 mins.

Tribal Legacies: Last Stand at Little Big Horn

A historical corrective to the events and circumstances behind one of the most famous and inaccurately reported battles in history. The program invokes the views of the Lakota Sioux, Cheyenne and Crow, developed through oral histories and drawings. 60 mins.
VHS: S18358. $19.95.

Vision of the Medicine Wheel (with Sun Bear)

Experience the Medicine Wheel Gathering with an understanding of the true essence of Sun Bear's vision. Inspired by his insight into the Earth Change prophecies and desire to create personal and planetary healing, this program is filled with interviews on ceremony, healing and Earth Changes, along with a dedication to the seventh generation. Features the ceremonies, drums and songs of Brooke Medicine Eagle, Wallace Black Elk, Brant Secunda and major Native and Earth Teachers from around the world. 60 mins.
VHS: S18096. $29.95.

Walk in Balance

Sun Bear, a Chippewa medicine man, writer, teacher and philosopher, adopts his teachings and practices in developing a vital, well-balanced, stress-free life through traditional and contemporary healing techniques. 60 mins.
VHS: S18091. $34.95.

The War Against the Indians

Produced by CBC, this beautifully crafted three-volume documentary production from award-winning filmmaker Harry Rasky combines moving imagery and historical and archival material to explore the impact on the First Nations of North America of the so-called discovery of the New World. This film provides an important historical perspective as North Americans re-examine the significance of Christopher Columbus' voyages 500 years ago. Volumes include *The Feather and the Cross*, *The Hunter Becomes the Hunted* and the *Dispossessed*. Winner of the Gold Angel Award for Best North American Documentary of the Year and 1992 winner of the Great Plains Film Festival Humanities Prize. "An epic masterpiece" (Smithsonian Institution).
VHS: S30127. $39.99.
Harry Rasky, Canada, 1992, 170 mins.

The Winds of Time

Narrated by Robert Urich, this film explores the ancient Basketmaker and Pueblo cultures, more commonly known as the Anasazi, who inhabited the Four Corners region for more than 14 centuries. Walk through the scattered Anasazi ruins of national monuments and parks like Hovenweep, Mesa Verde and Chaco Canyon. 60 mins.
VHS: S32410. $14.95.

Winnebago Women: Songs & Stories

Contemporary Native American women share their traditions in art and music through this video. The result is a moving tape, perfect for all types of libraries. 19 mins. Resource guide available.
Video.
VHS: S25768. $95.00.
Resource Guide.
VHS: S25781. $45.00.

Wisconsin Powwow and Naamikaaged: Dancer for the People

Illustrates the way in which powwows today incorporate historical traditions and modern innovations. The first video, *Wisconsin Powwow*, is a general treatment of the powwow itself as it has come to be held by Ojibwe people in northern Wisconsin. The second, *Naamikaaged*, follows a young Ojibwe as he prepares for, dances and sings at powwows in northern Wisconsin. Includes 40-page booklet. Two-video set. 68 mins.
VHS: S34817. $49.95.

With Hand in Heart

A portrait of southwestern Native American artists and their work, ranging from vases and bowls to hand-woven Navajo blankets and storyteller figures. With Lucy Lewis, Jody Falwel, Margaret Tefoya, Tony Roller, Fanny Nampeyo, Thomas Polacca, Mary Reed and Helen Cordero. 30 mins.
VHS: S31850. $24.95.

Wolf Nation

The Northern Arapaho Wolf Society performs their native "Wolf Dance" in celebration of the historic reintroduction of the wolf to Yellowstone National Park. Called one of the greatest triumphs of this decade, it was filmed by world-renowned wildlife photographer Jim Brandenburg. 30 mins.
VHS: S27656. $19.95.

Woven by the Grandmothers

Pottery making is one of the most enduring Native American traditions. The Southwest Indian women who create these sacred vessels preserve a centuries-old tradition while paving the way for contemporary artists. Set against the breathtaking landscape of the American southwest, this PBS documentary showcases the art of master Native American potters, the traditions they preserve and the precedent they set for modern artists. 30 mins.
VHS: S34635. $19.95.

Yanomami

Considered the last intact indigenous culture in the Americas, the Yanomami are now threatened by the encroachment of gold mining, development and disease. This documentary provides an in depth look at the Yanomami with the help of a group of anthropologists, doctors and journalists. 58 mins.
VHS: S21572. $95.00.

RELIGION

According to Kossoff

David Kossoff, master storyteller and Biblical scholar, magically recounts some of the best-loved stories of the Old Testament—simply, earnestly. Phenomenally successful on British television, this series is the antithesis of overblown Biblical epics.
Story of Adam and Eve.
VHS: S05570. $19.95.
Story of David.
VHS: S05573. $19.95.
Story of Elijah.
VHS: S05579. $19.95.
Story of Gideon.
VHS: S05575. $19.95.
Story of Jacob.
VHS: S05571. $19.95.
Story of Jonah.
VHS: S05572. $59.95.
Story of Joshua.
VHS: S05577. $19.95.
Story of Ruth.
VHS: S05574. $19.95.
Story of Samson.
VHS: S05576. $19.95.
Story of Samuel.
VHS: S05578. $19.95.
Story of Tobias.
VHS: S05580. $19.95.

Ancient Mysteries

Using modern technology, scientific analysis, high-tech evidence and recent archaeological developments, the films in the *Ancient Mysteries* series are on the cutting edge of discovery.
Ark of the Covenant. This real-life search for the Ark of the Covenant is based on new interpretations of the Bible. The possible whereabouts of this ancient artifact remain a mystery that must still be solved. This tape offers new answers to the age-old question: whatever became of this sacred repository? 50 mins.
VHS: S21687. $19.95.
Enigma of the Dead Sea Scrolls. In 1947, a shepherd boy found the Dead Sea Scrolls. Originally hailed as a window to the origins of Christianity, they were soon removed from public scrutiny. This is the story of the discovery, authenticity and cover-up that make these artifacts so intriguing. 50 mins.
VHS: S23106. $19.95.
Shroud of Turin. This artifact is held by many to be the burial shroud of Jesus Christ. Investigations into the history and the composition of this shroud are documented on this video. Conflicting results may well ensure that the true nature of this cloth remains a mystery. USA, 1995, 50 mins.
VHS: S26100. $19.95.
Who Wrote the Bible?: Probing the Eternal Mysteries Behind the Origins of the Holy Scriptures. Richard Kiley and Jean Simmons host this serious documentary filmed on location in the Holy Land. Leading Biblical scholars discuss the latest scientific research on the world's most widely read book and tackle questions regarding Moses, the Torah, the Dead Sea Scrolls and more. The theological insights and scientific facts on the Holy Scriptures will leave the faithful inspired and the scholarly fascinated. Two-volume set. 1994-1995, 150 mins.
VHS: S27203. $29.95.

Ancient Tales from a Promised Land

In this adaptation of 14 Old Testament stories, shot on location in the Holy Land, the gifted British actor Tony Robinson brings a storyteller's flair and passion to each staged telling.
Vol. I: Joshua Smashes Jericho/Joshua in Trouble Valley. In the first story, the Israelites, led by Joshua, emerge from the desert after 40 years to assume control of the land of Canaan. Joshua's strike against Canaanite towns is interrupted by his difficulties with a dishonest soldier and a corrupt mayor. 30 mins.
VHS: S18298. $19.95.
Vol. II: Deborah and the Headbanger/Gideon Gets His Wolly Wet. The Israelites turn to Deborh to repel the Canaanite offensive. In the second story, Gideon destroys the Canaanites' Corn Goddess. 30 mins.
VHS: S18299. $19.95.
Vol. III: Gideon's Exploding Pickle Pots/Samson Gets Knotted. Under the direction of Gideon, the disadvantaged Israelite army routs the Canaanites, awaiting the landing of the Philistines. In the second program, the able bodied though weak minded Samson must deal with the repercussions of marrying a Philistine woman. 30 mins.
VHS: S18300. $19.95.
Vol. IV: Samson Gets a Haircut/Samuel and the Spooky Goxbox. Delilah betrays Samson by revealing the nature of his superhuman strength. In the second story, Samuel is crowned the leader of the Israelites, and the Ark of the Covenant is stolen by the Philistines. 30 mins.
VHS: S18301. $19.95.
Vol. V: Saul Rips Up His Camel/David Gets a Good Gig. After elected to find a proper Israeli kingdom, Saul is disowned by the prophet Samuel for his delusions of grandeur. Greatness is expected from the harp-playing shepherd David. 30 mins.
VHS: S18302. $19.95.
Vol. VI: David and the Hairy Man Mountain/Saul Goes Bonkers. David is immortalized following his stunning defeat of the Philistine giant, Goliath, which enrages Saul. In the second story, Saul is humiliated by David's influence and orchestrates his removal from power. 30 mins.
VHS: S18303. $19.95.
Vol. VII: Saul Bumps into a Witch/David Gets to Number One. Saul seeks answers from the Witch of Endor but is unnerved by what he finds. In the second story, David's ascendancy is complete and the Israelites settle in Jerusalem, though their comfort is short-lived. 30 mins.
VHS: S18304. $19.95.
Ancient Tales from a Promised Land. Boxed Set.
VHS: S18305. $119.70.

Archaeology: Mysteries of the Holy Land

Scientists and historians take their cue from the Hebrew Bible to see if they can unlock some of the Holy Land's most confounding secrets. This fascinating excursion is from the Discovery Channel. 80 mins.
VHS: S25085. $49.00.

Ave Maria

Though revered by millions, little is actually known about the Virgin Mary. This documentary explores the history of this religious figure and her continuing influence, particularly among women. 51 mins.
VHS: S24925. $29.95.

Basil in Blunderland

In this film by Miles England, Cardinal Basil Hume, The Roman Catholic Archbishop of Westminster, talks openly about prayer, life after death, and his own moments of doubt and despair, and re-enacts a game from his childhood which had a profound impact upon his approach to spiritual life. 60 mins.
VHS: S35134. $19.95.

The Bible on Video: The Book of Genesis

A dramatic collection of vignettes dramatizing the biblical history and poetic storytelling of the *Book of Genesis*. The program reimagines the days of creation, Adam and Eve's removal from the Garden of Eden, the haunting tale of Cain and Abel and the steadfast heroism of Noah. It is available in two versions, the King James (KJV) and Revised Standard (RSV), and in two languages, English and Spanish.
RSV—English.
VHS: S19705. $79.95.
RSV—Spanish.
VHS: S19706. $79.95.
KJV—English.
VHS: S19707. $79.95.
KJV—Spanish.
VHS: S19708. $79.95.

The Bible on Video: The Gospel of Luke
The Genesis Project's daunting attempt to reconstruct the *Gospel of Luke* using authentic details, including a word-for-word biblical text created in the original languages—Hebrew, Greek and Aramaic—narrated by Orson Welles, Alexander Scourby and Jose Ferrer. The film recreates the Easter story, from the birth of Jesus to his crucifixion at Golgotha. The program is available in two versions, the King James (KJV) and Revised Standard (RSV), and in two languages, English and Spanish.
RSV—English.
VHS: S19701. $79.95.
RSV—Spanish.
VHS: S19702. $79.95.
KJV—English.
VHS: S19703. $79.95.
KJV—Spanish.
VHS: S19704. $79.95.

Billy Graham
American evangelist Billy Graham has been spreading the word of God for over 40 years, and has served as a confidant to U.S. Presidents, elevating him to a spiritual level matched only by the pope. This *A & E Biography* video offers an enlightening portrait of one of the world's most popular and powerful religious leaders. 50 mins.
VHS: S28494. $19.95.

Blood and Honey
The British actor and author Tony Robinson (*The Black Adder*) is in the Holy Land to narrate a series of gripping, stylized retellings of Old Testament stories.
Volume 1. 30 mins.
VHS: S17184. $14.95.
Volume 2. 30 mins.
VHS: S17185. $14.95.
Volume 3. 30 mins.
VHS: S17186. $14.95.
Volume 4. 30 mins.
VHS: S17187. $14.95.
Volume 5. 30 mins.
VHS: S17188. $14.95.
Volume 6. 30 mins.
VHS: S17189. $14.95.
Volume 7. 30 mins.
VHS: S17190. $14.95.
Complete Set. 210 mins.
VHS: S17191. $99.65.

Brides of Christ
Brenda Fricker (*My Left Foot*) stars in a searing, award-winning, British drama that captures the restless desperation of a reclusive society and its encounters with the outside world. From student Rosemary's rejection of rigid sexual moral codes to Sister Paul's decision to leave the convent for a radical priest, this is a critically-acclaimed, riveting production. Three tapes in a boxed set. Total length: 300 mins.
VHS: S21903. $59.95.

The Crucifixion/How Jesus Died: The Final 18 Hours
Medical experts Dr. John Bonica and Dr. Frederick T. Zugibe join Yale historian Ramsay MacMullen for this in-depth look at the final 18 hours in the life of Jesus Christ. The forensic and historic facts provide the basis for this accurate glimpse of that historic event. Directed by John Dauer, USA.
VHS: S27724. $29.95.

Discovering the Feminine
In 1990, two years before his death, Father Bede Griffiths suffered a stroke. This personal crisis allowed him to understand the importance of the feminine in all aspects of life. Through his humor and with great humility, he explains his insight in this lecture. 32 mins.
VHS: S21853. $29.95.

From a Far Country: Pope John Paul II
Sam Neill stars in this beautiful and inspiring historical film about the man who came from Poland to ascend the throne of St. Peter and become loved and revered as Pope John Paul II.
VHS: S33392. $89.95.
Krzysztof Zanussi, Italy/Poland/Great Britain, 1981, 120 mins.

The Gates of Jerusalem
The gates of this ancient city are rife with historical and religious significance. The Golden Gate, in particular, is of vital interest to millions of religious people the world over. This documentary is broken into two parts: *The Spirit of the City—From Abraham to the Roman Conquest* and *In Search of Peace—From the Crusades to the 21st Century*. Together they tell the tale of a city that continues to fascinate through its unique heritage. Narrated by Richard Kiley, 120 mins.
VHS: S27826. $39.95.

Genesis: A Living Conversation
Bill Moyers hosts this five-tape series which explores, in a serious but open fashion, important questions raised by the Bible. Moyers has gathered thoughtful and entertaining individuals—Biblical scholars, writers, artists, psychotherapists, composers, lawyers, translators—to discuss, debate and discover what relevance the Biblical stories have for us today. Each episode focuses on a different tale—from the Creation to fratricide to reconciliation, and they are brought alive by such inquisitive and entertaining intellects as John Barth, Oscar Hijuelos and Mary Gordon.
VHS: S29546. $119.00.

Greatest Heroes of the Bible
Enjoy the greatest stories ever told in this lavish series of biblical epics. Each tape is 50 mins.
Greatest Heroes of the Bible: Abraham's Sacrifice. A man must save his son from execution at the hands of an evil king, and only the power of his faith in God can help him. 50 mins.
VHS: S33150. $14.99.
Greatest Heroes of the Bible: David & Goliath. A young boy fights a victorious battle against a Philistine giant, with the strength and encouragement of prayer. 50 mins.
VHS: S33157. $14.99.
Greatest Heroes of the Bible: Joseph in Egypt. Sold as a slave by his his brothers, Joseph's faith changes his life and leads him to a dramatic reunion. 50 mins.
VHS: S33153. $14.99.
Greatest Heroes of the Bible: Samson and Delilah. Given the gift of tremendous strength, Samson's power is threatened when he meets the lovely yet deceptive Delilah. 50 mins.
VHS: S33155. $14.99.
Greatest Heroes of the Bible: Sodom and Gomorrah. Lot must lead his people away from wickedness. They cannot look back or they will forever become pillars of salt. 50 mins.
VHS: S33151. $14.99.
Greatest Heroes of the Bible: The Ten Commandments. High upon Mount Sinai God gave Moses the Ten Commandments. Now Moses must bring them to the Israelites, who have fallen into sin. 50 mins.
VHS: S33149. $14.99.
Greatest Heroes of the Bible: The Story of Noah. Instructed by God to build an ark, Noah gathers a male and female of each species and prepares for a flood that will destroy the world. 50 mins.
VHS: S33154. $14.99.
Greatest Heroes of the Bible: The Story of Moses. He delivered his people from the Pharoah's bondage. Now he must save them from the Red Sea. 50 mins.
VHS: S33156. $14.99.

The Hajj: One American's Pilgrimage to Mecca
In this ABC News Nightline program, writer Michael Wolfe documents his trip to Islam's holiest shrine during the Islamic pilgrimage Hajj and explains the origins and meanings of the various rituals. 22 mins.
VHS: S34367. $14.98.

Hanged on a Twisted Cross
Biblical theologian Dietrich Bonhoeffer was executed by the Nazis just days before the Allies defeated Germany in World War II. Using rare archival footage, documents, and visits to original locations, we get an intimate portrait of a man whose life and writings grow in their influence and speak powerfully to issues of our own day some 50 years after his death. 120 mins.
VHS: S34523. $24.95.

The History and Interpretation of the Bible
Father Bede Griffiths explores methods by which the Bible was recorded, and how changes in Christian thinking affect its interpretation. 40 mins.
VHS: S21854. $29.95.

The Holy Koran
The Holy Koran is a penetrating study of the holy book of Islam which explains for the western mind why this religion is such a force in the world today. *Islamic Science* shows in detail how the people of the Moslem world have contributed to today's civilization and culture. *The Religious Experience* compares the world's religions.
VHS: S03982. $29.95.

Holy Land & Holy City
The Holy Land at Christmas offers a heart-warming look at the holy land during the holy season when many Christian sects gather to share a common legacy. *The World of the Vatican II* gives us an artist's chronicle of the activities in the Holy City of Rome during the reign of Pope John XXIII.
VHS: S03983. $29.95.

The Holy Quest: In Search of Biblical Relics
This four-part series follows the work of reknowned authors, scientists and archeologists who have searched the Holy Land and beyond for traces of ancient religious artificats. Tapes include: *Quest for the Lost Ark of the Covenant*, *The Turin Shroud*, *Castle of the Holy Grail* and *The Dead Sea Scrolls*.
VHS: S28475. $89.95.

How Do You Spell God?
A heartwarming journey of faith, based on the best-selling book by Rabbi Marc Gellman and Monsignor Thomas Hartman, featuring funny, insightful and surprising interviews with children of many religions. Animated stories feature the voices of Maya Angelou, Deepak Chopra, Griffin Dunne, Fyush Finkel, Joe Mantegna, Chris Rock, Fred Savage, Marlo Thomas and Alfre Woodard. 31 mins.
VHS: S33132. $12.95.

A Human Search: The Life of Father Bede Griffiths
Benedictine monk Father Bede, a great mystic and visionary, is revealed in this intimate portrait. His profound union of Eastern mysticism, Western religions and modern science offers a unique and inspired perspective. Through his exceptional learning and deep spirituality he speaks directly to the human spirit. 60 mins.
VHS: S21852. $29.95.

In Search of Angels
Debra Winger narrates this exploration of the myths, meanings and allure of these otherworldly creatures. Shot on locations around the world, images of angels from all eras are used to elucidate their enduring powers. Interviews with celebrities, including playwright Tony Kushner and singer Rickie Lee Jones, make this a fascinating documentary. 60 mins.
VHS: S22960. $29.98.

In the Company of Angels: Biblical Truths About God's Glorious Creatures
Ten respected scholars spanning the Catholic, Evangelical, Orthodox and Jewish faiths are joined here to investigate the nature of these spiritual figures. Angels are spoken of in the Bible, and this documentary begins with Biblical times in order to answer basic questions about the nature and significance of angels. The result is a moving and informative video. Produced and written by Janet Russo and Sue Kiner. 60 mins.
VHS: S27487. $24.95.

Inside the Vatican, with Sir Peter Ustinov
From inside Vatican City and across Europe, Ustinov leads this four-volume video history of one of the world's most wealthy, powerful and art-laden institutions. Each volume is 50 mins.
VHS: S23937. $59.95.

Islam: A Closer Look
A thought-provoking exploration of Islam. Imam Hamza Yusuf, Shaikh Abdullah Hakim, Dr. John Esposito, Nancy Ai and basketball star Hakeem Olajuwon share their understanding of this faith. 30 mins.
VHS: S32986. $12.95.

Islamic Mysticism: The Sufi Way
Acclaimed filmmaker Elda Hartley is joined by author Huston Smith (*The Religions of Man*) in this revealing look at one of the most mysterious of all religious sects. Shot on location in Morocco, Hartley's breathtaking images feature stunning Muslim art and architecture, rarely seen religious rituals and the fascinating whirling dervishes of Turkey. 30 mins.
VHS: S33856. $19.98.

Island Soldiers: The History of the Celtic Saints
In this two-part series Anglican Canon Martin Shaw traces the roots of Celtic Christianity through the lives of the men and women who kindled its fire in the British Isles during the Dark Ages. Shaw explores the length and breadth of the ancient land to uncover the source of today's renewed interest in the Celtic spiritual traditions-meditation, prayer and music rooted in the ministries of the Celtic saints. Each tape is 60 mins.
VHS: S31214. $39.95.

Jesus and His Times
A three-sided laser disk that vividly portrays the dusty roads, people, villages and ancient cities of the Holy Land as they appeared during the time of Jesus. On-site footage was specifically filmed to depict the feeling of Jesus' life and message. Produced by *Reader's Digest*. 180 mins.
Laser: CLV. LD72360. $59.95.

Jesus from the Gospel (KJV)
This collection of films based on the King James Version of the Bible is narrated by Alexander Scourby. These are word-for-word re-enactments of the Scripture. Nothing has been added or subtracted. It's as if Jesus were reliving the events and teachings that form the core of His Gospels.

Jesus from the Gospel: The Birth.
VHS: S21721. $14.95.
Jesus from the Gospel: The Parables.
VHS: S21722. $14.95.
Jesus from the Gospel: The Passion.
VHS: S21723. $29.95.
Jesus from the Gospel: The Set.
VHS: S21724. $39.95.

Jesus from the Gospel (RSV)

This collection of films based on the Revised Standard Version Bible is narrated by Orson Welles. These are word-for-word re-enactments of the Scripture. Nothing has been added or subtracted. It's as if Jesus were reliving the events and teachings that form the core of the Gospels.
Jesus from the Gospel: The Birth.
VHS: S21717. $14.95.
Jesus from the Gospel: The Parables.
VHS: S21718. $14.95.
Jesus from the Gospel: The Passion.
VHS: S21719. $14.95.
Jesus from the Gospel: The Set.
VHS: S21720. $39.95.

Jesus—His Life

A&E's Biography series captures the essence of the life of Jesus. The mysteries and myths surrounding his life are examined by leading scholars and historians. In the Holy Land, new archeological explorations yield fresh insights that round out this thoroughly fresh approach to an enduring story. 100 mins.
VHS: S27642. $19.95.

John Wycliffe: The Morning Star

An Oxford scholar, John Wycliffe was one of Europe's most renowned philosophers. He uses biblical teachings to call the medieval church to repent. Later, exiled from Oxford, he accomplishes his greatest work: the translation of the Bible. Multiple festival winner; winner, Best Film, Christian Film Distributor's Association. 75 mins.
VHS: S34520. $19.95.

Journey Through the Bible Lands

Watch the Bible come to life in this video tour of the Holy Land. Follow the path of Moses and the Israelites through the desert of Sinai. Continue into Negev, past the ancient walls of Hebron, to Bethlehem, the birthplace of Jesus. Retrace the Stations of the Cross along the via Dolorossa to the Church of the Holy Sepulchre. 45 mins.
VHS: S10775. $24.95.

The Life and Times of Jesus

Armand Assante narrates this series; Betty Buckley provides readings from the Gospel for this unique production.
VHS: S22550. $19.98.
Who Was Jesus? Through an examination of the teachings and the events that made up Jesus' life, the nature of this extraordinary historical figure is thoroughly explored. His unique philosophy offers solace to millions.
VHS: S22551. $19.98.
The Life and Times of Jesus, Gift Pack.
VHS: S22553. $49.98.

Lives of Jesus

This series explores the story of Jesus and the origins of Christianity. Visiting historical sites in Europe and the Middle East, this three-volume set sheds new light on the mysteries surrounding the founder of a religion that has shaped the world. Tapes include *Jesus the Jew, Jesus the Rebel* and *The Hidden Jesus*. Each tape is 50 minutes.
VHS: S33682. $59.95.

Living Islam

A tour around the history, the faith(s) and the cultures of Islam with focus on what it means to be a Muslim today. The programs capture the excitement and ecstasy of great Muslim festivals, and the beautiful and evocative places of the Islamic world.
Islam and Modernity. This program looks at the tensions within Islamic states as they attempt to make their laws and practices compatible with the 21st century while remaining true to the spirit of the faith. 50 mins.
VHS: S20465. $29.95.
Islam in the Minority. Over 40% of the world's Muslims live as minorities, but is it possible to live a true Muslim life outside the Islamic world? This program asks whether Muslims suffer particular discrimination and whether life in a secular society compromises their faith. 50 mins.
VHS: S20463. $29.95.
The Challenge of the Past. The three empires' greatness and subsequent decline explain many differences in Muslim thinking as the Ottoman empire confronted Europe and Christianity, the Mughals achieved a synthesis with Hinduism, while the Saffavid dynasty was characterized by the shi'a/sunni split. 50 mins.
VHS: S20462. $29.95.
The Last Crusade. As many nations both East and West, from Algeria to Malaysia, face an Islamic revival, this program looks at the revolutionary and reforming spirit of Muslims. Why is a need for change sweeping through Muslim societies? What kind of change do the radicals want? And do they wish to achieve it by peace or violent means? 50 mins.
VHS: S20466. $29.95.
The Muslim Family. Explores the position of women under shari'a law in Egypt and Iran and asks how much is laid down by the faith and how much is added by the confines of local or tribal custom. In Indonesia, Muslim women are seen in jeans and short skirts working alongside those in the jilbab. Is this Islam or a heresy? 50 mins.
VHS: S20464. $29.95.
The Prophet, the Book and the Desert. An introduction to the essentials of Islam, which is deeply woven around the life of Muhammad, the Prophet of Allah. The program finds a living saint in the dunes of Timbuktu converting villagers to Islam. 50 mins.
VHS: S20461. $29.95.
Living Islam, Complete. All six volumes in one set.
VHS: S20467. $149.95.

Lost Years of Jesus

There are 18 years missing in the Biblical account of the life of Jesus. These years are explored in this acclaimed documentary, originally produced for television.
VHS: S06249. $29.95.
Richard Bock, USA, 1986, 93 mins.

The Making of a Modern Mystic

This is an in-depth look at Andrew Harvey, the youngest ever Fellow of All Souls Oxford. He is a best-selling novelist, poet and mystic, who was recently profiled in the *New York Times Magazine*. 59 mins.
VHS: S21847. $29.95.

Man of Peace: A Video Portrait of Pope John Paul II

A sensitive biography of the humble man who has great influence over the lives all who see and hear him, the "Jet-Age Pope" who reaffirms the message of Jesus Christ. This video takes the viewer inside the Vatican and to private audiences with Prince Charles and Princess Diana, opera star Pavarotti and Father Martin Jenco, as well as on the Pope's visit to Mother Teresa in India, and the face-to-face meeting with his assailant in which he forgives him. USA, 1986, 58 mins.
VHS: S04747. $29.95.

Martin Luther

Nial MacGinnis of the Old Vic stars as one of the prominent leaders of the Protestant Reformation. Unlike most of the early church reformers, Martin Luther was not burned at the stake and lived to see his work spread and prosper. The compelling dramatization covers most of the major developments.
VHS: S03947. $29.95.
Irving Pichel, Great Britain, 1953, 105 mins.

Martin Luther, His Life and Time

Produced by the Lutheran Film Division, this film traces the birth, youth and great reformation within the Church. Silent with music score. USA, 1924, 101 mins.
VHS: S04367. $29.95.

Mary Magdalene: An Intimate Portrait

Penelope Ann Miller hosts this examination of the mysterious woman follower of Jesus. She was there even at his death, and yet is not thought of as one of his close disciples. Instead, she is remembered as the bad girl, the prostitute of the New Testament. This video explores her story and the important role sexuality and power play in shaping her reputation. USA, 1995, 43 mins.
VHS: S27006. $19.98.

Mary of Nazareth

Though she is rarely mentioned in the Gospels, she is perhaps the most important and most revered woman in history. This is the amazing story of the 13-year-old virgin whose inexplicable pregnancy after becoming engaged to Joseph changed the fate of the world. 502 mins.
VHS: S31755. $19.95.

Merton: A Film Biography

The first film biography of Thomas Merton—writer, religious philosopher, and Trappist monk—in this acclaimed examination of his life and work. Contains interviews with those who knew him, including the Dalai Lama, Lawrence Ferlinghetti, Ernesto Cardenal, and Joan Baez. "A brilliant and creative masterpiece."
VHS: S09441. $29.95.
Paul Wilkes, USA, 1984, 57 mins.

Mother Teresa: In the Name of God's Poor

Geraldine Chaplin gives an outstanding performance as the tiny woman from Albania who captured the hearts and minds of the world as she dedicated her life to the dying and destitute and transformed the world with her faith, courage and love. Filmed on location in Sri Lanka. With David Byrd (*Lost Highway*).
VHS: S32666. $19.98.
Kevin Connor, USA, 1997, 93 mins.

Mysteries from the Bible

This film explores the biblical wonders and powers of God as described through the miracles of Moses and Jesus. Many of their works are convincingly recreated for the screen. 96 mins.
VHS: S16574. $19.95.

Mysteries of the Ancient World Gift Set

Darrin McGavin, Dennis Weaver and William Devane host this series, which explores a number of age-old mysteries. Science has been baffled by the religious and spiritual mysteries examined in these four volumes: *Mysteries of the Ancient World (Shroud of Turin, Pyramids, Nostradamus), The Incredible Discovery of Noah's Ark, Ancient Secrets of the Bible* and *Ancient Secrets of the Bible, Part 2*. Four-volume set.
VHS: S23750. $54.98.

Mysteries of the Bible

Uncover the lost secrets of the ancient world and explore new archaeological discoveries and the unknown history of the world's most influential text with this collection of seven of the Bible's greatest stories, filmed on location in the Holy Land.
Biblical Angels.
VHS: S30845. $14.95.
Cain and Abel.
VHS: S30844. $14.95.
Heaven and Hell.
VHS: S30848. $14.95.
Herod the Great.
VHS: S30847. $14.95.
The Last Supper.
VHS: S30846. $14.95.
The Bible's Greatest Secrets.
VHS: S30849. $14.95.
The Last Revolt.
VHS: S30850. $14.95.
Seven Tape Set.
VHS: S30851. $59.95.

Mysteries of the Bible: The Story Continues

A journey of discovery into the origins, enigmas and contradictions of the scriptures continues in the second installment of A&E's video series on the Bible. The latest scientific findings and archeological discoveries shed new light on enduring mysteries. Shot throughout the Holy Land, this series explores both prophets and stories from the old testament as well as the very last days of Jesus as recorded in the New Testament. 50 mins each.
Volume 1: Queen Esther.
VHS: S26580. $14.95.
Volume 2: The Apocalypse.
VHS: S26581. $14.95.
Volume 3: Execution of Jesus.
VHS: S26582. $14.95.
Volume 4: The Philistines.
VHS: S26583. $14.95.
Volume 5: Abraham.
VHS: S26584. $14.95.
Volume 6: Prophets.
VHS: S26585. $14.95.
Volume 7: Joseph.
VHS: S26586. $14.95.
The Greatest Mysteries of the Bible: The Story Continues Set.
VHS: S26587. $59.95.

Mysteries of the Dead Sea Scrolls

Two tapes.
Mysteries of the Dead Sea Scrolls: Exposed. For years the secrets contained in The Dead Sea scrolls have been withheld from the public. Now for the first time, hear accurate translations of never-before-released parchments found in the caves of Quran, which could change our views of the past and future. 72 mins.
VHS: S34227. $24.95.
Mysteries of the Dead Sea Scrolls: Exposed 2. This controversial program explores the translations of these important early Jewish and Christian writings and the so-called "cover-up" of these scrolls which continues to this day. 40 mins.
VHS: S34228. $19.95.

The Mysterious Man of the Shroud

Is the Shroud of Turin the burial wrapping of Jesus Christ or a Medieval hoax? This film takes an intriguing journey through the realms of science, archeology, history, art and religion, tracing the ongoing attempt to solve the mysteries surrounding the most-studied archeological textile in history. 60 mins.
VHS: S33235. $14.98.

Mystery of the Sacred Shroud

The ancient cloth imprinted with an image of Christ—is it a medieval hoax or proof of Jesus' crucifixion? Richard Burton narrates this investigation into the Shroud of Turin. 86 mins.
VHS: S16572. $29.98.

The Naked Truth

Jordan Maxwell, Derek Partridge and Bill Jenkins destroy the wall of lies engineered by organized religion, to obscure the truth about early spiritual wisdom. Judaism, Christianity and Islam have all participated in this deception to consolidate their own power in this world.
VHS: S21232. $34.95.

The Old Testament Collection

A & E Biography created this six-volume video series based on the Old Testament. All the drama and import of specific figures, including "King David," "Moses," "Noah," "Adam and Eve," "Solomon and Sheba" and "Samson and Delilah," are at the center of each tape. 360 mins.
VHS: S29904. $99.95.

Opiates of the Masses: Religion in the USSR

The battle between church and state was never more profound than in the Soviet block. This film, made just before the Gorbachev reforms, seems to indicate that the church was winning the battle. 105 mins.
VHS: S12716. $24.98.

Passion of the Saints

Travel through 2,000 years since the time of Christ and across three continents to experience the lives and deaths of some extraordinary individuals, on this three-tape set from The Learning Channel. Witness the rise of martyrdom from Stephen, the first martyr, to Joan of Arc and Thomas Becket in Volume 1, *The Blood of the Martyrs* (50 mins.). Meet Catherine of Sienna, Saint Francis of Assisi, Saint Augustine and Saint Thomas Aquinas on Volume II, *Hermits, Monks and Madmen* (50 mins.). On Volume III, *Mystics and Miracles*, follow the lives and deaths of those who have known the divine, travel to a French monastery where theologians and academics have been seeking answers to the questions of sainthood for 300 years, and go behind the scenes at the Vatican to peek inside the politics of sainthood on "The Road to Sainthood" (100 mins.).
VHS: S30834. $89.95.

People of the Book

Biblical legends come alive in this award-winning five-volume series. Filmed on location in the Holy Land, these portraits of the most compelling figures of the Bible provoke a spirited inquiry of contemporary issues and inspire the viewer to explore an exciting range of moral and philosophical possiblities. Volumes include Abraham, Moses, Ruth, Esther and Matityahu the Maccabee. 112 mins.
VHS: S30027. $79.95.

Pharaohs and Kings: A Biblical Quest

Egyptologist David Rohl conducts his search for historical truth by beginning with the stories of the Bible. He shows the factual side of the religious figures King Saul, King David and King Solomon, as well as Joshua and the patriarch Joseph. From the Discovery Channel. 150 mins.
VHS: S27824. $29.95.

The Pope in America

Covers Pope John Paul II's historic visit to Denver in 1993. Produced by CNN. 60 mins.
VHS: S20510. $14.98.

Pope John Paul II

The full-length feature about the life of Pope John Paul II, covering a span of 40 years to his election to the Papacy in 1978 as the first non-Italian Pope in over four centuries. Albert Finney stars as the Pope.
VHS: S04497. $79.95.
Herbert Wise, USA, 1984, 147 mins.

Pope John Paul II: Seven Days of Eternity

A lavish keepsake of the celebration of Holy Week in Rome hosted by Joseph Campanella. Includes the pomp and pageantry of everything from Palm Sunday to the somber rite of Good Friday, to glorious Easter Sunday. 48 mins.
VHS: S13172. $19.98.

Pope John Paul II: Statesman of Faith

Before he inhabited the Vatican, this religious leader kept the Catholic faith alive behind the iron curtain. This video biography from A&E tells his whole story, beginning in a Polish village and leading to his succession as Pope. 50 mins.
VHS: S23935. $19.95.

Priests of Passion

This documentary focuses on the vow of celibacy taken by a number of Catholic priests who had to confront their commitment to the church when they fell in love. David Rice, himself a former priest, went from Germany to Brazil to New Jersey as he traced these troubled men.
VHS: S20589. $29.95.
Nick Gray, USA, 51 mins.

The Rabbit Ears Collection

The universal traditions of storytelling and music are charmingly celebrated in the animated programs of the Rabbit Ears *We All Have Tales* series. Each narrated by famous actors like Kathleen Turner and Denzel Washington, these entertaining programs showcase the folklores of peoples around the world and are set to the sounds of various musicians. Grammy and Parents' Choice awards have been given to Rabbit Ears.

Joseph and His Brothers. Musician and actor Ruben Blades tells the inspiring story of a brother betrayed. Though mistreated by his family, Joseph overcomes their treachery and forgives them. Music by Strunz and Farah.
VHS: S24055. $19.98.

Moses in Egypt. Danny Glover narrates this animated version of the delivery of the Israelites from slavery. Grammy Award-winning Gospel musicians Sounds of Blackness perform the musical score in this episode from *The Greatest Stories Ever Told* series.
VHS: S21258. $19.98.

Moses the Lawgiver. Another episode in the *The Greatest Stories Ever Told* series, this cartoon continues the story of the Israelites and their new found freedom. Moses received the Ten Commandments and after 40 years led his people to the Promised Land. Narrated by Ben Kingsley.
VHS: S21259. $19.98.

The Creation. Amy Grant tells the story of the creation of the world by God in seven days. Children will enjoy this adaptation from the first pages of the Bible. Bela Fleck and The Flecktones provide the music.
VHS: S24054. $19.98.

The Lion and the Lamb. The animated Christmas story of a fierce lion who escapes from the circus and finds refuge with a meek lamb in a stable. Narrated by Hollywood legends Christopher Reeve and Amy Grant. Music by Lyle Mays. 23 minutes.
VHS: S24056. $19.98.

Radiant Life

Hildegard, a powerful Benedictine Abbess in the 12th century, began having visions about the sanctity of nature. Her words describe "The Web of Creation." In addition, she composed liturgical chants for women singers. These works have been brought together on this video to create a complete meditation. 40 mins.
VHS: S29467. $19.95.

Rapture of Being: Pir Vilayat Inayat Khan

The Sufi path, says Pir Vilayat, is one of merging our individual existence with the divine reality. The dancing of Sufis is an expression of the dynamic shifting equilibriums of life, striving from moment to moment toward the higher states of being. In Part II of this program, Pir Vilayat focuses on details of Sufi meditation practices. 90 mins.
VHS: S13321. $49.95.

The Riddle of the Dead Sea Scrolls

This feature-length documentary probes the mysteries of the *Bible*. It offers startling new perspectives on the most miraculous stories. Unfathomable exploits, such as the turning of water into wine or the very nature of Jesus and Mary, have emerged in the scrolls in more rational terms that are accesible to everyone. 80 mins.
VHS: S22966. $19.95.

Roots and Wings: A Jewish Congregation

Too few Christians understand the Jewish Faith. This video introduces the living community of Judaism, a religion with thousands of years of history and tradition, that has managed to survive in predominantly Christian societies. 28 mins.
VHS: S22476. $19.95.

Saints and Sinners

This historical documentary explores the rich and compelling history of the Roman Catholic Church and the Papacy, revealing the crucial roles and human dimensions of the Popes, from St. Peter to Pope John Paul II. Six-volume set includes *Upon This Rock, Between Two Empires, Set over Nations, Protest and Division, The Pope and the People* and *The Oracles of God*. Each tape is 52 mins.
VHS: S33681. $79.95.

Seeking God: The Way of the Monk at the Monastery of Christ in the Desert

The simple patterns of the monastic existence are interwoven with candid interviews of the monks themselves. The result is a fascinating expose of this hidden way of life dominated by a fervent belief in God. 58 mins.
VHS: S26813. $24.95.

Seven Signs of Christ's Return

According to scriptural predictions, seven momentous events will herald the second coming of Jesus Christ. One—the establishment of the State of Israel—is already part of history. Could the others be occurring now? This fascinating program explores the meaning of the "Seven Signs" and examines contemporary events that may hold the promise of their fulfillment. One hour.
VHS: S30963. $29.95.

Silent Witness

Documentary based on the book *The Shroud of Turin*. Medical examiners, theologians, physicists and historians trace the probable history of this burial cloth and attempt to reconstruct the events of the last days of Jesus Christ.
VHS: S01201. $69.95.
D.W. Rolfe, USA, 55 mins.

Six Little Angels

Angels are everywhere, but they are especially visible in this video. Six children explain, through both action and song, the hidden aspects of everyday life as apprehended by angels. 30 mins.
VHS: S26814. $9.95.

Song of the Holy Land

Inspired footage, favorite Christian hymns and Hebrew songs of praise capture the spirit, beauty and sacred heritage of Israel. The timeless grandeur and majesty of the Holy Land comes alive in this musical celebration. 65 mins.
VHS: S23137. $29.95.

Speaking with Your Angels: A Guide

In this PBS special, authors and facilitators Trudy Griswold and Barbara Mark conduct a workshop about the techniques found in their book *Angelspeake: How to Talk with Your Angels*. Their workshops have been successful for five years, but require only a simple seven-step process. 70 mins.
VHS: S29469. $19.95.

The Story of David

Rivalry between the enterprising David and his daunting foe, Goliath, sets in motion one of the Bible's best remembered stories. Timothy Bottoms stars as King David, the most famous underdog of recorded history. Released on two videocassettes, 191 mins.
VHS: S20681. $29.95.

Story of Islam

Over three years in the making, this is a brilliant journey through Islam's history. We are introduced to the culture, philosophy and staples of this way of life, a religion that is gathering tremendous momentum in the west: today they have over one billion devotees. 120 mins.
VHS: S13170. $24.98.

The Story of Jacob and Joseph

Set in the land of the Bible, this famous tale of two brothers is brought to life. Jealousy and envy are poisonous traits, but forgiveness holds out hope even between the most divided of siblings. Featuring Colleen Dewhurst and Keith Mitchell. 96 mins.
VHS: S20680. $19.95.

Testament

Writer and archeologist John Romer hosts this fascinating series that explores the cultural and historical origins and authorship of the most influential book ever written, the Bible. Each volume is 52 mins.

As It Was in the Beginning. Explores the development of ideas about God and holiness from the East to the God of Moses and the Exodus, and addresses historical fact in Old Testament Stories.
VHS: S09481. $29.95.

Chronicles and Kings. The rise and fall of ancient Israel and the role of Jehovah in the development of the Jewish nation. The period between the establishment of the kingdom in the Promised Land and the exile of the Jews in Babylon.
VHS: S09482. $29.95.

Gospel Truth. The historical remains of the time, place and perhaps the life of Jesus and how the Christian Bible came into being.
VHS: S09484. $29.95.

Mightier than the Sword. The historical context into which Jesus was born, the background against which the New Testament was written, the period in which the Old Testament achieved its final shape.
VHS: S09483. $29.95.

Paradise Lost. The evolution of the Bible from unquestioned sacred book to object for study, and the historical and cultural influences that generated this changing point of view. Beginning with the 14th century Renaissance poet Petrarch, proceeding to Martin Luther, and concluding with the impact of scientific knowledge in the 19th century.
VHS: S09487. $29.95.

Power and the Glory. The sole source of learning during the Dark Ages, the Bible was used to justify social order. The artistry lavished on it made these stories and characters central to medieval culture. This program concludes in 1453, when Constantinople fell and Gutenberg printed his first Bible.
VHS: S09486. $29.95.

Thine Is the Kingdom. The story of Christianity from the transformation of the Roman Empire into a Christian one; the conversion of Constantine, the correspondence between Sts. Jerome and Augustine; how Bible stories came to be used.
VHS: S09485. $29.95.

Thomas Berry: Dreamer of the Universe

Ecotheologian Berry is a highly regarded American monk whose writings have inspired a whole generation of environmentalists. This controversial figure is revealed in an intimate conversation. He is perhaps one of the greatest spiritual thinkers of our time. 57 mins.
VHS: S21848. $29.95.

The Unexplained: Prophets and Doom

From the pages of the Old Testament to today, explore stories of prophecy with leading experts, including authors Eva Shaw (*Eve of Destruction*) and James Rani (*Flim Flam*). 50 mins.
VHS: S34898. $14.95.

The Unexplained: The Exorcists

It is an ancient Catholic ritual that seems to belong in the deep past, yet exorcism survives to this day. Venture into the dark heart of this controversial subject. 50 mins.
VHS: S34895. $14.95.

The Unexplained: The Power of Prayer

This probing look at four real-life cases of miraculous healing includes testimony from scientists, ministers and people who claim to have been cured by faith. 50 mins.
VHS: S34897. $14.95.

Video Outlines of Asian Religions

An in-depth series which looks at the principal beliefs of Hindu and Buddhist countries. Produced by scholars Nancy Moore Gettleman and Richard Sherburne.
Volume 1: Absorption in Brahman. The story of Hinduism-ancient India, Aryans—from polytheism to monist God. Karma-Rebirth-Caste. Religions: Liberation vs. Salvation. Three Paths: Action-Devotion-Knowledge. Four stages of life: Student-householder-forest dweller-sannyasin. 30 mins.
VHS: S23350. $69.95.
Volume 2: The Great Awakening. The rise of Buddhism in India. Siddhartha Hautama Four Truths No Soul. Monastic life. Theravada and Mahayana: Arhats & Bodhisattvas. Yoga Meditation and Emptiness. Decline in India. 45 mins.
VHS: S23351. $69.95.
Volume 3: Diamond Path. Hinduism and Buddhism intermingle in Nepal. Early history; later: Newars-Malla and Shah dynasties. Rana control-restoration. Tantric Buddhism, the Swift path, Mandala-Mantra-Mudra. Visualization and Thankas ritual objects. 45 mins.
VHS: S23352. $69.95.
Volume 4: Dalai Lama's and Tulku's Living Bodhisattvas. Mahayana Buddhism in Tibet. Early history and shamanist religion (Bon). Conversion of early kings and growth of Buddhist monastic orders. Tibetan translation of Buddhist scriptures. Kanjur and Tengyur. Mongol influence and Buddhocracy by Dalai and Panchen lamas. Jesuit missionaries: first Westerners in the Forbidden Kingdom. 45 mins.
VHS: S23353. $69.95.
Volume 5: Incarnate Buddha—Kings of the Dragon. Buddhism in Bhutan. Early history: the outpost of Tibetan monastic sects; 17th-century beginnings of new nation; Shabdrung, the monk-tulku-king founder; Dharma-rajas and Deb-rajas; division of secular and religious powers; Dzons: the monastery-fortress governance; unification and first modern education. 45 mins.
VHS: S23354. $69.95.
Companion Text: Himalayan Journey of Buddhism. This provides an effective written reference to reinforce the Video Outline of Asian Religions video series.
VHS: S23355. $69.95.

Voyages: The Journey of the Magi

The Biblical journey of the Magi has inspired artists for nearly 2,000 years. This program recreates their actual route, setting the event in both its cultural and archeological contexts. As sites in the journey of the Wise Men are seen, artifacts and coins dating from the period offer additional insight into an event which generated a wealth of art. Narrated by art historian and archeologist Karl Katz; filmed in Jerusalem and Bethlehem. 30 mins.
VHS: S04653. $29.95.

Walk in Crusader Jerusalem

A prominent archeologist and a Dominican abbot retrace the steps of a pilgrim to Crusader Jerusalem. Their explorations uncover both an important period of the city's history as well as the place of Jerusalem in the mind of twelfth century Christendom. 34 mins.
VHS: S10465. $29.95.

Where Jesus Walked

A video journey through Nazareth, Jericho, Capernaum and Jerusalem, capturing the beauty of the Holy Land, as it follows the footsteps of Jesus, his baptism at the Jordan River, Baptism on the Mount, and his final walk through the streets of Jerusalem. USA, 60 mins.
VHS: S04695. $29.95.

Who Am I? Why Am I Here?

Ordinary Christians, Jews, Hindus, Buddhists, Taoists, Muslims and Sufis approach these questions in this video. The result is a timeless distillation of wisdom from many world religions around the vital truths of life. Thomas Moore, author of *Care of the Soul*, coordinates this wide-ranging discussion. 60 mins.
VHS: S29468. $19.95.

The Wisdom of a Prophet (2 Lectures)

"A New Vision of Reality in the Light of Modern Science" is an exploration of the relationship between science and spirituality. "A New Vision of Reality in the Light of Christian Mysticism and Hindu Advait" goes beyond the dogma of religions and scientific rationalism to an unexpected essence.
VHS: S21855. $29.95.

The Wisdom of Faith with Huston Smith

Hinduism, Buddhism, Confucianism, Christianity, Judaism and Islam, six of the world's great religions, are all examined and compared in this five-video set. It's *A Bill Moyers Special* that uses art, architecture, music and poetry to illustrate the common heart of religious experience.
VHS: S27605. $119.95.

Within Thy Gates, O Jerusalem: The City and the Temple

Following Jewish pilgrims to Jerusalem, at the time of the birth of Christianity, the film unfolds the Holy City with its many sites. The description of the sites and events is based on Joseph Flavius, the rich archeological findings and a mini model of Jerusalem. 32 mins.
VHS: S10466. $29.95.

Worship the King

Stunning visuals, passages from Scripture and classic hymns create an inspirational experience. This video includes excerpts from the 21st Psalm, the Sermon on the Mount, and hymns, including "Amazing Grace", "A Mighty Fortress Is Our God" and "O Worship the King". 55 mins.
VHS: S23136. $29.95.

Zwingli and Calvin

This program covers the Swiss Reformation, its key centers of Zurich and Geneva, and its central leaders, Zwingli and Calvin. Zwingli instituted sweeping reforms. Calvin provided crucial leadership. 28 mins.
VHS: S34521. $19.95.

BIOGRAPHY & MEMOIRS

A&E Biography: Houdini—The Great Escape

An expert contortionist and master of illusion, The Great Houdini fascinated vaudeville audiences around the world. Among other tricks, he escaped from a submerged crate, walked through a brick wall and promised to come back from the dead if it were possible. His fascinating story as both a showman and a celebrity is told on this video. 50 mins.
VHS: S29417. $19.95.

A&E Biography: Nostradamus, Prophet of Doom

Over four centuries the dark predictions of this medieval physician have inspired fear and debate. Some maintain he predicted such widespread and unconnected events as the French Revolution, the rise of Hitler and JFK's assassination. From his work as a healer during the plague, to the veracity of his predictions, all is examined on this videocassette. 50 mins.
VHS: S29418. $19.95.

Abraham Lincoln

James McPherson, Princeton University historian and Pulitzer Prize winner for his *Battle Cry of Freedom*, hosts this fascinating story of Abraham Lincoln from his boyhood to the White House. 35 mins.
VHS: S12190. $19.95.

Al Capone: Scarface

This *A&E Biography* tells the bullet-riddled, rags-to-riches story of the undisputed Emperor of Chicago with rare photographs, films and exclusive interviews. 50 mins.
VHS: S32992. $19.95.

Albert Einstein: How I See the World

William Hurt narrates this program which chronicles the ways in which the world's most famous Nobel Prize winner became its most eloquent advocate for peace. Much of it is told in Einstein's own words, excerpted from his diaries, personal letters and writings. PBS, 60 mins.
VHS: S15637. $19.98.

Albert Einstein: The Education of a Genius

Einstein failed exams, cut classes—and set the world of modern physics on its ear! Here is his story, filled with vivid images of the ordinary occurrences that led him to his theories. 44 mins.
VHS: S05739. $39.95.

Amazing Howard Hughes

Millionaire, flyer, playboy, film mogul—Howard Hughes had it all. The story of the legendary eccentric comes alive with all the mystery that made him an American hero. 119 mins.
VHS: S04541. $19.95.

Amelia Earhart

Diane Keaton and Rutger Hauer star in this biography of America's most famed woman aviator. Her disappearance left the nation stunned. Even so the legend of a strong woman who dared to do exactly what she dreamed of lives on. Her story is more fascinating than fiction and more inspiring than fantasy because she really did make history. 95 mins.
VHS: S21825. $92.98.

Amelia Earhart: The Price of Courage

Kathy Bates narrates the story of America's most highly acclaimed woman hero. Earhart was the first woman to fly across the Atlantic solo. Combining a taste for daredevil antics with her charismatic presence, she became a national hero. Her untimely and mysterious demise makes her story an enduring and fascinating tale. B&W, 60 mins.
VHS: S23050. $19.95.

American Lifestyle Series: Inventors

This series offers a view of truly great Americans. These lives stand as testament to the virtues and values of individuality, creativity, and leadership. Creative explorers on the technological frontier have shaped not only this country but the world. This series offers three great examples of this inventive spirit.
Benjamin Franklin: Citizen-Sage of a New Age. Hugh Downs explores the genius of Franklin, one of the most important scientists, inventors and writers of his day. 24 mins.
VHS: S23551. $49.95.
Laser: LD74780. $99.95.
Alexander Graham Bell. Biographical detail abounds in this program about the American legend. Hugh Downs narrates a look at this teacher of the deaf, inventor, scientist and poet. 24 mins.
VHS: S23552. $49.95.
Laser: LD74781. $99.95.
Thomas Edison's Glenmount. Edison called his magnificent Victorian mansion his workbench. Here he perfected the phonograph, the motion picture camera, and incandescent and florescent lighting. 23 mins.
VHS: S23553. $49.95.
Laser: LD74782. $99.95.

American Lifestyle Series: Military Leaders

This series offers a view of truly great Americans. These lives stand as testament to the virtues and values of individuality, creativity, and leadership. E.G. Marshall hosts these two video biographies of great American leaders.
Sam Houston and Texas: A Giant Man for a Giant Land. Rich in intriguing personal and political facts, this program presents Houston, the first president of the Republic of Texas. 24 mins.
VHS: S23545. $49.95.
Laser: LD74775. $99.95.
Stratford Lee and Robert E. Lee. This video offers a profile of Lee, a general many considered to be the greatest military mind ever produced by the American armed forces. A tour of his family home is also included. 24 mins.
VHS: S23546. $49.95.
Laser: LD74776. $99.95.

American Lifestyle Series: U.S. Presidents

This series offers a view of truly great Americans. These lives stand as testament to the virtues and values of individuality, creativity, and leadership. This collection of six biographical tapes about the great presidents of the US is hosted by E.G. Marshall.
Love, Liberty, and the Pursuit of Conscience: John Adams and Massachusetts America. The story of the first Vice President and the second President is intertwined with the founding of the U.S. 24 mins.
VHS: S23539. $49.95.
Thomas Jefferson's Monticello. Jefferson's home in Charlottesville, Virginia, is presented as a setting where he exercised his many skills and interests. 24 mins.
VHS: S23540. $49.95.
Laser: LD74770. $99.95.
Theodore Roosevelt's Sagamore Hill. This rambling, informal house on Long Island's northern shore reflects the many aspects of the 26th president, Theodore Roosevelt. 23 mins.
VHS: S23541. $49.95.
Laser: LD74771. $99.95.
Woodrow Wilson: Peace and War and the Professor President. This program presents the career and loves of the scholar president. 23 mins.
VHS: S23542. $49.95.
Laser: LD74772. $99.95.

Andrew Jackson's Hermitage. This program visits the home President Andrew Jackson planned, developed and lived in with his beloved Rachel. 23 mins.
VHS: S23543. $49.95.
Laser: LD74773. $99.95.
Franklin D. Roosevelt's Hyde Park. FDR's home near the Hudson River is featured on this video. There are reminders of his childhood, his early career, his struggle with polio and his years as President. 24 mins.
VHS: S23544. $49.95.
Laser: LD74774. $99.95.

Andrew Carnegie: The Original Man of Steel

Hugh Downs hosts this version of Carnegie's life story. This industrialist's legacy still influences the country through his many philanthropic enterprises, including libraries, universities, institutes and more. 24 mins.
VHS: S23554. $49.95.
Laser: LD74783. $99.95.

The Beauty Queens

The cosmetic, beauty and treatment industry affects nearly everyone's life. This series portrays three exceptional women of the 20th century, all of whom founded vast empires by cooking up formulas on their kitchen stoves.
Volume 1: Helena Rubinstein. Born in 1870 into an impoverished Polish family, Helena Rubinstein became a shrewd business woman, married a Russian prince and lived to the age of 95. Glamorous, tempestuous and exotic, Rubinstein had a unique sense of personal style and she triumphed over extreme odds to be successful. 60 mins.
VHS: S10300. $29.95.
Volume 2: Elizabeth Arden. Elizabeth Arden's fundamental belief was that beauty was an intelligent cooperation between nature and science, a partnership to develop a woman's natural assets. She was the first person to really develop the beauty salon and health farm business. This portrait traces Arden's success and reveals her as a woman whose fame and temper hid an insecure and fragile personality—one who loved horses more than she did people. 60 mins.
VHS: S10301. $29.95.
Volume 3: Estee Lauder. The richest self-made woman in the world, now in her eighties, Estee Lauder is still the inspiration behind the business. She is a promotional genius and a living legend—the last of the old style, grand slam beauty queens whose lives were beauty and who made fortunes from pots of cream. This film looks at the career and style of this remarkable woman whose company now earns an estimated $1.3 billion a year.
VHS: S10302. $29.95.

Biography

Programs first broadcast on *Arts and Entertainment*, which uses interviews, archival footage and photographs to trace the lives of modern legends:
Elizabeth Taylor.
VHS: S20437. $19.95.
Elvis: Story of a Legend.
VHS: S20438. $19.95.
George Bush: His WWII Years.
VHS: S20443. $19.95.
Jackie Robinson.
VHS: S20442. $19.95.
Jacqueline Kennedy Onassis.
VHS: S20439. $19.95.
Joe DiMaggio.
VHS: S20440. $19.95.
John Gotti: A Mafia Story.
VHS: S20441. $19.95.
Ronald Reagan: The Many Lives.
VHS: S20444. $19.95.

Buckminster Fuller: Grandfather of the Future

A last interview with the great inventor, architect and visionary. Fuller discusses the "invisible" new reality, which has recently made it possible to maintain the planet's entire population at a higher standard of living than anyone has ever known. 25 mins.
VHS: S08305. $29.95.

Bugsy Siegel: Gambling on the Mob

This *A&E Biography* tells the story of the gangster playboy, from his stormy relationship with Virginia Hill to his founding of Las Vegas and his mysterious murder. 50 mins.
VHS: S32991. $19.95.

The Churchills

Spanning two centuries and three generations, *The Churchills* chronicles the public and private lives of one of Britain's most celebrated political dynasties and the 20th-century statesman whose remarkable achievements brought glory to his nation and family name. Parts include *Aristocratic Adventures*, *Moment of Destiny* and *Born a Churchill*. 150 mins.
VHS: S34330. $49.95.

Colin Powell: A General's General

Produced by CNN, the life story of Colin Powell, the first African-American to become Chairman of the Joint Chiefs of Staff. 60 mins.
VHS: S20512. $14.98.

Colin Powell: A Soldier's Campaign

This biographical documentary from A&E tells the story of the highly popular and charismatic general. Born to immigrant parents, he grew up in the Bronx and rose through the ranks in the military to lead the Allied forces in the Gulf War. Includes interviews with his family and friends as well as rare archival footage.
VHS: S27212. $19.95.
Bill Harris, USA, 1995, 50 mins.

The Complete Churchill

The definitive four-part profile of the English statesman, politician and military leader, in a special collector's edition boxed set. Written and narrated by Martin Gilbert, Churchill's official biographer, the program covers the amazing spectrum of his life, mixing interviews, commentary, research and archival footage. Directed by Maris Appugliese. 200 mins. "Historically comprehensive and fact-packed" (*The Wall Street Journal*).
VHS: S17073. $59.95.
Laser: CLV. LD72075. $69.95.

Conquest of Everest

A beautifully filmed documentary about the Sir Edmund Hillary expedition to Mt. Everest. The film also chronicles the history of the mountain, its discovery and naming and previous attempts to reach the summit, as well as Hillary's elaborate preparations for the climb, and the final, triumphant reach to the summit. Academy Award nominee. England, 1953, 78 mins.
VHS: S05601. $19.95.

Don't Call Me Bugsy

This movie shows the rise and fall of Benjamin Siegel, arguably the flashiest gangster in American history and the man who built Las Vegas. Interviews, archival footage and contemporary photographs reveal the man "with a face for the movies and a nose for crime." 70 mins.
VHS: S17026. $19.98.

Donald Trump

This modern Midas elevated the business of deal-making to an art form and came to epitomize a glitzy, greedy era, only to see his fortune and fame threatened by changing times. 50 mins.
VHS: S30117. $19.95.

Dwight D. Eisenhower: From Soldier to President

This video reveals the life of this statesman's early life and shows how it prepared him for the highest elected office in the land. 19 mins.
VHS: S23564. $49.95.

Dwight D. Eisenhower: Library and Museum

From documents, pictures, special displays and exhibitions throughout the library, this video tells a story about President Eisenhower's personal life and how his presidency affected the history of the U.S. 58 mins.
VHS: S23425. $24.95.

Dwight D. Eisenhower: The Presidential Years

In addition to trouble overseas there was trouble at home. This president faced the challenge of enforcing school desegregation. 19 mins.
VHS: S23565. $49.95.

Einstein Revealed

New revelations from his archives paint a surprising portrait of the physicist as a passionate young man in this NOVA journey into the life and thoughts of a genius through interviews with "Einstein" (Andrew Sachs, *Fawlty Towers*), insight from experts and whimsical computer animation. 120 mins.
VHS: S31419. $19.95.

Eisenhower—A Place in History

Before Dwight David Eisenhower served as president of the United States, he was better known for his military career as a Five Star General during World War II. This U.S. government documentary tells the story of that life in color and black and white footage. Filmed at the Eisenhower Library in Abilene, Kansas. 52 mins.
VHS: S09522. $19.95.

Eisenhower: Soldier/Statesman

David MacCullough narrates this two-tape set about one of America's most highly regarded military heroes and presidents. In Part One, *Soldier*, Ike's early years in Kansas unfold. His education, early career and participation in WW II are all here. Part Two traces his career as a statesman, from McCarthy through the beginnings of the Cold War. B&W, 150 mins.
VHS: S23049. $39.95.

Eleanor Roosevelt Story

This award-winning documentary traces Eleanor Roosevelt's overcoming of personal obstacles to shape a humanitarian agenda. Narrated by Archibald Macleish, Francis Cole and Eric Sevareid.
VHS: S17646. $29.95.
Richard Kaplan, USA, 1965, 91 mins.

Eleanor, First Lady of the World

Jean Stapleton stars in this biography of Eleanor Roosevelt. With E.G. Marshall, Coral Browne, Joyce Van Patten and Gail Strickland.
VHS: S17487. $19.98.
John Erman, USA, 1982, 100 mins.

Famous Americans of the 20th Century: The Story of Babe Ruth

No sports hero in American history has thrilled fans as "The Babe" did. He was the greatest baseball player who ever played. Part of the acclaimed documentary series. USA, 55 mins.
VHS: S14916. $29.95.

Famous Americans of the 20th Century: The Story of Charles Lindbergh

In 1927, Charles Lindbergh made the first non-stop, solo, trans-Atlantic flight to Paris in 33.5 hours. This insightful documentary examines the ups and downs of his dramatic life. USA, 55 mins.
VHS: S14911. $29.95.

Famous Americans of the 20th Century: The Story of Douglas MacArthur

In WWII, Douglas MacArthur commanded the U.S. Forces in the Far East and accepted the Japanese surrender aboard the U.S.S. Missouri. Includes actual footage of events, and interviews. USA, 55 mins.
VHS: S14910. $29.95.

Famous Americans of the 20th Century: The Story of Dwight D. Eisenhower

This is the story of victory in WWII and the "Eisenhower years" (1952-60), a period that shaped the second half of the 20th century. A fascinating historical documentary. USA, 55 mins.
VHS: S14915. $29.95.

Famous Americans of the 20th Century: The Story of Franklin Delano Roosevelt

This president's tough-minded attitude and relief programs altered the conduct of American life throughout the 20th century. A powerful documentary of the man and his incredible influence. USA, 100 mins.
VHS: S14918. $29.95.

Famous Americans of the 20th Century: The Story of G.I. Joe

The story of young men who learned how to fight and were dying for freedom in lands across the Atlantic and Pacific oceans. Part of the renowned documentary series. USA, 55 mins.
VHS: S14914. $29.95.

Famous Americans of the 20th Century: The Story of Harry S Truman

President Truman is the man who approved the dropping of two atomic bombs on Japan, in August 1945; he felt it was the only way to save the lives of 300,000 American G.I.s. Learn more about that decision from this special documentary. USA, 55 mins.
VHS: S14919. $29.95.

Famous Americans of the 20th Century: The Story of Helen Keller

A story of courage and faith; Helen Keller, shut off from the world of sight and sound, grew into a highly intelligent and sensitive woman who wrote, spoke and labored incessantly for the betterment of others. A documentary portrait. USA, 55 mins.
VHS: S14917. $29.95.

Famous Americans of the 20th Century: The Story of Henry Ford

Henry Ford introduced mass ownership of automobiles and sparked the 20th century industrial revolution in America. A fascinating video documentary. USA, 55 mins.
VHS: S14913. $29.95.

Famous Americans of the 20th Century: The Story of Knute Rockne

From the sandlots of Chicago, Knute Rockne became the most well-known college coach in American football history. A documentary portrait. USA, 55 mins.
VHS: S14920. $29.95.

Famous Americans of the 20th Century: The Story of Thomas Edison
Eager to release man from toil and tedium, Edison would patent over 1,000 inventions during his lifetime. A compelling video documentary of the man and world-shaking work. USA, 55 mins.
VHS: S14912. $29.95.

FDR
Emmy Award-winning producer David Grubin wrote and produced this collection of four 30-minute videos about America's great president, Franklin Delano Roosevelt, which offers a fresh, incisive and at times surprising view of this key historical figure. Originally produced for PBS' *The American Experience*. Historian David McCullough narrates.
Fear Itself. Begins with Roosevelt's paralysis from polio at the age of 39 and follows his relentless struggle to rehabilitate himself. The segment ends with Roosevelt achieving the highest office in the land in a landslide victory.
VHS: S24838. $19.95.
The Center of the World. Explores Roosevelt's family background, looking for clues as to how the coddled child of rich parents confounded those who dismissed him as an ambitious lightweight.
VHS: S24839. $19.95.
The Grandest Job in the World. Focuses on the first two terms of Roosevelt's presidency and documents how his programs and personal style restored hope to Americans who were gripped by despair.
VHS: S24837. $19.95.
The Juggler. This segment is devoted to the wartime years, making use of FDR's remarkable correspondence with Winston Churchill to chart the cunning way FDR maneuvered support for England before leading his country through the greatest war in history.
VHS: S24698. $19.95.
FDR, The Boxed Set. Includes all four titles.
VHS: S24840. $69.95.

First Ladies
Produced by ABC News, this humorous and historical program examines the public and private lives of 45 first ladies. From the tender love story of John and Abigail Adams to Betty Ford's candid discussions about her alcoholism, *First Ladies* studies the women behind the presidents. 60 mins.
VHS: S12269. $19.98.
Laser: LD70229. $34.95.

First Ladies
From Martha Washington to Barbara Bush, this program introduces you to some of the most distinguished women who have been the nation's highest unofficial officials. Visit the Smithsonian's unique collection of First Ladies' gowns, accessories and furnishings and learn how they are being preserved. 1989, 60 mins.
VHS: S14542. $29.95.

Ford: The Man and the Machine
Cliff Robertson stars in this critical biography of auto magnate Henry Ford. Hope Lange stars as Ford's wife and Heather Thomas as his mistress.
VHS: S17711. $14.98.
Allan Eastman, USA, 1987, 200 mins.

Frontline: Hillary's Class
Six of Hillary Rodham Clinton's classmates from the Wellesley College Class of 1969 talk about coming into their own at a key moment in the trajectory of women's progress. They explain significant turning points, the paths they chose and the price exacted from them for their decisions.
VHS: S24886. $19.95.

The Gangsters: Bugsy, Dutch and Al
Bugsy Siegel, Dutch Shultz and Al Capone controlled and corrupted the American dream with their syndicated crime organizations. Running bootleg liquor, brothels, and extortion and gambling houses, they infiltrated the government and police force, drawing their iron grip even tighter around the throats of a terrorized nation. Included in this bloody expose is rare and explicit footage revealing their ruthless rampages, as well as Bonnie and Clyde's, John Dillinger's and others. 58 mins.
VHS: S15923. $19.95.

General Douglas MacArthur
His simple promise, "I will return," signaled a tenacious fighting quality which made him a vital force in the U.S. war effort during World War II. This *A & E Biography* traces his life from childhood through his career, where he ended by going head-to-head with President Truman. 50 mins.
VHS: S29912. $19.95.

General Omar Bradley
Learn how World War II General Omar Bradley transformed America's raw recruits into the finest fighting force in history in this *A & E Biography*. 50 mins.
VHS: S30098. $19.95.

Harry S. Truman: His Life and Library
Follows Truman from his early years on a farm to his service in WWI to his eventual rise to the highest office in the land. Visit the Harry S. Truman Library and Museum in Independence, Missouri.
VHS: S34073. $29.95.

Harry S. Truman: Library and Museum
This video tour of the library's artifacts and exhibitions will impart the feeling of a personally narrated tour. Often it offers a more detailed view of the exhibits than could be gained from an actual visit to the site itself. 57 mins.
VHS: S23426. $24.95.

Harry S. Truman: Suddenly, Mr. President
Though his presidency held the promise of continuing policies, it ushered in a new age. Truman became the first man to use a nuclear bomb. 20 mins.
VHS: S23562. $49.95.

Harry S. Truman: The Challenges of Office
Between 1948 and 1952, Truman faced down the challenge of a new aggressor and shaped the policies of a new and bitter cold war. 20 mins.
VHS: S23563. $49.95.

Helen Keller: Separate Views
The Helen Keller story is a colorful dramatization of the life of that remarkable woman and her teacher, Annie Sullivan. Part two has Katherine Cornell, Martha Graham, and President Dwight Eisenhower narrating her fascinating biography.
VHS: S02063. $19.95.

Hillary Rodham Clinton: Changing the Rules
This First Lady stirs public opinion as few other political figures can. She is one of Washington's most intriguing and controversial players, who has welded her largely ceremonial position into one of unrivaled influence. This biography looks at the unique personality behind the politician. 50 mins.
VHS: S21684. $19.95.

Hoffa: The True Story
A documentary portrait of James R. Hoffa. The program chronicles Hoffa's rise from obscure union official to president of the International Brotherhood of Teamsters, his war with Attorney General Robert Kennedy, questions of mob influence and infiltration, his prison stay for racketeering and jury fraud, and the events surrounding his disappearance in July 1975. 50 mins.
VHS: S18109. $19.95.

Houdini
This haunting journey details the life of a man whose name and legend continues to fascinate: master escape artist Harry Houdini. Never-before-seen footage, interviews with historians and associates, and recently uncovered papers provide this riveting biography with insights into the mystery surrounding Houdini and what drove him to seek worldwide acclaim. 61 mins.
VHS: S28519. $19.98.

Houdini, The Life of the World's Greatest Escapologist
Houdini's career as a magician, illusionist and spiritualist is revealed in this film exploration of his life. He flirted with death so often that many of his fans still believe he will come back. This film begins with a seance at Niagara Falls. Then through photos, dramatizations and interviews it traces the career of this charismatic dreamer. 60 mins.
VHS: S26217. $19.95.

Howard Stern Exposed
Meet the the controversial man who calls himself the "King of All Media," Howard Stern, in this *A & E Biography* that Stern asked his fans to boycott! The host of a top-rated national radio program and TV show, the author of two record-breaking autobiographies, and star of his own autobiographical movie, Stern is known for his outrageous blend of fearless interviews and in-your-face, off-color comedy. Follow the original "shock jock" from his shy, awkward youth on Long Island to his notorious run-ins with the FCC. Celebrities recall their time in Howard's hot seat, friends tell their favorite Stern stories, and rare clips highlight some of his wildest material.
VHS: S30946. $9.99.
Bill Harris, USA, 1996, 50 mins.

Hugh Hefner: Once Upon a Time
An entertaining portrait of Hugh Hefner, the controversial founder and publisher of *Playboy* magazine. The filmmakers use the occasion of Hefner's recent wedding to a former Playmate to assess his life and work. Produced by the team of David Lynch and Mark Frost. Narrated by James Coburn.
VHS: S18322. $89.95.
Robert Heath, USA, 1992, 90 mins.

Indomitable Teddy Roosevelt
Remarkable documentary footage combined with dramatization, with narration by George C. Scott, music by John Philip Sousa. "History with a wallop and a heart" (Tom Shales, *Washington Post*).
VHS: S01888. $79.95.
Harrison Engle, USA, 1983, 94 mins.

Jackie Chan
In this *A&E Biography*, Hong Kong action movie producer, writer, actor, director and stuntman Jackie Chan talks about his childhood in Peking Opera School where he learned his skills, and his long battle to make it big in America. With clips. 40 mins.
VHS: S33422. $14.95.

Jim Thorpe—All American
Also known as *Man of Bronze*, this touching biography stars Burt Lancaster as the multi-talented Native American athlete who became an Olympic champion and who almost single-handedly put pro football on the map. A film about triumph and tragedy, as Thorpe eventually succumbs to drink.
VHS: S15988. $19.98.
Laser: LD74706. $34.98.
Michael Curtiz, USA, 1951, 107 mins.

Lindbergh's Great Race: Are There Any Mechanics Here?
This award-winning story of Charles Lindbergh's transatlantic triumph is composed entirely of rare newsreel and motion picture film, including never-before-seen footage and little-known sound recordings. 90 mins.
VHS: S34074. $29.95.

Lord of the Universe
The Alfred I. Dupont award-winning documentary on the Guru Maharij Ji's attempt to levitate the Houston Astrodome. USA.
VHS: S15195. $24.95.

Lucky Luciano: Chairman of the Mob
This *A&E Biography* traces the 30-year-career of New York Mafia boss Charles "Lucky" Luciano with rare interviews and archival footage. 50 mins.
VHS: S32990. $19.95.

MacArthur
A large scale biography of the strategist and general that traces his life and work from World War II to the Korean War, when he was dismissed by Harry Truman for insubordination and defying direct orders. With Gregory Peck as the eponymous general, Ed Flanders, Ed O'Herlihy, Sandy Kenyon and Art Fleming.
VHS: S31093. $19.95.
Laser: LD70052. $39.98.
Joseph Sargent, USA, 1977, 130 mins.

Michael Idvorsky Pupin
Pupin became one of the most widely respected mathematicians of his time. His inventions in the field of X-rays continue to shape this enduring technology. Born in a village near Belgrade, the story of his emigration to the U.S. and his education both here and in Europe became the subject of his Pulitzer-Prize winning autobiography. This documentary traces the trajectory of this amazing individual.
VHS: S21538. $24.95.

Milton Hershey: The Chocolate King
In this A&E biography, the origins of one of America's most successful business empires are revealed in the story of a man from a humble background. He was born on a farm and quit school at the fourth grade. Despite the odds, he built a business that sold confections to the ordinary person. Hershey differed from his contemporaries in that he treated his workers with respect. From the A&E *Biography* series.
VHS: S27170. $19.98.
Don Horan, USA, 1995, 50 mins.

The Model T Man from Michigan, America: Henry Ford and His Horseless Carriage

Ford's motor car and assembly line methods transformed manufacturing and modern life. This video explores the complex personality behind these innovations and shows the interiors of his many homes. Hosted by E.G. Marshall. 24 mins.
VHS: S23555. $49.95.
Laser: LD74784. $99.95.

Monty Roberts: A Real Horse Whisperer

The "riveting and inspirational story" (*New York Times*) of Monty Roberts, Queen Elizabeth II's chosen horse trainer and author of the bestseller, *Monty Roberts: The Man Who Listens to Horses*, upon which the movie, *The Horse Whisperer*, starring Robert Redford, was based. Tells the story of Roberts' remarkable life, following him on a three-day expedition during which he faces the ultimate horse-breaking challenge: taming a wild mustang.
VHS: S34084. $14.98.
John Groom, Great Britain, 1997, 48 mins.

Mother Teresa

A highly acclaimed, moving portrait of Mother Teresa, directed by the independent team of Ann and Jeanette Petrie, with narration by Richard Attenborough. "Enough to charm a cynic….One of those films that make you pleased to be a human being" (Peter Stack, *The San Francisco Chronicle*).
VHS: S03429. $19.95.
Ann Petrie/Jenette Petrie, USA, 1986

Mother Teresa: A Life of Devotion

This *A & E Biography* of the woman who was hailed as a living saint tells the story of Mother Teresa's crusade to help the poor, from her early years in the Missionaries of Charity to her role as a leading representative of the poor and downtrodden. Prominent clergymen, family members and close associates recall their experiences with her around the world. 50 mins.
VHS: S32637. $19.95.

Mother Teresa: In the Name of God's Poor

Geraldine Chaplin gives an outstanding performance as the tiny woman from Albania who captured the hearts and minds of the world as she dedicated her life to the dying and destitute and transformed the world with her faith, courage and love. Filmed on location in Sri Lanka. With David Byrd (*Lost Highway*).
VHS: S32666. $19.98.
Kevin Connor, USA, 1997, 93 mins.

Mussolini: Italy's Nightmare

In this *A & E Biography*, rare photos and films tell the story of Mussolini's life, from his days as a schoolyard bully to his creation of the dreaded Black Shirt Brigades. Experts reveal how his alliance with Hitler ultimately destroyed his country and led to his execution and mutilation by Italian partisans. Contemporary observers explore his renewed popularity and the shocking return of Fascism to Italy today. 50 mins.
VHS: S32632. $19.95.

N Is a Number: A Portrait of Paul Erdos

A man with no home and no job, Paul Erdos was the most prolific mathematician who ever lived. Erdos, who died in 1996 at the age of 83, inspired generations of mathematicians throughout the world with his insightful approach and wry humor. This whimsical documentary follows him for four years through four countries, presenting his mathematical quest and its personal and philosophical dimensions. Animated sequences illustrate the kinds of mathematical problems that Erdos pursued.
Home Video.
VHS: S31782. $49.95.
Public Performance.
VHS: S31783. $200.00.
George Paul Csicsery, USA, 1993, 57 mins.

Nikola Tesla: The Genius Who Lit the World

Tesla was the amazing Serbian inventor who emigrated from the Balkans to the US just before the turn of the century. His inventions include fluorescent light, the laser beam, wireless communication, wireless transmission of electricity and—perhaps his greatest achievement—alternating current. This biography is a tribute to his ingenuity.
VHS: S21537. $24.95.

The Nixon Interviews with David Frost

A five-volume collection of David Frost's famous, controversial interviews with former president Richard Nixon. The programs look at the wide-scale domestic, international and personal repercussions of the Nixon administration, including Vietnam, the war at home, the Silent Majority, Nixon's foreign policy in China, Russia, the Middle East, Central America, the implications of Watergate and the cover-up, Spiro Agnew's resignation, Nixon's relationship with Henry Kissinger, the missing footage of the Watergate tapes, John and Martha Mitchell and the ideological composition and makeup of the Supreme Court.
Volume 1: Watergate.
VHS: S17248. $19.98.
Volume 2: The World.
VHS: S17249. $19.98.
Volume 3: War at Home and Abroad.
VHS: S17250. $19.98.
Volume 4: The Final Days.
VHS: S17251. $19.98.
Volume 5: The Missing 18½ Minutes and More.
VHS: S17252. $19.98.

Nostradamus: A Voice from the Past

Examines the life and intrigue of the French professor, physician, astrologer, mathematician and scholar who lived from 1503-1566 and predicted the French Revolution, both world wars, the rise and fall of the Third Reich, the Kennedy assassinations, the moon landing and more. 51 mins.
VHS: S32669. $12.99.

P.T. Barnum: America's Greatest Showman

Barnum carved out a unique place in American folklore with his mix of hype, entertainment and natural history. This Discovery Channel documentary details his life and his work. It's all here, from the little general, Tom Thumb, to the massive Jumbo the Elephant. 90 mins.
VHS: S27819. $19.95.

Patton: A Genius for War

A&E's Biography series reveals the life of this controversial World War II General. His brilliant military maneuvers broke Hitler's Thousand Year Reich, but his unorthodox ways disturbed his own Allied colleagues. 100 mins.
VHS: S27601. $19.95.

Paul Harvey's The Rest of the Story

Popular radio host Paul Harvey relates anecdotes, stories and personal accounts from his true life radio series, *The Rest of the Story*. 60 mins.
VHS: S17848. $19.95.

Paul Revere: The Midnight Rider

Not only did Paul Revere announce the coming of the British in his famed midnight ride, he actually led the Sons of Liberty and helped organize the Boston Tea Party. In addition to his civic work, he crafted fine silver, which led him into a career as a successful industrialist. This A&E biography shows all sides of this amazing historic figure. From the A&E *Biography* series. USA, 1995, 50 mins.
VHS: S27172. $19.98.

Portraits of American Presidents

Beginning with the first man to occupy the office, to the current president, this documentary presents the men who filled the office of President of the United States. This exceptional three video collection places all the presidents in the context of their times, gives a brief assessment of their character, the events leading up to their election, their families, and the conflicting social and political influences at work on them. Volume 1: *The Presidents of a New Nation—1789-1829*. Volume 2: *The Presidents of a National Struggle—1829-1901*. Volume 3: *The Presidents of a World Power—1901-1992*.
VHS: S17263. $59.95.

Profiles of Power

A series of tapes on 20th Century leaders—men who had immeasurable impact on history.
Profiles of Power: Franklin D. Roosevelt. A fascinating account of FDR's legacy from the Depression to the terrifying World War II. 40 mins.
VHS: S11142. $19.95.
Profiles of Power: Gandhi. Utilizing rare footage, the life of this century's eloquent spokesman for nonviolence brilliantly comes alive. 45 mins.
VHS: S11147. $19.95.
Profiles of Power: Hitler. This highly collectable video chronicles the fascinating rise and fall of one of history's most controversial leaders. 45 mins.
VHS: S11146. $19.95.
Profiles of Power: Lenin. Utilizing rare footage, Lenin's life unfolds against the backdrop of Russia's Revolution. 45 mins.
VHS: S11145. $19.95.
Profiles of Power: Mussolini. Il Duce was the second most hated villain of the century; from his humble origins to his rise to ultimate power in Italy. 45 mins.
VHS: S11143. $19.95.
Profiles of Power: Winston Churchill. Learn how Churchill alone stood firm when all the world seemed to cower before Hitler. 45 mins.
VHS: S11144. $19.95.

Public Enemies on the Rock

Narrated by Rod Steiger, this program looks at America's most famous criminals—Al "Scarface" Capone, George "Machine Gun" Kelly, Alvin "Creepy" Karpis, Arthur "Doc" Barker, and "The Birdman" Robert Stroud—on America's most famous prison island, Alcatraz. With stories by guards and the ex-cons who shared the prison with them. 50 mins.
VHS: S34563. $19.98.

The Real Stories of Capone, Dillinger and Bonnie & Clyde

From New York to Chicago, these accounts bring to life three uniquely American stories and the infamous personalities behind them, captured in rare footage and newsreel accounts of the gangster era of the roaring 20s and the restless 30s. 75 mins.
VHS: S23138. $29.95.

Red Baron

An informative and engaging look at the legendary personality of aviation, Manfred von Richthofen, the Ace of Aces, nemesis of Allied flyers, and the greatest aerial tactician of World War I. Through interviews with the last surviving pilots, rare World War I footage, dogfights, crashes, and the Red Baron's last flight and controversial death are explored. 60 mins.
VHS: S09915. $29.95.

Richard M. Nixon Remembered

After the hype and confused facts surrounding Oliver Stone's epic drama *Nixon*, a documentary with the actual historical facts is a vital antidote to the growing pressures of infotainment. This CNN documentary shows Richard M. Nixon as a flawed and intriguing individual. Featuring insights from such political figures as President Bill Clinton and Henry Kissinger.
VHS: S27513. $14.98.

Richard M. Nixon: His Life and Times

ABC News crafted this essential video biography of the American president known around the world for both his achievements and his failures. All the key times of his life are covered, including his career prior to the White House, his presidency, Watergate and his final years as an elder statesman. 60 mins.
VHS: S29484. $9.95.

Richard Nixon Reflects

Like a phoenix rising from the ashes, former President Richard Nixon returns again to center stage in this candid and revealing 90-minute video memoir. Utilizing never before seen footage from his own personal archives, and extensive interviews conducted by Morton Kondracke, *Richard Nixon Reflects* provides enlightening and often entertaining anecdotes from his rather colorful political life. Includes his personal thoughts on Kennedy, Reagan, Bush and Gorbachev, as well as his opinions on his own handling of Watergate. 90 mins.
VHS: S13605. $24.98.

Richard Nixon—Checkers, Old Glory, Resignation

A brief look at the former president as seen in three media events. *Checkers* is a 30-minute paid political announcement aired during the 1952 Presidential campaign. For those who don't remember, Checkers was a pet cocker spaniel. The other segments cover a short Flag Day speech in 1957 and his resignation speech in 1974. USA, 1952-74, 45 mins.
VHS: S05509. $24.95.

Richard Nixon: Man and President

A&E's Biography series looks at the life of one of America's most controversial presidents. Born on a modest California ranch, Nixon rose to prominence despite a number of overwhelming setbacks. In retrospect, his lifetime achievements balance brilliant political successes with nearly unimaginable disaster. 100 mins.
VHS: S27602. $19.95.

Santa Claus

A & E Biography looks at the legend of the jolly old man in the red suit who brings gifts and good cheer—a man who once lived, and lives on in the hearts and imaginations of children and adults all over the world. 50 mins.
VHS: S30101. $19.95.

Sir Terence Conran

Terence Conran, the man who has changed the face of home and style and created a business empire in the process, talks about his life and career. Head of a retail empire including *Habitat, Mothercase, BHS* and *Richard Shops*, this documentary examines the man behind this astounding design revolution and the widespread influence of Conran's ideas on modern living. 55 mins.
VHS: S07606. $39.95.

The Speeches of Famous Women: From Suffragette to Senator

Elizabeth Stanton, Eleanor Roosevelt, Betty Ford, Betty Friedan, Carol Mosely Braun and Barbara Boxer have all courageously fought for the rights of women. They are just a few of the women featured in this singular collection of inspiring oratory. From *The Speeches Collection*. USA, 1995, 56 mins.
VHS: S27279. $19.98.

The Speeches of General Douglas MacArthur

Heroic General Douglas MacArthur was the most dynamic military speaker of the 20th century. Relive his bold "I shall return" speech, his reflections on the arms race and much more. 55 mins.
VHS: S12311. $19.98.

The Speeches of Gerald Ford

Chosen to succeed Spiro Agnew as Vice President, he eventually replaced Richard Nixon as President as well. Speeches from Ford's presidential career show his acceding to office, the pardoning of Nixon, his honoring of Queen Elizabeth during her visit to the U.S., his acceptance of the Republican nomination for President and, finally, his farewell to Congress and the nation. From *The Speeches Collection*. USA, 1995, 55 mins.
VHS: S27277. $19.98.

The Speeches of Harry S. Truman

He "gave 'em hell" when he led the American people through the Korean war and crusaded against communism without compromise. This fascinating cassette documents the speeches at the beginning of the Cold War era of Harry S. Truman. 55 mins.
VHS: S12310. $19.98.

The Speeches of Jimmy Carter

Jimmy Carter was the 39th President of the United States. This collection of speeches features his views on a variety of issues, ranging from support for human rights and international peace to the troubling energy crisis of the late 1970s. From *The Speeches Collection*. USA, 1995, 55 mins.
VHS: S27276. $19.98.

The Speeches of Lyndon B. Johnson

Lyndon B. Johnson's term as President is documented on this video through a series of speeches he gave while holding the highest office of this country. Much is included, from his continuation of the Kennedy legacy of supporting civil rights to his decision not to run for reelection as President. From *The Speeches Collection*. USA, 1995, 57 mins.
VHS: S27275. $19.98.

The Speeches of Richard M. Nixon

The tumultuous Nixon era is recreated through Nixon's speeches in Communist China to his sad resignation press conference. 55 mins.
VHS: S12306. $19.98.

The Speeches of Ronald Reagan

"The Great Communicator" inspired many with his oratorical ease. This video showcases highlights of his speaking career, beginning with a 1964 speech lauding Barry Goldwater for President and continuing through to such gems as his debate with former CIA director George Bush. The "Evil Empire" and "Star Wars" speeches, as well as his final words as President, are also included. From *The Speeches Collection*. USA, 1995, 69 mins.
VHS: S27274. $19.98.

The Story of Will Rogers

A biography of the irreverent political humorist. This program traces Rogers' idiosyncratic life from the rugged individualist whose self-deprecating humor concealed a harsh critique of American society to his death in an Alaskan plane crash. Narrated by Bob Hope. "An altogether superior biography" (*New York Times*). 60 mins.
VHS: S19246. $19.95.

Thomas Jefferson: In Pursuit of Liberty

This is a fascinating portrait of Jefferson and his legacy. As one of the U.S.' founding statesmen he had a profound impact on the young nation. Period paintings, documents and archival footage are combined with images of Monticello and other sites to explain his legacy. President Jimmy Carter, Supreme Court Justice Sandra Day O'Conner and George F. Will all lend their perspectives on this political visionary.
VHS: S24406. $29.95.

Thomas Jefferson: Philosopher of Freedom

This biography tells the amazing history behind one of the country's most intriguing founding fathers. He drafted the Declaration of Independence, fought tirelessly for free speech and U.S. expansion, and even excelled in science and architecture. This video examines whether he really sired many children with his slave and engaged in a troubling affair while working for the U.S. in Paris. From the A&E *Biography* series.
VHS: S27171. $19.98.
Adam Friedman/Monte Markham, USA, 1995, 50 mins.

A Tribute to Charles Kuralt

In this moving tribute, *CBS Sunday Morning* host Charles Osgood takes us from the early days when Charles Kuralt brought a touch of compassion to his coverage of the Vietnam war, to the groundbreaking series *On the Road with Charles Kuralt*, a treasury of living history, good people and breathtaking beauty. Included are excerpts from some of his most memorable episodes.
VHS: S32541. $14.98.

Truman

Gary Sinise is superb as one of the United States' most pivotal presidents. The rise to prominence of this simple farmer, shopkeeper and county politician coincided with the growing influence of America. He made key decisions and stood by them, including his decision to open the nuclear age with the bombing of Hiroshima and Nagasaki. USA, 1995, 130 mins.
VHS: S26998. $19.98.

Where Have You Gone Joe DiMaggio?

An entertaining documentary on the life and times of baseball hero Joe DiMaggio, featuring never-before-seen film footage and rare archival photos and interviews with baseball greats Bob Feller, Reggie Jackson and Pete Rose; DiMaggio teammates Jerry Coleman, Phil Rizzuto, and Tommy Henrich; and high-profile fans George Bush and Mario Cuomo. 63 mins.
VHS: S33131. $14.95.

Will Rogers

A wise and wistful look at America's favorite son, who for 25 years endeared himself to the nation with his sense of humor. 23 mins.
VHS: S06423. $19.98.

Will Rogers: Champion of the People

Honesty, wry humor and a down-to-earth philosophy endeared this American to the entire nation. Starring Robert Hays. 54 mins.
VHS: S06426. $12.98.

World Without Walls—Beryl Markham's African Memoir

A remarkable documentary about an equally remarkable woman, Beryl Markham—aviatrix, race horse trainer, elephant tracker, irresistible woman—who led a life of unparalleled romance and adventure as the "other" woman in the love triangle between Dennis Finshatten and Karen Blixen (*Out of Africa*). This documentary captures the spectacular scenery of Africa, and offers a unique insight into the English society of Kenya in the 1920's. Winner of the special jury prize at the San Francisco International Film Festival. 60 mins.
VHS: S04368. $29.95.

You May Call Her Madam Secretary

Frances Perkins, the first woman to hold high public office in the nation, is almost unknown today. Yet she was a leading social reformer, a driving force behind protective laws on which our lives depend, an inspiring figure in American and women's history. The film traces the rise of social conscience in this country: from the outrage that followed the Triangle Shirtwaist Fire in 1911 to the revolutionary legislation of the New Deal. In this moving and often witty documentary, actress Frances Sternhagen presents Perkins' complex character on camera, using the words from her oral history and papers. Includes Public Performance Rights. 57 mins.
VHS: S09263. $49.95.

You're the Top—The Cole Porter Story

Some of the most unique, romantic and wittiest songs ever written were products of Cole Porter's genius. Clearly one of the greatest composers to date, his wit and sophisticated style are still the standards to which today's composers and lyricists aspire. To commemorate the 100th anniversary of the late Cole Porter's birth, this profile provides an entertaining look at the man who embraced an elite lifestyle—and chronicled the world of high society. Performances include: Fred Astaire and Ginger Rogers, Judy Garland and Gene Kelly, Grace Kelly and Bing Crosby, and many more. 56 mins.
VHS: S14106. $19.98.
DVD: DV60282. $24.95.

Zona Gale: 1874-1938

The first woman to win a Pulitzer Prize in drama is the subject of this fascinating video. This author's success can be a source of inspiration to all writers. 15 mins. Resource guide available.
Resource Guide.
VHS: S25783. $45.00.
Video.
VHS: S25770. $95.00.

THE KENNEDYS

Assassinated: The Last Days of King and Kennedy

Focuses on the last months in the lives of Rev. Martin Luther King Jr. and Robert Kennedy, men whose decisions put them on a collision course with history. 90 mins.
VHS: S34597. $19.98.

The Assassination of JFK (Dennis Mueller)

This intriguing film reveals how rogue elements of the CIA and FBI may have allied themselves with organized crime and Texas oil money in a plot to kill the president. Utilizes rare archival footage and original documents.
VHS: S16792. $79.98.
Dennis Mueller, USA, 1992, 78 mins.

Best Evidence: Disguise and Deception in the Assassination of John F. Kennedy

Author David S. Lifton hosts this "research video" into the JFK assassination, focusing on the autopsy and the critical 12 hours following the shooting. Lifton claims that the President's body was secretly intercepted, the wounds altered, autopsy findings faked, and that the assassination conspiracy reached the highest levels of the U.S. government. 30 mins.
VHS: S12162. $14.95.

Beyond JFK: The Question of Conspiracy

A provocative documentary by award-winning filmmaker Barbara Kopple (*Harlan County, U.S.A.*; *American Dream*) investigates the issues and background materials introduced in Oliver Stone's film *JFK*, offering new research and interviews with the main participants. Narrated by CBS journalist Ike Pappas.
VHS: S17878. $19.98.
Barbara Kopple, USA, 1991, 90 mins.

Confession of an Assassin: The Murder of JFK

Prisoner James E. Files of the Joliet State Penitentiary admits to having been a part of the murder of JFK. This video interview contains another plausible explanation which could unravel the mystery surrounding this puzzling issue. Though Files died prematurely, his confession goes some way toward an accounting of what actually happened. 76 mins.
VHS: S29806. $19.98.

Four Days in November

A tribute to John F. Kennedy, drawn from more than 8 million feet of newsreel, amateur footage, tapes and photos, this tape vividly chronicles the events surrounding his death and the gunning down of his assassin. 123 mins.
VHS: S07476. $29.95.

Grey Gardens

An eccentric mother and daughter are hidden away in a decaying East Hampton mansion; the mother is Edith Bouvier Beale, the daughter, Edie—aunt and cousin of Jacqueline Bouvier Kennedy. Called "hilarious, horrifying and tragic," and "as compelling a drama as Tennessee Williams might hope to achieve," *Grey Gardens* is a funny, moving descent into American classic decay.
VHS: S07438. $79.95.
Maysles Brothers, USA, 1976, 94 mins.

He Must Have Something

This is the real story of Jim Garrison, the New Orleans law man who investigated the assassination of JFK on his own time. 88 mins.
VHS: S22396. $49.95.

Jack: The Last Kennedy Film

John Kennedy narrates this personal portrait of one of the century's most beloved and charismatic figures. Rare family and historic archival footage tell the story of the milestones that marked the progress of his personal and public lives.
VHS: S21351. $14.98.

Jackie: A Tribute to the First Lady

Jacqueline Kennedy Onassis is legendary for her charm and poise, but behind the public persona was a warm, elegant and intensely private person. This Discovery Channel documentary uses archival footage, home movies and the words of family members to reveal the person behind the myth. 55 mins.
VHS: S27820. $19.95.

Jacqueline Kennedy Onassis Remembered

This charming women continued to transform herself throughout a lifetime shaped by some of the most momentous events of our time. Beginning as a reporter, she quickly adapted to the role of a politician's wife and ultimately first lady. Part One offers an autobiographical overview while parts Two and Three are original early broadcasts consisting of a White House tour conducted by the First Lady herself, and an interview with the Kennedy family just before Jack entered the White House.
VHS: S21352. $14.98.

JFK (Gift Set)

A beautifully packaged, three-cassette collection contains the director's cut of Oliver Stone's *JFK*, with 17 minutes of additional footage, and Barbara Kopple's video documentary, *Beyond JFK: The Question of Conspiracy*, a further probing of the issues and connections introduced by the film.
VHS: S17879. $39.98.
Laser: *JFK*—CAV; *Beyond JFK*—CLV. **LD71836. $149.98.**

The JFK Assassination: The Jim Garrison Tapes

Jim Garrison faces the camera to tell the suppressed story surrounding the fateful day of November 22, 1963. Includes actual footage of the crime, recordings of the plotters, new witnesses, new evidence and a complete examination of the record. "If you thought *JFK* was important and you want the factual background to the maligned Garrison investigation, see this film" (Oliver Stone). 1991, 90 mins.
VHS: S16751. $19.98.

The JFK Conspiracy

Hosted by James Earl Jones, *The JFK Conspiracy* exams the events of the day. The program teams the shared opinions of government officials, eye witnesses and director Oliver Stone with expert testimony, photographs, documents and evidence. Includes the complete Zapruder film and six minutes of footage from the House Select Committee on Assassination. 98 mins.
VHS: S16713. $24.98.

JFK in Ireland

In June 1963, JFK made an historic trip to Ireland, where he was given a hero's welcome in every locale he visited. This special program includes never-before-seen footage of JFK that enables the viewer to share the journey of an American president paying homage to his family's birthplace. 42 mins.
VHS: S30683. $19.95.

JFK: The Day the Nation Cried—November 22, 1963

James Earl Jones reviews the brief life of John F. Kennedy—his triumphs, failures, contribution to history. The moving documentary combines the tragic events of Kennedy's assassination with the remembrances of those who knew him best. 52 mins.
VHS: S10790. $19.95.

JFK: The End of Camelot

In this dramatic and historic documentary from the Discovery Channel, witnesses of JFK's fateful end speak about the experience of this momentous event. The result is a moving document of memory and loss. 90 mins.
VHS: S25076. $19.95.

John F. Kennedy and the Nazi Spy

Much has been learned about JFK's sexual conduct, most of it inconsequential. This tape examines the possibility of leaks that could have occurred due to his infidelities. The subject of the JFK affair had her own agenda. Was she successful? 50 mins.
VHS: S13101. $24.98.

John F. Kennedy's Lost Pathway to Peace

Narrated by Robert Vaughn, a moving portrait of the Kennedy presidential legacy—Kennedy's emphasis on the strategy of world peace, with rare and historical film clips bringing alive the Kennedy message.
VHS: S07141. $29.95.
Dr. Joseph A. Bagnall, USA, 1985, 30 mins.

John F. Kennedy—The Commemorative Album

A three-part presentation on the life and times of JFK put together by CBS News. Walter Cronkite, Dan Rather and others review the life and death of the man and talk to his mother, Rose Kennedy, for insight into the earlier years. Twenty-five years after the motorcade in Dallas, Kennedy comes alive again on video. USA, 1982, 110 mins.
VHS: S07682. $19.98.
Laser: LD70254. $59.95.

John F. Kennedy: A Personal Story

In this *A & E Biography*, the pivotal moments of Kennedy's life are revisited through archival footage and interviews with famous journalists, Hollywood actors and White House staffers. 100 mins.
VHS: S32194. $19.95.

John F. Kennedy: Challenges and Tragedy

Despite his tragically short time in the White House, President Kennedy managed to achieve a great deal, as this video shows. 18 mins.
VHS: S23567. $49.95.

John F. Kennedy: The New Generation

The unique personality of this charismatic president is evoked, and the issues he faced as a leader are examined. 23 mins.
VHS: S23566. $49.95.

Kennedy's Ireland

Part of the great immigrant wave of the 1800's during the Irish potato famine, the Kennedy family moved to America in search of a better life. This tape is an examination of one great family's ethnic heritage. 71 mins.
VHS: S13100. $29.98.

Kennedys

This is the definitive look at America's most powerful and controversial family. Using rare footage, the history of the family is traced to the present with the emergence of a new generation of Kennedys. 100 mins.
VHS: S13099. $19.98.

The Kennedys (American Experience)

A no-holds-barred investigation into the Kennedys, the political dynasty whose charismatic, provocative and firm hold on our political, social and economic institutions is arguably untouched by any rival American family. Produced in association with WGBH/ Boston and London's Thames Television.
The Kennedys #1 (American Experience). 120 mins.
VHS: S17344. $19.95.
The Kennedys #2 (American Experience). 120 mins.
VHS: S17345. $19.95.
The Kennedys (American Experience), Complete Set. 240 mins.
VHS: S17346. $39.95.

Kennedys Don't Cry

A definitive look at America's first family, this biography traces their rise to prominence from the days of Joe Kennedy's empire building to the political rise of Jack, Bobby and Teddy. Narrated by Cliff Robertson. 100 mins.
VHS: S02313. $59.95.

The Kennedys of Massachusetts

William Peterson, Annette O'Toole, Charles Durning, Steven Weber and Tracy Pollan star in this film adaptation of Doris Kearn Goodwin's best-selling novel, *The Fitzgeralds and The Kennedys*. This epic film recounts major events in the life of the Kennedy family, from Joe Kennedy's courtship of Rose to the inauguration of J.F.K. 278 mins.
VHS: S26393. $39.98.

The Men Who Killed Kennedy

A new theory about JFK's murder is at the center of this A&E documentary. It posits that Robert Kennedy knew something of the assassination plot because it was modeled on his own plot to kill Castro. Interviews, including one with a colonel who admits to being trained for eliminating witnesses, and image technology that reveals how autopsy photos were faked, make this a must-see video. 50 mins.
VHS: S27600. $19.95.

Oswald: The Backyard Photographs

One of the most controversial issues in the JFK assassination is the authenticity of the "backyard photographs" of Lee Harvey Oswald, which Oswald himself insisted were fakes. This provocative program sheds new light on the crime of the century. 50 mins.
VHS: S30684. $19.95.

Plot to Kill Robert Kennedy

On the anniversary of Robert Kennedy's assassination, this film contradicts the single-assassin theory, alleging that investigators ignored conflicting eyewitness accounts, disregarded testimony and destroyed evidence. USA, 1988, 95 mins.
VHS: S07347. $59.95.

Reasonable Doubt

Rare film and interview footage fill this documentary on the assassination of President John F. Kennedy, giving credibility to the theory that there was more than a single gunman involved in the tragedy that shook the nation. 60 mins.
VHS: S12950. $29.95.

Rivals: J.F.K. vs. Khruschev

When President John Kennedy refused to let Soviet Premier Khruschev move nuclear missiles to Cuba in 1962, two superpowers wrestled for control while the world teetered on the brink of destruction. With interviews and rare footage. 46 mins.
VHS: S33163. $9.95.

Robert Kennedy and His Times

This well acted biography stars Brad Davis, as the young Bobby Kennedy, alongside Ned Beatty, Veronica Cartwright and Jack Warden, in this terrific look at the Kennedy clan. The double-cassette dramatic biography is based on the best-selling book by Pulitzer-Prize winner and Kennedy confidante Arthur M. Schlessinger, Jr. 309 mins.
VHS: S25753. $24.95.

Say Goodbye to the President

Reports on the true circumstances surrounding the death of Marilyn Monroe and the cover-up which followed for 25 years. Would the mob's knowledge of Marilyn's affairs with the Kennedys have led to blackmail, holding the American Government hostage? 71 mins.
VHS: S31821. $19.98.

The Speeches of John F. Kennedy

President Kennedy's greatest speeches in a unique video collection.
VHS: S07030. $19.95.

The Speeches of Robert F. Kennedy

The Senator from New York was one of the most charismatic speakers of our time. Now you can own his eulogy at his brother John's funeral, his ironic reflections on Vietnam, and more. 55 mins.
VHS: S12307. $19.98.

Ted Kennedy

He's been called the conscience of Congress, a liberal libertine, and the last great hope of America's foremost political dynasty. This *A & E Biography* looks at the real Ted Kennedy. 50 mins.
VHS: S30107. $19.95.

A Tour of the White House

Jacqueline Kennedy is seen at that unique time in her life when she was at the center of the mystique that was Camelot. Here she shows viewers her home, The White House. 60 mins.
VHS: S23795. $24.95.

Two Men in Dallas

In this 1987 documentary, author and leading Kennedy assassination theorist Mark Lane *(Rush to Judgment, Plausible Denial)* interviews Roger Craig, the Dallas deputy sheriff, who recounts his eyewitness version of the events on November 22, 1963, and Craig's subsequent charges that his testimony (which contradicts large portions of the Warren Commission) were suppressed.
VHS: S17006. $29.95.

POLITICS & CONTEMPORARY EVENTS

1993: A Year in Review

A look back at the tumultuous events that made history in 1993. Produced by CNN. 60 mins.
VHS: S20513. $14.98.

Are We Scaring Ourselves to Death?

John Stoessel originally made this documentary for ABC news. Now this examination of public hysteria around a number of issues is available for home viewing. From crime to cancer to consumer reporting, this journalist examines the scary statistics that litter the airwaves. 50 mins.
VHS: S24324. $19.98.

Arming Dictators

Throughout the 1980's, while the U.S. government opposed dictatorships in the Soviet Bloc, it also supplied over $80 million to ruthless dictators elsewhere. Indonesia, Zaire, Saudi Arabia and El Salvador are just some of the places examined in this documentary, where U.S. tax dollars were used to brutally repress innocent people. 28 mins.
VHS: S21590. $29.95.

Best of Nightline

Assassination Attempt Against President Reagan. 60 mins.
VHS: S14020. $14.98.
Assassination Attempt Against Pope John Paul II. 85 mins.
VHS: S14021. $14.98.
Challenger Disaster. 60 mins.
VHS: S14040. $14.98.
Freeing of the Hostages. 150 mins.
VHS: S14019. $14.98.
Highlights. Celebrate a decade of memorable moments from the ground-breaking, late-night news forum. Footage of the most controversial interviews conducted by the irrepressible Ted Koppel are the focus of this special. 50 mins.
VHS: S12680. $19.98.
Judge O'Conner Nominated for Supreme Court. 30 mins.
VHS: S14022. $14.98.
Oliver North. 30 mins.
VHS: S14047. $14.98.
President Reagan's Farewell Address. 30 mins.
VHS: S14057. $14.98.
Ronald Reagan Elected President. 120 mins.
VHS: S14016. $14.98.
The First Nightline. 30 mins.
VHS: S14015. $14.98.
U.S. Invades Panama. 60 mins.
VHS: S14062. $14.98.

Beyond Goodwill

Teenagers from the two super powers join forces to combat problems neglected during the Cold War. Restoring forests in Costa Rica, helping survivors of the Armenian earthquake, even providing relief for the homeless of Washington State are just some of the ways these young people hope to overcome distrust through joint action. 58 mins.
VHS: S21587. $59.95.

The Bill of Rights in Action: Capital Punishment

The case of a convicted murderer provokes a number of questions about capital punishment. Does it deter crime? Is it cruel and unusual punishment? When is it appropriate to the crime? 23 mins.
VHS: S23690. $79.95.

The Bill of Rights in Action: De Facto Segregation
School busing is a contentious issue. This film shows how problems arise when the law tries to counteract the effects of de facto segregation. 22 mins.
VHS: S23692. $79.95.

The Bill of Rights in Action: Due Process of Law
The case of a student who is summarily suspended illustrates the problems of eliminating due process in order to avoid violence and anarchy. The student participated in a campus demonstration. Now viewers must decide if he was denied his rights through immediate suspension. Or was the safety of others more important? 23 mins.
VHS: S23687. $79.95.

The Bill of Rights in Action: Equal Opportunity
An arbitrator is presented with a case where a black worker is promoted over a white worker even though the white worker has greater seniority. This program is left open-ended for the viewer to decide. 22 mins.
VHS: S23689. $79.95.

The Bill of Rights in Action: Freedom of Religion
A woman refuses a blood transfusion for religious reasons, even though it may save her life and preserve the health of her developing fetus. Lawyers debate the free exercise of religious practice in the face of this dangerous situation. 23 mins.
VHS: S23694. $79.95.

The Bill of Rights in Action: Freedom of Speech
Viewers can decide who is right in this case about an unpopular speaker. Lawyers argue the constitutional issues before a court of appeals by weighing the rights of the individual against the community's need for law and order. 18 mins.
VHS: S23685. $79.95.

The Bill of Rights in Action: Freedom of the Press
No law can abridge the freedom of the press. Does this grant reporters the right to refuse information to criminal investigations? This video explores these issues through a case about just such a reporter. 23 mins.
VHS: S23691. $79.95.

The Bill of Rights in Action: Juvenile Law
Two brothers, ages 15 and 18, are treated dramatically differently upon arrest. This scenario demonstrates the way adult and juvenile law vary. Should juveniles be treated as adults under the law? Viewers confront this question in this film. 23 mins.
VHS: S23688. $79.95.

The Bill of Rights in Action: The Privilege Against Self-Incrimination
Accused criminals are protected from forced or coerced confessions by the 5th amendment. Now advanced technologies challenge the importance of this constitutional right. Lawyers present opposing sides around this contentious issue in this dramatic, open-ended program. 22 mins.
VHS: S23696. $79.95.

The Bill of Rights in Action: The Right to Privacy
Does electronic police surveillance violate the constitutional right to privacy? Law enforcement has always had to weigh the importance of the right to privacy against their ability to protect the public good. 23 mins.
VHS: S23695. $79.95.

The Bill of Rights in Action: The Story of a Trial
Two young men are accused of a misdemeanor offense. Following their progress through arrest, arraignment and trial, the importance of due process and constitutional safeguards is revealed. 21 mins.
VHS: S23686. $79.95.

The Bill of Rights in Action: Women's Rights
A high school girl is prohibited by a state law from swimming on a boy's team. Between the 14th amendment and its promise of equal protection, and the physical differences between men and women, there lies a contentious area explored by lawyers who argue this case. 22 mins.
VHS: S23693. $79.95.

Biting the Bullet
A moving profile of workers and community and industrial leaders in areas hard hit by military cutbacks, from a former ammunition plant on the Gulf Coast of Mississippi to the empty naval shipyards of Southern California. A timely and provocative program. USA, 1991, 28 mins.
VHS: S15207. $39.95.

The Blame Game: Are We a Country of Victims?
John Stoessel, a journalist with ABC news, examines what he calls the victim movement. He probes the failures of social security, the limits of lawsuits and the diminishment of self-reliance and individual responsibility. 50 mins.
VHS: S24325. $19.98.

Blood Makes the Grass Grow: Conscientious Objectors and the Gulf War
This program interviews four men and two women who were among the 2,500 U.S. soldiers who attempted to become conscientous objectors during the Gulf War. This video raises critical questions for those considering enlistment, for service people contemplating conscientous objection, and for anyone concerned with basic issues of militarism in a democratic society. High school to adult. 1997, 46 mins.
VHS: S31916. $49.95.

Blowing the Whistle: How to Protect Yourself and Win
This training video teaches potential whistleblowers their rights, demonstrates effective methods of whistleblowing and explains what assistance is available. Meet other courageous whistleblowers and learn from their mistakes. High school to adult. 1994, 35 mins.
VHS: S31922. $49.95.

The Bottom Line
This program looks at the daily life and difficulties faced by the elderly. Two stories are intertwined, both posing a series of moral and ethical dilemmas on the distinction between life and the quality of life. 30 mins.
VHS: S17932. $49.95.

Campaign Against the Death Penalty
Amnesty International produced this documentary examining the issues surrounding the death penalty and the campaign by human rights organizations to repeal it.
VHS: S07764. $20.00.

Changing the Focus of Foreign Aid
This program considers the benefits of fostering economic stability of other countries. With commentary by Donna Culpepper of the Civic Education Project, Bryan Johnson of the Heritage Foundation and Julia Taft of Interaction.
VHS: S31918. $49.95.

Changing the Law
American life is governed by the law. This program examines complex legal issues confronting our contemporary society. Are laws inflexible or does interpretation of the law offer society's changing needs room to grow? 23 mins.
VHS: S23735. $79.95.

Childhood in America
"Educators, bureaucrats and advocates heatedly discuss the roles of family, government and community in reversing the problems of teen pregnancies, dropouts and child care in America" *(Booklist)*. The program also covers five experimental programs in the United States. 90 mins.
VHS: S19384. $29.95.

The CIA Contra Crack Connection—Parts I and II
Learn the awful facts about the CIA/Contra/Crack connection. Hear award-winning investigative journalist Dennis Bernstein and former DEA agents Celerino Castillo and Micheal Levine as they blow the lid off U.S. government drug involvement. Hosted by Jerry Brown. Each part is 60 mins.
VHS: S33832. $24.95.
Claire Burch, USA, 1997, 120 mins.

CIA: America's Secret Warriors
Granted unprecedented access, the Discovery Channel provides a revealing look at the extraordinary secrecy that allowed the CIA to protect U.S. interests, but also concealed botched operations and involvement in coups, arms distributions and assassinations in its 50-year history. Narrated by Liev Schreiber. 150 mins.
VHS: S31722. $29.95.

CIA: The Secret Files
This four-part, collector's boxed set is a behind-the-scenes portrait of the Central Intelligence Agency and its intriguing cast of characters. The show chronicles covert missions, unsanctioned wars, diabolical coups and illegal assassinations. With unprecedented access into the inner workings of the CIA, this program reveals the nature of the work of the "organization dedicated to secrecy and survival." Narrated by Jack Perkins. 200 mins.
VHS: S17902. $59.95.

CNN Video: Arms Race on America's Streets
In this riveting documentary, produced by America's number one all news network, the violence caused by the arms race on America's streets is examined in depth. It is an invaluable contribution to the ongoing debate around the role of guns in our society. 50 mins.
VHS: S21107. $14.98.

CNN Video: Work in Progress
America's workplace is being transformed by evolving technology and the new global interdependency. The result is greater stress as workers strive to compete under threat of losing their livelihood. This documentary explores these factors as they impact the workaday world. 45 mins.
VHS: S21109. $14.98.

Cocaine...The Source and the Consequences
This film chillingly portrays narco terrorism: how cocaine is grown by the mountainous native tribes in Colombia, sold through huge drug cartels that control entire governments, and ultimately finances third world unrest. 45 mins.
VHS: S09201. $39.95.

Committed to Choice: Women of Faith Speak Out on Reproductive Freedom
Covers a range of issues which illustrate the depth and complexity of freedom of choice for persons of faith. 36 mins.
VHS: S31650. $39.95.

Conversation with Ross Perot
This 75-minute interview shows where Ross Perot stands on a variety of issues as an American, a Texas businessman and a potential world leader. His faith in common sense and traditional values are expressed, as are his efforts to free MIA's in Southeast Asia.
VHS: S16707. $19.98.
Sue Ann Taylor, USA, 1992, 75 mins.

The Cosmic Joke
A compelling documentary on the consequences of the global population explosion. Experts predict the population will double in the next 100 years. This two-part program looks at the issues and solutions. The first program looks at innovative efforts in Mexico and Indonesia to control birth rates. The second program examines women's roles and education and their relation to overpopulation. 120 mins.
VHS: S19375. $49.95.

The Cost of Caring
Addressing the financial and emotional impact of long term care for the elderly, the stories of three married couples and their families reveal limitations in our national health care system. A dramatically important study to individuals coping with current policies affecting health care. 30 mins.
VHS: S16386. $39.95.

Culture of Aging
Attitudes toward aging and the aged vary from culture to culture. This program looks at how older people remain determined to lead active and productive lives in a world that seems to place a greater value on the pleasures of youth than on the wisdom and experience of age. Produced by Maryknoll Media. 28 mins.
VHS: S09068. $24.95.

Dialogues with Elie Wiesel

A fascinating five-part series on the challenging issues of our times. Taking on current controversies, Nobel Prize winner Elie Wiesel and *Open Mind* host Richard D. Heffner lead an exciting inquiry into the promising possibilities that lie ahead. Each tape includes two programs: Volume 1: *Am I My Brother's Keeper* and *The Use and Misuse of Memory*; Volume 2: *Nationalism and World Peace* and *Taking Life: An Act of Mercy?*; Volume 3: *Political Correctness* and *Genetic Engineering*; Volume 4: *Religion and Politics* and *The Intellectual in Our Lives*; and Volume 5: *Capital Punishment* and *The Role of the State*. 270 mins.
VHS: S34242. $119.95.

The Election

The concluding video polls a wide range of voters and leads a discussion about social, political and economic difficulties of the country.
VHS: S16885. $19.95.

Enemy Mine

Gil Rossellini presents images of six modern European countries in conflict in this series which "give[s] voice to ordinary people whose lives are forever altered by ethnic violence."
Albania: White Faces. This film was the first Western film shot in Albania. It shows the horrors of family feuding which has been a constant problem in the Balkans for centuries. One man acts to stop the violence. 55 mins.
VHS: S26725. $29.95.
Cyprus: The Moment Time Stood Still. The memories and nightmares of the Greek Cypriots who have been separated from their homeland by the Turkish invasion of 1974 inspired this sensitive and provocative film. 55 mins.
VHS: S26722. $29.95.
Germany: Cracks in the Land. This film explores the psychological aftermath of the falling of the Berlin wall. Two people who now share the same city have an ironic and sad affinity. 55 mins.
VHS: S26724. $29.95.
Hungary: Where the Water Is Deep. A murder outlines the hatred between Hungarians and their Gypsy neighbors. Mistrust and anger divide this beautiful land. 55 mins.
VHS: S26723. $29.95.
Italy: South of Italy. Giuseppe's bank once offered hope to small local farmers, but mobsters have forced his hand. Now Giuseppe must face the specter of a takeover from a Northern institution certain to be less sympathetic to local needs. 55 mins.
VHS: S26720. $29.95.
Northern Ireland: The Kickhams. An unusual football team is at the heart of this controversial story. The Kickhams are at the heart of Belfast, and as a result, have no playing field of their own. 55 mins.
VHS: S26721. $29.95.

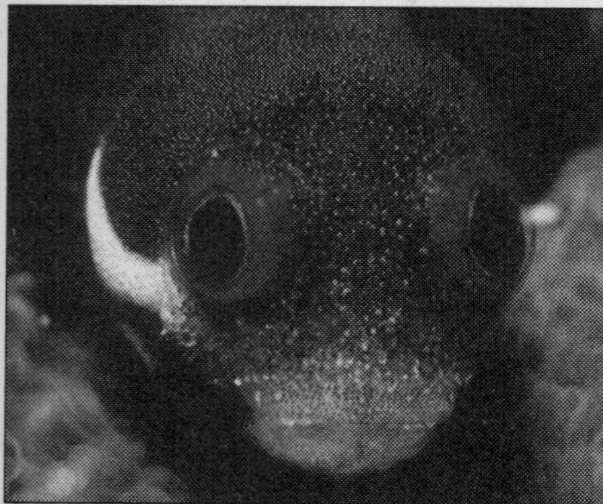

The Expanding Nuclear Club

Though the arms race between the U.S. and the USSR appears to be over, 15 other nations are possible new members of this exclusive club. The proliferation of these deadly weapons may actually be encouraged by the spread of nuclear power plants throughout the world, a process supported by the U.S. government. This documentary illuminates the dimensions of this growing problem with the help of key advisors, including former arms control negotiator Paul Warneke. 28 mins.
VHS: S21583. $25.00.

Family of Women

Women's peace encampments are vital sources of power in today's feminist movement. Meet the women who follow this dream in the 90's. USA, 36 mins.
VHS: S26821. $29.95.

Fragile Balance (1955-1961)

The Cold War and arms race spur technological innovation that keeps the world on edge. Sputnik, the Soviet satellite, brings a new dimension to this competition. Soon a newly elected President Kennedy will redefine American military policy in order to pursue a goal in outer space. 24 mins.
VHS: S23598. $99.95.

Harlem Grace

What happens when a Harvard graduate with a promising future, from a prominent family, decides to move into Harlem to help the homeless? This film, based on the life of Joseph Holland, New York State's Commissioner of Housing, chronicles the impact of one individual on the lives of homeless men. 31 mins.
VHS: S33289. $19.95.

In the Life

This award-winning TV series reflects the rich diversity and accomplishments of the gay community nationwide. Covers politics, health, global issues, art, culture, current events, and comics. 85 mins.
VHS: S34560. $29.95.

Kids in the Crossfire: Violence in America: Answering Children's Questions

Peter Jennings moderates this live special which examines violence in our society through the eyes of America's youth. 70 mins.
VHS: S22990. $19.98.

Life Remembers 1993

Life magazine's retrospective of the personalities and events that made the year 1993 a memorable year: Audrey Hepburn, Arthur Ashe, Thurgood Marshall, Rudolph Nureyev, Dizzy Gillespie, Lillian Gish, and many more. 60 mins.
VHS: S20532. $14.98.

Man and the State: Burke and Paine on Revolution

Locked in debate, Burke and Paine state their conflicting views on man, political change, and liberty. Events from the French Revolution are dramatically re-enacted in front of them, underscoring the importance of their concerns. 28 mins.
VHS: S23699. $79.95.

Man and the State: Machiavelli on Political Power

Niccolo Machiavelli debates his influential ideas on political power. The resulting film will stimulate discussion on contemporary problems in government, history and literature. 28 mins.
VHS: S23697. $79.95.

Man and the State: Marx and Rockefeller on Capitalism

Pushed into the 20th century, these 19th-century figures debate the evolution of their opposing philosophies, communism and capitalism. 26 mins.
VHS: S23702. $79.95.

Mandela and DeKlerk

Sidney Poitier gives a compelling performance as African National Congress co-founder Nelson Mandela, whose commitment to the cause of freedom took him from political prisoner to the presidency of South Africa. Michael Caine stars as moderate minister F.W. DeKlerk, elected after Mandela's tactics led to the ousting of conservative president P.W. Botha. With Tina Lifford as Winnie Mandela.
VHS: S31745. $19.98.
Laser: LD76299. $39.99.
Joseph Sargent, USA, 1997, 114 mins.

Manufacturing Consent: Noam Chomsky and the Media

This remarkable Canadian documentary is a riveting look at the political life and times of the controversial author, linguist and radical philosopher, Noam Chomsky. Chomsky provides shocking examples of media deception as he analyzes the media and democratic societies. A film which has achieved cult status in its remarkable call to Chomsky's charge for viewers to "extricate themselves from this web of deceit by undertaking a course of intellectual self-defense."
VHS: S21851. $39.95.
Mark Achbar/Peter Wintonick, Canada, 1993, 180 mins.

May Day—May Day

Filmed in seven countries on International Labour Day, 1987, this video is about the abuse of trade unionists' human rights and their struggle to make their voices heard and achieve official recognition. The video places special emphasis on Guatemala. Produced by Amnesty International. 1987, 30 mins.
VHS: S09780. $19.95.

The Military on Campus

Nearly 300 universities receive millions in research funds from the military, with some 60 campuses getting over 3 million dollars each year. Seventy percent of computer science research money from the federal government also comes from the military. What role should the military play in the intellectual life of America's colleges and universities now that the cold war is over? 28 mins.
VHS: S21589. $25.00.

Modern America Patriot: Mark Hatfield

Republican senator from Oregon Mark Hatfield talks about war: his personal experiences in World War II and his opposition to the Vietnam Gulf Wars. Not a pacifist, Hatfield believes in a well-trained military, but he is very critical of the economic motives of war, military merchants and their impact on foreign policy, military assistance and arms sales. High school to adult. 1997, 27 mins.
VHS: S31915. $360.00.

My Name Is Abbie: A Portrait of Abbie Hoffman

Abbie Hoffman documents the trial of the Chicago 7 in his first interview after seven years in hiding. 60 mins.
VHS: S31851. $24.95.

New Foundations: Visions for Democratic Socialism

A lucid exposition that locates the ideas of Socialism in America's past and future. "A lively film that shows Socialism as a way of living, not an 'ism'" (Barbara Garson, author of *The Electronic Sweatshop*). 30 mins.
VHS: S31652. $49.95.

New Immigrants

Immigration is a continuing American story, and each period brings different faces and different elements to a growing America. Who the newest immigrants are, and how they join American society in the last decade of the 20th century is the focus of this program. 28 mins.
VHS: S10783. $29.95.

New US-USSR Relationship

Barbara Marx Hubbard, leading futurist speaker, currently serves as host for those who travel to the USSR to establish groups fostering the concept of the Global Family. In this forum she explores US and USSR relations and their impact on the Global Family. 75 mins.
VHS: S10224. $29.95.

The Nomination

This program re-examines the fortunes and failures of the winning candidates from both parties, and considers the prospect of an independent challenger and its impact on the selection of the president.
VHS: S16884. $19.95.

Oliver North: Memo to History

No doubt, one of the memos not shredded. Actually, this is a compilation of excerpts of the testimony at the Congressional Iran-Contra hearings. USA, 1987, 90 mins.
VHS: S04501. $19.95.

Out of the Silence: Fighting for Human Rights

In 1948, the Declaration of Human Rights ushered in a new era in human rights awareness. This documentary chronicles the global struggle waged on behalf of all people everywhere. 55 mins.
VHS: S23650. $69.95.

A Perfect Candidate

Sometimes horrifying, often hilarious, *A Perfect Candidate* is a twisted journey into the underbelly of American politics. When former Marine Oliver North re-emerged from the Iran-Contra scandal to run for the U.S. Senate, the filmmakers were granted astonishing access to the backroom games played by the candidates, their handlers and the press. "The best American documentary since *Hoop Dreams*.... Invigorating, entertaining and essential" *(Washington Post)*.
VHS: S32358. $59.95.
R.J. Cutler/David Van Taylor, USA, 1996, 105 mins.

Peter Jennings Reporting: Men, Sex and Rape

Peter Jennings and ABC News travel to Palm Beach, Florida, site of the highly publicized William Kennedy Smith rape trial, to raise questions about men and rape for which no easy answers exist. 75 mins.
VHS: S16795. $29.98.

The Powers of the Presidency: Armed Intervention

Military intervention is a course of action often chosen by the President despite conflicting and continually changing intelligence information. How can the President respond swiftly to complex international situations? This question is posed for the viewer, who must decide when intervention is appropriate. 23 mins.
VHS: S23738. $79.95.

The Powers of the Presidency: Economic Controls

In this open-ended program the powers of the President are examined in regard to the imposition of wage and price controls. The scenario goes like this: there is runaway inflation and the Congress does nothing. Can the President set limits on the economy and what will the effects of this control be? 23 mins.

VHS: S23737. $79.95.

President Clinton: Answering Children's Questions, 1993

In a special town meeting, live from the White House with Peter Jennings, children in the audience and from all over the country have the opportunity to ask questions and voice their concerns to President Bill Clinton. 105 mins.

VHS: S22988. $19.98.

President Clinton: Answering Children's Questions, 1994

One year later, children have another chance to express their opinions and concerns to President Clinton, with Peter Jennings as the moderator. 90 mins.

VHS: S22989. $19.98.

Preventive Diplomacy

Examines the untold story of the elements that avert the tragedy of civil war. Case studies of Burundi in central Africa and Macedonia in the South Balkans are analyzed by Jimmy Carter and other governmental and non-governmental leaders. For those concerned with peace in an era when most of the world's wars are civil wars, this is an extremely hopeful presentation.

VHS: S31919. $49.95.

The Primary

Three documentaries from the innovative program *The '90s* that provide a kaleidoscopic view of the inner dynamics of the American political process. *The Primary* considers the events, activities and strategic importance of Arkansas governor Bill Clinton's primary victory in Illinois opposite Carol Mosely Braun's stunning, historically unprecedented contest for the Democratic nomination in the U.S. Senate. "A video tour de force," wrote the *Chicago Tribune's* Rick Kogan.

VHS: S16883. $29.95.

The Prize

An eight-part documentary based on Daniel Yergin's book on the relationship between oil, money and politics. The documentary opens with the initial well drilled in 1859 Pennsylvania, and traces the western democracies' increasing dependence on oil, the foundation of "oil economies," and the various global and regional wars fought over its control, including the Iraqi's invasion of Kuwait and the aftermath of the Gulf War. Narrated by Donald Sutherland, the program interweaves first-person accounts, interviews, letters and personal memoirs to create a dazzling and provocative vision. Two programs per tape. Each tape is approximately 60 mins.

The Prize, Vol. 1: The Trust Busters/The Oil Wars.
VHS: S17720. $49.95.
The Prize, Vol. 2: The Black Giant/Oil, War and Strategy.
VHS: S17721. $49.95.
The Prize, Vol. 3: Fill'er Up/A New Center of Gravity.
VHS: S17722. $49.95.
The Prize, Vol. 4: The Oil Weapon/Oil's New World Order.
VHS: S17723. $49.95.
The Prize, Complete Set.
VHS: S17724. $99.95.

Secret Weapons

This six-volume, 13-part series takes a fact-filled look at the frenzy and fury of war-fueled advances in the shrouded technology of battle, exploring the secret development of the physical and tactical weapons of modern war. Hosted by John Palmer, the series cuts across the phenomenon of war, visiting key military installations and uncovering secret events, devices and tactics. Parts include: The Jet Revolution, The Fabulous Flops, The Fighting Elite, The Foot Soldier, Hide and Seek, Waves of Steel, The Shark Hunters, The Nuclear Hammer, The Expendables, Rapid Fire, The Armor Busters, The Sharpshooters, and Firestorm. 5 hrs., 48 mins.

VHS: S30251. $79.98.

Stopping War Before It Starts

Enhanced with on-the-scene visuals and fascinating historical footage, leading practitioners—including Brian Atwood of USAID and Louise Diamond from the Institute for Multi-Track Diplomacy-provide an overview of the important new field of preventive diplomacy.

VHS: S31917. $49.95.

Talks by Michael Parenti

Michael Parenti is the brilliant observer of press and media and its manipulation of contemporary politics, reality and values, and the author of books including *Inventing Reality, Democracy for the Few, Power and the Powerless, The Sword and the Dollar* and *Make Believe Media: The Politics of Entertainment*. In this series of videotapes, he discusses some of the dominant issues of our time.

Crimes of Empire: Bush's War in the Middle East. Takes a close look at the excuses given for intervention in the Gulf and the real, underlying reasons (updated version).
VHS: S15595. $19.95.
Democracy and U.S. Intervention. Looks at the differences between a Marxist and liberal analysis of political life, and the myth of "national security."
VHS: S15589. $19.95.
Human Nature and Politics. Looks at the political dimensions of "What is Human Nature?" A critique of the conservative concepts.
VHS: S15592. $19.95.
Imperialism and the Bush Hypocrisy. A critique of Bush's foreign and domestic policies, including the invasion of Panama.
VHS: S15593. $19.95.
Imperialism, Drugs and Social Control. Parenti discusses the link between US intervention and the CIA's use of drugs abroad and at home.
VHS: S15594. $19.95.
Inventing Reality. Parenti discusses the monopoly ownership of the media, news distortions and ideological control.
VHS: S15586. $19.95.
Michael Parenti Interview. Includes discussions of Corporatism and the US political scene, as well as media distortion of the Gulf War.
VHS: S15596. $19.95.
Monopoly Culture and Academic Freedom. The class basis of our "independent" cultural, legal and educational institutions.
VHS: S15587. $19.95.
Rambo and the Swarthy Hordes. A talk Michael Parenti gave in Hollywood on the political images of the entertainment media. Treats actual movies that propagate imperialistic and racist themes.
VHS: S15591. $19.95.
The Political Uses of Religion. Parenti examines the ways in which the Right use religion to manipulate people; contains kind words about liberation theology.
VHS: S15588. $19.95.
The Sword and the Dollar. The history of imperialism and the forced mal-development of the Third World are examined.
VHS: S15590. $19.95.

Terrorism: The New World War

Beirut, London, Paris: these are the battlegrounds of the modern world. Their goals may be political or religious, but the brutal reality of terrorist activities has spread through the world in epidemic proportions. From ABC News. 60 mins.

VHS: S12683. $24.98.

Torture in the Eighties

An overview of the use of torture by governments around the world, produced as a part of Amnesty International's Campaign to end the use of torture of prisoners and detainees around the world. 1985, 14 mins.

VHS: S06889. $15.00.

TVTV: Four More Years

A documentary on the anarchic events surrounding the 1972 Republican National Convention in Miami, framed through the guerrilla tactics of the outlaw television activists at TVTV, who trained their cameras on the pure spectacle of the absurd. B&W, 60 mins.

VHS: S15557. $34.95.

United States Elections: How We Vote

All elements of the voting process, including registration, voting, tabulation, and procedures that protect the rights of voters and candidate are explored in this film. 14 mins.

VHS: S23736. $79.95.

Walk with the People

Why would people leave their own country, their families and even profitable careers to serve the poor in Asia, Africa, and Latin America? In this film, a Maryknoll priest, Sister, Brother and lay missioner speak of what motivates them, and of the joys and heartaches of giving themselves to those in need. Produced by Maryknoll Media. 28 mins.

VHS: S04936. $24.95.

Wall Street Journal Video: Emerging Powers

Four one-hour guides to the emerging economic powerhouses of China, Mexico, Brazil and India are joined in this informative video set. It offers insider information to these fast-growing markets with detailed analysis of the risks, from political instability and roller-coaster currency to a lack of current and reliable information. Investors will get a unique view on these tempting but unknown developing economies.

VHS: S27658. $79.95.
David Royle, USA, 1996

What Is the Third World?

Does the term "third world" still have any meaning? What are the obligations of developed nations toward developing countries? What does faith demand of us as individuals with respect to our brothers and sisters in the "Third World" nations? And what are the real needs of these countries? Produced by Maryknoll Media. 28 mins.

VHS: S09069. $24.95.

Women in Construction

Five women, a carpenter, an architect, a sheetmetalworker and plumbing and electrical apprentices, discuss the challenges they face in the traditionally male world of construction. 15 mins.

VHS: S22155. $126.50.

Women in Policing

Six police officers with differing specialties and varying levels of experience present their views on this unique career. It's definitely a job with a future; one of these women has been at it for over 20 years. 15 mins. Resource guide available.

Resource Guide.
VHS: S25782. $45.00.
Video.
VHS: S25769. $95.00.

Women's Options: The Experience and Wisdom of Seven Low Income Women

Straightforward, often funny stories and thoughts of seven low-income women combine to shatter myths about poverty, domestic violence, men, public assistance and race. 60 mins.

VHS: S31649. $59.95.

ENVIRONMENTAL & GLOBAL ISSUES

Acid Rain

This program explains clearly how acid rain is created and what is being done to better understand its effects on the environment. Winner of Gold Medal at the International Film and TV Festival in New York. 36 mins.

VHS: S12268. $104.00.

After the Warming

James Burke moderates this series on the aftermath of the Greenhouse Effect. "Fast-paced production, visually interesting and full of ideas to mull over and to act on" *(Washington Post)*.

After the Warming: Tape One. Burke suggests the ecological impact of what various warming scenarios beginning in the year 2050 will contain. Burke shows "how life on earth has often altered by changing weather patterns." 60 mins.
VHS: S18059. $29.95.
After the Warming: Tape Two. Burke studies the means that could be employed to respond to the environmental crisis, particularly the impact of global warming on food supplies and the effects of increased rainfall and deforestation. 60 mins.
VHS: S18060. $29.95.
After the Warming: Complete Set.
VHS: S18061. $49.95.

Along the Erie Canal

Tour the Erie Canal, past and present, with Tom Grasso, President of the New York State Canal Society, as he explores the beauty and history of this great artificial river and its rebirth as a timeless attraction for visitors from around the world.

VHS: S33895. $24.95.
Bruce Pacho Lane, USA, 1998, 37 mins.

The Amazing Coral Reef

Created especially for elementary-age children, this program provides an introduction to the wonder and importance of the world's coral reefs, along with the environmental problems harming them. Includes study guides. 20 mins.

VHS: S33773. $59.95.

America's Defense Monitor: Bringing the Troops Home

A major portion of our military budget goes to support 500,000 American troops stationed abroad at over 300 foreign military bases. Bush administration supporters advocate keeping sizeable forces overseas, while other experts believe, in light of recent world events, that it is time to dramatically reduce the U.S. military presence around the world. 1990, 29 mins.

VHS: S13962. $29.95.

America's Defense Monitor: National Security in the 90's

With the Cold War officially over, what constitutes our national security? This provocative, forward-thinking episode asks the experts how we can secure a strong America—economically, socially, and militarily. 1990, 29 mins.

VHS: S13958. $29.95.

America's Defense Monitor: The Great Arms Debate

What should the size, role, and cost of our armed forces be now in the post-Cold War era? Is there any hope for a "peace dividend?" Some call for a smaller military and restraint in the weapons programs. Former Defense Secretary Cheney makes the case for staying the course. 1990, 29 mins.

VHS: S13961. $29.95.

America's Defense Monitor: The Language of War

"Pre-Dawn Vertical Insertion." "Violence Processing." "Permanent Pre-hostility." Does the military use language to clarify or camouflage the reality of war and the preparations for war? Though sometimes humorous, this program raises very serious questions about the critical impact of language on public debate and public policy. 1990, 29 mins.
VHS: S13960. $29.95.

America's Defense Monitor: The UN's Blue Helmets

The United Nation's peacekeeping forces have played a quiet but important role in many parts of the world, helping to monitor and prevent conflicts between warring countries or factions. As the Cold War ends, what will be the world role for the UN? 1990, 29 mins.
VHS: S13959. $29.95.

Atchafalaya

This video documentary offers a history of the Mississippi River system. Man has changed its course and the basin where it enters the Gulf of Mexico. Wilderness expert C.C. Lockwood presents detailed environmental information about this key ecosystem. 26 mins.
VHS: S22387. $54.95.

The Atom and Eve

Produced in 1965 by a consortium of utility companies to promote electricity use and nuclear power, this blend of male chauvinism and conspicuous consumption now provokes both outrage and uproarious laughter as the film follows a scantily-clad housewife through her all-electric day. Proven popular with womens' and anti-nuclear groups, as well as in classes where the nuclear propaganda battle is a subject. 15 mins.
VHS: S31102. $19.95.

Atomic Memories

Before the United States and the Soviet Union learned to live together in peace and harmony, there was a time when mutually assured destruction was a major concern. This nostalgic documentary looks back on an era when the U.S. government felt it was necessary to produce films like *Duck and Cover, The Effects of Atomic Bomb Explosions* and *Survival under Atomic Attack*. Also featured is footage of the A-bomb test at the Bikini Atoll.
VHS: S13314. $19.95.

Battle for the Trees

A multiple award winner, this is a highly effective look at the impact of clearcutting, the potential for alternatives that balance economic needs with forest preservation, and the role of multinational corporations which are increasingly logging old growth forests. 57 mins.
VHS: S23372. $95.00.

Bound by the Wind

This video document presents the dramatic, international impact of nuclear testing on the people who live downwind from the U.S., Soviet and French test sites—people who have suffered extremely high rates of cancer. Includes interviews with Andrei Sakharov and others. USA, 1991, 40 mins.
VHS: S15205. $75.00.

Building Bombs

A rich, personal look at the social and environmental impact of the Savannah River Plant in South Carolina, where weapons-grade plutonium and tritium are manufactured. This is a thoughtful film on an important topic that has proven to be an effective catalyst with a wide-range of audiences. 1989, 54 mins.
VHS: S13957. $95.00.

The Business of Hunger

In many Third World countries, cash crops are exported while the poor go hungry. This phenomenon, one of the major causes of world hunger, is examined in Latin America, Africa, Asia, and the U.S.A. Winner of American Film Festival. 28 mins. Produced by Maryknoll Media.
VHS: S04922. $24.95.

Buster and Me

Robin Goodrow stars as Robin in this award-winning program. Today's children are increasingly aware of the prospect of nuclear war and this awareness affects their lives. *Buster and Me* uses puppets to address these feelings, bring them out in the open, give children the sense that they are not alone and give them a feeling of hope and power.
VHS: S03811. $24.95.
Christina Metcalf, USA, 1983, 28 mins.

Call for Peace: The Military Budget and You

Based on a moving speech by Congressman Ronald V. Dellums, with narration by Harry Belafonte, the film asks, "Do we (the American people) want to live or do we want to die? If we want to live, we must make our every act a furtherance of world peace." Alice Walker, author of *The Color Purple* said, "If we wish to die, all that is required is a continuation of ourselves as we are. Ponder the message of this film and choose to act. Choose to live."
VHS: S03804. $45.00.
Steve Rauh, USA, 1983, 28 mins.

Canary of the Ocean: America's Troubled Reef

Produced by award-winning filmmakers, this engaging film mixes first-person accounts of the Florida reefs before their decline with a look at the variety of human activities found to be causing their ill health. It portrays the stunning beauty of America's fragile undersea kingdom, investigates the serious threats to its health, and profiles some of the concerned people working to preserve it for future generations. Grade 8 to adult. 56 mins.
VHS: S31911. $89.00.

Centerpiece for Peace

In this talk, former astronaut Brian O'Leary explores the possibilities of future space programs. Here he expands on his statement, "we are experiencing a quantum leap in our awareness of ourselves as citizens of the universe, and as leaders of a new society whose exploits hover at the edge of our imagination." 52 mins.
VHS: S10223. $29.95.

Changing Tides Along the Mediterranean

One of the world's most historic seas is dying. This moving documentary follows a group of young people from 14 nations as they come together to learn about these environmental problems and seek solutions. An inspiring example to youth. 23 mins.
VHS: S10890. $45.00.

Chernobyl

The graphic and otherwise unavailable facts about the after-effects of Chernobyl—the blast site, the people and areas affected, and the questions: What are the statistical risks? Who will develop cancer? Whose children will be mutants? The Chernobyl accident is expected to cause an additional 20,000 to 200,000 deaths in Western Europe.
VHS: S05281. $29.95.

Choice or Chance II

The Pentagon spends over $1.5 billion a year for advertising aimed at filling the ranks of the military with young recruits. But for many, the military may be the wrong choice. This colorful, factual presentation explores such questions as: What are a recruiter's promises really worth? Does military training help in civilian life? What are the potential problem areas recruiters ignore? 20 mins.
VHS: S10891. $75.00.

Choices for the Future

John Denver hosts this inspiring new look at options for a peaceful, sustainable future. Featured are perspectives offered by Ted Turner, Ram Dass, astronaut Rust Schweickart, Jean-Michel Cousteau, Robert Muller, Dr. Robert Bourne and others. From the first Choices for the Future Symposium held at Snowmass, Colorado in 1986. Produced by he Windstar Foundation. 45 mins.
VHS: S04313. $29.95.

Civilized Defense Plan

A thought-provoking program which illustrates an important proposal for using international economic pressure to help eliminate weapons of mass destruction and reduce armed aggression. Graphic techniques and interviews with experts including Lloyd J. Dumas, Professor of Political Economy at the University of Texas, and Benjamin Ferencz, former chief prosecutor at the Nuremberg War crimes trials. 30 mins.
VHS: S10883. $29.95.

Cleaning Up Toxics at Home

This program gives simple and practical advice on how we can reduce pollution from households and protect our families from the toxic hazards found in our homes. An important, hands-on program for anyone concerned about the potential hazards posed by the chemicals we all use daily. 1990, 30 mins.
VHS: S13945. $59.95.

Cleaning Up Toxics in Business

Small businesses of all kinds are making remarkable changes to protect our environment. This program shows businessmen and women a variety of innovative solutions to comply with increasingly strict environmental regulations. 1990, 30 mins.
VHS: S13946. $59.95.

Common Ground: The Battle for Barton Springs

This award-winning and uplifting documentary shows how the citizens of Austin used the democratic process to protect their endangered natural springs. This is an especially heartening and positive example for social activists. Study guide included. High school to adult. 1994, 28 mins.
VHS: S31913. $69.95.

Common Table

Focus on a new understanding of indigenous cultures and practices in the Philippines and Africa. 28 mins.
VHS: S04923. $24.95.

Connect: A New Ecological Paradigm

Presented by YES! (Youth for Environmental Sanity) and hosted by R.E.M.'s Michael Stipe, *Connect* features leading youth activists from 20 countries to show how youth activism is improving the world's environmental and social problems. Grades 7-12. 1996, 23 mins.
VHS: S31900. $39.95.

Conserving America: Champions of Wildlife

Ospreys in Massachusetts, turtles in Texas, baby bears in Oregon—wherever species are endangered, concerned conservationists are working to restore lost habitat and provide sanctuary for injured birds and animals. 1988, 58 mins.
VHS: S13948. $39.95.

Conserving America: The Challenge on the Coast

Nearly 75% of Americans live within 50 miles of the coast. Yet nearly half of the country's coastal wetlands have disappeared. It's clear today that we all must do our part to protect these invaluable resources. 1989, 58 mins.
VHS: S13950. $39.95.

Conserving America: The Rivers

Only 1% of America's rivers are protected by the Federal Wild and Scenic Rivers Act. Some concerned citizens are lobbying governments to pass protective legislation to keep our rivers safe from pollution, contamination, dams, channelization, and industrial development. 1988, 58 mins.
VHS: S13949. $39.95.

Conserving America: The Wetlands

America's swamps and marshes are our richest and least understood landscapes. 300,000 acres of wetlands disappear each year—filled in to build airports, industrial plants, and housing. But attitudes are changing, and people are beginning to work together to protect these unique habitats. 1990, 58 mins.
VHS: S13951. $39.95.

Coral Reefs: Rainforests of the Sea

Created especially for middle and high school age, this program provides an excellent introduction to the science, ecology and importance of coral reefs, as well as an overview of the serious environmetal problems confronting them. 20 mins.
VHS: S33780. $59.95.

Coyoteland

Jay April used a hand-held camera to document this story about the competition between wildlife and urbanization. A coyote carries away a pet dog, leading residents to call on a trapper. His view of wild life is contrasted with an elderly woman who articulates a defense in favor of the coyote. The result is a humorous and provocative film about the conflicts of contemporary life. 17 mins.
VHS: S21582. $59.95.

Danger at the Beach

Ted Danson explores the 10,000 miles of coastline under siege by rot, decay, dead animals and medical waste. The film documents the destruction of marine life.
VHS: S16879. $14.98.

Dash McTrash and the Pollution Solution

Designed for primary grades, *Dash McTrash* is an excellent course in ecological awareness and action. This collection features five episodes, including his adventures with the Bogs, Anna Mae, Uncle Don, the Big Cleanup, and "E for Ecology."
VHS: S14173. $159.95.

Day After Trinity

This haunting examination of the dawn of the nuclear age focuses on the dramatic events surrounding the development of the first atomic bomb. Featuring interviews with scientists and soldiers, and rare, archival footage, it provides a gripping profile of J. Robert Oppenheimer, the bomb's principal architect, and offers a penetrating commentary on the nature of scientific inquiry, the McCarthy era, and nuclear proliferation.
VHS: S00307. $39.95.
Laser: LD75026. $49.95.
Jon Else, USA, 1981, 88 mins.

Deadly Deception

G.E. does more than "bring good things to life." It also is the industry leader in producing nuclear arms components. This challenging video questions the role of corporate responsibility given the deadly influence exerted by this firm's many nuclear installations. Winner of the Academy Award for Best Documentary.
VHS: S21586. $50.00.
Debra Chasnoff, USA, 1991, 29 mins.

Deafsmith, A Nuclear Folktale

One day Texas farmer John Smith returned home to find a mysterious crew of people placing seismographic cables on his land. That was the start of Deafsmith County's struggle to prevent all of the nation's high-level nuclear waste from being buried beneath their farms. 1990, 43 mins.
VHS: S13953. $79.00.

Defending America: The Price We Pay

A thorough, timely examination of the causes, costs and consequences of military spending. This film takes a close look at a variety of issues, including military waste, procurement policies, the effects on research, contribution to the national debt, impact on jobs, and the trade-offs with social programs. An insightful study. 1989, 58 mins.
VHS: S13964. $75.00.

Direct Connection

Fifteen teenagers from Sierra Mounain High School, California, videotape a message of hope for peace and mutual understanding to an equal number of Soviet students. Produced by Michael Killigrew, 30 mins.
VHS: S04311. $45.00.

Disarmament: A Public Opinion Poll

In June, 1982, there were rallies held throughout the world in support of the U.N. Conference on Disarmament. Video artist Skip Blumberg and hundreds of crew members collaborated on the most expansive video project to date. They recorded more than 3,000 interviews in 60 locations around the world. This tape features the most interesting, most humorous and most eccentric of these interviews with individuals of all races, colors, professions, offering a panorama of characters expressing their hopes, fears and concerns about the nuclear issue. 1982, 30 mins.
VHS: S08527. $29.95.

Does the U.S. Need Nuclear Weapons?

A thought-provoking assessment of our nuclear stockpile of 17,000 weapons at an annual cost of $30 billion. A wide range of political experts and military personnel provides a compelling argument for ridding ourselves of these weapons of mass destruction. 25 mins.
VHS: S23391. $35.00.

A Dream of Peace

In 1987 the entire country of New Zealand became a nuclear free zone, banning nuclear ships from the country's ports. *A Dream of Peace* is a closer look at the motivations and historical developments that led to New Zealand's nuclear-free declaration. Through archival news footage and interviews with key leaders, including former Prime Minister David Lange, the video describes the events surrounding the declaration and its significance for other countries. Produced by the New Zealand Foundation for Peace Studies. 12 mins.
VHS: S11486. $29.95.

Early Warnings

This 1981 film captures the movement against the Seabrook atomic plant at its peak, featuring a 20,000-person rally on the nuclear site, with apearances by Jackson Browne, Dr. John Gofman, Dick Gregory, Amory Lovins, Dr. Benjamin Spock, Pete Seeger and others. 20 mins.
VHS: S31101. $19.95.

The Earth at Risk Environmental Video Series

Former MTV host Kevin Seal presents this fascinating and fun, 10-volume set which examines important environment issues of our time. Science is both important and enjoyable. Each volume is 30 mins.

Acid Rain.
VHS: S24425. $39.95.
Clean Air.
VHS: S24426. $39.95.
Clean Water.
VHS: S24427. $39.95.
Degradation of the Land.
VHS: S24428. $39.95.
Extinction.
VHS: S24429. $39.95.
Global Warming.
VHS: S24430. $39.95.
Nuclear Energy/Nuclear Waste.
VHS: S24431. $39.95.
The Ozone Layer.
VHS: S24432. $39.95.
The Rainforest.
VHS: S24433. $39.95.
Recycling.
VHS: S24434. $39.95.
The Earth at Risk Environmental Video Series. 10-volume set.
VHS: S24435. $349.50.

Earth First! The Struggle for the Australian Rainforest

Highlights the plight of our oldest living link with the past, the majestic rain forests. Set in Australia, the program looks at a 70 square kilometer stand of rainforest, which is all that remains from an age when Australia was the center of a mighty supercontinent called Gondwanaland, covered by a magnificent emerald rainforest. It is also the story of people who went to the most extraordinary lengths to save these rain forests—who stirred the conscience of a nation through their dramatic, risk-taking actions. 58 mins.
VHS: S11489. $39.95.

The Earth Is the Lord's: Ecology as a Religious Concern

Ecologists David Ehrenfeld and Wes Jackson of the Land Institute talk about ways to control environmental damage. Rabbi Ismar Schorsch then explains how Judaism can preserve creation and not abuse it. 60 mins.
VHS: S24501. $29.95.

Eclipse of the Man-Made Sun

The imagery and language used to describe nuclear energy and nuclear weapons are redolent with metaphysical and divinely derived metaphors. This documentary explores how these technologies were presented in ways that continue to impact contemporary society. Animation, archival footage, special effects and commentary from assorted experts illuminate this fascinating idea. 50 mins.
VHS: S21585. $95.00.

Ecocide

This 1982 film vividly reports on the results of unprecedented tactics during the Vietnam War as it shows the threat which a war strategy aimed at the ecology poses. 23 mins.
VHS: S31094. $29.95.

Ecology of the Urban Environment

This program discusses concepts of ecology in relation to improving daily urban life, including issues of sanitation, water supply, air pollution, population, housing patterns and urban wildlife. 28 mins.
VHS: S20282. $29.95.

The Edge of History

Twelve distinguished men and women, including Admiral Noel Gayler, former commander of the Pacific fleet, stress the crucial need for cooperation in international affairs, both in arms controls talks and in citizen diplomacy. Filmed at the Stanford Symposium on the Prevention of Nuclear War. Winner at many film festivals.
VHS: S03795. $29.95.
Ian Thiermann/Vivien Verdon-Roe, USA, 1984, 28 mins.

Experimental Animals

Some 300,000 military personnel were deliberately exposed to nuclear blasts during WWII in an effort to determine whether soldiers could fight and survive the blast. Now coping with serious health problems, these individuals are not receiving the aid they need from the government that used them as human guinea pigs. A compelling story combining archival footage of soldiers and sailors during exposure tests and personal interviews. 35 mins.
VHS: S23389. $79.00.

Exploring Ecology

This program instructs children on the need to preserve the environment. Students are asked to process information and organize solutions to problems pertaining to natural resources, endangered species, ecosystems, non-renewable energy sources and alternative energy resources. For children in grades 4-6.

Air, Water & Soil Resources. An examination of our vital resources—air, water and soil—that explains their importance. The program also shows solutions to pollution and depletion of these resources. 15 mins.
VHS: S19963. $36.95.

Energy Resources. This program studies the importance of nonrenewable energy resources—including fossil fuels. The program examines how the fuels are formed, measured and processed. 13 mins.
VHS: S19965. $36.95.

Future Resources. Emerging technology and valuable energy resources developed for future use, including solar, hydroelectric, wind and geothermal, are contrasted through the advantages and disadvantages they pose to the environment. 13 mins.
VHS: S19966. $36.95.

Wildlife Resources. This program studies wildlife and plant resources, including endangered species. The concepts of eco-systems and habitats and niches are examined. 13 mins.
VHS: S19964. $36.95.

Exploring Ecology, Set.
VHS: S19967. $129.00.

First Strike: Portrait of an Activist

Early one Sunday morning, 28-year-old Susan Komisaruk entered Vandenburg Air Base and spent two uninterrupted hours damaging military computer equipment linked to first-strike missile guidance systems. *First Strike* is a compelling portrait of individual commitment, tracing Komisaruk's evolution from a 22-year-old MBA student at the University of California to her arrest, trial and imprisonment. Produced by Doug Dibble. 38 mins.
VHS: S10885. $39.95.

Folktales for Peace

Three folktales about peace-making, reconciliation and friendship are delivered by world-class storytellers. Tales from West Africa, Appalachia and the Iroquois are told in a compelling cinematic style, in this award-winning video. For all ages. 1996, 22 mins.
VHS: S31901. $29.95.

Fueling the Future

Originally produced for PBS, this comprehensive series looks at energy use in four major areas: transportation, farming, housing and disposable products. Along the way viewers will realize how our values and dreams are shaped by current energy usage, often without regard for the future. Each episode is 58 mins. In *Running on Empty*, lively archival footage recreates the dramatic rise of the automobile as a primary means of transportation within this century. Viable alternative fuels are then examined along with the prospects for revitalizing public transportation. *Hot Wiring America's Farms* relates how heavy fossil fuel use has allowed American farms to become among the most productive on the planet. Yet this very success may ultimately destroy the lands upon which we depend for survival. This episode examines the impact of energy intensive agriculture and presents more energy-efficient alternatives. *No Deposit, No Return* demonstrates how America's throw-away lifestyle provides many conveniences, but how much energy are we simply throwing out with the trash? This video reveals the enormous costs of this wastefulness and shows how we can get to the core of the waste problem. And *No Place Like Home* discusses how today's suburban communities force residents to be continually on the go, consuming large quantities of fuel and human energy in the process. This episode shows how these communities evolved in the era of cheap energy and what some designers are doing to counteract this trend.
VHS: S21567. $299.00.

Future in the Cradle

Using the Plan of Action, an agreement forged at the United Nations Cairo Populaton Conference, as a way of introducing the issue of our population future, this hard-hitting program paints a vivid picture of where the world stands today in the race between education and catastrophe. Ages 14 to adult. 1996, 20 mins.
VHS: S31921. $59.95.

Generation Earth

This video and 46-page guide present an inspiring look at a wide variety of hands-on student environmental education and action programs in America's urban and rural high schools. Students are involved in a range of creative activities in their schools, including environmental audits of campuses and local businesses, monitoring water quality, gardening and composting, mentoring younger students, seeking environmental justice, and creating sideshows, documentaries and newspapers. "Extremely useful, timely, entertaining.... Offers an array of fabulous ideas for making school curricula relevant, effective, and fun. Highly recommended" *(Video Librarian)*. 40 mins.
VHS: S31212. $39.95.

Genetic Time Bomb

Because of a dramatic decline in crop diversity, the world may be facing a serious shortage in the food supply. A look at the agricultural changes that could lead to catastrophe, the importance of maintaining biodiversity and the increase in "seed savers"—those individuals who are cultivating thousands of rare and threatened species of fruits and vegetables. 50 mins.
VHS: S23378. $150.00.

Get It Together

A positive, fast-paced look at the contributions of young people of all races to transform their communities and protect the environment. Produced by Youth for Youth, the video profiles several organizations, including Detroit Summer, youth working to improve America's inner cities; YouthBuild in New York, which builds low-income housing; and young Mexican-American women in California speaking out against pollution. 28 mins.
VHS: S23363. $59.95.

Ghosts Along the Freeway

The building of the freeway system displaces thousands of homeowners. This is a concise, highly effective look at the impact on two neighborhoods of the arrival of a superhighway. Historic photographs and personal interviews with former residents merge to create a memorable, prize-winning video on the environment, transportation and urban development. 10 mins.
VHS: S23385. $79.00.

Global Brain

World-renowned philosopher, scientist and humanitarian Peter Russell presents an empowering and optimistic vision of humanity's potential. This captivating program is used by U.S. diplomats, English and Swedish television, and multinational corporations in management development programs. Based on Peter Russell's best-selling book.
VHS: S03810. $39.95.
Chris Hall, Great Britain, 1985, 35 mins.

Global Dumping Ground: The International Traffic in Hazardous Waste

Few Americans realize that the hazardous waste we generate here is one of our country's leading exports to third world nations. This PBS Frontline special report reveals how toxic exports have become big business—and a serious health hazard to the citizens of foreign nations. 1990, 60 mins.
VHS: S13947. $99.95.

Green Plans

Presents a hopeful and empowering look at how two countries have supported national plans for sustainable development. Competing interests in the Netherlands and New Zealand were brought together to hammer out a comprehensive national environmental policy-or Green Plan. This program profiles how this new approach works and looks at efforts to adopt Green Plans underway in the U.S. and in other countries. 56 mins.
VHS: S31213. $95.00.

Greenbucks: The Challenge of Sustainable Development

Major corporations have responded to environmental regulations with concrete steps that recognize the limits of development. Volkswagen and ABB are two firms who are developing cleaner, renewable technologies compatible with both the environment and profitability. This tape will help inspire other business people to understand the relationship of the environment to the future of economic development. 55 mins.
VHS: S21577. $150.00.

Greenhouse Crisis: The American Response

Based on research by the Union of Concerned Scientists, this video details the potential consequences of global warming, and stresses the need for energy efficiency and renewable forms of energy. Specific ways individuals can help to resolve this critical environmental problem are highlighted. Produced by the Union of Concerned Scientists. 11 mins.
VHS: S12320. $20.00.

The Greening of Cuba

Profiles Cuban farmers and scientists working to reinvent a sustainable agriculture, based on ecological principals and local knowledge rather than imported agricultural inputs. High school to adult. Spanish with English subtitles. 1995, 38 mins.
VHS: S31907. $69.95.

Greenpeace's Greatest Hits

Featuring the daring true-life adventures of the dedicated Greenpeace volunteers who risk arrest, assault, and even their lives to stop pollution, slow the nuclear arms race and save wildlife. There are no special effects here—just real men and women putting themselves through some of the most hair-raising exploits ever seen. 60 mins.
VHS: S14095. $29.95.

Growing Like a Weed

Green, weed-free lawns are a North American obsession at odds with the environment that are only sustainable through extreme chemical dependence. This program encourages alternative methods by revealing how damaging lawn maintenance can be and by showcasing different, easier to maintain ground-covering plants. 29 mins.
VHS: S21579. $59.95.

Hawaii in Transition

Some citizens in Hawaii are at the forefront of developing a sustainable vision for America. Practices of sustainable agriculture, composting and integrated land use are all part of a program which encourages harmony with the forces of nature, while providing models for necessary change for all 50 states. 28 mins.
VHS: S31210. $95.00.

Heading for Shore: The Struggle to Save America's Coasts

Looks at the impact rising population is having on our coastal areas and the policy choices that can help protect our fragile shorelines. Looks at sewage pollution in Boston harbor, rapid growth and toxic pollution in Puget Sound, and the massive loss of vital wetlands in Louisiana. 29 mins.
VHS: S33771. $89.95.

Heroes of the Earth

An inspiring testimony to the power of individual action, this story profiles people who are fighting to protect the environment, often at great personal risk. Hosted by Ed Begley, Jr. 45 mins.
VHS: S23374. $59.95.

How Then Shall We Live?

This is a unique, independently-produced television series nationally broadcast on PBS, focused on the issues of consciousness and human survival.
America's Secret Nuclear Policy. Daniel Ellsberg, whose release of *The Pentagon Papers* helped to end the Vietnam War, reconstructs a hidden history of American nuclear diplomacy. "The United States has used its nuclear weapons about a dozen times…secretly. Used them the way a gun is used when you point it at somebody's head in a confrontation, whether you pull the trigger or not. The American people didn't know much of what was happening. We were lied to throughout that process." 56 mins.
VHS: S04758. $49.95.
Caring for an Endangered Planet. Dr. Helen Caldicott, M.D., founder of Physicians for Social Responsibility, proposes options for protecting and preserving life on earth: "The diagnosis is that we have a terminally ill planet. When terminally ill patients come into the emergency room, we work on them, we put them in intensive care, and very occasionally, one survives with absolutely dedicated work and a total commitment to their salvation. But there's no short cut. You've got to really make a total commitment. And the commitment is to save the planet." 50 mins.
VHS: S04757. $49.95.
Dialogue for Human Survival. Ram Dass and Daniel Ellsberg explore the interrelationships of their spiritual and political paths toward peace. Ellsberg: "I take as my preoccupation the postponing and avoiding of a nuclear war." Dass: "I also would like to have my actions reduce the probability of some kind of holocaust." 58 mins.
VHS: S04759. $49.95.

Hunger and Land at Home and Overseas

Third World farmers have long faced the problem of being forced off their land by expanding agribusiness corporations. Today many American farmers are losing their land to high debts, high interest, high costs. The family farm is being replaced by the corporate farm. What are the relationships between this trend here and the situation of farmers in Asia, Africa and Latin America? Produced by Maryknoll Media. 28 mins.
VHS: S06267. $24.95.

The Infinite Voyage: Crisis in the Atmosphere

Learn about this fragile planet and what can be done to save it in this absorbing and timely program. 58 mins.
VHS: S16463. $14.98.

The Infinite Voyage: Fires of the Mind

This exciting voyage takes you on a trip into the complex universe of the human brain. Find out how we think, learn and create. 58 mins.
VHS: S16464. $14.98.

The Infinite Voyage: Sail On, Voyager

Share the joy of discovery as the "Voyager" spacecraft travels over four billion miles, gathering previously unknown facts about the solar system. 58 mins.
VHS: S16465. $14.98.

A Jewish Perspective on the Environment

In this documentary produced by the Jewish Theological Seminary of America and the Coalition on the Environment and Jewish Life, you'll take a fascinating journey through the Bible and along the Appalachian Trail as experts in the fields of science, religion and philosophy hike, camp and explore the world of nature and share their thoughts and concerns on the intersection of Judaism, the environment and justice. One hour.
VHS: S30960. $34.95.

The Keepers of Eden

An environmentally aware video that provides a guided tour of the innovative efforts by important zoo and park administrators and scientists to fight off the rapid decline of various species of wildlife.
VHS: S17731. $14.98.

Kimbark: Focus on Environmental Education

Parents, teachers and administrators interested in how environmental education can be incorporated into all aspects of the primary school curriculum will find this program which examines the system set up at the Kimbark Elementary School in San Bernadino, California both stimulating and inspiring. 1988, 30 mins.
VHS: S13940. $35.00.

Large Dams, False Promises

The direct result of building dams worldwide is the major destruction of vast ecosystems and uprooting of ancient cultures who live along those areas being dammed. Are large dams a wise way to manage waterways or could smaller scale alternatives be explored in order to maintain existing cultures that are being so drastically affected? 36 mins.
VHS: S23384. $89.00.

Last Epidemic

Called "overwhelming," "harrowing," and "devastating" by newspapers including the *San Francisco Chronicle, Washington Post* and *Video Review*, this powerful film conveys in plain language the effects of one or more nuclear weapons on a civilian population, while using visuals which actually show the effects of a nuclear explosion. It describes the drastic damage to the environment and the long-range devastation to the planet.
VHS: S03780. $29.95.
Eric Thiermann/Ian Thiermann, USA, 1981, 28 mins.

The Last Resort

This 1978 film chronicles the roots of the long-ranging controversy and mass actions against nuclear power construction. An exciting and essential primer in understanding the atomic controversy and the local and global issues that are behind it. "An important documentary. Until someone comes up with a workable answer to atomic wastes, pictures like this should be a must for public education" (Archer Winston, *NY*). 60 mins.
VHS: S31096. $29.95.

Life on Earth Perhaps

At times whimsical, at times terrifyingly blunt, this film looks at the unthinkable—Nuclear War—in a way that brings the issues into sharp focus. Cleverly put together mixing animated and documentary footage, this British production confronts the history of war.
VHS: S04309. $45.00.
Oliver Postgate, 29 mins.

Living with Disaster

A documentary that considers the groundbreaking methods scientists are developing to more accurately gauge natural catastrophes such as earthquakes, volcanoes and hurricanes.
VHS: S17732. $14.98.

Logging Siberia

One of the world's most important environmental battles is taking place in the largest remaining ancient forest on earth. A portrait of the beauty of the Siberian forest, the dangers it faces, and forest policy alternatives that could help preserve the Taiga. 28 mins.
VHS: S23371. $125.00.

Losing Control?

Bill Kurtis hosts this program, which questions whether a nuclear war could begin by accident, even with warmer relations between the U.S. and the Soviet Union. The heart of the film is a frightening, plausible scenario that starts in the Middle East and escalates to an unintended confrontation between the two superpowers. Among the experts featured are former Defense Secretary Robert McNamara, Senator Sam Nunn, former Assistant Secretary of Defense Richard Perle and MIT computer scientist Joseph Weizenbaum. 58 mins.
VHS: S11487. $45.00.

Lovejoy's Nuclear War
Awarded the John Grierson award, this 1975 documentary classic follows Sam Lovejoy as he topples a nuclear power plant project tower in Montague, Massachusetts, and turns himself in to the police. "A very thoughtful and provocative account of an original and stubborn one-man war against nuclear power. Muted and underplayed, it is one of the few genuinely consciousness-changing and organically political films of the last few years" (Amos Vogel, *Film Comment*). 60 mins.
VHS: S31095. $29.95.
Daniel Keller, 1977

Magnificent Fish: Forgotten Giants
Deep sea and archival footage dispell myths and present shocking statistics on the lives of sharks, tunas and billfish, the apex predators of the ocean food chain. 15 mins.
VHS: S33778. $49.95.

Many Faces of Homelessness
Homelessness is a worldwide and growing phenomenon. The problems of homeless people are poorly understood and are challenging societies and individuals in new ways. Being homeless can mean a lot more than being houseless. It is also a symptom of value breakdowns in society. Special insights from those involved with homeless people bring to life video features from Hong Kong and Bolivia. Produced by Maryknoll Media. 28 mins.
VHS: S06266. $24.95.

March for Disarmament
A documentary that captures the spirit and essence of the historic June 12, 1982, March for Disarmament. From extensive coverage of the event, the tape features Joan Baez, Theodore Bikel, Dr. Helen Caldicott, Dick Gregory, Abbie Hoffman, Coretta Scott King, Holly Near, Susan Sarandon, and a crowd of nearly a million. Produced by Willow Mixed Media. USA, 1982, 28 mins.
VHS: S07413. $34.95.

The Media and the Image of War
A look at how America's image is perceived in terms of war and violence. Is the portrayal of war on film and TV creating a false sense of history and values? Leading experts discuss the media and its creation of contemporary myths of American warmongers as heroes. 26 mins.
VHS: S23394. $361.00.

Mile Zero: The Sage Hour
A remarkable story of four Canadian high school students who decided they had to do something to promote nuclear disarmament. So they rounded up a used station wagon and organized a cross-country speaking tour. Their goal was to reach one out of every 20 high school students. The film follows their nine-month adventure as they travel and speak coast-to-coast to 120,000 students in 362 schools, ending with a celebration at "Mile Zero" on the Pacific Coast. Co-produced by the National Film Board of Canada. 48 mins.
VHS: S10887. $39.95.

The Military and the Environment
Is the Pentagon protecting us or poisoning us? The military uses and disposes of huge quantities of the most deadly substances known: nuclear wastes, nerve gas, and hundreds of toxic chemicals. Yet the handling of these substances is often done secretly and without any civilian regulation or oversight. State representatives and journalists shed light on the military's soiled record in this area. A remarkable study. 1990, 29 mins.
VHS: S13944. $25.00.

Need for Christian Peacemaking
Father George Zabelka, chaplain for the men who dropped atomic bombs on Hiroshima and Nagasaki, is featured in this moving statement about his conversion to peacemaking, the basis for Christian peacemaking, and his personal testimony against nuclear madness.
VHS: S03807. $19.95.
A. Nelson/Eric Thiermann, USA, 1986, 28 mins.

The Non-Proliferation Treaty: Dead at 25?
This highly informative video examines the Nuclear Non-Proliferation Treaty on the eve of its expiration date, 1995. The treaty has helped stem the spread of nuclear weapons and is looked at in ways in which it may be improved. 26 mins.
VHS: S23393. $35.00.

Nuclear Bombs in Our Future
An investigation into the world's nuclear weapon supply, what should be done about further acquisition of weapons, and what role the U.S. would play in preventing their spread. Interviews with a range of experts with opposing views on these important issues. 28 mins.
VHS: S23392. $35.00.

The Nuclear Threat at Home
A comprehensive look at the dangers generated by bomb factories, waste created by them, atmospheric nuclear testing, and intentional radiation releases. The need to clean up these sites is imperative, the cost staggering at $300 million. 26 mins.
VHS: S23390. $35.00.

Nuclear Winter: Changing Our Way of Thinking
The most important study of our time by leading scientists reveals that the use of a small fraction of the world's nuclear arsenal would have such devastating climactic consequences that civilization as we know it would be destroyed and the human species would probably become extinct. Dr. Carl Sagan discusses the results of the research into the global consequences of nuclear war.
VHS: S03801. $35.00.

Nuclear Winter: Growing...
A mini-documentary including a six-minute segment incorporating computer graphics and scientific information on the consequences of nuclear war. Designed for workshops, classrooms, or TV as a brief introduction on the subject. 20 mins.
VHS: S03802. $45.00.

Oceanography: Dr. Sylvia Earle
Chief scientist for the National Oceanic and Atmospheric Administration Sylvia Earle, who has spent thousands of hours under water, explains the vital role that plants and animals play in sustaining the ocean's ecosystem. 50 mins.
VHS: S33776. $24.95.

On Wings of a Dream
Presents both ethical and practical pathways that can lead to a better future and a saner present. Producer Dawn Griffin merges intuitive and rational messages in this colorful program, inspiring the viewer to let human instincts play a stronger role in the world's future. High school to adult. 1995, 34 mins.
VHS: S31912. $69.95.

Our Biosphere: The Earth in Our Hands
Robert Redford takes you on a tour of the Smithsonian's National Museum of Natural History and looks at models which scientists have created to help unlock the mysteries of our planet and its fragile ecology. 1991, 55 mins.
VHS: S14546. $29.95.
Laser: CAV. LD72179. $34.95.

Our Fragile Earth: Energy Efficiency and Renewables
First there is a brief history of energy use and the limits of fossil fuel. Then this documentary explores renewable energy resources, including solar energy, wind power, geothermal power, hydropower and biomass. This award-winning work also tells students how to make a difference right now, through sensible conservation techniques. 22 mins.
VHS: S21566. $65.00.

Our Threatened Heritage
Every minute more than 50 acres of tropical forest are destroyed or seriously degraded. Several species a day are lost to extinction as a result. This tape, produced by The National Wildlife Federation, provides a concise overview of the destruction of rain forests and what can be done to stop it. Images of the fascinating wildlife and towering trees are vividly presented along with comments from global experts about the causes and potential solutions to the destruction. 19 mins.
VHS: S10889. $29.95.

Out of the Way Cafe
A fictional film for adults that explores serious questions about the changing American landscape with a light and poignant touch. With imagery that critics have compared to the paintings of Edward Hopper, *Out of the Way Cafe* has been honored by the Uppsala Short Film Festival in Sweden and broadcast on national Swedish television and PBS. High school to adult. 1995, 51 mins.
VHS: S31914. $59.95.

Ozone and the Politics of Medicine
A documentary on the harmful effects of the depletion of the ozone layer and the controversial therapies employed in Europe but banned in the United States and Canada. 30 mins.
VHS: S20153. $29.95.

Ozone: Cancer of the Sky
The destruction of the Earth's ozone layer is one of the most critical environmental issues of our time. What is causing depletion of this fragile layer? How serious a threat does it pose to life on the planet? What can be done to reverse this threat? 40 mins.
VHS: S23367. $79.95.

The Paper Colony
The state of Maine boasts the largest uninhabited area in the lower 48 yet it also has the largest corporate land ownership of any state. Shocking aerial shots of massive clear-cutting interspersed with perspectives of foresters, loggers and industry representatives portray a composite picture of out-of-balance over-harvesting and raise the question of how to develop sustainable forests. High school to adult. 1996, 27 mins.
VHS: S31923. $69.95.

The Peace Tapes
This chronicle follows the peace movement from the '50s to the present. Featuring a myriad of controversial personalities, the program showcases the infamous Smothers Brothers' *Draft Dodgers Rag*. 60 mins.
VHS: S16200. $19.98.

People of Faith and the Arms Race
Produced by the Presbyterian Peacemaking Program, a unique, self-directing video workshop designed to help people of differing perspectives engage in dialog about the arms race. Six different sessions are included on the tape: *Peace in the Bible, Telling Personal Nuclear Age Stories, Biblical-Theological Perspectives, What Do We Know About the Arms Race?, What Is the Church's Role?* and *Doing Peacemaking*. 105 mins.
VHS: S10884. $39.95.

People to People
The story of "Target Seattle" and its citizens, who decide to talk and visit with the citizens of their sister city of Tashkent in the Soviet Union. Captured through the eyes of a young photographer, the pilgrimage for peace proceeds across the seas to Moscow, Leningrad, Samarkand and eventually to Tashkent.
VHS: S03806. $45.00.
Marlow Boyer, USA, 1985, 28 mins.

Planting Seeds for Peace
A timely documentary promoting intercultural dialog and understanding in the Middle East. The program focuses on the relationships among four Arab, Jewish and Palestinian teenagers who come together in the United States to share their cultures, break down stereotypes, and present their perspectives on the Middle East conflict to American young people. Along the way, they develop close friendships and a better understanding of each other's cultures. 23 mins.
VHS: S10892. $75.00.

Poligon
Thousands of residents living near the Soviet nuclear test site of Semipalatinsk were harmed by ambitious Soviet nuclear arms tests. This extraordinary film, shot just before the fall of USSR, reveals the extent of the damage inflicted on this region as well as the rationale behind the development of ever more deadly arms. The last interview given by Andrei Sakharov is also included. 58 mins.
VHS: S21584. $95.00.

Prophets and Loss
This documentary features a range of the world's most informed and profound thinkers on the environmental crisis and the path to a viable future: Carl Sagan, Paul Ehrlich, Bill Hare, Kenyan Professor Richard Oding, Soviet Physicist Ronald Sagdeev and many more. A tough examination of global issues and a clear agenda for what needs to be done. Introduction by actor-environmentalist Robert Redford. USA, 1991, 49 mins.
VHS: S15198. $79.00.

Protect-a-Dolphin Pod
A complete guide to dolphin behavior, anatomy and habitat with an emphasis on a pod of Atlantic spotted dolphins, exploring the interrelationships between individual dolphins, their environment and humans. 28 mins.
VHS: S33777. $59.95.

Protectors and Polluters
A horrifying look at the unregulated disposal of toxic waste at military bases across the country. Experts tour the worst offenders, including an air force base, munitions plants, a chemical weapons facility and other sites. 28 mins.
VHS: S23382. $35.00.

Question of Power
A moving and definitive media history of the nuclear power controversy, with inspirational portraits of successful grassroots opposition to the "peaceful atom."
VHS: S03813. $79.00.
David L. Brown, USA, 1986, 60 mins.

Real Sanctuary
A peaceful, musical, wordless exploration of shimmering waters and beckoning coral reefs, this soothing journey has been used to stimulate expressive movement, writing and art, and to enhance concentration before academic projects, creative work or standardized testing. 48 mins.
VHS: S33774. $24.95.

Regard for the Planet
A portrait of the global village, captured through more than 50,000 photographs by the photojournalist Marc Granger, from the Grand Canyon to Pakistan and the Far East.
Laser: LD70307. $99.95.

Reliability and Risk: Computers and Nuclear War

Produced by an organization of computer professionals, this short documentary explores our increasing dependence upon computers to make crucial military decisions. The unreliability inherent in complex systems is examined and chilling examples of typical failures are chronicled. Produced by Jonathan Schwarz for Computer Professionals for Social Responsibility. 20 mins.
VHS: S04310. $35.00.

Rhonda Abrams: Lament of the Sugar Bush Man

Acid rain destroys both the forest ecosystem and sugar maples. This documentary chronicles the woes of a maple sugar farmer who together with his family is seeing a way of life destroyed. The destruction they face bodes ill for other environments and other people who are not directly tied to the land. 1987, 12 mins.
VHS: S22586. $65.00.

Right Human Relations

A thought-provoking look at the development of "human rights" from the time of Moses through the 20th Century. With a special focus on the creation of the United Nations in 1945 and the subsequent adoption of the "Universal Declaration of Human Rights." 1990, 28 mins.
VHS: S13963. $75.00.

Rights & Wrongs: Human Rights in the World Today

Charlayne Hunter-Gault narrates this five-volume series that provides an in-depth look at human rights issues in the world today.

The Power of Human Rights. An introduction to human rights issues. Includes segments on the history of human rights, peace solutions and a human rights high school in a Brooklyn 9th grade class. 20 mins.
VHS: S23395. $49.95.

The World's Children. The human rights of children are explored in this insightful video featuring the stories of a 13-year-old African American boy in Washington, D.C., a 15-year-old girl from India and the seven million street children of Brazil. 26 mins.
VHS: S23396. $49.95.

Women Under Attack. Two of the most terrifying human rights issues facing women in several countries are explored. Featured are an investigation into how rape is systematically used as a weapon of war, the forced mutilation of female genitals for cultural and religious reasons and the emerging women's movement. 30 mins.
VHS: S23397. $59.95.

U.S. & Canada. Concerns of human rights abuses within the U.S. and Canada are revealed. Highlighted are civil rights of the 60's, tribal lands of James Bay, a taxpayer-funded military training school in Georgia and native Hawaiians—victims of history who are fighting for the right to live on their native lands. 32 mins.
VHS: S23398. $49.95.

Around the World. Records of the major human rights hot spots around the world and the ongoing debate over how to support human rights most effectively. China, Sarajevo and Somalia are examined. 30 mins.
VHS: S23399. $49.95.

Five-tape set.
VHS: S23400. $199.00.

River That Harms

Documents the largest radioactive waste spill in U.S. history—a national tragedy that has received little media attention. With the sound of a thunderclap, 94 million gallons of water contaminated with uranium mining waste broke through a United Nuclear Corporation storage dam in 1979 and poured into the Puerco River in New Mexico. This film tells the story of this tragedy and the toll that it continues to take on the Navajos, who have lost the use of their water and witnessed the sickness and death of their animals.
VHS: S12323. $39.95.
Colleen Keane, USA, 1987, 45 mins.

The Rotten Truth

This winner of the Media and Methods Awards Portfolio explores ways to reduce solid waste. A tour of the world's largest landfill reveals fascinating details about the problems posed by garbage, and the promise of recycling.
VHS: S23270. $34.95.

The Rush to Burn

This film examines whether the practice of waste incineration is safe, whether the government is adequately regulating this process, and the alternatives to toxic burning. 1989, 35 mins.
VHS: S13943. $55.00.

Save Our Planet

A young student receives elemental lessons in what needs to be done to preserve and sustain the environment. Armed with this knowledge, the young man sets about informing his classmates, friends and family about their own involvement and responsibilities. 30 mins.
VHS: S20281. $39.95.

Save the Earth: A How-To Video

A lively hour-long look at the practical, everyday things individuals can do to help restore the environment. With cameo appearances by celebrities such as Chevy Chase and Charlton Heston. 1990, 60 mins.
VHS: S13938. $19.95.

Save the Planet

A fast-paced capsule history of the atomic age and the debate over nuclear power, first released for the Musicians United for Safe Energy concert in 1979. 18 mins.
VHS: S31100. $19.95.

Scrapping Chemical Weapons

This documentary looks at ways the U.S. and the Soviet Union can destroy their highly toxic chemical weapons arsenals now that the Cold War is over. USA, 1991, 28 mins.
VHS: S15201. $25.00.

Secret World of the CIA

A distinguished CIA agent reveals the chilling secrets of a career in international espionage. *The Secret World of the CIA* presents the explosive personal story of former agent John Stockwell, winner of the CIA's Medal of Merit and the National Security Council coordinator of the covert war in Angola under Henry Kissinger. Stockwell provides a rare inside look at the life on the front lines of covert operations and ultimately makes a plea for radically altering how our government conducts clandestine operations around the world. 35 mins.
VHS: S11493. $49.95.

Secrets of Science: Our Sea and Sky

This two-part program provides a concise overview of the characteristics of the world's oceans and the many forms of life that dwell there. With video and animated graphics, concepts are explained, including currents, waves, tides, ocean floor geology, mineral and oxygen flow, plankton and marine zones. 48 mins.
VHS: S33775. $49.95.

Secrets of the Bay

This glowing film reveals the magnificent wildlife hidden among the six million human inhabitants of the San Francisco Bay area. The film shows the fragility of the Bay environment in the face of urbanization, and urges that this unique national treasure be protected and preserved for future generations. Narrated by TV personality, Jan Yanehiro. All ages. 1990, 28 mins.
VHS: S31924. $49.95.

Solid Solutions: Rural Waste Confronts the Waste Crisis

No longer strictly a big city problem, mounting solid waste has become a major problem in our country's rural areas. This film presents a positive look at how four rural communities have arrived at creative solutions to the growing problems of waste management. 30 mins.
VHS: S23381. $79.00.

Spaceship Earth: Our Global Environment

This unique program demonstrates the amazing interdependence of human, natural, an technological systems. Hosted entirely by young people, it is an excellent discussion starter: fast-paced, factual, educational, and entertaining. Good for teenage and adult audiences. 1990, 25 mins.
VHS: S13936. $39.95.

Star Wars: A Search for Security

A critical look at the proposed Strategic Defense initiative, featuring leading supporters and critics of the Star Wars defense system. In a fast moving, visually exciting and informative presentation, the film explores the key questions about the Star Wars plan. Narrated by Ed Begley Jr.
VHS: S03793. $35.00.
Ian Thiermann, USA, 1986, 28 mins.

Starving for Sugar

For centuries peasant workers have sweated in tropical heat to satisfy the world's sweet tooth. Now even the impoverished existence of sugarcane workers is being reduced to a greater state of misery as scientists and large corporations turn out a cheaper sweetener in the form of high fructose corn sugar. *Starving for Sugar* probes the brave new world of biotechnology and looks at the human and social price of this scientific progress in a call for a new sense of social responsibility to accompany scientific advances. Produced by Maryknoll Media. 60 mins.
VHS: S07720. $49.95.

A Step Away from War

Paul Newman leads the audience through a video on ending all nuclear explosions by discussing the role of nuclear weapons explosions in fueling the arms buildup, why a U.S./Soviet test ban would avert possible nuclear war; among those featured are Admiral Gene La Rocque; Congressman James Leach; Dr. Glenn Seaborg, former chairman of the Atomic Energy Commission; and Robert Stuart, chairman emeritus of National Can Company.
VHS: S03794. $35.00.
Cntr. for Defense Inf'n., USA, 1986, 28 mins.

Strategic Cooperation Initiative

Retired Air Force General Jack Kidd draws on his over 48 years of military perspective to develop a constructive platform for world peace. He offers a six-part strategy for radical change in the way world powers interact that eschews SDI and nuclear arms in favor of international cooperation in space exploration. 90 mins.
VHS: S10222. $29.95.

Survival of Spaceship Earth

Commissioned by the United Nations Conference on the Human Environment, *Spaceship Earth* was nominated for ten Emmy awards and has been the #1 environmental film in the nation. Narrated by Raymond Burr, hosted by Hugh Downs, and introduced by Rue McClanahan. "The finest ecological film we have seen" (BBC, London). Kit Parker Video is donating a portion of the sales proceeds from this tape to the UN Environment Program. 63 mins.
VHS: S13731. $24.95.
Laser: LD71767. $34.95.

Sustainable Lies, Attainable Dreams

This program takes you to Indonesia, Kenya and Mexico, where family planning programs are putting the brakes on rapid human population growth, which leads to desertification, wildlife habitat destruction, overconsumption of resources and deterioration of water and air quality. Produced by the National Wildlife Association. Grades 6-adult. 1996, 28 mins.
VHS: S31920. $59.95.

Thinking Like a Watershed

Environmental restoration is explained and demonstrated in this inspiring model of citizen initiative in a small coastal community in Northern California. 27 mins.
VHS: S33779. $89.95.

This Island Earth

Produced by the National Audobon Society, this educational and entertaining program features Kenny Loggins, Catherine Oxenburg, Gloria Estefan and Shanice sharing their environmental concerns through music. The program also provides viewers with important "Eco-tips" they can take to protect the environment. Includes 8-page teacher's guide. Grades 4-10. 1992, 53 mins.
VHS: S31902. $59.95.

Three Mile Island Revisited

An exploration of the devastating outcome of America's worst nuclear disaster, the incidence of rising cancer deaths and birth defects are documented. As the owners of the nuclear power plant quietly reach monetary settlements with ex-residents, they publicly claim that no one was harmed. Award winner. 30 mins.
VHS: S23387. $59.95.

Through the Eyes of the Forest

From the unique perspective gained by a successful preservation movement, this documentary shows the intrinsic value of old-growth forests. Bowen Gulch is an old-growth forest in the Colorado Rockies that was saved through a variety of tactics, including demonstrations, letter-writing and economic boycotts. This story illustrates the controversy that has grown up around these invaluable resources. 59 mins.
VHS: S21573. $39.95.

Times Beach, Missouri

The first town condemned by the federal government for toxic waste contamination, this film recounts the town's story through interviews with former residents and government officials. Significant questions focus on the relationship between government officials and the chemical industry, as well as the media's part in downplaying the dangers of dioxin. Multiple award winner. 57 mins.
VHS: S23379. $89.95.

To What End?

This timely analysis, narrated by Marvin Kalb, explores the four major long-term policy options our nation could pursue in an attempt to reduce the risk of nuclear war while maintaining national security. Interviews with 15 leading experts, policy makers, government officials and scientists, as well as the Soviet government perspective by a top arms control adviser to Mikhail Gorbachev. Among those featured are Robert McNamara, former Secretary of Defense, Randall Forsberg, Institute for Defense and Disarmament Studies and others. 58 mins.
VHS: S10882. $99.95.

Toxic Racism

Poor and minority populations suffer most from industrial and toxic pollution, yet benefit least from clean-up programs, according to a variety of studies. This devastating look at discrimination profiles three communities fighting for their health, safety and human rights. 56 mins.
VHS: S23380. $149.00.

Trees, Toilets, and Transformation

This is the story of a recycling specialist who expects to share his expertise with the citizens of El Salvador. Instead, he is impressed with the many practical and ingenious methods which the common people are using to reclaim their land, their water and their forests. 28 mins.
VHS: S31211. $89.00.

Tunnel Visions: Into the Sea of Uncertainty

Two-volume set includes *History: The Temptation of Technology*, which examines the current controversy over the series of events that led to the turnaround of Boston Harbor, once America's most most polluted waterfront, and *Science: Reliability and Risk*, which reveals painful choices imbedded in all public works projects and considers alternatives faced by every municipality adjacent to a body of water. Each tape is 28 mins.
VHS: S33772. $99.95.

U.S. Campaign Against the Death Penalty

A look at the historical background and current uses of the death penalty in the U.S., an arbitrary and racially discriminatory practice which violates human rights. Produced by Amnesty International. 1987, 28 mins.
VHS: S06888. $20.00.

The Water Cycle

A portrait of the continuing battle over water, history of water wars, and the underlying issues of resource use, development, and individual action. Provokes questions into the issues of the proper use of this treasured natural resource. 28 mins.
VHS: S23375. $79.00.

We All Live Downstream

America's most historic river, the Mississippi, has become a 2300-mile toxic waterway. This documentary explores the problems and the stories of people who live along the river, many of whom are now fighting to save the Mighty Mississippi. USA, 1990, 30 mins.
VHS: S15202. $39.95.

We Can Make a Difference

Concerned about the environmental crisis, 12 high school students decided to make a video that would inspire other young people to save their planet. The students worked on the project for an entire school year, interviewing hundreds of children ages 4-18. A testimony to the power of young people. 1989, 16 mins.
VHS: S13941. $25.00.

Weapons Bazaar

An eye-opening look at how weapons makers actually sell guns, tanks, aircraft and bombs to the Pentagon and Congress. Admiral La Rocque, Director of Center for Defense Information, leads the tour of a trade show with a difference. Among the amazing facts revealed are why the Falklands War was a "good opportunity" for the British Aerospace Corporation, and how razzle-dazzle games and displays promote cruise missiles, Pershing II and Trident submarines.
VHS: S03798. $35.00.
Cntr. for Defense Inf'n., USA, 1985, 28 mins.

Weapons in Space

A thoughtful analysis of the feasibility and consequences of space-based defenses. Four distinguished Americans—Dr. Henry Kendall, physicist; Dr. Carl Sagan, astronomer; Dr. Richard Garwin, physicist and National Defense Consultant; and Admiral Noel Gayler, former commander-in-chief of the Pacific Fleet—comment on these questions based on a televised tele-conference on space weapons.
VHS: S03800. $45.00.
Union Concerned Scientists, USA, 1984, 28 min.

What Soviet Children Are Saying About Nuclear War

A group of American psychiatrists led by Eric Chivian, M.D., and John Mack, M.D., visited two Soviet Pioneer camps and interviewed Soviet girls and boys aged 10-15. The result is an extraordinary documentary which is informative, refreshing and inspiring.
VHS: S03796. $45.00.
Int'l. Phys. for Prev. Nuc. War, 1983, 22 mins.

When Governments Kill

Produced by Amnesty International with college students in mind, this video examines the death penalty both internationally and in the United States. It answers the tough questions and lets students know how they can participate in the struggle for abolition. 1989, 24 mins.
VHS: S12783. $20.00.

When the People Lead

Twenty-three Americans from Northern California—doctors, lawyers, a city planner, homemakers, firefighters, school teachers, nurses, business men and women —decide to visit the Soviet Union and make friends. Their adventures, confrontations, and human encounters give the viewer a deeper understanding of modern-day Soviet life. Produced by Sharon Tennison, 40 mins.
VHS: S04312. $35.00.

When the Salmon Runs Dry

Salmon were once abundant in the Columbia river of the Pacific Northwest. Today competing interests, Native Americans, farmers, fishers and power managers must all find a way to balance their demands on this mighty river in order to ensure that the salmon survive. 51 mins.
VHS: S21581. $85.00.

When the Spill Hit Homer

Homer is a quiet fishing community that was devastated by the Exxon Valdez oil spill. This community, and other nearby Alaskan Native villages, are still trying to recover from this event and the inadequate clean-up efforts that followed. Dramatic home video footage and angry interviews offer a searing indictment of development in pristine environmental areas. 27 mins.
VHS: S21575. $85.00.

Where Have All the Dolphins Gone?

In the last 30 years, the dolphin world has been devastated by the tuna industry, which continues to use the deadly "purse seine" nets that needlessly entrap dolphins. Over 6 million spinner, spotted, and common dolphins have been killed by U.S. and foreign fishing fleets. Relentless, widespread destruction is pushing some dolphin communities to the brink of extinction. *Where Have All the Dolphins Gone?* documents the confrontation between major multi-national companies and environmental groups, which see the plight of the dolphins as symbolic of the crisis facing many species today. Narrated by George C. Scott. Produced by the Marine Mammal Fund. 58 mins.
VHS: S12322. $59.95.

Where There Is Hatred

Recent events in the world have shown that nonviolence means much more than turning the other cheek. From Chile to the Philippines, from Palestine to Eastern Europe, people have forced major changes using the tactics of nonviolence. This video is a dramatic witness to the power of people who use nonviolence as an effective strategy for peacemaking. *Where There Is Hatred* looks at both the moral and practical aspects of this strategy and suggests its application to turn societies around. Produced by Maryknoll Media. 56 mins.
VHS: S11714. $39.95.

The White Hole in Time

Peter Russell, of the award-winning video *The Global Brain*, weaves his characteristic blend of physics, psychology and philosophy to paint a new picture of humanity and the times we are passing through. With hundreds of images that span the breadth of creation and music by Vangelis. Jr. High School to Adult. 1996, 30 mins.
VHS: S31910. $39.95.

Wilderness: The Last Stand

Narrated by Susan Sarandon, this is a powerful look at the status of America's last remaining virgin forests. It examines the impact of Forest Service policies, documenting the devastating harm caused by clearcutting. 53 mins.
VHS: S23373. $95.00.

Will Our Children Thank Us?

Dr. Benjamin Spock, active in the anti-nuclear movement, narrates this documentary about three New Englanders and how the controversy over the build-up of nuclear armaments has affected their lives. Produced by The Documentary Guild. USA, 1984, 58 mins.
VHS: S07412. $44.95.

Wind: Energy for the 90's and Beyond

How can we harness the power of the wind? In California we already are. Wind power provides enough energy for a city the size of San Francisco for one full year. Combining graphics, animation and interviews with leading experts, this documentary explores the nationwide potential for wind energy and the obstacles holding back this renewable resource. 24 mins.
VHS: S21570. $59.95.

Working for Peace: The Nuclear Issue

The U.S. Catholic bishops defined the nuclear arms race as more than a political issue and said that the questions surrounding it are moral ones. This documentary discusses how the nuclear race involves more than the U.S. and U.S.S.R.; that it destroys people as it filters down to the poorest of the Third World. Produced by Maryknoll Media. 28 mins.
VHS: S06261. $24.95.

World of Refugees

Millions of people across the world live exiled as refugees, while most of the world remains unaware of their situation. The causes may differ, but their plight and their problems are similar. Concerned leaders examine what people of faith and good will can and are doing to aid these people. Visual segments include refugee camps in Mexico and Macao. Produced by Maryknoll Media. 28 mins.
VHS: S06268. $24.95.

The Yes! Tour: Working for Change

Youth for Environmental Safety (Yes!) is a concerned group of teenage environmentalists who crisscross the country in a cramped old station wagon delivering their message to 200,000 students a year. Their goal is to inform young people about environmental issues. 29 mins.
VHS: S23364. $59.95.

You Can Beat the A-Bomb

You Can Beat the A-Bomb is just the first of four films from the 1950's collected on this video. If this film is strangely funny, *One Plane, One Bomb* with Edward R. Murrow is simply chilling. *Warning Red* and *The House in the Middle* round out this collection, made in a time when many believed it was possible to survive nuclear attack. 60 mins.
VHS: S24075. $19.95.

You Can't Grow Home Again

This Emmy Award-winning documentary explores the richness and diversity of Costa Rica's rain forests. Their destruction impoverishes the biodiversity of the planet and poses a threat to human survival.
VHS: S23272. $49.95.

EDUCATION & HISTORY

1970: Year of Protest

Nixon bombs Cambodia, Kent State, the Equal Rights Amendment, the Chicago 7, Chappaquiddick. 48 mins.
VHS: S13146. $19.98.

1971: Year of Disillusionment

Pentagon Papers are printed in the Washington Post, riots wage at Attica, hunger wars in Bangladesh, expose on the My Lai massacre. 48 mins.
VHS: S13145. $19.98.

1972: Year of Summits

Nixon beats McGovern, Olympians are held hostage, SALT talks begin, George Wallace is shot, Bobby Fischer is the American chess champion. 48 mins.
VHS: S13144. $19.98.

1973: Year of Watergate

U.S. troops withdraw from Vietnam, Yom Kippur War wages, Watergate grand jury proceedings are televised, Agnew resigns. 48 mins.
VHS: S13143. $19.98.

1974: Year of Resignation

Nixon resigns and Ford pardons him, anti-busing demonstrations in Boston, Gay rights demonstrations in New York, streaking and Hank Aaron. 48 mins.
VHS: S13142. $19.98.

1975: Year after the Fall

New York City talks bankruptcy, Saigon falls to Communism, Thatcher becomes Prime Minister, Suez canal re-opens, Patty Hearst is arrested, UN equates Zionism with racism. 48 mins.
VHS: S13141. $19.98.

1976: Year of the Bicentennial

Carter is elected president, Viking spacecraft lands on Mars, Legionnaire's disease, mud wrestling, Idi Amin. 48 mins.
VHS: S13140. $19.98.

1977: Year of the Southern President

Sadat and Begin start peace talks, New York has a blackout, Gary Gilmore is executed, punk rock, *Rocky* wins an Academy Award, CNN is launched, Elvis dies. 48 mins.
VHS: S13182. $19.98.

1978: Year of Moral Dilemmas

Proposition 13 wins in California, Nazis march in Skokie, Camp David accords are drawn, Jonestown, jogging, disco and roller skating, Rev. Sun Myung Moon. 48 mins.
VHS: S13183. $19.98.

1979: Year of Overthrow

Chinese invade Vietnam, Amin is overthrown, Sandinistas oust Somoza, the Shah flees, Skylab falls, Thurman Munson dies, Three Mile Island almost explodes. 48 mins.
VHS: S13184. $19.98.

Above and Beyond the Call of Duty

The history of the Congressional Medal of Honor. Combining rare combat footage and interviews with recipients, this documentary provides an intriguing account of America's greatest heroes and the extraordinary actions for which they received the Medal of Honor. 120 mins.
VHS: S09199. $49.95.

Alcatraz: America's Toughest Prison

The toughest prison in American history in this documentary tracing the island's infamous career through Al Capone, Machine Gun Kelly, the Birdman of Alcatraz and others. Interviews with ex-cons are interwoven against the backdrop of the violence which marked the prison. Narrated by William Conrad. 54 mins.
VHS: S05174. $29.95.

America Grows Up (1850-1900s)

An Industrial Nation and *A World Power* trace America's course from a nation of farms and villages to status of one of the leading industrial nations of the world in a matter of decades. The American system of manufacturing is analyzed here along with a developing new foreign policy.
VHS: S03976. $64.95.

American Foundation Series

A series of 30 minute tapes specifically designed for junior and senior high school students, which explores the political and philosophical foundations of American society. 30 mins each.
American Ideas in the Twentieth Century.
VHS: S06745. $29.95.
Birth of a Nation: The Thirteen Colonies.
VHS: S06742. $29.95.
Colonists Become Citizens: The Evolution of Freedom.
VHS: S06743. $29.95.
Technology and Environment: The Economic Development of America.
VHS: S06744. $29.95.

American Heroes Series

30 minutes each.
18th Century—The Age of Revolution. Includes George Washington, Benjamin Franklin, Patrick Henry and Thomas Jefferson.
VHS: S06735. $29.95.
19th Century—Growth of America. Includes Lewis and Clark, Daniel Boone, Andrew Jackson and Abraham Lincoln.
VHS: S06736. $29.95.
20th Century—Recent Times. Includes Woodrow Wilson, Franklin D. Roosevelt, John F. Kennedy and Martin Luther King.
VHS: S06737. $29.95.

American History for Children

Children's education experts have developed this series about major issues in American history. These lively videos incorporate music, animation, stories and dramatization in order to make history come alive. Diverse viewpoints are included to convey the various elements that make up American society. Each episode of this 12-volume set is 25 minutes long.
American History for Children: African-American Life. African-American life from slavery to the Emancipation Proclamation, and the legacy of Dr. Martin Luther King, Jr., are joined in this video.
VHS: S26751. $29.95.
American History for Children: American Independence. Everything from the Declaration of Independence to a biography of Thomas Jefferson is shown in this episode. Trips to Liberty Hall and the Liberty Bell are also included, and it shows how a child's day might have been under British rule.
VHS: S26749. $29.95.
American History for Children: Early Settlers. This video concentrates on the settling of New England with a discussion of the Mayflower and the Mayflower Compact. It then explains the origin of the Thanksgiving holiday. A child's view of colonial Williamsburg rounds out this look at the early settlers.
VHS: S26748. $29.95.
American History for Children: Equal Rights for All. The Bill of Rights, the Abolitionist movement, the woman's suffrage movement and biographies of Abraham Lincoln and Susan B. Anthony provide vital background for this enduring American concern.
VHS: S26752. $29.95.
American History for Children: Immigration to the U.S. Beginning with an exposition of immigrant desires, this video goes on to explain the drama of the Atlantic passage from Europe. It includes a story of an immigrant child's experience. Diversity is addressed with a discussion of early Chinese immigration and newer immigrants.
VHS: S26755. $29.95.
American History for Children: Native American Life. This video begins with life in North America before European contact. It continues on to detail an overview of Native American history that includes seminal events like the Trail of Tears. It concludes with a look at contemporary Native American life.
VHS: S26747. $29.95.
American History for Children: National Observances. National holidays from Veteran's Day to Labor Day are fully discussed in this video. Election Day and the history of American elections receive special attention.
VHS: S26757. $29.95.
American History for Children: U.S. Songs and Poems. Patriotic songs like "The Star Spangled Banner," "America the Beautiful," "My Country 'Tis of Thee," "Yankee Doodle" and more are explained in this final episode.
VHS: S26758. $29.95.
American History for Children: United States Constitution. Along with the story of the Constitution, biographies of George Washington and Ben Franklin, as well as the history of the great Seal, illuminate this key moment in American history.
VHS: S26750. $29.95.
American History for Children: United States Flag. From the origins of the flag to the current code of proper flag handling, everything about this vital American symbol is discussed here. Betsy Ross' role in the flag's creation, the National Anthem and the Pledge of Allegiance are also explained.
VHS: S26753. $29.95.
American History for Children: United States Expansion. Pioneer life and the experiences of a child pioneer make this volume particularly exciting for devotees of the Western frontier. The achievements of Lewis and Clark as well as the forced relocations of Native Americans and other vital issues are also addressed in this video.
VHS: S26754. $29.95.
American History for Children: Washington D.C. Important structures in Washington illustrate the story of this capitol city's development. The White House, The Capitol, the Lincoln, Jefferson and Vietnam Memorials and the Supreme Court building are included.
VHS: S26756. $29.95.
American History for Children. The complete 12-volume set.
VHS: S26759. $359.40.

American History: A Bilingual Study

A special series of tapes, available in two versions: Spanish and English. These unique programs were adapted from film strips or slide presentations, and cover the development of the American continent.
Becoming a Modern Nation. The Spanish-American War and World War I. English narration.
VHS: S06374. $29.95.
Becoming a Modern Nation. The Spanish-American War and World War I. Spanish narration.
VHS: S06375. $29.95.
Discovery and Exploration. Columbus and the Spanish explorers. John Cabot and the English explorers. The French in New France. Henry Hudson and New Amsterdam. Spanish narration.
VHS: S06380. $29.95.
Discovery and Exploration. Columbus and the Spanish explorers. John Cabot and the English explorers. The French in New France. Henry Hudson and New Amsterdam. English narration.
VHS: S06381. $29.95.
Divided House—The Second American Revolution. Historical background, the events of the Civil War, Civil War personalities, the legacy and aftermath of the Second American revolution. English narration.
VHS: S08930. $29.95.
Divided House—The Second American Revolution. Historical background, the events of the Civil War, Civil War personalities, the legacy and aftermath of the Second American revolution. Spanish narration.
VHS: S08931. $29.95.
Expansion and Growth: 19th Century America. West to the Mississippi, The Louisiana Territory, Conquest of New Spain, Manifest Destiny—To The Pacific. English narration.
VHS: S06370. $29.95.
Expansion and Growth: 19th Century America. West to the Mississippi, The Louisiana Territory, Conquest of New Spain, Manifest Destiny—To The Pacific. Spanish narration.
VHS: S06371. $29.95.
First American Revolution: 1750-1789. Background. Causes of the 1776 revolt. Revolutionary War events. Results of the first American revolution—the Constitution. English narration.
VHS: S06382. $29.95.
First American Revolution: 1750-1789. Background. Causes of the 1776 revolt. Revolutionary War events. Results of the first American revolution—the Constitution. Spanish narration.
VHS: S06383. $29.95.
Industrial America—The Third American Revolution. Early industry in America. The American industrial revolution. Labor unions and an industrialized society, modern technology and its impact on the world. English narration.
VHS: S06372. $29.95.
Industrial America—The Third American Revolution. Early industry in America. The American industrial revolution. Labor unions and an industrialized society, modern technology and its impact on the world. Spanish narration.
VHS: S06373. $29.95.
Transformation of American Society. Changing life styles. Rise of the cities. Civil rights. Communications for people and industry. English narration.
VHS: S06378. $29.95.
Transformation of American Society. Changing life styles. Rise of the cities. Civil rights. Communications for people and industry. Spanish narration.
VHS: S06379. $29.95.
Twentieth Century America. The Great Depression. World War II. Emergence of the United States in the world community. The future in science and space. English narration.
VHS: S06376. $29.95.
Twentieth Century America. The Great Depression. World War II. Emergence of the United States in the world community. The future in science and space. Spanish narration.
VHS: S06377. $29.95.

Americans Courageous (1600-1950s)

The Gloucesterman is a celebration of the people of this historic Massachusetts town over a 400-year period, a rousing story told in song and dance and heroic action at sea. Paired with *Not for Ourselves Alone*, a record of victory in four U.S. military crises, here is a great tribute to American courage and resourcefulness.
VHS: S03970. $64.95.

Attack: Battle of New Britain

Created by the U.S. Army Signal Corps, this unique documentary covers the exceptionally bloody Marine Assault on New Britain in the Pacific. 56 mins.
VHS: S05626. $19.95.

Before the Industrial Revolution

Video sequences of numerous hand crafts and trades, including soap making, bread making, sheep shearing, wheel wrighting, horseshoeing and more. 18 mins.
VHS: S15532. $45.00.

Best of Nightline

Achille Lauro Hijacked. 30 mins.
VHS: S14038. $14.98.
Artificial Heart. 30 mins.
VHS: S14026. $14.98.
Baby Fae. 30 mins.
VHS: S14033. $14.98.
General Manuel Noriega Indicted. 30 mins.
VHS: S14049. $14.98.
Geraldine Ferraro. 30 mins.
VHS: S14031. $14.98.
Jackie Robinson. 70 mins.
VHS: S14045. $14.98.
Jim & Tammy Faye Bakker. 80 mins.
VHS: S14046. $14.98.
Jimmy Swaggart. 55 mins.
VHS: S14051. $14.98.
John Belushi's Career. 30 mins.
VHS: S14024. $14.98.
John Lennon Murdered. 30 mins.
VHS: S14018. $14.98.
Ku Klux Klan. 30 mins.
VHS: S14017. $14.98.
T.V. Evangelists. 75 mins.
VHS: S14044. $14.98.
The Titanic. 30 mins.
VHS: S14043. $19.98.

Between the Wars, 1918-1941

A unique, eight-volume series about the world between the two World Wars, hosted by Eric Sevareid.
Between the Wars, 1918-1941, Vol. 2. The First Salt Talks/America in the Pacific. 60 mins.
VHS: S11906. $19.99.
Between the Wars, 1918-1941, Vol. 3. Radio, Racism and Foreign Power/The Great Depression. 60 mins.
VHS: S11907. $19.99.
Between the Wars, 1918-1941, Vol. 4. FDR and Hitler: Rise to Power/The Dynamics of Power. 60 mins.
VHS: S11908. $19.99.
Between the Wars, 1918-1941, Vol. 5. Recognition of Russia/Latin America: Intervention in Our Backyard. 60 mins.
VHS: S11909. $19.99.
Between the Wars, 1918-1941, Vol. 6. Italian-Ethiopian War/The Spanish Civil War. 60 mins.
VHS: S11910. $19.99.
Between the Wars, 1918-1941, Vol. 7. The Phony War/FDR and Churchill: The Human Partnership. 60 mins.
VHS: S11911. $19.99.
Between the Wars, 1918-1941, Vol. 8. Japan Invades China/War Comes to Pearl Harbor. 60 mins.
VHS: S11912. $19.99.
Between the Wars, 1918-1941, Vol. 1. Versailles: The Lost Peace/Return to Isolationism. 60 mins.
VHS: S11914. $19.99.
The entire 8-volume series.
VHS: S11913. $169.99.

Brute Force: The Definitive History of War Technology

George C. Scott presents the evolution of military hardware honed from primitive inception to high-tech perfection. From the Arts & Entertainment Network's highly acclaimed series, this collection is compiled in two deluxe boxed sets.
Air Weapons. *Fighters, Bombers, Helicopters.* The first armed aircraft were little more than glorified barnstormers. Today's sophisticated flying machines require highly trained top 26 guns, who must be fearless amidst the flak. Three cassettes, 50 minutes each.
VHS: S15837. $44.95.
Ground Weapons. *Tanks, Artillery, Infantry.* Watch the turrets turn through 70 years of battle. Learn the history of the only weapon systems impervious to weather or electronic interference. Speak with foot soldiers having fought as far back as WWII. Three cassettes, 50 minutes each.
VHS: S15838. $44.95.

Capitol to Capitol
This dramatic news special provides coverage of a unique live event: discussions held between the White House and the Kremlin, the United States and Soviet Union via the news media, broadcasts shown simultaneously in both countries. An essential program in understanding the goals and lifestyles of our world counterpart. 55 mins.
VHS: S13180. $19.98.

City out of Wilderness: Washington
A definitive history of Washington, D.C., utilizing the prints, documents, daguerrotypes and Matthew Arnold photographs as well as spectacular aerial photography to evoke the spirit of the capital city. Produced by the U.S. Capitol Historical society. 28 mins.
VHS: S03737. $19.95.

Colonial America (1500-1600)
Recalled here are *The Beginnings* and *The Way of Life* in America's earliest days, when France, Spain and Great Britain were fighting for the riches of the virgin continent. Illustrated here are customs and traditions which set patterns for life as we live it in the United States today.
VHS: S03971. $64.95.

Columbus
This extraordinary series, produced to commemorate the anniversary of Columbus' arrival in America, covers the man and the history of his travels in seven separate volumes. Public performance rights included.
First Voyage. The ships, the crews, the means of navigation and the first landings in the New World are featured on this tape. 35 mins.
VHS: S12642. $125.00.
God and Gold. The business side of discovery and the relentless missionary zeal of Columbus and his followers are the focus of this tape. 35 mins.
VHS: S12645. $125.00.
La Genovesita Di Columbo. Leading scholars and experts of the greater Genoa area discuss, *in Italian*, the Genoese ancestry, birth and citizenship of Columbus.
VHS: S12647. $175.00.
Later Voyages. The lands and cultures Columbus encountered after the Americas. Also investigated are his fall from power, his later years and the summary of his lasting contributions. 35 mins.
VHS: S12646. $125.00.
New World. Historians, linguists, and modern explorers re-create the pre-Columbian Indians of the Caribbean; their cultures, conflicts, languages, and the colonies Columbus established in their midst. 35 mins.
VHS: S12644. $125.00.
Search for La Navidad. Long a mystery, the location for Columbus' ill-fated first settlement is actively investigated by scientists, technicians and others. 35 mins.
VHS: S12643. $125.00.

Democracy in a Different Voice
When President Clinton withdrew Lani Guinier's nomination for assistant attorney general for civil rights, the distinguished legal scholar, civil rights attorney and tenured University of Pennsylvania law professor was denied a Congressional hearing and the opportunity to illuminate her theories on race and voting. Guinier here outlines her views on democracy and invites a discussion on its meaning in a diverse society. 37 mins.
VHS: S28443. $195.00.

The Fabulous 60's
The ten volumes of this series trace the epic 1960's, year by year. Narrated by Peter Jennings. 60 minutes each.
Volume 1: 1960. Kennedy vs. Nixon, Princess Margaret marries, the U-2 incident, Voerward assassination attempt, Elvis goes into the army.
VHS: S02963. $19.95.
Volume 2: 1961. The Bay of Pigs, Roger Maris' 61st home run, Kennedy Inauguration, Eichmann Trial, the pill, the twist, the romance between Burton and Taylor.
VHS: S02964. $19.95.
Volume 3: 1962. James Merideth of the University of Mississippi, Thalidomide tragedy, the Cuban missile crisis, John Glenn, the China-India border war, the death of Marilyn Monroe.
VHS: S02965. $19.95.
Volume 4: 1963. Smoking scare, Peace Corps, the assassination of President Kennedy, the Playboy Magazine phenomenon, the March on Washington, the Great Train Robbery.
VHS: S02966. $19.95.
Volume 5: 1964. The Gulf of Tonkin, Beatles invade the U.S., New York World's Fair, Teddy Kennedy's plane crash, the murder of three civil rights workers in Mississippi.
VHS: S02967. $19.95.
Volume 6: 1965. Selma March, Watts, murder of Malcolm X, Sinatra-Farrow courtship, miniskirts, Bob Dylan and the Rolling Stones, the blackout in the Northeast.
VHS: S02968. $19.95.
Volume 7: 1966. Warren report controversy, Indira Gandhi in India, Aberfan disaster, Reagan in California, Maddox and Bond in Georgia, Batman, bomb lost in Spain.
VHS: S02969. $19.95.
Volume 8: 1967. Hippies in Haight-Asbury, Expo '67, Queen Mary's last voyage, Cassius Clay refuses to be drafted, riots in Detroit, Che Guevara assassinated in Bolivia, Bonnie and Clyde.
VHS: S02970. $19.95.
Volume 9: 1968. Tiny Tim, the first heart transplants, Jackie and Ari, Martin Luther King assassination, Robert Kennedy's death, Chicago Democratic convention, Nixon elected.
VHS: S02971. $19.95.
Volume 10: 1969. Woodstock, Apollo moon landing, Tricia Nixon profile, World Series—Mets win; Prince Charles' investiture, Nixon's inauguration.
VHS: S02972. $19.95.

Fields of Armor
The Discovery Channel's series reveals the history of armed machines that transformed the nature of warfare in the 20th century. From the soldiers who were there and fought in the great tank battles you will experience what these machines meant for the most savage land battles in living memory.
Volume I: Desert Attack. The sands of North Africa and the Middle East were the setting for two decisive tank battles: the battle of El Alamein in World War I, and the fight for the Golan Heights in the October War. See how these machines increased the efficiency of man's most deadly enterprise, war. 90 mins.
VHS: S20696. $14.95.
Volume II: Birth of Blitzkrieg. In this episode the growth of tank technology from 1916-1942 is seen as a development that preceded the know-how needed to deploy these machines most effectively. That is, until Hitler's feared Wehrmacht perfected the strategy. 90 mins.
VHS: S20697. $14.95.
Volume III: Battle of Armor. With the advent of nuclear arms at the close of World War II, many thought tanks had become obsolete. In *Battle of Armor* these war machines prove their enduring capacity in the Korean War. Even today tanks line both sides of the border that separates these countries, an testament to the usefulness of this technology. 90 mins.
VHS: S20698. $14.95.
Volume IV: Cold War to Gulf War. Armored strategy continues to evolve in different situations around the globe. Vietnam, Afghanistan, and the Gulf War all hold painful lessons about the advancement of armored vehicle warfare. 90 mins.
VHS: S20699. $14.95.
Deluxe Boxed Set. Over six hours in length, this collection contains all four volumes of the series *Fields of Armor*. Taken together, these insightful documentaries offer the war buff an unparalleled look at the history of tanks and the effects they had on war.
VHS: S20700. $54.95.

Footloose in History—Grades 5-12
A fast-moving, entertaining view of history combines art, architecture, fads and fashions, dealing with art as a consequence of historical, economic, social and political thinking of various periods.
VHS: S09089. $149.00.

The Game of Monopoly (1870-1914)
Industrial Giants and *Trust Busters* examine the rise to wealth and power of the industrial titans like Carnegie, Rockefeller, and Vanderbilt. Here is the story of how President Theodore Roosevelt fought the monopolists and enforced the principle that corporations are no more above the law than the humblest citizen.
VHS: S03977. $64.95.

Gathering Strength (1840-1914)
Immigration and *The Pacific Northwest* explore the differences between the "old" immigrants from northern Europe and the "new" immigrants, the waves of settlers from eastern and southern Europe. In rich detail here is the story of how the new manpower was found for the needs of the nation's burgeoning industries.
VHS: S03975. $64.95.

Great American Frontiers
Explore the history of America's last great frontiers—Utah, Arizona, Colorado, New Mexico, Washington, Oregon, Northern California and Alaska—in this three-volume set. Includes *America's Last Frontier: Alaska* (60 mins.), covering from the earliest Siberian migrations to Alaska to the Gold seekers in the late 1800s and to the Japanese invasion of the Aleutian Islands in World War II; *America's Canyon Country* (60 mins.), which explores America's western destiny and the land where many great Hollywood westerns were made; and *America's Great Northwest* (55 mins.), covering the Lewis and Clark trail and the early imigrants who traveled to the Oregon Trail.
VHS: S33892. $59.95.

Great Commanders
Filmed on locations throughout the world, a look at six individuals who were military greats. Leading experts talk about their achievements, with 3D computer animation used to illustrate each commander's particular skills.
Alexander the Great—The Battle of Issus. At the time of his death, at age 32, Alexander had conquered more of the known world than anyone before or since, and had established himself as a great commander and conqueror. 45 mins.
VHS: S20454. $24.95.
Georgi Zhukov—The Battle of Berlin. The Battle of Berlin, which finally destroyed the Nazi regime, was a difficult military objective and Zhukov's ultimate triumph, which led to him being called the greatest commander of the Second World War. 45 mins.
VHS: S20459. $24.95.
Horatio Nelson—Battle of Trafalgar. At Trafalgar, Nelson secured a mastery of the seas that brought the expansion of the British Empire. 45 mins.
VHS: S20456. $24.95.
Julius Caesar—The Battle of Alesia. At the Battle of Alesia, Caesar used technological superiority and tactical cunning against a force which outnumbered him more than five to one in his quest for Gaul. 45 mins.
VHS: S20458. $24.95.
Napoleon Bonaparte—The Battle of Austerlitz. At Austerlitz, Napoleon won a spectacular victory against Austria and Russia which justifies his reputation as the greatest modern commander. 45 mins.
VHS: S20457. $24.95.
Ulysses S. Grant—The Battle of the Wilderness. At the beginning of the Civil War, Ulysses S. Grant worked in a store, but within four years he commanded the Union Armies, and in The Battle of the Wilderness established his military genius in an indecisive tangle in a dense forest which became a vital strategic victory. 45 mins.
VHS: S20455. $24.95.
Great Commanders, Complete. The six-volume set of the *Great Commanders* series.
VHS: S20460. $119.95.

Great Days of History
A new series which culls rare footage of world archives to provide a comprehensive history of major events of the 20th century.
The Battle of Verdun. This program retraces the battle that became synonymous with trench warfare in World War I. Archival footage makes clear the enormous sacrifice in lives by the French defenders and German attackers. 26 mins.
VHS: S09426. $29.95.

Great Debates: JFK vs. Richard Nixon
The 1960 Presidential debates—two of history's greatest figures square off in a series of debates that are as fresh and exciting today as they were when they were broadcast. 60 mins.
VHS: S12693. $24.98.

Historical Heritage Series
The Missions. Told in the form of a diary, the daily life of old California missions, their construction and daily life, and an exploration of the missions of the southwest. 35 mins.
VHS: S05816. $19.95.
The Trappers. The major thrust west of the fur trappers, beaver and buffalo hunts, and the westward push to California. 31 mins.
VHS: S05817. $19.95.

History of the Twentieth Century, Volume 1
1900-1909. The newest technological fad is the moving picture. McKinley is assassinated. Teddy Roosevelt becomes President. An earthquake destroys San Francisco. This is a chronicle of the first decade of our century. 60 mins.
VHS: S12699. $19.98.

History of the Twentieth Century, Volume 2
1910-1919. Roosevelt organizes the "Bull Moose" party. The Lusitania is torpedoed off the Irish coast, 1200 people are killed. World War I begins. 60 mins.
VHS: S12700. $19.98.

History of the Twentieth Century, Volume 3
1920-1929. World War I ends, America's veterans try to resume their lives. Prohibition is established. Al Capone wreaks havoc in Chicago. The stock market crashes, and Babe Ruth hits 61 home runs. 60 mins.
VHS: S12701. $19.98.

History of the Twentieth Century, Volume 4
1930-1939. Fifteen million American are out of work due to the depression. Prohibition is repealed. Hitler is elected Prime Minister of Germany. DiMaggio plays for the Yankees, who win four World Series in a row. 60 mins.
VHS: S12702. $19.98.

History of the Twentieth Century, Volume 5

1940-1949. Pearl Harbor is bombed by the Japanese. World War II rages. The Nazis institutionalize death camps like Auschwitz. FDR dies. An atomic bomb is detonated over Japan in 1945. 60 mins.
VHS: S12703. $19.98.

History of the Twentieth Century, Volume 6

1950-1959. A cold war wages between the US and the USSR. Hungarian liberals are crushed by Russians in a 10-day revolution. Castro rules Cuba. Television comes to town. Eisenhower and Nixon team up. 60 mins.
VHS: S12704. $19.98.

History of the Twentieth Century, Volume 7

1960-1964. Kennedy and Nixon square off on TV. Bay of Pigs and the Berlin Wall is built. Roger Maris hits 61 home runs. JFK tours Dallas in an open convertible. 60 mins.
VHS: S12705. $19.98.

History of the Twentieth Century, Volume 8

1965-1969. Protesters fight the war at home. Violence rocks the '68 Democratic Convention. Martin Luther King is shot and killed. Apollo 11 lands on the moon. 60 mins.
VHS: S12706. $19.98.

History of the Twentieth Century, Volume 9

1970-1979. The National Guard kills four students at Kent State. America invades Cambodia. Nixon resigns. Iranians storm the embassy in Tehran and take Americans hostage. 60 mins.
VHS: S12707. $19.98.

Images of the '80s

The Reagan years…the Space Shuttle…Jim and Tammy…AIDS…the Berlin Wall. Join host Peter Jennings for a dramatic and comprehensive replay of the people, places and happenings that shaped a decade. From ABC News. 55 mins.
VHS: S12678. $19.98.

Independence: Birth of a Free Nation

Narrated by E.G. Marshall, this award-winning program recreates the dramatic events that led to the Declaration of Independence and the establishment of the Constitution. Ben Franklin, Thomas Jefferson, John Adams and George Washington tell the historic events that took place in Philadelphia during the late 70's. 28 mins.
VHS: S09181. $29.95.

Independence: Texas Gains Its Freedom

1836, Washington, Texas. In this dramatic reenactment, Sam Houston and other heroes of Texan history meet to declare Texas a free nation from Mexico. Official State Film of the Texas Sesqui-centennial. 30 mins.
VHS: S06674. $29.95.

Inside the White House

President George Bush and Barbara Bush are your guides for this intimate insider's tour of the White House's historical hallways. This private video tour will also take you inside Lincoln's "haunted" bedroom and the private second floor and into rooms never seen by most Americans. 50 mins.
VHS: S12270. $19.98.

Justice Factory

Court TV follows judges, assistant district attorneys, public defenders and defense attorneys through their everyday experience. Teens will see what it's like to lead the life of a legal professional, visit a law school, and look at the roles played by bailiffs, court reporters, court clerks and the many others who make the legal system work. Episodes include *The Assistant District Attorney, The Public Defender, Judges, Juries and the Jury Selection Expert, Arrest/Representation, Punishment for Teen Offenders, Reform/Intervention, Conflict Resolution, Lawyers Who Rarely Go to Court, Unsung Heroes of the Courtroom, Mock Trials, Environmental Law* and *Teens in Prison*. Six-volume, 13 half-hour episode gift set. 6½ hours.
VHS: S32385. $119.95.

March of Time: Great Depression

Multiple Academy Award series on the Great Depression.
March of Time: Economy Blues. Army, Father Coughlin, Croix de Feu, Ethiopia, Bootleg Coal, CCC, Palestine, Neutrality, G.O.P. 81 mins.
VHS: S07553. $19.95.
March of Time: Prosperity Ahead? The Lunatic Fringe, U.S. Milky Way, Labor vs. Labor, The Football Business, The Presidency, New Schools for Old. 103 mins.
VHS: S07556. $19.95.
March of Time: Reality and America's Dreams. Conquering Cancer, Mormonism—1937, Midwinter Vacations, Birth of Swing, Enemies of Alcohol, Child Labor. 98 mins.
VHS: S07557. $19.95.
March of Time: Time Marches In. Sainoji, Speakeasy Street, Belisha Beacons, Buchsbaum, Fred Perkins, Metropolitan Opera, Germany, Huey Long. 85 mins.
VHS: S07552. $19.95.
March of Time: Trouble Beyond Our Shores. Japan-China, Narcotics, Townsend Plan, Pacific Islands, TVA, Diebler, Moscow, Hartman Discovery, Father Divine. 80 mins.
VHS: S07554. $19.95.
March of Time: War and Labor Woes. Veterans of Future Wars, Arson Squads in Action, Jockey Club, Field Trails, League of Nations Union, Railroads, Relief. 107 mins.
VHS: S07555. $19.95.
Complete Set.
VHS: S07551. $99.95.

March of Time: The Cold War

A four-volume set by March of Time chronicling the Cold War, winner of four Academy Awards as well as 48 national and international awards.
March of Time—Changing Attitudes. This volume deals with the Cold War and its beginnings. Reports on atomic power, political crises in Italy, revolutions in Greece, and a special section on "the Russia that nobody knows." 88 mins.
VHS: S09836. $19.95.
March of Time—Hostility Grows. The perilous times following World War II are chronicled, including America's new air power, an answer to Stalin, the battle for Germany, and a report on the atom, as well as new voices in Asia. 90 mins.
VHS: S09837. $19.95.
March of Time—Peace or War? The third in the Cold War series looks at Japan under General MacArthur, changing views in Russia, and the future of Sweden. Tensions rise in this newsreel series as the super powers jockey for position. 83 mins.
VHS: S09838. $19.95.
March of Time—Time Marches On. The world in turmoil as March of Time covers Formosa, Morocco and Iran, as well as a report on Yugoslavia's General Tito. Is he a new ally in securing world peace? 105 mins.
VHS: S09839. $19.95.
Gift Pack of 4 Volumes.
VHS: S09835. $69.95.

Masters of War

A 13-tape series.
Masters of War—Battle for North Africa. One of the crucial battles of WWII showcases the different styles of two great leaders: the methodical and calculating Field Marshall Bernard "Monty" Montgomery and the brilliantly daring "Desert Fox," General Erwin Rommel. 45 mins.
VHS: S33974. $19.98.
Masters of War—Battle for the Boot. From Salerno to Rome, U.S. General Mark Clark and British General Sir Harold Alexander slug their way up the Italian boot, facing crack German divisions commanded by wily Luftwaffe Field Marshall Albert Kesselring. 47 mins.
VHS: S33964. $19.98.
Masters of War—Blitzkrieg Battle: The Battle for France. Bold and innovative, General Heinz Guderian was the leading exponent of Germany's Blitzkrieg tactics. In 1944, U.S. General Omar Bradly employed huge "land fleets" of mechanized armor to take back France, using the very same Blitzkrieg tactics. 45 mins.
VHS: S33965. $19.98.
Masters of War—Day of Decision. Operation Overlord—the invasion of France. D-Day pitted the best Allied leaders—Eisenhower, Montgomery, Marshall and Bradley—against Axis warriors Rommel and Von Runstedt in a battle of what has been called "The Longest Day." 45 mins.
VHS: S33975. $19.98.
Masters of War—Endgame: The Cold Warriors. Civilization teetered on the edge of extinction as Kennedy and Krushev fought a deadly battle of brinksmanship. Relive the Cuban Missile Crisis, when the U.S. and the U.S.S.R. caused the world to hold its breath. 47 mins.
VHS: S33968. $19.98.
Masters of War—Guerilla Warfare: Vietnam. Peasant General Vo Nguyen Giap vs. U.S. General William Westmoreland—these men commanded armies that pounded and pursued each other throughout Indochina. See the consequences during Ia Drang in 1965, and the Tet Offensive in 1968. 46 mins.
VHS: S33971. $19.98.
Masters of War—In the Lair of the Bear. Zhukov, the brilliant and ruthless Russian General, stops the Nazi Panzers at the gates of Moscow. A year later, he masterminds the offensive that annihilates the methodical General von Paulus' 6th Army at Stalingrad. 46 mins.
VHS: S33963. $19.98.
Masters of War—Operation Pointblank. U.S. General Carl Spaatz and British Air Marshall Sir Arthur "Bomber" Harris direct the largest air campaign ever—the strategic bombing of Germany. Repelling the assault are the Luftwaffe fighters of Goering— "The Fat One." 46 mins.
VHS: S33970. $19.98.
Masters of War—Patton's Charge. Maverick, pistol-packing General George Patton mounts a rapid, full-scale assault behind the German lines, driving his tank corps night and day, racing to save the besieged 101st Airborne. 45 mins.
VHS: S33969. $19.98.
Masters of War—The Battle for Leyte Gulf. When Japanese Admiral Toyoda divides his forces, Admiral Halsey charges after the decoy carriers. But Admiral Sprague's carriers and Admiral Oldendorf's Battlewagons carry the day in the battle that broke the back of the Japanese Navy. 45 mins.
VHS: S33973. $19.98.
Masters of War—The Knights of Desert Storm. Believing no Arab nation would ever unite with "infidels," Saddam Hussein defied the world and invaded Kuwait. Watch General Schwarzkopf's coalition forces, including Arabs, Americans, French and British, shatter Hussein's illusions. 47 mins.
VHS: S33966. $19.98.
Masters of War—The Turning Point at Guadalcanal. Guadalcanal was the bloody seesaw campaign that began America's march across the Pacific to ultimate victory. Watch General Alexander Vandegrift and Admiral William F. "Bull" Halsey square off aginst the legendary Japanese Admiral Yamamoto. 44 mins.
VHS: S33972. $19.98.
Masters of War—Wolfpack: The Hidden Enemy. Watch German Admiral Carl Donetz lead his U-Boat wolfpacks in an effort to sever England's maritime lifeline. The English fight back with convoys, patrol planes and sophisticated code-breaking to ferret out the hidden enemy. 45 mins.
VHS: S33967. $19.98.

Mercenary Game

This film explores the private rites and rituals of a mercenary training camp. Filmed at a "merc" camp in Georgia, this frightening and fascinating documentary features rare footage of an actual mercenary raid. 60 mins.
VHS: S13177. $39.98.

Music, Memories & Milestones

Rare, archival, British newsreel footage captures four decades that changed the world.
1930's. The era of the Big Band, rise of Fascism in Europe, terrible worldwide depression, Edward and Mrs. Simpson, Jesse Owens makes history, Amelia Earhart, Adolf Hitler, and Woody Herman's "At the Woodchopper's Ball" is in every dance hall. 60 mins.
VHS: S12412. $19.95.
1940's. The fighting, bravely optimistic days of WWII, the politicians of the time—Churchill, Hitler, Roosevelt, Stalin—the days of rebuilding and hope after the war, the proclamation of the state of Israel. 60 mins.
VHS: S12413. $19.95.
1950's. Elvis, the 4-minute mile, Sputnik. Symbols of a world recovered from war, its energy restored as prosperity returned. Suez, Korean War, Hungarian Revolution. 60 mins.
VHS: S12414. $19.95.
1960's. The era of sexual liberation, flower power, the Cuban missile crisis, the Berlin Wall erected, Vietnam, the Mid-East 6-day war. 60 mins.
VHS: S12415. $19.95.
Music, Memories & Milestones 4-Pack. The 1930's, 40's, 50's, and 60's (4 cassettes) at a special price.
VHS: S12416. $75.81.

Mutiny on the Western Front (WWI)

Here for the first time is the untold story of *World War I* filmed on locations in France, Germany and "down under." This is a startling portrait of the 300,000 Australian Anzac volunteers, suffering the largest share of casualties of the war, who mutiny against their incompetent and callous French and British commanders.
VHS: S03980. $29.95.

A Newsreel Library of America in Sports

Except for the World War II reports, sports highlights were the most popular moments of the theatrical newsreel. Among the 79 stories featured in this collection, find Knute Rockne's "Go-Go" speech, Babe Ruth's special game in Wrigley Field, Jesse Owens in Hitler's Berlin, the Jack Dempsey story, Lou Gehrig's farewell and the first Super Bowl. 90 mins.
VHS: S15947. $29.95.

A Newsreel Library of America in the News

Newsreels were shown regularly in the nation's movie theaters from the early 1900s to the late 1960s when television preempted their role. Audiences depended on the newsreel to bring life to events around the nation and the world. This collection of 87 segments includes the Wright Brothers' first flight, the Stock Market crash of 1929, the Hindenburg disaster, the Scopes trial and Sinatra and the Bobby Soxers. 90 mins.
VHS: S15946. $29.95.

A Newsreel Library of American Nostalgia

After reporting national disasters, wars, politics and social upheavals, the newsreel usually ended with an odd story or personality reflecting the comic side of life. Find 107 examples of lighthearted trivia in this program, including the premiere of Mickey Mouse, Elvis in the Army, the "It" Girl of the '20s, the Bikini Sensation, when 1937 Miss America said "No" and Clark Gable, Rita Hayworth and Marilyn Monroe taking Hollywood by storm. 90 mins.
VHS: S15948. $29.95.

Portraits from the Past

Original archive film documentaries on the life and times of two outstanding historical personalities: *Ace of Aces* is a presentation of the Eddie Rickenbacker story, from World War I air race to 20th century hero; *FDR* is the Franklin D. Roosevelt story told through the newsreels of the day. 28 mins.
VHS: S10781. $29.95.

Presidents
Historical footage from the ABC News archives reveals the profoundly different styles and personalities of America's presidents. From George Washington to George Bush, from Andrew Jackson's rambunctious inauguration to the Reagan years, this program reveals little-known facts about the men who led and shaped the destiny of the country. 60 mins.
VHS: S12272. $19.98.

Reagan Years
A history of the life and times of Ronald Reagan, tracing his life from college football player to charismatic politician, including an examination of the two terms of his presidency, and his legacy. 75 mins.
VHS: S07717. $29.95.

Reagan's Way
Steal from the poor and give to the rich? No, this is a loving and respectful tribute to Ronald Reagan; family man, managerial wizard. For those who still have a color portrait of the president on your walls, this tape is for you. 52 mins.
VHS: S13102. $39.98.

The Roots of Democracy (1700s)
The dynamic forces which shaped America are revealed in studies of *The Economy* and the beliefs of the foresighted men who drafted *The Constitution*, and gave us the *Bill of Rights* and the amendments guaranteeing our rights to religious freedom, freedom of speech, of the press, of assembly and of equal justice under the law.
VHS: S03972. $64.95.

Sixties Headlines
Emphasizing the incredible amount of headline from the 1960's, this tape includes everything from Martin Luther King to Vietnam, Neil Armstrong to the Beatles, JFK to Woodstock. 30 mins.
VHS: S13150. $14.98.

This Is America
A history of America from 1917 to 1932, including the Big Crash and the Depression, a history of the first World War, as well as American presidents, through rare footage. Also on the same program is the film *The American Road*, a history of the automobile, reportedly directed by John Ford, and narrated by Raymond Massey. USA, 1932.
VHS: S09525. $29.95.

Time Warp: 1954
Ike and Mamie, The Honeymooners, Liberace, The Reagans, Marlon Brando, Betty Furness, Speedy Alka Seltzer, Creature from the Black Lagoon, the McCarthy Hearings, the Eniwetok Atoll, H-Bomb blast and more. 79 mins.
VHS: S13147. $19.98.

Time Warp: 1960
The Kennedys, Castro, Khrushchev, Elvis, Marilyn, Mickey Mantle, Nixon, Hitchcock, Jerry Lewis, Princess Margaret, the Debates, the Twist, the U-2 incident, Crisis in Algeria, South Africa and more. 83 mins.
VHS: S13148. $19.98.

Time Warp: 1964
The Johnsons, Roy Orbison, the Beatles, Malcolm X, Barry Goldwater, Cassius Clay, GI Joe, Carol Doda, Lester Maddox, Martin Luther King, Dick Van Dyke, Gulf of Tonkin, the Long Hot Summer, surfing and more. 85 mins.
VHS: S13149. $19.98.

Two Great Crusades (1935-1945)
The New Deal and *World War II* are the subject here, the two greatest crises to confront the nation since the Civil War. Emerging from the paralyzing depression of the 30's, America in the 40's enters a war on two fronts, against the Japanese and Nazi Germany, and highlights the unheralded efforts of Americans on the home front.
VHS: S03979. $64.95.

War of 1812
From the English attack on the U.S. frigate Chesapeake through the battle of Lake Erie and the creation of The Star Spangled Banner, this video history covers all of the crucial naval battles that were fought for control of the Atlantic coast and the supremacy of the Great Lakes. 21 mins.
VHS: S09490. $29.95.

Warring & Roaring (1914-1929)
World War I and *The 1920's*, with startling realism and boldness, reveal how the United States vacillated between isolationism and involvement and finally for the first time plunged into a European conflict which was followed by a decade of paradoxes called both "The Age of Normalcy" and "The Era of Wonderful Nonsense."
VHS: S03978. $64.95.

Where America Began: Jamestown, Colonial Williamsburg and Yorktown
Historic sites and life in Colonial America of 250 years ago-militia musters, fifes and drums, skilled craftsmen, authentic buildings, and the dramatic events of the important chapters of American history. 30 mins.
VHS: S10102. $29.95.

Within These Walls
An intimate program on the personal and political significance of the White House, its symbolism, its architectural history, and the various men and women who lived there, providing an important human scale and dimension. With an introduction by the First Lady and a closing speech by the president. 33 mins.
VHS: S17719. $19.95.

nature videos

A&E's Incredible World of Cats

A compresive history of cats, from ancient Egypt's feline gods to today's tabby, featuring expert tips on training and care. Two videos, 50 mins. each.
VHS: S31147. $29.95.

Adventure

Six tapes of exciting adventures from around the world. 60 minutes each.
Return to the Jade Sea. Archeologist Andrew Hartley explores Kenya's Lake Turkana, one of the least known regions on the African continent and a rich hunting ground for traces of an advanced Stone Age culture.
VHS: S14729. $19.95.
The Logan Challenge. Following in the footsteps of the first expedition up Mount Logan in 1925, an extraordinary achievement which was filmed, three adventurers set out to take their husky dog team to the summit.
VHS: S14727. $19.95.
The Wildman of China. An American anthropologist and a British crypto-zoologist search for the *yeren*, a huge ape-like creature said to prowl the remote regions of central China.
VHS: S14726. $24.95.
To the Island of the Aye-Aye. A search and rescue expedition into the remote interior of northeastern Madagascar with Gerald Durrell, the world's foremost animal conservationist.
VHS: S14724. $19.95.
Adventure: Complete Set. The complete set at a special price.
VHS: S19337. $124.95.

African Shark Safari

In treacherous waters, the great white shark lies in wait for a tasty morsel. This video documentary shows photographers studying the great whites who congregate to feed on young penguins and seals. 60 mins.
VHS: S26044. $19.95.

Alaska's Three Bears and the Alaska Mother Goose

Shelly Gill and Shannon Cartwright are Alaska's most popular children's book creators. These clever stories join charming illustrations with actual live footage of Alaska's abundant wildlife and breathtaking scenery. 45 mins.
VHS: S23083. $24.95.

Alaska's Whales and Wildlife

Alaska's southeast coast contains a treasure trove of unmatched natural wonders, including the world's largest temperate rainforest and massive glaciers. Naturalists guide the viewer through these ecosystems, revealing the unique plant and animal life contained in these areas. Brown bears, bald eagles and humpback whales are just some of the wildlife shown. 46 mins.
VHS: S21580. $59.95.

Alaska's Wildlife

On this Alaskan safari there is an abundance of unique wildlife. Brown bears gorge themselves on salmon, caribou wander the tundra, and the Dall sheep engage in their ritual mating rut. Whistling swans, bald eagles, puffins and walruses are seen in this exciting wildlife documentary. 30 mins.
VHS: S23968. $14.95.

Alaskan Safari

Fascinating adventure film travels through the North Country by airplane and dogsled to track moose and grizzly bear as well as seals, sea lions and walrus.
VHS: S02264. $19.95.
R. Hayes/B. Hayes, USA, 1986, 93 mins.

Alien Empire: We Are Not Alone

They surround you every day, and yet if you look closely you realize that they are utterly different and completely alien to everything you know. This video brings the secret world of insects to life with state-of-the-art macrophotography and digital effects. Three-tape set. Each tape is approximately 60 mins.
VHS: S27414. $49.99.

America's Western National Parks

From the Sierra Nevada of California to the Badlands of South Dakota, from the depths of the Grand Canyon to the peaks of the Olympic Mountains, you'll explore the very best of more than 40 national parks and monuments in a way you never imagined. USA, 60 mins.
VHS: S15078. $29.95.

The American West: Land of Beautiful Places

In this journey of images and harmonies some of the most beautiful scenery from the Western United States is joined with moving music for a unique video experience. Yosemite, Yellowstone, the Grand Canyon, Monument Valley and many other famous sites are included in this breathtaking work. 40 mins.
VHS: S21064. $19.95.

Among the Wild Chimpanzees

In 1960, Jane Goodall set out for Tanzania's remote Gombe Stream Game Reserve to study the behavior of man's closest living relative, the chimpanzee. With dedication and perseverance, she earned the trust of a wild chimp community, and has now spent two landmark decades observing their varied personalities and rich life. National Geographic. 59 mins.
VHS: S04887. $19.95.

Ancient Sea Turtles: The Last Voyage?

With fascinating footage, this documentary provides an overview of the extraordinary natural history of sea turtles, including their mysterious migrations and primeval egg-laying habits. Informative and entertaining. USA, 1991, 25 mins.
VHS: S15203. $59.95.

Animal Babies in the Wild

An entrancing look at baby animals from Africa to the Arctic, captured on this video which uses live photography, stories and songs, that capture the hearts of children 2-8.
VHS: S04135. $14.95.

Animal Tales: "Lost Cubs" and "The Bully"

These two adventure stories combine wildlife footage, fantasy storytelling and original music, and conclude with a visit to a zoo, where children learn more about the "animal actors" depicted in the stories. Teacher's activity guide included. Ages 3-10. 1996, 26 mins.
VHS: S31899. $39.95.

Animal Wonders from Down Under

A new series exploring the unique wildlife of Australia issued as a six-volume set.
Tiny Carnivores/Wombat. Many of the Australian marsupials are carnivores, small but fierce predators of insects, spiders. Looks at the native cats, the Tasmanian Devil, and Wombats—pig-like marsupials as endearing as the koala. 50 mins.
VHS: S07356. $14.95.
Complete Set.
VHS: Out of print. For rental only.

Animals of Africa: From the Sky to the Sea

The gregarious pink throated, web-footed cormorants as they breed and gather nesting materials; baby sea pups as they are born and cared for in a communal nursery; and the antics of the rare black-footed African penguins that live underground in burrows.
VHS: S09563. $29.95.

Animals of Africa: Hippos, Baboons and the African Elephant

Joan Embery hosts this look at baboons, hippos, and African elephants.
VHS: S01684. $29.95.

Animals of Africa: The Land of the Elephants

Experience a highly ritualized form of combat as two sables conduct a dance of dominance; watch hippos nibble on fragile hyacinths and frolic in the world's largest bathtub; and see playful baby elephants who only weigh a ton.
VHS: S09564. $29.95.

Antarctica

Representing the last great wilderness on Earth, Antarctica conceals a treasure trove of wildlife and rugged, beautiful terrain. From unlocking the secrets of ancient glacial ice to watching the underwater ballet of penguins swimming, this documentary captures the raw feel and power of nature. Filmed in IMAX. 40 mins.
VHS: S23972. $29.95.
Laser: LD75007. $39.95.

Ape Man: The Story of Human Evolution

Walter Cronkite hosts a riveting four-volume set tracing the story of mankind's ascent. Filmed on location in Africa and featuring the latest scientific evidence. The four volumes are: *The Human Puzzle, Giant Strides, All in the Mind* and *Science and Fiction*. Boxed set, 200 mins.
VHS: S21901. $79.95.
Laser: CLV. **LD74748. $79.95.**

Arctic Refuge: A Vanishing Wilderness

The concerns of the oil and gas industry, who want to drill across this 100-mile stretch of land, threaten the annual migrations of animals who gather every spring at the coastal plain of the Arctic National Wildlife Refuge. Narrated by Meryl Streep.
VHS: S16876. $14.98.

Ascent of the Chimps

A chimpanzee enclosure which mimics the conditions of the wild was built at the Arnhem Zoo in the Netherlands in 1971. Lorne Greene explores the life of the thriving chimpanzee community at the Zoo which, surprisingly, reflects many human social elements. USA, 22 mins.
VHS: S03095. $14.95.

Audubon Society Videoguides to the Birds of North America

Combines bird sights and sounds for simple and accurate identification of 505 North American species. Moving and still pictures show each bird's distinctive markings and behavior, with computer-animated range maps showing breeding and wintering areas for each species. Bird calls and sounds from the Cornell Laboratory of Ornithology complement the narration and visuals.
Volume 3: 77 species of pigeons and doves, cuckoos, owls, nighthawks, hummingbirds, swifts, trogons, kingfishers and woodpeckers. 61 mins.
VHS: S01672. $29.95.
Laser: LD72224. $35.95.
Volume 5: Part 2 of songbirds: 109 species of warblers, orioles and blackbirds, tanagers, grosbeaks, finches, buntings and sparrows. 80 mins.
VHS: S02959. $29.95.
Volume 2: 105 species of water birds, including herons and egrets, cranes, shorebirds, gulls, terns and alcids. 78 mins.
VHS: S03123. $29.95.
Laser: LD72223. $35.95.
Volume 1: 116 species of loons, grebes, pelicans and their allies, swans, geese and ducks, hawks, vultures and falcons, and the chicken-like birds (pheasants, grouse, quails, ptarmigans). 94 mins.
VHS: S03211. $29.95.
Laser: LD70847. $39.95.
Volume 4: 98 species of songbirds: flycatchers, larks, swallows, crows and jays, titmice and chickadees, nuthatches, creepers, wrens, thrushes, waxwings, shrikes, thrashers and vireos. 75 mins.
VHS: S05966. $29.95.
Laser: LD72225. $35.95.

Audubon: Greed and Wildlife: Poaching in America

Richard Chamberlain narrates the story of grizzlies, bald eagles, alligators and thousands of other threatened or endangered species that are killed in senseless slaughter each year. In shocking and horrifying footage, witness the tragic waste of our wildlife and discover what is being done to stop illegal hunting. 60 mins.
VHS: S12133. $14.98.

Audubon: Sharks
Peter Benchley narrates the story of the shark—reviled, feared and destroyed through the ages, and now finally earning the respect and appreciation it deserves. Discover the emerging truths of this misunderstood species, including remarkable applications in cancer treatment and human skin grafting. 60 mins.
VHS: S12132. $14.98.

Australian Ark Documentary Series
A look at the fascinating land of Australia and the unique animal world that inhabits that land.
Amazing Marsupials. Astonishing footage of Tasmanian devils, kangaroos, koalas and wombats, the numbat, which is shown feasting on termites, as well as rare footage of the now-extinct marsupial wolf. 79 mins.
VHS: S03815. $19.95.
Changing Face of Australia. A geological history told through the rock formations found there. Some of the land is inconceivably old, such as the vast Western Shield which rose from the sea three billion years ago and contains fossils dating from the dawn of life. Spectacular scenery and vivid contrasts highlight this program. 54 mins.
VHS: S03816. $19.95.
Coming of Man. A program which examines man's 50,000 year stay in Australia, with particular attention to carved symbols which inexplicably resemble carvings in Sibera and South America. 67 mins.
VHS: S03817. $19.95.
Farthest West. An examination of the eerie windswept scrubland in Western Australia and the life that thrives in this almost alien area. The plump bottle-trunked monsters called baobabs, technicolor parrots and cockateels, lizards and elusive numbats make for an interesting program. 50 mins.
VHS: S03818. $19.95.
Green World. A look at the Australian rain forest and the unique plant and animal life that call it home. View the world's tallest hardwood trees soaring over 300 feet into the air, bats the size of a small fox that travel in flocks of 25,000, and giant flightless birds. 52 mins.
VHS: S03819. $19.95.

Avalanche
Watch a powder avalanche hurtle down a mountain at 200 mph, snapping trees like matchsticks, and hang on as skiers race for their lives before rivers of snow.
VHS: S34281. $14.98.

Avalanche Awareness
Snow avalanches are the single greatest hazard to the unwary back-country traveller. Combining spectacular live footage with practical safety tips, this film clearly presents the fundamentals of avalanche safety in a simple and straightforward way. Endorsed by the National Mountain Rescue Association and the U.S. Forest Service. 1988, 28 mins.
VHS: S13699. $29.95.

Baboona
Fabled explorers and documentary filmmakers Osa and Martin Johnson share their encounters on an African safari, where they discovered the largest baboon community any explorer had ever encountered. The camera captures the lifestyle of this highly intelligent member of the monkey family with an intimacy and agility never before accomplished.
VHS: S31879. $19.95.
Martin Johnson/Osa Johnson, USA, 1935, 73 mins.

BBC Wildlife Special Volume 2
Tidbits: The blue tit is a welcome guest in every garden; no bird table or nest box is complete without one. This beautiful film examines the private life of this familiar bird. It shows how the male feeds and cares for its mate, how their first tiny nestling is born, and how they avoid such hazards as a cat and a sparrow hawk. It is an affectionate look at the blue tit, everybody's favorite bird. *Nightlife*: In the dead of night is the time we sleep but for many animals nighttime is far from dead. It's the hour when the barn owl pounces on the luckless vole, the fox stalks his prey, beetles mate and the nightingale sings. Through the eyes and ears of these nocturnal animals this fascinating film unfolds and tells the story of one night in the English countryside. 55 minutes.
VHS: S07593. $24.95.

BBC Wildlife Specials: Aliens from Inner Space/The Fastest Claw in the West
Cuttlefish, squid and octopus—do these unusual ocean creatures "talk" to each other? Are they perhaps trying to contact us? *Aliens from Inner Space* allows us to judge for ourselves. *The Fastest Claw in the West* shows us pugnacious, belligerent and apparently fearless Mantis shrimp audacious enough to engage in battle with octopus twice their size and 20 times their weight. Special camera techniques and exceptionally high speed photography examine the behavior of this remarkable underwater creature. Narrated by David Attenborough. 48 mins.
VHS: S11765. $19.94.

BBC Wildlife Specials: Birds of a Sun God/In-Flight Movie
David Attenborough narrates these two programs. The first focuses on the birds that can hover motionless, fly backwards and even upside down—hummingbirds. They lay the smallest eggs, have the fastest wingbeats, and the most dazzling plumage. *In-Flight Movie* is the story of how birds fly. Using a remarkable new filming technique, the camera takes to the air for the experience of a lifetime. This unique film enables you to fly in the clouds with a flock of geese. 58 mins.
VHS: S10289. $24.95.

BBC Wildlife Specials: On the Tracks of the Wild Otter/The Mouse's Tale
The story of a rare man searching for a rare animal. The animal is the otter; the scene is the Shetlands. The stars of the film are the wild otters themselves, living their free and natural lives in these remote and beautiful islands. *The Mouse's Tale* follows the adventures of four species of mice in and around a country cottage in Wiltshire, England. Narrated by David Attenborough. 83 mins.
VHS: S11763. $19.94.

Beastly Behavior
The wild but true sexual antics and bizarre mating rituals of more than 30 animals, insects, birds and sea creatures are hilariously animated and explained. Uproariously funny, often dangerous, always fascinating. With sidesplitting narration and special insights by the British "Professor" Roger Knightly, *Beastly Behavior* will have you roaring with laughter as all the shocking, intimate details unfold.
VHS: S30481. $19.95.
Andy Wyatt, Great Britain, 1996, 45 mins.

Beyond the Ring of Fire
Lawrence Blair explores monkey forests, colorful native rituals, headhunter tribes, mysterious villages and giant eels in underwater reefs, in this return journey to remote lands and tribes that are being slowly infiltrated by the modern world. 58 mins.
VHS: S28619. $19.95.

The Big Wet
Australian monsoons unleash dynamic changes on the environment. This video details the effects of cyclones and electrical storms, which are inevitably followed by dry spells and fire. Together this pattern of wet and dry sets the tone for a unique ecosystem. 60 mins. From the Discovery Channel.
VHS: S25070. $19.95.

The Biggest Bears
All kinds of bears in their wild habitat are shown in this exciting documentary narrated by a five-year-old Alaskan boy. The makers travelled across Alaska, Canada and Russia in order to create this unparalleled musical adventure.
VHS: S22160. $14.95.

Binocular Vision
A wonderfully entertaining look at the National Audubon Society's Christmas Bird Count. A documentary about bird watchers and birding, a lighthearted yet intimate look at the people who share the passion. *Binocular Vision* looks at the Annual Christmas Bird Count, in which some 40,000 people throughout the U.S. and Canada watch and count birds.
VHS: S09438. $24.95.
Robert Machover, USA, 1988, 26 mins.

Birds
This ten-part series is a fascinating portrait of various birds of prey. The series includes programs on bird watching, the variety of birds, seabirds, migration, basket weaving and nest building, eagles, storks, swans and owls.
Birds: A Little Owl's Story.
VHS: S17297. $29.95.
Birds: Concerning Swans.
VHS: S17295. $29.95.
Birds: Eagles International/Eagles: The Majestic Hunters/ Where Eagles Fly.
VHS: S17294. $29.95.
Birds: Getting to Know Birds.
VHS: S17288. $29.95.
Birds: Seabirds.
VHS: S17291. $29.95.
Birds: Talons, Beaks and Nests.
VHS: S17289. $29.95.
Birds: The Feathered Athletes.
VHS: S17293. $29.95.
Birds: The Masterbuilders.
VHS: S17292. $29.95.
Birds: The Migration of Birds—Fight for Survival.
VHS: S17290. $29.95.
Birds: The Year of the Stork.
VHS: S17296. $29.95.

Bo-Ru the Ape Boy
This fascinating documentary delves into the relationships that grow between humans and animals. Major C. Court produced and directed this unique effort. 35 mins.
VHS: S23792. $24.95.

Bride of the Beast
Osa and Martin Johnson created this unusual documentary that was shot on location in Africa. 57 mins.
VHS: S23793. $24.95.

Brumby: Horse Run Wild
Narrator Bryan Brown presents a compelling look at the Brumbies, wild horses of Australia who have had limited interaction with humans. A symbol of the wilderness and a nostalgic link to the past, they are also an environmental threat and an object of cruelty. 54 mins.
VHS: S34724. $19.98.

Canyon Dreams
The majestic Grand Canyon captured by director Jan Nickman with rare perception and sensitivity. Original music by Tangerine Dream. 45 mins.
VHS: S10960. $29.95.

Carlsbad Caverns & Guadalupe Mountains National Parks
An entirely new video program featuring the Carlsbad Caverns, New Cave and nearby Guadalupe Mountains National Park, exploring how caverns are formed, with detailed closeups of formations, bat flight.
VHS: S06665. $29.95.

Christian the Lion
Ten years after the making of *Born Free*, this docudrama finds Bill Travers and Virginia McKenna once again involved with the welfare of a member of the lion family. They help a London Zoo-born animal back to the wilds of Kenya. A sequel of sorts to *Lion at World's End*.
VHS: S12840. $29.95.
Bill Travers, Great Britain, 1976, 89 mins.

Coastal Habitat Set
Castaways of Galapagos, Orca Whales and Mermaid Tales and *Penguins in Paradise* are all part of this three-volume set from the Discovery Channel's *Mother Nature: Tales of Discovery* series. Together these videos document unique coastal landscapes in varying climates.
VHS: S25088. $39.95.

Commune with the Dolphins
This film takes the viewer into the deep and up in the air with Nature's most lyrical and magnificent creatures. Filmed by Emmy award-winning cinematographer Rober Riger and underscored musically by composer/ arranger Carlos Alornar, this footage brings the power, compassion, energy and serenity of dolphins. 25 mins.
VHS: S07729. $29.95.

Cousteau 2—Bering Sea: Twilight of the Alaskan Hunter
Jacques and Jean-Michel Cousteau study the hunting traditions of an ancient people colliding with the modern ways of life and the struggle to preserve the different species unique to this ice-encrusted region. 48 mins.
VHS: S13558. $19.98.
Laser: LD71566. $29.95.

Cousteau 2—Borneo II: Forests Without Land
Jacques and Jean-Michel Cousteau investigate the incomparable beauty and fragility of the third largest island in the world. The abundant mangrove thickets that comprise the island hold a wealth of fish and other underwater life. 48 mins.
VHS: S13560. $19.98.

Cousteau 2—Haiti: Waters of Sorrow
Jacques and Jean-Michel Cousteau investigate Haiti. It was once a lush island, abundant in natural resources. Today it is dying a slow death caused by massive overpopulation, and its predicament reveals trends forthcoming to Third World countries the world over. 48 mins.
VHS: S13557. $19.98.
Laser: LD71565. $29.95.

Cousteau 2—Riders of the Wind

The turbo-sail system developed by Jacques Cousteau, Lucien Malavard and Bertrand Charrier operates much like conventional sailing, but with heightened efficiency and the hope of revolutionizing the shipping industry of the future. 48 mins.
VHS: S13562. $19.98.
Laser: LD71567. $29.95.

Cousteau 2—Thailand: Convicts of the Sea

Jacques and Jean-Michel Cousteau explore the effects of undersea tin-ore mining, including vast canyons on the ocean floor and clouds of sliding mud, creating regions uninhabitable by any marine life, including seaweed. 48 mins.
VHS: S13559. $19.98.

Cousteau 2—Western Australia: Out West Down Under

Jacques and Jean-Michel Cousteau study the encroachment of humanity on the fragile western coastline of Australia threatening ocean communities of tremendous vitality and untold wealth. 48 mins.
VHS: S13561. $19.98.

Cousteau 2—Series Gift Pack

Contains all six titles listed above plus a "Save the Planet" computer disk which includes graphic illustrations, a global-warming scenario game, resources for environmental action, energy-saving tips and shopping guidelines. Available for either IBM or Apple Macintosh computers and their compatibles. 388 mins.
VHS: S13563. $119.98.

The Cousteau Odyssey

Mediterranean: Cradle or Coffin? Calypso studies the impact of industry, urbanization, tourism and fishing on the fragile beauty and bounty of the virtually landlocked Mediterranean region. 58 mins.
VHS: S10943. $24.98.
Time Bomb at Fifty Fathoms.
VHS: S10944. $24.98.

Cousteau: Alaska: Outrage at Valdez

In a Cousteau Society special report, Jean-Michel Cousteau takes us on a voyage to investigate first-hand the devastating impact of the 1989 *Exxon Valdez* oil spill in Alaska. 57 mins.
VHS: S13025. $19.98.

Cousteau: Amazon: Snowstorm in the Jungle and Rigging for the Amazon

Penetrate the dark mysteries of the Amazon basin and confront the awesome power of the source of cocaine. Then see how the Cousteaus prepared for their most challenging expedition. 90 mins.
VHS: S13028. $19.98.

Cousteau: Journey to a Thousand Rivers

Join Cousteau on a monumental expedition into the vast and mysterious realm of the Amazon River system. 98 mins.
VHS: S14736. $19.98.

Cousteau: Lilliput in Antarctica

Cousteau is accompanied by six children from around the world on a spectacular odyssey to Antarctica, where they are greeted by huge glaciers, humpback whales, penguins and elephant seals. 48 mins.
VHS: S13026. $19.98.

Cousteau: Papua New Guinea: The Center of Fire

In Papua New Guinea Cousteau divers explore the remains of violent World War II battles: a 500-foot Japanese freighter and a famous B-17 Flying Fortress, still remarkably intact. 60 mins.
VHS: S13027. $19.98.

Cousteau: Pioneers of the Sea

A special biographical film salute to Captain Cousteau upon his 75th birthday, featuring rare photographs and remarkable footage from some of his greatest expeditions. 60 mins.
VHS: S13024. $19.98.

Cousteau: River of the Future

How man is adversely influencing the Amazon's delicate and vitally important ecosystem, and how, perhaps, he can save it. 98 mins.
VHS: S14738. $19.98.

Cousteau: Tahiti Fire Waters

Cousteau pilots the *Calypso* to the beautiful islands surrounding Tahiti in the South Pacific. With stunning photography, his team examines the effects upon nature and the economies of local cultures of continued testing of nuclear weapons. 60 mins.
VHS: S13029. $19.98.

Cousteau: The Great White Shark

Jean-Michel Cousteau and his team of divers and scientists embark on an ambitious expedition to track and film the great white shark.
VHS: S17738. $19.98.

Cousteau: The New Eldorado—Invaders and Exiles

A fascinating examination of the Amazon's inhabitants and their struggle with the ever-invading modern world. 98 mins.
VHS: S14737. $29.95.

Cradle in the Sea

With endearing stories of the ocean's most adorable baby animals, this elegantly photographed series follows six infants—a spotted dolphin, sea otter, harbor seal, gray whale, killer whale and manatee-from their first breath to their discovery of the fascinating ocean around them. Three volumes, 50 mins. each.
VHS: S33362. $49.95.

Creatures Great and Small

James Whitmore and James Earl Jones narrate this fascinating look into the past and present of dinosaurs, which ruled the world for 140 million years, and insects, which predate the dinosaurs by at least 100 million years. 1989, 60 mins.
VHS: S14541. $29.95.

Crocodile Territory

Glimpse 200 million years of evolutionary perfection in action as you travel to billabongs and flood plains of the vast Northern Territory wilderness; take a fascinating look at the ecosystem from the rainy season to the struggles of the dry months; and go jaw to jaw with Australia's giant Australian salt crocodile: a 20-foot, cold-blooded mammoth weighing over a ton. Narrated by Brenda Vaccaro.
VHS: S30589. $19.95.
USA, 1996, 60 mins.

Curse of T. Rex

Follow the trail of legal and illegal fossil-dealing in South Dakota, as government agencies, fossil hunters and landowners argue over who owns the best *Tyrannosaurus rex* specimen ever found. 60 mins.
VHS: S31420. $19.95.

Death on the Wing

Lorne Greene hosts this program about the migration of the majestic Golden Eagle from summer in Idaho to winter in Texas, as the devoted Golden Eagle parents, mated for life, strive to feed and protect their offspring.
VHS: S06328. $14.95.
Charles Greene/Stephen W. Dewar, USA, 1984, 30 mins.

Demons of the Deep

From the Bahamas comes this gripping firsthand account of spectacular physical action photography. Shark and barracuda feeding frenzies are revealed in close camera work, made possible by free-swimming divers, unhindered by safety cages. The basics of shark and barracuda biology are also made clear in this video, thereby separating fact from fiction. 60 mins.
VHS: S21796. $19.95.

Desert Under Siege

A beautifully shot production that provides a concise overview of desert ecology and an examination of the human endeavors that threaten this fragile ecosystem. USA, 1991, 28 mins.
VHS: S15204. $79.00.

Desert Vision

The magical Southwest captured in breathtaking imagery with original music by David Lanz and Paul Speer. 50 mins.
VHS: S10958. $29.95.

Dinosaurs

The Smithsonian Institution's own collection of artifacts is key to this documentary about the new controversies surrounding the mammoth beasts from the past. The lives of these creatures as well as their extinction and the way information is uncovered about them is all shown in this fascinating video.
VHS: S21268. $29.95.

The Dinosaurs

This fascinating four-part set follows the story of dinosaurs, those mammoth creatures who are known to us only through fossils. Fortunately scientists the world over have painstakingly recreated their stories. Dr. John Ostrun, the paleontologist who inspired the character Alan Grant in *Jurassic Park*, is featured.
Flesh on the Bones. The mysteries start to unravel. Where did dinosaurs live, how fast did they move, and were they hot- or cold-blooded? Find out some astonishing answers to questions about a 200-million-year-old mystery.
VHS: S21750. $14.98.
The Death of the Dinosaur. The most fascinating and puzzling question of all is, "Why did the dinosaurs disappear?" Share in the theories of the cause of their demise, which range from massive meteors to violent volcanoes to disease.
VHS: S21752. $14.98.
The Monsters Emerge. A fascinating look at how a skeptical world first reacted to the proposed existence of dinosaurs. Join lively bone-hunts and an expedition with a real-life Indiana Jones in this exciting video.
VHS: S21749. $14.98.
The Nature of the Beast. Travel around the world with scientists in their quest to find answers to how dinosaurs originated, and how these animals came to dominate the entire planet for over 140 million years. From Argentina to Nova Scotia to the Western U.S., learn about recent discoveries, such as the existence of "good lizard mothers."
VHS: S21751. $14.98.
The Complete Set.
VHS: S21753. $39.98.

The Discoverers

Reverberating with the passion to discover our world, this video charts the earliest voyages that mapped the earth. It continues up into the present day by examining contemporary space launches. The challenges, lessons and exhilaration of mankind's unending quests are charted in *The Discoverers*. 38 mins. Filmed in IMAX.
Laser: LD74733. $39.95.

Discovering Gardens

An entertaining series on England's most beautiful and elaborate gardens, the series shows the care and skill brought to each house and garden. Hosted by Gyles Brandrell and Michele Brown.
Vol. 1: Trelissick, Cornwall/East Lambrook, Somerset. At the foot of Trelissick house and garden, we're introduced to the famous Cornish garden, its effervescent spring glory richly planted with summer favorites.
VHS: S17956. $29.95.
Vol. 2: Cotehele, Cornwall/Docton Mill, Devon. A contemporary study of the Cotehele House, which overlooks the River Tamar, with its medieval history and glory. The second part looks at the efforts of Stephen and Irish Pugh and their garden crafted in the hills of the coastal North Devon.
VHS: S17957. $29.95.
Vol. 3: Bicton Park, Devon/Mapperton, Dorset. A visually spectacular view of the contemporary oriental garden, the Palm House, created by Bill Hearne, and an 18th century Italianate renaissance garden. The second part looks at an exquisite Italianate garden, a 17th-century water garden and Victor Montague's wild valley garden.
VHS: S17958. $29.95.
Vol. 4: Stourhead, Wiltshire/Glendurgan, Cornwall. This stunning landscape epitomizes the 18th-century English idea. The second part looks at the components of the wild areas of a beautiful hidden valley, and the mazes at Glendurgan.
VHS: S17959. $29.95.
Vol. 5: Tresco, Isles of Scilly/Mount Edgcumbe, Cornwall. Brandell and Brown study the amazing Abbey Gardens, the world's sole garden-heliport. In the second piece they interact with Gods in the Italian Garden and a geyser in the New Zealand garden.
VHS: S17960. $29.95.
Vol. 6: St. Michael's Mount, Cornwall/Trewithen, Cornwall. Follow Lord St. Leven on the perilous, storm-lashed garden in the first part, and then move to England's finest spring garden, a setting overladen with rhododendrons, camellias and magnolias.
VHS: S17961. $29.95.

Dolphin Adventure

In this fascinating underwater adventure, dolphins are captured on film in the open ocean for the first time. These intelligent creatures are revealed as never before in this film, winner of the "Cup of the Prime Minister of Italy Award" at the Milan Film Festival. Special appearance by Buckminster Fuller.
VHS: S23671. $19.95.
Michael Wiese, USA, 1994, 60 mins.

Dolphins

Commune with the dolphins. Enjoy graceful acrobatics and sensuous swimming in the ocean at the Dolphin Research Center, Grassy Key, Florida. Lush music by Private Music Artist Carlos Alomar to the filmed images by Robert Riger. 25 mins.
VHS: S10242. $29.95.

Dolphins, Close Encounters

George Page narrates this exploration of the research focused on the abilities of these large sea mammals. Study shows that they are highly intelligent and aware creatures who are also capable of great affection. 60 mins.
VHS: S24376. $19.95.

Drought
A highly evocative film which examines the dry seasons and their place in the rhythm of the Australian climate. The cycle of drought, fire and flood is part of the natural order rather than a series of unpredictable catastrophies. The film explores the Australian aborigine's attitude to drought and examines the theories of its causes—sunspots, volcanic eruptions, eccentricities of our planet's orbit. 58 mins.
VHS: S10292. $24.95.

Ducks Unlimited's Videoguide to Waterfowl and Game Birds
For the hunter and naturalist, bird identification is a must. *Ducks Unlimited's Videoguide to Waterfowl and Game Birds* gives a comprehensive system of sight and sound identification for our 43 species of waterfowl and 21 upland game birds of North America. Breath-taking footage, still photographs and computer-animated video graphics simulating the birds' appearance under low-light conditions with wingbeats calibrated to actual speed for each species focus today's technology on identifying birds in flight.
VHS: S03998. $39.95.
Laser: LD70958. $39.95.

Earth Bridge
The Earth Bridge Project is an innovative, nature-based leadership development program that brings together high school students of different cultures and helps them develop a deepened respect for nature, for their own cultural heritage and for the culture of others. 28 mins.
VHS: S23366. $59.95.

Earth Dance
David Fortney's visual poem about nature and beauty, "tall grasses dancing in the wind, water cascading wildly and clouds moving across the sky in silent majesty." 30 mins.
Laser: LD70244. $24.95.

Earth Day Special
This is the celebrity-strewn television special that celebrated the 20th anniversary of Earth Day. Everyone from Candice Bergen to Carl Sagan partakes, profits go to the People of the Earth Foundation. 95 mins.
VHS: S12751. $9.95.

Earth Dreaming
Georgianne Cowan's mythological journey reveals the texture, rhythm and shape of the earth, punctuated by Steve Roach's haunting, ethereal score. 23 mins.
Laser: LD70241. $24.95.

Earthquake! Disaster in L.A.
Experience the first-hand devastation of a major quake, including actual footage taken during the 1987 Whittier Quake. A Cal Tech seismologist discusses the effects of a larger future quake in Southern California. 53 mins.
VHS: S10028. $29.95.

Echo of the Elephants
Echo is the matriarch of a family of African elephants. Her calf Ely was born unable to walk. This nature documentary reveals the lives of these great animals in startling detail, allowing each creature to appear as a complete individual.
VHS: S24373. $19.95.

Eco-Rap: Voices from the Hood
A multi-ethnic group of young men and women learn about local environmental hazards and express their concerns using the urban poetry of rap music. The video features the best of Eco-Rap music with contemporary graphics. 38 mins.
VHS: S23362. $59.95.

Enchanted Forest
A wildlife oasis full of amazing animals, this tape focuses on the red deer, known for their extraordinary antlers. Directed by wildlife filmmaker Peter Lalovic, narrated by Lorne Greene. 30 mins.
VHS: S05002. $14.95.

Endangered
Largely because of human activity, our planet loses 100 species each day. This video provides a clear introduction to how human activities are endangering thousands of species, why protecting nature's diversity is critical to us all and how the Endangered Species Act works to help us do that. 30 mins.
VHS: S23365. $29.95.

The Ends of the Earth
Western Australia is home to spellbinding creatures who inhabit a dry and foreboding landscape. The thorny devil, the frilled lizard, the banjo ray and the sinister saltwater crocodile are just some of the more intriguing animals featured in this video. 60 mins. From the Discovery Channel.
VHS: S25073. $19.95.

Eruption of Mt. St. Helens
Witness the explosive eruption of Mt. St. Helens and its devastating aftermath as photographed by men who narrowly escaped the Mountain's wrath. Enter the devastated area only hours after the eruption and witness the incredible destruction. 30 mins.
VHS: S05736. $29.95.

Explorers: A Century of Dis2covery
Produced to commemorate the Centennial anniversary of the National Geographic Society, this tribute to the pioneers covers their contributions that have made the wonders of the world accessible. 60 mins.
VHS: S07394. $19.95.

Eyewitness
This fascinating PBS nature series is unlike any other available. It combines state of the art computer animation to explore how each animal evolved and how it actually works. In addition it includes wildlife segments that reveal each creature's relationship to its environment. Perhaps the most interesting segments are those which explain how man uses animals to express some of the most noble concepts. Each episode is 30 mins.

Eyewitness Amphibian.
VHS: S24962. $12.95.
Eyewitness Bird.
VHS: S24958. $12.95.
Eyewitness Cat.
VHS: S24959. $12.95.
Eyewitness Dinosaur.
VHS: S24964. $12.95.
Eyewitness Dog.
VHS: S24960. $12.95.
Eyewitness Elephant.
VHS: S24965. $12.95.
Eyewitness Fish.
VHS: S24963. $12.95.
Eyewitness Horse.
VHS: S24966. $12.95.
Eyewitness Insect.
VHS: S24968. $12.95.
Eyewitness Jungle.
VHS: S24969. $12.95.
Eyewitness Reptile.
VHS: S24961. $12.95.
Eyewitness Shark.
VHS: S24967. $12.95.
Eyewitness Skeleton.
VHS: S24970. $12.95.

Eyewitness Living Earth
Experience the beauty and intrigue of nature's most spectacular wonders through live-action photography and stunning video footage with this 13-part series. Fast-moving and stimulating, the series is packed with information, anecdotes and humor to create an entertaining experience for all viewers.

Ape.
VHS: S30664. $12.95.
Arctic & Antarctic.
VHS: S30665. $12.95.
Butterfly & Moth.
VHS: S30666. $12.95.
Desert.
VHS: S30667. $12.95.
Mammal.
VHS: S30668. $12.95.
Pond & River.
VHS: S30669. $12.95.
Prehistoric Life.
VHS: S30670. $12.95.
Rock & Mineral.
VHS: S30671. $12.95.
Seashore.
VHS: S30672. $12.95.
Shell.
VHS: S30673. $12.95.
Tree.
VHS: S30674. $12.95.
Volcano.
VHS: S30675. $12.95.
Weather.
VHS: S30676. $12.95.

The Filming of the Leopard Son
Observe the complexities of wildlife filmmaking as you go behind the scenes of Discovery Channel Pictures' first wildlife feature film, *The Leopard Son*, and follow renowned filmmaker and naturalist Hugo van Lawick and his crew as they devote two years to tracking and filming the adventures of a young leopard growing up on the Serengeti Plain. Witness Stewart Copeland's (The Police) creation of the musical score, then listen as a 60-piece orchestra brings the music to life.
VHS: S30590. $14.95.
Holly Barden Stadtler, USA, 1996, 50 mins.

Finite Oceans
This Discovery Channel video about environmental risk to the world oceans was made in conjunction with the Smithsonian Institution/Times Mirror exhibit. Dr. Roger Payne explores political, economic and environmental aspects of this pressing concern.
VHS: S25097. $19.95.

Fire
Get behind the scenes and then into the middle of a raging inferno with a fire-fighting crew as they battle a furious and deadly forest fire. Amazing footage highlights the destructive power of these walls of fire.
VHS: S34282. $14.98.

The Fire Below Us
May 18, 1980, was the day that the Mount St. Helens volcano exploded without any warning. This documentary combines dramatic eyewitness accounts, spectacular footage of the devastation, and clear scientific explanations of this natural event. 68 mins.
VHS: S25738. $24.95.

First Time Garden
For millions of new home owners and enthusiastic gardeners, this video is an essential aid to creating a beautiful and practical garden. The information-packed video traces the complete development of a bare and muddy building site into a flourishing garden. A BBC production. 90 mins.
VHS: S10282. $19.94.

Fish (Pet Care)
Dr. Michael Fox hosts this video featuring Joe Yaiullo, senior aquarist at the New York Aquarium, with tips on setting up a fresh water aquarium, tank size, filtration assembly, conditioning the tank, choosing the fish, maintaining good water, feeding, and more. 30 mins.
VHS: S09627. $14.95.

Flight over the Equator
At the Earth's Equator, a wide range of cultures are experiencing growing interdependence through the effects of globalization. Once seen by Europeans as a vast torrid zone, this multifaceted span of the globe is fast adapting to the 21st century. This Discovery Channel film, narrated by Stacy Keach, travels from Africa to America to Asia. 90 mins.
VHS: S29424. $19.95.

The Floating World
A portrait of undersea life and visuals choreographed to the works of Bach, Debussy, Elgar, Franck, Handel, Harvey, Offenbach and Tchaikovsky. 45 mins.
Laser: LD70247. $29.95.

Flood
Discovery brings you rare footage of flash floods and rising tides, the world's biggest natural killers. Watch as raging torrents strike, trapping victims and jeopardizing the lives of rescuers.
VHS: S34283. $14.98.

Following the Tundra Wolf
Robert Redford narrates this award-winning account of the feral tundra wolf. The filmmakers document the animal's rituals and behavioral patterns. 48 mins.
VHS: S12158. $14.98.

Forest Habitat Set
This three-volume set from the Discovery Channel's *Mother Nature: Tales of Discovery* series features *When Bears Go Fishing*, *The Business of Beavers* and *Antlers Big and Small*. Together these tapes offer an exhaustive look at the life of the forest.
VHS: S25086. $39.95.

The Forest Through the Trees
Northern California's majestic redwood forests are an irreplaceable national treasure. While the world's attention is on the devastation of rainforests, here in the U.S. the last remaining stands of virgin redwoods are being destroyed at a much faster rate. This a thoughtful, visually spectacular film on a complex issue of national importance. 1990, 58 mins.
VHS: S13935. $85.00.

The Free Willy Story: Keiko's Journey Home
Go behind the scenes with the Discovery Channel to experience the drama of the journey to freedom of Keiko, the real-life orca who inspired the *Free Willy* films. Critically acclaimed actress Rene Russo narrates Keiko's life story, from his capture and journey from Iceland, to his captivity in Canada and Mexico, his high-stakes move to Oregon for rehabilitation, and the emotional bond that developed between Keiko and his trainer Karla Corral.
VHS: S30835. $19.95.
1996, 50 mins.

Friendly Gray Whales
A journey to Mexico's lagoons for an encounter with these friendly whales and for a study of their behavior, including underwater. 30 mins.
VHS: S10921. $29.95.

Galapagos: Beyond Darwin

Charles Darwin's historic voyage to the Galapagos islands forever changed our view of the world, but he only scratched the surface. Climb into a state-of-the-art submersible and plunge 3,000 feet beneath the surface as history's first deep-diving expedition to the Galapagos probes where no camera has gone before. Be part of the expedition scientists will be writing about for years as you share the discovery of over two dozen new species and capture creatures never before seen or even named.
VHS: S30591. $19.95.
David Clarke/Al Giddings, USA, 1996, 100 mins.

Galapagos: My Fragile World (National Audubon)

Narrated by Cliff Robertson. An extraordinary journey to the magical, almost prehistoric world of the Gapalagos Islands through the eyes and photographic lens of lifetime resident and world-renowned photographer Tui De Roy. 60 mins.
VHS: S09002. $14.98.

Gardens of the World

Audrey Hepburn hosts this six-part series that looks at more than 50 gardens for their historical, cultural and aesthetic principals. With narration by Hepburn and Michael York.
Country Gardens. This program studies the pleasures of country gardens, with their pungent sense of smell, taste and touch. Audrey Hepburn looks at imposing gardens such as the Giardino del Ninfa, cottage gardens in England and farmhouse gardens connected to Chilcombe House in Dorset (UK). Commentary by garden designers John Brookes and Ryan Gainey. 27 mins.
VHS: S20325. $24.95.
Flower Gardens. Claude Monet's garden at Giverny showcases the proper display of flowers. The color schemes beautifully contrast with the grace and elegance of the borders specific to the Tintinhull House in Somerset, England. The program also studies the native flora of America's Southwest. With special commentary by Penelope Hobhouse. 27 mins.
VHS: S20324. $24.95.
Formal Gardens. Audrey Hepburn shows the evolution of formal design, visiting the luscious gardens of Renaissance-period Italy, the luminous 17th-century gardens of France, and England's elaborate 20th-century gardens. With guest commentary by garden authority Penelope Hobhouse. 27 mins.
VHS: S20323. $24.95.
Public Gardens and Trees. Audrey Hepburn travels to the elegantly restored gardens at Mt. Vernon, formerly owned by George Washington. Hepburn also discusses the diversity and vast number of public gardens in Paris, including the "pocket parks," the grand royal gardens. 27 mins.
VHS: S20326. $24.95.
Roses and Rose Gardens. Audrey Hepburn studies the historical importance of the rose, which has a deep symbolic meaning relevant to legend, romance and beauty. With a lecture by author Graham Stuart Thomas. 27 mins.
VHS: S20321. $24.95.
Tulips and Spring Bulbs. Audrey Hepburn reveals the vast history of bulbs and their connection to the history of Holland. The program shows the bulb's transformation from sleeping bulb to full bloom. 27 mins.
VHS: S20322. $24.95.
Gardens of the World, Set. The complete set of six programs is a collector's edition preserved in a beautiful box set.
VHS: S20327. $139.95.

Gems and Minerals

This program explores the Smithsonian's vaults, containing some of the rarest gems in the world, including a 4.6-billion-year-old meteorite and the legendary 45½ carat Hope diamond. 1989, 45 mins.
VHS: S14544. $29.95.
Laser: LD70228. $34.95.

Giant Sequoias

Largest of all living things! Learn about these amazing trees and their relationships with other forest inhabitants. Experience the splendor of the Giant Sequoia groves found in Sequoia and Yosemite National Parks. 30 mins.
VHS: S06669. $29.95.

Gift of the Whales

The fascinating story of a young, Native American boy's rediscovery of life. The arrival of the whales was a gift…just for him, with the video capturing spectacular, never before seen photography of the largest creatures to grace the earth, in a blend of entertainment and education. 30 mins.
VHS: S10961. $29.95.
Laser: LD71004. $24.95.

The Great Barrier Reef

This highly acclaimed production is a spellbinding glimpse under the sea, off the coast of Australia on the Great Barrier Reef. Prince Philip narrates the story of the undersea life and ecological balance of this beautiful reef. 57 minutes.
VHS: S03291. $29.95.

The Great Bears of Alaska

Intimate behavior of the Great Bear is shown on this video with startling clarity. It's like coming face to face with one of these magnificent creatures in the wild, only much safer. 60 mins. From the Discovery Channel.
VHS: S25071. $19.95.

Great Canadian Parks

The natural landscapes and diverse wildlife of Canada's national and provincial parks are presented in three volumes: *Kluane National Park Reserve, Yukon Saguenay-St. Lawrence Marine Park, Quebec, Ts'il-os Provincial Park, British Columbia Parks of Fundy New Brunswick*, and *Waterton Lakes National Park, Alberta Cypress Hills Interprovincial Park, Alberta/Saskatchewan*. Each tape is 48 minutes.
VHS: S31708. $39.95.

Great Dinosaurs Set

A collection of four programs about the massive beasts who roamed in prehistoric times, including profiles of the Brontosaurus, Stegosaurus, Triceratops and Tyrannosaurus. 35 mins.
VHS: S20055. $159.95.

Great White

This video brings the great white shark closer than ever before. Renowned as the most fearsome killing machine on earth, this animal's awesome force is a wonder of nature. A Discovery Channel production. 90 mins.
VHS: S25082. $19.95.

Grizzly & Man: Uneasy Truce (National Audubon)

Can grizzlies and man live peacefully together? This is the question explored in this award-winning Audubon special about the uneasy coexistence of man and bear, narrated by Robert Redford.
VHS: S09561. $14.98.

Help Save Planet Earth

Ted Danson hosts this guide full of everyday tips on how to protect and save the environment (and often save money at the same time). How to conserve water, heat and electricity, preserve trees and conserve energy are among the hundreds of suggestions. Features Beau Bridges, Lloyd Bridges, Jamie Lee Curtis, Cheech Marin and many others.
VHS: S13052. $14.95.

Hidden World

This spectacular animated 3D stereogram video takes viewers from a warp-speed trek through deep space to the gentle waters of the coral reef, on a swim with dolphins to an amusement park ride, and more. Narrated by Peter Jones. 30 mins.
VHS: S28520. $17.99.

Housefly: An Everyday Monster

With spectacular macrophotography, learn how the inconspicuous housefly followed mankind throughout the world, and throughout time. Experience in extreme realism how these insects propagate, feed, and avoid extinction and extermination. 45 mins.
VHS: S34675. $19.98.

Hunters of Chubut

Lorne Greene travels to the rugged Atlantic Coast of Argentina where sea lions and penguins battle and breed in a packed, frenzied colony. In this beautiful, violent world, even these large hunters fall prey to the biggest, most powerful predators on earth—the Killer Whale. USA, 22 mins.
VHS: S03091. $14.95.

Huntress

Lorne Greene narrates this tape about a young cougar's odyssey for independence.
VHS: S10039. $14.95.

Hurricane

Trace the destructive path of Hurricane Andrew and join North Carolina residents preparing for the arrivals of Bertha and Fran.
VHS: S34284. $14.98.

I Dig Fossils

A father and his son go exploring in the Mazon Creek region of Illinois. There they uncover fossils of leaves that were probably chewed on by prehistoric reptiles. This video offers clear information about the search for fossils and explains how these imprints of the past are made. 25 mins.
VHS: S23856. $19.95.

If Dolphins Could Talk

Dolphins have survived natural calamities, but now they're confronted by their greatest threat—man. This program looks at the efforts by scientists and biologists to "protect the closest relative of man in the seas." Narrated by Michael Douglas.
VHS: S16877. $14.98.

In a Time of Headlong Progress

Over 90% of the lush rainforests in Brazil's Bahia have been destroyed. This destruction now threatens the economic well-being of the region as well as the habitat of the golden-headed lion tamarin. This is a lively, comprehensive look at the complex economic and social issues behind deforestation and the hopeful, innovative work of pioneering Brazilian conservationist Cristina Alves. 45 mins.
VHS: S23369. $125.00.

In Celebration of Trees

Trees are the world's oldest living things. Their majesty and grandeur make this video from the Discovery Channel a true delight to watch. Somehow the serenity of towering trees seems to defy time itself. 60 mins.
VHS: S25081. $19.95.

In Good Hands: Culture and Agriculture in the Lacandon Rainforest

While inefficient agricultural methods are destroying many of the world's rainforests, the Lacandon Maya of Chiapas in Southern Mexico have been practicing a sustainable form of rainforest farming for centuries. Dr. James Nations, an ecological anthropologist, shows how the Lacandon farm in the forest, and how culture, mythology and religion influence their agricultural methods. 27 mins.
VHS: S23368. $99.95.

In Search of the Golden Hammerhead

In the murky waters at the mouth of the Orinoco River along Venezuela's coast lives the recently discovered golden hammerhead shark. This Discovery Channel film explores theories about the unique golden coloration of this impressive sea creature. 45 mins.
VHS: S29428. $19.95.

In the Company of Whales

Come travel in the company of the largest animals to ever live on earth…powerful creatures of extraordinary grace and intelligence…masters of the watery realm where they have existed for over 30 million years. Featured on The Discovery Channel. 90 mins.
VHS: S17011. $24.95.

In the Kingdom of the Dolphins

A fascinating look at the dolphin, filmed in the clear waters of a remote corner of the Carribean, as journalist Hardy Jones and marine biologist Julia Whitty spend seven summers filming these magical creatures in their natural habitat. Spectacular underwater photography. 50 mins.
VHS: S03427. $24.95.

In the Path of a Killer Volcano

Stay with scientists at the Phillippines' Mount Pinatubo and see some astonishing footage of the world's largest volcanic eruption in 80 years. From NOVA. 60 mins.
VHS: S31434. $19.95.

In the Wild: Dolphins with Robin Williams

Robin Williams hosts this intimate portrait of creatures many believe to be highly intelligent and affectionate. Plenty of information about dolphins is provided by experts, but the most intriguing aspect of this video is the personal rapport Williams cultivates with them. 60 mins.
VHS: S27775. $19.98.

In the Wild: Grey Whales with Christopher Reeve

Grey whales were once nearly extinct. Fortunately, their numbers have increased from a low of a few hundred to approximately 22,000. Reeve took the trip of a lifetime just before his accident, following these animals along their difficult migration from Siberia to Baja. 60 mins.
VHS: S27776. $19.98.

In the Wild: Pandas with Debra Winger

Pandas were shrouded in mystery until very recently. Even today, as they come close to extinction, little is known about these reclusive animals. Winger and her son travel the route used by the first Western woman to find pandas. After a long journey, they discover that Professor Pan Wenshi has successfully protected a panda and her young cub from danger. 60 mins.
VHS: S27777. $19.98.

The Incredible Story of Dogs

This three-tape series follows the story of dogs from ancient times all the way to the present. All kinds of breeds and their origins are showcased, including Labradors, Maltese, and German Shepherds. *Vol. I, Fatal Attraction* traces the evolution of dogs into domesticity. *Vol. II, Matters of Life and Death: Gods and Gladiators* celebrates the many roles of dogs today. Then *Vol. III, A Question of Breeding: What Price Friendship?* examines people's obsession with man's best friend.
VHS: S21535. $59.95.

The Infinite Voyage: Great Dinosaur Hunt
The Infinite Voyage series takes viewers on a fascinating trip to unlock the mysteries of how the dinosaur lived—*not* how it perished. 60 mins.
VHS: S12186. $14.98.

The Infinite Voyage: The Future of the Past
Artist and scientists pool their resources to develops ways to preserve civilization's heritage for future generations. 58 mins.
VHS: S19201. $14.98.

The Infinite Voyage: The Living Clock
This exciting blend of science and technology studies the intricate biology of time and detail. 58 mins.
VHS: S19202. $14.98.

The Infinite Voyage: Unseen Worlds
Some of the Unseen Worlds in this *Infinite Voyage* program are a black hole in the Milky Way galaxy, the interior of a human heart, and an atomic accelerator. 60 mins.
VHS: S12188. $14.98.

Inky, Dinky Spider
Lorne Greene narrates this tape about the *Bola* spider as she begins her "weapon"—a long strand of sticky silk weighted every few inches with a unique, pear-like drop of silk. When the bola is completed, the spider sends out an odor to attract males, who will be caught in her web. 30 mins.
VHS: S05001. $14.95.

Insects
Insects make up over 80% percent of all animal life on earth. Learn how they have evolved and adapted to survive for eons.
Laser: LD70227. $34.95.

Inside Hawaiian Volcanoes
Backed up by awesome graphics and stunning live action footage, this video is a colorful, devastating portrait of the volcanic activity on a tropical island. Narrated by Roger Mudd. 25 mins.
Laser: CAV. **LD72263. $29.95.**

Invasion of the Dinosaurs
A program that attempts to consider unresolved questions about the activities, patterns and mental processes of the dinosaurs, covering their dominance and extinction. The scientists employ the technological aid of Dinamation—lifelike robots—to interpret the animals' movements. 30 mins.
VHS: S18715. $9.95.

Island of the Dragons
Komodo Dragons are direct descendants of dinosaurs. These formidable, man-eating monsters are one of the most incredible inhabitants found on the Indonesian Archipelago. Some of the animals' most surprising secrets are revealed in this video. 60 mins. From the Discovery Channel.
VHS: S25072. $19.95.

Island of Whales
Experts brave perilous waterways to pursue the gray, humpback killer whales on Vancouver Island. Narrated by Gregory Peck. 55 mins.
VHS: S18240. $19.95.

It's a Male's World
The unusual sexual dynamics of the Hamadryas, a species of baboon whose social hierarchy operates as a male tyranny, is explored in this nature documentary hosted by Lorne Greene. 30 mins.
VHS: S06325. $14.95.

Jellies and Other Ocean Drifters
Leonard Nimoy narrates this collaborative documentary from Sea Studios and The Monterey Bay Aquarium Research Institute. Never-before-seen creatures from the deep, such as predatory comb jellies, web-weaving larvaceans and the spectacular 30-foot-long siphonophores make this video a unique window into a dark world. 35 mins.
VHS: S27781. $19.95.

Journey into Life
An Academy Award nominee in 1990, this powerfully moving film captures the most amazing moments of creation on the remarkable journey that ends with the miracle of birth. 30 mins.
VHS: S23144. $14.95.

Just Call Me Kitty
A charming video which is all about cats—dubbed the "Everything you ever wanted to know about cats guide for the home viewer." With Persians, calicoes, and hundreds of loveable cats. 60 mins.
VHS: S11114. $14.95.

Kangaroos Under Fire
Three million kangaroos are slaughtered annually and the video investigates the uncertain future of Australia's national symbol. 25 mins.
VHS: S06496. $49.95.

Kangaroos: Faces in the Mob
This award-winning film is the engaging, true story of life within a mob of Eastern Grey kangaroos, from birth to the dramatic and sometimes deadly battles between adult males. Stunning detail and superb photography provide the most compelling account of the kangaroo society ever filmed.
VHS: S32911. $19.95.
Jan Aldenhove/Glen Carruthers, Australia, 1992, 58 mins.

Kuiseb the Vanishing River/Kalahari Bigfoot (BBC Wildlife Special)
For many months of the year, all that can be seen of the modern Kuiseb river is the dry bed snaking its empty way from Southwest Africa to the Atlantic Ocean. Only with flash flooding or other special rainfall conditions does the surface riverbed become a waterway. It has to wait for the life-giving waters as do all the animals that depend on it. Nearby in the grasslands which fringe the Kalahari desert lives an animal which looks as if it could be a cross between a rabbit and a kangaroo. In fact, it's the spring hare, a rodent, and for its size it has just about the biggest feet around. 55 mins.
VHS: S12393. $19.94.

Land of the Birds
Unique and beautifully feathered, the cassowary, lyrebird and bowerbird take flight in one's imagination, as well as in the wide blue sky in this look at nature's first aeronautical pilots.
VHS: S05236. $29.95.

Land of the Leopard
John Varty, born and raised in Africa, and his trusted friend Elmon Mhlongo develop a unique relationship with a family of wild leopards. Gripping and compelling sequences filmed over five years describe the territorial behavior of the female leopard, her mothering of cubs, and the stalking skills the cubs must learn in order to survive. 60 mins.
VHS: S04696. $29.95.

Late Great Planet Earth
Orson Welles narrates this chilling exploration of the end of the human race. Based on the cult book by Hal Lindsey. 87 mins.
VHS: S08728. $14.95.

Life in the Desert
Nothing moves under the infernal mid-day sun of Australia's desert outback. At dusk, however, the desert blossoms with mammals, birds and reptiles. A desperate struggle for survival among the heartiest of creatures is about to begin.
VHS: S05239. $19.95.

Life in the Southern Seas
Come face to face with a curious pack of sea lions or find out that a hole in the ground is really a snug little home to a mutton bird and a tiger snake. A fascinating look at Australia's wilderness.
VHS: S05240. $19.95.

Lightning
Meet lightning-strike survivors; witness a "lightning sprite;" visit with Dr. Lightning; and learn why lightning's beauty is matched only by its danger.
VHS: S34285. $14.98.

The Lion's Kingdom
Created with the support of the World Wildlife Fund, this box set from The Discovery Channel presents a firsthand look at the varied habitats where lions roam and examines the role that the King of Beasts plays in each. The series earned The Dove Foundation's "Family Approval" seal. Tapes include *The Plains, The Deserts* and *The Forests and Highlands*. Each tape is 51 minutes.
VHS: S30958. $39.95.

The Living Edens
Six tapes.
The Living Edens—Bhutan: The Last Shangri-La. Bhutan, the Land of the Thunder Dragon, is the only remaining Buddhist Himalayan Kingdom. Shrouded in timeless mystery, Bhutan is one of the few surviving regions whose secrets have passed undisturbed through the millennia. 60 mins.
VHS: S34591. $19.95.
The Living Edens—Denali: Alaska's Great Wilderness. 60 mins.
VHS: S34592. $19.95.
The Living Edens—Etosha: Africa's Untamed Wilderness. Travel to Africa's Etosha, a vast and ancient land of seasonal paradox. During the bloom of the wet season, springboks, elephants, lions, leopards, cheetahs, jackals, zebras and giraffe thrive. But heat, drought and thirst put all life at risk. 60 mins.
VHS: S34590. $19.95.
The Living Edens—Manu: Peru's Hidden Rain Forest. Journey to the great river Manu, the life blood for one of the world's great secrets—the Manu Biosphere Reserve. This Eden is the richest Amazonian wilderness on earth. Discover this tropical paradise where 90 percent of the flora and fauna have yet to be identified. 60 mins.
VHS: S34589. $19.95.
The Living Edens—Namib: Africa's Burning Shore. 60 mins.
VHS: S34594. $19.95.
The Living Edens—Patagonia: Life at the End of the Earth. 60 mins.
VHS: S34593. $19.95.

Loch Ness Discovered
This video seeks to answer the question, "Is there a prehistoric creature hiding in the murky depths of Loch Ness?" Scientists brave ridicule in the first serious investigation of the underwater lair of this mysterious beast. From the Discovery Channel.
VHS: S22540. $19.95.

Lost Worlds/Vanished Lives
David Attenborough uses fossils to boldly recapture the daily activity of dinosaurs, providing a valuable look at the evolution of the earth. "Attenborough is affable and often amazing" *(New York Post)*. 240 mins.
VHS: S19382. $99.95.

A Love Story: The Canada Goose
The wetlands of North America, the breeding grounds for one of the largest, most intelligent and adaptable birds on earth, this is the powerful story of love and devotion as the birds raise their young in the face of constant danger from racoons, minks and man. Narrated by Lorne Greene. 30 mins.
VHS: S04999. $14.95.

Luray Caverns
The largest and most popular caverns in eastern America; explores how the Luray caverns in Virginia were formed, and includes an autumn excursion to Luray's neighboring attraction, Shenandoah National Park. 30 mins.
VHS: S09183. $29.95.

The Magnificent Whales
In this video, more than 20 different species of whales and dolphins are showcased. Shot around North America and Hawaii. 60 mins.
VHS: S18428. $29.95.

Mammoth Cave National Park, Kentucky
The mysterious world of Mammoth cave, the longest cave on Earth, including its unique formations such as helicites, gypsum flowers, soda straws and flowstone. 30 mins.
VHS: S10044. $29.95.

Man of the Trees
Moved by his great love of life, Richard St. Barbe Baker dedicated most of his 92 years to preserving the world's forests. *Man of the Trees* presents the remarkable life of this vibrant New Zealander who travelled the world in defense of trees—a cause he saw as essential to planetary survival. St. Barbe Baker is shown at work spreading his love of trees to New Zealand, North America and African tribes, whom he inspired to create a ceremonial dance for tree planting. Through his efforts, billions of trees were planted, and his life serves as an inspiration for anyone concerned about the impact of deforestation on the ecosphere. 26 mins.
VHS: S11488. $29.95.

The Man Who Loves Sharks
Stan Waterman is one of the world's finest underwater cinematographers. Some of the most memorable adventures and exotic creatures of his career are captured in this journey through dangerous waters. 90 mins.
VHS: S21795. $19.95.

Marmot Mountain/Yellowstone Below Zero (BBC Wildlife Special)

The Austrian Tyrol in spring is an idyllic land of flower-filled meadows and glistening peaks. The hills are alive with the sound of marmots. For in the brief season ahead, these playful rodents, who are likened to overweight squirrels, struggle to gain the nourishment that will enable them to survive another eight harsh months under the snow. *Yellowstone Below Zero* explores the incredible beauty and dramatic change in lifestyle that takes place within the park during the first few weeks of winter.
VHS: S12394. $19.94.

Master Hunter of the Night

The fabled night predator—the great horned owl—is examined in this documentary led by Kay Mc Keever, a pioneer in the rehabilitation of owls, as Kay helps an injured owl. Narrated by Lorne Greene. USA, 22 mins.
VHS: S03092. $14.95.

Microcosmos

This revealing, shocking and fascinating look at the mysterious world of insects through the miracle of microphotography mesmerized audiences at Cannes. Watch as these fantastic creatures struggle with nature's most urgent issues.
VHS: S32348. $14.99.
Laser: LD76352. $39.99.
Claude Nurdsany/Marie Perennou, France, 1996, 75 mins.

Monster Forces of Nature

Tornados, hurricanes, erupting volcanos, earthquakes and floods are shown in all their awe-inspiring force by this collection of scientific films. High tech equipment on planes, boats and satellites were used by NASA to gather this educational material. 90 mins.
VHS: S24692. $39.95.

Mountain Habitat Set

Mountains harbor a variety of creatures. This three-volume set from the Discovery Channel's *Mother Nature: Tales of Discovery* series features videos that show some of the fascinating inhabitants of these upper climes. *Good Neighbor Ground Squirrel, When Goats Go Climbing* and *Curious Cougar Kittens* are included.
VHS: S25089. $39.95.

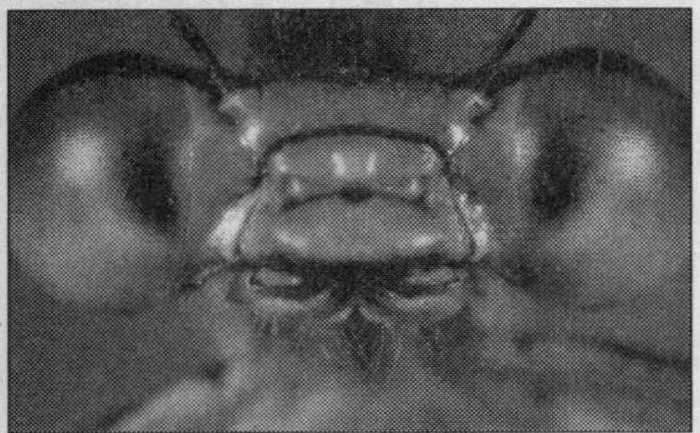

Mutual of Omaha's Spirit of Adventure Series

Wildlife expert Jim Fowler hosts this series, produced by Emmy Award winner John Wilcox, which displays incredible, rare footage of endangered species in their own habitats, allowing the viewer to be a part of these exotic and sometimes dangerous expeditions. Guest hosts include Peggy Fleming, Christopher Cross, Peter Benchley, and Diana Nyad.
Mount Everest American Firsts. 50 mins.
VHS: S14070. $19.98.
Struggle to Survive—China's Giant Panda. 50 mins.
VHS: S14071. $19.98.
Challenging China's Yangtze, Part I & II. 90 mins.
VHS: S14072. $19.98.
Beneath the Sea—The Galapagos. 50 mins.
VHS: S14073. $19.98.
Uncovering China's Hidden Wildlife. 50 mins.
VHS: S14074. $19.98.
Twilight of the Gorilla. 50 mins.
VHS: S14075. $19.98.
Headhunter's Legacy. 50 mins.
VHS: S14076. $19.98.
Africa's Poaching Wars. 60 mins.
VHS: S14077. $19.98.
Antarctic Odyssey. 50 mins.
VHS: S14078. $19.98.
Voices in the Wild. 50 mins.
VHS: S14079. $19.98.
Rafting into Siberia. 50 mins.
VHS: S14080. $19.98.
Whales and Dolphins. 50 mins.
VHS: S14081. $19.98.

Mystery of the Animal Pathfinders

NOVA travels to bird feeding grounds in Brazil, bat caves in Mexico, and eel habitats in Maine to understand the mystery of animal migration. 60 mins.
VHS: S28653. $19.95.

National Geographic Geo Kids: Bear Cubs, Baby Ducks, and Kooky Kookaburras

Sunny Honeypossum, Bobby Bushbaby and Balzac de Chameleon tell how different wild animals grow from infancy to young adulthood. The footage of a mother monkey caring for her baby is unforgettable.
VHS: S21961. $12.95.

National Geographic Geo Kids: Cool Cats, Raindrops, and Things That Live in Holes

While playing hide-and-seek, Sunny Honeypossum and Bobby Bushbaby discover a tree hole. Balzac de Chameleon then explains to them the variety of animals that make their home in these natural crevices.
VHS: S21962. $12.95.

National Geographic Geo Kids: Flying Trying and Honking Around

The delightful characters Sunny Honeypossum, Bobby Bushbaby and Balzac de Chameleon host this fascinating look at birds. These characters are all created by the maker of the Muppet Babies. Together they help kids explore the world of flight.
VHS: S21960. $12.95.

National Geographic Video

The National Geographic Society has always been renowned for their award-winning television specials; now these great programs are available on home video! 60 minutes each.
African Wildlife. Filmed in Etosha National Park in Namibia over a two-year period, *African Wildlife* captures animal behavior in extraordinarily close range.
VHS: S02061. $19.95.
Creatures of the Namib Desert. Burgess Meredith narrates this look at Africa's Namib desert, a vast wilderness of sand, sun and open spaces where nature has learned to adapt and flourish.
VHS: S03053. $19.95.
Iceland River Challenge. Follow 12 adventurers as they run a wild Icelandic river through glacial caverns, violent gales, and crashing rapids, and see breathtaking footage of man against nature.
VHS: S02055. $19.95.
Land of the Tiger. Enter the mysterious world of the tiger, one of earth's most feared predators. Experience their beauty and strength as you visit their jungle home.
VHS: S02056. $19.95.
Polar Bear Alert. Jason Robards narrates a journey to Churchill, Manitoba, where the residents have learned to live with a unique wildlife problem. Each fall, the largest, most deadly carnivore in the Arctic migrates through this isolated Canadian village on an annual northward trek.
VHS: S03055. $19.95.
Save the Panda. Join scientists as they track these rare creatures through bamboo-forested mountain ranges in central China. Narrated by Richard Basehart.
VHS: S02062. $19.95.
The Gorilla. Meet Koko, the world's most famous gorilla, in this engaging look at the mountain gorilla of central Africa. She's able to communicate by American sign language, telling everyone exactly what she'd like!
VHS: S02058. $19.95.
The Sharks. This famous *Geographic* film takes you underwater into the fascinating world of sharks—350 different species, of which only 20 are dangerous to humans. Learn the truth about these terrifying big fish!
VHS: S02057. $19.95.
Yukon Passage. Embark on a danger-filled journey through the Alaskan Yukon, as four adventurers face the Arctic circle as they travel 1,800 miles on foot, skis, raft, and dogsled. Jimmy Stewart narrates.
VHS: S02059. $19.95.

National Geographic Video: Africa's Stolen River

In the Savuti region of Botswana, one of nature's unfathomable mysteries plays itself out when a river slowly begins to disappear. Thought once to have been a lake, the channel appeared in 1957 and vanished again in 1982, creating a struggle for the animals whose lives depend upon the channel. 60 mins.
VHS: S09275. $19.95.

National Geographic Video: African Animal Oasis

A precarious excursion into the depths of Africa's wild animal kingdom, to Tanzania's Ngorngoro Crater, where the abundant supply of water alters an extinct volcanic crater into a spectacular wildlife oasis. 60 mins.
VHS: S19342. $19.95.

National Geographic Video: America's Endangered Species: Don't Say Good-bye

Photographer Susan Middleton and David Luttschwager are in a race against the clock to capture powerful portraits of America's most threatened creatures. Join them on an unforgettable adventure that takes them from the California Sierra to the deep South, from the woods of North Carolina to the Pacific's shores. 60 mins.
VHS: S34452. $19.95.

National Geographic Video: Antarctic Wildlife Adventure

The 50-foot schooner *Damien II* sets off to the most remote continent, Antarctica. Its rocky coasts and azure seas are home to fascinating wildlife, including penguins, humpback whales, elephant seals and more. 60 mins.
VHS: S25899. $19.95.

National Geographic Video: Beauty and the Beasts: A Leopard's Story

Follow the fascinating lives of a great cat and a curious warthog, intertwined since birth, against the dramatic backdrop of the South African wilderness. 60 mins.
VHS: S32507. $19.98.

National Geographic Video: Braving Alaska

Martin Sheen narrates this documentary about the pioneers in America's largest state. They hunt for survival. Groceries and mail are delivered by plane. Warmth is precious as the temperature drops to 60 degrees below zero during the hard winter. Within this harsh environment however, there is an unmatched beauty. 60 mins.
VHS: S22039. $19.95.

National Geographic Video: Cats: Caressing the Tiger

Though house cats are beloved pets, their behavior is not so far removed from their ferocious cousins in the wild. This video explores the mystery of the ordinary housecat to uncover basic facts. Once and for all it is clearly explained how cats always manage to land on their feet. 60 mins.
VHS: S23949. $19.95.

National Geographic Video: Creatures of the Mangrove

Explores the unique wildlife community on the lush coast of Borneo. Produced by National Geographic. 60 mins.
VHS: S07393. $19.95.

National Geographic Video: Crocodiles: Here Be Dragons

This program ventures into the treacherous Grumeti River in Africa to capture footage of the ferocious crocodiles. 60 mins.
VHS: S18892. $19.95.

National Geographic Video: Cyclone!

Tornadoes from the Midwest's "Tornado Alley," Hurricane Andrew in Florida, and powerful typhoons in the Pacific are all shown in this fascinating exploration of cyclone storms. Scientists are still struggling with how to track and predict these powerful, killer weather systems.
VHS: S27662. $19.95.
Richard J. Wells, USA, 1995, 60 mins.

National Geographic Video: Dinosaur Hunters

The discovery that rocked the scientific world. Join an expedition in search of ancient dinosaurs. Unearth the fossilized embryo of an Oviraptor and skeletons that reveal an astonishing story. 60 mins.
VHS: S32508. $19.98.

National Geographic Video: Egypt: Secrets of the Pharoahs

Witness ancient mysteries revealed as you investigate pyramid building and the afterlife and watch as scientists re-create the ritual of mummification. 60 mins.
VHS: S34465. $19.95.

National Geographic Video: Elephant

The largest, strongest and among the most intelligent animals to walk this planet, the elephant is examined in this in-depth look at a truly magnificent creature. 60 mins.
VHS: S11653. $19.95.

National Geographic Video: Eternal Enemies: Lions and Hyenas

This documentary about the battle between lions and spotted hyenas, as they fight for territory in northern Botswana, is remarkable for the eerie, nighttime footage. 60 mins.
VHS: S19343. $19.95.

National Geographic Video: Giant Bears of Kodiak Island

This is a documentary about the largest carnivores on Earth. They hunt for salmon in the rich rivers in order to gorge themselves for the hard winter. In this harsh environment they raise their cubs with surprising tenderness. 60 mins.
VHS: S22038. $19.95.

National Geographic Video: Great Explorers Gift Box

A compelling ethnographic study collects four works: Al Reinert's documentary about the Apollo space missions, *For All Mankind*; the historic climb of the world's highest summit, *Return to Everest*; a documentary about the 100-year travel expedition, *The Explorers: A Century of Discovery*; and the fearless, brilliant cinematographers who risked their lives to create their art, *Cameramen Who Dared*.
VHS: S18843. $79.95.

National Geographic Video: Great Whales

Slaughtered by man to near extinction, these benign undersea creatures are beautifully documented in this National Geographic exploration.
VHS: S06297. $19.95.

National Geographic Video: Hawaii: Strangers in Paradise

Documents the painstaking efforts of conservationists to preserve the natural and wildlife habitats of the ancient green turtle, the monk seal or Hawaiian honeycreeper threatened in the Hawaiian Islands.
VHS: S18842. $19.95.

National Geographic Video: Himalayan River Run

A death-defying ride down a wild Mt. Everest river as the National Geographic explores the daredevils who take a thrilling adventure.
VHS: S05886. $19.95.

National Geographic Video: Hunt for the Great White Shark

Great white sharks are featured in this video in all their fury and grandeur. They are seen in their natural surroundings and the experience of a shark attack victim makes clear the awesome force these creatures possess. 55 mins.
VHS: S24677. $19.95.

National Geographic Video: Invisible World

Each moment events take place that the eye cannot perceive because these occurrences are too small, too fast, too slow, or beyond the spectrum of visible light. Some of the captivating sights that will forever alter our perception and knowledge of our world are in this National Geographic documentary. 60 mins.
VHS: S06611. $19.95.

National Geographic Video: Jewels of the Caribbean

Coral reefs shelter a world of incredible but hidden beauty. There are schools of brightly colored fish amid the sandy plains and sea grasses of these unique underwater ecosystems. Special attention is given to dolphins, manatees and other rare creatures. 55 mins.
VHS: S24678. $19.95.

National Geographic Video: Killer Whales: Wolves of the Sea

This documentary looks at how killer whales pursue their prey for food gathering. The program includes some stunning underwater documentary footage of whales on the attack. 60 mins.
VHS: S19915. $19.95.
Laser: LD72019. $29.95.

National Geographic Video: King Cobra

Tread into the jungle realm of a legendary serpent whose bite delivers enough venom to kill 100 people. 60 mins.
VHS: S34463. $19.95.

National Geographic Video: Last Feast of the Crocodiles

During a punishing drought a multitude of diverse creatures is drawn to the receding waters of the Luvuvhu River. Baboons, impala, elephants, lions and water birds are all drawn to these crocodile-infested waters. This video captures the drama of the resulting clashes between the thirsty creatures and the hungry crocodiles. 60 mins.
VHS: S29207. $19.95.

National Geographic Video: Lions of Darkness

Renowned filmmakers Dereck and Beverly Joubert filmed this story of a growing lion pride in Botswana. It begins as three young, aggressive outsiders invade and depose the pride's aged leader. Soon there are new cubs attesting to the vigor of this change. One cub's struggle to survive was especially harrowing and yet allowing nature to take its own course proves especially rewarding.
VHS: S21807. $19.95.
Laser: LD74633. $34.95.

National Geographic Video: Lions of the African Night

A startling look at 30 African lions as they stalk their prey at night, fending off their constant enemy—hunger—in this National Geographic look at wildlife in Africa. 60 mins.
VHS: S06609. $19.95.

National Geographic Video: Mysteries of Mankind

The subject: the human race. The questions: who are we, and where did we come from? Controversies about how we evolved still abound. Explored here is the mystery, taking the viewers around the world and back in time millions of years in search for answers. 60 mins.
VHS: S09276. $19.95.

National Geographic Video: Nature's Fury!

Earthquakes, hurricanes and floods are powerful natural occurrences that have a drastic impact on human lives. This video features heroic individuals fighting everything from earthquakes in San Francisco and Tokyo to floods in France and China to tornadoes in the American Midwest to hurricanes in Bangladesh and Florida.
VHS: S27663. $19.95.
Jaime Bernanke, USA, 1994, 60 mins.

National Geographic Video: Ocean Drifters

The powerful currents of the open ocean carry a surfeit of unusual animals that can travel up to 100 miles a day. Loggerhead turtles, Portuguese men-of-war, seahorses and other remarkable drifters are featured in this wildlife video. 55 mins.
VHS: S24676. $19.95.

National Geographic Video: Puma: Lion of the Andes

Acclaimed filmmaker Hugh Miles captures magnificent, never-before-seen images of this spectacular predator of the Andes. 60 mins.
VHS: S32506. $19.98.

National Geographic Video: Rain Forest

An exploration of a Central American rain forest, highlighting the delicate balance of some of the world's most unusual flora and fauna.
VHS: S03856. $19.95.

National Geographic Video: Reptiles and Amphibians

National Geographic searches for exotic reptiles such as the komodo dragon, the largest of all lizards; encounters the crocodile, which has remained relatively unchanged since the era of the dinosaur; and tracks the evolutionary link to our past by examining the creatures that have long inspired fascination and fear. 60 mins.
VHS: S11655. $29.95.

National Geographic Video: Rhino War

This National Geographic special program explores the desperate fight to save the rhino, an endangered species, from extinction. 60 mins.
VHS: S07391. $19.95.

National Geographic Video: Rocky Mountain Beaver Pond

Tireless worker, exceptional parent, and highly skilled builder, the beaver has earned its reputation as nature's great architect and engineer. 60 mins.
VHS: S08056. $19.95.

National Geographic Video: Search for the Great Apes

Dian Fossey is featured in this documentary on her pioneering fieldwork with Africa's mountain gorillas. 60 mins.
VHS: S09930. $19.95.

National Geographic Video: Season of the Cheetah

On the great open plains of the Serengeti, one of nature's fastest animals, the cheetah, hunts its prey in a never-ending quest for survival. This National Geographic documentary follows three cheetah brothers as they work together on the hunt.
VHS: S20822. $19.95.

National Geographic Video: Secret Leopard

Enter the private world of the wild leopard. In this intimate profile, you will observe the stealth of this elusive big cat amidst other predators such as the lion, hyena and cheetah—and discover the leopard's survival instinct. 60 mins.
VHS: S08058. $19.95.

National Geographic Video: Secrets of the Wild Panda

In central China a research team has spent ten years studying the panda in the wild. Their work is critical to the survival of this unique creature. Among their crucial findings is a body of research tracking the nurturing of a newborn panda. 60 mins.
VHS: S25897. $19.95.

National Geographic Video: Shark Encounters

Underwater filmmaker Mike deGruy reenacts the sequences of a vicious shark attack he suffered in his efforts to capture the world of sharks. The program also blends in new material to provide an eerie context for the sharks' aggression. 60 mins.
VHS: S19916. $19.95.

National Geographic Video: Strange Creatures of the Night

Astonishing nocturnal scenes of the eerie vampire bat, the great horned owl and wild hyena, in the world of darkness. 60 mins.
VHS: S10243. $19.95.

National Geographic Video: Survivors of the Skeleton Coast

Southwestern Africa's Namib desert offers one of the Earth's harshest climates. Despite scorching temperatures and flash floods, nature's creatures adapt and survive. National Geographic shows how in new footage shot on location in this inhospitable landscape.
VHS: S20823. $19.95.

National Geographic Video: The Grizzlies

This National Geographic documentary explores the fascinating world of the feared monarch of the wild, following their life cycle.
VHS: S05885. $19.95.

National Geographic Video: The Photographers

This video takes you around the world with some of the world's best photographers as they reflect on their art. You'll hear the secrets of these award-winning photographers, how they get those breathtaking shots, the dangers they face, and the lives they lead for the love of their craft. 60 mins.
VHS: S34451. $19.95.

National Geographic Video: The Predators Collection

A four-program collection of National Geographic Videos, including *African Animal Oasis; Eternal Enemies: Lions and Hyenas; Crocodiles*; and *Grizzlies*.
VHS: S19344. $79.95.

National Geographic Video: Those Wonderful Dogs

These beloved pets are also tireless helpers to their human masters. They help uncover earthquake victims, star in movies, and even act as messengers in time of war. All these feats are included in this tribute to "man's best friend". 60 mins.
VHS: S23950. $19.95.

National Geographic Video: Tigers of the Snow

Venture into the dense forests of coastal Siberia to track the biggest cat on earth, the elusive Siberian tiger, and join a team of Russian and American scientists risking their lives to save this endangered and dangerous creature. Nominated for five Emmys.
VHS: S32403. $19.98.

National Geographic Video: Volcano

A heartbreaking piece about the death-defying pursuits of filmmakers and naturalists Maurice and Katia Krafft, who actively pursued volcanic activity and were killed during an eruption. 60 mins.
VHS: S18891. $19.95.

National Geographic Video: Webs of Intrigue

Enter the world of an ancient creature that has become an expert weaver, hunter, and master of adaptation. 60 mins.
VHS: S34464. $19.95.

National Geographic Video: White Wolf

Follow a pack of wild arctic wolves through their remote and unforgiving wilderness in this National Geographic program about the fascinating creature. 60 mins.
VHS: S09932. $19.95.

National Geographic Video: Wild Survivors

Wild animals from Africa to the Caribbean deploy clever methods to hide their presence. Some blend into the background while others masquerade as other less harmful things. In this wildlife documentary from National Geographic, learn the secrets of these crafty, often invisible creatures.
VHS: S20821. $19.95.

National Geographic Video: Wildlife Warriors

African filmmakers Dereck and Beverly Joubert capture the fierce offensive waged against a band of wildlife poachers in Botswana. The government of Botswana deployed a small army to defend its wildlife heritage from these determined poachers. This film captures the drama of the heroic struggle to defend Africa's animals. 60 mins.
VHS: S29208. $19.95.

National Geographic Video: Wings over the Serengeti

Vultures and other scavengers are often reviled, but these creatures are an integral element of the Serengeti plain, where they live. This wildlife film explores the important role played by these creatures in the beautiful African savannah. 60 mins.
VHS: S29209. $19.95.

National Geographic Video: Zebra: Patterns in the Grass

A program about the spectacle of the great zebra migration in Botswana: a 300-mile journey studded with glorious scenery. The film also traces the evolution of the foal into a full grown zebra. 60 mins.
VHS: S18841. $19.95.

National Geographic— World's Last Great Places— Arctic Kingdom: Life at the Edge

Stalk the arctic ice with its fiercest predator, the polar bear, as it prowls one of the most forbidding places on the planet, a hidden kingdom of magnificent creatures.
VHS: S34596. $19.98.

National Geographic— World's Last Great Places— Yellowstone: Realm of the Coyote

Explore the back-country of Yellowstone National Park and discover an untamed wilderness most visitors never see—through the eyes of a coyote.
VHS: S34595. $19.98.

National Parks: America's Natural Heritage

Landscapes protected across the span of our history are featured on this video. From the simple beauty of open spaces to pastoral scenes of majesty, the various features of pristine wilderness collected on this tape make for breathtaking viewing. Features music by many artists, including Tangerine Dream. 40 mins.
VHS: S29548. $9.98.

The National Zoo

Take a private tour of the Smithsonian's living animals collection. Join seven-year-old Jenny and her friend Max as they meet the most famous and unusual residents of the National Zoo. 1989, 50 mins.
VHS: S14545. $29.95.
Laser: LD70225. $34.95.

Natural States

The lush Pacific Northwest in a blend of scenic cinematography and original music by David Lanz and Paul Speer. 45 mins.
VHS: S10959. $29.95.

Nature Archive Series

Six of the most popular episodes from PBS' landmark wildlife series. Each tape is 60 mins.
Designed for Living. Looks at the abundance of architectural feats of some of nature's most ingenious creatures. Many of these remarkable nests, tunnels and webs have inspired and served as models for man.
VHS: S31248. $19.95.
In-Flight Movie & Birds of the Sun God. Remarkable new film techniques are used to simulate the sensation of birds in flight. *In-Flight Movie* shows the world through the eyes of soaring hawks and storks, while *Birds of the Sun God* observes up close the hummingbird's aerial miracle.
VHS: S31247. $19.95.
Lords of Hokkaido. Spends a year with a family of red foxes and their wildlife neighbors: silka deer, red squirrels and red crowned cranes, as all struggle to survive the harsh winter on Japan's northernmost island, Hokkaido.
VHS: S31251. $19.95.
Lost World of the Medusa. Enters the complex community of marine life that thrives among the coral reefs of the tropical archipelago of Palau, home to strange oceanic creatures such as the giant clam and saltwater crocodile, as well as spectacular hordes of jellyfish.
VHS: S31249. $19.95.
Secrets of an African Jungle. Probes the hidden mystery of Korup, Africa's last great tropical rain forest, where interdependent plants struggle for survival.
VHS: S31252. $19.95.
Spirits of the Forest. Visits the remote island of Madagascar to enter the world of the lemur, a unique, monkey-like primate found nowhere else on earth.
VHS: S31250. $19.95.

The Nature Connection

Part of the prize-winning series in which Dr. David Suzuki takes children on an enchanting adventure with invaluable lessons and first-hand perspectives of how science and nature are related to human behavior and what everyone can do to protect the environment. 360 mins.
The Nature Connection, Vol. 1. In *Buying a Rainforest* Dr. Suzuki and a group of children buy private tracts of the rainforest and discover how their investment has preserved its beauty. In *Urban Ecology* Dr. Suzuki and the children from a Toronto suburb intermix with city kids to examine nature within an urban setting. 60 mins.
VHS: S19665. $19.95.
The Nature Connection, Vol. 2. In the first part, *Fishing the Ocean*, Dr. Suzuki and the children examine the life and work of a Newfoundland fisherman. In the second part, *Where Our Food Comes From*, the group receives lessons in farm life, including milking, weeding and harvesting. 60 mins.
VHS: S19666. $19.95.
The Nature Connection, Vol. 3. In *Merv's Forest* the group visits a 150-acre farm to learn how careful selective logging and forest management preserve forest industries without ecological damage. In *Water Works* Dr. Suzuki and his group examine the Great Lakes basin to study the role of water in the biosphere. 60 mins.
VHS: S19667. $19.95.
The Nature Connection, Vol. 4. In *The Badlands* the group explores fossil evidence in Dinosaur Provincial Park. In *A Winter Walk* the children take a dazzling walk to imagine how animals preserve their winter homes in hostile or threatening areas. 60 mins.
VHS: S19668. $19.95.
The Nature Connection, Vol. 5. In *Carmanah* the group explores the temperate rainforest in Carmanah Valley on Vancouver Island. In *Grasslands* the group discovers a vast 900-acre research ranch in the Albertan foothills. 60 mins.
VHS: S19669. $19.95.
The Nature Connection, Vol. 6. In *Tide Pools* Dr. Suzuki and his daughters bring a group of children to visit their cottage, where they study tide pools which teem with marine life. In *Cattail Country*, set in a marsh within a large industrial space, the group finds a wide variety of plants and animals. 60 mins.
VHS: S19670. $19.95.

Nature of Sex

This six-part series developed by the television series *Nature* tours the realm of animal and human sexuality as it travels the globe filming courtship displays and fights for dominance, mating, birthing, and caring for young. 60 minutes each.
A Time and a Place. Explores how the sun, moon and seasons of nature profoundly influence courtship, mating and birth.
VHS: S20431. $19.95.
A Miracle in the Making. Graphically shows the ingenious ways in which animals mate, prepare for birth and deliver their young.
VHS: S20434. $19.95.
Sex and the Human Animal. The origins of human sexuality are investigated by looking at other social animals and the various ways in which different cultures define sexual roles.
VHS: S20433. $19.95.
The Primal Instinct. Looks at the remarkable variety of ways the sexual urge is expressed among the Earth's countless species.
VHS: S20430. $19.95.
The Sex Contract. Focuses on how animals select partners and explores the duration of that contract, which might last a moment or a lifetime.
VHS: S20432. $19.95.
The Young Ones. Takes a look at life after sex, exploring the bond between parent and offspring.
VHS: S20435. $19.95.
Nature of Sex, Complete Set. The six-volume set.
VHS: S20436. $99.95.

Nature Perfected: The Story of the Garden

This enlightening documentary series is devoted to the art of gardening throughout history. From the ancient gardens of Pompeii to contemporary New York, it promises to open new vistas for all those engaged in perfecting nature.
Tape I. Program One: Paradise on Earth. Program Two: Ancient Spirits: China and Japan.
VHS: S25665. $29.95.
Tape II. Program Three: The Heritage of Rome. Program Four: Garlands of Repose.
VHS: S25666. $29.95.
Tape III. Program Five: Gardens of Conquest. Program Six: New Perspectives.
VHS: S25667. $29.95.
Tape IV. Program Seven: The Landscaping of England. Program Eight: Moving On.
VHS: S25668. $29.95.
Tape V. Program Nine: Glory and Grandeur. Program Ten: The Machine and the Garden.
VHS: S25669. $29.95.
Tape VI. Program Eleven: Grounds for Change. Program Twelve: The Genius of the Place.
VHS: S25670. $29.95.
Nature Perfected: The Story of the Garden, Set.
VHS: S25671. $119.95.

Nature's Fury: A Decade of Disasters

From ABC News comes this stunning spectacle of nature's more destructive impulses. Witness the earthquakes, tornadoes, floods, raging fires and bitter cold that have tested man's endurance in the past decade. 60 mins.
VHS: S12682. $24.98.

Nature's Great African Moments

This beautifully photographed documentary displays the wildlife riches of Africa. Lions on the hunt, wildebeest migrating, flamingoes in flight and prowling crocodiles are seen as they exist in the wild. Narrated by Avery Brooks. 60 mins.
VHS: S24374. $19.95.

Nature's Symphony

A program that interweaves beautiful, poetic images of nature scored to the works of Tchaikovsky, Strauss, Mozart and Puccini. 60 mins.
VHS: S30962. $29.95.
Laser: LD70237. $34.95.

North of Capricorn

Home to two of the world's highest waterfalls, incredibly long snakes, fat toads and giant butterflies, this is a fascinating look at the unique wilderness of Australia's northern territories, a land barely explored.
VHS: S05241. $19.95.

Nova—All American Bear

What enables the American black bear to go without food and water for six months? Looks at the bear's hibernation, habitat, eating and mating patterns. 60 mins.
VHS: S09404. $14.98.

Nova—Animal Hospital

An offbeat, humorous and sad portrait of pets, their owners and the veterinarians who treat our animals' ailments. From race horses under the knife for cancer treatment, to Manhattan hounds on Prozac, to anorexic boa constrictors, see how cutting edge veterinary medicine is saving animals' lives. 60 mins.
VHS: S33095. $19.95.

Nova—Avalanche!

Nova travels to the Swiss Alps, Montana and Alaska with the men and women at the cutting edge of avalanche science. 60 mins.
VHS: S33073. $19.95.

Nova—Buried in Ash

Ten million years ago, an enormous volcanic eruption buried much of what is now Nebraska in up to ten feet of ash, preserving countless skeletons of prehistoric big-game animals. *Nova* joins paleontologist and Nebraska native Mike Voorhies, the discoverer of this treasure trove, to learn what life was like way before buffalo roamed the west. 60 mins.
VHS: S33075. $19.95.

Nova—Can Elephants Be Saved?

An investigation of the epic struggle involved in the survival of elephants in Africa. The program warns that unless immediate intervention by wildlife authorities and scientists takes place and anti-poaching laws are enacted, the animals could become extinct. 60 mins.
VHS: S19117. $14.98.

Nova—Cities of Coral
The Caribbean coral reef is a beautiful and chaotic metropolis teeming with life, where hundreds of different species of fish vie for survival. This program uses spectacular photography to unravel the mysteries of the underwater world. 60 mins.
VHS: S11247. $14.98.

Nova—Cracking the Ice Age
Trek to Tibet with a renegade band of researchers bent on proving that the Himalayas are the cause of the Ice Age. 60 mins.
VHS: S33078. $19.95.

Nova—Diving for Pearls
Revel in the luster of these desirable gems from the depths of ocean to the riches of Fifth Avenue as you travel around the world to exotic locations where rare pearls are harvested by divers, and to farms where huge numbers of pearls are grown. 60 mins.
VHS: S33096. $19.95.

Nova—Everest: The Death Zone
Nova treks with a group of Himalayan climbers in their quest to reach the summit of Everest, along the way exploring in never-before-conducted tests of how extremes of weather and altitude affect the human mind and body. 60 mins.
VHS: S33097. $19.95.

Nova—In the Land of the Polar Bears
Take a wondrous look at a unique Arctic landscape and its diverse population in this Nova Series program. 60 mins.
VHS: S09818. $14.98.

Nova—Killer Quake!
Even though L.A. is still recovering, newly discovered faults could lead to more devastating natural disasters. This documentary explores the science that seeks to explain earthquakes.
VHS: S24875. $19.95.

Nova—Kingdom of the Seahorse
Tour the magical and complex world of the seahorse, from an underwater enclave in Australia (where their mating dance is caught on film for the first time) to the bustling apothecary shops of Hong Kong to a village in the Philippines dependent on the seahorse for survival. 60 mins.
VHS: S33082. $19.95.

Nova—Little Creatures Who Run the World
Through amazing close-up photography, Howard University's Edward Wilson reveals the hidden world of ants. It's a world governed by violent predation, tactical warfare and intimate partnerships.
VHS: S24878. $19.95.

Nova—Signs of the Apes, Songs of the Whales
Do animals understand us? Or do they learn required responses to get rewards? This special *Nova* program explores language in the animal world and their awe-inspiring ability to communicate with themselves, and with man. 60 mins.
VHS: S06968. $29.98.

Nova—T. rex Exposed
Sit in on a suspenseful dig to uncover the first complete *T. rex* ever found, and hear what scientists say about how this mysterious beast lived and what kind of cosmic zap may have made it die. 60 mins.
VHS: S33085. $19.95.

Nova—The Bermuda Triangle
Nova takes a hard look at this watery graveyard which has claimed so many lives and caused so much immense fascination, as this program explores the mystery of the strange occurrences which have resulted in thousands of mysterious disappearances. 60 mins.
VHS: S06967. $29.98.

Nova—The Shape of Things
A dazzling look at the world of nature up close and personal. Using time-lapse photography, computer animation and microphotography, Nova examines a drop of water, the construction of snowflakes and how crystals are formed. Also an inside look at a beehive in action. 60 mins.
VHS: S07578. $19.95.

Nova—Visions of the Deep
The popular television science series goes below sea level to explore the fascinating world of underwater photography and moviemaking. *Nova* explores the world of Al Giddings and his work on such films as *The Deep* and *For Your Eyes Only*. Find out the hazards of asking a shark to do retakes. USA, 60 mins.
VHS: S06026. $29.98.

Nova—Warnings from the Ice
Could the world be facing a catastrophic rise in sea levels as a result of the rapid break-up of the huge Antartic ice sheets, which hold 70% of the world's fresh water? Scientists are racing to understand whether the recent calving of a Connecticut-sized iceberg signals the beginning of a giant meltdown. 60 mins.
VHS: S33101. $19.95.

Nova—Yellowstone's Burning Question
Nova uncovers the astounding story of the fires that affected over a million acres of Yellowstone National Park in 1988, examines the controversy that surrounded the park's "let burn" policy, and reveals nature's miraculous process of rebirth. 60 mins.
VHS: S11652. $14.98.

Nursery Habitat Set
The Discovery Channel presents this three-volume set from their *Mother Nature: Tales of Discovery* series which explore young animals. The *Nursery Habitat Set* includes *Springtime Toddler Tales, Babes in the Woods* and *Bringing Up Baby*. Kids will love this look at a variety of cuddly animals.
VHS: S25087. $39.95.

The Ocean Blue: Man's Relationship to the Sea
This four-part series looks at the different ways that the sea affects humankind today. The imagination, weather, war and even health are broad areas where the sea continues to offer important input into the modern world.
The Sea of Imagination. The sea has always held a strong fascination for mankind. This program explores the realm of imagination between Melville's *Moby Dick* and Jules Verne's *20,000 Leagues Under the Sea*, that is between fear, superstition and reality. 53 mins.
VHS: S24916. $19.95.
Water and Weather. El Nino is a weather system that grows every year beginning around Christmas time. This video explores its physical underpinnings and its effects on man and culture. All the best efforts to curb this weather system's strength have failed. 53 mins.
VHS: S24917. $19.95.
Struggle for the Seas. Today modern navies have technology that appears to dwarf the human capacities of their staff. This video traces a history of important naval battles from ancient times into the present, when the US cruiser Vincennes downed a civilian Iranian airliner. 53 mins.
VHS: S24918. $19.95.
The Healing Sea. The sea is the source of life on the planet. Now scientists explore its depths and uncover important answers to some of life's mysteries. From Alzheimer's disease to cancer and chemical warfare, the sea holds many surprising possibilities that will affect how we live. 53 mins.
VHS: S24919. $19.95.
Four-Part Set.
VHS: S24920. $79.95.

Ocean Symphony
An original musical score is combined with breathtaking underwater photography. From the icy Antarctic to the warm waters of the Caribbean the viewer is invited to marvel at the wonders of the deep. Eleven segments include jelly fish, sharks and a variety of whales.
VHS: S03923. $29.95.
Al Giddings, USA, 1987, 47 mins.

Oceans of Air
Earth's four dominant climate types are revealed in this Discovery Channel documentary—the Olympic Peninsula of Washington, a lush rainforest, alpine glaciers and arid deserts of the prairies serve as examples. 60 mins.
VHS: S25079. $19.95.

Olympic National Park: Wilderness Heritage
Experience the essence of Olympic National Park: glacier-carved mountains, rugged Pacific coastline and lush rain forest. You'll also discover, close-up, the native plant and animal life which resides in this beautiful region—known to many as the jewel of the Northwest. USA, 30 mins.
VHS: S15079. $29.95.

On the Edge of Extinction: Panthers and Cheetahs
Loretta Swit narrates this entertaining and fascinating view of two imperiled animals and what is being done to protect them from extinction. 60 mins.
VHS: S08290. $14.98.

Orangutans—The High Society
This film blends in-depth footage of wild orangutans with a portrait of the South East Asian rainforest where they live. See how orangs interact at a rare social gathering, how they attract a mate, why they spend so much time alone, how their never-ending quest for food dictates their every move, and, for the first time on film, how wild orangs use tools like humans. Narrated by Brenda Vaccaro.
VHS: S30588. $19.95.
USA, 1996, 50 mins.

Orca: Killer Whale or Gentle Giant
Orcas—called killer whales—are more feared than understood. This film gives us an unusual window into the world of these magnificent marine mammals and challenges popular misconceptions about so-called "killer whales." An outstanding program for all ages. 1990, 26 mins.
VHS: S13952. $59.95.

Our Natural Heritage Series
Baby Animals. "Moose Baby," which follows a baby moose from infancy to adulthood; "Tembo—The Baby Elephant", the story of a baby elephant, and "Now I Am Bigger," the exploration of the growth of a baby chick. 42 mins.
VHS: S05818. $19.95.
Environments. "A Stream Environment" explores the beginnings and substance of streams, and "Ark", the exploration of environments corrupted by pollution and destruction, and how we might prevent a bleak environmental future. 29 mins.
VHS: S05819. $19.95.
Living Together. "Birds in Your Backyard," shows how to attract birds with a feeding tray, bath and nesting structure; "A Park Community" explores the building of parks as a defense against the concrete nature of cities, and "Communities of Living Things" explores the relationship between growing things and their surroundings. 36 mins.
VHS: S05820. $19.95.
Pretty Insects. "Butterflies Are" teaches the principles of collecting and studying butterflies; "The Aphid Eaters" follows Eve as she finds a cluster of yellow insect eggs that she collects and hatches, and watches eat aphids. 30 mins.
VHS: S05824. $19.95.
Seashores. "The Atlantic Coast" follows the Coast from the Bay of Fundy with gigantic tides, to the rockbound New England shores, the marshes of the Chesapeake to the Florida Keys; "The Pacific Coast" explores the diversity of the Coast's sandy beaches, shoreline flowers. 25 mins.
VHS: S05822. $19.95.
Survival of the Fittest. In "Greenhouse," a young boy discovers the beauty of flowers and the pain that the destruction of beauty causes; in "The Last Pigeon," a young boy participates in racing with homing pigeons. 26 mins.
VHS: S05825. $19.95.
The Mountains. "The Rocky Mountains" discovers the open fields, forests, meadows and rivers of the Rockies; "The Mountains" is a celebration of the diverse geological formations of mountains. 31 mins.
VHS: S05821. $19.95.
The Plains. "The Desert" explores the flora and fauna of the extreme climates; "The Prairie," the animals, insect and plant life in this ecologically precious environment; "The Meadow" the ecosystem of the spring and summer's inhabitants. 43 mins.
VHS: S05823. $19.95.
Western Birds and Flowers. "Waterbirds of the Western Flyways" follows the feeding, nesting of rare western waterbirds; "Wildflowers of the West" is a panorama of floral gems of the West. 27 mins.
VHS: S05826. $19.95.

Paleo World
This three-volume series from Discovery brings the largest and smallest creatures from prehistory to life. Dinosaurs and other creatures are examined using the latest theories, with cutting-edge 3-D graphics, and robotic models from the Dinamation International Society.
Paleo World, Volume 1: Rise of the Predators. This video has it all, from the tiny creatures who discovered that survival was just a swallow away, to the huge flesh-eating dinosaurs: the snake-quick velociraptor, poison-spitting dilophosaurus and that king of the jungle, *T. rex*.
VHS: S23019. $14.95.
Paleo World, Volume 2: Sea Monsters. Early mammals swam among giant squid and enormous sharks in the primordial seas. Some established themselves on land and prospered. Others made the return trip to becomes today's whales and dolphins.
VHS: S23020. $14.95.
Paleo World, Volume 3: Mysteries of Evolution. Is evolution more complex than we believe? Was *Homo sapiens* the only human species? Just what did kill the dinosaurs? In this volume these exciting questions are thoroughly explored.
VHS: S23021. $14.95.
Paleo World Deluxe Boxed Set.
VHS: S23022. $59.95.

Penguin World
From the storm-driven isles of the southern coastal oceans to the frozen tundra of Antarctica, this video provides a rare glimpse into various penguin habitats, from the four-pound and smaller Fairies to the 90-pound Emperors. 45 mins.
VHS: S18429. $29.95.
Laser: CAV. **LD74460. $34.95.**

People of the Forest
Follow 20 years of love and rivalry within a tribe of chimpanzees from the forests surrounding Lake Tanganyika. Based on the research of naturalist Jane Goodall, this rich tapestry of emotion and drama, narrated by Donald Sutherland, is captured by wildlife photographer Hugo van Lawick. 90 mins.
VHS: S17014. $24.95.

A Pipeline and Animals

This is a whimsical look at the wildlife along the route of the trans-Alaska pipeline. Mel Blanc narrates as footage depicts bears, beavers, moose, musk oxen, foxes, ducks, geese and more against the breath-taking Alaskan landscape. 28 mins.
VHS: S23971. $19.95.

Pity the Pilot Whale

The pilot whale is unprotected by international whaling regulations. This powerful video examines their nature and fate and how two countries treat these intelligent creatures differently. Narrated by James Coburn. 50 mins.
VHS: S23377. $59.95.

Planet of Life

A variety of perspectives is used in this four-part series to unravel the mystery of life's origins. Among the views seen here, new imaging techniques offer some of the most amazing insights. Explore the beginnings of life in *The Birth of Earth* and *Ancient Oceans*. From the Discovery Channel. 90 mins.
VHS: S29430. $89.95.

Predators of the Wild

A look at nature's most dangerous animals. These realistic documentaries were shot on location. 312 mins.
Predators of the Wild: African Survival. A waterhole in Africa is like Piccadilly Circus in London or Times Square in New York. Sooner or later, all creatures show up. Some come to drink or bathe. Others come to hunt. Giraffes and elephants are fearsome but lions are crafty predators. 52 mins.
VHS: S22339. $19.95.
Predators of the Wild: Bats. In some areas these swarming creatures of the dark consume up to 30,000 pounds of insects nightly. Nearly 25% percent of all mammals are bats. And yet only three bat species are true vampires, that require blood for sustenance. 51 mins.
VHS: S22342. $19.95.
Predators of the Wild: Cheetah and Leopard.
VHS: S19220. $19.95.
Laser: LD71902. $24.98.
Predators of the Wild: Crocodiles and Alligators. Perhaps a primal memory gives these scaly creatures—virtually unchanged since Earth was dominated by dinosaurs—their fierce savagery. From the water's edge to its murky depths these animals await their prey with endless patience. 49 mins.
VHS: S22340. $19.95.
Predators of the Wild: Giant Tarantula. Soft, even pleasant to the touch, but at what price? The giant tarantula is the largest and one of the most venomous spiders in the world. While waiting near its three-foot burrow, it conserves its energy and then pounces on insects, frogs, snakes, birds and rodents. 51 mins.
VHS: S22343. $19.95.
Predators of the Wild: Grizzly Bear.
VHS: S19221. $19.95.
Laser: LD71903. $24.98.
Predators of the Wild: Hunters and the Hunted.
VHS: S19218. $19.95.
Laser: LD71900. $24.98.
Predators of the Wild: Killer Whale.
VHS: S19219. $19.95.
Laser: LD71901. $24.98.
Predators of the Wild: Lion.
VHS: S19216. $19.95.
Laser: LD71898. $24.98.
Predators of the Wild: Shark.
VHS: S19217. $19.95.
Laser: LD71899. $24.98.
Predators of the Wild: Snake. Fearsome and fascinating, these creatures are responsible for the deaths of 40,000 people each year. Some 2000 species, 85% percent of them harmless to man, slither across the land or swim in the ocean deep. See how an anaconda can smother a much larger animal—in this instance an alligator! 52 mins.
VHS: S22341. $19.95.
Predators of the Wild: Wolf. Bone numbing howls sear the night sky. The eerie cries, slightly out of tune, drift from one to the other, keeping these animals in touch over a wide area. It's time for the hunt and the pack must be called together. Deer and livestock alike are not safe from these clever predators.
VHS: S22344. $19.95.
Predators of the Wild: Gift Pack. Includes *Cheetah and Leopard, Grizzly Bear, Hunters and the Hunted, Killer Whale, Lion* and *Shark*.
VHS: S19222. $119.93.
Laser: LD71904. $99.98.

Prehistoric Beasts

Four videos delve into the myth and power of prehistoric animals that ruled the Earth more than 65 million years ago. With their massive size and astonishing physical skills, they altered the ecological balance. Intended for children in grades 1-6.
Archaeopteryx. What was the exact nature of this beast, bird or dinosaur? This tree climber could float from tree branches to escape danger or catch prey but its vast wings were used to trap insects. 10 mins.
VHS: S20046. $44.95.
Plesiosaurus. This air-breathing marine reptile is believed to be the first giant reptile. Its bones were discovered and studied after lying dormant beneath the sea for millions of years. 10 mins.
VHS: S20047. $44.95.
Pteranodon. Scientists have been fascinated by this amazing beast, which descended from reptiles, had an amazing wing span of 23 feet and could fly. 12 mins.
VHS: S20048. $44.95.
Woolly Mammoth. A plant-eating, tusked creature of the Ice Age, this mammal had an elaborate, two-layer coat of hair for keeping warm. 11 mins.
VHS: S20049. $44.95.
Prehistoric Beasts, Set. This set contains four titles: *Archaeopteryx, Plesiosaurus, Pteranodon* and *Woolly Mammoth*. 43 mins.
VHS: S20050. $159.95.

The Private Life of Plants

Sir Richard Attenborough hosts this BBC production. It looks at plants all over the world, from Borneo to Tasmania, in order to reveal some intriguing secrets. Plants have unique methods that help them perceive and respond to their surroundings.
Volume 1: Branching Out. Plants can see and count and even communicate with one another. That's how they manage to live in harmony with each other. Their function goes well beyond producing oxygen and food for other organisms.
VHS: S26980. $19.98.
Volume 2: Putting Down Roots. In this volume, the intricate security systems which ensure plant development and growth are examined. Deadly poisons, sharp barbs and menacing spikes are just some of the weapons used by plants to protect their leaves from mutilation.
VHS: S26981. $19.98.
Volume 3: The Birds and the Bees. Flowers direct insects and animals to their pollen centers. Some plants attract their partners to the pollen with appealing blooms which actually point out their prize and simultaneously ensure pollination.
VHS: S26982. $19.98.
Volume 4: Plant Politics. Plant interactions mirror those of animals and people. Since there is always a limited supply of energy, water, oxygen and minerals, each plant's positioning is critical for its survival.
VHS: S26983. $19.98.
Volume 5: Living Together. Plants do compete for survival. In some instances however, plants actually develop symbiotic relations that generate a necessary co-dependence.
VHS: S26984. $19.98.
Volume 6: It's a Jungle Out There. Plants survive in places where humans have not found ways to exist. These sturdy plants maintain a ferocious appetite for survival that allows them to thrive in brutally harsh environments.
VHS: S26985. $19.98.
The Private Life of Plants: Collector's Edition. The complete six-volume set.
VHS: S26986. $79.98.

Private Lives of Dolphins

Observe the deep-sea drama of dolphins, the ocean's most charming and intelligent mammals, in this NOVA video. 60 mins.
VHS: S28655. $19.95.

Procreation in the Wild

From Antarctica to Africa and Asia, this video reveals exactly how a number of animals, including hippos, giraffes, elephants, tigers, monkeys and more, procreate. This is the wildlife video that actually shows the wild thing. 90 mins.
VHS: S24693. $39.95.

Queen of the Elephants

Author Mark Shand undergoes a 300-mile odyssey tracing the migratory route of the endangered Indian elephant. These mammoth creatures are capable of both great affection and unmatched destruction. Of course their greatest challenge lies not in their natural environment but in the ever-encroaching reach of man. 90 mins.
VHS: S20902. $19.95.

Quest for the Dolphin Spirit

A first-person account from producers Liz and Steve Weiss, who, with their one-year-old daughter in tow, travel the world's beaches and ocean communities to learn about the peculiar and fascinating relations between dolphins and humans. 46 mins.
VHS: S17608. $24.95.

Quest

Three-tape set. *Dancing with Rhinos*—Glenn Tatham, the last hope of the beleaguered Black Rhino, journeys deep into the African bush to view the last of these creatures still living in the wild. As Chief Warden of Zimbabwe's National Parks, Tatham and his rangers have held the line here for the past three years, not having lost a single animal to poachers. *Last of the Stone Agers: Part 2*—On the second leg of this journey, Herve de Maigret continues on into the central highlands in search of the more peace-loving pygmy tribes that he first encountered in 1969. *Bali: The Dance of Life*—Explore Balinese religious rituals, where dance and music accompany all phases of life, from the time a baby's feet touch the earth, to teenage tooth filing, to elaborate weddings and funerals. Each tape is 50 mins.
VHS: S34399. $39.98.

Rain Forests: Proving Their Worth

With stunning visuals, rare archival footage, first-person accounts, and an original soundtrack, this documentary provides a provocative look at a crucial effort to save the rain forests and the people who inhabit them. Forceful work creatively presented. 1990, 31 mins.
VHS: S13934. $85.00.

Realm of the Alligator

The mysterious wilderness of Okefenokee, 700 miles of swampland on the Georgia-Florida border, eerie, forbidden, darkly beautiful, and brilliantly explored in this National Geographic documentary, which follows scientists as they study the behavior of the giant and powerful alligator. 59 mins.
VHS: S04885. $19.95.

Rescuing Baby Whales

Watch the dramatic rescue of young, stranded pilot whales with NOVA to learn what is behind this puzzling phenomenon. 60 mins.
VHS: S28654. $19.95.

Return of the Great Whale

Filmed in the "national park of ocean," this documentary is an environmental success story about the re-emergence of humpback and blue whales into the coastal waters of northern California, where fishing and whaling industries once hunted these magnificent mammals to the brink of extinction. 50 mins.
VHS: S04150. $39.95.

Return of the Wolves

This program chronicles the controversial reintroduction of the wolf into Yellowstone National Park, and explores human conceptions and misconceptions of wolves. With unique footage of wolves in the wild. 60 mins.
VHS: S32408. $14.95.

River of Stone: The Powell Expedition

Narrated by Robert Redford, this award-winning documentary retraces John Wesley Powell's historic 1869 pioneering trips down the Colorado and Green Rivers. The film includes some of the first photographs ever taken of the Grand Canyon river territories. 60 mins.
VHS: S32409. $14.95.

Roadrunner Clown of the Desert/ Punk Puffins and Hard Rock (BBC Wildlife Special)

The Road Runner, that lovable cartoon character, actually exists. A real bird that cannot fly, but can zip around the desert at speeds of up to 30 miles per hour in hot pursuit of insects, mice and reptiles. *Punk Puffins* ventures off to the island of St. Lararia off the coast of Alaska where more than a half million birds make their summer home. The most spectacular are the tufted puffins—dumpy, clown-like birds with white faces, orange beaks and wild plumes on their heads. 55 mins.
VHS: S12392. $19.94.

San Francisco Earthquake

A complete account of the 15 seconds when the San Francisco Bay Area stood on the brink of annihilation, and the deadly aftermath of the 7.1 quake. This tape features dramatic footage of the heroes and victims of this natural disaster. From ABC News. 60 mins.
VHS: S12679. $14.98.

Savage and Beautiful

A breathtaking look at the animal kingdom, narrated by Donald Sutherland, with a compelling soundtrack by Vangelis.
VHS: S06552. $14.95.

Savage Skies

In this four-tape set, Al Roker of NBC's *Today* show explains some of the most powerful weather systems plaguing the face of the earth. The savagery and beauty of these systems is awe-inspiring. Each episode is approximately 60 minutes long.
VHS: S29466. $79.98.

Saviors of the Forest
Tired of filming TV commercials, two Los Angeles "camera guys" decide to do their part for the environment by exposing the villains responsible for destroying the rain forests. Along the way they meet a range of paradoxical characters, including poor people who cut down forests to survive, environmentalists trying to import an "ecological" sawmill, timber companies campaigning for reforestation and Hollywood producers who use rain forest plywood to build their sets. 90 mins.
VHS: S23370. $95.00.

A Sea Otter Story: Warm Hearts and Cold Water
The heartwarming tale of orphaned sea otters is at the center of this insightful documentary. The Monterey Bay Aquarium rears these animals and trains them so that they can be released into the wild. George Page narrates. 60 mins.
VHS: S24375. $19.95.

Sea Turtles: Ancient Nomads (National Audubon)
Jane Alexander narrates this program featuring stunning wildlife and underwater photography which constitutes an intimate look at the behavior of wild sea turtles and their perilous fight for survival. 60 mins.
VHS: S09559. $14.98.

Secrets of the Desert Sea
The story of how life is sustained in the Sea of Cortez. Through unique photography, viewers see the interconnectedness of life in this sea and see how each creature fits into the larger ecosystem. Produced by the award-winning team of Hardy Jones and Julia Whitty. 50 mins.
VHS: S07591. $24.95.

Shark Attack Files
Shark attack victims who survived speak about their experiences in this surprising video. Also the stories of those who weren't so lucky are told. This video attempts to discover if these attacks are deliberate and malicious or just a case of mistaken identity. 60 mins.
VHS: S26047. $19.95.

Shark Bait
Shark attacks are on the rise world-wide. A leader in shark research is struggling to find a safe, practical chemical repellant that can save both divers and sharks from harm. 60 mins.
VHS: S26045. $19.95.

Shark Hunter
This dramatic video demonstrates how Vic Hislop tracks and catches sharks—whalers, hammerheads, tiger sharks, the Great Whites. Vic reveals the truth about sharks, through spectacular underwater shark segments. 60 mins.
VHS: S09917. $29.95.

Sharks of the Red Triangle
Roddy McDowell narrates a Discovery Channel documentary about the habits of the Great White Shark. Red Triangle refers to a key patch of the ocean where these creatures breed and feed. This documentary explores the role of these sharks in the California ecosystem, and the threat, if any, that they pose to humans. 45 mins.
VHS: S29427. $39.95.

Sharks: Predators or Prey?
A fascinating look at shark behavior, revealing the serious threat to some shark populations through overfishing. Mixing humor with hard facts, *Sharks* dispels some of the common myths about these complex creatures of the deep. 20 mins.
VHS: S23376. $79.95.

Slaves of the Harvest
Documentary on the hunting of fur seals on the Priboff Islands off the coast of Alaska. Produced by Greenpeace. 25 mins.
VHS: S06497. $49.95.

Small World
Insects seem alien to man at first glance, yet on closer inspection they share many human traits. This examination of the habitat of the miniature, filled with industrious, sociable and sexually active creatures is a remarkable wildlife documentary.
VHS: S05243. $19.95.

Smithsonian World: Zoo
The National Zoological Park has been a vital institution for 100 years. This video celebrates Washington D.C.'s link to the larger natural world. It also allows Zoo Director Michael Robertson to share his vision of a futuristic biopark. 58 mins.
VHS: S27375. $19.98.

The Snow Wolves
Narrated by Joseph Campanella, this powerful film features rare and intimate footage of nature's most mysterious canines in the wild at Yellowstone and Denali National Parks and the Canadian Arctic. 60 mins.
VHS: S32407. $19.95.

Splendors of the Sea
The sea contains many bizarre creatures. A number of the most exotic are captured in this video featuring stunning underwater photography. 60 mins. From the Discovery Channel.
VHS: S25074. $19.95.

The Story of America's Great Volcanoes
From deep within the earth, the most violent natural act manifests itself in Alaska, Washington, Oregon, Idaho, Hawaii, Arizona and California. Learn the exciting histories of these geologic wonders through spectacular photography and a concise, entertaining narrative. 56 mins.
VHS: S16636. $29.95.

Super Shark Collection
This three-volume set from the Discovery Channel explores the underwater world where sharks rule supreme as the most feared predators. *Great White, Demons of the Deep* and *The Man Who Loves Sharks* capture these brutal animals in all their ferocity. 180 mins.
VHS: S25083. $54.95.

Survival in the Wild
The widely respected British Broadcasting Company is well known for its commitment to the production of excellent documentaries. Now for the first time a series of BBC wild life films are available. A wide range of the earth's creatures are featured in this series as they struggle to survive.
Deadly Illusions. Not all deadly hunters use speed or brute strength to find their quarry. Some use cunning, stealth, or even disguise. Chameleons meld into their background while a snapping turtle lures victims with false offers of food. This documentary uncovers the secret weapons of the world's wild life.
VHS: S20703. $14.95.
Pack Hunters. Many of the world's most ferocious animals hunt in packs, including grizzly bears, vampire bats, and white wolves. In this film the social and communication skills are revealed that allow these powerful animals to join their abilities for the common goal of survival.
VHS: S20701. $14.95.
Predators and Prey. Solitary hunters have an intricate relationship with those animals that they feed upon, their prey. In this episode tigers, sharks, cheetahs and leopards are all seen honing their unique skills as they seek sustenance in a cruel war of survival.
VHS: S20702. $14.95.

Symphony to America the Beautiful
This musical journey across America captures the beauty of the changing seasons set to the music of Brahms, Vivaldi, Mozart and other classical composers. Two-volume set, 120 mins.
VHS: S23135. $39.95.

Tidal Wave
Imagine an unstoppable wall of water, racing to shore at 500 mph, reaching heights of nearly 100 feet. Amazing rare footage and survivor stories help explain the mysterious phenomenon.
VHS: S34286. $14.98.

Tornado
Join stormchasers who drive right to the edge of tornadoes to capture nature's ultimate rage in this rare footage with heartstopping images.
VHS: S34287. $14.98.

Tornado Chasers
Most people flee these awesome natural phenomena. With winds that rage up to 300 miles an hour, tornadoes can reduce entire towns to mere kindling. This video shows a group of people who risk their lives and cruise "Tornado Alley" in Oklahoma to capture images of twisters close-up. Narrated by Bill Kurtis.
VHS: S26096. $19.95.

Tornado! Hurricane! Flood! Won ders of Weather
Every year thousands of American lives are uprooted and lost to our most violent storm systems. Join professional storm chasers and charge into the eye of the storm to witness nature's brute force firsthand. Through unforgettable footage you'll experience a category 5 hurricane, see twisters spinning up to 300 miles per hour, watch deadly lightening bolts ignite the sky and hear one survivor's story, and track devastating flash floods from the first raindrop until people are clinging to treetops as their cars and homes float away.
VHS: S30592. $19.95.
Yavar Abbas/Richard Burke/Martin Gorse, USA, 1996, 90 mins.

Trailside
Fourteen episodes from the award-winning, critically acclaimed TV series featuring leading outdoor experts, guides and instructors in extraordinary adventures and destinations around the world as they bring their knowledge to novice and expert alike. Each tape is 30 mins.
Trailside—Desert Hiking in Big Bend, Texas.
VHS: S32779. $19.95.
Trailside—Jungle Hiking in Costa Rica.
VHS: S32788. $19.95.
Trailside—Kayak Sailing the Exuma Islands, Bahamas.
VHS: S32789. $19.95.
Trailside—More Wilderness 911.
VHS: S32782. $19.95.
Trailside—Mountain Biking Colorado's 10th Mountain Trail.
VHS: S32790. $19.95.
Trailside—Mountaineering the Grand Teton.
VHS: S32791. $19.95.
Trailside—Paddling and Poling Louisiana's Bayou Country.
VHS: S32783. $19.95.
Trailside—Rock Climbing in the Adirondacks.
VHS: S32784. $19.95.
Trailside—Sea Kayaking with Orcas.
VHS: S32785. $19.95.
Trailside—Ski Touring California's High Sierra.
VHS: S32786. $19.95.
Trailside—Thru-Hiking the Appalachian Trail.
VHS: S32780. $19.95.
Trailside—Trekking in Iceland.
VHS: S32781. $19.95.
Trailside—Whitewater Canoeing the Chattooga River.
VHS: S32792. $19.95.
Trailside—Winter Camping in Yellowstone National Park.
VHS: S32787. $19.95.

Trials of Life
Sir David Attenborough, the renowned naturalist, leads an exploration of the mysteries of animal behavior in this acclaimed, 12-part documentary series. The winner of two Ace Awards, this series is often more fantastic than any invention of the imagination.
Arriving.
VHS: S15609. $19.98.
Continuing the Line.
VHS: S17749. $19.98.
Courting.
VHS: S17748. $19.98.
Fighting.
VHS: S17745. $19.98.
Finding Food.
VHS: S15611. $19.98.
Finding the Way.
VHS: S15613. $19.98.
Friends & Rivals.
VHS: S17746. $19.98.
Growing Up.
VHS: S15610. $19.98.
Home Making.
VHS: S15614. $19.98.
Hunting/Escaping.
VHS: S15612. $19.98.
Living Together.
VHS: S17744. $19.98.
Talking to Strangers.
VHS: S17747. $19.98.
Trials of Life, Collector's Gift Set.
VHS: S15615. $199.98.
Laser: LD74965. $199.99.

Tropical Kingdom of Belize
This National Geographic Video takes the armchair traveler to the Central American nation of Belize. Formerly British Honduras, this tiny nation is said to feature one of the most diverse natural environments in the world. See for yourself. 60 mins.
VHS: S03677. $19.95.

Tropical Rainforest
This IMAX documentary film explores the incredible diversity of life found in the world's rain forests, as well as the problems faced by these fragile ecosystems. 90% of the world's species are found here and yet many of these may become extinct before they are even discovered. Filmed in Australia, Central and South America, and Asia. 40 mins.
VHS: S22666. $29.95.
Laser: LD74550. $39.95.

Tropical Sweets
Bill Patterson's fresh mosaic of music, the sounds and rhythms of nature and a cascading symphony of tropical images and quixotic delights. 40 mins.
Laser: LD70245. $29.95.

The Ultimate Guide
Combining advanced research with the latest in film technology, this program from The Discovery Channel is the most comprehensive science/natural history series to be shown on television. Each episode presents detailed information accompanied by startling visuals and stunning images as it takes an innovative approach to scientifically exploring each animal, from its physiological composition to its behavioral patterns. Each tape is 50 mins.
Elephants.
VHS: S31934. $19.95.
Sharks.
VHS: S31935. $19.95.
Snakes.
VHS: S31936. $19.95.

The Ultimate Guide: T. Rex

The Discovery Channel created this video documentary, which goes some way toward demolishing the myths built up around this massive creature. It is all done from the perspective of a *T. rex* that may have been a scavenger, a bird-like runner and a doting father. 50 mins.
VHS: S29901. $19.95.

The Ultimate Journey

Stunning microphotography by Lennart Nilsson *(The Miracle of Life)* shows how the developing human embryo reveals links to other species, reflecting a shared ancestry that harks back to the dawn of creation. From NOVA. 60 mins.
VHS: S31438. $19.95.

The Unknown World

Magnified to monster size, the microphotography of Lennart Nilsson *(The Miracle of Life)* catches creepy crawlers in the act. From NOVA. 60 mins.
VHS: S31439. $19.95.

Unseen World of Chiricahua

Explores the scenic beauty and natural history of Chiricahua National Monument in Arizona. Learn how the plants and animals have learned to adapt to this evolving geological fantasyland and depend on each other to survive. 30 mins.
VHS: S09184. $29.95.

Untamed Africa

Narrated by John Hurt, this two-volume documentary captures the great African migration of grazing animals. *Volume I: The Great Migration Begins* and *Volume II: Survival on the Savannah* show how wildebeests fare with the predators and dangers that haunt them as they wander from the lush Masai Mara to the Serengeti Plain. 120 mins.
VHS: S27827. $39.95.

The Untamed Wild

This award-winning program from The Discovery Channel by acclaimed filmmaker Will Taylor surveys daily life-and-death struggles among Africa's diverse wildlife on three tapes: *Royal Blood, Rivers of Life* and *The Big Five of Africa*. 52 minutes each.
VHS: S30959. $39.95.

Vanishing Dawn Chorus

The pristine sounds of nature are captured in this visually and aurally stunning film as Gordon Hempton, the Sound Tracker, circles the globe, visiting locations on six continents where human noises are nonexistent. 58 mins.
VHS: S31885. $24.95.

Volcano

See a volcanic eruption in progress, photographed at close range, and experience the force, heat, lava flow, and fire that is created. 29 mins.
VHS: S05734. $29.95.

Volcanoes of Hawaii

Spectacular eruption footage, including the recent eruption which overran Kalapana Village and entered the sea, highlights this fascinating program that shows the many moods of Hawaii's Mauna Loa and Kilauea volcanoes. 30 mins.
VHS: S08459. $29.95.

Volcanos: Cauldrons of Fury

This program examines the natural phenomenon of volcanos through stunning footage, vintage newsreels, still photographs and drawings; consults with teams of geologists, geophysicists and seismologists; revisits the disasters accompanying the eruptions of Mt. Vesuvias, Agung, Krakatoa, Mt. Pinatubo and Mt. St. Helens; and interviews survivors of the 1980 Mt. St. Helens eruption. 55 mins.
VHS: S31876. $19.98.

Voyage of the Great Southern Ark

Australia's unique geological forms and exotic animals and plants have intrigued generations. This program takes audiences on a sweeping journey through the history of the Australian continent and its inhabitants, from 4.2 billion years ago to modern times. Gleaning information from the latest technology and the most respected experts in the field, this enthralling video presents a panoramic survey of our planet's development. Everywhere in Australia the primeval and the modern co-exist, forming a dramatic visual history of the earth's evolution. 138 mins.
VHS: S10288. $39.95.

Voyage to Save the Whales

An award-winning documentary of Greenpeace's early campaign to save the whale in 1975 and 1976. 30 mins.
VHS: S06498. $49.95.

Walk in the Forest

Journey into the heart of America's rain forests, the old-growth forests of the Pacific Northwest. See the remarkable diversity of life hidden there. Feel the warmth of summer, the terror of fire, the blessing of rain. This beautiful portrait details the delicate balance of plants and animals that make this region a living whole. "Outstanding" *(Booklist)*. First Prize winner, Chicago Film Festival. 1976, 28 mins.
VHS: S13697. $24.95.

Water Journey

Jon Child's aquatic journey from thunder storm through forest, marsh, pond, lake, and river. Winner of Film as Environment award. Natural sounds of water, birds and insects. An ambient escapade. 60 mins.
VHS: S10241. $29.95.

Waterfalls and Wildlife

Two of Canada's most magnificent parks—British Columbia's Wells Grey, a spectacular waterfalls park, and Ontario's Algonquin wilderness sanctuary—are showcased. 48 mins.
VHS: S31707. $19.95.

Whale for the Killing

Strong performances by Peter Strauss and Richard Widmark plus a poignant lesson in ecology distinguish this story about one man's attempt to save a stranded whale. 145 mins.
VHS: S10100. $59.98.

Whales! (National Audubon)

Johnny Carson narrates this moving look at whales—after years of senseless slaughter, the whale is not the focus of international preservation efforts. Audubon investigates this change in attitude and features some spectacular whale-watching, with unique underwater photography. 60 mins.
VHS: S09560. $14.98.

Whalesong: Whales and Dolphins of the Pacific

Narrated by Lloyd Bridges, this documentary explores underworld sea life. 40 mins.
VHS: S17221. $24.95.

Wild Alaska

Dale Johnson leads this rare wildlife video shot in the Alpine tundra in the shadow of Mt. McKinley, following the migrating caribou, musk ox, and a dramatic life struggle between a caribou and grizzly. 60 mins.
VHS: S05968. $29.95.

Wild Australia on Video

A wildlife adventure down under: the world of the koala, kangaroo, platypus, echidna, numbat and crocodile, as well as a rare segment of the Tasmanian tiger, now extinct. 60 mins.
VHS: S09908. $29.95.

Wild Discovery

This program from The Discovery Channel journeys into dark jungles, searing deserts, treacherous mountains and ocean depths to reveal the exotic world around them and the remarkable creatures who inhabit them. Each tape is 50 mins.
Cheetahs: The Winning Streak.
VHS: S31937. $19.95.
Crocodile Territory.
VHS: S31938. $19.95.
Dragons of Komodo.
VHS: S31939. $19.95.
Gorillas: Tender Giants.
VHS: S31940. $19.95.

Wild India

The safari of a lifetime is featured on this video from the Discovery Channel. In the teaming jungles of the Himalayas lurk a variety of rare and fascinating creatures. The camera crew goes all out to stalk these animals. 90 mins.
VHS: S25077. $19.95.

The Wild World Series: Daisy Discovers the World

A young sea lion is simply curious. In this beautifully photographed wildlife film, curiosity is all it takes for this young animal to start an exciting adventure. 15 mins.
VHS: S23462. $49.95.

Wildflowers of the Cajun Prairies

Prairie grasses and flowers once reached to shoulder height. Now the remnants of this ecosystem must be rescued in southwest Louisiana. 28 mins.
VHS: S22394. $44.95.

Wilds of Madagascar

The island of Madagascar was separated from the mainland of Africa more than 165 million years ago; its flora and fauna have evolved in near isolation. This trek to remote sunken forests discovers the crowned lemur, the leaf-tailed geeko and the souimanga sunbird. 60 mins.
VHS: S10245. $19.95.

The WIPP Trail

The acronym for the Waste Isolation Pilot Project, this video, narrated by Robert Redford, explores the current nuclear waste controversy. As a massive backlog of close to 300 million cubic feet of nuclear waste piles up at U.S. defense facilities, pressure is mounting to open the Waste Isolation Pilot Plant in southeastern New Mexico. Technical review of WIPP, waste transportation, emergency response, public information and democratic process are the issues addressed in this citizen-produced, engaging dialog which focuses on one of the dominant political, ecological and safety issues of our time. 60 mins.
VHS: S08790. $24.95.

The Wolf Pack

On *The Snow Wolf* you'll see footage of nature's most mysterious canines in the wild at Yellowstone, Denali National Park and the Canadian Arctic. *Return of the Wolves* seeks to explain and deploy human conceptions of wolves, chronicling the controversial attempts to reintroduce the wolf into Yellowstone National Park. Two cassettes. 120 mins.
VHS: S34716. $19.95.

Wolves

Wolves examines the ecological contributions of these animals. Narrated by Robert Redford.
VHS: S16875. $14.98.

Wonders of God's Creation

This documentary series of three videos looks at the mysteries and beauty of the creation of the universe. The programs are *Planet Earth: Sanctuary of Life*, a panoramic view of the ecological, environmental and physical beauty of the earth; *The Animal Kingdom: Great Are Thy Works*, an observation of animals and species; *Human Life: The Crown of Creation*, a piece about the interlocking human mysteries, the brain, the hand and skeletal system and the components of the heart. Available in two editions, the Deluxe Edition with a gold-embossed slipcase with Creation booklet, and Standard Edition, with Creation booklet. Wonders of God's Creation. Deluxe Edition.
VHS: S17267. $79.95.

Wood Stork: Barometer of the Everglades (National Audubon)

Narrated by Richard Crenna. The wood stork, a fragile figure whose delicate existence mirrors that of all the wildlife in Florida's Everglades is now an endangered species. 60 mins.
VHS: S09003. $14.98.

World of Discovery: Beautiful Killers

Naturalist filmmaker Nicolas Noxon presents a kaleidoscopic work about the habits and lifestyle of the killer whales moored off the coast of British Columbia. The program studies the controversial confinement and commercialization of theme parks and aquariums. 50 mins.
VHS: S19309. $19.98.

World of Discovery: Cougar: Ghost of the Rockies

Wildlife filmmaker Jim Dutcher and mountain lion specialist Dr. Morris Hornocker undertake a rugged two-year expedition to track a mountain lion and her kittens. 50 mins.
VHS: S19307. $19.98.

World of Discovery: Realm of the Serpent

This exotic video examines the daily rituals of the snake. The program features Burmese cobra charmers, the emergence of the green tree python in the rain forest, a Texas rattle snake round up and the identification of a fer-de-lance in Central America. 50 mins.
VHS: S19310. $19.98.

World of Discovery: Shark Chronicles

Naturalist filmmaker Al Giddings deploys underwater photography to document the ferocious nature and predatory instincts of the shark. 50 mins.
VHS: S19305. $19.98.

World of Discovery: The Secret Life of 118 Green Street

Billions of uninvited houseguests invade the average home every day. This universe swarming with life is not visible to the naked eye, but it can be revealed through the wonder of microscopic photography. 50 mins.
VHS: S22518. $19.98.

World of Discovery: Wildebeest: Race for Life

These stately creatures run a gauntlet of life, birth and death. The African plain they inhabit is plagued by predators from crocodiles to lions. 50 mins.
VHS: S22517. $19.98.

World of Discovery: Wolf: Return of a Legend

Wildlife photographer and wolf expert Jim Dutcher captures the camera-shy wolf up close. These intriguing creatures are shown in their natural habitat for the first time. 50 mins.
VHS: S22516. $19.98.

World of Herbs

A five-part, three volume program studies the origins, history and multiple uses of herbs, based on the book by Lesley Bremness. "An excellent series, and a surefire circulator in public libraries" *(Video Librarian)*. 200 mins.
VHS: S17382. $79.95.

The World of the Koala

A fascinating look at Australia's most adorable animal, this program explores the lifestyle of this amazing marsupial, from its unique characteristics, to the history of its life down under, to its relationships with other forest dwellers. 25 mins.
VHS: S35021. $14.95.

Yellowstone to Yukon

This beautifully photographed documentary offers an in-depth look at the wild heart of the Northern Rockies, called the Serengeti of North America. Beginning in Yellowstone and moving up into the Yukon Territory, it showcases grizzlies, cougars, elk, caribou, wolves, bighorn sheep and the world's last remaining herds of bison. 48 mins.
VHS: S32664. $19.95.

Yellowstone-Teton Wildlife

Set amidst the breathtaking scenery of Yellowstone and Grand Teton National Parks, this program follows the wildlife through the changing seasons, including grizzly and black bears, owls, elk, moose, coyotes, bald eagle, porcupine and others. 45 mins.
VHS: S10924. $29.95.

Yesterday's Heroes

Venture to scenic Australia and experience the harsh and fatal reality of horses, donkeys and camels whose strong backs helped build the island continent. Yesterday's heroes are today's courageous warriors fighting for life against a civilization bent on their destruction. Lorne Greene hosts. 30 mins.
VHS: S06324. $14.95.

SPORTS & THE OUTDOORS

100 Years of Olympic Glory

The wondrous feats of the modern Olympics have been compiled on this two-tape, three-hour-long set. Contemporary figures such as Nadia Comaneci, Mark Spitz and Mary Lou Retton, as well Olympians from long ago like Jesse Owens, have brought the world together through triumphant athletic feats. Now the story of their efforts is compellingly told in this documentary through priceless archival footage. 180 mins.
VHS: S27505. $29.98.

1986 Tour de France: LeMond and Hinault Challenge

This British produced documentary captures the grueling and historic challenge between Bernard Hinault and Greg LeMond. This is the race that placed an American rider in the forefront of the cycling world. Commentary by Phil Liggett. 53 mins.
VHS: S16215. $29.95.

1987 Tour of Ireland: Nissan Classic

Running three hours in length, this video gives the viewer a complete look at one of pro cycling's best races. The action is fast paced, and the in-depth interviews with Sean Kelly, Stephen Roche and Greg LeMond are enlightening. 180 mins.
VHS: S08926. $59.95.

1988 Iditabike Race: Bicycling on Snow

This race pushes the sport to its outer limits. Conditions can range from slush and 40 degrees to a blizzard at 40 below, riding over snow covered lakes and dog-sled paths both day and night. This exciting race is gaining in popularity and now you can experience it first hand. 25 mins.
VHS: S09222. $24.95.

1989 World Championship: LeMond's Victory

Balancing pure action and great sports drama, this video showcases footage from previous LeMond victories in both amateur and professional cycling. In the recent World Championship, Fignon makes a desperate bid for victory, but LeMond provides the brilliant counter. Directed by Kent Gordis. 48 mins.
VHS: S16221. $29.95.

1990 Paris-Roubaix: A Photo Finish!

Motorcycle and helicopter cameras reveal the critical action of this truly thrilling race. Phil Liggett offers a steady stream of fascinating anecdotes and insights, as well as an encyclopedic knowledge of the riders. 98 mins.
VHS: S16217. $39.95.

1990 Tour de France: Greg LeMond—The Best Yet!

This no-nonsense, insightful portrait relives the moments that led to LeMond's third Tour victory. "Virtually every major break is covered...some of the best high-speed descent shots we've ever seen" *(Bicycling)*. With commentary from Paul Liggett. 102 mins.
VHS: S16213. $39.95.

1990 World Cycling Championships: The Complete Story!

Previously unseen highlights from this remarkable two week event consists of road races, time trials, and velodrome action. Includes moments of glory for Connie Young and Michael Hubner, and an interview with World Champion Rudy Dhaenens. With commentary by Paul Liggett. 60 mins.
VHS: S16220. $29.95.

1991 Liege-Bastogne-Liege: Cycling's Oldest Classic

The oldest bike race is fought in the Belgian Ardennes among the world's top riders. This account of the 1991 Liege-Bastogne-Liege captures Moreno Argentin's fourth win at this famous classic. Written by commentator Phil Liggett. 90 mins.
VHS: S16218. $39.95.

1991 Paris-Roubaix: A Fight to the Finish!

After losing the toughest classic race of all by a millimeter the previous year, Canadian Steve Bauer returns to the Hell of Northern France to try again for victory. This grueling course follows over 267 kilometers, including 22 sections on ancient cobblestones. Introduced and narrated by Phil Liggett. 90 mins.
VHS: S16216. $39.95.

1991 Tour de France: Miguel Indurian—The New Tour Champion!

The 1991 Tour introduced Spaniard Miguel Indurian as the newest, and most surprising, winner since Laurent Fignon in 1983. Witness the agony of Greg LaMond as he battles against illness and exhaustion in his attempt to defend his crown. See all the decisive moves made in the Pyrenees as three men-Indurian, Chiapucci and Bugno—set the Tour afire with their strength and determination. Commentary by Paul Liggett. 90 mins.
VHS: S16212. $39.95.

1991 World Cycling Championships: One of Cycling's Greatest Prizes

See Italian Gianni Bugno win an exciting sprint finish to capture the men's professional road race at the World Cycling Championships in Stuttgart, Germany. Commentary by Phil Liggett. 60 mins.
VHS: S16219. $29.95.

1992 Paris-Roubaix

Cyclists Kelly, Van Hooydonck, LeMond, Argentin, Sorensen, Bugno and others compete on a trail that stretches more than 250 km over ancient cobblestone. 90 mins.
VHS: S16558. $39.95.

1992 Tour of Flanders

One of the greatest single-day cycling races covers 272 km over bone-crushing cobblestones though the winding hills of Belgium. Legendary star Sean Kelly battles Van Hooydonck, LeMond, Argentin, Sorensen, Bugno and other greats. 90 mins.
VHS: S16557. $39.95.

1994 Winter Olympic Highlights

The very best of winter sports will be available on this collection of highlights from the 1994 Olympic Games set in Lillehammer, Norway. Everything from the opening and closing ceremonies to all the most-watched competitions in skating, skiing, hockey, and more will be included in this timely video. 60 mins.
VHS: S20669. $19.98.

1994 Winter Olympics Figure Skating Competition and Figure Skating Exhibition Gift Set

Figure skating fans will be engrossed by this two-tape collection containing the gold medal-winning performances of all the Olympic Champions. America's greatest hopefuls, like 1988 gold medalist Brian Boitano, are sure to inspire with their unmatched talents.
VHS: S20670. $39.98.

23 Days in July: Tour de France

The film follows Australian star Phil Anderson in his attempt to win the 1983 Tour de France. Anderson, riding for the Peugeot Team, discusses his training and strategy for winning cycling's most famous race. Cycling journalist John Wilcokson provides analysis, day-to-day coverage of the race and its leading riders.
VHS: S04467. $34.95.
Tim Sullivan, Great Britain, 50 mins.

America Screams

Vincent Price has found a new way to make people scream: roller coasters. Hold on for plenty of laughs, chills and thrills as the master of horror presents the ultimate scream machines: the 13-story Loch Ness Monster, upside-down backwards King Kobra, double-track Rebel Yell and triple-loop Mindbender. Plus the highest, longest and fastest coaster in the world, Colossus. From Coney Island to Disneyland, the bone-rattling best in amusement parks. 30 mins.
VHS: S12382. $14.95.

America's Greatest Olympians

Edwin Moses, Jackie Joyner-Kersee, Jesse Owens, Mark Spitz, Greg Louganis, Bruce Jenner and Muhammad Ali are just some of the athletic superstars who have made the United States a super-competitor at all Olympic competitions. The history of the games is inextricably entwined with the success of these Americans. That history is recreated on this video. 120 mins.
VHS: S27506. $19.98.

American Challenge: In the Observer Singlehanded TransAtlantic Race

The intimate on-board story of seven solo sailors facing an ultimate challenge: The Observer Singlehanded TransAtlantic Race. Automatic cameras installed on their boats recorded unique close-up views of men and women facing constant danger. 3,000 miles of pounding to windward strips away the veneer to reveal the human spirit alone against the inexorable power of the sea. "The most exciting sea documentary I have ever seen" (William F. Buckley Jr.). 57 mins.
VHS: S06345. $49.95.

Arc Across the Atlantic

An international view of sailing; 204 boats converge in Las Palmas to start the first Atlantic Rally for Cruisers. 3700 miles later, the boats finish in Barbados. This is the spirited tape of the sailors, families, and amateur crews in the tense race. 52 mins.
VHS: S05946. $29.95.

Around Alone

53-year old businessman Dodge Morgan decides to sail around the world without stopping, alone. This inspiring adventure story shows how he realized that dream aboard the *American Promise*. Morgan confronts his fears, copes with loneliness and gear problems, fierce gales and mountainous seas of the southern Ocean, and finally comes home after 150 days at sea, having shattered the old record and becoming the first American to sail around the world solo. 58 mins.,
VHS: S06344. $59.95.

Around Cape Horn

In 1929, the last great days of commercial sail were passing. During that year, Captain Irving Johnson sailed aboard the massive bark *Peking*. He narrates this program filming the crew's daily activities, as well as spectacular scenes during a wild storm as the ship rounded the feared Cape Horn. 37 mins.
VHS: S05942. $29.95.

Artistry on Ice

American Olympic silver medalist Nancy Kerrigan and Olympic gold medalist Brian Boitano are just two of the international figure skating stars featured in this collection of beautiful performances. This video offers a unique opportunity to see the world's greatest skaters doing routines never seen on TV.
VHS: S24818. $19.98.

Babe Ruth

Perhaps the greatest sports hero in American history, Babe Ruth possessed a combination of power and charisma that made him unique. An *A & E Biography*.
VHS: S30115. $19.95.

Baseball

Ken Burns *(Civil War)* turns his attention to the American national pastime in this 18-hour epic which spans 150 years of the game that is America. Released on nine tapes in a collector's boxed set.
VHS: S21896. $149.98.
Laser: LD74841. $299.99.
Ken Burns, USA, 1994, 1080 mins.

Baseball Card Collector
Millions of baseball card hobbyists will love this program narrated by Mel Allen, the voice of the New York Yankees, with much information on new and classic cards, including buying, trading, rating and collecting. 40 mins.
VHS: S09101. $19.99.

Baseball in the News
Newsreels from 1951 to 1967 are the source for this nostalgic look at baseball. America's favorite pastime remains the stuff of lore. Now some of the most talked about sporting incidents from the past are available for viewing once again, in this boxed set.
VHS: S21683. $44.95.

Baseball in the News Series
Some of baseball's greatest moments in the World Series, All Star games, spring training and off-diamond highlights in three volumes tracing the recent history of baseball. Each program is approx. 60 mins.
Baseball in the News Volume 1: 1951-1955. Giants' Thomson fires the shot heard round the world; Joltin' Joe Di Maggio strokes the last home run; Bye Bye Beantown: Braves move to Milwaukee; and the Dodgers take the series from the Yankees.
VHS: S11119. $29.95.
Baseball in the News Volume 2: 1956-1960. Don Larsen hurls the perfect game in title contest; Dodgers play the last game at Brooklyn's Ebbetts Field; White Sox win the first pennant in 40 years; Bobby Richardson smashes series slam for Yankees; and Mazeroski's blast brings Pirates world championship.
VHS: S11120. $29.95.
Baseball in the News Volume 3: 1961-1967. Willie Mays blasts four homers in a single game; Casey Stengel takes Mets to the first spring training; Cards trump Yanks in Series; Orioles sweet Dodgers for World Championship.
VHS: S11121. $29.95.

Baseball's Greatest Hits
An all-star collection of music videos celebrating America's great national pastime, with the all-star lineup featuring *I Love Mickey* with Mickey Mantle and Teresa Brewer; Dave Frishberg's *Van Lingle Mungo*; Terry Cashman's *Willie, Mickey and the Duke*; Bruce Springstone's *Take Me Out to the Ball Game*; rare, vintage TV commercials featuring baseball's greatest stars and footage from the vaults of major baseball. 30 mins.
VHS: S12184. $14.95.

Born to Run
The story of Sebastian Coe, his training program, racing strategy and motivation, the isolation and constant pain that are an intrinsic part of his mental and physical preparation for every race.
VHS: S05545. $39.95.

The Boys of Summer
An affectionate and informative documentary on the Brooklyn Dodgers. Recall the memories made in Ebbetts Field. See once again the exploits of Duke Snider, Roy Campanella, Carl Erskine and Preacher Roe. Flatbush was never the same after they let the Bums leave; now the good old days are available on tape. 1983, 90 mins.
VHS: S02619. $19.98.

Budo Sai: The Spirit of the Samurai
A program about various martial arts styles and techniques that have emerged in the 20th century. Shot at the Budo Sai Festival, the program features 12 masters demonstrating Kendo, Karate, Aikido and Capoeira, a form of Brazilian street fighting. 70 mins.
VHS: S19733. $29.95.

Champion Acrobats of China
Performances by the women acrobats of China, who have dedicated years to mastering the most dangerous routines.
Champion Acrobats of China: Flying Lotus.
VHS: S16729. $19.98.
Champion Acrobats of China: Steel Silk.
VHS: S16730. $19.98.

Comeback
A documentary on the life of German boxer Max Schmeling, following his career from the early years of boxing to his later match for the World Championship against America's Joe Louis. German silent and sound.
VHS: S07502. $29.95.

The Cycling Experience
A documentary of spectacular California location photography and New Age music that takes the form of a travelogue, told from the cyclists' perspective. 52 mins.
Laser: LD70255. $29.95.

Daredevils: All Time Great Death-Defying Acts
From Carl Wallenda to Evel Knievel, the famed daredevils of the 20th century have turned danger into an American art form. Motorcycle jumper Robbie Knievel (Evel's son), tightrope artist Enrico Wallenda (Carl's son), Niagara Falls jumper Steve Trotter and wing-walker Lee Oman perform amazing record-setting stunts staged just for this production. Special "lipstick cameras" capture the action as the stuntmen see it. Also features rare footage of stunts from the past, including some of the most incredible successes and spectacular disasters ever seen. Hosted by Regis Philbin.
VHS: S30594. $19.95.
1996, 100 mins.

David Carradine's Kung Fu and Tai Chi Workouts
This class for beginners uses the principles of Kung Fu and Tai Chi workouts to strengthen the connection between mental and body awareness. 116 mins.
Laser: LD71950. $39.95.

Discovery Sport
Strange and unique sports from around the world are featured in this video. From the World Tug of War at the Irish Hurling Finals to Finland's fast version of baseball, this tape displays endurance and ability unimagined by the average sports viewer. This is one place to find both Sumo wrestlers and the Eskimo Olympics. From the Discovery Channel. 60 mins.
VHS: S29900. $19.95.

Double Exposure
John and Dan Egan join Rob and Eric DesLauriers for this ski extravaganza. Together they outrun avalanches in Wyoming, tackle 14,000' peaks in Russia and explore the most difficult terrain in Romania, Turkey, Yugoslavia and North America.
VHS: S22052. $19.95.

The Dream Team
This documentary chronicles the story of the greatest basketball team in Olympic history. Twelve of the game's most gifted players, including Michael Jordan, Larry Bird and Magic Johnson, put aside personal agendas and monetary rewards to capture the greatest single reward in sports. 73 mins.
VHS: S33253. $19.95.

Endless Summer
Join Robert August and Mike Hynson as they follow the summer season to Senegal, Ghana, Nigeria, South Africa, Australia, New Zealand, Tahiti, Hawaii and California in search of the perfect wave. Still the ultimate surf film!
VHS: S14250. $19.96.
Bruce Brown, USA, 1964, 90 mins.

Eurocycling—Motorola Team
For two weeks, Paul Liggett went behind the usually closed doors of one of the world's top teams to see how they prepare for the season's two most important classics: Paris-Roubaix and Liege-Bastogne-Liege. "Packed with spontaneous comments and full of information on tactics and training, this is a must for every cycling fan" *(Velo News)*. 90 mins.
VHS: S16222. $34.95.

The Falcon Gentle
A video survey of the history and practice of falconry. The training of the Peregrine falcon, using dogs and falcons for hunting grouse, the relationship between falcon and falconer, etc. 33 mins.
VHS: S15538. $35.00.

Fast Cars
The exhilaration of speed meets the challenges of aerodynamic design as champion driver Bobby Rahal and a team of experts race to ready his custom car for the Indianapolis 500. From NOVA. 60 mins.
VHS: S31427. $19.95.

Fire on the Track: The Steve Prefontaine Story
The story of champion distance runner Steve Prefontaine's life, which embodied the spirit of athletic excellence. Meet the man hailed by *Sports Illustrated* as America's Distance Prodigy, through rare footage and the memories of those who knew him best—his teammates, coaches, family and friends.
VHS: S32401. $19.95.

Fitness Fables: #1
The Cat Who Had to Be Best. Narrated by Tony Randall, these fables include simple exercises designed by the Directors of Conditioning, U.S. Olympic Ski Team. Music by Phil Baron. For ages 3-8. USA.
VHS: S14953. $19.95.

Fitness Fables: #2
Detective Squirrel/Missing Tree. Narrated by Tony Randall, these fables include simple exercises designed by the Directors of Conditioning, U.S. Olympic Ski Team. Music by Phil Baron. For ages 3-8. USA.
VHS: S14954. $19.95.

Fitness Fables: #3
Monkey Who Only Watched T.V. Narrated by Tony Randall, these fables include simple exercises designed by the Directors of Conditioning, U.S. Olympic Ski Team. Music by Phil Baron. For ages 3-8. USA.
VHS: S14955. $19.95.

Friendship Sloop: A Heritage Retained
Two Maine boat builders are dedicated to preserving the Friendship sloop—a graceful, classic, able and rugged boat first built in the 1800's as a sturdy fishing vessel. One builder uses the old craft of shaping wood by hand, the other uses modern materials of fiberglass and epoxy. The annual homecoming of sloop owners is a slice of Americana in their bonding of love for the Friendship sloop and keeping alive the heritage. Winner of many awards. 28 mins.
VHS: S06348. $39.95.

Full Cycle: A World Odyssey
Cyclists travel nine countries in this mammoth trek with an environmental twist. Mark Schulze and Patty Mooney lead the tour through the U.S.A., Canada, Costa Rica, Greece, Switzerland, Great Britain, Tahiti, Australia and India. Along the way cultural, historical and geographical information is revealed, along with glimpses of natural scenery. 108 mins.
VHS: S25624. $39.95.

Gay Games II: Highlights
This program features outstanding scenes from this nine-day event. Includes the parade of 3500 athletes, the inspirational keynote address by the late Dr. Tom Waddell and San Francisco Mayor Diane Feinstein. There are highlights of all 18 sports events with interviews of both men and women athletes. 60 mins.
VHS: S16841. $39.95.

Gay Games IV from A to Q
Highlights include *In the Life* coverage from the Opening Ceremonies as well as *Dyke TV & Network Q* footage showing hunks competing for gold. *Gay Entertainment Television* provides a view of the history and the organization behind the games while *Gay Cable Network* shows the closing ceremonies of this historic event. 60 mins.
VHS: S21702. $24.95.

Golden Decade of Baseball 1947-1957
Brent Mussberger narrates two programs covering the unforgettable era of baseball.
Golden Decade of Baseball Part 1. Covers Jackie Robinson's arrival, Di Maggio's comeback, the shot heard round the world, and Bill Bevan's no hitter. 30 mins.
VHS: S12159. $14.95.
Golden Decade of Baseball Part 2. Covers Willie Mays, Mickey Mantle's greatest catch ever made, and the Dodgers and Giants leaving New York. 30 mins.
VHS: S12160. $14.95.

Great Moments at the Winter Games
An overview of the most outstanding performances at the Winter Olympics, featuring such great athletes as Sonja Henie, Jean-Claude Killy and Dorothy Hammill. 47 mins.
VHS: S05889. $14.95.

Greatest Goals World Cup USA '94
This video features a stunning 56 goals from the World Cup matches in the U.S. Team members from many countries are seen at their best, including Houghton (Ireland), Dahlin (Sweden), Romario (Brazil), Salenko (Russia), Wynalda (U.S.A.), Batistuta (Argentina) and many more. 45 mins.
VHS: S23434. $14.95.

Greatest Sports Follies
Crammed full of accidents and mistakes just waiting to happen in football, basketball, baseball, tennis and ice-skating with Football's Hall-of-Fame Fumbles, College Basketball's Outrageous Coaches, Bloopers on Ice, Tennis in Turmoil and Baseball Gone Bats. 45 mins.
VHS: S12350. $14.98.

Hank Aaron: Chasing the Dream
Hanks Aaron's stats make this one of the greatest players of all time. He battled racism and hatred but still managed to overtake Babe Ruth's homerun record. Now his amazing story is available on video. 95 mins.
VHS: S25039. $14.98.

The History of Baseball Card Collecting

Beginning as well as established baseball card enthusiasts will enjoy this entertaining and informative program loaded with fun facts, amazing stories and inside secrets about America's favorite hobby. Teaches how and what to collect for optimizing the value of a collection. Features many rare baseball cards as well as a video tour of the Baseball Hall of Fame in Cooperstown, NY. Also includes a pack of 15 genuine, collectable baseball cards.
VHS: S31154. $19.95.

Holst: The Planets, Featuring the Duchesnays

Olympic sensations Paul and Isabelle Duchesnays perform their figure skating artistry to the symphonic music of Gustav Holst, as choreographed by Lar Lubovitch. Solo, ensemble ice dance and precision group skating are all incorporated in this video. Also features figure-skating champion Brian Orser. 55 mins.
VHS: S23867. $19.95.

Idols of the Game

Three videos track the evolution and contributions of key American sports heroes. Through their stories across a range of different sports, the fascinating development of the modern super athlete comes into view. Each video is 95 mins.
Babes in Boyland. Women have slowly won respect in the male-dominated world of American sports. The unlevel playing fields and the obstacles faced by pivotal female sports superstars are recounted in this video.
VHS: S27765. $19.98.
Inventing the All-American. Formerly amateurs who rose on skill and luck alone dominated American sports. The current American athlete, however, relies on a level of professionalism once unimagined. This transformation is outlined in the first video of the series.
VHS: S27764. $19.98.
Love and Money. Big business and the promise of big money have captured the soul of sports. Once players were loyal to fans and their hometown; now marketing is a vital indicator of how careers and teams will develop.
VHS: S27766. $19.98.
Idols of the Game: Three-Pack.
VHS: S27767. $39.98.

The Immortals

The performances of Sonja Henie of Norway, Uhlrich Wehling of East Germany, Burger Ruud of Norway, Toni Sailer of Austria and Billy Fiske of the U.S. have assured them sports immortality. This is the story of these great athletes. 47 mins.
VHS: S05890. $14.95.

The Impossible Hour: Ole Ritter & Eddie Merckx

The Impossible Hour follows Danish racing star Ole Ritter as he tries to regain his record for the hour ride. He had set the record in 1968, only to have it shattered by Eddie Merckx in 1972. A film about human limits and the quest for the heroic.
VHS: S04468. $29.95.
Jorgen Leth, Denmark, 48 mins.

Joe Louis

A challenging glimpse of the "Brown Bomber" who became the youngest heavyweight champ at the age of 23, including Louis' KO of Max Schmeling. 24 mins.
VHS: S06422. $14.98.

Joe Louis—For All Time

A documentary with plenty of punch that doesn't duck and weave when it comes to the less attractive parts of the life of The Brown Bomber. The legendary heavyweight boxing champ, who was born Joseph Louis Barrow, successfully defended his title 25 times. He was also the victim of cocaine, racism and the I.R.S. Color and B&W.
VHS: S08118. $29.95.
Peter Tatum, USA, 1985, 89 mins.

The Journey of the African-American Athlete

Recounts the history of the African-American athletes who took on the struggle to meet their fellow competitors on a level playing field. Witness some of the world's greatest athletes as they make sports history: boxing's Jack Johnson, Joe Louis and Muhammad Ali; basketball's Dr. J and Michael Jordan; tennis stars Althea Gibson and Arthur Ashe; baseball's Negro Leagues and the breakthrough of Jackie Robinson; and more. Narrated by Samuel L. Jackson. 119 mins.
VHS: S33144. $19.98.
Laser: LD76441. $34.98.

King of the Hill

A look at big league baseball from the inside, from the experience of Ferguson Jenkins, one of the few Canadian-born players to make the major leagues. Filmed over the last two years Fergie played for the Chicago Cubs before being traded to the Texas Rangers, this story captures the frustrations, the satisfaction and much of the humorous side of baseball. Produced by the National Film Board of Canada.
VHS: S04365. $29.95.
W. Canning/Donald Brittain, Canada, 57 mins.

L.L. Bean Guides

Several excellent guides to activities in the outdoors, produced by the famous house of L.L. Bean.
L.L. Bean Guide to Fly Fishing.
VHS: S05302. $29.95.
L.L. Bean Guide to Outdoor Photography.
VHS: S05303. $29.95.

La Course en Tete: The Eddie Merckx Story

This outstanding film follows star Eddie Merckx at the peak of his career through the challenge of Europe's best races from the World Championships to the Tour de France. A rare portrait of "The Babe Ruth of Cycling," and an extraordinary document of human endurance and courage.
VHS: S04466. $59.95.
Joel Santoni, France/Denmark, 110 mins.

The Last Hurrah

Only 10 months after his 11-round defeat to Larry Holmes, Muhammed Ali stepped into the ring against Jamaican-born Trevor Berbick for what would be his last bout. Billed as "the Drama in Bahama," this 10-round brawl fought December 11, 1981, was Ali's fifth loss in a 21-year career. Two-tape set covers the Ali-Berbick match and features a rare pre-fight press conference and interview footage. 127 mins.
VHS: S34359. $19.95.

Legends of the Ring

Muhammad Ali, Jack Johnson and Sugar Ray Robinson are all captured on video in this three-part series. These biographies use abundant footage of fights and interviews to catalogue the careers of the greatest boxing champions. 215 mins.
VHS: S29545. $79.98.

Little League's Official How-to-Play-Baseball Video

The definitive video look at baseball— "a four-bagger!" 70 mins.
VHS: S12161. $19.95.

A Man Named Lombardi

Vince Lombardi gave to the game of football and to the men he led a philosophy of life that became a legend. Filled with interview, this tape is narrated by George C. Scott. 55 mins.
VHS: S13072. $29.98.

Marathon: A History of the Great Race

It all began with a legendary messenger who ran to the Greek city of Marathon. His legend inspired the reintroduction of this event to the modern world in the 1896 Olympics. Since then the marathon has become popular the world over. This documentary shows the winning runners and the glamorous events that exemplify this grueling test of endurance. 52 mins.
VHS: S28064. $19.95.

Mike Tyson: The Inside Story

Forty-one wins, one loss and thirty-five knockouts are the facts behind this star boxer's rise to fame. Before his troubled relationship with Robin Givens took him out of the ring, his promoter, Don King, had managed to place Tyson firmly in the spotlight. This is his story.
VHS: S25629. $19.98.

Muhammad Ali vs. Zora Folley

From Madison Square Garden, a World Heavyweight Bout fought on March 22, 1967. Don Duphy reports the blow-by-blow. Win Elliot supplies the color commentary. Pre-fight training films and interviews are shown, as is a post-fight interview with Ali and his father. USA, 1967, 68 mins.
VHS: S05455. $29.95.

Muhammad Ali: The Whole Story

This six-volume set follows the great heavyweight champion from the 1960 Olympics as 18-year-old gold-medalist Cassius Clay to his exile as a conscientious objector during the Vietnam War. With three hours of highlights from Ali's most important fights, including bouts with Ken Norton and George Foreman, and his two historic confrontations with "Smokin' Joe Frazier." Tapes include *The Beginning: Olympic Gold, The Youngest Heavyweight Champion, Exile, The Road Back, The Rumble in the Jungle* and *The Thrilla in Manilla*. 348 mins.
VHS: S31278. $109.98.

Mystic Origins of the Martial Arts

The world's most accomplished practioners of these ancient arts demonstrate their stunning skills in this action-packed program that crosses the Orient to uncover the *Mystic Origins of the Martial Arts*. 100 mins.
VHS: S34899. $19.95.

National Geographic Video: Return to Everest

In May, 1953, Sir Edmund Hillary and Tenzing Norgay became the first men to conquer the world's highest peak. Now, more than 30 years later, they return to Mount Everest to celebrate their historic ascent. 60 mins.
VHS: S10244. $19.95.

National Pastime: A History of Major League Baseball

A five-video set celebrates baseball from its beginnings to the present, showcasing the greatest players, moments and records. 345-minute boxed set.
VHS: S21971. $69.98.

Not So Great Moments in Sports, Take Three

More of the most memorable mishaps, madness and mayhem sports has ever seen. Host: Tim McCarver. 45 mins.
VHS: S12560. $14.99.

Official History of Baseball

This two-tape set is a comprehensive review of baseball's history, with rare footage, new and exclusive interviews, tracing baseball from 1869 to the present. 155 mins.
VHS: S21970. $24.98.

Olympiad Series

Jesse Owens Returns to Berlin. Using actual film highlights of the fateful 1936 Olympics and Owens' personal, on-camera recollections, Bud Greenspan, the host, retells the story of one of sports' greatest triumphs—in which the 22-year old Owens defeated Hitler's showcase for the "master race." Emmy Awards. USA, 1964, 46 mins.
VHS: S06635. $14.95.
The Marathon. The thrilling history of Olympics' most grueling competition. Highlights include the event's ancient origins, Abebe Bikila striding barefoot to victory in Rome, and Joan Benoit's historic win in the first-ever Women's Olympic marathon. USA, 1974, 46 mins.
VHS: S06636. $14.95.
They Didn't Have a Chance. Inspiring stories including the survivor of a near-fatal plane crash who returned to Olympic greatness…the marathon champion who ran for Japan but claimed history for his occupied Korean homeland…the gold-medal comeback of the sprinter labeled "an old man." USA, 1979, 46 mins.
VHS: S06637. $14.95.

On Any Sunday

The quintessential Academy Award-winning motorcycle film by Bruce Brown. A dizzying and intoxicating experience that puts you in the driver's seat with rugged road riders. Remastered director's edition featuring a special tribute to Steve McQueen.
VHS: S31549. $19.95.
Bruce Brown, USA, 1972, 96 mins.

Once There Was a Ballpark

Martin Sheen hosts this informative and entertaining look at the history of baseball stadiums. From the humble beginnings in the streets through the original wooden bleachers, and on to more modern concrete structures, it's all here, including a look at some of the most beloved structures still standing, like Wrigley Field. 108 mins.
VHS: S21707. $19.98.

Only the Ball Was White

A superior television documentary on the formation and rise of the baseball Negro Leagues and the great ballplayers who were denied a chance to play in the racially segregated Major Leagues. The program features interviews with Satchel Paige, Roy Campanella, Buck Leonard, Jimmy Crutchfield, David Malarcher, Effa Manley and Quincy Troupe. Narrated by Paul Winfield. 30 mins.
VHS: S20421. $19.98.

The Other Side of the Mountain

Jill Kinmont was an Olympic hopeful until she suffered a skiing accident that left her paralyzed. Marilyn Hassett stars in this true life story of courage and recovery. With Beau Bridges, Dabney Coleman and Belinda J. Montgomery.
VHS: S07806. $59.95.
Larry Peerce, USA, 1975, 101 mins.

The Other Side of the Mountain, Part 2

Jill Kinmont was a shoo-in for the Olympics in downhill skiing until a sporting accident occurred. In Part 2 of her true-life story, she must overcome depression and the death of the man who helped her recover. Features Marilyn Hasset and Timothy Bottoms.
VHS: S21766. $19.98.
Larry Peerce, USA, 1978, 99 mins.

Play Chess! The United States Chess Federation Guide

Learn how to play and how to improve your game plan with expert tips and tricks from the U.S. Chess Federation. 60 mins.
VHS: S07424. $19.99.

Play Soccer, Jack Charlton's Way: The Collection Set

All three volumes feature instruction by the famed English soccer star, Jack Charlton. He played for the winning English team at the World Cup event in 1966 and coached the Irish team in 1994. Now his expertise is available for everyone. 170 mins.
VHS: S24783. $59.98.

Power Moves
Emmy Award-winning director Jan C. Nickman explores the human form and its spectacular achievements in the world of sports. Greg Louganis is just one of the athletes whose movements yield their intricate beauty to this powerful cinematographic work. A rock climber, a skier and a snow-boarder are also featured. 40 mins.
VHS: S24131. $19.98.
Laser: LD75420. $29.99.

Return to the Snow Zone
The new James Angrove/Jon Long ski film takes the viewer to the edge of his/her seat and back again. From the high alpine reaches of Kashmir, India, to the menacing north wall of Mount Currie in the Coastal Range of British Columbia, Canada, their new action-packed documentary covers three continents. Soundtrack includes music by Yello and Midnight Oil.
VHS: S15327. $39.95.
Angrove/Long, Canada, 1990, 65 mins.

River of the Red Ape
This classic whitewater river journey took place in Sumatra, as a crack team of wilderness explorers from Sobek made the first attempt to navigate the wild Alas River. William Devane narrates this exciting trip into the world's largest orangutan rain forest wilderness. 57 minutes.
VHS: S03531. $39.95.

Sails and Sailors: J Boats '37
Three short films: in *Sails and Sailors*, a period newsreel film in color has been preserved and improved to show a glimpse of the famous race of 1937; in *Weetamoe*, a fantastic sail aboard the Clinton Crane designed *Weetamoe*, and *Yachting in the Thirties* shows famous boats and races of the 30's. 46 mins.
VHS: S05941. $24.95.

Seaflight/Windflight
Champion surfers from Hawaii and Southern California challenge Waimea Bay's 20' waves, shoot the Banzai Pipeline and perform 360° flips on their sailboards in two spectacular films on the sports of surfing and windsurfing. 1985, 26 mins.
VHS: S14450. $19.95.

The Secrets of the Warrior's Power
The ancient teachings, practices and rituals surrounding the world's most awesome martial arts are revealed by Grandmaster Chan Pui, Master Dennis Brown, Master Pan Quing Fu, Shaolin Monk Shi Yan Ming and the legendary Bruce Lee. 50 mins.
VHS: S31634. $19.98.

Soviet Athletes—Summer Sports
The United States boycotted the Summer Olympics of 1980, but the games went on nonetheless. These are Soviet films about the famous games. 70 mins.
VHS: S12721. $19.95.

Soviet Athletes—The Gymnasts
The extraordinary performances of many Soviet super-gymnasts at Olympic competitions have inspired international youth to adopt an unhindered devotion to training and competition. 65 mins.
VHS: S12720. $19.98.

Soviet Athletes—Winter Sports
The rigid, vigorous coaching techniques that make Soviet athletes champions are documented thoroughly. This tape also introduces strange regional games, including a polo-like game where teams fight over a dead goat. 60 mins.
VHS: S12722. $19.95.

Sports Illustrated 25th Anniversary Swimsuit Video
A winner all the way, a behind-the-scenes look at the making of the 25th anniversary swimsuit issue.
VHS: S09307. $19.99.

Stars and Water Carriers
A concise, colorful chronicle of the Giro d'Italia. This extraordinary film by the world's foremost bicycle-race filmmaker recreates the magic of the moment, and brings the Giro's thrills and disappointments home to every viewer.
VHS: S04465. $49.95.
Jorgen Leth, Denmark, 90 mins.

Steeper and Deeper
More than beautiful scenery and great skiers, this film follows men on downhill trajectories that take your breath away. It truly captures stunts that are steeper and deeper than anything ever done before.
VHS: S22051. $19.95.

Stride to Glory
This documentary chronicles the Olympic performances of a vast array of exceptional black athletes since the beginning of the century, from household names like Jesse Owens and Jackie Joyner-Kersee to unsung heroes such as John Baxter Taylor and DeHart Hubbard. 73 mins.
VHS: S33252. $19.95.

A Sunday in Hell
Probably the finest cycling film ever made, *A Sunday in Hell* follows the Paris-Roubaix road race, an event which taxes the energies of Europe's finest riders.
VHS: S02009. $59.95.
Jorgen Leth, France, 110 mins.

Super Duper Baseball Bloopers 2
A two-tape set that includes on-the-field antics, off-the-wall wackiness and baseball's clubhouse clowns. Each video is 40 minutes and includes such moments as Comedian Bill Murray explaining baseball to a foreigner.
VHS: S21972. $14.95.

Thorpe's Gold
In 1912, Jim Thorpe won both the Decathlon and Pentathlon in Sweden. Six months later, it was discovered he had played minor league baseball for $2.00 a game. His name was removed from the Olympic record book but his heroic legacy lives on. 75 mins.
VHS: S34196. $19.95.

Those Who Endured
About a rare group of Winter Games athletes who, unable to accept defeat, persisted in competing at the Olympics until the elusive gold medal was won. Among the athletes in this program are Eugenio Monti of Italy, the bobsledder who won two gold medals in 1968, skiers Andrea Mead Lawrence of the United States and Rosi Mittermaier of West Germany. 47 mins.
VHS: S05891. $14.95.

To Win at All Costs: The Story of the America's Cup
A lively, informative, and often amusing look at the yacht race which has found clubs, men, and countries challenging for the most prestigious trophy in yachting. Beginning with the re-enactment of the first race in 1851, it follows through the lifting of the Cup from American grasp in 1983; with much archival footage. 56 mins.
VHS: S05934. $29.95.

Torvill & Dean with the Russian All-Stars
Jayne Torvill and Christopher Dean have thrilled audiences world-wide since their unparalleled triumphs in the Olympic ice-skating championships. In this breathtaking extravaganza from the tour that broke box office records, Torvill and Dean join forces with Russia's top professional skaters. 78 mins.
VHS: S16136. $24.98.

The Tour du Pont: Hammer and Hell
Highlights from America's premiere competition pits Americans against top Europeans on familiar ground, providing high-powered action and drama over the course of this eleven day stage race. 90 mins.
VHS: S16223. $29.95.

The Trial of Red Riding Hood: A Fantasy on Ice
A charming musical fairy tale on ice, this video blends the skating artistry of Canadian Olympic Silver Medalist Elizabeth Manley, as Red Riding Hood, and the comic talents of Alan Thicke, as Phineas T. Wolf. 50 mins.
VHS: S23140. $19.95.

TVTV Goes to the Super Bowl
Bill Murray and Christopher Guest are the irreverent hosts of this hilarious program that deconstructs the hypocrisy and greed of sport's most famous game, centered around the 1976 game between the Dallas Cowboys and Pittsburgh Steelers, focusing on the players, their wives, coaches, owners and the media. 60 mins.
VHS: S15194. $24.95.

Ultimate Athlete: Pushing the Limits
The Discovery Channel produced this video, which uncovers the will to succeed that is part of every great athlete's makeup. This is essential, given that today's competition is faster, stronger and bigger than ever before. Track and field, cycling, tennis and gymnastics are examined. 100 mins.
VHS: S29899. $19.95.

Ultimate Challenge: Around the World Alone
Seventeen sailors set out from Newport at the start of the First solo race around the world that would take eight months to complete. Each man must look within himself to find the will and the courage to continue. Ten of the 17 starters cross the finish line—for each it is a victory. 58 mins.
VHS: S06346. $59.95.

Ways at Wallace and Sons and The Bank Dory
The ill-fated coasting schooner *John F. Levitt* went down on her maiden voyage; the story here is of the New England shipbuilders taking us from the laying of the keel through the launching; *The Bank Dory* documents the building of one of the famous Bank dories. 58 mins.
VHS: S05943. $39.95.

Where Have You Gone Joe DiMaggio?
An entertaining documentary on the life and times of baseball hero Joe DiMaggio, featuring never-before-seen film footage and rare archival photos and interviews with baseball greats Bob Feller, Reggie Jackson and Pete Rose; DiMaggio teammates Jerry Coleman, Phil Rizzuto, and Tommy Henrich; and high-profile fans George Bush and Mario Cuomo. 63 mins.
VHS: S33131. $14.95.

Yachting in the Thirties
Four programs using rare archival footage to detail the adventure, spirit and energy of this peculiar sport, including pieces on racing strategy and the various transatlantic courses, boats and personalities that define the sport's allure and prestige. 45 mins.
VHS: S05945. $24.95.

TRAVEL

Acadia National Park & Cape Cod National Seashore
Explore glacier carved Acadia, where forest-draped mountains descend to the sea. Travel to charming Cape Cod, a special blend of natural and historical heritage. 30 mins.
VHS: S06667. $29.95.
Laser: LD70251. $29.95.

Alaska Stories
W.C. Thompson wrote and narrated this fascinating travelogue about his trip to the largest state. There are three stories that offer the perfect excuse to leave the road and explore sights that few tourists ever see, such as glacial calving and sites of the historic Gold Rush. 47 mins.
VHS: S24915. $24.95.

America's Great National Parks
A lavishly produced, three-volume, slipcased set of four videos documenting the great parks in the National Park System: *The Story of Yellowstone, The Story of Yosemite, The Story of Grand Canyon*, and a special *Hidden Treasures of America's National Parks*. 270 minutes total.
VHS: S13347. $89.95.
Laser: LD70236. $59.95.

Audubon Zoo
This walking tour of the New Orleans zoo is great for kids. 30 mins.
VHS: S22401. $35.95.

Barbados, A Culture in Progress
A panoramic and personal view of Barbados, narrated by Claudette Colbert. Ms. Colbert has a home on the island and through her eyes you feel and see the beauty of the island's natural environment, the work of the native artists and relaxed life style of the inhabitants. Directed by Angel Hurtado. Narrated in English. 15 mins.
VHS: S06774. $40.00.

Belgrade Ancient and New
This insightful film reveals the history of this key city, that sits at the confluence of two great rivers. As a result of this fortuitous site, the metropolis is also the place where two great civilizations meet.
VHS: S24594. $19.95.

Bent's Old Fort N.H.S. & Great Sand Dunes National Monument
Bent's Fort, a Castle on the Plain, and the Great Sand Dunes in Colorado—geology in motion. 46 mins.
VHS: S06671. $29.95.

Big Bend National Park, Texas
Discover the tremendous variety of wildlife and plant communities, the park's spectacular hiking trails and its incredible geology. 30 mins.
VHS: S06675. $29.95.

The Big Dig
A comprehensive view of a major public works project is on view in this video. The depression of the central artery and the building of the third tunnel under Boston Harbor is a fascinating enterprise.
VHS: S25009. $19.95.

Bourbon Street
This is a fun look at the historic neon strip in New Orleans known as Bourbon Street. Fascinating archival footage reveals the story behind the most famous collection of bars, nightclubs and honkytonks in the nation. 60 mins.
VHS: S22397. $41.95.

Bryce, Zion & Grand Canyon's North Rim
This program lets you visit the most popular features of these three treasured national parks, with the emphasis on Bryce and Zion in Utah. 25 mins.
VHS: S06660. $29.95.

Built on the Rock: The Southern Appalachians
Features over 60 old-time mountain churches in four magnificent seasons in the Blue Ridge and Great Smoky Mountains. Includes Baptist, Methodist, Presbyterian and Episcopalian, all against the scenic background of the Appalachian Mountains. 60 mins.
VHS: S32674. $19.95.

Byzantium: The Lost Empire
This two-tape mini-series from The Discovery Channel investigates the lost culture of the Byzantine Empire, which once spanned Europe and the Middle East. Historian John Romer takes the viewer on journeys through Istanbul, Greece, Italy, Spain, Russia and North Africa, including the Byzantine treasures of St. Mark's Cathedral in Venice and the newly accessible collections of Kiev, Leningrad and Moscow. 100 mins.
VHS: S31945. $29.95.

Canal Street: Great Wide Way
The culture and history of this New Orleans thoroughfare is the subject of this interesting documentary. It's a memorable trip aided by photographs from the past. 30 mins.
VHS: S22399. $41.95.

Canyon de Chelly & Hubell Trading Post
Explore deep red-rock canyons, ancient Anasazi cliff dwellings and age-old Navajo tradition with visits to two national park areas in an exploration of the geology of the canyon, and visits to Antelope House, White House, and Navajo craftsmen at work. 30 mins.
VHS: S10928. $29.95.

Cape Cod: The Sands of Time
Tells about the formation of Cape Cod by ice, wind and waves, accounts for the forces of erosion, and looks at the wooden ships, the men of iron, the story of Henry David Thoreau and his writings of Cape Cod, and a fascinating look at why the Italian inventor Marconi chose Cape Cod to be the site of the first wireless radio station to transmit a message between the U.S. and Europe. 43 mins.
VHS: S10923. $29.95.

Castles of Scotland
This three-volume set tours the spectacular Scottish countryside, visiting many of the nation's most notable landmarks. Features Edinburgh Castle, Stirling Castle, Eileen Donan, Glamis, Fort George, and Kinloch Castle. Each volume is 50 mins.
VHS: S34265. $39.95.

The Chronicle Travel Library
Alaska. This surprising state boasts Grizzly bears, caribous, moose, glaciers, humpback whales, salmon, and trees worth $10,000. Visit Anchorage, Ketchikan, Sitka, Juneau, and Fairbanks; see the Waterfall Resort, a sports fisherman's paradise. It's a state you won't forget. 55 mins.
VHS: S05726. $29.95.
America's Secret Places. Here's a video for you explorers who want to escape civilization, to find your own fairylands and lands of Oz; places where the nearest road is 40 miles away. You'll find your secret refuge in places smooth and rough, dry and wet, high and low, barren and abundant; from Maine to Florida, up through the Heartland to the Northern Coast of California. 54 mins.
VHS: S05719. $29.95.
Australia. The former home of the America's cup, Australia is the oldest, flattest, and driest continent. Yet it boasts more snow than Switzerland. This travel adventure takes you to see the world's supply of opals, to wild camel country, a Koala bear sanctuary and the mystical Olga mountains in an absolute paradise. 60 mins.
VHS: S05713. $29.95.
California's North Coast. This haunting production captures the Gold Coast, visits the Sonoma Valley, Cape Mendocino, and the giant redwoods. 60 mins.
VHS: S05720. $29.95.
Family Outings: Northern California. This video explores the range of places to go and things to do for adventurous families in Northern California's water wonderlands, forest adventures, worlds of natural wonders, airborne thrills, and more. 60 mins.
VHS: S05546. $29.95.
Hong Kong. This crisp, quick-paced video hustles through the heart of the Orient—Hong Kong. See the three principal areas-Hong Kong Island, Kowloon, and the New Territories—that combine the mystique of ancient China, the elegance of Colonial Britain, and the energy of the New World. 48 mins.
VHS: S05718. $29.95.
New Zealand. See placid lakes, Alpine peaks, totem poles, tomatoes that grow on trees, the famous flightless Kiwi bird, and much more. This colorful tape surveys beautiful New Zealand, and does not forget the scenic North and South Islands. 56 mins.
VHS: S05721. $29.95.
Paris and the Seine. Take this elegant and enchanting 500-mile journey down the Seine River from its source near Dijon. The river meanders through some of the most beautiful landscapes of France until it reaches Paris, where you'll see the city's famous sights and go on some off-beat excursions, finally arriving at Le Havre. 58 mins.
VHS: S05722. $29.95.
Rome. Visit famed Roman attractions such as the Colosseum, Trevi Fountain, Piazza Di Spagna, and the Vatican. This video is a virtual catalog of Rome and its people, an excellent preview of what you'll see there—and what you will never forget. 57 mins.
VHS: S05723. $29.95.
Spain. Roman, Islamic, and Arabic influences are apparent in the mixture of Spain's people and its architecture. The land of such legends as Don Juan, Don Quixote, and Carmen is all part of this video filled with enlightening information and entertaining historical facts. 55 mins.
VHS: S05724. $29.95.

Colorado's Narrow Gauge Railroads
On the late 1800s, daring engineers carved railroads through the Rockies to link the mountain boomtowns of Colorado. The colorful past is relived along the four remaining narrow gauge railroads still operating. 55 mins.
VHS: S09943. $29.95.

Complete Yellowstone
This video tour of Yellowstone through all the seasons captures all of the magnificent park's scenic, thermal and wildlife attractions, including spectacular geyser eruptions, bubbling hot pools, roaring rivers and waterfalls. 60 mins.
VHS: S09944. $29.95.

Cruising the Chesapeake Bay and Potomac River
Designed for recreational boaters, a visual introduction to two of the most popular waterways anywhere, with a rich sampling of the best known sights and destinations of these scenic and historic waters. 30 mins.
VHS: S11123. $29.95.

Death Valley
Learn of Death Valley's geological treasures and of man's struggle to survive here. 26 mins.
VHS: S06664. $29.95.

Denali Wilderness, Alaska
Set amidst the pristine wilderness of Denali National Park, this award-winning program lets you join moose, wolves, grizzly bears and caribou in a four-season struggle for survival. 30 mins.
VHS: S06661. $29.95.

Discover California
From the fabulous coastline to the towering Sierra, from the sun-drenched cities and deserts to the inspiring scenery of Yosemite, Sequoia, Kings Canyon and the Redwoods. 60 mins.
VHS: S06692. $29.95.

Discover Portugal!
A comprehensive look at the hustle and bustle of Lisbon, and the violent volcanic landscape of the Azores, in a joyous look at Portugal today. 60 mins.
VHS: S23348. $29.95.

Egyptian Adventures
The mysteries and exotic beauty of Egypt in an exploration of the pyramids of Giza, Cairo, Alexandria, and Esmailia; a visit to the Sinai Peninsula with its vast deserts and beaches; and Mount Sinai, where Moses is said to have received the Ten Commandments. This adventure also includes a river boat down the Nile from Aswan to Luxor and Thebes, as well as a visit to the ancient temples at Abu Simbel, Philae, Luxor and Kamak. 20 mins.
VHS: S05872. $24.95.

European Balloon Adventures
Ten years ago, Buddy Bombard created a new concept in travel: the balloon vacation. These aerial nature walks tour over fortified castles, private chateaux and architectural wonders of medieval villages, often at altitudes that allow the traveler to speak with people on the farms and villages below. Delight in the lolling scenery as pleasure seekers of all ages roam the clouds above and explore the sights below in this enchanting jaunt across Europe.
VHS: S15844. $19.95.

Everglades: Big Cypress, Biscayne, Fort Jefferson
A tour of four national park areas, with a look at the variety of plant and animal life. 56 mins.
VHS: S10920. $29.95.

Explore Colorado
Capture the breath-taking scenery and pioneer spirit of Colorado, including her natural wonders, mining towns, scenic railroads and historic sites. 60 mins.
VHS: S06683. $29.95.

Exploring Antarctica
Now you can visit the frozen continent that holds 90 percent of the world's fresh water without worrying about frostbite or runaway dog teams. Questar Home Video presents a detailed geographic and historical tour of a land mass where the ice can be three miles deep. See killer whales at play and penguins at home, as well as some very unusual marine life. 60 mins.
VHS: S13264. $29.95.

Florida! America's Vacationland
Enjoy Florida's natural splendor, unique wildlife, rich history and many exciting attractions. 60 mins.
VHS: S06685. $29.95.

Fodor's Video Guides
Each of these guides, from the creators of the best-selling travel guides, is 75 minutes.
Fodor's Bangkok.
VHS: S10341. $29.95.
Fodor's Hawaii.
VHS: S10030. $29.95.
Fodor's Hungary.
VHS: S10340. $29.95.
Fodor's London.
VHS: S05018. $29.95.
Fodor's Mexico.
VHS: S04958. $29.95.
Fodor's Singapore.
VHS: S10342. $29.95.

Glacier Bay
Glacier Bay National Park is the site of amazing scenery and abundant wildlife. Towering ice pinnacles and natural ice sculptures lay behind cavorting whales and flying seabirds. 35 mins.
VHS: S24225. $14.95.

Glacier National Park, Montana
This is a land of majestic mountains and deep, blue lakes; a land of sweeping panoramas and glacier-carved valleys. This is where the grizzly bear roams and bald eagles soar. 30 mins.
VHS: S06701. $29.95.

Glimpses of Martinique
Lively, upbeat introduction to the people, culture, and geography of this multicultural Caribbean department of France. Interviews with Martinicans promote cultural awareness. Tapescript of English narration with brief French interviews and lesson plans included. 22 mins.
VHS: S34475. $39.95.

Glimpses of the Indian Ocean—Reunion Island
Warmly engaging interviews with teens introduce the people and geography of this Creole department of France. Cultural diversity and the need for mutual respect and tolerance are highlighted. Includes tapescript of English narration and French interviews, lesson plans for two levels, questions in French and English. English narration. 35 mins.
VHS: S34476. $39.95.

Grand Canyon & Petrified Forest
Capture the Grand Canyon experience. Spectacular vistas, summer thunderstorms, raft and mule expeditions, plus Petrified Forest National Park—Arizona's prehistoric wonder. 45 mins.
VHS: S06663. $29.95.

Grand Canyon National Park
One of Nature's spectacular sights showing the Canyon's South Rim from season to season, at sunrise and sunset, including a helicopter trip to out-of-the-way waterfalls and monuments.
VHS: S06017. $29.95.

The Grand Tour: Legendary Resorts of the World
Relive the golden age of travel and visit some of the most opulent resorts ever built with this exqusite set. It's a privileged glimpse at a life reserved for the chosen few. Set of five videos. 550 mins.
VHS: S34858. $99.99.

The Great Alaska Train Adventure
Originally constructed to haul ore from the gold fields of Fairbanks to the seaport at Anchorage, the Alaska Railroad is now a major tourist attraction. This two-tape set features the world-famous Iditarod Dog Sled Race; Alaska's famous bush pilots; Denali National Park and Preserve; Mt. McKinley, America's most majestic peak; an Alaskan flag train; Fairbanks, Alaska's gold-mining, riverboat capital; and the village of Talkeetna, the town said to be the model for TV's *Northern Exposure*. Each tape is 45 mins.
VHS: S31209. $29.95.

Great Castles of Europe

Return to a time when a man's castle was his home, his livelihood and maybe even his only safe refuge. Some of the structures examined in this fascinating series were built as fortifications, while other were intended as private, sumptuous retreats.
Vol. 1: France and Spain. The castles of Spain date from early medieval times. Some were built to resist the Moors while others were strengthened and beautified by these Islamic invaders. The French castle Chambord, built for a king's brief encounter with a countess, and the fortress at Chenocceau, a massive keep built on a man-made island, are included in this tour. 90 mins.
VHS: S21152. $19.95.
Vol. 2: Germany and Romania. Along the Rhine some of Europe's most spectacular scenery can be found, including a range of castles built on these shores to keep watch over the river. In Bavaria, the late 19th-century fantasy, "mad" King Ludwig's Neuschwanstein, is a fairybook wonder that inspired Walt Disney's magic kingdom. Finally, Brancastle, the home of Dracula, offers an authentic gothic setting filled with evocative shadows. 90 mins.
VHS: S21153. $19.95.
Vol. 3: British Isles. From England's Warwick castle to the Scottish Isle of Skye, and all the way to Ireland's Bunratty castle, this volume shows the famed strongholds of these seafaring Islands where the bloody past is never fully lost as long as these magnificent structures still stand. 90 mins.
VHS: S21154. $19.95.
Three-Volume Deluxe Boxed Set.
VHS: S21155. $54.95.

Great Cities of Europe

This grand tour of Europe's most renowned cities includes glimpses of London, Dublin, Amsterdam, Munich, Vienna, Salzburg, Madrid, Paris, Athens and Rome. Viewers see romantic castles, picturesque canals, lively piazzas, splendid parks. 60 mins.
VHS: S10780. $24.95.

Great Smoky Mountains

Discover the natural wonders and pioneer spirit of three national park areas with this tour of the Great Smokies, The Blue Ridge Parkway, and the mountain beauty of Shenandoah. Includes visits to many historical sites and Appalachian folk centers. 60 mins.
VHS: S10927. $29.95.
Laser: LD70250. $29.95.

Guardians of the Night

A documentary which studies the evolution of the Lighthouse. Shot on location in the United States, France, Britain and Canada, the program laments the replacement of lighthouses with more sophisticated technology. 52 mins.
VHS: S19671. $24.95.

Hawaii: The Pacific Paradise

This two-tape set includes *Hawaii: Paradise Sought* and *Hawaii: Paradise Found*. 1000 years of history and drama make up the traditions of these idyllic islands, from the original Polynesian settlers to today's climate of tourism and travel, based on an amalgam of Eastern and Western cultures. 120 mins.
VHS: S21068. $39.95.

Hawaiian Paradise

A picturesque journey to six of the islands, interconnected with images, sounds and music, "as vibrant as the island itself." 92 mins.
Laser: LD70238. $34.95.

Historic San Simeon Castle

A home movie that weaves together footage of famous Hollywood stars and personalities at this palatial California estate.
VHS: S18899. $19.95.

Historic FTraveler Great Destinations

This exciting series, hosted by Bill Boggs, takes you to the world's great historic destinations, giving you a personal sense of the people and events that have shaped the world. Each tape is 50 mins.
Historic Traveler Great Destinations—Robert E. Lee Country. Takes viewers in the footsteps of the great general, from Richmond to Harpers Ferry, including the battlefields of Antietam and Gettysburg and the Appomattox Court House.
VHS: S32732. $19.95.
Historic Traveler Great Destinations—The Path to Independence. In *Washington the General* you'll visit Valley Forge Historic Park, Washington Crossing Historic Park on the Delaware River, and the Old Barracks Museum. In *Colonial Virginia*, you'll visit the New World: Jamestown, Colonial Williamsburg and Yorktown.
VHS: S32733. $19.95.
Historic Traveler Great Destinations—Exploring the West. In *Historic Rockies* visit Grand Junction, Colorado, where history goes back to the dinosaurs; the Mesa Verde ruins of the ancient Anasazi; and the Durango-Silverton Railroad. Explore the settlements of the first Europeans, from Old Town in Albuquerque to Sante Fe to Mission San Xavier del Bac and view the ruins of the Anasazi Indians at Aztec Ruins National Monument in *The Southwest*.
VHS: S32734. $19.95.
Historic Traveler Great Destinations—To Win the War. Visit the historic places of World War II. In *Normandy Beachheads* you'll visit Omaha, Utah and Sword, St. Mere Eglise and the cemeteries of soldiers. In *Wartime Britain* you'll go to Cabinet War Rooms and St. Paul's Cathedral in London, the RAF Museum, the Imperial War Museum and Bletchley Park.
VHS: S32735. $19.95.
Historic Traveler Great Destinations—Grant and Sherman. In *Grant and the Civil War* you'll visit many of the battlefields where Grant exhibited his military genius, including Vicksburg National Military Park, Shiloh Military Park and Chickamauga & Chattanooga Military Park. In *Sherman's March to the Sea* you'll visit Andersonville National Historic Site and many battlefield sites where Sherman pounded the Confederates into retreat in Georgia.
VHS: S32736. $19.95.
Historic Traveler Great Destinations—Roots of American Entertainment. *Old Hollywood* takes viewers to many locations in today's Los Angeles that preserve the heritage of the film industry, including the Warner Bros. back lot to Old Tucson in Arizona, where many great westerns were filmed. In *Birthplace of American Music* you'll travel to the places that spawned the blues and led to jazz and country music, from the backroads of Mississippi and the Delta Blues Museum to Graceland, Beale Street and Sun Studios in Memphis.
VHS: S32737. $19.95.
Historic Traveler Great Destinations—Gold Rush and Gun Fights. *Gold Rush* visits the restored structures and museums of Sacramento, California, the Marshall Gold Discovery State Historic Park where the rush started and the Columbia State Historic Park. In *The Gun Fighters* follow in the footsteps of many of the notorious characters of American history from the O.K. Corral in Tombstone to Tucson, Wilcox, Arizona and Lincoln State Monument.
VHS: S32738. $19.95.

Hitchhiking Vietnam: Letters from the Trail

Karin Muller, a 28-year-old former management consultant, leads a fascinating solo trek through an enchanted Vietnam far off the tourist map, from the hustling backstreets of Saigon and Hanoi to a remote Hmong tribal mountain village few foreigners have ever seen. A PBS WGBH Boston Special. 60 mins.
VHS: S33087. $19.95.

Honduras: Gateway to Central America

Explore the history and culture of a nation that provides insights into human development in both ancient and modern times. Visit the capital at Tegucigalpa and the bustling city of San Pedro and ponder the mysteries of the ancient Mayan civilization at the center of Copan. Includes study guide. 32 mins.
VHS: S31241. $29.95.

How to See Hollywood

An affectionate look at Hollywood, from the silent screen to the Golden Era, for tourists from the movie buff to the cultivated museum-goer. You'll see the Walk of Fame, the Hollywood sign, the Chinese Theater, Sunset Strip, Rodeo Drive, Universal Studios, Venice, the Gene Autry Western Museum, the Hollywood Bowl, the Warner Bros. backlot, homes of the stars, the Tournament of Roses, Disneyland and more.
VHS: S32728. $19.95.
Clay Francisco, USA, 1993, 80 mins.

If These Walls Could Speak

Vincent Price hosts this entertaining series of the mysteries and secrets of some of the world's great castles, palaces and historical sites. Each tape is 30 minutes.
Edinburgh Castle.
VHS: S05110. $19.95.
Fushimi Castle.
VHS: S05111. $19.95.
Kilmainham Jail.
VHS: S05114. $19.95.
Kronborg Castle.
VHS: S05115. $19.95.
Mt. Vernon.
VHS: S05116. $19.95.
Virginia City.
VHS: S05123. $19.95.

Into the Thin Air of Everest: Mountain of Dreams, Mountain of Doom

The definitive documentary of the history and mystery of Mt. Everest, this three-volume set is the incredible story of the world's highest mountain and the adventurers who tempt fate to reach its deadly 5½-mile summit. *Part I—Everest: The Quest* includes the incredible stories of the early climbers, including George Leigh Mallory and Sir Edmund Hillary's legendary summit climb. *Part II—Everest: Tempting Fate* explores triumphant (and tragic) expeditions of the modern era and takes an in-depth view of the terrible events of 1996, the deadliest year in the history of Mt. Everest. *Part III—The Conquest of Everest* is the thrilling Academy Award-nominated documentary about the 1953 British expedition that was the first to reach Mt. Everest's summit. 170 mins.
VHS: S32731. $49.95.

James L. Fitzpatrick's Traveltalks

Assembles 11 of the original *Traveltalks* as released by MGM 1930-1933. In these early sound travelogues, location footage provides a fascinating window into the pre-jet world of 70 years ago. Includes "Glimpses of Eiren," "Siam to Korea," "Romantic Argentina," "Japan in Cherry Blossom Time," "A Day in Venice," and more.
VHS: S34307. $24.95.
James A. Fitpatrick, USA, 1930-33, 91 mins.

Jerusalem: City of Heaven

This program from The Discovery Channel presents a portrait of the complex city claimed by Jews, Muslims and Christians. Filled with the voices of Jerusalem's diverse residents, this documentary uses personal stories and powerful images to show how Jerusalem's remarkable past resonates in the lives of its people today and how anticipation of the Day of Judgement shapes ordinary life as nowhere else on earth. 90 mins.
VHS: S31941. $19.95.

Knott's Berry Farm, California

This is where the Old West meets the 20th century—head on! Ride a steam locomotive, a stage coach, or a thrill ride like the Corkscrew. Great family fun. 38 mins.
VHS: S06684. $29.95.

Kodak Travel Series

Olympic Range. From snow-covered peaks to peaceful streams, immerse yourself in the beauty of Washington state's famous rain forest, with firs and cedars as tall as skyscrapers.
Laser: LD70252. $29.95.

L.A. Journal, Vol. 1

An impressionistic tapestry of Los Angeles that is conveyed through a collection of photographs that document the pleasures and diversity in daily city life. The program captures the glamorous hot spots and urban blight. On three digital soundtracks are an original score by Carl Stone, a selection of early California music and poetry readings by Angelenos.
Laser: LD71930. $24.95.

Lakewold: Where the Blue Poppy Grows

A tour of Washington State's renowned Lakewold Gardens, which were finely crafted by landscape architects Thomas Church and the Olmsted brothers. 58 mins.
VHS: S19672. $29.95.

Las Vegas & the Enchanted Desert

The most up-to-date video available on the hottest and fastest-growing travel destination in the country—an exciting oasis of extravagance, entertainment and fun. Stereo. USA, 45 mins.
VHS: S15082. $29.95.

Las Vegas and Hoover Dam

Experience fabulous Las Vegas—including gambling, hotels, the Strip, showgirls. Marvel at the incredible design and grandeur of mighty Hoover Dam. Plus, witness the Great Colorado River Flood of 1983. 25 mins.
VHS: S06691. $29.95.

Laura McKenzie's Travel Tips

A video guide hosted by Laura McKenzie, a noted travel expert, which answers the questions where to go, what hotel to stay at, how to pack, where to find the night life, and much more.
Alaska.
VHS: S04614. $24.95.
Arizona.
VHS: S04612. $24.95.
Austria. Vienna's Lippizan stallions, Salzburg, the city of Mozart, Innsbruck's Olympic village, ski resorts and Austria's famous castles.
VHS: S04992. $24.95.
Australia.
VHS: S07361. $24.95.
Boston.
VHS: S04615. $24.95.
Eastern Canada.
VHS: S11207. $19.95.
Egypt.
VHS: S02038. $24.95.
English Countryside and Scotland.
VHS: S11209. $19.95.
Florida.
VHS: S07324. $24.95.
Hawaii.
VHS: S02039. $24.95.
Hong Kong. Kowloon, Wan Chai, Causeway Bay, Aberdeen, Repulse Bay, Macao.
VHS: S04995. $24.95.
Ireland. Includes information on Dublin, Blarney, Cork, Limerick, Shannon.
VHS: S02040. $24.95.
Las Vegas. Surrounding day trips to casinos, revues, calico, Hoover Dam.
VHS: S04993. $24.95.
London. Devoted to all the spots both within London and also within a day's journey, such as Windsor Castle, Stratford-on-Avon and Warwick Castle.
VHS: S02041. $24.95.

Los Angeles. Includes the Hollywod celebrity home tours, Palm Springs, the Southern California beaches and more.
VHS: S02042. $24.95.
Mainland China.
VHS: S11210. $19.95.
Mexican Beaches.
VHS: S04613. $24.95.
Morocco. Information about Casablanca, Rabat, Marrakesh, and day trips to Agadir and Taroudannt.
VHS: S02043. $24.95.
Munich and Bavaria. An introduction to King Ludwig's castle, the Salt Mines of Berchresgaden, Bavarian beer halls, medieval towns.
VHS: S04990. $24.95.
Netherlands.
VHS: S11205. $19.95.
New York City.
VHS: S04616. $24.95.
New Orleans. The French quarter, Bourbon Street jazz, creole cuisine, the Mississippi River ferries, plantations.
VHS: S04991. $24.95.
New Zealand.
VHS: S07325. $24.95.
Paris.
VHS: S02044. $24.95.
Queensland, Australia.
VHS: S11208. $19.95.
Rome. The guide to the Eternal City includes information on Vatican City, Pompeii, and the Amalfi Coast.
VHS: S02045. $24.95.
San Francisco. Learn about the famous sights such as the Golden Gate Bridge, Ghirardelli Square, Fisherman's Wharf and surrounding points of interest.
VHS: S02046. $24.95.
Spain. Includes information on Madrid, Granada and Toledo, as well as Tangiers, Morocco and Costa del Sol.
VHS: S02047. $24.95.
Switzerland.
VHS: S02048. $24.95.
Tahiti and French Polynesia.
VHS: S11206. $19.95.
The Caribbean.
VHS: S07323. $24.95.
The French Riviera.
VHS: S11211. $19.95.
Venice. St. Mark's square, the Doge's palace, the famed canals and gondolas, Venetial glassworks.
VHS: S04994. $24.95.
Washington, D.C.
VHS: S04617. $24.95.
Western Canada.
VHS: S07326. $24.95.

Mount Rainier

Washington state's Mt. Rainier National Park is the crown jewel of the Cascade peaks. Lush forests of cedar, hemlock and fir flourish on its volcano-born slopes. 28 mins.
VHS: S06668. $29.95.

Mt. Rushmore and The Black Hills of South Dakota

Explore Mt. Rushmore and the surrounding Black Hills with all its unique natural wonders and Old West heritage. See the Badlands, Custer State Park, Wind Cave and more. 30 mins.
VHS: S06700. $29.95.

Mt. Rushmore— Four Faces on a Mountain

In this inspiring National Park Service film, you will see the faces of Presidents Washington, Jefferson, Lincoln and Roosevelt being carved from Mt. Rushmore in rare black and white film. 30 mins.
VHS: S06666. $29.95.

Mush, You Malamutes!

Father Bernard R. Hubbard compiled this ethnographic film about his journey in search of a fabled tropical valley allegedly located in the heart of Alaska. It contains unique footage of this harsh landscape and the people who live there. 68 mins.
VHS: S24082. $24.95.

Mystic Lands

Includes *Mystic Lands—Anasazi: The Ancient Ones/Taj Mahal: Heaven on Earth; Mystic Lands—Bali: Island of 1,000 Temples/Haiti: Dance of the Spirit; Mystic Lands—Varanasi: City of Light/Australia: Dreamtime; Mystic Lands—Thunder Dragon/Maya: Messages in Stone; Mystic Lands—Burma: Triumph of the Spirit/Jerusalem: Mosaic of Faith*; and *Mystic Lands—Peru: Kingdom in the Clouds/Egypt: Cycle of Life/Greece: Isle of Revelation*. 300 mins.
VHS: S33740. $89.95.

National Geographic Video: 30 Years of National Geographic Specials

For over 30 years, National Geographic has brought the most fascinating scientific discoveries to television. This video shows the best of this tradition. Jacques Cousteau, Louis and Mary Leakey, and Jane Goodall are among the scientific personalities seen in this compilation tape. Its scope ranges from the heights of the Himalayas to the ocean's nearly unfathomable depths. 90 mins.
VHS: S29919. $19.95.

National Monuments of Southern Arizona

Explore the splendid scenery and fascinating natural and cultural history of eight National Park Service locations in Southern Arizona, including Saguaro, Organ Pipe Cactus, Tonto and Tumacacori. 30 mins.
VHS: S06672. $29.95.

A New England Clambake

This regional culinary tradition can be prepared on the beach, on the back yard barbecue, on the stove, and even in the microwave. It's all explained on this video.
VHS: S25008. $14.95.

Over America

Aerial photography spanning the entire US is joined with an original Hi-Fi stereo musical score. The result is this unique video experience. High definition cameras show amazing detail of the coasts, mountains and great expanses of wilderness that are the unique heritage of this land. 80 mins.
VHS: S25736. $24.95.

Over New England

A vivid travelogue of the beauty, splendor, grace and tradition of New England, examining its unique history, geography and landscape. 60 mins.
VHS: S19393. $19.95.

Over Washington

This video studies the beauty and history of Washington State. The program is "backed by a lush musical score" *(Booklist)*. 60 mins.
VHS: S19390. $19.95.

Pikes Peak Country, with Colorado Springs

Explore the area's scenic wonders and visit over 40 of its finest attractions, including museums, historic sites and rustic towns. 50 mins.
VHS: S06697. $29.95.

Reader's Digest: Great Splendors of the World

Three-volume collectors edition as seen on The Disney Channel. "Splendors of Nature" follows the course of the seasons to explore five of nature's greatest events. "Ancient Splendors" explores four of the most magnificent sites in human antiquity: Egypt's temples at Thebes, The Acropolis in Athens, Guatemala's temple-pyramids at Tikal and Cambodia's Angkor Wat. "Imperial Splendors" tells the stories of great empires and their rulers and the secret world hidden behind palace doors.
VHS: S30459. $59.95.

Rivers of France

Take a luxury cruise on the Seine and experience picturesque Honfleur, the Bayeux tapestry, Monet's Giverny, Normandy's D-Day beaches, Joan of Arc's Rouen, Mont St. Michel, Brittany folklore, Carnac's monolith, ballooning the Loire Valley Chateaux, a canal trip through Burgundy's vineyards, the Louvre's new pyramid entrance, the Musee D'Orsay, and the new Bastille Opera House.
VHS: S32729. $49.95.
Clay Francisco, USA, 1993, 80 mins.

Rocky Mountain National Park

Discover the Crown Jewel of Colorado—a land of towering peaks, where fully one-third of the park is above the tree line. See some of North America's most splendid mountain lakes and drive spectacular Trail Ridge Road—the highest continuous highway in the U.S. 30 mins.
VHS: S06673. $29.95.

Route 66

This nostalgic program takes a trip along America's beloved highway, from Chicago to Los Angeles, exposing the now "hidden" America modern freeway riders never see. 105 mins.
VHS: S32292. $19.95.

The Route 66 Collection

This two-tape look at "America's Mother Road" includes the award-winning and critically acclaimed *Route 66: An American Odyssey* (55 mins.), highlighting the most spectacular stretches of open highway in America to the unforgettable motels, dazzling neon, and road cafes; and *Route 66: A Cruise Down Main Street* (45 mins.), featuring supermodel Hunter Reno travelling from Chicago to L.A. in a tribute to the the all-weather road that came to symbolize roadside culture in the 20th century.
VHS: S32204. $29.95.

Russia: Then & Now

Travel through Moscow, St. Petersburg, Ukraine, Yalta, Sochi and Samarkand, and see the Trans-Siberian Railroad, Lake Baikal, and more with veteran travel filmmaker Clay Francisco before and after the breakup of the Soviet Union. "Anyone who wants to know more about Russia should not miss Francisco's work" *(ABC News, Hollywood)*.
VHS: S32727. $19.95.
Clay Francisco, USA, 1994, 90 mins.

San Simeon: Hearst's Castle

Ken Murray tours the magnificent castle that was once the playground of the wealthy—including the furniture, sculpture and art. 28 mins.
VHS: S09972. $12.95.

Scenic Seattle

Tour Seattle's scenic, historical and cultural attractions, as well as the beautiful surrounding area. 30 mins.
VHS: S06682. $29.95.

Scenic Wonders of America

Three programs, *Atlantic Vistas, Pacific Frontiers* and *American West*, offer a naturalist portrait of the landscape, mountains and water. 180 mins.
Laser: LD70230. $49.95.

Seasons of the Heart

This is a journey through Fairbanks and Alaska's untamed interior. Every season in the "Golden Heart" of this state is magical. Summer festivals, wildlife, the Northern Lights, dog sleds and more are on view. 28 mins.
VHS: S24223. $14.95.

Shenandoah Valley of the Virginias

Discover why Shenandoah Valley is known as the crowning glory of the Virginias; explore the Blue Ridge Mountains, the countryside of George Washington, Stonewall Jackson, Robert E. Lee and Woodrow Wilson, and visit the battlefields and museums of the Civil War. 30 mins.
VHS: S10925. $29.95.

Shenandoah—The Gift

Shenandoah National Park is a symbol of renewal, hidden away in the sleepy hollows of Virginia's mountains. Through black and white footage, see Shenandoah as it was developed in the 1920's and 30's. 20 mins.
VHS: S06670. $29.95.

Southern California

From San Diego to Santa Barbara, including L.A. and Hollywood, this stimulating film whisks you to the most exciting scenic, cultural and tourist attractions in the Southland. 30 mins.
VHS: S06693. $29.95.

St. Charles Avenue: Mansions and Monarchs

The history and beauty of America's grandest boulevard is revealed in this documentary about New Orleans' most fashionable area. 30 mins.
VHS: S22398. $41.95.

St. Charles Streetcar

Peter Fountain narrates this lively historical look at the world's oldest street railway along New Orleans' most history-laden boulevard. 30 mins.
VHS: S22400. $49.95.

The Story of America's Canyon Country

This program concerns the landscape carved out by the Colorado River, the "Grand Circle," the breathtaking scenery and 11 national parks around Utah, Arizona, Colorado and New Mexico that comprise the mythology and history of the American west. The areas covered include Monument Valley, Bryce Canyon, Cedar Breaks, Capitol Reef and the Grand Canyon. 60 mins.
VHS: S17264. $29.95.

The Story of America's Great Northwest

Spanning its entire history, dating back 200 million years, this program considers the beauty of this area and its formation from nature, fire, glaciers and water. The work also features episodes about the conflicts between Native Americans and the settlers, gold seekers, entrepreneurs, and travelers. 60 mins.
VHS: S17266. $29.95.

The Story of America's Historic Inns

A travelogue of Americana which visits the inns, taverns and various stagecoaches and offers telling anecdotes about local history, architectural wonder and scenic high points. The program features visits to St. Francis Inn, Stillman's Inn, St. James Hotel, San Ysidro Ranch, Robert Morris Inn, Monmouth Plantation, and Wolf Creek Tavern. 60 mins.
VHS: S20188. $29.95.

The Story of America's Last Frontier: Alaska

This program chronicles the history and emergence of Alaska, from prehistoric to the post-atomic and its status as the last frontier, a cultural gateway, with its national parks, preserves and monuments. The epic work includes sections on the caribou crossing at Kobuk, the Eskimo and Indian battles, Mt. McKinley, North America's tallest peak, the "forgotten war" during World War II, the Gold Rush, and its U.S. purchase in 1863. 60 mins.
VHS: S17265. $29.95.

SuperCities

SuperCities is a series of beautifully photographed, professionally produced short films which bring the world's favorite cities to life in your living room. All titles are available in hi-fi stereo.
Amsterdam. This canal-lined city is known both for its beauty and its traditionally liberal outlook. It attracts young people from the world over by offering all the pleasures of modern life in a civilized and understanding setting. 30 mins.
VHS: S26111. $9.95.
Bangkok. A vast, modern city has sprung up between the temples of old Bangkok. This video shows a place marked by vivid contrasts and vibrant energy. 30 mins.
VHS: S26112. $9.95.
Barcelona. The Catalonian capital maintains a strong sense of identity and history balanced with a contemporary flair. As host to the 1992 Olympics, this city took the opportunity to prove both its attractiveness and openness to foreign visitors. 30 mins.
VHS: S26113. $9.95.
Berlin. A turbulent and central role in the 20th century has defined the face of this unique historic city. Today Berlin joins a multiplicity of styles at the heart of a newly unified Europe. 30 mins.
VHS: S26125. $14.95.
Berne & Lucerne. These two Swiss cities combine a medieval legacy with vibrant, contemporary urban life. Berne is both a perfectly preserved medieval town and the capital of Switzerland, and Lucerne has the best preserved city walls still standing in Europe. 30 mins.
VHS: S26126. $9.95.
Budapest. The Hungarian capital betrays a zest for life unbowed by the passage of centuries. Much has been preserved and restored in this Central European city on the Danube. 30 mins.
VHS: S26127. $9.95.
Cairo. Africa's largest city is home to Pharonic treasures, Muslim edifices of unmatched grandeur and a busy, modern way of life. The Nile and the Pyramids appear eternal amid the bustle. 30 mins.
VHS: S26128. $9.95.
Florence. The city of the Renaissance lures visitors with architectural and artistic treasures. It's all on view in this video, from Michelangelo to Vasari, Donatello and Giotto. 30 mins.
VHS: S26114. $9.95.
Hong Kong. The gateway to China is a vast, modern metropolis, noted for its density. Amidst the crowds lie a variety of attractions, including some of the best shopping available. 30 mins.
VHS: S26115. $9.95.
Istanbul. The fabled Constantinople combines the best of East and West. This former capital of the Roman Empire maintains a unique historical legacy. 30 mins.
VHS: S26116. $9.95.
Johannesburg. South Africa's commercial capital is a lively setting for museums, galleries, theaters and markets. The city's diversity is key to its vibrancy. 30 mins.
VHS: S26129. $9.95.
Lisbon. Once the richest city in Europe, Lisbon still offers an air of relaxed elegance. Though destroyed by an earthquake in the mid-18th century, it remains a favorite destination for travelers. 30 mins.
VHS: S26117. $9.95.
London. The capital of the once mighty British Empire combines a rich legacy with an unmatched cosmopolitan style. London's monuments are beautifully displayed in this video. 30 mins.
VHS: S26118. $9.95.
Madrid. From the Prado, one of the world's greatest art museums, to the nightlife around the Puenta del Sol, Madrid offers something for every visitor. 30 mins.
VHS: S26130. $9.95.
Marrakesh & Fez. Both of these cities have spanned centuries to emerge as vibrant, lively places that still offer much to the contemporary world. 30 mins.
VHS: S26131. $9.95.
Mexico City. The largest city on Earth proudly preserves a heritage that combines an Aztec legacy, Spanish colonial influence, and the contemporary verve of modern Mexico. 30 mins.
VHS: S26132. $9.95.
Munich. Beerhalls are not the only sites offered by the Bavarian capital. There are palaces, baroque churches and peerless museums in this city of riches. 30 mins.
VHS: S26133. $9.95.
New York. The "city that never sleeps" is the perfect place for a whirlwind video tour. Skyscrapers cram together in this dynamic, American, "can-do" setting. 30 mins.
VHS: S26119. $9.95.
Paris. With boulevards and monuments unmatched the world over, the "City of Light" is the ideal European metropolis, and is wonderfully documented on this video. 30 mins.
VHS: S26120. $9.95.
Prague. The city of a thousand spires survived the terrors of World War II and the depredations of a moribund communist government. As a result, it offers treasures from another era. 30 mins.
VHS: S26134. $9.95.
Rio de Janeiro. Rio's Carnival and the Copacabana beach have fixed this city in the popular imagination as an exotic and vibrant destination. This video shows the uninhibited spirit of the city which invented the Bossa Nova. 30 mins.
VHS: S26121. $9.95.
Rome. From ancient times to the present, Rome has played a vital role in world history. The video shows Rome's treasures from the ancient world, the medieval era, the Renaissance and more. 30 mins.
VHS: S26122. $9.95.
St. Petersburg. Founded by Tsar Peter the Great to orient Russia toward Europe, this city offers a lovely melange of European influences, with sumptuous palaces and majestic canals which still stand despite a turbulent history. 30 mins.
VHS: S26123. $9.95.
Stockholm. Built on 14 islands, this Nordic city seems to float on water. Despite its ethereal appearance, it contains a host of solid and elegant sites both old and new. 30 mins.
VHS: S26135. $9.95.
Venice. Along ancient canals, gondolas float by magnificent sites such as the Basilica of San Marco, the Doge's Palace and the Campanile. 30 mins.
VHS: S26124. $9.95.
Vienna. Architectural majesty is evident in a variety of buildings at the heart of the old Hapsburg Empire. The Ringstrasse Boulevard circles one of the most beautiful cities in Europe. 30 mins.
VHS: S26136. $9.95.

Surprising Amsterdam

Capture the essence of one of the world's great cities. Some of the major sights include Dam Square, the Jordaan, and Vondel Park. Visit Anne Frank's house, then take a leisurely cruise down the quaint canals. 30 mins.
VHS: S10767. $24.95.

Switzerland's Glacier Express

All aboard for the famous "Glacier Express" rail trip through the Swiss Alps. Travel by train from St. Moritz to Zermatt, stopping for breathtaking views and scenic villages. It's a trip to remember! 52 mins.
VHS: S05762. $29.95.

Switzerland, the Alpine Wonderland

Journey to Switzerland, famous for clocks, rich chocolate and breathtaking scenery. Explore the Jungfrau mountain area and hear yodelers in Grindelwald. Visit Neuchatel, one of the country's watchmaking centers, then shop in elegant Lausanne. Shiver in the dungeon of the Chateau de Chillon. Visit the international city of Geneva and marvel at Zermatt's magnificent neighbor-the Matterhorn. 55 mins.
VHS: S10770. $24.95.

Tales from the Map Room

Even if X doesn't always mark the spot, maps can illuminate both the past and the present. This series explores the enormous variety of maps both ancient and modern, and includes the related history and politics that shaped mapmaking. Each of the six half-hour programs focuses on a single theme.
Metropolis. Every aspect of city life requires maps. Tourism, transportation, emergency services, planning and of course politics depend on them. London is the model for this look at the relationship between history, the growth of a great city and the art of mapmaking.
VHS: S21528. $69.95.
On the Road. From medieval pilgrims to today's car atlases, maps chart the explosion of human travel. This program traces the evolution of maps from the time of Charles II to contemporary atlases. Map reading skills and unconventional tactile maps are also covered.
VHS: S21527. $69.95.
On the Rocks. For centuries navies lost more ships on the rocks offshore than they did to enemies. In Normandy before D-Day there was a plot to chart the beaches of this vital coastline. Maritime maps are still vital as the sea continually shifts its beds and shorelines.
VHS: S21529. $69.95.
Paths of Glory (Fog of War). From the Battle of Culloden to the Gulf War, maps can spell the difference between victory and defeat. The private collection of the Duke of Cumberland, the fortifications designed for Louis XIV at Mauberge and even the maps used in World War I, make this abundantly clear.
VHS: S21526. $69.95.
Plumb Pudding in Danger. Forty percent of Third World boundaries are said to be the work of Britain and France. Early maps were used to settle local property disputes. Then it was realized maps could enhance the power of the state. Collecting taxes, establishing borders, and even defining areas of colonization are important functions made easier by maps.
VHS: S21525. $69.95.
A Tissue of Lies. All map design is a compromise, because the Earth is not flat. A designer must know what to include and what to omit. The confines, conventions, imagination and politics employed in mapmaking are the theme of this episode.
VHS: S21524. $69.95.
Tales from the Map Room. The complete six-volume set.
VHS: S21530. $375.00.

Teton Country

Set in Wyoming's Grand Teton National Park. No roads, no cars—just the fantastic wilderness and wildlife for which the park is noted. 30 mins.
VHS: S06699. $29.95.

Touring Alaska

Fascinating view of the uniqueness of Alaska from the wilderness of the great parks to the life of the people in the cities and countryside. Includes cruise information and coastal fjords and glaciers. USA, 56 mins.
VHS: S03325. $29.95.

Touring America's Ghost Towns

This video brings alive 11 of America's deserted ghost towns. It's all here—a collection of anecdotes and history of America's past, gone but never to be forgotten. Ghost towns include Buckskin Joe, CO; Coloma, CA; Virginia City, NV and eight more. USA, 1991, 60 mins.
VHS: S15517. $29.95.

Touring America's Historic Inns

A one-of-a-kind video that features nine very special historic inns that are still in operation in the United States; it also explores the exciting history of each longstanding venue, including the famous people who have visited there. Includes the Beekman Arms in New York and the St. James Hotel in New Mexico. USA, 1992, 60 mins.
VHS: S15518. $29.95.

Touring America's National Parks

A journey through 17 of the nation's greatest natural treasures, including Yellowstone, the Everglades, Mesa Verde, and the Great Smokies. USA, 56 mins.
VHS: S03290. $29.95.

Touring Exciting Europe

Travel to eight countries and be a part of Europe's most colorful festivals in *Touring Great Festivals of Europe*. Visit Europe's great cities in *Touring London, Paris & Rome*. Two-volume set. 130 mins.
VHS: S34715. $34.95.

Touring Hawaii

An unusual video that goes beyond the most popular sights to areas seldom seen, such as Waimea Canyon, Wailua River, coral reef diving and Volcanoes National Park. USA, 32 mins.
VHS: S03326. $29.95.

Touring Switzerland

Visit the home of the Geneva Conventions, the International Red Cross, the International Olympic Committee, Dada and the music box and see Montreux, the Jungfrau, the Matterhorn, Geneva, Lake Geneva, Bern, Basel, Appenzell, St. Moritz, Lugano, Zermatt, Interlaken, Lucerne and Zurich. 60 mins.
VHS: S32915. $19.95.

Trailside

Fourteen episodes from the award-winning, critically acclaimed TV series featuring leading outdoor experts, guides and instructors in extraordinary adventures and destinations around the world as they bring their knowledge to novice and expert alike. Each tape is 30 mins.
Trailside—Desert Hiking in Big Bend, Texas.
VHS: S32779. $19.95.
Trailside—Jungle Hiking in Costa Rica.
VHS: S32788. $19.95.
Trailside—Kayak Sailing the Exuma Islands, Bahamas.
VHS: S32789. $19.95.
Trailside—More Wilderness 911.
VHS: S32782. $19.95.

Trailside—Mountain Biking Colorado's 10th Mountain Trail.
VHS: S32790. $19.95.
Trailside—Mountaineering the Grand Teton.
VHS: S32791. $19.95.
Trailside—Paddling and Poling Louisiana's Bayou Country.
VHS: S32783. $19.95.
Trailside—Rock Climbing in the Adirondacks.
VHS: S32784. $19.95.
Trailside—Sea Kayaking with Orcas.
VHS: S32785. $19.95.
Trailside—Ski Touring California's High Sierra.
VHS: S32786. $19.95.
Trailside—Thru-Hiking the Appalachian Trail.
VHS: S32780. $19.95.
Trailside—Trekking in Iceland.
VHS: S32781. $19.95.
Trailside—Whitewater Canoeing the Chattooga River.
VHS: S32792. $19.95.
Trailside—Winter Camping in Yellowstone National Park.
VHS: S32787. $19.95.

Travel the World

Rick Steves hosts this award-winning PBS series which explores with experience, enthusiasm and humor the history and culture of Europe's most intriguing destinations. Each program is designed around an actual itinerary, with gorgeous filmed scenery and invaluable budget-conscious touring tips.
Travel the World: Austria. Includes Vienna and the Danube, Salzburg and the Lakes District. 55 mins.
VHS: S33292. $24.95.
Travel the World: Eastern Cities. Includes Prague, Istanbul and Budapest. 52 mins.
VHS: S33293. $24.95.
Travel the World: France (Burgundy, Provence and the Loire). 55 mins.
VHS: S33294. $24.95.
Travel the World: France (Paris, Normandy and Brittany). 52 mins.
VHS: S33296. $24.95.
Travel the World: France (The Dordogne Region, The French Riviera). 52 mins.
VHS: S33295. $24.95.
Travel the World: Germany (Munich and Bavaria, Berlin and Potsdam). 52 mins.
VHS: S33297. $24.95.
Travel the World: Germany (The Rine and Mosel, The Romantic Road). 52 mins.
VHS: S33298. $24.95.
Travel the World: Great Britain (London, Edinburgh). 52 mins.
VHS: S33299. $24.95.
Travel the World: Great Britain (North Wales Cotswold Villages and Bath). 52 mins.
VHS: S33300. $24.95.
Travel the World: Greece. Includes Athens and the Peloponnese, Greek Islands. 52 mins.
VHS: S33301. $24.95.
Travel the World: Ireland. Includes Western Ireland, Dublin and Belfast. 51 mins.
VHS: S33302. $24.95.
Travel the World: Italy (Hilltowns of Tuscany, The Italian Riviera). 55 mins.
VHS: S33303. $24.95.
Travel the World: Italy (Rome, Naples and the Amalfi Coast). 52 mins.
VHS: S33304. $24.95.
Travel the World: Italy (Venice, Florence). 52 mins.
VHS: S33305. $24.95.
Travel the World: Portugal. The Algarve, Southern Coast, Lisbon. 52 mins.
VHS: S33307. $24.95.
Travel the World: Spain. Toledo and Madrid, Seville and Andalusia. 55 mins.
VHS: S33308. $24.95.
Travel the World: Switzerland. Berner Alps, Western Switzerland. 52 mins.
VHS: S33309. $24.95.
Travel the World: The Low Countries. Includes Holland, Belgium and Luxembourg. 52 mins.
VHS: S33306. $24.95.
Travel the World: West Coast, Central Turkey. 52 mins.
VHS: S33310. $24.95.

Treasures of the Green Belt: Gates of the City

Narrated by Bay Area Backroads host Jerry Graham, with an Emmy Award-winning music score by Gary Remal, this breathtakingly photographed program spotlights the beautiful and productive land of the California countryside around San Francisco Bay. All ages. 1987, 28 mins.
VHS: S31909. $49.95.

Video Visits: New England, America's Living Heritage

Hear notorious tales at Salem's Witch Museum, glimpse the daily lives of colonial settlers at Plimoth Plantation, walk Boston's cobblestone streets, replay pivotal Revolutionary War events at Minute Man National Historical Park, go lobstering in Atlantic waters, tour Ben & Jerry's ice cream headquarters, and more in this entertaining and educational tape. 55 mins.
VHS: S28500. $24.95.

Virginia Plantations—Mount Vernon, Monticello and Other Great Houses of Old Virginia

Explores the world of colonial Virginia's great estates, focusing on two of America's most famous homes, George Washington's Mount Vernon, located on the banks of the Potomac, and Thomas Jefferson's mountaintop Monticello. A handful of other historic plantations in Tidewater, Virginia, including Stratford Hall, birthplace of Robert E. Lee, and Sherwood Forest Plantation, are also glimpsed. 30 mins.
VHS: S11124. $19.95.

Virginia's Civil War Parks

From the war's first major battle at Bull Run to the final surrender at Appomattox, Virginia was the arena where North and South fought many of their bloodiest battles. This program gives a full account of the events and visits the battlefields at Manassas, Richmond, Fredericksburg, Chancellorsville, Wilderness, Spotsylvania, Petersburg and Appomattox. 55 mins.
VHS: S10926. $29.95.

Voices from the Ice, Alaska

This is a land still dominated by active glaciers, where you will hear the roar of crashing ice and see the exquisite beauty of a timeless yet constantly changing land. 20 mins.
VHS: S06677. $29.95.

Washington Monuments

Robert Prosky narrates this informative and picturesque tour of our capital's major landmarks, including the White House, the Vietnam War Memorial, the Supreme Court and Library of Congress. 30 mins.
VHS: S08460. $19.95.

Washington, D.C.

Explore Washington's rich heritage, magnificent architecture, historical treasures, and honored memorials and monuments. Tour inside the Smithsonian Museums and the Library of Congress. Visit the White House, the Capitol, the Lincoln and Vietnam Memorials, and much more. 30 mins.
VHS: S06695. $29.95.

Washington, D.C.: An Inspiring Tour

A complete guide to Washington's rich historical heritage, magnificent buildings, national museums, memorials and monuments. 55 mins.
VHS: S10922. $29.95.

Whitewater Adventures

Orange Torpedo Trips. The company that pioneered commercial use of inflatable kayaks on whitewater rivers invites you to command your own kayak on a wild taste of river recreation. *California Whitewater.* Whitewater Voyages handles day trips in California and extended expeditions on other continents. If you're looking for free-reined adventure or a relaxing dream ride, a whitewater vacation is the sure find.
VHS: S15848. $19.95.

Yellowstone & Grand Teton

Discover the wonders and wildlife in two of America's most inspiring parks. Yellowstone, a geological showcase, features the most spectacular geyser field in the world, Old Faithful, and emerald hot pools. 42 mins.
VHS: S06659. $29.95.

Yosemite National Park

60-minute tape shows the parks' popular valley area from a rafting trip down the Merced River to the mighty waterfalls, in spring, fall, and winter. Classical music and natural sounds accompany the scenery.
VHS: S06015. $29.95.

Yosemite—Seasons & Splendor

Finally, a video program equal to the splendor of Yosemite! See unsurpassed scenic beauty and learn of Yosemite's fascinating geological and natural wonders. 40 mins.
VHS: S06662. $29.95.

Yosemite: The Fate of Heaven

Robert Redford narrates this breathtaking look at "the most beautiful valley in the world" on the occasion of Yosemite's 100th anniversary. The amazing natural wonder is seen through the eyes of whose who struggle to preserve it—the rangers, trail builders, fire-fighters and naturalists.
VHS: S12005. $14.98.
Laser: LD71221. $29.95.
Jon Else/John Korty, USA, 1989, 61 mins.

Zion Canyon—Treasure of the Gods

IMAX technology, coupled with Dolby Surround audio, captures the splendor of Zion Canyon and the Southwest. A bird's eye view of this landscape enlivens the tales and myths which were inspired by this majestic scenery. USA, 38 mins.
Laser: LD75008. $39.95.

AIDS

AIDS 101: Tammy Talks with Teenagers

Tammy Boccomino explains exactly how one can and cannot contract HIV. She has been asymptomatic for over 10 years. In this video she is accompanied by Dr. James Jarvis in a discussion format that helps reassure kids even as it informs them how to combat this serious disease. 44 mins.
VHS: S25806. $169.95.

AIDS—What You Need to Know

The Surgeon General's report to the world on AIDS attempts to separate myths from reality in covering the devastating disease. 60 mins.
VHS: S09202. $39.95.

AIDS: A Test of the Nation

AIDS impacts on many of the problems facing women, children and families in America today. This videotape addresses the larger issues of reproductive rights, access to quality health care and the standard of living for many women and children in our society. Produced by Gay Men Health Crisis. 28 mins.
VHS: S11422. $19.95.

AIDS: Allie's Story

Allie Gertz claims she was exposed to HIV from spending one night with a friend. She is a young, heterosexual, non drug user who belies all stereotypes about people with AIDS. Before Allie died she urged people to learn from her example. Now her family continues her mission. This ABC *20/20* presentation includes a discussion of the risk faced by college students. 14 mins.
VHS: S25811. $129.95.

AIDS: Alternative Therapies and the Struggle for Legalization

This program examines legalized treatments and alternative therapies and drugs—contrasting their effectiveness—and the government regulation of their use. 76 mins.
VHS: S20152. $29.95.

AIDS: Bleach, Teach and Outreach

The issue of needle exchange in New York City has long been a contentious one. This videotape documents New York City's needle exchange program in its first year. Interviews with representatives of groups such as the Association of Drug Abuse, Prevention and Treatment discuss the issues involved in trying to stem the spread of HIV among intravenous drug users in New York City. Produced by Gay Men Health Crisis. 24 mins.
VHS: S11423. $19.95.

AIDS: Doctors, Liars and Women: AIDS Activists Say "No" to Cosmo

In January 1988, a group of women from the AIDS Coalition to Unleash Power organized a protest against *Cosmopolitan* magazine for publishing an article that gave seriously misleading information to women about AIDS. *Doctors, Liars and Women* documents the process of organizing AIDS activists around issues pertinent to women. Produced by Gay Men Health Crisis. 23 mins.
VHS: S11424. $19.95.

AIDS: Everything You Should Know

Whoopi Goldberg joins Dr. Alexander Levine to present the facts about how one can and cannot contract HIV. They also explain how AIDS destroys the body's immune system. 28 mins.
VHS: S25802. $149.95.
Laser: LD75002. $169.95.

AIDS: Prostitutes, Risk and AIDS

Prostitutes are frequently scapegoated as the vectors of HIV transmission. This fallacy is often based upon prejudice that evolves out of stereotypical representations we see in the media. This videotape provides an analysis of these images in the context of sex workers and health care professionals who are actively educating the public about safer sex and IV drug use. Produced by Gay Men Health Crisis. 28 mins.
VHS: S11425. $19.95.

AIDS: PWA Power

A diverse group of people with AIDS/ARC talk about their experiences, giving valuable insight to those recently diagnosed with AIDS. First-person accounts about the birth of the PWA self-empowerment movement are included. Produced by Gay Men Health Crisis.
VHS: S11426. $25.00.

AIDS: Seize Control of the FDA

On October 11, 1988 at 7:00 a.m., hundreds of AIDS activists from around the U.S. seized control of the Food and Drug Administration in Rockville, Maryland. This tape documents the action and addresses the issues that motivated this non-violent direct action. Produced by Gay Men Health Crisis. 28 mins.
VHS: S11428. $19.95.

AIDS: What Are the Risks
This program provides a clear explanation of Acquired Immuno-Deficiency Syndrome and various methods of transmission. Social and psychological aspects of this disease are also explored from the perspective of the family and friends of people with AIDS, as well as from the perspectives of PWA's themselves. 30 mins.
VHS: S25814. $144.95.

AIDS: Women and AIDS
"Women take care of everyone, who takes care of women?" Although women have been dying of AIDS since 1981, little attention has been paid to their particular situation. *Women and AIDS* explores the underlying issues of how AIDS highlights problems such as racism, sexism, child care and lack of adequate health care for women. Produced by Gay Men Health Crisis. 28 mins.
VHS: S11430. $25.00.

AIDS: Work Your Body
The purpose of this video is to help those who are HIV positive, asymptomatic or otherwise, to develop strategies for living with HIV infection. By aggressively pursuing prophylactic treatments and diligently maintaining one's health, an HIV positive person can take steps to prevent the development of AIDS and actively pursue a healthy existence. Produced by Gay Men Health Crisis. 28 mins.
VHS: S11431. $25.00.

Asi Me Gusta
Latino men offer perspectives on family, "coming out," substance abuse and gay identity. 18 mins.
VHS: S28418. $24.95.

Beginnings: You Won't Get AIDS
Animation, live action sequences, songs and the Surgeon General's guidelines about HIV and AIDS are joined in this video, to reassure kids about this serious disease. Nothing that they do on any normal day exposes them to the dangers of this disease. 14 mins.
VHS: S25805. $79.95.
Laser: LD75001. $99.95.

Best of Nightline
AIDS. 30 mins.
VHS: S14027. $14.98.
Rock Hudson Suffers from AIDS. 30 mins.
VHS: S14036. $14.98.
Ryan White. 60 mins.
VHS: S14052. $14.98.

Clean Needles Save Lives
This video documents the illegal efforts of militant activists with ACT-UP and their needle exchange program in New York. The program combines interviews with recovering drug users discussing how to reduce risk and incorporate safer sex practices. 28 mins.
VHS: S18775. $20.00.

Come Sit by Me: AIDS Education
This story by Dr. Margaret Merrifield explores the fears and emotions of young children who learn about AIDS and HIV when a young boy is shunned by his peers. 8 mins.
VHS: S25803. $69.95.

Come Sit by Me: AIDS Education and Thumbs Up for Kids: AIDS Education
This first story is by Dr. Margaret Merrifield. It explores the fears and emotions of young children who learn about AIDS and HIV when a young boy is shunned by his peers. 8 mins. Then former *Romper Room* teacher Ruby Petersen Unger leads a children's discussion about HIV, AIDS and the transmission of the virus. She introduces an HIV-positive youngster with whom the kids can enjoy playing and whom they can also touch. 23 mins.
Laser: LD75003. $129.95.

Current Flow
Taken from the popular work *Safer Sex Shorts*, this explicit sexual program demonstrates safer sex practices for sexually active gay women. 5 minutes.
VHS: S18776. $15.00.

Edith Springer on Harm Reduction
Edith Springer provides insight on how harm reduction has worked in her training of street youth peer educators in New York City, in this humorous, fast-paced training video. 26 mins.
VHS: S28414. $25.00.

Facts About AIDS
This program dispels persistent myths about AIDS. It also stresses the belief that limiting sexual partners can be helpful in avoiding contact. Condoms, spermicides and government findings about AZT therapy and the danger of HIV infection for pregnant women are also discussed. 11 mins.
VHS: S25813. $129.95.

Fear of Disclosure
Phil Zwickler and David Wojnarowicz explore the psychological and social implications of informing a potential lover you are HIV-positive. 5 minutes.
VHS: S18777. $10.00.

Fit!
A landmark exercise video launched by and for gay men, this rigorous exercise program studies the relationship of aerobics and stress reduction movements on the immune system. The program combines a cardiovascular workout with the tenets of yoga and relaxation. 50 mins.
VHS: S18261. $29.95.

Growing Up in the Age of AIDS
This ABC News Special is hosted by Peter Jennings and features leading experts in health and medicine and questions by a studio audience. 75 mins.
VHS: S16088. $19.98.

Hope for the Future: Confronting HIV in Children and Adolescents
Four families recall the pain they felt upon learning their children were HIV-positive. Information about advances in pediatric AIDS and the comfort these stories provide may prove helpful to others. 15 mins.
VHS: S25812. $129.95.

An Informed Approach to HIV Antibody Testing
An informative and sensitive video that considers the personal and social consequences of testing. From the GMHC's *Living with AIDS* cable program. 22 mins.
VHS: S18774. $25.00.

Is This the Cure?
A comprehensive and timely, non-clinical look at the new issues surrounding recent breakthroughs in HIV and AIDS treatment and care. It raises questions and provides answers about the long-term impact of protease inhibitors, triple-combination "cocktails" and new immune modulation therapies. Leading medical experts reveal emerging strategies for ongoing management of HIV infection and long-term survivors share their insights on facing the new challenges that come with continuing to get better. Features many HIV/AIDS resources, including websites, hotlines, and national and local support organizations. 1996. 30 mins.
VHS: S30497. $19.98.

"It Is What It Is"
An important educational video that discusses teen sexuality, HIV prevention and social isolation, the program is split into three 20-minute segments. The program is accompanied by a discussion guide. "This is the first AIDS education video I've seen that realistically addresses the complex issue of teen sexuality, coming out and AIDS" (Rev. Margaret A. Reinfeld, American Foundation for AIDS Research).
VHS: S18781. $50.00.

Just Say kNOw to AIDS: Abstinence
Teens will learn about HIV and AIDS from doctors and health care experts. Facts are provided by these experts while HIV-positive individuals describe their experiences with the virus. 47 mins.
VHS: S25807. $169.95.

Just Say kNOw to AIDS: Safer Sex
Teens will learn about HIV and AIDS from doctors and health care experts. Facts are provided by these experts while HIV-positive individuals describe their experiences with the virus. 47 mins.
VHS: S25808. $169.95.

Listen Up!
This video provides teenagers with clear information about AIDS. They learn about the difference between HIV and AIDS, methods of transmission, and popular myths spread about the virus. Rap music is provided by Hard Corps. 11 mins.
VHS: S25810. $129.95.

Living Proof
A group of lesbians and gay men dealing with the aftermath of their alcohol and drug addictions speak about the issues related to their communities regarding substance abuse and HIV status in the context of recovery. 28 mins.
VHS: S18779. $50.00.

Living Proof: HIV and the Pursuit of Happiness
Based on Carolyn Jones' photo project of the same name, this documentary follows the lives of subjects seen in that landmark exhibit and book, *Living Proof*. It will change the way people perceive Persons Living with AIDS, that is, PWAs. Men, women and children show that they have not given up but continue to fight and live.
VHS: S22454. $29.95.
Kermit Cole, USA, 1993, 72 mins.

No Rewind
In this fast-paced, award-winning video by Paula Mozen, peer educators and HIV-infected youth speak frankly about sexual and social issues and the importance of abstinence, safe sex and communication toward the prevention of the disease. "*No Rewind* is an excellent video for teens. The individuals in the production bring a sense of reality to the issue of AIDS and teens and help them to start thinking about responsible behavior. I hope as many young people as possible see this video" (Mervyn F. Silverman, M.D., President, American Foundation for AIDS Research). 23 mins.
VHS: S28442. $150.00.

The Plan (Addictions—HIV)
Robert and Eileen have addictive personalities which make their experiences with HIV helpful for those struggling with both chemical dependency and the HIV virus. This video charts their progress from dependency and denial to recovery, and the struggle with this chronic syndrome caused by HIV. 38 mins.
VHS: S25809. $169.95.

Points to Change
Practitioners and patients discuss the philosophy and practice of ear point acupuncture in drug treatment, needle exchange and AIDS services. 25 mins.
VHS: S28412. $25.00.

Positive
The New York City gay community's response to the AIDS crisis is powerfully documented in *Positive*. Rosa von Praunheim has captured the spirit of activism generated by playwright Larry Kramer, musician and co-founder of People With AIDS Coalition (PWA) Michael Callen, and New York filmmaker and journalist Phil Zwickler. They have chosen to act and speak out, refusing to be "AIDS victims." Having neither the time nor the patience to mince words, their groups, like ACT-UP and Queer Nation, demand a response to the epidemic that has threatened to annihilate them. An immensely important historical document.
VHS: S14152. $29.95.
Rosa von Praunheim/Phil Zwickler, USA, 1990, 80 mins.

Positive 20s
Poignant but often humorous, this documentary focuses on a support group for young people dealing with HIV infection. Young people are very much at risk for infection. This documentary offers vital information for everyone. USA, 30 mins.
VHS: S26818. $24.95.

Positive Faith
This documentary tells the story of four avowed Christians who have the HIV virus. One explains how his church reacted to his status. Another relates how a Navy-administered HIV test led to his discharge. One is a survivor since 1979, and the final story belongs to a woman who was infected at age 13. 28 mins.
VHS: S22055. $29.95.

Safer Encounter (Encuentro sin Riesgo)
This is an erotic and explicit video specifically targeted to Latino gay men. It all begins when two sexy men meet at a bar. A variety of techniques are shown that will maker safer sex easier to understand, and just as importantly, a hot time. From New York's Gay Men's Health Crises. 15 mins.
VHS: S19484. $15.00.

Same Stuff, Different Day
An intergenerational discussion on gay identity, community, substance use and HIV and AIDS is presented in this collaboration with Gay Men of African Descent. 20 mins.
VHS: S28417. $15.00.

Steps Toward Change
Four individuals speak about their experiences as participants of Substance Use & Counseling Education's (SUCE) ongoing peer education group for HIV-positive gay men. 20 mins.
VHS: S28416. $15.00.

Talk About It
Six HIV-negative or nontested gay men speak candidly about isolation, oral sex and other issues related to remaining HIV-free. 19 mins.
VHS: S28415. $15.00.

Thumbs Up for Kids: AIDS Education

Former *Romper Room* teacher Ruby Petersen Unger leads this children's discussion about HIV,AIDS and the transmission of the virus. She introduces an HIV-positive youngster with whom the kids can enjoy playing and whom they can also touch. 23 mins.
VHS: S25804. $79.95.

Time Out— The Truth About HIV, AIDS and You

This educational film about AIDS awareness, prevention, and responsibility stars legendary basketball player Magic Johnson and actor and talk show host Arsenio Hall and was directed by Malcolm-Jamal Warner. Features guest appearances by Paula Abdul, Luke Perry, Jasmine Guy, Tom Cruise, Kirstie Alley and others. 42 mins.
VHS: S17105. $19.95.

Video Against AIDS, Volumes 1, 2 & 3

This series of three programs brings together the response of independent film and video makers to the AIDS crisis. *Video against AIDS #1*: *PWA Power* contains *Survival of the Delirious* by Michael Balser and Andy Fabo, which invokes metaphors from Native American mythology and weaves them into a narrative concerned with the often hallucinatory effect the epidemic has on people living with AIDS (14 mins.) and *Work Your Body*, produced by the New York City Gay Men's Health Crisis, offering a variety of life-affirming testimonies from HIV antibody positive people. The second section is concerned with discrimination and contains Amber Hollibaugh and Alisa Lebow's *Second Epidemic*, an informative documentary on discrimination cases negotiated by New York City's Human Rights Commission through the lives of two people living with AIDS. *AIDS and Women* contains several works: *Safe Sex Slut*, a pro-safe sex education reminder from Carol Leigh, a member of the activist prostitutes group, COYOTE; *Cori: A Struggle for Life* (18 mins), which recounts the heroic battle of one woman to care for her baby daughter who has been infected with AIDS from a blood transfusion; and Jean Carlomusto and Maria Maggenti's *Doctors, Liars and Women: AIDS Activists Say "No" to Cosmo* (23 mins.), which documents the angry protest made against *Cosmopolitan* magazine by women from AIDS Coalition to Unleash Power, a protest against the magazine for publishing dangerously misleading information concerning the risk of AIDS to women. *Video against AIDS #2*: The three sections of this program are titled *Resistance, Mourning* and *Community Education*. Canadian producer John Greyson's *The AIDS Epidemic* adopts a music-video format to preach against "ADS"—acquired dread of sex. Barbara Hammer's *Snow Job-The Media Hysteria of AIDS* (8 mins.) critiques the representation of AIDS in the popular press, where the distortions amount to a "snow job" that justifies the continuation of society's practices of homophobia and sexual discrimination. In *We Are NOT Republicans* Adam Hassuk and Robert Huff document the disruption of the 1988 Republican presidential convention by AIDS activists; *Stiff Sheets*, produced by John Goss, similarly indicts public officials and politicians for lack of adequate and humane care of AIDS patients in Los Angeles by documenting a mock fashion show staged by ACT UP activists. *Mildred Pearson: When You Love a Person* recounts a mother's dedication to her son when she learns he is gay and gravely ill from AIDS; *The Inaugural Display of the Names Project Quilt* commemorates the unparalleled public memorial when the Quilt's first 1,920 panels (one for each person dead from AIDS) were unfolded in Washington, D.C. *Danny* (20 mins.), is a heartfelt and complex commemoration of a young man: the stages of Danny's illness are visualized as he discusses his life, his family, and the disease. *Se Met Ko*, by Patricia Benoit, is a model fictional analysis of attitudes and misconceptions about AIDS within a Haitian-American neighborhood. *Video against AIDS #3*: The three sections of this program deal with Loss, Analysis and Activism. Emjay Wilson's *A Plague Has Swept My City* is an associate evocation of the fear and confusion generated by the epidemic. Ann Akiko Moriyasu's *Gab* focuses on a dear friend who died of AIDS; Andre Burke's *A* intricately weaves layers of sound and image to question the threat to sexual desire and identity posed by AIDS. British producer Isaac Julien's *This Is Not an AIDS Advertisement* offers a lyrical and meditative celebration of life and sexuality. Tom Kalin's *They Are Lost to Vision Altogether* is a poetic retaliation against right-wing homophobia and anti-AIDS hysteria; Pratibha Parmar's *Reframing AIDS* offers a wide-ranging global analysis of the AIDS epidemic. Youth Against Monsterz' *Another Man* is a short retort to the Jerry Falwells of the world; *Testing the Limits*, produced by the collective of the same name, documents the range of activist responses to the AIDS crisis. Set of three tapes, produced by the Video Data Bank.
VHS: S16265. $150.00.

Voices from the Front

Shot across North America and Britain, this documentary explains both the rationale and the causes espoused by a generation of AIDS activists. This tape offers a singular opportunity to hear from activists themselves about the nature of their work. It was all about ending the AIDS crises, which is now a worldwide epidemic.
VHS: S27911. $39.98.

Walt Odets on Primary Prevention for Gay Men

Nationally recognized psychologist Walt Odets, author of *In the Shadow of the Epidemic: Being HIV-Negative in the Age of AIDS*, is interviewed in this training video for counselors. 27 mins.
VHS: S28413. $25.00.

What Ramon Did

Esai Morales leads an all-star cast in this drama about a Latino and former IV drug user who returns home. The film begins at a wedding and goes on to explore the feelings of fear and pain that are caused by the lead character's HIV status within his community. Also features an information segment featuring former U.S. Surgeon General C. Everett Koop. 30 mins.
VHS: S25815. $149.95.

SCIENCE

Beyond T. Rex

Did *T. rex* have competition? Recent evidence could damage this superbeast's reputation as the largest meat-eater ever to stalk the earth.
VHS: S34279. $19.95.

Birth of the Lamaze Method

Lamaze, a French physician, developed his method after observing the breathing techniques used by Soviet women preparing for delivery. This amazing film goes right to the source, providing insight into the same birthing techniques that so impressed Dr. Lamaze. 50 mins.
VHS: S12726. $19.98.

Body Atlas Boxed Set

New techniques reveal the interior of the body and all its amazing abilities. Everything is visible, including muscle, bone, skin, the respiratory system, glands and hormones, the senses, the brain, the heart and the reproductive system. This series of six videos was first screened by the Learning Channel.
VHS: S25836. $149.95.

The Bombing of America

NOVA follows investigators using the latest forensic techniques and psychological insights to crack such notorious cases as the World Trade Center and the Unabomber, as well as the proliferation of lesser-known, tragic incidents. 60 mins.
VHS: S31425. $19.95.

Brain Sex

Are men and women really different? Provocative new research offers intriguing evidence that gender differences may actually result from physical differences at the level of the mind. This documentary explores some of the latest research in this area and its weighty implications. Three-volume set, 135 mins.
VHS: S26052. $39.95.

The Brain

Amazing images of the human brain at work and investigations of the brain's mysterious powers in a unique, 3-volume set.
Vol. 1: Evolution & Perception. Travel to the dawn of time and explore the texture of thought of our remote ancestors.
VHS: S23011. $19.95.
Vol. 2: Memory/Miraculous Mind. True tales of damaged brains reveal the intricacies of memory and the remarkable ability of the brain to recover and function.
VHS: S23012. $19.95.
Vol. 3: Matter over Mind. Consciousness, creativity, the emotions, our sense of self—are these all products of biochemistry? Science explores the role of the neurotransmitter serotonin.
VHS: S23013. $19.95.
The Brain, Complete Set. Deluxe boxed set of three volumes.
VHS: S23014. $49.95.

Bug City

Kids will have fun as they learn about all aspects of bug life on this 10-volume set featuring the most dramatic microscopic photography of bugs ever shot. Each episode is hosted by Christina Ricci *(The Addams Family)*, Dr. Art Evans, renowned entomologist and Insect Zoo Director for the Natural History Museum of Los Angeles County, and the mischievous, loveable puppet Bugsy Seagull. Volumes include: *Ants, Aquatic Insects, Bees, Beetles, Butterflies & Moths, Crickets, Grasshoppers & Friends, Flies & Mosquitoes, House & Backyard Insects, Ladybugs & Fireflies* and *Spiders & Scorpions*. Includes teacher's guide. Each tape is 23 mins.
VHS: S33239. $299.50.

The Building Blocks of Life

Clones and genetic engineering, biogenic industries as growth stocks: clearly the age of the computer is giving way to the age of genetics. As a result, *Cell Structure I* and *II* offer an exciting package, anticipating tomorrow's headlines as they examine the basic unit of all life, the cell, of which there are 60 trillion in a single human body.
VHS: S03988. $64.95.

Cellular Automata

A video demonstration, with award-winning science writer Rudy Rucker, of the popular CA Lab cellular automata software. Rapidfire images of hallucinatory beauty. 30 mins.
VHS: S13896. $29.95.

The Coming Plague

This Cable Ace award winner uncovers the frightening reality of a world out of balance where microbes outwit science. 180 mins.
VHS: S34600. $29.98.

Compassionate Use

This in-depth profile explores the use of medical marijuana from the point of view of people who rely on it day to day to relieve their pain and suffering. Also profiles the San Francisco Cannabis Buyers Club, formerly the world's largest medical marijuana emporium.
VHS: S30451. $11.95.
Kent Sugnet, USA, 1996, 20 mins.

Connections 3: Journey on the Web

This humorous and upbeat science series shows that history is filled with seemingly unrelated discoveries that are actually connected in the most surprising ways. Host James Burke delights viewers as he explores the effects and origins of inventions and events that shape the modern world. Volumes include *Feedback, What's in a Name?* and *Drop the Apple*. Three one-hour tapes.
VHS: S32384. $59.95.

Continental Drift

This provocative and entertaining 1980 film uses music, dance and comic scenes to introduce beginning science students and the general public to the history of crustal evolution. 30 mins.
VHS: S31098. $29.95.

Cosmic Travelers Series

Three-volume set uses state-of-the-art 3-D animation, deep-space photographs and computer-generated images to explore asteroids, comets and meteors. Volumes include *Comets & Asteroids, Sudden Impact: Meteors* and *Final Target: Planet Earth*. Each tape is 50 mins.
VHS: S34820. $39.95.

Dinosaur!

Walter Cronkite hosts this four-part series that's part travelogue, part detective story, interweaving state-of-the-art graphics, animation and astonishing special visual effects to explore the dinosaurs.
Birth of a Legend—Tale of an Egg.
VHS: S18769. $19.95.
The First Clue—Tale of a Tooth.
VHS: S18767. $19.95.
Dinosaur! Boxed set of four tapes, or one laser disc. 200 mins.
VHS: S18771. $69.95.
Laser: LD70226. $69.95.

Disney Presents Bill Nye the Science Guy: Dinosaurs, Those Big Boneheads

What large ferocious creatures are loved by every kid on the planet? Dinosaurs of course, and Bill Nye is just the guy to explain to kids the science behind these prehistoric creatures. In-home experiments and special guests help make this another kid-pleasing science adventure. 47 mins.
VHS: S22337. $12.99.

Disney Presents Bill Nye the Science Guy: Outer Space Way Out There

Kids love the puns, jokes and cool science facts that Bill Nye tells. This video is so way out, it's stratospheric. It presents the hard science on outer space in an MTV like format with in-home experiments and special guests. 47 mins.
VHS: S22336. $12.99.

Disney Presents Bill Nye the Science Guy: The Human Body

Bill will take kids on a journey to the inner most parts of the human body. There is no more fun way to explore the cardiovascular system or the nervous system. 47 mins.
VHS: S22338. $12.99.

Ebola: The Plague Fighters

Travel behind the quarantine line with NOVA and the scientists battling to contain the devastatingly deadly Ebola virus. 60 mins.
VHS: S28649. $19.95.

Emergency: Health Care in America— A National Town Meeting

Host Ted Koppel travels to Chicago to discuss the growing problems pointing to the lack of a nationwide comprehensive health care plan. A panel of experts field questions raised by members of a studio audience. 120 mins.
VHS: S16796. $29.98.

Engine Power

Greasy mechanic, gasoline fanatic and *Cracker* star Robbie Coltrane looks at the engines that changed the world, in this six-episode, three-tape set. Episodes include *The V8, The Steam Engine, The Diesel Engine, The Supercharger, The Two Stroke* and *The Jet Engine*.
VHS: S32386. $59.95.

Expansion of Life

Discover the chain of life with this look at the evolutionary spiral. Begin with single-cell life and progress to invertebrates, fish, amphibians, reptiles, then finally explore primates and modern man. 59 minutes.
VHS: S03987. $64.95.

Extreme Machines

Sit behind the wheel of the fastest cars in the world, man a submarine during war maneuvers and plunge into the world of high-tech machinery with this exhilarating three-volume series which helps viewers understand the inner workings of the most powerful—and sometimes the most destructive—inventions ever created. Volumes include *Wheels of Steel/Race Cars/ Rollercoasters, Superplanes/Spaceplanes/Rockets* and *Diving Deep/Choppers/Hovercraft*. 450 mins.
VHS: S31943. $49.95.

Fire from the Sky

Examines the myths surrounding cosmic events and examines the consequences of being hit again. 60 mins.
VHS: S34599. $19.98.

Forces of Life

Here is a four-part study of the essential properties which make up our physical universe. Considered in turn are the *Origin of the Elements, Chemical Change*, the *Origin of Rocks and Mountains* and the dynamics of *Magnetism and Electricity*. This group of films represents a primer for physical science studies.
VHS: S03989. $64.95.

Great Minds of Medicine

Go one-on-one with five of the world's top specialists chosen by the editors of *Health Magazine*. They offer valuable facts on health issues that concern the entire family. The five-volume set includes *Heart Disease* (47 mins.), with Dr. William Castelli; *Cancer* (49 mins.), with Dr. Susan Love; *Infectious Diseases* (46 mins.), with Dr. Karl Johnson; *Mental Illness* (48 mins.), with Dr. Kay Redfield Jamison; and *Emergency Medicine* (45 mins.), with Dr. Peter Rosen. Hosted by Laurie Garrett, Pulitzer Prize-winning reporter and author of *The Coming Plague*. 235 mins.
VHS: S32749. $79.98.

Great Minds of Science

Spend time with the men and women who have transformed and defined science from astronomy to virology. This six-volume set includes *Dinosaurs* (40 mins.), with Dr. Robert Bakker; *Viruses* (44 mins.), with Dr. Robert C. Gallo; *Evolution* (45 mins.), with Dr. Jared Diamond; *Oceanography* (50 mins.), with Dr. Sylvia Earle; *Astronomy* (42 mins.), with Dr. Sallie Balunas; and *Artificial Intelligence* (36 mins.), with Dr. Marvin Minsky. Hosted by Paul Hoffman, former editor-in-chief of *Discover Magazine*. 257 mins.
VHS: S32747. $79.98.

The Great Quake of '89

Produced by ABC News Interactive and hosted by anchor Diane Sawyer, this program investigates the phenomenal destructive capacities of earthquakes, studying the 1989 Loma Prieta earthquake that hit Northern California and the 1906 San Francisco quake.
Laser: LD70112. $49.95.

The Greatest Adventure

NASA footage helps reconstruct the history of space exploration that culminated in the 1969 landing on the moon. From the invention of liquid fuel and Werner Von Braun's experiments with rockets all the way to Neil Armstrong's big step for mankind, the history of scientific discovery is revealed. Narrated by Orson Welles. 54 mins.
VHS: S21098. $14.98.

Heart to Heart: The Truth About Heart Disease

Heart disease is the number one killer of both men and women. This video reveals the facts and disproves the fictions about this silent killer.
VHS: S25007. $14.95.

The Human Sexes

From The Learning Channel. Prepare to be surprised, appalled, confused and intrigued as famed anthropologist Desmond Morris hosts an eye-opening six-part series that challenges the way we look at our sexuality.
VHS: S34908. $89.98.

Hunt for the Serial Arsonist

Follow fire sleuths and the NOVA film crew as they discover the mysterious source of a series of Los Angeles fires and capture an unusual suspect. 60 mins.
VHS: S28651. $19.95.

The Infinite Voyage: Life in Balance

Part of the acclaimed science series. Would you indiscriminately destroy your own home? Undoubtedly, the answer is no. But that is precisely what mankind is doing to Earth. The long-term effects of our disturbances to the ecosystem are unknown, but some researchers say they could be deadly. This program explores the many ways humans of the 20th century are altering evolution. 58 mins.
VHS: S14993. $14.98.

The Infinite Voyage: Miracles by Design

This program studies the personal repercussions of how breakthroughs in science impact our daily lives. 58 mins.
VHS: S19203. $14.98.

The Infinite Voyage: The Champion Within

Part of the acclaimed science series. Explore exercise and physiology to discover the reasons some bodies gain or lose abilities, the mysteries of performance levels, and the impact of aging. Using athletes as living laboratories, scientists are making important discoveries that may affect your life in some unexpected ways. 58 mins.
VHS: S14992. $14.98.

The Infinite Voyage: To the Edge of the Earth

Part of the acclaimed science series. Go with scientists to five far-flung locations where they are using the latest tools to answer some of the planet's oldest questions. Their discoveries could impact how we treat fragile ecosystems in years to come. 58 mins.
VHS: S14994. $14.98.

An Interview with David Bohm: Quantum Physics and Philosophy

David Bohm is a brilliant physicist who blends physics with philosophy. He sees the universe as an undivided wholeness which can only be comprehended with capabilities beyond rational thought. Intuition, insight and intelligence are the human faculties which can grant one experience of this wholeness. 52 mins.
VHS: S26717. $29.95.

Kaboom!

With high-speed photography and dramatic reconstructions, NOVA examines the history of explosives and their role in accidents, war and terrorism. 60 mins.
VHS: S31421. $19.95.

Life on Earth

A natural history written and hosted by David Attenborough—a four hour program on two cassettes. This video encyclopedia spans in detail the complete story of evolution, was filmed in over 100 locations in more than 30 countries, and features amazing wildlife photography. Produced by the BBC. 225 mins.
VHS: S03285. $39.95.

Lifesense

The actual perception of animal senses is beautifully transposed in this award-winning documentary from the BBC. Now people can understand how a host of animals, from the average dog to microscopic parasites, view the world and human beings. 175 mins.
VHS: S26033. $39.98.

Machine Dreams

This wide-ranging film explores mankind's love affair with the machine. From a Marilyn Monroe robot to artificial intelligence, this film traces the enduring fascination and obsession that drives innovation in robotics, cybertechnology and supercomputers.
VHS: S14150. $59.95.
Peter Krieg, Germany, 1989, 87 mins.

Metamorphosis

Rupert Sheldrake, the originator of theory on morphogenetic fields; Ralph Abraham, a mathematics expert on chaos, and Terence McKenna, a shamanologist and ethno-pharmacologist, debate the relationship between chaos, creativity and imagination in this expansive video seminar. 88 mins.
VHS: S26180. $29.95.

Meteorite Impact

Filled with amazing computer graphics, pictures from *Voyager II*, footage of ancient meteor craters and particle specimens from around the world, *Meteorite Impact* tells a fascinating story of science, legend, myth and danger. *Volume 1: Menace from the Sky; Volume 2: Witnesses from Beyond the Times*. Each tape is 84 mins.
VHS: S34578. $19.95.

Mind of a Serial Killer

NOVA follows the FBI's psychological detectives as they race against time to penetrate the mind of a serial killer and stop him from striking again. 60 mins.
VHS: S31426. $19.95.

Miracle of Life

An incredible voyage through the human body as a new life begins. With magnification of up to half a million times, the video actually documents what happens at the moment of conception, and follows the development of the embryo, fetus, and finally, birth. 60 mins.
VHS: S04355. $19.95.
Laser: LD70302. $75.00.

Miracle of Taxila

The true story of an ingenious technique of "assembly line surgery" perfected by Dr. Noval Christy, an American doctor who went to Pakistan in 1949 for a six-month stay and ended up dedicating over 40 years of his life. 47 mins.
VHS: S34522. $19.95.

The Miracle Planet

A six-part series on the mysteries and beauty of the planet. "Serious science delivered like jewels of knowledge amid images and music that create an epic experience" *(Seattle Post Intelligence)*. Narrated by Bill Kurtis.

Life from the Sea. This episode looks at the beauty, depth and size of the blue oceans that cover two thirds of the planet. 60 mins.
VHS: S18235. $29.95.

Patterns in the Air. This program considers the formation of the ozone layer, the emergence of plants and wildlife and the impact of the atmosphere on the life and nature of the planet. 60 mins.
VHS: S18236. $29.95.

Riddles of Sand and Ice. This video looks at the extreme changes in climate. It notes how tropical plants once grew at the South Pole and considers whether these vast changes in temperature and climate might strike again. 60 mins.
VHS: S18237. $29.95.

The Heat Within. This program explores the heat the earth releases from its interior, responsible for breaking continents and the vast mineral deposits. 60 mins.
VHS: S18234. $29.95.

The Home Planet. This program considers the value systems and efforts of humans to safeguard and protect the resources of the planet. 60 mins.
VHS: S18238. $29.95.

The Third Planet. Craters represent the unknown clues about collisions with meteorites. Can we unlock the mystery about the disappearance of the dinosaurs? 60 mins.
VHS: S18233. $29.95.

The Miracle Planet, Set. "A stellar series" *(Booklist)*. 360 mins.
VHS: S19379. $149.95.

Mysteries of Deep Space

Combines live-action sequences, state-of-the-art computer animationand spectacular high-resolution images from the Hubble Space Telescope to present the newest achievements in modern astronomy and a stunning new perspective of the universe. Three-volume set. Three hours.
VHS: S34616. $49.98.

National Geographic Video

The National Geographic Society has always been renowned for their award-winning television specials; now these great programs are available on home video! 60 minutes each.

Miniature Miracle: The Computer Chip. With the help of computers and robots, medical science, aviation and the arts have made tremendous breakthroughs. This fascinating National Geographic special takes a look at what has made it possible: the tiny computer chip.
VHS: S03054. $19.95.

The Incredible Human Machine. Go on a fantastic journey through the inner world of the human body and see, through sophisticated microcamera techniques, the microscopic world inside us.
VHS: S02008. $14.95.

Nova—Adventures in Science: Hurricane!

Follow scientists into the eye of the world's most deadly storms in this amazing documentary. Between walls of hurling clouds ten miles high lies a valley of clear blue sky. First-hand accounts of Hurricane Camille, the most destructive storm to ever strike the United States, and of Hurricane Gilbert, one of the worst hurricanes ever, round out his absorbing look at these powerful weather systems.
VHS: S26910. $19.95.
Larry Engel/Thomas Lucas, USA, 1989, 60 mins.

Nova—Adventures in Science: In Search of Human Origins

Three episodes (*The Story of Lucy, Surviving in Africa* and *The Creative Revolution*) from *Nova* tell the story of the evolutionary past of humanity. From the growth of sexual politics to the birth of technology, all purportedly had a significant impact on the growth of human beings. Three-tape set. Each episode is 60 mins.
VHS: S27325. $59.85.

Nova—Adventures in Science: Making of a Doctor

Beneath the skin of every person is a miraculous world, one explored in this three-part series. *Miracle of Life* starts the series, exploring conception and continuing to follow the progress of a fetus through its wondrous development. In *Universe Within*, a tour of the human body via micro-photography is on offer, while the final installment, *What's New About Menopause*, explores the possibilities and controversies surrounding technological developments that can postpone or even reverse the effects of menopause.
VHS: S27098. $19.95.

Nova—Adventures in Science: Mystery of the Senses

This five-part series explores the five senses through a variety of intriguing segments. From the quietest place on earth, to one of the most fragrant, the five senses shape our perceptions of the world around us. This video shows the richness of the sensual environment.
VHS: S27327. $69.95.

Nova—Adventures in Science: Tornado!

Over one thousand tornadoes, some travelling as fast as 70 miles an hour, occur in the United States every year. The inside of these dynamos can reach 300 miles an hour. *Nova* follows a "chase team": scientists who track these storms.
VHS: S26911. $19.95.
Larry Engel/Thomas Lucas, USA, 1985, 60 mins.

Nova—Coma

In a gripping, real-life drama, *Nova* follows famous neurosurgeon Jam Ghajar as he struggles to save a boy with a massive head trauma, using simple but crucial techniques that are dangerously absent from most hospitals across the country. 60 mins.
VHS: S33077. $19.95.

Nova—Cut to the Heart

Nova covers a controversial surgical technique that could be a breakthrough in treating heart failure. 60 mins.
VHS: S33079. $19.95.

Nova—Danger in the Jet Stream

Come on board with *Nova* as three global challengers attempt non-stop journeys around the world in hot air balloons. 60 mins.
VHS: S33080. $19.95.

Nova—Earthquake

"Only fools, charlatans and liars predict earthquakes…" This exciting analysis challenges an age-old expression with in-depth accounts of possible future predictions of the world's most frightening natural disaster. 1991, 60 mins.
VHS: S16818. $14.98.

Nova—Faster Than Sound

Nova tells the story of those who risked all to make aviation history to break the sound barrier, including Chuck Yeager, who, on October 14, 1947, was the first pilot to fly faster than sound. 60 mins.
VHS: S33081. $19.95.

Nova—The Case of the Flying Dinosaur!

Join *Nova* and biologist Jacques Gauthier in the great debate over whether birds and dinosaurs are related. 60 mins.
VHS: S33076. $19.95.

Nova—The Science of Murder

Statistics say there will be two murders in this country in the next hour. NOVA attempts to find out why we kill ten times more often in the United States than in any other so-called civilized nation in the world. America's medical detectives take on a disturbing case and tell who done it and who will become another statistic. 60 mins.
VHS: S07580. $29.98.

Nova—The Universe Within

This video takes viewers on a journey through the human body. Microscopic photography and stunning graphics make this invisible realm visible.
VHS: S24879. $19.95.

Nova—What's New About Menopause?

New research has transformed our understanding of this stage in the aging process. Now controversy brews as scientists enable women to postpone menopause or even to bear children long after its onset.
VHS: S24876. $19.95.

Nova—Wonders of Plastic Surgery

The techniques of medicine's miracle workers are examined in this fascinating Nova series program. 60 mins.
VHS: S09819. $14.98.

Origin of Life (& Scopes Footage)

Evolution and *Beginnings of Life* start with Darwinian Theory and go on to illustrate the different stages of animal and human development from the beginnings of fossil history. As an update for the contemporary controversy, actual footage of the Scopes Trial with Clarence Darrow and William Jennings Bryan from the Rohauer Collection is included.
VHS: S03773. $64.95.

Origins of Man: Complete Set

Both *Retracing Man's Steps* and *The Big Bang and Beyond* at a special discount.
VHS: S20536. $39.95.

Origins of Man: Retracing Man's Steps

From fossils and bones, paleontologists have pieced together a family tree of man's ancestors. This program follows the rise of symbolic thinking and the development of speech from gestural language in an attempt to trace man's efforts to adapt in the journey of *Homo sapiens*. 33 mins.
VHS: S20534. $19.95.

Origins of Man: The Big Bang and Beyond

An examination of how life began, this program looks at five billion years of evolution in an attempt to understand the structure of the universe. The key to its survival may lie in avoiding the threat from man's own cultural evolution—tool-making, symbolic thought and adaptability. 30 mins.
VHS: S20535. $19.95.

Planet Earth: 7-Volume Boxed Set

Various aspects of the wondrous planet we call home are explored in this inventive and fascinating Emmy Award-winning series. Everything from the conundrums of climate to the Earth's position in the cosmos to the fate of this blue planet are discussed in depth in these videos. Each tape is approximately one hour. Narrated by Richard Kiley. 403 mins.
VHS: S27326. $99.98.

The Quantum Universe

Twentieth-century physics has been shaken to its core by unexpected new theories in quantum mechanics. Through visits to the Harvard Smithsonian Center for Astrophysics and the Stanford Linear Accelerator Center, this video shows how scientists explore these new possibilities. Nobel laureates Sheldon Glashow and Burtin Richter are also featured in a fascinating discussion. 58 mins.
VHS: S29540. $19.98.

Reproduction of Life

Reproduction of Life tastefully and scientifically presents the entire process of human reproduction from conception through prenatal development to birth itself. With *Kittens Are Born*, younger viewers learn first-hand about birth and are helped to develop an enlightened and positive attitude toward the natural phenomenon.
VHS: S03993. $19.95.

The Savage Garden

Wisecracking gardener Leslie Nielsen hosts this look at sex and violence in the insect world. National Geographic Video, using the most advanced microphotography techniques available, offers up a breathtaking, horrifying, close-up view of this savage world in your own backyard. "A Hollywood thriller, laced with scenes of violence, action, stunts, and comedy" *(New York Daily News)*.
VHS: S33044. $19.98.
George D. Dodge/Kathleen M. Dodge/Chase Newhart, USA, 1997, 60 mins.

Science in Action

This award-winning series covers six areas of science in an enlightening and engaging manner. A must-have for schools and libraries and an invaluable aid for hands-on science classes. 18 mins. each.
Color and Light. Explores the origins of color, the basis of primary colors and how light and color impact our perceptions of objects around us.
VHS: S31855. $19.95.
Lenses and Mirrors. Defines types of mirrors and lenses and the different ways light is refracted and reflected from lighthouses to telescopes.
VHS: S31856. $19.95.
Pieces of the Past. Documents how sunken artifacts are scientifically traced, located and retrieved and their importance in determining how ancient people lived. The legendary *Atocha* shipwreck is featured.
VHS: S31860. $19.95.
Pollution. Details the three types of pollution (air, water and noise), how they're created, environmental effects, and methods to reduce, control and recycle waste.
VHS: S31858. $19.95.
Rocks and Minerals. Illustrates the three basic rock formations, the "rock cycle" and how rocks and minerals are used in our daily lives.
VHS: S31859. $19.95.
Solar Energy. Demonstrates how the power of the Sun is captured, transferred and stored to provide a multitude of uses.
VHS: S31857. $19.95.

Science Primer

These special science programs help children understand the five senses, the animal world and the four elements that compose matter. Designed for children from kindergarten through 3rd grade.
Earth, Air, Water, Fire. From ancient civilization, the four basic elements make up matter. This video helps children understand the elements of the world they inhabit. 19 mins.
VHS: S19955. $49.95.
The Five Senses. The five senses are called the "windows of the world," which process signals to the brain and keep us attuned to our environment. This program helps children understand the feelings and information their senses convey. 27 mins.
VHS: S19956. $49.95.
Habitats. Children are introduced to the habitat of plants and animals. The program studies plants and animals in their natural environments, above and below ground, in the sea and in the air. 35 mins.
VHS: S19957. $49.95.
Science Primer, Set. A collection of three programs. 110 mins.
VHS: S19958. $129.00.

Secrets of the Code

The magic of the genetic code is explained through animated graphics. This video explains how different codes make each species and each individual different.
VHS: S23271. $34.95.

Shape of the World Set

A six-tape educational set about cartography, or mapping, from ancient civilization to contemporary times. These "sophisticated, well-edited programs combine exploration, science, religion [and] math" *(Booklist)*. 360 mins.
VHS: S19380. $149.95.

Smithsonian World

A broad intellectual journey into history, science, nature and travel, following the aims and principles of the Smithsonian Institute. The series is a kaleidoscopic and impressionistic account of scientific and technological accomplishment which examines different relations—man to society, the individual to art, and social and cultural movements and their historical context.
Smithsonian World: A Desk in the Jungle. A sympathetic and thrilling document about scientists who specialize in idiosyncratic and quirky subject matter, going beyond traditional science. 60 mins.
VHS: S19194. $14.98.
Smithsonian World: Crossing the Distance. This program studies compelling achievements in science, art and technology and the determination and will of the people responsible. 54 mins.
VHS: S19197. $14.98.
Smithsonian World: Designs for Living. This work looks at man's resourcefulness and valor and his ability to adapt to wildly disparate events, situations and demands. 52 mins.
VHS: S19199. $14.98.
Smithsonian World: On the Shoulders of Giants. This program traces the practices and methods of a scientific sleuth. 58 mins.
VHS: S19193. $14.98.
Smithsonian World: The Last Flower. This documentary examines the painstaking efforts of scientists and activists to devise measures to save vanishing or extinct treasures. 55 mins.
VHS: S19198. $14.98.

Smithsonian World: Tales of Human Dawn

Journey through time and across the continents to explore fascinating and complex stories of human evolution. Anthropologists Richard Potts and Stephan Jay Gould combine storytelling and scientific evidence into insights about being human.
VHS: S29538. $19.98.

Smithsonian World: Web of Life

Marvel at molecular genetics and examine the ethical dilemmas that stem from our new discoveries. *Web of Life* confronts some of the serious issues facing our genetic engineers, through thought-provoking interviews with leading scientists, educators and philosophers.
VHS: S29536. $19.98.

Stephen Hawking's Universe

The world-renowned scientist brings to life one of the most fundamental questions of our time—"Where do we come from?"—on this captivating and easy-to-understand voyage of discovery. Three-volume set. Six hours.
VHS: S34615. $59.98.

Surviving the Big One: How to Prepare for a Major Earthquake

Host Henry Johnson provides a detailed guide to preparing for a major earthquake. The program also provides coping strategies for the difficult weeks after the first major shockwaves.
VHS: S16395. $19.95.

T. Rex: The Real World

Enter the real world of *Tyrannosaurus rex*, the largest carnivore to walk the face of the earth, by traveling to the actual sites where five skeletons have been excavated since 1990. Scientists take you from the dusty prairie into their laboratories as they uncover ancient bones and exciting secrets. Then visit the Black Hills Institute of Geological Research in Hill City, South Dakota, the largest private fossil preparatory on the planet, which is responsible for excavating one-quarter of all significant *T. rex* specimens found to date. 35 mins.
VHS: S31032. $19.95.

Treasures of the Earth

This three-tape boxed set explores the most remarkable materials on earth and how over millennia, they have affected men and women for better or worse. Volumes: *Gold, Diamonds*, and *Pearls & Amber*. Each volume is 52 mins.
VHS: S34070. $49.95.

Understanding Science

This series explains basic scientific principles using clear diagrams and easy-to-follow instructions. Children will be led through fascinating demonstrations that demystify the wonders of science.

Understanding Science, Vol. 1: Scientific Problem Solving. This video explains the correct procedures for solving a quandary the scientific way. A simple experiment is demonstrated that can be easily recreated in the classroom. Lab safety procedures are also presented. 17 mins.
VHS: S22142. $39.95.

Understanding Science, Vol. 2: Matter. Matter's physical and general properties are defined and described in this video. Phase transformations, including gas laws, are included. 22 mins.
VHS: S22143. $39.95.

Understanding Science, Vol. 3: Energy. Dr. Science explains heat energy, how it moves, what substances conduct it, and its relationship to temperature. The wave model is also discussed. 22 mins.
VHS: S22144. $39.95.

Understanding Science, Vol. 4: Ecosystems. Six biomes are compared, with explanations of how plants and animals disperse and interact. The cycles and rhythms of all living things are the focus of this volume.
VHS: S22145. $39.95.

Understanding Science, Vol. 5: Classification of Living Things. The kingdoms which define living organisms are discussed, including the evolutionary adaptations that affect Monera, Protista and Fungi.
VHS: S22146. $39.95.

Understanding Science, Vol. 6: Weather Systems. Weather patterns, atmospheric factors, heat transfers and global wind patterns are all explained in this episode. A historical overview presents the evolution of weather over the course of global climactic change.
VHS: S22147. $39.95.

The Series of Six Volumes.
VHS: S22148. $239.70.

The Video Encyclopedia of Psychoactive Drugs

Scientists, law enforcement agents, counselors, drug historians and professors are brought together in this comprehensive 10-volume set. It provides the most up-to-date information on drug education available. Each volume is 30 mins.

Alcohol and Alcoholism.
VHS: S24473. $39.95.

Alcohol: Teenage Drinking.
VHS: S24474. $39.95.

Amphetamines: Danger in the Fast Lane.
VHS: S24475. $39.95.

Barbiturates: Sleeping Potion or Intoxicant?
VHS: S24476. $39.95.

Cocaine and Crack: The New Epidemic.
VHS: S24477. $39.95.

Heroin: The Street Narcotic.
VHS: S24478. $39.95.

Marijuana: Its Effects on Mind and Body.
VHS: S24479. $39.95.

Nicotine: An Old-Fashioned Addiction.
VHS: S24480. $39.95.

Prescription Narcotics: The Addictive Painkillers.
VHS: S24481. $39.95.

Teenage Depression and Suicide.
VHS: S24482. $39.95.

The Video Encyclopedia of Psychoactive Drugs. The complete 10-volume set.
VHS: S24483. $399.50.

Viruses and Bacteria: The Story of the Warm Wet Spots

Educator and TV personality Ruby Peterson explains how germs cause disease. She shows how the body's interior can nurture and fight off disease. Humor, popular music, demonstrations and computer graphics makes this educational video easy to understand. 21 mins.
VHS: S25801. $149.95.

World Population

This program is a striking depiction of actual population growth from 1 A.D. to the present and of projected future growth to the year 2020. The visual presentation makes the statistical information exciting and easily understood. 1990, 7 mins.
VHS: S13939. $29.95.

Your Family's Health

This series examines some broad, important areas of health, in easy-to-understand language, through six steps. It explores relations between doctors and patients, over-the-counter medicine, headaches, stress, sports injuries and preventative medicine.

Tape 1. This program includes *How to Talk to Your Doctor* and *Over-the-Counter Medicines*. The first segment talks the viewer through appropriate use of the medical system, while the second segment clarifies the many medications available to non-professionals. 53 mins.
VHS: S24921. $29.95.

Tape 2. *Dealing with Headaches* offers practical advice on these common and paralyzing maladies. *Stress* is about a widespread condition that can be alleviated with a variety of techniques. 54 mins.
VHS: S24922. $29.95.

Tape 3. *Kids, Parents, and Sports* addresses the pros and cons of youth sports with expertise provided by coaches and professional athletes. *Preventing Injuries* talks about common sense and risk-taking before outlining preventative measures in five areas. 52 mins.
VHS: S24923. $29.95.

Three-Tape Set.
VHS: S24929. $75.00.

MATHEMATICS

Child's Play Video Flash Cards—Math

An innovative new series of video programs designed to help students learn mathematics, combining basic instructional methods with high tech. The programs are designed to enable students to master the fundamentals of addition, subtraction, multiplication and division. Each program is divided into a training, reinforcement and drill segment. The programs were specifically developed for elementary school students, grades 2-6, and all four programs are available in English and Spanish versions.

Addition (English).
VHS: S06282. $11.95.

Addition (Spanish).
VHS: S06283. $11.95.

Multiplication (English).
VHS: S06284. $11.95.

Multiplication (Spanish).
VHS: S06285. $11.95.

Subtraction (English).
VHS: S06286. $11.95.

Subtraction (Spanish).
VHS: S06287. $11.95.

Division (English)
VHS: S06288. $11.95.

Division (Spanish)
VHS: S06289. $11.95.

Consumer Math

A program for understanding math and its practical applications, including Decimals, Fractions and Percents in the home and business, banking, budgeting, insurance, taxes, profits, discounts, commissions and investments. Study guide included. 120 mins.
VHS: S17478. $39.95.

Expecting Miracles

Four couples candidly explore their problems with infertility over a three year period. A look at the medical processes and techniques doctors use to help increase the chances of having a child. 60 mins.
VHS: S16392. $39.95.

Intermediate Algebra

These videos instruct students in rational numbers, rational expressions, real numbers and radicals, relations and functions, exponential functions, logarithmic functions and quadratic equations. Three-tape set, 360 mins.
VHS: S17479. $119.95.

Math Primer

Lollipop Dragon and Box teach kids important lessons and theories about math and numbers, offering practical instruction on the numbers 0-9, including the concept of a number line, how to understand coins and bills and how to read and set different clocks and watches. Designed for kindergarten through 3rd grade.

Box Introduces Numbers. Students learn how numbers represent a specific quantity, and are given illustrated examples of numerals 0-9 for practical usage and better understanding. 27 mins.
VHS: S19948. $60.95.

Money and Time Adventures of the Lollipop Dragon—I. This important video instructs children about money-counting skills and techniques, explaining the value of dollars and cents. 34 mins.
VHS: S19946. $60.95.

Money and Time Adventures of the Lollipop Dragon—II. Time-skills lessons and exercises show young viewers how to correctly tell time in hours, half-hours and minutes. The program also discusses the proper ways to use time. 34 mins.
VHS: S19947. $60.95.

Math Primer, Set. A set of three programs about number systems and practical applications. 85 mins.
VHS: S19949. $159.00.

Math...Who Needs It?

Meet the famous calculus teacher Jaime Escalante (who inspired the film *Stand and Deliver*), some of his students, plus Bill Cosby, Dizzy Gillespie and other guest celebrities, in this TV special. Ages 8+. 60 minutes.
VHS: S24980. $19.95.

Mathematics Series

Instructors guide these comprehensive video review courses, which can be used either in the classroom or studied independently.

Arithmetic Review. 120 mins.
VHS: S08755. $39.95.

Calculus I. 2 tape set, 240 mins.
VHS: S08760. $79.95.

Calculus II. 2 tape set, 240 mins.
VHS: S08761. $79.95.

Decimals. 120 mins.
VHS: S08757. $39.95.

Elementary Algebra. Ten comprehensive lessons, in a 3 tape, 360-minute set.
VHS: S08759. $159.95.

Fractions. 2 tape set, 240 mins.
VHS: S08756. $79.95.

Percents. 120 mins.
VHS: S08758. $39.95.

Probability. 2 tape set, 240 mins.
VHS: S08762. $79.95.

Statistics. 2 tape set, 240 mins.
VHS: S08763. $119.95.

Pre-Calculus

A preparation video on the prerequisites of the more difficult calculus courses. Topics considered are theory of equations, transcendental functions, polar coordinates, conics, sequences, series, matrix algebra and determinants. Study guide included. Four-tape set, 480 mins.
VHS: S17481. $159.95.

Trigonometry

This program details problems and examples of trigonometric functions, graphs, applications, equations and identities. Two-tape set, 240 mins.
VHS: S17480. $79.95.

SPACE EXPLORATION

America in Space: The First 25 Years

This is NASA's best. 25 years of history-making space exploration compressed into one dynamic program. From the 1958 Explorer 1 launch to the Shuttle Challenger STS-7 flight—and everything in-between—it's all here for you to enjoy. 50 mins.
VHS: S06708. $29.95.

Apollo 13—The Untold Story

Genuine footage of the disastrous Apollo 13 space mission gives this video documentary an incredibly immediate feeling. Interviews with the astronauts who were aboard the completely dead spacecraft and the engineers on the ground convey not just the facts, but the feelings of those involved. Billy Mumy, from *Lost In Space*, hosts. 50 mins.
VHS: S26374. $19.95.

The Apollo Legacy

Beginning with the Apollo space missions, this video explores where that legacy of space exploration will lead. Japan, Russia and the United States all have the commitment to continue exploring our solar system. Inhabited space stations and even peopled missions to Mars lie in the not too distant future. 45 mins.

VHS: S26762. $14.98.

The Astronomers: Collector's Set

We have learned more about the universe in the last ten years than we have in the last several centuries combined; this series imparts that recently discovered knowledge. Narrated by acclaimed actor Richard Chamberlain, *The Astronomers* was produced with the largest grant ever for a single public TV series, and it took over five years to complete. This collector's edition includes all six of the fascinating programs in the popular PBS series. 360 mins. Six videocassettes.

VHS: S13816. $79.98.
Laser: LD70845. $124.95.

Blue Planet

Using photographic evidence collected by astronauts on five space shuttle missions, *Blue Planet* is a breathtaking view of Earth from deep space. The program also examines the ecological systems that shape the Earth's future. "A stunning look at our planet as a living being—beautiful, volatile and extremely vulnerable" *(The Washington Post)*. 42 mins.

VHS: S19741. $29.95.
Laser: LD71942. $39.95.

Blueprint for Space

This program charts the evolution of spaceflight, focusing on the visionaries and dreamers who designed, developed and paved the way for space travel. The film merges rare paintings, archival footage and computer animation to examine the earliest conceptions, such as ancient Chinese rockets and today's scientific breakthroughs. Narrated by astronaut Alan Shepard. 58 mins.

VHS: S19740. $24.95.

Conquest

A thrilling look at man's shining achievements in space. See how the dream of traveling to the moon was realized by scientists as we trace back to World War II planning and progress, to modern day technology. 180 mins.

VHS: S12735. $59.98.

Contact UFO: Alien Abductions

First in a series dedicated to evaluating evidence regarding UFOs, *Alien Abductions* reveals theories from a number of leading experts, including Boston Planetarium astronomer Walter Webb, *Intruders and Missing Time* author Budd Hopkins, Center for UFO Studies President Mark Rodeghier and Betty Hill, a UFO abductee. 90 mins.

VHS: S16201. $19.98.
Laser: CLV. **LD74642. $29.98.**

Cosmos 9: The Lives of the Stars

Using computer animation and amazing astronomical art, astronomer and Cosmos host Dr. Carl Sagan shows how stars are born, live, die and sometimes collapse to form neutron stars and black holes. Viewers then journey to the future to witness the last perfect day on Earth, 5 billion years from now, after which the Sun will engulf our planet in its fires.

VHS: S10699. $19.98.

Cosmos 13: Who Speaks for Earth?

Through the use of startling special effects we retrace the 15-billion-year journey from the Big Bang to the present. The tragic story of the martyrdom of Hypatia, the woman scientist of ancient Alexandria, is told. This is the famous *Cosmos* episode on nuclear war in which Dr. Sagan argues that our responsibility for survival is owed not just to ourselves but also to the Cosmos, ancient and vast, from which we spring.

VHS: S10703. $19.98.

Cosmos Gift Pack B

Episodes 6-9 of *Cosmos* plus the Cosmos paperback for free.

VHS: S10706. $79.98.

Creation of the Universe

Award-winning science journalist Timothy Ferris hosts this widely acclaimed exploration of some of the most challenging theories in contemporary science. Dazzling special effects, music by Brian Eno, and an interview with Dr. Stephen Hawking. *Science* magazine hails it as "...nothing short of a masterpiece." 90 mins.

VHS: S12940. $19.98.
Laser: CLV. **LD70104. $49.95.**

Destination: Universe

Tackles America's involvement in space exploration from the past, present and future. 44 mins.

Laser: LD70248. $29.95.

The Dream Is Alive

Narrated by Walter Cronkite, this is arguably the best space documentary ever made. Over 25 million viewers have enjoyed this film in the giant IMAX theaters countrywide—an experience the astronauts say is "the closest to being there." Take a window seat on the space shuttle and experience man's dream of living and working in space. Hi-Fi Surround Stereo. USA, 40 mins.

VHS: S15076. $29.95.
Laser: LD70274. $39.95.

Earth to Space for Peace

Dr. Carol Rosin, president of the Institute for Security and Cooperation in space, actively works with others to bring about a joint space program with the Soviets to stop the Strategic Defense Initiative. Here she explains how space programs help to unite the world in contrast to the way military programs divide it. 90 mins.

VHS: S10221. $29.95.

Exploration: Space

Four films—*Mysteries of the Universe, Astro Smiles, Mercury Exploration* and *Challenger Explosion*—show the achievements of NASA. This collection reveals the mysteries of space. 120 mins.

VHS: S24691. $39.95.

Eyes in the Sky

Satellites serve myriad human needs, from tracking endangered species to charting weather patterns. The Discovery Channel produced this documentary which explains the functions of these new global telecommunications tools. 100 mins.

VHS: S29421. $19.95.

Filling in the Blanks

This documentary takes its viewers behind the frenzied efforts to restore the Smithsonian's Air and Space Museum, the site's most popular tourist attraction.

VHS: S16872. $14.98.

Flight of the Dream Team

An exhilarating portrait of the world's finest skydivers performing their ballet of movement and "aerobatics" to R.J. Miller's musical score.

Laser: LD70249. $34.95.

Flyers

Flyers has earned a permanent place in film history for its unforgettable stunt flying sequences. A stuntman falls from the wing of one airplane and is rescued in mid-air by a companion plane, a Corsair crashes on the deck of a carrier, and an F-15 test flight clocks in at 2½ times the speed of sound. From the IMAX Motion Picture, in Surround Sound. 34 mins.

Laser: CAV. **LD71493. $39.95.**

For All Mankind

From 1968 to 1972, 24 astronauts traveled to the moon. This is their story, told in their words, in their voices, using the images of their experiences. Winner of the Grand Prize at Utah's Sundance Film Festival in 1989.

Laser: CLV. **LD70986. $52.95.**
Laser: CAV. **LD70987. $99.95.**

From Disaster to Discovery: The Challenger Explosion

The story of the *Challenger* explosion and the seven who died, as well as the investigation into the fiasco. Finally, the rebirth of the shuttle system is highlighted and America's return to space. From ABC News. 60 mins.

VHS: S12689. $24.98.

From Here to Infinity

Patrick Stewart hosts this video exploration that travels to the known ends of the universe and beyond. State-of-the-art computer graphics and never-before-seen spacescapes make this documentary a must for sci-fi fans and trekkers. 43 mins.

VHS: S25833. $14.95.

Hail Columbia!

From its opening shots of the Kennedy Center launch, this documentary examines the 1981 maiden voyage of Columbia, the first space shuttle. 40 mins.

Laser: LD71945. $39.95.

History of Flight and The Golden Days of Flight

Two NASA programs in one. The first examines man's quest to fly farther, faster and higher as well as the technology that enabled him to do so; the second takes us back to the first days of powered flight as aviation pioneer Paul Garver relates his experiences with Orville Wright, Charles Lindbergh, Glenn Curtis, Amelia Earhart and Howard Hughes. 56 mins.

VHS: S06705. $29.95.

Hoagland's Mars, Vol. I, The NASA/Cydonia Briefings

Richard Hoagland presents new theories of the tetrahedral geometries of the Cydonian structures—which he believes are evidence that intelligent life existed on Mars. 83 mins.

VHS: S20162. $34.95.

Hoagland's Mars, Vol. II, The U.N. Briefing, the Terrestrial Connection

Drawing on computer-enhanced photos from NASA's 1976 Viking mission, Richard Hoagland explores the relationship between the "face," a pyramid-like structure surrounding Mar's Cydonia region, and some ancient Earth monuments, including the Sphinx. 80 mins.

VHS: S18037. $44.95.

Hoagland's Mars, Vol. III, The Moon/Mars Connection

Are there ancient alien bases on the moon? Richard Hoagland presents evidence of extraterrestrial intelligence in this comprehensive three-hour video. He links moon bases to those bases he discovered on mars.

VHS: S24694. $49.95.

Hubble Space Telescope: Rescue in Space

Follow the astronauts of NASA during one their most daring and important space flights ever, the retrieval and repair of the Hubble space telescope. Images from this complex machine offer dramatically improved views deep into outer space. This documentary follows the mission from pre-flight preparation all the way through to the successful completion of this historic task. 50 mins.

VHS: S21774. $24.95.

The Infinity Series: Part 1—The Solar System

Using moving images and photographs captured from NASA and other leading observatories, this program considers the solar system from the perspective of alien guides, looking at the sun and its relationship to the planets and their moons, the asteroids and comets and their working systems. The program also looks at the formation of the solar system and the planets. 60 mins.

VHS: S18469. $19.95.

The Infinity Series: Part 2—Deep Space

This program looks at the formation of the universe, its growth and development, the evolution and death of various types of stars, and the status, destination and eventual death of the universe. 60 mins.

VHS: S18470. $19.95.

The Infinity Series: Part 3—The Light Beyond Light and Life

Part 3 examines the dark edges of the universe, the probability of extraterrestrial existence and what their life might entail. 60 mins.

VHS: S18471. $19.95.

The Infinity Series: Part 4—The Crystal Space/Time Ship

The final segment considers the metaphysical "soul" of the universe and everything that falls under its realm. With music by the Celestial Mechanics. 45 mins.

VHS: S18472. $19.95.

Jupiter, Saturn and Uranus

The Voyager Missions in this film produced by the Jet Propulsion Laboratory for NASA, taking the viewer on a billion-mile journey to the giant planets, exploring the planets, moons, magnetic fields, geology and weather through the eyes of Voyager 1 and 2. 58 mins.

VHS: S06710. $29.95.

Jupiter, Saturn, Uranus & Neptune

An all-new video program featuring the very latest images, information and computer animation from the missions to the outer planets, including Voyager's last stop in our Solar System—Neptune. USA, 30 mins.

VHS: S15077. $29.95.

Kennedy Space Center: Window to the Universe

Tour NASA's awesome launch facilities and exhibits and re-live many of the history-making missions which blasted off here. 30 mins.

VHS: S06687. $29.95.

Lift Off to Space

This program gives a complete history of the rivalry between the U.S. and the Soviet Union to be the first on the moon, using spectacular footage of Glenn's first orbit and Armstrong's first steps. 60 mins.
VHS: S13115. $19.98.

Liftoff

Patrick Stewart narrates this exciting behind-the-scenes documentary, which follows the crew of the spacecraft Columbia on a successful mission. These astronauts repair a satellite and retrieve the stranded Long Duration Facility from a dangerously low orbit. From their dramatic perspective, forest fires in the Amazon and even their nighttime landing provide a dazzling new experience. 50 mins.
VHS: S21874. $19.98.

Man on the Moon

Culled from 32 hours of CBS footage of the mission to the moon, this program includes a retrospective interview with Walter Cronkite and all of the three astronauts, as well as a look back at President Kennedy's historic 1960's speech that set the stage for that decade's space exploration program.
VHS: S09604. $19.95.

Mars Lives

Footage of new evidence and animations explore the controversy of life on Mars. 46 mins.
VHS: S31403. $19.95.

Mercury Spacecraft Missions and Legacy of Gemini

The drama of the first years of America's space programs with two historical NASA programs. The Mercury and Gemini missions gave us many firsts in space, and the videos explore space veterans in action—John Glenn, Ed White, Virgil Grissom, and many others. 56 mins.
VHS: S06707. $29.95.

Meteorites

Tens of hundreds of small meteorites strike the earth every year. These messengers from the heavens could tell us the secrets to the formation of the solar system. Or one large one could destroy the world as we know it. These objects, worshipped by the Anasazi, are thoroughly explored in this fascinating documentary package, with computer graphics and images from Voyager II. 84 mins.
VHS: S22455. $29.95.

Moon Shot

In this documentary, new footage never seen before shows the behind the scenes story of this historic challenge that changed forever man's relationship to outer space. It was not just a race between nations, but a race between the men who flew, the astronauts themselves. 189 mins.
VHS: S21209. $19.98.

National Geographic Video: For All Mankind

Al Reinert's documentary uses the footage of the Apollo flights as found art, from John Kennedy's bold proclamation of the New Frontier to a stylized rumination on the vast expansiveness, infinity and peculiar serenity of space.
VHS: S18840. $19.95.
Al Reinert, USA, 1989, 80 mins.

The New Solar System

The space age has revealed hitherto unsuspected secrets about our own corner of the universe. This documentary brings those discoveries together. The inner planets, gas giants, a comet crashing into Jupiter, asteroids, volcanoes and more are explored in this fascinating video. 60 mins.
VHS: S23973. $24.95.

Nova— Countdown to the Invisible Universe

The entire universe is revealed in a whole new way. A spacecraft called IRAS explores the infrared wavelength beyond the rainbow and maps this previously hidden region of the sky.
VHS: S24883. $19.95.

Nova—Death of a Star

On February 23, 1987, one of the most violent events since the creation of the universe was observed by a Canadian astronomer, and then by scientists worldwide. It was the first supernova visible at close range in nearly 400 years.
VHS: S24884. $19.95.

Nova—Eclipse of the Century

During the total solar eclipse of July 11, 1991, scientists struggled to pack all the scientific experiments and measurements possible into a brief span. The eclipse lasted just four minutes and luckily it was visible from the advanced observatories of Mauna Kea.
VHS: S24885. $19.95.

Nova—One Small Step

How did America win the Space Race? A look at the first orbit around the Earth, the Mercury and Apollo missions, and the Russian and American space race. 60 mins.
VHS: S09405. $14.98.

Nova—Rescue Mission in Space

This video follows the astronauts of the Space Shuttle mission to repair the Hubble Space Telescope. In addition, this video shows the stunning work performed by the telescope since its repair.
VHS: S24877. $19.95.

Nova—Russian Right Stuff: The Mission

This episode chronicles the arduous training of cosmonauts involved in the Soviet Space Station MIR. 1991, 60 mins.
VHS: S16817. $14.98.

On Robot Wings: A Flight Through the Solar System

Features footage from Jet Propulsion Laboratory; you'll fly *On Robot Wings* over planets and moons as if aboard a high-speed, low-flying spacecraft and explore—close-up—the features of Earth, Venus, Mars and Uranus' moon Miranda. 30 mins.
VHS: S16627. $24.95.

One Giant Leap

The untold, inside story of the Apollo 11 moon mission is revealed in this documentary from the Discovery Channel. Young, brazen scientists entered into one of the greatest calculated risks in history in order to conquer the trip to the moon.
VHS: S23225. $19.95.

One Small Step for Man

A captivating look at the story of the Apollo missions, culminating with Armstrong's historic walk on the moon.
60 minutes.
VHS: S02293. $39.95.

Planet Mars and Mercury

Two NASA programs tracing man's sometimes imaginative theories of Mars, from its discovery in 1669 to the historic Viking landing on its surface. The second program explores the planet Mercury in startling detail, with photographs and findings from the Mariner 10 mission. 52 mins.
VHS: S06706. $29.95.

The Planets

A wonderful depiction of the planets from the perspective of photographs taken from the U.S. and Soviet space flights, computer animation and digital special effects. The program is scored by Isao Tomita and heavily influenced by Gustav Holst's musical suite, "The Planets." "Factual, fascinating, beautiful and just plain fun" *(The Planets)*. 56 mins.
VHS: S17628. $19.98.
Laser: CAV. **LD72222. $29.95.**

The Planets Deluxe Collector's Edition

A special collector's edition of the space program *The Planets*, with some supplementary materials, including four color posters by Geoffrey Chandler, a facts booklet, Peterson First Guides *Astronomy*, and the U.S. Space Camp catalog. 56 mins.
VHS: S17629. $34.98.

Racing for the Moon: America's Glory Days in Space

The story of America's race for space; from the shock of Sputnik to John Glenn's first orbit to Armstrong's first steps on the moon. From ABC News.
VHS: S12685. $24.98.

Satellite Imaging: The Jet Propulsion Laboratory

These four movies demonstrate a variety of remarkable data visualization techniques. They include a startling aerial ride over a three-dimensional Southern California landscape and a simulated flight over the towering mountains and steep canyons of Miranda, a moon of Uranus. 20 mins.
VHS: S13897. $19.95.

Satellite Rescue in Space: Shuttle Flights 41C & 51A

Join the shuttle crew as they narrate the most interesting and spectacular scenes to date depicting life aboard the space shuttle. 42 mins.
VHS: S06686. $29.95.

Smithsonian Air and Space, Dreams of Flight: Beyond the Moon...

It all began with man's first steps on the lunar surface during the Apollo 11 mission. Now dreams of exploring worlds beyond our solar system fire the imagination. This video discovers the reality within the dream. 50 mins.
Laser: LD74751. $34.95.

Smithsonian Air and Space, Dreams of Flight: To the Moon...

This video is another chapter in the never-ending saga of mankind's dreams of flight. Visionaries like H.G. Wells paved the way for man's adventures in space. In this story, science fiction becomes science fact. 50 mins.
Laser: LD74750. $34.95.

Solar Empire

Armed with science, history and contemporary pop culture, this three-volume, six-episode program from The Discovery Channel journeys through the wonders of outer space to bring to life the story of our solar system and its planets with stunning space photography and high-quality computer animation. Volumes include *A Star Is Born/Alien Neighbors, Space Trek/Impact 3* and *Heavens Above/Edge of Darkness*. 100 mins.
VHS: S31942. $49.95.

Space Age Program

A six-part documentary series on space exploration. Narrated by Patrick Stewart, the program considers the quest for Mars, celestial sentinels, satellites, the moon and the origins of the universe, as well as a philosophical and scientific inquiry into the nature of heaven.
Space Age Program 1: Quest for Planet Mars.
VHS: S17712. $24.95.
Space Age Program 2: Celestial Sentinels.
VHS: S17713. $24.95.
Space Age Program 3: The Unexpected Universe.
VHS: S17714. $24.95.
Space Age Program 4: To the Moon and Beyond.
VHS: S17715. $24.95.
Space Age Program 5: Mission to Planet Earth.
VHS: S17716. $24.95.
Space Age Program 6: What's a Heaven For?
VHS: S17717. $24.95.

Space Dreaming

Marianne Dolan's expressive, sensual and quite beautiful celestial ballet of images, movement, sound, dance and the origins of creation, in collaboration with composer Steve Roach. 30 mins.
Laser: LD70242. $24.95.

Space Race

From the Soviet point of view. When the USSR put a rocket named Sputnik in the air, the United States came to attention. This program portrays the enthusiasm for space exploration, and the movie-star-like celebrity of Yuri Gagarin, the astronaut who captured the attention of the nation and the world. 100 mins.
VHS: S12712. $24.95.

The Space Shuttle

From Mission Control in Houston, the Discovery Channel brings the story of America's premier spacecraft. The technicians and scientists that keep the shuttle working and flying have an immense and complicated task. They must not only get it off the ground but they must bring it back intact.
VHS: S23224. $19.95.

Space Shuttle: Flights STS-1 Through STS-8

Enjoy the triumphs of the first eight shuttle flights. Features two NASA films—*Opening New Frontiers* and *We Deliver*—summarizing the accomplishments of flights 1 through 8. Includes spectacular views from space, satellite deployments, experiments and more. 60 mins.
VHS: S06709. $29.95.

Spies Above

Intelligence-gathering satellites changed the course of history. This documentary from the Discovery Channel was produced with the cooperation of the CIA and the secretive NRO. Actual photos from spy satellites and top secret locations are part of this expose of these powerful tools of espionage. 50 mins.
VHS: S29420. $39.95.

Stargazers

For 100 years the Lowell Observatory in Flagstaff, Arizona, has been the site of important scientific discoveries. From Percival Lowell's declaration that Mars had been shaped by advanced civilizations, to the discovery of Pluto, this institution has served science. The Discovery Channel produced this video to celebrate their centennial celebration. Patrick Stewart narrates. 60 mins.
VHS: S29422. $19.95.

Symphony to the Planets

Leonard Nimoy narrates this double video set which examines the history of our galaxy and man's exploration of space. Two episodes, *Part One: A Star to Call Home* and *Part Two: Mysteries Beyond Our Reach*, combine footage and resources from NASA and the National Air and Space Museum in Washington, D.C. Classical music comprises the score. Two-tape set, 120 mins.
VHS: S26366. $29.95.

Time and Light

Part of the PBS series drawing on the resources of the Smithsonian Institution, *Time and Light* explores time as measured by man, plants and animals, peering into the vast stretches of space to the origins of time as reflected in Earth's most distant stars.
VHS: S16871. $14.98.

To Be an Astronaut

From the archives of ABC News, this overview of America's space program starts with the preparation for the seven original Mercury astronauts, through the daring odysseys of Apollo, to today's Shuttle experience. 45 mins.
VHS: S10851. $14.95.

Universe (Mastervision)

A comprehensive look at what mankind knows today about our sun and solar system as well as the seemingly infinite number of other stars and galaxies in all universal space and time. An awe inspiring look at the heavens in all their majesty and mystery.
VHS: S03985. $64.95.

Universe (Shatner)

Journey through our solar system and beyond to the Milky Way with William Shatner as he takes you on an information-packed tour of the Universe. Learn the theories behind black holes, pulsars, and other space phenomena. 30 minutes.
VHS: S03774. $29.95.

Uranus: I Will See Such Things

Ancient moons with 16-mile-high cliffs and surface temperatures 300 degrees below zero. The geology, the weather, the moons, the magnetic fields—even the operation of Voyager 2—all are explored. 29 mins.
VHS: S06679. $29.95.

Voyage to the Outer Planets and Beyond

Isaac Asimov presents this musical video voyage in outer space—in a classical music video which features rare NASA and JPL footage set to the music of Gustav Holst's *The Planets*. This musical video voyage through space includes a NASA-prepared brochure, "A Look at the Planets", "Space Almanac", and a list of astronomical events between now and the year 2001. 54 mins.
VHS: S06321. $39.95.

The Voyager Odyssey

A journey through infinity, the outer reaches of the solar system, captured in this documentary combining space photography, computer animation, and special digital effects, in the four-billion-mile trip from Jupiter to Neptune. "A gorgeous, inspirational experience that's stunning in its audio quality and video excellence" *(Entertainment Weekly)*. 44 mins.
Laser: LD70246. $34.95.

A Walk Through History

This exhaustive look at the Apollo 11 space mission documents the first human space walk. Spectacular photography of the Earth and the landscape features of the Moon add to the excitement. It all culminates with the planting of the American flag on lunar soil. 22 mins.
VHS: S26761. $9.98.

We Remember: The Space Shuttle Pioneers 1981-1986

The first and only complete documentary on the landmark adventures of America's Space Shuttle during the first five years, from Columbia's first launch to Challenger's final mission. A unique historic program. 58 mins.
VHS: S08137. $29.95.

Where None Has Gone Before

A subjective view of the Voyager's around the world flight, and the development of the space telescope and its extraordinary capacity to see seven times greater into space and examine previously hidden underwater caves.
VHS: S16873. $14.98.

TRANSPORTATION

The 10 Greatest American Cars

A look at the evolution of the design, styling and engineering of the best American cars. The program assembles a group of experts, automotive writers, collectors and critics to debate and discuss the craftsmanship, speed and muscle of the greatest machines. Photographed by Bill Anwelier. Narrated by Jack Perkins. 50 mins.
VHS: S19345. $19.95.

21st Century Jet

Boeing's 777 represents a $5 billion undertaking in technological, organizational and marketing terms. This documentary shows the first critical year of progress in the manufacturing of this flying marvel. 58 mins.
VHS: S25734. $19.95.

777: First Flight

The Boeing 777 is the largest, most complex aircraft ever built. It is the first to be designed electronically. This video exposes the drama of its test period. All aspects of the process, from the top corporate level to the workers who build and maintain it, are on view. This reflects a new corporate attitude of no secrets and no rivalry. 57 mins.
VHS: S25735. $19.95.

The Air Mail Story

Produced in collaboration with the Smithsonian Institutions' National Postal Museum and the U.S. Postal Service, this program looks at the pioneering efforts in air mail postage and its contribution to modern aviation. 40 mins.
VHS: S17178. $19.95.

Always Ready: The U.S. Coast Guard Story

Founded in 1789 to end smuggling, this is the story of the invaluable arm of the U.S. Navy. 45 mins.
VHS: S13133. $29.98.

The American Experience: The Wright Stuff

Though they were only the proprietors of a small bicycle shop in Dayton, Ohio, the Wright Brothers surprised the world with their ingenuity. In the process, they also outdid the world's best scientific minds. This video tells of their achievement. 60 mins.
VHS: S29913. $19.95.

Amtrak's X2000 Demonstration

The need for development and refining new equipment to serve the Northeast Corridor paved the way for the sleek, high-speed X2000, a cutting-edge Amtrak train that astounded people with its futuristic design, speed and comfort. 30 mins.
VHS: S20085. $19.95.

Anchors Away: The U.S. Navy Story

From its birth more than two centuries ago to its accomplishments in Vietnam, this is an historical account of the Navy and its missions. 45 mins.
VHS: S13132. $29.98.

Antique Farm Tractors

Explores the history of this primary tool of agriculture and engine for social change and takes viewers to farms, tractor shows and collector craftsmen. 60 mins.
VHS: S34071. $19.95.

Battleship

Explore some of the mighty dreadnoughts that helped propel the world into war: *Bismarck*, with almost half its weight in armour, and *Yamato*, whose suicide mission ended in a mushroom cloud visible for 50 miles. See how fate of war often hinges on the brute strength of the battleship: from the bitter legacy of the *Prince of Wales* and *Repulse*, the first battleships sunk by aircraft, to the aging USS *Missouri*, a survivor of WWII, recently fortified with modernized firepower to emerge as an invincible Gulf War force. From the Discovery Channel. 100 mins.
VHS: S31832. $19.95.

Bicycle: A Celebration of the Invention

This new video from the BBC celebrates every aspect of the evolution of the bike, from its earliest form to the achievements of Eddie Merckx and Greg LeMond at the Tour de France. 115 mins.
VHS: S16559. $34.95.

Blue Angels

Dennis Quaid narrates as the *Blue Angels*, a top-notch flight team, demonstrate precision flying using the most advanced military jets. The F-18 Hornet offers an unforgettable ride. Music by Queen, Billy Joel and Los Lobos is included. 100 mins.
VHS: S22088. $29.95.

Blue Angels: Around the World at the Speed of Sound

The thrill, precision and aerial artistry of the Navy's Blue Angels. Host Dennis Quaid opens the cockpit on this legendary squadron as they take off on their first European tour in 20 years. Footage includes the Angels over Russia, where they encounter MIG fighters, and the team's illustrious history, revealed through archival footage. 100 mins.
VHS: S21902. $29.95.

Branchline Railway

The late Sir John Betjeman presents this little known film which captures the atmosphere of the 24-mile stretch of the now vanished Somerset and Dorset railway. It celebrates a working, living railway complete with dirty locomotives, clean stations with flowers, and austere gas-lit waiting rooms, in a return to a vanished age. 47 mins.
VHS: S07612. $19.94.

British Rail Journeys

Four volumes covering the British Isles from the unique vantage point of British Rail are included in this set. Within each region a wide-ranging itinerary shows the alternating dramatic and gentle landscapes which are famous the world over. Included are *Northern England: Settle to Carlisle, North Wales: Chester to Aberystwyth, Central Highlands: Edinburgh to the Isle of Skye* and *South West: Exeter to Penzance*. Each video is 55 mins.
VHS: S27641. $79.80.

The Bugatti

Ettore Bugatti and his famous cars are detailed in this two-volume video set. Both the interesting story of this industrialist and the evolution of his cars, from the 10 prototype to the Type 57G, are included. 100 mins.
VHS: S29991. $49.95.

Carrier: Fortress at Sea

The *Discovery Channel* brings a month aboard an actual aircraft carrier to light in this illuminating video. On multiple stories, 5800 men and women work day and night to keep a deadly arsenal of conventional and nuclear weapons ready for use. 100 mins.
VHS: S26051. $24.95.

Choppers

This program follows the colorful evolution of the helicopter, from initial conception to today's complex machines. Includes information on how choppers were used in times of war. 60 mins.
VHS: S13124. $19.98.

Christmas Trains

In this festive video, nine different venues are visited where you'll see everything from operating steam locomotives to toy trains and special garden railroads decorated for the holidays. The sounds of familiar carols and joyful Christmas music enhance the stunning visual images. It's the greatest variety of Christmas trains ever recorded on video.
VHS: S30474. $19.95.

Citizen Soldiers: The U.S. Army Story

Using rare, restored footage and photographs, the triumphs over the British through the present are interwoven into a comprehensive history of America's armed victories. 45 mins.
VHS: S13134. $29.98.

Cleared for Takeoff

Fred Levine leads kids through the nation's busiest airport, Chicago's O'Hare. An actual United Airlines pilot takes kids into the control tower, the luggage sorting area and the front row seat of a jet.
VHS: S25688. $19.95.

Col. Culpeper's Flying Circus

Deep in the heart of Texas lies the airfield of the Confederate Air Force, where a dedicated group of volunteers have restored and preserved vintage 1939-45 war planes in flying condition. Their skillfully recreated air battles feature Messerschmitts, Spitfires, Mustangs and Flying Fortresses. 50 mins.
VHS: S03418. $19.94.

Dawn of the Jet Age: The First 25 Years

This program traces the first 25 years of the jet plane, beginning with pilots and designers of the 30's, to the first breaking of the sound barrier, to wartime jet use. 60 mins.
VHS: S13121. $19.98.

Driving the Dream

Harrod Blank, who took us into the world of art cars with his epic *Wild Wheels*, now focuses on the Grass Bus, the Hamburger Harley, and the camera van in a dauntless look at American car culture.
VHS: S34145. $29.95.
Harrod Blank, USA, 1998, 29 mins.

Early Birds

An interesting, informative look into the world of automotive nostalgia, highlighting the 1955, 1956 and 1957 models of the Thunderbird—a product of the Ford Motor Company. Burt Reynolds and Glen Campbell are out for a quick spin while Ronald Hughes narrates an interview with Thunderbird restoration expert Jim Weatherly. 41 mins.

VHS: S11115. $14.95.

The Ferrari Collection

The legendary Ferrari automobile has continually been at the forefront of technical innovation and style. This ultimate Ferrari video collection highlights the details of seven legendary models and contains thrilling behind-the-wheel driving footage. 210 mins.

VHS: S30065. $99.95.

Flights of Courage

Features stunning aerials of vintage biplanes of the U.S. Air Mail Service from 1918 to 1927, from the Eastern forests to the Rocky Mountains. With archival footage. 55 mins.

VHS: S32200. $19.95.

Floating Palaces

Early in the 20th century the mighty maritime nations competed to build the most advanced and opulent oceanliners. This four-part series tells the story of these spectacular ships, including the *Titanic*, the *Andrea Doria*, the *Lusitania*, the *Normandie* and others. Each episode is hosted from aboard the *QE II* during her 999th Atlantic crossing and is approximately 50 mins. long.

VHS: S29398. $59.95.

Flying Machines

Meet the Smithsonian staff dedicated to preserving the history of aviation. This exhilarating look at the National Air and Space Museum presents cockpit-views of the Wright Flyer, the Spirit of St. Louis and the Enola Gay. 1989, 60 mins.

VHS: S14543. $29.95.
Laser: LD70224. $34.95.

Flying the Blimp

Revisit the giant airships that ruled the skies—before the *Hindenburg* disaster dashed their promise—and find out how latter-day blimp builders are resurrecting these lighter-than-airmachines. From NOVA. 60 mins.

VHS: S31430. $19.95.

Formula 1 Saga

An exciting series that takes us into the world of circuits, champions and their cars from the beginning of Formula 1 racing until today. Rare footage features the legends of Formula 1 racing, including Stirling Moss, Alain Prost, Jackie Stewart, Ayrton Senna, Niki Lauda, Nigel Mansell and others. Great cars in action: Renault, BMW, Mercedes, Ferrari, Fiat, Alfa Romeo and more.

Volume 1: The Cars. Parts 1 and 2 of "The Legendary Cars" looks at their specialists and manufacturers. 90 mins.
VHS: S21918. $19.98.

Volume 2: The Drivers. A look at the great drivers and their rivalries. 90 mins.
VHS: S21919. $19.98.

Volume 3: The Thrill of Formula 1. The dangers and art of Formula 1 racing and its economics. 90 mins.
VHS: S21920. $19.98.

Volume 4: The Grand Prix. The Grand Prix weekend, the Monaco Grand Prix and the turbo era of Formula 1 racing. 90 mins.
VHS: S21921. $19.98.

Formula 1 Saga, Complete Set. A pre-packed, 4-volume set.
VHS: S21922. $79.80.

From the Wake of the Bow

Our maritime heritage, from pirogues and skiffs to tankers. Hosted by Louisiana Governor Edwards. 59 mins.

VHS: S22389. $42.50.

Ghost Trains of the Old West Volume 1

The first volume in this series introduces the breathtaking beauty of the landscape dominated by early steam locomotives. The iron horse was responsible for the development of the wilderness. 60 mins.

VHS: S24484. $19.95.

Ghost Trains of the Old West Volume 2

The second volume in this series picks up where Volume 1 left off. 60 mins.

VHS: S24485. $19.95.

The Golden Age of the Automobile

See many autos from past years and discover the reasons for the demise of marquees such as La Salle, Auburn, and Pierce Arrows, and learn about the development of many of today's engineering advances. 55 minutes.

VHS: S02250. $29.95.

The Great Alaska Train Adventure

Originally constructed to haul ore from the gold fields of Fairbanks to the seaport at Anchorage, the Alaska Railroad is now a major tourist attraction. This two-tape set features the world-famous Iditarod Dog Sled Race; Alaska's famous bush pilots; Denali National Park and Preserve; Mt. McKinley, America's most majestic peak; an Alaskan flag train; Fairbanks, Alaska's gold-mining, riverboat capital; and the village of Talkeetna, the town said to be the model for TV's *Northern Exposure*. Each tape is 45 mins.

VHS: S31209. $29.95.

Great American Eastern Train Rides

Two volumes reveal the itineraries of classic and historic train routes in key Eastern states. From Blue Mountain, Pennsylvania, to Cumberland, Maryland, some of the most scenic countryside and quaint train technology is shown in this comprehensive video set. 120 mins.

VHS: S26367. $29.95.

Great American Train Rides

Vintage steam and diesel locomotives, cabooses, electric trolleys and interurbans bring unforgettable experiences to this video. Sixteen truly American adventures are shown from the Colorado Rockies to California's Redwood coast. Two-volume set, 120 mins.

VHS: S23134. $29.95.

Great Railway Journeys

This series travels along some of the world's most spectacular rail systems. Each program visits a different country, including Ireland, Pakistan, Russia, Brazil, South Africa and China. Great feats of engineering, romantic landscapes and the charm of trains are joined in this collection. 50 minutes each.

Capetown to the Lost City. Hosted by author Rian Malan.
VHS: S23216. $19.95.

Derry to Kerry. Hosted by Michael Palin.
VHS: S23212. $19.95.

Hong Kong to Ulaanbaatar. Hosted by Clive Anderson.
VHS: S23217. $19.95.

Karachi to Kyber Pass. Hosted by Mark Tully.
VHS: S23215. $19.95.

Santos to Santa Cruz. Hosted by poet and novelist Lisa St. Aubin de Teran.
VHS: S23214. $19.95.

St. Petersburg to Tashkent. Hosted by prima ballerina Natalia Makarova.
VHS: S23213. $19.95.

Six-Volume Set.
VHS: S23218. $99.95.

Great Railway Journeys of the World: Flying Scotsman

O.S. Nick, railway expert, is the guide to this video survey of today's steam railway scene. This video focuses on two locomotive personalities from the history of steam: the 4472 Flying Scotsman on its last non-stop London to Edinburgh run, and an impressive 1/8 scale model of the largest steam locomotive ever built, the Union Pacific Big Boy. A BBC production. 98 mins.

VHS: S10296. $19.94.

Great Railway Journeys of the World: India

Brian Thompson is the guide armed with a 30 pound rail pass and only a hazy notion of destination as he boards the '85 Down Madras Mail and heads south. On his leisurely five-day journey from the noise and heat of Bombay to the calm of Cochin he passes through four states, crosses the dusty Deccan plain and visits Ooctamund, a cool hill retreat built by the British in the days of the Empire. Produced by the BBC. 60 mins.

VHS: S10298. $29.95.

The Great Ships

This definitive sailing collectible on video includes the complete history of the most influential sailing ships ever built. Includes stunning computer graphics, rare archival footage and expert interviews. The three-volume set includes *The Whalers*, *The Galleons* and *The Clippers*. Each tape is 50 mins.

VHS: S31148. $49.95.

Great Train Journeys of Australia: The Indian Pacific

Vivid landscapes, exotic creatures and mystical destinations are some of the highlights of this 2,700-mile rail journey from Sydney to Perth. On board Australia's crown jewel of trains, the heart of the Outback emerges in the Nullarbor Plain as well as the ghost town of Silverton, where *Mad Max* was filmed, in this stark look at Australia's frontier days. Two-tape set, 100 minutes.

VHS: S28524. $29.95.

The Great Train Stations of America

Go back in time to a romantic bygone era with this program that journeys through seven American railroad stations, including Union Stations in Washington, DC, St. Louis and Los Angeles. You'll see the exquisite architecture of these magnificent buildings and hear historical and social commentary. With period footage, archival stills and interviews. 50 mins.

VHS: S32914. $19.95.

Heritage to Glory: The U.S. Marine Corps Story

Real footage describes the action and events the Marines have seen in the two World Wars. This is the history of brave marines. 45 mins.

VHS: S13130. $29.98.

The Hindenburg

Two volumes tell the story behind the creation of the preeminent dirigible that inspired the world. Count Zeppelin was a true visionary, but his creation came to a fiery end which forever eclipsed the brilliance of his invention. Interviews with survivors and eyewitnesses recreate the catastrophe and explore the validity of a curious theory. Did a bomb destroy this flying machine? Each tape is 50 mins.

VHS: S29909. $29.95.

History of Naval Aviation

Fifty years of Naval Aviation is covered in this program. Includes interviews with pilots, footage of the Wright brothers' first public test flights and rare filmed accounts of World War I and II air battles fought over the Atlantic and South Pacific. 84 mins.

VHS: S13128. $29.98.

The History of the Volkswagen

Though a popular counter culture icon, the bug was actually designed with the political aims of National Socialism in mind. Hitler opened the Volkswagen factory personally in 1938. This video shows how, despite this inauspicious start, the beetle was transformed into the beloved bug. 30 mins.

VHS: S24833. $14.95.

The History of the World's Fastest Trains

Experience the global search for railroad speed, from the breakthrough of Stephenson's "Rocket" and the first 100 mph steam locomotive to the ultimate hight-speed TGV. Then look ahead to the shapes and technologies of the future. 75 mins.

VHS: S30487. $19.95.

Indian Motorcycle Memories

Hear the stories of Indian Chief motorcycle enthusiasts and learn the history of the Indian Motorcycle Company, from its phenomenal worldwide success, to the rivalry with Harley Davison, to its unexpected failure after World War II. 40 mins.

VHS: S34749. $19.95.

Irving Johnson High Seas Adventurer

Highlights Johnson's exciting life beginning with his introduction to the sea aboard the *Peking* in 1929. Seven of Johnson's round-the-world voyages aboard the brigantine *Yankee* are charted, illustrated with National Geographic's striking footage of stops in South Pacific Islands. 43 mins.

VHS: S05944. $34.95.

Jets: The New Generation

War in Vietnam required a new generation of fighter planes. From the Voodoo Reconnaissance to the deadly napalm bombers, this program studies these aircraft and the role they played. 60 mins.

VHS: S13120. $19.98.

Kitty Hawk

This program examines the competition that took place prior to the Wright brothers' historic flight at Kitty Hawk, the flight itself, and the evolution of engine-powered planes. 60 mins.

VHS: S13125. $19.98.

Last of the Giants: Vol. 1: Union Pacific's Big Boys

A 1959 documentary that traces the social and industrial development of the biggest locomotive ever designed, the self-named "Big Boy," which pioneered the development of Union Pacific steam power. 25 mins.

VHS: S20082. $19.95.

Last of the Giants: Vol. 2: The Cheyenne Shops

A follow-up to *Last of the Giants*, incorporating much of the unused footage that was shot by Union Pacific cameramen over a three-year period in the 50s. The film features interviews with contemporary Union Pacific workers who discuss their experiences on the famous locomotives. 60 mins.

VHS: S20083. $39.95.

Last Train Across Canada

Murray Sayles, the veteran war correspondent, travels across the Canadian Dream, 7000 miles of transcontinental railways. Along the way he encounters a vast array of Canadians, including Native Americans, mounties, fishermen from the maritime provinces and cowboys in the prairie. The wildlife is breathtaking. 110 mins.

VHS: S23119. $29.95.

Lindbergh's Great Race: Are There Any Mechanics Here?

This award-winning story of Charles Lindbergh's transatlantic triumph is composed entirely of rare newsreel and motion picture film, including never-before-seen footage and little-known sound recordings. 90 mins.
VHS: S34074. $29.95.

Locomotion: The Amazing World of Trains

This set of four tapes includes: *Vol. 1, Engines of Enterprise*, the story of America's first big business; *Vol. 2, Taming the Iron Monster*, a history of how early railway construction literally moved mountains; *Vol. 3, The War Machines*, a chronicle of trains from the Civil War to the Second World War; and *Vol. 4, Magic Machines and Mobile People*, which shows how trains change society, including a look at the fastest trains running today.
VHS: S21249. $79.95.

Marathon of Steam

This four-volume series will appeal to all train fans. The series criss-crosses the country in search of the most exciting, nostalgic and historic trains. 120 mins.
Volume 1. Two documentaries, *Narrow Rails Still Shine* and *Rotary Snowplow through the Rockies*, are included in this volume. They take the viewer through Colorado and New Mexico.
VHS: S22151. $19.95.
Volume 2. These three short films show the Illinois Railway Museum and follow a train ride up to the top of Bear Mountain. The 4-6-2 Pacific is also featured.
VHS: S22152. $19.95.
Volume 3. Spectacular scenery and classic railroads are showcased in this collection of three films: *BCR Steam, NKP Autumn Spectacular* and *819 Arkansas Steam*.
VHS: S22153. $19.95.
Volume 4. The 90-minute film *Steam in St. Louis* captures the excitement of four steam locomotives which operate for the St. Louis NRHS convention. Then *Sierra Railways* tours the historic facilities of this well-known railroad.
VHS: S22154. $19.95.

Mighty Steam Series

This collection examines the steam-powered locomotives that defined the building of the American frontier. The series includes the Norfolk Western, the Canadian Steam, Cotton Belt and Union Pacific. 180 mins.
Canadian Steam.
VHS: S20089. $19.95.
Cotton Belt 819.
VHS: S20090. $19.95.
Norfolk Western 1218.
VHS: S20088. $19.95.
S.P. Daylight 4449.
VHS: S20091. $19.95.
Union Pacific 844.
VHS: S20092. $19.95.
Union Pacific 3985.
VHS: S20093. $19.95.
Mighty Steam Series, Set. A collection of six tapes.
VHS: S20094. $239.00.

Modern Warplanes

The most sophisticated fighter jets plan their attack strategies with the aid of radar, sonar and satellites. This program shows how the modern war plane evolved with each war to become powerful, high-tech machines. 60 mins.
VHS: S13122. $19.98.

Moving Beyond Auto America

Seventeen of the nation's foremost transportation experts critically analyze our love affair with the car and ask how much longer we can rely on this energy-intensive method of transportation. Alternatives like electric cars, magnetic trains, light rail systems and low-tech as well as highly futuristic approaches are all explored in this video. 28 mins.
VHS: S21569. $59.95.

National Geographic Video: Love Those Trains

Celebrate a slice of history and ride the rails of the world in this look at the romance, majesty and adventure of trains, from steam engines to sleek diesels. 60 mins.
VHS: S11408. $19.95.

National Geographic Video: Superliners: Twilight of an Era

Experience life aboard the magnificent and luxurious *Queen Elizabeth II* in a nostalgic look at the great vessels of a time gone by. 60 mins.
VHS: S08057. $19.95.

National Geographic Video: The Great Indian Railway

Steam engines have been transforming the Indian landscape since 1853. Now endangered by progress, the massive and powerful engines are on view in this video. For over a century they have performed myriad tasks, like climbing into the Himalayas or bringing commuters into central Bombay. 111 mins.
VHS: S25898. $19.95.

The New Ford

Originally shot in the late 1920's, this footage demonstrates how the Model A Ford was assembled and tested. All the major components are covered and the car's many abilities are revealed through grueling road circuits. New music has been added to this originally silent film.
VHS: S22108. $39.95.

Nova—Aircraft Carrier!

Round-the-clock life aboard the aircraft carrier Independence is captured on this video. A wealth of technology and know how makes flying at sea possible.
VHS: S24880. $19.95.

Nova—Daredevils of the Sky

Preparing to compete in the 1992 World Aerobatic Championship, the members of the US team practice snap rolls, loops, humpty bumps and hammerheads. Stunning in-air photography captures these skill-sharpening escapades.
VHS: S24881. $19.95.

Nova—Mysterious Crash of Flight 201

Flight 201 crashes in a remote Panamanian jungle. This video charts the investigation waged by federal authorities to determine the cause of the accident. The case offers a daunting puzzle that requires close scrutiny of twisted and charred remains.
VHS: S24882. $19.95.

Nova—Supersonic Spies

A massive espionage effort during the Cold War enabled the Soviet Union to beat the West with the first supersonic passenger airliner. *Nova* reveals the cause behind the fatal Konkordski disaster at the 1973 Paris Air Show, which put the Soviet's work on the jet in a deep freeze. Now the Konkordski is being resurrected in a NASA initiative to build the second generation of supersonic jets. 60 mins.
VHS: S33100. $19.95.

Nova—The Blimp Is Back

This documentary examines the evolution of the modern dirigible, and the scientific and mathematic principles required to sustain lift, flight and movement, from the famous Goodyear blimp to the strange and bizarre Cyclocrane. 60 mins.
VHS: S19116. $19.98.

Nova—War from the Air

Nova takes an in-depth look at the creation and destruction of bombs. Includes authentic war footage, films of actual bombings, and the bombing strategy. 60 mins.
VHS: S11248. $14.98.

The Orient Express

See the rise, decline and re-birth of the Orient Express, the world's most celebrated train, in this fascinating video. Home to royalty and racketeers, stars and statesmen, courtesans and charlatans, the Orient Express linked the great capitals of Western Europe with the Danube, the Balkans and lands far beyond. Includes rare archival scenes of the golden age of rail travel, interviews with staff, and unique behind-the-scenes footage to tell how the train is run, victualled and maintained on both sides of the channel. 60 mins.
VHS: S30188. $14.95.

Railway Adventures Across Europe: Volume 1

Bernie Kopell ("Doc" from television's *The Love Boat*) hosts these three enchanting railway trips. The Scottish Highlands are on view in *Bagpipes, Trains and Highland Games*, while *Next Stop—The English Riviera* heads South. Finally *The William Tell Express* gives an Alpine view of Switzerland. 66 mins.
VHS: S27488. $19.98.

Railway Adventures Across Europe: Volume 2

Bernie Kopell takes viewers on two tours of Great Britain in *Adventures Across Time* and *Wild, Wild Wales*. Then, in *Mainline to the Matterhorn*, a view of the stateliest Swiss mountain is the chief attraction. 66 mins.
VHS: S27489. $19.98.

Red Green's of Cars and Men

A hilarious bumper-to-bumper trip down memory lane with PBS' Red Green, his nephew Harold and the Possum Lodge gang, lined with car lore and Red's own driving tips. 60 mins.
VHS: S34256. $19.95.

Return of the Scorcher

This spirited celebration of the bicycle asks why this cheap, clean, quiet and healthy method of transportation isn't more widely used in America. Filmed in China, Europe and the U.S., this documentary explores the reasons behind the varying popularity of the bicycle in these different areas. It just might inspire a redefinition of the very idea of progress.
VHS: S21568. $85.00.

Riding the Rails: The American Experience

At the height of the Great Depression, more than 250,000 teenagers were living on the road in America. Many criss-crossed the country by hopping freight trains, although it was both dangerous and illegal. This award-winning documentary interweaves the evocative stories of ten men and women who left home in their youth.
VHS: S34588. $29.95.
Michael Uys/Lexy Lovell, USA, 1998, 72 mins.

The Rocket Men

Narrated by Ed Harris, this program tells the story of Robert Goddard, who successfully fired the world's first liquid-fueled rocket, and other scientific visionaries that developed powerful rockets that changed history. 60 mins.
VHS: S34076. $19.95.

The Rockies by Rail

Traveling aboard the American Orient Express from Denver to Portland, this remarkable rail adventure offers a luxurious train ride through the heart of the West. 55 mins.
VHS: S34714. $19.95.

Romancing the Classics

Over 125 classic cars, custom models and hot rods are showcased in this video. Music from the 50's and 60's accompanies these cars, resulting in a great music video for classic car enthusiasts. 40 mins.
VHS: S24832. $14.95.

S.O.S. Titanic

On April 10, 1912, the world's most luxurious liner set on her maiden voyage. *S.O.S. Titanic* tells her story from leaving Southampton until her tragic and sudden end four days later. This docu-drama features a mix of archival footage and artifacts with a cast including David Janssen, Cloris Leachman, Susan St. James, David Warner, Ian Holm and Beverly Ross.
VHS: S13046. $19.95.
Billy Hale, USA, 1990, 109 mins.

Sea Power: A Global Journey

Six episodes center around the voyage of a vessel that represents one of the various aspects of man's relationship with the sea: trade, defense, ownership of resources, the quest for knowledge and passenger travel. A U.S.-Japanese-British-Portuguese-Dutch co-production.
Program 1: Lifeblood. Oceans are the arteries of the world and oil is today's lifeblood. Centuries ago it was grain, gold or copper. This program defines how this lifeblood affects the rise and fall of empires.
VHS: S21963. $29.95.
Program 2: Ruling the Waves. Navies are the means by which nations control their coasts and interests. This program examines the evolution of naval force and demonstrates how navies fit into the present geopolitical environment.
VHS: S21964. $29.95.
Program 3: Trade Winds, Trade Wars. Commerce and competition, trade wars and tariffs. Consumer goods glow easily from Asia to the West via the efficiency, speed and low cost of container freight. This is a look at the innovation and economics of sea power.
VHS: S21965. $29.95.
Program 4: Passage to Paradise. Since the earliest voyages of discovery, man has braved the seas in pursuit of dreams of pleasure, adventure and freedom. Yet while some escape the realities of life aboard luxurious pleasure cruises, others risk the perils of the open sea in a desperate bid to fulfill their dreams.
VHS: S21966. $29.95.
Program 5: Who Owns the Oceans? Over 70% of the planet's surface is covered by ocean, and below it lie untold resources. Yet unchecked exploitation can create environmental catastrophe.
VHS: S21967. $29.95.

Program 6: A Depth of Knowledge. Those who know best how to use the seas have the greatest power over them. Today, power lies in the ability to protect and preserve as well as to use and control the seas. This program examines the new information and technology that allow man to monitor and map the global ocean.
VHS: S21968. $29.95.
Sea Power: A Global Journey, Complete Set. The six-volume, boxed set.
VHS: S21969. $149.95.

Seapower
A history of the modern navy, this documentary vividly recreates the excitement and danger of the struggle for control of the seas using unique archival footage as well as new material of British and U.S. naval vessels at sea. Produced by the BBC. 109 mins.
VHS: S03395. $19.94.

Search for the Titanic
Orson Welles narrates this fascinating search for the *Titanic* as scientists and oceanographers use sonar readings to discover the ship that sank in the North Atlantic in 1912. Also includes *Return to the Titanic*, narrated by James Drury, in which the team returns a year later to film the sunken ship for the first time.
198 mins.
VHS: S33335. $14.95.

SeaWings
The fastest and deadliest planes ever launched from an aircraft carrier are featured in this *Discovery Channel* documentary series. These aircraft make use of any stretch of open sea, turning it into a staging area for sophisticated air power. Three-volume set: each 60 mins.
VHS: S26050. $39.95.

Secrets of the Titanic
National Geographic covers the spectacular underwater discovery of the "unsinkable" *Titanic* on the floor of the Atlantic Ocean. 60 mins.
VHS: S02014. $14.95.

Shipwreck!
Fatal Collision investigates the debatable causes that led to the terrifying crash and sinking of the *Andrea Doria*. Experience the terror of the greatest submarine rescue ever in *Deep Sea Rescue*, and meet the USS *Squalus* crew members who survived. Bravery, fright, and mystery are onboard when a midnight cruise to paradise leaves 87 passengers dead on the *Yarmouth Castle*, in *Floating Inferno*. Three-tape set.
VHS: S34280. $39.98.

Spruce Goose and RMS Queen Mary
A must for aviation and maritime buffs! Experience a complete tour of these two marvels of engineering and learn of their fascinating history. 53 mins.
VHS: S06689. $29.95.

Steam Across America: Vol. I: The East
A view of Norfolk and Western, the last major type of steam powered locomotives that dominated railway transportation through the first half of the 20th century. 35 mins.
VHS: S20086. $39.95.

Steam Across America: Vol. II: The West
A glimpse at the vanishing moments of steam-driven locomotives, in particular the Union Pacific "Challengers" and "Big Boys."
35 mins.
VHS: S20087. $39.95.

Steam Days 2
Railroad enthusiasts should relish this BBC production that is, not surprisingly, a sequel to *Steam Days*. Travel once more on the Great Western Railway, a distinguished line that still transports thousands of holiday goers to the Cornish Riviera. Spend an hour with freight trains that belch smoke and recall simpler times. England, 60 mins.
VHS: S09863. $19.94.

Steam Days: Travels with a Duchess and the Fishing Line
Railroad enthusiast Miles Kington relives the boyhood pleasures in this celebration of the steam age, encountering some of the great engines, famous lines and wonderfully eccentric people who keep steam alive in Britain. *Travels with a Duchess* examines The Duchess of Hamilton, one of the most famous passenger trains built in the 30's. *The Fishing Line* is the West Highland Fishing line built to transport herring at the end of the 19th century. 60 mins.
VHS: S07611. $19.94.

Steam Kings and Iron Horses
Historical railroad footage is at the center of this video, where you can enjoy a trip on the fabled Coast Daylight. The famous steamers *Tom Thumb, The Atlantic, Memnon, Royal Blue 1310, Britannia, DeWitt Clinton, Camelback* and more are all seen on this tape. B&W. Silent with musical score.
VHS: S27483. $19.95.

Story of Naval Air Power
Through the years, the U.S. Navy has excelled in making their planes faster, higher and able to go farther than ever before. This program traces the innovations that were made in design, radar, and landing gear. 60 mins.
VHS: S13117. $19.98.

Submarine: Steel Boats, Iron Men
The challenges and interactions faced by 130 officers and personnel confined in the restricted spaces of a submarine. The program features interviews with submarine commanders, provides an overview of the strategic uses of the craft and contains a special interview with author and naval authority Tom Clancy. 59 mins.
VHS: S18569. $29.95.

Subway: The Empire Beneath New York's Streets
Beneath the fierce commotion on the streets of the Big Apple lies an astonishing network of tunnels, turnstiles and technology. This video explores the subterranean labyrinth of New York, including the finances of this system and the mysterious money train. Experimental rail cars and even the legendary disasters of this, the world's largest subway system, are also shown. 50 mins.
VHS: S21546. $19.95.

Supercharged: The Grand Prix Car
In 1924, a British Sunbeam defeated the speed restrictions set by Grand Prix regulations by super-charging the engine. This was the beginning of one of the greatest eras in the history of motor racing. Bugatti, Alfa Romeo, Maserati and Mercedes Benz all appeared in a series of dramatic and sometimes dangerous races. Using unique film and lovingly restored cars, this program recreates the Golden Age of motor racing. A BBC production.
50 mins.
VHS: S10299. $19.94.

Swiss Rail Journeys
From the vantage points afforded by Swiss rail lines these videos explore the history and sights of the land at the heart of Europe. From beautiful lakes and valleys to some of the most breathtaking alpine scenery anywhere, there is unmatched adventure along these routes.
The Albula Line, Chur to St. Moritz. 50 mins.
VHS: S20916. $19.95.
The Appenzell Railway, Gossau to St. Gallen. 50 mins.
VHS: S20924. $19.95.
The Arosa Line. 50 mins.
VHS: S20919. $19.95.
The Bodensee-Toggenburg Railway, Lake Zurich to Lake Constance. 50 mins.
VHS: S20925. $19.95.
The Breunig Line, Part 1, Interlaken to Meiringen. 50 mins.
VHS: S20920. $19.95.
The Breunig Line, Part 2, Meiringen to Luzerne. 50 mins.
VHS: S20921. $19.95.
The Davos Line, Landquart to Davos and Filisur. 50 mins.
VHS: S20917. $19.95.
The Emmental Railways, Montier to Thun. 50 mins.
VHS: S20923. $19.95.
The MOB, Montreaux to Zweisimmen. 50 mins.
VHS: S20918. $19.95.
Six-Volume Boxed Set. Contains the Albula, Davos, MOB, Arosa and Breunig Line tapes.
VHS: S20922. $99.95.

Tanks: Monsters in Motion
This program is a complete history of tank warfare, from their first appearance as armored tractors to their heyday in World War II, where they were instrumental in the Invasion of Poland, North Africa, and the Battle of Kursk. 50 mins.
VHS: S13127. $29.98.

Those Magnificent Men in Their Flying Machines
A rousing documentary history of the daredevils and pioneers of airplanes, from the Wright Brothers to the pilots of World War II.
60 mins.
VHS: S02983. $39.95.

Three Men and a Balloon
Follow one of the foremost teams in a race against time, technology and competition as they fly around the world in a balloon. From NOVA. 60 mins.
VHS: S31429. $19.95.

Titanic
In this two-volume set, the Discovery Channel uncovers the truth about the sinking of the *Titanic*, through an extraordinary research and recovery expedition and using state-of-the-art imaging techniques, computer animation and reenactments. Volumes include *The Investigation Begins* and *Anatomy of a Disaster*. Narrated by Martin Sheen. 150 mins.
VHS: S31723. $29.95.

Titanic
This four-volume set is the most complete chronicle of that fated ocean liner, the *Titanic*. From its construction and christening to the gala maiden voyage, and on to the terror of its final night, the entire tale of this doomed vessel is told. The series concludes with the dramatic discovery of the wreck in deep seas.
VHS: S22182. $39.95.
Laser: CLV. **LD74749. $79.95.**

Titanic in a Tub
Using the famous *Forbes Magazine* collection of over 300 rare toy boats to explore the history of both full-size sailing vessels and their miniature counterparts, this is a charming chronological account of the rapid development of maritime technology from the 1890s to the 1930s. 28 mins.
VHS: S31883. $29.95.

Titanic's Lost Sister
NOVA searches for the wreck of the *Britannic* and explores the clues as to how it sank, four years after its sister, the *Titanic* went down, despite an overhaul to meet post-*Titanic* standards.
60 mins.
VHS: S31424. $19.95.

Titanic: A Question of Murder
This tragic event, the sinking of an unsinkable oceanliner, is finally the subject of a TV inquiry. Journalist Peter Williams examines some key issues, including the lack of life boats and a boat drill, and missing government files. 52 mins.
VHS: S25844. $19.95.

Titanic: The Nightmare and the Dream
Dr. Robert Ballard led the expedition to locate and film the watery grave that contains the wreckage of the *Titanic*. Discovered on September 1, 1985, under 2½ miles of ocean, this documentary offers breathtaking footage from the sea floor.
52 mins.
VHS: S25845. $19.95.

Titanica
A look at the events and circumstances behind the most notorious shipwreck in naval history, the *Titanic*, which, on its maiden voyage, struck an iceberg and sank, April 15, 1912. Naturalist director Stephen Lowe shot the film during the expedition of the Akademik Keldysh to the site of the Titanic's sinking in the North Atlantic. 94 mins.
VHS: S34819. $19.95.
Laser: LD71947. $69.95.

Top Gun over Moscow
Meet the rugged pilots of the Russian Air Force and take a close-up look at the heart-stopping maneuvers that still awe Western flyers. From NOVA. 60 mins.
VHS: S31431. $19.95.

Train Now Departing
When the steam locomotive was abandoned in the 60's, a piece of history disappeared, but nothing could dampen the fire of the steam enthusiast. About a thousand trains survived the scrap heap; some are in museums, others are back on the lines in pristine condition—a breath of the past and a noisy reminder that the spirit of the steam age lives on. Produced by the BBC.
Train Now Departing Part One. 87 mins.
VHS: S12388. $19.94.
Train Now Departing Part Two. 86 mins.
VHS: S12389. $19.94.

Treasures of a Lost Voyage
A rich, historic shipwreck gives up its long lost treasure to a group of high tech adventurers and a submersible robot. Gold worth millions draws them in, resulting in this entertaining documentary. 60 mins. From the Discovery Channel.
VHS: S25075. $19.95.

Trolley
This program is a nostalgic, sentimental tribute to the ingenuity and perseverance in the construction and deployment of America's street cars. 60 mins.
VHS: S17179. $19.95.

Union Pacific's 40th Anniversary Steam Excursion
On the 40th anniversary of the debut steam excursion on the Union Pacific Railroad, the Rocky Mountain Railroad Club sponsored a historic retracing of the original route. The trip originated in Denver and ended in Laramie, Wyoming. 60 mins.
VHS: S20084. $29.95.

Visual History of Cars
A three-volume extensive history of cars with facts, rare car footage from yesterday and today.
Visual History of Cars—Volume 1. Covers Jeep, Volkswagen, Firebird and Thunderbird. 115 mins.
VHS: S11254. $59.95.
Visual History of Cars—Volume 2. Covers Lincoln, Cadillac, Mercedes Benz and Jaguar. 115 mins.
VHS: S11255. $59.95.

Visual History of Cars—Volume 3. Covers Aston Martin, Corvette, BMW and Mustang. 115 mins.
VHS: S11256. $59.95.

Wheels a' Rolling

This pageant play was produced for the 1934 Chicago Railroad Fair. It is a unique stage production, preserved on film, that tries to capture the epic sweep of America's railroads and their progress across the continent. 30 mins.
VHS: S24078. $14.95.

Wild Blue Yonder: The U.S. Air Force Story

From the "flyboys" of the first warplanes (1909), to dogfights of the World Wars, to precision bombing, Enola Gay and the jet age, this is the history of American aviation warfare. 45 mins.
VHS: S13131. $29.95.

Wings of the Red Star

Now that the Cold War is over, Russian MIG's can be documented in this three-volume set from the Discovery Channel. *Vol. 1: Duel over Korea, Vol. 2: The Phantom's Foe* and *Vol. 3: The Foxbat* show precisely why these brutal fighters were so feared. 180 mins.
VHS: S25091. $59.95.

Wings over the Gulf, Vol. 1: First Strike: F-15 Eagle, F-117A, Nighthawk

The Discovery Channel obtained recently declassified footage which shows the F-15 Eagle, the F-117A and the Nighthawk in action during the Gulf War. This is a look at the real strategy deployed by these fighters. 60 mins.
VHS: S25094. $9.95.

Wings over the Gulf, Vol. 2: In Harm's Way: Tornado, A-6 Intruder

The Tornado and A-6 Intruder were two of the aircraft that made military history in the Gulf War. Now the Discovery Channel can show the effective technology that defeated Saddam Hussein. 60 mins.
VHS: S25095. $9.95.

Wings over the Gulf, Vol. 3: The Final Assault: F-16 Falcon, A-10 Thunderbolt

In Operation Desert Storm, both the F-16 Falcon and the A-10 Thunderbolt II were indispensable fighting machines. The Discovery Channel shows the role played by these amazing aircraft, using actual footage from the war. 60 mins.
VHS: S25096. $9.95.

Wings over the Gulf: Complete Set

This three volume set includes *First Strike: F-15 Eagle, F-117A, Nighthawk, In Harm's Way: Tornado, A-6 Intruder* and *The Final Assault: F-16 Falcon, A-10 Thunderbolt*. 180 mins.
VHS: S26152. $24.95.

Wings over the World

From the Wright Brothers' wobbly take-off to beyond the sound barrier, this 13-part series tells the stories of the great aircraft-commercial aircraft, war planes, helicopters, supersonic jets-and of their inventors, combining interviews with the aircraft pioneers, stories of struggle, heart-stopping success and heart-breaking failure, and spectacular aerial photography of both yesterday and today. Narrated by Richard Todd.

A Tale of Two German Giants. The story of Claude Dornier and Willy Messerschmidt from the days of Count Zeppelin through the fighter aircraft of World War II to their success in postwar European aviation. 49 mins.
VHS: S13371. $24.95.

Boeing: The Red Barn. From William Boeing's first seaplane to World War Two to Boeing Aircraft's post-war emergence as a leader in passenger transport. 49 mins.
VHS: S13370. $24.95.

Fokker: A Dream Fulfilled. From Anthony Fokker's first company in Germany to its move to Holland during World War I to Fokker Aircraft's role in World War II—on both sides. 49 mins.
VHS: S13373. $24.95.

Higher, Further and Faster. The race to build and beat the Concorde. 49 mins.
VHS: S13377. $24.95.

Igor Sikorsky: A Man and His Dream. From the beginnings of Russian aviation to modern helicopters. 49 mins.
VHS: S13369. $24.95.

In Defense of Neutrality. The history of Swedish aviation and how Sweden became a combat-ready country with no military runways. 49 mins.
VHS: S13374. $24.95.

Legacy of a Legend Builder. Roy Chadwick's accomplishments, from his early work with Alliot Verden Roe to the Avro Lancaster bombers. 49 mins.
VHS: S13375. $24.95.

McDonnell-Douglas: A Tale of Two Giants. The early years of this giant of aviation. 49 mins.
VHS: S13368. $24.95.

The Dassault Dream. From the earliest days of French aviation to the present. 49 mins.
VHS: S13378. $24.95.

The Dream Becomes the Disaster. Great Britain's early passenger aircraft from the de Havilland Comet to the Nimrod. 49 mins.
VHS: S13376. $24.95.

The Lockheed Legend. From the Lockheed brothers' start in a garage in 1910 to spy planes. 49 mins.
VHS: S13372. $24.95.

Wings over Water: History of American Naval Aviation

Subtitled *The Complete Video History of American Naval Aviation*, this program considers the historical, strategic and personal role of naval aviation in America's emergence as a world power. The program explores the vast historical arc, from Teddy Roosevelt's Rough Riders through the present, dealing with technological development, foreign relations, international tension and wartime experiences. 59 mins.
VHS: S18570. $29.95.

World of Discovery: Red Express: The Trans-Siberian Railroad

An ethnographic travelogue captured through Russia's Trans-Siberian Express. This work follows 6000 miles and seven time zones, capturing a history, time and place that has remained closed. 50 mins.
VHS: S19308. $19.98.

World of Discovery: Tall Ship: High Sea Adventure

An adventure aboard *The Danmark*, a tall ship. Set in the raging North Atlantic, the program examines the technical responsibilities of sailing, joining the 80 cadets dealing with 13-story masts and 12,000 feet of rope and wires. 50 mins.
VHS: S19306. $19.98.

X-Planes

This is a program about experimental planes and the men who flew them. Includes daring feats by test pilots, the Wright brothers, Chuck Yeager and NASA pilots. 60 mins.
VHS: S13118. $19.98.

COMPUTERS

The Best of Sex Bytes

This tape from HBO shows what people share in cyberspace, from the pleasures of food and sex, and artists who bodycast human sculptures, to the pleasures of public nudity. 60 mins.
VHS: S31617. $14.95.

Bits and Bytes Set

A comprehensive series designed to demystify the computer and other technology and make their functions and capabilities more accessible and easier to learn. Designed by computer training experts, the series looks at emerging technologies, the principles behind computer use and introductions to basic programming. 180 mins.
VHS: S19376. $149.95.

Chaos: A Video Demonstration

In this video, Rudy Rucker shows a wide range of chaotic graphics produced by CHAOS:The Software. A wonderful introduction to chaos theory. 30 mins.
VHS: S13903. $29.95.

The Creative Spirit Complete Set

This engaging work attempts to examine the relationship of creativity and output. Produced by IBM, the provocative series examines creativity in a number of disparate fields, and how to further it for your own potential. 240 mins.
VHS: S19378. $99.95.

D-Base for D-Base III, An Introduction

Conquer the world of computer software. Learn how to set up files, enter information, add, edit and delete data from your data base, as well as retrieve and display your data. For the first time user, little or no experience is required. 30 mins.
VHS: S12576. $14.95.

DOS—Disc Operating System, An Introduction

The heart of your computer, learn how to use your computer faster and more efficiently via the DOS. Learn how to log in, set time and date, use directory commands, format, copy and erase discs, copy and delete files. Professional instructors give practical examples. 30 mins.
VHS: S12574. $39.95.

The Dream Machine

This popular series is a look at high-tech computer graphics, surveying state-of-the-art developments in hardware and software.

Volume 1: Visual Computer.
Laser: LD70107. $49.95.
Volume 2: Computer Dreams.
Laser: LD70108. $49.95.
Volume 3: Computer Visions.
Laser: LD70122. $49.95.

Fractal Lumination

Beau Lee is an artist explorer of hyper-dimensional realities who combines computer-generated designs based on fractal mathematics with music from diverse sources. William Aura, Craig Chaquico, The Soto Band and EKO are just some of the musical contributors heard on this unique video. 50 mins.
VHS: S23865. $19.95.

From Information to Wisdom

Information management is subject to immense technological change and innovation. Nevertheless, wisdom remains an elusive but vital counterpoint to the growing body of electronically stored data. Differences between information and wisdom are at the center of this intriguing video. 58 mins.
VHS: S29542. $19.98.

Heart Attack Theater

Escape mainstream mediocrity and tune in to this unique prime-time TV series by Lucky Charm Studio and Kelly Hughes, the folks who brought you the outrageous and popular *La Cage aux Zombies*. You'll enter a world of glamour, sex and violence "reminiscent of *Twin Peaks*" *(University Herald)*, and supported by a lively and hip cult following. Episodes (which aired from 1991 to 1993) include *Gut Reaction, Frog, and Inconvenient Whore, Beast, Miserably, Blow!, Pen Pal, Eternity* and *Curse*.
VHS: S32017. $39.95.
Kelly Hughes, USA, 1991-1993, 120 mins.

How to Produce a CD-ROM

An introduction to the steps involved in producing a CD-ROM, from concept to development to production. Several examples of CD-ROM productions are included. 20 mins.
VHS: S22790. $149.00.

Lotus 123, An Introduction

How to use the world's most popular spread sheet program. Learn how to set up spread, enter text and numerical information, use formulas and ranges. Also provided is instruction on cell format and cell edit entries, as well as erasing cells and saving spreadsheets. 30 mins.
VHS: S12575. $19.95.

Lotus 123, Database

Will teach you to understand database concepts such as entering information into your database; add, edit and delete data; retrieve and display data. Work through all database features with easy, step-by-step examples.
VHS: S12580. $14.95.

Lotus 123, Graphs

We will show you how to use graph features of Lotus 123. You will define data ranges, create pie charts, bar charts and stacked bar charts. The power of graphs explained with easy, step-by-step examples.
VHS: S12579. $14.95.

National Center for Supercomputing Applications

Animated visualizations which represent the state-of-the-art in scientific computing. Includes a computer simulation of the global climactic effects of increased greenhouse gases and a study of the landscape dynamics of Yellowstone National Park. 60 mins.
VHS: S13898. $25.00.

Nova—The KGB, The Computer and Me

Nova follows computer sleuth Clifford Stoll as he tracks down a data thief through a maze of military and research computers. 60 mins.
VHS: S34748. $19.95.

Spacetime Visualization

These 3D visual effects allow the viewer to "see" objects moving at near light speed velocities through computer simulation techniques. 20 mins.
VHS: S13899. $20.00.

Staking a Claim in Cyberspace

Converging technologies in computers, telephones and interactive TV offer a new challenge for community organizers. They are working to ensure that the Information Superhighway will be accessible for all people, leaving no one left out of the information revolution. 30 mins.
VHS: S23105. $19.95.

Triumph of the Nerds

Bob Cringley wrote and hosted this three-part adaptation of his book *Accidental Empires*. Aside from chronicling the triumph of techno nerds Bill Gates of Microsoft and Steve Jobs, co-founder of Apple, this video offers an irreverent history of the relatively new but incredibly powerful home computer industry. It includes incredible stories about innovations and achievments that were left on the wayside to billions of dollars in income.
VHS: S29445. $49.95.

The Video Guide to the Internet

This informative visual overview of the internet features graphics and demonstrations of key tools such as e-mail, World Wide Web and Mosaic. The history and more importantly the future of this growing technology is explained and demystified for the home viewer. 45 mins.
VHS: S24311. $19.95.

Virtual Reality

A compendium presenting an overview of the exciting field of virtual reality. This tape features demonstrations from research laboratories that are at the forefront of this exciting new technology. Discover what the future has in store. 60 mins.
VHS: S13902. $29.95.

Wordperfect Quickstart

Thirty minutes to introduce novices to the wonders of WordPerfect, including practical examples, help menus, keyboard functions, and how to edit, delete and insert text. 30 mins.
VHS: S11521. $14.95.

Wordstar, An Introduction

If you need to get up and running on Wordstar, then this is the instruction program for you. Learn Wordstar's special functions: creating and saving a document, editing, inserting and deleting text, reformatting your document. 30 mins.
VHS: S12578. $19.95

personal growth

The 12 Steps

A video collection of five tapes and workbook of the process developed by Alcoholics Anonymous and used in other recovery programs. Recovering addicts explain each step, stressing the benefits of recovery.
VHS: S18654. $149.95.

Abbey Semel, M.S., R.D., Lic. A, and Stephen Rechtschaffen, M.D.: Nutrition for Life

We are what we eat. This video is an informative guide for achieving wellness through food. The effects of various foods are discussed as they affect both the mind and the body. Suggestions are made that can be followed at home or even in restaurants. 110 mins.
VHS: S23211. $39.95.

Addiction and Responsibility

Francis Seeburger is the respected chair of the Philosophy Department at the University of Denver. He has written about the spiritual craving that underlies all addictions. Like the Saint, the addict has devoted him or herself completely to one thing, and these longings can lead to spiritual redemption. 60 mins.
VHS: S23620. $34.95.

Addiction, Attachment, and Spiritual Crisis

Christina Grof describes her struggle with alcoholism, which led to her unique spiritual insights. Addiction results from a yearning for spiritual union. The crises associated with this yearning can lead to higher states of personality integration. Grof is the author of *The Thirst for Wholeness*. 60 mins.
VHS: S23629. $34.95.

Adoption: Your Guide to Success

Explores various adoption methods as well as the emotional ups and downs experienced by adoptive parents and birth mothers. Host Jobeth Williams dispels many of the myths surrounding adoption. Features interviews with attorneys, agency officials, counselors and psychologists. 75 mins.
VHS: S16391. $39.95.

The Adventure of Self-Discovery

With Stanislav Grof, MD. The innovative psychotherapist and author of *Beyond the Brain* and *Realms of the Human Unconscious* describes the stages of the birth process and how they relate to attitudes we develop later in life. 90 mins.
VHS: S08623. $49.95.

Adventure of the Spirit

Richard Bach has written such important books as *Jonathan Livingston Seagull*. In this video he shares his insights about the relationship between fact and fiction. Reality is ultimately much deeper than the physical world apprehended by the senses. 60 mins.
VHS: S23618. $34.95.

Affirmations for Getting Well Again

O. Carl Simonton, M.D. is a highly regarded physician and author whose insights are embodied in this multimedia approach to combating stress and pressure. Images from beautiful areas such as the isle of Kauai and music from assorted artists, including Yanni, help link the mind, the central nervous system and the immune system to promote well-being and health. 38 mins.
VHS: S29549. $24.95.

Affirmations for Living Beyond Cancer

Dr. Bernie Siegel is the well-recognized author and lecturer whose practice offers hope to those living with cancer. Inner balance can lead to greater strength and a state of wellness. This video combines the latest techniques, supported by medical research, to regaining wellness with natural sounds and positive affirmations.
VHS: S27475. $24.95.
Jan C. Nickman, USA, 1995, 30 mins.

Age Is No Barrier

Meet the U of Agers, a touring gymnastics team comprised of 21 men and women ranging in age from 55 to 77, on the cutting edge of the seniors wellness movement.
VHS: S32716. $24.95.
Francis Damberger, Canada, 1993, 24 mins.

Alan Watts: The Art of Meditation

Filmmaker Elda Hartley made a number of films with Alan Watts from 1965 until his death in 1973. This video brings the best of those works together. Watts demonstrates meditative disciplines, including posture, breathing and concentration. Also included is Hartley's film *Meditation: The Inward Journey*.
VHS: S26138. $19.95.
Elda Hartley, USA, 1965-1973, 50 mins.

Alchemy & the Crystal Cave

Explore the inner world of spirit through the masterful guidance of renowned healer and teacher Deepak Chopra. Based on his book *The Way of the Wizard*, this unique program guides the viewer on a spiritual journey using an enlightening series of readings based on *Merlin and the Arthurian Knights*. In *Alchemy: The Art of Spiritual Transformation*, the viewer is challenged to change the stuff of everyday existence into pure spirit. In *The Crystal Cave: Lessons from the Teaching of Merlin*, the Wizard takes Arthur to the realm of pure spirit—the place beyond opposites that is within each one of us. Both lessons feature readings by Robert Guillaume, Martin Sheen and Joanna Cassidy, with commentary by Deepak Chopra. 1 hour and 40 minutes on two videocassettes.
VHS: S30957. $35.98.

Alternative Medicine Natural Home Remedies

This video will help you learn how to treat more than 50 common health conditions using inexpensive, natural methods. Dr. Jay Gordon shows how to use ordinary ingredients such as garlic, honey and ginger root for relief from conditions like acne, allergies, anxiety, toothaches and warts. 52 mins.
VHS: S22687. $29.95.

Angel Stories, Volume 1

Angels have emerged as legitimate harbingers of messages from another reality. Interviews reveal actual encounters between people and these mythic figures that some thought existed only in scripture. 60 mins.
VHS: S22748. $19.95.

Angel Stories, Volume 2

Angels seem to proliferate as more and more people come forward to claim direct contact with these spiritual entities. This volume continues to explore the reality of angels in our midst. 60 mins.
VHS: S22749. $19.95.

Another Trip with Ram Dass

Meet Dr. Richard Alpert, known as Ram Dass, who worked with Timothy Leary at Harvard and later Millbrook, experimenting with psychedelics.
VHS: S33805. $24.95.
Claire Burch, USA, 1996, 45 mins.

Art and Science of Human Transformation

Jean Houston, the author of *The Possible Human, The Search for the Beloved* and *Godseed*, presents three new tapes on human potential.
Walking the Life Journey. The vision of sacred stewardship, the discovery of "The Possible Society," with a vivid recollection of Jean Houston's mentor, Margaret Mead, discussion of the legend of the Grail, and a vision of humanity as "the beings who live for all life." 90 mins.
VHS: S10144. $39.95.
Creating a World That Works. Jean Houston sets the perspective of what it's like to be here now—at this critical point in human history. Using processes—the crossing of the Crystal Bridge and its empowerment, heart-to-heart linking, and the ancient dance of Enos Mythos—participants discover ingredients they need to fulfill themselves as planetary stewards. 102 mins.
VHS: S10146. $39.95.

The Art of Aikido

This harmonious system of defense blends the movement of an attacker into his own downfall. Dr. Lee, Ah Loi and 7th Dan articulate Shikko (knee walking), techniques from a kneeling position, bowing etiquette, parrying, hitting, blocking, throwing and breakfalling training. 45 mins.
VHS: S26847. $24.95.

Asana: Dance of the Yogis: Music by Sting and Jah Wobble

Jivamukti Yoga directors Sharon Gannon and David Life explore yoga and dance as a single discipline, combining modern dramatic performance in a music video format. With music by Sting and Jah Wobble. 30 mins.
VHS: S34253. $19.95.

Awakening Your Body's Energies

With George Leonard. This aikido trainer and author of *The Silent Pulse* demonstrates several awareness exercises in which the viewer can participate, including balancing, centering and transforming pain to energy. 90 mins.
VHS: S08628. $49.95.

Balance and Coordination for Seniors

Using movements from T'ai-Chi, Master Bob Klein and Jean Goulet demonstrate how to be more flexible and avoid falls. This instruction will help seniors prevent strains and accidents. 70 mins.
VHS: S23667. $19.95.

Becoming Orgasmic

Nineteen out of twenty women are said to be helped by the techniques revealed in this video. Increasing desire and comfort can open up new pathways to orgasm and greater fulfillment. 83 mins.
VHS: S25055. $29.95.

Benefits of Long-Term Meditation

With Shinzen Young. Meditation practices can lead to permanent changes in awareness of the self and the transcendence of the ego, says an ordained Buddhist Monk and scholar of Buddhism. 30 mins.
VHS: S08644. $29.95.

Bernie Siegel, M.D.: How to Never Grow Old and Die Young at Heart

Drawing upon his unique approach with people facing chronic or catastrophic illness, Dr. Siegel shares new information about living healthy and dying young at heart. He is the author of the best-selling book, *Love, Medicine, and Miracles*. 65 mins.
VHS: S23202. $39.95.

Beyond the Looking Glass: Self-Esteem and Body Image

Produced with high school students and their parents in mind, *Beyond the Looking Glass* features candid commentary from teenagers and the guidance of clinical psychologist and author Dr. Rita Freedman. Covering such topics as Looks, Your Body, Media, Gender, Love, Feeling Connected, Role Models, Empowerment and Uniqueness, the film gives a comprehensive overview of the elements that make up a person's self-esteem. 30 mins.
VHS: S32341. $49.95.

The Big O

Nationally recognized sex educator Dr. Marty Klein leads viewers through the latest findings on orgasms, enhanced with explicit footage of attractive couples reaching the highest peaks of pleasure. Women will learn why they need to avoid faking it; tips on what will please a partner, styles of arousal and ways to create multiple orgasms for men and women. 60 mins.
VHS: S31268. $29.95.

Bioenergy: A Healing Art

An intelligent, mind-stretching video, this tape explores the unique ability of bioenergy to facilitate healing and our own bioelectric being. Poignant stories from clients and interviews with Polish healer Mietek Wirkus, as well as researchers Dr. Robert Becker, Elmer Green, PhD., and Steve Fahrion, give a complete picture of this amazing phenomenon. 46 mins.
VHS: S22688. $29.95.

Body and Soul: The Complete Workout
Handsome David Torres is joined by a group of sexy workout partners as he guides the viewer through a day of complete fitness. This attractive trainer from Los Angeles explains the importance of body-building techniques, aerobic exercise, good nutrition and a positive outlook. 60 mins.
VHS: S23128. $29.95.

Boundaries of the Soul: Explorations in Jungian Analysis
With June Singer, Ph.D. Jungian analysis focuses on unconscious archetypes that operate beneath cultural conditioning, says this analyst and author of *Boundaries of the Soul*. Transformation, she says, must emerge from within this dynamic interplay of images. 90 mins.
VHS: S08621. $49.95.

A Call to Greatness
Isana Mada believes that many people are experiencing an awakening but that the isolation of the ego keeps us from full awareness. In this video she describes the essential process of surrender that leads to spiritual alignment with the higher Self. 60 mins.
VHS: S23627. $34.95.

Callanetics
Callan Pinkney, author of the best-selling book, demonstrates her innovative deep-muscle exercise technique that "sheds years off your figure in hours without putting pressure on your back." 60 mins.
VHS: S10956. $24.95.

Chen Style T'ai-chi-Ch'uan
Step-by-step instructions of the "cannon fist" form, where the soft exterior disguises great power, are found in this video. Many camera angles are used to ease the learning experience and self-defense applications are shown for each movement. Features Master Tseng and Yun Xiang. 90 mins.
VHS: S26826. $19.95.

Childhood Complete Set
This revealing series examines the difficulties and hardships of growing up, collected from experiments with 12 families on five continents, that features expert opinions on children and families. 360 mins.
VHS: S19381. $149.95.

Chinese Chi-Gung Health
This ancient Chinese health exercise combines slow movements, special breathing techniques and concentration to bring vitality and health to the body. Movements based on the snake and tiger, as well as the philosophy behind this healing method, are explored. 60 mins.
VHS: S22701. $24.95.

Chinese Herbs for Health
This video explains the cooking of medicinal Chinese herbs and teas, even the creation of an herbal health kit. It is designed for newcomers. Acupuncturists Harriet Beinfield and Efrem Korngold, authors of the definitive text on Chinese herbs, *Between Heaven and Earth*, and Chef/Zen master Ed Brown are featured. 59 mins.
VHS: S22697. $24.95.

Chinese Kickboxing
Complete instructions for the full contact T'ai-chi-Ch'uan system of kickboxing are included in this video. Punching, kicking, grappling, ground fighting and the use of animal styles, such as the snake, tiger, monkey, crane and drunken movements are all explained by Master Bob Klein. 2-tape set, 230 mins.
VHS: S26825. $19.95.

Chinese Kung-fu
Master Tseng is certified by the Taiwanese government. He demonstrates step-by-step instructions which explain the snake, tiger, monkey, crane, drunken and mantis styles. With Yun Xiang. 50 mins.
VHS: S26832. $19.95.

Colin Wilson: The High and the Low
In this moving program Colin Wilson shares with us his personal struggle in dealing with states of panic and depression; in Part II he elaborates on his Laurel and Hardy theory of consciousness as a model for attaining optimal mental functioning. 90 mins.
VHS: S13322. $49.95.

Coming Down from the Mountain: The Men's Movement
New from bestselling author John Lee is a groundbreaking video which explores the essence of the Men's Movement today and shows how men can break destructive cycles and begin living fuller lives. Joining John are Shepard Bliss, Jed Diamond and Dan Jones. 54 mins.
VHS: S18088. $24.95.

Compassion in Action
With Ram Dass. Ram Dass probes the nature of helping relationships. He suggests that when we look deeply into human beings, no matter how desperate the situation, we are able to honor and learn from them. 90 mins.
VHS: S08630. $49.95.

The Conference Faculty: Aging Conference Highlights
A compilation of key moments from the Omega's Culture in Transition Conference is found on this video. It provides an overview and panel discussion that ties many issues together. Ram Dass, Marion Woodman, Rabbi Zalman Schachter, Mary Catherine Bateson, gerontologist Harry Moody, and Sufi Master and Omega cofounder Pir Vilayat Khanmins all offer their views. 117 mins.
VHS: S23204. $29.95.

Conscious Living/Conscious Dying
With Stephen Levine. Genuine healing occurs when we take ourselves mercifully into our own hearts and accept the totality of our lives. A poet and meditation teacher, Levine is the author of *Healing into Life and Death* and *Who Dies?*. 90 mins.
VHS: S08631. $49.95.

A Conversation with Thomas Moore
Thomas Moore, author of the bestsellers *Care of the Soul* and *Soul Mates*, offers inspiration in the last place anyone would think to look; within the self. His lectures help people to accept themselves rather than to improve themselves. 60 mins.
VHS: S26137. $19.95.

The Couple's Guide to Great Sex over 40, Volume 1
This informative and erotic series explores sex in mid-life and beyond. Four real couples discuss the pros and cons of sex in their 40's, 50's and 60's. Techniques to facilitate communication and experimentation, the use of toys, and positions that accommodate back problems are included. Even erection difficulties and oral sex are addressed. 60 mins.
VHS: S26418. $34.95.

The Couple's Guide to Great Sex over 40, Volume 2
In this video, health topics like exercise and diet are discussed as they affect sex. Interviews with couples also reveal the changes brought on by aging, including menopause. In addition, penile injections, vacuum devices for erections and positions that facilitate deep penetration are shown, all in an explicit and erotic manner. 60 mins.
VHS: S26419. $34.95.

Covert Bailey's Smart Exercise: Burning Fat, Getting Fit
Bailey is the author of the book *The New Fit or Fat*. Now this prolific author shares his tips for healthful toning and exercise in this video. He can help you achieve your right to a healthy body. 82 mins.
VHS: S23944. $14.98.

Crystal Vista
Visual effects and space music combine to create a fantasy otherworldly experience. Music track.
VHS: Out of print. For rental only.
Laser: LD70243. $24.95.
Iasos, USA, 1982, 30 mins.

Cultivating Mindfulness
With Charles T. Tart. The underlying cause of most social and personal problems is lack of mindfulness. The author of *Waking Up* discusses how difficult it is to translate meditative awareness to daily life. 30 mins.
VHS: S08645. $29.95.

The Da Vinci Body Series: Vol. 1
Subtitled *A Workout for the Renaissance Man of the 90s*, this program takes the viewer through rigorous movements, exercises and routines to explore the best means to achieve maximum strength and conditioning for the upper body. With a step-by-step narration.
VHS: S18260. $24.95.

DaVinci Body Series, Vol. 4: Stretch
Seven fully nude male athletes demonstrate Eastern techniques of body stretching for a sharper mind, a more supple physique and a drive to conquer all challenges. 42 mins.
VHS: S30138. $24.95.

Death: The Trip of a Lifetime
The original PBS series is an odyssey in search of life's profound mystery. Greg Palmer hosts this look at how human cultures respond to the universal experience of death. A unique and compelling aspect of *Death: The Trip of a Lifetime* is Palmer's use of humor interspersed with pathos. Four one-hour programs make up the series.
Going for Glory.
VHS: S20478. $29.95.
Letting Go.
VHS: S20477. $29.95.
The Chasm.
VHS: S20475. $29.95.
The Good Death.
VHS: S20476. $29.95.
Death: The Trip of a Lifetime, Set. The four-volume set.
VHS: S20479. $99.95.

Deepak Chopra: Body, Mind and Soul
Chopra's view on the nexus between these three vital elements of human existence has been read by nearly six million readers in his five best sellers. This two-tape set brings his unique teachings to an easy-to-follow video format. 120 mins.
VHS: S27759. $39.98.

Designed Brain
Bob Samples, director of Solstice Seminars and author of seven books, mixes humor with content in covering natural and cultural approaches to reality, and the different qualities of apprehending and comprehending mind. He illustrates the important roles played by intuition, intelligence and creativity. 102 mins.
VHS: S10143. $39.95.

Develop Your Psychic Powers
Medium and clairvoyant Litany Burns shows you how to use your innate psychic power with easy, relaxing exercises to help you sharpen and build confidence in your own intuition. You'll learn about "preliminaries" to eliminate stress, gut feelings, sensing vs. feeling, clairvoyance, auras, psychic healing, "mediumship" and telepathy. 55 mins.
VHS: S32718. $19.95.

Diet for a New America: Your Health, Your Planet
Host John Robbins takes us on a journey into the great American food machine, drawing ideas from his Pulitzer Prize nominated book. In simple, startling pictures, he reveals the dramatic impact of our daily food choices on the health of both our bodies and the environment. 60 mins.
VHS: S16388. $19.95.

Discovering Everyday Spirituality
Thomas Moore, author of the best sellers *Care of the Soul*and *Soulmates*, hosts this four-video set. Interviews with five individuals reveal how one can garner greater satisfaction in everyday life through a deeper knowledge of humanity. 180 mins.
VHS: S27760. $79.98.

Discovering the Mystical Yucatan: Activating the Energy of the Heart
Psychotherapist, channeller and past-life facilitator Susan Drew visits the sacred sites of Chichen Itza, the Loltun Caves, Uxmal, Kabah, Sayil, Cabo and Tulum. The journey takes place during the acceleration of the Time Shift energy. 60 mins.
VHS: S20157. $24.95.

Discovering Unforgettable Sex
This three-volume program captures the secrets of sexual intimacy with *Five Steps to Unforgettable Sex, Secrets of History's Greatest Lovers* and *The Art of Seduction (What Turns On a Woman)*. Each tape is 60 mins.
VHS: S32225. $59.95.

Discovering Your Expressive Body
Basic concepts in dance training utilizing Bartenieff fundamentals, with Peggy Hackney and Irmgard Bartenieff. This comprehensive demonstration provides a basis for expanded knowledge of movement principles that lead to an articulate, more expressive body. USA, 1981, 60 mins.
VHS: S15337. $49.95.

Dr. Bernie Siegel
Dr. Siegel, a surgeon and teacher at Yale New Haven Hospital and prominent author of two best selling books, *Love, Medicine and Miracles* and *Peace, Love and Healing*, outlines the way patients can respond to the crisis of illness. He helps them to assume more control over their lives, resolve conflicts in their relationships, and then focus more energy toward healing. USA, 75 mins.
VHS: S15606. $29.95.

Dr. Ji Liang Chen: Ba Duan Jin Qi Gong (Eight Pieces of Brocade)

Qi Gong is the ancient Chinese system of mind, breath and body that develops and refines the Qi, the vital force. Dr. Chen is a Shaolin master from the Beijing Traditional Chinese Medical Hospital. Eight exercises are explained by Dr. Chen in this video, that build strength and wisdom by harnessing Qi. 78 mins.
VHS: S23206. $36.00.

Dr. Sandra Scantling's Ordinary Couples, Extraordinary Sex

Ordinary Couples, Extraordinary Sex goes beyond self-imposed limits to explore new vistas in sexuality, giving couples the tools to transform ordinary sex into extraordinary sex.
Discovering Extraordinary Sex. Dr. Scantling is a licensed clinical psychologist and certified sex therapist. She shares her research in this video with the help of three couples. They go beyond self-imposed limits to reach new vistas in sexuality. 60 mins.
VHS: S23938. $29.95.
Getting Creative with Sex. Beyond the routine which often characterizes sex for many long-term couples, there lies a realm of creative sex. This video presents advanced exercises and suggestions to help couples have more fun with each other. 60 mins.
VHS: S23939. $29.95.
Keeping Sex Extraordinary. Dr. Scantling engages in one-on-one sessions with her patients. This permits viewers to see how her suggestions lead to dramatic, real-life improvements in sexual intimacy. 60 mins.
VHS: S23940. $29.95.

Drugs and the Law

Steven B. Duke, a distinguished law professor, points out that the many problems associated with drugs actually result from the prohibition of drugs. Death by violence and overdose, theft, health risks and law enforcement expenditures are just some of the problems that result from current drug policies. 60 mins.
VHS: S23628. $34.95.

Eagle Claw Kung-fu

This extremely vigorous Kung-fu style is demonstrated by Master Tseng and Yun Xiang. Step-by-step instructions explain the defense application of each movement. 56 mins.
VHS: S26824. $19.95.

Ebony/Jet Guide to Black Excellence Program 1: The Entrepreneurs

In this charismatic, revealing series about African-American achievement and empowerment, this program profiles the will and determination of three successful entrepreneurs: publisher John H. Johnson; Maxima Corporation CEO Joshua I. Smith; and actress and television commentator Oprah Winfrey. 35 mins.
VHS: S17100. $14.95.

Edible and Medicinal Herbs Vol. I

Dr. Sharol Tilgner introduces a variety of wild edible and medicinal herbs. Identifying and collecting these plants for food and medicine are a vital technique amply illustrated by this video. Perfect for beginners or the seasoned herbalist. 60 mins.
VHS: S22698. $29.95.

Edible and Medicinal Herbs Vol. II

In Volume II, Dr. Sharol Tilgner covers 20 new plants. From the woods to an herb garden, there are detailed instructions on gathering and preparing these edible and medicinal plants. 60 mins.
VHS: S22699. $29.95.

Emotionally Free

Based on the book by Dr. David Viscott, this how-to video presents a program for self-actualization based on letting go of the past to live in the moment. 60 mins.
VHS: S20470. $19.95.

Emotions of Life

Here three critical mental crises are examined: *Aggression* deals with our fears and frustrations in commonplace situations; *Depression* is a study of abnormal behavior; *Addiction* deals with alcoholism as a model of drug dependence with its attendant impact on the family and society.
VHS: S03992. $64.95.

Ending the Tyranny of the Inner Patriarch

In this thought-provoking tape, based on the groundbreaking book *Daughters of the Shadow King: Ending the Tyranny of Your Inner Patriarch*, Dr. Sidra Levi Stone explores the origins of the "Inner Patriarch" and demonstrates how he affects our lives, both positively and negatively. She then shows ways in which women can free themselves from his domination while maintaining respect and appreciation for the gifts that he brings. 52 mins.
VHS: S30703. $29.95.

Essentials of Karate with Chris Thompson

In addition to a brief history of Karate, basic step-by-step instruction emphasizes the power of this martial art. Punching, blocking, sparring, stance training, free fighting and the five basic Kata are shown at various film speeds. 45 mins.
VHS: S26850. $24.95.

The Euro Guide to Sexual Fitness: Sexercise

Exercises are demonstrated in this video which promise to enhance sexual capability and sexual desire. Actual couples show caresses and massage methods that sensitize the body. Renewed interest, greater energy and responsiveness along with new and less inhibited communication should result. 65 mins.
VHS: S26417. $29.95.

An Evening with Dr. Bernie Siegel

"It can be a lifesaver," says Ann Landers. Dr. Siegel is a surgeon who wrote the best-selling book *Love, Medicine and Miracles*. His basic themes are the healing qualities of love and peace of mind. His techniques utilizing dreams, drawings, music, patient participation and responsibility are helping to change the way medicine is taught and practiced. The tape includes stories of hope, discussion of the role of the subconscious, and a guided imagery exercise with music. "If you or someone you care about has a life-threatening illness, this video will give you hope." 108 mins.
VHS: S10138. $39.95.

Evolution of the Magical Child

A three-session video by Joseph Chilton Pearce, a leading expert and spokesman on the development of human intelligence from infancy to adulthood. Pearce re-examines concepts of childbirth, rearing and schooling, stresses the critical issue of bonding and early imprinting. He looks at trends and practices in Western society which damage our creative potential, and follows the maturity of the magical child into adolescence and the challenges of adult life.
Evolution of the Magical Child—Volume 1. *The New Physics* and *Intelligence and Intellect*. 86 mins.
VHS: S10139. $39.95.
Evolution of the Magical Child—Volume 2. *Emotions and Relationships* and *Stages in Human Development*. 88 mins.
VHS: S10140. $39.95.
Evolution of the Magical Child—Volume 3. *Bonding and Integration* and *Imagery, Symbol and Metaphor*. 99 mins.
VHS: S10141. $39.95.

Explorations into Consciousness

Deepak Chopra has brought alternative medicine into the mainstream. His meditation therapies combine the forces of the mind and the body into a single wellspring of health. This best-selling author shows how the spiritual and the physical are linked. 35 mins.
VHS: S26801. $14.95.

Eye-Tripping Psychedelics

A three-volume series that approximates, through computer color-generated images, the sensation of psychedelic experiences. Each video is equipped with a pair of neon laser light disrupting glasses. 40 mins. each.
Vol. 1: Mesmerize.
VHS: S18050. $19.95.
Vol. 2: Brain Bliss.
VHS: S18051. $19.95.
Vol. 3: Hue Heaven.
VHS: S18052. $19.95.

Fat City

Host Roger Bingham explains several theories on why some people gain weight and others do not, and gives pointers on how to trigger weight loss. 30 mins.
VHS: S16389. $19.95.

Fit or Fat for the 90s

The video version of Covert Bailey's best-selling books, *Fit or Fat* and *The New Fit or Fat*. Bailey explains the relationship between good eating and body mechanics, and tells you how to get fit and stay fit.
VHS: S15622. $14.98.

Food for Thought

This program examines the environmental impact of America's love for beef: how it affects water resources, top soil, grain supplies, global warming and the fate of the rainforests. Hosted by Roger Bingham. 30 mins.
VHS: S16390. $19.95.

From Here to Alternity: Adventures of a Scientist

With John C. Lilly, MD. The author of *Center of the Cyclone* and *The Mind of the Dolphin* reveals a life of deep inner exploration, suggesting that within the province of the mind every limit is a belief system to be tested and transcended. 90 mins.
VHS: S08624. $49.95.

From Light to Enlightenment

In the sequel to his book *Light: Medicine of the Future*, Dr. Jacob Liberman challenges assertions that diseases are cured only through medicine. He sets up the guidelines for a new science that re-imagines the way personal experience impacts our ability to heal ourselves. 114 mins.
VHS: S20161. $29.95.

Fun with Herbs

Beverly Fennell shares her lifetime experience, previously available only to Hyssop Hill students. Planning and planting a garden, harvesting, drying, preserving and using herbs for gourmet meals are all covered in this video. Wreath making, potpourri and herbal cosmetics are also demonstrated. 60 mins.
VHS: S22700. $29.95.

Future of Humanity

A dialog between Krishnamurti and David Bohm which took place in England in 1983. Starting with the questions "Are psychologists really concerned with the future of man? Are they concerned with the human being conforming to the present society or going beyond that?", the conversation embarks on the incredible journey of the unconditioned mind and asks if the consciousness of mankind can be changed through time. 60 mins.
VHS: S12481. $29.95.

Gabrielle Roth: The Wave

The Wave imagines rhythms as the key to seeing life as energy, motion and movement. 40 mins.
VHS: S20222. $24.95.

Geomancy: Consciousness and Sacred Sites

Based on a 12-year study of sacred sites, John Steele describes how the heart is a "living organism". He describes sacred geometry, the levels of consciousness, forgetting who we are and how to remember. 59 mins.
VHS: S10393. $39.95.

Get Off the Karmic Wheel

Aileen Nobles presents a workshop in this video which illustrates the techniques put forward in her best-selling book, *Get Off the Karmic Wheel*. These spiritual journeys will clear the emotional body and release limiting belief systems, allowing a merger with a higher self. 120 mins.
VHS: S22703. $33.00.

Gifts from the Healing Earth, Volume I

Ellen Hopman leads this magical walk through a New England forest in spring, gathering ingredients. Then she prepares these elements in her kitchen. Finally, Hopman reveals how she found her way to the healing powers of herbalism. 70 mins.
VHS: S22942. $29.95.

Go for It!

A presentation by Oscar-winning filmmaker Vivienne Verdon-Roe at John Denver's "Choices for the Future" Conference. An inspiring story of how one person can overcome inhibitions and succeed in making a difference. Relating her own personal experiences, Vivienne encourages people to get involved in ending the arms race and other issues of importance. 42 mins.
VHS: S11494. $24.95.

The Good Sex Guide—Series No. 1

Margi Clarke hosts this television series compiled on three videos that is unafraid of asking questions about that most intimate of human activities: sex. The series combines factual information with the advice of health experts and the sexual experiences of ordinary people, all in a fun and engaging format. Sexual habits, size, sexual confidence and sexual etiquette are just some of the issues covered in these tapes.
VHS: S27348. $59.98.
Mike Adams/Richard Trayler-Smith/Martin Head, Great Britain, 1995, 175 mins.

The Good Sex Guide—Series No. 2

Margi Clarke is back for this second compilation of the unabashed series, once again available in a three-tape set. The importance of sex, mismatched sex drives, finding the perfect mate, love triangles, hidden triggers of sexual attraction, sexual fidelity, monogamy and more are discussed on these tapes.
VHS: S27349. $59.98.
Mike Adams/Richard Trayler-Smith/Martin Head, Great Britain, 1995, 175 mins.

Green Winter

A warm, intimate look at growing old gracefully. Features the collective wisdom of many cultures. Senior award-winning filmmaker Elda Hartley examines issues such as retirement vs. continuing work, dealing with a spouse in declining health, considering nursing homes, and attitudes toward death and dying.
VHS: S32720. $24.95.
Elda Hartley, USA, 1994, 30 mins.

The Guide to Advanced Sexual Positions

Explicit demonstrations using a variety of positions and even furniture make this video a surefire way to expand a sexual repertoire. Specific erogenous zones respond to positions that also permit deeper penetration. Overall intense sexual excitement and heightened intimacy are possible with the techniques shown here. 30 mins.
VHS: S264[illegible]0. $19.95.

A Guide to Rational Living: The Principles of Rational-Motive Therapy

With Albert Ellis, Ph.D. Working to change your personal philosophy is a valid therapeutic technique which can lead to genuine growth. Albert Ellis, author of more than 50 books, is one of the most influential figures in modern psychology. 90 mins.
VHS: S08625. $49.95.

Healing and the Mind: Healing from Within

Bill Moyers studies the controversial methodology of Jon Kabat-Zinn, who teaches Buddhist meditation techniques to alleviate pain. Moyers also examines the work of David Spiegel, a therapist who believes group psychotherapy prolongs the lives of women suffering from advanced cases of breast cancer. 58 mins.
VHS: S18636. $29.95.

Healing and the Mind: The Art of Healing

Bill Moyers visits Boston, Dallas and rural Oregon to study whether emotional stability lessens patients' vulnerability to disease and improves their chances of recovery. Moyers looks at a counseling program for an open-heart patient and her family, an intensive care unit for premature babies where nurses help mothers connect with their children, and a hospital that has radically changed its physical settings and services to aid patients in their physical and emotional healing. 58 mins.
VHS: S18637. $29.95.

Healing and the Mind: The Mind Body Connection

In a series of interviews with prominent specialists, Bill Moyers studies the mysterious connections between the mind and body. Psychologist Margaret Kemeny talks about how state of mind influences the immune system. Neuroscientist David Felten talks about how a patient's response to his condition affects how the body responds. Neuroscientist Candace Pert, who discovered the opiate receptor, relates how chemicals travel between the mind and body. 58 mins.
VHS: S18635. $29.95.

Healing and the Mind: The Mystery of Chi

Journalist Bill Moyers travels to China to examine the relationship of the mind and body, from the perspective of an ancient civilization. Chinese culture is dominated by Taoism, a philosophy governed by the yin-yang, two interdependent though opposite forces of nature that influence life. The traditional, unconventional nature of Chinese medicine—the use of herbs, acupuncture, massage and meditation—is to balance the flow of the chi, a mysterious energy that rages through the body. 58 mins.
VHS: S18634. $29.95.

Healing and the Mind: Wounded Healers

At a cancer retreat in Bolinas, California, Bill Moyers looks at the center's philosophy of helping patients cope with and accept their condition. Moyers follows the individual acts of a group of people who relate their individual stories and engage in a variety of activities, including yoga, meditation, relaxation and prayer, to overcome their fear, rage, hopelessness and despair. 58 mins.
VHS: S18638. $29.95.

Healing and the Mind, Set

A five-tape boxed set of Bill Moyers' important series that reimagines different means of considering the mind and body.
VHS: S18639. $129.95.

Healing and the Unconscious

Dr Brugh Joy says the unconscious is composed of multiple, autonomous personalties. These personalities affect the state of our health. Esoteric rites and initiations were designed to call forth particular personalities from the unconscious at appropriate stages of development. 90 mins.
VHS: S13328. $49.95.

A Healing Journey

Sree Chakravarti was a sickly housewife who became a spiritual healer. She claims that the pace of modern life does not allow us time to appreciate one another and that this in turn leads to illness. 60 mins.
VHS: S23616. $34.95.

The Healing Mind

Dr. Chopra grew up in India where he watched his physician father work. From this early exposure to the art of healing he developed a keen interest and a unique approach. He diagnoses diseases by touching the pulse. From his own healing center, Dr. Chopra instructs patients how meditation, yoga, music and purification therapies can help the body regain control. 60 mins.
VHS: S22689. $29.95.

Healing with Ancient Sound

A panel discussion held at the 4th National Unity in Yoga conference with panelists David Frowley, Cathryn Wersen and Eleanor Leatham discussing the history and uses of sound, the relationship of sound to the cosmos, and use of sound in meditations. 90 mins.
VHS: S10216. $29.95.

Healing with Shaolin Acupressure

Migraines, sinus tension headaches, ear infections, back pains, menstrual cramps and more can be healed through acupressure techniques. Master Robert Lyons, along with a minor student, shows how to find these pressure points and apply the appropriate power. 110 mins.
VHS: S26836. $19.95.

Healing Yourself with Mental Imagery

With Martin Rossman, MD. Mental imagery can provide a valuable adjunct to traditional medicine. The author of *Healing Yourself* shows how to dialog with one's symptoms and to interact with an "inner advisor" who can provide personal health guidance. 90 mins.
VHS: S08632. $49.95.

Health and Your Whole Being

With Kenneth R. Pelletier, Ph.D. What constitutes a balanced lifestyle? How can diet, exercise and stress management combine to produce optimal states of health? One of the world's foremost health authorities focuses on the details of developing a personal holistic health program. 90 mins.
VHS: S08619. $49.95.

Health Power

Health Power is a practical guide for feeling and looking better. Body composition, flexibility, strength, endurance and cardiovascular efficiency can be evaluated in your own home. Then a special fitness program can be designed just for you. Marc Sorenson, Ed.D., of the National Institute of Fitness and Neal Barnard, M.D., President of the Physician's Committee for Responsible Medicine are both featured. 45 mins.
VHS: S22692. $19.95.

Healthy Aging

Healthy Aging shows you how you can have more control over your longevity than you might think. Offering simple ways to prolong good health, the program outlines methods of diet, exercise, and stress control that contribute to a sounder lifestyle. Hosted by Ken Pelletier. Also includes a resource guide, 60 mins.
VHS: S16387. $39.95.

Herbal Preparations for Home Remedies

Holistic health educator Kay Moon Dreamer demonstrates the effective use of herbs in the preparation of folk remedies. 55 mins.
VHS: S20156. $24.95.

Homeopathic Care for Infants and Children

Nationally known pediatrician Dr. Lendon Smith discusses the most commonly used homeopathic remedies for bedwetting, colds, chicken pox, measles, ear infections, flu, teething, constipation, sore throats, diarrhea, etc. A remedy chart for easy diagnosis is included. 45 mins.
VHS: S22694. $24.95.

Homeopathic Care for Pets

Narrated by the nationally recognized consultant and lecturer on veterinary homeopathy Dr. Christine Chambreau, this video explains the most-used homeopathic veterinary methods. All five remedies discussed are found to be highly effective for feline acne and other skin ailments, arthritis, nervousness and digestive disorders. 45 mins.
VHS: S22695. $24.95.

Homeopathic Care for the Family

David E. Karp explains the 14 most commonly used homeopathic remedies. These are good for such routine ailments as bruises, cuts, scrapes, burns, shock, food-poisoning, motion sickness and more. 45 mins.
VHS: S22693. $24.95.

How Good Do We Have to Be: A New Understanding of Guilt and Forgiveness

Best-selling author Rabbi Harold Kushner (*When Bad Things Happen to Good People*) explores how to deal successfully with our inherent imperfections. Issues include parent/child relationships, husbands and wives, guilt and forgiveness, sibling rivalry, and why we should choose happiness over righteousness. 70 mins.
VHS: S32699. $24.98.

How Serious Is This?

Loretta LaRoche, comedienne and stress expert, reveals how individual thoughts can become the foundation for the highly illogical yet steadfast rules by which people live—rules that, according to LaRoche, can also be changed. A PBS WGBH Boston Special. 80 mins.
VHS: S33089. $19.95.

How Then Shall We Live?

This is a unique, independently-produced television series nationally broadcast on PBS, focused on the issues of consciousness and human survival, available for the first time on home video.

Awakening to Life Through Truthful Relationship and On Pain, Perfection and the Work to Relieve Suffering. Ram Dass, the author of *Miracle of Love* and *How Can I Help?* discusses social action, personal relationship, and the cultivation of a compassionate heart: "One dies as one lives…Once that starts to fall into place, then the question is how you use the moment to moment experiences of your life as a vehicle for awakening." 58 mins.
VHS: S04755. $49.95.

Finding a Path to an Open Heart and Wisdom Has No Fear of Death. Ram Dass explores the awakening of a higher consciousness: "There is a way of shifting consciousness so that you can see what we are is a collection of souls. And you can look further than that and see that we are all one in the form of the many. You see that a starving person or a dying person or a frightened person is you. You dive into service. The whole trip of "What's good for me? What do I want? What do I need? just becomes less interesting. And that's where the power is that changes the universe." 58 mins.
VHS: S04756. $49.95.

From Tragedy to Grace: Stages in the Process of Dying and The Experience of Dying: A Guided Meditation. Stephen Levine offers a transformational experience of the dying process: "The stages of dying are states of mind that occur during the process of letting go, during the process of acknowledging loss. It has a lot to do with ego death, the death of those things that block the heart." 51 mins.
VHS: S04754. $49.95.

No Other Generation: Twelve Voices from the 37th Year of the Nuclear Age. Ram Dass, Daniel Ellsberg, Dr. Helen Caldicott and nine other leading teachers and activists illuminate a mode of consciousness that combines spiritual wisdom, political awareness and psychological understanding. Appearing are Phillip Deere, Patricia Ellsberg, Chellis Glendinning, Ken Keyes Jr., Joanna Macy, Theodore Roszak, Swami Satchidananda, John Steiner and Diane Thomas. 54 mins.
VHS: S04760. $49.95.

Opening to Grief: The Threshold Task and Purification by Fire: The Passage Through Pain. Stephen Levine, author of *A Gradual Awakening*, examines the healing nature of grief and the art of living with loss and impermanence. "What we've come together to do, all of us, is to stop postponing death. To come into the very presence of death. To confront death so profoundly that we take it within us, and therefore can go beyond it. As long as we're postponing death, we're postponing life" (Stephen Levine). 54 mins.
VHS: S04753. $49.95.

How to Conduct a Dream Workshop: A Practical Introduction

With Jeremy Taylor. Dream workshops are based on the premise that all dreams are in the service of health and wholeness. Jeremy Taylor, author of *Dreamwork*, is a leading advocate of leaderless dream workshops. 90 mins.
VHS: S08626. $49.95.

How to Live Between Office Visits, with Dr. Bernie Siegel

Dr. Siegel teaches how to embrace life, NOW, teaching how to overcome disease, emotional wounds and negative self-images to achieve peace. 80 mins.
VHS: S23332. $29.95.

How to Reawaken Your Sexual Powers

Becoming a better partner and lover or gaining a more rewarding relationship are possible through focusing on the fundamental powers of nature. Five attractive couples demonstrate techniques for increasing physical strength and enhancing emotional, mental and sexual energy. Better communication and trust will result from these techniques. 53 mins.
VHS: S22710. $39.95.

How to Spar Against Karate

Master Robert Lyons details exactly how to spar against Karate in tournaments. Blocking punches and kicks while delivering devastating attacks is vital. One-on-one instruction makes it all easy to follow. 80 mins.

VHS: S26840. $19.95.

How to Spar Against Tae Kwon Do

Master Robert Lyons spars with a Black Belt Tae Kwon Do expert. Detailed instruction on theory, footwork, punches, kicks and combinations is included. 80 mins.

VHS: S26841. $19.95.

How to Stop the One You Love from Drinking and Using Drugs Hosted by Mariette Hartley, an insightful program that shows how to stop tragedy and start the healing by bringing together selected family, friends and the substance abuser in a situation called Intervention. 56 mins.

VHS: S09899. $24.95.

Hsing-I

Basic and intermediate training methods of this internal martial art are shown in this video. In addition, the philosophy of the five elements, the circulation of energy and the basic techniques and short form are included. 45 mins.

VHS: S26848. $19.95.

Human Dilemma: Explorations in Existential Psychotherapy

With Rolly May, Ph.D. The renowned author of *Love and Will* proposes that genuine growth comes from confronting the pain of existence rather than escaping into banal pleasures. Genuine joy emerges from appreciation of life's dilemmas. 90 mins.

VHS: S08618. $49.95.

I Love You, Let's Work It Out

A self-help video from Dr. David Viscott about overcoming obstacles to intimacy in the personal quest for love, commitment and emotional security.

VHS: S20471. $19.95.

Interconnectedness and Social Policy

Stephen Schwartz, author of *The Secret Vaults of Time*, founded the Society for the Anthropology of Consciousness. His understanding of prayer can help people fit into the fabric of nature. 60 mins.

VHS: S23630. $34.95.

Internal Power ("Chi") in the Martial Arts

Internal energy training has been shrouded in secrecy. Generating and channeling this force is demonstrated in this video for practical self-defense applications. Master Bob Klein covers such topics as neutralizing the opponent's force, penetrating the defense and how to achieve maximum power and speed with the minimum effort. 60 mins.

VHS: S26835. $29.95.

An Interview with Stephen Levine: Healing and Dying

As the author of *Healing into Life and Death, Meetings at the Edge* and *Who Dies*, Levine has been acclaimed as the most inspirational teacher on death, dying and healing of our time. He gives forthright advice on how to deal with this tragic but fundamental aspect of human life.

VHS: S22968. $39.95.

Intimacy and Sexual Ecstasy

This highly acclaimed video presents the finest methods known for creating deep feelings of love and sexual fulfillment in an intimate relationship. "Attractive" couples tastefully demonstrate ways to create more fun and romance in your Love Life. "...presents the keys to great sex.... The tone is light and supportive, the information practical" (*Self Magazine*).

VHS: S15291. $39.95.

Introduction to Aromatherapy

A perfect visual introduction to the world of scent, this video is helpful for home or business use. Live classroom excerpts plus selections on history, distillation and plant identification, as well as actual consultations and massage demonstrations, reveal the tried and true techniques of effective oil application. 95 mins.

VHS: S22696. $29.95.

Japanese Shiatsu Massage Made Simple

This detailed instructional video includes stretching exercises for the masseur and techniques for massaging every part of the body. These techniques offer a tried and true method for achieving inner peace. 120 mins.

VHS: S23651. $19.95.

Jazzercise

Judy Sheppard Missett hosts a complete, physiologically sound sequence of 18 routines that include a warm-up, stretching and special cardio-vascular and muscle toning exercises.

VHS: S10965. $19.95.

Jean Houston: A Passion for the Possible/Body Mind Exercises with Jean Houston

This two-tape set features the wisdom of Jean Houston, explorer of human capacities, philosopher and best-selling author. On "Jean Houston: A Passion for the Possible," Houston weaves together evocative myths and stories of great lives, drawing on her study of human potential. 55 mins. In the companion video, "Body Mind Exercises with Jean Houston," she leads the viewer in a series of exercises to help activate the kinesthetic body: "the body of muscular imagination." 42 mins. Two tapes.

VHS: S30624. $34.95.

Joan Halifax: Elder as Healer

Anthropologist, Buddhist and shaman Joan Halifax has lived in communities with elder teachers in remote areas of the world. In this workshop at the Omega Conference on Aging, she discusses how to develop and understand the potential elders in all of us. 105 mins.

VHS: S20223. $39.95.

The Journey Back: Professionals Recovering from Addiction

Much of the attention given to drug addiction is centered around the underemployed and criminal; the problem of drug and alcohol abuse in professional life is easily overlooked. These are the personal stories of a doctor, lawyer, policeman and pilot who have broken the shackles of addiction and successfully fought their way back to a happier, more fulfilling life. 60 mins.

VHS: S16384. $39.95.

Ju Jutsu—Traditional Japanese Unarmed Combat with James Shortt

Originally this art was used to disarm Samurai. Traditional fighting techniques of the respected Ryoi Shinto Ryu School are used on this video. Technique and instruction for defense against weapons are displayed through many examples. 45 mins.

VHS: S26849. $24.95.

Keeping the Passion

Clinical psychologist Dr Wendy LeDoux explores how married couples can maintain a vibrant, romantic and rewarding sexual relationship. Deals gracefully and frankly with strategies couples use to keep or recapture romance. 50 mins.

VHS: S32721. $19.95.

Kung-fu Exercise Workouts

Two vigorous Kung-fu workouts and warm-ups are included on this videotape. Flexibility, fluidity, speed and stamina, as well as self defense ability, can all be enhanced by these regimens. Snake, tiger, monkey, crane and drunken Kung-fu movements are all clearly demonstrated by Master Bob Klein. 120 mins.

VHS: S26823. $19.95.

Leadership from Within

What is the difference between management and leadership? James M. Kouzes, president of Tom Peters Group Learning Systems, suggests that in order to live in a manner which exemplifies their values, leaders must become clear about their own priorities. He offers several exercises for values clarification and self-understanding. 90 mins.

VHS: S13325. $49.95.

Letters to a Dying Friend

Anton Grosz explains how the death of a friend prompted him to compile evidence concerning what happens when we die. He skillfully guides us through the stages presented in the classic Buddhist text *The Tibetan Book of the Dead*. 60 mins.

VHS: S18089. $29.95.

Life After Life: Understanding Near-Death Experience

With Raymond A. Moody, MD. Do near-death experiences represent an authentic encounter with a world beyond? Best-selling author Raymond Moody explores the nature and significance of these profound experiences for both those whose lives brush against death and their loved ones. 90 mins.

VHS: S08620. $49.95.

Living as a Peaceful Warrior

With Dan Millman. The author of *Way of the Peaceful Warrior* shows that the focused attention of the athlete can be applied to all facets of daily life—from eating and walking to working and relating to others. 90 mins.

VHS: S08627. $49.95.

Living with High Blood Pressure

Hosted by tennis legend and heart attack victim Arthur Ashe, this highly acclaimed video presents vital information about how to control high blood pressure, using clever animation, realistically reenacted vignettes, case histories and a knowledgeable commentary. 59 mins.

VHS: S10137. $34.95.

Louise L. Hay: Receiving Prosperity

Taken from a provocative session with her audience, author and teacher Louise L. Hay explores issues of identity, fulfillment, relationships and recognition, and how to achieve them.

VHS: S17607. $19.95.

Love and Romance

This program looks back at 100 years of love and the changing fortunes of the institution of marriage. Chronicles the ways people have flirted, wooed and courted in this century.

VHS: S30415. $39.95.

Love Skills

A guide to the pleasures of sex introduced by Dr. Joshua Golden, demonstrated by five couples. Explicit sexual activity. 56 mins.

VHS: S07371. $29.98.

The Lover's Guide to Sexual Creativity

The five senses can and do function as aphrodisiacs in this explicit video. Two couples demonstrate foreplay enhanced by erotic scents and flavors, as well as seductive sights and sounds. This video can spark the erotic imagination. 30 mins.

VHS: S26421. $19.95.

Lucid Dreaming

Lucid dreams are dreams in which you are aware of the dreaming state. Dr. Stephen LaBerge is a researcher at Stanford who has written extensively on this subject. In this video he explains techniques that can lead to reduced stress, problem solving and anxiety reduction. 60 mins.

VHS: S23613. $34.95.

Lucky Vanous: The Ultimate Fat-Burning System

Work out with the Lucky Vanous, the Diet Coke poster boy who is infamous for the television commercial in which he bared his chest to the delight of the women working in the office next door.

VHS: S23866. $14.98.

A Magical Journey

With Terrence McKenna. Three complete half-hour programs featuring a leading thinker in the area of alternative realities, including *Hallucinogens and Culture, Time and the I Ching* and *The Human Future*. 90 mins.

VHS: S08633. $49.95.

Mantra Meditation for Beginners with Wolfgang Arndt

In the Yoga of the mind, the goal is to focus on the highest and attain a state of joy and bliss. This non-sectarian video displays the methods and mantras of this simple but transforming practice in an easy-to-follow manner. 90 mins.

VHS: S22959. $24.98.

Marion Woodman: King Lear As an Image in Eldering

Shakespeare's *King Lear* faces the storms of fate and powerlessness associated with old age. He is initiated into the soul values that lead to his inner Queen. This Jungian analysis deploys this model for a new understanding of aging that honors femininity, nature and soul. 43 mins.

VHS: S23203. $39.95.

The Meditation Tool Kit

Whether you're a beginner or a Zen Master, you can calm your mind with this three-tape program, featuring spectacular nature photography, beautiful original music and thoughtful aphorisms from sources as diverse as Mohammed, Charles Mingus, Lao-tzu and Eleanor Roosevelt. Volumes include *Forest*, Water, and *Sky*.

VHS: S34543. $39.98.

Memory Skills

Greg Proops sets out to find amazing facts about memory and to try out different memory techniques in a unique BBC series about how memory works.

Memory Skills, Vol. 1: Associations. Total recall, the secrets of memory improvement, a look at hypnosis as a tool to recovering childhood memories, the thoughts of Roger Cooper (who spent five years in an Iranian jail), and the strange world of 1950's American neurosurgeon Wilder Penfield.

VHS: S21974. $13.95.

Memory Skills, Vol. 2: Sequences. Using a traditional memory technique of creating images in the mind, Greg Proops tries to remember the sequence of jokes for his stand-up comedy act.

VHS: S21976. $13.95.

Memory Skills, Vol. 3: Names/Faces. Proops forces a group of trainee security guards to employ police technology to try to reproduce his face from their memories. Learn how to remember faces and names.

VHS: S21978. $13.95.

Memory Skills, Vol. 4: Numbers. The program explains how to remember numbers and factual information based on association, and features advice from memory champion Dominic O'Brien.

VHS: S21975. $13.95.

Memory Skills, Vol. 5: Places. Proops takes us on a lightning tour of the main theories of forgetting. Learn how to make good use of external memory aids. Hear why the cast of a long-running play are still forgetting their lines and see vacationers helped to locate their cars at the airport after a long vacation in the sun.
VHS: S21977. $13.95.

Memory Skills, Vol. 6: Creating Lasting Impressions. Proops meets with advertising creative directors to discuss how they would advertise a TV series about memory in a way that would make people remember to watch it. Why we stand a better chance of getting people to remember what we are saying if we can amuse them.
VHS: S21979. $13.95.

Memory Skills: Complete Set. The six-tape set.
VHS: S21980. $59.95.

Memory, Suggestion and Abuse

Dr. Michael Apko explains how memory reconstructs the past. Through this understanding Dr. Apko shows that the trauma of past sexual abuse can be created through the reconstructive possibilities of memory. 60 mins.
VHS: S23617. $34.95.

Men Are from Mars, Women Are from Venus—But We Have to Live on Earth

John Gray, the author of the best-selling book, *Men Are from Mars, Women Are from Venus*, offers his insights into male and female differences for better understanding on how men and women can fulfill each other's needs and fall in love again. 90 mins.
VHS: S34343. $19.98.

Metaphoria

An award-winning documentary that examines processes of the brain during dreams and conditions altered by virtual reality and other artificial intelligence. The hosts who grapple with ideas and concepts behind computer animation and scientific inquiry are Dr. John C. Lilly (who invented the isolation tank), MIT professor Marvin Minsky, Native American Sam Sapiel and computer poet Michael Newman.
VHS: S18232. $19.95.

Metaphysics and Modern Science

Willis Harman is president of the Institute of Noetic Sciences. Dr. Harman believes that the integration of human consciousness into the body of human knowledge will lead to new directions in the study of life and death. 60 mins.
VHS: S23614. $34.95.

Mind as a Myth

With U.G. Krishnamurti. This disquieting Indian skeptic and author of *The Mystique of Enlightenment* asks whether the mind exists as a distinct entity apart from our thoughts about it? 30 mins.
VHS: S08638. $29.95.

Mind Power

With Bernie Zilbergeld. You can transform and improve your life by harnessing the power of your mind, according to the author of *Mind Power*. He suggests a number of powerful techniques for self actualizations. 30 mins.
VHS: S08653. $29.95.

Mind-Body Problem

With Julian Isaacs. This experimental psychologist doubts we will ever explain the mind in terms of neurological functioning. This view, he says, is inconsistent with the valid evidence of parasychology. 30 mins.
VHS: S08639. $29.95.

Minds, Brains and Science

With John Searle. The author of *Intentionality* challenges the notion that the human mind operates like a computer, pointing out that many human faculties are not achievable through artificial intelligence. 30 mins.
VHS: S08640. $29.95.

Money and Marriage

Clinical psychologist Dr. Wendy LeDoux probes the key financial issues in marriage: partnership, control, independence and coping with change. 50 mins.
VHS: S32722. $19.95.

The Montauk Project: Experiments in Time

In 1943 the Philadelphia Project was begun, a 40-year research endeavor that involved invisibility, psychotronics (mind control) and the actual manipulation of time itself. Three researchers give first-hand accounts, and show the abandoned site on Long Island where this extraordinary series of experiments occurred. 95 mins.
VHS: S22705. $29.95.

Mystery of Incarnation

With Richard Grossinger. To understand our spiritual origins we must look to nature—for our most intimate relationship is with our own biology. The author of *Planet Medicine* discusses the biology of consciousness. 30 mins.
VHS: S08649. $29.95.

Natural Healing with Crystals

Dr. Richman, a chiropractor and expert on nutrition and herbs, uses crystals for balancing and healing the body. 60 mins.
VHS: S10212. $29.95.

Near Death Experience

Death is feared but near death experience teaches us that this need not be so. Extraordinary personal accounts from four people and top researchers like Kenneth Ring and Melvin Morse clarify this amazing phenomenon. 105 mins.
VHS: S22704. $29.95.

The Next Epoch

The Next Epoch presents hopeful evidence that we are at a critical point in our evolution and suggests that if we are to move into the next epoch, we must consciously nurture new values and attitudes that emphasize cooperation to solve our global problems. Featuring interviews with Dr. Jonas Salk and others. USA, 1991, 28 mins.
VHS: S15206. $39.95.

Nothing to Lose: Fat Lip Reader's Theatre

Fat and feisty women speak, act and sing about being fat in '80s America. Dramatic vignettes, snappy answers to street taunts, poetry, song and comedy will provoke laughter, tears and anger. The message is fat positive and challenges the diet-obsessed, fat-hating culture we live in. 30 mins.
VHS: S16838. $29.95.

Nude Stretching

You haven't experienced the full pleasure of stretching until you have seen and practiced stretching in the nude, with this fully instructional stretching tape presented in the nude. 45 mins.
VHS: S30134. $19.98.

Nude Tai Chi

Whether to learn the many benefits of this art, or to simply enjoy the beauty of the naked human form, viewers will find many hours of enjoyment that energizes the body, soothes the mind and delights the spirit, in this fully instructional tape. 40 mins.
VHS: S30133. $19.98.

Nude Yoga

Four beautiful women demonstrate the ancient exercises of Yoga completely nude. These techniques develop strength and flexibility, increase circulation and align the spinal column. This tape makes it easy to learn this enjoyable and relaxing health regimen.
VHS: S26523. $19.98.

Number and Meaning

With Arthur M. Young. The author of *Geometry of Meaning* has developed a "theory of process" which integrates science with ancient teachings. Numbers, says Young, are more than abstract representations of quantity. 30 mins.
VHS: S08648. $29.95.

Of Sound Mind and Body

A group of experts, including Deepak Chopra, Bernie Siegel, Don Campbell, Ray Lynch, Steven Halpern and Jill Purce, investigate the way sound enforces or establishes healing. 70 mins.
VHS: S20164. $39.95.

On the Nature of Love

Eastern philosopher and wise man Krishnamurti explains his wise philosophy of love and loving in this thought-provoking program. 58 mins.
VHS: S12208. $29.95.

On the Wild Side... Meeting with Remarkable Women

Wild women are living their lives by reclaiming a creative spirit. Once unfettered by society, they become freer and more open. In this video, inspiring women share their wisdom. They are real live models of a new way of being, women who encourage other women to step out from under limiting ideas. 30 mins.
VHS: S22972. $24.98.

One Light Healing Touch

This "how to" documentary presents workshops, teachings, techniques and postures with internationally known hands-on spiritual healer Ron Lavin, who draws on teachings from Native Americans, Sufis, Rosicrucians, Tibetans, esoteric traditions and cutting-edge, present-day holisitic and medical practitioners. It explores the nature of spirit, illness and healing and includes numerous healings and interviews. "Ron Lavin interweaves Divine Inspiration with heartfelt compassion to create transformational healing experiences" (Peter Russell).
VHS: S31086. $29.95.
1997, 60 mins.

Opening to Angels

The angelic realm is open to those individuals who can attune themselves to the higher spiritual realm where these creatures hover. Inspirational advice from a number of respected new age spiritual teachers and healers will show the way to finding this positive influence in everyday life. 60 mins.
VHS: S21229. $29.95.

Pakua Chang

Master Ji, a direct descendant of Sun Lu-t'ang, demonstrates this internal martial art. This video includes the basic stepping and walking circle, eight palm techniques, direction changes and the full Swimming Dragon form. 55 mins.
VHS: S26846. $19.95.

Pattern and Transformation

With Jill Purce. The author of *The Mystic Spiral* traces her investigations into patterning in nature and form. The program contains a demonstration of an ancient Mongolian "polyphonic" chanting technique. 30 mins.
VHS: S08647. $29.95.

The Philosophy of Tantric Yoga

Swami Chetanananda shows that tantric yoga is not about sex but about focusing on life energy (kundalini). The ultimate goal remains a unity of consciousness. This teacher has written extensively on the subject and shares his knowledge in this enlightening video. 60 mins.
VHS: S23615. $34.95.

Planetary Birth

Barbara Marx Hubbard sees a positive future involving a quantum change in consciousness. Humans will achieve this higher state through a fuller awareness of the larger planetary being. She sees great religious figures as templates that can aid this evolution. 60 mins.
VHS: S23624. $34.95.

The Power of Dreams

A journey into the world of dreaming. 60 minutes each.

The Power of Dreams: Search for Meaning. After 90 minutes of sleep, we enter the world of dreams. The latest scientific methods are joined with an artist's dreamscapes to uncover insights about the hows and whys of the chemical cocktail that transports us each night into a place of fantastic wonder or utter horror.
VHS: S22962. $29.95.

The Power of Dreams: The Creative Spark. How do dreams mold us? From Ancient Greece to modern times doctors have used dreams to heal. Look inside the world of dreams using the latest 3-D holograms and brain mapping available. Dreams hold the key to progress and beauty.
VHS: S22964. $29.95.

Practical Self Defense

Master Bob Klein shows that even average people can defend themselves. Muscles are not vital if you can use your opponent's force against him. Klein reveals how to control the attacker's attention and then balance and neutralize his force. It's perfect for women and children. 90 mins.
VHS: S26831. $29.95.

Praying Mantis Kung-fu

The Northern Mayflower mantis form is show from two angles in natural surroundings. Master Bob Klein demonstrates step-by-step instructions which explain the defense applications of the mantis stance. 94 mins.
VHS: S26830. $19.95.

Prejudice: Answering Children's Questions

Host Peter Jennings leads a studio audience of children on an exploration of prejudice—or what he calls "the child of ignorance." 75 mins.
VHS: S16794. $19.98.

Presence of the Past

With Rubert Sheldrake. Were there any "laws of the universe" at the time of the big bang?" This Oxford trained biologist and author of *A New Science of Life* says that all laws developed as "habits" over time. 30 mins.
VHS: S08646. $29.95.

Primordial Tradition
With Huston Smith. The profound author of *Religions of Man* delineates common threads in all spiritual traditions. Modern western society, he says, is deviating from an understanding of the soul and spirit. 30 mins.
VHS: S08636. $29.95.

The Problem with Food
Examines how real people deal with eating disorders. You'll meet counselors, parents, teenagers and young adults dealing with eating disorders. 27 mins.
VHS: S32714. $19.95.

The Psychodynamics of Liberation
With Kathleen Speeth, Ph.D. True liberation involves attaining an awareness of our unity and interconnectedness, says this clinical psychologist and author of *The Gurdjieff Work* and *Gurdjieff: Seeker after Truth*. 90 mins.
VHS: S08622. $49.95.

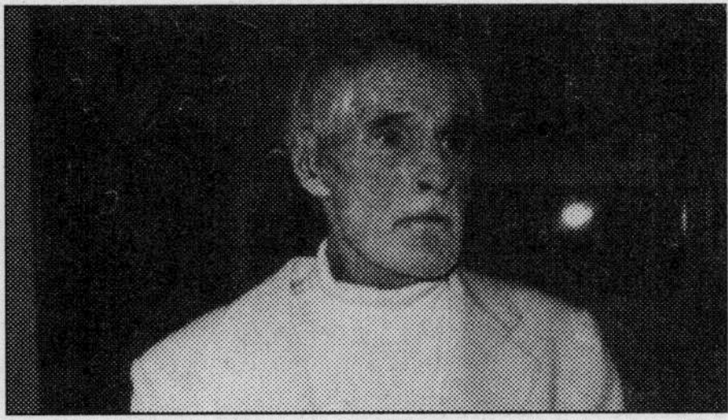

Push Hands (Kung-fu's Greatest Training Secret)
A unique Chinese two person exercise which develops fluidity, internal energy (chi), concentration and the ability to neutralize aggression is clearly demonstrated by Master Bob Klein in this video. Complete instructions for defense applications are included. 120 mins.
VHS: S26829. $19.95.

Pushed to the Edge
A *20/20* special edition focusing on the growing numbers of women who are fighting back against abusive partners and rapists. 50 mins.
VHS: S15880. $19.98.

Qualities of High Performance
With Lee Pulos. This innovative psychologist describes work with outstanding achievers in athletics and business, pointing out that qualities of success can be developed in all individuals. 30 mins.
VHS: S08651. $29.95.

Quantum Healing: Toward Perfect Health
Dr. Deepak Chopra explains his groundbreaking views on total "mind/body" healing. Includes rare footage of other pioneers in the field and a special "guided meditation."
VHS: S32715. $19.95.
Elda Hartley, USA, 1994, 40 mins.

A Question of Authority
A host of moral, ethic, religious and personal decisions are weighed when a mother, in an advanced state of pregnancy, is declared "brain dead" from the complications of a fall. The hospital wants to deliver her child, though her husband, fearing irreversible brain damage, refuses. 25 mins.
VHS: S17931. $49.95.

Quiet Garden
Visits to a quiet garden for relaxation, for active visualization through the Neuro-Linguistic Programming method, and for tranquil sights and sounds for enjoyment. Created by Yvan Miron. 60 mins.
VHS: S10232. $29.95.

Rabbi Zalman Schachter, Life Harvest: The Missing Piece to Wholeness
All must pass from simply aging to sage-ing. Ordained in the Lubavitcher community, but knowledgeable about many faiths, Schachter explains the integration of life experience into a wholeness of being. 35 mins.
VHS: S23200. $29.95.

Ram Dass: Aging and Awakening the Potential of Change
Change is the most constant aspect of life, and yet everyone resists change, especially aging. Ram Dass maps the path of conscious aging, showing how to substitute joy for fear and wonderment for dismay. His teaching offers those of any age a transforming vision of the years to come. 63 mins.
VHS: S23198. $39.95.

Ram Dass: Facing Death
The certainty of dying affects everyone. Ram Dass illuminates the journey toward death and beyond with gentle understanding, knowledge, insight and humor. This video documents a workshop from the Omega's Culture in Transition Conference. It's a valuable guide for those facing death, particularly those who see death as an enemy. 105 mins.
VHS: S23205. $39.95.

Recovering the Soul: A Scientific and Spiritual Search
Dr. Larry Dossey examines the relationship between healing and consciousness in a penetrating exploration at the crossroads of medicine and mysticism, religion and physics. Dossey's synthesis of ideas leads him to the threshold of a new era in medicine and uses information from many quarters—from the Spindrift experiment's documented effects of directed and non-directed prayer on growth and healing to the findings of Candace Pert, former director of the National Institutes of Health. 60 mins.
VHS: S12483. $29.95.

Reflections in a Forest
Three moments in a forest for relaxation: the first guides to relaxation, the second offers access to inner resources, the third provides a soothing ambience without dialog. 60 mins.
VHS: S10231. $29.95.

Relax
A program on the techniques of stress management, introducing fresh visuals and sounds. 60 mins.
Laser: LD70253. $29.95.

Revitalize Your Body
Master Bob Klein describes a program of exercises appropriate to recovering from injury. All levels are catered to in this video. 90 mins.
VHS: S23661. $19.95.

Riane Eisler: Reclaiming Our Past, Recreating our Future: Reflections on The Chalice and the Blade
At the dawn of modern civilization, says Riane Eisler, humanity shifted from a partnership model of social interaction to a dominator model. In this lucid discussion, she discusses many of the ideas behind her ground-breaking book, *The Chalice and the Blade*. 90 mins.
VHS: S13323. $49.95.

Rolling Thunder: The Unity of Man and Nature
Intertribal medicine man Rolling Thunder contrasts the notion of life in harmony with nature with the idea of mankind as dominator over nature. He describes the natural powers of native peoples, describes his role as a healer using shamanistic methods, and also describes his journeys to the other world of spirits. 90 mins.
VHS: S13324. $49.95.

Sacred Passions
Set in the beautiful area around Maui, this erotic travelogue is a spiritual journey into the mind, following Gavin Dillard and a group of young men who believe in Tantric rituals and the redemptive and fulfilling nature of erotic technique. It's "a sensual guide to the erotic that invites us to leave guilt and fear behind, and celebrate the sacred passions within."
VHS: S17794. $29.95.
Scott Craig, USA, 1990, 60 mins.

Sacred Sex: A Guide to Intimacy and Loving
In the ancient tantric beliefs, the hidden potency of sexual loving is the seed of all creativity and transcendence. Six couples demonstrate the key to sacred sex. It allows for greater intimacy and pleasure. Through tantric principles love-making becomes a transcendent ritual. 70 mins.
VHS: S22969. $29.98.

Saki Santorelli, Ed.D.: Responding to Stress
Dr. Santorelli is Associate Director of the Stress Reduction Center at the University of Massachussetts Medical Center. His proven techniques for stress management include meditation, relaxation, sensory awareness, centering and creative problem solving. 115 mins.
VHS: S23207. $39.95.

Satori
Satori, the sudden flash of enlightenment sought by Zen Buddhists, is only attainable through an intuitive, non-rational way of thinking. This video shows the effects of this belief at a Zen monastery, a business school, a street festival, and a Shinto ceremony inside a factory. 30 mins.
VHS: S26139. $19.95.

The Second Timothy Leary Tape
Claire Burch filmed Timothy Leary in San Francisco in 1995 and 1996. Pieces include *Ghost of the San Francisco Oracle Meets Timothy Leary*, *If Leary Was Dreaming*, *How Tim Leary Changed My Life*, *Second Thoughts of Tim Leary*, and *Tim Leary Remembers the Summer of Love*.
VHS: S33807. $24.95.
Claire Burch, USA, 1996, 150 mins.

Secrets of EuroMassage
Provocative, sensual massage techniques from the continent of romance, Europe. This informative and authoritative video tape was developed in consultation with leading massage experts.
VHS: S14003. $29.99.

Secrets of Female Sexual Ecstacy
Hosted by Charles and Caroline Muir, America's foremost western educators of the ancient Indian artform of tantric sex, this tastefully explicit tape featuring actual tantric couples is designed to teach both men and women how to use sexual energy for increased intimacy, harmony and pleasure. Contains sections on increasing sexual intimacy, sexual healing, touch and kissing, freeing female orgasm, methods of pelvic movement, energy exchange meditations and the truth about amrita (female ejaculation). "Charles and Caroline are emissaries from the future, leaders for a generation that desires an end to the battle of the sexes and the begining of a new form of relationship" (*Whole Life Times*).
VHS: S30765. $39.95.

Self and Society
With Jane Rubin. How we can live a meaningful life in a social milieu that lacks clear values? One response, says philosopher Rubin, is to define oneself by accepting as a role model one who is truly committed. 30 mins.
VHS: S08637. $29.95.

Self and Universe
With Arthur M. Young. How can there be separate things in a universe that is interconnected? The author of *The Reflexive Universe* suggests that we can be separate beings in a universe created by God. 30 mins.
VHS: S08635. $29.95.

Self Defense with Pressure Points
For anyone who wants to learn self-defense against larger opponents, this video demonstrates exactly how it is done. Reaching pressure points in actual fighting and grappling situations can be integrated with other fighting techniques. Master Robert Lyons is featured. 70 mins.
VHS: S26827. $19.95.

Self-Defense for Children
Breaking holds from stronger attackers, attacking out of headlocks, groundfighting, footwork, kicks, punches, blocks and combinations are all included in this video. Master Robert Lyons can give your child the skills needed to feel more confident and unafraid. 75 mins.
VHS: S26838. $19.95.

Self-Help Stress Reduction
Michael Reed Gach, founder of the Accupressure Institute's international professional training program, shares specific explanations and demonstrations for accupressure and trigger points to relieve tension and headaches, and to increase concentration and memory. 58 mins.
VHS: S10214. $29.95.

The Seth Phenomena
The energy personality essence, Seth, spoke through author Jane Roberts for over 20 years. In an exclusive interview with Jane's husband Robert Butts, this story is finally revealed. 40 photos and paintings by Rob and Jane and the only known footage of Jane speaking as Seth are featured. 70 mins.
VHS: S22706. $29.95.

The Seven Spiritual Laws of Success: A Practical Guide to the Fulfillment of Our Dreams
A companion to his best-selling book *The Seven Spiritual Laws of Success*, this video expounds on Dr. Deepak Chopra's concept that success is the universal desire to achieve a "progressive expansion of the state of happiness." Dr. Chopra talks about the state of happiness and the elements of his philosophy through his seven easy-to-comprehend principles for "success."
VHS: S27188. $19.98.

Sexual Positions for Lovers
Four typical couples illustrate a full catalog of lovemaking positions in explicit detail. G-spot and clitoral stimulation, along with instructions for those deeper penetration, are all clearly shown. Other positions for those facing arthritis, back problems, pregnancy, or obesity are also included. 53 mins.
VHS: S25056. $29.95.

Shaolin Chun Hop Kuen

This system is a common link between all the martial arts. It uses moves from Kung-fu, Karate and Tae Kwon Do. Master Robert Lyons demonstrates moves that will help any martial arts student. 80 mins.

VHS: S26839. $19.95.

Shaolin Fighting Crane Kung-fu

Step-by-step instructions with Master Robert Lyons show footwork, weight distribution and sources of power key to this style. This comprehensive video features applications shown at slow and full speed. 120 mins.

VHS: S26844. $19.95.

Shaolin Northern Tiger Kung-fu

This comprehensive video features Master Robert Lyons describing step-by-step instructions. Footwork, weight distribution and sources of power are explained. Applications are shown at slow and full speed. 120 mins.

VHS: S26843. $19.95.

Shaolin Sabre

The beautiful, swashbuckling Mayflower Sabre form, complete with leaps, whirlwind slashes and piercing strikes, is demonstrated in this video by Master Bob Klein. This inertial form is both fluid and explosive. Complete instructions and self defense applications are included. 60 mins.

VHS: S26834. $19.95.

Sharing the Joy of Nature

Designed by leading naturalist Joseph Cornell, *Sharing the Joy of Nature* is a video workshop on the awareness and appreciation of outdoor wilderness. Children and adults alike will cultivate enthusiasm and respect for our environment using his eight-step method. Through a process called "flow learning", you will find a method of awakening others to the techniques and games Cornell has developed. The Sierra Nevada mountains provide an inspired backdrop for this perfect introduction to nature activities. 40 mins.

VHS: S15685. $22.95.

Shiatsu Massage—Advanced

Accupressure and meridians are integral to Asian medical theory and diagnosis. These detailed demonstrations reveal the value of Shiatsu techniques. 120 mins.

VHS: S23663. $19.95.

A Short History of Nudity and a Short History of Love

These jaunty spoofs celebrate the year of "The Naked People of Berkeley," a time when they walked about like Adams and Eves in the Garden of Eden, explaining that their cheerful decision to bare all was protected by the First Amedenement.

VHS: S33842. $24.95.

Claire Burch, USA, 1992, 50 mins.

Snake Style Kung-fu

Master Tseng and Yun Xiang demonstrate step-by-step instructions which explain the form and defense applications of this style. This unusually beautiful style uses vibrations from the body to generate power. 90 mins.

VHS: S26833. $19.95.

Speaking of Sex: It's More Than Just Talk

This video contains the most current and reliable information about sex. Typical couples show how to deepen intimacy, with explicit instructions and demonstrations. There is also expert guidance from five top sex educators. 60 mins.

VHS: S25054. $29.95.

Spirituality and the Intellect

With Jacob Needleman. The essential tension between our material and spiritual natures is often forgotten as we pursue contemporary concerns, says the author of *The Heart of Philosophy* and *The New Religions*. 30 mins.

VHS: S08634. $29.95.

Spontaneous Healing

Dr. Andrew Weil, one of the most articulate and important leaders in the field of health and healing, shows how spontaneous healing has worked to resolve life-threatening diseases, severe trauma and chronic pain. Dr. Weil teaches us the power and the wisdom to draw on the sources of health we hold within, working with the body's natural defenses to manage illness. 72 mins.

VHS: S30559. $19.95.

Staying Faithful

Clinical psychologist Dr. Wendy LeDoux examines how to maintain the trust married couples need to avoid affairs and how partners can successfully deal with infidelity. 50 mins.

VHS: S32723. $19.95.

Stephan Rechtschaffen, M.D.: Holistic Health—A Guide for Living

This program was developed during a Wellness Weekend on the Omega campus. It offers a view of holistic health and suggests ways to achieve it. Diet, exercise, lifestyle, attitude and evolving concepts of longevity are all featured. 95 mins.

VHS: S23208. $39.95.

A Still, Small Voice

Chicago news anchor and journalist Bill Kurtis hosts this program about mystical experiences and transcendent moments. 60 mins.

VHS: S17182. $19.95.

Stress Management

With Janelle M. Barlow. This human development consultant and author of *The Stress Manager* offers suggestions for both becoming aware of how stress influences our bodies and for discharging its effects. 30 mins.

VHS: S08650. $29.95.

Stress Reduction Exercises

Stress leads to many ailments, some of which are life-threatening. Master Bob Klein outlines a basic stress reduction program in this video. 74 mins.

VHS: S23659. $24.95.

Stretching Your Whole Body

Jean Goulet explains how to relax the body in order to eliminate aches and prevent injury. 75 mins.

VHS: S23660. $19.95.

Super Abdomens Workout

This video is designed to emphasize exercises concentrating on the abdomen. It is useful for anyone involved in sports, dance or martial arts. 45 mins.

VHS: S23665. $19.95.

T'ai-Chi Chuan Kung-fu

Master Bob Klein shows step-by-step instructions of the ancient Chinese movements that are the basis of Kung-fu. Self-defense applications for each movement, weight distribution, breathing, the use of chi (internal energy) and the beginning "push hands" exercise are all explained. 120 mins.

VHS: S26822. $19.95.

T'ai-Chi Chuan: Chinese Moving Meditation

Master Bob Klein demonstrates the movements of the Yang short form from two angles, in a natural setting, with beginning level instructions. 48 mins.

VHS: S23657. $19.95.

T'ai-Chi Chuan: Movements of Power and Health

Master Bob Klein demonstrates the movements of the Yang short form, emphasizing basic coordination, the flow of energy (chi) and concentration exercises, all leading to stress reduction. 120 mins.

VHS: S23658. $29.95.

T'ai-Chi for Inner Beauty, with Jean Goulet

Jean Goulet demonstrates the 20-movement Yang short form. Along the way she explains the spiritual and physical ideals behind each movement. It will help the viewer move with greater grace and natural beauty. 60 mins.

VHS: S23656. $19.95.

T'ai-Chi for Seniors

Master Xue Dejun demonstrates the movements of the Yang long form for seniors. These techniques can rejuvenate seniors by revitalizing the body. 45 mins.

VHS: S23666. $24.95.

T'ai-Chi Massage

Learn how to give a pleasurable and relaxing massage based on the movements of T'ai-Chi. Accupressure, stretching, face massage, breathing techniques and even foot massage are covered. 60 mins.

VHS: S23662. $19.95.

T'ai-Chi Sword Forms

Master Bob Klein reveals the art of graceful sword movements from the Yang sword form to the intermediate fighting form in this video. Step-by-step instructions, defense applications, sword applications and free style sword fighting practice are all included. 120 mins.

VHS: S26828. $19.95.

T'ai-Chi-Ch'uan (Chen Man-Ching's Short Form)

This video includes preparatory exercises, basic training methods, a discussion of posture variations in the different styles, a demonstration of form and detailed training in the individual movements. 55 mins.

VHS: S26851. $24.95.

T'ai-Chi: The Inner Teachings, with Master Bob Klein: Body Awareness

In-depth training of the Yang short form, a slow, relaxing exercise, is featured in this video. These movements are practiced throughout China to stimulate energy and promote health. Master Bob Klein also explains the principals behind this form of exercise. 97 mins.

VHS: S23652. $19.95.

T'ai-Chi: The Inner Teachings, with Master Bob Klein: Chinese Chi-Gung Health Exercises

These enjoyable exercises combine relaxing, flowing movements with breathing and concentration techniques. Stress reduction strengthens the immune system, enhances the senses and promotes clearer thinking. 56 mins.

VHS: S23655. $19.95.

T'ai-Chi: The Inner Teachings, with Master Bob Klein: Harmonious Relationships

Enjoyable two-person exercises can help people open up to one another. Ultimately this can relieve stress and eliminate deep-seated fears. 45 mins.

VHS: S23654. $19.95.

T'ai-Chi: The Inner Teachings, with Master Bob Klein: Harmony of Mind and Body

This video explores the relationship between the mind and internal energy. The Yang form can be used to achieve a complete harmony of the mind. 52 mins.

VHS: S23653. $19.95.

Tai Chi for Health

Innovative exercises to tone muscles, improve flexibility and reduce stress. An excitingly different workout. 60 mins.

VHS: S08722. $9.98.

Tai Chi: 6 Forms 6 Easy Lessons

Dr. Paul Lam, a Tai Chi master and medical doctor, has combined the best of Eastern and Western traditions. He has distilled the 24 most popular forms of Tai Chi into 6 Forms that are perfect for beginners. Also includes a bonus set of "three in one" Qi Gong exercises. 100 mins.

VHS: S32700. $24.98.

Talking to Angels

This beautiful and inspiring film offers insight into how to face a life-threatening illness, as we meet Dr. Irene Goodale and her husband, Robert Perkins, who discovered unknown resources and a stronger love by coming to terms with her illness. 60 mins.

VHS: S31436. $19.95.

Tantra Love: Eastern Secrets of Intimacy and Ecstasy for Western Lovers

This professional, non-explicit (no nudity), instructional video explains in simple language and dramatic visuals how to make sexual energy and romantic love positive, even spiritual. "Excellent introduction to the Tantric Way" (*Better World* magazine). 60 mins.

VHS: S15290. $29.95.

Tantra: The Art of Conscious Loving

Charles and Caroline Muir, the foremost Western educators of this ancient Indian art form, bring the secrets of better sex and intimacy to western audiences. 70 mins.

VHS: S30764. $39.95.

The Tao of Practice

Created by Michael Murphy and human potential pioneer George Leonard, this daily, 40-minute practice for people with busy lives features exercises and imagery for body, mind, heart and soul. Drawing on both ancient wisdom and modern science, combining yoga, meditation, Eastern and holistic philosophies, this series of exercises is designed to help individuals reach goals of increased awareness, health and energies. "Leonard and Murphy are at the cutting edge, investigating the experiences of committed practice" (James Redfield, author of the best-selling book *The Celestine Prophecy*). 58 mins.

VHS: S30008. $29.95.

Teachings of the Masters

Jonette Crowley channels White Eagle to expound on the four states of the Master: Truth, Love, Invisibility and Compassion. Through these words of wisdom and guided meditation, you can touch the Master within yourself. 70 mins.

VHS: S22961. $24.95.

Thai Kickboxing

Thai kickboxing at its best is demonstrated by Master Robert Lyons on this video. Learn theory, stances, footwork, kicks, punches and elbow, leg and arm blocks through one-on-one instruction. Great for street self-defense. 110 mins.

VHS: S26837. $19.95.

The Secrets of Self-Pleasuring and Mutual Masturbation

Using different techniques and tools ranging from fingers to vibrators and jets of water, this exciting guide will help women learn masturbation skills that can help them become more readily orgasmic. Men will learn how self-pleasuring can be a long-lasting experience. 30 mins.

VHS: S31378. $29.95.

Thinking Allowed

An extraordinary series of conversations with leading thinkers on the cutting edge of knowledge and discovery. Each tape is 30 minutes, and is hosted by Dr. Jeffrey Mishlove, psychotherapist and television and radio interviewer.

Approaches to Growth: East and West. There are striking parallels between western psychotherapeutic methods such as gestalt therapy and the approaches of Sufism and Buddhism. In this discussion, Claudio Naranjo, psychiatrist and author of *The One Quest*, describes his personal experiences with the Arica training system. 30 mins.

VHS: S07902. $29.95.

Becoming More Fully Human. The problems of society result less from an intrinsic evil in human nature than from our failure to stop repeating behavior patterns from the past. Change, says Virginia Satir, begins with learning to accept and understand the many parts of yourself. Ms. Satir, one of the most influential psychologists today, is the author of *Conjoint Family Therapy, Peoplemaking, Self Esteem* and other books. 30 mins.

VHS: S07846. $29.95.

Beyond the Post-Modern Mind. The modern western world view is dominated by the materialist values of science. According to Huston Smith, this withdrawal of emphasis from human values—and from essential elements such as meaning, quality and purpose—has led to widespread alienation and social discontent. Dr. Smith is former professor of religion at MIT, and author of *The Religions of Man* and *Beyond the Post-Modern Mind*. 30 mins.

VHS: S07908. $29.95.

Challenging Assumptions. Donald Michael, Ph.D., former policy analyst for the National Science Foundation and the Joint Chiefs of Staff and the author of *The Next Generation* and *The Uncertain Society*, suggests that we are frequently misled by the certainties offered by politicians and social reformers, adding that by admitting our uncertainties we can begin to learn. 30 mins.

VHS: S07861. $29.95.

Common Threads in Mysticism. Robert Frager, founder of the California Institute for Transpersonal Psychology, shares his wide experience as a student and participant in diverse spiritual traditions, including Sufism, aikido. 30 mins.

VHS: S07903. $29.95.

Communication and Congruence. Virginia Satir, influential psychologist and founder of family therapy, describes how internalized "rules" for social behavior limit our communication. Ms. Satir demonstrates various communication styles-deprecation, blaming, intellectualizing and irrelevance—and how they are used to cover up feelings of low self-esteem. 30 mins.

VHS: S07859. $29.95.

Communication as Healing. All healing comes from a non-verbal "knowingness" within each of us, says Patricia Sun, spiritual teacher. Ms. Sun explores the nature of the healing process and demonstrates her use of sound as a method of focusing on her own healing consciousness. 30 mins.

VHS: S07863. $29.95.

Consciousness and Hyperspace. Nineteenth century theologians developed the idea of multiple dimensions to explain the idea of God in scientific language. Physicist Saul-Paul Sirag discusses recent theories of multiple dimensions, which have been fabricated to account for sub-atomic interactions, and the implications of these theories for the psychology and technology of the 21st century. 30 mins.

VHS: S07868. $29.95.

Consciousness and Quantum Reality. The mysteries of sub-atomic physics offers startling new perspectives on the human mind. Nick Herbert, author of *Quantum Reality*, points out that no matter how one interprets the equations of quantum physics the results lead to amazing and paradoxical concepts. Perhaps time runs backward as well as forward. Perhaps multiple independent universes are created each second. 30 mins.

VHS: S07869. $29.95.

Consciousness and Computers. William Whitson is currently involved in creating computer databases containing the world's great ethical and humanitarian teachings. Foreign affairs specialist and former Rand Corporation executive, he describes the role of computers in the democratization of knowledge claiming that "gaming" capabilities once limited to the military and industrial elite are now available to those of us seeking world peace. 30 mins.

VHS: S07877. $29.95.

Consciousness and the Martial Arts. One of the goals of martial artists is to cultivate an awareness both of their own subtle physiological rhythms and those of others. George Leonard, an aikido instructor and one of the founders of the consciousness movement, is the author of *The Ultimate Athlete*. 30 mins.

VHS: S07878. $29.95.

Course in Miracles. A home study system to unlearn the attitudes that separate the individual from his/her potential for spiritual unity, lead by Judith Skutch Whitson, president of the Foundation for Inner Peace. 30 mins.

VHS: S07899. $29.95.

Creativity in Business. In today's competitive environment, humanistic values are essential at every level of the corporation, according to Stanford professor Michael Ray. Dr. Ray, author of *Advertising and Communication Management*, describes how to apply principles of consciousness expansion, intuition and creativity in the business world. 30 mins.

VHS: S07872. $29.95.

Cult of Information. One of America's foremost social critics, Theodore Roszak, the author of *The Making of the Counter-Culture*, delivers a scathing indictment of the over-selling of computer and high-tech ideology to the American public under the argument that we are in the danger of becoming lost in the erroneous fascination with the information processing model of the mind. 30 mins.

VHS: S07874. $29.95.

Dark Side of Excellence. Business training techniques often focus mindlessly on "positive thinking", glossing over the need for executives to engage in soul-searching and self-renewal. John O'Neil, president of the California School of Professional Psychology, discusses the unfortunate trend in business to treat success as an all-consuming end in itself. 30 mins.

VHS: S07871. $29.95.

Developing and Applying Psychic Abilities. Kevin Riverson, psychic trance medium, gained attention as the focus of Shirley MacLaine's *Dancing in the Light*. In this program, Kevin predicts that the use of psychic intuitives for solving scientific and social problems will become an integral part of our culture. 30 mins.

VHS: S07898. $29.95.

Emerging New Culture. Dr. Fritjof Capra, the best-selling author of *The Tao of Physics* and *The Turning Point*, discusses the new holistic culture that has emerged in the late 20th century, arguing that the biological sciences, quantum physics and systems theory will provide a theoretical foundation which will supersede the decaying culture based on a linear, mechanistic world view. 30 mins.

VHS: S07886. $29.95.

Evolution: The Great Chain of Being. Philosopher Arthur M. Young, inventor of the Bell helicopter, describes three different types of evolution: physical evolution of the form of the body, evolution of the group soul of a species, and personal evolution. 30 mins.

VHS: S07897. $29.95.

Explanations of the Supernatural. Michael Scriven, Ph.D., calls to task those who maintain that all psychic claims must be either fraud or error. Dr. Scriven is a multi-disciplinary scholar who has made significant contributions to mathematics, logic, philosophy of science, ethics, education, psychology and parapsychology. 30 mins.

VHS: S07883. $29.95.

Global Mind-Changes. There is increasing global emphasis on the inner life of the mind. Futurist Willis Harman suggests that a new set of values, emerging spontaneously in many social strata and in different parts of the world, is having an impact in the world of business and corporate training. 30 mins.

VHS: S07887. $29.95.

Governance, Uncertainty and Compassion. Donald Michael, emeritus professor of University of Michigan, says that when we can acknowledge the existential realities of our uncertainty, our need for community and our isolation in the face of death, we are led to a position of compassion from which genuine long-range planning may proceed. 30 mins.

VHS: S07889. $29.95.

Health in the Workplace. Many businesses are beginning to appreciate the importance of optimal psychological and physical health within the workforce. Kenneth Pelletier, author of *Mind as Healer/Mind as Slayer* and other books, suggests that workers are no longer viewed as replaceable, but as the company's greatest asset. 30 mins.

VHS: S07870. $29.95.

Holographic Brain. With a better understanding of neurological functioning, says Dr. Harl Pribram, we may find the groundwork for a new approach to understanding spiritual and mystical experiences. Dr. Pribram, professor of neuropsychology at Stanford, is the author of *Languages of the Brain*. 30 mins.

VHS: S07895. $29.95.

Incorporating Creativity. Innovation, at every level of the corporation structure, is possible, argues William Miller, management consultant and author of *The Creative Edge*. Every individual, says Miller, has the capacity to overcome creative blocks by looking for answers which satisfy the desires and values of the heart. 30 mins.

VHS: S07873. $29.95.

Inner Mechanisms of Healing. Important breakthroughs in the field of neuroimmunology suggest that the human nervous system and the immune system are intimately linked. Brendan O'Regan, vice-president of research for the Institute of Noetic Sciences, notes the shift of emphasis in healing research from documenting the role of mind in healing to searching for an understanding of how and why healing occurs. 30 mins.

VHS: S07865. $29.95.

Learning to Use ESP. If you've read *Psychic Discoveries behind the Iron Curtain*, you are aware of the pioneering work of Czechoslovakian parapsychologist Dr. Milan Ryzl. Here he shares his personal experiences as a hypnotist and researcher, describing his training methods and their practical applications. 30 mins.

VHS: S07884. $29.95.

Metaphors of Transformation. Ralph Metzner is well known as a consciousness explorer. Here he stresses the importance of metaphor in guiding and understanding personal development. He focuses on the many forms of the metaphor of death and rebirth and of the journey. Dr. Metzner is author of *Opening to Inner Light, Maps of Consciousness*, and co-author of *The Psychedelic Experience*. 30 mins.

VHS: S07849. $29.95.

Mind over Machine. Human intuition and perception are basic and essential phenomena of consciousness. As such, they will never be replicated by computers. This is the challenging notion of Hubert Dreyfus, architect of the artificial intelligence establishment, and professor at University of California/Berkeley. 30 mins.

VHS: S07876. $29.95.

Mind-Body Connection. Eleanor Criswell, psychologist and managing editor of *Somatics*, points out that the mind-body connection can be approached through many disciplines, suggesting enormous possibilities for controlling mind and body. 30 mins.

VHS: S07881. $29.95.

New Science of Life. Biologist Rupert Sheldrake, author of *A New Science of Life* and *The Presence of the Past*, has stimulated and even startled the scientific world by challenging the mechanistic thinking in the life sciences. Dr. Sheldrake proposes a bold alternative to the idea that genetic programming is solely responsible for diversity of form, development of behavior and the development of mind in living creatures. 30 mins.

VHS: S07867. $29.95.

On Dreams and Dreaming. Patricia Garfield, Ph.D., author of *Creative Dreaming* and *Women's Bodies, Women's Dreams*, offers various methods of working with dreams to make them a source of positive value and growth. 30 mins.

VHS: S07851. $29.95.

Past Life Regression and Spirit Depossession. Edith Fiore, fascinating author of *You Have Been Here Before* and *The Unquiet Dead*, discusses her transformation from a conventional behavior therapist to a specialist in the application of spiritual principles of reincarnation and spirit possession to psychotherapy. 30 mins.

VHS: S07892. $29.95.

Personality Development and the Psyche. Helen Palmer, Ph.D., founder of the Center for the Investigation and Training of Intuition, shows how to open your mind to a range of intuitive and psychic experiences. 30 mins.

VHS: S07856. $29.95.

Physics and Consciousness. Witty and profound, physicist Fred Alan Wolf is the author of the National Book Award-winning *Taking the Quantum Leap* as well as *Starwave* and *Body Quantum*. Dr. Wolf's far-ranging thinking extends the understanding of quantum physics as it applies to your body and mind, suggesting that you are inextricably connected with all that exists in the physical universe. 30 mins.

VHS: S07866. $29.95.

Power of Ritual. Anna Halprin, director of the Tamalpa Institute, draws on her own experience battling cancer to discuss the psychological value of body movement and symbolic action in recognizing inner negativity and transforming its power into a healing experience. 30 mins.

VHS: S07852. $29.95.

Practice of Meditation. Buddhist teacher of Vipasana (mindfulness) meditation and author of *Living Masters of Buddhism* Jack Kornfield, Ph.D., shows how to quiet the mind so we become aware of our unconscious tensions and how to heal those tensions. 30 mins.

VHS: S07855. $29.95.

Psychic and Spiritual Healing. Can the methods and ideas of native spiritual healers be incorporated into modern psychological and medical practice? Psychologist Stanley Kripper tells of his experiences with native shamans and healers in the Americas and Asia. Dr. Krippner is the author of *Human Possibilities* and *Realms of Healing*. 30 mins.

VHS: S07862. $29.95.

Psychokinesis, or Mind over Matter. Dr. Julian Isaacs, professor of parapsychology at John F. Kennedy University, shows how to learn psychokineses through the attainment of zen-like concentration, and both focus on and indifference to the experimental task. 30 mins.

VHS: S07885. $29.95.

Psychological and Spiritual Blindspots. Patricia Sun, spiritual teacher and expert in conflict resolution, suggests that through a return to innocence you can rediscover your connection with the world in a healing manner. 30 mins.

VHS: S07858. $29.95.

Psychology of Religious Experience. One of the most widely read writers in the field of philosophy and religion, Huston Smith's classic book, *The Religions of Man*, has sold over two million copies. In this program, Dr. Smith discusses the relation between psychedelic experience and religious practice, the god within and the cultivation of psychic experiences within religious and shamanic traditions. 30 mins.
VHS: S07843. $29.95.

Psychotherapy and Spiritual Paths. Dr. Seymour Boorstein, the editor of *Transpersonal Psychotherapy*, discusses his transformation from a conventional and atheistic psychiatrist to a student of spirituality. 30 mins.
VHS: S07891. $29.95.

Science and Religion. While conventional religion and science are often in conflict, there is a growing convergence between non-reductionistic science and internally oriented religious traditions. Willis Harman points out that this movement reflects an important new area of public interest.
VHS: S07906. $29.95.

Science and Spiritual Traditions. Western science and traditional spiritual practice are both dedicated to the search for truth. Charles Tart, professor of psychology at the University of California, suggests that we may someday be able to specify which types of spiritual discipline would be most beneficial for difference people. 30 mins.
VHS: S07905. $29.95.

Self-Observation. Countless factors can mitigate against self-observation in Western society. Charles Tart, noted psychologist and author of *Waking Up*, suggests you begin by learning to focus on seemingly trivial details such as bodily sensations. 30 mins.
VHS: S07847. $29.95.

Sound and Healing. The use of sound in healing is based on the principle that the entire universe is created of vibrations and can be influenced through these vibrations. Jill Purce, the author of *The Mystic Spiral*, discusses the role of sound in traditional cultures as a means of harmonizing and healing the human body. 30 mins.
VHS: S07864. $29.95.

Spirit and Soma. The human organism and biosphere are part of one system, says Stanley Keleman, a leading pioneer of psychotherapy from a somatic perspective. The author of numerous books including *Emotional Anatomy*, he discusses the unity of spirit and soma (the body). 30 mins.
VHS: S07880. $29.95.

Spiritual Channeling. Alan Vaughan, one of America's best-known and most tested psychic intuitives, describes the channeling process. 30 mins.
VHS: S07900. $29.95.

Spiritual Training. Irina Tweedie, author of *Daughter of Fire*, a diary of her intensive spiritual training in India with a Sufi master, describes the bliss, peace and love—and the despair, hatred and loneliness—of her years of training in the Sufi tradition. 30 mins.
VHS: S07857. $29.95.

Spirituality and Psychology. True psychology is incomplete without an understanding of the spiritual yearnings of human beings. Frances Vaughan, a transpersonal psychotherapist, stresses that all spiritual traditions ultimately offer a means toward transcendence of the limited self.
VHS: S07890. $29.95.

Staying Alive: Psychology of Human Survival. We cannot live authentic lives without feeling touched by the major problems of the planet. Roger Walsh, professor of psychiatry at U.C. Irvine urges that by becoming aware of the roots of these problems in ourselves, we can begin to heal our culture of its dangerously insane condition. 30 mins.
VHS: S07888. $29.95.

Sufi Path. The Sufis are inheritors of a tradition which has influenced many world religions. Mrs. Irina Tweedle, a Sufi teacher, describes the teachings and devotional practice of the Sufis. 30 mins.
VHS: S07904. $29.95.

Thinking About Thinking. Michael Scriven, Ph.D., is a philosopher and multi-disciplinary scholar whose specialty is the process of thinking itself. He describes how individuals and organizations can examine the logic of their own decisions. Dr. Scriven is the author of *The Logic of Evaluation* and other books. 30 mins.
VHS: S07860. $29.95.

Time and Destiny. The qualitative and cyclical nature of time is the subject of this discussion with mathematician, physicist and philosopher Charles Muses, author of *Destiny and Control in Human Systems*. 30 mins.
VHS: S07896. $29.95.

Tools for Thought. Howard Theingold, author of *Tools for Thought: The History and Future of Mind-Expanding Technology*, says that the revolution in personal computers is yet to occur. In the next ten years personal computers will be sufficiently powerful to realize the dreams of many innovators who write about "fantasy amplifiers," and "computerized villages." 30 mins.
VHS: S07875. $29.95.

Toward a New Paradigm of the Unconscious. In extraordinary circumstances your mind is capable of accessing information from anywhere in time or space, according to evidence provided by Stanislav Grof. Author of *The Realms of the Human Unconscious*, Dr. Grof is an innovative psychotherapist who has attempted to integrate the divergent schools of Freud, Jung, and Reich with insights from the leading edge of contemporary physics and biology. 30 mins.
VHS: S07845. $29.95.

Transcending Limitations. James Fadiman, author of *Be All That You Are* offers several techniques to help individuals recognize and discard attachments to old attitudes and outworn ideas. A distinguished psychotherapist, Dr. Fadiman is the past president of the Association for Transpersonal Psychology. 30 mins.
VHS: S07848. $29.95.

Transforming the Human Body. Michael Murphy has spent years cataloging the ways in which human abilities can be transcended and the human body transformed. Founder of the Esalen Institute and the author of the *Psychic Side of Sports*, he describes how to consciously control physical evolution through religious and athletic disciplines, biofeedback and medicine. 30 mins.
VHS: S07879. $29.95.

Understanding Extra-Sensory Perception. One of America's foremost parapsychology researches, Dr. Charles Tart, discusses factors that facilitate ESP performance in the laboratory and in the world. 30 mins.
VHS: S07882. $29.95.

Understanding Mythology. Joseph Campbell, one of the world's foremost mythologists and interpreters of myth, in a provocative discussion as he argues against literal interpretation of ancient myth, claiming that modern science provides the raw material for future myths which can serve to unite all humankind as one biological and spiritual unit. 30 mins.
VHS: S07842. $29.95.

Universal Organism. The so-called laws of nature may actually be more like habits and instincts than immutable and inviolable principles, says Rupert Sheldrake Ph.D., biologist and author of the controversial *A New Science of Life*. From his perspective, all of creation may be viewed as a living organism. 30 mins.
VHS: S07894. $29.95.

Value and Purpose in Science. Consciousness, rather than being a property which emerges at higher orders of complexity, is a basic principle intrinsic to every level of creation, according to this program with philosopher Arthur M. Young. 30 mins.
VHS: S07907. $29.95.

Visionary Experience or Psychosis? The psychiatric community errs in treating visionary experience as a form of mental illness, says Jungian psychotherapist John Weir Perry, the author of many books, including *The Heart of History* and *The Far Side of Madness*. 30 mins.
VHS: S07893. $29.95.

Waking Up. Charles Tart, Ph.D., author of *Altered States of Consciousness*, suggests how to begin to wake up by allowing awareness to become conscious of itself. 30 mins.
VHS: S27049. $29.95.

What Is Chaneling? Arthur Hastings, Ph.D., explores the phenomenon known variously as spirit communication, trance mediumship or chaneling. 30 mins.
VHS: S07901. $29.95.

Working with Creative Energy. Shakti Gawan, author of the best-selling *Creative Visualization*, explains how to use visualized images as blueprints for events that manifest in our lives, providing instructions for a basic visualization technique. 30 mins.
VHS: S07850. $29.95.

Working with Dreams. Jeremy Taylor, founder of the movement for leaderless dream work groups and the author of *Dream Work*, points out that dreams are held in disrepute by mainstream institutions because they challenge closed systems of thought. He suggests that techniques such as lucid dreaming be used for purposes of healing and overcoming addictions. 30 mins.
VHS: S07853. $29.95.

The Thirteen Stones of the Universal Wheel

Maria Heller guides newcomers to the Universal Wheel, a movement that recognizes the interconnectedness of all things. This movement does not take the place of any culture or religion. Instead it teaches one how to realize the self without the separations between species, races, genders or ideologies. 60 mins.
VHS: S22967. $29.98.

Three Levels of Power and How to Use Them

Caroline Myss, Ph.D. explains that power and the loss of power are central ingredients in every health issue. She reveals the process of strengthening and invigorating your life through the natural and inherent energy of power. 70 mins.
VHS: S34706. $19.98.

Time & The More It Changes

Alan Watts is a charismatic philosopher and Zen mystic. This series of informal video talks finds him musing on the meaning of time and change, causality, ambition and the effect of the present on the past. 50 mins.
VHS: S26181. $29.95.

Time and Transformation

Peter Russell is a visionary writer and filmmaker who maintains that humans are part of a continual progression toward greater self-awareness. However, only a shift in consciousness will avert disaster. He believes we must create universal spiritual wisdom. 60 mins.
VHS: S23622. $34.95.

The Timothy Leary San Francisco Memorial

Documents an unusual memorial service for Timothy Leary at the First Unitarian church in San Francisco on June 12, 1996. Noted speakers Ram Dass, Robert Anton Wilson, Ralph Metzner, Frank Barron, Michael Horowitz, Cynthia Palmer, Diane Di Prima, Richard Katz, R.U. Sirius, Nina Graboi, Robert Forte, Country Joe McDonald, Paul Kantner, Diana Tremble, Barbara Imhoff, and family members Rosemary Leary, Deidra and Zach Leary.
VHS: S33808. $24.95.
Claire Burch, USA, 1997, 58 mins.

The Total Self

Hal Stone, Ph.D., author of *Embracing Heaven and Earth*, discusses what is the nature of the self. He proposes that we are not unitary beings, but consist of many autonomous sub-personalities and energy complexes. 90 mins.
VHS: S13327. $49.95.

Touch of Love...The Massage

A simple and beautiful way to learn the techniques of full body massage. Couples demonstrate how to stroke and relax each area of the body as the program invites you to experience the art of sensual massage.
VHS: S10955. $29.95.

Training Techniques of the Shaolin

A candid interview with Master Robert Lyons describes life behind the mysterious walls of the Shaolin Temple. Daily routines and constant physical and mental training are required. Chi-gung power and fighting techniques are explained. 70 mins.
VHS: S26842. $19.95.

Tranquility Through Tai Chi

Baiqing Li and Mei H. Li teach the 24-movement, simplified version of this healing martial art. A brief history of Tai Chi, together with careful, simple and repeated instruction, guarantee the viewer easy facility with these techniques. From stress reduction to lower blood pressure, the health effects of this exercise are invaluable. 50 mins.
VHS: S22230. $29.95.

The Transformation of Man

J. Krishnamurti, physicist David Bohm and psychiatrist David Shainberg debate the future of mankind's evolving consciousness in this video. They brilliantly expound on the possibility of a radical transformation of human beings and the way they see the world. 240 mins.
VHS: S26182. $39.95.

The Truth About Impotence

In an unblushingly honest look at real patients, real causes, and real treatments, NOVA pulls the veil on a rarely discussed but widespread problem. 60 mins.
VHS: S34586. $19.95.

Unlocking Your Body: Regaining Youth Through Somatic Awareness

According to Thomas Hanna, founder of the discipline of somatics, many of the effects of aging—aching muscles and joints, stooped postures, stiffness and weakness—are unnecessary and reversible. He explains how to establish body awareness and release contracted muscles through simple exercises. 90 mins.
VHS: S13326. $49.95.

Unlocking Your Subconscious Wisdom

Dr. Marcia Emory is an author and teacher who outlines steps that help unlock the intuitive mind. This series of exercises will eliminate obstacles that lead to distortions. 60 mins.
VHS: S23621. $34.95.

The Unquiet Dead: An Introduction to Spirit Depossession Therapy

With Edith Fiore, Ph.D. What connection do we have with the souls of the departed? Psychologist Edith Fiore describes diagnosis and treatment of apparent spirit depossession and leads us through an actual depossession technique. 90 mins.
VHS: S08629. $49.95.

Virtual Reality

Dr. Timothy Leary lectures on the multiple possibilities of how to operate, teleport the brain and interconnect with other tele-persons and virtual reality, the technology capable of producing the impression of alternate worlds or experiences. 95 mins.
VHS: S18034. $29.95.

Voices of a New Age

Today's foremost spiritual teachers share their ideas about creating a better tomorrow. This wide-ranging program explores the frontiers in health, science, spirituality and human consciousness. Narrated by Richie Havens.
VHS: S32717. $24.95.
Elda Hartley, USA, 1994, 60 mins.

Voices of Spirit

Elwood Babbitt, a farmer who lives deep in the hills of western Massachusetts, is also a trance medium. This 1975 film features skeptics and believers alike as it pursues a psychic detective story in search of both a dead friend and the real nature of Babbitt as he summons the spirits of Mark Twain, Walt Disney, Sir Arthur Conan Doyle, Jesus Christ and others while in a trance. 60 mins.
VHS: S31099. $29.95.

Waking Up the Power Within: The Freedom to Heal

Deepak Chopra takes viewers from modern quantum physics to ancient Vedic philosophy in search of perfect physical health and spiritual health and happiness. Unbounded freedom, relinquishing the known and stepping into the unknown is key. 60 mins.
VHS: S22690. $29.95.

The Way of the Wizard

This video from Deepak Chopra holds the key to love, personal fulfillment and spiritual growth. The road to magic begins with the pure potential that lies in everyone's hearts and minds. Based on the best-selling book *The Way of the Wizard*. 80 mins.
VHS: S27319. $19.95.

Wellness Series: Positive Imagery

This self-improvement series is based on the important concept of Imagery, the bridge between mind and body. Recent research has shown that mental images are involved in whether we stay well or become ill. The series combines the research of Dr. Jeanne Achterberg and Dr. G. Frank Lawlis with the creative skills of visual music artist Jon Mark.
Success Achievement.
VHS: S10233. $29.95.
Depression Manager.
VHS: S10234. $29.95.
Pain Manager.
VHS: S10235. $29.95.
Stop Smoking.
VHS: S10236. $29.95.
Stress Manager.
VHS: S10237. $29.95.
Weight Manager.
VHS: S10238. $29.95.

What Is Kundalini?

With Lee Sannella. This medical doctor and author of *Kundalini: Psychosis or Transcendence?* describes the changes in the nervous system that can result from intensive spiritual disciplines. 30 mins.
VHS: S08643. $29.95.

What Is Yoga?

Jivamukti Yoga Center directors Sharon Gannon and David Life, Academy Award-winning actor and yoga student Willem DaFoe, and devotional singer Bhagavan Das and others explore yoga as a religion, stress reducer and muscle builder. Soundtrack features Bill Laswell, Jai Uttal, Krishna Das and others. 56 mins.
VHS: S34252. $24.95.

What Makes Work Meaningful?

With Dennis T. Jaffe. Workers today are demanding a sense of self-actualization on the job. The author of *Take This Job and Love It* suggests how we can find meaning, commitment and passion in our work. 30 mins.
VHS: S08652. $29.95.

When Bad Things Happen to Good People

Harold Kushner provides this video presentation of the cornerstone ideas and philosophy of his theories and teachings. 60 mins.
VHS: S17180. $14.95.

When Food Becomes an Obsession: Overcoming Eating Disorders

Recommended by Eating Disoders Awareness & Prevention and highly regarded by the American Anorexia Bulimia Association, this film features Emma, a 17-year-old recovering anorexic, as she openly discusses her struggle with this eating disorder, and her concerned parents as they witness their daughter's rapid weight loss. Also features insight from Susanna Feder, a recovered bulimic who is now a psychologist and counselor specializing in eating disorders. 30 mins.
VHS: S32342. $49.95.

White Crane Kung-fu

This ancient, spectacular style is demonstrated by expert Bob Stannells. The "Siu Hok Kune" basic set is seen at various speeds including a helpful slow motion analysis of every aspect. History, fist forms, kicking techniques, stance exercises and a two-man sparring set are also featured in this video. 45 mins.
VHS: S26845. $24.95.

Why People Don't Heal and How They Can

In her no-nonsense, high-voltage style, Caroline Myss, Ph.D., provides insights that foster hope and inspiration, unlocking the doors to health and healing. With humor and compassion, sheexplains the cultural blocks to healing and shows how to improve your health with the revolutionary five steps to healing. 76 mins.
VHS: S34705. $19.98.

Women's Health Series

An informative eight-volume series on women's bodies and women's health.
Women's Health Series: After Pregnancy: A New Start. In the first few weeks after giving birth there are some important facts all young parents should know. This video explains the facts clearly and without inspiring fear. 34 mins.
VHS: S24253. $19.98.
Women's Health Series: Breast Cancer: Replacing Fear with Facts. In addition to explaining the risks caused by breast cancer, this video demonstrates the proper way to conduct your own examination. 37 mins.
VHS: S24255. $19.98.
Women's Health Series: Contraception: Know Your Options. This is a clear review of contraceptive methods for both men and women. 39 mins.
VHS: S24256. $19.98.
Women's Health Series: Infertility: The New Solutions. After explaining some of the causes of infertility in men and women, this video explores some of the treatment options currently available to treat this condition. 30 mins.
VHS: S24252. $19.98.
Women's Health Series: Menopause: Guidelines to a Healthy Life. This informative video explains the effects of menopause, including its symptoms and the physical changes endured by a maturing body. 31 mins.
VHS: S24251. $19.98.
Women's Health Series: Menstruation: Understanding Your Body. This video covers menarche, the menstrual cycle-including what is considered normal and abnormal—and PMS. 28 mins.
VHS: S24258. $19.98.
Women's Health Series: Pregnancy: Nine Special Months. The nine months of pregnancy require some basic health methods that can help insure both the health of the woman and her baby. 40 mins.
VHS: S24257. $19.98.
Women's Health Series: Sexually Transmitted Diseases: The Keys to Prevention. Understanding the transmission, prevention and recognition of these infectious diseases can help combat these maladies, which often inspire considerable anxiety. 39 mins.
VHS: S24254. $19.98.

Yang Long Form of T'ai-Chi Chuan

Master Bob Klein demonstrates the movements of the Yang long form from two different angles. Instructions are given for weight distribution, breathing and the names of movements. 75 mins.
VHS: S23664. $19.95.

You Can Heal Your Life

Based on the principles and ideas formulated by author, teacher and metaphysical counselor Louis L. Hay, this video deals with acquiring self-worth, self-esteem and self-definition.
VHS: S17606. $24.95.

PARENTING & THE HOME

The Art of Dining: The Business Lunch

Manners expert Marjabelle Young Stewart offers insights and proper strategies for pulling off the politically important business lunch. Mrs. Stewart offers advice on choosing the restaurant, ordering the meal, managing difficult foods and the correct etiquette of tipping. 27 mins.
VHS: S20191. $14.95.

The Art of Dining: The Formal Dinner

Marjabelle Young Stewart shows how to plan, prepare and orchestrate a formal dinner: writing the invitations, handling the proper seating arrangements, using utensils, making toasts and making a refined exit. 36 mins.
VHS: S20192. $14.95.

A Baby's World

This three-volume set explores the growth of babies from infants into walking, talking and thinking human beings. It offers compelling insights into the growth process, which remains a miraculous transformation. Each volume is 45 mins.
Vol. 1: A Whole New World.
VHS: S26053. $14.95.
Vol. 2: The Language of Being.
VHS: S26054. $14.95.
Vol. 3: Reason and Relationships.
VHS: S26055. $14.95.
Three-Volume Set.
VHS: S26056. $39.95.

Child Development: The First Two Years

A comprehensive guide to your children's emotional, spiritual and physical development. This program is designed to impart confidence and valuable teaching tools to young parents. The development is broken into four parts: 0-3 months, 3-6 months, 6-12 months and 12-24 months. The topics covered include physical growth, touching, diapering, language development, sounds and communications, mobility and motor skills and playing with other children. 47 mins.
VHS: S19174. $19.98.

Creative Parenting: The First Twelve Months

This program distills a series of expert opinions on the proper methods and instructions in the raising of babies during their vital first year. Hosted by Beau Bridges.
VHS: S19578. $9.95.

The Discovery Year

This program, hosted by Christopher Reeve, shows how babies learn to focus their senses, roll over, grasp objects, crawl, explore and finally stand up and walk unaided. Three sets of parents respond to the different personalities of their infant. 46 mins.
VHS: S20537. $29.95.

Far Eastern Cookery

A celebration of the myriad of distinctive flavors of the Far East, this video presents 16 of Madhur Jaffrey's own favorite dishes from Thailand, Japan, Korea, Hong Kong, the Philippines, Malaysia, Vietnam and Indonesia. 60 mins. A BBC Production.
VHS: S10280. $29.95.

Four Seasons in Polish Cooking

How to prepare the most delicious Polish dishes; includes a booklet full of recipes. The program is hosted by Katarzyna Pospieszynska. 110 mins. Narration in English.
VHS: S11382. $29.95.

The Gifts of Fathering

Dr. Ron Klinger, President of the Center for Successful Fathering, hosts this video about parenting for kids up to the age of 10. He details the importance of an active father role and explains how it can be achieved and maintained. 32 mins.
VHS: S26026. $19.98.

Great Chefs of the West

Visit the kitchens of some of the hottest chefs west of the Mississippi and their secrets to an array of culinary masterpieces as well as down home favorites.
VHS: S10159. $19.95.

Great Chefs: A Holiday Table

A Great Chefs video sampler of traditional Christmas and holiday dishes with a companion recipe booklet. Includes Christmas Pudding from England, a French Yule Log, a German Roast Goose and a whole suckling pig prepared Cajun style. 10 recipes.
VHS: S10156. $19.95.

Great Chefs: Appetizers

Eleven of the finest chefs in America reveal their techniques preparing appetizers ranging from Pepper Oysters to Empress Mushrooms.
VHS: S10157. $19.95.

Great Chefs: Desserts

Twelve spectacular desserts from twelve of the finest chefs in America—from New Orleans' Bananas Foster to Chicago's rich chocolate and Bourbon Pecan Cake. 12 recipes.
VHS: S10158. $19.95.

Great Chefs: New Orleans Jazz Brunch

Features historical footage of early creole cooking, a section on coffee and its relationship to New Orleans, as well as the creole version of a Japanese tea ceremony. Then you enjoy the famous Breakfast at Brennan's, and a companion recipe booklet. 60 mins.
VHS: S10155. $19.95.

Helping Your Baby Sleep Through the Night

This practical guide to parenting provides insights, suggestions and effective ways for helping a child sleep uninterrupted. "The information is presented in a way that educates, informs and encourages the new parent" (*Journal of the American Medical Association*).
VHS: S19577. $9.95.

Hot off the Grill

Hosted by celebrated TV journalist David Rosengarten, some of the country's top chefs uncover their searing secrets to grilling mouth-watering appetizers, entrees and a "feast fit for friends." A PBS WGBH Boston Special. 60 mins.
VHS: S33088. $19.95.

I Am Your Child

Hosted by two-time Academy Award-winner Tom Hanks, this in-depth special looks at new parenting and childhood development programs in the community of Hampton, Virginia. Written, directed and executive produced by Rob Reiner, and featuring Mel Brooks, Billy Crystal, Michael J. Fox, Charlton Heston, Jon Lovitz, Rosie O'Donnell, Shaquille O'Neal, Tracy Pollan, General Colin Powell, Carl Reiner, Martin Short, Roseanne, Alex Trebek, Robin Williams, Oprah Winfrey, President Bill Clinton and First Lady Hillary Rodham Clinton. 45 mins.
VHS: S33675. $19.98.

Jewish Mothers Video Cookbook

Now, for the first time, the secrets of traditional Jewish cooking, previously passed only from mother to daughter, are revealed for all to enjoy. This cassette leads you step by step through 16 delicious kosher recipes including appetizers, side dishes, main courses and desserts. Comes complete with a recipe booklet. 90 mins.
VHS: S06573. $34.95.

Ken Hom's Chinese Cookery

Ken Hom takes the lid off Chinese cookery and reveals the secrets of popular Chinese dishes, showing how they can be prepared without special equipment or unusual ingredients. A BBC production. 60 mins.
VHS: S10278. $19.94.

A Kid's Guide to Divorce

More than half of the children under the age of 18 are affected by divorce. This program helps children deal with the emotional and psychological repercussions associated with the strain and trauma of divorce.
VHS: S20027. $125.00.

A Kid's Guide to Drug, Alcohol and Smoking Awareness

Prepared for children from kindergarten through third grade, this program points out the aspects of drug, alcohol and tobacco abuse among children. The program examines substance abuse in factual, clear presentations.
VHS: S20028. $145.00.

Kids, Sex, and Choices

An in-depth look at the highly controversial issue of sex education in our schools. Should abstinence or birth control be taught, and are these subjects appropriate for students at all? This award-winning documentary lets you "sit-in" on classes and hear what educators, parents and kids have to say. 60 mins.
VHS: S16394. $39.95.

Life's First Feelings

Watch close-up with researchers as they seek to understand babies' emotional responses, clues about developing personality traits, and how parents help with socialization. 60 mins.
VHS: S28652. $19.95.

Madhur Jaffrey's Indian Cookery

Fabulous, foolproof recipes for anyone who loves the exotic taste of good Indian food, in this practical, step-by-step video. Madhur Jaffrey, using ingredients which are readily available, shows how to cook eight wonderfully authentic Indian dishes, including Tandoori Style Chicken. A BBC production. 60 mins.
VHS: S10279. $19.94.

Mediterranean Cookery

The cuisine of intense flavors, brilliant colors and simple, clean tastes which evoke images of the sun and the sea, in two volumes produced by the BBC.
Volume 2: Egypt, Turkey, Morocco and Greece. The culinary diversity of the region is indicated by the wide range of traditional specialties demonstrated by top chefs and in the home. 90 mins.
VHS: S10309. $19.94.

Mr. Baby Proofer

Danny "Mr. Baby Proofer" McNeill leads a room-by-room guide to providing a child-safe environment. McNeill is recognized nationwide as the foremost authority on child safety. 30 mins.
VHS: S16585. $14.95.

New and Improved Kids

Host Loni Anderson takes us to the heart of what it means to raise loving, responsible children. 1989, 47 mins.
VHS: S14452. $29.95.

Newborn Care

A reassuring program that guides parents through the basic skills they need to care for their infants. Includes a 20-page booklet that explains many subjects new parents will encounter during the first months of their child's life. 1989, 43 mins.
VHS: S14448. $24.95.

On Fire: A Family Guide to Fire Safety

Host Henry Johnson demonstrates simple, easy-to-remember techniques on how to fight, control, or escape from fires. Includes home safeguards, travel precautions, tips on use of fire safety equipment and a resource guide.
VHS: S16396. $19.95.

On the House: Restoring a Victorian House

Welcome to Number 50, once a dirty, neglected Victorian house, but under the loving care of "On the House," Britain's equivalent of PBS's "This Old House," it is restored to all its former glory. The informative video takes you through each detailed step. A BBC production. 98 mins.
VHS: S10283. $29.95.

Parenting for Today

Psychologist Dr. Lee Hausner, a noted authority on effective parenting and co-author of the acclaimed *Homework Without Tears*, offers simple, effective techniques you can use to maintain discipline with your children, particularly in adolescence. 70 mins.
VHS: S32702. $19.95.

Pat Paulsen on Wine

Legendary comedian, presidential candidate and winemaker Pat Paulsen in a funny—and very informative—video on wine in his three cheers for the red, white and rose! "Pat clearly demonstrates he knows as much about wine as he does about the Presidency," says Tommy Smothers.
VHS: S08120. $19.95.

Perfect Baby

An in-depth examination of state-of-the-art genetic engineering, a science which could cure genetically-transmitted disease, but could also signal a frightening future where genes are tested and manipulated at whim. This outstanding program prepares us for the ethical choices of the not-too-distant future: just how perfect do we want our children to be? 59 mins.
VHS: S13181. $19.98.

Stop Struggling with Your Child

Learn how to identify and resolve conflict with this four-step approach featuring national parenting experts Evonne Weinhaus and Karen Friedman, co-authors of the award-winning best-seller of the same name. 30 mins.
VHS: S33767. $29.95.

T. Berry Brazelton: The Changing Family and Its Implications

Brazelton's books on child-rearing are found in American homes across the country. Now he expounds on the dangers posed to families by the challenge of working parents. This is an important topic where Brazelton's insights are particularly troubling. 50 mins.
VHS: S24927. $29.95.

Vintage: A History of Wine by Hugh Johnson

One of the world's great wine experts presents this definitive, four-volume history of wine.
Vintage: A History of Wine Volume 1. Hugh Johnson explores the wines of today's Middle East, tracing the history of wine from its prized status in ancient Egypt to its prohibition in Islam. In northern Spain, Johnson discusses the history of Bacchanalian rites as Catholic parishioners douse themselves with wine in Dionysian frenzy. Then Johnson scrutinizes the grape-growing regions and marvels of the ancient houses of Greece, and finally discusses the debate in Germany between beer and wine by analyzing German wines. 116 mins.
VHS: S11185. $29.95.
Vintage: A History of Wine Volume 2. Wines of the torch-lit catacombs of Saint Emilion and the great sherry houses of Spain that are directly descended from Medieval tradition. On the golden slopes of Cote d'Or, Johnson tastes the region's savory wines, explaining how heat, rain and air mold a wine's character. Finally, the story of champagne, from its "invention" by Dom Perignon to celebrations at Maxim's. 116 mins.
VHS: S11186. $29.95.
Vintage: A History of Wine Volume 3. Wine and War: Madeira and Port—how war and politics have shaped the destiny of many of the wines now considered classics; Power of the Purse: Bordeaux Wines—how can a single region produce such diverse wines? The Devastator: Phylloxera—the insatiable parasite that destroyed Europe's vineyards in the late 19th century; Johnson reveals why today almost all European wines are grafted onto American stems. 116 mins.
VHS: S11187. $29.95.
Vintage: A History of Wine Volume 4. Migrating Vine: Wine in Australia; The Grape Goes West: California Wines—the evolution of some now great wines; and Vin Nouveau: Today and Tomorrow—the technology that will improve the future of wine making, why vineyards will thrive in the monsoon-drenched areas of Japan and how a winery in Tuscany was completely automated. 116 mins.
VHS: S11188. $29.95.

What's a Parent to Do?

John Stoessel explores the trials and tribulations of parenting in this compilation of his *20/20* reports. 50 mins.
VHS: S15882. $19.98.

When Mom and Dad Break Up

Hosted by Alan Thicke and developed in conjunction with family experts, a reassuring and entertaining program that tackles the questions children of divorced parents frequently ask, with kid-to-kid straight talk, music and animation. 32 mins.
VHS: S09898. $24.95.

TEST PREPARATION

GED Math Review

A video instruction to prepare for the General Educational Development test, including Arithmetic, Charts and Graphs, Probability and Statistics, Algebra and Geometry. Study guide included. 120 mins.
VHS: S17476. $39.95.

GMAT Math Review

A comprehensive video review course on the Graduate Management Admission Test includes sections on Arithmetic, Algebra, Geometry, Word Problems and Data Sufficiency. Study guide included. 120 mins.
VHS: S17473. $79.95.

GMAT Verbal Review

A video review of the GMAT verbal section details Analytical Reasoning, Reading Comprehension, and Sentence Correction. Study guide included. 135 mins.
VHS: S17474. $79.95.

LSAT

An in-depth video review that analyzes the Law School Admission Test entrance exam, with special emphasis on Reading Comprehension, Reasoning Analytically, Logical Analysis and Writing Sample Techniques. Study guide included. Two-tape set, 240 mins.
VHS: S17475. $79.95.

SAT/Analogies

An in-depth review of how analogy questions are deployed in standardized testing and the means to achieve a high score. The program details the logic behind analogy questions and how to recognize and attack relationships and patterns. Study guide included. 120 mins.
VHS: S17470. $39.95.

SAT/Reading Comprehension

A review of the skills and strategies students should master for reading comprehension on the SAT, PSAT, ACT and other standardized testing. Study guide included. 120 mins.
VHS: S17469. $39.95.

Secrets of Writing the College Admission Essay

A written essay is an important part of the college admission process. 60 mins.
VHS: S08764. $39.95.

Test Preparation Series

Experienced teachers, working at the chalkboard, guide students through intensive review courses crammed with important tips, insider test-taking strategies, and confidence building hints. The comprehensive reviews stress problem solving and are designed to prepare for even the most difficult and challenging questions.
ACT Math Review. High school seniors take the American College Testing Assessment for college admission. 120 mins.
VHS: S08737. $39.95.
ACT Verbal Review. 120 mins.
VHS: S08738. $39.95.
ASVAB Review. The Armed Services Voluntary Aptitude Battery tests. 120 mins.
VHS: S08749. $39.95.
Basic English/ESL. 120 mins.
VHS: S08753. $79.95.

Firefighter Exams Review. 120 mins.
VHS: S08751. $39.95.
GRE Math Review. Review for the Graduate Record Exam for admission to graduate school. 120 mins.
VHS: S08741. $119.95.
GRE Verbal Review. 120 mins.
VHS: S08742. $119.95.
MAT Review. College graduates take the Miller Analogies Test for admission to graduate school. 73 mins.
VHS: S08740. $39.95.
Math and Verbal Review for Civil Service Exams. For federal, state and city jobs. 120 mins.
VHS: S08748. $39.95.
NTE Review. Prospective teachers take the National Teacher Examination Core Battery in order to attain a license. 110 mins.
VHS: S08745. $39.95.
Police Officer Exams Review. 120 mins.
VHS: S08750. $39.95.
Post Office Exams Review. 120 mins.
VHS: S08752. $39.95.
SAT-PSAT Math Review. High school juniors and seniors take the Scholastic and Preliminary Scholastic Aptitude Test for college admission. 120 mins.
VHS: S08733. $39.95.
SAT-PSAT Verbal Review. 120 mins.
VHS: S08734. $39.95.

TOEFL Review

A comprehensive study of the Test of English as a Foreign Language with emphasis on comprehension, structure, written expression, vocabulary and reading. Study guide included. Three-tape set, 360 mins.
VHS: S17472. $119.95.

LANGUAGE ARTS

Basic Grammar Series

The three films in this series feature a robot, humans, and an assortment of whimsical objects that teach lessons in grammar. Each is 8 mins.
Modifiers (Adjectives and Adverbs).
VHS: S23465. $49.95.

Nouns.

VHS: S23463. $49.95.

Verbs.

VHS: S23464. $49.95.

Beginning American Sign Language Video Course

Join the Bravos, an upbeat modern family with a deaf father, hearing impaired mother and two fun-loving children. American Sign Language instructor Billy Seago guides the adventure, highlighting the grammatical and cultural aspects of ASL. Each lesson includes introduction to new vocabulary, visits with the Bravo family, cultural notes, grammatical notes, vocabulary review sessions and practice sessions. Produced by Sign Enhancers.
Lesson 1: Meet the Bravo Family.
VHS: S23409. $69.95.
Lesson 2: Breakfast with the Bravos. Breakfast and dining.
VHS: S23410. $69.95.
Lesson 3: Where's the TV Remote?
VHS: S23411. $69.95.
Lesson 4: Let's Go Food Shopping!
VHS: S23412. $69.95.
Lesson 5: Review Tape.
VHS: S23413. $69.95.
Lesson 6: Read Any Good Fingers Lately?
VHS: S23414. $69.95.
Lesson 7: A School Daze.
VHS: S23415. $69.95.
Lesson 8: A School Daze—The Sequel.
VHS: S23416. $69.95.
Lesson 9: Dollar Signs.
VHS: S23417. $69.95.
Lesson 10: Review Tape.
VHS: S23418. $69.95.
Lesson 11: Playing in the Park.
VHS: S23419. $69.95.
Lesson 12: The Doctor Is In!
VHS: S23420. $69.95.
Lesson 13: Business as Usual.
VHS: S23421. $69.95.
Lesson 14: Let's Go Clothes Shopping.
VHS: S23422. $69.95.
Lesson 15: Review Tape.
VHS: S23423. $69.95.
Lesson 16: The People Behind the Bravo Family.
VHS: S23424. $69.95.

C'est la Vie

These five slice-of-life vignettes give insight into the people, places and products of French-speaking countries, while helping beginning and intermediate viewers improve comprehension and communication skills. With 64 pages of tape scripts and exercises. French narration. Each part is 35 mins.
C'est la Vie: Part 1. Features shoppers in the open-air markets of Provence, a painter in Aix-en-Provence and the story of *Les Filles du Rois*.
VHS: S33270. $49.95.
C'est la Vie: Part 2. Shows Roquefort, Martinique and a canine beauty shop.
VHS: S33271. $49.95.
C'est la Vie: Parts 1 & 2.
VHS: S33272. $89.95.

Child's Play Video Flash Cards—Spell Well

An innovative new series of video programs designed to help students learn spelling, combining basic instructional methods with high tech. The programs develop competency in correct spelling of words that do not fit the phonic rules. The programs were developed by Harold Weitzberg and Dr. Richard Zweig, who is an experienced language remediation expert who has developed numerous diagnostic remediation programs over the last 20 years. The programs provide a multi-modality approach for input and reinforcement that include listening, seeing, and writing tasks. Each program is 30 minutes, and the programs are geared toward individuals of all age groups.
Spell Well 1.
VHS: S06290. $11.95.
Spell Well 2.
VHS: S06291. $11.95.
Spell Well 3.
VHS: S06292. $11.95.
Spell Well 4.
VHS: S06293. $11.95.

Functional Reading—I Can Read Signs

For beginning readers who will recognize many familiar signs, this program generates that all-important first feeling of success leading toward positive learning attitudes overall. Simple stills of common street and commercial signs can be a boon, especially in urban elementary and foreign language classrooms. They can be used to develop functional reading skills, build vocabulary, and reinforce motor skills in primary and intermediate reading. 30 mins.
VHS: S10317. $29.95.

Intermediate English/ESL

An important and valuable 25-lesson, interactive course that allows the viewer to listen to, speak, read and write English, finding a grammatical approach in the details and events of everyday life. Study guide included. Two-tape set, 240 mins.
VHS: S17486. $79.95.

Language Stories

A collection of educational videos about language, thought and action. The works concentrate on sentence structure and proper usage.
A Cache of Jewels and Other Collective Nouns. The text is created from collective nouns and enlivened by bright, beautifully colored drawings. 11 mins.
VHS: S20068. $44.95.
Kites Sail High. This video breaks down verbs in ebullient, musical verses. "The verses are accompanied by bold, gaily colored graphics that are especially striking for their skillful use of pattern and design" (*Publisher's Weekly*). 11 mins.
VHS: S20070. $44.95.
Many Luscious Lollipops. Subtitled *A Book about Adjectives*, this work points out, "adjectives [are] terrific when you want to be specific…" 8 mins.
VHS: S20069. $44.95.
Merry-Go-Round. This book about nouns highlights the different functions nouns serve. 16 mins.
VHS: S20071. $44.95.
Language Stories, Set. A collection of four programs. 46 mins.
VHS: S20072. $159.95.

Learning About Me

In this educational series, an eccentric witch and a giant green dragon join forces to instruct children on the need for honesty, forgiveness, responsibility, developing self-worth and respect and having the capacity to listen and communicate with their peers. "A lively, up-to-date program for the primary grades, designed to help children explore their own individuality in ways that will develop their capacity for making responsible choices" (*Booklist*). Designed for kindergarten through 3rd grade.
A Is for Autonomy. Children learn how to unlock the mysteries of their own identities by solving intricate riddles. A special game called "Hidden Treasure" enables them to discover what is unique and special about their lives. 16 mins.
VHS: S19943. $37.95.
B Is for Belonging. By telling frightening stories around a campfire, children learn to bond, share personal experiences and make friendships. 18 mins.
VHS: S19944. $37.95.
Ipsilwhich Adventures. Inability to communicate almost destroys an important cookout, until Lollipop Dragon and Apple Blossom intervene and teach the children how to get along. 23 mins.
VHS: S19942. $37.95.
Learning About Me, Set. A set of three programs. 55 mins.
VHS: S19945. $99.00.

Library Skills

Designed for middle school, high school and college students, this video program instructs on preparing and writing a research paper, from inception to completion, enhanced by colorful video graphics.
Finding Sources of Information.
VHS: S17483. $39.95.
Selecting and Defining a Topic.
VHS: S17482. $39.95.
Taking Notes and Organizing Your Ideas.
VHS: S17484. $39.95.
Writing the Paper.
VHS: S17485. $39.95.

Peter Elbow on Writing

Peter Elbow, one of the country's foremost teachers of writing, talks to students about the process of writing and provides personal insight into how to work through writing problems. Useful for students and teachers alike, this video will demystify the writing process as it offers encouragement and support for writers. 43 mins.
VHS: S28445. $225.00.

The Power of the Word

This PBS-sponsored series from the Bill Moyers Collection includes readings by some the most internationally acclaimed poets living and working today. They are featured in a number of settings and given the opportunity to discuss not just their work, but the importance and vitality of this immortal artform.
Ancestral Voices. Garret Kaoru Hongo reflects on his Japanese-American heritage in much of his work, while Native American poets Joy Haro and Mary Tallmountain draw on the strengths of their traditions. Together these three bring out the importance of diverse traditions in the realm of poetry. 60 mins.
VHS: S21224. $29.95.
Dancing on the Edge of the Road. Stanley Kunitz is one of America's leading poets. His work is tempered by advice learned over a lifetime of composing. This profile offers a close look at the man and his work, including his strong belief in reading aloud. 60 mins.
VHS: S21226. $29.95.
The Living Language. The living tradition of oral poetry is accentuated by two poets, James Autrey and Quincy Troupe. Autrey writes about the business world and the South of his youth. He often brings his work to places like business meetings and even church. Troupe is a professor of Third World literature who reads to all kinds of audiences, even prisoners. 60 mins.
VHS: S21223. $29.95.
The Simple Acts of Life. This program was filmed at the Geraldine R. Dodge Poetry Festival. Every other year, poets gather there to discuss and read their work to each other and students. Robert Bly, Galway Kinnel, Sharon Olds, Octavio Paz and William Stafford are included. 60 mins.
VHS: S21222. $29.95.
Voices of Memory. Li-Young is a famed poet whose work explores the ties he maintains with Chinese culture, even though he has never lived in China. For Gerald Stern, memory offers a path to his Jewish heritage, which he then reconstructs in his work. Poetry readings and extensive interviews with both men are included. 60 mins.
VHS: S21225. $29.95.
Where the Souls Live. Robert Bly, Lucille Clifton and W.S. Merwin are all featured reading and discussing their work. Bly's emphasis on the spiritual nature of poetry makes him a vital voice on the state of the human soul. Clifton draws on her experiences as a black woman to craft her art, while Merwin examines human relationships and our ties to nature. 60 mins.
VHS: S21227. $29.95.
Complete Six-Volume Set.
VHS: S22595. $119.95.

Quickwick: Your Library Guide

Quickwick, a very special lightning bug, teaches young children how to use their local library. Includes the use of puppets, colorful drawings, and live-action photography in an actual library setting. Five instructional episodes.
VHS: S14207. $179.95.

Story of English

The highly acclaimed televisions series hosted by award-winning reporter Robert MacNeil, in a remarkable journey through the history of the English language. Mounted in a five-cassette series. Program 1: *An English Speaking World*—More than 320 million people speak it as their first language. How has it risen to such prominence? Program 2: *Mother Tongue*—Follows the origin of English from its Anglo-Saxon roots. Program 3: *A Muse of Fire*—Shakespeare's words and the King James Bible represent the full flowering of English. Program 4: *The Guid Scots Tongue*—Traces the remarkable effect the Scots have had on the spread and sound of English. Program 5: *Black on White*—Examines the beginnings of Black English. Program 6: *Pioneers! O Pioneers!*—Walt Whitman's phrase evokes the spirit behind the evolution of early American English. Program 7: *The Muvver Tongue*—19th century British colonialism played an important role in the spread of English throughout the world. Program 8: *The Loaded Weapon*—Investigates the Irish influence on the language. Program 9: *Next Year's Words: A Look into the Future*—Latin, now considered "dead", was once a universal language. Does a similar fate await English? Available only as a complete set.
VHS: S08492. $99.95.

Strunk & White: The Elements of Style

Finally on video—the classic guide to clear, effective writing. Now you can learn the fundamentals of precise writing in under two hours, just by watching and listening. Plus, a free copy of the *Elements of Style* book is included as a handy reference guide. Featuring Charles Osgood. 112 mins.
VHS: S13879. $29.99.

Teacher Training Series

This teacher-to-teacher series features master teachers giving new or experienced teachers a creative and focused approach to the teaching of great classics in the classroom. Each video includes complete lesson plans with aims, motivations, objectives, discussion questions and homework assignments.
Teaching Hamlet. 30 mins.
VHS: S08766. $39.95.
Teaching Macbeth. 50 mins.
VHS: S08767. $39.95.
Teaching Romeo and Juliet. 30 mins.
VHS: S08768. $39.95.
Teaching Julius Caesar. 30 mins.
VHS: S08769. $39.95.
Teaching Othello. 30 mins.
VHS: S08770. $39.95.
Teaching The Great Gatsby. 25 mins.
VHS: S08775. $39.95.

OTHER EDUCATIONAL VIDEOS

American Cultures for Children

Actress Phylicia Rashad introduces children to this 12-volume multicultural series that explores the rich tapestry of world cultures thriving in America today. Volumes include *African-American Heritage, Arab-American Heritage, Central-American Heritage, Chinese-American Heritage, Irish-American Heritage, Japanese-American Heritage, Jewish-American Heritage, Korean-American Heritage, Mexican-American Heritage, Native American Heritage, Puerto Rican Heritage* and *Vietnamese-American Heritage*.
VHS: S31743. $359.40.

Animation in the Classroom

Art teachers Danny Knepper and Jill Smith demonstrate basic devices and show how to make them and how they illustrate "persistance of vision," which allows the eye to blend images and create an illusion of motion. Devices include the thaumatrope, phenakistoscope, zoetrope and flip book. 20 mins.
VHS: S32709. $29.95.

Beyond Blame: Challenging Violence in the Media

This comprehensive series offers a number of well-reasoned steps that can help children understand and counteract the overwhelming media fascination with violence. Children are directly addressed, but caregivers of all type are also catered to. Finally this vital issue can be dealt with through concrete, positive means developed by media literacy experts and violence prevention specialists. The set contains five videos, handouts, lesson plans and outlines.
VHS: S26326. $249.95.

Biggest and the Best

Three short discussion starter films on topics facing teenagers: *Heartburn* challenges teens to examine some common misconceptions about love, *Eagle Beak* helps teens see that self-image is often founded on wrong input, and *Face Value*, winner of five international awards, is a provocative look at peer pressure. 26 mins.
VHS: S09796. $59.95.

Close to Home: Moyers on Addiction

Bill Moyer's groundbreaking five-part PBS television series on addiction visits recovering addicts and treatment programs to throw light on coping with personal tragedies.
Close to Home: Moyers on Addiction—Portrait of Addiction. Nine recovering drug and/or alcohol addicts tell their stories. 60 mins.
VHS: S33958. $29.95.
Close to Home: Moyers on Addiction—The Hijacked Brain. Bill Moyers goes inside the laboratory to follow researchers engaged in charting an "image of desire in the brain." 60 mins.
VHS: S33959. $29.95.
Close to Home: Moyers on Addiction—Changing Lives. Interviews recovering addicts and sits in on a group therapy session in Ridgeview Institute near Atlanta, and visits Project Safe, an innovative treatment program that reaches out to disadvantaged mothers who are addicts and their children. 90 mins.
VHS: S33960. $29.95.
Close to Home: Moyers on Addiction—The Next Generation. Examines community and family prevention efforts to curb drug and nicotine addiction. 60 mins.
VHS: S33961. $29.95.
Close to Home: Moyers on Addiction—The Politics of Addiction. Looks at Arizona's recent struggle to find an alternative to current policies for recovering addicts. Proposition 200 proposed a reassessment of the status of nonviolent drug addicts now serving time, and emphasized treatment over incarceration. 60 mins.
VHS: S33962. $29.95.
Close to Home: Moyers on Addiction—Complete Set. 330 mins.
VHS: S33957. $119.95.

Common Miracles: The New American Revolution in Learning

This groundbreaking ABC News Special looks at communities all across the country that are discovering how to liberate the potential in every child. Correspondents Peter Jennings and Bill Blakemore reveal ways of enabling students to uncover their special strengths and become eager learners. 60 mins.
VHS: S31779. $19.98.

The Date Rape Backlash

Academy Award-winning screenwriter Callie Khouri (*Thelma and Louise*) hosts this lively discussion with Susan Faludi (*Backlash*), Mary Koss, Neil Malamuth, Katha Pollitt and others, on the origins of the media backlash against progress made in the campaign to stop sexual violence against women. 60 mins.
VHS: S28440. $195.00.

Degrassi Jr. High/High—Health Education Curriculum

This frank but funny 70-part dramatic series reveals the joys, crises and perplexities of the adolescent years and is targeted at middle through high school students, their teachers, and their parents. Set in a city neighborhood with families from mixed ethnic and economic backgrounds, this award-winning drama series is designed to reflect teenagers' own lives through stories portraying the emotionally charged problems and tough decisions that confront the Degrassi kids. Six-tape series includes *Relationships, Date Abuse, Teen Pregnancy, HIV/AIDS, Alcoholism,* and *Sexual Orientation*. Also includes background information, lesson handouts and reading and resource lists.
VHS: S34587. $99.95.

Doing Business

Documentary offers a behind-the-scenes look at the pleasures and the difficulties of operating a small, self-managed business. Public performance rights included.
VHS: S33386. $29.95.
Howard Libov, USA, 1981, 15 mins.

Drug Free Kids

This instructional program is designed to aid parents in recognizing and dealing with childhood drug abuse. Familiar faces who are advising that kids say no to drugs include Ken Howard, Jane Alexander, Ned Beatty, Marla Gibbs and Melissa Gilbert. USA, 1987, 70 mins.
VHS: S03641. $19.95.

The Electronic Storyteller: Television and the Cultivation of Values

For the first time on video, George Gerbner, founder of the Cultural Indicators Project at the University of Pennsylvania, explains the results of his 40-year study of television, reveals the complex effects of the media on society, and examines the stories the media tells about gender, class, risk, health and racial stereotyping. 40 mins.
VHS: S28436. $195.00.

Emergency! EMS to the Rescue

Go behind the scenes with New York City's Emergency Medical Service—the largest EMS in the world—where over 2,000 men and women respond to 1.3 million calls a year. You'll never hear an ambulance siren the same way again. Narrated by Bill Kurtis.
VHS: S30593. $19.95.
Pamela Yoder, USA, 1996, 50 mins.

Fireworks: The Magic of Pyrotechnics

George Plimpton joins the first family of fireworks, the Gruccis, as they light up the night sky with their awesome pyrotechnical displays. History, ceremony, technology and fun span the globe in this collection of firework events from China, Spain and Disney World.
VHS: S24535. $29.95.

The Geography Tutor

This series by Tell Me Why video contains six volumes that cover various elements of geography. It explains all those different principles that define the face of the Earth. Nationally acclaimed geography instructors make this series a helpful tool for any teacher or student.
Volume 1: Map and Globe Terms. 18 mins.
VHS: S22135. $49.95.
Volume 2: Types of Maps and Map Projections. 18 mins.
VHS: S22136. $49.95.
Volume 3: Map Skills. 18 mins.
VHS: S22137. $49.95.
Volume 4: Earth's Physical Features. 18 mins.
VHS: S22138. $49.95.
Volume 5: Weather and Climate. 18 mins.
VHS: S22139. $49.95.
Volume 6: Global Problems and Issues. 18 mins.
VHS: S22140. $49.95.
Complete Set.
VHS: S22141. $299.70.

Great Minds of Business

Meet the titans of business who offer valuable information in a way that is understandable, accessible and easily absorbed. This five-volume set includes *Entrepreneurs* (38 mins.), with Fred Smith; *Finance* (42 mins.), with Paul Volcker; *Investing* (36 mins.), with Peter Lynch; *Management* (40 mins.), with Andrew Grove; and *Marketing* (46 mins.), with Pleasant T. Rowling. Hosted by Gretchen Morgenson, senior editor of *Forbes Magazine*. 202 mins.
VHS: S32748. $79.98.

Gumbo

This innovative and tasty cuisine stretches throughout Acadiana into New Orleans. 30 mins.
VHS: S22391. $39.95.

Guns

Peter Jennings hosts this frightening expose on firearms in America. *Guns* depicts the bloody effect handguns, semiautomatic weapons and other firearms have had on society, including the deaths of some 30,000 people every year. 120 mins.
VHS: S12289. $19.98.

In the House

Three autobiographical stories written and performed by teenagers in a children's psychiatric hospital. The experiences they relate will stimulate discussion amongst other teen viewers as well as medical professionals dealing with young patients. Public performance rights included.
VHS: S33381. $99.99.
Lisa Rinzler/Peter Stasny, USA, 1997, 15 mins.

Information Superhighway Robbery: The Crisis of the Cultural Environment

George Gerbner exposes the way in which corporate powers control the "information superhighway" and reveals how global marketing strategies affect the national cultures of countries. 40 mins.
VHS: S28437. $195.00.

Inside the Secret Service

At the heart of America's oldest elite law enforcement agency is a tradition of service. Its major job is to protect the President. This inside glimpse of the secretive institution provides a rare view of the attitudes and ideals that shape it. Along with the history of the Secret Service, this video contains the first public statement by the agent who blames himself for the assasination of JFK. 90 mins.
VHS: S25637. $19.95.

Jancis Robinson's Wine Course

This BBC program demystifies the sometimes intimidating world of wine. Hosted by international expert Jancis Robinson, editor of *The Oxford Companion to Wine*, this five-volume series gives you a lighthearted grape-by-grape introduction. *The Wine Advocate* calls Robinson "witty, brilliant, authoritative…of all the wine writers in the world today, she may well be the most gifted." Five hours.
VHS: S32752. $99.95.

The Killing Screens

Dr. Jean Kilbourne guides audiences through an interview with America's foremost communication scholar, Dr. George Gerbner, founder of the Cultural Indicators Project. Illustrated with violent images from popular films and television programs and drawing on the Project's research, this film explores the psychological, political, social and developmental effects of growing up within a cultural environment of pervasive violent representation. "If every American could see *The Killing Screens* there would ensue a revolution in the content of popular media" (Prof. Neil Postman, NYU, author, *Amusing Ourselves to Death*). 37 mins.
VHS: S28435. $195.00.

Pack of Lies

Jean Kilbourne and Rick Pollay expose tobacco industry claims that they are not seeking to addict children to nicotine. "Powerful, persuasive, informative and entertaining. An essential part of any tobacco educational program" (Dr. Blake Cady, Chairperson, Coalition for a Healthy Future). 35 mins.
VHS: S28438. $225.00.

Public Enemies of the '20s & '30s

FBI police film, archival footage and rare photographs combine to present this close-up of America's most notorious gangsters: Al Capone, John Dillinger, Bonnie and Clyde, Legs Diamond, Dutch Schultz, Pretty Boy Floyd and Machine Gun Kelly. 75 mins.
VHS: S33891. $19.95.

Raising Face: A Menstrual Journey

This documentary features intimate discussions among women, as well as a class of fourth- and fifth-grade girls, about their menstruation experiences, including their first period, what they were told by their mothers and grandmothers, and how this information is passed on from generation to generation. Encourages frank discussion of this universal but rarely discussed female experience.
VHS: S34431. $150.00.
Wendy Surinsky, USA, 1997, 40 mins.

The Schlessinger Teen Health Video Series

Sex, abortion, homosexuality, date rape and abuse are all sensitive issues dealt with in this unique guide to health and education for teens. Experts from the University of Pennsylvania, the Children's Hospital of Philadelphia and Temple University School of Medicine emphasize prevention and coping in a non-judgmental manner. Each volume is 30 mins.

Abusive Relationships. Interviews with abused individuals, an abuser and a therapist reveal the brutal cycle of emotion which constitutes abusive behavior. Grades 8-12.
VHS: S24409. $39.95.

AIDS. People living with AIDS share their experiences with this syndrome and their views on sex, condoms and life. Grades 7-12.
VHS: S24410. $39.95.

Birth Control. All varieties of birth control are examined, including abstinence and sex without intercourse. Grades 7-12.
VHS: S24411. $39.95.

Cancer. Interviews with experts and cancer patients reveal the many types, causes and treatments for cancer. Grades 7-12.
VHS: S24412. $39.95.

Child Abuse. Recognizing child abuse and what to do about it are covered in this volume. In addition, the potential damage caused to innocent adults accused of abuse is examined. Grades 7-12.
VHS: S24413. $39.95.

Eating Disorders. Interviews with youngsters who experienced anorexia nervosa and bulimia are balanced with therapists discussing these dangerous disorders. Grades 7-12.
VHS: S24414. $39.95.

Nutrition/Diet. Expert advice on nutrition is loaded with important tips and key do's and don'ts. Grades 5-9.
VHS: S24415. $39.95.

Peer Pressure. Kids will benefit from these useful tools that help them resist pressure by reinforcing their own individuality. Grades 5-9.
VHS: S24416. $39.95.

Puberty. Emotional and physical changes that occur during puberty are explained in this volume. Grades 5-9.
VHS: S24417. $39.95.

Self-Esteem. The difference between high and low self-esteem is explained, along with methods to improve one's own self-image. Grades 7-12.
VHS: S24418. $39.95.

Sexual Harassment. Distinctions between harassment and appropriate behavior are discussed so that concepts like date rape and healthy affection are rendered more understandable. Grades 7-12.
VHS: S24419. $39.95.

Sports Medicine. Two expert doctors provide tips on how to avoid and recognize injury. Grades 7-12.
VHS: S24420. $39.95.

STDs (Sexually Transmitted Diseases). The prevention and identification of STDs is explained, together with the option of abstinence. Grades 8 -12.
VHS: S24421. $39.95.

Teen Pregnancy. Teen mothers discuss pregnancy and motherhood. Adoption and abortion are also explained. Grades 7-12.
VHS: S24422. $39.95.

Teen Sexuality. This is an open and frank look at teen sexuality. Sexual intercourse, abstinence, homosexuality, sex without intercourse, birth control, disease prevention and more topics are included. Grades 7-12.
VHS: S24423. $39.95.

The Schlessinger Teen Health Video Series. 15-volume set.
VHS: S24424. $599.25.

Sexual Harassment

Jean Kilbourne hosts this discussion, addressed to both men and women, on the nature of sexual harassment and its psychological, legal and communicational ramifications. Includes interviews with students, faculty and experts. 23 mins.
VHS: S28439. $195.00.

Slim Hopes

Award-winning filmmaker and noted lecturer Dr. Jean Kilbourne, Ed.D., analyzes how female bodies are depicted in advertising imagery and the devastating effects of that imagery on women's health. Addresses the relationship between these images and the obsession of girls and women with dieting and thinness which may lead to life-threatening eating disorders such as anorexia and bulimia. 30 mins.
VHS: S28447. $250.00.

Teen Sexuality in a Culture of Confusion

This powerful documentary by award-winning photojournalist and documentarian Dan Habib features discussions by eight people, age 16-24, on the forces in their lives that influence their decisions about sex. Author Prof. Susan Bardo (*Unbearable Weight: Feminism, Western Culture and the Body*) and five other prominent cultural scholars examine the messages popular culture communicates about sexuality, gender, the body and beauty. 40 mins.
VHS: S28441. $189.00.

The Unexplained: Cannibals

From South Seas headhunters to the chilling case of Jeffrey Dahmer, this is an unflinching investigation into the long and mysterious history of cannibalism. 50 mins
VHS: S34896. $14.95.

The Waldorf Promise

Since the founding of the first Waldorf school in America in 1928 in New York, Waldorf has become the fastest-growing alternative to public education in the U.S. Eight public school teachers talk about their Waldorf-inspired education programs. Winner of the CINE Golden Eagle Award and a Bronze Apple Award. 53 mins.
VHS: S35126. $39.95.

Woof! Woof! Uncle Matty's Guide to Dog Training

Matthew Margolis, dog trainer to the stars, uses a humane, innovative approach to show you how to master everything from picking the right puppy to making him feel at home, from basic obedience training to common behavioral problems. A PBS WGBH Boston Special. 60 mins.
VHS: S33094. $19.95.

OCCULT/NEW AGE

Ancient Mysteries

Using modern technology, scientific analysis, high-tech evidence and recent archaeological developments, the films in the *Ancient Mysteries* series are on the cutting edge of discovery.

Bigfoot. Does Yeti exist? Is Sasquatch only an imaginary creature? This investigation is set on finding the answers to the questions posed by the riddle of this elusive creature, seen only at the most outer reaches of untamed wilderness. 50 mins.
VHS: S21685. $19.95.

Vampires. The world of the undead, from corpses with pulses to graves where no vegetation will grow, is the focus of this fascinating video. Unraveling the mystery of these legendary creatures is not a task for the faint-hearted. 50 mins.
VHS: S21686. $19.95.

Witchcraft in America. From the witchcraft of Salem, Massachusetts, to 19th-century Caribbean voodoo and even modern-day ritual ceremony, all these practices offer evidence of the power mustered by the dark arts. In this video, filmed live, the secrets of witchcraft are unveiled as never before. 50 mins.
VHS: S21688. $19.95.

Aroma Massage

Beautifully filmed, this video teaches the techniques and benefits of massage with essential oils. It explains the correct and safe way to give or receive a massage. This video demonstrates effleurage, kneading, vibration and percussion strokes. 60 mins.
VHS: S22702. $24.95.

Arthur C. Clarke: World of Strange Powers

Two episodes, *Warnings from the Future* and *Have We Lived Before?* make this video an exciting foray into the mysteries of the human mind. Clarke, author of *2001*, looks at startling instances of clairvoyance, prophecy and memories of past lives. 56 mins.
VHS: S26368. $19.95.

Beyond Belief

This film documents actual experiments in ESP, reincarnation, faith healing and other spiritual and psychic phenomena. A frighteningly real expose of unexplainable mysteries that will keep you on the edge of your seat. 94 mins.
VHS: S16575. $19.95.

Beyond Bizarre

Take a trip around the world in search of outrageous events, unexplained phenomena, macabre people and weird places with this highest rated documentary series on the Discovery Channel. Hosted by Jay Robinson (*Bram Stoker's Dracula*). Each episode is 47 mins.

Beyond Bizarre—Episode 1. Includes pentecostal serpent handlers, witches of Wicca, rocks that move, an anti-aging machine and modern-day mummification.
VHS: S34826. $14.98.

Beyond Bizarre—Episode 2. Includes self-made freaks, modern-day primitives, cryptozoology, ghostly visitations and forensic sleuths.
VHS: S34827. $14.98.

Beyond Bizarre—Episode 3. Includes bizarre healing practices, shoeshine shamanic ritual, bizarre natural phenomena and the weird world of pets.
VHS: S34828. $14.98.

Beyond Bizarre—Episode 4. Includes weird food, trepanning (ancient brain surgery), bizarre museums, ancient creations, America's Stonehenge and bizarre houses.
VHS: S34829. $14.98.

Beyond Bizarre—Episode 5. Includes Phuket Vegetarian Festival, crystal skulls, voodoo, Sedona's Vortexes and bizarre artist Dr. Evermore.
VHS: S34830. $14.98.

Beyond Bizarre—Episode 6. Includes Fragonard Museum, spontaneous human combustion, UFOs, alien implants and the urban myth of Texas ghost children.
VHS: S34831. $14.98.

Beyond Bizarre—Episode 7. Includes weird anthropology, Chupacabra, zombies, bizarre audio phenomena and the curse of bizarre Bodie.
VHS: S34832. $14.98.

Do You Believe in Miracles?

Written and produced by Hanoch Teller, this video docu-drama celebrates divine providence and features the miraculous stories of lives saved, destinies changed and fortunes reversed. It may make a believer out of you. 62 mins.
VHS: S32077. $29.95.

Experiments That Could Change the World

Unconventional scientist Dr. Rupert Sheldrake explores everyday phenomena, the results of which are shaking up the scientific world. Discusses psychic links between pets and their owners, why you can feel when someone is staring at you and how pigeons home. 60 mins.
VHS: S32701. $19.95.

Haunted Houses

This spine-tingling program from A & E visits the most fascinating haunted houses in America to learn the secrets of their notorious, unquiet spirits. With eyewitness interviews, expert analysis and dramatic recreations. 100 mins.
VHS: S32182. $19.95.

Miracles and Other Wonders

Darren McGavin hosts this five-volume program exploring extraordinary but factual events and unexplained phenomena which justify the faith and hope inherent in the supernatural and parapsychological. Each volume is 50 minutes.
VHS: S31776. $99.98.

Myths, Mysteries and Mysticism

This series of five tapes is an exciting journalistic look at age-old myths and mysteries. Tape titles include: *Mystery of the Lamb of God*, *Compostella/The Next Step*, *The Golem*, *The Nazca Lines: Pathway to the Gods* and *The Giza Pyramids: The Tribute to Osiris*.
VHS: S30409. $99.95.

Round Trip

Meet five men and women whose near-death experiences will give you great comfort and insight into one of life's greatest mysteries. You'll also hear from a philosopher, a parapsychologist and a theologian, who will help interpret these remarkable events.
VHS: S32697. $19.95.
Timothy O'Reilly, USA, 1996, 40 mins.

Secrets of the Psychics

Follow master magician James Randi as he uncovers the secrets of those born with mysterious powers of the mind that can move objects at will, read a person's thoughts, or cure physical ailments. From NOVA.
VHS: S31432. $19.95.

Strictly Supernatural

The definitive guide to a range of supernatural practices and how they really work. Combining stunning visuals with atmospheric, original music, each video explores the origins and history of the supernatural with insights from leading practitioners, interviews with scholars and scientists, and dramatic reenactments. Narrated by Christopher Lee. Volumes: *Seance*, *Astrology* and *Tarot*.
VHS: S31176. $39.98.

Telegrams from the Dead

In 1848, two young girls heard strange rapping noises in their otherwise quiet upstate New York hometown. This simple incident started the spiritualism craze that spread throughout the US. Ellen Burstyn narrates this documentary, which uses re-enactments and archival resources to chart the growth of the spiritualism phenomenon. 60 mins.
VHS: S24695. $19.95.

Three Minutes to Power and Peace

Martial arts master Lawrence Tan introduces an amazing, three-minute technique that invigorates your body, mind and spirit. "The Universal Form" is based on principles of yoga and tai chi, but is much quicker and easier to do. Three-tape set includes *Three Minutes to Power, Three Minutes to Peace, Three Minutes to Prepare*. 60 mins.
VHS: S32726. $29.95.

UNIDENTIFIED FLYING OBJECTS

Area 51: America's Most Secret Base

This comprehensive documentary investigates the mystery which attracts UFOlogists and the curious alike to this desolate region in the Nevada desert. Features never-before-seen footage of flying objects at Area 51. 54 mins.
VHS: S31626. $24.98.

Chariots of the Gods

Controversial and revealing film adapted from Erich Von Daeniken's best-selling book, dealing with the theory that many ancient civilizations developed advanced knowledge brought to earth by extra-terrestrial visitors. A cult hit. 90 mins.
VHS: S11501. $19.95.
Laser: LD70915. $39.95.

Countdown to Alien Nation

Investigative journalist Michael Lindemann reports on the various phases of the government's UFO cover-up since 1947, and discusses the serious consequences of alien-human interaction, and "how you can prepare for the unprecedented changes ahead." 115 mins.
VHS: S18043. $29.95.

Crop Circle Update

The British founder of the Circle Phenomenon Research, Colin Andrews, presents additional evidence to support his claims on the historical developments of the evolving "crop circles." 120 mins.
VHS: S18038. $29.95.

The Extraterrestrial Influence

A channeled workshop develops theories on the way early human beliefs were influenced and evolved by their extraterrestrial ancestors. 90 mins.
VHS: S20170. $29.95.

Farewell Good Brothers

The Discovery Channel has collected these tales from people who claim to have been aboard UFO's. This is an offbeat and hilarious look at extraterrestrial contactees—a cult for our own times.
VHS: S22541. $29.95.

The Flying Saucer Mystery

The mysteries of UFO's are investigated in this early sci-fi documentary. Completely camp and sensationalistic in its approach, it has an appealing sense of fun that has been lost ever since the invention of ET. There are also 30 minutes of sci-fi trailers added to round out the feeling of the era.
VHS: S23151. $29.95.

Flying Saucers

This program argues the government has extensive knowledge of the existence of UFOs, and charges they're suppressing it from the public. 90 mins.
VHS: S18041. $29.95.

Geosophy

Why did the ancients build sacred sites around our planet-circles, pyramids, henges, standing stones? Why did they make massive use of crystals? construct leys? develop geomancy and use sacred geometry all over the world? The world-renowned researchers and philosophers carrying on pioneer work in Earth Mysteries in Britain are developing a new science—geosophy-rediscovering knowledge from the remote past. 95 mins.
VHS: S08530. $29.95.

The Grand Deception of 1995

The director of the Civilian Intelligence Network argues that a secret international government will orchestrate an extraterrestrial event in 1995 to initiate an oppressive New World Order. 100 mins.
VHS: S18039. $29.95.

Hidden Memories: Are You a UFO Abductee?

One of the foremost authorities on UFO abduction, Budd Hopkins, examines the symptoms adults and children report experiencing in cases of abduction. 90 mins.
VHS: S20165. $29.95.

Human Encounters with Aliens

John Mack is a professor of psychiatry at Harvard. He argues that physical evidence makes memories of alien encounters fundamentally different from other similar recollections. Dr. Mack is the author of *Abduction: Human Encounters with Aliens*. 60 mins.
VHS: S23619. $34.95.

Kidnapped by UFOs

Hear UFO eyewitness accounts and learn what lies behind the incredible claims of UFO abductions in this NOVA video. 60 mins.
VHS: S28648. $19.95.

Mysteries of the Gods

Hosted by William Shatner, this is a follow up to *Chariots of the Gods*, based on the bestseller by Eric Von Daniken.
VHS: S34471. $19.95.
USA, 1979, 87 mins.

The Mystery of Crop Circles: Messages from Another World?

Michael Hesemann, the publisher of Germany's leading UFO magazine, produced this documentary that investigates the unsolved enigmas of England's Crop Circle phenomena. The work features interviews with authorities Colin Andrews, Pat Delgado, John Michell and George Winfield. 120 mins.
VHS: S20171. $39.95.

Nova—UFOs: Are We Alone?

From the most popular and enlightening television science series comes the home video version you can play any time you like. This cassette explores the fascinating world of unidentified flying objects. *Nova* claims to have an answer to this puzzling phenomenon. What do they know that you don't? Rent this tape and find out. USA, 60 mins.
VHS: S06025. $29.98.

One on One on UFOs

A three-volume video interview series that explores the possibilities of UFOs, the existence of an alien presence, government complicity, the psychological consequences of people who maintain they were abducted, and Colin Andrews discussing the phenomenon of "crop circles" (pictograms). 190 mins.
One on One on UFOs: Vol. 1.
VHS: S18045. $29.95.
One on One on UFOs: Vol. 2.
VHS: S18046. $29.95.
One on One on UFOs: Vol. 3.
VHS: S18047. $29.95.

Oz Encounters: UFOs in Australia

An amazing cross-section of case studies of ordinary people's accounts of multiple UFO sightings, encounters, and abductions in Australia. Incorporates people's presentations of stories in their own words with the latest 3-D animation and exciting dramatizations. 60 mins.
VHS: S34562. $19.98.

The Pleiadian Connection

Swiss farmer Eduard "Billy" Meier's collection of personal encounters with cosmonauts from *The Pleiades*. The program discusses Pleiadian messages "about Earth's history, man's spiritual development and laws of creation." 60 mins.
VHS: S18044. $39.95.

Preparing for Contact

Lecturer Lyssa Channeling Germane believes contact between Earth and alien beings is an inevitable occurrence, and offers insights into how society might relate to different extraterrestrial civilizations. 50 mins.
VHS: S20169. $24.95.

The Second Coming of Science

Dr. Brian O'Leary, a former astronaut and physicist, investigates the linkage between science and the paranormal, examining psychokinesis, the existence of UFOs, crop circles, free energy and the manifestations of Sai Baba. 90 mins.
VHS: S20166. $29.95.

Strange Harvests 1993

Linda Moultaon Howe is well known for her television appearances on *UFO Report*. Now she investigates in depth the strange killings of animals reported all over the world in 1993. Police are puzzled. All that is certain is that strange moving lights accompanied these bizzare deaths. 60 mins.
VHS: S22971. $29.98.

UFOs and the Alien Presence

Michael Lindemann cites UFO photographs, film clips and eyewitness testimony to authenticate his claims the government has knowingly misled the public about the presence of UFOs. 35 mins.
VHS: S20158. $19.95.

UFOs and the New World Order

Michael Lindemann, an investigative journalist, explores alien presences and discusses his research, claiming the existence of "alien beings" is covered up by a secret government organization, as part of a plan to unleash a New World Order. 60 mins.
VHS: S18042. $24.95.

UFOs and Underground Bases

UFO investigator Bill Hamilton hosts this program, which maintains UFOs and other unexplained phenomena are linked to government sites that reported house underground bases and combine alien and military personnel. 120 mins.
VHS: S20168. $34.95.

UFOs: Encounters and Abductions

Since the first sighting in 1947, accounts of extraterrestrial encounters and kidnappings have proliferated. This video explores the theories behind these visitations. Is there any truth to these accounts or are they simply imaginary responses to Cold War hysteria? Photographs, film, eyewitness accounts and faithful recreations are all featured in this ultimate UFO dossier. 100 mins.
VHS: S29907. $19.95.

UFOs: The Miracle of the Unknown

This is the most comprehensive program ever produced on this interplanetary phenomenon. It features sightings from around the world, expert interviews, eyewitness accounts plus actual photographs of UFOs. There is even the story of a US government cover-up. Two-volume set, 120 mins.
VHS: S23139. $39.95.

UFOs: The Secret Evidence

Michael Hesemann produced this work which tries to validate the existence of UFOs through 44 different film and video clips throughout the world that purport to be various sightings. 110 mins.
VHS: S20167. $49.95.

Undeniable Evidence

Colin Andrews, the British founder of the Circle Phenomenon Research, presents evidence of the authenticity of crop circle phenomena. He showcases the practical features of genuine formations and shots of circles evolving from a single shape to huge symbolic formations. 60 mins.
VHS: S18036. $35.00.

Update on Alien Phenomena

This program offers updated information on crop circles, alien communications, animal metamorphoses, and the facts behind an alleged UFO crash retrieval case. 110 mins.
VHS: S18040. $29.95.

Whispers from Space

This "engagingly deadpan" (Dennis Harvey, *Variety*) documentary looks at UFO lore and one rather disreputable "researcher" in particular: Gray Parker, a self-stylized "expert" on strange phenomena, who not only didn't believe in Unidentified Flying Objects, but may have perpetrated a UFO-related hoax or two himself. Stills, home movies, location shooting and interviewees, ranging from Parker's surviving relatives to a former male lover, business associates, amateur sleuths and a local folklorist, offer their insight into the man from rural West Virginia who specialized in the flying saucer trade.
VHS: S31123. $19.99.
Ralph Coon, USA, 1996, 105 mins.

Who's Out There?

Is there intelligent life on other planets? Do they know we exist? Orson Welles narrates this special, which includes interviews with experts, including Dr. Carl Sagan. 55 mins.
VHS: S09254. $39.95.

cd-roms

Adventure Kid, Vol. 1

Computer whiz Norizaku discovers a World War II-era computer that he thinks will be a fun piece of history to play with. Unfortunately, his curiosity unwittingly releases the encoded spirit of the machine's evil creator, Massago, freed to fulfill his dreams of vengeance against his wife and the army officer who raped her. Anime. Japanese with English subtitles.

MAC. Req: System 7 or higher. 68020, 68030, 68040, or Power PC CPU and CD ROM drive. 4 MB RAM, 256 color monitor (or better). Quicktime 1.5 or better (included).

WIN. Req: Windows 3.1 and MS DOS 5.0 or higher. 80386SZ MHz or higher CPU and CD ROM drive. 4MB RAM, SVGA with at least 256 color display. Soundblaster compatible sound card. Quicktime 1.1 or better (included).

CD-ROM: CD90068. $24.95.

Japan, 75 mins.

Adventure Pack

Includes the titles *Wayzata World Factbook 1994 Edition, Internet Surfer: Getting Started, Who Killed Sam Rupert?, Quick Art Designer 1, Virtual Universe, Journey to the Planets, SpaceTime and Art, Font Pro 3: Designer Type, Windsurfing Portfolio CD* and *MusicScapes Professional*.

DOS. Req: DOS 4.0 or higher; 1 Mb free RAM; hard drive; CD-Rom drive.

MAC. Req: Mac 7.1 or higher; 1 Mb free RAM; hard drive; CD-Rom drive.

WIN. Req: Windows 3.1 or higher; 1 Mb free RAM; hard drive; CD-Rom drive.

CD-ROM: CD90050. $39.00.

Aesop's Fables

Acclaimed actor Danny Glover and jazz great Ron Carter combine their unique talents in this charming and contemporary telling of 24 of Aesop's timeless tales, including *The Tortoise and the Hare, The Wolf in Sheep's Clothing* and *The Lion and the Mouse*. Aesop's enduring wit and wisdom are illustrated with stunning animation, magnificent graphics and vibrant colors. Includes morals, origins and history of the fables. Children can watch the fables and play the animated story morals, or they can scroll through the stories picture by picture. Games and stories combine to provide hours of entertainment with 60 challenging mazes and 36 sliding puzzles with three levels of difficulty.

MAC. Req: Color Macintosh (Mac II or greater); 256 color display or greater; 4MB of RAM; System 7.0 or later. Recommended System: double-speed CD-ROM drive; 25MHz 68030 microprocessor or better; joystick optional.

WIN. Req: 386/33MHz or higher CPU (486SX recommended); 4MB of RAM; Windows 3.1 or later; VGA video adapter; 256 color VGA display; Windows-compatible sound card; double-speed CD-ROM drive; mouse (joystick is not supported).

CD-ROM: CD90202. $19.95.

All My Hummingbirds Have Alibis

Composer and performer Morton Subotnick presents two breathtaking musical pieces, "All My Hummingbirds Have Alibis" and "Five Scenes from an Imaginary Ballet", written expressly for CD-ROM use. They are combined with images and text by surrealist Max Ernst and commentary from Subotnick.

MAC. Req: Any Macintosh with color display; System 7; CD-ROM drive; no more than 3.2 Mb available RAM (5 Mb installed); 640x480 resolution (13") color monitor; speakers or headphones if CD-ROM drive is external.

CD-ROM: CD90027. $39.95.

Morton Subotnick

Amanda Stories

Kids and parents alike love the mischievous Inigo the Cat and Your Faithful Camel, which are only two of the ten charming stories which *The New York Times* "highly recommended for children". Amanda Goodenough's colorful animations offer lessons about love, friendship and loyalty.

MAC. Req: Any Macintosh with color display; system 7; CD-ROM drive; no more than 2.2MB available RAM (4MB installed).

WIN. Req: 25-MHz 486SX or higher processor; MS-DOS 5 or later; 640x480, 16-color display (256-color recommended); 4MB RAM (8MB recommended).

CD-ROM: CD90006. $59.95.

Amanda Goodenough, USA

American Heritage: The Civil War

Based on the Pulitzer Prize-winning *American Heritage Picture History of the Civil War* by Bruce Catton, this two-disc CD-ROM package is loaded with information on the American Civil War. Featured are the complete texts of the classic American novels *Uncle Tom's Cabin* and *The Red Badge of Courage*, along with several short stories by author Ambrose Bierce, the works of dozens of other poets and artists, and more. In addition, this CD-ROM features photographs, artwork, maps and video clips, essays on the issues of the time, along with biographies of the people who shaped the era, a look into the military strategies of the Union and the Confederacy, and a game in which the user can experience the Presidency of the United States through the eyes of either Abraham Lincoln or Jefferson Davis.

MAC. Req: Street date: March 20, 1996. System requirements will be available shortly thereafter.

WIN. Req: 486 DX 33 or higher, 8Mb of RAM, 8Mb hard drive space, SVGA graphics 640 x 480, 256-color monitor, double speed CD-ROM drive (or faster), MPC compatible sound card, a mouse (or comparable pointing device), Windows version 3.1 or 3.11, and DOS 3.3 or higher.

CD-ROM: CD90108. $69.95.

USA

American Medical Association Family Medical Guide

The five-million-copy best-seller comes to CD-ROM. This authoritative guide to your family's health features AMA-approved interactive self-diagnosis charts and information on the prominent health issues of our times.

MAC. Available for Macintosh platforms.

WIN. Available for Windows platforms.

CD-ROM: CD90225. $49.95.

American Poetry: The Nineteenth Century

Over 1,000 poems by nearly 150 poets. Dickinson, Longfellow, Emerson and Poe, among others, are included. Six hours of audio recordings, indexes of all the poets, titles and first lines, biographical notes and photos of 60 poets, extensive annotations and performances by Garrison Keillor, Cynthia Ozick and others.

MAC. Req: 68030 processor (examples: Performa 575; Quadra; Centris) or better; 7.0 operating system or later; 8 MB RAM; 640x480 color monitor or 13" display; Double-speed CD-ROM drive.

WIN. Req: 486SX-33 or higher processor; 640x480, 256-color display (accelerator recommended); 8 MB RAM; MPC2-compatible CD-ROM drive; Sound card (16-bit) with speakers or headphones; Windows 3.1 or Windows 95.

CD-ROM: CD90130. $39.95.

The American Sign Language Dictionary on CD-ROM

American Sign Language (ASL) is the primary form of communication for nearly 1 million deaf people in the United States. This remarkable CD-ROM is an invaluable tool for anyone learning ASL and a convenient reference for proficient ASL speakers. Presents video clips showing how to make 2,181 signs, arranged into 21 subject categories. Also includes an overview of ASL's 300-year history and usage, a guide for finger spelling of the alphabet's 26 letters, and a "Skills" section with practice games using the dictionary's video clips.

MAC. Req: Not available at present.

WIN. Req: Not available at present.

CD-ROM: CD90180. $69.99.

Amnesty Interactive

Sponsored by the human rights watchdog organization Amnesty International, this hybrid CD-ROM gives an overview of human rights and human rights violations, from ancient times through the 20th century. Highlights include the ideas of noted thinkers and political figures, multicultural imagery, art, music, and many other valuable reference materials for teachers and students alike. Features include an atlas of world human rights conditions, stories by former political prisoners, a world music soundtrack and more. Winner of the Interactive Media Festival Award.

MAC. Req: 68030 processor (examples: Performa 575; Quadra; Centris) or better; 7.0 operating system or later; 8 MB RAM; 640x480 color monitor or 13" display; Double-speed CD-ROM drive.

WIN. Req: 486SX-25 or higher processor; 640x480, 256-color display; 4MB RAM (8MB recommended); MPC compatible CD-ROM drive; Sound card (8-bit) with speakers or headphones; Microsoft Windows 3.1 or Windows 95.

CD-ROM: CD90080. $19.95.

USA

The Anglo-Saxons

Discover England and its Anglo-Saxon history, art, literature and way of life. Meet kings and queens and tour kingdoms, castles, cemeteries, churches and museums. With hundreds of photographs and illustrations from the British museum, a comprehensive index, maps of Anglos-Saxon medieval sites and the complete text of *Beowulf* and the *Anglo-Saxon Chronicle*.

WIN. Req: 386SX; 12MHz+; 2X speed CD-ROM; 4MB recom; SVGA 256 colors; DOS 3.1+; sound card; mouse.

CD-ROM: CD90242. $29.99.

Animals in Danger

Includes up-to-date information on numbers of many endangered species and reasons for their plight, movie sequences showing animals in their native habitat, information on where to see endangered animals in U.S. zoos and wildlife parks, a searchable database of North American endangered and theatened animals and project work for students, and maps of the world's major biomes and discussion of their features, climates and wildlife.

MAC. Req: 13" monitor or larger; color (256 minimum), 4MB RAM, hard drive, CD-ROM hard drive.

WIN. Req: 13" monitor or larger; 386 (or better) processor; 4MB RAM (8 MB recommended); Sound blaster compatible sound card; Super VGA graphics card (minimum 640 x 480 x 256 color resolution); Windows 3.1 and Windows 95 compatible. .

CD-ROM: CD90253. $29.95.

Animals-Life-Habitat-Ecosystem

A captivating glimpse into the mysterious and majestic animal kingdom, featuring over 100 animals, 200 full-color images, over 50 full-motion video clips, an interactive memory game, 200 pages of text and a glossary of zoological terms.

MAC. Available for Macintosh platforms.

WIN. Available for Windows platforms.

CD-ROM: CD90230. $49.99.

Antonin Dvorak: Symphony No. 9 "From the New World"

The Vienna Philharmonic's audio CD recording of Antonin Dvorak's 1892 symphony, inspired by the vitality of the American people, is accompanied by the entire score, which rolls before you as the music plays (the first of its kind on CD-ROM). Also included is extensive research on the history and social climate of Dvorak's time.

MAC. Req: Any Macintosh with color display; System 7; CD-ROM drive; no more than 2.2MB available RAM (4MB installed); speakers or headphones if CD-ROM is external.

CD-ROM: CD90018. $79.95.

Robert Winter

Art and Music: Evolutions

This four-CD-ROM series uses art and music to tell the story of Western civilization from the medieval era to the present. Musical excerpts from renowned compositions complement magnificent paintings, sculpture and architectural treasures. Volumes include the Eighteenth Century, the Baroque, the Renaissance, and the Medieval Era. Each features a self-playing multimedia presentation that combines musical and visual sequences to illustrate the cultural spirit of the era presented. Also includes hundreds of images, a customized electronic glossary, and 100 interactive questions to enhance users' understanding of the subject.

MAC. Available for Macintosh platforms.

WIN. Available for Windows platforms.

CD-ROM: CD90147. $39.98.

As You Like It

This CD-ROM version of Shakespeare's comedy features an easy-to-read commentary that provides a synopsis on each line of the text. Also features detailed character profiles, a glossary and hypertext link, and rare pictures.

WIN. Req: CD-ROM; 4MB RAM; VGA 256 colors; Win 3.1; Sound Card; Mouse.

CD-ROM: CD90255. $179.99.

Baseball's Greatest Hits

Filled with rare video clips and more than six hours of audio recordings from the greatest moments in baseball, this CD-ROM takes you through more than 60 high points, with box scores of important games, team histories, career statistics, still photos of baseball's greatest players, columns by Pulitzer Prize-winner Red Smith, and introductions by Mel Allen.

MAC. Req: Any Macintosh with color display; System 7; CD-ROM drive; no more than 2.2 Mb available RAM (4 Mb installed).

WIN. Req: 25-MHz 486SX or higher processor; MS-DOS 5 or later; 640x480, 256-color display; 4 Mb RAM (8 Mb recommended).

CD-ROM: CD90043. $59.95.

Jeff Kisseloff, USA

The Beat Experience: The Red Hot Organization

A portrait of the artists—writers, musicians, poets, filmmakers—who gave birth to the 1950's artistic community. An experience meant to immerse the user in the ethos of the Beat Generation—who and what they were—sexuality, drug use, art. Includes selections from books by Ginsberg, Burroughs, Kerouac; music by Monk, Parker, Davis and Coltrane, and over 50 images from the Whitney exhibition of "Beat Culture and the New America: 1950-1965."

MAC. Req: 68030 processor (examples: Performa 575; Quadra; Centris) or better; 7.0 operating system or later; 8 MB RAM; 640x480 color monitor or 13" display; Double-speed CD-ROM drive.

WIN. Req: 486SX-33 or higher processor; 640x480, 256-color display (accelerator recommended); 8 MB RAM; MPC2-compatible CD-ROM drive; Sound card (16-bit) with speakers or headphones; Windows 3.1 or Windows 95.

CD-ROM: CD90117. $39.95.

Beethoven Lives Upstairs

Based on the popular Classical Kids audio series. This interactive CD (kids can try their hand at playing some of his symphony pieces) features opportunities to learn about Beethoven's life and personality, and to play fun games which supply musical facts. With gorgeous video clips from the live-action film of the same name, this is a seamless blend of historical fact, fiction and imagination.

WIN. Req: Requires 4MB RAM, 4MB available hard-disk space.

CD-ROM: CD90109. $901.09.

Berlitz Live! (Japanese)

A quick tour guide for travelers to Japan who wish to learn key words and phrases, as well as cultural tips. Divided into 12 sections: Language Essentials, Basic Expressions, Arrival, Hotels, Business, Using the Phone for Business, Eating Out, Traveling Around, Shopping, Entertainment and Leisure, Getting to Know Japan, and Reference, which covers such topics as currency, street signs, telling time, and phrases to use in emergencies. The Sensei (teacher) guide provides narration, and his lip movements are synchronized with his speech to aid in pronunciation. Dialog scenes are accompanied by transliterized English in roman letters. If your computer has a microphone, you may also record yourself to check pronunciation using the program. Users can also play Tokyo Subway, a game in which they answer quiz questions to move around a map of the Tokyo subway system. A 15,000-word Japanese-English English-Japanese dictionary is also provided.

MAC. Available for Macintosh platforms.

WIN. Available for Windows platforms.

CD-ROM: CD90181. $69.99.

Berlitz Live! (Spanish)

A quick tour guide for travelers to Spanish-speaking countries who wish to learn key words and phrases, as well as cultural tips. Divided into 10 sections: Language Essentials, Basic Expressions, Spanish Grammar, Arrival, Hotels, Business, Phoning, Eating Out, Shopping, and Country Information, which provides a short summary on every Latin American country. Users can also play Mexico City Adventure Game. Animated on-screen guide, Rosalinda, provides narration. If your computer has a microphone, you may also record yourself to check pronunciation using the program. A 15,000-word Spanish-English English-Spanish dictionary is also provided.

MAC. Available for Macintosh platforms.

WIN. Available for Windows platforms.

CD-ROM: CD90182. $69.99.

Beyond Roswell

The alien crash at Roswell in July 1947 is the best-known UFO incident in the world. This CD-ROM features digital footage of the world-famous alien autopsy film, the full, searchable, text of the book, hundreds of indexed pages supporting documentation, video clips, and a screensaver.

WIN. Req: Windows 3.x and Windows 95 compatible; Quick Time for Windows.

CD-ROM: CD90263. $29.95.

Beyond the Wall: Stories Behind the Vietnam Wall

Armed Forces Radio D.J. Adrian Cronauer narrates this thought-provoking look at the stories behind the Vietnam Veterans Memorial in Washington, D.C. Veterans' memories and reflections on the war are augmented by newsreel footage, historical photographs, and recordings and newspaper articles about the war and the military buildup that preceded it.

MAC. Req: System 7.0 or higher; 7.01 system requirement.

OTHER. Req: Multimedia PC.

CD-ROM: CD90102. $59.98.

Bird

Explore the biology, behavior and cultural significance of all bird life with this virtual reality multimedia guide.

MAC. Available for Macintosh platforms.

WIN. Available for Windows platforms.

CD-ROM: CD90220. $39.95.

Brer Rabbit and the Wonderful Tar Baby

This classic children's story is now interactive and teaches reading comprehension skills to children four and younger and five and older. Features enchanting narration by acclaimed actor Danny Glover and music by legendary bluesman Taj Mahal. Choose one of two age levels for games, display the story text on-screen so kids see the words as they hear them, select activities related to the story and much more. Includes a detailed parents' guide to help enrich childrens' learning experiences.

MAC. Req: Macintosh LCII or higher (68030/16MHz or better recommended); 640 x 480 resolution (13") with 256 color display or greater; CD-ROM drive (double-speed recommended); 5MB of RAM (8MB recommended); System 7.0.1 or better. Recommended System: double-speed CD-ROM drive; 25MHz 68030 microprocessor or better; joystick optional.

WIN. Req: 386DX/33MHz CPU (486 recommended); 8MB or RAM total; Windows 3.1 or higher; 640 x 480 display with SVGA graphics, 256 colors; Windows compatible sound card; CD-ROM drive (double-speed recommended); mouse.

CD-ROM: CD90201. $19.95.

Butterflies of the World

Includes narrated video and a picture menu system to allow easy access to some 250 species of butterflies, often illustrated at life size. With chapters covering life cycle, body plan and ecology.

MAC. Req: 13" monitor or larger; color (256 minimum), 4MB RAM, hard drive, CD-ROM hard drive.

WIN. Req: 13" monitor or larger; 386 (or better) processor; 4MB RAM (8 MB recommended); Sound blaster compatible sound card; Super VGA graphics card (minimum 640 x 480 x 256 color resolution); Windows 3.1 and Windows 95 compatible. .

CD-ROM: CD90247. $29.95.

Cartoon Jukebox

Kids sing, dance and color along with this musical coloring book featuring ten classic songs, including "Wheels on the Bus," "Mary Had a Little Lamb," "Home on the Range," "Pop Goes the Weasel," "The Alphabet Song," "De Colores" and more. Kids "paint" up to 50 pages and then play back the cartoons in the colors they selected.

MAC. Req: Color Macintosh with 256 color display or better; 6MB of RAM (8MB recommended); CD-ROM drive (double-speed recommended); System 7.0 or higher. .

WIN. Req: 386SX 25MHz CPU; 4MB of RAM (8MB recommended); Windows 3.1 or higher; VGA display; Windows compatible sound card; CD-ROM drive (double-speed recommended); mouse.

CD-ROM: CD90206. $19.99.

Cartoon Network `Toon Jam!

Kids create their own music videos with special magic effects and 25 different music themes to choose from. Children can audition for and cast, select music for, direct and save their videos and create their own personal film festivals. The delightful *Cartoon Network `Toon Jam!* is hosted by Moxy, the Cartoon Network host, and features 18 other well-known characters, such as the Jetsons, Yogi Bear, Huckleberry Hound and more. Starring Bobcat Goldthwait as the voice of Moxy. Suitable for ages 4-13 years.

WIN. Req: 386 SX 25 MHz or better, 4 MB RAM, 2 megs available of hard drive, DOS 6 or later Windows 3.1 or later, single speed CD-ROM drive or better, 16-bit digital sound card, video card display (640 x 480 resolution) with 256 colors, mouse.

CD-ROM: CD90073. $44.98.

Cartopedia

Combining the cartographic resources of an atlas, the comprehensive information of an encyclopedia and the analytic and statistical depth of an almanac, this electronic guide to the nations of the world is unlike any other multimedia atlas. Over 7,000 pop-up windows present uniquely detailed overviews of every country, as well as specific up-to-date information on such topics as population, natural resources and climate. "The photographs, text and graphics are models of succinctness and clarity" *(BookPage)*.

MAC. Available for Macintosh platforms.

WIN. Available for Windows platforms.

CD-ROM: CD90222. $59.95.

Castle

Don the "disguise" of a page, knight, or servant to discover the mysteries of a 14th-century castle. Part interactive learning adventure, part educational experience, *Castle* offers a unique 3-D opportunity to uncover the castle's secrets and explore life in feudal Europe.

MAC. Available for Macintosh platforms.

WIN. Available for Windows platforms.

CD-ROM: CD90216. $39.95.

Cat

From roars to purrs, these virtual felines will fascinate all as they come to life on your computer screen in this multimedia guide to cats.

MAC. Available for Macintosh platforms.

WIN. Available for Windows platforms.

CD-ROM: CD90221. $39.95.

Children's Songbook: Music from Around the World

This CD-ROM features 15 traditional musical favorites from around the world. Each recording is accompanied by charming animated illustrations, lyrics and background information. Features vocalists from ten countries singing in their native languages, an instrumental version of each song so children can sing along, lively games which teach children to recognize music and lyrics, historical and cultural information about each song, and lyrics in English and in the song's original language.

MAC. Available for Macintosh platforms.

WIN. Available for Windows platforms.

CD-ROM: CD90198. $29.95.

Chronicle of the 20th Century

Witness firsthand the century's sweep, from the rise of the motor car to the fall of the Berlin Wall, with this ultimate record of our times. Listen to figures such as Winston Churchill and Martin Luther King Jr. deliver their epoch-making speeches and browse the news screens with entries for every day of the 20th century. Includes over 100 video clips, more than 2,000 photographs, and over two million words.

MAC. Available for Macintosh platforms.

WIN. Available for Windows platforms.

CD-ROM: CD90215. $59.95.

Cinema Volta

Artist and narrator Jim Petrillo looks at the diverse accomplishments and lives of the great electrical inventors of the 19th century juxtaposed with the history of Sicily, Shelley and Byron, James Joyce, the cave paintings of Lascaux, *Frankenstein*, and Petrillo's own childhood. The result is a provocative look at the technology which surrounds us and what we have become—a treat for the eye and mind alike.

MAC. Req: Any Macintosh with color display; System 7; CD-ROM drive; no more than 3.2MB available RAM (5MB installed); 640x480 resolution (13") color monitor.

WIN. Req: 486SX-33 or higher processor; 640x480, 256-color display (accelerator recommended); 8MB RAM; MPC2-compatible CD-ROM drive; sound card (16-bit) with speakers or headphones; Windows 3.1 or Windows 95.

CD-ROM: CD90028. $39.95.

Jim Petrillo

Comic Book Confidential

This CD-ROM features Ron Mann's critically acclaimed film *Comic Book Confidential* in its entirety and includes over 120 pages of comics by artists such as Stan Lee, William Gaines, Lynda Barry, R. Crumb and Art Spiegelman, as well as biographies of each artist, lists of their published works, and a new introduction by Scott McCloud, author of *Understanding Comics. Comic Book Confidential* spans the history of the comics from the 1930s to the present, and is the only comprehensive documentary of comics and their creators ever made.

MAC. Req: Any color-capable Macintosh (25-MHz 68030 processor or better recommended): System 7; not more than 6.2MB of available RAM (8MB installed); 13" color monitor; CD-ROM drive.

WIN. Req: 486SX-33 or higher processor; 640x480, 256-color display (accelerator recommended); 8MB RAM; MPC2-compatible CD-ROM drive; sound card (16-bit) with speakers or headphones; Windows 3.1 or Windows 95.

CD-ROM: CD90014. $39.95.

Ron Mann, USA

The Complete Maus

Art Spiegelman won the Pulitzer Prize for his gripping comic book saga of his parents' survival of the Holocaust, *Maus*, in which the Jews are mice and the Nazis are cats. This CD-ROM includes 18 hours with his father, thousands of color sketches, many never seen in public before, and interviews with Spiegelman himself, discussing what went into the making of *Maus*. Each page of the text is linked to historical documents such as maps, prisoners' drawings and photographs.

MAC. Req: Any color capable Macintosh (25-MHz 68030 processor or better recommended): System 7; not more than 6.2MB of available RAM (8MB installed); 13" color monitor; CD-ROM drive.

WIN. Req: 486SX-33 or higher processor; 640x480, 256-color display (accelerator recommended); 8MB RAM; MPC2-compatible CD-ROM drive; sound card (16-bit) with speakers or headphones; Windows 3.1 or Windows 95.

CD-ROM: CD90033. $49.95.

Art Spiegelman

Compton's Encyclopedia of American History

Comprehensive reference of U.S. history, including the actual words of people throughout history, over 300 documents, pictures, videos and speeches. Includes the complete text of *American History: A Survey*, by renowned historian Alan Brinkley.

WIN. Req: 486SX; 25MHz; 8MB recom; SVGA 256 colors; DOS 3.1+; Win 3.1+; sound card; mouse.

CD-ROM: CD90243. $39.99.

Countdown (Visual Almanac Series, Vol. 1)

Countdown uses three challenging games to build intuition and math skills, using new approaches to teaching young minds mathematical concepts. Players can increase the difficulty level of problems as they increase their skills.

MAC. Req: Any Macintosh with color display; System 7; CD-ROM drive; no more than 2.2MB available RAM (4MB installed).

WIN. Req: 486SX-33 or higher processor; 640x480, 256-color display (accelerator recommended); 8MB RAM; MPC2-compatible CD-ROM drive; sound card (16-bit) with speakers or headphones; Windows 3.1 or Windows 95.

CD-ROM: CD90010. $29.95.

M. Nanny & R. Mohl

Countries of Intrigue: Egypt-Greece-Mediterranean

Experience the beauty, legend and history of Greece and its islands, travel through time to visit the mysteries of Egypt and set sail to discover the great civilizations of the Mediterranean on this set of three CD-ROMs.

WIN. Available for Windows platforms.

CD-ROM: CD90228. $49.99.

Criterion Goes to the Movies

Containing clips from the more than 140 films in Voyager's Criterion Collection of laser disc films, this CD-ROM spans from *Some Like It Hot* to *King Kong* to *Blade Runner* to *The Adventures of Baron von Munchausen*. Entries include film credits, essays on the individual films, still photographs of the stars, original theatrical trailers, production photos and more.

MAC. Req: Any Macintosh with color display; System 7; CD-ROM drive; no more than 3.2MB available RAM (5MB installed); 640x480 resolution (13") color monitor.

WIN. Req: 25-MHz 486SX or higher processor; MS-DOS 5 or later; 640x480, 256-color display; 4MB RAM (8MB recommended).

CD-ROM: CD90013. $24.95.

Critical Mass: America's Race to Build the Atomic Bomb

Tracing the atomic bomb from its advent to its enormous, controversial and devastating impact, the unique content and exceptional quality of this CD-ROM offers compelling insight into the culture, science and technology that plunged the world into the atomic age.

MAC. Available for Macintosh platforms.

WIN. Available for Windows platforms.

CD-ROM: CD90184. $59.99.

The Crucible CD-ROM

This CD-ROM is a study guide for anyone wanting to learn more about Arthur Miller's popular play, the playwright, and about the witch hunts of the 1690s in Salem, Massachusetts, as well as the McCarthy Communist "witch hunts" of the 1950s, for which *The Crucible* remains a powerful allegory. Features seven major sections, including the full text of the play, essays, video clips, and an interview with the playwright from June 1992.

WIN. Available for Windows platforms.

CD-ROM: CD90172. $65.00.

Curious George Comes Home

Children can create and print a book full of adventures with Curious George in this CD-ROM based on the children's classic by H.A. Rey.

WIN. Available for Windows platforms.

CD-ROM: CD90138. $49.99.

The Day After Trinity: J. Robert Oppenheimer and the Atomic Bomb

Based on the Academy Award-nominated documentary by Jon Else, this hybrid CD-ROM explores the life and mind of J. Robert Oppenheimer, the charismatic yet tragic man who launched the United States and the rest of the world into the nuclear age. Featuring rare footage and first person interviews with participants from the first atomic test over 50 years ago in New Mexico, biographical information on all participants, Jon Else's complete film, declassified military and FBI documents, commentary by Else and by historian Michael Renov, a glossary of terms and more.

MAC. Req: 68030 processor (examples: Performa 575; Quadra; Centris) or better; 7.0 operating system or later; 8 MB RAM; 640x480 color monitor or 13" display; Double-speed CD-ROM drive.

WIN. Req: 486SX-33 or higher processor; 640x480, 256-color display (accelerator recommended); 8 MB RAM; MPC2-compatible CD-ROM drive; Sound card (16-bit) with speakers or headphones; Windows 3.1 or Windows 95.

CD-ROM: CD90085. $29.95.

Jon Else, USA

Dinosaurs

Enter the incredible world of the dinosaur and see the two huge, animated 3-D models that dominate the newest floor of this interactive museum. Special viewing screens allow virtual visitors to explore how these beasts lived and hunted. You can even descend into the archeological Discovery Pit to uncover fossilized bones of dinosaurs and bring them back to life.

MAC. Available for Macintosh platforms.

WIN. Available for Windows platforms.

CD-ROM: CD90219. $39.95.

Dr. Sulphur's Night Lab

This colorful, virtual chemistry lab turns chemistry into a fun learning experience for 9- to 14-year-olds as they conduct experiments and try to rescue Dr. Sulphur and his missing formulas. Chemical principles and relationships are explored with some of the doctor's uniquely bred animals, such as Alkaline Alligator.

MAC. Available for Macintosh platforms.

WIN. Available for Windows platforms.

CD-ROM: CD90170. $49.99.

Eastwood

A retrospective of Clint Eastwood's career as both an actor and director. This two-CD set contains over 200 video and audio clips including dozens of film clips, slide shows, interviews and countless behind-the-scene surprises. Offering hours of entertainment, this set is bound to thrill the Eastwood afficionado as well as the general movie fan.

WIN. Req: 486DX/66, 8MB RAM, Vesa local-bus or PCi video, 2X ROM drive, 16-bit Windows-compatible sound card.

CD-ROM: CD90112. $69.98.

Encyclopedia of U.S. Endangered Species

These comprehensive multimedia reports cover more than 20,000 hypertext pages on more than 700 endangered animal and plant species in the United States which can be accessed by state, scientific classification, common name and scientific name. Includes details on the origin of a species, its natural habitat, and where and why it is endangered in America. Features more than 35,000 color photos, locator and state maps, name pronunciations and selected animal sounds. Also includes *Webster's New World Dictionary*.

DOS. Available for DOS platforms.

MAC. Available for Macintosh platforms.

WIN. Available for Windows platforms.

CD-ROM: CD90144. $39.99.

Encyclopedia of U.S. Postage Stamps

More than 5,000 hypertext pages present large, full-color photos of the 2,400 face-different U.S. postage stamps ever issued. Includes historical background, discussions and introductions by leading philatelic experts. Produced with Richard L. Sine, former editorial director of the nation's largest philatelic publisher. Also includes *Webster's New World Dictionary*.

DOS. Available for DOS platforms.

MAC. Available for Macintosh platforms.

WIN. Available for Windows platforms.

CD-ROM: CD90145. $39.99.

Ephemeral Films: 1931-1960

A two-part series capturing tales from the dawn of the American Consumer Age, documenting the revealing, absurd and perverse films of educators, marketers and others. Part 1 is entitled *1931-1945: To New Horizons*, and Part 2 is *1946-1960: You Can't Get There from Here*. Filmmaker Rick Prelinger is a film scholar and anthropologist whose other works include *Call It Home* and *Television Toys*.

MAC. Req: Any Macintosh with color display; System 7; CD-ROM drive; no more than 2.2MB available RAM (4MB installed).

WIN. Req: 25-MHz 480SX or higher processor; MS-DOS 5 or later; 640x480, 256-color display; 4MB RAM (8MB recommended).

CD-ROM: CD90016. $39.95.

Rick Prelinger, USA

The Escape of Marvin the Ape

Children join bookworms Wendy, Albert and Pablo as they follow Marvin on an adventure-packed multi-media romp through New York City. Interactive games build concentration skills and vocabulary in four languages. Enhanced with voices by Jonathan Winters.

DOS. Req: 5.0 or higher.

MAC. Req: Double-speed CD-ROM drive; color monitor; system 7.0 or higher, LC III series or better; 8 MB RAM; 4 MB hard disk space available.

WIN. Req: Double-speed CD-ROM drive, VGA 256-color monitor; Windows 3.1; 486 or Pentium processor; 8- or 16-bit sound blaster or compatible sound card; 8 MB RAM; 4 MB hard disk space available.

CD-ROM: CD90191. $29.95.

Exotic Japan

An interactive guide to Japanese customs and language with over 150 lessons and quizzes, instructive animations, traditional Japanese games and woodcuts, and information on everything from the bullet train to business cards. Both male and female native Japanese speakers guide you through proper pronunciation as you record and play your own voice speaking Japanese. From Nikki Yokokura, Japanese language professor at McMaster University in Toronto.

MAC. Req: Macintosh Plus or better (any Mac produced since 1986) running system 6.0.7 or later; CD-ROM drive; 1.5 Mb of available RAM. If running system 6, must have at least 2 Mb RAM installed; if running System 7, must have at least 3 Mb. Requires speakers or headphones if CD-ROM drive is external.

WIN. Req: 386SX or higher processor; MS-DOS 3.3 or later; 640x480, 256-color display; 4 Mb RAM.

CD-ROM: CD90042. $59.95.

Nikki Yokokura

Explorer Pack

Contains the titles *Tony Quinn's Virtual Galaxy, Beyond the Wall of Stars: Quest One of the Taran Trilogy, Sound Library Pro, World of Motion, Loon Magic, Matt & Joe's Cool Screen Backgrounds, Font Pro 2: Types of Distinction, epsPRO 1: Design Elements, CD FilmFest: Comedy Classics,* and *Photo Pro Select: The Best of Photo Pro*.

MAC. Req: Mac 7.1 or higher; 2 Mb free RAM; hard drive; CD-Rom drive.

WIN. Req: Windows 3.1 or higher; 2 Mb free RAM; hard drive; CD-Rom drive.

CD-ROM: CD90051. $39.00.

Eyewitness Encyclopedia of Science 2.0

This revised multimedia reference guide to science and technology adds half a million additional words of text and new graphics animation, as well as video sequences and sound clips.

MAC. Available for Macintosh platforms.

WIN. Available for Windows platforms.

CD-ROM: CD90223. $49.95.

Eyewitness Encyclopedia of Space and the Universe

Tis multimedia guide to space and the universe flies around the moon, examines the life and death of stars and reveals the inside of a space station. There is also a dramatic recreation of the big bang theory.

MAC. Available for Macintosh platforms.

WIN. Available for Windows platforms.

CD-ROM: CD90224. $49.95.

FDR

Cinematic tours capture the most dramatic events of the presidency of FDR during this century's greatest turning points. Interactive exploration of the locations significant to the Roosevelts, including the White House and Hyde Park, reveal the forces and personalities which shaped Franklin and Eleanor's lives. A timeline and innovative contextual pathways bring to light the progression of FDR's life in relationship to world events.

MAC. Available for Macintosh platforms.

WIN. Available for Windows platforms.

CD-ROM: CD90212. $49.99.

The First Emperor of China

This fascinating CD-ROM combines archival film footage of the first days of the excavation of the tomb of the First Emperor of China, Qin Shi Huang Di, with archival materials, a tour through the Qin Museum of Warriors and Horses, over 2,000 slides, and commentary from distinguished scholars to tell the story of this amazing archaeological find. It features a bilingual Chinese/English soundtrack, a glossary of terms, an audio guide to Chinese pronunciation of terms, maps, a timeline, and much more.

MAC. Req: Any color capable Macintosh (25-MHz 68030 processor or better recommended): System 7; not more than 6.2 Mb of available RAM (8 Mb installed); 13" color monitor; CD-ROM drive.

CD-ROM: CD90030. $79.95.

Dr. Ching-chih Chen

First Person: Donald Norman, Defending Human Attributes in the Age of the Machine
Design theorist Donald Norman examines technology in terms of the plight of the human race. Join him as he examines a Macintosh desktop, points out its good points and its bad points, and ties these into the problems humans face by living in the technological age. This so-called "guru of interface design" insists that humanity must come before technology. Thought provoking. From the *First Person* CD-ROM series.

MAC. Req: 68030 processor (examples: Performa 575; Quadra; Centris) or better; 7.0 operating system or later; 8MB RAM; 640x480 color monitor or 13" display; double-speed CD-ROM drive.

WIN. Req: 486SX-33 or higher processor; 640x480, 256-color display (accelerator recommended); 8MB RAM; MPC2-compatible CD-ROM drive; Sound card (16-bit) with speakers or headphones; Windows 3.1 or Windows 95.

CD-ROM: CD90083. $39.95.

USA

First Person: Marvin Minsky, The Society of Mind

Marvin Minsky's theories come to life as he walks, talks and jumps across the page, challenging conventional notions of what makes us tick in a program that combines over 100 minutes of original video, 200 color graphics and 1100 pages of text, including the complete *Society of Mind*. Minsky is the co-founder of the MIT Media Laboratory.

MAC. Req: Any color-capable Macintosh (25-MHz 68030 processor or better recommended); System 7; not more than 6.2MB of available RAM (8MB installed); 13" color monitor; CD-ROM drive.

CD-ROM: CD90001. $49.95.

First Person: Mumia Abu-Jamal, Live from Death Row

Mumia Abu-Jamal is an award-winning Philadelphia journalist who has been on death row since 1982 for the killing of a Philadelphia police officer. Convicted and sentenced under extremely questionable circumstances, Abu-Jamal speaks about the lives and treatment of African-Americans in the United States, the judicial system, life in America's prisons and more. This hybrid CD-ROM features the entire text of Abu-Jamal's autobiography *Live from Death Row*, video and audio interviews with Abu-Jamal, an overview of his life, highlights of his political involvements, other of his writings and more.

MAC. Req: 68030 processor (examples: Performa 575; Quadra; Centris) or better; 7.0 operating system or later; 8 MB RAM; 640x480 color monitor or 13" display; Double-speed CD-ROM drive.

WIN. Req: 486SX-33 or higher processor; 640x480, 256-color display (accelerator recommended); 8 MB RAM; MPC2-compatible CD-ROM drive; Sound card (16-bit) with speakers or headphones; Windows 3.1 or Windows 95.

CD-ROM: CD90084. $29.95.

USA

First Person: Stephen Jay Gould, On Evolution

Best-selling author and evolutionary biologist Stephen Jay Gould tackles evolution and natural history in a lecture delivered for this CD-ROM, in which he poses three intriguing riddles about Charles Darwin. A wealth of additional material includes the best of Gould's published work on the subject and relevant writings by Darwin and other explorers of the Victorian era.

MAC. Req: Any color-capable Macintosh (25-MHz 68030 processor or better recommended); System 7; not more than 6.2MB or available RAM (8MB installed); 13" color monitor; CD-ROM drive.

WIN. Req: 486SX-33 or higher processor; 640x480, 256-color display (accelerator recommended); 8MB RAM; MPC2-compatible CD-ROM drive; sound card (16-bit) with speakers or headphones; Windows 3.1 or Windows 95.

CD-ROM: CD90002. $39.95.

For All Mankind

Between 1968 and 1972, 24 astronauts left Earth for the moon. Culled from 80 hours of interviews, a 79-minute film (complete here) tells the story of the first "extraterrestrial humans." Also included are lunar maps, illustrations, mission histories and astronaut biographies. Hundreds of images from NASA archives.

MAC. Req: 68030 processor (examples: Performa 575; Quadra; Centris) or better; 7.0 operating system or later; 8 MB RAM; 640x480 color monitor or 13" display; Double-speed CD-ROM drive.

WIN. Req: 486SX-33 or higher processor; 640x480, 256-color display (accelerator recommended); 8 MB RAM; MPC2-compatible CD-ROM drive; Sound card (16-bit) with speakers or headphones; Windows 3.1 or Windows 95.

CD-ROM: CD90129. $39.95.

Four Footed Friends

Multilingual bookworms guide children through ten beautifully illustrated and animated animal rhymes. Video and interactive lessons teach children about animals, spelling and vocabulary.

DOS. Available for DOS platforms.
MAC. Available for Macintosh platforms.
WIN. Available for Windows platforms.
CD-ROM: CD90193. $29.95.

Franz Schubert: "The Trout" Quintet

American music critic and author Alan Rich offers a personal look at "The Trout" Quintet, including the original song "Die Forelle" in both English and German, and the Trout Cookbook.

MAC. Req: Macintosh Plus or better (any Mac produced since 1986) running system 6.0.7 or later; CD-ROM drive; 1.5 Mb of available RAM. If running system 6, must have at least 2 Mb RAM installed; If running System 7, must have at least 3 Mb. Requires speakers or headphones if CD-ROM drive is external.

CD-ROM: CD90025. $59.95.

Alan Rich, USA

French Pronunciation Tutor

This hybrid CD-ROM simplifies the process of learning French, because it allows students to listen to French as spoken by a native speaker, then record themselves speaking French and compare their speech to that of a native French speaker. This educational CD-ROM features interactive help, hints to explain the finer points of pronunciation, detailed animations of the speech process, interactive exercise screens, pronunciation tests for tracking your progress, audio and video of native speakers and more. From The Learning Company.

MAC. Req: Runs on all Macintosh computers equipped with a CD-ROM drive, a 256-color monitor, 680.30/25MHz or better processor, and System 7. Requires 4 MB of memory. Requires a microphone or MacRecorder.

WIN. Req: System 386 or higher; Multimedia PC with CD-ROM drive; Requires 386/25MHz or better, 4 MB RAM, Windows 3.1 or higher, doublespeed CD-ROM drive, Windows compatible sound card, VGA or better, plus a microphone.

CD-ROM: CD90095. $59.98.

Gettysburg Multimedia Battle Simulation

Shelby Foote, noted Civil War Historian, narrates this innovative CD-ROM, which features an historically correct simulation of the battle at Gettysburg. Also featured are video clips from the acclaimed epic *Gettysburg*. This historical simulation can be used in either historical or free play.

WIN. Req: MPC IBM or 100% compatible 386SX/25Mhz, MS Windows 3.1, 4 Megabytes RAM, Double-speed CD-ROM, VGA 256-color graphics, Soundblaster-compatible sound card.

CD-ROM: CD90072. $69.98.

Great Paintings—Renaissance to Impressionism: The Frick Collection

This CD-ROM highlights 138 paintings by 64 different artists from the renowned Frick Collection of New York. Each image features historical background and descriptive information and is displayed in a full-screen format. Includes an online tour of the Frick Collection, sharp, clear images, and more.

MAC. Req: LCII or above (040 CPU or above strongly recommended). 5MB RAM (8-10MB for 16- or 24-bit color). Color Monitor (640 x 480) and 8-bit color (16- or 24-bit color strongly recommended). Double-Speed CD-ROM Drive. System 7.0 or better. Mouse.

WIN. Req: 486/25 or above. 8MB RAM. VGA Monitor (640 x 480) and Video Card running at 256 colors. Double-Speed CD-ROM Drive. Windows 3.1. Windows Compatible Sound Card. Mouse.

CD-ROM: CD90105. $59.95.

Greatest Moments of Our Time

Features milestones in entertainment, science, sports and world events. Contains film footage of the Wright Brothers at Kitty Hawk, Edison in his laboratory, Charles Lindbergh, Albert Einstein, the Beatles and a star's birth. Covers such great leaders in history as Gandhi, Roosevelt, Mandela and Kennedy.

WIN. Req: 486DX 33MHz; 68040; 4X speed CD-ROM recom.; 8MB RAM; 256 colors; Win. 3.1; Sys 7.1; Sound Card; Mouse.

CD-ROM: CD90246. $49.99.

Green Eggs and Ham

This adaptation of the #1-selling Dr. Seuss book takes the original story's charm one step further. Meticulously animated from hundreds of sketches, it's filled with delightful new scenes, surprises and activities. Includes original storybook, games and illustrated parent handbook.

MAC. Available for Macintosh platforms.
WIN. Available for Windows platforms.
CD-ROM: CD90211. $49.98.

Guide to Classical Music

Experience over four hours of some of the best musical pieces ever writtten, all performed by virtuoso European musicians and orchestras. Provides detailed descriptions of over 200 compositions, with accompanying excerpts. Contains information regarding the births, deaths, compositions and performances of the great composers of the Baroque, Classical, Romantic and Modern Periods.

WIN. Req: 486SX; 25MHz; 2X speed CD-ROM; 8MB recom; SVGA 256 colors; Win. 3.1+; Win 95; sound card; mouse.

CD-ROM: CD90235. $39.98.

Guide to the Orchestra

An interactive tour of the evolution of the orchestra, its greatest composers, the purpose and placement of each instrument, the role of the conductor and more, Contains recording of compositions, video interviews, detailed illustrations and a 17-minute concert film and orchestra game.

WIN. Req: 486DX; 2x CD-ROM; 8MB RAM; SVGA; 64k colors; DOS 5.0; Win 3.1+; W95; 16-bit sound card; Mouse.

CD-ROM: CD90234. $39.95.

The Guinness Encyclopedia

This comprehensive, interactive encyclopedia contains articles, illustrations, maps, animations, over 1,000 photographs, more than 30 language samples, and more. *The Guinness Encyclopedia* is thematically arranged, offers in-depth explanations of facts, including animated demonstrations of the way things work, and focuses on such topics as "The Nature of the Universe," "The Human Organism," "Religion and Philosophy," "Language and Literature," "Music and Dance" and "The Countries of the World," among others.

MAC. Req: Mac 7.1 or higher; 1 Mb free RAM; hard drive; CD-Rom drive.

WIN. Req: Windows 3.1 or higher; 1 Mb free RAM; hard drive; CD-Rom drive.

CD-ROM: CD90049. $39.00.

USA

Hablemos Ingles 6.0

This highly-interactive, self-paced language program helps students speak and understand everyday English words and phrases quickly. Includes video of native speakers and speech recognition and record/playback features. Includes grammar exploration and translations in Spanish, allowing students to study English from their native Spanish.

MAC. Available for Macintosh platforms.
WIN. Available for Windows platforms.
CD-ROM: CD90158. $149.00.

Haight-Ashbury in the Sixties

In the 1960s, San Francisco was a Mecca to the new youth culture. This hybrid CD-ROM takes a look back at the 1960s Haight-Ashbury scene through artwork, articles, photographs, poetry and commentary from Haight-Ashbury's own 1960s counterculture newspaper, *The San Francisco Oracle*. Also included are video clips, text, narration, music and more.

OTHER. Req: Multimedia PC.

CD-ROM: CD90089. $54.98.

USA

Hamlet

This CD-ROM version of Shakespeare's famous drama features an index button that provides instant access to every piece of information in the entire database. Digital, stereo recording allows the users to hear the thunder of hoofbeats and the clash of swords.

WIN. Req: CD-ROM; 4MB RAM; VGA 256 colors; Win 3.1; Sound Card; Mouse.

CD-ROM: CD90256. $179.99.

Hanna-Barbera's Cartoon Carnival

Visit the cartoon world of Hanna-Barbera and play games with your favorite characters: Fred Flintstone, Yogi Bear, George Jetson, Huckleberry Hound, Top Cat and Scooby Doo. Characters juggle and duck, snatch and crash in delightful animations throughout a zany variety of games, including Sound Match, Balloon Catch, Haunted Maze, Trivia Game, Gift Match and Space Race. The fun and games grow with children through ten levels of difficulty as they learn important coordination and logic skills.

MAC. Req: Minimal system: color Macintosh with 256 color display; CD-ROM drive with 4MB RAM; System 7.0 or better. Recommended system: double-speed CD-ROM drive; 25MHz 68030 microprocessor or better; joystick optional.

WIN. Req: Minimal system: MPC1 compliant; CD-ROM drive with 4MB RAM. Recommended system: double-speed CD-ROM drive; 386DX or better processor; joystick optional.

CD-ROM: CD90205. $19.95.

A Hard Day's Night

The first Beatles' film is interactive and shown in its entirety. Also includes the original script, two short films, clips from the early work of director Richard Lester, an essay on the Beatles and the history of rock n' roll, profiles of the band, cast, and crew, and the movie's original theatrical trailer.

MAC. Req: Any Macintosh with color display; System 7; CD-ROM drive; no more than 3.2MB available RAM (5MB installed).

WIN. Req: Not available at present.

CD-ROM: CD90012. $39.95.

Richard Lester, Great Britain, 1964

Haunted House

Lively animations, eerie sounds and a rich musical score bring Jan Pienkowski's highly acclaimed pop-up book, *Haunted House*, to life. Ten spooky rooms full of mysterious surprises and creepy games will captivate children every time they enter. Fully orchestrated musical score includes works by Beethoven, Handel, Gilbert & Sullivan, and others.

MAC. Req: 68030 33 MHz or better; 68040 25 MHz or better; System 7.1 or later; 5MB of RAM; 3MB hard disk free space; 640x480 256 colors; double-speed CD-ROM drive.

WIN. Req: 486SX 25 MHz or better; DOS version 5.0 or later; Windows 3.1 or later; 8MB of RAM; 2MB hard disk space free; SVGA, 640x480 256 colors; double-speed CD-ROM drive; Windows 95.

CD-ROM: CD90210. $49.99.

History of Medicine

This elegant multimedia reference set details important events in the history of medicine, defines medical terms and has a database of little-known facts. Also includes medical histories of famous people, including Moses, Adolf Hitler, John Wayne and Rock Hudson.

WIN. Req: 486SX33 or higher processor; 256-color SVGA display; 8 MB RAM; MPC2-compatible CD-ROM drive; sound card; 4MB free disk space.

CD-ROM: CD90162. $44.98.

History of Music Collection

This five-part collection chronicles the evolution of Western classical music through American folk music of the modern era, focusing on the genius of its musicians, the development of instruments, and turning points in music that affected all of civilization. Enhanced with additional reference materials, including *Webster's New World Dictionary*, which features over 150,000 entries, the *American Concise Encyclopedia*, which features over 15,000 entries and 21 subjects, and original source documents, including the Old and New Testaments, the Declaration of Independence, the Magna Carta, the U.S. Constitution and the Emancipation Proclamation.

MAC. Available for Macintosh platforms.

WIN. Available for Windows platforms.

CD-ROM: CD90140. $39.98.

History of the World

An unrivaled source of knowledge on civilizations, historical events and the people who have shaped history. Travel to any part of the world, at any time in history, through a unique interface that allows access to hundreds of articles, selected artifacts, video sequences and animation, as well as more than 700 photos and illustrations.

MAC. Req: 4MB RAM; 256 colors; Sys 7.0+.

WIN. Req: 386DX; 33MHz+; 4MB RAM; SVGA 256 colors; Win 3.1+; sound card; mouse.

CD-ROM: CD90244. $49.99.

How the Rhinoceros Got His Skin

This blend of fantasy and reality in Rudyard Kipling's classic children's story of the gluttonous rhinoceros who got his comeuppance makes for enjoyable bilingual storytelling, thanks to the talents of Jack Nicholson, who narrates the English version, and Raul Julia, who narrates the Spanish version. Jazz singer-composer Bobby McFerrin supplies the unique musical score. Choose one of two age levels for games, display the story text on-screen so kids see the words as they hear them, select activities related to the story and much more. Includes a detailed parents' guide to help enrich childrens' learning experiences.

MAC. Req: Macintosh LCII or higher (68030/16MHz or better recommended); 640 x 480 resolution (13") with 256 color display or greater; CD-ROM drive (double-speed recommended); 5MB of RAM (8MB recommended); System 7.0.1 or later.

WIN. Req: 386DX/33MHz or higher CPU (486 recommended); 8MB of RAM total; Windows 3.1 or later; 640 x 480 display with SVGA graphics; Windows-compatible sound card; double-speed CD-ROM drive.

CD-ROM: CD90203. $19.95.

I Photograph to Remember

I Photograph to Remember is the family memoir of renowned Latin American photographer Pedro Meyer. Narrated by Meyer in both English and Spanish, he documents his parents' last years of life, using the computer as a powerful medium for expression. His photographic work has appeared in more than 125 exhibitions, and is on display in over 20 museums worldwide. His published works include *Espejo de Espinas (Mirror of Thorns)*.

MAC. Req: Any Macintosh with color display; System 7; CD-ROM drive; no more than 2.2 Mb available RAM (4 Mb installed); 640x480 resolution (13") color monitor; speakers or headphones if CD-ROM drive is external; 10-20 Mb of hard drive space; multiple configurations or special requirements possible.

WIN. Req: 386SX or higher processor; MS-DOS 3.3 or later; 640x480, 256-color display; 4 Mb RAM.

CD-ROM: CD90031. $39.95.

Pedro Meyer

If Monks Had Macs: A Hearty Stew of Interactive Books, Games, Art

An interactive look at Henry David Thoreau's life and ideas, electronic editions of *Walden, The Scarlet Letter* and *JFK Witness* among others, Bruegel's masterpiece "Tower of Babel" examined in detail via the Painting Navigator, and games ranging from an existential art puzzle, a medieval adventure to the Monks' Memory Challenge!

MAC. Req: 68030 processor (examples; Performa 575; Quadra; Centris) or better; 7.0 operating system or later; 8 MB RAM; 640x480 color monitor or 13" display; Double-speed CD-ROM drive.

CD-ROM: CD90131. $34.95.

Igor Stravinsky: The Rite of Spring

This CD-ROM contains the energy and creativity of Igor Stravinsky and invites you to listen to the music of Stravinsky's "The Rite of Spring" as scholar and pianist Robert Winter's commentary on each theme scrolls by. There is also a detailed glossary of musical terms and theory, and a guide to the life and times of Stravinsky.

MAC. Req: Macintosh Plus or better (any Mac produced since 1986) running system 6.0.7 or later; CD-ROM drive; 1.5MB of available RAM; if running system 6, must have at least 2MB RAM installed; if running System 7, must have at least 3MB. Requires speakers or headphones if CD-ROM drive is external.

CD-ROM: CD90021. $79.95.

Robert Winter

The Indian in the Cupboard

Based on the award-winning children's book series and critically acclaimed movie, this magical learning adventure will sharpen children's listening, logic and problem-solving skills. Ten toy figures come to life as Iroquois guide Little Bear leads children on an enchanting journey into the culture and customs of mid-18th century Iroquois life.

MAC. Available for Macintosh platforms.

WIN. Req: Windows '95 or higher.

CD-ROM: CD90136. $49.98.

Invention Studio

With the help of brainy, off-beat host Doc Howard, kids nine and up can design, build and test their own inventions in this interactive CD-ROM from the Discovery Channel. Kids have fun while they develop critical thinking and problem-solving skills in this fully-equipped, gadget-filled, virtual testing ground and patent office. Go from blueprint to functioning 3-D images in the Garage, build a moving gadget in the Gadgetorium, construct real machines in the Machine Shop, and fire up power sources in the powerhouse arcade game.

WIN. Req: 256 color display; 8MB RAM (16MB recommended); double-speed CD-ROM drive; Windows compatible audio board; Microsoft Windows 3.1 or Windows 95.

CD-ROM: CD90165. $39.95.

Invisible Universe

Dodging Centaurus A, reclining on the Andromeda Galaxy, exploding into the Veil Nebula, Dr. Fiorella Terenzi brings it all to you in this entertaining and informative study of the universe beyond human sight. Dr. Terenzi uses star maps, movies, music and poetry to show you the evolution of stars, black holes, and glimpses of the origins of the universe itself.

MAC. Req: 68030 processor (i.e. Performa 575;Quadra;Centris)or better; 7.0 operating system or later; 8 MB RAM; 640x480 color monitor or 13" display; Double-speed CD-ROM drive.

WIN. Req: 486SX-33 or higher processor; 640x480, 256-color display (accelerator recommended); 8MB RAM; MPC2-compatible CD-ROM drive; Sound card (16-bit) with speakers or headphones; Windows 3.1 or Windows 95.

CD-ROM: CD90128. $39.95.

Isaac Asimov's Library of the Universe

This seven-title multimedia series explores the farthest reaches of the universe through the knowledge and imagination of scientific authority Isaac Asimov. Volumes include Astronomy, the Inner Planets, the Outer Planets, the Solar System, Space Exploration, Space Speculation, and the Universe.

MAC. Available for Macintosh platforms.

WIN. Available for Windows platforms.

CD-ROM: CD90146. $54.98.

A Jack Kerouac ROMnibus

Go on the road with Jack Kerouac and his Beat buddies with this interactive adventure that no Kerouac fan should be without. Includes the complete text of *The Dharma Bums*, laced with annotations; a "Kerouac sampler" containing 28 performances of selections from Kerouac works; a timeline of Kerouac's life; a "Beat family tree" illustrating the relationships between key Beat figures; selections from Keroac texts, excerpts from his journals and letters; and audio and video clips and photographs.

DOS. Req: 5.0 or higher.

MAC. Req: Double-speed CD-ROM drive; color monitor; system 7.0 or higher, LC III series or better; 8 MB RAM; 4 MB hard disk space available.

WIN. Req: Double-speed CD-ROM drive, VGA 256-color monitor; Windows 3.1; 486 or Pentium processor; 8- or 16-bit sound blaster or compatible sound card; 8 MB RAM; 4 MB hard disk space available.

CD-ROM: CD90190. $49.95.

Jerusalem: An Interactive Pilgrimage to the Holy City

Retrace the Holy City's glorious history, from the New Testament to the present. Discover the shrines, relics, landmarks and people. Explore its spiritual heritage..from the Roman Era, through the Crusades and Islamic periods, to contemporary times. Hundreds of photographs, animations, video and audio clips, and even an interactive game for children. This priceless CD is interesting for all—for the scholar, the pilgrim and the armchair traveller!

MAC. Available for Macintosh platforms.

WIN. Available for Windows platforms.

CD-ROM: CD90113. $39.98.

The Journey of Thomas Blue Eagle

This CD-ROM will transport you to the world of a young Lakota warrior born on the Plains of 1868. "Uncommon artistry combined with thoughtful research have produced a work of rare quality and merit" *(Publishers Weekly)*.

WIN. Req: Windows 3.1, 486, 4MB.

CD-ROM: CD90185. $49.95.

Julius Caeser

This CD-ROM version of Shakespeare's historical drama features pop-up definitions to explain the meanings of unusual words that may be unfamiliar to users. Also allows users to browse the Image Gallery, which gives access to over 100 engravings from the 17th, 18th and 19th centuries. Images portray actors in costume, famous scenes and Shakespeare himself.

WIN. Req: CD-ROM; 4MB RAM; VGA 256 colors; Win 3.1; Sound Card; Mouse.

CD-ROM: CD90257. $179.99.

Kon-Tiki

Hundreds of pages of text from Thor Heyerdahl's famous expeditions—the Ra, the Tigris and the Kon-Tiki—are included in this fascinating CD-ROM, with films taken onboard the ocean voyages and at archeological digs. Heyerdahl himself pops up to add explanations, and anecdotes, maps and diagrams contribute as well.

MAC. Req: 68030 processor (examples: Performa 575; Quadra; Centris) or better; 7.0 operating system or later; 8 MB RAM; 640x480 color monitor or 13" display; Double-speed CD-ROM drive.

WIN. Req: 486SX-33 or higher processor; 640x480, 256-color display (accelerator recommended); 8 MB RAM; MPC2-compatible CD-ROM drive; Sound card (16-bit) with speakers or headphones; Windows 3.1 or Windows 95.

CD-ROM: CD90125. $39.95.

Thor Heyerdahl

La Blue Girl, Volume 1

This CD-ROM features episodes 1 and 2 of the story of Miko Mido, an 18-year-old Ninja-in-training. Centuries ago his clan made a deal with the underworld forces, and now those forces are getting a new boss. Miko is suddenly called upon to protect the family business and keep the lustful Shikima away from the humans. Anime, Japanese with English subtitles.

DOS. Req: Windows 3.1 and MS DOS 5.0 or higher; 80386SX MHz or higher CPU and CD ROM drive; 4 Mb RAM; SVGA with at least 256 color display; Soundblaster compatible sound card; Quicktime 1.1 or better (included).

MAC. Req: System 7 or higher; 68020, 68030, 68040, or Power PC CPU and CD ROM drive; 4 Mb RAM; 256 color monitor (or better); Quicktime 1.5 or better (included).

WIN. Req: Windows 3.1 and MS DOS 5.0 or higher; 80386SX MHz or higher CPU and CD ROM drive; 4 Mb RAM; SVGA with at least 256 color display; Soundblaster compatible sound card; Quicktime 1.1 or better (included).

CD-ROM: CD90063. $24.95.

90 mins.

Last Chance to See

A spellbinding photographic chronicle of the many species of the world that are on the verge of extinction, including dozens of elephants, egrets, lemurs and more. The CD-ROM includes the entire text of the book *Last Chance to See*, plus over six hours of audio indexed to the text, over 700 photographs, information about each species and its current status, audio segments from the BBC radio series of the book, and more.

MAC. Req: Any Macintosh with color display; System 7; CD-ROM drive; no more than 2.2 Mb available RAM (4 Mb installed); speakers or headphones if CD-ROM drive is external.

WIN. Req: 386SX or higher processor; MS-DOS 3.3 or later; 640x480, 256-color display; 4 Mb RAM.

CD-ROM: CD90037. $59.95.

D. Adams & M. Carwar

Le Grand Louvre

Features a complete tour of the Louvre, 500 full-color paintings, live sounds, over 50 animated video clips, 350 illustrations and a visit to the new addition.

WIN. Available for Windows platforms.

CD-ROM: CD90226. $49.99.

Learn to Speak English 6.0

This highly-interactive, self-paced language program helps students speak and understand everyday English words and phrases quickly. Includes video of native speakers and speech recognition and record/playback features. Voices and text are entirely in English, making the program ideal for students who have some understanding of English and wish to further develop their fluency.

MAC. Available for Macintosh platforms.

WIN. Available for Windows platforms.

CD-ROM: CD90157. $149.00.

Learn to Speak French 4.0

This highly-interactive, self-paced language program helps students speak and understand everyday French words and phrases quickly. Includes video of native speakers and speech recognition and record/playback features.

MAC. Available for Macintosh platforms.

WIN. Available for Windows platforms.

CD-ROM: CD90160. $149.00.

Learn to Speak German 6.0

This highly-interactive, self-paced language program helps students speak and understand everyday German words and phrases quickly. Includes video of native speakers and speech recognition and record/playback features. Suitable for beginning to intermediate level foreign language students.

MAC. Available for Macintosh platforms.

WIN. Available for Windows platforms.

CD-ROM: CD90159. $149.00.

Learn to Speak Spanish 6.0

This highly-interactive, self-paced language program helps students speak and understand everyday Spanish words and phrases quickly. Includes video of native speakers and speech recognition and record/playback features.

MAC. Available for Macintosh platforms.

WIN. Available for Windows platforms.

CD-ROM: CD90156. $149.00.

Left at East Gate

With more material evidence of an alien landing than was ever found at Roswell, the Bentwaters incident occurred less than 20 years ago in Great Britain. This CD-ROM contains the complete text of the book *Left at East Gate*, an eyewitness account of the incident by Larry Warren and Peter Robbins, supporting documents, pictures, video and audio interviews, UFO organizations info, and the video shot at the base and forest area. Screensaver included with both video clips and images.

WIN. Req: Windows 3.x and Windows 95 compatible. Quicktime for Windows.

CD-ROM: CD90264. $29.95.

The Legend of Dracula: Truth and Terror

Sink your fangs into this complete collection of facts and bone-chilling fiction of the most notorious member of the vampire race—Dracula. See the earliest vampire film ever made, test your knowledge of vampire trivia, and learn about incidents of vampire hysteria. Narrated and compiled by Dracula expert Dr. Raymond McNally, this CD-ROM reveals how scientists and historians explain this mythical creature and how writers and filmmakers have made him a celebrity. Includes the annotated text of Bram Stoker's *Dracula*; the classic Murnau film, *Nosferatu*, with a commentary track by Dr. McNally; the life history of the "real" Dracula, Vlad the Impaler, including photographs, drawings, and re-enactments; film clips from some of the most ridiculous vampire movies ever made; and a comprehensive library of vampire legends from around the world.

MAC. Available for Macintosh platforms.

WIN. Available for Windows platforms.

CD-ROM: CD90196. $39.95.

Leonardo da Vinci

The writings and drawings of the *Codex Leicester* serve as a window into the thoughts of the most fascinating artist and scientist of the Italian Renaissance, illuminating how his examination of nature inspired his paintings and inventions. A detailed study of the entire manuscript, complete with innovative viewing and translation tools, as well as cinematic tours, works of art, interactive experiments and expert commentary, explore Leonardo's visionary observations and his profound influence on the modern world.

MAC. Available for Macintosh platforms.

WIN. Available for Windows platforms.

CD-ROM: CD90213. $49.99.

Leonardo the Inventor

While most people are familiar with Leonardo da Vinci's legacy of paintings and artwork, not everyone is aware that he was also a talented inventor, centuries ahead of his time. This hybrid CD-ROM takes drawing of inventions by da Vinci and animates them, showing what they might have looked like in action, both during da Vinci's lifetime and today. Rated "four mice" by *MacUser*.

MAC. Req: System 7.0 or higher; 7.01 system requirement.

OTHER. Req: Multimedia PC.

CD-ROM: CD90098. $49.98.

Library of the Future, Third Edition

Contains the full text of 1750 literary works from 205 authors, including works by William Shakespeare, poetry by William Butler Yeats, fairy tales by Hans Christian Andersen, philosophy by Immanuel Kant, and novels by Joseph Conrad. Features an extensive, multi-feature search system for sorting through the text to quickly find a specific reference. Includes a helpful, two-sentence introduction to aid in navigation.

WIN. Available for Windows platforms.

CD-ROM: CD90177. $99.98.

Life in the Desert

Includes a wide array of photographs and video of desert regions and desert wildlife, together with extensive maps of the world's deserts and animations explaining how deserts and their features are formed and maintained. An encyclopedia section details many of the plant and animal species of desert regions and includes video sequences of desert animals and desert terrain. Also covers the desert people of the American southwest and other desert regions.

MAC. Req: 13" monitor or larger; color (256 minimum), 4MB RAM, hard drive, CD-ROM hard drive.

WIN. Req: 13" monitor or larger; 386 (or better) processor; 4MB RAM (8 MB recommended); Sound blaster compatible sound card; Super VGA graphics card (minimum 640 x 480 x 256 color resolution); Windows 3.1 and Windows 95 compatible. .

CD-ROM: CD90252. $29.95.

Like the Dickens

Includes full text of Dickens's 17 novels and 56 short stories, John Forster's *The Life of Charles Dickens* (numerous editions), and Dickens's obituary in the *London Times*.

WIN. Req: Not available at present.

CD-ROM: CD90115. $39.95.

Love, Medicine & Miracles

Bernie Siegel has touched millions of people with his message for living. Now, his informative workshop seminar can be customized to suit the individual needs of those who are ill, who are caring for someone who is sick, or who simply need inspiration to live a healthy and happy life.

MAC. Req: 7.0 operating system or later.

WIN. Req: Windows 3.1, 486, 8MB.

CD-ROM: CD90187. $49.95.

Ludwig van Beethoven: Symphony No. 9

This CD-ROM contains the energy and creativity of Ludwig van Beethoven and invites you to listen to the music of Beethoven's *Symphony No. 9* as scholar and pianist Robert Winter's commentary on each theme scrolls by. There is also a detailed glossary of musical terms and theory, and a guide to the life and times of Beethoven.

MAC. Req: Macintosh Plus or better (any Mac produced since 1986) running system 6.0.7 or later; CD-ROM drive; 1.5MB of available RAM. If running system 6, must have at least 2MB RAM installed; if running System 7, must have at least 3MB. Requires speakers or headphones if CD-ROM drive is external.

CD-ROM: CD90019. $79.95.

Robert Winter

The Madness of Roland

Described by its creator as the world's first interactive multimedia novel, this CD-ROM retells the legend of Roland, a knight in the service of Charlemagne, from multiple perspectives. It is set in Paris in 778 and takes Roland through seven chapters of bloodshed, insanity and betrayal. Each chapter begins with a display of up to five tarot cards representing the characters contributing to the story. Users click for several pages of text accompanied by music or audio narration, poetry, history, or animated video clips.

MAC. Req: Macintosh 2.

WIN. Req: Windows 2.

CD-ROM: CD90173. $29.95.

Making Music

The first true composing space for children. Allows kids to enter notes by painting on the screen, and modify volume, tempo and instrumentation. Lets kids save their compositions, too! Alter melody and rhythm, transpose or change six simple tunes to learn about structure and repetition. Games involve playing from novice musician to maestro using their own compositions.

MAC. Req: 68030 processor (examples: Performa 575; Quadra; Centris) or better; 7.0 operating system or later; 8 MB RAM; 640x480 color monitor or 13" display; Double-speed CD-ROM drive.

WIN. Req: 486SX-33 or higher processor; 640x480, 256-color display (accelerator recommended); 8 MB RAM; MPC2-compatible CD-ROM drive; Sound card (16-bit) with speakers or headphones; Windows 3.1 or Windows 95.

CD-ROM: CD90126. $39.95.

Mammals of Africa

This interactive encyclopedia on the wildlife of Africa features award-winning photography with video and narration on the major mammal families. Each species is discussed in depth and illustrated in color, and features a distribution map, body plan, ecology, classification and life cycles.

MAC. Req: 13" monitor or larger; color (256 minimum), 4MB RAM, hard drive, CD-ROM hard drive.

WIN. Req: 13" monitor or larger; 386 (or better) processor; 4MB RAM (8 MB recommended); Sound blaster compatible sound card; Super VGA graphics card (minimum 640 x 480 x 256 color resolution); Windows 3.1 and Windows 95 compatible. .

CD-ROM: CD90249. $29.95.

Masterworks of Japanese Painting: The Etsuko and Joe Price Collection

This CD-ROM features over 1,100 full-color images from the Etsuki and Joe Price collection—outside of Japan, the largest private collection of scrolls and screens from the Edo period. What makes the Edo period remarkable is that during that time, Japan closed its ports to the outside world, allowing Japanese art to grow and flourish without the influence of outsiders. With an introductory movie and in-depth commentary on each image.

MAC. Req: LCII or above (040 CPU or above strongly recommended). 5MB RAM (8-10MB for 16- or 24-bit color). Color Monitor (640 x 480) and 8-bit color (16- or 24-bit color strongly recommended). Double-Speed CD-ROM Drive. System 7.0 or better. Mouse.

WIN. Req: 486/25 or above. 8MB RAM. VGA Monitor (640 x 480) and Video Card running at 256 colors. Double-Speed CD-ROM Drive. Windows 3.1. Windows Compatible Sound Card. Mouse.

CD-ROM: CD90103. $59.95.

Merchant of Venice

This interactive version of Shakespeare's play features pop-up definitions which explain meanings of unusual words. A theme page catalogs the play's principal themes and allows the user to easily locate poetic, dramatic and other literary devices. With digital sound.

WIN. Req: CD-ROM; 4MB RAM; VGA 256 colors; Win 3.1; Sound Card; Mouse.

CD-ROM: CD90258. $179.99.

The Metropolitan Museum of Art: Fun with Architecture

This delightful rubber stamp set from the Metropolitan Museum of Art has been transformed into a CD-ROM. Features over 30 shapes, 16 landscapes to use as backdrops; over a dozen templates, from simple houses to buildings by Frank Lloyd Wright and LeCorbusier; 18 textures including stone, wood, stucco and concrete; and an introduction to design by architect David Eisen.

MAC. Available for Macintosh platforms.

WIN. Available for Windows platforms.

CD-ROM: CD90195. $24.95.

A Midsummer Night's Dream

In this marvelous interactive treatment of Shakespeare's whimsical play, the full text is accompanied by tools that help understand its themes, language, characters and more. Digital stereo recording features professional voices and sound effects.

WIN. . Req: CD-ROM; 4MB RAM; VGA 256 colors; Win 3.1; Sound Card; Mouse.

CD-ROM: CD90259. $179.99.

Modern Art: A Visit to the Foundation of Marguerite & Aimé Maeght

Marguerite and Aimé Maeght had hoped to create an environment architecturally worthy of the greatest works by Joan Miro, Georges Braque, Marc Chagall and other renowned 20th century artists. Works by these and other artists are featured in this hybrid CD-ROM, which takes the user on a guided tour through a detailed presentation of the masterpieces of 20th century art.

MAC. Req: System 7.0 or higher; 7.01 system requirement.

WIN. Req: 4 MB RAM; System 386 or higher; Windows 3.1 or higher; Multimedia PC with CD-ROM drive.

CD-ROM: CD90097. $49.95.

Monty Python and the Quest for the Holy Grail

The famous British comedy troupe is back on a riotous quest CD-ROM which reworks the 1975 movie into a multimedia game that pokes fun at multimedia games. Players navigate through nine sequences based on the film, using logic and luck to collect "inventory" items, view scenes from the movie, and eventually win the Grail. Under the direction of Python Eric Idle, the game also features animation by Terry Gilliam that was cut from the movie.

MAC. Available for Macintosh platforms.

WIN. Available for Windows platforms.

CD-ROM: CD90167. $74.99.

Much Ado About Nothing

Shakespeare's timeless tale springs to life in this interactive CD-ROM. Contains a glossary and hypertext link, making research quick and easy. Commentary provides side-by-side synopsis of each line of text. Text is accompanied by a digital recording featuring a professional cast, authentic period music and sound effects in a radio theatre-style production.

WIN. Req: CD-ROM; 4MB RAM; VGA 256 colors; Win 3.1; Sound Card; Mouse.

CD-ROM: CD90260. $179.99.

The Muppets CD-ROM: Muppets Inside

The Muppets are lost inside your PC! Set Kermit, Miss Piggy, Animal, Dr. Bunsen Honeydew, Beaker, Statler and Waldorf free by locating and playing a series of games at different skill levels. Includes over an hour of new audio and video footage, five new songs, and dozens of classic clips from *The Muppet Show*.

WIN. Req: Windows '95 or higher.

CD-ROM: CD90133. $59.98.

Mythology

Four-part series uses colorful artwork to introduce students to mythology. Includes a glossary of important terms, an encyclopedia of related topics, a compendium of key myths, 40 interactive activities, anagrams, puzzles and educational games. Sections include: What Are Myths?, The Greek Myths: Character and Content, The Greek Myths: Sources and Styles, and The Roman Gods and Goddesses.

MAC. Available for Macintosh platforms.

WIN. Available for Windows platforms.

CD-ROM: CD90151. $69.99.

Myths and Legends Vols. 1 & 2

Discover your greatest hopes and deepest fears between fantasy and reality on Volume 1, *Myths and Mythical Creatures*. You'll see what no one has seen for 2,000 years on Volume 2, *Legendary Lands/Lost Cities*.

WIN. Available for Windows platforms.

CD-ROM: CD90227. $49.99.

National Museum of American Art

This authoritative, highly informative and incredibly comprehensive program compiled by the Smithsonian Institution's National Museum of American Art presents a rich portrait of the art and artists who have captured our cultural heritage in a variety of mediums. An intuititive menu and a convenient navigator allow you to wander through this fantastic collection of more than 750 objects spanning 250 years—colonial through 20th century—and covering a diverse range of genres.

DOS. Available for DOS platforms.

MAC. Available for Macintosh platforms.

WIN. Available for Windows platforms.

CD-ROM: CD90231. $39.99.

Natural History of Yellowstone

This ecology-centered CD-ROM looks at the formation, history and geology of Yellowstone Park, with its awe-inspiring mountains, forests, plains and thermal features. Catalogs the wildlife of the region, with photography and videos, and features a number of interactive maps and animations to clarify Yellowstone's story,

MAC. Req: 13" monitor or larger; color (256 minimum), 4MB RAM, hard drive, CD-ROM hard drive.

WIN. Req: 13" monitor or larger; 386 (or better) processor; 4MB RAM (8 MB recommended); Sound blaster compatible sound card; Super VGA graphics card (minimum 640 x 480 x 256 color resolution); Windows 3.1 and Windows 95 compatible. .

CD-ROM: CD90254. $29.95.

The New Family Bible

This respectful and artistic presentation of the New Revised Standard Version of the Bible includes all 39 books of the Old Testament, from Genesis to Malachi, divided into chapter and verse, presented in eight sections: The Beginning, The Patriarchs, In Egypt, The Exodus, The Promised Land, The Monarchy, The Monarchy Divided, and Exile and Restoration. Also presents a selection of 40 Bible stories, such as Adam and Eve and the trial of Job. Many include slide shows with narrations and a series of still pictures, each running several minutes. Includes a helpful pronunciation guide to Hebrew and English pronunciations of Old Testament names.

MAC. Available for Macintosh platforms.

WIN. Available for Windows platforms.

CD-ROM: CD90175. $29.99.

New Voices New Visions

This compilation CD-ROM contains selections from the 24 winners of a computer art contest. The contest generated over 500 entries from independent artists in 18 different countries. *New Voices New Visions* contains the three grand prize winners, one artist who received an honorable mention, and 21 noteworthy entries.

MAC. Req: 68030 processor (examples: Performa 575; Quadra; Centris) or better; 7.0 operating system or later; 8 MB RAM; 640x480 color monitor or 13" display; Double-speed CD-ROM drive.

CD-ROM: CD90081. $29.95.

A Night to Remember

The definitive full-length British film about the 1912 sinking of the Titanic, *A Night to Remember*, is included, along with scene-by-scene commentary by Titanic experts Don Lynch and Ken Marschall, a blueprint of the shop detailing areas and rooms appearing in the film, a passenger log featuring characters based on real-life passengers and crew, a timeline tracking the course of the ship from Southampton to the iceberg, and Smart Search, a searchable text track for the entire film. Also includes a bonus disc featuring Ray Johnson's 60-minute 1993 documentary, *The Making of "A Night to Remember"*, featuring producer William MacQuitty's rare archival footage of the sets, the miniature boats, and the tank in which much of the movie was shot, and the original theatrical trailer.

MAC. Available for Macintosh platforms.

WIN. Available for Windows platforms.

CD-ROM: CD90164. $29.95.

Nixon, The CD-ROM

Learn more about President Richard M. Nixon and the Watergate era by viewing documents, biographies, videoclips and interviews. Narrated by Alexander Butterfield, deputy assistant to Nixon, this title features insights and commentary from several sources who knew Nixon, biographies of 250 people in Nixon's life, complete Watergate trial transcripts, including the "Nixon tapes," 10,000 pages of previously unpublished documents, more than 20 minutes of Nixon videoclip footage, an interactive screenplay of Oliver Stone's *Nixon*, and interviews with the filmmaker on the liberties he took to create his controversial film.

MAC. Available for Macintosh platforms.

WIN. Available for Windows platforms.

CD-ROM: CD90171. $39.99.

Ocean Life/Great Barrier Reef

Extensive depiction of over 200 species of fish is accompanied by text, range maps, photographs and movies. Contains nearly three hours of narrated, underwater video and maps of Australia's Great Barrier Reef.

WIN. Req: 68040; 2X speed CD-ROM; 8MB RAM; VGA 256 colors; DOS 5.1+; Win 3.1: Sys 7.0 +Sound Card.

CD-ROM: CD90236. $49.99.

Ocean Life/Hawaiian Islands

Comprehensive text, range maps, photographs and full-color videos for over 90 species. Browse by photo, name or keyword. Includes interactive maps and a morphology section describing anatomical variations. With an easy-to-use visual index of marine life families.

WIN. Req: 68040; 2X speed CD-ROM; 8MB RAM; VGA 256 colors; DOS 5.1+; Win 3.1: Sys 7.0 +Sound Card.

CD-ROM: CD90237. $49.99.

Ocean Life/Micronesia

Detailed maps of Micronesia, original underwater video footage and extensive still photography of more than 150 species. Covers fish behaviors, mating, predidation, camouflage, brooding and nesting.

WIN. Req: 68040; 2X speed CD-ROM; 8MB RAM; VGA 256 colors; DOS 5.1+; Win 3.1: Sys 7.0 +Sound Card.

CD-ROM: CD90238. $49.99.

Ocean Life/Western Pacific 2.0

Covers more than 30 families and 100 species of the world's most elusive creatures, in their natural environment in the tropical reefs of the Vanuatu, Fiji and Tonga. More than an hour of underwater video and photography.

WIN. Req: 68040; 2X speed CD-ROM; 8MB RAM; VGA 256 colors; DOS 5.1+; Win 3.1: Sys 7.0 +Sound Card.

CD-ROM: CD90239. $49.99.

Of Mice and Men

Incorporates the text of the novel, 80 photos, six musical numbers from the 1958 Broadway musical, selected Steinbeck correspondence and criticism. The complete text of Jackson J. Benson's *The True Adventures of John Steinbeck, Writer: A Biography* is also included.

MAC. Available for Macintosh platforms.

WIN. Available for Windows platforms.

CD-ROM: CD90114. $49.95.

Operation: Weather Disaster

Dr. Rainwater, once a mild-mannered meteorologist, has turned into the Evil Weatherman and is causing global weather disasters. With the help of Team Extreme, kids ages 10 and up learn what it takes to keep nature in balance. From the Discovery Channel.

MAC. Req: Not available at present.

WIN. Req: 486SX or higher processor; 256-color display; 8MB RAM; double-speed CD-ROM; Windows compatible sound card; Windows 3.1 or Windows 95.

CD-ROM: CD90132. $39.95.

Our Secret Century: Archival Films from the Darker Side of the American Dream, Volumes 1 & 2

This hybrid CD-ROM includes the first two volumes in the 12-part *Our Secret Century: Archival Films from the Darker Side of the American Dream* series. *Volume 1: The Rainbow Is Yours* contains six color films which look at how consumerism and marketing in the 1950s were able to create an American obsession with form and design. *Volume 2: Capitalist Realism* contains three B&W films from the 1930s which borrow heavily from Soviet-style imagery of heroism. These portrayals of workers in corporate films serve to show the human aspects of factory life and mass production. This captivating CD-ROM also includes lectures, supplementary materials, commentary from filmmaker and media archaeologist Rick Prelinger and more.

MAC. Req: A "quadra" or better; Any Macintosh with a CD-ROM drive; At least 8 MB of RAM (5,500K free).

WIN. Req: 486SX-33 or higher processor; 640x480, 256-color display (accelerator recommended); 8 MB RAM; MPC2 compatible CD-ROM drive and sound card with speakers or headphones; Microsoft Windows 3.1; MS-DOS 5.0 or later.

CD-ROM: CD90065. $34.95.

Rick Prelinger, USA, 1995

Our Secret Century: Archival Films from the Darker Side of the American dream, Volumes 3 & 4

Film scholar and media archaeologist Rick Prelinger continues his exploration of American history and society with the third and fourth installments of his *Our Secret Century: Archival Films from the Darker Side of the American Dream* series. This hybrid CD-ROM begins with *Volume 3: The Behavior Offensive*, an in-depth look at the American post-war mentality and the attempt to instill "family values" into American hearts and homes. The eight films featured document the national crusade of the 1950s for social guidance and social control. In *Volume 4: Menace and Jeopardy*, seven "safety" films warn of the dangers haste and carelessness can cause as they prey on unconscious fears about everyday "risks" Americans encounter at home and on the job.

MAC. Req: A "quadra" or better; Any Macintosh with a CD-ROM drive; At least 8 MB of RAM (5,500K free).

WIN. Req: 486SX-33 or higher processor; 640x480, 256-color display (accelerator recommended); 8 MB RAM; MPC2 compatible CD-ROM drive and sound card with speakers or headphones; Microsoft Windows 3.1; MS-DOS 5.0 or later.

CD-ROM: CD90066. $34.95.

Rick Prelinger, USA, 1995

Our Solar System

Travel on a fully-narrated tour of our solar system—its comets, its asteroids, its planets and their moons—from the torrid world of Venus to the freezing atmosphere of Neptune. Made in cooperation with the Jet Propulsion Laboratory (JPL), the United States Geological Survey and NASA, this hybrid CD-ROM features images never before seen by the general public and is noted for the exceptional quality of its sound and photographs. This "layman's guide to the solar system" includes a space glossary, hundreds of photographs and fascinating facts, music, special effects, and more.

MAC. Req: Any Macintosh computer with 256+ color, Color monitor; XA compatible CD-ROM drive; Macintosh system 6.0.7 or higher with a CD-ROM driver, foreign file access extension.

WIN. Req: IBM PC AT or compatible 80386 or 80486; VGA display or better (minimum 256+ color for acceptable display); DOS 3.3 or higher; Microsoft Windows System 3.0 or higher. OTHER. Req: Kodak Photo CD, Phillips & Magnavox CD-1, Panasonic 3DO or other Photo CD compatible systems; or TV-Based Players: Sega Saturn, Panasonic 3DO, Phillips CD-i, Kodak Photo CD players and all Photo CD compatible players.

CD-ROM: CD90064. $29.95.

USA, 1995

Painters Painting

Based on the critically acclaimed film by Emile de Antonio, this is a vibrant collective portrait of the legendary figures who powered the tumultuous post-war art scene. Examples of each artist's work, full transcripts of interviews and the 100-minute film are included. Rauschenberg, Rivers, Warhol, Johns, Motherwell, Stella and many more are featured.

MAC. Req: 68030 processor (examples: Performa 575; Quadra; Centris) or better; 7.0 operating system or later; 8 MB RAM; 640x480 color monitor or 13" display; Double-speed CD-ROM drive.

WIN. Req: 486SX-33 or higher processor; 640x480, 256-color display (accelerator recommended); 8 MB RAM; MPC2-compatible CD-ROM drive; Sound card (16-bit) with speakers or headphones; Windows 3.1 or Windows 95.

CD-ROM: CD90118. $39.95.

The Parts of Speech

Eight-part series defines and explains the rules of usage for all the major parts of speech. In addition to an original narrative and colorful artwork, the program contains interactive features, eight sections of exercises and questions to test students' knowledge of parts of speech, and dozens of ancillary activities, games, puzzles and projects.

MAC. Available for Macintosh platforms.

WIN. Available for Windows platforms.

CD-ROM: CD90152. $69.99.

A Passion for Art: Renoir, Cézanne, Matisse and Dr. Barnes

Explore Dr. Barnes' rarely seen collection of post-impressionist paintings. Paintings by Renoir, Cézanne, Matisse and many other artists are shown in stunning detail, revealing the creativity and passion that went into creating these pieces. These controversial works have been the talk of the art world since the beginning of the 20th century and are now available to be explored and discovered.

MAC. Req: System 7.0 or higher; 7.01 system requirement.

WIN. Req: 4 MB RAM; System 386 or higher; Windows 3.1 or higher; Multimedia PC with CD-ROM drive.

CD-ROM: CD90101. $59.98.

Pathways Through Jerusalem

This hybrid CD-ROM takes the user on a tour of Jerusalem, from the Old City to the more modern East Jerusalem and West Jerusalem. Visit the Western Wall, the Via Delarosa, the Old City's Jewish, Muslim, Christian and Armenian Quarters, the Dome of the Rock and more. View a timeline of 3,000 years of Jerusalem's history or move between eras and watch the face of the city change. Featuring brilliantly crafted video, meticulously re-created historical sites, carefully preserved ruins from the Crusades and more.

MAC. Available for Macintosh platforms.

WIN. Available for Windows platforms.

CD-ROM: CD90099. $49.98.

Paul Cezanne: Portrait of My World

Wander around the studio of one of the greatest originators of modern art and observe the scenes that inspired him, the galleries that exhibited his favorite works and the bistros where he dined, as stirring narration reveals the artist's thoughts and reflections. Friends and acquaintances share their memories of the great painter and a detailed biography presents the progression of Cezanne's paintings alongside events in his personal life.

MAC. Available for Macintosh platforms.

WIN. Available for Windows platforms.

CD-ROM: CD90139. $69.99.

Pecos Bill

The legend of the fearless buckaroo raised by coyotes is told by Robin Williams with original music by Ry Cooder, evoking a Texas of crusty cowboys and campfire tales. This interactive experience teaches children reading comprehension skills. Choose one of two age levels for games, display the story text on-screen so kids see the words as they hear them, select activities related to the story and much more. Includes a detailed parents' guide to help enrich childrens' learning experiences.

MAC. Req: Macintosh LCII or higher (68030/16MHz or better recommended); 640 x 480 resolution (13") with 256 color display or greater; CD-ROM drive (double-speed recommended); 5MB of RAM (8MB recommended); System 7.0.1 or later.

WIN. Req: 386DX/33MHz CPU (486 recommended); 8MB of RAM total; Windows 3.1 or higher; 640 x 480 display with SVGA graphics; 256 colors; Windows-compatible sound card; double-speed CD-ROM drive; mouse.

CD-ROM: CD90204. $19.95.

Photopaedia Vol. 1: 100 Japanese Photographers, 1993

Edited by critic Shuhei Takahashi, this hybrid CD-ROM features over 900 photographs by 100 of the best modern Japanese photographers. Ranging from fashion and advertising to documentary and art, these images represent a wide variety of artistic styles and approaches. Includes a detailed analysis of the work of each photographer, business addresses for all photographers featured in the program, and more.

MAC. Available for Macintosh platforms.

WIN. Available for Windows platforms.

CD-ROM: CD90086. $59.95.

Shuhei Takahashi, Japan, 1993

Photopaedia Vol. 2: Faces of Summer by Koichi Inakoshi
This hybrid CD-ROM features over 400 photographs, many never before published, by renowned artist Koichi Inakoshi. Taken during his travels throughout the world, this retrospective collection is full of evocative images of the experiences of his journeys. Also included are accompanying literature, a recent biography of Inakoshi, a critical study of his work, and an autobiographical essay. Edited by noted critic Shuhei Takahashi.

MAC. Available for Macintosh platforms.

WIN. Available for Windows platforms.

CD-ROM: CD90087. $59.95.

Photopaedia Vol. 3: Still Lifes by Diane Wesson

British photographer Diane Wesson's still lifes of such familiar objects as stones, feathers, flowers and fruits are highlighted in this hybrid CD-ROM. Over 100 of her images, full of textured transparency, masterfully layered light and delicate composition, are included. This project, edited by Shuhei Takahashi, also includes his essays *Women Photographers* and *History of Photography*.

MAC. Available for Macintosh platforms.

WIN. Available for Windows platforms.

CD-ROM: CD90088. $59.95.

Planetary Taxi (Visual Almanac Series, Vol. 2)

Thousands of facts about our solar system come to life in this challenging game of discovery. Find out where a golf ball will fly the farthest, bounce the highest, or freeze the fastest. See the spectacular QuickTime movies of recent NASA missions.

MAC. Req: Any Macintosh with color display; System 7; CD-ROM drive; no more than 2.2MB available RAM (4MB installed).

WIN. Req: 486SX-33 or higher processor; 640x480, 256-color display (accelerator recommended); 8MB RAM; MPC2-compatible CD-ROM drive; sound card (16-bit) with speakers or headphones; Windows 3.1 or Windows 95.

CD-ROM: CD90009. $39.95.

M. Nanny & R. Mohl, USA

Poetry in Motion

Eighteen modern poets, including Helen Adam, Miguel Algarin, Amiri Baraka, Ted Berrigan, Charles Bukowski, William S. Burroughs, John Cage, Jim Carroll, Jayne Cortez, Christopher Dewdney, Kenward Elmslie, Allen Ginsberg, John Giorno, Ed Sanders, Ntozake Shange, Gary Snyder, Tom Waits and Anne Waldman, perform their work and talk about what inspires them. The video is linked with the complete text of each poem so you can read along.

MAC. Req: Any Macintosh with color display; System 7; CD-ROM drive; no more than 2.2MB available RAM (4MB installed).

WIN. Req: 25-MHz 486SX or higher processor; MS-DOS 5 or later; 640x480, 256-color display; 4MB RAM (8MB recommended).

CD-ROM: CD90015. $29.95.

Ron Mann, USA

Poetry in Motion II

Twelve noted authors performs their works and talk about what inspires them. Taking up where *Poetry in Motion* left off, this hybrid CD-ROM includes work by poets Jim Carroll (author of *The Basketball Diaries*), Spalding Gray (author of *Swimming to Cambodia*), Diane di Prima (author of *Memoirs of a Beatnik*), Allen Ginsberg (author of *Howl*), Amiri Baraka, Charles Bukowski, Tom Waits, Cookie Mueller, Anne Waldman, Peter Orlovsky and more. "The readings bring the works alive, revealing intonations a solitary reader might not otherwise notice" *(PC Magazine)*.

MAC. Req: 68030 processor (examples: Performa 575; Quadra; Centris) or better; 7.0 operating system or later; 8 MB RAM; 640x480 color monitor or 13" display; Double-speed CD-ROM drive.

WIN. Req: 486SX-33 or higher processor; 640x480, 256-color display (accelerator recommended); 8 MB RAM; MPC2-compatible CD-ROM drive; Sound card (16-bit) with speakers or headphones; Windows 3.1 or Windows 95.

CD-ROM: CD90077. $29.98.

Ron Mann, USA

Portraits of American Presidents

This informative CD-ROM covers more than 200 years of American Presidents, from George Washington to Bill Clinton, and everyone in between. *Portraits of American Presidents* is broken down into three smaller sections: *The Presidents of a New Nation, 1789-1829, The Presidents of a National Struggle, 1829-1901* and *The Presidents of a World Power, 1901-Present*. Includes 30 minutes of NBC News footage, more than 300 rare archival photographs and illustrations, commentary by noted scholars, interactive timelines and trivia game challenges to help make learning fun.

WIN. Req: CD-ROM drive, double speed (recommended), 4 Mb RAM, 3 Mb free hard disk space, EGA or SVGA sound device compatible with Microsoft Windows (recommended), mouse compatible with Microsoft Windows.

CD-ROM: CD90074. $49.95.

Puppet Motel

It's never-ending performance art with Laurie Anderson, the artist known for constantly pushing the boundaries of music, technology and expression. *Puppet Motel* offers the full range of Laurie Anderson's imagination through videos, music, text and excerpts from her recent *Stories from the Nerve Bible* piece. This CD-ROM is the first one to tie directly into World Wide Web and can be used to download new Laurie Anderson videos. Set design by Hsin-Chien Huang.

MAC. Req: 68030 processor (examples: Performa 575; Quadra; Centris) or better; 7.0 operating system or later; 8MB RAM; 640x480 color monitor or 13" display; double-speed CD-ROM drive.

CD-ROM: CD90076. $39.95.

L Anderson & H Huang, USA

Quick Time the CD

A CD-ROM series consisting of the winners of three annual International Quick Time Film Festivals. Contains excerpts from the categories of humor, narrative, animation, education, interactive, music video, commercial, micromovies, experimental and documentaries.

WIN. Req: 68040; 2X speed CD-ROM; 8MB RAM; VGA 256 colors; DOS 5.1+; Win 3.1: Sys 7.0 +Sound Card.

CD-ROM: CD90241. $49.99.

The Rainforest

A complete educational guide to the rainforests of the world featuring 60 minutes of narrated video and animations, over 400 color photographs and paintings, and hundreds of text pages. Includes sections on rainforest ecology, peoples and debates, interviews with rainforest experts, a full index to keywords, and an interactive village section showing everyday objects that come from the rainforest.

MAC. Req: 13" monitor or larger; color (256 minimum), 4MB RAM, hard drive, CD-ROM hard drive.

WIN. Req: 13" monitor or larger; 386 (or better) processor; 4MB RAM (8 MB recommended); Sound blaster compatible sound card; Super VGA graphics card (minimum 640 x 480 x 256 color resolution); Windows 3.1 and Windows 95 compatible..

CD-ROM: CD90250. $29.95.

Record of Lodoss War, Volume 1

This full-length CD-ROM contains episodes 1-3 of the story of Lodoss, the accursed island. The battle for the future of Lodoss begins as six people are drawn together to save the island from an evil far worse than any of the fires and wars that have ravaged it in the past thousand years. Anime, Japanese with English subtitles.

DOS. Req: Windows 3.1 and MS DOS 5.0 or higher; 80386SX MHz or higher CPU and CD ROM drive; 4 Mb RAM; SVGA with at least 256 color display; Soundblaster compatible sound card; Quicktime 1.1 or better (included).

MAC. Req: System 7 or higher; 68020, 68030, 68040, or Power PC CPU and CD ROM drive; 4 Mb RAM; 256 color monitor (or better); Quicktime 1.5 or better (included).

WIN. Req: Windows 3.1 and MS DOS 5.0 or higher; 80386SX MHz or higher CPU and CD ROM drive; 4 Mb RAM; SVGA with at least 256 color display; Soundblaster compatible sound card; Quicktime 1.1 or better (included).

CD-ROM: CD90062. $24.95.

80 mins.

Religions of the World

This fascinating review of the forms of worship, scriptures, artifacts, festivals, and sacred places for the world's major religions features comparative views, self-assessment tools and a useful index to explore Judaism, Buddhism, Islam, Christianity, Hinduism, Confucianism, Shinto and Sikhism.
WIN. Req: Windows 3.1, 386, 4MB.
CD-ROM: CD90186. $49.95.

Renaissance Masters Vol. 1

An interactive experience with the art of the late Gothic through the early Italian Renaissance, including thousands of paintings, sculpture, architecture and mosaics. With biographies on Botticelli, Piero della Francesca, Giotto and their contemporaries.
WIN. Req: 386+; 25MHz+; 4MB RAM+; SVGA 256 colors; Win 3.1+; Sound Card; Mouse.
CD-ROM: CD90232. $49.98.

Renaissance Masters Vol. 2

Learn about the Italian Renaissance, Mannerist and Baroque periods and study the works of Michelangelo, Raphael, Titian and their contemporaries with hundreds of paintings, mosaics, sculpture and architecture. Includes artists' biographies. Search functions by artist, title, medium, date, object and school.
WIN. Req: 386+; 25MHz+; 4MB RAM+; SVGA 256 colors; Win 3.1+; Sound Card; Mouse..
CD-ROM: CD90233. $49.98.

The Residents: Freak Show

The Residents, based in San Francisco, have created innovative music, videos and performance art since 1972. Their famous quirk is that no one ever sees their faces or learns their true identities, and this is no exception. Animator Jim Ludtke breathes life into The Residents through Tex the Barker, Herman the Human Mole, Harry the Head, Wanda the Worm Woman, Jelly Jack and Benny the Bump, and you peek into their beyond-the-freak-show lives and discover fetishes, fantasies, rituals and tragic secrets.
MAC. Req: Any color-capable Macintosh (25-MHz 68030 processor or better recommended); System 7; not more than 6.2MB of available RAM (8MB installed); 13" color monitor; CD-ROM drive.
WIN. Req: 486SX-33 or higher processor; 640x480, 256-color display (accelerator recommended); 8MB RAM; MPC2-compatible CD-ROM drive; sound card (16-bit) with speakers or headphones; Windows 3.1 or Windows 95.
CD-ROM: CD90032. $39.95.
Jim Ludtke, USA

Richard Strauss: Three Tone Poems

A sweeping, lavish look at Richard Strauss' tribute to Romantic myths and heroes from Russell Steinberg, an author and composer who teaches music at UCLA.
MAC. Req: Macintosh Plus or better (any Mac produced since 1986) running system 6.0.7 or later; CD-ROM drive; 1.5 Mb of available RAM. If running system 6, must have at least 2 Mb RAM installed; if running System 7, must have at least 3 Mb. Requires speakers or headphones if CD-ROM drive is external.
CD-ROM: CD90026. $59.95.
Russell Steinberg, USA

Road to Ancient Egypt

Explore ancient Egypt with hundreds of interactive elements, original narrative and visuals, two matching exercises, a comprehensive glossary of important terms, an encyclopedia of related subject areas, key maps, historical timelines, and dozens of ancillary materials.
MAC. Available for Macintosh platforms.
WIN. Available for Windows platforms.
CD-ROM: CD90155. $30.00.

Road to Ancient Greece

Explore ancient Greece with hundreds of interactive elements, original narrative and visuals, two matching exercises, a comprehensive glossary of important terms, an encyclopedia of related subject areas, key maps, historical timelines, and dozens of ancillary materials.
MAC. Available for Macintosh platforms.
WIN. Available for Windows platforms.
CD-ROM: CD90153. $30.00.

Road to Ancient Rome

Explore ancient Rome with hundreds of interactive elements, original narrative and visuals, two matching exercises, a comprehensive glossary of important terms, an encyclopedia of related subject areas, key maps, historical timelines, and dozens of ancillary materials.
MAC. Available for Macintosh platforms.
WIN. Available for Windows platforms.
CD-ROM: CD90154. $30.00.

Robert Mapplethorpe: An Overview

An edited overview of the work of controversial photographer Robert Mapplethorpe. While many of the late artist's better known works have not been included, this CD-ROM gives a good introduction to Mapplethorpe's graceful and evocative floral photographs, his insightful celebrity portraits, and some of his less widely known early images. Suitable for all ages.
MAC. Req: 68030 Processor or better. 8 MB RAM. 24-bit Graphics Card strongly recommended. Double-Speed CD-ROM Drive. System 6.05 or higher with 32-bit QuickDraw (7.0 recommended).
WIN. Req: 8 MB RAM. Microsoft Windows 3.1. 256 Color S-VGA Minimum. 24-bit Graphics Card strongly recommended. Double-Speed CD-ROM drive.
CD-ROM: CD90104. $59.95.

Robert Winter's Crazy for Ragtime

Overflowing with more than 60 interactive rags, rare film footage, artwork of sheet music covers, and over 200 articles, this CD-ROM lets users engage in America's love affair with ragtime music and American life during the early 20th century. Includes a "Make Your Own Rag" section which allows users to create their own ragtime music.
MAC. Available for Macintosh platforms.
WIN. Available for Windows platforms.
CD-ROM: CD90148. $59.99.

Rodney's Wonder Window

Artist Rodney Alan Greenblat's 24 hands-on colorful stories include "Probe and Poke Pet Shop", "Data Shorts", "Chip and Peg's Adventures in Shapeland", and more. Children and adults alike will love these interactive episodes in this inventive playland of art and sound.
MAC. Req: Any Macintosh with color display; System 7; CD-ROM drive; 640x480 resolution (13") color monitor; speakers or headphones if CD-ROM drive is external; supports System 6.07.
WIN. Req: 25-MHz 486SX or higher processor; MS-DOS 5 or later; 640x480, 256-color display; 4MB RAM (8MB recommended).
CD-ROM: CD90007. $39.95.

Romeo and Juliet

Experience Shakespeare's tragedy with all the immediacy and vividness of a live performance with this interactive learning tool which features pop-up definitions, a theme page, character profiles and an index button which accesses the entire play's database.
WIN. Req: CD-ROM; 4MB RAM; VGA 256 colors; Win 3.1; Sound Card; Mouse.
CD-ROM: CD90261. $179.99.

Sacred and Secular: The Aerial Photography of Marilyn Bridges

Photographs of ceremonial places, shot from an altitude of 300 feet, of six featured sites—Egypt, Mexico, Peru, the United States, Greece and Britain. Includes background information about the culture and landscape of each site. Zoom feature allows examination of 100 richly textured B&W photographs in detail, and five guided tours link the photographs thematically. Audio commentary from Marilyn Bridges, the photographer.
MAC. Req: 68030 processor (examples: Performa 575; Quadra; Centris) or better; 7.0 operating system or later; 8 MB RAM; 640x480 color monitor or 13" display; Double-speed CD-ROM drive.
WIN. Req: 486SX-33 or higher processor; 640x480, 256-color display (accelerator recommended); 8 MB RAM; MPC2-compatible CD-ROM drive; Sound card (16-bit) with speakers or headphones; Windows 3.1 or Windows 95.
CD-ROM: CD90121. $39.95.

Salt of the Earth

Features the complete film *Salt of the Earth*, along with the short film *The Hollywood Ten*.... Filmed during the height of the McCarthy Era by blacklisted filmmakers, this film is a moving portrait of the 1951 zinc miners' strike in Silver City, New Mexico. This version includes the original screenplay and notes by Michael Wilson, production photographs, critical and historical essays, reviews of the film, and source materials in English, Spanish, French and German.
MAC. Req: Any color-capable Macintosh (25-MHz 68030 processor or better recommended); System 7; no more than 6.2MB of available RAM (8MB installed); 13" color monitor; CD-ROM drive.
CD-ROM: CD90011. $49.95.
M. Wilson, Herbert Biberman

San Francisco and Its Environs

Take a tour of beautiful San Francisco, a focus of major global tourism on this CD-ROM. Five different trips are included: the city, including downtown, the Embarcadero, Chinatown, Fisherman's Wharf, Palace of Fine Arts, The Marina and Golden Gate Park; Sausalito, Tiburon, Muir Woods and Stinson Beach; Sonoma and Napa, including a view of over 20 of the most beautiful wineries; the North Coast; and the south, including Filoli Gardens, Stanford University and Stanford Shopping Center, Monterey, 17 Mile Drive, Point Lobos, Carmel and Big Sur. Includes many historical details.
MAC. Req: Centris, Quadra, Power P.C., 8 MB.
WIN. Req: 486 and Pentium; 8MB RAM; Windows 3.1.1 or Windows 95.
CD-ROM: CD90194. $29.95.

The Shakespeare Collection

This three-CD-ROM collection explores the life and times of the world's greatest playwright, William Shakespeare. Contains discussions of the Bard's contributions to literature, a selection of Shakespearean sonnets, and authentic Elizabethan songs. Features a self-playing multimedia presentation, hundreds of images, a customized electronic glossary, and 100 interactive questions to enhance users' understanding of Shakespeare.
MAC. Available for Macintosh platforms.
WIN. Available for Windows platforms.
CD-ROM: CD90141. $29.99.

Shakespeare's Macbeth

This brilliant edition prepared by UCLA Professor A.R. Braunmuller provides instant annotation, the entire Royal Shakespeare Company performance, clips from Roman Polanski and Orson Welles' film versions or Kurosawa's *Throne of Blood*. The new edition of the play contains 1,500 annotations and a 24,000 word commentary with the RSC in Trevor Nunn's production, with Ian McKellan and Judi Dench as the Macbeths. Includes a gallery of QuickTime clips from other performances of *Macbeth* and concordance and textual analysis.
MAC. Req: 68030 processor (examples: Performa 575; Quadra; Centris) or better; 7.0 operating system or later; 8MB RAM; 640x480 color monitor or 13" display; double-speed CD-ROM drive.
WIN. Req: 486SX-33 or higher processor; 640x480, 256-color display (accelerator recommended); 8MB RAM; MPC2-compatible CD-ROM drive; sound card (16-bit) with speakers or headphones; Windows 3.1 or Windows 95.
CD-ROM: CD90003. $49.95.

Shining Flower

Available outside of Japan for the first time, *Shining Flower* combines mesmerizing music, rich animations, images from oil paintings and more. This "interactive haiku" aids your mind as it wanders through a metaphorical journey to the Flower, the source of all power and true enlightenment.
MAC. Req: Any Macintosh with color display; System 7; CD-ROM drive; no more than 3.2 Mb available RAM (5 Mb installed).
CD-ROM: CD90029. $39.95.
Japan

A Silly Noisy House

Peggy Weil's children's adventure of secret passageways, a teddy bear's birthday party, magic wands and a piano-playing spider are only a few of the many surprises. Children move from room to room clicking on hundreds of objects to uncover animation, tongue twisters, nursery rhymes, songs and sound effects. For ages three and older; no reading required.
MAC. Req: Any Macintosh with color display; System 7; CD-ROM drive; no more than 2.2MB available RAM (4MB installed).
WIN. Req: 25-MHz 486SX or higher processor; MS-DOS 5 or later; 640x480, 16-color display (256-color recommended); 4MB RAM (8MB recommended).
CD-ROM: CD90005. $59.95.
Peggy Weil

The Simpsons Cartoon Studio

Cowabunga, man! Create your own episodes of *The Simpsons* with 17 animated characters and voices from the show, more than 35 backgrounds, 250 moving and stationary props, 20 special effects, colorful fades, textures and patterns, and music.
MAC. Available for Macintosh platforms.
WIN. Available for Windows platforms.
CD-ROM: CD90134. $59.95.

SkyTrip America

Irene Bedard *(Pocahontas)* narrates this interactive look at the United States from the air. Kids control their choice of either a space-age hoverjet, a Wright Brothers-style "sputter-clunker" or a hot air balloon on an adventure through American history and geography. History comes alive when recounted by such pioneers as Christopher Columbus, Mark Twain, Harriet Tubman and Neil Armstrong, and the 3-D graphics and informative video clips give kids a memorable and informative tour of such sites as the Statue of Liberty, Mount Rushmore, the Grand Canyon and the Alamo. Other features include "The Pony Express game," a 3-D Old West Ghost Town, home of "the Mining Maze Game" and "Hangman Trivia," and cultural perspectives from celebrities such as pro basketball player Chris Weber, tennis pro Michael Chang and magician Penn Jilette of the infamous combo Penn & Teller. Suitable for children ages 9 & up.

MAC. Req: System hardware: Performa, Centris, Quadra or PowerPC. System software: System 7.0. Memory: 8MB RAM. Monitor: 256 colors. CD-ROM drive: Double speed (2x). Sound card: N/A. Input device: mouse.

WIN. Req: System hardware: 486 33Mhz or faster, Hard Drive. System software: Microsoft Windows 3.1 or Windows 95, MS/PC DOS 3.1. Memory: 8 MB of RAM. Monitor: VGA Monitor (256 colors). CD-ROM drive: Double speed (2x). Sound card: Windows compatible. Input device: mouse. .

CD-ROM: CD90107. $39.95.

USA, 1996

So I've Heard, Vol. 1: Bach and Before

Clips from two millennia of music are accompanied by commentary from American music critic Alan Rich, spanning from ancient Greek rituals to the passionate complexities of Bach and Handel. Also features search tools that will find all references to a particular composer, work, or glossary definition.

MAC. Req: Macintosh Plus or better (any Mac produced since 1986) running system 6.0.7 or later; CD-ROM drive; 1.5MB of available RAM. If running system 6, must have at least 2MB RAM installed; if running System 7, must have at least 3MB. Requires speakers or headphones if CD-ROM drive is external.

CD-ROM: CD90022. $24.95.

Alan Rich, USA

So I've Heard, Vol. 2: The Classical Ideal

American music critic Alan Rich comments on the Eighteenth Century's momentous changes in music, as exemplified by Mozart and Haydn. Special search tools will help you find all references to a particular composer, work, or glossary definition.

MAC. Req: Macintosh Plus or better (any Mac produced since 1986) running system 6.0.7 or later; CD-ROM drive; 1.5MB of available RAM. If running system 6, must have at least 2MB RAM installed; if running System 7, must have at least 3MB. Requires speakers or headphones if CD-ROM drive is external.

CD-ROM: CD90023. $24.95.

Alan Rich, USA

So I've Heard, Vol. 3: Beethoven & Beyond

Clips from the late classical era are accompanied by American music critic Alan Rich's commentaries on the profound impact of Beethoven's masterful compositions. In addition, special search tools help you find all reference to a particular composer, work, or glossary definition.

MAC. Req: Macintosh Plus or better (any Mac produced since 1986) running system 6.0.7 or later; CD-ROM drive; 1.5MB of available RAM. If running system 6, must have at least 2MB RAM installed; if running System 7, must have at least 3MB. Requires speakers or headphones if CD-ROM drive is external. Or, any Macintosh with color display; System 7; CD-ROM drive.

WIN. Req: 386SX or higher processor; MS-DOS 3.3 or later; 640x480 16-color display; 4MB RAM.

CD-ROM: CD90024. $24.95.

Alan Rich, USA

Sound Toys

Part toy, part musical instrument, make music by experimenting with different sounds and visuals. A fusion of wacky and whimsical instruments allows the beginner to compose, record, and save compositions of any length—up to six in one session. Weird and intensely gratifying.

MAC. Req: 68030 processor (examples Performa 575; Quadra; Centris or better); 7.0 operating system or later; 8 MB RAM; 640x480 color monitor or 13" display; Double-speed CD-ROM drive.

WIN. Req: 486SX-33 or higher processor; 640x480, 256-color display (accelerator recommended); 8 MB RAM; MPC2-compatible CD-ROM drive; Sound card (16-bit) with speakers or headphones; Windows 3.1 or Windows 95.

CD-ROM: CD90127. $39.95.

Space: A Visual History Manned Flight

The definitive multimedia almanac of American space missions. Contains over 1-1/2 hours of narrated movies, covering the best from the NASA film archives. With full text-search capability, timelines and movie indices.

WIN. Req: 68040; 2X speed CD-ROM; 8MB RAM; VGA 256 colors; DOS 5.1+; Win 3.1: Sys 7.0 +Sound Card.

CD-ROM: CD90240. $49.99.

Spanish Pronunciation Tutor

This hybrid CD-ROM aids students either learning Spanish for the first time, or simply fine tuning their Spanish speaking skills. *Spanish Pronunciation Tutor* allows students to listen to Spanish being spoken by a native speaker, record themselves speaking, and then compare the two. This educational CD-ROM features interactive help, hints to explain the finer points of Spanish pronunciation, detailed animations of the speech process, interactive exercise screens, pronunciation tests for tracking your progress, video and audio of native Spanish speakers and more. From The Learning Company.

MAC. Req: Runs on all Macintosh computers equipped with a CD-ROM drive, a 256-color monitor, 680.30/25MHz or better processor, and System 7. Requires 4 MB of memory. Requires a microphone or MacRecorder.

WIN. Req: System 386 or higher; Multimedia PC with CD-ROM drive; Requires 386/25MHz or better, 4 MB RAM, Windows 3.1 or higher, doublespeed CD-ROM drive, Windows compatible sound card, VGA or better, plus a microphone.

CD-ROM: CD90096. $59.98.

Spinal Tap

The CD-ROM companion to Rob Reiner's hilarious rockumentary spoof *This Is Spinal Tap*. This hybrid CD-ROM picks up where the film left off, and is the first CD-ROM to offer three concurrent, synched audio tracks. Includes two audio tracks discussing the making of the film, an hour of QuickTime video that features outtakes, video clips and the working script from the film, a Smart Search feature, 16-bit Dolby sound, commentary from Rob Reiner and more. "Get yourself a copy of this witty, ingenious and deliciously nasty package" *(Premiere Magazine)*. Two disc set.

MAC. Req: 68030 processor (examples: Performa 575; Quadra; Centris) or better; 7.0 operating system or later; 8 MB RAM; 640x480 color monitor or 13" display; Double-speed CD-ROM drive.

WIN. Req: 486SX-33 or higher processor; 640x480, 256-color display (accelerator recommended); 8 MB RAM; MPC2-compatible CD-ROM drive; Sound card (16-bit) with speakers or headphones; Windows 3.1 or Windows 95.

CD-ROM: CD90078. $29.95.

Rob Reiner, USA

Stars of the Louvre: 4,000 Years of Greatness

This in-depth tour of the famous Louvre Museum is a stunning and elegant guide to hundreds of the world's most beloved treasures. Over 200 works of art are celebrated here, including works by masters such as Da Vinci, Gericault, Botticelli, Raphael, Van Dyck, Rodin and Reubens. Learn the complete stories behind such masterpieces as the "Mona Lisa," "The Raft of the Medusa," the "Seated Scribe," the "Victory of Samothrace" and the "Venus de Milo." State-of-the-art CD-ROM technology allows you to highlight sections of paintings for closer study and to view sculptures from all 360 degrees. A 4,000 year timeline, spanning five of the richest periods of art history, shows the ties between art, politics, and culture. Also included are over three hours of music and two hours of narration, comprehensive biographies of the artists whose works are featured, and a complete index. From *The Great Artists Collection* series.

MAC. Req: Apple Macintosh LC or later model with at least 4 MB of RAM for the application. 640 x 480, 256 color graphics. System 7.0 or later. 32-Bit QuickDraw, Quicktime 2.0. Apple-compatible double-speed (300 Kps) CD-ROM drive.

WIN. Req: 386sx or better processor, 8 MB of RAM, Double-speed (300 Kps) CD-ROM drive, Microsoft Winodws compatible sound card, Super VGA graphics (640 x 480, 256 colors). Microsoft Windows version 3.1. MS-DOS version 5.0 or later, MS-DOS CD-ROM extensions. Stereo headphones or speakers. Minimum 1.5 MB free hard disk space.

OTHER. Req: ONLY available as a PC/MAC Hybrid.

CD-ROM: CD90106. $39.98.

USA/France, 1995

Stickybear Spelling

Children will enjoy delightful games and spelling activities which combine learning with the excitement and surprises of an interactive arcade. Offers hours of engaging, interactive amusement. Parents, teachers and children can customize the spelling games, choosing from thousands of words.

MAC. Req: System 7.0 or later; 6MB of RAM; 256 color display or better (or 256 grays); CD-ROM drive.

WIN. Req: Hard drive; SVGA display; Windows 3.11 or later; MSCDEX 2.2 or later; 386SX/16MHz or better; 4MB of RAM; MPC compatible CD-ROM drive; Windows-compatible sound card; will run under Windows '95.

CD-ROM: CD90207. $19.95.

Stradiwackius: The Counting Concert

Zany antics in this interactive storybook, chock full of numbers, music, games, color-in pictures, and surprises, will challenge and engage kids for hours. Children will learn about musical instruments and can even create their own tunes. Named a 1994 *American Bookseller* new media "Bookseller's Choice."

DOS. Req: 5.0 or higher.

MAC. Req: Double-speed CD-ROM drive; color monitor; system 7.0 or higher, LC III series or better; 8 MB RAM; 4 MB hard disk space available.

WIN. Req: Double-speed CD-ROM drive, VGA 256-color monitor; Windows 3.1; 486 or Pentium processor; 8- or 16-bit sound blaster or compatible sound card; 8 MB RAM; 4 MB hard disk space available.

CD-ROM: CD90192. $29.95.

Take Five

The original stress-reduction CD-ROM! This program guides you through four different ways to soothe aching muscles and features 45 video demonstrations of exercises to restore energy and flexibility. Also included is "Visual Vacation", a series of beautiful landscapes to relax your eyes, "Music of the Spheres", an audio program of the surf in the Amazon rain forest, and "The Mind's Eye", a guided imagery program.

MAC. Req: Any Macintosh with color display; System 7; CD-ROM drive; no more than 3.2MB available RAM (5MB installed).

WIN. Req: 486SX-25 or higher processor; 640x480, 256-color display; 4MB RAM (8MB recommended); MPC-compatible CD-ROM drive; sound card (8-bit) with speakers or headphones; Microsoft Windows 3.1 or Windows 95.

CD-ROM: CD90045. $29.95.

Dina Silver, USA

Taming of the Shrew

This interactive version of Shakespeare's biting drama includes pop-up word definitions and indexing, character profiles and a digital stereo recording featuring professional cast voicing and authentic period music.

WIN. Req: CD-ROM; 4MB RAM; VGA 256 colors; Win 3.1; Sound Card; Mouse.

CD-ROM: CD90262. $179.99.

Theatre of the Imagination

During the golden age of radio, Orson Welles was a formidable talent who dazzled listeners with the likes of *War of the Worlds* and *Heart of Darkness*. This hybrid CD-ROM features 15 of Orson Welles' programs from his 1930s and 1940s radio show *Radio Stories by Orson Welles and the Mercury Theatre*. Also featured are program notes and transcripts of every program; over six hours of audio recordings; supplementary articles, videos and clippings on Orson Welles, his programs, and the early history of video; and more.

MAC. Req: 68030 processor (examples: Performa 575; Quadra; Centris) or better; 7.0 operating system or later; 8 MB RAM; 640x480 color monitor or 13" display; Double-speed CD-ROM drive.

WIN. Req: 486SX-33 or higher processor; 640x480, 256-color display (accelerator recommended); 8 MB RAM; MPC2-compatible CD-ROM drive; Sound card (16-bit) with speakers or headphones; Windows 3.1 or Windows 95.

CD-ROM: CD90079. $29.98.

USA

Think & Talk French

Learn French with the "Berlitz Method," the self-teaching program used by the U.S. foreign service to teach useful words and phrases in record time. This interactive, hybrid CD-ROM allows a phrase to be heard as many times as desired by simply clicking the mouse. Also, record yourself speaking and compare your French to the native speaker's. Includes 50 language lessons, a vocabulary of over 1,000 words, an online, bilingual dictionary, and more. From Berlitz.

MAC. Req: System 7.0 or higher; 7.01 system requirement.

OTHER. Req: Multimedia PC.

CD-ROM: CD90090. $199.00.

Think & Talk German

Now the "Berlitz Method," the self-teaching program used by the U.S. foreign service to teach useful words and phrases in record time, is available on CD-ROM. This interactive, hybrid CD-ROM allows a phrase to be heard as many times as desired by simply clicking the mouse. Also, record yourself speaking German and compare your German to that of a native speaker. Includes 50 language lessons, a vocabulary of over 1,000 words, an online, bilingual dictionary, and more. From Berlitz.

MAC. Req: System 7.0 or higher; 7.01 system requirement.

OTHER. Req: Multimedia PC.

CD-ROM: CD90091. $199.00.

Think & Talk Italian

You can learn to speak Italian like a native with the "Berlitz Method," the self-teaching program used by the U.S. foreign service to teach useful words and phrases in record time. This interactive, hybrid CD-ROM allows a phrase to be heard as many times as desired by simply clicking the mouse. Also, record yourself speaking and compare your Italian to that of a native speaker. Includes 50 language lessons, a vocabulary of over 1,000 words, an online, bilingual dictionary, and more. From Berlitz.
MAC. Req: System 7.0 or higher; 7.01 system requirement.
OTHER. Req: Multimedia PC.
CD-ROM: CD90092. $199.00.

Think & Talk Spanish

Learning Spanish will feel effortless with the "Berlitz Method," the self-teaching program used by the U.S. foreign service to teach useful words and phrases in record time. This interactive, hybrid CD-ROM allows a phrase to be heard as many times as desired by simply clicking the mouse. Also, record yourself speaking and compare your Spanish to a native speaker's. Includes 50 language lessons, a vocabulary of over 1,000 words, an online, bilingual dictionary, and more. From Berlitz.
MAC. Req: System 7.0 or higher; 7.01 system requirement.
OTHER. Req: Multimedia PC.
CD-ROM: CD90093. $199.00.

Tommy—The Interactive Adventure

Explore Pete Townsend's legendary rock opera *Tommy* from a musical, cinematic and theatrical perspective, and experience this compelling story on an amazing journey of sight and sound. Includes over one hour of audio and visual interviews, star-studded live performances, clips from the movie, the '89 tour and the Broadway show, hundreds of full-color and black-and-white images, and original concert and movie posters.
MAC. Available for Macintosh platforms.
WIN. Req: Windows '95 or higher.
CD-ROM: CD90137. $49.99.

Toon Works

This multimedia-based drawing program teaches children how to design, color, manipulate and print cartoons. Covers the use of painting, drawing, distortion tools and color. Includes over 50 templates for making cartoons and 100 professionally designed characters to play with.
WIN. Req: 386 33 MHz; CD-ROM; 8MB RAM recom.; 256 colors ; Win. 3.1; Windows 95; Sound Card.
CD-ROM: CD90245. $49.99.

Toy Story Animated Storybook

Players can explore the world of *Toy Story*, Disney's full-length computer-animated cartoon, through an interactive storybook and arcade-style computer games.
MAC. Req: 68040 processor or better; 7.1 operating system or later; 640x480 256 color display monitor; double-speed CD-ROM drive.
WIN. Req: 486DX50 or higher processor; 256-color display; 8MB RAM; 8-bit Windows-compatible sound card; Windows 3.1 or Windows 95; 10MB free disk space.
CD-ROM: CD90161. $59.99.

Treasures of the Museum of Natural History

Scientific and anthropological background on 50 of the Museum's greatest treasures, from the Tasmanian wolf to a dinosaur mummy to Margaret Mead. Games, teacher's guide, a 3-D tour of the new Dinosaur Hall and the Hall of African Mammals. Over one hour of historic and descriptive film footage.
MAC. Req: 68030 processor (examples: Performa 575; Quadra; Centris) or better; 7.0 operating system or later; 8 MB RAM; 640x480 color monitor or 13" display; Double-speed CD-ROM drive.
WIN. Req: 486SX-33 or higher processor; 640x480, 256-color display (accelerator recommended); 8 MB RAM; MPC2-compatible CD-ROM drive; Sound card (16-bit) with speakers or headphones; Windows 3.1 or Windows 95.
CD-ROM: CD90124. $39.95.

Tripleplay Plus! (French)

Departing from the grammar and vocabulary memorization typical of most language instruction textbooks, the *Playing with Language* series seeks to teach French through a series of games that grows more challenging as the student gains skill. One thousand words and phrases are taught, allowing students to see and hear only French, with no English help unless they turn to the instruction manual. Students choose one of three modes: oral comprehension games which require the student to listen to audio cues and enter answers on the keyboard; reading games which also use the keyboard for answers; and speaking games which use a microphone for speech recognition. Students then choose one of six game subjects: Food, Numbers, Home & Office, Places & Transportation, People & Clothing, or Activities. They then finally choose one of 33 games divided into three difficulty levels. This is an especially appealing learning tool for children.
WIN. Available for Windows platforms.
CD-ROM: CD90178. $99.00.

Tripleplay Plus! (Spanish)

Departing from the grammar and vocabulary memorization typical of most language instruction textbooks, the *Playing with Language* series seeks to teach Spanish through a series of games that grows more challenging as the student gains skill. One thousand words and phrases are taught, allowing students to see and hear only Spanish, with no English help unless they turn to the instruction manual. Students choose one of three modes: oral comprehension games which require the student to listen to audio cues and enter answers on the keyboard; reading games which also use the keyboard for answers; and speaking games which use a microphone for speech recognition. Students then choose one of six game subjects: Food, Numbers, Home & Office, Places & Transportation, People & Clothing, or Activities. They then finally choose one of 33 games divided into three difficulty levels. This is an especially appealing learning tool for children.
WIN. Available for Windows platforms.
CD-ROM: CD90179. $99.00.

Trouble Is My Business: The Raymond Chandler Library

Offers the complete Raymond Chandler works, an interactive map of Chandler's L.A., video clips and stills from movies made of his works, some of Chandler's correspondence which relates to his fiction writing. Each book is preceded by a movie still, and searching navigation and printing are easy and evident.
WIN. Available for Windows platforms.
CD-ROM: CD90116. $79.98.

Truths & Fictions

This pictorial essay focuses on the work of photographer Pedro Meyer. It is "a journey from documentary to digital photography" as Meyer discusses the methods he uses to compose images and talks about the process through which his works reach completion. "...this disc is truly interactive in a way few multimedia CD-ROMs are: it makes you think" *(USA Today)*. This Macintosh CD-ROM features bilingual (English and Spanish) narration, over 2,000 photographs, a "Digital Studio" hosted by Pedro Meyer and more.
MAC. Req: 68030 processor (examples: Performa 575; Quadra; Centris) or better; 7.0 operating system or later; 8 MB RAM; 640x480 color monitor or 13" display; Double-speed CD-ROM drive.
CD-ROM: CD90082. $39.95.
Pedro Meyer

Twain's World

This powerful resource contains virtually the entire written work of Mark Twain (1835-1910), considered one of the greatest American authors. Users can instantly search on specific words and phrases in Twain's works, letters and life. Included is the full text of *The Adventures of Tom Sawyer, The Adventures of Huckleberry Finn, A Connecticut Yankee in King Arthur's Court* and *The Prince and the Pauper*; 120 short stories, including *The Notorious Jumping Frog of Calaveras County*; eight nonfiction books, including *Life on the Mississippi* and *The Innocents Abroad*; 49 essays; and 91 speeches, as well as numerous letters and a selection of biographical essays about Twain. Multimedia content includes a small gallery of photos; 11 video clips, including a one-minute 1909 newsreel of Twain; and 23 brief narrations of text excerpts.
WIN. Available for Windows platforms.
CD-ROM: CD90174. $39.98.

Ultimate 3-D Skeleton

Take an amazing 3-D tour through the body's fascinating skeletal system with this educational, enlightening and fun CD. Rotate and flip each bone, do research and take a quiz on terminology and function.
MAC. Available for Macintosh platforms.
WIN. Available for Windows platforms.
CD-ROM: CD90218. $39.95.

The Ultimate Human Body 2.0

Peel back the layers and go on your own "incredible journey" with this updated multimedia guide to the body and how it works. Groundbreaking 3-D technology simulates a body "fly-through" and reveals all the major physiological elements. You can even combine body systems to observe how they interact.
MAC. Available for Macintosh platforms.
WIN. Available for Windows platforms.
CD-ROM: CD90217. $49.95.

Understanding McLuhan: The Life and Work of Marshall McLuhan

Complete text of McLuhan's *Understanding Media* and *The Gutenberg Galaxy*, a "Probes" section to learn about McLuhan's main theories, an extensive biography, complete audio and text transcript of a McLuhan lecture and video footage of Neil Postman, Camille Paglia and others commenting on McLuhan's theories.
MAC. Req: 68030 processor (examples: Performa 575; Quadra; Centris) or better; 7.0 operating system or later; 8MB RAM; 640x480 color monitor or 13" display; Double-speed CD-ROM drive.
WIN. Req: 486SX-33 or higher processor; 640x480, 256-color display (accelerator recommended); 8 MB RAM; MPC2-compatible CD-ROM drive; Sound card (16-bit) with speakers or headphones; Windows 3.1 or Windows 95.
CD-ROM: CD90119. $39.95.

Urotsukidoji III: Return of the Overfiend 1

The world is ravaged by a savage monster called Nagumo. Now, 20 years later, a new world order has evolved and is headed by the Demon Beasts. Tokyo and its ruler, Caesar, are at constant war with the Demon Beasts. Elsewhere in the story, the Overfiend is born decades earlier than he is supposed to be because he becomes aware of an evil presence. Anime. In English.
MAC. Req: System 7 or higher. 68020, 68030, 68040, or Power PC CPU and CD ROM drive. 4 MB RAM, 256 color monitor (or better). Quicktime 1.5 or better (included).
WIN. Req: Windows 3.1 and MS DOS 5.0 or higher. 80386SZ MHz or higher CPU and CD ROM drive. 4MB RAM, SVGA with at least 256 color display. Soundblaster compatible sound card. Quicktime 1.1 or better (included).
CD-ROM: CD90067. $24.95.
Japan, 60 mins.

Using Macromedia Director

The complete guide to version 3.1.3 of Director, the bestselling guide to the graphics authoring tool. A comprehensive source for new authors and seasoned professionals alike, this CD-ROM offers over 80 movies (in both QuickTime and Director formats), Lingo scripts, and more.
MAC. Req: Macintosh Plus or better (any Mac produced since 1986) running system 6.0.7 or later; CD-ROM drive; 1.5 Mb of available RAM. If running system 6, must have at least 2 Mb RAM installed; if running system 7, must have at least 3 Mb. Or, any Macintosh with color display; System 7; CD-ROM drive.
CD-ROM: CD90046. $49.95.

T. Bove & C. Rhodes

Van Gogh: Starry Night: A History of Matter and a Matter of History
This hybrid CD-ROM's foundation is Vincent Van Gogh's famous painting "Starry Night." Research done at UCLA's Griffith Observatory determined that the painting was most probably a representation of the pre-dawn sky over Saint Rémy on June 19, 1889. Art history professor Albert Boime used that information as a starting point to create a CD-ROM that features audio, over 200 images, Van Gogh's personal correspondence, illustrations, photographs and more.
MAC. Req: 68030 processor (examples: Performa 575; Quadra; Centris) or better; 7.0 operating system or later; 8 MB RAM; 640x480 color monitor or 13" display; Double-speed CD-ROM drive.
WIN. Req: 486SX-33 or higher processor; 640x480, 256-color display (accelerator recommended); 8 MB RAM; MPC2-compatible CD-ROM drive; Sound card (16-bit) with speakers or headphones; Windows 3.1 or Windows 95.
CD-ROM: CD90075. $39.98.
Albert Boime, USA

The Visual Almanac Complete

The complete package includes the same videodisc found in the original *Almanac*, featuring 7,000 image resources, a full hour of sound, and both still images and motion video. Also included is a 200-page guide which explains the contents of both the video and software, and suggests activities for classroom use. The updated software includes a data-management system for finding images based on key words, lets you manipulate and present sounds and images, and includes a list of suggested classroom activities.
MAC. Req: Macintosh Plus or better (any Mac produced since 1986) running system 6.0.7 or later; CD-ROM drive; 1.5 Mb of available RAM. If running system 6, must have at least 2 Mb RAM installed; if running System 7, must have at least 3 Mb. Multiple configurations or special requirements possible; supports System 6.0.7.
CD-ROM: CD90044. $149.95.
USA, 1994

The Visual Almanac Upgrade

Originally released in 1990, *The Visual Almanac* has become an essential teaching and learning tool in classrooms across the country, perfect for all disciplines and grade levels. This update makes *The Visual Almanac* compatible with today's improved Macintosh hardware and software, and includes a data-management system that finds and organizes according to key words, sample compositions, suggested classroom activities and HyperCard 2.1.
MAC. Req: Macintosh Plus or better (any Mac produced since 1986) running system 6.0.7 or later; CD-ROM drive; 1.5MB of available RAM. If running system 6, must have at least 2MB RAM installed; if running System 7, must have at least 3MB. Multiple configurations or special requirements possible; supports System 6.0.7.
CD-ROM: CD90035. $49.95.
USA, 1994

Volcanoes: Life on the Age

This CD-ROM is an irresistible interactive experience for students of all ages. Thrilling cinematic documentaries and an extensive reference section explore the science, history and indomitable lure of the world's most active volcanoes.
MAC. Req: System 7.1, 68030, 8MB.
WIN. Req: Windows 3.1, 486, 8MB.
CD-ROM: CD90183. $49.95.

War in the Pacific

Fought over two-thirds of the world's surface, the War in the Pacific was a conflict of staggering magnitude and monumental importance. Discover the strategies, technologies and personalities that shaped this awesome encounter in this CD-ROM.

WIN. Req: Windows 3.1, 486, 8MB.

CD-ROM: CD90188. $49.99.

Washington, DC

Discover America on this interactive grand tour of the nation's capitol and important historic areas, buildings, museums, monuments and memorials. Fully narrated, this CD-ROM captures the spirit of freedom and democracy with interactive maps; a 40-minute tour; interiors and exteriors of every major attraction; DC history, facts and statistics; 250 photos and graphics; portraits and achievements of the presidents; regional tours of Monticello, Jamestown, Yorktown, Mount Vernon, Georgetown and colonial Williamsburg; Civil War highlights and Lincoln's assassination.

MAC. Req: 256 color monitor; 7.0 operating system or later; XA compatible, double-speed CD-ROM drive.

WIN. Req: 80386 or 80486 IBM PC compatible; 256-color display; CD-quality sound (16-bit); Windows 3.0 or higher.

OTHER. Req: TV-based players such as Sega Saturn, Kodak Photo CD, Phillips CD-i, Panasonic 3DO, and other Photo CD compatible systems.

CD-ROM: CD90163. $24.95.

The Way Things Work

David Macaulay's acclaimed *The Way Things Work* has become one of the most popular and best-loved CD-ROMs since its debut in 1994. This new version features a tour of the Inventors Workshop, conducted by Macaulay himself, plus an online link to the unique "Mammoth.net" featuring the Mammoth Inventors Club.

MAC. Req: Version 1.0.

WIN. Req: Version 1.0.

CD-ROM: CD90214. $49.95.

Whales and Dolphins

Every one of the 70 known species of whales and dolphins is described and illustrated in this volume. Features distribution maps and whale sounds, plus videos, photography and award-winning whale and dolphin paintings. Also includes several fully narrated sections that describe whale biology, including echolocation, migration, the mystery of whale strandings, and details on whale conservation.

MAC. Req: 13" monitor or larger; color (256 minimum), 4MB RAM, hard drive, CD-ROM hard drive.

WIN. Req: 13" monitor or larger; 386 (or better) processor; 4MB RAM (8 MB recommended); Sound blaster compatible sound card; Super VGA graphics card (minimum 640 x 480 x 256 color resolution); Windows 3.1 and Windows 95 compatible..

CD-ROM: CD90248. $29.95.

Who Built America? American Social History Project

Based on a definitive two-volume history, authors Roy Rosenzweig and Steve Brier have extended their text with thousands of source documents—audio, video and text. Read 20 years of a Norwegian immigrant's poignant letters home, listen to a young boy's account of a lynching in rural Florida in 1902 or to William Jennings Bryan's famous "Cross of God" speech. Thousands of historical documents including pictures, letters, photographs, archival audio and films, graphs, games and quizzes, the world's first crossword puzzle, and extensive research tools including search, index and notebook.

MAC. Req: Color capable, 25-MHz or better, 13" monitor, CD-ROM drive.

CD-ROM: CD90004. $99.95.

Who Built America? Education Edition

This edition of *Who Built America?* features five copies of the CD-ROM along with specially prepared Expanded Book editions of five works of the period, an extensive teaching guide, lesson plans, student activities, and suggestions for uses across the curriculum. This program is suitable for students grades 9 through college and allows them access to thousands of primary sources, including original diaries, letters, photographs, archival audio and oral histories and films.

MAC. Req: Any color-capable Macintosh (25-MHz 68030 processor or better recommended): System 7; not more than 6.2 Mb of available RAM (8 Mb installed); 13" color monitor; CD-ROM drive. Or, all Powerbooks and Duos, and all desktop Macintoshes driving 13" monitors; 1.5 Mb of available RAM. If running system 6.0.7 or 6.0.8, must have at least 2 Mb RAM installed; if running System 7, must have at least 3 Mb installed.

CD-ROM: CD90034. $350.00.

R. Rosenzweig, S. Br, USA

With Open Eyes: Images from the Art Institute of Chicago

Includes a laserdisc and Mac software, designed especially for young students, to offer an entertaining introduction to the world of art. This program includes over 200 works of art selected from the Art Institute of Chicago's collection and each is accompanied by music, sound effects, poetry and spoken information about the work, allowing pre-readers to explore artworks independently. Also includes jigsaw puzzles, connect the dots, hide and seek games, magnified details and more.

MAC. Req: 68030 processor (examples: Performa 575; Quadra; Centris) or better; 7.0 operating system or later; 8MB RAM; 640x480 color monitor or 13" display; double-speed CD-ROM drive.

WIN. Req: 486SX-33 or higher processor; 640x480, 256-color display (accelerator recommended); 8MB RAM; MPC2-compatible CD-ROM drive; sound card (16-bit) with speakers or headphones; Windows 3.1 or Windows 95.

CD-ROM: CD90036. $39.95.

Witness to the Future

Branda Miller's documentary of environmental activism, *Witness the Future*, furthers the dialog begun by Rachel Carson's *Silent Spring*, the book that catalyzed the environmental movement. Together, they support the ongoing struggle to protect our communities and our health. Includes the entire documentary, with full transcripts of the film's original interviews; the best-selling *Silent Spring*, with an introduction for new readers; information about activist groups and organizations; and links to its own World Wide Web page and other relevant sites.

MAC. Available for Macintosh platforms.

WIN. Available for Windows platforms.

CD-ROM: CD90200. $39.95.

Wolfgang Amadeus Mozart: The "Dissonant" Quartet

This CD-ROM contains the energy and creativity of Wolfgang Amadeus Mozart and invites you to listen to the music of Mozart's "Dissonant" Quartet as scholar and pianist Robert Winter's commentary on each theme scrolls by. There is also a detailed glossary of musical terms and theory, and a guide to the life and times of Mozart.

MAC. Req: Macintosh Plus or better (any Mac produced since 1986) running system 6.0.7 or later; CD-ROM drive; 1.5MB of available RAM. If running system 6, must have at least 2MB RAM installed; if running System 7, must have at least 3MB. Requires speakers or headphones if CD-ROM drive is external.

CD-ROM: CD90020. $59.95.

Robert Winter

A World Alive

James Earl Jones narrates this interactive documentary which covers everything from the humpback whale to leaf-cutter ants to the Pacific Ocean to Northern elephant seals. The documentary is linked to an interactive program that showcases the more than 100 species featured in the movie.

MAC. Req: Any Macintosh with color display; System 7; CD-ROM drive; no more than 2.2MB available RAM (4MB installed).

WIN. Req: 486SX-25 or higher processor; 640x480, 256-color display; 4MB RAM (8MB recommended); MPC-compatible CD-ROM drive; sound card (8-bit) with speakers or headphones; Microsoft Windows 3.1 or Windows 95.

CD-ROM: CD90008. $39.95.

39 mins.

The World of Reptiles

Includes five introductory chapters detailing the life history, ecology and body structure of reptiles, as well as specialized chapters which discuss each group of reptiles: the turtles, lizards, snakes, worm lizards, crocodillians and tuatara. Features narrated video sequences, a knowledge quiz and interactive index.

MAC. Req: 13" monitor or larger; color (256 minimum), 4MB RAM, hard drive, CD-ROM hard drive.

WIN. Req: 13" monitor or larger; 386 (or better) processor; 4MB RAM (8 MB recommended); Sound blaster compatible sound card; Super VGA graphics card (minimum 640 x 480 x 256 color resolution); Windows 3.1 and Windows 95 compatible..

CD-ROM: CD90251. $29.95.

World War I

This interactive experience puts you in the trenches of World War I with 25 minutes of film, over 750 photographs, 300 supplemental/mission cards and 150 minutes of audio commentary, and offers revealing insights into how this event laid the foundation for historic developments through the end of the 20th century.

WIN. Available for Windows platforms.

CD-ROM: CD90149. $44.98.

World War II

This interactive two-disk program puts you on the battlefields of WWII with over 40 minutes of film footage, six hours of commentary, 370 supplemental/mission cards and 1,100 photographs.

WIN. Available for Windows platforms.

CD-ROM: CD90150. $44.98.

World War II: Global Conflict

This CD-ROM gives amateur historians everything they need to understand the causes and consequences of the last global war. A superb multimedia experience using extensive video sequences to introduce the five phases of the war.

WIN. Req: Windows 3.1, 486, 8MB.

CD-ROM: CD90189. $49.99.

short film index

SHORT FILM	COMPILATION TAPE	PAGE
$1,000 Prize	The Abbott and Costello Television Show, Tape 4	414
100% Canadian	The Short Films of Mary Pickford	404
100% Nerve	The Films of Leo Maloney	368
1002nd Ruse, The	Early Russian Cinema, Vol. 07: Evgenii Bauer	85
123 Coco	Droits au Coeur (Rights from the Heart)5	709
16th Century Russian Wedding,	Early Russian Cinema, Vol. 02: Folklore and Legend	85
1776 (The Hessian Renegades)	The Short Films of Mary Pickford	404
1776 (The Hessian Renegades)	Griffith Shorts (1909)	412
1970	The Birth of theFilms of Scott Bartlett, Vol. 1:	485
20,000 Leaks Under the Sea	Mega Man: 20,000 Leaks Under the Sea	698
245 Days	Plymptoons: The Complete Works of Bill Plympton	715
25 Ways to Quit Smoking	Animation Celebration Vol. 2	705
25 Ways to Quit Smoking	Plymptoons: The Complete Works of Bill Plympton	715
28	Brunch/28	428
47 Seconds	William Wegman Reel 3	491
5 Dim/mind	Works of Ken Feingold—Names in Search of a Body	492
78 Tours	International Tournee of Animation Volume 3	712
8 x 8	Hans Richter: Give Chance a Chance	63, 485
9 Seconds and A Half	Too Outrageous Animation	717
97th Day, The	Nostalgia World War II Video Library #11	771
A	Video Against AIDS, Volumes 1, 2 & 3	835
A-car-tune Portrait	Little Lulu (Cartoonies)	685
A.I.D.S.C.R.E.A.M	A.I.D.S.C.R.E.A.M., Ecce Homo and Final Solutions	456, 482
Abdul the Bulbul Ameer	MGM Cartoon Classics: Happy Harmonies	686
Abet and Abtu	William Wegman Reel 1	491
Abominable Snow Rabbit, The	Looney Tunes After Dark	685
ABSCAM (Framed)	Chip Lord: Selected Works	428
Absence	Susan Rynard	488
Academy Leader Variations	Griffiti	710
Academy Leader Variations	International Tournee of Animation Volume 2	712
Ace in the Hole	Woody Woodpecker 50th Anniversary Vol. 2	690
Ace of Light	Tony Vegas' Animated Acidburn Flashback Tabu	717
Aces of Aces	Portraits from the Past	810
Achilles	Boys in Love	457
Acid Rain	Plymptoons: The Complete Works of Bill Plympton	715
Acrobatty Bunny	Bugs Bunny Classics	678
Acrobatty Bunny	Bugs Bunny's Comedy Classics 7	678
Action Antics	Cartoon Classics Vol. 6: Early Animation	680
Actor's Home	The Abbott and Costello Television Show, Tape 1	414
Actor, The	Rockin' Ronnie	281
Adagio	Live Short Films by Larry Jordan	718
Adam	Creature Comforts	708
Adam	Outrageous Animation Vol. 2	714
Adam	Spike & Mike's Festival of Animation Vol. 2	716
Adam Powers	Computer Animation Classics 4	708
Adam Raises Cain	Cartoon Classics Vol. 6: Early Animation	680
Adam's Other Rib	Spike & Mike's Sick & Twisted Festival of Animation	716
Adam's Smile	Picturebook Classics: Complete Set	639
Admiral Bataille	Writing in Water and Admiral Bataille & the S.S. Esoterica	480
Advantage of Having Warts, The	Moron Movies	508
Adventure of Norwood Builder	Sherlock Holmes Spellbinders	642
Adventure of the Dancing Man,	Sherlock Holmes' Greatest Cases	642
Adventure of the Lion's Mane	Sherlock Holmes Spellbinders	642
Adventure of the Reigate Puzzl	Sherlock Holmes Spellbinders	642
Adventure of the Solitary Cycl	Sherlock Holmes Spellbinders	642
Adventure of the Three Student	Sherlock Holmes Spellbinders	642
Adventurer, The	Charlie Chaplin Early Years II	407
Adventurer, The	Classic Chaplin, Charlie Chaplin at Mutual Studios	407
Adventurer, The	The Count and the Adventurer	407
Adventures Across Time	Railway Adventures Across Europe: Volume 2	843
Adventures Best Friend	Jonny Quest: Bandit—Adventure's Best Friend	698
Adventures of An *	Hubley Studio: Voyage to Next	711
Adventures of Billy	Griffith Shorts (1911-1912)	413
Adventures of Dolly	Griffith Shorts (1908-09)	412
Adventures of Priory School	Sherlock Holmes Cliffhangers	642
After Art	Potato Wolf Coleslaw	435
Agnes Keedan's Secret Plan	Puppets & Demons: Films by Patrick McGuinn	436
Ain't Nature Grand?	Cartoon Classics Vol. 5: The Other Studios	680
Air Pockets	Airplane Comedies	410
Air Race, The	Cartoons That Time Forgot Vol. 4: Willie Whopper's Fantastic Adventures	681
Air Travel	William Wegman Reel 4	491
Airborne Airhead	Tazmania: Taz-Tronaut	704
Aisle Six	CineBLAST! Vol. 3	428
Aisles of Doom	Squeal of Death	282
Al-lad-in His Lamp	Wince upon a Time: Foolhardy Fairy Tales & Looney Legends	690
Aladdin	NFBC: The Tender Tale of Cinderella Penguin	714
Aladdin & His Wonderful Lamp	Cartoons That Time Forgot Vol. 5: Free-Form Fairytales	681
Aladdin and His Lamp	Ub Iwerks' Famous Fairytales	689
Alan Watts: Meditation	Alan Watts: The Art of Meditation	847
Alarm Clock A and B	William Wegman Reel 7	491
Albert's Bad Word	Shelley Duvall's Bedtime Stories (Collection)	657
Alchemist of the Surreal	Alchemist of the Surreal	705
Aleutians, The	Wartime Cartoons	717
Alexeieff at the Pinboard	Alexeieff & Parker	482, 705
Ali Baba	Cartoon Classics in Color #1: Comicolor/Van Beuren	679
Ali Baba	Cartoons That Time Forgot Vol. 4: Willie Whopper's Fantastic Adventures	681
Ali Baba Bound	Cartoon Collection Vol. 3: Coal Black & De Sebben Dwarfs	680
Ali Baba Bound	Pioneers in Animation Vol. 3	714
Ali Baba Bunny	Bugs Bunny/Roadrunner Movie	679
Alias St. Nick	MGM Cartoon Magic	686
Alice Chop Suey	The Disney Primitive Collection: Alice	691
Alice in the Jungle	The Disney Primitive Collection: Alice	691
Alice in Wonderland	Great & Minor Animation Volume 3	684
Alice Jailbird	The Disney Primitive Collection: Alice	691
Alice on the Farm	Animation Vol. 1: The Beginning	706
Alice Orphan	The Disney Primitive Collection: Alice	691
Alice Rattled by Rats	The Disney Primitive Collection: Alice	691
Alice Rattled by Rats	Disney's Beginnings	692
Alice Solves a Puzzle	The Disney Primitive Collection: Alice	691
Alice the Toreader	Cartoon Classics Vol. 3: The Early Pioneers	680
Alice the Toreader	Weird Cartoons Vol. 2	717
Alice The Toreador	Cartoon Classics in Color #3: Wartime Warner Bros.	679
Alice the Toreador	The Disney Primitive Collection: Alice	691
Alice the Whaler	The Genesis of Animation, Volume One	710
Alice's Baloon Race	Early Animation Vol. 1	709
Alice's Eggplant	The Disney Primitive Collection: Alice	691
Alice's Eggplant	Animation Vol. 2	706
Alice's Tin Pony	The Disney Primitive Collection: Alice	691
Alice's Tin Pony	Great & Minor Animation Volume 1	684
Aliens from Inner Space	BBC Wildlife Specials: Aliens from Inner Space/ The Fastest Claw in the West	813
Alkali Ike's Auto	Slapstick Encyclopedia—Vol. 1: In the Beginning	411
All A Bir-r-d	Sylvester & Tweety: The Best Yeows of Our Lives	688
All Aboard	Films of Harold Lloyd—Volume 2	409
All Aboard	Harold Lloyd Comedies Vol. 1	410
All American Newsreel	Rare Black Short Subjects	448
All Dolled Up	Charley Chase Vol. 1	410
All My Relations	International Tournee of Animation Volume 4	712
All Night Long	All Night Long and Smile Please	410
All Night Long	Tramp, Tramp, Tramp	405
All Orientals Look the Same	Video Art, Tape One	489
All the Boys Named Patrick	Classic Foreign Shorts—Volume 2	153
All This and Rabbit Stew	Cartoon Collection Vol. 1: Porky in Wackyland	680
All Wet	Charley Chase and Ben Turpin	410
All Wet	Charley Chase Jimmy Jump Series	410
All Women Are Equal	All Women Are Equal & Pentagon Peace March	456, 482
All Women are Joan of Arcs	Letterist Films—Woman, Women!	432
All's Well	Gabby (Cartoonies)	684
Allal	Halfmoon	63, 304
Allegretto	The Films of Oskar Fischinger—Optical Poetry	710
Alley Cat, The	MGM Cartoon Classics: Happy Harmonies	686
Alley O Alley	Art Com Video 02: Waveforms: Video Japan	482
Allez Oop	Buster Keaton Talkies, Vol. 3	408
Allied Armor	Allied Fighting Machines of World War II	765
Allied Bombers	Allied Fighting Machines of World War II	765
Allied Fighters	Allied Fighting Machines of World War II	765
Allierten Band	Klaus Von Bruch: Black Box I	486
Along Came Auntie	Films of Oliver Hardy	410
Along Came Daffy	Daffy Duck: Just Plain Daffy	682
Alphabet	Avant Garde Program #11	482
Alphabet	NFBC: The Sand Castle	714
Alter Ego	Masters of Russian Animation: Volume	82, 713
Alterations	Animation for Fallen Catholics	706
Always Kickin	Great & Minor Animation Volume 4	684
Amazonia	Hubley Collection Vol. 2	711
America in the Pacific	Between the Wars, 1918-1941, Vol. 2	808
American West	Scenic Wonders of America	831
Amida	Amida/A Mosaic for the Kali Yuga/Arches/Body Count/ Hey Joe	482
Amore Baciami	Spike & Mike's Festival of Animation Vol. 2	716
Amos, The Story of an Old Dog	Shelley Duvall's Bedtime Stories: Moe the Dog in Tropical Paradise	657
Amphibian Blues	CineBLAST! Vol. 3	428
An American Sequence	Sara Hornbacher Early Works	488
An Autumn Wind	CineBLAST! Vol. 2	483
An Energy Carol	NFBC: An Animated Christmas	714
An Ill Wind	Cartoon Classics Vol. 5: The Other Studios	680
An Itch in Time	Pioneers in Animation Vol. 3	714
An Unseen Enemy	A Corner in Wheat and Selected Biograph Shorts	412
An Unseen Enemy	D.W. Griffith's Years of Discovery	412
An Urban Tragedy	Best of the Fests 1990	706
Anatole	Alice in Wonderland in Paris	705
Ancient Secrets of the Bible	Mysteries of the Ancient World Gift Set	791
And You Act Like One, Too	First Works Volume One	334
Anemic Cinema	Avant Garde Program #11	482
Anemic Cinema	Avant Garde Shorts/France	483
Angel of the Alps	Astro Boy Volume 12	722
Anijam	International Tournee of Animation Volume 1	711
Animal Kingdom	Wonders of God's Creation (Deluxe Edition)	824
Animal Kingdom: Great Are Thy Works	Wonders of God's Creation (Standard Edition)	824
Animal's Picnic Day, The	Spinning Tops and Tickle Bops	670
Animals Should Wear Underwear	Moron Movies	508
Animated Grouch Chaser, The	Cartoon Classics Vol. 7: Early Animation	680
Animated International	International Tournee of Animation Volume 4	712
Anna & Bella	International Tournee of Animation Volume 1	711
Annie	Female Misbehavior	63, 459
Annie Oakley	Shelley Duvall's Tall Tales and Legends	658
Anniversary	NFBC: Leonard Maltin's Animation Favorites from the National Film Board of Canada	714
Another Fine Mess	Laurel and Hardy on the Lam	274
Another Great Day!	Nice Girls...Films by and About Women	434
Another Great Moment	Outrageous Animation Vol. 2	714
Another Use for Bad Presidents	Moron Movies	508
Another Use for Tough Meat	Moron Movies	508
Answer, The	First Works Volume One	334
Ant and the Grasshopper, The	Early Russian Cinema, Vol. 03: Starewicz's Fantasies	85
Anthem	Boys' Shorts	457
Antlers Big and Small	Forest Habitat Set	815
Antosha Ruined by a Corset	Early Russian Cinema, Vol. 09: High Society	85

SHORT FILM	COMPILATION TAPE	PAGE
Ants in the Plants	Cartoon Classics in Color #2: Fleischer/Warners	679
Anything for Jazz: Kalo Byard	Three Piano Portraits	616
Anything Goes	Mabel Normand, Vol. 1	411
Apartheid Aside	Mitch Corber Works	487
Apes of Wrath	Stars of Space Jam—Bugs Bunny	687
Apes of Wrath	Stars of Space Jam: 5-Tape Boxed Set	687
Apparition, The	Grand Melies (Franju) and Melies' Short Films	20
Appearing Nitely	Lily Tomlin 3-Pack	462, 535
Apprentice, The	The National Film Board of Canada's Animation Festival	714
April Maze	Cartoon Classics Vol. 5: The Other Studio	680
April Maze	Classic Shorts Compilation #14: Felix the Cat	682
Aptom's Attack: Reactivate	Guyver: Volume 6, The Terminal Battle	732
Arabiantics	Early Animation Vol. 1	709
Arcaatan Mata, An	Griffith Shorts (1909-1910)	412
Archaeology of the Cinema	Origins of the Motion Picture	337
Architecture of Transcendence	Art on Film/Film on Art, Program 4: Film Voice/Art Voice	545
Arctic Giant	Superman (50th Anniversary)	688
Are You My Mother?	Are You My Mother? English Narration	629
Are You My Mother?	Are You My Mother? Spanish Narration	629
Aries Jones the Team	Gaiking	729
Aristo-cat, The	Golden Age of Looney Tunes: Vol. 05, Chuck Jones	684
Armchair Inventions	Sextoons: An Erotic Animation Festival	715
Army of One, An	Jonny Quest: Race Bannon—An Army of One	698
Arnold Escapes from Church	International Tournee of Animation Volume 3	712
Arnold Waltz, The	International Tournee of Animation Volume 4	712
Around & About	Video Art: Gary Hill	490
Art Film	Critical Art Ensemble	483
Art Gallery	MGM Cartoon Classics: Happy Harmonies	686
Art in Ancient Greece	Ancient Greece Volume 1	784
Art of Lotte Reiniger, The	Lotte Reiniger Compilation	713
Arts and Flowers	Woody Woodpecker 50th Anniversary Vol. 2	690
Artspace Computer-Controlled	The Pleasures of the Uninhibited Excess	567
As a Boy Dreams	Griffith Shorts (1911)	413
As Luck Would Have It	These Girls Won't Talk	405
Ascent of Man, The	The Ascent of Man/In the Absence of Heroes	482
Ask Dr. Stupid	Ren & Stimpy Vol. 2: The Stupidest Stories	701
Ask Father	Films of Harold Lloyd—Volume 2	409
Ass and the Stick, The	European Folk Tales, Volume 38	646
Astro Smiles	Exploration: Space	839
Astro Taz	Tazmania: Taz-Tronaut	704
At Land	Maya Deren Experimental Films	487
At Maxwell Street	Palazzolo's Chicago Vol. 2	476
At One View	International Tournee of Animation Volume 5	712
At the Devil's Ball	Great & Minor Animation Volume 2	684
At the Rongside	Early Comedies Volume 2	410
At the Rose Leaf	Secrets of Love, Classics of Erotic Literature Vol. 2	510
Atalanta	Heroines and Goddesses of the Greek Myths	784
Athene and Arachne	Heroines and Goddesses of the Greek Myths	784
Atlantic Vistas	Scenic Wonders of America	831
Atom Strikes, The	Nostalgia World War II Video Library #05	771
Attack of the Tree People	Jonny Quest: Bandit—Adventure's Best Friend	698
Au bord du lac	Patrick Bokanowski—Courts-Metrages	8
Au Revoir Mon Frigidaire	The Cheese Stands Alone	707
Audio Tape and Video Tape	William Wegman Reel 5	491
Augusta Feeds Her Child	International Tournee of Animation Volume 2	712
Augusta Kneading	International Tournee of Animation Volume 3	712
Augustine	Secrets of Love, Classics of Erotic Literature: Vol. 2	510
Aurora Accepts the Challenge	Spaceketeers	746
Aus der Ferne - The Memo Book	Matthias Muller—Selected Films	433
Auto Fire Life	Chip Lord: Selected Works	428
Auto Ride	Max Fleischer Presents Koko the Clown	685
Autobiography	Men in Shorts	463
Automan	Figures	484
Autumnal	Stan Brakhage—Hand-Painted Films	488
Average Guy	William Wegman Reel 5	491
Awakenings	A Glorious Accident	782
Awful Orphan, The	Porky Pig Tales	687
Awful Tooth	Dental Follies	267
Axis Armor	Axis Fighting Machines of World War II	766
Axis Bombers	Axis Fighting Machines of World War II	766
Axis Fighters	Axis Fighting Machines of World War II	766
Ayersrock	Takahiko Iimura: A Journey to Ayersrock	488
Babar and the Bicycle	Best of Babar, Vol. 1	630
Babar and the Cheese Fondue	Best of Babar, Vol. 1	630
Babar Gets Sunstroke	Best of Babar, Vol. 1	630
Babes in the Woods	Nursery Habitat Set	821
Baby Bottleneck	Porky!	687
Baby Story	Bruno Bozzetto: Animator, Vol. 1	707
Babylon	New British Animation: The Best from Channel 4	714
Babysitter, The	Naughty Nostalgia #2	508
Bacchus, The God of Wine	Ancient Greece Volume 2	784
Back Stage	Buster and Fatty	408
Backyard	Ross McElwee Films	477
Bad Liver, Broken Heart	CineBLAST! Vol. 2	483
Bad Luck Blackie	Tex Avery's Screwball Classics 1	688
Badge of Honor	Gigantor Retrospective 30 Vol. 1	730
Badums and Goodums	Animation Propaganda	706
Bag of Winds, The	European Folk Tales, Volume 5	646
Bagpipes, Trains and Highland	Railway Adventures Across Europe: Volume 1	843
Bagpuss	BBC Children's Favorites	629
Bakery, The	Heavy Hardy	411
Bakery, The	Larry Semon #3	411
Balance	International Tournee of Animation Volume 4	712
Balance	The World's Greatest Animation	718
Ball and Can	William Wegman Reel 6	491
Ball Drop	William Wegman Reel 5	491
Ball Game, The	Tom & Jerry & Friends #1	688
Ball Game, The	Van Beuren Studio, Volume #2	689
Ball of Yarn	Masters of Russian Animation: Volume 7	82, 713
Ballad of John Henry, The	Cartoon Collection Vol. 5: Racial Cartoons	680
Ballerina on a Boat	Masters of Russian Animation: Volume 1	82, 713
Ballerina on a Boat	Masters of Russian Animation: Volume 4	82, 713
Ballet Mecanique	Avant Garde & Experimental Film	482
Ballonatic, The	Blacksmith and Balloonatic	408
Balloon Guy	Computer Animation Classics	708
Balloon Head	Best of the Fests 1991	706

SHORT FILM	COMPILATION TAPE	PAGE
Balloon Land	Cartoons That Time Forgot Vol. 3: Things That Go Bump in the Night	681
Balloonatic	Buster Keaton (1917-22)	408
Balloonatic	Buster Keaton Festival Volume 3	408
Balloonatic	Seven Chances	409
Balloonatic	Buster Keaton	408
Ballroom Dancer, The	Rockin' Ronnie	281
Balognie Birdman, The	National Film Board of Canada's Animation Festival	714
Bambi Meets Godzilla	Experimental Avant Garde Series Volume 19 (Very Serious Fun)	484
Bambi Meets Godzilla	The Rocketship Reel	715
Bambi Meets Godzilla	Spike & Mike's Festival of Animation Vol. 1	716
Bank Dory, The	Ways at Wallace and Sons and The Bank Dory	828
Bank, The	Classic Chaplin, Charlie Chaplin at Essanay Studios	407
Bank, The	Emerging Chaplin	407
Bank, The	Essanay #2	407
Bank, The	Rare Chaplin	408
Banquet Busters	Woody Woodpecker 50th Anniversary Vol. 1	690
Baptism of Fire	Nostalgia World War II Video Library #7	771
Barbarian Forces	Ancient Warriors	784
Barbary Coast Bunny	Stars of Space Jam: Five-Tape Boxed Set	687
Barbary Coast Bunny	Stars of Space Jam—Bugs Bunny	687
Barber Shop, The	W.C. Fields: 6 Short Films	286
Barbie	Film Musicals	430
Barbie	Tina L'hotsky: Barbie and Snakewoman	489
Bargain Counter Attack	Cartoon Collection Vol. 8: Private Snafu	680
Barney Bear's Victory Garden	MGM Cartoon Classics: Happy Harmonies	686
Barney Oldfield's Race for Life	Slapstick Encyclopedia—Vol. 2: Keystone Tonight!	411
Barney Oldfield's Race for Life	Early Comedies Volume 1	410
Barney Oldfield's Race for Life	Mabel Normand Comedies, Vol. 2	411
Barnyard Babies	MGM Cartoon Classics: Happy Harmonies	686
Barnyard Bunk	Tom & Jerry & Friends #3	688
Barnyard Melody	Van Beuren Studio, Volume #1	689
Baron Munchhausen's Dream	Melies III: The Search for Munchhausen	22
Baron, The	Mack Sennett: The Biograph Years	411
Barry Harris: Passing It On	Three Piano Portraits	616
Bars & Stripes	Thirties Magic Vol. 1	716
Bartered Bride, The	The Bartered Bride and The Last Waltz	27, 577
Bashful	Harold Lloyd Comedies Vol. 2	410
Bashful Whirlwind	Early Westerns #2	398
Bath, The	Tom Chomont: A Two-Volume Collection, Volume I	466, 489
Battle at Elderbush Gulch, The	The Musketeers of Pig Alley and Selected Biograph Shorts	413
Battle at Elderbush Gulch, The	D.W. Griffith's Years of Discovery	412
Battle at Elderbush Gulch, The	The Short Films of D.W. Griffith—Volume 1	413
Battle at the Bottom	Gigantor Vol. 1	730
Battle of Elderbush Gulch, The	Griffith Shorts (1913-1914)	413
Battle of Elderbush Gulch, The	D.W. Griffith Triple Feature	412
Battle of Kerjenets	Masters of Russian Animation: Volume 5	82, 713
Battle of San Pietro	The Battle of San Pietro/Marines Have Landed	766
Battle of the Century	Slapstick Encyclopedia—Vol. 6: Hal Roach: The Lot of Fun	411
Battle Royal	Films of Oliver Hardy	410
Battle Wreckage	Nostalgia World War II Video Library #1	770
Battle, The	Griffith Shorts (1911-1912)	413
Battle, The	The Short Films of D.W. Griffith—Volume 1	413
Battle, The	Vietnam: Time of the Locust	778
Battling Bosko	Cartoon Classics Vol. 1: Looney Tunes & Merrie Melodies	680
Battling Butler	Art of Buster Keaton—Box 2	408
Battling Butler	Battling Butler	408
Battling Travers	Early Westerns #2	398
Baudrillard's Lasso	Critical Art Ensemble	483
Be Human	Best of Betty Boop	677
Be My King	Selected Shorts #2	403
Be My Wife	Slapstick Encyclopedia—Vol. 1: In the Beginning	411
Be Reasonable	Forgotten Comedians	411
Beach Blanket Babies	Rugrats: Tales from the Crib	641, 702
Beach Comber	Great & Minor Animation Volume 3	684
Beachcomber	Pioneers in Animation Vol. 2	714
Beachcombers	Thirties Magic Vol. 1	716
Beaker and Homeslice Get Out	Too Outrageous Animation	717
Bear and the Beavers, The	MGM Cartoon Classics: Happy Harmonies	686
Bear and the Fly, The	Joey Runs Away and Other Stories	653
Bear for Punishment, A	Looney Tunes Assorted Nuts	685
Bear of a Story, A	Tom Mix Short Subjects	405
Bear That Couldn't Sleep, The	MGM Cartoon Classics: Happy Harmonies	686
Bear's X-ones	NFBC: An Animated Christmas	714
Beast at Bay, A	Griffith Shorts (1912, #1)	413
Beast in the Bathtub, The	Picturebook Classics: Complete Set	639
Beast of Monsieur Racine, The	Rosie's Walk and Other Stories	656
Beat It	Videotapes of Elizabeth Sher, V. 1-11, What's Inside These Shorts?	491
Beauty and the Beast	Disney Canta con Nosotros	672
Beauty and the Beast	Katharine Hepburn: World of Stories	647
Beauty Contest	The Abbott and Costello Television Show, Tape 5	414
Beavis and Butthead in Peace, Love & Understanding	Spike & Mike's Sick & Twisted Festival of Animation, Vol. 1	716
Bed, The	Films of James Broughton, Volume 1: Erotic Celebration	492
Bedevilled Rabbit	Stars of Space Jam: Five-Tape Boxed Set	687
Bedroom, The	International Tournee of Animation Volume 4	712
Beep Beep	Chariots of Fur	682
Begone Dull Care	NFBC: Leonard Maltin's Animation Favorites from the National Film Boards of Canada	714
Behind the Screen	Charlie Chaplin Early Years IV	407
Behind the Screen	Classic Chaplin, Charlie Chaplin at Mutual Studios	407
Behind the Screen	Early Russian Cinema: Before the Revolution, Vol. 10: The End of an Era	85
Bellhop, The	The Bellhop/The Noon Whistle	395
Bellhop, The	Heavy Hardy	411
Bellhop, The	Larry Semon #1	411
Ben Hur	Classic Photoplays	396
Bent Time	Perceptual Landscapes	464, 492
Best Nest, The	Are You My Mother? English Narration	629
Best Nest, The	Are You My Mother? Spanish Narration	629
Best of Buelah, The	Kukla, Fran and Ollie: Tis the Season to be Ollie	653
Best of Fletcher, The	Kukla, Fran and Ollie: Madame O's Merry Musicale	653
Best of Kukla, The	Kukla, Fran and Ollie: Get on the Dragon Wagon	653
Best of Madame, The	Kukla, Fran and Ollie: Be a Clown, Be a Clown	653
Best of Ollie, The	Kukla, Fran and Ollie: Kukla Discovers America	653

SHORT FILM	COMPILATION TAPE	PAGE
Best, The	Babe Hardy: Early Training	410
Betty and Henry	Cartoon Collection Vol. 8: Private Snafu	680
Betty Boop & Grampy	Cartoon Collection Vol. 7: Tokyo Jokio	680
Betty Boop in Crazy Town	Bambi Meets Godzilla and Other Weird Cartoons	677
Betty Boop's Crazy Inventions	Weird Cartoons Vol. 2	717
Betty Boop's Halloween Party	Cartoon Holidays	680
Betty Boop's Rise to Fame	Cartoon Collection Vol. 1: Porky in Wackyland	680
Betty in Blunderland	Cartoon Collection Vol. 4: Warner Bros. & Fleischer	680
Betty in Blunderland	Thirties Magic Vol. 2	717
Betty Minds a Baby	Betty Boop's Dizzy Dozen	678
Between Showers	Keystones #1	407
Between the Lines	Video Art: Antonio Muntadas	489
Beware the Red Moon	Grandizer	731
Bewitched Bunny	Looney Tunes After Dark	685
Bewitched Matches	Attack of the Cohl Pumpkins	706
Beyond the Walls	CineBLAST! Vol. 3	428
Biblical-Theological Perspective	People of Faith and the Arms Race	805
Bicoastal and Exec. Air Travel	Chip Lord: Selected Works	428
Big Baby	Animation Celebration Vol. 4	706
Big Bad Wolf, The	Pioneers in Animation Vol. 3	714
Big Bang, The	International Tournee of Animation Volume 5	712
Big Bird Brings Spring	Five Sesame Street Stories	652
Big Drip	Little Lulu (Cartoonies)	685
Big Fat World of Science	Spike & Mike's Festival of Animation Vol. 2	716
Big Fat World of Science, The	The Cheese Stands Alone	707
Big Flame Up, The	Paramount/Fleischer Studios Volume 3	686
Big Moments from Big Pictures	Hollywood Spoofs	411
Big Moments From Little Pictures	Slapstick Encyclopedia—Vol. 6: Hal Roach: The Lot of Fun	411
Big Shave, The	Italian American/The Big Shave	253
Big Shot, The	Ren & Stimpy Vol. 2: The Stupidest Stories	701
Big Snit, The	The National Film Board of Canada's Animation Festival	714
Big Top	Spike & Mike's Sick & Twisted Festival of Animation	716
Big Top Bunny	Bugs Bunny: Hare Beyond Compare	679
Bill and Pete	Shelley Duvall's Bedtime Stories: Elizabeth and Larry and Bill and Pete	657
Bill of Hare	Stars of Space Jam: Five-Tape Boxed Set	687
Billboard Frolics	Cartoon Collection Vol. 3: Coal Black & De Sebben Dwarfs	680
Billion Dollar Limited	Superman (50th Anniversary)	688
Billy & Bobby	Liquid Television 2	698
Billy Goat's Whiskers	Fox Terrytoons	684
Billy Nayer Show, The	International Tournee of Animation Volume 6	712
Billy Turner's Secret	Boys' Shorts	457
Bingo's Troubles	The Abbott and Costello Television Show, Tape 3	414
Bird Lives	Jazz Shorts	612
Birds Anonymous	The Looney Looney Looney Bugs Bunny Movie	685
Birds of a Feather	I'm Not Oscar's Friend Anymore and Other Stories	635
Birds of a Sun God	BBC Wildlife Specials: Birds of a Sun God/In-Flight Movie	813
Birdy Birdy	Too Outrageous Animation	717
Birth of Astroboy	Astro Boy Volume 1	722
Birth of Brian, The	Spike & Mike's Sick & Twisted Festival of Animation Vol. 1	716
Birth's Child	Video Art: Noel Harding	490
Birthday Gand, The	Jane Hissey's Old Bear Stories: Happy Birthday Old Bear	653
Birthday Party	Mickey Mouse: The Black & White Years	693
Bit Snit, The	Incredible Manitoba Animation	711
Bitter Half, The	Daffy Duck's Thanks-For-Giving Special	682
Bitz Butz	International Tournee of Animation Volume 1	711
Black & Decker Hedgetrimmer Murders, The	Karl Krogstad Films	432
Black Dog	New British Animation: The Best from Channel 4	714
Black Ice	Stan Brakhage—Hand-Painted Films	488
Black Music Videos from the 19	That's Black Entertainment: African-American Contributions in Film and Music 1903-1944	455
Black on White	Story of English	860
Black Sheep Boy	Black Sheep Boy and Decodings	457
Blackberry Subway Jam	NFBC: Cartoon Festival: The Cat Came Back	714
Blackfly	The National Film Board of Canada's Animation Festival	714
Blacksmith, The	Buster Keaton Festival Volume 1	408
Blacksmith, The	Buster Keaton (1917-22)	408
Blacksmith, The	Blacksmith and Balloonatic	408
Blacksmith, The	College	409
Blacksmith, The	Great Stone Face—Buster Keaton—Vol. 1	409
Bladder Trouble	Spike & Mike's Sick & Twisted Festival of Animation Vol. 1	716
Blake Ball	Hubley Collection Vol. 1	711
Blind Love	Griffith Shorts (1912, #2)	413
Blindscape	Spike & Mike's Festival of Animation Vol. 3	716
Blinky Bill's Fund Run	Adventures of Blinky Bill: Blinky's Fire Brigade/Fund Run	628
Blinky Bill's Zoo	Adventures of Blinky Bill: Blinky Bill's Zoo/Magician	628
Blinky's Fire Brigade	Adventures of Blinky Bill: Blinky's Fire Brigade/Fund Run	628
Blitz Wolf	Tex Avery's Screwball Classics 4	688
Blondes Revenge	Ben Turpin #1	410
Blow Me Down	Cartoon Collection Vol. 4: Warner Bros. & Fleischer	680
Blue Blazes	Buster Keaton Talkies, Vol. 3	408
Blue Cat Blues	Tom & Jerry's Festival of Fun	689
Blue Danube, The	MGM Cartoon Classics: Happy Harmonies	686
Blue Kisses and Marshmallows	Letterist Films—Woman, Women!	432
Blue Man Down	Amazing Stories: Book 4	414
Blue Moon	Mediamystics	487
Blue Moses	Stan Brakhage Selected Films: Vol. 2	488
Blue Movie	6 Films by Mark Street	482
Blue Rhythm	Mickey Mouse: The Black & White Years	693
Blueberries For Sal	Corduroy Bear	651
Bluebird Penguin	CineBLAST! Vol. 3	428
Boat, The	Buster Keaton Festival Volume 2	408
Boat, The	Slapstick Encyclopedia—Vol. 4: Keaton, Arbuckle & Al St. John	411
Bob Kick, The	More Melies	22
Bob the Frog in	Greentoons: Environmentally Aware Animation	710
Bob's Hot Story	Naughty Nostalgia #1	508
Bobby Bumps	Origins of American Animation	714
Bobby Bumps Puts a Beanery On	Animation Vol. 1: The Beginning	706
Bobby Bumps Puts a Beanery On	Cartoon Classics Vol. 3: The Early Pioneers	680
Bobby the Coward	Griffith Shorts (1911)	413
Body Beautiful	The British Animation Invasion	707
Body Count	Amida/A Mosaic for the Kali Yuga/Arches/Body Count/ Hey Joe	482
Bogus Man, The	Cinema of Transgression	483
Bogus Man, The	Nick Zedd: Steal This Video	434

SHORT FILM	COMPILATION TAPE	PAGE
Bold King Cole	Best of the Van Beuren Studio	677
Bondage	Female Misbehavior	63, 459
Bongo	Fun and Fancy Free	692
Boo Moon	Paramount/Famous Studios Volume 2	686
Boobs in the Woods	Films of Harry Langdon Volume 2	410
Boobs in the Woods	Langdon at Sennett	411
Boobs a Lot	Sextoons: An Erotic Animation Festival	715
Boogie-Woogie Dreams	That's Black Entertainment: African-American Contributions in Film and Music 1903-1944	455
Book of Days	The Films of Meredith Monk	485, 567
Bookworm, The	MGM Cartoon Classics: Happy Harmonies	686
Boom	CineBLAST! Vol. 2	483
Boom Boom	Cartoon Collection Vol. 7: Tokyo Jokio	680
Boomtown	Plymptoons: The Complete Works of Bill Plympton	715
Bored Cuckoo	Little Lulu and Friends	685
Bored of Education	Cartoon Collection Vol. 6: The Ducktators	680
Bored of Education	Paramount/Famous Studios Volume 1	686
Born to Peck	Woody Woodpecker 50th Anniversary Vol. 1	690
Born With No Mouth	William Wegman Reel 3	491
Bosko at the Beach	All Singing, All Dancing	676
Bosko Shipwrecked	Cartoon Collection Vol. 6: The Ducktators	680
Bosko the Speed King	Cartoon Collection Vol. 3: Coal Black & De Sebben Dwarfs	680
Bosko's Easter Eggs	MGM Cartoon Classics: Happy Harmonies	686
Bosko's Soda Fountain	Cartoon Collection Vol. 6: The Ducktators	680
Boston Quackie	Stars of Space Jam: Five-Tape Boxed Set	687
Botco	Computer Animation Classics	708
Bottle Cap Blues	Tazmania: Taz-Tronaut	704
Bottles	MGM Cartoon Classics: Happy Harmonies	686
Bottom's Dream	International Tournee of Animation Volume 1	711
Bout with a Trout, A	Cartoon Collection Vol. 8: Private Snafu	680
Box Office Bunny	Bugs Bunny: Winner by a Hare	679
Box, The	NFBC: The Box	714
Boy and the Snow Goose, The	The Dingles	632
Boy and the Wolf	MGM Cartoon Classics: Happy Harmonies	686
Boy Meets Dog	Cartoon Classics Vol. 5: The Other Studios	680
Boy Meets Dog	Great & Minor Animation Volume 2	684
Boy Named Cocoy, A	Rich Boy, Poor Boy	145, 464
Boy Who Called Wolf	Aesop & His Friends	645
Bra Unhooking Champion, The	More Moron Movies	508
Brad Dharma: Psychadelic Detec	Liquid Television 2	698
Brain Drain	Clarissa Explains It All: "Take My Brother, Please"	631
Brassieres of Uranus	A Performance by Jack Smith	487, 567
Brat, The	Films of Harold Lloyd—Volume 5	410
Brats	Laurel and Hardy and the Family	274
Brave Irene	Norman the Doorman and Other Stories	639
Brave Little Tailor, The	Mickey Loves Minnie	693
Brave Tin Soldier, The	Cartoons That Time Forgot Vol. 5: Free-Form Fairytales	681
Break	International Tournee of Animation Volume 2	712
Breakdown	International Tournee of Animation Volume 5	712
Breakfast Tips	Ren & Stimpy Vol. 1: The Classics	701
Bremen Town Musicians, The	Blue Ribbon Stories Vol. 2	650
Bremertown Musicians, The	Cartoons That Time Forgot Vol. 1: All Singing! All Dancing!	681
Brian's Brain	Spike & Mike's Sick & Twisted Festival of Animation, Vol. 2	716
Bride and Gloom	The Adventures of Popeye, Vol. 2	676
Bride Stripped Bare, The	Tom Palazzolo: Films from the Sixties	478
Bridge	Rare Dutch and Belgian Experimental Program	31, 488
Bridge, The	American Avant-Garde Films	482
Brigand Brothers	Early Russian Cinema: Before the Revolution, Vol. 2: Folklore and Legend	85
Brilliance	Computer Animation Classics	708
Bring 'Em Back Half Shot	Tom & Jerry & Friends #7	688
Bring Me the Head of Geraldo	Small Gauge Shotgun	488
Bringing up Baby	Nursery Habitat Set	821
Britannia	Spike & Mike's Festival of Animation Vol. 3	716
Broccoli Abuse	More Moron Movies	508
Broken Heart	Nice Girls...Films by and About Women	434
Bromo and Juliet	Charley Chase Vol. 2	410
Bronco Billy's Sentence	Bronco Billy Anderson	396
Brother Brat	Porky!	687
Brother Jetto	Astro Boy Volume 7	722
Brother's Great Escape, The	Sohryuden Vol. 5: Episodes 9 and 10	746
Brouhaha	The Best of the New York Underground, Year 2	483
Brownie Bucks the Jungle	Cartoon Classics Vol. 5: The Other Studios	680
Brunch	Brunch/28	428
Brute Force	Griffith Shorts (1913-1914)	413
Bubblebath	William Wegman Reel 3	491
Bubbles	Koko the Clown, 1915-27	712
Buccaneer Bunny	Starring Bugs Bunny!	687
Buccaneer Bunny	Bugs Bunny's Zaniest Toons	679
Buckingham Palace	Pictures Don't Tell You Anything: Selected Films of Ann Marie Flemming	211, 487
Bug Carnival	Fox Terrytoons	684
Bug Vaudeville	Classic Shorts Compilation #12: Winsor McCay	682
Bug Vaudeville	A Tribute to Winsor McCay	717
Bugs and Daffy: Carnival	Bugs & Daffy's Carnival of the Animals	678
Bugs Bunny and the Three Bears	Bugs!	679
Bugs Bunny Bond Rally	Cartoon Collection Vol. 5: Racial Cartoons	680
Bugs Bunny Rides Again	Bugs Bunny's Zaniest Toons	679
Building a Building	Mickey Mouse: The Black & White Years	693
Built	Hard	460
Bulleteers, The	Superman (50th Anniversary)	688
Bulleteers, The	Color Adventures of Superman	682
Bully for Bugs	Bugs Bunny: Winner by a Hare	679
Bully, The	Cartoons That Time Forgot Vol. 2: Down & Out with Flip the Frog	681
Bumble-Boogie	Classics in Clay	707
Bumbledown	Bumbledown/Sound of Maggie	415
Bunker Hill Bunny	Bugs Bunny: Hare Beyond Compare	679
Burglar's Dilemma, The	The Musketeers of Pig Alley and Selected Biograph Shorts	413
Burglar's Dilemma, The	D.W. Griffith's Years of Discovery	412
Burglar's Dilemma, The	The Musketeers of Pig Alley and Selected Biograph Shorts	413
Burglar's Dilemma, The	Griffith Shorts (1912, #3)	413
Buried Treasure	Sextoons: An Erotic Animation Festival	715
Buried Treasure	The Wind in the Willows, Volume #3	644, 718
Burlesque on Carmen	Essanay #3	407
Bus Stop	Tony Vegas' Animated Acidburn Flashback Tabu	717
Business of Beavers, The	Forest Habitat Set	815

SHORT FILM	COMPILATION TAPE	PAGE
Buster and Babs Go Hawaiian	Tiny Toon Island Adventures	688
Buster Keaton Detective	Great Stone Face—Buster Keaton—Vol. 2	409
Busy Bodies	Laurel and Hardy at Work	274
Busy Buddies	Comedy Shorts #4	410
Busy Day, A	Keystones #2	407
But would you take her back?	The Athena Awards 1996	456
Butcher Boy	Buster and Fatty	408
Butterfly, The	The Rocketship Reel	715
Butterscotch & Soda	Paramount/Famous Studios Volume 1	686
Buy Now—Pay Later	Problems for Young Consumers	670
Buying a House	William Wegman Reel 5	491
By Land and Air	Aesop's Fables Volume 3	676
By the Sea	Classic Chaplin, Charlie Chaplin at Essanay Studio	407
By the Sea	Essanay #2	407
Bye, Bye Bluebeard	Porky Pig: Days of Swine and Roses	687
Cabinet of Jan Svankmajer, The	The Brothers Quay Vol. 1	707
Cactus Makes Perfect	The Three Stooges: Whoops I'm an Indian	284
Cactus Swing	NFBC: Cartoon Festival: Cactus Swing	714
Cadillac Ranch	Cadillac Ranch/Media Burn	483
Calamitous Elopement, A	Griffith Shorts (1908-09)	412
Calcutta Adventure	Jonny Quest: Hadji—Mysteries of the East	698
Caldonia	Black Jazz and Blues	609
Calico Dragon, The	MGM Cartoon Classics: Happy Harmonies	686
California Whitewater	Whitewater Adventures	833
California Zones	War Dance	439
Call at Corazon	Halfmoon	63, 304
Call Waiting	CineBLAST! Vol. 2	483
Calling Dr. Porky	Cartoon Collection Vol. 3: Coal Black & De Sebben Dwarfs	680
Calling Man Ray	William Wegman Reel 4	491
Camel Who Took a Walk, The	Danny and the Dinosaur and Other Stories	651
Cameraman at War	Wartime Combat	479
Cameraman's Revenge, The	The Cameraman's Revenge: The Amazing Puppet Animation of Ladislaw Starewicz	707
Cameraman, The	Doughboys	409
Campaign	Tom Palazzolo: Films from the Sixties	478
Camping Out	Mickey Mouse: The Black & White Years	693
Campus Carmen, The	These Girls Won't Talk	405
Canary Row	Stars of Space Jam: Five-Tape Boxed Set	687
Candlemaker, The	Classic Cartoon Christmas Treasures	682
Candyland	Tom & Jerry & Friends #1	688
Candy Town	Great & Minor Animation Volume 1	684
Cannonnball	Cannonball/Dizzy Heights	410
Cape On	William Wegman Reel 1	491
Caps for Sale	Five Stories for the Very Young	652
Captain Hareblower	Bugs Bunny: Winner by a Hare	679
Captain Kidder	Aesop's Film Fables	676
Captain Kidding	Best of George Pal	677
Captain's Christmas, The	Tom & Jerry's The Night Before Christmas	689
Car Came Back, The	NFBC: Cartoon Festival: The Cat Came Back	714
Carabosse	Short Animations by Larry Jordan	718
Caretaker's Daughter	Comedy Shorts #4	410
Carmelita Tropicana: Your Kun	Girl Friends (Shorts)	229, 460
Carnival	Figures	484
Carnival	International Tournee of Animation Volume 2	712
Carnival of Misplaced Devotion	The Pleasures of the Uninhibited Excess	567
Carousel	Simultaneous	488
Carried Away	Incredible Manitoba Animation	711
Cartoongate	Cartoongate!	681
Case of Identity, A	Sherlock Holmes Cliffhangers	642
Case of the Missing Hare	Cartoon Collection Vol. 2: Classic Warner Bros.	680
Case of the Stuttering Pig	Porky Pig: Ham on Wry	687
Case of the Stuttering Pig	Cartoon Collection Vol. 4: Warner Bros. & Fleischer	680
Casey at the Bat	Four for Thrills, Edgar Allan Poe, Etc.	633
Casey at the Bat	Shelley Duvall's Tall Tales and Legends	658
Casey's Revenge	Human Race Club: A Story About Fights Between Brothers and Sisters	635
Casper	William Wegman Reel 1	491
Castro Street	Tung, To Parsifal & Castro Street	489
Cat & Company	Masters of Russian Animation: Volume 4	713
Cat and Rat	International Tournee of Animation: Volume 4	712
Cat Came Back, The	Incredible Animation Collection: Vol. 1	711
Cat Came Back, The	NFBC: Leonard Maltin's Animation Favorites from the National Film Board of Canada	714
Cat Came Back, The	Incredible Manitoba Animation	711
Cat Came Back, The	The National Film Board of Canada's Animation Festival	714
Cat Nip	I Became a Lesbian and Others Too	460
Cat Strikes Back	Incredible Manitoba Animation	711
Cat that Ate the Golden Hairball	Ren & Stimpy Vol. 3: The Stinkiest Stories	701
Cat's Canary	Van Beuren Studio, Volume #2	689
Cat's Cradle	Stan Brakhage Selected Films: Vol. 2	488
Cat's Cradle	Incredible Animation Collection: Vol. 2	711
Cat's Dilemma, The	Tom & Jerry & Friends #3	688
Cat, Cow, and Beautiful Fish,	Spike & Mike's Sick & Twisted Festival of Animation, Vol. 2	716
Catharsis	Karl Krogstad: Idiot Savant & Catharsis	432
Catour	NFBC: Every Child	714
Caught in a Cabaret	Classic Chaplin, Charlie Chaplin at Keystone Studio	407
Caught in a Cabaret	Keystones #2	407
Caught in the Can	Third Sex Sinema Volume 5—Consenting Adults	466, 511
Caught Looking	Caught Looking & North of Vortex	457
Cavalcade of Music	Great & Minor Animation Volume 2	684
Celebration on Victory Day	Soviet War Stories from World War II	772
Celebrity Author	Chip Lord: Selected Works	428
Censored!	Cartoon Collection Vol. 8: Private Snafu	680
Centaurs, The	Winsor McCay: Animation Legend	718
Central Highlands: Edinburgh	British Rail Journeys	841
Century of Progress - Chicago	Cityscape Compilations	470
Certain Grace, A	Dyke Drama	458
Cezanne	M/W/F Music Video One	433
Chaconne	Balanchine: Prodigal Son/Chaconne	568
Chain Gang, The	Mickey Mouse: The Black & White Years	693
Chainsaw Bob in a Cult Classic	Spike & Mike's Sick & Twisted Festival of Animation, Vol. 2	716
Chakra	Samadhi and Other Films	488
Challenger Explosion	Exploration: Space	839
Chameleon Cat, The	European Folk Tales, Volume 4	646
Champion	Aesop's Fables Volume 3	676
Champion, The	Classic Chaplin, Charlie Chaplin at Essanay Studio	407
Champion, The	Essanay #1	407
Change Myself	Computer Animation Festival Vol. 1.0	708
Change of Spirit, A	Griffith Shorts (1912, #2)	413
Changes	Five Stories for the Very Young	652
Channel Swimmer, The	Forgotten Comedians	411
Chaos in the Classroom	Peanuts: Charlie Brown & Snoopy Show Vol. 6	700
Chapter of an Ogre's Lament	Ogre Slayer 2: Grim Fairy Tale	738
Chapter of the Ogre Witch	Ogre Slayer 2: Grim Fairy Tale	738
Char, En Oversattning	Art Com Video 1: Scandinavia	482
Charade	Spike & Mike's Festival of Animation Vol. 1	716
Charade	International Tournee of Animation Volume 1	711
Charade	The World's Greatest Animation	718
Charity Bazaar	The Abbott and Costello Television Show, Tape 5	414
Charleen	Ross McElwee Films	477
Charleston	Avant Garde Shorts/France	483
Charleston	Renoir Silent Shorts	26
Charlie Needs a Cloak	Rosie's Walk and Other Stories	656
Charlie's Boogie Woogie	Best of the Fests: For Kids	706
Chartres Series	Stan Brakhage—Hand-Painted Films	488
Chase (Bonaparte in the Mist)	New Dominion Tank Police Vol. 2: Episodes 3 and 4	738
Chasing Choo Choos	Slapstick Encyclopedia—Vol. 7: The Rage Is On 1917-1927	411
Chasing the Chaser	Directed by Stan Laurel	410
Chef, The	Harold Lloyd's Comedy Classics	410
Chemical Change	Forces of Life	836
Chemist, The	Buster Keaton Talkies, Vol. 1	408
Cherub	Squeal of Death	282
Chick and Double Chick	Cartoon Collection Vol. 8: Private Snafu	680
Chick and Double Chick	Little Lulu and Friends	685
Chicken a la King	Pioneers in Animation Vol. 3	714
Chicken Soup with Rice	The Maurice Sendak Library	654
Chicken, The	Short Subject Potpouri	477
Child of the Big City, A	Early Russian Cinema, Vol. 07: Evgenii Bauer	85
Child's Alphabet, A	Sextoons: An Erotic Animation Festival	715
Children of Light, The	Wheeler Dixon: Selected Films	491
Children of the Damned	Village of the Damned/Children of the Damned (1960)	501
Chimaera, The	Monsters of the Greek Myths	637
China Doll	Terrytoons: The Cats & Mice of Paul Terry	716
China Jones	Porky Pig Tales	687
Chinaman	Max Fleischer Presents Koko the Clown	685
Chinaman's Chance, A	Cartoons That Time Forgot Vol. 3: Things That Go Bump in the Night	681
Chinese Nightingale, The	MGM Cartoon Classics: Happy Harmonies	686
Choo Choo	Shelley Duvall's Bedtime Stories: Little Toot and The Loch Ness Monster and Choo Choo	657
Christmans Racoons, The	Christmas Carousel	630
Christmas Carol	Bugs Bunny's Looney Christmas Tales	679
Christmas Comes But Once	Cartoon Holidays	680
Christmas Comes But Once	Classic Cartoon Christmas Treasures	682
Christmas Comes But Once	Christmas Cartoon Classic	682
Christmas Cracker	NFBC—Cartoon Festival: The Sweater	714
Christmas Cracker, The	A Christmas Gift	707
Christmas Dream, A	Christmas Cartoon Classic	682
Christmas Eve	Early Russian Cinema: Before the Revolution, Vol. 3: Starewicz's Fantasies	87
Christmas Feast, The	European Folk Tales, Volume 3	646
Christmas Night	Cartoons That Time Forgot Vol. 6: The Odd & The Outrageous	681
Christmas Toy Shop	Christmas Cartoon Classic	682
Christmas Toyshop	Cartoon Classics Vol. 9: Early Pioneers	680
Christmas Visitor, The	Classic Cartoon Christmas Treasures	682
Chromosaurus	Computer Animation Classics	708
Cigarette Blues	Six Short Films of Les Blank, 1960-1985	480
Cinderella	Lotte Reiniger Compilation	713
Cinderella Barber, The	European Folk Tales, Volume 4	646
Cinderella Cinders	The Comediennes, Volume 1	397
Cinema Director	Harold Lloyd's Comedy Classics	410
Cinema Director, The	Films of Harold Lloyd—Volume 1	409
Circus	Circus/Day of Pleasure	407
Circus Baby, The	Max's Chocolate Chicken	654
Circus Today	Slapstick Encyclopedia—Vol. 7: The Rage Is On 1917-1927	411
City of Stars	Touring the Silent Studios	405
City of the Dead and the World	Julian Samuel Trilogy	474
City Slicker, The	Films of Harold Lloyd—Volume 2	409
City, The	The City/The Power and the Land	470
Clangers	BBC Children's Favorites	629
Clash of Minds, Parts 1 & 2	A Glorious Accident	782
Classic Space Ghost	Jonny Quest: Bandit—Adventure's Best Friend	698
Classic Space Ghost	Jonny Quest: Dr. Zin—Master of Evil	698
Classic Space Ghost	Jonny Quest: Hadji—Mysteries of the East	698
Classic Space Ghost	Jonny Quest: Race Bannon—An Army of One	698
Classical Warriors	Ancient Warriors	784
Classmates	Soviet War Stories from World War II	772
Cleanliness Brings Health	Animation Propaganda	706
Clever Dummy, A	Ben Turpin #1	410
Clever Dummy, A	Charley Chase and Ben Turpin	410
Clockmaker's Dream	More Melies	22
Clodhopper, The	Larry Semon #2	411
Clodhopper, The	Larry Semon #1	411
Cloisters: The Glories	Metropolitan Museum Boxed Set	553
Close Call, A	Tom & Jerry & Friends #7	688
Close Call, A	Van Beuren Studio, Volume #2	689
Close Shave, A	Wallace & Gromit Collection	717
Cloudland	Hubley Collection Vol. 3	711
Clown of God, The	Christmas Stories	631
Clown's Little Brother	Max Fleischer Presents Koko the Clown	685
Club, The	Griffiti	710
Club, The	Outrageous Animation Vol. 2	714
Coach for Cinderella, A	Great & Minor Animation Volume 3	684
Coal Face	Benjamin Britten	469
Cocktail Waiter	William Wegman Reel 4	491
Cohen Save the Flag	Mabel Normand Comedies, Vol. 2	411
Coin Toss	William Wegman Reel 2	491
Collars and Cuffs	Versatile Mr. Laurel	412
Collective Oedipal Revolution	Critical Art Ensemble	483
College	Art of Buster Keaton—Box 3	408
Color Box	Documentary Masterpieces by John Grierson	471
Color of Love, The	The Dead Man and The Color of Love	483

SHORT FILM	COMPILATION TAPE	PAGE
Come In	William Wegman Reel 1	491
Comic Zoom, A	Computer Animation Classics	708
Comicalamities	Felix the Cat: Sound & Silent	683
Commissioned Work	Griffiti	710
Concrete People	M/W/F Music Video One	433
Conductor, The	Rockin' Ronnie	281
Coney Island	Buster and Fatty	408
Confidence	Griffith Shorts (1908-09)	412
Conflict City	New Dominion Tank Police Vol. 3: Episodes 5 and 6	738
Confusions of a Nutsy Spy	Cartoon Collection Vol. 3: Coal Black & De Sebben Dwarfs	680
Congo Jazz	Cartoon Collection Vol. 5: Racial Cartoons	680
Conqueror Worm	Earthworm Jim: Conqueror Worm/Day of the Fish	696
Conquest of the North Pole, The	Marvelous Melies	22
Conquest of the North Pole, The	Films of Georges Melies, Volume 1	20
Conquest of the North Pole, The	Grand Melies (Franju) and Melies' Short Films	20
Consciousness	A Glorious Accident	782
Constable, The	Glenn Gould Plays Beethoven	590
Constant State of Departure	Nice Girls...Films by and About Women	434
Contact	Masters of Russian Animation: Volume 3	82, 713
Contest, The	Secrets of Love, Classics of Erotic Literature: Vol. 3	510
Contract	William Wegman Reel 1	491
Conujction Junction	Schoolhouse Rock: Grammar Rock	702
Conversation Pieces	New British Animation: The Best from Channel 4	714
Conversation Pieces: Early Bird	International Tournee of Animation Volume 1	711
Convict 13	Steamboat Bill Jr.	409
Coo Coo Bird, The	Woody Woodpecker 50th Anniversary Vol. 2	690
Cook in Trouble, The	More Melies	22
Cookie Carnival	Great & Minor Animation Volume 4	684
Cool Black and De Sebben Dwarfs	Cartoon Collection Vol. 3: Coal Black & De Sebben Dwarfs	680
Copernicus	Films of Charles and Ray Eames, Volume 4	485
Copper Beeches, The	The "Silent" Mr. Sherlock Holmes	187
Cops	Buster Keaton (1917-22)	408
Cops	Buster Keaton Festival Volume 1	408
Cops	Great Stone Face—Buster Keaton—Vol. 2	409
Cops	Buster Keaton	408
Copyright	William Wegman Reel 5	491
Corduroy	Corduroy Bear	651
Cori: A Struggle for Life	Video Against AIDS, Volumes 1, 2 & 3	835
Coriolis Effect	Kisses in the Dark	234
Cornell 1965	Live Short Films by Larry Jordan	718
Corner in Wheat, A	Griffith Shorts (1909-1910)	412
Corner in Wheat, A	A Corner in Wheat and Selected Biograph Shorts	412
Corner in Wheat, A	D.W. Griffith's Years of Discovery	412
Corny Casanovas	The Three Stooges: Corny Casanovas	284
Corny Concerto	Cartoon Collection Vol. 1: Porky in Wackyland	680
Corny Concerto, A	Golden Age of Looney Tunes: Vol. 4, Bob Clampett	684
Coronation, The	Third Sex Sinema Volume 2—The Song of the Loon	466
Costumes on Review	Gay for a Day	459, 472
Count and Easy Street, The	Charlie Chaplin Early Years I	407
Count, The	Classic Chaplin, Charlie Chaplin at Mutual Studios	407
Count, The	The Count and the Adventurer	407
Counter Fancy, A	CineBLAST! Vol. 2	483
Counterfeit Cat	Tex Avery's Screwball Classics 4	688
Country Cupid	Griffith Shorts (1911)	413
Country Doctor, The	Griffith Shorts (1909)	412
Country Villa, A	Secrets of Love, Classics of Erotic Literature: Vol. 1	510
County Hospital	Laurel and Hardy: Stan "Helps" Ollie	274
Courage of Collier, The	Films of Edmund Cobb	398
Courthouse Crooks	Lloyd and Chase at Keystone	411
Cow and Chicken	Jonny Quest: Dr. Zin—Master of Evil	698
Cow Who Fell in the Canal, The	Joey Runs Away and Other Stories	653
Cow, The	International Tournee of Animation Volume 4	712
Cowboy Cabaret	Van Beuren Studio, Volume #2	689
Cowgirl Sweethearts	The Athena Award 1996	456
Cowpuncher	Cartoon Classics Vol. 7: Early Animation	680
Cows, The	The Roots	52
Cramps	Cartoon Classics Vol. 7: Early Animation	680
Crazy Inventions	Cartoon Collection Vol. 8: Private Snafu	680
Crazy Like a Fox	Charley Chase Vol. 2	410
Crazy Mixed-Up Pup	Man's Best Friend	685
Crazy Town	Paramount/Famous Studios Volume 2	686
Creation, The	God's Trombones—A Trilogy	452
Creative Revolution, The	Nova—Adventures in Science: In Search of Human Origins	837
Creature Comforts	Creature Comforts	708
Creature Comforts	Spike & Mike's Festival of Animation Vol. 2	716
Creature Comforts	The World's Greatest Animation	718
Creature Comforts at Home	Spike & Mike's Festival of Animation Vol. 2	716
Credit	Video Art: Antonio Muntadas	489
Creole	I'm Not Oscar's Friend Anymore and Other Stories	635
Cricket	Art Com Video 1: Scandinavia	482
Crime of Dr. Crespi	Fugitive Road and Crime of Dr. Crespi	369
Crime Time Comix	Video Art: Dana Atchley & Eric Metcalfe	490
Critical Path	Karl Krogstad: The Gigabyte Trilogy	432
Criticize	William Wegman Reel 4	491
Crooked Finger	William Wegman Reel 3	491
Crooked Stick	William Wegman Reel 3	491
Crosby, Columbo & Vallee	All Singing, All Dancing	676
Crosby, Columbo & Vallee	Cartoon Collection Vol. 4: Warner Bros. & Fleischer	680
Cross Country Run	Aesop's Fables Volume 2	676
Cross-eyed Love	Ben Turpin #1	410
Crossroads of Life	Griffith Shorts (1908-09)	412
Cruise Cat	Tom & Jerry on Parade	689
Crusader Rabit	Pioneers in Animation Vol. 2	714
Crushed World, A	Animation Celebration Vol. 2	705
Cuckoo Clock, The	Tex Avery's Screwball Classics 4	688
Cuckoo Murder Case, The	Cartoons That Time Forgot Vol. 3: Things That Go Bump in the Night	681
Cuckoo Murder Case, The	The Monster Walks	526
Cuckoo, The	Animaland (9 Titles)	705
Culture Wars	The Question of Equality	464
Cumberland Story, The	Listen to Britain	474, 769
Cunt Dykula	She's Safe	465
Cupid Gets His Man	Cartoons That Time Forgot Vol. 7: Rainbow Parades	681
Cure, The	Unknown Chaplin, My Happiest Years	408
Cure for Pokeritis, A	Slapstick Encyclopedia—Vol. 1: In the Beginning.	411
Cure, The	Charlie Chaplin Early Years III	407
Cure, The	Classic Chaplin, Charlie Chaplin at Mutual Studios	407
Cure, The	Pioneers in Animation Vol. 1	714
Curious Cougar Kittens	Mountain Habitat Set	818
Curious George Rides a Bike	Doctor De Soto and Other Stories	632
Current Flow	She's Safe	465
Curtain Pole, The	Griffith Shorts (1908-09)	412
Custard Pies	Tom & Jerry & Friends #1	688
Custard Pies	Van Beuren Studio, Volume #1	689
Customers Wanted	Cartoon Collection Vol. 1: Porky in Wackyland	680
Cut and In	William Wegman Reel 1	491
Cut-Up Kamera	Liquid Television 2	698
Cyclops Cave, The	Heroes of the Greek Myths	784
Daffy Commando, The	Cartoon Collection Vol. 2: Classic Warner Bros.	680
Daffy Duck & the Dinosaur	Thirties Magic Vol. 2	717
Daffy Duck & the Dinosaur	Cartoon Collection Vol. 2: Classic Warner Bros.	680
Daffy Duck & the Dinosaur	Cartoon Classics in Color #4: Classic Warner Bros.	680
Daffy Duck in Hollywood	Daffy!	683
Daffy Duck in the Daffy Doc	Cartoon Collection Vol. 3: Coal Black & De Sebben Dwarfs	680
Daffy Duck Slept Here	Daffy Duck: Just Plain Daffy	682
Daffy Duckaroo	Cartoon Collection Vol. 1: Porky in Wackyland	680
Daffy Gone	Bugs & Daffy: The Wartime Cartoons	678
Daffy's Southern Exposure	Cartoon Collection Vol. 2: Classic Warner Bros.	680
Damnation of Faust	Video Art: Damnation of Faust Trilogy	490
Damnation of the Monster, The	Melies III: The Search for Munchhausen	22
Dance in Cyberspace	Eye Candy	484
Dance of the Sacred Applicatio	A Performance by Jack Smith	487, 567
Dance of the Stumblers	Computer Animation Classics	708
Dance of the Weed	MGM Cartoon Classics: Happy Harmonies	686
Dancing	Animation Celebration Vol. 4	706
Dancing on the Moon	Fleischer Color Classics	683
Dancing Tape	William Wegman Reel 5	491
Danger Ahead	Slapstick Encyclopedia—Vol. 7: The Rage Is On 1917-1927	411
Dangerous Dr. Diamond	Gigantor Vol. 3	730
Danny	Video Against AIDS, Volumes 1, 2 & 3	835
Danny and the Dinosaur	Danny and the Dinosaur and Other Stories	651
Dark Places	Holocaust (Sontag)	775
Dark Star	First Works Volume One	334
Darkness of Light Darkness	Scenes from the Surreal	715
Darling Wars	Clarissa Explains It All: "Take My Brother, Please"	631
Dash through the Clouds	Early Comedies Volume 1	410
Dash through the Clouds	Mack Sennett: The Biograph Years	411
Dating Do's and Don'ts	Sex Education Films of the 40's	510
David	Festival of Britain	471
David and the Hairy Man	Ancient Tales from a Promised Land, Vol. VI:	789
David Gets a Good Gig	Ancient Tales from a Promised Land, Vol. V:	789
David Gets to Number One	Ancient Tales from a Promised Land, Vol. VII:	789
Dawn and Twilight	Matinee Idols: The Gentlemen	401
Day at the Zoo, A	Cartoon Classics Vol. 9: Early Pioneers	680
Day Dreams	Great Stone Face—Buster Keaton—Vol. 1	409
Day Dreams	Buster Keaton	408
Day in the Country, A	Naughty Nostalgia #2	508
Day in Vietnam, A	Vietnam: Time of the Locust	778
Day Jimmy's Boa Ate the Wash	The Day Jimmy's Boa Ate the Wash	632
Day of Freedom	Terror of the Third Reich	772
Day of Freedom—Our Fighting Forces	Day of Freedom—Our Fighting Forces	68, 767
Day of Pleasure	Circus/Day of Pleasure	407
Day of the Fish	Earthworm Jim: Conqueror Worm/Day of the Fish	696
Day with the FBI, A	Short Subject Potpouri	477
Daybreak & Whiteye	Stan Brakhage Selected Films: Vol. 1	488
Daybreak Express	Jazz Shorts	612
Daydreams	Early Russian Cinema, Vol. 07: Evgenii Bauer	85
Daydreams	Buster Keaton Festival Volume 3	408
Daydreams	Steamboat Bill Jr.	409
Dead Boys Club, The	Boys' Shorts	457
Dead Man, The	The Dead Man and The Color of Love	483
Dead, The	Stan Brakhage Selected Films: Vol. 2	488
Deadtime Story	New British Animation: The Best from Channel 4	714
Dealing with Headaches	Your Family's Health, Tape 2	838
Dear Diary	Alvin and the Chipmunks: Love Potion #9	628
Death by Stalinism	Scenes from the Surreal	715
Death in Venice, CA	Boys in Love	457
Death of a Rat	Pascal Aubier Films	487
Death of Magma	Ambassador Magma Vol. 6: Episodes 12-13	720
Death Weed	Drug Propaganda and Satire Compilation	505
Death's Marathon	Griffith Shorts (1913)	413
Death's Marathon	D.W. Griffith's Years of Discovery	412
Death's Marathon	The Musketeers of Pig Alley and Selected Biograph Shorts	413
Deborah and the Headbanger	Ancient Tales from a Promised Land, Vol. II	789
December Lights	A Christmas Gift	707
Decodings	Black Sheep Boy and Decodings	457
Deduce	Porky Pig: Ham on Wry	687
Deer Tax	Tazmania: Taz-Maniac	703
Deinstag	The Best of the New York Underground, Year 2	483
Deja Vu	Computer Animation Classics	708
Dejeuner du matin	Patrick Bokanowski—Courts-Metrages	8
Delayed Date	Disney Love Tales	691
Delivery Man	Tony Vegas' Animated Acidburn Flashback Tabu	717
Delphi 1830	Delphi 1830 & Next Time Everything Will Be Better	483
Demeter and Persephone	Heroines and Goddesses of the Greek Myths	784
Dentist, The	Dental Follies	267
Dentist, The	W.C. Fields: 6 Short Films	286
Deodorant	Best of William Wegman	483
Deodorant	William Wegman Reel 3	491
Departure of a Great Old Man	Early Russian Cinema Before the Revoltuion: Vol. 8: Iakov Protazanov	85
Der Fuebrer's Face	Cartoons Go to War	681
Der Western Lebt	Just Hold Still	486
Dervish Machine	Mediamystics	487
Desert Victory	Wartime Combat	479
Design Q & A	Films of Charles and Ray Eames, Volume 4	485
Desistfilm	Stan Brakhage Selected Films: Vol. 1	488
Desperate Scoundrel	Comedy Classics of Mack Sennett and Hal Roach	410
Desperate Scoundrel, A	Early Comedies Volume 1	410
Destination Moon	Best of George Pal	677
Destro All Blondes	Destroy All Blondes/The Naked Hipstress/Sick Sick Sister	429
Destroy the Dam	Johnny Sokko and His Flying Robot: Episodes 5 and 6	734
Destruction, Inc.	Superman (50th Anniversary)	688
Detectress, The	The Comediennes, Volume 1	397

SHORT FILM	COMPILATION TAPE	PAGE
Detectress, The	Slapstick Encyclopedia—Vol. 3: Funny Girls	411
Detergent Salesman, The	Rockin' Ronnie	281
Devil May Hare	Stars of Space Jam: Five-Tape Boxed Set	687
Devotions	Films of James Broughton, Volume 4: Autobiographical Mysteries	492
Dexter's Laboratory	Jonny Quest: Race Bannon—An Army of One	698
Diagram Film	The Paul Glabicki Animation Tape	714
Dialog	Outrageous Animation Vol. 2	714
Diamond Mind	Video Art: Les Levine	490
Diamond Smugglers, The	Gigantor Vol. 3	730
Diary For Timothy, A	Listen to Britain	474, 769
Diary of a Sergeant	Nostalgia World War II Video Library #5	771
Dick Whittington's Cat	Cartoons That Time Forgot Vol. 5: Free-Form Fairytales	681
Dick Whittington's Cat	Ub Iwerks' Famous Fairytales	689
Dig	Hubley Studio: The Hole	711
Dig That Dog	Man's Best Friend	685
Digital Speech	Digital Speech and Pressures of the Text	484
Diignus Vindice Nodus	Sara Hornbacher Early Works	488
Dimensions of Dialogue	Alchemist of the Surreal	705
Dinah	Paramount/Fleischer Studios Volume 2	686
Ding Dog Daddy	Cartoon Collection Vol. 6: The Ducktators	680
Ding Dong Doggie	Thirties Magic Vol. 2	717
Dingbat Land	Great & Minor Animation Volume 4	684
Dingles	NFBC: Animation for Kids Vol. 1	714
Dingles	The Dingles	632
Dingles, The	NFBC: Cartoon Festival: The Cat Came Back	714
Dinkinsville	Tompkins Square Park, 1989/Dinkinsville	479
Dinko's Day	Spike & Mike's Festival of Animation Vol. 2	716
Dino Drive	Cadillacs and Dinosaurs: Rogue & Dino Drive	679
Dinosaur and the Missing Link	Cartoon Classics Vol. 3: The Early Pioneers	680
Dinosaur and the Missing Link	Animation Vol. 1: The Beginning	706
Dinosaur and the Missing Link	Willis O'Brien Primitives	717
Dinosaur and the Missing Link	Cartoon Classics in Color #3: Wartime Warner Bros.	679
Dinosaur and the Missing Link	The Lost World (1925)	400
Dirty Birdy	Spike & Mike's Festival of Animation Vol. 3	716
Dirty Work	Laurel and Hardy Spooktacular	274
Disco Years, The	Boy's Life	457
Discoveries	Spike & Mike's Sick & Twisted Festival of Animation, Vol. 1	716
Disorder in the Court	The Three Stooges	284
Displaced Dice	CineBLAST! Vol. 3	428
Dissatisfied Cobbler	Aesop's Fables Volume 3	676
Disturbing the Universe	A Glorious Accident	782
Ditch in Time, A	Tiny Toon BIG Adventures	688
Ditto	Buster Keaton Talkies, Vol. 6	408
Diving Board	William Wegman Reel 2	491
Dixie Days	Tom & Jerry & Friends #4	688
Dizzy Day, A	Tom & Jerry & Friends #2	688
Dizzy Heights	Cannonball/Dizzy Heights	410
Dizzy Heights and Daring Heart	Comedy of Chester Conklin	410
Dizzy Red Riding Hood	Cartoon Collection Vol. 4: Warner Bros. & Fleischer	680
Do You Want To?	William Wegman Reel 3	491
Doctor De Soto	Doctor De Soto and Other Stories	632
Doctor Joke	William Wegman Reel 7	491
Doctor's Secret, The	Marvelous Melies	22
Doctors, Liars and Women: AIDS Activists Say "No" to Cosmo	Video Against AIDS, Volumes 1, 2 & 3	833, 835
Dodge Your Debts	Films of Harold Lloyd—Volume 3	410
Dog & the Devil, The	International Tournee of Animation Volume 2	712
Dog and Turtle Story, The	Tazmania: Taz-Manimals	704
Dog Collared	Porky Pig Tales	687
Dog Duet	William Wegman Reel 6	491
Dog Gone South	Looney Tunes Assorted Nuts	685
Dog Napper, The	Mickey Mouse: The Black & White Years	693
Dog Pile	Spike & Mike's Sick & Twisted Festival of Animation, Vol. 1	716
Dog Pile II	Spike & Mike's Sick & Twisted Festival of Animation, Vol. 2	716
Dog Show Off	Little Lulu (Cartoonies)	685
Dog Shy	Charley Chase Vol. 2	410
Dog Tax Dodgers	Man's Best Friend	685
Dog's Life, A	Chaplin Revue	407
Dogma Palace	Astro Boy Volume 7	722
Dogonne Tired	Great & Minor Animation Volume 1	684
Dogs of War	Slapstick Encyclopedia—Vol. 6: Hal Roach: The Lot of Fun	411
Doing Peacemaking	People of Faith and the Arms Race	805
Doll House	Lesbian Humor	461, 492
Dome Doctor	Larry Semon #2	411
Don from Lakewood	Don from Lakewood/You Talk, I Buy	429
Don Quixote	Cartoons That Time Forgot Vol. 4: Willie Whopper's Fantastic Adventures	681
Don Quixote	Classic Stories in Spanish	672
Don't Axe Me	Daffy Duck: Duck Victory	682
Don't Shove	Early Comedies Volume 2	410
Don't Shove	Films of Harold Lloyd—Volume 3	410
Donald's Double Trouble	Mickey Loves Minnie	693
Donkey Tricks	Aesop's Fables Volume 3	676
Donkey Tricks	Tom & Jerry & Friends #7	688
Door to Door	Droits au Coeur (Rights from the Heart)	709
Door, The	William Wegman Reel 1	491
Dora's Dunkin Donuts	Shirley Temple and Friends	282
Double Cinched	The Films of Leo Maloney	368
Double Danger	Jonny Quest: Race Bannon—An Army of One	698
Double Entente	Teasers	466
Double Strength	Lesbian Sexuality	462, 492
Double, The	The Works of Ken Feingold—Names in Search of a Body	492
Doublecross	Variety Is the Spice of Life	489
Doug	Frightfest, Nickelodeon	696
Doug's Dinner Date	Doug Vol. 2: Patti, You're the Mayonnaise for Me	709
Doug's Fair Lady	Doug Vol. 2: Patti, You're the Mayonnaise for Me	709
Doug's Out in Left Field	Doug Vol. 2: Patti, You're the Mayonnaise for Me	709
Dough and Dynamite	Keystones #3	407
Dove, The	Experimental Avant Garde Series Volume 19 (Very Serious Fun)	484
Dove, The	Classic Foreign Shorts—Volume 1	153
Down from Mach 2	Dangard Ace	726
Down on the River	She's Safe	465
Down Time	William Wegman Reel 4	491
Downhearted Duckling	Tom & Jerry's Comic Capers	689
Dr. Bed Bug	Best of the Fests 1990	706

SHORT FILM	COMPILATION TAPE	PAGE
Dr. Devil and Mr. Hare	Stars of Space Jam: Five-Tape Boxed Set	687
Dr. Devil and Mr. Hare	Bugs Bunny: Truth or Hare	679
Dr. Paglia	Female Misbehavior	63, 459
Dr. Simon	Alvin and the Chipmunks: Love Potion #9	628
Dr. Stupid	Ren & Stimpy: Nothing But Shorts	701
Dracalon	Johnny Sokko and His Flying Robot: Episodes 1 and 2	734
Dragon	Johnny Sokko and His Flying Robot: Episodes 7 and 8	734
Dragon Formation...Switch On	Starvengers	748
Dragon's Teeth, The	Monsters of the Greek Myths	637
Drama in a Gypsy Camp	Early Russian Cinema: Before the Revolution, Vol. 2: Folklore and Legend	85
Draw	The Tune	717
Drawing Lesson	More Melies	22
Drawing Lesson #2	Plymptoons: The Complete Works of Bill Plympton	715
Drawing on My Mind	International Tournee of Animation Volume 2	712
Dreaded Wheat	Moron Movies	508
Dream	Classic Shorts Compilation #12: Winsor McCay	682
Dream Documentary	House of Un-American Activities	473
Dream Flower	Experimental Avant Garde Series Volume 23	484
Dream of a Rarebit Fiend	American Avant-Garde Films	482
Dream of a Rarebit Fiend	Animation Vol. 2	706
Dreammaker	CineBLAST! Vol. 3	428
Dreams From China	House of Un-American Activities	473
Dress Curtain	William Wegman Reel 1	491
Drifters	E.M.B. Classics	471
Drinking Milk	William Wegman Reel 5	491
Drinking Water	Wartime Cartoons	717
Droids: The Pirates and the Prince	Star Wars Droids: The Pirates and The Prince	703
Drop It	William Wegman Reel 7	491
Drugstore, The	The Abbott and Costello Television Show, Tape 4	414
Drummer Hoff	Five Stories for the Very Young	652
Drummer of the Eighth	Films of Thomas Ince	398
Drumstix	Pictures Don't Tell You Anything: Selected Films of Ann Marie Fleming	211, 487
Drunkard's Reformation, A	Griffith Shorts (1908-09)	412
Dry and Thirsty	Slapstick Encyclopedia—Vol. 8: Tons of Fun: Comedy's Anarchic Fringe	411
Dual Function	William Wegman Reel 3	491
Duck Amuck	Bugs Bunny/Roadrunner Movie	679
Duck Amuck	Daffy Duck: Duck Victory	682
Duck and Cover	Atomic Memories	802
Duck Dinner	The Abbott and Costello Television Show, Tape 1	414
Duck Dodgers	Daffy Duck's Thanks-For-Giving Special	682
Duck Dodgers	Daffy Duck: Duck Victory	682
Duck Hunt	Mickey Mouse: The Black & White Years	693
Duck in the Dark	Tiny Toon Fiendishly Funny Adventures	688
Duck Soup to Nuts	Daffy Duck: Just Plain Daffy	682
Duck! Rabbit! Duck!	Daffy Duck: Duck Victory	682
Duck, Babysitter	Maurice Sendak's Little Bear—Parties & Picnics	637
Duckators, The	Cartoon Collection Vol. 6: The Ducktators	680
Ducking the Devil	Stars of Space Jam: Five-Tape Boxed Set	687
Ducksters, The	Porky Pig: Ham on Wry	687
Duel Over Korea	Wings of the Red Star	845
Duet	Best of William Wegman	483
Duo Concertantes	Short Animations by Larry Jordan	718
Dutch Nelson	CineBLAST! Vol. 3	428
Duxorcist, The	Bugs Bunny's Creature Features	678
Duxorcist, The	Daffy Duck's Quackbusters	682
Dyke TV & Network Q	Gay Games IV from A to Q	459, 826
Dyketactics	Lesbian Sexuality	462, 492
Dynamics Of Power, The	Between the Wars, 1918-1941, Vol. 4	808
Eagle Ceak	Biggest and the Best	860
Early Worm Gets the Bird, The	Cartoon Collection Vol. 7: Tokyo Jokio	680
Earth Quake!	Fearless Fortune Hunter	683
Easter Yeggs	Bugs Bunny's Comedy Classics	678
Eastern Westerner	Harold Lloyd Comedies Vol. 3	410
Easy Does It	Animation Propaganda	706
Easy Street	Classic Chaplin, Charlie Chaplin at Mutual Studios	407
Easy Street	Emerging Chaplin	407
Eating on the Cuff	Cartoon Collection Vol. 3: Coal Black & De Sebben Dwarfs	680
Eaux d'Artifice	Fireworks	485
Ecco Homo	A.I.D.S.C.R.E.A.M., Ecce Homo and Final Solutions	456, 482
Echo Anthem	6 Films by Mark Street	482
Eclipse, The	Films of Georges Melies, Volume 1	20
Effects of Atomic Bomb Explosion	Atomic Memories	802
Egg Salad	CineBLAST! Vol. 3	428
Eggnog	Karl Krogstad Films	432
Eggs	Hubley Studio: Voyage to Next	711
Ego	Bruno Bozzetto: Animator, Vol. 1	707
Eisenhower Spots	Cartoongate!	681
Elastic Party	Art Com Video 1: Scandinavia	482
Elbert's Bad Word	Shelley Duvall's Bedtime Stories: Elbert's Bad Word and Weird Parents	657
Elbows	William Wegman Reel 1	491
Eldorado	Outrageous Animation Vol. 2	714
Electric Horse	Buster Keaton Festival Volume 2	408
Electric House	College	409
Electrical Earthquake	Superman (50th Anniversary)	688
Elephants	Video Art: Noel Harding	490
Eleventh Hour	Superman (50th Anniversary)	688
Elizabeth and Larry	Shelley Duvall's Bedtime Stories: Elizabeth and Larry and Bill and Pete	657
Ella Cinders	Ella Cinders and Mormon Maid	398
Ellis Island	Cityscape Compilations	470
Ellis Island	The Films of Meredith Monk	485, 567
Elmer's Candid Camera	Elmer!	683
Emak Bakia	Avant Garde Program #14	483
Emak Bakia	Avant Garde Shorts/France	483
Emak Bakia	Man Ray Video	486
Emergence of Eunice	Nice Girls...Films by and About Women	434
Emily's Song	CineBLAST! Vol. 3	428
Emperor's New Clothes, The	The Emperor's New Clothes and Other Folktales	646
Emperor's New Clothes, The	Katharine Hepburn: World of Stories	647
Emperor's New Clothes, The	Victor Borge Tells Hans Christian Andersen Stories	649
Emporer and Dish	William Wegman Reel 3	491
Empty Roll	Spike & Mike's Sick & Twisted Festival of Animation, Vol. 3	716
Enchanted Square, The	Paramount/Famous Studios Volume 1	686

SHORT FILM	COMPILATION TAPE	PAGE
Enchanted Well, The	Grand Melies (Franju) and Melies' Short Films	20
Enchanted Well, The	Marvelous Melies	22
End Memory	Letterist Films—Woman, Women!	432
End of Summer	Award Winning French Shorts	2
End the Dreaming	New Dominion Tank Police Vol. 3: Episodes 5 and 6	738
Endangered	Optical Nerves	463, 492
Energies	Jim Davis: Volume #2	486
Energy and How to Get It	It's Clean—It Just Looks Dirty	486
Energy Carol, The	NFBC—Cartoon Festival: The Sweater	714
Energy Carol, The	A Christmas Gift	707
Energy Carol, The	NFBC: Christmas Cracker	714
English Speaking World, An	Story of English	860
Enjoy Yourself: It's Later	Palazzolo's Chicago	476
Enoch Arden	Griffith Shorts (1911)	413
Enoch Arden	The Short Films of D.W. Griffith—Volume 4	413
Enormous Lies	European Folk Tales, Volume 5	646
Enough to Do	Films of Oliver Hardy	410
Enter Captain Mask	Dangard Ace	726
Enter Life	Hubley Collection Vol. 1	711
Entertainment and Industry	Rare Black Short Subjects	448
Entr'acte	Avant Garde Program #2	482
Entr'acte	Le Petit Theatre de Jean Renoir	26
Ephemeral Solidity	Stan Brakhage—Hand-Painted Films	488
Epic of Gilgamesh	The Brothers Quay Vol. 2	707
Equinox Dance/Polyglot Robot	Sara Hornbacher Early Works	488
Erection	Guido Manuli: Animator	710
Erection	Outrageous Animation Vol. 2	714
Ernestine: Peak Experiences	Lily Tomlin 3-Pack	462, 535
Erogeny	Films of James Broughton, Volume 1: Erotic Celebrations	492
Erotic Psyche	Potato Wolf Spring 1984	435
Et Cetera	Alchemist of the Surreal	705
Eugene	Kovacs & Keaton	409, 535
Eugene the Jeep	Cartoon Collection Vol. 1: Porky in Wackyland	680
Eurhythmy	Computer Animation Classics	708
Eve's Love Letters	Comedy Shorts #4	410
Every Child	NFBC: Every Child	714
Every Child	Incredible Animation Collection: Vol. 2	711
Every Dog's Guide to Complete	NFBC: Cartoon Festival: Cactus Swing	714
Every Dog's Guide to Home Safe	NFBC: Animation for Kids Vol. 1	714
Every Dog's Guide to Playground	NFBC: Animation for Kids Vol. 1	714
Every Dog's Guide to Playground	The National Film Board of Canada's Animation Festival	714
Every Inch a Man	Matinee Idols: The Gentlemen	401
Everything Turns, Everything	Hans Richter: Early Avant-Garde Films	485
Evil Cleric, The	Tear Jerker	489
Evils of Alcohol, The	Cartoon Classics Vol. 6: Early Animation	680
Evils of Alcohol, The	The Genesis of Animation, Volume One	710
Evolution	Incredible Animation Collection: Vol. 2	711
Evolution	Puppets & Demons: Films by Patrick McGuinn	436
Ex Voto	Viva Eu! & Ex Voto	467, 491
Exhumation	Gulag Archipelago	92
Excursion to the Bridge	Women from Down Under	467
Excursions	6 Films by Mark Street	482
Exercise for Fat Ears	Moron Movies	508
Existentialist, The	Classic Foreign Shorts—Volume 1	153
Expiration Date	Too Outrageous Animation	717
Exposition	Fatty Arbuckle	410
Exterior Night	Three Short Films (Mark Rappaport)	438
Extra Man & the Milk Fed Lion	Early Westerns #2	398
Extraordinary Illusions	Grand Melies (Franju) and Melies' Short Films	20
Eyes of Ray	William Wegman Reel 6	491
Eyes Without Blood	It's Clean—It Just Looks Dirty	486
F.D.R.	Portraits from the Past	810
F.D.R. & Hitler: Rise to Power	Between the Wars, 1918-1941, Vol. 4	808
Fable of the Alley Cat	Aesop's Fables Volume 1	676
Fable of the Jolly Rounders	Aesop's Film Fables	676
Face on the Barroom Floor	Keystones #3	407
Face Value	Biggest and the Best	860
Faerie Film	Men in Shorts, Volume 2	463
Fahnen Junker	Fahnen Junker	69, 767
Failure	Griffith Shorts (1911-1912)	413
Fair Haired Hare, The	Bugs Bunny: Winner by a Hare	679
Fair Haired Hare, The	Bugs Bunny: Truth or Hare	679
Fair Play	Computer Animation Classics	708
Fair Weather Friend, The	Human Race Club: A Story About Making Friends, a Story About Prejudice and Discrimination	635
Faith and Patience	Best of the Fests, 5th Annual	706
Fall of the House of Usher	American Avant-Garde	482
Fallacies of Hope, The	Civilization, Programs 11 & 12	781
Falling Hare	Cartoon Classics in Color #2: Fleischer/Warners	679
Falling Hare	Cartoon Collection Vol. 2: Classic Warner Bros.	680
Falling Hare	Bugs Bunny's Comedy Classics	678
False Vases	Felix the Cat: Sound & Silent	683
False Vases	Thirties Magic Vol. 2	717
Family for Maria, A	Droits au Coeur (Rights from the Heart)	709
Family Life	Selected Shorts #2	403
Family Life	Slapstick Encyclopedia—Vol. 8: Tons of Fun: Comedy's Anarchic Fringe	411
Family Portrait	Festival of Britain	471
Fan-Tasy	CineBLAST! Vol. 3	428
Fan-tasy	Computer Animation Showcase	708
Fanaround	Best of the Fests: For Kids	706
Fancy Dress Parade	Jane Hissey's Old Bear Stories: Happy Birthday Old Bear	653
Fantabiblical	Guido Manuli: Animator	710
Fantasmagoria	Animation Vol. 1: The Beginning	706
Fantasy on London Life, A	Animaland	705
Farm Foolery	Paramount/Fleischer Studios Volume 3	686
Farmer Al Falfa's Wayward Pup	Cartoon Classics Vol. 3: The Early Pioneers	680
Fast and Furry-ous	Stars of Space Jam: Five-Tape Boxed Set	687
Fast Food	Classics in Clay	707
Fast Food Matador	International Tournee of Animation Volume 5	712
Fastest Claw in the West, The	BBC Wildlife Specials: Aliens from Inner Space/ The Fastest Claw in the West	813
Fat and the Lean	Fat and the Lean	97
Fat and the Lean	Classic Foreign Shorts—Volume 2	153
Fatal Attraction	The Incredible Story of Dogs	816
Fatal Glass of Beer, The	W.C. Fields: 6 Short Films	286
Fatal Mallet, The	Keystones #2	407
Fates Turning	Griffith Shorts (1910-1911)	413
Fatherhood of Buck McKee	Early Westerns #1	397
Father's Hatband	Norma Talmadge Films	402
Fatt's Plucky Pup	Arbuckle Volume 3	410
Fatty & Mabel at San Francisco	Mabel Normand, Vol. 1	411
Fatty & Mabel at the San Diego	Arbuckle Volume 3	410
Fatty & Mabel at the San Diego	Fatty Arbuckle	410
Fatty & Mabel's Simple Life	Arbuckle Volume 3	410
Fatty & Mabel's Simple Life	Fatty Arbuckle	410
Fatty & Mabel's Smash Day	Arbuckle Volume 3	410
Fatty and Mabel Adrift	Mabel Normand Comedies, Vol. 1	411
Fatty and Mabel Adrift	Slapstick Encyclopedia—Vol. 4: Keaton, Arbuckle & Al St. John	411
Fatty and the Law	Arbuckle Volume 3	410
Fatty at Coney Island	Buster Keaton	408
Fatty's Faithful Fido	Fatty Arbuckle	410
Fatty's New Role	Arbuckle Volume 3	410
Fatty's New Role	Fatty Arbuckle	410
Faust	Video Art: Damnation of Faust Trilogy	490
Faxion	X-Rated: Movieyeur	439
FDR and Churchill	Between the Wars, 1918-1941, Vol. 7	808
Fearless Harry	Adventures of Hairbreadth Harry	395
Feathered Follies	Tom & Jerry & Friends #1	688
Feeling Anything Being Existing	Four Directions: Selections from MIX 94— The NY Lesbian & Gay Film Festival	459
Feet of Mud	Films of Harry Langdon Volume 2	410
Feet of Song	New British Animation: The Best from Channel 4	714
Feet of Song	Spike & Mike's Festival of Animation Vol. 1	716
Feline Follies (1919)	Felix!	683
Felix All Puzzled	Classic Shorts Compilation #14: Felix the Cat	682
Felix and the Goose that Laid	Cartoons That Time Forgot Vol. 7: Rainbow Parades	681
Felix Busts a Bustle	Felix the Cat—Silent—Volume 2	683
Felix Dines and Pines	Classic Shorts Compilation #14: Felix the Cat	682
Felix Gets Broadcast	Classic Shorts Compilation #14: Felix the Cat	682
Felix Goes West	Classic Shorts Compilation #14: Felix the Cat	682
Felix in Fairyland	Animation Vol. 2	706
Felix in Fairyland	Classic Shorts Compilation #14: Felix the Cat	682
Felix in Fairyland	Felix the Cat—Silent—Volume 1	683
Felix in Hollywood	Animation Vol. 1: The Beginning	706
Felix in Hollywood	Felix!	683
Felix in Hollywood	Felix the Cat—Silent—Volume 1	683
Felix Minds the Kid	Felix the Cat: Sound & Silent	683
Felix Pines	Felix the Cat—Silent—Volume 1	683
Felix Revolts	Felix the Cat: Sound & Silent	683
Felix Saves the Day	Felix!	683
Felix Switches Witches	Felix the Cat—Silent—Volume 2	683
Felix the Cat and the Goose	Cartoon Collection Vol. 6: The Ducktators	680
Felix the Cat in Bold King Cole	Cartoons That Time Forgot Vol. 7: Rainbow Parades	681
Felix the Cat: April Maze	Cartoon Classics Vol. 5: The Other Studios	680
Felix Turns the Tide	Classic Shorts Compilation #14: Felix the Cat	682
Felix Turns the Tide	Felix the Cat—Silent—Volume 2	683
Felix Whoos Whoppie	Felix the Cat—Silent—Volume 1	683
Felix Wins Out	Felix the Cat—Silent—Volume 1	683
Felix Woos Whoopee	Felix!	683
Female of the Species, The	The Short Films of Mary Pickford	404
Female of the Species, The	Griffith Shorts (1912, #1)	413
Female of the Species, The	D.W. Griffith's Years of Discovery	412
Females Is Fickle	Cartoon Collection Vol. 4: Warner Bros. & Fleischer	680
Ferdinand the Bull	Willie, The Operatic Whale	694
Fiberglass Chairs, The	Films of Charles and Ray Eames, Volume 4	485
Fiddlers Three	The Three Stooges: Wee Wee Monsieur	284
Fiddlesticks!	Cartoons That Time Forgot Vol. 1: All Singing! All Dancing!	681
Fiddlin' Around	Babe Hardy: Early Training	410
Field of Honor	First Works Volume One	334
Fieldmouse, The	MGM Cartoon Classics: Happy Harmonies	686
Fields of Honey	Tiny Toon Adventures Vol. 3: Tiny Toons in Two-Tone Town	688
Fifth Army Report	Nostalgia World War II Video Library #11	771
Fight for the Sky, The	Nostalgia World War II Video Library #9	771
Fight it Out	Early Westerns #1	397
Fighting Blood	Griffith Shorts (1911)	413
Fighting Fluid	Charley Chase Jimmy Jump Series	410
Fighting Tools	Wartime Cartoons	717
Filly, The	The Roots	52
Film Film Film	Masters of Russian Animation: Volume 1	82, 713
Film Film Film	Masters of Russian Animation: Volume 6—The Works	82, 713
Film Johnny, A	Keystones #1	407
Film Spectators are Quiet Vamp	M/W/F Music Video One	433
Film Study (Filmstudie)	Hans Richter: Early Avant-Garde Films	485
Film with Three Dancers	Films by Ed Emshwiller	484
Film-Wipe-Film	The Paul Glabicki Animation Tape	714
Final Assault: F-16 Falcon	Wings over the Gulf: Complete Set	845
Final Call	Erotique	430
Final Solutions	A.I.D.S.C.R.E.A.M., Ecce Homo and Final Solutions	456, 482
Fine Feathered Friend	Tom & Jerry's Cartoon Cavalcade	689
Finger Food	Spike & Mike's Sick & Twisted Festival of Animation, Vol. 2	716
Fire Fighters	Mickey Mouse: The Black & White Years	693
Fire Station, The	Angela's Airplane (plus The Fire Station)	649
Fire Walking in Greece	Ancient Greece Volume 2	784
Firechief	William Wegman Reel 1	491
Firedogs	Ren & Stimpy in Disguise	701
Fireman's Life, A	Tom & Jerry & Friends #3	688
Fireman, The	Classic Chaplin, Charlie Chaplin at Mutual Studios	407
Fireman, The	Charlie Chaplin Early Years IV	407
Fireworks	Fireworks	485
Firing Range	Masters of Russian Animation: Volume 7	82, 713
First Aid	Wartime Cartoons	717
First Romantic Picture, The	Art on Film/Film on Art, Program 2: Film Sense/Art Sense	545
First Salt Talks	Between the Wars, 1918-1941, Vol. 2	808
First Snow, The	Fox Terrytoons	684
First Strike: F-15 Eagle	Wings over the Gulf: Complete Set	845
Fish Factory In Astrakhan, A	Early Russian Cinema: Before the Revolution, Vol. 1: Beginnings	85
Fisher Folks	Griffith Shorts (1910-1911)	413
Fisherman's Luck	Tom & Jerry & Friends #7	688
Fishing Bear, The	MGM Cartoon Classics: Happy Harmonies	686
Fishing Line, The	Steam Days: Travels with a Duchess and the Fishing Line	844
Fishmind	CineBLAST! Vol. 1	483

SHORT FILM	COMPILATION TAPE	PAGE
Fit to be Tied	Tom & Jerry's Comic Capers	689
Five Chinese Brother, The	The Mysterious Tadpole and Other Stories	638
Five Improvisations	The Paul Glabicki Animation Tape	714
Five Secrets in a Box	Picturebook Classics: Complete Set	639
Flamethrowers, The	Matthias Muller—Selected Films	433
Flashback	Pascal Aubier Films	487
Flat Heads	Great & Minor Animation Volume 2	684
Fleet that Came to Stay, The	Nostalgia World War II Video Library #6	771
Flesh of Morning	Stan Brakhage Selected Films: Vol. 1	488
Flieger Am Feind (Nazi Newsreel)	Nazis...Lest We Forget!	770
Flip about Flip	Small Gauge Shotgun	488
Flip Flap	Great & Minor Animation Volume 4	684
Flip's Circus	Winsor McCay: Animation Legend	718
Flipper	Art Com Video 14: Rebel Girls	482
Flo's Discipline	Matinee Idols: The Ladies	401
Floating	New Directors: New Short Films	487
Floorwalker, The	Charlie Chaplin Early Years III	407
Floorwalker, The	Classic Chaplin, Charlie Chaplin at Mutual Studios	407
Floorwalker, The	Emerging Chaplin	407
Florida Enchantment, A	The Patchwork Girl of Oz/A Florida Enchantment	402
Fluttering Hearts	Slapstick Encyclopedia—Vol. 6: Hal Roach: The Lot of Fun	411
Flying Bear, The	MGM Cartoon Classics: Happy Harmonies	686
Flying Fur	Griffiti	710
Flying Hoofs	Aesop's Fables Volume 1	676
Flying House	A Tribute to Winsor McCay	717
Flying House, The	Animation Vol. 2	706
Flying Sorceress	Tom & Jerry's Comic Capers	689
Foney Fables	Cartoon Collection Vol. 6: The Ducktators	680
Food for Thought	Tazmania: Taz-Maniac	703
Fool Coverage	Stars of Space Jam: Five-Tape Boxed Set	687
Fool's Choice, The	Orguss 02, Vol. 1	739
Foolish Frog, The	Strega Nonna and Other Stories	649
Foot Book, The	One Fish Two Fish Red Fish Blue Fish, Spanish Narration	655
Foot Book, The	One Fish Two Fish Red Fish Blue Fish, English Narration	655
For His Son	The Female of the Species & Selected Biograph Shorts (Volume III)	412
For His Son	Griffith Shorts (1911-1912)	413
For His Son	D.W. Griffith's Years of Discovery	412
For Luck	Early Russian Cinema, Vol. 10: The End of an Era	85
Force of Terror	Gigantor Vol. 3	730
Forgotten Sweeties	Charley Chase Vol. 1	410
Fork on a Filling	Karl Krogstad: Temple, Fork & Jack in the Fox	432
Forty Winks	Early Animation Vol. 2	709
Forty Winks	Felix the Cat—Silent—Volume 2	683
Forty Winks	Felix the Cat: Sound & Silent	683
Forward March Hare	Stars of Space Jam: Five-Tape Boxed Set	687
Four Dragon Kings Take	Sohryuden Vol. 6: Episodes 11 and 12	746
Four Gun Bandit	Early Westerns #1	397
Four in the Afternoon	Films of James Broughton, Volume 2: Rituals of Play	492
Four Wishes, The	Too Outrageous Animation	717
Four Wishes, The	Outrageous Animation Vol. 1	714
Fourteen Rats & a Rat-Catcher	The Three Robbers and Other Stories	643
Fourteen Rats & a Rat-Catcher	The Day Jimmy's Boa Ate the Wash	632
Fox and the Crow, The	Aesop & His Friends	645
Fox Hunt	Fox Terrytoons	684
Fox-Trot Finesse	Slapstick Encyclopedia—Vol. 1: In the Beginning	411
Foxhat, The	Wings of the Red Star	845
Fractasia	Eye Candy	484
Fraidy Cat	Charley Chase Jimmy Jump Series	410
Framed	Homage to May 19th/Framed	473
Frank Lloyd Wright: Taliesin-E	Jim Davis: Volume #1	486
Frank Lloyd Wright: Taliesin-W	Jim Davis: Volume #1	486
Frankenweenie	Frankenweenie	255
Frannie's Christmas	Spike & Mike's Festival of Animation Vol. 3	716
Frantic Atlantic	Timon and Pumbaa's Wild Adventures: Quit Buggin' Me	694
Frauds & Frenzies	Stan Laurel: At the Beginning	411
Frauds and Frenzies	Larry Semon #3	411
Freddie the Freshman	All Singing, All Dancing	676
Freddie the Freshman	Early Warner Brothers Cartoons	683
Freddie the Freshman	Cartoon Classics Vol. 1: Looney Tunes & Merrie Melodies	680
Fredericksburg	Civil War Journal, Set II	779
Freedom Comes High	Nostalgia World War II Video Library #11	771
French Performance	Simultaneous	488
Frescade	Karl Krogstad: Eggnog, Gazebo, Frescade	432
Fresh Hare	Cartoon Collection Vol. 2: Classic Warner Bros.	680
Fresh Hare	Cartoon Classics in Color #4: Classic Warner Bros.	680
Fresh Vegetable Mystery, The	Fleischer Color Classics	683
Fresh Vegetable Mystery, The	Cartoon Classics Vol. 9: Early Pioneers	680
Fresh Vegetable Mystery, The	Paramount/Fleischer Studios Volume 1	686
Friend Of Dorothy, A	Boy's Life	457
Friendly Ghost, The	Glenn Gould Plays Beethoven	590
Friendly Ghost, The	Cartoon Collection Vol. 1: Porky in Wackyland	680
Friendly Ghost, The	Paramount/Famous Studios Volume 1	686
Friends	Griffith Shorts (1912, #2)	413
Fright Before Christmas, The	Stars of Space Jam: Five-Tape Boxed Set	687
Fright to the Finish	The Adventures of Popeye, Vol. 2	676
Frog Crossing	CineBLAST! Vol. 2	483
Frog Prince, The	Classic Stories for Children	651
Frog Prince, The	Lotte Reiniger Compilation	713
Frog, The	International Tournee of Animation Volume 2	712
Frogland	The Cameraman's Revenge: The Amazing Puppet Animation of Ladislaw Starewicz	707
From Chaos to Chronos	Dawn of the Greek Gods	784
From Hand to Mouth	Films of Harold Lloyd—Volume 5	410
Frowning Prince, The	Alice in Wonderland in Paris	705
Frozen North	Battling Butler	408
Frozen North	Buster Keaton Festival Volume 2	408
Fugitive Road	Fugitive Road and Crime of Dr. Crespi	369
Fugitive, The	Griffith Shorts (1910-1911)	413
Full Circle	Video Art: Gary Hill	490
Full of Grace	Outrageous Animation Vol. 1	714
Funderary Painting of Roman	Art on Film/Film on Art, Program 1: Balance: Film/Art	545
Funeral of Vera Kholodnaia	Early Russian Cinema: Before the Revolution, Vol. 09: High Society	85
Fungus Eroticus	Mediamystics	487
Funny Face	Cartoon Classics Vol. 9: Early Pioneers	680
Funny Face	Cartoons That Time Forgot Vol. 2: Down & Out with Flip the Frog	681

SHORT FILM	COMPILATION TAPE	PAGE
Funshine State	Gabby (Cartoonies)	684
Furniture	William Wegman Reel 6	491
Further Adventures of Super	Sextoons: An Erotic Animation Festival	715
Future Shock	Eye Candy	484
Futuritzy	Classic Shorts Compilation #14: Felix the Cat	682
Futuritzy	Felix!	683
Gab	Video Against AIDS, Volumes 1, 2 & 3	835
Gabby Goes Fishing	Great & Minor Animation Volume 4	684
Gahan Wilson's	International Tournee of Animation Volume 6	712
Gai Dimanche	Gai Dimanche/Swing to the Left	28
Galaxy Guy	CineBLAST! Vol. 3	428
Gallopin' Gaucho	Mickey Mouse: The Black & White Years	693
Galloping Hooves	Tom & Jerry & Friends #4	688
Gambler, The	Gold of Naples	38
Gangor, The Monster	Astro Boy Volume 6	722
Gangster, The	Rockin' Ronnie	281
Garage, The	Buster Keaton (1917-22)	408
Garage, The	Buster Keaton Festival Volume 3	408
Garage, The	Slapstick Encyclopedia—Vol. 4: Keaton, Arbuckle & Al St. John	411
Garbage in Garbage Out	International Tournee of Animation Volume 2	712
Garden	Tom Chomont: A Two-Volume Collection, Volume II	466, 489
Gardener of Eden, The	Films of James Broughton, Volume 5: Parables of Wonder	492
Gargoyle Vine	Johnny Sokko and His Flying Robot: Episodes 3 and 4	734
Gaucho, The	Douglas Fairbanks Sr. Collection	397
Gay Cable Network	Gay Games IV from A to Q	459, 826
Gay Entertainment Television	Gay Games IV from A to Q	459, 826
Gay for a Day	Gay for a Day	459, 472
Gazebo By the Sea	Karl Krogstad: Eggnog, Gazebo, Frescade	432
Gee Whiz-z-z-z	Stars of Space Jam: Five-Tape Boxed Set	687
General, The	Art of Buster Keaton—Box 3	408
General, The	Buster Keaton	408
Generation Q	The Question of Equality	464
Generic Metal Titan	CineBLAST! Vol. 2	483
Gents Without Cents	The Three Stooges: A Pain in the Pullman	284
Geologic Time	Best of the Fests 1990	706
George and Rosemary	National Film Board of Canada's Animation Festival	714
Georgie	What's Under My Bed and Other Creepy Stories	659
Gertie	Animation Vol. 2	706
Gertie	Cartoon Classics Vol. 7: Early Animation	680
Gertie on Tour	Winsor McCay: Animation Legend	718
Gertie the Dinosaur	Animation Vol. 1: The Beginning	706
Gertie the Dinosaur	Classic Shorts Compilation #12: Winsor McCay	682
Gertie the Dinosaur	A Tribute to Winsor McCay	717
Gertie the Dinosaur	Winsor McCay: Animation Legend	718
Get a Haircut	International Tournee of Animation Volume 6	712
Get a Job	National Film Board of Canada's Animation Festival	714
Get a Job	Incredible Animation Collection: Vol. 2	711
Get Lost! Little Doggy	Man's Best Friend	685
Get Out and Get Under	Slapstick Encyclopedia—Vol. 6: Hal Roach: The Lot of Fun	411
Get Ready to March	Chip Lord: Selected Works	428
Get Rich Quick, Porky	Cartoon Collection Vol. 8: Private Snafu	680
Get Rich Quick, Porky	Cartoon Classics Vol. 2: Warner Brothers	680
Get Your Adverbs Here	Schoolhouse Rock: Grammar Rock	702
Get Your Man	Early Westerns #2	398
Getting a Job	The Abbott and Costello Television Show, Tape 2	414
Getting Started	NFBC: Leonard Maltin's Animation Favorites from the National Film Board of Canada	714
Getting Started	Incredible Manitoba Animation	711
Getting There	International Tournee of Animation Volume 5	712
Getting to Know Maurice Sendak	The Maurice Sendak Library	654
Ghost of the Canyon, The	Railroad Dramas	403
Ghost Talks, The	The Three Stooges: Heavenly Daze	284
Ghost Town: The Fort Lee Story	Touring the Silent Studios	405
Ghost, The	Pinchas Zukerman: Here to Make Music/The Ghost	593
Ghosts Before Breakfast	Experimental Avant Garde Series Volume 20 (The Secret Lives of Inanimate Objects)	484
Ghosts Before Breakfast	Hans Richter: Give Chance a Chance	63, 485
Ghosts Before Breakfast	Hans Richter: Early Avant-Garde Films	485
Giant Cobra, The	Gigantor Retrospective 30 Vol. 5	730
Giant Land	Mickey Mouse: The Black & White Years	693
Giant Woman & the Lightning	Magicians of the Earth	552
Gibson Goddess, The	Griffith Shorts (1909)	412
Gideon Gets His Wolly Wet	Ancient Tales from a Promised Land, Vol. II: Deborah	789
Gideon's Exploding Pickle Pots	Ancient Tales from a Promised Land, Vol. III: Gideon	789
Gift of the Black Folk	Portraits in Black	453
Gift of Zeo	Astro Boy Volume 5	722
Gift-Wrapped Aporia	Critical Art Ensemble	483
Gigantic Task	Ambassador Magma Vol. 3: Episodes 6-7	720
Ginger Nutt's Bee Brother	Animaland	705
Ginger Nutt's Forest Dragon	Animaland	705
Giorgione's Tempest	Art on Film/Film on Art, Program 2: Film Sense/Art Sense	545
Girl and Her Trust, A	Griffith Shorts (1912, #1)	413
Girl at the Cupola, The	Matinee Idols: The Ladies	401
Girl from Moush, The	CineBLAST! Vol. 1	483
Girl in Her Trust, The	D.W. Griffith's Years of Discovery	412
Girl on the Eiffel Tower	Nadia Movie Compilation	737
Girl Who Lives on Heaven Hill	It's Clean—It Just Looks Dirty	486
Girl's Folly, A	Touring the Silent Studios	405
Girl's Night Out	International Tournee of Animation Volume 2	712
Girlfriend	Masters of Russian Animation: Volume 1	82, 713
Girls and Daddy, The	The Short Films of D.W. Griffith—Volume 3	413
Girls Can't Help It!	Maneaters: A Trilogy	486
Girls Will Be Boys	Funny Guys and Gals of the Talkies	269
Girls Will Be Boys	She's Safe	465
Gisele Kerozene	International Tournee of Animation Volume 4	712
Giving Away	Nice Girls...Films by and About Women	434
Glad Rags to Riches	Shirley Temple's Baby Burlesks	282
Glider	Computer Animation Classics	708
Gloucesterman, The	Americans Courageous (1600-1950s)	808
Go Down Death	God's Trombones—A Trilogy	452
Go to Hell	Cinema of Transgression	483
Go to Hell	Wide World of Lydia Lunch	439
Go West	Art of Buster Keaton—Box 2	408
Go!	Men in Shorts, Volume 2	463
Go, Dog Go	Are You My Mother? English Narration	629
Go, Dog Go	Are You My Mother? Spanish Narration	629

SHORT FILM	COMPILATION TAPE	PAGE
Goal Rush, The	Paramount/Famous Studios Volume 1	686
Goat	Three Ages	409
Gobs of Fun	Gabby (Cartoonies)	684
God Within, The	Griffith Shorts (1912, #3)	413
Goddess of Sagebrush Gulch	D.W. Griffith Triple Feature	412
Goddess of Sagebrush Gulch	Griffith Shorts (1912, #1)	413
Gods and Gladiators	The Incredible Story of Dogs	816
Goggles	Stories from the Black Tradition	642
Going Bye-bye!	Laurel and Hardy on the Lam	274
Going Home	Cartoon Collection Vol. 8: Private Snafu	680
Gold Series, The	Computer Animation Classics	708
Goldbrick, The	Cartoon Collection Vol. 8: Private Snafu	680
Golden Fleece, The	Heroes of the Greek Myths	784
Golden Positions	Films of James Broughton, Volume 5: Parables of Wonder	492
Goldfinger	Art Com Video 14: Rebel Girls	482
Goldilocks and The Three Bears	MGM Cartoon Classics: Happy Harmonies	686
Goldilocks and The Three Bears	The James Marshall Library	636
Goldilocks and The Three Bears	Wings: A Tale of Two Chickens and Other Stories by James Marshall	644
Golf Specialist, The	Funny Guys and Gals of the Talkies	269
Golf Specialist, The	W.C. Fields: 6 Short Films	286
Gombrich Themes	Art on Film/Film on Art, Program 5: Film/Art: Subject and Expert	545
Gone to Pieces	Tazmania: Taz-Maniac	703
Good Advice	Classics in Clay	707
Good Neighbor Ground Squirrel	Mountain Habitat Set	818
Good Night Elmer	Elmer!	683
Good Night Nurse	Buster and Fatty	408
Good Omen, The	Holocaust (Sontag)	775
Good Scout	Cartoons That Time Forgot Vol. 4: Willie Whopper's Fantastic Adventures	681
Goodrich Dirt	Cartoon Classics Vol. 7: Early Animation	680
Goods	Films of Charles and Ray Eames, Volume 4	485
Goofy Goat Antics	Thirties Magic Vol. 2	717
Goofy Goofy Gander	Paramount/Fleischer Studios Volume 3	686
Goose That Laid the Golden Egg	Best of the Van Beuren Studio	677
Gopher Spinach	The Adventures of Popeye, Vol. 2	676
Gorgon's Head, The	Monsters of the Greek Myths	637
Gorilla My Dreams	Bugs!	679
Gorilla Mystery	Mickey Mouse: The Black & White Years	693
Government Strategy	Ambassador Magma Vol. 2: Episodes 4-5	720
Gran'ma	Puppets & Demons: Films by Patrick McGuinn	436
Grand Annual Show	The Wind in the Willows, Volume #4	644, 718
Grand Day Out, A	Wallace & Gromit Collection	717
Grand Slam Opera	Buster Keaton Talkies, Vol. 2	408
Grand Uproar	Fox Terrytoons	684
Grandeur and Obedience	Civilization, Programs 7 & 8	396, 781
Grandfather's Clock	Cartoon Classics Vol. 8: Early Thirties	680
Granton Trawler	Documentary Masterpieces by John Grierson	471
Granton Trawler	England in the Thirties	471
Grasshopper	Bruno Bozzetto: Animator, Vol. 1	707
Grasshoppers	Spike & Mike's Festival of Animation Vol. 2	716
Gravity	International Tournee of Animation Volume 2	712
Grazers, The	Catch Me If You Can	651
Grease My Axle	Hard	460
Great Adventure, The	The Films of Arne Sucksdorff: The Great Adventure Plus Short Subjects	75, 472
Great British Moments	Outrageous Animation Vol. 1	714
Great Depression, The	Between the Wars, 1918-1941, Vol. 3	808
Great Exploit, The	Soviet War Stories from World War II	772
Great Guns	Disney's Beginnings	692
Great Hunt, The	Gigantor Retrospective 30 Vol. 5	730
Great Rocket Robbery, The	Astro Boy Volume 4	722
Great Sea Monster, The	Johnny Sokko and His Flying Robot: Episodes 1 and 2	734
Great Steamer	The Wind in the Willows, Volume #3	644, 718
Great Thaw, The	Civilization, Programs 1 & 2	781
Great Toy Robbery, The	A Christmas Gift	707
Great Toy Robbery, The	NFBC: An Animated Christmas	714
Great Toy Robbery, The	NFBC—Cartoon Festival: The Sweater	714
Great Toy Robbery, The	NFBC: Christmas Cracker	714
Great White Man-Eatting Shark,	The Day Jimmy's Boa Ate the Wash	632
Greater than Sherlock Holmes	Films of Stan Laurel Volume 1	410
Green Man, The	Computer Animation Showcase	708
Green Mountain, The	European Folk Tales, Volume 3	646
Greenhouse	Secrets of Love, Classics of Erotic Literature: Vol. 1	510
Gremlins from the Kremlins	Bugs & Daffy: The Wartime Cartoons	678
Grey Wolf & Little Riding Hood	International Tournee of Animation Volume 5	712
Grin and Share It	Droopy & Company	709
Gring Gallet's Reward	Too Outrageous Animation	717
Grinning Evil Death	Computer Animation Festival Vol. 1.0	708
Grocery Clerk, The	Larry Semon #3	411
Grocery Clerk, The	Slapstick Encyclopedia—Vol. 8: Tons of Fun: Comedy's Anarchic Fringe	411
Groucho Marx, Carole Landis	Funny Guys and Gals of the Talkies	269
Growl	William Wegman Reel 4	491
Gruesome Twosome	Tweety & Sylvester	689
Guano!	Too Outrageous Animation	717
Guid Scots Tongue, The	Story of English	860
Guided Muscle	Roadrunner & Wile E. Coyote: The Scrapes of Wrath	687
Gulag Archipelago	Gulag Archipelago	92
Gulliver Mickey	Mickey Mouse: The Black & White Years	693
Gun, Zipper, Snot	Spike & Mike's Sick & Twisted Festival of Animation	716
Gunsmoke Editing Film	Origins of the Motion Picture	337
Gus' Backward Way	Syd Chaplin at Keystone	412
Gussle the Golfer	Syd Chaplin at Keystone	412
Gussle Tied to Trouble	Syd Chaplin at Keystone	412
Gussle's Day of Rest	Syd Chaplin at Keystone	412
Gussle's Wayward Path	Syd Chaplin at Keystone	412
Gymnopedies	Short Animations by Larry Jordan	718
Gypped in Egypt	Cartoon Collection Vol. 8: Private Snafu	680
Gypped in Egypt	Tom & Jerry & Friends #2	688
H20	Experimental Avant Garde Series Volume 20 (The Secret Lives of Inanimate Objects)	484
Ha-Ha-Ha	Cartoon Collection Vol. 4: Warner Bros. & Fleischer	680
Hair-Raising Hare	Bugs Bunny: Hollywood Legend	679
Hairdresser, The	Films of Harold Lloyd—Volume 5	410
Half a Man	Films of Stan Laurel Volume 1	410

SHORT FILM	COMPILATION TAPE	PAGE
Hallucinogens and Culture	A Magical Journey	851
Hand, The	Four for Thrills, Edgar Allan Poe, Etc.	633
Handmirror/Brush Set	Art Com Video 14: Rebel Girls	482
Handy	William Wegman Reel 1	491
Hangman, The	Four for Thrills, Edgar Allan Poe, Etc.	633
Hangman, The	Holocaust (Sontag)	775
Hansel and Gretel	Babes in the Woods	395
Hansel and Gretel	Lotte Reiniger Compilation	713
Hansel and Gretel	Ray Harryhausen Compilation	715
Haploid Affair	Outrageous Animation Vol. 1	714
Happy Anniversary	Experimental Avant Garde Series Volume 22	484
Happy Birthday Moon	Happy Birthday Moon and Other Stories	647
Happy Days	Cartoons That Time Forgot Vol. 4: Willie Whopper's Fantastic Adventures	681
Happy Hoboes	Tom & Jerry & Friends #1	688
Happy Hoboes	Van Beuren Studio, Volume #1	689
Happy Jack: A Hero	Mack Sennett: The Biograph Years	411
Happy Lion, The	Danny and the Dinosaur and Other Stories	651
Happy Owls, The	The Pigs' Wedding and Other Stories	640
Happy Song	William Wegman Reel 1	491
Happy You and Merry Me	Glenn Gould Plays Beethoven	590
Hard Boiled Eggs	Films of Oliver Hardy	410
Hard Edition	Too Outrageous Animation	717
Hard Luck	College	409
Hard Woman	Computer Animation Classics	708
Hare Devil Hare	Bugs Bunny Classics	678
Hare Grows in Manhattan, A	Bugs Bunny: Hollywood Legend	679
Hare Meets Hare	Bugs & Daffy: The Wartime Cartoons	678
Hare Ribbin'	Bugs!	679
Hare Splitter	Stars of Space Jam: Five-Tape Boxed Set	687
Hare Splitter	Stars of Space Jam—Bugs Bunny	687
Hare Tonic	Starring Bugs Bunny!	687
Hare Trigger	Bugs Bunny's Zaniest Toons	679
Hare-Brained Hypnotist	Elmer!	683
Hare-Brained Hypnotist, The	Bugs Bunny's Comedy Classics	678
Hare-Raising Night	Tiny Toon Fiendishly Funny Adventures	688
Hare-Um Scare-Um	Cartoon Collection Vol. 7: Tokyo Jokio	680
Haredevil Hare	Bugs Bunny's Comedy Classics	678
Hareway to the Stars	Bugs Bunny: Truth or Hare	679
Harlem Wednesday	Hubley Studio: Voyage to Next	711
Harold and the Purple Crayon	Blue Ribbon Stories Vol. 2	650
Harold's Fairy Tale	Five Stories for the Very Young	652
Harrowing & Tryst Haunt, The	Stan Brakhage—Hand-Painted Films	488
Harvest Town	Best of the Fests 1991	706
Hasher's Delirium	Weird Cartoons Vol. 1	717
Hat, The	Hubley Studio: The Hole	711
Hat, The	Doctor De Soto and Other Stories	632
Hatch up Your Troubles	Tom & Jerry's Comic Capers	689
Haul in One, A	The Adventures of Popeye, Vol. 2	676
Haunted House	Battling Butler	408
Haunted Ship, The	Tom & Jerry & Friends #2	688
Haunted Spooks	Films of Harold Lloyd—Volume 1	409
Haunted Spooks	His Royal Slyness and Haunted Spooks	410
Haunted Spooks	Harold Lloyd Comedies Vol. 1	410
Haunting We Will Go, A	Paramount/Famous Studios Volume 2	686
Haunting We Will Go, A	Thirties Magic Vol. 1	716
Have We Lived Before?	Arthur C. Clarke: World of Strange Powers	861
Hawaii: Paradise Found	Hawaii: The Pacific Paradise	830
Hawaii: Paradise Sought	Hawaii: The Pacific Paradise	830
Hawaiian Punch	Computer Animation Classics	708
Hayseed Romance	Buster Keaton Talkies, Vol. 7	408
He Cooked His Goose	The Three Stooges: Corny Casanovas	284
He's in Again	Slapstick Encyclopedia—Vol. 5: Chaplin and Co.: The Music Hall Tradition	411
Head	Griffiti	710
Headless Horseman, The	Cartoons That Time Forgot Vol. 3: Things That Go Bump in the Night	681
Headless Horseman, The	Ub Iwerks' Famous Fairytales	689
Heard the News	It's Clean—It Just Looks Dirty	486
Heartburn	Biggest and the Best	860
Hearts and Arrows	Sextoons: An Erotic Animation Festival	715
Hearts and Flowers	Slapstick Encyclopedia—Vol. 3: Funny Girls	411
Hearts of Age	Avant Garde & Experimental Film	482
Hearts of Age	Classic Foreign Shorts—Volume 2	153
Heat Wave	I Became a Lesbian and Others Too	460
Heaven is What I've Done	Pier Marton: Collected Works: 1979-84	487
Heavenly Daze	The Three Stooges: Heavenly Daze	284
Heavens, The	Tom Chomont: A Two-Volume Collection, Volume I	466, 489
Heavy Metal	Films of Scott Bartlett, Vol. 2: The Future of Human Mythology	485
Hector and Achilles	Heroes of the Greek Myths	784
Hector's Hectic Life	Classic Cartoon Christmas Treasures	682
Hector's Hectic Life	Cartoon Holidays	680
Hector's Hectic Life	Christmas Cartoon Classic	682
Hedgehog in the Fog	Masters of Russian Animation: Volume 5	82, 713
Hell	Video Art: Ardele Lister	489
Hell's Fire	Cartoons That Time Forgot Vol. 3: Things That Go Bump in the Night	681
Hell's Hinges	Cradle of Courage	397
Hell-Bent for Election	Cartoongate!	681
Helpful Sisterhood, The	Norma Talmadge Films	402
Helpmates	Laurel and Hardy: Stan "Helps" Ollie	274
Helter Shelter	Man's Best Friend	685
Henpecked Duck	Cartoon Collection Vol. 2: Classic Warner Bros.	680
Hepcat Symphony	Paramount/Fleischer Studios Volume 2	686
Her Boyfriend	Heavy Hardy	411
Her Boyfriend	Larry Semon #2	411
Her Bridal Nightmare	These Girls Won't Talk	405
Her First Biscuits	Griffith Shorts (1908-09)	412
Her First Biscuits	The Short Films of Mary Pickford	404
Her First Flame	The Comediennes, Volume 2	397
Her Terrible Ordeal	Griffith Shorts (1909-1910)	412
Her Terrible Ordeal	The Short Films of D.W. Griffith—Volume 1	413
Hercules and the Golden Apples	Heroes of the Greek Myths	784
Here Kitty Kitty Pts 1&2	Tazmania: Taz-Manimals	704
Here to Make Music	Pinchas Zukerman: Here to Make Music/The Ghost	593
Hermes Bird	Films of James Broughton, Volume 1: Erotic Celebrations	492

SHORT FILM	COMPILATION TAPE	PAGE
Hero as an Artist, The	Civilization, Programs 5 & 6	781
Hero for Hire	High-Flying Hero	693
Heroic Exploit	Soviet War Stories from World War II	772
Heroic Materialism	Civilization, Program 13	781
Heron and Crane	Masters of Russian Animation: Volume 5	82, 713
Herr Meets Hare	Bugs Bunny: Hollywood Legend	679
Heterosexual Love	M/W/F Music Video One	433
Hey Hey Fever	MGM Cartoon Classics: Happy Harmonies	686
Hey Joe	Amida/A Mosaic for the Kali Yuga/Arches/Body Count/ Hey Joe	482
Hi-De-Ho	That's Black Entertainment: African-American Contributions in Film and Music 1903-1944	455
Hidden Treasures of America's	America's Great National Parks	828
Hidden Utensil	William Wegman Reel 1	491
Hide	Don from Lakewood/You Talk, I Buy	429
High and Dizzy	Harold Lloyd Comedies Vol. 2	410
High and the Flighty, The	Stars of Space Jam: Five-Tape Boxed Set	687
High Fidelity	Computer Animation Classics	708
High Kukus	Films of James Broughton, Volume 5: Parables of Wonder	492
High Price to Pay	Human Race Club: A Story About Self-Esteem, a Story About Earning Money	635
High Sign	The Saphead	409
Hillary's Birthday	The Abbott and Costello Television Show, Tape 1	414
Hillary's Father	The Abbott and Costello Television Show, Tape 3	414
Hillbilly Hare	Looney Tunes Curtain Calls	685
Hippie Temptation, The	Experimental Avant Garde Series Volume 23	484
His Bitter Pill	The Tollgate	297, 405
His Favorite Pastime	Keystones #1	407
His Girl	Griffith Shorts (1911)	413
His Majesty, the Scarecrow	L. Frank Baum's Silent Film Collection of Oz	400
His Mother's Son	Griffith Shorts (1913)	413
His Mouse Friday	Tom & Jerry on Parade	689
His New Job	Classic Chaplin, Charlie Chaplin at Essanay Studio	407
His New Job	Essanay #1	407
His New Profession	Keystones #3	407
His Royal Slyness	Films of Harold Lloyd—Volume 3	410
His Royal Slyness	Harold Lloyd Comedies Vol. 3	410
His Trust	Griffith Shorts (1910-1911)	413
His Trust	D.W. Griffith's Years of Discovery	412
His Trust	A Corner in Wheat and Selected Biograph Shorts	412
His Trust and His Trust Fulfilled	The Short Films of D.W. Griffith—Volume 1	413
His Wooden Wedding	Charley Chase Vol. 1	410
Hitler and Stalin	The Schwartzkopf Four-Pack	763
Hitler Youth	Terror of the Third Reich	772
Hitting the Rails	Aesop's Fables Volume 1	676
Hitting the Trail for Hallelujah	All Singing, All Dancing	676
Hobo on Train	William Wegman Reel 5	491
Hogan Out West	Early Comedies Volume 1	410
Hogwild	Laurel and Hardy: Stan "Helps" Ollie	274
Hokum Hotel	Tom & Jerry & Friends #3	688
Hokus Pokus	The Three Stooges: Heavenly Daze	284
Hold Anything	Cartoon Collection Vol. 3: Coal Black & De Sebben Dwarfs	680
Hole in One, A	Spike & Mike's Sick & Twisted Festival of Animation, Vol. 2	716
Holiday for Drumsticks	Stars of Space Jam: Five-Tape Boxed Set	687
Hollow Liberty	The Question of Equality	464
Hollywood Capers	Cartoon Collection Vol. 6: The Ducktators	680
Hollywood Daffy	Daffy Duck: Just Plain Daffy	682
Hollywood Steps Out	Cartoon Collection Vol. 1: Porky in Wackyland	680
Hollywood Steps Out	Great & Minor Animation Volume 1	684
Holy Koran, The	The Holy Koran	790
Holy Land at Christmas, The	Holy Land & Holy City	790
Homage to May	Homage to May 19th/Framed	473
Home Honey, I'm High	Spike & Mike's Sick & Twisted Festival of Animation, Vol. 3	716
Home on the Range	MGM Cartoon Classics: Happy Harmonies	686
Home Stories	Matthias Muller—Selected Films	433
Home Sweet Home	Aesop's Fables Volume 2	676
Home Sweet Home	Judith of Bethula/Home Sweet Home	413
Home Tweet Home	Sylvester & Tweety: The Best Yeows of Our Lives	688
Homeless Hare	Stars of Space Jam: Five-Tape Boxed Set	687
Homeless Hare	Stars of Space Jam—Bugs Bunny	687
Honeyland	MGM Cartoon Classics: Happy Harmonies	686
Honky Tonk Bud	Jazz Shorts	612
Hook, Line and Stinker	Chariots of Fur	682
Hook, Line and Stinker	Stars of Space Jam: Five-Tape Boxed Set	687
Hooligan Whodunit, The	Astro Boy Volume 9	722
Hooray for Sandbox Land	The Rocketship Reel	715
Hop to It	Hardy and Ray	411
Hopalong Casualty	Roadrunner & Wile E. Coyote: The Scrapes of Wrath	687
Hopi Prophecy, The	A Common Destiny:	470
Horndog	Spike & Mike's Sick & Twisted Festival of Animation, Vol. 2	716
Horton Hears a Who	Dr. Seuss Video Festival	683
Hot and Nasty	Sneakin' and Peekin'	478
Hot Cross Bunny	Stars of Space Jam: Five-Tape Boxed Set	687
Hot Cross Bunny	Stars of Space Jam—Bugs Bunny	687
Hot Love	Corpse Fucking Art	505
Hot Rod Hearse	Three Films by Chris Frieri	438
Hot Sake	William Wegman Reel 1	491
Hot Wiring America's Farms	Fueling the Future	803
Hot-Rod and Reel!	Stars of Space Jam: Five-Tape Boxed Set	687
Hotel Monterey	Akermania, Volume One	29
House Boat	Films of Stan Laurel Volume 3	410
House Cleaning Time	Tom & Jerry & Friends #1	688
House in the Middle, The	You Can Beat the A-Bomb	807
House of Darkness, The	Griffith Shorts (1913)	413
House of Darkness, The	The Female of the Species & Selected Biograph Shorts (Volume III)	412
House of Darkness, The	D.W. Griffith's Years of Discovery	412
House of Kolomna, The	Early Russian Cinema: Before the Revolution, Vol. 05: Chardynin's Pushkin	85
House of Un-American Activities	House of Un-American Activities	473
House that Jack Built, The	Greentoons: Environmentally Aware Animation	710
House with Closed Shutters	Griffith Shorts (1909-1910)	412
House-Cat, The	Animaland (9 Titles)	705
Housecats	Best of the Fests: For Kids	706
Houses Belong to those who Live	Video Art: Noel Harding	490
Housing Problems	Classic Documentaries: People and Places	470
Housing Problems	Land Without Bread	47
How a Mosquito Operates	Winsor McCay: Animation Legend	718
How Came Israel?	Holocaust (Sontag)	775
How Much is That Window	Spike & Mike's Sick & Twisted Festival of Animation, Vol. 1	716
How the Camel Got His Hump	Just So Stories, Set I	653
How the Grinch Stole Christmas	Dr. Seuss Video Festival	683
How the Loon	Greentoons: Environmentally Aware Animation	710
How the Rhinoceros Got His Skin	Just So Stories, Set I	653
How the Whale Got His Throat	Just So Stories, Set I	653
How They Stopped the Run	Matinee Idols: The Ladies	401
How to Aggravate	Moron Movies	508
How to Clean the Toilet	Moron Movies	508
How to Exercise If You're Ugly	Moron Movies	508
How to get Fatter	More Moron Movies	508
How to Hold a Husband	They Wear No Clothes	511
How to Kiss	Plymptoons: The Complete Works of Bill Plympton	715
How to Kiss	Spike & Mike's Festival of Animation Vol. 1	716
How to Talk to Your Doctor	Your Family's Health, Tape 1	838
How Weary Goes Wooing	Tom Mix Short Subjects	405
Howling Hollywood	Hollywood Spoofs	411
Hug Me	I'm Not Oscar's Friend Anymore and Other Stories	635
Hullabaloo Land	Astro Boy Volume 10	722
Hum	Kartemquin Films, Vol. 3: Trick Bag	474
Human Future, The	A Magical Journey	851
Human Race, The	Art Com Video 1: Scandinavia	482
Human Rights	Plymptoons: The Complete Works of Bill Plympton	715
Human Voice, The	Amore	38
Human Waste	M/W/F Music Video One	433
Humorous Phases of Funny Faces	Animation Vol. 1: The Beginning	706
Humorous Phases of Funny Faces	Cartoon Classics Vol. 6: Early Animation	680
Humorous Phases of Funny Faces	The Genesis of Animation, Volume One	710
Humpty Dumpty	Cartoons That Time Forgot Vol. 1: All Singing! All Dancing!	681
Hungreed	CineBLAST! Vol. 1	483
Hungry Hearts	Babe Hardy: Early Training	410
Hungry Wolf, The	Droopy & Company	709
Hunky and Spunky	Paramount/Fleischer Studios Volume 1	686
Hunt	Masters of Russian Animation: Volume 1	82, 713
Hunt	Masters of Russian Animation: Volume 4	82, 713
Hunt	Masters of Russian Animation: Volume 6—The Works	82, 713
Hunter and the Forest—A Story	The Films of Arne Sucksdorff: The Great Adventure Plus Short Subjects	75, 472
Hut Sluts	Spike & Mike's Sick & Twisted Festival of Animation, Vol. 3	716
Hyde and Hare	Looney Tunes After Dark	685
I Became a Lesbian	I Became a Lesbian and Others Too	460
I Can Hardly Wait	Dental Follies	267
I Don't Care	The Adventures of Popeye, Vol. 2	676
I Haven't Got a Hart	Porky!	687
I Love a Parade	Cartoon Collection Vol. 4: Warner Bros. & Fleischer	680
I Love a Parade	Early Warner Brothers Cartoons	683
I Love My Work	Pictures Don't Tell You Anything: Selected Films of Ann Marie Fleming	211, 487
I Love You Mom	Art Com Video 14: Rebel Girls	482
I Never Ho'd For My Father	Spike & Mike's Sick & Twisted Festival of Animation, Vol. 3	716
I Shit on God	Whoregasm	491
I Should See	International Tournee of Animation Volume 5	712
I Ski Love Ski You Ski	Cartoon Collection Vol. 1: Porky in Wackyland	680
I Surrender Dear	Bing at Sennett Vol. 2	263
I Taw a Putty Tat	Bugs Bunny Superstar	678
I Thaw a Putty Tat	Tweety & Sylvester	689
I Think I Was an Alcoholic	International Tournee of Animation Volume 6	712
I Was a Contestant at Mother's	Sneakin' and Peekin'	478
I'll Be Glad When You're Dead	Cartoon Collection Vol. 5: Racial Cartoons	680
I'll Be the Sportsman	Larry Semon #2	411
I'm Afraid to Come Home	Cartoon Collection Vol. 4: Warner Bros. & Fleischer	680
I'm Hungry, I'm Cold	Akermania, Volume One	29
I'm in the Army Now	Cartoon Collection Vol. 1: Porky in Wackyland	680
I'm Just Curious	Little Lulu (Cartoonies)	685
I'm Not Oscar's Friend Anymore	I'm Not Oscar's Friend Anymore and Other Stories	635
I'm On My Way	Films of Harold Lloyd—Volume 2	409
I'm On My Way	Harold Lloyd Comedies Vol. 2	410
I'm On My Way	Harold Lloyd's Comedy Classics	410
IBM Math Peep Shows	Films of Charles and Ray Eames, Volume 4	485
Iddy Biddy Beat Boy	Spike & Mike's Festival of Animation Vol. 3	716
Idiot Savant	Karl Krogstad: Idiot Savant & Catharsis	432
Idle Class, The	The Kid/The Idle Class	407
Idle Eyes	Eyes of Ben Turpin Are upon You!	410
Idle Eyes	Selected Shorts #2	403
If Only to Be	Incredible Animation Collection: Vol. 1	711
IFE	Dyke Drama	458
Illusions of Shameless Abundance	The Pleasures of the Uninhibited Excess	567
Immigrant, The	Charlie Chaplin Early Years I	407
Immigrant, The	Classic Chaplin, Charlie Chaplin at Mutual Studios	407
Immigrant, The	Unknown Chaplin, My Happiest Years	408
Impatient Patient, The	Daffy Duck: Tales from the Duckside	682
Impetigo	Tony Vegas' Animated Acidburn Flashback Tabu	717
Impulses	Jim Davis: Volume #2	486
In a Cartoon Studio	Cartoon Collection Vol. 7: Tokyo Jokio	680
In a Cartoon Studio	Cartoons That Time Forgot Vol. 6: The Odd & The Outrageous	681
In a Summer Garden	Live Short Films by Larry Jordan	718
In Again—Out Again	Aesop's Film Fables	676
In Darkest Africa	Cartoon Classics Vol. 5: The Other Studios	680
In Dutch	Felix the Cat: Sound & Silent	683
In Dutch	Disney Sweetheart Stories	692
In Harm's Way: Tornado	Wings over the Gulf: Complete Set	845
In Old Madrid	The Short Films of Mary Pickford	404
In Shadow City	The Works of Ken Feingold—Fictions	491
In Society	The Abbott and Costello Television Show, Tape 5	414
In the Absence of Heroes	The Ascent of Man/In the Absence of Heroes	482
In the Border States	The Female of the Species & Selected Biograph Shorts (Volume III)	412
In the Border States	Griffith Shorts (1909-1910)	412
In the Border States	D.W. Griffith's Years of Discovery	412
In the Cup	William Wegman Reel 2	491
In the Life	Gay Games IV from A to Q	459, 826
In the Night Kitchen	The Maurice Sendak Library	654
In the Park	Essanay #1	407
In the Street	Cityscape Compilations	470

SHORT FILM	COMPILATION TAPE	PAGE
In the Switch Tower	A Tale of Two Cities/In the Switch Tower	405
In Transit	Best of the Fests 1991	706
In Vaudeville	Aesop's Fables Volume 3	676
In Vaudeville	Tom & Jerry & Friends #3	688
In View of Her Fatal Inclination	Men in Shorts	463
In Wanna Be Your Lover	Guido Manuli: Animator	710
In-Flight Movie	BBC Wildlife Specials: Birds of a Sun God/In-flight Movie	813
Inaugural Display, The	Video Against AIDS, Volumes 1, 2 & 3	835
Inca Gold Fever	Astro Boy Volume 10	722
Incredible Discovery of Noah's	Mysteries of the Ancient World Gift Set	791
Incubus	Guido Manuli: Animator	710
Incubus	International Tournee of Animation Volume 1	711
Indefinite Concrete Material	Critical Art Ensemble	483
Indoor Outing	Glenn Gould Plays Beethoven	590
Industrial Britain	Documentary Masterpieces by John Grierson	471
Industrial Britain	E.M.B. Classics	471
Infernal Caldron, The	Melies III: The Search for Munchhausen	22
Inflation (Inflation)	Hans Richter: Early Avant-Garde Films	485
Info for People Who Can Take	Videotapes of Elizabeth Sher, V. 1-11, I.V. Magazine #3	491
Information Withheld	Juan Downey	486
Inki and the Mynah Bird	Weird Cartoons Vol. 2	717
Inn Where No Man Rests, The	More Melies	22
Inner Sanctum	Tom Chomont: A Two-Volume Collection, Volume II	466, 489
Insect's Christmas, An	The Cameraman's Revenge: The Amazing Puppet Animation of Ladislaw Starewicz	707
Inside Fighting China	Nostalgia World War II Video Library #6	771
Inside Job, An	Outrageous Animation Vol. 1	714
Instant Sex	Outrageous Animation Vol. 1	714
Instruments of the Orchestra	Benjamin Britten	469
Insultin' the Sultan	Cartoons That Time Forgot Vol. 4: Willie Whopper's Fantastic Adventures	681
Interjections	Schoolhouse Rock: Grammar Rock	702
International Sweethearts	International Sweethearts of Rhythm/Tiny & Ruby: Hell-Divin' Women	461, 611
Into the European Mirror	Julian Samuel Trilogy	474
Invaders, The	Films of Thomas Ince	398
Invasion of the Ballroom People	Really Strange Stories of the Totally Unknown	509
Invasion of the Bunny Snatcher	Bugs Bunny's Creature Features	678
Invincible Warrior	Spaceketeers	746
Invisible Revenge	Cartoon Classics Vol. 7: Early Animation	680
Invocation of My Demon Brother	Lucifer Rising	486
Irises, The	National Film Board of Canada's Animation Festival	714
Iron Mule, The	Slapstick Encyclopedia—Vol. 4: Keaton, Arbuckle & Al St. John	411
Irony (The Abyss of Speech)	The Works of Ken Feingold—Fictions	491
Is That Jazz?	Jazz Shorts	612
Islamic Science	The Holy Koran	790
Island	Masters of Russian Animation: Volume 2	82, 713
Island	Masters of Russian Animation: Volume 6—The Works	82, 713
Island of Song, The	Danny and the Dinosaur and Other Stories	651
Island of the Skog, The	The Three Robbers and Other Stories	643
Ism, Ism	Cinema of Transgression	483
Isn't Life Wonderful	D.W. Griffith's Years of Discovery	412
It Can't Last	Nostalgia World War II Video Library #1	770
It's a Bird	Weird Cartoons Vol. 2	717
It's a Gift	Slapstick Encyclopedia—Vol. 6: Hal Roach: The Lot of Fun	411
It's a Greek Life!	Cartoons That Time Forgot Vol. 7: Rainbow Parades	681
It's a Hap-Hap-Happy Day	Paramount/Fleischer Studios Volume 3	686
It's a Hap-Hap-Happy Day	Cartoon Collection Vol. 6: The Ducktators	680
It's a Hap-Hap-Happy Day	Gabby (Cartoonies)	684
It's a Lovely Day	Animaland	705
It's an O.K. Life	Animation Celebration Vol. 1	705
It's an OK Life	Griffiti	710
It's Got Me Again	Cartoon Classics Vol. 1: Looney Tunes & Merrie Melodies	680
It's Got Me Again	Cartoon Collection Vol. 7: Tokyo Jokio	680
It's Just Not You, Murray	First Works Volume One	334
It's Me Again	Pictures Don't Tell You Anything: Selected Films of Ann Marie Fleming	211, 487
It's Murder She Says	Cartoon Collection Vol. 8: Private Snafu	680
It's That Team Spirit, Charlie	Peanuts: Charlie Brown & Snoopy Show Vol. 7	700
Italian American	Italian American/The Big Shave	253
Italian-Ethiopian War	Between the Wars, 1918-1941, Vol. 6	808
Italy Turns Around	Love in the City	41
Ivor the Engine	BBC Children's Favorites	629
J'aurais Dit Glenn Gould	Video Art: Rober Racine	490
Jabberwocky	Alchemist of the Surreal	705
Jabbock	Tom Chomont: A Two-Volume Collection, Volume I	466, 489
Jac Mac & Rad Boy...Go	Outrageous Animation Vol. 2	714
Jack & the Beanstalk	Cartoons That Time Forgot Vol. 5: Free-Form Fairytales	681
Jack and the Beanstalk	Peanuts: Charlie Brown & Snoopy Show Vol. 7	700
Jack and the Beanstalk	Classic Stories for Children	651
Jack and the Beanstalk	Katharine Hepburn: World of Stories	647
Jack and the Beanstalk	Ub Iwerks' Famous Fairytales	689
Jack Frost	Cartoons That Time Forgot Vol. 3: Things That Go Bump in the Night	681
Jack in the Fox	Karl Krogstad: Temple, Fork & Jack in the Fox	432
Jack in the Fox	Sextoons: An Erotic Animation Festival	715
Jack the Ripper	Jack the Ripper (Karloff)	524
Jail Brakers, The	Tom & Jerry & Friends #2	688
Jailbait	Buster Keaton Talkies, Vol. 6	408
Jale's Not Happy	Pictures Don't Tell You Anything: Selected Films of Ann Marie Fleming	211, 487
Jamaica No Problem	Classics in Clay	707
Jan Svankmajer: The Animator	Scenes from the Surreal	715
Japan Invades China	Between the Wars, 1918-1941, Vol. 8	808
Japoteurs, The	Cartoon Collection Vol. 5: Racial Cartoons	680
Japoteurs, The	Superman (50th Anniversary)	688
Japoteurs, The	Color Adventures of Superman	682
Jason and the Argonauts	Ray Harryhausen Compilation	715
Jasper	Best of George Pal	677
Jasper & The Haunted House	Great & Minor Animation Volume 2	684
Jay Duck	Guido Manuli: Animator	710
Jazz Band, The	Mabel Normand, Vol. 1	411
Jean Jean and the Evil Cat	Spike & Mike's Festival of Animation Vol. 2	716
Jerky Turkey	Cartoon Classics in Color #2: Fleischer/Warners	679
Jerky Turkey	Great & Minor Animation Volume 2	684
Jerry and Jumbo	Tom & Jerry: Starring Tom & Jerry!	689
Jerry and the Lion	Tom & Jerry's Cartoon Cavalcade	689
Jerry's	Palazzolo's Chicago	476
Jerry's Cousin	Tom & Jerry's Cartoon Cavalcade	689
JFK Workout, The	Experimental Avant Garde Series Volume 19 (Very Serious Fun)	484
Jill Jacks Off	She's Safe	465
Jimmy Who?	Cartoongate!	681
Jingle Jive	Cartoon Collection Vol. 5: Racial Cartoons	680
Jitney Elopement, A	Essanay #1	407
Joe	Kisses in the Dark	234
Joe & Basket: Mostly Sports	CineBLAST! Vol. 3	428
Joe Glow the Firefly	Cartoon Collection Vol. 5: Racial Cartoons	680
Joey Runs Away	Joey Runs Away and Other Stories	653
John Rance, Gentleman	Norma Talmadge Films	402
Johnny Appleseed	Shelley Duvall's Tall Tales and Legends	658
Johnny Bravo	Jonny Quest: Hadji—Mysteries of the East	698
Johnny-A Modern Interpretation	Art Com Video 1: Scandinavia	482
Joint Wipers	Cartoons That Time Forgot Vol. 6: The Odd & The Outrageous	681
Joke	William Wegman Reel 6	491
Jollity Farm	The British Animation Invasion	707
Jolly Jilter	Ben Turpin #1	410
Jonah and the Great Fish	The Mysterious Tadpole and Other Stories	638
Jones Have Amateur Theatrics	Griffith Shorts (1908-09)	412
Joshua in Trouble Valley	Ancient Tales from a Promised Land, Vol. I	789
Joshua Smashes Jericho	Ancient Tales from a Promised Land, Vol. I	789
Journey to the Afternoon	Works	718
Journey to the Center of Acme	Tiny Toon BIG Adventures	688
Jours de Plaine	The National Film Board of Canada's Animation Festival	714
Joyous Microbes, The	Attack of the Cohl Pumpkins	706
Juan in New York	Mitch Corber Works	487
Judge for a Day	Cartoon Collection Vol. 8: Private Snafu	680
Judge for a Day	Betty Boop's Dizzy Dozen	678
Judgment Day	Cinema of Transgression	483
Judith of Bethula	Judith of Bethula/Home Sweet Home	413
Juggling	Videotapes of Elizabeth Sher, What's Inside These Shorts?	491
JuJu Shampoo	CineBLAST! Vol. 3	428
Juke Bar	Incredible Animation Collection: Vol. 1	711
Juke Bar	The National Film Board of Canada's Animation Festival	714
Jump, The	Outrageous Animation Vol. 2	714
Jumped Out	Video Art: David Askevold	490
Jumpin' Jupiter	Looney Tunes After Dark	685
Jumpin' Jupiter	Porky Pig Tales	687
Jumpin' the Gun	Women from Down Under	467
Jumping	International Tournee of Animation Volume 1	711
Jungle Drums	Color Adventures of Superman	682
Jungle Drums	Superman (50th Anniversary)	688
Jungle Fool	Van Beuren Studio, Volume #1	689
Jungle Sports	Aesop's Fables Volume 2	676
Jupiter's Thunderbolt	More Melies	22
Just Desserts	Women from Down Under	467
Just Neighbors	Films of Harold Lloyd—Volume 1	409
Just Rambling Along	Stan Laurel: At the Beginning	411
Juste Le Temp	Robert Cahen: L'Invitation au Voyage/Juste le Temps	488
Kakania	International Tournee of Animation Volume 4	712
Kalahari Bigfoot	Kuiseb the Vanishing River/Kalahari Bigfoot (BBC Wildlife Special)	817
Katalina and Katalin	European Folk Tales, Volume 6	646
Katzenhammer Kids	Origins of American Animation	714
Keep Off	Forgotten Comedians	411
Keeping up with the Jonses	Origins of American Animation	714
Keystone Hotel	Ben Turpin #1	410
KGB	Mitch Corber Works	487
Kick in Time	Paramount/Fleischer Studios Volume 3	686
Kid Auto Races	Emerging Chaplin	407
Kid in Africa	Shirley Temple's Baby Burlesks	282
Kid Speed	Films of Oliver Hardy	410
Kid Stuff	Incredible Animation Collection: Vol. 1	711
Kid's Auto Race	Keystones #1	407
Kid, The	The Kid/The Idle Class	407
Kiddin Kate	Comedy Shorts #4	410
Kids in the Shoe, The	Paramount/Fleischer Studios Volume 2	686
Kids, Parents, and Sports	Your Family's Health, Tape 3	838
Kill or Cure	Films of Stan Laurel Volume 2	410
Kill or Cure	Versatile Mr. Laurel	412
Killer's Wife	The Abbott and Costello Television Show, Tape 5	414
Kilroy Was Here	Rare Black Short Subjects	448
King Dong	Moron Movies	508
King for a Day	Gabby (Cartoonies)	684
King Midas	Puppet Masters	715
King of Sex	Cinema of Transgression	483
King's Tailor	Ub Iwerks' Famous Fairytales	689
Kingdom of the Fairies	Marvelous Melies	22
Kings of the Water	Magicians of the Earth	552
Kiss	Men in Shorts	463
Kiss Me Goodbye	Wide World of Lydia Lunch	439
Kiss, The	William Wegman Reel 2	491
Kittens are Born	Reproduction of Life	837
Kitty Kornered	Porky!	687
Klondike Kid, The	Mickey Mouse: The Black & White Years	693
Knickknack	Tiny Toy Stories	717
Knights on Bikes	Experimental Avant Garde Series Volume 22	484
Knighty-Knight Bugs	The Looney Looney Looney Bugs Bunny Movie	685
Knockout, The	Keystones #2	407
Know For Sure	Sex Education Films of the 40's	510
Know Thy Wife	Slapstick Encyclopedia—Vol. 3: Funny Girls	411
Ko-Ko	Griffiti	710
Koko in Reverse	Koko the Clown, Volume 2	685
Koko Kills Time	Koko the Clown, Volume 2	685
Koko Smokes	Koko the Clown, Volume 2	685
Koko's Balloons	Koko the Clown, Volume 2	685
Koko's Barnyard	Koko the Clown, Volume 2	685
Koko's Cartoon Factory	Max Fleischer Presents Koko the Clown	685
Koko's Kid	Koko the Clown, Volume 2	685
Koko's Storm	Koko the Clown, Volume 2	685
Koto Buki	Art Com Video 2: Waveforms: Video Japan	482

SHORT FILM	COMPILATION TAPE	PAGE
Krazy Kat	Animation Vol. 2	706
Krazy Kat	Origins of American Animation	714
Kreise	The Films of Oskar Fischinger—Optical Poetry	710
Kristopher Kolumbus	Cartoon Collection Vol. 3: Coal Black & De Sebben Dwarfs	680
Kuiseb the Vanishing River	Kuiseb the Vanishing River/Kalahari Bigfoot (BBC Wildlife Special)	817
L'Apparition	Pascal Aubier Films	487
L'Etoile de Mer	Avant Garde Program #2	482
L'Etoile de Mer	Man Ray Video	486
L'Histoire du Soldat Inconnu	Experimental Avant Garde Series Volume 21 (An Attack on Social, Sexual, and Political Order)	484
L'il Eightball in Silly Supers	Thirties Magic Vol. 1	716
L'Ingenue	Lesbovision	462
L'Invitation au Voyage	Robert Cahen: L'Invitation au Voyage/Juste le Temps	488
L'ombre de la Pomme	Sextoons: An Erotic Animation Festival	715
LA 84	Simultaneous	488
La Femme qui se poudre	Patrick Bokanowski—Courts-Metrages	8
La Folie du Dr. Tube	Avant Garde Shorts/France	483
La Jetee	Avant Garde Program #12	482
La Jetee	La Jetee/An Occurrence at Owl Creek Bridge	4, 10
La Maison Tellier	Le Plaisir	27
La Modele	Le Plaisir	27
La Pista	Spike & Mike's Festival of Animation Vol. 2	716
La Plage	Patrick Bokanowski—Courts-Metrages	8
La Rateleur	Animation Vol. 1: The Beginning	706
La Ravissement	She's Safe	465
La Ricotta	Rogopag	10, 37, 39, 41
La The a la Menthe	Award Winning French Shorts	2
Labor Day - East Chicago	Palazzolo's Chicago Vol. 2	476
Labyrinth	Neo-Tokyo	737
Lady and the Apple, The	European Folk Tales, Volume 2	646
Lady and the Lamp	Animation Celebration Vol. 2	705
Lady Lazarus	New Directors: New Short Films	487
Lady Play Your Mandolin	Early Warner Brothers Cartoons	683
Lady Roxanne	Secrets of Love, Classics of Erotic Literature: Vol. 6	510
Lafftoons	Slapstick Encyclopedia—Vol. 6: Hal Roach: The Lot of Fun	411
Lamb in a Jam, A	Little Lulu and Friends	685
Lambert, the Sheepish Lion	Willie, The Operatic Whale	694
Lambeth Walk Nazi Style	Experimental Avant Garde Series Volume 19 (Very Serious Fun)	484
Lame Brains	Comedy of Chester Conklin	410
Land of the Lost	Paramount/Famous Studios Volume 1	686
Land Without Bread	Un Chien Andalou/Land Without Bread	47
Language of the Heart	Picture Windows	242
Last Clean Shirt, The	Pull My Daisy (The Beat Generation)	435, 476
Last Deal, The	Griffith Shorts (1909-1910)	412
Last Drop of Water	Griffith Shorts (1911)	413
Last Hunt	Masters of Russian Animation: Volume 4	82, 713
Last of the Line	Films of Thomas Ince	398
Last Trick, The	Alchemist of the Surreal	705
Last Waltz, The	The Bartered Bride and The Last Waltz	27, 577
Last Year in Vietnam	First Works Volume One	334
Latin America; Intervention In	Between the Wars, 1918-1941, Vol. 5	808
Laugh-o-Grams	Animation Vol. 1: The Beginning	706
Laughing Gas	Dental Follies	267
Laughing Gas	Charlie Chaplin's Keystone Comedies	407
Laughing Gas	Keystones #3	407
Laughing Mirror, The	European Folk Tales, Volume 6	646
Launchpad's Civil War	High-Flying Hero	693
Laundromat	William Wegman Reel 4	491
Laurel and Hardy Murder Case	Laurel and Hardy Spooktacular	274
Law of the Jungle	Timon and Pumbaa's Wild Adventures: Live and Learn	694
LBS	Computer Animation Classics	708
Le Cendre	Pascal Aubier Films	487
Le Circuse Electrique	Le Petit Theatre de Jean Renoir	26
Le Dernier Reveillon	Le Petit Theatre de Jean Renoir	26
Le Masque	Le Plaisir	27
Le Poisson D'amour	I Became a Lesbian and Others Too	460
Le Poulet	Award Winning French Shorts	2
Le Retour a la Raison	Man Ray Video	486
Le Roi D'Yvetot	Le Petit Theatre de Jean Renoir	26
Lea Press on Limbs	Spike & Mike's Festival of Animation Vol. 1	716
Lean Mean Machine	Human Race Club: A Story About Fights Between Brothers and Sisters	635
Leaving the 20th Century	Video Art: Leaving the 20th Century and Perfect Leader	490
Legend of Sleepy Hallow, The	The Adventures of Ichabod & Mr. Toad	690
Legend of Sleepy Hollow	Shelley Duvall's Tall Tales and Legends	658
Lemon Grove Kids Go Hollywood	The Lemon Grove Kids	507
Lemon Grove Kids Meet	The Lemon Grove Kids	507
Lemon Grove Kids, The	The Lemon Grove Kids	507
Lena and the Geese	Griffith Shorts (1912, #1)	413
Lentil	Norman the Doorman and Other Stories	639
Leonardo's Deluge	Art on Film/Film on Art, Program 3: Film Form/Art Form	545
Leopold the See-Through Crumb	The Three Robbers and Other Stories	643
Lerch Hairpiece	William Wegman Reel 5	491
Les Mistons	Classic Foreign Shorts—Volume 2	153
Les Mysteres du Chateau du De	Man Ray Video	486
Les Petits Cons	Pascal Aubier Films	487
Les Saisons Quatre a Quatre	International Tournee of Animation Volume 5	712
Lesser Evil	Griffith Shorts (1912, #1)	413
Let There Be Light	Rugrats: A Baby's Gotta Do What a Baby's Gotta Do	641, 701
Let's Chop Soo-E!	Too Outrageous Animation	717
Let's Go to the Movies	Origins of the Motion Picture	337
Let's Talk About Sex	Erotique	430
Letter on Light Blue Stationer	Human Race Club: A Story About Self-Esteem, a Story About Earning Money	635
Letter to Amy, A	The Ezra Jack Keats Library	633
Letter to Amy, A	The Pigs' Wedding and Other Stories	640
Letter, The	Frog and Toad Are Friends	652
Letter, The	William Wegman Reel 4	491
Lezzie Life	Lesbovision	462
Liberated Don Quixote	Masters of Russian Animation: Volume 2	82, 713
Liberty	Slapstick Encyclopedia—Vol. 6: Hal Roach: The Lot of Fun	411
License to Kill	Spike & Mike's Festival of Animation Vol. 2	716
Life and Death of 9421	Avant Garde Program #12	482
Life and Death of a Hollywood	American Avant-Garde	482
Life and Death of an Architect	Trio	489

SHORT FILM	COMPILATION TAPE	PAGE
Life for a Life, A	Early Russian Cinema: Before the Revolution, Vol. 9: High Society	85
Life in Cartoons: Red Hot	Early Animation Vol. 1	709
Life is Flashing (Before Your Eyes)	Tony Vegas' Animated Acidburn Flashback Tabu	717
Life Lessons	New York Stories	260, 288
Life with Zoe	New York Stories	260, 288
Lifelines	Films by Ed Emshwiller	484
Lift, The	International Tournee of Animation Volume 5	712
Light and Heavy	CineBLAST! Vol. 3	428
Light Darkness	Animation Celebration Vol. 3	705
Light of Experience, The	Civilization, Programs 7 & 8	781
Light that Came, The	Griffith Shorts (1909)	412
Light Trails	William Wegman Reel 1	491
Lighthouse Keeping	Thirties Magic Vol. 2	717
Lights Before Dawn	International Tournee of Animation Volume 3	712
Like a Breeze	Jim Davis: Volume #2	486
Lilo Wanders Gives Up	Men in Shorts	463
Lilting Towards Chaos	6 Films by Mark Street	482
Lily of the Tenements	Griffith Shorts (1910-1911)	413
Limbo District	Figures	484
Limit the Tube Way	New Dominion Tank Police Vol. 2: Episodes 3 and 4	738
Limnologic Jargon	Critical Art Ensemble	483
Lincoln and Gettysburg	Civil War Journal, Set II	779
Lineage	Griffiti	710
Lines of White on a Sullen Sea	Griffith Shorts (1909)	412
Lion and Ox	Masters of Russian Animation: Volume 6—The Works	82, 713
Lion and the Mouse	The Dingles	632
Lion Tamer, The	Cartoon Classics Vol. 8: Early Thirties	680
Lion Tamer, The	Tom & Jerry & Friends #4	688
Lion, The	Animaland (9 Titles)	705
Lion, The	British Animation Vol. 2	707
Liquid Selves	Computer Animation Festival Vol. 2.0	708
Listen The Body	Art Com Video 2: Waveforms: Video Japan	482
Listen to Britain	Listen to Britain	474, 769
Listener, The	Best of the Fests, 5th Annual	706
Little Bear's Sweet Tooth	Maurice Sendak's Little Bear—Parties & Picnics	637
Little Beau Porky	Cartoon Collection Vol. 3: Coal Black & De Sebben Dwarfs	680
Little Bird Told Me, A	Cartoon Classics Vol. 5: The Other Studios	680
Little Black Sambo	Cartoon Classics in Color #1: Comicolor/Van Beuren	679
Little Black Sambo	Cartoon Collection Vol. 5: Racial Cartoons	680
Little Boy Blue	Cartoons That Time Forgot Vol. 5: Free-Form Fairytales	681
Little Brown Burro, The	Christmas Carousel	630
Little Brown Jug	Little Lulu (Cartoonies)	685
Little Buck Cheezer	MGM Cartoon Classics: Happy Harmonies	686
Little Cake of Horrors	Tiny Toon Fiendishly Funny Adventures	688
Little Cheezer	MGM Cartoon Classics: Happy Harmonies	686
Little Chimney Sweep	Lotte Reiniger Compilation	713
Little Death, The	Computer Animation Classics	708
Little Drummer Boy	Christmas Stories	631
Little Fugitives, The	Nadia Movie Compilation	737
Little Genitalia	Sextoons: An Erotic Animation Festival	715
Little Goldfish, The	MGM Cartoon Classics: Happy Harmonies	686
Little Match Girl	Renoir Silent Shorts	26
Little Mermaid, The	Disney Canta con Nosotros	672
Little Miss Muffet	Ray Harryhausen Compilation	715
Little Mole, The	MGM Cartoon Classics: Happy Harmonies	686
Little Ms. Muffet	Sextoons: An Erotic Animation Festival	715
Little Nemo	Animation Vol. 1: The Beginning	706
Little Nemo	Classic Shorts Compilation #12: Winsor McCay	682
Little Nemo	Pioneers in Animation Vol. 1	714
Little Nemo	A Tribute to Winsor McCay	717
Little Nemo	Winsor McCay: Animation Legend	718
Little Nobody	Best of Betty Boop	677
Little Orphan Airdale	Porky!	687
Little Quacker	Tom & Jerry's Festival of Fun	689
Little Red Hen, The	Blue Ribbon Stories Vol. 1	650
Little Red Hen, The	Cartoons That Time Forgot Vol. 1: All Singing! All Dancing!	681
Little Red Hen, The	More Stories for the Very Young	655
Little Red Riding Hood	The Dingles	632
Little Red Riding Hood	Too Outrageous Animation	717
Little Red Riding Hood	Ray Harryhausen Compilation	715
Little Red Rodent Hood	Wince upon a Time: Foolhardy Fairy Tales & Looney Legends	690
Little Routine, A	Griffiti	710
Little Rude Riding Hood	Too Outrageous Animation	717
Little School Mouse	Tom & Jerry on Parade	689
Little Tease, The	The Short Films of D.W. Griffith—Volume 2	413
Little Toad to the Rescue	Poky's Favorite Stories	656
Little Toot and the Loch Ness	Shelley Duvall's Bedtime Stories: Little Toot and the Loch Ness Monster and Choo Choo	657
Little Wolf	International Tournee of Animation Volume 6	712
Little Women in Transit	Girl Friends (Shorts)	229, 460
Live Gost, The	Laurel and Hardy Spooktacular	274
Live Wires and Love Sparks	Slapstick Encyclopedia—Vol. 5: Chaplin and Co.: The Music Hall Tradition	411
Liver, Lust, or Louie	Too Outrageous Animation	717
Living in a Mobile Home	International Tournee of Animation Volume 3	712
Lloyd Loses His Lunch	Spike & Mike's Sick & Twisted Festival of Animation, Vol. 3	716
Lloyd's Lunchbox	Spike & Mike's Sick & Twisted Festival of Animation, Vol. 2	716
Loaded Weapon, The	Story of English	860
Local Talent	Early Animation Vol. 1	709
Locomotion	Computer Animation Festival Vol. 1.0	708
Log	Ren & Stimpy: Nothing But Shorts	701
Log	Ren & Stimpy Vol. 1: The Classics	701
Log Driver's Waltz	NFBC: Every Child	714
Log Driver's Waltz, The	NFBC: Cartoon Festival: The Cat Came Back	714
Log Driver's Waltz, The	NFBC: Leonard Maltin's Animation Favorites from the National Film Board of Canada	714
Log, The	Spike & Mike's Festival of Animation Vol. 2	716
Lola's Promise	D.W. Griffith Triple Feature	412
Lolly, Lolly, Lolly	Schoolhouse Rock: Grammar Rock	702
Lone Star State, The	Paramount/Fleischer Studios Volume 3	686
Lone Stranger, The	Cartoon Collection Vol. 5: Racial Cartoons	680
Lonedale Operator	The Short Films of D.W. Griffith—Volume 2	413
Lonedale Operator, The	Griffith Shorts (1911)	413
Lonely Villa	The Short Films of Mary Pickford	404
Lonesome Stranger, The	MGM Cartoon Classics: Happy Harmonies	686

SHORT FILM	COMPILATION TAPE	PAGE
Long Beach Earthquake	Cityscape Compilations	470
Long Pants	Long Pants	351
Long Road, The	Griffith Shorts (1909-1911)	413
Looking for Sally	Charley Chase Vol. 2	410
Looking for Trouble	Comedy Classics of Mack Sennett and Hal Roach	410
Looking for Trouble	Snub Pollard...A Short But Funny Man	411
Loony Tom	Films of James Broughton, Volume 2: Rituals of Play	492
Looping	Kisses in the Dark	234
Loose in a Caboose	Little Lulu and Friends	685
Loose in the Caboose	Cartoon Collection Vol. 6: The Ducktators	680
Loose in the Caboose	Great & Minor Animation Volume 3	684
Lost Button, A	Frog and Toad Are Friends	652
Lost World, The	Willis O'Brien Primitives	717
Lot in Sodom	American Avant-Garde	482
Lot in Sodom	American Avant-Garde Films	482
Lot in Sodom	Experimental Avant Garde Series Volume 21 (An Attack on Social, Sexual, and Political Order	484
Lot in Sodom	Third Sex Sinema Volume 2—The Song of the Loon	466
Lou Falls for Ruby	The Abbott and Costello Television Show, Tape 3	414
Lou's Birthday	The Abbott and Costello Television Show, Tape 2	414
Lou's Marriage	The Abbott and Costello Television Show, Tape 5	414
Love	Slapstick Encyclopedia—Vol. 6: Hal Roach: The Lot of Fun	411
Love Amongst Machines	Video Works: Miroslaw Rogala (1980-86)	491
Love at First Sight	Outrageous Animation Vol. 1	714
Love Cheerfully Arranged	Love in the City	41
Love in the Fast Lane	Plymptoons: The Complete Works of Bill Plympton	715
Love in the Hills	Griffith Shorts (1909-1911)	413
Love It, Leave It	Tom Palazzolo: Films from the Sixties	478
Love Loot and Crash	Comedy Classics of Mack Sennett and Hal Roach	410
Love Nest on Wheels	Buster Keaton Talkies, Vol. 1	408
Love of a Mother, The	Love in the City	41
Love Show	Potato Wolf Coleslaw	435
Love Story, A	Letterist Films—Woman, Women!	432
Love Strikes Hard	Teasers	466
Love Teller	Just Hold Still	486
Love, Loot and Crash	Early Comedies Volume 1	410
Love, Loot and Crash	Lloyd and Chase at Keystone	411
Lovelorn Giant, The	European Folk Tales, Volume 1	646
Loves of Franistan	Experimental Avant Garde Series Volume 19 (Very Serious Fun)	484
Loves of Franistan	Classic Foreign Shorts—Volume 1	153
Loves Water	William Wegman Reel 5	491
Loving	Stan Brakhage Selected Films: Vol. 1	488
Lowell Moves to New York	Variety Is the Spice of Life	489
Lucas—The Ear	Plymptoons: The Complete Works of Bill Plympton	715
Luchare	Variety Is the Spice of Life	489
Lucifer Rising	Lucifer Rising	486
Lucky Dog	Laurel and Hardy: The Legend Begins	411
Lucky Star	Films of Harry Langdon Volume 2	410
Lucky Stars	Baby Face Harry Langdon	410
Lucky T-shirt	William Wegman Reel 3	491
Lucretia	NFBC—Cartoon Festival: The Sweater	714
Luke's Movie Muddle	Lloyd and Chase at Keystone	411
Lulu at the Zoo	Little Lulu (Cartoonies)	685
Lulu's Doctor	Matinee Idols: The Ladies	401
Lump, The	The National Film Board of Canada's Animation Festival	714
Lunch	Tony Vegas' Animated Acidburn Flashback Tabu	737
Luncheon	International Tournee of Animation Volume 1	711
Lupo the Butcher	Outrageous Animation Vol. 1	714
Luxo, Jr.	Tiny Toy Stories	717
Lynch	Franck Goldberg: Sampler	8
Ma: Space and Time in the Garden	Art on Film/Film on Art, Program 1: Balance: Film/Art	545
Mabel & Fatty's Wash Day	Fatty Arbuckle	410
Mabel at the Wheel	Keystones #1	407
Mabel Lost	Arbuckle Volume 3	410
Mabel's Busy Day	Classic Chaplin, Charlie Chaplin at Keystone Studio	407
Mabel's Busy Day	Keystones #2	407
Mabel's Dramatic Career	Slapstick Encyclopedia—Vol. 1: In the Beginning	411
Mabel's Married Life	Charlie Chaplin's Keystone Comedies	407
Mabel's Married Life	Keystones #2	407
Mabel's Married Life	Tillie's Punctured Romance	412
Mabel's Strange Predicament	Keystones #1	407
Mabel, Mabel	Arbuckle Volume 3	410
Macabre Nightmare	Coffin Joe's Visions of Terror	518
Macha's Curse	Best of the Fests 1990	706
Machine Room	Hard	460
Mad Beltway, The	Astro Boy Volume 8	722
Mad Doctor, The	Great & Minor Animation Volume 1	684
Mad Doctor, The	Mickey Mouse: The Black & White Years	693
Mad Doctors of Borneo	Too Outrageous Animation	717
Mad Maestro, The	MGM Cartoon Classics: Happy Harmonies	686
Madcap	Best of the Fests 1991	706
Madeline & The Bad Hat	Alice in Wonderland in Paris	705
Madeline & The Gypsies	Alice in Wonderland in Paris	705
Madeline and the Bad Hat	Madeline's Rescue	654
Madeline and the Gypsies	Madeline's Rescue	654
Madeline's Rescue	Madeline's Rescue	654
Magenta Geryon	Live Short Films by Larry Jordan	718
Magic	Simultaneous	488
Magic Art	Tom & Jerry & Friends #4	688
Magic Cloak of Oz, The	L. Frank Baum's Silent Film Collection of Oz	400
Magic Flute, The	NFBC—Cartoon Festival: The Sweater	714
Magic Flute, The	A Christmas Gift	707
Magic Flute, The	NFBC: Every Child	714
Magic Globe, The	Johny Sokko and His Flying Robot: Episodes 1 and 2	734
Magic Lantern, The	More Melies	22
Magic Mummy, The	Tom & Jerry & Friends #7	688
Magic Punch Card, The	Astro Boy Volume 4	722
Magician	The Adventures of Blinky Bill: Blinky Bill's Zoo/Magician	628
Magnetic Telescope	Superman (50th Anniversary)	688
Magnetic Telescope, The	Color Adventures of Superman	682
Mail Pilot, The	Mickey Mouse: The Black & White Years	693
Makin' Up	Makin' Up	64
Making a Living	Classic Chaplin, Charlie Chaplin at Keystone Studio	407
Making a Living	Charlie Chaplin's Keystone Comedies	407
Making a Living	Keystones #1	407
Making of Bronco Billy	Bronco Billy Anderson	396
Making of Gunsmith Cats	Gunsmith Cats 1: Special Edition	731
Making of Red Green, The	The Best of Red Green	414
Making of the Tune	The Tune	717
Making Offon	Films of Scott Bartlett, Vol. 2: The Future of Human Mythology	485
Making Serpent	Films of Scott Bartlett, Vol. 3: The Process of Creation	485
Making Stars	Cartoon Collection Vol. 4: Warner Bros. & Fleischer	680
Malaria Mike	Cartoon Collection Vol. 8: Private Snafu	680
Male Nudists, The	Third Sex Sinema Volume 5—Consenting Adults	466, 511
Malice in the Palace	The Three Stooges	284
Man About Town	Stan About Town	411
Man About Town	Films of Stan Laurel Volume 2	410
Man and His World, A	Bruno Bozzetto: Animator, Vol. 1	707
Man Descending	Best of the Fests 1991	706
Man from Nowhere, The	Early Westerns #1	397
Man from Tia Juana	Early Westerns #1	397
Man in the Moon	Early Animation Vol. 2	709
Man Tamer	Films of Edmund Cobb	398
Man Who Yelled, The	International Tournee of Animation Volume 6	712
Man with a Punch, The	Early Westerns #2	398
Man with the Twisted Lip, The	The "Silent" Mr. Sherlock Holmes	187
Man's Best Friend	Man's Best Friend	685
Man's Genesis	Griffith Shorts (1912, #1)	413
Man's Genesis	The Short Films of D.W. Griffith—Volume 2	413
Man's Pest Friend	Little Lulu (Cartoonies)	685
Man—The Measure of all Things	Civilization, Programs 3 & 4	781
Mandarin Mix-Up	Stan About Town	411
Mandragora	Secrets of Love, Classics of Erotic Literature: Vol. 3	510
Manhattan	Cityscape Compilations	470
Maniac	Maniac and Protect Your Daughter	508
Manicure Lady, The	Mack Sennett: The Biograph Years	411
Manipulation	Spike & Mike's Festival of Animation Vol. 2	716
Manly Games	Scenes from the Surreal	715
Many Moons	Alice in Wonderland in Paris	705
Many Ray	William Wegman Reel 3	491
Marbles	William Wegman Reel 5	491
Marcello, I'm So Bored	First Works Volume One	334
Marie	CineBLAST! Vol. 3	428
Marines Have Landed	The Battle of San Pietro/Marines Have Landed	766
Mark Rappaport: The TV Spinoff	Three Short Films (Mark Rappaport)	438
Marmot Mountain	Marmot Mountain/Yellowstone Below Zero (BBC Wildlife Special)	352
Marquette Park I	Chicago Nazis	470
Marquette Park II	Chicago Nazis	470
Martina's Playhouse	Martina's Playhouse and The Scary Movie	487
Marty the Monk	Thirties Magic Vol. 1	716
Martyr, The	Animated Classics of Japanese Literature: The Martyr/ The Priest of Mt. Kouya	720
Mary of Mile 18	NFBC: The Box	714
Mary's Little Lamb	Cartoons That Time Forgot Vol. 1: All Singing! All Dancing!	681
Mary's Little Lamb	Ub Iwerks' Famous Fairytales	689
Mascot, The	The Cameraman's Revenge: The Amazing Puppet Animation of Ladislaw Starewicz	707
Mascot, The	Ladislas Starevitch	712
Mascot, The	Puppet Masters	715
Masque of the Red Death	Four for Thrills, Edgar Allan Poe, Etc.	633
Masquerade	Short Animations by Larry Jordan	718
Masquerader, The	Classic Chaplin, Charlie Chaplin at Keystone Studio	407
Masquerader, The	Keystones #3	407
Massacre	Griffith Shorts (1912, #3)	413
Massage Chair	Best of William Wegman	483
Massage Chair	William Wegman Reel 3	491
Master of Evil	Jonny Quest: Dr. Zin—Master of Evil	698
Masterpieces of the Met	Metropolitan Museum Boxed Set	553
Masters of the Djinni	Fearless Fortune Hunter	683
Matador	CineBLAST! Vol. 3	428
Matrimonial Agency, The	Love in the City	41
Matters of Life and Death	The Incredible Story of Dogs	816
Max	Female Misbehavior	63, 459
Max's Chocolate Chicken	Max's Chocolate Chicken	654
Max's Christmas	More Stories for the Very Young	655
Max's Place	Computer Animation Classics	708
Maxi Cat's Lunch	Outrageous Animation Vol. 2	714
May 19th	Potato Wolf Spring 1984	435
Maya	Dyke Drama	458
Me and Joe	Four Directions: Selections from MIX 94— The NY Lesbian & Gay Film Festival	459
Me and My Pal	Laurel and Hardy: Stan "Helps" Ollie	274
Measurements of Oxford, The	Best of the Fests 1990	706
Mebel's New Hero	Mabel Normand Comedies, Vol. 2	411
Mechanical Cow	Disney's Beginnings	692
Mechanical Man	Thirties Magic Vol. 1	716
Mechanical Man, The	Cartoon Classics Vol. 8: Early Thirties	680
Mechanical Monsters, The	Color Adventures of Superman	682
Mechanical Monsters, The	Superman (50th Anniversary)	688
Media Burn	Cadillac Ranch/Media Burn	483
Mediation on Violence	Maya Deren Experimental Films	487
Mediations	Video Art: Gary Hill	490
Medina	Films of Scott Bartlett, Vol. 2: The Future of Human Mythology	485
Meditation: The Inward Journey	Alan Watts: The Art of Meditation	847
Megacycles	Computer Animation Classics	708
Melomaniac	Films of Georges Melies, Volume 1	20
Mended Lute-Sealed Room	Griffith Shorts (1909)	412
Menschen	Art Com Video 1: Scandinavia	482
Menses	Lesbian Humor	461, 492
Merchant Bashirov's Daughter	Early Russian Cinema: Before the Revolution, Vol. 4: Provincial Variations	85
Merchants and Masterpieces	Metropolitan Museum Boxed Set	553
Mercury Exploration	Exploration: Space	839
Merkala Beach	Halfmoon	63, 304
Mermaid, The	More Melies	22
Merrily Yours	Shirley Temple and Friends	282
Merry Christmas	Christmas Cartoon Classic	682
Meshes of the Afternoon	Maya Deren Experimental Films	487
Message of the Violin, The	Griffith Shorts (1910-1911)	413
Metal Dogs of India	Best of the Fests: For Kids	706

SHORT FILM	COMPILATION TAPE	PAGE
Metal Modern Romance	M/W/F Music Video One	433
Metamorphoses	NFBC: The Tender Tale of Cinderella Penguin	714
Mexican Joyride	Daffy!	683
MGM Studio Tour	Touring the Silent Studios	405
Mickey and the Beanstalk	Fun and Fancy Free	692
Mickey Cuts Up	Mickey Mouse: The Black & White Years	693
Mickey Steps Out	Mickey Mouse: The Black & White Years	693
Mickey's Delayed Date	Disney Love Tales	691
Mickey's Follies	Mickey Mouse: The Black & White Years	693
Mickey's Gala Premiere	Mickey Mouse: The Black & White Years	693
Mickey's Nightmare	Mickey Mouse: The Black & White Years	693
Mickey's Orphans	Mickey Mouse: The Black & White Years	693
Mickey's Revue	Mickey Mouse: The Black & White Years	693
Mickey's Rival	Disney Sweetheart Stories	692
Mickey's Service Station	Mickey Mouse: The Black & White Years	693
Mickey's Song	Cartoon Collection Vol. 5: Racial Cartoons	680
Microphone	William Wegman Reel 1	491
Middle Grays	Best of the Fests 1990	706
Midnight at the Old Mill	Early Comedies Volume 2	410
Midsummer Night's Dream	Oh My Goddess!: Hybrid LD #1	739
Mighty Like a Moose	Slapstick Encyclopedia—Vol. 3: Funny Girls	411
Mighty Mouse in Wolf!	Pioneers in Animation Vol. 3	714
Miguel, Ma Belle	Boys in Love	457
Mildred Pearson: When You Love	Video Against AIDS, Volumes 1, 2 & 3	835
Milk Floor Piece	Best of William Wegman	483
Milk/Floor	William Wegman Reel 1	491
Milkman, The	Cartoons That Time Forgot Vol. 2: Down & Out with Flip the Frog	681
Milky Way, The	MGM Cartoon Classics: Happy Harmonies	686
Million Dollar Refund	The Abbott and Costello Television Show, Tape 1	414
Mindscape	NFBC: Leonard Maltin's Animation Favorites from the National Film Board of Canada	714
Mining in Ancient Greece	Ancient Greece Volume 1	784
Minotaur, The	Monsters of the Greek Myths	637
Minute the Moocher	Cartoon Collection Vol. 1: Porky in Wackyland	680
Miracle, The	Amore	38
Mirror of Reduction	Critical Art Ensemble	483
Mirror, Mirror	Amazing Stories: Book 4	414
Mirror, The	Tom Chomont: A Two-Volume Collection, Volume II	466, 489
Misappropriation	Critical Art Ensemble	483
Mischievous Kid, The	More Melies	22
Miser's Heart, The	Griffith Shorts (1911-1912)	413
Miss Fatty's Seaside Lovers	Lloyd and Chase at Keystone	411
Miss Fatty's Seaside Lovers	Fatty Arbuckle	410
Missed Fortune, A	The Three Stooges: Corny Casanovas	284
Missing Something Somewhere	6 Films by Mark Street	482
Mission at the Middle	Astro Boy Volume 8	722
Mission, The	Amazing Stories: Book 1	414
Mite Makes Right, The	Paramount/Famous Studios Volume 2	686
Mitt the Prince	Snub Pollard...A Short But Funny Man	411
Mixed Blood	Video Art, Tape Two	489
Mixed Majic	Buster Keaton Talkies, Vol. 3	408
Mixed Nuts	Stan Laurel: At the Beginning	411
Mixed Nuts	Films of Stan Laurel Volume 1	410
Mixed Nuts	Films of Stan Laurel Volume 4	410
Mixed Relations	Naughty Nostalgia #1	508
Moa Moa	International Tournee of Animation Volume 1	711
Mobiliu Fedele	Animation Vol. 1: The Beginning	706
Modeling	Cartoon Classics Vol. 6: Early Animation	680
Modelling/Bubbles	Animation Vol. 1: The Beginning	706
Modern Atlanta, A	Matinee Idols: The Ladies	401
Modern Love	Variety Is the Spice of Life	489
Modern Prodigal	Griffith Shorts (1909-1910)	412
Moe the Dog in Tropical Paradise	Shelley Duvall's Bedtime Stories: Moe the Dog in Tropical Paradise	657
Mojica No Mojo	Three Films by Chris Frieri	438
Mole's Cousin	The Wind in the Willows, Volume #3	644, 718
Molly Moo Cow & Rib Van Winkle	Cartoons That Time Forgot Vol. 6: The Odd & The Outrageous	681
Molly Moo Cow & Rip Van Winkle	Cartoon Classics Vol. 8: Early Thirties	680
Molly Moo Cow & The Butterflie	Cartoons That Time Forgot Vol. 7: Rainbow Parades	681
Molly Moo Cow & The Indians	Cartoons That Time Forgot Vol. 7: Rainbow Parades	681
Molly Moo-cow and the Butterflies	Cartoon Classics in Color #1: Comicolor/Van Beuren	679
Moments at the Rock	Takahiko Iimura: A Journey to Ayersrock	488
Mondo Familiae	Critical Art Ensemble	483
Monk and the Fish, The	Spike & Mike's Festival of Animation Vol. 3	716
Monkey Business	William Wegman Reel 2	491
Monster in the Garage	Rugrats: A Baby's Gotta Do What a Baby's Gotta Do	641, 701
Monster Machine, The	Astro Boy Volume 1	722
Monster, The	Films of Georges Melies, Volume 1	20
Monty	The Day Jimmy's Boa Ate the Wash	632
Moo Moo Cow & Robinson Crusoe	Cartoons That Time Forgot Vol. 7: Rainbow Parades	681
Moon 1969	Films of Scott Bartlett, Vol. 1: The Birth of the Counter Culture	485
Moonbird	Hubley Collection Vol. 3	711
Moonlight and Cherry Blossoms	Oh My Goddess!: Hybrid LD #1	739
Moonlight For Two	Cartoon Classics Vol. 1: Looney Tunes & Merrie Melodies	680
Moonlight for Two	Cartoon Collection Vol. 7: Tokyo Jokio	680
Moonlight Madness	Aladdin & Jasmine's Moonlight Magic	676, 690
Moonlight Sonata	Short Animations by Larry Jordan	718
More Otaku No Video	Otaku No Video	739
Mormon Maid	Ella Cinders and Mormon Maid	398
Morpheus Mike	Cartoon Classics Vol. 6: Early Animation	680
Morpheus Mike	The Genesis of Animation, Volume One	710
Morris Has a Cold	Morris the Moose	655
Morris the Midget Moose	The Reluctant Dragon	694
Morris the Moose Goes to Schoo	Morris the Moose	655
Morris's Disappearing Bag	Christmas Stories	631
Mosaic for the Kali Yuga, A	Amida/A Mosaic for the Kali Yuga/Arches/Body Count/ Hey Joe	482
Mosque in Time, A	Art on Film/Film on Art, Program 3: Film Form/Art Form	545
Most Beautiful Breasts	Makin' Up	64
Most Wonderful Egg in the Worl	Joey Runs Away and Other Stories	653
Mother and Her Love	Ambassador Magma Vol. 5: Episodes 10-11	720
Mother Goose Land	Cartoon Collection Vol. 4: Warner Bros. & Fleischer	680
Mother Tongue	Story of English	860
Mother's Day	Films of James Broughton, Volume 2: Rituals of Play	492
Mothering Heart	Griffith Shorts (1913)	413
Mothering Heart, The	A Corner in Wheat and Selected Biograph Shorts	412
Mothering Heart, The	D.W. Griffith's Years of Discovery	412
Mothering Heart, The	A Corner in Wheat and Selected Biograph Shorts	412
Motion Painting #1	The Films of Oskar Fischinger—Optical Poetry	710
Mountains and the Dynamics	Forces of Life	836
Mouse Cleaning	Tom & Jerry: Starring Tom & Jerry!	689
Mouse Wreckers	Looney Tunes Assorted Nuts	685
Mouse's Tale, The	BBC Wildlife Specials: On the Tracks of the Wild Otter/ The Mouse's Tale	813
Movie Mad	Cartoons That Time Forgot Vol. 2: Down & Out with Flip the Frog	681
Movie Star, A	Slapstick Encyclopedia—Vol. 2: Keystone Tonight!	411
Mowgli's Brothers	The Jungle Books, Set I	636
Mr. Duck Steps Out	Disney Love Tales	691
Mr. Flip	Slapstick Encyclopedia—Vol. 1: In the Beginning	411
Mr. Frog Went A-Courting	NFBC: The Tender Tale of Cinderella Penguin	714
Mr. Gloom	Outrageous Animation Vol. 2	714
Mr. Heartthrob	Alvin and the Chipmunks: Love Potion #9	628
Mr. Hiccup	Guido Manuli: Animator	710
Mr. Magic	Amazing Stories: Book 4	414
Mr. Resistor	International Tournee of Animation Volume 6	712
Mr. Too	Animation Celebration Vol. 3	705
Mrs. Ladybug	MGM Cartoon Classics: Happy Harmonies	686
Mt. Fuji	Art Com Video 2: Waveforms: Video Japan	482
Mud and Sand	Hollywood Spoofs	411
Mud Bath, A	Early Comedies Volume 1	410
Muddy Romance, A	Mabel Normand Comedies, Vol. 2	411
Muddy Romance, A	Slapstick Encyclopedia—Vol. 2: Keystone Tonight!	411
Mufaro's Beautiful Daughters	Stories from the Black Tradition	642
Mugzy's First Sweetheart	Griffith Shorts (1909-1910)	412
Multiple Orgasm	Lesbian Sexuality	462, 492
Mum's the Word	Charley Chase Vol. 2	410
Mummy Strikes	Superman (50th Anniversary)	688
Mummy Strikes, The	Color Adventures of Superman	682
Muratti Gets in the Act	The Films of Oskar Fischinger—Optical Poetry	710
Murder That Never Happened	Jack the Ripper (Karloff)	524
Muscle Tussie	Daffy Duck: Duck Victory	682
Muse of Fire, A	Story of English	860
Musgrave Ritual, The	Sherlock Holmes Cliffhangers	642
Music Box, The	Laurel and Hardy at Work	274
Musica-Lulu	Paramount/Famous Studios Volume 1	686
Musical Lulu	Cartoon Collection Vol. 6: The Ducktators	680
Musical Memories	Paramount/Fleischer Studios Volume 2	686
Musicians of Bremen, The	Katharine Hepburn: World of Stories	647
Musketeers of Pig Alley, The	Griffith Shorts (1912, #3)	413
Musketeers of Pig Alley, The	The Short Films of D.W. Griffith—Volume 2	413
Musketeers of Pig Alley, The	D.W. Griffith's Years of Discovery	412
Musketeers of Pig Alley, The	The Musketeers of Pig Alley and Selected Biograph Shorts	413
Mutable Fire	Cinema of Transgression	483
Mutilator II	Spike & Mike's Sick & Twisted Festival of Animation, Vol. 2	716
Mutiny on the Bunny	Bugs Bunny: Hare Beyond Compare	679
Mutiny on the Bunny	Yosemite Sam: The Good, The Bad and the Ornery	690
Mutts about Racing	Droopy & Company	709
Muvver Tongue, The	Story of English	860
My Birthday Cake	Best of the Fests, 5th Annual	706
My Boyfriend Gave Me Peaches	Pictures Don't Tell You Anything: Selected Films of Ann Marie Fleming	211, 487
My Bunny Lies over the Sea	Bugs Bunny: Winner by a Hare	679
My Favorite Duck	Porky!	687
My First Suit	Clay Farmers	458
My Gaijin Tengoky	Art Com Video 2: Waveforms: Video Japan	482
My Green Crocodile	CineBLAST! Vol. 3	428
My Little Duckaroo	Porky Pig Tales	687
My Polish Waiter	Boys in Love	457
My Wife's Relations	Three Ages	409
Mysteres du Chateau du De	Avant Garde Program #14	483
Mysteries Beyond	Symphony to the Planets	841
Mysteries of the Ancient World	Mysteries of the Ancient World Gift Set	791
Mysteries of the East	Jonny Quest: Hadji—Mysteries of the East	698
Mysteries of the Universe	Exploration: Space	839
Mysterious Sea Monster, The	Nadia Movie Compilation	737
Mysterious Tadpole, The	The Mysterious Tadpole and Other Stories	638
Mystery of the Amless Dam	Astro Boy Volume 3	722
Mystery of the Leaping Fish	Drug Propaganda and Satire Compilation	505
Mystery of the Lizard Men	Jonny Quest: Race Bannon—An Army of One	698
Mystery of the Metal Men	Astro Boy Volume 6	722
Mystic Lamb	Rare Dutch and Belgian Experimental Program	31, 488
Nail Business	William Wegman Reel 4	491
Naked Hands	Bronco Billy Anderson	396
Naked Hipstress	Destroy All Blondes/The Naked Hipstress/Sick Sick Sister	429
Nanna & L'il Puss Puss	Too Outrageous Animation	717
Napping House, The	Happy Birthday Moon and Other Stories	647
Napping House, The	More Stories for the Very Young	655
Narrow Road, The	Griffith Shorts (1912, #2)	413
Nation Aflame	Nation Aflame and Probation	508
Native Food	Wartime Cartoons	717
Natural Born Gambler, A	Slapstick Encyclopedia—Vol. 1: In the Beginning	411
Naughts	Stan Brakhage—Hand-Painted Films	488
Naughty But Mice	Little Lulu and Friends	685
Naughty But Nice	Paramount/Fleischer Studios Volume 3	686
Naughty Nurse	Paul Bartel's Secret Cinema	435
Nautilus to the Rescue	Nadia Movie Compilation	737
Navigator	Art of Buster Keaton—Box 2	408
Navy Steward	The Black Military Experience	450
Near Dublin	Films of Stan Laurel Volume 4	410
Near Dublin	Versatile Mr. Laurel	412
Near to the Earth	Griffith Shorts (1913)	413
Negative Man	Spike & Mike's Festival of Animation Vol. 2	716
Negro in Sports	Rare Black Short Subjects	448
Negro Sailor	The Black Military Experience	450
Neighbors	Seven Chances	409
Nekromantik	Corpse Fucking Art	505
Neoimpressionist Painter	Attack of the Cohl Pumpkins	706
Neptune Nonsense	Cartoons That Time Forgot Vol. 6: The Odd & The Outrageous	681
Neptune Nonsense	Great & Minor Animation Volume 1	684

SHORT FILM	COMPILATION TAPE	PAGE
Neptune's Nonsense	Best of the Van Beuren Studio	677
Never Change	Just Hold Still	486
Never Waken	Harold Lloyd Comedies Vol. 2	410
New and Used Car Salesman	William Wegman Reel 4	491
New Car, The	Cartoons That Time Forgot Vol. 2: Down & Out with Flip the Frog	681
New Earth	Classic Documentaries: People and Places	470
New Earth	Rare Dutch and Belgian Experimental Program	31, 488
New Fangled	Griffiti	710
New Frontier, The	The Power and the Land: Four Documentary Portraits of the Great Depression	476
New Janitor, The	Charlie Chaplin's Keystone Comedies	407
New Janitor, The	Keystones #3	407
New Refrigerator, The	Lassie: Mother Knows Best	636
New Science of Life	A Glorious Accident	782
New Shoes	Nice Girls...Films by and About Women	434
New Shoes	Pictures Don't Tell You Anything: Selected Films of Ann Marie Fleming	211, 487
New World, The	Rogopag	10, 37, 39, 41
New Year, Pts. 1 & 2	Video Art, Tape One	489
New York Hat, The	Griffith Shorts (1912, #3)	413
New York Hat, The	The Short Films of Mary Pickford	404
New York Hat, The	A Corner in Wheat and Selected Biograph Shorts	412
New York Hat, The	D.W. Griffith's Years of Discovery	412
Newman Laugh-O-Grams	Cartoon Classics Vol. 3: The Early Pioneers	680
Next Door	Spike & Mike's Festival of Animation Vol. 2	716
Next Stop—The English Riviera	Railway Adventures Across Europe: Volume 1	843
Next Time Everything Will Be	The Day You Love Me	49
Next Year's Words: A Look Into	Story of English	860
Nice Girls Don't Do It	Nice Girls...Films by and About Women	434
Nicklehopper, The	Mabel Normand Comedies, Vol. 1	411
Nifty Nineties	Disney Sweetheart Stories	692
Niggernight	Cinema of Transgression	483
Night Before Christmas, The	Tom & Jerry's The Night Before Christmas	689
Night in the Show, A	Classic Chaplin, Charlie Chaplin at Essanay Studio	407
Night in the Show, A	Essanay #3	407
Night in the Show, A	Rare Chaplin	408
Night in the Show, A	Slapstick Encyclopedia—Vol. 5: Chaplin and Co.: The Music Hall Tradition	411
Night Mail	Benjamin Britten	469
Night Mail	Classic Documentaries: People and Places	470
Night Mail	The Plow That Broke the Plains/Night Mail	476
Night Music	Stan Brakhage—Hand-Painted Films	488
Night of the Living Duck	Bugs Bunny's Creature Features	678
Night of the Living Duck	Daffy Duck's Quackbusters	682
Night of the Living Duck	Looney Tunes After Dark	685
Night of the Living Pets	Tiny Toon Fiendishly Funny Adventures	688
Night on Bald Mountain	Alexeieff & Parker	482, 705
Night Out, A	Essanay #1	407
Night Watchman, The	Golden Age of Looney Tunes: Vol. 5, Chuck Jones	684
Nightingale, The	Katharine Hepburn: World of Stories	647
Nightlife	BBC Wildlife Special Volume 2	813
No Deposit, No Return	Fueling the Future	803
No Neck Joe	Spike & Mike's Sick & Twisted Festival of Animation, Vol. 3	716
No No Nooky T.V.	Lesbian Humor	461, 492
No Pain, No Gain	Best of the Fests 1990	706
No Place Like Home	Fueling the Future	803
No Place Like Jail	Laurel and Hardy Solo Flights	411
No Sell Out	M/W/F Music Video One	433
No Sellout	Franck Goldberg: Sampler	8
No Sign of Life	Men in Shorts, Volume 2	463
No Smoking in this Theater	It's Clean—It Just Looks Dirty	486
No Substitute	Cartoongate!	681
No Toon is an Island	Tiny Toon Island Adventures	688
Noah Knew His Ark	Tom & Jerry & Friends #3	688
Noah Knew His Ark	Van Beuren Studio, Volume #2	689
Noah's Outing	Fox Terrytoons	684
Nocturna Artificiala	The Brothers Quay Vol. 2	707
Nocturne	William Wegman Reel 5	491
Non Stop Fright, The	Weird Cartoons Vol. 2	717
Non-Stop Freight	Classic Shorts Compilation #14: Felix the Cat	682
Non-Stop Kid	Films of Harold Lloyd—Volume 1	409
Non-Stop Kid, The	Harold Lloyd Comedies Vol. 1	410
Noodle Ear	Plymptoons: The Complete Works of Bill Plympton	715
Noon Whistle, The	The Bellhop/The Noon Whistle	395
Noon Whistle, The	Stanley on the Job	412
Noon Whistle-Oranges and Lemon	Early Comedies Volume 2	410
Norman the Doorman	Norman the Doorman and Other Stories	639
North of Vortex	Caught Looking & North of Vortex	457
North Sea	England in the Thirties	471
North Wales: Chester	British Rail Journeys	841
North Wind and the Sun, The	NFBC: The Sand Castle	714
Northern England: Settle	British Rail Journeys	841
Nose (Le Nez), The	Alexeieff & Parker	482, 705
Nose to the Wind	Ladislas Starevitch	712
Nosy	William Wegman Reel 1	491
Not a Shadow of a Doubt	Tazmania: Taz-Maniac	703
Not For Ourselves Alone	Americans Courageous (1600-1950s)	808
Not Now	Cartoon Collection Vol. 8: Private Snafu	680
Not So Fast Songololo	More Stories for the Very Young	655
Not Without My Handbag	Creature Comforts	708
Notes to You	Cartoon Collection Vol. 2: Classic Warner Bros.	680
Notes to You	Pioneers in Animation Vol. 3	714
Now is the Time for All Good	Cartoongate!	681
Now We Live on Clifton	Kartemquin Films, Vol. 2: Winnie Wright, Age 11	474
Now You Tell One	Slapstick Encyclopedia—Vol. 8: Tons of Fun: Comedy's Anarchic Fringe	411
Nucleaon	Johnny Sokko and His Flying Robot: Episodes 1 and 2	734
Numen Lumen	Wheeler Dixon: Selected Films	491
Nunja Monster, The	Johnny Sokko and His Flying Robot: Episodes 7 and 8	734
Nuremburg Und Sein Lehre	Nazis...Lest We Forget!	770
Nurse Maid, The	Cartoons That Time Forgot Vol. 2: Down & Out with Flip the Frog	681
Nurse Stimpy	Ren & Stimpy Vol. 3: The Stinkiest Stories	701
Nutman's Got the Blues: Cyrus	Three Piano Portraits	616
Nutshell Library: Alligators	The Maurice Sendak Library	654
Object Conversation	The Paul Glabicki Animation Tape	714

SHORT FILM	COMPILATION TAPE	PAGE
Observational Hazard	Outrageous Animation Vol. 2	714
Occurrence at Owl Creek Bridge	La Jetee/An Occurrence at Owl Creek Bridge	4, 10
Occurrence at Owl Creek Bridge	An Occurrence at Owl Creek Bridge	22, 301
Oceantics	Cartoon Collection Vol. 7: Tokyo Jokio	680
Oceantics	Early Animation Vol. 2	709
Oceantics	Felix the Cat: Sound & Silent	683
Ode to G.I. Joe	International Tournee of Animation Volume 5	712
Oedipus Wrecks	New York Stories	260, 288
Of Stars and Men	Hubley Studio: Of Men and Demons	711
Offen	Films of Scott Bartlett, Vol. 1: The Birth of the Counter Culture	485
Office Boy, The	Cartoons That Time Forgot Vol. 2: Down & Out with Flip the Frog	681
Office Space	Animation Celebration Vol. 4	706
Officer Pooch	Droopy & Company	709
Often an Orphan	Porky Pig: Ham on Wry	687
Oh Crappy Day	Spike & Mike's Sick & Twisted Festival of Animation: Vol. 2	716
Oh Dad Ii	Greentoons: Environmentally Aware Animation	710
Oh, Doctor!	Slapstick Encyclopedia—Vol. 4: Keaton, Arbuckle & Al St. John	411
Oh, My Achin' Tooth	Dental Follies	267
Oh, The Thanks You Can Think	One Fish Two Fish Red Fish Blue Fish, Spanish Narration	655
Oh, The Thanks You Can Think	One Fish Two Fish Red Fish Blue Fish, English Narration	655
Oil and Water	Griffith Shorts (1912, #3)	413
Oily Bird, The	Felix the Cat: Sound & Silent	683
Old Anything	Cartoon Classics Vol. 8: Early Thirties	680
Old Anything	Weird Cartoons Vol. 2	717
Old Box, An	NFBC: An Animated Christmas	714
Old Box, An	A Christmas Gift	707
Old Glory	Golden Age of Looney Tunes: Vol. 5, Chuck Jones	684
Old Grey Hare	Bugs Bunny Superstar	678
Old Hokum Bucket	Tom & Jerry & Friends #7	688
Old Manor House	British Animation Vol. 2	707
Old Mother Hubbard	Cartoons That Time Forgot Vol. 1: All Singing! All Dancing!	681
Old Plantation, The	MGM Cartoon Classics: Happy Harmonies	686
Old Shell Game, The	Paramount/Fleischer Studios Volume 2	686
Old Stair	Masters of Russian Animation: Volume 2	82, 713
Oliver the Eighth	Laurel and Hardy Spooktacular	274
On the Ball	William Wegman Reel 4	491
On the Fire	Films of Harold Lloyd—Volume 1	409
On the Front Page	Films of Stan Laurel Volume 1	410
On the Job	Films of Stan Laurel Volume 1	410
On the Tracks of the Wild Otter	BBC Wildlife Specials: On the Tracks of the Wild Otter/ The Mouse's Tale	813
Once Upon a Time	Short Animations by Larry Jordan	718
One A.M.	Charlie Chaplin Early Years II	407
One A.M.	Classic Chaplin, Charlie Chaplin at Mutual Studios	407
One Droopy Knight	Droopy & Company	709
One Fish Two Fish Red Fish	One Fish Two Fish Red Fish Blue Fish, Spanish Narration	655
One Fish Two Fish Red Fish	One Fish Two Fish Red Fish Blue Fish, English Narration	655
One Froggy Evening	Looney Tunes Curtain Calls	685
One Good Turn	Felix the Cat—Silent—Volume 2	683
One Good Turn	Aesop's Film Fables	676
One Good Turn	Laurel and Hardy on the Lam	274
One Ham's Family	Tom & Jerry's The Night Before Christmas	689
One is Business the Other Crime	Griffith Shorts (1912, #2)	413
One is Business the Other Crime	D.W. Griffith's Years of Discovery	412
One is Business the Other Crime	The Musketeers of Pig Alley and Selected Biograph Shorts	413
One Man's Instrument	Spike & Mike's Sick & Twisted Festival of Animation Vol. 1	716
One Million Mammoth Snails	Astro Boy Volume 2	722
One More Chance	Bing at Sennett Vol. 2	263
One More Chance	Betty Boop's Dizzy Dozen	678
One More Time	Cartoon Classics Vol. 2: Warner Brothers	680
One More Time	Cartoon Collection Vol. 4: Warner Bros. & Fleischer	680
One Nation Under TV	Tony Vegas' Animated Acidburn Flashback Tabu	717
One Night Stand, A	Comedy of Chester Conklin	410
One of the Family	Charley Chase Jimmy Jump Series	410
One of those Days	Plymptoons: The Complete Works of Bill Plympton	715
One of those Days	Outrageous Animation Vol. 1	714
One Plane, One Bomb	You Can Beat the A-Bomb	807
One Run Elmer	Buster Keaton Talkies, Vol. 1	408
One Too Many	Slapstick Encyclopedia—Vol. 1: In the Beginning	411
One Two Many	Babe Hardy: Early Training	410
One Was Johnny	The Maurice Sendak Library	654
One Week	The Saphead	409
One Wet Night	Slapstick Encyclopedia—Vol. 3: Funny Girls	411
One-Eyed Boy, The	The Roots	52
Only Me	Slapstick Encyclopedia—Vol. 5: Chaplin and Co.: The Music Hall Tradition	411
Only the Cat Saw it	Greentoons: Environmentally Aware Animation	710
Open Road Again	The Wind in the Willows, Volume #4	644, 718
Open Sesame	Mediamystics	487
Opening New Frontiers	Space Shuttle: Flights STS-1 Through STS-8	840
Opening Night	Cartoons That Time Forgot Vol. 6: The Odd & The Outrageous	681
Opera	Guido Manuli: Animator	710
Opera Industriel	Computer Animation Classics	708
Operating Manual for Spaceship	CineBLAST! Vol. 3	428
Operation	The Best of the New York Underground, Year 2,	483
Operation Rabbit	Chariots of Fur	682
Opium Den, The	Naughty Nostalgia #2	508
Optic Nerve, The	Optical Nerves	463, 492
Oracle of Delphi, The	More Melies	22
Oral Hygiene	International Tournee of Animation Volume 5	712
Orange Torpedo Trips	Whitewater Adventures	833
Orange, The	Droits au Coeur (Rights from the Heart)	709
Oranges and Lemons	Slapstick Encyclopedia—Vol. 6: Hal Roach: The Lot of Fun	411
Oranges and Lemons	Films of Stan Laurel Volume 2	410
Oranges and Lemons	Stanley on the Job	412
Order to Stop Construction	Neo-Tokyo	737
Ordinary Day of SS-Man Schmidt	Holocaust, Polish Jews (Holocoust, Zydzi Polscy)	775
Organ House	Too Outrageous Animation	717
Origin of Rocks	Forces of Life	836
Origin of the Elements	Forces of Life	836
Origins of the Motion Picture	Origins of the Motion Picture	337
Orphan's Benefit	Mickey Mouse: The Black & White Years	693
Ostrich, The	Animaland (9 Titles)	705

SHORT FILM	COMPILATION TAPE	PAGE
Oswals & the Mechanical Cow	Animation Vol. 1:The Beginning	706
Otaku No Video	Otaku No Video	739
Ottawa '90 Signal Films	The National Film Board of Canada's Animation Festival	714
Ouija Board	Koko the Clown, 1915-27	712
Our Hospitality/Sherlock Jr.	Art of Buster Keaton—Box 1	408
Our Lady	The Roots	52
Our Lady of the Spheres	Short Animations by Larry Jordan	718
Our Trip	Lesbian Humor	461, 492
Out in the Garden	Out in the Garden & You	464, 487
Out of Bound	Slapstick Encyclopedia—Vol. 7:The Rage Is On	411
Out of Control	Video Art: Noel Harding	490
Out of Order	Sextoons:An Erotic Animation Festival	715
Out of the Inkwell	Animation Vol. 1:The Beginning	706
Out Rage 69	The Question of Equality	464
Out to Punch	The Adventures of Popeye, Vol. 2	676
Out West	Buster and Fatty	408
Outdoor Indoor	Felix the Cat—Silent—Volume 2	683
Outdoor Indoor	Felix the Cat: Sound & Silent	683
Over the Drink	William Wegman Reel 5	491
Over-the-counter Medicines	Your Family's Health, Tape 1	838
Owl and the Lemming, The	NFBC: The Sand Castle	714
Owl and the Pussy Cat, The	Happy Birthday Moon and Other Stories	647
Owl and the Pussy-Cat, The	The Pigs' Wedding and Other Stories	640
Owl and the Raven, The	NFBC: The Tender Tale of Cinderella Penguin	714
Pacific 231	Avant Garde Program #11	482
Pacific Frontiers	Scenic Wonders of America	831
Paid Love	Love in the City	41
Pain in the Pullman, A	The Three Stooges: A Pain in the Pullman	284
Painted Earth: The Art	Art on Film/Film on Art, Program 4: Film Voice/Art Voice	545
Painted Lady, The	Griffith Shorts (1912, #3)	413
Painted Lady, The	D.W. Griffith's Years of Discovery	412
Painted Lady, The	The Musketeers of Pig Alley and Selected Biograph Shorts	413
Palace of Arabian Nights	Films of Georges Melies, Volume 1	20
Paleface, The	Buster Keaton Festival Volume 1	408
Paleface, The	Great Stone Face—Buster Keaton—Vol. 1	409
Palm Sunday	Karl Krogstad: Black & Decker Hedgetrimmer Murders	432
Palooka from Paducha	Buster Keaton Talkies, Vol. 6	408
Panama	Corduroy Bear	651
Pandora	Heroines and Goddesses of the Greek Myths	784
Panspermia	Spike & Mike's Festival of Animation Vol. 2	716
Pantry Panic	Great & Minor Animation Volume 3	684
Pantry Panic	Pioneers in Animation Vol. 2	714
Paorky's Pig's Feat	Daffy Duck's Thanks-For-Giving Special	682
Papa	Droits au Coeur (Rights from the Heart)	709
Paper Doll, The	Matinee Idols: The Ladies	401
Paperhanger's Helper	Films of Oliver Hardy	410
Paperhanger's Helper	Hardy and Ray	411
Para-Sight	The National Film Board of Canada's Animation Festival	714
Parataxis	Tony Vegas' Animated Acidburn Flashback Tabu	717
Pardon My Clutch	The Three Stooges: Wee Wee Monsieur	284
Pardon My Pups	Funny Guys and Gals of the Talkies	269
Parents	Kartemquin Films, Vol. 2: Winnie Wright, Age 11	474
Paris to Monte Carlo	Grand Melies (Franju) and Melies' Short Films	20
Paris to Monte Carlo	Marvelous Melies	22
Parisian Blinds	Optical Nerves	463, 492
Parlez Voo Woo	The Adventures of Popeye, Vol. 2	676
Particle Dreams	Spike & Mike's Festival of Animation Vol. 1	716
Party at Owl's House	Maurice Sendak's Little Bear—Parties & Picnics	637
Party Line	Karl Krogstad: Black & Decker Hedgetrimmer Murders	432
Pas a Deux	International Tournee of Animation Volume 3	712
Pas De Deux	NFBC: Leonard Maltin's Animation Favorites from the National Film Board of Canada	714
Passion	Jurgen Reble—Passion	432
Patchwork Blanket, The	Poky's Favorite Stories	656
Patchwork Girl of Oz, The	L. Frank Baum's Silent Film Collection of Oz	400
Patchwork Girl of Oz, The	The Patchwork Girl of Oz/A Florida Enchantment	402
Pathways of Life	Griffith Shorts (1913-1914)	413
Patricia Gives Birth	Short Animations by Larry Jordan	718
Patrick	Doctor De Soto and Other Stories	632
Patrick's Dinosaurs	Shelley Duvall's Bedtime Stories (Collection)	657
Paul Lawrence Dunbar	Portraits in Black	453
Pawnshop, The	Charlie Chaplin Early Years II	407
Pawnshop, The	Classic Chaplin, Charlie Chaplin at Mutual Studios	407
Pay Your Dues	Films of Harold Lloyd—Volume 3	410
Payum Portraits, The	Art on Film/Film on Art, Program 1: Balance: Film/Art	545
Peace in the Bible	People of Faith and the Arms Race	805
Peace of Mind	Karl Krogstad: The Gigabyte Trilogy	432
Peace on Earth	MGM Cartoon Classics: Happy Harmonies	686
Peace on Earth	MGM Cartoon Magic	686
Peach	Women from Down Under	467
Peach Peach Pear Plum	Max's Chocolate Chicken	654
Pear Tree, The	European Folk Tales, Volume 4	646
Peasants' Lot, The	Early Russian Cinema: Before the Revolution, Vol. 6: Class Distinctions	85
Peepshow	Experimental Avant Garde Series Volume 22	484
Pencil Test	Computer Animation Classics	708
Pentagon Peace March	All Women Are Equal & Pentagon Peace March	456, 482
People, People, People	Hubley Collection Vol. 2	711
Peppermint Patty's School Days	Peanuts: Charlie Brown & Snoopy Show Vol. 9	701
Peppy	Computer Animation Classics	708
Perfect Day	Laurel and Hardy and the Family	274
Perfect Leader	Video Art: Leaving the 20th Century and Perfect Leader	490
Perfect Pair	Variety Is the Spice of Life	489
Perpetual Motion	Max Fleischer Presents Koko the Clown	685
Person to Bunny	Stars of Space Jam: Five-Tape Boxed Set	687
Personal Cleanliness	Wartime Cartoons	717
Perspective or Anamorphosis	Art on Film/Film on Art, Program 4: Film Voice/Art Voice	545
Pertaining to Chicago	Jim Davis: Volume #1	486
Pertaining to John Marin	Jim Davis: Volume #2	486
Pest Man Wins	The Three Stooges: Vagabond Loafers	284
Pest that Came to Dinner, The	Porky Pig Tales	687
Pet Names	Lesbovision	462
Pet Peeve	Tom & Jerry on Parade	689
Pet Show	The Ezra Jack Keats Library	633
Pet Store, The	Mickey Mouse: The Black & White Years	693
Pet, The	Classic Shorts Compilation #12: Winsor McCay	682
Peter Pan	Disney Canta con Nosotros	672

SHORT FILM	COMPILATION TAPE	PAGE
Peter's Chair	The Ezra Jack Keats Library	633
Peter's Chair	Happy Birthday Moon and Other Stories	647
Petey's Wake	Spike & Mike's Sick & Twisted Festival of Animation, Vol. 2	716
Pett and Pott	England in the Thirties	471
Petunia	More Stories for the Very Young	655
Phables	Origins of American Animation	714
Phantom's Foe, The	Wings of the Red Star	845
Pharmacist, The	W.C. Fields: 6 Short Films	286
Philosophy	Potato Wolf Spring 1984	435
Phoenix Bird	Astro Boy 30th Anniversary, Vol. 1	722
Phony War, The	Between the Wars, 1918-1941, Vol. 7	808
Phuk Yew	Spike & Mike's Sick & Twisted Festival of Animation, Vol. 3	716
Piano Hands	William Wegman Reel 7	491
Piano Tooners	Cartoon Collection Vol. 7: Tokyo Jokio	680
Piano Tooners	Cartoons That Time Forgot Vol. 6: The Odd & The Outrageous	681
Piano Tuners	Van Beuren Studio, Volume #1	689
Pick and Shovel	Films of Stan Laurel Volume 1	410
Pick and Shovel	Stanley on the Job	412
Picnic	Aesop's Fables Volume 3	676
Picnic	Early Animation Vol. 1	709
Picnic	Max's Chocolate Chicken	654
Picnic on Pudding Hill	Maurice Sendak's Little Bear—Parties & Picnics	637
Picture for Harold's Room	Harold and the Purple Crayon and Other Harold Stories	634
Pictures from Memory	International Tournee of Animation Volume 4	712
Picturing Oriental Girls:	Video Art, Tape Two	489
Pie-Covered Wagon, The	Shirley Temple's Baby Burlesks	282
Pie-Eyed	Slapstick Encyclopedia—Vol. 5: Chaplin and Co.: The Music Hall Tradition	411
Pied Piper Porky	Wince upon a Time: Foolhardy Fairy Tales & Looney Legends	690
Pierre	The Maurice Sendak Library	654
Pigs in a Polka	Pioneers in Animation Vol. 2	714
Pigs' Wedding, The	The Pigs' Wedding and Other Stories	640
Pilgrim, The	Chaplin Revue	407
Pilot, The	Rockin' Ronnie	281
Pink Komkommer	Spike & Mike's Sick & Twisted Festival of Animation, Vol. 1	716
Pioneer Days	Mickey Mouse: The Black & White Years	693
Pioneers of X-Ray Technology:	Pictures Don't Tell You Anything: Selected Films of Ann Marie Fleming	211, 487
Pioneers! O Pioneers!	Story of English	860
Pipe Dreams	MGM Cartoon Classics: Happy Harmonies	686
Pippa Passes	Griffith Shorts (1909)	412
Pirates (The Lift)	Too Outrageous Animation	717
Pirates from Below	Jonny Quest: Hadji—Mysteries of the East	698
Pizza on Credit	Gold of Naples	38
Place Mattes	Optical Nerves	463, 492
Plague Has Swept My City, A	Video Against AIDS, Volumes 1, 2 & 3	835
Plane Crazy	Mickey Mouse: The Black & White Years	693
Plane Dumb	Cartoon Collection Vol. 5: Racial Cartoons	680
Plane Dumb	Tom & Jerry & Friends #4	688
Planet Earth: Sanctuary of Life	Wonders of God's Creation (Standard Edition)	824
Planet of Love, The	Ambassador Magma Vol. 6: Episodes 12-13	720
Planet of the Tickle Bops, The	Spinning Tops and Tickle Bops	670
Platypus	Animaland (9 Titles)	705
Platypus	British Animation Vol. 2	707
Play Ball	Van Beuren Studio, Volume #2	689
Play Safe	Paramount/Fleischer Studios Volume 1	686
Playhouse	Buster Keaton (1917-22)	408
Playing the Part	Girl Friends	229, 460
Pleasant Hill USA	Best of the New York Underground	427
Pleasure Film	Pictures Don't Tell You Anything: Selected Films of Ann Marie Fleming	211, 487
Plow that Broke the Plains	Classic Documentaries: The Power and the Land	470
Plow that Broke the Plains	The Plow That Broke the Plains/Night Mail	476
Plow that Broke the Plains	The River and The Plow That Broke the Plains	477
Plow that Broke the Plains	The Power and the Land: Four Documentary Portraits of the Great Depression	476
Plunger Series	William Wegman Reel 1	491
Plus One Minus One	Guido Manuli: Animator	710
Plus One, Minus One	International Tournee of Animation Volume 2	712
Pluto's Heart Throb	Disney Love Tales	691
Plymptoons	Animation Celebration Vol. 3	705
Plymptoons	Plymptoons: The Complete Works of Bill Plympton	715
Plymptoons	International Tournee of Animation Volume 4	712
Pocket Bookman	Best of William Wegman	483
Pocketbook Man	William Wegman Reel 1	491
Poetic Jaundice	Spike & Mike's Sick & Twisted Festival of Animation, Vol. 2	716
Points	The Rocketship Reel	715
Poky Little Puppy, The	Poky's Favorite Stories	656
Police	Essanay #3	407
Police Academy	The Abbott and Costello Television Show, Tape 5	414
Police State	Nick Zedd: Steal This Video	434
Polish Dance '80	Video Works: Miroslaw Rogala (1980-86)	491
Political Basketball	Cartoongate!	681
Polka-Dot Puss	Tom & Jerry's Comic Capers	689
Polly-Tics	Early Animation Vol. 2	709
Polly-tics	Classic Shorts Compilation #14: Felix the Cat	682
Polly-tix in Washington	Shirley Temple's Baby Burlesks	282
Poly-tics	Felix the Cat: Sound & Silent	683
Polychris Hapus	Films of Charles and Ray Eames, Volume 4	485
Pond and Waterfall	Perceptual Landscapes	464, 492
Pool Days	Boy's Life	457
Pool Sharks	Bill Fields and Will Rogers	396
Pool Sharks	W.C. Fields: 6 Short Films	286
Pools	Perceptual Landscapes	464, 492
Poop Deck Pappy	Cartoon Collection Vol. 1: Porky in Wackyland	680
Poor Fish	Charley Chase Jimmy Jump Series	410
Poor Little Me	MGM Cartoon Classics: Happy Harmonies	686
Popeye & His Wonderful Lamp	Popeye the Sailor	687
Popeye for President	Popeye for President	687
Popeye for President	Cartoongate!	681
Popeye Meets Ali Baba	Popeye the Sailor	687
Popeye the Sailor Meets Sinbad	Popeye the Sailor	687
Porcelain Cat, The	Picturebook Classics: Complete Set	639
Porky in Wackyland	Cartoon Collection Vol. 1: Porky in Wackyland	680
Porky Phony Express	Cartoon Collection Vol. 3: Coal Black & De Sebben Dwarfs	680

SHORT FILM	COMPILATION TAPE	PAGE
Porky Pig's Feat	Cartoon Classics Vol. 2: Warner Brothers	680
Porky's Detective Agency	Porky Pig: Days of Swine and Roses	687
Porky's Garden	Cartoon Collection Vol. 6: The Ducktators	680
Porky's Hare Hunt	Cartoon Collection Vol. 5: Racial Cartoons	680
Porky's Hired Hand	Cartoon Collection Vol. 6: The Ducktators	680
Porky's Midnight Matinee	Cartoon Collection Vol. 2: Classic Warner Bros.	680
Porky's Movie Mystery	Cartoon Collection Vol. 5: Racial Cartoons	680
Porky's Party	Porky Pig: Days of Swine and Roses	687
Porky's Pastry Pirates	Cartoon Collection Vol. 2: Classic Warner Bros.	680
Porky's Picnic	Cartoon Collection Vol. 3: Coal Black & De Sebben Dwarfs	680
Porky's Pooch	Cartoon Collection Vol. 5: Racial Cartoons	680
Porky's Preview	Cartoon Classics Vol. 2: Warner Brothers	680
Porky's Preview	Cartoon Collection Vol. 2: Classic Warner Bros.	680
Porky's Preview	Pioneers in Animation Vol. 2	714
Porky's Railroad	Cartoon Collection Vol. 2: Classic Warner Bros.	680
Post No Bills	Best of the Fests 1991	706
Postcards	Three Short Films (Mark Rappaport)	438
Potato Hunter	International Tournee of Animation Volume 5	712
Powder and Smoke	Charley Chase Jimmy Jump Series	410
Powdered Toastman	Ren & Stimpy: Nothing But Shorts	701
Powdered Toastman	Ren & Stimpy Vol. 3: The Stinkiest Stories	701
Power and the Land, The	Classic Documentaries: The Power and the Land	470
Power and the Land, The	The City/The Power and the Land	470
Power and the Land, The	The Power and the Land: Four Documentary Portraits of the Great Depression	476
Powers of Ten	Films of Charles and Ray Eames, Volume 1	485
Powers of the Olympians, The	Dawn of the Greek Gods	784
Prayer, The	Outrageous Animation Vol. 2	714
Predators	Catch Me If You Can	651
Prehistoric Beast	International Tournee of Animation Volume 6	712
Prehistoric Poultry	The Lost World (1925)	400
Prehistoric Poultry Creation	Willis O'Brien Primitives	717
Prelude to Eden	CineBLAST! Vol. 3	428
Presidents of a National Struggle	Portraits of American Presidents	796, 870
Presidents of a New Nation	Portraits of American Presidents	796, 870
Presidents of a World Power	Portraits of American Presidents	796, 870
Pressures of the Text	Digital Speech and Pressures of the Text	484
Presto Change-O	Cartoon Classics Vol. 9: Early Pioneers	680
Presto-Change-O	Cartoon Collection Vol. 6: The Ducktators	680
Preventing Injuries Talks	Your Family's Health, Tape 3	838
Previous Lives	Plymptoons: The Complete Works of Bill Plympton	715
Price of Cictory, The	Nostalgia World War II Video Library #9	771
Priest of Mt. Kouya, The	Animated Classics of Japanese Literature: Martyr/ The Priest of Mt. Kouya	720
Primal Call	Griffith Shorts (1911)	413
Primiti Too Taa	Spike & Mike's Festival of Animation Vol. 1	716
Princess and the Goat Boy, The	European Folk Tales, Volume 5	646
Princess and the Pea	Victor Borge Tells Hans Christian Andersen Stories	649
Princess Nicotine	Cartoon Classics Vol. 6: Early Animation	680
Princess Nicotine	The Genesis of Animation, Volume One	710
Princess Tarankova	Early Russian Cinema: Before the Revolution, Vol. 1: Beginnings	85
Prisoner of Zenda	His Royal Slyness and Haunted Spooks	410
Prisoner, The	Bronco Billy Anderson	396
Private	Forgotten Comedians	411
Private Eye Pooch	Man's Best Friend	685
Private Life of the Gannetts	Documentary Masterpieces by John Grierson	471
Private Snafu	Nostalgia World War II Video Library #8	771
Probation	Nation Aflame and Probation	508
Prodigal Son	Balanchine: Prodigal Son/Chaconne	568
Prodigal Son	God's Trombones—A Trilogy	452
Product	William Wegman Reel 2	491
Professor Bonehead	Animation Vol. 1: The Beginning	706
Progress: Los Angeles	Cityscape Compilations	470
Promised Land	Franck Goldberg: Sampler	8
Property Man, The	Keystones #3	407
Protect Your Daughter	Maniac and Protect Your Daughter	508
Protest and Communication	Civilization, Programs 5 & 6	781
Psychophony	Works	718
Publicity Pays	Charley Chase and Ben Turpin	410
Publicity Pays	Charley Chase Vol. 1	410
Puddy Tat Twouble	Stars of Space Jam: Five-Tape Boxed Set	687
Puff	CineBLAST! Vol. 3	428
Puke a Pound	Spike & Mike's Sick & Twisted Festival of Animation, Vol. 3	716
Pull My Daisy	Pull My Daisy (The Beat Generation)	435, 476
Pumpkin Madness	Best of the Fests: For Kids	706
Pumpkin Race, The	Attack of the Cohl Pumpkins	706
Punch and Judy	Alchemist of the Surreal	705
Pupil, The	Secrets of Love, Classics of Erotic Literature: Vol. 4	510
Puppet	William Wegman Reel 1	491
Puppy Love	Aesop's Fables Volume 2	676
Puppy Love	Mickey Mouse: The Black & White Years	693
Puppy Tale	Tom & Jerry's Comic Capers	689
Purely Human Sleep	The Works of Ken Feingold— Water Falling from One World to Another	492
Pursuit	Cadillacs and Dinosaurs: Wild Child & Pursuit	679
Pursuit of Happiness, The	Civilization, Programs 9 & 10	781
Push Comes to Shove	International Tournee of Animation Volume 5	712
Push-Button Kitty	Tom & Jerry on Parade	689
Pusher, The	Drug Propaganda and Satire Compilation	505
Puss in Boots	Cartoon Classics Vol. 3: The Early Pioneers	680
Puss in Boots	Cartoons That Time Forgot Vol. 5: Free-Form Fairytales	681
Puss in Boots	Ub Iwerks' Famous Fairytales	689
Puss N Boots	Animation Vol. 1: The Beginning	706
Pussycat	Tom & Jerry's Festival of Fun	689
Puzzled Pals	Cartoon Classics Vol. 9: Early Pioneers	680
Pyramids	William Wegman Reel 4	491
Quad Libet	Outrageous Animation Vol. 2	714
Quail Hunt	Thirties Magic Vol. 1	716
Queen Elizabeth	Salome and Queen Elizabeth	403
Queen Mercy	Best of the New York Underground	427
Queen of Hearts, The	Cartoons That Time Forgot Vol. 5: Free-Form Fairytales	681
Queen of Spades, The	Early Russian Cinema: Before the Revolution, Vol. 08	85
Queen of Spades, The	Early Russian Cinema: Before the Revolution, Vol. 05	85
Queen Was in the Parlor, The	Cartoon Classics Vol. 1: Looney Tunes & Merrie Melodies	680
Quest: A Long Ray's Journey	Computer Animation Classics	708
Quest: A Long Ray's Journey	Animation Celebration Vol. 1	705
Question of Breeding	The Incredible Story of Dogs	816
Questions to Another Nation	Video Works: Miroslaw Rogala (1980-86)	491
Quiet Please	Tom & Jerry: Starring Tom & Jerry!	689
Quiniscopio	International Tournee of Animation Volume 3	712
Quintessential Warrior, The	Ambassador Magma Vol. 3: Episodes 6-7	720
Quiver City	Mitch Corber Works	487
R.E.M.	Art Com Video 1: Scandinavia	482
R.F.D. 10,000 B.C.	Willis O'Brien Primitives	717
R.F.D. 10,000 B.C.	The Lost World (1925)	400
R.S.V.P.	Boys' Shorts	457
Rabbit Every Monday	Yosemite Sam: The Good, The Bad and the Ornery	690
Rabbit Hood	Bugs Bunny: Winner by a Hare	679
Rabbit of Seville	Looney Tunes Curtain Calls	685
Rabbit Punch	Bugs Bunny Classics	678
Rabbit Transit	Bugs!	679
Rabbit Transit	Bugs Bunny's Zaniest Toons	679
Rabbit's Boom	Fireworks	485
Rabbitson Crusoe	Wince upon a Time: Foolhardy Fairy Tales & Looney Legends	690
Race Symphony	Hans Richter: Early Avant-Garde Films	485
Racketeer Rabbit	Bugs Bunny's Comedy Classics	678
Racketeer, The	Gold of Naples	38
Radar Screen	William Wegman Reel 4	491
Radio Racket	Tom & Jerry & Friends #3	688
Radio, Racism & Foreign Power	Between the Wars, 1918-1941, Vol. 3	808
Raft of Medusa: Three Voices	Julian Samuel Trilogy	474
Rage and Depression	William Wegman Reel 3	491
Rage of the Earth	Ambassador Magma Vol. 5: Episodes 10-11	720
Raggedy Ann & Raggedy Andy	Glenn Gould Plays Beethoven	590
Raggedy Ann & Raggedy Andy	Paramount/Famous Studios Volume 2	686
Raggety Rose	Directed by Stan Laurel	410
Ragtime Romeo	Cartoons That Time Forgot Vol. 2: Down & Out with Flip the Frog	681
Railrodder, The	The Railrodder/Buster Keaton Rides Again	409
Rain	Avant Garde & Experimental Film	482
Rain	Rain and Uberfall	488
Rain	Rare Dutch and Belgian Experimental Program	31, 488
Raise Treat	William Wegman Reel 3	491
Rakthavira	Too Outrageous Animation	717
Rampage of the Iron Dragon	Sohryuden Vol. 4: Episodes 7 and 8	746
Randy's Sick	William Wegman Reel 1	491
Range Grown Chicken, The	Rogopag	10, 37, 39, 41
Raoul Barre's Cartoons on Tour	Pioneers in Animation Vol. 1	714
Rapid Eye Movements	Tony Vegas' Animated Acidburn Flashback Tabu	717
Rapunzel	Classic Stories for Children	651
Rapunzel	Ray Harryhausen Compilation	715
Rare Chaplin Snippet	Slapstick Encyclopedia—Vol. 5: Chaplin and Co.: The Music Hall Tradition	411
Rasslin' Match, The	Tom & Jerry & Friends #4	688
Rasslin' Round	Cartoons That Time Forgot Vol. 4: Willie Whopper's Fantastic Adventures	681
Raster Relief/Video Canvas	Sara Hornbacher Early Works	488
Rat's Revenge	Aesop's Fables Volume 3	676
Rats Knuckles	Charley Chase Jimmy Jump Series	410
Razor Head	Tom Chomont: A Two-Volume Collection, Volume I	466, 489
Re-entry	Samadhi and Other Films	488
Ready, Woolen and Able	Chariots of Fur	682
Reagan Commercials	War Dance	439
Reagan Occhio	Cartoongate!	681
Real Inside	Incredible Animation Collection: Vol. 2	711
Real or Robots	Rugrats: Tales from the Crib	641, 702
Reasons to be Glad	Tony Vegas' Animated Acidburn Flashback Tabu	717
Recognition of Russia	Between the Wars, 1918-1941, Vol. 5	808
Recreation	Keystones #3	407
Red Balloon	Red Balloon/White Mane	23, 640
Red Headed Baby	Cartoon Classics Vol. 1: Looney Tunes & Merrie Melodies	680
Red Hot Sands	Aesop's Fables Volume 1	676
Red Riding Hood	The James Marshall Library	636
Red Riding Hood	Charley Chase Jimmy Jump Series	410
Red Riding Hood	Wings: A Tale of Two Chickens and Other Stories by James Marshall	644
Red Souvenir	Franck Goldberg: Sampler	8
Red's Dream	Tiny Toy Stories	717
Redman's View, The	The Female of the Species & Selected Biograph Shorts (Volume III)	412
Redman's View, The	D.W. Griffith's Years of Discovery	412
Redskin Blues	Cartoon Collection Vol. 7: Tokyo Jokio	680
Redwood Sap, The	Woody Woodpecker 50th Anniversary Vol. 1	690
Reel, The	William Wegman Reel 6	491
Reflections on Black	Stan Brakhage Selected Films: Vol. 1	488
Reformers, The	Griffith Shorts (1913-1914)	413
Regarde-Moi	Teasers	466
Rehearsals of Extinct Anatomie	The Brothers Quay Vol. 2	707
Reign of Zeus, The	Dawn of the Greek Gods	784
Relax	Boys' Shorts	457
Relax	New Directors: New Short Films	487
Reluctant Dragon	The Reluctant Dragon	694
Religious Experience, The	The Holy Koran	790
Remember Pearl Harbor	The Schwartzkopf Four-Pack	763
Remember When	Langdon at Sennett	411
Remote Faces: Outerpretation	Video Works: Miroslaw Rogala (1980-86)	491
Ren and Stimpy	Frightfest, Nickelodeon	696
Ren's Pecs	Ren & Stimpy in Disguise	701
Ren's Toothache	Ren & Stimpy Vol. 3: The Stinkiest Stories	701
Renunciation, The	Griffith Shorts (1909)	412
Reproductions of Life	Reproduction of Life	837
Requiem for 500 Thousand	Holocaust, Polish Jews (Holocoust, Zydzi Polscy)	775
Resonance	Boys' Shorts	457
Resurrection	Griffith Shorts (1908-09)	412
Resurrectors, The	Puppets & Demons: Films by Patrick McGuinn	436
Retour a la Raison	Avant Garde Program #14	483
Return of Cleopatra	Astro Boy Volume 9	722
Return of the Spider	Gigantor Vol. 2	730
Return to Isolationism	Between the Wars, 1918-1941, Vol. 1	808
Reunion, The	Pioneers in Animation Vol. 1	714
Revenge of the Four Brothers	Sohryuden Vol. 4: Episodes 7 and 8	746
Revenge of the Kinematograph	Animation Vol. 1: The Beginning	706

SHORT FILM	COMPILATION TAPE	PAGE
Revenue Man, The	Griffith Shorts (1911)	413
Revolutionary, The	Early Russian Cinema: Before the Revolution, Vol. 10: The End of an Era	85
RFD 10,000	Cartoon Classics Vol. 6: Early Animation	680
Rhea	Video Art: David Askevold	490
Rhythm 21 (Rhythmus 21)	Hans Richter: Give Chance a Chance	63, 485
Rhythm 21 (Rhythmus 21)	Hans Richter: Early Avant-Garde Films	485
Rhythm 23 (Rhythmus 23)	Hans Richter: Early Avant-Garde Films	485
Rhythmus 21	Experimental Avant Garde Series Volume 20 (The Secret Lives of Inanimate Objects)	484
Richter on Film	Hans Richter: Early Avant-Garde Films	485
Rick the Dick in Hospital	Spike & Mike's Sick & Twisted Festival of Animation, Vol. 3	716
Riddle of the Gold	Jonny Quest: Dr. Zin—Master of Evil	698
Ride to the Abyss, The	International Tournee of Animation Volume 6	712
Rien Que Les Heures	Classic Foreign Shorts—Volume 2	153
Right Down the Middle	Gaiking	729
Rikki-tikki-tavi	The Jungle Books, Set I	636
Ring Up the Curtain	Harold Lloyd Comedies Vol. 1	410
Ring up the Curtain	Early Comedies Volume 2	410
Ring up the Curtain	Films of Harold Lloyd—Volume 1	409
Ring, The	William Wegman Reel 1	491
Rink, The	Charlie Chaplin Early Years IV	407
Rink, The	Classic Chaplin, Charlie Chaplin at Mutual Studios	407
Rink, The	Emerging Chaplin	407
Rink, The	Slapstick Encyclopedia—Vol. 5: Chaplin and Co.: The Music Hall Tradition	411
Risk and Roughnecks	Larry Semon #2	411
Ritual in Transfigured Time	Maya Deren Experimental Films	487
Rival Railroad Plot	Railroad Dramas	403
River, The	Classic Documentaries: The Power and the Land	470
River, The	The Power and the Land: Four Documentary Portraits of the Great Depression	476
River, The	The River and The Plow That Broke the Plains	477
Roameo	Early Animation Vol. 1	709
Robert E. Lee	Civil War Journal, Set II	779
Robin Hoek	Ren & Stimpy Vol. 2: The Stupidest Stories	701
Robin Hood	Douglas Fairbanks Sr Collection	397
Robot Back to Action	Grandizer	731
Robot Olympics, The	Astro Boy Volume 11	722
Robot, The	Jonny Quest: Dr. Zin—Master of Evil	698
Rockin' Thru the Rockies	The Three Stooges: Whoops I'm an Indian	284
Rocky	Liquid Television 2	698
Rogue	Cadillacs and Dinosaurs: Rogue & Dino Drive	679
Roman Scandal, A	The Comediennes, Volume 2	397
Romance and Beauty	Civilization, Programs 3 & 4	781
Romance of Western Hills	Griffith Shorts (1909-1911)	413
Romance Sentimentale	Classic Foreign Shorts—Volume 3: Un Chant d'Amour, Romance Sentimentale	19
Romance with Double Bass	Early Russian Cinema: Before the Revolution, Vol. 1: Beginnings	85
Romeo & Juliet	International Tournee of Animation Volume 1	711
Romeo in Rhythm	MGM Cartoon Classics: Happy Harmonies	686
Romeo Robin, A	Van Beuren Studio, Volume #2	689
Rondino	Outrageous Animation Vol. 1	714
Room Runners	Cartoons That Time Forgot Vol. 2: Down & Out with Flip the Frog	681
Rooster and the Eagle	Aesop's Fables Volume 1	676
Rooster, The	Best of the Fests: For Kids	706
Ropin' Fool, The	Bill Fields and Will Rogers	396
Rosa Mi Amour	Best of the New York Underground	427
Rose, The	Griffith Shorts (1909-1910)	412
Rosie's Walk	Rosie's Walk and Other Stories	656
Roughest Africa	Films of Stan Laurel Volume 1	410
Roughest Africa	Films of Stan Laurel Volume 3	410
Rounders, The	Classic Chaplin, Charlie Chaplin at Keystone Studio	407
Rounders, The	Keystones #3	407
Rounders, The	Slapstick Encyclopedia—Vol. 4: Keaton, Arbuckle & Al St. John	411
Rowdy Ann	Slapstick Encyclopedia—Vol. 3: Funny Girls	411
Royal Canadian Kiltered Yaksme	Ren & Stimpy on Duty	701
Royal Flush	Outrageous Animation Vol. 2	714
Rudolph the Red Nosed	Christmas Cartoon Classic	682
Rudolph the Red Nosed Reindeer	Fleischer Color Classics	683
Rudolph the Rednosed Reindeer	Cartoon Holidays	680
Rudolph's Revenge	Adventures of Hairbreadth Harry	395
Ruff	Jane Hissey's Old Bear Stories: Happy Birthday Old Bear	653
Rugrats	Frightfest, Nickelodeon	696
Rumba	Best of the Fests 1990	706
Rumble	M/W/F Music Video One	433
Rumors	Cartoon Collection Vol. 8: Private Snafu	680
Rumours	Wartime Cartoons	717
Rumpelstiltskin	Classic Stories for Children	651
Rumpelstiltskin	Fables and Fairy Tales, Fairy Tale Masterpieces	646
Rumpelstilzchen	Jurgen Reble—Passion	432
Rumzababalaars	Works	718
Runaway Balloon	Aesop's Fables Volume 1	676
Runaway Blackie	Tom & Jerry & Friends #7	688
Running Around Like a Chicken	Six Short Films of Les Blank, 1960-1985	480
Running Man, The	Neo-Tokyo	737
Running on Empty	Fueling the Future	803
Rural Romance	Aesop's Film Fables	676
Rusalka	Early Russian Cinema: Before the Revolution, Vol. 2: Folklore and Legend	85
Sabda	Sabda and Sombra a Sombra	488
Sacred Art of Tibet, The	The Sacred Art of Tibet/The Visible Compendium	149, 718
Saddle Daze	Cartoon Collection Vol. 7: Tokyo Jokio	680
Safe Sex is Hot Sex	She's Safe	465
Safe Sex Slut	Video Against AIDS, Volumes 1, 2 & 3	835
Safe Soap	She's Safe	465
Safer Sister	She's Safe	465
Sage Brush Tom	Tom Mix Short Subjects	405
Sahara Hare	Yosemite Sam: The Good, The Bad and the Ornery	690
Sailor Dog, The	Poky's Favorite Stories	656
Sails and Sailors	Sails and Sailors: J Boats '37	828
Saint in London, The	The Saint Volume II: Film Series 1939-1940	177
Saint in New York, The	The Saint Volume I: Film Series 1938-1939	177
Saint in Palm Springs, The	The Saint Volume IV: Film Series 1941-1943	177
Saint Meets the Tiger, The	The Saint Volume IV: Film Series 1941-1943	177
Saint Strikes Back, The	The Saint Volume I: Film Series 1938-1939	177
Saint Takes Over, The	The Saint Volume III: Film Series 1940-1941	177
Saint's Double Trouble, The	The Saint Volume II: Film Series 1939-1940	177
Saint's Vacation, The	The Saint Volume III: Film Series 1940-1941	177
Sally's Sweet Babboo	Peanuts: Charlie Brown & Snoopy Show Vol. 9	701
Salome	American Avant-Garde Films	482
Salome	Salome and Queen Elizabeth	403
Samadhi	Samadhi and Other Films	488
Same Shirt	William Wegman Reel 2	491
Samson Gets a Haircut	Ancient Tales from a Promised Land, Vol. IV	789
Samson Gets Knotted	Ancient Tales from a Promised Land, Vol. III	789
Samuel and the Spooky Goxbox	Ancient Tales from a Promised Land, Vol. IV	789
San Francisco by Golden Gate	Cityscape Compilations	470
San Pietro	Nostalgia World War II Video Library #10	771
Sand	It's Clean—It Just Looks Dirty	486
Sand Castle, The	NFBC: Cartoon Festival: Cactus Swing	714
Sand Dance	International Tournee of Animation Volume 4	712
Sandman, The	International Tournee of Animation Volume 6	712
Sands O'Dee, The	Griffith Shorts (1912, #1)	413
Sandwich, The	Bruno Bozzetto: Animator, Vol. 1	707
Sandy Claws	Stars of Space Jam: Five-Tape Boxed Set	687
Sanforized	William Wegman Reel 2	491
Santa's Pocket Watch	Christmas Carousel	630
Santa's Surprise	Classic Cartoon Christmas Treasures	682
Santa's Surprise	Cartoon Holidays	680
Santeuse de l'Ange	Pascal Aubier Films	487
Saphead, The	The Saphead	409
Saphead, The	Art of Buster Keaton—Box 1	408
Satan's Game	Puppets & Demons: Films by Patrick McGuinn	436
Saturday Afternoon	Films of Harry Langdon Volume 1	410
Saturday Afternoon	Langdon at Sennett	411
Saturday Afternoon	Long Pants	351
Saturday Afternoon	Slapstick Encyclopedia—Vol. 2: Keystone Tonight!	411
Saul Bumps into a Witch	Ancient Tales from a Promised Land, Vol. VII	789
Saul Goes Bonkers	Ancient Tales from a Promised Land, Vol. VI	789
Saul Rips Up His Camel	Ancient Tales from a Promised Land, Vol. V	789
Saute Ma Ville	Akermania, Volume One	29
Save the Ship	Versatile Mr. Laurel	412
Saved from Himself	Griffith Shorts (1911-1912)	413
Saw Movies	William Wegman Reel 4	491
Sawdust & Salome	Norma Talmadge Films	402
Sawdust Baby	Adventures of Hairbreadth Harry	395
Sawmill, The	Larry Semon #1	411
Say Thankyou, Please	Puppets & Demons: Films by Patrick McGuinn	436
Scalp Trouble	Cartoon Collection Vol. 3: Coal Black & De Sebben Dwarfs	680
Scandal in Bohemia, A	Sherlock Holmes' Greatest Cases	642
Scarlet Pumpernickel	Looney Tunes Curtain Calls	685
Scars of Memory	Video Art: Helen Doyle	490
Scary Movie, The	Martina's Playhouse and The Scary Movie	487
Scattered Remains	Films of James Broughton, Volume 4: Autobiographical Mysteries	492
Schichlegruber Doing the Lambe	Why We Fight, No. 2: The Nazis Strike	774
Schitt for President	Moron Movies	508
School Teacher and the Waif	Griffith Shorts (1912, #2)	413
Schwartzkopf in Vietnam	The Schwartzkopf Four-Pack	763
Scotty Finds A Home	Great & Minor Animation Volume 4	684
Scout with Gout, A	Little Lulu and Friends	685
Scout with the Gout, A	Cartoon Collection Vol. 8: Private Snafu	680
Scram!	Laurel and Hardy on the Lam	274
Scrap Happy	Cartoon Classics Vol. 2: Warner Brothers	680
Scrap Happy Daffy	Cartoon Collection Vol. 1: Porky in Wackyland	680
Scrap Happy Daffy	Weird Cartoons Vol. 2	717
Scrappily Married	Great & Minor Animation Volume 4	684
Scratch Video	Video Art, Tape One	489
Screaming Chigger Productions	Best of the New York Underground	427
Screenplay	Spike & Mike's Festival of Animation Vol. 3	716
Screw, A	It's Clean—It Just Looks Dirty	486
Scrub Me Mama with a Boogie	Weird Cartoons Vol. 1	717
Scrub Me Mammy with a Boogie	Cartoon Classics Vol. 9: Early Pioneers	680
Scum and Slime	It's Clean—It Just Looks Dirty	486
Se Met Ko	Video Against AIDS, Volumes 1, 2 & 3	835
Sealed Room, The	A Corner in Wheat and Selected Biograph Shorts	412
Sealed Room, The	D.W. Griffith's Years of Discovery	412
Sealed Room, The	A Corner in Wheat and Selected Biograph Shorts	412
Seapreme Court	Paramount/Famous Studios Volume 2	686
Search for Intelligent Life	Lily Tomlin 3-Pack	462, 535
Seashell and the Clergyman	Avant Garde Program #12	482
Seashell and the Clergyman	Germaine Dulac: The Smiling Madame Beudet and Seashell and the Clergyman	485
Seasons	Masters of Russian Animation: Volume 5	82, 713
Seawards the Great Ships	Documentary Masterpieces by John Grierson	471
Second Class Mail	Animation Celebration Vol. 1	705
Second Epidemic	Video Against AIDS, Volumes 1, 2 & 3	835
Secret Agent	Superman (50th Anniversary)	688
Secret Cinema	Paul Bartel's Secret Cinema	435
Secret Valley	Gigantor Vol. 2	730
Secret Video Membership Oath	Ren & Stimpy in Disguise	701
Seed Reel #1	Sextoons: An Erotic Animation Festival	715
Self Portrait	Plymptoons: The Complete Works of Bill Plympton	715
Selkie Girl, The	The Pigs' Wedding and Other Stories	640
Seni's Children	Magicians of the Earth	552
Serene Composition Suggestive	Video Art: Noel Harding	490
Serenissima	Guido Manuli: Animator	710
Serial Metaphysics	Wheeler Dixon: Selected Films	491
Serpent	Films of Scott Bartlett, Vol. 2: The Future of Human Mythology	485
Servant Girl's Legacy	Laurel and Hardy Solo Flights	411
Set in Motion	International Tournee of Animation Volume 2	712
Settled at the Seaside	Early Comedies Volume 1	410
Seven Chances	Art of Buster Keaton—Box 2	408
Seven Flames, The	European Folk Tales, Volume 6	646
Seventh Seal	Six Short Films of Les Blank, 1960-1985	480
Seventh Voyage of Sinbad	Ray Harryhausen Compilation	715
Sex	X-Rated: Movieyeur	439
Shadow of the Hunter, The	The Films of Arne Sucksdorff: The Great Adventure Plus Short Subjects	75, 472

SHORT FILM	COMPILATION TAPE	PAGE
Shadows	William Wegman Reel 1	491
Shadows on the Snow	The Films of Arne Sucksdorff: The Great Adventure Plus Short Subjects	75, 472
Shadrach	International Tournee of Animation Volume 4	712
Shanghaied	Classic Chaplin, Charlie Chaplin at Essanay Studio	407
Shanghaied	Essanay #3	407
Shanghaied	Rare Chaplin	408
Shanty Where Santy Claus Lives	Cartoon Classics Vol. 8: Early Thirties	680
Sharpe's Downtown New York	M/W/F Music Video One	433
Sharpshooter	Terrytoons: The Cats & Mice of Paul Terry	716
She Sick Sailor	Cartoon Collection Vol. 1: Porky in Wackyland	680
Sheep in the Deep, A	Looney Tunes Assorted Nuts	685
Sheep Wrecked	Droopy & Company	709
Sheep's Meadow	CineBLAST! Vol. 1	483
Sherriff of Stone Gulch	Early Westerns #1	397
Shifters	Juan Downey	486
Ship Ahoy	Terrytoons: The Cats & Mice of Paul Terry	716
Ship Ahoy	Tom & Jerry & Friends #1	688
Shipwreck in Space	Astro Boy Volume 5	722
Shithaus	Cinema of Transgression	483
Shoot it Baby	Third Sex Sinema Volume 1—Vapors	466
Short Kilts	Laurel and Hardy Solo Flights	411
Short Orders	Stanley on the Job	412
Short Vacation	Terrytoons: The Cats & Mice of Paul Terry	716
Should Tall Men Marry?	Films of Stan Laurel Volume 1	410
Shoulder Arms	Chaplin Revue	407
Show Biz	Sextoons: An Erotic Animation Festival	715
Show Business	Forgotten Comedians	411
Show, The	Larry Semon #1	411
Showdown	Superman (50th Anniversary)	688
Showtime	Videotapes of Elizabeth Sher, V. 1-11, I.V. Magazine #2	491
Sick Sick Sister	Destroy All Blondes/The Naked Hipstress/Sick Sick Sister	429
Side of the Road, The	CineBLAST! Vol. 1	483
Sigmund	International Tournee of Animation Volume 1	711
Silence	Holocaust, Polish Jews (Holocoust, Zydzi Polscy)	775
Silent Heroes	Films of Thomas Ince	398
Silent Partner, The	Great Stone Face—Buster Keaton—Vol. 1	409
Silent Witnesses, The	Early Russian Cinema: Before the Revolution, Vol. 6: Class Distinctions	85
Silver Blaze	Sherlock Holmes' Greatest Cases	642
Silver Comet	Astro Boy Volume 11	722
Silvery Moon	Cartoons That Time Forgot Vol. 6: The Odd & The Outrageous	681
Simon Pure Beer	A Few Moments with Buster Keaton and Laurel & Hardy	268
Simonland	Cinema of Transgression	483
Simple Simon	Cartoon Classics in Color #1: Comicolor/Van Beuren	679
Simple Simon	Cartoons That Time Forgot Vol. 5: Free-Form Fairytales	681
Simplified Confusions	Video Art: Noel Harding	490
Sinbad the Sailor	Cartoon Classics in Color #1: Comicolor/Van Beuren	679
Sinbad the Sailor	Cartoons That Time Forgot Vol. 4: Willie Whopper's Fantastic Adventures	681
Sing a Song of Six Pants	The Three Stooges	284
Sing Beast Sing	The Rocketship Reel	715
Sing, Bing, Sing	Bing at Sennett Vol. 2	263
Sing-a-long with Popeye	Cartoon Collection Vol. 5: Racial Cartoons	680
Sing-Song of Old Man Kangaroo	Just So Stories, Set I	653
Singing Ding a Lings	Spike & Mike's Festival of Animation Vol. 2	716
Singing Teacher	Masters of Russian Animation: Volume 2	82, 713
Sinister Harvest	Drug Propaganda and Satire Compilation	505
Sinkin in the Bathtup	Cartoon Collection Vol. 7: Tokyo Jokio	680
Sinking of the Lusitania, The	Pioneers in Animation Vol. 1	714
Sinking of the Lusitania, The	Animation Vol. 1: The Beginning	706
Sinking of the Lusitania, The	Classic Shorts Compilation #12: Winsor McCay	682
Sinking of the Lusitania, The	Winsor McCay: Animation Legend	718
Sirius Remembered	Stan Brakhage Selected Films: Vol. 2	488
Sissie and Blake	Scar of Shame	448
Six Point Nine	Best of the Fests 1991	706
Skin of our Teeth	Civilization, Programs 1 & 2	781
Skip It	Best of the Fests: For Kids	706
Skippy the Dog Food Taster	Too Outrageous Animation	717
Skulls & Sculls	Early Animation Vol. 2	709
Sky is Blue, The	NFBC: The Tender Tale of Cinderella Penguin	714
Sky Pirates	Best of George Pal	677
Skywhales	International Tournee of Animation Volume 1	711
Slaughter Day	Spike & Mike's Sick & Twisted Festival of Animation, Vol. 2	716
Sleepy Haven	Matthias Muller—Selected Films	433
Sleepy Time Down South	Cartoon Collection Vol. 4: Warner Bros. & Fleischer	680
Sleuth	Larry Semon #2	411
Sleuth, The	Stan About Town	411
Slick Sleuth	Pioneers in Animation Vol. 1	714
Slick Sleuths	Early Animation Vol. 2	709
Slightly Daffy	Daffy!	683
Small Fry	Paramount/Fleischer Studios Volume 1	686
Small Fry	Weird Cartoons Vol. 2	717
Small Town Idol	Eyes of Ben Turpin Are upon You!	410
Small Town Sheriff	Animation Vol. 1: The Beginning	706
Smallest Particle	The Works of Ken Feingold—Fictions	491
Smile of Reason	Civilization, Programs 9 & 10	781
Smile Please	All Night Long and Smile Please	410
Smile, Darn Ya, Smile	All Singing, All Dancing	676
Smile, Darn Ya, Smile	Cartoon Classics Vol. 2: Warner Brothers	680
Smile, Darn Ya, Smile	Cartoon Collection Vol. 4: Warner Bros. & Fleischer	680
Smiling Madame Beudet	Germaine Dulac	485
Smiling Madame Beudet, The	Avant Garde Shorts/France	483
Smith's Army Life	Smith Family Series	404
Smith's Cook	Smith Family Series	404
Smith's Customer	Smith Family Series	404
Smith's Fishing Trip	Smith Family Series	404
Smith's New Home	Smith Family Series	404
Smith's Picnic	Smith Family Series	404
Smithy	Films of Stan Laurel Volume 4	410
Smithy	Stanley on the Job	412
Smogging	Greentoons: Environmentally Aware Animation	710
Smoke	Four Directions: Selections from MIX 94—The NY Lesbian & Gay Film Festival	459
Smoked Out	The Films of Leo Maloney	368
Smoking	William Wegman Reel 7	491

SHORT FILM	COMPILATION TAPE	PAGE
Smothering Dreams	Smothering Dreams and Thousands Watch	488
Snafuperman	Cartoon Collection Vol. 7: Tokyo Jokio	680
Snafuperman	Superman	688
Snafurman	Wartime Cartoons	717
Snake Theatre	Too Outrageous Animation	717
Snakewoman	Film Musicals	430
Snakewoman	Tina L'hotsky: Barbie and Snakewoman	489
Snap Happy	Cartoon Collection Vol. 5: Racial Cartoons	680
Sneakin' and Peekin'	Sneakin' and Peekin'	478
Sniffles Takes a Trip	Golden Age of Looney Tunes: Vol. 5, Chuck Jones	684
Snob Fever	Films of Harold Lloyd—Volume 3	410
Snookles	Spike & Mike's Festival of Animation Vol. 1	716
Snoopy and the Giant	Peanuts: Charlie Brown & Snoopy Show Vol. 7	700
Snoopy's Brother Spike	Peanuts: Charlie Brown & Snoopy Show Vol. 8	700
Snoopy's Football Career	Peanuts: Charlie Brown & Snoopy Show Vol. 6	700
Snoopy's Robot	Peanuts: Charlie Brown & Snoopy Show Vol. 8	700
Snow Business	Stars of Space Jam: Five-Tape Boxed Set	687
Snow Foolin'	Cartoon Holidays	680
Snow Time	Tom & Jerry & Friends #2	688
Snow White	Disney Canta con Nosotros	672
Snow White and the Seven Dwarfs	Sextoons: An Erotic Animation Festival	715
Snowflakes	William Wegman Reel 4	491
Snowy Day, The	The Ezra Jack Keats Library	633
So Far So...	Pictures Don't Tell You Anything: Selected Films of Ann Marie Fleming	211, 487
So Many People	Puppets & Demons: Films by Patrick McGuinn	436
So Near Yet So Far	Griffith Shorts (1912, #2)	413
Soaring Blue Dragon King	Sohryuden Vol. 6: Episodes 11 and 12	746
Social Experiment	Nice Girls...Films by and About Women	434
Society Dog Show	Mickey Loves Minnie	693
Soda Squirt	Cartoons That Time Forgot Vol. 3: Things That Go Bump in the Night	681
Soilers, The	Stan "Tex" Laurel Rides Again	411
Soir Bleu	Picture Windows	242
Sold at Auction	Risky Business (1928)	403
Soldier Man	Films of Harry Langdon Volume 1	410
Soldiers of the East	Ancient Warriors	784
Soldiers, The	Films of Stan Laurel Volume 3	410
Solly's Diner	Basement Tape	427
Solly's Diner	How to Survive	431
Solly's Diner	Kisses in the Dark	234
Soma Sema	Mediamystics	487
Sombra a Sombra	Sabda and Sombra a Sombra	488
Some Enchanted Genie	Aladdin & Jasmine's Moonlight Magic	676, 690
Something in Her Eye	Laurel and Hardy Solo Flights	411
Somewhere in Dreamland	Cartoon Classics in Color #1: Comicolor/Van Beuren	679
Somewhere in Dreamland	Paramount/Fleischer Studios Volume 1	686
Somewhere in Springtime	Christmas Cartoon Classic	682
Son's Return, The	Griffith Shorts (1909-1911)	413
Song from an Angel	Best of the Fests 1990	706
Song of Ceylon	Classic Documentaries: People and Places	470
Song of Ceylon	E.M.B. Classics	471
Song of Songs	Picture Windows	242
Song of the Birds	Paramount/Fleischer Studios Volume 2	686
Song of the Godbody	Films of James Broughton, Volume 1: Erotic Celebrations	492
Song of the Prairie	Puppet Masters	715
Sorcerer's Apprentice	Tales of Frankenstein	530
Sorrows of the Unfaithful	Griffith Shorts (1909-1911)	413
SOS	Guido Manuli: Animator	710
Sound Collector, The	NFBC: Animation for Kids Vol. 1	714
Sound of Maggie, The	Bumbledown/Sound of Maggie	415
Sound of One	Films of Scott Bartlett, Vol. 2: The Future of Human Mythology	485
Soundings	Figures	484
Soup Song, The	Cartoons That Time Forgot Vol. 1: All Singing! All Dancing!	681
South Pole or Bust	Fox Terrytoons	684
South West: Exeter to Penzance	British Rail Journeys	841
Southbound Duckling	Tom & Jerry's Cartoon Cavalcade	689
Space Madness	Ren & Stimpy Vol. 1: The Classics	701
Space Plant, A	Johnny Sokko and His Flying Robot: Episodes 3 and 4	734
Spaghetti Snot	Spike & Mike's Sick & Twisted Festival of Animation, Vol. 2	716
Spanish Civil War, The	Between the Wars, 1918-1941, Vol. 6	808
Spanking Breezes	The Comediennes, Volume 1	397
Spanking, The	Secrets of Love, Classics of Erotic Literature: Vol. 4	510
Spartacus Rex	Best of the Fests 1990	706
Special Delivery	Incredible Animation Collection: Vol. 1	711
Spectator, The	Love in the City	41
Speed Reading	William Wegman Reel 3	491
Speeder	Computer Animation Classics	708
Spelling Lesson, The	William Wegman Reel 4	491
Spelling Lesson, The	Best of William Wegman	483
Spider Jan.16.91	Tom Chomont: A Two-Volume Collection, Volume II	466, 489
Spider's Revenge	Gigantor Vol. 2	730
Spies	Cartoon Collection Vol. 8: Private Snafu	680
Spill Your Seed	Men in Shorts, Volume 2	463
Spinach Roadster	Cartoon Collection Vol. 4: Warner Bros. & Fleischer	680
Spinning Tops	Spinning Tops and Tickle Bops	670
Spirit of '43, The	Great & Minor Animation Volume 3	684
Spirit of '43, The	Cartoon Collection Vol. 1: Porky in Wackyland	680
Spiritual Constructions	The Films of Oskar Fischinger—Optical Poetry	710
Spiritualist Photographer	More Melies	22
Spokes	Men in Shorts, Volume 2	463
Spooks	Cartoons That Time Forgot Vol. 3: Things That Go Bump in the Night	681
Spooks	The Face at the Window	521
Sport of Kings	Aesop's Fables Volume 3	676
Sportsman, The	Larry Semon #3	411
Spot Finds a Key	Where's Spot	659
Spot Goes Splash	Where's Spot	659
Spring	Frog and Toad Are Friends	652
Spring Fever	Harold Lloyd Comedies Vol. 3	410
Springtime Toddler Tales	Nursery Habitat Set	821
Squalid Salad	Maneaters: A Trilogy	486
Square Meal	The Abbott and Costello Television Show, Tape 4	414
Square of Light, The	International Tournee of Animation Volume 6	712
Squaw's Love, A	Griffith Shorts (1911-1912)	413
Squeal of Death	Squeal of Death	282

SHORT FILM	COMPILATION TAPE	PAGE
Srt of Lotte Reiniger	Lotte Reiniger Compilation	713
St. Louis Blues, The	That's Black Entertainment: African-American Contributions in Film and Dance 1903-1944	455
St. Louis Blues, The	Black Jazz and Blues	609
Stagecoach Driver and the Girl	Tom Mix Short Subjects	405
Stain, The	International Tournee of Animation Volume 6	712
Stalking	William Wegman Reel 5	491
Stanley and Stella in	Computer Animation Classics	708
Star Border, The	Keystones #1	407
Star of Bethlehem	Classic Cartoon Christmas Treasures	682
Star to Call Home, A	Symphony to the Planets	841
Star-Spangled Banner	Animation Celebration Vol. 3	705
Stars of the Circus	Terrytoons: The Cats & Mice of Paul Terry	716
State of Grace	Karl Krogstad: The Gigabyte Trilogy	432
Stationmaster	Films of Oliver Hardy	410
Stealing Altitude	Best of the Fests 1991	706
Steamboat Bill Jr.	Art of Buster Keaton—Box 3	408
Steamboat Willie	Mickey Mouse: The Black & White Years	693
Stella!	Puppets & Demons: Films by Patrick McGuinn	436
Stellar	Stan Brakhage—Hand-Painted Films	488
Stenka Razin Current	Early Russian Cinema: Before the Revolution, Vol. 1: Beginnings	85
Steps of the Ballet	Benjamin Britten	469
Stereo Systems	William Wegman Reel 6	491
Sternenschauer	Matthias Muller—Selected Films	433
Stich and Tooth	William Wegman Reel 3	491
Stick Around	Hardy and Ray	411
Stiff Sheets	Stiff Sheets	465
Stiff Sheets	Video Against AIDS, Volumes 1, 2 & 3	835
Still Life of Postcards, A	Nice Girls...Films by and About Women	434
Stimpy's Big Day	Ren & Stimpy Vol. 2: The Stupidest Stories	701
Stimpy's Inventions	Ren & Stimpy Vol. 1: The Classics	701
Stolen Goods	Charley Chase Vol. 1	410
Stolen Skates	The Abbott and Costello Television Show, Tape 2	414
Stomach Pump	CineBLAST! Vol. 3	428
Stomach Song	Best of William Wegman	483
Stomach Song	William Wegman Reel 1	491
Stone Circles	Perceptual Landscapes	464, 492
Stop That Noise	Best of Betty Boop	677
Stop! Look! And Hasten!	Roadrunner & Wile E. Coyote: The Scrapes of Wrath	687
Stork Naked	Daffy Duck: Tales from the Duckside	682
Storm of the White Dragon King	Sohryuden Vol. 5: Episodes 9 and 10	746
Story about Ping, The	Rosie's Walk and Other Stories	656
Story of a Transport	Nostalgia World War II Video Library #10	771
Story of Christmas	A Christmas Gift	707
Story of Christmas, The	NFBC—Cartoon Festival: The Sweater	714
Story of Christmas, The	NFBC: Christmas Cracker	714
Story of Cinderella, The	NFBC: The Box	714
Story of Grand Canyon	America's Great National Parks	828
Story of King Midas	Ray Harryhausen Compilation	715
Story of Lucy, The	Nova—Adventures in Science: In Search of Human Origins	837
Story of Yellowstone, The	America's Great National Parks	828
Story of Yosemite, The	America's Great National Parks	828
Story, A	Spike & Mike's Festival of Animation Vol. 1	716
Story, The	Frog and Toad Are Friends	652
Story—A Story, A	Stories from the Black Tradition	642
Story—A Story, A	Strega Nonna and Other Stories	649
Strange Case of Balthazar, The	CineBLAST! Vol. 3	428
Strange Island of Dr. Wily	Mega Man: 20,000 Leaks Under the Sea	698
Strange Meeting, A	Griffith Shorts (1909-1911)	413
Strange Monster, A	Johnny Sokko and His Flying Robot: Episodes 3 and 4	734
Stratos-Fear	Cartoons That Time Forgot Vol. 3: Things That Go Bump in the Night	681
Straw and String	William Wegman Reel 2	491
Stream	Computer Animation Festival Vol. 2.0	708
Street of Crocodiles	The Brothers Quay Vol. 1	707
Street Sweeper	Spike & Mike's Festival of Animation Vol. 2	716
Street Vendor, The	Problems for Young Consumers	670
Street, The	NFBC: Leonard Maltin's Animation Favorites from the National Film Board of Canada	714
Streetsweeper	Spike & Mike's Festival of Animation Vol. 3	716
Stress	Your Family's Health, Tape 2	838
Strife with Father	Looney Tunes Assorted Nuts	685
String of the Spider	Gigantor Vol. 1	730
Strings	National Film Board of Canada's Animation Festival	714
Striptease	Outrageous Animation Vol. 1	714
Stripy	Guido Manuli: Animator	710
Strong Men Keep A-Comin' On	Promised Land	435
Strong Revenge, A	Mabel Normand, Vol. 1	411
Struggle at the South Pole	Gigantor Vol. 1	730
Struggle for Survival	The Films of Arne Sucksdorff: The Great Adventure Plus Short Subjects	75, 472
Struggle, The	Films of Thomas Ince	398
Stubbs	Spike & Mike's Sick & Twisted Festival of Animation, Vol. 2	716
Study #7	The Films of Oskar Fischinger—Optical Poetry	710
Study #8	The Films of Oskar Fischinger—Optical Poetry	710
Study in Choreography	Maya Deren Experimental Films	487
Study in Color and Black & White	Stan Brakhage—Hand-Painted Films	488
Stuntman, The	Larry Semon #1	411
Stupidsitious Cat, The	Pioneers in Animation Vol. 3	714
Stupor Duck	Stars of Space Jam: Five-Tape Boxed Set	687
Subo and the White Horse	The Emperor's New Clothes and Other Folktales	646
Success	International Tournee of Animation Volume 2	712
Suddenly It's Spring	Paramount/Famous Studios Volume 2	686
Sufferin' Cats	Tom & Jerry's Festival of Fun	689
Sugar Delight	Plymptoons: The Complete Works of Bill Plympton	715
Suicide, A	Cinema of Transgression	483
Sultan Pepper	Cartoon Classics Vol. 8: Early Thirties	680
Summer Legend	NFBC: Cartoon Festival: The Cat Came Back	714
Summertime	Cartoons That Time Forgot Vol. 1: All Singing! All Dancing!	681
Sunbeam, The	Animation Celebration Vol. 1	705
Sunbeam, The	Griffith Shorts (1912, #1)	413
Sunbeam, The	D.W. Griffith's Years of Discovery	412
Sunbeam, The	Musketeers of Pig Alley and Selected Biograph Shorts	413
Sundae in New York	The World's Greatest Animation	718
Sunday Afternoon	Baby Face Harry Langdon	410
Sunny Italy	Terrytoons: The Cats & Mice of Paul Terry	716
Sunnyside	A Woman of Paris	408
Sunshine Makers, The	Cartoons That Time Forgot Vol. 6: The Odd & The Outrageous	681
Sunshine Sue	Griffith Shorts (1910-1911)	413
Super Brain	Astro Boy Volume 3	722
Super Lulu	Little Lulu and Friends	685
Super-Grover	Five Sesame Street Stories	652
Super-Hooper-Dyne Lizzies	Slapstick Encyclopedia—Vol. 2: Keystone Tonight!	411
Superdyke	Lesbian Humor	461, 492
Superman	Color Adventures of Superman	682
Superman	Superman (50th Anniversary)	688
Superman the Psychiatrist	More Moron Movies	508
Surface is Illusion	Art on Film/Film on Art, Program 5: Film/Art: Subject and Expert	545
Surprise	Animation Vol. 2	706
Survival of the Delirious	Video Against AIDS, Volumes 1, 2 & 3	835
Surviving in Africa	Nova—Adventures in Science: In Search of Human Origins	837
Suspect No. 1	Trio	489
Swat the Fly	Cartoon Classics Vol. 6: Early Animation	680
Swat the Fly	The Genesis of Animation, Volume One	710
Sweater, The	NFBC—Cartoon Festival: The Sweater	714
Sweater, The	A Christmas Gift	707
Sweater, The	NFBC: Leonard Maltin's Animation Favorites from the National Film Board of Canada	714
Swedish One	Simultaneous	488
Swedish Two	Simultaneous	488
Sweet Adeline	Aesop's Fables Volume 2	676
Sweet and Twenty	Griffith Shorts (1909)	412
Sweet Dreams Luv	Outrageous Animation Vol. 2	714
Sweet Memories	Mary Pickford—The Early Years	401
Sweet Memories	The Short Films of Mary Pickford	404
Swim, A	Frog and Toad Are Friends	652
Swineherd, The	The Ugly Duckling (Children's Circle)	649
Swing Cleaning	Great & Minor Animation Volume 2	684
Swing Shift Cinderella	Tex Avery's Screwball Classics 1	688
Swing to the Left	Gai Dimanche/Swing to the Left	28
Swing Wedding	MGM Cartoon Classics: Happy Harmonies	686
Swiss Misfit	Man's Best Friend	685
Swiss Missed	Timon and Pumbaa's Wild Adventures: Quit Buggin' Me	694
Switch Tower, The	Griffith Shorts (1913-1914)	413
Switch Tower, The	The Short Films of D.W. Griffith—Volume 2	413
SX-70	Films of Charles and Ray Eames, Volume 4	485
Symbolize	William Wegman Reel 4	491
Symphonie Diagonale	Avant Garde Program #2	482
Symphony in Black	Black Jazz and Blues	609
Symphony in Slang	Tex Avery's Screwball Classics 1	688
Sync Touch	Lesbian Humor	461, 492
Synchronicity	Simultaneous	488
T'was Henry's Fault	The Comediennes, Volume 2	397
Taboo Parlor	Erotique	430
Tails	William Wegman Reel 4	491
Take Me to Chicago	The Promised Land (Documentary)	454, 435
Taking Medicine	Wartime Cartoons	717
Tale of Antonia, The	Tales of Paris	23
Tale of Benjamin Bunny, The	Treasury of Animal Stories, Set I	643
Tale of Ella, The	Tales of Paris	23
Tale of Francoise, The	Tales of Paris	23
Tale of Jeremy Fisher, The	Treasury of Animal Stories, Set I	643
Tale of Peter Rabbit, The	Treasury of Animal Stories, Set I	643
Tale of Sophie, The	Tales of Paris	23
Tale of Squirrel Nutkin, The	Treasury of Animal Stories, Set I	643
Tale of Tales	Masters of Russian Animation: Volume 5	82, 713
Tale of the Frozen Ghost	Are You Afraid of the Dark?	629
Tale of the Shiny Red Bicycle	Are You Afraid of the Dark?	629
Tale of the Vienna Woods	MGM Cartoon Classics: Happy Harmonies	686
Tale of Two Chickens, A	The James Marshall Library	636
Tale of Two Cities, A	A Tale of Two Cities/In the Switch Tower	405
Tale of Two Kitties, A	Cartoon Collection Vol. 7: Tokyo Jokio	680
Tale of Two Kitties, A	Cartoon Classics in Color #4: Classic Warner Bros.	680
Talking Magpies, The	Great & Minor Animation Volume 1	684
Talking Magpies, The	Cartoon Collection Vol. 6: The Ducktators	680
Tall Time Tales	Hubley Collection Vol. 3	711
Tammy and Can of Plums	William Wegman Reel 5	491
Tampon	Too Outrageous Animation	717
Tango Tangles	Keystones #1	407
Tantalizing Fly	Koko the Clown, 1915-27	712
Tapes	Pier Marton: Collected Works: 1979-84	487
Target Japan	Nostalgia World War II Video Library #6	771
Tars and Stripes	Buster Keaton Talkies, Vol. 2	408
Tarts & Flowers	Paramount/Fleischer Studios Volume 3	686
Tattercoats	Katharine Hepburn: World of Stories	647
Tattoed Lady of Riverview	Palazzolo's Chicago	476
Taylor Chain I	Taylor Chain I and II	478
Taz and the Terodactyl	Tazmania: Taz-Tronaut	704
Teaching Hickville to Sing	Matinee Idols: The Ladies	401
Tear Jerker	Tear Jerker	489
Techno-Cracked	Cartoons That Time Forgot Vol. 3: Things That Go Bump in the Night	681
Technological Threat	Computer Animation Festival Vol. 2.0	708
Technological Threat	International Tournee of Animation Volume 3	712
Teddy at the Throttle	Early Comedies Volume 1	410
Teddy at the Throttle	Slapstick Encyclopedia—Vol. 7: The Rage Is On	411
Tee Time	Felix the Cat: Sound & Silent	683
Teenage Father	First Works Volume One	334
Teeny-tiny and the Witch-Woman	What's Under My Bed and Other Creepy Stories	659
Telepathos	Pier Marton: Collected Works: 1979-84	487
Telephone Girl and Lady	Griffith Shorts (1912, #3)	413
Telling Personal Nuclear Age	People of Faith and the Arms Race	805
Temple on a Stick	Karl Krogstad: Temple, Fork & Jack in the Fox	432
Ten Minute Egg	Charley Chase Jimmy Jump Series	410
Tender Game	Hubley Studio: Voyage to Next	711
Tender Tale of Cinderella, Penguin	NFBC: The Tender Tale of Cinderella Penguin	714
Tender Tale of Cinderella, Penguin	NFBC: Animation for Kids Vol. 1	714
Tender Tale of Cinderella, The	NFBC: Cartoon Festival: Cactus Swing	714
Tennis	Spike & Mike's Sick & Twisted Festival of Animation, Vol. 2	716
Tennis Chums	Tom & Jerry's Festival of Fun	689
Teresa	Gold of Naples	38

SHORT FILM	COMPILATION TAPE	PAGE
Termites of 1938	The Three Stooges: A Pain in the Pullman	284
Terrance Baum: Intergalactic A	Puppets & Demons: Films by Patrick McGuinn	436
Terrence Davies Trilogy: Child	Terence Davies Trilogy	164
Terrence Davies Trilogy: Death	Terence Davies Trilogy	164
Terrence Davies Trilogy: Madon	Terence Davies Trilogy	164
Terrible Time Gun, The	Astro Boy Volume 2	722
Terrible Turkish Executioners	Films of Georges Melies, Volume 1	20
Terrible Turkish Executioners	Melies III: The Search for Munchhausen	22
Terror Island	Jonny Quest: Bandit—Adventure's Best Friend	698
Terror of the Third Reich	Terror of the Third Reich	772
Terror on the Midway	Superman (50th Anniversary)	688
Test of Love	Secrets of Love, Classics of Erotic Literature: Vol. 5	510
Testament	Films of James Broughton, Volume 4: Autobiographical Mysteries	492
Thanatopsis	Films by Ed Emshwiller	484
Thanks for the Mammaries	Spike & Mike's Sick & Twisted Festival of Animation ...Vol 1	716
That's Forever	Teasers	466
Their First Mistake	Laurel and Hardy and the Family	274
Them	The British Animation Invasion	707
Theodore and Juliet	Alvin and the Chipmunks: Love Potion #9	628
Theology	Computer Animation Festival Vol. 2.0	708
There Ain't No Santa Claus	Charley Chase Vol. 1	410
There Was a Dog	Masters of Russian Animation: Volume 6—The Works	32, 713
There's a Nightmare in My Closet	Shelley Duvall's Bedtime Stories (Collection)	657
There's an Alligator Under	Shelley Duvall's Bedtime Stories (Collection)	657
There's Something in My Attic	Shelley Duvall's Bedtime Stories (Collection)	657
They All Fall	Hardy and Ray	411
They are Lost Vision Altogether	Video Against AIDS, Volumes 1, 2 & 3	835
They Wear No Clothes	They Wear No Clothes	511
Thief of Baghdad	Douglas Fairbanks Sr Collection	397
Thigh Line Lyre Triangular	Stan Brakhage Selected Films: Vol. 2	488
Thing What Lurked in the Tub	Spike & Mike's Festival of Animation Vol. 1	716
Things We Said Today	Dyke Drama	458
Third Sex, The	Third Sex Sinema Volume 1—Vapors	466
This and That	Simultaneous	488
This is It	Films of James Broughton, Volume 5: Parables of Wonder	492
This is Not an Advertisement	Video Art: Antonio Muntadas	489
This Is Not an AIDS Ad	Video Against AIDS, Volumes 1, 2 & 3	835
This is Your Brain on Animation	Too Outrageous Animation	717
Those Awful Hats	Griffith Shorts (1909-1911)	413
Those Awful Hats	D.W. Griffith's Years of Discovery	412
Those Awful Hats	A Corner in Wheat and Selected Biograph Shorts	412
Those Beautiful Dames	Cartoon Collection Vol. 3: Coal Black & De Sebben Dwarfs	680
Those Love Fangs	Keystones #3	407
Thousands Watch	Smothering Dreams and Thousands Watch	488
Three Ages	Art of Buster Keaton—Box 1	408
Three Bears, The	Cartoons That Time Forgot Vol. 5: Free-Form Fairytales	681
Three Billy Goats Gruff, The	Blue Ribbon Stories Vol. 1	650
Three Dark Horses	The Three Stooges: Vagabond Loafers	284
Three Drugs	Chip Lord: Selected Works	428
Three Homerics	Stan Brakhage—Hand-Painted Films	488
Three Little Kittens	Cartoon Classics Vol. 8: Early Thirties	680
Three Little Kittens	Tom & Jerry & Friends #3	688
Three Little Pigs, The	Happy Birthday Moon and Other Stories	647
Three Little Pigs, The	The James Marshall Library	636
Three Little Pigs, The	Wings: A Tale of Two Chickens and Other Stories by James Marshall	644
Three Muskateers, The	Douglas Fairbanks Sr Collection	397
Three of a Kind	Slapstick Encyclopedia—Vol. 8: Tons of Fun: Comedy's Anarchic Fringe	411
Three on a Limb	Buster Keaton Talkies, Vol. 2	408
Three Robbers, The	The Three Robbers and Other Stories	643
Three Robbers, The	What's Under My Bed and Other Creepy Stories	659
Three Robotiers	Astro Boy Volume 12	722
Three Wishes, The	Lotte Reiniger Compilation	713
Through an Open Window	Best of the Fests, 5th Annual	706
Through Darking Vales	Griffith Shorts (1911-1912)	413
Thrust in Me	Nick Zedd: Steal This Video	434
Thrust in Me	Wide World of Lydia Lunch	439
Thumb Fun	Porky Pig: Days of Swine and Roses	687
Tick	CineBLAST! Vol. 2	483
Tick vs. Chairface Chippendale	The Tick	704
Tick vs. the Idea Man, The	The Tick	704
Tidbits	BBC Wildlife Special Volume 2	813
Tiger! Tiger!	The Jungle Books, Set I	636
Tightrope Tricks	Tom & Jerry & Friends #1	688
Tikki Tikki Tembo	Strega Nonna and Other Stories	649
Tillie's Punctured Romance	Mabel Normand Comedies, Vol. 1	411
Time and the I Ching	A Magical Journey	851
Time for a Beer	How to Survive	431
Time for Love, A	CineBLAST! Vol. 3	428
Time of the Angels	Hubley Collection Vol. 2	711
Time of the Locust	Vietnam: Time of the Locust	778
Timely Interception	Griffith Shorts (1913)	413
Timid Toreador, The	Pioneers in Animation Vol. 3	714
Timid Young Man	Buster Keaton Talkies, Vol. 7	408
Tin Toy	Tiny Toy Stories	717
Tiny & Ruby: Hell-Divin' Women	International Sweethearts of Rhythm/ Tiny & Ruby: Hell-Divin' Women	461, 611
Tinkle Terror	CineBLAST! Vol. 3	428
Tintype Tangle	Fatty Arbuckle	410
Tiny	CineBLAST! Vol. 3	428
Titans vs. Olympians	Dawn of the Greek Gods	784
To Duck or Not to Duck	Cartoon Collection Vol. 2: Classic Warner Bros	680
To Parsifal	Tung, To Parsifal & Castro Street	489
To See the World	Droits au Coeur (Rights from the Heart)	709
To Spring	MGM Cartoon Classics: Happy Harmonies	686
To Spring	Thirties Magic Vol. 1	716
Toccata for Toy Trains	Films of Charles and Ray Eames, Volume 2	485
Toilet Bowl	Outrageous Animation Vol. 2	714
Tokyo Jokio	Cartoon Collection Vol. 7: Tokyo Jokio	680
Tom Thumb	Cartoon Classics Vol. 5: The Other Studios	680
Tom Thumb	Cartoons That Time Forgot Vol. 4: Willie Whopper's Fantastic Adventures	681
Tom Thumb	Best of George Pal	677
Tom Turk & Duffy	Cartoon Collection Vol. 3: Coal Black & De Sebben Dwarfs	680
Tom Turkey and His Harmonica	MGM Cartoon Classics: Happy Harmonies	686

SHORT FILM	COMPILATION TAPE	PAGE
Tom's Designs on Jerry	Tom & Jerry on Parade	689
Tompkins Square Park, 1989	Tompkins Square Park, 1989/Dinkinsville	479
Tony de Peltrie	International Tournee of Animation Volume 1	711
Tony de Peltrie	Computer Animation Classics	708
Toomai of the Elephants	The Jungle Books, Set I	636
Toonerville Ahoy	Best of the Van Beuren Studio	677
Toonerville Picnic	Cartoons That Time Forgot Vol. 6: Odd & The Outrageous	681
Toonerville Picnic	Best of the Van Beuren Studio	677
Toonerville Trolley	Cartoons That Time Forgot Vol. 7: Rainbow Parades	681
Toonerville Trolley	Best of the Van Beuren Studio	677
Toonerville Trolley	Cartoon Classics in Color #1: Comicolor/Van Beuren	679
Top of the World	Teasers	466
Tortoise and the Hare, The	Fables and Fairy Tales, Fairy Tale Masterpieces	646
Tortoise Bets the Hare	Bugs Bunny's Zaniest Toons	679
Tortoise Wins by a Hare	Bugs Bunny's Zaniest Toons	679
Tosio	CineBLAST! Vol. 3	428
Total Loss	Ben Turpin #1	410
Touch of Deceit, A	International Tournee of Animation Volume 4	712
Touchbase	CineBLAST! Vol. 3	428
Touchdown Mickey	Mickey Mouse: The Black & White Years	693
Touchdown Tommy	Rugrats: A Baby's Gotta Do What a Baby's Gotta Do	641, 701
Touche	Tom & Jerry's Festival of Fun	689
Tough	CineBLAST! Vol. 1	483
Tourist	Optical Nerves	463, 492
Towed in a Hole	Laurel and Hardy at Work	274
Tower of Mice, The	European Folk Tales, Volume 1	646
Town Mouse & the Country Mouse	NFBC: Every Child	714
Toy Palace	Rugrats: Tales from the Crib	641, 702
Toy Story: The Adventures of	Tiny Toy Stories	717
Toyland Broadcast	MGM Cartoon Classics: Happy Harmonies	686
Toyland Broadcast	Tom & Jerry's The Night Before Christmas	689
Toyland Caper	Classic Cartoon Christmas Treasures	682
Toys Will Be Toys	Classic Cartoon Christmas Treasures	682
Trailer Life	Fox Terrytoons	684
Train Gang	International Tournee of Animation Volume 4	712
Tramp, The	Classic Chaplin, Charlie Chaplin at Essanay Studio	407
Tramp, The	Emerging Chaplin	407
Tramp, The	Essanay #2	407
Tramp, The	Charlie Chaplin's Keystone Comedies	407
Tramp, The	The Tramp and a Woman	408
Transformation of Mike, The	Griffith Shorts (1911-1912)	413
Transformation of Mike, The	The Short Films of D.W. Griffith—Volume 4	413
Transformed Humans, The	Johnny Sokko and His Flying Robot: Episodes 5 and 6	734
Travels of a Dollar Bill	Best of the Fests: For Kids	706
Travels of an Ant	Masters of Russian Animation: Volume 4	82, 713
Travels of an Ant	Masters of Russian Animation: Volume 6—The Works	82, 713
Travels with a Duchess	Steam Days: Travels with a Duchess and the Fishing Line	844
Treat Bottle	William Wegman Reel 2	491
Treat Table	William Wegman Reel 5	491
Tree Cornered Tweety	Stars of Space Jam: Five-Tape Boxed Set	687
Tree in a Test Tube	Laurel and Hardy's Magic Lantern Show	411
Triangle	Best of the Fests 1990	706
Triassac Parking Lot	Spike & Mike's Sick & Twisted Festival of Animation, Vol. 2	716
Trick Bag	Kartemquin Films, Vol. 3: Trick Bag	474
Trick Shooting with K. Duncan	Crossroad Avenger/Trick Shooting with Kenne Duncan	514
Trikfilm 3	Griffiti	710
Trip Across Country	William Wegman Reel 4	491
Trip to the Moon, A	Grand Melies (Franju) and Melies' Short Films	20
Trip to the Moon, A	Marvelous Melies	22
Trip to the Moon, A	Films of Georges Melies, Volume 1	20
Trip, The	The Ezra Jack Keats Library	633
Triple Trouble (aka The Bond)	Essanay #3	407
Trivial Pursuit	Plymptoons: The Complete Works of Bill Plympton	715
Trolley Ahoy!	Cartoons That Time Forgot Vol. 7: Rainbow Parades	681
Troubles on the Ark	Aesop's Fables Volume 2	676
Troublesome Secretary	Mabel Normand Comedies, Vol. 2	411
Truce Hurts, The	Tom & Jerry's Festival of Fun	689
Truck Wrestler, The	Moron Movies	508
True Story of Lili Marlene	Listen to Britain	474, 769
Trumpeter, The	European Folk Tales, Volume 1	646
Truth in the Lord	It's Clean—It Just Looks Dirty	486
Tuba Tooter	Cartoons That Time Forgot Vol. 6: The Odd & The Outrageous	681
Tubby the Tuba	Paramount/Fleischer Studios Volume 2	686
Tube Talk	William Wegman Reel 6	491
Tukiki and His Search	Christmas Carousel	630
Tune	The Tune	717
Tung	Tung, To Parsifal & Castro Street	489
Tuning In	Tom & Jerry & Friends #2	688
Tunnel Workers, The	The Short Films of D.W. Griffith—Volume 3	413
Turd is a Man's Best Friend, A	Moron Movies	508
Turn On, The	Plymptoons: The Complete Works of Bill Plympton	715
Turning the Tables	Mack Sennett: The Biograph Years	411
TV of Tomorrow	Tex Avery's Screwball Classics 4	688
TV Tango	Droits au Coeur (Rights from the Heart)	709
Twas Henry's Fault	The Comediennes: Vol. 2	397
Twas the Night Before Christmas	Bugs Bunny's Looney Christmas Tales	679
Tweet and Sour	Sylvester & Tweety: The Best Yeows of Our Lives	688
Tweet Zoo	Stars of Space Jam: Five-Tape Boxed Set	687
Tweety Pie	Tweety & Sylvester	689
Twelve Days of Christmas, The	Christmas Stories	631
Twelve Months	The Velveteen Rabbit (Claymation)	717
Twenty Minutes Of Love	Keystones #2	407
Twenty-eight	M/W/F Music Video One	433
Twice Two	Laurel and Hardy and the Family	274
Two Centuries of Black Am Art	Portraits in Black	453
Two Daughters of Eve	Griffith Shorts (1912, #2)	413
Two Figures	Figures	484
Two Fister	Films of Edmund Cobb	398
Two Gun Gussie	Harold Lloyd's Comedy Classics	410
Two Gun Gussie	Films of Harold Lloyd—Volume 2	409
Two Gun Gussie	Harold Lloyd Comedies Vol. 3	410
Two Gun Mickey	Mickey Mouse: The Black & White Years	693
Two in Twenty	Variety Is the Spice of Life	489
Two Lamps	Best of William Wegman	483
Two Little Pups	MGM Cartoon Classics: Happy Harmonies	686

SHORT FILM	COMPILATION TAPE	PAGE
Two Mamorus, The	Ambassador Magma Vol. 2: Episodes 4-5	720
Two Men and a Wardrobe	Classic Foreign Shorts—Volume 2	153
Two Men and a Wardrobe	Two Men and a Wardrobe	98
Two Orphans	Classic Photoplays	396
Two Paths	Griffith Shorts (1910-1911)	413
Two Portraits	Peter Thompson Films	487
Two Sisters	National Film Board of Canada's Animation Festival	714
Two Wagons, Both Covered	King of the Wild Horses	400
Two-Lip Time	Early Animation Vol. 1	709
Two-Penny Magic	Hans Richter: Early Avant-Garde Films	485
Two-tone Town	Tiny Toon Adventures Vol. 3: Tiny Toons in Two-Tone Town	688
Tyrox	Johnny Sokko and His Flying Robot: Episodes 3 and 4	734
Uberfall	Avant Garde & Experimental Film	482
Uberfall	Rain and Uberfall	488
Uganda Be an Elephant	Timon and Pumbaa's Wild Adventures: Live and Learn	694
Ugly Duckling, The	The Ugly Duckling (Children's Circle)	649
Ugly Duckling, The	Victor Borge Tells Hans Christian Andersen Stories	649
Umbrella	Rare Dutch and Belgian Experimental Program	31, 488
Un Chant D'amour	Classic Foreign Shorts—Volume 3: Un Chant d'Amour, Romance Sentimentale	19, 457
Un Chien Andalou	Un Chien Andalou/Land Without Bread	47
Un Chien Andalou	Avant Garde & Experimental Film	482
Un Chien Delicieux	The Works of Ken Feingold—Fictions	491
Uncensored Movies	Hollywood Spoofs	411
Unchanging Sea, The	D.W. Griffith's Years of Discovery	412
Unchanging Sea, The	A Corner in Wheat and Selected Biograph Shorts	412
Uncle Bozzo	The Abbott and Costello Television Show, Tape 2	414
Uncle Ruppert	The Abbott and Costello Television Show, Tape 3	414
Uncle Tom's Cabin	Spartacus (1910/Silent)	154
Unclean	It's Clean—It Just Looks Dirty	486
Uncommon Ground	The Athena Award 1996	456
Under Burning Skies	Griffith Shorts (1912, #2)	413
Under Royal Patronage	Matinee Idols: The Gentlemen	401
Underground World	Superman (50th Anniversary)	688
Unforgettable Pen Pal	Human Race Club: A Story About Making Friends, a Story About Prejudice and Discrimination	635
Unholy Three, The	West of Zanzibar/The Unholy Three	406
Uninvited Pest, The	MGM Cartoon Classics: Happy Harmonies	686
Unity through Strength	Pier Marton: Collected Works: 1979-84	487
Universal Citizen	Peter Thompson Films	487
Universal Hotel	Peter Thompson Films	487
Universal Infiltrators	Lydia Lunch: Malicious Intent	433
Universal Studio Tour	Touring the Silent Studios	405
Unlucky Boy, The	European Folk Tales, Volume 2	646
Unresolved Mysteries	Really Strange Stories of the Totally Unknown	509
Unruly Hare, The	Cartoon Collection Vol. 7: Tokyo Jokio	680
Unsavory Avery	Animation Celebration Vol. 4	706
Unseen Enemy	Griffith Shorts (1912, #2)	413
Unseen Enemy	A Corner in Wheat and Selected Biograph Shorts	412
Unseen Enemy	The Short Films of D.W. Griffith—Volume 2	413
Unsuspecting Stranger	The Films of Leo Maloney	368
Untamed World	Ren & Stimpy Vol. 1: The Classics	701
Untitled Ii	Art Com Video 14: Rebel Girls	482
Untitled—A Tape About Memory	Susan Rynard	488
Unwelcome Guest, The	Griffith Shorts (1913)	413
Up in the Air	Aesop's Fables Volume 1	676
Ups 'n Downs	Cartoon Classics Vol. 9: Early Pioneers	680
Upside Down	Hubley Collection Vol. 1	711
Upstanding Sitter, The	Daffy!	683
Urashima Taro	Urashima Taro & Cabbages and Kings	643
Urban Steal	Nice Girls...Films by and About Women	434
Urban Wildlife	Potato Wolf Coleslaw	435
Urbanissmo	Hubley Studio: Voyage to Next	711
Urchin	Ariel's Undersea Adventures: Whale of a Tale	690
Use Instructions	Too Outrageous Animation	717
Using His Brain	Tom Mix Short Subjects	405
USS-VD: the Ship Of Shame	Sex Education Films of the 40's	510
Usurer, The	Griffith Shorts (1909-1910)	412
Vagabond Loafers	The Three Stooges: Vagabond Loafers	284
Vagabond, The	Charlie Chaplin Early Years III	407
Vagabond, The	Classic Chaplin, Charlie Chaplin at Mutual Studios	407
Valient Tailor, The	Cartoons That Time Forgot Vol. 5: Free-Form Fairytales	681
Vampire Vale	Astro Boy 30th Anniversary, Vol. 1	722
Vanished World of Gloves, The	Experimental Avant Garde Series Volume 20 (The Secret Lives of Inanimate Objects)	484
Vapors	Third Sex Sinema Volume 1—Vapors	466
Venice Vamp	Tom & Jerry & Friends #2	688
Ventriloquism	William Wegman Reel 1	491
Venus Adonis	Tom Palazzolo: Films from the Sixties	478
Venus of Venice	Aesop's Fables Volume 2	676
Verdunstucke	Klaus Von Bruch: Black Box I	486
Versailles; the Lost Peace	Between the Wars, 1918-1941	808
Very Eye of Night	Maya Deren Experimental Films	487
Very Very Long Time Ago, A	International Tournee of Animation Volume 4	712
Vice Versa	Too Outrageous Animation	717
Vice Versa	Outrageous Animation Vol. 1	714
Video	William Wegman Reel 6	491
Viewmaster	Griffiti	710
Village Barber, The	Cartoons That Time Forgot Vol. 1: All Singing! All Dancing!	681
Village of Round and Square	Stories from the Black Tradition	642
Village Smithy, The	Cartoons That Time Forgot Vol. 1: All Singing! All Dancing!	681
Villain Foiled, A	Mack Sennett: The Biograph Years	411
Villain, The	Babe Hardy: Early Training	410
Violin Maker of Cremona	Griffith Shorts (1908-09)	412
Violin Maker of Cremona	The Short Films of Mary Pickford	404
Virginity	Rogopag	10, 37, 39, 41
Virus	Four Directions: Selections from MIX 94—The NY Lesbian & Gay Film Festival	459
Visible Compendium, The	The Sacred Art of Tibet/The Visible Compendium	149, 718
Visions From the Amazon	Spike & Mike's Festival of Animation Vol. 2	716
Visions of a City	Live Short Films by Larry Jordan	718
Visit to the Smithsonian, A	Short Subject Potpouri	477
Vitamin Hay	Great & Minor Animation Volume 3	684
Viva Eu!	Viva Eu! & Ex Voto	467, 491
Viva Willie	Cartoons That Time Forgot Vol. 4: Willie Whopper's Fantastic Adventures	681
Vixen and the Hare, The	European Folk Tales, Volume 2	646
Voice of the Nightingale	The Cameraman's Revenge: The Amazing Puppet Animation of Ladislaw Starewicz	707
Volcano	Superman (50th Anniversary)	688
Vykrutasy	International Tournee of Animation Volume 4	712
W.O.W. Women of the World	Hubley Collection Vol. 2	711
Wabbit Who Came to Supper, The	Cartoon Classics in Color #4: Classic Warner Bros.	680
Wabbit Who Came to Supper, The	Cartoon Collection Vol. 2: Classic Warner Bros.	680
Wackiki Wabbit	Cartoon Collection Vol. 2: Classic Warner Bros.	680
Wacky Wabbit, The	Cartoon Collection Vol. 2: Classic Warner Bros.	680
Wacky Wabbit, The	Elmer!	683
Wager of Three Wives	Secrets of Love, Classics of Erotic Literature: Vol. 6	510
Waif's Welcome, A	Best of the Van Beuren Studio	677
Waif's Welcome, A	Cartoons That Time Forgot Vol. 7: Rainbow Parades	681
Wake Up	William Wegman Reel 4	491
Walking Around	CineBLAST! Vol. 3	428
Walking in Both Worlds	A Common Destiny:	470
Walking the Mountain	Video Art, Tape Two	489
Wallace + Theresa	Video Art: Jan Peacock	490
Walls in the Woods	Best of the Fests 1991	706
Wanderer, The	Griffith Shorts (1913)	413
Wandering Papas	Directed by Stan Laurel	410
Wandering Willies	Slapstick Encyclopedia—Vol. 2: Keystone Tonight!	411
Wanted KK	Karl Krogstad: Idiot Savant & Catharsis	432
Wanting for Bridge	Best of the Fests 1991	706
War Bride, The	Aesop's Film Fables	676
War Comes to Pearl Harbor	Between the Wars, 1918-1941, Vol. 8	808
War Dance	War Dance	439
War Reporters, The	Civil War Journal, Set II	779
Ward March Hare	Stars of Space Jam—Bugs Bunny	687
Warm Reception in L.A., A	International Tournee of Animation Volume 4	712
Warning Red	You Can Beat the A-Bomb	807
Warnings from the Future	Arthur C. Clarke: World of Strange Powers	861
Wars Speed Up, The	Nostalgia World War II Video Library #1	182, 770
Wastes Away	Spike & Mike's Sick & Twisted Festival of Animation, Vol. 3	716
Wat's Pig	Creature Comforts	708
Watch with Mother	CineBLAST! Vol. 1	483
Watching Her Sleep	Girl Friends	229, 460
Water Circle	Films of James Broughton, Volume 5: Parables of Wonder	492
Water Falling from One World	Works of Ken Feingold—Water Falling from One World to Another	492
Water Nymph, The	Mabel Normand, Vol. 1	411
Water Wagons	Slapstick Encyclopedia—Vol. 7: The Rage Is On	411
Water, Water Every Hare	Looney Tunes After Dark	685
Waverley Steps	Festival of Britain	471
Waving	Pictures Don't Tell You Anything: Selected Films of Ann Marie Fleming	211, 487
Wayfarers All	The Wind in the Willows, Volume #4	644, 718
Ways at Wallace and Sons	Ways at Wallace and Sons and The Bank Dory	828
We are Not Republicans	Video Against AIDS, Volumes 1, 2 & 3	835
We Deliver	Space Shuttle: Flights STS-1 Through STS-8	840
We Love It	International Tournee of Animation Volume 6	712
We Said We'd Come Back	Nostalgia World War II Video Library #11	771
We're In the Honey	Great & Minor Animation Volume 4	684
Weak and Wide Astray	New Directors: New Short Films	487
Wedding Day	Early Russian Cinema: Before the Revolution, Vol. 04: Provincial Variations	85
Wedding Ring, The	Amazing Stories: Book 1	414
Wedding Show	M/W/F Music Video One	433
Wee Men, The	Paramount/Famous Studios Volume 2	686
Wee Wee Monsieur	The Three Stooges: Wee Wee Monsieur	284
Weetamoe	Sails and Sailors: J Boats '37	828
Weird Bird	Too Outrageous Animation	717
Weird Parents	Shelley Duvall's Bedtime Stories (Collection)	657
Weird Parents	Shelley Duvall's Bedtime Stories: Elbert's Bad Word and Weird Parents	657
Well	Larry Semon #2	411
Well Deserved Punishment, A	Secrets of Love, Classics of Erotic Literature: Vol. 5	510
Well Oiled	The Abbott and Costello Television Show, Tape 5	414
Well Oiled	Woody Woodpecker 50th Anniversary Vol. 2	690
West of Hot Dog	Stan "Tex" Laurel Rides Again	411
West of Zanzibar	West of Zanzibar/The Unholy Three	406
Western	Spike & Mike's Festival of Animation Vol. 1	716
Western Whoppee	Tom & Jerry & Friends #2	688
Westward Whoa	Great & Minor Animation Volume 1	684
Westward Whoa	Thirties Magic Vol. 2	717
Whale of a Tale	Ariel's Undersea Adventures: Whale of a Tale	690
What a Life!	Cartoons That Time Forgot Vol. 2: Down & Out with Flip the Frog	681
What Do We Know About the Arms	People of Faith and the Arms Race	805
What Do You Pay?	Problems for Young Consumers	670
What Drink Did	Griffith Shorts (1908-09)	412
What Happened to Mary	Matinee Idols: The Ladies	401
What Happened to Patrick	Shelley Duvall's Bedtime Stories (Collection)	657
What is the Church's Role	People of Faith and the Arms Race	805
What Makes a Battle	Nostalgia World War II Video Library #11	771
What Makes Daffy Duck?	Elmer!	683
What Price Fleadom	Tex Avery's Screwball Classics 4	688
What Shall We Do with Our Old?	Griffith Shorts (1909-1911)	413
What Shall We Do With Our Old?	Female of the Species & Selected Biograph Shorts (Vol. III)	412
What Shall We Do with Our Old?	D.W. Griffith's Years of Discovery	412
What Shall We Do with Our Old?	The Short Films of D.W. Griffith—Volume 4	413
What the Fuck are These Red Squares	Kartemquin Films, Vol. 3: Trick Bag	474
What's a Nice Girl Like You	First Works Volume 1	334
What's Buzzin' Buzzard?	Tex Avery's Screwball Classics 4	688
What's Cookin' Doc?	Bugs Bunny Superstar	678
What's to Do	Shirley Temple and Friends	282
What's Under My Bed	What's Under My Bed and Other Creepy Stories	659
What's Up Doc?	Looney Tunes Curtain Calls	685
When a Man Loves	Griffith Shorts (1910-1911)	413
When Bats are Quiet	International Tournee of Animation Volume 3	712
When Bears Go Fishing	Forest Habitat Set	815
When Goats Go Climbing	Mountain Habitat Set	818
When Love Fails	Love in the City	41
When Quackle Did Hyde	Hollywood Spoofs	411
When the Owling Has Come	Puppets & Demons: Films by Patrick McGuinn	436
When Worlds Collide	Best of George Pal	677
Where Angles Fear to Tread	Orguss 02, Vol. 1	739

SHORT FILM	COMPILATION TAPE	PAGE
Where the Wild Things Are	The Maurice Sendak Library	654
Where There's a Will	Jack the Ripper (Karloff)	524
Whistle for Willie	The Ezra Jack Keats Library	633
Whistle for Willie	Five Stories for the Very Young	652
White Mane	Red Balloon/White Mane	23, 640
White Wings	Stan About Town	411
Who Am I?	Hubley Collection Vol. 1	711
Who Killed Who?	Tex Avery's Screwball Classics 1	688
Who'll Fly Poseidon	Starvengers	748
Whoopee Party, The	Mickey Mouse: The Black & White Years	693
Whoops I'm an Indian	The Three Stooges: Whoops I'm an Indian	284
Whoregasm	Nick Zedd: Steal This Video	434
Whoregasm	Whoregasm	491
Why I'll Never Trust You	Teasers	466
Why Mosquitoes Buzz	The Emperor's New Clothes and Other Folktales	646
Why Mosquitoes Buzz	Stories from the Black Tradition	642
Why Pick in Me	Films of Harold Lloyd—Volume 2	409
Why Pick on Me	Films of Harold Lloyd—Volume 1	409
Why We Fight	Best of the Fests 1991	706
Why We Murder	Lydia Lunch: Malicious Intent	433
Why Worry	Selected Shorts #2	403
Wicked City	Aesop's Fables Volume 1	676
Wideo Rabbit	Bugs Bunny: Truth or Hare	679
Wife Tamers	Forgotten Comedians	411
Wife Wanted	The Abbott and Costello Television Show, Tape 4	414
Wild and Wooly Hare	Yosemite Sam: The Good, The Bad and the Ornery	690
Wild Child	Cadillacs and Dinosaurs: Wild Child & Pursuit	679
Wild Engine, The	Railroad Dramas	403
Wild Hoose Chase	Tom & Jerry & Friends #7	688
Wild Side	Hard	460
Wild West, The	Terrytoons: The Cats & Mice of Paul Terry	716
Wild World of Lydia Lunch	Nick Zedd: Steal This Video	434
Wild, Wild Wales	Railway Adventures Across Europe: Volume 2	843
Will-Be-Weds	Matinee Idols: The Ladies	401
Willi's Nightmare	Cartoon Classics Vol. 7: Early Animation	680
William Tell Express, The	Railway Adventures Across Europe: Volume 1	843
William Wegman in Chinese	William Wegman Reel 1	491
Willie the Operatic Whale	Willie, The Operatic Whale	694
Willie Whopper in Hell	Cartoons That Time Forgot Vol. 3: Things That Go Bump in the Night	681
Win Place or Showboat	Gabby (Cartoonies)	684
Wind in the Willows, The	The Adventures of Ichabod & Mr. Toad	690
Window to Heaven, A	Art on Film/Film on Art, Program 2: Film Sense/Art Sense	545
Window Water Baby Moving	Stan Brakhage Selected Films: Vol. 2	488
Window, The	Three Films by Chris Frieri	438
Windy City	Hubley Collection Vol. 3	711
Wine, Women and Sauerkraut	Comedy Shorts #4	410
Winged Scrooge, The	Animation Propaganda	706
Wings: a Tale of Two Chickens	Wings: A Tale of Two Chickens and Other Stories by James Marshall	644
Winky the Watchman	Animation Propaganda	706
Winnie Wright	Kartemquin Films, Vol. 2: Winnie Wright, Age 11	474
Winning Back His Love	Griffith Shorts (1910-1911)	413
Winter	Spike & Mike's Festival of Animation Vol. 1	716
Winter Carousel	Cameraman's Revenge: The Amazing Puppet Animation of Ladislaw Starewicz	707
Winter Carousel	Ladislas Starevitch	712
Winter Draws On	Glenn Gould Plays Beethoven	590
Winter Light	Live Short Films by Larry Jordan	718
Winter Steele	Liquid Television 2	698
Winterwheat	6 Films by Mark Street	482
Wireless Lizzies	Forgotten Comedians	411
Wise Guys Prefer Brunettes	Directed by Stan Laurel	410
Wise Quackers	Daffy Duck: Tales from the Duckside	682
Witch's Revenge, The	Melies III: The Search for Munchhausen	22
With the Cowboys	Felix the Cat: Sound & Silent	683
With the Enemy's Help	Griffith Shorts (1909-1911)	413
With the Good Witch	Tear Jerker	489
Within Dialogue	Susan Rynard	488
Witness or Timid Expectation	Letterist Films—Woman, Women!	432
Wittgenstein's Vienna	A Glorious Accident	782
Wizard, The	The Mysterious Tadpole and Other Stories	638
Woeful Willie	Spike & Mike's Sick & Twisted Festival of Animation, Vol. 2	716
Wolf and Calf	Masters of Russian Animation: Volume 7	82, 713
Wolf and the Crane	Aesop's Fables Volume 2	676
Wolf and the Kid	Aesop's Film Fables	676
Wolf in Sheep's Clothing, The	Fables and Fairy Tales, Fairy Tale Masterpieces	646
Woman is Not What She Used to	Letterist Films—Woman, Women!	432
Woman of Paris, A	A Woman of Paris	408
Woman Scorned, A	Griffith Shorts (1909-1911)	413
Woman, A	Classic Chaplin, Charlie Chaplin at Essanay Studio	407
Woman, A	Essanay #2	407
Woman, A	The Tramp and a Woman	408
Women I Love	Lesbian Sexuality	462, 492
Wonder Ring, The	Stan Brakhage Selected Films: Vol. 1	488
Wonton Soup	Erotique	430
Woody Woodpecker Cracked Nut	Woody Woodpecker 50th Anniversary Vol. 1	690
Words, Words, Words	International Tournee of Animation Volume 6	712
Work	Work and Police	408
Work	Essanay #2	407
Work Your Body	Video Against AIDS, Volumes 1, 2 & 3	835
Work's Ant	Computer Animation Classics	708
World of the Vatican II, The	Holy Land & Holy City	790
World	Samadhi and Other Films	488
World in Danger	Gigantor Retrospective 30 Vol. 1	730
World Peace	Maneaters: A Trilogy	486
Worm Movie	Cinema of Transgression	483
Worship of Nature, The	Civilization, Programs 11 & 12	781
Wrestling Match	The Abbott and Costello Television Show, Tape 6	414
Wrestling with Trouble	Kovacs & Keaton	409, 535
Writer, The	International Tournee of Animation Volume 3	712
Writing Degree Z	Sara Hornbacher Early Works	488
Writing in Water	Writing in Water and Admiral Bataille & the S.S. Esoterica	480
Wrong Gift, The	Lassie: Mother Knows Best	636
Wrong Hole	Spike & Mike's Sick & Twisted Festival of Animation, Vol. 2	716
Wrong Mr. Fox, The	Slapstick Encyclopedia—Vol. 1: In the Beginning	411
Wrong Trousers, The	Wallace & Gromit Collection	717
Wrong Type, The	International Tournee of Animation Volume 5	712
Wynken & Blynken & Nod	Karl Krogstad: Eggnog, Gazebo, Frescade	432
Yachting in the Thirties	Sails and Sailors: J Boats '37	828
Yak Shaving Day	Ren & Stimpy: Stinky Little Christmas	701
Yankee Doodle Daffy	Cartoon Collection Vol. 7: Tokyo Jokio	680
Yankee Doodle Daffy	Daffy!	683
Yankee Doodle Dandy	Cartoon Collection Vol. 6: The Ducktators	680
Ye Olden Days	Mickey Mouse: The Black & White Years	693
Year of the General, The	The Schwartzkopf Four-Pack	763
Yellow, M	Video Art: Noel Harding	490
Yellowstone Below Zero	Marmot Mountain/Yellowstone Below Zero (BBC Wildlife Special)	818
Yes Timmy, There is a Santa	Too Outrageous Animation	717
Yes We Can	Hubley Collection Vol. 2	711
Yes, Yes, Nanette	Directed by Stan Laurel	410
Yodeling Yokels	All Singing, All Dancing	676
Yodeling Yokels	Cartoon Classics Vol. 2: Warner Brothers	680
You	Out in the Garden & You	464, 487
You Can Beat the A-Bomb	You Can Beat the A-Bomb	807
You Can't Teach an Old Dog	Outrageous Animation Vol. 2	714
You Don't Know What You're	All Singing, All Dancing	676
You Don't Know What You're	Cartoon Classics Vol. 1: Looney Tunes & Merrie Melodies	680
You Killed Me First	Cinema of Transgression	483
You Only Live Once Editing	Origins of the Motion Picture	337
You Ought to be in Pictures	Porky Pig: Ham on Wry	687
You Rascal You	Cartoon Collection Vol. 5: Racial Cartoons	680
You Say	Porky Pig: Ham on Wry	687
You Take Care Now	Pictures Don't Tell You Anything: Selected Films of Ann Marie Fleming	211, 487
You Take Care Now	Nice Girls...Films by and About Women	434
You Talk, I Buy	Don from Lakewood/You Talk, I Buy	429
You're a Sap, Mr. Jap	Cartoon Collection Vol. 4: Warner Bros. & Fleischer	680
You're Darn Tootin	Slapstick Encyclopedia—Vol. 6: Hal Roach: The Lot of Fun	411
You're Not Built That Way	Cartoon Collection Vol. 8: Private Snafu	680
You're Too Careless With Your	Cartoon Classics Vol. 1: Looney Tunes & Merrie Melodies	680
Young Man's Dream & a Woman's	Magicians of the Earth	552
Young Oldfield	Charley Chase Jimmy Jump Series	410
Your Astronauts	Palazzolo's Chicago	476
Your Face	Plymptoons: The Complete Works of Bill Plympton	715
Your Face	International Tournee of Animation Volume 2	712
Yukon Jake	Slapstick Encyclopedia—Vol. 8: Tons of Fun: Comedy's Anarchic Fringe	411
Zinky Boys Go Underground	CineBLAST! Vol. 1	483
Zip 'n Snort	Chariots of Fur	682
Zip 'N' Short	Stars of Space Jam: Five-Tape Boxed Set	687
Zoo, The	Experimental Avant Garde Series Volume 22	484
Zoom and Bored	Stars of Space Jam: Five-Tape Boxed Set	687
Zwisch	Outrageous Animation Vol. 2	714
Zzang Toumb Toumb	Trio	489

director index

Aalmuhammed, Jefri
Brother Minister 450
Aaron, Jane
Set in Motion (Int. Animation 2) 712
Traveling Light (Animation C.1) 705
Aau, Chan Kooi
3 Wishes 118
Abbas, Yavar
Tornado! Hurricane! Flood! Wonders of Weather 823
Abbas-Mustan
Baazigar 146
Abbott, George
Damn Yankees 321
Abel, Alan and Jeanne
Is There Sex After Death? 272
Abel, Robert
Elvis on Tour 536
Abrahams, Jim
Airplane! 261
First Do No Harm 227
More! Police Squad! 419
Police Squad! Help Wanted! 421
Welcome Home, Roxy Carmichael 286
Acconci, Vito
Video Art: Red Tapes 490
Achard, Marcel
Days of Our Years 19
Achbar, Mark
Manufacturing Consent:
Noam Chomsky and the Media 475, 800
Acin, Jovan
Hey Babu Riba 103
Ackerman, Robert Allen
Safe Passage 245
Ackland, Rodney
Thursday's Child 179
Acomba, David
Hank Williams: The Show He Never Gave 323
Adams, Catlin
Sticky Fingers 437
Adams, Mike
The Good Sex Guide—Series No. 1 849
The Good Sex Guide—Series No. 2 849
Adamson, Al
Blood of Ghastly Terror 517
The Female Bunch 506
Horror of the Blood Monsters 523
Adato, Perry Miller
Gertrude Stein: When This You See, Remember Me 304
Addiss, Jus
The Jungle Trap 374
Adelson, Alan
Lodz Ghetto 474
Adige, Pierre
Elvis on Tour 536
Joe Cocker: Mad Dogs & Englishmen 621
Adler, Jerry
National Lampoon's Class of '86 277
Adler, Joseph
Sex and the College Girl 510
Adlon, Percy
Bagdad Cafe 63
Celeste 63
The Last Five Days 64
Rosalie Goes Shopping 65
Salmonberries 65, 465
Younger and Younger 288
Adlum, Ed
Invasion of the Blood Farmers 507
Adolphson, Elvin
The Count of the Old Town 75
Adomenaite, Niyole
House Built on Sand 81
Agee, James
In the Street 486
Aginsky, Yasha
Cajun Visits 601
Les Blues de Balfa 602
Ahearn, Charlie
Deadly Art of Survival 471
Twins 438
Wild Style 439
Ahlberg, Mac
Around the World with Fanny Hill 503
Fanny Hill 506
I, A Woman 76
Ahwesh, Peggy
The Dead Man and The Color of Love 483
Martina's Playhouse and The Scary Movie 487
Strange Weather 488
Ainsworth, John
Pattern for Plunder (Curse of San Michel) 527
Akerman, Chantal
Akermania, Volume One 29
A Couch in New York 29
The Eighties (Akerman) 29
Je, Tu, Il, Elle 29
News from Home 30
Night and Day (Nuit et Jour) 30
Rendezvous d'Anna 30
Toute Une Nuit 30
Window Shopping 30
Akerman, Ed
Primiti Too Taa (Spike/Mike 1) 716
Akkad, Moustapha
Lion of the Desert 116
The Message 116
Alazraki, Benito
The Roots (Gonzales) 116
Alberti, Irene von
Halfmoon 63, 304
Albicocco, Jean-Gabriel
The Wanderer 7
Aldashin, Mikhail
The Hunter (Animation C.4) 706
Poumse (Animation C.3) 705
Aldenhove, Jan
Kangaroos: Faces in the Mob 817
Aldighieri, M.
Borders 427
Aldrich, Robert
Apache 290
Attack 358
Autumn Leaves 358
The Big Knife 360
Dirty Dozen 366
Flight of the Phoenix 368
Four for Texas 369
The Frisco Kid 228
Hush, Hush, Sweet Charlotte 523
Kiss Me Deadly 375
Sodom and Gomorrah 356
Vera Cruz 297
What Ever Happened to Baby Jane? 531
The Witness (Charles Bronson) 393
Alea, Tomas Gutierrez
Death of a Bureaucrat 53
Guantanamera 53
The Last Supper (Cuba) 53
Letters from the Park 53
Memories of Underdevelopment 53
Strawberry & Chocolate 53
Up to a Certain Point 53
Alessandrini, Goffredo
We the Living 42
Alexandrov, Grigori
Circus 80
Jazz Comedy (Jolly Fellows) 82
Orlova Three-Pack 82
Que Viva Mexico 86
Romance Sentimentale
(Classic Foreign Shorts #3) 19
Volga-Volga 84
Alexeieff, Alexander/Parker, Claire
Alexander Alexeieff 482, 705
Alexeieff & Parker Films 482
Algrant, Dan
Three Piano Portraits 616
Alk, Howard
Janis 620
Alkabetz, Gil
Bitz Butz (Int. Animation 1) 711
Allegret, Marc
Blanche Fury 171
Fanny (France) 26
Just Another Pretty Face 20
Lady Chatterley's Lover (French) 21
Love of Three Queens 21
Zou Zou 24
Allegret, Yves
Dedee d'Anvers 20
The Proud Ones (Les Orgueilleux) 23
Seven Deadly Sins (episode) 6, 39
Allen, Fred
Ride Him Cowboy 295
Allen, Irwin
Five Weeks in a Balloon 663
The Lost World (1960) 498
The Towering Inferno 250
Voyage to the Bottom of the Sea 501
Allen, John D.
Mona's Pets 637
Allen, Kevin
Twin Town 164
Allen, Lewis
Another Time Another Place (1958) 357
The Perfect Marriage 279
Suddenly 388
The Uninvited 530
Allen, Russell
The Valley of Hate 406
Allen, Woody
Alice (Allen) 288
Annie Hall 288
Another Woman 288
Bananas 288
Bullets over Broadway 288
Crimes and Misdemeanors 288
Deconstructing Harry 288
Everyone Says I Love You 288
Everything You Always Wanted to Know About Sex
(But Were Afraid to Ask) 288
Husbands and Wives 288
Interiors 288
Love and Death 288
Manhattan 288
Manhattan Murder Mystery 288
Mighty Aphrodite 288
New York Stories 260, 288
Oedipus Wrecks (New York Stories) 288
Purple Rose of Cairo 289
Radio Days 289
September 289
Shadows and Fog 289
Sleeper 289
Stardust Memories 289
What's Up Tiger Lily? 289
Zelig 289
Allio, Rene
The Shameless Old Lady 23
Allione, Costanzo
Fried Shoes, Cooked Diamonds 304
Allouache, Merzak
Lumiere & Company 5, 336
Salut Cousin 8
Almendros, Nestor
Improper Conduct 58, 460
Almereyda, Michael
Nadja 434
Almodovar, Pedro
Dark Habits 46
The Flower of My Secret 46
High Heels 46
Kika 46
Labyrinth of Passion 46
Law of Desire 46
Live Flesh 46
Matador 46
Pepi, Luci, Bom and Other Girls 46
Tie Me Up, Tie Me Down 46
What Have I Done to Deserve This? 46
Women on the Verge of a Nervous Breakdown 46
Almy, Max
Video Art: Leaving the 20th Century
and Perfect Leader 490
Alpert, Jon
Nowhere to Hide 475
Altman, Robert
Aria 158, 577
Beyond Therapy 254
Brewster McCloud 254
Buffalo Bill and the Indians or Sitting Bull's
History Lesson 254
Caine Mutiny Court-Martial 254
Countdown 254
Fool for Love 254
The Gingerbread Man (Thriller) 254
James Dean Story 254
Kansas City 254
Long Goodbye 254
M*A*S*H 254
Making of Short Cuts 336
McCabe and Mrs. Miller 254
Nashville 254
The Player 254
Popeye 254
Quintet 254
Ready to Wear (Pret-a-Porter) 254
Robert Altman's Jazz '34: Remembering Kansas City
Swing 614
The Room 254
Secret Honor 254
Short Cuts 254
Streamers 254
Tanner '88 254
That Cold Day in the Park 254
Thieves Like Us 254
Wedding 254
Alton, Robert
Merton of the Movies 276
Pagan Love Song 327
Amaral, Suzana
Hour of the Star 54
Ambrose, Joe
Destroy All Rational Thought 303
Amelio, Gianni
Lamerica 33

Open Doors 33
Amenta, Pino
All the Rivers Run 205
Ames, Alfred
From Stump to Ship: A 1930 Logging Film 759
Amiel, Jon
Copycat 223
The Singing Detective 197
Sommersby 247
Amodeo, Rachel
What About Me 439
Amrohi, Kamaal
Pakeezah 148
Amurri, Franco
Monkey Trouble 238
Anand, Mukul
God Is My Witness (Khuda Gawah) 147
Anand, Mukul S.
Agneepath (Path of Fire) 146
Anand, Vijay
Jewel Thief 147
Ananiades, J.
Adam (Outrageous 2) 714
Anders, Allison
Four Rooms 430, 441
Gas Food Lodging 430
Grace of My Heart 431
Mi Vida Loca: My Crazy Life 59, 433
Anderson III, Paul
Shopping 163
Anderson, Andy
Positive I.D. 242
Anderson, Christina Bjork & Lena
Linnea in Monet's Garden 664, 712
Anderson, David
Deadsy (Spike/Mike Sick 1) 716
Door (British Animation) 707
Anderson, John M.
King of Jazz 325
Anderson, Lindsay
Britannia Hospital 159
If... 174
O Lucky Man! 162
This Sporting Life 179
The Whales of August 164
Anderson, Michael
1984 (1956 Version) 171
Around the World in 80 Days (1956) 358
Captains Courageous (1995) 221
The Dam Busters 172
The Naked Edge 380
Operation Crossbow 771
Shake Hands with the Devil 529
Shoes of the Fisherman 356
The Wreck of the Mary Deare 394
Anderson, Paul Thomas
Boogie Nights 427
Hard Eight 230
Anderson, Steve
South Central 446
Anderson, Walter
In the Name of Brotherhood 232
Anderson, Wes
Bottle Rocket 427
Andr, Raoul
Man and Child 507
Andreacchio, Mario
Napoleon 665
Andrew, Ian
Dolphins (British Animation) 707
Andrieux, Roger
L'Amour en Herbe (Budding Love) 4
La Petite Sirene 4
Angelico, Irene
Dark Lullabies 775
Angelo, Yves
Colonel Chabert 2
Angelopoulos, Theo
Landscape in the Mist 105
Lumiere & Company 5, 336
Ulysses' Gaze 105
Anger, Kenneth
Fireworks 485
Inauguration of the Pleasure Dome 486
Lucifer Rising 486
Angsten, David
Notes from a Lady at a Dinner Party 301
Annakin, Ken
Battle of the Bulge (Fonda) 359
Call of the Wild (1972) 221
Land of Fury 175
The Longest Day 377
New Adventures of Pippi Longstocking 665
Those Daring Young Men in Their Jaunty Jalopies 390
Those Magnificent Men in
Their Flying Machines 283
Three Men in a Boat 185
Annaud, Jean-Jacques
The Bear 16
The Lover 16
Quest for Fire 16
Seven Years in Tibet (1997) 16
Annaud, Monique
Road to Ruin 436
Anspaugh, David
Fresh Horses 228
Hoosiers 231
Moonlight and Valentino 238
Antamoro, Guilio
The Christus 40, 153
Frate Francisco 41, 153
Antczak, Jerzy
The Countess Cosel (Hrabina Cosel) 91
Nights and Days 93
Antel, Frantz
Tower of the Screaming Virgins 530
Anthony, Joseph
Career 362
The Matchmaker 275
Rainmaker (Nash) 384
Antin, Manuel
Don Segundo Sombra 50
Far Away and Long Ago (Alla Lejos y Hace Tiempo) 50
Antoine, Andre
La Terre 21
Antoine, Philippe
Manu Dibango: King Makossa 603
Anton, Amerigo
Caesar the Conquerer 42
Antonelli, John
Kerouac 305
Antonio, Lou
Last Prostitute 235
Antonioni, Michelangelo
Blow-Up 35
Eclipse 35
Il Grido 35
L'Avventura 35
La Notte 36
Mystery of Oberwald 36
Red Desert 36
When Love Fails (Love in the City) 714
Zabriskie Point 36
Antonucci, Danny
Lupo the Butcher (Outrageous 1) 714
Lupo the Butcher (Spike/Mike Sick 1) 716
Antsey, Edgar
Classic Documentaries: People and Places 470
Granton Trawler (Documentary Masterpieces) 471
Housing Problems (Classic Documentaries) 470
Anwary, Ackyl
Angel of Fury 124
Apon, Annette
Crocodiles in Amsterdam 30, 458
Apted, Michael
28 Up 468
35 Up 468
Blink 219
Coal Miner's Daughter 321
Critical Condition 266
Extreme Measures 226
Gorillas in the Mist 229
Incident at Oglala 787
The Long Way Home 474
Moving the Mountain 135, 475
Nell 239
Thunderheart 789
Aqua, Karen
Kakania (Int. Animation 4) 712
Araki, Gregg
The Doom Generation 429, 458
The Living End 433
Nowhere 435, 463
Totally F***ed Up 438
Aranda, Vicente
Intruso 44
Lumiere & Company 5, 336
Aranovitch, Semeon
The Anna Akhmatova File 80
I Was Stalin's Bodyguard 81
I Worked for Stalin 81
People's Gala Concert 83
Stalin: By Those Who Knew Him 83
Arau, Alfonso
Like Water for Chocolate 51
A Walk in the Clouds 251
Arcand, Denys
Decline of the American Empire 213
Jesus of Montreal 213
Love and Human Remains 213
Archainbaud, George
The Lady Refuses 375
The Silver Horde 386
Woman of the Town 298
Archard, Marcel
Paris Waltz (La Valse de Paris) 618
Archer, W.
Jac Mac & Rad Boy...Go! (Outrageous 2) 714
Ardavin, Cesar
Lazarillo 45
Ardolino, Emile
Chances Are 265
Dirty Dancing 225
Gypsy (1993/Midler) 323
Sister Act 282
Argento, Dario
The Bird with the Crystal Plumage 40, 68
Suspiria 529
Argueta, Luis
The Silence of Neto 52
Aristarain, Adolfo
La Discoteca del Amor 51
A Place in the World 52
Stranger 248
Time for Revenge 52
Arkin, Alan
Little Murders 274
Arkush, Allan
DeathSport 505
Rock 'n' Roll High School 328
Arliss, Leslie
The Night Has Eyes (Terror House) 176
Wicked Lady 185
Armendariz, Montxo
Letters from Alou 45
Armitage, George
Grosse Pointe Blank 270
Armstrong, Gillian
The Last Days of Chez Nous 206
Little Women (1994/Ryder) 236
Little Women Gift Set 236
Mrs. Soffel 239
Oscar and Lucinda 206
Starstruck 207
Armstrong, Michael
Mark of the Devil (Collectors Edition) 525
Armstrong, Moira
How Many Miles to Babylon 161
A Village Affair 198, 467
Armstrong, Robin
Pastime 242
Armstrong, Ron
Bugged 504
Arnold, Jack
Bachelor in Paradise 358
Creature from the Black Lagoon 519
A Global Affair 269
High School Confidential 506
Incredible Shrinking Man 497
It Came from Beneath the Sea/20 Million Miles to Earth ...498
It Came from Outer Space 498
Man in the Shadow 294
Monster on the Campus 526
The Mouse That Roared 184
No Name on the Bullet 294
Revenge of the Creature 528
Tarantula 500
Arnold, Newton
Hands of a Stranger 522
Aronson, Jerry
The Life and Times of Allen Ginsberg 305
Arrabal, Fernando
Odyssey of the Pacific (The Emperor of Peru) 211
Arsenault, Jeffrey
Night Owl 240
Artenstein, Isaac
Break of Dawn 428
Arteta, Miguel
Star Maps 437
Arthur, Karen
True Women 250
Arthuys, Bertrand
Tom and Lola 7
Arutnuan, Grigor
Theatre Square (Glasnost Film Fest V.6) 81
Arzner, Dorothy
Bride Wore Red 361
Craig's Wife 364
The Wild Party (Clara Bow) 412
Ascher, Steven
Troublesome Creek: A Midwestern 479
Ashby, Hal
Being There 263
Bound for Glory 220
Coming Home 223
Harold and Maude 270
The Landlord 273
The Last Detail 273
Shampoo 282
Ashby, Tim
Ninja Assassins 130
Ashcroft, Ronnie
The Astounding She-Monster 494
Ashi
Go Shogun: The Time Etranger 731
Ashley, Christopher
Jeffrey 461
Ashley, Robert
Atalanta Strategy 482
Music Word Fire and I Would Do It Again:
The Lessons 487
Asif, K.
Mughal-E-Azam 148
Askevold, David
Video Art: David Askevold 490
Askoldov, Alexander
Commissar 80
Asquith, Anthony
The Browning Version (1951) 172
The Demi-Paradise 182
Fanny by Gaslight 173
I Stand Condemned 174
The Importance of Being Earnest 312
The Millionairess 184
Pygmalion 177
The VIP's 179
We Dive at Dawn 179
The Winslow Boy 179
The Woman in Question 179
Assayas, Olivier
Irma Vep 8

Astley, N. & J. Newitt
The Jump (Outrageous 2) 714
Astley, Neville
Living in a Mobile Home (Int.Animation 3) 712
Astruc, Alexandre
Sartre by Himself (Sartre par Lui Meme) 6
Atamanov, Lev
Ballerina on a Boat (Masters of Russian An. 1) 82, 713
Singing Teacher (Masters of Russian Animation 2) 82, 713
Atchley, Dana/Metcalfe, Eric
Crime Time Comix Presents Steel & Flesh (Vide Art) 490
Attenborough, Richard
Bridge Too Far 159
Chaplin 407
Cry Freedom 150
Gandhi 160
Shadowlands 163
Young Winston 165
Attwood, David
Wild West 298
Au, Tony
Christ of Nanking 119
Dream Lovers 120
Aubert, Elisabeth
Drawing the Line: A Portrait of Keith Haring 548
Aubier, Pascal
Pascal Aubier Films 487
Aucion, G.M.
Oh Calcutta! 314
Audiard, Jacques
A Self-Made Hero 8
Audley, Michael
Mark of the Hawk 448
Auer, John H.
City That Never Sleeps 364
Crime of Dr. Crespi 519
Fugitive Road and Crime of Dr. Crespi 369
Seven Days Ashore 281
Wheel of Fortune 297
August, Bille
The Best Intentions 75
The House of the Spirits 231
Jerusalem (Bergman) 76
Smilla's Sense of Snow 77
Aujolat, Norbert
Lascaux Revisited 551
Aured, Carlos
Horror Rises from the Tomb 523
Aurel, Jean
The Women 7
Auric, Georges
Days of Our Years 19
Auster, Paul
Blue in the Face 427
Austin, Chris
Brother with Perfect Timing 601
Austin, Michael
Princess Caraboo 280
Austin, Ray
Zorro: A Conspiracy of Blood 253
Ausubel, Ken
Hoxsey: How Healing Becomes a Crime 473
Autant-Lara, Claude
The Count of Monte Cristo (Louis Jourdan) 19
Devil in the Flesh 20
The Red and the Black 23
The Red Inn (L'Auberge Rouge) 17
Sylvia and the Phantom 23
Auzins, Igor
We of the Never Never 207
Avary, Roger
Killing Zoe 234
Avati, Pupi
Bix 32, 609
The Story of Boys and Girls 34
Avedis, Hikmet
The Teacher 249
Averback, Hy
A Guide for the Married Woman 230
I Love You, Alice B. Toklas 183
Where Were You When the Lights Went Out? 287
Avery, Tex
The Early Worm (Black 3) 707
Tex Avery's Screwball Classics 688
Avila, Jac
Krik? Krak! Tales of a Nightmare 54
Avildsen, John G.
8 Seconds 290
The Formula 228
Happy New Year (Falk) 230
Joe 233
Lean on Me 235
Save the Tiger 245
Avnet, Jon
Fried Green Tomatoes 228
Red Corner 244
Up Close & Personal 286
Axel, Gabriel
Babette's Feast 75
Lumiere & Company 5, 336
Royal Deceit 245
Axelrod, George
Lord Love a Duck 274
Ayala, Fernando
Argentinisima I 49
Aymes, Julian
Great Expectations (BBC) 192
Jane Eyre (BBC) 193
The Lady's Not for Burning 161, 312
Azpurua, Carlos
Shoot to Kill 52
Azuley, Jom Tob
The Jew 48
B, Beth
Two Small Bodies 438
Babakitis, Peter
Classic Stories for Children 651
Babbit, Jamie & Ari Gold
Frog Crossing (CineBLAST 3) 483
Babbs, O.B.
Timothy Leary's Last Trip 478
Babenco, Hector
At Play in the Fields of The Lord 218
Ironweed 233
Kiss of the Spider Woman 234
Pixote 54
Babin, Charles
Twinkletoes 405
Bablet, Denis
Theatre of Tadeusz Kantor 99, 315
Bach, Jean
A Great Day in Harlem 472, 611
Bachmann, Gideon
Ciao Federico! 36
Bacon, Kevin
Losing Chase 236
Bacon, Lloyd
42nd Street 319
Action in the North Atlantic 356
Boy Meets Girl (Cagney) 264
Brother Orchid 361
Devil Dogs of the Air 267
The Fighting Sullivans 368
Footlight Parade 322
Footsteps in the Dark 268
Fuller Brush Girl 269
The Fuller Brush Man/The Fuller Brush Girl 269
It Happens Every Spring 272
Kept Husbands 374
Knute Rockne, All American 375
Marked Woman 378
Miss Grant Takes Richmond 276
The Oklahoma Kid 294
The Singing Fool 329
Bacso, Peter
Oh, Bloody Life! 102
The Witness (Hungarian) 103
Badger, Clarence
Hands Up (Silent) 399
It 400
Paths to Paradise 402
The Ropin' Fool, With Will Rogers 281
Teddy at the Throttle 412
Badham, John
Bingo Long Traveling All-Stars and Motor Kings 263
Blue Thunder 220
Drop Zone 226
Nick of Time 239
Saturday Night Fever 245
Wargames 251
Whose Life Is It Anyway? 252
Baggot, King
The Notorious Lady 402
Tumbleweeds 297
Bagnall, Dr. Joseph A.
John F. Kennedy's Lost Pathway to Peace 798
Bahr, Fax
Hearts of Darkness: A Filmmaker's Apocalypse 259, 334
Bail, Chuck
Cleopatra Jones and the Casino of Gold 532
Bailey, John
China Moon 222
Bailey, R.C.
Beezbo 629
Baillargeon, Paule
The Sex of the Stars 213
Baillie, Bruce
Tung, To Parsifal & Castro Street 489
Baird, Joel
Tear Jerker 489
Bairnsfather, Bruce
Carry On Sergeant (1928/Silent) 210
Bairstow, Jonathan
Prophet and Loss (British Animation) 805
Bajon, Filip
A Daimler Benz Limousine 95
Little Pendulum 95
The Magnate 95
Sauna 94
Baker, Fred
Lenny Bruce Without Tears 535
Baker, Graham
Impulse (Horror) 523
Baker, Hendrick
The Toytown Story Adventures 643, 717
Baker, Kelley
You'll Change (Best Fest 5th Annual) 706
Baker, Michael
An Affair in Mind 158
Baker, Robert S.
Jack the Ripper (Paterson) 524
Baker, Roy Ward
The Anniversary 171
Asylum 516
The Legend of the Seven Golden Vampires 175, 525
A Night to Remember 176, 869
The October Man 176
Quatermass and the Pit 499
The Weaker Sex 179
Baker, Sharon K.
Cartoons Go to War 681
Bakshi, Ralph
American Pop 618, 705
Cool World 708
Coonskin 708
Heavy Traffic 710
Hey Good Lookin' 710
Street-Fight 716
Wizards 718
Baky, Josef von
Baron Munchhausen 68
Balaban, Bob
The Last Good Time 235
Parents 279
Balaban, Burt
The Stranger from Venus 500
Baladon, Rafael
The Man and the Monster 525
Balasko, Josiane
French Twist 3
Balch, Antony
Towers Open Fire 489
Balcon, Michael
Seven Sinners (Doomed Cargo) 178
Baldi, Ferdinando
David and Goliath 42
Balducci, Richard
Scandal Man 6
Baldwin, Craig
O No Coronado 487
Sonic Outlaws 478
Baldwin, Ruth Ann
Forty-Nine Seventeen 398
Women Who Made the Movies 339
Bale, Paul Trevor
The Littlest Viking 76
Balewa, Saddik
Kasarmu Ce: This Land Is Ours 150
Ballard, Carroll
The Black Stallion 662
Fly Away Home 228
Never Cry Wolf 665
Wind (Modine) 252
Balletbo-Coll, Marta
Costa Brava (Family Album) 44
Bambilla, Marco
Excess Baggage 226
Band, Albert
I Bury the Living 523
Zoltan: Hound of Dracula 531
Bani-eternad, Rakhshan
Nargess 106
Bank, Mirra
Enormous Changes at the Last Minute 429
Nobody's Girls 240
Banks, B.
Tibet in Exile 150
Banks, Cindy
Finger Food (Spike/Mike Sick 2) 716
Puke a Pound (Spike/Mike Sick 2) 716
Thanks for the Mammaries (Spike/Mike Sick 1) 716
Banks, Monty
Great Guns 270
Bannah, Mike
One Man's Intrument (Spike/Mike Sick 1) 716
Bannon, Fred C.
Ghost of Zorro 369
Barabash, Uri
Beyond the Walls 107
Late Summer Blues 108
Baran, Jack
Destiny Turns on the Radio 225
Baranski, Andrzej
Taboo 94
Barben, Katrin
Around the World the Lesbian Way 456
Barber-Fleming, Peter
Coming Through 159
Barclay, Paul
America's Dream 443
Bardin, Gari
Grey Wolf & Little Red Riding Hood (Int.Animtn 5) 712
Vykrutasy (Int.Animation 4) 712
Bareja, Stanislaw
Man/Woman Wanted 93
Teddy-Bear 94
What Are You Going to Do to Me, If You Catch Me? 95
Barkas, Geoffrey
Q Ships 403
Barker, Clive
Hellraiser/Special Edition 523
Lord of Illusions 525
Barker, Cordell
The Cat Came Back (NFBCanada) 714
Barker, Mike
The Tenant of Wildfell Hall 164
Barker, Reginald
The Italian 400
Barkin, Edward S.
Rift 244

Barnes, Rick
The Enquirers 429
Barnes, Stephen
Capital P (Int.Animation 5) 712
Barnet, Boris
Girl with the Hatbox 85
Patriots....83
Barnett, Ivan
Fall of the House of Usher (Tendeter) 521
Barnett, Rex
Benjamin E. Mays: Mentor of Martin Luther King, Jr. 449
The Cultural Philosophy of Paul Robeson 451
Ida B. Wells....452
Barnette, Neema
Run for the Dream: The Gail Devers Story 245, 454
Spirit Lost 247
Barnstone, Lisa
Works....718
Barrera, Mario
The Party Line....60
Barreto, Bruno
Amor Bandido....53
Carried Away 221
Dona Flor and Her Two Husbands....53
Four Days in September 54
Happily Ever After 54
Show of Force....246
The Story of Fausta 54
Barreto, Fabio
Luzia 54
Barrett, Lezli-Ann
Business as Usual 159
Barrett, Ruth
Images: A Lesbian Love Story....460
Barrett, Shirley
Love Serenade....206
Barron, Arthur
Jolly Corner 301
Barron, Steve
The Adventures of Pinocchio 661
Merlin 237
Barron, Zelda
Secret Places....163
Shag 510
Barry, Christopher
The Brain of Morbius (Collector's Edition) 199
The Rescue/The Romans....201
Barry, Martin
Juke Bar (NFBCanada) 714
Barry, Tony
The Real Charlotte....195
Barsky, Bud
Coast Patrol....396
Barta, Jiri
Vanished World of Gloves (Experimental Ser. 20) 484
Bartel, Paul
Death Race 2000 513
Eating Raoul....267
Lust in the Dust 275
Paul Bartel's Secret Cinema 435
Private Parts (Bartel)....280
Scenes from the Class Struggle in Beverly Hills....281
Bartlett, Craig
The Arnold Waltz (Int.Animation 4) 712
Bartlett, Freude
Folly (Short Personal Films)....437
Bartlett, Hall
The Caretakers 363
Barton, Charles
Abbott and Costello: Mexican Hayride 261
Africa Screams 261
Buck Privates Come Home....265
Bud Abbott and Lou Costello Meet the Killer....265
Dance With Me, Henry....266
Harmon of Michigan....371
Ma and Pa Kettle at the Fair....275
The Noose Hangs High....278
The Shaggy Dog....694
The Wistful Widow of Wagon Gap—Abbott and Costello ..287
Bartosch, Berthold
The Idea....711
Bashore, Juliet
Kamikaze Hearts....461
Batalov, Alexei
The Overcoat....83
Battaglia, Skip
The Animated Star Spangled Banner (Animation C.3)....705
Geologic Time (Best Fest 90)....706
Parataxis (Acidburn)....717
Battersby, Roy
The Moth 162
Bauer, Evgenii
The 1002nd Ruse (Early Russian #7) 85
Child of the Big City (Early Russian #7) 85
Daydreams (Early Russian #7) 85
Revolutionary (Early Russian #10)....85
Bauer, Randy
Lava Jr. (Animation C.3) 705
Bauer, Yevgeni
Death of a Swan....85
Baum, L. Frank
L. Frank Baum's Silent Film Collection of Oz....400
Bauman, Suzanne
Light of the Gods 552
Baumbach, Noah
Kicking and Screaming....432
Bava, Lamberto
Demons 2 520
Bava, Mario
Baron Blood....516
Black Sabbath 517
Black Sunday....517
Blood and Black Lace....517
Danger: Diabolik 519
The Devil's Commandment....520
Dr. Goldfoot's the Girl Bombs....505
Hatchet for a Honeymoon 522
Hercules in the Haunted World 42
Kill, Baby, Kill....524
Lisa and the Devil 525
Planet of the Vampires....499
What! 531
Baxter, Jack
Brother Minister 450
Baxter, John
Love on the Dole 175
Bay, Michael
The Rock 244
Bear, Liza
Force of Circumstance 430
Oued Nefifik: A Foreign Movie....435
Beatty, Maria
The Black Glove 456
Box of Laughter: The Dueling Pages 457
Gang of Souls....304
Beatty, Warren
Dick Tracy 225
Reds 244
Beaudin, Jean
Being at Home with Claude....213
Beaudine, William
Apeman 516
Bela Lugosi Meets a Brooklyn Gorilla 516
Billy the Kid Versus Dracula....517
Blues Busters 264
Bowery Buckaroos....264
Desperate Cargo 365
Ghost Chasers....269
Ghosts on the Loose (East End Kids Meet Bela Lugosi)....506
Hardboiled Mahoney 270
Little Annie Rooney 400
The Rose Bowl Story 385
Sparrows....404
Spook Busters....282
Spotlight Scandals....329
Beaumont, Harry
Beau Brummel (Barrymore) 395
Broadway Melody (1929) 320
Dance Fools Dance....365
Laughing Sinners 376
Our Dancing Daughters....402
When's Your Birthday?....287
Beaver, Chris
Dark Circle....471
Beccaglia, Derlis Maria
An Elephant Named Illusion (Un Elefante Color Illusion)..672
Beck, George
Behave Yourself 359
Becker, Harold
City Hall 222
Malice 237
Sea of Love....245
Becker, Jacques
Ali Baba and the Forty Thieves (France)....19
Grisbi (Hands Off the Loot)....20
Modigliani (Montparnasse 19)....22
Becker, Jean
One Deadly Summer....6
Beckford, Keeling
Belly Pain 54
Beebe, Ford
Ace Drummond....537
The Films of Leo Maloney 368
Flash Gordon Conquers the Universe 537
The Invisible Man's Revenge 524
My Dog Shep 665
Night Monster....526
The Phantom Creeps....527
The Shadow of the Eagle....386
Sky Raiders 539
Stampede....296
Beems, Mary
Seed Reel #1 (Sextoons)....715
Beeson, Charles
The Pale Horse 163
Behar, Andrew
Tie-Died: Rock 'n' Roll's Most Deadicated Fans....623
Behi, Ridha
Secret Obsession 6
Beineix, Jean-Jacques
Diva 3
Bejar, Alfredo
Getting to Heaven 57
Bekeski, Sandor
Lights Before Dawn (Int.Animation 3....712
Bekolo, Jean-Pierre
Quartier Mozart 150
Bell, Douglas
Theater of Blood....530
Bell, Martin
American Heart 426
Hidden in America....231
Streetwise (Seattle)....478
Bell, Monta
The Torrent 405
Bellamy, Earl
Walking Tall: The Trilogy....251
Bellocchio, Marco
The Conviction....32
Devil in the Flesh 32
The Eyes, the Mouth 33
Henry IV (1985) 33
Bellon, Yannick
Colette: Of the Goncourt Academy....19
Belmont, Vera
Red Kiss....6
Beloff, Zoe
A Trip to the Land of Knowledge 489
Belson, Jordan
Samadhi and Other Films....488
Belvaux, Remy
Man Bites Dog 29
Belyayev, Igor
Trial II (Glasnost Film Fest V.10) 81
Bemberg, Maria-Luisa
Camila (Argentina)....49
I Don't Want to Talk About It 44
I the Worst of All 50
Miss Mary....51
Ben Dov, Yaacov
Films of Yaacov Ben Dov 109
Benayoun, Robert
Serious About Pleasure 18
Bender, Jack
Two Kinds of Love....251
Benedeck, Catharine
Maya (Dyke Drama)....458
Benedek, Laszlo
Daring Game....365
Namu, The Killer Whale 665
The Night Visitor....240, 527
Port of New York 383
The Wild One....393
Benedict, Stephen
The Best of Red Green 414
Benegal, Shyam
Antarnaad 146
Benigni, Roberto
Johnny Stecchino....33
The Monster 33
Benjamin, Richard
Little Nikita....236
Made in America....275
Mrs. Winterbourne....277
My Favorite Year 277
My Stepmother Is an Alien....277
Bennett, Bill
Kiss or Kill 206
Bennett, Compton
After the Ball....171
Glory at Sea 174
The Seventh Veil 178
That Forsyte Woman....390
The Years Between 179
Bennett, Edward
A Woman at War....253
Bennett, Rodney
Monsignor Quixote 162
Sense and Sensibility (1986)....301
Bennett, Spencer
Atomic Submarine....494
Black Widow (Cliffhanger Serials #5) 537
Hawk of the Hills....399
Marked Money....401
Perils of the Darkest Jungle 538
Bennett, Stephanie
Women in Rock 623
Benoit-Levy, Jean
La Maternelle 21
Benson, Leon
Flipper's New Adventure 663
Bentley, Thomas
David Copperfield 153
The Living Dead 175
Benton, Robert
Kramer vs. Kramer....234
Nobody's Fool....240
Places in the Heart....242
Benz, Obie
Heavy Petting....472
Ber, Ryszard
Hotel Lux....92
Iron Hand 92
The Stranger 94
Thais 94
Beranger, George
Burn 'em Up Barnes (1921/Silent)....396
Beremenyi, Geza
The Midas Touch....102
Beresford, Bruce
Aria....158, 577
Black Robe....210
Breaker Morant....205
Don's Party 205
Driving Miss Daisy 226
The Getting of Wisdom....206
Mister Johnson....238
Paradise Road....241
Rich in Love....244
Tender Mercies 249

Bergen, Andrew
Candide in the Americas 428
Bergen, Brian
Sex Is Sex 436, 477
Berger, Pamela
The Imported Bridegroom 232
Bergman, Andrew
Freshman 269
It Could Happen to You 272
Striptease 283
Bergman, Daniel
Sunday's Children 77
Bergman, David
The 81st Blow 774
Bergman, Ingmar
After the Rehearsal 77
All These Women 77
Autumn Sonata 77
Brink of Life 77
Cries and Whispers 77
Devil's Eye 78
Devil's Wanton 78
Document: Fanny and Alexander 78
Dreams 78
From the Life of the Marionettes 78
Hour of the Wolf 78
A Lesson in Love 78
The Magic Flute 78
The Magician (1958) 78
Monika 78
Night Is My Future 78
Persona 78
The Ritual 78
Sawdust and Tinsel 78
Scenes from a Marriage 78
Secrets of Women 78
Serpent's Egg 78
Seventh Seal 78
Shame 78
Silence 78
Smiles of a Summer Night 78
Summer Interlude 78
Three Strange Loves 78
Through a Glass Darkly 78
Virgin Spring 78
Wild Strawberries 78
Winter Light 78
Bergman, Martin
A Weekend in the Country 286
Berkeley, Busby
Babes in Arms 320
Babes on Broadway 320
For Me and My Gal 322
Gold Diggers of 1935 323
Strike Up the Band 329
Take Me Out to the Ball Game 330
They Made Me a Criminal 390
Berle, Milton
Milton Berle Invites You to a Night at La Cage 535
Berlin, Abby
Blondie Knows Best 264
Berliner, Alain
Ma Vie en Rose 5
Berlinger, Joe
Brother's Keeper 469
Paradise Lost 476
Berman, Daniel
Renee Rosnes: Jazz Pianist 614
Three Piano Portraits 616
Berman, Monty
Jack the Ripper (Paterson) 524
Bernanke, Jaime
National Geographic Video: Nature's Fury! 819
Bernard, Paul
Frontier in Space 200
Bernaza, Luis Felipe
Butterflies on the Scaffold (Mariposas en el Andamio) 457
Bernds, Edward
Blondie Hits the Jackpot 264
Clipped Wings 266
Return of the Fly 499
The Three Stooges in Orbit 284
The Three Stooges Meet Hercules 284
Berne, Josef
Mirele Efros 112
Bernhard, Jack
The Second Face 386
Bernhardt, Curtis
Beau Brummel (Granger/Taylor) 171
Conflict 364
Interrupted Melody 324
Kisses for My President 273
The Merry Widow (1952) 326
Miss Sadie Thompson 379
Sirocco 386
A Stolen Life 388
Woman Men Yearn For 71
Bernstein, Armyan
Cross My Heart (American) 226
Bernstein, Walter
Little Miss Marker 274
Berri, Claude
The First Time 17
Germinal 3
Jean de Florette 4
Jean de Florette/Manon of the Spring 4
Le Poulet (Award Winning French Shorts) 2
Manon of the Spring 5
Uranus 7
Berry, Ian
Joey 206
Berry, John
Maya (Film) 665
Pantaloons (Don Juan) 22
Tamango 389
Berry, Paul
The Sandman (Int. Animation 6) 712
Bertolucci, Bernardo
1900 35
Before the Revolution 35
The Conformist 35
The Grim Reaper 35
The Last Emperor 35
Last Tango in Paris 35
Little Buddha 35
Partner 35
The Sheltering Sky 35
The Spider's Stratagem 35
Stealing Beauty 35
Tragedy of a Ridiculous Man 35
Bertram, William
The Smoking Trail 296, 404
Bertrin, Francesco
Diamond Plaza 44
Berwick, Irvin
Monster of Piedras Blancas 526
Berwick, Wayne
Microwave Massacre 508
Beshears, James
Homework 231
Bessie, Dan
Turnabout: The Story of the Yale Puppeteers 466, 479
Besson, Luc
The Fifth Element 3, 496
La Femme Nikita 8
The Professional 8
Subway 9
Betancour, Antonio J.
Cronica del Alba 44
Beuys, Joseph
Videotape with Joseph Beuys 558
Beyer, John
The Bill Evans Trio 609
The Dexter Gordon Quartet 610
Great Guitarists 611
The Phil Woods Quartet 614
Beyzai, Bahram
Bashu, The Little Stranger 106
Travellers 107
Bharadwaj, Radha
Closet Land 222
Bhatt, Mahesh
Arth 146
Sir 148
Bhatt, Vikram
Jaanam 147
Bhavnani, Moan
China on the March 135
Biao, Yuen
The Kid from Tibet 121
Peacock Prince 130
Biberman, Herbert
Salt of the Earth (CDROM) 871
Biberman, Herbert J.
Salt of the Earth 385, 871
Bielicky, M.
Die Fettecke 484
Bier, Suzanne
Freud Leaving Home 75
Bigelow, Kathryn
Blue Steel (Jamie Lee Curtis) 220
Strange Days 500
Bill, Tony
Beyond the Call 219
Five Corners 268
Oliver Twist (1997/Bill) 693
Billon, Pierre
Ruy Blas 23
Binder, John
Uforia 438
Binder, Mike
Indian Summer 272
Binder, Steve
Diana Ross Live 610
Bingham, Edfrid
Riders of the Purple Sage (1925) 403
Binney, Josh
Boardinghouse Blues 447
Hi-De-Ho 448
Killer Diller 448
Binyon, Claude
Here Come the Girls 271
Bird, Antonia
Mad Love (Bird) 237
Priest 163
Bird, Brad
The Family Dog (Amazing Stories: Book 2) 696
Bird, Richard
Men of Ireland 204
Bird, Stewart
Home Free All! 431
Birkin, Andrew
The Cement Garden 159
Birnbaum, Dara
Video Art: Damnation of Faust Trilogy 490
Birri, Fernando
A Very Old Man with Enormous Wings 53
Birt, Daniel
Interrupted Journey 174
Three Weird Sisters 179
Bischoff, Sam
The Last Mile 375
Bishop, John M.
New England Dances: Squares, Quadrilles, Step Dances 574
New England Fiddles: Playing Down the Devil 605
Bishow, Pat
El Frenetico & Go-Girl 505
Blache, Herbert
The Saphead 409
Secrets of the Night 403
The Untamable 406
Black, Edward
Frozen Limits 182
Black, Eric
The Witching 531
Black, Noel
Golden Honeymoon 300
I'm a Fool 300
Black, Trevor
Goldy, The Last of the Golden Bears 663
Goldy II: Saga of the Golden Bear 663
Blackton, J. Stuart
Film Parade 333
Genesis of Animation V.1 710
Blair, David
Wax, or the Discovery of the Television Among the Bees 439
Blair, Jon
Anne Frank Remembered 468, 774
Blair, Les
Bad Behavior 181
Blair, Lorne
Lempad of Bali 552
Blake, Alfonso Corona
Samson vs. the Vampire Women 528
Blake, Ben K.
Two Sisters 113
Blake, Joel
The Stones of Blood 201
Blake, Michael
Laughing Horse 432
Blakemore, Michael
Country Life 205
Blanc, Michel
Dead Tired (Grosse Fatigue) 17
Blancato, Ken
Stewardess School 510
Blank, Harrod
Driving the Dream 841
In the Land of the Owl Turds 432
Wild Wheels 479
Blank, Jonathan
Sex, Drugs and Democracy 437
Blank, Les
Always for Pleasure 480
The Best of Blank 480
A Blank Buffet 480
Blues Accordin' to Lightnin' Hopkins 480
Burden of Dreams 480
Chicken Real 480
Christopher Tree 480
Chulas Fronteras 480
Cigarette Blues 480
Dizzy 480
Dry Wood 480
Gap-Toothed Women 480
Garlic Is As Good As Ten Mothers 480
God Respects Us When We Work, But Loves Us When We Dance 480
Hot Pepper 480
In Heaven There Is No Beer 480
Innocents Abroad 480
J'Ai Ete au Bal: I Went to the Dance 480
Marc and Ann 480
Puamana 480
Six Short Films of Les Blank, 1960-1985 480
Spend It All 480
Sprout Wings and Fly 480
A Well Spent Life 480
Werner Herzog Eats His Shoe 480
Yum, Yum, Yum! 481
Blasco, Ricardo
Gunfight at Red Sands (Gringo) 293
Blasetti, Alessandro
1860 40
Fabiola 40
The Iron Crown 41
What a Woman! 42
Blashfield, Jim
Suspicious Circumstances (Animation C.2) 705
Blasioli, Joseph
Blast 'Em 558
Blechman, R.O.
The Soldier's Tale (Animation) 716
Blier, Bertrand
Beau Pere 11
Buffet Froid 11
Get Out Your Handkerchiefs 11
Menage 11
My Man 11
Too Beautiful for You 12

Bluemke, Ralph C.
I Was a Teenage Mummy (1962) 523
Blumenfeld, Pavel
Tereza 100
Bluth, Don
All Dogs Go to Heaven 676
American Tail, An 661
Banjo the Woodpile Cat 706
The Land Before Time 1 685
The Pebble and the Penguin 686
Rock-A-Doodle 687
The Secret of NIMH 687
Thumbelina 667, 688
A Troll in Central Park 717
Blystone, John G.
Dick Turpin 397
Great Guy 370
Bock, Richard
Lost Years of Jesus 791
Bodrov, Sergei
Freedom Is Paradise 81
Prisoner of the Mountains 83
Boese, Carl
The Golem 69
Boetticher, Budd
Bullfighter and the Lady 362
Nostalgia World War II Video Library #06 771
Red Ball Express 384
The Rise and Fall of Legs Diamond 385
A Time for Dying 391
Bogart, Paul
Broadway Bound 264
Cancel My Reservation 265
The Canterville Ghost (1986/Gielgud) 181
The Heidi Chronicles 312
A House Without a Christmas Tree 231
Marlowe 378
The Three Sisters 315
Torch Song Trilogy 315
Bogayevicz, Yurek
Three of Hearts 466
Bogdanovich, Peter
Daisy Miller 224
The Last Picture Show 235
Mask (1985) 237
Paper Moon 241
Peter Bogdanovich and Henry Jaglom 337
Picture Windows 242
Rescuers: Stories of Courage—Two Women 477, 776
Targets 389
They All Laughed 283
A Thing Called Love 249
What's Up Doc 287
Bohlen, Anne
Blood in the Face 469
Bohus, Ted A.
Vampire Vixens from Venus 512
Boianos, Jose Antonio
Born in America 290
Boisrand, Michel
That Naughty Girl 18, 23
Boisrond, Michel
Will You Dance with Me? 24
Boisset, Yves
Dupont Lajoie (Rape of Innocence) 3
Boivin, Jerome
Barjo 16
Baxter 7
Bokanowski, Patrick
Courts-Metrages 8
L'Ange 8
Bokenkamp, Jon
After Sunset: The Life & Times of the Drive-In Theater 332
Boleslawski, Richard
Last of Mrs. Cheyney 375
Les Miserables (1935/Fredric March) 376
Painted Veil 382
Rasputin and the Empress 384
Theodora Goes Wild 283
Boll, Christopher
Der Sprinter 63
Bolognini, Mauro
Il Bell'Antonio 41
Bolt, Ben
An Unsuitable Job for a Woman 198
Boluk, Kam
Brave Young Girls 125
Bond III, James
Def by Temptation 519
Bond, Rose
Macha's Curse (Best Fest 90) 706
Bondarchuk, Sergei
War and Peace 84, 198, 393, 586
Bone, John T.
Hindsight 231
Bonnard, Mario
Rossini 328
Bonney, Jo
Fun House 534
Bonzel, Andre
Man Bites Dog 29
Bookwalter, J.R.
The Dead Next Door 519
Kingdom of the Vampires 524
Ozone 527
Zombie Cop 531
Boorman, John
Beyond Rangoon 219
Deliverance 225
Emerald Forest 226
Excalibur 226
Lumiere & Company 5, 336
Point Blank 383
Zardoz 502
Bootzin, Dan
Six Point Nine (Best Fest 91) 706
Borden, Lizzie
Born in Flames 427
Erotique 430
Love Crimes 433
Bork, Miroslaw
Consul 91
Borman, Arthur
And God Spoke 262
Borowczyk, Walerian
The Story of Sin 95
Borsos, Phillip
Dr. Bethune 210
Far from Home: The Adventures of Yellow Dog 663
Borthwick, Dave
The Secret Adventures of Tom Thumb 715
Bortman, Michael
Crooked Hearts 223
Borzage, Frank
Desire (USA) 365
A Farewell to Arms 367
Flirtation Walk 322
His Butler's Sister 324
History Is Made at Night 372
I've Always Loved You 373
Mannequin 378
Moonrise 379
The Mortal Storm 379
Seventh Heaven 403
Shining Hour 386
Smilin' Through (1941) 329
Stage Door Canteen 387
Strange Cargo 388
Three Comrades 390
Until They Get Me 406
Bose, Satyen
Friendship 147
Bosio, Gianfranco De
Moses (Lancaster) 356
Boskovich, John
Without You I'm Nothing 316
Bosukovsky, Sergei
Tomorrow Is a Holiday (Glasnost Film Fest V.12) 81
Boszormenyi, Geza
Recsk 1953 Documentary of a Hungarian Secret Labor Camp 103
Botes, Costa
Forgotten Silver 208
Boughedir, Ferid
Halfaouine—Boy of the Terraces 116
Bouiss, Elizabeth
No Time for Tears—Vietnam: The Women Who Served 778
Boulting, John
Brighton Rock 171
The Guinea Pig 174
Heavens Above 183
Journey Together 175
Lucky Jim 184
Private's Progress 177
Boulting, Roy
Brothers-in-Law 181
Bourgoujian, Lisa
Ellis Island (Documentary) 758
Bourguignon, Serge
Head over Heels (Bardot) 20
Sundays and Cybele 23
Bourne, Matthew
Tchaikovsky's Swan Lake (Male Cast) 576
Bourne, St. Clair
Big City Blues 443
In Motion: Amiri Baraka 445, 473
Bourque, Kevin
In Transit (Best Fest 91) 706
Simply Divine (Animation for Fallen Catholics) 706
Bowers, George
Body and Soul (1981) 220
Bowser, Kenneth
Frank Capra's American Dream 350
Box, Muriel
Truth About Women 179
Boyd, Daniel
Chillers 504
Invasion of the Space Preachers 233
Boyd, Joe
The Jimi Hendrix Story 621
Boyd, Melba Joyce
The Black Unicorn: Dudley Randall and the Broadside Press 300, 450
Boydstun, M.
The Gate to the Mind's Eye 710
Boydstun, Michael
Beyond the Mind's Eye 706
Imaginit 635
Televoid 438
Boyer, Jean
Crazy for Love 19
Extenuating Circumstances 17
Fernandel the Dressmaker 17
Senechal the Magnificent 18
Boyer, Marlow
People to People 805
Boyle, Danny
A Life Less Ordinary 184
Shallow Grave 163
Trainspotting 164
Bozetto, Bruno
Baeus (Int. Animation 2) 712
Best of Bruno Bozetto 707
The Big Bang (Int. Animation 5) 712
Bruno Bozetto: Animator 707
Dancing (Animation C.4) 706
Eldorado (Outrageous 2) 714
Grasshoppers (Spike/Mike 2) 716
Moa Moa (Int. Animation 1) 705
Mr. Tao (Animation C.3) 705
Sigmund (Int. Animation 1) 705
Striptease (Outrageous 1) 714
Bozzetto, Bruno
Allegro Non Troppo 705
Mr. Rossi's Dreams 713
Brabant, Charles
Respectful Prostitute 23
Brabin, Charles J.
The Mask of Fu Manchu 525
The Raven (1915/Silent) 403
Bracho, Julio
Crepuscolo 49
Bradbury, Robert N.
Behind Two Guns 290, 395
Big Calibre 516
Blue Steel (John Wayne) 290
Man from Utah 294
Riders of the Desert 295
Riders of the Range/Storm over Wyoming 295
The Star Packer 296
West of the Divide 297
Braddock, Reb
Curdled 224
Bradshaw, Randy
Song Spinner 666
Brady, David W.
Renee Rosnes: Jazz Pianist 614
Brahm, John
Guest in the House 371
Miracle of Our Lady of Fatima 379
Singapore 386
Wintertime 393
Brakhage, Stan
Stan Brakhage Selected Films: Vol. 1 488
Stan Brakhage Selected Films: Vol. 2 488
Stan Brakhage—Hand-Painted Films 488
Brambilla, Marco
Demolition Man 495
Brame, Bill
Miss Melody Jones 508
Branagh, Kenneth
Dead Again 224
Hamlet (1996) 312
Henry V (Branagh) 312
Mary Shelley's Frankenstein 525
A Midwinter's Tale 162
Much Ado About Nothing 314, 869
Peter's Friends 184
Brandeis, Madeline
The Star Prince 404
Brando, Marlon
One-Eyed Jacks 295
Brandstrom, Charlotte
A Business Affair 265
Brannon, Fred
The Crimson Ghost 537
Federal Agents vs. Underworld Inc. (Cliffhanger Serials #5) 537
Flying Disc Men from Mars (Cliffhanger Serials #5) 537
The Invisible Monster (Cliffhanger Serials #5) 538
Jungle Drums of Africa (Cliffhanger Serials #5) 538
King of the Rocketmen (Lost Planet Airmen) 538
Radar Men from the Moon 499
Radar Patrol vs. Spy King (Cliffhanger Serials #5) 539
Zombies of the Stratosphere (Satan's Satellites) 539
Brass, Tinto
Caligula 32
Brasso, Enrique
In Memoriam 44
Brault, Michel
Paper Wedding 213
Bravo, Edgar Michael
I'll Love You Forever...Tonight 460
Breakston, George
Geisha Girl 496
The Manster 525
Brealey, Gil
Test of Love 207
Bregstein, Philo
Otto Klemperer's Long Journey Through His Times 593
Whoever Says the Truth Shall Die 37
Breillat, Catherine
36 Filette 2
Breitbart, Eric
A World on Display 765
Brel, Jacques
Franz 3
Brennan, Neal
Half-Baked 270

Brenon, Herbert
Dancing Mothers 397
The Spanish Dancer 404
Brescia, Alfonso
The War of the Robots 501
White Fang and the Hunter 667
Bressan, Arthur J.
Abuse 456, 468
Bresson, Robert
The Devil, Probably 15
Diary of a Country Priest 15
L'Argent 15
Lancelot of the Lake 15
Les Dames du Bois de Boulogne 15
A Man Escaped 15
Mouchette 15
Pickpocket 15
Une Femme Douce 15
Brest, Martin
Beverly Hills Cop 263
Midnight Run 237
Scent of a Woman (1992) 245
Bretherton, Howard
Boys' Reformatory 361
Brett, Leonard
The Last Reunion 175
Brewster, Joe
The Keeper 234, 445
Briant, Michael
The Green Death 200
Revenge of the Cybermen 201
Brickman, Paul
Men Don't Leave 237
Risky Business (1983) 280
Bridges, Alan
Out of Season 163
Pudd'nhead Wilson 309
Bridges, James
China Syndrome 222
The Paper Chase 241
Perfect 242
September 30, 1995 246
Urban Cowboy 251
Bright, Matthew
Freeway 228
Brill, Steven
Heavyweights 692
Brilliant, Barry
Little Genitalia (Sextoons) 715
Brismee, Jean
Devil's Nightmare 520
Brittain, Donald
King of the Hill (Canning) 827
Briz, Joseph
White Commanche 298
Brocka, Lino
Macho Dancer 145, 462
Brockway, Merrill
The Balanchine Essays: Passe and Attitude 568
The Balanchine Essays: Port de Bras and Epaulement 568
Choreography by Balanchine: Selections from Jewels/Stravinsky Violin Concerto 569
Martha Graham Dance Company 573
Brodax, Al
Sunshine Porcupine 716
Broder, H.M.
Zoll Zeyn (Let It Be) 113
Broderick, Matthew
Infinity 233
Bromski, Jacek
La Cuisine Polonaise 93
Bromski, Jack
The Art of Loving 90
Brook, Clive
On Approval 184
Brook, Peter
Lord of the Flies 175
The Mahabharata (1989/166 mins.) 313
The Mahabharata (1992/318 mins.) 313
Marat/Sade (The Persecution and Assassination of Jean-Paul Marat) 313
Meetings with Remarkable Men 162
Moderato Cantabile 22
Brookner, Howard
Bloodhounds of Broadway 427
Burroughs 302
Brooks Jr., Lowry
Just Dam' Lucky 445
Brooks, Adam
Red Riding Hood (Isabella Rossellini) 649
Brooks, Albert
Defending Your Life 267
Lost in America 275
Modern Romance 276
Mother 276
Real Life 280
Brooks, David
The Wind Is Driving Him Towards the Open Sea 439, 491
Brooks, James L.
As Good As It Gets 262
Broadcast News 264
I'll Do Anything 271
Terms of Endearment 249
Brooks, Joseph
If I Ever See You Again 232
You Light Up My Life 253
Brooks, Mel
Blazing Saddles 264
High Anxiety 271
The History of the World, Part One 271
Life Stinks 274
The Producers 280
Silent Movie 282
The Twelve Chairs 285
Young Frankenstein 288
Brooks, Richard
Battle Circus 359
Bite the Bullet 360
Blackboard Jungle 360
Brothers Karamazov 361
Cat on a Hot Tin Roof (1958) 310
Catered Affair 265
Elmer Gantry 367
The Happy Ending 371
In Cold Blood (1967) 373
Last Time I Saw Paris 375
Looking for Mr. Goodbar 236
Lord Jim 175
Sweet Bird of Youth (1962) 389
Broomfield, Nick
Aileen Wuornos: The Selling of a Serial Killer 468
Dark Obsession 159
Heidi Fleiss: Hollywood Madam 472
Monster in a Box 313
Brose, Lawrence F.
An Individual Desires Solution & War Songs 461, 486
Broughton, James
Autobiographical Mysteries 492
Dreamwood 492
Erotic Celebrations 492
Parables of Wonder 492
Pleasure Garden 492
Rituals of Play 492
Broullon, C.
Stephane Grappelli—Live in San Francisco—1985 615
Brown, Bruce
Endless Night 173
Endless Summer 826
On Any Sunday 827
Brown, Clarence
Ah, Wilderness 310
Angels in the Outfield (1951) 357
Anna Christie (1930/Garbo) 357
Anna Karenina (1935/Garbo) 357
Conquest (Garbo/Boyer) 364
The Eagle 397
Edison, the Man 367
Flesh and the Devil 398
A Free Soul 369
Goose Woman 399
Gorgeous Hussy 370
Human Comedy 372
Inspiration 373
Intruder in the Dust 373
The Last of the Mohicans (1920) 235
The Light of Faith 400
National Velvet 665
Of Human Hearts 381
Plymouth Adventure 383
Possessed (1931) 383
Possessed (1947) 383
The Rains Came 384
Romance 385
Smouldering Fires 404
Song of Love 387
They Met in Bombay 390
To Please a Lady 391
The White Cliffs of Dover 393
Wife vs. Secretary 393
Woman of Affairs 406
The Yearling (1946) 667
Brown, David L.
Question of Power 805
Brown, G.
The Dark Light of Dawn 56
Brown, Georg Stanford
Miracle of the Heart: A Boy's Town Story 238
Brown, Harry J.
The Fighting Legion 398
One Punch O'Day 402
Brown, Jim
The Weavers: Wasn't That a Time 606
Brown, Karl
Ballet for Children and Adults 568
Flames 368
Brown, Melville
Behind Office Doors 359
Brown, Thomas
Night of the Living Dead 25th Anniversary Documentary 526
Brownell, Cara
Cave Girls 483
Browning, Tod
The Devil Doll 520
Dracula (Lugosi) 520
Freaks 522
Mark of the Vampire 525
Outside the Law 402
The Unholy Three (Silent/1925) 406
The Unknown 406
White Tiger 406
Brownlow, Kevin/Gill, David
Cinema Europe: The Other Hollywood 333
Brownrigg, S.F.
Don't Look in the Basement 520
Brozovich, Tom
No Pain No Gain (Best Fest 90) 706
Bruce, James
Dirty Money 429
Bruce, Ken
Lullaby (Spike/Mike Sick 1) 716
Bruch, Klaus von
Klaus Von Bruch: Black Box I 486
Bruckman, Clyde
The Cameraman 409
The General 409
Bruneau, Jean Pierre
In South Louisiana/Dedans le Sud de la Louisiane 602
Brunel, Adrian
The Lion Has Wings 180
Old Spanish Custom 409
Brusati, Franco
Bread and Chocolate 32
The Sleazy Uncle 34
Brusselin, Alf
Germany in Autumn 66
Brustellin, Alf
Germany in Autumn 66
Bryden, Bill
Aria 158, 577
Brynych, Zbynek
Transport from Paradise 100
Buchanan, Larry
Creature of Destruction 519
Goodbye, Norma Jean 229
Mars Needs Women 498
Buchowetzki, Dimitri
Danton (aka All for a Woman) 68
Othello (1922/Silent) 314
The Swan (1925) 389
Buckner, Noel
The Good Fight 48, 472
Bucquet, Harold S.
Adventures of Tartu 171
Dragon Seed 366
On Borrowed Time 314
Without Love (Spencer Tracy) 287
Bucquoy, Jan
The Sexual Life of the Belgians 29
Buczkowski, Leonard
Florian 91
Buell, Jed
Lucky Ghost 275
Bugajski, Ryszard
Clearcut 210
Interrogation 95
A Woman and a Woman 95
Bulajic, Veljko
Day That Shook the World (Sarajevsky atentat) 103
Buld, Wolfgang
Girls Bite Back 620
Punk and Its After Shocks 622
Bun, Yuen
Tough Beauty and the Sloppy Slob 133
Bunin, Lou
Alice in Wonderland 705
Bunuel, Luis
Age of Gold 46
Belle de Jour 46
The Criminal Life of Archibaldo de la Cruz 46
Death in the Garden 46
Diary of a Chambermaid (Bunuel) 46
The Discreet Charm of the Bourgeoisie 46
El (This Strange Passion) 46
El Bruto 47
The Exterminating Angel 47
Fever Mounts in El Pao 47
The Great Madcap (El Gran Calavera) 47
Illusion Travels by Streetcar 47
Land Without Bread 47
Los Olvidados 47
Mexican Bus Ride 47
Milky Way (Bunuel) 47
Nazarin 47
Phantom of Liberty 47
Simon of the Desert 47
Susana 47
That Obscure Object of Desire 47
Tristana 47
Un Chien Andalou (Avant Garde & Experimental Films) 47
Un Chien Andalou/Land Without Bread 47
Viridiana 47
A Woman Without Love 47
Wuthering Heights (1953) 47
The Young One 47
Buravsky, Alexander
Sacred Cargo 245
Burch, Claire
Alfonia 608
The Amazing Art of Beauford Delaney: From David Leming's Reading 302
Another Trip with Ram Dass 847
Atrocities of the Drug War: Ram Dass Speaks Out 781
Celebrate for the Rain: Featuring the Music of Elizabeth Burch 604
The CIA Contra Crack Connection—Parts I and II 799
Country Joe McDonald at Provo Park: Earth Day Concert with Wild Mango and Others 604
Country Joe McDonald: Concerts at People's Park 604
Elegy for a Street Survivor (Yume) 471

Entering Oakland 451
A Festival of Bay Area Music (Relix Concert) 605
The Ghost of James Baldwin at Glide Memorial 304
The Ghost of Solid Gold Illusion Meets Danny Boy 472
Ghost of the San Francisco Oracle Meets Timothy Leary 304
Guilty Until Proven Not Guilty— Napoleon's Revenge 472
Hello Goodbye Bob Sparks 473
Highlights of Atrocities of the Drug War 782
The History of American Funeral Directing 760
Homeless in the Nineties (The Video) 473
I Can't Give You Anything But Love/ Solid Gold Illusion 561
The James Baldwin Anthology 304
Kenny & Georgia: The Story of a Homeless African-American Couple 453
Lethal Weapons: The Visual Art of Barton Benes 561
Memoirs of a Barbed Wire Surgeon: An Interview with Elmer Shabart 770
A New Connection: The Video 782
Poetry on Telegraph Avenue 306
Remembering the Summer of Love and Other Songs 622
The Second Timothy Leary Tape 853
A Short History of Nudity and a Short History of Love 854
Solid Gold Illusion, Variations I, II and III 561
Streetwise (San Francisco) 783
Telegraph Avenue Street Musicians: The Concert at Ashkenaz 606
Thumbed a Ride to Heaven: The Music of Alfonia Tims and Others 606
The Timothy Leary San Francisco Memorial 856
To Save Jack Kerouac's Daughter 307
The Wavy Gravy Birthday Benefit for Seva Foundation 623
Burch, Noel
What Do Those Old Films Mean? 154, 339
Burckhardt, Jacob
Duet for Spies/Frankie Lymon's Nephew Story 429
It Don't Pay To Be an Honest Citizen 432
Landlord Blues 432
Burckhardt, Rudy
Rudy Burckhardt 488, 559
Burge, Stuart
Julius Caesar (Heston/Gielgud) 312
The Mikado (D'Oyly Carte) 583
Othello (1965) 163
Burgos, Robert
Horse Dealer's Daughter 300
Burke, Andrew
Odile & Yvette at the Edge of the World 240
Burke, Richard
Tornado! Hurricane! Flood! Wonders of Weather 823
Burnett, Charles
The Glass Shield 444
Nightjohn 445
To Sleep with Anger 446
Burns, Bonnie
Vincent (Nimoy) 316
Burns, Edward
The Brothers McMullen 428
No Looking Back 434
She's the One 437
Burns, Ken
Baseball 825
The Civil War (Ken Burns/PBS) 779
Lewis & Clark 761
Thomas Jefferson 764
Vezelay 479
Burris, David
Side of the Road (CineBLAST 1) 483
Burroughs, Jackie
A Winter Tan 439
Burroughs, Jim
Quest, Box 1 783
Burrowes, Geoff
Return to Snowy River 207
Burstall, Tim
Kangaroo 206
Burton, Claudia Z.
This Land Is Your Land: The Animated Kids' Songs of Woody Guthrie 606
Burton, David
Lady by Choice 375
Burton, Geoff
The Sum of Us 207, 465
Burton, Richard
Doctor Faustus 160
Burton, Tim
Batman (1989) 255
Batman Returns 255
Beetlejuice 255
Ed Wood 255, 514
Edward Scissorhands 255
Frankenweenie 255
Mars Attacks 255
The Nightmare Before Christmas 686
The Nightmare Before Christmas Collector's Edition 686
Pee-Wee's Big Adventure 255
Burton, Tom
This Land Is Your Land: The Animated Kids' Songs of Woody Guthrie 606
Buscemi, Steve
Trees Lounge 438
Bussman, Tom
Whoops Apocalypse 185
Bute, Mary Ellen
Mary Ellen Bute 487
Butler, David
April in Paris 320
Bright Eyes 320
By the Light of the Silvery Moon 321
Calamity Jane 321
Captain January 321
Caught in the Draft 265
A Connecticut Yankee (Will Rogers) 309
Doubting Thomas 366
It's a Great Feeling 325
King Richard and the Crusaders 374
The Little Colonel 325
Littlest Rebel 325
Look for the Silver Lining 326
Lullaby of Broadway 326
Pigskin Parade 279
Princess and the Pirate 280
The Road to Morocco 281
San Antonio 296
The Story of Seabiscuit 666
Tea for Two 330
Thank Your Lucky Stars 330
They Got Me Covered 283
Butler, Frank
Flying Elephants 410
Butler, George
In the Blood 473
Pumping Iron 476
Pumping Iron II: The Women 476
Butterfield, David
Hemingway...In the Autumn 304
Buttgereit, Jorg
Schramm 65, 510
Buzaglo, Haim
Fictitious Marriage 107
Buzzell, Edward
At the Circus 262
Best Foot Forward 320
Easy to Wed 322
Go West 269
Honolulu 271
Neptune's Daughter 327
Omaha Trail 294
Ship Ahoy 328
Song of the Thin Man 282
Woman of Distinction 287
Bykov, Rolan
Scarecrow 83
Byrd, Phillip
Anna Russell Farewell Concert 595
Byrne, David
True Stories 285
Byrum, John
Heart Beat 230
The Razor's Edge (1984) 243
Cabanne, Christy
Annapolis 395
Dixie Jamboree 322
Jane Eyre (1934) 373
Lamb (1915) 400
The Mummy's Hand 526
Reggie Mixes In 403
Scared to Death 528
Cabanne, William Christy
Sold for Marriage 404
Cabrera, Sergio
Details of a Duel 49
Cachuela, Mike
Dinko's Day (Spike/Mike 2) 716
Cacoyannis, Michael
Attila 74 105
The Girl in Black 105
A Matter of Dignity 105
Stella (Mercouri) 105
Zorba the Greek 105
Cafarelli, Vincent/Kugel, Candy
Fast Food Matador (Int. Animation 5) 712
A Warm Reception in L.A. (Int. Animation 4) 712
We Love It (Int. Animation 6) 712
Cahen, Robert
Robert Cahen: L'Invitation au Voyage/ Juste le Temps 488
Cahn, Edward L.
Invisible Invaders 498
It! The Terror from Beyond Space 498
Suicide Batallion 389
Voodoo Woman 531
Caiano, Mario
Nightmare Castle 527
Cain, Christopher
The Amazing Panda Adventure 661
Stone Boy 666
That Was Then...This Is Now 249
Young Guns 298
Caird, Jim/Goddard, Jim
Life and Adventures of Nicholas Nickleby 28
Cako, Ferenc
Zeno Reads a Newspaper (Animation C.3) 705
Calenda, Antonio
One Russian Summer 163
Callahan, John
I Think I Was An Alcoholic (Int. Animation 6) 712
Callas, Peter
Peter Callas: Night's High Noon: An Anti-Terrain 487
Callow, Simon
Ballad of the Sad Cafe 219
Cameron, James
Alien Trilogy 494
Aliens 494
Terminator, The 500
Terminator 2: Judgment Day 501
Titanic (1997/USA) 249
Cameron, William
Invaders from Mars (1953) 497
Camp, Joe
Benji 662
Benji Takes a Dive at Marineland 662
Benji the Hunted 662
Benji's Very Own Christmas Story 662
For the Love of Benji 663
Campanile, Pasquale Festa
The Libertine (La Matriarca) 41, 507
When Women Had Tails 34
Campbell, Colin
Little Orphan Annie (1918) 400
Campbell, Dick
Glitter Goddess of the Sunset Strip 506
Campbell, Dirk
The Country Diary of an Edwardian Lady 191
Campbell, Douglas
Season of Fear 246
Campbell, Graeme
Murder One 239
Campbell, Martin
Cast a Deadly Spell 518
Edge of Darkness 160
Goldeneye 168
Campbell, Nicholas
Stepping Razor Red X: The Peter Tosh Story 55
Campion, Anna
Loaded 208
Campion, Jane
An Angel at My Table 208
The Piano 208
Sweetie 207
Two Friends 209
Campogalliani, Carlo
Musica Proibita 41
Camps, Liz
Smoke (Four Directions) 459
Campus, Michael
The Mack 533
Camus, Marcel
Black Orpheus 53
Camuzat, Jerome
Pin-Ups: A Picture History The of America's Dream Girls 337
Cange, Brian D.
Counter Fancy (CineBLAST 3) 428
Canning, W.
King of the Hill 827
Cannon, Dyan
End of Innocence 226
Cannon, Raymond
Samurai 509
Cantsin, Monty
Anti-Credo 544
Capra, Bernt
Mindwalk 238
Capra, Frank
American Madness 350
Arsenic and Old Lace 350
Bell Science Series: Hemo the Magnificent 677
Bell Science Series: Our Mr. Sun 677
Bell Science Series: The Strange Case of the Cosmic Rays 677
Bell Science Series: Unchained Goddess 677
The Bitter Tea of General Yen 350
Broadway Bill 350
Frank Capra AFI Lifetime Achievement Award 332
Frank Capra's American Dream 350
Here Comes the Groom 351
A Hole in the Head 351
It Happened One Night 351
It's a Wonderful Life 351
Ladies of Leisure 351
Lady for a Day 351
Langdon at Sennett 411
Long Pants 351
Lost Horizon 351
Meet John Doe 351
The Miracle Woman 351
Mr. Deeds Goes to Town 351
Mr. Smith Goes to Washington 351
Negro Soldier 351, 453
Platinum Blonde 351
Pocketful of Miracles 351
Riding High 351
State of the Union 351
The Strong Man 351
That Certain Thing 351
You Can't Take It with You 351
Capuano, Antonio
Vito and the Others 34
Capurso, David
Emily's Song (CineBLAST!) 428
Carafelli, Vincent/Kugel, Candy
Snowie and the Seven Dorps (Animation C.3) 705
Carbonnaux, Norbert
Candide 19
Cardiff, Jack
Dark of the Sun 173
The Long Ships 175
My Geisha 277
Carducci, Mark Patrick
Flying Saucers over Hollywood 334
Carew, Topper
Talkin' Dirty After Dark 446
Carewe, Edwin
Evangeline 398

Carland, Tammy Rae
Odd Girl Out....463
Carle, Gilles
Blood of the Hunter....213
In Trouble....213
Carlei, Carlo
Flight of the Innocent....33
Carlino, Lewis John
Great Santini....230
Sailor Who Fell from Grace with the Sea....163
Carlsen, Henning
Hunger (Sweden)....76
Wolf at the Door....77
A World of Strangers....77
Carne, Marcel
Bizarre Bizarre....24
Children of Paradise....24
Daybreak (Le Jour Se Leve)....24
Les Visiteurs du Soir....24
The Marvelous Visit....24
Misty Wharf (Quai des Brumes)....24
Caro, Marc
The City of Lost Children....2
Delicatessen....17
Caron, Glenn Gordon
Clean and Sober....222
Love Affair (1994)....236
Wilder Napalm....287
Carpenter, Jeff/Lambert, Mary
Rapid Eye Movements (Acidburn)....717
Carpenter, John
Assault on Precinct 13....218
Body Bags....517
Christine....518
Dark Star....495
Escape from L.A.....226
Escape from New York....496
The Fog....521
Halloween (Fiction)....522
In the Mouth of Madness....497
Memoirs of an Invisible Man....276
Prince of Darkness....527
Starman....500
They Live....501
Village of the Damned....501
Carr, Bernard
Who Killed Doc Robin....287
Carra, Lawrence
Tragedy of Antony and Cleopatra....315
Carra, Lucille
The Inland Sea....138
Carreras, Michael
The Lost Continent (Porter)....175
Shatter....178, 443
Carrigan, Ana
Roses in December....60, 477
Carroll, Larry
Sam Kinison: Why Did We Laugh?....536
Carruthers, Glen
Kangaroos: Faces in the Mob....817
Carson, David
Star Trek Generations....500
Carstairs, John Paddy
Sleeping Car to Trieste....178
Tony Draws a Horse....179
Carter, Bill
Miss Sarajevo....475
Carter, John
Zombie Island Massacre....531
Carter, Michael
Homage to Hermann Nitsch (Apologies to Don Garlits)....567
Carver, H.P.
The Silent Enemy (1930)....211
Carver, Steve
The Arena....532
Big Bad Mama....513
The Tell-Tale Heart (1973)....530
Casady, Chris
Pencil Dance (Animation C.2)....705
Shadrach (Int. Animation 4)....712
Caslor, Brad
Get A Job (Incredible Animiation 2)....711
Get a Job (NFBCanada)....714
Cass, Henry
Glass Mountain....160
Last Holiday....175
Young Wives' Tale....185
Cassavetes, John
Big Trouble....440
A Child Is Waiting....440
Faces....440
Gloria....440
The Killing of a Chinese Bookie....440
Opening Night....440
Shadows (1959)....440
A Woman Under the Influence....440
Cassavetes, Nick
She's So Lovely....437
Unhook the Stars....438
Cassenti, Frank
Archie Shepp: I Am Jazz...It's My Life....608
Cast, Leon
When We Were Kings....479
Castellani, Renato
Romeo and Juliet (Laurence Harvey)....314
Castellari, Enzo G.
Cold Eyes of Fear (Gli occhi freddi della paura)....518
Castle Jr., Nick
Tap....249
Castle, Nick
Mr. Wrong....277
Castle, William
The Americano....290
The House on Haunted Hill....523
The Night Walker....527
Strait-Jacket....529
The Tingler....530
Castro, Rich
Hustler White....460
Cates, Gilbert
Hobson's Choice (1983)....312
I Never Sang for My Father....232
Summer Wishes, Winter Dreams....248
Catoline, A.J.
Timothy Leary's Last Trip....478
Caton-Jones, Michael
Doc Hollywood....267
Memphis Belle (1990/Caton-Jones)....237
Rob Roy....244
This Boy's Life....249
Cattaneo, Peter
The Full Monty....182
Cavalcanti, Alberto
Coal Face (Benjamin Britten)....469
Dead of Night....173
The Life and Adventures of Nicholas Nickleby....28
Night Mail (Benjamin Britten)....469
Pett and Pott (England in 30s)....471
Rien Que les Heures....28
Rien que les heures (Classic Foreign #2)....153
Went the Day Well?....28
Cavani, Liliana
Beyond Obsession....32
Night Porter....33, 463
Cavara, Paolo
Malamondo....507
Cayo, E./Kounen J.
Gisele Kerozene (Int. Animation 4)....712
Cech, Vladimir
New Pastures....100
Cella, Len
More Moron Movies....508
Moron Movies....508
Cellon-Jones, James
Fortunes of War....192
Cervera Jr., Jorge
Julio and His Angel....50
Chabrol, Claude
Betty....12
Blood Relative....12
Club Extinction....12
The Eye of Vichy....12
Horse of Pride....12
Innocents with Dirty Hands....12
L'Enfer....12
La Ceremonie....12
La Rupture....12
Le Beau Serge....12
Le Boucher....12
Les Biches....12
Les Bonnes Femmes (The Good Girls)....12
Les Cousins....13
Madame Bovary....13
Piece of Pleasure....13
Story of Women....13
Ten Days' Wonder....13
Who's Got the Black Box?....13
Chadha, Gurinder
Bhaji on the Beach....181
Chaffey, Don
Dentist in the Chair....182
Gift of Love....229
Jason and the Argonauts....42, 174
Chahine, Youssef
Lumiere & Company....5, 336
Chaikin, Joseph
The Open Theater: Terminal....314
Chakhnazarov, Karen
Jazzman....82
Chan, Anthony
A Fishy Story....120
Chan, Benny
Man Wanted....130
Chan, David
Three Piano Portraits....616
Chan, Dennis
Perfect Match....123
Chan, Evans
Crossings....119
Chan, Gordon
Fight Back to School....120
First Option....127
Fist of Legend....127
Chan, Jackie
The Armour of God....133
Bloodpact....133
Dragon Lord....134
Jackie Chan and the 36 Crazy Fists....134
Jackie Chan's Police Force....134
Operation Condor....134
Project A (Part I)....134
The Young Master....135
Chan, Joyce
Crossings....119
Chan, Peter
Alan & Eric — Between Hello and Goodbye....118
Who's the Woman, Who's the Man....124
Chan, Philip
Mr. Sunshine....122
Chan, Tony
Combination Platter....455
Chaney, Tom
Frostbiter....506
Chang, Llee Han
My Better Half....122
Chang, William
China Heat....126
Chanuel, Charles
In the Wake of the Bounty....206
Chaplin, Charles
Burlesque of Carmen....407
Chaplin....407
Chaplin Revue....407
Charlie Chaplin Early Years I....407
Charlie Chaplin Early Years II....407
Charlie Chaplin Early Years III....407
Charlie Chaplin Early Years IV....407
Charlie Chaplin's Keystone Comedies....407
Circus/Day of Pleasure....407
City Lights....407
Count and the Adventurer, The....407
A Countess from Hong Kong....407
Emerging Chaplin....407
Essanay #1....407
Essanay #2....407
Essanay #3....407
The Gold Rush....407
The Great Dictator....407
Keystones #1....407
Keystones #2....407
Keystones #3....407
The Kid/The Idle Class....407
King in New York....408
Limelight....408
Modern Times....408
Monsieur Verdoux....408
Rare Chaplin....408
The Tramp and a Woman....408
Unknown Chaplin....408
A Woman of Paris....408
Work and Police....408
Chapnick, G.
Outside in Sight: Music of the United Front....614
Chappelle, Dave
Half-Baked....270
Charell, Erik
Congress Dances....68
Chasnoff, Debra
Deadly Deception....471, 803
Chatiliez, Etienne
Life Is a Long Quiet River....5
Tatie Danielle....18
Chau-Sun, Anthony Wong
New Tenant....122
Chaudet, Louis
In the Tentacles of the North....399
Chaudhri, Amin Q.
Unremarkable Life....251
Chauvel, Charles
Forty Thousand Horsemen....206
Chavarri, Jaime
I'm the One You're Looking For....44
Cheang, Shu Lea
Freshkill....160
Chechik, Jeremiah
Benny & Joon....263
Diabolique (1996)....225
Tall Tale....667
Checinski, Sylwester
All Friends Here....90
Take It Easy....94
Cheh, Chang
Assassin, The....125
Street Gangs of Hong Kong....132
Chekmayan, Ara
Forever James Dean....334
Chelsom, Peter
Funny Bones....269
Hear My Song....161, 324
Chen, Betty
Marguerite (Short Personal Films)....437
Chen, Chu-Huang
My Beloved....122
Chenal, Pierre
Crime and Punishment (French)....19
Man from Nowhere....22
Native Son (African American Films)....447
Cheng, Kent
Heartbeat 100....121
Why Me?....124
Chenzira, Ayoka
Alma's Rainbow....443
Cher
If These Walls Could Talk....232
Cherchiio, Fernando
Head of Tyrant....42
Chereau, Patrice
L'Homme Blesse (The Wounded Man)....4, 461
Queen Margot....6
Cherniack, David
Heart of Tibet....149

Chesebro, George
Wolf Blood 406
Chetwynd, Lionel
Hanoi Hilton 230
Cheung, Alton
Catman in Lethal Track 125
Catman's Boxer's Blow 125
Kickboxer from Hell 128
Thunder Ninja Kids: The Hunt for the Devil Boxer 132
Cheung, Chan Siu
Ninth of September, The Cursed Day 122
Cheung, Jacob
Cageman 119
Cheung, Mabel
An Autumn's Tale 118
Cheves, Manuel
And Now Miguel 468
Chi, Lee Lik
Flirting Scholar 120
Chi-Leung, Jacob Cheung
The Returning 123
Chi-Li, Tang
Butterfly and Sword 119
Chi-Man, Chung
Deception 119
Royal Warriors 131
Chi-Man, David Chung
Magnificent Warriors 129
Chi-Ngai, Li
Doctor Mack (aka Mack the Knife) 120
He Ain't Heavy, He's My Father 121
Heaven Can't Wait 121
Tom, Dick & Hairy 124
Chi-Wai, Eric Tsang
Aces Go Places II 124
Aces Go Places III (Our Man from Bond Street) 124
Handsome Siblings 128
Lucky Stars 129
Those Were the Days 124
Tigers, The 133
Chi-Yuk, Cheung
Couples, Couples, Couples 119
Chia-Yung, Liu
Black Wall 119
Chiang, Jeff
Lethal Match 129
Chiang, John
Will of Iron 135
Chin, Hsin
Jackie Chan: Ten Fingers of Death 134
Chin-Chung, Chan
Heroes Among Heroes (aka The Iron Beggar) 121
Ching-Fong, Ling
The Private Eye Blues 131
Ching-Wah, Wong
Enigma of Love 120
The Last Blood 129
Chiodo Brothers
Dino Alley (Animation C. 1) 705
Chionglo, Mel
Midnight Dancers 145, 463
Chiu, Che Wing
Roar of the Vietnamese 123
Chiu, Lee
Angel of Kickboxer 124
Mission Kill 130
Shaolin Avengers 131
Chiu, Samson
Rose (Hong Kong) 123
Chmielewski, Tadeusz
Eve Wants to Sleep 91
The Faithful River 91
Cho, Renee
Jazz Is My Native Language 612
Chodorov, Pip
End Memory (Letterist Films) 432
Choi, Nam Lai
Peacock Prince 130
Choi, Nam Nai
Erotic Ghost Story 120
The Seventh Curse 123
Chomsky, Marvin J.
Anastasia: The Mystery of Anna 217
Holocaust 775
Victory at Entebbe 251
Chopra, B.R.
Dhund (Fog) 147
Chopra, Joyce
Lemon Sisters 235
Chopra, Vidhu Vinod
1942: A Love Story 146
Chopra, Yash
Kabhi-Kabhi 147
Mashall (The Torch) 147
Trishul 148
Chow, Cindy
Lethal Panther 2 129
Chow, Peter
Pickles Make Me Cry 131
Chow, Wing
Close Escape 126
Christ, Joe
Acid Is Groovy Kill the Pigs 426
Speed Freaks with Guns 437
Christensen, Benjamin
The Devil's Circus 397
Witchcraft Through the Ages 77
Christensen, Bent
The Only Way 76, 776
Christensen, Soren Ole
Fearless Frida and the Secret Spies 663
Christian, Roger
Nostradamus 240
Christopher, Mark
Boys' Shorts 457
Chuan, Yan
Seeding of a Ghost 131
Chubakova, Tatyana
Homecoming (Glasnost Film Fest V.8) 81
Chueh, Chang
The One-Armed Swordsman 130
Chuen, Lam Wah
Xing Qi Gong Zhi Tan Bi 124
Chuen-Yee, Cha
Legal Innocence 121
Chuen-Yi, Cha
Middle Man 130
Chueng, Alfred
Talk To Me, Dicky 124
Chui, Pak Lam
Crystal Hunt 126
Chukrai, Grigori
Ballad of a Soldier 80
Chun, Lee
Lady Killer (Hong Kong) 129
Chun-Man, Yuen
Forbidden Arsenal 127
Chun-Wai, Jeff Lau
The Eagle-Shooting Heroes 127
Chun-Yeun, Wong
Hard to Die 128
Chun-Yeung, Brandy Yuen
The Sword Stained with Royal Blood 132
Chung, David
I Love Maria (aka Roboforce) 128
It's a Drink! It's a Bomb! 128
Chung, Peter
Aeon Flux 695
Aeon Flux: Mission Infinite 695
Chung, Sun
City War 126
Chung-Sun, Tsui
Tough Beauty and the Sloppy Slob 133
Ciccoritti, Gerard
Paris, France 211
Cimber, Matt
Jayne Mansfield: Single Room Furnished/ The Female Jungle 507
Cimino, Michael
The Deer Hunter 225
Heaven's Gate 293
The Sicilian 246
Ciolfi, Adam
Attic in the Blue 706
Civirani, Osvaldo
Hercules Against the Sons of the Sun 42
Clair, Rene
A Nous la Liberte 24
And Then There Were None 24
Beauties of the Night (Les Belles de Nuit) 24
Beauty and the Devil (La Beaute du Diable) 24
Crazy Ray 24
Entr'acte (Avant Garde Program #2) 482
Forever and a Day 170
I Married a Witch 24
The Italian Straw Hat 24
Le Million 24
Le Voyage Imaginaire 24
Les Grandes Manoeuvres 24
Quatorze Juillet 24
Rene Clair (doc) 25
Two Timid Souls (Les Deux Timides) 25
Under the Roofs of Paris 25
Clampett, Bob
Golden Age of Warner Brothers Cartoons 684
Clarehout, Paul
Scaredy Cat (Animation C.2) 705
Clark, Anthony
The Hemp Revolution 473
Clark, Bob
Christmas Story 662
Tribute 212
Clark, Colbert
The Three Musketeers (1933/Wayne) 390
The Whispering Shadow 539
Clark, James B.
A Dog of Flanders 663
Flipper 663
Island of the Blue Dolphins 664
Misty 665
Clark, Jim
Madhouse 525
Clark, Larry
Kids 432
Clark, Lawrence Gordon
Jamaica Inn 193
Clark, Louise
A Winter Tan 439
Clark, Matt
Da 311
Clarke, David
Galapagos: Beyond Darwin 816
Clarke, Robert
Elvira's Midnight Madness: The Hideous Sun Demon 521
Clarke, Shirley
The Connection 311
Clavell, James
To Sir, With Love 179
Clay, Carl
Let's Get Bizzee 445
Clayton, Jack
Great Gatsby 230
The Innocents 174
The Lonely Passion of Judith Hearne 161
The Pumpkin Eater 177
Room at the Top 177
Clegg, Tom
Mountbatten: The Last Viceroy 170, 762
Clein, John
Keep Punching 374
Clemens, William
Nancy Drew Reporter 380
Clement, Dick
Bullshot 181
Porridge 195
Water 185
Clement, Rene
And Hope to Die 210
The Deadly Trap (Death Scream) 7
Forbidden Games 20
Gervaise 20
Is Paris Burning? 20
Purple Noon (Plein Soleil) 23
Walls of Malapaga 24
Clements, Ron
Hercules 42, 634, 693
Clifford, Graeme
Frances 228
Clift, Denison
Phantom Ship (Mystery of the Mary Celeste) 177
Clifton, Elmer
Assassin of Youth 503
Cyclone of the Saddle 537
Down to the Sea in Ships 397
Let 'Er Go Gallegher 400
Not Wanted 381
Pilot X (Death in the Air) 499
Shame (Not Wanted) (Lupino) 386
Cline, Eddie
The Bank Dick 262
My Little Chickadee 277
Never Give a Sucker an Even Break 277
Private Buckaroo 328
Three Ages 409
The The Villain Still Pursued Her 409
Cloche, Maurice
Monsieur Vincent 22
Clokey, Art
Davey & Goliath: Caring for Others 708
Davey & Goliath: Christmas Lost & Found 708
Davey & Goliath: Forgiveness 708
Davey & Goliath: Halloween WHO DID IT? 708
Davey & Goliath: Happy Easter 708
Davey & Goliath: Helping Others 709
Davey & Goliath: Lost & Found: The Movie 709
Davey & Goliath: New Year Promise 709
Davey & Goliath: School: Who Needs It? 709
Davey & Goliath: Summer Camp to the Rescue 709
Davey & Goliath: Thanksgiving Special 709
Davey & Goliath: Trusting 709
Gumby: The Movie 684
Cloos, Hans Peter
Germany in Autumn 66
Clough, Chris
Dragonfire 200
Clouse, Robert
Black Belt Jones 532
China O'Brien 2 126
Enter the Dragon 127
Enter the Dragon—25th Anniversary Special Edition 127
Clouzot, Henri-Georges
Diabolique (1955) 25
Jenny Lamour 25
Karajan: Early Images, Vol. 2 (1965-66) 25, 591
Manon (Film) 25
The Raven (1943/Clouzot) (Le Corbeau) 25
The Wages of Fear 25
Coates, John
The Snowman 716
Cochran, Stacy
Boys 220
My New Gun 434
Cocteau, Jean
Beauty and the Beast 27
Blood of a Poet 27
Days of Our Years 19
The Eagle Has Two Heads (L'Aigle A Deux Tetes) 27
Les Enfants Terribles and Les Parents Terribles 25, 27
Les Parents Terribles 27
Orpheus 27
Testament of Orpheus 27
Coe, Fred
A Thousand Clowns 390
Coe, George/Lpver, Anthony
The Dove (Classic Foreign Shorts V.1) 153
Coe, Wayne
Grim Prairie Tales 230
Coen, Ethan
The Big Lebowski 441
Fargo 441
Fargo Collectors Set 441

Coen, Joel
Barton Fink 441
The Big Lebowski 441
Blood Simple 441
Fargo 441
Fargo Collectors Set 441
Hudsucker Proxy 441
Miller's Crossing 441
Raising Arizona 441
Coghill, Nevill
Doctor Faustus 160
Cohen, Avi
The Battle of the Chairmanship 107
Cohen, Eli
The Quarrel 211
The Summer of Aviya 777
Under the Domim Tree 108
Cohen, John
That High Lonesome Sound 606
Cohen, Larry
Black Caesar 532
God Told Me To 522
Hell Up in Harlem 532
It Lives Again 524
It's Alive 524
Q the Winged Serpent 509
Return to Salem's Lot 528
Wicked Stepmother 287
Cohen, Pamela
Dateline: San Salvador 56
Cohen, Peter
The Architecture of Doom 565, 766
Cohen, Rob
Dragon: The Bruce Lee Story 127
Dragonheart 225
A Small Circle of Friends 247
Cohen-Stitt, Ethan
Dr. Ded Bug (Best Fest 90) 706
Cohl, Emile
Attack of the Cohl Pumpkins 706
French Animation Festival 710
Cohn, Bennett
Midnight Faces 401
Where the North Holds Sway 406
Coke, Cyril
Pride and Prejudice (1985/BBC) 195
Cokliss, Harley
Chicago Blues 610
Colcord, Webster
Bladder Trouble (Spike/Mike Sick 1) 716
Slaughter Day (Spike/Mike Sick 2) 716
Cole, Kermit
Living Proof: HIV and the Pursuit of Happiness 834
Cole, Marcus
From the Mixed-Up Files of Mrs. Basil E. Frankweiler 663
Coles, John David
Signs of Life (B. Bridges) 246
Coletti, Duilio
Heart and Soul (Italian Drama) 41
Lure of the Sila 41
Coletti, Enrico
Honey Sweet Love 33
Colizzi, Giuseppe
Ace High 290
Colla, Richard A.
Don't Look Back: The Story of Leroy 451
Olly Olly Oxen Free 240
Collachia, Jeanne
Odd Birds 435
Collard, Cyril
Savage Nights 6, 465
Collier, James F.
Hiding Place 231
The Prodigal (1983) 243
Collins, Bob
Pat Paulsen for President 535
Collins, Lewis D.
The Desert Trail 292
Hoosier Schoolmaster 372
Collins, Vincent
200 (Acidburn) 717
Life is Flashing (Before Your Eyes) (Acidburn) 717
Collinson, Peter
The Italian Job 183
Collum, Jason Paul
5 Dark Souls 503
Colo, Papo
Exit in 3 549
Colomo, Fernando
Skyline 45
Starknight 45
Columbus, Chris
Adventures in Babysitting 261
Heartbreak Hotel 536
Mrs. Doubtfire 277
Nine Months 278
Comencini, Luigi
Bread, Love, and Dreams 38
Heidi (1953) 663
Comfort, Lance
Courageous Mr. Penn 172
Great Day 174
Conant, Justin
Beaker and Homeslice Get Out of Hand 717
Condie, Richard
The Apprentice (NFBCanada) 714
The Big Snit (NFBCanada) 714
Condon, Bill
Sister, Sister 246
Coney, John
Space Is the Place 615
Coninx, Stijn
Daens 29
Conklin, Gary
L.A.—Suggested by Art of Ruscha 551
Paul Bowles in Morocco 306
Conn, Nicole
Claire of the Moon 457
Cynara 458
Moments: Making of Claire of the Moon 337
Connell, W. Merle
Devil's Sleep 173
Connelly, Marc
The Green Pastures 371
Connor, Kevin
Mother Teresa: In the Name of God's Poor 791, 796
The Old Curiosity Shop 162
Conrad, Mikel
Flying Saucer 496
Contat, Michel
Sartre by Himself (Sartre par Lui Meme) 6
Conway, Jack
Boom Town 361
Brown of Harvard 396
Dragon Seed 366
The Girl from Missouri 369
Honky Tonk 271
Hucksters 372
Julia Misbehaves 273
Let Freedom Ring 325
Libeled Lady 274
Love Crazy 377
Our Modern Maidens 402
Red Headed Woman 280
Saratoga 281
A Tale of Two Cities (1935/Ronald Colman) 389
Tarzan and His Mate 539
Too Hot to Handle 391
Twelve Miles Out 405
Viva Villa! 392
Conway, James L.
Donner Pass: The Road to Survival 298
The Last of the Mohicans (1985) 235
Cook, Fielder
Big Hand for the Little Lady 290
Hideaways 663
Homecoming (Neal) 231
I Know Why the Caged Bird Sings 445
The Member of the Wedding (1997) 237
Patterns 421
Seize the Day 246
Too Far to Go 285
Cooley, Tita
Moebius Play (Animation C.1) 705
Coolidge, Martha
Angie 262
Joy of Sex 273
Lost in Yonkers 236
Plain Clothes 279
Rambling Rose 243
Three Wishes 284
Valley Girl 251
Coon, Ralph
Whispers from Space 862
Cooney, Robert
Alien Nation 217
God's Police 430
Coonley, Don
Purdy's Station 454
Cooper, George
The Shadow 178
Cooper, Merian
Chang 396
Grass 399
Cooper, Stuart
The Disappearance 210
The Long Hot Summer 236
Coppola, Eleanor
Hearts of Darkness: A Filmmaker's Apocalypse 259, 334
Coppola, Francis F.
Apocalypse Now (Remastered) 259
Bram Stoker's Dracula 259
The Conversation 259
Dementia 13 ....259, 520
Finian's Rainbow 259
The Godfather Part I 259
The Godfather Part II 259
The Godfather Part III 259
The Godfather, Collection 259
Hearts of Darkness: Filmmaker's Apocalypse 259, 334
Life with Zoe (New York Stories) 260, 288
New York Stories 260, 288
Outsiders 260
Peggy Sue Got Married 260
The Rain People 260
The Rainmaker 260
Rumble Fish 260
Tonight for Sure 260
Tucker: The Man and His Dream 260
You're a Big Boy Now 260
Coraci, Frank
The Wedding Singer 286
Corber, Mitch
Best of Radio Thin Air 566
James Schuyler: Interview/Reading 305
Mitch Corber Works 487
Pre-Real Estate 555
The Real Estate Show 555
The Wedding Show 439
Corbiau, Gerard
Farinelli 3, 29
The Music Teacher 5, 29
Corbucci, Sergio
Companeros 291
Corcoran, Bill
Sherlock Holmes and the Incident at Victoria Falls 186
Corcoran, Jay
Life and Death on the A-List 462
Cordova, Fred De
Bedtime for Bonzo 263
For the Love of Mary 368
Frankie and Johnny (Presley) 536
I'll Take Sweden 271
Cordova, Leander de
She (1925) 154
Corey Yuen/Wai, Lai Daai
Saviour of the Soul II 123
Corman, Roger
Atlas 513
Attack of the Crab Monsters 513
Bucket of Blood 513
Carnival Rock 513
Creature from the Haunted Sea 443, 513
Haunted Palace 522
It Conquered the World 513
Last Woman on Earth 513
Little Shop of Horrors (Original) 513
The Masque of the Red Death 514
Shame (The Intruder) 514
St. Valentine's Day Massacre 514
Swamp Women 514
Tales of Terror 514
Teenage Caveman 514
The Terror 514
Tomb of Ligeia 514
Tower of London (1962/Vincent Price) 514
The Undead 514
Von Richtofen and Brown 514
Wasp Woman 514
The Wild Ride 514
X—The Man with the X-Ray Eyes 514
Corneau, Alain
All the Mornings in the World 2
Fort Saganne 3
Lumiere & Company 5, 336
Cornelius, Henry
The Galloping Major 182
I Am a Camera 174
Passport to Pimlico 184
Cornell, John
Crocodile Dundee II 205
Cornfield, Hubert
Plunder Road 383
Cornfield, Stuart
The Night of the Following Day 380
Corona, Alfonso
Strange Ways 52
Corra, Henry
Umbrellas 479, 558
Corrente, Michael
American Buffalo 217
Federal Hill 227
Corrigan, Lloyd
The Dancing Pirate 321
Cort, Bud
Ted & Venus 283
Coscarelli, Don A.
Phantasm II: The Ball Is Back 527
Phantasm III: Lord of the Dead 499
Costa-Gavras
Betrayed (1988) 105
Conseil de Famille 105
Costa Gavras Talks with Marcel Ophuls 16, 105
Hanna K. 105
Lumiere & Company 5, 336
Mad City 106
Missing 106
Music Box (Costa-Gavras) 106
Z 102
Costner, Kevin
Dances with Wolves (Deluxe Collector's Set) 292
Dances with Wolves (Special Expanded Edition) 292
Cottafavi, Vittorio
Hercules and the Captive Women 42
Couffer, Jack
Living Free 161
Ring of Bright Water 665
Cousino, Niki
Fat of the Land 430
Couturie, Bill
Dear America: Letters Home from Vietnam 778
Covert, John
The Blind Lead 427
Cowan, William J.
Oliver Twist 381
Cox, Alex
Highway Patrolman 431
Repo Man 436
Walker 251
The Winner 252

Cox, Paul
Vincent (Cox) 207
A Woman's Tale 207
Cozarinsky, Edgardo
Jean Cocteau: Autobiography of an Unknown 27
Crabtree, Arthur
Fiend Without a Face 521
Horrors of the Black Museum 174, 523
Craft, William J.
Hero for a Night 399
Craig, Scott
Sacred Passions 853
Crain, William
Blacula 532
Crama, Nico
Animation in The Netherlands 706
Cramer, Ronnie
Back Street Jane 503
Even Hitler Had a Girlfriend 506
Crane, Kenneth D.
The Manster 525
Monster from Green Hell 526
Craven, Jay
High Water 431
Craven, Wes
A Nightmare on Elm Street 527
The People Under the Stairs 527
Scream 528
Scream 2 528
Serpent and the Rainbow 529
Wes Craven's New Nightmare 531
Crevenna, Alfredo B.
Neutron vs. the Maniac 508
Crichton, Charles
Against the Wind (Great Britain) 171
Battle of the Sexes 181
Dead of Night 173
A Fish Called Wanda 182
Hue and Cry 183
The Lavender Hill Mob 184
Crichton, Michael
The Great Train Robbery 160
Westworld 502
Crisp, Donald
Don Q, Son of Zorro 397
Fighting Eagle 398
The Navigator 409
The Street of Forgotten Women 404
The Young April 407
Cristofer, Michael
Gia 229
Croghan, Emma-Kate
Love and Other Catastrophes 275
Cromwell, John
Algiers 357
Ann Vickers 357
Anna and the King of Siam 357
Dead Reckoning 365
Goddess, The 370
Little Lord Fauntleroy (1936) 376
Made for Each Other 377
Of Human Bondage (Howard/Davis) 381
Prisoner of Zenda (1937) 383
So Ends Our Night 387
Son of Fury 387
Cronenberg, David
Crash 212
Dead Ringers 212
The Dead Zone 212
The Fly (1986) 212
M. Butterfly 212
Naked Lunch 212
Scanners 212
Shivers 212
Videodrome 213
Crosland, Alan
Beloved Rogue 395
Don Juan 397
Is Life Worth Living? 400
The Jazz Singer 325
Crouch, William Forest
Reet, Petite and Gone 448
Crowe, Cameron
Jerry Maguire 272
Say Anything 281
Singles 282
Cruikshank, Sally
Quasi's Cabaret Trailer (Animation C.1) 705
Cruze, James
Covered Wagon 397
The Fighting Coward 398
The Great Gabbo 370
Hawthorne of the USA 399
Leap Year 411
Mr. Skitch 379
Old Ironsides 402
The Roaring Road 403
Crystal, Billy
Forget Paris 268
Mr. Saturday Night 276
Csicsery, George Paul
N Is a Number: A Portrait of Paul Erdos 796
Cuaron, Alfonso
Great Expectations (Hawke/Paltrow) 229
The Little Princess 664
Cukor, George
Adam's Rib 349
Bhowani Junction 349
A Bill of Divorcement 349
Born Yesterday 349
Camille 349
The Corn Is Green 350
David Copperfield 350
Dinner at Eight 350
A Double Life 350
Gaslight 350
Holiday 350
Justine 350
Keeper of the Flame 350
Les Girls 350
Let's Make Love 350
A Life of Her Own 350
Little Women 350
The Marrying Kind 350
My Fair Lady 350
Pat and Mike 350
The Philadelphia Story 350
Romeo and Juliet 350
Song Without End 350
A Star Is Born 350
Susan and God 350
Travels with My Aunt 350
Two-Faced Woman 350
A Woman's Face 350
The Woman 350
Cummings, Howard
Courtship—An American Romance 223
Cummings, Irving
Broken Hearts of Broadway 396
Curly Top 663
The Dolly Sisters 322
Double Dynamite 366
Down Argentine Way 322
Everything Happens at Night 367
Flesh and Blood (Silent) 398
Little Miss Broadway 325
Louisiana Purchase 326
The Poor Little Rich Girl (1936) 327
Springtime in the Rockies 329
The Story of Alexander Graham Bell 388
Cummins, Stephen
Boys' Shorts 457
Cunha, Richard E.
Elvira's Midnight Madness: Frankenstein's Daughter 521
Elvira's Midnight Madness: She Demons 521
Giant from the Unknown 506
Missile to the Moon 498
Curiel, Federico
Neutron and the Black Mask
(Neutron el Enmascarado Negro) 508
Neutron vs. the Amazing Dr. Caronte 508
Neutron vs. the Death Robots 508
Curran, Daniel
All the Love in the World 426
Curtis, Dan
Dracula (Palance) 520
The Night Strangler 420
Scream of the Wolf 529
The Turn of the Screw 250
War and Remembrance 423
Winds of War 423
Curtis, Edward S.
In the Land of the War Canoes 399, 787
Curtis, Jack
The Flesh Eaters 521
Curtiz, Michael
Adventures of Huckleberry Finn (Hodges/Moore), The 308
The Adventures of Robin Hood 356
Angels with Dirty Faces 357
A Breath of Scandal 361
The Cabin in the Cotton 362
Captain Blood 362
Captains of the Clouds 362
Casablanca (2 LDs) 363
The Charge of the Light Brigade (1936) 363
Comancheros 291
Dive Bomber 366
Doctor X 520
Dodge City 292
Egyptian 367
Female 268
Flamingo Road 368
Force of Arms 368
Four Daughters 369
I'll See You in My Dreams 324
The Jazz Singer 325
Jim Thorpe—All American 795
Kennel Murder Case 374
Kid Galahad 374
Life with Father 274
Mildred Pierce 379
Moon of Israel 74
My Dream Is Yours 326
Mystery of the Wax Museum 526
Night and Day 327
Noah's Ark 638
Passage to Marseilles 382
Proud Rebel 383
Romance on the High Seas 328
Santa Fe Trail 385
Sea Hawk 385
The Sea Wolf (1941) 386
Sodom & Gomorrah 74
The Strange Love of Molly Louvain 388
This Is the Army 330
Trouble Along the Way 285
Virginia City 297
We're No Angels 286
White Christmas 331
Yankee Doodle Dandy 331
Young Man with a Horn 394
Cusumano, Rudolph
Wild Ones on Wheels 512
Cutler, R.J.
A Perfect Candidate 476, 800
Cutts, Graham
Return of the Rat 154
Cvitanovich, Frank
Scotland Yard 170
Cypher, D. Julie
Teresa's Tattoo 283
Cypriano, Tania
Viva Eu! & Ex Voto 467, 491
Czinner, Paul
As You Like It 310, 864
Catherine the Great 172
Dreaming Lips 173
The Rise of Catherine the Great 177
Romeo and Juliet (Nureyev) 575
D'Amato, Joe
Emmanuelle Queen of the Desert 32
D'Angiolillo, Luis Cesar
Killing Grandpa 51
D'Arrast, Harry d'Abbadie
Raffles (USA/1930) 384
D'Aruia, Mark
Smoke 247
Da Campo, Gianni
The Flavor of Corn 33, 459
Da Costa, Morton
Auntie Mame 358
The Music Man 326
da Silva, Raul
Rime of the Ancient Mariner (Redgrave) 715
Dahl, John
The Last Seduction 235
Red Rock West 244
Unforgettable 251
Dakota, Reno
American Fabulous 217
Daley, Martin
Something to Sing About (Music) 207
Dali, Salvador
Un Chien Andalou (Avant Garde &
Experimental Films) 47, 482
Dallamano, Massimo
Dorian Gray 520
Dalsheim, Friedrich
The Wedding of Palo 783
Dalva, Robert
The Black Stallion Returns 662
Daly, William R.
Uncle Tom's Cabin (1914) 405
Damberger, Francis
Age Is No Barrier 847
Damiani, Damiano
A Bullet for the General 40
Daniel, Rod
Beethoven's 2nd 662
Like Father Like Son 274
Daniela, Georgi
Autumn Marathon 80
A Summer to Remember (USSR, 1960) 83
Daniels, Harold
Sword of Venus 389
Terror in the Haunted House 530
Danniel, Danniel
Egg 31
Danska, Herbert
Sweet Love, Bitter 438
Dante, Joe
Amazon Women on the Moon 262
The 'Burbs 265
Gremlins 230
Matinee 237
Twilight Zone—The Movie 258, 501
Darabont, Frank
The Shawshank Redemption 246
Dardenne, Jean-Pierre
La Promesse 4, 29
Dardenne, Luc
La Promesse 4, 29
Dash, Julie
Daughters of the Dust 444
Dassin, Jules
The Canterville Ghost (1943/Laughton) 265
The Naked City 380
Never on Sunday 380
Reunion in France 384
Rififi 23
Topkapi 391
Where the Hot Wind Blows 42
Davenport, Tom
Ashpet: An American Cinderella 645
Bearskin (Or the Man Who Didn't Wash for Seven Years) 645
The Frog King 646
The Goose Girl 647
Hansel and Gretel, An Appalachian Version 647
Jack and the Dentist's Daughter 647
Mutzmag 638
Rapunzel, Rapunzel 648

Willa: An American Snow White 667
Daves, Delmer
The Badlanders 290
Broken Arrow (Stewart) 291
Dark Passage 365
Demetrius and the Gladiators 355
Destination Tokyo 366
Hollywood Canteen 324
Kings Go Forth 375
Never Let Me Go 380
Parrish 382
Red House 528
Rome Adventure 385
A Summer Place 389
Task Force 389
David, Charles
Lady on a Train 273
David, Hugh
Jude the Obscure 193
David, Mario
Shattered Cross 52
Davids, Paul
Timothy Leary's Dead 478
Davidson, Boaz
Going Bananas 269
Going Steady 107
Davidson, Martin
Eddie and the Cruisers 226
Davies, Gareth
Oliver Twist 174
P.D. James: A Mind to Murder 195
Davies, John
Kim (1984) 234
Davies, Terence
The Long Day Closes 161
The Neon Bible 162
Terence Davies Trilogy 164
Davies, Valentine
The Benny Goodman Story 320
Davis, Andrew
The Fugitive (Harrison Ford) 229
Steal Big, Steal Little 283
Davis, Barry
Don't Hang Up 182
Davis, Beau
Laser Mission 129
Davis, Desmond
The Clash of the Titans 159
The Sign of Four (Richardson) 187
Davis, Eddie
Panic in the City 435
Davis, Jim
Jim Davis: Volume #1 486
Jim Davis: Volume #2 486
Davis, Kate
Girl Talk 472
Davis, Michael Paul
Beanstalk 662
Davis, Ossie
Cotton Comes to Harlem 444
Davudneshad, Alireza
Need, The 106
Dawn, Norman
Tundra 392
Dawn, Vincent
Caged Women 504
Dawson, Anthony
Castle of Blood 518
Go, Go, Go, Go World! 506
The Long Hair of Death 525
Day, Dennis
Dennis Day: Oh Nothing 484
Day, Robert
Corridors of Blood 518
The Haunted Strangler 174
She (1965) 178
Dayan, Josee
Simone de Beauvoir (Subtitled) 6
Dayton, Lyman
Baker's Hawk 662
de Antonio, Emile
1968: America Is Hard to See 481
In the King of Prussia 481
McCarthy: Death of a Witchhunter 481
Millhouse: A White Comedy 481
Mr. Hoover & I 481
Painters Painting 481, 554
de Antonio, Emile
Painters Painting (CDROM) 870
de Antonio, Emile
Plot to Kill JFK: Rush to Judgment 481
Vietnam: In the Year of the Pig 481, 778
De Beifer, Evert
Characters (Animation C. 1) 705
De Bont, Jan
Speed 247
Twister 250
de Broca, Philippe
Cartouche 16
Dear Detective (Tendre Poulet) 17
The Green House 3
King of Hearts 17
That Man from Rio 18
de Chalonge, Christian
Dr. Petiot 7
de Concine, Ennio
Hitler: The Last Ten Days 161
de Felice, Lionello
Constantine and the Cross 364
De Filippo, Eduardo
Seven Deadly Sins (episode) 6
de Gastyne, Marc
The Marvelous Life of Joan of Arc 22
de Heer, Rolf
Dingo 205
The Quiet Room 206
de Jong, Ate
A Flight of Rainbirds 31
de la Bouillerie, Hubert
The Right to Remain Silent 280
de la Torre, Raul
Pubis Angelical 52
De Latour, Charles
Impulse (Drama) 174
de Lussanet, Paul
The Dear Boys 30, 458
De Niro, Robert
A Bronx Tale 221
De Nooiker, Paul
RRINGG! (Animation C.4) 706
De Noojier, Paul
I Should See (Int. Animation 5) 712
De Oliveira, Manuel
The Convent 48
de Santis, Giuseppe
Bitter Rice 40
de Seta, Vittorio
Bandits of Orgosolo 40
de Sica, Vittorio
After the Fox 37
The Bicycle Thief 37
The Children Are Watching Us 38
The Garden of the Finzi-Continis 38
Gold of Naples 38
Indiscretion of An American Wife 38
It Happened in the Park 38
Miracle in Milan 38
Roof 38
Shoeshine 38
Two Women 38
Umberto D. 38
Yesterday, Today and Tomorrow 38
De Wit, Michael
The Monk and the Fish (Spike/Mike 3) 716
Dean, Basil
21 Days 171
Lorna Doone (1934) 175
Dear, William
Angels in the Outfield (1994) 262
Harry and the Hendersons 270
Dearden, Basil
The Bells Go Down 171
The Blue Lamp 171
Captive Heart 172
Dead of Night 173
Frieda 173
Khartoum 175
League of Gentlemen 175
The Man Who Haunted Himself 176
Saraband 170
Smallest Show on Earth 184
Train of Events 179
Victim 179
Who Done It? 185
Dearden, James
Pascali's Island 163
Decoin, Henri
License to Kill (Nick Carter) 376
DeCoteau, Dave
Dr. Alien! 505
DeFalco, Martin
Cold Journey 210
DeFelitta, Raymond
Bronx Cheers 428
DeGrasse, Joseph
Scarlet Car 403
Degregori, Felipe
We're All Stars 53
Dehlavi, Jamil
Born of Fire 158
Dein, Edward
Curse of the Undead 519
The Leech Woman 524
Deitch, Donna
Desert Hearts 429, 458
Women of Brewster Place 455
Deitch, Gene
Five Stories for the Very Young 652
The Ugly Duckling (Children's Circle) 649
DeKuyper, Eric
Pink Ulysses 464
Del Monte, Peter
Invitation au Voyage 3
Julia and Julia 33
Del Ruth, Roy
Smile Please (All Night Long..) 410
Del Toro, Guillermo
Cronos 49
Mimic 238
Delannoy, Jean
Eternal Return 20
The Hunchback of Notre Dame (1957) 20
La Symphonie Pastorale 21
This Special Friendship 7, 466
Delon, Nathalie
Sweet Lies 248
Delpeut, Peter
The Forbidden Quest 31
Lyrical Nitrate 31
DeMille, Cecil B.
Carmen 354, 578
Cecil B. DeMille: The Greatest Showman on Earth 354
The Cheat 354
Cleopatra (Colbert) 354
The Crusades 354
The Greatest Show on Earth 354
Joan the Woman 354
King of Kings 354
Little American 354
Madam Satan 355
Male and Female 355
Manslaughter 355
Plainsman 355
Reap the Wild Wind 355
Road to Yesterday 355
Samson and Delilah 355
Sign of the Cross 355
The Spoilers 355
The Story of Dr. Wassell 355
The Ten Commandments 355
The Ten Commandments 355
The Ten Commandments:
40th Anniversary Collector's Edition 355
The Unconquered 355
Union Pacific 355
The Volga Boatman 355
The Whispering Chorus 355
Why Change Your Wife 355
Demme, Jonathan
Caged Heat 255
Citizen's Band 255
Cousin Bobby 255
Married to the Mob 255
Philadelphia 255
The Silence of the Lambs 255
Subway Stories 248, 255
Swimming to Cambodia 255
Swing Shift 255
Who Am I This Time? 255
Demme, Ted
Beautiful Girls 219
Ref, The 280
Subway Stories 248, 255
Dempsey, Shawna
Around the World the Lesbian Way 456
Demy, Jacques
Lola 5
The Umbrellas of Cherbourg 24
Denis, Claire
Chocolat 7
I Can't Sleep 8
Nenette and Boni 8
No Fear, No Die 8
Denis, Jean-Pierre
Field of Honor (French) 8
Densham, Pen
Moll Flanders (USA) 306
Denslow, Phil
Madcap (Animation C.4) 706
Madcap (Best Fest 91) 706
DePalma, Brian
Body Double 220
Bonfire of the Vanities 220
Carlito's Way 221
Carrie 517
Casualties of War 221
The Fury 229
Hi, Mom! 231
Mission: Impossible 238
Obsession (USA) 240
Phantom of Paradise 509
The Untouchables 251
Wise Guys 287
Depardieu, Gerard
Tartuffe (1984/Depardieu) 7
Depardon, Raymonod
Lumiere & Company 5, 336
Dereddere, Dominique
Suite 16 31
Wait Until Spring Bandini 251
Deren, Maya
Divine Horsemen: The Living Gods of Haiti 54, 484
Maya Deren Experimental Films 487
DeRochemont, Louis
Ramparts We Watch 763
des Roziers, Hugues
Blue Jeans 2, 457
Desai, Manmohan
Mard 147
Desplechin, Arnaud
My Sex Life (Or How to Get Into an Argument) 8
Deubel, Robert
Norman Rockwell's World...An American Dream 554
Deutch, Howard
Grumpier Old Men 270
Some Kind of Wonderful 247
Deval, Jacques
Club des Femmes 19
DeValois, Geoffrey
Computer Dreams (Dream Machine Vol. 2) 708

Devenish, Ross
Bleak House....189
Devers, Claire
Noir et Blanc....8
Deville, Michel
La Lectrice....4
Voyage en Douce....7
Devine, David
Beethoven Lives Upstairs....662, 864
Liszt's Rhapsody....636
Rossini's Ghost....640
DeVito, Danny
Hoffa....231
Matilda....664
Throw Momma from the Train....284
War of the Roses....286
Devyatkin, Dimitri
Video from Russia....89
Dewar, Stephen W.
Death on the Wing....814
Diamond, Matthew
The Balanchine Celebration: Part One....568
The Balanchine Celebration: Part Two....568
DiCillo, Tom
Box of Moonlight....428
Johnny Suede....432
Living in Oblivion....433
The Real Blonde....436
Dickerson, Ernest R.
Juice....445
Dickinson, Thorold
Gaslight....173
Hill 24 Doesn't Answer....107
The Prime Minister....177
Dickson, Paul
David (Festival of Britain)....471
Didden, Marc
Istanbul....233
Diegues, Carlos
Bye Bye Brazil....53
Quilombo....54
Xica....54
Diegues, Carlos Carlos
Tieta di Agresta....54
Dienar, Baruch
Take Two....108
Dieterle, William
The Devil and Daniel Webster....366
Doctor Ehrlich's Magic Bullet....366
Elephant Walk....367
Fashions....322
The Hunchback of Notre Dame (1939)....372
Kismet (1944)....375
The Life of Emile Zola....376
Love Letters (Jones/1945)....377
Omar Khayyam....381
Salome (Hayworth)....385
Satan Met a Lady....385
Scarlet Dawn....385
September Affair....386
Story of Louis Pasteur....388
Dillon, John Francis
Millie....379
Suds....404
Dilworth, John
Dirdy Birdy (Spike/Mike 3)....716
Dirty Birdy (Spike/Mike Sick 2)....716
Dimon, Elizabeth
Master Misery....433
DiNapoli, Victor
Sesame Street: Sing Yourself Sillier at the Movies....657
Dindo, Richard
Ernesto Che Guevara: The Bolivian Diary....30, 56
Dippe, Mark A.Z.
Spawn (Live Action)—The Director's Cut....500
Disney, Walt
Disney's Beginnings....692
Snow White and the Seven Dwarfs....694
Dixon, Denver
Pioneer's Gold....402
Dixon, Wheeler
Wheeler Dixon: Selected Films....491
Dixon, Wheeler Winston
What Can I Do?....252
Djordjadze, Nana
A Chef in Love....80
Dlugacz, Judy
The Changer: A Record of Times....604
Dmytryk, Edward
Alvarez Kelly....290
Anzio....358
Broken Lance....291
The Caine Mutiny....362
Captive Wild Woman....517
Crossfire (USA)....364
The Mountain....379
Murder My Sweet....380
Raintree County....384
Shalako....296
Soldier of Fortune....387
Walk on the Wild Side....393
Warlock....297
Where Love Has Gone....393
The Young Lions....774
Dmytryk, George
Her First Romance....270
Doblmeier, Martin
Thomas Jefferson: A View from the Mountain....764
Dobson, Kevin
Gold Diggers: The Secret of Bear Mountain....663
Miracle in the Wilderness....294
Docter, Pete
Next Door (Spike/Mike 2)....716
Winter (Spike/Mike 1)....716
Dodge, George D.
The Savage Garden....837
Dodge, Kathleen M.
The Savage Garden....837
Dohrn, Walt
Petey's Wake (Spike/Mike Sick 2)....716
Doillon, Jacques
Ponette....6
Domalik, Andrzej
Siegfried (Polish)....94
Domaradzki, Jerzy
Cupid's Bow....95
Great Race....95
Legend of the White Horse....664
Donaldson, Roger
Cocktail....222
The Getaway (1993)....229
White Sands....252
Donehue, Vincent J.
Lonelyhearts....377
Peter Pan (Martin)....327
Sunrise at Campobello....389
Donen, Stanley
Arabesque....358
Charade....363
Damn Yankees....321
Deep in My Heart....322
Funny Face....322
Give a Girl a Break....323
The Grass Is Greener....270
Indiscreet (1958/Grant)....272
It's Always Fair Weather....325
The Little Prince (Musical)....325
Love Is Better Than Ever....275
Royal Wedding....328
Seven Brides for Seven Brothers....328
Singin' in the Rain....329
Surprise Package....389
Two for the Road....392
Donev, Donio
Come Back to Sorrento (Animation C. 1)....705
Dong, Arthur
Coming Out Under Fire....455, 458
Dong-Kit, Michael Mak
Sex and Zen....123
Donner, Clive
Luv....275
Oliver Twist....240
Rogue Male....177
The Scarlet Pimpernel (1982/Anthony Andrews)....245
The Thief of Baghdad....390
What's New Pussycat....287
Donner, Richard
Conspiracy Theory....223
Goonies....270
Ladyhawke....235
Lethal Weapon....236
Lethal Weapon 2....236
Lethal Weapon 3....236
Lola (The Statutory Affair; Twinky)....376
The Omen....527
Radio Flyer....243
Scrooged....281
Superman: The Movie....248
The Toy....285
Donohoe, Gerald
27 Pieces of Me....426, 456
Donohue, Jack
Assault on a Queen....358
Lucky Me....326
Marriage on the Rocks....275
Watch the Birdie....286
The Yellow Cab Man....288
Donovan, Martin
Apartment Zero....218
Mad at the Moon....294
Donovan, Paul
George's Island....663
I Worship His Shadow....210, 497
Donskoi, Mark
My Apprenticeship (Gorky Trilogy)....81
My Childhood (Gorky Trilogy)....81
Donskoy, Mark
My Apprenticeship (Gorky Trilogy)....81
Dore, Mary
The Good Fight....48, 472
Dorfman, Herbert
Stan Getz: A Musical Odyssey....615
Dorfman, Stanley
Max Roach: Jazz in America....613
Dornhelm, Robert
Children of Theatre Street....569
Cold Feet....291
Echo Park....226
Dorr, John
Approaching Omega....426
Dorothy and Alan at Norma Place....429
Dorrie, Doris
Me and Him....64
Men....64
dos Santos, Nelson Pereira
How Tasty Was My Little Frenchman....54
Memories of Prison....54
Doucette, Robert
Triangle (Best Fest 90)....706
Douglas, Gordon
Black Arrow....360
Bombers B-52....361
Broadway Limited....361
Call Me Bwana....265
Chuka....291
Follow That Dream....536
In Like Flint....272
Kiss Tomorrow Goodbye....375
Lady in Cement....375
The McConnell Story....378
Only the Valiant....295
Rio Conchos....295
Robin and the 7 Hoods....328
Saps at Sea....281
Slaughter's Big Ripoff....533
Them!....501
Tony Rome....391
Up Periscope....392
Young at Heart....331
Zenobia....288
Douglas, Kirk
Posse (Kirk Douglas/1975)....295
Doumani, Lorenzo
Storybook....642
Dovzhenko, Alexander
Arsenal....85
Earth....85
Zvenigora....86
Dow, Sergio
The Day You Love Me....49
Dowling, Kevin
The Sum of Us....207, 465
Downey Sr., Robert
Hugo Pool....232
Downey, Juan
Bachdisc....483
J.S. Bach....486
Juan Downey....486
Downey, Robert
Moment to Moment....379
Putney Swope....436
Rented Lips....280
Up the Academy (Mad Magazine Presents Up the Academy)....286
Doyle, Helen
Video Art: Helen Doyle....490
Drach, Michel
Les Violons du Bal....5
Dragic, Nedjeljko
Pictures From Memory (Int. Animation 4)....712
Dragojevic, Srdjan
Pretty Village, Pretty Flame....103
Draskovic, Boro
Vukovar....103
Drazan, Anthony
Imaginary Crimes....232
Zebrahead....440
Dreifuss, Arthur
Double Deal....448
Murder on Lennox Ave....448
Sunday Sinners....449
Dreville, Jean
Lafayette....21
Drew, Les
The Balognie Birdman (NFBCanada)....714
Every Dog's Guide to the Playground (NFBCanada)....714
Drew, Sidney
Playing Dead....402
Dreyer, Carl Theodor
Day of Wrath....79
Gertrude....79
Leaves from Satan's Book....79
Master of the House....79
Ordet....79
Passion of Joan of Arc....79
Vampyr....79
Dridi, Karim
Bye Bye....2
Pigalle....8
Driessen, Paul
Animation in the Netherlands....706
Cat's Cradle (Incredible Animiation 2)....711
Getting There (Int. Animation 5)....712
Oh What a Knight (Animation C.1)....705
Paul Driessen: Animator....714
Pink Komkommer (Spike/Mike Sick 1)....716
Train Gang (Int. Animation 4)....712
The Writer (Int. Animation 3)....712
Driver, John
Alice in Wonderland (1982/Musical)....661
Drury, David
Prime Suspect 3....195
Dryfoos, Susan W.
The Line King....552
Dubin, Charles
Cinderella (Rodgers & Hammerstein)....321
Dubos, David
Rodrigue: A Man & His Dog....477
Dubroux, Daniele
The Seducer's Diary (Le Journal du Seducteur)....6

Duchamp, Marcel
Anemic Cinema (Avant Garde Program #11) 482
Duchemin, Remy
A la Mode 2
Dudko, A.
The Kirov Ballet in Tchaikovsky's Sleeping Beauty 572
Duesing, James
Impetigo (Acidburn) 717
Duggan, John
The Leading Man 161
Dugowson, Martine
Mina Tannenbaum 8
Duguay, Christian
The Assignment 218
Duigan, John
Flirting (Australia) 205
The Journey of August King 234
Romero 52
Sirens 207
Wide Sargasso Sea 207, 252
Duke, Bill
America's Dream 443
Deep Cover 444
Hoodlum 231
The Killing Floor 432
Rage in Harlem 446
Sister Act II: Back in the Habit 282
Duke, Daryl
The Silent Partner 211
The Thorn Birds 422
Dulac, Germaine
Germaine Dulac: The Smiling Madame Beudet and Seashell and the Clergyman 485
Seashell and the Clergyman (Avant Garde #12) 482
Dunlap, Scott
Winning the Futurity 406
Dunlop, Dick
A Long Time Till Dawn 419
Dunye, Cheryl
The Watermelon Woman 439
Duplantier, Stephen
Vivre pour Manger 479
Dupont, E.A.
Moulin Rouge 154
Variety 71
Dupont, Jaques
Wild Rapture 153
Durant, Alberto
Alias, La Gringa 49
El Grito 50
Dutilleux, Jean-Pierre
Raoni 60
Duvall, Robert
The Apostle 426
Duvivier, Julien
Anna Karenina (1948/Leigh) 171
The Burning Court 19
Diabolically Yours 20
Golgotha 20, 355
The Great Waltz (Strauss) 323
Le Golem: The Legend of Prague 21
Little World of Don Camillo 21
Lydia 377
The Man in a Raincoat 17
Maria Chapdelaine 22
Panique 22
Pepe le Moko 23
Poil de Carotte 23
Tales of Manhattan 389
Dwan, Alan
Driftwood 367
Dwan, Allan
Calendar Girl 321
The Gorilla (Lugosi) 270
Heidi (1937) 663
I Dream of Jeannie 324
Iron Mask 399
Manhandled 401
Manhattan Madness 378
Northwest Outpost 381
Rebecca of Sunnybrook Farm 328
Robin Hood (Fairbanks) 403
The Sands of Iwo Jima 772
The Three Musketeers (1939/Ameche) 330
Young People 668
Dwass, Michael
Lunch (Acidburn) 717
Dworsky, Rudolf/Wather-Fein, Rudolf
Wilhelm Tell 71
Dyakonov, Vladimir
The Temple (Glasnost Film Festival V.2) 81
Dyer, Julia
Late Bloomers 461
Dykhovichny, Ivan
Moscow Parade 82
Dziki, Waldemar
Young Magician 668
Eady, David
Faces in the Dark 173
Three Cases of Murder 179
Eason, B. Reeves
Test of Donald Norton 405
Eastman, Allan
Ford: The Man and the Machine 795
Eastwood, Clint
Absolute Power 256
Bird 256, 864
Breezy 256
The Bridges of Madison County 256
Bronco Billy 256
Clint Eastwood AFI Lifetime Achievement Award 332
Eastwood 865
The Eiger Sanction 256
Heartbreak Ridge 256
High Plains Drifter 256
Midnight in the Garden of Good and Evil 256
Outlaw Josey Wales 256
Pale Rider 256
A Perfect World 256
Play Misty for Me 257
The Rookie 257
Unforgiven (1992) 257
White Hunter, Black Heart 257
Eberhardt, Thom
Without a Clue 185
Ecare, Desire
Faces of Women 150
Echevarria, Nicolas
Cabeza de Vaca 49
Ecklund, Greg
Lloyd's Lunchbox (Spike/Mike Sick 2) 716
Ecklund, Gregory
Lloyd Loses His Lunch (Spike/Mike Sick 2) 716
Economou, Michael
John Hus 355
Edel, Uli
Last Exit to Brooklyn 235
Rasputin: Dark Servant of Destiny 88, 163
Eder, Harriet
Mein Krieg (My Private War) 64, 770
Edgren, Gustaf
Walpurgis Night 77
Edison Studio
Raoul Barre's Cartoons on Tour (Pioneers 1) 714
Edwards, Blake
10 353
Blind Date 353
Breakfast at Tiffany's 353
Breakfast at Tiffany's: Collector's Edition 353
Curse of the Pink Panther 354
Days of Wine and Roses 354
The Great Race (Edwards) 354
The Man Who Loved Women 354
Micki and Maude 354
Operation Petticoat 354
The Party 354
The Perfect Furlough 354
The Pink Panther 354
The Pink Panther Strikes Again 354
Return of the Pink Panther 354
Revenge of the Pink Panther 354
S.O.B. 354
A Shot in the Dark 354
Sunset 354
Trail of the Pink Panther 354
Victor/Victoria 354
Wild Rovers 354
Edwards, Dave
Shakespeare Vol. 1: The Twelfth Night 715
Shakespeare Vol. 2: A Midsummer Night's Dream 715
Shakespeare Vol. 3: Romeo and Juliet 715
Shakespeare Vol. 4: Hamlet 715
Shakespeare Vol. 5: The Tempest 715
Shakespeare Vol. 6: Macbeth 715
Edwards, George
Attic 218
Edwards, Harry
All Night Long 262
His First Flame 399
Langdon at Sennett 411
Tramp, Tramp, Tramp 405
Edwards, Harry et al.
These Girls Won't Talk 405
Edwards, Henry
The Private Secretary 184
Scrooge 178
Edwards, Hilton
Orson Welles' Ghost Story 344
Edwards, Peter
A Mind to Kill 162
Egeli, Arthur Bjorn
Unconditional Love 438
Eggeling, Victor
Symphonie Diagonale (Avant Garde Program #2) 482
Eggleston, Colin
Sky Pirates 207
Egoyan, Atom
The Adjuster 212
Calendar 212
Exotica 212
Family Viewing 212
Next of Kin 212
Speaking Parts 212
The Sweet Hereafter 212
Ehrlich, Jacquot
The 81st Blow 774
Einstein, Cassandra
Little Red Riding Hood (Too Outrageous) 717
Eisenstark, Doug
Everyone Sings/Cantemos Todos! 602
Eisenstein, Sergei
Alexander Nevsky 86
Alexander Nevsky (New Score) 86
The Battleship Potemkin 86
General Line 86
Ivan the Terrible, Part I 86
Ivan the Terrible, Part II 86
Ivan the Terrible, Parts 1 & 2 86
Que Viva Mexico 86
Romance Sentimentale 19, 457
Strike 86
Ten Days That Shook the World 86
Thunder over Mexico 86
Eisner, Vladimir
Marshall Blucher: A Portrait (Glasnost V.9) 81
Ekk, Nicolai
Road to Life 83
Ekman, Hasse
Blueprint for a Million 75
Elbert, Lawrence
Days of Pentecost 458
Eldridge, John
Waverley Steps (Festival of Britain) 471
Elek, Judit
Maria's Day 102
The Memories of a River 102
Elgort, Arthur
Colorado Cowboy: The Bruce Ford Story 470
Texas Tenor: The Illinois Jacquet Story 616
Elias, Michael
Lush Life 237
Elikann, Larry
Blue River 220
One Against the Wind 241
The Story Lady 248
Elissalde, Serge
Street Sweeper (Spike/Mike 2) 716
Streetsweeper (Spike/Mike 3) 716
Elkins, Steven
Medusa Challenger 433
Elliot, Clyde E.
Jungle Cavalcade 374
Elliott, Aiyana
Tough (Cineblast 1) 483
Elliott, Paul
Resistance 206
Elliott, Stephen
The Adventures of Priscilla, Queen of the Desert 205, 456
Ellis, Bernard
Boob's A Lot (Sextoons) 715
Else, Jon
Day After Trinity 471, 803
Yosemite: The Fate of Heaven 833
Elton, Arthur
Classic Documentaries: People and Places 470
Housing Problems (Classic Documentaries) 470
Elvey, Maurice
Beware of Pity 171
The Clairvoyant 172
Harassed Hero 183
Kiepura in My Song for You 183
Phantom Fiend 177
A Spy of Napoleon 178
Trans-Atlantic Tunnel 179
Emerson, John
His Picture in the Papers 411
The Mystery of the Leaping Fish and Chess Fever 86
Old Heidelberg 402
Reaching for the Moon 403
The Social Secretary 404
Wild and Woolly 406
Emmerich, Roland
Independence Day (Sci-Fi) 497
Stargate 500
Emshwiller, Ed
Films by Ed Emshwiller 484
En, Zhang Zi
Serenade in the Mist 123
Endfield, Cy
The Mysterious Island (1961) 176
Sea Fury 385
Try and Get Me 392
Zulu 180
Endoh, Tajuji
Satanika 745
Engel, Erich
Blum Affair 68
Engel, Larry
Nova—Adventures in Science: Hurricane! 837
Nova—Adventures in Science: Tornado! 837
Engel, Michael
Xingu: Land of No Shame 784
Engel, Morris
The Little Fugitive 376
Lovers and Lollipops 377
Weddings and Babies 393
Engle, Harrison
Benny Carter: Symphony in Riffs 609
Indomitable Teddy Roosevelt 795
English, John
The Adventures of Captain Marvel 537
Daredevils of the Red Circle 495
Fighting Devil Dogs (The Tornado of Doom) 537
Jungle Girl 538
The Mysterious Dr. Satan 538
Utah 297
Zorro Rides Again (Feature) 394
Zorro Rides Again (Serial) 539
English, Ron
Ron English 556

Englund, George H.
The Ugly American 392
Enrico, Robert
Jailbird's Vacation 20
The Last Adventure 21
An Occurrence at Owl Creek Bridge 22, 301
Enright, Ray
Coroner Creek 291
Dames 321
Earthworm Tractors 267
Gung Ho! 768
Iron Major 373
South of St. Louis 296
The Spoilers (1942) 387
Enyedi, Ildiko
Magic Hunter 102
My Twentieth Century 102
Ephron, Nora
Michael 237
Sleepless in Seattle 282
Epps II, Karl P.
Kin Folks 273
Epstein, Jean
La Chute de la Maison Usher 21, 486
Epstein, Marie
La Maternelle 21
Epstein, Rob
The Celluloid Closet 333, 457
Times of Harvey Milk 478
Erice, Victor
Dream of Light (Quince Tree of the Sun) 44
Spirit of the Beehive 45
Eriksen, Gordon
The Big Dis 427
Erman, John
Breathing Lessons 220
An Early Frost 458
Eleanor, First Lady of the World 794
Stella (Midler) 248
A Streetcar Named Desire (1984) 315
Ermler, Frederic
No Greater Love 82
Eros, Bradley
Mediamystics 487
Erskine, Chester
Androcles and the Lion 357
Call It Murder 362
The Egg and I 267
Escamilla, Teo
Tu Solo 45, 466
Escheverria, Juan Carlos
A Mixed-Up Adventure 51
Eskenazi, Diane
Gulliver's Travels 634
Esper, Dwain
Maniac and Protect Your Daughter 508
Estevez, Emilio
The War at Home (Drama) 251
Esway, Alexandre
Mauvaise Graine 346
Etaix, Pierre
Happy Anniversary (Experimental Series 22) 484
Evans, David Mickey
The Sandlot 666
Evans, John
The Black Godfather 532
Evans, Kim
Andy Warhol 544
Evans, Marc
Thicker Than Water 164
Evans, Maurice
Macbeth 97, 344, 573
Export, Valie
Invisible Adversaries 74
Menschenfrauen 74
The Practice of Love 74
Eyre, Richard
Singleton's Pluck 164
Faber, Christian
Bail Jumper 218
Fabri, Zoltan
The Fifth Seal 101
Fadiman, Dorothy
When Abortion Was Illegal: Untold Stories 479
Faenza, Roberto
The Bachelor 218
Faiman, Peter
Crocodile Dundee 205
Fain, David
Oral Hygiene (Int. Animation 5) 712
Fairchild, William
John & Julie 183
Fairfax, Ferdinand
Spymaker: The Secret Life of Ian Fleming 307
Fairly, Gene
Andrew Wyeth: The Helga Pictures 544
Fakuda, Jun
Son of Godzilla 499
Falk, Feliks
Hero of the Year 95
Top Dog 95
Fan, Ho
Yu Pui Tsuen 124
Fan-Kei, Frankie Chan
The Outlaw Brothers 130
Fanaka, Jamaa
Black Sister's Revenge 532
Penitentiary II 445
Penitentiary III 445
Soul Vengeance 533
Street Wars 446
Fanck, Arnold
White Hell of Pitz Palu 71
Fansten, Jacques
Cross My Heart (French) 17
Farino, Ernest
Josh Kirby...Time Warrior! Journey to the Magic Cavern ..664
Farm, Ant
Cadillac Ranch/Media Burn 483
Farmanara, Bahman
Prince Ehtejab 106
Farnsworth, Esther
Women Speak Up: A Collection of Women's Voices from Around the World 765, 783
Farrell, Perry
Gift 430
Farrelly, Bobby
Kingpin 273
Farrelly, Peter
Dumb and Dumber 267
Kingpin 273
Farrow, John
The Big Clock 360
China 363
Commandos Strike at Dawn 364
Copper Canyon 291
Hondo 293
John Paul Jones 374
Sea Chase 385
Two Years Before the Mast 392
Wake Island 392
Fassbinder, Rainer W.
Ali: Fear Eats the Soul 66
The American Soldier 66
Beware of a Holy Whore 66
The Bitter Tears of Petra Von Kant 66
Chinese Roulette 66
Effi Briest 66
Fox and His Friends 66
Germany in Autumn 66
Gods of the Plague 66
I Only Want You to Love Me (Ich Will Doch Nur, Dass Ihr Mich Lieb) 66
In a Year of Thirteen Moons 66
The Marriage of Maria Braun 66
Merchant of Four Seasons 66
Mother Kusters Goes to Heaven 66
Satan's Brew 66
Shadow of Angels (collaborator) 66
The Stationmaster's Wife 66
Why Does Herr R. Run Amok? 66
Fati, Tsui
Cheetah on Fire 125
Faver, Hector
La Memoria del Agua 45
Favio, Leonardo
Chronicle of a Boy Alone 49
Featherstone, Don
David Hockney: Portrait of an Artist 547
Fedorenko, Eugene
Every Child (Incredible Animiation 2) 711
Fefer, Sylvie
Software (Animation C.3) 705
Fei, Chen Yi
Evening Liaison 120
Fei, Xie
Girl from Hunan 117
Women from the Lake of Scented Souls 117
Feingold, Ken
The Works of Ken Feingold—Distance of the Outsider 491
The Works of Ken Feingold—Fictions 491
The Works of Ken Feingold—Life in Exile 492
The Works of Ken Feingold—Names in Search of a Body ..492
The Works of Ken Feingold—Water Falling from One World to Another 492
Feist, Felix E.
Battles with Chief Pontiac 290
Donovan's Brain 520
Guilty of Treason 371
The Man Who Cheated Himself 378
Western Classics Collection: Vengeance Valley and The Big Trees 297
Fekete, Ibolya
Bolshe Vita 101
Feldman, Dennis
Real Men 243
Feldman, Marty
The Last Remake of Beau Geste 273
Fellini, Federico
8-1/2 36
Amarcord 36
City of Women 36
The Clowns 36
Fellini Satyricon 36
Fellini's Roma 36
Fellini: A Director's Notebook 36
Ginger and Fred 36
I Vitelloni 36
Il Bidone 36
Intervista 36
Juliet of the Spirits 36
La Dolce Vita 36
La Strada 36
The Matrimonial Agency (Love in the City) 41
Nights of Cabiria 37
Orchestra Rehearsal 37
Spirits of the Dead 37
Variety Lights 37
White Sheik 37
Fend, Peter
Italy Wins World War III: 1990 Summit 473
Moving a River 487
Feng, Ni
The Chinese Dragon Poses as a Hero 119
Ferguson, Graeme
Love Goddesses 336
Ferguson, Michael
The Glory Boys 229
Ferland, Guy
Telling Lies in America 249
Fernandez, Emilio
Maria Candelaria 51
The Pearl 52
The Torch 53, 391
Fernie, Lynne
Fiction and Other Truths: A Film About Jane Rule 459
Ferrara, Abel
The Addiction 426
The Bad Lieutenant 426
Body Snatchers 427
Dangerous Game 429
The Funeral 430
Ms. 45 434
Subway Stories 248, 255
Ferraro, John
Sesame Street: Do the Alphabet 657
Ferrer, Jose
Return to Peyton Place 384
Ferrer, Mel
Green Mansions 371
Ferreri, Marco
La Grande Bouffe 4
Ferrin, Frank
Sabaka (The Hindu) 528
Ferris, Costas
Rembetiko 105
Ferroni, Giorgio
Bacchantes 310
Fessenden, Larry
Experienced Movers 430
Habit 431
Hollow Venus: Diary of a Go-Go Dancer 431
My Sheroes, My Sheroes 434
No Telling 434
Stars & Scars 567
Feuer, Donya
The Dancer 75, 471
Feuillade, Louis
Juve Contre Fantomas 20
Les Vampires 21
Feyder, Jacques
Carnival in Flanders 19
Crainquebille 19
The Kiss 400
Fiaschi, Giulio
Rigoletto (Gobbi/Dubbed) 585
Fichman, Ina
Moving Mountains: The Montreal Yiddish Theatre in the U.S.S.R. 112
Fielder, Gary
Kiss the Girls 234
Fields, Michael
Bright Angel 221
Figgis, Mike
The Browning Version (1994) 159
Leaving Las Vegas 235
Mr. Jones 239
One Night Stand 241
Stormy Monday 164
Filipski, Ryszard
Coup d'Etat 91
Filowych, Miniatur
David & The Magic Pearl 709
Finch, Charles
Circle of Passion 159
Finch, Nigel
The Lost Language of the Cranes 162, 462
Stonewall 465
Fincher, David
Alien Trilogy 494
Alien3 494
Seven 246
Findlay, Seaton
Janis 620
Finegan, John P.
Girls School Screamer 522
Fiore, Robert
Pumping Iron 476
Firth, Michael
Heart of the Stag 208
Fischinger, Oskar
Films of Oskar Fischinger 710
Oskar Fischinger 487, 686
Fischli, Peter
The Way Things Go 562
Fishel, D. Deirdre
Risk 436
Fisher, Terence
The Brides of Dracula 517
Curse of the Werewolf 519
The Devil Rides Out (a.k.a. The Devil's Bride) 520

Dracula: Prince of Darkness 521
Four Sided Triangle 173
Frankenstein Created Woman 522
Frankenstein Must Be Destroyed! 522
Horror of Dracula 523
Island Terror 524
The Phantom of the Opera (1962/Lom) 527
Sherlock Holmes and the Deadly Necklace 186

Fishman, M.
Puerto Cabezas: Our Sister City 60

Fitzgerald, Dallas N.
My Lady of Whims 401

FitzGerald, Jon
Apart from Hugh 456

Fitzmaurice, George
As You Desire Me 358
Lilac Time 400
Mata Hari 378
Raffles (USA/1930) 384
Son of the Sheik 404
Suzy 389

Fitzpatrick, James A.
James L. Fitzpatrick's Traveltalks 830
The Lady of the Lake 153

Flaherty, Paul
Who's Harry Crumb? 287

Flaherty, Robert
Elephant Boy 173
Louisiana Story 474
Man of Aran 204, 475
Moana, A Romance of the Golden Age 475
Nanook of the North 475
Tabu 73
Titan—Story of Michelangelo 557

Flanagan, Fionnula
James Joyce's Women 202

Fleischer, Dave
Fleischer Color Classics 683
Popeye the Sailor 687

Fleischer, Max
Evolution 398
Max Fleischer's Superman 685
Superman (50th Anniversary) 688
Superman: The Complete Cartoon Collection 688

Fleischer, Richard
10 Rillington Place 158
Barabbas 355
Between Heaven and Hell 359
Call Out the Marines/Clay Pigeons 362
Compulsion 364
Doctor Dolittle 322
The Fantastic Voyage 496
The Jazz Singer 325
The New Centurions 239
Soylent Green 500
Tora! Tora! Tora! 250
Vikings 392

Fleming, Andrew
The Craft 518
Threesome 249

Fleming, Anne Marie
Pictures Don't Tell You Anything:
Selected Films of Ann Marie Fleming 211, 487

Fleming, Victor
Adventure 356, 812
Bombshell 361
Captains Courageous (1937) 362
Dr. Jekyll and Mr. Hyde (Tracy) 520
Gone with the Wind 370
A Guy Named Joe 371
Hula 399
Joan of Arc 374
Mantrap 401
The Mollycoddle 401
Reckless 384
Red Dust 384
Test Pilot 390
Tortilla Flat 391
Treasure Island (1934, Beery) 392
Ultimate Oz (Collector's Edition) 331
When the Clouds Roll By 412
The Wizard of Oz 331

Flemyng, Gordon
Doctor Who and the Daleks 200

Fletcher, Mandie
Deadly Advice 159

Florey, Robert
The Beast with Five Fingers 516
The Cocoanuts 266
Ex-Lady 367
The Incredible Doktor Markesan 523
Johnny One-Eye 374
The Murders in the Rue Morgue (1932) 526
Outpost in Morocco 382

Floriniotis
Marching on to Glory 105

Flynn, John
Brainscan 517
The Outfit 241

Fockela, Jorg
Spokes (Men in Shorts V.2) 463

Fogel, Eric
Expiration Date (Too Outrageous) 717
Mutilator II (Spike/Mike Sick 2) 716

Fok, Clarence
Thunder Cop 132

Foley, James
Fear 227
Glengarry Glen Ross 311
Two Bits 250

Folman, Ari
Saint Clara 108

Fonda, Peter
Idaho Transfer 497
Wanda Nevada 297

Fong, Allen
Ah Ying 118

Fons, Angelino
Fortunata y Jacinta 44
Marianela 45

Fons, Jorge
Midaq Alley (El Callegon de los Milagros) 51

Fontaine, Anne
Augustin 2

Fontaine, Dick
David, Moffet, Ornette 610
Sound?? 615

Fontaine, Richard
Sins of Rachel 465

Fonti, Steven
Yes Timmy, There Is A Santa Claus (Too Outrageous) 717

Foray, J.
You Can't Teach An Old Dog New Tricks 714

Forbes, Bryan
The Endless Game 226
King Rat 374
The Madwoman of Chaillot 313
Seance on a Wet Afternoon 178
The Stepford Wives 529
The Wrong Box 185

Ford, Aleksandar
Border Street 90
Children Must Laugh 91
First Day of Freedom 91
Knights of the Teutonic Order 92

Ford, Charles E.
Jacare 473

Ford, Clarence
The Naked Killer 122

Ford, Francis
Officer 444 402
Power God 402

Ford, John
Arrowsmith 340
Drums Along the Mohawk 340
Fort Apache 340
The Grapes of Wrath 340
Hangman's House 340
The History of World War II: Battle of Midway 340, 768
The History of World War II: December 7th 340, 768
The Horse Soldiers 340
How Green Was My Valley 340
How the West Was Won 293, 340
Hurricane 340
The Informer (1935) 340
John Ford: AFI Lifetime Achievement Award 332
Judge Priest 340
The Last Hurrah 340
Long Grey Line 340
Long Voyage Home 340
Man Who Shot Liberty Valance 340
Mister Roberts 340
Mogambo 340
My Darling Clementine 340
The Quiet Man 340
Rio Grande 340
The Searchers 340
Sergeant Rutledge 340
Seven Women 340
Stagecoach 340
Straight Shooting 340
The Sun Shines Bright 340
They Were Expendable 341
Three Godfathers 341
Two by John Ford 341
Two Rode Together 341
Wee Willie Winkie 341
What Price Glory? (1952) 341
The Whole Town's Talking 341
Wings of Eagles 341
Young Mr. Lincoln 341

Ford, Phillip R.
Vegas in Space 466, 512

Forde, Walter
Forbidden Music 322

Forder, Timothy
The Mystery of Edwin Drood (1993) 301

Foreman, Richard
Strong Medicine 438

Forest, Matt
Snapper Showreel (British Animation) 707

Forestieri, Maurizio
Salome (Animation C.2) 705

Forman, Milos
Amadeus 100
Competition 100
Filmmakers on Their Craft 333
Firemen's Ball 100
Hair 100
Loves of a Blonde 100
One Flew Over the Cuckoo's Nest 100
The People vs. Larry Flynt 100
Ragtime 100
Valmont 100

Forman, Tom
Fighting American 398
Shadows (1922) 403
The Virginian (1923/Silent) 406

Forouzesh, Ebrahim
The Key (Iran) 106

Forrester, Jeff
My Man Norton 419

Forster, Russ
So Wrong They're Right 618

Forsyth, Bill
Being Human 219
Comfort and Joy 182
Gregory's Girl 183
Housekeeping 231
Local Hero 184
That Sinking Feeling 185

Fortier, Robert
Devil at Your Heels 471

Fortney, David
Natural Light: Windance 487

Fosse, Bob
All That Jazz 319
Cabaret 321
Lenny 235
Niagara Niagara 239
Pippin 327
Star 80 247
Sweet Charity 330

Fosselius, Ernie
Hardware Wars 497

Foster, Giles
Hotel Dulac 192
Silas Marner (BBC) 197

Foster, Jodie
Home for the Holidays 271
Little Man Tate 236

Foster, Lewis R.
Cavalry Charge 363
Crashout 364
Unaccustomed As We Are 285

Foster, Norman
Mr. Moto's Last Warning 379
Rachel and the Stranger 295

Fowler, Gene
I Married a Monster from Outer Space 497
I Was a Teenage Werewolf 523

Fox, Eytan
Song of the Siren 108

Fox, Wallace
Bowery at Midnight 517
The Corpse Vanishes 518
Inner Sanctum: Dead Man's Eyes/Pillow of Death 524

Foy, Bryan
Lights of New York 376

Fraker, William
Monte Walsh 294

Frakes, Jonathan
Star Trek First Contact 500

France, Chuck
Jazz in Exile 612

Franciolini, Gianni
Pardon My Trunk 41

Francis, Coleman
The Beast of Yucca Flats 494

Francis, Freddie
Doctor and the Devils 160
Dracula Has Risen from the Grave 520
Evil of Frankenstein 521
Nightmare (1963) 176
Paranoiac 176
The Skull 529
Trog 512

Francisco, Clay
How to See Hollywood 336, 830
Rivers of France 29, 831
Russia: Then & Now 88, 831

Francisi, Pietro
Hercules (Live Action) 42
Hercules Unchained 42
The Queen of Sheba 41

Franco, Jess
Awful Dr. Orlof 516
Castle of Fu Manchu 518
Count Dracula 518
Deadly Sanctuary 2
Dr. Orlof's Monster 520
Oasis of the Zombies
(La Tumba de los Muertos Vivientos) 527

Francovich, Allan
Houses Are Full of Smoke 473
Inside the CIA 1: History 473
Inside the CIA 2: Assassination 473
Inside the CIA 3: Subversion 473

Franju, Georges
Blood of the Beasts 19
Dream of Wild Horses 2, 19
Eyes Without a Face 521
Grand Melies 20
Head Against the Wall 20
Horror Chamber of Dr. Faustus 523
Judex 20
Le Grand Melies: The Great Melies,
Father of Fiction Films 21

Frank, Charles
The Inheritance (Uncle Silas) 174

Frank, Christopher
Josepha 4
L'Annee des Meduses 4
Frank, Hertz
Final Verdict (Glasnost Film Fest V.11) 81
Frank, Melvin
Above and Beyond 356
Buona Sera, Mrs. Campbell 265
Court Jester 266
Duchess and the Dirtwater Fox 267
The Facts of Life 268
Jayhawkers 373
Li'l Abner 325
The Prisoner of Second Avenue 280
Frank, Robert
Candy Mountain 210
Frankel, Cyril
On the Fiddle 184
Frankel, David
Miami Rhapsody 276
Frankenheimer, John
Against the Wall 216
All Fall Down 357
Andersonville 217
Birdman of Alcatraz 360
Burning Season, The 211
Days of Wine and Roses 311
French Connection 2 228
George Wallace 229
Grand Prix 370
The Manchurian Candidate 378
Seconds 386
Seven Days in May 386
Train 772
Young Savages 394
Franklin, Carl
Devil in a Blue Dress 444
Laurel Avenue 445
One False Move 445
Franklin, Charles
Babes in the Woods 395
Franklin, Chester M.
Going Straight 399
Toll of the Sea 405
Vanity Fair (1932) 392
Franklin, Howard
Larger Than Life 273
Franklin, Richard
Patrick (Australia) 206
Franklin, Sidney
The Barretts of Wimpole Street 359
Brass 396
The Dark Angel (Oberon) 365
The Duchess of Buffalo 397
The Forbidden City 398
The Good Earth 370
The Guardsman 270
Heart o' the Hills 399
Primitive Lover 402
Private Lives 314
Smilin' Through (1932) 387
Wild Orchids 406
Fraser, Christopher
Summer City 207
Fraser, Harry
Chained for Life 504
From Broadway to Cheyenne 292
Randy Rides Alone 295
Spirit of Youth 449
Frawley, Ray
Mumia: A Case for Reasonable Doubt? 475
Frears, Stephen
Dangerous Liaisons 166
The Grifters 166
Gumshoe 166
Hero 166
Mary Reilly 166
My Beautiful Laundrette 166
Saigon: Year of the Cat 166
Sammy and Rosie Get Laid 166
The Snapper 166
The Van 166
Freda, Ricardo
The Devil's Commandment 520
The Ghost (Italy) 522
Magnificent Adventurer 41
Samson and the 7 Miracles of the World 42
Sins of Rome 42
The White Warrior 512
Freeland, Thornton
Jericho 448
They Call It Sin 390
Whoopee 331
Freeman, Jerold
Native Son (1986) 445
Freeman, Mark
The Yiddishe Gauchos 116
Freeman, Morgan
Bopha! 443
Freeman, Morgan J.
Boom (CineBLAST 2) 483
Fregonese, Hugo
Apaches Last Battle (Old Shatterhand) 290
Blowing Wild 361
Death Ray of Dr. Mabuse 505
Decameron Nights 173
Man in the Attic 378
Freier, Matthias
Fishmind (CineBLAST 1) 483
Freleng, Fritz
Golden Age of Warner Brothers Cartoons 684
Looney Looney Looney Bugs Bunny Movie 685
French, Harold
Adam and Evelyn 19
The Day Will Dawn 173
Secret Mission 178
Frend, Charles
The Cruel Sea 172
Run for Your Money 385
Scott of the Antarctic 178
The Third Key 178
Fresnay, Pierre
Days of Our Years 19
Freund, Karl
The Mummy 526
Freundlich, Bart
The Myth of Fingerprints 239
Freundlich, Ken
Three Piano Portraits 616
Fric, Martin
The Hard Life of an Adventurer 99
Fricke, Ron
Baraka 469
Chronos 483
Fridge, Roy
Hearts and Arrows (Sextoons) 715
Fridriksson, Fridrik Thor
Children of Nature 75
Cold Fever 75
Fried, Randall
Heaven Is a Playground 230
Fried, Yan
The Twelfth Night (1956/Russia) 83
Friedenberg, Richard
The Deerslayer (Forrest/1978) 663
The Education of Little Tree 226, 786
Mr. and Mrs. Loving 239
Friedgen, Bud
That's Entertainment III 330
Friedkin, William
12 Angry Men 216
Blue Chips 220
Boys in the Band 457
Cruising 224
The Exorcist—25th Anniversary Edition 521
The Exorcist—25th Anniversary Edition Set 521
The French Connection 228
Good Times 370
Jade 233
The Night They Raided Minsky's 381
The People vs. Paul Crump 476
Rampage 243
Sorcerer 247
Friedlander, Louis
The Raven (1935/Karloff/Lugosi) 528
Friedman, Adam
Thomas Jefferson: Philosopher of Freedom 797
Friedman, Anthony
Bartleby 158
Friedman, Jeffrey
The Celluloid Closet 333, 457
Friedman, Peter
Silverlake Life: The View from Here 465
Friedman, Richard
Scared Stiff 528
Friend, Chan
Happy Bigamist 120
Friendman, Serge
Nehru 149
Frieri, Chris
The Stranger (Frieri) 437
Three Films by Chris Frieri 438
Frieri, Christopher C.
I Was a Teenage Mummy (1992) 523
Frizzel, John
A Winter Tan 439
Froelich, Keith
The Toilers and the Wayfarers 466
Frost, Lee
Black Enforcers 532
Black Gestapo 532
Frumin, Boris
Black and White 80
Boris Frumin Three-Pack 80
The Errors of Youth (Wild Oats) 80
Viva Castro! 83
Frumkes, Roy
George Romero: Document of the Dead 334
Fuentes, Fernando de
Dona Barbara 50
El Compadre Mendoza 50
Vamanos con Pancho Villa 53
Fuest, Robert
The Abominable Dr. Phibes 516
The Devil's Rain 520
Dr. Phibes Rises Again 520
Wuthering Heights (1970/Dalton/Marshall) 302
Fukasaku, Kinji
Black Lizard 137, 457
Fukuda, Jun
Godzilla vs. Gigan 497
Godzilla vs. Mechagodzilla 497
Godzilla vs. Megalon 497
Godzilla vs. the Sea Monster 497
Secret of the Telegian 499
Fukusaku, Kinji
Tora! Tora! Tora! 250
Fulci, Lucio
The Black Cat (1986/Patrick Magee) 517
Zombie 531
Fuller, Charles
Sky Is Gray 446
Fuller, Sam
Baron of Arizona 341
The Big Red One 341
China Gate 341
Dead Pigeon on Beethoven Street 341
The Naked Kiss 341
Pick Up on South Street 341
Shock Corridor 341
The Steel Helmet 341
Underworld, U.S.A. 341
Fuller, Samuel
Merrill's Marauders 341
Fumiko, Hayashi
Animated Classics of Japanese Literature: Wandering Days/Growing 721
Fung, Chow
Phantom War 130
Fung, Raymond
For Your Heart Only 120
Fuqua, Antoine
The Replacement Killers 244
Furie, Sidney J.
The Appaloosa 290
Hit! 532
Lady Sings the Blues 325
The Naked Runner 380
Furukawa, Taku
Tarzan (Animation C.4) 706
Fywell, Tim
Ice House 161
Gabel, Martin
The Lost Moment 377
Gabrea, Radu
A Man Like Eva 66
Gade, Sven
Hamlet (1921) 69
Gadette, Fredric
This Is Not a Test 501
Gaffney, Stuart
Virus (Four Directions) 459
Gage, Beth
Fire on the Mountain 472, 767
Gage, George
Fire on the Mountain 472, 767
Gagne, Michael
A Touch of Deceit (Int. Animation 4) 712
Gainville, Rene
The Associate 19
Le Complot 4
Galeen, Henrik
Alraune (aka Unholy Love) 68
Student of Prague (1926) 71
Gallagher, John
The Deli 429
Gallone, Carmine
Corelli in Tosca 578
Il Trovatore (Pederzini) 581
Puccini—Two Loves Had I 593
Gallu, Samuel
Blood Fiend (aka Theatre of Death) 517
Galvadon, Robert
Golden Cockerel (El Gallo de Oro) 50
Ganani, Gideon
Crossfire (Israel) 107
Gance, Abel
Abel Gance's Beethoven 19
Battle of Austerlitz 19
End of the World 20
J'Accuse (Silent) 20
J'Accuse (Sound) 20
La Folie du Dr Tube (Avant Garde Shorts France) 483
La Roue (Wheel of Fate) 21
Moore and Thill in Louise 22
Napoleon 22
Torture of Silence 24
Gang, Feng Xiao
Gone Forever with My Love 120
Gannaway, Albert C.
Daniel Boone Trail Blazer 292
Garcia, Jerry
Grateful Dead Movie 620
Garcia, Nicole
Every Other Weekend 3
Gardan, Juliusz
Is Lucyna a Girl? 92
Gardner, Danielle
Soul in the Hole 437
Gardner, Herb
I'm Not Rappaport 272
Gardner, Richard Harding
Sherlock the Undercover Dog 666
Gardner, Robert
Clarence and Angel 444
Garfein, Jack
The Strange One 388
Garmes, Lee
Actors and Sin 356
Garnett, Tay
Bataan 359

Cause for Alarm 363
Cheers for Miss Bishop 363
China Seas....363
A Connecticut Yankee in King Arthur's Court 309
Eternally Yours 367
Flying Fool, The....398
Mrs. Parkington....379
One Minute to Zero....381
The Postman Always Rings Twice (1946) 383
Seven Sinners (Dietrich/Wayne)....386
Slightly Honorable 387
The Valley of Decision 392
Garnier, Katia Von
Makin' Up....64
Garris, Mick
Quicksilver Highway 243
The Stand....247
Garson, Harry
The Worldly Madonna....406
Gartside, Philip
Contraband Spain 172
Gasnier, Louis
El Tango en Broadway....50
Reefer Madness....509
Topaze (1933/French) 27
Gasper, Mark
Empty Bed 459
Gates, Jim
Hey Abbott!....271
Milton Berle Invites You to a Night at La Cage 535
Gates, Martin
Mole's Christmas 637
Gatewood, Charles
Weird America 512
Gatlif, Tony
Latcho Drom....4
Gau, David
Fanaround (Best Fest Kids)....706
Gaup, Nils
Pathfinder (Norway)....76
Gavaldon, Roberto
La Dama de las Camelias....51
La Rosa Blanca 51
Macario 51
Gaviria, Victor
Rodrigo D: No Future 52
Gavrilko, Yelena
Girlfriend (Masters of Russian Animation 1)....82
Gayton, Charles
Music of the West: A Tribute to the Singing Cowboys 337
Gazdag, Gyula
A Hungarian Fairy Tale....102
Stand Off....102
Gazecki, William
Waco: The Rules of Engagement 479
Gebhardt, Steve
Bill Monroe: Father of Bluegrass Music....604
Gebski, Jozef
Gulag Archipelago 92
Geesing, Goop
Animation in the Netherlands 706
Geffner, David
Wild Blade 467
Gei-Yin, Stephen Shin
White Lotus Cult....133
Gelev, Sotir
The Chicken (Animation C. 1)....705
General Idea
Video Art: Shut the Fuck Up 490
Video Art: Test Tube....490
Genet, Jean
Un Chant d'Amour (Classic Foreign Shorts #3)....19
Genina, Augusto
Cyrano de Bergerac (Genina) 40
Prix de Beaute 23
Genini, Izza
Embroidered Canticles 110
Genji, Nakamura
Beautiful Mystery 137, 456
Gentilomo, Giacomo
Hercules Against the Moon Men....42
George, George W.
James Dean Story (Altman)....254
George, Peter
Surf Nazis Must Die 511
George, Terry
Some Mother's Son 164
Georgiadis, Vassilis
Red Lanterns....105
Gerard, Jerry
Deep Throat....505
Gerasimov, Sergei
Leo Tolstoy....82
Gerima, Haile
Ashes and Embers....443
Bush Mama 444
Child of Resistance and Hour Glass....444
Harvest: 3,000 Years....150
Sankofa 446
Gering, Marion
Thunder in the City 185
Germi, Pietro
Divorce—Italian Style....40
Four Ways Out 40
Seduced and Abandoned 41
Gerolmo, Chris
Citizen X....222
Gerson, Skip
God Respects Us When We Work, But Loves Us When We Dance 480
A Well Spent Life....480
Gert, Vanyoska
Krik? Krak! Tales of a Nightmare 54
Gerz, Jochen
Gerz Jochen Ti Amo 485
Gessner, Nicolas
Someone Behind the Door 7
Geurs, Karl
Pooh's Grand Adventure 693
Ghai, Subhash
Hero (India)....147
Karma 147
Vidhaata 148
Ghaudet, Louis
Eyes Right! 398
Giacobetti, Francis
Emmanuelle 2 3
Giammona, Sal
Walls in the Woods (Best Fest 91)....706
Gianini, Giulio
Five Lionni Classics 633, 710
Giannaris, Constantine
Caught Looking & North of Vortex 457
Gibbons, Rodney
Louisa May Alcott's Little Men 236
Gibson, Alan
Charmer, The....159
Dracula A.D. 1972 520
The Satanic Rites of Dracula 177, 528
The Woman Called Golda 110
Gibson, Angus
7 Up in South Africa 150
Gibson, Brian
Breaking Glass 159
The Josephine Baker Story 453
Murderers Among Us: The Simon Wiesenthal Story....776
Poltergeist II 527
What's Love Got to Do with It....331
Gibson, Mel
Braveheart (1995)....220
The Man Without a Face 237
Giddings, Al
Galapagos: Beyond Darwin....816
Ocean Symphony 821
Gielgud, John
Richard Burton's Hamlet 314
Gilbert, Brian
French Lesson....160
Not Without My Daughter 240
Tom & Viv 164
Gilbert, Lewis
Alfie 181
Cast a Dark Shadow....172
A Cry from the Streets 172
Damn the Defiant! 172
Educating Rita....182
Ferry to Hong Kong....182
Moonraker 169
Operation Daybreak 241
The Sea Shall Not Have Them....178
The Seventh Dawn 386
Shirley Valentine 163
The Spy Who Loved Me....169
Tough Guy 179
You Only Live Twice 169
Gilbert, Peter
Hoop Dreams 473
Giles, David
A Murder Is Announced....194
Vanity Fair (1967) 198
Gillen, Jeff
Deranged 505
Gillespie, Jim
I Know What You Did Last Summer 232
Gilliam, Terry
12 Monkeys 168
The Adventures of Baron Munchhausen....168
Brazil....168
The Fisher King....168
Monty Python and the Holy Grail....168
Time Bandits....168
Gilliat, Sidney
Green for Danger....174
Millions Like Us....176
Only Two Can Play....184
Gilling, John
Flesh and the Fiends (Mania)....521
The Mummy's Shroud....526
The Plague of the Zombies....527
The Reptile 528
Vampire over London 531
Gilmore, Stuart
Half Breed....293
The Virginian (1946)....297
Gilpin, Margret
Butterflies on the Scaffold (Mariposas en el Andamio) 457
Gilroy, Tom
Touchbase (CineBLAST!) 428
Gioanola, Vincenzo
9 Seconds and a Half (Too Outrageous) 717
Giovanni, Marita
Bar Girls....456
Giraldi, Franco
A Minute to Pray, A Second to Die 294
Girard, Bernard
Dead Heat on a Merry-Go-Round 267
Girard, Francois
Thirty-Two Short Films About Glenn Gould....212
Girard, Michael Paul
Different Strokes 458, 505
Girault, Jean
Le Gendarme a New York....21
Le Gendarme de St. Tropez....21
Pilgrimage to Rome 23
Girdler, William
Grizzly 522
Sheba, Baby....533
Girod, Francis
Lumeire & Company....5, 336
Girod, Francois
The Elegant Criminal (L'Elegant Criminel) 3
The Infernal Trio....17
L'Etat Sauvage 4
Gisler, Marcel
The Blue Hour 63
Gissberg, Jan
Peter-No-Tail 639
Gist, Robert
Della 365
Glabicki, Paul
The Paul Glabicki Animation Tape 714
Gladsjo, Leslie Asako
Deliberate Evolution of a War Zone/ A Calculated Forecast of Ultimate Doom, The 483
The Pleasures of the Uninhibited Excess 567
Gladstone, Howard
The Race for Mayor 476
Gladys, Leszek
Two That Stole the Moon 99
Glassman, Arnold
Visions of Light....339
Glatter, Lesli Linka
Now and Then 240
Glatter, Leslie Linka
The Proposition....243
Glatzer, Richard
Grief....460
Glen, John
Christopher Columbus: The Discovery....222
For Your Eyes Only 168
License to Kill (James Bond) 168
The Living Daylights....169
Octopussy....169
Glenister, John
Blunt: The Fourth Man 158
Glenville, Peter
Beckett....171
Hotel Paradiso....271
Me and the Colonel 276
The Prisoner (Movie)....177
Summer and Smoke....315
Glickenhaus, James
The Protector 134
Glikofridis, Panos
With Glittering Eyes 105
Glimcher, Arne
The Mambo Kings 59
Glinski, Robert
Poisonous Plants....93
Glut, Donald F.
Dinosaur Valley Girls....505
Gnatovich, Gavrilo
Lazar (Animation C.2)....705
Pre-Hysterical Daze (Animation C.4)....706
Go, Lui Jun
Killer Angels....129
Godard, Jean-Luc
All the Boys Named Patrick (Classic Foreign #2) 153
Alphaville....9
Aria....158, 577
Band of Outsiders....9
Breathless 9
Comment Ca Va? (How Is It Going?) 9
Detective 9
First Name: Carmen 9
Godard/Truffaut Shorts....9, 14
Ici et Ailleurs (Here and Elsewhere) 9
JLG/JLG....9
King Lear 9
Le Gai Savoir....9
Le Petit Soldat....9
A Married Woman....9
Masculine Feminine....9
My Life to Live 9
Numero Deux....9
Oh Woe Is Me (Helas Pour Moi) 9
Passion....9
Pierrot le Fou....10
Rogopag....10, 37, 39, 41
Sympathy for the Devil 10
Two or Three Things I Know About Her....10
Weekend....10
A Woman Is a Woman 10
Goddard, Jim
The Impossible Spy 232
A Tale of Two Cities (1980/Chris Sarandon) 248
Godfrey, Bob
Instant Sex (Outrageous 1)....714
Godfrey, Peter
Christmas in Connecticut....265
Cry Wolf....365

Escape Me Never....367
The Two Mrs. Carrolls....392
Godmilow, Jill
Far from Poland....98, 442
The Popovich Brothers of South Chicago....442
Roy Cohn/Jack Smith....442
What's Underground About Marshmallows: Ron Vawter Performs Jack Smith....442, 567
Godoy, Armando Robles
The Green Wall....50
Goggin, Dan/Stern, David
Nunsense....327
Golan, Menahem
Diamond Shaft (aka Diamonds)....532
Eagles Attack at Dawn....107
Hanna's War....775
Kazablan....108
Lupo....108
Mack the Knife....313
Operation Jonathan....108
Gold, Adam
American Messiah....503
Gold, Harmony
Robotech Vol. 01....743
Robotech Vol. 02....743
Robotech Vol. 03....743
Robotech Vol. 04....743
Robotech Vol. 05....743
Robotech Vol. 06....743
Robotech Vol. 07....743
Robotech Vol. 08....743
Robotech Vol. 09....743
Robotech Vol. 10....743
Robotech Vol. 11....743
Robotech Vol. 12....743
Robotech Vol. 13....743
Robotech Vol. 14....743
Robotech Vol. 15....743
Robotech Vol. 16....743
Robotech Vol. 17....743
Robotech Vol. 18....743
Robotech Vol. 19....743
Robotech Vol. 20....743
Robotech Vol. 21....743
Robotech Vol. 22....743
Robotech Vol. 23....743
Robotech Vol. 24....743
Robotech Vol. 25....743
Robotech Vol. 26....743
Robotech Vol. 27....743
Robotech Vol. 28....743
Robotech Vol. 29....743
Robotech Vol. 30....743
Robotech Vol. 31....743
Robotech Vol. 32....743
Robotech Vol. 33....743
Robotech Vol. 34....744
Robotech Vol. 35....744
Robotech Vol. 36....744
Robotech Vol. 37....744
Robotech Vol. 38....744
Robotech Vol. 39....744
Robotech Vol. 40....744
Robotech Vol. 41....744
Robotech Vol. 42....744
Robotech, Macross LD #2....744
Robotech, Macross LD #3....744
Robotech, Macross LD #4....744
Robotech, Macross LD #5....744
Robotech, Macross LD #6....744
Robotech, Macross LD #7....744
Robotech, Macross LD #8....744
Robotech, Macross LD #9....744
Gold, Jack
Catholics....355
A Deadly Game....159
Escape from Sobibor....226
Into the Blue....161
Little Lord Fauntleroy (1980)....664
Naked Civil Servant....162, 463
The Return of the Native....163
The Tenth Man....249
Goldberg, Franck
Franck Goldberg: Sampler....8
How to Squash a Squat....473
Goldberg, Gary
Gary Goldberg—Four Films: Plates, Mesmer, Usher and TV Head....567
Plates....464, 488
Goldberg, Gary David
Dad....224
Goldin, Sidney
East and West....112
His Wife's Lover....112
Uncle Moses....113
Goldstein, Alvin
The Unquiet Death of Julius and Ethel Rosenberg....479, 764
Goldstein, Bruce
Hollywood Outtakes....506
Goldstein, Leonard
Comanche Territory....291
Goldstone, James
Brother John....221
Kent State....760
They Only Kill Their Masters....249
Winning....393
Goldstone, Richard
No Man Is an Island....381
Goldwasser, Jacob
Over the Ocean....108
Goleszowski, Richard
Ident (British Animation)....707
Gomer, Steve
Barney's Great Adventure—The Movie....662
Sweet Lorraine....248
Gomez, Andrea
Bus Stop (Acidburn)....717
Gomez, Jaime Osorio
Confessing to Laura....49
Gomez, Nick
Illtown....431
Laws of Gravity....432
New Jersey Drive....239
Gonopolsky, Igor
Scenes of a Fountain (Glasnost Film Fest V.4)....81
Gonzalez, A.P.
Clay Farmers....458
Gonzalez, Servando
The Fool Killer....368
Yanco....53
Goodhew, Philip
Intimate Relations....183
Goodman, Barak
Daley: The Last Boss....471
Goodman, Karen
Buckminster Fuller: Thinking Out Loud....469, 565
Goodwins, Leslie
The Mummy's Curse....526
Gordon, Bert I.
The Amazing Colossal Man....516
Beginning of the End....359
Earth vs. the Spider....495
Fantastic Puppet People....496
The Magic Sword....377
The War of the Colossal Beast....531
Gordon, Bette
Variety (Gordon)....439
Gordon, Gerald
Young Hearts, Broken Dreams, Episode 1: The Delivery Boy....467
Young Hearts, Broken Dreams, Episode 2: The Search....467
Young Hearts, Broken Dreams, Episode 3: He Loves Me He Loves Me Not....467
Gordon, Keith
A Midnight Clear....237
Mother Night....238
Gordon, Michael
Boys' Night Out....361
Cyrano de Bergerac (Ferrer)....311
The Impossible Years....272
Pillow Talk....279
Portrait in Black....383
Texas Across the River....296
Gordon, Robert
It Came from Beneath the Sea....498
The Joe Louis Story....374
Gordon, Steve
Arthur....262
Gordy, Berry
Mahogany....445
Goren, Amit
Echoes of Conflict....110
Goretta, Claude
The Invitation....30
The Lacemaker....30
Gorlenko, Alexander
Old Stair (Masters of Russian Animation 2)....82, 713
Gormley, Charles
Gospel According to Vic....183
Gorris, Marleen
Antonia's Line....30
Mrs. Dalloway....162
A Question of Silence....31
Gorse, Martin
Tornado! Hurricane! Flood! Wonders of Weather....823
Gosha, Hideo
Hunter in the Dark....137
Goskind, Shaul
Our Children....113
Goskind, Shaul and Yizhak
Jewish Life in Bialystock....112
Jewish Life in Cracow....112
Jewish Life in Lvov....112
Goskind, Shaul and Yizkah
Jews of Poland....112
Gosling, Andrew
Light Princess....647
Gosling, Maureen
Dry Wood....480
J'Ai Ete au Bal: I Went to the Dance....480
Goss, John
Out Takes....464
Stiff Sheets....465
Wild Life....467
Wrecked for Life: The Trip and Magic of Trocadero Transfer....467
Gothar, Peter
A Priceless Day....102
Gottlieb, Carl
Amazon Women on the Moon....262
Gottlieb, Franz
Curse of the Yellow Snake....519
Gottlieb, Lisa
Cadillac Ranch....221
Gottlieb, Michael
A Kid in King Arthur's Court....664
Gould, Heywood
Mistrial....238
Goulding, Alfred
A Chump at Oxford....265
His Royal Slyness and Haunted Spooks....410
Goulding, Edmund
Dark Victory....365
The Dawn Patrol....365
Forever and a Day....170
Grand Hotel....370
The Great Lie....370
The Old Maid....381
The Razor's Edge (1946)....384
Riptide....385
That Certain Woman....390
We're Not Married....286
Gouri, Haim
The 81st Blow....774
Gout, Alberto
Cuando Viajan las Estrellas....49
Govenar, Alan
Cigarette Blues....480
Stoney Knows How....478
Gover, Victor M.
Curse of the Wraydons....505
Gowers, Bruce
Eddie Murphy Delirious....534
Grabo, Niels
The Hideaway....75
Gradowski, Krzysztof
Akademia Podroze Pana (Mr. Blot's Academy/ Travels of Mr. Blot)....90
Grady, Jerry
The Life and Times of Deacon A.L. Wiley....453
Graef-Marino, Gustavo
Johnny 100 Pesos....50
Graeff, Tom
Teenagers from Outer Space....500
Grafstrom, Anders
The Long Island Four....433
Graham, William A.
George Washington: The Forging of a Nation....417
Get Christie Love....532
Gore Vidal's Billy The Kid....292
The Man Who Captured Eichmann....237
Montana....294
Orphan Train....241
Proud Men....295
Waterhole #3....393
Where the Lilies Bloom....644
Gram, Leif
The Mysterious Island (1987)....638
Grammatikov, Vladimir
Land of Faraway (Mio in the Land of Faraway)....664
Grangier, Gilles
Duke of the Derby....20
Granier-Deferre, Pierre
The Last Train....4
Le Chat....17
Widow Couderc....18
A Woman at Her Window....7
Grant, Gregory
Ode to GI Joe (Int. Animation 5)....712
Grant, James Edward
Angel and the Badman....290
Grant, Lee
Down and Out in America....471
Tell Me a Riddle....249
When Women Kill....479
Grauman, Walter
633 Squadron....356
Lady in a Cage....375
Graver, Gary
Working with Orson Welles....345
Graves, Alex
Crude Oasis....428
Grawert, Gunter
Whisky and Sofa (Operation Moonlight)....66
Gray, David
Pumkin Madness II (Best Fest Kids)....706
Gray, F. Gary
Set It Off....246
Gray, John
An American Story....217
Born to Be Wild....220
The Day Lincoln Was Shot....224
A Place for Annie....242
Gray, Nick
Priests of Passion....792
Greaves, Daniel
Manipulation (Spike/Mike 2)....716
Greaves, William
Black Power in America: Myth or Reality?....450
Booker T. Washington: The Life and the Legacy....450
Frederick Douglass: An American Life....452
From These Roots....452
Just Doin' It....453
Greco, Celeste
Return to Aguacayo....60
Grede, Kjell
Good Evening Mr. Wallenberg....75
Green, Alfred E.
Baby Face....358

Copacabana 266
Dangerous....365
Disraeli....366
Ella Cinders....398
The Fabulous Dorseys 322
Invasion USA....507
The Jackie Robinson Story 452
Jolson Story 325
Man Who Had Everything....401
Silk Husbands and Calico Wives 404
A Thousand and One Nights....330
Top Banana 285
Green, David
Buster 159
Green, Guy
Diamond Head....366
A Patch of Blue 382
Sea of Sand....178
Green, Jack
Traveller....250
Green, Joseph
Elvira's Midnight Madness: The Brain That Wouldn't Die 521
The Jester (Der Purimshpiler) 112
Legend of Sea Wolf....664
Letter to Mother 112
Little Mother....507
Yidl with a Fiddle 113
Greenaway, Peter
26 Bathrooms 165
The Cook, The Thief, His Wife and Her Lover 165
Death in the Seine 165
Drowning by Numbers....165
Lumiere & Company....5, 336
The Pillow Book....165
Prospero's Books 165
Greenberg, Alan
Land of the Look Behind 602
Greenberg, Mark
Unbroken Circle—Vermont Music: The Tradition Change 606
Greene, Charles
Death on the Wing....814
Greene, Danford
Secret Diary of Sigmund Freud....281
Greene, David
After the Promise....216
Bella Mafia 219
The Count of Monte Cristo (Richard Chamberlain)....223
Godspell 323
Godspell and Filming of Godspell....323, 334
Gray Lady Down 229
Madame Sin 237
Greenfield, Amy
Antigone: Rites of Passion 482, 566
Videotape for a Woman and a Man....491, 567
Greenspan, Bud
Wilma 455
Greenwald, Maggie
The Ballad of Little Jo 290
The Kill-Off....234
Greenwald, Robert
Forgotten Prisoners 228
Xanadu....331
Gregg, Colin
Lamb (1995) 161
To the Lighthouse 197, 307
Gregoretti, Ugo
Rogopag....10, 37, 39, 41
Greif, Leslie
Keys to Tulsa 234
Gremillon, Jean
Pattes Blanches 23
Stormy Waters (Remorques) 23
Grenier, Vincent
Out in the Garden & You 464, 487
Greville, Edmond T.
Beat Girl....171
Hands of Orlac....522
Liars, The....21
Princess Tam Tam....23
The Romantic Age 177
Greyson, John
Autobiography (Men in Shorts) 463
Urinal....466
Zero Patience 212, 467
Greytak, Sharon
Hearing Voices 431
Grgic, Z.
Maxi's Cat's Lunch (Outrageous 2)....714
Grierson, John
Documentary Masterpieces by John Grierson 471
Drifters (E.M.B. Classics) 471
Industrial Britain (Documentary Masterpieces) 471
Gries, Tom
Breakheart Pass....291
The Migrants....238
QB VII 421
Will Penny 298
Grieve, Andrew
Lorna Doone (1990) 162
Grieve, Neil
Man Descending (Best Fest 91) 706
Griffi, Giuseppe Patroni
Collector's Item 32
The Driver's Seat 40
Griffin, George
The Club (Outrageous 2)....714
Griffiti 710
It's an OK Life (Animation C.1) 705
New Fangled (Animation C.3)....705
Griffith, Charles B.
Eat My Dust (USA) 505
Griffith, D.W.
Abraham Lincoln 412
America 412
Avenging Conscience 412
The Birth of a Nation....412
Broken Blossoms 412
D.W. Griffith Triple Feature 412
D.W. Griffith's Years of Discovery 412
Dream Street....412
The Female of the Species & Selected Biograph Shorts (Volume III)....412
Greatest Question....412
Griffith Shorts (1908-09) 412
Griffith Shorts (1909) 412
Griffith Shorts (1909-1910) 412
Griffith Shorts (1909-1911) 413
Griffith Shorts (1910-1911) 413
Griffith Shorts (1911) 413
Griffith Shorts (1911-1912) 413
Griffith Shorts (1912, #1)....413
Griffith Shorts (1912, #2)....413
Griffith Shorts (1912, #3)....413
Griffith Shorts (1913) 413
Griffith Shorts (1913-1914) 413
Hearts of the World....413
Home Sweet Home....413
Idol Dancer....413
Intolerance 413
Isn't Life Wonderful 413
Judith of Bethula....413
Judith of Bethula/Home Sweet Home 413
Love Flower....413
Mother and the Law 413
Musketeers of Pig Alley....413
Orphans of the Storm....413
Romance of Happy Valley....413
Sally of the Sawdust....413
The Short Films of D.W. Griffith—Volume 1 413
The Short Films of D.W. Griffith—Volume 2 413
The Short Films of D.W. Griffith—Volume 3 413
The Short Films of D.W. Griffith—Volume 4 413
Sorrows of Satan....413
The Struggle 413
True Heart Susie 413
Way Down East....413
White Rose 413
Griffith, Edward H.
The Animal Kingdom....357
Griffiths, Kevin
Jane Hissey's Old Bear Stories: Friends, Friends, Friends 653
Jane Hissey's Old Bear Stories: Happy Birthday Old Bear....653
Grimaldi, Aurelio
Acla's Descent into Floristella....32, 456
Grimault, Paul
The Curious Adventures of Mr. Wonderbird 672
Grimblat, Pierre
Secrets of Love, Classics of Erotic Literature: Vol. 4....510
Secrets of Love, Classics of Erotic Literature: Vol. 5....510
Secrets of Love, Classics of Erotic Literature: Vol. 6....510
Grimshaw, Mike
Little Rude Riding Hood (Too Outrageous)....717
Grinde, Nick
Hitler Dead or Alive 372
The Man They Could Not Hang....525
Stone of Silver Creek 296
Grint, Alan
The Secret Garden (1987) 666
Grlic, Rajko
Charuga 103
In the Jaws of Life....103
Melody Haunts My Reverie (You Only Love Once)....103
That Summer of White Roses 103
Groberg, Lee
Trail of Hope: The Story of the Mormon Trail 764
Grodecki, Wiktor
Body Without Soul 457
Mandragora 100, 462
Not Angels, But Angels....100, 463
Grofe Jr., Ferde
The Proud and the Damned 243
Groom, John
Monty Roberts: A Real Horse Whisperer....796
Grooms, Red
Red Grooms and Fat Feet....488, 555
Grosbard, Ulu
Georgia (Jennifer Jason Leigh)....430
Straight Time....248
The Subject Was Roses 388
True Confessions....250
Gross, Natan
Our Children 113
Gross, Yoram
Camel Boy....662, 707
Dot & Santa Claus 663, 709
Dot & The Bunny 663, 709
Grossman, David
Frog 633
Gruber, Krzysztof
Greta....92
Gruber, Markus
My First Name Is Maceo 621
Grune, Karl
The Prisoner of Corbal 177
Street 71
Grunewald, Allan
Nightmare Castle 527
Gryn, Naomi
Chasing Shadows....775
The Sabbath Bride 115
The Star, The Castle and the Butterfly....116
Guard, Candy
Fantastic Person (Animation C.4)....706
Moanalogue (British Animation)....707
What About Me (British Animation) 707
Wishful Thinking (British Animation) 707
The Wrong Type (Int. Animation 5) 712
Guazzoni, Enrico
Quo Vadis (1912) 41
Guenette, Robert
Here's Looking at You, Warner Bros. 334
Guercio, James W.
Electra Glide in Blue....226
Guerra, Ruy
Erendira 50
Fable of the Beautiful Pigeon Fancier 50
Guerraz, Sergio
After Darkness 158
Guerrero, Juan
Narda or the Summer 52
Guest, Christopher
The Big Picture....263
Waiting for Guffman....286
Guest, Robert
Fatal Confinement 160
Guest, Val
Break in the Circle....171
Carry On Admiral....181
Dance Little Lady....172
The Day the Earth Caught Fire 495
Expresso Bongo....173
Quatermass 1: The Quatermass Experiment....499
Quatermass 2: Enemy from Space 499
The Runaway Bus 177
Up the Creek 185
When Dinosaurs Ruled the Earth 502
Guggenheim, Charles
The Great St. Louis Bank Robbery 370
Guglielmetti, Giorgio
Fumo (Animation C.3)....705
Guida, Louis
Saturday Night, Sunday Morning: The Travels of Gatemouth Moore....608, 615
Guillermin, John
Blue Max....361
The Bridge at Remagen 361
Death on the Nile 160
King Kong Lives....524
Shaft in Africa....533
Skyjacked....386
The Towering Inferno....250
Waltz of the Toreadors 185
Guiol, Fred
Battling Orioles....395
Guitry, Sacha
The Fabulous Versailles....20
Napoleon (Guitry)....22
The Pearls of the Crown....23
The Story of a Cheat....23
Guney, Yilmaz
Baba—The Father....106
The Wall....106
Yol....106
Gunkan, Kaitei
Super Atragon 1 748
Super Atragon 2 748
Gunn, Bill
Ganja and Hess 444
Gunn, Gilbert
Girls at Sea....182
Guriev, Alexander
Cat & Company (Masters #3) 713
Gush, Bryan
Why We Fight (Best Fest 91)....706
Gustafson, Julie
Trial of the Avco Ploughshares 764
Guthrie, Tyrone
Oedipus Rex 314
Gutierrez Aragon, Manuel
Demons in the Garden 44
Gutman, Walter
Clothed in Muscle: A Dance of the Body 483
The March on Paris 1914 of General Von Kluck & His Memory of Jess....486
Gutteridge, Tom
Sleeping Beauty on Ice 575
Guttman, Amos
Amazing Grace (Drama) 107
Drifting 458
Guy-Blache, Alice
Women Who Made the Movies....339
Guymer, Christiane
Witness of Timid Expectations (Letterist Films)....432
Guzman, Tony
Philosophy in the Bedroom....509
Guzzetti, Alfred
Pictures from a Revolution 60
Gvozdanovic, R.
The Prayer (Outrageous 2) 714

Gyarmathy, Livia
Recsk 1953 Documentary of a Hungarian Secret Labor Camp.....103
Gyllenhaal, Stephen
A Dangerous Woman.....224
Homegrown.....431
Losing Isaiah.....236
Paris Trout.....241
Waterland.....252
Ha, Huang
Descendant of Wing Chun.....126
Haanstra, Bert
Zoo (Experimental Series 22).....484
Haas, Philip
Angels and Insects.....158
Day on the Grand Canal with the Emperor of China.....547
Magicians of the Earth.....552
The Music of Chance.....434
The Singing Sculpture.....556
Hackford, Taylor
Against All Odds.....216
Batman Forever.....219
Chuck Berry: Hail! Hail! Rock and Roll.....619
Dolores Claiborne.....225
Teenage Father (First Works).....334
White Nights.....252
Hadrich, Rolf
Stop Train 349 (Delay at Marienborn).....71
Hadyn, Richard
Mr. Music.....326
Haggard, Piers
The Blood on Satan's Claw.....517
The Fiendish Plot of Dr. Fu Manchu.....521
Haid, Charles
Buffalo Soldiers (Glover).....221
Iron Will.....664
Riders of the Purple Sage (1995).....295
Haig, Roul
The Wacky World of Doctor Morgus.....512
Haines, Fred
Steppenwolf.....248
Haines, Randa
Children of a Lesser God.....222
Jilting of Granny Weatherall.....301
Wrestling Ernest Hemingway.....253
Haines, Richard
Class of Nuke 'em High.....504
Halas, John
The Three Musketeers (1977).....717
Hale, Alan
Braveheart (1925).....396
Risky Business (1928).....403
Hale, Billy
S.O.S. Titanic.....843
Hale, Sonnie
Head over Heels (Matthews).....183
Sailing Along.....184
Haley Jr., Jack
That's Dancing.....330
That's Entertainment.....330
Hall, Alexander
Because You're Mine.....320
Doctor Takes a Wife.....366
Down to Earth (Hayworth).....366
Forever, Darling.....268
Goin' to Town.....269
The Great Lover.....270
Here Comes Mr. Jordan.....271
I Am the Law.....372
They All Kissed the Bride.....283
Hall, Chris
Global Brain.....804
Hall, Godfrey
Honor and Glory.....128
Lethal Extortion.....129
Hall, Mark
The Wind in the Willows, Volume #1.....644, 718
The Wind in the Willows, Volume #2.....644, 718
The Wind in the Willows, Volume #3.....644, 718
The Wind in the Willows, Volume #4.....644, 718
Hall, Peter
Jacob.....355
A Midsummer Night's Dream.....313
Never Talk to Strangers.....239
Orpheus Descending.....241
Hallis, Ophera
Chopi Music of Mozambique and Banguza Timbila.....601
Music of the Spirits.....603
Hallis, Ron
Chopi Music of Mozambique and Banguza Timbila.....601
Music of the Spirits.....603
Hallstrom, Lasse
The Children of Noisy Village.....75, 662
Lumiere & Company.....5, 336
More About the Children of Noisy Village.....76, 665
My Life as a Dog.....76
Once Around.....240
Something to Talk About.....247
What's Eating Gilbert Grape.....252
Halperin, Victor
I Conquer the Sea.....372
Nation Aflame.....508
Party Girl (Dangerous Business).....402
Revolt of the Zombies.....528
Supernatural.....389
White Zombie.....531
Hamburg, John
Tick (CineBLAST 2).....483
Hamer, Robert
Detective.....173
Kind Hearts and Coronets.....183
School for Scoundrels.....184
To Paris with Love.....185
Hamilton, Dean
The Road Home.....666
Hamilton, Guy
Battle of Britain (Olivier).....158
The Colditz Story.....172
The Devil's Disciple.....182
Diamonds Are Forever.....168
Evil Under the Sun.....173
Funeral in Berlin.....173
Goldfinger.....168
Live and Let Die.....168
Man with the Golden Gun.....169
Mirror Crack'd.....162
Hamilton, Nancy
Helen Keller in Her Story.....472
Hamilton, Strathford
Diving In.....225
Hamilton, William
Call Out the Marines.....362
Hammer, Barbara
Lesbian Humor.....461, 492
Lesbian Sexuality.....462, 492
Nitrate Kisses.....434, 492
Optical Nerves.....463, 492
Perceptual Landscapes.....464, 492
Hammond, Peter
The Dark Angel (O'Toole).....519
Hamolya, Gabor
Western (Spike/Mike 1).....716
Hampton, Benjamin B.
Heart's Haven.....399
Hampton, Christopher
Carrington.....159
The Secret Agent.....163
Hamrick, Lynn
Chess Kids.....470
Hancock, John
Bang the Drum Slowly (De Niro).....219
Prancer.....665
Haneke, Michael
Lumiere & Company.....5, 336
The Seventh Continent.....74
Hani, Susumu
Bad Boys (Hani).....137
Nanami, First Love.....138
She and He.....139
Hankin, Larry
Basement Tape.....427
How to Survive.....431
Hankison, Ron
Dr. Zoology: The Tamarin Mystery.....632
Hanks, Tom
That Thing You Do!.....283
Hansel, Marion
Between Heaven and Earth.....2
Hansen, Dane
Mine Eyes Have Seen the Glory: The Women's Army Corps.....770
Hansen, Paul
Bloody Korea: The Real Story.....757
We Were There: Jewish Liberators of the Nazi Concentration Camps.....777
Hansen, Rolf
Devil in Silk.....68
Hanson, Curtis
The Bedroom Window.....219
L.A. Confidential.....234
The River Wild.....244
Harding, Noel
Video Art: Noel Harding.....490
Harding, Sarah
Reckless (Richards).....195
Hardman, Holly
White Trash at Heart.....439
Hardwick, Mary
Yiddish: The Mame-Loshn (The Mother Tongue).....113
Hardwicke, Cedric
Forever and a Day.....170
Hardy, Joseph
Great Expectations (York/Miles).....300
Hardy, Robin
The Wicker Man.....531
Hardy, Rod
The Yearling (1994).....667
Hare, David
Strapless.....164
Hark, Tsui
A Better Tomorrow—Part III.....125
The Blade.....125
The Butterfly Murders.....119
Green Snake.....120
I Love Maria (aka Roboforce).....128
Once Upon a Time in China III, Parts A & B.....130
Once Upon a Time in China V.....130
Peking Opera Blues.....130
Tri-Star.....124
Twin Dragons.....135
Zu: Warriors of the Magic Mountain.....133
Hark, Tsui/Ko, Clifton/Cheung, Joe
The Banquet.....118
Harlan, Richard
Mercy Plane.....379
Harlan, Veit
Die Goldene Stadt.....69
Jud Suess.....69, 769
Kolberg.....69
Harlin, Renny
Cliffhanger.....222
Cutthroat Island.....224
Harman, Hugh
Animation Propaganda.....706
Harmon, Larry
Bozo the Clown Vol. 1: Ding Dong Dandy Adventures.....695
Bozo the Clown Vol. 2: Wowie Kazowie Clown Tales.....695
Bozo the Clown Vol. 3: Just Keep Laughing.....695
Bozo the Clown Vol. 4: Crazy Clown Capers.....695
Laurel & Hardy in Camera Bugged.....698
Harrington, Curtis
Night Tide.....434
Planet of Blood (Queen of Blood).....499
What's the Matter with Helen?.....512
Harris Jr., Wendell B.
Chameleon Street.....444
Harris, Bill
Colin Powell: A Soldier's Campaign.....451, 794
Howard Stern Exposed.....795
Yitzhak Rabin.....110
Harris, Damian
Bad Company.....218
Harris, Harry
Alice in Wonderland (1985/Live Action).....216
Alice in Wonderland Set.....216
Alice Through the Looking Glass.....216
Harris, Hilary
Hilary Harris.....485
Seawards the Great Ships (Documentary Masterpieces).....471
Harris, James B.
The Bedford Incident.....359
Harris, Kirk
Loser.....433
Harris, Leslie
Just Another Girl on the I.R.T......445
Harris, Mark Jonathan
The Long Way Home.....474, 776
Harris, Stirlin
The Little Horse That Could.....203, 637
Harris, Trent
Rubin & Ed.....245
Harrison, Hugh
Dream Man.....567
Jerker.....461
On Common Ground.....463
Harrison, John
Tales from the Darkside: The Movie.....530
Harrison, John Kent
City Boy.....660
Old Man.....240
The Sound and the Silence.....247
Harrison, Matthew
Kicked in the Head.....432
Rhythm Thief.....436
Harrison, Oliver
Amore Baciami (Spike/Mike 2).....716
Harrison, Richard L.
Drawing on Life.....548
Harron, Mary
I Shot Andy Warhol.....431
Harryhausen, Ray
Ray Harryhausen Compilation.....715
Hart, Harvey
Fortune and Men's Eyes.....311
The Pyx (The Hooker Cult Murders).....211
Hart, William S.
The Disciple.....397
The Fugitive (The Taking of Luke McVane).....398
Hell's Hinges.....399
Hartford, David M.
Nomads of the North.....402
Hartl, Karl
FP-1 Doesn't Answer.....69
Hartley, Elda
Alan Watts: The Art of Meditation.....847
Green Winter.....849
Quantum Healing: Toward Perfect Health.....853
Voices of a New Age.....857
Hartley, Hal
Amateur.....442
Flirt.....442
Surviving Desire.....442
Trust.....442
The Unbelievable Truth.....442
Hartman, Don
Mr. Imperium.....379
Harvey, Anthony
Eagle Wing.....292
The Lion in Winter.....175
They Might Be Giants.....283
Harvey, Herk
Carnival of Souls.....517
Has, Wojciech J.
The Doll (Poland).....91
The Saragossa Manuscript.....94
Hashimoto, Kohji
Godzilla 1985.....496
Haskin, Byron
Armored Command.....358
Captain Sinbad.....362

Denver and Rio Grande 292
His Majesty O'Keefe....372
Killer Bait (Too Late for Tears)....507
Long John Silver....664
The Naked Jungle....380
War of the Worlds....501
Hastrup, J.
Dreaming of Paradise....709
Hata, Masanori
Adventures of Milo and Otis....661
Hathaway, Henry
13 Rue Madeleine....356
Call Northside 777....362
Circus World....291
Dark Corner....365
Five Card Stud....292
Go West, Young Man....269
The House on 92nd Street....372
How the West Was Won....293, 340
Johnny Apollo....374
The Last Safari....375
Legend of the Lost....376
Lives of a Bengal Lancer....376
Nevada Smith....294
Niagara....380
North to Alaska....381
Prince Valiant (1954)....383
Racers....383
Raid on Rommel....771
Rawhide....295
Real Glory....384
Seven Thieves....282
Sons of Katie Elder....296
Souls at Sea....387
Spawn of the North....387
Sundown....389
To the Last Man....297
The Trail of the Lonesome Pine....391
True Grit....297
Wing and a Prayer....393
Hatta, Kayo
Picture Bride....435
Hauff, Reinhard
Knife in the Head....64
Haupe, Wlodzimierz
Dr. Judym....91
Hauser, Rick
The Scarlet Letter (Hauser)....301
Haverstick, Mary
Shades of Black....465
Hawkins, Stephen
Blown Away....220
Hawks, Howard
Air Force....341
Ball of Fire....341
Barbary Coast....341
Big Sleep, The....341
Bringing Up Baby....341
Ceiling Zero....341
Come and Get It....341, 343
Criminal Code....341
El Dorado....341
Gentlemen Prefer Blondes....341
A Girl in Every Port....342
His Girl Friday....342
Howard Hawks: American Artist....336, 342
I Was a Male War Bride....342
Land of the Pharaohs....342
Man's Favorite Sport....342
Only Angels Have Wings....342
Red River....342
Rio Bravo....342
Rio Lobo....342
Scarface: The Shame of a Nation....342
Sergeant York....342
Song Is Born....342
To Have and Have Not....342
Today We Live....342
Twentieth Century....342
Hawn, Goldie
Hope....231
Hay, Lee Tai
Flirting (Hong Kong)....120
Hayashi, Mitsuru
Theatre of Indifference....557
Haydn, Richard
Dear Wife....365
Hayers, Sidney
Circus of Horrors....518
Hayes, B.
Alaskan Safari....812
Hayes, Michael
The Androids of Tara....199
Hayes, R.
Alaskan Safari....812
Hayman, David
A Woman's Guide to Adultery....165
Haynes, Todd
Poison....435, 464
Safe....436
Hayward, Rudall C.
The Last Stand....208
Haywood-Carter, Annette
Foxfire....228
Hazan, Jack
A Bigger Splash....546
The Clash: Rude Boy....619
Head, John
The Jimi Hendrix Story....621
Head, Martin
The Good Sex Guide—Series No. 1....849
The Good Sex Guide—Series No. 2....849
Heath, Robert
Hugh Hefner: Once Upon a Time....795
Hebert, Bernar
Faces of Dance....571
Hecht, Ben
Actors and Sin....356
Angels over Broadway....262
Heckerling, Amy
Clueless....266
Look Who's Talking....274
National Lampoon's European Vacation....277
Heeley, David
The Universal Story....339
Heerman, Victor
Animal Crackers....262
Heffner, Avram
But Where Is Daniel Wax?....107
Laura Adler's Last Love Affair....108
Hegedus, Chris
The War Room....479
Heifitz, Josef
Baltic Deputy....80
Lady with the Dog....82
Heisler, Stuart
Along Came Jones....290
Blue Skies....320
The Burning Hills....291
Chain Lightning....363
The Glass Key....369
I Died a Thousand Times....372
The Monster and the Girl....526
Smash-Up: The Story of a Woman....387
The Star....388
Tokyo Joe....391
Tulsa....392
Hellbron, Olle
Pippi Longstocking....665, 715
Heller, Barbara
Little Women in Transit (Girl Friends)....460
Hellings, Sara
The Mark of the Rani....200
Hellman, Monte
Beast from Haunted Cave....443
China 9, Liberty 37....443
Creature from the Haunted Sea....443, 513
Ride in the Whirlwind....443
Shatter....178, 443
Shooting....443
Helsop, Richard
Floating (New Directors)....487
Hemmings, David
Dark Horse....224
Just a Gigolo....64
Wild Little Bunch....164
Henabery, Joseph
Cobra....396
His Majesty, the American....399
The Man from Painted Post....401
Henderson, John
The Borrowers (1993)....662
Henderson, Kirk
Cat and Mouse (Animation C. 1)....705
Henkel, Kim
Texas Chainsaw Massacre: The Next Generation....511
Henreid, Paul
Battle Shock....359
Dead Ringer....365
Henson, Brian
Muppet Treasure Island....655
Muppet Treasure Island Sing-Alongs....655
Things That Fly Sing-Alongs....658
Henson, Jim
The Labyrinth....234
Henszelman, Stefan Christian
Friends Forever....75
Henzell, Perry
Harder They Come....54
Herbert, Andrew
Third Sex Sinema Volume 2—The Song of the Loon....466
Herbert, James
Figures....484
Hercules, Bob
Briefcases and Bomb Shelters....469
Did They Buy It?: Nicaragua's 1990 Elections....56
Herek, Stephen
101 Dalmatians (1996)....690
Mr. Holland's Opus....239
The Three Musketeers (1993/Sheen)....284
Herman, Al
The Whispering Shadow....539
Herman, Albert
The Big Chance....360
Herman, Jean
Honor Among Thieves....231
Herman, Mark
Brassed Off!....181
Herman-Wurmfeld, Charles
Fanci's Persuasion....459
Hermosillo, Jaime H.
Dona Herlinda and Her Son....50
Mary My Dearest....51
The Summer of Miss Forbes....52
Hernandez, Gaspar
Poker....435
Herralde, Gonzalo
Last Evenings with Teresa (Ultimas Tardes con Teresa)....45
Herrington, Rowdy
Jack's Back....524
Hershman, Joel
Hold Me Thrill Me Kiss Me....271
Herz, Michael
Sgt. Kabukiman, N.Y.P.D.....510
Troma's War (Director's Cut)....512
Herzfeld, John
Don King: Only in America....225
Two Days in the Valley....250
Herzog, Werner
Aguirre: The Wrath of God....67
Burden of Dreams....480
Heart of Glass....67
Herdsmen of the Sun....67
The Mystery of Kaspar Hauser....67
Nosferatu the Vampyre....67
Signs of Life (Herzog)....67
Stroszek....67
Werner Herzog Eats His Shoe....480
Where the Green Ants Dream....67
Woyzeck (Herzog)....67
Hessler, Gordon
Cry of the Banshee....519
Girl in a Swing....75
Golden Voyage of Sinbad....634
The Murders in the Rue Morgue (1971)....526
The Oblong Box....527
Scream and Scream Again....528
Heston, Charlton
A Man for All Seasons....237
Heston, Fraser C.
Alaska....216
The Crucifer of Blood....186
Needful Things....526
Treasure Island....250
Heusch, Paolo
The Day the Sky Exploded....68
Hewitt, David L.
Journey to the Center of Time....498
Monsters Crash the Pajama Party....526
Hewitt, Peter
The Borrowers (1998)....662
Tom and Huck....694
Heyerdahl, Thor
Kon-Tiki....782, 867
Heynemann, Laurent
The Old Lady Who Walked in the Sea....6
Hibbs, Jesse
To Hell and Back....772
Walk the Proud Land....297
Hick, Jochen
Via Appia....65, 467
Hickenlooper, George
Hearts of Darkness: A Filmmaker's Apocalypse....259, 334
The Low Life....433
Some Folks Call It a Sling Blade....437
Hickey, Aidan
An Inside Job (Outrageous 1)....714
Hickox, Anthony
Prince Valiant (1997)....163
Hickox, Douglas
Brannigan....159
The Hound of the Baskervilles (Richardson)....186
Hicks, Scott
Shine....207
Hideaki, Ooba
Genesis Survivor Gaiarth: Stage 3....730
Higashi, Yoichi
Village of Dreams....140
Higgin, Howard
The Racketeer....384
Skyscraper....404
Higgins, Colin
The Best Little Whorehouse in Texas....320
Hiken, Nat
The Love God....275
Hildenbrandt, Dan
Zydeco Gumbo....604
Hilferty, Robert
Stop the Church....465
Hill, Bob
Shadow of Chinatown (The Yellow Phantom)....539
Hill, Gary
Video Art: Gary Hill....490
Hill, George Roy
Butch Cassidy and the Sundance Kid....291
Hawaii....371
Little Romance....236
Min & Bill....379
Period of Adjustment....382
Slaughterhouse Five....246
The Sting....248
Toys in the Attic....315
The World According to Garp....253
The World of Henry Orient....288
Hill, George W.
The Big House....360
Hill, Jack
The Big Bird Cage (Women's Penitentiary II)....532
Big Doll House....504
Coffy....532
Foxy Brown....532

The Snake People (Isle of the Snake People) 529
Spider Baby 529
Switchblade Sisters 511

Hill, James
Black Beauty (1971) 662
Born Free 662
A Study in Terror 529
Trial and Error (The Dock Brief) 185

Hill, Jerome
Albert Schweitzer 468
Dr. Carl G. Jung or Lapis Philosophorum 442
Film Portrait 484

Hill, Sinclair
Greek Street 174

Hill, Walter
48 Hours 261
Another 48 Hours 217
Geronimo (Drama) 292
Johnny Handsome 233
Long Riders 294
Trespass 250
Warriors 251
Wild Bill 298

Hillenburg, Stephen
The Green Beret (Animation C.4) 706

Hiller, Arthur
The Americanization of Emily 357
The Babe 218
The Hospital 271
The In-Laws 272
Lonely Guy 274
Love Story 237
Making Love 462
Man of La Mancha 326
The Out-of-Towners 278
Plaza Suite 279
Promise Her Anything 280
See No Evil, Hear No Evil 281
Silver Streak 282
Teachers 283
Tobruk 391
The Wheeler Dealers 287

Hillyer, Lambert
Cradle of Courage 397
Dracula's Daughter 520
Hat Box Mystery 371
Invisible Ray 524
Shock (Chaney) 404
The Tollgate 297, 405

Hilton, Arthur
Cat Women of the Moon 495

Hin-Sung, Billy Tang
Red to Kill 123
Run and Kill 131

Hines, Charles
The Crackerjack 397
Live Wire 400
Speed Spook 404

Hines, Hank
What Ever Happened to… 531

Hines, Johnny
Burn 'em Up Barnes (1921/Silent) 396

Hinton, Chris
Blackfly (NFBCanada) 714
A Nice Day in the County (Animation C.3) 705

Hinzman, Bill
The Majorettes 525

Hiroshi, Inagaki
Incident at Blood Pass 138

Hiroyuki, Oki
I Like You, I Like You Very Much 138, 460

Hiscott, Leslie S.
The Triumph of Sherlock Holmes 187

Hitchcock, Alfred
Alfred Hitchcock TV 351
Alfred Hitchcock: AFI Lifetime Achievement 332
Alfred Hitchcock: Master of Suspense 332, 351
The Birds 351
Blackmail 351
Bon Voyage & Aventure Malgache 351
Champagne 351
Dial M for Murder 352
Easy Virtue 352
Family Plot 352
The Farmer's Wife 352
Foreign Correspondent 352
Frenzy 352
Hollywood Babylon 334
I Confess 352
Jamaica Inn (1939) 352
Juno and the Paycock 352
The Lady Vanishes 352
Lifeboat 352
Lodger 352
Man Who Knew Too Much (1934) 352
Man Who Knew Too Much (1955) 352
Manxman 352
Marnie 352
Murder 352
North by Northwest 352
Notorious 352
Number Seventeen 352
Paradine Case 352
Psycho 352
Rear Window 352
Rebecca (1940) 352
Rich and Strange 352
The Ring 352
Rope 352
Sabotage 352
Saboteur 352
Secret Agent 352
Shadow of a Doubt 353
Skin Game 353
Stage Fright 353
Strangers on a Train (American Version) 353
Strangers on a Train (British Version) 353
Suspicion 353
The Thirty-Nine Steps 353
To Catch a Thief 353
Topaz 353
Torn Curtain 353
The Trouble with Harry 353
Vertigo 353
The Wrong Man 353
Young and Innocent 353

Hittle, Timothy
Potato Hunter (Int. Animation 5) 712

Hixson, Peter
Tennis (Spike/Mike Sick 2) 716

Ho, Godfrey
Fatal Target 120
Lethal Panther 129

Ho, Ma Wai
Feel 100% 120

Ho, Yim
The Day the Sun Turned Cold 117

Ho-Ping, Yuang
Drunken Tai-Chi 127

Ho-Sun, Peter Chan
He Ain't Heavy, He's My Father 121
He's a Woman, She's a Man 121
Tom, Dick & Hairy 124

Hobbs, Lyndall
Back to the Beach 503

Hoblit, Gregory
Primal Fear 243
Roe vs. Wade 421

Hodges, Mike
Get Carter 174
Morons from Outer Space 498
Prayer for the Dying 242

Hodgson, Johnathan
Johnathan Hodgson Showreel (British Animation) 707

Hodson, Christopher
The Marquise 313

Hoffman, Hermann
The Invisible Boy 497
It's a Dog's Life 373

Hoffman, Jerzy
Beautiful Stranger 90
Colonel Wolodyjowski 91
The Deluge 91
Leper 93
The Quack 94

Hoffman, John
The Inner Sanctum: Calling Dr. Death/ Strange Confession 523

Hoffman, Kurt
The Confessions of Felix Krull 68

Hoffman, Michael
One Fine Day 278
Promised Land (Drama) 435
Restoration 244

Hofmeyr, Gray
Yankee Zulu 288

Hofsiss, Jack
Cat on a Hot Tin Roof (1984) 311

Hogan, James
Arrest Bulldog Drummond 362
Bulldog Drummond Escapes 361
Bulldog Drummond's Bride 362
Bulldog Drummond's Peril 361
Bulldog Drummond's Secret Police 362

Hogan, James P.
Broken Mask 396
Capital Punishment 396
The Final Extra 398
The Mad Ghoul 525

Hogan, P.J.
Muriel's Wedding 206
My Best Friend's Wedding 277

Holcomb, Rod
Blind Justice 219
China Beach 416

Holden, Lansing C.
She (1935) 386

Holland, Agnieszka
Angry Harvest 96
Europa Europa 96
Fever 96
A Lonely Woman 96
Olivier Olivier 96
Provincial Actors 96
The Secret Garden (1993) 666
To Kill a Priest 96
Total Eclipse 96
Washington Square 96

Holland, John
A Night in Havana 614

Holland, Luke
Good Morning Mr. Hitler 768

Hollander, Eli
Deadly Drifter 532

Holleb, Alan
Candy Stripe Nurses 504

Holloway, Ron
Paradjanov: A Requiem 84

Holofcener, Nicole
Walking and Talking 286

Holt, Seth
The Nanny 176
Scream of Fear 528

Holubar, Allen
Heart of Humanity 153

Honda, Inoshiro
Dagora, the Space Monster 495
Ghidrah the 3-Headed Monster 496
Godzilla 5-Pack 496
Godzilla vs. Monster Zero 497
Godzilla vs. Mothra 497
Godzilla's Revenge 497
Godzilla, King of the Monsters 497
Half Human 522
King Kong vs. Godzilla 498
Mothra 498
Rodan 499
Terror of Mechagodzilla 501
War of the Gargantuas 501

Honda, Ishiro
Destroy All Monsters 505

Hook, Harry
Kitchen Toto 161
Lord of the Flies (Harry Hook) 236

Hooks, Kevin
Glory & Honor 229, 452
Passenger 57 241
Roots: The Gift 454
Strictly Business 283

Hooper, Tobe
Body Bags 517
Invaders from Mars (1986) 497
Lifeforce 161
Poltergeist 258, 527
Salem's Lot: The Movie 528
The Texas Chainsaw Massacre 530

Hoover, Mike
Solo 437

Hopkins, Anthony
August 181

Hopkins, Arthur
His Double Life 372

Hopkins, Billy
I Love You, I Love You Not 232

Hopkins, Stephen
The Ghost and the Darkness 229

Hopper, Dennis
Backtrack 218
Chasers 222
Colors 222
Easy Rider 429
Hot Spot 231
Out of the Blue 241

Hopper, E. Mason
Blonde for a Night 396
Getting Gertie's Garter 398
Square Shoulders 404

Hopper, Jerry
Pony Express 295

Horan, Don
Milton Hershey: The Chocolate King 795
United States Naval Academy: 150 Years in Annapolis 764

Horn, Andrew
Doomed Love 429

Hornbacher, Sara
Sara Hornbacher Early Works 488

Horne, James W.
The Bohemian Girl 264
Bonnie Scotland 264
College 409

Horner, Harry
Beware My Lovely 359
Red Planet Mars 499

Horner, Henry
New Faces 327

Horton, Peter
Amazon Women on the Moon 262
The Cure 224

Hossein, Robert
Double Agents 20
I Killed Rasputin 20

Hossman, Robert
Yellowneck 394

Hostettler, Joe
Paramount Comedy Theater: Volume 1-3 535

Houck Jr., Joy N.
Creature from Black Lake 518

Hough, John
Treasure Island (1972, Welles) 179

Houldey, Michael
Edith Piaf: I Regret Nothing 28

Houle, Lisa
Puss Bucket 509

Houseman, John
Clarence Darrow 311

Hovde, Ellen
Enormous Changes at the Last Minute 429

Hoven, Adrian
Mark of the Devil, Part II 525

How, C. Yun
Diary of the Big Man 126

Howard, David
The Crimson Romance 364
Daniel Boone 292
Park Avenue Logger 382
Howard, Leslie
The Gentle Sex 369
Pimpernel Smith 177
Spitfire 178
Howard, Ron
Apollo 13 218
Backdraft 218
Cocoon 266
Far and Away 227
Grand Theft Auto 229
Paper, The 241
Ransom 243
Willow 667
Howard, William K.
Back Door to Heaven 358
Evelyn Prentice 367
Fire over England 173
Johnny Come Lately 374
Little Odessa 236
Princess Comes Across 280
A Ship Comes In 404
White Gold 406
Hoyt, Harry O.
The Lost World (1925) 400
The Return of Boston Blackie 403
Hsiang Li, Han
Flower Drums of Fung Yang 120
Hsiao-hsien, Hou
Dust in the Wind 136
A Time to Live and a Time to Die 136
Hsin, Chin
Master with Cracked Fingers 134
Hsu, Dachin
Pale Blood 527
Hsu, Hsia
Beauty Investigator 125
Hu, King
Fate of Lee Khan 127
Swordsman 132
The Valiant Ones 133
Huang, George
Swimming with Sharks 283
Hubbard, Jim
Homosexual Desire in Minnesota 460
Memento Mori 487
A Valentine for Nelson & Two Marches 466, 489
Hubley, Emily
Blake Ball (Hubley Collection 1) 711
Delivery Man (Acidburn) 717
Enough (Best Fest 5th Annual) 706
Hubley Collection Vol. 1 711
Hubley, Faith
The Cosmic Eye (Hubley Studio) 711
Dream Tales: The Sacred Ways Collection 709
Enter Life (Hubley Collection 1) 711
Hubley Collection Vol. 1 711
Hubley Collection Vol. 2 711
Hubley Collection Vol. 3 711
Hubley Studio: Of Men and Demons 711
Hubley Studio: The Cosmic Eye 711
Hubley Studio: The Hole 711
Hubley Studio: Voyage to Next 711
Upside Down (Hubley Collection 1) 711
Who Am I? (Hubley Collection 1) 711
Hubley, John
Hubley Collection Vol. 2 711
Hubley Collection Vol. 3 711
Hubley Studio: Of Men and Demons 711
Hubley Studio: The Hole 711
Hubley Studio: Voyage to Next 711
Hubley, John & Faith
A Doonesbury Special 709
Everybody Rides the Carousel 709
Hubley, John/Faith
Adventures of An * (Hubley Studio) 711
Amazonia (Hubley Collection 2) 711
Cloudland (Hubley Collection 3) 711
Dig (Hubley Studio) 711
Eggs (Hubley Studio) 711
Harlem Wednesday (Hubley Studio) 711
The Hat (Hubley Studio) 711
The Hole (Hubley Studio) 711
Moonbird (Hubley Collection 3) 711
Of Men and Demons (Hubley Studio) 711
Of Stars & Men (Hubley Studio) 711
People, People, People (Hubley Collection 2) 711
Tall Time Tales (Hubley Collection 3) 711
Tender Game (Hubley Studio) 711
Time of the Angels (Hubley Collection 2) 711
Urbanissimo (Hubley Studio) 711
Voyage to Next (Hubley Studio) 711
W.O.W. Women of the World (Hubley Collection 2) 711
Windy Day (Hubley Collection 3) 711
Yes We Can (Hubley Collection 2) 711
Hudlin Brothers
Bebe's Kids 706
Hudlin, Reginald
Boomerang (Eddie Murphy) 443
The Great White Hype 230
House Party 444
Hudson, Hugh
Chariots of Fire 159
Lost Angels 236
Lumiere & Company 5, 336
Hue, David
Karate Wars 128
Huestis, Marc
Men in Love 463
Sex Is... ....465, 477
Hughes Brothers, The
Dead Presidents 224
Menace II Society 445
Hughes, Bronwen
Harriet the Spy 663
Hughes, Howard
Hell's Angels 371
Outlaw 295
Power 402
Hughes, John
The Breakfast Club 220
Planes, Trains and Automobiles 279
Pretty in Pink 279
Hughes, Kelly
Heart Attack Theater 845
La Cage aux Zombies 461
Hughes, Ken
The Atomic Man 494
Chitty Chitty Bang Bang 662
Cromwell 223
Long Haul 175
Sextette 282
The Trials of Oscar Wilde 179, 466
Hughes, Terry
Barnum (Crawford/Britain) 310
Monty Python Live at the Hollywood Bowl 199
Mrs. Santa Claus 665
Hughes-Freeland, Tessa
Playboy & Rhonda Goes to Hollywood 488
Hui, Ann
Song of the Exile 136
Zodiac Killers 133
Hui, Michael
The Contract (Hong Kong) 119
Teppanyaki 124
Humberstone, H. Bruce
Charlie Chan at the Opera 363
The Crooked Circle 266
The Desert Song 322
Goodbye Love 270
Hello, Frisco, Hello 324
I Wake Up Screaming 373
Iceland 272
Pin-Up Girl 279
Sun Valley Serenade 329
Ten Wanted Men 296
To the Shores of Tripoli 391
Wonder Man 287
Hume, Kenneth
Go Go Big Beat 620
Hung, Lam Chi
Escort Girls 120
Hung, Samo
Don't Give a Damn 126
Dragons Forever 134
Eastern Condors 127
Heart of the Dragon 134
The Iron-Fisted Monk 128
The Moon Warriors 130
Mr. Nice Guy 134
My Lucky Stars (Jackie Chan) 134
On the Run 122
Panty Hose Hero 130
Paper Marriage 123
Pedicab Driver 130
The Prodigal Son 131
Shanghai Express (Hong Kong) 131
Slickers vs. Killers 132
Sworn Brother 132
Wheels on Meals 135
Winners and Sinners 135
Hung, Tran Anh
Cyclo 145
The Scent of Green Papaya 6, 145
Hunsinger, Tom
Boyfriends 457
Hunt, Charles J.
Queen of the Chorus 403
Hunt, Peter
1776 319
Life on the Mississippi 309
On Her Majesty's Secret Service 169
Hunter, Max
The Bloody Pit of Horror 517
Hunter, Neil
Boyfriends 457
Hunter, T. Hayes
The Ghoul 522
Hunter, Tim
The Saint of Fort Washington 245
Huntington, Lawrence
Tower of Terror 530
Huraux, M.
Batouka: The First International Festival of Percussion 601
Hurley, James F.
The Psychic 509
Hurst, Brian Desmond
A Christmas Carol (1951/Sim) 172
Hungry Hill 174
The Lion Has Wings 180
Malta Story 176
River of Unrest (Ourselves Alone) 177
Hurst, Paul
Battling Bunyon 395
Midnight Message 401
Hurtado, Angel
Delta Solar and the Four Seasons, English Narration 548
Dominican Republic, Cradle of the Americas, English Narration 54
Francisco Oller 549
Guatemala, Land of Color 57
Honduras, A World into Itself 57
La Antigua-Guatemala: An American Monument 58
The Legend of El Dorado 58
Moire 553
Points of Convergence 783
Poleo and Poetic Figuration 555
The Pyramids of the Sun and the Moon 60
Reality and Hallucinations 555
Rhythms of Haiti 55
The Roar of the Gods 556
Soto, A New Vision of the Art 557
Torres-Garcia and the Universal Constructivism 557
The World of a Primitive Painter 558
Husain, Nasir
Zamaaneko Dikanahai 148
Huse, Michael F.
A Rat's Tale 665
Huseyin, Metin
Henry Fielding's Tom Jones 192
Hussein, Waris
Arch of Triumph (Hopkins) 188
Fall from Grace 160
Quackser Fortune Has a Cousin in the Bronx 280
The Shell Seekers 246
Summer House 185
Huston, Anjelica
Bastard Out of Carolina 427
Huston, Danny
Becoming Colette 427
Mr. North 239
Huston, John
Across the Pacific 348
The African Queen 348
The African Queen Commemorative Edition 348
Annie 348
The Asphalt Jungle, ...348
Beat the Devil 348
The Bible 348
Casino Royale 348
The Dead 348
Fat City (Huston) 348
Heaven Knows, Mr Allison 348
In This Our Life 348
Independence 349
John Huston: The Man, The Movies, The Maverick 349
Juarez 349
Key Largo 349
Let There Be Light 349
The Life and Times of Judge Roy Bean 349
List of Adrian Messenger 349
The Mackintosh Man 349
The Maltese Falcon 349
The Man Who Would Be King 349
Misfits 349
Moby Dick (1956) 349
Moulin Rouge (Huston) 349
Night of the Iguana 349
Phobia 349
Red Badge of Courage 349
Reflections in a Golden Eye 349
Treasure of the Sierra Madre 349
Under the Volcano 349
The Unforgiven (1960) 349
Victory (Escape to Victory) 349
Wise Blood 349
Huszarik, Zoltan
Sindbad 102
Hutchison, Charles
Lightning Hutch 400
Huth, Harold
The Thoroughbred 390
Hutton, Brian G.
Kelly's Heroes 234
Hutton, Larry
City Ninja 126
Hutton, Robert
Slime People 529
Huxley, Julian
Private Life of the Gannets (Documentary Master) 471
Huyck, Willard
French Postcards 269
Hwa, Po-Fa
Angel Force 124
Hyams, Nessa
Leader of the Band 274
Hyams, Peter
Hanover Street 230
Outland 499
The Relic 528
Running Scared 245
Hylkema, Hans
Last Date: Eric Dolphy 612
Hytner, Nicholas
The Crucible (1996) 311
The Madness of King George 162
Iasos
Crystal Vista 848

Ibanez, Juan
Dance of Death 519
The Snake People (Isle of the Snake People) 529
Torture Zone 530
Ichaso, Leon
Bitter Sugar 49
El Super 50
Sugar Hill 248
Ichikawa, Kon
An Actor's Revenge 141
Being Two Isn't Easy 141
The Burmese Harp 141
Enjo 141
Fires on the Plain 141
Makioka Sisters 141
Odd Obsession 141
Tokyo Olympiad 141
Ichiyo, Higuchi
Animated Classics of Japanese Literature: Wandering Days/Growing 721
Idle, Eric
Monty Python and the Quest for the Holy Grail 869
The Rutles: All You Need Is Cash 199
Iglesia, Eloy de la
Colegas 44, 458
El Diputado 44, 458
El Sacerdote (The Priest) 44, 458
Los Placeres Ocultos 45, 462
Iimura, Takahiko
Takahiko Iimura: Concept Tapes (1975-87) 489
Takahiko Iimura: John Cage Performs James Joyce 489
MA: Space/Time-In the Garden of Ryoan-ji 486
Ikehiro, Kazuo
Zatoichi: Masseur Ichi and a Chest of Gold 140
Zatoichi: Zatoichi's Flashing Sword 140
Ilic, Dragan
Fifth, Park & Madison 471
Imamura, Shohei
The Ballad of Narayama 141
Black Rain 141
Eijanaika 141
Vengeance Is Mine 141
Imhoof, Markus
The Boat Is Full 30
Inagaki, Hiroshi
Chushingura (The Loyal 47 Retainers) 137
Rikisha-Man 139
Samurai Banners 139
Samurai I 139
Samurai II 139
Samurai III 139
Ince, Thomas H.
Civilization (a.k.a. He Who Returned) 396
The Coward (Silent) 397
D'Artagnan 397
Infascelli, Fiorella
Zuppa di Pesce (Fish Soup) 35
Ingraham, Lloyd
American Aristocracy 395
Ingram, Rex
Conquering Power 397
The Four Horsemen of the Apocalypse (1921) 398
Inouye, Akira
The Blind Swordsman's Revenge 137
Intrator, Jerald
Satan in High Heels 509
Striporama 511
Iosseliani, Otar
Chasing Butterflies 2
Iovenko, Chris
Lydia Lunch: Malicious Intent 433
Ireland, Dan
The Whole Wide World 252
Ireland, O'Dale
High School Caesar 506
Iribe, Paul
Night Club 401
Irvin, John
City of Industry 222
Crazy Horse 223
The Dogs of War 160
A Month by the Lake 238
Robin Hood: The Movie 244
Turtle Diary 164
Widow's Peak 202
Irving, George
Raffles, The Amateur Racksman (USA/1917) 403
Irving, Judy
Dark Circle 471
Irving, Richard
Jesse Owens Story 452
Ishii, Sogo
Angel Dust 137
Ishii, Teruo
Blind Woman's Curse 137
Isitan, Isaac
By Any Means Necessary 451
Israel, Ira
Hungreed (CineBLAST 1) 483
Israel, Neal
Americathon 262
Tunnel Vision 536
Itagaki, Keisuke
Grappler Baki 731
Itami, Juzo
The Funeral (Itami) 140
Minbo—Or the Gentle Art of Japanese Extortion 140
Tampopo 140
A Taxing Woman 140
A Taxing Woman's Return 141
Ivanov Vano
Magic Horse 82, 713
Ivens, Joris
Bridge (Rare Dutch & Belgian) 31, 488
Classic Documentaries: People and Places 470
Classic Documentaries: The Power and the Land 470
New Earth (Rare Dutch & Belgian) 31, 488
Power and the Land 476
Power and the Land: Four Documentary Portraits of the Great Depression 476
Rain (Avant Garde & Experimental Films) 488
Rain (Rare Dutch and Belgian) 31, 488
Spanish Earth 478
Ives, Stephen
The West 299
Ivory, James
Autobiography of a Princess 258
The Bostonians 258
The Europeans 259
The Householder 259
Howards End 259
Jefferson in Paris 259
Lumiere & Company 5, 336
Maurice 259
Mr. and Mrs. Bridge 259
Noon Wine 259
Quartet 259
Remains of the Day 259
Room with a View 259
Roseland 259
Savages 259
Slaves of New York 259
Surviving Picasso 259
Iwerks, Ub
Cartoons That Time Forgot Vol. 1: All Singing! All Dancing! 681
Cartoons That Time Forgot Vol. 2: Down & Out with Flip the Frog 681
Cartoons That Time Forgot Vol. 3: Things That Go Bump in the Night 681
Cartoons That Time Forgot Vol. 4: Willie Whopper's Fantastic Adventures 681
Cartoons That Time Forgot Vol. 5: Free-Form Fairytales 681
Flip the Frog Vol. 1 683
Flip the Frog Vol. 2 684
Flip the Frog Vol. 3 684
Flip the Frog Vol. 4 684
Flip the Frog Vol. 5 684
Ub Iwerks Comicolor Classics 717
Ub Iwerks' Famous Fairytales 689
Jackson, David S.
Detonator 225
Jackson, George
House Party 2: The Pajama Jam 444
Jackson, Mick
Chattahoochee 222
Clean Slate 266
Threads 501
Jackson, Peter
Dead Alive 208
Forgotten Silver 208
The Frighteners 228
Heavenly Creatures 208
Meet the Feebles 208, 713
Jacobovici, Simcha
Deadly Currents 110
Jacobs, Alan
Nina Takes a Lover 240
Jacobs, Evan
Safety in Numbers 436
The Toll Collector 438
Walking Between the Raindrops 439
Jacobs, Scott
Las Vegas Tapes (America in Black & White) 468
Pugs 'N Pols (America in Black and White) 468
Real Realness of Higher Highness (America in Black & White) 468
The Santa Tapes 477
Jacoby, George
Tales from Vienna Woods 330
Jacopetti, Gualtiero
Mondo Cane 508
Mondo Cane 2 508
Jacque, Christian
Fanfan la Tulipe 20
Lady Hamilton 375
Nana 22
The Pearls of the Crown 23
Jacquot, Benoit
Jacques Lacan's Psychoanalysis Part One 3, 785
A Single Girl 6
Jaeckin, Just
Emmanuelle 3
Story of O 511
Jaglom, Henry
Always (Jaglom) 217
Babyfever 218
Eating 429
Last Summer in the Hamptons 235
New Year's Day...Time to Move On 239
Peter Bogdanovich and Henry Jaglom 337
Someone to Love 247
Tracks 250
Venice/Venice 251
Jakubowska, Wanda
The Last Stage 93
James, Pedr
Martin Chuzzlewit 194
James, Steve
Hoop Dreams 473
Prefontaine 435
Jameson, Jerry
The Bat People 516
Jancso, Miklos
Hungarian Rhapsody 102
The Red and the White 102
Round Up 102
Jankel, Annabel
D.O.A. 224
Jansen, Gail
Lasting Impressions 551
Jarcho, B./Manning M.
A Very Very Long Time Ago (Int. Animation 4) 712
Jarman, Derek
The Angelic Conversation 167
Aria 158, 577
Blue 167
Caravaggio 167
Edward II 167
The Garden 167
Jubilee 167
Last of England 168
Sebastiane 168
War Requiem 168
Wittgenstein 168
Jarmusch, Jim
Dead Man 442
Down by Law 442
Mystery Train 442
Night on Earth 442
Stranger Than Paradise 442
Jarrold, Julian
Painted Lady 195
Jarrott, Richard
Anne of the Thousand Days 171
Jarvik, Laurence
Who Shall Live and Who Shall Die? 777
Jarvis, Peter
Incas Remembered 58
Jasny, Vojtech
All My Good Countrymen 99
Cassandra Cat (When the Cat Comes) 99
The Great Land of Small 663
Jason, Leigh
Lady for a Night 375
Mad Miss Manton 275
Jaubert, Alain
Gustave Caillebotte or the Adventures of the Gaze 549
Jean, Mark
Homecoming (Bancroft) 231
Jean, Vadim
Leon the Pig Farmer 184
Jefferson, Roland S.
Perfume 242
Jeles, Andras
The Annunciation 101
The Little Valentino 102
Jen-Tai, Donny Yu
Shogun and Little Kitchen 132
Jenkins, Ken
Illumination 92, 485
Jenkins, Michael
Sweet Talker 207
Jennings, Humphrey
Diary for Timothy (Wartime Moments) 479
Family Portrait (Festival of Britain) 471
Fires Were Started (Wartime Homefront) 479
Listen to Britain 474, 769
Listen to Britain (Wartime Moments) 479
London Can Take It (Wartime Homefront) 479
The True Story of Lili Marlene 479
Jerrett, Shereen
Kid Nerd 474
Jessner, Leopold
Backstairs 68
Jessua, Alain
Killing Game 21
Life Upside Down 21
Jeunet, Jean-Marie
Delicatessen 17
Jeunet, Jean-Pierre
Alien Resurrection 217
The City of Lost Children 2
Jewison, Norman
40 Pounds of Trouble 356
Agnes of God 310
And Justice for All 262
Cincinnati Kid 363
Fiddler on the Roof 322
In the Heat of the Night 373
Jesus Christ Superstar 325
Moonstruck 276
Only You 278
Other People's Money 241
Picture Windows 242
Send Me No Flowers 281
Soldier's Story 301
Thomas Crown Affair 390
The Thrill of It All! 284
Jhally, Sut
Dreamworlds: Desire/Sex/Power in Rock Video 785

Jianxin, Huang
The Wooden Man's Bride 118
Jimenez, Neal
The Waterdance 251
Jimenez-Leal, Orlando
8-A Ochoa 49
El Super 50
Jin, Wang
Women Flowers 124
Jing, Wong
Casino Tycoon II (Part A) 125
Flying Dagger 120
God of Gamblers 128
God of Gamblers II 128
Holy Weapon 121
Kung Fu [Cult] Master 129
Last Hero in China 129
The New Legend of Shaolin 122
Royal Tramp 131
Royal Tramp II 131
Jiras, Robert
I Am the Cheese 431
Jiro, Akagawa
Animated Classics of Japanese Literature: Incident in the Bedroom 720
Joannon, Leo
Utopia 286
Joanou, Phil
Heaven's Prisoners 230
State of Grace 248
U2: Rattle and Hum 623
Jodorowsky, Alejandro
Santa Sangre 52
Joff, Alex
Bomb for a Dictator 19
Joffe, Arthur
Alberto Express 16
Joffe, Mark
Cosi 205
The Efficiency Expert 205
Joffe, Roland
Fat Man and Little Boy 227
Killing Fields 234
The Mission 238
Johansen, Ernst
You Are Not Alone 77, 467
Johnson, Alan
To Be or Not to Be (Brooks) 285
Johnson, Cindy Lou
Trusting Beatrice 250
Johnson, David
Cut-Out Animation 708
Drop Squad 226
Johnson, Jack
Maskmaker 563
Johnson, Karen
Orange (Short Personal Films) 437
Johnson, Lamont
The Broken Chain 221
Crisis at Central High 223
Execution of Private Slovik 226
Paul's Case 301
Johnson, Martin
Baboona 469, 813
Simba 477
Johnson, Nunnally
Man in the Gray Flannel Suit 378
The Three Faces of Eve 390
Johnson, Osa
Baboona 469, 813
Simba 477
Johnson, Patrick Read
Angus 262
Johnson, Raymond K.
The Reckless Way 384
Johnson, Sherann
Middle Grays (Best Fest 90) 706
Johnson, W. Ray
Riding for Life 403
Johnston, Aaron Kim
For the Moment 210
The Last Winter 211
Johnston, Andrew
Churchill and the Cabinet War Rooms 169
Johnston, Joe
Jumanji (Feature) 664
Johnstone, Jyll
Martha & Ethel 475
Jonas, Joan
Joan Jonas: Vertical Roll 486
Jonasson, Oskar
Remote Control 76
Jones, Buck
Law for Tombstone 293
Jones, Chuck
Betty Boop's Crazy Inventions (Weird Cartoons 2) 717
The Cricket in Times Square 708
Dr. Seuss: Horton Hears a Who 683
Dr. Seuss: How the Grinch Stole Christmas 683
Golden Age of Looney Tunes V.5 685
Golden Age of Warner Brothers Cartoons 684
Inki and the Mynah Bird (Weird Cartoons 2) 717
Mowgli's Brothers 686
Private S.N.A.F.U. 687
Rikki-Tikki-Tavi 687
Superior Duck 687
Tom & Jerry: The Art of Tom & Jerry V.3 689
The White Seal 690
Jones, David
84 Charing Cross Road 158
Christmas Wife 222
Jacknife 233
Look Back in Anger—Kenneth Branagh 312
The Trial (1993) 164
Jones, F. Richard
Bulldog Drummond (Colman) 361
The Extra Girl 398
The Gaucho 398
Mickey 401
Jones, Harmon
As Young As You Feel 358
Pride of St. Louis 383
Jones, James Cellan
Harnessing Peacocks 161
The Vacillations of Poppy Carew 164
Jones, L.Q.
Boy and His Dog 495
Jones, Peter
Stuff Stephanie in the Incinerator 511
Jones, Richard
Aliens, Dragons, Monsters & Me 494
Yankee Doodle in Berlin 407
Jones, Terry
Life of Brian 198
Monty Python's Meaning of Life 199
Personal Services 199
Jones, William
Finished 459
Massillon 462
Jordan, Glenn
Barbarians at the Gate 263
Displaced Person 300
Les Miserables (1978/Anthony Perkins) 235
O Pioneers! 240
Picture of Dorian Gray (1974/GB) 235
Sarah, Plain and Tall (1991) 666
A Streetcar Named Desire (1995) 315
Jordan, Jeanne
Troublesome Creek: A Midwestern 479
Jordan, Larry
H.D. Trilogy 718
Live Short Films by Larry Jordan 718
Rime of the Ancient Mariner (Welles) 718
The Sacred Art of Tibet/ The Visible Compendium 718
Short Animations by Larry Jordan 718
Sophie's Place 718
Jordan, Neil
The Crying Game 202
High Spirits 183
Interview with the Vampire 233
Michael Collins 202
Mona Lisa 162
We're No Angels (1989) 286
Jorfald, Knut W.
The Littlest Viking 76
Joritz, Cathy
Negative Man (Spike/Mike 2) 716
Joslin, Tom
Silverlake Life: The View from Here 465
Jost, Jon
All the Vermeers in New York 441
Angel City 441
Bell Diamond 441
Chameleon 441
Jon Jost's Frameup 441
Last Chants for a Slow Dance 441
Plain Talk and Common Sense 441
Rembrandt Laughing 441
Slow Moves 441
Speaking Directly 441
Stagefright 441
Sure Fire 441
Jourdan, Pierre
Phedre 23
Jrvilaturi, Ilkka
City Unplugged 86
Judge, Mike
Beavis and Butthead in Peace & Love & Understanding 716
Office Space (Animation C.4) 706
Julian, Rupert
Merry-Go-Round 348
The Phantom of the Opera (1925/Chaney) 402
Walking Back 406
Julien, Isaac
Looking for Langston 453
Junli, Zheng
Crows and Sparrows 117
Juran, Nathan
20 Million Miles to Earth 494
The 7th Voyage of Sinbad 356
The Black Castle 517
Brain from Planet Arous 495
The Deadly Mantis 495
First Men in the Moon 496
H.G. Wells' First Men in the Moon 497
It Came from Beneath the Sea/ 20 Million Miles to Earth 498
Jack the Giant Killer 664
Law and Order 293
Jurgenson, Jens
New York Videos 487
Jutra, Claude
Mon Oncle Antoine 213
Jutzi, Piel
Mother Krausen's Journey into Happiness 70
Ka-Chun, Cheung
Mainland Dundee 122
Ka-Wing, Lau
Those Merry Souls 124
Kabore, Gaston
Lumiere & Company 5, 336
Wend Kuuni (God's Gift) 150
Kachyna, Karel
The Cow 99
The Last Butterfly 100
Kaczender, George
Chanel Solitaire 2
Kadar, Jan
Adrift 101
Blue Hotel 101
Freedom Road 101, 452
The Shop on Main Street 101
Kadokawa, Haruki
The Blade of Kamui 723
Kafien, Pierre
The a la menthe (Award Winning French Shorts) 2
Kageyama, S.
Zeguy, Parts 1 & 2 753
Kahn, Richard C.
Bronze Buckaroo 448
Son of Ingagi 448
Two-Gun Man from Harlem 449
Kai-Keung, Lai
Love, Guns, and Glass 129
Kaige, Chen
Farewell My Concubine 117
Life on a String 117
Yellow Earth 118
Kaiserman, Connie
My Little Girl 239
Kalatozov, Mikhail
The Cranes Are Flying 80
I Am Cuba 81
The Red Tent 83
Turksib/Salt for Svanetia 86
Kalin, Tom
Swoon 466
Kalliher, Kevin
Home, Honey, I'm High (Spike/Mike Sick 2) 716
Kalvert, Scott
The Basketball Diaries 219
Kamanetsky, Mikhail
Wolf and Calf (Masters of Russian Animation 7) 83, 713
Kambanellis
Cannon and Nightingale 105
Kampmann, Steven
Stealing Home 248
Kan, Yeung
The Beautiful Swordswoman 125
Kan-Ping, Yu
Outcasts 136, 464
Kane, Joseph
Dakota 292
Flame of the Barbary Coast 368
Hoodlum Empire 372
Jubilee Trail 293
The Maverick Queen 294
Kanefsky, Rolfe
My Family Treasure 665
Kaneko, Shusuke
Summer Vacation: 1999 139
Kanev, Boyo
A Crushed World (Animation C.2) 705
Kanevski, Vitaly
Freeze, Die, Come to Life 81
Kanew, Jeff
Tough Guys 250
Kang, Jacky
The Gingko Bed 136
Kanievska, Marek
Less Than Zero 235
Kanin, Garson
Bachelor Mother 262
Next Time I Marry 278
Tom, Dick and Harry 285
Kao, Phillip
Angel's Mission 125
Kaplan, Ed
Primal Secrets 243
Kaplan, Jonathan
The Accused 216
Immediate Family 232
In Cold Blood (1996) 232
Over the Edge 241
Picture Windows 242
Truck Turner 533
Kaplan, Mindy
Devotion (Kaplan) 458
Kaplan, Nelly
Nea 5
Kaplan, Richard
Assignment: Rescue 426
Eleanor Roosevelt Story 794
The Exiles 471
Kapoor, Raj
Aashiq 146
Awara 146
Bobby 146
Shree 420 148
Kar-Wai, Wong
As Tears Go By 118
Ashes of Time 118

Chungking Express 119
Days of Being Wild 119
Fallen Angels 120
Happy Together 121, 460
Karaev, Alexei
Welcome (Animation C.3) 705
Karasik, Yuri
Seagull 83
Karavayev, Valentine
Last Hunt (Masters of Russian Animation 2) 83, 713
Kardos, Leslie
Small Town Girl 329
Karel, Russ
Almonds and Raisins: A History of the Yiddish Cinema 111
Karim-Masihi, Varuzh
The Last Act 106
Karlson, Phil
Charlie Chan: The Shanghai Cobra 363
Kansas City Confidential 374
Ladies of the Chorus 325
Tight Spot 391
Walking Tall: The Trilogy 251
Karmann, San
Omnibus (Best Fest 5th Annual) 706
Karn, Bill
Ma Barker's Killer Brood 377
Kartemquin Films
Chicago Maternity Center Story 470
Golub 472
Hum 255 (Kartemquin Films #3) 474
Inquiring Nuns (Kartemquin Films) 474
Last Pullman Car 474
Now We Live on Clifton (Kartemquin 2) 474
Parents (Kartemquin Films #2) 474
Taylor Chain I and II 478
Trick Bag (Kartemquin Films #3) 474
What the Fuck Are the Red Squares (Kartemquin 3) 474
Winnie Wright, Age 11 (Kartemquin Films 2) 474
Kasakov, Velislav
Cuckoo (Animation C.1) 705
Kasdan, Jake
Zero Effect 288
Kasdan, Lawrence
The Accidental Tourist 216
The Big Chill 219
Body Heat 220
French Kiss 269
Grand Canyon 229
Silverado 296
Wyatt Earp 298
Kass, Sam Henry
The Search for One-Eye Jimmy 436
Kassovitz, Mathieu
Cafe au Lait 16
Hate (La Haine) 3
Kast, Pierre
Girl in His Pocket 496
Kastner, Daphna
French Exit 228
Kato, Nancy
Visions from the Amazon (Spike/Mike 2) 716
Katselas, Milton
Butterflies Are Free 362
Report to the Commissioner 244
Katz, Joel
Dear Carry 429
Katzin, Lee
The Bastard: Part I of the Kent Family Chronicles 414
Le Mans 235
Kaufman, George S.
The Senator Was Indiscreet 281
Kaufman, Jimmy
Whiskers 667
Kaufman, Lloyd
The Battle of Love's Return 503
Sgt. Kabukiman, N.Y.P.D. 510
Troma's War (Director's Cut) 512
Tromeo & Juliet 512
Kaufman, Philip
Great Northfield Minnesota Raid 293
Henry & June 230
Invasion of the Body Snatchers (1978) 497
The Right Stuff 244
Rising Sun 244
Unbearable Lightness of Being 251
White Dawn 252
Kaurismaki, Aki
Ariel 79
La Vie de Boheme 79
Leningrad Cowboys Go America 79
The Match Factory Girl 79
Kaurismaki, Mika
Amazon 79
Tigrero: A Film That Was Never Made 79, 478
Zombie and the Ghost Train 79
Kautner, Erich
Ludwig II 69
Kautner, Helmut
Captain from Koepenick 68
Clothes Make the Man 68
Girl from Flanders 69
Romance in a Minor Key 70
Under the Bridge 71
Kavun, Olag
Lessons at the End of Spring 82, 462
Kawalerowicz, Jerzy
Austeria 90
Death of the President 91
Mother Joan of the Angels 93
Night Train 93
Pharaoh 93
Kay, Chin Man
Sex and Zen II, Parts A & B 123
Kay, Gilbert L.
White Commanche 298
Kay, Stephen
The Last Time I Committed Suicide 235, 305
Kazan, Elia
America America 357
The Arrangement 358
Baby Doll 358
East of Eden 367
Elia Kazan: A Director's Journey 333
Face in the Crowd 367
Gentleman's Agreement 369
Last Tycoon 235
On the Waterfront 381
Panic in the Streets 382
Pinky 382
Sea of Grass 296
Splendor in the Grass 387
A Streetcar Named Desire: Director's Cut (1951) 315
A Tree Grows in Brooklyn 392
The Visitors 251
Kazan, Nicholas
Dream Lover 225
Keach, James
The Stars Fell on Henrietta 248
Keane, Colleen
River That Harms 806
Keating, David
Summer Fling 283
Keaton, Buster
Battling Butler 408
Buster Keaton (1917-22) 408
Buster Keaton Talkies, Vol. 1 408
Buster Keaton Talkies, Vol. 2 408
Buster Keaton Talkies, Vol. 3 408
Buster Keaton Talkies, Vol. 6 408
Buster Keaton Talkies, Vol. 7 408
The Cameraman /Spite Marriage 409
The General 409
Go West (1925) 409
Our Hospitality/Sherlock Jr. 409
Three Ages 409
Keaton, Diane
The Girl with the Crazy Brother 229
Heaven 472
Unstrung Heroes 285
Wild Flower 439
Keays, Vernon
Whirlwind Raiders 298
Keays-Byrne, Hugh
Resistance 206
Keeve, Douglas
Unzipped 479
Kehoe, Mark
Destroy All Blondes/The Naked Hipstress/ Sick Sick Sister 429
Revenge of the Amazons/Metal Madam 436
Keighley, William
Bride Came C.O.D. 264
Brother Rat 265
Bullets or Ballots 362
Each Dawn I Die 367
The Fighting 69th 368
George Washington Slept Here 269
The Green Pastures 371
Ladies They Talk About 375
The Man Who Came to Dinner 275
The Master of Ballantrae 378
The Prince and the Pauper (1937) 309
Street with No Name 388
Keith, Harvey
Mondo New York 434
Keller, Daniel
Abe Ajay 544
Cannabis Rising 469
Lovejoy's Nuclear War 805
Keller, Frederick King
The Eyes of Amaryllis 227
Vamping 251
Keller, H. Len
IFE (Dyke Drama) 458
Keller, Harry
The Brass Bottle 361
The Major and the Minor 377
Tammy and the Doctor 389
Kelljan, Bob
Scream, Blacula, Scream 533
Kellogg, Ray
Elvira's Midnight Madness: Giant Gila Monster 521
Killer Shrews 524
Kelly, Albert
Campus Nights 396
Kelly, Gene
Cheyenne Social Club 291
Hello, Dolly! 324
Invitation to the Dance 572
It's Always Fair Weather 325
Singin' in the Rain 329
That's Entertainment II 330
The Tunnel of Love 285
Kelly, Rory
Sleep with Me 282
Kemp, Jack
Miracle in Harlem 448
Kenji, Misumi
Lone Wolf and Cub—Baby Cart at the River Styx 138
Lone Wolf and Cub—Baby Cart in Peril 138
Lone Wolf and Cub—Baby Cart in the Land of Demons 138
Lone Wolf and Cub—Baby Cart to Hades 138
Lone Wolf and Cub—Sword of Vengeance 138
The Razor—Sword of Justice 138
Kenji, Tsuruta
Spirit of Wonder: Miss China's Ring 747
Kennedy, Burt
The Good Guys and the Bad Guys 292
Hannie Caulder 293
Return of the Seven 295
Support Your Local Gunfighter 296
Train Robbers 250
The Trouble with Spies 285
The War Wagon 297
Young Billy Young 394
Kent, Billy
Egg Salad (CineBLAST!) 428
Kentis, Chris
Grind 431
Kenton, Eric
Fight for the Title 368
Kenton, Erle C.
Bare Knees 395
The Ghost of Frankenstein 522
The Girl in the Pullman 399
House of Dracula 523
House of Frankenstein 523
Island of Lost Souls 524
Melody for Three 378
Pardon My Sarong—Abbott and Costello 279
Remedy for Riches 384
They Meet Again 390
Kerbosch, Roeland
For a Lost Soldier 31, 459
Kern, James V.
Never Say Goodbye 278
Second Woman 386
Kern, Peter
Street Kid 65
Kern, Richard
Lydia Lunch: Malicious Intent 433
Kerrigan, Lodge
Clean, Shaven 428
Kershner, Irvin
The Hoodlum Priest 372
Never Say Never Again 169
The Return of a Man Called Horse 295
Up the Sandbox 286
Keshishian, Alek
Madonna: Truth or Dare 475, 621
Kessler, Bruce
Gay Deceivers 459
Keung, Lai Kay
Sex and Zen III 123
Keung, Lau Fu
Sweet Peach 123
Keung, Lau Wai
Young and Dangerous II, Parts A & B 133
Young and Dangerous III 133
Kezdi-Kovacs, Zsolt
The Nice Neighbor 102
Khan, Mehboob
Amar 146
Andaz (A Matter of Style) (Beau Monde) 146
Mother India (Bharat Mata) 148
Khitruk, Fyodor
Film Film Film (Masters of Russian Animation 1) 82, 713
Khleifi, George
You, Me, Jerusalem 108
Khosla, Raj
Who Was She? 148
Khovorova, Nadezhda
Are You Going to the Ball? (Glasnost Film F V.12) 81
Kiarostami, Abbas
Life and Nothing More 106
Lumiere & Company 5, 336
Where Is the Friend's Home? 107
Kidawa, Janusz
Most Eligible Bachelor 93
Kidron, Beeban
Antonia and Jane 181
Oranges Are Not the Only Fruit 195, 463
Shades of Fear 163
Swept from the Sea 164
To Wong Foo, Thanks for Everything! Julie Newmar 285, 466
Used People 286
Kieslowski, Krzysztof
Blind Chance 95
Blue 95
Camera Buff (Amator) 95
The Double Life of Veronique 95
No End (Without End) 96
Red 96
Subsidiaries (Personel) 96
White 96
Kihachi, Okamoto
Samurai Assassin 139
Kijowski, Janusz
Kung-Fu 95
Masquerade 95

Kikione, Gerard
Buried Alive 517
Edge of Sanity 505
Kikuchi, Hideyuki
Demon City Shinjuku 726
Kim, Kidduck
Yongary Monster from the Deep 136
Kim-Ming, Jamie Luk
Hello! Who Is It? 121
Kimm, Barry
The Measurements of Oxford (Best Fest 90) 706
Kimmel, Bruce
First Nudie Musical 506
Kimmins, Anthony
Bonnie Prince Charlie 171
Mine Own Executioner 176
Kin, Lo
Heartbeat 100 121
Spider Woman 132
Kindhem, Gorham
Hungers of the Soul: Be Gardiner, Stone Carver 550
Kiner, Darren
Bob the Frog in 'Burp' (Best Fest 5th Annual) 706
King Jr., Woodie
Death of a Prophet 451
King, Allan Winton
Silence of the North 246
King, Allen
Termini Station 212
King, Burton
Man from Beyond 401
King, George
Crimes at the Dark House 519
Crimes of Stephen Hawke 172
The Demon Barber of Fleet Street 520
The Face at the Window 521
Ticket of Leave Man 511
Tomorrow We Live 179
King, Henry
12 O'Clock High 356
Alexander's Ragtime Band 319
Beloved Infidel 359
The Black Swan 360
Bravados 291
Captain from Castile 362
David and Bathsheba 355
The Gunfighter 293
Hell Harbor 371
In Old Chicago 373
Lloyd's of London 175
Love Is a Many Splendored Thing 377
Marie Galante 378
Romola 403
She Goes to War 403
Snows of Kilimanjaro 387
Song of Bernadette 356
Stanley and Livingstone 388
Tol'able David 405
The White Sister 406
Wilson 393
A Yank in the RAF 394
King, Lisa
Odd Gals Out 463
King, Louis
Bulldog Drummond Comes Back 361
Bulldog Drummond in Africa 362
Bulldog Drummond's Revenge 361
Drifting Souls 366
King, Rick
Forced March 228
Hard Choices 230
Hot Shot (1986 Film) 231
King, Zalman
Delta of Venus 505
King-Sang, Edward Tang
Red Zone 131
Kinoshita, Keisuke
Narayama Bushi-ko 138
Kinsella, Stephen
March in April 462
Kinugasa, Teinosuke
Gate of Hell 137
A Page of Madness 138
Kirchheimer, Manfred
Stations of the Elevated 437
We Were So Beloved 777
Kirkland, David
Tomboy 405
Kirkwood, Ray
The Shadow of Silk Lennox 386
Kirsanov, Dimitri
Menilmontant 22, 487
Kirschner, Klaus
Mozart: A Childhood Chronicle 64
Kishon, Ephaim
Sallah 108
Kitchell, Mark
Berkeley in the Sixties 469
Kiwerski, Krzysztof
The Kingdom of Green Glade 92
Klane, Robert
Thank God It's Friday 511
Klapisch, Cedric
Lumiere & Company 5, 336
When the Cat's Away 7
Kleifi, Michel
Wedding in Galilee 108
Klein, Dusan
Summons for the Queen 100
Klein, Jim
Seeing Red 477
Kleiser, Randall
The Boy in the Plastic Bubble 220
Grease 323
It's My Party 233
Klick, Roland
Let It Rock 235
Klimov, Elem
Come and See 80
Klimovsky, Leon
Werewolf vs. the Vampire Woman 531
Kline, Herbert
The Fighter 368
The Forgotten Village 57, 369
Klingler, Werner
Titanic (1943/Germany) 71
Klotzel, Andre
Savage Capitalism 54
Kloves, Steven
Fabulous Baker Boys 227
Flesh and Bone 228
Klug, Rob
Eric Bogosian: Confessions of a Porn Star 567
Kluge, Alexander
Germany in Autumn 66
Klushantsev, Pavel
Planeta Burg 83, 499
Knight, Arthur
Wild, Wild World of Jayne Mansfield 512
Knight, William
My Four Years in Germany 401
Knowles, Bernard
The Magic Bow 175
Norman Conquest 176
Ko, Blackie
Curry and Pepper 126
Ko, Clifton
Happy Ghost IV 120
Ko, Clifton C.S.
City Squeeze 119
Daddy, Father, and Pa Pa 119
Ko, Danny
Bloody Friday 125
Ko, Philip
Angel on Fire 125
The Cyprus Tigers 126
Kickfighter 129
Killer's Romance 129
Ko, Phillip
Guardian Angel 128
Ko, Phillip
Interpol Connection 128
Ko, Phillip
Power Connection 131
Ultracop 2000 124
Kobayashi, Masaki
Harikiri 137
Human Condition 137
Kwaidan 138
Samurai Rebellion 139
Kobler, Erich
Snow White (Kobler/Germany) 666
Koch, Howard W.
Frankenstein 1970 522
Koch, Philip
Pink Nights 435
Koepp, David
The Trigger Effect 250
Koff, David
Black Man's Land Trilogy, Vol. 1, White Man's Country 151
Black Man's Land Trilogy, Vol. 2, Mau Mau 151
Black Man's Land Trilogy, Vol. 3, Kenyatta 152
Blacks Britannica 469
Occupied Palestine 475
Koglin, Robert
First in the Philippines: A Film History of the Second Oregon Volunteer Regiment 146
Kohn, Yariv
Harry Weinberg's Notebook 460
Kokkinos, Ana
Only the Brave 206, 463
Kollek, Amos
Double Edge 225
Forever Lulu 228
Whore 2 512
Koller, Xavier
Journey of Hope 30
Squanto: A Warrior's Tale 694
Koltai, Robert
We Never Die 103
Konchalovsky, Andrei
Duet for One 84
Inner Circle 84
Lumiere & Company 5, 336
Odyssey, The 301, 785
Runaway Train 84
Shy People 84
Siberiade 84
Kondratiuk, Andrzej
Big-Bang 90
Kong, Don
Ninja Empire 130
Koninck, Atelier
The Brothers Quay Vol. 1 707
The Brothers Quay Vol. 2 707
Koopman, Maarten
The Bedroom (Int. Animation 4) 712
Koplin, Raimund
Fast Buck 63
Kopp, B.
Mr. Gloom (Outrageous 2) 714
Observational Hazard (Outrageous 2) 714
Kopple, Barbara
American Dream 468
Beyond JFK: The Question of Conspiracy 797
Harlan County U.S.A. 472
Korchevsky, Vadim
Liberated Don Quixote (Masters of Russian Animation 2) 82, 713
Korda, Alexander
Divorce of Lady X 182
Ideal Husband, An 183
The Lion Has Wings 180
Marius 27
Private Life of Don Juan 383
The Private Life of Henry VIII 177
The Thief of Baghdad (Korda) 390
Korda, Vincent
Challenge 172
Korda, Zoltan
Cash (For Love or Money) 182
Cry, The Beloved Country (1951) 172
Elephant Boy 173
If I Were Rich 174
The Jungle Book (Sabu) 175
Sahara 772
Sanders of the River 448
Kore-eda, Hirokazu
Maborosi 138
Korine, Harmony
Gummo 431
Korty, John
Autobiography of Miss Jane Pittman 449
Eye on the Sparrow 227
Redwood Curtain 244
Yosemite: The Fate of Heaven 833
Kory, Michael/Conn, Peter
Bohenead (Animation C.3) 705
Kosinski, Bogdan
Parada Wspomnien 98
Kosmatis, George P.
Tombstone 297
Kosminsky, Peter
Emily Bronte's Wuthering Heights 160
Koster, Henry
The Bishop's Wife 264
D-Day, The Sixth of June 365
Dear Brigitte 365
Desiree 365
First Love 322
Flower Drum Song 322
Harvey 270
Inspector General 312
It Started with Eve 272
A Man Called Peter 377
Mr. Hobbs Takes a Vacation 276
The Naked Maja 380
No Highway in the Sky 381
One Hundred Men and a Girl 327
Rage of Paris 384
The Robe 356
The Singing Nun 329
Stars and Stripes Forever 329
Story of Ruth 356
Three Smart Girls 330
Three Smart Girls Grow Up 330
Two Sisters from Boston 331
The Virgin Queen 392
Kotcheff, Ted
The Apprenticeship of Duddy Kravitz 210
Billy Two Hats 290
Joshua Then and Now 211
Who Is Killing the Great Chefs of Europe? 212
Winter People 212
Koth, Brett
Happy Hour (Animation C. 1) 705
Kotkowski, Andrzej
Citizen P. 91
In an Old Manor House 92
Kou, Chen Kun
Marriage 122
Kousuke, F.
You're Under Arrest! Ep. 1: And So They Met 753
You're Under Arrest! Ep. 2: Tokyo Typhoon Rally 753
You're Under Arrest! Ep. 3: Love's Highway Stars 753
You're Under Arrest! Ep. 4: On the Road Again 753
You're Under Arrest! Hybrid Laserdisc #1 753
You're Under Arrest! Hybrid Laserdisc #2 753
Koutsky, Pavel
Love at First Sight (Outrageous 1) 714
Kovacs, Andras
Cold Days 101
Kowalski, Bernard L.
Attack of the Giant Leeches 516
Krakatoa: East of Java 375
Night of the Blood Beast 499
Sssssss 500
Kozintsev, Grigori
Don Quixote (Kozintsev) 80
King Lear (Kozintsev) 82
New Babylon (Novyi Vavilon) 82

SVD—Club of the Big Deed 86
Kraft, D.
Puerto Cabezas: Our Sister City 60
Kragh-Jacobsen, Soeren
Emma's Shadow 75
Kramer, Lance
Singing Ding a Lings (Spike/Mike 2) 716
Kramer, Robert
Starting Place 7, 478
Kramer, Stanley
Bless the Beasts and Children 219
Defiant Ones 365
Guess Who's Coming to Dinner 371
Inherit the Wind 373
It's a Mad, Mad, Mad, Mad World 272
Judgment at Nuremberg 374
Not As a Stranger 381
On the Beach 381
Pressure Point 383
The Pride and the Passion 383
The Secret of Santa Vittoria 386
Ship of Fools 386
Krantz, Steve
The Nine Lives of Fritz the Cat 686
Krasilovsky, Alexis
Beale Street 609
Blood 427
End of the Art World 548
Exile 775
Mr. Boogie Woogie 613
Krasna, Norman
The Big Hangover 360
Krauze, Antoni
Aquarium 90
Krawicz, Mieczyslaw
I Lied 92
Jadzia 92
Sportsman Against His Will 94
Kreck, Joachim
Chord Sharp 707
Kress, Harold F.
The Painted Hills 665
Krieg, Peter
Machine Dreams 836
Kriegman, Mitchell
My Neighborhood 434
Krishna, Srinivas
Masala 211
Krishnama, Suri
A Man of No Importance 162
Kristofovich, Vyacheslav
Adam's Rib (Russia) 80
Kroesen, Janice
Desire: An Erotic Fantasy Play 458
Krogstad, Karl
Jack in the Fox (Sextoons) 715
Karl Krogstad Films 432
Karl Krogstad: Seven-Tape Boxed Set 432
Krohn, Bill
It's All True 344
Kroll, Nathan
The Guns of August 760
Krom, Frank
To Play or to Die 31
Kroyer, Bill
FernGully I: The Last Rainforest 683
Technological Threat (Int. Animation 3) 712
Krueger, Lisa
Best Offer 630
Manny & Lo 433
Krumins, Daine
Divine Miracle (Animation for Fallen Catholics) 706
Krumme, Raimond
Rope Dance (Animation C.1) 705
Krzystek, Waldemar
Dismissed from Life 91
Kubrick, Stanley
2001: A Space Odyssey 255
2001: A Space Odyssey (25th Anniversary Edition) 255
Barry Lyndon 255
A Clockwork Orange (Film) 256
Conversation with Arthur C. Clarke 256, 333
Dr. Strangelove 256
Full Metal Jacket 256
Killer's Kiss 256
The Killing 256
Lolita 256
Paths of Glory 256
Primer for 2001: A Space Odyssey 256
The Shining 256
Spartacus (1960/Kubrick) 256
Kuby, Clemens
Ladakh: In Harmony with the Spirit 149
Tibet: The Survival of the Spirit 150
Kuchar, Mike
Cupid's Infirmary 483
Kuen, Yeung
Fortune Hunters 120
Kufus, Thomas
Mein Krieg (My Private War) 64, 770
Kugel, Candy
Snowie and the Seven Dorps 705
Kukasaku, Kinji
The Green Slime 522
Kuleshov, Leveviks
Chess Fever/By the Law 85
The Extraordinary Adventures of Mr. West in the Land of the Bolsheviks 85
Kulijanov, Lev
Crime and Punishment (Russian) 80
Kulik, Buzz
Around the World in 80 Days (1989) 218
From Here to Eternity (Remake) 229
The Lindbergh Kidnapping Case 236
Kumar, Vinod
Mere Hazoor 148
Kumel, Harry
Daughters of Darkness (Director's Cut) 519
Kunhardt, Peter W.
Lincoln (Vidal) 236
Kuo, Joseph
Born Invincible 125
The Old Master 122
Kurahara, Koreyoshi
Hiroshima 231
Kuran, Peter
Trinity and Beyond: The Atomic Bomb Movie 479
Kurchevsky, Vadim
My Green Crocodile (Masters of Russian Animation 7) 82, 713
Kureishi, Hanif
London Kills Me 161
Kuroda, Yoshiyuki
Majin, The Monster of Terror 525
Return of the Giant Majin 509
Kurosawa, Akira
The Bad Sleep Well 142
Dersu Uzala 142
Dodes'ka-den 142
Dreams 142
Drunken Angel 142
The Hidden Fortress 142
High and Low 142
I Live in Fear 142
The Idiot 142
Ikiru 142
Kagemusha 142
The Lower Depths 142
Men Who Tread on Tiger's Tail 142
No Regrets for Our Youth 142
Quiet Duel 142
Ran 142, 314
Rashomon 142
Record of a Living Being 142
Red Beard 142
Rhapsody in August 142
Sanjuro 142
Sanshiro Sugata 142
Scandal 142
Seven Samurai 142
Stray Dog 143
Throne of Blood 143
Yojimbo 143
Kurotsuchi, Mitsuo
Traffic Jam 140
Kurtz, Bob
Drawing On My Mind (Int. Animation 2) 712
Kurtz, Ken
The Phantom of the Opera (1990/Hirshfeld Theater) 327
Kurys, Diane
Entre Nous 3
Love After Love 5
Peppermint Soda 6
Kushnevrov, S.
The Log (Spike/Mike 2) 716
Kustov, Boris
Against the Current (Glasnost Film Festival V.1) 81
Kusturica, Emir
Arizona Dream 104
Do You Remember Dolly Bell? 104
Time of the Gypsies 104
When Father Was Away on Business 104
Kuzminski, Kazimierz
On the Neman River 93
Kuzminski, Zbigniew
Agent #1 90
Between the Cup and the Lip 90
Kwai, Corey Yuen
Bodyguard from Beijing 125
My Father Is a Hero 130
Righting Wrongs (aka Above the Law) 131
Kwan, Cheung Mei
Struggle for Avengence 123
Kwan, O Chi
Girls Gang 120
Kwan, Stanley
Love unto Waste 121
Rouge 123
Kwan, Teddy Robin
Legend of Wisely 121
Kwapis, Ken
Vibes 286
Kwiatkowska, Maria
Ordonka 98
Kwong, Lee Yan
What Price Survival? 133
Kyriakis, William
Dark Odyssey 505
L'Herbier, Marcel
L'Inhumaine 21
L'hotsky, Tina
Film Musicals 430
Tina L'hotsky: Barbie and Snakewoman 489
La Bruce, Bruce
Hustler White 460
Super 8-1/2 ....212, 465
La Cava, Gregory
Big News 360
Fifth Avenue Girl 268
Gabriel over the White House 369
His First Command 399
My Man Godfrey 277
New School Teacher 401
Labrune, Jeanne
Sand and Blood 8
Labs, Survival Research
Virtues of Negative Fascination 567
LaBute, Neil
In the Company of Men 431
Lachman, Harry
Castle in the Desert 363
Charlie Chan in Rio 363
Murder Over New York 363
Lachnit, Ewa
Andrzej Wajda, A Portrait 96
Lacombe, Georges
Seven Deadly Sins (episode) 6, 39
Lagos, Taso
American Messiah 503
Lahiff, Craig
Heaven's Burning 206
Lahire, Sandra
Lady Lazarus (New Directors) 487
Lai, Albert
Bitter Taste of Blood 119
Lai, Guy Y.C.
Point of No Return 131
Lai, Ivan
The Imp 121
Thank You Sir 124
Lai-To, Herman Yau
Chez 'n' Ham 119
The Untold Story 124
Laloux, Rene
Fantastic Planet 710
Light Years 712
Lam, David
Call Girl 1988 119
Prince of Portland Street 131
Lam, Ringo
City on Fire 126
Full Contact 127
Prison on Fire 131
Touch and Go (Hong Kong) 133
Wild Search 133
Lam, Tsui Pak
Thunder Run 132
Lamb, Tom/Brisson, Dan
Poetic Jaundice (Spike/Mike Sick 2) 716
Lambert, Mary
Siesta 246
Lambert, Steve
The Best of Red Green 414
Lamont, Charles
Abbott and Costello Comin' Round the Mountain 261
Abbott and Costello Go to Mars 261
Abbott and Costello in the Foreign Legion 261
Abbott and Costello Meet the Invisible Man 261
Abbott and Costello Meet the Keystone Kops 261
Abbott and Costello Meet the Mummy 261
Bagdad 358
Flame of Araby 368
The Kettles in the Ozarks 273
Little Red Schoolhouse 376
Ma and Pa Kettle 275
Ma and Pa Kettle at Home 275
Ma and Pa Kettle Go to Town 275
Ma and Pa Kettle on Vacation 275
Road Agent 385
Salome Where She Danced 266
Shirley Temple's Baby Burlesks 282
Lamorisse, Albert
Bim, the Little Donkey and Dream of the Wild Horses 2, 19
Red Balloon 23, 640
Voyage en Ballon 644
Lamprecht, Gerhard
Barcarole 68
Lamy, Benoit
La Vie Est Belle (Life Is Rosy) 150
Lancaster, Burt
The Kentuckian 374
Landers, Lew
Aladdin and His Magic Lamp (Live Action) 645
Annabel Takes a Tour/Maid's Night Out 262
Return of the Vampire 528
Torpedo Alley 391
U-Boat Prisoner 392
Landis, James
Deadwood 292
The Sadist 528
Landis, John
Amazon Women on the Moon 262
Animal House 262
The Blues Brothers 264
Coming to America 266
Innocent Blood 233
Kentucky Fried Movie 507
Trading Places 285
Twilight Zone—The Movie 258, 501

Landres, Paul
The Return of Dracula 528
Landreth, Christopher
The Listener (Best Fest 5th Annual) 706
Landy, Ruth
Dark Circle 471
Lane, Bruce Pacho
Along the Erie Canal 801
The Black Tulip 87
The Eagle's Children 56
Inside Afghanistan 111
Stoney Knows How 478
The Tree of Knowledge 61
Tree of Life 61
Lane, Charles
True Identity 446
Lanfield, Sidney
The Hound of the Baskervilles (Rathbone) 186
The Lemon Drop Kid 274
My Favorite Blonde 277
One in a Million 381
Second Fiddle 328
Skirts Ahoy! 329
Sorrowful Jones 282
Station West 296
Thin Ice 390
Where There's Life 287
You'll Never Get Rich 331
Lang, Fritz
The Big Heat (USA) 71
Clash by Night 71
Cloak and Dagger 71
Crimes of Dr. Mabuse 71
Destiny 71
Doctor Mabuse 72
Dr. Mabuse, the Gambler, Part I 72
Dr. Mabuse, the Gambler, Part II 72
Dr. Mabuse, the Gambler, Parts I & II 72
The Fatal Passion of Dr. Mabuse 72
Fury (Lang) 72
Hangmen Also Die 72
House by the River 72
The Indian Tomb 72
Kriemhilde's Revenge 72
Liliom 72
M 72
Metropolis 72
Ministry of Fear 72
Moonfleet 72
The Return of Frank James 72
Scarlet Street 72
Secret Beyond the Door 72
Siegfried (Lang) 72
Spiders 72
Spies (Spione) 72
The Testament of Dr. Mabuse 72
The Thousand Eyes of Dr. Mabuse (Eyes of Evil) 72
The Tiger of Eschnapur 72
Western Union 72
Woman in the Moon 72
The Woman in the Window 72
You and Me 73
Lang, Krzysztof
The Trial (Poland) 94
Lang, Richard
James A. Michener's Texas 233
Kung Fu the Movie 129, 234
Lang, Teresa
License to Kill (Spike/Mike 2) 716
Lang, Walter
Blue Bird 361
But Not for Me 362
Can-Can 321
Desk Set 267
The Jackpot 272
The King and I 325
The Little Princess (Lang/1939) 376
Moon over Miami 326
Red Kimono 403
Snow White and the Three Stooges 282
Song of the Islands 329
There's No Business Like Show Business 330
Week-End in Havana 331
Langan, John
Nancy Drew Reporter 380
Langley, Noel
Adventures of Sadie 181
The Pickwick Papers 177
The Search for Bridey Murphy 386
Langlois, Denis
L'Escorte 4, 461
Langton, Simon
Jane Austen's Pride and Prejudice 193
Langway, Douglas
Raising Heroes 464
Lantz, Walter
Man's Best Friend 685
Wild and Woody 690
The World of Andy Panda 718
Lanzmann, Claude
Shoah 477, 776
Lapicki, Andrzej
Suspended 94
Lapine, James
Passion (Lapine) 327
Large, Brian
Stiffelio (Domingo) 585
Larkin, Christopher
A Very Natural Thing 466
Larry, Sheldon
Keeping the Promise 234
Larsen, Robert W.
The Narcotic Story 508
Lasota, Gregorz
Champion Always Loses 90
Jaguar 1936 92
Secret Detective 94
Lasseby, Stig
Peter-No-Tail 639
Lasseter, John
Lady and the Lamp (Animation C.2) 705
Tiny Toy Stories 717
Lathan, Stan
Almos' a Man 300
Go Tell It on the Mountain 444
Uncle Tom's Cabin (1987/Bruce Dern) 301
Lattuada, Alberto
Anna (Italy) 40
Christopher Columbus (1985) 32
Italy Turns Around (Love in the City) 41
Variety Lights 37
Lau, David
Runaway Blues 123
Lau, Herman
Cop Image 126
Lau, Jeff
Operation Pink Squad 122
Operation Pink Squad II 122
Lau, Ricky
Raped by an Angel (aka Naked Killer 2) 131
Lauenstein, C. & W.
Balance (Int. Animation 4) 712
Laufer, Erez
Solitary Star: Zehava Ben 109
Laughlin, Michael
Strange Behavior 209
Laughton, Charles
The Night of the Hunter 380
Launder, Frank
Belles of St. Trinians 181
Blue Murder at St. Trinian's 181
Captain Boycott 172
The Happiest Days of Your Life 183
Laurel, Stan
Directed by Stan Laurel 410
Raggedy Rose 403
Laurent, Emmanuel
Portrait of Gustave Caillebotte in the Country 555
Lauterier, Fernand
Nais 27
Lautner, Georges
Icy Breasts 3
La Cage aux Folles III 17
Lautrec, Linda/Legend, Johnny
My Breakfast with Blassie 277
Lauzon, Jean-Claude
Leolo 213
Night Zoo 213
Lavacherry, Vincent
Gring Gallet's Reward (Too Outrageous) 717
Laven, Arnold
The Glory Guys (Western) 292
The Monster That Challenged the World 498
Rough Night in Jericho 295
Law, Alex
Painted Faces 134
Law, Clara
Autumn Moon 118
Erotique 430
The Reincarnation of Golden Lotus 117
Temptation of a Monk 117
Law, Joe
The Crippled Masters 126
Law, Rocky
Dragons of the Orient 127
Law, Williamson
Lethal Girls 2 129
Lawrence, Denny
Archer's Adventure 629
Lawrence, Diarmuid
Emma (Beckinsale) 226
Lawrence, Quentin
Crawling Eye 495
Lawrence, Ray
Bliss (Australia) 205
Lazarkiewicz, Magdalena
By Touch 90
The Trip 94
Lazarkiewicz, Piotr
The Trip 94
Lazzard, Marc
A Lobster Tale (Best Fest 5th Annual) 706
Le Borg, Reginald
The Diary of a Madman 520
Inner Sanctum: Calling Dr. Death/
Strange Confession, The 523
The Inner Sanctum: Dead Man's Eyes/ Pillow of Death 524
The Inner Sanctum: Weird Woman/Frozen Ghost 524
The Mummy's Ghost 526
The White Orchid 393
Le Chanois, Jean-Paul
L'Ecole Buissoniere 21
Le Cas du Dr. Laurent 21
Les Miserables 21
Passion for Life 22
Le Piouffle, Georges
Still Life (Animation C.3) 705
Le Roy, Mervyn
Bad Seed, The 358
Blossoms in the Dust 360
East Side, West Side 367
Gold Diggers of 1933 323
Gypsy (1962/Wood) 323
I Am a Fugitive from a Chain Gang 372
Lovely to Look At 326
Quo Vadis (1951) 356
Rose Marie (1954) 328
Thirty Seconds over Tokyo 390
Three Men on a Horse 284
Three on a Match 391
Leach, Wilford
Pirates of Penzance 327
Leacock, Philip
Angel City 217
Curse of King Tut's Tomb 519
Leacock, Robert
Catwalk 470
Leader, Anton
Children of the Damned 172
Leaf, Caroline
Two Sisters (NFBCanada) 113
Leaf, David
The Unknown Marx Brothers 285, 339
Lean, David
Blithe Spirit 180, 310
The Bridge on the River Kwai 180
Doctor Zhivago 180
Great Expectations (Lean) 180
Hobson's Choice (1953) 180
In Which We Serve 180
Lawrence of Arabia 180
Lawrence of Arabia (Criterion) 180
Oliver Twist (1948/Lean) 180
A Passage to India 180
The Passionate Friends (One Woman's Story) 180
Ryan's Daughter 180
Summertime (Summer Madness) 180
This Happy Breed 180
Lear, Norman
Cold Turkey 504
Lech, Zygmunt
Sarah's House 94
Leconte, Patrice
French Fried Vacation (Les Bronzes) 17
The Hairdresser's Husband 8
Lumiere & Company 5, 336
Monsieur Hire 8
Ridicule 6
Leder, Alan
Mama Florence and Papa Cock 475
Leder, Mimi
The Peacemaker 242
Lederman, David Ross
Phantom of the West 538
The Range Feud/Two Fisted Law 295
Texas Cyclone 296
Leduc, Paul
Barrocco 49
Frida 50
Reed: Mexico Insurgente 52
Lee, Ang
Eat Drink Man Woman 136
The Ice Storm 232
Pushing Hands 455
Sense and Sensibility (1995) 301
The Wedding Banquet 455, 467
Lee, Charles
Thunder Ninja Kids: In the Golden Adventure 132
Thunder Ninja Kids: Wonderful Mission 132
Lee, Danny
Road Warriors 131
Lee, Iara
Synthetic Pleasures 478
Lee, Jack
A Town Like Alice (1956) 179
Lee, Lik-Chi
Master Wong v. Master Wong 122
Lee, Norman
Bulldog Drummond at Bay 172
Chamber of Horrors (The Door with Seven Locks) 518
Lee, Quentin
Flow 430, 459
Lee, Raymond
Blue Lightning 119
Swordsman III (aka The East Is Red) 132
Lee, Rowland V.
Captain Kidd 362
Love from a Stranger 175
One Rainy Afternoon 381
Son of Frankenstein 529
Son of Monte Cristo 387
The Toast of New York 391
Tower of London (1939/Boris Karloff) 391
Lee, Spike
The Answer (First Works) 334
Clockers 446
Crooklyn 447
Do The Right Thing 447
Get on the Bus 447
Girl 6 447
Jungle Fever 447

Lumiere & Company 5, 336
Malcolm X (Lee) 447
Mo' Better Blues 447
School Daze 447
She's Gotta Have It 447
Lee, Iara
An Autumn Wind (CineBLAST 2) 483
Leehman, Linda
Women Speak Up: A Collection of Women's Voices from Around the World 765, 783
Lefebvre, Genevieve
Le Jupon Rouge 4, 461
Left, Abraham
Where Is My Child? 116
Leg, Lung
Worm Movie (Cinema of Transgression) 483
LeGault, Gary
Roadsinger 436
Leger, Fernand
Ballet Mecanique (Avant Garde & Experimental Films 482
Lehman, Ernest
Portnoy's Complaint 279
Lehmann, Michael
Heathers 270
Meet the Applegates 276
The Truth About Cats and Dogs 285
Lehotay, Zoltan
Success (Int. Animation 2) 712
Leifer, Neil
Trading Hearts 250
Leigh, Mike
Abigail's Party 165
Bleak Moments 165
Career Girls 165
Four Days in July 165
Grown Ups 165
Hard Labor 165
Home Sweet Home 165
Kiss of Death (Great Britain) 165
Life Is Sweet 165
Meantime 165
Naked 165
Nuts in May 166
Secrets and Lies 166
Who's Who 166
Leighter, Jackson
Rita Hayworth's Champagne Safari 338
Leiner, Danny
Time Expired 438
Leisen, Mitchell
The Big Broadcast of 1938 263
Easy Living 267
Golden Earrings 370
Hands Across the Table 270
The Lady Is Willing 273
Midnight 379
Remember the Night 280
Swing High, Swing Low 330
To Each His Own 391
Leiser, Erwin
Germany Awake 69
Mein Kampf 770
Leivick, David
Gospel 607
Lejtes, Jozef
The Border (Poland) 90
Leland, David
Checking Out 182
Lelouch, Claude
Bandits 16
Les Miserables (1995/Jean-Paul Belmondo) 4
Lumiere & Company 5, 336
A Man and a Woman 5
A Man and a Woman—20 Years Later 5
Lemaitre, Maurice
A Love Story (Letterist Films) 432
Lemaitre, Suzanne
All Women Are Joan of Arcs (Letterist Films) 432
Leman, Juda
Land of Promise 109
Lemmons, Kasi
Eve's Bayou 430
Lemont, John
The Duel (Errol Flynn) 367
The Frightened City 173
Leni, Paul
The Cat and the Canary 396, 518
The Man Who Laughs 401
Waxworks 71
Lenzi, Umberto
The Greatest Battle 768
Leo, Malcolm
This Is Elvis 537
Leon, Gerardo de
Terror Is a Man 501
Vampire People 531
Women in Cages 534
Leonard, Arthur
Boy! What a Girl! 447
Devil's Daughter 448
Sepia Cinderella 448
Leonard, Brett
The Lawnmower Man 498
Virtuosity 501
Leonard, Jack E.
The World of Abbott and Costello 288
Leonard, Leon
Omoo Omoo, The Shark God 508
Leonard, Robert Z.
Broadway Serenade 321
Dancing Lady 321
Dutchess of Idaho 267
Firefly, The 322
Girl of the Golden West 323
The Great Ziegfeld 323
In the Good Old Summertime 324
The King's Thief 375
Mademoiselle Midnight 401
Maytime 326
A Mormon Maid 401
Nancy Goes to Rio 326
New Moon 327
Pride and Prejudice (1940/MGM) 383
Strange Interlude (1932) 315
Susan Lennox: Her Fall and Rise 389
Weekend at the Waldorf 286
When Ladies Meet 393
Ziegfeld Girl 331
Leone, Sergio
Fistful of Dollars 39
A Fistful of Dynamite 39
For a Few Dollars More 39
The Good, The Bad and the Ugly 40
Once Upon a Time in America 40
Once Upon a Time in the West 40
Leong, Po Chih
He Lives By Night 128
Leong, Raymond & Teresa Woo
Midnight Angels 130
Lerner, Carl
Black Like Me 360
Lerner, Irving
Studs Lonigan 388
Lerner, Joseph
C-Man 362
Lerner, Murray
From Mao to Mozart 589
Jimi Hendrix Live at the Isle of Wight, 1970 620
Message to Love: The Isle of Wight Festival: The Movie 621
Lerner, Richard
What Happened to Kerouac? (1985) 308
Lerner, Yitzhak
Jewish Life in Vilna 112
Leroi, Francis
Emmanuelle 2 3
LeRoy, Mervyn
Anthony Adverse 358
Any Number Can Play 358
The Devil at 4 o'Clock 366
FBI Story 368
Homecoming (Gable) 372
Johnny Eager 374
Latin Lovers 273
Little Caesar 376
Little Women (1949/Taylor) 376
Madame Curie 377
A Majority of One 377
Million-Dollar Mermaid 326
Moment to Moment 379
Random Harvest 384
Waterloo Bridge 393
Lesage, Julia
El Crucero 56
In Plain English 473
Las Nicas and Home Life 58
Troubadours: A Musical Performance by Groupo Camayoc 61
Leshin, Liz
Freefall 430
Lesiewicz, Witold
King Boleslaus the Bold 92
Leslie, Alfred
Pull My Daisy (The Beat Generation) 435, 476
Leslie, David
My Sheroes, My Sheroes 434
Stars & Scars 567
Lessac, Michael
House of Cards (USA) 231
Lester, Richard
Butch and Sundance: The Early Days 291
Cuba 224
The Four Musketeers 182
A Funny Thing Happened on the Way to the Forum 322
A Hard Day's Night 323, 623, 866
Help! 183, 324
How I Won the War 183
The Knack…and How to Get It 183
Petulia 177
The Return of the Musketeers 184
Richard Lester 338, 488
Ritz 280, 464
Robin and Marian 163
Superman II 248
The Three Musketeers (1974/York) 185
Leszczylowski, Michal
Directed by Andrei Tarkovsky 84
Leszczynski, Witold
Personal Search 93
Letch, Eric von
Sex in the Comics 541
Leth, Jorgen
The Impossible Hour: Ole Ritter & Eddie Merckx 827
Stars and Water Carriers 828
A Sunday in Hell 828
Letts, Barry
Carnival of Monsters 199
Gulliver in Lilliput 160
Letts, Berry
The Android Invasion 199
Leung, Chan Chun
Yes Madam 133
Leung, Clarence Fok Yiu
They Came To Rob Hong Kong 124
Leung, Fok Yiu
The Naked Killer 122
Leung, Kam Kwok
4 Faces of Eve 118
Leung, Kwan Ching
Spring Comes Again 132
Leung, Lau Kar
Drunken Master II, Parts A & B 134
Leung, Raymond
Angel 2 118
First Time is the Last Time 120
Leung, Raymond/Woo, Teresa
Midnight Angels II 130
Leung, Tony
Gun of Dragon 128
Levant, Brian
Beethoven (Grodin) 263
Leven, Jeremy
Don Juan DeMarco 267
Levey, William
Blackenstein 532
Monaco Forever 463
Levin, Harry
Jolson Sings Again 325
Levin, Henry
Desperadoes 292
Farmer Takes a Wife 367
Man from Colorado 294
Where the Boys Are 287
Wonderful World of the Brothers Grimm 649
Levin, Meyer
Falashas 114
The Illegals 775
The Unafraid 110
Levine, Les
Video Art: Les Levine 490
Levinson, Barry
Avalon 218
Bugsy 221
Diner 225
Disclosure 225
Good Morning Vietnam 229
Rain Man 243
Sleepers 246
Sphere 247
Toys 285
Wag the Dog 286
Young Sherlock Holmes 187
Levitan, Israeli Nadav
Intimate Story 108
Levitow, Abe
Gay Purr-ee 710
Levitt, Helen
In the Street 486
Levy, Jeffery
Inside Monkey Zetterland 432
Levy, Ralph
Bedtime Story 263
A Christmas Carol 172, 321, 363, 682, 707
Levy, Raoul J.
Hail Mafia 20
Lewin, Albert
The Moon and Sixpence 379
Pandora and the Flying Dutchman 382
Picture of Dorian Gray (1945/USA) 382
The Private Affairs of Bel Ami 383
Lewin, Ben
The Favor, The Watch and the Very Big Fish 182
Georgia (Judy Davis) 206
Lewis, Al
Our Miss Brooks 278
Lewis, Audrey King
The Gifted 496
Lewis, Everett
The Natural History of Parking Lots 434
Lewis, Herschell Gordon
2000 Maniacs 503
Blast-Off Girls 504
Blood Feast 504
Boinng 504
The Girl, the Body and the Pill 506
The Gruesome Twosome 506
How to Make a Doll 507
Jimmy, The Boy Wonder 507
Just for the Hell of It 507
Living Venus 507
Lucky Pierre 507
Moonshine Mountain 508
The Prime Time (Cult) 509
Scum of the Earth 510
She-Devils on Wheels 510
Something Weird 510
Suburban Roulette 511
A Taste of Blood 511
This Stuff'll Kill You 511
The Wizard of Gore 512

Lewis, Jerry
The Bellboy 263
Big Mouth 263
Cinderfella 265
Cracking Up 266
The Errand Boy 268
The Family Jewels 268
Ladies' Man 273
The Nutty Professor (1963) 278
The Patsy 279
Lewis, Jonathan
The Treaty 204
Lewis, Joseph H.
Gun Crazy 371
The Invisible Ghost 524
The Lawless Street 294
Pride of the Bowery 279
Retreat, Hell! 384
Terror in a Texas Town 296
Lewis, Mark
Cane Toads: An Unnatural History 205
Rat 476
Lewis, Robert
Summer to Remember (USA, 1985) 248
Lewison, Sarah
Fat of the Land 430
Li, D.Yin
The Story of Xinghua 117
Li, Kao
The Mermaid 122
Libov, Howard
Doing Business 860
Lichy, Atahualpa
Black River 49
Liconti, Carlo
Good Night, Michelangelo 270
Liebeneizer, Wolfgang
Ironhand 64
Liebenwein, Renate
Paolo Veronese: Between Art and Inquisition 554
Light, Charles
Cannabis Rising 469
Lignini, Fabio
When Bats Are Quiet (Int.Animation 3) 712
Lilien, Jadina
Marie (CineBLAST!) 428
Lima Jr., Walter
The Dolphin 53
Liman, Doug
Swingers 283
Linday-Hogg, Michael
Master Harold and the Boys 313
Lindberg, Per
June Night 76
Linder, Maud
Man in the Silk Hat 22, 154
Linder, Max
Max Linder 22, 154
Seven Years Bad Luck 411
The Three Must-Get-Theirs 412
Lindsay-Hogg, Michael
As Is 456
Frankie Starlight 228
The Habitation of Dragons 230
Nasty Habits 277
The Object of Beauty 162
The Rolling Stones Rock & Roll Circus 622
Lindstrom, Jon
Dreaming of Rita 75
Lindtberg, Leopold
Four in a Jeep 30
The Last Chance 30
Link, Matthew
Male Escorts of San Francisco 462
Linklater, Richard
Before Sunrise 427
Dazed and Confused 429
The Newton Boys 434
Slacker 437
SubUrbia 438
Liotta, Jean
Mediamystics 487
Lipsky, Jeff
Childhood's End 428
Lister, Ardele
Video Art: Ardele Lister 489
Litten, Peter
The Art of Cruising Men 456
Litten, Peter Mackenzie
Heaven's a Drag 460
Little, Dwight H.
The Phantom of the Opera (1989/Englund) 527
Little, Rick
Larry Smith/Apollo Belvedere 432
Little, Rik
The Church of Shooting Yourself 428
Littman, Lynne
Testament 438, 792
Litvak, Anatole
All This and Heaven Too 357
Anastasia (Brynner) 357
City for Conquest 364
Five Miles to Midnight 368
Goodbye Again 370
Mayerling (1936) 22
Night of the Generals 176
Sisters, The 386
Snake Pit 387
Sorry, Wrong Number 387
Liu, Chia Liang
Tiger on the Beat II 133
Livingston, Jennie
Paris Is Burning 464, 476
Livingston, Joe
Robo Vampire 131
Lizzani, Carlo
Paid Love (Love in the City) 41
Lloyd, Frank
Blood on the Sun 360
Cavalcade 363
Forever and a Day 170
Howards of Virginia 372
If I Were King 272
Mutiny on the Bounty (Laughton) 380
Oliver Twist (1922/Lloyd) 402
Spieler, The 404
A Tale of Two Worlds (Water Lily) 405
Lo, Ming-Yau
Song of China 117
Lo, Tony C.K.
Devil Hunters 126
Loach, Ken
Family Life 91, 166
Hidden Agenda 166
Ladybird Ladybird 166
Land and Freedom 166
Raining Stones 166
Riff Raff 166
Locke, Sondra
Ratboy 243
Lockwood, Roy
Mutiny of the Elsinore 176
Lodge, David
Childhood of a Phrophet (British Animation) 707
Loeb, Janet
Quiet One 476
Loeb, Janice
In the Street 486
Loftis, Norman
Messenger (Loftis) 445
Small Time 446
Logan, Joshua
Camelot (Musical) 321
Ensign Pulver 268
Fanny (USA) 367
Paint Your Wagon 327
Picnic 382
Sayonara 385
South Pacific (Gaynor) 329
Tall Story 389
Loi, Anthony
Wastes Away (Spike/Mike Sick 2) 716
Lombardi, Francisco J.
The City of the Dogs (La Ciudad de los Perros) 49
Lomnicki, Jan
Just Beyond This Forest 92
Operation Arsenal 93
Loncraine, Richard
Bellman and True 158
Brimstone and Treacle 159
The Missionary 199
Richard III 163
The Wedding Gift 164
London, Jerry
The Scarlet and the Black 245
Shogun 144, 422
Long, Philomene
The Beats: An Existential Comedy 302
Longo, Robert
Johnny Mnemonic 210
Lord, Chip
The Aroma of Enchantment 144, 482
Chip Lord: Selected Works 428
The Motorist 434
Not Top Gun 435
Lord, Del
Trapped by Television 392
Lord, Peter
Adam (Spike/Mike 2) 716
Going Equipped (British Animation) 707
War Story (Animation C.3) 705
Lorentz, Pare
Plow That Broke the Plains 476
The River (Classic Documentaries) 470
The River and The Plow That Broke the Plains 477
Losey, Joseph
Blind Date 353
Don Giovanni 353, 579
The Go-Between 353
Joseph Losey and Adolfus Mekas 353
King and Country 175
Mr. Klein 353
Road to the South 353
Sleeping Tiger 353
Time Without Pity 353
Lotenau, Emil
The Shooting Party (Russian) 83
Louden, Chris
Woeful Willie (Spike/Mike Sick 2) 716
Lounguine, Pavel
Luna Park 82
Taxi Blues 83
Lourie, Eugene
The Beast from 20,000 Fathoms 494
The Giant Behemoth 496
Gorgo 174, 497
Lovell, Lexy
Riding the Rails: The American Experience 843
Lowell, Alayn
Grow Dutch 472
Lowenstein, Richard
Dogs in Space 205
Lowery, Dick
Rascals and Robbers—The Secret Adventures of Tom Sawyer and Huck 309
Lowney, Declan
Time Will Tell: Bob Marley 604
Lowy, Craig
Many Wonder 433
Loy, Nanni
Where's Piccone? 34
Lubin, Arthur
Ali Baba and the Forty Thieves (USA) 357
Black Friday 517
Buck Privates 265
Francis Goes to the Races 268
Francis in the Navy 268
Francis Joins the WACS 269
Francis the Talking Mule 269
Impact 373
In the Navy 272
Keep 'Em Flying 273
Lady Godiva 375
The Phantom of the Opera (1943/Rains) 527
Ride 'Em Cowboy—Abbott and Costello 280
Lubitsch, Ernst
Angel 345
Bluebeard's Eighth Wife 345
The Eyes of the Mummy 345
Gypsy Blood 345
Heaven Can Wait 345
Lady Windermere's Fan 345
The Lubitsch Touch 345
Marriage Circle 345
The Merry Widow (1934) 345
Meyer aus Berlin 345
Ninotchka 345
One Arabian Night 345
The Oyster Princess 70
Passion (Lubitsch) 345
The Shop Around the Corner 345
So This Is Paris 345
The Student Prince in Old Heidelberg 345
That Uncertain Feeling 345
To Be or Not to Be 345
Lucas, George
American Graffiti 217
Star Wars 500
THX 1138 501
Lucas, Meredith
Blood Orgy of the Leather Girls 504
Lucas, Thomas
Nova—Adventures in Science: Hurricane! 837
Nova—Adventures in Science: Tornado! 837
Lucinski, Andrzej
Wilanow—King Jan III Sobieski Residence 99
Ludwig, Edward
Big Jim McLain 360
Fighting Seabees 368
Swiss Family Robinson (Ludwig) 667
That Certain Age 330
Wake of the Red Witch 393
Lugossy, Laszlo
Flowers of Reverie 102
Luhrmann, Baz
Strictly Ballroom 207
William Shakespeare's Romeo & Juliet 316
Lui, Wong Sing
Angry Young Man 125
Luk, Jamie
Crossline 119
Lukasiewicz, Jerzy
Faustyna 91
Lumet, Sidney
Critical Care 223
Daniel 224
Death Trap 224
Dog Day Afternoon 225
Equus 311
Fail Safe 367
Family Business 268
Fugitive Kind 369
Garbo Talks 229
The Group 371
The Hill 174
The Last of the Mobile Hot-Shots 235
Long Day's Journey into Night (1962/Hepburn) 312
Morning After 238
Murder on The Orient Express 162
Network 239
Night Falls on Manhattan 240
The Pawnbroker 382
Q & A 243
Running on Empty 245
Serpico 246
Sidney Lumet: From Theater to Film 315, 338
A Stranger Among Us 248
Twelve Angry Men 392
The Verdict 251
Wiz 331

Lumiere, Pierre and August
Lumiere Brothers' First Films 22, 153
Luna, Bigas
Anguish....217
Jamon, Jamon....45
Lumiere & Company....5, 336
Lupino, Ida
The Bigamist....360
The Hitch-Hiker....372
The Trouble with Angels....285
Women Who Made the Movies....339
Lustgarten, Steve
American Taboo....426
Lustig, William
Maniac Cop....525
Maniac/Special Edition....525
Vigilante....251
Luther, Salvo
Forget Mozart....63
Luyet, Claude
The Square of Light (Int. Animation 6)....712
Luzuriaga, Camilo
La Tigra....51
Lyde, Ted
The Windy City....252
Lydecker, Howard
Fighting Seabees....368
Lye, Len
Color Box (Documentary Masterpieces)....471
Free Radicals Vol. 1....710
Lambeth Walk Nazi Style (Experimental Series 19)....484
Len Lye....486, 712
Lynch, David
Alphabet (Avant Garde Program #11)....482
Blue Velvet....257
Dune....257
Lost Highway....257
Lumiere & Company....5, 336
Pretty as a Picture: Art of David Lynch....257
Twin Peaks....257
Twin Peaks Pilot....257
Twin Peaks: Fire Walk with Me....257
Wild at Heart....257
Lynch, Jennifer Chambers
Boxing Helena....428
Lynch, Paul
Prom Night....527
Lynd, Laurie
Boys' Shorts....457
Together and Apart....466
Lyne, Adrian
9-1/2 Weeks....216
Fatal Attraction (Director's Cut)....227
Flashdance....227
Foxes....228
Jacob's Ladder....233
Lynn, Harry
Where Is My Child?....116
Lynn, Henry
Mothers of Today....112
Lynn, Jonathan
Greedy....270
My Cousin Vinny....277
Nuns on the Run....184
Sgt. Bilko....282
Trial and Error....285
Lyon, Danny
Born to Film....481
Dear Mark....481
El Mojado....481
El Otro Lado (The Other Side)....481
Little Boy....481
Llanito....481
Los Ninos Abandonados (The Abandoned Children)....481
Media Man....481
Social Sciences 127....481
Willie....481
Lyon, Francis D.
Castle of Evil....518
Cult of the Cobra....519
Lyon, Nancy Weiss
Media Man....481
Willie....481
Lyons, Johnathon
The Rooster (Best Fest Kids)....706
Ma, Wu
Circus Kids....126
The Dead and the Deadly....126
MacAdams, Lewis
Fun House....534
What Happened to Kerouac? (1985)....308
Macartney, Syd
The Canterville Ghost (1995/Stewart)....265
Prince Brat and the Whipping Boy....665
MacDonald, David
Bad Lord Byron....358
Christopher Columbus (1949)....172
Devil Girl from Mars....495
Moonraker (1957/MacDonald)....172
Never Too Late to Mend....176
This England....179
MacDonald, Heather
Ballot Measure 9....456, 469
MacDonald, Hettie
Beautiful Thing....158
MacDonald, Peter
Mo' Money....276
The Neverending Story III: Return to Fantasia....665
MacDougall, Ronald
Queen Bee....383
Machaty, Gustav
Ecstasy....69
Erotikon....99
Machover, Robert
Binocular Vision....813
Machulski, Juliusz
Deja Vu....95
Kingsize....95
Sexmission....94
Mack, Earle
Children of Theatre Street....569
Mackendrick, Alexander
Ladykillers....183
Man in the White Suit....184
Sweet Smell of Success....389
Whiskey Galore....185
MacKenzie, John
Fourth Protocol....160
Infiltrator, The....232
The Long Good Friday....161
MacKenzie, Will
Hobo's Christmas....231
MacKinnon, Gilles
The Playboys....163
Small Faces....164
Trojan Eddie....164
Maclaine, Christopher
The End....484
MacLean, Alison
Crush....208
MacNaughton, Ian
And Now for Something Completely Different....198
MacRae, Henry
Tarzan the Tiger....539
Macy, William H.
Lip Service....274
Madden, John
Ethan Frome....300
Her Majesty Mrs. Brown....161
Maddin, Guy
Careful....210
Tales from the Gimli Hospital....212
Maddow, Ben
The Savage Eye....385
Madison, Cleo
Women Who Made the Movies....339
Maeck, Klaus
William S. Burroughs: Commissioner of the Sewers....308
Magalhaes, Ana Maria
Erotique....430
Maggenti, Maria
The Incredibly True Adventure of Two Girls in Love....461
Magliano, Benjamin
The Secret Service....763
Magni, Luigi
In the Name of the Pope-King....33
Magnoli, Albert
Purple Rain....328
Magyar, Dezso
Rappaccini's Daughter....301
Mahendra, Balu
Sadma....148
Maier, Robert
Love Letter to Edy....507, 514
Mailer, Norman
Tough Guys Don't Dance....250
Mainka, Maximiliane
Germany in Autumn....66
Mainka-Jellinghaus, Beate
Germany in Autumn....66
Majano, Anton Giulio
Atom Age Vampire....516
Majewski, Janusz
H. M. Deserters....92
Hotel Pacific....92
Mak, Peter
Wicked City (Hong Kong)....117
Makavejev, Dusan
Coca-Cola Kid....104
Gorilla Bathes at Noon....104
Innocence Unprotected....104
Love Affair: Or, the Case of the Missing Switchboard Operator....104
Man Is Not a Bird....104
Montenegro....104
A Night of Love....104
Sweet Movie....104
WR: Mysteries of the Organism....104
Makhmalbaf, Mohsen
Cyclist, The....106
Once Upon a Time, Cinema....106
The Peddler....106
Makin, Kelly
Brain Candy....264
Makk, Karoly
Another Way....101
Cat's Play....101
Lilly in Love....102
Love....102
A Very Moral Night....102
Malaparte, Curzio
The Forbidden Christ....40
Malasomma, Nunzio
Revolt of the Slaves....42
Malenotti, Roberto
Slave Trade in the World Today....510
Malick, Terence
Badlands....218
Days of Heaven....224
Malle, Louis
Alamo Bay....13
Atlantic City....13
Au Revoir les Enfants (Goodbye, Children)....13
Calcutta....13
Damage....13
Elevator to the Gallows....13
The Fire Within....13
The Lovers (French)....13
May Fools....13
Murmur of the Heart....13
My Dinner with Andre....13
Pretty Baby....13
Spirits of the Dead....37
Vanya on 42nd Street....13
A Very Private Affair....13
Viva Maria....13
Zazie dans le Metro....13
Mallet, David
David Bowie—The Glass Spider Tour....619
Mallinson, Matthew
Dragon and the Cobra: The Collector's Edition....333
Fist of Fear Touch of Death....506
Malone, Mark
Bulletproof Heart....221
Maloney, Paul
I Live with Me Dad....206
Mamalakis, Mark
Art of Haiti....545
Mambety, Djibril Diop
Hyenas....150
Touki Bouki....150
Mamedov, Murat
Early on Sunday (Glasnost Film Festival V.3)....81
Mamet, David
Homicide....231
Oleanna....314
The Spanish Prisoner....437
Things Change....283
Mamin, Yuri
Sideburns....83
Window to Paris....84
Mamoulian, Rouben
Becky Sharp....359
Dr. Jekyll and Mr. Hyde (March)....520
Golden Boy (Drama)....370
Mark of Zorro (1940)....378
Queen Christina....383
Silk Stockings....329
Summer Holiday....329
Man Ray
Emak Bakia (Avant Garde #14)....483
L'Etoile de Mer (Man Ray Video)....486
Les Mysteres du Chateau du De....486
Retour a la Raison (Avant Garde #14)....483
Man, Chan Hung
You Make Me Laugh....124
Man, Lee Wai
To Be No. 1....133
Man, Low
Hearty Response....128
Man, Ng Dick
Death Rim....126
Man-Kit, Poon
City Kids....126
Shanghai Grand....131
Sword of Many Loves....124
Manabe, Johji
Capricorn....725
Manchevski, Milcho
Before the Rain....158
Mandel, Robert
Independence Day (Romantic Drama)....232
School Ties....245
Sunshine's on the Way....248
Mandoki, Luis
Gaby—A True Story....229
When a Man Loves a Woman....252
White Palace....252
Mandrayar, Dharan
Ele, My Friend....663
Manduke, Joseph
Cornbread, Earl and Me....223
Gumshoe Kid....230
Mangold, James
Cop Land....223
Heavy....431
Maniaci, Teodoro
One Nation Under God....476
Mankiewicz, Joseph L.
All About Eve....357
Barefoot Contessa....359
Cleopatra (Taylor)....364
Five Fingers....368
The Ghost and Mrs. Muir....369
Guys and Dolls....323
House of Strangers....372
Julius Caesar (MGM/Brando)....312
Letter to Three Wives....376
No Way Out....381
People Will Talk....382
Sleuth....315

Suddenly Last Summer....388
There Was a Crooked Man....297
Mankiewicz, Tom
Dragnet....267
Mann, Abby
King....453
Mann, Amir
Warsaw Story....777
Mann, Anthony
Bend of the River....290
Black Book (Reign of Terror)....360
Dandy in Aspic....224
El Cid....367
Fall of the Roman Empire....367
Glenn Miller Story....323
God's Little Acre....370
Great Flamarion....370
The Heroes of Telemark....768
Man from Laramie....294
Man of the West....294
The Naked Spur....294
Railroaded....384
Raw Deal....384
Savage Wilderness....296
Serenade....328
T-Men....389
Tin Star, The....297
Winchester '73....298
Mann, Daniel
Butterfield 8....362
Come Back, Little Sheba....364
Dream of Kings....366
I'll Cry Tomorrow....373
Last Angry Man....375
Our Man Flint....278
The Rose Tattoo....314
Teahouse of the August Moon....389
Mann, Delbert
All Quiet on the Western Front (1979)....217
April Morning....218
David Copperfield (Mann/1970)....173
Desire Under the Elms....311
Fitzwilly....268
Marty (Borgnine)....378
The Pink Jungle....382
That Touch of Mink....283
Mann, Edward
Cauldron of Blood....518
Mann, Michael
Heat (Mann)....230
The Last of the Mohicans (1992)....235
Mann, Ron
Comic Book Confidential....541, 864
Poetry in Motion....306, 870
Twist....576
Manoussakis, Manoussos
The Enchantress....105
Mansfield, Scott
Women First & Foremost: Volume 1:....765
Women First & Foremost: Volume 2:....765
Women First & Foremost: Volume 3:....765
Mantello, Joe
Love! Valour! Compassion!....462
Manuli, Guido
Erection (Outrageous 2)....714
Guido Manuli: Animator....710
Incubus (Int. Animation 1)....711
Plus One, Minus One (Int. Animation 2)....712
Use Instructions (Too Outrageous)....717
Volere Volare....34
Manzor, Rene
Legends of the North....235
Marano, Eric
The Age of Insects....426
March, Alex
Firehouse....444
Mastermind....275
Marconi, David
The Harvest (Marconi)....522
Marcus, Larry
A Link in the Chain....376
Marczewski, Wojciech
Housemaster....95
Mardirossian, Margaret
Robbie Burkett: A Line of Balance....314
Margheriti, Antonio
Assignment Outer Space....494
Margolin, Stuart
The Glitter Dome....229
Margolis, Jeff
Richard Pryor Live! In Concert....535
Marie, Dina
Rhinoskin: The Making of a Movie Star....464
Marin, Edwin L.
A Christmas Carol (1938/Owen)....363
Death Kiss....365
Everybody Sing....322
Listen, Darling....325
A Study in Scarlet....187
Marins, Jose Mojica
At Midnight I'll Take Your Soul....516
Awakenings of the Beast....516
The Bloody Exorcism of Coffin Joe....517
Coffin Joe's Visions of Terror....518
The End of Man....521
Hallucinations of a Deranged Mind....522
Perversion....527
Strange World of Coffin Joe....529
Marker, Chris
La Jetee....10
Le Joli Mai....10
Sans Soleil....10
Marker, Russ
The Yesterday Machine....502
Markham, Monte
Thomas Jefferson: Philosopher of Freedom....797
Markle, Fletcher
The Incredible Journey....693
Markle, Peter
Nightbreaker....240
The Personals....242
Markovic, Goran
Tito and Me....103
Markowitz, Robert
Afterburn....216
Decoration Day....225
The Tuskegee Airmen....250, 455
Marks Jr., John
No Man Is an Island....381
Marks, Arthur
Bucktown....532
Detroit 9000....532
Friday Foster....532
J.D.'s Revenge....533
Monkey Hustle....533
Marks, Harrison
As Nature Intended....503
Marks, Ross
Twilight of the Golds....250
Markson, Morley
Growing Up in America....472
Marquand, Richard
Eye of the Needle....227
Hearts of Fire....230
Jagged Edge....233
Star Wars—The Return of the Jedi....500
Marre, Jeremy
Ladyboys....461
Marshall, Cindy
Life of Song: Portrait of Ruth Rubin....112
Marshall, Garry
Beaches....219
Frankie and Johnny (Pfeiffer/Pacino)....269
Marshall, George
Blue Dahlia....361
Boy Did I Get a Wrong Number....264
Destry Rides Again....292
Eight on the Lam....268
Fancy Pants....268
The Gazebo....269
The Ghost Breakers....269
The Goldwyn Follies....323
Houdini (Curtis/Leigh)....372
How the West Was Won....293, 340
The Mating Game....276
Monsieur Beaucaire....276
My Friend Irma....277
Never a Dull Moment....277
Off Limits....278
Pack Up Your Troubles....278
Papa's Delicate Condition....382
The Perils of Pauline (1947)....279
Scared Stiff....281
Show Them No Mercy....386
Star Spangled Rhythm....329
Marshall, Penny
Awakenings....218
Big....263
The Preacher's Wife....279
Marshall, Robert
Conquerors....758
Marshall, Stuart
Desire (Great Britain)....458
Marshall, William
The Phantom Planet....499
Marston, Theodore
She (1911)....154
Martell, Alphonse
Gigolettes of Paris....369
Martin, Charles
My Dear Secretary....277
Martin, D'Urville
Dolemite....532
Fass Black....532
Martin, Darnell
I Like It Like That....57
Martin, E.R.
Jungle Princess....400
Martin, Edwin L.
Invisible Agent....524
Martin, Eugenio
Horror Express....523
Martin, Frank
Behind the Mask....202
Martin, Paul
Black Roses....68, 171
Martin, Steven M.
Theremin: An Electronic Odyssey....478
Martine, Marie
11th and B: East Village Summer of Love....618
Martinez Jr., Rene
The Guy from Harlem....532
Martini, Richard
Cannes Man....428
Martino, Alberto de
The Medusa Against the Son of Hercules....42
Martinson, Leslie
Batman (1966)....503
Marton, Andrew
Clarence the Cross-Eyed Lion....662
Green Fire....371
Gypsy Colt....663
Men of the Fighting Lady....379
Marton, Pier
Pier Marton (are we and/or do we) Like Men....487
Pier Marton: Collected Works: 1979-84....487
Pier Marton: Say I'm a Jew....488
Marx, Fred
Dream Documentary (House of Un-American)....473
Dreams from China (House of Un-American)....473
Marx, Frederick
Hoop Dreams....473
House of Un-American Activities....473
Marziano-Tinoco, Rafael
The Track of the Ants....53
Masahiso, Sadanaga
Sure Death....140
Masakazu, Y.
My My Mai Vol. 1....737
My My Mai Vol. 2....737
Masamune, S.
New Dominion Tank Police Vol. 1: Episodes 1 and 2....738
New Dominion Tank Police Vol. 2: Episodes 3 and 4....738
New Dominion Tank Police Vol. 3: Episodes 5 and 6....738
Mascelli, Joseph V.
The Atomic Brain (Monstrosity)....503
Maselli, Francesco
Time of Indifference....41
Mashimo, Koichi
Dominion Tank Police Act I....727
Dominion Tank Police Act II....727
Dominion Tank Police Act III....727
Dominion Tank Police Act IV....727
Dominion Tank Police Pt. 1: Acts I & II....727
Dominion Tank Police Pt. 2: Acts III & IV....727
Maslin, Nigel
Conquerors....758
Mason, Edward McQ
Waterfront....207
Mason, Herbert
Lady in Distress....175
Mason, Lowell
Night of the Day of the…....508
Mason, William
Paddle to the Sea....211, 639
Massi, Stelvio
Black Cobra....532
Masterson, Peter
Arctic Blue....218
Convicts....223
Lily Dale....236
The Trip to Bountiful....250
Mastrocinque, Camillo
An Angel for Satan....516
Crypt of Horror....519
Full Hearts and Empty Pockets....41
Masuda, Toshio
Tora! Tora! Tora!....250
Matarazzo, Raffaello
Verdi (The Opera)....41, 586
Mate, Rudolph
The Black Shield of Falworth....360
Branded (Ladd)....291
D.O.A. (Original)....365
The Dark Past....365
The Deep Six....365
The Green Glove....371
The Violent Men....297
When Worlds Collide....502
Mather, Bill
Them (British Animation)....707
Mathiesen, Muir
Instruments of the Orchestra (Benjamin Britten)....469
Steps of the Ballet (Benjamin Britten)....469
Mathieu, Betsy
Heart's Desire....460
Matmor, Daniel
Urban Jungle....533
Matsubayashi, Shuei
I Bombed Pearl Harbor....137
Matsushita, Toshi
Cuba Amor....56
Matthau, Charles
The Grass Harp....229
Matthau, Walter
Gangster Story....369
Matthews, John
Mouse Soup....637
Pocahontas (Stop-Motion Animation)....640
Mattox, Janis
Book of Shadows....569
Mattox, Walt
The Bela Lugosi Collection: Devil Bat/ Scared to Death....516
Mattson, Arne
The Doll (Sweden)....75
Maurer, Norman
The Three Stooges Go Around the World in a Daze....284
The Three Stooges: The Outlaws....284
Mawra, Joseph P.
Chained Girls....457
White Slaves of Chinatown....512

Maxwell, Garth
Jack Be Nimble 208
Maxwell, Ronald F.
Gettysburg (Martin Sheen) 779
May, Elaine
Heartbreak Kid 270
Mikey and Nicky 276
A New Leaf 278
May, Joe
Homecoming (Silent) 69
The House of the Seven Gables 372
The Invisible Man Returns 524
May, Paul
Dr. Mabuse vs. Scotland Yard 505
May, Ted
Sesame Street: Quiet Time 657
Maybach, Chris
Art City: Making It in Manhattan 545
Mayer, Daisy Von Scherler
Party Girl (Mayer) 279
Mayersberg, Paul
Nightfall 499
Mayo, Archie
The Adventures of Marco Polo 356
Angel on My Shoulder (1946) 262
Archie Mayo Collection: Angel on My Shoulder and Svengali 358
Crash Dive 364
Illicit 373
Night After Night 380
Orchestra Wives 327
Petrified Forest 382
Svengali 389
They Shall Have Music 330
Mayo, Zac/Boggs, Fernella
Big Top (Spike & Mike's) 716
Rick the Dick in Hospital Hell (Spike/Mike Sick 2) 716
Maysles, Albert
Umbrellas 479, 558
Maysles, Albert & David
Christo in Paris 470, 547
Christo's Valley Curtain 470, 547
Gimme Shelter 620
Grey Gardens 797
Islands (Maysles Brothers) 337, 475
Running Fence 477, 556
Salesman 477
Maysles, Albert and David
Maysles Brothers: Direct Cinema 337, 475
Mayson, Michael
Boys' Shorts 457
Mazursky, Paul
Alex in Wonderland 216
Bob & Carol & Ted & Alice 361
Faithful 268
Harry and Tonto 230
Moon over Parador 276
Moscow on the Hudson 238
Next Stop, Greenwich Village 278
The Tempest 315
An Unmarried Woman 251
Willie and Phil 287
McAbee, Cory/Lurie, Bobby
The Billy Nayer Show (Int. Animation 6) 712
McAfee, Bob
Phuk Yew (Spike/Mike Sick 2) 716
McBrearty, Don
A Child's Christmas in Wales 662
McBride, Jim
David Holzman's Diary 471
Glen or Randa 496
The Wrong Man (McBride) 253
McCabe, Mitch
Playing the Part (Girl Friends) 460
McCall, Rod
Lewis & Clark & George 236
McCann, Tim
Desolation Angels 429
McCarey, Kevin
Gunfighters of the West 230
McCarey, Leo
An Affair to Remember 357
The Awful Truth 262
Belle of the Nineties 263
The Bells of St. Mary's 320
Duck Soup 267
Going My Way 323
Good Sam 370
Indiscreet (1931/Swanson) 373
Kid from Spain 273
Love Affair (1939) 377
The Milky Way (McCarey) 276
Ruggles of Red Gap 281
Six of a Kind 282
McCarey, Ray
Sunset Range 296
You Can't Fool Your Wife 394
McCarthy, Katherine
Civilians in War—Then and After: Poland and World War II 766
McCay, Winsor
Classic Shorts Compilation #12: Winsor McCay 682
Little Nemo (Pioneers 1) 714
The Sinking of The Lusitania (Pioneers 1) 714
A Tribute to Winsor McCay 717
Winsor McCay: Animation Legend 718
McClain, John
Cairo 321
McClanahan, Preston
Chester Zardis: The Spirit of New Orleans 610
McClary, J. Michael
Annie O 217
Curse of the Starving Class 311
McClure, H.P.
New Frontier (Power and the Land) 476
McCracken, Craig
No Neck Joe (Spike/Mike Sick 2) 716
McCrae, Scooter
Shatter Dead 529
McCubbin, Peter
Home for Christmas 231
McCullough, Jim
Where the Red Fern Grows, Part II 667
McDonald, Bruce
Highway 61 210
McDonald, Frank
One Body Too Many 508
Treasure of Fear (aka Scared Stiff) 530
McDonald, Gary
The Sea Wolf (1997) 245
McDowell, Roddy
Tam Lin 178
McElwee, Ross
Ross McElwee Films 477
Sherman's March 477
Six O'Clock News 478
Time Indefinite 478
McEveety, Vincent
Firecreek 292
Smoke (Disney) 666
McFadden, Hamilton
Stand Up and Cheer 329
McFall, Kathleen
Counterclockwise 428
McFerran, Mary
Homage to May 19th/Framed 473
McGann, William
Dr. Christian Meets the Women 366
In Old California 293
McGaugh, Wilbur
Three Pals 405
McGehee, Scott
Suture 438
McGlynn, Don
Charles Mingus: Triumph of the Underdog 610
McGowan, Dorrell
Tokyo File 391
McGowan, J.P.
Blood and Steel 396
Canyon of the Missing Men 291
Hunted Men 399
The Hurricane Express 372
Lost Express 400
Mistaken Orders 401
Red Signals 403
Webs of Steel 406
McGowan, Robert
The Old Swimmin' Hole 381
McGowan, Stuart E.
Tokyo File 391
McGrath, Douglas
Emma (Paltrow) 226
McGrath, Joseph
The Great McGonagall 183
The Magic Christian 184
McGuinn, Patrick
Desert Spirits 429
Puppets & Demons: Films by Patrick McGuinn 436
Suroh: The Alien Hitchhiker 500
McHenry, Doug
House Party 2: The Pajama Jam 444
Jason's Lyric 445
McIntosh, Michael
Aliens Cut My Hair 503
McKay, Craig
Subway Stories 248, 255
McKay, Jim
Girls Town 229
Lighthearted Nation 433
McKenney, Phil
Travels of a Dollar Bill (Best Fest Kids) 706
McKeough, Rita
Rita McKeough: An Excavation 556
McKimson, Robert
PT 109 771
McKinney, Brandon
Chainsaw Bob in a Cult Classic (Spike/Mike Sick 2) 716
Performance Art Starring Chainsaw Bob (Spike/Mike) 716
McKinney, Miles
Spaghetti Snot (Spike/Mike Sick 2) 716
McLagan, M.
Tibet in Exile 150
McLaglen, Andrew V.
Bandolero! 290
Blue and the Gray 779
Breakthrough 171
Cahill—U.S. Marshall 291
Chisum 291
McLintock! (Restored Producer's Cut) 294
The Rare Breed 295
The Sea Wolves 163
Shenandoah 386
The Undefeated 392
McLaren, Norman
Creative Process: Norman McLaren 708
McLaughlin, Sheila
Committed 428
She Must Be Seeing Things 437, 465
McLean, Steve
Postcards from America 464
McLenighan, Valjean
Las Vegas Tapes (America in Black & White) 468
Pugs 'N Pols (America in Black and White) 468
McLeod, Norman Z.
Alias Jesse James 262
Casanova's Big Night 265
Here Comes Cookie 271
Horse Feathers 271
Kid from Brooklyn 273
Lady Be Good 325
Let's Dance 325
Little Men 376
Monkey Business 276
Never Wave at a WAC 278
Paleface 278
Panama Hattie 327
The Road to Rio 281
The Secret Life of Walter Mitty 281
McLoughlin, Tom
Journey 234
McLuhan, Teri
The Shadow Catcher: Edward S. Curtis and the North American Indian 788
McNaughton, John
Borrower 494
Mad Dog and Glory 237
Normal Life 240
Sex, Drugs, Rock & Roll 437
Wild Things 252
McTiernan, John
The Hunt for Red October 232
Meckler, Nancy
Sister My Sister 164
Medak, Peter
The Changeling 518
Day in the Death of Joe Egg 182
The Hunchback (1997) 232
The Krays 161
Let Him Have It 161
Romeo Is Bleeding 245
The Ruling Class 184
Medem, Julio
The Red Squirrel 45
Medford, Don
I'm a Fool and The Wild Bunch 418
Medvedkin, Alexander
Happiness 85
Meffre, Pomme
Grain of Sand 3
Megahey, Leslie
The Advocate 158
Megahy, Francis
The Disappearance of Kevin Johnson 225
Mehrjui, Darioush
Hamoon 106
The Tenants 107
Mehta, Deepa
Camilla (USA) 221
Fire (Drama) 210
Mehta, Ketan
Spices 148
Meisel, Myron
It's All True 344
Meiselas, Susan
Pictures from a Revolution 60
Mekas, Adolfas
Hallelujah the Hills 431
Mekas, Adolfus
Joseph Losey and Adolfus Mekas 353
Mekas, Jonas
cup/saucer/two dancers/radio 442
Dr. Carl G. Jung or Lapis Philosophorum 442
Guns of the Trees 442
He Stands in a Desert Counting the Seconds of His Life 442
In Between 442
Interview with Jonas Mekas 336
Lost, Lost, Lost 442
Notes for Jerome 442
Paradise Not Yet Lost (aka Oona's Third Year) 442
Reminiscences of a Journey to Lithuania 443
Scenes from the Life of Andy Warhol 443
Walden (aka Diaries, Notes & Sketches) 443
Zefiro Torna or Scenes from the Life of George Maciunas 443
Melancon, Andre
Bach and Broccoli 662
Melendez, Bill
Dick Deadeye 709
Melford, George
The Charlatan 396
Dracula (Spanish) 520
East of Borneo 367
Moran of the Lady Letty 401
The Sheik 404
Melies, Georges
Films of Georges Melies Vol. 1 20
Grand Melies and Melies' Short Films 20
Marvelous Melies 22
More Melies 22

Melkonian, James
The Jerky Boys: The Movie 272
The Stoned Age 248
Mellencamp, John Cougar
Falling from Grace 227
Melville, Jean-Pierre
Bob le Flambeur 25
Le Doulos 25
Le Samourai 25
Le Silence de la Mer 25
Leon Morin, Priest 25
Les Enfants Terribles 25
Les Enfants Terribles and Les Parents Terribles 25, 27
Menaul, Christopher
A Dangerous Man: Lawrence After Arabia 159
Fatherland 227
Feast of July 160
Mendelsohn, Eric
Through an Open Window (Best Fest 5th Annual) 706
Mendes, Lothar
Man Who Could Work Miracles 176
Moonlight Sonata 176, 326
Moonlight Sonata (Romance) 176
Mendez, Fernando
The Vampire 530
Menell, Jo
Mandela (Documentary) 152
Menendez, Ramon
Stand and Deliver 61
Menkes, Nina
The Bloody Child 427
Great Sadness of Zohara 472
Magdalena Viraga 433
Queen of Diamonds 436
Mennees, Matt
Fan-Tasy (CineBLAST!) 428
Menotti, Giancarlo
The Medium 583
Menshov, Vladimir
Moscow Does Not Believe in Tears 82
Menzel, Jiri
Closely Watched Trains 99
Larks on a String 100
My Sweet Little Village 100
Menzies, William C.
Drums in the Deep South 367
Things to Come 501
Mercero, Antonio
Don Juan, My Love 44
Merchant, Ismail
In Custody 147
Lumiere & Company 5, 336
The Proprietor 243
Meredith, Burgess
Man on the Eiffel Tower 378
Merhage, E. Elias
Begotten 427
Merino, J.L.
Scream of the Demon Lover 529
Merlet, Agnes
Son of the Shark 8
Merrill, Nathaniel
Hansel and Gretel (Met Opera) 580
Merriwether, Nicholas
Elvira's Midnight Madness: EEGAH! 521
Mervish, Dan
omaha (the movie) 435
Meske, Ellen
Animation in the Netherlands 706
Meszaros, Marta
Adoption 101
The Girl (Hungarian) 102
Riddance 102
Metcalf, Christina
Buster and Me 802
Metter, Alan
Cold Dog Soup 266
Moving 276
Metzger, Radley
The Alley Cats 456, 503
Dark Odyssey 505
The Lickerish Quartet 507
Little Mother 507
Score 465, 510
Therese and Isabelle 7, 466
Metzner, Erno
Uberfall (Avant Garde & Experimental Films) 482
Meyer, Jean
Le Bourgeois Gentilhomme 21
Meyer, Muffie
Enormous Changes at the Last Minute 429
Meyer, Nicholas
Star Trek II: Wrath of Khan 500
Star Trek VI: The Undiscovered Country 500
Volunteers 286
Meyer, Russ
Beneath the Valley of the Ultravixens 513
Beyond the Valley of the Dolls 513
Blacksnake! 513
Cherry, Harry and Raquel 513
Common-Law Cabin 513
Eve and the Handyman 513
Faster Pussycat! Kill! Kill! 513
Finders, Keepers, Lovers, Weepers 513
Good Morning...And Goodbye 513
Immoral Mr. Teas 513
Lorna 513
Mondo Topless 513
Motor Psycho 513
Mudhoney 513
Russ Meyer's Up! 513
Supervixens 513
Vixen 513
Wild Gals of the Naked West 513
Meyers, Sidney
Quiet One 476
The Savage Eye 385
Meza, Eric
House Party 3 444
Michaels, Barbara Rose
Watching Her Sleep (Girl Friends) 460
Micheaux, Oscar
Body and Soul (African American Films) 447
Girl from Chicago (African American Film) 447
God's Step Children 448
Lying Lips (African-American Film) 447
Murder in Harlem 448
Swing 449
Ten Minutes to Live 449
Veiled Aristocrats 449
Within Our Gates 449
Michel, Andre
The Sorceress 23
Michell, Roger
The Buddha of Suburbia 190
Jane Austen's Persuasion (Film) 161, 193
Michio, Takeyama
Animated Classics of Japanese Literature: Harp of Burma, Pts 1 & 2 720
Mieville, Anne-Marie
Comment Ca Va? (How Is It Going?) 9
Migeat, F.
Batouka: The First International Festival of Percussion 601
Miguet, F.
Percy Mayfield: Poet Laureate of the Blues 614
Mihalka, George
Bullet to Beijing 210
The Crossbow 663
Mihaylov, Eugeny
Canary Season 104
Mike, D.J.
Comet Butterfly and Sword 119
Mikesch, Elfi
Seduction: The Cruel Woman 65, 465
Mikhalkov, Nikita
Burnt by the Sun 80
Close to Eden 80
Dark Eyes 80
Oblomov 82
Unfinished Piece for a Mechanical Piano, An 83
Milani, Tahmineh
The Legend of a Sigh 106
Milestone, Lewis
All Quiet on the Western Front (1930) 357
Arch of Triumph (Bergman) 358
Edge of Darkness (1943/Flynn) 367
Front Page (1931) 369
Garden of Eden 398
General Died at Dawn 369
Hallelujah, I'm a Bum 323
Mutiny on the Bounty (Brando) 380
The North Star 381
Ocean's 11 381
Pork Chop Hill 383
Rain 384
Red Pony 384
Strange Love of Martha Ivers 388
They Who Dare 178
A Walk in the Sun 773
Milici, Jennifer
Sex Is Sex 436, 477
Milio, Jim
The Real Las Vegas 763
Milius, John
Marcello, I'm So Bored (First Works) 334
Rough Riders 245
The Wind and the Lion 252
Millan, Lorri
Around the World the Lesbian Way 456
Milland, Ray
A Man Alone 294
Panic in Year Zero 499
Millar, Gavin
Dreamchild 225
Millar, Stuart
When the Legends Die 297
Miller, Allan
High Fidelity 590
Small Wonders 478
Miller, Anthony
An American Werewolf in Paris 217
Miller, Chris
Lea Press on Limbs (Spike/Mike 1) 716
Miller, Claude
The Accompanist 16
The Best Way 2, 456
The Little Thief 5
Lumiere & Company 5, 336
This Sweet Sickness 7
Miller, David
Back Street 358
Captain Newman, M.D. 362
Diane 366
Executive Action 226
Flying Tigers 368
Lonely Are the Brave 294
Love Happy 275
Midnight Lace 379
Opposite Sex 327
Our Very Own 381
The Story of Esther Costello 388
Sudden Fear 388
Miller, George
All the Rivers Run 205
Andre 661
Lorenzo's Oil 236
Mad Max Beyond Thunderdome 206
Man from Snowy River 206
Miracle Down Under 206
The Neverending Story II: The Next Chapter 665
Road Warrior 207
Twilight Zone—The Movie 258, 501
The Witches of Eastwick 252
Zeus and Roxanne 668
Miller, Jason
That Championship Season 315
Miller, Michael
Jackson County Jail 233
National Lampoon's Class Reunion 277
Miller, Neal
Under the Biltmore Clock 301
Miller, Robert Ellis
Any Wednesday 217
The Heart Is a Lonely Hunter 371
Miller-Monzon, John
Things We Said Today (Dyke Drama) 458
Milligan, Andy
The Naked Witch 526
Millot, Eric
Djabote: Sengalese Drumming & Song from Master Drummer Doudou N'D 152
Mills, Michael
Evolution (Incredible Animation 2) 711
Mills, Reginald
Tales of Beatrix Potter (Ballet) 576
Milton, Robert
Devotion 366
Minassians, Serj
Stream of Social Intercourse 438
Miner, Allen
Stranded 388
Miner, Steve
My Father the Hero 277
Wild Hearts Can't Be Broken 667
Ming-Liang, Tsai
Vive l'Amour 136
Minghella, Anthony
The English Patient 226
Mr. Wonderful 239
Truly, Madly, Deeply 164
Mingozzi, Gianfranco
Bellissimo: Images of the Italian Cinema 32
The Last Diva 33, 336
Minnelli, Vincente
An American in Paris 319
Bad and the Beautiful 358
The Band Wagon 320
Bells Are Ringing 320
Brigadoon 320
Cabin in the Sky 362
The Clock 321
Cobweb 364
The Courtship of Eddie's Father 266
Designing Woman 365
Father of the Bride (Spencer Tracy) 268
Father's Little Dividend 268
The Four Horsemen of the Apocalypse (1961) 369
Gigi 323
Home from the Hill 372
I Dood It 324
Kismet (1955) 325
Long, Long Trailer 274
Lust for Life 377
Madame Bovary 377
Meet Me in St. Louis 326
Minnelli on Minnelli 337
On a Clear Day You Can See Forever 327
The Reluctant Debutante 280
Tea & Sympathy 315
Two Weeks in Another Town 392
Undercurrent 392
Yolanda and the Thief 331
Ziegfeld Follies 331
Minnich, Rick
Delphi 1830 & Next Time Everything Will Be Better 483
Minnis, Jon
Charade (Int. Animation 1) 711, 716
Minsker, Ethan
Anything Boys Can Do 618
Miroshnichenko, Sergei
And the Past Seems But a Dream (Glasnost V.6) 81
Mirzoyan, Vladimir
The Tailor (Glasnost Film Festival V.3) 81
Misumi, Kenji
Return of the Giant Majin 509
Sleepy Eyes of Death—Sword of Fire 139
Zatoichi Challenged! 140
Zatoichi: The Blind Swordsman and the Chess Expert 140
Zatoichi: The Blind Swordsman Samaritan 140
Zatoichi: The Life and Opinion of Masseur Ichi 140
Zatoichi: The Return of Masseur Ichi 140

Mita, Ryusuke
Dragon Half Parts 1 and 2 728
Mitchell, Bruce
Dynamite Dan 397
Phantom Flyer 402
Won in the Clouds 406
Mitchell, Eric
Kidnapped 432
Red Italy 436
Mitchell, George
Wolf Blood 406
Mitchell, Howard
Hidden Aces 399
Mitchell, Mike
Frannies Christmas (Spike/Mike 3) 716
Mitchell, Oswald
The Greed of William Hart 522
House of Darkness 523
Mitry, Jean
Pacific 231 (Avant Garde Program #11) 482
Mitterand, Frederic
Madame Butterfly 5, 583
Mittler, Leo
Novotna in The Bartered Bride and The Last Waltz 27
Miyazaki, Hayao
Kiki's Delivery Service 734
Mizoguchi, Kenji
Chikamatsu Monogatari (Crucified Lovers) 143
A Geisha 143
Life of Oharu 143
Osaka Elegy 143
Princess Yang Kwei Fei 143
Sansho the Bailiff 143
Sisters of Gion 143
Story of the Last Chrysanthemum 143
Street of Shame 143
Taira Clan Saga 143
Ugetsu 143
Utamaro and His Five Women 143
Mizrahi, Moshe
House on Chelouche Street 107
I Love You Rosa 108
La Vie Continue 4
Madame Rosa 5
Moch, Ryszard
I Am Who I Am 92
Mock, Freida Lee
Maya Lin: A Strong Clear Vision 475, 778
Moffatt, Peter
The King's Demons/The Five Doctors 200
Moguy, Leonide
Action in Arabia 356
Whistle Stop 393
Mohre, Terry
Studio Melee Sampler 561
Works, 1978-79 718
Mokhtari, Ebrahim
Zinat 107
Moland, Hans Petter
Zero Kelvin 77
Molander, Gustaf
Dollar 75
Intermezzo (Bergman/Sweden) 76
Only One Night 76
Swedenhielms 77
A Woman's Face (1938/Bergman) 77
Moleon, Rafael
Baton Rouge 44
Molinaro, Edouard
A Pain in the A.. 16
Back to the Wall 19
Beaumarchais 2
La Cage aux Folles 17
La Cage aux Folles II 17
Mondell, A. & C. Salzman
West of Hester Street 116
Monger, Christopher
The Englishman Who Went up a Hill But Came Down a Mountain 182
Just Like a Woman 183
Monicelli, Mario
Big Deal on Madonna Street 40
Laugh for Joy (Risate di Gioia) 41
Lovers and Liars 33
The Organizer 41
Monk, Egon
Oppermann Family 64
Monk, Meredith
Films of Meredith Monk 485, 567
Monson, Carl
Please Don't Eat My Mother 279
Montagne, Edward
McHale's Navy 276
McHale's Navy Joins the Air Force 276
Montagne, Edward J.
How to Frame a Figg 271
The Reluctant Astronaut 280
Montaldo, Giuliano
Sacco and Vanzetti 34
Montell, Preben
Spartacus (Bolshoi/Vasiliev) 575
Monter, Jose Luis
It's Raining Money 44
Montero, Robert
Mondo Balardo 508
Monster of the Island (Island Monster) 526
Montgomery, George
From Hell to Borneo 369
Guerillas in Pink Lace 371
Samar 385
Satan's Harvest 245
Steel Claw 388
Montgomery, Jennifer
Art for Teachers of Children 426
Montgomery, Patrick
The Man You Loved to Hate 348
Montgomery, Robert
Gallant Hours 369
Lady in the Lake 375
Moon, Sarah
Lumiere & Company 5, 336
Moore, Alan
Raptures of the Deep 436
Reptile Mind 436
Moore, Frank
Beehive 483
Moore, Gary
Armchair Inventions (Sextoons) 715
Moore, Michael
Canadian Bacon 428
Paradise, Hawaiian Style 537
Roger & Me 477
TV Nation 422
Moore, Robert
Chapter Two 222
The Cheap Detective 265
Murder by Death 277
Moore, Rudy Ray
The Legend of Dolemite: Rudy Ray Moore 533
Moore, Simon
Under Suspicion 251
Moore, Tom
Night Mother 314
Moore, Vin
The Drag-Net 366
Moorhouse, Jocelyn
How to Make an American Quilt 232
Proof 206
A Thousand Acres 249
Mora, Philippe
Death of a Soldier 205
Mad Dog Morgan 206
Pterodactyl Woman from Beverly Hills 509
Mora, Phillipe
Brother Can You Spare a Dime? 469
Morahan, Christopher
After Pilkington 158
Clockwise 198
Heat of the Day 161
Unnatural Pursuits 164
Morais, Jose Alvano
The Jester 48
Morales, Jose Diaz
Loyola, the Soldier Saint 48
Morayta, Miguel
Invasion of the Vampires 524
Mordillat, Gerard
My Life and Times with Antonin Artaud 5
Moretti, Nanni
Caro Diario (Dear Diary) 32
Palombella Rossa 34
Moreuil, Francois
Love Play 21
Morgan, Andrew
Little Lord Fauntleroy (1995) 161
Swallows and Amazons Forever!: Coot Club 667
Swallows and Amazons Forever!: The Big Six 667
Morgan, Charles
Stick It in Your Ear 510
Morgenstern, Janusz
Legend of the White Horse 664
Polish Ways 93
W Hour 94
Moriarty, John
Dream Boys Revue 458
Moritsugu, Jon
Hippie Porn 431
Mod Fuck Explosion 434
Moro, Santiago
Katy Meets the Aliens 672, 712
Morris, Ernest
The Tell-Tale Heart (1963) 530
Morris, Errol
A Brief History of Time 481
Fast, Cheap & Out of Control 481
Morris, Richard
Big Jim 360
Morris, Wendy
An Urban Tragedy (Best Fest 90) 706
Morrissey, Paul
Beethoven's Nephew 514
Dracula (Warhol) 514
Frankenstein (Warhol) 514
Morse, Hollingsworth
Crash of the Moons 495
Morse, Terry
British Intelligence 361
Danny Boy 365
Unknown World (Sci-Fi) 501
Morton, Rocky
D.O.A. (Remake) 224
Mosbacher, Dee
Straight from the Heart 465, 478
Mosbacher, Dr. Dee
All God's Children 449, 456
Moses, Harry
Assault at West Point 218
Moshenson, Han
Wooden Gun 108
Mosher, Gregory
A Life in the Theater 312
Our Town (1988/Eric Stoltz) 314
Moshinsky, Elijah
Genghis Cohn 192
The Green Man 192
Moskalyk, Antonin
Dita Saxova 99
Mosquera, Gustavo
Times to Come 53
Moss, Carlton
Portraits in Black 453
Moss, Dann
Memories of Hollywood, Vol. 1 337
Moszuk, Stanislaw
Caesarian Section 90
Motta, Marcello
The Strange Hostel of Naked Pleasures 511
Mottola, Greg
The Daytrippers 266
Motyl, H.D.
The Voyage of LaAmistad: A Quest for Freedom 455
Motyleff, Ilya
Cantor's Son 112
Moudy, Peg McClure
Housecats (Best Fest Kids) 706
Mouradian, Sarky
Forty Days of Musa Dagh 759
Mouris, Frank
Frank Film 710
Movic
Super Deformed Double Feature 748
Mowbray, Edward
Video Art: Not Dead Yet 490
Moxey, John
Circus of Fear 172
Moxey, John Llewelyn
Horror Hotel 523
The Night Stalker 420
Moyle, Allan
Empire Records 429
Pump Up the Volume 243
Moyne, Lennie
The Hand of Fear 200
Mrazek, David
My Prague Spring 101
Muccigrosso, John
The Jousters 636
Mudge, Jean
Emily Dickinson: A Certain Slant of Light 303
Herman Melville: Consider the Sea 304
Mudie, Peter
Another Great Moment (Outrageous 2) 714
Great British Moments (Outrageous 1) 714
Mueller, Dennis
The Assassination of JFK 797
Mueller, Eric
World & Time Enough 467
Mueller, Ray
The Wonderful, Horrible Life of Leni Riefenstahl 66, 480
Mugge, Robert
Cool Runnings: The Reggae Movie 601
Entertaining the Troops: American Entertainers in World War II 767
George Crumb: The Voice of the Whale 617
Gospel According to Al Green 607
Hawaiian Rainbow: The Magic and the Music of the Islands 602
Kumu Hula: Keepers of a Culture 602
Ruben Blades 60
Saxophone Colossus 615
Muir, Madeline
West Coast Crones: A Glimpse into the Lives of Nine Old Lesbians 467
Muk-Sing, Benny Chan
Happy Hour 120
Mukherjee, Hrishikesh
Abhimaan 146
Anand 146
Mulcahy, Russell
Highlander: The Director's Cut 231
Ricochet 244
Mullen, Sean
Horndog (Spike/Mike Sick 2) 716
Oh Crappy Day (Spike/Mike Sick 2) 716
Muller, Matthias
Matthias Muller—Selected Films 433
Muller, Traugott
Friedemann Bach 69
Mullett, Peter
Situation Critical: The USS Forrestal 778
Mulligan, Robert
Baby, The Rain Must Fall 358
Clara's Heart 222
Great Imposter 370
Inside Daisy Clover 373
Love with a Proper Stranger 377
Man in the Moon 237
Summer of '42 389
To Kill a Mockingbird 391
Up the Down Staircase 392
Munch, Christopher

The Hours and Times 431, 460
Mune, Ian
The End of the Golden Weather 208
Munger, Chris
Kiss of the Tarantula 524
Muniz, Angel
Nueba Yol 52, 55
Munk, Andrzej
Bad Luck 90
Eroica 91
Man on the Track 93
The Passenger (Munk) 93
Munoz-Briggs, Simona
El Charanguero: Jaime Torres, the Charango Player 56, 602
Muntadas, Antonio
Video Art: Antonio Muntadas 489
Murakami, Ryu
Tokyo Decadence 140, 511
Murnau, Friedrich W.
The Burning Soil 73
City Girl 73
Faust (Murnau) 73
Haunted Castle 73
The Last Laugh 73
Nosferatu 73
Nosferatu: The First Vampire 73
Sunrise 73
Tabu 73
Tartuffe (1925/Jannings) 73
Murphy, Dudley
Emperor Jones 448
Murphy, Eddie
Harlem Nights 444
Murphy, Geoff
The Last Outlaw (1994) 235
Utu: The Director's Cut 209
Murphy, Tab
Last of the Dogmen 235
Murray, Ian
Video Art: Come on Touch It
(Study No. 4 for a Personality Inventory Channel) 490
Murray, Joe
The Chore 705
Murray, Ken
Hollywood Without Make-Up 335
Murray, Scott
Beyond Innocence 205
Murua, Lautaro
Winter Barracks 53
Musker, John
Hercules 42, 634, 693
Mweze, Ngangura
La Vie Est Belle (Life Is Rosy) 150
Myles, Bruce
Ground Zero 206
Nabili, Marva
Nightsongs 434
The Sealed Soil (Khak-e Sar Beh Morh) 107
Nadel, Arthur
Clambake 536
Naderi, Amir
The Runner 107
Nagai, Go
Iron Virgin Jun 733
Shuten Doji—The Star Hand Kid 1 745
Shuten Doji—The Star Hand Kid 2 745
Shuten Doji—The Star Hand Kid 3 745
Shuten Doji—The Star Hand Kid 4 745
Violence Jack Part 3: Slum King 752
Nagaich, Ravee
Mere Jeevan Saathi 148
Nagaoka, Akinori
Record of Lodoss War, Gift Box 743
Nagy, Gyula
Finger Wave (Animation C.2) 705
Nair, Mira
Kama Sutra 147
Mississippi Masala 433
The Perez Family 279
Nakagawa, Nobuo
Ghost of Yotsuya 137
Nakajima, Takehiro
Okoge 138
Nakano, Desmond
White Man's Burden 252
Nakazawa, Keiji
Barefoot Gen 722
Nakis, Algas
Show Biz (Sextoons) 715
Nallon, James
Blood Hook 517
Nalls, Gayil
Walking in Both Worlds (A Common Destiny) 470
Nam, Lee Tse
The Tattoo Connection 124
Naranjo, Lisandro Duque
Miracle in Rome 45
Nardo, Don
Stuff Stephanie in the Incinerator 511
Nares, James
Rome '78 488
Narizzano, Silvio
24 Hours in a Woman's Life 356
Blue 290
The Body in the Library 189
Georgy Girl 182
Why Shoot the Teacher? 212
Naruse, Mikio
Late Chrysanthemums 138
When a Woman Ascends the Stairs 140
Nathan, John
Passover: Traditions of Freedom 115
Nava, Gregory
My Family 434
Selena 61, 328
Naylor, Timothy
Generic Metan Titan (CineBLAST 2) 483
Nazarov, Eduard
Hunt (Masters of Russian Animation 1) 713
Travels of an Ant (Masters #3) 713
Nazarro, Ray
Dog Eat Dog 505
Law of the Canyon 293
Nazimova, Alla
Salome 403
Neal, Peter
Jimi Hendrix: Experience 621
Neame, Ronald
Chalk Garden 311
Filmmakers on Their Craft 333
Gambit 369
The Golden Salamander 174
Horse's Mouth, The 183
I Could Go on Singing 324
The Man Who Never Was 176
Odessa File 162
The Poseidon Adventure 242
The Prime of Miss Jean Brodie 177
The Promoter 184
Tunes of Glory 179
Windom's Way 179
Nechvatal, Joseph
When Things Get Rough on Easy Street,
Ovid and Shorts 439
Needham, Hal
The Villain 297
Needleman, Neil Ira
Red Ribbons 464
Negrepontis, Yiannis
Lysistrata 313
Negroponte, Michel
Jupiter's Wife 474
Negulesco, Jean
The Best of Everything 359
Daddy Long Legs 321
How to Marry a Millionaire 271
Humoresque 372
Johnny Belinda 374
Mask of Dimitrios 378
Phone Call from a Stranger 382
Road House 385
Three Came Home 390
Three Coins in the Fountain 283
Titanic (1953/USA) 391
Woman's World 287
Neidik, Abbey Jack
Dark Lullabies 775
Neilan, Marshall
Chloe 504
Stella Maris 404
Swing It Professor 330
The Vagabond Lover 331
Neilan, Mickey
Chloe/Love Is Calling You/Sun 396
Neill, Roy William
Black Angel 360
Black Room 360
Dr. Syn 366
Frankenstein Meets the Wolfman 522
Sherlock Holmes and the Spider Woman 186
Neilson, James
Gentle Giant 633
Neiter, Hans
Seven Years in Tibet (1957) 178
Nekes, Werner
Film Before Film 63
Nelson, A.
Need for Christian Peacemaking 805
Nelson, Gary
Noble House 194
Nelson, Gene
Harum Scarum 536
Kissin' Cousins 325
Nelson, Gunvor
My Name Is Una (Short Personal Films) 437
Nelson, Jack
The Call of the Wilderness 396
Nelson, Jessie
Corrina, Corrina 223
Nelson, Ralph
Christmas Lilies of the Field 222
Duel at Diablo 292
Father Goose 268
A Hero Ain't Nothin' but a Sandwich 231
Lilies of the Field 376
Requiem for a Heavyweight (1962) 384
The Wilby Conspiracy 533
Nelson, Sam
Sagebrush Trail 295
Nelson, Tim Blake
Eye of God 227
Nemec, Jan
Code Name Ruby 101
Diamonds of the Night 101
Oratorio for Prague 101
A Report on the Party and the Guests 101
Nesheim, Berit
Sondagsengler (The Other Side of Sunday) 77
Nettlebeck, Sandra
A Certain Grace (Dyke Drama) 458
Neuland, Marc
Bambi Meets Godzilla (Experimental Series 19) 484
Neumann, Kurt
Carnival Story 363
The Fly (1958) 521
Kronos 498
Let's Sing Again 376
Make a Wish 326
Rocketship X-M 499
Son of Ali Baba 387
Newberry, Jim
Writing in Water and Admiral Bataille
& the S.S. Esoterica 480
Newbrough, Cheryl
Goodbye Emma Jo 460
Newby, Chris
Relax (New Directors) 487
Newby, Christopher
Boys' Shorts 457
Newell, Mike
An Awfully Big Adventure 158
Donnie Brasco 225
Enchanted April 160
Four Weddings and a Funeral 182
Newfield, Sam
The Black Raven 517
Dead Men Walk 519
Federal Agent 368
Lost Continent (Romero) 498
The Mad Monster 525
Monster Maker 526
Racing Luck 383
Terror of Tiny Town 511
Newhart, Chase
The Savage Garden 837
Newland, Marv
Anijam (Int. Animation 1) 711
Bambi Meets Godzilla (Spike/Mike 1) 716
Newman, Joseph M.
Love Nest 377
This Island Earth (Sci-Fi) 501
Newman, Paul
The Glass Menagerie (American) 311
Sometimes a Great Notion 247
Newmeyer, Fred
General Spanky 269
Harold Lloyd: Girl Shy 410
Night Bird 401
Perfect Clown 411
Newmeyer, Fred C.
A Sailor-Made Man 410
Newsom, Ted
Frankenstein—A Cinematic Scrapbook 522
Ngai, Chan Wui
Way of the Black Dragon 533
Ngai, Kong
The Great Jetfoil Robbery 128
Nibbelink, Phil
An American Tail: Fievel Goes West 661
Niblo, Fred
Ben-Hur (Novarro) 395
Blood and Sand (Valentino) 396
Camille (Niblo/1921) 396
Dangerous Hours 397
Mark of Zorro (1920) 401
Mysterious Lady 380
Sex 403
The Temptress 405
The Three Musketeers (1921/Fairbanks) 405
Niccol, Andrew
Gattaca 496
Niccoli, Casey
Gift 430
Nichetti, Maurizio
The Icicle Thief 33
Stephano Quantestorie 34
Volere Volare 34
Nichol, Alex
The Screaming Skull 529
Nicholas, Gregor
Broken English 208
Nicholls, George
Anne of Green Gables (RKO) 661
The Return of Peter Grimm 384
Nichols, George
She (1911) 154
Nichols, Mike
The Birdcage 263
Carnal Knowledge 221
Catch-22 265
The Fortune 228
The Graduate 370
The Graduate, 25th Anniversary Edition 370
Heartburn 230
Postcards from the Edge 279
Primary Colors 279
Regarding Henry 244
Silkwood 246
Who's Afraid of Virginia Woolf? 393
Wolf 531
Working Girl 288

Nicholson, Jack
Jack Nicholson: AFI Lifetime Achievement 332
The Two Jakes 251
Nickell, Paul
Coriolanus 311
Nickman, Jan C.
Affirmations for Living Beyond Cancer 847
Planetary Traveler 715
Third Stone from the Sun 667
Nicolaou, Ted
Fowl Play 663
Leapin' Leprechauns 664
Nicolella, John
Finish Line 227
Kull the Conqueror 234
Nielsen, Lasse
You Are Not Alone 77, 467
Nielsen, Niels
Gods of Beauty: A Portrait of the Visionary Artist: Mona Boulware Webb, The 549
Nierenberg, George
Say Amen, Somebody 608
Nigh, William
The Ape 516
Black Dragons 360
Doomed to Die 366
The Fatal Hour 367
Hoosier Schoolboy 372
Mr. Wong in Chinatown 379
Mr. Wong, Detective 379
Mysterious Mr. Wong 380
The Mystery of Mr. Wong 380
Nihomatsu, Dazui
X from Outer Space 502
Nilsson, Rob
Heat and Sunlight 431
Signal 7 437
Nimoy, Leonard
Good Mother 229
Star Trek III: Search for Spock 500
Star Trek IV: The Voyage Home 500
Star Trek IV: The Voyage Home (Director's Cut) 500
Three Men and a Baby 284
Vincent 316
Ninio, Ron
Auditions 107
Nishizawa, Nobutaka
Adventures of an American Rabbit 676
Nitolli, Tony
I Never Ho'd for My Father (Spike/Mike Sick 2) 716
Niv, Orna Ben-Dor
Because of That War 775
Newland 108
Noble, Nigel
Voices of Sarafina 151
Noguchi, Haruyasu
Monster from a Prehistoric Planet 498
Nolbandov, Sergei
Ships with Wings 178
Undercover 179
Nolte, William
Duke Is Tops (African American Films) 447
Nolte, William L.
The Bronze Venus 321
Noojier, Paul
At One View (Int. Animation 5) 712
Noonan, Chris
Babe 662
Noonan, Tom
What Happened Was... 439
Wife, The 439
Norstein, Yuri
Battle of Kerjenets (Masters #5) 713
Tale of Tales (Masters #3) 713
North, Don
War in El Cedro: American Veterans in Nicaragua 62
Norton, Bill L.
Gargoyles 506
Nosaka, Akiyuki
Grave of the Fireflies 137, 731
Nosseck, Max
Dillinger 366
Overture to Glory 113
Nossiter, Jonathan
Resident Alien 436, 464
Novaro, Maria
Danzon 49
Novik, William
Travels of Marco Polo 667
Novy, Wade
In Between 431
Nowicki, Marek
Chatelaine's Daughter 91
Noxon, Nicolas L.
Dear Mr. Gable 333
Noy, Wilfred
Midnight Girl 401
Noyce, Phillip
Blind Fury 219
Clear and Present Danger 222
Dead Calm 205
Patriot Games 242
Nuckolls III, Charles Butler
Kwanzaa: An African-American Cultural Holiday 453
Nugent, Elliott
Give Me a Sailor 269
Love in Bloom 275
The Male Animal 275
My Favorite Brunette 277
My Girl Tisa 380
Never Say Die 278
Splendor 387
Up in Arms 331
Welcome Stranger 286
Nunez, Victor
Ruby in Paradise 436
Ulee's Gold 438
Nunn, Trevor
Lady Jane 161
The Twelfth Night (1996/Great Britain) 164, 316
Nupen, Christopher
Itzhak Perlman: Virtuoso Violinist 591
Nurdsany, Claude
Microcosmos 818
Nussbaum, Raphael
From Czar to Stalin 87
Nutley, Colin
House of Angels 76
The Last Dance 76
Nuytten, Bruno
Camille Claudel 2
Nyby, Christian
First to Fight 368
Thing, The 501
Nykvist, Carl-Gustaf
The Women on the Roof 77
Nykvist, Sven
The Ox 76
O'Brien, Glenn
T.V. Party 422
O'Brien, Jim
Dressmaker 160
Foreign Affairs 268
Rebecca (1996) 163
O'Brien, John
The Big Dis 427
Vermont Is for Lovers 439
O'Brien, Willis
Dinosaur and the Missing Link (O'Brien Primitives) 717
Prehistoric Poultry Creation (O'Brien Primitives) 717
RFD 10,000 (O'Brien Primitives) 717
O'Callaghan, Maurice
Broken Harvest 202
O'Connolly, James
Tower of Evil 530
Valley of the Gwangi 501
O'Connor, Frank
Devil's Island 397
Free to Love 398
O'Connor, Pat
Cal 202
Circle of Friends 266
Fools of Fortune 228
Inventing the Abbotts 233
Stars and Bars 247
O'Connor, W.A.
Cocaine Fiends 504
O'Connor, William
Ten Nights in a Barroom 405
O'Ferrall, George Moore
Three Cases of Murder 179
O'Hara, Gerry
Maroc 7 378
O'Horgan, Tom
Futz 311
O'Neal, Ron
Superfly TNT 533
O'Neil, Lawrence
Breast Men 220
O'Neil, Robert Vincent
Avenging Angel 218
O'Neill, Pat
Water and Power 439
O'Reilly, Timothy
Round Trip 861
O'Steen, Sam
Queen of the Stardust Ballroom 243
Sparkle 247
O'Sullivan, Thaddeus
December Bride 202
Nothing Personal 162
Obata, Masayoshi
Organ House (Too Outrageous) 717
Oblowitz, Michael
King Blank 432
This World, Then the Fireworks 249
Oboler, Arch
One Plus One 509
Obukhovich, Nikolai
Dialogues (Glasnost Film Fest V.7) 81
Ocelot, Michael
The Four Wishes (Outrageous 1) 717
The Four Wishes (Too Outrageous) 717
Ochs, Jacki
Vietnam: The Secret Agent 778
Odenbach, Marcel
Marcel Odenbach: In the Peripheral Vision of the Witness 486
Oedekerk, Steve
Ace Ventura: When Nature Calls 261
Oftedal, Mark
Wrong Hole (Spike/Mike Sick 2) 716
Ofteringer, Susanne
Nico Icon 621
Ogorodnikov, Valeri
The Burglar 80
Ogrodnik, Mo
Ripe 244
Oh, Hyun Mi
La Senorita Lee 432
Ohgai, Mori
Animated Classics of Japanese Literature: Izu Dancer/Dancing Girl 720
Ohio, Denise
Amazing World 456, 503
Oidi, Gib T.
Portrait in Red 242
Okada, Megumu
Shadow Skill 745
Shadow Skill Part 2 745
Okamoto, Kihachi
Red Lion 139
The Sword of Doom 140
Okao, Takahiro
Ayane's High Kick 722
Okawara, Kunio
Armored Trooper Votoms, Stage 1 721
Armored Trooper Votoms, Stage 2 721
Armored Trooper Votoms, Stage 3 722
Armored Trooper Votoms, Stage 4 722
Okuyama, Kazuyoshi
The Mystery of Rampo 138
Olcott, Sidney
Claw 396
From the Manger to the Cross 398
Ranson's Folly 403
Oldman, Gary
Nil by Mouth 162
Oldman, Michael
A Jumping Night in the Garden of Eden 114
Olea, Pedro
The Fencing Master 44
Zafarinas 45
Oliansky, Joel
The Competition 223
Oliver, Enrique
Photo Album 60, 435
Oliver, Mark
Klip 432
Sergio Moyano: Living the Dance 556
Olivera, Hector
Argentinisima I 49
El Muerto 50
Fridays of Eternity 50
Funny Dirty Little War 50
A Shadow You Soon Will Be 52
Two to Tango 53
Olivier, Laurence
Hamlet (1948) 312
Henry V 312
The Prince and the Showgirl 280
Richard III (1956) 314
Ollive, Richard
Night Visitors (British Animation) 707
Olmi, Ermanno
Fiances (I Fidanzati) 40
The Tree of Wooden Clogs 34
Olmos, Edward James
American Me 217
Olson, Jenni
Homo Promo 460
Omori, Kazuki
Godzilla vs. Biollante 496
Onodera, Midi
A Performance by Jack Smith 487, 567
Ophuls, Marcel
Costa Gavras Talks with Marcel Ophuls 16, 105
Hotel Terminus: The Life and Times of Klaus Barbie 16, 473
Sorrow and the Pity 16
Ophuls, Max
Bartered Bride 27
Caught 27
De Mayerling a Sarajevo 27
Earrings of Madame De... 27
La Ronde 27
La Signora di Tutti 27
Le Plaisir 27
Letter from an Unknown Woman 27
Liebelei 27
Lola Montes 27
Novotna in The Bartered Bride and The Last Waltz 27
Ordyriski, Ryszard
Dziesieciu z Pawiaka 91
Orme, Stuart
Hands of a Murderer 186
Ivanhoe (1996) 193
The Sculptress 163
Ormerod, James
Frankenstein (Gielgud) 522
Ormond, Ron
Mesa of Lost Women 498
Ornstein, Bruce
Jack and His Friends 233
Orr, James
Man of the House 693
Orsini, Valintino
Smugglers 34
Oseledchik, Vladimir
This Is How We Live (Glasnost Film Fest V.8) 81
Oshima, Nagisa

Cruel Story of Youth 141
Empire of Passion (aka In the Realm of Passion) 141
In the Realm of the Senses 141
Max Mon Amour 141
Merry Christmas Mr. Lawrence 141
The Sun's Burial 141
Violence at Noon 141
Ossorio, Amando de
Return of the Blind Dead 528
Tombs of the Blind Dead 45, 530
Osten, Suzanne
Mozart Brothers 76
Oswald, Gerd
Crime of Passion 364
A Kiss Before Dying (1955) 375
Paris Holiday 279
Oswald, Richard
Cesare Borgia 68
The Lovable Cheat 409
My Song Goes 'Round the World 70
Weird Tales 71
Othenin-Girard, Dominique
After Darkness 158
Ottoson, Lar Henrik
Gorilla (Swedish) 75
Ouedraogo, Idrissa
Tilai 150
Ouedraogo, Ismail
Lumiere & Company 5, 336
Oury, Gerard
The Brain 16, 835
Delusions of Grandeur 17
La Grande Vadrouille 17
The Sucker (Le Corniauds) 18
Owen, Cliff
Bawdy Adventures of Tom Jones 158
Wrong Arm of the Law 185
Oxenberg, Jan
Thank You and Goodnight 438, 466
Oz, Frank
Dirty Rotten Scoundrels 267
In and Out 232
The Indian in the Cupboard 663, 867
Little Shop of Horrors (Musical) 325
What About Bob? 286
Ozawa, Sakae
The Street Fighter 139
Ozgenturk, Ali
The Horse 106
Ozu, Yasujiro
An Autumn Afternoon 143
Drifting Weeds 143
Early Summer 143
Equinox Flower 143
Good Morning (Ohayo) 143
A Hostel in Tokyo (An Inn in Tokyo; Tokyo No Yado) 143
Late Spring 143
Record of a Tenement Gentleman 144
Tokyo Story 144
Pabst, G.W.
Diary of a Lost Girl 68
Don Quixote (Pabst) 69
Joyless Street 69
Kameradschaft 69
The Love of Jeanne Ney 69
Pandora's Box 70
Paracelsus 70
Secrets of a Soul 71
The Threepenny Opera (1931) 71
Westfront 1918 71
White Hell of Pitz Palu 71
Pace, David/Bellomo, Victor
Don't Touch That Dial (Best Fest 5th Annual) 706
Pacino, Al
Looking for Richard 312, 474
Packard, Frank
In Your Face 533
Padron, Juan
Quinoscopo #2 (Animation C.2) 705
Quinoscopo (Int. Animation 3) 706, 712
Page, Anthony
Missiles of October 238
Monte Carlo 194
Nightmare Years 240
Page, Marcy
Paradisia (Animation C.2) 705
Paggi, Gianni
Operafest 584
Pagliero, Marcel
Respectful Prostitute 23
Pagnol, Marcel
Angele 26
Baker's Wife 26
Cesar 26
Harvest (Pagnol) 26
Le Schpountz 26
Letters from My Windmill 27
Topaze (1951/French) 27
The Well-Digger's Daughter 27
Paik, Nam Jun
Nam Jun Paik 487
Paine, Tom
Weak and Wide Astray (New Directors) 487
Pak, Lau Chung
Yellow Rain 133
Pakula, Alan J.
All the President's Men 217
Comes a Horseman 291
Consenting Adults 223
The Devil's Own 225
Klute 234
Orphans 241
Pelican Brief 242
Presumed Innocent 242
Sophie's Choice 247
Sterile Cuckoo 248
Pal, George
Animation in the Netherlands 706
Atlantis, The Lost Continent 494
Best of George Pal 677
George Pal Puppetoons 710
John Henry & The Inky Poo (Black 3) 707
Pupettoon Movie 687
Seven Faces of Dr. Lao 386
Time Machine 501
Tom Thumb (Peter Sellers) 667
Palazzolo, Tom
Caligari's Cure 428
Chicago Nazis 470
Gay for a Day 459, 472
Palazzolo's Chicago 476
Palazzolo's Chicago Vol. 2 476
Sneakin' and Peekin' 478
Tom Palazzolo: Films from the Sixties 478
Palcy, Euzhan
A Dry White Season 151
Sugar Cane Alley 55
Palmer, Stephen
Blindscape (Spike/Mike 3) 716
Palmer, Tony
200 Motels 503
Palud, Herve
Little Indian, Big City 17
Panahi, Jafar
White Balloon 107
Panama, Norman
Court Jester 266
How to Commit Marriage 271
The Road to Hong Kong 281
Panfilov, Gleb
The Theme 83
Panganiban, Will/Smith, Aaron
Snake Theatre (Too Outrageous) 717
Papastathis, Lakis
When the Greeks 105
Papatakis, Nico
Les Abysses 21
Papic, Krsto
The Secret of Nikola Tesla 103
Paradjanov, Sergei
Ashik Kerib 84
The Color of Pomegranates 84
The Legend of Suram Fortress 84
Shadows of Forgotten Ancestors 84
Paranjpye, Sai
Katha (The Tale) (The Fable) 147
Parel, Jabbar
Threshold (aka Dawn) (Umbartha/Subah) 148
Parikka, Pekka
The Winter War 77
Paris, Dominic
Dracula's Last Rites 520
Paris, Jerry
Don't Raise the Bridge, Lower the River 267
Viva Max 286
Paris, Marguerite
All Women Are Equal & Pentagon Peace March 456, 482
Park, Chul-Soo
301/302 136
Park, Nick
Creature Comforts (British Animation) 707
Creature Comforts (Spike/Mike 2) 716
Creature Comforts at Home (Spike/Mike 2) 716
Wallace & Gromit Collection 717
Wallace & Gromit Laserdisc 717
Wallace & Gromit: A Close Shave 717
Wallace & Gromit: A Grand Day Out 717
Wallace & Gromit: The Wrong Trousers 717
Parker, Alan
Angel Heart 217
Birdy 219
Bugsy Malone 321
Come See the Paradise 223
The Commitments 321
Evita 322
Fame 322
Midnight Express 237
Mississippi Burning 238
Pink Floyd: The Wall 622
The Road to Wellville 281
Shoot the Moon 246
Parker, Albert
The Black Pirate 396
Late Extra 175
The Love of Sunya 400
Shifting Sands 404
Parker, John
Daughter of Horror 519
Parker, Oliver
Othello (1996) 314
Parker, Robert
Left Right 552
Parkinson, H.B.
Trapped by the Mormons 154
Parks Jr., Gordon
Superfly 533
Parks, Gordon
The Learning Tree 445
Shaft 533
Shaft's Big Score 533
Parolini, Gianfranco
Fury of Hercules 42
Samson 42
The Three Avengers (Alan Steele) 501
Parr, Larry
Soldier's Tale (Drama) 247
Parrish, Robert
The Bobo 181
Cry Danger 364
Fire Down Below 173
Journey to the Far Side of the Sun 498
Mississippi Blues 11, 613
Parsons, Nick
Dead Heart 205
Pascal, Gabriel
Caesar and Cleopatra 310
Major Barbara 313
Pascal, Michel
Francois Truffaut: Stolen Portraits 14, 334
Pasikowski, Wladyslaw
Pigs 95
Paskaljevic, Goran
Someone Else's America 103
Pasolini, Pier Paolo
Accatone! 37
Arabian Nights 37
The Canterbury Tales 37
The Decameron 37
The Gospel According to St. Matthew 37
Hawks and Sparrows 37
Love Meetings 37
Mamma Roma 37
Medea 37
Oedipus Rex 37
Pigsty 37
Rogopag 10, 37, 39, 41
Salo: 120 Days of Sodom 37
Teorema 37
Passendorfer, Jerzy
Janosik 92
Passer, Ivan
Born to Win 220
Cutter's Way 224
Stalin 89
Pasternak, Joseph
Black Square (Glasnost Film Fest V.7) 81
Pastrone, Giovanni
Cabiria 40, 153
Pate, Jonas
Deceiver 224
Pate, Joshua
Deceiver 224
Pate, Michael
Tim 207
Paterson, Andrew
Video Art: Hygiene 490
Paterson, Andrew J.
Andrew J. Paterson: Controlled Environments 544
Pathe Freres
Pathe Freres Vol. 1 22
Pathe Freres Vol. 2 23
Paton, Stuart
20,000 Leagues Under the Sea 395
Mystery Trooper (Trail of the Royal Mounted) 538
Patterson, Clayton
Joe Coleman 551
Nick Zedd 434
Tompkins Square Park Police Riot 478
Tompkins Square Park, 1989/Dinkinsville 479
Pattison, Michael
Ground Zero 206
Patton-Spruill, Robert
Squeeze 437
Paull, Laura
Havana Nagila: The Jews in Cuba 114
Pavia, Mark
The Night Flier 240
Pavlatova, Michaela
Word Word Words (Int. Animation 6) 712
Pavlov, Mikhail
Bam Zone (Glasnost Film Festival V.3) 81
Pavlov, Yuri
Creation of Adam 80, 458
Paymar, Michelle
And Another Honky Tonk Girl Says She Will 426
Payne, Alexander
Citizen Ruth 222
Payne, Pam
Six Shorts 437
Pays, Armand
Alley Tramp 503
Payson, John
Joe's Apartment 272
Peacock, Jan
Video Art: Jan Peacock 490
Pearce, Richard
A Family Thing 227
Leap of Faith 235
The Long Walk Home 453
Pearson, George

Midnight at Madame Tussaud's 526
Pecas, Max
Daniella by Night 19
Erotic Touch of Hot Skin 505
Her and She and Him 3
Peck, Ron
Empire State 160
Nighthawks 463
Strip Jack Naked 465
Peckinpah, Sam
The Ballad of Cable Hogue 347
Bring Me the Head of Alfredo Garcia 347
Convoy (Peckinpah, 1978) 347
The Deadly Companions 347
The Getaway (1972) 347
Junior Bonner 347
Major Dundee 347
Pat Garrett and Billy the Kid 347
Ride the High Country 347
Straw Dogs 347
The Wild Bunch (Peckinpah, Boxed Set) 347
The Wild Bunch (Peckinpah, Director's Cut) 347
Peebles, Mario Van
New Jack City 445
Posse (Mario Van Peebles/1993) 295
Peebles, Melvin Van
Don't Play Us Cheap 444
Greased Lightning 444
La Permission 445
Melvin Van Peebles' Classified X 445, 453
Story of a Three-Day Pass 446
Sweet Sweetback's Baadassss Song 446
Tales of Erotica 249
Watermelon Man 446
Peerce, Larry
Ash Wednesday 218
The Court-Martial of Jackie Robinson 451
Elvis and Me 536
Goodbye Columbus 370
The Other Side of the Mountain, Part 1 ....241, 827
The Other Side of the Mountain, Part 2 ....241, 827
Queenie 338
Separate Peace 246
Wired 252
Peeters, Barbara
Humanoids from the Deep (Monster) 497
Peled, Micha
Inside God's Bunker 109
Will My Mother Go Back to Berlin? 108
Peled, Micha X.
You, Me, Jerusalem 108
Pelissier, Anthony
Personal Affair 177
Peltier, Melissa Jo
The Real Las Vegas 763
Penn, Arthur
Alice's Restaurant 257
Bonnie and Clyde 257
The Chase (Brando) 257
Dead of Winter 257
Inside 258
Left-Handed Gun 258
Lumiere & Company 5, 336
Mickey One 258
The Miracle Worker 258
The Missouri Breaks 258
Penn and Teller Get Killed 258
Penn, Leonard
Dark Secret of Harvest Home 224
Judgment in Berlin 234
Penn, Sean
The Crossing Guard 223
The Indian Runner 232
Pennebaker, D.A.
Don't Look Back 471, 620
Little Richard: Keep on Rockin' 474, 621
Monterey Pop 475, 621
The War Room 479
Penney, Joseph
Torpedo Run 391
Pentes, Dorne
The Closest Thing to Heaven 428
Peploe, Clare
Rough Magic 245
Peredo, R.
Die Fettecke 484
Peregini, Frank
Scar of Shame 448
Scar of Shame (African American Film) 447
Pereira, Manuel Gomez
Mouth to Mouth (Boca a Boca) 45
Pereira, Miguel
La Boca del Lobo 51
Veronico Cruz 53
Perelsztejn, Diane
Escape to the Rising Sun 775
Perennou, Marie
Microcosmos 818
Perez, Jack
America's Deadliest Home Video 426
Perez, Severo
And the Earth Did Not Swallow Him
(...y no se lo trago la tierra) 55, 426
Perier, Etienne
Zeppelin 165
Perinan, Paco
Against the Wind (Spain) 44
Perry, Frank
Compromising Positions 223
Doc 292
Mommie Dearest 238
Rancho Deluxe 295
The Swimmer 389
Perry, Gordon
Innocents in Paris 183
Pesce, P.J.
The Desperate Trail 292
Pesic, Slobodan
The Harms Case 103
Petelski, Czeslaw
Base of the Dead People 90
Petelski, Ewa & Czeslaw
The Birthday 90
Peters, Brooke L.
Anatomy of a Psycho 503
The Unearthly 530
Peters, Erwin Bahan
Ebony Pearls 444
Peters, Guido
Ciske the Rat 30
Petersen, Wolfgang
Air Force One 216
Black and White as Day and Night 63
Das Boot: The Director's Cut 63
In the Line of Fire 232
The Neverending Story 665
Outbreak 241
Shattered (1991) 246
Petkov, Rumen
Okay Tex (Animation C.4) 706
Petraska, Brian
TimePiece 466
Petricic, Dujan
Romeo & Juliet (Int. Animation 1) 711
Petrie, Ann
Mother Teresa 796
Petrie, Daniel
Bay Boy 210
The Bramble Bush 361
Calm at Sunset 221
Fort Apache, the Bronx 228
Lassie 664
Raisin in the Sun (1971/Poitier) 454
Resurrection 244
Rocket Gibraltar 245
The Spy with the Cold Nose 164
Stolen Hours 178
Petrie, Donald
Grumpy Old Men 270
Mystic Pizza 277
Petrie, Glen
$8.50/A Barrel! Huit Piastres et Demiei and Cajun Visits 468
Petrie, Jeanette
Mother Teresa 796
Petroff, B.
Friends: A Closer Look at the Enemy 87
Petrov, Alexander
The Cow (Int. Animation 4) 712
Petrov, Anatoly
Firing Range (Masters #7) 713
Petrov, Vladimir
Inspector General 82
Peter the First Part One 83
Peter the First Part Two 83
Petrucha, Stephan
Really Strange Stories of the Totally Unknown 509
Petrycki, Jacek
Parada Wspomnien 98
Pettibon, Raymond
Sir Drone 437
The Whole World Is Watching - Weatherman '69 439
Pevney, Joseph
Cash McCall 363
Istanbul 373
Man of a Thousand Faces 378
Meet Danny Wilson 326
The Strange Door 388
Tammy and the Bachelor 389
Peyser, Ruth
One Nation Under TV (Acidburn) 717
Phelps, D. Gary
New York Nights 239
Philibert, Nicolas
City Louvre (La Ville Louvre) 547
In the Land of the Deaf 8, 473
Philipp, Harald
Punishment Battalion 999 70
Philipps, Todd
Hated: GG Allin and the Murder Junkies 620
Philips, Rick
Tear Jerker 489
Phillips, Lee
Barnum (Lancaster/USA) 219
Phillips, Maurice
Another You 262
Pialat, Maurice
Loulou 10
Police 10
Under the Sun of Satan 10
Van Gogh 10
Picazo, Miguel
Extramuros 44, 459
Picha
Shame of the Jungle 715
Pichel, Irving
Destination Moon 495
The Great Rupert 323
Martin Luther (MacGinnis) 791
The Miracle of the Bells 379
The Most Dangerous Game 379
Mr. Peabody and the Mermaid 276
O.S.S. 381
Quicksand 383
She (1935) 386
Something in the Wind 387
Tomorrow Is Forever 391
Pick, Lupu
Shattered (1921) 71
Piekutowski, Andrzej
Miners '88 98
Piersen, Claude
Justine de Sade 4
Piersol, Virge
Virge Piersol Short Pieces 623
Pierson, Brian
Manhattan Naturally and Stories from Brooklyn 433
Pierson, Frank
Citizen Cohn 222
King of the Gypsies 234
Lakota Woman 787
The Looking Glass War 162
A Star Is Born (1976/Streisand) 329
Pies, Dennis
Ace of Light (Acidburn) 717
Pigors, Eric
Let's Chop Soo-E! (Too Outrageous) 717
Pilafian, Peter
Jimi Plays Berkeley 621
Pillsbury, Sam
Starlight Hotel 209
Pine, William H.
Aerial Gunner 356
Swamp Fire 389
Pineyro, Marcelo
Wild Horses 45
Ping, Chu Yen
Fantasy Mission Force 134
Island of Fire 134
Slave of the Sword 132
Ping, He
Red Firecracker Green Firecracker 117
Ping, Yuen Wo
In the Line of Duty 4 (aka The Witness) 128
The Miracle Fighters 130
Tai Chi II 132
Wing Chun 133
Pink, Sidney
Reptilicus 499
Pintilie, Lucian
Lumiere & Company 5, 336
An Unforgettable Summer 104
Pintilie, Lucien
Oak, The 104
Ward Six 103
Pires, Gerard
Act of Aggression 2
Pirosh, Robert
Go for Broke! 370
Valley of the Kings 392
Pirro, Mark
Curse of the Queerwolf 458
Piscator, Erwin
Revolt of the Fishermen 83
Pita, Dan
Stone Wedding 104
Pitchul, Vassili
Little Vera 82
Pitrie, Glen
Yellow Fever/La Fievre Jaune 440
Pitt, Susan
Crocus (Sextoons) 715
Piwoski, Mark
A Trip down the River 94
Piwowarski, Radoslaw
Train to Hollywood 95
Piwowski, Marek
Foul Play 95
Place, Lou
Daddy-O 505
Plotnick, Danny
I'm Not Fascinating—The Movie! 431
Pipsqueak Pfollies 435
Plympton, Bill
25 Ways to Quit Smoking (Animation C.2) 705
How to Kiss (Spike/Mike 1) 716
J. Lyle 712
One of Those Days (Outrageous 1) 714
Plymptoons (Animation C.3) 705
Plymptoons (Int. Animation 4) 712
Plymptoons: The Complete Works of Bill Plympton 715
Push Comes to Shove (Int. Animation 5) 712
The Tune 717
Wiseman (Animation C.3) 705
Your Face (Int. Animation 2) 712
Po-Chi, Leung
Hong Kong 1941 121
Shanghai 1920 123
Podeswa, Jeremy
Eclipse 210
Podniek, Yuri

Is It Easy to Be Young....82
Poe, Amos
Foreigner....430
Poelvoorde, Benoit
Man Bites Dog....29
Pohjola, Ilppo
Daddy and the Muscle Academy: A Documentary on the Art, Life and Times of Tom of Finland....458
Poire, Jean-Marie
The Visitors....18
Poirer, R.
Stephane Grappelli—Live in San Francisco—1985....615
Poirier, Paris
Last Call at Maud's....461, 474
Poitier, Sidney
Buck and the Preacher....443
Fast Forward....227
Ghost Dad....444
Let's Do It Again....445
A Piece of the Action....445
Stir Crazy....446
Uptown Saturday Night....446
Polanski, Roman
Bitter Moon....97
Chinatown....97
Death and the Maiden....97
Diary of Forbidden Dreams....97
Fat and the Lean....97
Fat and the Lean (Classic Foreign #2)....153
Fearless Vampire Killers....97
Frantic....97
Knife in the Water....97
Macbeth....97
Mammals....97
Pirates....97
Repulsion....98
Rosemary's Baby....98
The Tenant....98
Tess....98
Two Men and a Wardrobe....98
Two Men and a Wardrobe (Classic Foreign #2)....153
What!....98
Politsch, Barbara
28th Instance of June 1914, 10:50 AM, The....456
Pollack, Jeff
Booty Call....264
Pollack, Sharon
Everything Relative....459
Pollack, Sidney
Castle Keep....363
Pollack, Sydney
Absence of Malice....216
The Electric Horseman....226
The Firm....227
Havana....230
Jeremiah Johnson....233
Out of Africa....241
Sabrina (1995)....281
The Scalphunters....296
The Slender Thread....387
They Shoot Horses, Don't They?....390
This Property Is Condemned....390
Tootsie....285
The Way We Were....252
Pollard, Bud
Beware....447
Black King (African American Film)....447
Look Out Sister....448
Tall, Tan and Terrific....449
Pollard, Harry
California Straight Ahead....396
Pollexfen, Jack
The Indestructible Man....523
Pollock, George
Broth of a Boy....202
Murder Ahoy....176
Polonsky, Abraham
Force of Evil (Garfield)....368
Polop, Francisco Lara
Murder Mansion....526
Polselli, Renato
The Reincarnation of Isabel....528
Pommer, Erich
Beachcomber....181
Pompucci, Leone
Mille Bolle Blu....33
Pontecorvo, Gillo
Battle of Algiers....40
Burn!....32
Kapo....41
Ponting, Herbert G.
90 Degrees South: With Scott to the Antarctic....153, 171
Pontius, Rich
The Yiddish Cinema....113
Ponzi, Maurizio
Aurora....32
The Pool Hustlers....34
Pool, Lea
The Savage Woman....211
Straight for the Heart....211
Pope, Angela
Captives....221
Hollow Reed....231
Pope, Tim
The Crow: City of Angels....224
Popkin, Leo
Gang War....448
Popzlatev, Peter
The Countess....104
Poreba, Bohdan
Major Hubal....93
Portillo, Rafael Lopez
Face of the Screaming Werewolf....521
Portillo, Ralph
Naked Lies....239
Posch, Michael
Mongo Makongo (Animation C.1)....705
Posner, Bill
Teenage Strangler....511
Posner, Geoffrey
Victoria Wood: As Seen on TV....198
Post, Ted
Beneath the Planet of the Apes....494
Go Tell the Spartans....229
Hang 'em High....293
The Legend of Tom Dooley....294
Yuma....298
Postgate, Oliver
Life on Earth Perhaps....804
Potter, H.C.
Beloved Enemy....359
The Cowboy and the Lady....364
The Miniver Story....379
Mr. Blandings Builds His Dream House....276
Second Chorus....328
The Shopworn Angel....386
Three for the Show....330
You Gotta Stay Happy....394
Potter, Richard
David and Goliath....42
Potter, Sally
Orlando....163, 463, 584
The Tango Lesson....164
Potterton, Gerald
Heavy Metal....710
The Railrodder....409
Powell, Aubrey
Tap Dogs....576
Powell, Dick
Conqueror....364
The Enemy Below....367
Split Second....387
Powell, Frank
A Fool There Was....398
Powell, Michael
The 49th Parallel....180
Black Narcissus....180
A Canterbury Tale....180
Edge of the World....180
The Elusive Pimpernel....180
I Know Where I'm Going....180
Life and Death of Colonel Blimp....180
The Lion Has Wings....180
One of Our Aircraft Is Missing....180
Peeping Tom....181
Red Shoes....181
The Small Back Room....181
Stairway to Heaven....181
Tales of Hoffman....181
Powell, Paul
All Night....395
Pollyanna (1920/USA)....402
Powell, Tristam
American Friends....158
Power, John
Alice to Nowhere....205
All My Sons (1986)....310
Father....205
Prashad, Udayan
Brothers in Trouble....148, 159
Prate, Jean-Yves
Regina....244
Praunheim, Rosa von
Anita, Dances of Vice....63
I Am My Own Woman....64, 460
Neurosia....64, 463
Positive....65, 834
Silence=Death....65, 465
A Virus Knows No Morals....65, 467
Pray, Doug
Hype!....620
Preminger, Otto
Advise and Consent....356
Anatomy of a Filmmaker....332
Anatomy of a Murder....357
Bonjour Tristesse....361
The Cardinal....355
Carmen Jones....448
Court-Martial of Billy Mitchell....364
Exodus....367
Forever Amber....369
The Human Factor....232
In Harm's Way....373
Laura....376
Man with the Golden Arm....378
The Moon Is Blue....276
River of No Return....295
Rosebud....245
Saint Joan....385
Pressburger, Emeric
Black Narcissus....180
A Canterbury Tale....180
The Elusive Pimpernel....180
Life and Death of Colonel Blimp....180
Red Shoes (Powell)....181
The Small Back Room....181
Stairway to Heaven....181
Pressburger, Fred
Crowded Paradise....364
Pressman, Michael
Some Kind of Hero....247
Preston, Gaylene
War Stories Our Mothers Never Told Us....479, 773
Prevert, Pierre
Voyage Surprise....24
Prezioso, Vincent
I'll Always Be Anthony....460
Price, B. Lawrence
Teenage Devil Dolls....511
Price, Will
Rock, Rock, Rock....622
Priestly, Joanna
All My Relations (Int. Animation 4)....712
Prieto, Joseph G.
Shanty Tramp....510
Primus, Barry
Mistress (USA)....276
Prince
Graffiti Bridge....323
Under the Cherry Moon....331
Proctor, Elaine
Friends (South African)....151
Proshkin, Alexander
To See Paris and Die....83
Protazanov, Iakov
Departure of Great Old Man (Early Russian 8)....85
Queen of Spades (Early Russian #8)....85
Protazanov, Yakov
Aelita: Queen of Mars....85
Father Sergius....85
Proyas, Alex
The Crow (Brandon Lee)....119
Dark City (USA)....495
Prussian, M.
Percy Mayfield: Poet Laureate of the Blues....614
Pryor, Richard
Jo Jo Dancer, Your Life Is Calling....445
Przybylski, Jan Nowina
Ty Co w Ostrej Swiecisz Bramie....94
Ptushko, Alexander
The Magic Voyage of Sinbad (Sadko)....647, 713
Sword and the Dragon....83, 716
Pudovkin, Vsevolod
Chess Fever/By the Law....85
Deserter....85
End of St. Petersburg....85
Mother....86
The Mystery of the Leaping Fish and Chess Fever....86
Storm over Asia....86
Puenzo, Luis
The Official Story....52
Old Gringo....60
Punch, Monkey
The Castle of Cagliostro....725
Lupin III: The Mystery of Mamo....735
Pupillo, Masimo
Terror-Creatures From the Grave....511
Pupillo, Massimo
Terror Creatures from the Grave (Cemetery of the Living Dead)....530
Purdy, Jon
Reflections in the Dark....244
Purrer, Ursula
Flaming Ears....63, 459
Purves, Barry
Next (British Animation)....707
Screenplay (Spike/Mike 3)....716
Purves, Bary
Achilles (Boy's Life)....457
Pyun, Albert
Captain America....221
Quade, Richard
Sand Dance (Int. Animation 4)....712
Quakenbush, Corky
Smaller World....706
Quay Brothers
The Brothers Quay V. 1....707
Brothers Quay V. 2....707
The Cabinet of Jan Svankmajer (Brothers Quay 1)....707
The Street of Crocodiles (Brothers Quay 1)....707
Quell, Frank De
Elixir of Love....579
Quigley, George P.
Murder with Music....448
Quine, Richard
Bell, Book and Candle....263
Full of Life....369
How to Murder Your Wife....271
My Sister Eileen....326
Paris When It Sizzles....279
Sex and the Single Girl....282
The Solid Gold Cadillac....387
Strangers When We Meet....388
World of Suzie Wong....394
Quinn, Anthony
The Buccaneer....361
Quinn, Joanna
Body Beautiful (British Animation)....707
Britannia (Spike/Mike 3)....716
Quinn, John

Goldy, The Last of the Golden Bears 663
Quintero, Jose
Roman Spring of Mrs. Stone 385
Rabenalt, Arthur Maria
Unnatural 530
Racine, Rober
Video Art: Rober Racine 490
Rademakers, Fons
The Assault 30
Radev, Zlatin
Canfilm (Animation C.4) 706
Radford, Michael
1984 (1984 Version) 300
Il Postino 33
Radtke, Edward
bottom land 427
Radvanyi, Geza von
Uncle Tom's Cabin (1969/Herbert Lom) 308
Women in Prison 42
Women Without Names 42
Raeburn, Michael
Jit 150
Rafelson, Bob
Black Widow (1986) 219
Blood & Wine 220
Five Easy Pieces 227
Head (USA) 506
King of Marvin Gardens 234
Man Trouble 275
Mountains of the Moon 239
The Postman Always Rings Twice (1981) 242
Tales of Erotica 249
Rafferty, Kevin
The Atomic Cafe 469
Blood in the Face 469
Feed 471
Rafkin, Alan
The Ghost and Mr. Chicken 269
The Shakiest Gun in the West 282
Rai, Rajiv
Mohra 148
Raimi, Sam
Army of Darkness 516
Evil Dead 2: Dead by Dawn 521
The Quick and the Dead 295
Raizman, Yuli
Private Life 83
Rakoff, Alvin
Voyage Round My Father 198
Ramis, Harold
Groundhog Day 270
Multiplicity 277
Stuart Saves His Family 283
Rampo, Edogawa
Animated Classics of Japanese Literature: Walker in the Attic/Psychological Test/Red Room 721
Randas, Lance
Galaxy of the Dinosaurs 522
Randel, Tony
One Good Turn 241
Randol, George
Midnight Shadow 448
Ranga, Dana
East Side Story (Documentary) 63
Rankin, Scott
Simultaneous 488
Ranody, Lazlo
Nobody's Daughter 102
Ransen, Mort
Margaret's Museum 211
Ransick, Whitney
My Birthday Cake (Best Fest 5th Annual) 706
Rao, T. Rama
Jeevan Dhara 147
Raphael, Frederic
Women & Men - Stories of Seduction 302
Rappaport, Mark
Casual Relations 428
Chain Letters 428
From the Journals of Jean Seberg 430
Imposters 431
Local Color 433
Mozart in Love 434
Postcards (Three Short Films) 438
Rock Hudson's Home Movies 465, 477
Scenic Route, The 436
Spinoff (Three Short Films) 438
Three Short Films 438
The TV Spinoff (Three Short Films) 438
Rappeneau, Jean-Paul
Belmondo Is the Swashbuckler 16
Cyrano de Bergerac (Depardieu) 2
The Horseman on the Roof 3
Rapper, Irving
The Adventures of Mark Twain: Fredric March 309
The Brave One 361
The Corn Is Green (Davis) 364
Marjorie Morningstar 378
Now Voyager 381
Rhapsody in Blue 328
Rash, Steve
The Buddy Holly Story 221
Rasky, Harry
Homage to Chagall 550
The War Against the Indians 789
Rasmussen, Knud
The Wedding of Palo 783
Rasmussen, Lars
The Littlest Viking 76
Rathborne, Tina
Zelly and Me 253
Rathod, David
West Is West 439
Ratoff, Gregory
Footlight Serenade 322
The Heat's On 324
Oscar Wilde 176
Rose of Washington Square 328
Ratony, Akos Von
The Phoney American 70
Rauh, Steve
Call for Peace: The Military Budget and You 802
Rawi, Ousama
The Housekeeper 210
Rawlins, John
Arabian Nights 358
Ray, Albert
The Intruder 507
Shriek in the Night 386
Thirteenth Guest 390
Ray, Bernard B.
Broken Strings 448
Speed Reporter 387
Ray, Fred Olen
Haunting Fear 522
Night Shade 240
Wizards of the Demon Sword 512
Ray, Man
Avant Garde Program #14 483
Man Ray Video 486
Ray, Nicholas
55 Days at Peking 346
Flying Leathernecks 346
In a Lonely Place 346
Johnny Guitar 346
King of Kings 346
Knock on Any Door 347
Party Girl 347
Rebel Without a Cause 347
Ray, Sandip
The Broken Journey 146
Target 148
Ray, Satyajit
The Adversary 146
Aparajito 146
Charulata (The Lonely Wife) 146
The Chess Players (Shatranj Ke Khiladi) 146
Days and Nights in the Forest 146
Devi 147
Distant Thunder 147
Jalsaghar (The Music Room) 147
Jana Aranya (The Middleman) 147
Mahanagar (The Big City) 147
Pather Panchali 148
Satyajit Ray's Apu Trilogy 148
The Stranger (Agantuk) 148
Two Daughters 148
The World of Apu 148
Raymaker, Herman C.
Adventure Girl 356
Trailing the Killer 667
Raymond, Jack
Devil's Hand (Carnival of Sinners) 520
The Speckled Band (Massey) 187
When Knights Were Bold 185
Re, John Lawrence
Dominoes: Portrait of a Decade 620
Reble, Jurgen
Jurgen Reble—Passion 432
Redford, Robert
Milagro Beanfield War 59
Ordinary People 241
Quiz Show 243
A River Runs Through It 244
Reed, Carol
Agony and the Ecstasy 357
Climbing High 182
The Fallen Idol 173
The Immortal Battalion (The Way Ahead) 174
The Key 374
A Kid for Two Farthings 175
Kipps 183
Night Train to Munich 176
Odd Man Out 176
Oliver!—30th Anniversary Edition 327
The Stars Look Down 178
The Third Man 179
Trapeze 392
The Way Ahead 179
The Young Mr. Pitt 180
Reed, Theodore
The Nut 402
Rees, Clive
When the Whales Came 252
Reeve, Christopher
In the Gloaming 232
Reeve, Geoffrey
Souvenir 211
Reeves, B.
Law for Tombstone 293
Reeves, Daniel
Amida/A Mosaic for the Kali Yuga/Arches/ Body Count/Hey Joe 482
Sabda and Sombra a Sombra 488
Smothering Dreams and Thousands Watch 488
Reeves, Matt
The Pallbearer 241
Reeves, Michael
The Conqueror Worm 518
She Beast (Revenge of the Blood Beast) 529
Reggio, Godfrey
Anima Mundi 468
Koyaanisqatsi 474
Regnoli, Piero
The Playgirls and the Vampire 527
Regueiro, Francisco
Padre Nuestro 45
Reichardt, Kelly
River of Grass 436
Reichenbach, Carlos
Buccaneer Soul 53
Reichenbach, Francois
F for Fake 344
Reichert, Julia
Seeing Red 477
Reichert, Mark
Union City 439
Reichman, Rachel
Work 467
Reichmann, Thomas
Mingus 613
Reid, Alastair
Nostromo 194
Reid, Dorothy Davenport
Linda 400
Reid, Frances
All God's Children 449, 456
The Changer: A Record of Times 604
Straight from the Heart 465, 478
Reid, Tim
Once Upon a Time When We Were Colored 241, 445
Reilly, John
Trial of the Avco Ploughshares 764
Reiner, Carl
Bert Rigby You're a Fool 320
Dead Men Don't Wear Plaid 267
Where's Poppa? 287
Reiner, Rob
The American President 217
A Few Good Men 227
Ghosts of Mississippi 229
Misery 238
The Princess Bride 280
Stand by Me 247
When Harry Met Sally 287
Reinert, Al
National Geographic Video: For All Mankind 840
Reinert, Robert
Opium 70
Reinhardt, Gottfried
Rebel Flight to Cuba 70
Town Without Pity 391
Reinhardt, John
Cuesta Abajo 49
Tango Bar 52
Reinhardt, Max
A Midsummer Night's Dream 313
Reiniger, Lotte
Adventures of Prince Achmed 704
Reinke, Steve
Steve Reinke: The Hundred Videos 557
Reinl, Harald
Invisible Dr. Mabuse (The Invisible Horror) 497
The Last Tomahawk 293
Return of Dr. Mabuse (The Phantom Meets the Return of Dr. Mabuse) 528
Reis, Irving
All My Sons (1948) 357
Enchantment 367
New Mexico 294
Roseanna McCoy 385
Three Husbands 390
Reisner, Charles F.
Manhattan Merry-Go-Round 326
Steamboat Bill Jr. 409
Reisz, Karel
Everybody Wins 226
French Lieutenant's Woman 160
The Gambler 229
Isadora 174
Saturday Night and Sunday Morning 177
Who'll Stop the Rain 252
Reitman, Ivan
Dave 266
Ghostbusters 269
Reitz, Edgar
Germany in Autumn 66
Heimat 64
Heimat II 64
Heimat Set 64
Relph, Michael
Who Done It? 185
Renan, Sergio
Crecor de Golpe (Growing Up) 49
Rene, Norman
Longtime Companion 462
Prelude to a Kiss 279
Reckless (Rene) 280

Renoir, Jean
Boudu Saved from Drowning 25
Charleston (Avant Garde Shorts France) 25
Crime of Monsieur Lange 25
Day in the Country 25
Diary of a Chambermaid 25
Elena and Her Men 26
Elusive Corporal 26
French Can Can 26
The Golden Coach 26
Grand Illusion 26
La Bete Humaine 26
La Chienne 26
La Marseillaise 26
La Petite Marchande d'Allumettes 26
Le Petit Theatre de Jean Renoir 26
Lower Depths 26
Madame Bovary 26
Picnic on the Grass 26
Renoir Silent Shorts 26
The River 26
Rules of the Game 26
The Southerner 26
Testament of Dr. Cordelier 26
Toni 26
Tournament 26
Renton, Nicholas
Far from the Madding Crowd (1998) 191
Resnais, Alain
Hiroshima, Mon Amour 12
La Guerre Est Finie 12
Last Year at Marienbad 12
Mon Oncle d'Amerique 12
Muriel 12
Night and Fog 12, 776
Providence 12
Stavisky 12
Revier, Harry
Child Bride 504
Rey, Christina
Change the Frame 457
Inn Trouble 461
Reyes, E.
The Dark Light of Dawn 56
Reynolds, Kevin
187 216
Robin Hood, Prince of Thieves 244
Waterworld 502
Rhodes, Michael
The Fourth Wise Man 228
Heidi (Disney) 692
Rhodes, Michael Ray
Entertaining Angels: The Dorothy Day Story 226
Rhue, Dr. Sylvia
All God's Children 449, 456
Ribowska, Malka
Simone de Beauvoir (Subtitled) 6
Ricard, Dominique
Tadpole and the Whale 667
Rice, Ron
The Queen of Sheba Meets the Atom Man 488
Rich, David Lowell
Madame X (1966) 377
The Three Stooges: Have Rocket Will Travel 284
Rich, John
Boeing Boeing 264
Roustabout 537
Rich, Matty
Straight Out of Brooklyn 446
Rich, Richard
The Swan Princess III and the Mystery of the Enchanted Treasure 649
Richard, Pierre
The Daydreamer (Le Distrait) 17
Tall Blond Man with One Black Shoe 18
Richards, C.M. Pennington
Ladies Who Do 183
Richards, David
Reckless (Richards/Harding) 195
Richards, Dick
Farewell My Lovely 160
Richards, Lloyd
Paul Robeson (James Earl Jones) 314
The Piano Lesson 314
Richardson, James
Cat and Rat (Int. Animation 4) 712
Richardson, John
Dusty 205
Richardson, Peter
Eat the Rich 182
Pope Must Diet 509
Richardson, Tony
Blue Sky 220
The Border (USA) 220
The Charge of the Light Brigade (1968) 172
The Entertainer 311
Hamlet (1969/Williamson) 312
Joseph Andrews 161
Loneliness of the Long Distance Runner 175
Loved One 275
Mademoiselle 5
Penalty Phase 242
Shadow on the Sun 197
Taste of Honey 178
Tom Jones 185
Women & Men - Stories of Seduction 302
Richert, William
The Man in the Iron Mask (1998) 237
Richol, Helene
Blue Kisses and Marshmallows (Letterist Films) 432
Woman Is Not What She Used to Be (Letterist Films) 432
Richter, Hans
8 x 8 (A Chess Sonata in 8 Movements) 482
Ghosts Before Breakfast (Experimental Series 20) 484
Hans Richter: Early Avant-Garde Films 485
Hans Richter: Give Chance a Chance 63, 485
Rhythmus 21 (Experimental Series 20) 484
Rickman, Alan
The Winter Guest 165
Ridgeway, James
Blood in the Face 469
Feed 471
Ridley, Philip
Reflecting Skin 244
Riefenstahl, Leni
Blue Light 68
Day of Freedom—Our Fighting Forces 68, 767
Olympia: Festival of Beauty 70, 476
Olympia: Festival of the People 70, 476
Olympia: Parts One and Two 70, 476
Sacred Mountain/White Flame 70
Tiefland 71
Triumph of the Will 71, 479
White Flame, The 71
Women Who Made the Movies 339
Wonderful Horrible Life of Leni Riefenstahl 66, 480
Riesner, Charles
The Big Store 263
Lost in a Harem 274
Riesner, Dean
Bill and Coo 360
Riffel, Jim
Howard Stern: Shut Up and Listen 473
Riggs, Marlon
Anthem (Boys' Shorts) 457
Boys' Shorts 457
Tongues Untied 466
Righelli, Gennaro
Peddlin' in Society 41
Rikli, Dr. Martin
Gorch Fock 768
Riklis, Dina Zvi
Shiv'a 108
Riklis, Eran
Cup Final 107
Rilla, Wolf
Bachelor of Hearts 181
The Scamp (Strange Affection) 178
Village of the Damned 501
Rimkus, Steven
Around the World the Lesbian Way 456
Rimminen, Marjut
The Stain (Int. Animation 6) 712
Rin, Borge
Anna & Bella (Int. Animation 1) 712
Ring, Borge
Animation in the Netherlands 706
Rinzler, Lisa
In the House 860
Rios-Bustamante, Antonio
Images of Mexican Los Angeles 57
Ripley, Arthur
The Chase (Lorre) 363
Prisoner of Japan 383
Thunder Road 391
Ripploh, Frank
Taxi Zum Klo 65, 466
Ripstein, Arturo
Place Without Limits 52
Risi, Dino
Running Away 34
Scent of a Woman (Profumo di Donna) (1974) 34
The Spectator (Love in the City) 41
The Tiger and the Pussycat 511
Risi, Marco
Forever Mary 33
Ritchie, Michael
Candidate 221
Downhill Racer 366
The Golden Child 270
The Positively True Adventures of the Alleged Texas Cheerleader-Murdering Mom 279
Semi-Tough 281
Smile 247
Ritelis, Viktors
Crucible of Horror 519
Ritt, Martin
The Black Orchid 360
Conrack 223
Cross Creek 223
The Front 288
The Great White Hope 370
Hombre 293
Hud 372
Molly Maguires 379
Murphy's Romance 277
Norma Rae 240
Nuts 240
Paris Blues 382
Pete 'n' Tillie 279
Sounder 666
Spy Who Came in from the Cold 387
Stanley and Iris 247
Ritzenberg, Frederick A.
Gospel 607
Rivalta, Giorgio
Last Glory of Troy (The Avenger) 42
Rivette, Jacques
Celine and Julie Go Boating 10
Divertimento 10
Joan the Maid—The Battles 10
Joan the Maid—The Prisons 10
Joan the Maid: Complete Set 10
La Belle Noiseuse 10
Lumiere & Company 5, 336
The Nun (La Religieuse) 10
Paris Belongs to Us 11
Up/Down/Fragile 11
Rizzo, Fran
Sullivan's Last Call 438
Roach, Hal
Chasing Laughter 265
The Devil's Brother 267
His Royal Slyness and Haunted Spooks 410
King of the Wild Horses 400
White Sheep 406
Roach, Jay
Austin Powers: International Man of Mystery 262
Robbins, Jerome
West Side Story 331
Robbins, Matthew
Batteries Not Included 263
Bingo 662
Robbins, Tim
Bob Roberts 427
Dead Man Walking 224
Robe, Mike
Son of the Morning Star 422
Robert, Yves
My Father's Glory 5
My Mother's Castle 5
Return of the Tall Blond Man with One Black Shoe 17
Salut d'Artiste (Salute the Artist) 18
Roberts, Charles E.
Hurry, Charlie, Hurry (Seven Days..) 281
Roberts, Daryll
How U Like Me Now 444
Sweet Perfection 446
Roberts, John
War of the Buttons 185
Robertson, Andrew
The Best of Red Green 414
Robertson, John S.
Dr. Jekyll and Mr. Hyde (Barrymore) 520
Little Orphan Annie (1932) 376
Our Little Girl 665
Shore Leave 404
The Single Standard 404
Soul-Fire 404
Tess of the Storm Country 405
Robinson, Arthur
The Informer (1929) 174
Manon Lescaut (Drama) 70
Warning Shadows 71
Robinson, Bruce
How to Get Ahead in Advertising 183
Jennifer 8 233
Withnail and I 185
Robinson, Phil Alden
Field of Dreams 227
Robinson, Richard
Black Vengeance 532
Robinson, Todd
Wild Bill: Hollywood Maverick 339
Robinson, Walter
Love Show 433
Robson, Mark
Avalanche Express 218
The Bridges at Toko-Ri 361
Champion 363
The Harder They Fall 371
Home of the Brave 769
I Want You 373
The Inn of the Sixth Happiness 174
My Foolish Heart 380
Peyton Place 382
Prize 383
Return to Paradise 384
Valley of the Dolls 512
Von Ryan's Express 392
Rocco, Marc
Dream a Little Dream 267
Murder in the First 239
Rocco, Pat
Kiss 463
Mondo Rocco (aka It's a Gay World) 463
One Adventure 463
We Were There 467
Rocha, Glauber
Black God, White Devil 53
Terra em Transe 54
Rochant, Eric
The Fifth Monkey 227
Love Without Pity 5
Rochlin, Sheldon
Paradise Now 314
Signals Through the Flames 315
Vali: Witch of Positano 479
Rock, Joe
Cotton Queen 182
Rockwell, Alexandre

Four Rooms 430, 441
In the Soup 432
Roddam, Franc
Aria 158, 577
K2 234
Moby Dick (1998) 238
Quadrophenia 622
Rodes, Jennifer
Making of "Bar Girls" 462
Rodriguez, Ismael
Los Hermanos del Hierro 51
Rodriguez, Maria Elena
Regina Coeli (Animation for Fallen Catholics) 706
Rodriguez, Robert
Desperado 292
El Mariachi 429
Four Rooms 430, 441
From Dusk till Dawn 430
Roadracers 436
Roeg, Nicolas
Aria 158, 577
Castaway 166
Don't Look Now 166
Eureka 166
Full Body Massage 166
Heart of Darkness 166
The Man Who Fell to Earth 166
Performance 167
Sweet Bird of Youth (1989) 167
Track 29 167
Two Deaths 167
Walkabout 167
The Witches 167
Roemer, Michael
Nothing But a Man 445
The Plot Against Harry 435
Roffman, Julian
The Bloody Brood 504
Mask (1961/Elvira) 525
Rogala, Miroslaw
Macbeth: The Witches Scenes 486
Nature Is Leaving Us 487
Video Works: Miroslaw Rogala (1980-86) 491
Rogell, Albert S.
The Admiral Was a Lady 356
Cyclone Cavalier 397
The Tip Off 391
War of the Wildcats 393
Rogers, Charles
March of the Wooden Soldiers 275
Rogers, Richard P.
Pictures from a Revolution 60
Rogozhkin, Aleksandr
The Chekist 80
Rohmer, Eric
Chloe in the Afternoon 13
Claire's Knee 13
Eric Rohmer: The Moral Tales Box Set 13
Four Adventures of Reinette and Mirabelle 13
Full Moon in Paris 14
A Girl at the Monceau Bakery/Suzanne's Career 14
La Collectionneuse 14
My Night at Maud's 14
Pauline at the Beach 14
Rendevous in Paris 14
A Tale of Springtime 14
A Tale of Winter 14
Rohrer, Bob
The Man from the Pru 193
Roland, George
The Eternal Jew 767
Roland, Jurgen
The Green Archer 69
Rolfe, D.W.
Silent Witness 792
Roman, Film
Bruno the Kid 707
A Garfield Christmas 696
Garfield Gets a Life 696
Garfield Goes Hollywood 696
Garfield in the Rough 697
Garfield's Feline Fantasies 697
Garfield's Halloween Adventure 697
Garfield's Thanksgiving 697
Garfield: His Nine Lives 697
Tom & Jerry: The Movie 689
Romero, Eddie
Black Mama, White Mama 532
Terror Is a Man 501
Romero, George
George Romero: Document of the Dead 334
Romero, George A.
The Crazies (Code Name Trixie) 518
Creepshow 519
Dawn of the Dead (Director's Cut) 519
Day of the Dead (Horror) 519
Martin 525
Night of the Living Dead 526
Season of the Witch 529
Rondeau, Charles R.
The Devil's Partner 520
Rondi, Brunello
Emmanuelle in Egypt 32
Ronisz, Wincenty
Thank You Poles 99
Roodt, Darrell
Cry, The Beloved Country (1995) 151
Place of Weeping 151
Rooks, Conrad
Chappaqua 567
Room, Abram
Bed and Sofa 85
Root, Wells
The Bold Caballero: A Zorro Adventure 361
Roquemore, Cliff
Dolemite 2: Human Tornado 532
Petey Wheatstraw 533
Rosa, Michal
Hot Thursday 92
Rose, Bernard
Anna Karenina (1996/Marceau) 217
Candyman 517
Immortal Beloved 232
Rose, Peter
Digital Speech and Pressures of the Text 484
The Man Who Could Not See Far Enough 486
Rose, Sherman A.
Target Earth 500
Rosen, Lee
The Peacock Fan 402
Rosen, Martin
Watership Down 717
Rosen, Phil
Beggars in Ermine 359
Black Beauty (1933) 662
Charlie Chan: Meeting at Midnight 363
Charlie Chan: The Chinese Cat 363
Charlie Chan: The Jade Mask 363
Charlie Chan: The Scarlet Clue 363
Charlie Chan: The Secret Service 363
Meeting at Midnight (aka Black Magic) 378
Mystery of Marie Roget 380
Phantom Broadcast 382
Phantom of Chinatown 382
The Sphinx 387
Spooks Run Wild 282
Tango (Franklin Pangborn) 389
Rosenbach, Ulrike
Ulrike Rosenbach: Osho-Samadhi 489
Rosenberg, Stuart
Cool Hand Luke 364
Pocket Money 295
The Pope of Greenwich Village 279
Rosenbloom, Dale
Shiloh 666
Rosenblum, Nina
America & Lewis Hine 468, 558
Through the Wire 478
Rosenblum, Ralph
Any Friend of Nicholas Nickleby Is a Friend of Mine 661
Greatest Man in the World 300
Man That Corrupted Hadleyburg 309
Rosenfeld, Keva
Twenty Bucks 285
Rosenfeld, Seth Zvi
Brother's Kiss 221
Rosenthal, Ed
Grow Dutch 472
Rosenthal, Rick
Bad Boys 218
Rosi, Francesco
Bizet's Carmen 578
Rosler, Martha
Video Art: Vital Statistics of a Citizen, Simply Obtained 491
Ross, Benjamin
The Young Poisoner's Handbook 165
Ross, Carl
Belly Pain 54
Ross, Frank
The Lady Says No 273
Ross, Herbert
Boys on the Side 220
California Suite 265
Dancers 570
Footloose 322
Funny Lady 322
The Goodbye Girl 270
Goodbye, Mr. Chips (Great Britain) 323
Nijinsky 574
Pennies from Heaven 327
Play It Again, Sam 289
The Secret of My Success 281
Steel Magnolias 248
The Sunshine Boys 283
Turning Point 250
Undercover Blues 251
Ross, Nat
April Fool 395
Rossellini, Roberto
Age of the Medici 38
Amore 38
Blaise Pascal 38
Era Notte a Roma 38
Europa 51 38
Fear 38
Flowers of St. Francis 38
General Della Rovere 38
Germany Year Zero 38
Machine to Kill Bad People 38
Man with a Cross (L'Uomo della Croce) 38
Miracle 39
Open City 39
Paisan 39
Return of the Pilot (Un Pilota Ritorna) 39
The Rise of Louis XIV 39
Rogopag 10, 37, 39, 41
Seven Deadly Sins (episode) 39
Stromboli 39
Vanina Vanini 39
Voyage in Italy (Strangers) 39
Rossen, Robert
Alexander the Great 357
All the King's Men 357
Island in the Sun 373
Lilith 376
Mambo 377
They Came to Cordura 297
Rossi, Jeri Cain
Black Hearts Bleed Red 427
Rossif, Frederic
Wall in Jerusalem 110
Rosson, Arthur
The Last Outlaw (1927) 400
Rostrup, Kaspar
Memories of a Marriage 76
Roszell, Stephen
Other Prisoners 476
Writing in Water and Admiral Bataille & the S.S. Esoterica 480
Rotha, Paul
De Overval (Resistance) 30
Life of Adolf Hitler 474, 769
Rothmund, Sigi
Julia (France) 4
Rouan, Brigitte
Overseas 6
Rouch, Jean
Le Jaguar 16
Les Maitres Fous 16
The Lion Hunters 16
Rouffio, Jacques
La Passante 4
Rouleau, Raymond
The Crucible (1957) 19
Roussimof, Ari
Trail of Blood 512, 530
Roussin, Andre
Days of Our Years 19
Rowinski, Roland
Bottom Rock 90
Rowland, Richard A.
Burning Daylight 396
Rowland, Roy
The 5000 Fingers of Dr. T 356
Bugles in the Afternoon 291
Girl Hunters 506
Hit the Deck 324
Meet Me in Las Vegas 326
Our Vines Have Tender Grapes 381
Seven Hills of Rome 328
A Stranger in Town 388
Two Weeks with Love 331
Royer, Larry
Skippy the Dog Food Taster (Too Outrageous) 717
Royle, David
Wall Street Journal Video: Emerging Powers 801
Rozema, Patricia
When Night Is Falling 212, 467
Rozewicz, Stanislaw
Woman in the Hat 95
Rozsa, Janosz
Sunday Daughters 102
Ruane, John
Death in Brunswick 205
Rubbo, Michael
The Peanut Butter Solution 665
Ruben, J. Walter
Ace of Aces 356
Java Head 174
Riffraff (1936/Tracy) 384
Ruben, Joseph
Money Train 238
Sleeping with the Enemy 246
The Stepfather 248
Rubie, Howard
Lion's Den 206, 433
Rubin, Alex
Who Is Henry Jaglom? 339
Rubino, John
Lotto Land 275
Rubinstein, Amnon
The Heritage (Ha-Yerusha) 107
Nadia (Israel) 108
Rucker, Joseph
With Byrd at the South Pole 406
Rudolph, Alan
Afterglow 257
Choose Me 257
Equinox 257
Love at Large 257
The Moderns 257
Mortal Thoughts 257
Mrs. Parker and the Vicious Circle 257
Songwriter 257
Trouble in Mind 257
Ruggles, Wesley
Arizona 290
Cimarron 291
I'm No Angel 272
London Town 184

No Man of Her Own 278
The Plastic Age....402
Somewhere I'll Find You....387
Ruiz, Raul
The Golden Boat....11
Hypothesis of the Stolen Painting....11
Life Is a Dream....11
On Top of the Whale....11
Three Lives and Only One Death 11
Rupe, Katja
Germany in Autumn 66
Rupp, Christy
City Wildlife: Mice, Rats & Roaches....547
Rush, Richard
Color of Night (Director's Cut) 222
Hell's Angels on Wheels....506
Russell, Charles
Eraser....226
Russell, Chuck
Blob, The....517
The Mask (1994/Carrey)....275
Russell, David O.
Flirting with Disaster....268
Spanking the Monkey....437
Russell, Erica
Feet of Song (Spike/Mike 1)....716
Russell, Ken
Altered States....167
Aria....158, 577
Boyfriend....167
Crimes of Passion 167
Dante's Inferno....167
The Devils....167
Gothic....167
Isadora....167
Ken Russell....336
Knights on Bikes (Experimental Series #22)....484
The Lair of the White Worm 167
Lisztomania 167, 325
Mahler....167
The Music Lovers 167
Peepshow (Experimental Series #22)....484
Prisoner of Honor....167
Tales of Erotica 249
Valentino....167
Whore....167
Women & Men - Stories of Seduction....302
Women in Love....167
Russell, Paddy
Little Women (1970/BBC)....193
Russell, Peter
Peter Russell: The Global Brain 487
Russell, William D.
Best of the Badmen 359
Ruth, Roy Del
The Alligator People 516
Blessed Event....264
Blonde Crazy 264
Born to Dance 320
Broadway Melody of 1936....320
Broadway Melody of 1938....320
Broadway Rhythm 320
Bureau of Missing Persons....362
The Chocolate Soldier....321
Du Barry Was a Lady....322
Employees' Entrance....268
Happy Landing....371
Kid Millions....325
Lady Killer (USA)....375
My Lucky Star (Sonja Henie)....380
On Moonlight Bay....327
On the Avenue....327
Phantom of the Rue Morgue 527
Topper Returns....285
The West Point Story 331
Rutt, Todd/McConnell, Arn
Shock! Shock! Shock!....489
Ruttmann, Walter
Berlin, Symphony of a Great City....68, 483
Ryan, Frank
Call Out the Marines....362
Can't Help Singing....321
The Clay Pigeons (Call Out the Marines) 362
Ryan, Terence
The Brylcreem Boys 159
Ryan, Terry
Going Home 210
Rybkowski, Jan
Career of Nikodem Dyzma 90
Gniazdo 92
The Peasants 93
Polanicki's Family 93
Rydell, Mark
The Cowboys 291
Crime of the Century 223
Intersection 233
On Golden Pond....240
The Reivers....384
The River 244
The Rose (USA) 245
Rye, Stellan
The Student of Prague (1913) 71
Rymer, Judy
Who Killed Baby Azaria 207
Rymer, Michael
Angel Baby....158
Rynard, Su
Su Rynard: What Wants to Be Spoken, What Remains to Be Said....557
Rynne, Frank
Destroy All Rational Thought 303
Ryunosuke, Akutagawa
Animated Classics of Japanese Literature: Martyr/ Priest of Mt. Kouya....720
Rzeszewski, Janusz
Hallo, Fred the Beard 92
Love Can Take It All....93
Special Mission 94
The Twenties, The Thirties 94
Rzeznik, Francine
One Nation Under God 476
Sabiston, Bob
ASIFA's Children's Beat (Animation C.2) 705
Sachs, Ira
Delta, The....458
Sachs, William
The Incredible Melting Man 497
Sadanah, Vijay
Aulad....146
Sadwith, James
Sinatra....618
Sadykov, Bako
Adonis XIV (Glasnost Film Fest V.10)....81
Saffa, Joan
Journey of Carlos Fuentes: Crossing Borders....58
Sagal, Boris
Girl Happy 536
Masada (Peter O'Toole) 109
Sagan, Leontine
Maedchen in Uniform 70, 462
Saint-Jean, Raymond
Telefoto....560
Sakayants, Robert
The Button (Animation C.4)....706
Saks, Eric
Don from Lakewood/You Talk, I Buy 429
Forevermore: Biography of a Leach Lord....430
Saks, Gene
Barefoot in the Park....263
Brighton Beach Memoirs....264
Cactus Flower....265
Last of the Red Hot Lovers 273
Mame....326
Odd Couple 278
Salandra, Eugene
Faerie Film (Men in Shorts V.2)....463
Sale, Richard
Abandon Ship! 356
Let's Make It Legal 274
Salekarios, Alekos
Aunt from Chicago 104
Salicki, Miroslaw
This Is Warsaw 99
Salitt, Dan
Polly Perverse Strikes Again!....435
Salkin, Leo
The 2000-Year-Old Man 676
Salkow, Sidney
City Without Men 364
The Last Man on Earth....524
Sitting Bull 296
Twice Told Tales....530
Salle, David
Search and Destroy....246
Salles Jr., Walter
Exposure....226
Salloum, Jayce
The Ascent of Man/In the Absence of Heroes 482
Introduction to the End of an Argument 486
This Is Not Beirut/There Was and There Was Not....489
Up to the South 489
Salva, Victor
Powder 242
Salvador, Jaime
Boom in the Moon....408
Salvatores, Gabriele
Mediterraneo 33
Salvo, Calogero
Terranova....34
Salwen, Hal
Denise Calls Up 267
Salzmann, Laurence
Last Jews of Radauti (Song of Radauti) 115
Samanta, Shakti
Kashmir Ki Kali 147
Samperi, Salvatore
Ernesto....32, 459
Malicious 33
Samuel, Julian
Julian Samuel Trilogy 474
San Paulo, Piedro de
Rich Boy, Poor Boy 145, 464
Sanchez, Jose
La Paz....51
Sander, Helke
All-Round Reduced Personality 63
Sanders, Denis
Elvis—That's the Way It Is 536
One Man's Way 381
Revenge of the Bee Girls 509
Sanders-Brahms, Helma
Germany Pale Mother....63
Lumiere & Company....5, 336
Sandgren, Ake
Slingshot 77
Sandor, Pal
Daniel Takes the Train 101
Sandrich, Mark
Aggie Appleby, Maker of Men 261
Gay Divorcee 322
Here Come the WAVES 271
Melody Cruise....326
Shall We Dance 328
So Proudly We Hail....387
Top Hat....330
Sanford, Arlene
A Very Brady Sequel....286
Sanforth, Clifford
Murder by Television 508
Sang, To Hoi
Wai's Romance 124
Sanger, Jonathan
Down Came a Blackbird....225
Santell, Alfred
Hairy Ape....371
Internes Can't Take Money 373
Jack London....304
Orchids and Ermine....402
That Brennan Girl 390
Winterset....316
Santi, Giancarlo
The Grand Duel 293
Santiago, Cirio H.
The Muthers 508
Santley, Joseph
The Cocoanuts 266
Music in My Heart 380
Santoni, Joel
La Course en Tete: The Eddie Merckx Story....827
Santucci, Walter
The Cat, Cow and Beautiful Fish (Spike/Mike Sick 2) 716
Jean Jean and the Evil Cat (Spike/Mike 2)....716
Saperstein, David
Killing Affair....234
Saraf, Irving
In the Shadow of the Stars....473, 581
Sarafian, Deran
Back in the USSR 218
Sarafian, Richard C.
Man in the Wilderness....237
Man Who Loved Cat Dancing 294
Sardina, Sheryl
Eternity (Animation C.2) 705
Sargent, Joseph
Abraham 355
Caroline?....221
Colossus: The Forbin Project 495
Day One....417
MacArthur 795
Mandela and DeKlerk 800
Miss Evers' Boys 238, 453
Miss Rose White....238
My Antonia....239
Skylark 666
The Taking of Pelham 1 2 3 248
Tomorrow's Child....249
Tribes....250
Sarno, Jonathan
Ramona....436
Sasaki, Tomiyo
Video Art: Tomiyo Sasaki 490
Sasdy, Peter
Taste the Blood of Dracula 530
Sass, Barbara
Apple Tree of Paradise 90
Girls of Nowopilki 92
Without Love (Barbara Sass)....95
Sathyu, M.S.
Garam Hava (Hot Winds)....147
Sato, Hajime
Body Snatcher from Hell (Goke) 494
Sato, Junya
The Silk Road (Japanese)....139
Sau-Leung, Blackie Ko
Days of Being Dumb....119
Saunders, George
Intimate Deception 233
Saunders, Joyan
Video Art: Here in the Southwest 490
Saura, Carlos
Ay, Carmela 45
Blood Wedding....45
Cria! 45
Elisa Vida Mia 45
Garden of Delights 45
The Hunt 45
Outrage....46
Sevillanas 46
The Stilts (Los Zancos) 46
Sautet, Claude
Les Choses de la Vie....4
Mado....5
Nelly and Monsieur Arnaud 5
A Simple Story 6
Un Coeur en Hiver....7
Vincent, Francois, Paul & the Others 7
Sauvage, Pierre
Weapons of the Spirit 7
Sauvajon, Marc Gilbert
A Royal Affair 17
Savchenko, Igor

Guerilla Brigade 85
Saville, Philip
Shadey 163
Wonderland 165
Saville, Victor
Conspirator....172
Dark Journey 173
Evergreen....173
Forever and a Day....170
Green Dolphin Street 371
The Iron Duke 174
Kim (1950) 374
South Riding 178
Storm in a Teacup 185
Tonight and Every Night....330
Savoca, Nancy
Dogfight....225
Household Saints....271
If These Walls Could Talk 232
Savona, Leopoldo
The Mongols....42
Sayers, Eric
Common Law Wife 505
Sayles, John
Baby, It's You 440
The Brother from Another Planet....440
City of Hope 440
Eight Men Out 440
Lone Star....440
Matewan....440
Men with Guns....440
Passion Fish 440
The Secret of Roan Inish 440
Scarpelli, Umberto
Giant of Metropolis....496
Scarpulla, Caren
Liver, Lust, or Louie (Too Outrageous)....717
Scattini, Luigi
Primitive Love....509
Schachter, Steven
The Water Engine 316
Schaefer, Armand
The Hurricane Express....372
Sixteen Fathoms Deep....386
The Three Musketeers (1933/Wayne) 390
Schaefer, George
The Bunker....221
A Piano for Mrs. Cimino....242
Schaeffer, Eric
My Life's in Turnaround 277
Schafer, Marianne
Tears in Florence 65
Schaffner, Franklin J.
Best Man, The....359
Islands in the Stream 233
Nicholas and Alexandra (Drama) 162
Papillon....241
Patton 382
Planet of the Apes....499
Schall, Heinz
Hamlet (1921) 69
Schatzberg, Jerry
Lumiere & Company....5, 336
Scarecrow....245
Scheinfeld, John
The Unknown Marx Brothers....285, 339
Schell, Maximilian
Castle....864
First Love....74
Schenkel, Carl
The Mighty Quinn 238
Schenkman, Richard
The Pompatus of Love....435
Schepisi, Fred
A Cry in the Dark....205
Fierce Creatures....182
I.Q....272
Iceman....232
Plenty....163
Roxanne 281
The Russia House 245
Six Degrees of Separation....246
Scher, Jeffrey
Milk of Amnesia (Best Fest 5th Annual) 706
Scher, Jeffrey Noyes
Reasons to be Glad (Acidburn) 717
Schertzinger, Victor
Birth of the Blues....320
The Clodhopper....396
One Night of Love....327
Rhythm on the River 328
The Road to Singapore 281
The Road to Zanzibar 281
Something to Sing About 329
Uptown New York....392
What Happened to Rosa? 406
Schibli, Paul
The Nutcracker Prince 714
Schickel, Richard
Alfred Hitchcock: Master of Suspense....332, 351
Elia Kazan: A Director's Journey 333
Inside Hitchcock 352
Schiffer, Sheldon
Dad's Last Flight....428
Schiffman, Suzanne
Sorceress....7
Schiller, Greta
International Sweethearts of Rhythm/
Tiny & Ruby: Hell-Divin' Women....461, 611
Paris Was a Woman....464, 476
Waking Up: A Lesson in Love....467
Schindel, Morton
Mike Mulligan and His Steam Shovel....654
Schipek, Dietmar
Flaming Ears....63, 459
Schirk, Heinz
Wannsee Conference....65
Schivazappia, Piero
The Frightened Woman 33
Schlaich, Frieder
Halfmoon 63, 304
Schlamme, Thomas
Kingfish: A Story of Huey P. Long....234
Mambo Mouth....313
Miss Firecracker....276
Schlatter, George
Norman...Is That You? 278
Schlesinger, John
Billy Liar....158
Cold Comfort Farm....266
Darling....173
Day of the Locust....224
Eye for an Eye (USA)....226
The Falcon and the Snowman....227
Far from the Madding Crowd (1967) 173
The Innocent....233
Madame Sousatzka....162
Midnight Cowboy (25th Anniversary)....379
Sunday Bloody Sunday 164, 465
Yanks....253
Schlondorff, Volker
Death of a Salesman....311
Germany in Autumn 66
Handmaid's Tale....161
Michael Nyman Songbook: Ute Lemper 73
Palmetto....435
Swann in Love 65
The Tin Drum 65
Voyager....65
Schloss, Arleen
Glenn Branca: Symphony No. 4 589
Schlossberg, Julian
Sex and Justice....763
Schlow, Steven
Force of Evil (Eichmann) 775
Schmeichen, Richard
Times of Harvey Milk....478
Schmid, Daniel
Shadow of Angels....66
Tosca's Kiss....34
Schmidlapp, David
Not Quite Love....435
Schmidt, Peter C.
Fall of the Berlin Wall....73
Schmidt, Richard
1988....426
American Orpheus 426
Emerald Cities....429
Schmidt, Rick
A Man, a Woman and a Killer....433
Morgan's Cake....434
Schnabel, Julian
Basquiat....427
Schnaffner, Franklin J.
Our Town (1977/Robby Benson)....314
Schnall, John
Goodnight Norma...(Animation C.2)....705
Reading Room (Animation C.3)....705
Unsavory Avery (Animation C.4)....706
Schneider, Eric
Adam's Other Rib (Spike/Mike Sick 2) 716
Schoedsack, Ernest
Chang 396
Grass 399
Schoedsack, Ernest B.
Dr. Cyclops....495
King Kong (60th Anniversary Edition) 524
Mighty Joe Young....379
The Most Dangerous Game 379
Son of Kong....529
Schoendoerffer, Pierre
The 317th Platoon 2, 777
Anderson Platoon 2, 777
Le Crabe Tambour....4
Schofield, Wendy
Tibet: A Seed for Transformation....150
Schonfeld, Victor
Animals Film....468
Shattered Dreams 477
Schrader, Paul
American Gigolo....217
Cat People (1982)....518
The Comfort of Strangers....223
Light of Day....236
Light Sleeper....236
Mishima: A Life in Four Chapters....238
Witch Hunt....252
Schreyer, John F.
Naked Youth....508
Schroeder, Barbet
Barfly....15
Before and After....15
Charles Bukowski Tapes 15
Desperate Measures....15
Kiss of Death (USA/1994)....16
Reversal of Fortune 16
Single White Female 16
Schroeder, Tom
Harvist Town (Best Fest 91)....706
Schubert, Peter
Germany in Autumn 66
Schulmann, Patrick
Et la Tendresse?...Bordel!....17
Et la Tendresse?...Bordel! #2....17
Rendez-Moi Ma Peau....6
Schultz, Michael
Cooley High....444
Disorderlies 444
Greased Lightning 444
Krush Groove 445
Sgt. Pepper's Lonely Heart's Club Band 328
Schumacher, Joel
Batman & Robin 219
The Client....222
Cousins....266
Falling Down 227
The Incredible Shrinking Woman....272
The Lost Boys 236
St. Elmo's Fire....247
A Time to Kill....249
Schunzel, Reinhold
Balalaika....320
Fortune's Fool....69
Schure, Alexander
Tubby the Tuba 659
Schuster, Harold
Dinner at The Ritz....173
Finger Man....368
Marine Raiders....769
My Friend Flicka 665
Schutte, Jan
Dragon Chow 63
Schwartz, Howard
Dream Boys Revue 458
Schwartz, Maurice
Tevye the Dairyman....113
Schwartz, Peter
All Dressed Up and No Place to Go....468
Schweitert, Stefan
A Tickle in the Heart....604
Schwizgebel, George
78 Tours (Int. Animation 3) 712
Schwizgebel, Georges
The Ride to the Abyss (Int. Animation 6) 712
Scola, Ettore
The Family 36
Le Bal....36
Macaroni....36
Passione d'Amore 36
Scorsese, Martin
After Hours (Comedy)....253
The Age of Innocence....253
Alice Doesn't Live Here Anymore....253
Cape Fear (Remake) 253
Casino....253
The Color of Money 253
Goodfellas....253
It's Not Just You, Murray (First Works)....334
Italian American/The Big Shave....253
King of Comedy....253
Kundun....253
Last Temptation of Christ....253
Last Waltz....253
Life Lessons (New York Stories) 260
Martin Scorsese AFI Lifetime Achievement Award....332
Mean Streets 253
New York Stories....260, 288
New York, New York 253, 327
Raging Bull....253
Taxi Driver....254
What's a Nice Girl Like You (First Works)....334
Who's That Knocking at My Door?....254
Scott, Bonnie
Milk Cow. Eat Cheese. 637
Scott, Cynthia
Strangers in Good Company....211
Scott, Peter Graham
The Headless Ghost 174, 523
Scott, Ridley
1492: Conquest of Paradise....216
Alien....494
Alien Trilogy....494
Blade Runner....494
Duellists....160
Someone to Watch over Me....247
Thelma and Louise....249
White Squall 252
Scott, Tony
Beverly Hills Cop 2 263
Crimson Tide 223
The Fan....227
The Hunger (Deneuve)....460, 523
Top Gun....249
True Romance 441
Scotto, Aubrey
Uncle Moses 113
Scroczynski, Aleksander
Vice Versa (Too Outrageous) 717
Scuilli, Michael
Quest (Animation C.1) 705
Seaman, Bill

Video Art: Telling Motions 490
Searle, Francis
The Caretaker's Daughter 181
Sears, Fred F.
Earth vs. the Flying Saucers 495
Seaton, George
36 Hours 356
The Big Lift 360
The Country Girl (1954) 364
Miracle on 34th Street 379
Showdown 296
Teacher's Pet 283
Sebastian, Jonathan
Voyage to a Prehistoric Planet 501
Sebelious, Gregg
Day the Earth Froze 495
Sedgwick, Edward
Beware Spooks! 263
Sedgwick, Edward H.
Air Raid Wardens 261
Doughboys 409
Free and Easy 409
Gladiator 269
Ma and Pa Kettle Back on the Farm 275
Movie Struck (Pick a Star) 326
Parlor, Bedroom and Bath 409
Pick a Star 279
Riding on Air 280
Seven Chances 409
A Southern Yankee 282
Speak Easily 409
Spite Marriage 409
What! No Beer? 409
Seed, Paul
The Affair 216
Seeger, Mike
Talking Feet 606
Sehr, Peter
Kaspar Hauser 64
Sei, Xie
A Mongolian Tale 117
Seidelman, Arthur Allan
Harvest of Fire 230
The Summer of Ben Tyler 248
Tragedy of Macbeth 315
Seidelman, Susan
And You Act Like One, Too (First Works) 334
Cookie 266
Desperately Seeking Susan 267
Smithereens 437
Tales of Erotica 249
Seiden, Joseph
Eli Eli 112
God, Man and Devil 112
Paradise in Harlem 448
Seiderburg, Mark
Little Miss Muffet (Sextoons) 715
Seig, Matthew
Sarah Vaughan: The Divine One 615
Seiler, Lewis
Breakthrough 766
Doll Face 322
Guadalcanal Diary 768
Pittsburgh 382
The Tanks Are Coming 772
The Winning Team 393
Seiter, William
Borderline 361
Seiter, William A.
Belle of the Yukon 320
Big Business Girl 359
Cheerful Fraud 396
Daddies 397
Dimples 322
I'm a Fool and The Wild Bunch 418
It's a Date 324
It's a Pleasure 373
Lady Takes a Chance 273
Little Giant 274
Make Haste to Live 377
Nice Girl? 278
One Touch of Venus 327
Sons of the Desert 282
Stowaway 329
Susannah of the Mounties 666
Up in Central Park 392
The Wild Bunch (Seiter) 393
You Were Never Lovelier 331
Seitz, George B.
Drums of Jeopardy 521
The Last of the Mohicans (1936) 375
Life Begins for Andy Hardy/Andy Hardy's Secretary 274
The Vanishing American 406
Sekely, Steve
Day of the Triffids 495
The Scar (Hollow Triumph) 385
Selander, Lesley
Fighter Attack 368
Selander, Leslie
Flat Top 368
Flight to Mars 496
Self, Jim
Beehive 483
Seller, Lewis
Charlie Chan in Paris 363
Selpin, Herbert
Titanic (1943/Germany) 71
Seltzer, David
Lucas 237
Selwyn, Edgar
The Sin of Madelon Claudet 386
Skyscraper Souls 386
Selznick, Arna
Care Bears Movie 662
Semon, Larry
L. Frank Baum's Silent Film Collection of Oz 400
Sawmill and Dome Doctor 411
The Wizard of Oz (1925/Semon) 406
Sen, Mrinal
Genesis 147
Sena, Dominic
Kalifornia 234
Sennett, Mack
Bing—The Sennett Shorts 320
Tillie's Punctured Romance 412
Serafy, Sam
Watch with Mother (CineBLAST 1) 483
Serard, Michel
Soldier Duroc...It's Your Party 6
Serebriakov, Nikolai
Ball of Yarn (Masters #7) 82, 713
Seregi, Laszlo
Beggar Student 101
Sereny, Eva
Foreign Student 228
Sergeyev, K.
The Kirov Ballet in Tchaikovsky's Sleeping Beauty 572
Serious, Yahoo
Young Einstein 207
Serra, M.M.
L'Amour Fou 461
Serreau, Coline
Mama, There's a Man in Your Bed 17
Three Men and a Cradle 18
Setbon, Phillip
Mr. Frost 239
Seto, Javier
The Castilian 363
Sewell, Vernon
Blood Beast Terror 517
Shadyac, Tom
Liar Liar 274
The Nutty Professor (1996) 278
Shafer, Dirk
Man of the Year 462
Shaffer, Anthony
Absolution 158
Shah, Krishna
River Niger 446
Shan, Yu Ming
Zen of Sword 133
Shanley, John Patrick
Joe Versus the Volcano 272
Shannon, Jay
Uptown Angel 512
Shantaram, V.
Do Ankhen Barah Haath 147
Shaohong, Li
Blush 117
Shapiro, Craig
The Boardwalk Club 427
Shapiro, Joseph
Horodok 112
Shapiro, Paul
The Lotus Eaters 211
Sharma, Vijay
In Praise of Mother Santoshi 147
Sharman, Jim
Rocky Horror Picture Show 509
Sharon, Clark
John Wayne: On Board with the Duke 336
Sharp, Don
Kiss of the Vampire 524
Rasputin: The Mad Monk 528
Sharp, Ian
Thomas Hardy's Tess of the D'Urbervilles 197
Sharp, Willoughby
Joseph Beuys, Public Dialogues 551
Willoughby Sharp's Downtown New York 491
Shatner, William
Star Trek V: The Final Frontier 500
Shavelson, Melville
Cast a Giant Shadow 363
Houseboat 271
It Started in Naples 272
It Started with a Kiss 272
Seven Little Foys 282
Yours, Mine and Ours 288
Shaw, Anthony
Mrs. 'Arris Goes to Paris 162
Shea, Mike
And This Is Free 468, 608
Shear, Barry
Deadly Trackers 292
Shearer, Harry
Portrait of a White Marriage 279
Shebib, Donald
Pathfinder (USA) 242
Sheets, Todd
Bimbos B.C. 494
Dominion 520
Goblin 522
Prehistoric Bimbos in Armageddon City 509
Sorority Babes in the Dance-a-thon of Death 510
Zombie Rampage 531
Sheirl, Angela Hans
Flaming Ears 63, 459
Sheldon, James
The Bells of Cockaigne & Broadway Trust 414
Harvest 417
Sheldon, Sidney
Dream Wife 267
Shelton, Lois
Ernie Andrews: Blues for Central Avenue 610
Shelton, Ron
Cobb 222
Tin Cup 285
White Men Can't Jump 287
Shemer, Yaron
Pilgrimage of Remembrance: Jews in Poland Today 115
Shepard, Gerald S.
Heroes Die Young 371
Shepard, Richard
Linguini Incident 236
Shepard, Sam
Far North 260
Silent Tongue 260
Sher, Elizabeth
Fingers That Tickle and Delight 472
Interviews with Artists, Program 4: Three Installation Artists 550
Just Another Weekend 432
Videotapes of Elizabeth Sher V. 1-11 491
Sher, Jack
The Three Worlds of Gulliver 667
Sheridan, Jim
The Boxer 202
The Field 202
In the Name of the Father 202
My Left Foot 202
Sheridan, Michael J.
That's Entertainment III 330
Sherin, Edwin
The Father Clements Story 452
Valdez Is Coming 297
Sherman, George
Big Jake 290
The Desert Trail 292
Last of the Redmen 293
Tomahawk 297
War Arrow 297
Sherman, Lowell
Bachelor Apartment 262
Royal Bed 385
She Done Him Wrong 282
Three Broadway Girls 283
Sherman, Stuart
Me and Joe (Four Directions) 459
Sherman, Vincent
Adventures of Don Juan 356
Affair in Trinidad 357
All Through the Night 357
Cervantes 47
Harriet Craig 371
The Hasty Heart 174
Lone Star 294
Mr. Skeffington 379
Sherwood, Bill
Parting Glances 464
Sherwood, John
The Creature Walks Among Us 519
The Monolith Monsters 498
Shevchenko, Vladimir
Chernobyl: Chronicle of Difficult Weeks 81
Shibata, M.
Blue Sonnet Vol. 1 724
Blue Sonnet Vol. 2 724
Shiflett, John
Dazzle 709
Shils, Barry
Wigstock: The Movie 439, 467
Shima, Koji
Warning from Space 501
Shin, Stephen
BB30 118
Heart into Hearts 121
Shindo, Kaneto
Island 138
Onibaba 138
Shing, Chan Muk
Big Bullet 125
Shing, Tong Wai
Dangerous Duty 126
Shing-Hon, Lau
Hunted in Hong Kong 128
Yes Madam 5 133
Shinoda, Masahiro
Double Suicide 137
Gonza the Spearman 137
Shire, Talia
One Night Stand 241
Shirow, Masamune
Black Magic M-66 723
Ghost in the Shell 730
Shoemaker, G.
Friends: A Closer Look at the Enemy 87
Sholder, Jack
The Hidden 497
Sholem, Lee

The Doomsday Machine 495
Hell Ship Mutiny 371
Ma and Pa Kettle at Waikiki 275
Pharaoh's Curse 527
The Redhead from Wyoming 295
Superman & the Mole Men 511
Tobor the Great 501

Shore, Sig
The Return of Superfly 533

Shores, Lynn
Charlie Chan at the Wax Museum 363
The Shadow Strikes 510

Shub, Esther
Fall of the Romanov Dynasty 85

Shui Fan/Fung, Stanley
Love Soldier of Fortune 121

Shum, Mina
Double Happiness 210

Shumlin, Herman
Watch on the Rhine 393

Shun, Yip Wai
Mongkok Story 130

Shyer, Charles
Baby Boom 262

Sichel, Alex
All Over Me 426

Sicre, Jose Gomez
Alejandro Obregon Paints a Fresco, English Narration 544
The Art of Central America and Panama, English Narration 545
Chancay, The Forgotten Art 546
Nine Artists of Puerto Rico 554
Vicus 783

Sidney, George
Anchors Aweigh 319
Bathing Beauty 263
Bye Bye Birdie 321
Cass Timberlane 363
The Eddy Duchin Story 322
Half a Sixpence 183
The Harvey Girls 323
Holiday in Mexico 372
Jupiter's Darling 374
Key to the City 374
Pal Joey 327
Scaramouche 385
Show Boat (1951) 328
Thousands Cheer 330
The Three Musketeers (1948/Kelly) 391
Viva Las Vegas 537
Young Bess 394

Sidney, Scott
Charley's Aunt 396
Nervous Wreck 401
Tarzan of the Apes 405

Siegel, David
Suture 438

Siegel, Don
An Annapolis Story 357
The Beguiled 219
Black Windmill 158
Dirty Harry 225
The Duel at Silver Creek 292
Invasion of the Body Snatchers (1956) 497
Killers 374
Madigan 377
Private Hell #36 383
Riot in Cell Block 11 384
The Shootist 296
Telefon 249

Siegel, Lois
Lip Gloss 462

Sienski, Maciej
At the Bottom of the Hell (Dno piekta) 98

Sievernich, Lillian
The Dubliners 348

Sign-Pui, K.
An Eye for an Eye 127

Sih-Ming, Ko
The Kidnap of Wong Chak Fai 121

Sihanouk, H.M. Norodom
An Ambition Reduced to Ashes 144
The Last Days of Colonel Savath 145
Peasants in Distress 145

Sijan, Slobodan
The Marathon Family 103
Who's Singing Over There? 104

Sijie, Dai
China, My Sorrow 117

Sikora, Jim
Bring Me the Head of Geraldo Rivera 504

Silber, Glenn
War at Home (Documentary) 778

Silberg, Joel
Rappin' 328

Silberg, Yoel
Kuni Lemel in Tel Aviv 108

Silberling, Brad
Casper 662

Silberman, J.
The Way of the Little Dragon 133

Silbey, Paul (Ramana Das)
Citizen Diplomat 470

Siler, Megan
The Midwife's Tale 463

Sills, Sam
The Good Fight 48, 472

Silver, Joan Micklin
Bernice Bobs Her Hair 300
Big Girls Don't Cry 263
Chilly Scenes of Winter 265
Crossing Delancey 266
Hester Street 231
In the Presence of Mine Enemies 232

Silver, Marisa
Permanent Record 242

Silver, Scott
Johns 461

Silverman, David
Strange Case...(Animation C.1) 705

Silverstein, Elliot
Cat Ballou 291

Simenon, Marc
By the Blood of Others 2

Simmons, Katina
Clemintine Hunter 547

Simon, Frank
The Queen 464

Simon, Juan Piquer
Supersonic Man 500

Simon, Kirk
Buckminster Fuller: Thinking Out Loud 469, 565

Simon, Lisa
Sesame Street Kids' Guide to Life: Learning to Share 656
Sesame Street Kids' Guide to Life: Telling the Truth 656

Simon, Murray E.
Great Cantors of the Golden Age 114

Simon, S. Sylvan
Abbott and Costello in Hollywood 261
The Fuller Brush Man/The Fuller Brush Girl 269
Rio Rita 280
Son of Lassie 666
Whistling in Brooklyn 287
Whistling in Dixie 287
Whistling in the Dark 287

Simoneau, Yves
Blind Trust 213
Memphis 237
Til Death Us Do Part 249

Simpson, Kelli
Around the World the Lesbian Way 456

Sims, Karl
Panspermia (Spike/Mike 2) 716
Particle Dreams (Spike/Mike 1) 716

Sin-Keng, Chen
White Lotus Cult 133

Sinatra, Frank
None But the Brave 770

Sing, Cheung Chi
Love & Sex Among the Ruins 121

Sing, Tsui Kwong
A Lustful Night 122

Sing, Yee Tung
Full Throttle 127
The Lunatics 122

Sing-Pui, O
My Flying Wife 122

Singer, Bryan
Lion's Den 206, 433
The Usual Suspects 251

Singer, Gail
Wisecracks 212

Singleton, John
Boyz N The Hood 443
Higher Learning 444
Poetic Justice 446
Rosewood 446

Singleton, Ralph S.
Graveyard Shift 522

Sinise, Gary
Miles from Home 238
Of Mice and Men (Malkovich) 240

Sinkel, Bernhard
Germany in Autumn 66

Sinofsky, Bruce
Brother's Keeper 469
Paradise Lost 476

Sinyor, Gary
Leon the Pig Farmer 184

Siodmak, Curt
Bride of the Gorilla 517
The Devil's Messenger 520
Menschen am Sontag (People on Sunday) 401
Murder in the Mirror 526

Siodmak, Robert
The Crimson Pirate 364
Criss Cross 364
Custer of the West 292
The Dark Mirror 365
The Killers 374
Menschen am Sontag (People on Sunday) 401
Phantom Lady 382
The Rough and the Smooth (Portrait of a Sinner) 177
Son of Dracula 529
The Strange Affair of Uncle Harry 388

Sippy, Ramesh
Flames of the Sun (Sholay) 147

Siriscevic, Drazen
Placido Domingo: His 25th Anniversary Concert at the Roman Amphitheater of Verona 599

Sirk, Douglas
All I Desire 342
All That Heaven Allows 342
Battle Hymn 342
Imitation of Life (1959) 342
Magnificent Obsession 342
The Tarnished Angels 342
Written on the Wind 342
Zu Neuen Ufern 342

Sito, Tom
Propagandance (Animation C.2) 705

Siu, Stanley
Winner Takes All 133

Siu-Tung, Ching
Dragon Inn 127

Sivan, Uri
Saint Clara 108

Siversten, T.
Zwisch (Outrageous 2) 714

Sjoberg, Alf
Miss Julie 76
Torment 77

Sjoman, Vilgot
I Am Curious—Yellow 76

Sjostrom, Victor
He Who Gets Slapped 79
Outlaw and His Wife 79
Phantom Chariot 79
Secret of the Monastery 79
Under the Red Robe 79
Victor Sjostrom 339
The Wind (Gish) 79

Skabard, Tatyana
The Limit (Glasnost Film Fest V.5) 81

Sklar, Roberta
The Open Theater: Terminal 314

Skoggard, Ross
Conversation with Roy Lichtenstein and The New German Art 547

Skolimowski, Jerzy
Hands Up (Polish) 97
The Lightship 97
The Shout 97
Torrents of Spring 97

Slak, Franci
When I Close My Eyes 104

Slapczynski, R.
Off on a Comet 639, 714

Slater, Guy
A Pocketful of Rye 195

Slater, Mel
Radioland Murders 243

Slesicki, Wladyslaw
Gypsies 92
In Desert and Wilderness 92

Sloan, Edward
Surrender 404

Sloan, Holly Goldberg
The Big Green 691

Sloane, Paul
Coming of Amos 397
Consolation Marriage 364
Eve's Leaves 398
Half Shot at Sunrise 270
Made for Love 401

Sloman, Edward
Lost Zeppelin 377

Sloman, Edward S.
The Ghost of Rosy Taylor 398

Sluizer, George
Utz 164
The Vanishing 31

Smallcombe, John
An African Dream 158

Smight, Jack
The Illustrated Man 497
Midway 237
The Secret War of Harry Frigg 281

Smilow, Margaret
Music for the Movies: The Hollywood Sound 337, 617

Smith, Aaron
Molly (Too Outrageous) 717

Smith, Brooke
Sheep's Meadow (CineBLAST 1) 483

Smith, Clifford
The Back Trail 395

Smith, Cynthia
Images: A Lesbian Love Story 460

Smith, Dan
Discoveries (Spike/Mike Sick 1) 416

Smith, Dave
A Hole in One (Spike/Mike Sick 2) 416

Smith, Harry
Harry Smith: Early Abstractions 710
Heaven and Earth Magic 485

Smith, Jack
Flaming Creatures 459, 485
Normal Love 463, 487
A Performance by Jack Smith 487, 567

Smith, John N.
The Boys of St. Vincent 210
Masculine Mystique 211

Smith, Kevin
Chasing Amy 428
Clerks 428
Floundering 430

Smith, Mel
The Tall Guy 185

Smith, Michael

Video Art: It Starts at Home 490
Smith, Mike
Get A Haircut (Int. Animation 6) 712
Mike Smith Showreel (British Animation) 707
Smith, Noel Mason
Fighting Pilot 173
Smithee, Alan
An Alan Smithee Film: Burn Hollywood Burn 216
Bloodsucking Pharaohs in Pittsburgh 504
Call of the Wild (1993) 662
The Indiscreet Mrs. Jarvis 373
Snider, Bill
Skip It (Best Fest Kids) 706
Snowden, Alison/Fine, David
The Boss (Animation C.4) 706
Second Class Mail (Animation C.1) 705
Snyder, Robert
Willem de Kooning: Artist 558
The World of Buckminster Fuller 566
So, Philip
Eat My Dust (Hong Kong) 127
Soavi, Michelle
Cemetery Man (aka Of Death, Of Love) 32
The Devil's Daughter 520
Soderbergh, Steven
Gray's Anatomy 443
Kafka 443
King of the Hill 443
sex, lies and videotape 443
Steven Soderbergh's Schizopolis 443
The Underneath 443
Soe, Valerie
Video Art, Tape One 489
Video Art, Tape Two 489
Sofian, Sheila
Faith & Patience (Best Fest 5th Annual) 706
Softley, Iain
BackBeat 158
The Wings of the Dove 165
Sokurov, Alexander
Evening Sacrifice (Glasnost Film Fest V.11) 81
Second Circle 83
Solan, Peter
Boxer and Death 99
Solares, Gilberto Martinez
Face of the Screaming Werewolf 521
Solberg, Helena
Carmen Miranda: Bananas Is My Business 470
Sole, Alfred
Alice, Sweet Alice 216
Sollima, Sergio
Sandokan and the Pirates of Malaysia 42
Solondz, Todd
Welcome to the Dollhouse 439
Solt, Andrew
Imagine: John Lennon 620
This Is Elvis 537
Sommers, Stephen
The Adventures of Huck Finn (Disney) 308
The Jungle Book (Disney/1994) 6, 93
Sonder, Carsten
Pretty Boy 76, 464
Sonnenfeld, Barry
Addams Family 261
Addams Family Values 261
Get Shorty 269
Men in Black 276
Sontag, Susan
Agnes Varda and Susan Sontag: Love Cannibals 14
Sopher, Sharon
Witness to Apartheid 153
Sorensen, Steven
Pirate's Dagger 640
Soseki, Natsume
Animated Classics of Japanese Literature: Botchan, Parts 1 & 2 720
Sota, Bruno Ve
Jayne Mansfield: Single Room Furnished/ The Female Jungle 507
Sottnick, Mark
Elephant's Child 646
Steadfast Tin Soldier 649
The Ugly Duckling (Cher) 649
The Velveteen Rabbit (Streep) 649
Soule, Beatrice
Djabote: Sengalese Drumming & Song from Master Drummer Doudou N'D 152, 602
Spacey, Kevin
Albino Alligator 216
Spalding, Philip
New Orleans: Til the Butcher Cuts Him Down 614
Spangler, Larry
Joshua 533
Spangler, Larry G.
Joshua the Black Rider 293
Spara, Robert
The Badge 426
Spears, Ross
An Afternoon with Father Flye 468
Agee 468
The Electric Valley 471
Long Shadows: The Legacy of the American Civil War 780
To Render a Life: 478
Speck, Wieland
Westler: East of the Wall 65, 467
Spector, Johanna
2,000 Years of Freedom and Honor: The Cochini Jews of India 148
About the Jews of Yemen: A Vanishing Culture 113
Without the Past 116
Spence, Richard
Different for Girls 160
Spence, Thomas
A Child's Alphabet (Sextoons) 715
Spencer, Don
Little Toot 654
Spencer, Patricia
Dreamers of the Day 458
Spheeris, Penelope
Decline of Western Civilization— Part II—The Metal Years 620
Wayne's World 286
Spielberg, Steven
Always 258
Amistad 258, 449
Close Encounters of the Third Kind (Director's Cut) 258
The Color Purple 258
Duel 258
E.T. the Extra-Terrestrial 258
Empire of the Sun 258
Hook 258
Indiana Jones and the Last Crusade 258
Indiana Jones and the Temple of Doom 258
Jaws 258
Jurassic Park 258
The Lost World (1997) 258
Raiders of the Lost Ark 258
Schindler's List 245, 258
Steven Spielberg AFI Lifetime Achievement Award 332
Twilight Zone—The Movie 258, 501
Spiers, Bob
That Darn Cat 694
Spigland, Ethan
The Strange Case of Balthazar (CineBLAST!) 428
Spitzer, Nicholas
Zydeco 604
Sporn, Michael
Abel's Island 704
Christmas Stories 631
It Zwibble: Earthday Birthday 653
Jazz Time Tale 636
Nonsense and Lullabyes: Nursery Rhymes 655
Nonsense and Lullabyes: Poems for Children 655
Red Shoes (Animation) 649
Story of the Dancing Frog 649
Whitewash 455, 644
Sporup, Murray Douglas
Rock, Baby, Rock It 509
Spotten, John
Buster Keaton Rides Again 409
Spottiswode, Roger
Hiroshima 231
Tomorrow Never Dies 169
Spottiswoode, Roger
And the Band Played On 456
Sprenkel, Kenn
TimePiece 466
Spring, Jim
New York Videos 487
Springsteen, R.G.
Hostile Guns 293
Oklahoma Annie 381
The Red Menace 384
When Gangland Strikes 393
Spry, Robin
Obsessed 211
Squire, Anthony
Mission in Morocco 379
Squitieri, Pasquale
Corleone 32
The Third Solution 249
Sroczynski, Aleksander
Vice Versa (Outrageous 1) 717
St. Clair, Malcolm
Are Parents People? 395
The Bullfighters 265
Grand Duchess and the Waiter 399
The Show-Off 404
Stabile, Salvatore
Gravesend 431
Stacey, Terry
Bad Liver, Broken Heart (CineBLAST 2) 483
Stadtler, Holly Barden
The Filming of the Leopard Son 333, 815
Stahl, John M.
Father Was a Fullback 268
Imitation of Life (1934) 373
Keys of the Kingdom 374
Leave Her to Heaven 376
A Letter of Introduction 376
Stamets, Bill
Chicago Politics: A Theatre of Power 470
Stanley, Herb
Confessions of a Psycho Cat 505
Stanley, Mike
Dead Is Dead 519
Stanley, Richard
Hardware 230
Stanojevic, Stanislav
Notorious Nobodies (Illustres Inconnus) 6
Stanton, Andrew
A Story (Spike/Mike 1) 716
Stanton, Richard
American Pluck 395
Stanze, Eric
The Scare Game 528
Stapleford, Betty
The Zombie Army 531
Starewicz, Ladislas
The Cameraman's Revenge: The Amazing Puppet Animation of Ladislaw Starewicz 707
Ladislas Starevitch 712
Starewicz, Vladimir
Starewicz's Fantasies (Early Russian Cinema 3) 85
Stark, Cassandra
Lost Films of Cassandra Stark 433
Staroselksy, Edward
My Family Treasure 665
Starr, Steven
Joey Breaker 272
Starrett, Jack
Cleopatra Jones 532
Race with the Devil 527
Walking Tall: The Trilogy 251
Starski, Ludwik
Forbidden Songs 91
Stasny, Peter
In the House 860
Stathacos, Chrysanne
Chrysanne Stathacos: India 2063 547
Staub, Ralph
Mandarin Mystery 378
Staudte, Wolfgang
Der Untertan (The Subject) 68
Murderers Are Among Us 70
The Threepenny Opera (1962) 71
Staveley, Andrew
Strangers in Paradise (British Animation) 707
Staveley, Joan
Wanting for Bridge (Best Fest 91) 706
Staven, Karl
This is Your Brain on Animation (Too Outrageous) 717
Steckler, Ray Dennis
Blood Shack (Director's Cut) 504
Body Fever 504
The Hollywood Strangler Meets the Skid Row Slasher 506
The Incredibly Strange Creatures Who Stopped Living and Became Mixed Up Zombies 507
Las Vegas Serial Killer 507
The Lemon Grove Kids 507
Rat Fink a Boo-Boo 509
The Thrill Killers 511
Wild Guitar 512
Steele, Phillip W.
Haunted Hills: Ghost Stories 472
Steen Jr., Harald Heide
Monk in Oslo 613
Steensland, Mark
Last Way Out 235
Stegmuller, Renate
Fast Buck 63
Stein, Paul L.
Mimi 176
The Outsider 176
Tauber in Blossom Time 330
Stein, Peter L.
The Castro 457
Steinberg, Michael
Bodies, Rest & Motion 427
The Waterdance 251
Steinberg, Mimi
Call Waiting (CineBLAST 2) 483
Steinberger, Harlan
Tibor Jankay—The Art of Survival 557, 777
Steiner, Charles
Nothing to Lose 98
Steiner, Ralph
The City 470
H2O (Experimental Series 20) 484
Steinhoff, Hans
Hitler Youth Quex 768
The Old and the Young King 70
Stelling, Jos
Rembrandt—1669 ....31, 555
Stenhouse, Bob
The Frog, The Dog, & The Devil (Int. Animation 2) 712
Steno
Flatfoot 33
Stephani, Frederick
Flash Gordon—Rocketship 496
Sterling, Joseph
The Case of the Mukkinese Battle Horn 181
Sterling, William
Alice's Adventures in Wonderland 158
Stern, Bert
Jazz on a Summer's Day 612
Stern, Steve
Breaking the Surface: The Greg Louganis Story 457
Stern, Tom
Freaked 269
Sternberg, Josef von
Anatahan 347
Blonde Venus 347
The Blue Angel (English) 347
The Blue Angel (German) 347
Crime and Punishment 347
Dishonored 347
The Docks of New York 347
Epic That Never Was 333
I Kiss Your Hand, Madame 347

Jet Pilot 347
Last Command 347
Macao 347
Morocco 347
The Scarlet Empress 348
Shanghai Express 348
The Shanghai Gesture 348
Underworld 348
Stevens Jr., George
George Stevens: A Filmmaker's Journey 343, 768
Separate But Equal 454
Stevens, David
A Town Like Alice (1980) 207
Stevens, George
A Damsel in Distress 342
Diary of Anne Frank 342
George Stevens: A Filmmaker's Journey 343, 768
George Stevens: D-Day to Berlin 343, 768
Giant 343
Greatest Story Ever Told 343
I Remember Mama 343
Kentucky Kernels 343
The More the Merrier 343
Penny Serenade 343
A Place in the Sun 343
Shane 343
Swing Time 343
Talk of the Town 343
Woman of the Year 343
Stevens, Mark
Cry Vengeance 365
Stevens, Robert
Never Love a Stranger 380
Stevenson, Robert
Dishonored Lady 366
Forever and a Day 170
King Solomon's Mines 175
The Man Who Lived Again 525
My Forbidden Past 380
Non Stop—New York 176
Old Yeller—40th Anniversary Limited Edition 693
The Shaggy D.A. 694
Tom Brown's Schooldays 179
Walk Softly, Stranger 393
Stigliano, Roger
Fun Down There 459
Stiller, Ben
The Cable Guy 265
Reality Bites 280
Stiller, Mauritz
Hotel Imperial 399
Sir Arne's Treasure 77
Story of Gosta Berling 77
Thomas Graal's Best Child 77
Thomas Graal's Best Film 77
The Treasure of Arne 77
Stillman, Whit
Barcelona (Stillman) 426
Metropolitan 433
Stine, R.L.
Goosebumps: The Haunted Mask 697
Stix, John
The Great St. Louis Bank Robbery 370
Stoloff, Ben
Affairs of Annabel 261
It's a Joke, Son! 272
Night of Terror 526
Palooka 278
Stone, Andrew L.
Her Favorite Patient (aka Bedside Manner) 270
Julie 374
The Last Voyage 376
Stormy Weather 329
Stone, Bernard
Roses in December 60, 477
Stone, Cordelia
Yiddish: The Mame-Loshn (The Mother Tongue) 113
Stone, David
Jollity Farm (British Animation) 707
Stone, Julien
Waiting for Max (Best Fest 5th Annual) 706
Stone, Norman
Shadowlands 163
Stone, Oliver
Born on the 4th of July 220
The Doors 620
Heaven and Earth (American) 230
JFK (Director's Cut) 233
Last Year in Vietnam (First Works) 334
Natural Born Killers 441
Nixon 240
Platoon 242
Salvador 245
Talk Radio 249
U-Turn 251
Wall Street 251
Stoppard, Tom
Rosencrantz & Guildenstern Are Dead 301
Storck, Henri
L'Histoire du Soldat Inconnu (Experimental #21) 484
Masters of the Congo Jungle 152, 475
Storm, Jerome
The Busher 396
Sweet Adeline 405
Story, Richard
Some Letters to a Young Poet 211
Strachwitz, Chis
J'Ai Ete au Bal: I Went to the Dance 480
Strand, Chick
Angel Blue Sweet Wings (Short Personal Films) 437
Strand, Paul
Native Land 475
Strate, Walter
Violated 512
Strayer, Frank
Blondie 264
Blondie Has Trouble 264
Blondie in Society 264
Blondie's Blessed Event 264
Condemned to Live 518
The Daring Young Man 266
It's a Great Life 272
The Monster Walks 526
The Vampire Bat 531
Street, Mark
6 Films By Mark Street 482
Streisand, Barbra
The Mirror Has Two Faces 238
The Prince of Tides 243
Yentl 331
Streitfeld, Susan
Female Perversions 459
Strick, Joseph
The Balcony 310
Portrait of an Artist as a Young Man 242
The Savage Eye 385
Tropic of Cancer 250
Ulysses 392
Strock, Herbert L.
Blood of Dracula 517
Crawling Hand 518
Stroheim, Erich von
Blind Husbands 348
Foolish Wives 348
Greed 348
Man You Loved to Hate 348
The Merry Widow (1925) 348
The Merry Widow (German Version) 348
Merry-Go-Round 348
Queen Kelly 348
The Wedding March 348
Stroud, Juliet
Snookles (Int. Animation 2) 712
Snookles (Spike/Mike 1) 716
Stuart, Mel
If It's Tuesday, This Must Be Belgium 272
Willie Wonka and the Chocolate Factory 667
Stumphaus, Jurgen
Chameleon Cameraman (Changing Roles) 766
The Eye of the Third Reich 767
The Silent Service: The Story of Submarine Warfare in the Pacific 772
Sturges, John
Bad Day at Black Rock 358
By Love Possessed 362
The Capture 291
The Eagle Has Landed 767
Escape from Fort Bravo 292
The Great Escape 370
Gunfight at The O.K. Corral 293
The Hallelujah Trail 293
The Law and Jake Wade 293
Magnificent Seven 294
The Magnificent Yankee 377
Marooned 498
Never So Few 770
The Old Man and the Sea (1958) 381
Sturges, Preston
Beautiful Blonde from Bashful Bend 346
Christmas in July 346
The Great McGinty 346
Hail the Conquering Hero 346
The Lady Eve 346
Miracle of Morgan's Creek 346
Palm Beach Story 346
Sin of Harold Diddlebock 346, 410
Sullivan's Travels 346
Unfaithfully Yours (1948) 346
Sturridge, Charles
Aria 158, 577
FairyTale 160
A Foreign Field 160
Gulliver's Travels 230
A Handful of Dust 160
Where Angels Fear to Tread 164
Subiela, Eliseo
Dark Side of the Heart 49
Man Facing Southeast 51
Sucksdorff, Arne
The Films of Arne Sucksdorff: The Great Adventure Plus Short Subjects 75, 472
Sughrue, John
Louvre (Boyer) 552
Sugnet, Kent
Compassionate Use 835
Suleiman, Elia
Introduction to the End of an Argument 486
Sullivan, A. Edward
The Bermuda Affair 359
Sullivan, Christopher
Landscape with the Fall of Icarus (Anim. for Fall) 706
Sullivan, Daniel
The Substance of Fire 248
Sullivan, James R.
Venus of the South Seas 406
Sullivan, Kevin
Anne of Avonlea 661
Anne of Green Gables (Disney) 690
Lantern Hill 664
Looking for Miracles 664
Sullivan, Kevin Rodney
America's Dream 443
Sullivan, Pat
Felix the Cat Silent Films Vol. 1 683
Felix the Cat Vol. 1 683
Felix the Cat Vol. 2 683
Felix the Cat: Sound & Silent 683
Felix! 683
Sullivan, Tim
23 Days in July: Tour de France 825
Sum, Ko Chi
Paradise Hotel 123
Summers, Jeremy
The House of 1000 Dolls 523
Summers, Walter
Human Monster (Dark Eyes of London) 523
Sun, Chan Ho
The Age of Miracles 118
Sun, Shirley
Iron and Silk 455
Sung, Addy
Bloody Hero 125
Sung-Kei, Chiu
Pink Bomb 123
Suo, Masayuki
Shall We Dance? 139
Surette, Christian
Learning to Paint with Carolyn Berry 563
Surin, Fred
Bride Is Much Too Beautiful 19
Surinsky, Wendy
Raising Face: A Menstrual Journey 861
Woman of the Wolf 253
Surjik, Stephen
Weapons of Mass Destraction 286
Suso, Henry
DeathSport 505
Sussfeld, Jean-Claude
Elle Voit des Nains Partout 3
Sussler, Betsy
Tripe 489
Sutcliffe, Jim
East Side Story (Art) 548
Sutherland, A. Edward
Behind the Front 395
Beyond Tomorrow 359
Every Day's a Holiday 268
Flying Deuces 268
Follow the Boys 368
International House 272
The Invisible Woman 524
It's the Old Army Game 400
Mr. Robinson Crusoe 379
Murders in the Zoo 380
One Night in the Tropics 327
Palmy Days 327
We're in the Navy Now 406
Sutherland, David
Jack Levine: Feast of Pure Reason 551
Sutherland, John
An American Retrospective Through Animation 705
Sutherland, Kiefer
Truth or Consequences N.M. 250
Sutherland, S.
Percy Mayfield: Poet Laureate of the Blues 614
Sutre, Daniel
Les Daisons Quatre a Quatre (Int. Animation 5) 712
Suzuki, Seijun
Branded to Kill 137
Tokyo Drifter 140
Svankmajer, Jan
Alchemist of the Surreal 705
Alice 705
Darkness, Light, Darkness (Animation C.3) 705
Faust 710
Scenes from the Surreal 715
Svatek, Peter
Call of the Wild (1997) 221
Sverak, Jan
The Elementary School 99
Kolya 100
Swackhammer, E.W.
The Dain Curse 224
Man and Boy 664
Swanson, Donald
The Magic Garden (The Pennywhistle Blues) 151
Swanson, Valerie
Charlie's Boogie Woogie (Best Fest Kids) 706
Sweenen, Peter
Animation Has No Borders (Animation C. 1) 705
Swets, Ben
Tinka's Planet 643
Swift, David
How to Succeed in Business Without Really Trying 324
Interns 233
Under the Yum-Yum Tree 285
Swimmer, Saul
The Concert for Bangladesh 619
Swirnoff, Brad
Tunnel Vision 536
Swirnoff, Bradley R.

Prime Time....280
Swords, Sarah
Siren....465
Syberberg, Hans Jurgen
Parsifal....64, 584
Szabo, Ildiko
Maidsplay....313
Szabo, Istvan
25, Firemen's Street....103
Father....103
Hanussen....103
Meeting Venus....103
Szalspski, James
Heartworn Highways....605
Szanialawski, E.Z.
1000 Years of Polish Cavalry....98
General Sosabowski....92
Szarek, Waldemar
Call Me Rockefeller....90
Szaro, Henryk
Three Stooges (Polish)....94
The Vow....113
Szebego, S.
Little Prince (Polish)....93
Szebego, T.
Little Prince (Polish)....93
Szirtes, Andras
After the Revolution....101
Szmagier, Krzysztof
As Crosses Are Measure of Freedom....98
Szomjas, Gyorgy
Bad Guys....101
Szorda, Csaba
Rondino (Outrageous 1)....714
Szoreny, Reszo
A Happy New Year!....102
Sztwiernia, Jerzy
The Comedienne....91
Merry Christmas....93
Szulzinger, Boris
Shame of the Jungle....715
Szwarc, Jeannot
The Murders in the Rue Morgue (1986)....526
Santa Claus: The Movie....666
Tahimik, Kidlat
Perfumed Nightmare....145
Turumba....146
Tai, Robert
Legend of the Drunken Tiger....129
Tak, Chan Kin
Muto Bontie....122
Tak-Sum, Teddy Chan
Twenty Something (5pm-9am)....124
Takada, Yuzo
Blue Seed, Collection 1....723
Blue Seed, Collection 2....723
Blue Seed, Vol. 01....723
Blue Seed, Vol. 02....723
Blue Seed, Vol. 03....723
Blue Seed, Vol. 04: The Kushinada Project....723
Blue Seed, Vol. 05: A Date with Danger....723
Blue Seed, Vol. 06: Impending Disaster....723
Blue Seed, Vol. 07: Rebirth....723
Blue Seed, Vol. 08: Sea Devils....723
Blue Seed, Vol. 09: When Gods Walk the Earth....724
Blue Seed, Vol. 10: Fate & Destiny....724
Blue Seed, Vol. 11: Sacrifice....724
Blue Seed, Vol. 12: Betrayal....724
Blue Seed, Vol. 13: Nightfall....724
Takahashi, Rumiko
Mermaid's Scar....736
Rumik World: Maris the Chojo....745
Rumik World: Mermaid Forest....745
Rumik World: The Laughing Target....745
Takahata, Isao
Grave of the Fireflies....137, 731
Takahiko, Imura
Takahiko Iimura: A Journey to Ayersrock....488
Takeshima, S.
Dark Warrior 1: First Strike....726
Dark Warrior 2: Jihad....726
Talalay, Rachel
Tank Girl....249
Talankin, Igor
A Summer to Remember (USSR, 1960)....83
Tchaikovsky....83
Talkington, C.M.
Love & a .45....433
Tallas, Greg
Prehistoric Women....509
Talmadge, Richard
Project Moonbase....499
Tam, Patrick
Final Victory....120
My Heart Is That Eternal Rose....122
Tamahori, Lee
The Edge....226
Mulholland Falls....239
Once Were Warriors....208
Tanaka, Shigeo
Gamera vs. Barugon....496
Tanaka, Tokuzo
Masseur Ichi Enters Again....138
Sleepy Eyes of Death—The Chinese Jade....139
Zatoichi: The Blind Swordsman's Vengeance....140
Tandon, Lekh
Amrapali....146
Tang, Billy
Dr. Lam[b]....126
Dragon Fight....126
Sexy & Dangerous....123
Street Angels....132
Street of Fury....132
Tanner, Alain
In the White City....30
Jonah Who Will Be 25 in the Year 2000....30
La Salamandre....30
Messidor....30
Tarantino, Paul
Courting Courtney....266
Tarantino, Quentin
Four Rooms....430, 441
Jackie Brown....441
Pulp Fiction....441
Reservoir Dogs....441
Tarasov, Vladimir
Contact (Masters #3)....82, 713
Tardos, Aaron
Birdy Birdy (Too Outrageous)....717
Tarkovsky, Andrei
Andrei Rublev....84
Mirror, The....84
My Name Is Ivan....84
Nostalghia....84
The Sacrifice....84
Solaris....84
Stalker....84
Tarr, Bela
Almanac of Fall....101
Tartaglia, Jerry
A.I.D.S.C.R.E.A.M.....456, 482
Holy Mary, Remembrance & Vocation....460, 485
Tash, Max
Runnin' Kind....436
Tashlin, Frank
Alphabet Murders....171
Artists and Models....358
Disorderly Orderly....267
Fuller Brush Man....269
The Geisha Boy....269
Girl Can't Help It....269
The Glass Bottom Boat....269
Hollywood or Bust....271
The Private Navy of Sgt. O'Farrel....280
Son of Paleface....282
Will Success Spoil Rock Hunter....287
Tassios, Pavlos
Heavy Melon....105
Parangelia....105
Special Request....105
Tasso, Armando
Placido Domingo: His 25th Anniversary Concert at the Roman Amphitheater of Verona....599
Tatarsky, Alexander
The Lift (Int. Animation 5)....712
Pirates (The Lift) (Too Outrageous)....717
Tati, Jacques
Gai Dimanche/Swing to the Left....28
Jour de Fete....28
Mon Oncle....28
Mr. Hulot's Holiday....28
Parade....28
Playtime....28
Traffic....28
Tato, Anna Maria
The Night and the Moment....162
Tatum, Peter
Joe Louis—For All Time....827
Taurog, Norman
The Adventures of Tom Sawyer (Kelly/Brennan)....309
Blue Hawaii....536
Boys Town....361
Broadway Melody of 1940....320
Bundle of Joy....321
Caddy, The....265
Double Trouble....536
Dr. Goldfoot and the Bikini Machine....505
G.I. Blues....536
Girl Crazy....323
Jumping Jacks....273
Little Nelly Kelly....325
Live a Little, Love a Little....536
Mad About Music....326
Men of Boys Town....378
Mrs. Wiggs of the Cabbage Patch....277
Palm Springs Weekend....509
Pardners....278
Presenting Lily Mars....328
Rhythm on the Range....328
Rich, Young and Pretty....328
Speedway....537
Spinout....537
Strike Me Pink....329
That Midnight Kiss....330
The Toast of New Orleans....330
We're Not Dressing....393
Words and Music....331
Young Tom Edison....394
Tauscher, Patti
Alterations (Animation for Fallen Catholics)....706
Tavella, Dino
The Embalmer....521
Taverna, Kathryn
Lodz Ghetto....474
Tavernier, Bertrand
Capitaine Conan....11
The Clockmaker....11
Coup de Torchon....11
Daddy Nostalgie....11
Judge and the Assassin....11
L.627....11
Life and Nothing But....11
The Lumiere Brothers' First Films....22, 153
Mississippi Blues....11, 613
Round Midnight....11
Spoiled Children....11
A Sunday in the Country....11
Taviani, Paolo
Allonsanfan....35
Fiorile (Wild Flower)....35
Night of the Shooting Stars....35
Padre Padrone....35
St. Michael Had a Rooster....35
Taviani, Vittorio
Allonsanfan....35
Fiorile (Wild Flower)....35
Night of the Shooting Stars....35
Padre Padrone....35
St. Michael Had a Rooster....35
Taylor, Alan
Palookaville....435
Taylor, Don
My Wicked Wicked Ways....239
Ride the Wild Surf....509
Tom Sawyer....309
Wild Women....252
Taylor, Donald
Battle for Music....587
Taylor, Finn
Dream with the Fishes....429
Taylor, Joan
Redlands....436
Taylor, Jud
Christmas Coal Mine Miracle....222
The Old Man and the Sea (1990)....163
Secrets (USA)....246
Taylor, Judson
Foxfire (Taylor)....228
Taylor, Ray
Adventures of Smilin' Jack....537
Flash Gordon Conquers the Universe....537
The Ivory Handled Gun....293
The Return of Chandu (Abridged)....528
Sky Raiders....539
Taylor, Sam
Ambassador Bill....357
Coquette....364
Harold Lloyd: Girl Shy....410
Kiki....374
Nothing But Trouble....278
The Tempest....405
Taylor, Sue Ann
Conversation with Ross Perot....799
Taylor, William Desmond
Nurse Marjorie....402
Tchernia, Pierre
The Holes (Les Gaspards)....3
Teague, Lewis
Cat's Eye....518
T Bone n Weasel....248
Techine, Andre
Barocco....2
My Favorite Season (Ma Saison Preferee)....5
Rendez Vous....6
Scene of the Crime....6
Thieves....7
Wild Reeds....7
Teich, Roger/Starr, John
Stealing Altitude (Best Fest 91)....706
Temple, Julien
Absolute Beginners: The Musical....158
Aria....158, 577
The Great Rock and Roll Swindle (The Sex Pistols)....620
Running out of Luck....622
Templeton, Gary
Corduroy Bear....651
Tennant, Andy
Fools Rush In....268
Tenney, Del
Elvira's Midnight Madness: I Eat Your Skin....521
Tennyson, Pen
Convoy....172
Tennyson, Penrose
Black Artists of the Silver Screen— Proud Valley....360, 450
Terasawa, Buichi
Raven Tengu Kabuto....742
Terry, Paul
Aesop's Film Fables....676
Camouflage (Animation)....707
Cartoonal Knowledge: Confessions of Farmer Gray....680
Cartoonal Knowledge: Farmer Gray & The Mice....680
Cartoonal Knowledge: Farmer Gray Goes to the Dogs....680
Cartoonal Knowledge: Farmer Gray Looks at Life....680
Cartoonal Knowledge: The Return of Farmer Gray....680
Cat's Meow: Kitty Kartoons by Paul Terry....681
Terwilliger, George
Married?....401
Teshigahara, Hiroshi
Antonio Gaudi....141, 565
Rikyu....141

Woman in the Dunes....142
Tessari, Duccio
Zorro (Delon)....24
Teton, John
B'raesheet....706
Tetzlaff, Ted
The Young Land....298
Tevaarwerk, Liz
Feeling Anything Being Existing (Four Directions)....459
Tevet, Akiva
Atalia....107
Tewkesbury, Joan
Cold Sassy Tree....222
Tewkesbury, Peter
Stay Away Joe....537
Trouble with Girls (a.k.a. How to Get into It)....537
Tewksbury, Peter
Sunday in New York....389
Tezuka, Osamu
Jumping (Int. Animation 1)....711
Legend of the Forest....735
Thacker, David
Broken Glass....159
Thayer, Otis B.
Tracy the Outlaw....405
Thew, Harvey
Confessions of a Vice Baron....505
Thiele, Rolf
Tonio Kroger....65
Thiermann, Eric
Last Epidemic....804
Need for Christian Peacemaking....805
Thiermann, Ian
The Edge of History....803
Last Epidemic....804
MacMichael on Nicaragua....58
Star Wars: A Search for Security....806
What About the Russians?....89
Thies, Christopher
Winterbeast....531
Thomas, Betty
The Brady Bunch....264
The Late Shift....273
Private Parts....280
Thomas, Gerald
Carry On Nurse....181
Thomas, Michael
Third Sex Sinema Volume 3—The Meatrack....466
Thomas, Ralph
The Clouded Yellow....172
Doctor at Large....182
Doctor at Sea....182
A Tale of Two Cities (1967/Bogarde)....178
Thomas, Ralph L.
A Young Connecticut Yankee in King Arthur's Court....309
Young Ivanhoe....667
Thomason, Harry
Encounter with the Unknown....521
Thomopoulos, Andreas
End of the Game (South Wind)....105
Thompson, Brett
Adventures in Dinosaur City....628
The Haunted World of Edward D. Wood, Jr....334, 515
Thompson, Caroline
Black Beauty (1994)....662
Buddy....221
Thompson, J. Lee
Battle for the Planet of the Apes....494
Cape Fear....362
Conquest of the Planet of the Apes....495
Escape from the Planet of the Apes....496
Flame over India....173
Guns of Navarone....768
Huckleberry Finn (1974/Musical)....309
Taras Bulba....389
White Buffalo....298
Thompson, Miles
The Birth of Brian (Spike/Mike Sick 2)....716
Brian's Brain (Spike/Mike Sick 2)....716
Dog Pile (Spike/Mike Sick 1)....716
Empty Roll (Spike/Mike Sick 2)....716
Gun, Zipper, Snot (Spike/Mike Sick 2)....716
Stubbs (Spike/Mike Sick 2)....716
Thompson, Peter
Peter Thompson Films....487
Thomsen, Christian Braad
Ladies on the Rocks....76
Thornby, Robert
That Girl Montana....405
Thornhill, Michael
The Everlasting Secret Family....205
Thornton, Billy Bob
Sling Blade....437
Thorpe, Richard
Above Suspicion....356
The Adventures of Huckleberry Finn (Rooney)....308
All the Brothers Were Valiant....357
Athena....320
Challenge to Lassie....662
A Date with Judy....321
Double Wedding....366
Fun in Acapulco....536
The Girl Who Had Everything....369
The Great Caruso....597
The Honeymoon Machine....271
The Horizontal Lieutenant....372
Ivanhoe (1952, USA)....373
Jailhouse Rock....536
Knights of the Round Table....375
Malaya....377
Night Must Fall....380
On an Island with You....327
Prisoner of Zenda (1952)....383
Probation (Nation Aflame)....508
The Prodigal (1955)....356
The Student Prince....329
The Sun Comes Up....666
Tarzan Escapes....539
Tarzan Finds a Son....539
Tarzan's New York Adventure....539
Tarzan's Secret Treasure....539
The Thin Man Goes Home....283
Three Little Words....330
Thrill of a Romance....284
Two Girls and a Sailor....331
Vengeance Valley....297
Western Classics Collection: Vengeance Valley and The Big Trees....297
White Cargo....393
Thorsen, Jens Jorgen
Quiet Days in Clichy....76
Thurow, Nancy
Islander....233
Tibaldi, Antonio
On My Own....211
Tickel, Paul
Zinky Boys Go Underground (CineBLAST 1)....483
Tierney, Pat
Don from Lakewood/You Talk, I Buy....429
Tiffany, Richard
Gerbert Is Ben Franklin....633
Gerbert Is Marco Polo....633
Gerbert Is Mozart....633
Gerbert Is Tom Sawyer....633
Tilby, Wendy
Strings (NFBCanada)....714
Till, Eric
The Challengers....662
Clarence....266
Hot Millions....271
Oh, What a Night....211
Tillman Jr., George
Soul Food....247, 446
Tillman, Lynn
Committed....428
Tilroe, Nikki
Dot and Dash, Volume 1....651
Tinnell, Robert
Kids of the Round Table....664
Tippett, Bill
Prehistoric Beast (Animation C.3)....705
Tippett, Phil
Prehistoric Beast (Int. Animation 6)....706
Tirola, Douglas
A Reason to Believe....243
Title, Stacy
The Last Supper (USA)....273
Tlatli, Moufida
Silences of the Palace....116
To, Johnny
All About Ah-Long....118
The Big Heat (Hong Kong)....125
The Fun, The Luck, and the Tycoon....120
Heroic Trio....128
Seven Years Itch (Hong Kong)....123
Toback, James
The Big Bang....469
Toccafundo, G.
La Pista (Spike/Mike 2)....716
Tofano, Gilberto
Siege....108
Tognazzi, Ricky
La Scorta....33
Tokar, Norman
Where the Red Fern Grows....667
Tolkin, Michael
The New Age....239
The Rapture....243
Tom, Konrad
Forgotten Melody....91
Prince Joseph's Soldier....93
Tominicki, Jan
The Great Betrayal....92
Tonelli, Renato
An American Songster....604
Tong, Stanley
First Strike....134
Rumble in the Bronx....134
Supercop....134
Tong, Terry
Seven Warriors....131
Tonti, Aldo
The Unfaithfuls....41
Toonder, Martin
Animation in the Netherlands....706
Toporoff, Ralph
American Blue Note....426
Topper, Burt
Hell Squad....389
The Strangler....388
Tornatore, Giuseppe
Cinema Paradiso....32
Everybody's Fine....32
A Pure Formality....6
The Star Maker....34
Torossian, Garine
Girl from Moush (CineBLAST 1)....483
Torre Nilsson, Leopoldo
Diary of the War of Pigs....50
Martin Fierro....51
Painted Lips (Boquitas Pintadas)....52
The Seven Madmen (Los Siete Locos)....52
Torre, Pablo
The Love of Silent Movies....51
Torrealba, Jose
Limites....559
Torrent, Jordi
Interview with Jonas Mekas....336
Will Eisner....541
Torres, Fina
Celestial Clockwork....49
Oriane....52
Tors, Ivan
Zebra in the Kitchen....668
Toshiya, Fujita
Lady Snowblood—Love Song of Vengeance....138
Toth, Andre de
House of Wax....523
Man in the Saddle....294
Pitfall....382
Ramrod....295
Springfield Rifle....296
The Stranger Wore a Gun....296
Totten, Robert
Huckleberry Finn (1975/Howard)....309
Toubiana, Serge
Francois Truffaut: Stolen Portraits....14, 334
Tourneur, Jacques
Canyon Passage....291
Cat People (1942)....518
Circle of Danger....172
The Comedy of Terrors....518
Curse of the Demon....519
Flame and the Arrow....368
Giant of Marathon....42
Tourneur, Maurice
Devil's Hand (Carnival of Sinners)....520
A Girl's Folly....399
The Last of the Mohicans (1920)....400
Lorna Doone (1922)....400
The Poor Little Rich Girl (1917)....402
Pride of the Clan....402
The Ship of Lost Men....71
Trilby....405
Volpone....24
The Whip....406
Wishing Ring....406
Towne, Robert
Personal Best....464
Townsend, Robert
Eddie Murphy: Raw....534
The Five Heartbeats....444
Meteor Man....445
Toye, Wendy
Three Cases of Murder....179
Toynton, Ian
Piece of Cake: Complete Set....195, 771
Toyoda, Shiro
Mistress....138
Snow Country....139
Trachtmann, Benno
Jumper....64
Tramont, Jean-Claude
All Night Long....262
Trasatti, Luciano
The Unfaithfuls....41
Trauberg, Leonid
New Babylon (Novyi Vavilon)....82
SVD—Club of the Big Deed....86
Travers, Bill
Christian the Lion....813
Travis, Sean
Depth Charge....429
Trayler-Smith, Richard
The Good Sex Guide—Series No. 1....849
The Good Sex Guide—Series No. 2....849
Tregenza, Rob
Talking to Strangers....438
Trench, Marianne
Cyberpunk....471
Trenchard-Smith, Brian
The Man from Hong Kong....129
Trenker, Luis
Challenge....172
Der Berg Ruft....69
Der Feuerteufel....69
Der Kaiser von Kalifornien....69
Der Rebell....69
Der Sohn der Wiessen Berge....69
Der Verlorene Sohn....69
Duell in den Bergen....69
Flucht in der Dolomiten....69
His People....69
In Banne des Monte Miracolo....69
Trent, Barbara
The Panama Deception....476
Trent, John
The Bushbaby....159
Treut, Monika
Erotique....430
Female Misbehavior....63, 459

My Father Is Coming 64, 463
Seduction: The Cruel Woman 65, 465
Virgin Machine 65, 467
Trier, Lars von
Breaking the Waves 75
The Element of Crime 75
The Kingdom 76
Zentropa 77
Trintignant, Nadine
Lumiere & Company 5, 336
Next Summer 5
Tripician, J.
Borders 427
Trivas, Victor
The Head (West Germany) 523
Troche, Rose
Go Fish 430, 460
Troell, Jan
The Emigrants 79
Hamsun 79
The New Land 79
Zandy's Bride 79
Troyano, Ela
Carmelita Tropicana (Girl Friends) 460
Trueba, Fernando
Belle Epoque 44
Lumiere & Company 5, 336
Twisted Obsession 250
Two Much 285
Truffaut, Francois
The 400 Blows 14
The Bride Wore Black 14
Confidentially Yours 14
Day for Night 14
Fahrenheit 451 14
Francois Truffaut: Stolen Portraits 14, 334
Godard/Truffaut Shorts 9, 14
Jules and Jim 14
The Last Metro 14
Les Mistons (Classic Foreign #2) 153
Love on the Run 14
The Man Who Loved Women 15
Mississippi Mermaid 15
Shoot the Piano Player 15
Small Change 15
The Soft Skin 15
Story of Adele H. 15
Two English Girls 15
The Wild Child 15
The Woman Next Door 15
Truffaut, Michelle
Ralph's Arm 436
Trumbull, Douglas
Brainstorm 220
Silent Running 499
Trystan, Leon
Upstairs 94
Tsi-liang, Chan
Lai Shi: China's Last Eunuch 121
Tsing, Wang
Mr. Possessed 122
Tsu, Hdeng
Rumble in Hong Kong 134
Tsukamoto, Shinya
Tetsuo I: The Iron Man 140
Tetsuo II: Body Hammer 140
Tokyo Fist 140
Tsuneo, Tomita
Animated Classics of Japanese Literature:
Shanshiro the Judoist 720
Tucci, Stanley
Big Night 427
Tuchner, Michael
Hunchback (1982) 232
Tucker, Anand
Saint-Ex 163
Tucker, David
Bramwell, Series 3 189
A Year in Provence 302
Tucker, George
Traffic in Souls 405
Tucker, Phil
Dance Hall Racket 429
Robot Monster 499
Tully, Montgomery
Dead Lucky 173
The Electronic Monster (Escapement) 495
A Life at Stake (aka Key Man) 376
Tumanshishvili, Mikhail
Incident at Map Grid 36-80 82
Tumelya, Mikhail
The Song of Wolfgang...(Animation C.4) 706
Tun, Tong Yee
Love in Mists 121
Tung, Ching Siu
A Chinese Ghost Story 119
A Chinese Ghost Story Part II 119
A Chinese Ghost Story Part III 119
Duel to the Death 127
Executioners 127
The Raid 123
Swordsman II 132
Witch from Nepal 124
Wonder Seven 133
Tung-shing, Yee
People's Hero 130
Turell, Saul
Love Goddesses 336
Turin, Viktor
Turksib/Salt for Svanetia 86
Turk, Ellen Fisher
Split: Portrait of a Drag Queen 465
Turner, Paul
Hedd Wyn 161
Turner, Richard
Violet's Visit 207
Turner, Tommy
Where Evil Dwells (The Trailer) 439
Turteltaub, Jon
Phenomenon 242
While You Were Sleeping 287
Turturro, John
Mac 433
Tuttle, Frank
Love 'Em and Leave 'Em 400
Lucky Devil 401
Roman Scandals 328
This Gun for Hire 390
Waikiki Wedding 331
Twist, Derek
Green Grow the Rushes 183
Police Dog 177
Twohy, David
The Arrival 494
Tzavellas, George
Antigone 310
Tzimas, Nikos
Man with the Red Carnation 105
Ucicky, Gustav
The Broken Jug 68
Cafe Electric 68
Morgenrot 70
Ullmann, Liv
Lumiere & Company 5, 336
Sofie 77
Ulloa, Juanma Bajo
Butterfly Wings 44
Ulmer, Edgar G.
Amazing Transparent Man 516
American Matchmaker (Amerikaner Shadchen) 112
Beyond the Time Barrier 494
The Black Cat (1934/Lugosi/Karloff) 517
Bluebeard 361
Captain Sirocco 362
Carnegie Hall 321
Damaged Lives 505
Detour (1946) 366
Green Fields 112
Jive Junction 507
Journey Beneath the Desert (L'Atlantide) 498
The Light Ahead 112
Menschen am Sontag (People on Sunday) 401
Monsoon 379
Moon Over Harlem (African American Film) 447
Naked Venus 508
The Singing Blacksmith 113
St. Benny the Dip 387
Strange Illusion 388
Strange Woman 388
Underwood, Ron
City Slickers 266
Ungar, George
The Champagne Safari 470
Uno, Michael Toshiyuki
Blind Spot 219
Without Warning: The James Brady Story 252
Unwin, Dave
The Wind in the Willows (Redgrave) 667, 718
Unwin, Paul
Bramwell, Series 3 189
Urchs, Wolfgang
Stowaways on the Ark 716
Urquhart, Gordon
Hard 460
Man for Man, Volume I 462
Man for Man, Volume II 462
Man for Man, Volume III 462
Man for Man, Volume IV 462
Urson, Frank
Night Club 401
Urueto, Chano
El Corsario Negro 50
The Witch's Mirror 531
Ustinov, Peter
Lady L 183
Uys, Jamie
The Gods Must Be Crazy 151
The Gods Must Be Crazy II 151
Uys, Michael
Riding the Rails: The American Experience 843
Vadim, Roger
And God Created Woman (Original) 2
And God Created Woman (Remake) 217
Barbarella 2
Blood and Roses 19
Les Liaisons Dangereuses (Original) 21
That Naughty Girl/Love on a Pillow 18
Ms. Don Juan (Don Juan 73) 22
Pretty Maids All in a Row 243
Spirits of the Dead 37
Warrior's Rest 24
Vajda, Ladislao
Miracle of Marcelino 45
Valas, Chris
The Fly 2 521
Valdez, Luis
Zoot Suit 62, 331
Vale, Travers
Betsy Ross 395
Valere, Jean
Time Out for Love 24
Vallois, Philippe
We Were One Man 7, 467
Van Bebber, Jim
My Sweet Satan 508
Van Den Berg, Rudolf
Cold Light of Day 159
Van der Keuken, Johan
Big Ben: Ben Webster in Europe 609
The Eye Above the Well 31
Van der Meulen, F.
Zoll Zeyn (Let It Be) 113
Van Dijk, Ferrit
Animation in the Netherlands 706
Van Dormael, Jaco
The Eighth Day 29
Lumiere & Company 5, 336
Toto the Hero 29
Van Dyke, W.S.
After the Thin Man 261
Another Thin Man 262
Battling Fool 410
Bitter Sweet (MacDonald) 320
Forsaking All Others 268
I Live My Life 372
I Love You Again 373
I Married an Angel 324
Journey for Margaret 175
Love on the Run (1936) 377
Manhattan Melodrama 378
Marie Antoinette 378
Naughty Marietta (1935) 326
Personal Property 382
Rosalie 328
Rose Marie (1936) 328
San Francisco (Gable/Tracy) 385
Shadow of the Thin Man 282
Sweethearts 330
Tarzan, The Ape Man 389
The Thin Man 283
Trader Horn 391
Van Dyke, Willard
The City 470
Van Goethem, Nicole
Full of Grace (Outrageous 1) 714
Van Gogh, Theo
1-900 30
Van Horn, Buddy
Any Which Way You Can 217
The Dead Pool 224
Pink Cadillac 242
Van Lawick, Hugo
The Leopard Son 664
Van Sant, Gus
Drugstore Cowboy 440
Even Cowgirls Get the Blues 440, 459
Good Will Hunting 440
My Own Private Idaho 440, 463
To Die For 440
Van Taylor, David
A Perfect Candidate 476, 800
Van Valkenburg, Rick
Video Void VIII 623
Vanderbeek, Stan
Stan Vanderbeek: The Computer Generation 488
Vanderbeekiana! 489
VanWagenen, Sterling
Alan and Naomi 426
Varaday, Brian
Eritrean Artists in War and Peace 152
Varda, Agnes
Agnes Varda and Susan Sontag: Love Cannibals 14
Cleo from 5 to 7 14
Jacquot de Nantes 14
Le Bonheur 14
Lion's Love 14
Vagabond 14
Varga, Csaba
Agusta Feeds Her Child (Int. Animation 2) 712
Augusta Kneading (Int. Animation 3) 712
Augusta Makes Herself Breakfast (Animation C. 1) 705
Luncheon (Int. Animation 1) 711
Varnel, Marcel
The Gasbags 182
O-Kay for Sound 184
Oh, Mr. Porter! 176
Vasilyev, Georgi
Chapayev 85
Vasilyev, Serge
Chapayev 85
Vasulka, Woody
Art of Memory 482
Commission 483
Veber, Francis
La Chevre 17
Vedres, Nicole
Paris 1900 22
Vega, Felipe
Umbrella for Three (Paraguas Para Tres) 45
Vega, Pastor

Portrait of Teresa 52
Vegas, Tony
Le Beatnik Sophistique (Best Fest 5th Annual) 706
Verbinski, Gore
Mousehunt 665
Verdon-Roe, Vivien
The Edge of History 803
What About the Russians? 89
Women—For America, for the World 479
Verdone, Carlo
Acqua e Sapone 32
Verhoeven, Michael
Killing Cars 64
The Nasty Girl 64
Verhoeven, Paul
Basic Instinct 219
Basic Instinct (Director's Cut) 219
The Eternal Waltz 69
Flesh and Blood 228
The Fourth Man 31
Keetje Tippel 31
Robocop 499
Showgirls 246
Spetters (Dubbed) 31
Spetters (Subtitled) 31
Starship Troopers 500
Turkish Delights 31
Verneuil, Henri
Forbidden Fruit 17
Guns for San Sebastian 293
Sheep Has Five Legs 18
Veroiu, Mircea
Stone Wedding 104
Verow, Todd
Frisk 430
Vertov, Dziga
Enthusiasm 86
Kino Pravda and Enthusiasm 86
Man with the Movie Camera 86
Three Songs of Lenin 86
VeSota, Bruno
The Brain Eaters 495
Vester, Paul
Picnic (British Animation) 707
Sunbeam (Animation C.1) 705
Vianey, Michel
Special Police 9
Vicario, Marco
Go, Go, Go, Go World! 506
Vidor, Charles
The Bridge (American Avant Garde Films) 482
Cover Girl 321
Gilda 369
Hans Christian Andersen 323
The Lady in Question 375
Love Me or Leave Me 326
The Loves of Carmen 326
Rhapsody 384
A Song to Remember 329
The Swan (1956) 389
Vidor, King
Beyond the Forest 359
The Big Parade 395
Bird of Paradise 360
The Champ 363
Citadel 172
Comrade X 364
The Crowd 397
Duel in the Sun 292
Fountainhead 369
Hallelujah! 323
Jack-Knife Man 400
Japanese War Bride 373
La Boheme 400
Love Never Dies 400
Man Without a Star 294
Northwest Passage 294
Our Daily Bread 381
Show People 404
The Sky Pilot 404
Song Without End 350
Stella Dallas 388
Street Scene 388
War and Peace 393
The Wedding Night 393
Vielle, Sophie
Four Fashion Horses 560
Vienne, Gerard
Monkey People (aka Monkey Folks, Le Peuple Singe) 5
Viertel, Berthold
Passing of the Third Floor Back 177
Rhodes of Africa 177
Vigne, Daniel
Return of Martin Guerre 6
Vignola, Robert
The Scarlet Letter 385
Vigo, Clement
Rude 211
Vigo, Jean
A Propos de Nice 25
L'Atalante 25
Zero for Conduct 25
Villa, Franz
X-Rated: Movieyeur 439
Villalobos, Reynaldo
Conagher 291
Villard, Dimitri
Once Bitten 278
Villaronga, Agustin
In a Glass Cage 44, 460
Moonchild 45
Vilsmaier, Joseph
Brother of Sleep 63
Stalingrad 65, 772
Vincent, Christian
La Discrete 17
Vincent, Chuck
Deranged 225
Hollywood Hot Tubs 271
Sensations 328
Vincent, James
A Woman in Grey 406
Vinton, Will
A Claymation Christmas Celebration 707
A Claymation Comedy of Horrors 707
A Claymation Easter 708
The Little Prince (Claymation) 664, 713
Martin the Cobbler 713
Mr. Register (Int. Animation 6) 712
Rip Van Winkle (Claymation) 715
The Star Child 642, 716
The Velveteen Rabbit (Claymation) 717
Will Vinton's Festival of Claymation 717
Virgoer, Tony
The King's Demons/The Five Doctors 200
Visconti, Luchino
Conversation Piece 39
The Damned 39
Death in Venice 39
The Innocent 39
Ludwig 39
Ossessione 39
Rocco and His Brothers 39
Sandra of a Thousand Delights 39
Senso 39
White Nights 39
Vitail, Fredrico
Guano! (Too Outrageous) 717
Vitale, Tony
Kiss Me, Guido 461
Vitezy, Laszlo
Red Earth 102
Vittoria, Stephen
Black and White 219
Vogel, Virgil W.
Beulah Land 219
The Kettles on Old MacDonald's Farm 273
The Land Unknown 498
The Mole People 498
Vogl, Harold
Candide in the Americas 428
Vohrer, Alfred
Dead Eyes of London 519
Volkoff, Alexandre
Loves of Casanova 21, 153
Volkov, Alexander
Kean 153
von Trotta, Margarethe
Marianne and Juliane 64
The Promise 65
Rosa Luxemburg 65
The Second Awakening of Christa Klages 65
Sheer Madness 65
Sisters, Or the Balance of Happiness 65
Vorhaus, Bernard
The Amazing Mr. X (The Spiritualist) 357
Broken Melody 171
Lady from Louisiana 375
Three Faces West 390
Way Down South 449
Vorkapich, Slavko
Life and Death of a Hollywood Extra (American Avant-Garde) 482
Votocek, Otakar
Wings of Fame 165
Vunak, D.
Dialog (Outrageous 2) 714
Wachowski, Andy
Bound 427, 457
Wachowski, Larry
Bound 427, 457
Wachsmann, Daniel
Hamsin (Eastern Wind) 107
Wacks, Jonathan
Powwow Highway 242
Wada, Shinji
Sukeban Deka 1 748
Sukeban Deka 2 748
Waddell, Amy
The Reluctant Muse 476
Wade, Doris Renee
Da Projects 444
Wadleigh, Michael
Wolfen 531
Woodstock 623
Waggner, George
The Climax 518
The Fighting Kentuckian 368
Man-Made Monster 525
Operation Pacific 381
Red Nightmare 509
Wolf Call 393
Wolf Man 531
Wagner, Suzanne
The World Within 786
Wah, Tsui Po
The Wild Couple 133
Wai, Kai-Fei
Peace Hotel 123
Wai, Kwok Siu
Obsession (Hong Kong) 122
Wai, Lau Kun
Mr. Vampire 122
Mr. Vampire II 122
Mr. Vampire III 122
Mr. Vampire IV 122
Wai, Shin Chi
The Fatalist 127
Wai, Sin Chi
Banana Club 118
Wai, Stephen Tung
Fox Hunter 127
Wai-Ching, Ku
The Cruel Kind 119
Wai-Keung, Andrew Lau
Ghost Lantern 120
Wai-Man, Raymond Lee
Dragon Inn 127
Wain, Dan
Aisle Six (CineBLAST!) 428
Wainwright, Rupert
Blank Check 264
Wajda, Andrzej
Andrzej Wajda, A Portrait 96
Ashes and Diamonds 96
Birch Wood 96
The Conductor (John Gielgud) 96
Fury Is a Woman (The Siberian Lady Maceth) 96
A Generation 96
Hunting Flies 96
Innocent Sorcerers 96
Kanal 96
Korczak 97
Land of Promise 97
Layer Cake 97
Lotna 97
Maids of Wilko 97
Man of Iron 97
Man of Marble 97
Samson 97
The Wedding 97
Without Anesthesia 97
Waletzky, Josh
Music for the Movies: Bernard Herrmann 337, 617
Music for the Movies: The Hollywood Sound 337, 617
Walker, Clay
Post No Bills (Best Fest 91) 706
Walker, Giles
90 Days 210
Masculine Mystique 211
Ordinary Magic 211
Walker, Hal
At War with the Army 262
The Road to Bali 281
The Road to Utopia 281
Walker, John
Strand: Under the Dark Cloth 560
A Winter Tan 439
Walker, Nancy
Can't Stop the Music 321, 457
Walker, Stuart
The Eagle and the Hawk 367
Great Expectations (Hale/Wyatt) 370
The Mystery of Edwin Drood (1935) 380
Werewolf of London 531
Wallace, Randall
The Man in the Iron Mask (1997) 237
Wallace, Richard
Bombardier 361
It's in the Bag 272
The Little Minister 376
Wallace, Stephen
For Love Alone 206
Prisoners of the Sun 206
Wallace, Tommy Lee
Stephen King's It 529
Wallen, Sigurd
The Count of the Old Town 75
Wallin, Michael
Black Sheep Boy and Decodings 457
Wallis, Hal B.
The Stooge 283
Walsh, Jack
The Second Coming 465
Walsh, John
Ed's Next Move 429
Walsh, Raoul
Along the Great Divide 290
Background to Danger 358
Band of Angels 359
Battle Cry 359
Blackbeard the Pirate 360
Captain Horatio Hornblower 362
College Swing 321
Dark Command 292
Desperate Journey 366
Distant Drums 366
Esther and the King 355
Gentleman Jim 369
Going Hollywood 323
Gun Fury 293

High Sierra 372
The Horn Blows at Midnight 271
The King and Four Queens 374
Klondike Annie 375
The Lawless Breed 294
A Lion Is in the Streets 376
The Man I Love 378
Northern Pursuit 381
Objective, Burma! 381
Pursued 295
Regeneration 403
Roaring Twenties 385
Sadie Thompson 403
Silver River 296
Strawberry Blonde 283
The Tall Men 296
They Died with Their Boots On 297
They Drive by Night 390
The Thief of Baghdad 405
Uncertain Glory 392
What Price Glory? (1926) 406
White Heat 393
The World in His Arms 394

Walsh, Steve
Where Did I Come From? 644

Walter, Bozena
History of Poland in Painting 550

Walters, Charles
Ask Any Girl 358
Barkleys of Broadway 320
Belle of New York 320
Dangerous When Wet 365
Don't Go Near the Water 267
Easter Parade 322
Easy to Love 322
Glass Slipper 634
Good News 323
High Society 324
Jumbo 325
Lili 325
Please Don't Eat the Daisies 279
The Tender Trap 330
Texas Carnival 390
Torch Song 391
The Unsinkable Molly Brown 331
Walk, Don't Run 286

Wam, Svend
Lakki: The Boy Who Grew Wings 76
Sebastian 77, 465

Wan, Zhang Siu
Deadend of Besiegers 126

Wanamaker, Sam
Catlow 291
Sinbad and the Eye of the Tiger 666

Wang, Newton
Mission to Kill 130

Wang, Peter
The Great Wall 455
The Laser Man 455

Wang, Wayne
Blue in the Face 427
Chan Is Missing 455
Eat a Bowl of Tea 455
The Joy Luck Club 455
A Man, a Woman and a Killer 433
Slam Dance 455
Smoke (Harvey Keitel) 455

Warchol, Grzegorz
I Like Bats 92

Ward, David
Cannery Row 221

Ward, Jay
George of the Jungle Triple-Pack 697
George of the Jungle: Gullible Travels 697
George of the Jungle: In George We Trust 697
George of the Jungle: It's a Mad, Mad, Mad, Mad Jungle 697
George of the Jungle: The Man from J.U.N.G.L.E. 697
Jay Ward & Bill Scott TV Commercials Vol. 1 712
Jay Ward & Bill Scott TV Commercials Vol. 2 712

Ward, Shirley
Soviet School Day: Styles in Soviet Education 89

Ward, Vincent
Map of the Human Heart 208
Navigator: A Time Travel Adventure 208
Vigil 209

Wardwell, Judith
Film Flyer (Short Personal Films) 437

Ware, Clyde
No Drums, No Bugles 240

Wargnier, Regis
Indochine 3
Lumiere & Company 5, 336

Warner, Jack
Bell Science Series: About Time 677
Bell Science Series: Gateway to the Mind 677
Bell Science Series: The Alphabet Conspiracy 677
Bell Science Series: The Thread of Life 677

Warnow, Catherine
Paul Bowles: The Complete Outsider 306

Warren, Charles Marquis
Arrowhead 290
Little Big Horn 376

Warren, Jerry
Face of the Screaming Werewolf 521
The Incredible Petrified World 497
Man Beast 525
Teenage Zombies 530

The Wild World of Batwoman 512

Warriner, Gray
The Art of Nature: Reflections on the Grand Design 558

Was, Don
Brian Wilson: I Just Wasn't Made for These Times 619

Wasson, David
Thing What Lurked in the Tub (Spike/Mike 1) 716

Waszynski, Michal
The Dybbuk 112
His Excellency the Shop Assistant 92
It'll Be Better 92
Mother's Heart 93
Second Youth 94
The Tramps 94

Waters, Charles
Summer Stock 329

Waters, Jack
Brains by Revlon 483

Waters, John
Cry Baby 514
Desperate Living 514
Divine 514
Hairspray 514
Nevada 294
No Smoking in This Theater (It's Clean...) 486
Pink Flamingos 514
Polyester 514
Serial Mom 514

Waters, Mark
The House of Yes 271

Watkins, Greg
A Little Stiff 433

Watkins, Peter
Battle of Culloden 168
Edvard Munch 168, 548

Watson, Charlie Fletcher
Bluefields Express (British Animation) 707

Watson, James/Webber, Melville
Fall of the House of Usher (American Avant Garde) 482

Watt, Harry
Classic Documentaries: People and Places 470
Night Mail (Benjamin Britten) 469
North Sea (England in 30s) 471
Target for Tonight (Wartime Moments) 479

Wayans, Keenen Ivory
I'm Gonna Git You Sucka 533

Wayne, John
The Alamo (Original) 290
The Alamo (Restored) 290
Green Berets 370

Webb, Harry S.
Mystery Trooper (Trail of the Royal Mounted) 538

Webb, Kenneth
Just Suppose 400

Webb, Millard
Glorifying the American Girl 323

Webb, Robert
Beneath the 12-Mile Reef 359

Webb, Robert D.
Love Me Tender 537

Weber, Bruce
Broken Noses 469
Chet Baker: Let's Get Lost 610

Weber, Lois
Blot 396
Chapter in Her Life 396
Lot in Sodom (American Avant Garde) 482
Women Who Made the Movies 339

Webster, Colcord
Mad Doctors of Borneo (Too Outrageous) 717

Wechsberg, Orin
Starlight—A Musical Movie 329

Weeks, Andrew
Split: Portrait of a Drag Queen 465

Wegener, Paul
Golem, The 69

Wegman, William
Alphabet Soup 649
Best of William Wegman 483
Fay's 12 Days of Christmas 633
The Hardly Boys in Hardly Gold 634
William Wegman Reel 1 491
William Wegman Reel 2 491
William Wegman Reel 3 491
William Wegman Reel 4 491
William Wegman Reel 5 491
William Wegman Reel 6 491
William Wegman Reel 7 491
William Wegman's Mother Goose 644

Wegmunsen, Hons
History of Pornography 506

Wehrli, Penelope
Alice Dropped the Mirror and It Broke 426
In a Storm Even Dinosaurs Trip & Invasion of the Amazons 567

Wei, Lo
Naughty! Naughty! 122
Seaman No. 7 131

Weick, Werner
Carl Gustav Jung: Artist of the Soul 785

Weidenmann, Alfred
Adorable Julia 19
Der Stern von Africa 68

Weigl, Peter
Werther 586

Weiland, Paul

For Roseanna 228

Weill, Claudia
Critical Choices 223
Girl Friends 229

Weill, Sam
Class of Nuke 'em High 504

Wein, Chuck
Rainbow Bridge 622

Weinberger, Tanya
Creating Animation on a Computer 708

Weinbren, Graham
Umbrellas 479, 558

Weiner, Charles
Rumba (Best Fest 90) 706

Weinreich, Regina
Paul Bowles: The Complete Outsider 306

Weir, Peter
The Cars That Ate Paris 207
Dead Poets Society 207
Fearless 208
Filmmakers on Their Craft 333
Gallipoli 208
Green Card 208
Last Wave 208
The Mosquito Coast 208
Picnic at Hanging Rock 208
Witness (Harrison Ford) 208
Year of Living Dangerously 208

Weis, Don
The Affairs of Dobie Gillis 319
Billie 263
The Gene Krupa Story 369
I Love Melvin 324

Weis, Gary
The Jimi Hendrix Story 621

Weisenborn, Gordon
Water Is Wet 659

Weiss, Andrea
International Sweethearts of Rhythm/ Tiny & Ruby: Hell-Divin' Women 461, 611

Weiss, David
The Way Things Go 562

Weiss, Jiri
The Coward (Czech) 99
Murder Czech Style 100
Romeo, Juliet and Darkness (Sweet Light in a Dark Room) 100
Wolf Trap 100

Weiss, Rob
Amongst Friends 217

Weiss, Robert K.
Amazon Women on the Moon 262

Weissbrod, Ellen
Listen Up: The Lives of Quincy Jones 613

Weissman, Aerlyn
Fiction and Other Truths: A Film About Jane Rule 459
Forbidden Love: The Unashamed Stories of Lesbian Lives 459
A Winter Tan 439

Weissman, David
Song From an Angel (Best Fest 90) 706

Welch, Craig
Disconnected (Animation C. 1) 705

Weldon, John
The Lump (NFB Canada) 714
Para-Sight (NFB Canada) 714

Weldon, John/Verrall, David
Real Inside Out (Incredible An. #2) 711

Wellens, Mike
The Cheese Stands Alone 707

Welles, Orson
Chimes at Midnight/Falstaff 344
Citizen Kane 344
Citizen Kane (50th Anniversary Edition) 344
F for Fake 344
Hearts of Age (Avant Garde & Experimental Films) 482
Hearts of Age (Classic Foreign #2) 153
The Immortal Story 344
It's All True 344
Journey into Fear 344
Lady from Shanghai 344
Macbeth 344
The Magnificent Ambersons 344
Mr. Arkadin (Confidential Report) 344
Orson Welles AFI Lifetime Achievement Award 332
Othello 344
The Stranger 344
Theatre of the Imagination 872
Touch of Evil 344
The Trial 345
Working With Orson Welles 345

Wellesley, Gordon
The Silver Fleet 772

Wellins, Mike
Big Fat World of Science (Spike/Mike 2) 716
Phulll Phrontal Phingers (Spike/Mike Sick 2) 716
Triassic Parking Lot (Spike/Mike Sick 2) 716

Wellins, Mike/Swain, Mark
This Is Not Frank's Planet (Animation C.3) 705

Wellman, William
Across the Wide Missouri 356
Battleground 359
Beau Geste 359
Beggars of Life 395
Blood Alley 360
Buffalo Bill 291
Dangerous Paradise 365

Goodbye, My Lady 370
The Great Man's Lady 370
Heroes for Sale 371
Lady of Burlesque 375
Magic Town 275
Next Voice You Hear 380
Night Nurse 380
Nothing Sacred 278
The Ox-Bow Incident 382
The Public Enemy 383
The Purchase Price 383
A Star Is Born (1937/Gaynor) 388
Wings 406
Wells, David
Fairgrounds 430
Wells, Peter
The Mighty Civic 208
Wells, Richard J.
National Geographic Video: Cyclone! 818
Wells, Simon
An American Tail: Fievel Goes West 661
Wen-Hua, Li
Golden Dart Hero 128
Wenders, Wim
The American Friend 67
The End of Violence 67
Faraway, So Close 67
Lisbon Story 67
Lumiere & Company 5, 336
Notebook on Cities and Clothes 67
Paris, Texas 67
Until the End of the World 67
Wings of Desire 67
Werden, Rodney
Video Art: Blue Moon 489
Werker, Alfred
He Walked by Night 371
Shock (Price) 386
Werner, Gosta
Victor Sjostrom 339
Werner, Peter
Barn Burning 300
Wertmuller, Lina
Belle Starr 32
Ciao, Professore 32
Love and Anarchy 64
A Night Full of Rain 33
The Seduction of Mimi 34
Seven Beauties 34
Sotto...Sotto 34
Summer Night (With Greek Profile, Almond Eyes and Scent of Basil) 34
Swept Away 34
Wescott, Margaret
Behind the Veil: Nuns 469
West, Big
Macross II: The Movie 735
Macross Plus Part 1 735
Macross Plus Part 2 735
Macross Plus Part 3 735
Macross Plus Part 4 735
Macross Plus: The Movie 735
Orguss 02, Vol. 1 739
Orguss 02, Vol. 2 739
Orguss 02, Vol. 3 739
Super Dimensional Fortress Macross 749
West, Roland
The Bat (1926) 395, 516
The Bat Whispers 516
West, Simon
Con Air 223
Weston & Grant
Wreck of Julie Plante (Animation C.1) 705
Wetzl, Fulvio
Rorret 34
Wexler, Haskell
Latino 235
Medium Cool 378
Whale, James
Bride of Frankenstein 517
Frankenstein—The Restored Version 522
The Invisible Man 192, 524
The Old Dark House 527
Show Boat (1936) 328
Wives Under Suspicion 393
Whatham, Claude
All Creatures Great & Small (1 tape) 188
Wheatley, David
The Wingless Bird 198
Wheeler, Anne
Loyalties 211
Wheeler, Michael
Finale Dance (Animation for Fallen Catholics) 706
Intermission Song (Animation for Fallen C.) 706
Opening Dance (Animation for Fallen Catholics) 706
Whelan, Tim
Action for Slander 171
Badman's Territory 290
Clouds over Europe 172
Higher and Higher 324
The Mill on the Floss (1936) 176
Sidewalks of London 178
St. Martin's Lane 178
Step Lively 329
Whitaker, Forest
Strapped 446
Waiting to Exhale 446
White, Chel
Metal Dogs of India (Best Fest Kids) 706
Photocopy Cha Cha (Int. Animation 5) 712
White, J. Kathleen
Dr. Jekyll and Ms. Hyde 429
White, Jules
Sidewalks of New York 409
The Three Stooges: Stop! Look! and Laugh! 284
White, Sally
The Wedding Show 439
White, Sam
People Are Funny 279
White, Wally
Lie Down with Dogs 462
Whitefield, Eric
Balloon Head (Best Fest 91) 706
Whitehead, Justine/Ingalls, Scott
Tampon (Too Outrageous Animation) 717
Whitman, Philip H.
His Private Secretary 372
Whitney Sr., John
John Whitney, Sr. 486
Whorf, Richard
It Happened in Brooklyn 324
Till the Clouds Roll By 330
Whyte, Michael
The Railway Station Man 243
Wickes, David
Frankenstein (Bergin/Quaid) 522
Wicki, Bernhard
The Bridge (Die Brucke) 63
Morituri 379
Widarski, Marek
Commando 91
Widen, Gregory
The Prophecy 243
Widerberg, Bo
Elvira Madigan 75
The Man from Mallorca 76
Man on the Roof 76
Wiene, Robert
Cabinet of Dr. Caligari 68
Wiese, Michael
Dolphin Adventure 814
Wilbur, Crane
The Bat (1959) 516
Wilcox, Fred M.
Courage of Lassie 663
Forbidden Planet 496
Hills of Home 663
Lassie Come Home 664
The Secret Garden (1949) 666
Three Daring Daughters 330
Wilcox, Herbert
Bitter Sweet (Neagle) 171
The Courtneys of Curzon Street 172
Forever and a Day 170
The King's Rhapsody 175
Let's Make Up 175
Lilacs in the Spring 184
Maytime in Mayfair 184
No No Nanette 327
Trouble in the Glen 179
Wild, Osker
Twin Cheeks: Who Killed the Homecoming King? 466
Wilde, Cornel
Sword of Lancelot 178
Wilde, Ted
Battling Orioles 395
Wilder, Billy
The Apartment 345
Avanti! 345
Billy Wilder AFI Lifetime Achievement Award 332
Buddy Buddy 345
Double Indemnity 345
The Emperor Waltz 345
Fedora 345
Five Graves to Cairo 345
Fortune Cookie 345
Irma La Douce 345
Kiss Me, Stupid 345
The Lost Weekend 346
Love in the Afternoon 346
Mauvaise Graine 346
One, Two, Three 346
The Private Life of Sherlock Holmes 346
Sabrina (1954) 346
Seven Year Itch 346
Some Like It Hot 346
Spirit of St. Louis 346
Stalag 17 346
Sunset Boulevard 346
Witness for the Prosecution 346
Wilder, W. Lee
Killers from Space 524
Phantom from Space 499
The Snow Creature 529
Wiles, Gordon
Charlie Chan's Secret 363
Wilhelm, Bettina
All of Me (Wilhelm) 63, 456
Wilhite, Ingrid
Lesbovision 462
Wilkes, Paul
Merton: A Film Biography 791
Willat, Irvin
False Faces 398
Willemartt, Jacques
Lascaux Revisited 551
Willems, Mo
Iddy Biddy Beat Boy (Spike/Mike 3) 716
The Man Who Yelled (Int. Animation 6) 712
Williams Jr., Spencer
Blood of Jesus (African American Film) 447
Marching On 448
Williams, Emlyn
Last Days of Dolwyn 175
Williams, Linda
Maxwell Street Blues 475
Williams, Paul
Miss Right 276
Williams, Richard
A Christmas Carol (1972/Sim) 707
The Thief and the Cobbler 667, 716
Williams, Spencer
Dirty Gertie from Harlem 448
Girl in Room 20 448
Juke Joint 448
Williams, Stephen
Soul Survivor 247
Williams, Sue
China: A Century of Revolution 135
Williamson, Fred
Adios Amigos 531
Foxtrap 532
The Messenger 533
Mr. Mean 533
Willis, F. McGrew
Blonde for a Night 396
Willis, J. Elder
Song of Freedom 447
Wills, J. Elder
Big Fella 171
Wilmer, Val
Jazz Is Our Religion 612
Wilson, Andy
Playing God 242
Wilson, Gahan
Gahan Wilson's Diner (Int. Animation 6) 712
Wilson, Hugh
First Wives Club 268
Police Academy 279
Wilson, Richard
Invitation to a Gunfighter 293
It's All True 344
Winant, Scott
'Til There Was You 285
Wincer, Simon
Free Willy 663
The Lighthorsemen 206
The Phantom 242
Phar Lap 206
Windom, Lawrence
Heading Home 399
Windust, Bretaigne
The Enforcer 367
June Bride 273
The Pied Piper of Hamelin (Johnson/Rains) 665
Winter Meeting 393
Winer, Lucy
Silent Pioneers 465, 477
Wing, Lau Kar
City Cops 126
Skinny Tiger and Fatty Dragon 132
Wing-Keung, Andy Chin
Semi-Gods and Semi-Devils 131
Winick, Gary
Sweet Nothing 248
Winkler, Irwin
Guilty by Suspicion 230
The Net 239
Night and the City 239
Winkless, Terence H.
Berlin Conspiracy 219
Winner, Michael
Appointment with Death 218
Chato's Land 291
Lawman 294
Winston, Ron
The Gamblers 369
Winter, Alex
Freaked 269
Winterbottom, Michael
Butterfly Kiss 159
Jude 161
Welcome to Sarajevo 252
Wintonick, Peter
Manufacturing Consent: Noam Chomsky and the Media 475, 800
The New Cinema 337
Wionczek, Roman
Enigma Secret 91
Wise, Herbert
Breaking the Code 310, 457
Castle of the Living Dead 518
Pope John Paul II 792
The Woman in Black 198
Wise, Robert
Andromeda Strain 494
Audrey Rose 516
The Day the Earth Stood Still 495
Desert Rats 365
Executive Suite 367

The Haunting 522
Helen of Troy 371
I Want to Live 373
Mademoiselle Fifi (Film) 377
Odds Against Tomorrow 381
Run Silent Run Deep 771
The Sand Pebbles 385
Somebody up There Likes Me 387
The Sound of Music 329
Star Trek I: The Motion Picture 500
Star! 329
This Could Be the Night 283
Three Secrets 391
Two for the Seesaw 316
Until They Sail 392
West Side Story 331

Wishman, Doris
Bad Girls Go to Hell 503
Deadly Weapons 505
Double Agent 73 505
The Immoral Three 507
Nude on the Moon 508
Too Much, Too Often 511

Wiszniewski, Tomasz
The Scoundrel 95

Witcher, Theodore
Love Jones 236

Withers, Denise
Alternate Route 468

Witney, William
The Adventures of Captain Marvel 537
The Crimson Ghost 537
Daredevils of the Red Circle 495
Fighting Devil Dogs (The Tornado of Doom) 537
Jungle Girl 538
King of the Texas Rangers 538
Master of the World (Vincent Price) 498
The Mysterious Dr. Satan 538
Under California Stars 297
Zorro Rides Again (Feature) 394
Zorro Rides Again (Serial) 539

Wohl, Ira
Best Boy 469

Wojcik, Jerzy
Karate Polish Style 92

Wojcik, Wojciech
The Bermuda Triangle 90
Private Investigation 94

Wojnarowicz, David
Where Evil Dwells (The Trailer) 439

Wojtyszko, Maciej
Master and Margarita 93

Wolcott, James L.
The Wild Women of Wongo 512

Wolens, Doug
Weed 479

Wolf, Fred
Adventures of an American Rabbit 676

Wolf, Perry
Kamikaze 769

Wolfe, Michael
Niggernight 434

Wolkstein, Diane
The Story of Inanna, Queen of Heaven and Earth 783

Wolman, Dan
Hide and Seek 107
My Michael 108

Wolodarsky, Solly
Voices from Sepharad 116

Wolper, David
I Will Fight No More Forever 787

Wolper, David L.
The Devil's Brigade 366

Won, Dai
Red Hawk 743

Wong, Jing
Crocodile Hunter 126

Wong, Kirk
Crime Story 134
Organized Crime & Triad Bureau 130

Wong, Parkman
Final Justice 127

Wong, Paul
Video Art: Prime Cuts 490

Wong, Taylor
Born Invincible (Wong) 125
The Inside Story (Triad: The Inside Story) 128
No More Love, No More Death 130

Wong, Yeung Yee
Path of Glory 117

Woo, John
A Better Tomorrow 125
A Better Tomorrow—Part II 125
Broken Arrow (Travolta) 221
Bullet in the Head 125
Face/Off 227
The Hand of Death (aka Countdown in Kung-Fu) 134
Hard Boiled 128
Hard Target 128
Heroes Shed No Tears 121
The Killer 129
Last Hurrah for Chivalry 129
Run Tiger Run 123

Woo, Teresa
Angel 2 118

Woo-Ping, Yuen
Drunken Master (aka Drunken Monkey in a Tiger's Eye) 134
The Fiery Dragon Kid 127
Ghost Foot 120
Heroes Among Heroes (aka The Iron Beggar) 121
Iron Monkey 128
The Magnificent Butcher 129
Snake in the Eagle's Shadow 134
The Tai Chi Master 132
Tiger Cage 2 133

Wood Jr., Ed
Bride of the Monster 514
Crossroad Avenger/Trick Shooting with Kenne Duncan 514
Elvira's Midnight Madness: Night of the Ghouls 515
Glen or Glenda 515
Jail Bait 515
Married Too Young 515
Necromania 515
Orgy of the Dead 515
Plan 9 from Outer Space 515
Sinister Urge 515
Take It Out in Trade—The Outtakes 515
The Violent Years 515

Wood Jr., Edward D.
Haunted World of Edward D. Wood, Jr. 334, 515

Wood, Bret
Kingdom of Shadows 336

Wood, Sam
Casanova Brown 265
Command Decision 364
A Day at the Races 266
The Devil and Miss Jones 366
For Whom the Bell Tolls 368
Goodbye, Mr. Chips (USA) 370
Guest Wife 270
Heartbeat 371
Hold Your Man 271
King's Row 374
Kitty Foyle 375
Let 'Em Have It 376
Madame X (1937) 377
Navy Blue and Gold 380
A Night at the Opera 278
Our Town (1940/William Holden) 314
Outside in Sight: Music of the United Front 614
Peck's Bad Boy 411
Saratoga Trunk 385
Sins of the Children 386
The Stratton Story 388

Woodcock, Peter
Babette in Return of the Secret Society 503
Dominique in Daughters of Lesbos 458

Woodman, William
The Tempest 315
Tragedy of King Richard II 315

Woodward, Joanne
Come Along with Me 223

Wool, Abbe
Roadside Prophets 436

Wooster, Ann Sargent
Carmen 566
Dialectics of Romance 484

Worden, Donna
Tinka's Planet 643

Workman, Chuck
Cuba Crossing 224

Workman, Jeremy
Who Is Henry Jaglom? 339

Worne, Duke
Ships of the Night 404

Wornum, Barbara
M.F.K. 305

Worsley, Wallace
The Hunchback of Notre Dame (1923) 399
The Penalty 402, 527

Worthington, William
Tong Man 405

Wortmann, Sonke
Maybe...Maybe Not 64

Wosiewicz, Leszek
Kornblumenblau 92

Wozniak, Terry
Garbage In, Garbage Out (Int. Animation 2) 712

Wray, John Griffith
Anna Christie (1923/Silent) 395
Beau Ravel 395
Hail the Woman 399
Soul of the Beast 404

Wright, Basil
Classic Documentaries: People and Places 470
Song of Ceylon 478
Song of Ceylon (Classic Documentaries) 470

Wright, Geoffrey
Romper Stomper 207

Wright, Mack V.
Haunted Gold 293
The Man from Monterey 377
Somewhere in Sonora 296
Winds of the Wasteland 298

Wright, Tenny
The Big Stampede 290
The Telegraph Trail 296

Wu, David
The Bride with White Hair 2 119

Wu, Lo Chau
Ninja Heat 130

Wui-Ngai, Billy Chan
License to Streal 129

Wurlitzer, Rudy
Candy Mountain 210

Wyatt, Andy
Beastly Behavior 181, 813

Wyler, William
Ben-Hur (Heston) 343
Ben-Hur (Heston, 35th Anniversary Edition) 343
The Best Years of Our Lives 343
Big Country 343
Carrie 343
The Children's Hour 343
Collector 343
Come and Get It 341, 343
Dead End 343
Desperate Hours 343
Dodsworth 343
Funny Girl 343
The Heiress 343
How to Steal a Million 343
Jezebel 343
The Letter 343
Little Foxes 343
The Love Trap 344
Memphis Belle 344
Mrs. Miniver 344
Roman Holiday 344
These Three 344
Thunderbolt 344
The Westerner 344
Wuthering Heights (1939/Olivier) 344

Wyndham-Davis, Jayne
Pollyanna (1973/BBC) 640

Wynorski, Jim
Big Bad Mama II 504

Xhonneux, Henri
Marquis 8

Xiaodong, Cheng
Swordsman III (aka The East Is Red) 132

Xiaolian, Peng
Women's Story 118

Xiaowen, Zhou
Ermo 117

Xie, Jin
Stage Sisters 117

Yada, Kimoyoshi
The Adventures of a Blind Man 137
Masseur Ichi, The Fugitive (Zato Ichi Kyojotabi) 138

Yakin, Boaz
Fresh 430

Yanagimachi, Mitsuo
Himatsuri 137
Shadow of China 139

Yang, Edward
That Day, On the Beach 136

Yang, Kong
Spider Force 132

Yang-ming, Tsay
Flower Love (aka Love Is Grown with Flowers) 136

Yarborough, Jean
The Bela Lugosi Collection: Devil Bat/Scared to Death 516

Yarbrough, Jean
Devil Bat 520
Here Come the Co-Eds 270
House of Horrors 523
In Society 272
Jack and the Beanstalk 272
King of the Zombies 524
Lost in Alaska 274

Yasuda, Kimoyoshi
The Blind Swordsman's Cane Sword 137
Majin, The Monster of Terror 525
Sleepy Eyes of Death—Full Circle Killing 139
Zatoichi: The Blind Swordsman and the Fugitives 140

Yasuda, Kumiyoshi
Zatoichi: Masseur Ichi on the Road 140

Yasunari, Kawabata
Animated Classics of Japanese Literature:
Izu Dancer/Dancing Girl 720

Yasuzo, Masumara
The Razor—The Snare 139

Yates, Peter
Breaking Away 220
Bullitt 362
The Dresser 160
For Pete's Sake 268
Krull 498
Mother, Jugs and Speed 276
Roommates 281
The Run of the Country 202
Suspect 248

Yau, Herman
Adventurous Treasure Island 118
Best of the Best 125
Ebola Syndrome 120
War of the Underworld 133

Yau-Sin, Danny Lee
Dr. Lam[b] 126

Yee, Cha Tsuen
Once Upon a Time in Triad Society II 130

Yee, Chuk Ki
Fatal Chase 127

Yeshurun, Isaac
Noa at Seventeen 108

Yevtushenko, Yevgeny
Kindergarten 82

Yimou, Zhang

Ju Dou....118
Raise the Red Lantern....118
Red Sorghum....118
Shanghai Triad....118
The Story of Qiu Ju....118
To Live....118

Ying, Ye
Red Cherry....117

Yiu, Ma Tin
The Six Devil Women....132

Yiu-leung, Fok
The Iceman Cometh....128

Ylisela, James
The Race for Mayor....476

Yoder, Pamela
Emergency! EMS to the Rescue....860

Yong-kyun, Bae
Why Has Bodhi-Dharma Left for the East?....136

Yorkin, Bud
Arthur 2: On the Rocks....262
Divorce American Style....267
Never Too Late....278
Start the Revolution Without Me....282

Yoshida, Yoshihige
Lumiere & Company....5, 336

Yoshio, Inyoue
The Razor—Who's Got the Gold....139

Yoshiyuki, Kuroda
Lone Wolf and Cub: White Heaven and Hell....138

Young, Harold
Dreaming Out Loud....366
The Inner Sanctum: Weird Woman/Frozen Ghost....524
The Mummy's Tomb....526
The Scarlet Pimpernel (1934/Leslie Howard)....385

Young, Jacob
Dancing Outlaw....471

Young, James
The Bells....395, 516
Unchastened Woman....405

Young, Lance
Bliss (USA)....220

Young, Paul
Ballyhoo Baby....426

Young, Robert
Charlotte Bronte's Jane Eyre....159
Fierce Creatures....182
Romance with a Double Bass....199
Soldier's Home....301

Young, Robert M.
Caught....222
Dominick and Eugene....225
One Trick Pony....241
Rich Kids....280
Triumph of the Spirit....250

Young, Roger
Double Crossed....225
Joseph....355
Moses....356

Young, Susan
Carnival (Int. Animation 2)....705
Susan Young Showreel (British Animation)....707

Young, Susan/Smith, Mike
Umbabaurauma (Animation C.2)....705

Young, Terence
The Amorous Adventures of Moll Flanders....181
Black Tights....569
Corridor of Mirrors....172
Dr. No....168
From Russia with Love....168
Mayerling (1968)....176
Nino Martini in One Night with You....184
Red Sun....295
Thunderball....169
Triple Cross....179
Wait Until Dark....392
Woman Hater....185

Yu, Albert
Kickboxer—The Fighter, the Winner....129

Yu, Ronnie
The Bride with White Hair....119
The Occupant....122

Yu, Ronny
Legacy of Rage....129

Yu, Wang
Beach of the War Gods....125

Yuasa, Noriaki
Gamera vs. Barugon....496
Gamera vs. Gaos....496
Gamera vs. Guiron....496
Gamera vs. Zigra....496

Yuen, Corey
How to Pick Girls Up....121
Saviour of the Soul....123

Yuen, Peter
Shaolin Kung-Fu Kids....132

Yuen, Woo-Ping
Drunken Fist Boxing....134
Eagle Shadow Fists....134

Yukio, Mishima
Animated Classics of Japanese Literature: The Sound of Waves....721

Yule, Paul
Damned in the USA....471
Good Morning Mr. Hitler....768

Yung, Peter Wia-Chuen
Life After Life....121

Yutkevich, Sergei
Othello (1955/Yutkevich)....83

Yuzo, Yamamoto
Animated Classics of Japanese Literature: A Roadside Stone, Pts 1....720

Zabalza, Jose Maria
The Fury of the Wolfman....522

Zagdansky, Andrei
Interpretation of Dreams....82

Zahedi, Caveh
I Don't Hate Las Vegas Anymore....431
A Little Stiff....433

Zajaczkowski, Andrzej
Workers '80 (Robotnicy '80)....99

Zaks, Jerry
Marvin's Room....237

Zallman, Steven
Searching for Bobby Fischer....246

Zaluski, Roman
Egg-Nog (Kogel Mogel)....91
Oh Charles....93

Zampa, Luigi
Tigers in Lipstick....34
Woman of Rome....42

Zampi, Mario
Five Golden Hours....182
The Naked Truth (Comedy)....184

Zanada, Jorge
Tango: Our Dance....52, 576

Zanuck, Lili Fini
Rush....245

Zanussi, Krzysztof
Balance....90
Camouflage....90
Contract....91
Family Life....91
From a Far Country: Pope John Paul II....790
Illumination....92
The Silent Touch....94
The Structure of Crystal....94

Zaorski, Janusz
Baritone....95
Mother of Kings....95
Soccer Poker....94

Zapata, Ariel
Latin American Trails: Guatemala....58

Zappa, Frank
200 Motels....503
Video from Hell....512

Zaritsky, Raul
Maxwell Street Blues....475

Zarkhi, Alexander
Anna Karenina (1967/Russia)....80, 300
Baltic Deputy....80

Zauberman, Yolande
Ivan and Abraham....3, 776

Zavattini, Cesare
Love of a Mother (Love in the City)....41

Zbonek, Edwin
The Mad Executioners....525

Zedd, Nick
Bogus Man & Go To Hell (Cinema of Transgression)....483
Geek Maggot Bingo....430
Nick Zedd: Steal This Video....434
Police State....435
They Eat Scum....438
War Is Menstrual Envy—Parts I, II and III....439
Whoregasm....491
Wide World of Lydia Lunch....439

Zeffirelli, Franco
Brother Sun, Sister Moon....32, 457
Hamlet (1990/Gibson)....312
Jane Eyre (1995)....233
Jesus of Nazareth....355
La Traviata (Domingo)....582
Romeo and Juliet....314
The Taming of the Shrew....315

Zegio, Primo
Mission Stardust....498

Zehrer, Paul
Blessing....219

Zeisler, Alfred
Amazing Adventure....181

Zelinsky, Rafael
Fun....430

Zeman, Karel
Fabulous Adventures of Baron Munchhausen....99, 709
On the Comet....100, 714

Zemeckis, Robert
Back to the Future....262
Back to the Future II....262
Contact....495
Field of Honor (First Works)....334
Forrest Gump....228
I Wanna Hold Your Hand....324
Used Cars....286

Zhang, Yimou
Lumiere & Company....5, 336

Zhelyabuzhsky, Yuri
The Cigarette Girl of Mosselprom....85

Zhuangzhuang, Tian
The Blue Kite....117
The Horse Thief....117

Zidi, Claude
Stuntwoman....7

Zieba, Wieslaw
David & the Magic Pearl....709

Zieff, Howard
Dream Team....267
Hearts of the West....293
The Main Event....275
Private Benjamin....280
Slither....246
Unfaithfully Yours (1984)....285

Ziehm, Howard
Flesh Gordon....506

Zinnemann, Fred
Behold a Pale Horse....359
The Day of the Jackal....159
Eyes of the Night....367
From Here to Eternity....369
High Noon....293
Julia (USA)....234
A Man for All Seasons (Scofield)....176
Member of the Wedding (1953)....378
Men....378
Menschen am Sontag (People on Sunday)....401
Nun's Story....381
The Seventh Cross....386
Sundowners....389

Zlotoff, Lee David
The Spitfire Grill....437

Zohar, Uri
Three Days and a Child....108

Zucker, David
Airplane!....261
More! Police Squad!....419
Naked Gun....277
Police Squad! Help Wanted!....421

Zucker, Jerry
Airplane!....261
First Knight....227
Ghost....269
More! Police Squad!....419
Police Squad! Help Wanted!....421

Zucker, Ralph
Terror Creatures from the Grave (Cemetery of the Living Dead)....530

Zuckerman, Steve
North Shore Fish....240

Zurinaga, Marcos
The Disappearance of Garcia Lorca....56, 225

Zurlini, Valerio
Black Jesus....40
Girl with a Suitcase....41
Le Soldatesse....41

Zweig, Alan
The Darling Family....210

Zwerin, Charlotte
The Sculpture of Spaces....556
Straight No Chaser: Thelonious Monk....615

Zwick, Edward
About Last Night…....216
Glory....452
Legends of the Fall....235

Zwickler, Phil
Positive....65, 834
Silence=Death....65, 465

Zwigoff, Terry
Crumb....470, 541

title index

Numbers

1-900 30
10 353
10 Greatest American Cars, The 841
10 Rillington Place 158
100 Years of Comedy 261, 332
100 Years of Horror 332, 516
100 Years of Olympic Glory 825
1000 Years of Polish Cavalry 98
101 Dalmatians 690
1071 5th Avenue: Frank Lloyd Wright and the Guggenheim Museum 565
10th Mountain Division Ridge Runners, The 765
11th and B: East Village Summer of Love 618
12 Angry Men 216
12 Monkeys 168
12 O'Clock High 356
12 Steps, The 847
13 Rue Madeleine 356
1492: Conquest of Paradise 216
15th Century: Renaissance in Full Bloom 544
1641 and the Curse of Cromwell 202
16mm Camera, The 316
17 Days of Terror: The Hijack of TWA 847 110
1776 319
17th Karrmapa's Return to Tsurphu, The 149
1860 40
187 216
1900 35
1942: A Love Story 146
1964 World's Fair, The 756
1968: America Is Hard to See 481
1970: Year of Protest 807
1971: Year of Disillusionment 807
1972: Year of Summits 807
1973: Year of Watergate 807
1974: Year of Resignation 807
1975: Year after the Fall 807
1976: Year of the Bicentennial 807
1977: Year of the Southern President 807
1978: Year of Moral Dilemmas 807
1979: Year of Overthrow 807
1984 ....171, 300
1986 Tour de France: LeMond and Hinault Challenge 825
1987 Tour of Ireland: Nissan Classic 825
1988 426
1988 Iditabike Race: Bicycling on Snow 825
1989 World Championship: LeMond's Victory 825
1990 Paris-Roubaix: A Photo Finish! 825
1990 Tour de France: Greg LeMond—The Best Yet! 825
1990 World Cycling Championships: The Complete Story! 825
1991 Liege-Bastogne-Liege: Cycling's Oldest Classic 825
1991 Paris-Roubaix: A Fight to the Finish! 825
1991 Tour de France: Miguel Indurian—The New Tour Champion! 825
1991 World Cycling Championships: One of Cycling's Greatest Prizes 825
1992 Paris-Roubaix 825
1992 Tour of Flanders 825
1993: A Year in Review 798
1994 Winter Olympic Highlights 825
1994 Winter Olympics Figure Skating Competition and Figure Skating Exhibition Gift Set 825
2000-Year-Old Man, The 676
2,000 Years of Freedom and Honor: The Cochini Jews of India 113, 148
20,000 Leagues Under the Sea- 395
20,000 Lenguas de Viaje Submarino 671
20 Million Miles to Earth 494
200 Motels 503
2000 Maniacs 503
2001: A Space Odyssey (25th Anniversary Edition) 255
2001: A Space Odyssey 255
20th Century American Art: Whitney Museum of American Art 544
20th Century Art at the Metropolitan Museum 544
20th Century Fox: The First 50 Years 332
21 Days 171
21st Century Jet 841
23 Days in July: Tour de France 825
24 Hours in a Woman's Life 356
25, Firemen's Street 103
25 Classic Cartoons 676
26 Bathrooms 165
27 Pieces of Me 426, 456
28th Instance of June 1914, 10:50 AM, The 456
28 Up 468
317th Platoon, The 2, 777
3 by Martha Graham 568
3 Wishes 118
3 X 3 Eyes Compilation 719
3 X 3 Eyes Part 1: Altered States 719
3 X 3 Eyes Part 2: Yakumo 719
3 X 3 Eyes Part 3: Life and Death 719
3 X 3 Eyes Part 4: Blind Flight 719
3-D Video Visions: Vol. 1, Deep Space Videoscapes 503
3-D Video Visions: Vol. 2, Stereogram Videoscapes 503
301/302 136
317th Platoon, The 2, 777
33-1/3 Revolutions per Monkee 618
35 Up 468
36 Filette 2
36 Hours 356
4 Faces of Eve 118
40 Pounds of Trouble 356
40 Years of MJQ 608
400 Blows, The 14
42nd Street 319
444 Days to Freedom: What Really Happened in Iran 110
47 Ronin 143
48 Hours 261
49th Parallel, The 180
5 Dark Souls 503
500 Nations 786
5000 Fingers of Dr. T, The 356
55 Days at Peking 346
6 Films by Mark Street 482
60 Minutes: 25 Years 756
60 Years with Bob Hope 261
633 Squadron 356
7 Up in South Africa 150
7 Up in the Soviet Union 87
75 Years of Award Winners 332
777: First Flight 841
7th Voyage of Sinbad, The 356
$8.50/A Barrel! Huit Piastres et Demie and Cajun Visits 468
8 Man 719
8 Man After Vol. 1: City of Fear 719
8 Man After Vol. 2: End Run 719
8 Man After Vol. 3: Mr. Hallowe'en 719
8 Man After Vol. 4: Sachiko's Decision 719
8 Man After: Perfect Collection 719
8 Seconds 290
8-A Ochoa 49
8½ 36
81st Blow, The 107, 774
84 Charing Cross Road 158
8th Man Vol. 1 719
8th Man Vol. 2 719
8th Man Vol. 3 719
8th Man Vol. 4 719
8x8 (A Chess Sonata in 8 Movements) 482
90 Days 210
90 Degrees South: With Scott to the Antarctic 153, 171
9½ Weeks 216

A

A&E Biography: Houdini—The Great Escape 793
A&E Biography: Nostradamus, Prophet of Doom 793
A&E Biography: The Three Stooges 332
A&E's Incredible World of Cats 812
A.I.D.S.C.R.E.A.M., Ecce Homo and Final Solutions 456, 482
A la Mode 2
A.M. Klein: The Poet as Landscape 302
A Nous la Liberte 24
A Propos de Nice 25
AaaHH!!! Real Monsters: Meet the Monsters 694
AaaHH!!! Real Monsters: Monsters' Night Out 695
Aaron's Magic Village 704
Aashiq 146
Abandon Ship! 356
Abbado in Berlin: The First Year 586
Abbey Grange, The 185
Abbey Lincoln: You Gotta Pay the Band 608
Abbey Semel, M.S., R.D., Lic.A, and Stephen Rechtschaffen, M.D.: Nutrition for Life 847
Abbott and Costello 261
Abbott and Costello Comin' Round the Mountain 261
Abbott and Costello Go to Mars 261
Abbott and Costello in Hollywood 261
Abbott and Costello in the Foreign Legion 261
Abbott and Costello Meet the Invisible Man 261
Abbott and Costello Meet the Keystone Kops 261
Abbott and Costello Meet the Mummy 261
Abbott and Costello Television Show, The 414
Abbott and Costello Vol. I Who's on First 261
Abbott and Costello: Mexican Hayride 261
ABC No Rio, Open Mike 302
ABC Stage 67: Truman Capote's A Christmas Memory 414
Abduction from the Seraglio (Dresden) 577
Abduction from the Seraglio (Glyndebourne) 577
Abe Ajay 544
Abel Gance at Work 19
Abel Gance's Beethoven 19
Abel's Island 704
AbFab Moments 188
Abhimaan 146
Abigail's Party 165
Abominable Dr. Phibes, The 516
Aboriginal Art: Past, Present and Future 209
"About Last Night..." 216
About Painting 98
About the Jews of Yemen: A Vanishing Culture 113
Above and Beyond 356
Above and Beyond the Call of Duty 808
Above Suspicion 356
Abraham 355
Abraham Lincoln— Westinghouse Studio One 414
Abraham Lincoln 412, 793
Absence of Malice 216
Absolute Beginners: The Musical 158
Absolute Power 256
Absolutely Fabulous Collection 188
Absolutely Fabulous Volume One, Part 1 188
Absolutely Fabulous Volume One, Part 2 188
Absolutely Fabulous Volume Three, Part 1 188
Absolutely Fabulous Volume Three, Part 2 188
Absolutely Fabulous Volume Two, Part 1 188
Absolutely Fabulous Volume Two, Part 2 188
Absolutely Fabulous: The Last Shout 188
Absolutely the Best of the Soupy Sales Show 414
Absolution 158
Abu Simbel 332
Abuela's Weave 55, 628
Abuse 456, 468
Academia Museum of Venice 544
Acadia National Park & Cape Cod National Seashore 828
Accatone! 37
Accent on the Offbeat 608
Accidental Tourist, The 216
Accompanist, The 16
According to Kossoff 789
Accused, The 216
Ace Drummond 537
Ace High 290
Ace of Aces 356
Ace Ventura: When Nature Calls 261
Aces 756
Aces Go Places II 124
Aces Go Places III (Our Man from Bond Street) 124
Aces: Story of the First Air War 756
Acid Is Groovy Kill the Pigs 426
Acid Rain 801
Acla's Descent into Floristella 32, 456
Acoustic Guitar Musicianship 623
Acqua e Sapone 32
Across the Pacific 348
Across the Wide Missouri 356
Acrylic 562
Act of Aggression 2
Act of Faith 774
Action for Slander 171
Action in Arabia 356
Action in the North Atlantic 356
Actor's Revenge, An 141
Actors and Sin 356
Actors on Acting 310
AD Police Files Hybrid LD #1 719
AD Police Files Hybrid LD #2 719
AD Police Files Laserdisc 719
AD Police: File #1: Phantom Woman 719
AD Police: File #2: The Ripper 719
AD Police: File #3: The Man Who Bites His Tongue 719
Adam and Evelyn 19
Adam's Rib 80, 349
Addams Family 261
Addams Family Values 261
Addiction, Attachment, and Spiritual Crisis 847
Addiction, The 426
Addiction and Responsibility 847
Adelante Mujeres! 55
Adios Amigos 531
Adjuster, The 212
Admiral Nimitz Story 765
Admiral Was a Lady, The 356
Adolph Hitler's Home Movies 765
Adoption 101
Adoption: Your Guide to Success 847
Adorable Julia 19
Adriadne auf Naxos (Strauss) 577
Adriana Lecouvreur 577
Adrienne Rich 302
Adrift 101
Advanced Television Lighting: A Seminar with Bill Millar, BBC-TV 316
Advanced Voice Workout for the Actor 316
Adventure 356, 812
Adventure Girl 356
Adventure Kid, Vol. 1 863
Adventure of Self-Discovery, The 847
Adventure of the Spirit 847
Adventure Pack 863
Adventures from the Book of Virtues 628
Adventures in Babysitting 261
Adventures in Dinosaur City 628

Adventures of a Blind Man, The....137
Adventures of a Two-Minute Werewolf, The....628
Adventures of an American Rabbit....676
Adventures of Babar....628
Adventures of Baron Munchhausen, The....168
Adventures of Batman & Robin: Batman....676
Adventures of Batman & Robin: Fire and Ice....676
Adventures of Batman & Robin: Poison Ivy....676
Adventures of Batman & Robin: Robin....676
Adventures of Batman & Robin: The Joker....676
Adventures of Batman & Robin: The Penguin....676
Adventures of Batman & Robin: The Riddler....676
Adventures of Batman & Robin: Two-Face....676
Adventures of Blinky Bill: Blinky Bill's Zoo/Magician, The....628
Adventures of Blinky Bill: Blinky's Fire Brigade/Fund Run, The....628
Adventures of Captain Marvel, The....537
Adventures of Chico, The....628
Adventures of Corduroy, The....628
Adventures of Don Juan....356
Adventures of Don Quixote....595
Adventures of Droopy....676
Adventures of Frank and Jesse James, The....537
Adventures of Hairbreadth Harry....395
Adventures of Huck Finn, The....690
Adventures of Huck Finn (Disney), The....308
Adventures of Huckleberry Finn (Hodges/Moore), The....308
Adventures of Huckleberry Finn (Rooney), The....308
Adventures of Ichabod & Mr. Toad, The....690
Adventures of Jay Jay the Jet Plane, The....649
Adventures of Marco Polo, The....356
Adventures of Mark Twain: Fredric March, The....309
Adventures of Milo and Otis....661
Adventures of Peer Gynt, The....645
Adventures of Pinocchio, The....661
Adventures of Popeye, Vol. 2, The....676
Adventures of Prince Achmed....704
Adventures of Priscilla, Queen of the Desert, The....205, 456
Adventures of Rex & Rinty, The....537
Adventures of Robin Hood, The....356
Adventures of Sadie....181
Adventures of Smilin' Jack....537
Adventures of Tartu....171
Adventures of the Old West....298
Adventures of Tintin: Cigars of the Pharaoh, The....628
Adventures of Tintin: The Secret of the Unicorn, The....628
Adventures of Tom Sawyer (Kelly/Brennan), The....309
Adventures of Wayan and the Three R's, The....628
Adventurous Treasure Island....118
Adversary, The....146
Advise and Consent....356
Advocate, The....158
Aelita: Queen of Mars....85
Aeon Flux....695
Aeon Flux: Mission Infinite....695
Aeon Flux: Operative Terminus....695
Aerial Gunner....356
Aesop & His Friends....645
Aesop's Fables & Associates Vol. 1....676
Aesop's Fables....863
Aesop's Fables Volume 1....676
Aesop's Fables Volume 2....676
Aesop's Fables Volume 3....676
Aesop's Film Fables....676
Affair, The....216
Affair in Mind, An....158
Affair in Trinidad....357
Affair to Remember, An....357
Affairs of Annabel....261
Affairs of Dobie Gillis, The....319
Affirmations for Getting Well Again....847
Affirmations for Living Beyond Cancer....847
Affliction....503
AFI Life Achievement Awards, The....332
Africa Between Myth and Reality....151, 544
Africa Screams....261
Africa Speaks to the World....151
Africa: Part I....151
Africa: Part II....151
Africa: Part III....151
Africa: Part IV....151
African Americans in WWII: A Legacy of Patriotism and Valor....449, 765
African Art, Women, History....151, 544
African Art....151, 544
African Dance and Drumming....600
African Dream, An....158
African Drumming....600
African Guitar....601
African in America, An....781
African Journey....660
African Queen, The....348
African Queen (Commemorative Edition), The....348
African Ritual and Initiation....151
African Safaris....151
African Shark Safari....812
African Story Magic....449, 645
African-American Art: Past and Present....544
African-American Artists: Affirmation Today....544
African-American Film Heritage Series I....447
African-American Film Heritage Series I and II....447
African-American Film Heritage Series II....447
African-American Heroes of World War II, Tuskegee Fighter Pilots and Black War Time Radio....449
Afrika Bambaata and Family: Electric Dance Hop....601
Afro-Classic Folk Tales, Vol. I....449, 645
Afro-Classic Folk Tales, Vol. II....449, 645
Afro-Classic Mother Goose....449, 645
Afros Macks 'n Zodiacs....531
After Darkness....158
After Hours....253, 608
After Mein Kampf?....765
After Pilkington....158
After Sunset: The Life & Times of the Drive-In Theater....332
After the Ball....171
After the Cloud Lifted: Hiroshima's Stories of Recovery....144, 765
After the Fox....37
After the Promise....216
After the Rehearsal....77
After the Revolution....101
After the Storm: The American Exile of Bela Bartok....586
After the Thin Man....261
After the Velvet Revolution....101
After the Warming....801
Afterburn....216
Afterglow....257
Aftermath of the War with Iraq, The....110
Afternoon with Father Flye, An....468
Agadati: Screen of an Artist....109
Against All Odds....216
Against the Wall....216
Against the Wind....44, 171
Agatha Christie's Miss Marple....188
Agatha Christie's Miss Marple II....188
Agatha Christie's Poirot....188
Age Is No Barrier....847
Age of Anxiety (1952-1958)....756
Age of Gold....46
Age of Innocence, The....253
Age of Insects, The....426
Age of Miracles, The....118
Age of the Medici....38
Agee....468
Agent #1....90
Aggie Appleby, Maker of Men....261
Agneepath (Path of Fire)....146
Agnes of God....310
Agnes Varda and Susan Sontag: Lions and Cannibals....14
Agony and the Ecstasy....357
Agriculture Hall of Fame....756
Agrippina....577
Aguirre: The Wrath of God....67
Ah, Wilderness....310
Ah Ying....118
Ahi-Nama in Cuba....601
Ai City (Love City)....719
Aida (Downes)....577
Aida (Gencer, Cossotto, Bergonzi)....577
Aida (La Scala)....577
Aida (Metropolitan Opera)....577
Aida (Royal Opera)....577
Aida File....577
AIDS 101: Tammy Talks with Teenagers....833
AIDS—What You Need to Know....833
AIDS: A Test of the Nation....833
AIDS: Allie's Story....833
AIDS: Alternative Therapies and the Struggle for Legalization....833
AIDS: Bleach, Teach and Outreach....833
AIDS: Doctors, Liars and Women: AIDS Activists Say "No"....833
AIDS: Everything You Should Know....833
AIDS: Prostitutes, Risk and AIDS....833
AIDS: PWA Power....833
AIDS: Seize Control of the FDA....833
AIDS: What Are the Risks....834
AIDS: Women and AIDS....834
AIDS: Work Your Body....834
Aileen Wuornos: The Selling of a Serial Killer....468
Air Force....341
Air Force One....216
Air Force One: Flight II: The Planes and the Presidents....756
Air Force Training Films....765
Air Mail Story, The....841
Air Raid Wardens....261
Airplane Comedies....410
Airplane!....261
Airto & Flora Purim: The Latin Jazz All Stars....608
Airzone Solution, The....199
Akademia Podroze Pana (Mr. Blot's Academy/ Travels of Mr. Blot)....90
Akai Hayate Vol. 1: Episodes 1 and 2....719
Akai Hayate Vol. 2: Episodes 3 and 4....719
Akermania, Volume One....29
Akira....719
Akira Laserdisc....719
Akira Production Report....719
Al Capone: Scarface....793
Al Green...Everything's Gonna Be Alright....606
Al Green: On Fire in Tokyo....606
Al Jolson Collection, The....319
Alabaster's Song....628
Aladdin & Jasmine's Moonlight Magic....676, 690
Aladdin and His Magic Lamp....645
Aladdin and the King of Thieves....690
Aladdin and the Magical Lamp....671
Alakazam the Great!....720
Alamo, The....756
Alamo (Original), The....290
Alamo (Restored), The....290
Alamo Bay....13
Alan & Eric— Between Hello and Goodbye....118
Alan and Naomi....426
Alan Smithee Film: Burn Hollywood Burn, An....216
Alan Stivell....601
Alan Watts: The Art of Meditation....847
Alaska....216
Alaska's Three Bears and the Alaska Mother Goose....812
Alaska's Whales and Wildlife....812
Alaska's Wildlife....812
Alaska Stories....828
Alaskan Safari....812
Albert Einstein: How I See the World....793
Albert Einstein: The Education of a Genius....793
Albert Herring....577
Albert King....608
Albert Schweitzer....468
Alberta Hunter: My Castle's Rocking....608
Alberto Express....16
Albino Alligator....216
Alcatraz: America's Toughest Prison....808
Alchemist of the Surreal....705
Alchemy & the Crystal Cave....847
Aldo Ciccolini....586
Alef...Bet...Blast-Off!....113
Alejandro Obregon Paints a Fresco....544
Alejandro's Gift....628
Alex Haley's Queen....449
Alex in Wonderland....216
Alexander, Who Used to Be Rich Last Sunday....628
Alexander Alexeieff....482, 705
Alexander and the Terrible, Horrible, No Good, Very Bad Day....628
Alexander Nevsky....86
Alexander's Ragtime Band....319
Alexander the Great....357, 784
Alexeieff & Parker....482, 705
Alexis Smith: Life in America....544
Alf Bicknell's Personal Beatles Diary....618
Alfie....181
Alfonia....608
Alfred Hitchcock....351
Alfred Hitchcock TV....351
Alfred Hitchcock: Master of Suspense....332, 351
Algiers....357
Ali Baba and the Forty Thieves....19, 357
Ali: Fear Eats the Soul....66
Alias, La Gringa....49
Alias Jesse James....262
Alice, Sweet Alice....216
Alice....288, 705
Alice Doesn't Live Here Anymore....253
Alice Dropped the Mirror and It Broke....426
Alice in Acidland....503
Alice in Wonderland....216, 661, 690, 705
Alice in Wonderland Archive Edition....690
Alice in Wonderland in Paris....705
Alice in Wonderland Set....216
Alice in Wonderland: A Dance Fantasy....568
Alice's Adventures in Wonderland....158
Alice's Restaurant....257
Alice Through the Looking Glass....216
Alice to Nowhere....205
Alice Walker....449
Alicia....568
Alicia en el Pais de las Maravillas....671
Alien....494
Alien Empire: We Are Not Alone....812
Alien Nation....217
Alien Resurrection....217
Alien Terror....494
Alien Trilogy....494
Alien3....494
Aliens, Dragons, Monsters & Me....494
Aliens....494
Aliens Cut My Hair....503
All About ABC's....649
All About Ah-Long....118
All About Eve....357
All About Kids' Safety....668
All Color News—Sampler....414
All Creatures Great & Small (1 tape)....188
All Creatures Great & Small (8 tapes)....188
All Dogs Go to Heaven 2....676
All Dogs Go to Heaven....676
All Dressed Up and No Place to Go....468
All Fall Down....357
All for the Winner....118
All Friends Here....90
All God's Children....449, 456
All I Desire....342
All I See....628
All I Want for Christmas....661
All Men Are Brothers— Blood of the Leopard....124
All My Children: Behind the Scenes....414
All My Good Countrymen....99
All My Hummingbirds Have Alibis....863
All My Sons....310, 357
All Night....395
All Night Long....262
All Night Long and Smile Please....410
All of Me....63, 456
All Over Me....426
All Quiet on the Western Front....217, 357
All's Well, End's Well....118
All Singing, All Dancing....676
All Star Cartoon Parade....676
All That Bach....586
All That Heaven Allows....342
All That Jazz....319
All the Best from Russia....568
All the Brothers Were Valiant....357
All the Colors of the Earth....628
All the Great Operas in Ten Minutes....577, 705
All the King's Men....357

All the Love in the World....426
All the Money in the World....628
All the Mornings in the World....2
All the President's Men....217
All the Rivers Run....205
All the Troubles in the World....628
All the Vermeers in New York....441
All These Women....77
All This and Heaven Too....357
All Through the Night....357
All Women Are Equal & Pentagon Peace March....456, 482
All-Round Reduced Personality....63
All-Star Gospel Show, The....606
All-Star Toast to the Improv....534
Alle Brider: The Flying Bulgar Klezmer Band....601
Allegra's Window— Sing Along with Allegra & Lindi....649
Allegro Non Troppo....705
Allen & Allen: Live in Florida....606
Allen Ginsberg....302
Allen Ginsberg Meets Nanao Sakaki....302
Allen T.D. Wiggin....606
Alles Gute!....154
Alley Cats, The....456, 503
Alley Tramp....503
Allied Fighting Machines of World War II....765
Alligator Hunting: A Louisiana Legacy....756
Alligator People, The....516
Allonsanfan....35
Alma's Rainbow....443
Almanac of Fall....101
Almonds and Raisins: A History of the Yiddish Cinema....111
Almos' a Man....300
Almost Partners....660
Along Came Jones....290
Along the Erie Canal....801
Along the Great Divide....290
Alphabet Library....668
Alphabet Murders....171
Alphabet Soup....649
Alphaville....9
Alraune (aka Unholy Love)....68
Altered States....167
Altering Discourse: The Works of Helen and Newton Harrison....544
Alternate Route....468
Alternative Medicine Natural Home Remedies....847
Alvarez Kelly....290
Alvin and the Chipmunks: Love Potion #9....628
Always....217, 258
Always for Pleasure....480
Always Ready: The U.S. Coast Guard Story....841
Amadeus....100
Amahl and the Night Visitors....577
Amanda Stories....863
Amar....146
Amarcord....36
Amateur....442
Amatzia: The Bar Kochba Caves....109
Amazing Adventure....181
Amazing Art of Beauford Delaney: From David Leming's Reading from his Biography of James Baldwin, The....302
Amazing Bone and Other Stories, The....628
Amazing Colossal Man, The....516
Amazing Coral Reef, The....801
Amazing Grace....107, 456
Amazing Grace with Bill Moyers....606
Amazing Howard Hughes....793
Amazing Mr. X (The Spiritualist), The....357
Amazing Panda Adventure, The....661
Amazing Stories: Book 1....414
Amazing Stories: Book 4....414
Amazing Things, Vol. 1....668
Amazing Things, Vol. 2....668
Amazing Transparent Man....516
Amazing World....456, 503
Amazon....79
Amazon Women on the Moon....262
Amazonia: Voices from the Rainforest....55
Ambassador Bill....357
Ambassador Magma Vol. 1: Episodes 1-3....720
Ambassador Magma Vol. 2: Episodes 4-5....720
Ambassador Magma Vol. 3: Episodes 6-7....720
Ambassador Magma Vol. 4: Episodes 8-9....720
Ambassador Magma Vol. 5: Episodes 10-11....720
Ambassador Magma Vol. 6: Episodes 12-13....720
Ambition Reduced to Ashes, An....144
Amelia Earhart....793
Amelia Earhart: The Price of Courage....793
America & Lewis Hine....468, 558
America....412
America America....357
America and the Holocaust: Deceit & Indifference....774
America at War....765
America Fever....756
America Goes to War....766
America Grows Up (1850-1900s)....808
America Held Hostage: The Iran Crisis....110
America in Black & White....468
America in Portrait....302
America in Space: The First 25 Years....838
America Over There: The United States in World War I: 1917-18....756
America's Castles....781
America's Castles II....781
America's Civil War....779
America's Deadliest Home Video....426
America's Defense Monitor: Bringing the Troops Home....801
America's Defense Monitor: National Security in the 90's....801
America's Defense Monitor: The Great Arms Debate....801
America's Defense Monitor: The Language of War....802
America's Defense Monitor: The UN's Blue Helmets....802
America's Dream....443
America's Favorite Commercials....539
America's Favorite Jokes....534
America's Funniest Animal Foul-Ups....414
America's Funniest Kid Foul-Ups....414
America's Funniest TV Foul-Ups....414
America's Great National Parks....828
America's Greatest Olympians....825
America's Music: Blues 1....608
America's Music: Blues 2....608
America's Music: Bulk Pack....616
America's Music: Country & Western 1....604
America's Music: Country & Western 2....604
America's Music: Folk 1....604
America's Music: Folk 2....604
America's Music: Gospel 1....606
America's Music: Gospel 2....606
America's Music: Jazz Then Dixieland 1....608
America's Music: Jazz Then Dixieland 2....608
America's Music: Rhythm and Blues 1....608
America's Music: Rhythm and Blues 2....608
America's Music: Soul 1....608
America's Music: Soul 2....608
America's Western National Parks....812
America Screams....825
America: The Way We Were: The Home Front 1940-1945....766
American Aristocracy....395
American Art at the Huntington....544
American Avant-Garde....482
American Avant-Garde Films....482
American Ballet Theater Now....568
American Blue Note....426
American Buffalo....217
American Challenge: In the Observer Singlehanded TransAtlantic Race....825
American Cinema....332
American Craft Council: Fiber-Coiled Basketry....562
American Craft Council: Masks and Face Coverings....562
American Craft Council: Papermaking USA and The Handmade Paper Book....562
American Craft: Clay, Functional Pottery....544
American Craft: Clayworks....544
American Craft: Contemporary Ceramics....544
American Craft: Contemporary Clay—Diverse Soup Tureen Forms....544
American Cultures for Children....860
American Dream....468
American Dream Contest, The....629
American Experience: Spy in the Sky, The....756
American Experience: The Wright Stuff, The....756, 841
American Fabulous....217
American Foundation Series....808
American Friend, The....67
American Friends....158
American Gigolo....217
American Graffiti....217
American Gunmaker: John Moses Browning....756
American Heart....426
American Heritage: The Civil War....863
American Heroes Series....808
American History Birth of a Nation Series....756
American History for Children....808
American History: A Bilingual Study....808
American History: The Civil War....779
American Impressionist: Richard Earl Thompson....544
American in Paris, An....319
American Lifestyle Series: Inventors....793
American Lifestyle Series: Military Leaders....793
American Lifestyle Series: U.S. Presidents....793
American Lifestyle Series: Writers....302
American Madness....350
American Matchmaker (Amerikaner Shadchen)....112
American Me....217
American Medical Association Family Medical Guide....863
American Messiah....503
American Orpheus....426
American Pluck....395
American Poetry: The Nineteenth Century....863
American Pop....618, 705
American President, The....217
American Retrospective Through Animation, An....705
American Revolution, The....756
American Sign Language Dictionary on CD-ROM, The....863
American Soldier, The....66
American Songster, An....604
American Story, An....217
American Taboo....426
American Tail, An....661
American Tail 2-Pack, An....661
American Tail: Fievel Goes West, An....661
American Theater Conversations: The Actors Studio....310
American Werewolf in Paris, An....217
American West: Land of Beautiful Places, The....812
American Woman: Portraits of Courage, The....756
American Women of Achievement Video Collection....756
Americanization of Emily, The....357
Americano, The....290
Americans Courageous (1600-1950s)....808
Americans on Everest....756
Americathon....262
Amida/A Mosaic for the Kali Yuga/Arches/Body Count/ Hey Joe....482
AMIGA Animation: Volume 2....705
Amiri Baraka....449
Amish Folk, The....781
Amish: Not to Be Modern....468
Amistad....258, 449
Amnesty Interactive....863
Amnesty International Report on Iran....110
Among the Wild Chimpanzees....812
Amongst Friends....217
Amor Bandido....53
Amore....38
Amorous Adventures of Moll Flanders, The....181
Amos 'n' Andy: Anatomy of a Controversy....449
Amos Fortune, Free Man....629
Amrapali....146
Amtrak's X2000 Demonstration....841
Anais Observed....300
Anand....146
Anansi and the Talking Melon....629
Anarchy U.S.A.....756
Anastasia....357, 676
Anastasia—Dead or Alive?....87
Anastasia Sing-Along....676
Anastasia: The Mystery of Anna....217
Anatahan....347
Anatomy of a Filmmaker....332
Anatomy of a Murder....357
Anatomy of a Psycho....503
Anatomy of a Riot....756
Anchors Away: The U.S. Navy Story....841
Anchors Aweigh....319
Ancient Alien....705
Ancient America: Indians of the Northwest....786
Ancient America: Indians of the Southwest....786
Ancient Egypt....784
Ancient Futures: Learning from Ladakh....149
Ancient Greece....784
Ancient Greece Volume 1....784
Ancient Greece Volume 2....784
Ancient Indian Cultures of Northern Arizona....786
Ancient Mysteries....784, 789, 861
Ancient Romans: An Urban Lifestyle, The....784
Ancient Romans: Builders of an Empire, The....784
Ancient Romans: People of Leisure, The....784
Ancient Rome....784
Ancient Sea Turtles: The Last Voyage?....812
Ancient Tales from a Promised Land....789
Ancient Warriors....784
And a Nightingale Sang....414
And Another Honky Tonk Girl Says She Will....426
And God Created Woman....2, 217
And God Spoke....262
And Hope to Die....210
And Justice for All....262
And Now for Something Completely Different....198
And Now Miguel....468
And the Band Played On....456
And the Children Shall Lead....660
And the Earth Did Not Swallow Him....55, 426
And Then There Were None....24
And This Is Free....468, 608
Andaz (A Matter of Style) (Beau Monde)....146
Anderson Platoon....2, 777
Andersonville....217
Andre....661
Andre Rieu, From Holland with Love....586
Andre Rieu: The Vienna I Love, Waltzes from My Heart....586
Andre Serban: Experimental Theater....310
Andre Serban: The Greek Trilogy....310
Andrea Chenier (Royal Opera)....577
Andrei Rublev....84
Andrei Voznesensky....87
Andrew Carnegie: The Original Man of Steel....794
Andrew J. Paterson: Controlled Environments....544
Andrew Lloyd Webber: The Premiere Collection Encore....319
Andrew Wyeth: The Helga Pictures....544
Androcles and the Lion....357
Android Invasion, The....199
Androids of Tara, The....199
Andromeda Strain....494
Andrzej Wajda, A Portrait....96
Andrzej Wajda Trilogy....96
Andy Rooney Television Collection, The....414
Andy Rooney: His Best Minutes, Vol. 1....414
Andy Rooney: His Best Minutes, Vol. 2....414
Andy Warhol....544
Andy Warhol: The Scope of His Art....544
Andy Williams Christmas Show, The....616
Andy Williams in Concert at Branson....616
Angel 2....118
Angel....345
Angel and the Badman....290
Angel at My Table, An....208
Angel Baby....158
Angel Chants....616
Angel City....217, 441
Angel City....217, 441
Angel Cop—The Collection....720
Angel Cop Vol. 1: Special Security Force....720
Angel Cop Vol. 2: The Disfigured City....720
Angel Cop Vol. 3: The Death Warrant....720
Angel Cop Vol. 4: Pain....720
Angel Cop Vol. 5: Wrath of the Empire....720
Angel Cop Vol. 6: Doomsday....720
Angel Dust....137
Angel for Satan, An....516
Angel Force....124
Angel Heart....217

Angel in a Taxi 40
Angel of Fury....124
Angel of Kickboxer 124
Angel on Fire 125
Angel on My Shoulder....262
Angel Rama 302
Angel's Mission....125
Angel Stories, Volume 1 847
Angel Stories, Volume 2 847
Angela's Airplane (plus The Fire Station)....649
Angele 26
Angelic Conversation, The....167
Angelic Gospel Singers....606
Angels and Insects....158
Angels in the Outfield....262, 357
Angels over Broadway....262
Angels with Dirty Faces 357
Angelyne 468
Angie....262
Anglo-Saxons, The....863
Angry Harvest 96
Angry Young Man 125
Anguish 217
Angus 262
Anima Mundi....468
Animal Alphabet....668
Animal Babies in the Wild 812
Animal Crackers....262
Animal House....262
Animal Kingdom, The....357
Animal Tales: "Lost Cubs" and "The Bully" 812
Animal Wonders from Down Under....812
Animaland 705
Animals Are Beautiful People 629
Animals Film....468
Animals in Danger....863
Animals of Africa: From the Sky to the Sea....812
Animals of Africa: Hippos, Baboons and the African Elephant ...812
Animals of Africa: The Land of the Elephants 812
Animals of the Bible....629
Animals-Life-Habitat-Ecosystem....863
Animalympics....676
Animaniacs Sing-Along: Mostly in Toon 676
Animaniacs Sing-Along: Yakko's World 676
Animaniacs Stew 676
Animaniacs: A Pinky & The Brain Christmas....677
Animaniacs: Helloooo, Holidays! 677
Animaniacs: Pinky & The Brain: World Domination Tour....677
Animaniacs: Spooky Stuff....677
Animaniacs: The Warners Escape....677
Animaniacs: You Will Buy This Video! 677
Animated Classics of Japanese Literature Collection 1 144
Animated Classics of Japanese Literature Collection 2 144
Animated Classics of Japanese Literature: A Ghost Story/ The Theater of Life....720
Animated Classics of Japanese Literature: A Roadside Stone, Pts 1 & 2....720
Animated Classics of Japanese Literature: Ansunaro Story/Story of Koyasu Dog....720
Animated Classics of Japanese Literature: Botchan, Parts 1 & 2 720
Animated Classics of Japanese Literature: Harp of Burma, Pts 1 & 2....720
Animated Classics of Japanese Literature: Incident in the Bedroom Suburb /Voice from Heaven....720
Animated Classics of Japanese Literature: Shanshiro The Judoist, Parts 1, 2 & 3....720
Animated Classics of Japanese Literature: Tale of Shunkin/Friendship 721
Animated Classics of Japanese Literature: The Izu Dancer/The Dancing Girl....720
Animated Classics of Japanese Literature: The Martyr/The Priest of Mt. Kouya 720
Animated Classics of Japanese Literature: The Season of the Sun/Student Days/The Grave of the Wild Chrysanthemum....720
Animated Classics of Japanese Literature: The Sound of Waves, Pts 1 & 2....721
Animated Classics of Japanese Literature: The Wind Rises/The Fruit of Olympus 721
Animated Classics of Japanese Literature: Walker in the Attic/Psychological Test/Red Room....721
Animated Classics of Japanese Literature: Wandering Days/Growing Up 721
Animated Commercials #1....705
Animated Commercials #2....705
Animated Commercials #3....705
Animated Commercials #4....705
Animated Commercials #5....705
Animated Commercials #6....705
Animation Celebration Vol. 1....705
Animation Celebration Vol. 2....705
Animation Celebration Vol. 3....705
Animation Celebration Vol. 4....706
Animation Dreams 706
Animation for Fallen Catholics....706
Animation Game, The....706
Animation Games 316
Animation in the '30s 706
Animation in the Classroom....860
Animation in The Netherlands 706
Animation Propaganda....706
Animation Vol. 1: The Beginning....706
Animation Vol. 2 706
Anita, Dances of Vice 63
Ann Vickers 357
Anna, Schmidt & Oskar 671
Anna 40
Anna Akhmatova File, The 80
Anna and the King of Siam....357
Anna Christie....357, 395
Anna Karenina....80, 171, 217, 300, 357, 568
Anna Livia, Dublin: A City of Splendor....202
Anna Marie's Blanket....629
Anna Russell Farewell Concert 595
Anna Russell: The Clown Princess of Comedy....534, 577
Anna Sokolow 568
Annabel Takes a Tour/Maid's Night Out 262
Annabelle's Wish 706
Annapolis 395
Annapolis Story, An....357
Anne Frank Remembered....468, 774
Anne of Avonlea 661
Anne of Green Gables 661, 690
Anne of the Thousand Days 171
Anne Rice: Birth of the Vampire....302
Anne Waldman 302
Annie....348
Annie Hall 288
Annie Leibovitz: Celebrity Photographer....558
Annie O 217
Anniversary, The 171
Annunciation, The 101
Another 48 Hours 217
Another Evening with Fred Astaire 319
Another Thin Man 262
Another Time Another Place 357
Another Trip with Ram Dass 847
Another Way....101
Another Woman 288
Another You 262
Antarctica....812
Antarnaad....146
Anthony Adverse 358
Anthony and Cleopatra (Dalton/Redgrave)....310
Anthony Burgess on D.H. Lawrence....302
Anthony Quinn: An Original....332
Anti-Credo 544
Antigone....310
Antigone: Rites of Passion....482, 566
Antique Farm Tractors....841
Antiques Roadshow Collectors Edition 560
Antonia and Jane 181
Antonia's Line....30
Antonin Dvorak: Symphony No. 9 "From the New World" 863
Antonio Carlos Jobim: An All Star Tribute 601
Antonio Gaudi 141, 565
Antony and Cleopatra (Royal Shakespeare Company/ Patrick Stewart)....310
Antony and Cleopatra....40, 153
Any Friend of Nicholas Nickleby Is a Friend of Mine 661
Any Number Can Play 358
Any Wednesday 217
Any Which Way You Can 217
Anything Boys Can Do 618
Anything for Jazz 608
Anything I Catch 469
Anyuta 568
Anzio 358
Apache 290
Apaches Last Battle (Old Shatterhand)....290
Aparajito....146
Apart from Hugh 456
Apartment, The....345
Apartment Zero....218
Ape, The....516
Ape Man: The Story of Human Evolution 812
Apeman....516
Apocalypse Now (Remastered)....259
Apogee: Life in Motion 469
Apollo 13....218
Apollo 13—The Untold Story 838
Apollo Legacy, The....839
Apostle, The....426
Appalachia: No Man's Land 469
Appaloosa, The 290
Apple Tree of Paradise....90
Appleseed 721
Appointment in Tokyo 766
Appointment with Death....218
Apprentice to the Gods: Ruben Nakian 544
Apprenticeship of Duddy Kravitz, The....210
Approaching Omega 426
April Fool 395
April in Paris....320
April Morning....218
Aquaman (DC Superpowers Collection)....706
Aquarium 90
Arabella 577
Arabesque 358
Arabian Nights 37, 358
Arata Isozaki: Architecture from 1960-1990 545
Arbuckle Volume 3 410
Arc Across the Atlantic 825
Arc of Infinity....199
Arc-en-Ciel....671
Arcadia of My Youth 721
Arch of Triumph 188, 358
Archaeology: Mysteries of the Holy Land....789
Archeological Yucatan: Mexico 55
Archer's Adventure....629
Archie....188
Archie Mayo Collection: Angel on My Shoulder and Svengali 358
Archie Shepp: I Am Jazz...It's My Life....608
Architect's Journal....565
Architecture of Doom, The 565, 766
Arctic Blue....218
Arctic Refuge: A Vanishing Wilderness....812
Are Parents People?....395
Are We Scaring Ourselves to Death? 798
Are You Afraid of the Dark? "Ghostly Tales" 629
Are You Being Served?....188
Are You My Mother?....629
Area 51: America's Most Secret Base 862
Area 88 Act I: The Blue Skies of Betrayal 721
Area 88 Act II: The Requirements of Wolves....721
Area 88 Act III: Burning Mirage 721
Arena, The....532
Aretha Franklin: Live at Park West 608
Argentina....55
Argentina's Jews: Days of Awe....113
Argentinisima I....49
Arhoolie Records' 25th Anniversary Party....609
Aria 158, 577
Ariel 79, 721
Ariel Ramirez: Misa Criolla 595
Ariel's Undersea Adventures: Whale of a Tale 690
Arising from Flames 149
Aristocats, The 690
Arizona....290
Arizona Dream 104
Ark in Space, The....199
Armageddon....721
Armageddon Factor, The....199
Arming Dictators....798
Armistead Maupin's Tales of the City 456
Armitage III, Part 1: Electro Blood....721
Armitage III, Part 2 721
Armitage III, Part 3: Heart Core 721
Armitage III, Part 4: Bit of Love....721
Armitage III Polymatrix: The Movie....721
Armored Command 358
Armored Trooper Votoms, Stage 1 721
Armored Trooper Votoms, Stage 2....721
Armored Trooper Votoms, Stage 3....722
Armored Trooper Votoms, Stage 4....722
Armour of God, The 133
Army of Darkness....516
Army-Navy Screen Magazine....766
Arno Werner, Master Bookbinder....560
Aroma Massage....861
Aroma of Enchantment, The 144, 482
Around Alone 825
Around Cape Horn....825
Around the World in 80 Days 218, 358
Around the World the Lesbian Way 456
Around the World with Fanny Hill 503
Arrangement, The....358
Arrival, The 494
Arrowhead 290
Arrowsmith....340
Arsenal 85
Arsenic and Old Lace 350
Art Ache— The Game of Art and How to Play It....560
Art Ache—Art Is Long, Life Is Short? 560
Art Ache—The Complete Set....560
Art Ache—The Image of an Artist 560
Art and Life of Georgia O'Keefe, The....545
Art and Music: Evolutions....863
Art and Recreation in Latin America 545
Art and Science of Human Transformation 847
Art and Splendor: Michelangelo and the Sistine Chapel 545
Art Blakey and the Jazz Messengers: The Jazz Life....609
Art City: Making It in Manhattan 545
Art Com Video 14: Rebel Girls....482
Art Com Video 1: Scandinavia 482
Art Com Video 2: Waveforms: Video Japan....482
Art Com Video 4: Peter Callas....482
Art Ensemble of Chicago: Live from the Jazz Showcase....609
Art for Teachers of Children....426
Art in Its Soul: Provincetown Art Colony 560
Art in the Holocaust....774
Art Lessons for Children 668
Art Meets Science 781
Art of Aikido, The....847
Art of Andrew Wyeth, The 545
Art of Buster Keaton—Box 1 408
Art of Buster Keaton—Box 2 408
Art of Buster Keaton—Box 3 408
Art of Central America and Panama, The 545
Art of Conducting, The....586
Art of Conducting: Legendary Conductors of a Golden Era, The....586
Art of Cruising Men, The 456
Art of Dining: The Business Lunch, The 857
Art of Dining: The Formal Dinner, The....857
Art of Erotic Photography, The 558
Art of Fighting....722
Art of Fingerstyle Guitar, The....604
Art of Folk Art....545
Art of Haiti 545
Art of Illusion—One Hundred Years of Hollywood Special Effects, The....332
Art of Indonesia: Tales from the Shadow World....545
Art of Loving, The....90
Art of Memory....482
Art of Nature: Reflections on the Grand Design, The 558
Art of Navajo Weaving 560, 786
Art of Radio Advertising, The....316
Art of Singing, The....577
Art of the 20th Century Ballet, The 568

Art of the American West 545
Art of the Dogon 545
Art of the Fantastic 545
Art of the Western World 545
Art on Film/Film on Art 545
Art Out Doors: Andre Emmerich's Sculpture Farm 545
Art Smart Videotape Series 562
Art Treasures of Spain 545
Arth 146
Arthur 262
Arthur 2: On the Rocks 262
Arthur Ashe: Citizen of the World 449
Arthur C. Clarke: World of Strange Powers 861
Arthur Murray Dance Lesson Series, The 568
Arthur's Eyes 629
Arthur's Pet Business 629
Artistry on Ice 825
Artists and Models 358
Artists Are Special People... Just Like You! 562
Artists Talk (Los Artistas Hablan), The 545
Artmic, Japan, 1988, 60 mins. 732
Arts of Islam 545
Artur Rubinstein 587
Artur Rubinstein: Piano Concerto #3 and Piano Concerto #1 587
Arvis Strickling Jones: From the Inside Out 606
As Beautiful as I Can Make Them: The Art of Ken Done 546
As Crosses Are Measure of Freedom 98
As Frozen Music 577
As Good As It Gets 262
As Is 456
As Nature Intended 503
As Tears Go By 118
As You Desire Me 358
As You Like It 310, 864
As Young As You Feel 358
Asana: Dance of the Yogis: Music by Sting and Jah Wobble 847
Ascent of Man/In the Absence of Heroes, The 482
Ascent of the Chimps 812
Ash Wednesday 218
Ashes and Diamonds 96
Ashes and Embers 443
Ashes of Time 118
Ashik Kerib 84
Ashkenaz: Eastern European Jewry 113, 601
Ashkenazy Observed 587
Ashpet: An American Cinderella 645
Asi Me Gusta 834
Asia Close-Up 145
Ask Any Girl 358
Asphalt Jungle, The 348
Assassin, The 125
Assassin of Youth 503
Assassinated: The Last Days of King and Kennedy 797
Assassination of Dr. Martin Luther King, Jr., The 449
Assassination of JFK (Dennis Mueller), The 797
Assault, The 30
Assault at West Point 218
Assault on a Queen 358
Assault on Precinct 13 218
Assignment, The 218
Assignment Outer Space 494
Assignment: Rescue 426
Associate, The 19
Asterix 671
Asterix in Britain 671, 706
Asterix vs. Caesar 671, 706
Astounding She-Monster, The 494
Astro Boy 30th Anniversary, Vol. 1 722
Astro Boy 30th Anniversary, Vol. 2 722
Astro Boy 30th Anniversary, Vol. 3 722
Astro Boy 30th Anniversary, Vol. 4 722
Astro Boy 30th Anniversary, Vol. 5 722
Astro Boy LD #1 722
Astro Boy LD #2 722
Astro Boy Volume 1 722
Astro Boy Volume 2 722
Astro Boy Volume 3 722
Astro Boy Volume 4 722
Astro Boy Volume 5 722
Astro Boy Volume 6 722
Astro Boy Volume 7 722
Astro Boy Volume 8 722
Astro Boy Volume 9 722
Astro Boy Volume 10 722
Astro Boy Volume 11 722
Astro Boy Volume 12 722
Astro Boy: The Lost Episode 722
Astronomers: Collector's Set, The 839
Astronomy 101: A Family Adventure 629
Aswad "Live" 601
Asylum 516
At Home in the Coral Reef 629
At Midnight I'll Take Your Soul 516
At Play in the Fields of The Lord 218
At the Bottom of the Hell (Dno piekta) 98
At the Circus 262
At the Haunted End of the Day... A Profile of Sir William Walton 587
At the Jazz Band Ball 609
At War with the Army 262
Atalanta Strategy 482
Atalia 107
Atchafalaya 802
Athena 320
Athena Awards 1996, The 456
Athens and the Greek Spirit 784
Athol Fugard: Blood Knot 151, 310
Atlanta Cyclorama—The Battle of Atlanta 779
Atlantic City 13
Atlantis, The Lost Continent 494
Atlas 513
Atom Age Vampire 516
Atom and Eve, The 503, 802
Atomic Brain (Monstrosity), The 503
Atomic Cafe, The 469
Atomic Filmmakers, The 469
Atomic Man, The 494
Atomic Memories 802
Atomic Stampede 756
Atomic Submarine 494
Atrocities of the Drug War: Ram Dass Speaks Out 781
Atrocities of the Orient 766
Attack 358
Attack from Mars 494
Attack in the Pacific 766
Attack of the Cohl Pumpkins 706
Attack of the Crab Monsters 513
Attack of the Giant Leeches 516
Attack of the Supermonsters 722
Attack: Battle of New Britain 808
Attic 218
Attic in the Blue 706
Attila (La Scala) 577
Attila 74 105
Au Revoir les Enfants (Goodbye, Children) 13
Auditioning for the Actor 316
Auditions 107
Audrey Hepburn 332
Audrey Hepburn Remembered 332
Audrey Rose 516
Audubon Society Videoguides to the Birds of North America 812
Audubon Zoo 828
Audubon: Greed and Wildlife: Poaching in America 812
Audubon: Sharks 813
Auf Wiedersehen Pet 188
August 181
Augustin 2
Aulad 146
Aunt from Chicago 104
Auntie Mame 358
Aurobora Press: The Monoprint Studio 546
Aurora 32
Austeria 90
Austin Powers: International Man of Mystery 262
Australia: Secrets of the Land Down Under 209
Australian Ark Documentary Series 813
Australian Opera Series, The 577
Australian Way of Life, The 209
Austria, The Land of Music 74
Author to Author Video Series 302
Autobiography of a Princess 258
Autobiography of Miss Jane Pittman 449
Autumn Afternoon, An 143
Autumn Leaves 358
Autumn Marathon 80
Autumn Moon 118
Autumn's Tale, An 118
Autumn Sonata 77
Avalanche 813
Avalanche Awareness 813
Avalanche Express 218
Avalon 218
Avant Garde & Experimental Film 482
Avant Garde Program #2 482
Avant Garde Program #11 482
Avant Garde Program #12 482
Avant Garde Program #14 483
Avant Garde Shorts/France 483
Avantage 671
Avanti! 345
Ave Maria 40, 577, 789
Ave Maria 40, 577, 789
Ave Maria 40, 577, 789
Avengers, The 188
Avenging Angel 218
Avenging Conscience 412
Awakening & Frontios, The 199
Awakening Your Body's Energies 847
Awakenings 218
Awakenings of the Beast 516
Awara 146
Award Winning French Shorts 2
Awful Dr. Orlof 516
Awful Truth, The 262
Awfully Big Adventure, An 158
Axis Fighting Machines of World War II 766
Ay, Carmela 45
Ayane's High Kick 722
Aymaras of Bolivia 55
Aztecs, The 55, 199

B

B.B. King Live at Nick's 609
B.B. King Live in Africa 609
B'raesheet 706
B-29 Frozen in Time 756
Baazigar 146
Baba—The Father 106
Babar et le Pere Noel 671
Babar le Film 671
Babar's First Step 629
Babar: Babar Returns 629
Babar: The Movie 706
Babe, The 218
Babe 662
Babe Hardy: Early Training 410
Babe Ruth 825
Babel II Part 1: The Awakening 722
Babel II Part 2: First Blood 722
Babel II Part 3: Crossroads 722
Babel II Part 4: Final Conflict 722
Babel II Perfect Collection 722
Babes in Arms 320
Babes in the Woods 395
Babes in Toyland 677
Babes on Broadway 320
Babette in "The Return of the Secret Society" 503
Babette's Feast 75
Baboona 469, 813
Baby, The Rain Must Fall 358
Baby Animal Fun 649
Baby Animals Just Want to Have Fun 649
Baby Boom 262
Baby Boomer Television 539
Baby Doll 358
Baby Face 358
Baby Face Harry Langdon 410
Baby Goes... Songs for the Season 649
Baby Goes... Songs to Take Along 649
Baby's Bedtime 650
Baby's Morningtime 650
Baby's Storytime 650
Baby Songs 649
Baby Songs Series 649
Baby Vision 649
Baby-Sitter's Club Videos 629
Babyfever 218
Bacall on Bogart 332
Bacchantes 310
Bach and Broccoli 662
Bach's Christmas Oratorio 595
Bach's Fight for Freedom 629
Bach: Goldberg Variations 587
Bach: Mass in B Minor 587
Bach: Violin Concerto No. 2 587
Bachdisc 483
Bachelor, The 218
Bachelor Apartment 262
Bachelor in Paradise 358
Bachelor Mother 262
Bachelor of Hearts 181
Back Door to Heaven 358
Back in the USSR 218
Back Street 358
Back Street Jane 503
Back to Arafat 110
Back to the Beach 503
Back to the Forest 706
Back to the Future 262
Back to the Future II 262
Back to the Wall 19
Back Trail, The 395
BackBeat 158
Backdraft 218
Background to Danger 358
Backstage at the Kirov 568
Backstairs 68
Backtrack 218
Bad and the Beautiful 358
Bad Behavior 181
Bad Boys 137, 218
Bad Company 218
Bad Day at Black Rock 358
Bad Girls Go to Hell 503
Bad Guys 101
Bad Lieutenant, The 426
Bad Lord Byron 358
Bad Luck 90
Bad Seed, The 358
Bad Sleep Well, The 142
Badge, The 426
Badlanders, The 290
Badlands 218
Badman's Territory 290
Bagdad 358
Bagdad Cafe 63
Bail Jumper 218
Baker's Hawk 662
Baker's Wife 26
Balalaika 320
Balance 90
Balance and Coordination for Seniors 847
Balanchine Celebration: Part One, The 568
Balanchine Celebration: Part Two, The 568
Balanchine Essays: Arabesque, The 568
Balanchine Essays: Passe and Attitude, The 568
Balanchine Essays: Port de Bras and Epaulement, The 568
Balanchine Library, The 568
Balanchine: Dancing for Mr. B: Six Balanchine Ballerinas 568
Balanchine: Prodigal Son/Chaconne 568
Balanchine: Robert Schumann's Davidsbundlertanze 568
Balanchine: The Four Temperaments, Andante from Divertimento No. 15, Tzigane 568
Balcony, The 310
Bali: The Mask of Rangda 145
Balkan Express 103
Ball of Fire 341
Ballad of a Soldier 80
Ballad of Cable Hogue, The 347

Ballad of Little Jo, The 290
Ballad of Narayama, The 141
Ballad of the Sad Cafe 219
Ballad to Scotland 169
Ballads of Madison County, The 300
Ballerina: Karen Kain 568
Ballerina: Lynn Seymour 568
Ballerinas 568
Ballet Class for Beginners 568
Ballet Class—Intermediate-Advanced 568
Ballet Folklorico Nacional de Mexico 568
Ballet for Children and Adults 568
Ballet Legends: The Kirov's Ninel Alexandrovna Kurgapkina 568
Ballet Ruse 568
Ballet Russe 569
Ballet Shoes 629
Ballet Workout 569
Ballet Workout II, The 569
Ballot Measure 9 ....456, 469
Ballroom Dancing for Beginners 569
Ballroom Dancing: Advanced 569
Ballroom Dancing: Intermediate 569
Ballyhoo Baby 426
Balthus 546
Baltic Deputy 80
Balto 677
Bambi 690
Bambi Meets Godzilla and Other Weird Cartoons 677
Banana Club 118
Bananas 288
Bananas in Pajamas 650
Band of Angels 359
Band of Outsiders 9
Band Wagon, The 320
Band: The Authorized Video Biography, The 618
Bandits 16
Bandits of Orgosolo 40
Bandolero! 290
Bang the Drum Slowly 219
Banjo Picking Styles 623
Banjo the Woodpile Cat 706
Bank Dick, The 262
Bank on the Stars 414
Banks' Florilegium: The Flowering of the Pacific 560
Banquet, The 118
Banshee, The 645
BAOH 722
Bar Girls 456
Barabbas 355
Baraka 469
Barbados, A Culture in Progress 828
Barbara Frietchie 395
Barbara Hendricks 595
Barbarella 2
Barbarian 395
Barbarians at the Gate 263
Barbary Coast 341
Barbra Streisand: A Happening in Central Park 616
Barbra Streisand: Putting It Together—The Making of the Broadway Album 616
Barcarole 68
Barcelona 47, 426
Barcelona: Archive of Courtesy 47
Bare Knees 395
Barefoot Contessa 359
Barefoot Gen 722
Barefoot in the Park 263
Barfly 15
Baritone 95
Barjo 16
Barkleys of Broadway 320
Barn Burning 300
Barnes and Barnes Zabagabee 619
Barney and the Backyard Gang 650
Barney—Good Day Good Night 650
Barney Kessel 1962-1991 609
Barney's Adventure Bus 650
Barney's Great Adventure—The Movie 662
Barney's Imagination Island 650
Barney's Safety Video 650
Barney's Sense-sational Day 650
Barnum 219, 310
Barocco 2
Baron Blood 516
Baron Munchausen 68
Baron of Arizona 341
Barretts of Wimpole Street, The 359
Barrocco 49
Barry Harris: Passing It On 609
Barry Lopez 55
Barry Lyndon 255
Barry's Scrapbook: A Window into Art 629
Bartered Bride and The Last Waltz, The 27, 577
Bartholomew and the Oobleck 629
Bartleby 158
Barton Fink 441
Baryshnikov at Wolf Trap 569
Baryshnikov Dances Carmen 569
Baryshnikov Dances Sinatra 569
Base of the Dead People 90
Baseball 825
Baseball Card Collector 826
Baseball in the News 826
Baseball in the News Series 826
Baseball's Greatest Hits 826, 864
Basement Tape 427
Bashu, The Little Stranger 106
Basic Art by Video I: Painting 562
Basic Art by Video II: Drawing & Design 562
Basic Art by Video III: Color 562
Basic Chinese by Video 154
Basic Costumer, The 316
Basic Field Production: Lighting 316
Basic Field Production: Sound Recording 316
Basic Grammar Series 859
Basic Guitar Set-Up and Repair 623
Basic Hebrew 1 & 2 154
Basic Instinct (Director's Cut) 219
Basic Instinct 219
Basic Radio Skills Series 316
Basic Shooting 316
Basil Hears a Noise 629
Basil in Blunderland 789
Basketball Diaries, The 219
Basquiat 427
Bastard Out of Carolina 427
Bastard: Part I of the Kent Family Chronicles, The 414
Bat (1926), The 395, 516
Bat (1959), The 516
Bat People, The 516
Bat Whispers, The 516
Bataan 359
Bathing Beauty 263
Batik as Fine Art 562
Batman & Mr. Freeze: Subzero 677
Batman & Robin 219
Batman (DC Superpowers Collection) 677
Batman 255, 503
Batman Forever 219
Batman Returns 255
Batman/Superman Movie, The 677
Batman: Mask of the Phantasm 677
Batmania: From Comics to Screen 541
Baton Rouge 44
Batouka: The First International Festival of Percussion 601
Batteries Not Included 263
Battle Arena Toshinden 722
Battle Can-Can 722
Battle Circus 359
Battle Cry 359
Battle for Korea: How the War Was Won 756
Battle for Music 587
Battle for Survival: The Arab-Israeli Six Day War 113
Battle for the Falklands 55
Battle for the Planet of the Apes 494
Battle for the Trees 802
Battle Hymn 342
Battle of Algiers 40
Battle of Antietam 779
Battle of Arnhem, The 766
Battle of Austerlitz 19
Battle of Britain 158
Battle of Culloden 168
Battle of London 766
Battle of Love's Return, The 503
Battle of Midway, The 766
Battle of San Pietro/Marines Have Landed 766
Battle of the Alamo 756
Battle of the Bombs 504
Battle of the Bulge, The 766
Battle of the Bulge 359
Battle of the Chairmanship, The 107
Battle of the Sexes 181
Battle of Washington/Monocacy/Bill Shore 757
Battle Royal High School 723
Battle Shock 359
Battle Skipper 1 723
Battle Skipper 2 723
Battle Skipper 3 723
Battlefield 199, 766
Battleground 359
Battles with Chief Pontiac 290
Battleship 841
Battleship Potemkin 86
Battling Bunyon 395
Battling Butler 408
Battling Fool 410
Battling Orioles 395
Bawdy Adventures of Tom Jones 158
Baxter 7
Bay Boy 210
BB30 118
BBC Children's Favorites 629
BBC Wildlife Special Volume 2 813
BBC Wildlife Specials: Aliens from Inner Space/ The Fastest Claw in the West 813
BBC Wildlife Specials: Birds of a Sun God/In-Flight Movie 813
BBC Wildlife Specials: On the Tracks of the Wild Otter/ The Mouse's Tale 813
Be Forever Yamato 723
Beach of the War Gods 125
Beachcomber 181
Beaches 219
Beadmaking 562
Beady Bear 650
Beale Street 609
Beanstalk 662
Bear, The 16, 629
Bear in the Big Blue House 629
Bear Tribe Storytelling 786
Bear Who Slept Through Christmas, The 650
Bearskin (Or the Man Who Didn't Wash for Seven Years) 645
Beast from 20,000 Fathoms, The 494
Beast from Haunted Cave 443
Beast of Babylon Against the Son of Hercules 395
Beast of Yucca Flats, The 494
Beast with Five Fingers, The 516
Beastly Behavior 181, 813
Beat Experience: The Red Hot Organization, The 864
Beat Generation Show, The 302
Beat Generation: An American Dream 302
Beat Girl 171
Beat Legends: Allen Ginsberg 302
Beat Legends: Gregory Corso 302
Beat the Devil 348
Beatles' First U.S. Visit, The 619
Beatles, The 619
Beatles Anthology, The 619
Beatles Collection 619
Beatles Story: Days of Beatlemania 1962-1970, The 619
Beatrice Wood: Mama of Dada 546
Beats: An Existential Comedy, The 302
Beau Brummel 171, 395
Beau Geste 359
Beau Pere 11
Beau Ravel 395
Beaumarchais 2
Beauties of the Night (Les Belles de Nuit) 24
Beautiful Blonde from Bashful Bend 346
Beautiful Girls 219
Beautiful Mystery 137, 456
Beautiful Stranger 90
Beautiful Swordswoman, The 125
Beautiful Thing 158
Beauty and the Beast 27, 414, 646
Beauty and the Beast: Above, Below and Beyond 414
Beauty and the Beast: The Enchanted Christmas 690
Beauty and the Devil (La Beaute du Diable) 24
Beauty Investigator 125
Beauty Queens, The 794
Beavis and Butt-Head Do America 695
Beavis and Butt-Head Do Christmas 695
Beavis and Butt-Head: Chicks 'n' Stuff 695
Beavis and Butt-Head: Feel Our Pain 695
Beavis and Butt-Head: Innocence Lost 695
Beavis and Butt-Head: Law-Abiding Citizens 695
Beavis and Butt-Head: The Final Judgement 695
Beavis and Butt-Head: There Goes the Neighborhood 695
Beavis and Butt-Head: Work Sucks! 695
Bebe's Kids 706
Because of That War 107, 775
Because You're Mine 320
Beckett 171
Beckett Directs Beckett Collection 310
Beckett Directs Beckett: Endgame 310
Beckett Directs Beckett: Krapp's Last Tape 310
Beckett Directs Beckett: Waiting for Godot 310
Becky Sharp 359
Becoming Colette 427
Becoming Orgasmic 847
Bed and Sofa 85
Bedford Incident, The 359
Bedknobs & Broomsticks 690
Bedroom Window, The 219
Bedtime for Bonzo 263
Bedtime Story 263
Beebtots 629
Beehive 483
Beer Commercials 539
Beer Hunter, The 757
Beethoven, Schumann, Brahms 587
Beethoven 263
Beethoven Concerti 587
Beethoven—Klassix 13 587
Beethoven Lives Upstairs 662, 864
Beethoven's 2nd 662
Beethoven's Nephew 514
Beethoven: Missa Solemnis (Karajan) 595
Beethoven: Piano Concerto No. 1 and No. 2 (Zimmermann) 587
Beethoven: Piano Concerto No. 3 and Brahms: Piano Concerto No. 1 (Rubinstein) 587
Beethoven: Piano Concerto No. 3 and No. 4 (Zimmermann) 587
Beethoven: Piano Concerto No. 4 and No. 5 (Arrau) 587
Beethoven: Piano Concerto No. 5, "The Emperor" (Zimmermann) 587
Beethoven: Piano Sonatas 30, No. 31 and No. 32 (Serkin) 587
Beethoven: Piano Sonatas No. 21 and No. 23 (Barenboim) 587
Beethoven: Symphony No. 1, No. 2, No. 6 "Pastoral" and No. 8 (Karajan) 587
Beethoven: Symphony No. 1 and No. 2 (Bernstein) 587
Beethoven: Symphony No. 2 and No. 3 (Karajan) 587
Beethoven: Symphony No. 3 ("Eroica") and No. 7 (Bernstein) 587
Beethoven: Symphony No. 4, Symphony No. 5, "Coriolan" Overture, "Egmont" Overture 587
Beethoven: Symphony No. 4 and No. 7 (Kleiber) 587
Beethoven: Symphony No. 4 and No. 8 (Bernstein) 587
Beethoven: Symphony No. 5 and No. 6 (Bernstein) 587
Beethoven: Symphony No. 5/Solti 587
Beethoven: Symphony No. 6 and No. 7 (Karajan) 587
Beethoven: Symphony No. 6 and No. 8 (Harnoncourt) 587
Beethoven: Symphony No. 9 (Bernstein) 587
Beethoven: Symphony No. 9 (Karajan) 587
Beethoven: Violin Concerto (Karajan) 587
Beethoven: Waldstein and Appassionata (Barenboim) 587
Beetlejuice 255
Beezbo 629
Before and After 15
Before Gorbachev— From Stalin to Brezhnev 87
Before Sunrise 427
Before the Incas 55
Before the Industrial Revolution 808

Before the Rain....158
Before the Revolution....35
Before You Visit a Museum....560
Beggar's Opera, The....577
Beggar Student....101
Beggars in Ermine....359
Beggars of Life....395
Beginning American Sign Language Video Course....859
Beginning Bluegrass Piano....624
Beginning Blues Piano....624
Beginning Electric Bass....624
Beginning of the End....359
Beginnings: You Won't Get AIDS....834
Begotten....427
Beguiled, The....219
Behave Yourself....359
Behind Kremlin Walls....87
Behind Office Doors....359
Behind the Flag....110
Behind the Front....395
Behind the Mask....202
Behind the Scenes....546
Behind the Scenes with King Kong in Special Effects....332
Behind the Veil: Nuns....469
Behind Two Guns....290, 395
Behold a Pale Horse....359
Being at Home with Claude....213
Being Human....219
Being on TV: The Crash Course....316
Being There....263
Being Two Isn't Easy....141
Bela Lugosi Collection: Devil Bat/Scared to Death, The....516
Bela Lugosi Meets a Brooklyn Gorilla....516
Bela Lugosi: The Forgotten King....332
Belafonte Presents "Fincho"....151
Belgrade Ancient and New....828
Belize....55
Bell, Book and Candle....263
Bell Diamond....441
Bell hooks on Video: Cultural Criticism & Transformation....449, 785
Bell Science Series: About Time....677
Bell Science Series: Gateway to the Mind....677
Bell Science Series: Hemo the Magnificent....677
Bell Science Series: Our Mr. Sun....677
Bell Science Series: The Alphabet Conspiracy....677
Bell Science Series: The Strange Case of the Cosmic Rays....677
Bell Science Series: The Thread of Life....677
Bell Science Series: Unchained Goddess....677
Bella Mafia....219
Bellboy, The....263
Belle Case La Follette: 1859-1931....757
Belle de Jour....46
Belle Epoque....44
Belle of Amherst, The....310
Belle of New York....320
Belle of New York/I Love Melvin....320
Belle of the Nineties....263
Belle of the Yukon....320
Belle Starr....32
Belles of St. Trinians....181
Bellhop/The Noon Whistle, The....395
Bellini: La Sonnambula....577
Bellissimo: Images of the Italian Cinema....32
Bellman and True....158
Bells, The....395, 516
Bells Are Ringing....320
Bells Go Down, The....171
Bells of Cockaigne & Broadway Trust, The....414
Bells of St. Mary's, The....320
Belly Pain....54
Belmondo Is the Swashbuckler....16
Beloved Enemy....359
Beloved Infidel....359
Beloved Rogue....395
Ben and Me....690
Ben and Me/Bongo....691
Ben Jonson: The Alchemist....310
Ben Nicholson: Razor Edge....546
Ben Turpin #1....410
Ben Webster: The Brute and the Beautiful....609
Ben-Hur (35th Anniversary Edition)....343
Ben-Hur....343, 395
Bend of the River....290
Beneath the 12-Mile Reef....359
Beneath the Ghost Moon....629
Beneath the Planet of the Apes....494
Beneath the Valley of the Ultravixens....513
Benefits of Long-Term Meditation....847
Beniamino Gigli in Mamma....577
Benjamin and the Miracle of Hanukkah....113
Benjamin Britten....469
Benjamin E. Mays: Mentor of Martin Luther King, Jr.....449
Benjamin Franklin....757
Benjamin O. Davis, Jr.: American....449
Benji....662
Benji's Very Own Christmas Story....662
Benji Takes a Dive at Marineland....662
Benji the Hunted....662
Benny & Joon....263
Benny Andrew's The Invisible Line....449, 546
Benny Carter: Symphony in Riffs....609
Benny Goodman Story, The....320
Benny Goodman: At the Tivoli....609
Benny Hill....189
Benny Hill's World: New York....189
Bent's Old Fort N.H.S. & Great Sand Dunes National Monument....828
Bent Tree....112
Berenstain Bears Videos....650
Bergonzi in Luisa Miller....577
Berkeley in the Sixties....469
Berks Filmmakers: A Compilation Tape....483
Berlin, Symphony of a Great City....68, 483
Berlin Blockade and Airlift....73
Berlin Conspiracy....219
Berlin: Journey of a City....73
Berlioz: Requiem (Bernstein)....595
Berlioz: Symphonie Fantastique, Op. 14....588
Berlitz Live! (Japanese)....864
Berlitz Live! (Spanish)....864
Bermuda Affair, The....359
Bermuda Triangle, The....90
Bernard and the Genie....630
Bernice Bobs Her Hair....300
Bernie Siegel, M.D.: How to Never Grow Old and Die Young at Heart....847
Bert Jansch Conundrum....604
Bert Rigby You're a Fool....320
Berthe Morisot: The Forgotten Impressionist....546
Bertolt Brecht Practice Pieces....73, 310
Best Boy....469
Best Christmas Pageant....630
Best Christmas Surprise Ever, The....650
Best Classic Commercials from the 50's and 60's, Vol. 1....540
Best Classic Commercials from the 50's and 60's, Vol. 2....540
Best Defense, Vol. 1, The....456
Best Evidence: Disguise and Deception in the Assassination of John F. Kennedy....797
Best Foot Forward....320
Best Friend of the Cops....125
Best Friends Part I....630
Best Friends Part II....630
Best Intentions, The....75
Best Little Whorehouse in Texas, The....320
Best Man, The....359
Best of 120 Minutes, The....619
Best of Andy Hardy....263
Best of Babar, Vol. 1....630
Best of Babar, Vol. 2....630
Best of Beakman's World, The....668
Best of Betty Boop....677
Best of Blank, The....480
Best of British Film Comedy, The....189
Best of Bruno Bozzetto, The....706
Best of Cracker Mysteries, The....189
Best of Eddie Murphy— Saturday Night Live....534
Best of Ernie Kovacs, The....414
Best of Everything, The....359
Best of George Pal....677
Best of Kunicka....98
Best of Liquid Television, The....695
Best of Minnie Pearl: Let Minnie Steal Your Joke, The....534
Best of New Wave Theatre, Vol. 1, The....619
Best of New Wave Theatre, Vol. 2, The....619
Best of Nightline....110, 151, 332, 449, 766, 798, 808, 834
Best of Nightline: Akio Morita....144
Best of Nightline: Assassination of Indira Gandhi....148
Best of Nightline: Chernobyl Nuclear Disaster....87
Best of Nightline: East Germany Opens Its Borders....73
Best of Nightline: Marcos & Aquino....146
Best of Nightline: Student Protest in China....135
Best of On the Road with Charles Kuralt....414
Best of Radio Thin Air....566
Best of Real Sex, The....469
Best of Red Green, The....414
Best of Roger Rabbit....691
Best of Sex Bytes, The....414, 845
Best of Shabba Ranks, The....601
Best of Spike Jones—Volume 1....415
Best of Spike Jones—Volume 2....415
Best of Spike Jones—Volume 3....415
Best of Taxicab Confessions, The....469
Best of the 90's Home Video, The....415
Best of the Badmen....359
Best of the Best....125
Best of the Fests, 5th Annual....706
Best of the Fests 1990....706
Best of the Fests: For Kids....706
Best of The Kids in the Hall, The....534
Best of the Lenny Henry Show, The....189
Best of the Lovejoy Mysteries, The....189
Best of the New York Underground, Year 2, The....483
Best of the New York Underground....427
Best of the Not Necessarily the News....534
Best of the Real West Complete Set, The....298
Best of the Simpsons, Vol. 1, The....695
Best of the Simpsons, Vol. 2, The....695
Best of the Simpsons, Vol. 3, The....695
Best of the Simpsons, Vol. 4, The....695
Best of the Simpsons, Vol. 5, The....695
Best of the Simpsons, Vol. 6, The....695
Best of the Simpsons, Vol. 7, The....695
Best of the Simpsons, Vol. 8, The....695
Best of the Simpsons, Vol. 9, The....695
Best of the Simpsons, Vols. 1-3, 3-Pack, The....695
Best of the Simpsons, Vols. 4-6 3-Pack, The....695
Best of the Simpsons, Vols. 7-9 3-Pack, The....695
Best of the Two Ronnies, The....189
Best of the Van Beuren Studio....677
Best of Times (1920-1924), The....757
Best of What's Left... Not Only...But Also..., The....189
Best of William Wegman....483
Best of ZOOM—The Early Years, The....630
Best Offer....630
Best Valentine in the World, The....630
Best Way, The....2, 456
Best Years of Our Lives, The....343
Bethie's Really Silly Clubhouse....650
Bethlehem....110
Betrayed....105
Betsy Ross....395
Bette Davis (A & E Biography)....332
Bette Davis Collection, The....359
Bette Davis: The Bumpy Road to Stardom....332
Bette Midler's Mondo Beyond....534
Better Tomorrow, A....125
Better Tomorrow—Part II, A....125
Better Tomorrow—Part III, A....125
Betty....12
Betty Boop & Friends....677
Betty Boop Classics in Color....677
Betty Boop Collection Vol. 1....677
Betty Boop Confidential....677
Betty Boop Definitive Collection Vol. 1: The Birth of Betty....678
Betty Boop Definitive Collection Vol. 2: Pre-Code & Jazzy Guest Stars....678
Betty Boop Definitive Collection Vol. 3: Surrealism & Prime Betty....678
Betty Boop Definitive Collection Vol. 4: Musical Madness & Fairy Tales....678
Betty Boop Definitive Collection Vol. 5: Curtain Call & Betty and Grampy....678
Betty Boop Definitive Collection Vol. 6: Betty's Boys & New Friends....678
Betty Boop Definitive Collection Vol. 7: Betty's Travels & Betty and Pudgy 1....678
Betty Boop Definitive Collection Vol. 8: Betty and Pudgy & Pudgy and Pals....678
Betty Boop Definitive Collection: Boxed Set....678
Betty Boop's Dizzy Dozen....678
Between Heaven and Earth....2
Between Heaven and Hell....359
Between the Cup and the Lip....90
Between the Wars, (1918-1941)....808
Between the Wars (1918-1939)....757
Betye and Alison Saar....449
Beulah Land....219
Beulah Show, Vol. 1, The....447
Beulah Show, Vol. 2, The....447
Beverly Hillbillies Go Hollywood, The....415
Beverly Hills Cop 2....263
Beverly Hills Cop....263
Beware....447
Beware My Lovely....359
Beware of a Holy Whore....66
Beware of Pity....171
Beware Spooks!....263
Beyond Belief....861
Beyond Bizarre....861
Beyond Blame: Challenging Violence in the Media....860
Beyond Goodwill....798
Beyond Innocence....205
Beyond JFK: The Question of Conspiracy....797
Beyond Life with Timothy Leary....504
Beyond Obsession....32
Beyond Rangoon....219
Beyond Roswell....864
Beyond T. Rex....835
Beyond the Call....219
Beyond the Doors....619
Beyond the Forest....359
Beyond the Killing Fields....469
Beyond the Looking Glass: Self-Esteem and Body Image....847
Beyond the Mind's Eye....706
Beyond the Ring of Fire....813
Beyond the Time Barrier....494
Beyond the Valley of the Dolls....513
Beyond the Wall: Stories Behind the Vietnam Wall....864
Beyond the Walls....107
Beyond Therapy....254
Beyond Tomorrow....359
Beyond Tradition: Contemporary Indian Art and Its Evolution....546
Bhaji on the Beach....181
Bharamchari....146
Bhowani Junction....349
Bhutan: A Himalayan Cultural Diary....149
Bible, The....348
Bible on Video: The Book of Genesis, The....789
Bible on Video: The Gospel of Luke, The....790
Bicycle Thief, The....37
Bicycle: A Celebration of the Invention....841
Big....263
Big Bad Mama....513
Big Bad Mama II....504
Big Bang, The....469
Big Ben: Ben Webster in Europe....609
Big Bend National Park, Texas....828
Big Bird Cage (Women's Penitentiary II), The....532
Big Bird Gets Lost....650
Big Black "Live"....619
Big Breakdowns....504
Big Broadcast of 1938, The....263
Big Bullet....125
Big Business Girl....359
Big Calibre....516
Big Chance, The....360
Big Chill....219
Big City Blues....443
Big Clock, The....360
Big Country....343
Big Deal....90

Big Deal on Madonna Street....40
Big Dig, The....828
Big Dis, The....427
Big Doll House, The....504
Big Fat Fabulous Bear, The....630
Big Fella....171
Big Friendly Giant, The....706
Big Girls Don't Cry....263
Big Green, The....691
Big Hand for the Little Lady....290
Big Hangover, The....360
Big Heat, The....71, 125
Big House, The....360
Big Jake....290
Big Jim....360
Big Jim McLain....360
Big Knife, The....360
Big Lebowski, The....441
Big Lift, The....360
Big Moment, The....113
Big Mouth....263
Big News....360
Big Night....427
Big O, The....847
Big Parade....395
Big Picture, The....263
Big Red....650
Big Red One, The....341
Big Rigs: Close Up and Very Personal....650
Big Sleep, The....341
Big Stampede, The....290
Big Store, The....263
Big Store/Abbott and Costello in Hollywood, The....263
Big Timers, The....447
Big Trouble....440
Big Wars....723
Big Wet, The....813
Big-Bang....90
Bigamist, The....360
Bigger Splash, A....546
Biggest and the Best....860
Biggest Bears, The....630, 813
Bilingual Americans....55
Bill and Coo....360
Bill Cosby: Aesop's Fables....646
Bill Dana Show, The....415
Bill Evans Trio, The....609
Bill Fields and Will Rogers....396
Bill Monroe: Father of Bluegrass Music....604
Bill of Divorcement, A....349
Bill of Rights in Action: Capital Punishment, The....798
Bill of Rights in Action: De Facto Segregation, The....799
Bill of Rights in Action: Due Process of Law, The....799
Bill of Rights in Action: Equal Opportunity, The....799
Bill of Rights in Action: Freedom of Religion, The....799
Bill of Rights in Action: Freedom of Speech, The....799
Bill of Rights in Action: Freedom of the Press, The....799
Bill of Rights in Action: Juvenile Law, The....799
Bill of Rights in Action: The Privilege Against Self-Incrimination, The....799
Bill of Rights in Action: The Right to Privacy, The....799
Bill of Rights in Action: The Story of a Trial, The....799
Bill of Rights in Action: Women's Rights, The....799
Bill T. Jones: Dancing to the Promised Land....569
Billie....263
Billy Budd....578
Billy Graham....790
Billy Liar....158
Billy the Kid Versus Dracula....517
Billy Two Hats....290
Bim, the Little Donkey and Dream of the Wild Horses....2, 19
Bimbos B.C.....494
Bing at Sennett Vol. 2....263
Bing Crosby....332
Bing—The Sennett Shorts....320
Bingo....662
Bingo Long Traveling All-Stars and Motor Kings....263
Binocular Vision....813
Bio Hunter....723
Bioenergy: A Healing Art....847
Biography....794
Birch Wood....96
Bird....256, 864
Bird of Paradise....360
Bird with the Crystal Plumage, The....40, 68
Birdcage, The....263
Birdman of Alcatraz....360
Birds, The....351
Birdy....219
Birgit Nilsson: The Bell Telephone Hour....595
Birmingham Royal Ballet in Tchaikovsky's The Nutcracker, The....569
Birth of a Nation, The....412
Birth of the Blues....320
Birth of the Lamaze Method....835
Birth of the Renaissance: Giotto to Masaccio....546
Birthday, The....90
Birthday Dragon, The....650
Bishop Jeff Banks/Revival Mass Choir....606
Bishop's Wife, The....264
Bit of Fry and Laurie, A....189
Bite the Bullet....360
Biting the Bullet....799
Bits and Bytes Set....845
Bitter Moon....97
Bitter Rice....40
Bitter Sugar....49
Bitter Sweet....171, 320
Bitter Taste of Blood....119
Bitter Tea of General Yen, The....350
Bitter Tears of Petra Von Kant, The....66
Bix....32, 609
Bizarre Bizarre....24
Bizarre Music Television....619
Bizarre Sports and Incredible Feats....504
Bizet Concert....595
Bizet's Carmen....578
Bizet's Dream....320, 630
Black & White....80
Black Achievers Video Series....449
Black Adder Goes Forth: The Western Front of WWII, 1917....189
Black Adder I, Part I, The....189
Black Adder I, Part II, The....189
Black Adder II: The 16th Century....189
Black Adder's Christmas Carol....189
Black Adder the Third, Part I....189
Black Adder the Third, Part II....189
Black Americans of Achievement, The....450
Black Americans of Achievement Collection #2....450
Black and White....219
Black and White as Day and Night....63
Black Angel....360
Black Anthology Vol. 1: Cannibals, Carusoes & Uncle Toms....706
Black Anthology Vol. 2: Little 'Ol Bosko....706
Black Anthology Vol. 3: Ones Mammy Toad Me Not To Watch....707
Black Arrow....360
Black Artists of the Silver Screen—Harlem Variety Review (Showtime at the Apollo)....360, 450
Black Artists of the Silver Screen—Harlem Variety Review (Showtime at the Apollo)....360, 450
Black Artists of the Silver Screen—Proud Valley....360, 450
Black Artists of the Silver Screen—Proud Valley....360, 450
Black Artists Short Subjects, Volume One....447
Black Artists Short Subjects, Volume Three....447
Black Artists Short Subjects, Volume Two....447
Black Beauty (1933)....662
Black Beauty (1971)....662
Black Beauty (1994)....662
Black Belt Jones....532
Black Book (Reign of Terror)....360
Black Brigade....450
Black Caesar....532
Black Candle & The Black Velvet Gown, The....189
Black Castle, The....517
Black Cat, The....517
Black Cat....517
Black Cauldron, The....691
Black Cobra....532
Black Dragons....360
Black Easter....619
Black Enforcers....532
Black Friday....517
Black Gestapo....532
Black Glove, The....456
Black God, White Devil....53
Black Godfather, The....532
Black Hearts Bleed Red....427
Black Jack: Clinical Chart 1....723
Black Jack: Clinical Chart 2....723
Black Jack: Clinical Chart 3....723
Black Jack: Clinical Chart 4....723
Black Jack: Clinical Chart 5....723
Black Jack: Clinical Chart 6....723
Black Jack: Six Pack....723
Black Jazz and Blues....609
Black Jesus....40
Black Like Me....360
Black Lion....723
Black Lizard....137, 457
Black Magic M-66....723
Black Mama, White Mama....532
Black Man's Land Trilogy, Vol. 1, White Man's Country....151
Black Man's Land Trilogy, Vol. 2, Mau Mau....151
Black Man's Land Trilogy, Vol. 3, Kenyatta....152
Black Military Experience, The....450
Black Moses of Soul....609
Black Narcissus....180
Black Orchid, The....360
Black Orpheus....53
Black Panthers: Huey Newton....450
Black Pirate, The....396
Black Power in America: Myth or Reality?....450
Black Profiles....450
Black Rain....141
Black Raven, The....517
Black River....49
Black Robe....210
Black Room....360
Black Roses....68, 171
Black Sabbath....517
Black Sheep Boy and Decodings....457
Black Shield of Falworth, The....360
Black Sister's Revenge....532
Black Stallion, The....662
Black Stallion Returns, The....662
Black Studies: Then and Now....450
Black Sunday....517
Black Swan, The....360
Black Tights....569
Black Tulip, The....87
Black Unicorn: Dudley Randall and the Broadside Press, The....300, 450
Black Vengeance....532
Black Wall, The....119
Black Warriors of the Seminole....450, 781
Black Widow (Cliffhanger Serials #5)....537
Black Widow....219
Black Windmill....158
Blackbeard the Pirate....360
Blackboard Jungle....360
Blackenstein....532
Blackmail....351
Blacks Britannica....469
Blacksmith and Balloonatic....408
Blacksnake!....513
Blackstone on Tour....534
Blacula....532
Blade, The....125
Blade of Kamui, The....723
Blade Runner....494
Blaise Pascal....38
Blakes 7....189
Blame Game: Are We a Country of Victims?, The....799
Blanche Fury....171
Blank Buffet, A....480
Blank Check....264
Blarney Pilgrim— Celtic Fingerstyle Guitar, Vol. 2, The....604
Blast 'Em....558
Blast-Off Girls....504
Blat....189
Blaxploitation Cartoons....707
Blazing Saddles....264
Bleak House....189
Bleak Moments....165
Bless the Beasts and Children....219
Blessed Event....264
Blessing....219
Bli Sodot—Without Secrets....109
Blind Chance....95
Blind Date....353
Blind Fury....219
Blind Husbands....348
Blind Justice....219
Blind Lead, The....427
Blind Spot....219
Blind Swordsman's Cane Sword, The....137
Blind Swordsman's Revenge, The....137
Blind Trust....213
Blind Woman's Curse....137
Blink....219
Bliss....205, 220
Blithe Spirit....180, 310
Blitzkrieg, The Lightning War....766
Blizzard's Wonderful Wooden Toys....562
Blob, The....517
Blocking a Scene: Basic Staging with Actors....316
Blonde Crazy....264
Blonde for a Night....396
Blonde Venus....347
Blondie....264
Blondie Has Trouble....264
Blondie Hits the Jackpot....264
Blondie in Society....264
Blondie Knows Best....264
Blondie's Blessed Event....264
Blood & Iron: The Story of the German War Machine....766
Blood & Wine....220
Blood....427
Blood Alley....360
Blood and Black Lace....517
Blood and Honey....790
Blood and Roses....19
Blood and Sand....396
Blood and Steel....396
Blood Beast Terror....517
Blood Feast....504
Blood Fiend (aka Theatre of Death)....517
Blood Hook....517
Blood in the Face....469
Blood Makes the Grass Grow: Conscientious Objectors and the Gulf War....799
Blood Money: Nazi Gold....775
Blood of a Poet....27
Blood of Dracula....517
Blood of Ghastly Terror....517
Blood of the Beasts....19
Blood of the Hunter....213
Blood on Satan's Claw, The....517
Blood on the Sun....360
Blood Orgy of the Leather Girls....504
Blood Reign: Curse of the Yoma....723
Blood Relative....12
Blood Shack (Director's Cut)....504
Blood Simple....441
Blood Wedding....45
Bloodhounds of Broadway....427
Bloodpact....133
Bloodsucking Pharaohs in Pittsburgh....504
Bloody Brood, The....504
Bloody Child, The....427
Bloody Exorcism of Coffin Joe, The....517
Bloody Friday....125
Bloody Hero....125
Bloody Korea: The Real Story....757
Bloody Pit of Horror, The....517
Bloopers: Vol. 2....415
Bloopy's Buddies: Body Knowledge....650
Bloopy's Buddies: Yummy in Your Tummy....650
Blossoms in the Dust....360
Blot....396
Blow-Up....35

Blowing the Whistle: How to Protect Yourself and Win 799
Blowing Wild 361
Blown Away 220
Blue 95, 167, 290
Blue and the Gray 779
Blue Angel (English), The 347
Blue Angel (German), The 347
Blue Angel 569
Blue Angels 841
Blue Angels: Around the World at the Speed of Sound 841
Blue Bird 361
Blue Carbuncle, The 185
Blue Chips 220
Blue Dahlia 361
Blue Hawaii 536
Blue Hotel 101
Blue Hour, The 63
Blue in the Face 427
Blue Jeans 2, 457
Blue Jeans 2, 457
Blue Kite, The 117
Blue Lamp, The 171
Blue Light 68
Blue Lightning 119
Blue Max 361
Blue Men, The 300
Blue Murder at St. Trinian's 181
Blue Planet 839
Blue Ribbon Stories Vol. 1 650
Blue Ribbon Stories Vol. 2 650
Blue River 220
Blue Seed, Collection 1 723
Blue Seed, Collection 2 723
Blue Seed, Vol. 1 723
Blue Seed, Vol. 10: Fate & Destiny 724
Blue Seed, Vol. 11: Sacrifice 724
Blue Seed, Vol. 12: Betrayal 724
Blue Seed, Vol. 13: Nightfall 724
Blue Seed, Vol. 2 723
Blue Seed, Vol. 3 723
Blue Seed, Vol. 4: The Kushinada Project 723
Blue Seed, Vol. 5: A Date with Danger 723
Blue Seed, Vol. 6: Impending Disaster 723
Blue Seed, Vol. 7: Rebirth 723
Blue Seed, Vol. 8: Sea Devils 723
Blue Seed, Vol. 9: When Gods Walk the Earth 724
Blue Skies 320
Blue Sky 220
Blue Sonnet Vol. 1 724
Blue Sonnet Vol. 2 724
Blue Steel 220, 290
Blue Thunder 220
Blue Velvet 257
Blue Water: Great Naval Traditions 757
Bluebeard's Eighth Wife 345
Bluebeard 361
Bluebeard Goes to the Moon 408
Bluebeard's Castle 578
Bluegrass Mandolin 624
Blueprint for a Million 75
Blueprint for Space 839
Blues Accordin' to Lightnin' Hopkins 480
Blues Brothers, The 264
Blues Busters 264
Blues Legends: Son House & Bukka White 609
Blues Like Shower of Rain 609
Blues Masters, Vol. 1 609
Blues Masters, Vol. 2 609
Blues Up the Country 609
Bluesland: A Portrait in American Music 609
Bluetoes the Christmas Elf 650
Blum Affair 68
Blunt: The Fourth Man 158
Blush 117
Bo-Ru the Ape Boy 813
Boardinghouse Blues 447
Boardwalk Club, The 427
Boast of Kings 596
Boat Is Full, The 30
Bob & Carol & Ted & Alice 361
Bob Branaman: Everybody's a Buddha 546
Bob Brozman 601
Bob Goldthwait: Is He Like That All the Time? 534
Bob Hope Remembers World War II 766
Bob Hope: America's Ambassador of Comedy 264
Bob James Live 609
Bob le Flambeur 25
Bob Marley Legend 601
Bob Marley Story: Caribbean Nights, The 601
Bob Roberts 427
Bob Vila's Guide to Historic Homes 565
Bob Wilber Big Band: Bufadora Blow-up, The 609
Bobby 146
Bobby Jones Gospel 606
Bobby's World: Me and Roger 678
Bobby Short at the Cafe Carlyle 609
Bobo, The 181
Bodies, Rest & Motion 427
Body and Soul 189, 220
Body and Soul: The Complete Workout 848
Body Atlas Boxed Set 835
Body Bags 517
Body Double 220
Body Fever 504
Body Heat 220
Body in the Library, The 189
Body Snatcher from Hell (Goke) 494
Body Snatchers 427
Body Without Soul 457
Bodyguard from Beijing 125
Boeing Boeing 264
Bogart Collection, The 361
Bohemian Girl, The 264
Boinng 504
Bold Caballero: A Zorro Adventure, The 361
Bolero/Pictures at an Exhibition 588
Bollo Caper, The 630
Bolshe Vita 101
Bolshoi at the Bolshoi 569
Bolshoi Ballet, The 569
Bolshoi Prokofiev Gala 569
Bolshoi Soloists 569
Bolshoi: Les Sylphides 569
Bolt of Lightning, A 415
Bomb for a Dictator 19
Bombardier 361
Bombardier: The Real Story 766
Bomber Biker Mecha Pack 724
Bombers 766
Bombers B-52 361
Bombing of America, The 835
Bombshell 361
Bon Voyage & Aventure Malgache 351
Bon Voyage 109
Bond 007 Gift Set Volume 1 168
Bond 007 Gift Set Volume 2 168
Bonfire of the Vanities 220
Bongo 691
Bonjour de Paris 28
Bonjour les Amis! 671
Bonjour Tristesse 361
Bonnie and Clyde 257
Bonnie Prince Charlie 171
Bonnie Scotland 264
Bonnie Scotland/Pick a Star 264
Boogie in Blue 609
Boogie Nights 427
Book of Shadows 569
Booker 450
Booker T. Washington's Tuskegee America 450
Booker T. Washington: The Life and the Legacy 450
Boom in the Moon 408
Boom Town 361
Boomerang 443
Boop Oop A Doop 678
Booty Call 264
Bopha! 443
Border, The 90, 220
Border, The 90, 220
Border Clash Volume 1 601
Border Clash Volume 2 601
Border Street 90
Borderline 361
Borders 427
Boris Frumin Three-Pack 80
Born Free 662
Born in America 290
Born in Flames 427
Born Invincible 125
Born of Fire 158
Born on the 4th of July 220
Born to Be Wild 220
Born to Dance 320
Born to Film 481
Born to Run 826
Born to Swing 609
Born to Win 220
Born Yesterday 349
Borneo 469
Borrower 494
Borrowers (1993), The 662
Borrowers (1998), The 662
Boscombe Valley Mystery, The 185
Bosko Cartoons Vol. 1 678
Bosko Cartoons Vol. 2 678
Bosko Cartoons Vol. 3 678
Bosom Buddies, Vol. 1 415
Bosom Buddies, Vol. 2 415
Bosom Buddies, Vol. 3 415
Bosom Buddies, Vol. 4 415
Bostonians, The 258
Bottle Rocket 427
bottom land 427
Bottom Line, The 799
Bottom Rock 90
Boudu Saved from Drowning 25
Boulez in Salzburg 588
Bound 427, 457
Bound by the Wind 802
Bound for Glory 220
Bound for Nowhere: The St. Louis Episode 775
Boundaries of the Soul: Explorations in Jungian Analysis 848
Bounty Dog 724
Bourbon Street 828
Bowery at Midnight 517
Bowery Boys, The 415
Bowery Buckaroos 264
Box of Laughter: The Dueling Pages 457
Box of Moonlight 428
Boxer, The 202
Boxer and Death 99
Boxing Helena 428
Boy and His Dog, A 495
Boy Did I Get a Wrong Number 264
Boy in the Plastic Bubble, The 220
Boy Meets Girl 264
Boy's Life 457
Boy Scout Advancement Program: First Class 668
Boy Scout Advancement Program: Second Class 668
Boy Scout Advancement Program: Tenderfoot 668
Boy Who Cried Wolf, The 630
Boy Who Loved Trolls, The 660
Boy! What a Girl! 447
Boyfriend 167
Boyfriends 457
Boys' Night Out 361
Boys' Reformatory 361
Boys' Shorts 457
Boys 220
Boys from Brooklyn 504
Boys in Love 457
Boys in the Band 457
Boys of St. Vincent, The 210
Boys of Summer, The 826
Boys on the Side 220
Boys Town 361
Boyz N The Hood 443
Bozo the Clown Vol. 1: Ding Dong Dandy Adventures 695
Bozo the Clown Vol. 2: Wowie Kazowie Clown Tales 695
Bozo the Clown Vol. 3: Just Keep Laughing 695
Bozo the Clown Vol. 4: Crazy Clown Capers 695
Brady Bunch, The 264
Brady Bunch, Vol. 1, The 415
Brady Bunch, Vol. 2, The 415
Brady Bunch, Vol. 3, The 415
Brady Bunch, Vol. 4, The 415
Brahms—Klassix 13 588
Brahms Quartets 588
Brahms Sextets 588
Brahms: German Requiem (Ein Deutches Requiem) 588
Brahms: Piano Concerto No. 1 and No. 2 (Bernstein) 588
Brahms: Symphony No. 1 (Ozawa) 588
Brahms: Symphony No. 1 and No. 2 (Karajan) 588
Brahms: Symphony No. 3 and No. 4 (Karajan) 588
Brain, The 16, 835
Brain Candy 264
Brain Eaters, The 495
Brain from Planet Arous 495
Brain of Morbius (Collector's Edition), The 199
Brain Sex 835
Brains by Revlon 483
Brainscan 517
Brainstorm 220
Bram Stoker's Dracula 259
Bramble Bush, The 361
Bramwell, Series 1 189
Bramwell, Series 3 189
Branching Out: Tracing Your Jewish Roots 113
Branchline Railway 841
Branded 291
Branded to Kill 137
Branford Marsalis: Steep 609
Brannigan 159
Brass 396
Brass Bottle, The 361
Brassed Off! 181
Bravados 291
Brave Frog, The 662, 707
Brave Little Toaster, The 691
Brave Little Toaster Goes to Mars, The 691
Brave New Age (1903-1912), The 757
Brave One, The 361
Brave Young Girls 125
Braveheart 220, 396
Brazil 168
Brazil: Heart of South America 55
Bread, Love, and Dreams 38
Bread 190
Bread and Chocolate 32
Break in the Circle 171
Break of Dawn 428
Breaker Morant 205
Breakfast at Tiffany's 353
Breakfast at Tiffany's: Collector's Edition 353
Breakfast Club, The 220
Breakheart Pass 291
Breaking Away 220
Breaking Glass 159
Breaking into Hollywood 332
Breaking the Code 310, 457
Breaking the Surface: The Greg Louganis Story 457
Breaking the Waves 75
Breakout 757
Breakthrough 171, 766
Breakthrough: A Portrait of Aristides Demetrios 546
Breast Men 220
Breasts: A Documentary 469
Breath of Scandal, A 361
Breathe on Me: Rev. James Cleveland 606
Breathing Lessons 220
Breathless 9
Breezy 256
Brenda Brave 630
Brendel on Beethoven 588
Brer Rabbit and the Wonderful Tar Baby 646, 864
Brett Butler: The Child Ain't Right 534
Bretts, The 190
Brewster McCloud 254
Brian Eno: Imaginary Landscapes 601
Brian Wilson: "I just wasn't made for these times" 619
Brice Marden 546

Bride Came C.O.D. 264
Bride Is Much Too Beautiful 19
Bride of Frankenstein 517
Bride of the Beast 813
Bride of the Gorilla 517
Bride of the Monster 514
Bride with White Hair, The 119
Bride with White Hair 2, The 119
Bride Wore Black, The 14
Bride Wore Red 361
Brides of Christ 190, 790
Brides of Dracula, The 517
Brideshead Revisited 190
Bridge (Die Brucke), The 63
Bridge at Remagen, The 361
Bridge on the River Kwai, The 180
Bridge to Terabithia 660
Bridge Too Far 159
Bridges at Toko-Ri, The 361
Bridges of Madison County, The 256
Bridging the Silence 588
Brief History of Time, A 481
Briefcases and Bomb Shelters 469
Brigadoon 320
Brigham Young 757
Bright Angel 221
Bright Eyes 320
Brighter Garden, A 300
Brighton Beach Memoirs 264
Brighton Rock 171
Brimstone and Treacle 159
Bring Me the Head of Alfredo Garcia 347
Bring Me the Head of Geraldo Rivera 504
Bringing Up Baby 341
Brink of Life 77
Bristlelip 646
Britannia Hospital 159
British & Australian Cartoons 707
British Animation Invasion, The 707
British Animation Vol. 2 707
British Intelligence 361
British Military Pageantry 169
British Rail Journeys 841
British Theater in the United States: Backstage with Richardson and Gielgud 310
British Way of Life, The 169
Broadcast News 264
Broadway Bill 350
Broadway Bound 264
Broadway Limited 361
Broadway Melody 320
Broadway Melody of 1936 320
Broadway Melody of 1938 320
Broadway Melody of 1940 320
Broadway Rhythm 320
Broadway Serenade 321
Broken Arrow 221, 291
Broken Blossoms 412
Broken Chain, The 221
Broken English 208
Broken Glass 159
Broken Harvest 202
Broken Hearts of Broadway 396
Broken Journey, The 146
Broken Jug, The 68
Broken Lance 291
Broken Mask 396
Broken Melody 171
Broken Noses 469
Broken Strings 448
Bronco Billy 256
Bronco Billy Anderson 396
Bronco: Death of an Outlaw 415
Bronco: Shadow of Jesse James 415
Bronx Cheers 428
Bronx Tale, A 221
Bronze Buckaroo 448
Bronze Venus, The 321
Brooke Medicine Eagle: Dancing Awake the Drum 786
Broth of a Boy 202
Brother Cadfael 190
Brother Cadfael II 190
Brother Cadfael III 190
Brother Can You Spare a Dime? 469
Brother Future 660
Brother John 221
Brother Minister 450
Brother of Sleep 63
Brother Orchid 361
Brother Rat 265
Brother's Keeper 469
Brother's Kiss 221
Brother Sun, Sister Moon 32, 457
Brother with Perfect Timing 601
Brothers in Trouble 148, 159
Brothers Karamazov 361
Brothers McMullen, The 428
Brothers Quay Vol. 1, The 707
Brothers Quay Vol. 2, The 707
Brothers Schellenberg, The 68
Brothers-in-Law 181
Brown of Harvard 396
Brownie McGhee: Born with the Blues 609
Browning Version, The 159, 172
Bruce Edelstein: The Vessel 546
Bruce Lee and the Green Hornet 125, 415
Bruce Lee Gift Set 125
Bruce Lee: The Immortal Dragon 125
Bruce Lee: The Lost Interview 125
Bruce Partington Plans, The 185
Bruckner: Symphony No. 8 588
Bruckner: Symphony No. 9 588
Bruckner: Symphony No. 9 in D Minor, Te Deum (Vienna) 588
Brum: The Big Adventures of a Little Car 650
Brumby: Horse Run Wild 813
Brunch/28 428
Bruno Bozzetto: Animator, Vol. 1 707
Bruno the Kid 707
Bruno Walter: The Maestro, The Man 588
Brute Force: The Definitive History of War Technology 808
Bryce, Zion & Grand Canyon's North Rim 828
Brylcreem Boys, The 159
Bryony Brind's Ballet—The First Steps 569
Bubbe Meises, Bubbe Stories 113
Bubblegum Crash 1: Illegal Army 724
Bubblegum Crash 2: Geo Climbers 724
Bubblegum Crash 3: Meltdown 724
Bubblegum Crash LD 724
Bubblegum Crisis Collector's Boxed Set: Vol. 1-8 724
Bubblegum Crisis Collector's Suite 724
Bubblegum Crisis LD #1 724
Bubblegum Crisis LD #2 724
Bubblegum Crisis LD #3 724
Bubblegum Crisis LD #4 724
Bubblegum Crisis Music Video: Hurricane Live 2032 724
Bubblegum Crisis Vol. 1 724
Bubblegum Crisis Vol. 2: Born to Kill 724
Bubblegum Crisis Vol. 3: Blow-Up 724
Bubblegum Crisis Vol. 4: Revenge Road 724
Bubblegum Crisis Vol. 5: Moonlight Rambler 724
Bubblegum Crisis Vol. 6: Red Eyes 724
Bubblegum Crisis Vol. 7: Double Vision 724
Bubblegum Crisis Vol. 8: Scoop Chase 724
Buccaneer, The 361
Buccaneer Soul 53
Buccaneers, The 190
Buck and the Preacher 443
Buck Privates 265
Buck Privates Come Home 265
Bucket of Blood 513
Buckminster Fuller: Grandfather of the Future 794
Buckminster Fuller: Thinking Out Loud 469, 565
Bucktown 532
Bud Abbott and Lou Costello Meet Jerry Seinfeld 265
Bud Abbott and Lou Costello Meet the Killer 265
Buddha of Suburbia, The 190
Buddhism and Black Belts 149
Buddy 221
Buddy Barnes 609
Buddy Buddy 345
Buddy Holly Story, The 221
Budo Sai: The Spirit of the Samurai 826
Buffalo Bill 291
Buffalo Bill and the Indians or Sitting Bull's History Lesson 254
Buffalo Soldiers, The 450
Buffalo Soldiers 221, 450
Buffet Froid 11
Bug City 835
Bugatti, The 841
Bugged 504
Bugis Street 144, 457
Bugles in the Afternoon 291
Bugs & Daffy's Carnival of the Animals 678
Bugs & Daffy: The Wartime Cartoons 678
Bugs Bunny Classics 678
Bugs Bunny Classics/Starring Bugs Bunny Laser 678
Bugs Bunny in King Arthur's Court 678
Bugs Bunny Mystery Special, The 678
Bugs Bunny on Parade 678
Bugs Bunny's Bustin' Out All Over 678
Bugs Bunny's Comedy Classics 678
Bugs Bunny's Creature Features 678
Bugs Bunny's Cupid Capers 679
Bugs Bunny's Easter Funnies 679
Bugs Bunny's Festival of Fun 679
Bugs Bunny's Greatest Hits 679
Bugs Bunny's Hare-Brained Hits 679
Bugs Bunny's Hare-Raising Tales 679
Bugs Bunny's Howl-Oween Special 679
Bugs Bunny's Looney Christmas Tales 679
Bugs Bunny's Lunar Tunes 679
Bugs Bunny's Mad World of Television 679
Bugs Bunny's Mother's Day Special 679
Bugs Bunny's Overtures to Disaster 679
Bugs Bunny's Thanksgiving Diet 679
Bugs Bunny's Wild World of Sports 679
Bugs Bunny's World of Animals 695
Bugs Bunny's Zaniest Toons 679
Bugs Bunny Superstar 678
Bugs Bunny/Roadrunner Movie 679
Bugs Bunny: 1001 Rabbit Tales 679
Bugs Bunny: All-American Hero 679
Bugs Bunny: Hare Beyond Compare 679
Bugs Bunny: Here Comes Bugs 679
Bugs Bunny: Hollywood Legend 679
Bugs Bunny: Truth or Hare 679
Bugs Bunny: Winner by a Hare 679
Bugs Don't Bug Us 630
Bugs vs. Daffy: Battle of the Music Video Stars 679
Bugs vs. Elmer 679
Bugs! 679
Bugs: The Very Best of Bugs 679
Bugsy 221
Bugsy Malone 321
Bugsy Siegel: Gambling on the Mob 794
Building a Character 310
Building Blocks of Life, The 835
Building Bombs 802
Building Peace in the Midst of War 55
Built by Hand String Trio 609
Built on the Rock: The Southern Appalachians 565, 829
Built on the Rock: The Southern Appalachians 565, 829
Bujones in Class 569
Bujones: In His Image 569
Buju on Top 601
Bukowski at Bellevue 302
Bulldog Drummond 361
Bulldog Drummond at Bay 172
Bulldog Drummond Series 361
Bullet for the General, A 40
Bullet in the Head 125
Bullet to Beijing 210
Bulletproof Heart 221
Bullets or Ballots 362
Bullets over Broadway 288
Bullfighter and the Lady 362
Bullfighters, The 265
Bullitt 362
Bullshot 181
Bumbledown/Sound of Maggie 415
Bumbledown: The Life and Times of Ronald Reagan 415
Bump—My First Video 650
Bundle of Joy 321
Bunker, The 221
Bunraku 310
Buona Sera, Mrs. Campbell 265
'Burbs, The 265
Burchfield at the Met 546
Burchfield's Vision 546
Burden of Dreams 480
Bureau of Missing Persons 362
Burger Town 781
Burglar, The 80
Buried Alive 517
Buried Mirror, The 55
Buried Treasures: Volume 2—Reggae Classics 619
Buried Treasures: Volume 3—Rap Source 619
Burlesque in Harlem 448
Burlesque of Carmen 407
Burmese Harp, The 141
Burn 'em Up Barnes 396, 537
Burn Up W! File 1: Skin Dive 725
Burn Up W! File 2 725
Burn Up W! File 3: Policetown Assault Part 1 725
Burn Up W! File 4: Policetown Assault Part 2 725
Burn Up! 725
Burn! 32
Burning Court, The 19
Burning Daylight 396
Burning Hills, The 291
Burning Man Festival 566
Burning Poles: Cecil Taylor in Performance 588
Burning Rivers 55
Burning Season, The 221
Burning Soil, The 73
Burnt by the Sun 80
Buron B. Blackbear and Beyond the Stars 630
Burroughs 302
Bush Mama 444
Bushbaby, The 159
Busher, The 396
Bushwacked 504
Business Affair, A 265
Business as Usual 159
Business of Hunger, The 802
Buster 159
Buster and Chauncey's Silent Night 630
Buster and Fatty 408
Buster and Me 802
Buster Keaton 408
Buster Keaton (1917-22) 408
Buster Keaton: A Hard Act to Follow 408
Buster Keaton: The Metaphysics of His Films 408
Buster Keaton Festival Volume 1 408
Buster Keaton Festival Volume 2 408
Buster Keaton Festival Volume 3 408
Buster Keaton Show, The 408
Buster Keaton Show: Fishing Story & The Collapsible Clerk, The 408
Buster Keaton Talkies, Vol. 1 408
Buster Keaton Talkies, Vol. 2 408
Buster Keaton Talkies, Vol. 3 408
Buster Keaton Talkies, Vol. 6 408
Buster Keaton Talkies, Vol. 7 408
Busy World of Richard Scarry: Mr. Frumble's New Car, The 651
Busy World of Richard Scarry: Summer Picnic, The 651
Busy World of Richard Scarry: The Best Babysitter Ever, The 651
Busy World of Richard Scarry: The Busiest Firefighters Ever, The 651
Busy World of Richard Scarry: The Snowstorm, The 651
But Not for Me 362
But... Seriously 534
But Where Is Daniel Wax? 107
Butch and Sundance: The Early Days 291
Butch Cassidy and the Sundance Kid 291
Butterfield 8 362
Butterflies 190
Butterflies Are Free 362
Butterflies of the World 864
Butterflies on the Scaffold (Mariposas en el Andamio) 457
Butterfly and Sword 119

Butterfly Kiss.....159
Butterfly Murders, The.....119
Butterfly Wings.....44
By Any Means Necessary.....451
By Love Possessed.....362
By the Blood of Others.....2
By the Light of the Halloween Moon.....630
By the Light of the Silvery Moon.....321
By Touch.....90
Bye Bye.....2
Bye Bye Birdie.....321
Bye Bye Brazil.....53
Byzantium: The Lost Empire.....829

C

C'est la Vie.....859
C-Man.....362
Caballe Subjugates La Scala.....578
Cabaret.....321
Cabaret Voltaire Presents.....566
Cabeza de Vaca.....49
Cabin in the Cotton, The.....362
Cabin in the Sky.....362
Cabinet of Dr. Caligari.....68
Cabiria.....40, 153
Cable Guy, The.....265
Cactus Flower.....265
Caddie Woodlawn.....630, 660
Caddy, The.....265
Cadillac Desert: Water and the Transformation of Nature.....469
Cadillac Ranch.....221
Cadillac Ranch/Media Burn.....483
Cadillacs and Dinosaurs: Rogue & Dino Drive.....679
Cadillacs and Dinosaurs: Wild Child & Pursuit.....679
Caesar and Cleopatra.....310
Caesar the Conquerer.....42
Caesarian Section.....90
Cafe au Lait.....16
Cafe Electric.....68
Cage/Cunningham.....616
Caged Heat.....255
Caged Women.....504
Cageman.....119
Cahill—U.S. Marshall.....291
Caine Mutiny, The.....362
Caine Mutiny Court-Martial.....254
Cairo.....321
Cajun Country.....601
Cajun Crossroads.....757
Cajun Visits.....601
Cal.....202
Calamity Jane.....321
Calcutta.....13
Calendar.....212
Calendar Girl.....321
California in '49.....396
California Rock.....619
California Straight Ahead.....396
California Suite.....265
Caligari's Cure.....428
Caligula.....32
Caligula: The Untold Story.....221
Call and Response.....55
Call for Peace: The Military Budget and You.....802
Call Girl 1988.....119
Call It Courage.....630
Call It Murder.....362
Call Me Bwana.....265
Call Me Rockefeller.....90
Call Northside 777.....362
Call of the Wild (1972).....221
Call of the Wild (1997).....221
Call of the Wild.....662
Call of the Wilderness, The.....396
Call Out the Marines.....362
Call Out the Marines/The Clay Pigeons.....362
Call to Greatness, A.....848
Callanetics.....848
Calm at Sunset.....221
Calvin & The Colonel Vol. 1.....707
Calvin & The Colonel Vol. 2.....707
Cambodian Royal Ballet.....569
Camel Boy.....662, 707
Camelot.....321, 757
Camera Buff (Amator).....95
Cameraman, The.....409
Cameraman's Revenge: The Amazing Puppet Animation of Ladislaw Starewicz, The.....707
Cameraman/Spite Marriage, The.....409
Cameramen at War.....332, 766
Cameramen Who Dared.....332
Camila.....49
Camilla.....221
Camille.....349, 396
Camille Claudel.....2
Camouflage.....90, 707
Camp of Hope and Despair: Westerbork Concentration Camp, 1939-45.....775
Campaign Against the Death Penalty.....799
Campus Nights.....396
Can I Be Good?.....630
Can't Help Singing.....321
Can't Stop the Music.....321, 457
Can-Can.....321
Canadian Bacon.....428
Canadian Brass Live.....601
Canadian Brass: Home Movies.....588
Canadian Reggae Music Awards.....601
Canal Street: Great Wide Way.....829
Canary of the Ocean: America's Troubled Reef.....802
Canary Season.....104
Cancel My Reservation.....265
Candidate.....221
Candide.....19
Candide in the Americas.....428
Candide Royalle's The Gift.....504
Candle for St. Jude, A.....415
Candles, Snow and Mistletoe.....630
Candy Mountain.....210
Candy Stripe Nurses.....504
Candyman.....517
Cane Toads: An Unnatural History.....205
Cannabis Rising.....469
Cannery Row.....221
Cannes Man.....428
Cannon and Nightingale.....105
Cannonball/Dizzy Heights.....410
Canterbury Tale, A.....180
Canterbury Tales, The.....37
Canterville Ghost, The.....181, 265, 630, 660
Canterville Ghost (Stewart), The.....265
Cantor's Son.....112
Canyon de Chelly & Hubell Trading Post.....829
Canyon Dreams.....813
Canyon of the Missing Men and Wolfheart's Revenge.....291
Canyon Passage.....291
Cap'n O.G. Readmore Meets Dr. Jekyll and Mr. Hyde.....630
Cape Cod: The Sands of Time.....829
Cape Fear.....253, 362
Capitaine Conan.....11
Capital Punishment.....396
Capitol to Capitol.....809
Capricorn.....725
Captain America.....221
Captain Blood.....362
Captain Boycott.....172
Captain from Castile.....362
Captain from Koepenick.....68
Captain Horatio Hornblower.....362
Captain January.....321
Captain Kidd.....362
Captain Newman, M.D......362
Captain of the Forest.....707
Captain Sinbad.....362
Captain Sirocco.....362
Captains Courageous.....221, 362
Captains of the Clouds.....362
Captive Heart.....172
Captive Wild Woman.....517
Captives.....221
Capture, The.....291
Car 54: Where Are You?.....415
Car Commercials.....540
Caravaggio.....167
Caravaggio and the Baroque.....546
Caravaggio Conspiracy.....546
Cardboard Box, The.....185
Cardinal, The.....355
Care Bears Adventure in Wonderland.....662
Care Bears Movie II: A New Generation.....662
Career.....362
Career Girls.....165
Career of Nikodem Dyzma.....90
Careful.....210
Caretaker's Daughter, The.....181
Caretakers, The.....363
Caribbean Carnival.....601
Caribbean Kids.....671
Caribbean Music and Dance.....601
Carl Gustav Jung: Artist of the Soul.....785
Carla Bley and Steve Swallow: Very, Very Simple.....609
Carlito's Way.....221
Carlitos, Dani y Luis Alfredo.....671
Carlos Fuentes (Lannan Literary Videos).....56
Carlos Fuentes.....56
Carlos Kleiber: Mozart Symphony No. 36 and Brahms Symphony No. 2.....588
Carlsbad Caverns & Guadalupe Mountains National Parks.....813
Carmen (Bolshoi).....578
Carmen (Covent Garden).....578
Carmen (DeMille).....354, 578
Carmen (Met).....578
Carmen.....566, 569
Carmen Jones.....448
Carmen McRae Live.....610
Carmen Miranda: Bananas Is My Business.....470
Carmina Burana (Cardiff).....596
Carmina Burana (Polygram).....596
Carnal Knowledge.....221
Carnegie Hall.....321
Carnegie Hall Salutes the Jazz Masters.....610
Carnival in Flanders.....19
Carnival of Animals.....630
Carnival of Monsters.....199
Carnival of Souls.....517
Carnival Rock.....513
Carnival Story.....363
Caro Diario (Dear Diary).....32
Carole Farley in "The Telephone" and "La Voix Humaine".....578
Carole King in Concert.....604
Caroline?.....221
Carols for Christmas.....596
Carols from Christchurch, Oxford.....596
Carolyn Forche (2/12/90).....302
Carolyn Forche (5/24/94).....302
Carolyn Oberst: Small and Large Works.....546
Carpenters—Yesterday Once More.....619
Carrie.....343, 517
Carried Away.....221
Carrier: Fortress at Sea.....841
Carrington.....159
Carrot Highway, The.....630
Carrotblanca.....679
Carry On Admiral.....181
Carry On Nurse.....181
Carry On Sergeant.....210
Cars That Ate Paris, The.....207
Carteri in "La Traviata".....578
Cartoon Classics in Color #1: Comicolor/Van Beuren.....679
Cartoon Classics in Color #2: Fleischer/Warners.....679
Cartoon Classics in Color #3: Wartime Warner Bros......679
Cartoon Classics in Color #4: Classic Warner Bros......680
Cartoon Classics Vol. 1: Looney Tunes & Merrie Melodies.....680
Cartoon Classics Vol. 2: Warner Brothers.....680
Cartoon Classics Vol. 3: The Early Pioneers.....680
Cartoon Classics Vol. 5: The Other Studios.....680
Cartoon Classics Vol. 6: Early Animation.....680
Cartoon Classics Vol. 7: Early Animation.....680
Cartoon Classics Vol. 8: Early Thirties.....680
Cartoon Classics Vol. 9: Early Pioneers.....680
Cartoon Collection Vol. 1: Porky in Wackyland.....680
Cartoon Collection Vol. 2: Classic Warner Bros......680
Cartoon Collection Vol. 3: Coal Black & De Sebben Dwarfs.....680
Cartoon Collection Vol. 4: Warner Bros. & Fleischer.....680
Cartoon Collection Vol. 5: Racial Cartoons.....680
Cartoon Collection Vol. 6: The Ducktators.....680
Cartoon Collection Vol. 7: Tokyo Jokio.....680
Cartoon Collection Vol. 8: Private Snafu.....680
Cartoon Crazys.....680
Cartoon Holidays.....680
Cartoon Jukebox.....864
Cartoon Madness: The Fantastic Max Fleischer Cartoons.....680
Cartoon Network `Toon Jam!.....864
Cartoonal Knowledge: Confessions of Farmer Gray.....680
Cartoonal Knowledge: Farmer Gray & The Mice.....680
Cartoonal Knowledge: Farmer Gray Goes to the Dogs.....680
Cartoonal Knowledge: Farmer Gray Looks at Life.....680
Cartoonal Knowledge: The Return of Farmer Gray.....680
Cartoongate!.....681
Cartoons Cel-ing Commercials Vol. 1.....707
Cartoons Cel-ing Commercials Vol. 2.....707
Cartoons for Big Kids.....681
Cartoons Go to War.....681
Cartoons That Time Forgot, Laserdisc Set Vol. 2.....707
Cartoons That Time Forgot Vol. 1: All Singing! All Dancing!.....681
Cartoons That Time Forgot Vol. 2: Down & Out with Flip the Frog.....681
Cartoons That Time Forgot Vol. 3: Things That Go Bump in the Night.....681
Cartoons That Time Forgot Vol. 4: Willie Whopper's Fantastic Adventures.....681
Cartoons That Time Forgot Vol. 5: Free-Form Fairytales.....681
Cartoons That Time Forgot Vol. 6: The Odd & The Outrageous.....681
Cartoons That Time Forgot Vol. 7: Rainbow Parades.....681
Cartopedia.....864
Cartouche.....16
Cary Grant (Boxed Set).....363
Cary Grant: A Celebration.....332
Cary Grant: The Leading Man.....332
Caryl Phillips.....54, 303
Casablanca (50th Anniversary).....363
Casablanca.....363
Casanova Brown.....265
Casanova's Big Night.....265
Case of the Mukkinese Battle Horn, The.....181
Case Study House Program 1945-1966: An Anecdotal History & Commentary.....546
Casey Kasem's Rock and Roll Goldmine: The British Invasion.....619
Cash (For Love or Money).....182
Cash McCall.....363
Casimir the Great.....90
Casino.....253
Casino Royale.....348
Casino Tycoon II (Part A).....125
Cask of Amontillado, The.....300
Caspar David Friederich: The Borders of Time.....546
Casper.....662
Casper Cartoons Vol. 1.....681
Casper Cartoons Vol. 2.....681
Casper Cartoons Vol. 3.....681
Casper Cartoons Vol. 4.....681
Casper Cartoons Vol. 5.....681
Casper Meets Wendy.....681
Casper's Animal Friends.....681
Casper's Brave Acts.....681
Casper's City Trips.....681
Casper's Fairy Tales.....681
Casper's Favorite Days.....681
Casper's Friend Wendy.....681
Casper's Furry Friends.....681
Casper's Ghost Buddies.....681
Casper's Good Deeds.....681
Casper's Halloween.....681
Casper's Magic Touch.....681
Casper's Outdoor Sports.....681
Casper's Outer Space.....681
Casper's Secret Powers.....681
Casper's Tall Tales.....681
Casper's Travels.....681

Cass Timberlane 363
Cassandra Cat (When the Cat Comes) 99
Casshan: Robot Hunter: Perfect Collection 725
Cast a Dark Shadow 172
Cast a Deadly Spell 518
Cast a Giant Shadow 363
Cast Commercials 540
Castaway 166
Castilian, The 363
Castle 864
Castle Ghosts of England 169
Castle Keep 363
Castle of Blood 518
Castle of Cagliostro, The 725
Castle of Evil 518
Castle of Fu Manchu 518
Castle of the Living Dead 518
Castles of Scotland 829
Castro, The 457
Castrovalva 199
Casual Relations 428
Casualties of War 221
Cat 864
Cat and the Canary, The 396, 518
Cat and the Fiddler, The 651
Cat Ballou 291
Cat Girl Nuku Nuku Vol. 1: Episodes 1 and 2 725
Cat Girl Nuku Nuku Vol. 2: Episodes 3 and 4 725
Cat Girl Nuku Nuku Vol. 3: Episodes 5 and 6 725
Cat on a Hot Tin Roof (1958) 310
Cat on a Hot Tin Roof (1984) 311
Cat People (1942) 518
Cat People (1982) 518
Cat's Eye 518
Cat's Meow: Kitty Kartoons by Paul Terry 681
Cat's Play 101
Cat Women of the Moon 495
Catch Me If You Can 651
Catch-22 265
Catered Affair 265
Caterpillar's Wish, A 630
Catherine Cookson Collection Set 1 190
Catherine Cookson Collection Set 2 190
Catherine Cookson Collection Set 3 190
Catherine Cookson: The Glass Virgin 190
Catherine the Great 172
Catherine Wheel, The 569
Catholics 355
Catlow 291
Catman in Lethal Track 125
Catman's Boxer's Blow 125
Cats Don't Dance 681
Catwalk 470
Caught 27, 222
Caught in the Act 190
Caught in the Draft 265
Caught Looking & North of Vortex 457
Cauldron of Blood 518
Cause for Alarm 363
Cavalcade 363
Cavalcade of MGM Shorts 332
Cavaliers & Craftsmen— Colonial Williamsburg and Jamestown 757
Cavalleria Rusticana (Verrett/1990) 578
Cavalleria Rusticana and I Pagliaci 578
Cavalry Charge 363
Cave Girls 483
Caves of Androzani, The 199
Cecil B. DeMille: The Greatest Showman on Earth 354
Cecilia Bartoli—A Portrait 596
Ceiling Zero 341
Celebrate for the Rain: Featuring the Music of Elizabeth Burch 604
Celebrating Bird: The Triumph of Charlie Parker 610
Celebration in Vienna, A 588
Celebration—Royal Ballet 569
Celebrity Commercials 540
Celebrity Propaganda 333
Celeste 63
Celestial Clockwork 49
Celine and Julie Go Boating 10
Cellular Automata 835
Celluloid Closet, The 333, 457
Celtic Feet 202, 569
Celtic Monasteries 202
Celts: Rich Traditions and Ancient Myths, The 202
Cement Garden, The 159
Cemetery Man (aka Of Death, Of Love) 32
Centerpiece for Peace 802
Centre Georges Pompidou 546
Century of Black Cinema, A 333, 451
Century of Russian Music, A 588
Century of Science-Fiction, A 333, 495
Century of the Cinema: Journey 333
Century of Women, A 757
Ceramics 562
Ceramics: Handbuilding 562
Ceramics: Introduction to Throwing on the Potter's Wheel 562
Cereal Commercial Tapes 540
Cereal Commercials 540
Certain Age, A 785
Cervantes 47
Cervantes and Friend 47
Cesar 26
Cesare Borgia 68
Cezanne: The Riddle of the Bathers 546
Chagall 546
Chain Letters 428
Chain Lightning 363
Chained for Life 504
Chained Girls 457
Chalice and the Blade, The 853
Chalk Garden 311
Chalk-Stream Trout 169
Challenge 172
Challenge to Lassie 662
Challengers, The 662
Chamber of Horrors (The Door with Seven Locks) 518
Chameleon 441
Chameleon Cameraman (Changing Roles) 766
Chameleon Street 444
Champ, The 363
Champagne 351
Champagne Safari, The 470
Champion 363
Champion Acrobats of China 826
Champion Always Loses 90
Chan Is Missing 455
Chancay, The Forgotten Art 546
Chance for Peace, A 110
Chances Are 265
Chanel, Chanel 28
Chanel Solitaire 2
Chang 396
Change of Heart, A 149
Change the Frame 457
Changeling, The 518
Changer: A Record of Times, The 604
Changing the Focus of Foreign Aid 799
Changing the Law 799
Changing Tides Along the Mediterranean 802
Chanter pour S'Amuser 671
Chantmania 616
Chantons Disney Ensemble 671
Chanuka at Bubbe's 113, 630
Chanuka at Bubbe's, A 630
Chanukah Adventure, A 114
Chaos: A Video Demonstration 845
Chapayev 85
Chaplin 407
Chaplin Revue 407
Chappaqua 567
Chapter in Her Life 396
Chapter Two 222
Charade 363
Charge of the Light Brigade, The 172, 363
Chariots of Fire 159
Chariots of Fur 682
Chariots of the Gods 862
Charlatan, The 396
Charlemagne 757
Charles & Diana: For Better or Worse 169
Charles Bukowski Tapes 15
Charles Dickens 303
Charles Drew: Determined to Succeed 451
Charles Gounod's Romeo et Juliette 578
Charles Haughey's Ireland 202
Charles Ives: Good Dissonance Like a Man 588
Charles Kuralt: American Heritage 415
Charles Kuralt: Seasons of America 415
Charles Kuralt: Unforgettable People 415
Charles Mingus: Triumph of the Underdog 610
Charles Reid: Flowers in Watercolor 562
Charles Rennie Mackintosh: A Modern Man 565
Charles Santore Illustrates The Wizard of Oz 546
Charles the Clown 630
Charles Weidman: On His Own 569
Charley Chase and Ben Turpin 410
Charley Chase Jimmy Jump Series 410
Charley Chase Vol. 1 410
Charley Chase Vol. 2 410
Charley's Aunt 396
Charlie Chan Collection 363
Charlie Chan: Meeting at Midnight 363
Charlie Chan: The Chinese Cat 363
Charlie Chan: The Jade Mask 363
Charlie Chan: The Scarlet Clue 363
Charlie Chan: The Secret Service 363
Charlie Chan: The Shanghai Cobra 363
Charlie Chaplin 407
Charlie Chaplin Early Years I 407
Charlie Chaplin Early Years II 407
Charlie Chaplin Early Years III 407
Charlie Chaplin Early Years IV 407
Charlie Chaplin's Keystone Comedies 407
Charlie's Angels 415
Charlotte Bronte's Jane Eyre 159
Charlotte Forten's Mission 451
Charlotte Forten's Mission Half Slave, Half Free Part 2 451
Charlotte's Web 662
Charm of La Boheme, The 578
Charm of London, The 169
Charmer, The 159
Charterhouse at Parma 19
Charuga 103
Charulata (The Lonely Wife) 146
Chase, The 257, 363
Chase the Devil 601
Chasers 222
Chasing Amy 428
Chasing Butterflies 2
Chasing Laughter 265
Chasing Shadows 775
Chasing Those Depression Blues 265
Chatelaine's Daughter 91
Chato's Land 291
Chatsworth 169
Chattahoochee 222
Cheap Detective, The 265
Cheat, The 354
Cheating Flea 91
Checking Out 182
Checkmate 569
Cheerful Fraud 396
Cheers for Miss Bishop 363
Cheese Stands Alone, The 707
Cheetah on Fire 125
Chef in Love, A 80
Chef! 190
Chekist, The 80
Chen Style T'ai-chi-Ch'uan 848
Cheniere au Tigre: Island of the Marsh 757
Chernobyl 87, 802
Chernobyl 87, 802
Cherries and Cherry Pits 630
Cherry, Harry and Raquel 513
Chess Fever/By the Law 85
Chess Kids 470
Chess Players (Shatranj Ke Khiladi), The 146
Chester Himes: The Long Climb 451
Chester Zardis: The Spirit of New Orleans 610
Chet Atkins & Friends 604
Chet Atkins 1955-1975 604
Chet Baker: Let's Get Lost 610
Cheyenne Social Club 291
Cheyenne: The Iron Trail 415
Cheyenne: White Warrior 415
Chez 'n' Ham 119
Chicago 1968 470
Chicago and Its Gangsters 757
Chicago Blues 610
Chicago Latino Cinema Collection: I 49
Chicago Latino Cinema Collection: II 49
Chicago Maternity Center Story 470
Chicago Nazis 470
Chicago Politics: A Theatre of Power 470
Chicago's Riverfront: Where the Present Meets the Past 565
Chicago Sings— Gospel's Greatest Hymns, Vol. 1 606
Chicago Television 415
Chicano! History of the Mexican American Civil Rights Movement 56
Chick Corea Keyboard Workshop 610
Chick Corea: Electric Workshop 610
Chicken Minute (Not Just for Kids) 672
Chicken Real 480
Chicken Sunday 630
Chico Hamilton: The Jazz Life 610
Chieftains in China, The 601
Chikamatsu Monogatari (Crucified Lovers) 143
Child Bride 504
Child Development: The First Two Years 857
Child in Two Worlds 775
Child Is Waiting, A 440
Child of Mine: The Lullaby Video 668
Child of Resistance and Hour Glass 444
Child's Christmas in Wales, A 662
Child's Garden of Verses, A 630
Child's Play Video Flash Cards— Spell Well 859
Child's Play Video Flash Cards—Math 838
Childhood Complete Set 848
Childhood in America 799
Childhood's End 428
Children Are Watching Us, The 38
Children Must Laugh 91, 114
Children of a Lesser God 222
Children of Nature 75
Children of Noisy Village, The 75, 662
Children of Paradise 24
Children of the Damned 172
Children of the Earth Series: Asia Close-up, Japan and Cambodia 145
Children of Theatre Street 569
Children's Chants and Games 668
Children's Hour, The 343
Children's Songbook: Music from Around the World 864
Children's Stories from Africa 152, 646
Chilean Indian Legends 546
Chiller: "Here Comes the Mirror Man" 190
Chiller: "Number Six" 190
Chiller: "Prophecy" 190
Chiller: "The Man Who Didn't Believe in Ghosts" 190
Chiller: "Toby" 190
Chillers 504
Chilly Scenes of Winter 265
Chimera 725
Chimes at Midnight/Falstaff 344
China, My Sorrow 117
China 363
China 9, Liberty 37 443
China and the Forbidden City 135
China Beach 416
China Gate 341
China Heat 126
China Moon 222
China O'Brien 2 126
China on the March 135
China Rising 135
China Seas 363
China Syndrome 222
China—The Cold Red War 135
China: A Century of Revolution 135

Chinatown 97
Chinese Brush Painting 546
Chinese Chi-Gung Health 848
Chinese Dragon Poses as a Hero, The 119
Chinese Ghost Story, A 119
Chinese Ghost Story Part II, A 119
Chinese Ghost Story Part III, A 119
Chinese Herbs for Health 848
Chinese Kickboxing 848
Chinese Kung-fu 848
Chinese People: A Time of Change, The 135
Chinese Roulette 66
Chinese Way of Life, The 135
Chingis Khan 630
Chip Lord: Selected Works 428
Chisum 291
Chitty Chitty Bang Bang 662
Chloe 504
Chloe in the Afternoon 13
Chloe/Love Is Calling You/Sun 396
Chocolat 7
Chocolate Soldier, The 321
Choice or Chance II 802
Choices for the Future 802
Choo Choo Trains: Close Up and Very Personal 630
Choose Me 257
Choosing One's Way: Resistance in Auschwitz/Birkenau 775
Choosing Sides: I Remember Vietnam 778
Chopi Music of Mozambique and Banguza Timbila 601
Choppers 841
Chord Sharp 707
Choreography by Balanchine: Selections from Jewels/ Stravinsky Violin Concerto 569
Choreography of the Hands: The Work of Dorothy Taubman 624
Chris Burden: A Video Portrait 546
Christ of Nanking 119
Christabel 191
Christian Boltanski 546, 775
Christian the Lion 813
Christians and Christianity in Jerusalem 110
Christine 518
Christine's Secret 504
Christmas at Ripon Cathedral 588
Christmas Carol, A 172, 321, 363, 682, 707
Christmas Carols from England 596
Christmas Carousel 630
Christmas Cartoon Classic 682
Christmas Coal Mine Miracle 222
Christmas Collection, The 631
Christmas Gift, A 707
Christmas Goes Baroque 588
Christmas in Connecticut 265
Christmas in July 346
Christmas in Spain 47
Christmas Lilies of the Field 222
Christmas Reunion 631
Christmas Sing-Along Video Album 651
Christmas Star 631
Christmas Stories 631
Christmas Story 662
Christmas Time in Vienna 596
Christmas Trains 841
Christmas Unwrapped 631
Christmas Video (Germany) 73
Christmas Wife 222
Christmas with Eleanor Steber 596
Christmas with Jose Carreras 596
Christmas with Luciano Pavarotti 596
Christo in Paris 470, 547
Christo's Valley Curtain 470, 547
Christopher Columbus 32, 172
Christopher Columbus: The Discovery 222
Christopher Tree 480
Christus, The 40, 153
Chroma Key Techniques 316
Chromosome XL 547
Chronicle of a Boy Alone 49
Chronicle of the 20th Century 864
Chronicle Travel Library, The 829
Chronicles of Narnia, The 660
Chronos 483
Chrysanne Stathacos: India 2063 547
Chuck Amuck: The Movie 682
Chuck Berry: Hail! Hail! Rock and Roll 619
Chuck Berry: Live at the Roxy 619
Chuck Berry: Rock and Roll Music 619
Chuck Close 547
Chuka 291
Chulas Fronteras 480
Chump at Oxford, A 265
Chungking Express 119
Church of Shooting Yourself, The 428
Churchill and the Cabinet War Rooms 169
Churchills, The 757, 794
Chushingura (The Loyal 47 Retainers) 137
CIA Contra Crack Connection—Parts I and II, The 799
CIA: America's Secret Warriors 799
CIA: The Secret Files 799
Ciao, Professore 32
Ciao Federico! 36
Cigarette Blues 480
Cigarette Commercials 540
Cigarette Girl of Mosselprom, The 85
Cimarron 291
Cincinnati Kid 363
Cinder Path, The 191
Cinder-Elly 646
Cinderella (1950) 691
Cinderella (1997) 691
Cinderella (Berlin) 578
Cinderella (Bolshoi) 570
Cinderella (Glyndebourne) 578
Cinderella (Lyon Opera Ballet) 570
Cinderella 321, 646
Cinderella 321, 646
Cinderella: A Dance Fantasy 570
Cinderfella 265
CineBLAST! Vol. 1 483
CineBLAST! Vol. 2 483
CineBLAST! Vol. 3 428
Cinema Europe: The Other Hollywood 333
Cinema of Senegal 150
Cinema of Transgression 483
Cinema Paradiso 32
Cinema Volta 864
Cipango 757
Circle in the Square: The First Twenty-Five Years, The 311
Circle of Danger 172
Circle of Deceit 518
Circle of Friends 266
Circle of Passion 159
Circus 80
Circus Kids 126
Circus of Fear 172
Circus of Horrors 518
Circus World 291
Circus/Day of Pleasure 407
Circus: 200 Years of Circus in America 631
Cirque du Soleil: We Reinvent the Circus 567
Ciske the Rat 30
Citadel 172
Citizen Barnes: An American Dream 547
Citizen Cohn 222
Citizen Diplomat 470
Citizen Kane (50th Anniversary Edition) 344
Citizen Kane 344
Citizen P. 91
Citizen Ruth 222
Citizen's Band 255
Citizen Soldiers: The U.S. Army Story 841
Citizen Tanya 428
Citizen X 222
Cittee Cittee Cittee: The Poetry of Herschel Silverman with the Music of Perry Robinson 303
City Boy 660
City Cops 126
City for Conquest 364
City Girl 73
City Hall 222
City Kids 126
City Lights 407
City Louvre (La Ville Louvre) 547
City Ninja 126
City of Death 199
City of Industry 222
City of Lost Children, The 2
City of the Dogs (La Ciudad de los Perros), The 49
City of Women 36
City on Fire 126
City out of Wilderness: Washington 809
City Slickers 266
City Squeeze 119
City That Never Sleeps 364
City Unplugged 86
City War 126
City Wildlife: Mice, Rats & Roaches 547
City Without Men 364
City/The Power and the Land, The 470
Cityscape Compilations 470
Civil War, The 779
Civil War (Ken Burns/PBS), The 779
Civil War (Parade Video), The 779
Civil War Diary 779
Civil War Journal, Set II 779
Civil War Journal 779
Civil War Journal: The 54th Massachusetts 451, 779
Civil War Journey 779
Civil War Legends 779
Civil War: 125th Anniversary Series, The 779
Civil War: The Fiery Trial 779
Civilians in War—Then and After: Poland and World War II 766
Civilization (He Who Returned) 396, 781
Civilized Defense Plan 802
Claes Oldenburg 547
Claire of the Moon 457
Claire's Knee 13
Clairvoyant, The 172
Clambake 536
Clancy Brothers and Tommy Makem Reunion Concert, The 202
Clara's Heart 222
Clarence 266
Clarence and Angel 444
Clarence Darrow 311
Clarence the Cross-Eyed Lion 662
Clarissa Explains Dating 631
Clarissa Explains It All: "Take My Brother, Please" 631
Clarissa Explains It All: Ferguson Explains It All 631
Clark Gable 333
Clark Gable Collection, The 364
Clark Sisters 606
Clash by Night 71
Clash of the Titans, The 159
Clash: Rude Boy, The 619
Class Act 191
Class of Nuke 'em High 504
Classic Animation Commercials from the 50's and 60's, Vol. 1 540
Classic Books on Video 300
Classic Car Commercials from the 50's and 60's, Vol. 1 540
Classic Cartoon Christmas Treasures 682
Classic Cereal Commercials from the '50s & '60s 707
Classic Chaplin 407
Classic Christmas Stories 646
Classic Cigarette Commercials from the 50's and 60's, Vol. 1 540
Classic Commercials 540
Classic Commercials Volume 1 540
Classic Commercials Volume 2 540
Classic Commercials Volume 3 540
Classic Documentaries: People and Places 470
Classic Documentaries: The Power and the Land 470
Classic Doll Commercials of the 50's and 60's 540
Classic Foreign Shorts—Volume 1 153
Classic Foreign Shorts—Volume 2 153
Classic Foreign Shorts—Volume 3: Un Chant d'Amour, Romance Sentimentale 19, 457
Classic Kirov Performances 570
Classic Literary Stories, Vol. 1 300
Classic Literary Stories, Vol. 2 300
Classic Literary Stories, Vol. 3 300
Classic Photoplays 396
Classic Schiller's Reel Collection, The 534
Classic Sci-Fi Trailers Vol. 1 495
Classic Shorts Compilation #12: Winsor McCay 682
Classic Shorts Compilation #14: Felix the Cat 682
Classic Stories for Children 651
Classic Stories in Spanish 672
Classic TV Train Commercials 540
Classic Views Video Magazine, Volume 2 ....578, 588
Classical Christmas 588
Classical Images—A Concert in Nature 588
Classical Music from Moscow 588
Classics in Clay 707
Classics of the Soviet Cinema 85
Classroom Collection, The 558
Classroom Holidays 631
Claudio Arrau—Volumes 1, 2, 3, 4 588
Claudio Monteverdi: L'Orfeo 578
Claw 396
Claws of Axos, The 199
Clay Farmers 458
Clay in a Special Way 562
Claymation Christmas Celebration, A 707
Claymation Comedy of Horrors, A 707
Claymation Easter, A 708
Clea Waite: Stella Maris 483
Clean, Shaven 428
Clean and Sober 222
Clean Needles Save Lives 834
Clean Slate 266
Clean Your Room, Harvey Moon! 651
Cleaning Up Toxics at Home 802
Cleaning Up Toxics in Business 802
Clear and Present Danger 222
Clear Day 504
Clearcut 210
Cleared for Takeoff 841
Clementine's Enchanted Journey 631
Clemintine Hunter 547
Cleo from 5 to 7 14
Cleopatra 354, 364, 757
Cleopatra Jones 532
Cleopatra Jones and the Casino of Gold 532
Clerks 428
Cleveland Orchestra: A Portrait of George Szell, The 588
Cleveland Quartet, The 588
Client, The 222
Cliffhanger 222
Cliffhangers: Adventures from the Thrill Factory 537
Clifford's Fun with Numbers 651
Clifford's Fun With... Series 651
Clifford's Sing-Along Adventure 651
Clifton Chenier: The King of Zydeco 601
Climax, The 518
Climbing High 182
Clint Eastwood Western Box Set 256
Clipped Wings 266
Cloak and Dagger 71
Clock, The 321
Clockers 446
Clockmaker, The 11
Clockwise 198
Clockwork Orange, A 256, 495
Clodhopper, The 396
Cloisters: The Grandeur of Medieval Art 547
Close Encounters of the Third Kind (Director's Cut) 258
Close Escape 126
Close to Eden 80
Close to Home: Moyers on Addiction 860
Closely Watched Trains 99
Closest Thing to Heaven, The 428
Closet Land 222
Clothed in Muscle: A Dance of the Body 483
Clothes Make the Man 68
Clouded Yellow, The 172
Clouds of Joy 607
Clouds of War (1916-1917) 757
Clouds over Europe 172
Cloudy with a Chance of Meatballs 631
Clown of God, The 631
Clowning Around 2 660
Clowns, The 36
Club des Femmes 19

Club Extinction 12
Clueless 266
Clutch Cargo Vol. 2 695
Clutching Hand, The 537
CNN 1994: The Year in Review 757
CNN Video: Arms Race on America's Streets 799
CNN Video: Work in Progress 799
Coal Miner's Daughter 321
Coast Patrol 396
Coastal Habitat Set 813
Cobb 222
Cobham Meets Bellson 610
Cobra 396
Cobra Live 601
Cobweb 364
Coca-Cola Kid 104
Cocaine Fiends 504
Cocaine...The Source and the Consequences 799
Cocktail 222
Cocoanuts, The 266
Cocoon 266
Code Name Ruby 101
Coffin Joe's Visions of Terror 518
Coffy 532
Col. Culpeper's Flying Circus 841
Cold Comfort Farm 266
Cold Days 101
Cold Dog Soup 266
Cold Eyes of Fear (Gli occhi freddi della paura) 518
Cold Feet 291
Cold Fever 75
Cold Journey 210
Cold Light of Day 159
Cold Sassy Tree 222
Cold Turkey 504
Cold War 757
Colditz Story, The 172
Colegas 44, 458
Colette: Of the Goncourt Academy 19
Colin Baker Years, The 199
Colin Campbell 483
Colin Powell: A General's General 794
Colin Powell: A Soldier's Campaign 451, 794
Colin Wilson: The High and the Low 848
Collage Methods 562
Collecting America: Folk Art and the Shelburne Museum 547
Collection of Chow Yun Fat, A 126
Collector 343
Collector's Item 32
College 409
College Swing 321
Colombian Way of Life, The 56
Colonel Bleep Vol. 1 695
Colonel Bleep Vol. 2 695
Colonel Chabert 2
Colonel Wolodyjowski 91
Colonial America (1500-1600) 809
Colonial Life for Children 631
Colonial Williamsburg 757
Color Adventures of Superman 682
Color of Love, The 444
Color of Money, The 253
Color of Night (Director's Cut) 222
Color of Pomegranates, The 84
Color Perceptions 562
Color Purple, The 258
Color: The Artist's Inspiration 562
Colorado Cowboy: The Bruce Ford Story 470
Colorado's Narrow Gauge Railroads 829
Colors 222
Colors of Hope 56
Colossus: The Forbin Project 495
Colt Called Lucky, A 631
Coltrane Legacy 610
Columbia Cartoon Classics Vol. 2: Mr. Magoo 682
Columbia Cartoon Classics Vol. 3: Gerald McBoing Boing 682
Columbia Cartoon Classics Vol. 4: Cartoon Classics 682
Columbia Cartoon Classics Vol. 5: Mr. Magoo 682
Columbia Cartoon Classics Vol. 6: Cartoon Classics 682
Columbia Cartoon Classics Vol. 7: Mr. Magoo 682
Columbia Cartoon Classics Vol. 8: Mr. Magoo 682
Columbia Cartoon Classics Vol. 9: UPA Classics 682
Columbia Cartoon Classics Vol. 10: Mr. Magoo 682
Columbia Cartoon Classics Vol. 11: Lil' Abner 682
Columbia Cartoon Classics Vol. 12: Mr. Magoo 682
Columbus 809
Columbus Didn't Discover Us 470
Columbus: Man and Myth 758
Comanche Territory 291
Comancheros 291
Combat America 766
Combat for the Stage 316
Combat for the Stage and Screen 316
Combination Platter 455
Come Along with Me 223
Come and Get It 341, 343
Come and See 80
Come Back, Little Sheba 364
Come See the Paradise 223
Come Sit by Me: AIDS Education 834
Come Sit by Me: AIDS Education and Thumbs Up for Kids: AIDS Education 834
Come to Saint Lucia 54
Come Up Smiling 397
Comeback 826
Comedienne, The 91
Comediennes, Volume 1, The 397
Comediennes, Volume 2, The 397
Comedy Classics of Mack Sennett and Hal Roach 410
Comedy of Chester Conklin 410
Comedy of Max Linder 397
Comedy of Terrors, The 518
Comedy's Dirtiest Dozen 534
Comedy Shorts #4 410
Comes a Horseman 291
Comet Butterfly and Sword 119
Comfort and Joy 182
Comfort of Strangers, The 223
Comic Book Confidential 541, 864
Comic Book Greats: Overkill, The 541
Comic Book Greats: Rob Liefeld, The 541
Comic Book Greats: Sergio Aragones, The 541
Comic Book Greats: Todd McFarlane, The 541
Coming Down from the Mountain: The Men's Movement 848
Coming Home 223
Coming of Age (1924-1928) 758
Coming of Amos 397
Coming Out Is a Many Splendored Thing 458
Coming Out Under Fire 455, 458
Coming Plague, The 835
Coming Through 159
Coming to America 266
COMM3TV Vol. 1 ....616, 619
Command Decision 364
Commando 91
Commando's Tale 169
Commandos Strike at Dawn 364
Comment Ca Va? (How Is It Going?) 9
Commercial Art: Design, Vol. 3 560
Commercial Art: General, Vol. 1 560
Commercial Art: Media, Vol. 2 560
Commercial Best—2 540
Commercial Best 540
Commercial Jingles 540
Commercial Mania 540
Commercials from Around the World 540
Commies Are Coming, Commies Are Coming! 505
Commissar 80
Commission 483
Commissioned in Concert 607
Commitments, The 321
Committed 428
Committed to Choice: Women of Faith Speak Out on Reproductive Freedom 799
Common Destiny:, A 470
Common Ground: The Battle for Barton Springs 802
Common Law Wife 505
Common Miracles: The New American Revolution in Learning 860
Common Table 802
Common-Law Cabin 513
Commune with the Dolphins 813
Communications Update 483
Communism Boxed Set 758
Companeros 291
Compassion in Action 848
Compassionate Use 835
Competition, The 223
Competition 100
Compleat Beatles 619
Complete Adventure Kid, The 725
Complete Black Adder, The 191
Complete Camera Clinic, The 317
Complete Churchill, The 794
Complete Iczer-One, The 733
Complete Maus, The 865
Complete Yellowstone 829
Compromising Positions 223
Compton's Encyclopedia of American History 865
Compulsion 364
Computer Animation Celebration 708
Computer Animation Classics 708
Computer Animation Festival 708
Computer Animation Festival Vol. 1.0 708
Computer Animation Festival Vol. 2.0 708
Computer Animation Magic 708
Computer Animation Showcase 708
Computer Dreams (Dream Machine Vol. 2) 708
Computer Visions (Dream Machine Vol. 3) 708
Computer Visions 708
Comrade X 364
Con Air 223
Conagher 291
Concert Aid 588
Concert for Bangladesh, The 619
Concert in Pantomime, A 416
Condemned to Live 518
Conductor, The 96
Conductor 397
Coneheads, The 708
Coney Island of Lawrence Ferlinghetti, The 303
Conference Faculty: Aging Conference Highlights, The 848
Confessing to Laura 49
Confession of an Assassin: The Murder of JFK 797
Confessions of a Psycho Cat 505
Confessions of a Vice Baron 505
Confessions of Felix Krull, The 68
Confidentially Yours 14
Conflict 364
Conformist, The 35
Congress Dances 68
Connect: A New Ecological Paradigm 802
Connecticut Yankee (Will Rogers), A 309
Connecticut Yankee in King Arthur's Court (Bing Crosby), A 309
Connecticut Yankee in King Arthur's Court (Westinghouse Studio One), A 309
Connecting—Grades K-8 563
Connection, The 311
Connections 3: Journey on the Web 835
Connections 781
Connections: The Journey Continues 781
Conquering Power 397
Conqueror 364
Conqueror Worm, The 518
Conquerors 758
Conquest 364, 839
Conquest of Everest 794
Conquest of the Planet of the Apes 495
Conrack 223
Conscious Living/Conscious Dying 848
Conseil de Famille 105
Consenting Adults 223
Conserving America: Champions of Wildlife 802
Conserving America: The Challenge on the Coast 802
Conserving America: The Rivers 802
Conserving America: The Wetlands 802
Consolation Marriage 364
Conspiracy Theory 223
Conspirator 172
Constantine and the Cross 364
Construction Ahead 631
Construction of Hoover Dam 758
Consul 91
Consumer Math 838
Consuming Hunger: Getting the Story 470
Consuming Hunger: Selling the Feeling 470
Consuming Hunger: Shaping the Image 470
Contact 495
Contact UFO: Alien Abductions 839
Contacto 154
Contemporary and Native American Readings 786
Contest Fiddling Championship Style 624
Continental Drift 835
Contour Drawing 563
Contraband Spain 172
Contract, The 119
Contract 91
Controlling Watercolor 563
Convent, The 48
Conversation, The 259
Conversation Piece 39
Conversation with Arthur C. Clarke About "2001: A Space Odyssey" 256, 333
Conversation with George Burns, A 416
Conversation with Magic, A 631
Conversation with Richard Wilbur 303, 451
Conversation with Ross Perot 799
Conversation with Roy Lichtenstein and The New German Art 547
Conversation with Thomas Moore, A 848
Conversations Entre les Jeunes au Sujet des Jeunes 672
Conversations with Playwrights: Arthur Miller and Israel Horovitz 311
Conviction, The 32
Convicts 223
Convoy 172
Cook, The Thief, His Wife and Her Lover, The 165
Cookie 266
Cookie Monster's Best Bites 651
Cool Hand Luke 364
Cool It—Phil Cool 191
Cool Runnings: The Reggae Movie 601
Cool World 708
Cooler Than Country— The Bluegrass Mountaineers 604
Cooler Than Country— The Lewis Family 604
Cooley High 444
Coonskin 708
Cop Image 126
Cop Land 223
Copacabana 266
Coppelia (Ballets de San Juan) 570
Coppelia (Lyon National Opera Ballet) 570
Copper Beeches, The 185
Copper Canyon 291
Copycat 223
Coquette 364
Coral Reefs: Rainforests of the Sea 802
Corduroy Bear 651
Corelli in Tosca 578
Coriolanus—Westinghouse Studio One 311
Corleone 32
Corletto and Son 631
Corn Is Green, The 350, 364
Cornbread, Earl and Me 223
Corner in Wheat and Selected Biograph Shorts, A 412
Coroner Creek 291
Corpse Fucking Art 505
Corpse Vanishes, The 518
Corridor of Mirrors 172
Corridors of Blood 518
Corrina, Corrina 223
Cosi 205
Cosi Fan Tutte (Chatelet Theater) 578
Cosi Fan Tutte (Glyndebourne) 578
Cosi Fan Tutte (La Scala) 578
Cosi Fan Tutte (Vienna) 578
Cosmic Joke, The 799
Cosmic Travelers Series 835
Cosmos 13: Who Speaks for Earth? 839
Cosmos 9: The Lives of the Stars 839
Cosmos Gift Pack B 839
Cosquin, City of Folklore 56

Cost of Caring, The 799
Costa Brava (Family Album) 44
Costa-Gavras Talks with Marcel Ophuls: Political Films 16, 105
Costakis the Collector 560
Cotton Comes to Harlem 444
Cotton Queen 182
Couch in New York, A 29
Cougar 631
Count and the Adventurer, The 407
Count Dracula 518
Count of Monte Cristo, The 19, 223
Count of the Old Town, The 75
Countdown (Visual Almanac Series, Vol. 1) 865
Countdown 254
Countdown to Alien Nation 862
Counterclockwise 428
Countess, The 104
Countess Cosel (Hrabina Cosel), The 91
Countess from Hong Kong, A 407
Countries of Intrigue: Egypt-Greece-Mediterranean 865
Country Diary of an Edwardian Lady, The 191
Country Girl, The 364
Country Joe McDonald at Provo Park: Earth Day Concert with Wild Mango and Others 604
Country Joe McDonald: Concerts at People's Park 604
Country Life 205
Country Stars: A New Tradition 601
Coup d'Etat 91
Coup de Torchon 11
Couple's Guide to Great Sex over 40, Volume 1, The 848
Couple's Guide to Great Sex over 40, Volume 2, The 848
Couples, Couples, Couples 119
Courage of Lassie 663
Courage of Sarah Noble 631
Courage to Care 775
Courageous Mr. Penn 172
Court Jester 266
Court-Martial of Billy Mitchell 364
Court-Martial of Jackie Robinson, The 451
Courting Courtney 266
Courtneys of Curzon Street, The 172
Courtship—An American Romance 223
Courtship of Eddie's Father, The 266
Cousin Bobby 255
Cousins 266
Cousteau 2—Bering Sea: Twilight of the Alaskan Hunter 813
Cousteau 2—Borneo II: Forests Without Land 813
Cousteau 2—Haiti: Waters of Sorrow 813
Cousteau 2—Riders of the Wind 814
Cousteau 2—Series Gift Pack 814
Cousteau 2—Thailand: Convicts of the Sea 814
Cousteau 2—Western Australia: Out West Down Under 814
Cousteau Odyssey, The 781, 814
Cousteau: Alaska: Outrage at Valdez 814
Cousteau: Amazon: Snowstorm in the Jungle and Rigging for the Amazon 814
Cousteau: Journey to a Thousand Rivers 814
Cousteau: Lilliput in Antarctica 814
Cousteau: Papua New Guinea: The Center of Fire 814
Cousteau: Pioneers of the Sea 814
Cousteau: River of the Future 814
Cousteau: Tahiti Fire Waters 814
Cousteau: The Great White Shark 814
Cousteau: The New Eldorado— Invaders and Exiles 814
Covenant: People of the Living Law 114
Cover Girl 321
Covered Wagon 397
Covert Bailey's Smart Exercise: Burning Fat, Getting Fit 848
Coverup: Behind the Iran-Contra Affair 470
Cow, The 99
Coward, The 99, 397
Cowboy and the Lady, The 364
Cowboy Art 547
Cowboys, The 291
Cowboys of the Saturday Matinee 333
Coyoteland 802
Cracker 191
Cracker: To Be a Somebody 416
Crackerjack, The 397
Cracking Up 266
Cracow and Its University 98
Cradle in the Sea 814
Cradle of Courage 397
Craft, The 518
Craft of Acting: Auditioning, The 333
Craig's Wife 364
Crainquebille 19
Cranberry Birthday 651
Cranberry Easter 651
Cranberry Holidays: Christmas 651
Cranberry Holidays: Halloween 651
Cranberry Holidays: Thanksgiving 651
Cranberry Holidays: The Complete Set 651
Cranberry Holidays: Valentine 651
Cranberry Mystery 651
Cranberry Summer 651
Cranes Are Flying, The 80
Crash 212
Crash Corrigan: One More Chance 708
Crash Dive 364
Crash of the Moons 495
Crashout 364
Crawfish 758
Crawling Eye 495
Crawling Hand 518
Crazies (Code Name Trixie), The 518
Crazy for Love 19
Crazy Horse 223
Crazy Ray 24
Creating Abstract Art 563
Creating Animation on a Computer 708
Creating Nonobjective Paintings 563
Creating the Decorative Cloth 563
Creating with Ceramics 563
Creating with Watercolor 563
Creation of Adam 80, 458
Creation of the Universe 839
Creation of the Woodstock 1969 Music Festival: Birth of a Generation, The 619
Creative Act: Paths to Realization, The 547
Creative Dance for Preschoolers 651
Creative Drama & Improvisation 311
Creative Drama and Improvisation 317
Creative Movement: A Step Towards Intelligence 668
Creative Parenting: The First Twelve Months 857
Creative Partnership: The Actor and Director, A 317
Creative Process: Norman McLaren 708
Creative Spirit Complete Set, The 845
Creative Video Techniques 317
Creature Comforts 708
Creature from Black Lake 518
Creature from the Black Lagoon 519
Creature from the Haunted Sea 443, 513
Creature of Destruction 519
Creature Walks Among Us, The 519
Creatures Great and Small 814
Crecor de Golpe (Growing Up) 49
Creeping Man, The 185
Creepshow 519
Creole Giselle (Dance Theatre of Harlem) 570
Crepuscolo 49
Cria 45
Cricket in Times Square, The 708
Cricket on the Hearth 397
Cries and Whispers 77
Crime and Punishment 19, 80, 347
Crime Inc. 758
Crime of Dr. Crespi 519
Crime of Monsieur Lange 25
Crime of Passion 364
Crime of the Century 223
Crime Story 134
Crimes and Misdemeanors 288
Crimes at the Dark House 519
Crimes of Dr. Mabuse 71
Crimes of Passion 167
Crimes of Stephen Hawke 172
Criminal Code 341
Criminal Life of Archibaldo de la Cruz, The 46
Crimson Ghost, The 537
Crimson Pirate, The 364
Crimson Romance, The 364
Crimson Tide 223
Crippled Masters, The 126
Crisis at Central High 223
Criss Cross 364
Criterion Goes to the Movies 865
Critical Art Ensemble 483
Critical Care 223
Critical Choices 223
Critical Condition 266
Critical Mass: America's Race to Build the Atomic Bomb 865
Critter Songs 631
Crizmac Master Pack 563
Cro 651
Crocodile Dundee 205
Crocodile Dundee II 205
Crocodile Hunter 126
Crocodile Territory 814
Crocodiles in Amsterdam 30, 458
Cromwell 223
Cronica del Alba 44
Cronkite Remembers 758
Cronos 49
Crooked Circle, The 266
Crooked Hearts 223
Crooked Man, The 185
Crooklyn 447
Crop Circle Update 862
Crosby, Stills and Nash: Acoustic 619
Cross and the Star, The 775
Cross Creek 223
Cross My Heart 17, 266
Crossbow, The 663
Crosscurrents and C-Man 416
Crossfire 107, 364
Crossing Delancey 266
Crossing Guard, The 223
Crossings 119
Crossline 119
Crossroad Avenger/Trick Shooting with Kenne Duncan 514
Crossroads of the Cold War 89
Crow, The 119, 224
Crow: City of Angels, The 224
Crowd, The 397
Crowded Paradise 364
Crowning of the Browning 601
Crows and Sparrows 117
Crucible, The 19, 311
Crucible CD-ROM, The 865
Crucible of Horror 519
Crucifer of Blood, The 186
Crucifixion/How Jesus Died: The Final 18 Hours, The 790
Crude Oasis 428
Cruel Kind, The 119
Cruel Sea, The 172
Cruel Story of Youth 141
Cruising 224
Cruising the Chesapeake Bay and Potomac River 829
Crusade in Europe 766
Crusade in the Pacific 766
Crusades, The 354
Crusades 758
Crush 208
Crusher Joe: The Movie 725
Crusher Joe: The OVA's 725
Cry, The Beloved Country 151, 172
Cry Baby 514
Cry Danger 364
Cry Freedom 150
Cry from the Streets, A 172
Cry in the Dark, A 205
Cry of the Banshee 519
Cry of the Forgotten Land 209
Cry Vengeance 365
Cry Wolf 365
Crying Freeman Vol. 1: Portrait of a Killer 725
Crying Freeman Vol. 2 725
Crying Freeman Vol. 3 725
Crying Freeman Vol. 4 725
Crying Freeman Vol. 5 725
Crying Game, The 202
Crypt of Horror 519
Crystal Hunt 126
Crystal Triangle 725
Crystal Vista 848
Cuando Viajan las Estrellas 49
Cuba 224
Cuba Amor 56
Cuba Crossing 224
Cubism and Non-Objective Art 547
Cuenca, Ecuador 547
Cuesta Abajo 49
Cult of the Cobra 519
Cult of the Dead 519
Cultivating Mindfulness 848
Cultural Philosophy of Paul Robeson, The 451
Culture of Aging 799
Cup Final 107
cup/saucer/two dancers/radio 442
Cupid's Bow 95
Cupid's Infirmary 483
Curator's Choice 560
Curdled 224
Cure, The 224
Cure—Staring at the Sea 619
Curious Adventures of Mr. Wonderbird (La Bergere et Le Ramoneur), The 672, 708
Curious George 631
Curious George Comes Home 865
Curious Journey: The Fight for Irish Freedom 202
Curly Top 663
Current Flow 834
Curry and Pepper 126
Curse of Fenric, The 199
Curse of King Tut's Tomb 519
Curse of Peladon 199
Curse of T. Rex 814
Curse of the Demon 519
Curse of the Pink Panther 354
Curse of the Queerwolf 458
Curse of the Starving Class 311
Curse of the Undead 519
Curse of the Werewolf 519
Curse of the Wraydons 505
Curse of the Yellow Snake 519
Curtis Mayfield: Live at Ronnie Scott's 610
Custer of the West 292
Custer's Last Trooper 298
Cut-Out Animation 708
Cutter's Way 224
Cutthroat Island 224
Cutting Edge, The 619
Cyber City Oedo 808: Data One 725
Cyber City Oedo 808: Data Three 725
Cyber City Oedo 808: Data Two 725
Cyber Ninja 725
Cybermen—The Early Years 199
Cybernetics Guardian 726
Cyberpunk 471
Cyberscape 483
Cyborg 009: Legend of the Super Galaxy 726
Cycling Experience, The 826
Cyclist, The 106
Cyclo 145
Cyclone Cavalier 397
Cyclone of the Saddle 537
Cynara 458
Cyprus Tigers, The 126
Cyrano de Bergerac (Ferrer) 311
Cyrano de Bergerac 2, 40
Czeslaw Milosz 98

D

D'Artagnan 397
d'Aulaire's Holiday Biographies: Complete Set 631
d'Aulaire's: Abraham Lincoln 631
d'Aulaire's: Benjamin Franklin 631
d'Aulaire's: Christopher Columbus 631

d'Aulaire's: George Washington....631
D.O.A. 224, 365
D.P. 300
D.W. Griffith's Years of Discovery....412
D.W. Griffith Triple Feature....412
D.W. Griffith: Biograph Years....412
D.W. Griffith: Feature Film Years....412
D-Base for D-Base III, An Introduction....845
D-Day, The Sixth of June....365
D-Day: The Great Crusade....767
Da....311
Da Projects....444
Da Vinci Body Series: Vol. 1, The....848
Dad....224
Dad's Army....191
Dad's Last Flight....428
Daddies....397
Daddy, Father, and Pa Pa....119
Daddy and the Muscle Academy: A Documentary on the Art, Life and Times of Tom of Finland....458
Daddy Can't Read....631
Daddy Long Legs....321
Daddy Nostalgie....11
Daddy-O....505
Daemons, The....199
Daens....29
Daffy Duck & Co.....682
Daffy Duck's Easter Egg-Citement....682
Daffy Duck's Madcap Mania....682
Daffy Duck's Movie: Fantastic Island....682
Daffy Duck's Quackbusters....682
Daffy Duck's Thanks-For-Giving Special....682
Daffy Duck: Duck Victory....682
Daffy Duck: Just Plain Daffy....682
Daffy Duck: Tales from the Duckside....682
Daffy! & Porky!....683
Daffy!....683
Dagger of Kamui, The....726
Dagora, the Space Monster....495
Daimler Benz Limousine, A....95
Daimyo....144
Dain Curse, The....224
Daisy and Her Garden: A Dance Fantasy....570
Daisy Miller....224
Dakota....292
Dakota Conflict, The....786
Dalek Invasion of Earth Parts 1 & 2, The....199
Daleks, The....199
Daleks Boxed Set, The....200
Daleks Invasion Earth 2150 AD....200
Daleks—The Early Years....200
Daley: The Last Boss....471
Dallos....726
Dam Busters, The....172
Damage....13
Damaged Lives....505
Dame Kiri Te Kanawa....596
Dames....321
Dames Ahoy....397
Damn the Defiant!....172
Damn Yankees....321
Damned, The....39
Damned in the USA....471
Damsel in Distress, A....342
Dan Crow's Oops!....631
Dan Willis and the Pentecostals of Chicago....607
Dance and Myth, The World of Jean Erdman Part 1: The Early Dances....570
Dance and Myth, The World of Jean Erdman Part 2: The Group Dances....570
Dance and Myth, The World of Jean Erdman Part 3: The Later Solos....570
Dance Basics Plus Curriculum....570
Dance Black America....570
Dance Fools Dance....365
Dance Hall Racket....429
Dance Little Lady....172
Dance of Death....519
Dance of the Wheel....563
Dance Theater of Harlem....570
Dance with Me, Henry....266
Dancehall Queen....54
Dancehall Vibes....601
Dancer, The....75, 471
Dancers....570
Dances with Wolves (Deluxe Collector's Set)....292
Dances with Wolves (Special Expanded Edition)....292
Dancetime! 500 Years of Social Dance....570
Dancing....570
Dancing Hands: Visual Arts of Rita Blitt....547
Dancing Lady....321
Dancing Men, The....186
Dancing Mothers....397
Dancing Outlaw....471
Dancing Pirate, The....321
Dancing with the Indians....631
Dancougar, Vol. 8: Episodes 36-40....726
Dancougar Vol. 1: Episodes 1-5....726
Dancougar Vol. 2: Episodes 6-10....726
Dancougar Vol. 3: Episodes 11-15....726
Dancougar Vol. 4: Episodes 16-20....726
Dancougar Vol. 5: Episodes 21-25....726
Dancougar Vol. 6: Episodes 26-30....726
Dancougar Vol. 7: Episodess 31-35....726
Dandy in Aspic....224
Dangaio....726
Dangaioh....726
Dangaioh: Hyper-Combat Unit....726
Dangard Ace....726
Danger at the Beach....802
Danger Mouse Vol. 1: Trouble with Ghosts....708
Danger Mouse Vol. 2: Public Enemy No. 1....708
Danger Mouse Vol. 3: Chicken Run....708
Danger Mouse Vol. 4: The Day of Suds....708
Danger Mouse Vol. 5: Lord of the Bungle....708
Danger: Diabolik....519
Dangerous....365
Dangerous Brothers: World of Danger, The....191
Dangerous Duty....126
Dangerous Game....429
Dangerous Hours....397
Dangerous Liaisons....166
Dangerous Man: Lawrence After Arabia, A....159
Dangerous Paradise....365
Dangerous When Wet....365
Dangerous Woman, A....224
Daniel....224
Daniel and the Towers....631
Daniel Boone....292
Daniel Boone Trail Blazer....292
Daniel Takes the Train....101
Daniella by Night....19
Danny and the Dinosaur and Other Stories....651
Danny Boy....365
Dante's Inferno....167
Danton (aka All for a Woman)....68
Danylo Shumuk: Life Sentence....87
Danzon....49
Daphnis and Chloe....570
Daredevils of the Red Circle....495
Daredevils: All Time Great Death-Defying Acts....826
Daria....696
Daria—Disenfranchised....696
Daring Game....365
Daring Young Man, The....266
Dark Adapted Eye, A....191
Dark Angel, The....365, 519
Dark Circle....471
Dark City....495
Dark Command....292
Dark Corner....365
Dark Eyes....80
Dark Habits....46
Dark Horse....224
Dark Journey....173
Dark Light of Dawn, The....56
Dark Lullabies....775
Dark Mirror, The....365
Dark Myth Part 1, The....726
Dark Myth Part 2, The....726
Dark Obsession....159
Dark Odyssey....505
Dark of the Sun....173
Dark Passage....365
Dark Past, The....365
Dark Secret of Harvest Home....224
Dark Shadows 1: The Resurrection of Barnabas Collins....416
Dark Shadows 2: Three-Pack....416
Dark Shadows: Behind the Scenes....416
Dark Shadows: Music Videos....416
Dark Shadows: Vampires & Ghosts....416
Dark Shadows, Volumes 5-8....416
Dark Shadows, Volumes 9-12....416
Dark Shadows, Volumes 13-16....416
Dark Shadows, Volumes 17-20....416
Dark Shadows, Volumes 25-28....416
Dark Shadows, Volumes 29-32....416
Dark Shadows, Volumes 45-48....416
Dark Shadows, Volumes 49-52....416
Dark Shadows, Volumes 53-56....416
Dark Shadows, Volumes 57-60....416
Dark Shadows, Volumes 61-64....416
Dark Shadows, Volumes 65-68....416
Dark Shadows, Volumes 69-72....416
Dark Shadows, Volumes 73-76....416
Dark Shadows, Volumes 81-84....416
Dark Shadows, Volumes 85-88....416
Dark Shadows, Volumes 89-92....416
Dark Shadows, Volumes 93-96....416
Dark Shadows, Volumes 97-100....416
Dark Shadows, Volumes 101-104....416
Dark Shadows, Volumes 105-108....416
Dark Shadows, Volumes 109-112....416
Dark Shadows, Volumes 117-120....416
Dark Shadows, Volumes 121-124....416
Dark Side of the Heart....49
Dark Star....495
Dark Victory....365
Dark Warrior 2: Jihad....726
Dark Warrior: First Strike....726
Darkest Africa....537
Darkest Hour (1939-1941), The....767
Darkside Blues....726
Darling....173
Darling Buds of May— Holiday Special Collection Set, The....191
Darling Buds of May—Collection Set 1: The The Darling Buds of May, The....191
Darling Buds of May—Collection Set 2: Oh! To Be in England, The....191
Darling Buds of May—Collection Set 3: The Happiest Days of Your Life, The....191
Darling Family, The....210
Das Boot: The Director's Cut....63
Das Konzert....588
Dash McTrash and the Pollution Solution....803
Date Rape Backlash, The....860
Date with Judy, A....321
Dateline: San Salvador....56
Daughter of Horror....519
Daughter of the Regiment (Sills), The....578
Daughter of the Regiment (Sutherland), The....578
Daughters of Darkness (Director's Cut)....519
Daughters of Eve....153
Daughters of the Dust....444
Dave....266
Dave Garroway's Wide Wide World....417
Dave Holland Quartet: Vortex....610
Dave Van Ronk....604
Davey & Goliath: Caring for Others....708
Davey & Goliath: Christmas Lost & Found....708
Davey & Goliath: Forgiveness....708
Davey & Goliath: Halloween WHO DID IT?....708
Davey & Goliath: Happy Easter....708
Davey & Goliath: Helping Others....709
Davey & Goliath: Lost & Found: The Movie....709
Davey & Goliath: New Year Promise....709
Davey & Goliath: School: Who Needs It?....709
Davey & Goliath: Summer Camp to the Rescue....709
Davey & Goliath: Thanksgiving Special....709
Davey & Goliath: Trusting....709
David, Moffet, Ornette....610
David & The Magic Pearl....709
David and Bathsheba....355
David and Goliath....42
David Bowie—The Glass Spider Tour....619
David Carradine's Kung Fu and Tai Chi Workouts....826
David Copperfield....153, 173, 350
David Halberstam's The Fifties....758
David Hockney at the Tate....547
David Hockney: Portrait of an Artist....547
David Holzman's Diary....471
David Macaulay Series, The....565
David Mamet: The Playwright as Director....311
David Manzur Paints a Picture....547
David Oistrakh in Performance....589
David Oistrakh: Remembering a Musician....589
David Raymond: Art Out West....547
David Skinner: Paintings on Metal....547
David the Gnome—Volume 1....631
David Vinas y Mempo Giardinelli....56
David: The Passing Show....547
DaVinci Body Series, Vol. 4: Stretch....848
Davy Crockett and the River Pirates....646
Dawn of Sound, The....321
Dawn of the Dead (Director's Cut)....519
Dawn of the Greek Gods....784
Dawn of the Jet Age: The First 25 Years....841
Dawn Patrol, The....365
Day After Trinity....471, 803
Day After Trinity: J. Robert Oppenheimer and the Atomic Bomb, The....865
Day at the Races, A....266
Day at the Zoo, A....651
Day Before Yesterday, The....203
Day Boy and the Night Girl, The....631
Day for Night....14
Day in the Country....25
Day in the Country: Impressionism and the French Landscape, A....547
Day in the Country: Impressionism and the French Landscape (Kirk Douglas), A....547
Day in the Death of Joe Egg....182
Day in the Life of Ireland, A....203
Day in Warsaw, A....114
Day Jimmy's Boa Ate the Wash, The....632
Day Lincoln Was Shot, The....224
Day of Freedom—Our Fighting Forces....68, 767
Day of the Daleks, The....200
Day of the Dead....56, 519
Day of the Jackal, The....159
Day of the Locust....224
Day of the Triffids....495
Day of Wrath....79
Day on the Grand Canal with the Emperor of China (or surface is illusion but so is depth), A....547
Day One....417
Day That Shook the World (Sarajevsky atentat)....103
Day the Earth Caught Fire, The....495
Day the Earth Froze....495
Day the Earth Stood Still, The....495
Day the Sky Exploded, The....68
Day the Sun Turned Cold, The....117
Day Will Dawn, The....173
Day with Horses, A....651
Day with Lions and Other Cats, A....651
Day with Monkeys, A....651
Day with Whales, A....651
Day You Love Me, The....49
Daybreak (Le Jour Se Leve)....24
Daydreamer (Le Distrait), The....17
Daydreamer....709
Days and Nights in the Forest....146
Days of Being Dumb....119
Days of Being Wild....119
Days of Heaven....224
Days of Our Years, The....19
Days of Pentecost....458
Days of Wine and Roses....311, 354
Daytime's Greatest Weddings: All My Children....417

Daytime's Greatest Weddings: General Hospital....417
Daytime's Most Wanted....417
Daytrippers, The....266
Dazed and Confused....429
Dazzle....709
De Mayerling a Sarajevo....27
De Overval (Resistance)....30
Dead, The....348
Dead Again....224
Dead Alive....208
Dead and the Deadly, The....126
Dead Calm....205
Dead Can Dance: Toward the Within....619
Dead End....343
Dead Eyes of London....519
Dead Heart....205
Dead Heat on a Merry-Go-Round....267
Dead Is Dead....519
Dead Lucky....173
Dead Man....442
Dead Man and The Color of Love, The....483
Dead Man Walking....224
Dead Men Don't Wear Plaid....267
Dead Men Walk....519
Dead Next Door, The....519
Dead of Night....173
Dead of Winter....257
Dead Pigeon on Beethoven Street....341
Dead Poets Society....207
Dead Pool, The....224
Dead Presidents....224
Dead Reckoning....365
Dead Ringer....365
Dead Ringers....212
Dead Tired (Grosse Fatigue)....17
Dead Zone, The....212
Deadend of Besiegers....126
Deadly Advice....159
Deadly Art of Survival....471
Deadly Assassin, The....200
Deadly Companions, The....347
Deadly Currents....110
Deadly Deception....471, 803
Deadly Deception....471, 803
Deadly Dolls Collection....126
Deadly Drifter....532
Deadly Duels....758
Deadly Game, A....159
Deadly Mantis, The....495
Deadly Sanctuary....2
Deadly Target....126
Deadly Trackers....292
Deadly Trap (Death Scream), The....7
Deadly Weapons....505
Deadwood....292
Deafsmith, A Nuclear Folktale....803
Dealers in Death....758
Dean Martin & Jerry Lewis Comedy Collection....267
Dean Martin....333
Dear America: Letters Home from Vietnam....778
Dear Boys, The....30, 458
Dear Brigitte....365
Dear Carry....429
Dear Detective (Tendre Poulet)....17
Dear Mark....481
Dear Mr. Gable....333
Dear Mr. Henshaw....632
Dear Wife....365
Death and the Maiden....97
Death in Brunswick....205
Death in the Garden....46
Death in the Seine....165
Death in the West....471
Death in Venice....39, 578
Death Kiss....365
Death March of the Jews from the Camp at Flossenberg, The....775
Death of a Bureaucrat....53
Death of a Prophet....451
Death of a Salesman....311
Death of a Soldier....205
Death of a Swan....85
Death of Ales Martinu....101
Death of Che Guevara....56
Death of the President....91
Death on the Nile....160
Death on the Nile: The Assassination of Anwar Sadat....110
Death on the Wing....814
Death Race 2000....513
Death Ray of Dr. Mabuse....505
Death Rim....126
Death to the Daleks....200
Death Trap....224
Death Valley....829
Death: The Trip of a Lifetime....848
Death: The Ultimate Mystery....505
DeathSport....505
Debussy Etudes Performed and Discussed
by Mitsuko Uchida, The....589
Debutante Detective Corps....726
Decade (Miramar)....709
Decameron, The....37
Decameron Nights....173
Deceiver....224
December 7th, Midway, Bougainville....767
December Bride....202
Deception....119
Decline of the American Empire....213
Decline of Western Civilization— Part II—The Metal Years....620
Deconstructing Harry....288
Decoration Day....225
Decoy, The....560
Dedee d'Anvers....20
Deep Cover....444
Deep in My Heart....322
Deep Six, The....365
Deep Throat....505
Deepak Chopra: Body, Mind and Soul....848
Deer Hunter, The....225
Deerslayer, The....397, 663
Def by Temptation....519
Defender, The....417
Defending America: The Price We Pay....803
Defending Your Life....267
Defiant Ones....365
Definitive Dali: A Lifetime Retrospective....547
Degas, Erte & Chagall....548
Degas....547
Degas: The Unquiet Spirit....548
Degrassi Jr. High/High— Health Education Curriculum....860
Deja Vu....95
Del Monaco at His Most Thrilling....596
Del Monaco: The Singing Volcano....578
Delacroix: The Restless Eye....548
Deli, The....429
Deliberate Evolution of a War Zone/A Calculated Forecast of
Ultimate Doom, The....483
Delicanis....105
Delicatessen....17
Deliverance....225
Della....365
Delphi 1830 & Next Time Everything Will Be Better....483
Delta, The....458
Delta of Venus....505
Delta Solar and the Four Seasons....548
Deluge, The....91
Delusions of Grandeur....17
Deluxe Ariel 1....726
Deluxe Ariel 2....726
Dementia 13....259, 520
Demetrius and the Gladiators....355
Demi-Paradise, The....182
Demjanjuk Trial: The State of Israel vs. John Demjanjuk....775
Democracy in a Different Voice....809
Democratic Party, 1960-1992, The....758
Demolition Man....495
Demon Barber of Fleet Street, The....520
Demon City Shinjuku....726
Demons 2....520
Demons in the Garden....44
Demons of the Deep....814
Denali Wilderness, Alaska....829
Denis Leary: No Cure for Cancer....534
Denise Calls Up....267
Denise Levertov....303
Dennis Brown: The Living Legend....601
Dennis Day: Oh Nothing....484
Dennis Potter's Lipstick on Your Collar....191
Dennis Potter: The Last Interview....191
Dennis the Movie Star....417
Dental Follies....267
Dentist in the Chair....182
Denver and Rio Grande....292
Depth Charge....429
Der Ring....578
Der Rosenkavalier (Bavarian State)....578
Der Rosenkavalier (Schwarzkopf)....578
Der Rosenkavalier (Vienna)....578
Der Sprinter....63
Der Stern von Africa....68
Der Untertan (The Subject)....68
Deranged....225, 505
Derek Mahon....203
Dersu Uzala....142
Descendant of Wing Chun....126
Desert Hearts....429, 458
Desert Rats....365
Desert Song, The....322
Desert Spirits....429
Desert Trail, The....292
Desert Under Siege....814
Desert Victory....767
Desert Vision....814
Deserter....85
Design—An Introduction....317
Designed Brain....848
Designing and Building Your Desktop Video System....317
Designing Woman....365
Desire....365, 458
Desire Under the Elms....311
Desire: An Erotic Fantasy Play....458
Desiree....365
Desk Set....267
Desolation Angels....429
Desperado....292
Desperadoes....292
Desperate Cargo....365
Desperate Hours....343
Desperate Journey....366
Desperate Living....514
Desperate Measures....15
Desperate Teenage Love Dolls....505
Desperate Trail, The....292
Desperately Seeking Susan....267
Destination Moon....495
Destination Tokyo....366
Destination: Mozart—A Night at the Opera with Peter Sellars....578
Destination: Universe....839
Destiny....71
Destiny of the Daleks....200
Destiny Turns on the Radio....225
Destroy All Blondes/The Naked Hipstress/Sick Sick Sister....429
Destroy All Monsters....505
Destroy All Rational Thought....303
Destry Rides Again....292
Details of a Duel....49
Detective (aka Father Brown)....173
Detective....9
Detonator....225
Detonator Orgun, Part 1....726
Detonator Orgun, Part 2....726
Detonator Orgun, Part 3....726
Detour....366
Detroit 9000....532
Develop Your Psychic Powers....848
Devi....147
Devil, Probably, The....15
Devil and Daniel Webster, The....366
Devil and Miss Jones, The....366
Devil at 4 o'Clock, The....366
Devil at Your Heels....471
Devil Bat....520
Devil Dogs of the Air....267
Devil Doll, The....520
Devil Girl from Mars....495
Devil Got My Woman: Blues at Newport 1966....610
Devil Hunter Yohko 1....726
Devil Hunter Yohko 2 & 3....727
Devil Hunter Yohko 4 & 5....727
Devil Hunter Yohko 4-Ever!....727
Devil Hunter Yohko 5: The Death of Yohko....727
Devil Hunter Yohko 6....727
Devil Hunters....126
Devil in a Blue Dress....444
Devil in Silk....68
Devil in the Flesh....20, 32
Devil Man Vol. 1: Genesis....727
Devil Man Vol. 2: Siren, The Demon Bird....727
Devil Rides Out (a.k.a. The Devil's Bride), The....520
Devil's Brigade, The....366
Devil's Brother, The....267
Devil's Circus, The....397
Devil's Commandment, The....520
Devil's Daughter, The....520
Devil's Daughter....448
Devil's Disciple, The....182
Devil's Eye....78
Devil's Foot, The....186
Devil's Hand (Carnival of Sinners)....520
Devil's Island....397
Devil's Messenger, The....520
Devil's Nightmare....520
Devil's Own, The....225
Devil's Partner, The....520
Devil's Rain, The....520
Devil's Sleep....173
Devil's Wanton....78
Devils, The....167
Devo: The Complete Truth About De-Evolution....620
Devotion....366, 458
Dewess Cochran, Doll Artist....560
Dewey Balfa—The Tribute Concert....601
Dexter Gordon Quartet, The....610
Dhimmis: To Be a Jew in Arab Lands, The....109
Dhund (Fog)....147
Diabolically Yours....20
Diabolique....25, 225
Dial M for Murder....352
Dialectics of Romance....484
Dialogues with Elie Wiesel....800
Diamond Head....366
Diamond Plaza....44
Diamond Shaft (aka Diamonds)....532
Diamonds Are Forever....168
Diamonds of the Night....101
Diamonds on Wheels....632
Diana Ross Live....610
Diane....366
Diane Bish—Classic Organ Favorites....589
Diane Bish—Favorite Hymns of Faith....589
Diane Bish—J.S. Bach Favorites for Organ....589
Diane Bish—Mozart: The Man & His Music....589
Diane DiPrima: Recollections of My Life as a Woman....303
Diane Teramana: The Knitting Factory Show....484
Diary of a Chambermaid....25, 46
Diary of a Country Priest....15
Diary of a Lost Girl....68
Diary of a Madman, The....520
Diary of a Nudist....520
Diary of Anne Frank....342
Diary of Forbidden Dreams....97
Diary of the Big Man....126
Diary of the War of Pigs....50
Dick Deadeye....709
Dick Tracy....225, 537
Dick Turpin....397
Did They Buy It?: Nicaragua's 1990 Elections....56
Diderot....484
Die Deutsche Wochenschau #1
(The German Weekly Newsreel)....69, 767
Die Entfuhrung aus dem Serail (Bohm)....579
Die Entfuhrung aus dem Serail (Drottningholm)....579

Die Fettecke 484
Die Fledermaus (Schenk) 579
Die Fledermaus (Sutherland/Pavarotti) 579
Die Frau ohne Schatten 579
Die Goldene Stadt 69
Die Meistersinger von Nurnberg (Jerusalem/Bayreuth) 579
Die Meistersinger von Nurnberg (The Australian Opera) 579
Die Soldaten 579
Die Todliche Doris 484
Die Zauberflote (Araiza) 579
Die Zauberflote (Battle) 579
Diego Rivera/Los Murales del Palacio Nacional 548
Diet for a New America: Your Health, Your Planet 848
Different Drummer: Elvin Jones 610
Different for Girls 160
Different Strokes 458, 505
Dig Hole, Build House 632
Digital Speech and Pressures of the Text 484
Dil Deke Dehko 147
Dillinger 366
Dimples 322
Diner 225
Dingles, The 632
Dingo 205
Dinner at Eight 350
Dinner at the Ritz 173
Dinosaur 865
Dinosaur Valley Girls 505
Dinosaur! 835
Dinosaurs, The 814
Dinosaurs 814
Direct Art, Good Lovin' Guitar Man and Other Works 620
Direct Connection 803
Directed by Andrei Tarkovsky 84
Directed by Stan Laurel 410
Directing Process, The 317
Dirty Dancing 225
Dirty Dozen 366
Dirty Gertie from Harlem 448
Dirty Harry 225
Dirty Money 429
Dirty Pair Flash Act 1 727
Dirty Pair Flash Act 3 727
Dirty Pair: Affair on Nolandia 727
Dirty Pair: Flight 005 Conspiracy 727
Dirty Pair: Project Eden 727
Dirty Rotten Scoundrels 267
Disappearance, The 210
Disappearance of Garcia Lorca, The 56, 225
Disappearance of Kevin Johnson, The 225
Disappearance of Lady Frances Carfax, The 186
Disappearing World: Ongka's Big Moka, The Kawelka of Papua, New Guinea 781
Disappearing World: The Herders of Mongun-Taiga, The Tuvans of Mongolia 781
Disappearing World: The Island of Malaita, The Lau of the Solomon Islands 782
Disappearing World: The Kayapo, Indians of the Brazilian Rainforest 782
Disappearing World: The Masai Women, The Masai of Kenya 782
Disarmament: A Public Opinion Poll 803
Disarmament: Savage Republic 616
Disasters/Crime and Terrorism 758
Disciple, The 397
Disclosure 225
Disco Godfather 532
Discover California 829
Discover Portugal! 829
Discoverers, The 814
Discovering American Folk Music 604
Discovering American Indian Music 786
Discovering China and Tibet 135
Discovering Country and Western Music 604
Discovering Electronic Music 616
Discovering Everyday Spirituality 848
Discovering France 672
Discovering Gardens 814
Discovering Jazz 610
Discovering Russian Folk Music 87
Discovering the Feminine 790
Discovering the Music of Africa 601
Discovering the Music of India 602
Discovering the Music of Japan 144
Discovering the Music of Latin America 56
Discovering the Music of the Middle Ages 589
Discovering the Music of the Middle East 110
Discovering the Mystical Yucatan: Activating the Energy of the Heart 848
Discovering Unforgettable Sex 848
Discovering Your Expressive Body 848
Discovery, The 114
Discovery of the Americas, The 632
Discovery Sport 826
Discovery Stories 632
Discovery Year, The 857
Discreet Charm of the Bourgeoisie, The 46
Dishonored 347
Dishonored Lady 366
Dismissed from Life 91
Disney Animation 683, 691
Disney Canta con Nosotros 672
Disney Cartoon Classics Special Edition: Fun on the Job! 691
Disney Cartoon Classics Special Edition: GOOFY 691
Disney Cartoon Classics Special Edition: Happy Summer Days 691
Disney Cartoon Classics Special Edition: The Goofy World of Sports 691
Disney Cartoon Classics: Here's Donald/Here's Goofy 691
Disney Cartoon Classics: Here's Mickey/Here's Pluto 691
Disney Cartoon Classics Vol. 1: Here's Mickey! 691
Disney Cartoon Classics Vol. 2: Here's Donald! 691
Disney Cartoon Classics Vol. 3: Here's Goofy! 691
Disney Cartoon Classics Vol. 4: Silly Symphonies! 691
Disney Cartoon Classics Vol. 5: Here's Pluto! 691
Disney Cartoon Classics Vol. 6: Mickey & Minnie 691
Disney Cartoon Classics Vol. 7: Donald & Daisy 691
Disney Cartoon Classics Vol. 8: Animals by Two 691
Disney Cartoon Classics Vol. 9: Chip 'n Dale 691
Disney Cartoon Classics Vol. 10: Pluto & Fifi 691
Disney Cartoon Classics Vol. 11: Mickey & The Gang 691
Disney Cartoon Classics Vol. 12: Nuts About Chip 'n Dale 691
Disney Cartoon Classics Vol. 13: Donald's Scarey Tales 691
Disney Cartoon Classics Vol. 14: Halloween Haunts 691
Disney Christmas Gift, A 691
Dog of Flanders, A 663
Disney Love Tales 691
Disney Presents Bill Nye the Science Guy: Dinosaurs, Those Big Boneheads 632, 835
Disney Presents Bill Nye the Science Guy: Outer Space Way Out There 632, 835
Disney Presents Bill Nye the Science Guy: The Human Body 632, 835
Disney Presents the Best of Broadway Musicals 322
Disney Primitive Collection: Alice, The 691
Disney's Beginnings 692
Disney's Sing-Along Songs Vol. 1: Heigh Ho 692
Disney's Sing-Along Songs Vol. 2: Zip-A-Dee-Doo-Dah 692
Disney's Sing-Along Songs Vol. 3: You Can Fly! 692
Disney's Sing-Along Songs Vol. 4: The Bare Necessities 692
Disney's Sing-Along Songs Vol. 5: Fun with Music 692
Disney's Sing-Along Songs Vol. 6: Under the Sea 692
Disney's Sing-Along Songs Vol. 7: Disneyland Fun 692
Disney's Sing-Along Songs Vol. 8: Merry Christmas Songs 692
Disney's Sing-Along Songs Vol. 9: I Love to Laugh 692
Disney's Sing-Along Songs Vol. 10: Be Our Guest 692
Disney's Sing-Along Songs Vol. 11: Friend Like Me 692
Disney's Sing-Along Songs Vol. 12: 12 Days of Christmas 692
Disney's Sing-Along Songs: Be Our Guest/Fun with Music 692
Disney's Sing-Along Songs: Circle of Life (Lion King) 692
Disney's Sing-Along Songs: Colors of the Wind (Pocahontas) 692
Disney's Sing-Along Songs: Friend Like Me/Disneyland Fun 692
Disney's Sing-Along Songs: Pongo & Perdita 692
Disney's Sing-Along Songs: The Bare Neccessities/ You Can Fly 692
Disney's Sing-Along Songs: Topsy Turvy (Hunchback) 692
Disney's Sing-Along Songs: Under the Sea/I Love to Laugh 692
Disney's Sing-Along Songs: Zip-A-Dee-Doo-Dah. 692
Disney's Sing-Along Songs: Zip-A-Dee-Doo-Dah/Heigh Ho 692
Disney Sing-Alongs 683, 691
Disney Sweetheart Stories 692
Disorderlies 444
Disorderly Orderly 267
Displaced Person 300
Disraeli 366
Distant Drums 366
Distant Thunder 147
Dita Saxova 99
Diva 3
Dive Bomber 366
Divertimento 10
Divided Union, The 779
Divine 514
Divine Garbo, The 333
Divine Horsemen: The Living Gods of Haiti 54, 484
Diving In 225
Divorce American Style 267
Divorce Can Happen to the Nicest People 632
Divorce—Italian Style 40
Divorce of Lady X 182
Dixie Jamboree 322
Dizzy 480
Dizzy Gillespie: A Night in Chicago 610
Dizzy Gillespie: A Night in Tunisia 610
Dizzy Gillespie: Live in London 610
Djabote: Sengalese Drumming & Song from Master Drummer Doudou N'Diaye Rose 152, 602
Django, A Jazz Tribute 610
Djembefola 602
Do Ankhen Barah Haath 147
Do The Right Thing 447
Do You Believe in Miracles? 861
Do You Remember Dolly Bell? 104
Doc 292
Doc and Merle Watson 604
Doc Hollywood 267
Doc Watson: Doc's Guitar Jam Featuring Doc Watson, Tony Rice, Dan Crary, Steve Kaufman & Jack Lawrence 605
Doc Watson: Rare Performances 1963-1981 605
Doc Watson: Rare Performances 1982-1993 605
Docks of New York 347
Doctor and the Devils 160
Doctor at Large 182
Doctor at Sea 182
Doctor De Soto and Other Stories 632
Doctor Dolittle 322
Doctor Ehrlich's Magic Bullet 366
Doctor Faustus 160
Doctor Mabuse 72
Doctor Mack (aka Mack the Knife) 120
Doctor Takes a Wife 366
Doctor Who 191
Doctor Who and the Daleks 200
Doctor Who and the Silurians 200
Doctor Who: Timelash 201
Doctor X 520
Doctor Zhivago 180
Document: Fanny and Alexander 78
Documentary Masterpieces by John Grierson 471
Documentary Urge: Tom Arndt 558
Dodes'ka-den 142
Dodge City 292
Dodsworth 343
Does the U.S. Need Nuclear Weapons? 803
Dog Day Afternoon 225
Dog Days of Arthur Cane, The 632
Dog Eat Dog 505
Dog Soldier: Shadows of the Past 727
Dog Who Had Kittens, The 632
Dogfight 225
Dogs in Space 205
Dogs of War, The 160
Dogsong 632
Doing Business 860
Doing Things: Eating, Washing, In Motion 651
Dolemite 2: Human Tornado 532
Dolemite 532
Doll, The 75, 91
Doll Face 322
Dollar 75
Dolly Sisters, The 322
Dolores Claiborne 225
Dolphin, The 53
Dolphin Adventure 814
Dolphins, Close Encounters 814
Dolphins 814
Dominators, The 200
Dominican Republic, Cradle of the Americas 54
Dominick and Eugene 225
Dominion 520
Dominion II, Vol. 1 727
Dominion Tank Police Act I 727
Dominion Tank Police Act II 727
Dominion Tank Police Act III 727
Dominion Tank Police Act IV 727
Dominion Tank Police Pt. 1: Acts I & II 727
Dominion Tank Police Pt. 2: Acts III & IV 727
Dominique in "Daughters of Lesbos" 458
Dominoes: Portrait of a Decade 620
Don Carlo (Met) 579
Don Cherry's Multikulti 610
Don Cooper: Mother Nature's Songs 651
Don Daredevil Rides Again 537
Don from Lakewood/You Talk, I Buy 429
Don Giovanni (Glyndebourne) 579
Don Giovanni (Muti) 579
Don Giovanni (Ruggero Raimondi) 579
Don Giovanni (Salzburg) 579
Don Giovanni (Sellars) 579
Don Giovanni (Siepi) 579
Don Giovanni 353, 579
Don Juan, My Love 44
Don Juan 397
Don Juan DeMarco 267
Don King: Only in America 225
Don Pasquale 579
Don Q, Son of Zorro 397
Don Quijote 672
Don Quixote (Ananiashvili) 570
Don Quixote (Kirov Ballet) 570
Don Quixote (Nureyev) 570
Don Quixote 69, 80
Don's Party 205
Don Segundo Sombra 50
Don't Call Me Bugsy 794
Don't Give a Damn 126
Don't Go Near the Water 267
Don't Hang Up 182
Don't Leave Out the Cowboys 451
Don't Look Back 471, 620
Don't Look Back: The Story of Leroy "Satchel" Paige 451
Don't Look in the Basement 520
Don't Look Now 166
Don't Play Us Cheap 444
Don't Raise the Bridge, Lower the River 267
Don't Start Me to Talking... 311
Dona Barbara 50
Dona Flor and Her Two Husbands 53
Dona Herlinda and Her Son 50
Donald in Mathmagic Land 692
Donald Trump 794
Donkey's Dream, The 651
Donner Pass: The Road to Survival 298
Donnie Brasco 225
Donovan's Brain 520
Doom Generation, The 429, 458
Doomed Love 429
Doomed Megalopolis Part 1: The Haunting of Tokyo 727
Doomed Megalopolis Part 2: The Fall of Tokyo 727
Doomed Megalopolis Part 3: The Gods of Tokyo 727
Doomed Megalopolis Part 4: The Battle for Tokyo 727
Doomed to Die 366
Doomsday Machine, The 495
Doomsday Plan, The 758
Doonesbury Special, A 709
Door of Compassion: An Interview with Zen Meditation Master Thich Nhat Hanh 149
Doors, The 620
Doors of Perception, The 785
Dope, Guns and Fucking Up Your Videodeck, Vol. I 620
Dope, Guns and Fucking Up Your Videodeck, Vol. II 620
Dorian Gray 520

Dorothea Lange: A Visual Life 559
Dorothy and Alan at Norma Place 429
DOS—Disc Operating System, An Introduction 845
Dos Fallopia: Pretty Girls, Not Too Bright 458, 534
Dosvedanya Means Good-bye 114
Dot & Santa Claus 663, 709
Dot & The Bunny 663, 709
Dot and Dash, Volume 1 651
Double Agent 73 505
Double Agents 20
Double Crossed 225
Double Crossing: The Voyage of the St. Louis, The 775
Double Deal 448
Double Dynamite 366
Double Edge 225
Double Exposure 826
Double Happiness 210
Double Indemnity 345
Double Life, A 350
Double Life of Veronique, The 95
Double Suicide 137
Double Trouble 536
Double Wedding 366
Doubting Thomas 366
Doug Hall: Storm and Stress 484
Doug Vol. 1: How Did I Get into This Mess? 709
Doug Vol. 2: Patti, You're the Mayonnaise for Me 709
Doug: Christmas Story 709
Doughboys 409
Doughboys: Heroes of WWI, The 758
Douglas Fairbanks Sr. Collection, The 397
Douglas Miller Live in Houston 607
Down and Out in America 471
Down Argentine Way 322
Down Buttermilk Lane 652
Down by Law 442
Down Came a Blackbird 225
Down Memory Lane: Rev. James Cleveland 607
Down to Earth 366, 397
Down to the Sea in Ships 397
Down Under 205
Downbeat vs. Addies 602
Downfall of the Monarchies/The Surviving Monarchies 758
Downhill Racer 366
Dozen Dizzy Dogs, A 632
Dr. Alien! 505
Dr. Bernie Siegel 848
Dr. Bethune 210
Dr. Carl G. Jung or Lapis Philosophorum 442
Dr. Charles G. Hayes and the Cosmopolitan Church of Prayer 607
Dr. Christian Meets the Women 366
Dr. Cyclops 495
Dr. Demento's 20th Anniversary Collection 620
Dr. Devious: Dance in Cyberspace 709
Dr. Goldfoot and the Bikini Machine 505
Dr. Goldfoot's the Girl Bombs 505
Dr. Jekyll and Mr. Hyde (Barrymore) 520
Dr. Jekyll and Mr. Hyde (March) 520
Dr. Jekyll and Mr. Hyde (Tracy) 520
Dr. Jekyll and Ms. Hyde 429
Dr. Ji Liang Chen: Ba Duan Jin Qi Gong (Eight Pieces of Brocade) 849
Dr. John Teaches New Orleans Piano 610
Dr. John: New Orleans Swamp 610
Dr. Judym 91
Dr. Katz 534
Dr. Lam[b] 126
Dr. Mabuse, the Gambler, Part I 72
Dr. Mabuse, the Gambler, Part II 72
Dr. Mabuse, the Gambler, Parts I & II 72
Dr. Mabuse vs. Scotland Yard 505
Dr. Martin Luther King, Jr.: A Historical Perspective 451
Dr. No 168
Dr. Orlof's Monster 520
Dr. Petiot 7
Dr. Phibes Rises Again 520
Dr. Sandra Scantling's Ordinary Couples, Extraordinary Sex 849
Dr. Seuss' Daisy-Head Mayzie 683
Dr. Seuss' The Butter Battle Book 683
Dr. Seuss 652
Dr. Seuss Collection 683
Dr. Seuss Video Festival 683
Dr. Seuss: Green Eggs & Ham & Other Stories 683
Dr. Seuss: Grinch Night 683
Dr. Seuss: Horton Hears a Who 683
Dr. Seuss: How the Grinch Stole Christmas 683
Dr. Seuss: How the Grinch Stole Christmas/ Horton Hears a Who 709
Dr. Seuss: Pontoffel Rock and His Magic Piano 683
Dr. Seuss: The Cat in the Hat 683
Dr. Seuss: The Grinch Grinches the Cat in The Hat 683
Dr. Seuss: The Hoober-Bloob Highway 683
Dr. Seuss: The Lorax 683
Dr. Strangelove 256
Dr. Sulphur's Night Lab 865
Dr. Syn 366
Dr. Todt: Mission and Achievement 767
Dr. Zoology: The Tamarin Mystery 632
Dracula (Lugosi) 520
Dracula (Palance) 520
Dracula (Spanish Version) 520
Dracula 514
Dracula—A Cinematic Scrapbook 521
Dracula A.D. 1972 520
Dracula Has Risen from the Grave 520
Dracula's Daughter 520
Dracula's Last Rites 520
Dracula: A True Story 521
Dracula: Prince of Darkness 521
Drag-Net, The 366
Dragnet 267
Dragon and the Cobra: The Collector's Edition 333
Dragon Ball, Vol. 1: Secret of the Dragon Ball 728
Dragon Ball, Vol. 2: The Nimbus Cloud of Roshi 728
Dragon Ball, Vol. 3 728
Dragon Ball, Vol. 4 728
Dragon Ball, Vol. 5 728
Dragon Ball Z, Vol. 10: Rebirth 728
Dragon Ball Z, Vol. 11: Namek 728
Dragon Ball Z, Vol. 12: Betrayal 728
Dragon Ball Z, Vol. 13: Zarbon! 728
Dragon Ball Z, Vol. 1: Arrival 727
Dragon Ball Z, Vol. 2: The Saiyans 727
Dragon Ball Z, Vol. 3: Snake Way 727
Dragon Ball Z, Vol. 4 727
Dragon Ball Z, Vol. 5 727
Dragon Ball Z The Movie: The World's Strongest 728
Dragon Ball Z: The Movie: Dead Zone 728
Dragon Ball Z: The Movie: The Tree of Might 728
Dragon Ball: Curse of the Blood Rubies 728
Dragon Chow 63
Dragon Fight 126
Dragon Flyz: The Legend Begins 672, 709
Dragon Half Parts 1 and 2 728
Dragon Inn 127
Dragon Lord 134
Dragon Seed 366
Dragon Slayer 728
Dragon That Wasn't (Or Was He?), The 709
Dragon: The Bruce Lee Story 127
Dragonfire 200
Dragonfly's Tale 632, 786
Dragonheart 225
Dragonquest: Sacred Sites of Britain 169
Dragons Forever 134
Dragons of the Orient 127
Drake Case 397
Drama Training Videos I and II, The 317
Drawing and Sketching with Markers 563
Drawing I 563
Drawing II 563
Drawing III 563
Drawing in the Source: Lita Albuquerque 563
Drawing Landscapes with Pencil and Ink 563
Drawing Methods with Gail Price 563
Drawing on Life 548
Drawing the Line: A Portrait of Keith Haring 548
Drawing: Learning Professional Techniques 563
Dreadlocks and the Three Bears 646
Dream a Little Dream 267
Dream Awake, The 451
Dream Boys Revue 458
Dream Is Alive, The 839
Dream Lover 225
Dream Lovers 120
Dream Machine, The 845
Dream Man 567
Dream of Kings 366
Dream of Light (Quince Tree of the Sun) 44
Dream of Peace, A 803
Dream Street 412
Dream Tales: The Sacred Ways Collection 709
Dream Team, The 826
Dream Team 267
Dream Weaver 560
Dream Wife 267
Dream Window: Reflections on the Japanese Garden 548
Dream with the Fishes 429
Dreamchild 225
Dreamers of the Day 458
Dreaming Lips 173
Dreaming of Paradise 709
Dreaming of Rita 75
Dreaming Out Loud 366
Dreaming Universe, The 209
Dreams 78, 142
Dreamworlds: Desire/Sex/Power in Rock Video 785
Dressed to Kill 186
Dresser, The 160
Dressmaker 160
Drifting 107, 458
Drifting Souls 366
Drifting Weeds 143
Driftwood 367
Driver's Seat, The 40
Driving Miss Daisy 226
Driving the Dream 841
Droits au Coeur (Rights from the Heart) 709
Droopy & Company 709
Drop Kick 397
Drop Squad 226
Drop Zone 226
Drought 815
Drowning by Numbers 165
Drug Free Kids 860
Drug Propaganda and Satire Compilation 505
Drugs and the Law 849
Drugstore Cowboy 440
Drum Course for Beginners with Louie Bellson 624
Drums Along the Mohawk 340
Drums in the Deep South 367
Drums of Jeopardy 521
Drunken Angel 142
Drunken Master (aka Drunken Monkey in a Tiger's Eye) 134
Drunken Master II 134
Drunken Tai-Chi 127
Drunkenfist Boxing 134
Dry White Season, A 151
Dry Wood 480
Du Barry Was a Lady 322
Dub, The 317
Dubliners, The 348
Dubliners Live 203
Duchess and the Dirtwater Fox 267
Duchess of Buffalo, The 397
Duchess of Duke Street, The 191
Duck Soup 267
Ducks Unlimited's Videoguide to Waterfowl and Game Birds 815
Duel, The 367
Duel 258
Duel at Diablo 292
Duel at Silver Creek, The 292
Duel in the Sun 292
Duel to the Death 127
Duellists 160
Duet for One 84
Duet for Spies/Frankie Lymon's Nephew Story 429
Duke, The 292
Duke Ellington 610
Duke of the Derby 20
Dukes of Dixieland and Friends 610
Dumb and Dumber 267
Dumbo 692
Dune 257
Dupont Lajoie (Rape of Innocence) 3
Dust in the Wind 136
Dusty 205
Dutchess of Idaho 267
Dvorak in Prague: A Celebration 589
Dwelling Place, The 191
Dwight D. Eisenhower: From Soldier to President 794
Dwight D. Eisenhower: Library and Museum 794
Dwight D. Eisenhower: The Presidential Years 794
Dybbuk, The 112
Dying Detective, The 186
Dying for a Smoke 471
Dyke Drama 458
Dynamite Dan 397
Dziesieciu z Pawiaka 91

E

E.M.B. Classics 471
E.T. 258
E.Y.E.S. of Mars 728
E-Z Bread Dough Sculpture 668
Each Dawn I Die 367
Eagle, The 397
Eagle and the Hawk, The 367
Eagle Claw Kung-fu 849
Eagle Has Landed, The 767
Eagle Has Two Heads (L'Aigle A Deux Tetes), The 27
Eagle of the Night 397
Eagle's Children, The 56
Eagle's Nest: Hitler's Secret Center of Power, The 767
Eagle Shadow Fists 134
Eagle Wing 292
Eagle-Shooting Heroes, The 127
Eagles Attack at Dawn 107
Early Animation Vol. 1 709
Early Animation Vol. 2 709
Early Birds 842
Early Comedies Volume 1 410
Early Comedies Volume 2 410
Early Dance Part 1: From the Greeks to the Renaissance 570
Early Dance Part 2: The Baroque Era 570
Early Frost, An 458
Early Musical Instruments 589
Early Russian Cinema: Before the Revolution 85
Early Silent Movie Prevues 397
Early Summer 143
Early Warner Brothers Cartoons 683
Early Warnings 803
Early Westerns #1 397
Early Westerns #2 398
Earrings of Madame De... 27
Earth 85
Earth at Risk Environmental Video Series, The 803
Earth Bridge 815
Earth Dance 815
Earth Day Special 815
Earth Dreaming 815
Earth First! The Struggle for the Australian Rainforest 803
Earth Is the Lord's: Ecology as a Religious Concern, The 803
Earth to Space for Peace 839
Earth vs. the Flying Saucers 495
Earth vs. the Spider 495
Eartha Kitt: The Most Exciting Woman in the World 610
Earthian 728
Earthkeepers 152
Earthquake! Disaster in L.A. 815
Earthshock 200
Earthworm Jim: Assault and Battery/Trout! 696
Earthworm Jim: Book of Doom/The Egg Beater 696
Earthworm Jim: Bring Me the Head of Earthworm Jim/ Sword of Righteousness 696
Earthworm Jim: Conqueror Worm/Day of the Fish 696
Earthworm Tractors 267
East and West 112
East Meets West 173

East of Borneo ... 367
East of Eden ... 367
East Side, West Side ... 367
East Side Story ... 63, 333, 548
Easter Bunny, The ... 632
Easter Bunny Is Coming to Town, The ... 683
Easter Island ... 782
Easter Island: A Vanished Culture ... 782
Easter Parade ... 322
Easter Story Keepers, The ... 632
Eastern Condors ... 127
Eastern Heroes ... 127
Eastwood ... 865
Easy Living ... 267
Easy Rider ... 429
Easy to Love ... 322
Easy to Wed ... 322
Easy Virtue ... 352
Eat a Bowl of Tea ... 455
Eat Drink Man Woman ... 136
Eat My Dust ... 127, 505
Eat the Rich ... 182
Eating ... 429
Eating Raoul ... 267
Eavan Boland ... 203
Ebola Syndrome ... 120
Ebola: The Plague Fighters ... 835
Ebony Pearls ... 444
Ebony/Jet Guide to Black Excellence Program 1: The Entrepreneurs ... 849
Ebony/Jet Guide to Black Excellence Program 2: The Leaders ... 451
Ebony/Jet Guide to Black Excellence Program 3: The Entertainers ... 451
Echo of the Elephants ... 815
Echo Park ... 226
Echoes of Conflict ... 110
Echoes Without Saying ... 303
Eclipse ... 35, 210
Eclipse of the Man-Made Sun ... 803
Eco-Rap: Voices from the Hood ... 815
Ecocide ... 803
Ecology of the Urban Environment ... 803
Ecstasy ... 69
Ed & Chester Bible Stories ... 632
Ed & Chester Show ... 632
Ed McBain ... 303
Ed's Next Move ... 429
Ed Sullivan Show, The ... 417
Ed Wood ... 255, 514
Ed Wood Collection, The ... 515
Ed Wood Collection, Vol. 2, The ... 515
Ed Wood Story: The Plan 9 Companion, The ... 515
Ed Wood: Look Back in Angora ... 515
Eddie and the Cruisers ... 226
Eddie Fisher: A Singing Legend ... 617
Eddie Izzard: Glorious ... 534
Eddie Jefferson Live from Jazz Showcase ... 610
Eddie Murphy Delirious ... 534
Eddie Murphy: Raw ... 534
Eddy Duchin Story, The ... 322
Eden Valley ... 160
Edgar Allan Poe ... 303
Edgar Allan Poe: Architect of Dreams ... 303
Edgar Kennedy Slow Burn Festival ... 267
Edge, The ... 226
Edge of Darkness ... 160, 367
Edge of History, The ... 803
Edge of Sanity ... 505
Edge of the World ... 180
Edible and Medicinal Herbs Vol. I ... 849
Edible and Medicinal Herbs Vol. II ... 849
Edinburgh Military Tattoo 1987 ... 169
Edison, the Man ... 367
Edith Piaf: I Regret Nothing ... 28
Edith Piaf: La Vie en Rose ... 28
Edith Springer on Harm Reduction ... 834
Editing Exercise, An ... 317
Editing Techniques: Reducing Time ... 317
Edouard Manet ... 548
Edouard Manet: Painter of Modern Life ... 548
Edouardo Chillida ... 548
Eduardo Galeano ... 56, 303
Educating Rita ... 182
Education of Little Tree, The ... 226, 786
Edvard Munch ... 168, 548
Edward and Mrs. Simpson ... 169
Edward Hopper: The Silent Witness ... 548
Edward II ... 167
Edward R. Murrow: The Best of Person to Person ... 417
Edward Ruscha: Don't Want No Retro... ... 548
Edward Scissorhands ... 255
Edward the King ... 191
Eek! Stravaganza ... 696
Effi Briest ... 66
Efficiency Expert, The ... 205
Egberto Gismonti ... 56
Egg ... 31
Egg and I, The ... 267
Egg-Nog (Kogel Mogel) ... 91
Eggs Mark the Spot ... 632
Egyptian ... 367
Egyptian Adventures ... 829
Ei Ei Yoga ... 668
Eiffel Tower, The ... 28
Eiger Sanction, The ... 256
Eight on the Lam ... 268
Eight Super Stories from Sesame Street ... 652
Eight: The American Independence Movement, The ... 548
Eighteenth Century Woman, The ... 560
Eighth Day, The ... 29
Eighties, The ... 29, 758
Eijanaika ... 141
Einstein Revealed ... 794
Eisenhower—A Place in History ... 794
Eisenhower: Soldier/Statesman ... 794
Eisenstein ... 86
El (This Strange Passion) ... 46
El Alfabeto Espanol ... 154
El Bruto ... 47
El Charanguero: Jaime Torres, the Charango Player ... 56, 602
El Che: Investigating a Legend ... 56
El Cid ... 367
El Compadre Mendoza ... 50
El Corsario Negro ... 50
El Crucero ... 56
El Dia Que Me Queiras ... 50
El Diputado ... 44, 458
El Dorado ... 341
El Escorial and Toledo ... 48
El Frenetico & Go-Girl ... 505
El Gran Acontecimiento (The Great Apparition) ... 50
El Greco ... 548
El Grito ... 50
El Hazard Vol. 1: The First Night ... 728
El Hazard Vol. 2: The Second Night and Third Night ... 728
El Hazard Vol. 3: Episodes 5 and 6 ... 728
El Hazard Vol. 4: Episodes 6 and 7 ... 728
El Hazard 2, Vol. 1 ... 728
El Mariachi ... 429
El Matador ... 56
El Mojado ... 481
El Muerto ... 50
El Mundo del Talisman ... 50
El Otro Lado (The Other Side) ... 481
El Pequeno Tren (The Little Train) ... 672
El Sacerdote (The Priest) ... 44, 458
El Salvador: The Seeds of Liberty ... 56
El Super ... 50
El Tango en Broadway ... 50
El Teatro Museo Dali ... 548
Elayne Boosler ... 534
Elayne Boosler: Broadway Baby ... 534
Elayne Boosler: Live Nude Girls ... 534
Eldon Garnet: Today, Tonight, Tomorrow ... 484
Ele, My Friend ... 663
Eleanor, First Lady of the World ... 794
Eleanor Roosevelt ... 758
Eleanor Roosevelt Story ... 794
Election, The ... 800
Electra Glide in Blue ... 226
Electric Horseman, The ... 226
Electric Hot Tuna: Live at the Fillmore ... 610
Electric Valley, The ... 471
Electronic Monster (Escapement), The ... 495
Electronic Storyteller: Television and the Cultivation of Values, The ... 860
Elegant Criminal (L'Elegant Criminel), The ... 3
Elegy for a Street Survivor (Yume) ... 471
Elektra (Marton) ... 579
Elektra (Nilsson) ... 579
Element of Crime, The ... 75
Elementary Art Appreciation Videos—Understanding Painting Series ... 563
Elementary Guitar Practice and Theory with Barney Kessel ... 624
Elementary School, The ... 99
Elements and Principles of Design with Artist Tony Couch ... 563
Elena and Her Men ... 26
Elephant Boy ... 173
Elephant Named Illusion (Un Elefante Color Illusion), An ... 672
Elephant's Child ... 646
Elephant Walk ... 367
Elephants of Timbuktu, The ... 152
Elevator to the Gallows ... 13
Eli Eli ... 112
Elia Kazan: A Director's Journey ... 333
Eligible Bachelor, The ... 186
Elisa Vida Mia ... 45
Elisabeth Jappe: Documenta 8—Performance—Action—Ritual ... 484
Elixir of Love ... 579
Elizabeth Cotten ... 605
Elizabeth R. ... 191
Elko: The Cowboy Gathering ... 298
Ella Cinders ... 398
Ella Cinders and Mormon Maid ... 398
Ella Jenkins Live at the Smithsonian ... 652
Ella Jenkins: For the Family ... 652
Ellcia 2: Ghost Ship ... 728
Ellcia 3: Ironclads ... 728
Ellcia 4: Ship of God ... 728
Ellcia ... 728
Ellcia: The Legend Begins ... 729
Elle Voit des Nains Partout ... 3
Ellis Island ... 758
Elmer Fudd's School of Hard Knocks ... 683
Elmer Gantry ... 367
Elmer! ... 683
Elmo Says Boo! ... 652
Elmopalooza! ... 632
Elmore Leonard ... 303
Elroy's Toy ... 709
Elusive Corporal ... 26
Elusive Pimpernel, The ... 180
Elvin Jones Jazz Machine ... 610
Elvira Madigan ... 75
Elvira's Midnight Madness: EEGAH! ... 521
Elvira's Midnight Madness: Frankenstein's Daughter ... 521
Elvira's Midnight Madness: Giant Gila Monster ... 521
Elvira's Midnight Madness: I Eat Your Skin ... 521
Elvira's Midnight Madness: Night of the Ghouls ... 515
Elvira's Midnight Madness: She Demons ... 521
Elvira's Midnight Madness: The Brain That Wouldn't Die ... 521
Elvira's Midnight Madness: The Hideous Sun Demon ... 521
Elvis and Me ... 536
Elvis on Tour ... 536
Elvis Stories ... 536
Elvis—That's the Way It Is ... 536
Elvis: The Echo Will Never Die ... 536
Embalmer, The ... 521
Embroidered Canticles ... 110
Embryo ... 548
Emerald Cities ... 429
Emerald City of Oz ... 632
Emerald Forest ... 226
Emergency! EMS to the Rescue ... 860
Emergency: Health Care in America—A National Town Meeting ... 835
Emerging Chaplin ... 407
Emigrants, The ... 79
Emily Bronte's Wuthering Heights ... 160
Emily Dickinson: "A Certain Slant of Light" ... 303
Eminent Scholars Series ... 303
Emma ... 160, 226
Emma Amos: Action Line ... 451, 548
Emma's Shadow ... 75
Emmanuelle ... 3
Emmanuelle 2 ... 3
Emmanuelle in Egypt ... 32
Emmanuelle Queen of the Desert ... 32
Emotionally Free ... 849
Emotions of Life ... 849
Emperor Jones ... 448
Emperor's New Clothes and Other Folktales, The ... 646
Emperor Waltz, The ... 345
Empire in the Sun ... 56
Empire of Passion (aka In the Realm of Passion) ... 141
Empire of the Red Bear ... 87
Empire of the Rising Sun ... 144
Empire of the Sun ... 258
Empire Records ... 429
Empire State ... 160
Employees' Entrance ... 268
Empty Bed ... 459
Empty House, The ... 186
Empty Pot, The ... 632
Empty Space, The ... 311
Enchanted April ... 160
Enchanted Forest ... 815
Enchanted Landscapes, Volume 2 ... 484
Enchanted Tales: Beauty and the Beast ... 646
Enchanting Travels of Benjamin of Tudela, The ... 632
Enchantment ... 367
Enchantress, The ... 105
Encounter with the Unknown ... 521
Encyclopedia Brown: The Boy Detective—The Case of the Missing Time Capsule ... 632
Encyclopedia of U.S. Endangered Species ... 865
Encyclopedia of U.S. Postage Stamps ... 865
End, The ... 484
End of Innocence ... 226
End of Man, The ... 521
End of St. Petersburg ... 85
End of the Art World ... 548
End of the Game (South Wind) ... 105
End of the Game ... 632
End of the Golden Weather, The ... 208
End of the Ordeal (1943-1945) ... 767
End of the Trail ... 786
End of the World ... 20
End of Violence, The ... 67
Endangered ... 815
Ending the Tyranny of the Inner Patriarch ... 849
Endless Game, The ... 226
Endless Night ... 173
Endless Summer ... 826
Endless Summer: Donna Summer's Greatest Hits ... 617
Ends of the Earth, The ... 815
Enemy Below ... 367
Enemy Mine ... 800
Enforcer ... 367
Engine Power ... 835
England, Land of Splendor ... 169
England in the Thirties ... 471
England's Historic Treasures ... 169
English Patient, The ... 226
English Plus ... 154
Englishman's Home, An ... 169
Englishman Who Went up a Hill But Came Down a Mountain, The ... 182
Enigma of Love ... 120
Enigma Secret ... 91
Enjo ... 141
Enlightenment ... 200
Enola Gay and the Atomic Bombing of Japan ... 767
Enormous Changes at the Last Minute ... 429
Enquirers, The ... 429
Enrico Macias Live at the Olympia ... 620
Ensemble: A Home Video Course for Beginners in French ... 154
Ensign Pulver ... 268
Enter the Dragon—25th Anniversary Special Edition ... 127

Enter the Dragon....127
Entering Oakland....451
Entertainer, The....311
Entertaining Angels: The Dorothy Day Story....226
Entertaining the Troops: American Entertainers in World War II....767
Enthusiasm....86
Entre Nous....3
Entrepreneurs: An American Adventure, The....758
Environment Under Fire: Ecology and Politics in Central America....56
Ephemeral Films: 1931-1960....484, 865
Epic History of the Mexican Revolution....56
Epic That Never Was....333
Epic Voyages of History....758
Epicenter U.....471
Episodes 3 and 4....738
Episodes of the Hazards of Helen....398
Equality: A History of the Women's Movement in America....758
Equinox....257
Equinox Flower....143
Equus....311
Era Notte a Roma....38
Erase Una Vez....672
Eraser....226
Erendira....50
Eric Bogosian: Confessions of a Porn Star....567
Eric Rohmer: The Moral Tales Box Set....13
Erich Hawkins' America....570
Erick Friedman Plays Fritz Kreisler....589
Erik Bruhn Gala: World Ballet Competition....571
Erik the Viking....226
Eritrean Artists in War and Peace....152
Ermo....117
Ernani....579
Ernesto....32, 459
Ernesto Cardenal....56
Ernesto Che Guevara: The Bolivian Diary....30, 56
Ernie Andrews: Blues for Central Avenue....610
Ernst....632
Eroica....91
Erotic Ghost Story....120
Erotic Touch of Hot Skin....505
Erotikon....99
Erotikus: History of the Gay Movies....459
Erotique....430
Errand Boy, The....268
Errol Flynn Theatre....417
Errol Flynn: Portrait of a Swashbuckler....333
Errors of Youth (Wild Oats), The....80
Eruption of Mt. St. Helens....815
Es Increible! (Hanna-Barbera in Spanish)....672
Escape from Fort Bravo....292
Escape from L.A.....226
Escape from New York....496
Escape from Sobibor....226
Escape from the Planet of the Apes....496
Escape Me Never....367
Escape of Marvin the Ape, The....865
Escape to the Rising Sun....775
Escort Girls....120
Esoteric Nature of Music....602
"Espana Es..."—The Sights and Sounds of Modern Spain....48
Essanay #1....407
Essanay #2....407
Essanay #3....407
Essential Alan Watts: Man in Nature and Work as Play....782
Essential Ballet....571
Essential Opera....579
Essential Opera II....579
Essential Sutherland, The....579
Essentials—4000 Series, The....317
Essentials of Karate with Chris Thompson....849
Esso Salon of Young Artists....548
Esteban and the Ghost....632
Esther and the King....355
Estonia: A Tale of Two Nations....86
Et L'Amour....459
Et la Tendresse?...Bordel! #2....17 17
Etched in Stone: The Golden Age of Cuban Tobacco Art....57, 560
Eternal France....28
Eternal Jew, The....114, 767
Eternal Return....20
Eternal Tramp, The....407
Eternal Waltz, The....69
Eternally Yours....367
Ethan Frome....300
Ethel Kvalheim, Rosemaler....560
Etruscans, The....548
Eugene....114
Eugene O'Neill, Journey into Genius....304
Eugene Onegin (Bolshoi)....579
Eugene Onegin (Covent Garden)....579
Eugene Onegin (Kirov)....579
Eui Kyu Kim: The Elusive Figure....548
Eureeka's Castle: Sing Along with Eureeka....632
Eureka....166
Euro Guide to Sexual Fitness: Sexercise, The....849
Eurocycling—Motorola Team....826
Europa 51....38
Europa Europa....96
Europe: Toward the Twentieth Century....114
European Balloon Adventures....829
European Dance Theater....571
European Folk Tales....646
European Video Library....548
Europeans, The....259
Ev Viva Belcanto....596
Eva Marton in Concert....596
Eva Marton in Tosca....579
Evangeline....398
Eve and the Handyman....513
Eve's Bayou....430
Eve's Leaves....398
Eve Wants to Sleep....91
Evelyn Glennie in Rio/Fiesta....602
Evelyn Laye and Conchita Supervia in Evensong....596
Evelyn Prentice....367
Even Cowgirls Get the Blues....440, 459
Even Hitler Had a Girlfriend....506
Evening Liaison....120
Evening with Ballet Rambert, An....571
Evening with Dr. Bernie Siegel, An....849
Evening with Ed Sanders and the Fugs, An....304
Evening with Lena Horne, An....611
Evening with Marlene Dietrich....333
Evening with Placido Domingo....596
Evening with Royal Ballet, An....571
Evening with the Bolshoi Ballet, An....571
Everglades: Big Cypress, Biscayne, Fort Jefferson....829
Evergreen....173
Everlasting France....549
Everlasting Secret Family, The....205
Every Day's a Holiday....268
Every Other Weekend....3
Everybody Rides the Carousel....709
Everybody's Fine....32
Everybody Sing....322
Everybody Wins....226
Everyone Says I Love You....288
Everyone Sings/Cantemos Todos!....602
Everything Happens at Night....367
Everything Relative....459
Everything You Always Wanted to Know About Sex (But Were Afraid to Ask)....288
Evil Dead 2: Dead by Dawn....521
Evil of Frankenstein....521
Evil Under the Sun....173
Evita....322
Evita: Her Real Story....57
Evita: The Woman Behind the Myth....57
Evolution....398
Evolution of the Magical Child....849
Ewok Adventure....633
Ex-Lady....367
Excalibur....226
Excess Baggage....226
Execution of Private Slovik....226
Executioners....127
Executive Action....226
Executive Suite....367
Exile....775
Exiles, The....471
Exit in 3....549
Exodus....367
Exorcist—25th Anniversary Edition, The....521
Exotic Japan....865
Exotica....212
Expanding Nuclear Club, The....800
Expansion of Life....836
Expecting Miracles....838
Experience Brazil: The Northeast....57
Experience Ecuador and the Galapagos Islands....57
Experience Indonesia....110
Experience Morocco....152
Experience North India....148
Experience Pacific Islands— Fiji, Vanuatu and the Solomon Islands....209
Experience Ruta Maya....57
Experience Vietnam....145
Experience Zimbabwe, Botswana & Namibia....152
Experience: Perception, Interpretation, Illusion....484
Experienced Movers....430
Experimental Animals....803
Experimental Audio Research—Millennium Music: A Meta-Musical Portrait....617
Experimental Avant Garde Series Volume 19 (Very Serious Fun)....484
Experimental Avant Garde Series Volume 20 (The Secret Lives of Inanimate Objects)....484
Experimental Avant Garde Series Volume 21 (An Attack on Social, Sexual, and Political Order)....484
Experimental Avant Garde Series Volume 22....484
Experimental Avant Garde Series Volume 23....484
Experiments That Could Change the World....861
Exploration/Inventions....759
Exploration: Space....839
Explorations into Consciousness....849
Explore Colorado....829
Explore!....782
Explorer Pack....865
Explorer Woman Ray....729
Explorers: A Century of Discovery....815
Exploring Antarctica....829
Exploring Color Workshop: Vol. 1: Basic Color Mixing....563
Exploring Ecology....803
Exploring the Himalayas, Nepal & Kashmir....149
Exposure....226
Expresso Bongo....173
Extenuating Circumstances....17
Exterminating Angel, The....47
Extra Girl, The....398
Extramuros....44, 459
Extraordinary Adventures of Mr. West in the Land of the Bolsheviks, The....85
Extraterrestrial Influence, The....862
Extreme Machines....836
Extreme Measures....226
Eye Above the Well, The....31
Eye Candy....484
Eye for an Eye, An....127
Eye for an Eye....226
Eye of God....227
Eye of Painter: Judy Rifka and Frank Mann....549
Eye of the Needle....227
Eye of the Third Reich, The....767
Eye of Vichy, The....12
Eye on the Sparrow....227
Eye-Tripping Psychedelics....849
Eyes, the Mouth, The....33
Eyes in the Sky....839
Eyes of Amaryllis, The....227
Eyes of Ben Turpin Are upon You!....410
Eyes of the Mummy, The....345
Eyes of the Night....367
Eyes of Youth....398
Eyes on the Prize....451
Eyes Right!....398
Eyes Without a Face....521
Eyewitness....815
Eyewitness Encyclopedia of Science 2.0....865
Eyewitness Encyclopedia of Space and the Universe....865
Eyewitness Living Earth....815
Eyewitness South Africa....152
Ezra Jack Keats Library, The....633

F

F for Fake....344
F.P. 1 Doesn't Answer....496
Fabiola....40
Fable of the Beautiful Pigeon Fancier....50
Fables and Fairy Tales....646
Fabulas de la Selva....50
Fabulous 60's, The....809
Fabulous Adventures of Baron Munchhausen....99, 709
Fabulous Baker Boys....227
Fabulous Dorseys, The....322
Fabulous Versailles, The....20
Fabulous World of Jules Verne....709
Face at the Window, The....521
Face in the Crowd....367
Face of Russia, The....87
Face of the Screaming Werewolf....521
Face to Face....333
Face/Off....227
Faces....440
Faces in the Dark....173
Faces of Battle Series....779
Faces of Dance....571
Faces of Women....150
Facts About AIDS....834
Facts of Life, The....268
Faerie Tale Theatre....646
Fahnen Junker....69, 767
Fahrenheit 451....14
Fail Safe....367
Fairgrounds....430
Fairy Tale Classics....646
Fairy Tales from Exotic Lands....646
Fairyland....672
FairyTale....160
Faith Ringgold Paints Crown Heights....549
Faith Ringgold: The Last Story Quilt....549
Faithful....268
Faithful River, The....91
Falashas....114
Falcon and the Snowman, The....227
Falcon Gentle, The....826
Fall and Rise of Reginald Perrin, The....191
Fall from Grace....160
Fall of Communism....89
Fall of Freddie the Leaf, The....633
Fall of Saigon, The....778
Fall of the Berlin Wall....73
Fall of the House of Usher....521
Fall of the Roman Empire....367
Fall of the Romanov Dynasty....85
Fallen Angels....120
Fallen Idol, The....173
Falling Down....227
Falling from Grace....227
False Faces....398
Falstaff (Glyndebourne)....579
Falstaff (Zeffirelli)....579
Fame....322
Families We Choose, The....459
Family, The....36
Family Business....268
Family Circus Christmas, A....709
Family Circus Easter, A....709
Family Circus Special Valentine, A....709
Family Concert Featuring the Roches, A....633
Family Dog, Laserdisc Set....696
Family Dog (Amazing Stories: Book 2), The....696
Family Dog Vol. 1....696
Family Dog Vol. 2....696
Family Dog Vol. 3....696
Family Farm: Thomas Locker, The....633

Family Jewels,The 268
Family Life....91, 166
Family of Women....800
Family Plot....352
Family Thing,A 227
Family Viewing 212
Famous Americans of the 20th Century: The Story of Babe Ruth 794
Famous Americans of the 20th Century: The Story of Charles Lindbergh 794
Famous Americans of the 20th Century: The Story of Douglas MacArthur....794
Famous Americans of the 20th Century: The Story of Dwight D. Eisenhower 794
Famous Americans of the 20th Century: The Story of Franklin Delano Roosevelt....794
Famous Americans of the 20th Century: The Story of G.I. Joe....794
Famous Americans of the 20th Century: The Story of Harry S Truman 794
Famous Americans of the 20th Century: The Story of Helen Keller....794
Famous Americans of the 20th Century: The Story of Henry Ford....794
Famous Americans of the 20th Century: The Story of Knute Rockne 794
Famous Americans of the 20th Century: The Story of Thomas Edison 795
Famous Black Americans....451
Famous for 15 Minutes/Mad, Mad Century 758
Famous Third Army 767
Fan,The 227
Fanci's Persuasion 459
Fancy Pants 268
Fanfan la Tulipe 20
Fanny 26, 367
Fanny by Gaslight....173
Fanny Hill 506
Fantasia....692
Fantastic Four:The Origin of the Fantastic Four 696
Fantastic Planet 710
Fantastic Puppet People....496
Fantastic Voyage,The....496
Fantastic World of M.C. Escher,The....549
Fantasy Film Worlds of George Pal 683
Fantasy Garden Ballet Class,A 571
Fantasy Mission Force 134
Far and Away 227
Far Away and Long Ago (Alla Lejos y Hace Tiempo)....50
Far Away from the Shamrock Shore: A History of Irish Music in America 203
Far Eastern Cookery....857
Far from Home:The Adventures of Yellow Dog 663
Far from Poland 98, 442
Far from the Madding Crowd....173, 191
Far North....260
Far Pavilions,The....417
Faraway, So Close....67
Farewell Good Brothers....862
Farewell My Concubine 117
Farewell My Lovely....160
Farewell to Arms,A....367
Farewell to Yamato: In the Name of Love....729
Fargo 441
Fargo Collectors Set 441
Farinelli....3, 29
Farm Animals: Close Up and Very Personal 652
Farmer's Huge Carrot,The....633
Farmer's Wife,The 352
Farmer Takes a Wife....367
Farouk: Last of the Pharaohs 110
Fashions 322
Fass Black 532
Fast, Cheap & Out of Control....481
Fast Buck....63
Fast Cars....826
Fast Forward....227
Faster Pussycat! Kill! Kill!....513
Fat and the Lean....97
Fat Charlie's Circus....633
Fat City 348, 849
Fat Man and Little Boy....227
Fat of the Land 430
Fatal Attraction (Director's Cut) 227
Fatal Chase 127
Fatal Confinement....160
Fatal Fury 1-2 Punch 729
Fatal Fury 2:The New Battle 729
Fatal Fury Boxed Set 729
Fatal Fury: Legend of the Hungry Wolf....729
Fatal Fury:The Motion Picture 729
Fatal Hour,The....367
Fatal Inversion,A 191
Fatal Passion of Dr. Mabuse,The 72
Fatal Target 120
Fatalist,The....127
Fate of Lee Khan 127
Father....103, 205
Father Christmas 633
Father Clements Story,The....452
Father Goose....268
Father of the Bride 268
Father's Little Dividend 268
Father Sergius....85
Father Was a Fullback....268
Fatherland 227
Fatty Arbuckle 410
Faure/Poulenc Concert 596
Faust 73, 710
Faustyna 91
Fauvism and Expressionism 549
Fauvres: Plein Aire Painters,The 549
Favor,The Watch and the Very Big Fish,The 182
Fawlty Towers 191
Fay's 12 Days of Christmas....633
FBI Story....368
FBI War on Black America 452
FDR 759, 795, 865
Fear 38, 227
Fear and the Muse:The Story of Anna Akhmatova....87
Fear of Disclosure 834
Fearless....208
Fearless Fortune Hunter....683
Fearless Frida and the Secret Spies 663
Fearless Vampire Killers 97
Fears....98
Feast of July....160
Feast of the Gods,The 549
Feast of Irish Set Dances,A....571
Feature Film Lighting 317
Federal Agent....368
Federal Agents vs. Underworld Inc. (Cliffhanger Serials #5) 537
Federal Hill....227
Fedora 345
Feed....471
Feeding Frenzy 506
Feel 100%....120
Fela in Concert....602
Fela Live 602
Felix the Cat Silent Films Vol. 1 683
Felix the Cat—Silent—Volume 1 683
Felix the Cat—Silent—Volume 2 683
Felix the Cat Vol. 1....683
Felix the Cat Vol. 2....683
Felix the Cat: Sound & Silent....683
Felix!....683
Fellini's Roma....36
Fellini Satyricon....36
Fellini:A Director's Notebook 36
Female....268
Female Bunch,The 506
Female Misbehavior....63, 459
Female of the Species & Selected Biograph Shorts (Volume III),The....412
Female Perversions 459
Feminine— Ancient Vision, Modern Wisdom 787
Femme 506
Fencing Master,The....44
Ferdy the Ant....710
Fernandel the Dressmaker 17
Fernando de Szyszlo of Peru Paints a Picture....549
FernGully II:The Magical Rescue 683
FernGully:The Last Rainforest....683
Ferrari Collection,The....842
Ferry to Hong Kong 182
Fertile La Toyah Jackson Video Magazine:The Kinky Issue! 459
Festival of Bay Area Music (Relix Concert),A....605
Festival of Britain 471
Festivals and Holidays in Latin America 57
Festive Nuremberg (Festlisches Nurnberg) 767
Fever 96
Fever Mounts in El Pao....47
Few Good Men,A 227
Few Men Well-Conducted:The George Rogers Clark Story,A....298
Few Moments with Buster Keaton and Laurel & Hardy,A....268
Fiances (I Fidanzati) 40
Fiction and Other Truths:A Film About Jane Rule 459
Fictitious Marriage 107
Fiddler on the Roof....322
Fiddlin' Man:The Life and Times of Bob Wills....611
Fidelio (Covent Garden)....579
Fidelio (Glyndebourne)....579
Field,The 202
Field of Dreams 227
Field of Honor....8
Fields of Armor....809
Fiend Without a Face....521
Fiendish Plot of Dr. Fu Manchu,The....521
Fierce Creatures 182
Fiery Angel,The....579
Fiery Dragon Kid,The 127
Fiesta....57, 633
Fiesta Gitana!....571
Fifteen Streets,The 191
Fifth, Park & Madison 471
Fifth Avenue Girl 268
Fifth Element,The....3, 496
Fifth Monkey,The....227
Fifth Seal,The 101
Fig Tree,The....660
Fight Back to School 120
Fight for the Sky....767
Fight for the Title....368
Fight of the Sky 767
Fighter....368
Fighter Attack 368
Fighting 69th,The 368
Fighting American 398
Fighting Coward,The....398
Fighting Devil Dogs (The Tornado of Doom)....537
Fighting Eagle....398
Fighting Kentuckian,The....368
Fighting Legion,The 398
Fighting Marines,The 537
Fighting Pilot....173
Fighting Seabees....368
Fighting Sullivans,The....368
Figure Drawing and Painting with James Kirk 563
Figures....484
Filipino Americans: Discovering Their Past for the Future 146
Filling in the Blanks....839
Film Before Film....63
Film Genius: Orson Welles Gift Pack,A....344
Film Graphics....317
Film Musicals....430
Film Parade....333
Film Portrait 484
Film Reality and Film Fantasy....333
Filming Ballet....333, 571
Filming of the Leopard Son,The....333, 815
Filmmakers on Their Craft....333
Films by Ed Emshwiller....484
Films of Arne Sucksdorff:The Great Adventure Plus Short Subjects,The....75, 472
Films of Charles and Ray Eames....485
Films of Edmund Cobb....398
Films of Georges Melies,Volume 1 20
Films of Harold Lloyd—Volume 1 409
Films of Harold Lloyd—Volume 2....409
Films of Harold Lloyd—Volume 3 410
Films of Harold Lloyd—Volume 5....410
Films of Harry Langdon Volume 1....410
Films of Harry Langdon Volume 2....410
Films of James Broughton,The....492
Films of John Wayne....368
Films of Leo Maloney,The 368
Films of Meredith Monk,The 485, 567
Films of Oliver Hardy 410
Films of Oskar Fischinger— Optical Poetry,The....710
Films of Scott Bartlett,The 485
Films of Stan Laurel Volume 1 410
Films of Stan Laurel Volume 2....410
Films of Stan Laurel Volume 3 410
Films of Stan Laurel Volume 4 410
Films of Thomas Ince 398
Films of Yaacov Ben Dov: Father of the Hebrew Cinema,The....109
Final Cut,The....192
Final Extra,The....398
Final Fantasy,Vol. 1: Legend of the Crystals 729
Final Fantasy,Vol. 2 729
Final Justice....127
Final Problem,The....186
Final Romance Starring Jose Carreras 596
Final Victory 120
Final Yamato 729
Finders, Keepers, Lovers, Weepers....513
Fine Art of Separating People from Their Money,The 540
Fine Art: Education,Vol. 3 560
Fine Art: General,Vol. 1....560
Fine Art: Production,Vol. 2....560
Fine and Long Tradition,A 782
Fine White Dust....633
Finger Man 368
Fingermouse,Yoffy and Friends 652
Fingerpicking Blues of John Jackson,The 611
Fingers That Tickle and Delight....472
Fingerstyle Guitar....605
Finian's Rainbow....259
Finish Line....227
Finished....459
Finite Oceans 815
Finland, Fresh and Original 79
Fiorile (Wild Flower)....35
Fire 210, 815
Fire and Rescue....633
Fire Below Us,The....815
Fire Down Below 173
Fire Fighters 759
Fire from the Sky....836
Fire in the Steppe....91
Fire on the Mountain....472, 767
Fire on the Track:The Steve Prefontaine Story 826
Fire over England 173
Fire Storm over Dresden 767
Fire Within,The 13
Firearm Safety Onstage 317
Firebird....571
Firecreek 292
Firefly,The 322
Firehouse....444
Firemen's Ball 100
Fires of Kuwait 759
Fires on the Plain 141
Firestone Dances....571
Fireworks....485
Fireworks:The Magic of Pyrotechnics....860
Firm,The 227
First American Features....398
First and Second Grade Feelings....633
First Christmas,The....683
First Day of Freedom....91
First Do No Harm....227
First Draw Gift Set....417
First Easter Rabbit,The....683
First Emperor of China,The....135, 865
First in the Philippines:A Film History of the Second Oregon Volunteer Regiment....146
First Knight 227
First Ladies 795
First Love....74, 322
First Men in the Moon....496

First Modern Sculptor: Donatello, 1386-1466 549
First Name: Carmen 9
First Nudie Musical 506
First Option 127
First Person: Marvin Minsky, The Society of Mind 866
First Person: Mumia Abu-Jamal, Live from Death Row 866
First Person: Stephen Jay Gould, On Evolution 866
First Strike 134
First Strike: Portrait of an Activist 803
First Time, The 17
First Time Garden 815
First Time Is the Last Time 120
First to Fight 368
First Wives Club 268
First Works 334
First World Festival of Negro Arts, The 152
Fish (Pet Care) 815
Fish Called Wanda, A 182
Fisher King, The 168
Fishing Trip: I Love Lucy: Deep Sea Fishing and The Honeymooners: Something Fishy 417
Fishy Story, A 120
Fist of Fear Touch of Death 506
Fist of Legend 127
Fistful of Dollars 39
Fistful of Dynamite, A 39
Fists of Chan 134
Fit or Fat for the 90s 849
Fit! 834
Fitness Fables: #1 826
Fitness Fables: #2 826
Fitness Fables: #3 826
Fitzwilly 268
Five Card Stud 292
Five Corners 268
Five Dances by Martha Graham 571
Five Doctors, The 200
Five Easy Pieces 227
Five Fingers 368
Five Golden Hours 182
Five Graves to Cairo 345
Five Heartbeats, The 444
Five Lady Venoms 127
Five Lionni Classics 633, 710
Five Miles to Midnight 368
Five Sesame Street Stories 652
Five Stories for the Very Young 652
Five Weeks in a Balloon 663
Fizz and Martina 672
Flambards 192
Flame and the Arrow 368
Flame of Araby 368
Flame of the Barbary Coast 368
Flame over India 173
Flamenco 571
Flames 368
Flames in Ashes 775
Flames of Revolt: The Irgun 109
Flames of the Sun (Sholay) 147
Flaming Creatures 459, 485
Flaming Ears 63, 459
Flamingo Road 368
Flash Gordon Conquers the Universe 537
Flash Gordon—Rocketship 496
Flash Gordon: The Movie: Marooned on Mongo 710
Flash Gordon: To Save Earth 710
Flashbacks: Easy Lovin' 617
Flashbacks: Pop Parade 617
Flashbacks: Soul Sensations 617
Flashdance 227
Flat Top 368
Flatfoot 33
Flavor of Corn, The 33, 459
Flavors of South America 57
Fledgling 633
Fleet Firepower 759
Fleet Firepower: New Technology 759
Fleischer & Famous Studios 683
Fleischer Color Classics 683
Flesh and Blood 228, 398
Flesh and Bone 228
Flesh and the Devil 398
Flesh and the Fiends (Mania) 521
Flesh Eaters, The 521
Flesh Gordon 506
Flesh Merchant, The 506
Flickers 459
Flight of Dragons 710
Flight of Rainbirds, A 31
Flight of the Dream Team 839
Flight of the Innocent 33
Flight of the Phoenix 368
Flight over the Equator 815
Flight to Mars 496
Flight to the Finish, A 633
Flights of Courage 842
Flintstones Deluxe Laserdisc Set, The 696
Flintstones: A Flintstone Christmas, The 696
Flintstones: A Flintstones Christmas Carol, The 696
Flintstones: A Haunted House Is Not a Home, The 696
Flintstones: Babe in Bedrock, The 696
Flintstones: Bedrock 'n Roll, The 696
Flintstones: Christmas in Bedrock, The 696
Flintstones: Dino's Two Tales, The 696
Flintstones: Fearless Fred Strikes Again, The 696
Flintstones: Fred Takes the Field, The 696
Flintstones: Hooray for Hollyrock, The 696
Flintstones: How the Flintstones Saved Christmas, The 696
Flintstones: I Yabba-Dabba Do, The 696
Flintstones: Love Letters on the Rocks, The 696
Flintstones: Rocky Bye Babies, The 696
Flintstones: Wacky Inventions, The 696
Flip the Frog Vol. 1 683
Flip the Frog Vol. 2 684
Flip the Frog Vol. 3 684
Flip the Frog Vol. 4 684
Flip the Frog Vol. 5 684
Flipper 663
Flipper's New Adventure 663
Flirt 442
Flirtation Walk 322
Flirting 120, 205
Flirting Scholar 120
Flirting with Disaster 268
Floating Palaces 842
Floating World, The 815
Flood 815
Florence 42
Florence: Cradle of the Rennaissance 42
Florian 91
Florida! America's Vacationland 829
Floundering 430
Flow 430, 459
Flower Drum Song 322
Flower Drums of Fung Yang 120
Flower Love (aka Love Is Grown with Flowers) 136
Flower of My Secret, The 46
Flower Storm 646
Flowers and Gardens 560
Flowers from a Stranger 417
Flowers of Reverie 102
Flowers of St. Francis 38
Fluxfilm Anthology 485
Fly, The 212, 521
Fly Away Home 228
Fly II, The 521
Flyaway Pantaloons, The 633
Flyers 839
Flying Dagger 120
Flying Deuces 268
Flying Disc Men from Mars (Cliffhanger Serials #5) 537
Flying Elephants 410
Flying Fool, The 398
Flying Fruit Fly Circus, The 668
Flying Leathernecks 346
Flying Machines 842
Flying Saucer 496
Flying Saucer Mystery, The 862
Flying Saucers 862
Flying Saucers over Hollywood 334
Flying the Blimp 842
Flying Tigers 368
Fobia 1 729
Focus for the Future 785
Fodor's Video Guides 829
Fog, The 521
Folk City 25th Anniversary Concert 605
Folkloric Ballet of Mexico 571
Folks Like Us 152
Folktales for Peace 803
Follow My Leader 633
Follow That Bunny! 652
Follow That Dream 536
Follow That Fish 652
Follow That Goblin 710
Follow the Boys 368
Follow the Drinking Gourd 633
Following the Tundra Wolf 815
Fonda on Fonda 334
Fonteyn & Nureyev: The Perfect Partnership 571
Food for Thought 849
Fool for Love 254
Fool Killer, The 368
Fool of the World and the Flying Ship, The 633
Fool There Was, A 398
Foolish Wives 348
Fools of Fortune 228
Fools Rush In 268
Footlight Parade 322
Footlight Serenade 322
Footloose 322
Footloose in History—Grades 5-12 809
Footnotes: The Classics of Ballet 571
Footsteps in the Dark 268
For a Few Dollars More 39
For a Lost Soldier 31, 459
For All Mankind 839, 866
For Auld Lang Syne 268
For Better or Worse 684
For Love Alone 206
For Me and My Gal 322
For Pete's Sake 268
For Roseanna 228
For the Living: The Story of the U.S. Holocaust Memorial Museum 775
For the Love of Benji 663
For the Love of Mary 368
For the Moment 210
For Us, The Living: The Story of Medgar Evers 452
For Whom the Bell Tolls 368
For Your Eyes Only 168
For Your Heart Only 120
Forbidden Arsenal 127
Forbidden Christ, The 40
Forbidden City, The 398
Forbidden City: The Great Within 135
Forbidden Fruit 17
Forbidden Games 20
Forbidden Hollywood, The 368
Forbidden Love: The Unashamed Stories of Lesbian Lives 459
Forbidden Moon 496
Forbidden Music 322
Forbidden Photographs 472
Forbidden Planet 496
Forbidden Quest, The 31
Forbidden Songs 91
Force of Arms 368
Force of Circumstance 430
Force of Evil 368, 775
Forced March 228
Forces of Life 836
Ford Star Jubilee 417
Ford Star Jubilee Salute to Cole Porter 417
Ford: The Man and the Machine 795
Foreign Affairs 268
Foreign Correspondent 352
Foreign Field, A 160
Foreign Legion, The 759
Foreign Student 228
Foreigner 430
Forest Habitat Set 815
Forest Through the Trees, The 815
Forever, Darling 268
Forever Amber 369
Forever and a Day 170
Forever Fairytales— Hans Christian Andersen 646
Forever James Dean 334
Forever Lulu 228
Forever Mary 33
Forevermore: Biography of a Leach Lord 430
Forget Mozart 63
Forget Paris 268
Forgotten Comedians 411
Forgotten Melody 91
Forgotten Prisoners 228
Forgotten Silver 208
Forgotten Village, The 57, 369
Forms of Artistic Expression: Glass and Sculpture 560
Formula, The 228
Formula 1 Saga 842
Forrest Bales Presents Basic Latex Mold Making 563
Forrest Gump 228
Forsaking All Others 268
Fort Apache, the Bronx 228
Fort Apache 340
Fort Mose 452
Fort Saganne 3
Fortunata y Jacinta 44
Fortune, The 228
Fortune and Men's Eyes 311
Fortune Cookie 345
Fortune Hunters 120
Fortune's Fool 69
Fortunes of War 192
Forty Days of Musa Dagh 759
Forty Thousand Horsemen 206
Forty-Nine Seventeen 398
Foul Play 95
Fountainhead 369
Four Adventures of Reinette and Mirabelle 13
Four American Composers 589
Four Corners of Earth 787
Four Daughters 369
Four Days in July 165
Four Days in November 797
Four Days in September 54
Four Directions: Selections from MIX 94—The NY Lesbian & Gay Film Festival 459
Four Fashion Horses 560
Four Footed Friends 866
Four for Texas 369
Four for Thrills, Edgar Allan Poe, Etc. 633
Four Horsemen of the Apocalypse, The 369, 398
Four Hours a Year: The March of Time 759
Four in a Jeep 30
Four Musketeers, The 182
Four Noble Truths, The 149
Four Rooms 430, 441
Four Seasons, The 589
Four Seasons in Polish Cooking 857
Four Sided Triangle 173
Four Star Playhouse 417
Four Ways Out 40
Four Ways to Say Farewell 589
Four Weddings and a Funeral 182
Fourth King, The 633
Fourth Man, The 31
Fourth Protocol 160
Fourth Wise Man, The 228
Fowl Play 663
Fox and His Friends 66
Fox Hunter 127
Fox Leon and Others 672
Fox Terrytoons 684
Foxes 228
Foxfire 228
Foxtrap 532
Foxy Brown 532
FP-1 Doesn't Answer 69
Fractal Experience 710
Fractal Fantasy: The Art of Mathematics 710

Fractal Lumination 845
Fractal Universe 710
Fractasia 710
Fragile Balance (1955-1961) 800
Frame and Context: Richard Ross 549
France Nobody Knows 28
Frances 228
Francesca da Rimini 579
Franchise Affair, The 160
Francis Bacon 549
Francis Goes to the Races 268
Francis in the Navy 268
Francis Joins the WACS 269
Francis the Talking Mule 269
Francisco Oller 549
Franck Goldberg: Sampler 8
Francois Truffaut 14
Francois Truffaut: 25 Years, 25 Films 14
Francois Truffaut: Stolen Portraits 14, 334
Frank and Koen Theys, Lied Meines Landes II: Die Walkure 485
Frank Capra's American Dream 350
Frank Capra AFI Lifetime Achievement Award 332
Frank Film 710
Frank Gambale: Monster Licks and Speed Picking 624
Frank Lloyd Wright: The Office for Edgar J. Kaufmann 565
Frank Patterson: Ireland's Golden Voice 203
Frank Sinatra: His Life & Times 617
Frank Yankovic: America's Polka King 602
Frankenstein (Bergin/Quaid) 522
Frankenstein (Gielgud) 522
Frankenstein 1970 522
Frankenstein 514
Frankenstein—A Cinematic Scrapbook 522
Frankenstein Created Woman 522
Frankenstein Meets the Wolfman 522
Frankenstein Must Be Destroyed! 522
Frankenstein—The Restored Version 522
Frankenweenie 255
Frankie and Johnny 269, 536
Frankie Starlight 228
Franklin D. Roosevelt: The New Deal 767
Franklin D. Roosevelt: The War Years 767
Franklin D. Roosevelt: War Comes to America 767
Frans Hals of Antwerp 549
Frantic 97
Franz 3
Franz Schubert: "The Trout" Quintet 866
Frate Francisco 41, 153
Freaked 269
Freaks 522
Fred Astaire Dance Series 571
Freddie King in Concert 611
Freddie King: Free Stage 611
Freddie King: The!!!!Beat—1966 611
Freddie the Frog 710
Frederic Remington: The Truth of Other Days 549
Frederich Gulda/Mozart No End and the Paradise Band 589
Frederick Delius: A Village Romeo and Juliet 580
Frederick Douglass: An American Life 452
Frederick Douglass: When the Lion Wrote History 452
Frederick Law Olmsted and the Public Park in America 565
Fredro for Adults 91
Free and Easy 409
Free at Last 472
Free Radicals, Vol. 1 710
Free Soul, A 369
Free to Love 398
Free Willy 663
Free Willy Story: Keiko's Journey Home, The 815
Freedom Beat: The Video 620
Freedom Is Paradise 81
Freedom Road 101, 452
Freedom's Heritage— The Miracle of America 759
Freefall 430
Freeway 228
Freeze, Die, Come to Life 81
French & Saunders 192
French Animation Festival 710
French Can Can 26
French Connection, The 228
French Connection 2 228
French Exit 228
French Fairy Tales—Blanche Neige 672
French Fairy Tales—Le Petit Chaperon 672
French Folk Dances 571
French Folk Dancing Video, Volume 2 571
French Fried Vacation (Les Bronzes) 17
French Kiss 269
French Lesson 160
French Lieutenant's Woman 160
French Peek-a-Boo 506
French Postcards 269
French Pronunciation Tutor 866
French Singers 28
French Twist 3
French Way 20
Frenzy 352
Frescoes of Diego Rivera 549
Fresh, Vol. III 602
Fresh 430
Fresh Horses 228
Freshkill 160
Freshman 269
Freud Leaving Home 75
Frida 50
Frida Kahlo 549
Friday Foster 532
Fridays of Eternity 50
Fried Green Tomatoes 228
Fried Shoes, Cooked Diamonds 304
Frieda 173
Friedemann Bach 69
Friendly Gray Whales 815
Friends 151
Friends Forever 75
Friends: A Closer Look at the Enemy 87
Friendship 147
Friendship Sloop: A Heritage Retained 826
Frightened City, The 173
Frightened Woman, The 33
Frighteners, The 228
Frightfest, Nickelodeon 696
Frisco Kid, The 228
Frisk 430
Fritz the Cat 710
Fritz Wunderlich—Live 580
Frog 633
Frog and Toad Are Friends 652
Frog and Toad Together 652
Frog King, The 646
Frogs! 660
From a Far Country: Pope John Paul II 790
From Beijing with Love (aka From China with Love) 127
From Broadway to Cheyenne 292
From Czar to Stalin 87
From Disaster to Discovery: The Challenger Explosion 839
From Dusk till Dawn 430
From Hare to Eternity 684
From Hell to Borneo 369
From Here to Alternity: Adventures of a Scientist 849
From Here to Eternity 229, 369
From Here to Infinity 839
From Information to Wisdom 845
From Light to Enlightenment 849
From Mao to Mozart 589
From Russia with Love 168
From Stump to Ship: A 1930 Logging Film 759
From Sunup 152
From the Heart of the World: The Elder Brother's Warning 787
From the Journals of Jean Seberg 430
From the Life of the Marionettes 78
From the Manger to the Cross 398
From the Mixed-Up Files of Mrs. Basil E. Frankweiler 663
From the Wake of the Bow 842
From These Roots 452
From Weimar to Bonn 73
Fronczewski—Pietrzak— Smolen Cabaret 98
Front, The 288
Front Page 369
Frontier Heritage 298
Frontier in Space 200
Frontier Photographers, The 559
Frontier Progress 298
Frontline: Hillary's Class 795
Frontline: Waco 759
Frostbiter 506
Frosty Returns 696
Frosty's Winter Wonderland 696
Frosty the Snowman 696
Frozen Limits 182
Fueling the Future 803
Fugitive, The 229, 417
Fugitive (The Taking of Luke McVane), The 398
Fugitive Kind 369
Fugitive Road and Crime of Dr. Crespi 369
Fuhrer: Rise of a Madman 767
Fulfilling the Vision 787
Full Body Massage 166
Full Contact 127
Full Cycle: A World Odyssey 826
Full Hearts and Empty Pockets 41
Full Metal Jacket 256
Full Monty, The 182
Full Moon in Paris 14
Full of Life 369
Full Throttle 127
Fuller Brush Girl 269
Fuller Brush Man 269
Fuller Brush Man/The Fuller Brush Girl, The 269
Fun, The Luck, and the Tycoon, The 120
Fun 430
Fun and Fancy Free 692
Fun Down There 459
Fun House 534
Fun in a Box 668
Fun in Acapulco 536
Fun in the U.S.S.R. 87
Fun with Clay 668
Fun with Herbs 849
Functional Reading—I Can Read Signs 859
Functional Readings in Spanish— Signs in a Mexican City 154
Fundamentals of Scenic Painting 317
Funeral, The 140, 430
Funeral in Berlin 173
Funny Bones 269
Funny Dirty Little War 50
Funny Face 322
Funny Girl 343
Funny Guys and Gals of the Talkies 269
Funny Lady 322
Funny Thing Happened on the Way to the Forum, A 322
Furniture to Go 560
Fury, The 229
Fury 72
Fury Is a Woman (The Siberian Lady Macbeth) 96
Fury of Hercules 42
Fury of the Wolfman, The 522
Fusion Arts 549
Future in the Cradle 803
Future of Humanity 849
Future Shock 710
Futz 311

G

"G" Men 369
G.E. Theatre 417
G.I. Blues 536
G-Men vs. the Black Dragon 537
Gabby (Cartoonies) 684
Gable and Stewart in the Air Force 767
Gabriel Garcia Marquez 57
Gabriel over the White House 369
Gabrielle Roth: The Wave 849
Gaby—A True Story 229
Gadd Gang Live, The 611
Gadget 710
Gael Force: An Irish Music Event 571
Gai Dimanche/Swing to the Left 28
Gaiking 729
Gaite Parisienne 571
Gala Concert with Luciano Pavarotti 596
Gala Tribute to Tchaikovsky 589
Galapagos: Beyond Darwin 816
Galapagos: My Fragile World (National Audubon) 816
Galaxy Express 999: Adieu Galaxy Express 729
Galaxy Express 999: The Signature Edition 729
Galaxy Fraulein Yuna 2 729
Galaxy of the Dinosaurs 522
Gall Force 1: Eternal Story 729
Gall Force 2: Destruction 729
Gall Force 3: Stardust War 729
Gall Force Earth Chapter 1 729
Gall Force Earth Chapter 2 729
Gall Force Earth Chapter 3 729
Gall Force: New Era 1 729
Gall Force: New Era 2 729
Gallagher—Melon Crazy 534
Gallagher—Over Your Head 534
Gallagher—Stuck in the Sixties 534
Gallagher—The Bookkeeper 534
Gallagher—The Maddest 534
Gallant Hours 369
Gallavants 710
Gallipoli 208
Galloping Major, The 182
Gallowglass 192
Galway Kinnell 304
Gambit 369
Gambler, The 229
Gamblers, The 369
Gambling Man, The 192
Game of Monopoly (1870-1914), The 809
Gamera 496
Gamera vs. Barugon 496
Gamera vs. Gaos 496
Gamera vs. Guiron 496
Gamera vs. Zigra 496
Ganapati/A Spirit in the Bush 485
Gandhi 160
Gang of Souls 304
Gang War 448
Gangster Story 369
Gangsters: Bugsy, Dutch and Al, The 795
Ganja and Hess 444
Gap-Toothed Women 480
Garaga 730
Garam Hava (Hot Winds) 147
Garbo Talks 229
Garcia Marquez Collection, The 50
Garden, The 167
Garden of Abdul Gasazi 633
Garden of Delights 45
Garden of Eden 398
Garden of the Finzi-Continis, The 38
Gardens of the World 816
Garfield Christmas, A 696
Garfield Gets a Life 696
Garfield Goes Hollywood 696
Garfield in the Rough 697
Garfield on the Town 697
Garfield's Feline Fantasies 697
Garfield's Halloween Adventure 697
Garfield's Thanksgiving 697
Garfield: Babes & Bullets 697
Garfield: His Nine Lives 697
Gargoyles 506
Gargoyles: The Movie 692
Garlic Is As Good As Ten Mothers 480
Garth Fagin's Griot New York 571
Gary Cooper 334
Gary Cooper: American Life, American Legend 334
Gary Goldberg—Four Films: Plates, Mesmer, Usher and TV Head 567
Gary Hill: Watch Words, Vols. 1-3 485
Gary Snyder, Vols. 1 & 2 304
Gary Soto 304
Gas Food Lodging 430
Gasbags, The 182
Gaslight 173, 350

Gatchaman, Vol. 1: The Dragon King....730
Gatchaman, Vol. 2: The Red Specter....730
Gatchaman, Vol. 3: The Final Countdown....730
Gate of Hell....137
Gate to the Mind's Eye, The....710
Gates of Jerusalem, The....790
Gathered in Time....560
Gathering Strength (1840-1914)....809
Gattaca....496
Gaucho, The....398
Gaudi....549
Gay Deceivers....459
Gay Divorcee....322
Gay for a Day....459, 472
Gay Games II: Highlights....826
Gay Games IV from A to Q....459, 826
Gay Gay Hollywood....459
Gay Purr-ee....710
Gay Youth....459
Gazebo, The....269
GED Math Review....858
Geek Maggot Bingo....430
Gefilte Fish....114
Geisha, A....143
Geisha Boy, The....269
Geisha Girl....496
Gems and Minerals....816
Gender: The Enduring Paradox....785
Gene Autry....334
Gene Kelly Collection, The....322
Gene Krupa Story, The....369
General, The....409
General Bradley Story....759
General Della Rovere....38
General Died at Dawn....369
General Douglas MacArthur....795
General Line....86
General Marshall Story....768
General Omar Bradley....795
General Sosabowski....92
General Spanky....269
Generation, A....96
Generation Earth....803
Generations: A Chinese Family....135
Genesis....147
Genesis of Animation, Volume One, The....710
Genesis Survivor Gaiarth: Stage 1....730
Genesis Survivor Gaiarth: Stage 2....730
Genesis Survivor Gaiarth: Stage 3....730
Genesis: A Living Conversation....790
Genetic Time Bomb....803
Genghis Cohn....192
Genocyber Part 1: Birth of Genocyber....730
Genocyber Parts 2 & 3: Vajranoid Showdown....730
Genocyber Parts 4 & 5: The Legend of Ark de Grande....730
Gentle Giant....633
Gentle Sex, The....369
Gentleman Jim....369
Gentleman Jim Reeves: The Story of a Legend....605
Gentleman's Agreement....369
Gentlemen Prefer Blondes....341
Gentlemen Prefer Nature Girls....506
Geography Tutor, The....860
Geomancy: Consciousness and Sacred Sites....849
George Balanchine's The Nutcracker....571
George Bellows: Portrait of an American Artist....549
George Crumb: The Voice of the Whale....617
George Dunning....684
George Frederick Handel: Honour, Profit and Pleasure....589
George Gershwin Remembered....589
George Jones: Golden Hits....605
George of the Jungle Triple-Pack....697
George of the Jungle: Gullible Travels....697
George of the Jungle: In George We Trust....697
George of the Jungle: It's a Mad, Mad, Mad, Mad Jungle....697
George of the Jungle: The Man from J.U.N.G.L.E.....697
George Pal Puppetoons....710
George Romero: Document of the Dead....334
George's Island....663
George Shearing: Lullaby of Birdland....611
George Stevens: A Filmmaker's Journey....343, 768
George Stevens: D-Day to Berlin....343, 768
George Wallace....229
George Washington....759
George Washington Slept Here....269
George Washington: The Forging of a Nation....417
George Washington: The Man Who Wouldn't Be King....759
George Washington: The Unknown Years....759
Georgia....206, 430
Georgia O'Keefe....549
Georgia Ragsdale: Honey, Pass That Around....460
Georgy Girl....182
Geosophy....862
Gerald McBoing Boing: Dusty of the Circus....697
Gerald McBoing Boing: Favorite Animals....697
Gerald McBoing Boing: Favorite Painters....697
Gerald McBoing Boing: Favorite Sing-Along Songs....697
Gerald McBoing Boing: Favorite Stories & Tales....697
Gerald McBoing Boing: The Silly Twirliger Twins & Their Funny Friends....697
Gerbert Is Ben Franklin....633
Gerbert Is Marco Polo....633
Gerbert Is Mozart....633
Gerbert Is Tom Sawyer....633
Gericault: Men and Wild Horses....549
Germaine Dulac: The Smiling Madame Beudet and Seashell and the Clergyman....485
German Folk Dances....571
German Folk Dancing Video, Volume 2....571
German TV Commercials....73
German Way of Life, The....73
Germany, A Tapestry of Tradition....73
Germany Awake....69
Germany in Autumn....66
Germany Pale Mother....63
Germany Year Zero....38
Germinal....3
Geronimo....292, 787
Geronimo and the Apache Resistance....787
Geronimo: The Last Renegade....787
Gertrude....79
Gertrude Stein: When This You See, Remember Me....304
Gervaise....20
Gerz Jochen Ti Amo....485
Get an Education, My Son....105
Get Carter....174
Get Christie Love....532
Get It Together....803
Get Off the Karmic Wheel....849
Get on the Bus....447
Get Out Your Handkerchiefs....11
Get Ready for School....652
Get Shorty....269
Getaway, The....229, 347
Getting Around....472
Getting Gertie's Garter....398
Getting of Wisdom, The....206
Getting the Message Across....334
Getting to Heaven....57
Gettysburg (Documentary)....779
Gettysburg (Martin Sheen)....779
Gettysburg Battlefield Tour....779
Gettysburg Multimedia Battle Simulation....866
Gevatron—Sing Along, The....109
Ghidrah the 3-Headed Monster....496
Ghost, The....522
Ghost....269
Ghost and Mr. Chicken, The....269
Ghost and Mrs. Muir....369
Ghost and the Darkness, The....229
Ghost Breakers, The....269
Ghost Chasers....269
Ghost Dad....444
Ghost Dances....571
Ghost Foot....120
Ghost in the Shell....730
Ghost in the Shell—Special Edition....730
Ghost Lantern....120
Ghost Light....200
Ghost of Frankenstein, The....522
Ghost of James Baldwin at Glide Memorial, The....304
Ghost of Rosy Taylor, The....398
Ghost of Solid Gold Illusion Meets Danny Boy, The....472
Ghost of the San Francisco Oracle Meets Timothy Leary....304
Ghost of Versailles, The....580
Ghost of Yotsuya....137
Ghost of Zorro....369
Ghost Trains of the Old West Volume 1....842
Ghost Trains of the Old West Volume 2....842
Ghost Writer: Into the Comics....633
Ghost Writer: Who Burned Mr. Brinker's Store....634
Ghostbusters....269
Ghosts Along the Freeway....804
Ghosts of Mississippi....229
Ghosts on the Loose (East End Kids Meet Bela Lugosi)....506
Ghostwriter....668
Ghoul, The....522
Gia....229
Giant....343
Giant Behemoth, The....496
Giant from the Unknown....506
Giant Nile, The....110
Giant of Marathon....42
Giant of Metropolis....496
Giant Robo— The Night the Earth Stood Still, Vol. 1....730
Giant Robo, Vol. 1....730
Giant Robo, Vol. 1: Episodes 1 and 2....730
Giant Robo, Vol. 2....137
Giant Robo, Vol. 2: Episode 3: Magnetic Web Strategy....730
Giant Robo, Vol. 3: Episode 4: Twilight of the Superhero....730
Giant Robo, Vol. 4: Episode 5: The Truth of Bashtarlle....730
Giant Robo, Vol. 5: Episode 6: Conflict in the Snow Mtns.....730
Giant Sequoias....816
Gidget....417
Gielgud's Chekhov....87, 304
Gift....430
Gift of Love....229
Gift of the Whales....816
Gift of Winter, The....697
Gifted, The....496
Gifts from the Fire: The Ceramic Art of Brother Thomas....561
Gifts from the Healing Earth, Volume I.....849
Gifts of Fathering, The....857
Gigantor—30th Anniversary....731
Gigantor—30th Anniversary Vol. 2....731
Gigantor Retrospective 30 Vol. 1....730
Gigantor Retrospective 30 Vol. 2....730
Gigantor Retrospective 30 Vol. 3....730
Gigantor Retrospective 30 Vol. 4....730
Gigantor Retrospective 30 Vol. 5....730
Gigantor Vol. 1....730
Gigantor Vol. 2....730
Gigantor Vol. 3....730
Gigi....323
Gigli in Solo per te....580
Gigolettes of Paris....369
Gil Evans and His Orchestra....611
Gilbert & Sullivan: 12 Best-Known Operas....580
Gilbert Sorrentino....304
Gilda....369
Gilda Radner....534
Gimme Shelter....620
Ginger and Fred....36
Gingerbread Man, The....254, 646
Gingko Bed, The....136
Ginsberg Sings Blake....567
Giovanna d'Arco....580
Girl, The....102, 192
Girl, the Body and the Pill, The....506
Girl 6....447
Girl at the Monceau Bakery/Suzanne's Career, The....14
Girl Can't Help It....269
Girl Crazy....323
Girl Friends....229, 460
Girl from Flanders....69
Girl from Hunan....117
Girl from Missouri, The....369
Girl from Phantasia, The....731
Girl Happy....536
Girl Hunters....506
Girl in a Swing....75
Girl in Black, The....105
Girl in Every Port, A....342
Girl in His Pocket....496
Girl in Room 20....448
Girl in the Pullman, The....399
Girl of the Golden West....323
Girl of the Limberlost, A....660
Girl's Folly, A....399
Girl Talk....472
Girl Who Had Everything, The....369
Girl with a Suitcase....41
Girl with the Crazy Brother, The....229
Girl with the Hatbox....85
Girls at Sea....182
Girls Bite Back....620
Girls Gang....120
Girls of Nowopilki....92
Girls on Top....192
Girls School Screamer....522
Girls Town....229
Giselle (Alonso)....571
Giselle (Bolshoi)....571
Giselle (Bujones)....571
Giselle (Malahov)....571
Giselle (Nureyev)....572
Giselle...The Making of....572
Giulio Cesare....580
Giuseppe Verdi: Simon Boccanegra....580
Give a Girl a Break....323
Give Me a Sailor....269
Giving Thanks: A Native-American Good Morning Message....634, 787
Glacier Bay....829
Glacier National Park, Montana....829
Gladiator....269
Glasnost Film Festival....81
Glass Bottom Boat, The....269
Glass Key, The....369
Glass Menagerie, The....92, 311
Glass Mountain....160
Glass Shield, The....444
Glass Slipper....634
Glassnost Film Fest. Vol. 1-12....81
Glen or Glenda....515
Glen or Randa....496
Glengarry Glen Ross....311
Glenn Branca: Symphony No. 4....589
Glenn Gould Collection, The....589
Glenn Gould Collection: Laser....589
Glenn Gould Plays Beethoven....590
Glenn Gould's Greatest Hits....590
Glenn Gould: Two Portraits....590
Glenn Miller Story....323
Glenville School Computer Graphics....561
Glimpses of Martinique....829
Glimpses of the Indian Ocean— Reunion Island....829
Glimpses of West Africa....152
Glitter Dome, The....229
Glitter Goddess of the Sunset Strip....506
Global Affair, A....269
Global Brain....804
Global Dumping Ground: The International Traffic in Hazardous Waste....804
Globalstage....311, 668
Gloria....440
Glorifying the American Girl....323
Glorious Accident, A....782
Glorious Romantics, The....300
Glory & Honor....229, 452
Glory....452
Glory at Sea....174
Glory Boys, The....229
Glory Guys, The....292
Glory of Gospel, Vol. 1....607
Glory of Gospel, Vol. 2....607
Glory of Gospel, Vol. 3....607
Glory of Gospel, Vol. 4....607
Glory of Spain....590
Glyndebourne Festival Opera: A Gala Evening....580
GMAT Math Review....858

GMAT Verbal Review....858
Gniazdo....92
Go, Go, Go, Go World!....506
Go Fish....430, 460
Go for Broke!....370
Go for It!....849
Go Go Big Beat....620
Go Shogun: The Time Etranger....731
Go Tell It on the Mountain....444
Go Tell the Spartans....229
Go West, Young Man....269
Go West....269, 409
Go-Between, The....353
Goblin....522
God, Man and Devil....112
God Is My Witness (Khuda Gawah)....147
God of Gamblers....128
God of Gamblers II....128
God Respects Us When We Work, But Loves Us When We Dance....480
God's Little Acre....370
God's Police....430
God's Step Children....448
God's Trombones—A Trilogy....452
God Told Me To....522
Godard/Truffaut Shorts....9, 14
Goddess, The....370
Godfather, The....259
Godfather Collection, The....259
Godfather Part II, The....259
Godfather Part III, The....259
Godfather Trilogy: 1901-1980, The....259
Godmars....731
Gods Must Be Crazy, The....151
Gods Must Be Crazy II, The....151
Gods of Beauty: A Portrait of the Visionary Artist: Mona Boulware Webb, The....549
Gods of the Plague....66
Godspell....323
Godspell and the Filming of Godspell....323, 334
Godunov: The World to Dance In....572
Godzilla, King of the Monsters....497
Godzilla 1985....496
Godzilla 5-Pack....496
Godzilla's Revenge....497
Godzilla vs. Biollante....496
Godzilla vs. Gigan....497
Godzilla vs. Mechagodzilla....497
Godzilla vs. Megalon....497
Godzilla vs. Monster Zero....497
Godzilla vs. Mothra....497
Godzilla vs. the Sea Monster....497
Gogol: Diary of a Madman....87, 312
Goin' to Town....269
Going Bananas....269
Going Hollywood....323
Going Hollywood: The War Years....334
Going Home....210
Going My Way....323
Going on Fifty....590
Going Steady....107
Going Straight....399
Gold and Silver Gala, The....580
Gold Diggers of 1933....323
Gold Diggers: The Secret of Bear Mountain....663
Gold of Naples....38
Gold Rush, The....407
Golden Age of German Cinema, The....69
Golden Age of Looney Tunes Vol. 2....684
Golden Age of Looney Tunes Vol. 3....684
Golden Age of Looney Tunes Vol. 4....684
Golden Age of Looney Tunes Vol. 5....684
Golden Age of Looney Tunes: Vol. 5, Chuck Jones....684
Golden Age of the Automobile, The....842
Golden Age of Warner Brothers Cartoons....684
Golden Boat, The....11
Golden Boy 2....731, 370
Golden Boy....370, 731
Golden Boy 3: Danger! The Virgin's First Love!....731
Golden Boy 4: Swimming in the Sea of Love....731
Golden Boy 5: B@!!s to the Wall....731
Golden Boy 6: Animation Is Fun!....731
Golden Boy Collection 1....731
Golden Child, The....270
Golden Coach, The....26
Golden Cockerel (El Gallo de Oro)....50
Golden Dart Hero....128
Golden Decade of Baseball 1947-1957....826
Golden Domes of Moscow....87
Golden Earrings....370
Golden Goose, The....646
Golden Honeymoon....300
Golden Pince-Nez, The....186
Golden Ring, The....580
Golden Salamander, The....174
Golden T.V. Memories of the 50's, Volume 1....417
Golden T.V. Memories of the 50's, Volume 2....417
Golden T.V. Memories of the 50's, Volume 3....417
Golden Tales and Legends, Vol. 1....647
Golden Tales and Legends, Vol. 2....647
Golden Treasury of Nursery Rhymes, A....652
Golden Voyage of Sinbad....634
Goldeneye....168
Goldfinger....168
Goldy, The Last of the Golden Bears....663
Goldy II: Saga of the Golden Bear....663
Goldy III....663
Goldyn Follies, The....323
Golem, The....69
Golem (of L.A.), The....114
Golf Classic: I Love Lucy: The Golf Game and The Honeymooners: The Golfer....417
Golgo 13: Queen Bee....731
Golgotha....20, 355
Golub....472
Gone Forever with My Love....120
Gone with the Wind....370
Gonza the Spearman....137
Good, The Bad and the Ugly, The....40
Good Earth, The....370
Good Evening Mr. Wallenberg....75
Good Fight, The....48, 472
Good Guys and the Bad Guys, The....292
Good Heart, The....149
Good King Wenceslas....634
Good Mornin' Blues....611
Good Morning, Good Night: A Day on the Farm....652
Good Morning, Granny Rose!....652
Good Morning (Ohayo)....143
Good Morning...And Goodbye....513
Good Morning Miss Toliver....634
Good Morning Mr. Hitler....768
Good Morning Sunshine....652
Good Morning Vietnam....229
Good Mother....229
Good Neighbors Vol. 1....192
Good News....323
Good Night, Michelangelo....270
Good Night and Good Luck: The Edward R. Murrow Television Collection....417
Good Old Days....540
Good Sam....370
Good Sex Guide—Series No. 1, The....849
Good Sex Guide—Series No. 2, The....849
Good Thing About Spots, A....652
Good Times....370
Good Will Hunting....440
Goodbye, Mr. Chips....323, 370
Goodbye, My Lady....370
Goodbye, Norma Jean....229
Goodbye Again....370
Goodbye Bird, The....663
Goodbye Columbus....370
Goodbye Emma Jo....460
Goodbye Girl, The....270
Goodbye Love....270
Goodfellas....253
Goofy Movie, A....692
Goon Show Movie....192
Goonies....270
Goose Girl, The....647
Goose Woman....399
Goosebumps: The Haunted Mask....697
Goosebumps: The Werewolf of Fever Swamp....697
Gorch Fock....768
Gordon Parks: "Visions"....452
Gore Vidal....304
Gore Vidal's Billy The Kid....292
Gorgeous Hussy....370
Gorgo....174, 497
Gorilla, The....270
Gorilla....75
Gorilla Bathes at Noon....104
Gorilla Tapes: Death Valley Days/Lo Pay No Way!....485
Gorillas in the Mist....229
Gorky Trilogy, The....81
Gospel....607
Gospel According to Al Green....607
Gospel According to St. Matthew, The....37
Gospel According to Vic....183
Gospel Keynotes Live....607
Gospel Music Workshop of America—Men of Promise, The....607
Gospel's Best from Saturday Night Sing....607
Gothic....167
Gothic Art....549
Gotterdammerung....580
Grace Kelly Story, The....417
Grace Kelly—The American Princess....334
Grace of My Heart....431
Graduate, The....370
Graduate (25th Anniversary Edition), The....370
Graffiti Bridge....323
Graffiti Verite....549
Graffiti/Post-Graffiti....549
Grain of Sand....3
Grammar Music Videos....155
Grand Canyon & Petrified Forest....829
Grand Canyon....229
Grand Canyon National Park....829
Grand Deception of 1995, The....862
Grand Duchess and the Waiter....399
Grand Duel, The....293
Grand Duo: Itzhak Perlman and Pinchas Zukerman....590
Grand Hotel....370
Grand Illusion....26
Grand Melies (Franju) and Melies' Short Films....20
Grand Prix....370
Grand Theft Auto....229
Grand Tour: Legendary Resorts of the World, The....829
Grandes Festivales de Espana....48
Grandizer....731
Granpa....634
Grant and Lee....779
Grapes of Wrath, The....340
Graphic Arts Training Library....563
Grappler Baki....731
Grass....399
Grass Harp, The....229
Grass Is Greener, The....270
Grateful Dead Movie....620
Grave of the Fireflies....137, 731
Gravesend....431
Graveyard Shift....522
Gray Lady Down....229
Gray's Anatomy....443
Grease....323
Greased Lightning....444
Great & Minor Animation Volume 1....684
Great & Minor Animation Volume 2....684
Great & Minor Animation Volume 3....684
Great & Minor Animation Volume 4....684
Great Actors of the 20th Century: Vol. 1....334
Great Actors of the 20th Century: Vol. 2....334
Great Actors of the 20th Century: Vol. 3....334
Great Actresses of the 20th Century: Vol. 1....334
Great Actresses of the 20th Century: Vol. 2....334
Great Actresses of the 20th Century: Vol. 3....334
Great Alaska Train Adventure, The....829, 842
Great American Eastern Train Rides....842
Great American Frontiers....809
Great American Monuments: The Presidential Memorials....759
Great American Monuments: The War Memorials....759
Great American Monuments: The White House....759
Great American Speech Series: Lincoln's Gettysburg Address....759
Great American Speech Series: Patrick Henry's "Liberty or Death"....759
Great American Speech Series: Washington's Farewell....759
Great American Speeches....759
Great American Train Rides....842
Great Ape Activity Tape....668
Great Barrier Reef, The....816
Great Bears of Alaska, The....816
Great Betrayal, The....92
Great Bible Stories....634
Great Books....304
Great Books: Frankenstein: The Making of the Monster....304
Great Books: Le Morte d'Arthur: The Legend of the King....304
Great Books: Origin of Species: Beyond Genesis....304
Great British Documentary Movement, The....174, 472
Great Campaign (1917-1918), The....759
Great Campaigns of the Civil War: Touring Civil War Battlefields, Volumes I and II....779
Great Canadian Parks....816
Great Cantors of the Golden Age....114
Great Caruso, The....597
Great Castles of Europe....830
Great Chase, The....399
Great Chefs of the West....857
Great Chefs: A Holiday Table....857
Great Chefs: Appetizers....857
Great Chefs: Desserts....857
Great Chefs: New Orleans Jazz Brunch....857
Great Cities of Europe....830
Great Commanders....809
Great Conquest: The Romance of the Three Kingdoms....731
Great Crimes and Trials of the 20th Century: John Wayne Gacy, Richard Speck....759
Great Crimes and Trials of the 20th Century: Murph the Surf, The Boston Brink's Robbery....759
Great Crimes and Trials of the 20th Century: The Assassination of Martin Luther King, The Ku Klux Klan Killings....452, 759
Great Crimes and Trials of the 20th Century: The Massacre of the Tsar, Stalin and Katyn....87, 759
Great Crimes and Trials of the 20th Century: Trial of Adolf Eichmann, Hitler and the Nuremberg Trials....760, 775
Great Crimes of the Century....760
Great Day....174
Great Day for Singing, A....652
Great Day in Harlem, A....472, 611
Great Days of History....768, 809
Great Days of History: Exodus and the Birth of Israel....109
Great Days of History: Gandhi and India's Independence....148
Great Days of History: Prelude to Vietnam....778
Great Days of the Century Collector's Boxed Set....760
Great Debates: JFK vs. Richard Nixon....809
Great Depression, The....760
Great Dictator, The....407
Great Dinosaurs Set....816
Great Egyptians, The....760
Great Egyptians II, The....760
Great Escape, The....370
Great Escapes of World War II, The....768
Great Expectations....180, 192, 229, 300, 370, 692
Great Flamarion....370
Great Gabbo, The....370
Great Gatsby....230
Great Guitarists....611
Great Guitars....611
Great Guns....270
Great Guy....370
Great Hero from China....128
Great Hollywood Memories: Volume I....334
Great Hollywood Memories: Volume II....334
Great Imposter....370
Great Jetfoil Robbery, The....128
Great Kate....370
Great Land of Small, The....663
Great Lie, The....370
Great Lover, The....270
Great Madcap (El Gran Calavera), The....47
Great Man's Lady, The....370

Great McGinty, The 346
Great McGonagall, The 183
Great Minds of Business 860
Great Minds of Medicine 836
Great Minds of Science 836
Great Moments at the Winter Games 826
Great Moments from Serials 538
Great Music from Chicago 590
Great Northfield Minnesota Raid 293
Great Opera Gala for Armenia 580
Great Paintings—Renaissance to Impressionism: The Frick Collection 866
Great Palaces of the World 565
Great Pharaohs of Egypt, The 760
Great Quake of '89, The 836
Great Race, The 354
Great Race 95
Great Railway Journeys 842
Great Railway Journeys of the World: Flying Scotsman 842
Great Railway Journeys of the World: India 842
Great Rock and Roll Swindle (The Sex Pistols), The 620
Great Rupert, The 323
Great Sadness of Zohara 114, 472
Great Santini 230
Great Scenes from Der Ring des Nibelungen 580
Great Screenwriting 317
Great Ships, The 842
Great Singers from the CBC 580
Great Smoky Mountains 830
Great Solos with James Galway and Friends 590
Great St. Louis Bank Robbery, The 370
Great Stone Face— Buster Keaton—Volume 1 409
Great Stone Face— Buster Keaton—Volume 2 409
Great Tales in Asian Art 549
Great Train Journeys of Australia 209
Great Train Journeys of Australia: The Indian Pacific 842
Great Train Robbery, The 160
Great Train Stations of America, The 842
Great Union Presidents 779
Great Wall, The 455
Great Waltz, The 323, 580
Great West Collection, The 298
Great White 816
Great White Hope, The 370
Great White Hype, The 230
Great Ziegfeld, The 323
Greatest Adventure, The 836
Greatest Adventure: Daniel & The Lion's Den 697
Greatest Adventure: David & Goliath 697
Greatest Adventure: Jonah 697
Greatest Adventure: Joseph & His Brothers 697
Greatest Adventure: Joshua & The Battle of Jericho 697
Greatest Adventure: Moses 697
Greatest Adventure: Noah's Ark 697
Greatest Adventure: Queen Esther 697
Greatest Adventure: Samson & Delilah 697
Greatest Adventure: The Creation 697
Greatest Adventure: The Easter Story 697
Greatest Adventure: The Miracles of Jesus 697
Greatest Adventure: The Nativity 697
Greatest Battle, The 768
Greatest Goals World Cup USA '94 826
Greatest Heroes of the Bible 790
Greatest Man in the World 300
Greatest Moments of Our Time 866
Greatest Question 412
Greatest Show on Earth, The 354
Greatest Sports Follies 826
Greatest Story Ever Told 343
Greatest Thinkers Series 785
Greatest Week in Gospel 607
Greed 348
Greed of William Hart, The 522
Greedy 270
Greedy Man in the Moon, The 634
Greek Fire 784
Greek Interpreter, The 186
Greek Street 174
Green Archer, The 69
Green Berets 370
Green Card 208
Green Death, The 200
Green Dolphin Street 371
Green Eggs and Ham 866
Green Fields 112
Green Fire 371
Green Fire and Ice 572
Green for Danger 174
Green Glove, The 371
Green Grow the Rushes 183
Green House, The 3
Green Legend Ran 731
Green Man, The 192
Green Mansions 371
Green Pastures, The 371
Green Plans 804
Green Slime, The 522
Green Snake 120
Green Wall, The 50
Green Winter 849
Greenbucks: The Challenge of Sustainable Development 804
Greenhouse Crisis: The American Response 804
Greening of Cuba, The 57, 804
Greenpeace's Greatest Hits 804
Greentoons: Environmentally Aware Animation 710
Greg & Steve Live! In Concert 634
Greg & Steve Musical Adventures 634
Gregory Peck: His Own Man 334
Gregory's Girl 183
Gremlins 230
Grenada Revisited 57
Greta 92
Greta Garbo Collection, The 371
Grey Gardens 797
Grey: Digital Target 731
Greyling 634
Grief 460
Griffith Shorts (1908-09) 412
Griffith Shorts (1909) 412
Griffith Shorts (1909-1910) 412
Griffith Shorts (1909-1911) 413
Griffith Shorts (1910-1911) 413
Griffith Shorts (1911) 413
Griffith Shorts (1911-1912) 413
Griffith Shorts (1912, #1) 413
Griffith Shorts (1912, #2) 413
Griffith Shorts (1912, #3) 413
Griffith Shorts (1913) 413
Griffith Shorts (1913-1914) 413
Griffiti 710
Grifters, The 166
Grim Prairie Tales 230
Grim Reaper, The 35
Grind 431
Grisbi (Hands Off the Loot) 20
Grizzly & Man: Uneasy Truce (National Audubon) 816
Grizzly 522
Grokgazer 620
Groove Tube, The 534
Grosse Isle 203
Grosse Pointe Blank 270
Groucho Marx—Classic Television 270
Ground Zero 206
Groundhog Day 270
Group, The 371
Grover Washington, Jr. in Concert 611
Grow Dutch 472
Grow Live Monsters 620
Growing Like a Weed 804
Growing Up Gay and Lesbian 460
Growing Up in America 472
Growing Up in the Age of AIDS 834
Grown Ups 165
Gruesome Twosome, The 506
Grumpier Old Men 270
Grumpy Old Men 270
Gryphon 660
Guadalcanal & The Shores of Iwo Jima 768
Guadalcanal Diary 768
Guantanamera 53
Guardian Angel 128
Guardians of the Night 830
Guardsman, The 270
Guarneri Quartet, The 590
Guatemala, Land of Color 57
Guatemala: Jeramias and El Salvador: Flor 57
Guatemala: When the People Lead 57
Guelaguetza 57
Guerilla Brigade 85
Guerillas in Pink Lace 371
Guess Who's Coming to Dinner 371
Guest in the House 371
Guest Wife 270
Guffaw and Order: Looney Tunes Fight Crime 684
Guide for the Married Woman, A 230
Guide to Advanced Sexual Positions, The 850
Guide to Classical Music 866
Guide to Rational Living: The Principles of Rational-Motive Therapy, A 850
Guide to the Orchestra 866
Guido Manuli: Animator 710
Guillotine, The 760
Guilt and Repentance 114
Guilty by Suspicion 230
Guilty Men 768
Guilty of Treason 371
Guilty Until Proven Not Guilty—Napoleon's Revenge 472
Guinea Pig, The 174
Guinness Encyclopedia, The 866
Guitar Legends 620
Guitar of Rory Block, The 611
Guitarra 590
Gulag Archipelago 92
Gulf Bowl Cabaret, The 110
Gulf Crisis TV Project, The 111
Gulf of Danzig: German Once Again 768
Gulf War, The 111
Gullah Gullah Island—Feelings 452, 634
Gullah Gullah Island: Dance Along with the Daise Family 634
Gulliver in Lilliput 160
Gulliver's Travels 230, 634, 684
Gumbo 860
Gumby: The Movie 684
Gummo 431
Gumshoe 166
Gumshoe Kid 230
Gun Crazy 371
Gun Fury 293
Gun Is Loaded 506
Gun of Dragon 128
Gunbuster Vol. 1 731
Gunbuster Vol. 2 731
Gunbuster Vol. 3 731
Gunfight at Red Sands (Gringo) 293
Gunfight at The O.K. Corral 293
Gunfighter, The 293
Gunfighters of the West 230
Gung Ho! 768
Guns 860
Guns for San Sebastian 293
Guns of August, The 760
Guns of Navarone 768
Guns of the Civil War 779
Guns of the Trees 442
Gunsmith Cats 1: Episodes 1 and 2 731
Gunsmith Cats 1: Special Edition 731
Gunsmith Cats 2 731
Gunsmith Cats 3 731
Gustave Caillebotte or the Adventures of the Gaze 549
Guy from Harlem, The 532
Guy Named Joe, A 371
Guys and Dolls 323
Guyver Data 1: Genesis of the Guyver, The 731
Guyver Data 2: Battle of the Guyvers, The 732
Guyver Data 3: Mysterious Shadow, The 732
Guyver Data 4: Attack of the Hyper Zoanoid-Team 5, The 732
Guyver Data 5: Death of the Guyver, The 732
Guyver Data 6: Terminal Battle, The 732
Guyver Data 7: The Battle Begins, The 732
Guyver Data 8: The Lost Unit, The 732
Guyver Data 9: Transformation Tragedy, The 732
Guyver Data 10: Haunted Village, The 732
Guyver Data 11: Terminal Battle, The 732
Guyver Data 12: Reactivation, The 732
Gypsies 92
Gypsy (1962/Wood) 323
Gypsy (1993/Midler) 323
Gypsy Blood 345
Gypsy Colt 663
Gypsy Guitar: The Legacy of Django Reinhardt 611

H

H. M. Deserters 92
H.D. Trilogy 718
H.G. Wells' First Men in the Moon 497
H.H. The Dalai Lama on Campus 149
H.R. Pufnstuf Live at the Hollywood Bowl 634
Habiba: A Sufi Saint from Uzbekistan 87
Habit 431
Habitation of Dragons, The 230
Hablemos Ingles 6.0 866
Hades Project Zeorymer Vol. 1: Episodes 1 and 2 732
Hague School, The 549
Haight-Ashbury in the Sixties 866
Hail Caesar 784
Hail Columbia! 839
Hail Mafia 20
Hail the Conquering Hero 346
Hail the Woman 399
Hair 100
Hairdresser's Husband, The 8
Hairspray 514
Hairy Ape 371
Hajj: One American's Pilgrimage to Mecca, The 790
Hakkenden Vol. 1: Episodes 1 and 2 732
Hakkenden Vol. 2: Episodes 3 and 4 732
Hakkenden Vol. 3: Episodes 5 and 6 732
Hakkenden Vol. 4: Episode 7 and Digest 732
Hakkenden Vol. 5: Episodes 8 and 9 732
Hakkenden Vol. 6: Episodes 10 and 11 732
Hakkenden Vol. 7: Episodes 12 and 13 732
Halber Mensch 567
Hale House: Alive with Love 452
Half a Sixpence 183
Half Breed 293
Half Human 522
Half Shot at Sunrise 270
Half-Baked 270
Halfaouine—Boy of the Terraces 116
Halfmoon 63, 304
Hallelujah, I'm a Bum 323
Hallelujah the Hills 431
Hallelujah Trail, The 293
Hallelujah! 323
Hallelujah: A Celebration of Psalms 607
Hallelujah: A Gospel Celebration 607
Hallo, Fred the Beard 92
Hallo Spencer Presents Robin Hood and Sleeping Beauty 647
Halloween 522, 634
Halloween Tree, The 697
Hallucinations of a Deranged Mind 522
Hamlet (1948/Olivier) 312
Hamlet (1969/Williamson) 312
Hamlet (1990/Gibson) 312
Hamlet (1996/Branagh) 312
Hamlet 69, 866
Hamlet Ballet 572
Hammer Dulcimer, The 624
Hamoon 106
Hampton Hawes All Stars 611
Hamsin (Eastern Wind) 107
Hamsun 79
Hancock Set 192
Hand of Death (aka Countdown in Kung-Fu), The 134
Hand of Fear, The 200
Handel's Last Chance 634
Handful of Dust, A 160
Handmaid's Tale 161
Hands Across America 472

Hands Across the Table....270
Hands of a Murderer....186
Hands of a Stranger....522
Hands of Orlac....522
Hands Up....97, 399
Handsome Siblings....128
Hang 'em High....293
Hang Up Your Brightest Colors: The Life and Death of Michael Collins....203
Hanged on a Twisted Cross....790
Hangman's House....340
Hangmen Also Die....72
Hank Aaron: Chasing the Dream....826
Hank Williams: "The Show He Never Gave"....323
Hanna K.....105
Hanna's War....775
Hanna-Barbera's Cartoon Carnival....866
Hannie Caulder....293
Hanoi Hilton....230
Hanover Street....230
Hans Christian Andersen....323
Hans Hartung: A German Destiny....550
Hans Richter: Early Avant-Garde Films....485
Hans Richter: Give Chance a Chance....63, 485
Hans-Joachim Marseille: The Star of Africa....768
Hansel and Gretel, An Appalachian Version....647
Hansel and Gretel (Met)....580
Hansel and Gretel (Vienna)....580
Hanussen....103
Hanya: Portrait of a Pioneer....572
Happiest Days of Your Life, The....183
Happily Ever After....54
Happily Ever After Fairy Tales....647
Happiness....85
Happiness Patrol, The....200
Happy Bigamist....120
Happy Birdy....652
Happy Birthday Bugs!....684
Happy Birthday Moon and Other Stories....647
Happy Ending, The....371
Happy Ghost IV....120
Happy Hour....120
Happy Landing....371
Happy New Year....230
Happy New Year!, A....102
Happy Pooh Day....652
Happy Together....121, 460
Harassed Hero....183
Harbor Tugs at Work....634
Hard....460
Hard Boiled....128
Hard Choices....230
Hard Day's Night, A....323, 866
Hard Eight....230
Hard Labor....165
Hard Life of an Adventurer, The....99
Hard Target....128
Hard to Die....128
Hardboiled Mahoney....270
Harder They Come....54
Harder They Fall, The....371
Hardly Boys in Hardly Gold, The....634
Hardware....230
Hardware Wars....497
Hardy and Ray....411
Harikiri....137
Harlan County U.S.A.....472
Harlem Diary....452, 472
Harlem Grace....800
Harlem Hotshots....611
Harlem Nights....444
Harlem Swings Volume 1....611
Harlem Swings Volume 2....611
Harlem Swings Volume 3....611
Harlem Swings Volume 4....611
Harlem Swings Volume 5....611
Harmagedon....732
Harmon of Michigan....371
Harms Case, The....103
Harnessing Peacocks....161
Harold and Maude....270
Harold and the Purple Crayon and Other Harold Stories....634
Harold Clurman....312
Harold Lloyd Comedies Vol. 1....410
Harold Lloyd Comedies Vol. 2....410
Harold Lloyd Comedies Vol. 3....410
Harold Lloyd's Comedy Classics....410
Harold Lloyd: Girl Shy....410
Harp of My Country....203
Harriet Craig....371
Harriet the Spy....663
Harry and the Hendersons....270
Harry and the Lady Next Door....634
Harry and Tonto....230
Harry Callahan, Eleanor and Barbara....559
Harry S Truman....760
Harry S Truman: His Life and Library....760, 795
Harry S Truman: Library and Museum....795
Harry S Truman: Suddenly, Mr. President....795
Harry S Truman: The Challenges of Office....795
Harry Smith: Early Abstractions....710
Harry the Dirty Dog....634
Harry Weinberg's Notebook....460
Hartnell Years, The....200
Harum Scarum....536
Harvest, The....522
Harvest....26, 417
Harvest of Despair....86
Harvest of Fire....230
Harvest: 3,000 Years....150
Harvey....270
Harvey Girls, The....323
Hasidim, The....114
Hassidut: Hassidic Music....114, 602
Hasty Heart, The....174
Hat Box Mystery....371
Hatchet for a Honeymoon....522
Hate (La Haine)....3
Hated: GG Allin and the Murder Junkies....620
Haunted Castle....73
Haunted Gold....293
Haunted Hills: Ghost Stories....472
Haunted House....867
Haunted Houses....861
Haunted Palace....522
Haunted Strangler, The....174
Haunted World of Edward D. Wood, Jr., The....334, 515
Haunting, The....522
Haunting Fear....522
Haunting of Barney Palmer, The....660
Havana....230
Havana Nagila: The Jews in Cuba....114
Havana: Cigar of Connoisseurs, The....57
Hawaii....371
Hawaii in Transition....804
Hawaii: The Pacific Paradise....830
Hawaiian Paradise....830
Hawaiian Rainbow: The Magic and the Music of the Islands....602
Hawk of the Hills....399
Hawks and Sparrows....37
Hawthorne of the USA....399
Hayden Carruth....304
Haydn at Esterhaza Hogwood....590
Haydn: Cello Concerto No. 1 and No. 2....590
Haydn: The Creation (Bernstein)....597
Haydn: The Creation (Muti)....597
He Ain't Heavy, He's My Father....121
He Lives by Night....128
He Must Have Something....797
He's a Woman, She's a Man....121
He Stands in a Desert Counting the Seconds of His Life....442
He Walked by Night....371
He Who Gets Slapped....79
Head, The....523, 697
Head....506
Head Against the Wall....20
Head of Tyrant....42
Head over Heels....20, 183
Headgear, Japan, 1988, 60 mins.....739
Heading for Shore: The Struggle to Save America's Coasts....804
Heading Home....399
Headless Ghost, The....174, 523
Headless Horseman....399
Headline Stories....760
Healer, The....57
Healers, The....149
Healing and the Mind, Set....850
Healing and the Mind: Healing from Within....850
Healing and the Mind: The Art of Healing....850
Healing and the Mind: The Mind Body Connection....850
Healing and the Mind: The Mystery of Chi....850
Healing and the Mind: Wounded Healers....850
Healing and the Unconscious....850
Healing Journey, A....850
Healing Mind, The....850
Healing with Ancient Sound....850
Healing with Shaolin Acupressure....850
Healing Yourself with Mental Imagery....850
Health and Your Whole Being....850
Health Power....850
Healthy Aging....850
Hear My Song....161, 324
Hearing Voices....431
Heart and Soul....41, 620
Heart Attack Theater....845
Heart Beat....230
Heart into Hearts....121
Heart Is a Lonely Hunter, The....371
Heart o' the Hills....399
Heart of Darkness....166
Heart of Glass....67
Heart of Humanity....153
Heart of the Dragon....134
Heart of the Stag....208
Heart of Tibet....149
Heart's Desire....460
Heart's Desire and Forbidden Music....597
Heart's Haven....399
Heart to Heart: The Truth About Heart Disease....836
Heartbeat 100....121
Heartbeat....371
Heartbeat of America, The....760
Heartbreak Hotel....536
Heartbreak Kid....270
Heartbreak Ridge....256
Heartburn....230
Hearts of Darkness: A Filmmaker's Apocalypse....259, 334
Hearts of Fire....230
Hearts of the West....293
Hearts of the World....413
Heartworn Highways....605
Hearty Response....128
Heat....230
Heat and Sunlight....431
Heat of the Day....161
Heat's On, The....324
Heathers....270
Heaven....472
Heaven and Earth....230
Heaven and Earth Magic....485
Heaven Can't Wait....121
Heaven Can Wait....345
Heaven Is a Playground....230
Heaven Knows, Mr Allison....348
Heaven's a Drag....460
Heaven's Burning....206
Heaven's Gate....293
Heaven's Prisoners....230
Heavenly Creatures....208
Heavenly Host and The Sons of Calvary....607
Heavens Above....183
Heavy....431
Heavy Hardy....411
Heavy Melon....105
Heavy Metal....710
Heavy Petting....472
Heavy Traffic....710
Heavyweights....692
Hector's Bunyip....660
Hedd Wyn....161
Hedda Hopper's Hollywood....334
Heidi (1937)....663
Heidi (1953)....663
Heidi....672, 692
Heidi Chronicles, The....312
Heidi Fleiss: Hollywood Madam....472
Heifetz Master Classes....590
Heimat....64
Heimat II....64
Heimat Set....64
Heiress, The....343
Helen Keller in Her Story....472
Helen Keller: Separate Views....795
Helen of Troy....371
Hell Harbor....371
Hell Hounds of the Plains....399
Hell's Angels....371
Hell's Angels on Wheels....506
Hell's Hinges....399
Hell Ship Mutiny....371
Hell Up in Harlem....532
Hellish Flesh....523
Hello, Dolly!....324
Hello, Frisco, Hello....324
Hello Goodbye Bob Sparks....473
Hello Kitty....652
Hello! Who Is It?....121
Hellraiser/Special Edition....523
Helmut Newton: Frames from the Edge....559
Help Save Planet Earth....816
Help!....183, 324
Helping Your Baby Sleep Through the Night....857
Hemingway in Cuba....304
Hemingway...In the Autumn....304
Hemp Revolution, The....473
Hemp Video, The....473
Henri Cartier-Bresson....559
Henry & June....230
Henry (Portrait of a Serial Killer)....431
Henry and Mudge in Puddle Trouble....652
Henry and Mudge in the Green Time....652
Henry and Mudge Under the Yellow Moon....652
Henry Fielding's Tom Jones....192
Henry Hamilton: Graduate Ghost....634
Henry IV....33, 417
Henry Miller Odyssey....304
Henry Moore....550
Henry's Cat: The Birthday Caper....652
Henry V (Branagh)....312
Henry V (Olivier)....312
Her and She and Him....3
Her Favorite Patient (aka Bedside Manner)....270
Her First Romance....270
Her Majesty Mrs. Brown....161
Her Mother Before Her: Winnebago Women's Stories of Their Mothers & Grandmothers....787
Her Own Words: Pioneer Women's Diaries....760
Herbal Preparations for Home Remedies....850
Herbie Hancock Trio: Hurricane!....611
Hercules & Xena: The Animated Movie....685
Hercules....42, 634, 693
Hercules Against the Moon Men....42
Hercules Against the Sons of the Sun....42
Hercules and the Captive Women....42
Hercules in the Haunted World....42
Hercules Unchained....42
Herdsmen of the Sun....67
Here Come the Co-Eds....270
Here Come the Girls....271
Here Come the WAVES....271
Here Comes a Roller Coaster....634
Here Comes Cookie....271
Here Comes Droopy!....685
Here Comes Mr. Jordan....271
Here Comes Peter Cottontail....697
Here Comes the Cat and Other Cat Stories....634
Here Comes the Groom....351
Here Is Germany....768
Here Is Greenwood Vol. 1: Episodes 1 and 2....732
Here Is Greenwood Vol. 2: Episodes 3 and 4....733
Here Is Greenwood Vol. 3: Episodes 5 and 6....733

Here's Looking at You, Warner Bros. 334
Here We Go Again 634
Here We Go—Vol. 1 634
Heritage (Ha-Yerusha), The 107
Heritage of England, The 170
Heritage to Glory: The U.S. Marine Corps Story 842
Herman & Marguerite 634
Herman Hesse's Long Summer 304
Herman Melville: Consider the Sea 304
Hermann Scherchen: In Rehearsal—Bach's Art of the Fugue 590
Hermitage Masterpieces 550
Hermitage Museum of St. Petersburg—Series 1, The 550
Hermitage Museum of St. Petersburg—Series 2, The 550
Hermitage: A Russian Odyssey, The 550
Hero 147, 166
Hero Ain't Nothin' but a Sandwich, A 231
Hero for a Night 399
Hero of the Year 95
Hero's Journey 785
Heroes Among Heroes (aka The Iron Beggar) 121
Heroes Die Young 371
Heroes for Sale 371
Heroes of Telemark, The 768
Heroes of the Earth 804
Heroes of the Greek Myths 784
Heroes Shed No Tears 121
Heroic Legend of Arislan, Part 1 733
Heroic Legend of Arislan, Part 2 733
Heroic Legend of Arislan, Parts 3 & 4 733
Heroic Trio 128
Heroines and Goddesses of the Greek Myths 784
Hester Street 114, 231
Hey, What About Me? 652
Hey Abbott! 271
Hey Arnold!: Arnold's Christmas 698
Hey Arnold!: Love Stinks 698
Hey Arnold!: The Helga Stories 698
Hey Arnold!: Urban Adventures 698
Hey Babu Riba 103
Hey Good Lookin' 710
Hezekiah Walker and the Love Fellowship Crusade Choir 452
Hi, Mom! 231
Hi-De-Ho 448
Hi-Di-Hi 183
Hidden, The 497
Hidden Aces 399
Hidden Agenda 166
Hidden Army 768
Hidden Army: Women in World War II, The 760
Hidden Fortress, The 142
Hidden in America 231
Hidden Japan, The 144
Hidden Memories: Are You a UFO Abductee? 862
Hidden Treasures 561
Hidden World 816
Hide and Seek 107
Hideaway, The 75
Hideaways 663
Hiding Place 231
High and Low 142
High Anxiety 271
High Crusade, The 497
High Fidelity 590
High Heels 46
High Lonesome 605
High Noon 293
High Plains Drifter 256
High School Caesar 506
High School Confidential 506
High Sierra 372
High Society 324
High Spirits 183
High Water 431
High-Flying Hero 693
Higher and Higher 324
Higher Learning 444
Highlander: The Adventure Begins 710
Highlander: The Animated Series, The History Lesson 417, 710
Highlander: The Animated Series, The Suspended Village 418, 711
Highlander: The Animated Series, The Suspended Village 418, 711
Highlander: The Animated Series, The Valley of Thorn Pods 418, 711
Highlander: The Director's Cut 231
Highlights of Atrocities of the Drug War 782
Highway 61 210
Highway Patrolman 431
Highwaymen: On the Road Again, The 605
Hilary Harris 485
Hill, The 174
Hill 24 Doesn't Answer 107
Hill Number One 418
Hillary Rodham Clinton: Changing the Rules 795
Hills of Home 663
Himalayan Trekking: Sherpa Expeditions, Nepal 149
Himatsuri 137
Hindenburg, The 842
Hindsight 231
Hindustani Slide: The Indian Classical Guitar of Debashish Bhattacharya 148
Hippie Porn 431
Hiroshima, Mon Amour 12
Hiroshima - Nagasaki, August 1945 144, 768
Hiroshima 231
Hiroshima Maiden 660
His Butler's Sister 324
His Double Life 372
His Excellency the Shop Assistant 92
His First Command 399
His First Flame 399
His Girl Friday 342
His Majesty, the American 399
His Majesty O'Keefe 372
His Picture in the Papers 411
His Private Secretary 372
His Royal Slyness and Haunted Spooks 410
His Wife's Lover 112
Hispanic Folk Art and the Environment: A New Mexican Perspective 57
Hispanic Magazine's Guide to Hispanic Excellence 57
Hispanics of Achievement Video Collection 57
Historic San Simeon Castle 830
Historic Traveler Great Destinations 830
Historical Heritage Series 809
History and Interpretation of the Bible, The 790
History Is Made at Night 372
History of American Funeral Directing, The 760
History of Baseball Card Collecting, The 827
History of Blue Jeans, The 760
History of Chase in Film, Volume One: Comedy Chase, The 399
History of Flight and The Golden Days of Flight 839
History of Ireland 203
History of Medicine 867
History of Music Collection 867
History of Naval Aviation 842
History of Poland in Painting 550
History of Pornography 506
History of Santa Claus, The 782
History of Talk Radio, The 760
History of the '80s 782
History of the Amiga 711
History of the Bikini, The 760
History of the Civil Rights Movement in America, A 452
History of the Comics, The 541
History of the Condom, The 473
History of the Federal Republic of Germany 73
History of the Slavery in America, A 452
History of the Twentieth Century, Volume 1 809
History of the Twentieth Century, Volume 2 809
History of the Twentieth Century, Volume 3 809
History of the Twentieth Century, Volume 4 809
History of the Twentieth Century, Volume 5 810
History of the Twentieth Century, Volume 6 810
History of the Twentieth Century, Volume 7 810
History of the Twentieth Century, Volume 8 810
History of the Twentieth Century, Volume 9 810
History of the Volkswagen, The 842
History of the World, Part One, The 271
History of the World 867
History of the World's Fastest Trains, The 842
History of World War II: Battle of Midway, The 340, 768
History of World War II: December 7th, The 340, 768
History of World War II: December 7th, The 340, 768
History of World War II: Desert Victory, The 768
History's Turning Points 760
Hit the Deck 324
Hit! 532
Hitch-Hiker, The 372
Hitchhiker's Guide to the Galaxy, The 192
Hitchhikers, The 300
Hitchhiking Vietnam: Letters from the Trail 778, 830
Hitler 768
Hitler Dead or Alive 372
Hitler's Constructions 768
Hitler's Henchmen (MPI) 768
Hitler Tapes, The 506
Hitler Youth Quex 768
Hitler: The Final Chapter 768
Hitler: The Last Ten Days 161
Hitler: The Whole Story 768
Hoagland's Mars, Vol. I, The NASA/Cydonia Briefings 839
Hoagland's Mars, Vol. II, The U.N. Briefing, the Terrestrial Connection 839
Hoagland's Mars, Vol. III, The Moon/Mars Connection 839
Hobbit, The 711
Hobo's Christmas 231
Hoboken Chicken Controversy 660
Hobson's Choice 180, 312
Hoffa 231
Hoffa: The True Story 795
Hoffnung Festival Concert 590
Hogarth's Progress 550
Hola Amigos 672
Hold Me Thrill Me Kiss Me 271
Hold Up: An Editing Exercise, The 317
Hold Your Man 271
Hole in the Head, A 351
Holes (Les Gaspards), The 3
Holiday 350
Holiday Collection, The 634
Holiday in Mexico 372
Holiday of Ballet 572
Holidays for Children Video Series 635
Hollow Boy, The 300
Hollow Reed 231
Hollow Venus: Diary of a Go-Go Dancer 431
Hollywood Babylon 334
Hollywood Canteen 324
Hollywood Chronicles: Censorship— The Unseen Cinema/ Sex in the Movies 334
Hollywood Chronicles: In the Beginning/ The Studio System Takes Over 334
Hollywood Chronicles: Pen & Ink Movies/ The Evolution of Sound 335
Hollywood Chronicles: Poverty Row/The New Rebels 335
Hollywood Chronicles: Publicity Stunts & Coming Attractions/How Movies Are Made 335
Hollywood Chronicles: Riding into the Sunset/ The American Hero 335
Hollywood Chronicles: Scandal!/Mysteries & Secrets 335
Hollywood Chronicles: Stereotypes & Minorities/Familiar Faces, Unknown Names 335
Hollywood Chronicles: The Depression Years/ The Silent Witness 335
Hollywood Chronicles: The Futurists/The Wizards of the EFX 335
Hollywood Chronicles: The Great Detectives/ The Great Clowns 335
Hollywood Chronicles: The Search for God, Grails & Profits/ The Nightmare Factory 335
Hollywood Chronicles: Women with Clout/ Hollywood's Children 335
Hollywood Dinosaur Chronicles 506
Hollywood Dinosaurs 335
Hollywood Directors and Their Craft 317
Hollywood Goes to War 335
Hollywood Hookers 335
Hollywood Hot Tubs 271
Hollywood Mavericks 335
Hollywood Musicals of the '50s 324, 335
Hollywood on Trial 335
Hollywood or Bust 271
Hollywood Outtakes 506
Hollywood Party 324
Hollywood Revels 271
Hollywood Rhythm 324
Hollywood's Children 335
Hollywood Scandals and Tragedies 335
Hollywood Screenwriters and Their Craft 335
Hollywood Spoofs 411
Hollywood Strangler Meets the Skid Row Slasher, The 506
Hollywood—The Definitive Story 335
Hollywood Without Make-Up 335
Holocaust, Polish Jews (Holocoust, Zydzi Polscy) 775
Holocaust (Chomsky) 775
Holocaust (Sontag) 775
Holocaust and Yad Vashem: Displaced Persons, The 775
Holocaust as Seen Through the Eyes of a Survivor, The 775
Holocaust in Memory of Millions, The 775
Holst: The Planets, Featuring the Duchesnays 827
Holy Koran, The 790
Holy Land & Holy City 790
Holy Mary, Remembrance & Vocation 460, 485
Holy Quest: In Search of Biblical Relics, The 790
Holy Weapon 121
Homage to Chagall 550
Homage to Hermann Nitsch (Apologies to Don Garlits) 567
Homage to May 19th/Framed 473
Hombre 293
Home at Last 660
Home Away from Home: The Yanks in Ireland 203
Home for Christmas 231
Home for the Holidays 271
Home Free All! 431
Home from the Hill 372
Home of the Brave 485, 769
Home Sweet Home 165, 413
Homecoming (Bancroft) 231
Homecoming (Neal) 231
Homecoming 69, 372, 607
Homegrown 431
Homeland 109
Homeless in the Nineties (The Video) 473
Homeopathic Care for Infants and Children 850
Homeopathic Care for Pets 850
Homeopathic Care for the Family 850
Homer Price Stories 635
Homes of Frank Lloyd Wright, The 565
Homework 231
Homicide 231
Homo Promo 460
Homophobia in the Media and Society 1993 MIT Panel 460
Homophobia in the Workplace 460
Homosexual Desire in Minnesota 460
Hondo 293
Honduras, A World into Itself 57
Honduras: Carlos and Nicaragua: Balty 57
Honduras: Gateway to Central America 830
Honey Sweet Love 33
Honeymoon Machine, The 271
Honeymooners Hidden Episodes, The 418
Honeymooners—Honeybloopers!, The 418
Honeymooners Lost Episodes, The 418
Honeymooners Lost Episodes: 12-Volume Set, The 418
Honeymooners Valentine's Special, The 418
Honeymooners: The Best of the Lost Episodes, The 418
Hong Kong 1941 121
Hong Kong: A Family Portrait 145
Honi Coles & Cholly Atkins: Over the Top to Bebop 572
Honky Tonk 271
Honky Tonk Girl (Highway Hell) 507
Honolulu 271
Honor Among Thieves 231
Honor and Glory 128
Hoodlum 231
Hoodlum Empire 372
Hoodlum Priest, The 372
Hook 258
Hooked on Comix 541
Hoop Dreams 473
Hooray for Abbie! 300, 760
Hoosier Schoolboy 372
Hoosier Schoolmaster 372

Hoosiers 231
Hope 231
Hope for the Future: Confronting HIV in Children and Adolescents 834
Horace Pippin 452, 550
Horizontal Lieutenant, The 372
Horn Blows at Midnight, The 271
Horodok 112
Horror Chamber of Dr. Faustus 523
Horror Express 523
Horror Hotel 523
Horror of Dracula 523
Horror of It All 523
Horror of the Blood Monsters 523
Horror Rises from the Tomb 523
Horrors of the Black Museum 174, 523
Horse, The 106
Horse Dealer's Daughter 300
Horse Feathers 271
Horse of Pride 12
Horse's Mouth, The 183
Horse Soldiers, The 340
Horse Thief, The 117
Horseman on the Roof, The 3
Horses: Close Up and Very Personal 652
Horst P. Horst 559
Horszowski: Live at Carnegie Hall 590
Horton Dance Method 572
Hospital, The 271
Hostel in Tokyo (An Inn in Tokyo; Tokyo No Yado), A 143
Hostile Guns 293
Hot Bagels: The Hole Story 114
Hot Millions 271
Hot off the Grill 858
Hot Pepper 480
Hot Shot 231, 602
Hot Thursday 92
Hot Tuna: 25 Years and Runnin'— Live at Sweetwater 611
Hotel Dulac 192
Hotel Imperial 399
Hotel Lux 92
Hotel Pacific 92
Hotel Paradiso 271
Hotel Terminus: The Life and Times of Klaus Barbie 16, 473
Houdini, The Life of the World's Greatest Escapologist 795
Houdini 372, 795
Hound of the Baskervilles (Brett), The 186
Hound of the Baskervilles (Cushing), The 186
Hound of the Baskervilles (Rathbone), The 186
Hound of the Baskervilles (Richardson), The 186
Hour of the Star 54
Hour of the Wolf 78
Hours and Times, The 431, 460
House Built on Sand 81
House by the River 72
House of 1000 Dolls, The 523
House of Angels 76
House of Cards 192, 231
House of Darkness 523
House of Dies Drear, The 660
House of Dracula 523
House of Elliot, The 192
House of Frankenstein 523
House of Horrors 523
House of Magical Sounds, The 580
House of Strangers 372
House of the Seven Gables, The 372
House of the Spirits, The 231
House of Un-American Activities 473
House of Usher—Malice in Wonderland 617
House of Wax 523
House of Yes, The 271
House on 92nd Street, The 372
House on Chelouche Street 107
House on Haunted Hill, The 523
House Party 2: The Pajama Jam 444
House Party 3 444
House Party 444
House That Shadows Built, The 335
House with Knights, The 87
House Without a Christmas Tree, A 231
Houseboat 271
Housefly: An Everyday Monster 816
Household Saints 271
Householder, The 259
Housekeeper, The 210
Housekeeping 231
Housemaster 95
Houses Are Full of Smoke 473
How a Car Is Built 635
How Beaver Stole Fire 635, 787
How Bugs Bunny Won the West 685
How Do You Spell God? 790
How Good Do We Have to Be: A New Understanding of Guilt and Forgiveness 850
How Great Thou Art 607
How Green Was My Valley 340
How Hitler Lost the War 769
How I Won the War 183
How It's Done: From Baseball Bats to Potato Chips 635
How It's Done: From Roller Coasters to Ice Cream 635
How Many Miles to Babylon 161
How Serious Is This? 850
How Tasty Was My Little Frenchman 54
How the Rhinoceros Got His Skin 867
How the West Was Lost 298
How The West Was Lost II 299
How the West Was Won 293, 340
How Then Shall We Live? 804, 850
How to Be a Perfect Person in Just Three Days 661
How to Commit Marriage 271
How to Conduct a Dream Workshop: A Practical Introduction 850
How to Draw Comics the Marvel Way 563
How to Fold a Paper Crane 668
How to Frame a Figg 271
How to Get Ahead in Advertising 183
How to Hide Stories 635
How to Irritate People 198
How to Live Between Office Visits, with Dr. Bernie Siegel 850
How to Make a Doll 507
How to Make an American Quilt 232
How to Marry a Millionaire 271
How to Murder Your Wife 271
How to Pick Girls Up 121
How to Play Flutes of the Andes 624
How to Produce a CD-ROM 845
How to Reawaken Your Sexual Powers 850
How to See Hollywood 336, 830
How to Spar Against Karate 851
How to Spar Against Tae Kwon Do 851
How to Squash a Squat 473
How to Steal a Million 343
How to Succeed in Business Without Really Trying 324
How to Survive 431
How to Use a C-Stand 317
How to Visit an Art Museum 563
How U Like Me Now 444
Howard Hawks: American Artist 336, 342
Howard Hodgkin 550
Howard Stern Exposed 795
Howard Stern: Shut Up and Listen 473
Howard Terpning: The Storyteller 550, 787
Howardena Pindell: Atomizing Art 550
Howards End 259
Howards of Virginia 372
Hoxsey: How Healing Becomes a Crime 473
Hsing-I 851
Hubble Space Telescope: Rescue in Space 839
Huberman Festival 590
Hubley Collection Vol. 1 711
Hubley Collection Vol. 2 711
Hubley Collection Vol. 3 711
Hubley Studio: Of Men and Demons 711
Hubley Studio: The Cosmic Eye 711
Hubley Studio: The Hole 711
Hubley Studio: Voyage to Next 711
Huckleberry Finn (1974/Musical) 309
Huckleberry Finn (1975/Howard) 309
Hucksters 372
Hud 372
Hudson River and Its Painters, The 550
Hudsucker Proxy 441
Hue and Cry 183
Huggabug Club: I'm One of a Kind, The 652
Huggabug Club: School Days, The 652
Huggabug Club: You Can't Win 'em All, The 652
Hugh Hefner: Once Upon a Time 795
Hugh Shannon: Saloon Singer 611
Hugo Pool 232
Huit Piastres et Demie! 473
Hula 399
Hullabaloo (Chuck Berry et al.) 620
Hullabaloo (Simon & Garfunkel et al.) 620
Hullabaloo 653
Hum Paanch 147
Human Comedy 372
Human Condition 137
Human Dilemma: Explorations in Existential Psychotherapy 851
Human Encounters with Aliens 862
Human Factor, The 232
Human Monster (Dark Eyes of London) 523
Human Race Club: A Story About Fights Between Brothers and Sisters 635
Human Race Club: A Story About Making Friends, a Story About Prejudice and Discrimination 635
Human Race Club: A Story About Self-Esteem, a Story About Earning Money 635
Human Rights and Moral Practice: The Dalai Lama at Berkeley 149
Human Search: The Life of Father Bede Griffiths, A 790
Human Sexes, The 836
Humanoid, The 733
Humanoids from the Deep (Monster) 497
Humoresque 372
Hunchback (1982) 232
Hunchback (1997), The 232
Hunchback of Notre Dame, The 20, 28, 372, 399, 635, 693
Hundred Dresses 635
Hungarian Fairy Tale, A 102
Hungarian Rhapsody 102
Hungary, Land of Hospitality 103
Hunger, The 460, 523
Hunger 76
Hunger and Land at Home and Overseas 804
Hungers of the Soul: Be Gardiner, Stone Carver 550
Hungry Hill 174
Hungry I Reunion, The 534
Hunt, The 45
Hunt for Red October, The 232
Hunt for the Serial Arsonist 836
Hunted in Hong Kong 128
Hunted Men 399
Hunter in the Dark 137
Hunter: The Fox's Foul Play, The 698
Hunters and Gatherers 782
Hunters of Chubut 816
Hunting Flies 96
Huntress 816
Hurricane 340, 816
Hurricane Express, The 372
Husbands and Wives 288
Hush, Hush, Sweet Charlotte 523
Hustler White 460
Huston Smith: The Mystic's Journey Gift Box Set 149
Hutterites, The 473
Huxley Pig 653
Hyena of London 523
Hyenas 150
Hymn for a Nation 769
Hype! 620
Hyper Doll Act 1 733
Hyper Doll Act 2 733
Hypnotic Places, Exotic Spaces 485
Hypothesis of the Stolen Painting 11

I

I, A Woman 76
I, Claudius 192
I Am a Camera 174
I Am a Dancer 572
I Am a Fugitive from a Chain Gang 372
I Am Cuba 81
I Am Curious—Yellow 76
I Am My Own Woman 64, 460
I Am the Cheese 431
I Am the Law 372
I Am Who I Am 92
I Am Your Child 858
I Ask for Wonder: Experiencing God 114
I Became a Lesbian and Others Too 460
I Bombed Pearl Harbor 137
I Bury the Living 523
I Can Build 635
I Can Dance 668
I Can't Give You Anything But Love/ Solid Gold Illusion 561
I Can't Sleep 8
I Capuleti e I Montecchi 597
I Confess 352
I Conquer the Sea 372
I Could Go on Singing 324
I Died a Thousand Times 372
I Dig Fossils 816
I Don't Hate Las Vegas Anymore 431
I Don't Want to Talk About It 44
I Dood It 324
I Dream of Jeannie 324
I Have a Friend 635
I Killed Rasputin 20
I Kiss Your Hand, Madame 347
I Know What You Did Last Summer 232
I Know Where I'm Going 180
I Know Why the Caged Bird Sings 445
I Lied 92
I Like Bats 92
I Like It Like That 57
I Like You, I Like You Very Much 138, 460
I Live for Art—The Great Toscas 597
I Live in Fear 142
I Live My Life 372
I Live with Me Dad 206
I'll Always Be Anthony 460
I'll Cry Tomorrow 373
I'll Do Anything 271
I'll Fix Anthony 635
I'll Love You Forever...Tonight 460
I'll See You in My Dreams 324
I'll Take Sweden 271
I Love Big Machines 653
I Love Lucy 418
I Love Lucy's Zany Road Trip 418
I Love Lucy: Adventures in Europe 418
I Love Lucy: The Classics 418
I Love Lucy: The Very First Show 418
I Love Maria (aka Roboforce) 128
I Love Melvin 324
I Love Toy Trains 3-Video Set 653
I Love You, Alice B. Toklas 183
I Love You, I Love You Not 232
I Love You, Let's Work It Out 851
I Love You Again 373
I Love You Rosa 108
I'm a Ballerina Now 669
I'm a Civilian Here Myself! 769
I'm a Fool 300
I'm a Fool and The Wild Bunch 418
I'm from Hollywood: Andy Kaufman 271
I'm Gonna Git You Sucka 533
I'm No Angel 272
I'm Not Fascinating—The Movie! 431
I'm Not Oscar's Friend Anymore and Other Stories 635
I'm Not Rappaport 272
I'm the One You're Looking For 44
I Married a Monster from Outer Space 497
I Married a Witch 24
I Married an Angel 324
I Need a Hug! 635
I Never Sang for My Father 232

I Only Want You to Love Me (Ich Will Doch Nur, Dass Ihr Mich Liebt) 66
I Pagliacci (Gobbi/Allegro) 580
I Pagliacci (Gobbi/Video Yesteryear) 580
I Pagliacci (Zeffirelli) 580
I Photograph to Remember 867
I.Q. 272
I Remember Mama 343
I Saw Him in the Rice Field 135
I Shot Andy Warhol 431
I Sing for You Alone 41, 580
I Stand Condemned 174
I the Worst of All 50
I've Always Loved You 373
I Vespri Siciliani 580
I Vitelloni 36
I Wake Up Screaming 373
I Wanna Hold Your Hand 324
I Want My MTV 418
I Want to Be an Artist When I Grow Up 635
I Want to Live 373
I Want You 373
I Was a Male War Bride 342
I Was a Teenage Mummy (1962) 523
I Was a Teenage Serial Killer 507
I Was a Teenage Werewolf 523
I Was Stalin's Bodyguard 81
I Will Fight No More Forever 787
I Worked for Stalin 81
I Worship His Shadow 210, 497
Ice House 161
Ice Storm, The 232
Iceland 272
Iceman 232
Iceman Cometh, The 128
Ici et Ailleurs (Here and Elsewhere) 9
Icicle Thief, The 33
Icy Breasts 3
Iczelion! Acts 1 & 2 733
Iczer 3 Vol. 1 733
Iczer 3 Vol. 2 733
Iczer 3 Vol. 3 733
Iczer-One Vol. 1: Acts One & Two 733
Iczer-One Vol. 2: Act Three 733
Ida B. Wells 452
Ida B. Wells: A Passion for Justice 452
Idaho Transfer 497
Idea, The 711
Ideal Husband, An 183
Idiot, The 142
Idol Dancer 413
Idols of the Game 827
Idomeneo (Drottningholm) 580
Idomeneo (Met) 580
If 174
If Dolphins Could Talk 816
If I Ever See You Again 232
If I Were King 272
If I Were Rich 174
If It's Tuesday, This Must Be Belgium 272
If Monks Had Macs: A Hearty Stew of Interactive Books, Games, Art 867
If the People Will Lead 87
If These Walls Could Speak 830
If These Walls Could Talk 232
Igor Stravinsky 590
Igor Stravinsky's Symphony of Psalms 590
Igor Stravinsky: The Rite of Spring 867
II International Biennial of Painting: Cuenca-Ecuador 550
Ikiru 142
Il Ballarino: The Art of Renaissance Dance 572
Il Barbiere di Siviglia (La Scala) 580
Il Barbiere di Siviglia (Met) 580
Il Bell'Antonio 41
Il Bidone 36
Il Grido 35
Il Matrimonio Segreto 580
Il Postino 33
Il Re Pastore 580
Il Ritorno d'Ulisse in Patria 581
Il Tabarro/Pagliacci 581
Il Trovatore (Del Monaco) 581
Il Trovatore (Levine) 581
Il Trovatore (Pederzini) 581
Illegals, The 112, 775
Illicit 373
Illtown 431
Illumination 92, 485
Illusion Travels by Streetcar 47
Illusions 73
Illustrated Guide to Caricature 561
Illustrated Man, The 497
Illustrious Client, The 186
Ilona Vera's Ballet Class: Developing a Personal Style 572
Imaan 147
Image of the Fendahl 200
Imagenes Latino Americanas 57
Images 150 Years of Photography 559
Images de France 155
Images of Mexican Los Angeles 57
Images of the '80s 810
Images: A Lesbian Love Story 460
Imaginaria 711
Imaginary Crimes 232
Imagine That! 653
Imagine the Sound 611
Imagine: John Lennon 620
Imaginit 635
Imitation of Life 342, 373
Immediate Family 232
Immoral Mr. Teas 513
Immoral Three, The 507
Immortal Battalion (The Way Ahead), The 174
Immortal Beloved 232
Immortal Story, The 344
Immortals, The 827
Imogen Cunningham: Never Give Up 559
Imp, The 121
Impact 373
Impact Addict Videos 567
Implosions 611
Importance of Being Earnest, The 312
Imported Bridegroom, The 232
Impossible Hour: Ole Ritter & Eddie Merckx, The 827
Impossible Spy, The 232
Impossible Years, The 272
Imposters 431
Impressionism and Post Impressionism 550
Impressionism Boxed Set 550
Impressionism: A Visual Revolution 550
Impressionists on the Seine 550
Impressions of Hong Kong and Macau 145
Improper Conduct 58, 460
Impulse 174, 523
In a Brilliant Light: Van Gogh in Arles 550
In a Cartoon Studio 711
In a Glass Cage 44, 460
In a Land Called Israel 607
In a Lonely Place 346
In a Storm Even Dinosaurs Trip & Invasion of the Amazons 567
In a Time of Headlong Progress 816
In a Year of Thirteen Moons 66
In an Old Manor House 92
In and Out 232
In and Out: The Petrie Court at the Metropolitan 550
In Between 431, 442
In Celebration of the Piano 590
In Celebration of Trees 816
In Coal Country 635
In Cold Blood 232, 373
In Concert: Karl Bohm & Jon Vickers 590
In Custody 147
In Desert and Wilderness 92
In Good Hands: Culture and Agriculture in the Lacandon Rainforest 816
In Harm's Way 373
In Heaven There Is No Beer 480
In Like Flint 272
In Love 50
In Love with Paris 28
In Love with These Times 620
In Memoriam 44
In Motion: Amiri Baraka 445, 473
In My Own Backyard 635, 672
In Old California 293
In Old Chicago 373
In Plain English 473
In Praise of Mother Santoshi 147
In Search of Angels 790
In Search of Dr. Seuss 711
In Search of the Golden Hammerhead 816
In Search of the Missing Numbers 669
In Service to America 760
In Society 272
In South Louisiana/Dedans le Sud de la Louisiane 602
In the Blood 473
In the Company of Angels: Biblical Truths About God's Glorious Creatures 790
In the Company of Men 431
In the Company of Whales 816
In the Footsteps of Peter: The Museums & The Buildings of Vatican City 565
In the Gloaming 232
In the Good Old Summertime 324
In the Grip of Evil 336
In the Heat of the Night 373
In the House 860
In the Jaws of Life 103
In the King of Prussia 481
In the Kingdom of the Dolphins 816
In the Land of the Deaf 8, 473
In the Land of the Owl Turds 432
In the Land of the War Canoes 399, 787
In the Life 460, 800
In the Life: The Funny Tape 461, 534
In the Line of Duty 4 (aka The Witness) 128
In the Line of Fire 232
In the Mouth of Madness 497
In the Name of Brotherhood 232
In the Name of the Father 202
In the Name of the Pope-King 33
In the Navy 272
In the Path of a Killer Volcano 816
In the Presence of Mine Enemies 232
In the Realm of the Senses 141
In the Shadow of Angkor Wat 550
In the Shadow of the Stars 473, 581
In the Shadow of War/O My People! 58
In the Silence of the Night 98
In the Soup 432
In the Steel: A Portrait of Mark di Suvero 550
In the Steps of Chopin: Portrait by Byron Janis 590
In the Street 486
In the Tall, Tall Grass 653
In the Tentacles of the North 399
In the Wake of the Bounty 206
In the White City 30
In the Wild: Dolphins with Robin Williams 816
In the Wild: Grey Whales with Christopher Reeve 816
In the Wild: Pandas with Debra Winger 816
In This Our Life 348
In Trouble 213
In Which We Serve 180
In Your Face 533
In-Laws, The 272
Inauguration of the Pleasure Dome 486
Incas Remembered 58
Incident at Blood Pass 138
Incident at Map Grid 36-80 82
Incident at Oglala 787
Incredible Animation Collection: Vol. 1 711
Incredible Animation Collection: Vol. 2 711
Incredible Doktor Markesan, The 523
Incredible Hulk Laserdisc 711
Incredible Hulk: Return of the Beast, The 711
Incredible Journey, The 693
Incredible Manitoba Animation 711
Incredible Melting Man, The 497
Incredible Mr. Limpet, The 711
Incredible Petrified World, The 497
Incredible Shrinking Man 497
Incredible Shrinking Woman, The 272
Incredible Story of Dogs, The 816
Incredible Voyage of Bill Pinkney, The 452
Incredibly Strange Creatures Who Stopped Living and Became Mixed Up Zombies, The 507
Incredibly True Adventure of Two Girls in Love, The 461
Independence 349
Independence Day 232, 497
Independence: Birth of a Free Nation 810
Independence: Texas Gains Its Freedom 810
Indestructible Man, The 523
India, Land of Spirit and Mystique 149
India and the Infinite: The Soul of a People 148
Indian & His Homeland: American Images, 1590-1876, The 787
Indian in the Cupboard, The 663
Indian in the Cupboard, The 663, 867
Indian Motorcycle Memories 842
Indian Runner, The 232
Indian Summer 272
Indian Tomb, The 72
Indiana Jones and the Last Crusade 258
Indiana Jones and the Temple of Doom 258
Indians of North America, Collection I 787
Indians of North America, Collection II 787
Indigo Girls Watershed 461
Indiscreet 272, 373
Indiscreet Mrs. Jarvis, The 373
Indiscretion of An American Wife 38
Individual Desires Solution & War Songs, An 461, 486
Indochine 3
Indomitable Teddy Roosevelt 795
Infernal Trio, The 17
Inferno 200
Infiltrator, The 232
Infinite Voyage: Crisis in the Atmosphere, The 804
Infinite Voyage: Fires of the Mind, The 804
Infinite Voyage: Great Dinosaur Hunt, The 817
Infinite Voyage: Life in Balance, The 836
Infinite Voyage: Miracles by Design, The 836
Infinite Voyage: Sail On, Voyager, The 804
Infinite Voyage: The Champion Within, The 836
Infinite Voyage: The Future of the Past, The 817
Infinite Voyage: The Living Clock, The 817
Infinite Voyage: To the Edge of the Earth, The 836
Infinite Voyage: Unseen Worlds, The 817
Infinity 233
Infinity Series: Part 1—The Solar System, The 839
Infinity Series: Part 2—Deep Space, The 839
Infinity Series: Part 3—The Light Beyond Light and Life, The 839
Infinity Series: Part 4—The Crystal Space/Time Ship, The 839
Information Superhighway Robbery: The Crisis of the Cultural Environment 860
Informed Approach to HIV Antibody Testing, An 834
Informer, The 174, 340
Ingres: Slaves of Fashion 550
Ingrid Bergman: Portrait of a Star 336
Inherit the Wind 373
Inheritance (Uncle Silas), The 174
Inky, Dinky Spider 817
Inland Sea, The 138
Inn of the Sixth Happiness, The 174
Inn Trouble 461
Inner Circle 84
Inner Sanctum: Calling Dr. Death/Strange Confession, The 523
Inner Sanctum: Dead Man's Eyes/Pillow of Death, The 524
Inner Sanctum: Weird Woman/Frozen Ghost, The 524
Innocence Unprotected 104
Innocent, The 39, 233
Innocent Blood 233
Innocent Sorcerers 96
Innocents, The 174
Innocents Abroad 309, 480
Innocents in Paris 183
Innocents with Dirty Hands 12
Insects 817
Inside 258
Inside Afghanistan 111
Inside AMG (The Athletic Model Guild Story) 461
Inside Daisy Clover 373
Inside God's Bunker 109

Inside Hawaiian Volcanoes....817
Inside Hitchcock....352
Inside Monkey Zetterland....432
Inside Russia....87
Inside Story (Triad: The Inside Story), The....128
Inside Termite Terrace Vol. 1: Daffy the Commando....711
Inside Termite Terrace Vol. 2: Tokyo Jokio....711
Inside Termite Terrace Vol. 3: Jungle Jitters....711
Inside Termite Terrace Vol. 4: Bosko....711
Inside Termite Terrace Vol. 5....711
Inside the CIA: Assassination....473
Inside the CIA: History....473
Inside the CIA: Subversion....473
Inside the Secret Service....860
Inside the Vatican, with Sir Peter Ustinov....790
Inside the West Bank....111
Inside the White House....810
Inside Tips on Discovering Antiques....561
Inspector General....82, 312
Inspector Morse....192
Inspiration....373
Inspired by Bach: Yo-Yo Ma....590
Instrumental Artistry of Vishwa Mohan Bhatt, The....590
Interconnectedness and Social Policy....851
Interiors....288
Intermediate Algebra....838
Intermediate English/ESL....859
Intermezzo....76
Internal Power ("Chi") in the Martial Arts....851
International House....272
International Release: A Moving Pictures Magazine....153
International Sweethearts of Rhythm/Tiny & Ruby: Hell-Divin' Women....461, 611
International Tournee of Animation Volume 1....711
International Tournee of Animation Volume 2....712
International Tournee of Animation Volume 3....712
International Tournee of Animation Volume 4....712
International Tournee of Animation Volume 5....712
International Tournee of Animation Volume 6....712
Internes Can't Take Money....373
Interns....233
Interpol Connection....128
Interpretation of Dreams....82
Interrogation....95
Interrupted Journey....174
Interrupted Melody....324
Intersection....233
Interview & Reading: Kenward Elmslie....304
Interview & Reading: Ron Padgett....304
Interview Techniques....317
Interview with David Bohm: Quantum Physics and Philosophy, An....836
Interview with Jonas Mekas....336
Interview with Stephen Levine: Healing and Dying, An....851
Interview with the Vampire....233
Interviews with Artists, Program 4: Three Installation Artists....550
Intervista....36
Intifada (Palestinian Uprising): A Jewish Eye Witness, The....111
Intifada (Palestinian Uprising): A Jewish Eye Witness, The....114
Intimacy and Sexual Ecstasy....851
Intimate Deception....233
Intimate Lesson with Tony Rice, An....624
Intimate Relations....183
Intimate Story....108
Into the Blue....161
Into the Thin Air of Everest: Mountain of Dreams, Mountain of Doom....830
Intolerance....413
Introducing Don Quixote....48
Introduction to Aromatherapy....851
Introduction to Ballroom Dancing....572
Introduction to Floor Managing....317
Introduction to Television Lighting....317
Introduction to the End of an Argument....486
Intruder, The....507
Intruder in the Dust....373
Intruso....44
Invaders from Mars (1953)....497
Invaders from Mars (1986)....497
Invasion, The....200
Invasion of the Blood Farmers....507
Invasion of the Body Snatchers (1956)....497
Invasion of the Body Snatchers (1978)....497
Invasion of the Dinosaurs....817
Invasion of the Space Preachers....233
Invasion of the Vampires....524
Invasion USA....507
Inventing the Abbotts....233
Invention Studio....867
Invincible Brothers....42
Invincible Fighter....134
Invisible Adversaries....74
Invisible Agent....524
Invisible Boy, The....497
Invisible Dr. Mabuse (The Invisible Horror)....497
Invisible Ghost, The....524
Invisible Invaders....498
Invisible Man, The....192, 524
Invisible Man Returns, The....524
Invisible Man's Revenge, The....524
Invisible Monster (Cliffhanger Serials #5), The....538
Invisible Ray....524
Invisible Universe....867
Invisible War, The....769
Invisible Woman, The....524
Invitation, The....30
Invitation au Voyage....3
Invitation to a Gunfighter....293
Invitation to the Dance....572
Iowa: An American Portrait....760
Ira Says Goodbye....635
Ira Sleeps Over....635
Ireland's Emerald Treasures....203
Ireland: The Isle of Memories....203
Iria: Zeiram the Animation Vol. 1: Episodes 1 and 2....733
Iria: Zeiram the Animation Vol. 2: Episodes 3 and 4....733
Iria: Zeiram the Animation Vol. 3: Episodes 5 and 6....733
Irish Cinderella, The....399
Irish Country Calendar, An....203
Irish Country House, The....203
Irish Dance....203, 572
Irish Homecoming....203
Irish Humor of Noel V. Ginnity, The....203
Irish in America: From the Emerald Isle to the Promised Land, The....203
Irish in America: Long Journey Home, The....203
Irish Magic: Irish Music....203
Irish R.M., The....193
Irish Waterways....203
Irma La Douce....345
Irma Vep....8
Iron & Silk....455
Iron Crown, The....41
Iron Duke, The....174
Iron Hand....92
Iron Major....373
Iron Man: The Origin of Iron Man....698
Iron Mask....399
Iron Monkey....128
Iron Road, The....760
Iron Thunder....507
Iron Virgin Jun....733
Iron Will....664
Iron-Fisted Monk, The....128
Ironclads: The Monitor and the Merrimac....779
Ironhand....64
Ironweed....233
Irresponsible Captain Tylor 1: Most Irresponsible Man in Space, The....733
Irresponsible Captain Tylor 2: Bring Me the Head of Capt. Tylor!, The....733
Irresponsible Captain Tylor 3: Boldly Going Nowhere, The....733
Irresponsible Captain Tylor 4: Escape Times Three, The....733
Irresponsible Captain Tylor 5: Strange Love, The....733
Irresponsible Captain Tylor 6: Irresponsibly Responsible, The....733
Irresponsible Captain Tylor: A Farewell to Responsibility, The....733
Irresponsible Captain Tylor: Leave It to Tylor, The....733
Irresponsible Captain Tylor: Prepack 1, The....734
Irving Johnson High Seas Adventurer....842
Is It Easy to Be Young....82
Is Life Worth Living?....400
Is Lucyna a Girl?....92
Is Paris Burning?....20
Is There Sex After Death?....272
Is This the Cure?....834
Isaac Asimov's Library of the Universe....867
Isaac Bashevis Singer in America....112
Isaac Bashevis Singer: Champion of Yiddish Literature....112
Isaac Stern: A Life....590
Isabel Allende....58
Isabel Bishop: Portrait of an Artist....550
Isadora....167, 174
Isadora Duncan Dance....572
Isamu Noguchi....551
Ishi, The Last Yahi....787
Ishmael Reed....300
Islam: A Closer Look....790
Islamic Mysticism: The Sufi Way....790
Island....138
Island in the Sun....373
Island of Bliss, The....69
Island of Fire....134
Island of Lost Souls....524
Island of Puerto Rico, The....58
Island of the Blue Dolphins....664
Island of the Dragons....817
Island of Whales....817
Island Soldiers: The History of the Celtic Saints....203, 790
Island Soldiers: The History of the Celtic Saints....203, 790
Island Terror....524
Islander....233
Islands....233, 473, 551
Islands in the Stream....233
Islands of the Caribbean....54
Isn't Life Wonderful....413
Israel and the Occupied Territories....111
Israel in Dance: Shalom in Action....572
Israel in Egypt....590
Israel Philharmonic Welcomes Berlin Philharmonic....591
Israel's Folk Dance Festival....572
Israel Sings—Sing Along....109
Israel—This Land Is Yours!....109
Israel vs. the PLO: The Invasion of Lebanon....111
Israel: A Nation Is Born....109
Israel: The Holy Land....109
Israeli Writers....109
Istanbul....233, 373
It....400
It Ain't Half Hot Mum....193
It Came from Beneath the Sea....498
It Came from Beneath the Sea/20 Million Miles to Earth....498
It Came from Outer Space....498
It Conquered the World....513
It Could Always Be Worse....635
It Could Happen to You....272
It Don't Pay To Be an Honest Citizen....432
It Happened in Brooklyn....324
It Happened in the Park....38
It Happened One Night....351
It Happens Every Spring....272
"It Is What It Is"....834
It Lives Again....524
It'll Be Better....92
It Means That to Me....373
It's a Date....324
It's a Dog's Life....373
It's a Drink! It's a Bomb!....128
It's a Great Feeling....324
It's a Great Feeling/Thank Your Lucky Stars....325
It's a Great Life....272
It's a Joke, Son!....272
It's a Mad, Mad, Mad, Mad World....272
It's a Male's World....817
It's a Mean Old World & Born in the Blues....611
It's a Mystery, Charlie Brown....698
It's a Pleasure....373
It's a Wonderful Life....351
It's Alive....524
It's All True....344
It's Always Fair Weather....325
It's Clean—It Just Looks Dirty....486
It's Hullabaloo!....418, 620
It's in Every One of Us....635
It's in the Bag....272
It's Like This, Cat....635
It's Me, Claudia! & My Grandson Lew....635
It's My Party....233
It's Not Always Easy Being a Kid....635
It's Not Easy Being Green....653
It's Raining Money....44
It's the Muppets!....653
It's the Old Army Game....400
It Started in Naples....272
It Started with a Kiss....272
It Started with Eve....272
It Zwibble: Earthday Birthday....653
It! The Terror from Beyond Space....498
Italian, The....400
Italian American/The Big Shave....253
Italian Job, The....183
Italian Straw Hat, The....24
Italy Wins World War III: 1990 Summit....473
Itzhak Perlman: Virtuoso Violinist....591
Ivan and Abraham....3, 776
Ivan the Terrible, Part I....86
Ivan the Terrible, Part II....86
Ivan the Terrible, Parts I & II....86
Ivan the Terrible Ballet....572
Ivanhoe....193, 373, 672
Ivo Pogorelich: In Villa Contarini....591
IvoPogorelich in Castello Reale di Racconigi....591
Ivor the Engine....653
Ivory Handled Gun, The....293

J

J. Lyle....712
J'Accuse (Silent)....20
J'Accuse (Sound)....20
J'Ai Ete au Bal: I Went to the Dance....480
J.D.'s Revenge....533
J.P. Donleavy's Ireland....203
J.S. Bach....486
Jaanam....147
Jacare....473
Jacek Fedorowicz Cabaret Evening....98
Jack and His Friends....233
Jack and the Beanstalk....272
Jack and the Dentist's Daughter....647
Jack Be Nimble....208
Jack Benny Program, The....418
Jack Frost....664, 712
Jack Kerouac ROMnibus, A....867
Jack L. Warner: The Last Mogul....336
Jack Levine: Feast of Pure Reason....551
Jack Levine: Out of the Studio....551
Jack London....304
Jack's Back....524
Jack Sheldon and New Orleans....611
Jack the Giant Killer....664
Jack the Ripper (Karloff)....524
Jack the Ripper (Paterson)....524
Jack the Ripper: The Final Solution....524
Jack-Knife Man....400
Jack: The Last Kennedy Film....797
Jackie Brown....441
Jackie Chan....134, 795
Jackie Chan and the 36 Crazy Fists....134
Jackie Chan Best Hits....134
Jackie Chan's Police Force....134
Jackie Chan: My Story....134
Jackie Chan: Ten Fingers of Death....134
Jackie Mason....535
Jackie McLean on Mars....611
Jackie Robinson Story, The....452
Jackie Robinson: Breaking Barriers....452
Jackie: A Tribute to the First Lady....797
Jacknife....233
Jackpot, The....272
Jackson County Jail....233

Jackson Pollock 551
Jacob 355
Jacob Have I Loved 636, 661
Jacob Lawrence 452, 551
Jacob Lawrence:The Glory of Expression 452, 551
Jacob's Ladder 233
Jacqueline du Pre and the Elgar Cello Concerto 591
Jacqueline Kennedy Onassis Remembered 797
Jacques Brel 28
Jacques Lacan's Psychoanalysis Part One 3, 785
Jacques Lipchitz 551
Jacques Prevert 28
Jacquot de Nantes 14
Jade 233
Jadzia 92
Jagged Edge 233
Jaguar 1936 92
Jaguar Trax 636
Jail Bait 515
Jailbird's Vacation 20
Jailhouse Rock 536
Jalsaghar (The Music Room) 147
Jamaica Inn 193, 352
Jamaican Heritage 54
James & The Giant Peach 664, 685
James A. Michener's Texas 233
James Baldwin Anthology,The 304
James Brown & Guest B.B. King 620
James Brown 620
James Brown:The Lost James Brown Tapes 620
James C. Christensen:The Art of Imagination 551
James Cagney Collection,The 373
James Cagney Scrapbook 336
James Cagney:Top of the World 336
James Dean and Me 336
James Dean at High Speed\ 336
James Dean Story 254
James Dean:A Portrait 336
James Fenimore Cooper's Leatherstocking Tales: I & II 304
James Galway in Concert 605
James Hall & Worship and Praise: ...According to James Hall—Chap. III 607
James Joyce's Women 202
James L. Fitzpatrick's Traveltalks 830
James Marshall Library,The 636
James Schuyler: Interview/Reading 305
James Stewart:A Wonderful Life 336
Jammin' with the Blues Greats 611
Jamon, Jamon 45
Jan Peerce, Marian Anderson & Andres Segovia 597
Jan Pietrzak—Mr. Censor 98
Jan van Eyck:The Mystery of Painting 551
Jana Aranya (The Middleman) 147
Jancis Robinson's Wine Course 860
Jane Austen's Emma 193
Jane Austen's Persuasion 161, 193
Jane Austen's Pride and Prejudice 193
Jane Eyre (1934) 373
Jane Eyre (1944) 373
Jane Eyre (BBC) 193
Jane Eyre 233, 418
Jane Hissey's Old Bear Stories: Friends, Friends, Friends 653
Jane Hissey's Old Bear Stories: Happy Birthday Old Bear 653
Janet Baker Full Circle 597
Janey Junkfood's Fresh Adventure 636
Janis 620
Janosch 636
Janosik 92
Janovska Camp at Lvov,The 776
Japan 144
Japan:The Island Empire 144
Japanese Shiatsu Massage Made Simple 851
Japanese War Bride 373
Japanese:Yesterday and Today 144
Jason and the Argonauts 42, 174
Jason's Lyric 445
Jasper Johns: Ideas in Paint 551
Java Head 174
Jaws 258
Jay Jay the Jet Plane and His Flying Friends 672
Jay Leno:The American Dream 535
Jay O'Callahan:A Master Class in Storytelling 636
Jay Ward & Bill Scott TV Commercials Vol. 1 712
Jay Ward & Bill Scott TV Commercials Vol. 2 712
Jayhawkers 373
Jayne Mansfield: Single Room Furnished/The Female Jungle 507
Jazz 611
Jazz Africa: Herbie Hancock/Foday Musa Suso 611
Jazz Age,The 611
Jazz Class for Kids 624
Jazz Comedy (Jolly Fellows) 82
Jazz Dance Class with Gus Giordano 572
Jazz Hoofer: Baby Laurence 611
Jazz in America: Gerry Mulligan 612
Jazz in Exile 612
Jazz Is My Native Language 612
Jazz Is Our Religion 612
Jazz Masters:Vintage Getz 612
Jazz Odyssey: Beyond El Rocco 612
Jazz on a Summer's Day 612
Jazz Shorts 612
Jazz Singer (Crosland),The 325
Jazz Singer (Curtiz),The 325
Jazz Singer (Fleischer),The 325
Jazz Time Tale 636
Jazz Workout 572
Jazz: Earle Hines and Coleman Hawkins 612
Jazzball 612
Jazzercise 851
Jazzman 82
Je,Tu, Il, Elle 29
Jean Cocteau:Autobiography of an Unknown 27
Jean de Florette 4
Jean de Florette/Manon of the Spring 4
Jean Gabin 4, 336
Jean Genet 28
Jean Houston:A Passion for the Possible/Body Mind Exercises with Jean Houston 851
Jeanette MacDonald 336
Jeanette MacDonald in Performance 617
Jeevan Dhara 147
Jeeves & Wooster 193
Jeff Carpenter:The Real Thing 551
Jeff Way: Faces and Masks 551
Jefferson in Paris 259
Jeffrey 461
Jellies and Other Ocean Drifters 817
Jennifer 8 233
Jenny Lamour 25
Jenufa 581
Jeremiah Johnson 233
Jeremy Around the World 636
Jericho 448
Jerker 461
Jerky Boys:The Movie,The 272
Jerry Douglas' Dobro Techniques 624
Jerry Lee Lewis: I Am What I Am 620
Jerry Lewis 336
Jerry Maguire 272
Jerusalem 76, 109
Jerusalem's Cardo 109
Jerusalem Stories 111
Jerusalem Throughout the Ages 109
Jerusalem Today: City of Neighborhoods 109
Jerusalem:An Interactive Pilgrimage to the Holy City 867
Jerusalem: City of Heaven 114, 830
Jerusalem: Gates to the City 109
Jerzy Grotowski 312
Jesse James Rides Again 538
Jesse James Under the Black Flag 293
Jesse Owens Story 452
Jessi Sings Songs from Around the World 636
Jessye Norman:A Christmas Concert 597
Jester,The 48
Jester (Der Purimshpiler),The 112
Jesus,The Son of Man 572
Jesus and His Times 790
Jesus Christ Superstar 325
Jesus from the Gospel (KJV) 790
Jesus from the Gospel (RSV) 791
Jesus—His Life 791
Jesus of Montreal 213
Jesus of Nazareth (The Story of the Saviour's Life) 400
Jesus of Nazareth 355
Jesus Paid It All 607
Jet Pilot 347
Jets:The New Generation 842
Jetsons:The Movie 698
Jew,The 48
Jewel Thief 147
Jewish American Patriots 114
Jewish Communities of the Middle Ages 114
Jewish Holidays Video Guide,The 114
Jewish Life in Bialystok 112
Jewish Life in Cracow 112
Jewish Life in Lvov 112
Jewish Life in Vilna 112
Jewish Mothers Video Cookbook 858
Jewish Museum 551
Jewish Perspective on the Environment,A 114, 804
Jewish Soul Music:The Art of Giora Feldman 114
Jews of Boston,The 114
Jews of Djerba 114
Jews of Poland 112
Jezebel 343
JFK (Director's Cut) 233
JFK (Gift Set) 797
JFK Assassination:The Jim Garrison Tapes,The 798
JFK Conspiracy,The 798
JFK in Ireland 798
JFK:The Day the Nation Cried—November 22, 1963 798
JFK:The End of Camelot 798
Jig Don't Jog 203
Jilting of Granny Weatherall 301
Jim Bailey Experience,The 461
Jim Davis:Volume #1 486
Jim Davis:Volume #2 486
Jim McCann & The Morrisseys 605
Jim Reeves/Ray Price (with Ernest Tubb) 605
Jim Rose Circus Sideshow,The 486
Jim Thorpe—All American 795
Jimbo and the Jet-Set 636
Jimi Hendrix Live at the Isle of Wight, 1970 620
Jimi Hendrix Story,The 621
Jimi Hendrix: Experience 621
Jimi Hendrix: Woodstock 621
Jimi Plays Berkeley 621
Jimi Plays Monterey 621
Jiminy Cricket's Christmas 693
Jimmy,The Boy Wonder 507
Jimmy Stewart 336
Jing,A Chinese Girl 636
Jingle Bell Rap! 636
Jirimpimbira 152
Jit 150
Jive Junction 507
JLG/JLG 9
Jo Jo Dancer,Your Life Is Calling 445
Joan Baez (1941-Present)— Mexican-American Folksinger 58
Joan Crawford Collection,The 374
Joan Halifax: Elder as Healer 851
Joan Jonas:Vertical Roll 486
Joan Miro: Constellations— The Color of Poetry 551
Joan of Arc 374
Joan Rivers:Abroad in London 535
Joan Sutherland: Making "Lakme" 597
Joan Sutherland:The Age of Bel Canto 581
Joan the Maid: Complete Set 10
Joan the Maid:The Battles 10
Joan the Maid:The Prisons 10
Joan the Woman 354
Joe 233
Joe Cocker: Mad Dogs & Englishmen 621
Joe Coleman 551
Joe Cool Live 612
Joe Louis 827
Joe Louis—For All Time 827
Joe Louis Story,The 374
Joe Pass in Concert 612
Joe Piscopo Live! 535
Joe's Apartment 272
Joe Scruggs First Video 653
Joe Scruggs in Concert 653
Joe Versus the Volcano 272
Joe Williams:A Song Is Born 612
Joey 206
Joey Breaker 272
Joey Runs Away and Other Stories 653
John & Julie 183
John Baldessari: Some Stories 551
John Cage 617
John Cage: I Have Nothing to Say and I Am Saying It 617
John Cage: Man and Myth 591
John Edgar Wideman 452
John F. Kennedy— The Commemorative Album 798
John F. Kennedy and the Nazi Spy 798
John F. Kennedy's Lost Pathway to Peace 798
John F. Kennedy:A Personal Story 798
John F. Kennedy: Challenges and Tragedy 798
John F. Kennedy:The New Generation 798
John Fahey/Elizabeth Cotten: Rare Interviews and Performances from 1969 605
John Hartford 612
John Hus 355
John Huston:The Man,The Movies,The Maverick 349
John Kim Bell:A Profile of the First North American Indian Conductor 591
John Lee Hooker & Friends 612
John Lee Hooker: Rare Performances, 1960-1984 612
John Lennon:The Bed-In 621
John Marin's New York 551
John Paul Jones 374
John Piper: Piper's Way 551
John Renbourn & Stefan Grossman 602
John Renbourn Group 602
John the Fearless 712
John Waters Collection, No. 1,The 514
John Wayne RKO Collection,The 374
John Wayne: On Board with the Duke 336
John Whitney, Sr. 486
John Wycliffe:The Morning Star 791
Johnny 100 Pesos 50
Johnny Apollo 374
Johnny Belinda 374
Johnny Carson: His Favorite Moments 418
Johnny Come Lately 374
Johnny Eager 374
Johnny Guitar 346
Johnny Handsome 233
Johnny McEvoy in Concert 602
Johnny Mnemonic 210
Johnny One-Eye 374
Johnny Sokko and His Flying Robot: Episodes 1 and 2 734
Johnny Sokko and His Flying Robot: Episodes 3 and 4 734
Johnny Sokko and His Flying Robot: Episodes 5 and 6 734
Johnny Sokko and His Flying Robot: Episodes 7 and 8 734
Johnny Stecchino 33
Johnny Suede 432
Johns 461
Jolly Corner 301
Jolly Paupers 112
Jolson Sings Again 325
Jolson Story 325
Jon Jost's Frameup 441
Jon Vickers Sings Verdi and Puccini 597
Jonah Who Will Be 25 in the Year 2000 30
Jonny Quest,The Real Adventures: Escape to Questworld 698
Jonny Quest,The Real Adventures: Rage's Burning Wheel 698
Jonny Quest,The Real Adventures:The Alchemist 698
Jonny Quest,The Real Adventures:The Darkest Fathoms 698
Jonny Quest vs.The Cyber Insects 698
Jonny Quest: Bandit—Adventure's Best Friend 698
Jonny Quest: Dr. Zin—Master of Evil 698
Jonny Quest: Hadjí—Mysteries of the East 698
Jonny Quest: Race Bannon—An Army of One 698
Jorge Luis Borges 58
Jorge Luis Borges: Borges and I 58
Jose Carreras' Comeback Recital in Spain 597
Jose Carreras 597
Jose Carreras and Friends 597
Jose Carreras in Concert 597

Jose Carreras in Salzburg....597
Jose Carreras: A Life Story....597
Jose Carreras: A Tribute to Mario Lanza....597
Jose Carreras: Four Days with the Famous Tenor on the Road...597
Jose Carreras: Music Festival in Granada....597
Jose Greco in Performance....572
Josef von Sternberg....347
Joseph....355
Joseph Andrews....161
Joseph Beuys, Public Dialogues....551
Joseph Brodsky: A Maddening Space....87
Joseph Campbell: Mythos II....149
Joseph Chaikin and the Open Theater....312
Joseph Heller....305
Joseph Losey and Adolfus Mekas: The First New York Film Festival....353
Joseph Papp and the Public Theater: American Playwrights 1976....312
Joseph Schultz....776
Josepha....4
Josephine Baker Story, The....453
Josephine's Imagination....636
Josh Kirby...Time Warrior! Journey to the Magic Cavern....664
Joshua....533
Joshua's Masai Mask....669
Joshua the Black Rider....293
Joshua Then and Now....211
Jour de Fete....28
Journey, The....168
Journey....234
Journey Back to Africa....152
Journey Back to Ireland....203
Journey Back to Oz....712
Journey Back: Professionals Recovering from Addiction, The....851
Journey Beneath the Desert (L'Atlantide)....498
Journey for Margaret....175
Journey Home: The Animals of Farthing Wood....636
Journey into Fear....344
Journey into Life....817
Journey of August King, The....234
Journey of Butterfly, The....776
Journey of Carlos Fuentes: Crossing Borders....58
Journey of Hope....30
Journey of the African-American Athlete, The....453, 827
Journey of Thomas Blue Eagle, The....867
Journey Through Fairyland....712
Journey Through Jazz....612
Journey Through the Bible Lands....791
Journey to Freedom: The Immigrant Experience....760
Journey to the Center of Time....498
Journey to the Far Side of the Sun....498
Journey Together....175
Jousters, The....636
Joy Harjo....787
Joy Luck Club, The....455
Joy of Life, The....669
Joy of Sex....273
Joyce Khozloff: The Erotic Paintings....551
Joyless Street....69
Jozef Pilsudzki/Road to Independence....98
Ju Dou....118
Ju Jutsu—Traditional Japanese Unarmed Combat with James Shortt....851
Juan Carlos Onetti....58
Juan Downey....486
Juan Goytisolo....58
Juan Rulfo....58
Juarez....349
Jubilee....167
Jubilee Trail....293
Jud Suess....69, 769
Jude....161
Jude the Obscure....193
Judex....20
Judge....734
Judge and the Assassin....11
Judge Priest....340
Judgment at Nuremberg....374
Judgment Day....567
Judgment Day Theater: The Book of Manson....432
Judgment in Berlin....234
Judith of Bethula....413
Judith of Bethula/Home Sweet Home....413
Judy Garland (General Electric Theatre)....419
Judy Garland Scrapbook....336
Juggle Time....669
Juice....445
Juju Music: King Sunny Ade....602
Juke Joint....448
Jules and Jim....14
Jules Feiffer: Feiffer's Follies....551
Julia....4, 234
Julia and Julia....33
Julia Misbehaves....273
Julian Samuel Trilogy....474
Julie....374
Julie Andrews—Broadway: The Making of Broadway, The Music of Richard Rodgers....325
Julie: Old Time Tales of the Blue Ridge....474
Juliet of the Spirits....36
Julio and His Angel....50
Julio Cortazar....58
Julio Rosado del Valle....551
Julius Caesar (Heston/Gielgud)....312
Julius Caesar (MGM/Brando)....312
Julius Caesar....581
Julius Caeser....867
Jumanji....636, 664
Jumbo....325
Jumper....64
Jumping Jacks....273
Jumping Night in the Garden of Eden, A....114
Junction 88....448
June Anderson: The Passion of Bel Canto....581
June Bride....273
June Night....76
Jung on Film....785
Jungle Book (1967), The....693
Jungle Book (1994), The....693
Jungle Book (Sabu), The....175
Jungle Books, Set I, The....636
Jungle Cavalcade....374
Jungle Drums of Africa (Cliffhanger Serials #5)....538
Jungle Fever....447
Jungle for Joey, A....636
Jungle Girl....538
Jungle King....636
Jungle Princess....400
Jungle Trap, The....374
Junglies: First Day at School....636
Junior Bonner....347
Junior G-Men....538
Juno and the Paycock....352
Jupiter, Saturn, Uranus & Neptune....839
Jupiter, Saturn and Uranus....839
Jupiter's Darling....374
Jupiter's Wife....474
Jurassic Park....258
Jurgen Reble—Passion....432
Juri Koll: The Artifact in Art....551
Just a Gigolo....64
Just Another Girl on the I.R.T.....445
Just Another Pretty Face....20
Just Another Weekend....432
Just Between Me & God....474
Just Beyond This Forest....92
Just Call Me Kitty....817
Just Dam' Lucky....445
Just Doin' It....453
Just for the Hell of It....507
Just Grandma and Me....653
Just Hold Still....486
Just Like a Woman....183
Just Me and My Dad....653
Just Say kNOw to AIDS: Abstinence....834
Just Say kNOw to AIDS: Safer Sex....834
Just So Stories, Set I....653
Just Suppose....400
Justice Factory....810
Justine....350
Justine de Sade....4
Juve Contre Fantomas....20
JVC/Smithsonian Folkways Video Anthology of Music and Dance of Africa....572, 602
JVC/Smithsonian Folkways Video Anthology of Music and Dance of Europe....572, 602
JVC/Smithsonian Folkways Video Anthology of Music and Dance of the Americas....572, 602

K

K2....234
Kabhi-Kabhi....147
Kaboom!....836
Kabuki Classics: Onoe Baiko VII in The Salt Gatherer....144, 312
Kabuki Techniques....312
Kafka....443
Kafka: Nabokov on Kafka....101
Kagemusha....142
Kalachakra: The Wheel of Time....149
Kaleidoscope: Polish Folk Dance and Songs....98
Kalifornia....234
Kaliman, El Hombre Incredible (Kaliman, the Incredible Man)....672
Kama Sutra....147
Kameradschaft....69
Kamikaze....769
Kamikaze Hearts....461
Kamikaze: Death from the Sky....769
Kanal....96
Kangaroo....206
Kangaroos Under Fire....817
Kangaroos: Faces in the Mob....817
Kansas City....254
Kansas City Confidential....374
Kapalana: Death of a Hawaiian Village....145
Kapo....41
Karajan Conducts....591
Karajan in Salzburg....591
Karajan: Early Images, Vol. 2 (1965-66)....25, 591
Karate Kat: Aristokratic Kapers....712
Karate Polish Style....92
Karate Wars....128
Karel Ancerl: In Rehearsal and Performance....591
Karen Akers: On Stage at Wolf Trap....617
Karibu....152
Karl Bohm: The Birth of a Symphony....591
Karl Krogstad Films....432
Karma....147
Kartemquin Films, Vol. 1: Inquiring Nuns....474
Kartemquin Films, Vol. 2: Winnie Wright, Age 11....474
Kartemquin Films, Vol. 3: Trick Bag....474
Kartemquin Films: The Complete Set....474
Kasarmu Ce: This Land Is Ours....150
Kashmir Ki Kali....147
Kaspar Hauser....64
Kate Clinton: The Queen of Comedy....461
Katha (The Tale) (The Fable)....147
Katharine Hepburn....336
Katharine Hepburn Collection, The....374
Katharine Hepburn: World of Stories....647
Katherine Anne Porter: The Eye of Memory....305
Kathleen Battle at the Metropolitan Museum....597
Katy Meets the Aliens....672, 712
Katya Kabanova....581
Kavanagh Q.C.....193
Kay Boyle....305
Kazablan....108
Kazimir Malevich: Breaking Free of the Earth....551
Kazuo Ishiguro....144, 305
Kean....153
Keep 'Em Flying....273
Keep Punching....374
Keeper, The....234, 445
Keeper of the Flame....350
Keeper of Traken, The....200
Keepers of Eden, The....804
Keeping Quilt, The....636
Keeping the Passion....851
Keeping the Promise....234
Keeping Up Appearances....193
Keetje Tippel....31
Keiko Matsui: Light Above the Trees....617
Kelly's Heroes....234
Ken Burns' America....760
Ken Hom's Chinese Cookery....858
Ken Russell....336
Ken Southworth Basic Animation Kit, The....712
Kendo: The Path of the Sword....144
Kennedy's Ireland....798
Kennedy Space Center: Window to the Universe....839
Kennedys (American Experience), The....798
Kennedys....798
Kennedys Don't Cry....798
Kennedys of Massachusetts, The....798
Kennel Murder Case....374
Kenneth Noland: A Look at a Minimalist....551
Kenny & Georgia: The Story of a Homeless African-American Couple....453
Kenny Drew Live....612
Kent State....760
Kentuckian, The....374
Kentucky Fried Movie....507
Kentucky Kernels....343
Kenya Safari: Essence of Africa....152
Kenyan Youth: Preparing for the Future....152
Kept Husbands....374
Kerouac....305
Kerry....203
Keshet ve Anan—Cloud and Rainbow....115
Ketchup Vampires, The....685
Kettles in the Ozarks, The....273
Kettles on Old MacDonald's Farm, The....273
Kevin Burke and Michael O'Domhnaill....602
Kevin Turvey Investigates....193
Key, The....106, 374
Key Largo....349
Key the Metal Idol, Vol. 7: Knowing....734
Key to the City....374
Key: The Metal Idol, Vol. 1....734
Key: The Metal Idol, Vol. 2: Awakening....734
Key: The Metal Idol, Vol. 3: Believing....734
Key: The Metal Idol, Vol. 4: Dreaming....734
Key: The Metal Idol, Vol. 5: Searching....734
Keys of the Kingdom....374
Keys to Tulsa....234
Keystones #1....407
Keystones #2....407
Keystones #3....407
KGB: The Soviet Sword and Shield of Action....87
Khartoum....175
Khmer Court Dance: Cambodian Royal Court Dances....572
Khovanschina (Kirov)....581
Khovanschina (St. Petersburg)....581
Khovanschina (Vienna State Opera)....581
Khovanschina....572
Kickboxer from Hell....128
Kickboxer—The Fighter, the Winner....129
Kicked in the Head....432
Kickfighter....129
Kicking and Screaming....432
Kid for Two Farthings, A....175
Kid from Brooklyn....273
Kid from Spain....273
Kid from Tibet, The....121
Kid Galahad....374
Kid in King Arthur's Court, A....664
Kid Millions....325
Kid Nerd....474
Kid's Eye View of Ecology, A....636
Kid's Guide to Divorce, A....858
Kid's Guide to Drug, Alcohol and Smoking Awareness, A....858
Kid Who Loved Christmas, The....664
Kid-A-Vision....540
Kid/The Idle Class, The....407
Kidnap of Wong Chak Fai, The....121
Kidnapped....432
Kidnapped by UFOs....862
Kids, Sex, and Choices....858
Kids....432

Kids by the Bay 669
Kids Explore Mexico 58
Kids Get Cooking: The Egg 669
Kids in the Crossfire: Violence in America: Answering Children's Questions 800
Kids Kitchen: Making Good Eating Great Fun for Kids! 669
Kids Learning Through Fun 669
Kids Love the Circus 653
Kids of the Round Table 664
Kidsongs Music Video Stories 669
Kiepura in My Song for You 183
Kiev Ballet Collection, The 572
Kika 46
Kiki 374
Kiki's Delivery Service 734
Kill, Baby, Kill 524
Kill or Be Killed Collection 129
Kill-Off, The 234
Killdozer "Li'l Baby Huntin'" Live 621
Killer, The 129
Killer Angels 129
Killer Bait (Too Late for Tears) 507
Killer Diller 448
Killer's Kiss 256
Killer's Romance 129
Killer Shrews 524
Killers, The 374
Killers 374
Killers from Space 524
Killing, The 256
Killing Affair 234
Killing Cars 64
Killing Fields 234
Killing Floor, The 432
Killing Game 21
Killing Grandpa 51
Killing of a Chinese Bookie, The 440
Killing Screens, The 861
Killing Zoe 234
Killing/Killer's Kiss, The 256
Kim 234, 374
Kimagure Orange Road, Collector's Suite 734
Kimagure Orange Road, Laserdisc #1 734
Kimagure Orange Road, Laserdisc #2 734
Kimagure Orange Road, Laserdisc #3 734
Kimagure Orange Road Vol. 1 734
Kimagure Orange Road Vol. 2 734
Kimagure Orange Road Vol. 3 734
Kimagure Orange Road Vol. 4 734
Kimagure Orange Road Vol. 5: I Want to Return to That Day 734
Kimba The Lion Prince: Insect Invasion 734
Kimba The Lion Prince: Jungle Thief 734
Kimba The Lion Prince: Legend of the Claw 734
Kimba The Lion Prince: River Battle 734
Kimbark: Focus on Environmental Education 804
Kimera 734
Kin Folks 273
Kind Hearts and Coronets 183
Kinda 200
Kindergarten 82
Kindred Men of a Dark War 778
Kinetic Sculpture Windcarver 551
King 453
King and Country 175
King and Four Queens, The 374
King and I, The 325
King and the Fool, The 112
King Arthur 170
King Arthur and His Country— Southern England 170
King Blank 432
King Boleslaus the Bold 92
King in New York 408
King Kong (60th Anniversary Edition) 524
King Kong Lives 524
King Kong vs. Godzilla 498
King Lear (Kozintsev) 82
King Lear (Laurence Olivier) 312
King Lear (Orson Welles) 312
King Lear 9
King of Comedy 253
King of Hearts 17
King of Jazz 325
King of Kings 346, 354
King of Marvin Gardens 234
King of the Gypsies 234
King of the Hill 443, 827
King of the Rocketmen (Lost Planet Airmen) 538
King of the Texas Rangers 538
King of the Wild Horses 400
King of the Zombies 524
King Priam 581
King Rat 374
King Richard and the Crusaders 374
King's Christmas, The 597
King's College Choir: The Festival of Nine Lessons and Carols 597
King's Demons/The Five Doctors, The 200
King's Rhapsody, The 175
King's Row 374
King's Singers in Concert, The 597
King's Thief, The 375
King Solomon's Mines 175
King Tut: The Face of Tutankhamen 784
King Tut: Tomb of Treasure 784
Kingdom, The 76
Kingdom of Green Glade, The 92
Kingdom of Shadows 336
Kingdom of the Vampires 524
Kingfish: A Story of Huey P. Long 234
Kingpin 273
Kings Go Forth 375
Kingsize 95
Kingston Trio & Friends Reunion 605
Kino Pravda and Enthusiasm 86
Kino's Story Time, Vol. 1 653
Kino's Story Time, Vol. 2 653
Kino's Story Time, Vol. 3 653
Kipps 183
Kiri Te Kanawa at Christmas 581
Kiri Te Kanawa: My World of Opera 581
Kiri Te Kanawa: Royal Gala Concert 597
Kiri! Her Greatest Hits Live 597
Kirov Ballet in London 572
Kirov Ballet in Tchaikovsky's Sleeping Beauty, The 572
Kirov Ballet: Classical Ballet Night 572
Kirov Ballet: Coppelia, The 572
Kirov Ballet: Le Corsaire, The 572
Kirov Ballet: The Stone Flower, The 573
Kirov Soloists 573
Kishin Corps #1: Episode 1 734
Kishin Corps #2: Episodes 2 and 3 734
Kishin Corps #3: Episodes 4 and 5 734
Kishin Corps #4: Episodes 6 and 7 734
Kishin—The Symphony 734
Kismet 325, 375
Kiss, The 400
Kiss Before Dying, A 375
Kiss for a Killer 21
Kiss Me, Guido 461
Kiss Me, Stupid 345
Kiss Me Deadly 375
Kiss of Death 16, 165
Kiss of the Spider Woman 234
Kiss of the Tarantula 524
Kiss of the Vampire 524
Kiss or Kill 206
Kiss the Girls 234
Kiss Tomorrow Goodbye 375
Kisses 336
Kisses for My President 273
Kisses in the Dark 234
Kissin' Cousins 325
Kit ou Double 155
Kitchen Toto 161
Kitten Companions 653
Kitty Foyle 375
Kitty Hawk 842
Kizuna 461
Klaus Von Bruch: Black Box I 486
Klee 551
Klip 432
Klondike Annie 375
Klute 234
Knack...and How to Get It, The 183
Knife in the Head 64
Knife in the Water 97
Knight Travellers, The 636
Knights and Armor 561
Knights of the Round Table 375
Knights of the Teutonic Order 92
Knives of the Avenger 507
Knock on Any Door 347
Knots on a Counting Rope 636
Knott's Berry Farm, California 830
Knute Rockne, All American 375
Kodak Cinematography Master Class Series 317
Kodak Travel Series 830
Kodo: Heartbeat Drummers of Japan 144
Koko Taylor: Queen of the Blues 612
Koko the Clown, 1915-27 712
Koko the Clown, 1927-29 712
Koko the Clown, Volume 2 685
Kolberg 69
Kolya 100
Kon-Tiki 728, 867
Konitz: Portrait of Artist 612
Konkome—Nigerian Music 602
Konrad 661
KOR Whimsical Highways LD Set 735
Korczak 97
Korea: MacArthur's War 760
Korean War, The 760
Kornblumenblau 92
Kovacs & Keaton 409, 535
Koyaanisqatsi 474
Krakatoa: East of Java 375
Kramer vs. Kramer 234
Kratts' Creatures 669
Krays, The 161
Kremlin, The 87
Kriemhilde's Revenge 72
Krik? Krak! Tales of a Nightmare 54
Kronos 498
Krotons, The 200
Krull 498
Krush Groove 445
Kuiseb the Vanishing River/Kalahari Bigfoot (BBC Wildlife Special) 817
Kukla, Fran and Ollie: Be a Clown, Be a Clown 653
Kukla, Fran and Ollie: Get on the Dragon Wagon 653
Kukla, Fran and Ollie: Kukla Discovers America 653
Kukla, Fran and Ollie: Madame O's Merry Musicale 653
Kukla, Fran and Ollie: Tis the Season to be Ollie 653
Kull the Conqueror 234
Kumu Hula: Keepers of a Culture 602
Kundun 253
Kung Fu [Cult] Master 129
Kung Fu the Movie 129, 234
Kung-Fu 95
Kung-fu Exercise Workouts 851
Kuni Lemel in Tel Aviv 108
Kurt Bestor Christmas 617
Kwaidan 138
Kwanzaa: An African-American Cultural Holiday 453
Kwanzaa: Echoes of Africa 152
Kyoto Vivaldi: The Four Seasons 591

L

L. Barnes & Red Budd Choir: So Satisfied 607
L. Frank Baum's Silent Film Collection of Oz 400
L.627 11
L.A. All Stars: Hampton Hawes 612
L.A. Art Fair 1990: Another Quick Take 551
L.A. Confidential 234
L.A. Journal, Vol. 1 830
L.A. Law 419
L.A. Mass Choir 607
L.A.—Suggested by Art of Ruscha 551
L'Africaine 581
L'Amour en Herbe (Budding Love) 4
L'Amour Fou 461
L'Annee des Meduses 4
L'Argent 15
L'Art Vetraria (The Art of Glass) 561
L'Atalante 25
L'Avventura 35
L'Ecole Buissoniere 21
L'Elisir d'Amore 581
L'Enfant et les Sortileges 573
L'Enfer 12
L'Escorte 4, 461
L'espace des Francais 155
L'Etat Sauvage 4
L'Homme Blesse (The Wounded Man) 4, 461
L'Incoronazione di Poppea (Glyndebourne) 581
L'Incoronazione di Poppea (Zurich) 581
L'Inhumaine 21
L'Innocenza ed il Piacer 581
L.L. Bean Guides 827
La Antigua-Guatemala: An American Monument 58
La Bayadere (Kirov) 573
La Bayadere (Royal Ballet) 573
La Belle Epoque 782
La Belle Noiseuse 10
La Bete Humaine 26
La Blue Girl, Volume 1 867
La Boca del Lobo 51
La Boheme (Levine) 581
La Boheme (Omnibus) 581
La Boheme (Pavarotti) 581
La Boheme (San Francisco Opera) 581
La Boheme (The Australian Opera) 581
La Boheme (Zeffirelli) 581
La Boheme 400
La Cage aux Folles 17
La Cage aux Folles II 17
La Cage aux Folles III 17
La Cage aux Zombies 461
La Cambiale di Matrimonio 581
La Cenerentola (Bartoli) 581
La Cenerentola (Salzburg Festival) 581
La Cenerentola (von Stade) 581
La Ceremonie 12
La Chevre 17
La Chienne 26
La Chute de la Maison Usher 21, 486
La Clemenza di Tito (Drottningholm) 581
La Clemenza di Tito (Glyndebourne) 581
La Clemenza di Tito (Vienna Philharmonic) 582
La Collectionneuse 14
La Conquista 58
La Course en Tete: The Eddie Merckx Story 827
La Cucaracha 325
La Cuisine Polonaise 93
La Dama de las Camelias 51
La Discoteca del Amor 51
La Discrete 17
La Dolce Vita 36
La Donna del Lago 582
La Fanciulla del West 582
La Favorita 582
La Femme Nikita 8
La Forza del Destino 582
La Gazza Ladra 582
La Gioconda 582
La Gloria de Espana 48
La Gran Scena Opera Company 597
La Grande Bouffe 4
La Grande Notte a Verona 598
La Grande Vadrouille 17
La Guerre Est Finie 12
La Ibla del Tesoro 672
La Jetee 10
La Jetee/An Occurrence at Owl Creek Bridge 4, 10
La Lectrice 4
La Lengua (The Spanish Language) 48
La Marseillaise 26
La Maternelle 21
La Memoria del Agua 45

La Musique Folklorique.....672
La Notte.....36
La Passante.....4
La Patrilla del Tiempo—1 (Time Patrol—1).....51
La Paz.....51
La Permission.....445
La Petite Marchande d'Allumettes (The Little Matchgirl)/ La Jetee.....26
La Petite Sirene.....4
La Promesse.....4, 29
La Publicite en France—Volume 1.....672
La Publicite en France—Volume 2.....672
La Rana Valiente (The Brave Frog).....672
La Regenta.....51
La Ronde.....27
La Rosa Blanca.....51
La Roue (Wheel of Fate).....21
La Rupture.....12
La Salamandre.....30
La Scala di Seta.....582
La Scala: A Documentary of Performances.....582
La Scorta.....33
La Senorita Lee.....432
La Signora di Tutti.....27
La Strada.....36
La Stupenda: A Profile of Dame Joan Sutherland.....598
La Sylphide.....573
La Symphonie Pastorale.....21
La Terre.....21
La Tigra.....51
La Traviata (Covent Garden).....582
La Traviata (Glyndebourne).....582
La Traviata (Moffo).....582
La Traviata (Sills).....582
La Traviata (Zeffirelli/Domingo).....582
La Vie Continue.....4
La Vie de Boheme.....79
La Vie Est Belle (Life Is Rosy).....150
La Vie Parisienne.....582
Labyrinth, The.....234
Labyrinth of Passion.....46
Lacemaker, The.....30
Ladakh: In Harmony with the Spirit.....149
Ladies' Man.....273
Ladies of Leisure.....351
Ladies of the Chorus.....325
Ladies on the Rocks.....76
Ladies Sing the Blues.....612
Ladies They Talk About.....375
Ladies Who Do.....183
Ladislas Starevitch.....712
Lady Be Good.....325
Lady Be Good/Ship Ahoy.....325
Lady by Choice.....375
Lady Chatterley's Lover.....21
Lady Day: The Many Faces of Billie Holiday.....612
Lady Eve, The.....346
Lady for a Day.....351
Lady for a Night.....375
Lady from Louisiana.....375
Lady from Shanghai.....344
Lady Godiva.....375
Lady Hamilton.....375
Lady in a Cage.....375
Lady in Cement.....375
Lady in Distress.....175
Lady in Question, The.....375
Lady in the Lake.....375
Lady Is Willing, The.....273
Lady Jane.....161
Lady Killer.....129, 375
Lady L.....183
Lady of Burlesque.....375
Lady of the Camellias.....573
Lady of the Lake, The.....153
Lady on a Train.....273
Lady Refuses, The.....375
Lady's Not for Burning, The.....161, 312
Lady Says No, The.....273
Lady Sings the Blues.....325
Lady Snowblood— Love Song of Vengeance.....138
Lady Sun.....121
Lady Takes a Chance.....273
Lady Vanishes, The.....352
Lady Windermere's Fan.....345
Lady with the Dog.....82
Ladybird Ladybird.....166
Ladyboys.....461
Ladyhawke.....235
Ladykillers.....183
Lafayette.....21
Lai Shi: China's Last Eunuch.....121
Laibach: A Film from Slovenia.....602
Lair of the White Worm, The.....167
Lakefront: Parks and Plans, The.....566
Lakewold: Where the Blue Poppy Grows.....830
Lakki: The Boy Who Grew Wings.....76
Lakme.....582
Lakota Woman.....787
Lamb.....161, 400
Lamb Chop in the Land of No Numbers.....653
Lamerica.....33
Lancelot of the Lake.....15
Land & Landscape: Views of America's History & Culture.....551
Land and Freedom.....166
Land Before Time, The.....685
Land Before Time, Vols. I-IV, The.....685
Land Before Time II: The Great Valley Adventure, The.....685
Land Before Time III: The Time of the Great Giving, The.....685
Land Before Time IV: Journey Through the Mists, The.....685
Land Before Time V: The Mysterious Island, The.....685
Land Before Time: Sing-Along Songs, The.....685
Land of Faraway (Mio in the Land of Faraway).....664
Land of Fury.....175
Land of Pleasant Dreams, The.....653
Land of Promise.....97, 109
Land of Sweet Taps, The.....573, 669
Land of the Birds.....817
Land of the Conquistadors.....58
Land of the Leopard.....817
Land of the Look Behind.....602
Land of the Pharaohs.....342
Land of the White Eagle—Part 1.....98
Land of the White Eagle—Part 2.....98
Land of the White Eagle—Part 3.....98
Land Unknown, The.....498
Land Without Bread.....47
Landlock, Part 1.....138, 735
Landlord, The.....273
Landlord Blues.....432
Landmark.....669
Landowska: Uncommon Visionary.....591
Landscape in the Mist.....105
Landscapes of Frederic Edwin Church, The.....551
Langdon at Sennett.....411
Language and Consciousness.....782
Language in Life.....155
Language of Life: A Festival of Poets with Bill Moyers, The.....305
Language Primer.....669
Language Stories.....859
Language Tapes.....155
Lantern Hill.....664
Large Dams, False Promises.....804
Larger Than Life.....273
Larks on a String.....100
Larry Heinemann.....305
Larry Semon #1.....411
Larry Semon #2.....411
Larry Semon #3.....411
Larry Smith/Apollo Belvedere.....432
Las Aventuras de Mafalda.....155
Las Aventuras de Pinocchio.....672
Las Aventuras de Tom Sawyer.....672
Las Minas del Rey Solomon.....672
Las Nicas and Home Life.....58
Las Vegas & the Enchanted Desert.....830
Las Vegas and Hoover Dam.....830
Las Vegas Serial Killer.....507
Lascaux Revisited.....551
Laser Man, The.....455
Laser Mission.....129
Lash of the Penitents, The.....474
Lassie.....664
Lassie Come Home.....664
Lassie's Great Adventure.....636
Lassie: Mother Knows Best.....636
Lassie: To Fetch a Thief.....636
Lassie: To the Rescue.....636
Last Act, The.....106
Last Adventure, The.....21
Last Angry Man.....375
Last Blood, The.....129
Last Butterfly, The.....100
Last Call at Maud's.....461, 474
Last Chance, The.....30
Last Chance to See.....868
Last Chants for a Slow Dance.....441
Last Command.....347
Last Dance, The.....76
Last Date: Eric Dolphy.....612
Last Days of Chez Nous, The.....206
Last Days of Colonel Savath, The.....145
Last Days of Dolwyn.....175
Last Days of Planet Earth.....498
Last Detail, The.....273
Last Diva, The.....33, 336
Last Emperor, The.....35
Last Epidemic.....804
Last Evenings with Teresa (Ultimas Tardes con Teresa).....45
Last Exit to Brooklyn.....235
Last Five Days, The.....64
Last Glory of Troy (The Avenger).....42
Last Good Time, The.....235
Last Hero in China.....129
Last Holiday.....175
Last Hurrah, The.....340, 827
Last Hurrah for Chivalry.....129
Last Jews of Radauti (Song of Radauti).....115
Last Journey.....115
Last Klezmer, The.....112, 602
Last Laugh, The.....73
Last Man on Earth, The.....524
Last Metro, The.....14
Last Mile, The.....375
Last Night of the Proms: The 100th Season.....598
Last of England.....168
Last of Mrs. Cheyney.....375
Last of the Blue Devils.....612
Last of the Czars.....88
Last of the Dogmen.....235
Last of the Giants: Vol. 1: Union Pacific's Big Boys.....842
Last of the Giants: Vol. 2: The Cheyenne Shops.....842
Last of the Mobile Hot-Shots, The.....235
Last of the Mohicans, The.....375, 400, 538
Last of the Mohicans (1985), The.....235
Last of the Mohicans (1992), The.....235
Last of the Red Hot Lovers.....273
Last of the Redmen.....293
Last Outlaw, The.....235, 400
Last Picture Show, The.....235
Last Place on Earth, Collection Set, The.....193
Last Prostitute.....235
Last Pullman Car.....474
Last Remake of Beau Geste, The.....273
Last Resort, The.....804
Last Reunion, The.....175
Last Safari, The.....375
Last Sea.....776
Last Seduction, The.....235
Last Seven Months of Anne Frank, The.....776
Last Stage, The.....93
Last Stand, The.....208
Last Summer in the Hamptons.....235
Last Supper, The.....53, 273
Last Tango in Paris.....35
Last Temptation of Christ.....253
Last Time I Committed Suicide, The.....235, 305
Last Time I Saw Paris.....375
Last Tomahawk, The.....293
Last Train, The.....4
Last Train Across Canada.....842
Last Tycoon.....235
Last Unicorn, The.....712
Last Vampyre, The.....186
Last Voyage, The.....376
Last Waltz.....253
Last Wave.....208
Last Way Out.....235
Last Winter, The.....211
Last Woman on Earth.....513
Last Year at Marienbad.....12
Lasting Impressions.....551
Latcho Drom.....4
Late Bloomers.....461
Late Chrysanthemums.....138
Late Extra.....175
Late Great Planet Earth.....817
Late Shift, The.....273
Late Spring.....143
Late Summer Blues.....108
Latin American Historical Personalities.....58
Latin American Trails: Guatemala.....58
Latin Lovers.....273
Latino.....235
Latino Session.....621
Laugh for Joy (Risate di Gioia).....41
Laughing Horse.....432
Laughing Sinners.....376
Laura.....376
Laura Adler's Last Love Affair.....108
Laura McKenzie's Travel Tips.....830
Laurel & Hardy in Camera Bugged.....698
Laurel & Hardy in Spanish.....51, 273
Laurel and Hardy and the Family.....274
Laurel and Hardy at Work.....274
Laurel and Hardy on the Lam.....274
Laurel and Hardy's Laughing '20s.....274
Laurel and Hardy's Magic Lantern Show.....411
Laurel and Hardy Solo Flights.....411
Laurel and Hardy Spooktacular.....274
Laurel and Hardy: Rare Home Movies.....274
Laurel and Hardy: Stan "Helps" Ollie.....274
Laurel and Hardy: The Legend Begins.....411
Laurel Avenue.....445
Laurence Olivier: A Life.....312
Lavender Hill Mob, The.....184
Lavender Limelight.....336, 461
Law and Jake Wade, The.....293
Law and Order.....293
Law for Tombstone.....293
Law of Desire.....46
Law of the Canyon.....293
Law or Justice.....121
Lawless Breed, The.....294
Lawless Street, A.....294
Lawman.....294
Lawnmower Man, The.....498
Lawrence of Arabia (Criterion).....180
Lawrence of Arabia.....180
Lawrenceville Stories: 3-Pack Miniseries.....301
Lawrenceville Stories: Beginning of the Firm.....301
Lawrenceville Stories: Prodigious Hickey.....301
Lawrenceville Stories: The Return of Hickey.....301
Laws of Gravity.....432
Layer Cake.....97
Lazar Berman in Recital.....591
Lazarillo.....45
Le Bal.....36
Le Barbier de Seville.....582
Le Beau Serge.....12
Le Bonheur.....14
Le Boucher.....12
Le Bourgeois Gentilhomme.....21
Le Calendrier des Francais.....155
Le Cas du Dr. Laurent.....21
Le Chambon: La Colline aux Mille Enfants.....776
Le Chat.....17
Le Complot.....4
Le Crabe Tambour.....4
Le Doulos.....25
Le Gai Savoir.....9

Le Gendarme a New York 21
Le Gendarme de St.Tropez....21
Le Golem:The Legend of Prague....21
Le Grand Louvre....868
Le Grand Melies:The Great Melies, Father of Fiction Films....21
Le Grandi Primadonne....582
Le Jaguar....16
Le Joli Mai....10
Le Jupon Rouge 4, 461
Le Million 24
Le Mystere des Voix Bulgares:A Bird Is Singing....602
Le Noel de Mickey 672
Le Nozze di Figaro (Gardiner)....582
Le Nozze di Figaro (Lyon National Opera)....582
Le Petit Soldat....9
Le Petit Theatre de Jean Renoir 26
Le Plaisir....27
Le Quebec....213
Le Samourai....25
Le Schpountz 26
Le Silence de la Mer 25
Le Soldatesse 41
Le Tresor d'Histoires Classiques 155
Le Voyage Imaginaire....24
Lea Delaria:The Queen of Comedy....461
Leader of the Band 274
Leader of the People 636
Leaders: Jazz in Paris 1988,The 612
Leadership from Within 851
Leading Ladies....336
Leading Man,The....161
Leading Men....336
League of Gentlemen....175
Lean on Me....235
Leap of Faith....235
Leap Year 411
Leapin' Leprechauns....664
Learn the Art of Flamenco (Videos Flamencos de la Luz) 573
Learn to Cook the Easy Way with the Kitchen Divas: Preparing an African Feast 152
Learn to Play Autoharp 624
Learn to Speak English 6.0....868
Learn to Speak French 4.0 868
Learn to Speak German 6.0....868
Learn to Speak Spanish 6.0 868
Learning About Me....859
Learning Blues Piano— Intermediate Level 624
Learning the Bluegrass Fiddle 624
Learning to Fingerpick— Intermediate Level 624
Learning to Fingerpick—Level 1/2 624
Learning to Flatpick 624
Learning to Paint with Carolyn Berry 563
Learning to Play Blues Guitar—Part 1 624
Learning to Play Blues Guitar—Part 2....624
Learning Tree,The 445
Leatherneck 400
Leave Her to Heaven....376
Leaves from Satan's Book....79
Leaving Las Vegas 235
Lectures:Volumes 1-3,The....305
Led Zeppelin: Song Remains the Same....621
Leda:The Fantastic Adventures of Yohko....735
Lee Evans Live:The Ultimate Experience....535
Lee Miller:Through the Mirror....559
Lee Ritenour and Friends,Vol. 1 612
Lee Ritenour and Friends,Vol. 2 612
Leech Woman,The....524
Left at East Gate 868
Left Right....552
Left-Handed Gun 258
Legacy 782
Legacy of a Princess....170
Legacy of Rage 129
Legacy of the Generations 787
Legacy of the Mamluks 552
Legal Innocence....121
Legend of a Sigh,The....106
Legend of Black Thunder Mountain 664
Legend of Dolemite: Rudy Ray Moore,The....533
Legend of Dracula:Truth and Terror,The....868
Legend of El Dorado,The 58
Legend of Lemnear....735
Legend of Love 573
Legend of Sea Wolf 664
Legend of Sleepy Hollow,The 693
Legend of Suram Fortress,The 84
Legend of the Beverly Hillbillies,The 419
Legend of the Drunken Tiger 129
Legend of the Forest 735
Legend of the Lost....376
Legend of the North Wind 712
Legend of the Seven Golden Vampires,The....175, 525
Legend of the White Horse 664
Legend of Tom Dooley,The 294
Legend of Tsar Saltan....582
Legend of Wisely 121
Legendary Theatre Organists....617
Legendary Voices: Cantors of Yesteryear 115
Legends 336
Legends of Bottleneck Blues Guitar....612
Legends of Comedy....274
Legends of Country Blues Guitar 612
Legends of Country Blues Guitar:Volume 2....612
Legends of Country Guitar, Featuring Chet Atkins, Merle Travis, Mose Rager & Doc Watson....605
Legends of Flatpicking Guitar 624
Legends of Gospel....607
Legends of Ireland....203
Legends of Jazz Guitar,Volume I....624
Legends of Jazz Guitar,Volume II 624
Legends of Jazz Guitar,Volume III 612
Legends of Old Time Music 617
Legends of the 1Delta Blues....612
Legends of the Fall 235
Legends of the Isles 170
Legends of the North 235
Legends of the Ring....453, 827
Legends of Traditional Fingerstyle Guitar....605
Legong....474
Leisure Hive,The 200
Lemon Drop Kid,The 274
Lemon Grove Kids,The 507
Lemon Sisters 235
Lempad of Bali 552
Len Lye....486, 712
Leni Riefenstahl....64
Lenin and the Bolsheviks 88
Leningrad Cowboys Go America....79
Leningrad Legend,The 573
Lenny....235
Lenny Bruce 535
Lenny Bruce Without Tears 535
Leo the Lion Vol. 1:The First Adventure 735
Leo the Lion Vol. 2:The Map of Danger....735
Leo the Lion Vol. 3:The Blue Lion 735
Leo the Lion Vol. 4: Leo Becomes a Father 735
Leo the Lion Vol. 5:The Mighty Gorilla....735
Leo the Lion Vol. 6:The Golden Bow....735
Leo the Lion Vol. 7:The Case of the Moonlight Stone 735
Leo the Lion Vol. 8:The Saber-Toothed Tiger....735
Leo Tolstoy 82
Leolo 213
Leon Morin, Priest 25
Leon the Pig Farmer....184
Leonard Bernstein (Candide)....591
Leonard Bernstein Conducts Bernstein 591
Leonard Bernstein Conducts West Side Story 582
Leonard Bernstein in Paris:The Ravel Concerts....591
Leonard Bernstein in Vienna: Beethoven Piano Concerto No. 1 in C Major....591
Leonard Bernstein on Broadway 591
Leonard Bernstein Place,A Musical in Celebration of Leonard Bernstein's 75th Birthday 591
Leonard Bernstein's Young People's Concerts: The Collector's Edition....591
Leonard Bernstein: Schumann/Shostakovich 591
Leonard Bernstein: Serenade for Violin and Orchestra....591
Leonard Bernstein:The Gift of Music....591
Leonard Bernstein:The Rite of Spring in Rehearsal 591
Leonardo, Michelangelo, Raphael and Titian 552
Leonardo da Vinci....868
Leonardo the Inventor 868
Leonid Kogan 591
Leonor Fini 552
Leopard Son,The....664
Leopard Woman 400
Leper....93
Leprechauns' Christmas Gold,The 712
Les Abysses....21
Les Antilles: Guadeloupe and Martinique 28
Les Biches....12
Les Blues de Balfa....602
Les Bonnes Femmes (The Good Girls)....12
Les Brigands 582
Les Carabiniers....9
Les Chateaux de la Loire 28
Les Choses de la Vie 4
Les Clips Francophones 28
Les Contes d'Hoffmann....582
Les Cousins 13
Les Creoles....602
Les Dames du Bois de Boulogne 15
Les Enfants Terribles....25
Les Enfants Terribles and Les Parents Terribles....25, 27
Les Girls 350
Les Grandes Manoeuvres 24
Les Huguenots (The Australian Opera) 582
Les Jeunes Entrepreneurs....673
Les Liaisons Dangereuses 21
Les Maitres Fous 16
Les McCann Trio....613
Les Miserables 4, 21, 235, 312, 376, 636
Les Parents Terribles....27
Les Pompiers....673
Les Troyens....582
Les Vampires....21
Les Violons du Bal 5
Les Visiteurs du Soir 24
Lesbian Humor 461, 492
Lesbian Sexuality 462, 492
Lesbovision 462
Less Than Zero 235
Lesson in Love,A 78
Lessons at the End of Spring 82, 462
Lessons in Visual Language....317
Leszek Dlugosz—It Can Be You....98
Let 'Em Have It 376
Let 'Er Go Gallegher....400
Let Freedom Ring....325
Let Him Have It 161
Let It Rock....235
Let Me Be Brave 474
Let's Cotton Together 98
Let's Create a Better World....669
Let's Create Art Activities (For Ages 5-10)....563
Let's Create for Halloween 669
Let's Create for Pre-Schoolers 653
Let's Create for Thanksgiving 669
Let's Create Fun Jewelry for Boys and Girls....669
Let's Dance....325
Let's Do It Again 445
Let's Get Bizzee 445
Let's Have an Irish Party....203
Let's Make a Map....636
Let's Make It Legal....274
Let's Make Love 350
Let's Make Up....175
Let's Play the Piano and All Those Keyboards 624
Let's Sing Again....376
Let's Sing Along 669
Let There Be Light 349
Lethal Extortion 129
Lethal Girls 2....129
Lethal Match....129
Lethal Panther 129
Lethal Panther 2 129
Lethal Weapon 2....236
Lethal Weapon 3....236
Lethal Weapons:The Visual Art of Barton Benes....561
Letter,The....343
Letter from an Unknown Woman....27
Letter of Introduction,A....376
Letter to Mother....112
Letter to Three Wives 376
Letterist Films—Woman, Women! 432
Letters from Alou....45
Letters from My Windmill 27
Letters from the Park 53
Letters to a Dying Friend 851
Lettres de France....673
Lewis & Clark & George 236
Lewis & Clark....761
Li'l Abner....325
Li-Young Lee 135, 305
Liar Liar 274
Liars,The 21
Libeled Lady 274
Liberace....617
Liberace Collection 617
Liberation....776
Libertine (La Matriarca),The....41, 507
Liberty! The American Revolution....761
Library of the Future,Third Edition....868
Library Skills....859
License to Kill....168, 376
License to Steal 129
Lickerish Quartet,The....507
Lie Down with Dogs 462
Liebelei....27
Life After Life 121
Life After Life: Understanding Near-Death Experience....851
Life and Adventures of Nicholas Nickleby,The 28, 312
Life and Adventures of Santa Claus,The 712
Life and Death of Colonel Blimp 180
Life and Death on the A-List 462
Life and Nothing But....11
Life and Nothing More 106
Life and Times Box....474
Life and Times of Allen Ginsberg,The....305
Life and Times of Deacon A.L.Wiley,The 453
Life and Times of Jesus,The....791
Life and Times of Judge Roy Bean,The....349
Life and Times of Wyatt Earp 299
Life at Stake (aka Key Man),A 376
Life Begins for Andy Hardy/Andy Hardy's Private Secretary 274
Life Drawing Video Workshops by Ruth Block....563
Life in a California Mission in 1790....761
Life in a Gold-Mining Camp 1850 761
Life in a Midwestern Small Town 1910 761
Life in America 1800 761
Life in an Eastern Seaport Town 1870....761
Life in Small Hispanic Towns....58
Life in the 30's....761
Life in the Desert....817, 868
Life in the Moscow Circus 88
Life in the Southern Seas....817
Life in the Theater,A....312
Life in the Woodlands Before the White Man Came....787
Life Is a Dream 11
Life Is a Long Quiet River....5
Life Is Sweet 165
Life Less Ordinary,A....184
Life of Adolf Hitler 474, 769
Life of Brian....198
Life of Donizetti,The 582
Life of Emile Zola,The....376
Life of Her Own,A....350
Life of Leonardo da Vinci....552
Life of Oharu 143
Life of Python....198
Life of Riley:The Bendix Episodes,The 419
Life of Riley:The Gleason Episodes,The....419
Life of Song:A Portrait of Ruth Rubin,A 112
Life of Verdi,The....598
Life on a String 117
Life on Earth....836
Life on Earth Perhaps 804
Life on the Mississippi....309
Life Remembers 1993 800
Life's First Feelings 858
Life Stinks....274

Life Upside Down 21
Life with Elvis 536
Life with Father 274
Life with Louie: For Pete's Sake 685
Life with Louie: The Masked Chess Boy 685
Lifeboat 352
Lifeforce 161
Lifesense 836
Lifestyles of the Ramones 621
Lifetime Commitment: A Portrait of Karen Thompson 462, 474
Lift Off to Space 840
Lifting a Curtain: Conservation of Rubens' Crowning of St. Catherine 563
Lifting the Fog: Intrigue in the Middle East 111
Liftoff 840
Light Ahead, The 112
Light Dance 617
Light of Day 236
Light of Faith, The 400
Light of the Gods 552
Light Princess 647
Light Sleeper 236
Light Years 712
Lighthearted Nation 433
Lighthorsemen, The 206
Lighting Brice 400
Lighting in the Real World 317
Lightnin' Hopkins: Rare Performances 1960-79 613
Lightning 817
Lightning Hutch 400
Lights of New York 376
Lights: The Miracle of Chanukah 636
Lightship, The 97
LightWave 3D—4000 Series 317
Like Father Like Son 274
Like the Dickens 868
Like Water for Chocolate 51
Lilac Time 400
Lilacs in the Spring 184
Lili 325
Lilies of the Field 376
Liliom 72
Lilith 376
Lilith Summer, The 636
Lillie 193
Lilly in Love 102
Lily Dale 236
Lily Tomlin 3-Pack 462, 535
Limelight 408
Limites 559
Lincoln 236, 780
Lincoln Assassination, The 761
Linda 400
Linda Hogan 305
Lindbergh Kidnapping Case, The 236
Lindbergh's Great Race: Are There Any Mechanics Here? 795, 843
Line in the Sand: What Did America Win?, A 111
Line King, The 552
Linguini Incident 236
Link in the Chain, A 376
Linnea in Monet's Garden 664, 712
Lion, The Witch and the Wardrobe, The 664, 712
Lion Has Wings, The 180
Lion Hunters, The 16
Lion in Winter, The 175
Lion Is in the Streets, A 376
Lion King, The 693
Lion of the Desert 116
Lion's Den 206, 433
Lion's Kingdom, The 817
Lion's Love 14
Lionel Hampton 613
Lions of Dakar 152
Lip Gloss 462
Lip Service 274
Liquid Television 2 698
Lisa and the Devil 525
Lisbon Story 67
List of Adrian Messenger 349
Listen, Darling 325
Listen to Britain 474, 769
Listen Up! 834
Listen Up: The Lives of Quincy Jones 613
Listening for Clues: Wynton on Form 624
Listening to America: 20 Years with Bill Moyers 474
Liszt's Rhapsody 636
Lisztomania 167, 325
Little American 354
Little Annie Rooney 400
Little Ant, The 654
Little Bear 654
Little Big Horn 376
Little Boy 481
Little Buddha 35
Little Caesar 376
Little Colonel, The 325
Little Dorrit 161
Little Drummer Boy, Book II, The 698
Little Drummer Boy, The 698
Little Drummer Boy 591
Little Duck Tale, A 654
Little Engine That Could, The 654, 673
Little Fox, The 713
Little Foxes 343
Little Fugitive, The 376
Little Giant 274
Little Girl and Gunny Wolf, A 654
Little Horse That Could, The 203, 637
Little Humpbacked Horse, The 573
Little Indian, Big City 17
Little Ireland 204
Little League's Official How-to-Play-Baseball Video 827
Little Lord Fauntleroy 161, 376, 664
Little Lou and His Strange Little Zoo 637
Little Lulu (Cartoonies) 685
Little Lulu and Friends 685
Little Man Tate 236
Little Match Girl, The 647
Little Men 376
Little Mermaid, The 693
Little Mermaid Vol. 1: Whale of a Tale 698
Little Mermaid Vol. 2: Stormy, The Wild Seahorse 698
Little Mermaid Vol. 3: Double Bubble 698
Little Mermaid Vol. 4: In Harmony 698
Little Mermaid Vol. 5: Ariel's Gift 698
Little Mermaid: Ariel's Undersea Adventures Vol. 1 698
Little Mermaid: Ariel's Undersea Adventures Vol. 2 698
Little Minister, The 376
Little Miss Broadway 325
Little Miss Marker 274
Little Monk and the Tiger 637
Little Mother (Mamele) 112
Little Mother 507
Little Murders 274
Little Nelly Kelly 325
Little Nemo: Adventures in Slumberland 713
Little Nezha Fights Great Dragon Kings 637
Little Nikita 236
Little Odessa 236
Little Orphan Annie 376, 400
Little Pendulum 95
Little People Videos 654
Little Prince, The 325, 664, 713
Little Prince 93
Little Princess, The 376, 661, 664
Little Rascals Collection, The 538
Little Rascals: Divot's Diggers and Mama's Little Pirate 538
Little Rascals: Our Gang: Don't Lie 538
Little Rascals: Pinch Singer and Framing Youth 538
Little Red Schoolhouse 376
Little Richard: Keep on Rockin' 474, 621
Little Romance 236
Little Shop of Horrors 325, 513
Little Sister Rabbit 637
Little Stiff, A 433
Little Thief, The 5
Little Toot 654
Little Troll Prince, The 637
Little Valentino, The 102
Little Vera 82
Little Women (BBC) 193
Little Women 236, 350, 376, 419
Little Women Gift Set 236
Little World of Don Camillo 21
Littlest Angel, The 664
Littlest Rebel 325
Littlest Viking, The 76
Live a Little, Love a Little 536
Live and Let Die 168
Live at the Bradford 617
Live at the Village Vanguard Vol. 1 613
Live at the Village Vanguard Vol. 2 613
Live at the Village Vanguard Vol. 3 613
Live at the Village Vanguard Vol. 4 613
Live at the Village Vanguard Vol. 5 613
Live at the Village Vanguard Vol. 6 613
Live Flesh 46
Live from the Met Highlights Volume 1 582
Live Short Films by Larry Jordan 718
Live Skull "Skullf*ck" 621
Live to Tell 462
Live Wire 400
Lives of a Bengal Lancer 376
Lives of Jesus 791
Living and Working In Space: The Countdown Has Begun 637
Living as a Peaceful Warrior 851
Living Daylights, The 169
Living Dead, The 175
Living Edens, The 817
Living End, The 433
Living Free 161
Living in Oblivion 433
Living in the World Around Us Series 637
Living Islam 791
Living Language 155
Living Monuments in Jewish Spain 552
Living Proof 834
Living Proof: HIV and the Pursuit of Happiness 834
Living Venus 507
Living with Disaster 804
Living with High Blood Pressure 851
Llanito 481
Lloyd and Chase at Keystone 411
Lloyd's of London 175
Lo Frate 'nnamorato 582
Loaded 208
Local Color 433
Local Hero 184
Location Sound Recording 318
Loch Ness Discovered 817
Locke the Superman 735
Locomotion: The Amazing World of Trains 843
Lodger 352
Lodz Ghetto 115, 474
Lodz Ghetto 474
Logging Siberia 804
Logopolis 200
Lohengrin (Bayreuth) 582
Lohengrin (Met) 582
Lohengrin (Vienna State Opera) 582
Lola (The Statutory Affair; Twinky) 376
Lola 5
Lola Montes 27
Lolita 256
London Kills Me 161
London Town 184
London: City of Majesty 170
London: Flower of Cities Allo 170
Lone Star 294
Lone Star Kid, The 661
Lone Wolf and Cub— Baby Cart at the River Styx 138
Lone Wolf and Cub— Baby Cart in the Land of Demons 138
Lone Wolf and Cub— Sword of Vengeance 138
Lone Wolf and Cub—Baby Cart in Peril 138
Lone Wolf and Cub—Baby Cart to Hades 138
Lone Wolf and Cub: White Heaven and Hell 138
Loneliness of the Long Distance Runner 175
Lonely Are the Brave 294
Lonely Guy 274
Lonely Passion of Judith Hearne, The 161
Lonely Struggle: Marek Edelman, Last Hero of the Warsaw Ghetto Uprising, The 769
Lonely Woman, A 96
Lonelyhearts 377
Long, Long Trailer 274
Long Day Closes, The 161
Long Day's Journey into Night 312
Long Good Friday, The 161
Long Goodbye 254
Long Grey Line 340
Long Hair of Death, The 525
Long Haul 175
Long Hot Summer, The 236
Long Island Four, The 433
Long John Silver 664
Long Pants 351
Long Riders 294
Long Shadows: The Legacy of the American Civil War 780
Long Ships, The 175
Long Time Till Dawn, A 419
Long Voyage Home 340
Long Walk Home, The 453
Long Way Home, The 474, 776
Longest Day 377
Longest Hatred, The 115
Longitude & Looneytude: Globetrotting Looney Tunes Favorites 685
Longtime Companion 462
Look and Learn 654
Look Around Endangered Animals, A 637
Look Back in Anger—Kenneth Branagh 312
Look for the Silver Lining 326
Look Out Sister 448
Look What Happens at the Car Wash 637
Look Who's Talking 274
Looking at Music with Adrian Marthaler, Vol. 1 591
Looking for Langston 453
Looking for Miracles 664
Looking for Mr. Goodbar 236
Looking for Richard 312, 474
Looking Glass War, The 162
Looking Like the Enemy 455, 474
Looney Looney Looney Bugs Bunny Movie, The 685
Looney Tunes After Dark 685
Looney Tunes Assorted Nuts 685
Looney Tunes Curtain Calls 685
Looney Tunes Sing-Along 685
Looney Tunes Video Show Volume 1 685
Looney Tunes Video Show Volume 2 685
Looney Tunes Video Show Volume 3 685
Loop: Where the Skyscraper Began, The 566
Lord Jim 175
Lord Love a Duck 274
Lord of Illusions 525
Lord of the Dance (Irish) 573
Lord of the Flies 175, 236
Lord of the Universe 795
Lorenzo's Oil 236
Loretta Lynn 605
Lori Taschler: Little Objects 552
Lorna 513
Lorna Doone 162, 175, 400
Los Angeles Murals 552
Los Hermanos del Hierro 51
Los Ninos Abandonados (The Abandoned Children) 481
Los Olvidados 47
Los Placeres Ocultos 45, 462
Los Tres Mosqueteros 673
Loser 433
Losing Chase 236
Losing Control? 804
Losing Isaiah 236
Loss of an Enemy, The 89
Lost, Lost, Lost 442
Lost Angels 236
Lost Boys, The 236
Lost Children of Berlin, The 776
Lost City 538
Lost Continent, The 175
Lost Continent 498
Lost Express 400

Lost Films of Cassandra Stark, The 433
Lost Highway 257
Lost Horizon 351
Lost in a Harem 274
Lost in Alaska 274
Lost in America 275
Lost in Space 419
Lost in Yonkers 236
Lost Language of the Cranes, The 162, 462
Lost Man's River 305
Lost Moment, The 377
Lost Stooges, The 419
Lost Weekend, The 346
Lost World, The 258, 400, 498
Lost Worlds/Vanished Lives 817
Lost Years of Jesus 791
Lost Zeppelin 377
Lotna 97
Lotte Reiniger Compilation 713
Lotto Land 275
Lotus 123, An Introduction 845
Lotus 123, Database 845
Lotus 123, Graphs 845
Lotus Eaters, The 211
Lou Gehrig Story—Climax, The 419
Lou Rawls Show with Duke Ellington 613
Lou Reed 621
Lou Reed: Rock & Roll Heart 621
Louie Bellson and His Big Band 613
Louis Armstrong 613
Louis Armstrong: The Gentle Giant of Jazz 613
Louisa May Alcott's Little Men 236
Louise Gluck 305
Louise L. Hay: Receiving Prosperity 851
Louise Nevelson in Process 552
Louisiana Boys: Raised on Politics 761
Louisiana Purchase 326
Louisiana Story 474
Loulou 10
Louvre, The 552
Louvre (Boyer) 552
Louvre 200 552
Louvre: Thousands of Masterpieces, The 552
Lovable Cheat, The 409
Love, Death and Eros 785
Love 'Em and Leave 'Em 400
Love, Guns, and Glass 129
Love, Medicine & Miracles 868
Love & a .45 433
Love & Sex Among the Ruins 121
Love 102
Love Affair 236, 377
Love Affair: Or, the Case of the Missing Switchboard Operator 104
Love After Love 5
Love and Anarchy 64
Love and Death 288
Love and Human Remains 213
Love and Other Catastrophes 275
Love and Other Sorrows 301
Love and Romance 851
Love and the Frenchwoman 5
Love at Large 257
Love Can Take It All 93
Love Crazy 377
Love Crimes 433
Love Dolls Superstars 507
Love Flower 413
Love for Lydia 193
Love from a Stranger 175
Love God, The 275
Love Goddesses 336
Love Happy 275
Love in Bloom 275
Love in Mists 121
Love in the Afternoon 346
Love in the City 41
Love Is a Many Splendored Thing 377
Love Is Better Than Ever 275
Love Jones 236
Love Letter to Edy 507, 514
Love Letters 377
Love Lion 567
Love Me or Leave Me 326
Love Me Tender 537
Love Meetings 37
Love Nest 377
Love Never Dies 400
Love of Destiny 582
Love of Jeanne Ney, The 69
Love of Silent Movies, The 51
Love of Sunya, The 400
Love of Three Orchestras, The 591
Love of Three Queens 21
Love on the Dole 175
Love on the Run 14, 377
Love Play 21
Love Serenade 206
Love Show 433
Love Skills 851
Love Soldier of Fortune 121
Love Story 237
Love Story: The Canada Goose, A 817
Love Trap, The 344
Love unto Waste 121
Love with a Proper Stranger 377
Love Without Pity 5
Love! Valour! Compassion! 462
Loved One 275
Lovejoy's Nuclear War 805
Lovely to Look At 326
Lover, The 16
Lover's Guide to Sexual Creativity, The 851
Lovers, The 13
Lovers and Liars 33
Lovers and Lollipops 377
Loves of a Blonde 100
Loves of Carmen, The 326
Loves of Casanova 21, 153
Loves of Emma Bardac, The 591
Low Life, The 433
Lowell Fulson and Percy Mayfield 613
Lower Depths, The 142
Lower Depths 26
Loyalties 211
Loyola, the Soldier Saint 48
LSAT 858
Lubin Studios, The 400
Lubitsch Touch, The 345
Lucas 237
Lucia di Lammermoor (Moffo) 583
Lucia di Lammermoor (Sutherland) 582
Luciano Pavarotti—The Event 598
Lucid Dreaming 851
Lucifer Rising 486
Lucille Ball Redhead Set 275
Lucille Clifton 305
Lucky Devil 401
Lucky Ghost 275
Lucky Jim 184
Lucky Luciano: Chairman of the Mob 795
Lucky Me 326
Lucky Pierre 507
Lucky Stars 129
Lucky to Be Born in Russia 88
Lucky Vanous: The Ultimate Fat-Burning System 851
Lucrezia Borgia 583
Lucy and Desi: A Home Movie 419
Ludmila Semenyaka Bolshoi Ballerina 573
Ludwig 39
Ludwig II 69
Ludwig van Beethoven: Symphony No. 9 868
Lugosi Files, The 525
Luis J. Rodriguez 58
Luis Rafael Sanchez 58
Luis Trenker 69
Luis Trenker Films 69
Luisa Miller 583
Luisa Valenzuela 58
Lullaby of Broadway 326
Lumiere & Company 5, 336
Lumiere Brothers' First Films, The 22, 153
Luminous Visions 713
Luna Park 82
Luna Varga Vol. 1 735
Luna Varga Vol. 2 735
Lunatics, The 122
Lupin III #1: Albatross: Wings of Death 735
Lupin III #2: Aloha, Lupin 735
Lupin III's Greatest Capers 735
Lupin III: The Mystery of Mamo 735
Lupo 108
Luray Caverns 817
Lure of the Range 401
Lure of the Sila 41
Lush Life 237
Lust for Life 377
Lust in the Dust 275
Lustful Night, A 122
Luv 275
Luzia 54
Lydia 377
Lydia Lunch: Malicious Intent 433
Lyle, Lyle Crocodile: The House on East 88th Street 654
Lyric Language French 673
Lyric Language French Teacher's Guide 673
Lyric Language Spanish 673
Lyric Language Spanish Teacher's Guide 673
Lyrical Nitrate 31
Lyrics by Tim Rice 617
Lysistrata 105, 313

M

M. Butterfly 212
M 72
M.C. Higgins, The Great 637
M.F.K. 305
M*A*S*H 254
M/W/F Music Video One 433
Ma and Pa Kettle 275
Ma and Pa Kettle at Home 275
Ma and Pa Kettle at the Fair 275
Ma and Pa Kettle at Waikiki 275
Ma and Pa Kettle Back on the Farm 275
Ma and Pa Kettle Go to Town 275
Ma and Pa Kettle on Vacation 275
Ma Barker's Killer Brood 377
Ma's Motors 637
Ma Vie en Rose 5
MA: Space/Time—In the Garden of Ryoan-ji and AIUEONN Six Features 486
Mabel Mercer: A Singer's Singer 613
Mabel Mercer: Cabaret Artist "Forever and Always" 613
Mabel Normand, Vol. 1 411
Mabel Normand Comedies, Vol. 1 411
Mabel Normand Comedies, Vol. 2 411
Maborosi 138
Mac 433
Macao 347
Macario 51
Macaroni 36
MacArthur 795
Macbeth (Deutsche Opera) 583
Macbeth (Evans) 313
Macbeth (Glyndebourne) 583
Macbeth (Jayson) 313
Macbeth (Verdi) 583
Macbeth 97, 344, 573
Macbeth: The Witches Scenes 486
Macedonia, The Land of a God, Vol. 1: Aina, Aiges, Dion and Pella 784
Macedonia, The Land of a God, Vol. 2: Aina, Aiges, Dion and Pella 784
Machine Dreams 836
Machine Robo: Revenge of Cronos, Vol. 1 735
Machine Robo: Revenge of Cronos, Vol. 2 735
Machine to Kill Bad People 38
Macho Dancer 145, 462
Mack, The 533
Mack Sennett: The Biograph Years 411
Mack the Knife 313
Mackintosh Man, The 349
MacMichael on Nicaragua 58
Macmillan Video Almanac for Kids 669
Macross II: The Movie 735
Macross Plus Part 1 735
Macross Plus Part 2 735
Macross Plus Part 3 735
Macross Plus Part 4 735
Macross Plus: The Movie 735
Mad About Music 326
Mad at the Moon 294
Mad City 106
Mad Death, The 525
Mad Dog and Glory 237
Mad Dog Morgan 206
Mad Executioners, The 525
Mad Ghoul, The 525
Mad Love 237
Mad Max Beyond Thunderdome 206
Mad Miss Manton 275
Mad Monster, The 525
Mad Whirl 401
Madam Satan 355
Madama Butterfly (La Scala) 583
Madame Bovary 13, 26, 377
Madame Butterfly 5, 583
Madame Curie 377
Madame Rosa 5
Madame Satan 525
Madame Sin 237
Madame Sousatzka 162
Madame X (1937) 377
Madame X (1966) 377
Made for Each Other 377
Made for Love 401
Made in America 275
Madeline and the Easter Bonnet 654
Madeline and The Toy Factory 654
Madeline Collection 654
Madeline's Rescue 654
Mademoiselle 5
Mademoiselle Fifi 377, 573
Mademoiselle Midnight 401
Madhouse 525
Madhur Jaffrey's Indian Cookery 858
Madigan 377
Madness of King George, The 162
Madness of Roland, The 868
Mado 5
Mado Robin Live! 41, 583
Madonna: Truth or Dare 475, 621
Madox-01 736
Madox-01/Riding Bean Laserdisc 736
Madrid 48
Madwoman of Chaillot, The 313
Mae West and the Men Who Knew Her 336
Mae West Collection: Special Edition Boxed Set 275
Maedchen in Uniform 70, 462
Maek/Muscha/Shafer/Trimpop 486
Maestro and the Diva, The 598
Maestro's Company—Volume 1 583
Maestro's Company—Volume 2 583
Mafia: The History of the Mob in America 761
Magda Olivero: The Last Verismo Soprano 583
Magdalena Viraga 433
Maggie Kuhn: When Biography and History Intersect 761
Magic Bow, The 175
Magic Christian, The 184
Magic Eye II—The Video, Volume 2 486
Magic Eye—The Video, Volume 1 486
Magic Eye—The Video for Kids 637
Magic Flute (Australian Opera), The 583
Magic Flute (Gewandhaus Orchestra, Leipzig), The 583
Magic Flute (Glyndebourne), The 583
Magic Garden (The Pennywhistle Blues), The 151
Magic Horse 82, 713
Magic Hunter 102
Magic Moments 193

Magic of Lionel Trains 3-Video Set, The 637
Magic of the Bolshoi Ballet 573
Magic of the Kirov Ballet 573
Magic Pony, The 713
Magic School Bus, The 698
Magic Sword, The 377
Magic Thinking Cap, The 637
Magic Town 275
Magic Voyage, The 713
Magic Voyage of Sinbad (Sadko), The 647, 713
Magic Work-Shop of Reveron 552
Magical Coqui—Puerto Rico—Mi Tierra! 673
Magical Field Trip to the Denver Mint, A 637
Magical Field Trip to the Post Office, A 637
Magical Forest, The 713
Magical Journey, A 851
Magical Mystery Tour 621
Magical Princess Gigi 736
Magical Twilight: The HeX Files 736
Magician, The 78
Magicians of the Earth 552
Magnate, The 95
Magnificat for Solo, Chorus and Orchestra 598
Magnificent Adventurer 41
Magnificent Ambersons 344
Magnificent Butcher, The 129
Magnificent Fish: Forgotten Giants 805
Magnificent Obsession 342
Magnificent Seven 294
Magnificent Victoria de los Angeles, The 598
Magnificent Warriors 129
Magnificent Whales, The 817
Magnificent Yankee, The 377
Mahabharata (1989/166 mins.), The 313
Mahabharata (1992/318 mins.), The 313
Mahalia Jackson 607
Mahalia Jackson Collection, The 607
Mahalia Jackson: "Give God the Glory" 607
Mahalia Jackson: The Power and the Glory 607
Mahalia Sings the Songs of Christmas 607
Mahanagar (The Big City) 147
Mahler 167
Mahler: Symphony No. 1 and No. 4 591
Mahler: Symphony No. 3 591
Mahler: Symphony No. 3 in D Minor 592
Mahler: Symphony No. 4 in G 592
Mahler: Symphony No. 5 592
Mahler: Symphony No. 6 592
Mahler: Symphony No. 7 592
Mahler: Symphony No. 8 592
Mahler: Symphony No. 9 592
Mahogany 445
Maid Marian and Her Merry Men 193
Maids of Wilko 97
Maidsplay and Dreiske Discipline Lecture Demonstration 313
Main Event, The 275
Mainland Dundee 122
Maison Ikkoku, Vol. 1: Welcome to Maison Ikkoku 736
Maison Ikkoku, Vol. 2: Ronin Blues 736
Maison Ikkoku, Vol. 3: Spring Wasabi 736
Maison Ikkoku, Vol. 4: Soichiro's Shadow 736
Maison Ikkoku, Vol. 5: Playing Doubles 736
Maison Ikkoku, Vol. 6: Love Love Story 736
Maison Ikkoku, Vol. 7: Call Me Confused 736
Maison Ikkoku, Vol. 8: No Strings Attached 736
Maison Ikkoku, Vol. 9: A Winter's Yarn 736
Maison Ikkoku, Vol. 10: Home for the Holiday 736
Maison Ikkoku, Vol. 11: Kyoko & Soichiro 736
Maison Ikkoku: She's Leaving Home 736
Majestic Marches 592
Majesty: The History of the British Monarchy 170
Majin, The Monster of Terror 525
Major and the Minor, The 377
Major Barbara 313
Major Dundee 347
Major Hubal 93
Majorettes, The 525
Majority of One, A 377
Makarova Returns 573
Make a Puppet, Make a Friend 669
Make a Wish 326
Make Haste to Live 377
Make Way for Ducklings and Other Classic Stories by Robert McCloskey 654
Make Way for the Ping Pong Club 736
Make-Up for Theatre with Ellen Dennis 318
Make-Up Workshop, The 318
Makin' Up 64
Making a Video Program 318
Making Ballet: The Actress 573
Making Grimm Movies 318
Making Love 462
Making Masterpieces 552
Making Music 868
Making Music in the Classroom, Program 3, Ages 3-7 669
Making Music in the Classroom, Program 4, Ages 7-11 670
Making Music with Children, Program 1, Ages 3-7 670
Making Music with Children, Program 2, Ages 7-11 670
Making Music: The Emerson String Quartet 592
Making of "Bar Girls", The 462
Making of a Legend: Gone with the Wind 336
Making of a Modern Mystic, The 791
Making of a Musical, The 326
Making of Miss Saigon, The 313
Making of Short Cuts (Luck, Trust & Ketchup), The 336
Making of The Hitchhiker's Guide to the Galaxy, The 193
Making of the Holland Tunnel Drive-In Billboard, The 475
Making Opera: The Creation of Verdi's "La Forza del Destino" 583
Making Stained Glass Windows 563
Making Theatre: Rashomon 313
Makioka Sisters 141
Makropulos Case 583
Malagan Art of New Ireland 561
Malamondo 507
Malaya 377
Malcolm X 447, 453
Malcolm X: El Hajj Malik El Shabazz 453
Malcolm X: His Own Story As It Really Happened 453
Malcolm X: Make It Plain 453
Malcolm X: Nationalist or Humanist? 453
Male and Female 355
Male Animal, The 275
Male Escorts of San Francisco 462
!Male! (In Excelsis Corruptus Deluxe) 617
Malice 237
Malicious 33
Malt Whisky Trail 170
Malta Story 176
Maltese Falcon, The 349
Mama, There's a Man in Your Bed 17
Mama Florence and Papa Cock 475
Mamas & The Papas: Straight Shooter 621
Mambo 377
Mambo Kings, The 59
Mambo Mouth 313
Mame 326
Mamma Roma 37
Mammals 97
Mammals of Africa 868
Mammoth Cave National Park, Kentucky 817
Man, a Woman and a Killer, A 433
Man Alone, A 294
Man and a Woman, A 5
Man and a Woman—20 Years Later, A 5
Man and Boy 664
Man and Child 507
Man and the Monster, The 525
Man and the Snake/The Return, The 301
Man and the State: Burke and Paine on Revolution 800
Man and the State: Hamilton and Jefferson on Democracy 761
Man and the State: Machiavelli on Political Power 800
Man and the State: Marx and Rockefeller on Capitalism 800
Man and the State: Roosevelt and Hoover on the Economy 761
Man and the State: The Trial of Socrates 785
Man Beast 525
Man Behind the Muppets: The World of Jim Henson, The 475
Man Bites Dog 29
Man Called Peter, A 377
Man Escaped, A 15
Man Facing Southeast 51
Man for All Seasons, A 176, 237
Man for Man, Volume I 462
Man for Man, Volume II 462
Man for Man, Volume III 462
Man for Man, Volume IV 462
Man from Beyond 401
Man from Colorado 294
Man from Hong Kong, The 129
Man from Laramie 294
Man from Mallorca, The 76
Man from Monterey, The 377
Man from Nowhere 22
Man from Painted Post, The 401
Man from Snowy River 206
Man from the Pru, The 193
Man from U.N.C.L.E., The 419
Man from Utah 294
Man I Love, The 378
Man in a Raincoat, The 17
Man in the Attic 378
Man in the Gray Flannel Suit 378
Man in the Iron Mask (1997), The 237
Man in the Iron Mask (1998), The 237
Man in the Moon 237
Man in the Saddle 294
Man in the Shadow 294
Man in the Silk Hat 22, 154
Man in the White Suit 184
Man in the Wilderness 237
Man Is Not a Bird 104
Man Like Eva, A 66
Man Named Lombardi, A 827
Man of a Thousand Faces 378
Man of Aran 204, 475
Man of Iron 97
Man of La Mancha 326
Man of Marble 97
Man of No Importance, A 162
Man of Peace: A Video Portrait of Pope John Paul II 791
Man of the House 693
Man of the Trees 817
Man of the West 294
Man of the Year 462
Man on the Eiffel Tower 378
Man on the Moon 840
Man on the Roof 76
Man on the Track 93
Man Ray Video 486
Man Ray: The Bazaar Years 559
Man's Best Friend 685
Man's Favorite Sport 342
Man That Corrupted Hadleyburg 309
Man They Could Not Hang, The 525
Man Trouble 275
Man Wanted 130
Man Who Came to Dinner, The 275
Man Who Captured Eichmann, The 237
Man Who Cheated Himself, The 378
Man Who Could Not See Far Enough, The 486
Man Who Could Work Miracles 176
Man Who Cried, The 193
Man Who Fell to Earth, The 166
Man Who Had Everything 401
Man Who Haunted Himself, The 176
Man Who Knew Too Much (1934) 352
Man Who Knew Too Much (1955) 352
Man Who Laughs, The 401
Man Who Lived Again, The 525
Man Who Loved Cat Dancing 294
Man Who Loved Women, The 15, 354
Man Who Loves Sharks, The 817
Man Who Mistook His Wife for a Hat, The 583
Man Who Never Was, The 176
Man Who Saw Tomorrow, The 761
Man Who Shot Liberty Valance 340
Man Who Would Be King, The 349
Man with a Cross (L'Uomo della Croce) 38
Man with the Golden Arm 378
Man with the Golden Gun 169
Man with the Movie Camera 86
Man with the Red Carnation 105
Man with the Twisted Lip, The 186
Man Without a Face, The 237
Man Without a Star 294
Man You Loved to Hate, The 348
Man-Made Monster 525
Man/Woman Wanted 93
Manabu Mabe Paints a Picture 552
Mance Lipscomb in Concert 613
Manchurian Candidate, The 378
Mandala: World of Mystic Circle 149
Mandarin Mystery 378
Mandela 152
Mandela and DeKlerk 800
Mandela's Fight for Freedom 152
Mandela: The Man and His Country 152
Mandragora 100, 462
Maneaters of Tsavo 337
Maneaters: A Trilogy 486
Manhandled 401
Manhattan 288
Manhattan Madness 378
Manhattan Melodrama 378
Manhattan Merry-Go-Round 326
Manhattan Murder Mystery 288
Manhattan Naturally and Stories from Brooklyn 433
Manhunt in the African Jungle 538
Manhunt of Mystery Island 538
Maniac and Protect Your Daughter 508
Maniac Cop 525
Maniac/Special Edition 525
Mannequin 378
Manny & Lo 433
Manon 25
Manon Lescaut 70, 583
Manon of the Spring 5
Mansfield Park 193
Manslaughter 355
Manster, The 525
Mantra Meditation for Beginners with Wolfgang Arndt 851
Mantrap 401
Manu Dibango: King Makossa 603
Manuel Puig 59
Manufacturing Consent: Noam Chomsky and the Media 475, 800
Manxman 352
Manxmouse 713
Many Adventures of Winnie the Pooh, The 693
Many Faces of Homelessness 805
Many Through One 111
Many Wonder 433
Mao's Little Red Video 117
Map of the Human Heart 208
Mapp & Lucia 194
Mapp & Lucia II 194
Maps 1 & 2 736
Maps 3 & 4 736
Maps: Symbols and Terms 637
Maps: Where Am I? (3rd Edition) 637
Marat/Sade (The Persecution and Assassination of Jean-Paul Marat as Performed by the Inmates of the Asylum of Charenton Under the Direction of Marquis de Sade) 313
Marathon Family, The 103
Marathon of Steam 843
Marathon: A History of the Great Race 827
Marc and Ann 480
Marc Blitzstein: The Cradle Will Rock 313
Marc Brown's Play Rhymes 637
Marcel Duchamp: A Game of Chess 552
Marcel Odenbach: In the Peripheral Vision of the Witness 486
March for Disarmament 805
March in April 462
March of the Wooden Soldiers 275
March of Time: America at War 769
March of Time: American Lifestyles 761
March of Time: Great Depression 810
March of Time: Post War Problems and Solutions 769
March of Time: The Cold War 810
March of Time: Trouble Abroad 769
March of Time: War Breaks Out 769
March on Paris 1914 of General Von Kluck & His Memory of Jessie Holladay, The 486

March to the Fuhrer....769
Marching for Freedom: The 1993 March on Washington Video....462
Marching On....448
Marching On to Glory....105
Mard....147
Margaret Price: Ruckert Lieder....598
Margaret's Museum....211
Margot Fonteyn Story....573
Maria Callas Concert: 1962 Hamburg....598
Maria Callas: Life and Art....598
Maria Candelaria....51
Maria Chapdelaine....22
Maria's Day....102
Maria! Indian Pottery of San Ildefonso....561, 787
Marianela....45
Marianne and Juliane....64
Maricela....661
Marie Antoinette....378
Marie Galante....378
Marija Gimbutas: The World of the Goddess....782
Marilyn Files, The....337
Marilyn Monroe....337
Marilyn Monroe—Beyond the Legend....337
Marine Raiders....769
Marines Are Coming, The....769
Marines at Tarawa/To the Shores of Iwo Jima, The....769
Marines Have Landed....769
Marines in Combat....761
Mario Lanza: The American Caruso....598
Mario Vargas Llosa....59
Marion Woodman: King Lear As an Image in Eldering....851
Marisol....552
Marius....27
Marjorie Morningstar....378
Mark Morris Dance Group—The Hard Nut....573
Mark Munski: Funcrime and Art....561
Mark Naftalin's Blue Monday....613
Mark of Cain—Westinghouse Studio One....419
Mark of the Devil, Part II....525
Mark of the Devil (Collectors Edition)....525
Mark of the Hawk....448
Mark of the Rani, The....200
Mark of the Vampire....525
Mark of Zorro....378, 401
Mark Twain's America....309
Mark Twain's Connecticut Yankee....309
Mark Twain: A Musical Biography....309
Marked Money....401
Marked Woman....378
Market Day in a Changing Economy (Latin American Lifestyles)....59
Marlowe....378
Marmot Mountain/Yellowstone Below Zero (BBC Wildlife Special)....818
Marnie....352
Maroc 7....378
Marooned....498
Marquis....8
Marquise, The....313
Marriage....122
Marriage Circle....345
Marriage of Figaro, The....583
Marriage of Maria Braun, The....66
Marriage on the Rocks....275
Married?....401
Married to the Mob....255
Married Too Young....515
Married with a Star....776
Married Woman, A....9
Marrying Kind, The....350
Mars Attacks....255
Mars Lives....840
Mars Needs Women....498
Martha & Ethel....475
Martha Graham Dance Company....573
Martha Graham: An American Original in Performance....573
Martha Graham: The Dancer Revealed....573
Martial Arts Mayhem, Vol. 1....130
Martian Chronicles, Volumes 1-3....498
Martian Chronicles Series....498
Martin....525
Martin Chuzzlewit....194
Martin Fierro....51
Martin Luther, His Life and Time....791
Martin Luther....791
Martin Luther King, Jr.: I Have a Dream....453
Martin Luther King, Jr.: Legacy of a Dream....453
Martin Luther King Commemorative Collection....453
Martin Mull Live from North Ridgeville, Ohio....535
Martin Simpson in Concert....603
Martin Taylor in Concert....613
Martin the Cobbler....713
Martina's Playhouse and The Scary Movie....487
Marty....378
Marty—Goodyear TV Playhouse....313
Marty Robbins/Ernest Tubb....605
Marvelous Land of Oz, The....637
Marvelous Life of Joan of Arc, The....22
Marvelous Melies....22
Marvelous Toys of Dr. Athelstan Spilhaus, The....561
Marvelous Visit, The....24
Marvin's Room....237
Marvin the Martian & K9: 50 Years on Earth....685
Marvin the Martian: Space Tunes....685
Mary Cassatt: Impressionist from Philadelphia....552
Mary Ellen Bute....487
Mary Magdalene: An Intimate Portrait....791
Mary McLeod Bethune: The Spirit of a Champion....453
Mary My Dearest....51
Mary of Nazareth....791
Mary Pickford—The Early Years....401
Mary Poppins....693
Mary Reilly....166
Mary Shelley's Frankenstein....525
Mary Wigman 1886-1973....573
Maryinsky Ballet, The....573
Marzipan Pig, The....647
Masaccio: A View of Mankind....552
Masada....109
Masala....211
Masculine Feminine....9
Masculine Mystique....211
Mashall (The Torch)....147
Mask, The....275, 525
Mask....237
Mask of Dimitrios....378
Mask of Fu Manchu, The....525
Mask of the Dancing Princess, The....637
Masked Marvel....538
Maskmaker....563
Maskmaking Introduction....564
Maskmaking with Clay....564
Maskmaking with Paper....564
Maskmaking Workshop....564
Masks from Many Cultures....561
Masque of Mandragora, The....200
Masque of the Red Death, The....514
Masquerade....95
Masseur Ichi, The Fugitive (Zato Ichi Kyojotabi)....138
Masseur Ichi Enters Again....138
Massillon....462
Master and Margarita....93
Master Blackmailer, The....186
Master Blaster, Vol. I....603
Master Blaster, Vol. II....603
Master Harold and the Boys....313
Master Hunter of the Night....818
Master Key....538
Master Misery....433
Master of Ballantrae, The....378
Master of the House....79
Master of the World....498, 637
Master Poets Collection I, The....305
Master Poets Collection II, The....305
Master with Cracked Fingers....134
Master Wong v. Master Wong....122
Mastermind....275
Mastermind: Great Motor Race....194
Mastermind: Infernal Device....194
Masterpieces of British Art....552
Masterpieces of Italian Art: Greek to Gothic....552
Masterpieces of the Met....553
Masters of Animation Vol. 1: USA & Canada....713
Masters of Animation Vol. 2: Great Britain, Italy & France....713
Masters of Animation Vol. 3: USSR, Poland, Yugoslavia & Hungary....713
Masters of Animation Vol. 4: Japan & Computer Animation....713
Masters of Comic Blues: Mance Lipscomb and Lightnin' Hopkins....613
Masters of Comic Blues: Rev. Gary Davis and Sonny Terry....613
Masters of Comic Book Art....541
Masters of Illusion....553
Masters of Photography: Andre Kertesz....559
Masters of Photography: Diane Arbus....559
Masters of Photography: Edward Steichen....559
Masters of Russian Animation....82, 713
Masters of Tap....573
Masters of the Blues....613
Masters of the Congo Jungle....152, 475
Masters of the French Stage: Jean-Louis Barrault and Madeline Renaud....28, 313
Masters of War....769, 810
Masterworks of Japanese Painting: The Etsuko and Joe Price Collection....868
Masterworks of Painting....553
Mastery of the Flamenco Guitar....624
Mata Hari....378
Matador....46
Match Factory Girl, The....79
Matched Set of Razors, A....138
Matchmaker, The....275
Material Witness....617
Math Primer....838
Math Rock Countdown....670
Math...Who Needs It?....838
Mathematics Series....838
Mathnet: The Case of The Unnatural....637
Matilda....664
Matinee....237
Matinee Idols: The Gentlemen....401
Matinee Idols: The Ladies....401
Mating Game, The....276
Matisse Voyages....553
Matrimaniac....401
Matt the Gooseboy....713
Matta Wagnest and Nicolas Eder: Analog 10001....487
Matter of Dignity, A....105
Matter of Heart: The Extraordinary Journey of C.G. Jung into the Soul of Man....786
Matters of the Heart....607
Matthias Muller—Selected Films....433
Maurice....259
Maurice Chevalier....28
Maurice Sendak Library, The....654
Maurice Sendak's Little Bear— Parties & Picnics....637
Maurizio Nannucci: Not All at Once....487
Mauvaise Graine....346
Maverick Queen, The....294
Maverick: Duel at Sundown....419
Maverick: Shady Deal at Sunny Acres....419
Mawdryn Undead....200
Max and Helen: A True Story....776
Max Ernst....553
Max Ernst/Marcel Duchamp....553
Max Fleischer Presents Koko the Clown....685
Max Fleischer's Superman....685
Max Frisch....30, 313
Max Linder....22, 154
Max Mon Amour....141
Max Roach: Jazz in America....613
Max's Chocolate Chicken....654
Max's Christmas....637
Maxwell Anderson: Lost in the Stars....305
Maxwell Street Blues....475
Maxx, The....698
May Day—May Day....800
May Fools....13
Maya....665
Maya Collection, The....59
Maya Deren Experimental Films....487
Maya Lin: A Strong Clear Vision....475, 778
Maya: Temples, Tombs and Time, The....782
Mayan Mystery, The....59
Maybe...Maybe Not....64
Mayerling....22, 176, 573
Maysles Brothers: Direct Cinema, The....337, 475
Maytime....326
Maytime in Mayfair....184
Mazarin Stone, The....186
Mazowsze: The Polish Song and Dance Ensemble....573
Mazurka (Mazurka Pa Sengekanten)....76
McCabe and Mrs. Miller....254
McCarthy: Death of a Witchhunter....481
McConnell Story, The....378
McDonald's Gospelfest....607
McHale's Navy....276
McHale's Navy Joins the Air Force....276
McLintock! (Restored Producer's Cut)....294
MD Geist....736
MD Geist II: Death Force....736
Me and Him....64
Me and the Colonel....276
Me Yu an' Mi Taxi....55
Mean Streets....253
Mean to Be Free: John Brown's Black Nation Campaign....453
Meantime....165
Medal Maker, The....561
Medea....37, 313, 573
Media and the Image of War, The....805
Media Man....481
Mediamystics....487
Meditation Tool Kit, The....851
Mediterranean Cookery....858
Mediterraneo....33
Medium, The....583
Medium Cool....378
Medusa Against the Son of Hercules, The....42
Medusa Challenger....433
Medusa: Dare to Be Truthful....419
Meet Danny Wilson....326
Meet John Doe....351
Meet Marcel Marceau....313
Meet Me at Brooklyn and Soto....115
Meet Me in Las Vegas....326
Meet Me in St. Louis....326
Meet the Applegates....276
Meet the Caldecott Illustrator: Jerry Pinkney....561
Meet the Feebles....208, 713
Meet the Met....583
Meet Your Animal Friends....654
Meeting at Midnight (aka Black Magic)....378
Meeting Magdalene....462
Meeting Venus....103
Meetings with Remarkable Men....162
Mefistofele....583
Mega Man: 20,000 Leaks Under the Sea....698
Mega Man: Robosaur Park....698
Mega Man: The Beginning....699
Megami Paradise 1....736
Megami Paradise 2....736
Mein Kampf....770
Mein Krieg (My Private War)....64, 770
Meishu—Travels in Chinese Art....553
Mel Brooks Collector's Set....276
Mel Lewis and His Big Band....613
Melies III: The Search for Munchhausen....22
Melody Cruise....326
Melody for Three....378
Melody Haunts My Reverie (You Only Love Once)....103
Melody Time....693
Melvin Van Peebles' Classified X....445, 453
Member of the Wedding, The....237
Member of the Wedding....378
Memento Mori....487
Memoirs of a Barbed Wire Surgeon: An Interview with Elmer Shabart M.D., FACS....770
Memoirs of an Invisible Man....276
Memorias de un Mexicano....59
Memories of a Marriage....76
Memories of a River, The....102
Memories of Hollywood, Vol. 1....337

Memories of Monet....553
Memories of Prison....54
Memories of Underdevelopment....53
Memories: Music from The Yank Years, Volume 1, The....613
Memories: Music from The Yank Years, Volume 2, The....613
Memory, Suggestion and Abuse....852
Memory Skills....851
Memphis....237
Memphis Belle....237, 344
Men....64, 378
Men Against Tanks/Engineers to the Front....770
Men Against Tanks/Engineers to the Front....70
Men and Women: Talking Together....786
Men Are from Mars, Women Are from Venus—But We Have to Live on Earth....852
Men Don't Leave....237
Men in Black....276
Men in Love....463
Men in Shorts, Volume 2....463
Men in Shorts....463
Men of Boys Town....378
Men of Horses....59
Men of Ireland....204
Men of the Fighting Lady....379
Men Who Danced: The Story of Ted Shawn's Male Dancers 1933-1940, The....573
Men Who Killed Kennedy, The....798
Men Who Tread on Tiger's Tail....142
Men with Guns....440
Menace II Society....445
Menage....11
Mendelssohn Symphonies No. 3 & 4....592
Menilmontant....22, 487
Menschen am Sontag (People on Sunday)....401
Menschenfrauen....74
Mercenary Game....810
Merchant of Four Seasons....66
Merchant of Venice, The....313
Merchant of Venice....868
Merchants and Masterpieces....561
Mercury Spacecraft Missions and Legacy of Gemini....840
Mercy Plane....379
Mere Hazoor....148
Mere Jeevan Saathi....148
Merle Travis: Rare Performances 1946-1981....605
Merlin, Arthur & The Holy Grail....761
Merlin....237
Merlin and the Dragons....637
Merlin of the Crystal Cave....194
Mermaid, The....122
Mermaid's Scar....736
Merrill's Marauders....341
Merrily We Go Along....761
Merry Christmas....93
Merry Christmas Mr. Lawrence....141
Merry Christmas Space Case....637
Merry Widow, The....326, 345, 348
Merry Widow (German Version), The....348
Merry Widow (The Australian Opera), The....583
Merry Widow Ballet....573
Merry Wives of Windsor (Esquire 4+4), The....313
Merry-Go-Round....348
Merton of the Movies....276
Merton: A Film Biography....791
Mesa of Lost Women....498
Mesa Verde....787
Message, The....116
Message to Love: The Isle of Wight Festival: The Movie....621
Messe Solennelle....598
Messenger, The....533
Messenger....445
Messiah (Cardiff), The....598
Messiah (Marriner), The....598
Messidor....30
Messin' with the Blues....613
Met Centennial Gala....598
Metal Fighters Miku Vol. 1....736
Metal Fighters Miku Vol. 2....736
Metal Fighters Miku Vol. 3....737
Metal Fighters Miku Vol. 4....737
Metal Fighters Miku Vol. 5....737
Metal Fighters Miku Vol. 6....737
Metal Roots....621
Metamorphosis....836
Metaphoria....852
Metaphysics and Modern Science....852
Meteor Man....445
Meteorite Impact....836
Meteorites....840
Metropolis....72
Metropolitan....433
Metropolitan Cats....561
Metropolitan Museum Boxed Set....553
Metropolitan Museum of Art: Fun with Architecture, The....868
Metropolitan Opera Gala 1991: 25th Anniversary at Lincoln Center, The....583
Mexican Arts....553
Mexican Bus Ride....47
Mexican Colonial Tour, A....59
Mexican Festivals....59
Mexican Market....59
Mexican People and Culture....59
Mexican Pre-Hispanic Cultures....59
Mexican Pyramid Tour, A....59
Mexican River Cruise....59
Mexican Way of Life, The....59
Mexican Youth Today....59
Mexico, Journey to the Sun....59
Mexico....59
Mexico Before Cortez....59
Mexico City— Metropolis in the Mountains....59
Mexico Is...The Sights and Sounds of Modern Mexico....59
Mexico on Video....59
Meyer aus Berlin....345
MGM Cartoon Christmas....685
MGM Cartoon Classics: Happy Harmonies....686
MGM Cartoon Magic....686
MGM's Big Parade of Comedy....276
MGM: When the Lion Roars....337
Mi Vida Loca: My Crazy Life....59, 433
Miami Rhapsody....276
Michael....237
Michael Caine: Breaking the Mold....337
Michael Collins....202
Michael Collins: The Shadow of Bealnablath....204
Michael Crawford: A Touch of Music in the Night....617
Michael Feinstein & Friends....613
Michael Idvorsky Pupin....795
Michael Nyman Songbook: Ute Lemper....73
Michael Todd: Jazz....553
Michel Tournier....29
Michelangelo....553
Michelangelo: Self Portrait....553
Michigan Avenue: From Museums to the Magnificent Mile....566
Mickey & The Beanstalk....693
Mickey & The Beanstalk/Reluctant Dragon....693
Mickey....401
Mickey Loves Minnie....693
Mickey Mouse: The Black & White Years....693
Mickey One....258
Mickey's Christmas Carol....693
Mickey's Fun Songs: Beach Party....693
Mickey's Fun Songs: Campout....693
Mickey's Fun Songs: Circus....693
Micki and Maude....354
Microcosmos....818
Microwave Massacre....508
Mid-Eastern Dance: An Introduction....574
Midaq Alley (El Callegon de los Milagros)....51
Midas Touch, The....102
Middle Man, The....130
Middlemarch....194
Midnight....379
Midnight Angels....130
Midnight Angels II....130
Midnight at Madame Tussaud's....526
Midnight Clear, A....237
Midnight Cowboy (25th Anniversary)....379
Midnight Dancers....145, 463
Midnight Express....237
Midnight Faces....401
Midnight Girl....401
Midnight in the Garden of Good and Evil....256
Midnight Lace....379
Midnight Message....401
Midnight Ramble....448
Midnight Run....237
Midnight Shadow....448
Midori Live at Carnegie Hall....592
Midsummer Night's Dream, A....869
Midsummer Night's Dream (BBC), A....313
Midsummer Night's Dream (Peter Hall), A....313
Midsummer Night's Dream (Reinhardt), A....313
Midsummer Night's Dream....583
Midway....237
Midwife's Tale, The....463
Midwinter's Tale, A....162
Mig Alley....770
Mighty Aphrodite....288
Mighty Civic, The....208
Mighty Ducks: The Movie: The First Face-Off....693
Mighty Joe Young....379
Mighty Kong, The....713
Mighty Pawns, The....661
Mighty Quinn, The....238
Mighty River, The....637
Mighty Space Miners....737
Mighty Steam Series....843
Migrants, The....238
Miguel Pinero at Magic Gallery....59
Mikado (D'Oyly Carte), The....583
Mikado (Miller), The....583
Mike Douglas Show— John Lennon & Yoko Ono, The....419, 621
Mike Mainieri: The Jazz Life....613
Mike Mulligan and His Steam Shovel....654
Mike Seeger: Fret and Fiddle....605
Mike Tyson: The Inside Story....827
Mikey and Nicky....276
Mikhail Baryshnikov's Stories from My Childhood....647
Milagro Beanfield War....59
Mildred Pierce....379
Mile Zero: The Sage Hour....805
Miles from Home....238
Military and the Environment, The....805
Military Channel....761
Military on Campus, The....800
Milk Cow. Eat Cheese....637
Milky Way, The....276
Milky Way....47
Mill on the Floss, The....176, 194
Mille Bolle Blu....33
Millennium: Five-Tape Boxed Set....782
Miller's Crossing....441
Millhouse: A White Comedy....481
Millie....379
Million-Dollar Mermaid....326
Millionairess, The....184
Millions Like Us....176
Mills Brothers Story, The....617
Milos Forman: The Fourth New York Film Festival....100
Milton Berle....337
Milton Berle Invites You to a Night at La Cage....535
Milton Berle's Buick Hour Collector's Series....419
Milton Hershey: The Chocolate King....795
Mime over Matter....318
Mimi....176
Mimic....238
Min & Bill....379
Mina Tannenbaum....8
Minbo—Or the Gentle Art of Japanese Extortion....140
Mind as a Myth....852
Mind in Tibetan Buddhism....149
Mind of a Serial Killer....836
Mind Power....852
Mind Robber, The....200
Mind's Eye, The....713
Mind to Kill, A....162
Mind-Body Problem....852
Minds, Brains and Science....852
Mindwalk....238
Mine and Yours....654
Mine Eyes Have Seen the Glory: The Women's Army Corps....770
Mine Own Executioner....176
Miners '88....98
Ming Garden....135
Mingus....613
Mini Dragons Series, The....145
Ministry of Fear....72
Ministry: In Case You Didn't Feel Like Showing Up....621
Miniver Story, The....379
Minnelli on Minnelli....337
Minnie the Moocher....613
Minstrel Man....326
Minute to Pray, A Second to Die, A....294
Miracle....39
Miracle at Moreaux....661
Miracle Down Under....206
Miracle Fighters, The....130
Miracle in Harlem....448
Miracle in Milan....38
Miracle in Rome....45
Miracle in the Rain— Westinghouse Studio One....313
Miracle in the Wilderness....294
Miracle of Intervale Avenue....115, 475
Miracle of Life....836
Miracle of Marcelino....45
Miracle of Morgan's Creek....346
Miracle of Our Lady of Fatima....379
Miracle of Saint Therese....22
Miracle of Survival/The Birth of Israel....109
Miracle of Taxila....836
Miracle of the Bells, The....379
Miracle of the Heart: A Boy's Town Story....238
Miracle on 34th Street....379
Miracle Planet, The....836
Miracle Rider....538
Miracle Woman, The....351
Miracle Worker, The....258
Miracles and Other Wonders....861
Mirele Efros....112
Miro: Theatre of Dreams....553
Mirror, The....84
Mirror Crack'd....162
Mirror Has Two Faces, The....238
Mirtala....553
Misadventures of Buster Keaton, The....409
Misery....238
Misfits....349
Mishima: A Life in Four Chapters....238
Miss Evers' Boys....238, 453
Miss Ewa's Follies....93
Miss Firecracker....276
Miss Grant Takes Richmond....276
Miss Julie....76
Miss Mary....51
Miss Melody Jones....508
Miss Right....276
Miss Rose White....238
Miss Sadie Thompson....379
Miss Sarajevo....475
Missa Luba....603
Missile to the Moon....498
Missiles of October....238
Missing....106
Mission, The....238
Mission in Morocco....379
Mission Kill....130
Mission Stardust....498
Mission to Kill....130
Mission: Impossible....238
Missionary, The....199
Mississippi Blues....11, 613
Mississippi Burning....238
Mississippi Masala....433
Mississippi Mermaid....15
Missouri Breaks, The....258
Mistaken Identity....448
Mistaken Orders....401
Mister Johnson....238
Mister Roberts....340
Mister Rogers' Neighborhood: Circus Fun....654

Mister Rogers' Neighborhood: Going to School 654
Mister Rogers' Neighborhood: Kindness 654
Mister Rogers' Neighborhood: Learning Is Everywhere! 654
Mister Rogers' Neighborhood: Love 654
Mister Rogers' Neighborhood: Making Music 654
Mister Rogers' Neighborhood: Our Earth: Clean and Green 654
Mister Rogers' Neighborhood: The Doctor, Your Friend 654
Mister Rogers: Dinosaurs & Monsters 654
Mister Rogers: Music and Feelings 654
Mister Rogers: Musical Stories 654
Mister Rogers: What About Love 654
Mister Rogers: When Parents Are Away 654
Mistress 138, 276
Mistrial 238
Misty 665
Misty Wharf (Quai des Brumes) 24
Mitch Corber Works 487
Mitch Gaylord: The Men's Total Body Workout 463
Mitridate, Re di Ponto (Ponnelle) 583
Mitridate, Re di Ponto (Vick) 583
Mixed-Up Adventure, A 51
Mixer, The 194
Miyuki-Chan in Wonderland 737
Mizike Mama 603
Mlada 583
Mo' Better Blues 447
Mo' Money 276
Moana, A Romance of the Golden Age 475
Mob, The 761
Mob Law 761
Mobile: By Alexander Calder 553
Mobiles: Making Art That Moves 564
Moby Dick 238, 349
Mod Fuck Explosion 434
Mod Squad, The 419
Mod Squad Lost Pilot, The 419
Model T Man from Michigan, America: Henry Ford and His Horseless Carriage, The 796
Moderato Cantabile 22
Modern America Patriot: Mark Hatfield 800
Modern Art: A Visit to the Foundation of Marguerite & Aimé Maeght 869
Modern Jazz Quartet 613
Modern Language Instruction 155
Modern Marvels Series 566
Modern Masters: Louise Bourgeois, The 553
Modern Puerto Rico 59
Modern Romance 276
Modern Times 408
Modern Warplanes 843
Modern World: Ten Great Writers, The 305
Moderns, The 257
Modigliani (Montparnasse 19) 22
Mogambo 340
Mohra 148
Moira's Birthday (plus Blackberry Subway Jam) 654
Moire 553
Moiseyev Ballet 574
Moiseyev Dance Company: Gala Evening 574
Moldiver #1: Metamorforce 737
Moldiver #2: Overzone 737
Moldiver #3: Longing 737
Moldiver #4: Destruction 737
Moldiver #5: Intruder 737
Moldiver #6: Verity 737
Mole People, The 498
Mole's Christmas 637
Moll Flanders 194, 306
Molly Maguires 379
Molly's Pilgrim 115, 637
Mollycoddle, The 401
Mom, Dad...I'm Gay 463
Moment to Moment 379
Moments: The Making of Claire of the Moon 337
Mommie Dearest 238
Mommy's Office 655
Mon Ane: Au Clair de la Lune 29, 673
Mon Oncle 28
Mon Oncle Antoine 213
Mon Oncle d'Amerique 12
Mona Lisa 162
Mona's Pets 637
Monaco Forever 463
Mondo Africana (Original: Africana) 508
Mondo Balardo 508
Mondo Cane 508
Mondo Cane 2 508
Mondo Lugosi—A Vampire's Scrapbook 526
Mondo New York 434
Mondo Rocco (aka It's a Gay World) 463
Mondo Sleazo (The World of Sleaze) 508
Mondo Topless 513
Mondrian 553
Mondrian: From Naturalism to Abstraction 553
Monet Legacy of Light 553
Money and Marriage 852
Money Rock 637
Money Train 238
Mongkok Story 130
Mongolian Tale, A 117
Mongols, The 42
Monika 78
Monk in Oslo 613
Monkey Business 276
Monkey Hustle 533
Monkey Moves 670
Monkey People (aka Monkey Folks, Le Peuple Singe) 5
Monkey Trouble 238
Monolith Monsters, The 498
Monroe Wheeler and MOMA 553
Monsieur Beaucaire 276
Monsieur Hire 8
Monsieur Rene Magritte 553
Monsieur Verdoux 408
Monsieur Vincent 22
Monsignor Quixote 162
Monsoon 379
Monster, The 33
Monster and the Girl, The 526
Monster Forces of Nature 818
Monster from a Prehistoric Planet 498
Monster from Green Hell 526
Monster in a Box 313
Monster in My Pocket with The Schnozzes 655
Monster Maker 526
Monster of Peladon, The 200
Monster of Piedras Blancas 526
Monster of the Island (Island Monster) 526
Monster on the Campus 526
Monster That Challenged the World, The 498
Monster Walks, The 526
Monsters Crash the Pajama Party 526
Monsters of the Greek Myths 637
Monsters on the March 526
Mont St. Michel 29
Montana 294
Montauk Project: Experiments in Time, The 852
Monte Carlo 194
Monte Walsh 294
Montenegro 104
Monterey Pop 475, 621
Month by the Lake, A 238
Montparnasse Revisited 29
Montserrat Caballe and Jose Carreras in Moscow 598
Montserrat Caballe: The Woman, the Diva 598
Monty Python and the Holy Grail 168
Monty Python and the Quest for the Holy Grail 869
Monty Python Live at the Hollywood Bowl 199
Monty Python's Meaning of Life 199
Monty Roberts: A Real Horse Whisperer 796
Monument Valley: Navajo Homeland 787
Moon and Sixpence, The 379
Moon Drum (Twelve dream song evocations by John Whitney) 603
Moon Heart: The Magical World of Tuvinian Shamans 88
Moon Is Blue, The 276
Moon of Israel 74
Moon over Miami 326
Moon over Parador 276
Moon's Prayer: Wisdom of the Ages, The 787
Moon Shot 840
Moon Stallion 665
Moon Warriors, The 130
Moonchild 45
Moonfleet 72
Moonlight and Valentino 238
Moonlight Sonata 176, 326
Moonraker 169, 176
Moonrise 379
Moonshine Mountain 508
Moonstone, The 194
Moonstruck 276
Moore and Thill in Louise 22
Mop Top 655
Moran of the Lady Letty 401
More About the Children of Noisy Village 76, 665
More Jeeves & Wooster 194
More Melies 22
More Moron Movies 508
More Perfect Union: The Story of the U.S. Constitution, A 761
More Preschool Power 655
More Songs of Placido Domingo in Mexico, Vol. 2 598
More Stories for the Very Young 655
More Than 30 Years in the TARDIS 200
More Than Bows and Arrows 787
More Than Broken Glass: Memories of Kristallnacht 770
More the Merrier, The 343
More! Police Squad! 419
Morecambe & Wise Musical Extravaganzas 194
Morecambe & Wise: Lots and Lots 194
Morecambe & Wise: Lots More 194
Morgan's Cake 434
Morgenrot 70
Morituri 379
Mormon Maid, A 401
Morning After 238
Morocco 347
Morocco: The Music of Moroccan Jews 115
Moron Movies 508
Morons from Outer Space 498
Morris the Moose 655
Mortal Storm, The 379
Mortal Thoughts 257
Moscow and Leningrad, The Crown Jewels of Russia 88
Moscow Circus: Animals Under the Big Top, The 88
Moscow Circus: Dancing Bears and More, The 88
Moscow Does Not Believe in Tears 82
Moscow on the Hudson 238
Moscow Parade 82
Moscow Sax Quintet: The Jazznost Tour 613
Moscow Treasures and Traditions 553
Moscow Virtuosi, The 598
Moses (Kingsley) 356
Moses (Lancaster) 356
Moshe Dayan 109
Mosque 111
Mosquito Coast, The 208
Most Dangerous Game, The 379
Most Eligible Bachelor 93
Moth, The 162
Mother, Jugs and Speed 276
Mother 86, 276
Mother and the Law 413
Mother Goose 647
Mother India (Bharat Mata) 148
Mother Ireland 204
Mother Joan of the Angels 93
Mother Krausen's Journey into Happiness 70
Mother Kusters Goes to Heaven 66
Mother Night 238
Mother of Kings 95
Mother's Heart 93
Mother Teresa 796
Mother Teresa: A Life of Devotion 796
Mother Teresa: In the Name of God's Poor 791, 796
Mothers of Today 112
Mothra 498
Motion Picture History of the Korean War 761
Motor Psycho 513
Motorist, The 434
Mots Difficiles 155
Mouchette 15
Moulin Rouge 154, 349
Mount Rainier 831
Mount Vernon— Home of George Washington 761
Mountain, The 379
Mountain Habitat Set 818
Mountain in the Mind 553
Mountain Wolf Woman: 1884-1960 787
Mountains of the Moon 239
Mountbatten: The Last Viceroy 170, 762
Mouse & The Motorcycle, The 713
Mouse on the Mayflower 713
Mouse Soup 637
Mouse That Roared, The 184
Mousehunt 665
Moussorgsky/Holst/Debussy: Ormandy and the Philadelphia Orchestra 592
Mouth to Mouth (Boca a Boca) 45
Move Like the Animals 655
Moveable Feast: Profiles of Contemporary American Authors 306
Movement for the Actor 318
Movie in Your Face! 508
Movie Magic: Disasters at Sea 337
Movie Star's Daughter, A 638
Movie Struck (Pick a Star) 326
Movies About Movies 337
Movies of the '20s 337
Movies of the '30s 337
Movies of the '40s 337
Moving 276
Moving a River 487
Moving Beyond Auto America 843
Moving Machines 655
Moving Memories 455, 475
Moving Mountains: The Montreal Yiddish Theatre in the U.S.S.R. 112
Moving the Mountain 135, 475
Mowgli's Brothers 686
Mozart, Smetana, Dvorak, Janacek 592
Mozart (Biography) 592
Mozart (Performances) 592
Mozart Brothers 76
Mozart Ensemble Salzburg 592
Mozart in Love 434
Mozart—Klassix 13 592
Mozart Mass in C Minor, K.427 598
Mozart on Tour: Volume 1 (London—The First Journey) 592
Mozart on Tour: Volume 2 592
Mozart on Tour: Volume 3 592
Mozart on Tour: Volume 4 592
Mozart on Tour: Volume 5 592
Mozart Piano Concerto No. 23 K. 488 (Horowitz) 592
Mozart Piano Concertos No. 9, K. 271 and Jeunehomme 592
Mozart Quintets by the Emerson String Quintet 592
Mozart Story 592
Mozart/Barenboim Volume 1 592
Mozart/Barenboim Volume 3 592
Mozart: "Haffner" (Solti) 592
Mozart: A Childhood Chronicle 64
Mozart: Concert in Tarascon Castle 592
Mozart: Coronation Mass (Karajan) 598
Mozart: Die Zauberflote 583
Mozart: Divertimento. K. 334/Strauss: Also Sprach Zarathustra 592
Mozart: Great Mass in C Minor 598
Mozart: His Life and Loves 592
Mozart: Requiem (Bernstein) 598
Mozart: Requiem (Davis) 598
Mozart: Requiem (Karajan) 598
Mozart: Requiem K and Mass in C Minor 598
Mozart: Serenade K. 361 Gran Partita 592
Mozart: Serenade Posthorn/Serenade Notturno 592
Mozart: Symphonies 39-41 593
Mozart: The Dissonant Quartet 593
Mozart: The Requiem from Sarajevo 598
Mr. and Mrs. Bridge 259
Mr. and Mrs. Loving 239
Mr. Arkadin (Confidential Report) 344
Mr. Baby Proofer 858
Mr. Bean 194

Mr. Bill Collection, The....535
Mr. Blandings Builds His Dream House....276
Mr. Boogie Woogie....613
Mr. Bubble Gum....655
Mr. Corbett's Ghost....239
Mr. Deeds Goes to Town....351
Mr. Five Percent: Calouste Gulbenkian....553
Mr. Flathead....508
Mr. Frost....239
Mr. Hobbs Takes a Vacation....276
Mr. Holland's Opus....239
Mr. Hoover & I....481
Mr. Hulot's Holiday....28
Mr. Imperium....379
Mr. Jones....239
Mr. Klein....353
Mr. Lincoln's Springfield....780
Mr. Magoo in Sherwood Forest....699
Mr. Magoo in the King's Service....699
Mr. Magoo Literary Classics: Cyrano de Bergerac/ A Midsummer Night's Dream....699
Mr. Magoo Literary Classics: Don Quixote....699
Mr. Magoo Literary Classics: King Arthur/ The Count of Monte Christo....699
Mr. Magoo Literary Classics: Little Snow White....699
Mr. Magoo Literary Classics: Sherlock Holmes/ Dr. Frankenstein....699
Mr. Magoo Literary Classics: The Three Musketeers....699
Mr. Magoo...Man of Mystery....699
Mr. Magoo's Christmas Carol....699
Mr. Magoo Show Vol. 1....699
Mr. Magoo Show Vol. 2....699
Mr. Magoo Show Vol. 3....699
Mr. Magoo Show Vol. 4....699
Mr. Magoo Show Vol. 5....699
Mr. Magoo Show Vol. 7....699
Mr. Magoo Show Vol. 8....699
Mr. Magoo Show Vol. 9....699
Mr. Magoo Show Vol. 10....699
Mr. Magoo: Uncle Sam Magoo....699
Mr. Mean....533
Mr. Men: In the Great Alphabet Hunt....670
Mr. Monster....655
Mr. Moto's Last Warning....379
Mr. Music....326
Mr. Nice Guy....134
Mr. North....239
Mr. Peabody and the Mermaid....276
Mr. Popper's Penguins....655
Mr. Possessed....122
Mr. Robinson Crusoe....379
Mr. Rossi's Dreams....713
Mr. Saturday Night....276
Mr. Sears' Catalogue: The Sears Roebuck Company and Its Impact on Life in America 1890-1930....762
Mr. Skeffington....379
Mr. Skitch....379
Mr. Smith Goes to Washington....351
Mr. Sunshine....122
Mr. Toad's Wild Ride....693
Mr. Vampire....122
Mr. Vampire II....122
Mr. Vampire III....122
Mr. Vampire IV....122
Mr. Wonderful....239
Mr. Wong, Detective....379
Mr. Wong in Chinatown....379
Mr. Wrong....277
Mrs. 'Arris Goes to Paris....162
Mrs. Dalloway....162
Mrs. Doubtfire....277
Mrs. Fanny Lou Hamer....453
Mrs. Frisby and the Rats of Nimh....655
Mrs. Miniver....344
Mrs. Parker and the Vicious Circle....257
Mrs. Parkington....379
Mrs. Piggle-Wiggle....638
Mrs. Santa Claus....665
Mrs. Soffel....239
Mrs. Wiggs of the Cabbage Patch....277
Mrs. Winterbourne....277
Ms. 45....434
Ms. Don Juan (Don Juan 73)....22
Mt. Rushmore— Four Faces on a Mountain....831
Mt. Rushmore and The Black Hills of South Dakota....831
Much Ado About Nothing....314, 869
Mud Family, The....638
Muddy Waters....614
Mudhoney....513
Mughal-E-Azam....148
Muhammad Ali vs. Zora Folley....419, 827
Muhammad Ali: The Whole Story....827
Mulholland Falls....239
Multicamera Direction Planning....318
Multicultural Peoples of North America Series....762
Multimedia in Education....318
Multiple Futures....498
Multiplicity....277
Mumia: A Case for Reasonable Doubt?....475
Mummies and the Wonders of Ancient Egypt....784
Mummy, The....526
Mummy's Curse, The....526
Mummy's Ghost, The....526
Mummy's Hand, The....526
Mummy's Shroud, The....526
Mummy's Tomb, The....526
Muppet Babies: Be My Valentine....699
Muppet Treasure Island....655
Muppet Treasure Island Sing-Alongs....655
Muppets CD-ROM: Muppets Inside, The....869
Muppets on Wheels....655
Murder....352
Murder Ahoy....176
Murder by Death....277
Murder by Television....508
Murder Czech Style....100
Murder in Harlem....448
Murder in the First....239
Murder in the Mirror....526
Murder Is Announced, A....194
Murder Mansion....526
Murder My Sweet....380
Murder of a Moderate Man....194
Murder of the Century....762
Murder on Lennox Ave....448
Murder on The Orient Express....162
Murder One....239
Murder with Music....448
Murderers Among Us: The Simon Wiesenthal Story....776
Murderers Are Among Us....70
Murders in the Rue Morgue (1932), The....526
Murders in the Rue Morgue (1971), The....526
Murders in the Rue Morgue (1986), The....526
Murders in the Zoo....380
Muriel....12
Muriel's Wedding....206
Murky Water Caper, The....638
Murmel, Murmel, Murmel (plus The Boy in the Drawer)....655
Murmur of the Heart....13
Murphy's Romance....277
Murray Avenue: A Community in Transition....115
Murray Louis in Concert Volume 1: Dance Solos....574
Murray Perahia in Performance: The Aldeburgh Recital....593
Murray Perahia's Mozart....593
Musee d'Orsay....553
Museum City Videos: Paris, City of Light....29
Museum of Modern Art of Latin America, The....553
Museum Without Walls Series....553
Musgrave Ritual, The....186
Mush, You Malamutes!....831
Mushfest: Nickelodeon....699
Music, Memories & Milestones....810
Music and Comedy Masters (Volume 1)....614
Music and Comedy Masters (Volume 2)....614
Music and Comedy Masters (Volume 3)....614
Music and Comedy Masters (Volume 4)....614
Music and Comedy Masters (Volume 5)....614
Music and Comedy Masters (Volume 6)....614
Music and Magic....638
Music Box....106
Music Classics, Vol. 2....614
Music for Film....318
Music for Montserrat....621
Music for the Movies: Bernard Herrmann....337, 617
Music for the Movies: Georges Delerue....337
Music for the Movies: The Hollywood Sound....337, 617
Music for the Movies: Toru Takemitsu....337
Music from Wagner's Ring....583
Music in My Heart....380
Music Lovers, The....167
Music Man, The....326
Music Moves the Spirit....617
Music of Chance, The....434
Music of the Night....598
Music of the Spirits....603
Music of the West: A Tribute to the Singing Cowboys....337
Music Teacher, The....5, 29
Music with Roots in the Aether....617
Music Word Fire and I Would Do It Again: The Lessons....487
Musica Para Hot Sundays....603
Musica Proibita....41
Musical Masterpiece at Masada....598
Musical Tales....638
Musicians in Exile....603
Musketeers of Pig Alley and Selected Biograph Shorts, The....413
Muslims in America....782
Mussogorsky: Pictures at an Exhibition/Solti....593
Mussolini: Italy's Nightmare....796
Mussolini: Rise and Fall of a Dictator....770
Mussorgsky: Pictures at an Exhibition....592
Mustang: The Hidden Kingdom....149
Mutaburuka: Live! at Reggae Summerfest '93....603
Muthers, The....508
Mutiny of the Elsinore....176
Mutiny on the Bounty (Brando)....380
Mutiny on the Bounty (Laughton)....380
Mutiny on the Western Front (WWI)....810
Muto Bontie....122
Mutual of Omaha's Spirit of Adventure Series....818
Mutzmag....638
My Antonia....239
My Beautiful Laundrette....166
My Beloved....122
My Best Friend's Wedding....277
My Better Half....122
My Breakfast with Blassie....277
My Brother Sam Is Dead....638
My Cousin Vinny....277
My Darling Clementine....340
My Dear Marie....737
My Dear Secretary....277
My Dinner with Andre....13
My Dog Shep....665
My Dream Is Yours....326
My Fair Lady....350
My Family....434
My Family and Other Animals....638
My Family Treasure....665
My Father Is a Hero....130
My Father Is Coming....64, 463
My Father's Glory....5
My Father the Hero....277
My Favorite Blonde....277
My Favorite Brunette....277
My Favorite Opera: Alfredo Kraus, Werther....584
My Favorite Season (Ma Saison Preferee)....5
My Favorite Year....277
My First Activity Series....670
My First Name Is Maceo....621
My First Series....673
My Flying Wife....122
My Foolish Heart....380
My Forbidden Past....380
My Four Years in Germany....401
My Friend Flicka....665
My Friend Irma....277
My Friend Walter....661
My Geisha....277
My Girl Tisa....380
My Heart Is That Eternal Rose....122
My Heart's Delight....598
My Lady of Whims....401
My Left Foot....202
My Life and Times with Antonin Artaud....5
My Life as a Dog....76
My Life's in Turnaround....277
My Life to Live....9
My Little Chickadee....277
My Little Girl....239
My Lucky Star....380
My Lucky Stars....134
My Man....11
My Man Godfrey....277
My Man Norton....419
My Michael....108
My Mother's Castle....5
My My Mai Vol. 1....737
My My Mai Vol. 2....737
My Name Is Abbie: A Portrait of Abbie Hoffman....800
My Name Is Bill W....419
My Name Is Ivan....84
My Neighbor Totoro....737
My Neighborhood....434
My New Gun....434
My New York....670
My Night at Maud's....14
My Own Private Idaho....440, 463
My Prague Spring....101
My Principal Lives Next Door....638
My Russian Friends....88
My Sesame Street Home Video....655
My Sex Life (Or How to Get Into an Argument)....8
My Sheroes, My Sheroes....434
My Side of the Mountain....638
My Sister Eileen....326
My Song Goes 'Round the World....70
My Stepmother Is an Alien....277
My Surrender....508
My Sweet Little Village....100
My Sweet Satan....508
My Twentieth Century....102
My Wicked Wicked Ways....239
My Youth in Arcadia....737
Myrna Loy: So Nice to Come Home To....337
Mysteries and Splendors of Ancient Egypt, The....784
Mysteries from the Bible....791
Mysteries of Deep Space....836
Mysteries of Peru....59
Mysteries of the Ancient World Gift Set....791
Mysteries of the Bible....791
Mysteries of the Bible: The Story Continues....791
Mysteries of the Dead Sea Scrolls....791
Mysteries of the Gods....862
Mysterious Dr. Satan, The....538
Mysterious Egypt....111
Mysterious Island, The....176, 638
Mysterious Lady....380
Mysterious Man of the Shroud, The....791
Mysterious Mr. Wong....380
Mysterious Origins of Man: Jurassic Art, The....784
Mysterious Stranger....309
Mysterious Tadpole and Other Stories, The....638
Mystery, Mr. Ra....614
Mystery of Crop Circles: Messages from Another World?, The....862
Mystery of Edwin Drood, The....194, 301, 380
Mystery of Harris Burdick....638
Mystery of Incarnation....852
Mystery of Kaspar Hauser, The....67
Mystery of Marie Roget....380
Mystery of Mr. Wong, The....380
Mystery of Oberwald, The....36
Mystery of Rampo, The....138
Mystery of the Animal Pathfinders....818
Mystery of the Double Cross....401
Mystery of the Leaping Fish and Chess Fever, The....86
Mystery of the Riverboat....420
Mystery of the Sacred Shroud....791
Mystery of the Wax Museum....526
Mystery Science Theater 3000....420
Mystery Science Theater 3000: The Movie....277
Mystery Train....442

Mystery Trooper (Trail of the Royal Mounted) 538
Mystery Writer Series— Earl Emerson, The 306
Mystery Writer Series— Tony Hillerman, The 306
Mystery Writer Series—Aaron Elkins, The 306
Mystery Writer Series—J.A. Jance, The 306
Mystery Writer Series—Jane Yolen, The 306
Mystic Lands 831
Mystic Origins of the Martial Arts 827
Mystic Pizza 277
Mystical Malaysia, Land of Harmony 145
Myth of Fingerprints, The 239
Mythology 869
Mythos with Joseph Campbell 786
Myths, Mysteries and Mysticism 861
Myths and Legends Vols. 1 & 2 869
Myths of the Pharaohs 784

N

N. Humbert/W. Penzel: Step Across the Border 487
N Is a Number: A Portrait of Paul Erdos 796
Nadia 108
Nadia Movie Compilation 737
Nadja 434
Nagasaki Journey 144, 770
Nais 27
Naked 165
Naked City, The 380
Naked Civil Servant 162, 463
Naked Edge, The 380
Naked Gun 277
Naked Jungle, The 380
Naked Killer, The 122
Naked Kiss, The 341
Naked Lies 239
Naked Lunch 212
Naked Maja, The 380
Naked Runner, The 380
Naked Spur, The 294
Naked Truth, The 184, 791
Naked Venus 508
Naked Witch, The 526
Naked Youth 508
Nam Jun Paik 487
Namu, The Killer Whale 665
Nana 22
Nanami, First Love 138
Nancy Drew Reporter 380
Nancy Goes to Rio 326
Nancy Wilson at Carnegie Hall 614
Nanna & Lil' Puss Puss Show, The 713
Nanny, The 176
Nanook of the North 475
Napa Valley Farmhouse Restoration 566
Napoleon (Gance) 22
Napoleon (Guitry) 22
Napoleon 665
Narayama Bushi-ko 138
Narcotic Story, The 508
Narda or the Summer 52
Nargess 106
Narrow Road/Alias Jimmy Valentine, The 401
Nashville 254
Nasty Girl, The 64
Nasty Habits 277
Nat King Cole Story, The 614
Nat King Cole: The Unforgettable 614
Nathalie Sarraute 306
Nation Aflame and Probation 508
Nation Asunder, A 780
National Baptist Convention Mass Choir: Let's Go to Church 607
National Center for Supercomputing Applications 845
National Film Board of Canada's Animation Festival, The 714
National Gallery of Art 554
National Geographic— World's Last Great Places— Arctic Kingdom: Life at the Edge 820
National Geographic Geo Kids: Bear Cubs, Baby Ducks, and Kooky Kookaburras 638, 818
National Geographic Geo Kids: Camouflage, Cuttlefish, and Chameleons Changing Color 638
National Geographic Geo Kids: Chomping on Bugs, Swimming Sea Slugs, and Stuff that Makes Animals Special 638
National Geographic Geo Kids: Cool Cats, Raindrops, and Things That Live in Holes 638, 818
National Geographic Geo Kids: Flying Trying and Honking Around 638, 818
National Geographic Geo Kids: Tadpoles, Dragonflies and the Caterpillar's Big Change 638
National Geographic Really Wild Animals 638
National Geographic Video 818, 836
National Geographic Video: 30 Years of National Geographic Specials 831
National Geographic Video: Africa's Stolen River 818
National Geographic Video: African Animal Oasis 818
National Geographic Video: America's Endangered Species: Don't Say Good-bye 818
National Geographic Video: Antarctic Wildlife Adventure 818
National Geographic Video: Australia's Aborigines 209
National Geographic Video: Ballad of the Irish Horse 204
National Geographic Video: Beauty and the Beasts: A Leopard's Story 818
National Geographic Video: Braving Alaska 818
National Geographic Video: Cats: Caressing the Tiger 818
National Geographic Video: Creatures of the Mangrove 818
National Geographic Video: Crocodiles: Here Be Dragons 818
National Geographic Video: Cyclone! 818
National Geographic Video: Dinosaur Hunters 818
National Geographic Video: Egypt: Quest for Eternity 784
National Geographic Video: Egypt: Secrets of the Pharoahs 818
National Geographic Video: Elephant 818
National Geographic Video: Eternal Enemies: Lions and Hyenas 818
National Geographic Video: For All Mankind 840
National Geographic Video: Giant Bears of Kodiak Island 818
National Geographic Video: Great Explorers Gift Box 819
National Geographic Video: Great Whales 819
National Geographic Video: Hawaii: Strangers in Paradise 819
National Geographic Video: Himalayan River Run 819
National Geographic Video: Hunt for the Great White Shark 819
National Geographic Video: In the Shadow of Vesuvius 784
National Geographic Video: Inside the White House 762
National Geographic Video: Invisible World 819
National Geographic Video: Jewels of the Caribbean 819
National Geographic Video: Killer Whales: Wolves of the Sea 819
National Geographic Video: King Cobra 819
National Geographic Video: Last Feast of the Crocodiles 819
National Geographic Video: Last Voyage of the Lusitania 770
National Geographic Video: Lions of Darkness 819
National Geographic Video: Lions of the African Night 819
National Geographic Video: Living Treasures of Japan 144
National Geographic Video: Love Those Trains 843
National Geographic Video: Mysteries of Mankind 819
National Geographic Video: Nature's Fury! 819
National Geographic Video: Ocean Drifters 819
National Geographic Video: Puma: Lion of the Andes 819
National Geographic Video: Rain Forest 819
National Geographic Video: Reptiles and Amphibians 819
National Geographic Video: Return to Everest 827
National Geographic Video: Rhino War 819
National Geographic Video: Rocky Mountain Beaver Pond 819
National Geographic Video: Russia's Last Czar 88
National Geographic Video: Search for Battleship Bismarck 762
National Geographic Video: Search for the Great Apes 819
National Geographic Video: Season of the Cheetah 819
National Geographic Video: Secret Leopard 819
National Geographic Video: Secrets of the Wild Panda 819
National Geographic Video: Shark Encounters 819
National Geographic Video: Soviet Circus 88
National Geographic Video: Strange Creatures of the Night 819
National Geographic Video: Superliners: Twilight of an Era 843
National Geographic Video: Survivors of the Skeleton Coast 819
National Geographic Video: The Great Indian Railway 843
National Geographic Video: The Grizzlies 819
National Geographic Video: The Lost Fleet of Guadalcanal 770
National Geographic Video: The Photographers 819
National Geographic Video: The Predators Collection 819
National Geographic Video: Those Wonderful Dogs 819
National Geographic Video: Tigers of the Snow 819
National Geographic Video: Volcano 819
National Geographic Video: Webs of Intrigue 819
National Geographic Video: White Wolf 819
National Geographic Video: Wild Survivors 820
National Geographic Video: Wildlife Warriors 820
National Geographic Video: Wings over the Serengeti 820
National Geographic Video: Zebra: Patterns in the Grass 820
National Lampoon's Class of '86 277
National Lampoon's Class Reunion 277
National Lampoon's European Vacation 277
National Monuments of Southern Arizona 831
National Museum of American Art 869
National Parks: America's Natural Heritage 820
National Pastime: A History of Major League Baseball 827
National Velvet 665
National Zoo, The 820
Nationtime, Gary 453
Native American Herbology for Beginners 788
Native American Indian Artist Series 554, 788
Native American Indians 788
Native American Prophecy & Ceremony 788
Native American Ritual: Healing Way Song 788
Native American Sweat Lodge Ceremony 788
Native Americans, The 788
Native Americans—An Overview 788
Native Grace: Prints of the New World 1590-1876 554
Native Land 475
Native Land: Nomads of the Dawn 788
Native Son (1986) 445
Nativity Story, The 617
Nativity—Westinghouse Studio One, The 420
Natural Born Killers 441
Natural Healing with Crystals 852
Natural History of Parking Lots, The 434
Natural History of Yellowstone 869
Natural Light: Windance 487
Natural Selections 617
Natural States 820
Nature Archive Series 820
Nature Connection, The 820
Nature Is Leaving Us 487
Nature of Music 618
Nature of Sex 820
Nature of the Artist: Homer Winslow, The 554
Nature Perfected: The Story of the Garden 820
Nature's Fury: A Decade of Disasters 820
Nature's Great African Moments 820
Nature's Symphony 820
Nature Stories 638
Naughty Marietta (1935) 326
Naughty Marietta (1955) 326
Naughty Nostalgia #1 508
Naughty Nostalgia #2 508
Naughty! Naughty! 122
Navajo Code Talkers 788
Naval Treaty, The 186
Navigator, The 409
Navigator: A Time Travel Adventure 208
Navy Blue and Gold 380
Nazarin 47
Nazi Medicine 776
Nazi War Crime Trials 770
Nazi War Crimes 770
Nazi War Crimes: Babi-Yar 770
Nazis...Lest We Forget! 770
Nazis Strike 770
NBC White Papers 762
Nea 5
Near Death Experience 852
Necessary Parties 661
Necklace, The 22
Necromania 515
Need, The 106
Need for Christian Peacemaking 805
Needful Things 526
Negro Soldier 351, 453
Nehru 149
Neighbors to Nicaragua 59
Nell 239
Nello Santi, Guglielmo Tell 593
Nelly and Monsieur Arnaud 5
Nelson Mandela 70th Birthday Tribute 152
Nelson: Palette Knife Portraits 554
Nenette and Boni 8
Neo-Tokyo 737
Neoclassicism, Romanticism, Realism 554
Neon Bible, The 162
Neon Genesis Evangelion, Genesis 0:1 737
Neon Genesis Evangelion, Genesis 0:2 737
Neon Genesis Evangelion, Genesis 0:3 737
Neon Genesis Evangelion, Genesis 0:4 737
Neon Genesis Evangelion, Genesis 0:5: Magma Diver 737
Neon Genesis Evangelion, Genesis 0:6: Day Tokyo 3 Stood Still 737
Neon Genesis Evangelion, Genesis 0:7: Invasion 738
Neon Genesis Evangelion, Genesis 0:8: Lies & Silence 738
Neon Genesis Evangelion, Genesis 0:9: The Fourth Child 738
Neon Genesis Evangelion, Genesis 0:10: Weaving a Story 738
Neon Genesis Evangelion, Genesis 0:11 738
Neon Genesis Evangelion, Genesis 0:12: Rei III 738
Neon Genesis Evangelion, Genesis 0:13: A World Ending 738
Neon Genesis Evangelion: Deluxe Collection LD 738
Nepal: Land of the Gods 149
Neptune's Daughter 327
Nervous Wreck 401
Nestor, The Long-Eared Christmas Donkey 714
Net, The 239
Network 239
Neurosia 64, 463
Neutron and the Black Mask (Neutron el Enmascarado Negro) 508
Neutron vs. the Amazing Dr. Caronte 508
Neutron vs. the Death Robots (Los Automatas de la Muerte) 508
Neutron vs. the Maniac 508
Nevada 294
Nevada Smith 294
Never a Dull Moment 277
Never Cry Wolf 665
Never Give a Sucker an Even Break 277
Never Let Me Go 380
Never Love a Stranger 380
Never on Sunday 380
Never Say Die 278
Never Say Goodbye 278
Never Say Never Again 169
Never So Few 770
Never Talk to Strangers 239
Never Too Late 278
Never Too Late to Mend 176
Never Wave at a WAC 278
Neverending Story, The 665
Neverending Story II: The Next Chapter, The 665
Neverending Story III: Return to Fantasia, The 665
Neville Marriner Conducts the Academy of St. Martin in the Fields 593
New Adventures of Black Beauty, The 665
New Adventures of Peter Rabbit, The 655
New Adventures of Pippi Longstocking 665
New Adventures of Tarzan—Collector's Edition, The 538
New Age, The 239
New and Improved Kids 858
New Babylon (Novyi Vavilon) 82
New Beginnings (1895-1904) 762
New British Animation: The Best from Channel 4 714
New Centurions, The 239
New Cinema, The 337
New Coat for Anna 638
New Connection: The Video, A 782
New Digital Imaging, The 318
New Directors: New Short Films 487
New Dominion Tank Police Vol. 1: Episodes 1 and 2 738
New Dominion Tank Police Vol. 2: 738
New Dominion Tank Police Vol. 3: Episodes 5 and 6 738
New England Clambake, A 831
New England Dances: Squares, Quadrilles, Step Dances 574
New England Fiddles: Playing Down the Devil 605
New Europeans, The 762
New Faces 327
New Family Bible, The 869
New Films from Iran 106
New Ford, The 843
New Foundations: Visions for Democratic Socialism 800

New Immigrants ... 800
New Jack City ... 445
New Jersey Drive ... 239
New Jersey Mass Choir ... 607
New Land, The ... 79
New Leaf, A ... 278
New Legend of Shaolin, The ... 122
New Mexico ... 294
New Moon ... 327
New Music, The ... 614
New Orleans: Til the Butcher Cuts Him Down ... 614
New Pastures ... 100
New School Teacher ... 401
New Solar System, The ... 840
New Sousa Band ... 593
New Statesman, The ... 194
New Tenant ... 122
New US-USSR Relationship ... 800
New Voices New Visions ... 869
New Wave Hits of the '80s, Volume 1 ... 621
New Wave Hits of the '80s, Volume 2: Just Can't Get Enough ... 621
New Ways of Seeing: Picasso, Braque and the Cubist Revolution ... 554
New World of Music, A ... 593
New World Visions: American Art and the Metropolitan Museum ... 554
New Year's Day... Time to Move On ... 239
New Year's Eve Concert 1985 ... 593
New Year's Eve Concert 1987 ... 593
New Year's Eve Concert 1991—Beethoven in Berlin ... 593
New Year's Eve Concert 1992 ... 593
New Year's Eve Concert 1993 ... 593
New Year's Eve Concert 1994— Wagner Gala ... 593
New York, New York ... 253, 327
New York Nights ... 239
New York Restoration Choir: Thank You Jesus ... 608
New York Stories ... 260, 288
New York Stories ... 260, 288
New York the Way It Was ... 762
New York Videos ... 487
New Zealand Coast to Coast ... 209
New Zimbabwe, The ... 152
Newborn Care ... 858
Newland ... 108
Newport Jazz Festival ... 614
News from Home ... 30
News News ... 434
Newsreel Library of America in Sports, A ... 810
Newsreel Library of America in the News, A ... 810
Newsreel Library of American Nostalgia, A ... 810
Newsreel Library of World War II, The ... 770
Newton Boys, The ... 434
Next Epoch, The ... 852
Next of Kin ... 212
Next Step ... 475
Next Stop, Greenwich Village ... 278
Next Summer ... 5
Next Time I Marry ... 278
Next Voice You Hear ... 380
Next Week Promos ... 540
NFBC—Cartoon Festival: The Sweater ... 714
NFBC: An Animated Christmas ... 714
NFBC: Animation for Kids Vol. 1 ... 714
NFBC: Cartoon Festival: Cactus Swing ... 714
NFBC: Cartoon Festival: The Cat Came Back ... 714
NFBC: Christmas Cracker ... 714
NFBC: Every Child ... 714
NFBC: Leonard Maltin's Animation Favorites from the National Film Board of Canada ... 714
NFBC: The Box ... 714
NFBC: The Sand Castle ... 714
NFBC: The Sweater ... 714
NFBC: The Tender Tale of Cinderella Penguin ... 714
Niagara ... 380
Niagara Niagara ... 239
Niall Tobin Live ... 535
Nicaragua: For the First Time ... 59
Nice Girl? ... 278
Nice Girls... Films by and About Women ... 434
Nice Neighbor, The ... 102
Nicholas and Alexandra ... 88, 162
Nick Jr.: Allegra's Window: Storytime Sing-Along ... 655
Nick Jr.: Eureeka's Castle: Wide Awake at Eureeka's Castle ... 638
Nick Jr.: Gullah Gullah Island: Play Along with Binyah and Friends ... 638
Nick of Time ... 239
Nick Zedd ... 434
Nick Zedd: Steal This Video ... 434
Nickelodeon Presents How to Throw a Double Dare Party ... 670
Nicklehopper, The ... 401
Nico Icon ... 621
Nicolai Gedda in Concert, Volume 2 ... 584
Nicolai Ghiaurov ... 598
Nigerian Art—Kindred Spirits ... 152, 554
Niggernight ... 434
Night After Night ... 380
Night and Day (Nuit et Jour) ... 30
Night and Day ... 327
Night and Fog ... 12, 776
Night and the City ... 239
Night and the Moment, The ... 162
Night at the Opera, A ... 278
Night Before Christmas (Edwards), The ... 655
Night Before Christmas (Styner), The ... 655
Night Bird ... 401
Night Falls on Manhattan ... 240
Night Flier, The ... 240
Night Full of Rain, A ... 33
Night Has Eyes (Terror House), The ... 176
Night in Havana, A ... 614
Night Is My Future ... 78
Night Monster ... 526
'Night Mother ... 314
Night Must Fall ... 380
Night Nurse ... 380
Night of Love, A ... 104
Night of Terror ... 526
Night of the Blood Beast ... 499
Night of the Day of the... ... 508
Night of the Following Day, The ... 380
Night of the Generals ... 176
Night of the Hunter, The ... 380
Night of the Iguana ... 349
Night of the Living Dead 25th Anniversary Documentary ... 526
Night of the Living Dead ... 526
Night of the Shooting Stars ... 35
Night on Earth ... 442
Night on the Galactic Railroad ... 738
Night Owl ... 240
Night Porter ... 33, 463
Night Shade ... 240
Night Stalker, The ... 420
Night Strangler, The ... 420
Night They Killed Rasputin, The ... 527
Night They Raided Minsky's, The ... 381
Night Tide ... 434
Night to Remember, A ... 176, 869
Night Train ... 93
Night Train to Munich ... 176
Night Visitor, The ... 240, 527
Night Walker, The ... 527
Night Warriors— Darkstalkers' Revenge, Vol. 1 ... 738
Night Warriors— Darkstalkers' Revenge, Vol. 2 ... 738
Night Zoo ... 213
Nightbreaker ... 240
Nightfall ... 499
Nightfighters: The Tuskegee Airmen ... 453, 770
Nighthawks ... 463
Nightjohn ... 445
Nightmare ... 176, 776
Nightmare Before Christmas, The ... 686
Nightmare Before Christmas Collector's Edition, The ... 686
Nightmare Campus, Vol. 1: The Resurrection of the Demon Lord Esedess ... 738
Nightmare Campus, Vol. 2: The Resurrection of the Demon Lord Esedess ... 738
Nightmare Campus, Vol. 3: The Great Ambitions of the Gods ... 738
Nightmare Campus: Collector's Boxed Set ... 738
Nightmare Castle ... 527
Nightmare on Elm Street, A ... 527
Nightmare Years ... 240
Nights and Days ... 93
Nights of Cabiria ... 37
Nightsongs ... 434
Nijinsky ... 574
Nikola Tesla: The Genius Who Lit the World ... 796
Nil by Mouth ... 162
Nile: River of Gods ... 784
Nina Ananiashvili and International Stars, Vol. 1 ... 574
Nina Ananiashvili and International Stars, Vol. 2 ... 574
Nina Ananiashvili and International Stars, Vol. 3 ... 574
Nina Ananiashvili and International Stars, Vol. 4 ... 574
Nina's Strange Adventure ... 638
Nina Takes a Lover ... 240
Nine Artists of Puerto Rico ... 554
Nine Lives of Fritz the Cat, The ... 686
Nine Months ... 278
Ninja Assassins ... 130
Ninja Empire ... 130
Ninja Heat ... 130
Ninja Hunter ... 130
Ninja Man Rides Again, The ... 603
Ninja Scroll ... 738
Nino Martini in One Night with You ... 184
Ninotchka ... 345
Ninth of September, The Cursed Day ... 122
Nitrate Kisses ... 434, 492
Nixon, The CD-ROM ... 869
Nixon ... 240
Nixon Interviews with David Frost, The ... 796
No Alternative ... 621
No Drums, No Bugles ... 240
No End (Without End) ... 96
No Fear, No Die ... 8
No Greater Gift ... 638
No Greater Love ... 82
No Highway in the Sky ... 381
No Longer Colonies: Hong Kong 1997, Macau 1999 ... 145
No Looking Back ... 434
No Man Is an Island ... 381
No Man of Her Own ... 278
No Man's Law ... 401
No More Love, No More Death ... 130
No Name on the Bullet ... 294
No No Nanette ... 327
No Regrets for Our Youth ... 142
No Rewind ... 834
No Shmaltz! My Yiddisheh Cooking Video ... 115
No Telling ... 434
No Time for Sergeants ... 420
No Time for Tears—Vietnam: The Women Who Served ... 778
No Way Out ... 381
Noa at Seventeen ... 108
Noah's Ark ... 638
Nobel Jubilee Concert: Kiri Te Kanawa ... 584
Noble House ... 194
Nobody's Fool ... 240
Nobody's Girls ... 240
Nobody's Daughter ... 102
Noel ... 655
Noel a Paris ... 29
Noir et Blanc ... 8
Nomadic Indians of the West ... 788
Nomads of the North ... 402
Nomads of the Rainforest ... 59
Nomads of the Wind ... 783
Nomination, The ... 800
Non Stop—New York ... 176
Non Ti Scordar di Me ... 41, 584
Non-Proliferation Treaty: Dead at 25?, The ... 805
None But the Brave ... 770
Nonsense and Lullabyes: Nursery Rhymes ... 655
Nonsense and Lullabyes: Poems for Children ... 655
Noon Wine ... 259
Noose Hangs High, The ... 278
Norma (Australian Opera) ... 584
Norma (Canadian Opera) ... 584
Norma Rae ... 240
Norma Talmadge Films ... 402
Normal Life ... 240
Normal Love ... 463, 487
Norman and the Killer ... 301
Norman Blake & The Rising Fawn Ensemble ... 605
Norman Conquest ... 176
Norman Conquests: Table Manners, The ... 314
Norman... Is That You? ... 278
Norman Mailer ... 306
Norman Rockwell and the Saturday Evening Post ... 561
Norman Rockwell Christmas, A ... 638
Norman Rockwell's World... An American Dream ... 554
Norman Rockwell: An American Portrait ... 561
Norman the Doorman and Other Stories ... 639
Normandy Invasion ... 770
Normandy: The Great Crusade ... 770
North by Northwest ... 352
North of Capricorn ... 820
North Shore Fish ... 240
North Star, The ... 381
North to Alaska ... 381
Northanger Abbey ... 194
Northern Pursuit ... 381
Northwest Outpost ... 381
Northwest Passage ... 294
Norwood Builder, The ... 186
Nosferatu ... 73
Nosferatu the Vampyre ... 67
Nosferatu: The First Vampire ... 73
Nostalghia ... 84
Nostalgia World War II Video Library #1 ... 770
Nostalgia World War II Video Library #2 ... 770
Nostalgia World War II Video Library #3 ... 771
Nostalgia World War II Video Library #4 ... 771
Nostalgia World War II Video Library #5 ... 771
Nostalgia World War II Video Library #6 ... 771
Nostalgia World War II Video Library #7 ... 771
Nostalgia World War II Video Library #8 ... 771
Nostalgia World War II Video Library #9 ... 771
Nostalgia World War IIVideo Library #10 ... 771
Nostalgia World War IIVideo Library #11 ... 771
Nostalgia World War IIVideo Library #12 ... 771
Nostradamus ... 240
Nostradamus: A Voice from the Past ... 796
Nostromo ... 194
Not Angels, But Angels ... 100, 463
Not As a Stranger ... 381
Not Like Sheep to the Slaughter: The Story of the Bialystok Ghetto ... 776
Not Now, Bernard ... 639
"Not Now!" Said the Cow ... 655
Not Quite Love ... 435
Not So Great Moments in Sports, Take Three ... 827
Not Top Gun ... 435
Not Wanted ... 381
Not Without My Daughter ... 240
Notebook on Cities and Clothes ... 67
Notes Alive! Nutcracker: The Untold Story ... 574, 639
Notes for Jerome ... 442
Notes from a Lady at a Dinner Party ... 301
Nothing But a Man ... 445
Nothing But Trouble ... 278
Nothing Personal ... 162
Nothing Sacred ... 278
Nothing to Lose ... 98
Nothing to Lose: Fat Lip Reader's Theatre ... 852
Notorious ... 352
Notorious Jumping Frog of Calaveras County, The ... 309, 639
Notorious Lady, The ... 402
Notorious Nobodies (Illustres Inconnus) ... 6
Notre Dame, Cathedral of Amiens ... 566
Nouns ... 859
Nouvelle Experience: Cirque du Soleil ... 567
Nova— Countdown to the Invisible Universe ... 840
Nova—Adventures in Science: Hurricane! ... 837
Nova—Adventures in Science: In Search of Human Origins ... 837
Nova—Adventures in Science: Making of a Doctor ... 837
Nova—Adventures in Science: Mystery of the Senses ... 837
Nova—Adventures in Science: Tornado! ... 837
Nova—Aircraft Carrier! ... 843
Nova—All American Bear ... 820
Nova—Ancient Treasures from the Deep ... 784
Nova—Animal Hospital ... 820

Nova—Avalanche! ... 820
Nova—Bomb Squad ... 204
Nova—Buried in Ash ... 820
Nova—Can Elephants Be Saved? ... 820
Nova—Cities of Coral ... 821
Nova—Coma ... 837
Nova—Cracking the Ice Age ... 821
Nova—Cut to the Heart ... 837
Nova—Danger in the Jet Stream ... 837
Nova—Daredevils of the Sky ... 843
Nova—Death of a Star ... 840
Nova—Disguises of War ... 762
Nova—Diving for Pearls ... 821
Nova—Earthquake ... 837
Nova—Echoes of War ... 771
Nova—Eclipse of the Century ... 840
Nova—Everest: The Death Zone ... 821
Nova—Faster Than Sound ... 837
Nova—In the Land of the Polar Bears ... 821
Nova—Killer Quake! ... 821
Nova—Kingdom of the Seahorse ... 821
Nova—Little Creatures Who Run the World ... 821
Nova—Mysterious Crash of Flight 201 ... 843
Nova—Mysterious Mummies of China ... 784
Nova—One Small Step ... 840
Nova—Rescue Mission in Space ... 840
Nova—Russian Right Stuff: The Mission ... 88, 840
Nova—Search for the Lost Cave People ... 762, 785
Nova—Signs of the Apes, Songs of the Whales ... 821
Nova—Super Bridge ... 566
Nova—Supersonic Spies ... 843
Nova—T. rex Exposed ... 821
Nova—The Bermuda Triangle ... 821
Nova—The Blimp Is Back ... 843
Nova—The Case of the Flying Dinosaur! ... 837
Nova—The KGB, The Computer and Me ... 845
Nova—The Science of Murder ... 837
Nova—The Shape of Things ... 821
Nova—The Universe Within ... 837
Nova—Treasures of the Sunken City ... 785
Nova—UFOs: Are We Alone? ... 862
Nova—Visions of the Deep ... 821
Nova—War from the Air ... 843
Nova—Warnings from the Ice ... 821
Nova—What's New About Menopause? ... 837
Nova—Wonders of Plastic Surgery ... 837
Nova—Yellowstone's Burning Question ... 821
Nova Scotia International Tattoo 1997 ... 618
Novotna in The Bartered Bride and The Last Waltz ... 27
Now and Then ... 240
Now I Know My Aleph Bet ... 115
Now Voyager ... 381
Nowhere ... 435, 463
Nowhere to Hide ... 475
Nowogrodek ... 113
Nuclear Bombs in Our Future ... 805
Nuclear Threat at Home, The ... 805
Nuclear Winter: Changing Our Way of Thinking ... 805
Nuclear Winter: Growing... ... 805
Nude on the Moon ... 508
Nude Stretching ... 852
Nude Tai Chi ... 852
Nude Yoga ... 852
Nudes in Limbo ... 564
Nueba Yol ... 52, 55
Number and Meaning ... 852
Number Seventeen ... 352
Numero Deux ... 9
Nun (La Religeuse), The ... 10
Nun's Story ... 381
Nuns on the Run ... 184
Nunsense ... 327
Nuremburg ... 771
Nureyev and the Joffrey Ballet in Tribute to Nijinsky ... 574
Nurse Marjorie ... 402
Nursery Habitat Set ... 821
Nut, The ... 402
Nutcracker, The ... 639, 647
Nutcracker (Baryshnikov), The ... 574
Nutcracker (Bolshoi), The ... 574
Nutcracker (Kirov), The ... 574
Nutcracker (Nureyev), The ... 574
Nutcracker (Royal Ballet), The ... 574
Nutcracker (Russian State Theatre Academy of Classical Ballet), The ... 574
Nutcracker Prince, The ... 714
Nutcracker: Fantasy on Ice ... 574
Nuts ... 240
Nuts in May ... 166
Nutty Professor (1963), The ... 278
Nutty Professor (1996), The ... 278
Nuzzling with Nozzles: A Magical Adventure ... 639
NY/New Wave at P.S. 1 ... 559
Nyoka and the Tigermen ... 538

O

O Lucky Man! ... 162
O No Coronado ... 487
O Pioneers! ... 240
O.S.S. ... 381
O-Kay for Sound ... 184
Oak, The ... 104
Oasis in Time, An ... 115
Oasis of the Zombies (La Tumba de los Muertos Vivientos) ... 527
"Oba Koso": Nigerian Music and Dance Drama ... 152
Obeah Wedding ... 55
Object of Beauty, The ... 162
Objective, Burma! ... 381
Oblomov ... 82
Oblong Box, The ... 527
Obsessed ... 211
Obsession ... 122, 240
Occupant, The ... 122
Occupied Palestine ... 111, 475
Occurrence at Owl Creek Bridge, An ... 22, 301
Ocean Blue: Man's Relationship to the Sea, The ... 821
Ocean Life/Great Barrier Reef ... 869
Ocean Life/Hawaiian Islands ... 869
Ocean Life/Micronesia ... 869
Ocean Life/Western Pacific 2.0 ... 869
Ocean's 11 ... 381
Ocean Symphony ... 821
Oceanography: Dr. Sylvia Earle ... 805
Oceans of Air ... 821
Octavio Paz (Lannan Literary Videos) ... 60
Octavio Paz ... 60
October Man, The ... 176
Octopussy ... 169
Odd Birds ... 435
Odd Couple ... 278
Odd Gals Out ... 463
Odd Girl Out ... 463
Odd Man Out ... 176
Odd Obsession ... 141
Odds Against Tomorrow ... 381
Ode to Freedom ... 598
Odessa File ... 162
Odile & Yvette at the Edge of the World ... 240
Odin: Photon Space Sailor Starlight ... 738
Odyssey, The ... 301, 785
Odyssey into the Mind's Eye ... 714
Odyssey of the Pacific (The Emperor of Peru) ... 211
Oedipus Rex (Felicity Palmer) ... 584
Oedipus Rex (Jessye Norman) ... 584
Oedipus Rex ... 37, 314
Of Heroes & Helicopters ... 778
Of Human Bondage ... 381, 420
Of Human Hearts ... 381
Of Men and Music ... 593
Of Mice and Men ... 240, 869
Of Pure Blood ... 771
Of Sound Mind and Body ... 852
Off Limits ... 278
Off on a Comet ... 639, 714
Off Our Knees ... 204
Off-Line Editing ... 318
Officer 444 ... 402
Officer Buckle and Gloria ... 639
Official History of Baseball ... 827
Official Story, The ... 52
Ogre Slayer 2: Grim Fairy Tale ... 738
Ogre Slayer ... 738
Oh, Bloody Life! ... 102
Oh, Mr. Porter! ... 176
Oh, What a Night ... 211
Oh Calcutta! ... 314
Oh Charles ... 93
Oh Happy Day ... 608
Oh My Goddess! Collector's Suite ... 739
Oh My Goddess! Hybrid LD #1 ... 739
Oh My Goddess! Hybrid LD #2 ... 739
Oh My Goddess! Hybrid LD #3 ... 739
Oh My Goddess! Vol. 1: Moonlight & Cherry Blossoms ... 738
Oh My Goddess! Vol. 2: Midsummer Night's Dream ... 738
Oh My Goddess! Vol. 3: Burning Hearts on the Road ... 739
Oh My Goddess! Vol. 4: Evergreen Holy Night ... 739
Oh My Goddess! Vol. 5: For the Love of Goddess ... 739
Oh Woe Is Me (Helas Pour Moi) ... 9
Oil and Water: A Portrait of Gloriane Harris ... 554
Oil Painting: Simplifying Outdoor Painting ... 564
Oklahoma Annie ... 381
Oklahoma Kid, The ... 294
Okoge ... 138
Oktoberfest in Munich ... 73
Old and the Young King, The ... 70
Old Curiosity Shop, The ... 162, 639
Old Dark House, The ... 527
Old Forest, The ... 301
Old Gringo ... 60
Old Heidelberg ... 402
Old Ironsides ... 402
Old Lady Who Walked in the Sea, The ... 6
Old Maid, The ... 381
Old Man ... 240
Old Man and the Sea, The ... 163
Old Man and the Sea ... 381
Old Man of Lochnagar ... 639
Old Master, The ... 122
Old Spanish Custom ... 409
Old Swimmin' Hole, The ... 381
Old Testament Collection, The ... 792
Old Yeller— 40th Anniversary Limited Edition ... 693
Old-Fashioned Christmas ... 783
Oldest Living Confederate Widow Tells All, The ... 762
Oleanna ... 314
Olga's House of Shame ... 508
Oliver & Company ... 693
Oliver North: Memo to History ... 800
Oliver Twist ... 180, 194, 240, 381, 402, 686, 693
Oliver!—30th Anniversary Edition ... 327
Olivier Olivier ... 96
Olly Olly Oxen Free ... 240
Olympia: Festival of Beauty ... 70, 476
Olympia: Festival of the People ... 70, 476
Olympia: Parts One and Two ... 70, 476
Olympiad Series ... 827
Olympic National Park: Wilderness Heritage ... 821
omaha (the movie) ... 435
Omaha Trail ... 294
Omar Khayyam ... 381
Omen, The ... 527
Omoo Omoo, The Shark God ... 508
On a Clear Day You Can See Forever ... 327
On an Island with You ... 327
On Any Sunday ... 827
On Approval ... 184
On Assignment ... 559
On Being Gay ... 463
On Borrowed Time ... 314
On Christmas Eve ... 639
On Common Ground ... 463
On Fire: A Family Guide to Fire Safety ... 858
On Golden Pond ... 240
On Her Majesty's Secret Service ... 169
On Moonlight Bay ... 327
On My Own ... 211
On Our Way to School ... 655
On Robot Wings: A Flight Through the Solar System ... 840
On the Avenue ... 327
On the Beach ... 381
On the Comet ... 100, 714
On the Comet ... 100, 714
On the Edge of Extinction: Panthers and Cheetahs ... 821
On the Fiddle ... 184
On the House: Restoring a Victorian House ... 858
On the Nature of Love ... 852
On the Neman River ... 93
On the Pow Wow Trail ... 788
On the Rocks ... 554
On the Run ... 122
On the Town ... 327
On the Trail of Ed Wood ... 515
On the Waterfront ... 381
On the Wild Side... Meeting with Remarkable Women ... 852
On Top of the Whale ... 11
On Wings of a Dream ... 805
On Your Toes... The Making of ... 574
Once Around ... 240
Once at a Border... Aspects of Stravinsky ... 593
Once Bitten ... 278
Once There Was a Ballpark ... 566, 827
Once Upon a Brothers Grimm ... 647
Once upon a Forest ... 686
Once Upon a Time, Cinema ... 106
Once Upon a Time ... 152
Once Upon a Time in America ... 40
Once Upon a Time in China III ... 130
Once Upon a Time in China V ... 130
Once Upon a Time in the West ... 40
Once Upon a Time in Triad Society II ... 130
Once Upon a Time When We Were Colored ... 241, 445
Once Were Warriors ... 208
Once When I Was Scared ... 639
One, Two, Buckle My Shoe ... 655
One, Two, Three ... 346
One Adventure ... 463
One Against the Wind ... 241
One and Only Lola Beltran, The ... 60, 603
One Arabian Night ... 345
One Body Too Many ... 508
One Deadly Summer ... 6
One False Move ... 445
One Fine Day ... 278
One Fish Two Fish Red Fish Blue Fish ... 655
One Flew Over the Cuckoo's Nest ... 100
One Foot in the Grave: In Lutton Airport No-One Can Hear You Scream ... 194
One Foot in the Grave: Who Will Buy? ... 195
One for the Road ... 420
One Giant Leap ... 840
One Good Turn ... 241
One Hand Don't Clap ... 603
One Hundred Men and a Girl ... 327
One in a Million ... 381
One Light Healing Touch ... 852
One Man's Way ... 381
One Minute to Zero ... 381
One Nation Under God ... 476
One Night in the Tropics ... 327
One Night of Love ... 327
One Night Stand (Figgis) ... 241
One Night Stand (Shire) ... 241
One Night Stand: Lionel Hampton and an All-Star Jazz Ensemble ... 614
One Night with Blue Note, Part 1 ... 614
One of Our Aircraft Is Missing ... 180
One on One on UFOs ... 862
One Plus One ... 509
One Punch O'Day ... 402
One Rainy Afternoon ... 381
One Russian Summer ... 163
One Small Step for Man ... 840
One Step Beyond ... 420
One Terrific Thanksgiving ... 639
One Touch of Venus ... 327
One Trick Pony ... 241
One Word, Many Texts ... 115
One-Armed Swordsman, The ... 130
One-Eyed Jacks ... 295

One-Minute Bible Stories (New Testament) 656
One-Minute Bible Stories (Old Testament) 656
One-Pound Gospel 739
Onegin 574
Onibaba 138
Only Angels Have Wings 342
Only One Night 76
Only the Ball Was White 453, 827
Only the Brave 206, 463
Only the Valiant 295
Only Two Can Play 184
Only Way, The 76, 776
Only You 278
Open All Hours 195
Open City 39
Open Doors 33
Open Switch 402
Open Theater: Terminal, The 314
Open Window/Child's Play (Two from Saki) 301
Opening Night 440
Opening the Gates of Hell: American Liberators of the Nazi Concentration Camps 776
Opening the West (1860-1900) 299
Opening to Angels 852
Opera Favorites Sung by Placido Domingo and Kiri Te Kanawa 598
Opera Imaginaire 714
Opera Stars in Concert, Volume 1 599
Opera Stars in Concert, Volume 2 599
Opera Stars in Concert, Volume 3 599
Operafest 584
Operation Arsenal 93
Operation Condor 134
Operation Crossbow 771
Operation Daybreak 241
Operation Jonathan 108
Operation Moses: A Documentary 115
Operation Pacific 381
Operation Petticoat 354
Operation Pink Squad 122
Operation Pink Squad II 122
Operation: Weather Disaster 869
Opiates of the Masses: Religion in the USSR 88, 792
Opium 70
Oppermann Family 64
Opposite Sex 327
Optical Nerves 463, 492
Orange Cheeks 639
Oranges Are Not the Only Fruit 195, 463
Orangutans—The High Society 821
Oratorio for Prague 101
Orbitrons, The 499
Orca Whales and Mermaid Tales 639
Orca: Killer Whale or Gentle Giant 821
Orchestra Rehearsal 37
Orchestra Wives 327
Orchestral Tribute to the Beatles 621
Orchestre l'Opera de Paris 593
Orchids and Ermine 402
Order of the White Eagle 98
Ordet 79
Ordinary Magic 211
Ordinary People 241
Ordonka 98
Oregon 614
Orfeo ed Euridice (Kowalski) 584
Orfeo ed Euridice (Kupfer) 584
Organized Crime & Triad Bureau 130
Organizer, The 41
Orguss 02, Vol. 1 739
Orguss 02, Vol. 2 739
Orguss 02 Vol. 3 739
Orgy of the Dead 515
Oriane 52
Orient Express, The 843
Orient Express Panorama Music 593
Oriental Art—Grades 5-12 564
Origin of Life (& Scopes Footage) 837
Original Flash Gordon, The 538
Original Tales and Tunes 656
Origins of American Animation 714
Origins of Man: Complete Set 837
Origins of Man: Retracing Man's Steps 837
Origins of Man: The Big Bang and Beyond 837
Origins of the Motion Picture 337
Origins: The Two Traditions in Ireland, The 204
Orlando 163, 463
Orlando Furioso 584
Orlova Three-Pack 82
Orphan Boy of Vienna 70
Orphan Train 241
Orphans 241
Orphans of the Storm 413
Orpheus 27
Orpheus Descending 241
Orson Welles' Ghost Story 344
Orson Welles 344
Osaka Elegy 143
Oscar and Lucinda 206
Oscar Peterson: Music in the Key of Oscar 614
Oscar's Greatest Moments: 1971-1991 337
Oscar Wilde 176
Oskar Fischinger 487, 686
Ossessione 39
Ossian: American Boy/Tibetan Monk 149
Oswald: The Backyard Photographs 798
Otaku No Video 739
Otello (Berlin) 584
Otello (Del Monaco) 584
Otello (Domingo/Solti) 584
Otello (Vickers) 584
Othello (1922/Silent) 314
Othello (1996/Parker) 314
Othello 82, 163, 344
Other People's Money 241
Other Prisoners 476
Other Side of the Mountain, Part 2, The 241, 827
Other Side of the Mountain, The 241, 827
Other World of Winston Churchill 554
Otis Redding: Shake 621
Otto Dix: The Painter Is the Eyes of the World 554
Otto Klemperer's Long Journey Through His Times 593
Otto Messmer 686
Oued Nefifik: A Foreign Movie 435
Our Biosphere: The Earth in Our Hands 805
Our Century 762
Our Children 113
Our Daily Bread 381
Our Dancing Daughters 402
Our Fragile Earth: Energy Efficiency and Renewables 805
Our Hospitality/Sherlock Jr. 409
Our Job in Japan 771
Our Little Girl 665
Our Man Flint 278
Our Miss Brooks 278
Our Modern Maidens 402
Our Musical Heritage Series 603
Our Natural Heritage Series 821
Our Russian Front 88
Our Secret Century: Archival Films from the Darker Side of the American Dream, Volumes 1 & 2 869
Our Secret Century: Archival Films from the Darker Side of the American Dream, Volumes 3 & 4 869
Our Solar System 870
Our Soviet Allies, World War II 771
Our Threatened Heritage 805
Our Town (1940) 314
Our Town (1977) 314
Our Town (1988) 314
Our Very Own 381
Our Vines Have Tender Grapes 381
Out for Laughs 463
Out in Suburbia 463
Out in the Garden & You 464, 487
Out of Africa 241
Out of Ireland 204
Out of Season 163
Out of the Ashes (1945-1949) 771
Out of the Blacks Into the Blues 614
Out of the Blue 241
Out of the Silence: Fighting for Human Rights 800
Out of the Way Cafe 805
Out Takes 464
Out There 464
Out-of-Towners, The 278
Outbreak 241
Outcasts 136, 464
Outer Limits, The 421
Outer Limits Series, The 420
Outfit, The 241
Outland 499
Outlanders 739
Outlaw 295
Outlaw and His Wife 79
Outlaw Brothers, The 130
Outlaw Drive-In Vol. 1: Horror Comedy Double Feature 527
Outlaw Josey Wales 256
Outlaws and Lawmen 762
Outlaws: The Ten Most Wanted 299
Outpost in Morocco 382
Outpost of Progress, An 301
Outrage 46
Outrageous Animation Vol. 1 714
Outrageous Animation Vol. 2 714
Outside in Sight: Music of the United Front 614
Outside the Law 402
Outsider, The 176
Outsiders 260
Over America 831
Over New England 831
Over the Edge 241
Over the Ocean 108
Over There, 1914-1918 762
Over Washington 831
Overcoat, The 83
Overseas 6
Overture to Glory 113
Ovide and the Gang 714
Owl Moon and Other Stories 639
Ox, The 76
Ox-Bow Incident, The 382, 421
Oyster Princess, The 70
Oz Encounters: UFOs in Australia 862
Oz: The American Fairyland 306
Ozma of Oz 639
Ozone 527
Ozone and the Politics of Medicine 805
Ozone: Cancer of the Sky 805
Ozric Tentacles—Live at the Fridge 618

P

P.D. James: A Mind to Murder 195
P.D. James: Devices and Desires 195
P.D.Q. Bach's "The Abduction of Figaro" 599
P.G. Wodehouse's Jeeves and Wooster 195
P.O.W.—Americans in Enemy Hands: World War II, Korea and Vietnam 771
P.T. Barnum: America's Greatest Showman 796
Pablita Velarde: An Artist and Her People 554, 788
Pack of Lies 861
Pack of Wolves, A 138
Pack Up the Troubles 204
Pack Up Your Troubles 278
Paddle to the Sea 211, 639
Paddy Reilly Live 204
Paderewski's Return 98
Padre Nuestro 45
Padre Padrone 35
Pagan Love Song 327
Page of Madness, A 138
Pagemaster, The 686
Paha Sapa: The Struggle for the Black Hills 788
Pain in the A.., A 16
Paint with Strings 'n Things 564
Paint Without a Brush 564
Paint Your Wagon 327
Painted Faces 134
Painted Hills, The 665
Painted Lady 195
Painted Lips (Boquitas Pintadas) 52
Painted Stallion 538
Painted Veil 382
Painters Forum Scene Painting Library, The 318
Painters Painting 481, 554, 870
Painting Barns in Watercolor 564
Painting Streams, Rocks and Trees in Watercolor 564
Painting That Fools the Eye: Trompe L'Oeil 554
Painting with Stephen Quiller 564
Paisan 39
Pakeezah 148
Pakua Chang 852
Pal Joey 327
Palazzolo's Chicago 476
Palazzolo's Chicago Vol. 2 476
Pale Blood 527
Pale Horse, The 163
Pale Rider 256
Paleface 278
Paleo World 821
Palestinian Diaries 111
Pallbearer, The 241
Palm Beach Story 346
Palm Springs Weekend 509
Palmetto 435
Palmy Days 327
Palombella Rossa 34
Palooka 278
Palookaville 435
Pampered Youths 402
Pamplona/Viva San Fermin 48
Panama Deception, The 476
Panama Hattie 327
Panama Invasion Revisited, The 60
Panda & The Magic Serpent 739
Pandora and the Flying Dutchman 382
Pandora's Box 70
Panic in the City 435
Panic in the Streets 382
Panic in Year Zero 499
Panique 22
Pantaloons (Don Juan) 22
Panther Girl of the Kongo 538
Panty Hose Hero 130
Paolo Veronese: Between Art and Inquisition 554
Papa John Creach: Setting the Record Straight 614
Papa's Delicate Condition 382
Papal Concert to Commemorate the Holocaust 593
Papal Concert: A Musical Offering from the Vatican 593
Papazian Live 593
Paper, The 241
Paper and Silk: The Conservation of Asian Works of Art 561
Paper Bag Princess 639
Paper Chase, The 241
Paper Colony, The 805
Paper John 639
Paper Marriage 123
Paper Moon 241
Paper Play 564
Paper Wedding 213
Papermaking and Bookbinding 564
Papillon 241
Paracelsus 70
Parada Wspomnien 98
Parade 28
Paradine Case 352
Paradise, Hawaiian Style 537
Paradise Hotel 123
Paradise in Harlem 448
Paradise Lost 476
Paradise Not Yet Lost (aka Oona's Third Year) 442
Paradise Now 314
Paradise Road 241
Paradise Towers 200
Paradjanov: A Requiem 84
Paramount Comedy Theater: Volumes 1-3 535
Paramount Comedy Theater: Volume 4 535
Paramount Comedy Theater: Volume 5 535
Paramount/Famous Studios Volume 1 686
Paramount/Famous Studios Volume 2 686

Paramount/Fleischer Studios Volume 1 686
Paramount/Fleischer Studios Volume 2 686
Paramount/Fleischer Studios Volume 3 686
Parangelia 105
Paranoiac 176
Pardners 278
Pardon My Sarong—Abbott and Costello 279
Pardon My Trunk 41
Parenting for Today 858
Parents 279
Paris, France 211
Paris, Texas 67
Paris 1900 22
Paris Belongs to Us 11
Paris Blues 382
Paris Dances Diaghilev 574
Paris Holiday 279
Paris Is Burning 464, 476
Paris Opera Ballet: Cinderella, The 574
Paris Opera Ballet: Seven Ballets 574
Paris Opera Ballet: Six Ballets 574
Paris Reunion Band 614
Paris Trout 241
Paris Vu Par (Six in Paris) 6, 9
Paris Waltz (La Valse de Paris) 618
Paris Waltz 22
Paris Was a Woman 464, 476
Paris When It Sizzles 279
Park Avenue Logger 382
Parker Adderson Philosopher and The Music School 301
Parlor, Bedroom and Bath 409
Parpar Nechmad—Lovely Butterfly 109
Parrish 382
Parrot Sketch Not Included 199
Parsifal (Bayreuth) 584
Parsifal (Berlin) 584
Parsifal (Met) 584
Parsifal (Syberberg) 64, 584
Parting Glances 464
Partner 35
Partners in Crime 195
Partridge Family, The 421
Parts of Speech, The 870
Party, The 354
Party Girl (Dangerous Business) 402
Party Girl 279, 347
Party Line, The 60
Pas de Deux 574
Pascal Aubier Films 487
Pascali's Island 163
Passage to India, A 180
Passage to Marseilles 382
Passenger, The 93
Passenger 57 241
Passin' It On 453
Passing of the Third Floor Back 177
Passing Storm (1931-1933), The 762
Passion 9, 327, 345
Passion Fish 440
Passion for Art: Renoir, Cézanne, Matisse and Dr. Barnes, A 870
Passion for Life 22
Passion of Joan of Arc 79
Passion of the Saints 792
Passionate Friends (One Woman's Story), The 180
Passione d'Amore 36
Passover at Bubbe's 115
Passover Seder, A 115
Passover: Traditions of Freedom 115
Passport to Pimlico 184
Pastime 242
Pat and Mike 350
Pat Donohue in Concert at the Freight & Salvage 614
Pat Garrett and Billy the Kid 347
Pat Paulsen for President 535
Pat Paulsen on Wine 858
Pat Paulsen's Greatest Bits 535
Patch of Blue, A 382
Patchwork Girl of Oz/A Florida Enchantment, The 402
Patchwork: A Kaleidescope of Quilts 762
Pather Panchali 148
Path of Glory 117
Path of God 105
Pathe Freres Vol. 1 22
Pathe Freres Vol. 2 23
Pathfinder 76, 242
Paths of Glory 256
Paths to Paradise 402
Pathways Through Jerusalem 870
Patlabor 1 Movie 739
Patlabor 2 Movie 739
Patlabor Mobile Police New Files, Boxed Set 739
Patlabor Mobile Police New Files Vol. 1 739
Patlabor Mobile Police New Files Vol. 2 739
Patlabor Mobile Police New Files Vol. 3 739
Patlabor Mobile Police New Files Vol. 4 739
Patlabor Mobile Police New Files Vol. 5 739
Patlabor Mobile Police Original Series, Boxed Set 739
Patlabor Mobile Police Original Series Vol. 1 739
Patlabor Mobile Police Original Series Vol. 2 739
Patlabor: The Mobile Police—The TV Series: Vol. 1 739
Patricia Highsmith 306
Patrick 204, 206
Patrick Bokanowski— L'Ange (1977-1982) 8
Patrick Bokanowski—Courts-Metrages 8
Patriot Games 242
Patriots 83
Patsy, The 279
Pattern and Transformation 852
Pattern Development Video, The 318
Pattern for Plunder (Curse of San Michel) 527
Patterns 421
Pattes Blanches 23
Pattiann Rogers 306
Patton 382
Patton: A Genius for War 796
Patton: Old Blood and Guts 771
Patty Duke Show, The 421
Paul Anka '62 621
Paul Bartel's Secret Cinema 435
Paul Bowles in Morocco 306
Paul Bowles: The Complete Outsider 306
Paul Bunyan 693
Paul Cadmus: Enfant Terrible at 80 554
Paul Cezanne: Portrait of My World 870
Paul Cezanne: The Man and His Mountain 554
Paul Driessen: Animator 714
Paul Gauguin: The Savage Dream 554
Paul Glabicki Animation Tape, The 714
Paul Harvey's The Rest of the Story 796
Paul Reiser: 31/2 Blocks from Home 535
Paul Revere: The Messenger of Liberty 762
Paul Revere: The Midnight Rider 796
Paul Robeson 314, 453
Paul Robeson: On His Shoulders Many Stand 453
Paul's Case 301
Paul Taylor Dance Company 574
Paul West 306
Paule Marshall 306
Paulette Phillips and Geoffrey Shea: Work 487
Pauline at the Beach 14
Pavarotti & Friends 599
Pavarotti & Friends 2 599
Pavarotti & Friends Together for the Children of Bosnia 599
Pavarotti and Levine in Recital 599
Pavarotti and the Italian Tenor 599
Pavarotti in Central Park 584
Pavarotti in Concert in China 599
Pavarotti in Confidence with Peter Ustinov 599
Pavarotti in Hyde Park 599
Pavarotti—Master Class at Juilliard 599
Pavarotti Valentine, A 599
Pawnbroker, The 382
Paws, Claws, Feathers and Fins 639
Payoff in the Pacific 771
Paz Si Guerra No 60
PBS Kids Pack of Pals 639
Peace Begins Here 60
Peace Hotel 123
Peace Is Every Step 149
Peace Tapes, The 805
Peacemaker, The 242
Peach of a Girl 93
Peacock Fan, The 402
Peacock King—Spirit Warrior 1 739
Peacock King—Spirit Warrior 2 739
Peacock King—Spirit Warrior: Castle of Illusion 740
Peacock King—Spirit Warrior: Festival of the Ogres' Revival 740
Peacock Prince 130
Peanut Butter Solution, The 665
Peanuts Double Feature: Charlie Brown's All Stars & It's Spring Training, Charlie Brown 699
Peanuts Double Feature: He's Your Dog, Charlie Brown & A Charlie Brown Thanksgiving & You're Not Elected, Charlie Brown 699
Peanuts Double Feature: He's Your Dog, Charlie Brown & It's Flashbeagle, Charlie Brown 699
Peanuts Double Feature: Life's a Circus, Charlie Brown & Snoopy's Getting Married 699
Peanuts Double Feature: Play It Again, Charlie Brown & She's a Good Skate, Charlie Brown 699
Peanuts Double Feature: There's No Time for Love & Someday You'll Find Her 699
Peanuts Double Feature: What a Nightmare, Charlie Brown & It's Magic, Charlie Brown 699
Peanuts Double Feature: You're in Love, Charlie Brown & It's Your First Kiss, Charlie Brown 699
Peanuts Double Feature: You're Not Elected, Charlie Brown & It Was a Short Summer, Charlie Brown 699
Peanuts Double Feature: You're the Greatest, Charlie Brown & Snoopy's Reunion 699
Peanuts Feature Film: A Boy Named Charlie Brown 700
Peanuts Feature Film: Bon Voyage, Charlie Brown 700
Peanuts Feature Film: Race for Your Life, Charlie Brown 700
Peanuts Feature Film: Snoopy, Come Home 700
Peanuts Holiday Special: A Charlie Brown Christmas 700
Peanuts Holiday Special: A Charlie Brown Thanksgiving 700
Peanuts Holiday Special: Be My Valentine, Charlie Brown 700
Peanuts Holiday Special: Happy New Year, Charlie Brown 700
Peanuts Holiday Special: It's Arbor Day, Charlie Brown 700
Peanuts Holiday Special: It's the Easter Beagle, Charlie Brown ..700
Peanuts Holiday Special: It's the Great Pumpkin, Charlie Brown 700
Peanuts Special: A Charlie Brown Celebration 700
Peanuts Special: Is This Goodbye, Charlie Brown? 700
Peanuts Special: It's a Mystery, Charlie Brown! 700
Peanuts Special: It's an Adventure, Charlie Brown 700
Peanuts Special: It's Christmastime Again, Charlie Brown 700
Peanuts Special: It's the Girl in the Red Truck, Charlie Brown 700
Peanuts Special: It Was My Best Birthday Ever, Charlie Brown 700
Peanuts Special: Snoopy the Musical 700
Peanuts Special: What Have We Learned, Charlie Brown? 700
Peanuts Special: Why, Charlie Brown, Why? 700
Peanuts Special: You Don't Look 40, Charlie Brown! 700
Peanuts Special: You're a Good Man, Charlie Brown 700
Peanuts Special: You're a Good Sport, Charlie Brown 700
Peanuts: Charlie Brown & Snoopy Show Vol. 1 700
Peanuts: Charlie Brown & Snoopy Show Vol. 2 700
Peanuts: Charlie Brown & Snoopy Show Vol. 3 700
Peanuts: Charlie Brown & Snoopy Show Vol. 4 700
Peanuts: Charlie Brown & Snoopy Show Vol. 5 700
Peanuts: Charlie Brown & Snoopy Show Vol. 6 700
Peanuts: Charlie Brown & Snoopy Show Vol. 7 700
Peanuts: Charlie Brown & Snoopy Show Vol. 8 700
Peanuts: Charlie Brown & Snoopy Show Vol. 9 701
Peanuts: This Is America LD #1: The Great Inventors/ The Wright Brothers at Kitty Hawk 701
Peanuts: This Is America LD #2: Building the Transcontinental Railroad/The Mayflower Voyagers 701
Peanuts: This Is America Vol. 1: The Great Inventors 701
Peanuts: This Is America Vol. 2: The Wright Brothers at Kitty Hawk 701
Peanuts: This Is America Vol. 3: Building the Transcontinental Railroad 701
Peanuts: This Is America Vol. 4: The Mayflower Voyagers 701
Peanuts: This Is America Vol. 5: The NASA Space Station 701
Peanuts: This Is America Vol. 6: The Birth of the Constitution 701
Peanuts: This Is America Vol. 7: The Music and Heroes of America 701
Peanuts: This Is America Vol. 8: The Smithsonian & The Presidency 701
Pearl, The 52
Pearl Harbor: Two Hours That Shook the World 771
Pearls of the Crown, The 23
Peasants, The 93
Peasants in Distress 145
Pebble and the Penguin, The 686
Peck's Bad Boy 411
Pecos Bill 870
Peddler, The 106
Peddlin' in Society 41
Pedicab Driver 130
Pee-Wee's Big Adventure 255
Pee-Wee's Collector's Gift Set 421
Pee-Wee's Collector's Gift Set: Vols. 9-16 421
Pee-Wee's Playhouse Christmas Special 421
Peep and the Big Wide World 656
Peeping Beauty by Mary Jane Auch 639
Peeping Tom 181
Pegasus 639
Peggy Sue Got Married 260
Peking Opera Blues 130
Pelican Brief 242
Pelleas et Melisande 584
Penal Days, The 204
Penalty, The 402, 527
Penalty Phase 242
Pencil Drawing with Gail Price 564
Penguin World 821
Penitentiary II 445
Penitentiary III 445
Penn and Teller Get Killed 258
Pennies from Heaven 327
Penny Serenade 343
People 639
People Are Funny 279
People of Faith and the Arms Race 805
People of the 7th Fire 788
People of the Book 792
People of the Caribbean 60
People of the Forest 821
People's Gala Concert 83
People's Hero 130
People to People 805
People Under the Stairs, The 527
People vs. Larry Flynt, The 100
People vs. Paul Crump, The 476
People Will Talk 382
Pepe le Moko 23
Pepi, Luci, Bom and Other Girls 46
Pepito's Dream 639
Peppe the Lamplighter 639
Pepper and All the Legs 639
Peppermint Soda 6
Perceptual Landscapes 464, 492
Percy Mayfield: Poet Laureate of the Blues 614
Perez Family, The 279
Perfect 242
Perfect Baby 858
Perfect Candidate, A 476, 800
Perfect Clown 411
Perfect Furlough, The 354
Perfect Harmony 618
Perfect Marriage, The 279
Perfect Match 123
Perfect Spy, A 195
Perfect World, A 256
Performance 167
Performance by Jack Smith, A 487, 567
Performing at the San Francisco Museum of Modern Art Groundbreaking Ceremony 567
Performing Shakespeare 318
Perfume 242
Perfumed Handkerchief, The 584
Perfumed Nightmare 145
Pergolesi: La Serva Padrona 584
Perils of Pauline, The 279, 538
Perils of the Darkest Jungle 538
Perils of the Planet Mongo 499
Perils of the Rails 402
Period of Adjustment 382
Permanent Record 242

Persian Gulf: Images of a Conflict, The 111
Persistent Women Artists 554
Person to Person Interviews—Volume 1 337
Person to Person Interviews—Volume 2 337
Persona 78
Personal Affair 177
Personal Best 464
Personal Performance Techniques 318
Personal Property 382
Personal Search 93
Personal Services 199
Personals, The 242
Persuaders—London Conspiracy, The 421
Persuaders—Mission: Monte Carlo, The 421
Persuaders—Sporting Chance, The 421
Pertwee Years, The 201
Peru Virreinal 554
Peru: Inca Heritage 60
Perversion 527
Pete 'n' Tillie 279
Pete's Dragon 693
Pete Seeger's Family Concert 656
Peter, Paul and Mary: 25th Anniversary Concert 605
Peter and the Wolf (Animation) 647
Peter and the Wolf (Live Action and Animation) 647
Peter and the Wolf (Live Action and Puppetry) 647
Peter and the Wolf: Moscow Musical Theatre for Children 647
Peter Bogdanovich and Henry Jaglom: The Ninth New York Film Festival 337
Peter Brook 314
Peter Callas: Night's High Noon: An Anti-Terrain 487
Peter Elbow on Writing 859
Peter Gabriel: Secret World Live 622
Peter Grimes 584
Peter Gunn 421
Peter Jennings Reporting from the Killing Fields 145
Peter Jennings Reporting: Men, Sex and Rape 800
Peter Martins: A Dancer 574
Peter Pan 327, 673, 693
Peter Paul Rubens: Classical Synthesis-Prophet of Modern Painting 555
Peter Reading 170
Peter Russell: The Global Brain 487
Peter's Friends 184
Peter the First Part One 83
Peter the First Part Two 83
Peter Thompson Films 487
Peter Ustinov 337
Peter Ustinov: The Orchestra 639
Peter-No-Tail 639
Petey Wheatstraw 533
Petrified Forest 382
Petulia 177
Peyote Road 476, 788
Peyton Place 382
Phantasm II: The Ball Is Back 527
Phantasm III: Lord of the Dead 499
Phantom, The 242
Phantom Broadcast 382
Phantom Chariot 79
Phantom Creeps, The 527
Phantom Empire 538
Phantom Fiend 177
Phantom Flyer 402
Phantom from Space 499
Phantom Lady 382
Phantom of Chinatown 382
Phantom of Liberty 47
Phantom of Paradise 509
Phantom of the Opera, The 327, 402, 686
Phantom of the Opera (1943), The 527
Phantom of the Opera (1962), The 527
Phantom of the Opera (1989), The 527
Phantom of the Rue Morgue 527
Phantom of the West 538
Phantom Planet, The 499
Phantom Quest Corp. Vol. 1 740
Phantom Quest Corp. Vol. 2 740
Phantom Rider, The 539
Phantom Ship (Mystery of the Mary Celeste) 177
Phantom Tollbooth, The 665, 686
Phantom War 130
Phar Lap 206
Pharaoh 93
Pharaoh's Curse 527
Pharaohs and Kings: A Biblical Quest 792
Phedre 23
Phenomenon 242
Phil Coulter—The Live Experience 204
Phil Woods in Concert: With Joe Sudler's Swing Machine 614
Phil Woods Quartet, The 614
Philadelphia 255
Philadelphia Story, The 350
Philip Hall Likes Me, I Reckon 639
Philip Johnson: Self Portrait 566
Philip Levine 306
Philip Pearlstein Draws the Artist's Model 564
Philosophy in the Bedroom 509
Philosophy of Tantric Yoga, The 852
Phobia 349
Phoenix 2772 740
Phone Call from a Stranger 382
Phoney American, The 70
Photo Album 60, 435
Photographer's Secrets, The 559
Photography 559
Photography Video Series— The Classroom Collection 559
Photopaedia Vol. 1: 100 Japanese Photographers, 1993 870
Photopaedia Vol. 3: Still Lifes by Diane Wesson 870
Piano, The 208
Piano for Mrs. Cimino, A 242
Piano Legends 614
Piano Lesson, The 314
Picasso (Musee Picasso) 555
Picasso 555
Picasso: The Man and His Work 555
Pick a Star 279
Pick Up on South Street 341
Pickles Make Me Cry 131
Pickpocket 15
Pickwick Papers, The 177
Picnic 382
Picnic at Hanging Rock 208
Picnic on the Grass 26
Picture Book of Martin Luther King, Jr., A 639
Picture Bride 435
Picture of Dorian Gray 163, 382
Picture Windows 242
Picturebook Classics: Adam's Smile 639
Picturebook Classics: Complete Set 639
Picturebook Classics: Five Secrets in a Box 640
Picturebook Classics: The Porcelain Cat 640
Pictures 195
Pictures and Letters: A Video Picture Dictionary 656
Pictures Don't Tell You Anything: Selected Films of Ann Marie Fleming 211, 487
Pictures from a Revolution 60
Picuris Indians 788
Piece of Cake: Complete Set 195, 771
Piece of Pleasure 13
Piece of the Action, A 445
Pied Piper, The 647
Pied Piper of Hamelin, The 665
Pied Piper/Cinderella, The 647
Pier Marton (are we and/or do we) Like Men 487
Pier Marton: Collected Works: 1979-84 487
Pier Marton: Say I'm a Jew 115, 488
Pierre Bonnard 555
Pierre Bonnard and the Impressionist Vision 555
Pierrot le Fou 10
Piet Mondrian: Mr. Boogie Woogie Man 555
Pieter Brueghel the Elder: A Painter for All Time 555
Pigalle 8
Pigeon Feathers 301
Piggy Banks to Money Markets 640
Pigs' Wedding and Other Stories, The 640
Pigs 95
Pigs and David's Father 656
Pigskin Parade 279
Pigsty 37
Pikes Peak Country, with Colorado Springs 831
Pilgrim, The 98
Pilgrim Jubilees 608
Pilgrimage of Remembrance: Jews in Poland Today 115
Pilgrimage to Rome 23
Pillow Book, The 165
Pillow Talk 279
Pilobolus 574
Pilot X (Death in the Air) 499
Pimpenella: Nuestras Mejores Canciones (Our Favorite Songs) 48
Pimpernel Smith 177
Pin-Up Girl 279
Pin-Ups: A Picture History of America's Dream Girls, The 337
Pinatas, Posadas y Pastorelas 60
Pinchas Zukerman: Here to Make Music/The Ghost 593
Pink Bomb 123
Pink Cadillac 242
Pink Flamingos 514
Pink Floyd: The Wall 622
Pink Jungle, The 382
Pink Narcissus 464
Pink Nights 435
Pink Panther, The 354, 686
Pink Panther Animation Archive Vol. 1 686
Pink Panther's Laugh Festival 686
Pink Panther Strikes Again, The 354
Pink Panther: A Pink Christmas 686
Pink Panther: Jet Pink, The 686
Pink Panther: Pink Bananas, The 686
Pink Panther: Pink-A-Rella, The 686
Pink Panther: Prehistoric Pink, The 686
Pink Ulysses 464
Pinky 382
Pinky and the Brain: Cosmic Attractions 701
Pinky and the Brain: Mice of the Jungle 701
Pinocchio (Animated) 647
Pinocchio (Live Action) 647
Pinocchio's Christmas 686
Pioneer's Gold 402
Pioneers in Animation Vol. 1 714
Pioneers in Animation Vol. 2 714
Pioneers in Animation Vol. 3 714
Pipeline and Animals, A 822
Pippi Longstocking 665, 715
Pippin 327
Pipsqueak Pfollies 435
Pique Dame—The Queen of Spades 584
Pirate Planet, The 201
Pirate's Dagger 640
Pirates 97
Pirates of Penzance 327
Pirelli Calendar 559
Pitfall 382
Pittsburgh 382
Pity the Pilot Whale 822
Pixote 54
Place for Annie, A 242
Place in the Sun, A 343
Place in the World, A 52
Place of Weeping 151
Place to Call Home, A 60
Place to Stand, A 762
Place Without Limits 52
Places in the Heart 242
Places We Live: Complete Set 566
Places We Live: Dream Houses 566
Places We Live: Houses for Individualists 566
Places We Live: Way Out Architecture 566
Placido Domingo & Rostropovich 599
Placido Domingo—Zarzuela 599
Placido Domingo: A Musical Life 599
Placido Domingo: Gala De Reyes 584
Placido Domingo: His 25th Anniversary Concert at the Roman Amphitheater of Verona 599
Placido Domingo: Hommage a Sevilla 599
Placido Domingo: Live from Miami 599
Placido Grandisimo 599
Placido in Prague 599
Placido: A Year in the Life of Placido Domingo 599
Plague of the Zombies, The 527
Plain Clothes 279
Plain Talk and Common Sense 441
Plainsman 355
Plan (Addictions—HIV), The 834
Plan 9 from Outer Space 515
Planes, Trains and Automobiles 279
Planet Busters 740
Planet Earth: 7-Volume Boxed Set 837
Planet Mars and Mercury 840
Planet of Blood (Queen of Blood) 499
Planet of Evil 201
Planet of Life 822
Planet of the Apes 499
Planet of the Spiders 201
Planet of the Vampires 499
Planeta Burg 83, 499
Planetary Birth 852
Planetary Taxi (Visual Almanac Series, Vol. 2) 870
Planetary Traveler 715
Planets, The 840
Planets Deluxe Collector's Edition, The 840
Planting Seeds for Peace 805
Plastic Age, The 402
Plates 464, 488
Platinum Blonde 351
Platoon 242
"Play Bach"—The 1989 Munich Concert 593
Play Bluegrass Banjo by Ear 624
Play Chess! The United States Chess Federation Guide 827
Play It Again, Sam 289
Play Misty for Me 257
Play Soccer, Jack Charlton's Way: The Collection Set 827
Playboy & Rhonda Goes to Hollywood 488
Playboys, The 163
Player, The 254
Playgirls and the Vampire, The 527
Playhouse 90: Requiem for a Heavyweight 314
Playing Dead 402
Playing God 242
Playtime 28
Playwrights '56 314
Plaza Suite 279
Please Don't Eat My Mother 279
Please Don't Eat the Daisies 279
Please Save My Earth Vol. 1 740
Please Save My Earth Vol. 2 740
Please Save My Earth Vol. 3 740
Pleasures of the Uninhibited Excess, The 567
Pleiadian Connection, The 862
Plenty 163
Plisetskaya Dances 574
Plot Against Harry, The 435
Plot to Kill JFK: Rush to Judgment 481
Plot to Kill Robert Kennedy 798
Plow That Broke the Plains/Night Mail, The 476
Plunder Road 383
Plymouth Adventure 383
Plymptoons: The Complete Works of Bill Plympton 715
Pocahontas (Animation) 640
Pocahontas (Stop-Motion Animation) 640
Pocahontas 693
Pocahontas Special Edition 693
Pocahontas: Her True Story 640
Pocket Money 295
Pocketful of Miracles 351
Pocketful of Rye, A 195
Poems for Children 98
Poesie de la Francophonie 155
Poetic Justice 446
Poetry by Americans Series 306
Poetry Hall of Fame, The 306
Poetry in Motion 306, 870
Poetry in Motion II 870
Poetry in Times of War 306
Poetry of Landscape: Great Britain 170
Poetry on Telegraph Avenue 306
Poil de Carotte 23
Point, The 665, 686
Point Blank 383
Point of No Return 131
Pointe by Point 574

Pointer Sisters Live in Africa....622
Points in Space....574
Points of Convergence....783
Points to Change....834
Poison....435, 464
Poisonous Plants....93
Poker....435
Poky Little Puppy's First Christmas....656
Poky's Favorite Stories....656
Poland, A Proud Heritage....98
Polanicki's Family....93
Poldark....195
Pole to Pole....199
Poleo and Poetic Figuration....555
Police....10
Police Academy....279
Police Dog....177
Police Squad! Help Wanted!....421
Police State....435
Policing the Peace (1948-1951)....762
Poligon....88, 805
Poligon....88, 805
Polish Chamber Orchestra....593
Polish Christmas Carols....98
Polish Songs....98
Polish Ways....93
Politically Incorrect: A Special Visit with Camille Paglia....464, 535
Politically Incorrect: Political Improvement....535
Politically Incorrect: Politics Tonight....535
Politically Incorrect: Pulp Politics....535
Politically Incorrect: Really Roseanne....535
Polly Perverse Strikes Again!....435
Pollyanna....402, 640
Poltergeist....258, 527
Poltergeist II....527
Poltergeist Report....740
Polyester....514
Pompatus of Love, The....435
Ponette....6
Pontius Pilate— Westinghouse Studio One....421
Pony Express....295
Pooh's Grand Adventure....693
Pool Hustlers, The....34
Poor Little Rich Girl....327, 402
Pop Culture Classics from the 50's and 60's....540
Pope in America, The....792
Pope John Paul II....792
Pope John Paul II: Seven Days of Eternity....792
Pope John Paul II: Statesman of Faith....792
Pope Must Diet....509
Pope of Greenwich Village, The....279
Popes and Their Art: The Vatican Collection, The....555
Popeye....254
Popeye Cartoons & The History of Animation....686
Popeye for President....687
Popeye the Sailor....687
Popeye Vol. 1....687
Popovich Brothers of South Chicago, The....442
Population Explosion and Industrialization (Latin American Lifestyles)....60
Porgy: A Gullah Version....314, 446
Pork Chop Hill....383
Porky Pig & Co.....687
Porky Pig Tales....687
Porky Pig: Days of Swine and Roses....687
Porky Pig: Ham on Wry....687
Porky!....687
Porridge....195
Port of New York....383
Portnoy's Complaint....279
Portrait, The....640
Portrait in Black....383
Portrait in Red....242
Portrait of a Lady....195
Portrait of a White Marriage....279
Portrait of Africa....153
Portrait of an Artist as a Young Man....242
Portrait of Civilization....783
Portrait of England: Treasure Houses and Gardens....170
Portrait of Gustave Caillebotte in the Country....555
Portrait of Teresa....52
Portraits from the Past....810
Portraits in Black....453
Portraits in Watercolor with James Kirk: Elements of Design....564
Portraits in Watercolor with James Kirk: Magic of Light and Dark....564
Portraits of American Presidents....796, 870
Posada Navidena....673
Poseidon Adventure, The....242
Positive 20s....834
Positive....65, 834
Positive Faith....834
Positive I.D.....242
Positively True Adventures of the Alleged Texas Cheerleader-Murdering Mom, The....279
Posse (Douglas)....295
Posse (Van Peebles)....295
Possessed (1931)....383
Possessed (1947)....383
Post Synchronization: The Editor's Role....318
Postcards from America....464
Postcards from the Edge....279
Postman Always Rings Twice, The....242, 383
Postman Pat's 123 Story....656
Potato Wolf Coleslaw....435
Potato Wolf Showcase....435
Potato Wolf Spring 1984....435
Potter's Song: The Art and Philosophy of Paul Soldner....564
Pound Puppies and the Legend of Big Paw....665
Powder....242
Power....402
Power and Prejudice (1926-1928)....762
Power and the Land: Four Documentary Portraits of the Great Depression, The....476
Power Connection....131
Power Dolls....740
Power God....402
Power Moves....828
Power of Dreams, The....852
Power of Kroll, The....201
Power of Myth (Joseph Campbell)....786
Power of the Word, The....859
Powers of the Presidency: Armed Intervention, The....800
Powers of the Presidency: Economic Controls, The....801
Powwow Highway....242
Practical Self Defense....852
Practice of Love, The....74
Prairie Cabin: A Norwegian Pioneer Woman's Story....762
Prairie Home Companion: Last Show....421
Prairie Home Companion: The Second Annual Farewell Performance....421
Prairie Quilts: A Celebration of the Tall-Grass Prairies....763
Prancer....665
Prayer for Katarina Horovitzova, A....100
Prayer for the Dying....242
Praying Mantis Kung-fu....852
Pre-Calculus....838
Pre-Real Estate....555
Preacher's Wife, The....279
Predators of the Wild....822
Prefontaine....435
Prehistoric Beasts....822
Prehistoric Bimbos in Armageddon City....509
Prehistoric Women....509
Prejudice: Answering Children's Questions....852
Prelude....99
Prelude to a Kiss....279
Prelude to Revolution....453
Prelude to War (1935-1939)....771
Premiere of "A Star Is Born"....337
Preparing for Contact....862
Preschool Power #3....656
Preschool Power: Jacket Flips & Other Tips....656
Presence of the Goddess, The....783
Presence of the Past....852
Presenting Lily Mars....328
Preserving the Past to Ensure the Future....776
President Clinton: Answering Children's Questions, 1993....801
President Fights the Japs...And Dirt, The....540
Presidents....811
Presidents Collection, The....763
Pressure Point....383
Presumed Innocent....242
Pretty as a Picture: The Art of David Lynch....257
Pretty Baby....13
Pretty Boy....76, 464
Pretty in Pink....279
Pretty Maids All in a Row....243
Pretty Village, Pretty Flame....103
Preventive Diplomacy....801
Price of Peace (1917-1918), The....763
Priceless Day, A....102
Pride and Prejudice....195, 383
Pride and the Passion, The....383
Pride of St. Louis....383
Pride of the Bowery....279
Pride of the Clan....402
Priest....163
Priests of Passion....792
Primal Fear....243
Primal Mind, The....788
Primal Secrets....243
Primary, The....801
Primary Colors....279
Prime Minister, The....177
Prime of Miss Jean Brodie, The....177
Primer for 2001: "A Space Odyssey", A....256, 338
Prime Suspect....195
Prime Suspect 2....195
Prime Suspect 3....195
Prime Suspect 4....195
Prime Suspect 5: Errors of Judgment....195
Prime Time, The....509
Prime Time....280
Primitive Love....509
Primitive Lover....402
Primordial Tradition....853
Prince & The Pauper/Willie/Peter & The Wolf....694
Prince and the Pauper, The....309
Prince and the Showgirl, The....280
Prince Brat and the Whipping Boy....665
Prince Charles....170
Prince Cinders....647
Prince Ehtejab....106
Prince Igor (Haitink)....584
Prince Igor (Kirov)....584
Prince Joseph's Soldier....93
Prince of Darkness....527
Prince of Portland Street....131
Prince of Tides, The....243
Prince Valiant....163, 383
Prince: Sign "O" the Times....622
Princess & The Goblin....715
Princess and the Goblin, The....647
Princess and the Pirate....280
Princess and the Swineherd....648
Princess Bride, The....280
Princess Caraboo....280
Princess Comes Across....280
Princess Minerva....740
Princess Tam Tam....23
Princess Yang Kwei Fei....143
Printmaking....564
Printmaking Gadgets....670
Priory School, The....186
Prison on Fire....131
Prisoner, The....177
Prisoner of Corbal, The....177
Prisoner of Honor....167
Prisoner of Japan....383
Prisoner of Second Avenue, The....280
Prisoner of the Mountains....83
Prisoner of Zenda (1937)....383
Prisoner of Zenda (1952)....383
Prisoners of the Sun....206
Private Affairs of Bel Ami, The....383
Private Benjamin....280
Private Buckaroo....328
Private Eye Blues, The....131
Private Film Collection of Eva Braun....771
Private Hell #36....383
Private History of a Campaign That Failed....309
Private Investigation....94
Private Life....83
Private Life of Don Juan....383
Private Life of Henry VIII, The....177
Private Life of Plants, The....822
Private Life of Sherlock Holmes, The....346
Private Lives....314
Private Lives of Dolphins....822
Private Navy of Sgt. O'Farrel, The....280
Private Parts....280
Private S.N.A.F.U.....687
Private S.N.A.F.U. Cartoon Festival....687
Private S.N.A.F.U. Vol. 1....687
Private S.N.A.F.U. Vol. 2....687
Private's Progress....177
Private Secretary, The....184
Prix de Beaute....23
Prize, The....801
Prize....383
Problem of Thor Bridge, The....186
Problem with Food, The....853
Problems for Young Consumers....670
Procreation in the Wild....822
Prodigal, The....243, 356
Prodigal Son, The....131
Producers, The....280
Professional, The....8
Professor Bunruckle's Guide to Pixilation....715
Professor Iris....670
Profile of an Artist: Moriziu Gottlieb....555
Profiles of Power....796
Program for Vietnam Veterans....778
Prohibition Era, The....763
Project A (Part I)....134
Project A-Ko 2: Plot of the Daitokuji Financial Group....740
Project A-Ko 3: Cinderella Rhapsody....740
Project A-Ko 4: Final....740
Project A-Ko....740
Project A-Ko Vs. Battle 1: Grey Side....740
Project A-Ko vs. Battle 2: Blue Side....740
Project Moonbase....499
Project Tanzania: Part 1: A Response Beyond Charity....153
Project Tanzania: Part 2: A Response Beyond Charity....153
Prokofiev: Classical Symphony (Karajan)....593
Prokofiev: Romeo and Juliet....593
Prokofiev: Symphonie Classique (Celibidache)....593
Prom Night....527
Promise, The....65
Promise Her Anything....280
Promised Land, The....454
Promised Land....435
Promoter, The....184
Proof....206
Prophecy, The....243
Prophets and Loss....805
Proposition, The....243
Proprietor, The....243
Prospero's Books....165
Protect-a-Dolphin Pod....805
Protector, The....134
Protectors and Polluters....805
Proud and the Damned, The....243
Proud Men....295
Proud Ones (Les Orgueilleux), The....23
Proud Rebel....383
Proud Valley and Jericho (Dark Sands), The....448
Providence....12
Provincial Actors....96
Pryor's Place....640
Psychedelic High....622
Psychic, The....509
Psycho....352
Psycho Diver....740
Psychodynamics of Liberation, The....853
PT 109....771
Pterodactyl Woman from Beverly Hills....509
Puamana....480
Pubis Angelical....52
Public Enemies of the '20s & '30s....861

Public Enemies on the Rock 796
Public Enemy 383
Public Sculpture: America's Legacy 555
Puccini 599
Puccini—Two Loves Had I 593
Pudd'nhead Wilson 309
Puerto Cabezas: Our Sister City 60
Puerto Rican Painting: Between Past and Present 555
Puerto Rico: History and Culture 60
Puff the Magic Dragon 656
Pull My Daisy (The Beat Generation) 435, 476
Pulp Fiction 441
Pump Up the Volume 243
Pumping Iron 476
Pumping Iron II: The Women 476
Pumpkin Eater, The 177
Punishment Battalion 999 70
Punk and Its After Shocks 622
Punk Rock Movie, The 622
Pupettoon Movie 687
Puppet Animation 715
Puppet Masters 715
Puppets & Demons: Films by Patrick McGuinn 436
Purchase Price, The 383
Purdy's Station 454
Pure Formality, A 6
Pure Pete Seeger 605
Purple Death from Outer Space 499
Purple Monster Strikes 499
Purple Noon (Plein Soleil) 23
Purple Rain 328
Purple Rose of Cairo 289
Pursued 295
Push Hands (Kung-fu's Greatest Training Secret) 853
Pushed to the Edge 853
Pushing Hands 455
Puss Bucket 509
Puss in Boots 574
Pussy Galore: Maximum Penetration 622
Putney Swope 436
Puzzle Channel, Vol. 1 509
Puzzle Channel, Vol. 2 509
Puzzle Place, The 640
Puzzle Place: Accentuate the Positive, The 640
Puzzle Place: Rock Dreams, The 640
Puzzle Place: Sing-Along Songs, The 640
Puzzle Place: Tuned In, The 640
Pygmalion 177
Pyramid 566
Pyramids and the Cities of the Pharaohs, The 785
Pyramids of Mars 201
Pyramids of the Sun and the Moon, The 60
Pyx (The Hooker Cult Murders), The 211

Q

Q & A 243
Q Ships 403
Q the Winged Serpent 509
QB VII 421
Qeros: The Shape of Survival 60
Quack, The 94
Quackser Fortune Has a Cousin in the Bronx 280
Quadrophenia 622
Qualities of High Performance 853
Quantum Healing: Toward Perfect Health 853
Quantum Universe, The 837
Quark the Dragonslayer 665, 715
Quarrel, The 211
Quarterback Princess 640
Quartet 259, 593
Quartier Mozart 150
Quatermass 1: The Quatermass Experiment 499
Quatermass 2: Enemy from Space 499
Quatermass and the Pit 499
Quatorze Juillet 24
Que Viva Mexico 86
Queen, The 464
Queen Bee 383
Queen Christina 383
Queen Elizabeth II: 60 Glorious Years 170
Queen Kelly 348
Queen Margot 6
Queen Mother 170
Queen Mother's New Garden, The 170
Queen of Diamonds 436
Queen of Sheba, The 41
Queen of Sheba Meets the Atom Man, The 488
Queen of Spades (Bolshoi) 584
Queen of Spades (Glyndebourne) 584
Queen of the Chorus 403
Queen of the Elephants 822
Queen of the Stardust Ballroom 243
Queenie 338
Querelle 66
Queremos La Paz (We Want Peace) 60
Quest 783, 822
Quest for Camelot Sing-Along 687
Quest for Fire 16
Quest for the Dolphin Spirit 822
Quest for Wisdom 788
Question of Authority, A 853
Question of Conscience, A 60
Question of Equality, The 464
Question of Power 805
Question of Silence, A 31
Quick and the Dead, The 295
Quick Time the CD 870
Quicksand 383
Quicksilver Highway 243
Quickwick: Your Library Guide 859
Quiet Days in Clichy 76
Quiet Duel 142
Quiet Garden 853
Quiet Man, The 340
Quiet One 476
Quiet Room, The 206
Quilombo 54
Quilt on the Wall: Portrait of Jan Myers 561
Quincy Jones: A Celebration 614
Quintet 254
Quip with Yip and Friends 306
Quiz Show 243
Quo Vadis? 41
Quo Vadis (1951) 356

R

Rabbi Kook 109
Rabbi Zalman Schachter, Life Harvest: The Missing Piece to Wholeness 853
Rabbit Ears Collection, The 648, 792
Rabbit Ears Collection, The 648, 792
Race for Mayor, The 476
Race to Freedom: The Story of the Underground Railroad 454
Race with the Devil 527
Racers 383
Rachel and the Stranger 295
Racing for the Moon: America's Glory Days in Space 840
Racing Luck 383
Racketeer, The 384
Radar Men from the Moon 499
Radar Patrol vs. Spy King (Cliffhanger Serials #5) 539
Radiant Life 792
Radio Days 289
Radio Drama 318
Radio Flyer 243
Radio Production: Making a Radio Commercial 318
Radioland Murders 243
Raffi in Concert with the Rise and Shine Band 670
Raffles, The Amateur Racksman 403
Raffles 195, 384
Rag Nymph, The 195
Raga 149
Rage in Harlem 446
Rage of Paris 384
Raggedy Ann and Andy 561
Raggedy Rose 403
Raging Bull 253
Rags & Tangos (Rifkin) 603
Ragtime 100
Raid, The 123
Raid on Rommel 771
Raiders of the Lost Ark 258
Rail of the Star 740
Railroad Dramas 403
Railroaded 384
Railrodder/Buster Keaton Rides Again, The 409
Rails to Hell…and Back, The 776
Railway Adventures Across Europe: Volume 1 843
Railway Adventures Across Europe: Volume 2 843
Railway Station Man, The 243
Rain 384
Rain and Uberfall 488
Rain Forests: Proving Their Worth 822
Rain Man 243
Rain People, The 260
Rainbow Bridge 622
Rainbow of My Own, A 656
Rainbow Fish, The 640
Rainbow Parades Vol. 2 687
Rainbow: Live Between the Eyes 603
Raindance: The Experience of Light and Celebration 488
Rainforest, The 870
Rainforest for Children Series, The 640
Raining Stones 166
Rainmaker, The 260
Rainmaker 384
Rains Came, The 384
Raintree County 384
Rainy Day Magic Show 670
Raise the Red Lantern 118
Raised Catholic (Can You Tell?) 535
Raisin in the Sun (Glover) 454
Raisin in the Sun (Poitier) 454
Raising Arizona 441
Raising Face: A Menstrual Journey 861
Raising Heroes 464
Rake's Progress, The 584
Raku Ceramics with James Romberg 564
Ralph Ellison: The Self-Taught Writer 306
Ralph Kirkpatrick Plays Bach 593
Ralph's Arm 436
Ram Dass: Aging and Awakening the Potential of Change 853
Ram Dass: Facing Death 853
Rambam Cures the King/Uncle Pinchey Comes Home 115
Rambert Dance Company— Soldat & Pulcinella 574
Ramble to Cashel: Celtic Fingerstyle Guitar 204, 605
Ramble to Cashel: Celtic Fingerstyle Guitar 204, 605
Rambling Rose 243
Ramona 436
Rampage 243
Ramparts We Watch 763
Ramrod 295
Ran 142, 314
Rancho Deluxe 295
Random Harvest 384
Randy Rides Alone 295
Range Feud/Two Fisted Law, The 295
Ranma 1/2 Anything Goes, Special Collector's Boxed Set 741
Ranma 1/2 Anything Goes Vol. 1: Darling Charlotte 740
Ranma 1/2 Anything Goes Vol. 2: It's Fast or It's Free 740
Ranma 1/2 Anything Goes Vol. 3: Cat-Fu Fighting 740
Ranma 1/2 Anything Goes Vol. 4: Chestnuts Roasting on an Open Fire 740
Ranma 1/2 Anything Goes Vol. 5: Cold Competition 740
Ranma 1/2 Anything Goes Vol. 6: The Breaking Point 741
Ranma 1/2 Anything Goes Vol. 7: Fowl Play 741
Ranma 1/2 Anything Goes Vol. 8: The Evil Wakes 741
Ranma 1/2 Anything Goes Vol. 9: Goodbye "Girl-Type" 741
Ranma 1/2 Anything Goes Vol. 10: Tough Cookies 741
Ranma 1/2 Anything Goes Vol. 11: Ranma and Juliet 741
Ranma 1/2 Collector's Edition Vol. 1 741
Ranma 1/2 Collector's Edition Vol. 2 741
Ranma 1/2 Collector's Edition Vol. 3 741
Ranma 1/2 Collector's Edition Vol. 4 741
Ranma 1/2 Collector's Edition Vol. 5 741
Ranma 1/2 Collector's Edition Vol. 6 741
Ranma 1/2 Collector's Edition: The OAV's Vol. 1 741
Ranma 1/2 Collector's Edition: The OAV's Vol. 2 741
Ranma 1/2 Hard Battle Vol. 1: Ukyo Can Cook 741
Ranma 1/2 Hard Battle Vol. 2: Dim Sum Darling 741
Ranma 1/2 Hard Battle Vol. 3: Dharma Chameleon 741
Ranma 1/2 Hard Battle Vol. 4: Once Upon a Time in Jusenkyo 741
Ranma 1/2 Hard Battle Vol. 5: Pretty Womanhood 741
Ranma 1/2 Hard Battle Vol. 6: Suddenly Sasuke 741
Ranma 1/2 Hard Battle Vol. 7: Melancholy Baby 741
Ranma 1/2 Hard Battle Vol. 8: Back to Happosai 741
Ranma 1/2 Hard Battle Vol. 9: Da-Doo Ling-Ling, Lung-Lung 741
Ranma 1/2 Hard Battle Vol. 10: Smells Like Evil Spirit 742
Ranma 1/2 Hard Battle Vol. 11: Soap Gets in Your Eyes 742
Ranma 1/2 Hard Battle Vol. 12: Mirror Mirror 742
Ranma 1/2 Movie #1: Big Trouble in Nekonron China 742
Ranma 1/2 Movie #2: Nihao My Concubine 742
Ranma 1/2 OAV #1: Desperately Seeking Shampoo 742
Ranma 1/2 OAV #2: Like Water for Ranma 742
Ranma 1/2 OAV #3: Akane and Her Sisters 742
Ranma 1/2 OAV #4: An Akane to Remember 742
Ranma 1/2 OAV #5: One Grew over the Kuno's Nest 742
Ranma 1/2 OAV #6: Faster Kasumi, Kill! Kill! 742
Ranma 1/2 Outta Control: My Fiance, The Cat 742
Ranma 1/2 TV Series Vol. 1 742
Ranma 1/2 TV Series Vol. 2 742
Ranma 1/2 TV Series Vol. 3 742
Ranma 1/2 TV Series Vol. 4 742
Ranma 1/2 TV Series Vol. 5 742
Ranma 1/2 TV Series Vol. 6 742
Ranma 1/2 TV Series Vol. 7 742
Ranma 1/2 TV Series Vol. 8 742
Ranma 1/2 TV Series Vol. 9 742
Ranma 1/2: Immortal Kombat 742
Ransom 243
Ranson's Folly 403
Raoni 60
Raoul Dufy: Painter and Decorator 555
Raoul Wallenberg: Between the Lines 776
Rap Master Ronnie: A Report Card 535
Raped by an Angel (aka Naked Killer 2) 131
Raphael 555
Raphael Series 555
Rappaccini's Daughter 301
Rappin' 328
Rapture, The 243
Rapture of Being: Pir Vilayat Inayat Khan 792
Raptures of the Deep 436
Rapunzel, Rapunzel 648
Rare Black Short Subjects 448
Rare Breed, The 295
Rare Chaplin 408
Rare Dutch and Belgian Experimental Program 31, 488
Rascals and Robbers— The Secret Adventures of Tom Sawyer and Huck Finn 309
Rashomon 142
Rasputin and the Empress 384
Rasputin: Dark Servant of Destiny 88, 163
Rasputin: The Mad Monk 528
Rat 476
Rat Fink a Boo-Boo 509
Ratboy 243
Rat's Tale, A 665
Rauschenberg: Man at Work 555
Raven, The 403, 528
Raven (Le Corbeau), The 25
Raven Tengu Kabuto 742
Ravioli 673
Raw Deal 384
Rawhide 295
Ray Bradbury: An American Icon 306
Ray Bremser: The Jazz Poems 306
Ray Harryhausen Compilation 715
Raymonda (Bolshoi/Bessmertnova) 575
Raymonda (Bolshoi/Semenyaka) 575
Razor's Edge, The 243, 384
Razor—Sword of Justice, The 138
Razor—The Snare, The 139
Razor—Who's Got the Gold, The 139
Reaching for the Moon 403
Reader's Digest Children's Classics 648
Reader's Digest: Great Splendors of the World 831

Ready to Wear (Pret-a-Porter) 254
Reagan's Way 811
Reagan Years 811
Real Blonde, The 436
Real Charlotte, The 195
Real Estate Show, The 555
Real Glory 384
Real Las Vegas, The 763
Real Life 280
Real Malcolm X, The 454
Real Men 243
Real Patsy Cline, The 605
Real Richard Nixon, The 763
Real Sanctuary 805
Real Soulja 533
Real Stories of Capone, Dillinger and Bonnie & Clyde, The 796
Real Story Videos Series, The 656
Real Weegee, The 559
Real West, The 299
Real World Reunion: Inside Out, The 421
Real World: Vacations, The 421
Reality and Hallucinations 555
Reality Bites 280
Really Strange Stories of the Totally Unknown 509
Realm of the Alligator 822
Realms of the Russian Bear 88
Reap the Wild Wind 355
Rear Window 352
Reason to Believe, A 243
Reasonable Doubt 798
Rebecca 163, 352
Rebecca of Sunnybrook Farm 328
Rebel Flight to Cuba 70
Rebel Without a Cause 347
Rebellion of the Santos 555
Reboot: Talent Night 701
Reboot: The Great Brain Robbery 701
Recent Readings/NY 307
Rechenka's Eggs 640
Reckless 195, 280, 384
Reckless Way, The 384
Record of a Living Being 142
Record of a Tenement Gentleman 144
Record of Lodoss War, Gift Box 743
Record of Lodoss War, Volume 1 870
Record of Lodoss War Vol. 1 742
Record of Lodoss War Vol. 2 742
Record of Lodoss War Vol. 3 742
Record of Lodoss War Vol. 4 743
Record of Lodoss War Vol. 5 743
Record of Lodoss War Vol. 6 743
Recovering the Soul: A Scientific and Spiritual Search 853
Recsk 1953 Documentary of a Hungarian Secret Labor Camp ..103
Rector's Wife, The 196
Red 96, 509
Red and the Black, The 23
Red and the White, The 102
Red Badge of Courage 349
Red Ball Express 384
Red Balloon 23, 640
Red Balloon/White Mane 23, 640
Red Baron 796
Red Beard 142
Red Bull Division: 34th Infantry Division 763
Red Cherry 117
Red Circle, The 186
Red Corner 244
Red Desert 36
Red Dust 384
Red Dwarf 196
Red Earth 102
Red Empire 88
Red Firecracker Green Firecracker 117
Red Green's of Cars and Men 421, 843
Red Grooms and "Fat Feet" 488, 555
Red Grooms Talks about Dali Salad 555
Red Hawk 743
Red Headed Woman 280
Red Hot + Country 605
Red House 528
Red Inn (L'Auberge Rouge), The 17
Red Is Green: Jud Fine 555
Red Italy 436
Red Kimono 403
Red Kiss 6
Red Lanterns 105
Red Lion 139
Red Menace, The 384
Red Nightmare 509
Red Planet Mars 499
Red Pony 384
Red Ribbons 464
Red Riding Hood 649
Red River 342
Red Rock West 244
Red Shoes 181, 575, 649
Red Signals 403
Red Sorghum 118
Red Squirrel, The 45
Red Star Rising: The Dawn of the Gorbachev Era 88
Red Sun 295
Red Tent, The 83
Red to Kill 123
Red Zone 131
Red-Headed League, The 186
Redhead from Wyoming, The 295
Rediscovering a Forgotten Legacy 555
Rediscovering America 763
Redlands 436
Reds 244
Redwood Curtain 244
Reed Royalty 614
Reed: Mexico Insurgente 52
Reefer Madness 509
Reet, Petite and Gone 448
Ref, The 280
Reflecting Skin 244
Reflections in a Forest 853
Reflections in a Golden Eye 349
Reflections in the Dark 244
Reflections: A Moment in Time 464
Reflejos Latinos 673
Regard for the Planet 805
Regarding Henry 244
Regeneration 403
Reggae Beach Rock, Vol. II 603
Reggae Go-Go Style Dirty Dancing, Vol. III 603
Reggie Mixes In 403
Regina 244
Regression in Time 115
Reilly: The Ace of Spies 196
Reilly: The Ace of Spies Series 196
Reincarnation of Golden Lotus, The 117
Reincarnation of Isabel, The 528
Reincarnation of Khensur Rinpoche, The 149
Reir, Jugar, Hablar 673
Reivers, The 384
Relax 853
Reliability and Risk: Computers and Nuclear War 806
Relic, The 528
Religion and Culture in China 135
Religions of the World 871
Reluctant Astronaut, The 280
Reluctant Debutante, The 280
Reluctant Dragon, The 694
Reluctant Muse, The 476
Remains of the Day 259
Rembetiko 105
Rembrandt—1669 ....31, 555
Rembrandt and Velazquez: Two Faces of the Seventeenth Century 555
Rembrandt Laughing 441
Rembrandt's Beret 640
Remedy for Riches 384
Remember Pearl Harbor 771
Remember the Night 280
Remembering Edward Weston 559
Remembering Jacqueline du Pre 593
Remembering Marilyn 338
Remembering the Summer of Love and Other Songs 622
Remi Lange—Omelette 8
Remington & AVA: American Art 555
Reminiscences of a Journey to Lithuania 443
Remote Control 76
Ren & Stimpy in Disguise 701
Ren & Stimpy on Duty 701
Ren & Stimpy Vol. 1: The Classics 701
Ren & Stimpy Vol. 2: The Stupidest Stories 701
Ren & Stimpy Vol. 3: The Stinkiest Stories 701
Ren & Stimpy: As Stinky As They Wanna Be 701
Ren & Stimpy: Classics II 701
Ren & Stimpy: Essential Collection 701
Ren & Stimpy: Incredibly Stupid Stories 701
Ren & Stimpy: More Stinky Stories 701
Ren & Stimpy: Nothing But Shorts 701
Ren & Stimpy: Stinky Little Christmas 701
Renaissance Masters Vol. 1 871
Renaissance Masters Vol. 2 871
Renata Scotto in Concert 599
Renata Scotto: Prima Donna in Recital 599
Renata Tebaldi Live! 599
Renata Tebaldi/Louis Quilico: Concerto Italiano 584
Rendevous in Paris 14
Rendez Vous 6
Rendez-Moi Ma Peau 6
Rendezvous d'Anna 30
Rene Clair 25
Renee Rosnes: Jazz Pianist 614
Renegade Force 743
Renoir Silent Shorts 26
Rented Lips 280
Repercussions: A Celebration of African-American Music 454
Replacement Killers, The 244
Repo Man 436
Report from Iraq 111
Report from the Aleutians 771
Report on the Party and the Guests, A 101
Report to the Commissioner 244
Reproduction of Life 837
Reptile, The 528
Reptile Mind 436
Reptilicus 499
Republic Pictures Story, The 338
Republican Party, 1960-1992, The 763
Repulsion 98
Requiem (Webber) 599
Requiem for a Faith 149
Requiem for a Heavyweight (1962) 384
Requiem for Mozart, A 599
Rescue Party 640
Rescue/The Romans, The 201
Rescuers, The 694
Rescuers: Stories of Courage— Two Women 477, 776
Rescuers: Stories of Courage— Two Women 477, 776
Rescuing Baby Whales 822
Reservoir Dogs 441
Resident Alien 436, 464
Resident Patient, The 186
Residents: Freak Show, The 871
Residents: Twenty Twisted Questions, The 622
Resistance 206
Respectful Prostitute 23
Restoration 244
Resurrection 244
Resurrection of the Daleks 201
Retreat, Hell! 384
Return, The 115
Return of a Man Called Horse, The 295
Return of Boston Blackie, The 403
Return of Chandu, The 528
Return of Chandu (The Magician), The 539
Return of Dr. Mabuse (The Phantom Meets the Return of Dr. Mabuse) 528
Return of Dracula, The 528
Return of Frank James, The 72
Return of Jafar, The 694
Return of Martin Guerre 6
Return of Peter Grimm, The 384
Return of Superfly, The 533
Return of the Blind Dead 528
Return of the Borrowers, The 640
Return of the Dinosaurs 743
Return of the Fly 499
Return of the Giant Majin 509
Return of the Goddess for the New Millennium 567
Return of the Great Whale 822
Return of the Jedi, The 500
Return of the King 687
Return of the Maya 60
Return of the Musketeers, The 184
Return of the Native, The 163
Return of the Pilot (Un Pilota Ritorna) 39
Return of the Pink Panther 354
Return of the Rat 154
Return of the Sand Fairy, The 665
Return of the Scorcher 843
Return of the Seven 295
Return of the Tall Blond Man with One Black Shoe 17
Return of the Vampire 528
Return of the Wolves 822
Return of Ulysses, The 584
Return of Video Yesterbloop, The 540
Return to Aguacayo 60
Return to Iwo Jima 771
Return to My Shtetl Delatyn 115
Return to Paradise 384
Return to Peyton Place 384
Return to Salem's Lot 528
Return to Snowy River 207
Return to the Jewish Ghetto of Venice 115
Return to the Sacred Hoop 788
Return to the Snow Zone 828
Returning, The 123
Reunion in France 384
Rev. Clay Evans: I'm Going Through 608
Rev. Ernest Davis, Jr., and the Wilmington Chester Mass Choir: "He's Preparing Me" 608
Rev. F.C. Barnes and Co. 608
Rev. James Cleveland and the L.A. Gospel Messengers 608
Revelations 509
Revenge of the Amazons/Metal Madam 436
Revenge of the Bee Girls 509
Revenge of the Creature 528
Revenge of the Creature/The Creature Walks Among Us 528
Revenge of the Cybermen 201
Revenge of the Pink Panther 354
Revenge of the Tai-Chi Master 131
Reversal of Fortune 16
Revitalize Your Body 853
Revolt of Mother 301
Revolt of the Fishermen 83
Revolt of the Slaves 42
Revolt of the Zombies 528
Revolutionary War, The 763
RG Veda, Part 1 743
RG Veda, Part 2 743
Rhapsody 384
Rhapsody in August 142
Rhapsody Pathetique 594
Rhea Gall Force 743
Rhinoskin: The Making of a Movie Star 464
Rhodes 153, 196
Rhodes of Africa 177
Rhonda Abrams: Lament of the Sugar Bush Man 806
Rhapsody in Blue 328
Rhythm of Resistance 603
Rhythm Thief 436
Rhythms of Haiti 55
Rhythms of the World Anthology 603
Rhythm on the Range 328
Rhythm on the River 328
Riane Eisler: Reclaiming Our Past, Recreating our Future: Reflections 853
Ribos Operation, The 201
Ricardo Montalban's South America 60
Rich and Strange 352
Rich Boy, Poor Boy 145, 464
Rich in Love 244
Rich Kids 280
Rich Little—One's a Crowd 535
Rich Little's Christmas Carol 535

Rich Little's Robin Hood 421
Rich, Young and Pretty 328
Richard Avedon: Darkness and Light 559
Richard Burton's Hamlet 314
Richard III 163, 314
Richard Lester 338, 488
Richard Lewis—I'm Exhausted 535
Richard M. Nixon Remembered 796
Richard M. Nixon: His Life and Times 796
Richard Nanes in Recital in Moscow and Kiev 594
Richard Nanes—The Holocaust Symphony No. 3 594
Richard Nixon— Checkers, Old Glory, Resignation 796
Richard Nixon Reflects 796
Richard Nixon: Man and President 796
Richard Pousette-Dart: Thinking with the Brush 556
Richard Pryor Live! In Concert 535
Richard Pryor: Live & Smokin' 535
Richard Scarry Series 656
Richard Strauss: Arabella 584
Richard Strauss: Three Tone Poems 871
Richard Wagner Edition—Bayreuth Fest 584
Richard Wilbur 307
Richard Wright: Writing Is His Weapon 307
Rick Danko's Electric Bass Techniques 624
Rick Grundy Chorale 608
Rick Prol: Facing the Critics 556
Ricochet 244
Riddance 102
Riddle of the Dead Sea Scrolls, The 792
Ride 'Em Cowboy—Abbott and Costello 280
Ride Him Cowboy 295
Ride in the Whirlwind 443
Ride the High Country 347
Ride the Wild Surf 509
Ride the Wind 421
Riders of Death Valley 539
Riders of the Desert 295
Riders of the Purple Sage 295, 403
Riders of the Range/Storm over Wyoming 295
Ridicule 6
Riding Bean 743
Riding for Life 403
Riding High 351
Riding on Air 280
Riding the Rails: The American Experience 843
Riding the Waves: Andre Emmerich on Art 556
Rien Que les Heures 28
Riff Raff 166
Riffraff 384
Rififi 23
Rifleman, The 421
Rift 244
Right Human Relations 806
Right Stuff, The 244
Right to Remain Silent, The 280
Righteous Enemy, The 776
Righting Wrongs (aka Above the Law) 131
Rights & Wrongs: Human Rights in the World Today 806
Rights of Passage (1919-1920), The 763
Rigoletto (Gobbi) 585
Rigoletto (Miller) 585
Rigoletto (Pavarotti) 585
Rigoletto at Verona 585
Rikisha-Man 139
Rikki-Tikki-Tavi 687
Rikyu 141
Rime of the Ancient Mariner 314, 715, 718
Ring, The 352
Ring Cycle 585
Ring of Bright Water 665
Ringo Starr and His All-Starr Band 622
Rings Around the World 640
Rio Bravo 342
Rio Conchos 295
Rio Grande 340
Rio Lobo 342
Rio Rita 280
Riot in Cell Block 11 384
Rip Van Winkle 403, 640, 715
Ripe 244
Ripping Yarns 199
Riptide 385
Rise and Fall of Adolf Hitler (Films for the Humanities), The 771
Rise and Fall of Adolf Hitler (History Channel), The 771
Rise and Fall of Legs Diamond, The 385
Rise of Catherine the Great, The 177
Rise of Louis XIV, The 39
Rising Damp, Collection Set 1 196
Rising Damp, Collection Set 2 196
Rising Sun 244
Risk 436
Risky Business 280, 403
Rita Hayworth's Champagne Safari 338
Rita McKeough: An Excavation 556
Rites of Passion 509
Ritual, The 78
Ritual: Three Portraits of Jewish Life 115
Ritz 280, 464
Rivals: Capone vs. Ness 763
Rivals: J.F.K. vs. Khruschev 763, 798
Rivals: Karloff vs. Lugosi 338
Rivals: King vs. Wallace 763
Rivals: Manson vs. Bugliosi 763
Rivals: Monroe vs. Mansfield 338
River, The 26, 244
River and The Plow That Broke the Plains, The 477
River Niger 446
River of Grass 436
River of No Return 295
River of Stone: The Powell Expedition 822
River of the Red Ape 828
River of Unrest (Ourselves Alone) 177
River Runs Through It, A 244
River That Harms 806
River Wild, The 244
Riverdance—The Show 204, 575
Riverdance: A Journey 204, 575
Riverdance: Live from New York City 575
Rivers of France 29, 831
Road Agent 385
Road Home, The 666
Road House 385
Road to Ancient Egypt 871
Road to Ancient Greece 871
Road to Ancient Rome 871
Road to Bali, The 281
Road to Collector's Set, The 281
Road to Freedom: The Vernon Johns Story, The 454
Road to God Knows Where, The 622
Road to Hong Kong, The 281
Road to Independence, A 99
Road to Life 83
Road to Morocco, The 281
Road to Rio, The 281
Road to Rome/Thunderbolt 771
Road to Ruin 436
Road to Singapore, The 281
Road to the South 353
Road to the Stamping Ground 575
Road to Utopia, The 281
Road to Wannsee: Eleven Million Sentenced to Death, The 776
Road to Wellville, The 281
Road to Yesterday 355
Road to Zanzibar, The 281
Road Warrior 207
Road Warriors 131
Roadracers 436
Roadrunner & Wile E. Coyote's Crash Course 687
Roadrunner & Wile E. Coyote: The Scrapes of Wrath 687
Roadrunner Clown of the Desert/Punk Puffins and Hard Rock (BBC Wildlife Special) 822
Roadrunner vs. Wile E. Coyote: If at First You Don't Succeed 687
Roadside Prophets 436
Roadsinger 436
Roar of the Gods, The 556
Roar of the Vietnamese, The 123
Roaring Road, The 403
Roaring Twenties 385
Rob Roy 244
Robbie Burkett: A Line of Balance 314
Robe, The 356
Robert Altman's Jazz '34: Remembering Kansas City Swing 614
Robert Ashley: Perfect Lives 585
Robert Cahen: L'Invitation au Voyage/Juste le Temps 488
Robert Coles: Teacher 477
Robert Colescott: The One-Two Punch 454, 556
Robert Creeley 307
Robert Creeley: 70th Birthday Reading 307
Robert E. Lee 780
Robert Kennedy and His Times 798
Robert Klein 535
Robert Mapplethorpe: An Overview 871
Robert Mitchum: The Reluctant Star 338
Robert Motherwell and the New York School; Storming the Citadel 556
Robert Parker 556
Robert Ripley: Believe It or Not 509
Robert Schumann: Piano Concerto in A Minor, Op. 54; Pyotr Ilyich Tchaikovsky: Piano Concerto No. 1 in B Flat Minor, Op. 23 594
Robert Vickrey: Lyrical Realist 556
Robert Winter's Crazy for Ragtime 871
Roberto Devereux 585
Robin and Marian 163
Robin and the 7 Hoods 328
Robin Hood, Prince of Thieves 244
Robin Hood 403, 673, 694
Robin Hood: The Movie 244
Robin Williamson in Concert 204
Robinson Crusoe 403
Robinson Crusoe of Clipper Island 539
Robo Vampire 131
Robocop 499
Robot 201
Robot Monster 499
Robotech II: The Sentinels 744
Robotech Macross LD #2 744
Robotech Macross LD #3 744
Robotech Macross LD #4 744
Robotech Macross LD #5 744
Robotech Macross LD #6 744
Robotech Macross LD #7 744
Robotech Macross LD #8 744
Robotech Macross LD #9 744
Robotech Perfect Collection Macross Vol. 1 744
Robotech Perfect Collection Macross Vol. 2 744
Robotech Perfect Collection Macross Vol. 3 744
Robotech Perfect Collection Macross Vol. 4 744
Robotech Perfect Collection Macross Vol. 5 744
Robotech Perfect Collection Macross Vol. 6 744
Robotech Perfect Collection Macross Vol. 7 744
Robotech Perfect Collection Mospeada Vol. 1 744
Robotech Perfect Collection Mospeada Vol. 2 744
Robotech Perfect Collection Mospeada Vol. 3 744
Robotech Perfect Collection Mospeada Vol. 4 744
Robotech Perfect Collection Mospeada Vol. 5 744
Robotech Perfect Collection Mospeada Vol. 6 744
Robotech Perfect Collection Mospeada Vol. 7 744
Robotech Perfect Collection Southern Cross Vol. 1 744
Robotech Perfect Collection Southern Cross Vol. 2 744
Robotech Perfect Collection Southern Cross Vol. 3 744
Robotech Perfect Collection Southern Cross Vol. 4 744
Robotech Perfect Collection Southern Cross Vol. 5 744
Robotech Perfect Collection Southern Cross Vol. 6 744
Robotech Perfect Collection Southern Cross Vol. 7 744
Robotech Vol. 1 743
Robotech Vol. 2 743
Robotech Vol. 3 743
Robotech Vol. 4 743
Robotech Vol. 5 743
Robotech Vol. 6 743
Robotech Vol. 7 743
Robotech Vol. 8 743
Robotech Vol. 9 743
Robotech Vol. 10 743
Robotech Vol. 11 743
Robotech Vol. 12 743
Robotech Vol. 13 743
Robotech Vol. 14 743
Robotech Vol. 15 743
Robotech Vol. 16 743
Robotech Vol. 17 743
Robotech Vol. 18 743
Robotech Vol. 19 743
Robotech Vol. 20 743
Robotech Vol. 21 743
Robotech Vol. 22 743
Robotech Vol. 23 743
Robotech Vol. 24 743
Robotech Vol. 25 743
Robotech Vol. 26 743
Robotech Vol. 27 743
Robotech Vol. 28 743
Robotech Vol. 29 743
Robotech Vol. 30 743
Robotech Vol. 31 743
Robotech Vol. 32 743
Robotech Vol. 33 743
Robotech Vol. 34 744
Robotech Vol. 35 744
Robotech Vol. 36 744
Robotech Vol. 37 744
Robotech Vol. 38 744
Robotech Vol. 39 744
Robotech Vol. 40 744
Robotech Vol. 41 744
Robotech Vol. 42 744
Robots of Death, The 201
Rocco and His Brothers 39
Rock, Baby, Rock It 509
Rock 'n' Roll Mobster Girls 509
Rock 'n' Roll High School 328
Rock, Rock, Rock 622
Rock, The 244
Rock and Roll Rhythm Guitar 624
Rock Hudson's Home Movies 465, 477
Rock in the UK 622
Rock-A-Doodle 687
Rockers—It's Dangerous 603
Rocket Gibraltar 245
Rocket Men, The 843
Rocket Movie, The 567
Rocketship Reel, The 715
Rocketship X-M 499
Rockies by Rail, The 843
Rockin' Ronnie 281
Rocko's Modern Life: Machine Madness 701
Rocko's Modern Life: Modern Love 701
Rocko's Modern Life: Rocko's Modern Christmas 701
Rocko's Modern Life: With Friends Like These… 701
Rockroots 622
Rocky Horror Picture Show 509
Rocky Mountain National Park 831
Rodan 499
Rodgers and Hammerstein: The Sound of Movies 338
Rodney King Case: What the Jury Saw in California 454
Rodney's Wonder Window 871
Rodrigo D: No Future 52
Rodrigo: Concierto de Aranjuez Pepe Romero 594
Rodrigue: A Man & His Dog 477
Rodrigue: Acadian Artist 556
Roe vs. Wade 421
Roger & Me 477
Rogopag 10, 37, 39, 41
Rogue Male 177
Roland Reiss 556
Role of the Assistant Editor, The 318
Role of the Script Supervisor, The 318
Roll of the Thunder 640
Rolling Stones—25 x 5: The Continuing Adventures of the Rolling Stones 622
Rolling Stones Rock & Roll Circus, The 622
Rolling Thunder 771
Rolling Thunder: Healer of Meta Tantay 788
Rolling Thunder: The Unity of Man and Nature 853
Roman Holiday 344
Roman Scandals 328
Roman Spring of Mrs. Stone 385
Romance 385
Romance in a Minor Key 70

Romance of a People: The First 100 Years of Jewish Life in Chicago: 1833-1933 115
Romance of Dance, The 575
Romance of Happy Valley 413
Romance of the Wasteland 295, 403
Romance on the High Seas 328
Romance with a Double Bass 199
Romancing the Classics 843
Romanesque Art 556
Romantic Age, The 177
Romantic Road 73
Romany Trail, Part I, The 603
Romany Trail, Part II, The 603
Romare Bearden: Visual Jazz 454, 556
Rome '78 488
Rome, The Eternal City 43
Rome 43
Rome Adventure 385
Romeo, Juliet and Darkness (Sweet Light in a Dark Room) 100
Romeo and Juliet (Bolshoi Ballet 1975) 575
Romeo and Juliet (Bolshoi Ballet) 575
Romeo and Juliet (Laurence Harvey) 314
Romeo and Juliet (Nureyev) 575
Romeo and Juliet (Preljocaj) 575
Romeo and Juliet (Ulanova) 575
Romeo and Juliet (Zeffirelli) 314
Romeo and Juliet 350, 871
Romeo Is Bleeding 245
Romero 52
Rommel—The Desert Fox 771
Romola 403
Romper Room: Ask Miss Molly 656
Romper Room: Kimble's Birthday 656
Romper Room: Outta Space 656
Romper Stomper 207
Romulus and Remus 42
Ron Carter & Art Farmer: Live at Sweet Basil 614
Ron Carter Live: Double Bass 615
Ron English 556
Ron Reagan Is the President's Son/The New Homeowner's Guide to Happiness 535
Roof 38
Rookie, The 257
Room, The 254
Room at the Top 177
Room with a View 259
Roommates 281
Root into Europe 196
Roots, Rock, Reggae 603
Roots, The 52
Roots 454
Roots and Wings: A Jewish Congregation 792
Roots of Democracy (1700s), The 811
Roots of Gospel 608
Roots of Rhythm 60, 603
Roots Search 744
Roots: The Gift 454
Roots: The Next Generation 454
Rope 352
Ropin' Fool, With Will Rogers, The 281
Rorret 34
Rory Story, The 640
Rosa Luxemburg 65
Rosalie 328
Rosalie Goes Shopping 65
Rosalyn Tureck at the Teatro Colon 594
Rosalyn Tureck Plays Bach: Goldberg Variations 594
Rosamond Bernier: The Metropolitan Museum of Art Lecture Series 556
Rose, The 245
Rose 123
Rose Bowl Story, The 385
Rose for Emily, A 301
Rose Marie (1936) 328
Rose Marie (1954) 328
Rose of Washington Square 328
Rose Tattoo, The 314
Roseanna McCoy 385
Rosebud 245
Roseland 259
Rosemary Clooney's Demi-Centennial 618
Rosemary's Baby 98
Rosemary Twig 94
Rosencrantz & Guildenstern Are Dead 301
Rosenschontz: The Teddy Bears' Jamboree 656
Roses in December 60, 477
Rosewood 446
Rosie's Walk and Other Stories 656
Ross McElwee Films 477
Rossini 328
Rossini's Ghost 640
Rossini: La Cenerentola (Cinderella) 585
Rotten Truth, The 806
Rotund World of Botero, The 556
Rouge 123
Rough and the Smooth (Portrait of a Sinner), The 177
Rough Magic 245
Rough Night in Jericho 295
Rough Riders 245
Roujin Z 744
Round Midnight 11
Round Trip 861
Round Up 102
Rounders, The 385
Roustabout 537
Route 66 831
Route 66 Collection, The 831
Routes of Exile: A Moroccan Jewish Odyssey 115
Rover Dangerfield 715
Rowan Atkinson Live 196
Roxaboxen 641
Roxanne 281
Roy Ayers Live 615
Roy Cohn/Jack Smith 442
Roy Lichtenstein 556
Roy Lichtenstein: Reflections 556
Roy Rogers 338
Roy Rogers Show, Vol. 2 421
Roy Rogers Show, Vol. 4 421
Roy Rogers Show, Vol. 5 421
Roy Rogers Show, Vol. 6 421
Royal Affair, A 17
Royal Ballet in Tchaikovsky's The Sleeping Beauty, The 575
Royal Bed 385
Royal Castle in Warsaw 99
Royal Collection Set, The 170
Royal Deceit 245
Royal Family at War 170
Royal Federal Blues— The Black Civil War Soldiers 454, 780
Royal Opera House 585
Royal Scandal, A 196
Royal Secrets 763
Royal Tramp 131
Royal Tramp II 131
Royal Warriors 131
Royal Wedding 328
Royal Wedding: H.R.H. the Prince Andrew and Miss Sarah Ferguson 170
Royal Windsor and Eton 170
Royal Windsor Style, The 170
Rrrecords "Testament" Vol. II 622
RSW In Video 603
Rubber Tires 403
Ruben Blades 60
Rubin & Ed 245
Rubinstein Remembered 594
Ruby in Paradise 436
Rude 211
Rude: Rudy Ray Moore 535
Rudolf Arnheim: A Life in Art 556
Rudolf Nureyev 575
Rudolf Serkin Performs Beethoven 594
Rudolph & Frosty's Christmas in July 641, 701
Rudolph's Shiny New Year 641, 701
Rudolph the Red Nosed Reindeer 641, 701
Rudy Burckhardt 488, 559
Ruggero Raimondi 599
Ruggles of Red Gap 281
Rugrats—Mommy Mania 641, 701
Rugrats: A Baby's Gotta Do What a Baby's Gotta Do 641, 701
Rugrats: A Rugrats Chanukah 641, 702
Rugrats: A Rugrats Passover 641, 702
Rugrats: A Rugrats Vacation 641, 702
Rugrats: Angelica the Divine 641, 702
Rugrats: Bedtime Bash 641, 702
Rugrats: Chuckie the Brave 641, 702
Rugrats: Diapered Duo 641, 702
Rugrats: Dr. Tommy Pickles 641, 702
Rugrats: Grandpa's Favorite Stories 641, 702
Rugrats: Phil & Lil—Double Trouble 641, 702
Rugrats: Return of Reptar 641, 702
Rugrats: Tales from the Crib 641, 702
Rugrats Thanksgiving, A 641, 701
Rugrats: The Santa Experience 641, 702
Rugrats: Tommy Troubles 641, 702
Ruin Explorers 744
Rules of the Game 26
Ruling Class, The 184
Rumble Fish 260
Rumble in Hong Kong 134
Rumble in the Bronx 134
Rumik World: Firetripper 745
Rumik World: Maris the Chojo 745
Rumik World: Mermaid Forest 745
Rumik World: The Laughing Target 745
Rumpole of the Bailey 196
Run and Kill 131
Run for the Dream: The Gail Devers Story 245, 454
Run for Your Money 385
Run of the Country, The 202
Run Silent Run Deep 771
Run Tiger Run 123
Runaway 661
Runaway Blues 123
Runaway Bus, The 177
Runaway Ralph 641
Runaway Train 84
Runner, The 107
Runnin' Kind 436
Running Away 34
Running Fence 477, 556
Running on Empty 245
Running out of Luck 622
Running Scared 245
Rupan III: Legend of the Gold of Babylon 745
Rupan III: The Fuma Conspiracy 745
Rupert— Caring and Sharing with Friends 641
Rupert 641
Rupert and the Runaway Dragon 641
Rusalka 585
Rush 245
Rush to Burn, The 806
Russ Forster, USA, 1995, 92 mins. 618
Russ Meyer's Up! 513
Russ Meyer: The Vixen Collection 513
Russia House, The 245
Russia's War: Blood upon the Snow 763
Russia: Then & Now 88, 831
Russian Ballet: The Glorious Tradition, Vol. 1 575
Russian Ballet: The Glorious Tradition, Vol. 2 575
Russian Ballet: The Glorious Tradition, Vol. 3 575
Russian Folk and Dance 575
Russian Language, The 155
Russian People: Revolution and Evolution 88
Russian-German War, The 772
Ruth Heller's Nature Stories 641
Rutles: All You Need Is Cash, The 199
Ruy Blas 23
Ryan's Daughter 180

S

S.A.S.: The Soldier's Story 763
S.O.B. 354
S.O.S. Coastguard 539
S.O.S. Titanic 843
Sabaka (The Hindu) 528
Sabbath Bride, The 115
Sabda and Sombra a Sombra 488
Sabicas: El Maestro de Flamenco 48
Sabotage 352
Saboteur 352
Sabrina 281, 346
Sacco and Vanzetti 34
Sacred and Secular: The Aerial Photography of Marilyn Bridges 871
Sacred Art of Tibet/The Visible Compendium, The 149, 718
Sacred Cargo 245
Sacred Mountain/White Flame 70
Sacred Passions 853
Sacred Sex: A Guide to Intimacy and Loving 853
Sacred Sites: Prehistoric Monuments of Europe 785
Sacred Trances in Bali and Java 575
Sacrifice, The 84
Sadako 641
Sadat 111
Sadie Thompson 403
Sadist, The 528
Sadko 585
Sadma 148
Safe 436
Safe Passage 245
Safer Encounter (Encuentro sin Riesgo) 834
Safety in Numbers 436
Saga of World War II Boxed Set, The 772
Sagebrush Trail 295
Sahara 772
Saheb 148
Saigon: Year of the Cat 166
Sailing Along 184
Sailor Moon Vol. 1: A Moon Star Is Born 745
Sailor Moon Vol. 2: Scouts Unite! 745
Sailor Moon Vol. 3: Evil Eyes 745
Sailor Who Fell from Grace with the Sea 163
Sailor-Made Man, A 410
Sails and Sailors: J Boats '37 828
Saint, The 177, 196
Saint Clara 108
Saint Gaudens: Masque of the Golden Bowl 556
Saint Joan 385
Saint of Fort Washington, The 245
Saint-Ex 163
Saints and Sinners 792
Saki Santorelli, Ed.D.: Responding to Stress 853
Salamanca— The Heart of Spain's Golden Age 48
Salamandre: Chateaux of the Loire 29
Salem, Massachusetts Antique Federal/Victorian Renovation 566
Salem's Lot: The Movie 528
Salesman 477
Sallah 108
Sally of the Sawdust 413
Salmonberries 65, 465
Salo: 120 Days of Sodom 37
Salome (Ewing/Hall) 585
Salome (Malfitano/Weigl) 585
Salome (Stratas/Boehm) 585
Salome 385, 403
Salome and Queen Elizabeth 403
Salome Where She Danced 296
Salsa 61
Salt of the Earth 385, 871
Salut Cousin 8, 116
Salut d'Artiste (Salute the Artist) 18
Salvador 245
Sam Francis: Another Quick Look 556
Sam Kinison: Family Entertainment Hour 535
Sam Kinison: Why Did We Laugh? 536
Samadhi and Other Films 488
Samar 385
Same Stuff, Different Day 834
Sammy and Other Songs from Getting to Know Myself 656
Sammy and Rosie Get Laid 166
Sammy Davis Jr. 338
Samson & Sally: The Song of the Whales 666, 715
Samson 42, 97
Samson and Delilah 355
Samson and the 7 Miracles of the World 42
Samson et Dalila 585
Samson vs. the Vampire Women 528
Samurai 509

Samurai Assassin 139
Samurai Banners 139
Samurai I 139
Samurai II 139
Samurai III 139
Samurai Rebellion 139
Samurai Shodown: The Motion Picture 745
Samurai Trilogy: Complete Set 139
San Antonio 296
San Francisco 385
San Francisco and Its Environs 871
San Francisco Earthquake 822
San Francisco Sound 622
San Simeon: Hearst's Castle 831
Sanatan Dharma: Pilgrimage to the Source of Eternal Wisdom 149
Sand and Blood 8
Sand Fairy, The 666
Sand Pebbles 385
Sandbaggers, The 196
Sanders of the River 448
Sandlot, The 666
Sandokan and the Pirates of Malaysia 42
Sandra of a Thousand Delights 39
Sands of Iwo Jima, The 772
Sandstorm in the Gulf 111
Sanjuro 142
Sankofa 446
Sans Soleil 10
Sanshiro Sugata 142
Sansho the Bailiff 143
Santa Claus 796
Santa Claus and the Magic Drum 641
Santa Claus: The Movie 666
Santa Fe Trail 385
Santa Fe: Artists of New Mexico 556, 788
Santa Sangre 52
Santa Tapes, The 477
Saphead, The 409
Saps at Sea 281
Sara Hornbacher Early Works 488
Saraband 170
Saragossa Manuscript, The 94
Sarah, Plain and Tall 641, 666
Sarah and the Squirrel 666
Sarah's House 94
Sarah Vaughan: The Divine One 615
Saratoga 281
Saratoga Trunk 385
Sartre by Himself (Sartre par Lui Meme) 6
SAT/Analogies 858
SAT/Reading Comprehension 858
Satan in High Heels 509
Satan Met a Lady 385
Satan's Brew 66
Satan's Harvest 245
Satanic Rites of Dracula, The 177, 528
Satanika 745
Satellite Imaging: The Jet Propulsion Laboratory 840
Satellite Rescue in Space: Shuttle Flights 41C & 51A 840
Satie and Suzanne: The Passion of a Lifetime 594
Satori 853
Saturday Night, Sunday Morning: The Travels of Gatemouth Moore 608, 615
Saturday Night and Sunday Morning 177
Saturday Night Entertainment 536
Saturday Night Fever 245
Saturday Night Kid, The 403
Satyajit Ray's Apu Trilogy 148
Sauna 94
Savage and Beautiful 822
Savage Capitalism 54
Savage Eye, The 385
Savage Garden, The 837
Savage Nights 6, 465
Savage Skies 822
Savage Wilderness 296
Savage Woman, The 211
Savages 259
Savannah, Georgia Victorian Row House 566
Savannah Smiles 641
Save Our Planet 806
Save the Earth: A How-To Video 806
Save the Planet 806
Save the Tiger 245
Saviors of the Forest 823
Saviour of the Soul 123
Saviour of the Soul II 123
Savoniha: A Siberian 88
Sawdust and Tinsel 78
Sawmill and Dome Doctor 411
Saxophone Colossus 615
Say Amen, Somebody 608
Say Anything… 281
Say Goodbye to the President 798
Say It by Signing 155
Saying Kaddish 116
Sayonara 385
Scalphunters, The 296
Scamp (Strange Affection), The 178
Scandal 142
Scandal in Bohemia, A 186
Scandal Man 6
Scanners 212
Scar (Hollow Triumph), The 385
Scar of Shame 448
Scaramouche 385
Scare Game, The 528
Scarecrow 83, 245
Scared Stiff 281, 528
Scared to Death 528
Scarface: The Shame of a Nation 342
Scarlet and the Black, The 245
Scarlet Car 403
Scarlet Dawn 385
Scarlet Empress 348
Scarlet Letter, The 301, 385
Scarlet Letter— Westinghouse Studio One, The 422
Scarlet Pimpernel, The 245, 385
Scarlet Street 72
Scene of the Crime 6, 344
Scenes from a Marriage 78
Scenes from the Class Struggle in Beverly Hills 281
Scenes from the Life of Andy Warhol 443
Scenes from the Surreal 715
Scenic Route, The 436
Scenic Seattle 831
Scenic Wonders of America 831
Scent of a Woman (Profumo di Donna) 34
Scent of a Woman 245
Scent of Green Papaya, The 6, 145
Scharnhorst, Part 1: The Early Years, The 772
Schimmelstein 715
Schindler (The True Story) 776
Schindler 776
Schindler's List 245, 258
Schlessinger Teen Health Video Series, The 861
Schmidt: My Song Goes Round the World (Ein Lied Geht Um die Welt) 599
Scholastic Productions 641
School Daze 447
School for Scandal 314
School for Scoundrels 184
School of Assassins 61
School Ties 245
Schoolhouse Rock: America Rock 702
Schoolhouse Rock: Grammar Rock 702
Schoolhouse Rock: Multiplication Rock 702
Schoolhouse Rock: Science Rock 702
Schramm 65, 510
Schreck 528
Schubert—Klassix 13 594
Schubert: The Greatest Love and the Greatest Sorrow 594
Schubert: The Trout 594
Schwartzkopf Four-Pack, The 763
Sci-Fi Files, The 499
Science in Action 837
Science Primer 837
Scientific Visualization 715
Scooby's All Star Laff-A-Lympics: Heavens to Hilarity 702
Scooby's All Star Laff-A-Lympics: On Your Marks, Get Set—Go Scoobys! 702
Scooby's All Star Laff-A-Lympics: Something Smells Really Rotten 702
Scooby's All Star Laff-A-Lympics: Yippee for the Yogi Yahooeys! 702
Scooby-Doo and a Mummy Too 702
Scooby-Doo Goes Hollywood 702
Scooby-Doo in Arabian Nights 702
Scooby-Doo on Zombie Island 702
Scooby-Doo: A Gaggle of Galloping Ghosts 702
Scooby-Doo: A Halloween Hassle at Dracula's Castle 702
Scooby-Doo: Foul Play in Funland 702
Scooby-Doo: Mystery Mask Mix-Up 702
Scooby-Doo: Nutcracker Scoob 702
Scooby-Doo: That's Snow Ghost 702
Scooby-Doo: The Haunted House Hang-Up 702
Scooby-Doo: The Headless Horseman of Halloween 702
Scooby-Doo: Wedding Bell Boos 702
Scooby-Doo: Which Witch Is Which? 702
Score 465, 510
Scoring Films: Bernard Herrmann 338, 618
Scoring Films: Marvin Hamlisch 338, 618
Scotch & Wry 196
Scotland the Brave 170
Scotland Yard 170
Scotland Yard's Chamber of Crime 170
Scotland: World of Difference 170
Scott of the Antarctic 178
Scott Russell Sanders: Lannan Literary Video No. 63 307
Scoundrel, The 95
Scrambled Feet 536
Scrapping Chemical Weapons 806
Scream, Blacula, Scream 533
Scream 2 528
Scream 528
Scream and Scream Again 528
Scream of Fear 528
Scream of the Demon Lover 529
Scream of the Wolf 529
Screaming Skull, The 529
Screening Middlemarch 197
Script to Screen 318
Scrooge 178
Scrooged 281
Scuffy the Tugboat and Friends 641
Sculptress, The 163
Sculpture and the Creative Process 564
Sculpture of Spaces, The 556
Scum of the Earth 510
Sea Chase 385
Sea Devils, The 201
Sea Dream 641
Sea Fury 385
Sea Hawk 385
Sea of Galilee 111
Sea of Grass 296
Sea of Love 245
Sea of Sand 178
Sea Otter Story: Warm Hearts and Cold Water, A 823
Sea Power: A Global Journey 843
Sea Root 123
Sea Shall Not Have Them, The 178
Sea Turtles: Ancient Nomads (National Audubon) 823
Sea Wolf, The 386
Sea Wolf 245
Sea Wolves, The 163
Seabert: Good Guys Wear White 641
Seaflight/Windflight 828
Seagull 83
Seal Morning 641
Sealed Soil (Khak-e Sar Beh Morh), The 107
Seaman No. 7 131
Seamus Heaney 204
Sean Connery Collection, The 169
Seance on a Wet Afternoon 178
Seapower 844
Search and Destroy 246
Search for Ancient Americans, The 788
Search for Bridey Murphy, The 386
Search for Haunted Hollywood, The 338
Search for One-Eye Jimmy, The 436
Search for Robert Johnson, The 615
Search for the Titanic 844
Searchers, The 340
Searching for Bobby Fischer 246
Season of Fear 246
Season of the Witch 529
Season on the Water 641
Seasons and Holidays Around the World 641
Seasons of the Heart 831
SeaWings 844
Sebastian 77, 465
Sebastiane 168
Sebastiao Salgado 560
Second Awakening of Christa Klages, The 65
Second Chance, A 641
Second Chorus 328
Second Circle 83
Second Coming, The 465
Second Coming of Science, The 862
Second Face, The 386
Second Fiddle 328
Second Stain, The 186
Second Timothy Leary Tape, The 853
Second Woman 386
Second Youth 94
Seconds 386
Secret Adventures of Tom Thumb, The 715
Secret Agent, The 163
Secret Agent 352
Secret Agent Man 197
Secret Beyond the Door 72
Secret Detective 94
Secret Diary of Sigmund Freud 281
Secret Egypt: A Trance Journey 111
Secret Garden, The 96
Secret Garden (1949), The 666
Secret Garden (1987), The 666
Secret Garden (1993), The 666
Secret Garden (1994), The 666, 715
Secret Gardens of Ireland, The 204
Secret Honor 254
Secret Life of Adolf Hitler 772
Secret Life of Walter Mitty, The 281
Secret Mission 178
Secret Obsession 6
Secret of Blue Water, Vol. 1: The Adventure Begins, The 745
Secret of My Success, The 281
Secret of Nikola Tesla, The 103
Secret of NIMH, The 687
Secret of Roan Inish, The 440
Secret of Santa Vittoria, The 386
Secret of the Monastery 79
Secret of the Seal, The 666, 715
Secret of the Telegian 499
Secret Places 163
Secret Service, The 763
Secret Space, A 116
Secret War of Harry Frigg, The 281
Secret Weapons 801
Secret World of Alex Mack: In the Nick of Time, The 642
Secret World of Erotic Art 556
Secret World of the CIA 806
Secrets 246
Secrets and Lies 166
Secrets of a Soul 71
Secrets of Alcatraz 763
Secrets of EuroMassage 853
Secrets of Female Sexual Ecstacy 853
Secrets of Love, Classics of Erotic Literature: Vol. 1 510
Secrets of Love, Classics of Erotic Literature: Vol. 2 510
Secrets of Love, Classics of Erotic Literature: Vol. 3 510
Secrets of Love, Classics of Erotic Literature: Vol. 4 510
Secrets of Love, Classics of Erotic Literature: Vol. 5 510
Secrets of Love, Classics of Erotic Literature: Vol. 6 510
Secrets of Science: Our Sea and Sky 806
Secrets of Self-Pleasuring and Mutual Masturbation, The 855
Secrets of the Bay 806
Secrets of the Code 837
Secrets of the Desert Sea 823

Secrets of the Lost Empires Gift Set 785
Secrets of the Mummy 785
Secrets of the Night 403
Secrets of the Psychics 861
Secrets of the Rock: Return to Alcatraz 763
Secrets of the Titanic 844
Secrets of the Unknown 422
Secrets of the Warrior's Power, The 828
Secrets of Women 78
Secrets of Writing the College Admission Essay 858
Secular Meditation 150
Seduced and Abandoned 41
Seducer's Diary (Le Journal du Seducteur), The 6
Seduction of Mimi, The 34
Seduction: The Cruel Woman 65, 465
See for Yourself 488
See How They Grow 670
See No Evil, Hear No Evil 281
Seeding of a Ghost 131
Seeds of Death, The 201
Seeds of Destiny 477
Seeds of Discord (1933-1936) 772
Seeds of Doom, Parts 1 & 2 201
Seeing Red 477
Seeking God: The Way of the Monk at the Monastery of Christ in the Desert 792
Segovia at Los Olivos 594
Segovia Legacy, The 594
Segovia: The Song of the Guitar 594
Seiji Ozawa: Boston Symphony Orchestra 594
Seiji Ozawa: Russian Night 594
Seize the Day 246
Selected Shorts #2 403
Selena 61, 328
Self and Society 853
Self and Universe 853
Self Defense with Pressure Points 853
Self-Defense for Children 853
Self-Help Stress Reduction 853
Self-Made Hero, A 8
Semi-Gods and Semi-Devils 131
Semi-Tough 281
Semiramide 585
Senator Was Indiscreet, The 281
Send Me No Flowers 281
Senechal the Magnificent 18
Sensational Nightingales: Ministry in Song, The 608
Sensations 328
Sense and Sensibility 163, 301
Senso 39
Sensual Escape 510
Sentinels of Silence: The Ruins of Ancient Mexico 61
Separate But Equal 454
Separate Peace 246
Sepharad: Judeo-Spanish Music 116, 603
Sepia Cinderella 448
September 1939 211
September 289
September 30, 1995 246
September Affair 386
Serebrier Conducts Prokofiev 594
Serenade 328
Serenade in the Mist 123
Serendipity, The Pink Dragon 715
Sergeant Rutledge 340
Sergeant York 342
Serial Collection, The 539
Serial Mom 514
Serious About Pleasure 18
Serpent and the Rainbow 529
Serpent's Egg 78
Serpico 246
Sesame Songs 656
Sesame Street Home Video Visits 656
Sesame Street Kids' Guide to Life: Learning to Share 656
Sesame Street Kids' Guide to Life: Telling the Truth 656
Sesame Street Presents: Follow That Bird! 657
Sesame Street Specials 657
Sesame Street Start to Read Books 657
Sesame Street: Big Bird Sings! 657
Sesame Street: Do the Alphabet 657
Sesame Street: Elmo Saves Christmas 657
Sesame Street: Elmocize 657
Sesame Street: Plaza Sesamo 673
Sesame Street: Quiet Time 657
Sesame Street: Sing Yourself Sillier at the Movies 657
Sesame Street: Slimey's World Games 657
Set It Off 246
Seth Phenomena, The 853
Setting the Stage 318
Seurat: Point Counterpoint 556
Severf 246
Seven Beauties 34
Seven Brides for Seven Brothers 328
Seven Candles for Kwanzaa 454, 642
Seven Chances 409
Seven Days Ashore/Hurry, Charlie, Hurry 281
Seven Days in May 386
Seven Days in Paris 123
Seven Deadly Sins, The 585
Seven Deadly Sins 6, 39
Seven Faces of Dr. Lao 386
Seven Hills of Rome 328
Seven Little Foys 282
Seven Madmen (Los Siete Locos), The 52
Seven Ninja Kids 131
Seven Samurai 142
Seven Signs of Christ's Return 792
Seven Sinners (Doomed Cargo) 178
Seven Sinners 386
Seven Spiritual Laws of Success: A Practical Guide to the Fulfillment of Our Dreams, The 853
Seven Thieves 282
Seven Warriors 131
Seven Women 340
Seven Wonders of the Ancient World 785
Seven Year Itch 346
Seven Years Bad Luck 411
Seven Years in Tibet 16, 178
Seven Years Itch 123
Seventh Continent, The 74
Seventh Cross, The 386
Seventh Curse, The 123
Seventh Dawn, The 386
Seventh Heaven 403
Seventh Seal, The 78
Seventh Veil, The 178
Severo Sarduy 61
Sevillanas 46
Seville: Jewel of Andalusia 48
Sex, Drugs, Rock & Roll 437
Sex, Drugs and Democracy 437
sex, lies and videotape 443
Sex 403
Sex and Buttered Popcorn 338
Sex and Justice 763
Sex and the College Girl 510
Sex and the Single Girl 282
Sex and Zen 123
Sex and Zen II, Parts A & B 123
Sex and Zen III 123
Sex Education Films of the 40's 510
Sex in the Comics 541
Sex in the Soviet Union 88
Sex Is… 465, 477
Sex Is Sex 436, 477
Sex Madness 510
Sex of the Stars, The 213
Sexmission 94
Sextette 282
Sextoons: An Erotic Animation Festival 715
Sexual Harassment 861
Sexual Life of the Belgians, The 29
Sexual Positions for Lovers 853
Sexy & Dangerous 123
Sgt. Bilko 282
Sgt. Kabukiman, N.Y.P.D. 510
Sgt. Pepper's Lonely Heart's Club Band 328
Shada 201
Shades of Black 465
Shades of Fear 163
Shadey 163
Shadow, The 178
Shadow Catcher: Edward S. Curtis and the North American Indian, The 788
Shadow Ninja 131
Shadow of a Doubt 353
Shadow of Angels 66
Shadow of China 139
Shadow of Chinatown (The Yellow Phantom) 539
Shadow of Silk Lennox, The 386
Shadow of the Eagle, The 386
Shadow of the Thin Man 282
Shadow on the Sun 197
Shadow Skill 745
Shadow Skill Part 2 745
Shadow Strikes, The 510
Shadow You Soon Will Be, A 52
Shadowlands 163
Shadows 403, 440
Shadows and Fog 289
Shadows of Forgotten Ancestors 84
Shady Grove: Old Time Music from North Carolina, Kentucky & Virginia—featuring Kilby Snow, Dock Boggs, Tommy Jarrell & Roscoe Holcomb 615
Shaft 533
Shaft in Africa 533
Shaft's Big Score 533
Shag 510
Shaggy D.A., The 694
Shaggy Dog, The 694
Shake a Lizard Tail, Or Rust Belt Rump 510
Shake Hands with the Devil 529
Shakers, The 783
Shakers in America, The 783
Shakespeare by the English Theater Company 314
Shakespeare Collection, The 871
Shakespeare Dance Trilogy 575
Shakespeare's Globe Theater Restored: Much Ado About Something 314
Shakespeare's Macbeth 871
Shakespeare Vol. 1: The Twelfth Night 715
Shakespeare Vol. 2: A Midsummer Night's Dream 715
Shakespeare Vol. 3: Romeo and Juliet 715
Shakespeare Vol. 4: Hamlet 715
Shakespeare Vol. 5: The Tempest 715
Shakespeare Vol. 6: Macbeth 715
Shakiest Gun in the West, The 282
Shalako 296
Shall We Dance? 139, 328
Shallow Grave 163
Shalom of Safed 556
Shalom Sesame 673
Shalom Shabat 116
Shalom—Songs of Polish Jews 113
Shame, The 78
Shame (Not Wanted) 386
Shame (The Intruder) 514
Shame of the Jungle 715
Shameless Old Lady, The 23
Shampoo 282
Shamrock and the Rose, The 403
Shamu & You 642
Shane 343
Shanghai 1920 123
Shanghai Express 131, 348
Shanghai Gesture, The 348
Shanghai Grand 131
Shanghai Triad 118
Shanty Tramp 510
Shaolin Avengers 131
Shaolin Chun Hop Kuen 854
Shaolin Collection 131
Shaolin Fighting Crane Kung-fu 854
Shaolin Kung-Fu Kids 132
Shaolin Northern Tiger Kung-fu 854
Shaolin Sabre 854
Shape of the World Set 837
Shape Up 575
Shari Lewis: 101 Things for Kids to Do 657
Shari Lewis: Don't Wake Your Mom 657
Shari Lewis: Kooky Classics 657
Shari Lewis: Lamb Chop in the Haunted Studio 657
Sharing the Joy of Nature 854
Shark Attack Files 823
Shark Bait 823
Sharks of the Red Triangle 823
Sharks: Predators or Prey? 823
Sharon, Lois & Bram's Elephant Show 657
Sharon Olds 307
Sharpe's Collection I 197
Sharpe's Collection II 197
Sharpe's Collection III 197
Sharpe's Collection IV 197
Sharpe: The Legend 197
Shatter 178, 443
Shatter Dead 529
Shattered 71, 246
Shattered Cross 52
Shattered Dreams 109, 477
Shattered Mirror, The 88
Shawshank Redemption, The 246
She (1911) 154
She (1925) 154
She 178, 386
She and He 139
She Beast (Revenge of the Blood Beast) 529
She Done Him Wrong 282
She Goes to War 403
She Must Be Seeing Things 437, 465
She's Gotta Have It 447
She's Safe 465
She's So Lovely 437
She's the One 437
She Shoulda Said No 510
She-Devils on Wheels 510
Sheba, Baby 533
Shedding Some Light 318
Sheep Has Five Legs 18
Sheer Madness 65
Sheik, The 404
Shell Seekers, The 246
Shelley Duvall's Bedtime Stories (Collection) 657
Shelley Duvall's Bedtime Stories: Aunt Ippy's Museum of Junk 657
Shelley Duvall's Bedtime Stories: Bootsie Barker Bites 657
Shelley Duvall's Bedtime Stories: Elbert's Bad Word and Weird Parents 657
Shelley Duvall's Bedtime Stories: Elizabeth and Larry and Bill and Pete 657
Shelley Duvall's Bedtime Stories: Little Toot and the Loch Ness Monster and Choo Choo 657
Shelley Duvall's Bedtime Stories: Moe the Dog in Tropical Paradise 657
Shelley Duvall's Bedtime Stories: My New Neighbors 657
Shelley Duvall's Bedtime Stories: The Christmas Witch 657
Shelley Duvall's Bedtime Stories: The Little Rabbit Who Wanted Red Wings 658
Shelley Duvall's Bedtime Stories: Tugford Wanted to be Bad 658
Shelley Duvall's Tall Tales and Legends 658
Shelly Manne Quartet 615
Sheltering Sky, The 35
Shenandoah 386
Shenandoah—The Gift 831
Shenandoah Valley of the Virginias 831
Sherlock Holmes' Greatest Cases 642
Sherlock Holmes and the Deadly Necklace 186
Sherlock Holmes and the Incident at Victoria Falls 186
Sherlock Holmes and the Secret Weapon 186
Sherlock Holmes and the Spider Woman 186
Sherlock Holmes Cliffhangers 642
Sherlock Holmes Spellbinders 642
Sherlock Hound: Dr. Watson, I Presume? 745
Sherlock Hound: Moriarty Unleashed 745
Sherlock Hound: Tales of Mystery 745
Sherlock Hound: The Dogs of Bowserville 745
Sherlock Hound: The White Cliffs of Rover 745
Sherlock the Undercover Dog 666
Sherman's March 477
Sherrill Milnes' Homage to Verdi 599
Sherrill Milnes: An All-Star Gala 599

Shiatsu Massage—Advanced 854
Shifting Sands 404
Shifting Sands: A History of the Middle East, The....111
Shiloh 666
Shindig! British Invasion, Vol. 1 622
Shindig! British Invasion, Vol. 2 622
Shindig! Frat Party 622
Shindig! Groovy Gals....622
Shindig! Jackie Wilson 622
Shindig! Jerry Lee Lewis....622
Shindig! Legends of Rock 'n' Roll 622
Shindig! Motor City Magic 622
Shindig! Sixties Superstars 622
Shindig! Soul 622
Shindig! The Kinks 622
Shindig! The Righteous Brothers....622
Shine 207
Shining, The 256
Shining Flower 871
Shining Hour 386
Ship Ahoy 328
Ship Comes In, A 404
Ship of Fools....386
Ship of Lost Men, The 71
Ships of the Night 404
Ships with Wings....178
Shipwreck Island....666
Shipwreck! 844
Shirley Temple and Friends 282
Shirley Temple's Baby Burlesks 282
Shirley Temple's Sing and Dance Along....338
Shirley Temple Scrapbook....338
Shirley Valentine....163
Shirley Verret....599
Shiv'a....108
Shivers....212
Shoah....477, 776
Shock....386, 404
Shock Cinema Volumes 1-4 529
Shock Corridor....341
Shock of Futurism, The....556
Shock Out with Metro Media 603
Shodo, The Path of Writing....561
Shoes of the Fisherman....356
Shoeshine....38
Shogun....144, 422
Shogun and Little Kitchen....132
Shonan Bakusozoku: Bomber Bikers of Shonan 745
Shoot the Moon....246
Shoot the Piano Player 15
Shoot to Kill 52
Shoot to Thrill 338
Shooting....443
Shooting Africa....153
Shooting Party, The 83
Shootist, The....296
Shop Around the Corner, The....345
Shop on Main Street, The....101
Shopping....163
Shopworn Angel, The 386
Shore Leave....404
Short Animations by Larry Jordan 718
Short Cinema Journal, Issue #3 437
Short Cuts 254
Short Films of D.W. Griffith—Volume 1, The....413
Short Films of D.W. Griffith—Volume 2, The....413
Short Films of D.W. Griffith—Volume 3, The....413
Short Films of D.W. Griffith—Volume 4, The....413
Short Films of Mary Pickford, The 404
Short History of Nudity and a Short History of Love, A....854
Short Personal Films by Seven West Coast Women 437
Short Subject Potpouri 477
Shoscombe Old Place 186
Shot in the Dark, A....354
Shotguns and Accordions....61
Shout, The....97
Show Boat (1936) 328
Show Boat (1951) 328
Show of Force 246
Show People 404
Show Promos 2 540
Show Promos 540
Show Them No Mercy....386
Show-Off, The....404
Showdown 296
Showdown at Lonesome Pellet 642
Showgirls 246
Shree 420 148
Shriek in the Night....386
Shtetl: A Journal of the Holocaust....777
Shuhei Takahashi, Japan, 1993 870
Shurtleff on Acting 318
Shut My Big Mouth....282
Shuten Doji—The Star Hand Kid 1 745
Shuten Doji—The Star Hand Kid 2 745
Shuten Doji—The Star Hand Kid 3 745
Shuten Doji—The Star Hand Kid 4 745
Shvitz! My Yiddisheh Workout....116
Shy People....84
Si o No? 61
Siberiade 84
Sicilian, The....246
Sideburns 83
Sidewalks of London 178
Sidewalks of New York....409
Sidney Lumet: From Theater to Film....315, 338
Siege 108
Siegfried & Roy: Masters of the Impossible....702
Siegfried 72, 94, 585
Siena: Chronicles of a Medieval Commune 783
Siesta 246
Sights and Sounds of South America, The....61
Sign for Friends, The....670
Sign of Four (Brett), The....187
Sign of Four (Richardson), The 187
Sign of the Cross 355
Sign Songs: Fun Songs to Sign and Sing....658
Signal 7....437
Signals Through the Flames....315
Signs of Life 67, 246
Silas Marner 197, 642
Silence....78
Silence of Neto, The 52
Silence of the Lambs, The....255
Silence of the North....246
Silence=Death 65, 465
Silences of the Palace....116
Silent Enemy, The....211
Silent Era Trailers 540
"Silent" Mr. Sherlock Holmes, The....187
Silent Mouse....642
Silent Movie....282
Silent Night with Jose Carreras 600
Silent Partner, The....211
Silent Pioneers....465, 477
Silent Running....499
Silent Service, The 745
Silent Service: The Story of Submarine Warfare in the Pacific, The....772
Silent Tongue....260
Silent Touch, The 94
Silent Victory....772
Silent Witness....792
Silk Husbands and Calico Wives....404
Silk Road, The 139
Silk Road I, Set 2, The....136
Silk Road I: An Ancient World of Adventure, The 135
Silk Road II, The....136
Silk Stockings 329
Silkwood 246
Silly Noisy House, A....871
Silly Tales and Tunes 670
Silver Blaze 187
Silver Fleet, The 772
Silver Horde, The 386
Silver Nemesis....201
Silver River 296
Silver Streak....282
Silver Theatre....422
Silverado....296
Silverlake Life: The View from Here....465
Simba....477
Similar Differences: Betye and Alison Saar....556
Simon and Garfunkel: The Concert in Central Park....622
Simon Boccanegra (Milnes) 585
Simon Boccanegra (Te Kanawa) 585
Simon Bolivar 61
Simon of the Desert 47
Simon the Lamb 658
Simon Wiesenthal: Freedom Is Not a Gift from Heaven 777
Simone de Beauvoir....6, 29
Simple and the Complex, The 786
Simple Story, A....6
Simply Magic: Episode 2....658
Simply Magic: The Rainy Day Adventure 658
Simpsons Cartoon Studio, The....871
Simpsons Christmas Special, The 702
Simultaneous....488
Sin of Harold Diddlebock 346, 410
Sin of Madelon Claudet, The....386
Sin You Sinners....529
Sinai Commandos....772
Sinatra....618
Sinbad and the Eye of the Tiger....666
Sindbad 102
Sinful Nuns of Saint Valentine, The....529
Sing 'n' Sign for Fun! 670
Sing-Along at Bubbe's....116
Sing-Alongs....670
Singapore 386
Singapore: Crossroads of Asia 145
Singin' in the Rain 329
Singing Blacksmith, The....113
Singing Detective, The....197
Singing Fool, The 329
Singing for Tin Ears....624
Singing French Songs for Children (Les Petits Chanteurs de Paris)....673
Singing Nun, The 329
Singing Princess 649
Singing Sculpture, The....556
Singing Stream: A Black Family Chronicle, A....642
Single Girl, A....6
Single Standard, The 404
Single White Female 16
Singles....282
Singleton's Pluck 164
Sinister Urge....515
Sins of Rachel....465
Sins of Rome 42
Sins of the Children....386
Sioux Legends 788
Sippie 615
Sir 148
Sir Arne's Treasure 77
Sir Drone 437
Sir Terence Conran 796
Siren....465
Sirens....207
Sirocco 386
Sister, Sister....246
Sister Act....282
Sister Act II: Back in the Habit....282
Sister My Sister....164
Sister Wendy in Conversation with Bill Moyers 556
Sister Wendy's Story of Painting....197, 556
Sisters, Or the Balance of Happiness....65
Sisters, The....386
Sisters & Friends: Winnebago Women's Stories 788
Sisters of Gion....143
Sitcom Seminars, The 318
Sites Unseen: Off the Beaten Track in Jerusalem 111
Sitting Bull....296
Situation Critical: The USS Forrestal 778
Six Degrees of Separation 246
Six Devil Women, The....132
Six Little Angels....792
Six Napoleons, The....187
Six O'Clock News 478
Six of a Kind....282
Six Short Films of Les Blank, 1960-1985....480
Six Shorts (Pam Payne)....437
Six Stories About Little Heroes....642
Six Wives of Henry VIII 197
Sixteen Fathoms Deep 386
Sixties Headlines 811
Skating Safe for Kids....670
Skin Game 353
Skinny Tiger and Fatty Dragon 132
Skirts Ahoy! 329
Skull, The 529
Sky Is Gray....446
Sky Pilot, The....404
Sky Pirates 207
Sky Raiders 539
Skyjacked 386
Skylark....666
Skyline....45
Skyscraper....404
Skyscraper Souls....386
SkyTrip America 872
Slacker....437
Slam Dance 455
Slapstick Encyclopedia....411
Slaughter's Big Ripoff....533
Slaughterhouse Five 246
Slave of the Sword....132
Slave Ship 454
Slave Trade in the World Today 510
Slaves in Bondage....510
Slaves of New York....259
Slaves of the Harvest 823
Slayers LD 1....746
Slayers LD 2....746
Slayers LD 3....746
Slayers LD 4....746
Slayers LD 5....746
Slayers LD 6....746
Slayers—The Motion Picture 746
Slayers Vol. 1: Episodes 1-4....745
Slayers Vol. 2: Episodes 5-7....746
Slayers Vol. 3: Episodes 8-10....746
Slayers Vol. 4: Episodes 11-13....746
Slayers Vol. 5: Episodes 14-16....746
Slayers Vol. 6: Episodes 17-19....746
Sleazemania....510
Sleazemania Strikes Back 510
Sleazemania: The Good, the Bad and the Sleazy 510
Sleazy Uncle, The....34
Sleep with Me 282
Sleeper 289
Sleepers....246
Sleeping Beauty (Bujones) 575
Sleeping Beauty (Kirov/Fedotov)....575
Sleeping Beauty (Kirov/HBO) 575
Sleeping Beauty (Kirov/Zaklinsky)....575
Sleeping Beauty (National Ballet of Canada)....575
Sleeping Beauty....694
Sleeping Beauty on Ice....575
Sleeping Car to Trieste 178
Sleeping Tiger....353
Sleeping with the Enemy 246
Sleepless in Seattle 282
Sleepy Eyes of Death— Sword of Adventure 139
Sleepy Eyes of Death— The Chinese Jade....139
Sleepy Eyes of Death—Full Circle Killing 139
Sleepy Eyes of Death—Sword of Fire....139
Slender Thread, The....387
Sleuth 315
Slickers vs. Killers....132
Slightly Honorable....387
Slim Hopes 861
Slime People....529
Sling Blade....437
Slingshot....77
Slip Casting 564
Slither....246
Slow Moves 441
Small Back Room, The 181
Small Change....15
Small Circle of Friends, A....247

Small Faces 164
Small Gauge Shotgun 488
Small Steps, Big Strides: The Black Experience in Hollywood 338, 454
Small Time 446
Small Town Girl 329
Small Wonders 478
Small World 823
Smallest Show on Earth 184
Smart One, The 557
Smash-Up: The Story of a Woman 387
Smashing of the Reich, The 772
Smile 247
Smile for Auntie and Other Stories 658
Smiles of a Summer Night 78
Smilin' Through 329, 387
Smilla's Sense of Snow 77
Smith Family Series 404
Smithereens 437
Smithsonian Air and Space, Dreams of Flight: Beyond the Moon... 840
Smithsonian Air and Space, Dreams of Flight: To the Moon 840
Smithsonian Jazz Series, The 615
Smithsonian's Great Battles of the Civil War 780
Smithsonian World 763, 837
Smithsonian World: Tales of Human Dawn 837
Smithsonian World: The Living Smithsonian 783
Smithsonian World: The Vever Affair 557
Smithsonian World: The Wyeths: A Father and His Family 557
Smithsonian World: Web of Life 837
Smithsonian World: Zoo 823
Smoke 247, 455, 666
Smoking Trail, The 296, 404
Smothering Dreams and Thousands Watch 488
Smouldering Fires 404
Smugglers 34
Snake in the Eagle's Shadow 134
Snake People (Isle of the Snake People), The 529
Snake Pit 387
Snake Style Kung-fu 854
Snakedance 201
Snapper, The 166
Snare Drum Rudiments with Pat Petrillo 624
Sneakin' and Peekin' 478
Snick Vol. 1: Nick Snicks Friendship 702
Snick Vol. 2: Nick Snicks the Family 702
Snow Country 139
Snow Creature, The 529
Snow Queen, The 649, 666, 716
Snow White 666
Snow White and the Seven Dwarfs 694
Snow White and the Three Stooges 282
Snow Wolves, The 823
Snowman, The 716
Snows of Kilimanjaro 387
Snowy River, The McGregor Saga: The Race 666
Snub Pollard... A Short But Funny Man 411
So Dear to My Heart 694
So Ends Our Night 387
So I've Heard, Vol. 1: Bach and Before 872
So I've Heard, Vol. 2: The Classical Ideal 872
So I've Heard, Vol. 3: Beethoven & Beyond 872
So Many Miracles 777
So Proudly We Hail 387
So This Is Paris 345
So Wrong They're Right 618
So You Wanna Get Laid 197
So You Want to Be An Actor 318
Soccer Poker 94
Social Sciences 127 481
Social Secretary, The 404
Sodom & Gomorrah 74
Sodom and Gomorrah 356
Sofie 77
Soft Skin, The 15
Sohryuden Vol. 1: Episodes 1 and 2 746
Sohryuden Vol. 2: Episodes 3 and 4 746
Sohryuden Vol. 3: Episodes 5 and 6 746
Sohryuden Vol. 4: Episodes 7 and 8 746
Sohryuden Vol. 5: Episodes 9 and 10 746
Sohryuden Vol. 6: Episodes 11 and 12 746
Sol Bianca 2 746
Sol Bianca 746
Solar Empire 840
Solaris 84
Sold for Marriage 404
Soldier Duroc... It's Your Party 6
Soldier of Fortune 387
Soldier's Home 301
Soldier's Story 301
Soldier's Tale, The 716
Soldier's Tale (L'Histoire du Soldat)/Symphony of Psalms, The ..600
Soldier's Tale 247
Soldiers of Music 594
Soldner: Thrown and Altered Clay 557
Soleri's Cities: Architecture for Planet Earth and Beyond 566
Solid Gold Cadillac, The 387
Solid Gold Illusion, Variations I, II and III 561
Solid Solutions: Rural Waste Confronts the Waste Crisis 806
Solitary Cyclist, The 187
Solitary Star: Zehava Ben 109
Solo 437
Solo Flight: The Genius of Charlie Christian, 1919-1942 615
Solo Tribute: Keith Jarrett 615
Solomon Northrup's Odyssey 454
Solovky Power 88
Solti: The Chicago Symphony Orchestra 594
Some Folks Call It a Sling Blade 437
Some Kind of Hero 247
Some Kind of Wonderful 247
Some Letters to a Young Poet 211
Some Like It Hot 346
Some Mother's Son 164
Some Mothers Do 'Ave 'Em! 197
Somebody up There Likes Me 387
Someone Behind the Door 7
Someone Else's America 103
Someone to Love 247
Someone to Watch over Me 247
Something Good (plus Mortimer) 642
Something in the Wind 387
Something New Out of Africa 153
Something Special 670
Something Strong Within 455, 478
Something to Sing About 207, 329, 465
Something to Talk About 247
Something Weird 510
Sometimes a Great Notion 247
Sometimes I Wonder 642
Somewhere I'll Find You 387
Somewhere in Sonora 296
Sommersby 247
Son of Ali Baba 387
Son of Dracula 529
Son of Frankenstein 529
Son of Fury 387
Son of Godzilla 499
Son of Hercules in the Land of Darkness 42
Son of Ingagi 448
Son of Kong 529
Son of Lassie 666
Son of Monsters on the March 529
Son of Monte Cristo 387
Son of Paleface 282
Son of the Morning Star 422
Son of the Shark 8
Son of the Sheik 404
Son of Video Yesterbloop 540
Son of Zorro 539
Son Son 55
Sondagsengler (The Other Side of Sunday) 77
Song for Ireland 204
Song Is Born 342
Song of Bernadette 356
Song of Ceylon 478
Song of China 117
Song of Love 387
Song of Survival 772
Song of the Birds: A Biography of Pablo Casals 594
Song of the Exile 136
Song of the Holy Land 792
Song of the Islands 329
Song of the Siren 108
Song of the Thin Man 282
Song Spinner 666
Song to Remember, A 329
Song Without End 350
Songs and Dance by Slask (Slask Tanczy i Spiewa) 99
Songs of a Wayfarer/Songs on the Death of Children—Mahler 600
Songs of Mexico: Placido Domingo: Volume 1 600
Songs of the Civil War 780
Songwriter 257
Sonia Sanchez 61
Sonic Outlaws 478
Sonic Soldier Borgman 1: Last Battle 746
Sonic Soldier Borgman 2: Lover's Rain 746
Sonny Rollins Live at Loren 615
Sonny Terry & Brownie McGhee: Red River Blues 1948-1974 615
Sonny Terry: Whoopin' the Blues 1958-1974 615
Sons of Bwiregi 153
Sons of Katie Elder 296
Sons of the Desert 282
Sontaran Experiment/The Genesis of the Daleks, The 201
Sophie's Choice 247
Sophie's Place 718
Sorcerer 247
Sorceress, The 600
Sorceress (1956), The 23
Sorceress 7
Sorority Babes in the Dance-a-thon of Death 510
Sorrow and the Pity 16
Sorrow: The Nazi Legacy 777
Sorrowful Jones 282
Sorrows of Satan 413
Sorry, Wrong Number 387
Sosua 777
Soto, A New Vision of the Art 557
Sotto... Sotto 34
Soul 786
Soul Brothers of Kung Fu 533
Soul Food 247, 446
Soul in the Hole 437
Soul of the Beast 404
Soul Survivor 247
Soul Vengeance 533
FSoul-Fire 404
Souls at Sea 387
Sound?? 615
Sound and the Silence, The 247
Sound Around 642
Sound of Music, The 329
Sound Toys 872
Sounder 666
Sounds of Mexico, The 61
Sousa to Satchmo: Wynton on the Jazz Band 624
South Africa—The Black Red War 153
South Americans in Cordoba 783
South Central 446
South of St. Louis 296
South Pacific (London Sessions) 600
South Pacific 329
South Park 422
South Park Vol. 1 703
South Park Vol. 2 703
South Park Vol. 3 703
South Riding 178
South Sea Adventures 478
Southern California 831
Southern Yankee, A 282
Southerner, The 26
Souvenir 211
Soviet Armed Forces (I Serve the Soviet Union) 88
Soviet Army Chorus, Band and Dance Ensemble 575
Soviet Athletes—Summer Sports 828
Soviet Athletes—The Gymnasts 828
Soviet Athletes—Winter Sports 828
Soviet Bedtime Stories— Films for Children 642
Soviet Mind, The 89
Soviet School Day: Styles in Soviet Education 89
Soviet Secret Archives 89
Soviet Spy 7
Soviet War Stories from World War II 772
Soviets on Soviet Jewry 89
Soylent Green 500
Space Adventure Cobra 746
Space Age Program 840
Space Angel Vol. 1 703
Space Angel Vol. 2 703
Space Battleship Yamato 746
Space Battleship Yamato: The New Voyage 746
Space Case 642
Space Dreaming 840
Space Goofs 703
Space Is the Place 615
Space Jam 687
Space Patrol 500
Space Race 840
Space Shuttle, The 840
Space Shuttle: Flights STS-1 Through STS-8 840
Space Warriors 746
Space Warriors Baldios 746
Space: A Visual History Manned Flight 872
Spaceketeers 746
Spaceship Earth: Our Global Environment 806
Spacetime Visualization 845
Spain: Everything Under the Sun 48
Spanish Cartoon Classics 673
Spanish Civil War 48
Spanish Club: Fiesta! 61, 673
Spanish Club: Los Animales! 61, 673
Spanish Dancer, The 404
Spanish Earth 478
Spanish Emergency Lesson Plans: The Video 155
Spanish Folk Dances 575
Spanish Guitar, The 594
Spanish History— A Continent Conquered 48
Spanish History—The Heritage of Rome 48
Spanish Prisoner, The 437
Spanish Pronunciation Tutor 872
Spanish TV Commercials 48
Spanish TV Commercials—Volume 2 48
Spanking the Monkey 437
Sparkle 247
Sparrows 404
Spartacus (Bolshoi/Mukhamedov) 575
Spartacus (Bolshoi/Vasiliev) 575
Spartacus 154, 256
Spawn Edited Edition 703
Spawn of the North 387
Spawn—The Director's Cut 500
Spawn Uncut Collector's Edition 703
Speak Easily 409
Speak for Yourself: A Dynamic Vocal Workout 318
Speaking Directly 441
Speaking in Tongues 575
Speaking of Sex: It's More Than Just Talk 854
Speaking Parts 212
Speaking with Your Angels: A Guide 792
Spearhead from Space 201
Special British Comedy Boxed Set 184
Special Mission 94
Special of the Day 211
Special Police 9
Special Request 105
Speckled Band (Brett), The 187
Speckled Band (Massey), The 187
Speeches Collection, The 763
Speeches of Abraham Lincoln, The 780
Speeches of Adolf Hitler, The 772
Speeches of Famous Women: From Suffragette to Senator, The 796
Speeches of Franklin D. Roosevelt, The 763
Speeches of General Douglas MacArthur, The 796
Speeches of Gerald Ford, The 797
Speeches of Harry S. Truman, The 797
Speeches of Jimmy Carter, The 797
Speeches of John F. Kennedy, The 798
Speeches of Lyndon B. Johnson, The 797
Speeches of Martin Luther King, The 454
Speeches of Nelson Mandela, The 153
Speeches of Richard M. Nixon, The 797

Speeches of Robert F. Kennedy, The 798
Speeches of Ronald Reagan, The 797
Speeches of Winston Churchill, The 763
Speed 247
Speed Freaks with Guns 437
Speed Racer 703
Speed Racer Vol. 1: The Great Plan 747
Speed Racer Vol. 2: The Secret Engine 747
Speed Racer Vol. 3: The Fastest Car on Earth 747
Speed Racer Vol. 4: The Race Against Time 747
Speed Racer Vol. 5: Crash in the Jungle 747
Speed Racer Vol. 6: The Desperate Desert Race 747
Speed Racer Vol. 7: The Girl Daredevil 747
Speed Racer Vol. 8: The Royal Racer 747
Speed Racer Vol. 9: Challenge of the Masked Racer 747
Speed Racer Vol. 10: The Fire Race 747
Speed Racer Vol. 11: The Secret Invaders 747
Speed Racer Vol. 12: The Car with a Brain 747
Speed Racer: The Movie 747
Speed Reporter 387
Speed Spook 404
Speedway 537
Spencer Tracy Collection, The 387
Spencer Tracy Legacy, The 338
Spend It All 480
Spetters (Dubbed) 31
Spetters (Subtitled) 31
Sphere 247
Sphinx, The 387
Spices 148
Spider Baby 529
Spider Force 132
Spider's Stratagem, The 35
Spider Woman 132
Spider-Man: The Hobgoblin 703
Spiders 72
Spieler, The 404
Spies (Spione) 72
Spies Above 840
Spike & Mike's Festival of Animation Vol. 1 716
Spike & Mike's Festival of Animation Vol. 2 716
Spike & Mike's Festival of Animation Vol. 3 716
Spike & Mike's Sick & Twisted Festival of Animation Vol. 1 716
Spike & Mike's Sick & Twisted Festival of Animation Vol. 2 716
Spike & Mike's Sick & Twisted Festival of Animation Vol. 3 716
Spike Jones Story, The 618
Spinal Tap 872
Spinning Tops and Tickle Bops 670
Spinout 537
Spirit and Song: The 1997 North American Jewish Choral Festival 116
Spirit Lost 247
Spirit of Haida Guaii, The 557
Spirit of Mickey, The 694
Spirit of Samba 61
Spirit of St. Louis 346
Spirit of the Beehive 45
Spirit of the Mask, The 783
Spirit of Wonder: Miss China's Ring 747
Spirit of Youth 449
Spirit Rider 661
Spirits of the Dead 37
Spirits of the Rainforest 642
Spirituality and the Intellect 854
Spirituals in Concert 600
Spite Marriage 409
Spitfire 178
Spitfire Grill, The 437
Spitting Image: The Music Video 422
Splendor 387
Splendor in the Grass 387
Splendors of the Sea 823
Split Second 387
Split: Portrait of a Drag Queen 465
Spoiled Children 11
Spoilers, The 355, 387
Spontaneous Healing 854
Spook Busters 282
Spooks Run Wild 282
Spooky Stories 642
Spoonbill Swamp 642
Sports Illustrated 25th Anniversary Swimsuit Video 828
Sportsman Against His Will 94
Spot 673
Spot Goes to School 658
Spotlight Scandals 329
Spring Comes Again 132
Springfield Rifle 296
Springtime in the Rockies 329
Sprout Wings and Fly 480
Spruce Goose and RMS Queen Mary 844
Spy of Napoleon, A 178
Spy Smasher 539
Spy Who Came in from the Cold 387
Spy Who Loved Me, The 169
Spy with the Cold Nose, The 164
Spymaker: The Secret Life of Ian Fleming 307
Squanto: A Warrior's Tale 694
Square Shoulders 404
Squeal of Death 282
Squeeze 437
Squiggles, Dots and Lines 670
Sri Lanka: A Nation in Anguish 145
Ssssss 500
St. Benny the Dip 387
St. Charles Avenue: Mansions and Monarchs 831
St. Charles Streetcar 831
St. Elmo's Fire 247
St. John Passion 600
St. Martin's Lane 178
St. Matthew Passion 600
St. Michael Had a Rooster 35
St. Patrick's Cathedral, Dublin 204
St. Patrick: The Living Legend 204
St. Valentine's Day Massacre 514
Stage Door Canteen 387
Stage Fight Director, The 318
Stage Fright 353
Stage Sisters 117
Stagecoach 340
Stagefright 441
Stairway to Heaven 181
Stairway to the Mayan Gods 61
Stairways to the Gods: On the Trail of the Jaguar 61
Staking a Claim in Cyberspace 846
Stalag 17 346
Stalag Luft 178
Stalin 89
Stalin: By Those Who Knew Him 83
Stalingrad 65, 772
Stalker 84
Stalking the President 764
Stampede 296
Stan "Tex" Laurel Rides Again 411
Stan About Town 411
Stan Brakhage—Hand-Painted Films 488
Stan Brakhage Selected Films: Vol. 1 488
Stan Brakhage Selected Films: Vol. 2 488
Stan Getz: A Musical Odyssey 615
Stan Laurel: At the Beginning 411
Stan VanDerBeek: The Computer Generation 488
Stand, The 247
Stand and Deliver 61
Stand by Me 247
Stand Off 102
Stand Up and Cheer 329
Standards II: With Keith Jarrett 615
Stanislav Bunin in Tokyo 594
Stanislav Moniuszko— The Haunted Manor 99
Stanley and Iris 247
Stanley and Livingstone 388
Stanley Jordan: Magic Touch 615
Stanley on the Job 412
Stanley Turrentine: In Concert 615
Star, The 388
Star, The Castle and the Butterfly, The 116
Star 80 247
Star Blazers Volume 1 747
Star Blazers Volume 2 747
Star Blazers Volume 3 747
Star Blazers Volume 4 747
Star Blazers Volume 5 747
Star Blazers Volume 6 747
Star Blazers Volume 7 747
Star Blazers Volume 8 747
Star Blazers Volume 9 747
Star Blazers Volume 10 747
Star Blazers Volume 11 747
Star Blazers Volume 12 747
Star Blazers Volume 13 747
Star Blazers Volume 14 747
Star Blazers Volume 15 747
Star Blazers Volume 16 747
Star Blazers Volume 17 747
Star Blazers Volume 18 747
Star Blazers Volume 19 747
Star Blazers Volume 20 747
Star Blazers Volume 21 747
Star Blazers Volume 22 747
Star Blazers Volume 23 748
Star Blazers Volume 24 748
Star Blazers Volume 25 748
Star Blazers Volume 26 748
Star Blazers Volume 27 748
Star Blazers Volume 28 748
Star Blazers Volume 29 748
Star Blazers Volume 30 748
Star Blazers Volume 31 748
Star Blazers Volume 32 748
Star Blazers Volume 33 748
Star Blazers Volume 34 748
Star Blazers Volume 35 748
Star Blazers Volume 36 748
Star Blazers Volume 37 748
Star Blazers Volume 38 748
Star Blazers Volume 39 748
Star Child, The 642, 716
Star for Jeremy, A 642, 716
Star Is Born, A 329, 350, 388
Star Maker, The 34
Star Maps 437
Star Packer, The 296
Star Prince, The 404
Star Shorts 282
Star Spangled Rhythm 329
Star Trek Generations 500
Star Trek I: The Motion Picture 500
Star Trek II: Wrath of Khan 500
Star Trek III: Search for Spock 500
Star Trek IV: The Voyage Home (Director's Cut) 500
Star Trek IV: The Voyage Home 500
Star Trek V: The Final Frontier 500
Star Trek VI: The Undiscovered Country 500
Star Trek Volume 1 703
Star Trek Volume 2 703
Star Trek Volume 3 703
Star Trek Volume 4 703
Star Trek Volume 5 703
Star Trek Volume 6 703
Star Trek Volume 7 703
Star Trek Volume 8 703
Star Trek Volume 9 703
Star Trek Volume 10 703
Star Trek Volume 11 703
Star Trek: First Contact 500
Star Trek: The Cage 500
Star Wars 500
Star Wars Droids: The Pirates and The Prince 703
Star Wars Ewoks: The Haunted Village 703
Star Wars Trilogy 500
Star Wars: A Search for Security 806
Star Wrek Zone: The Unauthorized Parody 716
Star! 329
Stardust Memories 289
Stargate 500
Stargazers 841
Starknight 45
Starlight—A Musical Movie 329
Starlight Hotel 209
Starman 500
Starring Bette Davis: The TV Years 338
Starring Bugs Bunny! 687
Stars & Scars 567
Stars and Bars 247
Stars and Films That Made Hollywood the Film Capital of the World, The 338
Stars and Stripes Forever 329
Stars and Water Carriers 828
Stars Fell on Henrietta, The 248
Stars in the Eye 422
Stars Look Down, The 178
Stars of Space Jam: Bugs Bunny 687
Stars of Space Jam: Daffy Duck 687
Stars of Space Jam: Five-Tape Boxed Set 687
Stars of Space Jam: Roadrunner & Wile E. Coyote 687
Stars of Space Jam: Sylvester & Tweety 687
Stars of Space Jam: The Tazmanian Devil 687
Stars of the Louvre: 4,000 Years of Greatness 872
Stars of the Russian Ballet 575
Starship Troopers 500
Starstruck 207, 642
Start the Revolution Without Me 282
Starting Place 7, 478
Starvengers 748
Starving for Sugar 806
State of Grace 248
State of the Union 351
Station of Sorrow 777
Station West 296
Stationmaster's Wife, The 66
Stations of the Elevated 437
Stavisky 12
Stay Away Joe 537
Staying Faithful 854
Steadfast Tin Soldier 649
Steal Big, Steal Little 283
Stealing Beauty 35
Stealing Home 248
Steam Across America: Vol. I: The East 844
Steam Across America: Vol. II: The West 844
Steam Days 2 844
Steam Days: Travels with a Duchess and the Fishing Line 844
Steam Kings and Iron Horses 844
Steamboat Bill Jr. 409
Steel Claw 388
Steel Helmet, The 341
Steel Magnolias 248
Steeleye Span: A 20th Anniversary Celebration 605
Steeper and Deeper 828
Stefan Grossman 615
Stella 105
Stella 248
Stella Adler: Awake and Dream 319
Stella Dallas 388
Stella Maris 404
Step Away from War, A 806
Step into Ballet 576
Step Lively 329
Stepfather, The 248
Stepford Wives, The 529
Stephan Rechtschaffen, M.D.: Holistic Health—A Guide for Living 854
Stephane Grappelli— Live in San Francisco—1985 615
Stephane Grappelli in New Orleans 615
Stephano Quantestorie 34
Stephen Forsyth: Passages 488
Stephen Hawking's Universe 838
Stephen King's It 529
Stephen Sondheim: Anatomy of a Song 625
Steppenwolf 248
Stepping Razor Red X: The Peter Tosh Story 55
Steps Toward Change 834
Steptoe and Son 197
Sterile Cuckoo 248
Steve Allen's 75th Birthday Celebration 536
Steve Allen's Golden Age of Comedy 536
Steve Allen's Jazz Scene USA 615
Steve Lacy: Lift the Bandstand 615
Steve McQueen—Man on the Edge 338
Steve McQueen: Man Behind the Wheel 338
Steve Reinke: The Hundred Videos 557

Steve Smith, Part 1 625
Steve Smith, Part 2 625
Steven Soderbergh's Schizopolis 443
Stewardess School 510
Stick It in Your Ear 510
Sticky Fingers 437
Stickybear Spelling 872
Stiff Sheets 465
Stiffelio (Carreras) 585
Stiffelio (Domingo) 585
Still, Small Voice, A 854
Stillwell Road 772
Stilts (Los Zancos), The 46
Sting, The 248
Stingiest Man in Town, The 703
Stir Crazy 446
Stolen Freedom: Occupied Palestine 111
Stolen Hours 178
Stolen Life, A 388
Stolen Necklace, The 642
Stomp Out Loud 576
Stompin' at the Savoy: World of Slide Guitar, Volume 2 618
Stone Boy 666
Stone Flower, The 576
Stone of Silver Creek 296
Stone Temple Pilots: Live 622
Stone Wedding 104
Stoned Age, The 248
Stones of Blood, The 201
Stones River National Battlefield 780
Stonewall 25: Global Voices of Pride and Protest! 465
Stonewall 465
Stonewall Jackson 780
Stoney Knows How 478
Stooge, The 283
Stoogephile Trivia Movie, The 283
Stop, Look and Cook! 670
Stop at Nothing 404
Stop Struggling with Your Child 858
Stop the Church 465
Stop the World I Want to Get Off 329
Stop Train 349 (Delay at Marienborn) 71
Stopping War Before It Starts 801
Stories from Ireland 204
Stories from the Black Tradition 642
Stories to Remember: Bedtime 658
Stories to Remember: Rhymin' Time! 658
Stories to Remember: Singing Time! 658
Stories to Remember: Storytime! 658
Storm in a Teacup 185
Storm over Asia 86
Stormy Monday 164
Stormy Waters (Remorques) 23
Stormy Weather 329
Story Lady, The 248
Story of 15 Boys, The 716
Story of a Cheat, The 23
Story of a People 454
Story of a Silent Night 642
Story of a Three-Day Pass 446
Story of Adele H. 15
Story of Alexander Graham Bell, The 388
Story of America's Canyon Country, The 831
Story of America's Great Northwest, The 831
Story of America's Great Volcanoes, The 823
Story of America's Historic Inns, The 832
Story of America's Last Frontier: Alaska, The 832
Story of Boys and Girls, The 34
Story of Carol, The 600, 783
Story of David, The 792
Story of Dr. Wassell, The 355
Story of English 860
Story of Esther Costello, The 388
Story of Fashion Box Set, The 561
Story of Fashion Volume 1: Remembrance of Things Past 561
Story of Fashion Volume 2: The Art and Sport of Fashion 561
Story of Fashion Volume 3: The Age of Dissent 561
Story of Fausta, The 54
Story of Gosta Berling 77
Story of Inanna, Queen of Heaven and Earth, The 783
Story of Islam 792
Story of Jacob and Joseph, The 792
Story of Jazz, The 615
Story of Lassie, The 642
Story of Louis Pasteur 388
Story of Naval Air Power 844
Story of O 511
Story of Qiu Ju, The 118
Story of Rome and Pompeii, The 785
Story of Ruth 356
Story of Seabiscuit, The 666
Story of Sin, The 95
Story of Television, The 422
Story of the Clancy Brothers and Tommy Makem, The 204
Story of the Dancing Frog 649
Story of the Last Chrysanthemum 143
Story of the Statue of Liberty, The 764
Story of the Symphony, The 594
Story of the Vietnam Veterans Memorial: The Last Landing Zone, The 778
Story of Two Synagogues, The 116
Story of Will Rogers, The 797
Story of Women 13
Story of Xinghua, The 117
Storybook 642
Storytellers Collection, The 658
Storytelling Giant: The Talking Heads Retrospective 623
Storytelling with Sandy Jenkins: Learning and Sharing 642
Stowaway 329
Stowaways On The Ark 716
Stradiwackius: The Counting Concert 872
Straight for the Heart 211
Straight from the Heart 465, 478
Straight No Chaser: Thelonious Monk 615
Straight Out of Brooklyn 446
Straight Shooting 340
Straight Time 248
Strait-Jacket 529
Strand: Under the Dark Cloth 560
Stranded 388
Strange Affair of Uncle Harry, The 388
Strange Behavior 209
Strange Cargo 388
Strange Case of the End of Civilization as We Know It, The 197
Strange Days 500
Strange Door, The 388
Strange Harvests 1993 862
Strange Hostel of Naked Pleasures, The 511
Strange Illusion 388
Strange Interlude (1932) 315
Strange Love of Martha Ivers 388
Strange Love of Molly Louvain, The 388
Strange One, The 388
Strange Ways 52
Strange Weather 488
Strange Woman 388
Strange World of Coffin Joe 529
Stranger, The 94, 344, 437
Stranger (Agantuk), The 148
Stranger 248
Stranger Among Us, A 248
Stranger Double Feature: Summoned by Shadows/More Than a Messiah, The 201
Stranger from Venus, The 500
Stranger in Town, A 388
Stranger Than Paradise 442
Stranger Wore a Gun, The 296
Stranger: Eye of the Beholder, Part 2, The 201
Stranger: In Memory Alone, The 201
Strangers in Good Company 211
Strangers on a Train (American Version) 353
Strangers on a Train (British Version) 353
Strangers When We Meet 388
Strangler, The 388
Strapless 164
Strapped 446
Strasberg on Acting 315
Stratasphere 600
Strategic Cooperation Initiative 806
Stratton Story, The 388
Strauss: Death and Transfiguration 594
Strauss: Don Quixote 594
Strauss: Ein Heldenleben 594
Strauss: Eine Alpensinfonie 594
Strauss: The King of 3/4 Time 594
Straw Dogs 347
Strawberry & Chocolate 53
Strawberry Blonde 283
Stray Dog 143
Stream of Social Intercourse 438
Streamers 254
Street 71
Street Angels 132
Street Fight 716
Street Fighter, The 139
Street Fighter II, Vol. 10— Fight to the Finish, Final Round 139
Street Fighter II V, Vol. 1: Beginning of a Journey 748
Street Fighter II V, Vol. 2: Darkness at Kowloon 748
Street Fighter II V, Vol. 3: Revenge of Ashura 748
Street Fighter II V, Vol. 4: Dark Omen 748
Street Fighter II V, Vol. 5: Legend of Hadouken 748
Street Fighter II V, Vol. 6: The Unveiled Ruler 748
Street Fighter II V, Vol. 7: The True Ruler 748
Street Fighter II V, Vol. 8: Rising Dragon 748
Street Fighter II V, Vol. 9: Fight to the Finish 748
Street Fighter II V, Vol. 10: Episodes 28-29 748
Street Fighter II: The Animated Movie 748
Street Gangs of Hong Kong 132
Street Kid 65
Street of Forgotten Women, The 404
Street of Fury 132
Street of Shame 143
Street Scene 388
Street Wars 446
Street with No Name 388
Streetcar Named Desire (1984), A 315
Streetcar Named Desire (1995), A 315
Streetcar Named Desire: Director's Cut (1951), A 315
Streetwise 478, 783
Strega Nonna and Other Stories 649
Stress Management 854
Stress Reduction Exercises 854
Stretching the Canvas with Guest Host Peter Sellars 564
Stretching Your Whole Body 854
Strictly Ballroom 207
Strictly Business 283
Strictly G.I. 338
Strictly Speaking 511
Strictly Supernatural 862
Stride to Glory 454, 828
Strike 86
Strike Me Pink 329
Strike Up the Band 329
Strindberg and His Women: 3 One-Act Dramas 315
Strindberg's Miss Julie: Royal Shakespeare Company 315
Strip Jack Naked 465
Striporama 511
Striptease 283
Stromboli 39
Strong Man, The 351
Strong Medicine 438
Stroszek 67
Structure of Crystals, The 94
Structures from Silence 603
Struggle, The 413
Struggle for Avengence 123
Strunk & White: The Elements of Style 860
Stuart Saves His Family 283
Student of Prague (1913), The 71
Student of Prague (1926), The 71
Student Prince, The 329
Student Prince in Old Heidelberg, The 345
Studio Melee Sampler 561
Studio Seconds: The Assistant Sound Engineer Video 319
Studs Lonigan 388
Studs Terkel's Chicago 764
Study in Scarlet, A 187
Study in Terror, A 529
Stuff Stephanie in the Incinerator 511
Stunt: A Musical Motion Picture 123, 567
Stuntwoman 7
Su Rynard: What Wants to Be Spoken, What Remains to Be Said 557
Subject Is Light, The 319
Subject Was Roses, The 388
Submarine Warfare 772
Submarine: Steel Boats, Iron Men 844
Subsidiaries (Personel) 96
Substance of Fire, The 248
Suburban Roulette 511
SubUrbia 438
Subway 9
Subway Stories 248, 255
Subway: The Empire Beneath New York's Streets 844
Sucker (Le Corniauds), The 18
Sudden Fear 388
Suddenly 388
Suddenly Last Summer 388
Suds 404
Sugar Cane Alley 55
Sugar Hill 248
Suicide Battalion/Hell Squad 389
Suikoden—Demon Century 748
Suite 16 31
Sukeban Deka 1 748
Sukeban Deka 2 748
Sukhavati: Place of Bliss 783
Suleyman the Magnificent 783
Sullivan's Last Call 438
Sullivan's Travels 346
Sum of Us, The 207, 465
Sum of Us, The 207, 465
Summer and Smoke 315
Summer City 207
Summer Fling 283
Summer Holiday 329
Summer House 185
Summer Interlude 78
Summer Night (With Greek Profile, Almond Eyes and Scent of Basil) 34
Summer of '42 389
Summer of Aviya, The 777
Summer of Ben Tyler, The 248
Summer of Miss Forbes, The 52
Summer Place, A 389
Summer Stock 329
Summer to Remember, A 83
Summer to Remember 248
Summer Vacation: 1999 139
Summer Wine 197
Summer Wishes, Winter Dreams 248
Summer with Selik 666
Summertime (Summer Madness) 180
Summons for the Queen 100
Sun Bear on Power 788
Sun Bear: Earth Changes 788
Sun Comes Up, The 666
Sun Dagger, The 788
Sun Ra: A Joyful Noise 615
Sun's Burial, The 141
Sun Shines Bright 340
Sun the Wind and the Rain, The 642
Sun Valley Serenade 329
Sunday Bloody Sunday 164, 465
Sunday Daughters 102
Sunday in New York 389
Sunday in Hell, A 828
Sunday in the Country, A 11
Sunday's Children 77
Sunday Sinners 449
Sundays and Cybele 23
Sundown 389
Sundowners 389
Sunrise 73
Sunrise at Campobello 389
Sunset 354
Sunset Boulevard 346
Sunset Range 296
Sunshine Boys, The 283
Sunshine Porcupine 716

Sunshine's on the Way 248
Super 81/2 ....212, 465
Super Abdomens Workout 854
Super Atragon 1 748
Super Atragon 2 748
Super Clash Round I 603
Super Deformed Double Feature 748
Super Dimensional Fortress Macross 749
Super Drumming 616
Super Duper Baseball Bloopers 2 828
Super Heroes 422
Super Shark Collection 823
Super Soul Brother 533
Super Structures of the World 566
Super TV Bloopers 422
Superboy (DC Superpowers Collection) 703
Supercharged: The Grand Prix Car 844
SuperCities 832
Supercop 134
Superfly 533
Superfly TNT 533
Superior Duck 687
Superman & the Mole Men 511
Superman (50th Anniversary) 688
Superman (DC Superpowers Collection) 703
Superman 688
Superman Cartoons Vol. 1 703
Superman Cartoons Vol. 2 703
Superman II 248
Superman: The Complete Cartoon Collection 688
Superman: The Last Son of Krypton 703
Superman: The Movie 248
Supernatural 389
Supersonic Man 500
Superstar: The Life and Times of Andy Warhol 557
Supervixens 513
Support Your Local Gunfighter 296
Sure Death 140
Sure Death: Brown, You Bounder 749
Sure Fire 441
Surf Nazis Must Die 511
Suroh: The Alien Hitchhiker 500
Surprise Package 389
Surprising Amsterdam 832
Surrender 404
Survival 201
Survival in the Wild 823
Survival of Spaceship Earth 806
Survival Research Laboratories 567
Survival Spanish 155
Surviving Desire 442
Surviving Picasso 259
Surviving the Big One: How to Prepare for a Major Earthquake 838
Survivors 144, 772
Survivors of the Holocaust 777
Susan and God 350
Susan Lennox: Her Fall and Rise 389
Susan Rynard 488
Susana 47
Susannah of the Mounties 666
Suspect 248
Suspended 94
Suspicion 353
Suspiria 529
Sustainable Lies, Attainable Dreams 806
Sutherland, Horne, Bonynge Gala Concert 585
Suture 438
Suzanne Westenhoefer: HBO Comedy Special 465
Suzy 389
SVD—Club of the Big Deed 86
Svengali 389
Swallows and Amazons 666
Swallows and Amazons Forever!: Coot Club 667
Swallows and Amazons Forever!: The Big Six 667
Swamp Fire 389
Swamp Women 514
Swan, The 389
Swan 405
Swan Lake (Ananiashvili) 576
Swan Lake (Bolshoi/Mikhalchenko) 576
Swan Lake (Bolshoi/Plisetskaya) 576
Swan Lake (Kirov/Ivanov) 576
Swan Lake (London Fest/Makarova) 576
Swan Lake (Nureyev) 576
Swan Lake 642
Swan Princess, The 667, 716
Swan Princess III and the Mystery of the Enchanted Treasure, The 649
Swan Princess: Escape from Castle Mountain, The 649, 667, 716
Swann in Love 65
Swat Kats: Deadly Dr. Viper 703
Swat Kats: Metallikats Attack 703
Swat Kats: Strike of Dark Kat 703
Swedenhielms 77
Sweet 15 661
Sweet Adeline 405
Sweet Bird of Youth 167, 389
Sweet Charity 330
Sweet Hereafter, The 212
Sweet Lies 248
Sweet Lorraine 248
Sweet Love, Bitter 438
Sweet Movie 104
Sweet Nothing 248
Sweet Peach 123
Sweet Perfection 446
Sweet Smell of Success 389
Sweet Sweetback's Baadassss Song 446
Sweet Talker 207
Sweethearts 330
Sweetie 207
Swept Away 34
Swept from the Sea 164
Swimmer, The 389
Swimming to Cambodia 255
Swimming with Sharks 283
Swing 449
Swing High, Swing Low 330
Swing It Professor 330
Swing Shift 255
Swing Time 343
Swing: Best of the Big Bands Vol. 1 616
Swing: Best of the Big Bands Vol. 2 616
Swing: Best of the Big Bands Vol. 3 616
Swing: Best of the Big Bands Vol. 4 616
Swingers 283
Swingle Singers, The 600
Swiss Family Robinson 642, 667
Swiss Rail Journeys 844
Switchblade Sisters 511
Switzerland, the Alpine Wonderland 832
Switzerland's Glacier Express 832
Swoon 466
Sword and the Dragon 83, 716
Sword for Truth 749
Sword in the Stone, The 694
Sword of Doom, The 140
Sword of Lancelot 178
Sword of Many Loves 124
Sword of Venus 389
Sword Stained with Royal Blood, The 132
Swordsman 132
Swordsman II 132
Swordsman III (aka The East Is Red) 132
Sworn Brother 132
Sworn to the Drum: A Tribute to Francisco Aguabella 480
Sycamore People 99
Syd Chaplin at Keystone 412
Sykes 197
Sylvester & Tweety's Bad Ol' Putty Tat Blues 688
Sylvester & Tweety's Tale Feathers 688
Sylvester & Tweety: The Best Yeows of Our Lives 688
Sylvia and the Phantom 23
Sylvie Guillem 576
Sympathy for the Devil 10
Symphony for the Spire 600
Symphony in the Mountains 74
Symphony of Mexico 61
Symphony of Wonders 618
Symphony to America the Beautiful 823
Symphony to the Planets 841
Synthetic Pleasures 478

T

T. Berry Brazelton: The Changing Family and Its Implications 858
T. Bove & C. Rhodes 873
T. Rex: The Real World 838
T'ai-Chi Chuan Kung-fu 854
T'ai-Chi Chuan: Chinese Moving Meditation 854
T'ai-Chi Chuan: Movements of Power and Health 854
T'ai-Chi for Inner Beauty, with Jean Goulet 854
T'ai-Chi for Seniors 854
T'ai-Chi Massage 854
T'ai-Chi Sword Forms 854
T'ai-Chi-Ch'uan (Chen Man-Ching's Short Form) 854
T'ai-Chi: The Inner Teachings, with Master Bob Klein: Body Awareness 854
T'ai-Chi: The Inner Teachings, with Master Bob Klein: Chinese Chi-Gung Health Exercises 854
T'ai-Chi: The Inner Teachings, with Master Bob Klein: Harmonious Relationships 854
T'ai-Chi: The Inner Teachings, with Master Bob Klein: Harmony of Mind and Body 854
T'ain't Nothin' Changed 608
T Bone n Weasel 248
T.V. Classics, Vol. 1: Hollywood Half Hour & Public Defender 422
T.V. Classics, Vol. 2: Howdy Doody & Art Linkletter and the Kids 422
T.V. Classics, Vol. 3: Colonel March of Scotland Yard & Sherlock Holmes 422
T.V. Classics, Vol. 4: Arthur Godfrey's Talent Scouts & The Ed Wynn Show 422
T.V. Classics, Vol. 5: The Burns and Allen Show & Heaven for Betsy 422
T.V. Classics, Vol. 6: Armchair Detective & Public Prosecutor 422
T.V. Classics, Vol. 7: Four Star Playhouse & The Stars and The Story 422
T.V. Classics, Vol. 8: The Jack Benny Show 422
T.V. Classics, Vol. 9: The Cisco Kid & The Roy Rogers Show 422
T.V. Party 422
T-Men 389
Table Manners for Kids: Tots to Teens 670
Taboo 94
Tabu 73
Tackling the Monster: Wynton on Practice 625
Tadeusz Drozda Cabaret 99
Tadpole and the Whale 667
Tahitian Choir Volume II, The 618
Tahtonka 788
Tai Chi for Health 854
Tai Chi II 132
Tai Chi Master, The 132
Tai Chi: 6 Forms 6 Easy Lessons 150, 854
Tail of the Tiger 642
Tailor of Gloucester, The 658
Taira Clan Saga 143
Taiwan: Exotic Blossom of the Orient 145
Taj Mahal 616
Takahiko Imura: A Journey to Ayersrock 488
Takahiko Imura: Concept Tapes (1975-87) 489
Takahiko Imura: John Cage Performs James Joyce 489
Take a Letter Mr. Jones 197
Take Five 872
Take It Easy 94
Take It Out in Trade—The Outtakes 515
Take Me Out to the Ball Game 330
Take Two 108
Takegami: Guardian of Darkness, 3-Pack 749
Takegami: Guardian of Darkness Vol. 1: Shrine of the Eight-Headed Dragon 749
Takegami: Guardian of Darkness Vol. 2: Legend of the 800 Priestesses 749
Takegami: Guardian of Darkness Vol. 3: The Mystery of Hiruko 749
Taking Care of Terrific 661
Taking of Pelham 1 2 3, The 248
Tale of Genji, The 749
Tale of Springtime, A 14
Tale of Two Cities, A 178, 248, 389
Tale of Two Cities (Masterpiece Theatre), A 301
Tale of Two Cities/In the Switch Tower, A 405
Tale of Two Worlds (Water Lily), A 405
Tale of Winter 14
Tales from the Darkside: The Movie 530
Tales from the Gimli Hospital 212
Tales from the Latin American Indians 61
Tales from the Map Room 832
Tales from Vienna Woods 330
Tales of Beatrix Potter 576, 658
Tales of Beatrix Potter: Vol II 658
Tales of Erotica 249
Tales of Frankenstein 530
Tales of Hoffman 181
Tales of Manhattan 389
Tales of Paris 23
Tales of Terror 514
Tales of the Days of Awe 116
Tales of Washington Irving 642
Taliesin: The Tradition of Frank Lloyd Wright 566
Talk About It 834
Talk of the Town 343
Talk of the Town: Shabba Ranks 603
Talk Radio 249
Talk to Me, Dicky 124
Talk with Ann McGovern, A 307
Talk with Avi, A 307
Talk with Betsy Byars, A 307
Talk with Bruce Coville, A 307
Talk with E.L. Konigsburg, A 307
Talk with Jean Craighead George, A 307
Talk with Jean Fritz, A 307
Talk with Jerry Spinelli, A 307
Talk with Karla Kuskin, A 307
Talk with Lee Bennett Hopkins, A 307
Talk with Lynne Reid Banks, A 307
Talk with M.E. Kerr, A 307
Talk with Madeleine L'Engle, A 307
Talk with Matt Christopher, A 307
Talk with Nancy Willard, A 307
Talk with Natalie Babbitt, A 307
Talk with Paula Fox, A 307
Talk with Phyllis Reynolds Naylor, A 307
Talkin' Dirty After Dark 446
Talking Feet 606
Talking Reference Library, The 643
Talking to Angels 854
Talking to Strangers 438
Talks by Michael Parenti 801
Tall, Tan and Terrific 449
Tall Blond Man with One Black Shoe 18
Tall Blond Man with One Black Shoe/Return of the Tall Blond Man 18
Tall Guy, The 185
Tall Men, The 296
Tall Story 389
Tall Tale 667
Tall Tales: Annie Oakley 649
Tall Tales: Pecos Bill 649
Tallest Tree in the Forest, The 454
Talmage Farlow 616
Talmud and the Scholar, The 116
Talons of Weng-Chiang, The 201
Tam Lin 178
Tamango 389
Taming of the Shrew (Esquire 4+4), The 315
Taming of the Shrew (Westinghouse Studio), The 315
Taming of the Shrew (Zeffirelli), The 315
Taming of the Shrew 872
Tammy and the Bachelor 389
Tammy and the Doctor 389
Tampopo 140
Tango 389, 576
Tango Bar 52
Tango Lesson, The 164
Tango: Our Dance 52, 576
Tank Girl 249
Tanka 716
Tanks Are Coming, The 772

Tanks: Monsters in Motion....844
Tanner '88....254
Tannhauser (Davis)....585
Tannhauser (Marton)....585
Tannhauser (Mehta)....585
Tantra....150
Tantra Love: Eastern Secrets of Intimacy and Ecstasy for Western Lovers....854
Tantra of Gyuto....150
Tantra: The Art of Conscious Loving....854
Tao of Practice, The....855
Tap....249
Tap Dancing for Beginners....576
Tap Dogs....576
Tara the Stonecutter....643
Tarantula....500
Taras Bulba....389
Target....148
Target Earth....500
Target for Tonight....772
Targets....389
Tarnished Angels, The....342
Tarnished Dream (1929-1931), The....764
Tartuffe....7, 73
Tarzan, The Ape Man....389
Tarzan and His Mate....539
Tarzan Escapes....539
Tarzan Finds a Son....539
Tarzan of the Apes....405
Tarzan's New York Adventure....539
Tarzan's Secret Treasure....539
Tarzan the Tiger....539
Task Force....389
Taste of Blood, A....511
Taste of Freedom, A....89
Taste of Honey....178
Taste the Blood of Dracula....530
Tatie Danielle....18
Tattoo Connection, The....124
Tauber in Blossom Time....330
Tawny Scrawny Lion's Jungle Tales....658
Taxi Blues....83
Taxi Driver....254
Taxi Zum Klo....65, 466
Taxing Woman....140
Taxing Woman's Return, A....141
Taylor Chain I and II....478
Tazmania: Taz-Maniac....703
Tazmania: Taz-Manimals....704
Tazmania: Taz-Tronaut....704
Tchaikovsky....83
Tchaikovsky Competition: Violin & Piano....594
Tchaikovsky's Swan Lake (Male Cast)....576
Tchaikovsky: Symphony No. 4 and No. 5....594
Tchaikovsky: Symphony No. 6 ("Pathetique") & Piano Concerto No. 1....594
Tchaikovsky: Violin Concerto Op. 35....594
Tea & Sympathy....315
Tea for Two....330
Teacher, The....249
Teacher's Pet....283
Teacher Training Series....860
Teachers....283
Teaching Shakespeare: New Approaches from the Folger Shakespeare Library....319
Teachings of the Masters....855
Teahouse of the August Moon....389
Tear Jerker....489
Tears in Florence....65
Teaserama: David Friedman's Roadshow Rarities, Vol. 1....511
Teasers....466
Techniques of TV Interviewing....319
Techno Police 21C....749
Technologies of the Gods: The Case for Pre-Historic High Technology....783
Ted & Venus....283
Ted Kennedy....798
Teddy at the Throttle....412
Teddy Bears' Jamboree....658
Teddy Bears' Picnic, The....658
Teddy-Bear....94
Teen Sexuality in a Culture of Confusion....861
Teenage Caveman....514
Teenage Confidential....511
Teenage Devil Dolls....511
Teenage Strangler....511
Teenage Zombies....530
Teenage-A-Go-Go....541
Teenagers from Outer Space....500
Teiman: Music of Yemenite Jewry....116, 604
Tekkaman Vol. 1....749
Tekkaman Vol. 2....749
Tekkaman: Blade II, Stage 1....749
Tekkaman: Blade II, Stage 2: The Alien Intruder....749
Telefon....249
Telefoto....560
Telegrams from the Dead....862
Telegraph Avenue Street Musicians: The Concert at Ashkenaz....606
Telegraph Trail, The....296
Telemann: Recorded Suite Concerto Violins and Concerto for Horns....594
Telephone Tips for Kids, Volume 1....643
Teletubbies....658
Television Toys Vol. 1....541
Television Toys Vol. 2....541
Televoid....438
Tell Me a Riddle....249
Tell Me Why (Spanish)....674
Tell Me Why:....643
Tell-Tale Heart (1963), The....530
Tell-Tale Heart (1973), The....530
Telling Lies in America....249
Tempera....564
Tempest, The....405
Tempest (Mazursky), The....315
Tempest (Woodman), The....315
Temptation of a Monk....117
Temptress, The....405
Ten Commandments (1923), The....355
Ten Commandments (1956), The....355
Ten Commandments: 40th Anniversary Collector's Edition, The....355
Ten Days' Wonder....13
Ten Days That Shook the World....86, 89
Ten Little Indians....422
Ten Minutes to Live....449
Ten Nights in a Barroom....405
Ten Tall Soldiers....643
Ten Tenors....600
Ten Wanted Men....296
Tenant, The....98
Tenant of Wildfell Hall, The....164
Tenants, The....107
Tenchi Muyo— Magical Girl Pretty Sammy 3: Super Kiss....750
Tenchi Muyo! Episodes 8 & 9....749
Tenchi Muyo! Episodes 10 & 11....749
Tenchi Muyo! Episodes 12 & 13....749
Tenchi Muyo! In Love....750
Tenchi Muyo! Mihoshi Special....749
Tenchi Muyo! The Magical Girl Pretty Sammy 2....750
Tenchi Muyo! The Magical Girl Pretty Sammy....749
Tenchi Muyo! Vol. 1: The Reincarnation of Ryoko....749
Tenchi Muyo! Vol. 2: Here Comes Ayeka!....749
Tenchi Muyo! Vol. 3: Hello Ryo-Ohki....749
Tenchi Muyo! Vol. 4: Mihoshi Falls to the Land of Stars....749
Tenchi Muyo! Vol. 5: Kagato Attacks....749
Tenchi Muyo! Vol. 6: We Need Tenchi....749
Tenchi Muyo! Vol. 7: Ryo-ohki Special—The Night Before the Carnival....749
Tenchi the Movie 2: The Daughter of Darkness....750
Tenchi Universe, Vol. 1: Tenchi on Earth I....750
Tenchi Universe, Vol. 2: Tenchi on Earth II....750
Tenchi Universe, Vol. 3: Tenchi on Earth III....750
Tenchi Universe, Vol. 4: Time & Space....750
Tenchi Universe, Vol. 5: Space I....750
Tenchi Universe, Vol. 6: Space II....750
Tenchi Universe, Vol. 7: Space III....750
Tenchi Universe, Vol. 8....750
Tender Mercies....249
Tender Trap, The....330
Tennessee Tuxedo: Brushing Off a Toothache....704
Tenor Legends: Coleman Hawkins in Brussels, 1962....616
Tenor Titans....616
Tenth Good Thing About Barney, The....643
Tenth Man, The....249
Teorema....37
Teppanyaki....124
Terence Davies Trilogy....164
Teresa's Tattoo....283
Tereza....100
Terminator, The....500
Terminator 2: Judgment Day....501
Termini Station....212
Terminus....201
Terms of Endearment....249
Terra em Transe....54
Terranova....34
Terror, The....514
Terror by Night....187
Terror Creatures from the Grave (Cemetery of the Living Dead)....530
Terror in a Texas Town....296
Terror in the Haunted House....530
Terror in the Minefields....778
Terror Is a Man....501
Terror of Mechagodzilla....501
Terror of the Autons....201
Terror of the Third Reich....772
Terror of the Zygons....201
Terror of Tiny Town....511
Terror-Creatures From the Grave....511
Terrorism: The New World War....801
Terrorism: The Russian Connection....89
Terrytoons: The Cats & Mice of Paul Terry....716
Tess....98
Tess of the Storm Country....405
Test of Donald Norton....405
Test of Love....207
Test Pilot....390
Test Preparation Series....858
Testament....438, 792
Testament of Dr. Cordelier....26
Testament of Dr. Mabuse, The....72
Testament of Orpheus....27
Teton Country....832
Tetsuo II: Body Hammer....140
Tetsuo: The Iron Man....140
Tevye the Dairyman....113
Tex Avery's Screwball Classics 1....688
Tex Avery's Screwball Classics 2....688
Tex Avery's Screwball Classics 3....688
Tex Avery's Screwball Classics 4....688
Tex Avery's Screwball Classics LD....688
Tex Avery: All This and Tex Avery, Too!....688
Tex Avery: The Compleat Tex Avery....688
Tex-Mex....604
Texas Across the River....296
Texas Carnival....390
Texas Chainsaw Massacre, The....530
Texas Chainsaw Massacre: A Family Portrait, The....530
Texas Chainsaw Massacre: The Next Generation....511
Texas Cyclone....296
Texas Fiddle Legends....606
Texas Tenor: The Illinois Jacquet Story....616
Textile Magicians....144, 561
Thai Kickboxing....855
Thais....94
Thank God It's Friday....511
Thank You and Goodnight....438, 466
Thank You Poles....99
Thank You Sir....124
Thank Your Lucky Stars....330
Thanksgiving Day by Gail Gibbons....643
That Brennan Girl....390
That Certain Age....330
That Certain Thing....351
That Certain Woman....390
That Championship Season....315
That Cold Day in the Park....254
That Darn Cat....694
That Day, On the Beach....136
That Forsyte Woman....390
That Girl Montana....405
That High Lonesome Sound....606
That Man from Rio....18
That Midnight Kiss....330
That Naughty Girl and Love on a Pillow....18, 23
That Obscure Object of Desire....47
That's Black Entertainment: African-American Contributions in Film and Music 1903-1944....455
That's Dancing....330
That's Entertainment....330
That's Entertainment II....330
That's Entertainment III....330
That's Offensive....511
That's Singing....330
That Sinking Feeling....185
That Summer of White Roses....103
That Thing You Do!....283
That Touch of Mink....283
That Uncertain Feeling....345
That Was Then...This Is Now....249
Theater of Blood....530
Theatre of Indifference....557
Theatre of Tadeusz Kantor, The....99, 315
Theatre of the Imagination....872
Theatre of the Iron Curtain....315
Theatrical Trailers....541
Thelma and Louise....249
Them!....501
Theme, The....83
Then They Came for Me: Intolerance in Modern Germany....73
Theodora Goes Wild....283
Theodore Roosevelt....764
There Goes a Boat....658
There Goes a Bulldozer....658
There Goes a Fire Truck....658
There Goes a Helicopter....658
There Goes a Monster Truck....658
There Goes a Motorcycle....658
There Goes a Police Car....658
There Goes a Race Car....658
There Goes a Spaceship....658
There Goes a Train....658
There Goes a Truck....658
There Goes an Airplane....658
There Goes Barder....390
There'll Always Be Stars in the Sky....604
There's a Cricket in the Library....643
There's a Witch Under the Stairs....643
There's No Business Like Show Business....330
There's No Such Thing as a Chanukah Bush, Sandy Goldstein....116
There's No Such Thing as Woman's Work....764
There Was a Crooked Man....297
There Was No Room for You....99
Theremin: An Electronic Odyssey....478
Therese and Isabelle....7, 466
Theresienstadt: Gateway to Auschwitz....777
These Girls Won't Talk....405
These Three....344
They All Kissed the Bride....283
They All Laughed....283
They Call It Sin....390
They Came to Cordura....297
They Came to Rob Hong Kong....124
They Died with Their Boots On....297
They Drive by Night....390
They Eat Scum....438
They Got Me Covered....283
They Live....501
They Made Me a Criminal....390
They Meet Again....390
They Met in Bombay....390
They Might Be Giants....283
They Only Kill Their Masters....249
They Risked Their Lives: Rescuers of the Holocaust....777
They Saved Hitler's Brain....511
They Shall Have Music....330
They Shoot Horses, Don't They?....390
They Wear No Clothes....511
They Were 11....750

They Were Expendable 341
They Who Dare 178
Thicker Than Water 164
Thief and the Cobbler, The 667, 716
Thief of Baghdad, The 405
Thief of Baghdad (Donner), The 390
Thief of Baghdad (Korda), The 390
Thieves 7
Thieves Like Us 254
Thin Blue Line, The 197
Thin Ice 390
Thin Man, The 283
Thin Man Collection, The 283
Thin Man Goes Home, The 283
Thin White Rope: The Axis Calls 623
Thing, The 501
Thing Called Love, A 249
Things Change 283
Things That Fly Sing-Alongs 658
Things to Come 501
Things to Do in Denver When You're Dead 438
Think & Talk French 872
Think & Talk German 872
Think & Talk Italian 873
Think & Talk Spanish 873
Thinking Allowed 855
Thinking Like a Watershed 806
Third Key, The 178
Third Man, The 179
Third Sex, The 466, 511
Third Sex Sinema Volume 1—Vapors 466
Third Sex Sinema Volume 2—The Song of the Loon 466
Third Sex Sinema Volume 3—The Meatrack 466
Third Sex Sinema Volume 5: Consenting Adults 466, 511
Third Solution, The 249
Third Stone from the Sun 667
Thirteen Moons on Turtle's Back 643, 789
Thirteen Stones of the Universal Wheel, The 856
Thirteenth Guest 390
Thirties Magic Vol. 1 716
Thirties Magic Vol. 2 717
Thirty Seconds over Tokyo 390
Thirty-Nine Steps, The 353
Thirty-Two Short Films About Glenn Gould 212
This Boy's Life 249
This Could Be the Night 283
This England 179
This Gun for Hire 390
This Happy Breed 180
This House of Power 455
This Is America 811
This Is Elvis 537
This Is Mexico 61
This Is Not a Test 501
This Is Not Beirut/There Was and There Was Not 489
This Is the Army 330
This Is Warsaw 99
This Is Your Life 422
This Island Earth 501, 806
This Land Is Our Land 61
This Land Is Your Land: The Animated Kids' Songs of Woody Guthrie 606
This Night I Will Possess Your Corpse 530
This Nude World 511
This Old House—Milton, MA— Project One 1701-1718 566
This Old Pyramid 566
This Pretty Planet 670
This Property Is Condemned 390
This Special Friendship 7, 466
This Sporting Life 179
This Stuff'll Kill You 511
This Sweet Sickness 7
This World, Then the Fireworks 249
Thom Gunn 307
Thomas Berry: Dreamer of the Universe 792
Thomas Crown Affair 390
Thomas Eakins: A Motion Portrait 557
Thomas Graal's Best Child 77
Thomas Graal's Best Film 77
Thomas Hampson: I Hear America Singing 600
Thomas Hardy's Tess of the D'Urbervilles 197
Thomas Jefferson 764
Thomas Jefferson: A View from the Mountain 764
Thomas Jefferson: In Pursuit of Liberty 797
Thomas Jefferson: Philosopher of Freedom 797
Thomas the Tank Engine & Friends 658
Thor Heyerdahl: Explorer and Scientist 783
Thorn Birds, The 422
Thoroughbred, The 390
Thorpe's Gold 828
Those Crazy Americans 764
Those Daring Young Men in Their Jaunty Jalopies 390
Those Magnificent Men in Their Flying Machines 283, 844
Those Merry Souls 124
Those Obnoxious Aliens! 750
Those Were the Days 124
Those Who Endured 828
Thousand Acres, A 249
Thousand and One Nights, A 330
Thousand Clowns, A 390
Thousand Eyes of Dr. Mabuse (Eyes of Evil), The 72
Thousands Cheer 330
Threads 501
Threads of Survival 561
Threads of Tradition 61
Three 466
Three Ages 409
Three Avengers, The 501
Three Broadway Girls 283
Three Caballeros, The 694
Three Caballeros/Saludos Amigos LD 694
Three Came Home 390
Three Cases of Murder 179
Three Coins in the Fountain 283
Three Comrades 390
Three Daring Daughters 330
Three Daughters 511
Three Days and a Child 108
Three Doctors, The 201
Three Faces of Eve, The 390
Three Faces West 390
Three Films by Chris Frieri 438
Three for the Show 330
Three Gables, The 187
Three Godfathers 341
Three Husbands 390
Three Levels of Power and How to Use Them 856
Three Little Pigs 694
Three Little Words 330
Three Lives and Only One Death 11
Three Men and a Baby 284
Three Men and a Balloon 844
Three Men and a Cradle 18
Three Men in a Boat 185
Three Men on a Horse 284
Three Mile Island Revisited 806
Three Minutes to Power and Peace 862
Three Musketeers, The 185, 284, 330, 405, 717
Three Musketeers (1933), The 390
Three Musketeers (1948), The 391
Three Must-Get-Theirs, The 412
Three of a Kind 197
Three of Hearts 466
Three on a Match 391
Three Pals 405
Three Piano Portraits 616
Three Robbers and Other Stories, The 643
Three Secrets 391
Three Sesame Street Stories 659
Three Short Films (Mark Rappaport) 438
Three Sisters, The 315
Three Smart Girls 330
Three Smart Girls Grow Up 330
Three Songs of Lenin 86
Three Sopranos, The 600
Three Soviet Masters 86
Three Stooges, The 284
Three Stooges 94, 284
Three Stooges Comedy Classics, The 422
Three Stooges Go Around the World in a Daze, The 284
Three Stooges Hit Home 284
Three Stooges in Orbit, The 284
Three Stooges Meet Hercules, The 284
Three Stooges—More Nyuks 284
Three Stooges: A Pain in the Pullman, The 284
Three Stooges: Corny Casanovas, The 284
Three Stooges: Dizzy Doctors, The 284
Three Stooges: Dopey Dicks, The 284
Three Stooges: False Alarms, The 284
Three Stooges: Have Rocket Will Travel, The 284
Three Stooges: Heavenly Daze, The 284
Three Stooges: Hoi Polloi, The 284
Three Stooges: Listen Judge, The 284
Three Stooges: Out West, The 284
Three Stooges: Stop! Look! and Laugh!, The 284
Three Stooges: The Outlaws, The 284
Three Stooges: Vagabond Loafers, The 284
Three Stooges: Wee Wee Monsieur, The 284
Three Stooges: Whoops I'm an Indian, The 284
Three Strange Loves 78
Three Tenors, The 600
Three Tenors in Concert: Carreras, Domingo, Pavarotti, The 600
Three Tenors: Encore 600
Three Waltzes 23, 585
Three Weird Sisters 179
Three Wishes 284
Three Worlds of Gulliver, The 667
Threepenny Opera (1931), The 71
Threepenny Opera (1962), The 71
Threesome 249
Threshold (aka Dawn) (Umbartha/Subah) 148
Thrill Killers, The 511
Thrill of a Romance 284
Thrill of It All!, The 284
Thriller 422, 530
Throne of Blood 143
Through a Glass Darkly 78
Through Hell and High Water 772
Through the Breakers 405
Through the Eyes of the Forest 806
Through the Wire 478
Throw Momma from the Train 284
Thumbed a Ride to Heaven: The Music of Alfonia Tims and Others 606
Thumbelina 667, 688
Thumbs Up for Kids: AIDS Education 835
Thumpkin and the Easter Bunnies 659
Thunder Cake 643
Thunder Cop 132
Thunder in the City 185
Thunder Ninja Kids: In the Golden Adventure 132
Thunder Ninja Kids: Little Kickboxer 132
Thunder Ninja Kids: The Hunt for the Devil Boxer 132
Thunder Ninja Kids: Wonderful Mission 132
Thunder over Mexico 86
Thunder Road 391
Thunder Run 132
Thunderball 169
Thunderbird 6 643
Thunderbirds, The 478
Thunderbirds Are Go 643
Thunderbolt 344
Thunderheart 789
Thursday's Child 179
THX 1138 501
Tibet in Exile 150
Tibet's Holy Mountain 150
Tibet: A Seed for Transformation 150
Tibet: On the Edge of Change 783
Tibet: The Survival of the Spirit 150
Tibetan Buddhist Meditation 150
Tibetan Medicine 150
Tibor Jankay—The Art of Survival 557, 777
Tick, The 704
Tick vs. Arthur?, The 704
Ticket of Leave Man 511
Tickle in the Heart, A 116, 604
Tickle Tune Typhoon: Let's Be Friends 643
Tidal Wave 823
Tide of Life, The 197
Tie Me Up, Tie Me Down 46
Tie-Died: Rock 'n' Roll's Most Deadicated Fans 623
Tiefland 71
Tieta di Agresta 54
Tiger and the Pussycat, The 511
Tiger Cage 2 133
Tiger of Eschnapur, The 72
Tiger on the Beat II 133
Tigers, The 133
Tigers in Lipstick 34
Tight Spot 391
Tigrero: A Film That Was Never Made 79, 478
Tigris 41, 154
Til Death Us Do Part 249
'Til There Was You 285
Tilai 150
Till the Clouds Roll By 330
Tillie's Punctured Romance 412
Tillie Wakes Up 412
Tim 207
Tim Allen: Men Are Pigs 536
Tim Tyler's Luck 539
Time & The More It Changes 856
Time and Light 841
Time and the Rani 201
Time and Transformation 856
Time Bandits 168
Time Capsule: War in Europe 772
Time Capsule: War in the Pacific 772
Time Expired 438
Time Exposure 564
Time for Dying, A 391
Time for Revenge 52
Time Groove 616
Time Indefinite 478
Time Life's Lost Civilizations 785
Time Machine 501
Time of Indifference 41
Time of the Gypsies 104
Time Out— The Truth About HIV, AIDS and You 835
Time Out for Love 24
Time There Was... A Profile of Benjamin Britten, A 595
Time to Kill, A 249
Time to Live and a Time to Die, A 136
Time Warner Presents the History of Rock 'n' Roll 623
Time Warp: 1954 811
Time Warp: 1960 811
Time Warp: 1964 811
Time Warrior, The 201
Time Will Tell: Bob Marley 604
Time Without Pity 353
TimePiece 466
Times Ain't Like They Used to Be 606
Times Beach, Missouri 806
Times of Harvey Milk 478
Times to Come 53
Timmy's Gift 643
Timmy's Special Delivery 659
Timon and Pumbaa's Wild Adventures: Don't Get Mad, Get Happy 694
Timon and Pumbaa's Wild Adventures: Live and Learn 694
Timon and Pumbaa's Wild Adventures: Quit Buggin' Me 694
Timothy Leary's Dead 478
Timothy Leary's Last Trip 478
Timothy Leary San Francisco Memorial, The 856
Tin Cup 285
Tin Drum, The 65
Tin Soldier (Plummer), The 649
Tin Soldier (Struthers), The 649
Tin Star, The 297
Tina L'hotsky: Barbie and Snakewoman 489
Tingler, The 530
Tinka's Planet 643
Tintoretto 557
Tiny Toon Adventures Vol. 1: The Best of Buster & Babs 688
Tiny Toon Adventures Vol. 2: Tiny Toon Music Television 688
Tiny Toon Adventures Vol. 3: Tiny Toons in Two-Tone Town 688
Tiny Toon Adventures: How I Spent My Vacation 688
Tiny Toon BIG Adventures 688
Tiny Toon Fiendishly Funny Adventures 688
Tiny Toon Island Adventures 688

Tiny Toons: It's a Wonderful Christmas Special 688
Tiny Toons: Night Ghoulery 688
Tiny Toy Stories 717
Tip Off, The 391
Titan—Story of Michelangelo 557
Titanic (1996) 249
Titanic (1997) 249
Titanic (The Learning Channel) 764
Titanic 71, 391, 844
Titanic in a Tub 844
Titanic's Lost Sister 844
Titanic: A Question of Murder 844
Titanic: The Final Chapter 764
Titanic: The Nightmare and the Dream 844
Titanic: Treasure of the Deep 764
Titanica 844
Titian 557
Titian: The Prince of Painters 557
Tito and Me 103
To Bathe a Boa 659
To Be an Astronaut 841
To Be No. 1 133
To Be or Not to Be 285, 345
To Be Young, Gifted & Black 455
To Build a Fire 301
To Catch a Thief 353
To Die For 440
To Each His Own 391
To Have and Have Not 342
To Hell and Back 772
To Kill a Mockingbird 391
To Kill a Priest 96
To Live 118
To Paris with Love 185
To Play or to Die 31
To Play the King 197
To Please a Lady 391
To Render a Life: "Let Us Now Praise Famous Men" & the Documentary Vision 478
To Save Jack Kerouac's Daughter 307
To See Paris and Die 83
To Sir, With Love 179
To Sleep with Anger 446
To the Last Man 297
To the Lighthouse 197, 307
To the Manor Born 197
To the Shores of Iwo Jima 772
To the Shores of Tripoli 391
To What End? 806
To Win at All Costs: The Story of the America's Cup 828
To Wong Foo, Thanks for Everything! Julie Newmar 285, 466
Toast of New Orleans, The 330
Toast of New York, The 391
Toast to Lenny 536
Tobor the Great 501
Tobruk 391
Toccata for Toy Trains 717
Today Was a Terrible Day 659
Today We Live 342
Todd Rutt/Arn McConnell: Shock! Shock! Shock! 489
TOEFL Review 859
Together and Apart 466
Together at Last 777
Toilers and the Wayfarers, The 466
Tokyo Babylon 1 750
Tokyo Babylon 2 750
Tokyo Decadence 140, 511
Tokyo Drifter 140
Tokyo File 391
Tokyo Fist 140
Tokyo Joe 391
Tokyo Olympiad 141
Tokyo Private Police Vol. 1 750
Tokyo Private Police Vol. 2 750
Tokyo Revelation 750
Tokyo Story 144
Tokyo: The Last Megalopolis 750
Tol'able David 405
Toll Collector, The 438
Toll of the Sea 405
Tollgate, The 297, 405
Tolstoy 89
Tom, Dick & Hairy 124
Tom, Dick and Harry 285
Tom & Jerry & Friends #1 688
Tom & Jerry & Friends #2 688
Tom & Jerry & Friends #3 688
Tom & Jerry & Friends #4 688
Tom & Jerry & Friends #5 688
Tom & Jerry & Friends #6 688
Tom & Jerry & Friends #7 688
Tom & Jerry & Friends #8 688
Tom & Jerry & Friends #9 689
Tom & Jerry Classics 689
Tom & Jerry on Parade 689
Tom & Jerry's 50th Birthday Classics 1 689
Tom & Jerry's 50th Birthday Classics 2 689
Tom & Jerry's 50th Birthday Classics 3 689
Tom & Jerry's Cartoon Cavalcade 689
Tom & Jerry's Comic Capers 689
Tom & Jerry's Festival of Fun 689
Tom & Jerry's The Night Before Christmas 689
Tom & Jerry: Starring Tom & Jerry! 689
Tom & Jerry: The Art of Tom & Jerry Vol. 1 689
Tom & Jerry: The Art of Tom & Jerry Vol. 2 689
Tom & Jerry: The Art of Tom & Jerry Vol. 3 (The Chuck Jones Era) 689
Tom & Jerry: The Movie 689
Tom & Jerry: The Very Best of Tom & Jerry 689
Tom & Viv 164
Tom and Huck 694
Tom and Lola 7
Tom Baker Years, The 201
Tom Brown's Schooldays 179
Tom Chomont: A Two-Volume Collection 466, 489
Tom Jones 185
Tom Mix Short Subjects 405
Tom Palazzolo: Films from the Sixties 478
Tom Sawyer 309
Tom Thumb 667
Tom Thumb Meets Thumbelina 643
Tomahawk 297
Tomb of Ligeia 514
Tomb of the Cybermen, The 201
Tomboy 405
Tombs of the Blind Dead 45, 530
Tombstone 297
Tommy—The Interactive Adventure 873
Tomorrow Is Forever 391
Tomorrow Never Dies 169
Tomorrow's Child 249
Tomorrow We Live 179
Tompkins Square Park, 1989/Dinkinsville 479
Tompkins Square Park Police Riot 478
Tong Man 405
Tong Tana— A Journey into the Heart of Borneo 783
Tongues Untied 466
Toni 26
Toni Morrison 307
Tonight and Every Night 330
Tonight for Sure 260
Tonio Kroger 65
Tony Bennett: The Art of the Singer 618
Tony Draws a Horse 179
Tony Kenny's Ireland, The Green Island 204
Tony Rice: The Video Collection 606
Tony Rome 391
Tony Vegas' Animated Acidburn Flashback Tabu 717
Too Beautiful for You 12
Too Far to Go 285
Too Hot to Handle 391
Too Many Pumpkins 643
Too Much, Too Often 511
Too Outrageous Animation 717
Toon Up the Volume 689
Toon Works 873
Toon-A-Vision 541
Toonland USA 689
Toothbrush Family, The 643
Toots Thielmans in New Orleans 616
Tootsie 285
Top Banana 285
Top Dog 95
Top Fighter 135
Top Fighter II: Deadly China Dolls 133
Top Gun 249
Top Gun over Moscow 844
Top Hat 330
Topaz 353
Topaze (1933) 27
Topaze (1951) 27
Topkapi 391
Topper Returns 285
Tora! Tora! Tora! 250
Torch, The 53, 391
Torch Song 391
Torch Song Trilogy 315
Torment 77
Torn Curtain 353
Tornado 823
Tornado Chasers 823
Tornado! Hurricane! Flood! Wonders of Weather 823
Torpedo Alley 391
Torpedo Run 391
Torrent, The 405
Torrents of Spring 97
Torres-Garcia and the Universal Constructivism 557
Tortilla Flat 391
Torture in the Eighties 801
Torture of Silence 24
Torture Zone 530
Torvill & Dean with the Russian All-Stars 828
Tosca (Domingo/Behrens) 585
Tosca (Domingo/Malfitano) 585
Tosca (Domingo/Milnes) 585
Tosca (Marton) 585
Tosca (Tebaldi) 585
Tosca's Kiss 34
Toshiko Akiyoshi Jazz Orchestra: Strive for Jive, The 616
Total Eclipse 96
Total Self, The 856
Totally F***ed Up 438
Toto the Hero 29
Touch and Go 133
Touch of Evil 344
Touch of Frost, A 197
Touch of Love... The Massage 856
Touching Peace 150
Tough Beauty and the Sloppy Slob 133
Tough Guy 179
Tough Guys 250
Tough Guys Don't Dance 250
Touki Bouki 150
Toulouse-Lautrec 557
Tour du Pont: Hammer and Hell, The 828
Tour of the White House, A 798
Touring Alaska 832
Touring America's Ghost Towns 832
Touring America's Historic Inns 832
Touring America's National Parks 832
Touring Australia 209
Touring Austria 74
Touring Civil War Battlefields 780
Touring Egypt 111
Touring England 170
Touring Exciting Europe 832
Touring Hawaii 832
Touring Korea 145
Touring Mexico 61
Touring New Zealand 209
Touring Switzerland 832
Touring the Silent Studios 405
Tournament, The 561
Tournament 26
Toute Une Nuit 30
Toward the Terra 750
Tower of Evil 530
Tower of London 391, 514
Tower of London: The Official Guide 170
Tower of Terror 530
Tower of the Screaming Virgins 530
Towering Inferno, The 250
Towers Open Fire 489
Town Like Alice, A 179, 207
Town Meetings: Pearl Harbor 772
Town That Santa Forgot, The 704
Town Without Pity 391
Toxic Racism 806
Toy, The 285
Toy Story 694
Toy Story Animated Storybook 873
Toy Story Deluxe Collector's Edition 694
Toys 285
Toys in the Attic 315
Toytown Story Adventures, The 643, 717
Tracey Takes On... 422
Track 29 167
Track of the Ants, The 53
Tracks 250
Tracy and Hepburn Collection, The 391
Tracy the Outlaw 405
Trader Horn 391
Trader Hornee 512
Trader Tom and the China Seas 539
Tradesmen and Treasures: Gothic and Renaissance Nuremburg 561
Trading Hearts 250
Trading Places 285
Traditional Basketmaking with John McGuire 564
Traditional Music Classics 606
Traffic 28
Traffic in Souls 405
Traffic Jam 140
Tragedy of a Ridiculous Man 35
Tragedy of Antony and Cleopatra 315
Tragedy of King Lear, The 315
Tragedy of King Richard II 315
Tragedy of Macbeth 315
Tragedy of Othello the Moor of Venice 315
Tragedy of Romeo and Juliet, The 315
Trail of Blood 512, 530
Trail of Hope: The Story of the Mormon Trail 764
Trail of the Axe 405
Trail of the Lonesome Pine, The 391
Trail of the Pink Panther 354
Trailing the Killer 667
Trailside 823, 832
Trailsigns North: Poop, Paw & Hoof Prints 670
Train 772
Train Now Departing 844
Train of Events 179
Train Robbers 250
Train to Happiness, The 113
Train to Hollywood 95
Training Techniques of the Shaolin 856
Trainspotting 164
Traitors of the Blue Castle 140
Traitors to Hitler 73, 772
Tramaine Hawkins 608
Tramp, Tramp, Tramp 405
Tramp and a Woman, The 408
Tramps, The 94
Tranquility Through Tai Chi 856
Trans-Atlantic Tunnel 179
Transformation of Man, The 856
Transport from Paradise 100
Trapeze 392
Trapped by Television 392
Trapped by the Mormons 154
Travel the World 833
Traveller 250
Travellers 107
Travels of Marco Polo 667
Travels with My Aunt 350
Treasure Houses of Britain 170
Treasure Hunt 133
Treasure Island 179, 250, 392, 643, 717
Treasure of Arne, The 77
Treasure of Fear (aka Scared Stiff) 530
Treasure of the Sierra Madre, The 349
Treasures of a Lost Voyage 844

Treasures of the Earth 838
Treasures of the Green Belt: Gates of the City 833
Treasures of the Holy Land: Ancient Art from the Israel Museum 111
Treasures of the Museum of Natural History 873
Treasures of the National Postal Museum/Rarities and Oddities of the National Postal Museum 562
Treasures of the Twilight Zone 422
Treasures of the Vatican Museum and Sistine Chapel 557
Treasury of Animal Stories, Set I 643
Treasury of Children's Stories: Stories to Help Us Grow 659
Treating the Casualties of the Gulf War 764
Treaty, The 204
Trecento: Italian Art and Architecture in the Fourteenth Century, The 557
Tree Grows in Brooklyn, A 392
Tree of Knowledge, The 61
Tree of Life 61
Tree of Wooden Clogs, The 34
Treehouse People: Cannibal Justice 783
Trees, Toilets, and Transformation 806
Trees Lounge 438
Trek in Nepal, A 150
Trespass 250
Tri-Star 124
Trial, The 94, 164, 345
Trial and Error (The Dock Brief) 185
Trial and Error 285
Trial of Adolf Eichmann, The 777
Trial of Red Riding Hood: A Fantasy on Ice, The 828
Trial of the Avco Ploughshares 764
Trial of the Timelord Boxed Set, The 201
Trials of Life 823
Trials of Oscar Wilde, The 179, 466
Tribal Design Grades 4-12 643
Tribal Legacies: Last Stand at Little Big Horn 789
Tribes 250
Tribute 212
Tribute to Alvin Ailey, A 576
Tribute to Charles Kuralt, A 797
Tribute to Dar Robinson 338
Tribute to Hollywood Stuntmen 338
Tribute to John Coltrane 616
Tribute to Noel V. Ginnity 204
Tribute to Sidney Bechet 616
Tribute to Winsor McCay, A 717
Trigger Effect, The 250
Trigonometry 838
Trilby 405
Trinity and Beyond: The Atomic Bomb Movie 479
Trio 489
Trip, The 94
Trip down the River, A 94
Trip to Bountiful, The 250
Trip to Christmas 422
Trip to the Land of Knowledge, A 489
Trip to Where? 512
Tripe 489
Triple Cross 179
Tripleplay Plus! (French) 873
Tripleplay Plus! (Spanish) 873
Trishul 148
Tristan and Isolde 586
Tristana 47
Triumph of Sherlock Holmes, The 187
Triumph of the Nerds 846
Triumph of the Spirit 250
Triumph of the Will 71, 479
Trog 512
Trojan Eddie 164
Trolley 844
Trolls and the Christmas Express 659
Troll in Central Park, A 717
Troma's War (Director's Cut) 512
Tromeo & Juliet 512
Tropic of Cancer 250
Tropical Kingdom of Belize 823
Tropical Rainforest 823
Tropical Sweets 823
Troubadours of Folk Music 606
Troubadours: A Musical Performance by Groupo Camayoc 61
Trouble Along the Way 285
Trouble in Mind 257
Trouble in Tahiti 586
Trouble in the Glen 179
Trouble Is My Business: The Raymond Chandler Library 873
Trouble with Angels, The 285
Trouble with Girls (a.k.a. How to Get into It) 537
Trouble with Harry, The 353
Trouble with Spies, The 285
Troublesome Creek: A Midwestern 479
Troughton Years, The 202
Troy Game 576
Truck Song 659
Truck Turner 533
True Confessions 250
True Glory (Gen. Dwight D. Eisenhower) 772
True Grit 297
True Heart Susie 413
True Identity 446
True Romance 441
True Stories 285
True Story of 200 Motels 623
True Story of Frankenstein, The 530
True Story of Lili Marlene, The 479
True Women 250
Truly, Madly, Deeply 164
Truly Tasteless Jokes: The Video 512
Truman 797
Trumpet Course Beginner-Intermediate with Clark Terry 625
Trumpet Kings 616
Trust 442
Trusting Beatrice 250
Truth About Cats and Dogs, The 285
Truth About Impotence, The 856
Truth About Women 179
Truth or Consequences N.M. 250
Truths & Fictions 873
Try and Get Me 392
Tsar's Bride, The 576
Tsvi Nussbaum: Boy from Warsaw 777
Tu Solo 45, 466
Tubby the Tuba 659
Tucker: The Man and His Dream 260
Tulsa 392
Tumbleweeds 297
Tundra 392
Tune, The 717
Tunes of Glory 179
Tung, To Parsifal & Castro Street 489
Tunisian Victory 772
Tunnel of Love, The 285
Tunnel Vision 536
Tunnel Visions: Into the Sea of Uncertainty 807
Tupac Shakur: Thug Immortal 623
Turandot (Corelli) 586
Turandot (New York) 586
Turandot (San Francisco) 586
Turbulent End to a Tragic War: America's Final Hours in Vietnam 778
Turckhein et Sa Fete du Vin 29
Turgenev's Month in the Country 89
Turkish Delights 31
Turksib/Salt for Svanetia 86
Turn of the Screw, The 250, 586
Turnabout: The Story of the Yale Puppeteers 466, 479
Turner at the Tate 557
Turning Point (1941-1944), The 772
Turning Point 250
Turtle Diary 164
Turumba 146
Tuskegee Airmen, The 250, 455
Tuskegee Airmen: American Heroes 455
Tut: The Boy King 785
Tutankhamen: The Immortal Pharaoh 785
TV Commercials 61
TV Current Affairs Reporting 319
TV Makeup: The Basics 319
TV Nation 422
TV Newsroom: News Gathering 319
TV Newsroom: News Production 319
TV Party 489
TV's Best Adventures of Superman: Volume 1 423
TV's Best Adventures of Superman: Volume 2 423
TV und Texte 155
TVTV Goes to the Super Bowl 828
TVTV Looks at the Oscars 338
TVTV: Four More Years 801
Twain's World 873
'Twas the Night Before Christmas 717
Tweety & Sylvester 689
Twelfth Night, The 83, 164, 316
Twelve Angry Men 392
Twelve Chairs, The 285
Twelve Miles Out 405
Twelve O'Clock High, Vol. 1 623
Twelve O'Clock High, Vol. 2 623
Twenties, The Thirties, The 94
Twentieth Century 342
Twenty Bucks 285
Twenty Something (5pm-9am) 124
Twice Told Tales 530
Twice upon a Time 717
Twilight of the Cockroaches 750
Twilight of the Dark Master 750
Twilight of the Golds 250
Twilight Zone 423
Twilight Zone—The Movie 258, 501
Twin Cheeks: Who Killed the Homecoming King? 466
Twin Dilemma, The 202
Twin Dragons 135
Twin Peaks 257
Twin Peaks Collector's Series 423
Twin Peaks Pilot 257
Twin Peaks: Fire Walk with Me 257
Twin Town 164
Twinkle Twinkle Little Star 671
Twinkletoes 405
Twins 438
Twist 576
Twisted Cross, The 772
Twisted Obsession 250
Twisted Toons: The Warped Animation of Bill Plympton 717
Twister 250
Two Bits 250
Two Bits and Pepper 667
Two by John Ford 341
Two Daughters 148
Two Days in the Valley 250
Two Deaths 167
Two Doctors, The 202
Two English Girls 15
Two for the Road 392
Two for the Seesaw 316
Two Friends 209
Two from Beirut: Seta Manoukian and Missak Terzian 557
Two Girls and a Sailor 331
Two Great Crusades (1935-1945) 811
Two in Twenty 466
Two Jakes, The 251
Two Kinds of Love 251
Two Men and a Wardrobe 98
Two Men in Dallas 798
Two Mrs. Carrolls, The 392
Two Much 285
Two or Three Things I Know About Her 10
Two Rode Together 341
Two Ronnies 197
Two Sisters 113
Two Sisters from Boston 331
Two Small Bodies 438
Two Soldiers 301
Two Stars in the Galaxy 71
Two That Stole the Moon 99
Two Timid Souls (Les Deux Timides) 25
Two to Tango 53
Two Weeks in Another Town 392
Two Weeks with Love 331
Two Without a Cox 99
Two Women 38
Two Years Before the Mast 392
Two-Faced Woman 350
Two-Gun Man from Harlem 449
Ty Co w Ostrej Swiecisz Bramie 94
Tyranny of Adolf Hitler 773

U

U.S. Campaign Against the Death Penalty 807
U-Boat Prisoner 392
U-Turn 251
U2: Rattle and Hum 623
Ub Iwerks' Famous Fairytales 689
Ub Iwerks Comicolor Classics 717
Uffizi, Florence's Treasure House of Art 558
Uforia 438
UFOs and the Alien Presence 862
UFOs and the New World Order 862
UFOs and Underground Bases 862
UFOs: Encounters and Abductions 862
UFOs: The Miracle of the Unknown 862
UFOs: The Secret Evidence 862
Ugetsu 143
Ugly American, The 392
Ugly Duckling (Cher), The 649
Ugly Duckling (Children's Circle), The 649
Ulee's Gold 438
Ulrike Rosenbach: Osho—Samadhi 489
Ultimate 3-D Skeleton 873
Ultimate Athlete: Pushing the Limits 828
Ultimate Challenge: Around the World Alone 828
Ultimate Guide, The 823
Ultimate Guide: T. Rex, The 824
Ultimate Journey, The 824
Ultimate Oz (Collector's Edition) 331
Ultimate Swan Lake, The 576
Ultimate Teacher, The 750
Ultracop 2000 124
Ultraman II 750
Ultraman: The Adventure Begins 750
Ultraman: Towards the Future 750
Ulysses' Gaze 105
Ulysses 392
Ulysses S. Grant 780
Umberto D 38
Umbrella for Three (Paraguas Para Tres) 45
Umbrellas 479, 558
Umbrellas of Cherbourg, The 24
Un Ballo in Maschera (Pavarotti/Millo) 586
Un Ballo in Maschera (Pavarotti/Ricciarelli) 586
Un Chien Andalou/Land Without Bread 47
Un Coeur en Hiver 7
Un Dia Cualquiera 61
Un Premier Prix—Perdu, Un Robot 674
Unaccustomed As We Are 285
Unafraid, The 110
Unanswered Question: Six Talks at Harvard by Leonard Bernstein, The 595
Unbearable Lightness of Being 251
Unbearables: Brooklyn Bridge Readings 1995/1996, The 308
Unbelievable Truth, The 442
Unbroken Circle—Vermont Music: Tradition Change, The 606
Uncensored Voices: War of Peace in Ireland 204
Uncertain Glory 392
Unchastened Woman 405
Uncle Moses 113
Uncle Tom's Cabin (1903 & 1914) 405
Uncle Tom's Cabin (1914) 405
Uncle Tom's Cabin 301, 308
Unconditional Love 438
Unconquered, The 355
Uncovering Shakespeare: An Update 316
Undead, The 514
Undefeated, The 392
Undeniable Evidence 862
Under California Stars 297
Under Suspicion 251
Under the Arbor 586
Under the Biltmore Clock 301
Under the Bridge 71

Under the Cherry Moon....331
Under the Domim Tree....108
Under the Red Robe....79
Under the Roofs of Paris....25
Under the Sun of Satan....10
Under the Volcano....349
Under the Yum-Yum Tree....285
Undercover....179
Undercover Blues....251
Undercurrent....392
Underdog Vol. 1:The Great Gold Robbery....704
Underdogs:A Sports (War) Movie....110
Underneath,The....443
Undersea Kingdom....539
Understanding McLuhan:The Life and Work of Marshall McLuhan....873
Understanding Science....838
Understanding Shakespeare....316
Understanding Surrealism: Painters of the Dream....558
Understanding the Art of the Renaissance: Ideas and Ideals....558
Underworld, U.S.A....341
Underworld....348
Une Femme Douce....15
Unearthly,The....530
Unearthly Child,An....202
Unexplained: Cannibals,The....861
Unexplained: Prophets and Doom,The....792
Unexplained:The Exorcists,The....793
Unexplained:The Power of Prayer,The....793
Unfaithfully Yours....285, 346
Unfaithfuls,The....41
Unfinished Piece for a Mechanical Piano,An....83
Unforgettable....251
Unforgettable Summer,An....104
Unforgiven,The....349
Unforgiven....257
Unheard Voices....61
Unholy Three,The....406
Unhook the Stars....438
Uninvited,The....530
Union City....439
Union Pacific....355
Union Pacific's 40th Anniversary Steam Excursion....844
United States Elections: How We Vote....801
United States Naval Academy: 150 Years in Annapolis....764
United States of Poetry....308
Universal Mind of Bill Evans,The....616
Universal Story,The....339
Universe (Mastervision)....841
Universe (Shatner)....841
Unknown,The....406
Unknown Chaplin....408
Unknown Marx Brothers,The....285, 339
Unknown Secrets:Art and the Rosenberg Era....558
Unknown Soldier,The....773
Unknown World,The....824
Unknown World....501
Unlocking Your Body: Regaining Youth Through Somatic Awareness....856
Unlocking Your Subconscious Wisdom....856
Unmarried Woman,An....251
Unnatural....530
Unnatural Pursuits....164
Unofficial Dan Quayle Video,The....285
Unquiet Dead:An Introduction to Spirit Depossession Therapy,The....856
Unquiet Death of Julius and Ethel Rosenberg,The....479, 764
Unremarkable Life....251
Unseen World of Chiricahua....824
Unsinkable Molly Brown,The....331
Unstrung Heroes....285
Unsuitable Job for a Woman,An....198
Untamable,The....406
Untamed Africa....153, 824
Untamed Wild,The....824
Until in Our Hearts....99
Until the End of the World....67
Until They Get Me....406
Until They Sail....392
Untold Story,The....124
Untold West,The....299
Untouchables,The....251
Unzipped....479
Up Close & Personal....286
Up in Arms....331
Up in Central Park....392
Up Periscope....392
Up Pompeii....198
Up the Academy (Mad Magazine Presents Up the Academy)....286
Up the Creek....185
Up the Down Staircase....392
Up the Sandbox....286
Up to a Certain Point....53
Up to the South....489
Up/Down/Fragile....11
Update on Alien Phenomena....862
Upstairs....94
Upstairs Downstairs....198
Uptown Angel....512
Uptown New York....392
Uptown Saturday Night....446
Uranus....7
Uranus: I Will See Such Things....841
Urashima Taro & Cabbages and Kings....643
Urban Cowboy....251
Urban Heat....512
Urban Jungle....533
Urinal....466
Urotsukidoji III: Return of the Overfiend 1....873
Urusei Yatsura Movie 1: Only You....751
Urusei Yatsura Movie 2: Beautiful Dreamer....751
Urusei Yatsura Movie 3: Remember My Love....751
Urusei Yatsura Movie 4: Lum the Forever....751
Urusei Yatsura Movie 5:The Final Chapter....751
Urusei Yatsura Movie 6:Always My Darling....751
Urusei Yatsura OVA #1: Inaba the Dreammaker....751
Urusei Yatsura OVA #2: Raging Sherbert & I Howl at the Moon....751
Urusei Yatsura OVA #3: Catch the Heart & Goat and Cheese....751
Urusei Yatsura OVA #4: Date with a Spirit & Terror of Girly-Eyes Measles....751
Urusei Yatsura OVA #5: Nagisa's Fiance & Electric Household Guard....751
Urusei Yatsura OVA #6: Ryoko's Tea Party & Memorial Album....751
Urusei Yatsura TV Series Vol. 1....751
Urusei Yatsura TV Series Vol. 2....751
Urusei Yatsura TV Series Vol. 3....751
Urusei Yatsura TV Series Vol. 4....751
Urusei Yatsura TV Series Vol. 5....751
Urusei Yatsura TV Series Vol. 6....751
Urusei Yatsura TV Series Vol. 7....751
Urusei Yatsura TV Series Vol. 8....751
Urusei Yatsura TV Series Vol. 9....751
Urusei Yatsura TV Series Vol. 10....751
Urusei Yatsura TV Series Vol. 11....752
Urusei Yatsura TV Series Vol. 12....752
Urusei Yatsura TV Series Vol. 13....752
Urusei Yatsura TV Series Vol. 14....752
Urusei Yatsura TV Series Vol. 15....752
Urusei Yatsura TV Series Vol. 16....752
Urusei Yatsura TV Series Vol. 17....752
Urusei Yatsura TV Series Vol. 18....752
Urusei Yatsura TV Series Vol. 19....752
Used Cars....286
Used People....286
Ushio & Tora Vol. 1....752
Ushio & Tora Vol. 2....752
Ushio & Tora Vol. 3....752
Ushio & Tora Vol. 4....752
Ushio & Tora Vol. 5 & Super-Deformed Special....752
Using Macromedia Director....873
Usual Suspects,The....251
Utah....297
Utamaro and His Five Women....143
Ute Lemper Sings Kurt Weill....618
Utopia....286
Utu:The Director's Cut....209
Utz....164

V

V for Victory....773
Vacillations of Poppy Carew,The....164
Vagabond....14
Vagabond Lover,The....331
Val Lewton Collection,The....530
Valdez Is Coming....297
Valentine for Nelson & Two Marches,A....466, 489
Valentino....167
Vali: Witch of Positano....479
Valiant Ones,The....133
Valley Forge....764
Valley Girl....251
Valley of Decision,The....392
Valley of Hate,The....406
Valley of the Dolls....512
Valley of the Gwangi....501
Valley of the Kings....392
Valmont....100
Vamanos con Pancho Villa....53
Vamping....251
Vampire,The....530
Vampire Bat,The....531
Vampire Hunter D....752
Vampire over London....531
Vampire People....531
Vampire Princess Miyu #1....752
Vampire Princess Miyu #2....752
Vampire Princess Miyu Series....752
Vampire Vixens from Venus....512
Vampyr....79
Van,The....166
Van Beuren & Commonwealth....689
Van Beuren Cartoons #1:Tom & Jerry....689
Van Beuren Cartoons #2: Cubby Bear....689
Van Beuren Cartoons #3:The Little King....689
Van Beuren Studio,Volume #1....689
Van Beuren Studio,Volume #2....689
Van Gogh....10
Van Gogh Revisited....558
Van Gogh:A Museum for Vincent....558
Vanderbeekiana!: Stan VanDerBeek's Vision....489
Vanina Vanini....39
Vanishing,The....31
Vanishing American,The....406
Vanishing Dawn Chorus....824
Vanity Fair....198, 392
Vanya on 42nd Street....13
Varga Girls:The Esquire Magazine Images of Alberto Vargas....562
Varietease: David Friedman's Roadshow Rarities, Vol. 2....512
Variety....71, 439
Variety Is the Spice of Life....489
Variety Lights....37
Various Artists Featuring Raymond Kane Ki Ho'alu: That's Slack Key Guitar....604
Vassar Clements....616
Vassily Kandinsky....558
Vatican City:Art and Glory....43
Vaudeville Videos....316
Vegas in Space....466, 512
Vegetable Print Shop....671
Veiled Aristocrats....449
Velazquez:The Nobleman of Painting....558
Veldt,The....644
Velveteen Rabbit,The....717
Velveteen Rabbit (Plummer),The....649
Velveteen Rabbit (Streep),The....649
Vendetta for the Saint....198
Vengeance Is Mine....141
Vengeance on Varos....202
Vengeance Valley....297
Venice/Venice....251
Venice: Queen of the Adriatic....43
Venus of the South Seas....406
Venus Wars,The....752
Vera Cruz....297
Verbs....859
Verdi (The Opera)....41, 586
Verdi/Donizetti:An Evening with Joan Sutherland & Luciano Pavarotti....586
Verdi: Requiem (La Scala/von Karajan)....600
Verdi: Requiem (London/Abbado)....600
Verdi:The King of Melody....586
Verdict,The....251
Vermeer: Love, Light and Silence....558
Vermillion Editions....562
Vermont Is for Lovers....439
Veronico Cruz....53
Versailles....29
Versatile Mr. Laurel....412
Vertigo....353
Very Brady Sequel,A....286
Very Curious Girl,A....7
Very Easy Christmas Ornament,A....564
Very Easy Santa Design,A....564
Very Easy Santa Pillow,A....564
Very Moral Night,A....102
Very Natural Thing,A....466
Very Old Man with Enormous Wings,A....53
Very Private Affair,A....13
Vespers of the Blessed Virgin....600
Vezelay....479
Via Appia....65, 467
Vibes....286
Vibrant Mirror....558
Vicar of Dibley....198
Victim....179
Victor Borge Tells Hans Christian Andersen Stories....649
Victor Borge: Live from London....595
Victor Borge: On Stage with Audience Favorites....536
Victor Hernandez Cruz....61
Victor Sjostrom....339
Victor/Victoria....354
Victoria de los Angeles in Recital....600
Victoria Wood:As Seen on TV....198
Victory (Escape to Victory)....349
Victory at Entebbe....251
Victory at Sea,Volumes 1 to 6....773
Victory Gardens of WWII....773
Victory over the Sun:A Reconstruction of the 1913 Futurist Performance....586
Vicus....783
Vidal in Venice, Part One....43
Vidal in Venice, Part Two....43
Video Against AIDS,Volumes 1, 2 & 3....835
Video Art,Tape One....489
Video Art,Tape Two....489
Video Art:Antonio Muntadas....489
Video Art:Ardele Lister....489
Video Art: Blue Moon....489
Video Art: Come on Touch It (Study No. 4 for a Personality Inventory Channel)....490
Video Art: Damnation of Faust Trilogy....490
Video Art: Dana Atchley & Eric Metcalfe....490
Video Art: David Askevold....490
Video Art: Gary Hill....490
Video Art: Helen Doyle....490
Video Art: Here in the Southwest....490
Video Art: Hygiene....490
Video Art: It Starts at Home....490
Video Art: Jan Peacock....490
Video Art: Leaving the 20th Century and Perfect Leader....490
Video Art: Les Levine....490
Video Art: Noel Harding....490
Video Art: Not Dead Yet....490
Video Art: Prime Cuts....490
Video Art: Red Tapes....490
Video Art: Rober Racine....490
Video Art: Shut the Fuck Up....490
Video Art:Telling Motions....490
Video Art:Test Tube....490
Video Art:Tomiyo Sasaki....490
Video Art:Vital Statistics of a Citizen, Simply Obtained....491
Video Band War Dance....623
Video Congress No. 8....491
Video Congress No. 9....491
Video Dance/The Video Dance Lectures....319
Video Dictionary of Classical Ballet....576

Video Editing....319
Video Encyclopedia of Psychoactive Drugs, The....838
Video from Hell....512
Video from Russia....89
Video Guide to the Internet, The....846
Video Network Program One....623
Video Network Program Two....623
Video Outlines of Asian Religions....793
Video Post Production....319
Video Scriptwriting for Success and Profit....319
Video Storybreak....644
Video Visits: Argentina, Land of Natural Wonder....61
Video Visits: Baltic States— Lithuania, Latvia, Estonia....87
Video Visits: China, Ancient Rhythms and Modern Currents....136
Video Visits: Costa Rica, The Land of Pure Life....61
Video Visits: Cuba, Island of Dreams....61
Video Visits: Czechoslovakia, Triumph and Tradition....101
Video Visits: Denmark, The Jewel of Europe....79
Video Visits: Discovering Wales....170
Video Visits: Egypt, The Land of Ancient Wonders....111
Video Visits: Indonesia, The Jeweled Archipelago....145
Video Visits: Israel, A Land for Everyone....110
Video Visits: Jerusalem, 3,000 Years of Miracles....110
Video Visits: Jordan, The Desert Kingdom....111
Video Visits: Morocco, A Bridge Across Time....153
Video Visits: New England, America's Living Heritage....833
Video Visits: Peru, A Golden Treasure....62
Video Visits: Sweden, Nordic Treasure....79
Video Visits: Thailand, The Golden Kingdom....145
Video Visits: The Philippines, Pearls of the Pacific....146
Video Visits: Ukraine—Ancient Crossroads, Modern Dreams....86
Video Visits: Vietnam, Land of the Ascending Dragon....145
Video Visits: Zimbabwe, Africa's Wildlife Sanctuary....153
Video Void VIII....623
Video Works: Miroslaw Rogala (1980-86)....491
Videodrome....213
Videotape for a Woman and a Man....491, 567
Videotape with Joseph Beuys....558
Videotapes of Elizabeth Sher, Volumes 1-11, The....491
Vidhaata....148
Vienna 1900....74
Vienna Boys' Choir Sings Mozart at the Chapel of the Hofburg, Vienna....600
Vienna in Music....595
Vienna New Year's Concert 1991....595
Vietnam....778
Vietnam Experience....778
Vietnam Home Movies....778
Vietnam—The Hot Red War....778
Vietnam War Story III....778
Vietnam: A Television History....778
Vietnam: Chronicle of War....778
Vietnam: In the Year of the Pig....481, 778
Vietnam: Remember....778
Vietnam: The Secret Agent....778
Vietnam: The Ten Thousand Day War....778
Vietnam: They Were Young and Brave....764
Vietnam: Time of the Locust....778
Vietnam: Two Decades and a Wake Up....778
Vigil....209
Vigilante....251
Vikings....392
Village Affair, A....198, 467
Village of Dreams....140
Village of the Damned (1994)....501
Village of the Damned....501
Village of the Damned/Children of the Damned (1960)....501
Villain, The....297
Villain Still Pursued Her, The....409
Vincent, Francois, Paul & the Others....7
Vincent....207, 316
Vincent Trasov: My Five Years in a Nutshell....89
Vincent van Gogh: His Art and Life....558
Vintage: A History of Wine by Hugh Johnson....858
Violated....512
Violence at Noon....141
Violence Jack Part 3: Slum King....752
Violent Men, The....297
Violent Years, The....515
Violet's Visit....207
Vip My Brother Superman....717
VIP's, The....179
Virge Piersol Short Pieces....623
Virgin Machine....65, 467
Virgin Queen, The....392
Virgin Spring, The....78
Virginia City....297
Virginia Plantations— Mount Vernon, Monticello and Other Great Houses of Old Virginia....833
Virginia's Civil War Parks....833
Virginian, The....297, 406
Viridiana....47
Virtual 60's....764
Virtual Reality....846, 856
Virtues of Negative Fascination....567
Virtuiti Militari 1792-1992....99
Virtuosity....501
Virus Knows No Morals, A....65, 467
Viruses and Bacteria: The Story of the Warm Wet Spots....838
Visas That Saved Lives, The....777
Vision of the Medicine Wheel (with Sun Bear)....789
Vision Shared: A Tribute to Woody Guthrie & Leadbelly, A....606
Visions of Eden: A Jewish Perspective on the Environment....116
Visions of Gregorian Chants....600
Visions of Light....339
Visions of Russia: A Granddaughter Returns....89
Visions of the Arawaks....558
Visions of War....773
Visions: Jewish American Hall of Fame....116
Visit with Alan Jay Lerner, A....618
Visit with Arthur Schwartz, A....618
Visit with Burton Lane, A....618
Visit with Charles Strouse, A....618
Visit with E.Y. "Yip" Harburg, A....618
Visit with Kander and Ebb, A....618
Visit with Mitchell Parish, A....618
Visit with Sheldon Harnick, A....618
Visit with Tomie dePaola, A....562
Visitation/Black Orchid, The....202
Visite en France....29
Visitor, The....644
Visitors, The....18, 251
Visual Almanac Complete, The....873
Visual Almanac Upgrade, The....873
Visual History of Cars....844
Visualizing Memory...A Last Detail....777
Vito and the Others....34
Viva Castro!....83
Viva Eu! & Ex Voto....467, 491
Viva Las Vegas....537
Viva Maria....13
Viva Max....286
Viva Villa!....392
Vivaldi: Le Quattri Stagioni (The Four Seasons) (Nupen)....595
Vivaldi: The Four Seasons (Karajan)....595
Vivaldi: Violin Concerti....595
Vive L'Amour....136
Vivien Leigh: Scarlett and Beyond....339
Vivre pour Manger....479
Vixen....513
Vizcaya Museum and Gardens....558
Vladimir Ashkenazy....595
Vladimir Horowitz in Moscow....595
Vladimir Horowitz in Vienna....595
Vladimir Horowitz: A Reminiscence....595
Vladimir Horowitz: Rachmaninoff Piano Concerto No. 3....595
Voice from the Screen, The....339
Voice of the Voiceless....62
Voice Workout for the Actor....319
Voices and Visions....308
Voices and Visions: Elizabeth Bishop....308
Voices and Visions: Emily Dickinson....308
Voices and Visions: Ezra Pound....308
Voices and Visions: Hart Crane....308
Voices and Visions: Langston Hughes....308
Voices and Visions: Marianne Moore....308
Voices and Visions: Robert Frost....308
Voices and Visions: Robert Lowell....308
Voices and Visions: Sylvia Plath....308
Voices and Visions: T.S. Eliot....308
Voices and Visions: Wallace Stevens....308
Voices and Visions: Walt Whitman....308
Voices and Visions: William Carlos Williams....308
Voices from Sepharad....116
Voices from the Front....835
Voices from the Ice, Alaska....833
Voices in Celebration....558
Voices of a New Age....857
Voices of Sarafina....151
Voices of Spirit....857
Volcano....824
Volcanoes of Hawaii....824
Volcanoes: Life on the Age....873
Volcanos: Cauldrons of Fury....824
Volere Volare....34
Volga Boatman, The....355
Volga-Volga....84
Volpone....24
Voltage Fighter Gowcaizer Round 1....752
Voltage Fighter Gowcaizer Round 2....752
Volunteers....286
Von Richtofen and Brown....514
Von Ryan's Express....392
Voodoo Woman....531
Votes for Women?! 1913 U.S. Senate Testimony....764
Vow, The....113
Voyage en Ballon....644
Voyage en Douce....7
Voyage in Italy....39
Voyage of LaAmistad: A Quest for Freedom, The....455
Voyage of the Great Southern Ark....824
Voyage Round My Father....198
Voyage Surprise....24
Voyage to a Prehistoric Planet....501
Voyage to Save the Whales....824
Voyage to the Bottom of the Sea....501
Voyage to the Outer Planets and Beyond....841
Voyager....65
Voyager Odyssey, The....841
Voyages: The Journey of the Magi....562, 793
Vukovar....103
Vulcan, Son of Jupiter....42

W

W. Eugene Smith....560
W.C. Fields: 6 Short Films....286
W.C. Fields: On Stage, on Screen, on the Air....286
W Hour....94
W.S. Merwin....308
Wacky World of Doctor Morgus, The....512
Waco: The Rules of Engagement....479
Wag the Dog....286
Wages of Fear, The....25
Wagner Concert in Leipzig....595
Wagner in Bayreuth....600
Wagner: Scenes from "The Ring" at the Met....586
Wagner: The Complete Epic....595
Wai's Romance....124
Waikiki Wedding....331
Wait Until Dark....392
Wait Until Spring Bandini....251
Waiting for God I....198
Waiting for God II....198
Waiting for Grandma....644
Waiting for Guffman....286
Waiting to Exhale....446
Wake Island....392
Wake of the Red Witch....393
Waking Up the Power Within: The Freedom to Heal....857
Waking Up: A Lesson in Love....467
Walden (aka Diaries, Notes & Sketches)....443
Waldheim: Commission of Inquiry....773
Waldo Kitty: Even Cats Can Dream....689
Waldorf Promise, The....861
Walk, Don't Run....286
Walk in Balance....789
Walk in Crusader Jerusalem....793
Walk in the Clouds, A....251
Walk in the Forest....824
Walk in the Sun....773
Walk in the Wild, A....644
Walk on the Wild Side....393
Walk Softly, Stranger....393
Walk the Proud Land....297
Walk Through History, A....841
Walk with the People....801
Walkabout....167
Walker....251
Walkin' in the Shoes of the King....537
Walking and Talking....286
Walking Back....406
Walking Between the Raindrops....439
Walking on Air....661
Walking Tall: The Trilogy....251
Walking with the Buddha....150
Wall, The....106
Wall in Jerusalem....110
Wall Street....251
Wall Street Journal Video: Emerging Powers....801
Wallace & Gromit Collection....717
Wallace & Gromit Laserdisc....717
Wallace & Gromit: A Close Shave....717
Wallace & Gromit: A Grand Day Out....717
Wallace & Gromit: The Wrong Trousers....717
Walls in the City....316
Walls of Light: The History of Stained Glass....562
Walls of Malapaga....24
Walpurgis Night....77
Walt Disney Christmas, A....694
Walt Odets on Primary Prevention for Gay Men....835
Walt Whitman and the Civil War....308
Walter Hawkins and Love Alive IV....608
Waltz of the Toreadors....185
Waltzing Matilda....659
Waltzing Through the Hills....661
Wanda Nero Butler: New Born Soul....608
Wanda Nevada....297
Wanderer, The....7
Wanderers, El Hazard TV Series Quest #6, The....752
Wanderers, The....752
Wandering Jew, The....154
Wanna-Be's....752
Wannsee Conference....65
Wanted: The Perfect Guy....644
War & Civilization....764
War Against the Indians, The....789
War and Peace....84, 198, 393, 586
War and Remembrance....423
War Arrow....297
War at Home, The....251
War at Home....778
War Between the States (1800s)....780
War Chronicles Volumes 1-8—Pre-Pack....773
War Chronicles Volume 1— The Greatest Conflict....773
War Chronicles Volume 6— Bomber Offensive: Air War in Europe....773
War Chronicles Volume 8— The Battle of Germany....773
War Chronicles Volume 10— Jungle Warfare: New Guinea to Burma....773
War Chronicles Volume 12— The Bloody Ridges of Peleliu....773
War Chronicles Volume 13— Return to the Philippines....773
War Dance....439
War Games (Parts 1 & 2), The....202
War in El Cedro: American Veterans in Nicaragua....62
War in the Gulf: Answering Children's Questions....111
War in the Pacific....874
War Is Menstrual Envy—Parts I, II and III....439
War Machines, The....202
War Machines of Tomorrow....764
War of 1812....811
War of the Buttons....185
War of the Colossal Beast, The....531
War of the Gargantuas....501
War of the Robots, The....501
War of the Roses....286
War of the Underworld....133
War of the Wildcats....393
War of the Worlds....501
War on Land and Sea....773

War Requiem 168, 600
War Room, The 479
War Stories 773
War Stories Our Mothers Never Told Us 479, 773
War That Changed War Deluxe Boxed Set, The 764
War Wagon 297
War Years: Britain in World War II, The 773
Ward Six 103
Wargames 251
Warlock 297
Warlords 774
Warner Bros. Collection Vol. 1: Tokyo Jokio 690
Warner Bros. Collection Vol. 2: Wackiki Wabbit 690
Warner Bros. Collection Vol. 3: Private Snafu 690
Warner Bros. Collection Vol. 4: The Dover Boys 690
Warner Bros. Collection Vol. 5: Porky Pig 690
Warning from Space 501
Warning Shadows 71
Warring & Roaring (1914-1929) 811
Warrior's Rest 24
Warriors 251
Warriors of the Amazon 62
Warriors of the Deep 202
Wars in Peace 764
Warsaw Ghetto, The 777
Warsaw Story 777
Warsaw Uprising Chronicle (Kroniki Powstania Warszawskiego) 774
Wartime Cartoons 717
Wartime Combat 479
Wartime Homefront 479
Wartime Moments 479
Washington, D.C. 833
Washington, D.C.: An Inspiring Tour 833
Washington, DC 874
Washington Monuments 833
Washington Square 96
Wasp Woman 514
Watch on the Rhine 393
Watch the Birdie 286
Water 185
Water and Power 439
Water Cycle, The 807
Water Engine, The 316
Water Is Wet 659
Water Journey 824
Water Media Techniques: Acrylic and Casein 564
Water Media Techniques: Watercolor and Gouache 564
Watercolor I 565
Watercolor II 565
Watercolor III 565
Watercolor Painting Pt. 1: Wet and Spontaneous 565
Watercolor Painting Pt. 2: Taming the Wet Medium 565
Watercolor Symbols: Rocks, Puddles and Weeds 565
Watercolor Symbols: Trees and Water 565
Waterdance, The 251
Waterfalls and Wildlife 824
Waterfront 207
Watergate Scandal and Resignation of President Nixon 764
Watergate—The Deluxe Boxed Set 764
Watergate: The Secret Story 764
Waterhole #3 393
Waterland 252
Waterloo Bridge 393
Watermelon Man 446
Watermelon Woman, The 439
Watership Down 717
Waterworks 439
Waterworld 502
Wavy Gravy Birthday Benefit for Seva Foundation, The 623
Wax, or the Discovery of the Television Among the Bees 439
Waxworks 71
Way Ahead, The 179
Way Down East 413
Way Down South 449
Way of the Black Dragon 533
Way of the Little Dragon, The 133
Way of the Wizard, The 857
Way Pots Pour, The 565
Way Things Go, The 562
Way Things Work, The 874
Way We Were, The 252
Way West, The 299
Wayne's World 286
Ways at Wallace and Sons and The Bank Dory 828
We All Live Downstream 807
We Are Guatemalans 62
We Can Keep You Forever 778
We Can Make a Difference 807
We Can't Help It—We're Men 423
We Dive at Dawn 179
We Learn About the World 659
We Like the Blues: Vol. 1 616
We Like the Blues: Vol. 2 616
We Never Die 103
We of the Never Never 207
We're All Stars 53
We're Back! A Dinosaur's Story 690
We're in the Navy Now 406
We're No Angels 286
We're Not Dressing 393
We're Not Married 286
We're Off to See the Munchkins 339
We Remember: The Space Shuttle Pioneers 1981-1986 841
We Sing, Gospel's Greatest Hymns 608
We the Living 42
We've Come for Your Daughters 623
We Were One Man 7, 467
We Were So Beloved 777
We Were There 467
We Were There: Jewish Liberators of the Nazi Concentration Camps 777
Weaker Sex, The 179
Weapons Bazaar 807
Weapons in Space 807
Weapons of Mass Destraction 286
Weapons of the Spirit 7
Weathered and Torn 618
Weavers: Wasn't That a Time, The 606
Web Planet, The 202
Webb Pierce/Chet Atkins 606
Webb Pierce: Greatest Hits 606
Webs of Steel 406
Wedding, The 97
Wedding 254
Wedding Banquet, The 455, 467
Wedding Gift, The 164
Wedding in Galilee 108
Wedding March, The 348
Wedding Night, The 393
Wedding of Palo, The 783
Wedding Show, The 439
Wedding Singer, The 286
Weddings and Babies 393
Wee Sing Series 671
Wee Willie Winkie 341
Weed 479
Week in the Life of a Chinese Student, A 644
Week in the Life of a Mexican Student, A 62
Week That Shook the World: The Soviet Coup, The 89
Week-End in Havana 331
Weekend 10
Weekend at the Waldorf 286
Weekend in the Country, A 286
Wegman's World 560
Weird America 512
Weird Cartoons Vol. 1 717
Weird Cartoons Vol. 2 717
Weird Tales 71
Weird TV Chunk 1 423
Weird World of LSD 512
Welcome Back Wil Cwac Cwac 659
Welcome Home, Roxy Carmichael 286
Welcome Stranger 286
Welcome to My Nightmare 623
Welcome to Sarajevo 252
Welcome to the Dollhouse 439
Well Spent Life, A 480
Well-Digger's Daughter, The 27
Wellness Series: Positive Imagery 857
Wend Kuuni (God's Gift) 150
Went the Day Well? 28
Werewolf of London 531
Werewolf vs. the Vampire Woman 531
Werner Herzog Eats His Shoe 480
Werther 586
Wes Craven's New Nightmare 531
West, The 299
West & Soda 717
West Coast Crones: A Glimpse into the Lives of Nine Old Lesbians 467
West Is West 439
West of Hester Street 116
West of the Divide 297
West of the Imagination 299
West of Zanzibar/The Unholy Three 406
West Point Story, The 331
West Side Story 331
Western Classics Collection: Vengeance Valley and The Big Trees 297
Western Frontier: The First to Let Women Vote, The 765
Western Union 72
Westerner, The 344
Westfront 1918 71
Westler: East of the Wall 65, 467
Westworld 502
Whale for the Killing 824
Whales and Dolphins 874
Whales of August, The 164
Whales! (National Audubon) 824
Whalesong: Whales and Dolphins of the Pacific 824
What! Mario Bava 531
What a Woman! 42
What About Bob? 286
What About Me 439
What About the Russians? 89
What Are You Going to Do to Me, If You Catch Me? 95
What Can I Do? 252
What Do Those Old Films Mean? 154, 339
What Do You Want to Be When You Grow Up? Heavy Equipment Operator 659
What Do You Want to Be When You Grow Up? Railroaders 659
What Ever Happened to… 531
What Ever Happened to Baby Jane? 531
What Happened to Kerouac? (1985) 308
What Happened to Kerouac? (1996) 308
What Happened to Rosa? 406
What Happened Was… 439
What Have I Done to Deserve This? 46
What Is Kundalini? 857
What Is Multimedia? 319
What Is the Third World? 801
What Is Yoga? 857
What Makes Work Meaningful? 857
What Price Glory? 341, 406
What Price Survival? 133
What Ramon Did 835
What's a Parent to Do? 858
What's Eating Gilbert Grape 252
What's Love Got to Do with It 331
What's New Mr. Magoo? Volume 1 704
What's New Mr. Magoo? Volume 2 704
What's New Mr. Magoo? Volume 3 704
What's New Mr. Magoo? Volume 4 704
What's New Mr. Magoo? Volume 5 704
What's New Mr. Magoo? Volume 6 704
What's New Mr. Magoo? Volume 7 704
What's New Mr. Magoo? Volume 8 704
What's New Pussycat 287
What's the Matter with Helen? 512
"What's the Score?"—Text Analysis for the Actor 319
What's Under My Bed and Other Creepy Stories 659
What's Underground About Marshmallows: Ron Vawter Performs Jack Smith 442, 567
What's Up Doc 287
What's Up Tiger Lily? 289
What Sex Am I? 479
What Soviet Children Are Saying About Nuclear War 89, 807
What! 98, 531
What! No Beer? 409
Wheel of Fortune 297
Wheeler Dealers, The 287
Wheeler Dixon: Selected Films 491
Wheels a' Rolling 845
Wheels on Meals 135
When a Kid Is Gay 467
When a Man Loves a Woman 252
When a Woman Ascends the Stairs 140
When Abortion Was Illegal: Untold Stories 479
When Bad Things Happen to Good People 857
When Chicago Was Hollywood 339
When Comedy Was King 412
When Dinosaurs Ruled the Earth 502
When Father Was Away on Business 104
When Food Becomes an Obsession: Overcoming Eating Disorders 857
When Gangland Strikes 393
When Governments Kill 807
When Harry Met Sally 287
When I Close My Eyes 104
When Ireland Starved 204
When Knights Were Bold 185
When Ladies Meet 393
When Mom and Dad Break Up 858
When Night Is Falling 212, 467
When's Your Birthday? 287
When the Cat's Away 7
When the Clouds Roll By 412
When the Greeks 105
When the Legends Die 297
When the People Lead 807
When the Salmon Runs Dry 807
When the Spill Hit Homer 807
When the Whales Came 252
When the Wind Stops 644
When Things Get Rough on Easy Street, Ovid and Shorts 439
When We Were Kings 479
When Women Had Tails 34
When Women Kill 479
When Worlds Collide 502
Where America Began: Jamestown, Colonial Williamsburg and Yorktown 811
Where Angels Fear to Tread 164
Where Did I Come From? 644
Where Do I Start: Basic Set Construction 319
Where Eagles Fly: Portraits of Women in Power 150
Where Evil Dwells (The Trailer) 439
Where Have All the Dolphins Gone? 807
Where Have You Gone Joe DiMaggio? 797, 828
Where in the World/Kids Explore 644
Where Is My Child? 116
Where Is the Friend's Home? 107
Where Jesus Walked 793
Where Land Is Life 62
Where Love Has Gone 393
Where None Has Gone Before 841
Where's Piccone? 34
Where's Poppa? 287
Where's Spot 659
Where the Boys Are 287
Where the Girls Are 287
Where the Green Ants Dream 67
Where the Hot Wind Blows 42
Where the Lilies Bloom 644
Where the North Holds Sway 406
Where the Red Fern Grows 667
Where the Red Fern Grows, Part II 667
Where the Wild Things Are/Higglety Pigglety Pop! 659
Where There Is Hatred 807
Where There's Life 287
Where Were You When the Lights Went Out? 287
Which Way, Weather? 644
Whiffle Squeek 644
While You Were Sleeping 287
Whip, The 406
Whipping Boy, The 644
Whirlwind Raiders 298
Whiskers 667
Whiskey Galore 185
Whisky and Sofa (Operation Moonlight) 66
Whispering Chorus, The 355

Whispering Shadow, The 539
Whispers from Space 862
Whispers on the Wind 308
Whistle Stop 393
Whistlepunks & Sliverpickers: A Fun Look at Forestry 644
Whistling in Brooklyn 287
Whistling in Dixie 287
Whistling in the Dark 287
White 96
White Balloon 107
White Buffalo 298
White Cargo 393
White Christmas 331
White Cliffs of Dover, The 393
White Commanche 298
White Crane Kung-fu 857
White Dawn 252
White Eagle (Orzel Bialy) 99
White Fang and the Hunter 667
White Flame, The 71
White Gold 406
White Heat 393
White Hell of Pitz Palu 71
White Hole in Time, The 807
White Hunter, Black Heart 257
White Lotus Cult 133
White Man's Burden 252
White Men Can't Jump 287
White Night of Dance in Leningrad 576
White Nights 39, 252
White Orchid, The 393
White Palace 252
White Rose 413
White Sands 252
White Seal, The 690
White Sheep 406
White Sheik 37
White Sister, The 406
White Slaves of Chinatown 512
White Squall 252
White Tiger 406
White Trash at Heart 439
White Warrior, The 512
White Zombie 531
Whitewash 455, 644
Whitewater Adventures 833
Who Am I? Why Am I Here? 793
Who Am I This Time? 255
Who Built America? American Social History Project 874
Who Built America? Education Edition 874
Who Done It? 185
Who Framed Roger Rabbit? 690
Who Is Henry Jaglom? 339
Who Is Killing the Great Chefs of Europe? 212
Who Killed "Doc" Robbin? (Curley and His Gang in the Haunted Mansion) 287
Who Killed Baby Azaria 207
Who'll Stop the Rain 252
Who's Afraid of Opera 586
Who's Afraid of Virginia Woolf? 393
Who's Got the Black Box? 13
Who's Harry Crumb? 287
Who's Out There? 862
Who's Singing Over There? 104
Who's That Knocking at My Door? 254
Who's the Woman, Who's the Man, Parts A & B 124
Who's Who 166
Who Shall Live and Who Shall Die? 777
Who Was She? 148
Who Will Be My Friend? 659
Whodunnit: The Art of the Detective Story 308
Whoever Says the Truth Shall Die 37
Whole Town's Talking, The 341
Whole Wide World, The 252
Whole World Is Watching-Weatherman '69, The 439
Whoopee 331
Whoopi Goldberg: Fontaine...Why Am I Straight? 536
Whoops Apocalypse 185
Whore 167
Whore 2 512
Whoregasm 491
Whose Life Is It Anyway? 252
Why Change Your Wife 355
Why Does Herr R. Run Amok? 66
Why Has Bodhi-Dharma Left for the East? 136
Why Me? 124
Why People Don't Heal and How They Can 857
Why Shoot the Teacher? 212
Why Toes Tap: Wynton on Rhythm 625
Why We Fight 774
Wicked City 117
Wicked Lady 185
Wicked Stepmother 287
Wicker Man, The 531
Wide Sargasso Sea 207, 252
Wide World of Lydia Lunch 439
Widow Couderc 18
Widow's Peak 202
Wife, The 439
Wife vs. Secretary 393
Wigstock: The Movie 439, 467
Wilanow— King Jan III Sobieski Residence 99
Wilby Conspiracy, The 533
Wild, Wild World of Jayne Mansfield 512
Wild Alaska 824
Wild and Woody 690
Wild and Woolly 406
Wild at Heart 257
Wild Australia on Video 824
Wild Bill 298
Wild Bill: Hollywood Maverick 339
Wild Blade 467
Wild Blue Yonder: The U.S. Air Force Story 845
Wild Bunch, The 393
Wild Bunch (Boxed Set), The 347
Wild Bunch (Director's Cut), The 347
Wild Child, The 15
Wild Christmas Reindeer, The 644
Wild Couple, The 133
Wild Discovery 824
Wild Flower 439
Wild Gals of the Naked West 513
Wild Guitar 512
Wild Hearts Can't Be Broken 667
Wild Horses 45
Wild India 824
Wild Life 467
Wild Little Bunch 164
Wild One, The 393
Wild Ones on Wheels 512
Wild Ones: The Air Cavalry in Vietnam, The 778
Wild Orchids 406
Wild Palms 423
Wild Party, The 412
Wild Rapture 153
Wild Reeds 7
Wild Ride, The 514
Wild Rovers 354
Wild Search 133
Wild Side 252
Wild Strawberries 78
Wild Style 439
Wild Things 252
Wild West, The 765
Wild West 298
Wild Wheels 479
Wild Women 252
Wild Women of Wongo, The 512
Wild World of Batwoman, The 512
Wild World Series: Daisy Discovers the World, The 824
Wilder Napalm 287
Wilderness: The Last Stand 807
Wildflowers of the Cajun Prairies 824
Wildlife Decoy Carvers 562
Wildlife Fantasia 618
Wildlife Symphony 644
Wilds of Madagascar 824
Wilhelm Tell 71
Will Eisner 541
Will My Mother Go Back to Berlin? 108
Will of Iron 135
Will Our Children Thank Us? 807
Will Penny 298
Will Rogers 797
Will Rogers: Champion of the People 797
Will Success Spoil Rock Hunter 287
Will Vinton's Festival of Claymation 717
Will We Miss Them? Endangered Species 644
Will You Dance with Me? 24
Willa: An American Snow White 667
Willem de Kooning: Artist 558
Willem de Kooning: The Last Picture Show 558
William Holden: The Golden Boy 339
William Merritt Chase at Shinnecock 558
William S. Burroughs: Commissioner of the Sewers 308
William Shakespeare 308
William Shakespeare's Romeo & Juliet 316
William Shakespeare Series 316
William Tell 586
William Wegman Reel 1 491
William Wegman Reel 2 491
William Wegman Reel 3 491
William Wegman Reel 4 491
William Wegman Reel 5 491
William Wegman Reel 6 491
William Wegman Reel 7 491
William Wegman's Mother Goose 644
Willie, The Operatic Whale 694
Willie 481
Willie and Phil 287
Willie Dixon 616
Willie Wonka and the Chocolate Factory 667
Willis O'Brien Primitives 717
Willoughby Sharp's Downtown New York 491
Willoughby Sharp: The Bronze Commission 558
Willoughby Sharp: The Cutting Edge 558
Willow 667
Wilma 455
Wilson 393
Winans: Live in Concert, The 608
Winans: Return, The 608
Winans: The Lost Concert, The 608
Wince upon a Time: Foolhardy Fairy Tales & Looney Legends 690
Winchester '73 298
Wind, The 79
Wind 287
Wind and the Lion, The 252
Wind and Water 644
Wind in the Willows, The 667, 690, 694, 718
Wind in the Willows, Volume #1, The 644, 718
Wind in the Willows, Volume #2, The 644, 718
Wind in the Willows, Volume #3, The 644, 718
Wind in the Willows, Volume #4, The 644, 718
Wind in the Willows: Four Seasons Set, The 644
Wind Is Driving Him Towards the Open Sea, The 439, 491
Wind Named Amnesia, A 752
Wind: Energy for the 90's and Beyond 807
Windaria 752
Windcarver 562
Windom's Way 179
Window Shopping 30
Window to Paris 84
Winds of Change (1912-1916) 765
Winds of the Wasteland 298
Winds of Time, The 789
Winds of War 423
Windsors: A Royal Family, The 170
Windy City, The 252
Wing and a Prayer 393
Wing Chun 133
Wingless Bird, The 198
Wings 406
Wings of Desire 67
Wings of Eagles 341
Wings of Fame 165
Wings of Honneamise 752
Wings of the Dove, The 165
Wings of the Luftwaffe Fighter Attack 774
Wings of the Red Star 845
Wings over Europe 774
Wings over the Gulf, Vol. 1: First Strike: F-15 Eagle, F-117A, Nighthawk 845
Wings over the Gulf, Vol. 2: In Harm's Way: Tornado, A-6 Intruder 845
Wings over the Gulf, Vol. 3: The Final Assault: F-16 Falcon, A-10 Thunderbolt 845
Wings over the Gulf: Complete Set 845
Wings over the World 845
Wings over Water: History of American Naval Aviation 845
Wings: A Tale of Two Chickens and Other Stories by James Marshall 644
Winnebago Women: Songs & Stories 789
Winner, The 252
Winner's Gala Concert, The 595
Winner Takes All 133
Winners and Sinners 135
Winnie the Pooh & A Day for Eeyore 694
Winnie the Pooh & Christmas Too 694
Winnie the Pooh & The Blustery Day 694
Winnie the Pooh & The Honey Tree 694
Winnie the Pooh & Tigger Too 694
Winnie the Pooh 659
Winnie the Pooh: Clever Little Piglet 659
Winnie the Pooh: Imagine That, Christopher Robin! 659
Winnie the Pooh: Making Friends, Learning 659
Winnie the Pooh: Three Cheers for Eeyore & Rabbit! 659
Winnie the Pooh: Un-Valentine's Day 659
Winning 393
Winning Team, The 393
Winning the Futurity 406
Winslow Boy, The 179
Winsor McCay: Animation Legend 718
Winter Barracks 53
Winter Guest, The 165
Winter Light 78
Winter Meeting 393
Winter People 212
Winter's Soft Mantle 565
Winter Stallion, The 667
Winter Tan, A 439
Winter War, The 77
Winter Wolf 644
Winterbeast 531
Winterset 316
Wintertime 393
WIPP Trail, The 824
Wired 252
Wisconsin Powwow and Naamikaaged: Dancer for the People 789
Wisdom of a Prophet (2 Lectures), The 793
Wisdom of Faith with Huston Smith, The 793
Wisdom of the Dream: C.G. Jung and His Work in the World 786
Wisdom of the Gnomes: Klaus the Judge & The Stolen Mirror 649
Wise Blood 349
Wise Guys 287
Wisecracks 212
Wish for Wings That Work, A 704
Wish That Changed Christmas, The 645
Wishbone: Bone of Arc 645, 704
Wishbone: Frankenbone 645, 704
Wishbone: Homer Sweet Homer 645, 704
Wishbone: Salty Dog 645, 704
Wishbone: Terrified Terrier 645, 704
Wishbone: The Prince and the Pooch 645, 704
Wishbone: The Slobbery Hound 645, 704
Wishbone: Twisted Tail 645, 704
Wishing Ring 406
Wisteria Lodge, The 187
Wistful Widow of Wagon Gap-Abbott and Costello, The 287
Witch Doctor in Tails 512
Witch from Nepal 124
Witch Hunt 252
Witch's Hat, The 659
Witch's Mirror, The 531
Witch's Night Out 718
Witch Who Turned Pink, The 659
Witchcraft Through the Ages 77
Witches (a.k.a. The Devil's Own), The 531
Witches 167
Witches of Eastwick, The 252

Witching, The 531
With a Feminine Touch 308
With a Silent Mind 786
With Byrd at the South Pole 406
With Glittering Eyes 105
With Hand in Heart 562, 789
With My Red Fires/New Dance: Dance Works by Doris Humphrey 576
With Open Eyes: Images from the Art Institute of Chicago 874
Within Our Gates 449
Within These Walls 811
Within Thy Gates, O Jerusalem: The City and the Temple 793
Withnail and I 185
Without a Clue 185
Without Anesthesia 97
Without Love 95, 287
Without the Past 116
Without Warning: The James Brady Story 252
Without You I'm Nothing 316
Witness, The 103, 393
Witness 208
Witness for the Prosecution 346
Witness to Apartheid 153
Witness to Genocide 777
Witness to the Future 874
Witness to the Holocaust: Trial of Adolf Eichmann 777
Wittgenstein 168
Wives Under Suspicion 393
Wiz 331
Wizard of Gore, The 512
Wizard of Oz, The 331, 406
Wizards 718
Wizards of the Demon Sword 512
Wizkids: Careers in Science 671
Wojciech Mlynarski—Lyrical Evening 99
Wolf 531
Wolf at the Door 77
Wolf Blood 406
Wolf Call 393
Wolf Man 531
Wolf Nation 789
Wolf Pack, The 824
Wolf Trap 100
Wolfe Tones On the One Road 204
Wolfen 531
Wolfgang Amadeus Mozart 586
Wolfgang Amadeus Mozart: The "Dissonant" Quartet 874
Wolfman: A Cinematic Scrapbook 531
Wolves 824
Wolves of Kultur 406
Woman and a Woman, A 95
Woman at Her Window, A 7
Woman at War, A 253
Woman Called Golda, A 110
Woman Called Moses, A 455
Woman Hater 185
Woman in Black, The 198
Woman in Green 187
Woman in Grey, A 406
Woman in Question, The 179
Woman in the Dunes 142
Woman in the Hat 95
Woman in the Moon 72
Woman in the Window, The 72
Woman in White, The 198
Woman Is a Woman, A 10
Woman Men Yearn For 71
Woman Next Door, The 15
Woman of Affairs 406
Woman of Distinction 287
Woman of Paris, A 408
Woman of Rome 42
Woman of the Town 298
Woman of the Wolf 253
Woman of the Year 343
Woman's Face, A 77, 350
Woman's Guide to Adultery, A 165
Woman's Place, A 765
Woman's Tale, A 207
Woman's World 287
Woman Under the Influence, A 440
Woman Without Love, A 47
Wombles, The 645
Women, The 7, 350
Women & Men—Stories of Seduction 302
Women and the American Family 765
Women and the Beats: The Beat Generation Show, Volume II 308
Women and the Civil War 780
Women First & Foremost: Volume One: "Remember the Ladies" 765
Women First & Foremost: Volume Three: "A Lady in the Spotlight" 765
Women First & Foremost: Volume Two: "Touching the Clouds with Pen and Plane" 765
Women Flowers 124
Women—For America, for the World 479
Women from Down Under 467
Women from the Lake of Scented Souls 117
Women in American Life 765
Women in Cages 534
Women in Construction 801
Women in Love 167
Women in Policing 801
Women in Prison 42
Women in Rock 623
Women in Tanzania 153
Women of Brewster Place 455
Women on Cane River 765
Women on the Roof, The 77
Women on the Verge of a Nervous Breakdown 46
Women's Health Series 857
Women's Options: The Experience and Wisdom of Seven Low Income Women 801
Women's Story 118
Women Speak Up: A Collection of Women's Voices from Around the World 765, 783
Women Who Made the Movies 339
Women Without Names 42
Won in the Clouds 406
Wonder Man 287
Wonder Seven 133
Wonderful, Horrible Life of Leni Riefenstahl, The 66, 480
Wonderful World of the Brothers Grimm 649
Wonderland 165
Wonders of God's Creation 824
Wood Stork: Barometer of the Everglades (National Audubon) 824
Wooden Gun 108
Wooden Man's Bride, The 118
Woodstock 623
Woodstock 94 623
Woody Woodpecker 50th Anniversary Vol. 1 690
Woody Woodpecker 50th Anniversary Vol. 2 690
Woody Woodpecker Collector's Edition 690
Woof! Woof! Uncle Matty's Guide to Dog Training 861
Word Is Out: Stories of Some of Our Lives 467
Word's Up 253
Wordperfect Quickstart 846
Words and Music 331
Words by Heart 661
Words for the Dying 623
Wordstar, An Introduction 846
Work 467
Work and Police 408
Work in Process: The Furniture of Larry Hendricks 562
Workers '80 (Robotnicy '80) 99
Working Actor: Actors on Acting, The 319
Working Actor: Teachers on Acting, The 319
Working for Peace: The Nuclear Issue 807
Working Girl 288
Working Together 645
Working with Orson Welles 345
Workout with Daddy & Me 671
Workout with Mommy & Me 671
Works, 1978-79 718
Works 718
Works of Ken Feingold— Distance of the Outsider, The 491
Works of Ken Feingold— Life in Exile, The 492
Works of Ken Feingold— Names in Search of a Body, The 492
Works of Ken Feingold—Fictions, The 491
Works of Ken Feingold—Water Falling from One World to Another, The 492
Works of Ken Feingold: The Complete Set, The 492
Workshop in Oils with William Palluth 565
World & Time Enough 467
World According to Garp, The 253
World Alive, A 645, 874
World at War, The 774
World at War 774
World Folk Art: A Multicultural Approach 558
World Gone Mad 394
World in His Arms, The 394
World of a Primitive Painter, The 558
World of Abbott and Costello, The 288
World of Andy Panda, The 718
World of Anne Frank, The 777
World of Apu, The 148
World of Baby Animals, The 659
World of Buckminster Fuller, The 566
World of David the Gnome: Rabbits, Rabbits Everywhere 659
World of Discovery: Beautiful Killers 824
World of Discovery: Cougar: Ghost of the Rockies 824
World of Discovery: Realm of the Serpent 824
World of Discovery: Red Express: The Trans-Siberian Railroad 845
World of Discovery: Shark Chronicles 824
World of Discovery: Tall Ship: High Sea Adventure 845
World of Discovery: The Secret Life of 118 Green Street 824
World of Discovery: Wildebeest: Race for Life 824
World of Discovery: Wolf: Return of a Legend 825
World of Fingerstyle Jazz Guitar 606
World of Henry Orient, The 288
World of Herbs 825
World of Refugees 807
World of Reptiles, The 874
World of Sholom Aleichem, The 113
World of Strangers, A 77
World of Suzie Wong 394
World of the Koala, The 825
World on Display, A 765
World Population 838
World's Greatest Animation, The 718
World's Greatest Movie Challenge 513
World's Philosophies, The 786
World's Young Ballet 576
World Through Kids' Eyes, The 645
World War I 874
World War I Complete Set 765
World War II 874
World War II: A Personal Journey 774
World War II: From Breadlines to Boomtimes 774
World War II: Global Conflict 874
World War II: Hearst Metronome News 774
World War II: The Eastern Front 774
World War II: The War Chronicles 774
World Within, The 786
World Without Walls— Beryl Markham's African Memoir 797
Worldly Madonna, The 406
Worlds Below, The 645
WorldScape 565
Worship the King 793
Woven by the Grandmothers 789
Wozzeck 67, 586
WR: Mysteries of the Organism 104
Wrapped in Glory: Quilts and Bedcovers from 1700-1900 562
Wrath of the Ninja: The Yotoden Movie 752
Wreck of the Mary Deare, The 394
Wrecked for Life: The Trip and Magic of Trocadero Transfer 467
Wrestling Ernest Hemingway 253
Wrestling with Gorgeous George 423
Writing for Film 319
Writing for Radio 319
Writing for Television 319
Writing in Water and Admiral Bataille & the S.S. Esoterica 480
Written on the Wind 342
Wrong Arm of the Law 185
Wrong Box, The 185
Wrong Man, The 253, 353
Wuthering Heights— Westinghouse Studio One 423
Wuthering Heights 47, 302, 344
WWII: Beyond the Battle 774
Wyatt Earp 298
Wyatt Earp: Justice at the OK Corral 299
Wynton Marsalis: Blues and Swing 616

X

X from Outer Space 502
X—The Man with the X-Ray Eyes 514
X-Men: The Phoenix Saga Part 1: The Sacrifice 704
X-Men: The Phoenix Saga Part 2: The Dark Shroud 704
X-Planes 845
X-Rated: Movieyeur 439
Xanadu 331
Xerxes 586
Xica 54
Xing Qi Gong Zhi Tan Bi 124
Xingu: Land of No Shame 784
Xuxa Celebration with Cheech Marin 659
Xuxa: Fantastic Birthday Party 659

Y

Yachting in the Thirties 828
Yanco 53
Yang Long Form of T'ai-Chi Chuan 857
Yank in the RAF, A 394
Yankee Doodle Dandy 331
Yankee Doodle in Berlin 407
Yankee Samurai: The Little Iron Men 774
Yankee Thunder, Rebel Lightning! 780
Yankee Zulu 288
Yanks 253
Yanomami 789
Year in Provence, A 302
Year of Living Dangerously 208
Year of the Generals, The 765
Year Without a Santa Claus 704
Yearling (1946), The 667
Yearling (1994), The 667
Yearning: Jerusalem of the 19th Century 110
Years Between, The 179
Yehuda Amichai 116
Yehudi Menuhin 595
Yehudi Menuhin: Concert for the Pope 595
Yehudi Menuhin: Tribute to J.S. Bach (1685-1750) 595
Yellow Cab Man, The 288
Yellow Earth 118
Yellow Fever/La Fievre Jaune 440
Yellow Rain 133
Yellowneck 394
Yellowstone & Grand Teton 833
Yellowstone to Yukon 825
Yellowstone-Teton Wildlife 825
Yentl 331
Yes, I Can Help 659
Yes, I Can Share 659
Yes, Minister 198
Yes, Prime Minister: Official Secrets 198
Yes, Prime Minister: Power to the People 198
Yes, Prime Minister: The Bishop's Gambit 198
Yes, Prime Minister: The Grand Design/The Ministerial Broadcast/The Smoke Screen 198
Yes, Prime Minister: The Key/A Real Partnership/ A Victory for Democracy 198
Yes, Virginia, There Is a Santa Claus 704
Yes Madam 133
Yes Madam 5 133
Yes! Tour: Working for Change, The 807
Yessongs 623
Yesterday, Today and Tomorrow 38
Yesterday Machine, The 502
Yesterday's Heroes 825
Yevgeny Kissin in Tokyo 595
Yevgeny Kissin Plays 595
Yiddish Cinema, The 113
Yiddish: The Mame-Loshn (The Mother Tongue) 113
Yiddishe Gauchos, The 116
Yidl with a Fiddle 113
Yitzhak Rabin 110

Yogi Bear's All-Star Comedy Christmas Caper 704
Yogi the Easter Bear 704
Yojimbo 143
Yol 106
Yolanda and the Thief 331
Yonder 645
Yongary Monster from the Deep 136
Yosemite National Park 833
Yosemite Sam's Yeller Fever 690
Yosemite Sam: The Good, The Bad and the Ornery 690
Yosemite—Seasons & Splendor 833
Yosemite: The Fate of Heaven 833
Yotoden Chapter 1: Break Out 753
Yotoden Chapter 2: Demon's Cry 753
Yotoden Chapter 3: Flames of Anger 753
You, Me, Jerusalem 108
You and Me 73
You Are Not Alone 77, 467
You Bet Your Life 423
You Can Beat the A-Bomb 807
You Can Choose 645
You Can Do It 660
You Can Heal Your Life 857
You Can Play Guitar 625
You Can Play Jazz Piano 625
"You Can" Videos 671
You Can't Do That: The Making of A Hard Day's Night 623
You Can't Fool Your Wife 394
You Can't Grow Home Again 807
You Can't Take It with You 351
You Gotta Stay Happy 394
You Light Up My Life 253
You'll Never Get Rich 331
You Make Me Laugh 124
You May Call Her Madam Secretary 797
You on Kazoo! 671
You Only Live Twice 169
You're a Big Boy Now 260
You're the Top—The Cole Porter Story 797
You're Under Arrest! Ep. 1: And So They Met 753
You're Under Arrest! Ep. 2: Tokyo Typhoon Rally 753
You're Under Arrest! Ep. 3: Love's Highway Stars 753
You're Under Arrest! Ep. 4: On the Road Again 753
You're Under Arrest! Hybrid Laserdisc #1 753
You're Under Arrest! Hybrid Laserdisc #2 753
You Were Never Lovelier 331
Young and Dangerous II, Parts A & B 133
Young and Dangerous III 133
Young and Innocent 353
Young April, The 407
Young at Heart 331
Young at Heart Comedians, The 536
Young Bess 394
Young Billy Young 394
Young Caruso 600
Young Cinematographer 645
Young Connecticut Yankee in King Arthur's Court, A 309
Young Einstein 207
Young Frankenstein 288
Young Guns 298
Young Hearts, Broken Dreams, Episode 1: The Delivery Boy 467
Young Hearts, Broken Dreams, Episode 2: The Search 467
Young Hearts, Broken Dreams— Episode 3: He Loves Me He Loves Me Not 467
Young Ivanhoe 667
Young Land, The 298
Young Lions, The 774
Young Magician 668
Young Man with a Horn 394
Young Master, The 135
Young Mr. Lincoln 341
Young Mr. Pitt, The 180
Young One, The 47
Young Ones: Bambi, Nasty, Time, The 198
Young Ones: Cash, Interesting, Summer Holiday, The 198
Young Ones: Demolition, Bomb, Sick, The 198
Young Ones: Oil, Boring, Flood, The 198
Young People 668
Young People's Concerts 595
Young Poisoner's Handbook, The 165
Young Savages 394
Young Sherlock Holmes 187
Young Tom Edison 394
Young Winston 165
Young Wives' Tale 185
Younger and Younger 288
Your Family's Health 838
Your Show of Shows 423
Yours, Mine and Ours 288
Yu Pui Tsuen 124
Yu Yu Hakusho: The Movie 753
Yugoslavian Cinema 104
Yul Brynner: The Man Who Was King 339
Yum, Yum, Yum! 481
Yuma 298
Yuri Grigorovich: Master of the Bolshoi 576
Yvonne Jacquette: Autumn Expansion 565
Dr. Ching-chih Chen 866

Z

Z 106, 405, 863, 874
Z Was Zapped, The 660
Zabriskie Point 36
Zafarinas 45
Zamaaneko Dikanahai 148
Zambian Safari 153
Zamke: One Story, A Thousand Thoughts 116
Zandy's Bride 79
Zardoz 502
Zatoichi Challenged! 140
Zatoichi: Masseur Ichi and a Chest of Gold 140
Zatoichi: Masseur Ichi on the Road 140
Zatoichi: The Blind Swordsman and the Chess Expert 140
Zatoichi: The Blind Swordsman and the Fugitives 140
Zatoichi: The Blind Swordsman's Vengeance 140
Zatoichi: The Blind Swordsman Samaritan 140
Zatoichi: The Life and Opinion of Masseur Ichi 140
Zatoichi: The Return of Masseur Ichi 140
Zatoichi: Zatoichi's Flashing Sword 140
Zazie dans le Metro 13
Zebra in the Kitchen 668
Zebrahead 440
Zeezel the Zowie Zoon in the Color Chase 660
Zefiro Torna or Scenes from the Life of George Maciunas 443
Zeguy, Parts 1 & 2 753
Zelig 289
Zelly and Me 253
Zen and I: The Life of a Zen Priest 150
Zen of Sword 133
Zen: In Search of Enlightenment 150
Zen: The Best of Alan Watts 150
Zenki the Demon Prince Vol. 1 753
Zenki the Demon Prince Vol. 2 753
Zenki the Demon Prince Vol. 3 753
Zenki the Demon Prince Vol. 4 753
Zenki the Demon Prince Vol. 5 753
Zenki the Demon Prince Vol. 6 753
Zenobia 288
Zentropa 77
Zeppelin 165
Zeram 502
Zero Effect 288
Zero for Conduct 25
Zero Hour 645
Zero Imperative, The 198
Zero Kelvin 77
Zero Patience 212, 467
Zero Woman 140
Zeus and Roxanne 668
Ziegfeld Follies 331
Ziegfeld Girl 331
Ziggy's Gift 660
Zillion 1-5 Laserdisc 753
Zillion 753
Zillion: Burning Night 753
Zillion: The Beginning 753
Zillions TV: A Kid's Guide to Toys and Games 671
Zinat 107
Zion Canyon—Treasure of the Gods 833
Ziveli! Medicine for the Heart 604
Zlateh the Goat 116, 645
Zocalo—The Heart of Mexico 62
Zodiac Killers 133
Zoll Zeyn (Let It Be) 113
Zoltan: Hound of Dracula 531
Zombie '90: Extreme Pestilence 531
Zombie 531
Zombie and the Ghost Train 79
Zombie Army, The 531
Zombie Cop 531
Zombie Island Massacre 531
Zombie Rampage 531
Zombies of the Stratosphere (Satan's Satellites) 539
Zona Gale: 1874-1938 797
Zoobilee Zoo 660
Zoot Sims Quartet 616
Zoot Suit 62, 331
Zorba the Greek 105
Zorro (Delon) 24
Zorro 704
Zorro Rides Again 394, 539
Zorro's Black Whip 539
Zorro's Fighting Legion 539
Zorro: A Conspiracy of Blood 253
Zorro: The Legend Begins 253
Zou Zou 24
Zu Neuen Ufern 342
Zu: Warriors of the Magic Mountain 133
Zubin Mehta and Leontyne Price 600
Zulu 180
Zuppa di Pesce (Fish Soup) 35
Zvenigora 86
Zwingli and Calvin 793
Zydeco 604
Zydeco Gumbo 604
Zydeco: Nite 'n' Day 604